W9-BNW-407

The New Encyclopædia Britannica

Volume 28

MACROPÆDIA

Knowledge in Depth

FOUNDED 1768
15 TH EDITION

Encyclopædia Britannica, Inc.
Robert P. Gwinn, Chairman, Board of Directors
Peter B. Norton, President
Philip W. Goetz, Editor in Chief

Chicago
Auckland/Geneva/London/Madrid/Manila/Paris
Rome/Seoul/Sydney/Tokyo/Toronto

THE UNIVERSITY OF CHICAGO

"Let knowledge grow from more to more
and thus be human life enriched."

The *Encyclopædia Britannica* is published with the editorial advice of the faculties of the University of Chicago.

Additional advice is given by committees of members drawn from the faculties of the Australian National University, the universities of British Columbia (Can.), Cambridge (Eng.), Copenhagen (Den.), Edinburgh (Scot.), Florence (Italy), London (Eng.), Marburg (W.Ger.), Oxford (Eng.), the Ruhr (W.Ger.), Sussex (Eng.), Toronto (Can.), Victoria (Can.), and Waterloo (Can.); the Complutensian University of Madrid (Spain); the Max Planck Institute for Biophysical Chemistry (W.Ger.); the New University of Lisbon (Port.); the School of Higher Studies in Social Sciences (Fr.); Simon Fraser University (Can.); and the State University of Leiden (Neth.).

First Edition	1768–1771
Second Edition	1777–1784
Third Edition	1788–1797
Supplement	1801
Fourth Edition	1801–1809
Fifth Edition	1815
Sixth Edition	1820–1823
Supplement	1815–1824
Seventh Edition	1830–1842
Eighth Edition	1852–1860
Ninth Edition	1875–1889
Tenth Edition	1902–1903

Printed in U.S.A.

Library of Congress Catalog Card Number: 88-83263
International Standard Book Number: 0-85229-511-1

CONTENTS

Spain

Lying at the southwestern end of the European continent, Spain (España), or the Spanish State (Estado Español), occupies about 85 percent of the Iberian Peninsula. With Portugal, which forms its western boundary, it is shaped like the hide of a bull, the neck pointing toward Africa in the south and a large base formed by the Pyrenees Mountains and the Bay of Biscay in the north. It is separated from France by the small principality of Andorra and by the Pyrenees; and in the far south lies the small peninsula of Gibraltar, which has been under British sovereignty since 1713. Off Spain's eastern coast lie the Balearic Islands; the Canary Islands, in the Atlantic Ocean off the coast of Africa, are also a part of Spain. The cities of Ceuta and Melilla, in northern Morocco, have belonged to Spain for several centuries and are considered by Spain to be an integral part of that country, despite Moroccan claims to their suzerainty. The total area of the national territory of Spain is 194,900 square miles (504,782 square kilometres).

One of the most ancient countries in Europe, Spain was also long one of the most powerful and, from the 16th to the 19th century, ruled a large empire. Evidence of that empire is the continuing use of the Spanish language in 18 Latin-American states, Puerto Rico, and the Republic of Equatorial Guinea. Lying at the crossroads of Africa and Europe, and holding the key to the Mediterranean from the Atlantic, Spain retains traces of European, African, Mediterranean, and Atlantic cultures that make of it a distinctive country within western Europe.

Under the constitution adopted in 1978, Spain is a constitutional monarchy in which the king assumes a ceremonial position. Its economy is fully integrated in the Western world, with large-scale foreign investments, tourism, and trade relations with other countries of the Atlantic area. Spain is a member of the North Atlantic Treaty Organization (NATO) and maintains a close relationship with that organization through bilateral agreements with the United States. Spain is a member of the United Nations and its specialized agencies and belongs to the Council of Europe and most technical organizations of western Europe. It is tied to the European Economic Community (EEC) with a commercial agreement. Close diplomatic, cultural, and economic links are maintained with most Latin-American countries and international organizations, such as the Andean Pact, the Inter-American Development Bank, and the Organization of American States.

The article is divided into the following sections:

Physical and human geography

THE LAND

Relief. With the exception of the southern triangle closing toward the Strait of Gibraltar, the Iberian Peninsula forms an irregular quadrangle, bordered on the east and southeast by the Mediterranean and on the west, southwest, and most of the north by the Atlantic Ocean. Most of the peninsula is occupied by the Meseta, a large plateau with approximately the same boundaries as the historical Kingdom of Castile (Castilla). The average height of the plateau is 2,000 feet (610 metres), although its northern part is slightly higher than the southern section. The Meseta is almost completely surrounded by mountain ranges: the Cordillera Cantábrica (Cantabrian Mountains) in the north; the Sistema Ibérico (Iberian System) from the Cantábrica to the southeast; the Sierra Morena in the south; and the lower mountains on the border with Portugal in the northwest. The southern plateau descends gently in the direction of Portugal, whereas the transition from the northern plateau to Portugal is marked by rugged terrain and mountain ranges. The Meseta is divided by the Cordillera Carpetovetónica (also called the Sistema Central), which extends across the plateau to the north of Madrid and runs all the way from the Sistema Ibérico to Portugal.

The Meseta

Around the central plateau, five natural regions can be identified. First, in northeastern Spain, there is the valley of the Río Ebro, enclosed by the Sistema Ibérico in the west and southwest, the Pyrenees and the Cordillera Cantábrica in the north, and the mountains of Catalonia (Cataluña) and other coastal ranges in the east. Second, there is the valley of the Guadalquivir River in the south, which is separated from the plateau by the Sierra Morena and from the Mediterranean by the Sistema Penibético (Baetic Cordillera), including the Sierra Nevada in the southeast, but which has unimpeded passage to the Atlantic in the southwest. Third, there is the region of the coastal area of Valencia, in the east, descending from the southern Iberian ranges toward the Mediterranean. Catalonia, a mountainous region between the valley of the Ebro, the eastern Pyrenees, and the Mediterranean, forms the fourth natural region. Finally, there is northern Spain from the Pyrenees to the west, a rugged, mountainous country comprising several small regions separated from each other by high mountains.

Geologically, the peninsula forms a great massif (not to be confused with the Meseta, which it partly overlaps), bordered on the north, east, and south by mountain folds. This massif is a fragment of the former Hercynian continent, which formed across Europe at the close of the Carboniferous Period (about 345,000,000 to 280,000,000 years ago). During the Mesozoic Era (between 225,000,000 and 65,000,000 years ago), the Hercynian system was shattered, and large portions sank below the sea. During the Tertiary Period (between 65,000,000 and 2,500,000 years ago), deposits of the Jurassic and Cretaceous seas, together with the earlier Tertiary beds, were crushed against the old massif to form the ranges bordering the Meseta. Later movements contorted and fractured the peninsula to give it its present general shape.

The Hercynian massif

The Balearic Islands in the Mediterranean are composed of mountain ranges of moderate altitude, not exceeding 5,000 feet. The Canary Islands in the Atlantic, however, are of volcanic origin and contain the highest peak among the Spanish territories, the Teide (12,198 feet [3,718 metres]), located on the island of Tenerife.

Drainage and soils. The most important drainage systems are found in the plateau and the two large valleys of the Ebro and the Guadalquivir. The plateau has three main drainage systems, all flowing into the Atlantic: the Río Duero (Douro) in the northern plateau and the Tagus (Tajo) and Guadiana in the southern plateau. While the Duero and the Tagus follow an almost parallel course from the Iberian range to the west coast of Portugal, the Guadiana turns south at the border with Portugal and empties into the Gulf of Cadiz (Golfo de Cádiz) on the southern Atlantic coast. The Ebro, which has the greatest outflow of the peninsula's rivers, follows an almost straight course from the northern mountains to the Mediterranean, collecting waters from the Pyrenees and the Sistema Ibérico. The Guadalquivir flows from the east to the southwest, gathering waters from the Sierra Morena and the Sierra Nevada. In the southeastern region, the two most important rivers are the Júcar and the Segura.

Three main mineralogical regions can be distinguished in Spain. Crystalline rocks predominate in the central and peripheral basins, whereas the east and north have an abundance of limestones. The soils may be described as generally acid-humid in the northwest, calcareous in eastern and southern Spain, and siliceous in the Cantábrica, northern Iberian, Carpetovetónica, and Sierra Morena ranges as well as in the Duero Valley and the mountains of Zamora and Salamanca. As in most of the western Mediterranean, erosion has played a very important role in the degradation of the soils, especially in the high areas of the plateau and the eastern and southern zones. In addition to natural erosion, humans have contributed considerably through the destruction of forests. Since the 1920s, however, the government has carried out important projects to forestall further erosion.

Soil erosion

Climate. Spain is located in the temperate zone of the Northern Hemisphere, between the latitudes of 27° (for the Canary Islands) and 44° N. In general, Spain belongs climatically to the western Mediterranean. The peninsula is exposed both to the westerly North Atlantic winds, which dominate during most of the year, and to the warm, dry airstream that blows less frequently from the Sahara. The Pyrenees and the Cordillera Cantábrica, however, play an important role in the Spanish climate, for they constitute the northern boundary of the subtropical airstream during the summer months, thereby maintaining dry weather conditions over most of the country.

Three basic types of climate predominate within the peninsula: the coastal climate of the Atlantic and Mediterranean seaboards; the continental climate of the plateau and the valleys of the Ebro and the Guadalquivir; and the mountain climate of areas above 3,000 feet. Northern Spain, from Galicia to northern Catalonia, is characterized by moderate, even temperatures and high rainfall. Thus, La Coruña, in the northwest, ranges from 48° F (9° C) in winter to 64° F (18° C) in summer, while the annual rainfall is about 38 inches (965 millimetres). The plateau has a continental climate, with lower rainfall and greater temperature variations. Thus Albacete, in the southeast of the plateau, varies between 40° F (4° C) in the winter and 75° F (24° C) in the summer, while the annual rainfall is less than 15 inches (380 millimetres). The valleys of the Ebro and the Guadalquivir also have a continental climate, drier and colder in the Ebro and warmer and more humid in the Guadalquivir. Catalonia, Valencia, and the Balearic Islands enjoy more temperate weather, with higher rainfall in Catalonia, while the Canary Islands have a subtropical, Atlantic climate.

Plant and animal life. *Vegetation.* There are four main vegetation areas: north, centre, south, and southeast. Northern Spain, enjoying humid weather, is covered with deciduous forests and meadows. It is basically a green country, good for forestry and pastures, as well as the cultivation of corn (maize), apples, and other products that thrive in humid areas. The northern plateau and the Ebro Valley, with low levels of humidity and extreme temperatures, mainly produce grains. The upper Ebro Valley, the southern plateau, Andalusia, and the eastern regions produce olives and grapes. Valencia and the irrigated areas of Murcia are noted for their citrus fruits, particularly oranges, but rice is also grown in Valencia, and the production of fruits and vegetables in Murcia has been diversified. Semi-desert areas occur in the valley of the Ebro, around the city of Zaragoza, and in southeastern Spain in the province of Almería, where irrigation projects support the cultivation of flowers, early fruits, and vegetables.

Fruit-growing regions

Livestock. Cattle are raised in the north and in the mountainous areas of central and southern Spain. Sheep are the most common stock animals in the plateau region. Pigs are raised in most of Spain, particularly in the west and northwest. Goats are mostly raised in the south of the peninsula and in the islands. Mules and donkeys, once a part of the Spanish landscape, were vanishing in the late 20th century as a consequence of the mechanization of harvesting and transportation. Spanish-Arabian horses are raised on large estates in Andalusia (Andalucía), and fighting bulls are raised for profit in Andalusia and Castile. Camels are used for tourist purposes in some of the Canary Islands.

Wildlife. Its close links with Africa give Spain more African species than exist in the other Mediterranean peninsulas, while the Pyrenean barrier and extent of the country explains the number of indigenous species. The larger species of wildlife are almost extinct in Spain, although bears and wolves can still be found in the Pyrenees and some of the northern mountain areas. The Spanish ibex (*Capra pyrenaica*) is threatened with extinction, and most are found within preserves. Other types of wildlife, such as deer or wild pigs, can be found in preserves all over Spain. Minor game, such as partridge, grouse, duck, and rabbit or hare, abound throughout Spain. At Gibraltar is confined the Barbary ape, thought either to be indigenous or to have been imported by the Romans or Arabs; it is also present across the strait.

Fish. The Spanish coasts were once rich in fish and shellfish, particularly in the Atlantic and the Bay of Biscay. Overexploitation led, however, to the exhaustion of coastal fisheries within the Spanish territorial waters. This induced the government to adopt a 200-mile offshore fishing zone in 1978, within which Spain claimed the right to manage and exploit fisheries. Trout, luce, carp, and other inland fishes are still found in the rivers and water reservoirs protected by the state.

Settlement patterns. *Traditional regions.* Because of the geographical diversity and the great variety of climates and vegetation, as well as for historical reasons, regional differences are very important in Spain. Their political relevance increased with the approval in 1978 of a new constitution that foresaw a reorganization of the state on the basis of autonomous communities. The country is divided into 14 traditional regions, two of which are the Balearic Islands and the Canary Islands. The old Kingdom of Castile, which covered most of the plateau, included three regions that are still considered to be Castilian: León and Old Castile, in the northern plateau, and New Castile, in the southern plateau. (The province of Santander, located between the Cordillera Cantábrica and the Bay of Biscay, was historically part of Old Castile, although it differs widely from inland Castile in location, climate, and economic structure.) The former kingdom also included six other regions that are no longer considered to be Castilian: the Basque Provinces, Asturias, and Galicia, in the north; Extremadura, in the southern plateau, bordering Portugal; and Murcia and Andalusia in the south. The old Kingdom of Aragón, located on the eastern half of the peninsula, encompassed the four regions of Navarre, bordering France and the Basque country; Aragón, covering the lower course of the Ebro River and extending from the Pyrenees to the Sistema Ibérico; Catalonia, in the northeastern corner of Spain; and Valencia, in the coastal plains between the Sistema Ibérico and the Mediterranean Sea.

The coastal regions differ markedly from each other and from inland Spain. Differences in geography, history, social and economic structures, and especially language have all contributed to a variety of regional identities. Regional nationalism—even regional separatism—has developed wherever a native language other than Spanish is spoken, as in Catalonia, Galicia, and, above all, the Basque country (Vascongadas). And in regions in which only Spanish is spoken, such as Andalusia, the Canary Islands, and Aragón, an acute sense of social and cultural identity has been acquired. Consequently, a movement developed all over Spain to transform the traditionally centralized political system into a decentralized one with an almost federal structure. Thus, traditional regions became the basis for the political reorganization of the country.

Regional consciousness

One of the most sensitive issues in Spanish politics in the late 20th century was the apportionment of powers between the central government and the new autonomous communities recognized by the constitution of 1978. The regionalist trend that had prevailed during the 1970s had become counterbalanced by centralist forces that opposed any further transfer of powers to the regional governments. Thus, a tug-of-war between national and regional identities developed, threatening the stability of democratic institutions and putting in question the nature of the state itself. The strain was particularly noticeable in the Basque country, but was also apparent in Catalonia and other regional communities.

Human settlement. Spain is now a predominantly industrial country, with less than 20 percent of the economically active population involved in agriculture, forestry, or fishing. There has been a sharp movement from the country to the cities in the last 50 years. In 1930, only one-quarter of the population lived in cities, whereas more than half of the Spanish population was settled in an urban environment by the late 20th century. The economic and structural changes that took place in that period are of paramount importance to an understanding of modern Spain.

Traditional rural settlements vary widely from one region to the next. Northern and Mediterranean Spain and the islands follow a pattern of small settlements surrounded by agricultural land. On the other hand, the plateau and the valleys of the Ebro and the Guadalquivir are characterized by highly concentrated rural populations inhabiting large towns. These differences are connected with the history and the landscape of the different regions.

Most of the population lives in towns of 10,000 or more inhabitants. The size of towns does not, however, always reflect their economic activity. In southern Castile, Extremadura, Murcia, and Andalusia, large towns of 20,000 or 30,000 people may concentrate mainly on agricultural tasks, while smaller towns in the Basque country or Catalonia may be predominantly industrial. The two main urban centres are Madrid, the capital, in New Castile, and Barcelona, on the Catalonian coast. The population of the province of Barcelona exceeds that of the province of Madrid, while the metropolitan districts of Madrid and Barcelona are roughly equivalent. Other large urban concentrations include Greater Bilbao, which is in the Basque country; Greater Valencia, in the east; Zaragoza, in the Ebro Valley; and Seville (Sevilla), in the lower Guadalquivir Valley.

THE PEOPLE

Because of its position between two continents and its relative accessibility from the Mediterranean, Spain has been invaded and inhabited by many different peoples. In prehistoric times, peoples from North Africa and western Europe settled in the peninsula, including the Celts,

SPAIN Size of symbol indicates relative size of town

Elevations in metres

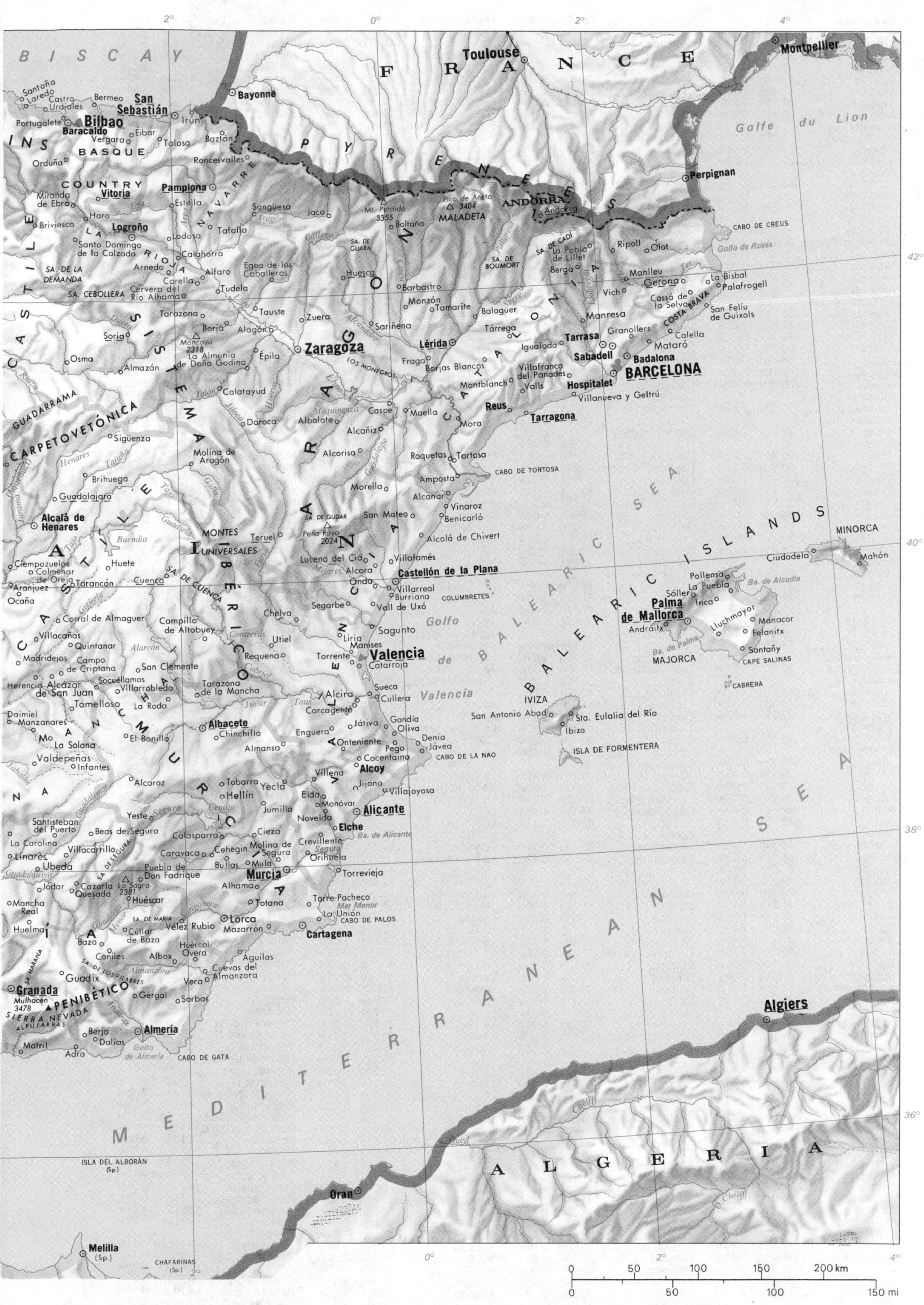
BISCAY
FRANCE
Toulouse
Montpellier
Golfe du Lion
Perpignan
Bayonne
San Sebastián
Bilbao
BASQUE COUNTRY
Vitoria
Pamplona
Logroño
PYRENEES
ANDORRA
Zaragoza
ARAGON
CATALONIA
BARCELONA
Tarragona
Lérida
SISTEMA IBÉRICO
CASTILLE
Teruel
Castellón de la Plana
Valencia
Golfo de Valencia
BALEARIC ISLANDS
BALEARIC SEA
MINORCA
Mahón
Palma de Mallorca
MAJORCA
IVIZA
Ibiza
Alicante
Murcia
Cartagena
Albacete
Granada
Almería
MEDITERRANEAN SEA
Algiers
Oran
ALGERIA
Melilla (Sp.)
0 50 100 150 200 km
0 50 100 150 mi

MAP INDEX

Cities and towns

Name	Lat.	Long.
Adra	36·44n	3·01w
Aguilar	37·31n	4·39w
Águilas	37·24n	1·35w
Alagón	41·46n	1·07w
Albacete	38·59n	1·51w
Alba de Tormes	40·49n	5·31w
Albalate [del Arzobispo]	41·07n	0·31w
Albox	37·23n	2·08w
Albuquerque	39·13n	7·00w
Alcalá de Chivert	40·18n	0·14e
Alcalá de Henares	40·29n	3·22w
Alcalá de los Gazules	36·28n	5·44w
Alcalá la Real	37·28n	3·56w
Alcanar	40·33n	0·29e
Alcañiz	41·03n	0·08w
Alcaraz	38·40n	2·29w
Alcaudete	37·36n	4·05w
Alcázar de San Juan	39·24n	3·12w
Alcira	39·09n	0·26w
Alcora	40·04n	0·12w
Alcorisa	40·53n	0·23w
Alcoy	38·42n	0·28w
Alfaro	42·11n	1·45w
Algeciras	36·08n	5·30w
Alhama [de Granada]	37·00n	3·59w
Alhama [de Murcia]	37·51n	1·25w
Alhaurín el Grande	36·38n	4·41w
Alicante	38·21n	0·29w
Allariz	42·11n	7·48w
Almadén	38·46n	4·50w
Almagro	38·53n	3·43w
Almansa	38·52n	1·05w
Almazán	41·29n	2·32w
Almendralejo	38·41n	6·24w
Almería	36·50n	2·27w
Almodóvar [del Campo]	38·43n	4·10w
Almonte	37·15n	6·31w
Almuñécar	36·43n	3·41w
Álora	36·48n	4·42w
Amposta	40·43n	0·35e
Andraitx	39·35n	2·25e
Andújar	38·03n	4·04w
Antequera	37·01n	4·33w
Aracena	37·53n	6·33w
Aranda de Duero	41·41n	3·41w
Aranjuez	40·02n	3·36w
Archidona	37·05n	4·23w
Arcos de la Frontera	36·45n	5·48w
Arenas de San Pedro	40·12n	5·05w
Arjona	37·56n	4·03w
Arnedo	42·13n	2·06w
Arroyo de la Luz	39·29n	6·35w
Arzúa	42·56n	8·09w
Astorga	42·27n	6·03w
Ávila [de los Caballeros]	40·39n	4·42w
Avilés	43·33n	5·55w
Ayamonte	37·13n	7·24w
Azuaga	38·16n	5·41w
Badajoz	38·53n	6·58w
Badalona	41·27n	2·15e
Baena	37·37n	4·19w
Bailén	38·06n	3·46w
Balaguer	41·47n	0·49e
Bande	42·02n	7·58w
Baracaldo	43·18n	2·59w
Barbastro	42·02n	0·08e
Barcarrota	38·31n	6·51w
Barcelona	41·23n	2·11e
Barruelo de Santullán	42·54n	4·18w
Baza	37·29n	2·46w
Baztán	43·15n	1·33w
Beas de Segura	38·15n	2·53w
Becerreá	42·51n	7·10w
Béjar	40·23n	5·46w
Belalcázar	38·34n	5·10w
Bélmez	38·16n	5·12w
Benavente	42·00n	5·41w
Benicarló	40·25n	0·26e
Berga	42·06n	1·51e
Berja	36·51n	2·57w
Bermeo	43·26n	2·43w
Betanzos	43·17n	8·12w
Bilbao	43·15n	2·58w
Boltaña	42·27n	0·04e
Boñar	42·52n	5·19w
Borja	41·50n	1·32w
Borjas Blancas	41·31n	0·52e
Bornos	36·48n	5·44w
Brihuega	40·48n	2·52w
Briviesca	42·33n	3·19w
Brozas	39·37n	6·46w
Bujalance	37·54n	4·22w
Bullas	38·03n	1·40w
Burgos	42·21n	3·42w
Burriana	39·53n	0·05w
Cabañaquinta	43·10n	5·38w
Cabeza del Buey	38·43n	5·13w
Cabra	37·28n	4·27w
Cáceres	39·29n	6·22w
Cádiz	36·32n	6·18w
Calahorra	42·18n	1·58w
Calañas	37·39n	6·53w
Calasparra	38·14n	1·42w
Calatayud	41·21n	1·38w
Calella	41·37n	2·40e
Campanario	38·52n	5·37w
Campillo de Altobuey	39·36n	1·48w
Campo de Criptana	39·24n	3·07w
Candeleda	40·09n	5·14w
Cangas	42·16n	8·47w
Cangas de Narcea	43·11n	6·33w
Caniles	37·26n	2·43w
Caravaca	38·06n	1·51w
Carballino	42·26n	8·04w
Carballo	43·13n	8·41w
Carcagente	39·08n	0·27w
Carmona	37·28n	5·38w
Carrión de los Condes	42·20n	4·36w
Cartagena	37·36n	0·59w
Caspe	41·14n	0·02w
Cassá de la Selva	41·53n	2·53e
Castellón de la Plana	39·59n	0·02w
Castro de Río	37·41n	4·28w
Castro Urdiales	43·23n	3·13w
Castuera	38·43n	5·33w
Catarroja	39·24n	0·24w
Cazalla de la Sierra	37·56n	5·45w
Cazorla	37·55n	3·00w
Cebreros	40·27n	4·28w
Cehegín	38·06n	1·48w
Cervantes	42·52n	7·04w
Cervera del Río Alhama	42·01n	1·57w
Ceuta	35·52n	5·20w
Chantada	42·37n	7·46w
Chelva	39·45n	0·59w
Chiclana [de la Frontera]	36·25n	6·08w
Chinchilla	38·55n	1·55w
Ciempozuelos	40·10n	3·37w
Cieza	38·14n	1·25w
Cistierna	42·48n	5·07w
Ciudadela	40·02n	3·50e
Ciudad Real	38·59n	3·56w
Ciudad Rodrigo	40·36n	6·32w
Cocentaina	38·45n	0·26w
Coín	36·40n	4·45w
Colmenar de Oreja	40·06n	3·23w
Colmenar Viejo	40·40n	3·46w
Constantina	37·52n	5·37w
Córdoba	37·53n	4·46w
Corella	42·07n	1·47w
Corral de Almaguer	39·46n	3·11w
Cortegana	37·55n	6·49w
Cortes [de la Frontera]	36·37n	5·20w
Crevillente	38·15n	0·48w
Cuéllar	41·25n	4·19w
Cuenca	40·04n	2·08w
Cuevas del Almanzora	37·18n	1·53w
Cúllar de Baza	37·35n	2·34w
Cullera	39·10n	0·15w
Daimiel	39·04n	3·37w
Dalías	36·49n	2·52w
Daroca	41·07n	1·25w
Denia	38·51n	0·07e
Don Benito	38·57n	5·52w
Dos Hermanas	37·17n	5·55w
Écija	37·32n	5·05w
Egea de los Caballeros	42·08n	1·08w
Éibar	43·11n	2·28w
El Arahal	37·16n	5·33w
El Barco [de Valdeorras]	42·25n	6·59w
El Bonillo	38·57n	2·32w
Elche	38·15n	0·42w
Elda	38·29n	0·47w
El Ferrol del Caudillo	43·29n	8·14w
El Puerto de Santa María	36·36n	6·13w
Enguera	38·59n	0·41w
Épila	41·36n	1·17w
Escairón	42·40n	7·40w
Estella	42·40n	2·02w
Estepa	37·18n	4·54w
Estepona	36·26n	5·08w
Fermoselle	41·19n	6·23w
Felanitx	39·28n	3·08e
Fernán-Núñez	37·40n	4·43w
Fonsagrada	43·08n	7·04w
Fraga	41·31n	0·21e
Fregenal de la Sierra	38·10n	6·39w
Friol	43·02n	7·47w
Fuensalida	40·03n	4·12w
Fuente de Cantos	38·15n	6·18w
Fuenteovejuna	38·16n	5·25w
Fuentesaúco	41·14n	5·30w
Gandía	38·58n	0·11w
Garrovillas	39·43n	6·33w
Gérgal	37·07n	2·33w
Gerona	41·59n	2·49e
Getafe	40·18n	3·43w
Gibraleón	37·23n	6·58w
Gijón	43·32n	5·40w
Ginzo [de Limia]	42·03n	7·43w
Gradefes	42·37n	5·13w
Grado	43·23n	6·04w
Granada	37·13n	3·41w
Granja de Torrehermosa	38·19n	5·35w
Granollers	41·37n	2·18e
Guadalajara	40·38n	3·10w
Guadalcanal	38·06n	5·49w
Guadix	37·18n	3·08w
Guareña	38·51n	6·06w
Haro	42·35n	2·51w
Hellín	38·31n	1·41w
Herencia	39·21n	3·22w
Hervás	40·16n	5·51w
Hinojosa [del Duque]	38·30n	5·09w
Hospitalet	41·22n	2·08e
Huelma	37·39n	3·27w
Huelva	37·16n	6·57w
Huércal-Overa	37·23n	1·57w
Huesca	42·08n	0·25w
Huéscar	37·49n	2·32w
Huete	40·08n	2·41w
Ibiza	38·54n	1·26e
Igualada	41·35n	1·38e
Inca	39·43n	2·54e
Infantes	38·44n	3·01w
Infiesto	43·21n	5·22w
Irún	43·21n	1·47w
Isla-Cristina	37·12n	7·19w
Jaca	42·34n	0·33w
Jaén	37·46n	3·47w
Játiva	38·59n	0·31w
Jávea	38·47n	0·10e
Jerez de la Frontera	36·41n	6·08w
Jerez de los Caballeros	38·19n	6·46w
Jijona	38·32n	0·30w
Jódar	37·50n	3·21w
Jumilla	38·29n	1·17w
La Almunia de Doña Godina	41·29n	1·22w
La Bisbal	41·57n	3·03e
La Carolina	38·15n	3·37w
La Coruña	43·22n	8·23w
La Estrada	42·41n	8·29w
La Guardia	41·54n	8·53w
Lalín	42·39n	8·07w
La Línea	36·10n	5·19w
La Palma [del Condado]	37·23n	6·33w
La Pobla de Lillet	42·15n	1·59e
La Puebla	39·46n	3·01e
La Puebla de Montalbán	39·52n	4·21w
Laredo	43·24n	3·25w
La Robla	42·48n	5·37w
La Roda	39·13n	2·09w
La Solana	38·56n	3·14w
La Unión	37·37n	0·52w
Lebrija	36·55n	6·04w
Ledesma	41·05n	6·00w
León	42·36n	5·34w
Lepe	37·15n	7·12w
Lérida	41·37n	0·37e
Lerma	42·02n	3·45w
Linares	38·05n	3·38w
Liria	39·38n	0·36w
Llanes	43·25n	4·45w
Llerena	38·14n	6·01w
Lluchmayor	39·29n	2·54e
Lodosa	42·25n	2·05w
Logroño	42·28n	2·27w
Logrosán	39·20n	5·29w
Loja	37·10n	4·09w
Lora [del Río]	37·39n	5·32w
Lorca	37·40n	1·42w
Los Santos [de Maimona]	38·27n	6·23w
Luarca	43·32n	6·32w
Lucena	37·24n	4·29w
Lucena del Cid	40·08n	0·17w
Lugo	43·00n	7·34w
Madrid	40·24n	3·41w
Madridejos	39·28n	3·32w
Maella	41·08n	0·09e
Mahón	39·53n	4·15e
Málaga	36·43n	4·25w
Malagón	39·10n	3·51w
Manacor	39·34n	3·12e
Mancha Real	37·47n	3·37w
Manises	39·29n	0·27w
Manlleu	42·00n	2·17e
Manresa	41·44n	1·50e
Manzanares	39·00n	3·22w
Marchena	37·20n	5·24w
Marín	42·23n	8·42w
Martos	37·43n	3·58w
Mataró	41·32n	2·27e
Mazarrón	37·36n	1·19w
Medina del Campo	41·18n	4·55w
Medina de Ríoseco	41·53n	5·02w
Medina Sidonia	36·27n	5·55w
Melilla	35·19n	2·57w
Mérida	38·55n	6·20w
Miajadas	39·09n	5·54w
Mieres	43·15n	5·46w
Minas de Ríontinto	37·42n	6·35w
Miranda de Ebro	42·41n	2·57w
Moguer	37·16n	6·50w
Molina de Aragón	40·51n	1·53w
Molina de Segura	38·03n	1·12w
Mondoñedo	42·26n	7·22w
Monforte de Lemos	42·31n	7·30w
Monóvar	38·25n	0·47w
Montánchez	39·13n	6·09w
Montblanch	41·22n	1·10e
Montefrío	37·19n	4·01w
Montellano	37·00n	5·34w
Montijo	38·55n	6·37w
Montoro	38·01n	4·23w
Monzón	41·55n	0·12e
Mora	39·41n	3·46w
Mora [de Ebro]	41·05n	0·38e
Morella	40·37n	0·06w
Morón de la Frontera	37·08n	5·27w
Motril	36·45n	3·31w
Mugia	43·06n	9·13w
Mula	38·03n	1·30w
Murcia	37·59n	1·07w
Muros	42·47n	9·02w
Nava del Rey	41·20n	5·05w
Navahermosa	39·38n	4·28w
Navalmoral de la Mata	39·54n	5·32w
Nerja	36·44n	3·52w
Nogueira	42·18n	7·31w
Novelda	38·23n	0·46w
Noya	42·47n	8·53w
Ocaña	39·56n	3·31w
Oliva	38·55n	0·07w
Oliva de Jerez	38·16n	6·55w
Olivenza	38·41n	7·06w
Olot	42·11n	2·29e
Olvera	36·56n	5·16w
Onda	39·58n	0·15w
Onteniente	38·49n	0·37w
Órdenes	43·04n	8·24w
Orduña	42·59n	3·00w
Orense	42·20n	7·51w
Orihuela	38·05n	0·57w
Ortigueira	43·41n	7·51w
Osma	41·35n	3·05w
Osuna	37·14n	5·07w
Oviedo	43·22n	5·50w
Palafrogell	41·55n	3·10e
Palencia	42·01n	4·32w
Palma del Río	37·42n	5·17w
Palma de Mallorca	39·34n	2·39e
Pamplona	42·49n	1·38w
Paredes de Nava	42·09n	4·41w
Pego	38·51n	0·07w
Peñafiel	41·36n	4·07w
Peñaranda de Bracamonte	40·54n	5·12w
Peñarroya-Pueblonuevo	38·18n	5·16w
Piedrabuena	39·02n	4·10w
Piélagos	43·22n	3·57w
Pinos-Puente	37·15n	3·45w
Plasencia	40·02n	6·05w
Pola de Allande	43·16n	6·37w
Pola de Laviana	43·15n	5·34w
Pollensa	39·53n	3·01e
Ponferrada	42·33n	6·35w
Pontevedra	42·26n	8·38w
Porcuna	37·52n	4·11w
Portugalete	43·19n	3·01w
Posadas	37·48n	5·06w
Pozoblanco	38·22n	4·51w
Pravia	43·29n	6·07w
Priego [de Córdoba]	37·26n	4·11w
Puebla de Don Fadrique	37·58n	2·26w
Puenteareas	42·11n	8·30w
Puente Ceso	43·14n	8·54w

MAP INDEX (continued)

Puentedeume....43·24n 8·10w
Puente-Genil....37·23n 4·47w
Puertollano......38·41n 4·07w
Quesada..........37·51n 3·04w
Quintana de la Serena.........38·44n 5·40w
Quintanar [de la Orden].........39·34n 3·03w
Quiroga..........42·29n 7·16w
Redondela.......42·17n 8·36w
Reinosa..........43·00n 4·08w
Requena.........39·29n 1·06w
Reus..............41·09n 1·07e
Ribadavia........42·17n 8·08w
Ribadeo..........43·32n 7·02w
Ribadesella......43·28n 5·04w
Ripoll.............41·29n 2·12e
Roncesvalles....43·01n 1·19w
Ronda.............36·44n 5·10w
Roquetas.........40·49n 0·30e
Rute...............37·19n 4·22w
Sabadell..........41·33n 2·06e
Sagunto..........39·41n 0·16w
Salamanca.......40·58n 5·39w
San Antonio Abad............38·58n 1·18e
San Clemente....39·24n 2·26w
San Felíu de Guixols..........41·47n 3·02e
San Fernando....36·28n 6·12w
Sangüesa.........42·35n 1·17w
San Ildefonso....40·54n 4·00w
San Lorenzo de El Escorial......40·35n 4·09w
Sanlúcar [de Barrameda]......36·47n 6·21w
San Mateo........40·28n 0·11e
San Roque.......36·13n 5·24w
San Sebastián...43·19n 1·59w
Santa Eugenia de Ribeira.......42·33n 9·00w
Santa Eulalia del Río...........38·59n 1·31e
Santa Fé..........37·11n 3·43w
Santander.........43·28n 3·48w
Santañy...........39·22n 3·07e
Santiago [de Compostela]....42·53n 8·33w
Santisteban del Puerto...........38·15n 3·12w
Santo Domingo de la Calzada...42·26n 2·57w
Santoña...........43·27n 3·27w
San Vicente de Alcántara.......39·21n 7·08w
Saragossa, see Zaragoza
Sariñena.........41·48n 0·10w
Sarria.............42·47n 7·24w
Segorbe..........39·51n 0·29w
Segovia...........40·57n 4·07w
Sevilla (Seville)..37·23n 5·59w
Siero..............43·23n 5·40w
Sigüenza.........41·04n 2·38w
Socuéllamos.....39·17n 2·48w
Sóller.............39·46n 2·42e
Sonseca..........39·42n 3·57w
Sorbas............37·07n 2·07w
Soria..............41·46n 2·28w
Sueca.............39·12n 0·19w
Tafalla............42·31n 1·40w
Talavera de la Reina..........39·57n 4·50w
Tamarite [de Litera]...........41·52n 0·26e
Tarancón.........40·01n 3·00w
Tarazona [de Aragón]..........41·54n 1·44w
Tarazona de la Mancha.........39·15n 1·55w
Tarifa.............36·01n 5·36w
Tarragona........41·07n 1·15e
Tarrasa...........41·34n 2·01e
Tárrega...........41·39n 1·09e
Tauste............41·55n 1·15w
Teruel............40·21n 1·06w
Tobarra...........38·35n 1·41w
Toledo............39·52n 4·01w
Tolosa............43·08n 2·04w
Tomelloso........39·10n 3·01w
Toro...............41·31n 5·24w
Torrejoncillo....39·54n 6·28w
Torrelavega......43·21n 4·03w
Torrente..........39·26n 0·28w
Torre-Pacheco...37·44n 0·57w
Torrevieja........37·59n 0·41w
Tortosa...........40·48n 0·31e
Totana............37·46n 1·30w
Trasparga........43·11n 7·51w
Trigueros.........37·23n 6·50w
Trujillo............39·28n 5·53w
Tudela............42·05n 1·36w
Úbeda............38·01n 3·22w
Ubrique...........36·41n 5·27w
Utiel...............39·34n 1·12w
Utrera............37·11n 5·47w
Valdepeñas......38·46n 3·23w
Valdoviño.......43·36n 8·08w
Valencia.........39·28n 0·22w
Valencia [de Alcántara]......39·25n 7·14w
Valladolid.......41·39n 4·43w
Vall de Uxó......39·49n 0·14w
Valls..............41·17n 1·15e
Valverde del Camino.........37·34n 6·45w
Vejer [de la Frontera].......36·15n 5·58w
Vélez-Málaga...36·47n 4·06w
Vélez Rubio....37·39n 2·04w
Vera..............37·15n 1·52w
Vergara..........43·07n 2·25w
Verín.............41·56n 7·26w
Viana del Bollo...42·11n 7·06w
Vich..............41·56n 2·15e
Vigo..............42·14n 8·43w
Villablino........42·56n 6·19w
Villacañas.......39·38n 3·20w
Villacarrillo......38·07n 3·05w
Villafamés.......40·07n 0·03w
Villafranca del Bierzo.........42·36n 6·48w
Villafranca de los Barros........38·34n 6·20w
Villafranca del Panadés.......41·21n 1·42e
Villagarcía [de Arosa]........42·36n 8·45w
Villajoyosa.......38·30n 0·14w
Villalba..........43·18n 7·41w
Villalpando......41·52n 5·24w
Villamartín.......36·52n 5·38w
Villanueva de Córdoba.........38·20n 4·37w
Villanueva de la Serena.........38·58n 5·48w
Villanueva y Geltrú............41·14n 1·44e
Villarreal........39·56n 0·06w
Villarrobledo....39·16n 2·36w
Villena...........38·38n 0·51w
Vinaroz..........40·28n 0·29e
Vitoria............42·51n 2·40w
Vivero............43·38n 7·35w
Yecla.............38·37n 1·07w
Yeste.............38·22n 2·18w
Zamora...........41·30n 5·45w
Zaragoza (Saragossa).....41·38n 0·53w
Zorita............39·17n 5·42w
Zuera.............41·52n 0·47w

Physical features and points of interest

Agueda, *river*....41·02n 6·56w
Alagón, *river*....39·44n 6·53w
Alarcón, *reservoir*..........39·36n 2·10w
Alberche, *river*...39·58n 4·46w
Alborán, Isla del, *island*..........35·58n 3·02w
Alboran Sea......36·00n 4·00w
Alcanadre, *river*..41·37n 0·12w
Alcudia, Bahía de, *bay*..........39·48n 3·13e
Aldeadavila, *reservoir*........41·10n 6·40w
Algeciras, Bahía de, see Gibraltar, Bay of
Alhucemas, *island*..........35·13n 3·53w
Alicante, Bahía de, *bay*..........38·18n 0·27w
Almanzora, *river*.37·14n 1·46w
Almería, see Andorax
Almería, Golfo de *gulf*............36·46n 2·30w
Almina, Punta, *point*...........35·54n 5·17w
Almonte, *river*....39·42n 6·28w
Alpujarras, *mountains*.......36·55n 3·15w
Andalucía (Andalusia), *historic region*...37·36n 4·30w
Andarax (Almería), *river*..36·48n 2·26w
Aneto, Pico de, *peak*............42·38n 0·40e
Aquilianos, Montes, *mountains*......42·27n 6·40w
Aragon, *historic region*.........41·00n 1·00w
Aragón, *river*....42·13n 1·44w
Arga, *river*.......42·18n 1·47w
Arlanza, *river*....42·06n 4·09w
Arlanzón, *river*...42·03n 4·17w
Asturias, *historic region*..........43·20n 6·00w
Atlantic Ocean...40·00n 10·00w
Baetic Cordillera, see Penibético, Sistema
Balearic Islands (Islas Baleares).39·30n 3·00e
Balearic Sea.....40·00n 2·00e
Basque Provinces (Vascongadas), *historic region*...43·00n 2·45w
Bembezar, *river*..37·45n 5·13w
Bermeja, Sierra, *mountains*.......36·28n 5·14w
Biscay, Bay of (Baie de Biscaye).......44·00n 4·00w
Boumort, Sierra de, *mountains*...42·13n 1·07e
Brava, Costa, *coast*...........41·45n 3,04e
Buendia, *reservoir*.........40·25n 2·43w
Bullaque, *river*...38·59n 4·17w
Cabrera, *island*...39·09n 2·56e
Cabriel, *river*.....39·14n 1·03w
Cadí, Sierra de, *mountains*.......42·17n 1·42e
Cádiz, Golfo de, *gulf*............36·50n 7·10w
Cantabrian Mountains (Cordillera Cantábrica).....43·00n 5·00w
Carpetovetónica, Cordillera (Cordillera Central), *mountains*........40·30n 5·00w
Carrión, *river*....41·53n 4·32w
Castilla la Nueva, see New Castile
Castilla la Vieja, see Old Castile
Catalonia (Cataluña), *historic region*...42·00n 2·00e
Cea, *river*........42·00n 5·36w
Cebollera, Sierra, *ridge*............42·00n 2·40w
Cega, *river*.......41·33n 4·46w
Cenajo, *reservoir*.38·20n 1·50w
Central, Cordillera, see Carpetovetónica, Cordillera
Cerredo, Torre de, *mountain*....43·10n 4·58w
Chafarinas, *islands*.........35·11n 2·26w
Chanza, *river*....37·33n 7·31w
Cijara, *reservoir*..39·18n 4·52w
Cinca, *river*......41·26n 0·21e
Columbretes, *islands*.........39·52n 0·40e
Contreras, *reservoir*........39·32n 1·30w
Creus, Cabo de, *cape*...........42·19n 3·19e
Cuenca, Serranía de, *mountains*...39·55n 1·50w
Culebra, Sierra de la, *mountains*...41·54n 6·20w
Demanda, Sierra de la, *mountains*.......42·15n 3·05w
Duero, *river*......41·02n 6·56w
Duratón, *river*....41·37n 4·07w
Ebro, *river*........40·43n 0·54e
Ega, *river*.........42·19n 1·55w
Eje, Sierra del, *mountains*.......42·18n 6·54e
Eria, *river*........42·03n 5·44w
Esgueva, *river*....41·40n 4·43w
Esla, *river*........41·29n 6·03w
Extremadura, *historic region*...39·00n 6·00w
Filabres, Sierra de los, *mountains*......37·13n 2·20w
Finisterre, Cabo de, *cape*.........42·53n 9·16w
Formentera, Isla de, *island*.......38·42n 1·28e
Galicia, *historic region*.........43·00n 8·00w
Gállego, *river*....41·39n 0·51w
Gallo, *river*......40·48n 2·09w
Gata, Cabo de, *cape*............36·43n 2·12w
Gata, Sierra de, *mountains*......40·14n 6·45w
Genil, *river*.......37·42n 5·19w
Gibraltar, Bay of (Bahía de Algeciras)......36·09n 5·25w
Gibraltar, Strait of........35·57n 5·36w
Gigüela, *river*....39·08n 3·44w
Gredos, Sierra de, *mountains*......40·18n 5·05w
Guadalete, *river*..36·35n 6·13w
Guadalhorce, *river*............36·41n 4·27w
Guadalimar, *river*............37·59n 3·44w
Guadalope, *river*.41·15n 0·03w
Guadalquivir, *river*............36·47n 6·22w
Guadalupe, Sierra de, *mountains*...39·26n 5·25w
Guadarrama, Sierra de, *mountains*.......40·55n 4·00w
Guadiana, *river*...37·14n 7·22w
Guadiana Menor, *river*............37·56n 3·15w
Guadiaro, *river*...36·17n 5·17w
Guadiato, *river*...37·48n 5·04w
Guadiela, *river*...40·22n 2·49w
Guara, Sierra de, *mountains*.......42·17n 0·10w
Gudar, Sierra de, *mountains*.......40·27n 0·42w
Harana, Sierra, *mountains*.......37·20n 3·30w
Henares, *river*....40·24n 3·30w
Huebra, *river*.....41·02n 6·48w
Huerva, *river*.....41·39n 0·52w
Ibérico, Sistema (Iberian Mountains).....40·30n 5·00w
Iviza, *island*.......39·00n 1·25e
Iznajar, *reservoir*.37·15n 4·30w
Jabalón, *river*....38·53n 4·05w
Jalón, *river*.......41·47n 1·04w
Jándula, *river*....38·03n 4·06w
Jarama, *river*.....40·02n 3·39w
Jiloca, *river*......41·21n 1·39w
Jistredo, Sierra de, *mountains*...42·45n 6·25w
Júcar, *river*.......39·09n 0·14w
La Mancha, *plain*............39·05n 3·00w
La Rioja, *historic region*...42·20n 2·20w
La Sagra, *mountain*........37·57n 2·34w
Las Marismas, *marsh*...........37·00n 6·15w
Leon (León), *historic region*...42·00n 6·00w
Libar, Sierra de...36·39n 5·22w
Llobregat, *river*...41·19n 2·09e
Los Monegros, *physical region*..41·29n 0·03w
Majorca (Mallorca), *island*..........39·30n 3·00e
Maladeta, *mountains*......42·40n 1·00e
Málaga, Bahía de, *bay*.........36·42n 4·24w
María, Sierra de, *mountains*......37·39n 2·14w
Menor, Mar, *lagoon*..........37·43n 0·48w
Mediterranean Sea...........37·30n 0·30e
Mequinenza, *reservoir*........41·15n 0·05w
Meseta Central (Meseta Iberica), *plateau*..........41·00n 4·00w
Mijares, *river*....39·55n 0·01w
Miño, *river*.......42·10n 8·10w
Minorca, *island*...40·00n 4·00e
Moncayo, *mountains*......41·46n 1·50w
Morena, Sierra, *mountains*......38·00n 5·00w
Mulhacén, *peak*..37·03n 3·19w
Murcia, *historic region*............38·30n 1·45w
Nalón, *river*......43·32n 6·04w
Nao, Cabo de la, *cape*............38·44n 0·14e
Nava, Laguna de la, *lake*.........42·03n 4·39w
Navarre (Navarra), *historic region*...43·00n 1·30w
Navia, *river*......43·33n 6·44w
Nevada, Sierra, *mountains*......37·05n 3·10w
New Castile (Castilla la Nueva), *historic region*...40·00n 3·45w
Noguera Pallaresa, *river*..42·15n 0·54e
Odiel, *river*......37·10n 6·54w
Old Castile (Castilla la Vieja), *historic region*...41·30n 4·00w
Órbigo, *river*.....41·58n 5·40w
Orellana, *reservoir*........39·00n 5·30w
Ortegal, Cabo, *cape*............43·45n 7·53w
Palma, Bahía de, *bay*............39·27n 2·35e
Palos, Cabo de, *cape*............37·38n 0·41w

in the north. The Mediterranean coast appears to have been settled by North Africans, whereas the Basques probably occupied a considerably larger area than the present Basque country. Ancient Greek and Phoenician settlements were established on the eastern and southern coasts, and Carthaginians founded large colonies in the southeast (around what is now Cartagena); but only the Romans were able to conquer the entire area, subjecting it to intensive Romanization. After the fall of the Roman Empire, Suebi, Vandals, and Alani razed the country. The Suebi consolidated a small kingdom in the northwest corner of the peninsula, but the whole peninsula eventually fell to the Visigoths. The Arabs invaded the peninsula in 711 and were not driven out of Spain until as late as 1492. These eight centuries of Arab influence, together with the prolonged Roman colonization, left a permanent imprint on the Spanish population. European influences dominate over non-European influences, however, and Spain is above all a Mediterranean European country that has many similarities to neighbouring countries such as France, Italy, and Portugal.

The Roman conquest

After almost five centuries of consolidation of the Spanish state, the population has become unified racially; and, with the possible exception of the wandering Gypsies, there are no recognizable racial minorities. Somehow, the Spanish population has incorporated into its genetic pool something from each of the succeeding invaders.

Linguistic groups. *Castilian.* Modern standard Spanish, or Castilian, is spoken throughout Spain. It is basically a Romance language, with some traces of other languages spoken in Spain before and after the Roman conquest, such as Celtic and Arabic. There are, however, important linguistic minorities within Spain—in the Mediterranean regions, in Galicia, and in the Basque country. Within the Castilian-speaking areas, there are some dialects spoken in remote places, such as the Bable of Asturias. There are also minor dialectal differences in Castilian vocabulary and pronunciation in the different regions. The best Castilian is reputed to be spoken in Old Castile, especially in the provinces of Burgos and Valladolid. The language spoken in southern Spain and the Canary Islands bears similarities to the Castilian of Latin America. Regional intonation and dialectal expressions can also be identified in the Castilian spoken in Catalonia, Galicia, and the Basque country. Castilian-speaking immigrants and their descendants living in Catalonia constitute a large and relatively underprivileged minority, particularly in the metropolitan area of Barcelona.

Catalan. Catalan is a Romance language closely related to the Provençal, or Occitan, language of southern France. It is spoken by a majority of the population in Catalonia, the Balearic Islands, and Valencia. The Valencian dialect of Catalan, however, has a strong Castilian influence. Catalan is a highly developed language, with a wealth of literary tradition in the areas of poetry, the novel, and drama. A strong revival of the language in recent years resulted in the naming of Catalan and Spanish as the official languages of Catalonia in the constitution of 1978.

Galician. Modern Portuguese originated in Galician (or Gallego), a Romance language that is still spoken in the Spanish region of Galicia. During the 13th century, Galician was used by the Castilian king Alfonso X the Wise as the literary language of his court, but it later lost its importance and was widely influenced by Castilian. Galician is now rarely spoken in the cities of Galicia, although it survives in the countryside and also among the Galician fishermen. Nonetheless, a revival of literary Galician began in the late 1800s, and the constitution of 1978 recognized Galician as an official language to be taught in local schools.

Basque. The most distinctive of the non-Castilian languages is found in the Basque country. Basque is neither of Romance nor of Indo-European derivation. Its origins are uncertain, but it was spoken in the peninsula before the Romans conquered Spain. Over the centuries, the Basque-speaking area shrank, and it is now spoken mostly in the countryside, in fishing villages, and in the small towns of the Basque country and Navarre and is rarely heard in the cities. The language was a vehicle for the assertion of Basque identity in the 1960s and '70s, however, and there was a revival of the language at the popular level and among intellectual circles. Basque became a local official language in 1978.

Ethnic groups. The Spanish population is basically homogeneous in race and culture, and the only true racial minority within Spain is that of the Gypsies. While a large number of Gypsies have been integrated with the general populace, there still remain a substantial number who lead a nomadic life and who can be seen on Spain's roads and streets, driving carts, begging, or peddling. Although there are no reliable statistics, they are estimated to number a few hundred thousand. The larger Gypsy communities are to be found in the cities of Granada, Madrid, Barcelona, and Murcia. Many of them have regular jobs and send their children to public or private schools, but, in general, they are considered to be a deprived minority, who are discriminated against and unable to achieve full integration in Spanish society.

The Gypsies

Unique ethnic features have been claimed for the populations of some of the Spanish regions, such as the Basque country and Andalusia. While some differences in the style of life and cultural traditions remain, the process of assimilation of the Spanish population has gone so far for so long a time that identification of ethnic groups can now be based only on language. Some of the most extreme Basque nationalists claim that there is a definite ethnic identity for the Basques, but exchanges between the Basque country and other parts of Spain have been so intense during the last two centuries that any original ethnic purity of the Basque population should now be considered to be much diluted.

Religious groups. *Roman Catholicism.* The majority of the Spanish population is Roman Catholic. Most Spaniards are baptized, married, and buried within the church. The process of industrialization and urbanization, however, has influenced the religious habits of the Spanish population, with a marked decrease in the church's influence upon everyday life. Under the constitution of 1978, the Catholic Church is no longer recognized as the established church of the state, although it still enjoys the government's financial support.

After the death in 1975 of Gen. Francisco Franco, who had been Spain's head of state from 1936, the Catholic Church supported the new democratic regime and thereby contributed greatly to an attitude of tolerance within Spanish society in general. The problem of relations between church and state, however, remained sensitive. Traditional anti-clerical attitudes became channelled during the late 20th century into the issues of divorce, abortion, and state financial support to private schools. The church's opposition to a proposed divorce law, and the general conservatism of Spanish bishops after the election of Pope John Paul II in 1978, led to a revival of old frictions between the church and liberal politicians, which reached its climax shortly before an unsuccessful coup d'état was attempted in February 1981. The dangerous constitutional situation provoked by the attempted coup in turn led the church and the political parties to search for new formulas of compromise between religious liberalization and the maintenance of traditional church privileges. By June 1981, divorce was legalized, and state support of private schools was barely challenged.

Religious minorities. Most of the non-Catholic minority population is Protestant. Among traditional Protestant churches, the most important are the Church of the Brethren and the Evangelical Baptist Church, with a few thousand members each. Since the middle decades of the 20th century, however, other groups have grown rapidly, and the Jehovah's Witnesses have become the most important Protestant sect. The Seventh-day Adventists claim a few thousand baptized members and several thousand additional adherents, and the Mormons claim about 1,000 members.

Eastern Orthodox and non-Christian groups are small. Among the non-Christians, the Jewish community is the most important.

Birth and mortality. The birth rate is about equal to the European average but is less than the figure for most developing countries. The long-range trend of the birth rate has been one of decline, especially since the mid-20th century, with a marked preference for small families. The natural rate of growth varies throughout the country, however, with the higher rates in the Canary Islands, Andalusia, Murcia, and the Basque country. The lowest birth rates are found in the plateau, especially in Old and New Castile.

Immigration and emigration. The traditional Spanish pattern of emigration to Latin America ended after the Spanish Civil War and World War II. During the 1950s and '60s, hundreds of thousands of Spaniards moved to western Europe, taking advantage of the economic boom. In the late 1970s, however, most of these emigrants returned to Spain, while western Europeans and Latin Americans settled in Spain, some temporarily, others permanently. Spain has granted asylum to many Latin-American political refugees. There are a few hundred thousand official foreign residents in Spain, and many others live in Spain without an official residence permit. Spaniards working in western Europe are estimated at between 250,000 and 500,000.

Internal migration

Internal migration became particularly important after the Civil War, showing the familiar industrial pattern of movement from the countryside to the cities. This has caused most Spanish cities to triple their population since the mid-1930s, whereas the population as a whole has grown by only 50 percent. Many small villages, especially those in the central plateau, became almost uninhabited and in a few cases were completely deserted. The main centres of attraction for internal migration were the cities of Madrid and Barcelona. Madrid attracted immigrants who had lived mostly in the centre and the northwest, while Barcelona drew its migrants from the east and the south. Other large cities, such as Bilbao, Valencia, Zaragoza, and Seville, also attracted large numbers of immigrants, as did most provincial capitals. The development of tourism drew migrants to the resort areas of the Costa Brava (Catalonia), Costa del Sol (Andalusia), the southeast (Alicante), and the Balearic and Canary islands. The economic slump of the late 20th century, however, brought internal migration to a halt, and in some cases the trend was reversed, with migrants returning to their places of origin in the countryside. The escalation of violence in the separatist movement pushed many non-Basques out of the Basque country.

Uneven population distribution

Distribution of the population. About two-thirds of the population of Spain is found in the coastal regions, while only about one-third inhabits the plateau and the valley of the Ebro, which are regions that account for more than half of the national territory. Thus, the distribution of the population is not evenly spread throughout the country. The coastal regions of the Basque country, Galicia, Catalonia, Valencia, and the Balearic and Canary islands have population densities that approach those of industrial western Europe, while the northern plateau, Navarre, and Aragón are almost deserted compared to western European standards. One-third of the inland population is concentrated in Madrid, accentuating the semi-deserted character of the central areas. The population within the coastal regions is more evenly distributed, although a substantial proportion is concentrated in the metropolitan area of Barcelona. Among the coastal regions only some areas of eastern Andalusia and Murcia approach the low densities of the plateau.

Most of Spain's population now inhabits cities with populations of 10,000 or more. Within the larger metropolitan areas, most people live in high-rise apartments in the cores of the cities, but suburbs developed during the 1960s and '70s, especially within the metropolitan districts of Madrid, Barcelona, and Bilbao.

General considerations. Because of its open spaces and moderately decreasing birth rate, Spain is not facing a population explosion. Industrialization and urbanization, however, have caused overpopulation and economic imbalance in Madrid, Barcelona, Bilbao, and other industrial areas, where pollution has become acute. The contamination of Spain's rivers and coastal waters threatens the nation's freshwater supplies and fish resources. A peculiar problem is posed by the massive influx of more than 30,000,000 tourists a year, especially during the summer months when the space available to Spaniards for recreation is reduced and public utilities are used to capacity. A decrease in tourism in the late 1970s and early '80s, and the consequent reduction in foreign currency revenues, led the government to develop new programs to improve the quality of life and to preserve natural resources in urban and industrial developments.

The Spanish economy was hard hit by the worldwide economic crisis of the 1970s. The crisis affected all aspects of Spanish life, including population growth, industrialization, and urbanization. The most immediate effect was a reduction in the exponential growth of production, which entailed a slowdown in industrial growth and an increase of the urban population.

The economic crisis appeared to have affected the growth of the population as well. The cumulative effects of inflation and unemployment, which were coupled with more permissive rules regarding contraception and a number of changes in social attitudes, led to a decrease in the birth rate. The increase of life expectancy, combined with the reduction of the birth rate, is expected to change Spain's demographic pyramid, bringing it more in line with those of other European countries; *i.e.,* a pyramid marked by a larger number of older people than younger people.

(M.Me.)

THE ECONOMY

In the 1960s and early 1970s Spain had one of the fastest growing economies in Europe and was in the process of transformation from an underdeveloped to a developed country. By the end of the 1970s, the country's gross national product per capita was almost as high as that of Italy. Since about the mid-1950s, when Spain emerged from a period of economic and political isolation, its development, especially in trade with other countries, has been notable. In 1958 it joined the International Monetary Fund, in 1959 the Organization for European Economic Cooperation (now the Organisation for Economic Co-operation and Development, or OECD), and in 1963 the General Agreement on Tariffs and Trade. Spain became an associate member of the European Economic Community (EEC) in 1970 and applied for full membership in the EEC in 1977. Despite this rapid growth, Spain still needs increasing industrial investment and modernization of equipment.

Coal mining

Resources. Spain has one of western Europe's largest coal-mining industries. Pits are situated chiefly in Asturias, but there are also some in the lower hills of the Sierra

Morena. Coal imports are mainly of coking coal, although the import of steam-raising coal is increasing. In the mid-1960s a radical reorganization of the industry was begun; uneconomic pits were closed, while investment was diverted to those having the greatest potential.

Discoveries of petroleum have so far proved disappointing, and the potential for commercial production from two natural gas fields—one in the Gulf of Cádiz and one at Jaca—is uncertain. The originally rich veins of hematite (rubious iron ore) of Bilbao are now nearly worked out, but Spain is relatively rich in other minerals, most of which are exported. Mercury is obtained from the ancient mines of Almadén in Ciudad Real, and there is also a good supply of tungsten, lead, zinc, potash, pyrites, and some uranium oxides.

Although Spain is a mountainous country in which, it might be thought, considerable hydroelectric power could be produced, the relatively low rainfall restricts capacity, and all profitable hydroelectric potential had been developed by the late 20th century. Spain is heavily dependent on imported petroleum.

Agriculture, forestry, and fishing. Although Spain is one of western Europe's largest agricultural producers, the barrenness of much of the countryside has always made agriculture and cattle rearing difficult. With the recent rapid increase of the manufacturing industry, it is not surprising that the proportion of national income provided by agriculture has steadily declined. Yet, despite the relative decline, agriculture has maintained a small real growth rate, the more notable in that the proportion of agricultural labourers is constantly diminishing.

The two main problems confronting Spanish agriculture are social and environmental; these involve, respectively, the *latifundia*, large estates owned by absentee landlords, and the still more intractable difficulty springing from the uncertain climatic conditions and the general infertility of the land. The *latifundia* are mainly in the south, in Extremadura and Andalusia, and although some attempt at division of them was begun in 1939, progress has not been great. More success has been achieved, however, in the amalgamation of small holdings into viable farm units.

Uncertain rainfall has a serious effect on crops, and land is mostly poor, with widespread soil erosion as a result of years of overtilling and overgrazing. Frost is frequently a formidable threat to the Valencian orange crop. With periodic widespread drought, irrigation has been an obvious necessity, and the earliest large canals and dams for this purpose, such as the Canal Imperial de Aragón on the Ebro, were built in the 18th century. Major irrigation projects have been carried out in the 20th century.

Barley and wheat are the two most important cereal crops in terms of land use and production. Despite government incentives for greater domestic production of corn (maize) and oil seeds, these are still imported in substantial quantities. Barley is grown in the southeast, while the wheat-producing areas are mainly in Old Castile, Aragón, New Castile, and Extremadura. The cereal lands, those which are less well irrigated, are farmed according to traditional practice, with a two-year rotation of crops. Pulses are a staple crop of the Meseta, while rice is grown in Valencia and the Ebro Delta. Potatoes, beans, and onions are also produced.

Spain's most successful adaptation to its difficult Mediterranean climate has been in citrus fruit production. Citrus fruit is grown mainly in Valencia and Castellón. Other areas specialize in other fruits; apples and pears are grown in the north and northwest, figs and almonds in Castellón and Alicante, and peaches and apricots in Murcia. The main crop of the *latifundia* is olives, almost the whole yield of which is made into oil. Grapes are grown especially in La Mancha, La Rioja, and the hills of Catalonia, Valencia, and Málaga. As the third largest wine-producing country in Europe, Spain has suffered from an overproduction of inferior wines. Brandy and sherry from Cádiz and Jerez de la Frontera and dessert wines from Valencia and Málaga remain in demand. Hemp, cotton, and tobacco are also grown, in comparatively small quantities.

Citrus fruit and wine production

Sheep and cattle rearing is very important, and Spain has one of Europe's largest sheep and goat populations. More than half the cattle are concentrated in the humid north, especially dairy cows in the Cordillera Cantábrica. Sheep, concentrated on the Meseta, are of three main breeds: the long-wooled churro, the short-wooled merino, and the manchegan. Goats are best suited to the arid conditions of the southeast, and pigs are reared in the Holm-oak woodlands of Extremadura.

Sheep, goats, and cattle

Some afforestation is practiced to counter soil erosion. Fishing is concentrated mainly on the northern and western Atlantic coasts and is particularly important in Galicia, where Vigo is the main fishing port. The catch comprises mainly sardines, anchovies, hake, cod, tunny, bream, mollusks, and crustaceans.

Industry. Although historical inertia and traditionalism long hampered the development of Spanish industry, the country's industrial growth rate since the mid-1950s has been one of the fastest in the world, and, in the late 20th century industry and construction contributed more than one-third of the total national output. Some manufacturing industries are long established and are supported by protectionist policies. The historical regional location of light industries still pertains: Manises, in Valencia province, is a centre for ceramic works; paper has been manufactured since Moorish times at Játiva, in the same province; Béjar, Segovia, Soria, and Burgos have long been woollen centres; and cotton manufactures are concentrated around Barcelona. Other light industries include a variety of textiles, clothing and footwear, food processing, liqueurs and wine, and light engineering. Chemical industries include the production of nitrogen fertilizers. During the late 20th century, massive investment was made in newer, high-technology industries.

Industrial growth

Heavy industries are largely centred in the north, where metallurgical works are found in Santander and the Basque country. Bilbao has been a steel centre since the Middle Ages. Madrid has engineering and metalworks, in addition to a range of light industry. One of the most successful and competitive of Spain's heavy industries in the 1960s and early 1970s was shipbuilding. As in other countries, shipbuilding was adversely affected by the recession of the mid-1970s, but a restructuring of that industry, and of the steel and textile industries, was undertaken.

Financial services. The central bank is the Banco de España, in the profits of which the government has participated since 1922. Many dealings of the commercial and savings banks are government regulated, although there has been some loosening of controls. The majority of corporate borrowers, both public and private, have recourse either to these banks or to the state-owned holding corporation created in 1941, the Instituto Nacional de Industria (INI). Largely because the public prefers to keep its savings on deposit rather than invest in securities, the banks control a large part of the issued capital of Spanish limited-liability companies. A considerable amount of private investment is also financed from abroad, and the Spanish stock market has thus remained relatively undeveloped. The most important sources are the United States, West Germany, Switzerland, the United Kingdom, and France. The most important sectors of the economy thus affected have been chemicals, the automobile industry, and real estate.

Trade. Importing considerably more than it exports, Spain has traditionally had a visible trade deficit. The deficits have been attributed to Spain's dependence on crude-oil imports for energy requirements. Trade is most frequent with member countries of the EEC, the United States, and Saudi Arabia. There is also some trade with Latin America. Food and agricultural exports, mainly citrus fruit, wines, fish products, and olive oil, account for about one-fifth of the total bulk of exports. Raw materials exported are mainly iron ores and pyrites, while cotton goods, textiles, and clothing also have a steady market. Engineering and heavy industrial exports, such as ships, automobiles, and electrical goods, are increasingly important. Some agricultural products have to be imported, notably cereals, animal products, and vegetable oils. Spain also imports raw cotton as well as textile products; petroleum and its products account for about one-third of the cost of imports. Engineering goods are also brought in.

Spain's rapid growth in the 1960s and early 1970s was made possible because imports were allowed to outstrip exports so greatly. The resultant gap was mainly financed in two striking ways. First, in the mid-1960s Spain became one of the world's most popular centres of tourism. Secondly, until the rise of unemployment in Europe began in 1973, Spain exported labour to other European countries, and workers' remittances sent home contributed substantially to the country's balance of payments.

Administration of the economy. *Private enterprise and the role of government.* Government influence over the economy is very strong in Spain. A large number of concerns are state-owned, including the railways, telephone services, and radio and television. The state also has large holdings of ordinary shares in a wide range of industrial companies, mostly through the medium of the INI. This corporation, run by the Ministry of Industry, owns wholly or in part some companies representing all facets of the industrial economy. In some industries, such as coal, basic steel, petroleum and petrochemicals, and automobile manufacture, INI's participation in individual firms has exerted an influence on the development of the sector as a whole.

Taxation and public spending. The collection of revenue by means of taxation was one of the least efficient features of the Spanish economy in the 1960s. Although incomes rose rapidly during the period, central government tax revenue did not rise proportionately. Legislation was introduced to enlarge the tax base and to improve the efficiency of collection. This led to a wholesale revision of the taxation structure.

Tax revision

Industrial development in the middle and late 20th century was stimulated by central government subsidies to certain designated regional development areas and by tax and other subsidies to favoured sectors of the economy, such as mining and automobile manufacturing. Social, health, and educational services were neglected until the late 1970s, when central government expenditure in these areas was substantially increased.

Trade unions and employers' associations. Spain's trade-union structure, the syndicalist system, was an integral feature of the country's political development since the end of the Civil War. Broadly speaking, most organized economic concerns, comprising mainly the manufacturing and service industries and a substantial section of agriculture, were covered by "syndicates." In theory, these syndicates represented simultaneously the interests of employers, workers, and the state, and their formal structure reflected the Fascist preoccupations of the 1930s and 1940s.

Early in 1971 the Spanish Parliament approved a new, government-sponsored basic law for trade-union activities. Although the vertical and comprehensive structure of the syndicates was retained—under the control of a Cabinet minister, the minister for syndical relations—the new law allowed management, technicians, and workers to set up independent associations. Workers could hold meetings and would be able to appeal in the courts against certain types of government decisions. But even in its new form, Spanish industrial and trade-union organization was still far from even approximating that of the countries of the European Economic Community.

The trade unions

In 1977, independent trade unions were legally recognized, and by 1981 there were three main trade unions—the Confederación Sindical de Comisiones Obreras, which has connections with the Communist Party; the Unión General de Trabajadores de España, which is linked with the major Socialist party; and the Unión Sindical Obrera. After 1977, labour legislation provided the basis for a new framework for labour relations and in 1980 a Workers Statute was enacted that covered a variety of labour issues.

Contemporary economic policies. From the late 1950s a group that came to be known as the technocrats tried to modernize and internationalize the Spanish economy. The convictions underlying their policies were that adjustment would be easier and more successful in the context of rapid, overall growth and that this would be stimulated by encouraging competition. The technocrats, whose power base was originally in the planning departments, were so successful that it became fashionable to believe that they had effective control of the economy, but their appearance of success stemmed partly from the fact that the overall performance of the economy was at that time reasonably satisfactory. Their influence on individual sections of the economy was often apparent rather than real, and their successful manipulation of overall policy did not mean that they had managed to reform particular monetary institutions and practices. They failed adequately to effect the reduction or elimination of subsidies, and particular business decisions remained subjected to far greater government regulation in Spain than in other Western industrialized economies.

Government economic policy statements have increasingly emphasized the need for lessening government intervention in the economy. Some progress in that direction was made. Industrial planning, for example, became subject to fewer regulations, and the number of prices controlled by the government was made much smaller than it had been. Greater liberalization of the financial system was also envisaged; in 1978, legislation was passed allowing foreign banks to operate in Spain, and, in 1981, banks were permitted to set their own interest rates on most credits.

In common with other European countries, Spain has had to contend with recession, inflation, unemployment, and balance of payments. Priority was initially given to curbing the rate of inflation. With unemployment figures very high, however, the government placed far greater emphasis on the need for incentives and investment that would result in the creation of more jobs.

(E.I.U.)

Transportation. The first system of communications established on the Iberian Peninsula dates back to Roman times, and traces of the extensive Roman road network still remain. A new system of highways was not built until the 18th century, during the reign of the first Bourbon kings. Since their capital, Madrid, was situated in the heart of the country, the new system took the form of radial highways extending to the periphery of the peninsula. During the 19th century and into the 20th, efforts were made to consolidate the system of public works. The maintenance and improvement of highways has been one of the chief features of successive plans for economic and social development that have been undertaken.

The Roman heritage

Roads. Of the national highway network, several thousand miles are classified as basic and complementary highways, and the remaining highways are regional. Additional public roads include municipal roads, rural roads, forestry roads, and roads leading to industrial and other projects.

The Red de Itinerarios Asfálticos (Redia; Network of Asphalt-Paved Roads) program was approved in 1967. Under this plan several thousand miles of frequently travelled state highways were given a coating of asphalt over coal brick and were widened for at least two lanes of traffic. In the late 20th century, the plan was expanded to include all basic highways. Construction of a motorway (expressway) network was initiated in 1967 to build several thousand miles of modern roadways.

The Redia program

Spain's highways carry some of the heaviest traffic in the world. Traffic congestion is especially critical along the coasts. The autonomous regions of Spain were granted the authority to manage the roads within their boundaries, the national government reserving control over certain national network roads.

Railroads. Spain was only the ninth European nation to undertake the construction of railroads, beginning with the lines between Barcelona and Mataró (1848) and between Madrid and Aranjuez (1851). During the second half of the 19th century, the national railroad system was gradually expanded, with Madrid as its centre. The legal arrangement under which the Spanish railroads operated was one of indirect government ownership, whereby the state granted concessions to private companies or individuals for the construction and management of the railroads during a 99-year period, after which the railroads with all their installations and rolling stock would become the perpetual property of the state. This arrangement was radically changed in 1941 by the passage of the law that established the Red Nacional de los Ferrocarriles Españoles (Renfe; National Network of Spanish Railroads). The Civil War of 1936–39 had done considerable damage to the railroads, and it was said that only the takeover of operations by the state could save them from economic disaster. The greater part of the rolling stock belonging to the railroads consisted of outmoded equipment. In 1964 a major long-term modernization plan was initiated. Outstanding among the new equipment introduced were the Talgo and the Talgo Pendular, light trains of Spanish design. The Renfe lines total several thousand miles of track, a substantial proportion of which is electrified. Madrid, Barcelona, and Seville have metropolitan subway networks.

Ports and maritime transportation. Spain's narrow and mountainous isthmus makes the country almost an island in terms of international trade, with the overwhelming majority of the country's imports and exports being carried by sea. Although the domestic transport of goods is done mainly by land, international trade is carried on by sea. Spain's merchant marine (not including the fishing fleet) was 13th in the world in total tonnage in 1980.

Spain's maritime traffic includes that of the fishing fleet, scheduled and unscheduled coastal shipping, the "Sovereignty Lines," and international lines that carry passengers and cargo. Before 1977, the "Sovereignty Lines" were national shipping concerns that provided coastal shipping, under government concessions, between the peninsula and the Balearic and Canary islands and the provinces of Ceuta and Melilla. The Transmediterranean Corporation had been granted an exclusive concession in 1922, but because of its need for heavy government subsidies despite the poor service given, the corporation was placed under government management and in 1977 became public property under the management of the National Institute of Industry. The most important international passenger and cargo lines are those that operate between Spain and Central and South America and the United States.

Spain's ports

Spain has many major ports that carry on a well-developed and coordinated regional maritime trade. The most important ports are those of Bilbao, Tarragona, Barcelona, Santa Cruz de Tenerife, Algeciras, Cartagena, Gijón, Las Palmas, Valencia, Huelva, Málaga, and Coruña. There are numerous smaller ports that carry on a large coastal trade in the peninsula and the islands. They are an important factor in Spain's socioeconomic structure, providing facilities for fishing, passenger transport, and aquatic sports.

The four autonomous ports of Barcelona, Bilbao, Huelva, and Valencia are run independently except for planning and finance. The other major ports are managed by autonomous government councils with more limited powers. The smaller ports are grouped into 20 administrative units. The coordination of the port system in Spain is the responsibility of the Dirección General de Puertos y Costas (General Administration of Ports and Coasts) of the Ministry of Public Works and Urbanism. Port facilities are financed by anchorage charges and government financing.

Air transport. The two national airlines of Spain, Iberia and Aviaco, are stock companies of which the National Institute of Industry holds the majority of shares. Several other airlines, which conduct unscheduled flights between cities, have tended in the late 20th century toward the creation of regional passenger and cargo services. Iberia, the company that best represents the country, employs many thousands of persons; its fleet of airplanes includes propeller planes used for small airports and short flights and jet aircraft.

Spain has many civil airports and military air bases that are open to civil aviation. International services are available at the majority of the civil airports and at the Reus military air base. Among the newest airports are the Foronda airport in Vitoria, serving the provinces of Navarra, Burgos, and Logroño, and the Queen Sofia airport in Tenerife-Sur. The Foronda airport functions as a regional airport, receiving all the air traffic of the region and channelling it to the others. The Madrid airport handles the greatest percentage of the total volume of passenger traffic; Palma de Mallorca is second, and Barcelona is third.

ADMINISTRATIVE AND SOCIAL CONDITIONS

Between 1938 and 1978, Spain had what was characterized as an open constitutional system in which a series of Fundamental Laws regulated all matters traditionally included in national constitutions. The Fundamental Laws were replaced by a new constitution that came into effect on December 29, 1978. The new document describes Spain's political system as a constitutional monarchy based on democracy, a respect for law, and a mercantile economy. The historical tension in Spain between a centralized government and regional autonomy was addressed by the constitution, which recognizes both the "indissoluble unity of the Spanish nation" and "the right to self-government of the nationalities and regions of which it is composed and solidarity among them all."

Government. *The Crown.* The king is the head of state and the highest representative of the government in international affairs. Among his domestic powers, he may ratify and promote new laws, summon or dissolve the legislature, call for general elections or referendums, propose candidates for the office of president of the government (prime minister), appoint or dismiss the president, and appoint or dismiss members of the Cabinet. The king is also the head of the armed forces; he has the power to declare war and to sign peace treaties.

The Cortes. The bicameral legislature of Spain, called the Cortes Generales, represents the Spanish people and guards their sovereignty. It is comprised of two houses—the Congress of Deputies, or Lower Chamber (Cámara Baja), and the Senate, or Upper Chamber (Cámara Alta). The members of the Congress are elected every four years by universal suffrage in provincial elections. The Senate is composed of four members from each of Spain's autonomous communities and insular provinces; they are also elected every four years.

Powers of the legislature

Both houses, the members of which have parliamentary inviolability and immunity, have the power of legislative initiative, which they share with the executive branch, the assemblies of the autonomous communities, and the people (a popular initiative requiring 500,000 signatures). The Congress, however, has the greatest legislative power. The period of time during which a bill initiated in the Congress can be modified by the Senate is limited to two months, or 20 days in case of emergency. Should the Congress not approve changes called for by the Senate, the bill, as written in the Congress, may be approved and promulgated by the king. Bills proposed by the Senate are sent to the Congress for the usual debate.

The Cortes must approve any international treaty, any law regarding personal rights, and any repeal or reform of any internal law. Either chamber may ask the executive branch for information or help and may demand that members of the executive branch attend their meetings and answer their questions.

The executive branch. The executive branch consists of the president, the vice presidents, and the heads of the various ministries. Through the exercise of its executive and regulatory powers, the executive branch directs international and national policies, civil and military administration, and the defense of the nation.

The presidency

A candidate for the presidency, usually put forth by the majority party in the Cortes, is proposed to the Cortes by the king. After receiving the approval of the Congress, he is named to the presidency by the king. The president and the members of his cabinet are responsible to the Congress and to the Supreme Court.

Members of the executive branch, though not necessarily part of the legislature, have access to meetings of the Cortes and its committees. The executive branch may ask Congress for a vote of confidence, which is granted by a simple majority vote. A motion of censure, requiring an absolute majority vote, results in the downfall of the government and the automatic appointment of the presidential candidate mentioned in the motion. The president may dissolve the Cortes and call for elections if a motion to censure his government is not pending.

Individual rights and liberties. The acknowledgement and protection of individual rights and liberties are as important to the definition of a state as a division of power and the principle that all power comes from the people. The Spanish constitution of 1978 recognizes these rights and freedoms, incorporating them into the law and providing channels for their guarantee and protection. The rights recognized include those to equality before the law, to life, to religious and ideological freedom, to personal freedom, to privacy, to the inviolability of a person's home, to freedom of residence and of movement, and to freedom of expression and education. They also include the freedom to meet and participate in associations, strikes, and petitions and the right to own property and to attain a good quality of life.

During a state of emergency, the government may suspend certain rights and liberties for a period of 30 to 60 days in all or part of the country. During a state of siege, the period of suspension is to be determined by the Congress. This suspension of rights does not decrease the government's political or legal responsibility for acts committed by its agents during normal or abnormal circumstances.

Autonomous communities. In the late 1970s and early 1980s Spain was in the process of developing a new system of local government. Under Title VIII of the constitution of 1978, "bordering provinces with common historic, cultural, and economic characteristics" may group together in autonomous communities. Each of these communities is to be given the power to govern itself, but this power must not violate the interests of Spain as a whole. The constitution allows for variation within the autonomous communities in accordance with a particular region's historical relationship with the central government. The central government, however, regulates the amount of autonomy to be granted to any particular community.

The granting of autonomous status

Autonomous status is granted following negotiations between the central government and the future community. These negotiations are initiated by the administrations of the provinces that will eventually comprise the new community. Two-thirds of the municipalities within the provinces, representing the majority of the population concerned, must agree to seek autonomous status. During the transition period, all levels of administrative and legislative action are maintained by the central government. By 1984, autonomous status had been granted to 17 "autonomous communities."

The provinces. The old provincial unit of local government, first introduced into Spain in 1883, was defined by the constitution of 1978 as a grouping of municipalities for the purpose of carrying out central government programs. Within each province is a Provincial Delegation of 24 to 51 members; the membership of a delegation is elected from among that province's municipal officials.

The municipalities. A municipality is a unit of local government, the autonomy and local jurisdiction of which are guaranteed by the constitution of 1978. Each municipality is governed by a municipal council, the members of which are elected by universal, direct suffrage by the inhabitants of the municipality. The municipal council elects a mayor, who is president of the council and chief administrator of the municipality, as well as the representative of the central government.

Large cities, such as Madrid and Barcelona, have special municipal governments in which the administrative and fiscal systems are strengthened, thereby making possible the administration and execution of such matters as urban planning.

The political process. Democratic plurality and universal suffrage are guaranteed in the constitution of 1978. The mosaic of peoples that makes up Spain is the basis for decentralized political participation, or autonomy.

Political parties are described in the constitution as expressing political pluralism, contributing to the formation and manifestation of the will of the people, and serving as the fundamental instrument of political participation.

Four major political parties

There were four major political parties in Spain in the early 1980s. The Unión de Centro Democrático (Democratic Centre Union; UCD), led by Adolfo Suárez, was a moderate coalition that took the parliamentary majority in the Cortes in 1977 and 1979. The Partido Socialista Obrero Español (Socialist Workers Party of Spain; PSOE), led by Felipe González, was the successor of the Partido Socialista (Socialist Party), founded by Pablo Iglesias 100 years ago; after the elections of 1977, it absorbed the Partido Socialista Popular (Popular Socialist Party), led by Tierno Galván. The PSOE was the opposition party until 1982, upholding the concept of socialist reform within the democratic framework. In the 1982 national elections the PSOE won a solid majority in the Cortes Generales and 46 percent of the popular vote, becoming the party in power. The Partido Comunista de España (Communist Party of Spain; PCE), led by Santiago Carrillo, was founded in 1921. Since 1968, it has moved away from the Soviet Union and attached itself to the concept of Eurocommunism. The Coalición Democrática (Democratic Coalition; CD), led by Manuel Fraga Iribarne, is basically a successor of the Alianza Popular; it was the most important conservative force in the 1977 election, representing the traditional right.

In addition to the countrywide parties, there are local nationalist parties in the autonomous communities of the Basque country, Catalonia, and Andalusia.

Justice. Spanish judicial structures alone possess the faculty of passing judgment and applying laws. Justice comes from the people and is administered in the name of the king through judges and magistrates who together form the independent judiciary.

The Supreme Court, with jurisdiction over the entire country, is the final arbiter in every question of justice except for matters relating to the constitution, which are referred to the Constitutional Tribunal. The president of the Supreme Court is proposed by the Consejo General del Poder Judicial (General Council of Judicial Power) and named by the king. The Supreme Court is comprised of six courts: the civil court, the penal court, three courts for administrative litigation, and one court for social and labour issues.

The National High Court, also with jurisdiction over the entire nation, is supplemental to the Supreme Court and the Territorial High Courts. It consists of tribunals for criminal matters and for administrative litigation.

The Supreme Courts of the autonomous communities, in which the local High Courts are integrated, are the highest courts within their communities. Their jurisdiction is subordinate to that of the national Supreme Court.

The Territorial High Courts are located in the country's 15 juridical districts. Each high court has a criminal and a civil tribunal, as do each of the Provincial High Courts.

There are more than 500 petty courts (*juzgados*) throughout Spain. Although some of them have separate criminal and civil jurisdictions, most have powers in both areas of the law. District courts hear civil and criminal cases in one or more municipalities; they are also responsible for the Civil Registry, which keeps a record of the civil status of local citizens. There are also courts for labour disputes and for juveniles.

Armed forces. The military forces of Spain include the army, the navy, and the air force, with reservists in each branch. The king is the commander in chief of the military forces; the president, in conjunction with the National Defense Board, is the national leader in times of war. The military forces are part of the Ministry of Defense, which formulates and executes national military policy. The supreme command of all the military forces includes the chiefs of staff of the army, navy, and air force; it is responsible for the regular maintenance and care of the armed forces.

Military service is compulsory for all Spanish males, except for those exempt by law. The length of service is between 15 and 18 months.

The national police corps is structurally and organizationally a military body. It is not part of the military forces, however, but is responsible to the Ministry of the Interior. It is charged with the prevention and repression of criminal acts committed in cities and other important urban areas. The civil guard (Guardia Civil), founded in 1844, is one of the oldest and most typical of Spain's police forces. It is part of the military forces, but in times of peace it is also responsible to the Ministry of the Interior. It is responsible for enforcing regulations regarding arms and explosives; for guarding Spain's ports, airports, coastline, frontiers, and prisons; and for maintaining civil order in times of natural disaster. (I.C.L.)

Education. The Spanish educational system, based on the General Law for Education (1970), is divided into the following units: preschool education; general basic education; *bachillerato* (see below); university education; professional training; and continuing education for adults. All these types of education are given in both public and private institutions.

The General Law for Education

The General Law for Education, which was directed toward a complete reform of the educational system, is being put into effect gradually and is expected to be fully in force by the 1990s. Associated reforms include free and obligatory basic general education for eight years; removal of rural–urban differentials in educational opportunity; equal access to the university; and university autonomy and the creation of new universities. Aid to students is also to be given in a broad variety of scholarships, loans, and other subsidies.

Preschool education. Preschool education comprises games, language activities, observation of nature, and similar activities. It is not compulsory and is divided into two stages—nursery schools for children between two and three years of age and for those between four and five.

General basic education. Designed for children between six and 13 years of age, general basic education is divided into two stages: in the first (for children between six and 10), the studies are of a general nature; in the second (for children from 11 to 13), subjects are divided into areas of knowledge and taught by specialized teachers. In both public and nonpublic institutions, general basic education is obligatory and without charge. Upon the successful completion of this program of studies, the pupils receive a diploma that allows them to go on to the *bachillerato* program. Those who do not qualify for that program receive a certificate for entrance into the first level of professional training.

The bachillerato. The *bachillerato* program of studies, which follows the general basic education program, covers a three-year period for pupils between 14 and 16. The curriculum includes required subjects and numerous electives. The title of *bachiller* enables the student to enter second-level professional schools or the pre-university course required before admission to the university proper.

The *bachiller* and entry to higher education

University and professional education. University education is preceded by an orientation course that lasts for one year and that is open to those who hold the *bachillerato* or who have completed their second-level professional studies. The course is planned and directed by the university but is taught in schools that offer the *bachillerato* or professional training.

University education proper may be undertaken in the universities or in advanced technical education schools. In the latter case, there are three cycles or programs of study: a first devoted to basic disciplines over a three-year period; a second, of specialization, which lasts for two years; and a third, of specialization and preparation for research and teaching.

Students who have completed their studies in a university or in the first cycle of an advanced technical school obtain the diploma that enables them to work in their field of competency. Those who complete studies through the second cycle receive the degree of licentiate (*licenciado*), engineer, or architect, allowing them to practice professionally or to continue their studies in the third cycle. The completion of studies in the third cycle, together with the writing and approval of a thesis, leads to the degree of doctor in the field of specialization.

In the late 20th century, Spain had many public universities, of which three were autonomous, and four private universities.

Other institutions. A variety of other educational institutions also exist in Spain. These include schools of fine arts, applied arts, and artistic crafts; the music conservatories; the schools of language; and the Institute for Teachers of Physical Education. "Labour universities" offer general, *bachillerato,* and technical education to the children of low-income workers. (E.L.O.M./I.C.L.)

Health and welfare. *Housing.* The administration of housing policy is carried out through the ministry for public works and town planning. Until 1976, government housing policy was aimed at the indiscriminate construction of large numbers of residential units to meet the needs of population growth. This policy led to much abuse and failed to take into account the economic capacity of the population.

Since 1976, government housing policy has been defined in programs that consider local housing needs and purchasing power. Legal measures have been taken to avoid abuses and to ensure that low-income housing is provided where needed. The government asserts pressure on private builders to ensure that public housing guidelines are followed.

Health and social security. Public health services are administered by the ministry of health and social security, the provincial delegations, and local administrative units. The government provides direct health services through health centres, general hospitals, surgical units, maternity centres, children's hospitals, and psychiatric units. In addition to the government health centres, there were several hundred private hospitals, church-run hospitals, Red Cross hospitals, and other health units.

Social security

The social security system protects everyone who works in any form of organized profession or trade, including commercial or industrial workers and those in special sectors such as agriculture, fishing, railroads, or mining. It does not include self-employed professionals.

Health assistance includes maternity and sickness benefits, hospital and medical cost assistance, and medicines that are free or provided at reduced cost. Financial assistance is provided for temporary disability, retirement, death, or unemployment and for economic protection of the family. Financial benefits and social services are provided by the National Institute of Social Security, the National Institute of Health, and the National Institute of Social Services. Social security is financed by workers' contributions, employer participation, and government contributions, the employers and the government providing the majority of the total cost.

Social conditions. The standard of living in Spain greatly increased in the middle and late 20th century, when the economy was centralized and wages were regulated by the Law of Collective Agreements of 1958. In that period, collective bargaining was based on compulsory unionization, with all managers and workers belonging to unions within the Trade Union Organization (Organización Sindical).

Since 1977, Spanish economic structures have greatly changed. The system of "vertical unionism" has been replaced by independent unions that now bear the brunt of salary negotiations, and the decentralization of the economy has begun. These structural economic changes, together with the world energy crisis and high rates of inflation and unemployment since the mid-1970s, have accentuated a sense of insecurity associated with the political changes. It was believed, however, that as democratization is consolidated the Spanish population will gain confidence and the economic situation will improve.

Weakening of social differences

Spain's social class structure has also undergone profound change since the mid-20th century. The great advances in industrialization and the increase in personal income and government-supplied social services produced a vertical growth in the country's social strata and an expansion of the so-called middle class. Differences between the rural and urban populations were reduced, further weakening the old class structure. Spanish society has invested a great deal in the creation and accumulation of human capital that, it is believed, will result in greater social equality. (I.C.L.)

CULTURAL LIFE

The cultural milieu. The Romanization of the greater part of the inhabitants of the Iberian Peninsula brought with it a diffusion of classical culture that was to influence permanently the cultural development of Spain as a nation. Specifically, the deep assimilation of the cultural ideals of Rome enabled them to survive the barbarian invasions that followed Rome's collapse.

During the ensuing centuries of Muslim domination and the entire period of the Reconquest (the expulsion of the Africans from Iberia), Spain continued to develop its unique culture by incorporating elements of both Islāmic–Oriental and Jewish civilizations. This amalgamation of cultures is, perhaps, the explanation for the development of the characteristic Spanish culture, which, while not removed from what is peculiarly European, does not correspond to it fully.

Serving as a meeting place for two distinct cultural worlds, the Islāmic–Oriental and the western European, Spain has performed an important task in the dissemination and extension of culture. The classic works of Greek antiquity were translated into Latin and later into Castilian; and a knowledge of both Muslim and Jewish culture was passed on to other European nations. The Castilian tongue, which was to become the national and official language, acquired vigour and maturity and soon became outstanding among all the languages of Europe. So strong did Spanish culture become that the term Golden Age—which, in Spain, comprises both the 16th and 17th centuries—can be applied not only to the political, literary, and artistic creations of the period but also to its outstanding achievements in theology, philosophy, law, and science.

Traditional Spanish culture, however, being deeply religious in character and specifically Roman Catholic in outlook, found itself farther and farther removed from the cultural life of the rest of Europe, as the latter (from the 18th century onward) assumed an increasingly secular quality. The critical nature of this stage in Spain's development is apparent in the conflict that arose during the 19th century between the nationalistic and the more European-oriented sectors of Spanish society. Spanish culture has also had an enormous effect on the New World.

In the prevailing Spanish viewpoint, Christian inspiration, a humanistic outlook that fosters appreciation of the worth of the individual, a certain eclecticism, and a striving toward universality of spirit are seen as characteristics of Spanish culture in every age. Contemporary Spain, it is felt, finds itself open to the most recent intellectual currents of the rest of Europe, and indeed further afield, but does not as a result intend to relinquish its own characteristic modes of thought and behaviour. It would seem that the mission of Spain continues to be that of creating peculiarly national forms of Western culture. (E.L.O.M.)

Architecture. Madrid and Barcelona are the principal centres of modern architecture in Spain. Major public buildings in Madrid have been designed by such architects as Francisco Javier Saez de Oiza, Alejandro de la Sota, José Antonio Corrales, Ramón Vázquez Molezún, and José Rafael Moneo. In Barcelona, the Catalonian Antonio Gaudí developed an expressive, sculptural style in numerous hotels, apartment houses, and churches in the late 19th and early 20th centuries. His unfinished church of the Sàgrada Familia, an idiosyncratic extrapolation of cathedral Gothic, remains a haunting feature of the city's skyline.

The major contemporary architects

Sculpture. Three great sculptors—Pablo Gargallo, Julio González, and Alberto Sánchez—mark the Spanish school of sculpture in the first half of the 20th century. Each developed a personal style that broke from tradition and paved the way for creativity. In the mid-20th century, José Planes, Cristino Mallo, Carlos Ferreira, and Jorge de Oteiza worked in traditional styles, while Angel Ferrant experimented with new forms. Pablo Serrano attained an integrated style in his search for a synthesis of abstract and representational forms.

The most universal figure of Spanish sculpture is Eduardo Chillida, who is noted for his metal, cement, wood, or alabaster figures. He has been followed by a new generation of abstract sculptors, including Miguel Berrocal, Martín Chirino, Francisco Barón, and José Luis Sánchez y Gabino, while minute representations of everyday life are sculptured by Julio and Francisco López and by Caulonga.

Painting. Spain also produced three major painters in the first half of the 20th century—Pablo Picasso, Joan Miró, and Salvador Dalí. Other talented painters of the period include Daniel Vázquez Díaz and Benjamín Palencia, as well as Francisco Arias, Augustín Redondela, and Manuel Mampaso of the Madrid school.

Since the opening in 1966 of the Museo Abstracto in Cuenca by Fernando Zobel, Gustavo Torner, and Marisa Rueda, the museum has been a centre for such new artists as José Ruiz de Rivera, Rafael Canogar, Manuel Millares, Luis Feito, and José Francés. Together with Antonio Saura, Manolo Mompó, José Guinovart Bertrán, José Guerrero Malagón, Pablo Palazuelo, Eusebio Sempere, and the Catalan group of Antonio Tapies, Modesto Cuixart, and Juan Ponç, they represent the best of contemporary Spanish art. (I.C.L.)

Music. The internationally significant generation of musicians to which Manuel de Falla, Joaquín Turina, Conrado del Campo, and Oscar Esplá belonged was succeeded by a generation of composers born at the turn of the 20th century. They include Federico Mompou, whose work follows the French impressionistic style; and Ernesto Halffter, often considered to be the truest of the disciples of Falla and who, like his master, has sought to combine both aristocratic and popular elements in his music. Composers whose work reveals a tendency to greater innovation include Xavier Montsalvage and Joaquín Homs. The same tendency is even more clearly expressed in the works of Cristóbal Halffter, Luis de Pablo, and Carmelo Bernaola, three figures of international renown in the world of avant-garde music. Other new composers in this field are Tomás Marco, Antón Garcia Abril, Manuel Castillo, and Ramón Barce.

Innovative composers

Among instrumentalists of major reputation are the guitarists Andrés Segovia, Narciso Yepes, and Regino Sainz de la Maza; the cellist Pedro Corostola; the violinists León Ara, Víctor Martín, and Gonzálo Comellas; the harpist Nicanor Zabaleta; and the pianists Rafael Orozco and Eduardo del Pueyo.

Spain's outstanding conductors include Odón Alonso, Antoni Ros Marbá, Enrique García Asensio, Jesús López Cobos, and Rafel Frübeck de Burgos. Major singers are Victoria de los Angeles, Montserrat Caballé, Teresa Berganza, Pilar Lorengar, Alfredo Kraus, and Plácido Domingo. Major orchestras are the National Orchestra, the Symphonic Orchestra of Spanish Radio and Television, and the Camerata of Madrid.

Literature. The illustrious traditions of Spanish literature continue to influence contemporary writers, and the *Don Quixote* of Cervantes has been characterized as the 17th-century prototype of the modern Spanish novel.

The Civil War (1936–39) represented a watershed in Spanish arts as well as politics, driving many artists in disparate fields into exile while substantially altering the focus for those who remained or emerged subsequently. Among its effects was the shift in predominance from poetry to the novel, though the Generation of 1927 movement in poetry, especially through such preeminent figures as Vicente Aleixandre (awarded the Nobel Prize for Literature in 1977) and Dámaso Alonso, continued to influence a host of postwar poets, including the great popular poet Miguel Hernández (who died in jail in 1940) and Luis Cernuda, Rafael Alberti, Luis Rosales, Salvador Espriu, Gabriel Celaya, Blas de Otero, and José Hierro. The best known of 20th-century Spanish poets outside their own country, however, remained the lyric poet Juan Ramón Jiménez, who was awarded the Nobel Prize for Literature in 1956 and died in exile in 1958, and Federico García Lorca, who is perhaps even more renowned as a dramatist. In both poetry and drama Lorca echoed an earlier Spain. His poetry is alive with the labyrinthine and sensuous imagery of a Moorish Spain of several centuries past. The few plays he wrote before he was murdered during the Civil War are both richly poetic and emotionally elemental in their actions, harkening back to the works of Lope de Vega and Pedro Calderón de la Barca, which helped the Spanish stage of the 17th-century Golden Age rival that of Elizabethan England in vigour and popular appeal.

Major poets

Major 20th-century novelists include Ramón Pérez de Ayala, who touched his philosophical themes with an Asturian humour; Gabriel Miró, who was occupied with more poetic themes; and Ramón José Sender, who returned to greater realism and social commentary; as well as Max Aub and Francisco Ayala. During the early 1940s the postwar novel began to emerge in the work of such writers as Rafael Sánchez Ferlosio and Carmen Martín Gaite, Miguel Delibes, Carmen Conde, Rosa Chancel, and Camilo José Cela and Carmen Laforet. They influenced a younger group including Jesús Fernández Santos, Juan Goytisolo, Luis Goytisolo-Gay, and Juan Marsé. Criticism, previously led by José Ortega y Gasset, champion of a pure, depersonalized art, passed to such younger observers as José Luis Cano and José María Castellet.

(E.L.O.M./I.C.L.)

Theatre. In the post-World War II era, Spanish theatre suffered from a scarcity of materials, an almost total lack of quality works and of thematic imagination, and a disregard for reaching large numbers of people. In response to this situation, the Ministry of Culture created the National Drama Centre in 1978 to bring major national and foreign works to the Spanish stage.

The Independent Theatre

Most interesting in Spanish theatre is the Independent Theatre (Teatro Independiente), which includes amateur and professional groups. Some, such as Tábano and the Teatre Lliure, are well known throughout the country, while others, such as the Cuadra de Sevilla and Els Joglars, have acquired an international reputation. Also of interest are the theatre festivals held in Almagro, Mérida, and Santander. There is a *zarzuela* (comic opera) season in Madrid, which is also the home of the National Ballet and the Classical Ballet.

Motion pictures. Motion pictures are very popular in Spain. In the late 20th century, the Spanish motion-picture industry produced many full-length films—of which a large proportion were joint ventures with Italian, Mexican, French, German, Venezuelan, or Argentinian companies—and short films. Only a small proportion of the films shown are Spanish productions, however. Spain's major motion-picture directors have included Luis Buñuel, who was in exile during the Franco regime, and Luis García Berlanga, Juan Antonio Bardem, and Carlos Saura.

Film festivals are held throughout Spain. Those held in San Sebastián, Barcelona, and Valladolid are of a general nature, while that of Gijón features children's films, those of Huesca and Bilbao feature documentaries and shorts, and that of Huelva features Iberoamerican films. (I.C.L.)

Folklore. *The fiesta.* The form of popular tradition that remains most intensely alive in the Spain of today is that of the fiesta, or popular festival, which never fails to have a certain amount of religious significance even though it may be essentially nonreligious in character. After having been preserved for centuries in a popular, spontaneous form, the festivals suffered from the crisis of traditional values of the 1960s and '70s. A revival of the festivals seemed to have occurred by the late 20th century, however. Each locality, no matter how small, has its own festival, celebrated in honour of a saint for whom the town feels a particular devotion. The list of local festivals is, as a result, almost interminable, but three outstanding ones are the Fallas of Valencia, the April fair of Seville, and the festivities honouring San Fermín in Pamplona. Although the festivals are found all over Spain, it is interesting to note that the coastal regions, despite the fact that they are more exposed to foreign influences, are precisely those that have best preserved their typical festivals.

Major local festivals

The bullfight. The bullfight, too, may be considered something of a hybrid celebration, since it possesses certain characteristics of a sport as well as those of a popular festival. It is customarily regarded, however, as the most typical of Spanish festivals and as the Spanish national fiesta par excellence, even though bullfighting is found in other countries, particularly those of Hispanic America. The tradition of bullfighting can be traced back to ancient times, but the present style of fighting the bull on foot dates back only to the 18th century.

Other aspects of traditional life. There are seemingly innumerable other forms of traditional activity, and many objects still used in daily living also have their roots deep in the past. Some change is taking place, but other activities continue to exist as they have in the past, notably in the remote rural areas. Spanish houses, for example, reflecting as they do both the varying regional climates and the exigencies of a preindustrial society, still continue to be constructed more or less as they were many years ago. On the other hand, the traditional or typical regional garb has undergone a slow evolution as to style, although certain costumes are still considered characteristic of the regions in which they originated.

Traditional arts and crafts, grouped together under their official name of *artesanía* (handicrafts), have become the object of government protection, designed to insure their continued existence in the face of the increasing mechanization of industry.

The academies and related bodies. Spanish cultural institutions have deep and rich roots in the nation's past. The oldest of the Spanish academies is the Royal Academy of Language, usually called the Royal Spanish Academy, which was established by King Philip V in 1713. Its primary purpose is "to cultivate and to set standards for the purity and elegance of the Castilian tongue." An essential aspect of this task involves the publication by the Academy of a Dictionary of the Language and other works, as well as the granting of prizes. Spain also possesses the internationally known Royal Academy of History; the Royal Academy of Fine Arts of San Fernando; the Royal Academy of Exact, Physical and National Sciences; the Royal Academy of Moral and Political Sciences; and the Royal National Academy of Medicine. All the academies form part of the Institute of Spain, founded in 1938 as a coordinating organization.

The Royal Spanish Academy

The Council for Scientific Research, created in 1939, directs research activities of a few hundred scientific centres located throughout the entire nation. The Institute of Iberoamerican Cooperation maintains cultural, economic, and linguistic ties with Latin-American countries. The institute maintains cultural exchange departments, possesses a commissariat in charge of expositions and also the important Hispanic Library, the collection of which numbers about 500,000 volumes. There are many institutes of Hispanic culture located in many countries of North and South America. These collaborate with the parent institute in Spain, which has several affiliated Hispanic-American cultural associations within the country itself.

The famous athenaeums (which carry on varied cultural activities) are located in 20 different Spanish cities. Founded in the 19th century as private political clubs, they have since been gradually transformed into groups influencing the artistic and literary life of their home city. The Casas de Cultura, through lectures, expositions, concerts, and libraries, perform analogous functions in smaller towns.

Museums. The great national art gallery is the world-famous Prado in Madrid. Installed in a magnificent building, it holds a unique place among the great museums of the world. Its collections and galleries have been enlarged in recent years by the acquisition of many Spanish paintings of the 19th century.

Other important museums include the Museo de la Real Academía de Bellas Artes de San Fernando and the Museo Arqueológico Nacional in Madrid, the Museo de Arte de Cataluña in Barcelona, and those of fine arts in Bilbao and Seville. Collections devoted to specific aspects of the art of Spain are found in other museums: thus, religious sculpture is housed in the Museo Nacional de Escultura Policromada in Valladolid; and the art of El Greco is to be found in his museum and house in Toledo.

The Army and Naval Museums in Madrid are interesting from the historical viewpoint, as is the Maritime Museum in the royal arsenals of Barcelona. In addition to numerous provincial and municipal museums, there are others belonging to the cathedrals, dioceses, and parishes. The various museums of the National Patrimony, housing collections that form part of the former royal patrimony, are also very significant. Finally, the country is rich in private museums, including the Cerralbo in Madrid and the Marés in Barcelona. New museums include the Sefardic Museum in Toledo; the Museum of Costume and the Picasso Museum in Barcelona; and the Museum of Abstract Art in Cuenca.

It is notable, however, that in a country that possesses great artistic and historic treasures and in which art, particularly religious art, is alive and active *in situ,* the activity of museums of necessity plays only a secondary role.

Libraries and archives. The most important of Spain's famous historical libraries is that of El Escorial, which served as a model for other European libraries until the 19th century. The Royal Library, established in the 18th century, was in the following century transformed into the National Library of Madrid. It has valuable collections that originally belonged to private libraries or to monasteries that were confiscated by the government. The Private Royal Library, or Palace Library, the libraries belonging to the royal academies, that of the Higher Council of Scientific Investigation, and the public libraries of the provinces form a broad library network throughout the entire country.

The Royal Library

In addition to a great number of smaller archives—regional, local, special, ecclesiastical, and private—Spain has four great general archives in which are assembled the historic documents of the nation. They are: the National Historical Archives, in Madrid; the General Archives of Simancas; the General Archives of the Indies, in Seville (which contains documents relating to the government of the Spanish overseas empire); and that of the Crown of Aragon (of supreme importance for the study of medieval history), in Barcelona.

Other cultural institutions. The National Orchestra, which was founded in the period immediately following the Civil War of 1936–39, has devoted itself chiefly to the promotion of interest in symphonic music. The Symphony Orchestra of Spanish Radio and Television, which gave its first concert in 1965, has, in its shorter existence, been able to reach a wide audience through the use of the communications media. Both of these orchestras are located in Madrid, as are two others with a long and brilliant history: the Symphony and the Philharmonic. Outside the capital, the principal Spanish orchestra is the municipally supported City Orchestra of Barcelona.

Spain has only one theatre for opera that has a regular season for its performances, the Lyceum Theatre in Barcelona, a private enterprise. The Festival of the Opera, however, which, in some respects, corresponds to a short opera season, is held every year in Madrid. Similar festivals, also of brief duration, are held in several of the provincial capitals.

The influence of private foundations

The March Foundation (founded 1955) is outstanding among foundations under private auspices. Its cultural activities include the giving of prizes, grants for research, scholarships for study in Spain or abroad, and annual contributions to the study of literature and the fine arts, as well as subsidies to institutions and enterprises interested in culture. It also publishes books. Other private foundations are the Barrié de la Maza, Rosillo, Urquijo, and Foessa foundations.

The number of literary prizes established has increased notably in recent years; the national prizes for literature remain, however, as the oldest and most distinguished. Other important prizes include the "Nadal" and the "Planeta" for the novel; the "Adonais" for poetry; and the "Cervantes" for foreign authors who write in Spanish.
(E.L.O.M./I.C.L.)

The press. The Spanish press was of fundamental importance to the transition from Franco's regime to democracy in the late 1970s. The repressive aspects of the Press Law of 1966 have since been abolished, and the constitution of 1978 guarantees freedom of the press within the ordinary limits of honour, privacy, self-respect, and the protection of children. Laws further defining press freedom were in the process of promulgation in the early 1980s.

The Spanish press is economically successful. Circulation has increased, and new types of newspapers and periodicals have appeared. Major newspapers in the late 20th century included *La Vanguardia Española* of Barcelona and *El País* and *A.B.C.* in Madrid.

Radio and television broadcasting. The first radio broadcasts made in Spain were carried out by an experimental station in Madrid in 1923. In the following year, the first two commercial radio stations were installed in Barcelona and Madrid. They were the country's only radio stations until the start of the Civil War in 1936. In 1937, a station called Radio Nacional de España (National Radio of Spain) began broadcasting from Salamanca, and after the Civil War had ended in 1939, a national radio broadcasting service was established, centred on the group of transmitters located in Arganda, in the province of Madrid. In 1951, when the Ministry of Information and Tourism was created, the government-operated radio and television stations were placed under its direction.

In 1960 the first station of Radio Peninsular devoted entirely to the broadcasting of music was set up, and stations of a similar type were later established in several of the provincial capitals. The first FM transmitter was installed in Madrid in 1957 by Radio Nacional de España, to be followed by several others of the same type.

The broadcasting of radio and television was restructured in the late 1970s and early '80s. A government plan was approved in 1978 to distribute new radio frequencies according to the provisions of the Geneva Conference of 1975. Another government plan included, among other matters, the broadcasting by both public and commercial stations of educational programs not supported by advertising. A law promulgated in 1980 redefined government radio and television broadcasting as a vehicle to disseminate information and educational and national and regional cultural programming, to promote public participation in the political process, to form public opinion, and to aid in the development of true and effective liberty and equality.

Radio and television broadcasting are regulated by Radiotelevisión Española (R.T.V.E.), a government body subject to civil law. R.T.V.E. is composed of an administrative council, made up of 12 members of the Cortes, and three advisory councils. The director general of R.T.V.E. is named by the government on the advice of the administrative council; he is charged with carrying out the directives of R.T.V.E. and with naming a territorial delegate in each of the autonomous communities.

Spanish television is transmitted on two channels, one of which reaches the majority of the country's population. Most of the programming is broadcast in colour. Television programming is financed by government grants, commercial advertising, and revenue from program sales.

Radio Nacional de España broadcasts three basic programs. The first offers information and entertainment. The second program is devoted to classical music, and the third to culture and education. There are also shortwave broadcasts to other countries in Spanish and foreign languages. Radio Nacional is totally supported by government grants and accepts no advertising.

Radio Cadena Española (Spanish Radio Network; RCE) is composed of the privately owned stations that were in operation before 1978. There are several other private radio networks, including that of the Roman Catholic Church. For statistical data, see the "Britannica World Data" section in the current *Britannica Book of the Year.*
(I.C.L.)

History

PRE-ROMAN SPAIN

Prehistory. The earliest human fossils found in the Iberian Peninsula are those of Neanderthaloid men, dating from about 200,000 BC, whose remains have been discovered at Gibraltar, Játiva (Valencia), and Bañolas (Gerona). But utensils found in Algeciras, Madrid, the Provincia de Soria, Lisbon, and elsewhere point to the existence of even earlier habitation. This indirect evidence suggests that the peninsula was inhabited as early as 500,000 BC. The most important sites are the camps of elephant hunters found at Madrid, Torralba, and Ambrona (Soria), where many animal bones have been discovered. The Neanderthaloids and other pre-*sapiens* disappeared with the last glaciation, when Old Stone Age (Paleolithic) cultures advanced in the peninsula.

The Paleolithic Period

One of the most remarkable achievements of the Late Paleolithic was in the realm of art. The famous Paleolithic cave paintings found at such sites as Pindal, Peña de Candamo, Castillo, El Pendo, Pasiega, Ribadesella, Altamira, and elsewhere in the peninsula represent a broad historical period extending roughly from 25,000 to 10,000 BC. The animals depicted in the paintings are cold-weather varieties—bison, bulls, horses, goats, wild boars, bears, lions, mammoths, reindeer, rabbits, and seals.

The transition to the Neolithic Period coincides with a climatic change the full effects of which came about gradually (beginning around 10,000 BC) and drove the food animals northward. The archaeological deposit at Muge, near Lisbon, undoubtedly belongs to the beginnings of this age, which, in its early stages, is sometimes called Mesolithic. Deposits of great quantities of ocean and river shells, Crustacea, and the remains of birds, fish, oxen, and swine attest to the diet of these early Neolithic men. In Santimamiñe (Vizcaya), a similar economic pattern is found. There are also two important cave sites near Valencia: at Las Cuevas del Oro and at Dos Aguas. At the height of the Neolithic Period, approximately between 4000 and 3000 BC, rock painting flourished in the region of the Levantina, appearing in the open air, sheltered by rock overhangs. Many isolated animal figures are depicted, but human beings are also seen, comprising narrative scenes of hunting, herding, dancing, fighting, and even honey gathering from a hive located on top of a rock. The figures are small and exhibit considerable movement and vitality. The men are shown using bows, and the women usually appear wearing only a long, bell-shaped skirt. The Neolithic Period in western Europe, however, lagged far behind that of the eastern Mediterranean. In the West, cave dwelling persisted, and although agriculture and husbandry were known, their practice was minimal. Settlements were quite rudimentary, being no more than simple groupings of shelters. This was an exclusively coastal culture and did not extend inland.

The age of metals

The Neolithic came to an abrupt end around 2500 BC with the beginning of the use of metals in the south. It was at this time that the first large population centres were formed, along with monumental burial sites; it was at this time also that agriculture, cattle raising, mining, and metallurgy (beginning with copper, then bronze) underwent a period of extraordinary development. It appears that these arts may have been brought from the Aegean, not, however, as the result of an invasion but apparently as the result of a sporadic penetration of "technicians." Concurrently, maritime trade flourished, thereby explaining the presence of artifacts from all over the Mediterranean, among them ivory, turquoise, obsidian, and amber (perhaps from the Baltic). The new economy brought forth a new social organization, founded in a type of monarchy, the support of which came from an aristocracy based on wealth, who lorded it over a more or less enslaved population. This culture, the Almería, ranged over the south of the peninsula, from Algarve to Cabo de la Nao and from the Strait of Gibraltar to the Tagus River, later extending up the coast and into the Meseta Central. The high point in the development of this culture was reached between 3000 and 2000 BC. The best known centres were those in the southeast (Almizaraque and Los Millares) and in the southwest (Vilanova de San Pedro and Zambujal). Settlements with round or oval houses were built on fortified hilltops, indicating a life of constant danger. In Los Millares, the people of the Almería culture raised wheat, barley, millet, rye, lentils, chick-peas, grapes, and olives; as domestic animals they had sheep, swine, oxen, horses, and dogs. Among their usable plants were linen and cotton for fabrics and esparto for baskets, shoe soles, ropes, and nets. At the same time, copper was being used. Contemporary with Los Millares was the mining centre at Almizaraque, where copper and silver were processed, as evidenced by crucibles and slag heaps found next to the mines. This was the culture that built large megalithic burial vaults with corbel-arched ceilings. These tombs are entered from the outside by a tunnel and are covered by a cone-shaped mound. Tombs of this type are found at El Romeral (Antequera), Matarrubilla (Seville), and Soto (Huelva), and there are partial remains at Alcalar (Algarve). In contrast, the dolmen at Viera (Antequera) consists of a rectangular chamber, and the famous "cave" at Menga (Antequera) is slightly oval. The latter is the most remarkable monument of its kind. In its construction, 31 enormous stone slabs were used, weighing a total of 1,600 tons. The flat roof was supported by three thick pillars. The dolmen culture spread through the rest of the peninsula and through Europe, giving rise to distinct dolmenic "provinces" in the central and Atlantic zones. These cultures also reached Italy, Corsica, Sardinia, and North Africa. Accompanying this expansion was an excellent ceramics industry characterized by campaniform, or bell-shaped, utensils, incised with geometric designs.

El Argar culture

Toward the beginning of the 2nd millennium, in the same region (Almería), El Argar culture appeared, in which the metallurgy of bronze, silver, and gold notably flourished. This industry was no longer in the hands of foreigners but constituted instead a native enterprise that produced for domestic consumption (weapons, jewelry, utensils) as well as for trade abroad. The result was a lively trade with other centres in the eastern Mediterranean. But there were substantial differences from previous cultures: dwellings had a rectangular floor plan, and the dead were buried individually in baskets or large urns beneath the floors of the houses, not in collective vaults, as in the previous epoch. Villages continued to be built on hilltops and were well fortified. Governed by kinglets or princes who were supported by an aristocracy, this culture, which at first was limited to the southeast, spread throughout the southern, the central, and the Levantina regions and reached the Balearic Islands. Its apogee came roughly between 1700 and 1000 BC. It was around this time that the kingdom of Tartessus appeared, along with the first Phoenician and Greek colonies.

Tartessus. Near the beginning of the 1st millennium, Spain entered written history. Passages in the Bible and in Greek and Latin texts refer to Tartessus (biblical Tarshish), an important centre of trade, especially in tin. The Tartessians were by this time sailing the Atlantic, southward along the African coast as well as northward in search of tin in the northeastern part of the peninsula and in the Cassiterides Islands (Scilly Islands). With this supply of tin and with the copper found around Huelva, a strong bronze industry developed that was mentioned by the Greeks. The Tartessians had a writing system, and while inscriptions have survived, they have not yet been translated. They also had a literature, but nothing of it remains. Their government was a hereditary monarchy, and while the names of several of the Tartessian kings are known, only one, Arganthonius, has historical status.

Arganthonius

Arganthonius, who reputedly lived 120 years, died in the middle of the 6th century BC, shortly before the Battle of Aleria (Alalia *c.* 540), whereby the Carthaginians gained control of the Mediterranean. His friendship with the Greeks and with the Phocians, to whom he loaned money to fortify their city against the Persians, brought reprisals against Tartessus by the Carthaginians. The exact location of Tartessus has yet to be established, and even the ancient writers themselves were in doubt about it. All that can be said at present is that it was undoubtedly situated along the coast between Huelva and the Strait of Gibraltar, perhaps in the direction of the mouth of the Guadalquivir or the Guadalete rivers.

Phoenician colonization. Textual sources reveal that Phoenicians from Tyre (Sūr, Lebanon) arrived on the peninsula shortly before 1100 BC, the traditional date of the founding of Gadir (Cádiz). This date, established by the Greek philosopher Poseidonius in Cádiz itself, is historically acceptable, though some historians place the Phoenician landing in the 8th century. The Phoenicians were attracted by the thriving trade in metals at Tartessus, the flourishing agriculture of Andalusia, and the rich fishing business of the coast that stimulated such allied industries as preserving, salt evaporation, and the extraction of purple dye from shellfish.

The Phoenician colonies founded after Gadir were Baria (Villaricos), Abdera (Adra), Sexi (Almuñécar), and Malaca (Málaga), all of which minted their own coins, although not until relatively late. Many processing and preserving plants for fish were established along the entire southern coast, and scattered agricultural centres were established inland. Ibiza was founded as a fishing colony by the Carthaginians in 654, though the dates of the founding of the rest of the colonies are not known. There is no definite information about Cádiz from before the 6th or 5th centuries. Hoards of jewelry and a human-shaped sarcophagus in the Phoenician style have been found in graves there, but nothing remains of the great Temple of Melqart (Hercules), and many other monuments have been lost to the destructive action of the sea along the Cádiz coast. At Baria many artifacts have been found, along with great numbers of painted ostrich eggs. Ibiza's many underground chambers at Puig des Molins have yielded terra-cotta objects, necklaces of glass paste beads, and Greek vases. Important statues of Tanit have been found in the temple at Cuyram, and terra-cottas of a very primitive type have been uncovered at Isla Plana. But the most spectacular finds have been made at the necropolis at Sexi, where Egyptian alabaster amphorae, dating from the 10th century, have been found in tombs from around 700 BC. Inland, engraved combs have been found in tombs at Carmona and Osuna; also important are the treasury found at La Aliseda (Cáceres) and at Sines and the many series of bronze pitchers found all over the western part of the peninsula, from the Strait of Gibraltar to the interior of Castilla (Castile). All the artifacts date from the 7th century BC.

After the fall of Tyre to the Assyrians, the Phoenician colonies were taken over or protected by the powerful Phoenician daughter city of Carthage in North Africa. The Carthaginians quickly turned the resources of the peninsula to the task of creating a staging area for attacks against Rome. Hamilcar landed in Spain in 237, taking possession of the entire south and southeast of the peninsula, where he founded Akra Leuke (Alicante). Shortly thereafter, Hasdrubal founded Carthago Nova (Cartagena), and Hannibal readied his attack against Rome after assuring the subjugation of the native peoples of both mesetas. In 219 Hannibal's successful siege of Saguntum (Sagunto), an ally of the Romans, precipitated the Second Punic War. The Carthaginian conquest of Spain provided the Carthaginians not only with the silver necessary to finance the wars but also with a nearly inexhaustible supply of mercenary soldiers. Hannibal crossed the Alps in 218, attacking the Romans on their home ground. But even as Hannibal ravaged the Italian peninsula, the Romans attacked the Carthaginians in Spain. In 218 the Roman general Publius Scipio landed at Emporia and achieved a temporary success. In 210, Scipio Africanus, the son and namesake of Publius Scipio, took command and won a series of brilliant victories. Scipio first took Tarraco, then Carthago Nova (209), and after a victory at Ilipa (Alcalá del Río, near Seville), he overran Cádiz (206), marking the end of Carthaginian domination in Spain.

The Punic Wars

Greek colonization. Thanks to the greater number of written accounts, much more is known about the Greek colonization. In the 9th and 8th centuries, Greeks were sailing the coasts of the peninsula, and their explorations paved the way for the subsequent arrival of the Phocians. According to the Greek historian Herodotus, the first Greek to reach Tartessus was Colaeus of Samos in the mid-7th century. As early as the 7th century, the Phocians founded Hemeroscopium (near Denia) and Mainake (near Málaga). These colonies maintained close contact with the Tartessians, whose king, Arganthonius, protected and aided them. It was probably also at this time, or shortly thereafter, that Meidakritos, Euthymenes, and Euphemus of Caria sailed along the Spanish coast. Toward 600 BC, the Phocians founded the city of Massilia (Marseille), opening the way for new settlements in the northeast. Emporiae (Ampurias) appeared at this time, and the Rhodian colony of Rhodae (Rosas) was populated by Phocians. Both cities minted their own coins, beginning in the 5th century. The Battle of Alalia (*c.* 540) brought not only the fall of the kingdom of Tartessus but also the collapse of the Greeks' two southernmost colonies, Mainake and Hemeroscopium. Later, with the arrival of Greeks from Sicily and Magna Graecia (southern Italy), contacts with the northeastern coast of Spain were re-established, and there followed the founding of Alonae (Benidorm?) and other trading centres. Of these colonies, only one, Emporiae, has been identified and excavated. Artifacts found there date from the end of the 7th century, and among them are abundant ceramics, representing all Greek styles, along with terra-cottas, figured bronzes, and coins. The most outstanding piece of sculpture is a large marble statue of Asclepius, dating from the 4th century. Few Greek inscriptions, however, have been found. Only the above-mentioned places are referred to as colonies, but textual evidence reveals a considerable number of Greek place names, all of them along the coast, which must refer to trading posts or even smaller population centres. Active trading flooded the Spanish coasts with Greek products. From the Pyrenees to the mouth of the Tagus, great numbers of Greek ceramics have been and continue to be discovered, ranging in date from the 7th century to the Hellenistic era. Many bronze statues, some of them quite large and dating as far back as the 6th century, have also been found, as well as two ancient Greek helmets, also made of bronze. Finally, coins from throughout the Greek world, from Massilia to the Crimea, have also been discovered. These coins span the entire period from the earliest mintings up until the Alexandrine era, with those from Greece, Sicily, and southern Italy in particular abundance.

The Iberians. The broad designation of Iberian culture is generally applied to the civilization that grew up in the south and east of the peninsula during the five or six centuries prior to the birth of Christ. The designation Iberian is derived from the usage of contemporary classical writers. From Neolithic times forward, there were no cultural changes that necessarily imply any change in the ethnic composition of the peninsula. The only important outside influences that brought about any change are those from the East, beginning with the Punic and, later, the Greek settlers. It may be assumed, therefore, that the Tartessians and other peoples who inhabited the Mediterranean coast of Spain were descended from the Neolithic and Chalcolithic peoples of the peninsula, whose direct ancestors may have been closely linked to prehistoric peoples who inhabited "white Africa" from the Red Sea to the Atlantic and the Canary Islands. During the 1st millennium, the ancient Iberians, the creators of the great cultural centre of Tartessus, were subject to the pressure of the Greek and Phoenician–Carthaginian colonization. These maritime influences gave rise in later years to a singular and progressive culture that may quite correctly be called Iberian.

Origins of the Iberians

Iron was in widespread use among the Iberians, who developed a complex economy based on agriculture, stock breeding, fishing, industry (mining, metallurgy, weapons, jewelry, preservatives, textiles, ceramics, thrown pottery), and including general commerce, both domestic and foreign. Cities grew apace, and almost all of the Iberian cities mentioned by ancient writers were highly developed before the Roman conquest. Houses were rectangular in shape. Cremation was universally practiced, and cemeteries often contain rich furnishings, such as Greek vessels, Punic artifacts, damascene weapons, and native pottery. Political organization was monarchical, with a king, princes, and dukes assisted by a council of elders. But there were also popular assemblies in times of stress. In general, these kings were politically independent, although sometimes a single king controlled many cities in military alliance. The Iberians possessed written laws, apparently in verse form, and were highly accomplished in several of the arts, including music and the dance.

Cities were built on well-defended hillocks; individual houses, with straw roofs, were made from rubblework and molded adobe bricks. To judge from the large stone cellars that have been found in Andalusia—in Tutugi (Galera, Granada), Tugia (Toya, Granada), Basti (Baza, Jaén), Almedinilla, Iponuba (Baena, Córdoba)—there must have been public buildings of monumental dimensions, although nothing remains of them. Stone sculpture shows a strong early Greek influence, attested to by the sphinxes found at Agost and El Salobral, the androcephalic bull from Balazote (Albacete), and griffins like the one found at Redován. Temples, particularly those at Albacete, have yielded hundreds of large human figurines, both male and female, in both standing and sitting positions. In general, these are votive statues, used to ward off evil. Among them, the most important are several heads, parts of full-length figures, and the "Gran Dama Oferente" from the Cerro de los Santos. Above all, there is the famous bust of

The "Lady of Elche"

the "Lady of Elche," apparently of late date, perhaps from the 1st century BC, adorned in gold.

It is known that large-scale mural painting was practiced, depicting scenes of hunting, fishing, warfare, and civil ceremonies, but only scant indications of its existence have survived. Some idea of what it was like may be seen in the painted ceramics from Azaila, Numantia, and Liria. This thrown pottery, of excellent workmanship and exhibiting a surprising variety of forms, first appeared with decorations consisting of simple straight-line and circle designs and geometric motifs. But in its final period, corresponding with the wars of resistance against the Roman conquest in the 2nd and 1st centuries BC, this ceramic art was characterized by the depiction of narrative scenes embracing a great variety of decorative motifs, ranging from war and large game hunting to domestic or popular scenes, such as processions, dances, and the earliest known bullfights. These scenes were rendered in a somewhat childlike linear style but with considerable narrative strength. Iberian ceramics were exported to southern France, Liguria, central Italy, Sicily, and North Africa in the 1st century.

Iberian silverwork and goldwork was exceptionally rich; silverwork predominated in the fashioning of vases, paterae (earthenware drinking saucers), and jewelry. Decorative patterns were inlaid on weapons, dishes, and the like, and at times Iberian inscriptions were added. The most important known Iberian treasures are those of Tivissa (Tarragona), which include a beautiful set of dishes, its various pieces nielloed, or engraved, with religious themes. Other Iberian treasures have been found at Abengibre, Salvacañete, Mogón, and Santisteban. Outstanding pieces of goldwork were found in the treasure of Santiago de la Espada (Jaén) and are similar to the jewelry worn by the "Lady of Elche."

The Iberian language

The Iberians developed early a system of writing. The Iberian alphabet has an older (6th–5th century) Western phase called Tartessian and a derived Eastern phase called Iberian. There are both Greek- and Phoenician-derived letter forms in the 28-character alphabet, most of which is of unknown origin. Many inscriptions exist, but few words—except place-names on the coinage, struck by many cities in the 3rd century—can be read. No bilingual inscriptions have been found. The Iberians retained their writing system until the Roman conquest, when the Latin alphabet came into use.

The Celts. While the Iberian culture of the south and the east flourished under the influence of colonizers from the eastern Mediterranean, in the central and western parts of the peninsula, the cultural level was still quite primitive and rooted in the Copper and Bronze ages. But the 9th through the 8th centuries witnessed the gradual and peaceful penetration of the peninsula by peoples from across the Pyrenees from central Europe. These peoples, named Celts by Greek and Roman writers, were primarily herdsmen and agriculturalists—and they were able to smelt iron. In spite of constant reinforcement from new migrations, these people were often absorbed into the native population. This gave rise in a mixed people known as the Celtiberians. In other cases, the native cultural identity was erased almost in its entirety and was supplanted not only by Celtic customs and beliefs but also by the Celtic language, as is attested by the vast number of place-names and family names in certain areas. This new culture never reached the level of the coastal Iberian culture. The Celts did not have their own system of writing; they did not strike coins; nor did they practice sculpture or painting. The Celts did, however, excel in pottery techniques and in ornamental design, characterized by elaborate geometrical patterns. Their weapons and jewelry were exceptionally well made, always from gold (bracelets, torques), and they had mastered such difficult techniques as damascene. The round-shaped dwelling was replaced by the rectangular floor plan. But in the northwest (Galicia, Asturias, and the north of Portugal), the Celtic culture remained virtually unaffected by the native culture it encountered. The houses continued to be built with a circular floor plan, and the dead were buried beneath the floor of the dwellings themselves, reminiscent of the prehistoric cultures found at Los Millares and El Argar. They remained in this area, at least with respect to the round floor plan, until the Middle Ages and have even been found surviving in modern times, although only in remote areas. This "Round House Culture" has also been referred to as the "Castro" culture, after the arrangement of towns on fortified hilltops.

ROMAN SPAIN

The conquest. Scipio's landing in Emporia (218) during the Second Punic War began the Roman conquest of Spain. The Carthaginians were expelled by 206, and over the next two centuries the Romans, against a grudging and stubborn resistance, extended their hegemony over the peninsula. It is significant that in the same year that Cádiz fell, Italica, the first Roman settlement, was established there.

Native uprisings

The harshness of the Roman conquest provoked a large-scale uprising among the Lusitanians (Lusitani) and the Celtiberians that threatened Rome's hegemony in the peninsula. Rome's vast resources and its superior command prevailed, however, first, with the assassination of the rebel leader Viriathus (Viriato) in 139, and, later, with the siege of Numantia, which fell only after a lengthy resistance that required Rome to use 60,000 men against a city of only 4,000 (133). The presence of Scipio Amilianus, the adopted grandson of the Scipio who defeated Hannibal, was even required before the city fell at last. In 138 the Romans arrived in Galicia (Gallaecia), in 121 they landed in the Baleares (Balearic Islands), and in 105 they drove out the Cimbrians and the Teutons, who had made their way into the peninsula.

Early in the 1st century BC, political wars between Marius and Sulla in Rome brought about the revolt of Sertorius, who was on the verge of creating in Spain an independent state. He had organized the native populations along Roman lines and had fought successfully against Metellus and Pompey, but the war became lengthy, and rivalries began to erode the original enthusiasm for the cause. The assassination of Sertorius allowed Pompey the final victory in this civil war in 72. The wars between Caesar and Pompey also had their repercussions in Spain. The Battle of Ilerda (Lérida), in 49, gave Caesar his decisive victory and put all of Spain into his hands. But Pompey's cause had many followers in Baetica (Pompey had died in 48), and Pompey's sons Sextus and Gnaeus took refuge there after the defeat at Thapsus (46). With the remaining members of the defeated armies in Spain and many partisans, they were able to build a powerful army. The sudden arrival of Caesar, however, put a quick end to this dangerous faction in the Battle of Munda (45), where Caesar won a decisive victory. Gnaeus died while fleeing, and Sextus succeeded in escaping from Spain. The armies that fought in these civil wars were made up for the most part of Spaniards, either as legionnaires or as auxiliaries. This fact, along with the great zeal among the adherents to either side of the issues, was evidence of the intense Romanization that had taken place in much of the country.

The Cantabrian War

The final stage of the Roman conquest was the Cantabrian War (29–19 BC) launched by the emperor Augustus. The assault on the Cantabrian mountains was carried out from three bases of operations: Segisama, for the eastern sector (Santander); Asturica, for the central (Asturias); and Bracara Augusta, for the western (Galicia). Seven legions participated, which, along with auxiliaries, amounted to some 70,000 men. The Emperor himself accompanied these forces, aided by the generals Agrippa, Carisius, and Antistius, while a naval squadron kept watch on the coast. After the Cantabrian War, the whole of Spain was under Roman domination, and peace was interrupted only by events occurring outside the country.

One such occurrence was the revolt of Galba against Nero in AD 68. The uprising was begun by Vindex in Gaul, but the central figure was Galba, at that time governor of Tarraconensis. After this uprising, the Roman legions took more responsibility than the Senate for naming the emperor, and they no longer took into account the place of the emperor's birth or his social class. The 2nd-century Roman emperors Trajan and Hadrian, both born in Spain, were the first two emperors of provincial origin to be elected by the Senate. An event of great importance during this time was the Moorish invasion of 172–175. Armies of Moors crossed the Strait of Gibraltar, invaded Baetica and Lusitania, and laid siege to Singlia Barba and Italica. At the end of the 2nd century, struggles took place for succession to the throne after the death of Commodus. Supporters of Albinus rallied part of the auxiliary forces of the Seventh Gemina Legion (Legio VII Gemina), then quartered in what is now León, against Septimus Severus. Around the middle of the 3rd century the Franks entered Spain, took Tarraco, and, after crossing the Strait of Gibraltar, drove into Mauretania, where they were eventually dispersed.

Administration. The Romans first divided provincial Hispania into two sections, Ulterior and Citerior, but Augustus soon altered this arrangement, creating three provinces: Hispania Tarraconensis, Hispania Baetica, and Hispania Lusitania. Their respective capitals were in Tarraco (Tarragona), Corduba (Córdoba), and Emertia Augusta (Mérida). In the late 3rd century, Diocletian made Spain into a single diocese and subdivided Tarraconensis into three new provinces: Tarraconensis, Carthaginiensis (along with the Baleares), and Gallaecia. In addition, he joined the new Provincia Mauretania Tingitana to the Diocesis Hispania, which took in all of northern Morocco.

The provinces

From F. Lot, *The End of the Ancient World*; Routledge & Kegan Paul Ltd., London (published in the U.S. by Barnes & Noble, Inc.)

Spain at the end of the 4th century AD.

Of the three Augustan provinces, Baetica, which was considered pacific, had senatorial status and was administered by the Roman Senate through a proconsul. There were no occupational troops in such a province; the others were "imperial" provinces and were thus governed through delegates appointed by the emperor and were controlled by occupational troops.

Justice was administered through *conventus juridici*. Baetica had four such administrative districts: Astigitanus, Cordubensis, Gaditanus, and Hispalensis. Tarraconensis had seven districts: Tarraconensis, Caesaraugustanus, Carthaginiensis, Cluniensis, Asturicensis, Lucensis, and Bracaraugustanus. Lusitania had three: Emeritensis, Scalabitanus, and Pacensis. There were thus a total of 14.

Roman forces in Spain

Complete information has not survived concerning the exact numbers and the composition of the forces that Rome sent into Spain during the conquest. Some 30,000 men, excluding native auxiliaries, took part in the battles of Viriathus and Numantia. In Augustus' reign, the record became more precise. In the Cantabrian War about 40,000 legionnaires were used; when joined by auxiliaries their number reached a total of about 70,000. With the wars over, the legions were slowly withdrawn, so that around the middle of the 1st century AD only one legion remained. It was later replaced by another one whose permanent base (garrison) was León.

The peninsula supplied the Roman Army with great numbers of auxiliaries in the first century of the empire. Somewhat more than 100 units, alae and cohorts, were composed of men recruited from the least Romanized regions of Spain—Lusitania, the far north, and the northern *meseta*. The majority of them saw action on the Rhine and Danube fronts, although they also fought in Britain, North Africa, and the East.

The decisive factor in the Romanization of Spain was the extension of Roman citizenship. At first colonists of Roman or Italian origin living in Roman colonies in Spain were considered citizens. These colonies were established chronologically as follows: seven were created before Caesar, six during his reign, and three between Caesar and Augustus. Fourteen colonies were then founded by Augustus himself, and four between Augustus and the Flavians. Geographically, the colonies were distributed in the following manner: 12 in Baetica, 16 in Tarraconensis, and five in Lusitania; that is, a total of some 33 colonial seats of government, including some that did not receive the official designation of "colony." It must be noted that the colonization did not follow a studied plan but was determined instead to a great extent by the availability of suitable expropriated territory. In the area where the most conflicts developed (the civil war between Pompey and Caesar, in particular), more punitive action was taken against certain cities, and, consequently, there was in these places more *ager publicus* ("public land") to be distributed among the Roman legionnaires. The total number of Roman colonists may have reached 60,000. But since transient natives of the peninsula could in various ways also obtain Roman citizenship, the total increased by a considerable number. At the beginning of the empire, there were already 24 municipalities of Roman citizens and 48 cities under the *jus Latii* (Latin right). When these figures are added to those for the 33 colonies, there is a total of 142 cities under Roman law, with a population that may have reached 250,000 to 300,000.

Cities

Beyond this there still remain, however, nearly 300 cities and great numbers of non-Romanized people who are not accounted for. The complete Romanization of the Hispanic territory was not achieved until the Edict of Vespasian (74), which extended rights of the empire to all those Spaniards who did not previously have them. The rest of the empire had to wait until the Edict of Caracalla (212), which made Roman citizens of all persons in the empire.

These political advances were accompanied by great steps forward in the process of urbanization. In Tarraconensis, the western borders of which were very little urbanized at the time of Augustus, there were 293 settlements, 179 of which had a capital and 114 of which were rural. A century and a half later, the number of cities had risen to 248, an increase of 69; and the number of rural localities had fallen to 27, a decrease of 87.

Society and culture. Native languages (Iberian and Celtic), and the Greek and Phoenician that were still spoken in what had been their colonies, had virtually disappeared by the end of the 1st century BC, at least in Baetica and in the important cities and Romanized provinces. Languages spoken in the more remote centres of population were much longer in disappearing, and Basque survives even into the 1970s as an example of one of the pre-Roman tongues of the peninsula. It can be said, however, that by the time of Caesar, Latin was the universal language for the cultivated citizens of the peninsula, and there soon developed a native Hispano-Roman literature.

Religion in the Roman period

With regard to religion, in addition to the gods and minor deities of the Roman pantheon, who were quickly identified with the gods of the native Hispanic peoples, there were also adherents of many exotic religions originating in Persia, Asia Minor, Egypt, and North Africa. The most widely practiced religion appears to have been the worship of Isis, followed by the worship of the Magna Mater. Several of these beliefs were brought into Spain before the Roman conquest (Melqart, Tanit-Caelestis, Magna Mater). The majority of the remaining ones were introduced during the empire.

There is no evidence as to how Christianity was first

introduced into Spain. It is quite possible that St. Paul visited Spain at some time between 63 and 67, but it is difficult to distinguish historical fact from legend concerning the "seven apostles." It is certain, however, that in the 2nd and 3rd centuries there were Christian communities throughout the peninsula. The most reliable documents on martyrs speak of persecutions of Christians in various locations under Prudentius. Shortly before (evidently), the Edict of Milan (313) called together the Council of Iliberri (Granada), which was attended by 19 bishops and 24 presbyters. The Nicene Council (325) was directed by Osio, the bishop of Corduba. The emperor Theodosius I (379–395), a Spaniard, made Christianity the only tolerated religion in the empire. The ascetic Priscillian spread the Manichean heresy throughout the western part of the peninsula during the second half of the 4th century, and the heresy persisted into the 6th century. Besides Priscillian, other Christian writers of note were Osio, Juvencus, Prudentius, and Orosius.

Roman remains

Archaeology has brought to light numerous monuments from this era—basilicas, amphitheatres, aqueducts, baths.

Monuments to Roman construction remain in many parts of the peninsula. Roman walls are to be found in Barcelona, Tarragona, Zaragoza, Idanha, Evora, and elsewhere. Bridges stand at Alcántara, Mérida, Piedras Albas, Alconétar, Chaves, Villa Formosa, Bibey, Salamanca, and Villa del Río, and aqueducts in Segovia, Mérida, and Tarragon. The entire peninsula is crossed by Roman roads, the principal ones going from Cádiz (the Via Augusta) along the Río Guadalquivir and continuing along the Levantina coast, from Cartagena north through Valencia and Tarragona to Narbonensis. Another road folows the Ebro from Tarragona to Galicia. Roman lighthouses are found at La Coruña and Caepionis Turris (Chipiona). Sites of military encampments are at León, Numantia, and elsewhere. Castles were built at Lousa and Benavente. Carmona has a necropolis, and there are mausoleums remaining at Tarragon, Fabara, Sádaba (two), Zalamea la Real, and Jumilla. Roman palaces and villas, many with mosaics, are found at Clunia, Milreu, Italica, and many other sites.

Roman art is also abundant throughout the peninsula. Principal centres for sculpture were Barcelona, Tarragona, Mérida, Italica, and Córdoba, while the centres for portrait work were at Italica, Córdoba, Cádiz, Tarragona, and Barcelona. There remain about 40 pagan sculptured sarcophagi, originating primarily in the south, the coast of the Levantina, and the central region. Mosaic work is common in all of the peninsula, with the exception of the northwest and the north.

Spaniards of great importance in the culture of Rome were writers such as the Senecas, Lucan, Mela, Martial, Quintilian, Columella, Canius Ruffus, Decianus, and Moderatus. Trajan, Hadrian, and Theodosius were Spanish emperors, and the Balbos and Lucius Licinius Sura were statesmen of note.

VISIGOTHIC SPAIN TO C. 500

There were many precedents to the great invasions by Germanic tribes of the beginning of the 5th century. Incursions by the Cimbrians and Teutons, the Franks, the Alemanni (Alamanni), and the Ostrogoths were signs of the growing threat to the empire. On the other hand, the peaceful infiltration and coexistence of the barbarians with the Romans along the interior border zones brought about the "barbarization" of the empire on every level, even in its high command. In 401 the Visigoths, under Alaric, crossed the Alps, descended on Italy, and in 410 sacked Rome. Other tribes, made up of Suebi, Alani, and Vandals, had crossed the Pyrenees the previous year (409). After two years of turmoil and anarchy, they at last ceased their movement, signing a treaty of alliance (*foedus*) with Rome that conceded them military settlements within the empire. The Suebi and the Asdingi Vandals settled in Galicia (Gallaecia), the Silingi Vandals in Baetica (Vandalusia = Andalusia), and the Alani in Lusitania and Carthaginiensis. Tarraconensis was occupied only after Ataulphus had been made king of the Visigoths and had invaded the Provincia, where he died the same year. The occupation of the peninsula by Germanic tribes was then complete. Wallia (415–419), through an agreement with Honorius, founded the kingdom of Tolosa in federation with Rome. With this agreement made, Wallia immediately attacked the Vandals and Alani of Andalusia and crushed them. The Vandals who survived joined with their Galician brothers and conquered Cartagena and Seville and, after sailing from Tarifa, crossed the Strait of Gibraltar under the command of Gaiseric (Genseric) and landed in North Africa (429). The Suebi, now in exclusive control of Galicia, established themselves there as an independent kingdom. They later divided the entire western region of the peninsula among their elite troops and extended their effective rule as far as the Tagus River. The kingdom of Galicia, as such, disappeared in 585.

Wallia

With Euric (466–484) the kingdom of Tolosa (Toulouse) became unified and independent from Rome. This kingdom's powers extended through the Galliae (except for the northern zone) and through the Hispaniae (except for Galicia, which continued, along with its Lusitanian possessions, to be a kingdom dependent on the Suebi). Euric was at that time the most powerful ruler in the West. He issued the first laws, which, because of the continuing predominance of Latin culture, were written in Latin, drawn up by Roman jurists, and were influenced heavily by Roman law (475). With the Alani and the Silingi Vandals having been defeated by Wallia and with the Asdingi Vandals in Africa, the only powers in the peninsula were the Suebi in the northwest and the Visigoths. Demographically and ethnically, they stood for very little, numbering only about 250,000, as compared with the 7,000,000 Hispano-Romans of the peninsula. But power was almost exclusively in their hands. They lived in relative harmony with the Hispanic people, a situation made possible largely by two great leaders, Orosius and Idatius, who strongly favoured the idea of a unified Spain under Visigothic protection.

When the Suebi and the Visigoths had arrived in Spain, they were to a great extent already Romanized; thus, there was no drastic cultural difference between the invaders and the invaded. Furthermore, for many years the Visigoths were considered allies and collaborators with the empire and, to a certain extent, its protectors. With the pact of 418, the Visigoths agreed to recognize the supreme authority of the Emperor and to submit to Roman political and administrative organization. The Visigoths arrived in Spain already bearing a certain political and social organization, although it is true that many aspects of it underwent important changes. They brought with them an elective monarchy that was assisted by a popular assembly made up of all free men who were eligible to go to war. The population of Visigothic Spain, however, was composed of two completely distinct societies. On one hand, there was the Hispano-Roman populace with its own laws, its Latin culture, and Catholic Christianity; and on the other hand, there were the Arian Visigothic invaders, who, even though they were a minority, held military power. They were ruled by a sovereign who, in theory, had authority only over his own people and not over the Hispano-Romans, since there was a code of Roman laws for these native people and a tradition of Visigothic common law for the invading people. Two-thirds of the land was redistributed into Visigothic hands, although vast territory remained unoccupied because of the scant numbers of the new colonists. A ban against marriage between Visigoths and Hispano-Romans lasted until its abolition by Leovigild (568–586). The Visigothic capital, which was originally in Tolosa, was transferred later to Toledo (Toletum) with the reign of Leovigild. (A.G. y B.)

THE VISIGOTHIC KINGDOM

Given their distinctive laws and customs and their profession of Arian Christianity, the Visigothic absorption by the Hispano-Roman population of perhaps 6,000,000 was not easy. Visigothic control of the peninsula remained incomplete so long as the Suebi (Suevi) maintained an independent kingdom in Galicia (Gallaecia) and the Basques refused submission to any external authority. Moreover, the Hispano-Romans in the southeast welcomed there the restoration of Byzantine rule early in the 6th century. Leovigild (568–586), the most capable of the Visigothic kings, who borrowed the Roman symbols and trappings of monarchy and ruled from a central position at Toledo (Toletum), made significant strides toward peninsular unification by conquering the Suebi and subjugating the Basques. Leovigild's attempt to convert the Hispano-Romans to Arianism, however, provoked a revolt in the southern province of Baetica under the leadership of his son, Hermenegild, who had accepted the Catholic religion. Rebel expectations of Byzantine help were unfulfilled, and so the uprising was finally crushed.

Conversion of Recared to orthodoxy

The evident futility of Leovigild's religious policy prompted his son, Recared (586–601), to convert to the Catholic faith professed by the majority of the people. His conversion, together with that of the Gothic nobles and bishops, removed one of the chief barriers to the assimilation of the two peoples. Thereafter, the Hispano-Romans, with less reason to be beguiled by Byzantium, developed a new and strong loyalty to the Visigothic monarchy. This facilitated the conquest of the last Byzantine strongholds in the peninsula during the reign of Swinthila (621–631). From then on, the Visigoths ruled over all of Spain.

The conversion also symbolized the triumph of Hispano-Roman civilization over the barbarians, and it helped to forge an alliance between the crown and the church. Realizing that the bishops were the leaders and spokesmen for the majority, the kings assumed the right to appoint them and to summon them to the Councils of Toledo. Those assemblies, though primarily ecclesiastical, had an extraordinary influence on the political life of the kingdom. After listening to the royal message describing problems of greatest concern, the prelates enacted appropriate canonical legislation as well as decrees relating to secular business, such as the election of the king or cases of treason. The bishops, in their councils, became a principal support of the monarchy, but in their quest for an ordered political regime, they lost some of their independence.

The monarchy was elective, partly because of aristocratic opposition to hereditary succession and partly because of a lack of natural heirs. Knowing the chronic Gothic tendency to assassinate the king, the bishops introduced the ceremony of anointing to give him a sacred character and to make known to all that he was under God's protection. In order to curtail the disorders attendant upon a royal election, they also elaborated an electoral procedure. The king ruled with the aid of a household (*officium palatinum*) based upon Roman models, and when important business required it, he took counsel with assemblies of magnates and other prominent persons (*aula regia*). Territorial administration was entrusted to dukes, counts, or judges. They were also responsible for the towns where self-government had long since decayed. Provinces and other administrative districts were essentially survivals from the Roman era. The economy was mainly agricultural, and there is scarcely any evidence of commercial or industrial activity.

The *Liber Judiciorum*

The influence of Roman civilization can also be noted in the steady subordination of Germanic law to the law of the Hispano-Roman majority. The *Liber Judiciorum*, a code of law promulgated around 654 by Recceswinth (649–672), in both its structure and its substance gives testimony to Roman influence. Intended to have territorial rather than personal application (as was the case with barbarian customary law), it reflected a persistent acceptance of Roman legal principles. Yet there are Germanic elements in the code, such as the ordeal of cold water. The *Liber Judiciorum* was one of the chief legacies of the Visigothic era and a tribute to the Hispano-Romans who were responsible for creating it.

The persistence of Roman tradition is also evident in the remarkable outburst of cultural activity in the 7th century. St. Isidore, bishop of Seville (Hispalis) from *c.* 600 to 636, friend and counsellor of kings, was a voluminous author who left his mark upon the entire medieval era. His works include a history of the Visigoths, a monastic rule, theological treatises, and, above all, the *Etymologies*, an encyclopaedic work that attempted to summarize the wisdom of the ancient world.

At the close of the 7th century, the Visigothic monarchy entered upon a critical time. The deposition, through trickery, of King Wamba (672–680), a competent ruler who tried to reform the military organization, indicated the trend of events. Numerous plots threatened his successors, who sought to blame the unrest upon the Jews, whom they tried to convert to Christianity or to reduce to slavery. Factionalism reached a climax when Witiza (700–710) died, hoping to leave the throne to his son; but Roderick, duke of Baetica (710–711), was acclaimed instead. Witiza's family apparently appealed to the Muslims in North Africa to help them overthrow Roderick. In response, Ṭāriq ibn Ziyād, the Muslim governor of Tangier, landed at Gibraltar (Calpe) in 711 and defeated King Roderick and the Visigoths near Río Guadalete on July 19. The conquest of the rest of Spain, left leaderless by the death of the king, followed quickly. The Visigothic kingdom perished, but its memory survived to inspire the kings of Asturias-Leon to attempt the reconquest of Spain.

CHRISTIAN SPAIN FROM THE MUSLIM INVASION TO C. 1260

The question of peninsular unity is central to the history of Christian Spain from the Muslim invasion in the 8th century to the advent of Ferdinand and Isabella in the late 15th. The Muslims destroyed what unity the Visigoths had been able to impose and introduced religious, cultural, legal, linguistic, and racial differences that impeded their assimilation by the natives. In the ensuing centuries, several Christian states emerged in the northern mountains; partly as a matter of self-preservation, partly for religious hostility, and partly to vindicate the Visigoths, they embarked upon the Reconquista (Reconquest). Their progress depended upon the strength of Muslim Spain at any given moment. In times of Muslim weakness or disintegration, the Christians usually made important gains. The kings of Asturias-Leon-Castile, eventually the largest state, aspired to dominance over the whole peninsula, but their ambitions were challenged and often thwarted by the rulers of Portugal, Navarre, and Aragon-Catalonia, which began to assume definitive form in the 11th and 12th centuries. The Reconquista was largely completed by the middle of the 13th century, with only the small Muslim kingdom of Granada (Gharnāṭah) surviving as tributary to Castile until 1492.

In the later Middle Ages, the problems of peninsular unity took on a new aspect as the kings of Castile tried to gain control of the other Christian states by marriage, diplomacy, and war. The Trastámara dynasty, which came to power in Castile in the late 14th century, consistently pursued this aim. It was achieved in part by Ferdinand and Isabella, whose marriage united Aragon and Castile. They also conquered Granada, thereby terminating the Reconquista, but their attempts to bring Portugal into a family union by marriage failed. In any case, the diversity of languages, laws, and traditions that had developed in the medieval centuries was not erased simply by the political union of kingdoms.

The Christian states, 711–1035. Christian resistance to the Muslim conquest began in the mountains of Asturias, where Visigothic nobles took refuge and joined the native mountaineers in opposing the invaders. Their leader was Pelayo (718–737), a Visigothic lord whose victory over the Muslims at Covadonga, around 722, later was hailed as the beginning of the Reconquista and the "salvation of Spain." Under King Alfonso I (739–757), the Asturians occupied Galicia, abandoned by rebelling Berber troops who had been garrisoned there. Farther south, he laid waste the Duero River Valley, which remained for many years a no-man's-land separating Christian and Muslim Spain. In the western Pyrenees, the Basques seem to have regained their independence; and the Franks, after expelling the Muslims from Septimania, began to penetrate into northeastern Spain. Charlemagne's attempt to take Saragossa (Saraqusṭah) in 778 failed, but his forces eventually moved into Catalonia, seizing Barcelona in 801. The Franks organized this region into several counties, later known collectively as the Spanish March. For several centuries, the March was linked by political and cultural ties to the Carolingian Empire and then to the Kingdom of France.

"Salvation of Spain"

While the Catalans tended to be oriented to the north, the Asturians looked southward and under Alfonso II (791–842) cautiously moved their capital to Oviedo, where they attempted to restore the institutions of the Visigothic monarchy.

Alfonso III

A breakdown of effective government in Muslim Spain in the late 9th century enabled Alfonso III (866–911) to cross enemy frontiers at will in search of plunder and to capture important places, notably Porto. Alfonso also began the process of colonizing the lands stretching southward to the Duero that had been depopulated for so long. On his eastern border, he erected many castles as protection against Muslim attacks, thus giving the area its name, Castile, and its distinctive character. The first extant Christian chronicles of the Reconquista were compiled during this period and sought to establish an essential continuity between the Visigothic and Asturian kingdoms. The Asturians saw themselves as the legitimate heirs of Visigothic power and tradition and consciously assumed responsibility for the reconquest of Muslim Spain. Future challenges to Asturian leadership were beginning to take shape, however, in the northeast, where a strong Basque kingdom, centred at Pamplona in Navarre, appeared under King Sancho I (905–926). In Catalonia, Count Wifred of Barcelona (873–898) took advantage of the disintegration of the Carolingian Empire to assert his independence and to secure control of several other counties. The dynasty he founded ruled in Catalonia until the 15th century.

Encouraged by the expansion of the Asturian kingdom and evident Muslim weakness, García I (911–914) moved his capital southward from Oviedo to the city of León. The optimism revealed by this action was shattered during the course of the 10th century as order and unity were restored in Muslim Spain under the rule of the caliphs of Córdoba (Qurṭabah). Muslim incursions into the Christian north were resumed and caused great destruction, though from time to time the Christians achieved some successes. Ramiro II (931–951) defeated the caliph ʿAbd ar-Raḥmān III at Simancas in 939, a truly remarkable feat. Yet within his own kingdom, Ramiro was faced with the growing defiance of the Castilians, who, as frontiersmen exposed to the hazards of daily conflict with the enemy, seem to have had little use for Leonese tradition and law. Their count, Fernán González (*c.* 930–970), successfully resisted the kings of Leon and laid the basis for Castilian independence.

As the century progressed, the Christian position steadily deteriorated. Muslim ascendancy was demonstrated clearly by the procession of envoys representing Ramiro III of Leon (966–984), Sancho II of Navarre (970–994), Count Borrell of Barcelona (*c.* 940–992), and Count Garci-Fernández of Castile (970–995), who came to Córdoba to offer homage and tribute to the caliph. Even in these depressed circumstances, the Leonese seem to have maintained the traditional Asturian claim to the Visigothic inheritance. As a more explicit assertion of peninsular hegemony, they elaborated a concept of a Hispanic empire centred at León. The theory no doubt served to bolster morale at the close of the century when all the Christian states suffered from the scourge of al-Manṣūr, who assumed dictatorial power in the caliphate. In order to distract the Muslims from his usurpation, he led armies on annual invasions of the north. In 985 he defeated Count Borrell and burned Barcelona; three years later he plundered León and many other towns.

The scourge of al-Manṣūr

The breakup of the caliphate following al-Manṣūr's death freed the Christian states from the threat of destruction. Count Ramón Borrell of Barcelona (992–1018) even gained a measure of retribution by intervening in the Muslim civil wars and sacking Córdoba in 1010. Alfonso V of Leon (999–1028) used the respite from war to repair his kingdom and in 1017, at a council held at León, promulgated the first general laws for the government of the realm. The cessation of Muslim attacks also encouraged a renewal of rivalry among the Christian states. For a few years, Sancho III the Great, king of Navarre (1000–35), succeeded in lording it over the rest of Christian Spain. During his reign, contacts with northern Christendom became more frequent. The pilgrimage route to Compostela, a principal avenue of French influence, was developed; the Cluniac reform of the monastic life was introduced, and feudal ideas began to affect the structure of aristocratic society. In pursuit of his own aggrandizement, Sancho III, who already held the counties of Aragon, Sobrarbe, and Ribagorza and numbered Count Berenguer Ramón I of Barcelona (1018–35) among his vassals, seized the county of Castile and threatened Bermudo III of Leon (1028–37). In 1034, Sancho occupied the city of León and assumed the title of emperor, but his triumph was cut short by his death in the following year.

The medieval empire, 1035–1157. Although Sancho III brought under his sway all the Christian states except Catalonia, he rejected the Leonese tradition of a unified, indivisible kingdom and regarded his dominions as a family patrimony to be shared among his sons. Thus, he gave the kingdom of Navarre to García III (1035–54); Ferdinand I (1035–65) received Castile; and Ramiro I (1035–63) obtained Aragon, to which he added Sobrarbe and Ribagorza in 1045 after the murder of a fourth brother, Gonzalo. As each of the sons bore the royal title, Castile and Aragon were elevated to the status of kingdoms. Although Bermudo III had regained possession of Leon, he was defeated and killed in 1037 by Ferdinand I, who annexed his kingdom and took the imperial title. For the next 30 years, he aspired to domination throughout Spain, overcoming his brothers on the battlefield, conquering Coimbra, and compelling the petty Muslim rulers (*reyes de taifas*) of Toledo (Ṭulayṭulah), Seville (Ishbīliyah), and Badajoz (Baṭalyaws) to pay him tribute.

Ferdinand's contemporary Count Ramón Berenguer I of Barcelona (1035–76) was actively developing Catalan interests and relationships among the lords of Languedoc, in southern France. He also promulgated the earliest legal texts included in the compilation of Catalan law known as the *Usatges de Barcelona* ("Usages of Barcelona").

At his death, Ferdinand I followed his father's custom and divided his kingdoms between his sons, giving Castile to Sancho II (1065–72) and Leon to Alfonso VI (1065–1109). Discord promptly arose and ended only with Sancho's murder in 1072. Alfonso VI thereupon reunited the two kingdoms, but he had to swear to the Castilian nobility that he had had no hand in his brother's death. Chief among the Castilians, who now became his vassals, was Rodrigo Díaz de Vivar, known to history as El Cid Campeador. Court jealousies eventually forced him into exile, and for a time he served the Muslim king of Saragossa before becoming the protector of the king of Valencia.

Alfonso VI

The division of Muslim Spain into several small kingdoms enabled Alfonso VI to levy tribute upon them, but he decided to conquer them and in 1085 received the surrender of Toledo, the fall of which had great symbolic importance because it had been the ancient seat of the Visigothic monarchy, and its possession strengthened the king's claims to hegemony in Spain. For this reason, he called himself "Emperor of Toledo," but he also used the title Emperor of the Two Religions to emphasize his ascendancy over both Christians and Muslims. The conquest brought his frontiers to the Tagus and resulted in the incorporation into his kingdom of large numbers of Muslims and Jews, who in times past usually had withdrawn to the south in the face of advancing Christian armies. Large numbers of Mozarabs, or Arabic-speaking Christians, also lived in Toledo and its environs. The interaction among these differing religious and cultural traditions became especially intense in the ensuing years.

The fall of Toledo alarmed the other petty kings in Muslim Spain, who invited the Almoravids, a fanatical Muslim sect in North Africa, to come to their aid. The Almoravids crushed the Christian army at Zalacca (az-Zallāqah) in 1086, but they also swallowed up the petty kingdoms. The reunification of Muslim Spain kept Alfonso VI on the defensive for the rest of his reign and made further progress in the Reconquista temporarily impossible. The Cid successfully defended Valencia against the Almoravids, but after his death in 1099 his followers had to abandon the city. The Almoravids were then able to occupy the whole of eastern Spain as far north as Saragossa.

The deeper Christian involvement in the world of Islām brought about by these events was counterbalanced by the steady growth of northern European influences, especially that of the papacy. Pope Gregory VII (1073–85), who spearheaded the general reform of the church, imposed uniformity of liturgical practice by insisting upon the abandonment of the ancient Mozarabic liturgy native to Spain and its replacement by the Roman. His assertion of papal sovereignty over Spain was not admitted by the Spanish rulers, and he did not press it. In addition, French monks and clerics discovered ecclesiastical fortunes in Spain, and French knights came to participate in greater numbers in the wars of the Reconquista. Two of them, the cousins Raymond and Henry of Burgundy, married the daughters of Alfonso VI, Urraca and Teresa, and so became the progenitors of dynasties that ruled in Leon and Portugal until the late 14th century.

After Alfonso VI's death, Urraca (1109–26), now widowed, succeeded him. She married Alfonso I of Aragon, "the Battler" (1104–34), but disharmony between them kept the kingdom in constant turmoil. Alfonso I eventually retired in disgust to his own kingdom. Urraca's son by Raymond of Burgundy, Alfonso VII (1126–57), restored the prestige of the Leonese monarchy and affirmed Leonese aspirations to predominance in Spain by being solemnly crowned as emperor in the cathedral of León in 1135. This was apparently the first and last imperial coronation in Spain. Within a few years, however, two formidable challenges to Leonese ascendancy appeared in the newly formed federation of Aragon and Catalonia and in the newly independent kingdom of Portugal.

Alfonso I of Aragon, after ending his marriage to Urraca, conquered Saragossa in 1118, thus advancing his frontiers to the Ebro. Shortly after, he made an extraordinary incursion into the heart of Muslim Spain to liberate the Mozarabs of Granada (Gharnāṭah), whom he settled in Aragon. Thereafter, the Mozarabic population in Muslim Spain seems to have been negligible. When he died, he bequeathed his realms to the military Orders of the Hospital, the Temple, and the Holy Sepulchre, but his people refused to accept this. The Navarrese, who had been subject to Aragonese rule since 1076, elected their own king, García IV (1134–50), and the Aragonese summoned the dead king's brother, Ramiro II (1134–37), from a monastery to become their king. He assumed the responsibility only long enough to marry and to father a child, Petronila, who could inherit the kingdom. She was betrothed in 1137 to Count Ramón Berenguer IV of Barcelona (1131–62), who was entrusted with the administration of the kingdom. The child by this marriage, Alfonso II (1162–96), united in his person the kingdom of Aragon and the country of Barcelona, a union of peoples with different traditions, interests, and languages, which survived innumerable vicissitudes throughout the medieval era. Catalonia developed as a maritime power, interested in expansion in the Mediterranean, while Aragon, a landlocked region, remained largely agricultural, dominated by a landed aristocracy. Each region retained its distinctive laws and institutions, and there was strong opposition on both sides to any attempt at assimilation. The term crown of Aragon appropriately describes the federation of the two territories.

The crown of Aragon

In the west, the county of Portugal, a part of the Kingdom of Leon, which Alfonso VI had given to Teresa and Henry of Burgundy, began to emerge as an independent state. Their son, Afonso I Henriques (1128–85), rejected Leonese overlordship and assumed the title of king, around 1139. In order to protect himself, he became a vassal of the papacy, pledging to pay an annual tribute; but the Pope did not explicitly recognize him as a king until 1179.

The Almoravid Empire, meanwhile, began to break up as a result of internal discord and the rise of the Almohads, another North African Muslim sect. Taking advantage of the Muslim civil wars, the Christian rulers penetrated deeply into Muslim Spain and made some significant conquests. In 1147, Afonso I, with the help of a crusading fleet from northern Europe, conquered Lisbon, while Alfonso VII and Ramón Berenguer IV, aided by Pisan ships, captured the great seaport of Almería on the southeastern coast. In the following year, the count of Barcelona seized Tortosa (Ṭurṭūshah) and Lérida (Lāridah), thereby completing the expansion of Catalonia and extending its frontiers to the mouth of the Ebro. The Almohads, however, after destroying Almoravid power, invaded Spain and reduced all the Muslim areas to their rule. In 1157 they reconquered Almería (al-Marīyah) and thereafter effectively checked any further Christian progress.

The rise of Castile and Aragon. Alfonso VII died in the same year. By dividing his realms between his sons, Sancho III (1157–58), to whom he gave Castile, and Ferdinand II (1157–88), who received Leon, he shattered the unity he had tried to impose upon the peninsula and ruined the concept of a Leonese empire. Although the Almohads kept the Christians on the defensive, Alfonso VIII of Castile (1158–1214) and Alfonso II of Aragon were confident enough of ultimate success to conclude a treaty in 1179 partitioning Muslim Spain. The territory of Valencia (Balansiyah) was reserved for Aragonese reconquest, while the rest of Andalusia fell to Castile. Rivalries among the Christian princes quickly arose, however, when Alfonso VIII tried to dominate his colleagues. Common action against the Almohads was impeded, and in 1195 they inflicted a humiliating defeat upon the king of Castile at Alarcos (al-Arak), south of Toledo. Realizing the seriousness of the Muslim threat, the other Christian kings made peace with Castile. In 1212, Alfonso VIII, supported by Sancho VII of Navarre (1194–1234) and Peter II of Aragon (1196–1213) and by contingents from Portugal and Leon, achieved a remarkable victory over the Almohads at Las Navas de Tolosa (al-ʿIqāb). His triumph opened the road to Christian penetration into Andalusia, and it sounded the death knell for the Almohad Empire.

Active participation in the Reconquista was only one aspect of Aragonese policy. The king of Aragon, as ruler of Catalonia, also had significant interests in southern France, where several lords were his vassals. The Albigensian heresy was spreading through the region, however, and Peter II, while no friend of heretics, concluded that his rights there were jeopardized by the crusade launched by Pope Innocent III against them. When Peter tried to rescue his brother-in-law, the count of Toulouse, he was defeated and killed by the crusaders at Muret in 1213. His death marked the beginning of the end of Catalan ambition and power in southern France.

Advance against the Almohads

The steady collapse of the Almohad Empire in the second quarter of the century enabled the Christian rulers to carry the Reconquista almost to completion. James I of Aragon (1213–76), after a turbulent minority, conquered Majorca (Mayūrqah) in 1229. This was the first important step in the overseas expansion of Catalonia and the first great manifestation of Catalan naval power. He then began the more arduous task of conquering the kingdom of Valencia, but he was distracted briefly by the possibility of annexing Navarre. When Sancho VII died without children, the Navarrese proclaimed his nephew, Count Theobald of Champagne (1234–53), as their king, and thereafter Navarre was drawn closer to French politics. Putting aside his ambitions in Navarre, James I received the surrender of the city of Valencia in 1238 and promulgated a code of law for his new realm, which formed the third constituent element in the crown of Aragon. For the first time, thousands of Muslims were incorporated into his dominions.

In the meantime, Alfonso IX of Leon (1188–1230) was advancing southward to the Guadiana (Wādī Ānā), taking Mérida (Māridah) and Badajoz in 1230 and opening the road to Seville. Upon his death, his son Ferdinand III, already king of Castile (1217–52), by virtue of inheritance from his mother, Berenguela, daughter of Alfonso VIII, was received as king of Leon, thus reuniting the two realms for good. With their combined resources, he conquered Córdoba in 1236, Murcia (Mursiyah) in 1243, Jaén (Jayyān) in 1246, and Seville in 1248. Only the Kingdom of Granada remained in Muslim hands, but it was subject to the payment of annual tribute to Castile. For this reason and because it did not constitute any evident threat, serious attempts to conquer it were seldom undertaken in the next two centuries.

Society, economy, and culture. In the first 300 years following the Muslim invasion, Christian society and institutions developed slowly, but substantial change came rapidly in the 12th and 13th centuries. Among the reasons for this were a general rise in population, increasing contacts with northern Europe, participation in the common European growth of trade and town life, and progress in the reconquest.

By the middle of the 13th century, the kingdoms of Leon-Castile, Aragon-Catalonia, Navarre, and Portugal had attained the frontiers they were to have, with only slight modification, until the close of the medieval era. The crown of Aragon was unique among them because it was a confederation of several distinct entities: the kingdoms of Aragon, Valencia, and Majorca, and the principality of Catalonia.

The principle of hereditary succession was established early, but the idea of election survived in the acclamation of the king when he was anointed and crowned in accordance with Visigothic tradition. Peter II of Aragon was crowned in Rome by the Pope, whose vassal he became, thereby subordinating his kingdom to papal suzerainty. The king ruled with the collaboration of his household, whose chief officers were the chancellor, ordinarily a prelate or cleric responsible for the dispatch of royal letters and the keeping of records, and the *mayordomo* and *alférez* (*majordom* and *senyaler* in Catalonia), magnates whose tasks were, respectively, the management of the household and royal estates and the command and organization of the army. Magnates also served as administrators of provinces and in Castile were known as *merinos* or, later, as *adelantados.* In Catalonia, the several counts originally governed their counties in the name of the Carolingian emperors, but they became in fact independent, and by the 11th century, the counts of Barcelona established an effective sovereignty over the principality. Vicars (*vegueros*), responsible for justice, and bailiffs (*batlles*), for taxes, administered Catalan territorial subdivisions. Bishops, magnates, monasteries, and military orders often enjoyed the privilege of immunity, whereby royal officials were forbidden to enter their estates to administer justice or to collect taxes, except in case of negligence. Among the most important immunities were those of the archbishop of Compostela in Galicia and those of the military orders in the region south of Toledo.

As the old Roman concept of the state had been obscured, private and personal relationships of a feudal character had considerable influence upon the governmental and military structure. The development of feudalism was greatest in Catalonia due to its contacts with France, but in the western states it was retarded and incomplete. The Catalan nobles were vassals of the count of Barcelona, to whom they owed military and court service in return for fiefs, and they often had vassals of their own. In the west, royal vassals had the same obligations, but ordinarily they did not receive fiefs nor did they give fiefs to their vassals. The magnates, known as *ricoshombres* (*i.e.,* rich or powerful men) in the west and as *barones* in Catalonia, usually were vassals of the king or count and served as his principal counsellors and as the backbone of the military organization. Nobles of secondary rank, called variously *infanzones, fijosdalgo, caballeros* or *cavallers,* usually were vassals of the magnates.

Inasmuch as the economy of the Christian states was mainly agricultural, the king and nobles of both ranks were landlords who derived the greater part of their income from the exploitation of landed estates. Peasants living on the estates cultivated the soil and paid a variety of rents and services to their lords. The burden fell heaviest upon the serfs (*solariegos* in Castile, *payeses de remensa* in Catalonia), who were effectively bound to the soil and denied freedom of movement. Catalan serfs, especially, were subject to abuse by their lords by means of the so-called evil usages. Leonese peasants occupying lands known as *behetrías* enjoyed the right of freely choosing their lord and of changing their allegiance as they wished, but this right was being limited in the 13th century. Peasants who were willing to accept the risks and the adventure of living on the frontier were the freest of all, and like pioneers in all ages, they developed a strong sense of personal worth and independence.

The serfs

As the Reconquista progressed, the crown encouraged the colonization of the Duero Valley by erecting fortified urban centres (*concejos*) with extensive rural areas dependent upon them. The people who settled there received charters (*fueros*) defining their liberties and giving them rights of self-government under their own elected magistrates (alcaldes). The economy of these towns was based not so much on industry and commerce as upon the raising of sheep and cattle and the booty taken by the urban militia in the wars of the Reconquista. Aragonese and Catalan towns enjoyed a lesser degree of autonomy, but the latter began to achieve a real importance as mercantile centres. The incorporation of such cities as Toledo, Saragossa, Lisbon, Córdoba, Valencia, and Seville greatly increased the urban population and contributed substantially to the development of trade and industry. Artisans appeared in greater numbers and began to organize guilds; a merchant class engaged in buying and selling on a large scale and commonly using money as a medium of exchange also emerged. The development of shipbuilding at such places as Santander and Barcelona made possible a native overseas-carrying trade.

The advance of the Reconquista also added large numbers of Muslims and Jews to the Christian kingdoms. The former, known as Mudéjares, were settled chiefly in rural areas, though there were always important Muslim quarters in the towns. The Jews lived mainly in the cities, where they were involved in trade and moneylending and were often employed as royal tax collectors. Both Muslims and Jews were permitted to practice their religions and to govern themselves according to Islāmic or Judaic law, but they were subject to the payment of regular tribute, and from time to time the Jews were assaulted by their Christian neighbours.

Government of the towns

In view of the growing administrative, military, and economic importance of the towns, the crown summoned their representatives to meet in the royal council with prelates and nobles. In 1188 at León, Alfonso IX held the first such assembly (*curia plena*), but similar gatherings began to be held regularly in the other states in the early 13th century. Meetings of the Cortes, as these assemblies were called, served a number of purposes, one of which was to enable the king to obtain consent for the levy of extraordinary taxation to meet ever increasing financial needs caused by the expansion of royal activities and responsibilities. Parliamentary growth in the peninsular kingdoms was a manifestation of a common European phenomenon, but it is noteworthy that it occurred earlier in Spain than elsewhere.

The Reconquista was also accompanied by the restoration of bishoprics or the expansion of older ones. Spain was divided ecclesiastically into five metropolitan sees: Toledo, which claimed the primacy, Tarragona, Braga, Compostela, and Seville. Papal intervention in their affairs became much more frequent in the 12th century. Monastic reforms emanating from Cluny and Citeaux in France profoundly affected religious life in the 11th and 12th centuries. Early in the 13th century, the mendicant orders, the Franciscans and Dominicans (whose founder was the Spaniard Domingo de Guzmán), spread through the peninsula. The military orders of the Temple and the Hospital, originating in the Holy Land, appeared in Spain in the 12th century, but in the second half of the century, several indigenous orders were founded—Calatrava, Alcántara, Santiago, and Avis. These knights tried to observe the monastic life, but they also provided much of the armed might responsible for the successes of the Reconquista.

The clergy were the guardians of the cultural tradition and the authors of the scant literary remains of the first centuries of the Reconquista. In the 8th century, the adoptionist controversy over the nature of the Trinity engendered many polemical works; the writings of the Mozarabs of Córdoba, Eulogio (died 859) and Alvaro (died 861), illustrate the difficulties faced by Christians living under Muslim rule. Under the influence of northern Europe, theology, philosophy, and Roman and canon law became formal subjects of study in the universities of Palencia and Salamanca, founded early in the 13th century by Alfonso VIII of Castile and Alfonso IX of Leon, respectively. The existence of the universities was problematical for some time, but eventually Salamanca attained international renown. In the meantime, a vernacular literature was developing, and around 1140 there appeared the first great epic in the Castilian tongue, *The Poem of the Cid.* The output of Spanish writers was still slim, however, though the historical works of Rodrigo Jiménez de Rada, archbishop of Toledo (died 1247), set the pattern for future generations of Spanish historians.

CHRISTIAN SPAIN, C. 1260–1479

Castile and Leon, 1252–1479. In the late medieval centuries, a power struggle developed between the kings of Castile, who sought to concentrate all authority in their hands, and the nobility, who tried to use the monarchy for their own aggrandizement. The struggle began during the reign of Alfonso X the Wise (1252–84), who is perhaps best known for the literary and scientific labours accomplished by the scholars who enjoyed his patronage. From a political standpoint, his reign ended in failure. Although he showed some interest in continuing the Reconquista and had to suppress a revolt by the Mudéjares of Andalusia and Murcia, he preferred to play a larger role upon the European scene. In 1257 he was elected Holy Roman emperor and spent most of his energy and resources in the next 17 years trying to overcome a rival candidate and to win papal recognition. His extraordinary need of money for this purpose eventually brought to a head a domestic crisis that had been developing since his first years in power.

Legal reform

Like his father, Ferdinand III, Alfonso perceived the need for a uniform royal law that would supersede all local and regional laws, such as the *fueros* of the towns and the Liber Judiciorum used in Leon (and translated into Castilian as the Fuero Juzgo on the orders of Ferdinand III). A code of law, known as the Fuero de las Leyes, intended to be common to the whole realm, was prepared; it was the earliest redaction of the Siete Partidas, the great code that received definitive form early in the 14th century. The new code drew heavily upon Roman law, but the King's attempt to impose it provoked outcries from the nobles and from the towns. In 1272 they forced him to confirm their traditional laws and customs and to abandon the attempt to create a single body of law for the kingdom. This disappointment was followed in 1274 by the Pope's final rejection of Alfonso X's claims to the empire. In 1275 Alfonso's eldest son and heir, Fernando de la Cerda, died, and the King recognized Fernando's son, Alfonso de la Cerda, as his successor. The King's second son, Sancho, refused to accept this decision, and, posing as the defender of the nobles against the crown, took up arms against his father. An assembly of nobles, prelates, and townsmen deprived Alfonso X of his right to rule and entrusted the government to Sancho, but civil war raged until the King's death.

Sancho IV (1284–95) had to contend with domestic and foreign opposition in support of his nephew, and he was also threatened by invasion from Morocco. The latter danger initiated a long struggle to control the Strait of Gibraltar and thus to close that invasion route. The minority of Ferdinand IV (1295–1312) saw a renewal of efforts on behalf of Alfonso de la Cerda, but he was finally persuaded to renounce his claims to any share in the royal inheritance. In 1309 the King captured Gibraltar (Jabal Ṭāriq), but the Muslims recovered it a quarter century later. Disorders recurred in the minority of Alfonso XI (1312–50), but when he came of age he crushed his opponents among the nobility with great brutality. For 25 years he waged war against Granada. In 1340, with help from the other Christian states, he won a great victory over the combined forces of Granada and Morocco at Río Salado, thereby putting an end to any further Moroccan attempts to gain a foothold in Spain. Four years later he seized Algeciras (al-Jazīraha al-Khaḍrā'), but his effort to take the adjacent fortress of Gibraltar ended with his death as a victim, like so many other thousands, of the Black Death.

Conflict between the crown and the nobility flared again in the reign of Peter I the Cruel (1350–69), whose half brother, Henry of Trastámara, an illegitimate son of Alfonso XI, challenged his right to rule. To further his aims, Henry secured French support, and in 1366, with a mercenary army commanded by Bertrand du Guesclin, he was able to expel Peter from the kingdom. The King, however, persuaded Edward, the Black Prince, to assist him in regaining his throne. The combined Anglo-Castilian forces routed Henry of Trastámara at Nájera in 1367. But once the Black Prince withdrew, Henry and du Guesclin returned; they defeated and killed Peter at Montiel in 1369.

Henry II (1369–79), the first of the Trastámara dynasty, had to defend his title against his neighbours in the peninsula and to overcome domestic opposition. But he succeeded in consolidating his position and was even able to supply ships to support his French allies against the English. One consequence of the French alliance was Castilian recognition of the Avignonese pope during the Great Western Schism. The ambitions of the Trastámara family to unify the peninsula were revealed when Henry's son John I (1379–90) claimed Portugal by right of marriage. His intervention evoked the spirit of nationalism among the Portuguese, who defeated him at Aljubarrota in 1385. In the next year, John of Gaunt, duke of Lancaster, who had married Peter I's daughter, claimed the Castilian throne and with Portuguese help invaded Galicia. The campaign failed, however, and he made peace in 1388, agreeing to the marriage of his daughter Catharine to Henry III, oldest son of John I. Thus the enmity between the two branches of the Castilian royal house was laid to rest.

Avignon papacy

During the minority of Henry III (1390–1406), the nobility again tried to further their own fortunes at the expense of the crown, but when the king came of age he effectively repressed them. The long reign of his son, John II (1406–54), proved to be disastrous to the prestige and authority of the crown. Stability was maintained during his minority by his uncle, Fernando de Antequera, who acted as regent until his election as king of Aragon in 1412. Fernando's sons, Henry and John of Navarre, continued to participate actively in Castilian affairs and tried to dominate the King, but the royal favourite Alvaro de Luna had already gained ascendancy over the King and successfully resisted these intrigues. For most of the reign, he was the effective instrument of royal power, and only in 1453 was the King persuaded to be rid of him and to order his execution.

Rivalry among the nobles for influence and power was intensified during the reign of Henry IV (1454–74). Juan Pacheco, marquess of Villena, long dominated the King, but others succeeded in winning royal favour. Henry's alleged impotence caused the magnates to cast doubt upon the legitimacy of the infanta Joan, who, it was charged, was the child of the queen and of Beltrán de la Cueva, one of the King's most recent favourites. In derision, the little girl was called La Beltraneja. Henry IV disowned her at Los Toros de Guisando in 1468 and recognized his sister Isabella as heir to the throne. Villena and his followers evidently hoped to be able to control her, but they were mistaken. Although she had promised not to marry without her brother's consent, she did precisely that in 1469. Her husband was Ferdinand, son and heir of the king of Aragon. Angered by this, Henry IV tried to deprive Isabella of her rights, but when he died, she was proclaimed as Queen Isabella I (1474–1504). Afonso V of Portugal, who was betrothed to Joan (La Beltraneja), invaded Castile on her behalf, but in 1479 she renounced her claims. In the same year, Ferdinand ascended the Aragonese throne, thus effecting the personal union of Aragon and Castile.

The infanta Joan

Castilian institutions, society, and culture. The reemergence in the 13th century of the idea of the state as a public institution, partly as a result of the revival of Roman law and the rediscovery of Aristotle's *Politics,* had important consequences for the development of the Castilian monarchy. As the embodiment of the state, the king (whom the Siete Partidas described as God's vicar on earth) tended to concentrate power in his own hands. The jurists who staffed and dominated the royal bureaucracy tried to push royal claims to authority as far as they would go. The influence of Roman law, though originally opposed, grew steadily, and when Alfonso XI promulgated the Ordenamiento de Alcalá in 1348, the place of Roman law and legal procedure in the courts was assured. The royal tribunal (*audiencia*) was reorganized in the reign of Henry II, but it did not receive definitive form until the end of the Middle Ages. The tendency toward centralization also prompted the crown to intervene more frequently in the government of the towns, where rivalry among factions was becoming endemic. The urban aristocracy, originating as a class of non-noble mounted warriors, had gained control of the government and tended to exclude the lower orders from participation, while seeking the status of nobility—with its attendant exemption from taxation—for themselves. In order to repress urban conflicts, the crown began to send corregidores (governors) to supersede local governmental officials; at first this was a temporary measure, but by the 15th century it had become a permanent arrangement.

The trend toward absolutism encountered opposition both from the nobility and from the Cortes. Under pressure from the Cortes, John I in 1386 organized a royal council (*consejo real*) composed of representatives from the three estates, who would have a permanent influence on royal policy. The experiment failed, chiefly because the nobility succeeded in gaining control of the council and in the 15th century used it for their own advantage. The magnates wielded great power in the territorial administration of the realm, for they held the posts of *adelantado mayor* (governor) in Castile, Murcia, and Andalusia. Moreover, the Trastámara kings gave the magnates extensive territorial lordships as well as lordships over some of the principal towns and cities. In so doing, the crown divested itself of control of some of the major bulwarks of royal power in the past. In general, a pro-aristocratic mentality pervaded Castilian society in the 15th century, encouraging the usurpation of royal authority by the magnates.

The Cortes

The Cortes played a prominent role in the political life of the kingdom, especially from about 1250 to 1350, and again during the reigns of the first two Trastámara kings, who needed its support to consolidate the dynasty. The Cortes met frequently to give consent to taxation (*servicio*) for fixed periods and for specific purposes. Ferdinand IV was compelled to declare formally that he could not levy an extraordinary tax without consent, and John I had to allow the Cortes to audit his accounts. Petitions presented by the Cortes and accepted by the king became the law of the land. The role of the Cortes was circumscribed in the reigns of John II and Henry IV, who abused the rights that the assembly had gained in the 14th century. The crown often appointed the procurators to represent the towns, and the number of towns summoned declined steadily. Many towns were not summoned because they were held in lordship by magnates who claimed to speak for them.

The Castilian economy, for the most part, remained agricultural and pastoral. Sheep and cattle grazing became extremely important as immense pasturelands were opened up in Extremadura and Andalusia. The Mesta, a national sheep-raising organization chartered by Alfonso X, wielded great influence. The manufacture of woollen cloth became an important industry in the towns, but on the whole the urban middle class was weak, and a powerful guild organization never really developed. The urban aristocracy, which had come to power in the wars of the Reconquista, was not inclined to engage in trade and crafts. A substantial maritime trade with England, Flanders, France, and Portugal was carried on by the ports of the Bay of Biscay. The Genoese maintained a large colony at Seville, the chief southern port, and had a great share in the carrying trade originating there.

The Black Death

The outbreak of the Black Death in the middle of the 14th century contributed to a radical decline in population and a steady succession of social and economic upheavals. In order to compel workers to accept the same wages as before the plague, Peter I enacted the Ordenamiento de Menestrales in 1351. Forty years later, social unrest vented itself in a great pogrom against the Jews, which quickly spread to many parts of the peninsula. Accepting Christianity rather than death, many Jewish converts (*conversos*) attained prominence in various aspects of public life, but they were always held in suspicion and accused of practicing Judaism in private. Deliberate attempts were made to exclude them from important positions by requiring them to prove *limpieza de sangre; i.e.,* that their ancestry was untainted by Jewish or Muslim blood.

Culturally, Castile was now fully integrated into western European life. Alfonso X gave great impetus to learning and to the development of Castilian as a literary language. Under his aegis, translations from the Arabic were undertaken, a "General Chronicle" of Spain was written, the Siete Partidas was compiled, and he personally gained renown as the author of the *Cantigas de Santa María,* a collection of more than 400 poems. His nephew Juan Manuel (died 1348) won lasting fame as the author of *El Libro de los enxiemplos del conde Lucanor et de Patronio* (a collection of Oriental fables), the *Libro de los estados* (a treatise on social classes), and numerous other works. His contemporary Juan Ruiz, the archpriest of Hita (died *c.* 1350), who wrote the *Libro de buen amor,* ranks as one of the greatest medieval poets. Interspersed with beautiful hymns in praise of the Virgin Mary are ribald and comic poems of love. A series of royal chronicles relates the history of this period. Perhaps the best among them are the chronicles of the reigns of Peter I, Henry II, John I, and Henry III by Pedro López de Ayala (died 1407), a brilliant writer who searched for motives and who realized the importance of social and institutional developments. In the 15th century, the influence of the Italian Renaissance was being felt at the court of John II, a patron of many poets and scholars. Among them were the marquess of Santillana (died 1458), whose lyric poems have great beauty; Jorge Manrique (died 1479), whose *Coplas,* written on the death of his father, are a reflection on the vanities of the world; and Fernán Pérez de Guzmán (died *c.* 1460), whose *Generaciones y semblanzas* is a series of sketches of the characters and personalities in the court of Henry III.

Aragon, Catalonia, and Valencia, 1276–1479. The aristocratic challenge to royal power that characterized Castilian history of the later Middle Ages was also evident in the kingdom of Aragon. The growing influence of Roman law and lawyers evoked protest in both Aragon and Catalonia. In 1265, at the Cortes of Egea, James I had to confirm traditional Aragonese laws and agree that the nobles should be tried by the *justicia,* a judge appointed by the king from the knightly class rather than from the ranks of professional jurists. The controversy reached an acute stage during the reign of Peter III the Great (1276–85), who received Aragon, Catalonia, and Valencia as his share in the inheritance while his younger brother James received the kingdom of Majorca.

Annexation of Sicily

Peter III conquered Sicily in 1282 in the wake of the rebellion against French rule known as the Sicilian Vespers. Peter's wife represented Hohenstaufen claims to both Naples and Sicily, in opposition to Charles of Anjou, to whom the papacy had awarded the kingdom. The annexation of Sicily was the second major step in the expansion of Catalonia into the Mediterranean, but it was also the cause of a long international conflict with serious domestic complications. The Pope excommunicated and deposed Peter III, offering his realm to a French prince. In the midst of these troubles, the Aragonese nobles formed a union to defend their liberties and in 1283 forced the King to grant the General Privilege. Confirming the right of the nobles to be judged by the *justicia,* the King also promised to convene the Cortes annually and to take its counsel in matters affecting the realm. He made similar promises in Catalonia and Valencia, but there he could count more fully on the support of his subjects. The crusade launched against him by the Pope and led by King Philip III of France ended in failure, but the problem of Sicily remained the primary concern of Peter's three sons.

Alfonso III (1285–91) inherited the peninsular dominions and also annexed Majorca because of his uncle's treachery during the crusade. His younger brother, James, inherited Sicily. Together, they struggled valiantly to overcome the formidable opposition of the papacy, the French, and the Angevins. The Aragonese nobles again threatened the

King and compelled him to issue two privileges in 1287, confirming the rights already ceded by his father and allowing them to appoint and to remove certain members of the royal council. James II (1291–1327) succeeded his brother as king of Aragon, but in order to obtain an undisputed title, he yielded his rights to Sicily in 1295 and also restored Majorca to his uncle James. In compensation, Pope Boniface VIII gave him title to Sardinia. The third brother, Frederick, was proclaimed king of Sicily, and in 1302 the Pope finally agreed to accept him. A force of *almogavares* (medieval Spanish mercenaries), who had fought in the Sicilian wars, found employment thereafter in the Byzantine Empire as the Grand Catalan Company and eventually established lordship over the duchy of Athens in 1311. Sicily and Athens, though not directly under the rule of the king of Aragon, remained outposts of Catalan influence and power.

James II, who achieved a favourable modification of his frontier with Murcia, occupied Sardinia only in 1325. Genoa contested Aragonese rights, and a series of wars on this account took place during the reigns of Alfonso IV (1327–36) and Peter IV the Ceremonious (1336–87). In 1343, Peter IV dispossessed his cousin, the king of Majorca, for disloyalty and reunited that kingdom to the crown of Aragon. A constitutional crisis arose in 1347 when the King proclaimed his daughter as heir to the throne, contrary to the ambitions of his brother, the Count of Urgel, who argued that only males could wear the crown. The Aragonese union, which had been relatively quiet in the preceding reign, renewed its challenge to royal authority and forced Peter to confirm the privileges granted by his predecessors. The Valencian nobility also formed a union and extorted similar concessions, but the ravages of the Black Death and the triumph of the royalists over the Aragonese at Epila in 1348 enabled the King to dissolve the union and to tear up its privileges. The union never appeared again.

The constitutional crisis of 1347

After midcentury, Peter IV had to defend his realm against a vigorous invasion by Peter I of Castile. He supported Henry of Trastámara's bid to gain the Castilian throne, but his subsequent efforts to secure territorial concessions from Henry II were unsuccessful. In 1377, however, he was able to reincorporate Sicily into the dominions of the crown of Aragon. Although Peter IV was inclined to neutrality in the Great Western Schism, his son John I (1387–96) recognized the Avignonese pope. Continued unrest in Sardinia and Sicily occupied much of his attention and that of his younger brother and successor, Martin I (1396–1410). The death of the latter without immediate heirs created the most critical situation ever to confront the crown of Aragon. Numerous claimants came forward, but none had wide support. In order to resolve the issue, the estates of Aragon, Valencia, and Catalonia appointed nine commissioners who met at Caspe. Their decision, the compromise of Caspe, published in 1412, declared that the throne belonged by right of inheritance to Fernando de Antequera, brother of King Henry III of Castile. Despite opposition from the Count of Urgel, Ferdinand I (1412–16) became the first of the Trastámara family to rule in Aragon and thereby prepared the way for the eventual union of Aragon and Castile. His principal accomplishment was the withdrawal of obedience from the Avignonese pope Benedict XIII, thus helping to bring the schism to an end.

His son, Alfonso V the Magnanimous (1416–58), generally neglected his peninsular realms to pursue ambitions in Italy. There he seized the Kingdom of Naples in 1442, aspiring to dominate the rest of Italy and even to extend his power into the eastern Mediterranean. His long absence from Aragon fostered a spirit of discontent that reached a crisis during the reign of his brother, John II (1458–79), who inherited the mainland kingdoms as well as Sicily. (Naples was given to Alfonso V's illegitimate son, Ferrante.) By his marriage in 1420, John had become king of Navarre, thus adding a third kingdom to the Trastámara holdings. Conflicts with his son, Prince Charles of Viana, alienated his subjects and aroused overt Catalan hostility. When Charles died suddenly in 1461, many supposed he had been poisoned. The Catalans, who had grown restive because of economic and social hardships, revolted and tried to find another king to rule over them. Meanwhile, Louis XI of France took advantage of the situation to occupy Roussillon and Cerdagne, thus laying the groundwork for future hostilities between France and Spain. By 1472, however, John II had succeeded in overcoming the Catalan revolt and was able to assist his daughter-in-law Isabella in securing the Castilian throne. When he died in 1479, his son Ferdinand succeeded as king of Aragon and Sardinia, and his daughter Eleanor inherited Navarre.

Aragonese institutions, society, and culture. During the late Middle Ages, the Aragonese confederation, amplified and at times dismembered or nearly so, consisted of the essential nucleus of Aragon, Catalonia, and Valencia. In 1319 James II declared the indissoluble union of these three states. From time to time, Majorca, Sicily, Sardinia, and Naples were added to, occasionally separated from, and finally reunited to the crown of Aragon. An attempt to sever parts of Valencia for the benefit of Peter IV's younger brother was opposed not only by the King but also by the people of Valencia. Only at the close of the Middle Ages was the Aragonese federation menaced by dissolution, when the Catalans rebelled against John II and tried to secede, without success. The crown of Aragon had been held as a fief of the papacy ever since Peter II in 1204; this allowed the papacy to intervene directly in Aragonese affairs and even to try to dispose of the throne.

As in Castile, the bureaucracy was much more complicated; it came to be dominated by jurists who encouraged royal absolutism. Peter IV, known as the Ceremonious, took special care to organize the administration around the four principal officials—the chancellor, the chamberlain, the majordomo, and the *mestre racional,* or chief financial officer. There was intense opposition in each of the several states to the employment of non-natives in administrative positions. Even after the suppression of the union of Aragonese nobles by Peter IV, the *justicia* continued to be the ordinary judge in litigation involving them, but he always served at the king's pleasure.

The king's oldest son usually was named as procurator general for all the realms and served as his father's lieutenant. In Valencia and Majorca, which the king visited only occasionally, a procurator or governor general became a permanent representative of the crown. The towns gained a much greater degree of self-government, though the crown was represented in them by a vicar or *justicia.* In Barcelona, a council of five acted as the executive authority, responsible to a larger *consell de cent,* or council of 100.

Revisions of the law

The Usages of Barcelona remained the basic law for Catalonia and Majorca, and in 1251 James I had to pledge that Roman law would not replace them. After the conquest of Valencia, he promulgated the Fori regni Valentiae (1240), a code of law—largely Roman—for use in that kingdom. The customary law of Aragon was compiled in the Code of Huesca, promulgated in 1247. As additions were made to it, a new compilation called the Fueros de Aragón was issued in the 15th century.

The states of the crown of Aragon developed a vigorous parliamentary structure. Each of the mainland states had a parliament, and from time to time the king convened a general assembly for all three. In 1283, at Barcelona, Peter III made two significant pledges of fundamental importance for Catalan constitutional development. He promised to convene an annual Corts "to treat of the good estate and reformation of the land," and he also promised not to make any general statute for Catalonia without the consent of the Corts. Although the assembly did not meet annually, it did gain great power in legislation, as the body of constitutions and *capitols de Corts* enacted in these gatherings makes clear. The parliaments in the three states also voted taxes. The Catalans, distrustful of the crown in this respect, created a commission of the Corts to control collection and expenditure of taxes authorized by the assembly. This commission became permanent in the latter part of the 14th century and was known as the Diputació del General de Catalunya, or simply the Generalitat. It represented the Catalan community when the Corts was not in session, and it assumed the responsibility for defending Catalan liberties against royal encroachments. Similar bodies were created in Aragon and Valencia early in the 15th century.

In Aragon proper, agriculture and pasturage were the chief economic activities. In lower Aragon and Valencia, farming was largely in the hands of the numerous class of Mudéjares, Muslims living under Christian rule and retaining many of their own institutions. The manufacture of woollen goods was the main industry in the towns of Catalonia, where a strong guild organization was developed. Barcelona and Valencia ranked among the major ports of the Mediterranean, trading with Tunis, Alexandria, Sicily, Sardinia, the Holy Land, and the Black Sea area. Settlements of Catalan merchants and consuls to represent their interests were found in many of the principal African ports. A compilation of Catalan maritime law, known as the *Llibre del consolat de mar* (*Book of the Consulate of the Sea*), was prepared about 1370 and quickly gained general acceptance in Europe.

After the Black Death worked its destruction, frequent social and economic crises disturbed the peace and resulted in such horrors as the massacre of the Jews in Valencia and other cities in 1391. The decline of trade, financial difficulties, and the failure of many private banks in the late 14th century added to the general misery. In Barcelona a popular party (the Busca) began to agitate against the ascendancy of the wealthy urban aristocracy (the Biga) and helped to bring on the Catalan revolt against John II. The *payeses de remensa* joined in the struggle in hopes of gaining their liberty.

Massacre of the Jews

The crown of Aragon enjoyed a flourishing cultural life in the late Middle Ages. James II, in 1300, founded the University of Lérida, the first in Aragonese territory, and others were later established at Huesca, Barcelona, and Saragossa. Outstanding representatives of the university tradition were the Dominicans St. Raymond of Peñafort (died 1275)—a great canonist—and St. Vincent Ferrer (died 1419), a preacher of exceptional eloquence. A series of historical works, generally regarded as gems of Catalan literature, helped to mold the vernacular as a literary language: *The Chronicle of James I*, purportedly written by the King himself; Bernat Desclot's *Chronicle of the Reign of King Pedro III;* Ramón Muntaner's *Chronicle*, recounting the adventures of the Catalan Company; and the *Chronicle of Peter IV*, of which the King claimed to be the author. The most prolific writer of the era, equally facile in Latin, Catalan, and Arabic, was Ramón Llull (died 1315). A philosopher, theologian, and mystic, he was also an active propagandist concerned about the recovery of the Holy Land and the conversion of the Muslims. His writings include *The Book of the Lover and the Beloved; Blanquerna*, a romance; and *The Book of the Order of Chivalry*. Francesc Eiximenis (died 1409) was best known for his *Lo Crestià*, an encyclopaedic work dealing with moral and political theory; and the poet Ausiàs March (died 1459) explored the psychological dimensions of love. (J.F.O'C.)

MUSLIM SPAIN

The conquest. During the 7th century, Byzantine strongholds in North Africa gave way before the Arab advance. Carthage fell near the end of the century, and in the early 8th century the caliph al-Walīd I appointed a new governor in the west, Mūsā ibn Nuṣayr, who annexed all North Africa as far as Tangier (Ṭanjah), leaving his general Ṭāriq ibn Ziyād to administer and Islāmize the native Berbers. Only Ceuta (Sabtah), which was supplied from Spain by the Goth Witiza, remained in Christian hands (see also NORTH AFRICA; ISLĀMIC WORLD).

But the Muslim invasion of Spain was the result of Visigoth invitation rather than Muslim initiative. The death of Witiza in 709 precipitated civil war in the Visigothic kingdom, in which the dispossessed family of Witiza and their partisans appealed to Mūsā for support against the usurper Roderick (see above *The Visigothic kingdom*). Ṭāriq crossed the Strait of Gibraltar with a Berber army and in 711 decisively defeated Roderick at a battle the precise location of which is disputed.

Ṭāriq

Ṭāriq, having accomplished his purpose, should have returned to Africa; but, believing that the legendary treasure of Solomon was located at Toledo (Ṭulayṭulah), he marched north and took the city. Much to his surprise, many Spaniards submitted to him voluntarily. In the following year, Mūsā himself brought an Arab army to the peninsula. Mūsā reduced Mérida (Māridah), the last stronghold of Roderick's followers, entered Toledo (Ṭulayṭulah) and Saragossa (Saraguṣṭah) (modern Zaragoza), and may have crossed the northern Meseta Central, forcing the Visigoths to submit or flee. Both Mūsā and Ṭāriq were recalled to the East by the Caliph; by the time of their departure most of the Iberian Peninsula was under their control.

The swift surrender of the peninsula to an army numbering at most 20,000 men appears to be accounted for by the fact that the Hispano-Visigoth society had not yet succeeded in achieving a compact and homogeneous integration. The Goths and Hispano-Romans preserved a clear consciousness of their differences, while lords and vassals found themselves in opposite camps because of profound economic and social factors. The Jews, harassed by the legal ordinances of Toledo, were particularly hostile toward the Christian government. Moreover, the Muslim conquest brought advantages to many elements of society: the burden of taxes was on the whole less onerous than it had been in the last years of the Visigoth epoch; serfs who converted to Islām advanced into the category of freedmen (*mawlās*) and enrolled among the dependents of some conquering noble; Jews were no longer persecuted and were placed on an equal footing with the Hispano-Romans and Goths who still remained within the Christian fold (the Mozarabs). Thus, in the first half of the 8th century, there was born a new and quite different society in Muslim Spain. The nobility of blood was now comprised of the Arab invaders ranked on the basis of the date of their arrival in the peninsula. The *baladiyyūn* were those Arabs who entered Spain in 712 under Mūsā ibn Nuṣayr; the Syrians were those who arrived in 740 under Balj. After the Arab aristocracy were the Berbers, who constituted the majority of the invading troops and whose numbers and influence constantly increased over the course of the centuries because of their continual influx from Africa. The Muslims, or *mawlā*s, and their descendants, the *muwallad*s, comprised by far the majority of the population, since, as indicated above, economic motives induced a considerable number of landowners to abandon Christianity. Then came the Mozarabs, whose numbers diminished in the course of the centuries; the Jews; and, on a lesser scale, Turkish and eastern European slaves who entered the peninsula later.

Muslim society

This new society was still in a period of gestation when decisive clashes took place between the Muslim troops, led by ʿAbd-ar-Raḥmān al-Ghāfiqī, and the army of the Franks, under Charles Martel at Poitiers (732). Between 711 and 756 Spain was ruled as part of the amirate dependency of Damascus. The period is so called because the governors of the peninsula were appointed, in the final analysis, by the Umayyad caliph at Damascus. This was a turbulent era, marked by continuous civil wars and by armed clashes between Arabs and Berbers. A major Berber uprising against the Arabs in Africa produced powerful repercussions in the peninsula. The Arab army that the caliph dispatched from Syria to subdue the Berber dissidents was defeated. The Syrian army under Balj was forced to seek refuge in Ceuta, whence it moved on to Spain, where its leaders seized power in Córdoba (Qurṭubah). This situation was altered with the establishment of an independent amirate (756) by ʿAbd ar-Raḥmān I ad-Dākkil, an Umayyad prince who, having succeeded in escaping from the slaughter of his family by the ʿAbbāsids, arrived at Córdoba and became politically independent of them (not religiously; he did not adopt the title of caliph).

The independent amirate. The dynasty of the Andalusian Umayyads (756–1031) marked the zenith of the Arabic civilization in Spain. Its history may be divided into two major periods—that of the independent amirate (756–929) and that of the caliphate (929–1031)—and may be interpreted as revolving around three persons of like name—ʿAbd ar-Raḥmān I (756–788), II (822–852), III (912–961)—and one dictator, al-Manṣūr (976–1002).

ʿAbd ar-Raḥmān I was the organizer of the new Arab

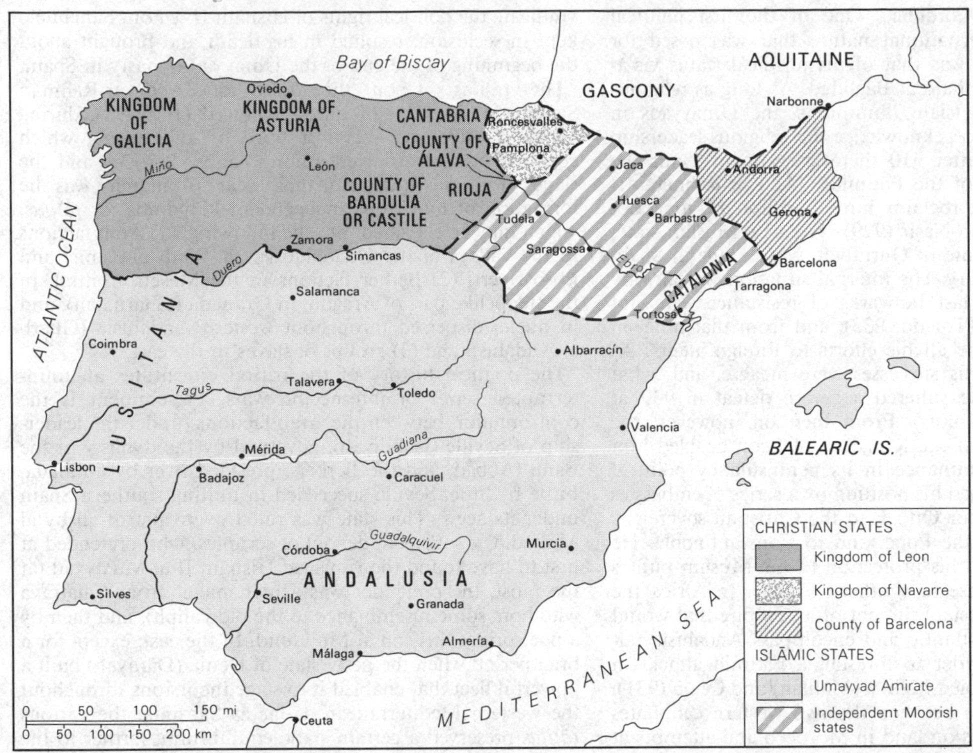

Christian and Islāmic states in Spain in 910.
Adapted from W. Shepherd, *Historical Atlas*; Barnes & Noble Books, New York

state. Cruel, energetic, and devoid of scruples, he vigorously checked all dissident elements in the peninsula. He endeavoured to base his power on the Eastern aristocracy affiliated with his house and heaped upon it property and riches, though he nonetheless treated it ruthlessly when it showed signs of rebellion; he protected the religious authorities who represented orthodoxy, and, through a series of punitive campaigns, he held in check the Christians of Asturias, who sought to reoccupy the desert to the north of the Duero. In the eastern part of the country he was troubled by intrigues of the ʿAbbāsids, and in the north he had to cope with the ambitions of Charlemagne, who menaced the valley of the Ebro (Ibruh). Charlemagne failed ignominiously in being forced to raise the siege of Saragossa and in the course of his retreat he suffered a defeat at Roncesvalles (778), which is celebrated in the great medieval epic *La Chanson de Roland.* The Franks had to be content with occupying the upper valleys of the Pyrenees. The Frankish advance ended with the Muslim seizure of Barcelona (Barshilūnah) in 801 and Old Catalonia.

ʿAbd ar-Raḥmān I's successors, Hishām I (788–796) and al-Ḥakam I (796–822), were confronted with severe internal dissidence among the Arab nobility. A rebellion in Toledo was put down savagely, and the internal warfare caused the amir to increase the numbers of Slav and Berber mercenaries and to impose new taxes to pay for them.

The reign of ʿAbd ar-Raḥmān II

ʿAbd ar-Raḥmān II inaugurated an era of great political and cultural splendour for Muslim Spain. The arrival in Spain of the Persian musician Ziryāb, for example, marked the beginning of a sharp "Orientalization," or, more precisely, of an "Iraquization" of customs that lent sophistication and refinement to the court. Certain technical advances were introduced, such as the technique of cutting rock crystal by ʿAbbās ibn Firnās and the importation of exotic seeds by the poet al-Ghazāl. ʿAbd ar-Raḥmān's greatest problems sprang from his restless vassals in the Ebro Valley, namely, the convert Banū Qasī family and, above all, before his death, from the Mozarabs, who, incited by extremist chiefs Alvaro and Eulogio (the latter, after his death, being canonized), sought to strengthen their ideas through the aura of martyrdom and began to revile publicly the Prophet Muḥammad—an action punishable by death (850). ʿAbd ar-Raḥmān II sought to persuade the "criminals" to retract, by alleging some pretext or by affirming that the insult had been proffered involuntarily. Failing in this effort, he was obliged to impose the death penalty. The "vogue" of seeking martyrdom voluntarily continued even after the death of the Amir. Both the latter and his successors, however, comported themselves with extraordinary tact and sought to soften the rough edges of friction, and this persecution, provoked by the Christians themselves, took a toll of 53 victims, the last of whom found themselves disavowed by their own ecclesiastical authorities.

In foreign policy ʿAbd ar-Raḥmān II conducted intensive diplomatic activity: he exchanged ambassadors with the Byzantine Empire and with the Frankish king Charles the Bald and maintained friendly relations with sovereigns of Tāhart, which supplied Spain with needed grain. He was able to confront the constantly growing incursions of the Northmen, whom he defeated in the vicinity of Seville. Furthermore, he established permanent defenses against the Viking invaders by the creation of two naval bases, one facing the Atlantic at Seville and another on the Mediterranean shore at Pechina near Almería.

His successors, Muḥammad I (852–886), al-Mundhir (886–888), and ʿAbd Allāh (888–912), were confronted with a new problem, which threatened to do away with the power of the Umayyads—and perhaps with Islām itself—in the peninsula: namely, the *muwallad*s, who, having become more and more conscious of their power, rose in revolt in the north of the peninsula, led by the powerful Banū Qasī clan, and in the south (879), by ʿUmar ibn Ḥafṣūn. The struggle against both these enemies was long and tragic—especially against the latter, who was well protected by the walls of the fortress of Bobastro near Córdoba. Ibn Ḥafṣūn was on the verge of delivering the final blow to the Umayyad dynasty, but he lacked the power to win the decisive Battle of Poley (891), which, if it did not put an end to his excursions, at least confined them to eastern Andalusia. ʿAbd Allāh was able to reduce the rebels one after the other, starting with the weakest, and, when he died, he left in the hands of his grandson, ʿAbd ar-Raḥmān III, more than sufficient means to challenge Ibn Ḥafṣūn successfully. The latter, moreover, committed the political stupidity of reverting to the Christianity of his Spanish ancestors, and, consequently, he was deserted by numerous *muwallad*s, who regarded themselves as good Muslims. When Ibn Ḥafṣūn died in 917 his sons were forced to capitulate, and in 928 ʿAbd ar-Raḥmān III was able to capture the hitherto impregnable fortress of Bobastro.

The Caliphate of Córdoba. One of the first political problems of an international nature that was posed for ʿAbd ar-Raḥmān III was that of his juridical status vis-à-vis the ʿAbbāsid caliphate at Baghdad. As long as religious unity existed in the Islām dominions, the Umayyads in Spain were content to acknowledge the religious leadership of Baghdad. When after 910 there grew up in Tunis the heterodox caliphate of the Fāṭimids, ʿAbd ar-Raḥmān III did not hesitate to proclaim himself caliph or to adopt the caliphal title of an-Nāṣir (929). The new Muslim state, known as the Caliphate of Qurṭubah, was to rule in Spain for little over a century. His internal situation was already almost assured; the last bulwarks of resistance were not long in capitulating (Toledo, 933), and from that time on he was able to devote all his efforts to foreign affairs. As to Christian Spain, his successes were meagre, and, what was more serious, he suffered a severe defeat in 939 at Simancas (Shānt Mānkus). From then on, however, the internal debilitation of the Kingdom of Leon enabled him to restore his predominance in its peninsula by political means. He consolidated his position by a series of embassies to the Roman emperor Otto I, to the Christian sovereigns of the peninsula, to the Pope, and to Constantinople. He furthermore extended his protection to the Muslim pirates who established a base in southern France. In Africa the Fāṭimids fought the establishment of an empire that would reach as far as the Atlantic and encompass Andalusia (al-Andalus). And, in order to forestall a Fāṭimid attack on Spain, an-Nāṣir occupied Melilla (Malīlah) and Ceuta (931). Intense naval warfare between the two western caliphates coincided with clashes on land in Morocco and attempts at subversive wars in the enemy states. In the latter area, an-Nāṣir came near to overthrowing the Fāṭimid caliphate by his support of the rebel Abū Yazīd; the conflict between the Umayyads and the Fāṭimids dragged on and ended when the latter conquered Egypt (969) and lost interest in Morocco, thus leaving a power vacuum that was rapidly filled by the Umayyads.

An-Nāṣir was succeeded by his son al-Ḥakam II (961–976), who adopted the caliphal title of al-Mustanṣir. His reign was peaceful, and he succeeded in resolving the problem of Morocco, thanks to the strategic ability of General Ghālib and the policy of the general of the African army, Abu ʿĀmir al-Maʿāfirī, later known as al-Manṣūr, the Victorious One (Almanzor).

Al-Manṣūr

On the death of al-Mustanṣir, his throne was occupied by his son, a minor, Hishām II al-Muʾayyad, who grew up under the tutelage of his mother, Aurora, and of the prime minister al-Muṣḥafī, who before long was liquidated by al-Manṣūr (governed 976–1002). The latter succeeded in eliminating all temporal power of the caliphs, whom he dominated, and acquired dictatorial power for himself.

He won complete control over Morocco, which he transformed into the viceroyalty of Córdoba, and he arrested the expansion of the Christian kings from the north through a series of raids—usually every six months—in which he sacked nearly every Christian capital. With the support of a professional army consisting predominantly of Berbers, many of them recent arrivals from Africa who obeyed him blindly, he managed to dispense with the Arab aristocracy, which for the most part was pro-Umayyad, and to hold in check the influence of the slaves, whose numbers had been increasing since an-Nāṣir had placed them in posts of high responsibility. But this balancing of forces—Arabic aristocracy, Berbers, and slaves—could only be sustained by the strong hand of a ruler such as himself.

Al-Manṣūr played the role of a grand lord. A protector of poets and scholars, he concealed his rationalism under a cloak of piety and was the darling of the *faqīh*s (scholars versed in the traditions of Islām); he contrived to attract to himself the outstanding poets of that era. At the time of his death, after a victorious campaign in Aragon, he succeeded in leaving a robust and well-organized state for his son al-Muẓaffar.

Al-Muẓaffar (1002–08) continued the policies of his father. He hemmed in Hishām II and fought against the Christians, but he died prematurely; his brother ʿAbd ar-Raḥmān Sanchuelo lacked the fortitude to maintain the structure built by his father. An uprising that sought to vindicate the political rights of Hishām II, whom Sanchuelo kept in seclusion, resulted in his death and brought about the beginning of the end of the Umayyad dynasty in Spain.

The *ṭāʾifas*. Upon the death of ʿAbd ar-Raḥmān Sanchuelo, 21 years of unrest followed (1009–31), during which al-Muʾayyad was lost trace of and during which constant clashes occurred among Arabs, Berbers, and the slaves. The consequence of those years of anarchy was the formation of numerous independent kingdoms, or *ṭāʾifas*, which may be classified into the following: (1) Arab factions in the valleys of the Guadalquivir (al-Wādī al-Kabīr) and Ebro rivers; (2) Berber factions in the Meseta Central, in the steppelike part of Aragon, in Granada (Gharnāṭah), and in nuclei dispersed throughout western Andalusia (Gharb al-Andalus); and (3) groups of slaves in the east.

The political history of the period constitutes an uninterrupted series of internecine wars. Pre-eminent is the confrontation between the Arab factions, under the leadership of Seville (Ishbīliyah), governed by the dynasty of the Banū ʿAbbād, and the Berbers, presided over by Granada. Little by little, Seville succeeded in uniting southern Spain under its aegis. This state was ruled over, first of all by al Muʿtaḍid, a sovereign devoid of scruples, who pretended at first to have found the vanished Hishām II al-Muʾayyad (at the most, the pretender was a mat maker from Calatrava who bore some resemblance to the old caliph), and then by a poet-prince, his son al-Muʿtamid. In the east, except for a brief period when the petty state of Denia (Dāniyah) built a powerful fleet that enabled it to stage incursions throughout the western Mediterranean as far as Sardinia, the various *ṭāʾifas* preserved a certain static equilibrium; farther to the north, the various *ṭāʾifas* also wasted their time in interminable internal quarrels.

This fragmentation facilitated the expansion of the Christian states of the north, which, lacking the demographic potential to repopulate the lands they had succeeded in occupying, wisely annexed only those that they were capable of repopulating and garrisoning. The Christian states also imposed a heavy economic burden of tribute on the *ṭāʾifas*. Christian armies forced the Andalusian petty kings to buy peace by paying annual tribute, the famous *parias.* This tribute, while it revitalized the economy of the Christian states, created sharp friction between the Muslim authorities and their subjects. The *ṭāʾifas* had constantly to increase the yield from their imposts, and they constantly laid new and heavier tax burdens on their subjects; when cash was lacking, they devaluated the currency, minting low-standard coins that were not accepted by the Christians. This, in turn, gave rise to new tax increases and to popular discontent, which was considerably aggravated by the clerical party of

Adapted from W. Shepherd, *Historical Atlas;* Barnes & Noble Books, New York

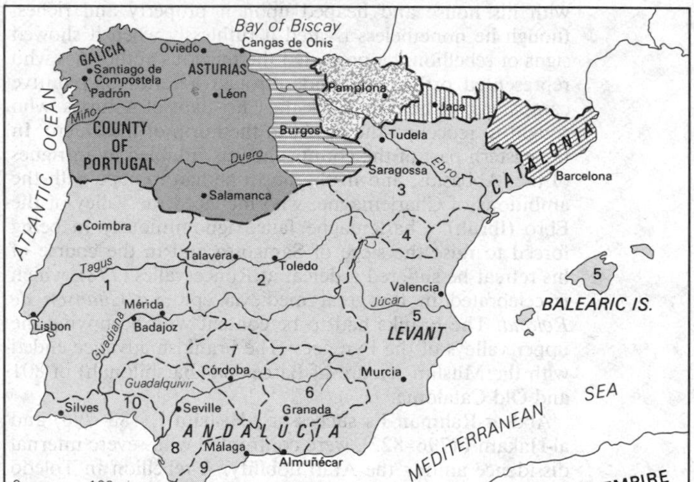

Spain in 1037.

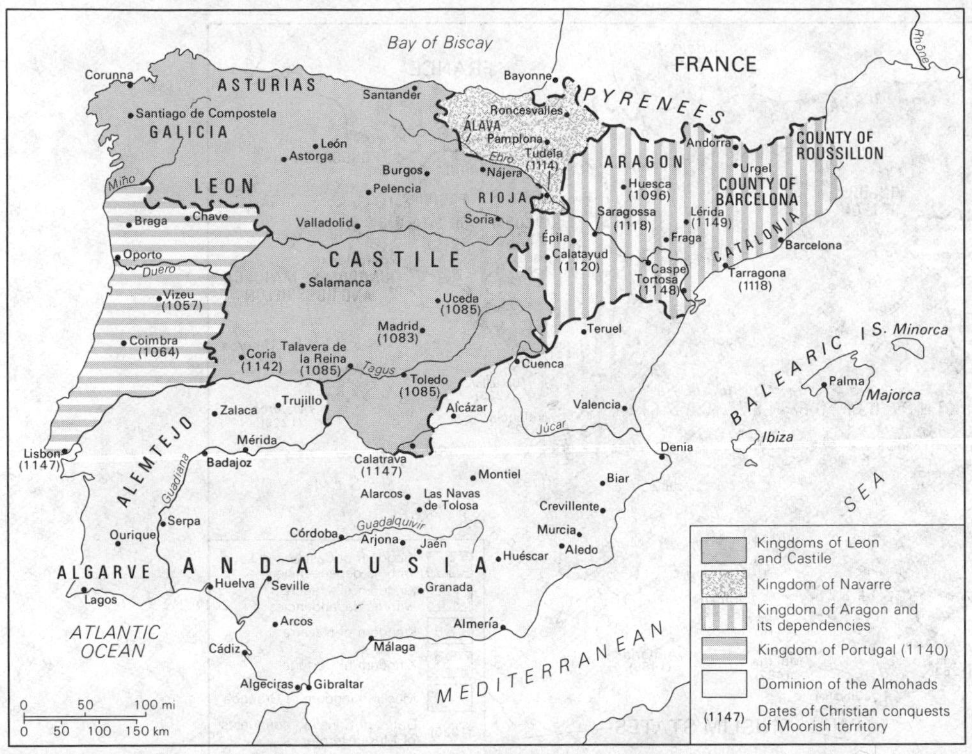

Spain in 1150.

From W. Shepherd, *Historical Atlas*, Harper & Row, Publishers (Barnes & Noble Books), New York; revision copyright © 1964 by Barnes & Noble, Inc.

the *faqīhs*. Furthermore, the petty local courts were characterized by extravagant luxury and lavish public outlays. This situation rendered Andalusia ripe for the foreign intervention that came when the Castilians occupied Toledo (1085), the key to the Meseta Central and to the peninsula. The factional chiefs, alarmed by the Christian advance, called in the help of the Almoravids.

The Almoravids. The Almoravid ruler Yūsuf ibn Tāshufīn entered the peninsula and by a slow advance reached the fields of az-Zallāqah, north of Badajoz (Baṭalyaws), where in 1086 he defeated a Castilian army under Alfonso VI; then he became an independent prince either unwilling or unable to exploit their victory. For four years Almoravid policy in Spain remained indecisive, but it appears that the siege of Aledo (1088) convinced Yūsuf ibn Tāshufīn of the urgent necessity of putting an end to the *ṭāʾifa*s if he were going to rescue Spanish Islām. In 1090–91, he deposed their rulers—except for Banū Hūd of Saragossa—and inflicted a series of defeats on the Christians. Only one of the chiefs of state, Rodrigo Díaz de Vivar (the Cid), exiled from his native Castile by King Alfonso VI, was able to resist the Africans, and he furthermore set himself up in an independent kingdom—a new *ṭāʾifa,* that of Valencia. The figure of the Cid—the Lord, a title that the Arabs conferred upon him—is quite curious: first he served as a mercenary under Alfonso VI; then he became an independent prince in the east, ruling over states that were entirely inhabited by Muslims. He led a retinue of men who were hardened in combat and who understood nothing of the ways of peace. He had the good fortune, however, of finding efficient administrators from among the Mozarabs residing in his states; further, his superb grasp of Almoravid tactics enabled him to overcome his numerical inferiority. Upon his death, Valencia remained under the control of his men until 1102, when they were forced to evacuate it and seek refuge in Castile. Following the fall of Valencia, the Almoravids were unopposed; and in 1110, under the leadership of ʿAlī ibn Yūsuf (1106–43), they were able to occupy Saragossa.

The Cid

The conquest of Saragossa, however, marked the beginning of the Almoravid decline. The Aragonese king Alfonso el Batallador (the Battler) and his stepson, Alfonso VII of Castile, launched renewed Christian assaults against the entire frontier of Islām in Spain. The Almoravids, who after 1121 experienced serious difficulties in Africa as a result of the preachings of a Berber reformer, Ibn Tūmart, could not successfully parry the blow; indeed, they had to hire Christian mercenaries to help them. In 1118 Saragossa fell into the hands of the Battler, who reconquered a large part of the valleys of the Jalón and of the Jiloca. A resounding Almoravid victory over the Aragonese at Fraga (Ifrāgah) in 1134 bore no fruit because the Almoravids lacked the resources to exploit their victory.

The Almohads. In Africa, the Almohads finally triumphed, and ʿAbd al-Muʾmin (1130–63), successor to Ibn Tūmart, was able to turn his attention to Spain and to undertake the integration of all the Muslim states—the second *ṭāʾifa*s—formed under the shield of the latest internecine wars caused by the Almoravid decline. Of these states, there stood out especially that under Ibn Mardanīsh (1147–72), who, with a largely Christian army, was successful in becoming the master of southeastern Spain.

The Almohads assumed the title of caliph, introduced a series of severe religious measures, and sought to strengthen their states through religious unification, in practice, by compelling the Jews and Christians to emigrate. Two great sovereigns, Abū Yaʿqūb Yūsuf (1163–84) and Abū Yūsuf Yaʿqūb al-Manṣūr (1184–99), raised western Islām to the zenith of its power. Taking advantage of the quarrels that divided the Christian kingdoms of Castile and Leon, al-Manṣūr defeated the sovereign of the former, Alfonso VIII, in 1195 at the Battle of Alarcos (al-Arak); but, despite this victory, he proved unable to exploit his triumph—repeating the fate that befell the Almoravids after al-Zallāqah. Years later, during the reign of his successor an-Naṣīr (1199–1214), the Christians avenged this defeat in the Battle of Las Navas de Tolosa (al-ʿIqāb). This battle created a power vacuum into which stepped some of the *ṭāʾifa*s, or petty kingdom states, prominent among which were those of Banū Hūd of Murcia (Mursiyah) and of the Naṣrids of Arjona (Arjūnah). The policies of the two states were quite divergent: Muḥammad ibn Hūd (1228–38) emphasized resistance on the part of the Muslims against the Christians who, led by Ferdinand III the Saint, were occupying the Guadalquivir Valley; Muḥammad I ibn al-Aḥmar (ruled in Granada 1238–73), on the other hand, acknowledged himself to be a vassal of the King of Castile and even helped him against his own co-religionists. This realistic policy enabled him to preserve in his possession the territory of what are the modern provinces of Málaga, Granada, and Almería, together with portions of neighbouring provinces.

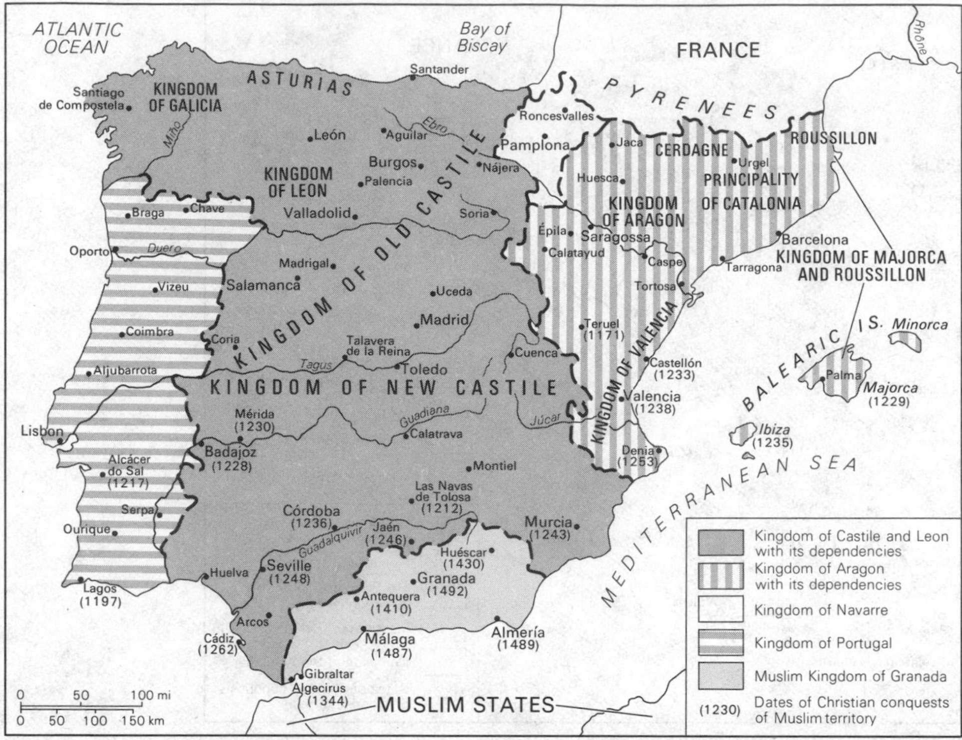

Spain in 1300.

Thus, after the middle of the 12th century and the reconquest of Jaén (Jayyān), Córdoba, Seville, and Murcia by the Castilians, and of Valencia and the Balearic Islands by the Aragonese under James I the Conqueror, no independent dominions of Islām remained in Spain with the exception of Granada and the tiny area of Crevillente (Qarbalyān), which soon disappeared.

Granada. The Naṣrid dynasty founded by Muḥammad ibn al-Aḥmar in Granada, however, was destined to endure for two and a half centuries. The Muslims of Granada lacked sufficient forces to constitute a genuine danger to the Christians, who limited themselves to collecting tribute and launching, from time to time, an attack against them, snatching from them some city or other. The people of Granada, for their part, always bore in mind what had happened in the cases of the Almoravids and the Almohads, who, having arrived from Africa as auxiliary troops, became masters in Spain. Vis-à-vis the new Moroccan empires, particularly the empire of the Banū Marīns, they maintained a policy of balance of power. They did permit the influx of volunteers from Africa to enroll in their army to fight against the Christians, but never permitted the crossing of the Strait of Gibraltar by massive organized contingents. The years between 1302 and 1340 are of an extraordinary complexity from a diplomatic as well as a military point of view. Both Morocco and Castile vied for the possession of the Granadine ports of Tarifa (Ṭarif) and Algeciras (al-Jazīrah al-Khaḍra'), ports that dominated the Strait. Granada, therefore, allied alternately with the Africans and Christians, hoping thus to maintain the balance of power. A fourth state, Catalonia, torn by discord under James II, aspired to obtain a larger slice of the Reconquista and intervened with its fleet and laid siege to Almería (al-Marīyah), under the pretext of a crusade (1309).

When Ismāʿīl I (1314–25) ascended the throne, another branch of the Naṣrid family gained the power. Ismāʿīl was able to check the reconquest ambitions of Alfonso XI—who later, in 1340, with the aid of the Portuguese, won a decisive victory over the Berber army of Abu'l-Ḥasan at the Battle of the Salado.

The reign of Muḥammad V

The defeat of the Berbers and the lack of interest in reconquest on the part of the successors of Alfonso XI created a favourable climate for Granada, which found itself free from political pressures of both Moroccans and Castilians. During the reign of Muḥammad V (1354–59; 1362–91) Granada reached its greatest splendour; its ministers included some of the most learned men of the epoch, such as the historian Ibn al-Khaṭīb, the physician Ibn Khātima, and the poet Ibn Zamraq. It protected Ibn Khaldūn, the great philosopher of history.

During this era there grew up also the institution of the "judge of the frontier," *juez de la frontera y de los fieles del rastro,* a Moorish official who heard Christian complaints against the Granadinos; this did much to reduce frontier incidents between Moors and Christians.

Little is known about the decline of the Naṣrid dynasty, since with Ibn al-Khaṭīb died the last great Muslim historian of Andalusia. The extant records and reports from the 15th century are as a rule from Christian sources or from the tales of travellers. The narrative poems that are of the utmost interest as historic sources for other periods in Muslim history are completely lacking in this era. The conventional verses of the king-poet Yūsuf III (1408–17) or the anonymous Arab poet of the romance *Abenamar, Abenamar, moro de la morería* do little to illuminate the history of this period. More illustrative, however, are the neglected verses of ʿAbd al-Karīm al-Qaysī (*c.* 1485), an esteemed member of Granada's middle class, who eschewed classic themes and wrote of such mundane phenomena as the increase in the cost of living or the decline in the power of the sovereign.

Foreign relations enjoyed a long period of tranquillity as a result of the ghastly losses of life from the Black Plague (1348–51) and, afterward, from the internal wars that weakened Christian Castile. Furthermore, border incidents were quickly disposed of by the "judge of the frontier and the faithful of the trail." Only an occasional confrontation served to remind the Muslims and Christians that the Reconquista had not yet come to an end. In the 15th century, however, the Reconquista proceeded apace. Prince Ferdinand seized Antequera (Antaqīrah) in 1410; Jimena and Huéscar fell in 1435, Huelma in 1438, and Gibraltar in 1462. One result of these events was that the people of Granada became increasingly less tolerant of Christians, and the Granadine *faqīh*s professed the most extreme xenophobia. This policy, common to both point to the existence of a Granadine school of law, which before long exerted an influence on the other side of the Strait; for the Moroccans, subjected to the constant pressure of the Portuguese—who had gained possession of their coastal areas (Ceuta, first, in

1415)—realized like the Granadinos that the only way to escape Christian hegemony was through the profession of the most rigorous Islāmic ideals and in the practice of the most extreme xenophobia. This policy, common to both sides of the Strait of Gibraltar, did not achieve equal results. It saved Morocco from the hands of its enemies, but in Granada it became the *casus belli* for the campaign that was to inaugurate the end of the Reconquista.

The end of Andalusian Islām

The sultan Muley Hacén (Abū al-Ḥasan ʿAlī) refused to pay the annual tribute he owed to the Catholic kings and seized the fortified town of Zahara (1481), thus launching hostilities that were destined to liquidate the last bastion of Andalusian Islām. The campaign proved to be difficult for the Christian army despite the discord that split the royal Granada family, and that was exploited in Machiavellian fashion by Ferdinand the Catholic: Boabdil (Arabic: Muḥammad Abū ʿAbd Allāh), son of Muley Hacén, rebelled in Guadix against his father and was recognized in Granada with the aid of the Abencerrajes, a powerful Granada family. Muley Hacén, however, who had taken refuge in Málaga, succeeded in recapturing the capital with the assistance of the Zegries, or border people. But he was successfully deposed by his brother, el Zagal (Abū ʿAbd Allāh Muḥammad az-Zaghall—the Valiant One), who was supported by the Venegas family.

Boabdil was captured by the Catholic kings during his attack at Lucena and, in order to regain his freedom, signed the Pact of Córdoba, in which he pledged himself to deliver the portion of the kingdom that was in the hands of el Zagal, in exchange for help from the Castilians to recover Granada, part of which (Alhambra) was still in the hands of Muley Hacén. The latter and el Zagal allied themselves against Boabdil, who had to flee and seek asylum in the court of the Catholic king. The death of Muley Hacén in 1485 enabled Boabdil, with the help of the inhabitants of Albaicin, to occupy the Alhambra. El Zagal, who had been routed by the Christians before Vélez Málaga, in 1487 retreated to Guadix and, being incapable of further resistance, delivered his states to the Catholic kings and emigrated to Tlemcén (1491). Taking advantage of this civil war, the Christians had seized Ronda, Marbella, Loja, Málaga, and Razo and were in a position to lay siege to Granada. When the siege began, the population divided into factions: one consisted of pacifists and the other of belligerent persons who, despite their quarrels, fiercely defended the city.

By the end of 1491, the situation became desperate, and Boabdil capitulated, but, before making the news public, he brought a detachment of Castilian troops into the Alhambra on the night of January 1–2, for the purpose of avoiding a disturbance on the part of his vassals that might render it impossible for him to comply with the terms of the pact. The official surrender, and with it the end of Muslim occupation of the peninsula, took place the following day, January 2, 1492.

Society. In discussing the influx of the Muslims into Spain, the various categories of the population that settled there were earlier pointed out: Arabs (*baladiyyūn* and Syrians), Berbers, *muwallad*s, Mozarabs, Jews, and slaves. The Muslim masses continued to increase during the early centuries of the occupation, because of the wave of conversions that markedly reduced the number of Christians. Precise figures cannot be given, but it is estimated that at the time of the conquest some 4,000,000 Spaniards inhabited the peninsula, while the total number of immigrant Arabs did not exceed 50,000. The population was primarily rural, and large cities were few in number. At the end of the 10th century one can estimate the following urban populations: Córdoba, 250,000; Toledo, 37,000; Almería, 27,000; Granada, 26,000; Saragossa, 17,000; Valencia, 15,000; and Málaga, 15,000.

At the peak of the administrative pyramid was the amir, caliph, sultan, or king, depending on the era, and all the functionaries exercised their power by delegation from the sovereign, who embodied within himself all executive, legislative, and judicial authority, even though at times he delegated power to a *ḥājib* (chamberlain) or, after the 11th century, to a prime minister (*dhū al-wizāratayn*). In the discharge of his functions he was assisted by various viziers. At times, there was, at the head of the various departments, a *kātib*, or official secretary. The provinces were governed by *wālī*s who enjoyed wide autonomy. There existed no uniform municipal organization, and the duties fulfilled by some officials cannot be considered as representative; such are, for example, the chief of police (*ṣāḥib al-shurta*) and the market inspector, known until the 10th century as *ṣāḥib al-sūq* (zabazoque) and later as *muḥtasib*. The Muslim cities of Spain, with their baths, parks, markets, mosques, and high cultural level, were quite different from and, some believe, superior to those of Christian Europe.

The military

The army was based on the voluntary recruitment of soldiers or on contracts with them from abroad. The units (*jund*), grouped according to the places of origin of their men, were strategically deployed along the borders and possessed extraordinary mobility at the time of the caliphate. Holding castles close to the enemy lands as their bases of operation, they were glad to welcome into their midst the Muslims, who were eager to die in combat, in order thus to open for themselves the gates of paradise. These volunteers, who became more and more numerous with the passage of time and about whom numerous details are known, were frequently second class soldiers, since they enrolled during years when they constituted a hindrance rather than a source of help. The *marina*, or navy, organized by ʿAbd ar-Raḥmān II, remained an effective force until the middle of the 14th century.

The entire state structure was supported, theoretically, on a foundation of the most rigid Islāmic orthodoxy and interpreted by the Mālikī school, which in Spain manifested special characteristics of hyperconservative nature. It is not known whether the school acquired these traits upon settling in the peninsula because intolerance was indigenous to the inhabitants there or whether it indoctrinated the Spanish Muslims in this manner, who transmitted it, in turn, to the Christian reconquerors.

The economy. The Moorish conquerors divided the lands seized from the Christians by force of arms and operated them, as a general rule, by means of "tenant farmer" leases. Possibly about the 10th century the woodlands achieved their widest expansion, and the cultivation of irrigated lands was encouraged by means of drastic regulations, which, however, were favourably received. Plants used in the manufacture of textile (flax, cotton, esparto grass, and silk) as well as those with medicinal properties were protected by the state.

In addition to agriculture, the raising of livestock (Christian sheep and Arabian horses) occupied a central position in the peninsular economy. As in the Roman period, lead, iron, gold, and mercury were mined. Domestic industry, which never went beyond the handicraft state, culminated in the production of luxury cloths such as silk (a state monopoly), in the tanning of hides (Cordoban leather), and in the export of ivory objects. Commerce was selective and carried on in products "of low weight and high value" that frequently reached the most remote regions of the known world. There are reports of Andalusian travellers as far as Sudan, central Europe, and even China.

The evolution of economic life was conditioned by political events; in proportion as the productive centres passed into Christian hands, the commercial vigour of the Muslims kept diminishing. No phenomenon is more illustrative of this than the confidence attached to the currency. In the 11th century, Barcelona was counterfeiting Muslim coins; in the 14th century, Granada was doing the same with Barcelona coins.

Culture of Muslim Spain. Arab civilization in the peninsula reached its zenith when the political power of the Arabs began to decline. In the 8th century, in the years immediately following the conquest, there are no traces of a cultural level higher than that attained by the Mozarabs who lived among the Arab conquerors. All available evidence points to the fact that in this period popular works of medicine, agriculture, astrology, and geography were translated from Latin into Arabic. Many of these texts must have been derived from the *Etymologies* of Isidore of Seville and from other Christian writers. In the 9th century, the situation was changed abruptly: the Andalusians, who travelled east in order to comply with the injunction to conduct a pilgrimage to Mecca at least once in their lifetimes, took advantage of their stay in those regions to enhance their knowledge, which they then introduced into their native country.

Literature. In the 9th century there flourished such court poets as ʿAbbās ibn Nāṣih, ʿAbbās ibn Firnās, Yaḥyā al-Ghazāl, and the knight Saʿīd ibn Jūdī. Towering above all these, however, is Ibn Hāniʾ, nicknamed the "Mutanabbī of the West," who by virtue of his religious ideas was obliged to forsake his native land and enter in the service of the Fāṭimid caliph al-Muʿizz. In the 10th century, another bardic tradition grew up around al-Manṣūr. Bards performed the functions of modern journalists; they accompanied their protector on war expeditions and celebrated his exploits in verse the singsong rhyme of which became engraved in the folk memory of the people of Andalusia. This occasional poetry did not always attain literary heights, but at times that was indeed the case. And al-Manṣūr himself chose as "poet-journalists" the foremost talents of his time—men such as Ibn Darrāj al-Qasṭallī, ar-Ramādī, Saʿīd of Baghdad, at-Ṭalīq, and numerous others. And it was in the 10th century that Ibn Faraj of Jaén deemed himself to possess sufficient background to compose the *Kitāb al-Hadāʾiq* ("Book of Orchards")—the first anthology of Andalusian poets. This was soon followed by another, that of the physician Ibn al-Kittānī.

Poetry

The highest peak in Islāmic literature in Spain was attained during the era of the *ṭāʾifas*, when the poet-king al-Muʿtamid established an embryo of an academy of belles lettres, which included the foremost Spanish intellects, as well as Sicilians who emigrated from their native land before its conquest by the Normans. Other petty kings in the peninsula endeavoured to compete with al-Muʿtamid but did not succeed in assembling a constellation of writers of comparable stature.

In the 12th century, in the Andalusian Levant, outstanding poets included Ibn Khafajā of Alcira and his nephew Ibn az-Zaqqāq. In the era of greatest decadence in the 13th century were Abū al-Baqāʾ of Ronda (*c.* 1285), Ibn al-Khaṭīb, Ibn Saʿīd al-Maghribī, and Ibn Zamraq, whose verses are preserved in the stuccos of the Alhambra.

Prose

In Arab literature, including that of contemporary times, poetry possesses greater vitality than prose. But, even so, it is necessary to mention Ibn Shuhayd (*c.* 1035), author of a work that lent inspiration to al-Maʿarrī for his *Risālat al-ghufrān* ("Epistle of Pardon"). The prolific Ibn Ḥazm of Córdoba (died 1064) wrote the delightful *Tawq al-ḥamāmah* ("The Ring of the Dove"), dealing with love and lovers, which is still popular today. The enormous output of Ibn Ḥazm is not possible to enumerate here. Nevertheless, it suffices to cite his *Kitāb al-fiṣal,* a history of religions that was not surpassed by Western scholars until well into the 19th century. Another polymath was the vizier-historian Ibn al-Khaṭīb (died 1375). Two 12th-century histories of literature, by Ibn Bassām and Ibn Khāqān, are excellent sources of information concerning the apogee of Andalusian letters. Often the best grammars and dictionaries of a language are written by authors living in the peripheral zones who endeavour to prevent gross errors being committed by their countrymen in the region. This perhaps explains why Andalusia, located at the western fringe of the Muslim world, produced works that to this day are used as texts in certain traditional Islāmic universities. Among these grammarians should be mentioned al-Zubaydi, tutor of Hishām II and Ibn Maḍā of Córdoba, who proposed a drastic reform of grammatical methods. Ibn Mālik of Jaén's didactic poem *Alfiyya* ("The Thousand Verses") constitutes an excellent handbook of grammar; and Abū Ḥayyan of Granada (died 1344), who emigrated to the east, wrote an outstanding commentary on the Quʾran as well as the first Turkish grammar. In the field of lexicology the blind Ibn Sīda of Denia (died 1066) is pre-eminent; he was also the author of a sort of "dictionary of ideas."

In the field of Quʾrānic science there stand out Abū ʿAmr of Denia and Ibn Fierro of Játiva, whose handbooks made possible the correct cantilation, or intonation of the chanting, of the Quʾrān. Also produced there were various collections of *ḥadith*s (traditions referring to the Prophet), but none of these was of particular importance. In this domain, the Andalusians were imitators of the East, and personalities such as Ibn ʿAbd al-Barr, a certain Ibn Rushd (the grandfather of Averroës), and an Ibn ʿĀṣim are of merely marginal interest.

The first extant chronicles in Muslim Spain, such as the *Taʾrīkh iftitāḥ al-Andalus* ("History of the Conquest of Spain"), by Ibn al-Qūṭiya, date back to the 10th century. In the *ṭāʾifa* era the pre-eminent Spanish historian is Ibn Ḥayyān of Córdoba (died 1076), whose *Muqtabis,* preserved for the most part, is an anthology of historic texts based to a great extent on the work of his predecessors. From the point of view of human interest are the *Memoirs* of the king Ziri ʿAbd Allāh, who was deposed by the Almoravids and who sought to justify in those memoirs his deeds as a statesman. In the Naṣrid era is found the frequently aforementioned Ibn al-Khaṭīb. The works of the North African historians Ibn Khaldūn and al-Maqqari (died 1631) supply much information concerning the Arab domination of Spain.

Science. In the mid-11th century, the *qāḍī* of Toledo, Ibn Ṣāʿid, composed a noteworthy handbook of history of science that contained much information on technical subjects. Mathematical sciences received little attention, but mention should be made of Maslama of Madrid (died 1008), who probably took part in the translation of Ptolemy's *Planispherium* and made some contributions to pure mathematics. Also during the heyday of Granada, there was al-Qalaṣādī, commentator on Ibn al-Bannāʾ, who did important work on fractions. Despite their lack of interest in the physical sciences, the Andalusians excelled in astronomy, both theoretical and practical. An array of these scholars sought to simplify the astrolabe, and finally al-Zarqālī (died 1087) achieved success by inventing the apparatus called the *azafea,* which was widely used until the 16th century. Al-Zarqālī also anticipated Kepler by suggesting that the orbits of the planets are not circular but ovoid. Jābir ibn Aflaḥ (12th century) criticized the Ptolemaic system.

Astrology was popular in Muslim Spain, and the Umayyad rulers, after 788, maintained an official astrologer in their courts. The most widely used astrological treatises were those of the Tunisian ʿAlī ibn Abī Rijāl and another anonymous scientist, who made a translation from Vulgar Latin into Arabic in the 8th century. This book was translated from Arabic into Spanish during the era of Alfonso under the title of *Libro de las Cruces* ("Book of the Crosses").

Natural science

The treatises on esoteric or occult subjects attribute to Maslama two works on natural science that are not properly his but may be ascribed to one of his pupils. They are *Ghāyat al-ḥakīm* ("The Goals of the Scholar"; also known as *Picatrix*) and *Rutbat al-ḥakim* ("The Step of the Scholar"). Greater interest is merited by the *Materia Medica,* a revision of the Eastern Arabic text of the 1st-century Greek physician Pedanius Dioscorides, ordered by an-Naṣir, on which Jews, Arabs, and Christians collaborated. Gradually, the Andalusian Arabs kept adding new medicinal "simples" (which described the properties of various medicinal plants) to those described by Dioscorides, and the last eminent essayist on the subject, Ibn al-Bayṭār (died 1248), describes more than 1,400 of these. The Arabs of Andalusia were familiar with the texts of the great Latin classics relating to natural science, and Ibn Wāfid, Ibn Baṣṣāl, and Ibn al-ʿAwwām (11th and 12th centuries) quote Varro, Virgil, and others. The most notable geographers in Muslim Spain were al-Bakrī (died 1094), who wrote the *Kitāb al-masālik wa-l-mamālik* ("Book of Highways and of Kingdoms"), and al-Idrīsī (died 1166), who was in the service of Roger II of Sicily and is the author of the leading universal geography composed by the Arabs. Somewhat later (1323) there appeared the first Arabic nautical map, possibly of Granadine origin. In technology, Muslim Spain was noted for its windmills and for its manufacture of paper. (J.V.G.)

UNITED SPAIN UNDER THE CATHOLIC KINGS

The union of Aragon and Castile. When Ferdinand II (1479–1516, also Ferdinand V of Castile from 1474) succeeded to the crown of Aragon in 1479, the union of Aragon (roughly east Spain) and Castile (roughly west Spain) was finally achieved, and the Trastámara became, after the Valois of France, the second most powerful monarchs in Europe. The different royal houses of the Iberian Peninsula had long thought in terms of a union of their crowns and had practiced intermarriage for generations. Nevertheless, the union of the crowns of Castile and Aragon was far from inevitable in the last quarter of the 15th century. A union between Castile and Portugal was equally feasible, and it has been argued that it would have made more sense, for it would have allowed the two western Hispanic kingdoms to concentrate on overseas exploration and expansion, and it would not have involved Castile in Aragon's traditional rivalry with France. The reasons that led John II of Aragon to arrange the marriage of his son and heir, Ferdinand, with Isabella of Castile, in 1469, were essentially tactical: he needed Castilian support against French aggression in the Pyrenees. In Castile an influential party of magnates, led by Archbishop Carillo of Toledo (who later reversed himself) and opposed to King Henry IV, supported the succession claims of the princess Isabella, the King's half sister, against those of his daughter, Joan. They were anxious for the help and leadership of the Aragonese prince and content with the alliance of a country in which the magnates had such far-reaching privileges as the Aragonese nobility. It needed a forged papal dispensation for the marriage, the blackmailing of Henry IV into (wrongly) denying the paternity of his daughter (Joan), and, finally, several years of bitter civil war before Ferdinand and Isabella defeated Joan's Castilian supporters and her husband, Afonso V of Portugal.

Reasons for union

Ferdinand and Isabella ruled jointly in both kingdoms and were known as the Reyes Católicos (Catholic Kings). It was, however, a union of crowns and not of kingdoms. In size, institutions, traditions, and, partly, even in language, the two kingdoms differed greatly. Within the Kingdom of Aragon, Aragon and Valencia (easternmost Spain, halfway up the coast) each had about 270,000 inhabitants, of whom some 20 percent and more than 30 percent, respectively, were Moors and Moriscos (Moors officially converted to Christianity). Catalonia (northeast Spain) had about 300,000 inhabitants. In each of these kingdoms the powers of the crown were severely limited. The barons ruled their estates like kings, dispensing arbitrary justice over their peasants. In Catalonia they had the right to wage private war. In Aragon anyone arrested by order of the king could put himself under the jurisdiction of a *justicia* who held his office for life and was therefore independent of the king's pleasure. It was this highest judge who crowned the kneeling king and made him swear to observe the *fueros,* the laws and privileges, of the kingdom. It is now known that the formula "We who are as good as you swear to you who are no better than we, to accept you as our king and sovereign lord, provided you accept all our liberties and laws; but if not, not" is a forgery, most probably of the mid-16th century. It does, however, summarize very well the relations between the kings of Aragon and the Aragonese nobility.

Ferdinand made no attempt to change this position; nor did he do so in Catalonia, where the crown had just emerged successfully from a long and confused civil war. The nobility and the urban aristocracy of Barcelona (Spain's northeast coast) had been faced by violent social movements of the peasants and the lower classes of the cities and were themselves riven by family and factional strife. The crown intervened, mainly on the side of the lower classes but, inevitably, in alliance with some of the noble factions and against the French who had taken the opportunity to occupy Cerdagne and Roussillon. In 1486 Ferdinand settled the Catalan problem by a compromise, the Sentencia de Guadalupe, which effectively abolished serfdom and the more oppressive feudal obligations of the peasants, in return for monetary payments to the lords. Otherwise, the political and legal privileges of the rural nobility and the urban aristocracy were left intact. Effectively, therefore, Ferdinand made no attempt to strengthen the powers of the crown and to give the principality a more efficient system of government. One hundred and fifty years later his successors were to pay a high price for this failure. In the meantime, Ferdinand had given Catalonia peace, a considerable degree of social stability, and the opportunity to make good the ravages of the civil wars and the losses of commercial markets to Italian competitors. This opportunity was only partially taken by the Catalans. They failed completely to prevent the Genoese from establishing a dominant position in the economy of Castile and, more especially, in the vital and rapidly expanding Atlantic trade of Seville (south Spain, 90 miles [140 kilometres] north of Gibraltar). The union of the crowns of Aragon and Castile therefore led to neither a political and institutional union nor to an economic integration of the Iberian Peninsula.

Catalonia's situation

Castile. Castile, too, was a poor country. Much of its soil was arid, and its agriculture was backward. The armed shepherds of the powerful sheep-owner's guild, the Mesta, drove their flocks over hundreds of miles, from summer to winter pastures and back again, spoiling much cultivated land. Despite the violent hostility of the landowners, the government upheld the Mesta privileges, since the Mesta paid generously for them and was supported by the merchants who exported the raw wool to the cloth industry of Flanders (modern Belgium). The power of the Mesta and the harm it did increased in the 16th century, for the Catholic Kings supported its privileges, anxious, as always, to increase their revenues by following the line of least resistance. Thus, the impoverished Spanish peasant was unable to buy the manufactures of his urban industries, and hence the Castilian towns remained comparatively small and their industries underdeveloped, compared with those of Italy and the Netherlands. Only the cities of Andalusia (south Spain) were relatively large, but, except for Seville, they were not primarily trading or manufacturing centres but were dominated by an urban nobility living on revenues from the surrounding countryside.

Underdeveloped Castilian industries

In the northern provinces of Castile there lived a large class of minor nobles, the hidalgos. The inhabitants of Guipúzcoa (by the westernmost French border) even claimed that they were all of noble birth. But the south, New Castile (southeast of Madrid), Extremadura (southwest of Madrid), and especially Andalusia—that is to say, those provinces most recently reconquered from the Moors—were the domain of the great nobility. There the families of the Enríquez, the Mendoza, the Guzmán, and others owned vast estates, sometimes covering almost half a province. They had grown rich during the 15th-century boom in wool exports to Flanders, at a time when there were more than 2,500,000 sheep in Castile, and it was they, with their hordes of vassals and retainers, who had attempted to dominate a constitutionally almost absolute, but politically weak, monarchy.

It was in this kingdom that the Catholic Kings determined to restore the power of the crown. Once this was achieved, or so it seemed, the liberties of the smaller kingdoms would become relatively minor problems. Like their contemporary, Henry VII of England, they had the advantage of their subjects' yearning for strong and effective government after many years of civil war. Thus, they could count on the support of the cities in restoring law and order, without having to make any important concessions to the Castilian Cortes. The Cortes of Toledo of 1480 accepted the appointment of corregidores, or royal officials, to supervise the administration of the principal towns. At the same time, both municipal efficiency and civic pride were enhanced by the obligation imposed on all towns to build a town hall (*ayuntamiento*).

With the great nobles it was necessary to move more cautiously. The Catholic Kings revoked usurpations of land and revenues by the nobility if these had occurred since 1464, but most of the great noble estates had been built up before that date and were effectively left intact. From a contemporary chronicler, Hernán Pérez del Pulgar, historians know how they proceeded piecemeal but systematically against the magnates, here using a nobleman's defiance of the law, there a breach of the peace or of a pledge, to take over or destroy his castles and thus his independent military power. Even more effective in dealing with the nobility was the enormous increase in royal patronage. Isabella was stage manager to Ferdinand's election as grand master of one after another of the three great orders of knighthood: Santiago, Calatrava, and Alcántara. This position allowed the King to distribute several hundred commanderships with their attached income from the huge estates of the orders. Equally important was royal control over all important ecclesiastical appointments, which the Catholic Kings insisted on with ruthless disregard of all papal claims to the contrary. In the Spanish dependencies in Italy, Ferdinand claimed the right of exequatur, according to which all papal bulls and breves (authorizing letters) could be published only with his permission. There exists a letter of Ferdinand to his viceroy in Naples, written in 1510, in which he upbraids the viceroy for permitting the Pope to publish a brief in Naples, threatens that he will renounce his own and his kingdoms' allegiance to the Holy See, and orders the viceroy to arrest the papal messenger, force him to declare he never published the brief, and then hang him. In Spain the Catholic Kings had no formal right of exequatur, but they and their Habsburg successors behaved very much as if they did. From now on the Spanish clergy had to look to the crown and not to Rome for advancement, and so did the great nobles who traditionally claimed the richest ecclesiastical benefices for their younger sons.

Perhaps most effective of all in reducing the political power of the high nobility was their virtual exclusion from the royal administration. The old royal council, a council of great nobles advising the king, was transformed into a bureaucratic body for the execution of royal policy, staffed by a prelate, three nobles, and eight or nine lawyers. These lawyers, mostly drawn from the poor hidalgo class, were entirely dependent on the royal will and became willing instruments of a more efficient and powerful central government. The Catholic Kings set up a Council of Finance (1480, but not fully developed until much later), the Council of the Hermandad (1476–98), the Council of the Inquisition (1483), and the Council of the Orders of Knighthood (for the administration of the property and patronage of the orders of Santiago, Calatrava, and Alcántara), and they reorganized the Council of Aragon. Charles I and Philip II were later to continue this work and to add further councils, notably those of the Indies (1524) and of Italy (1558).

When Isabella died, in 1504, the nobles appeared to be tamed and politically innocuous. In fact, their social position and its economic basis, their estates, had not been touched. Of the soil of Castile 97 percent was owned by 2 or 3 percent of the population, and some 50 percent of this was owned by a quite small number of families, mostly linked through intermarriage. In 1520 Charles I agreed to their demand for establishing a fixed hierarchy of rank, from the 25 grandees of Spain, through the rest of the titled nobility, down to some 60,000 hidalgos, or caballeros, and a similar number of urban nobility, all of them distinguished from the rest of the population, the *pecheros,* by far-reaching legal privileges and exemption from direct taxation. The Laws of Toro (1505), extending the right to entail family estates on the eldest child, further safeguarded the stability of noble property. The Catholic Kings had therefore shifted the balance of political power within the traditional ruling classes of Castile in favour of the crown, but they had not fundamentally altered the economic and social position of these classes.

Nobility's strong base

The Spanish Inquisition. With its large Moorish and Jewish populations, medieval Spain was the only multiracial and multireligious country in western Europe, and much of the development of Spanish civilization in religion, literature, art, and architecture during the later Middle Ages stemmed from this fact. The Jews had served Spain and its monarchs well, providing an active commercial class and an educated elite for many administrative posts. But, inevitably, their wealth created jealousy and their heterodoxy hatred in a population that traditionally saw itself as the defender of Christianity against the infidel. The Catholic Kings, ever good tacticians, profited from this feeling. In 1478 they first obtained a papal bull from Sixtus IV setting up the Inquisition to deal with the supposedly evil influence of the Jews and *conversos* (converted Jews). Since the Spanish Inquisition was constituted as a royal court, all appointments were made by the crown. Too late, Sixtus IV realized the enormous ecclesiastical powers that he had given away and the moral dangers inherent in an institution the proceedings of which were secret and that did not allow appeals to Rome.

With its army of lay familiars, who were exempt from normal jurisdiction and who acted both as bodyguards and as informers of the inquisitors, and with its combination of civil and ecclesiastical powers, the Spanish Inquisition became a formidable weapon in the armoury of royal absolutism. The Supreme Council of the Inquisition (or Suprema) was the only formal institution set up by the Catholic Kings for all their kingdoms together. Nevertheless, they thought of it primarily in religious and not in political terms. The Inquisition's secret procedures, its eagerness to accept denunciations, its use of torture, the absence of counsel for the accused, the lack of any right to confront hostile witnesses, and the practice of confiscating the property of those who were condemned and sharing it between the Inquisition, the crown, and the accusers—all this inspired great terror, as indeed it was meant to do. The number of those condemned for heresy was never very large and has often been exaggerated by Protestant writers. But during the reign of the Catholic Kings, several thousand *conversos* were condemned and burned for Judaizing practices. The whole family of the philosopher and Humanist Luis Vives was wiped out in this way. Many more thousands of *conversos* escaped similar fates only by fleeing the country. Many Catholics in Spain opposed the introduction of the Inquisition, and the Neapolitans and Milanese (who prided themselves on their Catholicism and who were supported by the popes) later successfully resisted the attempts by their Spanish rulers to impose the Spanish Inquisition on them. Even in Spain itself, it was the sumptuous autos-da-fé, or the ceremonial sentencings and executions of heretics, rather than the institution and its members that seem to have been popular. But most Spaniards never seem to have understood the horror and revulsion that this institution aroused in the rest of Europe.

The fate of the *conversos*

The first inquisitor general, Tomás de Torquemada, himself from a *converso* family, at once started a propaganda campaign against the Jews. In 1492 he persuaded the Catholic Kings to expel all Jews who refused to be baptized. Isabella and most of her contemporaries looked upon this explusion of about 170,000 of her subjects as a pious duty. At the moment when Spain needed all its economic resources to sustain its new European position and its overseas empire (see below), it was deprived of its economically most active citizens and laid open to exploitation by German and Italian financiers.

The conversos. Nevertheless, the explusion of 1492 did not signify the end of Jewish influence on Spanish history, as used to be thought until quite recently. It is not, however, easy to establish a clear-cut direction or pattern of this influence. At the end of the 15th century, there may have been up to 300,000 *conversos* in Spain, and the majority of these remained. They had constituted the educated urban bourgeoisie of Spain, and the richer families had frequently intermarried with the Spanish aristocracy and even transmitted their blood to the royal family itself. After 1492 their position remained precarious. Some reacted by stressing their Christian orthodoxy and denouncing other *conversos* to the Inquisition for Judaizing practices. Others embraced some form of less conventional, more spiritualized Christianity. Thus the followers of Sister Isabel de la Cruz, a Franciscan, organized the centres of the Illuminists (Alumbrados), mystics who believed that through inner purification their souls should submit to God's will and thus enter into direct communication with him. While they counted some of the high aristocracy among their numbers, most of the Illuminists seem to have been *conversos.* Again, it was among the *conversos* that Erasmianism (after Erasmus, a famous Humanist of the time), a more intellectual form of spiritualized Christianity, had its greatest successes in Spain. The Erasmians had powerful supporters at court in the early years of Charles I, when, as emperor, his policy was directed toward the healing of the religious schism by a general reform of the church. But in the 1530s and 1540s, the enemies of the Erasmians, especially the Dominican Order, launched a systematic campaign against them. The Inquisition annihilated them or forced them to flee the country, just as it had done in the case of the Illuminists as early as the 1520s. Nevertheless, the influence

Converso reactions

of Erasmus did not completely disappear from Spanish intellectual life, and it has been traced into the latter part of the 16th century.

But the majority of the *conversos* and their descendants probably became and remained orthodox Catholics, playing a prominent part in every aspect of Spanish religious and intellectual life. It has now become clear that without them the "Golden Century" of Spain would be inconceivable. They ranged from such saints as Teresa of Avila and St. John of God, one a mystical writer and founder of convents, the other an organizer of care for the sick, to Diego Laínez, a friend of St. Ignatius of Loyola and second general of the Jesuit Order. They included Fernando de Rojas, author of *La Celestina,* the first great literary work of the Spanish Renaissance, and, two generations later, Mateo Alemán, who wrote a picaresque novel, the *Guzmán de Alfarache;* and they could boast Luis de León, a Humanist and poet; a Dominican, Francisco de Vitoria, perhaps the greatest jurist of any country in the 16th century; and another famous Dominican, the defender of the American Indians and historian of the Indies, Bartolomé de Las Casas.

These, with Luis Vives, mentioned earlier, are only the most famous among the many distinguished *converso* names who played such a central and varied role in creating the cultural splendours of Spain's "Golden Century." It is an extraordinary phenomenon that had no parallel anywhere else in Europe before the 19th or even 20th century. Any attempt at an explanation is bound to be speculative, but the following may be suggested. The Spanish Jews and *conversos* formed a comparatively large section of the relatively small educated elite of Spain who were primarily responsible for the cultural achievements of the period. The *conversos,* moreover, having deliberately broken with the Jewish tradition of Talmudic (from the Talmud, the body of Jewish civil and canonical law) scholarship, found the glittering Renaissance world of Christian Spain ambivalently attractive and repellent but always stimulating. Their response to this stimulus was probably sharpened, their need to excel given a double urgency, by the hostility that they continued to meet from the "old" Christians. For these latter were very much aware of the ubiquity of the *conversos,* however much these were assimilated, and many resented it bitterly. Religious, racial, and even anti-aristocratic class prejudices combined to create the obsession with "purity of blood" (*limpieza de sangre*), which became characteristic of the Spaniards in the 16th and 17th centuries.

Converso contribution

It first crystallized with a statute of *limpieza,* imposed in 1547 on the cathedral chapter of Toledo, by which purity of ancestry from the taint both of *converso* blood and from any accusations of heresy by the Inquisition was made a condition of all future ecclesiastical appointments. The author of this statute was Archbishop Siliceo, a man of humble and hence, by definition, untainted origins, who had found himself despised by the aristocratic canons, many of whom, however, had *converso* blood in their veins. In 1556 Philip II gave his royal approval to the statute on the grounds that "all the heresies in Germany, France and Spain have been sown by descendants of Jews." As far as Germany and France were concerned, this remark was sheer fantasy, and it is especially ironic that, just at this time, Pope Paul IV, at war with Spain, described Philip II himself quite correctly as a Marrano, or descendant of Jews.

But statutes of *limpieza* now spread rapidly over Spain. They helped to perpetuate a set of values, the equation of pure ancestry, orthodoxy, and personal honour, which certainly helped to prevent the spread of heresies in Spain but which in the long run had a blighting effect on Spanish society, the more so as they were linked so closely with the basically corrupt institution of the Inquisition. For not only did they encourage the practice of denunciation, with inevitably corrupting and divisive effects, but they also educated generations of Spaniards to see their personal honour as a value depending on a set of circumstances substantially outside their own control or achievement.

Deadening effect of *limpieza* statutes

The conquest of Granada. The impact of the Moors on Spanish life and traditions had been rather different from that of the Jews. It was most evident, perhaps, in the position of women in southern Spain, who for long remained semi-veiled and in much greater seclusion than elsewhere in Christian Europe. It was evident also where Jewish influence was practically nonexistent, in the visual arts and especially in architecture. Not only did houses in southern Spain for a long time continue to be built facing inward, on to a patio, but a whole style of architecture, the Plateresque, derived from an imaginative fusion of the Moorish and the Christian: classical Renaissance structures were decorated with Gothic or Renaissance motifs but executed in the Moorish manner, as if a carpet had been hung over the outside wall of the building. This charming style, which was invented during the reign of the Catholic Kings, spread far and wide over Spain and eventually even to the New World.

To Ferdinand and Isabella, the Moorish problem presented itself in the first place in a political and military form, for the Moors still ruled their independent Kingdom of Granada (Spain's southeast corner). The Catholic Kings had to concentrate all their military resources and call on the enthusiastic support of their Castilian subjects to conquer the kingdom in a long and arduous campaign, which ended with the capture of Granada (some 130 miles east of Seville), the capital, in 1492. In this campaign Gonzalo Fernández de Córdoba, the "Great Captain," developed the tactics, training, and organization that made Spanish infantry almost unbeatable for 150 years. The Moors were granted generous terms and religious freedom. But, against the advice of the saintly Hernando de Talavera, the *converso* archbishop of Granada, who was trying to convert the Moors by precept and education, the Queen's confessor, Francisco (later Cardinal) Jiménez de Cisneros, introduced forced mass conversions. The Moors rebelled (1499–1500) and, after another defeat, were given the choice of conversion or expulsion. Jiménez and Isabella did not regard this new policy as a punishment of the Moors for rebellion, for Christian Baptism could never be that. It was rather that the rebellion released them from their previous undertaking, which they had entered into only with misgivings. Though many Moors chose conversion, the problem now became virtually insoluble. There were never enough Arab-speaking priests or money for education to make outward conversion a religious reality. The Moriscos remained an alien community, suspicious of and suspect to the "old" Christians. There was with the Moriscos very little of the intermarriage with Christians and of the deliberate acceptance of Spanish Christianity that, in spite of all the statutes of *limpieza,* allowed the *conversos* to become such an integral part of Spanish society.

Hopelessness of the Moorish position

Acquisition of Naples. Ferdinand's foreign policy was dominated by the traditional Aragonese rivalry with France along the Pyrenees and in Italy. Aragon still held Sicily and Sardinia from the much more extensive medieval Aragonese empire. French intervention in Italy, from 1494, gave Ferdinand his chance. Charles VIII of France, to secure his southern flank while he led his army into Italy, agreed to return to Ferdinand the counties of Cerdagne and Roussillon (Treaty of Barcelona, 1493), which Louis XI had seized during the Catalan civil wars, in 1463. But it was through Ferdinand's own diplomacy and through the generalship of Gonzalo de Córdoba that he acquired the Kingdom of Naples (1503). For the first time the union of Aragon and Castile had shown its strength, and Spain now rivalled France as the most powerful state in Europe. Ferdinand had carefully arranged the marriage of his children to strengthen his diplomatic position against France by alliances with Portugal, England, and Burgundy (which ruled the Netherlands). The unexpected deaths of the two eldest and their children, however, left the succession of Castile after Isabella's death (1504) to the third, Joan the Mad, and her husband, Philip I (the Handsome) of Castile, ruler of the Burgundian Netherlands. The Netherlands nobility were delighted to see this enormous accretion of power to their ruler and looked forward to the advantages that they might reap from it. They accompanied him to Castile, where a large section of the high nobility, in their turn, were anxious to acclaim him rather than the redoubtable Ferdinand. Ferdinand was therefore forced to recognize Philip's claims; but this latter died in 1506, and Ferdinand was left as uncontested ruler. His last great success was the annexation of the Spanish part of the Kingdom of Navarre in 1512.

Spain and the New World. While the exploration of the Atlantic coast of Africa had been mainly a Portuguese concern in the 15th century, the Castilians had not been entirely disinterested in such activities and had occupied the Canary Islands (off northwest Africa). In the Treaty of Alcáçovas (1479), when Afonso V of Portugal renounced his claims to the crown of Castile, he also recognized Castilian possession of the Canaries in return for Spanish recognition of Portuguese possession of the Azores (in the Atlantic Ocean west of Portugal), the Cape Verde Islands (off West Africa), and Madeira (north of the Canaries). The conquest of Granada allowed Castile, for the first time, to concentrate major resources and effort on overseas exploration. The support that Columbus received from Isabella was indicative of this new policy. In 1492 Columbus discovered the West Indies, and, in the next half century, the Spaniards conquered huge empires in America and made their first settlements in the Far East. From the beginning there were disputes with the Portuguese, who were conquering their own colonial empire. The Catholic Kings obtained a series of papal bulls (1493) from the Spanish pope Alexander VI and as a result concluded the Treaty of Tordesillas with Portugal (1494) to settle their respective claims. Everything west of an imaginary line 370 leagues (here, the league was just over three nautical miles) to the west of the Cape Verde Islands in the Atlantic was assigned to Spain; everything east went to Portugal. The rest of Europe saw no reason to accept the Pope's decision, and the result was constant and brutal warfare in the overseas colonies, even when the European governments were officially at peace (see also LATIN AMERICA).

Growing Castilian activity

Colonial policy. Unlike the other European colonists of that age, the Spaniards were vitally concerned with the moral problems of conquest, conversion, and government of heathen peoples. If the great majority of conquistadores ruthlessly pursued gold, power, and status, they took with them Dominican and Franciscan friars who set themselves to convert and educate the American Indians and, sometimes, to protect them from their Spanish masters. The Dominican Bartolomé de Las Casas fought long battles to modify at least the greatest evils of colonial exploitation. His debates with a theologian, Juan Ginés de Sepúlveda, and the writings of Francisco de Vitoria provide the first systematic discussions of the moral and legal problems of conquest and colonial rule. Their importance lay in their effects on Spanish colonial legislation. The Leyes Nuevas ("New Laws of the Indies") of 1542 were based largely on the arguments of Las Casas. While in the colonies these laws were honoured more in the breach than in the observance, yet they provided at least some protection for the Indians, and there was nothing like them in any of the other European overseas colonies of the period. Even Las Casas, however, supported the transatlantic slave trade of black Africans, until, late in his career, he came to recognize its evils.

The Atlantic trade. The crown insisted that all trade with the colonies should be carried on through Seville and should be reserved for Castilians on the argument that it was Castilian money and blood that had built the Spanish overseas empire. This trade was closely regulated by the Casa de Contratación (1503), or the House of Trade, in Seville. The city itself rapidly became one of the greatest trading centres in Europe, and its population rose from 25,000 in 1517 to 90,000 in 1594. Yet Castile was unable to supply all the manufactures that the colonists demanded and for which they paid in solid gold and silver. So far from seeing this trade as an opportunity for Castilian industry, the Cortes actually petitioned the crown in 1548 to prohibit exports to the Indies that, they claimed, were raising prices in Castile. The government did not accept this petition, but Castile had to import much of what its colonists needed from Italy and the Netherlands. The Castilian monopoly of trade with Spanish America in practice had only the effect of giving the rest of Europe the chance to compete on equal terms for the American trade with the monarchy's non-Castilian subjects. The organization and financing of the Spanish Atlantic trade were largely in the hands of Genoese and south German merchants. From the 1540s, when a new method of extracting silver from ore with the use of mercury was discovered, silver mining became a major industry in both Mexico and Peru, and silver shipments in rapidly increasing quantities soon surpassed the earlier gold shipments in value. Precious metal was exported from the Indies to Spain, partly as the crown's right of one-fifth (*quinto real*), but, more important, as payment for imports. The average annual quantities, as registered by the Casa de Contratación (not counting the unknown quantities that were smuggled), rose rapidly from about 1,000,000 pesos in the five-year period 1526–30, to 5,000,000 during 1541–54, and then to the peak of more than 35,000,000 during 1591–95. The growth of overall trade between Seville and the New World followed a very similar pattern, rising until 1550, then stagnating until the early 1560s, and rising again to a peak in the last decade of the 16th century. Prices, especially of agricultural produce, had started to rise in Spain, as in the rest of Europe, long before American silver was imported in considerable quantities. But, whatever the ultimate causes of the price revolution of the 16th century, there can be little doubt that American silver greatly aggravated the inflation in Spain in the second half of the 16th century. The theologians of the university of Salamanca (some 100 miles [160 kilometres] west–northwest to Madrid) in the 1550s were the first to see this connection and to formulate the earliest version of a quantity theory of money (in which money is worth more when scarce than when abundant). Very little of this American treasure seems to have been invested in economic production. Most of it was used for display by the court and ruling circles, to pay for Spanish imports, for the Spanish armies abroad, and to satisfy the government's German, Italian, and Netherlandish creditors. Thus Spain, with all the treasure of the New World at its command, remained a poor country.

Castile's demand for monopoly

The influx of silver from the New World

SPAIN UNDER THE HABSBURGS

Charles I. Ferdinand died on January 23, 1516, and the crowns of the Spanish kingdoms devolved on his grandson, Charles I (1516–56), the ruler of the Netherlands and heir to the Habsburg dominions in Austria and south Germany. This new union had not been planned in Spain, and, at first, it was deeply resented. Cardinal Jiménez, the regent until Charles's arrival in Spain, had to battle against the old antagonisms between nobles and towns that were flaring up again when the magnates took the opportunity of the regency to try to regain their old power. When Jiménez tried to raise a militia, nobles and cities both sabotaged the plan. The old hostilities between the different Spanish kingdoms were as bitter as ever, with the men of Navarre, for instance, claiming that they would rather accept a Turk than an Aragonese as governor of the fortress of Pamplona. Although the court at Brussels had been careful to hold its hand in the distribution of patronage, the Spaniards, nevertheless, accused the Netherlanders of greed and place hunting. It took Charles's Netherlandish ministers a year and a half to settle the Netherlandish government and to make agreements with France and England that would allow the boy-king to take possession of his new kingdom without outside interference. It was a considerable achievement, but for Spain the time was still too long. When Charles arrived in Spain, in September 1517, his supporters were already disillusioned, and the country was apprehensive of the rule of a foreigner. Charles himself, ugly, inexperienced, speaking no Spanish, and surrounded by Burgundian councillors and courtiers, did not initially make a good impression. The different Cortes of Castile, Aragon, and Catalonia granted his financial demands but attached to them much pointed advice and criticism.

The comunero movement. On June 28, 1519, Charles was elected Holy Roman emperor as Charles V and prepared to go to Germany. His chancellor, Mercurino

Gattinara, summoned the Castilian Cortes to Santiago in northwest Spain (April 1520) to demand more money, even though the former grant had not yet expired. The towns immediately made difficulties. The Toledans refused to appear; the others demanded the discussion of grievances before supply. By a mixture of bribery and concessions, the government finally induced a majority of the delegates (who had transferred from Santiago to La Coruña on the northwest coast of Spain) to vote the new grant. Many of the delegates were immediately disowned in their home towns, and one from Segovia was murdered by an enraged mob. As Charles set sail (May 20, 1520) the Castilian revolution had already begun.

Insurrection against Charles V

The towns, led by Toledo, formed a league and set up a revolutionary government. They claimed—more boldly even than the Third Estate during the French Revolution in 1789—that they were the kingdom and that the Cortes had the right to assemble without a royal summons and to discuss all matters relating to the welfare of the realm. There was talk of dethroning Charles in favour of his mother, Joan the Mad. The *comunero* leader, Juan de Padilla, actually captured the castle of Tordesillas (100 miles northwest of Madrid), where Joan was kept as prisoner; but the Queen, whether out of madness or calculation of the interests of the monarchy, would not commit herself to Padilla's proposals. The *comunero* movement spread rapidly through Castile, and the nobles did nothing to check it. They had not forgiven Charles his quest for the imperial title (which they thought inferior to that of king of Castile) nor his foreign councillors and courtiers. They resented above all his bestowal of the archbishopric of Toledo on a young Burgundian, Guillaume de Croy, and the appointment of his former tutor, Adrian of Utrecht (later Pope Adrian VI), as regent of Castile. Even the appointment of the admiral Fadrique Enríquez and the constable of Castile, Iñigo de Velasco, as Adrian's coregents did little to mollify the offended grandees. Only when the more radical and popular elements in the cities were gaining control of the *comunero* movement and beginning to spread it to the nobles' estates did the nobles combine to raise an army and defeat the *comunero* forces at Villalar (April 23, 1521).

The power of monarchy was thus restored in Castile, never to be seriously shaken again under the Habsburg kings. The towns kept much of their autonomy, but royal control in the town councils was safeguarded by the appointment of royal officials, the corregidores. The Cortes continued to function; but the deputies of the 18 "royal towns," which alone were summoned, were mostly members of the urban nobility, exempt from direct taxation and therefore not unduly concerned about voting the taxes the government asked for. As to their petitions, the King granted or ignored them as he saw fit. The nobles had won the civil war, but they could no longer break their alliance with the monarchy. The monarchy, now that it could manage the Cortes and afford a standing army, was the stronger partner. But when, in 1538, Charles I proposed a tax from which the nobles should not be exempt, there were immediate rumblings of revolt. Charles had to give way, but he never summoned the nobility again to the meetings of the Cortes. The monarchy had thus won its political victory in Castile only at the cost of letting the nobility contract out of the financial obligations of the state and the empire. The rising burden of taxes fell, therefore, on those least able to bear them and on the only classes whose activities and investments could have developed the Castilian economy.

The crown's expensive political triumph

The nobility. The traditions of the grandees and hidalgos, formed in the centuries of struggle against the Moors, made them even more averse to economic activities than the rest of the European nobility. They invested their money in land, without, however, improving agriculture, and preferred careers in the army, the church, and the civil service to the ignoble occupations of commerce. In the long run, the economic weakness of Spain, aggravated by its social traditions and its system of taxation, proved a serious handicap in Spain's struggle with its western European rivals. After Villalar, however, the Spanish nobility had come to accept Charles I. His championship of Catholic Christianity against the Muslim Turks and German heretics appealed to their own traditions of Christian warfare against the Moors. While Charles kept the grandees out of the central government of Spain itself, he had many prizes to offer in military commands, provincial governorships, and even viceroyalties in Italy and Spanish America. The hidalgos, trained as lawyers at Salamanca or as theologians at Alcalá de Henares (just east of Madrid), could look forward to dazzling careers in the King's councils and in the Spanish church. Even though Charles spent only 16 of the 40 years of his reign in Spain, the Spanish upper classes were beginning to accept and enjoy their monarch's position as the greatest ruler in Europe.

Charles I's foreign policy. Spain as a result, however, became involved in interminable wars. The necessity of defending southern Italy from the Turks brought Charles's empire into collision with the Ottoman Empire, with the central Mediterranean as the chief battle ground. Ferdinand's failure to complete the conquest of North Africa now brought a bitter revenge. The corsair leader Khayr ad-Dīn, known as Barbarossa, had made himself master of Algiers (1529) and acknowledged the suzerainty of the Sultan of Constantinople. Thus, the purely local problem of the Moorish raids on the Spanish south coast became merged into the much more formidable struggle with the Ottoman Empire. In 1535 Charles captured Tunis. It was, perhaps, his most satisfying triumph; for in this enterprise he manifestly appeared in his chosen role of "God's standard bearer," as he said himself. He now seriously considered carrying the war into the eastern Mediterranean, even conquering Constantinople itself. But in 1538 Barbarossa with a Turkish fleet defeated Charles's Genoese admiral, Andrea Doria, at Préveza (west Greece), and in 1541 the Emperor himself failed against Algiers. At the end of the reign, the balance of the two great naval powers in the Mediterranean, the Spanish and the Turkish, was still even.

Problems with the Turkish Empire

Rival Aragonese and Angevin (cousins of the ruling French house) claims to Naples also brought conflict with the French kings, against whom Charles fought four wars. His armies conquered Milan (north Italy) and reduced most of the still independent Italian states to Spanish satellites. An increasing part of the burden of these wars fell on Spain, and especially on Castile. The Spanish *tercios* (infantry regiments) were not only the Emperor's best troops, but it was in Castile that he could raise the largest part of his imperial revenues, and this, moreover, without having to account for the way he spent them, as he had to do with the taxes voted by the States General of the Netherlands. It is therefore not surprising that the empire in Europe with Charles V as head became gradually transformed into a Spanish, or, rather, Castilian, empire of Charles I. In the latter part of his reign, Spaniards and Hispanicized Italians monopolized all high positions in the empire south of the Alps and began to appear in Germany and the Netherlands. More and more they came to interpret the international and Catholic ideals of the Emperor in terms of the political predominance of Spain in Europe and overseas.

Philip II. When Charles abdicated his various lands (1555–56), Philip II (1556–98) succeeded to all his father's dominions except Germany. His empire in Europe, now without the imperial title, was still only a loose union of independent states recognizing the same head. Philip, a great traditionalist, was not the man to inspire his different subjects with a new unifying idea, though he improved the central administration of his empire by the creation of the Council of Italy (1558). But his own Castilian upbringing and preferences increased the tendency toward transforming the empire into a Castilian empire. Six of the nine viceroys Philip appointed to govern Sicily were Spaniards, as were all those of Naples, with the single exception of one Cardinal Granvelle, and 10 out of 13 governors of Milan. In the Spanish viceroyalties of Aragon, Catalonia, Valencia, and Navarre and in those of Mexico and Peru, none but Spaniards, and preferably Castilians, were ever thought of at all. These were the key figures in Philip II's empire, and they were backed by the commanders of the Spanish regiments. Fortresses were nearly always governed

Role of the Castilians in the armies

by Castilians. Only in the Low Countries was it necessary to appoint natives to military commands. When the viceroys and governors were appointed, they were given "secret" instructions—in short, ones not meant for purely propagandistic purposes. These instructions reflected the current commonplaces of Christian government that could be found in scores of "Mirrors of Princes" (handbooks of government popular at the time) published in the 16th century and that Philip had made his own. The governors were to represent the King—not the state or the Spanish Empire—as if he were present in person; it was stressed that they were not appointed for their own benefit but for that of the community they were sent to govern; they were to watch so that the King's subjects might sleep in peace and quiet and to dispense equal justice to rich and poor. Many of the Castilian grandees who were appointed to these high offices undoubtedly strove to live up to these precepts. In practice, however, their success depended largely on the strength of the local opposition they met: this was a great deal in Sicily, which had won the reputation of being "fatal to its viceroys," but very much less in Naples, about which at least one viceroy remarked that no one should wish to be viceroy there because of the pain he would have to suffer when he had to leave that post at the end of his term. A great part of the viceroys' difficulties, however, stemmed from the unreliability of the King himself. Philip was always anxious to maintain the dignity of their office, but he encouraged the local ministers and officials to report on their viceroys behind their backs, and he had no compunction about recalling a viceroy, governor, or minister when it suited him in this way to appease local opposition.

The King kept control over his viceroys and governors by weekly, sometimes daily, correspondence, carried by the excellent postal service that the House of Austria had organized in Europe. All important political decisions were thus taken in Madrid, and there the King relied almost entirely on Spaniards for advice. Only one non-Spaniard, Cardinal Granvelle of Franche-Comté, was ever summoned to Madrid to play a leading role in the King's inner councils (1579–86). It was Granvelle who had earlier, as the King's chief minister in the Netherlands, reminded his master of the international character of his empire. He advised a more international dispensation of royal patronage, as, for instance, the appointment of the Prince of Orange (William I the Silent) to the viceroyalty of Sicily so that Netherlanders and Italians would no longer think that the King regarded only the Spaniards as his "legitimate subjects." But Philip had refused to listen, and the bitter Castilian hostility at court to Granvelle ended by making the Cardinal's ministry in Madrid less and less effective in the last two or three years before his death in 1586.

Philip's refusal of non-Castilian appointments

Finance and imperial policy. Philip II on his accession inherited an unfinished war with France and a debt of some 20,000,000 ducats. While his ally England (to whose queen, Mary Tudor, Philip was married) lost Calais, Philip's own armies won considerable victories, and he was able to conclude the Peace of Cateau-Cambrésis (1559) with France, which confirmed Spanish possessions and hegemony in Italy and which left the frontiers of the Netherlands intact. But the financial position had become irretrievable, and Philip's governments, both in Madrid and in Brussels, had to declare a moratorium on their debts. It was the first of three such moratoriums in Philip II's reign—the other two were declared in 1575 and 1596—and it set the tone for the remainder of Habsburg rule in Spain, marked by growing disparity between the monarchy's imperial policies and the financial resources at its disposal to carry out these policies. For the rest of the 16th century this disparity was still largely masked by the fluctuating, but generally increasing, shipments of silver from the New World. These shipments inspired both the King and his German and Genoese creditors with the perennial hope of new treasure to pay off ever growing debts. But the armies and navies continued to swallow up more than the stream of American silver. In the end the financial burden of empire fell more and more on Castile, and it was this fact that came to determine the course of Spanish history for the next 100 years.

When Philip II returned to Spain, in 1559, he still had a naval war with the Turks on his hands, and, in the following year, his galleys suffered a humiliating and costly defeat at the island of Jarbah (off Tunisia's east coast). In 1566 the steadily deepening crisis of the Netherlands came to a head in an outbreak of image breaking. In that year Sultan Süleyman the Magnificent died, and, for a time, the Turkish danger faded into the background. Philip could therefore risk sending his commander, the Duke of Alba, with his best Spanish and Italian troops to the Netherlands (1567) in order to settle the problems of that dominion once and for all. Alba was to root out heresy, punish those responsible for the rebellion, and impose taxes sufficient to relieve Castile of the need to send any more financial help to the government in Brussels. It was the King's most terrible miscalculation, for rebellion now became revolt and involved Spain in an Eighty Years' War, 500 miles (800 kilometres) from its own borders (1568–1648). It was in the pursuit of this war that the Spanish Empire in Europe eventually foundered.

Repression in the Netherlands

The key to Philip II's and his successors' strategic thinking, however, was always France. This was reasonable; for France was potentially the strongest military power in Europe, and its hostility to Spanish greatness was absolute, despite occasional short periods of rapprochement. But, until 1595, France was paralyzed by a long succession of civil wars. Much as Philip II hated and feared a possible Huguenot (French Protestant) victory in France, he was content to see the civil wars continue, anxious, most often, to intervene on the side of the Catholics yet sometimes covertly offering help to the Huguenots. Until the late 1570s, the threat from the Turks rivalled in importance the problems of the Netherlands. Philip switched his limited resources from the Low Countries to the Mediterranean and back again, unable to achieve a decisive victory in either theatre. It was natural, therefore, that for 20 years after the Peace of Cateau-Cambrésis Spanish foreign policy remained on the defensive. There were, moreover, still formidable internal Iberian problems to be solved.

The Moriscos. The most immediate problem was that of the Moriscos of Granada. The attempt to Christianize and assimilate them had proceeded only very slowly. In the 1560s, the ineptitude and the mutual wrangling of the different public authorities in Andalusia brought government to a virtual standstill. The Captain General of Granada, in charge of defense and internal security, was quarrelling with the municipal council of Granada and with the *audiencia,* the supreme court for Andalusia, over precedence, rights of jurisdiction, and the ownership of some pastures. The *audiencia,* in its turn, quarrelled with the Inquisition over disputed rights of jurisdiction, as did the Captain General. He was supported by the Archbishop of Granada, who was, however, involved in a lawsuit with his cathedral chapter. Such disputes were typical of the Spanish system of government, and it was also characteristic that they became immediately involved in faction fights at Philip II's court. These were therefore rarely settled according to their merits but according to the prevailing political alignment at court. In this case the Governor General, who had usually acted as the protector of the Moriscos against the exploitation of the Christians, lost. The government in Madrid first sent a commission to inquire into titles of land, and this commission confiscated mainly Morisco land. In 1567 a decree was published forbidding the Moriscos the use of their Moorish names, dresses, and even of their Arabic language. Internal security was transferred from the governor general to the *audiencia.* This was the last straw, for now there was no one to protect the peaceful Morisco farmers from the murderous Morisco bandits of the sierra ("mountains"). On Christmas Day, 1568, they rose against the hated Christians. It took two years of ferocious campaigning, with dreadful atrocities committed by both sides, before the rebellion was put down. The Moriscos of Granada were then deported in small groups to different parts of Castile and settled in a last attempt to achieve assimilation. In the absence of systematic education and in the face of the hostility of the Christian population, this attempt was also doomed to failure.

Portugal and Aragon. There remained the question of the complete unification of the Iberian Peninsula. In the case of Portugal, Philip's opportunity came when his nephew, King Sebastian of Portugal, lost his life and a great Portuguese army in an ill-prepared crusade in Morocco at the Battle of the Three Kings in north Morocco (1578). During the short reign of Sebastian's old uncle, King Henry (1578–80), Philip carefully prepared his ground in Portugal by intrigue and bribery. Nevertheless, when Henry died the opposition to Castile was still so strong in Portugal and the attitude of France and England so threatening that it was necessary for Philip to send the Duke of Alba with an army to conquer Portugal in 1580. Philip respected the laws and privileges of his new subjects and left them to administer their own colonial empire. But the union increased rather than diminished the old hostility between the Castilians and the Portuguese.

Philip II's last action in the peninsula was against Aragon. It was precipitated by a court intrigue that led to the flight (1590) of the King's secretary, Antonio Pérez, to Aragon. Since Pérez was unlikely to be convicted in the *justicia's* court there, the King demanded his transfer to the court of the Inquisition. The populace of Saragossa (some 160 miles [260 kilometres] west of Barcelona) rioted, freed Pérez, and killed the King's special representative (1591). To the Aragonese it meant the defense of their liberties; to Philip it meant open rebellion. A Castilian army marched into Aragon (1591), and Philip made a number of constitutional changes. The *justicia* was, from now on, removable at royal pleasure; the viceroy could be a Castilian, and majority voting was substituted for the principle of unanimity in the Castilian Cortes. These changes gave the crown the ultimate power of decision in Aragon but preserved the kingdom's autonomy.

Aragonese liberties defended

Lepanto. In the Mediterranean the Spanish fleet was inferior to that of the Turks, and Philip had to remain on the defensive, even when the Turks were besieging Malta (1565). Their failure to capture the island from the Knights of St. John, who had leased it from Charles V as emperor, marked the end of their great offensive. Six years later, the combined Spanish, Venetian, and papal fleets—in alliance the numerical equals of the Turks—virtually annihilated the Turkish fleet at Lepanto (1571). The strategic effects of this great victory were negligible, but its moral effects were immense. It confirmed the Spaniards in their chosen role of champions of Christendom and explains much of their continued willingness to support their King's religious and imperial policies, even in the face of ruinous costs and mounting disasters. After Lepanto, however, it became clear that the stalemate in the Mediterranean could not be broken. In 1580 Spain signed a truce with the Porte (Turkish government).

The Armada. From about 1580 the Spanish government became convinced that the rebellion (1568–1609) and heresy in the Netherlands could not be crushed as long as the rebels received help from England and France. These countries, moreover, gave active support to the Portuguese pretender, Antonio, prior of Crato (mid-Portugal), and their privateers committed continual acts of piracy against Spanish trade in the Americas. Philip began to give financial aid to the League, the ultra-Catholic party in France. From 1586 he prepared the invasion of England. The Armada, which set sail from Lisbon in May 1588, numbered 130 ships and nearly 30,000 men, bravely and not at all incompetently commanded by the Duke of Medina-Sidonia. But it had been set an impossible task: that of convoying the army under Alessandro Farnese, Duque de Parma, from the Netherlands to England in the face of a better armed English fleet and without control of a single deepwater channel port. The defeat of the Armada was inevitable but not dishonourable.

Spanish intervention in France from 1590 was equally doomed to failure. The Duke of Parma, with his Spanish veterans, won great tactical victories, but Spain failed to prevent the succession of Henry of Navarre as Henry IV of France and the collapse of its ally, the League, when Henry became Catholic (1593).

Philip saw his role and that of Spain essentially as that of defender of the Catholic Church against the aggression of the heretics, an aggression that now seemed to have become mainly military and that therefore had to be met by military force. It was therefore essential that the King should safeguard and extend the power of Spain and the just claims of his house, such as those he claimed for his daughter for the throne of France. Every other consideration was subordinated to this obligation, even to the point at which the Spanish ambassador in Rome, the Count of Olivares, intervened in three successive conclaves in order to assure, by a mixture of promises and threats, the election of popes congenial to his master (conclaves of Urban VII, Gregory XIV, and Innocent IX, 1590–91). He just failed in the fourth, but crucial, election of Clement VIII, who was to receive Henry IV back into the Catholic Church (1595).

But, if Philip II could thus justify his aggressive policies to himself, both Spain's enemies and its allies were convinced that they were witnessing the quest for Spanish dominance over Europe. Many Spaniards themselves believed this; but, as the war dragged on and the costs mounted, even the faithful Castilian Cortes began to question the King's policy. After 1580, silver shipments from the New World to Seville reached new record levels, and this undoubtedly helped to persuade Philip II to embark on his grandiose schemes against England and France. Yet they only represented a quarter of his annual revenues. The rest was derived from taxation and from loans for which future revenues were pledged. The Armada campaign was said to have cost 10,000,000 ducats. The combined cost of the continuing naval war against England, the campaigns in the Netherlands, and the military intervention in France was even greater. In 1590 the Cortes accepted the royal demand for a new excise tax that was to raise 8,000,000 ducats in six years and that was appropriately nicknamed the *millones.* But by 1595, a deputy from Seville said bitterly that "the reason why taxes have been raised without noise is because they have not fallen on the rich who are those who have a voice . . . and the sweetness which they find, that is the blood of the poor." A year later, in 1596, Philip II's government declared its third bankruptcy (moratorium), but the *millones* were increased rather than lowered.

Spain had gambled its own prosperity and its American treasure on a decisive victory over the heretics in western Europe and with it its own hegemony over the Continent, and it had failed. Shortly before his death, Philip II concluded the Treaty of Vervins (1598) with France, which substantially re-established the position of 1559. Yet, if Spain failed in its highest ambitions, at the end of the 16th century it was still the greatest power in Europe. It had brought Christianity to millions overseas—and to most contemporaries, if they thought about it at all, it seemed worth the appalling price paid for it in terms of the lives and freedom of non-European peoples—and Protestantism, though not destroyed, had been contained. Spanish monks and mystics had given Catholicism a new content, and Spanish theologians and jurists had created the basis of international law. Spanish literature and art were only now entering their greatest period. Morally and economically there were dark sides to the picture, but to the Spaniards the 16th and early 17th centuries have always been their "Golden Century."

Philip's admission of defeat

Spain in 1600. It is not surprising that the enormous exertions of the last quarter of the 16th century, with its mixture of triumphs, disappointments, and miseries, should have been followed by a general mood of introspection and even disenchantment. This was particularly evident in economic and social thinking. The *arbitristas* (literally, "projectors") were writers who combined an economic analysis of the social ills of Spain with projects for economic recovery and social and moral regeneration. They saw clearly the central weakness of Spain, the attitude of mind that despised productive work and those who engaged in it. Far too many strove to live the life of a hidalgo. The treasures of Mexico and Peru, so far from stimulating investment and industrial production, had only encouraged men to look for shortcuts to riches and to live the life of *rentiers,* investing their money in the *censos,* the government annuities. These *censos* were the greatest plague and perdition of Spain, wrote González de Cellorigo, perhaps the most acute of the *arbitristas* of 1600. "It seems," he concluded, "as if we had wanted to turn these kingdoms into a republic of enchanted men, living outside the natural order."

The positive plans (among many fantasies) advocated by the *arbitristas* included the drastic cutting of government expenditure, the reform of the tax system, the encouragement of immigration into Castile, systematic and extensive irrigation, protection of industry, improvement of transport, and, finally, the sharing of the cost of empire among the constituent kingdoms of the monarchy. These were reasonable proposals, not unlike those put forward by mercantilist writers in the rest of Europe who treated economic activity as a means of increasing the power of the state. But it was not clear that the Castilian ruling classes would be capable and willing to act on them. Its attitudes were varied and often ambivalent, and this ambivalence is also reflected in the imaginative literature of the period.

Proposals for reform

Spain's Golden Age in literature. At one extreme there was the picaresque novel with its implicit satire of a society in which one could make one's way by cleverness and roguery rather than by honest work—that is, if one did not happen to be born a nobleman. Thus, the hidalgo in the *Lazarillo de Tormes* (published 1554), the first of the picaresque novels, is down and out but would rather starve than work, and he expects his servant, the boy Lazarillo, to scrounge for them both. In *Don Quixote* (published 1605 and 1615), the author, Cervantes, raised the picaresque novel to a completely new level of social and psychological insight. It is, among other things, a parable of Cellorigo's "republic of enchanted men," living in a world of illusions and tilting at windmills.

At the other extreme, there was the drama from exponents such as Lope de Vega to Tirso de Molina and Calderón. As with the picaresque novel, the comedy of the "Golden Century" was concerned with the contemporary social scene. The psychological problems faced by its characters arose nearly always directly out of social conflicts. But the social purpose of these plays was essentially conservative: the defense of the highly structured Spanish society of the time. This was achieved by insisting for all social ranks, from the king down to the peasants, on the special dignity and honour of their status. Thus Lope, for the first time, introduced the common people as fully rounded characters on the stage, allowing, for instance, to the daughter of a blacksmith the emotions of love formerly reserved on the stage to aristocratic ladies. Heredity and blood are the principles of a social order that in the comedies may be threatened but that are always reaffirmed in the end. Here may, perhaps, be seen a link with the visual arts of the age and with the Baroque style.

The "Golden Century" in architecture and painting. In the second half of the 16th century, in the more severe artistic climate of the Catholic Counter-Reformation, the playful Plateresque style of buildings fell into disfavour. Philip II preferred the unornamented and monumental classical architecture of Juan de Herrera, the greatest Spanish architect of the century. This could be very effective, as in Philip's monastic palace of El Escorial (20 miles [30 kilometres] northwest of Madrid), which embodied the gloomy and ascetic spirit of the King and also blended with the stark and forbidding landscape of the Sierra de Guadarrama (a range of mountains northwest of Madrid). But only too often the style produced an ugly and pompous monumentality, such as not infrequently afflicts the architecture of countries at the height of their imperial careers. But at the turn of the century this style gave way to the Baroque, which Spanish architects found no difficulty in acclimatizing in their country from Italy. This style could achieve monumentality without being pompous. It could display the grandeur of the church, or the monarchy, or anyone rich enough to build himself a palace. Perhaps most important of all, it was a style that, by its love of ornamentation and its essentially theatrical character, became immensely popular with the mass of the population.

Success of the Baroque style

The painting of the period does not lend itself as easily to a social interpretation; but certain patterns may still be observed. The greatest painter of the Spanish Counter-Reformation, the Cretan El Greco, made his home in Toledo, where the local aristocratic and ecclesiastical society (but not Philip II) seems to have fully appreciated his genius. El Greco's superb portraits, but above all his religious paintings, with their elongated figures rising like so many flames to heaven, seem like the embodiment of the most spiritual aspects of Spanish Catholicism.

El Greco left no school. The painters of the following generation, especially Murillo, had a different religious sensibility, more naturalistic than El Greco, more personal, and more romantic; and again, as did Baroque architecture, they appealed successfully to a popular religiosity. But the greatest of them, Velázquez, was hardly a religious painter at all. His subjects were the King with his family and court and, characteristic for the age and parallel with the drama of the period, the common people. All these he represented with a realism and psychological insight unmatched in the 17th century, except perhaps by Rembrandt.

The reign of Philip III. It was the tragedy of Spain that its ruling classes failed to respond to the social and political problems of the age as creatively as its writers and artists. For this failure there are at least some good reasons. In the first place, the system of royal government, as it was understood at the time, depended ultimately on the king's ability to lead and to make decisions. Philip II's very consciousness of his divinely imposed obligations in this respect, compounded by his almost pathological suspiciousness of the intentions and ambitions of other men, had led him to deprecate independent initiative by his ministers. Philip thus failed to educate an effective ruling class with a tradition of statesmanlike thinking and decision making.

Philip III (died 1621) was a devout, phlegmatic nonentity, totally incapable of carrying on his father's methods of personal government. He therefore had to have a minister who would do all his work for him, a *privado.* His choice, the Duke of Lerma, however, turned out to be a singularly unfortunate one. Amiable, incompetent, and, inevitably, under heavy attack from those who envied his position, Lerma strove to maintain himself by the lavish dispensation of royal patronage to the high nobility. He was not the man to translate the schemes of the *arbitristas* into effective reforms. During the reign of Philip III the government of Spain either became the victim of events that it did not attempt to control or allowed its hand to be forced by outsiders.

Lerma's incompetency

Not all events could have been controlled. In 1599–1600 an epidemic plague claimed some 500,000 victims in Castile. This sudden decimation of the labour force caused a sharp rise in wages that acted as another disincentive to capital investment by Spaniards. Yet the advantages that the labourers had reaped from the rise in wages were quickly offset by renewed inflation. This was the result of the government's decision to solve its perennial financial problems by the massive coinage of the *vellón,* a debased copper coinage. This did not prevent the need for another moratorium on government debts, in 1607, and in 1608 the King had to promise the Cortes of Castile not to issue any more *vellones* for 20 years. But by 1617 he had to ask the Cortes to allow another issue, and yet another one in 1621.

The expulsion of the Moriscos. The most serious social crisis of the reign was, however, entirely man-made. The great majority of the Moriscos lived in the Kingdom of Valencia. Like those of Andalusia, they had been forcibly but ineffectively converted to Christianity. Most of them were relatively poor farmers, agricultural labourers, or small tradesmen and hucksters. They were hated and despised by the poor Christian peasants but protected by the landowners for whom they provided industrious tenants and labourers.

For many years a controversy raged between those who wanted to "solve" the Morisco problem by expulsion and those who pleaded for time and money to achieve their genuine assimilation and Christianization. While the practical, economic aspects of these two views were not neglected, it was characteristic of the Spain of the period that the main emphasis of the debate was on the religious and moral problems involved. In 1609 Lerma's government ordered the expulsion of the Moriscos. By 1614 some 275,000 had been forced to leave Spain. The majority of Spaniards undoubtedly approved of the expulsion. About its economic effects there was at the time and there is still today considerable controversy. In Castile the effects were probably slight. In Aragon and Valencia, where the Moriscos had constituted between 20 and 30 percent of the population, they were certainly much greater. Some but by no means all Morisco land was resettled by "old" Christians. There was a shift from labour-intensive sugar and rice production to mulberry (silk) cultivation and viticulture (vines). The greatest difficulties were caused by the indebtedness of the Morisco peasants and the consequent losses suffered by their urban creditors. An ironic footnote to the expulsion was the plight of the Aragonese and Valencian inquisitions. Once hot for expulsion, they were now left without their major source of income, the composite fines for Moorish practices by which they had formerly milked the Morisco villages.

Effects of the expulsion

Spain and Europe. Neither Philip III nor Lerma were emotionally or intellectually capable of the fundamental reappraisal of foreign policy that Philip II's failures called for. Very few even of the *arbitristas* had seen this need sufficiently clearly. The court, the nobility, and, above all, the clergy and the King's confessors remained caught in the now hardening tradition of Spanish imperialism, simplistically interpreted as the cause of God. Once again, this attitude caused a serious misjudgment of the political forces in England: the absurd hope of placing the infanta Isabella on the English throne when Elizabeth I should die. In 1601 a small Spanish force was disembarked at Kinsale, in Ireland, to cooperate with the Irish rebels. The English army had no difficulty in forcing it to surrender.

Fortunately, the new government of James I was anxious for peace. On the Spanish side, the Treaty of London (1604), which ended 16 years of Anglo-Spanish war, was negotiated on the initiative of Philip II's son-in-law, the archduke Albert, to whom, in his last year, Philip II had handed over the nominal sovereignty of the Spanish Netherlands. It was also Albert and his Genoese general, Ambrogio Spinola, who virtually forced Madrid to negotiate with the Dutch rebels. Between 1604 and 1607, Spain sent unprecedentedly large sums to Flanders. Spinola captured Ostend (on modern Belgium's coast) and won victories in Friesland (north Holland). But it would take 300,000 ducats a month to continue the war successfully, he now wrote to Madrid. After the moratorium of 1607, Philip III was in no position to raise such sums; but still he could not bring himself to recognize the independence of his rebellious and heretical subjects. He compromised by concluding a truce for 12 years, to run from 1609.

In 1610 a new war with France threatened, but Henry IV was assassinated, and once more, for almost 20 years, Spain's most formidable opponent in Europe became preoccupied with its internal problems. The years from 1610 to 1630 were the last period in which Spain clearly dominated Europe. For the first of these two decades Europe enjoyed a kind of Pax Hispanica. Spanish armies controlled Italy, Flanders, and parts of the Rhineland. Spanish and Spanish-inclined Jesuits were confessors at the courts of the Austrian Habsburgs, of Poland, Bavaria, and of some of the minor German and Italian princes. Spanish subsidies, pensions, and bribes made clients even of Protestant politicians in England, Holland, and the Swiss cantons (although much less effectively so than Madrid hoped); and Spanish-paid spies fed the governments of Madrid and Brussels with valuable, if not always accurate, information about its potential enemies in the United Provinces (or Holland), England, and France. Yet, to a much greater degree than most contemporaries realized, this Spanish domination of Europe rested on default: the disunity and temporary weakness of Spain's political and religious opponents. The psychological effects on Spain of this position were wholly disastrous, for it confirmed the Castilian ruling classes in their imperialist attitudes.

While for Philip III and Lerma this attitude led, for reasons both of finance and temperament, to a largely defensive stance, it was quite otherwise for the Spanish representatives abroad. In the absence of an effective lead from Madrid, the Spanish grandees who were the King's viceroys and ambassadors in Europe took it upon themselves to advance Spanish interests as they saw them—that is, in terms of Spanish power. They fortified the route from Milan to the Tirol (now west Austria) through the Valtellina, the vital link with the Austrian Habsburgs; they annexed several small Italian lordships; they inveigled Dalmatian pirates (operating from what is now the Yugoslav coast), the Uskoks, to prey on the trade of Venice, and they even seem to have plotted the complete overthrow of that republic.

More fateful still were their activities in Prague and Brussels. At the courts of the emperors Rudolf II and Matthias, the ambassador Baltazar de Zúñiga organized an effective "Spanish" party. His successor, the Count of Oñate, negotiated the secret Treaty of Graz (1617) by which the Jesuit-educated archduke Ferdinand of Styria (later Emperor Ferdinand II) was designated as heir to Matthias. In return for giving up Philip III's claims to the Austrian succession, which Madrid had never seriously pursued in any case, Oñate obtained the promise of full Spanish sovereignty of the Tirol and Alsace (in modern east France), the two German pillars of the "Spanish Road" between Italy and the Netherlands. At the same time, the "Spanish" party in Prague managed the preelection of Ferdinand as king of Bohemia in case of Matthias' death. Zúñiga and Oñate had undoubtedly strengthened Spain's strategic position in central Europe; but they had also, for the first time since the abdication of Charles V, involved Spain again in the local politics of the Holy Roman Empire. For Philip IV, this involvement turned out to be even more disastrous than it had to Charles V. Spanish leadership, as practiced by the self-willed Castilian grandees abroad, had proved to be energetic and clever; but it was ultimately as devoid of true statesmanship as the slackness of the King and his *privado*.

Spain's position in central European politics

In 1617 Lerma's enemies at court finally managed to overthrow him. Zúñiga returned to Madrid and became the leading advocate of aggressive policies. The Marquis of Bedmar, former Spanish ambassador to Venice and the organizer of the anti-Venetian conspiracy, went as ambassador to Brussels and immediately began to press for the reopening of the war against the United Provinces. In 1621 Philip III died, and with him disappeared the last restraints on the neo-imperialists. Philip IV, a boy of 16, left the effective powers of kingship in the hands of his former gentleman of the chamber, the Count (later Count-Duke) of Olivares. Olivares shared his uncle Zúñiga's political views, and he soon dominated the Council of State.

Philip IV's reign. *Spain and the Thirty Years' War.* In 1620, following the defeat of Frederick V (the elector Palatine, or prince, from the Rhineland who had accepted the crown of Bohemia, now western Czechoslovakia, when offered it in 1618) and the Bohemians, Spanish troops from the Netherlands entered the "Winter King's" hereditary dominions of the Rhine Palatinate. Militarily, Spain was now in a favourable position to restart the war with the United Provinces at the expiration of the truce in 1621. The decision to do so was, however, taken on more general grounds. The Dutch had used the truce only to capture the carrying trade of western Europe and the Baltic with Spain, Zúñiga argued. On the oceans they had never observed the truce but continued their piracies against Spanish and Portuguese shipping. If they were allowed to continue, first the Indies would be lost, then the rest of Flanders, Italy, and, finally, Spain itself, for it would have lost the dominions that had made it great. These were very different grounds for resuming the war from those habitually advanced by Philip II. Little was said about religion or even the King's authority, while the protection of the overseas empire had become the central consideration in Spanish relations with the Dutch rebels." Olivares dismissed the counter-arguments of the Council of Finance. The young King, content to be told that he was not responsible for the debts of his predecessors, piously declared his intention not to burden his subjects any further. Neither he nor his ministers could foresee that a recent slump in silver shipments from America was not a temporary setback but heralded a rapid, long-term decline. The Dutch, it is true, were equally anxious for war, partly, at least, because of the vain hope that the Belgians would rebel against Spain and join the United Provinces.

Having decided on war, Olivares pursued a perfectly consistent strategy: communications between Spain and the Spanish Netherlands must be kept open at all costs, and the Dutch must be hit wherever they were most vulnerable. The first objective led Spain to cultivate the friendship of James I of England and even to contemplate the restoration of Frederick V to the Palatinate and the marriage of Philip IV's devoutly Catholic sister to the heretic Prince of Wales (later Charles I). It led to very close cooperation with the Austrian branch of the Habsburgs and the need to fight for the control of the Valtellina. The second objective, which followed the advance of the imperial armies under Wallenstein (an adventurer who made himself indispensable to the Habsburgs as a military organizer) to the Baltic, led to grandiose schemes of building an imperial Spanish fleet in the Baltic with Hanseatic (the Hanse towns on the Baltic were independent mercantile organizations) and Danish help in order to destroy the Dutch Baltic trade and with it the economic prosperity of the republic.

However rational and limited these aims and plans seemed in Spain, in the rest of Europe they appeared to show only too clearly the limitless ambitions of the House of Austria. The now habitual talk in Spanish court and military circles of restoring Spain's greatness did not help to persuade Europe otherwise. Spinola's and Wallenstein's victories in the mid-1620s convinced the Spanish Council of State that victory against the Dutch was possible and blinded them to the danger of raising up new and more powerful enemies. Thus, they let slip the last chances of a favourable peace. Yet, despite enormous sums sent annually from Castile to Flanders, the Spanish armies could not break Dutch resistance. They could not even supply their own provisions and ammunition without the covert help of Dutch merchants, who, in their turn, argued that this trade with the mortal enemy brought in the money needed to pay for the troops fighting this enemy. From 1630, when Sweden and France actively intervened in the war, Spain rapidly lost the initiative. Spanish armies could still win tactical victories in Italy and Germany, but the number and seriousness of Spanish reverses, especially at sea, were now steadily mounting.

Improved government under Olivares

The government of Olivares. Olivares was undoubtedly the most able politician directing the Spanish government since Cardinal Granvelle. All contemporaries remarked on the contrast between his energetic and bustling administration and the sleepy regime of Philip III and Lerma. The Catholic Kings, the Emperor, and Philip II had kept the high nobility, to a greater or lesser degree, out of the central government. Lerma had reversed this policy, and Olivares could not go back on this position, although he bitterly lamented the incompetence of his fellow aristocrats and sharply reduced the overgenerous flow of royal patronage to them. He could and did develop the system of committees (juntas) of experts within the councils, which took over a great deal of government business and made its administration more efficient.

In 1623 and 1624 Olivares presented to the King and Council of State a number of memorandums that were nothing less than plans for a far-reaching reform of government and society, on the lines advocated by the *arbitristas.* Like them, Olivares saw the need to change mental attitudes: restraints on the aristocratic love of splendour and display, the need to appreciate the dignity of work and productive economic activity, an end to the economically harmful and morally indefensible mania for *limpieza* (Olivares himself, through his grandmother, had *converso* blood flowing in his veins). On the more immediately practical level, Olivares' memorandums were concerned principally with finance; for, with an annual expenditure of 8,000,000 ducats, there was a deficit of 4,000,000. The Count-Duke proposed the abolition of some of the most harmful taxes, the *millones* and the *alcabala,* the sales tax, and their substitution by other, simpler, and more equitable taxes. Finally, Castile should not be expected to continue to bear almost alone the cost of the war. Like Granvelle, Olivares recognized that the King's non-Castilian dominions could only be expected to share in the burdens of empire if they could also enjoy its advantages, the honours, commands, and control over policy that had been all but completely reserved to the Castilians.

Hopelessness of reform

None of these plans was put into practice. The Spaniards were unwilling to change their mode of life and their ingrained beliefs at the behest of a royal favourite. Olivares did manage to arrange loans with a consortium of Portuguese Marrano businessmen, but he was bitterly attacked for this action. Philip IV consulted a committee of theologians about a proposed canalization of the Tagus River, flowing east–west across Spain and Portugal. They forbade it as an interference with God's design. The court itself gaily abandoned a short-lived austerity in the celebrations that followed the arrival of the Prince of Wales in his romantic but abortive quest for a Spanish bride (1623). The financial reforms foundered on the opposition of vested interests to taxation by the Cortes and on the opposition of the whole Castilian ruling class to the plan for the decentralization of the empire. Just as had happened to Granvelle's proposals, there was not even any serious discussion of Olivares' plan. In the 1560s the result of this failure had left Philip II with no alternative but Alba's policy of repression—which caused the revolt of the Netherlands; in the 1620s it left Olivares with no alternative but his Union of Arms—which caused the revolts of Catalonia and Portugal. The Union of Arms was a scheme for the creation of a reserve army of 140,000 men that was to be paid for by the dominions of the Spanish Empire in proportion to their estimated resources. But the non-Castilian dominions disliked this proposal because it infringed their liberties. They also distrusted Castilian intentions, and with some justice; for in 1625 Olivares had advised the King in a secret memorandum to "secretly plan and work to reduce these kingdoms of which Spain is composed to the style and laws of Castile."

The revolt of Catalonia. Apart from Portugal, Catalonia was the state with the greatest degree of autonomy. Its medieval form of government had not been changed since Ferdinand the Catholic had settled it in 1486. Its countryside, especially on the French border, was infested with smugglers and bandits and riven by local feuds. Its taxes were administered by the Diputació, a self-perpetuating and corrupt committee of the Catalan Corts that functioned during the long intervals between the meetings of that body. The viceroys, hemmed in on all sides by local privileges and without control over the finances of the province, were virtually powerless. In 1626 Philip IV summoned the Cortes of the realms of the crown of Aragon. Aragon and Valencia reluctantly voted some money but refused conscription of troops. Catalonia refused everything. Nevertheless, Olivares published the royal decree for the Union of Arms. Relations between Madrid and Catalonia deteriorated rapidly.

Increasing financial troubles

As the costs of warfare continued to soar, the government resumed the inflationary minting of *vellones* and had yet to declare another moratorium, in 1627. In 1628 the *vellón* coins were withdrawn, causing a collapse of prices and a business recession. The 1630s added new taxes in Castile and outright confiscations from private individuals, both of income from government annuities and of American silver imported in commercial transactions. Not surprisingly, Madrid was becoming obsessed with what it considered to be the injustice of Catalonia's immunity from taxation. In 1639 Olivares opened a campaign against southern France from Catalonia. It had no rational strategic objective except to pitchfork Catalonia into the war. If the Catalans had to defend their country, Olivares argued, they would have to support the army.

This logic was lost on the Catalans. The peasants, urged on by their clergy, refused to support the troops. During the winter the soldiers were billeted in the countryside. Soon there were clashes with the population, then riots and open rebellion. Too late, Olivares attempted to draw back and conciliate the Catalans. On June 7 the mob murdered the Viceroy in Barcelona. The higher nobility and the urban aristocracies were still most anxious for an accommodation; but the countryside was now completely out of control. The Diputació, which was the only remaining legal authority, was led by a strong-minded cleric named Pau Claris, canon of Urgel, located west of Barcelona, who was unwilling to make concessions. In the autumn of 1640 Olivares scraped together the last available troops and sent them against the Catalan rebels. Claris countered by transferring Catalan allegiance to the king of France, "as in the time of Charlemagne" (January 1641). French troops now entered Catalonia. Only when the renewed French civil wars (the Fronde) induced the French to withdraw their army were the Castilians able to reconquer Catalonia (1652). The Catalan upper classes, at least, were relieved, for they had found the French even less congenial masters than the Castilians. For once, Madrid did not repeat its previous mistakes: the liberties and privileges of Catalonia were fully restored.

The revolt of Portugal. The revolt of Catalonia gave the Portuguese their opportunity. The lower classes and the clergy had always hated the Castilians. The Portuguese aristocracy and the commercial classes, previously content with the patronage and the economic opportunities that the union with Spain had provided, had become dissatisfied during the last 20 years. They resented the introduction of Castilians into their government (1634), the ineffectiveness of Spanish naval support in the defence of Brazil against the Dutch, and the growing reaction of the Spanish colonies against Portuguese economic penetration during this period of contracting economic activity. Rather than allow themselves to be sent to fight the Catalan rebels, the Portuguese nobility decided to seize power in Lisbon and proclaimed the Duke of Bragança as King John IV of Portugal (December 1640). Madrid, with an aristocratic conspiracy in Andalusia on its hands (1641), no longer had the means to react.

Portuguese grievances

The last years of Philip IV. The disasters on Spain's periphery were matched by continued mismanagement of Spanish finances at the centre. Once more the government tampered with the *vellón* coinage and then reversed course into a sudden and catastrophic deflation (1641–42). In January 1643 the Castilian grandees were finally able to force Philip IV to dismiss Olivares. The King now decided to run his own government. He dissolved the juntas, and the councils resumed their authority. Soon, control of the government slipped into the hands of Olivares' nephew, Don Luis Méndez de Haro, a clever but colourless politician with neither his uncle's imperial vision nor his panache.

The defeats continued. The Great Condé (the French King's cousin) broke the Spanish *tercios* and their reputation for invincibility in the Battle of Rocroi, northeast France (1643). In 1647, popular revolutions broke out in Naples and Palermo (Sicily), and soon these two cities were in the hands of revolutionary governments. In Naples, at least, it was again the excessive taxation, imposed for Spain's war effort, that had precipitated the rebellion. The Spanish monarchy, wrote the Venetian ambassador to Madrid at the time, "resembled that great colossus that during an earthquake had collapsed in a few moments while everyone hurried along to enrich himself with the fragments."

In fact, Spain survived and even managed to hold on to much of its empire. The revolts of Naples and Sicily, directed as much against the local nobility as against Spain, were put down in 1648. When the Emperor conceded French claims to Alsace and the Rhine bridgeheads, the "Spanish Road" to the Netherlands was irrevocably cut, and the close alliance between the Spanish and the Austrian branch of the House of Habsburg came to an end. With Portugal in revolt and Brazil no longer an issue between the Dutch and the Spaniards, Philip IV drew the only possible conclusion from this situation and rapidly came to terms with the United Provinces, recognizing their full independence and agreeing to the closing of the Scheldt, a river emptying into the North Sea west of Antwerp (Treaty of Münster, January 1648). But Philip IV had not changed his basic policy. He wanted to have his hands free for a final effort against France, even after Catalonia had surrendered. Once again the temporary weakness of France during the Fronde confirmed the Spanish

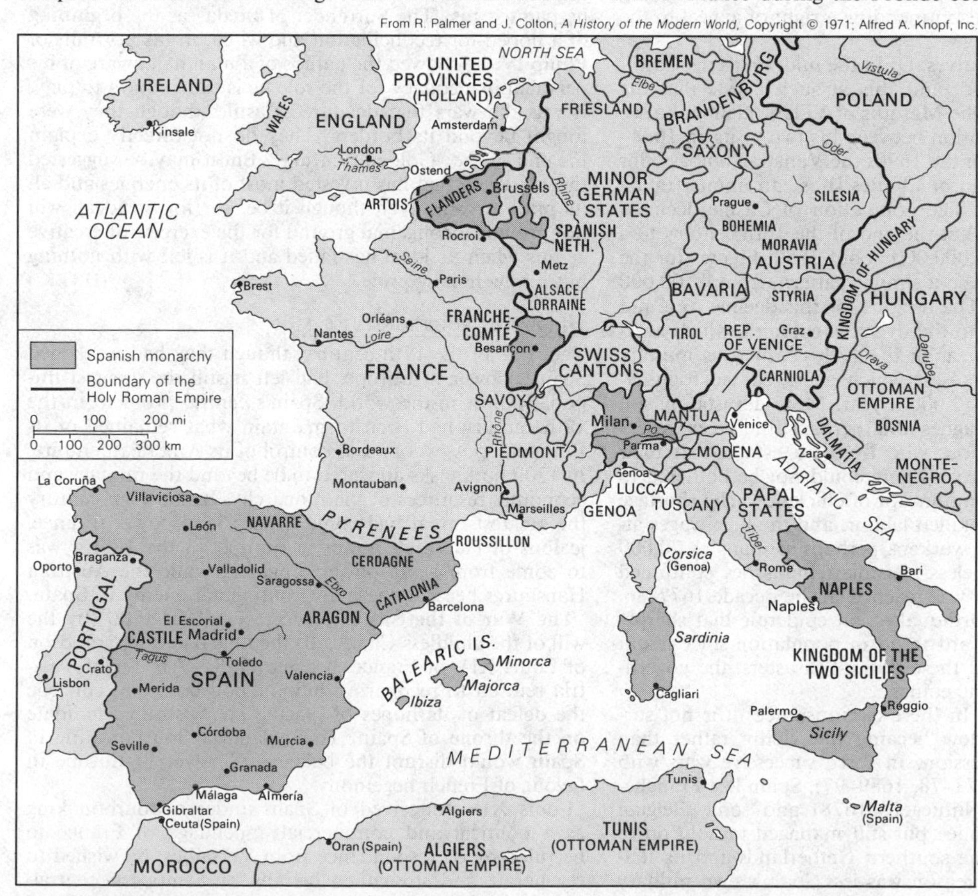

The European dominions of the Spanish Habsburgs in 1648.

court in its disastrous military policy. Haro passed up the chance of concluding a very favourable peace in 1656.

The war dragged on, with England joining France, capturing Jamaica, and contributing to the Spanish defeat in the Battle of the Dunes on the northern coast of France (1658). The Treaty of the Pyrenees (1659) cost Spain Artois (now northernmost France), Roussillon, and part of Cerdagne. More important than these relatively minor territorial losses was the realization throughout Europe that Spain's pretensions to hegemony had definitely and irremediably failed. The Spaniards themselves were slow to admit it. Philip IV had made concessions to France in order, once again, to have his hands free against the last unforgiven enemy, Portugal. There was no longer any rational basis for his hopes of success. All schemes for financial and tax reforms were still being blocked by vested interests, and the government had declared two more bankruptcies, in 1647 and 1653. Once more the Council of Finance issued a debased coinage to pay for the Portuguese campaign. But the Portuguese routed the last Spanish armies at Ameixial (1663) and at Villaviciosa on the north coast of Spain (1665). In 1668 Spain formally recognized the independence of Portugal.

The Treaty of the Pyrenees

Charles II. For 10 years Philip IV's widow, Maria Anna of Austria, acted as regent for the child Charles II (1665–1700). She allowed her government to be dominated by her confessor, the Austrian Jesuit Nithard. He was overthrown by John of Austria, an illegitimate son of Philip IV, who, however, proved quite incapable of providing effective leadership for the country. From then on, the high nobility dominated the government as effectively as it had done in the days of Philip III, playing court intrigues, first with the regent and, later, with the two successive wives of the incapable Charles II. The majority of these aristocrats were self-seeking and incompetent; but some, notably the Count of Oropesa, were men of considerable ability. They finally restored the coinage, in 1680, although not before they had caused another catastrophic deflation. They set up a committee for commerce that pursued orthodox mercantilist policies, encouraging trade and industry. They even took the unprecedented step of investigating the Inquisition and recommending a right of appeal to the secular courts.

Decline of Castile

But these were palliatives. Until the mid-1680s the Castilian economy declined, and this at such a rate that the French ambassador, the Marquis of Villars, claimed to see an appalling deterioration between his two visits, in 1668–69 and in 1671–73. In the 1690s the Venetian ambassador characterized the reign of Charles II as "an uninterrupted series of calamities." The population of Castile declined from about 6,500,000 at the end of the 16th century to a low point of under 5,000,000 about 1680. Figures for the whole of Spain followed a similar pattern, from 8,500,000 to about 6,600,000. The reasons for this decline were not so much emigration to the overseas colonies, which averaged 4,000–5,000 a year in the 17th century, as military casualties from all causes, which averaged the frightening figure of 10,000–12,000 a year. More devastating still were the recurrent plagues and, perhaps, the sheer misery of the rural population, who lived on estates that their noble and ecclesiastical owners could not be bothered to manage with even a minimum of efficiency. The shortage of labour, especially skilled labour, and the high wages attracted many foreign workers, perhaps as many as 70,000 Frenchmen. Nevertheless, Castilian industries continued to decline. The nadir was reached in the decade 1677–86, with crop failures, earthquakes, an epidemic that sharply reversed a slight upward trend in population since about 1650, and, on top of these natural disasters, the government's deflation of the coinage.

The French wars. In these circumstances it is not surprising that Spain now became the victim rather than the initiator of aggression. In three successive wars with France (1667–68, 1672–78, 1689–97), Spain lost Franche-Comté (Treaty of Nijmegen, 1678) and some Belgian frontier towns to France but still managed to hold on to the greater part of the southern Netherlands and its Italian dominions. The reason was less Spain's own military efforts, which were puny compared with those of the first half of the century, than the unwillingness of other European powers, especially the United Provinces, to see the Spanish dominions in Europe swallowed up by France. After the last and, for Spain, most disastrous of these wars, the War of the Grand Alliance (1689–97), Louis XIV himself restored Flanders and Catalonia, which his troops had occupied, for he now had his eye on the inheritance of the whole Spanish Empire.

The last years of the childless and evidently dying Charles II were occupied by the manoeuvres of the European powers for the Spanish succession or, alternatively, for the partition of the Spanish Empire. Amid cabals, intrigues, exorcisms of evil spirits, and blood feuds at court, while riots were going on in the streets of Madrid, the rule of the House of Austria came to an end with the death of Charles II, on November 1, 1700.

The decline of Spain. There can be no doubt about the economic and political decline of Spain in the 17th century and especially in its second half. Moreover, Calderón, Velázquez, and Murillo had no successors of remotely comparable stature. It need not be reasonable, however, to speak of decadence, as many non-Spaniards did at the time and later. The term decadence, except perhaps when applied to the person of Charles II, that last unhappy offspring of constant Habsburg intermarriage, does not explain the timing of the decline nor its duration. In the first place, the economic decline was mainly a Castilian phenomenon and did not affect Catalonia and Valencia to anything near the same degree. For Castile, it is perhaps best to see the problem of decline as the *arbitristas* saw it: in the depreciation by Castilians of economic activity, an attitude that was rooted deeply in Castile's past history but that was particularly baleful in a period of general European economic depression, such as the 17th century. To this must be added the aggressive militarism that was central to the Castilian aristocratic tradition and that led to the political hubris (overweening pride) of Spanish imperial policy, from Philip II to Philip IV. The Castilian ruling classes never produced, or perhaps gave no chance to, a leader who could break out of this tradition. Velázquez seems to have known it or felt it instinctively when he painted his "The Surrender of Breda" as the beginning of a hoped-for reconciliation and when, in his portraits of Philip IV, he showed the pathos of a man half aware of his personal inadequacy for the role he is called upon to play. It was the wars that devoured Castile, though they were fought beyond its borders. They do not directly explain the end of the "Golden Century." But it may be suggested that a society that has invested most of its energies and all its pride in war, even though it be war for an ideal, will not provide a congenial ground for the exercise of creative genius when its ideal has failed and it is left with nothing but a now hollow pride. (H.G.K.)

THE EARLY BOURBONS, 1700–53

The wars of the 17th century, though they had weakened Spain's power in Europe, had left it still the greatest imperial power in the world. Spain's central problem in the 17th century had been to maintain what remained of its European possessions and control of its American empire. In 1700 both tasks appeared to be beyond the military and economic resources of the monarchy. In the 17th century the greatest threat had come from a land power, France, jealous of Habsburg power in Europe; in the 18th it was to come from a sea power, England, while the Austrian Habsburgs became the main continental enemy of Spain.

The War of the Spanish Succession. In 1700 (by the will of the childless Charles II) the Duc d'Anjou, grandson of Louis XIV of France, became Philip V of Spain. Austria refused to recognize Philip, a Bourbon, and concede the defeat of its hopes of placing an Austrian candidate on the throne of Spain. To England, a Bourbon king in Spain would disrupt the balance of power in Europe in favour of French hegemony.

Louis XIV conceived of Spain under a Bourbon king as a political and commercial appendage of France to be ruled by correspondence from Versailles; he wished to regenerate and strengthen his ally by a modern centralized administration. This task was both complicated and facilitated by the War of the Spanish Succession (1701–14) when the allied armies of Britain and Austria invaded Spain in order to drive out Philip V and establish the "Austrian" candidate, the archduke Charles, on the throne. An efficient administration had to be created in order to extract resources from Spain for the war effort, and thus relieve pressure on the French treasury; at the same time financial shortages imperilled administrative reform while war taxation and war levies drove Catalonia and Aragon to revolt against the demands of the Bourbon dynasty.

Administrative reforms

The instruments of centralizing reform were French civil servants (Jean-Jacques Amelot, Louiv XIV's ambassador, and Jean-Henri-Louis Orry, a financial expert) and a handful of Spanish lawyer-administrators such as Melchor de Macanaz. They were supported by the queen, María Luisa of Savoy, and her friend the 60-year-old Princess of Ursins. The opponents of reform were those who suffered by it: the grandees who had dominated the cumbersome inefficient councils; the councils themselves; the regions like Catalonia, Aragon, and Valencia, in which the establishment of effective royal rule was seen as a Castilian, centralizing, imposition in conflict with the local privileges, or *fueros;* the church, whose position was threatened by the ferocious and doctrinaire regalism of Macanaz, who wished to subject the independent jurisdictions of the church (especially that of the papal nuncios and the Inquisition) to the absolute monarch.

The disaffection of all these elements easily turned to opposition to Philip V as king. Opposition to the new dynasty accentuated the determination of Bourbon civil servants to end special privileges that covered treasonable sympathy with the Austrian and English invaders.

Castile was ferociously loyal to the new dynasty throughout the war, in spite of severe financial difficulties (consequent on the loss of revenues from the Indies). The support of Castile and of France (until 1711) enabled Philip V to survive severe defeats and two occupations of Madrid. In 1705 the archduke Charles landed in Catalonia and took Barcelona. When Philip V tried to attack Catalonia through Aragon, the Aragonese, in the name of their *fueros,* revolted against the passage of Castilian troops.

It was this revolt, backed by the local nobility, that turned the King's advisers resolutely against local privileges and aristocratic treason. After the victory over the archduke Charles at Almansa (April 1707) the *fueros* of the kingdoms of Valencia and Aragon were abolished and the property of rebels confiscated. When the Archbishop of Valencia resisted attempts to make priests of doubtful loyalty appear before civil courts, the regalism of Macanaz was given full course.

This was the last direct triumph of the reformers. With the death of Queen María Luisa in 1714 and the arrival of Philip's new wife, Isabella (Elizabeth Farnese), court support for radical reform disappeared. Macanaz was condemned by the Inquisition, and a less rigid administration, more inclined to compromise with the church and the higher nobility, controlled the country's policy.

The last stages of the war were a Spanish concern. The allies deserted the archduke Charles; the French gave little help to Philip V. In 1714 Philip recaptured the Archduke's capital at Barcelona. By the Decree of Nueva Planta (1716) the *fueros* were abolished and Catalonia was integrated into Spain. Integration, criticized as it was by later generations of Catalans as the destruction of Catalan "nationality," was nevertheless a precondition for industrial revival; it gave Catalonia a domestic market in Spain and later an overseas market in America.

The integration of Catalonia into Spain

Paradoxically, a disastrous war had for the first time created a unitary Spanish state: except for the Basque Provinces and Navarre, Spain was under direct royal administration.

It was in its possessions outside Spain that Spain paid the price of defeat: the treaties of Maastricht and Utrecht (1713) stripped the country of its European possessions (Belgium, Luxembourg, Milan, Sardinia, and Naples) and gave Britain Gibraltar and the right to send one ship a year to trade with Spanish America.

"American" and "Italian" policies. Two tendencies can be discerned in Spanish policy until 1748: a desire for revenge and recovery in Italy, and an "Atlantic" policy; *i.e.,* the protection of America from British incursions and the revivification of Spanish colonial rule. Both policies demanded a strong army and navy. The "Italian" tendency is connected with Philip V's second wife, Isabella, and her desire to get Italian thrones for her sons. The instruments of her ambitions were two foreigners: the Italian cardinal Julio Alberoni, the exiled son of an Italian gardener, and the Dutch-born adventurer Johan Willem Riperdá. The attempt to recover its possessions in Italy involved Spain in an unsuccessful war with Austria, now the great power in Italy. Spain suffered a serious naval defeat at Capo Passero in 1718. Nevertheless, Isabella's persistence was rewarded when her son, the future Charles III, became the duke of Parma in 1731 and king of Naples in 1733, relinquishing his claims to Parma.

The American–Atlantic tendency was the work of Spanish ministers with a particular interest in the navy and foreign trade—José Patiño, Marqués de la Ensenada, and José de Carvajal y Lancáster. The "Italian" and "Atlantic" tendencies existed side by side in the late years of Philip V's reign. Atlantic rivalries in the form of a dispute over the interpretation of British trading privileges in Spanish America granted at Utrecht brought on the War of Jenkins' Ear (1739–43), during which the British sacked Porto Bello in the Caribbean. The Spanish fleet nevertheless was surprisingly effective and worsted Adm. Edward Vernon at Cartagena. The Italian–Mediterranean policy led directly to Spanish involvement in the War of the Austrian Succession (1740–48). It made possible an alliance of France and Spain against Austria, now the dominant power in Italy, giving Isabella the opportunity to settle her second son, Philip, in an Italian duchy. Spanish troops entered Milan (1745). Ferdinand VI (reigned 1746–59) was concerned with the domestic recovery of Spain rather than the extension of its power in Europe. He hoped to recover Gibraltar at the general peace that ended the War of the Austrian Succession. But the Anglo-French rapprochement made recovery of Gibraltar an impossibility at the Treaty of Aix-la-Chapelle (1748); the treaty merely strengthened Spain's position in Italy when Philip became duke of Parma, Piacenza, and Guastalla.

With Ferdinand VI the Atlantic tendency became dominant. Since Britain was Spain's great enemy in the Americas (as Austria had been in Italy) its "natural" ally was France as Ensenada and Carvajal had seen (hence a series of family pacts with France in 1733 and 1743). It was only in the last years of his reign that Ferdinand's minister, Ricardo Wall, attempted a policy of strict neutrality as the best means of saving Spain from the hostility of Britain, Austria, or France.

This American interest was reflected in increased trade (the old system of convoyed fleets was abandoned for individual sailings), the founding of privileged trading companies (1725), and the founding of new naval arsenals at Ferrod and Cartagena (1726). But the central weakness of Spain as an imperial power remained. The Spanish economy could not supply America with the consumer goods it needed in return for its increased exports. These were supplied either by British merchants through the "legitimate" trade from Cádiz or by smuggling. The Spanish navy, in spite of considerable efforts, could not suppress a contraband trade that, from the colonists' point of view, was a necessity.

The ministers of Ferdinand VI revived the reforming traditions weakened during the latter years of Philip V, whose lethargy deepened into chronic melancholia.

One of the most important imitations from French administrative practice was the use after 1749 of crown officers, or intendants, to rule in the provinces. The intendants strengthened royal control over local government, especially in its financial aspects; together with the captains general (set up by Philip V), they were responsible for a renewal of provincial public works. Carvajal reorganized the postal system; Ensenada, at one time the all-powerful minister of Ferdinand VI, was a great road builder; he opened the Seville tobacco factory, botanical gardens, and observatories; above all, he increased royal receipts by rationalization of the tax structure. The reforms of Ferdinand's successor, Charles III, though more dramatic, were a continuation of those of Ferdinand VI.

THE REIGN OF CHARLES III, 1759–88

Two features distinguished the Caroline reforms from those of the early Bourbons. First, Charles III was a "reformer's king" in that he consistently supported reforming ministers. This was surprising in a monarch who had no great intellectual gifts, was obsessed by hunting, and turned his court into the most boring society in Europe. Second, the civil servants were distinguished from their predecessors by their adherence to a philosophy of government derived from the commonplaces of the European Enlightenment.

Penetration of Enlightenment ideas

Nevertheless, there were sharp differences among the civil servants. The Conde de Aranda and Pablo de Olavide y Jáuregui were influenced by the French Philosophes; Gaspar Melchor de Jovellanos y Ramírez was a disciple of Adam Smith; Pedro Rodríguez Campomanes drew more directly on such Spanish reformers as Macanaz; José Moñino Floridablanca was a professional administrator. All would have taken as their slogan *Felicidad* ("Felicity")—a well-ordered monarchy based directly on the productivity of people who are made happy by the intelligent application of the principles of political economy. There were, however, impediments (*estorbos*), such as traditional privileges (*e.g.,* grazing rights held by a sheep breeders' corporation, the Mesta) or attitudes (*e.g.,* the prejudice of the nobility against the "mechanical trades"); they could not be allowed to stand in the way of greater prosperity and, therefore, of a higher tax income for the state.

Economic revival. The years after 1714 had seen a gradual economic recovery, quite marked in the last half of the 18th century. How much of this revival of the last half of the century was the work of conscious but often confused government policy must remain doubtful. Thus the famous decree (1783) "ennobling" the mechanical trades had little practical result; the attempt to establish government factories and replace religious charity by the productive employment of the poor was a relative failure. Government policy had little to do with the growth of population, which rose during the century from 8,000,000 to 12,000,000. The increased demand for food and the consequent sharp rise in prices encouraged agriculture, benefitting the large landowners of the south and the small farmers near growing towns such as Barcelona. The most remarkable feature of this economic revival was the emergence in Catalonia after 1745 of a modern textile industry, based on cotton. The industry benefitted from a protected market in Spain and the colonies. In the Basque Provinces the archaic iron industry began a slow process of modernization. In Galicia, Catalan immigrants established a flourishing fishing fleet. The brandy trade brought sudden prosperity to the ports of Catalonia and their hinterland.

Nevertheless, the financial reforms of the earlier years and the abolition of internal customs duties removed obstacles to the expansion of the internal market, and the opening of the American trade (see below) acted as a strong stimulant.

One important feature of these developments was that they took place not in the old Castilian core of the monarchy but in the peripheral regions; not in the countryside but in the towns. It was on the periphery that price rises were steepest, outstripping wages in Barcelona and thus creating the beginnings of a social problem. The role of Catalans in the economic revival lies at the origins of the Castilian stereotype of the Catalans as selfish, thrusting businessmen, indifferent to traditional values and exploiting their fellow Spaniards.

Imperial problems. To Charles III the key to prosperity lay in the Indies, for a prosperous Spain demanded an American market. He saw clearly that Spain alone could not preserve an overseas market closed to the outside world against Britain. Ricardo Wall's policy of strict neutrality had allowed Britain to make gains in Canada that must weaken France—the only other anti-British power in America. If Britain would respect Spain's possessions, or if Charles could mediate between France and Britain in such a way as to preserve the balance between them in America, then to commit Spain to the French alliance was a dynastic luxury. Once it was clear to Charles that British terms were non-negotiable, then the Family Compact with France of 1761 was a piece of realpolitik. It was signed by the "anglophile" Ricardo Wall.

The consequence of such an alliance was involvement in the Seven Years' War—too late to save France. In 1762 the British occupied Havana—the greatest single blow sustained by Spain in the war. Spain theoretically allowed no foreigners to share directly in the colonial trade: the effect of this had been to starve the colonies of necessary imports and to encourage smuggling. In 1762, 15 ships entered the port of Havana; during the 11 months of British occupation, 700. This was a dramatic indication to the colonists of the drawbacks of the Spanish monopoly, especially when that monopoly was exercised by what was, in European terms, an underdeveloped nation.

The Seven Years' War

The Treaty of Paris (1763) concluding the Seven Years' War destroyed France as an American power. Spain lost the territory between Florida and the Mississippi, in return gaining Louisiana from France. Spain also had to recognize Portuguese advances in the Río de la Plata (the fort of Sacramento) and the British right to cut mahogany in Central America. The Family Compact was therefore an immediate military failure, and it was only the revolt of the American colonies against Britain that enabled Spain to recover the ground it had lost; the successful alliance with France to aid the colonists resulted in the Treaty of Versailles (1783), which gave back Sacramento, the two Floridas, and Minorca. Not until later did it become apparent that an alliance of revenge with colonial insurgents is a shortsighted policy for an imperial power.

The problems of imperial defense were thus temporarily solved by British weakness after 1765. The positive side of Charles III's imperial policy was an attempt to create an efficiently administered colonial empire that would provide the crown with increased revenues and with a closed market for the exports of an expanding Spanish economy.

Reform of imperial administration

The rationalization of the administration of the Indies had started before Charles III with the creation of a new viceroyalty at Santa Fe de Bogotá (now Bogotá) in 1717. To protect the south against the British and against Portuguese incursions from Brazil, the Viceroyalty of La Plata was created in 1776. The centrepiece of Caroline reform was the introduction of the intendant system in the colonies to tighten up local administration. Most dramatic of all was the abolition of the monopoly of Cádiz, by which all trade to the colonies had to go through that port. Beginning in 1778 non-Castilian ports could trade directly with the colonies.

The new policies brought some immediate and striking results. Energetic viceroys and ministers and ruthless intendants doubled or tripled imperial revenues. The volume of Spanish goods in the American trade increased tenfold in 10 years, so that Britain became seriously concerned at the Spanish revival. But imperial free trade would not satisfy the growing demand from Creole producers for free trade with all nations. Nor did the colonial oligarchs desire efficient government and higher taxation; they preferred bad government that let them control their own affairs. They showed their discontent in a series of revolts in the 1780s; only the fear of the native Indians drove them back to allegiance to the Spanish crown.

Domestic reforms. The domestic reforms of Charles III are more interesting for what they intended than for what they accomplished. They were not directed, as has often been maintained, at fostering a "bourgeois revolution." The middle classes were too weak, in a predominantly agrarian country, for the role of a modernizing elite; nor did Charles III contemplate a frontal attack on the traditional nobility. The purpose of reform was to remove what seemed to civil servants to be "traditional" constrictions on economic growth and administrative anachronisms that prevented the efficient exercise of royal power.

Reorganizations of the machinery of central government made for greater executive efficiency, but complete rationalization was never achieved; the old machinery of the councils persisted, with the Council of Castile as the ultimate decision-making body. An attempt to establish royal control of municipalities (without which, reforms could not get past the oligarchic councils) was likewise only a partial success. Most of the public works that characterized the late 18th century were the achievement of vigorous captains general. The extensive civil functions of these military officials was the first sign of a hybrid military–civilian government that, in another form, was to be developed in the 19th century.

Nor was the economic structure of agrarian Spain modified. All the chief reformers believed that the great and extensively cultivated estates, especially in Andalusia and Extremadura, constituted the greatest bar to agricultural prosperity. The landless underemployed proletariat who worked the large estates began to alarm reformers. "Why in our villages and towns are these men without land and in the countryside land without men? Bring them together and all will be served." Property should be more widely distributed, it was felt; there should be a free market in land. Yet none of the reformers was radical enough to push through a wholesale assault on private property or on the civil entail (the juridical instrument by which the *latifundios,* or large estates, were preserved intact). Acts such as the limitation of future entail, which preserved great estate intact over generations (1789), the limitation of the privileges of the Mesta (1779), and the right to enclose olive groves and irrigated land (1788) showed that the reformers believed primarily in the right of private individuals to do what they liked with their own; the unrestricted pursuit of private profit, they believed, would bring public prosperity. *Corporate* property was the enemy: hence the proposal that common lands owned by municipalities and the crown should be sold for individual cultivation and hence the proposals to end ecclesiastical entail (mortmain).

The attack on the privileges of the greatest corporation in Spain, the church, was less radical than has sometimes been maintained. Charles III himself was a devoted Catholic—he dedicated Spain to the Immaculate Conception. Some of his servants were fashionable anticlericals.

The regalist attack on the church

Most were regalists; that is, they asserted the right of the crown to control over the church in civil matters. In the extreme regalists' view, the state should take care of charity and education; it should subject priests to civil jurisdiction for civil crimes and assert the traditional rights of the crown over church appointments.

The main attack of the regalists fell on the Jesuit order. In 1766 a serious riot in Madrid revealed some of the difficulties confronting the reformers. The abolition of fixed wheat prices during a bad harvest (a step that reflected the reformers' belief in the virtues of a free market) and an attempt to reform outlandish fashions in popular dress brought out the mob in Madrid. The Jesuits were alleged to have fostered the riot and were expelled from both Spain and America in 1767. The importance of this expulsion has been overestimated. Already expelled from France and Portugal, the Jesuits were bitterly criticized by rival orders and by the secular clergy: 42 of the 56 bishops approved of the expulsion. Again the expulsion was a *negative* achievement; more ambitious plans to set up a state university system and a state welfare organization failed.

The question arises of the extent to which the policies of Charles III resulted from the acceptance by his servant of the precepts of the Enlightenment. Certainly Aranda, the "Hammer of the Jesuits," and Olavide, whose flippant anti-clericalism was to be his undoing at the hands of the Inquisition, were what were called *esprits forts* (*i.e.,* French-influenced radicals); their views gave a sharp edge to traditional regalism. Jovellanos was a disciple of Adam Smith. Although his famous *Informe sobre la ley agraria* ("Report on the Agrarian Law") contains not a single original thought, the book is significant in that it attempts to apply dogmatic laissez-faire ideology to Spanish conditions. Here was one of the foundations of Spanish liberalism.

One of the aims of the Enlightenment was to produce a bourgeois society in which no traditional prejudices or traditional institutions should limit the pursuit of private profit—the foundation of national prosperity. But in Spain the social base was too narrow. In spite of economic changes over the century, the bourgeoisie was limited to the coastal towns, Barcelona and Cádiz in particular, with branches in Saragossa and the Basque country. Patriotic societies, organized with government encouragement from 1765 onward, were meant to provide the provincial basis for a progressive society and to familiarize Spaniards with European advances in technology and agriculture. They did not get much beyond the status of local reading rooms and debating societies.

Traditional Catholic society was still strong, if under attack from a minority of intellectuals and civil servants. As the reaction of the countryside after 1808 was to show, the church was still a great social power. The Duke of Wellington observed that "the real power in Spain is in the clergy. They kept the people right against France." To most of the clergy the new ideas of the Enlightenment were "foreign" and dangerous, and there could be no such thing as moderate progress encouraged by the king himself—the notion of a "revolution from above" that was to haunt subsequent Spanish history. Voltaire, Locke, and Rousseau were quite simply dangerous heretics, though the Inquisition proved powerless to prevent the clandestine circulation of their works. It was the clerical attacks on heretics as much as the subversive works themselves that familiarized a narrow stratum of society with new ideas. When the French Revolution exposed the dangers of progressive thought, the traditionalist cause was immensely strengthened and the Inquisition appeared to the crown itself to be a useful instrument to control the spread of dangerous ideas.

CHARLES IV AND THE FRENCH REVOLUTION

In 1788 Charles III, who had been the "nerve" of reform in the sense that he loyally supported able ministers, was succeeded by his son, Charles IV, a weak, amiable man dominated by a lascivious wife, María Luisa. Spain was ruled after 1792 by her favourite, Manuel de Godoy, a handsome, plump officer from the lower nobility.

The influence of Godoy

It was not merely that Godoy was incompetent and self-seeking; the French Revolutionary and Napoleonic Wars put unbearable pressures on a weak power. Reform was now dangerous. Neutrality was impossible; alliance with either France or the anti-Revolutionary coalitions engineered by Britain proved equally disastrous.

Floridablanca, the prime minister, disliked both the internal effects of the Revolution (the spread of radical as opposed to government guided reform) and its external consequences (the weakening of the anti-British alliance). His hostility to France was the cause of his dismissal. Aranda, a friend of France, was discredited by the excesses of the Revolution (1792). Godoy became prime minister at age 25 because the old ministers of Charles III had failed to devise a foreign policy. In domestic affairs, Godoy supported a mild version of the enlightened reformism of his predecessors; but, like them, he failed to find a satisfactory place for Spain in the Europe of the French Revolutionary and Napoleonic Wars (1800–15).

Spain had no alternative but to declare war on France after the execution of Louis XVI (1793). The war was popular but disastrous; in 1794 the French armies invaded Spain, taking Bilbao, San Sebastián, and Figueras. Godoy feared the spread of revolutionary propaganda in the wake of the French armies in Catalonia and the north (there was a republican conspiracy in 1795). Above all, he was convinced that Britain was the true enemy of Spain. Thus the Treaty of San Ildefonso (1796) represented a deliberate choice: the French alliance, irrespective of the nature of the French regime, as the only policy for a weak imperial power.

The consequences of this choice were disastrous. War with Britain became inevitable and cut off Spain from America, opening its colonial markets to Britain and the United States; Godoy invaded Portugal with success in the War of Oranges (1801) but the defeat of the Franco-Spanish fleet by the British at Trafalgar in 1805 and the "selfishness" of Napoleon caused him to seek a rapprochement with the allies. Had Napoleon lost the Battle of Jena (1806) against the Prussians, Godoy would have joined the Fourth Coalition against him.

Godoy's position was now extremely weak. He was unpopular at home. The court aristocracy disliked him as an upstart; severe inflation produced great hardship among the poorer classes; a campaign of gossip was mounted against him by those intellectuals whom he did not patronize. He now hoped, with French help, to dismember Portugal and to secure personal salvation in a principality. This curious hope was the basis of the Treaty of Fontainebleau (1807) by which Napoleon and the Spanish government agreed upon the conquest and partition of Portugal. When French troops on the way to Portugal occupied the fortresses of northern and central Spain and when Napoleon demanded territorial gains in Spain itself, Godoy's policy was bankrupt. It was obvious that Napoleon had lost all faith in Godoy and Spain as an ally: the "dirty intrigues" of the heir to the throne, Ferdinand, prince of Asturias, against his father and Godoy led Napoleon to think of drastic intervention in Spanish affairs.

Appointment of Joseph Bonaparte

The opportunity for direct intervention by Napoleon was given by the Revolt of Aranjuez (March 17, 1808), in which the partisans of Ferdinand (an alliance of discontented aristocrats and others opposed to Godoy) impelled the abdication of Charles IV and the dismissal of the favourite. Napoleon summoned both the old king and Ferdinand VII to Bayonne, where both were impelled to abdicate. The Spanish throne was offered to Napoleon's brother Joseph.

THE FRENCH INVASION AND THE WAR OF INDEPENDENCE, 1804–14

Joseph could count on the support of cautious, legalistic administrators and soldiers, of those who believed resistance to French power impossible, and of those who considered that Napoleon might "regenerate" Spain by modern reforms. These groups became convinced *afrancesados,* as members of the pro-French party were called. Relying on their support, Napoleon entirely underestimated the possibility of popular resistance to the occupation of Spain by French armies. Although the rising of May 2 in Madrid was suppressed, local risings against the French were successful wherever French military power was weak.

The War of Independence. After the deposition of King Ferdinand, "patriot" Spain outside the control of the French armies split into a number of autonomous provinces. Resistance centred in provincial committees (juntas) that organized armies. A Central Junta at Aranjuez sought to control this nascent federalism and the local levies, and Spanish regular troops defeated a French army of inferior, ill-supplied troops under Dupont at Bailén in July 1808. The French retired from Madrid. Napoleon himself invaded Spain and by 1809 was in control of most of the peninsula. The Spanish regular army, led by incompetent generals, suffered defeat after defeat.

The War of Independence, or, as the English call it, the Peninsular War, became for Napoleon the "Spanish ulcer," and he attributed his defeat in Europe to its requirements for men and money. He was defeated not by the inefficient Spanish regular army but by British troops under Wellington advancing from Portugal with the aid of Spanish guerrillas. The guerrillas represented popular resistance as against the supposed pro-French proclivities of the "possessing classes." As the main battles—Talavera (July 1809) and Vitoria (June 1813)—were fought by Wellington, the guerrillas pinned down French garrisons, intercepted dispatches, and isolated convoys.

The Constitution of Cádiz. The significance of the war years lies in the re-creation of a patriotic spirit to cover the bare bones of Bourbon administrative centralism and in the explicit formulation of a liberal ideology that was to be a dynamic factor in Spanish history.

The Central Junta and its successor, the Regency, were compelled to summon a Cortes (Parliament) in order to legitimize the situation created by the absence of Ferdinand VII, who was in France. Conservatives conceived of its task as the mere supply of the sinews of war on behalf of an absent king. The Cortes, when it met at Cádiz in 1810, was dominated by liberals who wished to go beyond the mere support of the war effort and establish a constitution that would make impossible the revival of rule by a favourite like Godoy. The Constitution of 1812 was to become the "sacred codex" of Latin liberalism.

The Constitution of Cádiz gave Spain a strictly limited monarchy (the king must work through his responsible ministers), a single-chamber Parliament with no special representation for the church or the nobility, and a modern centralized administrative system based on provinces and municipalities. All this had little basis in the medieval precedents quoted in the debates and was inspired by the constitutions of revolutionary France. Bourgeois individualism inspired legislation against entail, favouring instead the sale of common lands and the individual's right to dispose of his property as he might wish. The abolition of the Inquisition represented a mixture of historic regalism and modern anti-clericalism. This measure produced a conservative reaction, as did all liberal anticlericalism through to the Second Republic in the 1930s. This reaction gave a popular underpinning to Ferdinand VII's destruction of liberalism and all its works in 1814 (see below).

Abolition of the Inquisition

In addition to initiating a liberal tradition, the War of Independence bequeathed two problems: first, generals chafed at control by civilian juntas and on occasion overthrew them, thus initiating the phenomenon of the pronunciamento, or military revolution; second, the *afrancesados,* often men of liberal inclinations but tarred with the accusation of collaborationism with the French, were left as an indigestible element within liberalism itself.

FERDINAND VII, 1814–33

With the help of an army corps and of conservative sentiment that had been outraged by the liberalism of 1812, Ferdinand returned from exile in France to rule Spain as an absolute monarch. In 1820 he was forced by military sedition to return to constitutionalism (1820–23). For the last "ominous" decade of his reign he returned to a relatively enlightened form of ministerial despotism. The years 1814–20 were dominated by the attempt to reestablish Spanish rule in America and by the problem of maintaining an inflated wartime army with a permanent economic deficit.

The failure of liberalism. The solution of the Cádiz liberals to the imperial problem had been to make the colonies constitutionally part of metropolitan Spain by giving them representation in the Cortes. This did not stop the revolt of the colonies, where the Creoles wanted local self-government and free trade rather than liberal centralization. In 1814 it was not clear that the rebels under Simón Bolívar in the north and San Martín in the south would succeed; but all of Ferdinand's efforts to assemble a large army and a fleet to send to America failed. In 1820 the army that was to subdue the colonies revolted against the king in a pronunciamento organized by Major Riego y Núñez and supported by the local liberals organized in Masonic lodges.

The Revolution of 1820

The Revolution of 1820 brought into power the "jail birds"—liberals of the 1812 vintage who had been persecuted by Ferdinand VII. The Constitution of 1812 was reestablished together with other liberal legislation, including the sale of monastic property.

The liberal system failed once more because it was a minority creed sustained by a section of the army—the military radicals such as Riego—against a mounting conservative reaction that had been fed once more by an attack on the church, especially the monasteries. The liberals themselves split. The more conservative wing (led by Martínez de la Rosa, a dramatist) wished for a more moderate constitution, based on the French Charter of 1814, which would give better representation to the upper classes and would not be totally unacceptable to the King, as was the "prison" of the Constitution of 1812. The King gave no support whatsoever to this movement and, in a cowardly fashion, disowned a rising of the guards' regiments that backed it. Thus the extreme radicals (*exaltados*) gained control by means of demonstrations in the streets, organized by clubs run on the lines of the Jacobins of the French Revolution.

The conservative reaction developed in the north around the regency set up at Seo de Urgel. Without French help, the movement would not have been successful, but when Louis XVIII sent French troops (the "Hundred Thousand Sons of St. Louis"), the liberal armies disintegrated and the liberal system fell.

Once more revolution at home favoured revolution in the colonies. Mexican conservatives, who had no desire to be ruled by Spanish anti-clericals, successfully established an independent Mexico under Agustín de Iturbide (1822). Spanish military power in South America finally foundered on the decisive Battle of Ayacucho (1824). Of Spain's far-flung empire, only the islands of Cuba, Puerto Rico, and the Philippines remained.

The "ominous decade," 1823–33. The "ominous decade," as it was called by the persecuted liberals, began with a severe purge of liberals; but in its later stages the regime became increasingly unacceptable to extreme conservatives, who looked to the King's reactionary brother, Don Carlos. Ferdinand had to rely either on inefficient traditionalists who could raise no money on the European money markets or on the more liberal ministers who were able financiers. Ministers such as Luis López Ballesteros, a friend of the *afrancesados,* set the tone with a serious attempt at a government-fostered economic revival.

The Carlists

This return to 18th-century "ministerial despotism" did not satisfy the liberal exiles, who mounted ineffective invasions in 1824 and 1830. More important, the conservatives of Don Carlos' court faction accepted Ferdinand VII's rule only on condition that Don Carlos would inherit the crown. In 1829, Ferdinand married his niece María Cristina of Naples, who realized that her influence depended on the elimination of that of Don Carlos. In March 1830, her faction at court persuaded the King to exclude Don Carlos from the succession even if María Cristina produced a female heir. This attack on the rights of Don Carlos was the origin of the Carlist party and of the Carlist Wars, which were for over a half century to be a disrupting influence in Spain. After the defeat of an attempt to force María Cristina to recognize Don Carlos' rights during Ferdinand's illness (September 1832), María Cristina's faction was dominant at court. She succeeded in securing all important military commands in the hands of supporters of the claims of her daughter, Isabella. When, on September 29, 1833, Ferdinand died, Isabella was proclaimed queen, with María Cristina as regent. The First Carlist War (1833–39) broke out almost immediately.

ISABELLA II, 1833–68

The Carlist Wars. The dynastic war between Isabelline liberalism and Carlism was a savage civil war between urban liberalism and rural traditionalism, between the poorly paid and equipped regular army of the liberal governments, supporting Isabella, and the semi-guerrilla forces of the Carlists. The Carlist strength lay in the north, especially in the Basque Provinces and Navarre, where there was strong support for the *fueros* against liberal centralism and for the traditional Catholic order represented by the religious bigotry of Don Carlos and his circle. But the Carlists could not break out of their bases in the north to capture an important city. The great Carlist leader Tomás Zumalacárregui y de Imaz was killed in an attempt to capture Bilbao, and Don Carlos' expedition to Madrid failed (1837). In 1839 the Carlist commander staged a mutiny against the clerical court of Don Carlos and came to terms with Baldomero Espartero, the most successful of Isabella's generals.

María Cristina allied with liberalism out of military necessity, not from conviction. She would have preferred to grant administrative reforms rather than consent that her daughter should become a constitutional monarch. But the liberals alone could save her daughter's throne from the Carlists, and the minimum demand of all liberals was a constitution. As regent from 1833 to 1840, she therefore consistently supported conservative liberals against the radicals. The Royal Statute (1834) represented this alliance between respectable upper-middle-class liberals and the crown.

This conservative constitution, with its property franchise and the great powers it gave the crown in the choice of ministers, could not stop the drift toward the left implicit in liberalism itself. The radicals, who were the heirs of the *exaltados* of 1820–23, were installed in power first by a series of provincial town risings in 1835 and later, after a short-lived conservative reaction, by an army mutiny that forced María Cristina to accept the Constitution of 1812. The radical politicians, however, accepted a more moderate compromise constitution—that of 1837. Of more enduring importance was the sale of church lands to finance the war. The great disentailment carried out by Prime Minister Juan Alvarez Mendizábal and his successors altered profoundly the social structure of Spain by putting on the market large quantities of land, most of which was bought by large landowners or prosperous peasants.

Moderates, progressives, and the generals. The Carlist Wars left civilian politicians discredited, and generals became the arbiters of politics not, as in 1814–20, as intruders but as part of the political machinery. They became the "swords" of the two main political groups. The *moderados,* who were upper-middle-class oligarchic liberals fearful of democratic violence and upholders of the prerogatives of the crown, represented the conservative stream in liberalism. Their rivals, the *progresistas,* were the heirs of the *exaltados* and represented a lower stratum of the middle class; the *progresistas* were prepared to use the discontent of the urban masses in order to bring pressure on the crown to give them office. Their instrument was the Urban Militia. Espartero used his military faction and his supporters among the younger *progresista* politicians and their artisan followers in the great cities to oust María Cristina and establish himself as regent (1841–43). Espartero proved a disappointment to the radical *progresistas,* who now allied with his conservative opponents under his military and political rival, Ramón María Narváez. In 1843 Espartero was thrown out by a pronunciamento.

The pronunciamento of Narváez

Narváez jettisoned his *progresista* allies through a court intrigue, and between 1844 and 1854 he and his fellow generals dominated domestic politics as representatives of the *moderados.* Their administrative, educational, and financial measures and the formation of the Civil Guard were lasting achievements; but the generals could not stabilize their rule on the basis of their constitution of 1845, a conservative revision of 1837. The period was disturbed by a series of *progresista* military risings.

To the left of the *progresistas,* who were prepared to accept the monarchy if it gave them office, a Democratic Party developed; it was prepared to dethrone Isabella II, who was declared of age to rule in 1843. Never strong in numbers outside the towns, the Democrats radicalized politics. Orthodox *progresista* politicians were embarrassed by their extremist attitudes but could not neglect their potential role as urban revolutionaries.

It was not the Democrats but a group of discontented generals led by Leopoldo O'Donnell who successfully revolted in 1854. They were prepared to sacrifice the dynasty because the Queen and her mother favoured a rigid court conservatism that effectively excluded them from influence.

The rebellious military oligarchs were forced to call in civilian and radical support. This turned their pronunciamento into a mild revolution. Isabella survived only through Espartero's political timidity. Unprepared to accept the backing of the Democrats as the "George Washington of Spain," he accepted an alliance with O'Donnell, who was determined to arrest the drift to radicalism. In 1856 he broke with Espartero, defeated a demonstration in his favour, and dissolved the National Militia, the instrument of the left-wing Progressives. The radical thrust was thus defeated.

Economic expansion. The "revolutionary" period of 1854–56 saw no important constitutional change; but the further extension of disentailment and the new law for limited companies provided the legal structure for a rapid expansion of the economy. To promote this expansion, there were new injections of foreign credit—particularly French—and new banks. This capital made it possible to begin the railroad network that was to provide the transport infrastructure for a national market. The textile industry of Catalonia flourished, as a modern wool manufacture grew up; in the Basque Country, the second pole of an industrial economy developed slowly around iron. Agriculture, still a dominant sector of the economy, expanded as the church and common lands provided new fields for the easiest of cash crops—wheat; the growth of such towns as Barcelona created a market for vegetables, wines, and fruit.

Expansion resulted in the classic expression of 19th-century liberalism—the haute bourgeoisie of finance and industry. Members of this new class ranged from solid Catalan manufacturers demanding protective tariffs to safeguard their gains, to daring speculators such as the railway financier Marqués de Salamanca, who took an active part in political life and the urbanization of Madrid. It also included successful generals ready to forget their humble origins. Together with the large landowners, these groups formed the oligarchy of liberalism.

O'Donnell's Liberal Union

The government that presided over this prosperity was O'Donnell's Liberal Union, which was an attempt to fuse all dynastic parties in a broad-based coalition. It provided a long period of stable government (1856–63), and had the Progressive politicians been less afraid of losing their left wing to the Democrats and had the Queen been willing to grant Progressives power, the dynasty might have survived. Instead, she excluded the Progressives and forced them, first to withdraw formally from political life, then to contemplate revolution. Their "sword," General Prim y Prats (a chemist's son and a striking example of the social mobility of the liberal army), was a resolute conspirator and the ablest of the political generals of the 19th century. When Isabella's court ministers alienated O'Donnell's followers, a powerful coalition was formed, and Prim dropped his alliance with the Democrats. A slump caused by bad harvests, a series of mediocre ultra-conservative governments, and a growth in democratic agitation among university intellectuals (whose main concern was the hold of the church over education) gave wide support to the military rising against Isabella. Her armies would not defend her, and she was forced to leave for France in September 1868.

THE REVOLUTION OF 1868 AND THE REPUBLIC OF 1873

The revolution that led to the dethronement of Isabella was the work of army oligarchs led by Francisco Serrano y Domínguez and Progressive conspirators behind Prim. The Democrats became active in setting up juntas after the revolution: for the most part they rapidly became Federal Republicans under the influence of the theories of the French anarchist Pierre-Joseph Proudhon as presented by their leader, Pí y Margall. The Democratic intellectuals' main contribution was to add a radical democratic content to the demands of the military oligarchy.

The generals were determined to keep the leadership of the revolution in their own hands by channelling it into a constitutional monarchy. Although they had to concede universal suffrage in the Constitution of 1869, they ruthlessly suppressed republican risings in the summer of that year. Their problem was to find a constitutional monarch.

Amadeus, duke of Aosta

Prim's attempt to persuade a Hohenzollern to accept the throne was opposed by France and set off the Franco-German War in 1870. In November 1870, Amadeus, duke of Aosta, was elected king, and Prim, the kingmaker, was assassinated the day Amadeus entered Madrid.

Amadeus attempted to rule as a constitutional monarch. Opposed both by Republicans and by Carlists, he could form no stable government from the "September coalition" of former conservative Liberal Unionists, the ex-Progressives, and the moderate Democrats—now called Radicals. Once Amadeus called the Radicals to power, the conservatives deserted the dynasty. Amadeus abdicated after an attack by the Radicals on the army in February 1873. The Cortes proclaimed Spain a republic.

The Republic of 1873 came into existence to fill the political vacuum created by Amadeus' abdication. The Republican Party was neither strong nor united. When the Republican leaders, on legal scruples, refused to declare for a *federal* republic, the provincial Federal extremists revolted.

This Cantonalist revolt was serious in Cartagena, Alcoy, and Málaga. The Republican leaders had allowed attacks on the army that had reduced it to impotence. To conservatives and men of order, the country seemed on the verge of total dissolution; the Carlists were immensely strengthened by the "excesses" of Cantonalists. Too late, Emilio Castelar y Ripoll, the last president of the republic, tried to recapture the loyalty of the army. In January 1874, Gen. Manuel Pavia y Rodríguez de Alburquerque drove the Republican deputies from the Cortes building in the hope of creating a government of order. Pavia turned power over to Gen. Francisco Serrano to form a coalition government.

General Serrano took over as president of a unitary republic. His main task was victory over the Carlists, now a strong force in northern Spain. In this he failed, and on December 29, 1874, a young brigadier, Arsenio Martínez Campos, "declared" for Alfonso XII, the son of Isabella.

There was no resistance. The extreme threat of anarchy in 1873 had resulted in a strong conservative reaction, strengthened by the religious policies pursued since 1868. The Constitution of 1869 for the first time had allowed complete freedom of religion. In spite of a total failure to create political stability, the Revolution of 1868 bequeathed to Spain the model of a modern secular state based on universal suffrage. On the extreme left these years saw the effective penetration of anarchism, especially in rural Andalusia and in industrial Catalonia, where the lower classes deserted a long tradition of political action via the Democratic and Republican parties and moderate unionism. Though anarchists were persecuted after 1873, the movement was kept alive by small groups of enthusiasts.

The Cuban revolt

The worst problem of the years 1868–75 was posed by the independence movement in Cuba, which, along with Puerto Rico, was the last possession of Spain in America. Cubans had long resented the failure to reform rule by captains general, to grant some autonomy, and to ease the economic sacrifices that were imposed by the Spanish tariff system. The revolt that began in October 1868 made great demands on Spain in men (100,000 by 1870) and money. The Ten Years' War (1868–78) made difficulties for all governments in power in Spain after 1868 and forced abandonment of the most popular of the pledges made by the rebels in 1868: the abolition of the arbitrary and socially selective recruitment system. Like the Carlist wars, the Cuban War tended to favour the monarchical reaction.

THE RESTORED MONARCHY, 1875–1923

Once the Carlists had been defeated and the Cubans had accepted the peace settlement of El Zanjón (1878), the restored monarchy provided the most stable government Spain had known since 1833. This stability was sustained by respectable economic growth.

Stability, 1875–98. The architect of the restoration itself and of the Constitution of 1876 was Cánovas del Castillo. A superb politician, Cánovas had hoped for a civilian restoration; he accepted Martínez Campos' coup but used the young Alfonso XII to keep the military out of politics.

The Canovite system

The Canovite system was artificial in that it required the contrived rotation in office (*turno pacífico*) of a Liberal and a Conservative party; this in turn demanded governmental control of elections, which were run by caciques, or local political bosses, who controlled votes in their districts. Only in this way could the government selected by the king and the politicians in Madrid obtain a parliamentary majority; extensive corruption and the use of administrative pressures on electors were considered the only ways to make the parliamentary system work in an underdeveloped society. This system survived the death of Alfonso XII (1885) and only began to falter in the 1890s, toward the end of his wife's regency. The Carlist threat weakened with defeat, and the majority of Republicans in Spain were domesticated and reconciled to the use of "legal" means.

"Without being a rich country," wrote an economist in the early 1880s, "Spain has become comfortably off." This prosperity, which was untroubled by the claims of organized labour, was the result of the demand for iron ore after the invention of the Bessemer process (England and France invested heavily in mineral production), of the demand for Spanish wine after the devastations by phylloxera in France, and of the resumption of railway construction in Spain. The third largest wool industry in Europe grew up side by side with the older cotton mills in Catalonia. The boom did not break until the late 1880s, when an agricultural depression set in. A wave of economic pessimism preceded the political and intellectual reaction of 1898.

The loss of Cuba, Puerto Rico, and the Philippines in 1898 exposed the Spanish political system to severe criticism. No fiscal and political reform sufficient to satisfy Cuban demands could be effected within the framework of the monarchy, partly because of the pressure of the Spanish loyalist party in Cuba. A revolt in 1895 set off another costly war against Cuban guerrillas. The intervention of the United States could not be staved off by a last-minute grant of autonomy. Their humiliating and total naval defeat in 1898 became known to Spaniards as "the Disaster." Spain now lost the Philippines and the last of its possessions in the Americas at the very time when the great European powers were building their overseas empires.

War with the United States

Opposition movements, 1898–1923. Criticism of the restoration monarchy came from the Catalan and Basque regionalists, from a revived Republican Party, from the proletarian parties, from the army, from the more forward-looking of the Spanish politicians, and from the intellectuals.

Basque regionalism, though more akin in its ideas to extreme nationalist movements, was less a challenge than Catalan regionalism, which dominated Spanish politics until 1923. With its own Catalan language and a revived cultural tradition, it moved from a demand for protection of Catalan industry against "Castilian" free trade to a demand for political autonomy. The *Lliga Regionalista* (founded 1901), dominated by the Catalan industrialist Francesc Cambó i Batlle and the theoretician of Catalan nationalism, Prat de la Riba, demanded the end of the *turno* and a revival of regionalism within a genuine party system. Cambó wished to solve the Catalan question "within Spain"—*i.e.,* by legal means and in cooperation with monarchical politicians. The revival of Catalanism, however, set off a "Castilian" reaction in which moderate Catalans were accused of selfishness or of hiding separatist aims under "respectable" regionalism. In the 1907 election the united Catalan front, Solidaridad Catalana, defeated the parties of the system but then divided into a right (which accepted a solution within the monarchy) and a left (which was to drift to Republicanism). Cambó's cooperation with Madrid brought Catalonia no tangible concessions.

Republicanism, which had degenerated into local politicking and lived on its memories of 1873, was revived by the remarkable oratorical and organizational talents of Alejandro Lerroux, whose Radical Republican Party offered a program that appealed to the alienated working-class voter of Barcelona.

He was competing with a slow revival of anarchism, which veered between terrorism, educational propaganda, and union activity; the anarcho-syndicalist union, the Confederación Nacional del Trabajo (CNT), was founded in 1910. The Socialist movement with its union (the Unión General de Trabajadores, or UGT, founded 1888) was relatively weak except in the mining districts of the north and in Madrid, where it was dominated by its French-influenced founder, Pablo Iglesias. In 1909 the Socialists abandoned their boycott of "bourgeois" politics and allied themselves with the Republicans. This alliance was to give the party a political leverage in excess of its voting strength.

The Generation of '98

The intellectuals' protest embraced the writers of widely differing ideas collectively known as the Generation of '98. Joaquín Costa, a voluminous writer, was an especially harsh critic of *caciquismo;* he wanted a revived, effectively democratic, modernized Spain. His attempt to create a coalition of the "productive classes" against the political drones in the Unión Nacional failed. Miguel de Unamuno saw regeneration in terms of a return to "pure" Spanish values. All of the Generation of '98 distrusted politics as managed by professional politicians who, they said, were out of touch with the "real" Spain.

Among the politicians themselves, the conservative leaders Francisco Silvela and Antonio Maura and the democratic liberal José Canalejas sought to regenerate the system by widening the degree of political participation through "sincere" elections. They were opposed by the professional party members. Maura only succeeded in confusing the party structure by splitting the Conservative Party. The danger of "sincere" elections to the political establishment was revealed by the Republican victories in 1903.

Revolt in Morocco

The call up of troops for Morocco, where Spanish troops were engaged in operations protecting the Spanish coastal possessions, set off the Tragic Week of 1909 in Barcelona. Public order collapsed, and anarchists and Radical Republicans burned churches and convents. Maura was driven from office because Alfonso XIII (who ruled in his own right from 1902) accepted the Liberals' estimate of the harm Maura's firm repression would inflict on the monarchy. Rather than resist a Liberal Party that had allied with the Republican parties, the King held that the Liberals were a useful "lightning conductor," protecting the monarchy from the threat on the left. Ever since Maura's fall, the King's diagnosis had been challenged by conservatives.

World War I produced increased strains. Real wages fell, making the unions restive, and in 1917, junior officers formed juntas and struck for better conditions. The ensuing crisis was exploited by Catalan politicians, increasingly pressing for autonomy. The revolutionary coalition split up, and a general strike frightened Cambó and the Catalans, who threatened to call a national convention that would unite all critics of the monarchy. The formation of a national government under Maura ended the last serious attempt to regenerate the political system and to make it respond to reformist and Catalan demands. No subsequent government was strong enough to face the anarchist agitation in Catalonia and the Moroccan War.

Spain had been granted a protectorate in Morocco in 1912. In the effort to pacify it, economizing politicians were ready for compromise with the tribes, but the generals saw conquest as the only solution. A bid by Gen. Fernández Silvestre, reputedly backed by Alfonso XIII, for a crowning victory ended in the terrible massacre of Spanish troops at Annual in 1921. Opposition politicians were determined to expose the King's action and criticize the army.

Anarchist influences

World War I had given the anarcho-syndicalist movement great power. At the same time there grew a terrorist fringe, which the leaders of the CNT could not control. These leaders (Salvador Sequí and Angel Pestaña), though they shared the anarchist contempt for political action, wished to build unions powerful enough to challenge the employers by direct action. They mistrusted the libertarian tradition of spontaneous revolution as a means of toppling the bourgeois state. The great Barcelona strike of 1919 was the most impressive in Spanish history. When the employers' violent reaction discredited the moderates in the Confederación Nacional del Trabajo, it was followed by a wave of assassinations by gangsters employed by both the anarchists and the employers.

Thus, when Gen. Primo de Rivera staged his pronunciamento in September 1923, he could count on the support of the conservative classes fearful for social order. The Lliga, for instance, became more concerned about suppressing strikes than about Catalan autonomy, for which it had campaigned from 1915 to 1918. He could also count on the tacit alliance of Alfonso XIII, who was tired of politicians who could not provide him with effective governments.

PRIMO DE RIVERA (1923–30) AND THE SECOND REPUBLIC (1931–36)

Primo de Rivera. Primo de Rivera was a political improviser who believed his mission was to save Spain from the old politicians and to hand over government (after an interval of personal rule) to "clean" patriots. He failed to complete the process because his rule became increasingly unpopular, especially among the intellectuals and Catalans. The September 1923 coup by which he had gained power had been widely welcomed in Catalonia, where, as captain general, Primo had listened sympathetically to Catalan demands. Soon afterward, however, Primo became a Spanish patriot and permitted an "anti-Catalan crusade." His followers' attempts to build up a political party (the Patriotic Union) to run a regenerated Spain and to provide it with an ideology collapsed.

At first he ruled via the army. In spite of initial quarrels with the African commanders, whom he forced to retreat in Morocco, the Military Directory was responsible for final victory in the protectorate. The Spanish, collaborating for the first time with the French, landed at Alhucemas (al-Hoceima) in September 1925 and defeated the most successful tribal leader, Abd el-Krim. By 1927 the whole of the protectorate was successfully occupied.

The Civil Directory (1925–30) was responsible for a thorough overhaul of local government and for an ambitious public works program to increase irrigation, hydraulic power, and road building. Primo's economic nationalism entailed strict protectionist policies and an attack on foreign oil monopolies. The complicated bureaucratic control of industry did not endear him to capitalists after 1926; on the other hand he collaborated successfully with the UGT while suppressing the CNT. The Civil Directory failed in its main task: to win sufficient political support in the National Assembly summoned for 1928 to facilitate a return to quasi-constitutional government.

Throughout his early years Primo was favoured by an economic expansion based on favourable terms of trade for Spanish exports. By 1929 the peseta began to fall in value in spite of desperate measures to save it. Economic recession alone would not have ruined the dictator, but he lost the support of both the army and the King. The army turned against him as a result of his attempts to abolish the privileges of the artillery and engineer corps. The King believed that student protests, the growing discontent in Catalonia, and the increasing conspiracies of the "old" politicians imperilled the dynasty. On January 28, 1930, he forced Primo's resignation.

Alfonso acted too late. His earlier support of the dictatorship ruined him in the eyes of the politicians and public. The weak governments of Gen. Dámaso Berenguer and Adm. Juan Bautista Aznar could barely keep order. At San Sebastián (August 17, 1930) an alliance of former liberal monarchists, Catalan politicians, and Republicans agreed to overthrow the monarchy. The failure of a Republican military rising at Jaca (December 12, 1930) saved them from establishing a republic by force. The municipal elections of April 12, 1931, proved that the great cities were overwhelmingly Republican. Rather than face civil war and street demonstrations in Madrid, Alfonso XIII left Spain.

Abdication of Alfonso XIII

The Second Republic. The history of the Second Republic falls into four distinct phases: (1) the Provisional Government, which lasted until the religious issue forced its resignation in October 1931; (2) the governments of the Left Republicans and Socialists, which ruled from October 1931 and were defeated in the elections of November 1933; (3) the conservative government of the Radical Republicans and the Catholic right from November 1933 to February 1936, punctuated by the revolution of October 1934, and that ended with the electoral victory of the Popular Front in February 1936; and (4) the government of the Popular Front and "the descent into violence" that culminated in the military rising of July 1936.

The Provisional Government was a coalition government, presided over by Alcalá Zamora, whose Catholicism reassured moderate opinion. The coalition included all the groups represented at San Sebastian: Lerroux's Radicals, the Catalan left, the Socialists, and the Left Republicans dominated by Manuel Azaña y Diaz.

The elections to the Constituent Cortes strengthened the Socialists and Left Republicans and thus upset the parliamentary balance between moderate Catholic Republicans and the left. It was the left that imprinted its views on the constitution, especially its religious clauses. The historically conditioned anti-clericalism had led the government to tolerate an outburst of church burning (May 1931). The Socialists and Left Republicans inserted in the constitution an attack on religious education and the regular orders, which forced the resignation of Alcalá Zamora and Miguel Maura, his minister of the interior.

This direct and, it would seem, ill-advised clash with Catholic sentiment was to provide a base for the construction of a party of the right devoted to the reversal of the church settlement. This party, the creation of the Catholic politician José María Gil Robles, became Acción Popular; it was to become the main component of the right-wing electoral grouping, the Confederación Española de Derechas Autónomas (CEDA). To the left its "accidentalism" (the doctrine that forms of government were irrelevant provided the church could fulfill its mission) was suspect.

The Acción Popular

From October 1931 the government, with Azaña as premier, was in the hands of Left Republicans and Socialists, with the Catholic right, the Basque Catholics, the Navarrese Carlists, and Lerroux's Radicals in opposition. Azaña aimed to create a modern democracy; labour legislation would be the work of the Socialists, with the UGT leader, Largo Caballero, as minister of labour.

In April 1931 there was a danger that Catalonia might declare its independence within a federal state. Azaña's greatest achievement was the settlement of the Catalan question. He overcame conservative Republican opposition to limited home rule under the Generalidad, which was controlled by the Catalan left (Esquerra) under Luis Companys. Largo Caballero's legislation provided labour with a strong negotiating position but could not, in itself, mitigate the mounting unemployment, which was particularly serious in the *latifundios* of the southwest. Since new machinery for the settlement of labour disputes was dominated by the UGT, it was opposed by the CNT, now influenced by the extreme revolutionary apoliticism of an anarchist group, the Federación Anarquista Ibérica (FAI). Violent strikes were frequent.

Sedition from the right came to a head in General Sanjurjo's pronunciamento in Seville (August 10, 1932). Politically more dangerous than Sanjurjo's abortive coup, however, were the steady growth of Gil Robles' Acción Popular and the Socialists' desertion of the Azaña coalition, as Largo Caballero wearied of cooperation with "bourgeois" parties. In the elections of November 1933, therefore, the left was divided and the right relatively united in the electoral union of the CEDA. Given an electoral law that favoured electoral coalitions, the CEDA and Lerroux's Radicals, now a respectable middle class party, triumphed. The newly elected Cortes was dominated by Lerroux's Radicals and the CEDA. Lerroux could not govern without the support of Gil Robles. With power within sight, Gil Robles accentuated his legalism, to the distaste of the militant monarchists among his supporters. Nevertheless, his party was regarded by the Left Republicans and Socialists as a Catholic brand of the Fascist trends now winning out in western Europe.

Conservative reaction

When CEDA entered Lerroux's government the Socialists staged a revolution. Revolutionary councils were set up in the mining districts of Asturias, where there was considerable destruction of property. In Barcelona the revolution was the work of Catalan nationalists, who believed autonomy was imperilled by the actions of the Madrid government in overruling an agrarian law passed by the Generalidad. Unsupported by the CNT, it was quickly suppressed.

The October Revolution of 1934 is the dividing point in the Second Republic. The Socialists, fearing the fate of their Austrian and German brothers, had revolted against a legal government and thereby established in the minds of the right the fear of "Red" rebellion. In the subsequent repression by the army lay the emotional origins of the Popular Front against "Fascism"—a re-creation of the Azaña coalition of Left Republicans and Socialists in order to fight the elections of February 1936.

The Popular Front won the election of February 1936 by a narrow majority. Spain had become polarized, and the division was to intensify.

The Popular Front

The Popular Front government was exclusively Republican. Under Largo Caballero, the left Socialists put increasing pressure on the government, using revolutionary language if not intending revolution. Largo Caballero's revolutionary rhetoric concealed his hope that the orthodox Republicans could be eased from power, leaving the field open to a pure Socialist government, which his followers chose to call, in Leninist language, the "dictatorship of the proletariat."

Just as the fears of the "Fascism" of the right justified the defensive reaction of the Socialists, so the right argued that the Republican government was a prisoner of the revolutionary left (they could point to a rapid growth of Communist influence). The Falange, founded by José Antonio Primo de Rivera, the son of the dictator, was a nationalist anti-Marxist grouping appealing to youth ready to engage in street affrays with the Socialist Youth. Conservatives rallied behind the right-wing National Front, which openly appealed to the military to save Spain from Marxism.

The army was the key factor; by the early summer a young officers' conspiracy was backed by Mola, Manuel Goded, and, finally, Francisco Franco. The murder of Calvo Sotelo with the connivance of government security forces was the final outrage for the right and the army.

THE CIVIL WAR

The rising of the military started in Morocco on July 17, 1936, and spread to the garrisons of metropolitan Spain in the following days. The Civil War took place because the rising was successful only in Old Castile, in Navarre, where Carlist support was decisive, and, of the larger towns, in Saragossa, Seville, Córdoba, Valladolid, and Cádiz. Galicia soon went over to the Nationalists, as did most of Andalusia. Catalonia and the Basque Provinces were loyal to the government because the Republic guaranteed their autonomy. In Madrid and Barcelona, the security forces, helped by the workers who were armed belatedly by the government, defeated the officers. Thus, in broadest terms, the Republic held the centre, the Levant, Catalonia, and the Basque industrial zones; the Nationalists held the food-producing areas. One consequence was to be an increasingly acute food shortage in the Republican zone.

The role of the workers in defeating the rising made their organizations the power in the Republican zone. The legal government was by-passed or totally supplanted by local committees and trade unions; the workers' militia replaced the dissolved army. In many parts of Spain a social revolution took place in July 1936: factories and farms were collectivized. The English novelist George Orwell described Barcelona, where the CNT was all-powerful, as "a town where the working class was in the saddle." The success of working class control, in terms of increased production, is difficult to estimate.

Orwell on Barcelona

This revolution was distasteful to the Left Republicans and to the Communist Party, which rapidly grew in number and in political influence because it controlled the supply of arms from the Soviet Union. In the name of an efficient war effort and the preservation of "bourgeois" elements in the Popular Front, the Communists pressed for a popular army and central government control. In September–November 1936, the CNT was brought into the government of Catalonia and into Largo Caballero's ministry in Madrid—an astonishing step for a movement that had consistently rejected "bourgeois" politics. The CNT militants did not approve the leaders' "surrender" and the dismantling of the militia-backed revolution.

A small Marxist revolutionary party, the Partido Obrero de Unificación Marxista (POUM), which rejected the Popular Front in favour of a workers' government, set off a rebellion in Barcelona in May 1937. The Communists, Republicans, and anti-Caballero Socialists used this as an excuse to oust Largo Caballero, who proved insufficiently pliable to Communist demands. The government led by the Socialist doctor Juan Negrín was a Republican–Socialist–Communist concern. The great unions, the UGT and CNT, were replaced by the political parties.

The Communists were correct in arguing that the committee–militia system was militarily ineffective. General Franco's army, ferried over from Morocco, cut through the militia and arrived before Madrid by November 1936. The successful resistance of the city, which was stiffened by the arrival of the International Brigades and Soviet arms, meant that the Civil War would be prolonged for two years.

Victory would go to the side with the best army, with unified political control, and with adequate arms supply. The core of the Nationalist army was the African army commanded by General Franco. Given the confused political control in Republican Spain, the secure military and political command of Franco (from October 1936) was decisive. In April 1937 he incorporated the Falange into a unified movement under his leadership.

Both sides sought help from abroad. The republic consistently hoped that France and Great Britain would allow them to acquire arms. Partly because of fear of a general war, partly because of domestic pressures, both powers backed non-intervention (*i.e.,* self-imposed restriction of arms supply by all powers). General Franco appealed immediately to Hitler in Germany and to Mussolini in Italy, which supplied aircraft early in the war. The Germans, in return for mineral concessions, supplied the Condor Legion (100 combat planes), and the Italians sent ground troops; both supplied tanks and artillery.

The Western democracies protested but did nothing. The Soviet Union alone responded to the breakdown of non-intervention by supplying arms to the Republican side. Soviet supplies were of great importance (tanks, aircraft, and a military mission) after October 1936. The Communist International also organized the International Brigades. In 1938, Soviet supplies dropped off, and the balance of arms supply was decisively in favour of the Nationalists. Once the Popular Army replaced the militia, the republic held Madrid and defeated two flanking attacks in the battles of Jarama (February 1937) and Guadalajara (March 1937), where the International Brigades decisively defeated a motorized Italian corps.

After his failure at Madrid, General Franco transferred his effort to the north, where the bombing of Guernica, on April 26, 1937, by German planes outraged public opinion in the democracies: by October 1937, General Franco had captured the industrial zone, shortened his front, and won a decisive advantage.

When General Franco concentrated again on Madrid the Republican army staged its most effective offensive in the winter Battle of Teruel (launched December 15, 1937). General Franco recovered Teruel, drove to the sea, and committed his one strategic error in deciding on the difficult attack on Valencia. To relieve Valencia the Republicans attacked across the Ebro (July 24, 1938); once more they failed to exploit the breakthrough, and the bloody battle exhausted the Popular Army.

The final Nationalist campaign in Catalonia was relatively easy. On the Republican side, the feasibility of continued resistance, which was supported by the Communists and Negrín, caused acute political divisions. On March 7, 1939, a civil war broke out in Madrid between Communists and anti-Communists. On March 28 the Nationalist forces entered a starving capital.

FRANCO'S SPAIN, 1939–75

The first decade of General Franco's government was harsh. As a result of the Civil War roughly 1,000,000 Spaniards were dead or had emigrated. Fierce political repression was matched by economic hardship. General Franco's alliance with the Axis powers brought diplomatic isolation from the Western democracies. After 1950, growing foreign investment and change in economic policy brought an increase in material prosperity and a diminution of opposition activities.

Recovery after 1939 was made difficult by the destruction caused by the Civil War (especially of railway rolling stock), by a severe loss of skilled labour, by a series of bad droughts (especially 1949), by restrictions on the import of capital goods imposed by the European war, and by misguided attempts at state-controlled industrial development within a protected economy. The national income dropped back to the levels of 1900, and real wages fell. These were the years of near famine, of the black market, and of rural misery and flight to the towns.

Franco's relations with the democracies

General Franco's sympathies lay openly with Germany and Italy, to whom he gave moral and material support. He nevertheless demanded a high price for his military cooperation against the Western Allies, on whom he was dependent for food and oil imports. When it appeared likely that the Allies would win the war, in 1943, General Franco reaffirmed Spain's nominal neutrality, without gaining their benevolence.

The declared hostility of the dominant great powers after 1945 and the exclusion of Spain from the United Nations gave the opposition in Spain new life. Don Juan, the heir of Alfonso XIII, presented himself as a democratic alternative. Valiant but futile guerrilla activities, inspired largely by the Communist Party (1944–48), were easily suppressed.

General Franco met these difficulties, the most severe of his regime, with confidence. The Fuero de los Españoles (July 1945), guaranteeing personal freedoms (provided no attack was made on the government), was an attempt to establish a more democratic image. More significant was his alliance with the church, which was given control of education, and his reduction of the power of the Falange (which had supplied a national Fascist ideology). The ostracism of Spain by the United Nations was skillfully turned into a means of rallying support for General Franco in the name of national unity.

United States air and naval bases

General Franco's confidence came from his divination that, with the Cold War between the Western democracies and the Communist states, the United States could not sustain its hostility to Spain and that the Allies, while declaring for the democratic opposition, would not directly intervene to overthrow his regime. Hence the hopes of the opposition came to nothing. In 1953 an agreement with the United States gave General Franco considerable financial advantages in return for the establishment of four United States bases in Spain.

Thus by 1953, Spain appeared to be a stable state. Internal political control remained in General Franco's hands, ensured by his mastery of the army and his ability to play off the groups that supported him against each other. In these ministerial changes the Falange steadily lost power to the technocrats of the Opus Dei (a lay Catholic organization), which broke with the economic nationalism of the Falange in favour of a "normal" capitalist system, with market mechanisms replacing state control.

The new policies seemed justified by their success, which was aided by a rapid growth of tourism and foreign investment. As in many countries that have seen an economic miracle, spectacular expansion (a growth rate of 7.4 percent between 1962 and 1966) brought problems of inflation and a wages–cost spiral. Investment went mainly into industry and some spectacular irrigation projects; the Spanish countryside remained poor and its productivity low. The rural poor of the south emigrated to the factories of Europe or to the cities of Spain.

While the new prosperity brought a degree of social mobility that was novel to Spanish society and satisfied the middle classes, rising prices entailed a revival of labour troubles. The workers became disillusioned with the "official" syndicates run by the Falange. They set up workers' commissions outside the official framework, and there were serious strikes, in spite of legislation that forbade them. Sections of the church were sensitive to these discontents. While the episcopate, on the whole, held to the view that the church should support the state, younger priests saw the long-term dangers of such an alliance. Thus they were sympathetic to the workers' commissions. An even more intractable problem was that of Basque nationalism, and, again, some of the Basque lower clergy were sympathetic to the nationalists. The nationalist movement developed a terrorist wing.

During the final decade of Franco's life, and against a background of increasing economic and political ferment, the Caudillo moved in slow, determined steps to prepare Spain for the transfer of power. On November 22, 1966, he presented the Cortes with a new Organic Law of the State that provided for the office of premier (*presidente del gobierno*) and direct election of one-sixth of the Cortes' membership. Supplementary laws passed in June 1967 gave the Falange the powers of a legislative upper chamber. Adm. Luis Carrero Blanco was named vice premier, Franco himself serving as premier as well as chief of state (*jefe del estado*). Instead of Don Juan, his son, Juan Carlos de Borbón y Borbón, was named by Franco and approved by the Cortes (July 22, 1969) as prince of Spain and Franco's successor. Exactly two years later it was announced that Juan Carlos would assume the powers of head of state should Franco fall ill or be absent from Spain. On July 18, 1972, a law was passed naming Carrero Blanco interim premier upon Franco's death or retirement; he was made premier on June 9, 1973, Franco remaining as chief of state. Carrero Blanco was assassinated on December 20, 1973, by Basque nationalists and was succeeded nine days later by Carlos Arias Navarro, a former minister of the interior.

In a speech in February 1974 the new premier promised liberalization of the political system. Strict measures to maintain law and order were taken, however, including the first execution (March 2) of a political extremist since 1963. Franco's health began to fail, and Juan Carlos assumed the powers of chief of state from July to September. On December 20 a decree granted the right within certain limits to form political associations (except a Communist party).

The year 1975 was a momentous one for Spain. Increased terrorist activity by the Basque extremist organization led to a state of emergency in the provinces of Guipúzcoa and Vizcaya in April, anti-terrorist legislation in August, and the execution, despite worldwide protest, of five terrorists on September 27. On October 30 Juan Carlos became interim chief of state. Franco died on November 20, and Juan Carlos became king of Spain two days later.

SPAIN SINCE 1975

The accession opened a new political era leading to constitutional reform and the full transition to democracy. In April 1976 plans for reforming the constitution were announced. In July, Arias Navarro was replaced as premier by Adolfo Suárez González, who appointed a new, democratic-minded Cabinet. Following a program of transition to democracy, the Cortes on November 18 approved the Political Reform Law, setting elections for a bicameral legislature for June 15, 1977. In preparation, an electoral law of universal suffrage was passed (March 15, 1977), the National Movement (Falange) was disbanded (April 1), and the Communist Party was legalized (April 9).

During the elections several major and regional parties emerged, and a minority government was formed by an alliance of smaller, centrist groups; called the Unión Centro Democrático (UCD; Union of the Democratic Centre), it was led by Suárez. The new Cortes was opened by Juan Carlos on July 22, 1977, and it embarked upon a program of reform.

A new constitution was approved by the Cortes in November 1978 and by the electorate in December. Taking effect on December 29, it proclaimed Spain a parliamentary monarchy, took away the official status of the Roman Catholic Church, and guaranteed free enterprise and human and civil rights. Suárez resigned as premier and leader of the UCD in January 1981. On February 23, after the Cortes failed to confirm his successor, Leopoldo Calvo Sotelo y Bustelo, members of the Civil Guard staged a military coup that was ended only by the direct intervention of Juan Carlos. Sotelo was then confirmed and took office. (R.Ca./Ed.)

In October 1982 the Spanish parliamentary elections marked a monumental break with the Franco legacy, as a socialist majority was elected in the Cortes Generales. The PSOE received 46 percent of the popular vote and won a solid majority in the Cortes. The UCD, victors of the 1977 and 1979 elections, along with Prime Minister Leopoldo Calvo and his Cabinet were swept out of office. The primary beneficiaries of the election, besides the PSOE and its leader, Felipe González, were King Juan Carlos and the Popular Alliance, led by Manuel Fraga Iribarne. (Ed.)

Separatism

One of the most pressing problems continuing to face the government was that of the separatist movements. Limited autonomy was granted to Catalonia and to the Basque provinces in 1977; to the Balearic Islands, Castile–León (except for Madrid), and Estremadura in 1978; and to Andalusia and Galicia in 1980. By the early 1980s Catalonia, Galicia, and the Basque regions had elected regional parliaments. Tension, nonetheless, remained in the Basque region. The Basque terrorist organization, ETA, continued its policy of violence despite the central government's 10-point plan of 1983 to arrive at a peaceful settlement of the Basque problem and despite increased antiterrorist measures. The government did, however, achieve a breakthrough in 1984 in its efforts to control terrorism when France reversed its long-standing policy of granting asylum to ETA members.

Spain continued to follow a foreign policy that had been growing slowly more liberal during Franco's final years. The country had already divested itself of most of its colonial holdings, granting independence to Equatorial Guinea in 1968 and ceding Ifni to Morocco in 1969. In 1976 it ceded the Spanish Sahara to Morocco and Mauritania. Spain had begun commercial relations with the Communist countries by an agreement with Romania in 1967. Diplomatic activity had been extended to Latin America in 1971; a trade agreement was made with the Soviet Union in 1972; and formal diplomatic relations were established with East Germany and China in 1973. On January 1, 1986, after long negotiations, Spain gained admittance to the European Economic Community.

For later developments in the political history of Spain, see the *Britannica Book of the Year* section in the BRITANNICA WORLD DATA ANNUAL. (R.Ca./Ed.)

Andalusia

Andalusia (Spanish Andalucía) is a region with an area of 33,964 square miles (87,966 square kilometres), including most of Spain south of the Sierra Morena, corresponding roughly to the Roman province of Baetica and divided after 1833 into the eight provinces of Almería, Cádiz, Córdoba, Huelva, Jaén, Málaga, Sevilla, and Granada. The origins of the name are uncertain; scholars have connected it with the occupation of the country by the Vandals in the 5th century AD. The Arab form al-Andalus designated at various periods the whole peninsula, the area under Muslim rule, and the kingdoms of Seville, Córdoba, Jaén, and Granada. In 1981 the historic region of Andalusia became one of the 17 autonomous communities of Spain, including the present provinces of Almería, Málaga, Granada, Jaén, Córdoba, Sevilla, Huelva, and Cádiz.

PHYSICAL AND HUMAN GEOGRAPHY

Andalusia consists mostly of high, heavily eroded mountain chains and their foothills, broken in the west by the Guadalquivir depression and in the east by the Almería and Almanzora rivers. Settlement has been heaviest in the valleys and coastal plains and in the folds of the south-facing mountain spurs. The climate and fauna and flora, often varying considerably within a few miles from subtropical coastal type to alpine, correspond to those of certain parts of the North African littoral. Other shared features are flat-roofed houses, cave-dwelling communities, and the intensive cropping of irrigated hill terraces with the consequent proliferation of *minifundia* (small holdings), though stock-rearing *latifundia* are the rule in the plains. (K.Ga./Ed.)

Andalusia is one of the most distinctive major regions of the peninsula. Framed by the southern border of the Sierra Morena, the Campo do Montiel, the Murcian Steppes, and elsewhere by the sea, it is divided into two distinct sectors: the Guadalquivir Valley of Lower Andalusia, and the sub-Baetic and the Sistema Penibético of Upper Andalusia. Perhaps no other region of western Europe has had a richer cultural heritage, dating from the mineral exploitation and town life of the Tartessians and Romans. Of the major towns, almost all were Roman in origin and later intensely Arabicized. Compared with the rural peasantry of Castile, hard-working and resourceful, the Andalusian labourer is traditionally urban-minded and pleasure-loving. The economic strength of Andalusia has always been the balanced interests of mountain and plain, with complementary economies; thus the provinces of Sevilla and Granada tend to represent distinct interests.

The Andalusian Plain

Of the two, the Andalusian Plain is the more important, with a high population density around the city of Seville. Settlement is markedly nucleated, with the vast majority of the population living in large villages and towns. Significantly, the Guadalquivir Valley is the only extensive lowland in the peninsula that penetrates deeply into the interior from the coast. Its apex strikes 200 miles (320 kilometres) toward the northeast from the Gulf of Cádiz. From a width of about 100 miles (160 kilometres) at its mouth, it narrows to 60 miles (100 kilometres) at Seville and six miles (10 kilometres) at Ubeda, but to the south it is flanked by two other narrow depressions followed by the valleys of the Genil and Guadiana Menor. A marine trough until the late Quaternary, the Guadalquivir Valley contains fine sediments that have been carved into smoothly undulating relief, making it famed for its black soils. These are intensively cropped, with olives on the hill slopes. The marshes of Las Marismas and sand dunes of the Arenas Gordas are the only lands not utilized for agriculture. In Huelva, where cork forests and stock rearing are important, is a major afforestation scheme with eucalyptus forest, planted since 1940. Olive groves are very important in the other provinces; they cover a large proportion of the cultivated area of Jaén, Córdoba, and Sevilla; many have been planted since the 19th century. Vineyards are significant in the Condado of Huelva and Montilla in Córdoba. In the Campiña, most of the nation's cotton is grown. The chief towns are Seville and Huelva (both ports), Córdoba, and Jaén.

Upper Andalusia, though slightly smaller than the plain, is the dominant physical influence, bringing heavy rainfall on its southwestern flanks, and the source of the major tributaries of the Guadalquivir. Although the mountain ranges extend structurally for 500 miles (800 kilometres) from east-northeast to west-southwest and are 125 miles (200 kilometres) at their maximum width, they are much less compact than the Pyrenees. At their extremities they appear more like isolated mountain ranges emerging from a tangled relief of hills, plateaus, and plains. Termed the Sistema Penibético, the ranges can be divided into three zones: the sub-Baetic Mountains, which rise above the Andalusian Plain to 3,000–6,500 feet (910–2,000 metres) in three series of ranges; the central valleys and depressions traceable for about 110 miles (180 kilometres) between Antequera, Granada, and Baza; and the principal chain of Sierra Nevada. Rivers have trenched, deep valleys to the coast, and deforestation of the steep slopes has created new deltas.

In Cádiz as in the Andalusian Plain, *latifundia* (large landed estates) are an agrarian problem, with most of the province comprising estates of more than 620 acres (250 hectares) yet representing only a very small proportion of the total holdings. Family interests may form several great estates, the largest of which are under tree crops, especially olive groves. Specialized cultures such as the vineyards of Jerez de la Frontera and Málaga are in smaller holdings. Vegetables and cereals are irrigated in the intermontane basins of the Genil Valley, Arroyo de la Vega of Granada, Río de Guadix, and others. On the coast at Motril, Málaga, Torrox, Torre del Mar, and Adra sugarcane and bananas are grown. Tourism on the Costa del Sol is an important economic activity. Málaga, Granada, and Cádiz are the chief cities. (J.Ho.)

HISTORY

Andalusia's history was closely linked with that of the North African coast until the last decade of the 15th century, when the process of integration was partially suspended by the fall of Granada in 1492 to the monarchs of Castile and Aragon, who forbade their former Muslim subjects to communicate with Africa under pain of death, even after their conversion to Christianity. Both areas had been occupied successively by Punic, Roman, and Visigothic settlers; after the invasion of southern Spain from Tangier by Ṭāriq ibn Ziyād in 711, the Strait of Gibraltar virtually ceased to exist as a human frontier for the next eight centuries, even though political strife between

Spanish and African Muslim dynasties was often intense. In the 10th century the Caliphate of Córdoba drew its military strength largely from Berber mercenaries, just as Algiers in the 17th was garrisoned largely by deported Spanish Moriscos. Most of the distinguished figures of the Muslim period divided their lives between the two continents; for example, Averroës, the greatest of Spanish Muslim philosophers, who was born at Córdoba in 1126, was *qāḍī* of Seville and later of his native city, and, except for a few years of banishment, served after 1182 until his death as court physician in Marrakesh, where he did most of his writing.

Whereas the Andalusian contribution to North Africa in the medieval period was mainly cultural and artistic, the African Muslims repaid their coreligionists in Spain by reinvigorating their fighting power and religious zeal at times when discord and tolerance were weakening their resistance to the Christians. The invasions of Spain by the Almoravids in the 11th century and by the Almohads in the 12th prolonged the life of the petty but highly cultured Muslim principalities that arose from the ruins of the caliphate. These invasions also played a part as important as, though less direct than, that of the rivalry between the Christian monarchs in the birth of the Naṣrid sultanate of Granada in 1232. The defeat of the Marinids, one of the three great Berber groups, at the Salado (1340) and Palmones (1343) rivers, by Alfonso XI of Castile and Leon put an end to effective North African intervention in the peninsula; but the tide of the Christian reconquest of Spain was stemmed for a time by civil war in Castile, strife between crown and feudal nobility, and mutual distrust among the Christian princes.

Invasions by Almoravids and Almohads

For more than a century the Muslims who had thronged to Granada for asylum were saved by the slowing of the Christian advance. While their frontiers were the scene of a fluctuating guerrilla warfare which inspired the most colourful and moving of the Spanish ballads, their cities saw the revival of a score of fine crafts; Almería and Málaga traded with Italy and North Africa; the *vegas* and terraced slopes were cultivated to yield a wealth of fruits; the mulberry-planted mountainsides produced the finest silks in Europe; and even the poorest hillsides bore fast-growing crops of panic grass and millets. Above the thickly populated city of Granada itself, on an outlying spur of the Sierra Nevada, rose the fortress and palace of the Alhambra, flanked by the Generalife and other pleasure palaces, which fell into ruins soon after the reconquest.

Muslim institutions. The government of Muslim Spain, whether under the caliphs of Córdoba, the *ṭāʾifa* kings, or the sultans of Granada, was not radically different from that of the eastern caliphate. The office of ruler was nominally hereditary, though in practice he was frequently elected and deposed by military, aristocratic or merely local factions. A favourite of the ruler, or a military dictator who seized power, often took the title of hajib (chamberlain) and stood above the viziers (the ruler's delegates or ministers) who with the royal secretaries (kuttāb) formed the diwan or council of state. Local authority was delegated to civil and military governors called walis, each of whom administered a province or chief city, while on every frontier there was a military chief who enjoyed a large measure of independence. Armies consisted of paid mercenaries or were recruited on a tribal or clan basis and rewarded with the spoils of a raid; frontiers, however, were garrisoned by ascetic warrior sects, the Sufis, who corresponded to the military orders of the Christians.

Muslim law, which is canonical insofar as it derives ultimately from the Qurʾān, was administered by the *qāḍīs*, who were chosen from scholars versed in the traditions of Islām (the fakihs). As the office of *qāḍī* became increasingly onerous in Spain, criminal offenses were relegated to a special judge, the *sahib-al-shurtah,* while under the caliphate a magistrate residing in Córdoba, the *sahib-al-mazalim,* reviewed complaints against all public officials. In addition, most cities had a municipal justice, the *muhtasib* (Spanish *almotacén*), who directed the police, judged offenses against public morality, and retained after the reconquest his function of supervising markets, weights, and measures.

Administration of Muslim law

The income of the state was derived from the *zakah,* a tithe imposed originally on the incomes of individual Muslims, but later on the products of agriculture, industry, and commerce; from the capitation tax levied on non-Muslims, which declined after the expulsion of the Mozarabs; from rents on the state lands recorded in the chancellery registers, which became increasingly important; and from import and export duties, supervised by the officials of the revenue minister. In Granada under the Naṣrids the silk trade was an important source of revenue; silks could be bought and sold only in three marts, to which they were taken by elected deputies and stored until sold by the brokers. There was a variety of local taxes on consumer goods, public utilities, and irrigation, mostly devoted to defraying the personal expenses of the ruler's household. In addition, the pious bequeathed property to a public welfare fund that supported mosques, schools, leper houses, and lunatic asylums, provided maintenance for fakihs and students and ransoms for captives, and even served to repair roads, bridges, and defense works.

At the time of the reconquest, when Islāmic law was completely replaced by Roman and canon law, many administrative and fiscal institutions of the Muslims were guaranteed to them in their capitulations; in this way they were retained or copied by the Christians and survived until the advent of the Bourbon dynasty in Spain. This was especially true of municipal and guild regulations, which were often translated from the Arabic and incorporated in local *ordenanzas.*

Survival of Islāmic influence. While the most valuable contribution of Muslim Andalusia to the European heritage was in the realms of philosophy and literature, the most striking survivals of the Islāmic occupation to be seen in modern Spain are agricultural and domestic. Many of the crops grown in Andalusia were introduced by the Arabs (for example, sugarcane, apricots, and almonds—though two of the most characteristic features of the landscape, the maguey, or American aloe, and the prickly pear, come from the New World); and many of the elaborate irrigational constructions date from the Muslim period and have Arabic-derived names (*aljibe,* a well; *acequia,* a water channel; *noria,* a waterwheel). The traditional Andalusian house, though Roman in origin, owes many of its refinements to the Muslims. A spacious porch gives access to the central patio, decorated with blue tiles and horseshoe arches with stuccowork arabesques, in the centre of which a fountain plays among citron trees, flowering shrubs, and fragrant edgings of myrtle clipped in geometrical patterns. In summer, life revolves around the patio and the cool rooms leading off it; in winter the family moves upstairs to heavily carpeted rooms heated by a large round copper brazier standing in a polygonal surround of marquetry and burning, by a process of downward combustion, powdered charcoal made from olive stones. The house is covered by a flat roof and from the outside presents an unrevealing white facade broken only by a few small openings with elaborate wrought-iron grilles. Behind these the family lives in greater seclusion than is usual elsewhere in Europe, and guests other than kinsfolk are rarely invited. Modern Andalusian cooking obtains many of its ingredients from the New World; but the use of olive oil is associated primarily with the Muslims, for the Christians proved their faith by using lard until a comparatively recent date.

Much of what is accepted as typically Andalusian derives from periods before the Muslim conquest (as castanets and some flamenco dancing) or from later periods, being attributable to the influence of the New World, the Gypsies, the bandit and smuggler tradition of the 18th century, and the absentee landlords and political bosses of the 19th and 20th centuries. Perhaps the most lasting, though not the most immediately obvious, impress left by the Muslims on the Andalusian character is the gift for crystallizing the most fleeting emotion, aesthetic perception, or witty thought in improvised music and verse. (K.Ga.)

Aragon

Aragon was a constituent kingdom of the Spanish monarchy after 1479. The historic Kingdom of Aragon was roughly coextensive with the modern provinces of Huesca, Zaragoza, and Teruel and belonged to the Crown of Aragon, which also encompassed Catalonia, Valencia, and various French and Mediterranean territories. The economic, political, and cultural development of the Kingdom of Aragon lagged behind that of Catalonia and Valencia. In 1981 the historic region of Aragon became one of the 17 autonomous communities of Spain, including the provinces of Zaragoza, Huesca, and Teruel.

PHYSICAL AND HUMAN GEOGRAPHY

The north frontier of Aragon followed the Pyrenean water parting, from the peak of Anie (8,215 feet [2,504 metres]), the last of the great peaks toward the west, to the peak of the Aneto (11,168 feet [3,404 metres]) in the Maladetta group. Thus Aragon is backed by the western, or forward, echelon of the high Central Pyrenees, nearly to the point where the headwaters of the River Garonne separate it from the eastern. From this background of high peaks the descent to the lowlands of the Ebro is less rapid (average gradient 3½ in 100) than the descent toward the Garonne on the French side (seven in 100). The difference is due to the much greater development on the south side of topographical features parallel to the principal axis of the chain. Thus the River Aragon—finding at Jaca the soft marl that runs from east to west in a belt from Pamplona, in Navarre, to Boltaña—is diverted west and forms the broad valley of the Canal de Berdun; the influence of this belt is seen also in the course of the Cinca and of certain minor streams. East of Boltaña the rivers flow directly south, and the first of these, the Noguera Ribagorzana, gives the eastern boundary of Aragon. South of the belt of marl, a series of sierras—roughly aligned from west-north-west to east-south-east—of which the Sierra de Guara (6,791 feet [2,070 metres]) is the most important, runs from the River Aragon to the Sierra del Montsech (5,554 feet [1,693 metres]) in Catalonia; these sierras overlook the great, saucer-shaped central lowland on their south, across which runs the River Ebro. The heart of Aragon is this lowland and more strictly that part to which the descent from the crest of the Pyrenees is most obviously a descent by steps. The approaches to the defile by which the Ebro cuts its way from this enclosed basin through the Catalan coastal chain to the sea belong to Catalonia from Fayón downstream. The western boundary of Aragon runs more or less diagonally across the sierras bordering the central plateau so as to include within Aragon, in the south, the greater part of the sierra belt, while in the north the commanding Sierra del Moncayo (7,595 feet [2,315 metres]), immediately overlooking the Ebro lowland, forms an advanced bulwark of Castile. The descent from the central plateau is again by steps, and the border of Aragon is defined so as to cover the important structural depression, occupied in part by the River Jiloca, which runs from Calatayud, on the River Jalón, to Teruel. From the eastern limit of this depression the boundary runs to the Ebro at Fayón so as to include in Aragon the headwaters of the streams flowing to the Mediterranean. It is clear from the above that Aragon divides naturally into zones, parallel in the north to the Pyrenees and in the south to the border of the plateau. In the first zone, that of the high Pyrenean valleys, cultivated patches sustain scanty village populations; there is some mining—the cobalt mines are interesting—but the forest and the high summer pastures are the chief resources.

Topography

The next, the limestone zone to the south, includes picturesque scenic forms carved by the rivers; it is represented as high as the Pyrenean crest in the Monte Perdido (10,997 feet [3,352 metres]), one of the Three Sisters group. The zone is of no economic importance, but its strategic interest is obvious from the structure. Behind the protecting sierras to the south, Sierra di Guara, etc., beyond which the Muslims made no lasting conquest or impression, sprang up early in the Muslim period the countships of Aragon, with centre at Jaca, Sobrarbe, with centre at Ainsa, and Ribagorza, at first forming a single fief with Pallás. Until its establishment as an autonomous fief in 875, Ribagorza-Pallás was dependent on Toulouse through Cerdagne, and the influence of the easy Segre-Cerdagne pass across the Pyrenees extended as far westwards as the Ésera, the western boundary of Ribagorza. The separation of Pallás, the amalgamation (between 1034 and 1038) of Ribagorza with the western countships, which had always looked west to Navarre, and the declaration of Aragon as an independent kingdom (*c.* 1034) defined the boundaries of Upper Aragon as described above.

The lowland zone, which dips from an altitude of 1,640 feet (500 metres) to the Ebro (at 656 feet near Zaragoza) and rises again to the south toward the sierras, is by no means uniform. The frequency of local regional names, Monegros, Desierto de Calanda, Llano de Violada, indicates variations that express themselves sometimes in the nature of the soil (especially in the presence or absence of gypsum), but principally in the presence or absence of a non-brackish water supply. Huesca, in the north of the zone, on the old road from the coast by Lérida which, today as always, avoids the arid, waterless plateau of Los Monegros, was an important town long before Zaragoza, the natural centre of the lowlands. In the period following the final establishment by Augustus of Roman authority in the entire peninsula and with the new appreciation of the importance of the line of the Ebro as a baseline in strategical schemes envisaging the peninsula as a whole, Zaragoza became a most important nodal point of communications. Standing at the point of confluence with the Ebro of the Gallego valley, by which came the road from the Pyrenean pass of *Summus Portus*, and of the Huerva on the south, Zaragoza was also within 15 miles of the mouth of the Jalón, the entrance to the pass leading by the Sierra Ministra and the River Henares to the Tagus, and in Zaragoza was focussed the importance of the central lowland from which radiated all the routes to the interior of the peninsula. These advantages of site the city has always enjoyed, mutatis mutandis, in a degree corresponding with the degree of unification of the peninsular regions. The central lowland of Aragon had its most complete historical expression in the Muslim period as the kernel of the kingdom of Zaragoza. Not always able to maintain its independence of the Umayyads of Córdoba or of the Moroccan dynasties controlling the south, nor able always to control the north of its own area where the cities had climatic advantages and where Huesca had a much older tradition, the kingdom did not long survive the capture by Aragon of Monzón (1089) and of Huesca (1096); Zaragoza itself fell in 1118. The union of the enlarged kingdom of Aragon, now centred in Zaragoza, with the maritime state of Catalonia (1135) gave it a new Mediterranean outlook. The circumscription of Aragon by Castile both on the north, where the district of La Rioja and the plateau of Soria became finally Castilian, and on the south, where the conquest of Murcia for Castile drove a wedge between Valencia, held by the Aragonese, and the Muslims of Granada, forced eastward the expansion of Aragon and led to the foundation of the Aragonese empire.

Prominence of Zaragoza

The southern part of Aragon would form one single zone of hill country were it not for the strip of sheltered valleys along the line of the Jalón and of the depression marked by the towns of Calatayud, Daroca, and Teruel. With Albarracín, on the upper Guadalaviar, these towns formed the four communities that dominated the hill pastures for many centuries. The peach ripens in the valleys, where the irrigated lands are intensely cultivated; apart from these the sheep pastures on the hills are the principal resource.

The temperature of Lower Aragon is between that of Old Castile with its low mean winter temperatures and that of New Castile with its high mean summer temperatures. Northward from the Sierra de Guara the seasons are reduced more and more to long severe winters and short cool summers; in a lesser degree the same is true of the highlands of Aragon. The rainfall is small save on the Pyrenean front, and we note the approximate equality both of the winter and summer minima and of the spring and autumn maxima. The deficiency of the rainfall, which does not exceed 20 inches (500 millimetres) annually over the greater part of Aragon, and falls below 12 inches (300 millimetres) in the neighbourhood of Zaragoza, has made irrigation a prime necessity. Some of the more important canals are the Imperial canal with intake from the Ebro on the right bank below Tudila and terminating at El Burgo, below Zaragoza; the Canal de Tauste, on the opposite side of the river; the Canal de Aragon y Cataluña, with intake from the Ésera near Olvena, the principal canal terminating near the junction of the Rivers Segre and Cinca. One of the larger reservoirs is that of La Peña, on the River Gallego. The Moneva reservoir, on the River Aguas, is one of the largest in southern Aragon. (Ed.)

HISTORY

The original kingdom was brought into existence by a testamentary act of Sancho III of Navarre in 1035. Sancho left to his third son, Ramiro, the then small Pyrenean county of Aragon, elevating it to an independent kingdom. To this mountain domain (which took its name from the river flowing through Jaca, its capital) Ramiro (1035–63) was soon able to add the counties of Sobrarbe and Ribagorza, to the east. All the counties had long been under Frankish influence, an important bearing on the character of some Aragonese institutions. By 1104 the kings of Aragon had doubled the size of the original kingdom by conquests southward toward the Ebro. Zaragoza, capital of the Almoravid kingdom of the same name, fell to Alfonso I of Aragon (1104–34) in 1118, and the occupation of the valleys of the Jalón and Júcar rivers, to the south of Zaragoza and the Ebro, soon followed. These conquests, involving the absorption into Aragon of large numbers of Mudéjar and Mozarab farmers and artisans, greatly altered the social complexion of the country. The pattern of future operations against the Moors was fixed by the Treaty of Cazorla, signed by Alfonso II of Aragon (1162–96) and Alfonso VIII of Castile in 1179, which divided those parts of Spain remaining in Muslim hands into two zones—one for each kingdom to reconquer.

Early expansion of Aragon

In 1150 the ruler of Catalonia, Ramón Berenguer IV, count of Barcelona, married the heiress of the Kingdom of Aragon. Thus, until 1410, both countries came to be ruled by the Catalan house of Barcelona. The previous history of Catalonia, formerly the Frankish-dominated Spanish March, had been unlike that of Aragon. It possessed a unified legal code (in which feudal custom played a large part) and a written political constitution and was much more cosmopolitan and bourgeois in outlook than Aragon. Until 1412 Catalan influence dominated the union, with the Catalans tending to support the crown in its frequent constitutional struggles with the feudal Aragonese nobility. The union was of great value to the Catalans, who were able to devote themselves to commerce and maritime expansion, knowing that the financial and military responsibility of defending them from Castile would fall largely on the inhabitants of the Aragonese hinterland. Navarre, ruled by Aragon since 1076, became independent again in 1134; it once more came under the crown of Aragon in the reign of John II (king of Aragon from 1458 to 1479 and of Navarre from 1425).

At the time of their union, both Aragon and Catalonia had developed important territorial interests in southern France. These occupied much of the attention of the crown until Aragonese pretensions in France were finally abandoned in 1258. The only territory north of the Pyrenees that remained permanently attached to the Aragonese crown was the county of Roussillon. The occupation of the Balearic Islands took place in 1228 and the conquest of the rich Moorish kingdom of Valencia in 1238. Valencia, like the Balearics, was colonized by Catalans, though it retained a large Mudéjar population. It was administered as a separate kingdom of the crown of Aragon, with its own laws and parliament. Having thus completed the occupation of the Moorish territories allotted to Aragon by the Treaty of Cazorla, the Aragonese began expansion in the Mediterranean, made possible by the sea power of the Catalans. In 1282, after the Sicilian Vespers, Peter III (1276–85) was received by the Sicilians as their king, and thenceforward Sicily was ruled either directly by the kings of Aragon or by their relatives. Sardinia was incorporated into the Aragonese empire in 1320. A further accretion to Aragonese power came in 1442, when Alfonso V (1416–58) successfully concluded his long struggle to conquer the kingdom of Naples.

Between 1356 and 1369 Peter IV (1336–87) had been involved in a disastrous war with Castile. This war and its aftermath revealed that the powerful feudal nobles of Aragon tended to sympathize more with the Castilian magnates than with their own municipalist dynasty. Their chance came in 1412 when, after the extinction of the House of Barcelona in 1410, they procured the election of a a Castilian prince, Ferdinand of Trastámara, to the vacant throne against strong Catalan opposition. The final blow to Catalan supremacy came when Alfonso V of Aragon transferred his capital to Naples in 1443; though, later, the Catalans waged an unsuccessful civil war against Trastámaran rule. John II countered this resistance by arranging for his heir, Ferdinand, to marry Isabella, heiress of Henry IV of Castile. In 1479, therefore, on John's death, the countries of the Aragonese crown were united with Castile. Under this union the Aragonese countries retained their own political and administrative systems, despite certain modifications under Philip II, until the beginning of the 18th century, when, in consequence of the rebellion of the lands of the crown of Aragon during the War of the Spanish Succession, their constitutional privileges were abrogated by Philip V. As an administrative unit the old kingdom of Aragon proper survived until 1833, when the division of it into the three existing provinces took place. (P.E.R.)

Union with Castile

Asturias

Asturias once was a principality of Spain, created (1388) by John I of Leon and Castile when his eldest son Henry married the daughter of the Duke of Lancaster. The principality belonged to the eldest son of the sovereign; adminstratively the principality was chiefly merged in the province of Oviedo, to describe which Asturias still survives in popular usage as a regional term. In 1981 the historic region of Asturias became one of the 17 autonomous communities of Spain, including the province of Oviedo.

PHYSICAL AND HUMAN GEOGRAPHY

Clearly defined on three sides by mountain ranges, which make the district a rough oval, and on the fourth side by a long straight coastline, broken only by the projecting Cabo de Peñas, the Asturias are secluded from the rest of the peninsula and such outlook as they have is maritime. On the east the triple limestone massif of the Picos de Europa leaves only a narrow strip for passage to the coast of old Castile; on the south the Cantabrian mountains shut off the central plateau. On the west the lower Sierras de Rañadoiro and de Meira, running northeast to southwest, block the road to Galicia; between these sierras the boundary line of the Asturias runs without any special natural definition to the Ria de Rivadeo.

The abrupt descent from the Cantabrian crest in Peña Ubiña, brings down the rivers by steep courses set in deep valleys—in canyons, in the mountain limestone of the eastern Asturias—to the sea. A fan-shaped area drains to the Ria de Pravia by the converging Rivers Narcea and Nalón; the town of Pravia stands at the apex of the fan. Besides these rivers and their tributaries, the Navia and Sella are the only important streams. To the east of this fan, behind the coast between Avilés and Caravia, lies the area of successive marine invasions in geological times. To one of these invasions is due the natural trench that forms the central valley of the Asturias east of Oviedo and continues along the line of the old sea gulf narrowing out between the Picos de Europa and the Sierra de Cuera. This structural valley, neither the result of stream action nor occupied by any important stream, gives the principal interior line of communications in the Asturias. Along the coast the great Cantabrian platform, running from western Galicia to the mouth of the River Adour in France, is represented in the Asturias as elsewhere, by the gently rolling downs, 200 to 230 feet (61 to 70 metres) in height and cut usually in sheer cliffs toward the sea, into which the platform, segmented by the rivers from the interior, has been molded by the weather. Today the platform is thickly populated, and one single coastal road connects the long line of small towns set on successive heights. The intervening *rias* are clogged with silt and afford no good harbours. The relief, of mountain, valley, and coastal platform, the coal supply, and the humidity of the climate determine jointly the character of the Asturias. The impenetrable Picos de Europa, in whose fastnesses the chamois still roams, sheltered the Christian nucleus of resistance to the Muslims, which developed into the Kingdom of Oviedo and Asturias. In the early stages of this resistance the term Asturias (derived from the original inhabitants, the Astures, whose territory extended westward from Ribudesella and as far as the Douro) covered loosely the Cantabrian territory held by the Christians; there were Asturias in the Liébana valley and as far east as Santander (Asturia de Sancto Anderio), and the name lingered long east of the Picos in the term Asturia de Santillana (Sancta Illana). But the important movement was westward along the central valley, in which Cangas de Onís and Oviedo (alternating with Pravia) were successive headquarters or capitals of the small Christian state. After the capital of the enlarged state had been tranferred to Leon by Ordono II (914–924), the isolation of the Asturias and of Galicia, both from each other and from the repopulated territory on the central plateau, contributed to the weakness and lack of homogeneity of the Kingdom of Leon. The mountain barrier between Leon and the Asturias made Oviedo at a later date a refuge for the Leonese king Bermudo II during the raid of Almanzor.

Relief

The coal of the Asturias lies in distinct groups of small basins; the town of Tineo is the centre for the most westerly group, but the comparatively thick beds of anthracite coal have been little exploited there for lack of means of communication. The most important group at present is the central; here the coal lies in a series of folds of the mountain limestone, cut by the Rivers Caudal and Nalón, on which Mieres and Langres are respectively the centres of exploitation. The more northerly basins of Arnas and Ferroñes supply a soft coal. The coals of the Asturian basins form a descending scale of hardness from north to south. Iron ore is also extracted in the Asturias. Zinc ores are mined in the Picos de Europa. The altitude at which the zinc is found, however, prevents operations in winter; the iron ores have a high percentage of silica; the coal seams are relatively thin and irregular and they dip steeply, so that the costs both of production and of transport are high. Thus the mineral resources of the Asturias have served to industrialize considerable tracts of country without bringing any high degree of prosperity. With a humid climate and a high rainfall nowhere less than 40 inches (1,000 millimetres) per annum, the Asturias are predominantly pastoral and the cow is the chief domestic animal. Horses and mules are bred on the Asturian pastures but they are not worked, except in the mines. The absence of a regular period of drought, together with favourable temperature conditions makes maize (corn) the chief cereal cultivated; the soils do not, however, favour the cultivator, and America and the mines attract labour more than the farm. The marked summer minimum of rainfall is sufficient to make ordinary summer irrigation desirable, but the typical Asturian irrigation is the winter flooding of lands by running water, partly to maintain the soil temperature and partly to secure the benefit of the fertilizing deposit of mud.

HISTORY

Asturias was from 718 to 910 the only independent Christian kingdom in the Iberian Peninsula. The kingdom was formed by a number of Visigothic nobles and officials who, after the Muslim invasion of Spain, retired to this area, as high mountain ranges to the east, south, and west made it a small and easily defended enclave. They elected Pelayo, a Visothic noble, as king and set up a capital at Cangas de Onís. The new kingdom managed to survive repeated attacks by the armies of the amirate of Córdoba and extended its frontiers to include Galicia and Cantabria before the end of the 8th century. The capital was transferred first to Pravia (*c.* 780) and thence, in the reign of Alfonso II (791–842), to a strategically sited new city constructed for the purpose at Oviedo. During the reign of Alfonso III (866–910) the frontiers of Asturias were pushed south to the line of the Duero from the Atlantic to Osma. By this time, the kings of Asturias, with the aid of Mozarab (Christian) immigrants from the amirate, commanded sufficient manpower to garrison and repopulate the areas south of the Asturian mountains. The kings made alliances with dissident Muslim leaders and sometimes established a modus vivendi with the amirs of Córdoba but always retained their independence. An important factor in building up a sense of national identity was the discovery, early in 9th century, of the supposed tomb of St. James at Padrón, in Galicia. The shrine subsequently established at Santiago de Compostela was soon to become the spiritual centre of the nation. By the 10th century the kingdom was too large to be effectively controlled from the mountain capital at Oviedo, and García I (909–914) made Leon his administrative centre in 910.

Self-conscious Visigothicism was a feature of the Asturian kingdom, whose princes claimed direct descent from the Visigothic rulers of Spain and whose earliest chroniclers stressed the duty of the kingdom to proceed to the early and total reconquest of the whole peninsula. Church organization was reestablished on the Visigothic model, aided by the immigration of Mozarabic priests, and the many churches built in Asturias adhered closely to Visigothic architectural tradition. Similarly the secular administration of the Asturian kings continued, although in attenuated form, the system of the Visigothic rulers, and the *Forum judicum* remained the basis of Asturian law. Some Frankish influence is evident in the administration and in architecture, and there are traces of diplomatic contacts with Charlemagne and his successors, but, generally, the Asturian kingdom lived in total isolation from the rest of Christian Europe.

Visigothicism

Asturias was created a principality by John I of Castile for his eldest son, Henry, in 1388. This principality survived during the existence of the Spanish monarchy as a title (in modern times purely honorific) borne by the sovereign's eldest son. (P.E.R./Ed.)

Balearic Islands

The Balearic Islands (Islas Baleares) is an archipelago of five islands, with a number of islets, in the western Mediterranean. The islands are located about 50 to 190 miles (80 to 300 kilometres) off the east coast of Spain, of which they form a province. The archipelago, which lies between 38°40″ and 40°6″ N, and 1°22″ and 4°25″ E, comprises two distinct groups. The eastern and larger group, the Balearics proper, contains the two principal islands, Majorca (Spanish Mallorca) and Minorca (Menorca), and the small island of Cabrera, south of Majorca. The western group, formerly known as the Pine Islands (Las Pitiusas; ancient Pityusae), comprises Ibiza (Iviza) and Formentera, with several islets. In 1981 the Balearic Islands became one of the 17 autonomous communities of Spain.

PHYSICAL AND HUMAN GEOGRAPHY

The land. The Balearics are, structurally, the continuation of the Andalusian Mountains, which end on the Spanish mainland at Cabo de la Náo, a little more than 50 miles west of the Pityusae. They are the emergent portions of two submarine plateaus, which are separated from each other by a considerable marine depression. The seas separating Ibiza from Formentera and Majorca from Minorca are, however, relatively shallow, and a fall of the Mediterranean sea level of 300 feet (91 metres) would convert the Balearics into two islands. The edge of the northern submarine plateau is truncated abruptly by an east–west abyss more than 8,000 feet deep. Minorca's northwest–southeast axis lies obliquely to the direction of this fault zone; and the character and extent of the Palaeozoic formations of Devonian Age comprising the island suggest that Minorca is a remnant of the continental massif that formerly united Sardinia with Catalonia. The other islands of the Balearics are aligned on the southwest–northeast trend of the submarine plateaus and presumably are the expression of violent Alpine folding from the southeast. Rocks from Trias to Oligocene bear witness to these mountain-building movements, older formations being brought up also as inliers.

The resultant sierra of northwest Majorca, parallel to the coast, rises in the Torrellas or Puig Mayor to 4,734 feet; a minor highland zone in the southeast reaches almost 2,000 feet; and the core of Ibiza is crowned by La Atalaya, 1,558 feet. The rugged and precipitous cliff coastlines of both northwest Ibiza and northwest Majorca, often referred to as their Costa Brava, occur where these zones of high relief are adjacent to the sea. Elsewhere in Majorca and Ibiza there are broad belts of lowland, often of fertile Miocene soils or alluvium, surrounded or interrupted by undulating hills, boulder-strewn and scarred by the courses of torrents, which in flood spread their debris on the piedmont zone. Formentera has a more monotonous relief, consisting of two tablelands (the higher, La Mola, 630 feet) mainly of Quaternary deposits connected by a narrow isthmus of alluvium. Minorca has a more worn terrain, the highest of its small hills, Monte Toro, in the north centre, reaching an elevation of only 1,174 feet. This northern monotonous stony plateau runs to the sea in a northeast coast of much more dislocated relief, which contains many bays and capes and the deep inlet of Mahón. A fairly well-marked depression separates this plateau from the low southern tableland with its gently rolling surface cut by broad ravines with fertile alluvial bottoms. Cabrera, separated by a five-mile-wide strait from Majorca, is a semi-arid contiuation of the larger island's eastern hills.

Climate

Within a general pattern of Mediterranean climate characterized by winter rain and summer drought, there are marked variations from one island to another, and within each island, dependent largely on relief and aspect. Minorca, having no protecting range of mountains, is colder and wetter in winter (25 inches [635 millimetres] annually), and feels the effects of hot summer winds more than the other islands. The average summer temperature is 75° F (24° C), and that of winter 50° F (10° C). In Majorca there are marked differences between the rainy cooler northern mountains and the protected remainder of the island, which has an average rainfall of less than 20 inches and rarely suffers gales. Ibiza, Cabrera, and Formentera are even drier, with an annual precipitation of less than 15 inches. In all the islands the period May–August is almost rainless, the number of rainy days being less than 80 annually. There are, therefore, no permanent streams but a great number of torrent courses and ravined gullies which are filled spasmodically. Snow rarely falls, although frosts are not uncommon in the period January–March. In the mountains of Majorca snow may lie for several weeks until the spring thaw. Daytime summer temperatures frequently reach 90° in June, July, and August, but these are moderated by sea breezes, and the evenings are usually cool and often in the 50° range even in midsummer.

Agricultural and pastoral use of the lowland areas and the construction of hillside terraces for arable farming have limited natural vegetation to the rocky hilly lands, ravines, and terrain impracticable for farming. The exposed northern areas of Minorca are either treeless or support only stunted specimens, but the sheltered southern gullies (barrancas) have some pine woods, pomegranate orchards and even semitropical vegetation on their slopes. In the other islands Aleppo and Stone pine and some holm oak occur where rainfall and soils are sufficient, but great areas are covered with Mediterranean scrub vegetation, which includes juniper, oleander, myrtle, and rock roses. This *garigue* was formerly the undergrowth of a forest cover. The prevailing arboriculture of Majorca and Ibiza has resulted in a two-tier cover of the fertile parts of those islands (*huertas*), as cereals and legumes are grown in the orchards and groves of almond, olive, carob bean, and fig trees. Artificial meadows of lucerne occur in the most easily irrigated areas.

The people. The vast majority of the population of the Balearics live in Majorca, a large proportion of all the islanders residing in Palma alone. Most of the Majorcans and Minorcans are town-dwellers, but the reverse is true of Ibiza and Formentera where the majority of the people live in rural settlements. Cabrera and Formentera are thinly populated. Ethnically the people reflect the rich variety of their historical antecedents. The larger towns contain a majority of folk of Catalan descent, with Jewish and Italian minorities, but the country districts show in their physical types important admixtures of Moorish, Phoenician, Greek, and even Nordic characteristics, and some families can trace their ancestry to Moorish-Catalan progenitors. There are also small numbers of returned emigrants, from the mainland, from France, and from Latin America, the latter known as *americanos.* Castilian is the language of the cities, but in rural areas a Catalan dialect, with many resemblances to Provençal French and with several Arabic infusions, is the common tongue spoken. Some Majorcans returned from France and residing in Sóller speak French; and some forms of speech introduced by the British still survive in Minorca.

The economy. All the islands together form a Spanish province, with Palma as its capital. The city is also the military, judicial, and ecclesiastical headquarters of the province.

Agriculture

Arboriculture is the traditional industry of Majorca and Ibiza, cereals, legumes, and animal fodder crops being grown among the almond, carob, bean, fig, olive, and apricot trees, either on the irrigated *huerta* lowlands or on the intensely terraced hillsides. Minorca is more important for pastoralism but also produces good crops of ranges. Stock raising is widespread in all the islands, small groups of sheep, goats, and pigs being cared for by the women and children. *Feixes,* or reclaimed lands, adjacent to Ibiza city, are important sources of market-garden produce. This rural economy is essentially peasant-operated, much of the domestic furniture, foodstuffs, local customs, and arts exhibiting distinct self-sufficient characteristics. Almonds, figs, and apricots are exported, and there is a considerable local production of wines, olive oil, butter, cheese, and poultry.

For centuries Ibiza has been an important manufacturer of sea salt. Fishing provides much food for the islanders, and some fish is exported to the mainland. Timber-cutting, charcoal-burning, and small glass, pottery, footwear, and foodstuffs factories complete the industrial fabric, but many of these occupations are complementary and secondary to agriculture, having a labour supply that fluctuates with the demands of the farmland.

The tourist industry is an important part of the economy of all the islands, many thousands of visitors, especially from Spain, France, Great Britain, and Germany, being attracted by the climatic, scenic, and historic merits of the Balearics. The construction of hotels, guest houses, and villas, the provision of services, and the making and sale of souvenirs, especially fine lace and embroidery, provide employment and income.

Sea communications are maintained principally through Barcelona, and air services link Majorca and Minorca with many west European cities. (G.J.B.)

HISTORY

Archaeological artifacts. The earliest historical records describe the inhabitants of the Balearic Islands as cave dwellers. Natural and partly artificial caves abound in the limestone rock and have produced the few simple flint implements and incised pottery that can be assigned to the beginning of the Bronze Age and are the earliest records of human activity. Subterranean methods of living persisted, and the walled settlements of the inhabitants largely consisted of windowless rooms. Megalithic hill forts crown some of the hills.

Talayots. The earliest and best known monuments are the talayots (towers). They are still numerous and were formerly much more so, especially in the intensively cultivated island of Majorca, where great numbers were destroyed, particularly on the plains adjoining the southeast coast of the island. They are chambered towers of stone, with either a round or a rectangular plan. They were roofed, generally with the aid of a central pillar composed of circular superimposed slabs, and faced with clay to produce a monolithic appearance.

The masonry of the round towers is very rough, the walls being composed of immense rugged blocks of hammer-dressed limestone; but the four-cornered talayots, which are presumably later, show smaller masonry. Like the nuraghi of Sardinia, they served as fortified dwelling places; outbuildings are normally attached, and they are occasionally sited within villages enclosed by Cyclopean walls.

Taulas. With the talayots in Minorca are associated the so-called temples; these halls may well have been used for ceremonial purposes, but they certainly formed a normal element of the habitations associated with the talayots. Within the hall stands a taula (table), a rectangular slab of dressed stone that supports a second, horizontal, slab. These T-shaped taulas are central supports for roofing; there are often supplementary pillars between the taula and the outer wall and clay-covered pilasters against the wall and in the angles.

It seems certain that these most remarkable prehistoric remains in Majorca and Minorca are not likely to be much earlier than the middle of the 2nd millennium BC and represent a culture that continued with little change until Roman times.

Burial caves. Rock cut tombs and burial caves are found in many forms; those of the best known series, at San Vicente, on the northern extremity of Majorca, are cut into a sloping hillside. They resemble the burial grottoes of southern France near Arles and must indicate a common origin. Carvings in Majorcan caves confirm the relationship. Many caves of the same type, when sited on level ground, are approached by steps sunk in a trench, which was filled by blocking material to seal the tomb.

The *nau* grave

The *nau*, or *naveta* (Catalan, "ship"), so termed from its resemblance to an upturned boat, was also a type of grave. These are now found chiefly in Minorca and are elongated structures built, like the talayots, of immense closely fitted blocks of stone, with a rounded end and squared or slightly concave front; in this front face is a tiny door giving access from a forecourt through a passage to a long rectangular chamber roofed by large slabs. In the famous Nau d'Es Tudons the total length of the structure was about 60 feet, the width 24 feet, and the height about 25 feet. Structures of somewhat similar form in Majorca seem to have been used as dwellings.

Finds. Although the talayotic civilization seems to have continued without much modification, the position of the islands off the northern shore of the Mediterranean laid them open to continued influence from more eastern civilizations, as many finds attest. Important discoveries of bronze swords and single and double axes, antennae swords, heads and figures of bulls and other animals, small human figures from Sardinia or farther east, and many other objects bear witness to the foreign trade of the islanders over long periods of time. Local manufactures are represented by pots and shards. Most of the types seem to have persisted with little change until they are found mixed with Roman wares following the Roman occupation. (W.J.He./Ed.)

Invasions and occupations. There is historical evidence of at least 2,600 years of settlement, for the islands passed successively under the rule of Carthaginians, Romans, Vandals, Moors, and Spanish, all of whom have left their mark to some extent on the physical and cultural landscape. The islands are thus in many ways an epitome of Mediterranean insular history. Ibiza in particular was a strategic point, easily reached via the North African coast and providing a convenient base to raid the rich lands of Alicante, Valencia, and Majorca. Occupied for centuries by the Phoenicians and Carthaginians, Ibiza became a Roman colony in 123 BC. Under all these occupations its economic resources of lead, zinc, salt, foodstuffs, and purple dye (from marine mollusks) were sought by traders.

Founding of Palma

When the archipelago was conquered by Q. Caecilius Metellus in 123 BC, the largest city of the Balearics, Palma (the symbol of victory), was founded, and olive cultivation was introduced. Five centuries of peace, during which the islands supplied their new masters with Minorcan mules and the celebrated Balearic slingers, were broken by the arrival of the Vandals, who were followed by the troops of the Byzantine emperor Justinian. Though raided frequently both by Muslims and by Normans, the islands were not permanently conquered by the Caliphate of Córdoba until 903. The Moorish occupation led to many improvements in agriculture and irrigation, notably the introduction of windmills and waterwheels turned by animals, both devices being conspicuous features of the landscape today. James I of Aragon (the Conqueror) annexed Majorca and Ibiza in 1230–35, Minorca falling to his descendant Alfonso III in 1286. The islands formed a semiautonomous kingdom until 1349 and became a great base of medieval cartography and navigational science. Settlement was extended, agriculture was developed, and trade prospered.

In the War of the Spanish Succession the strategic value of the large landlocked harbour of Mahón attracted the attention of the participants, and its capture by the British in 1708 ushered in a century of dispute over its possession, which was not finally settled until the Spanish regained it in 1802 by the Peace of Amiens. In the Spanish Civil War (1936–38) points in the islands were seized by insurgent troops. Loyalist forces temporarily recaptured Ibiza, Formentera, and Minorca, the latter serving as an important base for their naval operations. (G.J.B./Ed.)

The Basque Provinces

The Basque Provinces (Provincias Vascongadas) are three small provinces, Guipúzcoa, Álava, and Vizcaya, that lie in north central Spain on the Bay of Biscay, adjoining the French border. In 1979 the three provinces formed the first autonomous community in Spain, the Basque Country (País Vasco). With an area of 2,803 square miles (7,261 square kilometres), approximately 90 miles (145 kilometres) wide from east to west and 45 miles (72 kilometres) from north to south, the Basque Country is one of the smaller autonomous communities of Spain. Isolated by the mountainous terrain, the Basques have maintained their linguistic and cultural uniqueness since the beginning of the Roman occupation in the 2nd century BC.

PHYSICAL AND HUMAN GEOGRAPHY

The Basque Provinces are bordered by France to the northeast, the provinces of Navarre to the east, La Rioja and Burgos to the south, Cantabria to the west, and the Bay of Biscay to the north. To the east the Pyrenees separate the Iberian Peninsula from the rest of the European continent and create a mountainous terrain that rapidly descends to the coast. To the south the Cantabrian Mountains run east–west through the provinces, separating the coast from the central plain of Álava and the provinces to the west. South of Álava's central plain lies the Ebro River, which defines the southern boundary of the province. Along the northern coast the Atlantic weather patterns prevail, characterized by heavy precipitation throughout the year, while in southern Álava, known as the Rioja Alavese, a warmer and drier climate permits the cultivation of both wine grapes and olives. Between the two regions lie the Cantabrian Mountains, which exhibit a more temperate climate.

Since the Spanish Civil War the Basque Provinces have undergone urbanization and heavy industrialization, with the result that the region around Bilbao, the capital of Vizcaya, has become the only significant rival to Barcelona as Spain's most industrialized area. With the subsequent depopulation of the rural areas, the traditional life of the Basques has changed dramatically since 1939.

The slopes of the Pyrenees were for centuries the domain of isolated farmers and shepherds. In the early 19th century, farmers began cultivating corn (maize) and potatoes after these two crops were imported from the United States. By the mid-20th century, cattle raising had largely supplanted sheep raising, and corn had become the primary crop. Wheat, barley, oats, and sugar beets are other principal crops. In the Rioja Alavese, situated at a lower elevation than the mountainous north, approximately one third of the the arable land is devoted to viticulture. The woodlands in the northern part of Álava are exploited for lumber, particularly oak. Vitoria, the provincial capital, is an industrial centre, where furniture, bicycles, and agricultural machinery are produced.

Álava

The two coastal provinces, Guipúzcoa and Vizcaya, are heavily industrialized. During the 19th century, iron and

Bilbao

steel production was concentrated around Bilbao, where iron was locally mined and shipped from the upriver port to the sea via the estuary called the Ria de Bilbao. Steel production reached its peak in Bilbao in the 1960s, when more than half of Spain's steel was produced there. Bilbao is also a centre for the chemical and metallurgical industries. Because the city is the most important port in Spain, it is also a financial centre and the traditional heart of various maritime industries, notably fishing and shipbuilding and repair. Along the coast, fishing, which once provided the primary means of livelihood, is now a secondary industry. Shipbuilding, a traditional activity of the Basques that began before the defeat of the Spanish Armada in 1588, when Spain was the major European naval power, has remained an important industry along the northern coast. Besides Bilbao, other shipbuilding centres are located at Santander and Gijón, Oviedo. Near the French border, the cities of Santander and San Sebastián, the capital of Guipúzcoa, have little heavy industry and are the centre of the region's tourism.

Certain genetic traits, including distinctive blood-type concentrations and skeletal differences, have led scholars to hypothesize that the Basques are descendants of an ancient Iberian people. The question of Basque origin is complicated by the Basque language, which bears no relation to Indo-European languages or to the few ancient fragments of Iberian writing that still exist.

Traditional Basque life centres around the *caserio,* the farm that houses a single family. Sometimes a few families form a small village, but the rural Basques are generally isolated, making for a strong patrimonial family life. This isolation has also allowed the Basques to maintain cultural separateness from their Spanish and French neighbours. Urbanization has attracted much of the rural population to the large coastal industrial centres; greater Bilbao accounts for four-fifths of the population of the three provinces. Agricultural production has thus declined, and many small villages have been depopulated. The urban centres have also attracted Spanish people from other provinces, so the traditions of Basque life and language have remained vital chiefly in the ever-dwindling rural enclaves.

HISTORY

Before the Roman invasion, the Basques occupied a large area of northern Spain, extending to the eastern edge of the Pyrenees, and part of southern France. When the Romans colonized the region in the 2nd and 1st centuries BC, many Basques assimilated Roman culture and language. Only the western Basques, living in relative isolation in the mountainous area of the present-day Basque Provinces, retained their distinct ethnicity and continued to speak their own language.

After the Roman Empire fell, these western Basques resisted all subsequent invaders, including the Visigoths, the Franks, the Normans, and the Moors, and they invaded in turn southwestern France. Basque self-government was conducted by local officials who were either appointed or elected. Delegates from each province gathered annually at the celebrated oak in Guernica to modify the *fueros,* or body of laws, that governed all three provinces. Despite the provinces' later alliances with Castile and Navarre, their political independence and the *fueros* were recognized by Spain until the 19th century. Although the Basques were required to swear allegiance to the Spanish crown, taxation was voluntary, and collection was determined by the Basques themselves. Basques served in the Spanish Army but only under Basque officers and only for the defense of the country. Elections for all local and provincial offices were conducted by the Basques, and they were free to engage in trade with foreign powers.

Self-government

After the Kingdom of Navarre broke from Castile and Aragon in 1035, the Basques found themselves situated between rival kingdoms. The region remained the subject of dispute until the three provinces were annexed to the Castilian crown. Guipúzcoa was the first to be annexed, in 1280, followed by Álava in 1332 and Vizcaya in 1379.

Basque autonomy was revived for a short time at the end of the Republican era in 1936. Basque Nationalists supported the Republicans based in Vizcaya and Guipúzcoa in order to pursue their own goal of political autonomy. Several attempts were made to enact an autonomy statute between 1931 and 1937, but the effort was thwarted until 1936, when an autonomous government was organized in Bilbao, which was controlled by the Republicans. Bilbao fell to the Nationalist forces soon after, in June 1937, and the nine-month-old government fled to France and then to Barcelona, which remained a Republican stronghold until the end of the Civil War. Proscriptions against speaking the Basque language or teaching Basque history suppressed Basque nationalism during Franco's regime but fuelled the growth of the extremist Basque separatist organization, the ETA (Basque Euzkadi ta Azkatasuna; "Basque Homeland and Liberty"). After Franco's death and the establishment of the autonomous community, the País Vasco, some measure of political autonomy was granted to the region, but the ETA continued its violent campaign in support of complete separation and social reform. (Ed.)

ETA

Canary Islands

The Canary Islands (Islas Canarias) is an archipelago in the Atlantic Ocean, between 27°39″ and 29°25″ N and 13°20″ and 18°12″ W. The minimum distance from the northwest African mainland is 67 miles (108 kilometres) between Fuerteventura and Cape Juby. In 1981 the Canary Islands, with the provinces of Santa Cruz de Tenerife and Las Palmas de Gran Canaria, became one of the 17 autonomous communities of Spain.

PHYSICAL AND HUMAN GEOGRAPHY

The land. Physically the Canaries fall into two groups: the western group includes Tenerife, Grand Canary, La Palma, Gomera, and Hierro and consists of isolated mountain peaks that rise from a deep ocean floor; the eastern group comprises Lanzarote, Fuerteventura, and six islets, surmounting a single submarine plateau less than 4,500 feet (1,400 metres) deep. After the researches of Christian Leopold von Buch in the early 19th century, the Canary

From *Madeira and the Canary Islands—A Concise Guide for the Visitor*

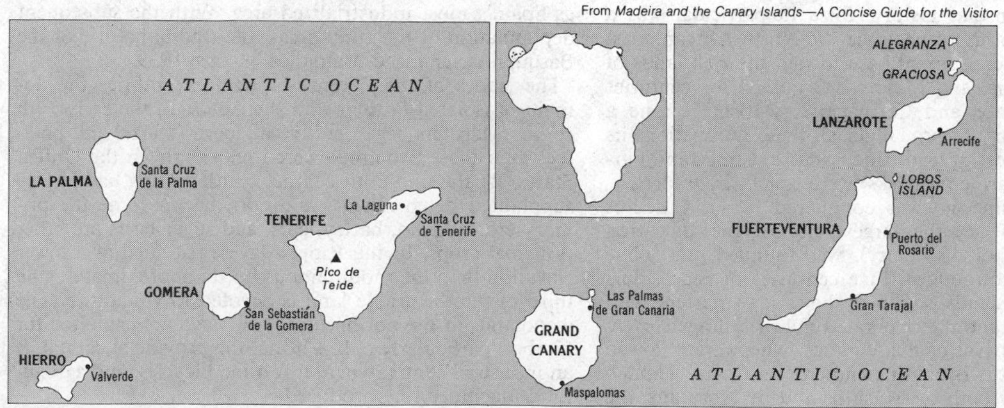

Major towns of the Canary Islands. Inset shows location of the islands off the coast of Cape Juby, Africa.

Islands, which are geologically associated with Madeira and the Azores, became classical ground to the student of volcanism. They are merely cones of ejection, formed by volcanic eruptions during and after the Tertiary Period. The lavas consist chiefly of basalts and trachytes.

The Canaries are situated at the eastern edge of a vast subtropical anticyclone and most of the year within the north–east trade wind. The trade wind blows strongly all summer but in winter may be interrupted by winds from between the west and southeast, occcasionally bringing hot, dusty weather and, rarely, locusts, from the mainland. In winter the passage of shallow depressions causes most of the archipelago's scanty rainfall. The climate is warm and dry. On the lower parts, February, the coolest month, has a mean temperature of 62° to 64° F (17° to 18° C), and August, the hottest month, has a mean temperature of 74° to 76° F (24° to 25° C), except in the eastern islands, which can be hot inland. Sunshine is abundant at all seasons, and rainfall, except on exposed parts of the western islands, is small and variable. The more populous districts have mean annual rainfalls of between six and 16 inches (150 and 400 millimetres), with about 50 to 60 rain days, but most of this falls in a few short, heavy storms in winter. The lower, eastern islands experience long droughts. Snow does not fall below about 3,000 feet (about 900 metres) and is unusual below 5,000 feet (1,500 metres). The Pico de Teide on Tenerife is often snowclad above 8,500 feet (2,600 metres) from November to April. This grand peak was the scene of a remarkable step in the progress of meteorology when in August 1856 the British astronomer Charles Piazzi Smyth (1819–1900) made two ascents that demonstrated the layering of the atmosphere in trade-wind areas.

Animal life

There were probably no indigenous mammals on the Canaries at the time of their discovery by Europeans. The dog, swine, goat, and sheep found there by the Spaniards had probably been introduced by earlier invading peoples from Africa. The ornithology is more interesting. About 220 species have been recorded, and, of these, 75 breed locally, and more than 40 are peculiar to this archipelago.

Of the 900 species of wild flowering plants found in the Canaries, just over 300 are indigenous. The latter show strong affinities with the vegetation of the Mediterranean and tropical East Africa and weak affinities with the vegetation of eastern Asia and the New World. The scanty rainfall and porous volcanic surfaces cause large tracts of the drier islands to be almost barren, yet the xerophytic plant life is of great interest, especially the cactuslike *Euphorbia,* of which about 25 species occur, and the famous dragon tree (*Dracaena draco*). The considerable height of the western islands, all exceeding 4,600 feet (1,400 metres), allows a wide range of subtropical and temperate plants to flourish. The following scheme for Tenerife illustrates the general zonal arrangement of vegetation with increase of altitude: (1) From sea level to 1,300 feet (400 metres) the climate resembles that of Egypt, and the characteristic plants of arid tracts are *Euphorbia* and *Sempervivum.* The better watered or irrigated lands yield crops such as bananas, oranges, coffee, dates, sugarcane, and tobacco. (2) From 1,300 to about 2,300 feet (700 metres) the climate resembles that of southern Italy, and the chief crops are wheat, barley, corn (maize), potatoes, and grapes. Where rainfall suffices, trees such as laurel, fig, walnut, almond, and eucalyptus thrive. (3) Between 2,300 and 4,000 feet (1,200 metres) is the main cloud layer, and the climate becomes appreciably cooler, except during southerly winds. Rather open formations and, in wetter places, quite dense stands of indigenous trees occur, including *Ardisia, Ilex, Rhamnus, Olea, Myrica,* and various species of laurel. (4) From 4,000 to about 6,000 feet (1,830 metres), athwart the normal edge of the cloud layer, the Canary pine (*Pinus canariensis*) is dominant, but tree heaths are fairly common. (5) Between 6,000 and 8,500 feet (2,600 metres), or above the cloud layer, the tree growth is replaced, first, by a narrow belt where *escobón* (*Cytisus proliferus*) and the gorselike *codeso* (Adenocarpus viscosus) provide important fodder supplies, and, then, by a wide zone where the pumice- and lava-strewn slopes are dotted with *retama,* a dark-green broom that bears white and pink flowers. (6) Above about 8,500 feet (2,600 metres) snow lies for many months, and vegetation is almost absent.

The people. The Guanches, who occupied the islands at the time of the Spanish invasion, no longer exist as a separate race. The present inhabitants, or Canarios, are scarcely distinguishable from the people of Spain. Spanish is the only language in use, and Spanish customs are stoutly maintained. Since 1900, when 80 percent of the Canarios could neither read nor write, education has progressed rapidly. Good schools are numerous, and there is a university (founded 1701) at La Laguna, Tenerife. The staple diet of many of the poorer people is composed of fish, potatoes, and *go fio,* which usually consists of corn or wheat roasted, salted, ground, and kneaded with water or milk.

Social conditions

In 1927 rivalry between the two chief ports, Las Palmas de Gran Canaria and Santa Cruz de Tenerife, caused the archipelago to be divided into two provinces. Appropriate civil and military provincial officials reside in both capitals. In addition, each of the seven main islands of the archipelago has its own council (*cabildo insular*) under a deputy civil governor. Roman Catholicism is the official religion; La Laguna and Las Palmas are episcopal sees in the archbishopric of Seville.

The economy. Because of the mild temperatures and richness of the volcanic soils, agriculture in the Canaries is usually profitable and varied. Until 1853 wine formed the staple product. In that year a grape disease caused by phylloxera (a plant louse) attacked the vineyards, and viticulture was soon largely replaced by cochineal production.

The cochineal insect, introduced in 1825, thrived on a local cactus. The boom imparted a lasting benefit to Canarian agriculture, as landowners undertook elaborate terracing and in places even broke up lava streams to expose the ancient soil buried beneath. The cochineal industry declined (because of competition from synthetic dyes) in the late 19th century in favour of the cultivation of sugarcane and later of bananas, tomatoes, potatoes, and various other vegetables and fruits. Potatoes, tomatoes, and bananas have become the main cash crops. Cuttlefish, sardines, mackerel, and anchovy are caught locally.

The Canaries lie athwart trade routes from Europe to South Africa and to Central and South America. Tourism, which is the chief industry, has grown rapidly on the five largest islands. The islands are connected by steamship services. Each of the two capital cities has an international airport and also maintains air services to Fuerteventura, Lanzarote, and La Palma.

HISTORY

The Romans learned of the Canaries through Juba, king of Mauretania, whose account of an expedition to the islands, made about 40 BC, was preserved by Plutarch and the elder Pliny. The latter mentions "Canaria, so called from the multitude of dogs [*canes*] of great size." Hierro, then the most westerly place known, was chosen in about AD 150 by Ptolemy for the prime meridian of longitude, and until the late 18th century some navigators continued to reckon from this line. In 1402 Gadifer de la Salle and Jean de Béthencourt sailed from La Rochelle and soon occupied Lanzarote. Béthencourt went to Cádiz for reinforcements and returned in 1404 with the title of king, which he had secured from Henry III of Castile. Thereupon he completed the conquest of Fuerteventura and Hierro, and in December 1406 he returned to Europe, leaving his nephew Maciot in charge of the islands. Eight years of misrule followed before Queen Catherine of Castile intervened. Between 1420 and 1460 a force sent by Prince Henry of Portugal subdued Gomera.

Spanish sovereignty

In 1479 the Treaty of Alcáçovas recognized Spanish sovereignty, and the bitter conquest of the three more populous islands then began. In 1483 the few hundred surviving Guanche warriors on Grand Canary surrendered; La Palma was finally conquered in 1491 and Tenerife in 1496. The islands were used by Columbus on his first transatlantic voyage and became an indispensable Spanish base on sea routes to America.

In 1833–34 the islands were linked by submarine cable to Europe and America. In 1936 Gen. Francisco Franco used the Canaries as the first base of the Nationalist revolution, going from there to Spanish Morocco.

(Ro.P.B./Ed.)

Castile

The name Castile refers to the central region of Spain, which occupies more than one-quarter of the area of peninsular Spain. Castile represents the limits reached at the end of the Middle Ages by the Kingdom of Castile proper and by the Moorish Kingdom of Toledo, which had been annexed to the Castilian crown at the end of the 11th century. The former is known as Old Castile (Castilla la Vieja). After the Middle Ages the name New Castile (Castilla la Nueva) was given to the former Kingdom of Toledo. The Sierra de Guadarrama forms the approximate dividing line between the two.

Between 1981 and 1983 Castile formed five autonomous communities. The historic region of Old Castile formed three autonomous communities. The largest part of the region became the autonomous community of Castile-León, which includes the modern provinces of Ávila, Soria, Valladolid, Burgos, León, Salamanca, Zamora, Palencia, and Segovia. The province of Santander, which lies north of the Cantabrian Mountains, became the autonomous community of Cantabria. The province of Logroño became the autonomous community of La Rioja. The region of New Castile formed two autonomous communities, Madrid and Castile-La Mancha, the latter comprising the modern provinces of Toledo, Ciudad Real, Cuenca, and Guadalajara.

PHYSICAL AND HUMAN GEOGRAPHY

Castile extends for about 300 miles (480 kilometres) from north to south and 160 miles from east to west. It consists of a vast central plateau, with an average altitude of about 2,500 feet (760 metres). This plateau has a natural frontier of high mountains on all sides, except on the borders of León and Murcia; it is also bisected by the Sierra de Guadarrama and Sierra de Grédos, which extend in a southwesterly direction across the central districts and form the dividing line between Old and New Castile. Geographically it also includes the high plains of León, toward the northwest, and of Murcia on the southeast. The existing frontier is marked on the north by the Cantabrian Mountains; on the east by the Sierra de la Demanda with its offshoots and by the Serrania de Cuenca; on the south by the Sierra Morena; and on the west by minor ranges that link the three more or less parallel chains of the Sierra de Grédos, Sierra de Guadalupe, and Sierra Morena. Three great rivers, the Douro, the Tagus, and Guadiana, flow westward into Portugal and finally reach the Atlantic; while the Ebro, which rises in the north of the kingdom, skirts the northeastern frontier on its way to the Mediterranean.

The climate of Old Castile is healthful but liable to severe cold and heat. Snow falls early and lies late in the mountains, and there is a heavy rainfall in the northwest. New Castile has a still more rigorous climate, for although the mean annual temperature is about 59° F (15° C), the summer heat in the valleys is peculiarly oppressive, and the highlands are swept by scorching or icy gales, laden with dust. The rainfall rarely exceeds 10 inches (254 millimetres) in a year.

Soil conditions in the central plateau

In both the Castiles the central plateau has a naturally fertile soil, but drought is common, owing to the insufficient volume of the rivers and the failure of the Spaniards to extend the fine system of irrigation that the Moors originated. Certain districts, indeed, in which a layer of heavy loam underlies the porous and friable surface, are able to retain the moisture that elsewhere is absorbed. Such land is found in Palencia and in the Mesa de Ocaña, where it yields abundant crops; and many of the northern mountains are well wooded. But vast tracts of land are useless except as pasture for sheep, and even the sheep are driven by the severe winters to migrate yearly into Extremadura. The normal Castilian landscape is an arid and sterile steppe, with scarcely a tree or spring of water; many of the villages are built of sunburnt unbaked bricks, which share the dusty brownish-gray tint of the soil. Especially characteristic is the great plain of La Mancha.

HISTORY

The name Castile—probably meaning "land of castles"—is first found in 800, when it was applied to a small district at the foot of the Cantabrian Mountains in the extreme north of the modern province of Burgos. This territory expanded during the 9th century but remained broken up into petty counties, whose rulers were nominated by the kings of Asturias and Leon, until these counties were united by Fernán González (932–970), the first count of all Castile. He contrived to make the new county hereditary in his family and thus secured a measure of autonomy for it under the kings of Leon. In the time of Fernán González the capital of the county was established at Burgos, where it was to remain, and expansion southward into Moorish territory occurred. Under counts García Fernández (*c.* 970–1005) and Sancho García (1005–17) the territory of Castile reached as far as the Douro (Spanish Duero) River. Relations with the kings of Leon, still nominally suzerains of Castile, were frequently bad.

The urge toward independence shown by the counts and people of Castile from the beginning has been variously explained. It seems likely that the regions conquered by the counts of Castile from the Moors were generally repopulated by emigrants from Cantabria, who had scarcely been affected by Arabic culture and custom, whereas in Leon there was a large immigration of Mozarabs from the Moorish areas further south, thus establishing marked social differences between the two regions. The country of Castile rejected the ancient Visigothic legal code (*Forum Judicum*), the basis of Leonese law, in preference for local customary law. Small, free proprietors were prominent among its people, and a considerable number of minor nobles (*infanzones*), rather than the traditional magnate families of Leon, made up the Castilian nobility. Later, however, the Castilians came to think of themselves as truer representatives than the Leonese of the Visigothic tradition.

The Visigothic tradition

In 1029 Castile lost its autonomy and passed into the hands of Sancho III (the Great) of Navarre. On his death (1035) he left it, as a kingdom, to his son, Ferdinand I. Under Ferdinand it was first united with Leon (1037–65), though the seniority of Leon in the partnership was still recognized. Castile was again united with Leon (1072–1157) under Alfonso VI and Alfonso VII, but thereafter the two kingdoms once more separated. The political and military hegemony of Castile over Leon was established by Alfonso VIII of Castile (1158–1214) who, in 1188, forced the king of Leon to do homage to him. By now, Castilian rule extended far south of the Tagus River and eastward to the modern frontiers of Aragon. The Leonese kings, however, never accepted the claims made by Castile to suzerainty, and Alfonso IX of Leon refused, in consequence, to support Alfonso VIII in his wars against the Almohads. Castilian pursuit of political hegemony over Leon, therefore, partially weakened the Christian front against the Muslims. In 1230 Ferdinand III, already king of Castile, succeeded to the Leonese throne, and both crowns were finally united under Castilian leadership.

An attempt by Castile to annex Portugal by force in 1383–85 failed, but a Castilian prince, Ferdinand of Trastámara, was successfully placed on the Aragonese throne, partly as a result of Castilian financial support and military force, in 1412. This move foreshadowed the personal union of the two crowns under Ferdinand and Isabella. The Kingdom of Navarre was annexed by Castile in 1515.

Castilian political hegemony in Spain

Castilian political hegemony in Spain was an accomplished fact from the middle of the 12th century, and the chanceries of European courts in the later Middle Ages frequently identify Castile with Hispania. The final conquest of most of Andalusia was carried out by Castilian armies in the time of Ferdinand III. The literary language of Spain after its unification was the Castilian vernacular, and the centre of political and administrative power since then has always been in Castile. Nevertheless, opposition to the political hegemony of Castile from the other regions, which enjoyed complete or partial independence in the Middle Ages, has always remained strong and is still a live political issue, especially since the centres of modern industrial strength in Spain are now largely outside Castile, which, for geographic reasons, is an economically backward area. It has been claimed that medieval Castile was, in all respects, a more progressive kingdom than its neighbours, with a more developed sense of the unity and destiny of Spain. Some of these claims seem exaggerated. The real reason for the dominating part that Castile has played in Spanish history may well have been the superior martial spirit and military organization of its people.

(P.E.R./Ed.)

Catalonia

Catalonia (Spanish Cataluña; Catalan Catalunya) is an autonomous community of Spain comprising the four modern provinces of Barcelona, Gerona, Lérida, and Tarragona, with an area of 12,328 square miles (31,929 square kilometres). It is the richest and most highly industrialized part of the country. Formerly a principality of the crown of Aragon, Catalonia has always played an important role in the history of the Iberian Peninsula and since the 17th century has been the centre of a separatist movement often dominating Spanish affairs.

PHYSICAL AND HUMAN GEOGRAPHY

Catalonia occupies a triangular area in the northeastern corner of Spain, bordered by France and Andorra in the north, by Aragon in the west, by Valencia in the south, and by the Mediterranean in the east. A mountainous zone, with more than one-third of its population concentrated in the city of Barcelona, Catalonia is cut off by mountains to the south and west; consequently for much of its history the region has exhibited closer ties with southern France than with the rest of Spain. Catalan, the native language, is spoken also in Roussillon, north of the Pyrenees, and is quite different from Castilian Spanish.

The coast, which is partly sandy, partly rocky, extends about 240 miles (190 kilometres); its chief harbours are those of the capital, Barcelona, of Mataró, of Rosas, and of Tarragona. The surface is much broken by spurs of the Pyrenees, the direction of which is generally south. Running southwest to northeast, and united on the north with one of the offsets of the Pyrenees, is the range of the Sierra Llena, which bisects Catalonia and forms its central watershed. The principal rivers are the Ter, the Llobrégat, and the Ebro, which all run into the Mediterranean. None of them is navigable. The climate, in spite of frequent mists and rains, sudden changes of temperature, and occasional great midday heat, is healthful and favourable to vegetation. The dwarf palm, orange, lime, and olive grow in the warmer tracts; and on the higher grounds the thorn apple, pomegranate, myrtle, esparto, and heaths flourish. There is much woodland, but meadows and pastures are rare. Corn, millet, rye, flax, licorice, and fruits of all sorts—especially nuts, almonds, oranges, figs, walnuts, and chestnuts—are produced. Wheat sufficient for one-fourth of the population is grown, and the vine is extensively cultivated. Few cattle but numbers of sheep, goats, and swine are reared. Game is plentiful, and the fisheries on the coast are excellent. The wines are for the most part rough and strong, though some are very good, especially when matured. They are much used to adulterate those of the Porto region of Portugal or, after undergoing the blending operation termed *compage,* are passed off as Bordeaux wines in France. The best of them, *priorato,* is chiefly known in England, under the disguise of second- or third-rate port; it was much used in the military hospitals of America during the Civil War.

The Catalonians are known for their national pride and strong revolutionary spirit. They are distinct in origin from the other inhabitants of Spain, from whom they differ in their dialect and costume. In their great energy and their love of enterprise they resemble the Basques. Irrigation, careful husbandry, and railroad communications have much developed the resources of their country, in themselves excellent; and there are many manufacturing towns and industrial establishments.

HISTORY

Catalonia was one of the first Roman possessions in Spain, forming the northeastern portion of Hispania Tarraconensis. Occupied during the 5th century by the Goths, it was taken by the Moors in 712, but Charlemagne began the reconquest later in the 8th century, establishing the March of Gothia as a Frankish outpost. Gerona was taken in 785 and Barcelona in 801. This part of Catalonia was then incorporated into the kingdom of the west Franks, but Frankish suzerainty over Catalonia became only nominal and was completely rejected during the reign of Count Borrell (died 991). From 1137, when Count Ramôn Berenguer IV was betrothed to Petronila, queen of Aragon, Catalonia and Aragon were united under the same ruler. In the 13th and 14th centuries Catalonia monopolized the trade of the western Mediterranean, and Catalan mercenaries intervened decisively in Italy and Greece. Catalan interests, which differed widely from those of Aragon, dominated the union until 1420, when the male line of the counts of Barcelona became extinct. Dissatisfaction in Catalonia with the new Trastámara dynasty increased after 1412 until, during the reign of John II, it developed into a full-scale, but unsuccessful, rebellion (1462–72).

Incorporation into the kingdom of the west Franks

During the 16th century, after the marriage of John II's son Ferdinand with Isabella of Castile had brought about the unification of Spain, Catalonia was relegated to a position of secondary importance in Spanish affairs. The Turks seriously interfered with trade in the western Mediterranean, on which Catalan prosperity depended; and the exploitation of Spanish America was reserved for Castile. By the 17th century the conflict of interests between Catalonia and Castile combined with the decline of the Spanish monarchy's prestige to produce the first of those separatist movements by which the history of Catalonia has since been characterized.

The trouble was caused by an economic crisis during the reign of Philip IV. To raise funds, the crown wanted to impose on the whole of Spain a degree of fiscal and administrative unity incompatible with the maintenance of the *fueros* of the lands of the crown of Aragon. The Catalans were determined to resist such efforts of centralization and regarded the shortage of money as due to waste caused by inefficiency at Madrid and rash expenditure on foreign wars. The deadlock was unresolved when, in 1635, war broke out between Spain and France. This aggravated the King's financial position and led to the billeting in Catalonia of "foreign" Castilian troops, whose behaviour initiated a secessionist revolt (June 1640). The rebellious Catalans placed themselves under the protection of the French king Louis XIII, and civil war ensued in which French support was mainly responsible for keeping the Catalan insurgents in the field. The fighting did not end until 1659 when, by the Treaty of the Pyrenees, Philip IV came to terms with the French.

In 1705, again motivated largely by a desire to ensure preservation of its *fueros,* Catalonia, together with Aragon and Valencia, declared its support for the archduke Charles in the War of the Spanish Succession. In 1714, however, Catalonia was completely subjugated by Philip V's forces, and its constitution and privileges were abrogated. Catalonia subsequently lost nearly all its previous autonomy, but it gained by the encouragement given by the Bourbons to industrial development, while the termination of Castile's monopoly of the trade with Spanish America provided a fresh impulse for Catalan commerce and shipping.

Catalan separatism reemerged in the 19th century in rural areas in the support given to Carlism and in the towns in the demands of the manufacturers for high tariffs against British and French competition. The Catalan resurgence, however, really began with the literary Renaixensa of the 1850s. This, at first, involved little more than competitions between Catalan poets and reviving medieval festivals such as the Jocs Florals, but during the 1860s, more serious efforts were made to revive the use of Catalan (then only spoken in rural areas) as a living language, including the establishment of a Catalan newspaper and a theatre for Catalan plays. Catalan nationalism became a serious political force after 1876, when the defeat of the Carlists led the church to transfer its support to the new,

Reemergence of Catalan separatism

rising movement for regional autonomy. It then became a predominantly right-wing movement.

The loss of Cuba in 1898, a dramatic revelation of Spain's political and economic decline, served to revive Catalonian separatism. The electoral victory won in 1901 by the new party, the Lliga Regionalista, showed that Catalan nationalism was politically a force of consequence, and the struggle for autonomy commenced in earnest. By 1913 a slight degree of home rule had been obtained under the *ley de mancomunidades,* but this measure was repealed 10 years later by Primo de Rivera, who attacked all manifestations of Catalan separatism. Primo de Rivera's policy led to the formation of a left-wing coalition party, the Esquerra Republicana, led by Francesc Macià. The Esquerra won a sweeping victory in the municipal elections of April 1931, and two days later Macià proclaimed a Catalan republic. Thereafter a compromise was worked out with the central republic established at Madrid, and in September 1932 the statute of autonomy for Catalonia was passed by the constituent Cortes. Catalonia played a prominent part in the history of the second republic in Spain and in the civil war of 1936–39. The nationalist victory in 1939 meant the loss of autonomy, and Gen. Francisco Franco's government adopted a repressive policy toward Catalan nationalism. Conversely, Catalonia was the most notable centre of opposition to Franco.

The establishment of democratic rule under the constitutional monarchy of Juan Carlos did not decrease Catalonia's desire for autonomy, and in September 1977 limited autonomy was granted to Catalonia. On October 25, 1979, autonomy was ratified by a regional plebiscite, thereby creating the autonomous community of Catalonia.

(B.J.R./Ed.)

Extremadura

Extremadura (Estremadura) is a region of western Spain, once economically important because of its rich winter pastures. Extremadura comprises the provinces of Cáceres and Badajoz, with an area of 16,062 square miles (41,600 square kilometres). It is to be distinguished from the Portuguese province of Estremadura, which occupies the central coastal region of Portugal. In 1981 Extremadura became one of the 17 autonomous communities of Spain.

PHYSICAL AND HUMAN GEOGRAPHY

Extremadura is bounded on the north by León and Old Castile, east by New Castile, south by Andalusia, and west by the Portuguese provinces of Beira and Alentejo, which separate it from Portuguese Estremadura. Extremadura consists mainly of a tableland separated from León and Old Castile by the lofty Sierra de Gredos, the plateau of Béjar, and the Sierra de Gata, which form an almost continuous barrier along the northern frontier, with summits ranging from 6,000 to more than 8,500 feet (1,830 to 2,590 metres) in altitude. On the south the comparatively low range of the Sierra Morena constitutes the frontier of Andalusia; on the east and west there is a still more gradual transition to the plateau of New Castile and the central plains of Portugal. The tableland of Extremadura is itself bisected from east to west by a line of mountains, the Sierras of San Pedro, Montánchez, and Guadalupe (4,000–6,000 feet), which separate its northern half, drained by the Tagus River, from its southern half, drained by the Guadiana. The Tagus and Guadiana flow from east to west through a monotonous country, often almost uninhabited and covered with a thin growth of shrubs and grass. A characteristic feature of this tableland is the vast heaths of gum cistus and lavender. The climate in summer is hot but not unhealthful, except in the swamps, which occur along the Guadiana. Sheep farming is the most important of Extremaduran industries. Immense herds of swine are bred and constitute a great source of food to the inhabitants, the pork, bacon, and hams being in high esteem. The beech, oak, and chestnut woods afford an abundance of food for swine, and there are numerous plantations of olive, cork, and fruit trees.

Tableland

In character and physical type, the people of this region are less easily classified than those of other Spanish provinces. Their failure to develop a distinctive local type of character and civilization is perhaps the result of the adverse economic history of their country. The two great waterways that form the natural outlet for Extremaduran commerce flow to the Atlantic through a foreign and, for centuries, a hostile territory.

HISTORY

Historically, this name—popularly supposed to derive from Latin *terra extrema et dura*—was given during static periods of the Christian reconquest of the Iberian Peninsula to whatever then happened to be the zones bordering on Moorish territory. Thus in the 10th and 11th centuries the border approximated to the line of the Duero, or Douro, River from Soria in the east to the Atlantic Coast near Coimbra. Then, during the reign of Alfonso VI of Leon and Castile, the name Extremadura was transferred (*c.* 1086) to a newly conquered region to the south, which included Salamanca, Segovia, and Ávila. Leon, following its southern expansion between 1157 and 1230, also had a province called Extremadura which stretched southward from Ciudad Rodrigo to beyond Badajoz. In the 12th and early 13th centuries, therefore, both Leon and Castile possessed Extremaduran provinces administered as separate entities by each kingdom. Later in the reign of Ferdinand III of Castile and Leon this separate administration was abandoned, and, from the later Middle Ages, the term was applied to a region only slightly larger than the combined area of the two modern provinces. (P.E.R./Ed.)

Galicia

Galicia (the ancient Gallaecia or Callaecia) is a former captaincy-general and a former kingdom, countship, and province in the northwestern angle of Spain. Galicia is bounded on the north by the Bay of Biscay, east by León and Asturias, south by Portugal, and west by the Atlantic Ocean. It has an area of 11,256 square miles (29,153 square kilometres). In 1833 Galicia was divided for administrative purposes into the provinces of La Coruña, Lugo, Orense, and Pontevedra. In 1981 the historic region of Galicia became one of the 17 autonomous communities of Spain, retaining its four provinces.

PHYSICAL AND HUMAN GEOGRAPHY

The highland north of the headwaters of the Miño forms the sole connecting link between the Cantabrians properly so called and the mountains of central and western Galicia. The average elevation of the province is considerable, and the maximum height (6,593 feet [2,009 metres]) is reached in the Peña Trevinca on the eastern border of Orense.

The principal river is the Miño (Portuguese Minho; Latin Minius; so named, it is said, from the minium, or vermilion, found in its bed). Rising near Mondoñedo, within 25 miles (40 kilometres) of the northern coast, the Miño enters the Atlantic near the port of Guardia, after a course of 170 miles south and southwest. Of its numerous affluents the most important is the Sil. Other rivers include the Tambre, the Ulla, and the Lerez, or Ler, which falls into the Atlantic by estuaries, or *rias,* called, respectively, Ria de Muros y Noya, Ria de Arosa, and Ria de Pontevedra.

According to Eratosthenes (276–196 BC) the entire population of the peninsula was at one time called Galatae. The region properly called Gallaecia, bounded on the south by Douro and on the east by the Navia, was first entered by the Roman legions under Decius Junius Brutus in 137–136 BC, but the final subjugation cannot be placed earlier than the time of Augustus (31 BC–AD 14).

Features of the coastline

The coastline of Galicia, extending to about 240 miles, is bold and deeply indented, presenting a large number of secure harbours. The Eo, which bounds Galicia on the east, has a deep estuary, the Rivadeo, or Ribadeo, which is a good harbour. Vivero Bay and the Ria del Barquero y Váres are of a similar character, while the harbour of Ferrol is an important naval station. On the opposite side of Betanzos Bay is the great port of Corunna, or Coruña. The principal port on the western coast is formed by the deep and sheltered Bay of Vigo, but there are also good roadsteads at Corcubion, at Marin, and at Carril.

The rainfall is exceptionally heavy, and snow lies on some of the high ground for a considerable portion of the year. Much timber is grown on the highlands, and the rich valley pastures support large herds of cattle and swine. In the lowland districts good crops of corn, wheat, barley, oats, and rye, as well as of turnips and potatoes, are obtained. The *dehesas,* or moorlands, abound in game, and fish are plentiful in all the streams. The mineral resources of the province, which are considerable, were known to some extent to the ancients. Strabo (*c.* 63 BC–AD 21) speaks of its gold and tin, and Pliny (AD 23–79) mentions the *gemma Gallaica,* a precious stone. Galicia is also remarkable for the number of its sulfur and other warm springs, the most important of which are those at Lugo and Orense.

HISTORY

In the Middle Ages Galicia was one of the constituent kingdoms of the crown of Castile. Its name is derived from the Gallaeci, who lived there when the region was conquered by the Roman legions *c.* 137 BC. The Gallaeci were probably not Iberians. Some historians consider that the region was heavily settled by Celts, but this has been disputed. In Roman and Visigothic times Galicia stretched south to the Douro and eastward to beyond the city of León. From *c.* 410 it was an independent kingdom under the Suebi until 585 when the latter were finally destroyed by Leovigild. After 711 its population was greatly increased by an influx of Visigothic refugee settlers who were able to establish themselves in its river basins. The language of Galicia is closely related to Portuguese, and the existence of a separate Galician-Portuguese language can be discerned by the early 11th century. By the 13th century there was a flourishing tradition of lyric poetry in Galicia, and, as a result, Galician-Portuguese became the language even of Castilian lyric poets until late in the 14th century.

Despite its clear ethnic, linguistic, and geographic differences from the rest of Spain, and its remoteness from the centre, Galicia rarely sought political independence. As a result of Alfonso III's division of his kingdom, it was ruled by Ordoño II as king (910–914), by Sancho I as a refugee (926–929), and by García, son of Ferdinand I, as king (1065–71). After 1369 it was unwilling to accept the usurpation of Henry II of Trastámara and, for a time, seemed disposed to accept Ferdinand of Portugal as king. Probably the possession of the national shrine of St. James of Compostela (Santiago de Compostela) from the 9th century attached the Galicians, for religious and economic reasons, firmly to the central kingdoms. In modern times there has been a revival of interest in the Galician language and culture. (P.E.R./Ed.)

León

León is a traditional region of Spain. In 1981 León became one of the provinces of the autonomous community of Castile-León.

PHYSICAL AND HUMAN GEOGRAPHY

In the northern part of the province is the high Cantabrian range, the highest peak of which is the Torre Cerredo (8,688 feet [2,648 metres]). This part of the province also contains the passes of Tarna, San Glorio, Pontón, and Pajares, which have links with Santander and Asturias. The natural regions are El Bierzo, a lowland where mining has replaced agriculture; La Montaña, comprising the judicial districts of Murias, Vecilla, and Riaño; and La Meseta, a dry desert with fertile strips, such as that along the Órbigo River. The climate is extreme continental. The main catchment area is the basin of the Esla, a tributary of the Duero (Douro), in which is situated the large dam at Ricobayo. Tributaries of the Esla are the Cea, Porma, Bernesga, and Órbigo. The second most important river basin is that of the Sil, which runs through Bierzo. Other rivers are the Sella and the Cares.

The main crops are cereals, flax, and hops, León being the most important producer of hops in Spain. Timber resources include oak, beech, and chestnut. Cattle, donkeys, and sheep are bred. There are deposits of anthracite, iron, bituminous coal, and mica; Ponferrada is a great coal- and iron-mining area. The considerable mineral resources offer prospects for industrial development. Chemical factories have been established for the manufacture of antibiotics.

The city of León

The city of León is the capital of the province and is located on the Bernesga, 83 miles (134 kilometres) north-northwest of Valladolid by road. It is on the Madrid–Oviedo road and railway; there are other railway lines to La Coruña and to Bilbao. It developed from the camp of the Roman seventh legion, its modern name being a corruption of the Latin *legio.* A monumental city with a wealth of artistic interest, it attracts large numbers of tourists. Especially remarkable are the fine Gothic cathedral, noteworthy for its stained-glass windows known as the Pulchra Leonina, the Romanesque collegiate church of San Isidoro, and the Renaissance-style church of San Marcos. After recapture from the Muslims, León became the capital of the Kingdom of Asturias and Leon in the 10th century when García I transferred his court there from Oviedo. An important market town on the pilgrimage route to Santiago, León exercised considerable political, cultural, and economic influence during the Middle Ages. The street names of the old part of the city recall the offices and structure of the medieval town. The economic life of the city declined in the 16th century and did not revive until the 19th with the development of mining. By the mid-20th century León was resurgent, with a new city and increasing industrialization.

HISTORY

In the later Middle Ages, the Kingdom of Leon covered the area of the modern provinces of León, Palencia, Valladolid, Zamora, and Salamanca, together with the Asturian province of Oviedo. The medieval kings of Leon also ruled Galicia and as much of the county of Portugal as had been reconquered before that country achieved independence in 1140. They were, in name at least, suzerains of the county of Castile until 1035. The group of dialects spoken and written in medieval Leon (Asturo-Leonese) were clearly demarcated from the language of Castile. Today these dialects survive strongly only in Asturias and, to some extent, in rural León as far south as Zamora. There is a popular literature and music of folktales, ballads, and other songs.

The rise of the medieval Leonese kingdom began with García I (909–914), who set up his court on the site of the former Roman permanent camp of the Legio VII Gemina. The period of Leonese hegemony in Christian Spain nominally lasted until the death of Alfonso VII (1157), but it had, long before, been seriously undermined by the conquests of Sancho the Great (1000–35) of Navarre and by the elevation, on his death, of Castile from county to kingdom. During the whole of the 10th century, when the Caliphate of Córdoba was at its most powerful, Leon lost ground in the struggle with the Moors, and its kings often had to accept a de facto submission to the caliphs. Leon, however, had inherited from the Asturian monarchy a strong attachment to Visigothic tradition, and its rulers, sometimes taking the title of emperor or king of all Spain, tried to further the Reconquest wherever possible. The second period in Leonese history runs from 1157 to 1230, when the kingdom was ruled, in separation from Castile, by its own kings Ferdinand II (1157–88) and Alfonso IX (1188–1230). Relations with Castile were rarely friendly, but Leon was stable during this time and won notable victories over the Moors in Leonese Extremadura. After the final union with Castile (1230), Leonese political and administrative institutions were, for a time, maintained, and the records of the Cortes show that some sense of the separate identity of Leon survived into the first half of the 14th century. In modern times, however, the revival of separatist feelings in various parts of Spain has awakened no response in Leon, now a predominantly agricultural and rather backward region.

Final union with Castile (1230)

During the first century of its existence there was a large influx of Mozarabic immigrants into Leon. These introduced strong Arabic linguistic and cultural influences into the kingdom. Modern Spanish historiography—concerned often to justify medieval Castilian separatism—has tended to portray medieval Leon as an archaizing, Byzantine type of state overready to compromise with the Moors. The evidence for this is not wholly convincing. Leon successfully bore the brunt of the caliphate's attacks and seems to have been the first peninsular kingdom to evolve popular parliamentary institutions. (P.E.R./M.B.F./Ed.)

Murcia

PHYSICAL AND HUMAN GEOGRAPHY

Murcia is part of the ancient kingdom of Murcia, made up of Albacete and Murcia, and in 1981 it became one of the 17 autonomous communities of Spain. It is situated mainly in the Penibetic mountain (Sistema Penibético) region. The Segura forms the basis for irrigation in the Murcian plain; its principal tributary is the Guadalentin. On the coast lies the Mar Menor, a large saltwater lagoon of 66 square miles (170 square kilometres). National highways and railways cross the province. It is an important producer of lemons and oranges. Other crops include esparto, hemp, cotton, saffron, and olives. There are rich deposits of zinc, lead, and sulfur; copper and tin are also mined. There is a large oil refinery at Escombreras on the coast. Other industries include the manufacture of chemicals and vegetable canning. Ports include the naval base at Cartagena, with the Bazan shipyards, and the fishing port at Mazarrón. There is a paratroop training base at Alcantarilla. Main towns include Lorca, Yecla, Cieza, and Caravaca.

The town of Murcia

The town of Murcia, the seat of a bishopric, is situated at the confluence of the Segura and Guadalentín (Sangonera) rivers, in a rich and fertile area known as the *huerta.* The Segura divides the city in two, the more important part lying on the left bank. The cathedral (Sta. Maria) dates from the 14th to 16th century but was restored in the 18th. It contains the fine chapel of the Vélez family (1507). In the Ermita de Jesús are the majority of the Passion sculptures of Francisco Salcillo; they attract many visitors during Holy Week. The University of Murcia was founded in 1915.

Murcia is a communications centre and an agricultural trade centre for citrus fruits, almonds, cereals, olive oil, and pepper cultivated in the *huerta.* The silk industry, which dates from Moorish times, is still carried on; manufactures of woollen, linen, and cotton goods, saltpetre, flour, leather, aluminum products, furniture, and hats have been established.

HISTORY

There was a town at Murcia before the Roman occupation of southern Spain in the 3rd century BC, but its name then, and during the Roman rule, is unknown. Its name is first mentioned in the histories and chronicles of the Muslims, and, according to the Arab geographer Yaqut, it was founded in 825 by the Umayyad amir of Córdoba, ʿAbd ar-Raḥmān II, who made it the capital of the province. After the fall of the Caliphate of Córdoba in 1031, it came under the control of Almería, and then of Valencia, until in 1063 its ruler, ʿAbd ar-Raḥmān ben Ṭāhir, declared himself independent.

The kingdom's very complicated history is consistent in representing a nationalistic interpretation of Islām. The ruler ʿAbd ar-Raḥmān ben Ṭāhir declared himself independent in 1063, though to preserve the fiction of the religious unity of the caliphate he took the title not of king (*malik*) but of minister (*hachib*). An attempt by the ruler of the *ṭāʾifa* (petty kingdom) of Seville to annex Murcia in 1079 failed because of a rebellion by the ruler's own vizier. For about 10 years thereafter Murcia played an intermediary role between the Almoravids and the Castilians, but in the end religious sympathies inclined it toward the former. The Almoravid caliph Yūsuf ibn Tāshufīn, who brought the quarrelling *ṭāʾifa*s under his control, took possession of Murcia in 1092, incorporating it into his empire.

The Almoravids imposed a completely military regime, which provoked discontent. In 1144 a former king of Zaragoza, Abu Ch'afar ben Hud (Zafadola), started a rising that became general. Involved internal struggles led Murcia to submit to Zafadola's authority, exercised by one of his lieutenants, Abd Allah ben Iyad, who administered the territory as a kingdom. Iyad contrived to unite Valencia and Murcia in a single kingdom after Zafadola's death. In 1147 Iyad was succeeded by Mohammed ben Mardanish. For 20 years, Mardanish led the struggle against a new invading force from North Africa, the Almohads. But a family quarrel, begun in 1168, led to the downfall of the kingdom, and, on dying, Mardanish recommended that his sons submit to the Almohads. In spite of this, Murcia retained an autonomous administrative system; it was conserved by the Castilians when they took possession of the territory, almost without a struggle, in 1243. (M.B.F./L.S.Fe./Ed.)

Navarre

Navarre (Navarra) is a traditional region of northern Spain. Originally formed by the Basques into a kingdom in the 9th century, it was not annexed to the Spanish crown until 1512. Under the Nationalist government it enjoyed a limited economic autonomy. In the remote districts, Lower and Upper Navarrese (Basque subdialects) and Navarro (Aragonese dialect) are still spoken. Navarre is one of the 17 autonomous communities of Spain and consists of Navarra province. It is bounded by the French Pyrenees to the north, Guipúzcoa province to the northwest, Álava and Logroño to the west, Zaragoza (Saragossa) to the south and southeast, and the Aragonese province of Huesca to the east.

PHYSICAL AND HUMAN GEOGRAPHY

Navarre has a great variety of scenery as it stretches from the western Pyrenees to the Ebro steppes. A tripartite division is clear: the Pyrenean sector, the central basins and hills, the southern plateaus and steppes. The Pyrenean sector consists of a tangled relief of forested mountains and well-watered valleys. The ranges consist largely of sandstones with rounded and more subdued relief (seldom exceeding 4,000 feet [1,200 metres]) than the central Pyrenees. The chief Pyrenean road pass is the Col de Roncesvalles (Puerto de Ibañeta; 3,468 feet), with two others to the northwest, the Puertos de Maya (Otsondo) and de Vera. The region is largely drained by the Bidasoa, an Atlantic stream. The lower basin, called Cinco Villas, has a relatively dense population in scattered hamlets. Iron workings have encouraged small metallurgical industries at Vera and Elizondo, linked by a narrow-gauge railway to Irún; but the dense stands of timber and pastoralism are the main sources of wealth.

The central depression, now utilized by the railway from Vitoria to Pamplona and then by a narrow-gauge line to Sangüesa on the Aragón river, has played a vital role in Navarrese history. It has united the diverse Pyrenean valleys and focussed commerce on the provincial capital, Pamplona. In this climatically transitional zone, cereal cultivation mingles with forest lands and stock rearing, and settlements become more nucleated into villages.

The southern half of Navarre consists essentially of foothills and steppes through which the valleys of the Ega, Arga, and Aragón run centripetally to the Ebro. The position of Tudela near the confluence of these valleys explains its role as a regional market town. The landscape is more arid and monotonous, with cultivation of cereals and large nucleated settlements; *e.g.,* Estella and Tafalla. Las Bárdenas on the southeastern borders is true steppe.

HISTORY

The Kingdom of Navarre

The Kingdom of Navarre was formed out of a part of the territory occupied by the Vascones (*i.e.,* the Basques and Gascons), who lived on the southern slope of the western Pyrenees and part of the shore of the Bay of Biscay. In the course of the 6th century there was a considerable emigration of Basques to the north of the Pyrenees. The cause is supposed to have been the pressure put upon them by the attacks of the Visigoth kings in Spain. The name of Navarre is derived by etymologists from *nava,* a flat valley surrounded by hills, and *erri,* a region or country. It began to appear as the name of part of Vasconia toward the end of the Visigoth epoch in Spain in the 7th century. Its early history is more than obscure. The first historic king of Navarre was Sancho Garcés, who ruled at Pamplona in the early years of the 10th century. Under him and his immediate successors, Navarre reached the height of its power and its extension. When the kingdom was at its height it included all the modern province of the name: the northern slope of the western Pyrenees called by the Spaniards the Ultrapuertos ("country beyond the passes"), and now known as French Navarre; the Basque Provinces; the Bureba, the valley between the Basque Mountains and the Montes de Oca to the north of Burgos; the Rioja and Tarazona in the upper valley of the Ebro. In the 12th century the kings of Castile gradually annexed the Rioja and Álava. About the year 1200 Alfonso VIII of Castile annexed the other two Basque provinces, Biscay (Vizcaya) and Guipúzcoa. Tarazona remained in possession of Aragon. After 1234 Navarre, though the crown was claimed by the kings of Aragon, passed by marriage to a succession of French rulers. In 1516 Spanish Navarre was finally annexed by Ferdinand the Catholic. French Navarre survived as an independent kingdom until it was united to the crown of France by Henry IV, founder of the Bourbon dynasty. From 1510 until 1833, when it was fully incorporated with Spain, Navarre was a viceroyalty.

The whole kingdom was mountainous except for the Tudela salient in the southeast, where the dry plains called Las Bárdenas provided an important grazing region. Though Navarre at an early date ceased to have a frontier with the Moors, a considerable Moorish population lived there, notably in Tudela. The Navarrese Moors were allowed to serve in the army and also provided a source of skilled artisans. Large Jewish aljamas (congregations) existed in the chief towns and were protected by the Navarrese kings when persecution became serious elsewhere. Another important element were the *francos*—mostly French and Gascon immigrants—who inhabited separate quarters in Pamplona and other towns. Their relations with the native Navarrese were often strained.

Despite its small size in the later Middle Ages, Navarre had an important part in international politics, not only because of its rulers' involvement in French affairs but also because it controlled the main pass into Spain in the western Pyrenees and was a buffer state between Gascony, Castile, and Aragon. The chief pilgrim roads from the north to Santiago de Compostela thus traversed it. From its earliest days to 1234, after which a succession of French dynasties ruled Navarre, the kingdom's history fell within a wholly Spanish context and was closely associated with that of Aragon. Afterward strong French political and institutional influences can be detected.

The route to Santiago de Compostela

Pamplona was Moorish territory after 711, but the Basque magnates of the region early achieved some degree of autonomy and (*c.* 798) one of them, Iñigo Arista, established himself as an independent ruler there and, for a time, accepted Frankish suzerainty. By the time of García Iñíguez (*c.* 860–880) this dynasty was strong enough to assume regal titles and to establish diplomatic and family relations with Asturias. Under Sancho Garcés (905–925) the rulers of Pamplona extended their dominions south of the Ebro, capturing Nájera and much of La Rioja. By a combination of diplomatic dexterity and military strength the kingdom survived, relatively unscathed, the heyday of the caliphate in the 10th century. During the reign of Sancho III the Great (1005–35), the Navarrese were able to establish a brief hegemony over all Christian Spain. Sancho's empire was, however, short-lived, and in 1076 Sancho Ramírez of Aragon (1063–94) occupied Pamplona.

Until 1134 Navarre was then ruled by the Aragonese crown. It recovered its independence when the Navarrese proclaimed García V the Restorer (1134–50) as king. An entirely new orientation was given to Navarrese history in 1234 when Sancho VII (1194–1234) was succeeded by his nephew, Theobald I (1234–53), count of Champagne, and a succession of French rulers with important possessions in France ruled the kingdom. Historically the most famous of these French rulers was Charles II the Bad (1349–87), count of Évreux, under whom Navarre became internationally of great importance because of the King's involvement in French politics and the spread of the Hundred Years' War to the kingdoms of the Iberian Peninsula. Charles himself had ambitions to recover for his kingdom the territories in Spain that had belonged to Sancho the Great. He has been criticized for the brazen way in which he constantly altered Navarrese foreign policy to meet rapidly changing foreign pressures. Charles managed, however, to retain the loyalty of his subjects and to preserve the independence of Navarre.

The reign of Charles III (1387–1425) was relatively tranquil, but John II of Aragon became ruler of Navarre by marriage (1425–79), and the kingdom was then the scene, for years, of civil war among his supporters, those of his son and heir, Charles, prince of Viana, and other factions favouring union with France or with Castile. In 1484 the throne passed to John II of Albret, but independence had now become impossible due to Navarre's position between two major, mutually hostile states, France and Spain. In 1512 Ferdinand the Catholic occupied the Spanish portion of Navarre, which was formally annexed to the Castilian crown in 1516 but retained its status, institutions, and law as an independent kingdom until the 1800s.

In the later Middle Ages Navarre was divided administratively into five *merindades*—La Ribera (Tudela), Sangüesa, Pamplona (La Montaña), Estella, and Allién Puertos; in the last the functions of royal *merinao* were carried out by the *castelán* of St. Jean-Pied-de-Port. Under the *merinos* were the *sozmerinos* and, in the towns, the *bailes.* The chief military officer of the kingdom was the *alférez.* The treasury was partly modelled on the French system under a *recibidor general* or *tesorero,* with *recibidores* in each *merindad.* The somewhat ambiguous international status of Navarre was reflected in its coinage; apart from local currency, French, Gascon, and Aragonese money circulated freely. The law was based on the *Fuero General de Navarra* (a body of customary law built up before 1155) but much modified in different localities by local *fueros.* Efforts by some of Navarre's French rulers to undermine customary law were effectively resisted. In the 14th century one-sixth of the whole population claimed *hidalguía* (noble descent) and the tax exemption that went with it. The Corte General of Navarre controlled, in theory, not only extraordinary subsidies but also ordinary taxation. Since, however, it was the king's prerogative to decide who should be summoned and when, the Navarrese parliament had little real power. Ecclesiastical jurisdiction in Navarre was complicated, the bishops of Dax and Bayonne (in Gascony), Tarazona (Aragon), and Calahorra (Castile) having, or claiming, authority over outlying regions. Shortage of manpower was a constant concern from a military point of view; the earliest *fueros* had not contemplated the existence of a formal army at all. Later the defense of the kingdom rested on a large number of small castles. To increase reserves in war the later kings (notably Charles II) enlisted large numbers of foreign knights and their retinues as *mesnaderos.* Navarrese culture in the late Middle Ages was much influenced by the pilgrim route, and French influences were naturally predominant.

(J.Ho./P.E.R./Ed.)

Valencia

Valencia was the name of an ancient kingdom in Spain. When the kingdom was incorporated into Aragon in 1238, it included the provinces of Castellón de la Plana, Valencia, and Alicante. Located on the eastern coast of Spain, the kingdom was bounded on the north by Catalonia, on the west by Aragon and New Castile, and on the south by Murcia. The modern province of Valencia has an area of 4,156 square miles (10,763 square kilometres). In 1982 Valencia, along with the provinces of Alicante and Castellón, became the Spanish autonomous region of Comunidad Valenciana.

PHYSICAL AND HUMAN GEOGRAPHY

The inhabitants are of very mixed race, owing to the successive occupation of the country by Iberians, Greeks, Carthaginians, Romans, Visigoths, and Moors. Their dialect resembles Catalan but is softer and contains a larger percentage of Arabic words.

The elaborate irrigation works and system of intensive agriculture, which have made the *huertas* ("gardens") of Valencia famous, were initiated by the Moors, as were the Elche date groves, Alicante vineyards, and Valencia orange plantations. The coast is skirted by considerable stretches of sand dune, and by a series of these the lagoon called the Albufera de Valencia is separated from the Mediterranean. The principal rivers are the Guadalaviar, or Turia, and the Júcar.

Principal rivers

The *vegas* ("plains") have an exceptionally fine, almost subtropical climate. In their low-lying portions rice is the favourite crop; elsewhere wheat, corn, and all kinds of fruit are raised; the mulberry is cultivated for silk; and wine and oil are produced. Esparto grass is grown in the less fertile areas. The fishing industry is considerable, and there are manufactures of silk, carpets, and tapestry, woollen, hemp, and linen fabrics, glass, pottery, and leather; there are also iron foundries, distilleries, cooperages, and oil refineries. The coast railway from Barcelona traverses the province. Valencia is the capital and principal seaport.

The province centres on the coastal plain of the Gulf of Valencia. It is limited to the south by the mountains of northern Alicante and less clearly to the north by the watershed of the Turia drainage. Westward, the interior plateaus rise in a series of faulted steps, representing the edge of the Meseta, trenched by the gorges of the middle course of the Júcar River and its tributary the Cabriel. The Turia follows a structural depression providing an easy route into Aragon, via the Teruel corridor. Much of the interior is wild, sparsely populated country, opening out onto the lower and richer lands of Requeña and Liria. The coastal plain (1,244 square miles [3,222 square kilometres]) is the largest in eastern Spain, and more than three-quarters of the province's wealth and most of its population are concentrated in this area.

With an average rainfall of only 14–15 inches (335–380 millimetres) the plain would be substeppe but for the irrigation works developed by the Moors and expanded over the centuries. Broadly speaking, there are three major systems of irrigation: the Vega of Valencia, under horticulture and watered by the Turia; the Ribera, irrigated from the Júcar since the Middle Ages and extended several times chiefly for orange groves and rice; and the bordering hill lands, irrigated by pump for orange growing. Near the coast, south of the city of Valencia, the lagoon La Albufera has been reclaimed for rice cultivation.

Besides the city of Valencia and its suburbs—Burjasót, Paterna, Manises, and Mislata—the other chief towns are Alcira, Carcagente, Játiva, Onteniente, Sueca, Cullera, Gandia, Oliva, Algemesi, Tabernes de Valldigna, Torrente, and Sagunto, concentrated mostly in the south of the plain.

HISTORY

The Kingdom of Valencia was a Muslim principality, independent at intervals from 1010 to 1238. When Umayyad power disintegrated in the reign of Hisham II, Valencia was ruled first by two irrigation officials, then by the slave general Labib, and subsequently by Abd al-Aziz al-Manṣūr (1021–61). Stabilized by the protection of the Hammudite caliphs of Córdoba and by friendship with Christian princes, his reign marks a period of peace and prosperity. His successor, however, a minor, ʿAbd al-Malik (1061–65), was attacked by Ferdinand I of Castile and Leon, who failed to capture Valencia but inflicted such a defeat on its defenders that they sought protection from al-Ma'mūn, the ruler of Toledo. Al-Ma'mūn deposed the minor, and from 1065 to 1075 Valencia formed part of his domains.

Leadership of Abū Bakr

The effeminacy of al-Kadir, al-Ma'mūn's successor, permitted the Valencians to reassert their independence under the leadership of the Toledan governor, Abū Bakr, who allied himself with Alfonso VI of Leon and Castile. But when the latter took Toledo in 1085, he installed al-Kadir as puppet ruler in Valencia with mercenary support. The following year when the mercenaries were recalled to stem the Almoravids, al-Kadir was left defenseless before his hostile subjects. Several potentates manoeuvred to depose him. The Count of Barcelona, allied with the Muslim ruler of Zaragoza, besieged Valencia (1089). To forestall them Alfonso offered the spoils of the city to the freebooter Rodrigo Díaz de Vivar, the Cid. On his approach the siege was lifted, but the Cid found it more politic to exact protection money from al-Kadir than to occupy the city. This was forced on him when the Valencians assassinated al-Kadir in 1092 and constituted themselves as a republic under Almoravid protection. The Cid ruled Valencia from 1094 to his death in 1099. When his widow was forced to relinquish the kingdom to the Almoravids in 1102, the Christians burned the city before evacuating it.

For the next 30 years Valencia was ruled by Almoravid governors, but in the confused period that preceded the arrival of the Almohads the city again recovered a measure of independence. The Valencians admitted as their overlords several ephemeral Murcian princelings, until the Valencian Ibn Mardanish seized control of both kingdoms in 1147. This prince, of Spanish origins, aroused popular opposition in Valencia by his alliances with the Christians, and in 1151 the Valencians, with Almohad support, revolted against him. The kingdom remained in the hands of local rulers, vassals of the Almohads, until it fell to James I of Aragon on September 28, 1238.

(J.Ho./K.Ga./Ed.)

BIBLIOGRAPHY

Physical and human geography. *General works:* The *Anuario Estadístico de España,* which is published annually by the Spanish government, contains general statistical information about the country. The *Enciclopedia Universal Ilustrada Europeo-Americana,* 70 vol. (1908–30; supplements, 1930–), provides detailed information about Spain, its regions, and its towns, especially in vol. 21, *España,* and under "España" in the supplements. PASCUAL MADOZ, *Diccionario geográfico-estadístico-histórico de España y sus posesiones de ultramar,* 16 vol. (1846–50), is still a valuable reference book despite the many years since its original publication. STEPHEN CLISSOLD, *Spain* (1969), and MATILDE MOLINER RUIZ, *España y los españoles* (1968), are informative books about the country and its regions; Spanish history is also treated.

The land: General information about Iberian geography may be found in books about the Mediterranean area, especially JAMES MCINTOSH HOUSTON, *The Western Mediterranean World: An Introduction to Its Regional Landscapes* (1964). MANUEL DE TERAN (ed.), *Geografía de España y Portugal* (1952–67), is the most complete work on the subject. J. VILA VALENTI, *La Península ibérica* (1968; new ed., 1978), gives a good, concise description of the country. HERMANN LAUTENSACH, *Iberische Halbinsel* (1964), constitutes a comprehensive geography of the Iberian Peninsula. WILLIAM BAYNE FISHER and HOWARD BOWEN-JONES, *Spain: An Introductory Geography* (1966), is a general manual. ADOLPH SCHULTEN, *Iberische Landeskunde. Geographie des antiken Spanien,* 2 vol. (1955–57), is an exhaustive scholarly work on the geography of the Iberian Peninsula in early historic times.

The people: The FUNDACION FOESSA, *Informe sociológico sobre la situación social de España* (1970), is a detailed survey of Spanish society, with extensive statistical information; it is periodically updated by *Síntesis actualizada.* JOSE CAZORLA, *Estratificación Social en España* (1973), is a discussion of classes in Spanish society. JUAN VELARDE FUERTES, *Economía y sociedad de la transition* (1978), is a discussion of Spain's economy and society in the years following the Franco regime. The most complete work on Spain's social structure is AMANDO DE MIGUEL, *Manual de estructura social de España* (1974). JULIO CARO BAROJA, *Los pueblos de España. Ensayo de etnología* (1946), is a well-documented account of the development of the Spanish people, from prehistoric times to present-day ethnological regions.

The economy: A general survey in English of the Spanish economy before the late 1970s is GEORGE HILLS, "Spain Under Franco: The Economic 'Miracle' 1959–67," in his *Spain* (1970). For the period of transition to democracy, see JOSE L. GARCIA DELGADO and JULIO SEGURA, *Reformismo y crisis económica* (1977); and RAMON TAMAMES, *Estructura Económica de España* (1980). The Organisation for Economic Co-operation and Development publishes occasional economic surveys of Spain in several languages, which contain much basic information. RODNEY H. MILLS, *The Spanish "Miracle": Growth and Change in the Spanish Economy, 1959 to mid-1965* (1966), is a staff economic study for the Board of Governors of the Federal Reserve System. RICHARD HUMBERT, *Spain* (1970), is published by the United States Bureau of International Commerce.

Transportation: *Las Obras Públicas* (annual), an account of the activities of the Ministry of Public Works for the year;

JOSE IGNACIO RAMOS TORRES and MARCOS MARTIN BLANCO, *El Transporte en España: Organización y magnitudes económicas* (1966), a study of the Spanish transportation system, with emphasis on economic and legal aspects; COMISARIA DEL (II) PLAN DE DESARROLLO ECONOMICO Y SOCIAL, *Transportes* (1967), an official analysis of the evolution, problems, objectives, investments, and operations of the Transport Division.

Administration and social conditions: *Anuario Político Español* (annual), a nonofficial publication, political in nature, that examines social and economic questions; OSCAR ALZAGA, *La constitución Española de 1978* (1978), an explanation of the basic principles of the Spanish constitution; *Informe económico* ("Economic Report"), a general review of the economy issued annually by the Bank of Bilbao; JOSE ANTONIO CARMONA GUILLEN, *Estructura electoral local de España* (1979), a description of Spain's local electoral structure; RAMON MARTIN MATEO, *Manual de derecho administrativo* (1980), a complete summary of the Spanish system of administration; RAUL MORODO, *Los partidos políticos en España* (1979), a description of Spain's political parties; for information on the formation of autonomous communities in Spain, see MINISTRY OF CULTURE, *Cultura Española y autonomías* (1980); MANUEL GARCIA PELAYO, *El tema de las nacionalidades* (1979); JOSE F. LORCA NAVARRETE, *Pluralismo, regionalismo, municipalismo* (1978); and ANTONIO RAMIRO, *Territorio nacional y constitución* (1978).

Cultural life and institutions: VALERIANO BOZAL, *Historia del arte en España* (1975), a history of the arts in Spain; CARLOS AREAN, *1971: Balance del arte joven en España* (1971), a brief treatment of recent tendencies in Spanish art, architecture, painting, and sculpture; ANIBAL ARIAS RUIZ, *La televisión española* (1970); and JUAN ANTONIO GAYA NUNO, *Historia y guía de los museos de España,* 2nd ed. (1968), an excellent overview of Spanish museums; and the same author's *La pintura española del siglo XX.* (1970); and JUAN LUIS ALBORG, *Historia de la literatura española,* 4 vol. (1972–80).

(M.Me./E.L.O.M.)

History. The principal bibliographical guide to Spanish history is BENITO SANCHEZ ALONSO, *Fuentes de la historia española e hispanoamericana,* 3rd ed., 3 vol. (1952). LUIS G. DE VALDEAVELLANO, *Historia de España,* vol. 1 (1952), is the best general history, but it extends so far only to 1212. The most comprehensive work eventually will be the collaborative *Historia de España* under the editorial direction of RAMON MENENDEZ PIDAL, of which five volumes have thus far appeared. Among the most important interpretive works is AMERICO CASTRO, *España en su historia* (1948; Eng. trans., *The Spaniards: An Introduction to Their History,* rev. ed., 1971), which centres on his thesis emphasizing the medieval interaction of Christians, Muslims, and Jews. CLAUDIO SANCHEZ-ALBORNOZ has taken sharp issue with Castro in his *España, un enigma histórico,* 2 vol. (1956). RAMON MENENDEZ PIDAL, *Historia de España,* vol. 1 (1947; Eng. trans., *The Spaniards in Their History,* 1950), is a judicious essay on the formation of the Spanish character. A highly readable and provocative overview of the trends of Spanish history is given by JAIME VICENS VIVES in his *Aproximación a la historia de España,* 5th ed. (1962; Eng. trans., *Approaches to the History of Spain,* 2nd ed. rev., 1970).

Ancient Spain: For prehistoric Spain, see LUIS PERICOT GARCIA, *La España primitiva* (1950); or ANTONIO GARCIA Y BELLIDO, *La península ibérica en los comienzos de su historia* (1953). GARCIA Y BELLIDO is also the author of works on the Carthaginians and Greeks in Spain: *Fenicios y Carthagineses en occidente* (1942) and *Hispania Graeca,* 3 vol. (1948). A useful work in English on the Roman period is C.H.V. SUTHERLAND, *The Romans in Spain, 217 B.C.–A.D. 117* (1939).

Medieval Christian Spain: In addition to the general works cited above, the following may be helpful: LUIS G. DE VALDEAVELLANO, *Curso de historia de las instituciones españolas. De los orígines al final de la edad media* (1968), an excellent survey of medieval institutions; ALFONSO GARCIA GALLO, *Manual de historia del derecho español,* 3rd ed. rev., 2 vol. (1967), especially valuable for its collection of documents relating to government and law. A useful work on its subject is JAIME VICENS VIVES, *Manual de historia económica de España,* 5th ed. (1967; Eng. trans., *An Economic History of Spain,* 1969). E.A. THOMPSON, *The Goths in Spain* (1969), is an informative study of the Visigothic kingdom. YITZHAK BAER, *A History of the Jews in Christian Spain,* 2 vol. (1961; originally published in Hebrew, 1959), treats one of the principal elements in medieval society and makes use of a wealth of sources. A classic work delineating the life of the Cid and placing him in the context of the 11th century is RAMON MENENDEZ PIDAL, *El Cid en la historia* (1921; Eng. trans., *The Cid and His Spain,* 1934). ROBERT I. BURNS, *The Crusader Kingdom of Valencia,* 2 vol. (1967), is a useful study of the settlement of Valencia after the Christian reconquest. See also EDWARD JAMES (ed.), *Visigothic Spain* (1980), a collection of essays.

Muslim Spain: The best work in English is W. MONTGOMERY WATT, *A History of Islamic Spain* (1965); see also E. LEVI-PROVENCAL, *Histoire de l'Espagne musulmane,* 2nd ed., 3 vol. (1950), and *L'Espagne musulmane au Xe siècle* (1932).

1479–1700: JOHN H. ELLIOTT, *Imperial Spain, 1469–1716* (1963), is the only single work covering precisely this period. JOHN LYNCH, *Spain Under the Habsburgs,* 2 vol. (1964–69), is based on modern research, especially in economic history. ROGER B. MERRIMAN, *The Rise of the Spanish Empire in the Old World and in the New,* vol. 2–4 (1918–34), covers the period from the Catholic Kings to Philip II. It is still useful as the most detailed political history of the period. The last volume, on Philip II, is especially good. ANTONIO DOMINGUEZ ORTIZ, *Crisis y decadencia de la España de los Austrias* (1969; Eng. trans., *The Golden Age of Spain, 1516–1659,* 1971), is a synthesis by one of the most distinguished contemporary Spanish scholars. HELMUT G. KOENIGSBERGER, *The Habsburgs and Europe, 1516–1660* (1971), attempts to view Spanish history in the perspective of European history. FERNAND BRAUDEL, *La Méditerranée et le monde méditerranéen à l'époque de Philippe II,* 2nd ed., 2 vol. (1966; Eng. trans. of vol. 1, *The Mediterranean and the Mediterranean World in the Age of Philip II,* 1972), is an economic and historical geography of the Mediterranean basin during the 16th century, in which Spain plays a central role. This book has become a classic since it first appeared (1949) and has been the basis for all further work on the period and area. WILLIAM H. PRESCOTT, *History of the Reign of Ferdinand and Isabella the Catholic,* 3 vol. (1838, many later editions), is still the fullest and most readable account in English. J.M. BATISTA I ROCA, "The Hispanic Kingdoms and the Catholic Kings," *The New Cambridge Modern History,* vol. 1 (1957), is an excellent short modern account. HENRY C. LEA, *A History of the Inquisition of Spain,* 4 vol. (1906–07), is still the fullest, and a very fair, account. PAUL J. HAUBEN (ed.), *The Spanish Inquisition* (1969), prints short extracts from authors with different viewpoints. JOSEPH PEREZ, *La révolution des "comunidades" de Castile, 1520–1521* (1970), is the most detailed account of the Comunero revolt. GARRETT MATTINGLY, *The Defeat of the Spanish Armada* (U.S. title, *The Armada;* 1959), is outstanding. JOHN H. ELLIOTT, *The Revolt of the Catalans: A Study in the Decline of Spain, 1598–1640* (1963), is the definitive work on this subject. JOHN H. PARRY, *The Spanish Seaborne Empire* (1966), is an excellent introduction to this subject. See also R.A. STRADLING, *Europe and the Decline of Spain: A Study of the Spanish System, 1580–1720* (1981); DAVID HOWARTH, *The Voyage of the Armada* (1981), an account from the Spanish perspective.

Spain since 1700: An informative introduction to the problems of modern Spain is GERALD BRENAN, *The Spanish Labyrinth,* 2nd ed. (1950). For an outline of political, economic, and social developments, see RAYMOND CARR, *Spain: 1808–1939* (1966). SALVADOR DE MADARIAGA, *Spain* (1958), is a stimulating general study by a liberal Spaniard. See also HENRY KAMEN, *The War of Succession in Spain, 1700–15* (1969). The reign of Charles III is covered by RICHARD HERR in *The Eighteenth Century Revolution in Spain* (1958). PIERRE VILAR, *La Catalogne dans l'Espagne moderne,* 3 vol. (1962), is a masterly treatment of late 18th-century Catalonia. EARL J. HAMILTON, *War and Prices in Spain, 1651–1800* (1947), is a study of the economy. ROBERT SOUTHEY, *History of the Peninsular War,* 3 vol. (1823–32), is still useful. For the army in politics, see ERIC CHRISTIANSEN, *The Origins of Military Power in Spain, 1800–1854* (1967); and STANLEY G. PAYNE, *Politics and the Military in Modern Spain* (1967). For mid-century politics see V.G. KIERNAN, *The Revolution of 1854 in Spanish History* (1966); and for the history of the republic, see C.A.M. HENNESSY, *The Federal Republic in Spain* (1962). ANTONIO RAMOS OLIVEIRA, *Politics, Economics and Men of Modern Spain, 1808–1946* (1946), is a useful guide. The best introduction is M. FERNANDEZ ALMAGRO, *Historia política de la España contemporánea* (1956). A Centre Left account of the republic is GABRIEL JACKSON, *The Spanish Republic and the Civil War, 1931–39* (1965). An excellent study of the politics of the Right is RICHARD ROBINSON, *The Origins of Franco's Spain* (1970). The history of the Civil War is fully treated in HUGH THOMAS, *The Spanish Civil War* (1961; rev. ed., 1977). For the internal history of the republic, BURNETT BOLLOTEN, *The Grand Camouflage* (1968), is excellent. The politics of Nationalist Spain are treated in STANLEY G. PAYNE, *Falange: A History of Spanish Fascism* (1961). For the development of the Franco régime, see J.W.D. TRYTHALL, *Franco: A Biography* (U.S. title, *El Caudillo: A Political Biography of Franco,* 1970); and GEORGE HILLS, *Franco: The Man and His Nation* (1967). For developments since 1975, see J. AMODIA, *Franco's Political Legacy* (1977), and F. GONZALEZ NAVARRO, *La nueva ley fundamental para la reforma política* (1976). Also of interest is RICHARD GUNTHER, *Public Policy in a No-Party State* (1980), an examination of government spending in the late 1960s and early 1970s.

Spanish Literature

The literature of Spain falls into three divisions according to language: Castilian, Catalan, and Galician. This article provides a brief historical account of the development of each of these three literatures and treats specifically the development of major genres. For a survey of the literature of the former Spanish colonies in the Americas, see LATIN-AMERICAN LITERATURE.

Although literature in the vernacular was not written until the medieval period, Spain had already made considerable contributions to literature. The two Senecas, Lucan, Martial, Quintilian, and Prudentius are among writers in Latin who lived in, or were born in, Spain before the separation of the Romance languages. For their writings, see LATIN LITERATURE. Later, the writings of Spanish Muslims and Jews form an important branch of Arabic and Hebrew literature.

The article is divided into the following main sections:

Castilian literature

MEDIEVAL PERIOD

The origins of vernacular writing. By the time of the Muslim invasion (beginning in 711), the Latin spoken in the Iberian Peninsula was in the process of transformation into Romance. The 10th-century glosses to Latin texts in manuscripts belonging to the monasteries of San Millán de la Cogolla and Silos, in La Rioja, reveal traces of a vernacular already substantially developed. The earliest texts in Mozarabic (the Romance dialect of Spaniards living under the Muslims) were recovered from Hebrew and from Arabic *muwashshaḥs* (poems in strophic form, with subjects such as panegyrics on love), the last strophe of which was the *markaz* (theme stanza). They provide evidence of a popular poetry that may have begun as early as the 10th century and explain much in the traditional Spanish lyric types (*e.g.,* the *villancico,* "carol") of the later Middle Ages and Renaissance. The *markaz* was generally a woman's love song, and the motif, in Romance, was a cry of passion on which the whole poem was based.

The rise of heroic poetry. The earliest surviving monument of Spanish literature, and one of its most distinctive masterpieces, was the *Poema* (or *Cantar*) *de mío Cid* ("Song of My Cid"), an epic poem of the mid-12th century (the existing manuscript is an imperfect copy of 1307). It tells of the fall from and restoration to royal favour of a Castilian noble, Rodrigo Díaz de Vivar (*c.* 1043–99), known by the Arabic title *sidi,* "lord." The setting and personages, the topographical detail, the realistic tone and treatment, and the proximity in time of the poet to his hero have led to the acceptance of historical authenticity as a characteristic of the poem and of the Castilian epic in general. The last two of the three sections were, however, wholly imaginative, and the mere six lines given to the Cid's taking of Valencia from the Muslims make it clear that the scale of values is subjective and that the work is essentially poetic in conception. It won fame, nevertheless, as a popular embodiment of the Castilian character and lived on in epic, chronicle, ballad, and drama. The only other surviving epic text, a fanciful *Cantar de Rodrigo* ("Song of Rodrigo"), tells of the Cid's early manhood, from which the later legend of the Cid took shape. Frequent allusions in vernacular chronicles to the heroic narratives of minstrels make it clear that many narrative poems must have been lost. The chroniclers accepted these as historically authentic and "prosified" them, so that themes and even fragments of text can be reconstructed. Heroic narratives about which some information is available include *Los siete infantes de Lara* ("The Seven Princes of Lara"), *El cerco de Zamora* ("The Siege of Zamora"), *Bernardo del Carpio,* and others treating themes integral to the feudal history of Castile that were closer to a remote Visigothic past than to any French epic.

Epic poem of the Cid

The beginnings of prose. A major influence on prose was exercised by Arabic. Oriental learning came to Spain with the capture (1085) of Toledo from the Muslims. The city became a centre of translation from Oriental languages. An anonymous translation from Arabic (1251) of the "beast fable" *Kalīlah wa Dimnah* was the first example of storytelling in Spanish. An Oriental romance of the Seven Sages, known as the *Sendebar,* was translated likewise through Arabic, and other collections of Eastern stories soon followed.

Alfonso the Wise. The middle of the 12th century saw the recovery of Córdoba, Valencia, and Seville by the Christians. A more propitious intellectual atmosphere resulted in the founding of universities, and under Alfonso X of Castile and Leon (reigned 1252–84) literature achieved prestige. Alfonso, in whose chancery Castilian replaced Latin, could be described as the father of Castilian prose. His vast enterprises of translation and compilation aimed at fusing all knowledge—classical, Oriental, Hebrew, and Christian—in the vernacular. The works, often under his personal editorship, included the great legal code Las Siete Partidas (Eng. trans., *The Seven Divisions of Law*), a mine of information on the life of the time, and compilations from Arabic sources such as treatises on astronomy, on

The *Crónica general* and the *General estoria*

the magical properties of precious stones, and on games, especially chess. With the *Crónica general,* a vast history of Spain, and the *General estoria,* an attempt at a universal history from the creation, Alfonso founded Spanish historiography. The former, carried by Alfonso to AD 711 and completed by his son Sancho IV, was the most influential single work of the Spanish Middle Ages. Himself a poet, Alfonso made one of the greatest collections of medieval poetry and music, the *Cantigas de Santa María* ("Songs to the Virgin"), in Galician, the then accepted language for lyric.

Learned narrative poetry. A new school of poetry, indebted to France and linked with the monastery and a literate public, became known as the *mester de clerecía* ("craft of the clergy"). Adapting the French Alexandrine in the "fourfold way"—*i.e.,* four-line single-rhyme stanza with a 14-syllable line—it dealt with religious, didactic, or pseudo-historical matter. It was best exemplified in Gonzalo de Berceo (*c.* 1195–*c.* 1268), the earliest Spanish poet known by name, who versified in the vernacular the lives of saints, miracles of the Virgin, and other devotional themes with an ingenuous candour and an accumulation of picturesque and affectionately observed detail.

The 14th century. The period of translation and compilation was succeeded by one of brilliant original creation, best represented in the prose of Alfonso's nephew Juan Manuel and in the poetry of Juan Ruiz, archpriest of Hita. Juan Manuel's *Libro de los enxiemplos del conde Lucanor et de Patronio* (*Count Lucanor: or, The Fifty Pleasant Stories of Patronio*), a collection of 50 moral tales, still drew on Arabic sources, but its individuality places it high in the beginnings of Spanish fiction.

Under the influence of the Arthurian, or Breton, cycle, which had been circulating in translation, there had appeared (*c.* 1305) the first Spanish romance of chivalry and the first Spanish novel, *El caballero Cifar* ("The Knight Cifar"), on the theme of St. Eustace, the Roman general miraculously converted to Christianity. About the same time the *Amadís de Gaula,* a chivalric romance related to the Arthurian cycle, the oldest known version of which was written in Spanish by Garci Rodríguez (or Ordóñez) de Montalvo, was circulating and was destined to hold the imagination throughout the 16th century through its sentimental idealism, lyrical atmosphere, and supernatural adventure.

The works of Juan Ruiz

Juan Ruiz was the most intensely alert and individual of early poets. His *Libro de buen amor* (1330, expanded 1343; "Book of Good Love"), a collection of disparate elements—Ovid, Aesop, the 12th-century Latin *Pamphilus de amore,* and the liturgy—suggested a Muslim way of thinking in the mingling of eroticism with devotion and an invitation to the reader to interpret for himself equivocal teachings. His Trotaconventos, ancestress of Celestina, was the first great character in Spanish literature. The Alexandrine metre he handled with new vigour and plasticity, and the text was interspersed with religious, pastoral-farcical, amorous, or satirical lyrics of great metrical variety.

More exotic elements occurred in the verse *Proverbios morales* (*c.* 1355) of Santob de Carrión de los Condes and in an Aragonese version of the story of Joseph, based on the Qur'ān and written in Arabic characters, which was the chief example of "barbarian" literature in Spanish. The *Proverbios* of Santob introduced the grave sententiousness of Hebrew poetry with its extreme aphoristic concision; Santob's sources were the Old Testament, the Talmud, and the Hebrew poet and Arabic philosopher Ibn Gabirol.

Pedro López de Ayala dominated the poetry and prose of the later 1300s with his *Rimado de palacio* ("Poem of Palace Life"), the last major relic of the "fourfold-way," and his chronicles of Peter I, Henry II of Trastamara, John I, and Henry III of Castile, which stimulated the writing of personal, contemporary history; an early humanist, he translated and imitated Livy and Boccaccio, Boethius, St. Gregory, and St. Isidore.

Italian influence on Castilian poetry

The 15th century. The early 15th century witnessed a renewal of poetry under Italian influence. The contrast was strong during the reign of John II between the anarchy of feudalism in its death throes and the cultivation of polite letters, which was becoming a mark of birth and breeding. Collections of poems such as the *Cancionero de Baena* ("Songbook of Baena") made for the King by Juan Alfonso de Baena (a converted Jew and a poet), containing 583 poems by 55 poets from the highest nobles to the humblest versifiers, showed not merely the decadence of the Galician-Portuguese troubadour but also the stirrings of more intellectual poetry using symbol, allegory, and classical allusion in the treatment of moral, philosophical, or political themes. Francisco Imperial, a Genoese settled in Seville and a leader of the new poetry, drew on Dante, while the Marqués de Santillana, poet, scholar, soldier, and statesman, collected masterpieces of foreign literatures and stimulated translation. His *Proemio e carta al condestable de Portugal* (1449; "Preface and Letter to the Constable of Portugal"), the earliest work of literary history and criticism in Spanish, drew on his reading in contemporary foreign languages and translated classics. Imperial had already sought to acclimatize the Italian hendecasyllable. Santillana's sonnets in the "Italian style" marked the beginnings of the formal enrichment of Spanish poetry. His role as precursor is still acknowledged, though the sonnets and long poems, which reflected his Italian-influenced training, are neglected in favour of his charming rustic songs of native inspiration.

Santillana's contribution

Juan de Mena's vast allegorical poem of the drama of history past, present, and future (*El laberinto de fortuna,* 1444; "The Labyrinth of Fortune"), a more conscious attempt to rival Dante, was weighed down by pedantry and over-Latinization of syntax and vocabulary.

An outstanding anonymous poem of the early part of the 15th century, the *Danza de la muerte* ("Dance of Death"), was the finest example of a theme then popular with poets, painters, and composers. Related to the earlier *Danse macabre* at Paris but written with greater satiric force, it introduced characters (*e.g.,* a rabbi) not included in the French cycle. It presented a cross section of society in the form of a dialogue between Death and his protesting victims and, although not intended for dramatic presentation, formed the basis for later drama.

THE ERA OF THE RENAISSANCE

The beginning of the Siglo de Oro. The unification of Spain in 1479 and Columbus' discovery of the New World (1492), following the introduction of printing (1474) and concurrent with the cultural traffic with Italy (Naples had been a dependency of Aragon since 1443), may be taken as opening the era of the Renaissance in Spain. In this period—known as the Siglo de Oro or "Golden Age"—Spanish literature reflected the wealth of new experience born of overseas adventure and the detached questioning attitude to the rediscovered norms of classical authority. The early Spanish humanists included the first grammarians and lexicographers of any Romance tongue. Juan Luis Vives, the brothers Juan and Alfonso de Valdés, and others were followers of Erasmus, whose writings circulated in translation from 1536 and whose influence was seen in the Counter-Reformation figure of St. Ignatius of Loyola, founder of the Society of Jesus, and later in a religious writer and poet, Fray Luis de León.

The masterpiece of the early Renaissance is the *Comedia de Calixto y Melibea* (1499), a novel in dialogue form published anonymously but attributed to a converted Jew, Fernando de Rojas. The dominant character, a procuress called Celestina, depicted with a realism unsurpassed in Spanish letters, gave this work the title by which it is most commonly known, *La Celestina.* The analysis of passion and the dramatic conflict that its pursuit involved were worked out with such psychological intensity as to make this the first masterpiece of Spanish prose and Spain's first realistic novel.

The significance of *La Celestina*

Poetry. Spanish ballads, or *romances,* link medieval heroic epic to 20th-century poetry and drama; they lie at the heart of the national consciousness; and their expansion and capacity for survival, from Salonika to Chile and from the Low Countries to North Africa, reflect the far-flung boundaries of Spain's prestige in its age of greatness. The earliest datable *romances* (mid-15th century) treated of frontier incidents or lyrical themes. The ballads on medieval heroic themes had importance because they formed everyman's source book on national history and character. Traditional ballads were collected in the Antwerp *Cancionero de romances* ("Ballad Songbook") and in the *Silva de varios romances* ("Miscellany of Various Ballads"), both *c.* 1550, and thereafter repeatedly. Soon the form (octosyllabic, alternate lines having a single assonance throughout) was exploited for lyrical purposes by the most famous poets of the age, and it has remained the chosen medium for popular narrative verse.

The earlier attempt to Italianize Spanish poetry had failed because Spanish language and verse techniques were still incapable of sustaining the burden. The Catalan Juan Boscán Almogáver, reintroducing Italian metres (see below *Catalan literature*), prepared the way for a much greater poet, Garcilaso de la Vega, with whom the lyric was reborn. To his mastery of poetic technique derived from medieval and classical poets he added an intense personal note in the use of characteristic Renaissance themes. His short poems, elegies, and sonnets largely determined the course of lyric poetry throughout the Siglo de Oro.

The rebirth of the lyric

Fray Luis de León, adopting some of Garcilaso's verse techniques, typified the "Salamanca school," with its emphasis on content rather than form. The poet and critic Fernando de Herrera headed a contrasting school of Seville, which, deriving equally from Garcilaso, was concerned rather with subtleties of refined sentiment; in a quartet of remarkable odes he gave vibrant expression to topical heroic themes. A defense of the short native metres was reinforced by the aforementioned traditional ballad collections (*romanceros*) and by the evolving drama.

For epic poetry the models were Ariosto and Tasso, but the themes and heroes were those of overseas conquest and expansion or defense of the empire and the faith. Alonso de Ercilla y Zúñiga came nearest to real achievement with his *Araucana* (published 1569–90), telling of native resistance to the Spanish conquest of Chile. Another typical example of the attempt at epic is Lope de Vega's *Dragontea* (1598), a verse history of Sir Francis Drake's last voyage and death.

Early drama. The origins of drama in Spain are to be sought, as elsewhere, in the church. The *Auto de los reyes magos* ("Play of the Three Wise Kings"), an incomplete play of an Epiphany cycle, is the only surviving text of medieval Spanish drama. The characterization of the Magi and of Herod and his advisers was realistic, and the medley of metres foreshadowed one aspect of later development of the drama in Spain.

A reference in King Alfonso X's legal code suggested also the existence of some form of secular drama in the 13th century, but no texts have survived. These *juegos* (short satiric entertainments given by traveling players) were the forerunners of the short plays and interludes—*pasos, entremeses, sainetes*—that formed one of Spain's main contributions to dramatic genres.

The dramas of Juan del Encina

Juan del Encina marked the emancipation of the drama from ecclesiastical ties by performances for a noble patron. His *Cancionero* (1496; "Songbook") contains pastoral-religious dramatic dialogues in a rustic dialect, but he soon turned to secular themes or vivid farce. Some of his plays showed a conception of drama changed by his long stay in Italy, in which native medievalism was transformed into Renaissance experimentation. Encina's Portuguese disciple Gil Vicente, a court poet at Lisbon who also wrote in Castilian, showed a great advance in naturalness of dialogue, acuteness of observation, and sense of situation.

The emergence of the drama from court to marketplace and the creation of a public were largely the work of Lope de Rueda, who toured Spain with his modest troupe and a repertoire of his own composition. His four prose comedies were clumsy, but the 10 *pasos* (comic interludes between the acts of longer plays) showed his dramatic merits, and he had the distinction of fathering the one-act play, which may be regarded as the most vital and popular dramatic form in Spain.

The first dramatist to realize the possibilities of the ballads in the theatre was Juan de la Cueva. His comedies and tragedies were mostly taken from classical antiquity, but in *Los siete infantes de Lara* ("The Seven Princes of Lara"), *El reto de Zamora* ("The Challenge of Zamora"), and *La libertad de España por Bernardo del Carpio* ("The Liberation of Spain by Bernardo del Carpio"), all published in 1588, he turned to early heroic stories already familiar in ballad; and thus, although not an accomplished dramatist, he helped to found a "national" drama.

Prose. *Historical writing.* Prose before the Counter-Reformation produced some notable dialogues, especially Alfonso de Valdés' *Diálogo de Mercurio y Carón* (1528; "Dialogue Between Mercury and Charon"). His brother Juan wrote a *Diálogo de la lengua* ("Dialogue About the Language") of great critical value. History continued to be cultivated, patriotism waxing higher as Spain's greatness cast its shadow over Europe; its last flowering was seen in Juan de Mariana's own translation into Spanish (from 1601) of his Latin history of Spain, which marked the triumph of the vernacular for all literary purposes.

The landmarks in historical writing, however, came from the New World and showed the transmitting of vital experience into literature with a vividness unknown in Spain. Columbus' letters and accounts of his voyages, the letters and accounts to Charles V of Hernán Cortés, and many other narratives by more humble conquistadores ("conquerors") opened up new horizons to the reader and, in the attempt to capture exotic landscapes in words, enlarged the resources of the language. The most engaging of such writings was the *Historia verdadera de la conquista de la Nueva España* (1632; *True History of the Conquest of New Spain*) by the explorer Bernal Díaz del Castillo. Bartolomé de Las Casas, the "Apostle of the Indies," wrote a *Brevísima relación de la destrucción de las Indias* (published 1552; "Very Brief Account of the Destruction of the Indies"; Eng. trans., *The Tears of the Indians*), criticizing Spanish colonial policy and the ill-treatment of the native population, which gave rise among Spain's enemies to the famous *leyenda negra,* or "black legend."

Narratives by the explorers

The novel. Popular taste in the novel was dominated for a century by the progeny of the medieval courtly romance *Amadís de Gaula.* These interminable romances kept alive certain ideals of medieval chivalry, but, having lost touch with life at every point, they represented pure escapism and in due course evoked such literary reactions as the pastoral novel. Naturalized from Italy and filled with nostalgia for an arcadian golden age, its shepherds were courtiers and poets who, like the knights-errant of chivalric romance, turned their backs on reality.

A more positive reaction was in the picaresque novel initiated in 1554 with the anonymous *Lazarillo de Tormes.* This genre, native to Spain and influential elsewhere, had as its hero a picaro ("rogue"), essentially an antihero, living by his wits and concerned only with staying alive, who, passing from master to master, depicted life from underneath. Important in guiding fiction back to direct observation of life, the picaresque formula contributed little to the development of the novel as an art form.

Don Quixote

Miguel de Cervantes, the preeminent figure in Spanish literature, produced in *Don Quixote* (part 1, 1605; part 2, 1615) the prototype of the modern novel. Nominally a satire on the moribund chivalric romance, Cervantes' conception allowed the presentation of reality on two levels: the "poetic truth" of Don Quixote and the "historic truth" of his squire, Sancho Panza. In the constant interaction of these rarely compatible attitudes, Cervantes revealed the novel's scope as a philosophical commentary on existence, and in the interplay of the two characters he established psychological realism in contrast with the static characterization of previous fiction. In the *Novelas ejemplares* (1613; "Exemplary Tales"), Cervantes particularized his claim to be the first to write *novelas* (short stories in the Italian manner) in Spanish by differentiating between those that interest by the action and those whose merit lies in the mode of telling.

Mystical writings. The great period of Spanish mysticism coincided with the Counter-Reformation, though it had antecedents, particularly in the expatriate Spanish Jew León Hebreo, whose *Dialoghi di amore* (1535; "The Dialogues of Love"), written in Italian, exercised a profound influence on 16th-century and later Spanish thought. The literary importance of the mystics derives from the fact that in trying to transcend limitations of language they liberated previously untapped resources of expression. In the writings of St. Teresa of Ávila, notably in her autobiography and letters, there were the gifts of a great novelist in embryo. In his prose as in his poetry, Fray Luis de León showed passionate devotion, sincerity, and profound feeling for nature in a style of singular purity. St. John of the Cross achieved preeminence through three poems expressing in exalted style the experience of mystic union.

The dramatic art of Lope de Vega

Later drama. The drama achieved its true splendour in the genius of Lope de Vega (in full, Lope Félix de Vega Carpio). Its manifesto was Lope's own treatise, *Arte nuevo de hacer comedias en este tiempo* (1609; "New Art of Writing Plays at This Time"), which rejected the Neoclassical "rules," opted for a blend of comedy and tragedy and metrical variety, and made public opinion the arbiter of good taste. The new *comedia* ("drama") was a "social" drama, ringing changes on the triple foundation of society: respect for crown, church, and the human personality, the last symbolized in the "point of honour" that Lope commended as the best theme of all. This was a matter of convention, "honour" being equivalent more or less to reputation. It was a drama less of character than of action and intrigue, which rarely grasped the essence of tragedy. What the great Spanish playwrights did possess was a remarkable sense of stagecraft and the ability to make the most intricate plot gripping.

Lope, who claimed authorship of more than 1,800 *comedias,* towered over his contemporaries. He had an unerring sense of what could move an audience to respond to a reflection on the stage of some of the ingredients of its country's greatness. Through Lope the drama became "national" in the truest sense. The two main categories of his work are the native historical and the *capa y espada* ("cloak-and-sword") plays of contemporary manners. Lope ransacked the literary past for heroic themes, chosen to illustrate aspects of the national character or of that social solidarity on which Spain rested.

The cloak-and-sword play, which dominated drama after Lope, was pure diversion, with much use of disguise, falling in and out of love, false alarms about honour, and a duplication of the plot by the humorous lackey and the lady's maid. It gave pleasure by its dexterity, sparkling dialogue, and entanglements in relations between the sexes and showed the pleasures of the moment in an irresponsible world.

The works of Tirso de Molina

The greatest of Lope's immediate successors was Tirso de Molina (pseudonym of Gabriel Téllez), whose *Burlador de Sevilla* (1630; "The Trickster of Seville") presented the Don Juan legend on stage for the first time. *La prudencia en la mujer* (1634; "Prudence in Woman") figured among the greatest of Spanish historical dramas, as did *El condenado por desconfiado* (1635; *The Doubter Damned*) among the theological, while Tirso's cloak-and-sword comedies were among the liveliest of the type. Mexican-born Juan Ruiz de Alarcón y Mendoza struck a distinctive note. His 20 plays were sober, studied, and imbued with serious moral purpose, and his *Verdad sospechosa* (1634; "The Truth Suspected") inspired the great French dramatist Pierre Corneille's *Menteur.* Corneille's famous *Le Cid* similarly had its source in the conflict between love and honour posed in *Las mocedades del Cid* ("The Youthful Exploits of the Cid") by Guillén de Castro y Bellvís.

Culteranismo and conceptismo. In poetry and prose the early 17th century in Spain was marked by the rise and spread of two interrelated stylistic movements. That known as *culteranismo,* the high-flown style of which Luis de Góngora y Argote was archpriest, resumed attempts to ennoble the language by re-Latinizing it. This process was not only carried to extremes in vocabulary, syntax, and word order, but expression was garbed in classical myth and allusion and complicated by every subtlety of metaphor. It was an attempt to achieve a poetry that, if rediscovered after hundreds of years, could be still fresh through the immortality of its Latinism. His example (*Soledades* [1613; "Solitudes"]) invited many untalented imitations. The other stylistic movement, *conceptismo,* played on ideas as *culteranismo* did on language. Aiming always at the semblance of profundity, the style was concise and epigrammatic and thus belonged to prose, especially satire, since it was much concerned with stripping appearances from reality. Its best outlet was the essay. Francisco Gómez de Quevedo y Villegas, the greatest satirist of his age and one of Spain's masters of language, was, in *Sueños* (1627; "Dreams"), an outstanding exponent. Baltasar Gracián y Morales reduced its refinement to an exact code in his *Agudeza y arte de ingenio* ("The Conceit, a Treatise on Style"), as he also tried to codify in a series of treatises the art of living. Gracián was certainly a thinker, and his allegorical novel *El criticón* (*The Critick*) was a pessimistic interpretation of life as a "daily dying."

The plays of Calderón. Pedro Calderón de la Barca adapted Lope de Vega's formula for producing a tightly structured drama in which formal artistry and poetic texture are closely wedded to depth of theme and unity of dramatic purpose. One of the world's outstanding dramatists, Calderón wrote plays that were as effective in the public playhouses as in the newly built court theatre of Buen Retiro. The elaborate stage techniques of the latter enabled Calderón to excel in mythological drama (*La estatua de Prometeo* [1669; "The Statue of Prometheus"]) and contribute to the rise of a type of musical comedy known as the zarzuela (*El jardín de Falerina* [1648; "The Garden of Falerina"]). Calderón was a fertile creator, and his numerous secular plays encompassed both comedy and tragedy. In his best comedies, the conventions of intrigue and suspense are modified to create a subtle critique of urban mores and generally accepted values, astride the joy of laughter and the foreboding of eventual tragedy (*La dama duende* [1629; *The Phantom Lady*]). His tragedies probe deeply into the human predicament, exploring problems of personal and collective guilt (*Las tres justicias en una* [*c.* 1637; *Three Judgments at a Blow*]), the bathos of limited vision and lack of communication (*El pintor de su deshonra* [*c.* 1645; *The Painter of His Own Dishonour*]), the destructiveness of certain social codes (*El médico de su honra* [1635; *The Surgeon of His Honour*]), and the clash between the constructive nature of reason and the destructive violence of self-centred passion (*La hija del aire* [1653; "The Daughter of the Air"]). Some of his best known plays are more appropriately classified as high drama, offering a positive though never simplistic vision. *El alcalde de Zalamea* (*c.* 1640; *The Mayor of Zalamea*), for example, rejects the supremacy of social honour and points to the inner nature of man's true worth and dignity. Philosophical problems of determinism and free will are vividly dramatized in *La vida es sueño* (1635; *Life Is a Dream*), in which the escape route from the confusion of life is shown to lie in an awareness of reality and self-knowledge.

Calderón's exploration and critique of natural values has its otherworldly counterpart in his overtly religious plays, whether in the mold of the Jesuit drama with its emphasis on conversion (*El mágico prodigioso* [1637; *The Wonder-Working Magician*]) and heroic saintliness (*El príncipe constante* [1629; *The Constant Prince*]) or in the medieval tradition of morality plays that he brought to a peak of artistic perfection in his *autos sacramentales.* These liturgical plays use formal abstractions and symbols in order to expound the specific drama of the human fall and Christian redemption, and they range in their artistry from the immediate metaphorical appeal of *El gran teatro del mundo* (*c.* 1635; *The Great Theatre of the World*) to the increasingly elaborate patterns of his later productions (*La nave del mercader* [1674; "The Merchant's Ship"]).

Calderón's *autos sacramentales*

After Calderón's death Spanish drama lay dead for 100 years. *Culteranismo* and *conceptismo,* though symptoms rather than causes of decline, played their part in stifling imaginative literature, and by the close of the century little remained of its former greatness.

THE 18TH CENTURY

With the establishment of the Bourbon dynasty after the War of the Spanish Succession (1701–14), renewal of the country's intellectual life began. Numerous academies were created, the most influential being the Real Academia de la Lengua Española (now the Real Academia Española), founded in 1713 to maintain the purity of the language. Men of letters began again to study abroad and discovered how far Spain had deviated from the intellectual course of western Europe. A new spirit of inquiry into the national heritage caused scholars to go back and unearth forgotten medieval literature. Gregorio Mayáns y Siscar wrote the first biographical study of Cervantes. A church historian, Enrique Flórez, embarking on a vast historical enterprise, *España sagrada,* helped resurrect the whole cultural background of medieval Christian Spain. Landmarks of even greater importance were the publication of the 12th-century epic *Poema de mío Cid,* the works of Gonzalo de Berceo, and Juan Ruiz' *Libro de buen amor,* all for the first time. From all this there resulted a debate between old and new that waged throughout the middle decades of the century, compelled both sides to reason out their positions, and marked the birth of a new critical approach to literature. Two names stand out: Ignacio de Luzán Claramunt, whose work on poetics launched the great Neoclassical polemic in Spain, and Benito Jerónimo Feijóo y Montenegro, a Benedictine monk who, in assailing error, prejudice, and superstition wherever he found them, made a monumental contribution to the intellectual emancipation of Spain. Imaginative prose produced the *Noches lúgubres* (published 1789–90; "Sad Nights") of José Cadalso Vázquez, looking forward to Romanticism, and the *Fray Gerundio* (1758) of José Francisco de Isla, a satire looking back to the picaresque novel.

First publication of the *Cid*

Poetry, moribund for nearly 100 years, raised a timid head in a small group at Salamanca, led by Diego González, which toward 1775 turned for inspiration to Fray Luis de León, just as two decades later a group at Seville sought to revive the glories of Herrera. Juan Meléndez Valdés, who learned to think from the English philosopher John Locke and to feel from the English poet Edward Young, best exemplified the combination of new influences at work. A conscious artificer rather than a great poet, he helped poetry through the painful apprenticeship necessary to its rehabilitation.

In drama, the second half of the century saw a great battle over the Neoclassical "rules" (meaning chiefly the unities of place, time, and action). *La Raquel* (1778), by Vicente Antonio García de la Huerta Muñoz, showed the capabilities of the reformist school. It fell to Ramón de la Cruz to bridge the gap by his resurrection of the earlier *paso* (one-act prose skit) and longer *entremeses* (interludes) of Lope de Rueda, Cervantes, and Luis Quiñones de Benavente. Based on satirical observation of the Madrid scene, his one-act sketches did not transgress the unities or offend the purist; at the same time they delighted the public and brought the drama back to commenting on life and society. Leandro Fernández de Moratín applied the lesson to the full-length play and produced comedies imbued with deep social seriousness which were yet good theatre. His dialogue in *La comedia nueva* (1792; "The New Comedy") and in *El sí de las niñas* (1806; *The Maiden's Consent*) ranks among the best prose of the 18th century.

THE 19TH CENTURY

The Romantic movement. Literature in Spain in the first third of the 19th century was still affected by the Napoleonic Wars and their long aftermath. Many liberals driven into exile by Ferdinand VII after 1823 sought refuge in France; and, when they returned to Spain after his death in 1833, they had been so influenced by French Romanticism that this date has been taken as the beginning of the Romantic movement in Spain. The ground had been prepared in Cádiz from 1814 onward in a debate initiated by a German, Johann Niklaus Böhl von Faber, on literary values; in Barcelona with the founding in 1823 of a review, *El europeo;* and in Madrid with Agustín Durán's essay in 1828 on the drama of the Siglo de Oro and his *Colección de romances antiguos* (1828–32). Romanticism in Spain was, in many respects, a return to the spirit of its own earlier classics. The formal characteristics of Spanish Romantic drama—mingling of genres, rejection of the unities, metrical variety—had characterized the drama of Lope de Vega and his contemporaries, who had, moreover, treated many of its themes.

Influence of French Romanticism

The movement arrived in Spain a generation later than elsewhere and had a short life. It never became a school or had a particular leader. José de Espronceda was the one Romantic who lived his Romanticism. His *Estudiante de Salamanca* (appeared in two parts, 1836 and 1837; "Student of Salamanca"), *Canciones* (1840; "Songs"), and an unfinished work, *El diablo mundo* (1840; "The Devilish World"), were the only subjective lyrics of value that the period produced, and they marked a milestone in the development of poetic form. A play, *Don Álvaro o la fuerza del sino* (1835; "Don Alvaro; or, The Force of Destiny"), by Ángel de Saavedra, duque de Rivas, and the preface, by the critic Antonio Alcalá Galiano, to Saavedra's narrative poem *El moro expósito* (1834; "The Foundling Moor"), came nearest to expressing a philosophy of Romanticism.

Three poets revealed how one of Romanticism's concerns was liberation of the individual personality. Gustavo Adolfo Bécquer, in 76 *Rimas* (published 1871; "Rhymes"), expressed his own tortured emotions; Ramón de Campoamor y Campoosorio wrote *Doloras* (1845; "Sufferings"), *Pequeños poemas* (1871; "Little Poems"), and *Humoradas* (new poetic forms of his invention, published in 1886), attempting to bring poetry back into the realm of ideas; and Gaspar Núñez de Arce wrote *Gritos del combate* (1875; "Combat Cries"), patriotic, declamatory exhortations defending democracy.

Costumbrismo. *Costumbrismo* was a movement that started earlier than Romanticism and flourished at the same time. It concerned realistic prose writing, often within a narrative framework. Both the *cuadro de costumbres* and the *artículo de costumbres* were short literary sketches on customs, manners, or character, but the *cuadro* inclined to description for its own sake, whereas the *artículo* was more critical and satirical. *Cartas de un pobrecito holgazán* (1820; "Letters from a Poor Idler"), by Sebastián de Miñano, was probably the first work of this kind, but the most important were by Mariano José de Larra, outstanding prose writer and most critical mind of his age, who dissected society pitilessly in *Artículos* (1835–37); by Ramón de Mesonero Romanos, whose *Escenas matritenses* (1836–42; "Scenes of Madrid") gave a vivid picture of contemporary life; and by Serafín Estébanez Calderón, who portrayed the manners, folklore, and history of Andalusia in *Escenas andaluzas* (1847; "Andalusian Sketches"). These writings and other similar pieces, with their realistic and regional elements, helped to prepare for a revival of the novel.

Realistic prose writing

Revival of the Spanish novel. For more than two centuries the novel, with which Spain had made its greatest contribution to literature, had been almost extinct. The first novels of the revival were more interesting for powers of observation and description (a continuation of *costumbrismo*) than for imaginative or narrative quality. A woman novelist, Fernán Caballero, determined the technique of observation that was to rehabilitate the novel in *La gaviota* (1849; *The Seagull*). In 1874 the great period of the regional novel began with *El sombrero de tres picos* (*The Three-Cornered Hat*), a sparkling tale of peasant malice by Pedro Antonio de Alarcón. Although local Realism prevailed too in Juan Valera's novels, they were also remarkable for their psychological insight and notes of cultured detachment. The greatest regional writer was José María de Pereda, whose Realism was a powerful re-creation of nature as the abiding reality, more important than the individual. *Sotileza* (1884; "Subtlety") and *Peñas arriba* (1893; "Up the Mountains") revealed his support for traditional values of religion, family, and country life. An attempt by Emilia, condesa de Pardo Bazán, in her novels of Galicia, *Los pazos de Ulloa* (1886; *The Son of a Bondwoman*) and *La madre naturaleza* (1887; "Mother Nature"), to combine a Spanish Christian outlook with French Naturalism made clear their incompatibility, and in later novels she returned to a genuinely Spanish Realism. Armando Palacio Valdés was the novelist of Asturias.

Besides this cult of regionalism, the fecundity in the novel of Benito Pérez Galdós created a world in itself. After living through one of the most turbulent chapters in Spanish history, he imaginatively re-created its antecedents, beginning with the war against Napoleon. The 46 novels of his *Episodios nacionales* (1873–79 and 1898–1912) embraced

The novels of Pérez Galdós

70 years of the country's story and taught generations of Spaniards much of what history they knew.

Postromantic drama. The drama, disoriented after a brief Romantic efflorescence, produced few outstanding works. Manuel Tamayo y Baus achieved fame by an isolated work, *Un drama nuevo* (1867; *A New Drama*), in which the characters are members of Shakespeare's company of actors (including Shakespeare himself). Adelardo López de Ayala pilloried bourgeois vices in *El tejado de vidrio* (1857; "The Glass Roof") and *Consuelo* (1870). The 1904 Nobel Prize for Literature set a seal on José Echegaray y Eizaguirre, whose 63 plays fall into two main groups. In the first, drama became melodrama with a constant striving after effect and a basic falsity of character, passion, and situation alike. The second comprised a serious, often tragic, drama of social problems. Joaquín Dicenta brought the drama nearer to earth with an unpleasantly realistic study of working-class conditions in *Juan José* (performed 1895).

THE MODERN PERIOD

The Generation of '98. For more than two decades before 1900, a mood of seething political and social analysis developed in Spain that gave in Ángel Ganivet's *Idearium español* (1897; *Spain, an Interpretation*) one of the most searching analyses of the Spanish character ever written. The imperial cycle, begun in 1492, ended in ignominy with the Spanish–American War of 1898, and thinking Spaniards embarked on a diagnosis of their country's ills and an attempt to shock the national mentality out of its *abulia*, or "lack of will." The novel was injected with a new seriousness of purpose, and the critical, psychological, and philosophical essay rose to new importance. Novelists and essayists constituted what Azorín (pseudonym of José Martínez Ruiz) called the Generation of '98, a group that regained respect for Spanish letters abroad.

Unamuno's analyses of the national problem

Miguel de Unamuno, who dominated the literary scene for a generation, studied the national problem acutely in the five essays in *En torno al casticismo* (1895; "On Spanish Purism") and in the *Vida de Don Quijote y Sancho* (1905; *The Life of Don Quixote and Sancho*). He examined the problem of immortality in his most important work, *Del sentimiento trágico de la vida* (1913; *The Tragic Sense of Life in Men and Peoples*). A provocative rather than a systematic thinker, he aimed at sowing spiritual disquiet. The novel was to him a medium for discussion of the fundamentals of personality; his own include *Niebla* (1914; *Mist*), *Abel Sánchez* (1917; Eng. trans., *Abel Sánchez*), and *Tres novelas ejemplares y un prólogo* (1920; "Three Cautionary Tales and a Prologue").

Azorín concerned himself with the reinterpretation of earlier literary values and of the Spanish countryside in, for example, *El alma castellana* (1900; "The Castilian Soul"), *La ruta de Don Quijote* (1905; "Don Quixote's Route"), and *Clásicos y modernos* (1913). An artist in criticism and a finely sensitive miniaturist, he contributed powerfully to the deflation of the rhetoric that had vitiated much 19th-century writing. A philosopher, José Ortega y Gasset, developed themes from criticism and psychology (*Meditaciones del Quijote* [1914; "Meditations on Quixote"]) to national problems (*La España invertebrada* [1921; *Invertebrate Spain*]), then to international (*El tema de nuestro tiempo* [1923; *The Modern Theme*] and *La rebelión de las masas* [1929; *The Revolt of the Masses*]).

Pío Baroja repudiated tradition, religion, and the cult of the individual and advocated social action. *La raza* ("The Race"), *La lucha por la vida* (1904; "The Struggle for Life"), and *Agonías de nuestro tiempo* (1926; "Agonies of Our Time") were fiercely vigorous attempts to arouse discontent with material conditions. As vigorous but possessing greater narrative skill was Vicente Blasco Ibáñez, who wrote on contemporary social problems from the standpoint of an anarchist, as in *La bodega* (1905; *The Wine Vault*) and *La horda* (1905; *The Mob*). He won international renown with *Los cuatro jinetes del apocalipsis* (1916; *The Four Horsemen of the Apocalypse*), a novel of World War I.

Novecentistas

The term *novecentistas* is applied to writers of the early 20th century who sought to renew intellectual and aesthetic standards after the passionate involvement of their immediate predecessors.

The novel. In Ramón Pérez de Ayala, the novel was at once a polished art form and a forum for philosophical discussion. *Belarmino y Apolonio* (1921; *Belarmino and Apolonio*), a projection of the old debate between faith and reason, made its characters almost symbolic, as did *Tigre Juan* (1926; *Tiger Juan*), on the traditional theme of honour. Gabriel Miró's perfect descriptive prose retarded the action of his novels, but he remained a supreme artist in words. The novel as a literary form fell under the influence of Ortega y Gasset, who in *La deshumanización del arte* (1925; *The Dehumanization of Art*) propounded principles of a pure, depersonalized art. Analyzing the novel as an art form, he predicted its decline. In the following decade Benjamín Jarnés and others attempted, without complete success, to apply a technique of pure art to the novel; Jarnés' works were outstanding examples of the Surrealist novel in Spain.

The Spanish Civil War (1936–39) drove into political exile some promising novelists whose narrative art matured abroad. Max Aub analyzed the civil conflict in an artistically and thematically impressive cycle of novels entitled *El laberinto mágico* (1943–68; "The Magic Labyrinth"). Ramón José Sender, whose pre-Civil War novels had been realistic and overtly sociopolitical, developed an interest in the mysterious and irrational. While his trilogy *Crónica del alba* (1942–66; "Chronicle of the Dawn") dwelt on the Civil War in a realistic manner, his magic, myth-dominated world of *Epitalamio del prieto Trinidad* (1942; *Dark Wedding*) or *Las criaturas saturnianas* (1968; "Saturnine Beings") pointed toward more universal concerns. Francisco Ayala abandoned his youthful aestheticism to cultivate Spanish and human themes in short stories and novels (*e.g.*, *Muertes de perro* [1958; *Death as a Way of Life*]) of multiple perspective and complex narrative techniques.

In the aftermath of the Civil War the narrative in Spain went into a relative decline, only occasionally arrested by such successes as the psychologically perceptive *La familia de Pascual Duarte* (1942; *The Family of Pascual Duarte*) of Camilo José Cela. This novel created a vogue for a form of harsh, sordid, unsentimental realism known as *tremendismo*. Always wedded to literary experimentation, Cela attempted more ambitious technical heights in his later novel *La colmena* (1951; *The Hive*), which provides a panorama of Madrid society during the post-Civil War period.

Cela and *tremendismo*

The sociopolitical trauma of the civil conflict with its cultural and economic uncertainty fostered a return of outmoded forms of Realism. Conventional reading was provided by such craftsmen as Juan Antonio de Zunzunegui and Ignacio Agustí. José María Gironella was more ambitious in his controversial epic trilogy on the Civil War: *Los cipreses creen en Dios* (1953; *The Cypresses Believe in God*), *Un millón de muertos* (1961; *The Million Dead*); and *Ha estallado la paz* (1966; *Peace After War*). Miguel Delibes conveyed a critical concern for a society whose natural values are under constant threat. Greater technical advance and thematic originality are evinced in his *Cinco horas con Mario* (1966; "Five Hours with Mario"), a powerful novel constructed almost entirely with interior monologue. During the 1950s a starker form of Social Realism became the dominant manner in the work of a group of competent, committed novelists (Ana María Matute, Rafael Sánchez Ferlosio, the brothers Juan and Luis Goytisolo, Jesús Fernández Santos, Juan García Hortelano, Carmen Martín Gaite, Ignacio Aldecoa, Jesús López Pacheco, Daniel Sueiro, and Elena Quiroga). The finest novel produced by a member of this group was Ferlosio's *El Jarama* (1956; "The Jarama"; Eng. trans., *The One Day of the Week*), in which the monotonous existence of urban youth is vividly re-created in the aimless conversations of the characters. By the 1960s, this form of direct, unadventurous Realism was a spent force. Luis Martín-Santos was the first to break the mold with his epoch-making *Tiempo de silencio* (1962; *Time of Silence*), in which the familiar topic of life in post-Civil War Spain was subjected to the elaboration of conscious artistry. Juan

New form of Social Realism

Goytisolo, whose early novels had been firmly anchored in Social Realism, ventured into increased introspectiveness and revolutionary experimentation with structure and language in his *Señas de identidad* (1966; *Marks of Identity*). In the same line of promising innovation is Juan Benet Goita, whose *Volverás a Región* (1967; "You Will Return to Región") combined density of form with myth and allegory.

Drama. With the new century, drama achieved renewed vigour under the stimulus of Jacinto Benavente y Martínez, a prolific playwright noted for his craftsmanship and wit. A social satirist preoccupied with ethics, Benavente stopped short of alienating the sympathies of his devoted upper-class public, as, for example, in *Los intereses creados* (1907; *The Bonds of Interest*). The bourgeois drama of Benavente and others shared some of its success with the poetic, nostalgic drama of Eduardo Marquina, and with the so-called *género chico—i.e.,* genre consisting of light dramatic or operatic one-act playlets. The popular, costumbrista setting of the latter dissolved into amusing inanities in the hands of the brothers Serafín and Joaquín Álvarez Quintero while reaching a more serious level in some of the satirical pieces of Carlos Arniches.

A most original, innovative playwright of the 1920s was Ramón María del Valle-Inclán, who attempted, without much success, to shake the theatre out of its bourgeois complacency and artistic mediocrity. In his dramatic productions, he inveighed against hypocrisy and corrupt values in poignant, taut scenes of mordant irony. *Luces de Bohemia* (1920; *Bohemian Lights*) illustrates both the theory and practice of *esperpento,* an aesthetic formula that sought to depict reality through a deliberately exaggerated mimesis of its grotesqueness. Also concerned with the renovation of the stage, Jacinto Grau added tragic dignity to his pessimistic view of an absurd reality in *El señor de Pigmalión* (1921).

García Lorca's drama

Federico García Lorca stood far above his contemporaries. His drama was poetic in more than the usual sense, presenting elemental passions with an intensity that made the characters poetic symbols of man's tragic impotence to arrest his fate. His dramatic poetry was modern yet traditional, personal yet universal, Surrealist yet childlike. His plays *Bodas de sangre* (1933; *Blood Wedding*), *Yerma* (1934; Eng. trans., *Yerma*), and *La casa de Bernarda Alba* (1936; *The House of Bernarda Alba*) depicted extremes of passion involving the traditional Spanish theme of honour.

Rafael Alberti's contribution to the movement of dramatic reform was characterized by an imaginative adaptation of classical forms of Spanish drama (*El hombre deshabitado* [1931; "The Uninhabited Man"], a modern allegorical *auto* in the manner of Calderón) and by the creation of poetic, fatalistic myths out of the realism of popular themes and folk motifs.

The renovation attempted by Valle-Inclán, Grau, Lorca, and Alberti had little effect on the commercial theatre and came to an abrupt end with the outbreak of the Civil War. Though there has been no lack of skillful playwrights to provide politically acceptable entertainment (Edgar Neville, José López Rubio, Víctor Ruiz Iriarte, and Alfonso Paso) or on occasion more soul-searching drama (Alejandro Casona and Joaquín Calvo Sotelo), no great dramatist has emerged since the mid-1940s. A figure of some importance, however, is Antonio Buero Vallejo, who has had some success in revitalizing the theatre. Subtle and imaginative, he uses myth, history, and contemporary life as dramatic metaphors in his exploration and critique of society—*En la ardiente oscuridad* (1950; "In the Burning Darkness"); *La tejedora de sueños* (1952; *The Dream Weaver*); and *Un soñador para un pueblo* (1958; "A Dreamer for a People"). Alfonso Sastre has rejected this formula in favour of a more direct, committed approach to social problems. The relaxation of censorship in the 1960s awoke an interest in the Theatre of the Absurd, its main exponent in Spain being Fernando Arrabal.

Modernismo

Poetry. Rubén Darío, Latin America's greatest poet, took *modernismo* to Spain in 1892. In general, Modernism was a reaction against 19th-century bourgeois materialism and a search for other and more specifically aesthetic values of life. Darío's Modernism greatly enriched the musical resources of Spanish verse, notably by a daring use of new rhythms and metres.

Modernism heralded a brilliant period for Spanish poetry that lasted for more than half a century. A new deeply introspective, aesthetically beautiful poetry emerged, and it proved to be truly cosmopolitan in its concern with the human condition without ceasing to respond to its Spanish circumstance and literary tradition. Antonio Machado explored memory through recurrent symbols of multiple evocation, the dimly drawn boundaries of dream and reality, time past and present, searching for permanency in the duration of consciousness. A consummate creator of introspective poems in *Soledades* (1903, augmented in 1907; "Solitudes"), Machado turned outward in *Campos de Castilla* (1912, augmented in 1917; "Fields of Castile") to produce powerful poems on the state of the country and the character of its people. Anguished by transient reality, Juan Ramón Jiménez sought salvation in an absorbing, manic dedication to *poesía desnuda* ("naked poetry"). In quest of a Platonic absolute, his measured, exact poetry reflected an increasing exultation in the mystical discovery of transcendence within the immanence of self and physical reality that he never totally forsook. Jiménez' voluminous output—*Rimas* (1902; "Rhymes"); *Sonetos espirituales* (1914–15; "Spiritual Sonnets"); *Diario de un poeta recién casado* (1917; "Diary of a Poet Recently Married"); and *Animal de fondo* (1947; "Animal of the Depth")—speaks of a lifetime spent in the pursuit of poetry and its modes of expression.

The *poesía desnuda* of Juan Ramón Jiménez

A group of outstanding poets, known collectively as the Generation of 1927, made its presence felt during the 1920s and '30s and for some decades thereafter. Following the lead of Machado and Jiménez, they took inspiration from the past (ballads, traditional songs, lyrics, and Góngora's poetry) as well as from the immediate, often ephemeral present (Surrealism and other "-isms") to produce well-integrated and intensely personal poetry. Images, free from the shackles of strict reason and logic, became central to the act of poetic creation.

Among the leading members of the group was Federico García Lorca. In every respect, Lorca was a poet of fundamentals whose work demonstrated the starkness of feeling and effect characteristic of the traditional song and ballad forms. In *Romancero gitano* (1928; *The Gypsy Ballads*), he created an illusion of popular poetry with a sophisticated use of myth and symbolic imagery that conveyed to the reader a mysterious, ambivalent vision of nature. Symbols and metaphors, always central to Lorca's poetry, approach the hermetic in *Poeta en Nueva York* (1940; *Poet in New York*), a Surrealist record of urban inhumanity and rootlessness written in 1929–30 at the time of his visit to the United States. Pedro Salinas sought "pure" poetry in a reduction of content and a heightened sensitivity to language. A profoundly personal experience of love in *La voz a ti debida* (1934; "The Voice Inspired by You"; Eng. trans., *Truth of Two and Other Poems*) leads to an exploration of the subtle interrelation between the solidity of external reality and the fleeting world of subjective perception.

Jorge Guillén's sustained poetic effort is contained in *Cántico* (1928; *Cántico: A Selection*). This work, organically enlarged in successive editions, is a disciplined hymn to the marvels of everyday reality. Guillén had the rare gift of transmuting sense impressions and emotions into conceptual and structural patterns while enhancing the humanity of the experience. Always alert to impending chaos, his later works (*Clamor* [1957–63; "Clamour"] and *Homenaje* [1967; "Homage"]) displayed a keener awareness of suffering and disorder.

Aleixandre and Alberti

Vicente Aleixandre, another prominent member of the Generation of 1927, attained maturity in the controlled creation of myth after a formless dabbling in the subconscious. In *La destrucción o el amor* (1935; "Destruction or Love"), he penetrated into human despair and cosmic violence. Similar to Lorca, Rafael Alberti began writing poetry by drawing on popular forms and folk elements. His playful poetry of *Marinero en tierra* (1925; "Sailor on Land"), however, soon gave way to the stylistic complexities of *Cal y canto* (1927; "Lime and Stone") and the sombre introspective mood of *Sobre los ángeles* (1929; *Concerning the Angels*), a controlled masterpiece born out of personal crisis. The poetry of Luis Cernuda, as suggested by the title of his collected works *La realidad y el deseo* (first published 1936; "Reality and Desire"), dwells on the gulf between harsh reality and a personal world of ideal aspirations. The tension, melancholy, and sense of alienation resulting from the unbridgeable gap between these realms pervades much of Cernuda's poetry.

Other poets worthy of mention in this brilliant period of Spanish poetry are Gerardo Diego, Dámaso Alonso, Emilio Prados, and Manuel Altolaguirre. The younger Miguel Hernández, whose promise was cut short by a tragic death, bridged the gap between the Generation of 1927 and the new wave of post-Civil War poets.

New directions in poetry

The Civil War and its traumatic aftermath resulted in an abandonment of pure poetry, already signaled in the 1930s, for a simpler approach to the problem of poetic communication. Discipline of form, devotion to clarity through direct imagery, and reduced lexis were stressed and the social and human content increased, though not always in an overtly political fashion. The contemporary period has yielded many notable names—Leopoldo Panero, Luis Rosales, Luis Vivanco, Gabriel Celaya, Blas de Otero, Vicente Gaos, José Ángel Valente, Claudio Rodríquez, among others—but no truly great voice has yet emerged in the second half of the century.

Catalan literature

The Catalan language is a branch of peninsular rather than of southern Gallo-Romance. It shows, nonetheless, many traces of kinship with Provençal, and the literature in its origins used the Occitan language (*langue d'oc*, the dialects of Old French spoken south of the Loire River) and the poetic forms cultivated by troubadours north of the Pyrenees.

MEDIEVAL PERIOD

Poetry. The early Catalan troubadours Guillem de Bergadà, Hug de Mataplana, Guillem de Cervera, and others were genuine Provençal poets. About 100 years later, in the late 14th century, Provençal influence apparently lessened, and poets turned to northern France for inspiration. They took over the long French narratives on romance themes such as the Arthurian cycle and used the *noves rimades* metre, a sequence of octosyllabic rhymed couplets. Several poets working in this tradition carried the new interest in the *langue d'oïl* (the dialects of Old French spoken north of the Loire) to the extent of incorporating passages of French poetry in their poems.

The great period of Catalan poetry

The great period of Catalan poetry was the 15th century, after John I of Aragon had established in 1393 a poetic academy in Barcelona on the model of the academy in Toulouse with *jocs florals* ("floral games," or poetry congresses), including literary competitions. This royal encouragement continued under Martin I and Ferdinand I and helped to emancipate the literary style from foreign influences. As the century advanced, Valencia emerged as a new focus of literary activity: a school of poetry developing there was noted for its characteristic use of eight-line decasyllabic verses with crossed, or "chained," rhymes and final four-line refrain, illustrating a turning away from French models and a new inspiration from Italy. The *cants d'amor* and *cants de mort* ("songs of love" and "songs of death") by Ausiàs March contained the finest verses ever written in Catalan, exerted influence in 16th-century Castile, and continue to influence modern Catalan poets. Jaume Roig's *Lo spill o llibre de les dones* (*c.* 1460; "The Mirror or Book of Women") was very different—a caustic satire on woman, written in more than 16,000 four-syllable lines, portraying contemporary Valencian life vividly. Johan Roiç de Corella, a Valencian lyricist, was perhaps the best representative of the Renaissance.

After the union of Aragon with Castile, the Castilian language predominated throughout Spain, spelling a long eclipse of Catalan literature. Nevertheless, Juan Boscán Almogáver inaugurated a new Castilian school of poetry, and Castilians regard him as a landmark in the history of their Renaissance; by the time Boscán's works were published (1543), Catalan poetry had been dead for 50 years.

Prose. Though the oldest document (the text of an oath by a bishop of Urgel) dates from *c.* 1100, literary prose did not begin until the end of the 13th century. It was written in the everyday speech found in charters from the time of James I's accession to the Aragonese throne in 1213; four great chronicles that survive represent the peak of medieval Catalan prose. The anonymous *Llibre dels feyts del rey en Jacme* ("Book of the Deeds of King James"), compiled after James I's death in 1276, and Ramon Muntaner's account of the Grand Catalan Company's expedition to the Morea in southern Greece and of James II's conquest of Sardinia were distinguished by skill of narration and quality of language. Bernat Desclot's chronicle deals with the reign of Peter I the Great; though the account of Peter IV the Ceremonious is ascribed to Bernat Desclot, it was planned and revised by the King himself.

The works of Ramon Llull

Ramon Llull was unequaled in his encyclopaedic production, in Catalan, Arabic, and Latin, covering every branch of medieval knowledge and thought. His exhaustive theological treatise *Llibre de contemplació en Déu* (*c.* 1272; "Book of the Contemplation of God") began Catalonia's golden age of literature, providing incidentally a mine of information on contemporary society. The *Llibre d'Evast e Blanquerna* (*c.* 1284; *Blanquerna; a Thirteenth Century Romance*) founded Catalan fiction. It included the *Llibre d'amic e amat* (*Book of the Lover and the Beloved*), a masterpiece of mysticism, while his *Fèlix* (*c.* 1288) and *Llibre de l'orde de cauaylería* (between 1275 and 1281; *The Book of the Order of Chivalry*) were instructive works in a narrative framework.

Bernat Metge began the "classical age" by translating Boccaccio's story of Griselda from Petrarch's Latin version and, clothing his scholastic learning with poetic imagination, achieved the stylistic masterpiece of Catalan prose. The chivalric romance *Tirant lo Blanc* (*c.* 1460) by Joanot Martorell was notable of its kind for the theme, drawn from Muntaner, of the real adventures of the Catalans in the Middle East. The anonymous late 14th-century *Curial e Güelfa* draws on Desclot and is the only other Catalan romance in this vein.

The beginnings of drama were represented by a 15th-century Assumption play, *Misteri d'Elch,* which is still performed annually at Elche on the Feast of the Assumption.

DECLINE: 16TH–18TH CENTURY

With the loss of political independence, literary and linguistic independence was also lost, and Catalan fell to the level of a patois, kept alive only in the countryside and in the pulpit. The 16th century furnishes a single poet worthy of the name: Pere Serafí, some of whose *Cants d'amor* (1565), written in imitation of Ausiàs March but less obscure, are graceful enough to merit remembrance. In prose, only scholars, chiefly antiquaries and historians, still wrote in Catalan. Forty years of research and abundant documentation give interest to the *Crònica universal del principat de Cathalunya,* a history of the Catalan kingdom, of Jeroni Pujadas, of which only the first part (1609) is in Catalan. Thereafter, the eclipse was almost complete. Catalan remained only as the language of folk song and ballad; in these—first collected in the *Romancerillo catalán* (1853; "Little Collection of Catalan Ballads") by Manuel Milà i Fontanals, the historian who played a considerable part in the Catalan revival—it lived on until the reawakening.

THE RENAIXENSA AND AFTER

In 1814 appeared the *Gramática y apologia de la llengua cathalana* ("Grammar and Apology of the Catalan Language") of Josep Pau Ballot i Torres, a forerunner of the literary and linguistic renascence (Renaixensa) that marked the Romantic period in Catalonia. The pioneers, however, saw the inadequacies of the ancient language for the expression of spiritual and intellectual ideas. The Institut d'Estudis Catalans, founded in Barcelona in 1907, has played a notable part in the deliberate enrichment and purifying of Catalan as a vehicle for contemporary thought.

Bonaventura Carles Aribau's patriotic *Oda a la pátria*

Major Romantic poets

(1832; "Ode to the Fatherland") and the poems of Joaquim Rubió i Ors and Victor Balaguer prepared the way for the mysticism of Jacintó Verdaguer Santaló, a great epic poet (*L'Atlántida* [1877], *Canigó* [1886]). Miguel Costa i Llobera cultivated a classical perfection of form. In Joan Maragall i Gorina, Catalonia found its first great modern poet who, in spiritual quality, exerted a powerful influence on later poets.

The foundations of modern Catalan prose were laid by the critical writings of Rubió i Ors, Francisco Pi i Margall, one of the four presidents of the Spanish Republic of 1873, and Josep Torras i Bages (*La tradició catalana* [1892; "The Catalan Tradition"]). One of the best and most influential writers in prose was the essayist Eugeni d'Ors (pseudonym "Xenius"), whose philosophical novel *La ben plantada* (1911; "Firmly Rooted") was one of the most notable works in modern Catalan literature.

Catalan dramatists have produced plays of considerable originality. Àngel Guimerà achieved a European reputation with *Terra baixa* (1896; "Lowlands"), which inspired a German and a French opera and was widely translated. The many social dramas of Ignasi Iglésias, inspired by the early works of Gerhart Hauptmann, included one near-masterpiece, *Els Vells* (1903). Adrià Gual, author of several works of fantasy, did his best work as director of the Teatre Intim, founded in Barcelona in 1898, which familiarized the public with the great drama of all countries and ages.

Further development of modern Catalan literature was delayed by the dictatorship (1923–30) of Miguel Primo de Rivera, who banned the use of any language other than Castilian, and by the Civil War of 1936–39. Many Catalan men of letters fled abroad, and those who remained found the political climate hardly conducive to productive literary activity.

Conditions in Catalonia improved only slightly during the postwar years as the government of Gen. Francisco Franco adopted a generally repressive policy toward Catalan culture. Although some Catalan writers chose to ignore the prevailing realities and cultivated what could be construed as a literature of artistic escape, the most influential poets of the period, Salvador Espriu and Pere Quart (pseudonym of Joan Oliver), began writing poetry that dealt with social issues in a decidedly Realistic mode. Other recent Catalan authors of note, such as the prose writers Mercè Rodoreda and Josep Maria Espinàs, also have largely grounded their works in contemporary social life.

Galician literature

Medieval poetry. Galician is closely related to Portuguese, and there is no separating the two languages in the three great repositories of medieval verse, the 14th-century *Cancioneiro* ("Songbook") *da Ajuda, Cancioneiro da Vaticana,* and *Colocci-Brancuti.* Indigenous lyric origins were overlaid by Provençal influence, and a dominance of emotion over thought identified Galician with subjective lyricism, so that for over a century Castilian poets made it their medium for lyrics. Of 116 names in the *Cancioneiro da Vaticana,* 75 have been tentatively identified as Galician; none achieved particular individuality. Macías El Enamorado (flourished mid-14th century) was the last Galician troubadour; Galicians thereafter wrote in Castilian, and, though there were echoes of their tradition, the Renaissance and Castilian political hegemony finally ended Galician literature until the 19th century.

The modern revival. The Romantic movement, like the Peninsular War, revived local feeling and interest in things Galician but not in the language. The *xogos froraes* ("floral games," or poetry congresses; an equivalent of Catalan and Provençal *jocs florals*) of 1861, with the first dictionary (1863) and first grammar (1864) of Galician, marked a change. Francisco Añón y Paz was the first notable poet in the resurrected idiom, his most stirring notes being love of country and of freedom. Rosalía de Castro, the greatest name in Galician literature, identified herself with the spirit and people of the Galician countryside in *Cantares gallegos* (1863; "Galician Songs"); her *Follas novas* (1880; "New Leaves"), introspective to the verge of despair, reflected deep personal sorrows. Eduardo Pondal y Abente, a bard of a dimly sensed heroic past, was concerned with nature and Celtic mythology. Valentín Lamas Carvajal has been remembered as the voice of the peasant.

Rosalía de Castro

Prose showed no comparable achievement. Aurelio Ribalta, Manuel Lugrís Freire, and Heraclio Pérez Placer wrote short stories but were overshadowed by novelists of stature—Emilia, condesa de Pardo Bazán, and Rosalía de Castro—who chose to write for a larger public in Castilian.

The 20th century has produced, especially since 1920, a continuing abundance of Galician poets, not yet sufficiently differentiated, who underline the identification of Galician literature with a markedly poetic regional temperament and language.

BIBLIOGRAPHY

Castilian: GERALD BRENAN, *The Literature of the Spanish People: From Roman Times to the Present,* 2nd ed. (1953, reprinted 1976); RICHARD E. CHANDLER and KESSEL SCHWARTZ, *A New History of Spanish Literature* (1961); GEORGE T. NORTHUP, *An Introduction to Spanish Literature,* 3rd ed. rev. by NICHOLSON B. ADAMS (1960), a good, readable history; PHILIP WARD (ed.), *The Oxford Companion to Spanish Literature* (1978); and FRANCISCO RICO (general ed.), *Historia y crítica de la literatura española,* 8 vol. (1980–84).

The following works focus on specific periods or trends of Spanish literary history: OTIS H. GREEN, *The Literary Mind of Medieval and Renaissance Spain* (1970), essays by an eminent scholar; A.D. DEYERMOND, *The Middle Ages* (1971), a very good introduction, with bibliography; OTIS H. GREEN, *Spain and the Western Tradition: The Castilian Mind in Literature from El Cid to Calderón,* 4 vol. (1963–66), readable and authoritative; R.O. JONES, *The Golden Age: Prose and Poetry: The Sixteenth and Seventeenth Centuries* (1971), an excellent introduction; EDWARD M. WILSON and DUNCAN MOIR, *The Golden Age: Drama* (1971), essential reading; JOHN A. COOK, *Neo-Classic Drama in Spain: Theory and Practice* (1959, reprinted 1974); ROBERT E. PELLISSIER, *The Neo-Classic Movement in Spain During the XVIII Century* (1918); NIGEL GLENDINNING, *The Eighteenth Century* (1972); DONALD L. SHAW, *The Nineteenth Century* (1972); E. ALLISON PEERS, *A History of the Romantic Movement in Spain,* 2 vol. (1940, reprinted 1964), a comprehensive account; L.B. WALTON, *Pérez Galdós and the Spanish Novel of the Nineteenth Century* (1927, reprinted 1970), a somewhat dated but still useful account; GONZALO TORRENTE BALLESTER, *Panorama de la literatura española contemporánea,* 3rd ed. (1965), studies and selections, and *Teatro español contemporáneo,* 2nd ed. (1968); RAMÓN CASTELLTORT, *La poesia lírica española del siglo XX* (1957); JUAN L. ALBORG, *Hora actual de la novela española,* 2 vol. (1958–62); PAUL ILIE, *The Surrealist Mode in Spanish Literature: An Interpretation of Basic Trends from Post-Romanticism to the Spanish Vanguard* (1968), the first examination of Spanish Surrealism, and *Literature and Inner Exile: Authoritarian Spain, 1939–1975* (1980); G.G. BROWN, *A Literary History of Spain,* vol. 6, *The Twentieth Century* (1972), one of the most thorough surveys in either English or Spanish.

Catalan: JOAN ARÚS, *Evolució de la poesia catalana* (1922); OCTAVI SALTOR, *Les idees literàries en la renaixença catalana* (1934); MARTÍN DE RIQUER, *Resumen de literatura catalana* (1947), and *Los Trovadores,* 3 vol. (1975, reissued 1983; originally published as *La lírica de los trovadores,* 1948), an anthology with notes; JOAN RUIZ I CALONJA, *Història de la literatura catalana* (1954); JOAN TRIADÚ (comp.), *Anthology of Catalan Lyric Poetry,* ed. by JOAN GILI (1953, reprinted 1976); and ARTHUR TERRY, *Catalan Literature* (1972).

Galician: ALVARO DE LAS CASAS (comp.), *Antología de la lírica gallega* (1928); ROSALÍA DE CASTRO, *Poems,* trans. by CHARLES DAVID LEY (1964); P. JOSÉ MOURIÑO, *La literatura medioeval en Galicia* (1929); and BENITO VARELA JÁCOME, *História de la literatura gallega* (1951).

(W.C.A./A.M.G.-G.)

Speech

While many animals possess voices of various types and inflections, man has learned to modulate his voice by articulating the laryngeal tone into audible oral speech. Vocal sound in itself is meaningless, until the conventional codes of a language have been learned, ordinarily first from the mother, then from other family members, and finally in school. "Sick," for example, means "ill" in English, while *sic* means "so" or "thus" in Latin. The difference between speech and language is one of application. Speech is the oral, audible expression of human language while talking. Writing and reading represent the use of human language through graphic symbols. The Morse code, naval flag signals, smoke signals of American Indians, African drum languages, and the almost extinct whistle language of the Pyrenees are all examples of special language usage without the need for oral speech. Each of these language systems has its own mode of transmission (electronic equipment, light, and air) and each is limited by darkness, distance, obstacles, etc.

Man became characteristically human when he learned to speak, perhaps 1,000,000 or more years ago, although the exact time will probably never be known. The ability to use symbolic and abstract spoken language is so far specifically human, though psychologists who have investigated the possibility of teaching spoken language to chimpanzees raised like human children in the family home have had results that, while limited, suggested that great affection and intensive training can teach a nonhuman some primitive beginnings of symbolic verbal behaviour (*e.g.*, sounds resembling "mama").

Man differs from the higher animals in several respects: he makes no mechanical use of his mouth in food gathering or tool making, and thus has freed his oral cavity for such activities as verbal articulation. He has developed manual dexterity, the preferred use of one leading and dominant hand for skilled manipulation, drawing, and (later) writing. Preferred laterality (left or right) of hand, foot, eye, face muscles, tongue, and even ears is linked to the development of a distinctively human (known in no other animal) dominance of one brain hemisphere over the other in speech learning. Many nerve pathways from either side of the brain cross to the other side of the body. Thus, the human brain became ready for specialized language function in the dominant hemisphere of the brain, usually the left hemisphere. It may be inferred that language had as its precursors such phenomena as tool making and cerebral dominance. Conversely, it would seem that prehistoric relics of fire, tools, weapons, and utensils indicate that the makers of such artifacts must have possessed some form of language. All human culture (and its propagation) appears to depend on some form of language to serve as the vehicle for teaching, persuasion, and tradition. Indeed, cultural impoverishment is observed in those with little or no language and speech: deaf-mutes, the mentally retarded, or the abnormally isolated. Without special instruction, learning is greatly impeded in deaf children, despite the potential for great intelligence that may be present. (Ed.)

The article is divided into the following sections:

The phonetics of speech

ARTICULATORY PHONETICS

The traditional method of describing speech sounds is in terms of the movements of the vocal organs that produce them. The main structures that are important in the production of speech are the lungs and the respiratory system, together with the vocal organs shown in Figure 1. The airstream from the lungs passes between the vocal cords, which are two small muscular folds located in the larynx at the top of the windpipe. The space between the vocal cords is known as the glottis. If the vocal cords are apart, as they are normally when breathing out, the air from the lungs will have a relatively free passage into the pharynx (see Figure 1) and the mouth. But if the vocal cords are adjusted so that there is a narrow passage between them, the airstream will cause them to be sucked together. As soon as they are together there will be no flow of air, and the pressure below them will be built up until they are blown apart again. The flow of air between them will then cause them to be sucked together again, and the vibratory cycle will continue. Sounds produced when the vocal cords are vibrating are said to be voiced, as opposed to those in which the vocal cords are apart, which are said to be voiceless.

Voiced and voiceless sounds

The air passages above the vocal cords are known collectively as the vocal tract. For phonetic purposes they may be divided into the oral tract within the mouth and the pharynx, and the nasal tract within the nose. Many speech sounds are characterized by movements of the lower articulators—*i.e.,* the tongue or the lower lip—toward the upper articulators within the oral tract. The upper surface includes several important structures from the point of view of speech production, such as the upper lip and the upper teeth; Figure 1 illustrates most of the terms that are commonly used. The alveolar ridge is a small protu-

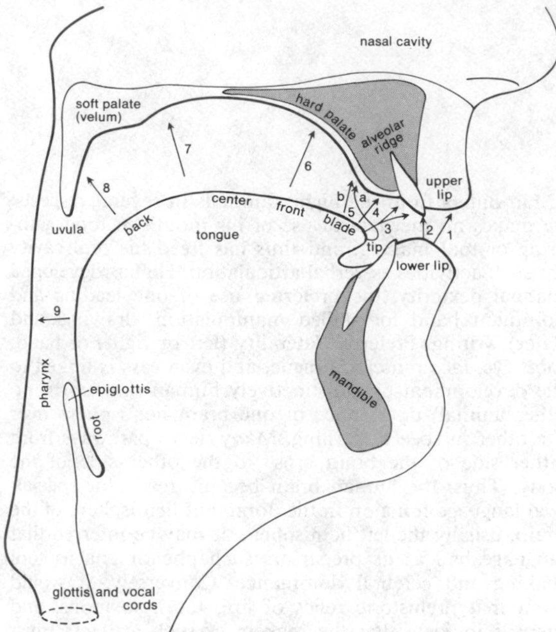

Figure 1: *Location of vocal organs and possible places of articulation.*
(1) Bilabial. (2) Labiodental. (3) Dental and interdental. (4) Alveolar. (5) Postalveolar. (a) retroflex. (b) palato-alveolar. (6) Palatal. (7) Velar. (8) Uvular. (9) Pharyngeal.

berance just behind the upper front teeth that can easily be felt with the tongue. The major part of the roof of the mouth is formed by the hard palate in the front, and the soft palate or velum at the back. The soft palate is a muscular flap that can be raised so as to shut off the nasal tract and prevent air from going out through the nose. When it is raised so that the soft palate is pressed against the back wall of the pharynx there is said to be a velic closure. At the lower end of the soft palate is a small hanging appendage known as the uvula.

As may be seen from Figure 1, there are also specific names for different parts of the tongue. The tip and blade are the most mobile parts. Behind the blade is the so-called front of the tongue; it is actually the forward part of the body of the tongue and lies underneath the hard palate when the tongue is at rest. The remainder of the body of the tongue may be divided into the centre, which is partly beneath the hard palate and partly beneath the soft palate; the back, which is beneath the soft palate; and the root, which is opposite the back wall of the pharynx.

The major division in speech sounds is that between vowels and consonants. Phoneticians have found it difficult to give a precise definition of the articulatory distinction between these two classes of sounds. Most authorities would agree that a vowel is a sound that is produced without any major constrictions in the vocal tract, so that there is a relatively free passage for the air. It is also syllabic. This description is unsatisfactory in that no adequate definition of the notion syllabic has yet been formulated.

Consonants. In the formation of consonants, the airstream through the vocal tract is obstructed in some way. Consonants can be classified according to the place and manner of this obstruction. Some of the possible places of articulation are indicated by the arrows going from one of the lower articulators to one of the upper articulators in Figure 1. The principal terms that are required in the description of English articulation, and the structures of the vocal tract that they involve are: bilabial, the two lips; dental, tongue tip or blade and the upper front teeth; alveolar, tongue tip or blade and the teeth ridge; retroflex, tongue tip and the back part of the teeth ridge; palato-alveolar, tongue blade and the back part of the teeth ridge; palatal, front of tongue and hard palate; and velar, back of tongue and soft palate. The additional places of articulation shown in Figure 1 are required in the description of other languages. Note that the terms for the various places of articulation denote both the portion

Classification of consonants

of the lower articulators (*i.e.,* lower lip and tongue) and the portion of the upper articulatory structures that are involved. Thus velar denotes a sound in which the back of the tongue and the soft palate are involved, and retroflex implies a sound involving the tip of the tongue and the back part of the alveolar ridge. If it is necessary to distinguish between sounds made with the tip of the tongue and those made with the blade, the terms apical (tip) and laminal (blade) may be used.

There are six basic manners of articulation that can be used at these places of articulation: stop, fricative, approximant, trill, tap, and lateral.

Stops. Stops involve closure of the articulators to obstruct the airstream. This manner of articulation can be considered in terms of nasal and oral stops. If the soft palate is down so that air can still go out through the nose, there is said to be a nasal stop. Sounds of this kind occur at the beginning of the words *my* and *nigh.* If, in addition to the articulatory closure in the mouth, the soft palate is raised so that the nasal tract is blocked off, then the airstream will be completely obstructed, the pressure in the mouth will be built up, and an oral stop will be formed. When the articulators open the airstream will be released with a plosive quality. This kind of sound occurs in the consonants in the words *pie, tie, kye, buy, die,* and *guy.* Many authorities refer to these two articulations as nasals, meaning nasal stops (closure of the articulators in the oral tract), and stops, meaning oral stops (raising of the soft palate to form a velic closure).

Fricatives. A fricative sound involves the close approximation of two articulators, so that the airstream is partially obstructed and a turbulent airflow is produced. The mechanisms used in the production of these sounds may be compared to the physical forces involved when the wind "whistles" round a corner. Examples are the initial sounds in the words *fie, thigh, sigh* and *shy.* Some authorities divide fricatives into slit and grooved fricatives, or rill and flat fricatives, depending on the shape of the constriction in the mouth required to produce them. Other authorities divide fricatives into sibilants, as in *sigh* and *shy,* and nonsibilants, as in *fie* and *thigh.* This division is based on acoustic criteria (see below).

Varieties of fricatives

Approximants. Approximants are produced when one articulator approaches another but does not make the vocal tract so narrow that a turbulent airstream results. The terms frictionless continuant, semivowel, and glide are sometimes used for some of the sounds made with this manner of articulation. The consonants in the words *we* and *you* are examples of approximants.

Trills. A trill results when an articulator is held loosely fairly close to another articulator, so that it is set into vibration by the airstream. The tongue tip and blade, the uvula, and the lips are the only articulators than can be used in this way. Tongue tip trills occur in some forms of Scottish English in words such as *rye* and *ire.* Uvular trills are comparatively rare but are used in some dialects of French, but not Parisian French. Trills of the lips are even rarer but do occur in a few African languages.

Taps. A tap is produced if one articulator is thrown against another, as when the loosely held tongue tip makes a single tap against the upper teeth or the alveolar ridge. The consonant in the middle of a word such as *letter* or *Betty* is often made in this way in American English. The term flap is also used to describe these sounds, but some authorities make a distinction between taps as defined here and flaps, in which the tip of the tongue is raised up and back and then strikes the alveolar ridge as it returns to a position behind the lower front teeth. Some languages—*e.g.,* Hausa, the principal language of Northern Nigeria—distinguish between words containing a flap and words containing a tap. The distinction between a trill and a tap is used in Spanish to distinguish between words such as *perro,* meaning "dog," and *pero,* meaning "but."

Laterals. When the airstream is obstructed in the midline of the oral tract, and there is incomplete closure between one or both sides of the tongue and the roof of the mouth, the resulting sound is classified as a lateral. The sounds at the beginning and end of the word *lull* are laterals in most forms of American English.

The production of many sounds involves more than one of these six basic manners of articulation. The sounds at the beginning and end of the word *church* are stops combined with fricatives. The articulators—tongue tip or blade, and alveolar ridge—come together for the stop, and then, instead of coming fully apart, they separate only slightly so that a fricative is made at the same place of articulation. This kind of combination is called an affricate. Lateral articulations may also occur in combination with other manners of articulation. The laterals in a word such as *lull* might more properly be called lateral approximants, in that the airstream passes out freely between the sides of the tongue and the roof of the mouth without a turbulent airstream being produced. But in some sounds in other languages the sides of the tongue are closer to the roof of the mouth and a lateral fricative occurs; an example is the sound spelled *ll* in Welsh words such as *llan* "church" and the name *Lluellyn*.

Affricates

Secondary articulations. When an approximant articulation occurs at the same time as another articulation is being made at a different place in the vocal tract, the approximant is said to form a secondary articulation. There are special terms for some of these possibilities. Added lip rounding is called labialization; it occurs in the formation of several English sounds—*e.g.,* during the pronunciation of the palato-alveolar fricative at the beginning of the word *shoe.* Raising of the front of the tongue while simultaneously making another articulation elsewhere in the vocal tract is called palatalization. It is the distinguishing characteristic of the soft consonants in Russian and also occurs, to a lesser extent, in English; *e.g.,* in the first consonant in the word *leaf.* Raising of the back of the tongue to form a secondary articulation is called velarization; it occurs in the last consonant in the word *feel,* which therefore does not contain the same sounds as those in the reverse order in the word *leaf.* Retracting of the root of the tongue while making another articulation is called pharyngealization; it occurs in Arabic in what are called emphatic consonants.

The states of the glottis, places of articulation, and manners of articulation discussed above are sufficient to distinguish between the major contrasts among the consonants of English and many other languages. But additional possibilities have to be taken into account in a more detailed description of English, or in descriptions of several other languages. Among these possibilities are variations in the timing of the states of the glottis. In addition to the contrast between the voiced and voiceless states of the glottis that occur during an articulation, there may be variations in the state of the glottis during the release of the articulation. Thus both the *p* in *pin* and that in *spin* are voiceless bilabial stops, but they differ in that the glottis remains in a voiceless position for a short time after the release of the bilabial stop in *pin,* whereas in *spin* the voicing starts as soon as the lips come apart. When there is a period of voicelessness during the release of an articulation, the sound is said to be aspirated. The main difference between the consonants in *pea* and *bee,* when these words are said in isolation, is not that the one is voiceless and the other voiced, but that the first is aspirated and the second is unaspirated. Some languages distinguish between both voiced–voiceless and aspirated–unaspirated sounds. Thus Thai has contrasts between voiceless aspirated stops, voiceless unaspirated stops, and voiced unaspirated stops.

States of the glottis

Several languages use more than just the voiced and voiceless states of the glottis. In Hindi and many of the other languages of India, some sounds are produced while the vocal cords are vibrating for part of their length but are apart, so that a considerable amount of air escapes between them at one end. This phenomenon is known as breathy voice, or murmur. Other languages have sounds in which the vocal cords are held tightly together so that only part of their length can vibrate. This kind of sound, which is usually very low pitched, is sometimes called creaky voice, or vocal fry. It is used to make contrasts between consonants in several American Indian languages. An additional glottal state that is widely used—*e.g.,* in the Austronesian (Malayo–Polynesian) languages of the Philippines—is a glottal stop, a tight closure of the two vocal cords. This articulation also occurs in many forms of English as the usual pronunciation of *t* in words such as *bitten* and *fatten.*

Types of airstream. In English, all sounds are produced with an airstream caused by the expiration of the air from the lungs. This is known as a pulmonic airstream. Other mechanisms for producing an airstream also occur. If there is a glottal stop and the closed glottis is moved rapidly upward or downward it can act like a piston pushing or pulling the air in the pharynx. This is the glottalic airstream mechanism. When there is an upward movement of the closed glottis the resulting sound is called an ejective. Amharic, the national language of Ethiopia, uses this mechanism to produce both ejective stops and fricatives, which contrast with the more usual stops and fricatives made with a pulmonic airstream mechanism. A downward movement of the glottis is used in the production of implosive sounds, which occur in many American Indian, African, and other languages. The use of movements of the tongue to suck air into the mouth is known as the velaric airstream mechanism; it occurs in the production of clicks, which are regular speech sounds in many languages of southern Africa.

To summarize, a consonant may be described by reference to seven factors: (1) state of the glottis, (2) secondary articulation (if any), (3) place of articulation, (4) type of airstream, (5) central or lateral articulation, (6) velic closure—oral or nasal, and (7) manner of articulation. Thus the consonant at the beginning of the word *swim* is a (1) voiceless, (2) labialized, (3) alveolar, (4) pulmonic, (5) central, (6) oral, (7) fricative. Unless a specific statement is made to the contrary, consonants are usually presumed to have a pulmonic airstream and no secondary articulation, and it is also assumed that they are not laterals or nasals. Consequently, points 2, 4, 5, and 6 are often disregarded and a three-term description—*e.g.,* voiceless alveolar fricative is sufficient.

Factors in consonant description

Vowels. Vowels traditionally have been specified in terms of the position of the highest point of the tongue and the position of the lips. Figure 2 shows these positions for eight different vowels. The highest point of the tongue is in the front of the mouth for the vowels in *heed, hid, head,* and *had.* Accordingly, these vowels are classified as front vowels, whereas the vowels in *hod, hawed, hood,* and *who'd* are classified as back vowels. The tongue is highest in the vowels in *heed* and *who'd,* which are therefore called high, or close, vowels, and lowest in the vowels in *had* and *hod,* which are called low, or open, vowels. The height of the tongue for the vowels in the other words is between these two extremes, and they are therefore called midvowels. Lip positions may be described as being rounded, as in *who'd,* or unrounded or spread, as in *heed.*

The specification of vowels in terms of the position of the highest point of the tongue is not entirely satisfactory for a number of reasons. In the first place, it disregards the fact that the shape of the tongue as a whole is very different in front vowels and in back vowels. Second, although the height of the tongue in front vowels varies by approximately equal amounts for what are called equidistant steps in vowel quality, this is just not factually true

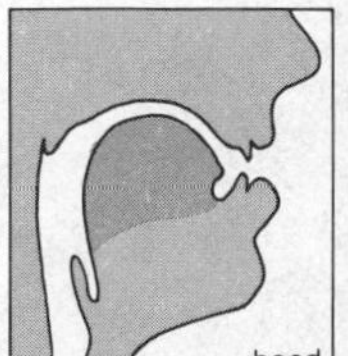

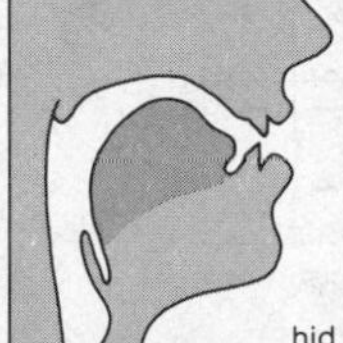

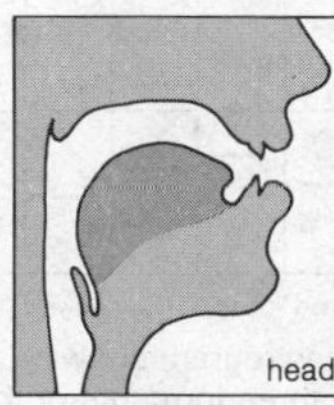

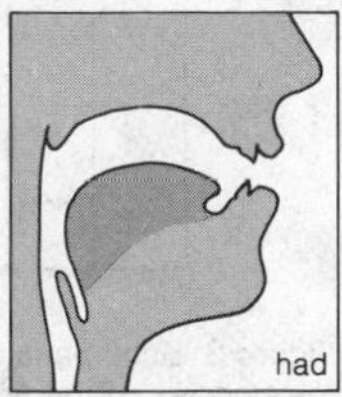

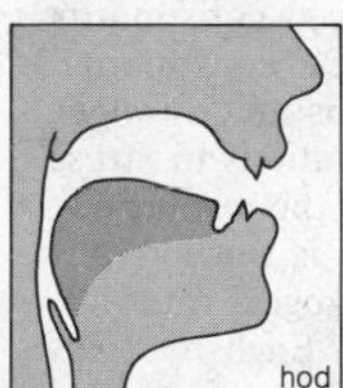

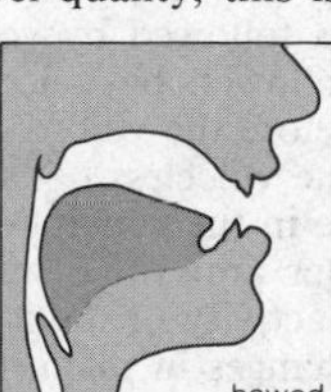

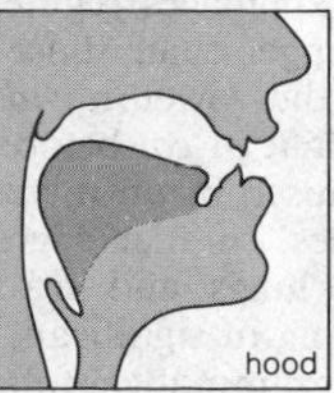

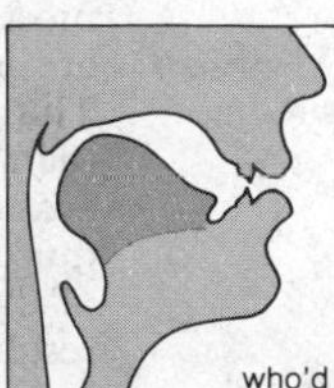

Figure 2: Tongue position for several vowel sounds.

in descriptions of back vowels. Third, the width of the pharynx varies considerably, and to some extent independently of the height of the tongue, in different vowels.

Tenseness and laxness

Some authorities use terms such as tense and lax to describe the degree of tension in the tongue muscles, particularly those muscles responsible for the bunching up of the tongue lengthways. Other authorities use the term tense to specify a greater degree of muscular activity, resulting in a greater deformation of the tongue from its neutral position. Tense vowels are longer than the corresponding lax vowels. The vowels in *heed* and *hayed* are tense, whereas those in *hid* and *head* are lax.

In many languages there is a strong tendency for front vowels to have spread lip positions, and back vowels to have lip rounding. As will be seen in the next section, this results in vowels that are acoustically maximally distinct. But many languages—*e.g.,* French and German—have front rounded vowels. Thus French has a contrast between a high front unrounded vowel in *vie,* "life," and a high front rounded vowel with a very similar tongue position in *vu,* "seen," as well as a high back rounded vowel in *vous,* "you." Unrounded back vowels also occur—*e.g.,* in Vietnamese.

Nasalized vowels, in which the soft palate is lowered so that part of the airstream goes out through the nose, occur in many languages. French distinguishes between several nasalized vowels and vowels made with similar tongue positions but with the soft palate raised. Low vowels in many forms of English are often nasalized, especially when they occur between nasal consonants, as in *man.*

Cardinal vowels

Because of the difficulty of observing the precise tongue positions that occur in vowels, a set of eight vowels known as the cardinal vowels has been devised to act as reference points. This set of vowels is defined partly in articulatory and partly in auditory terms. Cardinal vowel number one is defined as the highest and farthest front tongue position that can be made without producing a fricative sound; cardinal vowel number five is defined as the lowest and farthest back vowel. Cardinal vowels two, three, and four are a series of front vowels that form auditorily equidistant steps between cardinal vowels one and five; and cardinal vowels six, seven, and eight are a series of back vowels with the same sized auditory steps as in the front vowel series. Phoneticians who have been trained in the cardinal vowel system are able to make precise descriptions of the vowels of any language in terms of these reference points.

Suprasegmentals. Vowels and consonants can be considered to be the segments of which speech is composed. Together they form syllables, which in turn make up utterances. Superimposed on the syllables there are other features that are known as suprasegmentals. These include variations in stress (accent) and pitch (tone and intonation). Variations in length are also usually considered to be suprasegmental features, although they can affect single segments as well as whole syllables. All of the suprasegmental features are characterized by the fact that they must be described in relation to other items in the same utterance. It is the relative values of the pitch, length, or degree of stress of an item that are significant. The absolute values are never linguistically important, although they may be of importance paralinguistically, in that they convey information about the age and sex of the speaker, his emotional state, and his attitude.

Many languages—*e.g.,* Finnish and Estonian—use length distinctions, so that they have long and short vowels; a slightly smaller number of languages, among them Luganda (the language spoken by the largest tribe in Uganda) and Japanese, also have long and short consonants. In most languages segments followed by voiced consonants are longer than those followed by voiceless consonants. Thus the vowel in *cad* before the voiced *d* is much longer than that in *cat* before the voiceless *t.* Variations in stress are caused by an increase in the activity of the respiratory muscles, so that a greater amount of air is pushed out of the lungs, and in the activity of the laryngeal muscles, resulting in significant changes in pitch. In English, stress has a grammatical function, distinguishing between nouns and verbs, such as *an insult* versus *to insult.* It can also be used for contrastive emphasis, as in *I want a RED pen, not a black one.*

Pitch and intonation

Variations in laryngeal activity can occur independently of stress changes. The resulting pitch changes can affect the meaning of the sentence as a whole, or the meaning of the individual words. Pitch pattern is known as intonation. In English the meaning of a sentence such as *That's a cat* can be changed from a statement to a question by the substitution of a mainly rising for a mainly falling intonation. Pitch patterns that affect the meanings of individual words are known as tones and are common in many languages. In Chinese, for example, a syllable that is transliterated as *ma* means "mother" when said on a high tone, "hemp" on a midrising tone, "horse" on the falling-rising tone, and "scold" on a high-falling tone.

ACOUSTIC PHONETICS

Speech sounds consist of small variations in air pressure that can be sensed by the ear. Like other sounds, speech sounds can be divided into two major classes—those that have periodic wave forms (*i.e.,* regular fluctuations in air pressure) and those that do not. The first class consists of all the voiced sounds, because the vibrations of the vocal cords produce regular pulses of air pressure.

Fundamental frequency

From a listener's point of view, sounds may be said to vary in pitch, loudness, and quality. The pitch of a sound with a periodic wave form—*i.e.,* a voiced sound—is determined by its fundamental frequency, or rate of repetition of the cycles of air pressure. For a speaker with a bass voice, the fundamental frequency will probably be between 75 and 150 cycles per second. Cycles per second are also called hertz (Hz); this is the standard term for the unit in frequency measurements. A soprano may have a speaking voice in which the vocal cords vibrate to produce a fundamental frequency of over 400 hertz. The relative loudness of a voiced sound is largely dependent on the amplitude of the pulses of air pressure produced by the vibrating vocal cords. Pulses of air with a larger amplitude have a larger increase in air pressure.

The quality of a sound is determined by the smaller variations in air pressure that are superimposed on the major variations that recur at the fundamental frequency. These smaller variations in air pressure correspond to the overtones that occur above the fundamental frequency. Each time the vocal cords open and close there is a pulse of air from the lungs. These pulses act like sharp taps on the air in the vocal tract, which is accordingly set into vibration in a way that is determined by its size and shape. In a vowel sound, the air in the vocal tract vibrates at three or four frequencies simultaneously. These frequencies are the resonant frequencies of that particular vocal tract shape. Irrespective of the fundamental frequency that is determined by the rate of vibration of the vocal cords, the air in the vocal tract will resonate at these three or four overtone frequencies as long as the position of the vocal organs remains the same. In this way a vowel has its own characteristic auditory quality, which is the result of the specific variations in air pressure caused by the superimposing of the vocal tract shape on the fundamental frequency produced by the vocal cords.

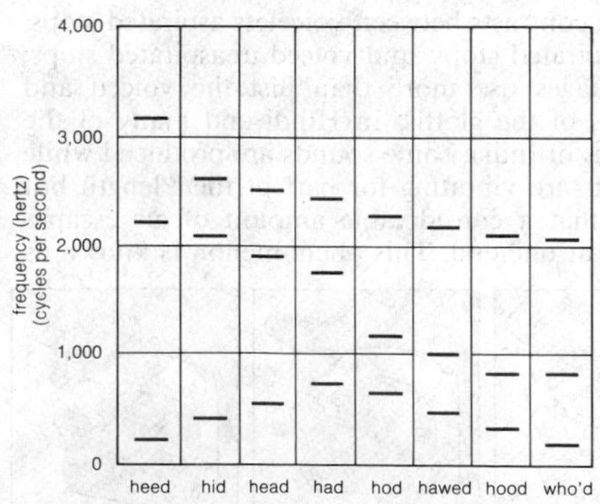

Figure 3: Schematic spectrogram showing frequencies of the first three formants of the vowels in similar English words.

Vowel formants. The resonant frequencies of the vocal tract are known as the formants. The frequencies of the first three formants of the vowels in the words *heed, hid, head, had, hod, hawed, hood,* and *who'd* are shown in Figure 3. Comparison with Figure 2 shows that there are no simple relationships between actual tongue positions and formant frequencies. There is, however, a good inverse correlation between one of the labels used to describe the tongue position and the frequency of the first, or lowest, formant. This formant is lowest in the so-called high vowels, and highest in the so-called low vowels. When phoneticians describe vowels as high or low, they probably are actually specifying the inverse of the frequency of the first formant.

Most people cannot hear the pitches of the individual formants in normal speech. In whispered speech, however, there are no regular variations in air pressure produced by the vocal cords, and the higher resonances of the vocal tract are more clearly audible. It is quite easy to hear the falling pitch of the second formant when whispering the series of words *heed, hid, head, had, hod, hawed, hood, who'd.* Conversely, the auditory effect of the second and higher formants is lessened when speaking in a creaky voice. Under such conditions, it is possible to hear the rise in pitch of the first formant during the first four of these words, and the fall in pitch during the last.

Consonant formants. Voiced consonants such as nasals and laterals also have specific vocal tract shapes that are characterized by the frequencies of the formants. They differ from vowels in that in their production the vocal tract is not a single tube. There is a side branch formed when the nasal tract is coupled in with the oral tract, or, in the case of laterals, when the oral tract itself is obstructed in the centre. The effect of these side branches is that the relative amplitudes of the formants are altered; it is as if one or more of the possible superimposed variations in air pressure had been lessened because it had been trapped in the cavity formed at the side. Nasals and laterals can therefore be specified in terms of their formant frequencies, just like vowels. But in a complete specification of these consonants the relative amplitudes of the formants also have to be given, because they are not completely predictable.

Other voiced consonants such as stops and approximants (semivowels) are more like vowels in that they can be characterized in part by the resonant frequencies—the formants—of their vocal tract shapes. They differ from vowels in that during a voiced stop closure there is very little acoustic energy, and during the release phase of a stop and the entire articulation of a semivowel the vocal tract shapes are changing comparatively rapidly. These transitional movements can be specified acoustically in terms of the movements of the formant frequencies.

Pitch of voiceless sounds

Voiceless sounds do not have a periodic wave form with a well-defined fundamental frequency. Nevertheless, some sensations of pitch accompany the variations in air pressure caused by the turbulent airflow that occurs during a voiceless fricative, or in the release phase of a voiceless stop. This is because the pressure variations are far from random. During the first consonant in *sea* these have a tendency to be at a higher centre frequency, and hence a higher pitch, than in the pronunciation of the first consonant in *she.* There is also a difference in the average amplitude of the wave form in different voiceless sounds. All voiceless sounds have much less energy—*i.e.,* a smaller amplitude—than voiced sounds pronounced with the same degree of effort. Other things being equal, the fricatives in *sin* and *shin* have more amplitude—*i.e.,* are louder—than those in *thin* and *fin.*

In summary, speech sounds are fairly well defined by nine acoustic factors. The first three factors include the frequencies of the first three formants; these are responsible for the major part of the information in speech. Characterizing the vocal tract shape, these formant frequencies specify vowels, nasals, laterals, and the transitional movements in voiced consonants. The frequencies of the fourth and higher formants do not vary significantly. The fourth factor is the fundamental frequency—roughly speaking, the pitch—of the larynx pulse in voiced sounds, and the fifth, the amplitude—roughly speaking, the loudness—of the larynx pulse. These last two factors account for suprasegmental information; *e.g.,* variations in stress and intonation. They also distinguish between voiced and voiceless sounds, in that the latter have no larynx pulse amplitude. The centre frequency of the high-frequency hissing noises in voiceless sounds constitutes the sixth acoustic factor, and the seventh is the amplitude of these high-frequency noises. These two factors characterize the major differences among voiceless sounds. In more accurate descriptions it would be necessary to specify more than just the centre frequency of the noise in fricative sounds. The eighth and ninth factors include the amplitudes of the second and third formants relative to the first formant; the amplitudes of the formants as a whole are determined by the larynx pulse amplitude. These latter factors are the least important in that they convey only supplementary information about nasals and laterals.

Sound spectrograph

Instruments for acoustic phonetics. The principal instrument used in acoustic phonetic studies is the sound spectrograph. This device gives a visible record of any kind of sound. A spectrographic analysis of the phrase *speech pictures* is shown in Figure 4. The time of occurrence of each item is given on the horizontal scale. The vertical scale shows the frequency components at each moment in time, the amplitude of the components being shown by the darkness of the mark. (Figure 3 diagrams the formant frequencies in a set of English vowels in the same way and might be regarded as a schematic spectrogram.) In the phrase *speech pictures* the first consonant has a comparatively random distribution of energy, but, as Figure 4 shows, it is mainly in the higher frequencies. The second consonant is a voiceless stop, which produces a short gap in the pattern. The next segment, the first vowel, has four formants that appear as dark bars with centre frequencies of 300, 2,000, 2,700, and 3,400 hertz. Each of the other segments has its own distinctive pattern.

By courtesy of Peter Ladefoged, University of California, Los Angeles

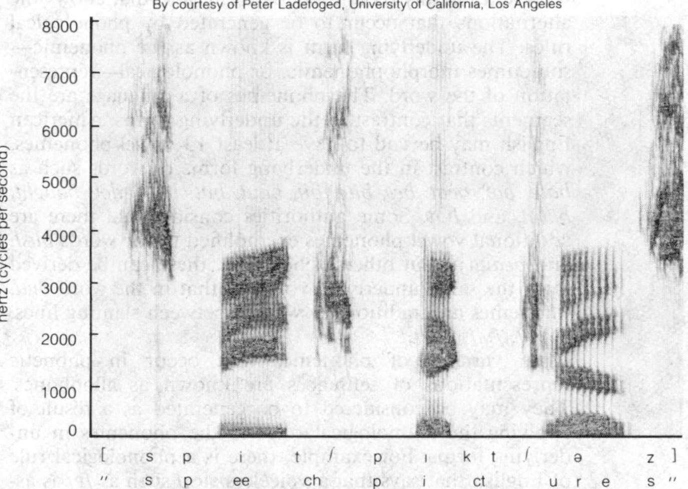

Figure 4: A spectrogram of the phrase "speech pictures." The horizontal dimension represents time, and the vertical scale represents frequency. The amplitude of the component frequencies at each moment in time is shown by the darkness of the mark.

Much information has also been gained from the use of speech synthesizers, which are instruments that take specifications of speech in terms of the acoustic factors summarized above and generate the corresponding sounds. Some speech synthesizers use electronic signal generators and amplifiers; others use digital computers to calculate the values of the required sound waves. Good synthetic speech is hard to distinguish from high-quality recordings of natural speech. The principal value of a speech synthesizer is its precisely controllable "voice" that an experimenter can vary in a systematic way to determine the perceptual effects of different acoustic specifications.

LINGUISTIC PHONETICS

Phonetics is part of linguistics in that one of the main aims of phonetics is to determine the categories that can

Relation of phonetics to linguistics

be used in explanatory description of languages. One way of looking at the grammar of a language is to consider it to be a set of statements that explains the relation between the meanings of all possible sentences in a language and the sounds of which they are composed. In this view, a grammar may be divided into three parts: the syntactic component, which is a set of rules describing the ways in which words may form sentences; the lexicon, which is a list of all the words and the categories to which they belong; and the phonological component, which is a set of rules that relates phonetic descriptions of sentences to the syntactic and lexical descriptions.

Phonological rules. In the lexicon of a language, each word is represented in its underlying, or basic, form, which discounts all of the alternations in pronunciation that are predictable by phonological rules. For example, there are phonological rules that will account for the variations in the placement of stress and the alternations of vowel quality that occur in sets of words such as *harmOny, harmOnic, harmOnious* and *melOdy, melOdic, melOdious.* The rules that predict the pronunciation of the capitalized *O*'s are general, rather than specific for each word, and the grammar should state such rules so that the regularities are revealed. Accordingly, each of these words must be entered in the lexicon in a way that represents simply its underlying form, and that allows the alternations that occur to be generated by phonological rules. The underlying form is known as the phonemic—sometimes morphophonemic, or phonological—representation of the word. The phonemes of a language are the segments that contrast in the underlying forms. American English may be said to have at least 13 vowel phonemes, which contrast in the underlying forms of words such as *bate, bat, beat, bet, bite, bit, bout, but, boat, dot, bought, balm,* and *boy.* Some authorities consider that there are additional vowel phonemes exemplified in the words *bush* and *beaut(y)*, but others believe that these can be derived from the same underlying vowel as that in the word *bud.* Phonemes are traditionally written between slanting lines, as /P/, /M/, or /L/.

The variants of phonemes that occur in phonetic representations of sentences are known as allophones. They may be considered to be generated as a result of applying the phonological rules to the phonemes in underlying forms. For example, there is a phonological rule of English that says that a voiceless stop such as /P/ is aspirated when it occurs at the beginning of a word (*e.g.*, in *pin*), but when it occurs after a voiceless alveolar fricative (*i.e.*, after/s/), it is unaspirated (*e.g.*, in *spin*). Thus the underlying phoneme /P/ has an aspirated and an unaspirated allophone, in addition to other allophones that are generated as a result of other rules that apply in other circumstances. Allophones are conventionally written inside brackets—*e.g.*, [p] or aspirated [pʰ].

In stating phonological rules it is necessary to refer to classes of phonemes. Consider part of the rule for the formation of the plural in English: there is an extra vowel in the suffix if the word ends in the same sound as occurs at the end of *horse, maze, fish, rouge, church,* or *judge.* The plural forms of words of this kind are one syllable longer than the singular forms. The phonological rules of English could simply list the phonemes that behave in the same way in the rules for plural formation; the rules for the possessive forms of nouns and for the 3rd person singular of the present tense of verbs are similar in this respect. The rules are more explanatory, however, if they show that these phonemes behave in a similar way because they form a natural class, or set, whose members are defined by a common property. In the case of these plural forms, the phonemes are all, and only, those that have a high-frequency fricative component; they may be called the sibilant, or strident, phonemes.

Classes of phonemes

Other phonological rules that refer to the natural classes of phonemes have already been mentioned. The rule concerning voiceless stops' being aspirated in some circumstances and unaspirated in others refers to the subset of phonemes that are both voiceless sounds and stops. Similarly, the variations in vowel length in *cat* and *cad* can be expressed with reference to the set of phonemes that are vowels, and also to the set that comprises both voiceless sounds and stops.

Features. Each of the phonemes that appears in the lexicon of a language may be classified in terms of a set of phonetic properties, or features. Phoneticians and linguists have been trying to develop a set of features that is sufficient to classify the phonemes in each of the languages of the world. A set of features of this kind would constitute the phonetic capabilities of man. To be descriptively adequate from a linguistic point of view, the set of features must be able to provide a different representation for each of the words that is phonologically distinct in a language; and if the feature set is to have any explanatory power it must also be able to classify phonemes into appropriate natural classes as required in the phonological rules of each language.

In the earlier work on feature sets, emphasis was placed on the fact that features were the smallest discrete components of language. Not much attention was paid to their role in classifying phonemes into the natural classes required in phonological rules. Instead, they were considered to be the units to which a listener attends when listening to speech. Features were justified by reference to their role in distinguishing phonemes in minimal sets of words such as *bill, pill, fill, mill, dill, sill, kill.*

Jakobson, Fant, and Halle features. As a result of studying the phonemic contrasts within a number of languages, Roman Jakobson, Gunnar Fant, and Morris Halle concluded in 1951 that segmental phonemes could be characterized in terms of 12 distinctive features. All of the features were binary, in the sense that a phoneme either had, or did not have, the phonetic attributes of the feature. Thus phonemes could be classified as being consonantal or not, voiced or not, nasal or not, and so on. In 1968, Noam Chomsky and Morris Halle stated that nearer 30 features are needed for a proper description of the phonetic, and linguistic, capabilities of man. In agreement with Jakobson, they claimed that each feature functions as a binary opposition that can be given the value of plus or minus in classifying the phonemes in underlying forms. But they suggested that the features may require more precise systematic phonetic specifications.

Binary quality of features

Chomsky–Halle features. Some of the binary features proposed by Chomsky and Halle are listed in Table 1. The

Table 1: Part of the Set of Features Proposed by Chomsky and Halle (1968)

Major class features	Cavity features
consonantal	nasal
syllabic	lateral
sonorant	anterior
Manner of articulation features	coronal
continuant	high
delayed release	low
tense	back
Source features	round
voice	
strident	

first group comprises major class features, because these features are required for dividing sounds into classes such as vowels, consonants, and semivowels. There are several problems in giving satisfactory definitions of the phonetic properties of these features, but there is no doubt that binary oppositions of this kind are needed for describing phonological patterns.

The next group, the manner of articulation features, includes continuant/noncontinuant (in which noncontinuant is exactly equivalent to the notion of stop as defined above), and delayed release (the comparatively slow parting of the articulators that occurs in an affricate). The source features refer to the action of the vocal cords (voice) or to fricative noise mechanisms (strident).

The cavity features include nasal and lateral, which are used in the same sense as they were in the section on articulatory phonetics, and the features that determine the place of articulation of consonants and the quality of vowels. The most important features specifying the place of articulation of consonants are anterior, made in the

Table 2: The Distinctive Feature Composition of Some English Segments

	i	u	e	ɑ	ɪ	w	r	l	p	t	d	θ	ð	n	s	z	ʃ	k	h
Syllabic	+	+	+	+	+	−	−	−	−	−	−	−	−	−	−	−	−	−	−
Consonantal	−	−	−	−	−	−	+	+	+	+	+	+	+	+	+	+	+	+	−
High	+	+	−	−	+	+	−	−	−	−	−	−	−	−	−	−	+	+	−
Back	−	+	−	+	−	+	−	−	−	−	−	−	−	−	−	−	−	+	−
Low	−	−	−	+	−	−	−	−	−	−	−	−	−	−	−	−	−	−	+
Anterior	−	−	−	−	−	−	−	+	+	+	+	+	+	+	+	+	−	−	−
Coronal	−	−	−	−	−	−	+	+	−	+	+	+	+	+	+	+	+	−	−
Round	−	+	−	−	−	+													
Tense	+	+	+	+	−	−													
Voice							+	+	−	−	+	−	+	+	−	+	−	−	−
Continuant							+	+	−	−	−	+	+	−	+	+	+	−	+
Nasal							−	−	−	−	−	−	−	+	−	−	−	−	−
Strident							−	−	−	−	−	−	−	−	+	+	+	−	−
Lateral							−	+	−	−	−	−	−	−	−	−	−	−	−

front of the mouth, and coronal, made with the tip or blade of the tongue raised toward the teeth or teeth ridge. These two features can be used to specify four places of articulation: bilabial (+anterior, −coronal); dental, or alveolar (+anterior, +coronal); postalveolar, or palato-alveolar (−anterior, +coronal); velar (−anterior, −coronal). There is still some disagreement concerning whether consonantal places of articulation are specified appropriately by binary oppositions of this kind.

Vowels and binary features

There is even more disagreement over the advisability of describing vowels in terms of binary features. Chomsky and Halle use the features high/nonhigh and low/nonlow to specify the height of the tongue, midtongue positions being considered to be simply those that are -high, -low; the feature back/nonback is employed to specify the front/back distinctions among vowels. But these three features can be combined to specify only six basic tongue positions: high front, high back, midfront, midback, low front, and low back. It is true that each of these possibilities can have tense/nontense (lax) variants and rounded/nonrounded (spread) variants. But the Chomsky–Halle feature system does not permit the specification within underlying forms of central vowels, nor of more than three degrees of tongue height. Moreover, their binary oppositions of vowel height do not make it clear that the difference between low vowels and midvowels is the same as that between midvowels and high vowels.

Table 2 shows the feature composition of a number of segments that occur in English. The phonetic symbols at the top of each column are used with the values discussed in the following section.

PHONETIC TRANSCRIPTION

There are many different kinds of phonetic transcription. In some circumstances a phonetic symbol can be simply an abbreviation for a phonetic description. The symbol [s] may then be regarded as exactly equivalent to the phrase "voiceless, alveolar, fricative." When a linguist tries to describe an unknown language he begins by writing it down using symbols in this way. Later, when he has learned about the function of sounds and the underlying forms in the language, he might make a more systematic transcription, known as a broad transcription, in which each phoneme is represented by a simple symbol.

Occasionally it is convenient to use a transcription in which some of the allophones are represented by specific symbols, or some of the phonemes are designated by the symbols for a more restricted set of categories. If, for example, the transcription were to be used in teaching pronunciation, the difference between the aspirated and unaspirated allophones of /ᴘ/ might be represented by transcribing *pan* as [pʰan] and *span* as [span]; or the vowel phoneme in each of these words might be designated by the more specific symbol [æ], which represents a low

Table 3: The International Phonetic Alphabet*
(revised to 1951)

	bilabial	labio-dental	dental and alveolar	retroflex	palato-alveolar	alveolo-palatal	palatal	velar	uvular	pharyngal	glottal
Consonants											
Plosive	p b		t d	ʈ ɖ			c ɟ	k g	q ɢ		ʔ
Nasal	m	ɱ	n	ɳ			ɲ	ŋ	ɴ		
Lateral fricative			ɬ ɮ								
Lateral nonfricative			l	ɭ			ʎ				
Rolled			r						ʀ		
Flapped			ɾ	ɽ					ʀ		
Fricative	ɸ β	f v	θ ð s z ɹ	ʂ ʐ	ʃ ʒ	ɕ ʑ	ç ʝ	x ɣ	χ ʁ	ħ ʕ	h ɦ
Frictionless continuants and semivowels	w ɥ	ʋ	ɹ				j (ɥ)	(w)	ʁ		

		front	central	back
Vowels				
Close	(y ʉ u)	i y	ɨ ʉ	ɯ u
Half-close	(ø o)	e ø		ɤ o
			ə	
Half-open	(œ ɔ)	ɛ œ		ʌ ɔ
		æ	ɐ	
Open	(ɒ)	a		ɑ ɒ

*Secondary articulations are shown by symbols in parentheses.

Other sounds—palatalized consonants: ƫ, ȡ, etc.; palatalized ʃ, ʒ: ʆ, ʓ. Velarized or pharyngalized consonants: ɫ, đ, ƶ, etc. Ejective consonants (with simultaneous glottal stop): p', t', etc. Implosive voiced consonants: ɓ, ɗ, etc. ɼ fricative trill. σ, ϱ (labialized θ, ð, or s, z). ʅ, ʓ (labialized ʃ, ʒ). ʇ, ʗ, ʖ (clicks, Zulu *c*, *q*, *x*). ɺ (a sound between r and l). ɴ Japanese syllabic nasal. ɧ (combination of x and ʃ). ʍ (voiceless w). ɩ, ʏ, ɷ (lowered varieties of i, y, u). ɜ (a variety of ə). ɵ (a vowel between ø and o).

Affricates are normally presented by groups of two consonants (ts, tʃ, d , etc.), but, when necessary, ligatures are used (ʦ, ʧ, ʤ, etc.), or the marks ͡ or ‿ (t͡s or t‿s, etc.). ͡ ‿ also denote synchronic articulation (m͡ŋ = simultaneous m and ŋ). c, ɟ may occasionally be used in place of tʃ, dʒ, and ƾ, ƻ for ts, dz. Aspirated plosives: ph, th, etc. r-coloured vowels: eɹ, aɹ, ɔɹ, etc., or eʴ, aʴ, ɔʴ, etc., or ɝ, ɑ˞, ɔ˞, etc.; r-coloured ə: əɹ or əʴ or ɹ or ə˞ or ɚ.

Length, stress, pitch—ː (full length). ˑ (half length). ˈ (stress, placed at beginning of the stressed syllable). ˌ (secondary stress). ¯ (high level pitch); ˍ (low level); ˊ (high rising); ˏ (low rising); ˋ (high falling); ˎ (low falling); ˆ (rise-fall); ˇ (fall-rise).

Modifiers— ˜ nasality. ̥ breath (l̥ = breathed l). ̬ voice (s̬ = z). ʻ slight aspiration following p, t, etc. ̫ labialization (n̫ = labialized n). ̪ dental articulation (t̪ = dental t). ˙ palatalization (ż = ʑ). ̣ specially close vowel (ẹ = a very close e). ̨ specially open vowel (ę = a rather open e). ˔ tongue raised (e˔ or e̝ = ẹ). ˕ tongue lowered (e˕ or e̞ = ę). ˖ tongue advanced (u˖ or u̟ = an advanced u, t̟ = t̪). - or ˗ tongue retracted (i- or =ɨ˖, t̠ = alveolar t). ˒ lips more rounded. ˓ lips more spread. Central vowels: ï (= ɨ), ü (= ʉ), ë (= ə˔), ö (= ɵ), ɛ̈, ɔ̈. ̩ (e.g. n̩) syllabic consonant. ̯ consonantal vowel. ʃˢ variety of ʃ resembling s, etc.

front vowel of a certain type. In a narrow transcription the symbols are more specific, either because allophones are differentiated, or because the phonetic quality of the sounds is shown more precisely.

Narrow transcription

The most widely used set of symbols is that of the International Phonetic Association (IPA). The latest version of the IPA chart is shown in Table 3. In general, the consonants have the same values as the corresponding letters in many European languages; the vowel symbols have similar values to the corresponding letters in a language such as Italian.

EXPERIMENTAL PHONETICS

Experimental phonetics employs the methods of investigation commonly used in other disciplines—*e.g.,* physics, physiology, and psychology—for measuring the physical and physiological dimensions of speech sounds and their perceptual characteristics. The sound spectrograph and speech synthesizers were mentioned in the section on acoustic phonetics. Other techniques include the use of X-rays; air-pressure and air-flow recording; palatography, a method of registering the contacts between the tongue and the roof of the mouth; and cinematography. All of these techniques have been used for studying the actions of the vocal organs.

Much of the work in experimental phonetics has been directed toward obtaining more accurate descriptions of the sounds that characterize different languages. There have also been several studies aimed at determining the relative importance of different features in signalling contrasts between sounds. But experimental phoneticians are probably most concerned with trying to discover the central cerebral processes involved in speech.

One issue of this kind that has been extensively discussed is the so-called motor theory of speech perception. There is a great deal of evidence that the way in which people speak greatly influences their perception of what is said to them. For example, speakers of Spanish cannot pronounce the different vowels in words such as *ship* and *sheep* in English. These people also have difficulty in hearing the difference between these two vowels. But when they have learned, by trial and error methods, to say them correctly, then they can easily hear the difference. Similarly, using synthetic speech stimuli it is possible to make a series of consonant sounds that go by acoustically equidistant steps from [b] through [d] to [g]. When listeners hear these synthetic sounds they do not consider the steps between them to be auditorily equidistant. The steps that correspond to the large articulatory movements between the consonants are heard as being much larger than the equal size acoustic steps that do not correspond to articulatory movements occurring in the listener's speech. Facts such as these have led some phoneticians to believe that the perception of speech is structured more in motor—articulatory—terms than in acoustic terms. Other phoneticians have claimed that the evidence does not really distinguish between these two possibilities but demonstrates simply that the perception of speech is structured in terms of linguistic categories.

Motor theory of speech perception

Another major problem is the size of the units that are involved in the perception of speech. Some authorities have claimed that a listener distinguishes between words by making a series of binary decisions concerning the features in each segment that he hears. Others hold that the listener takes in information in much larger temporal pieces and perhaps processes speech in terms of units of at least the size of a syllable. All authorities agree on the importance of context in the processing of information. Speech conveys information in a redundant way. Experiments have shown that a listener need attend to only a part of the information presented to him in order to understand all that is being said.

Perception and size of speech units

A related problem is that of the temporal structure of speech production. There may be very little structure, and a speaker may simply time the movements of his vocal organs by allowing each gesture to run its course before starting on the next one. Alternatively, he may impose a hierarchical structure on the gestures by requiring, for instance, each major stress in a sentence to occur at some predetermined moment, and the articulatory movements to be speeded up or slowed down depending on the number of movements that have to occur before the major stress. There is some evidence in favour of this latter possibility as a result of experiments in which a speaker is asked to say a given phrase first slowly and then fast. When he is speaking at a rate that is twice as fast as some other rate, then the interval between the major stresses is about halved. But the duration of each segment is not halved. The consonants are only slightly reduced in length, whereas the vowels are considerably shortened. Some authorities have used the results of experiments of this kind to argue that the stress group is the major unit in the temporal organization of speech.

(P.N.L./Ed.)

The physiology of speech

THE REGULATORS

Respiratory mechanisms. Human speech is served by a bellows-like respiratory activator, which furnishes the driving energy in the form of an airstream; a phonating sound generator in the larynx (low in the throat) to transform the energy; a sound-molding resonator in the pharynx (higher in the throat), where the individual voice pattern is shaped; and a speech-forming articulator in the oral cavity (mouth). Normally, but not necessarily, the four structures function in close coordination. Audible speech without any voice is possible during toneless whisper; there can be phonation without oral articulation as in some aspects of yodeling that depend on pharyngeal and laryngeal changes. Silent articulation without breath and voice may be used for lipreading.

An early achievement in experimental phonetics at about the end of the 19th century was a description of the differences between quiet breathing and phonic (speaking) respiration. An individual typically breathes approximately 18 to 20 times per minute during rest and much more frequently during periods of strenuous effort. Quiet respiration at rest as well as deep respiration during physical exertion are characterized by symmetry and synchrony of inhalation (inspiration) and exhalation (expiration). Inspiration and expiration are equally long, equally deep, and transport the same amount of air during the same period of time, approximately half a litre (one pint) of air per breath at rest in most adults. Recordings (made with a device called a pneumograph) of respiratory movements during rest depict a curve in which peaks are followed by valleys in fairly regular alternation.

Differences between quiet breathing and phonic respiration

Phonic respiration is different; inhalation is much deeper than it is during rest and much more rapid. After one takes this deep breath (one or two litres of air), phonic exhalation proceeds slowly and fairly regularly for as long as the spoken utterance lasts. Trained speakers and singers are able to phonate on one breath for at least 30 seconds, often for as much as 45 seconds, and exceptionally up to one minute. The period during which one can hold a tone on one breath with moderate effort is called the maximum phonation time; this potential depends on such factors as body physiology, state of health, age, body size, physical training, and the competence of the laryngeal voice generator—that is, the ability of the glottis (the vocal cords and the opening between them) to convert the moving energy of the breath stream into audible sound. A marked reduction in phonation time is characteristic of all the laryngeal diseases and disorders that weaken the precision of glottal closure, in which the cords (vocal folds) come close together, for phonation.

Respiratory movements when one is awake and asleep, at rest and at work, silent and speaking are under constant regulation by the nervous system. Specific respiratory centres within the brain stem regulate the details of respiratory mechanics according to the body needs of the moment. Conversely, the impact of emotions is heard immediately in the manner in which respiration drives the phonic generator; the timid voice of fear, the barking voice of fury, the feeble monotony of melancholy, or the raucous vehemence during agitation are examples. Conversely, many organic diseases of the nervous system or of the breathing mechanism are projected in the sound of the sufferer's voice. Some forms of nervous system disease make the voice sound tremulous; the voice of the asthmatic sounds laboured and short winded; certain types of disease affecting a part of the brain called the cerebellum cause respiration to be forced and strained so that the voice becomes extremely low and grunting. Such observations have led to the traditional practice of prescribing that vocal education begin with exercises in proper breathing.

Types of breathing

The mechanism of phonic breathing involves three types of respiration: (1) predominantly pectoral breathing (chiefly by elevation of the chest), (2) predominantly abdominal breathing (through marked movements of the abdominal wall), (3) optimal combination of both (with widening of the lower chest). The female uses upper chest respiration predominantly, the male relies primarily on abdominal breathing. Many voice coaches stress the ideal of a mixture of pectoral (chest) and abdominal breathing for economy of movement. Any exaggeration of one particular breathing habit is impractical and may damage the voice.

Brain functions. The question of what the brain does to make the mouth speak or the hand write is still incompletely understood despite a rapidly growing number of studies by specialists in many sciences, including neurology, psychology, psycholinguistics, neurophysiology, aphasiology, speech pathology, cybernetics, and others. A basic understanding, however, has emerged from such study. In evolution, one of the oldest structures in the brain is the so-called limbic system, which evolved as part of the olfactory (smell) sense. It traverses both hemispheres in a front to back direction, connecting many vitally important brain centres as if it were a basic mainline for the distribution of energy and information. The limbic system involves the so-called reticular activating system (structures in the brain stem), which represents the chief brain mechanism of arousal, such as from sleep or from rest to activity. In man, all activities of thinking and moving (as expressed by speaking or writing) require the guidance of the brain cortex.

The limbic system

In contrast to animals, man possesses several language centres in the dominant brain hemisphere (on the left side in a clearly right-handed person). It was previously believed that left-handers had their dominant hemisphere on the right side, but recent findings tend to show that many left-handed persons have the language centres more equally developed in both hemispheres or that the left side of the brain is indeed dominant. The foot of the third frontal convolution of the brain cortex, called Broca's area, is involved with motor elaboration of all movements for expressive language. Its destruction through disease or injury causes expressive aphasia, the inability to speak or write (see Figure 5). The posterior third of the upper temporal convolution represents Wernicke's area of receptive speech comprehension. Damage to this area produces receptive aphasia, the inability to understand what is spoken or written as if the patient had never known that language.

From N. Geschwind, *Science*, vol. 170, no. 3961, p. 941 (1970); Copyright 1970 by the American Association for the Advancement of Science

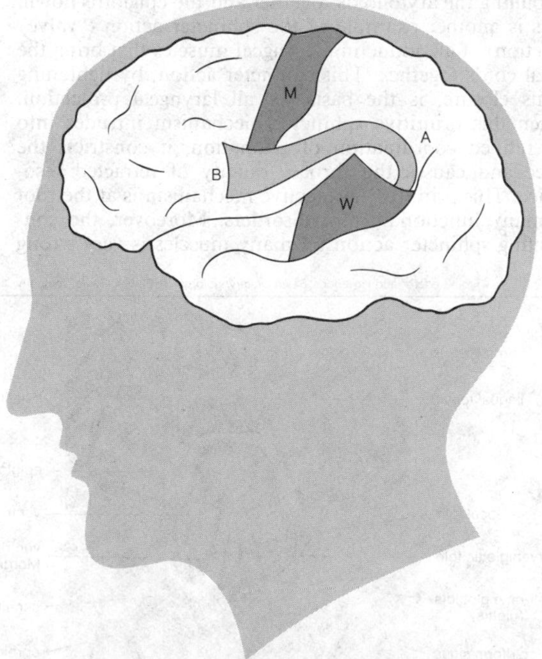

Figure 5: Lateral surface of left hemisphere of brain. B, Broca's area; M, motor cortex; W, Wernicke's area; A, arcuate fasciculus.

Broca's area surrounds and serves to regulate the function of other brain parts that initiate the complex patterns of bodily movement (somatomotor function) necessary for the performance of a given motor act. Swallowing is an inborn reflex (present at birth) in the somatomotor area for mouth, throat, and larynx. From these cells in the motor cortex of the brain emerge fibres that connect eventually with the cranial and spinal nerves that control the muscles of oral speech.

In the opposite direction, fibres from the inner ear have a first relay station in the so-called acoustic nuclei of the brain stem. From here the impulses from the ear ascend, via various regulating relay stations for the acoustic reflexes and directional hearing, to the cortical projection of the auditory fibres on the upper surface of the superior temporal convolution (on each side of the brain cortex). This is the cortical hearing centre where the effects of sound stimuli seem to become conscious and understandable. Surrounding this audito-sensory area of initial crude recognition, the inner and outer auditopsychic regions spread over the remainder of the temporal lobe of the brain, where sound signals of all kinds appear to be remembered, comprehended, and fully appreciated. Wernicke's area (the posterior part of the outer auditopsychic region) appears to be uniquely important for the comprehension of speech sounds.

The integrity of these language areas in the cortex seems insufficient for the smooth production and reception of language. The cortical centres are interconnected with various subcortical areas (deeper within the brain) such as those for emotional integration in the thalamus and for the coordination of movements in the cerebellum (hindbrain).

Feedback mechanisms

All creatures regulate their performance instantaneously comparing it with what it was intended to be through so-called feedback mechanisms involving the nervous system. Auditory feedback through the ear, for example, informs the speaker about the pitch, volume, and inflection of his voice, the accuracy of articulation, the selection of the appropriate words, and other audible features of his utterance. Another feedback system through the proprioceptive sense (represented by sensory structures within muscles, tendons, joints, and other moving parts) provides continual information on the position of these parts. Limitations of these systems curtail the quality of speech as observed in pathologic examples (deafness, paralysis, underdevelopment).

THE STRUCTURE OF THE LARYNX

The morphology (structure) of the larynx is studied according to the cartilages, muscles, nerves, blood vessels, and membranes of which it is composed.

Cartilages of the larynx. The frame or skeleton of the larynx is composed of several cartilages, three single and three pairs. Single cartilages are the shield-shaped thyroid in front, whose prominence forms the "Adam's apple" in the male; the cricoid cartilage below, which resembles a signet ring and connects the thyroid to the trachea or windpipe; and the leaf-shaped epiglottis, or laryngeal lid, on top. Among the paired cartilages are the two arytenoids, which ride on the cricoid plate and move the vocal cords sideways; the two corniculate cartilages of Santorini on top of the arytenoids; and the two cuneiform cartilages of Wrisberg. The cartilages are held together by ligaments and membranes, particularly around their joints. The larynx is connected below to the uppermost ring of the trachea (see Figure 6), while above it is connected by the thyrohyoid ligaments to the hyoid bone beneath the tongue. Most of the laryngeal cartilages ossify (turn to bone) to variable degrees with age under the influence of masculinizing hormones. This fact is an important sign in the X-ray diagnosis of certain vocal disorders. If a man

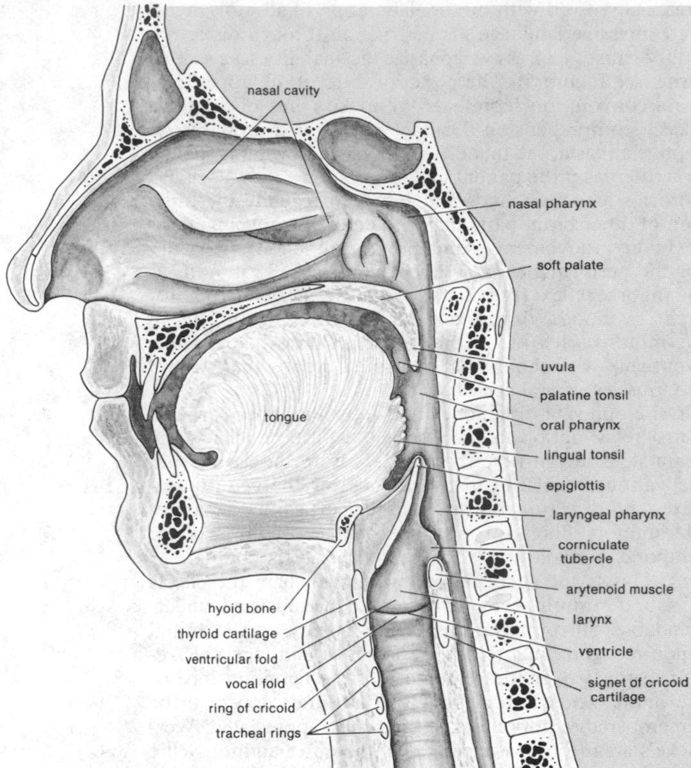

Figure 6: Sagittal section of head and neck.

shows less ossification than is normal for his age, he may be deficient in male hormones; this may also account for an effeminate sound in his voice. Conversely, when a woman shows increased laryngeal ossification, she may suffer from virilizing hormones, which might also explain any lowering and roughening in her voice.

Laryngeal muscles. There are two types of laryngeal muscles, the external (extrinsic) ones, which move the larynx as a whole, and the internal (intrinsic) ones, which move the vocal folds to shape the glottis. It is helpful to remember that the anatomical names of most such muscles are derived from their origin on one structure to their insertion on another.

The extrinsic muscles comprise the thyropharyngeus, which extends from the posterior border of the thyroid cartilage to the pharyngeal constrictor muscle, and the cricopharyngeus, which extends from the cricoid cartilage to the lower portion of the pharynx and the opening of the esophagus (the food tube that connects the mouth and the stomach). This cricopharyngeus muscle aids in the closing of the esophagus whenever it is not open for swallowing. Under the influence of emotional tension, the cricopharyngeus muscle may go into a spasm, which leads to a painful sensation of tightening in the throat that is usually described as a "lump in the throat." A disorder of this sort (which was previously referred to as globus hystericus) is now believed to be a sensation of cricopharyngeus spasm from emotional tension or imbalance as the result of excessive activity of the autonomic (involuntary) nervous system.

"Lump in the throat"

Extrinsic muscles. Although it is situated outside the laryngeal cartilages, the short cricothyroid muscle, a triangular muscle between the respective two cartilages, is traditionally discussed among the intrinsic (internal) muscles. Whenever this muscle contracts, the cricoid and thyroid cartilages are brought together anteriorly. This moves the anterior (forward) insertion of the vocal cords inside the thyroid wing forward, while their posterior (backward) insertion on the arytenoid cartilages is shifted backward. From this rotation results a marked elongation of the vocal folds clearly visible on X-ray films. This stretching action is the chief mechanism for raising the pitch of the sound generated and thus for the differentiation of vocal registers (*e.g.,* chest voice, falsetto). For embryologic reasons, the cricothyroid is the only laryngeal muscle that has its own nerve supply from the superior laryngeal nerve, a high branch of the vagus nerve (which issues from the brain stem). All other laryngeal muscles are innervated by the recurrent or inferior (low) laryngeal nerve, a low branch of the vagus nerve. This fact is important in the diagnosis of laryngeal paralysis because the resulting immobilization of the vocal cord and the remaining vocal function depend on the type of paralysis; *i.e.,* whether only the high or the low nerve or both of the laryngeal nerves are paralyzed on one side.

Intrinsic muscles. The intrinsic muscles include all of the following. The thyroarytenoid muscle extends from the inside of the anterior edge of the thyroid cartilage to the anterior vocal process of the arytenoid cartilage. This muscle may be separated into two portions, an internal part within the vocal cord and an external part between the vocal cord and the wing of the thyroid cartilage. For the most part, the fibres run parallel with the vocal cord. When they contract, they shorten the cord, make it thick, and round its edge. The external portion assists in bringing the vocal cords together, thus making glottal closure more tight.

The cricoarytenoid muscles

The cricoarytenoids are two muscle pairs: one lateral pair (to the side) and one posterior pair (backward). These two pairs of muscles have an antagonistic (opposing) action. The posterior cricoarytenoids are the muscles of inspiration that open the glottis. They arise from the posterior surface of the cricoid plate and are attached, in an upward, forward, and outward direction, to the lateral muscular process of the arytenoid cartilage. When these muscles contract, they rotate the arytenoid outward, thus opening the glottis. The lateral cricoarytenoids belong among the muscles of expiration, the adductor group. They arise from the lateral ring of the cricoid cartilage and insert into the muscular process of the arytenoid in an upward and backward direction. Contraction of the lateral cricoarytenoids rotates the arytenoid cartilages inward so that the vocal folds are brought together.

The two sides of the interarytenoid muscle are blended into one single mass, which extends from the muscular process of one arytenoid to that of the other. The action of this muscle is to pull together the posterior aspect of the arytenoid cartilages, thus closing the posterior portion of the cartilaginous glottis between the vocal processes of the arytenoids.

A fold from the top of the arytenoid to the lateral margin of the epiglottis on each side is supported by a bilateral band of muscle, the aryepiglotticus muscle. This semicircular structure aids in narrowing the laryngeal vestibule by pulling the arytenoids together and the epiglottis down. This is another example of the sphincter action ("valve" function) of all adducting laryngeal muscles that bring the vocal cords together. This sphincter action, by tightening of its closure, is the basis for all laryngeal protection. When this primitive sphincter mechanism intrudes into the refined coordination of phonation, it constricts the voice and causes the throaty quality of retracted resonance. This primitive, protective mechanism is at the root of many functional voice disorders. Moreover, the constricting sphincter action by many muscles is very strong

From Lederer and Hollender, *Basic Otolaryngology* (1956); F.A. Davis Company

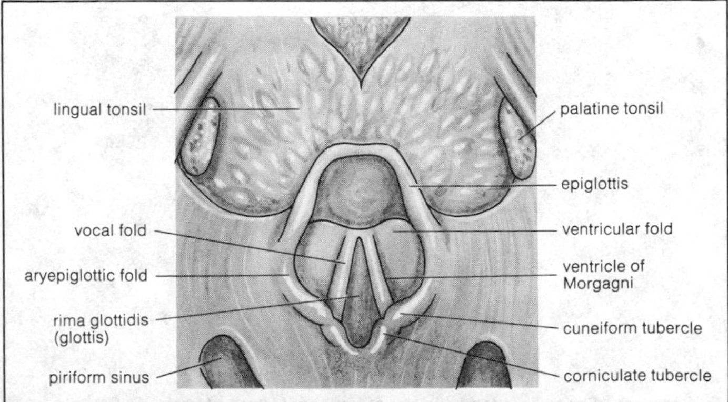

Figure 7: Laryngoscopic view of glottis and vocal cords (folds).

because it is opposed by only one muscle, the abducting posterior cricoarytenoid.

Vocal cords. The two true vocal cords (or folds) represent the chief mechanism of the larynx in its function as a valve for opening the airway for breathing and to close it during swallowing (see Figure 7). The vocal cords are supported by the thyroarytenoid ligaments, which extend from the vocal process of the arytenoid cartilages forward to the inside angle of the thyroid wings. This anterior insertion occurs on two closely adjacent points, the anterior commissure. The thyroarytenoid ligament is composed of elastic fibres that support the medial or free margin of the vocal cords.

The inner cavity of the larynx is covered by a continuous mucous membrane, which closely follows the outlines of all structures. Immediately above and slightly lateral to the vocal cords, the membrane expands into lateral excavations, one ventricle of Morgagni on each side. This recess opens anteriorly into a still smaller cavity, the laryngeal saccule or appendix. As the mucous membrane emerges again from the upper surface of each ventricle, it creates a second fold on each side—the ventricular fold, or false cord. These two ventricular folds are parallel to the vocal cords but slightly lateral to them so that the vocal cords remain uncovered when inspected with a mirror. The false cords close tightly during each sphincter action for swallowing; when this primitive mechanism is used for phonation, it causes the severe hoarseness of false-cord voice (ventricular dysphonia).

False vocal cords

The mucous membrane ascends on each side from the margins of the ventricular folds of the upper border of the laryngeal vestibule, forming the aryepiglottic folds. These folds extend from the apex of the arytenoids to the lateral margin of the epiglottis. Laterally from this ring enclosing the laryngeal vestibule, the mucous membrane descends downward to cover the upper-outer aspects of the larynx where the mucous membrane blends with the mucous lining of the piriform sinus of each side. These pear-shaped recesses mark the beginning of the entrance of the pharyngeal foodway into the esophagus.

The mucous membrane of the larynx consists of respiratory epithelium made up of ciliated columnar cells. Ciliated cells are so named because they bear hairlike projections that continuously undulate upward toward the oral cavity, moving mucus and polluting substances out of the airways. The true vocal cords, however, are exceptional in that they are covered by stratified squamous epithelium (squamous cells are flat or scalelike) as found in the alimentary tract. The arrangement is functional, since the vocal cords have to bear considerable mechanical strain during their rapid vibration for phonation, which occurs during many hours of the day. The transition from the respiratory to the stratified epithelium above and below the vocal cords is marked by superior and inferior arcuate (arched) lines. Unfortunately, such transitional epithelium also has the drawback of being easily disturbed by chronic irritation, which is one reason why the large majority of laryngeal cancers begin on the vocal cords. The mucous membrane of the larynx contains numerous mucous glands in all areas covered by respiratory epithelium, excepting again the vocal cords. These glands are especially numerous over the epiglottis and in the ventricles of Morgagni. The mucus secreted by these glands serves as a lubricant for the mucous membrane and prevents its drying in the constant airstream.

The vocal cords also mark the division of the larynx into an upper and lower compartment. These divisions reflect the development of the larynx from several embryonal components called branchial arches. The supraglottic portion differs from the one beneath the vocal cords in that the upper portion is innervated sensorially by the superior laryngeal nerve and the lower (infraglottic) portion by the recurrent (or inferior) laryngeal nerve. The lymphatics (*i.e.,* the vessels for the lymph flow) from the upper portion drain in an upward lateral direction, while the lower lymphatics drain in a lateral downward direction.

The space between the vocal cords is called rima glottidis, glottal chink, or simply glottis (Greek for tongue). When the vocal cords are separated (abducted) for respiration, the glottis assumes a triangular shape with the apex at the anterior commissure. During phonation, the vocal cords are brought together (adducted or approximated), so that they lie more or less parallel to each other. The glottis is the origin of voice, although not in the form of a "fluttering tongue" as the Greeks believed.

The vocal cords vary greatly in dimension, the variance depending on the size of the entire larynx, which in turn depends on age, sex, body size, and body type. Before puberty, the larynx of boys and girls is about equally small. During puberty, the male larynx grows considerably under the influence of the male hormones so that eventually it is approximately one-third larger than the female larynx. The larynx and the vocal cords thus reflect body size. In tall, heavy males the vocal cords may be as long as 25 millimetres (one inch), representing the low-pitched instrument of a bass voice. A high-pitched tenor voice is produced by vocal cords of the same length as in a low-voiced female contralto. The highest female voices are produced by the shortest vocal cords (14 millimetres), which are not much longer than the infantile vocal cords before puberty (10–12 millimetres). The larynx is, among other things, a musical instrument that follows the physical laws of acoustics fairly closely.

Dimensions of the vocal cords

Substitutes for the larynx. A growing number of middle-aged or older patients have had their larynx removed (laryngectomy) because of cancer. Laryngectomy requires the suturing of the remaining trachea into a hole above the sternum (breastbone), creating a permanent tracheal stoma (or aperture) through which the air enters and leaves the lungs. The oral cavity is reconnected directly to the esophagus. Having lost his pulmonary activator (air from the lungs) and laryngeal sound generator, such an alaryngeal patient is without a voice (aphonic) and becomes effectively speechless; the faint smacking noises made by the remaining oral structures for articulation are practically unintelligible. This type of pseudo-whispering through buccal (mouth) speech is discouraged to help the patient later relearn useful speech on his own. A frequently successful method of rehabilitation for such alaryngeal aphonia is the development of what is called esophageal or belching voice.

Alaryngeal aphonia

Esophageal voice. Some European birds and other animals can produce a voice in which air is actively aspirated into the esophagus and then eructated (belched), as many people can do without practice. The sound generator is formed by the upper esophageal sphincter (the cricopharyngcus muscle in man). As a replacement for vocal cord function, the substitute esophageal voice is very low in pitch, usually about 60 cycles per second in humans. Training usually elevates this grunting pitch to about 80 or 100 cycles.

Esophageal voice in man has been reported in the literature since at least 1841 when such a case was presented before the Academy of Sciences in Paris. After the perfection of the laryngectomy procedure at the end of the 19th century, systematic instruction in esophageal (belching) phonation was elaborated, and the principles of this vicarious phonation were explored. Laryngectomized persons in many countries often congregate socially in "Lost Cord Clubs" and exchange solutions of problems stemming from the alaryngeal condition.

Artificial larynx. Approximately one-third of all laryngectomized persons are unable to learn esophageal phonation for various reasons, such as age, general health, hearing loss, illiteracy, linguistic barriers, rural residence, or other social reasons. These persons, however, can use an artificial larynx to substitute for the vocal carrier wave of articulation. Numerous mechanical and pneumatic models have been invented, but the modern electric larynx is most serviceable. It consists of a plastic case about the size of a flashlight, containing ordinary batteries, a buzzing sound source, and a vibrating head that is held against the throat to let the sound enter the pharynx through the skin. Ordinary articulation thus becomes easily audible and intelligible. Other models lead the sound waves through a tube into the mouth or are encased in a special upper dental plate. More recent efforts aim at surgically inserting an electric sound source directly into the neck tissues to produce a more natural sound resembling that of normal speech.

THEORY OF VOICE PRODUCTION

Myoelastic theory

The physical production of voice has been explained for a long time by the myoelastic or aerodynamic theory, as follows: when the vocal cords are brought into the closed position of phonation by the adducting muscles, a coordinated expiratory effort sets in. Air in the lungs, compressed by the expiratory effort, is driven upward through the trachea against the undersurface of the vocal cords. As soon as the subglottic pressure has risen sufficiently to overcome the closing effort of the vocal cords, the glottis is burst open, a puff of air escapes, the subglottic pressure is reduced, and the elasticity of the glottis together with the effect of the moving air causes the adducted cords to snap shut. The subglottic pressure rises again and the entire cycle is repeated. These cycles of exploding air puffs occur as frequently as the physical interaction of the subglottic pressure with the glottic resistance permits. The latter is determined by the tension of the vocal cords and their closing force. The number of these cycles per second is small for tones of low pitch and much greater for high tones, as will be explained later. The resulting laryngeal fundamental tone thus varies greatly in audible pitch.

According to the myoelastic theory, the production of laryngeal voice is a mechanical phenomenon directed by aerodynamic principles and muscular coordination. The vocal cords vibrate purely passively in the blowing airstream and are merely maintained in their position of phonation by the adducting muscles as these are activated by the laryngeal nerves. This vibration is not an active phenomenon like the whirring of the wings of a flying insect. Evidence for the myoelastic theory can be demonstrated in various ways. High-speed motion pictures of the vocal cords have been made, photographing their vibration at the rate of 4,000 or more frames per second. When such a picture is then projected at regular film speeds of 16 or 24 frames per second, the available film length is greatly extended in duration so that each of the hundreds of vocal-cord vibrations per second can be seen in ultraslow motion. A tone of 250 cycles per second (cps or Hz), for example, filmed at 4,000 frames and played back at 16 frames per second will permit each of the 250 vibrations to be seen for one second. Other evidence supporting the myoelastic theory is found in observations such as the fact that a nearly normal voice can be produced despite bilateral (on both sides) vocal-cord paralysis.

Vocal registers. *The basic registers.* For many centuries the so-called vocal registers were well known to the classical masters of the bel canto style of singing, the basic registers being called chest voice, midvoice, and head voice. These terms are derived from observations, for example, that in the low-chest register the resonances are felt chiefly over the chest. When sitting on a wooden bench with a large male, one can feel the vibrations of his low voice being transmitted through the back of the bench. In the high head voice, the vibrations are felt chiefly over the skull. The practice of singing is based on several artistic subdivisions in both sexes, depending on factors as discussed below. Other vocal phenomena may be heard below and above normal register limits, such as extra low tones, the "vocal fry."

Transition between vocal registers

The natural transition between two adjacent registers may be compared to the gearshift of a car. The same absolute vehicle speed can be maintained by driving either with the engine turning fast while in low gear or with fewer engine revolutions in the next higher gear. The register mechanism of the human voice is quite similar in this respect. Where the registers overlap, a series of transitional tones may be sung with either of the adjacent registers. These tones of the same fundamental frequency, sound level, and basic sound category in different vocal registers have recently been defined as isoparametric tones. In the untrained male voice, the transition between the midvoice and the high falsetto sounds abrupt; this so-called register break is similar to the noisy gearshift in a run-down truck. One aim of vocal education is to teach smoothly equalized register transitions.

Loud phonation of any given tone shifts its register mechanism toward the next lower register; for example, a crescendo falsetto tone grows into loud head voice. Conversely, soft intonation raises the mechanism to the next higher type, as when a loud head tone fades into soft falsetto. This phenomenon is the physiologic basis of *messa di voce,* the technique of swelling tones. Thus, the characteristic mechanism of each register represents a continuum of intralaryngeal adjustments. In the male voice, the gradual and overlapping transitions of phonic function may be aligned as follows: low chest tones, loud–soft; transition; middle register, loud–soft; transition; loud head voice–soft artistic falsetto–thin natural falsetto. X-ray studies can show the difference between the loud male head voice and the soft male falsetto. The former employs the midvoice mechanism, the latter the falsetto mechanism. In the female voice, the two lower registers behave similarly, while head voice can be only loud or soft and may be followed by a fourth register, the flageolet or whistle register of the highest coloratura sopranos. The Italian term falsetto simply means false soprano, as in a castrato (castrated) singer. Hence, the normal female cannot have a falsetto voice.

Studies of register differences. Studies devoted to the problem of voice register may be divided into two groups: observations of the visible laryngeal mechanism and studies of the audible register differences.

Studies of the visible laryngeal mechanism for the production of different registers began with the laryngoscope. Modern laryngostroboscopes employ the oscillating light of a high-power fluorescent light source that is monitored by the laryngeal vibrations through a throat microphone. Such devices, when they flash on and off at just the right rate, make the vocal cord movements appear much slower than they actually are, so that the observer perceives a slow-motion pattern. High-speed cinematography (moviemaking) has elucidated many details of vocal cord function for the various registers. Radioscopic (X-ray) methods were introduced only a few years after the discovery of X-rays in 1895. Among these, lateral (from the side) radioscopy of the larynx reveals the mechanism of vocal cord tension; frontal X-ray films demonstrate the typical configuration of the vocal cords for each register. Mechanical recordings of the respiratory movements of the chest, originally with rubber belts and lately with electronic strain gauges, disclose the breathing patterns for the various registers. Breath support (*appoggio*) of singing instruction can be demonstrated through such recordings, as well as by radiography of the chest. Aerodynamic measurements of pressure, flow rate, and volume of the air exhaled during specific phonic tasks have produced additional details. Electromyography (study of muscle currents) involving the insertion of needle electrodes into certain laryngeal muscles permits the isolated recording of finely coordinated muscular effort during the singing in various registers.

Differences in sound-wave patterns

A second group of investigations concerns audible register differences as an acoustic phenomenon. Electroacoustic analysis demonstrates the specific sound-wave patterns (harmonic spectra) of each register. In general, the full chest voice is rich in higher harmonics, whereas the thin falsetto voice is composed chiefly of sound-wave energy distribution near the vocal fundamental (the relatively narrow band of wave frequencies that characterizes any particular voice). The subjective impressions of singers during the production of an ascending scale reflect the voluntary techniques of vocal breath control, such as with respiratory support (*appoggio*). Positioning of the larynx, suitable shaping of the pharyngo-oral resonator (vocal tract), proper placement of the tongue, and the specific tension of the soft palate belong among the learned techniques of register equalization. Definite vibrations may be felt in the thorax, in the area of the hard palate, or above the nose. These subjectively felt resonances depend on bone conduction of the laryngeal sound. Very little has as yet been done regarding the subjective evaluation of voice registers by listening judges. These perceptual factors are still little understood, but it appears that multiple acoustic perceptions operate in voice-register judgment.

It is clear that the vocal registers represent a continuum of

Table 4: Laryngeal Activity in Chest and Falsetto Register of the Male

	chest register	falsetto register
Position of larynx	low	elevated
Shape of cords	rounded, full	sharp-edged, thin
Length of cords	short	elongated
Tension of cords	low isotonic inner tension	great isometric outer tension
Ventricular folds	adducted	abducted
Ventricles	narrow	wide
Glottal closure	complete in each cycle	open oval slit
Length of glottis	full length of cords	short, anterior
Vibrations	broad, entire surface	narrow, marginal
Amplitude of vibration	wide	small
Frequency of vibration	low	high
Vocal pitch	low	high
Epiglottis	lowered	elevated
Supraglottic space	narrow	widened
Thyroarytenoid	very active	inactive
Cricothyroid	inactive below 150 Hz	very active
Harmonics	prominent higher harmonics	fundamental almost sinusoidal
Vocal timbre	full, resonant, loud	thin, weak, soft
Perceptual characteristic	masculine	juvenile, feminine
Function	speaking voice	special artistic effects

laryngeal adjustments in response to different respiratory-mechanical requirements necessary for the production of the individual frequency range. The poles of these adjustments at the opposites of chest voice and male falsetto voice illustrate the chief differences, as shown in Table 4; the midvoice occupies an intermediate position.

Vocal attributes. *Vocal frequency.* The voice has various attributes; these are chiefly frequency, harmonic structure, and intensity. The immediate result of vocal cord vibration is the fundamental tone of the voice, which determines its pitch. In physical terms, the frequency of vibration as the foremost vocal attribute corresponds to the number of air puffs per second, counted as cycles per second (cps or Hz). This frequency is determined by both stable and variable factors. The stable determinants of the individual voice range depend on the laryngeal dimensions as related to sex, age, and body type. The smaller a larynx, the higher its pitch range. Within this individually fixed range, variables that influence the pitch of a given phonation include: tension of the cord, force of glottal closure indicated by the glottal resistance, and expiratory air pressure. Growing tension of the cricothyroid muscle (as the external vocal cord tensor) increases the vocal pitch, and vice-versa. Increased glottal closure and expiratory effort add to this tensing effect under certain circumstances. For example, 100 vibrations per second produce a low chest tone of a low male voice, while 1,000 are close to the "high C" of a female soprano. An average vocal range normally encompasses two musical octaves (*e.g.,* 100 to 400 vibrations per second); trained singers may reach three or more octaves.

Voice types. Musical practice for centuries has recognized six basic voice types: bass, baritone, and tenor in the male, in contrast to contralto, mezzo-soprano, and soprano in the female. Sex, therefore, is one of the first determinants of voice type in the two categories. Body type and general physical constitution represent the second determinant of the individual voice type because the laryngeal dimensions vary in fairly strict conformity to whether the body type is large or husky or frail or small. A tall, athletic male usually has a large, spacious larynx. Repeated observations show that short, dainty females tend to have a small and delicately built larynx. The intermediate voice types of the male baritone and the female mezzo-soprano usually represent the corresponding intermediate body types. The art of singing recognizes additional subdivisions. The voice of a basso profundo is extremely low and heavy. The lyric tenor possesses a high, light, and flexible voice. Still higher and lighter is the counter tenor (as used in singing oratorios) who is the male counterpart of the highest female voice found in the extra high and light coloratura soprano. The dramatic voices employed in the Wagnerian operas represent intermediate forms between a male tenor (or high baritone) and a heroically masculine body type. The female dramatic soprano is usually heavily built; her strong mezzo-soprano voice can produce the high soprano tones.

The registers are related to voice types. As a general rule, the low voices possess a large range of chest voice with a much smaller range of head voice. The reverse holds for the high voice types, while baritone and mezzo-soprano assume an intermediate position. In the normal individual and the well-trained singer in particular, the midvoice encompasses one musical octave. As a further rule of thumb, the traditional and optimal transition tones follow a fairly stable and general pattern. As summarized in Figure 8, the three female voice types usually show the first transition from chest to midvoice at the tones d[1], e[1], and f[1], above middle c[1], respectively. The second transition between midvoice and head register in the three female voice types is almost precisely one octave higher. An extra-low contralto voice may prefer to shift the two transitions at

The relationship between registers and voice types

From *Archives of Otolaryngology*, vol. 62, p. 597; copyright 1955, American Medical Association

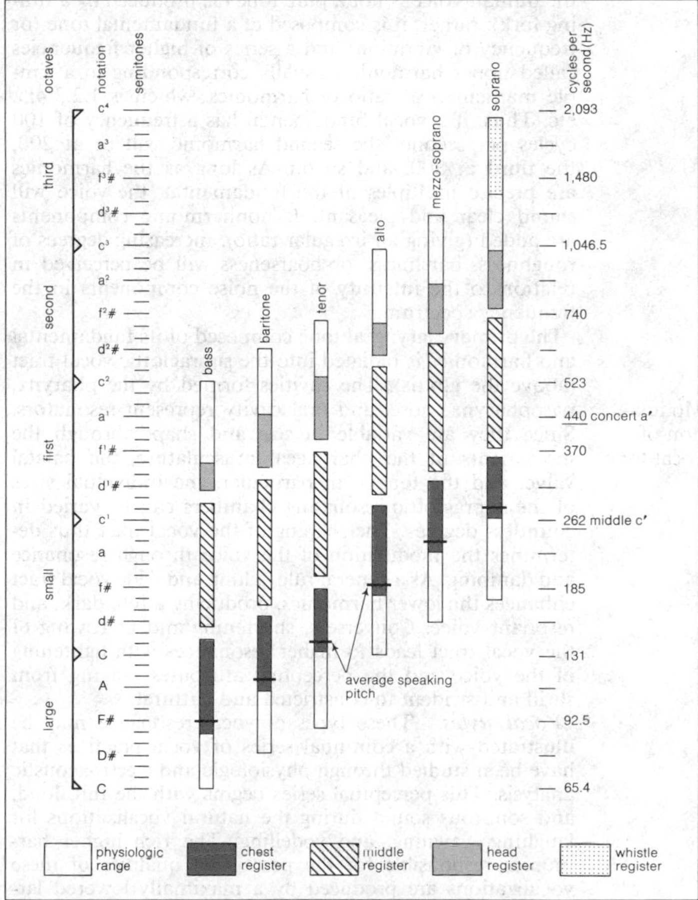

Figure 8: Relationships of registers, vocal range, average speaking pitch, and extreme tones of human voice. Octaves and notation according to von Helmholtz; frequencies based on standard concert a′ = 440 Hz.

slightly lower frequencies, whereas a very high coloratura soprano may prefer the two shifts a semitone (halftone) higher. The two transition tones of the three male voice types are situated almost precisely one octave lower than the respective six female transition tones. It should not be overlooked that the specific features in male voices sound approximately one octave lower than in the female voices of corresponding type. This octave phenomenon stems from the larger dimension of the adult male larynx. (The musical custom of writing the tenor part on the soprano stave in contrast to the correct notation of bass and baritone in the bass clef is a misleading tradition that derives from an old custom of four-part writing, for the tenor always sounds one octave lower than the soprano.)

Vocal ranges. As shown in Figure 8, the individual ranges of the singing voice extend from about 80 cycles per second in the low bass to about 1,050 cycles per second in the "high C" of the soprano (all values are approximated). The lowest note of serious musical literature is a low D with 73 cycles per second at the end of Osmin's aria in Mozart's *Abduction from the Seraglio,* and the highest is a high f^3 with almost 1,400 cycles per second sung by the Queen of the Night in Mozart's *Magic Flute.* Exceptionally high soprano tones are no longer sung with vocal cord vibration but are produced in the flageolet (or whistle) register simply by whistling through the narrow elliptical slit between the overtensed and motionless vocal cords. When citing the exceptional vocalistic feats of singers from the classical bel canto era, it should not be overlooked that musical pitch has been rising markedly since those days. Concert pitch is presently standardized at 440 cycles per second for the international tuning tone a^1. In the last half of the 18th century, the reference tone was at least one semitone lower.

Harmonic structure. A second attribute of vocal sound, harmonic structure, depends on the wave form produced by the vibrating vocal cords. Like any musical instrument, the human voice is not a pure tone (as produced by a tuning fork); rather, it is composed of a fundamental tone (or frequency of vibration) and a series of higher frequencies called upper harmonics, usually corresponding to a simple mathematical ratio of harmonics, which is 1:2:3:4:5, etc. Thus, if a vocal fundamental has a frequency of 100 cycles per second, the second harmonic will be at 200, the third at 300, and so on. As long as the harmonics are precise multiples of the fundamental, the voice will sound clear and pleasant. If nonharmonic components are added (giving an irregular ratio), increasing degrees of roughness, harshness, or hoarseness will be perceived in relation to the intensity of the noise components in the frequency spectrum.

The primary laryngeal tone composed of its fundamental and harmonics is radiated into the supraglottic vocal tract (above the glottis). The cavities formed by the pharynx, nasopharynx, nose, and oral cavity represent resonators. Since they are variable in size and shape through the movements of the pharyngeal musculature, the palatal valve, and the tongue in particular, the individual sizes of the supraglottic resonating chambers can be varied in countless degrees. The shaping of the vocal tract thus determines the modulation of the voice through resonance and damping. As a general rule, a long and wide vocal tract enhances the lower harmonics, producing a full, dark, and resonant voice. Conversely, shortening and narrowing of the vocal tract leads to higher resonances with lightening of the voice and the perceptual attributes ranging from shrill and strident to constricted and guttural.

Modulation of vocal tone

Vocal styles. These types of vocal resonance may be illustrated with a continual series of vocal practices that have been studied through physiologic and electroacoustic analysis. This perceptual series begins with the full, loud, and sonorous sound during the natural vocalizations for laughing, yawning, and yodelling. The rich higher harmonics responsible for the perceptual qualities of these vocalizations are produced by a maximally lowered larynx and greatly widened resonator. At the next step is the sonorous and full sound of so-called covered singing in the German opera style. Rich in higher harmonics (or overtones), this vocal style is performed with lowered larynx, elevated epiglottis, and widened throat cavity. A large group of open or uncovered singing styles lying in the centre of the series extends from the extremely uncovered, flat, and "white" openness of, for example, Spanish flamenco singing, over the flat style of popular singing, to the brightness of Italian bel canto. Approaching the other pole of the series, the large group of functional voice disorders results from constricted resonance of the vocal tract. It is typical of these hyperkinetic (overactive) vocal disorders that the voice is produced with marked laryngeal elevation, constriction of the laryngeal vestibule, and often with pronounced elementary sphincter action of the larynx. The extreme end of this functional series is characterized by the use of the larynx as a primitive sphincter organ as employed in ventriloquism. The maximally elevated and constricted larynx within a very narrow throat cavity produces the high-pitched, thin, muffled, and weak quality of ventriloquism, which is characterized by great reduction of the higher harmonics.

Use of the larynx in ventriloquism

Individual voice quality. Apart from the variable influences of the vocal tract on the momentary vocal resonance according to training and intention, the supraglottic resonator exerts a constant influence on the vocal quality by shaping its individual characteristics. Just as human faces differ in almost endless variations, the configuration of the supraglottic structures is also highly characteristic, having, in fact, been called the "inner face." The anatomical shape and the physiologic flexibility of the vocal tract serve to mold the individual vocal personality in at least two ways: by its inborn shape and by the learned behaviour of using it for communication. Any individual's mother tongue shapes his articulatory behaviour into certain patterns, which remain audible in all languages that he learns after puberty and constitute one aspect of the so-called foreign accent. It often is easy to recognize a speaker over the telephone after having listened to his voice a few times without necessarily having met him in person. The ability to recognize a given speaker solely by the quality and inflection of his voice is the basis of efforts to produce "voice prints" that should be as unmistakably identifying as fingerprints are.

Intensity. Vocal intensity, the third major vocal attribute, depends primarily on the amplitude of vocal cord vibrations and thus on the pressure of the subglottic airstream. The greater the expiratory effort, the greater the vocal volume. Another component of vocal intensity is the radiating efficiency of the sound generator and its superimposed resonator. The larynx has been compared to the physical shape of a horn. This construction is most efficient in acoustical practice, as seen in the shape of wind instruments, car horns, sirens, loudspeakers, etc. A well-shaped, wide, and flexible vocal tract enhances the projective potential of the voice. Conversely, a morphologically narrow, pathologically constricted, or emotionally tightened throat produces a muffled, constricted sound with poor carrying power.

Laughing and yawning

The inborn automatic reflexes of laughing and yawning illustrate the resonator action of the vocal organ. Together with a widely opened mouth, flat tongue, elevated palate, and maximally widened pharynx, the larynx assumes a lowered position with maximally elevated epiglottis. This configuration is ideal for the unimpeded radiation of the vocal cord vibrations so that the resulting sound is loud and bright, with a gaily ringing quality; it is the sound of happy laughter. The opposite is present with the painfully tight-throated, choked sobbing of someone crying in despair.

Singing and speaking. A major difference between singing and speaking is psychological in nature. Singing as a physiological performance is exhibited by the majority of human beings who have what seems to be an inborn musical sense that depends on appropriate development of their highest cortical (brain) centres for audition. Although the art of singing in a particular artistic style typically demands formal study, the untrained use of the voice for self-expression through singing develops spontaneously in late childhood and during the period following vocal maturation. Singing involves the use of inherited neural mechanisms that are regulated in part by deeper, subcortical (below the cortex) brain centres, particularly those related to emotional activity. Singing serves many as a way of emotional relief and is related to the social activities of human play. Although song among humans is not as intimately related to sexual propagation as it is in certain animals (*e.g.*, birds), people are still influenced by such sensual stimuli as love songs and madrigals, as well as ceremonial and religious performances.

The practice of spontaneous singing and of artistic song satisfies emotional needs, but it may not always communicate in a clear ideational sense. When a brain stroke causes aphasia (loss of language for communication), for example, the singing voice often remains normal or at least better preserved, so that some aphasics who cannot say a word can sing with good articulation. This observation has been used to explain that disorders causing aphasia may damage other brain areas than those used for singing. Another example is the severe stutterer who can sing or whisper with fluency. The same dichotomy of communicative speech and declamatory singing is often seen in cases of spastic dysphonia (a peculiar, grave voice disorder without demonstrable brain damage that causes a painfully choked and halting manner of speaking, while singing usually remains undisturbed).

Perceptual differences between speaking and singing

In the perceptual category, the principal differences between speaking and singing concern the rhythmic patterns. Speaking uses gliding vocal inflections with rapid pitch variations as well as frequent and abrupt intensity modifications for syllabic accentuation. The rhythmical pattern of stresses, unstressed syllables, and breathing pauses is dictated by the meaning of the sentence. The so-called prosodic features of speech (*i.e.*, its melodic inflections) follow the general, regional, and dialectal rules of a given language. In this sense, the essence of speaking is its continual flexibility, variability, and adaptability.

Singing differs from speaking in the following respects. The melody is followed in precise and discrete steps over customary musical intervals, which commonly are not smaller than semitones in Western music, though quarter and eighth tones are frequently used in Oriental and African music. The vowels are prolonged because they carry the melody. The rhythm of the fixed tonal steps follows the pattern prescribed by the composer and long notes may be sustained for special effects.

Exceptions to these general rules are found in the portamento, a gliding change between two pitch levels, of Western song, used sparingly as an embellishment. Parlando singing is a speaking type of song, used in the recitativo of Italian opera style. In these intentionally communicative preludes to formal arias—because they tell most of the story—the rhythm of the spoken word is incorporated into the melody, which, in turn, to a certain degree, follows the prosodic vocal inflection.

The melodic inflection of speech communicates considerable meaning in certain languages, such as in Africa and China. This problem of linguistic tonality, or word melody, requires the appropriate individual selection of various rising, sustained, or falling intervals to express the full meaning of a word. Chinese words are monosyllabic, and their multiple meanings cannot be understood without the appropriate prosodic inflection by the "tones" of the particular dialect. If Chinese is spoken without vocal inflection, such as when whispering, intelligibility is reduced by at least one-third.

SYNTHETIC PRODUCTION OF SPEECH SOUNDS

The essence of speech and its artificial re-creation has fascinated scientists for several centuries. Although some of the earlier speaking machines represented simple circus tricks or plain fraud, an Austrian amateur phonetician, in 1791, published a book describing a pneumomechanical device for the production of artificial speech sounds.

Speech synthesizers. A number of electronic speech synthesizers have been constructed in various phonetic laboratories in the latter half of the 20th century. Some of these are named the "Coder," "Voder," and "Vocoder," which are abbreviations for longer names (*e.g.*, "Voder" standing for Voice Operation Demonstrator). In essence, they are electrical analogues of the human vocal tract. Appropriately arranged electric circuits produce a voicelike tone, a modulator of the harmonic components of this fundamental tone, and a hissing-noise generator to produce the sibilant and other unvoiced consonant sounds. Resonating circuits furnish the energy concentrations within certain frequency areas to simulate the characteristic formants of each speech sound. The resulting speechlike sounds are highly controllable and amazingly natural as long as they are produced as continuants. For example, it is possible to imitate the various subtypes of the hard U.S. sound for R (as in "car") by moving a few levers or knobs. Difficulties become greater when many other attributes of fluent speech are to be imitated, such as coarticulation of adjacent sounds, fluctuating nasalization, and other segment features and transients of connected articulation. Speech synthesizers have, nevertheless, made a contribution to the study of the various physical characteristics that contribute to the perception and recognition of speech sounds.

Speech recognizers

The counterpart of speech synthesizers is the speech recognizer, a device that receives speech signals through a microphone or phono-optical device, analyzes the acoustic components, and transforms the signals into graphic symbols by typing them on paper. Modern models may incorporate computers to store some of the information that permits the device directly to type from dictation. Early models had great difficulties with the correct spelling of homophonous words (those that sound alike but differ in spelling and meaning) such as "to, too, two" or "threw, through, thru." Human transcribers usually have no difficulty with these distinctions because they listen to major parts of the sentence to recognize each word from the context and general situation. The computerized machines developed in the 1970s, however, had to be programmed for each detailed aspect of speech recognition that people normally learn through many years of general schooling and specialized training. Moreover, the machines could be effective only for very limited vocabularies and had to be adjusted to each individual speaker.

The pathology of speech

THE STUDY OF SPEECH DISORDERS

Prevalence of speech disorders. A comprehensive evaluation of knowledge and research in speech and hearing, published in 1969 by a section of the U.S. Public Health Service, under the title *Human Communication and Its Disorders—An Overview,* revealed that approximately 9,000,000 Americans were reported to have hearing impairments of handicapping magnitude; another 2,000,000 were said to suffer from central processing disorders from neurologic disease; and 10,000,000 to have speech disorders. The cost of coping with these problems was about $500,000,000 per year, while the annual deficit in earning power among such impaired persons approximated nearly $2,000,000,000. The same report estimated the prevalence of various speech disorders in the United States as shown in Table 5. The disorders of articulation among young children were numerically most frequent.

No data in similar detail are available from other countries; however, from experience in Germany, Austria, and other Central European countries, it may be said that

Table 5: Estimated Prevalence of Speech Defects in the United States

type of speech problem	ages 5–21 years		all ages	
	percent	number	percent	number
Functional articulatory	3.0	1,500,000	3.0	6,000,000
Stuttering	.7	350,000	.7	1,400,000
Voice	.2	100,000	.2	400,000
Cleft palate speech	.1	50,000	.1	200,000
Cerebral palsy speech	.2	100,000	.2	400,000
Retarded speech development	.3	150,000	.3	600,000
Impaired hearing (with speech defect)	.5	250,000	.5	1,000,000
Total	5.0	2,500,000	5.0	10,000,000

the incidence and prevalence of speech disorders follow similar patterns among other Western nations. Certain deviations from these trends are equally typical. The incidence of cleft palate is very high among American Indians, while it is much lower among Negroes than in Caucasians. Stuttering is more frequent in northern countries, such as in Scandinavia, than it is in southern regions—*e.g.*, Italy. Similar trends have been noted in the Far East. Nonorganic, functional, or emotional disorders of voice and speech reflect psychological tensions exerted by the environment. For such reasons, vocal nodules (growths on the vocal cords), contact ulcer, vocal fatigue, etc., occur with greater incidence in metropolitan areas and are conspicuously less frequent in rural regions.

Classification of speech disorders. In accordance with physiological considerations, disorders of communication are first classified into disorders of voice and phonic respiration, disorders of articulated speech, and disorders of language. It has been known for a long time that the majority of communication disorders are not caused by local lesions of the teeth, tongue, vocal cords, or regulating brain centres. Since these predominant disorders of voice and speech develop from derangements of the underlying physiological functions of breathing, use of the voice, speaking habits, or emotional disorders, this group has been labelled as functional. The remainder of the communication disorders with clearly recognizable structural abnormalities in the total speech mechanism has been termed organic.

Interaction of functional and organic disorders

While this empirical grouping has certain implications for the selection of the appropriate treatment, it is not satisfactory because organic structure and living function can never be separated. Certain functional disorders of the voice caused by its habitual abuse may very well lead to secondary structural changes, such as the growths (polyps and nodules) of the vocal cords, which develop as a result of vocal abuse. On the other hand, all of the obviously organic and structural lesions, such as loss of the tongue from accident or surgery, almost inevitably will be followed by emotional and other psychological reactions. In this case, the functional components are of secondary nature but to a great extent will influence the total picture of disturbance, including the patient's ability to adjust to his limitation, to relearn a new mode of appropriate function, and to make the best of his condition.

Within these major groups, the various types of communication disorders have for a long time, and in most parts of the world, been described by the listener's perceptual impression. Most languages employ specific words for the various types of abnormal speech, such as stuttering, stammering, cluttering, mumbling, lisping, whispering, and many others. The problem with such subjective and symptomatic labels is the fact that they try to define the final, audible result, the recognizable phenomenon, and not by any means the underlying basis. This general human tendency to describe disorders of communication by what the listener hears is analogous to the attempts of early medicine to classify diseases by the patient's symptoms that the diagnosing physician could see or hear or feel or perhaps smell. Before the great discoveries of the 19th century had erected a logical basis for medical pathology, the various diseases were classified as numerous types of fevers, congestions, dyscrasias, etc. Thus, malaria was originally thought to be caused by the evil emanations (miasma) of the bad air (*mal aria*) near swamps until it was recognized to be caused by a blood parasite transmitted by the mosquito.

The various approaches of medical, psychiatric, psychological, educational, behavioral, and other schools of speech pathology have made great advances in the recent past and better systems of classification continue to be proposed. They aim at grouping the observable symptoms of speech disorders according to the underlying origins instead of the listener's subjective impressions. While this is relatively easy in the case of language loss from, for example, a brain stroke because the destroyed brain areas can be identified at autopsy, it is more difficult in the case of the large group of so-called functional speech disorders for two reasons: first, they are definitely not caused by gross, easily visible organic lesions, and, second, many functional disorders are outgrown through maturation or appropriate learning (laboratory study of the involved tissues in such cases would reveal no detectable lesions). It is hoped that refined methods of study in the areas of both "functional" psychology and "organic" neurophysiology will eventually reveal the structural bases for the prevalent disorders of voice and speech.

Treatment and rehabilitation. The selection of methods in the medical treatment or educational rehabilitation of communication disorders depends primarily on the underlying basis for the disturbance. Any case of chronic hoarseness should be evaluated first by a laryngologist to establish a precise diagnosis. This is particularly important in the older age groups in which an incipient laryngeal cancer is often overlooked because the patient does not pay attention to his deteriorating voice. The prognosis of all cancers becomes rapidly poorer the longer the disease remains unrecognized. As soon as disease of the larynx is excluded as a cause of the vocal complaint, vocal rehabilitation by a competent speech pathologist should be considered.

Treatment by appropriate specialists

Malformations, diseases, or injuries of the peripheral speech mechanism are treated by appropriate specialists; the plastic surgeon repairs a cleft of the palate; the neurologist and internist treat the stroke patient until he has recovered sufficiently to be referred for re-education of his language abilities. The pediatrician treats the child with mental retardation, while the geneticist counsels the family regarding the possible inheritance of the disorder and its future avoidance. Deafness or severe hearing loss in early childhood is a typical cause for severe delay of language development and should be promptly recognized through appropriate examination by the ear surgeon (otologist) and hearing specialist (audiologist). Cases of childhood autism (withdrawal, severe eccentricities) or early schizophrenia are now being recognized with increasing frequency by speech pathologists, child psychiatrists, pediatricians, and clinical psychologists. This multitude of various professional interests in the recognition and rehabilitation of such exceptional children is well served by the coordination of these efforts in the modern team approach. But again, the largest group of disorders of voice and speech has causes other than these grossly organic lesions. They belong within the province of speech rehabilitation by experts in speech pathology and other functional practitioners.

Development of speech correction. That mankind has been troubled by speech afflictions since the beginning of recorded history can be gleaned from numerous remarks in the books of the Bible. Further, many scientific and medical writers from the time of antiquity to the Middle Ages reported observations of speech and voice disorders. The recommended remedies merely reflected the inadequacies of the philosophical or empirical notions of their times. Scientifically oriented speech pathology originated in Germany during the latter part of the 19th century, following closely the development of otolaryngology. Three names stand out in this respect: C.L. Merkel (*Anthropophonik;* 1857), Adolph Kussmaul (*The Disorders of Speech;* 1877), and Hermann Gutzmann, Sr., who became the first professor of speech pathology at the University of Berlin Medical School around 1900.

Experimental phonetics

During the same time, the new science of experimental phonetics was developed by Jean-Pierre Rousselot in Paris, who promptly recognized the great contributions that experimental phonetics could make to the study of normal and disturbed speech. This close collaboration of medical speech pathology with experimental phonetics has remained typical for the European continent where speech correction is customarily carried out under the direction of physicians in the ear, nose, and throat departments of the university hospitals. The designation of speech and voice pathology as logopedics and phoniatrics with its medical orientation subsequently reached many other civilized nations, notably in Japan and on the South American continent. The national organizations in most of these areas are now represented in the International Association of Logopedics and Phoniatrics, which was founded in Vienna in 1924.

The evolution of speech correction in the Anglo-Saxon countries followed a different trend. Although Great Britain has had a long tradition in general and experimental phonetics, its College of Speech Therapists was organized as an examining and supervisory body in 1945. Similar organizations followed in other areas of the British Commonwealth.

American speech pathology elected a different way. The American Speech and Hearing Association (ASHA), founded in 1925 in New York City, became the organizing, examining, and supervisory body for a rapidly growing membership, which surpassed 12,000 by 1970. More than 200 colleges and universities in the United States, many accredited by ASHA, offer degrees in speech pathology and audiology, some including work at the doctoral level. The large majority of ASHA members hold the master's degree and work as speech clinicians in the public school systems. A smaller number with master's degrees and a still smaller number with doctoral degrees staff the more than 300 clinics that deal with communication disorders and that are usually affiliated with hospitals, colleges, universities, and occasionally with civic organizations.

Soviet Russian speech correction originally followed the developments of European logopedics and phoniatrics and is now directed by the Department of Logopedics in the Government Institute of Defectology of the Academy of Pedagogical Sciences in Moscow. One facet of speech pathology in the U.S.S.R. is its emphasis on Pavlovian theory (conditioning and retraining) and intensive use of neuropsychiatric methods, including pharmacology, sleep therapy, and other intensive treatment programs during hospitalization. Similar trends operate in the eastern European countries under Russian influence, such as in Czechoslovakia, where the first independent medical department of logopedics and phoniatrics was organized at the Faculty of Medicine of Charles University in Prague.

MAJOR TYPES OF SPEECH DISORDERS

Voice disorders. In international terminology, disorders of the voice are described as dysphonia. Depending on the underlying cause, the various types of dysphonia are subdivided by the specifying adjective. Thus, a vocal disorder stemming from paralysis of the larynx is a paralytic dysphonia; injury (trauma) of the larynx may produce traumatic dysphonia; endocrine dysphonia reflects the voice changes resulting from disease of the various endocrine glands such as the pituitary. The various dysphonias of clearly organic origin from systemic disease (*e.g.*, muscular, nervous, or degenerative disease afflicting the entire body) or from local laryngeal changes differ in their visible symptomatology, as well as in the perceptual impression produced by the abnormal voice. Nevertheless, it has not yet been possible to define the acoustical alterations in the vocal spectrum that would allow a clear and objective differentiation among the subjective graduations of an abnormal voice as hoarse, harsh, husky, breathy, grating, gravelly, gritty, etc.

Because a large group of dysphonias have no visible laryngeal causes, they are grouped as nonorganic. Two main types of these so-called functional voice disorders may be distinguished: the habitual dysphonias that arise from faulty speaking habits and the psychogenic dysphonias that stem from emotional causes. Both of these types of dysphonia again occur in two basic subtypes, the hyperkinetic (overactive) and the hypokinetic (underactive) since emotional disorders interfere with voluntary vocal function by either causing excessive or depressed physiological activity. In the hyperkinetic disorders, the highly coordinated patterns of phonation regress to the primitive, forceful, and exaggerated sphincter action of the larynx as seen during gagging. The result is hyperkinetic dysphonia, the gratingly harsh vocal disorder due to excessive muscular action in a constricted larynx. In the second subtype, the movements for phonation regress even more deeply to the original function of respiration; the sluggish larynx remains more or less open, and the glottis is incompletely closed for phonation, leading to hypokinetic dysphonia with subdued, breathy huskiness.

Emotional causes

Disorders of language development. The most frequent speech disorders are those that disturb the child's acquisition or learning of language. While those concerned with modern terminology are striving for an improved classification according to the etiologic (causative) factors, it is still customary to classify these disorders on the basis of the complaint: absence of speech, baby talk, poorly intelligible articulation, lisping, etc. Recent studies of large numbers of children with such developmental language disorders have shown that at least two chief classes of these disorders may be distinguished: general language disability from genetic factors with a familial (inherited) pattern chiefly from the paternal side, and acquired language disorders due to damage sustained before, during, or shortly after birth (*i.e.*, perinatally).

These latter perinatal damages encompass the gamut of toxic, infectious, traumatic, nutritional, hormonal, and other damages that may hurt the growing fetus or young infant. Major and minor birth injury is not an infrequent factor. Hereditary factors also encompass a great variety of genetically predetermined influences, including familial tendency to exhibit slow language development, lesser endowment in the brain area for language, inferior function in the highest brain areas of auditory performance without organic damage to the ears, slow maturation of motor function (including clumsiness and deviation from normal cerebral dominance), and other signs of delayed cerebral growth. Additional environmental causes include poor language patterns used by the family, parental neglect, emotional maladjustment, general weakness from prolonged disease, as well as various socioeconomic, cultural, and other psychological influences.

While some otherwise perfectly normal children, particularly boys, may not elect to begin talking until age three, making good progress in every respect from then on, the absence of speech after age two may be caused by any of the conditions mentioned thus far and would appear to merit prompt investigation. If an organic cause can be detected, the symptomatic description of delayed language development then yields to a specific etiologic (causal) diagnosis. Although it is best to describe the absence of speech in early childhood as simply delayed language development, some American investigators tend to refer to this condition as congenital (present at birth) aphasia, a term rejected by most European scholars who argue that there cannot be an inborn or early acquired aphasia before a language has been learned.

Many children encounter unusual difficulties in mastering the patterns of articulation of their mother tongue and are said to manifest articulatory immaturity (infantile dyslalia). If no organic cause can be found, the probable cause may be delayed maturation of psychomotor skills.

Marked delays of language development are often followed by a period of inability to learn the rules of grammar and syntax at the usual age (dysgrammatism). Though this is often a sign of inherited language disability, it may reflect mental retardation or other types of brain damage.

Some children who have suffered such laboured language development may then go through a period of retarded reading and writing disability, a condition often defined as dyslexia. Again, there are two chief varieties: the primary or developmental reading and writing disability due to constitutional (organic) and hereditary factors, and a large secondary group of symptomatic reading disorders acquired through any of the influences that retard language development in general, including troubles with vision. Practically all investigators agree that primary or developmental dyslexia shows a marked hereditary tendency (is familial) and is typically associated with other disorders of psychomotor development, deviation from the prevalent right handedness, and poor function in the auditory area in the brain, often associated with lack of musical talent. Primary dyslexia is significantly associated with other developmental speech disorders.

Reading and writing disability

Articulatory disorders. *Cluttering.* Those who have followed large numbers of children with language disabilities for a long time are impressed by the fact that these various manifestations of an underlying developmental disorder often terminate in a peculiar impediment of speech that has been well known to European speech pathologists for many years but is not yet fully recognized in American speech literature: cluttering (or tachyphemia), the hasty, sloppy, erratic, stumbling, jerky, and poorly intelligible speech that may somewhat resemble stuttering (see below) but differs from it markedly in that the clutterer is usually unaware of it, remains unconcerned, and does not seem to fear speaking situations. Its association with other past or persistent signs of subnormal language development also differentiates congenital cluttering from emotional stuttering. Experts are strikingly unanimous in stressing the hereditary nature of cluttering.

Lisping. Although lisping belongs among the articulatory disorders and usually has the same causes as articulatory disorders (dyslalia) in general, it differs from other disorders of articulation in several respects. For one, lisping occurs in various varieties: with the tongue tip protruding between the front teeth, with a slurping noise in the cheek pouch, with the tongue too far back along the palatal midline, with excessive tongue pressure against the teeth; in several snorting and nasal subtypes, as well as through substitute hissing deep in the throat or even within the larynx, such as in cleft-palate speech. Moreover, the causes of lisping include a diverse group of particular conditions: abnormal number or position of teeth; imitation of other lispers; deficiency of palatal closure; slight hearing loss in the high frequencies; as well as several psychologic causes, such as effeminate affectation, infantile mannerisms, or mental disturbance. Lisping is less easily outgrown than the other infantile dyslalias and may persist into adult life if not corrected.

Causes of lisping

Stuttering, or stammering. Academically known as dysphemia, what is called stuttering in the United States is usually named stammering in Great Britain. While everyone seems to know what stuttering sounds like, experts do not agree about what really causes it. In the age groups after puberty, stuttering is the most frequent and conspicuous type of disturbed speech encountered. This is one reason why among the studies dealing with speech pathology in the world literature those devoted to stuttering are the largest single group. Despite numerous and intensive studies of the problem, findings and conclusions are far from unanimous. A great number of theories have been proposed to explain the origin and nature of stuttering, which range from the premise that subtle physical disturbances in the nervous system (so-called neurogenic asynchronies) are responsible to the opinion that psychological maladjustment alone is to blame. The report issued by the U.S. Public Health Service (see above *Prevalence of speech disorders*) concludes that "stuttering remains an enigma while illustrating the type of disorder which does not have either a clean-cut organic cause or a clearly habitual basis."

Research findings indicate (as is the case with many developmental speech disorders, particularly language disability, articulatory disorders, reading disability, and cluttering) that trouble with stuttering affects the male sex at least four times more frequently than the female. Hereditary predisposition has been noted in many studies of large groups of stutterers, with evidence for an inherited tendency found among as many as 40 percent of the stutterers studied. Some experts insist that stuttering is not a single disease entity but that it comprises several types of the disorder with different causes. According to such views, the familial occurrence of stuttering represents a combination of the stuttering symptom with a cluttering tendency that is inherited. Although imitation of another stutterer may form the basis for acquiring the habit, purely psychological explanations that stress parental attitudes in training their children fail to reveal why many stutterers have siblings (brothers or sisters) with perfectly normal speech.

Treatment of stuttering

The treatment of stuttering is difficult and often demands much skill and responsibility on the part of the therapist. The possibility of some specific medical cure seems remote at the present time. Even the most advanced methods of modern psychiatry have failed to produce superior results in treatment. For a time it was hoped that new psychopharmacological drugs (*e.g.,* tranquillizers) might facilitate and accelerate recovery from stuttering, but these efforts have been disappointing thus far. The typical program of management in this disorder is a strict program of psychotherapy (talking freely with a psychiatrist or psychologist so as to reduce emotional problems) supported by various applications of learning theory or behavioral theory (in retraining the stutterer) and other techniques depending on the therapist's position. It is widely agreed that the patient must acquire a better adjustment to the problems of his life and that he needs to develop a technique for controlling his symptoms and fears. Prognosis (predicted outcome of treatment) thus is held to depend greatly on the patient's motivation and perseverance. It is interesting to note that experienced investigators no longer aspire to a "cure" of stuttering through an etiologic (causal) approach. Instead of focussing on underlying causes, they aim at making the patient "symptom-free" via symptomatic therapy.

Prevention of stuttering may be aided through parent counselling. The normal, immature speech of many children is characterized by various nonfluencies; these include hesitations, syllable repetition, groping for the right word, and vocalizations between words such as "ah-ah." Some misguided parents castigate these normal signs of developing speech with various admonitions and, even worse, try to forbid the nonfluencies by mislabelling them as stuttering. In some children, this parental interference associates normal nonfluency with feelings of insecurity and fear, tending to make the child become a real stutterer. Much research has been devoted to this probable etiology for one type of stuttering; its elimination through parental guidance indeed has been reported to help in reducing the number of stutterers.

Dysphasia and aphasia. Dysphasia means the partial or total loss of language as a result of lesions in those parts of the brain that are directly related to language function. Stroke in elderly patients and head injury in younger ones are typical causes. Aphasia is seen most frequently when the left side of the brain is afflicted, as evidenced by paralysis of the right arm and leg. Evidence indicates that the left hemisphere is dominant in all right-handed individuals and in some left-handers as well. Some experts even believe that the left brain hemisphere is dominant for language in most individuals regardless of handedness and that dominance of the right brain is exceptional in some left-handers. According to other opinions, dominance for language is more evenly distributed in both hemispheres in left-handed persons. As explained before, two major brain areas are recognized as intimately associated with language function: Broca's area in the third frontal convolution and Wernicke's area in the posterior third of the upper temporal convolution. The angular gyrus at the junction of the temporal (side), parietal (top), and occipital (back) lobes of the brain is believed to be related to graphic language as used for reading and writing.

Aphasiology, the science of aphasic language loss, is studied by neurologists, neurosurgeons, some phoniatrists, certain speech pathologists, as well as some psychologists and linguists. This diversity of research background accounts, in part, for the great diversity in theoretical approaches to aphasia. Numerous classification schemes that have been proposed vary from simple groupings into a few main types of aphasia to complicated systems with many forms and subtypes of aphasic disturbances. Similar to research in stuttering, the literature on aphasia is exceptionally large and growing.

The phenomenon of aphasia

The essence of aphasia is the loss of memory for the meaning of language and its production. Thus, in the predominantly expressive or motor forms, the patient can no longer remember the intricate patterns for articulation; he can no longer form a word in speaking or writing, even though he may know what he wants to express. In the predominantly receptive or sensory forms, the patient can talk freely, sometimes excessively and incessantly (logorrhea), although with numerous errors and meaningless clichés, but he no longer comprehends what is said to him or what he tries to read. Those who recover from receptive forms of the disorder are likely to explain that during their aphasia spoken language sounded like an unintelligible, alien tongue. The degree to which there is combination of expressive and receptive symptoms varies greatly with the type and extent of brain lesion. There may be total loss of all language functions (global aphasia) to slight residual errors or misunderstandings when the brain damage is only slight or temporary. A major complication of aphasia is the frequent association with right hemiplegia, in which the paralyzed hand is no longer serviceable for writing. Retraining of the left hand for writing may then become necessary.

Management of aphasia has two goals: one, the physical recovery of the patient through treatment by the internist, neurologist, and possibly brain surgeon, and two, the re-education of the brain functions that remain, the aim being to help the patient relearn some use of language under the guidance of the speech pathologist. The better the recovery from the brain lesion, the more chances there are of prompt and complete return of language. When the brain losses are permanent, the patient must relearn each word, sentence, and phrase like the young child, albeit in a more cumbersome manner, apparently using brain parts that still function. He is repeatedly shown the picture of an object along with its printed name; these words are spoken to him by his teacher over and over in the hope that he will learn to repeat the word or phrase until he can say it spontaneously. Words that are relevant to the patient's everyday life are emphasized first with due consideration for his interests and past occupation; later he may advance to the use of abstract concepts and of higher levels of language. Various types of automated training programs are available, including a simple playback device that shows an inserted card with a picture on it, the name of the pictured object printed next to it, and the audible word recorded on a strip of magnetic tape. Devices of this type enable the patient to practice at his own pace.

Symptomatic speech disorders. Under this heading may be summarized various types of communication disorders that develop on the basis of known structural lesions or metabolic disturbances. Etiologic classifications group these impediments according to the types of organic diseases, as well as in respect to the afflicted effector organs (such as the tongue). Disturbed speech from lesions in the various parts of the nervous system is known as dysarthria. Mental retardation usually limits the development of linguistic ability to the same extent as it does intellectual capacity; this language disorder has been described as dyslogia. Mental disturbances can also manifest themselves in linguistic symptoms, such as in the peculiar (dysphrenic) mode of speech among sufferers of schizophrenia. Hearing loss dating from early childhood leads to a typical distortion of the speech pattern for which various names have been coined, such as audiogenic dyslalia. Visible defects in such oral articulators as the lips and teeth limit the mechanics of articulation and thus reduce the quality and intelligibility of speech; such speech problems are known collectively as dysglossia.

Dysarthria. Damage to those parts of the nervous system that regulate the actions of voice and speech cause distinctive alterations of the speech pattern. The most important disorder of this type is cerebral palsy from brain injury before, during, or soon after birth. The majority of cerebral palsy victims retain normal intelligence, but are handicapped by distortions of voluntary movements, including those for speaking. Just as walking may be stilted and jerky and arm movements crude and uncontrolled, the patterns of voice and speech will reflect the same distortions. Great advances in rehabilitation have been achieved in the recent past, such as with the well-known Bobath method, which is based on learned suppression of primitive reflexes.

Effects of cerebral palsy

Shaking palsy. Another type of dysarthria is observed in cases of Parkinson's disease. This affliction of the nervous system makes body movements either excessively rigid or tremulously repetitive, such as with the so-called "pill-rolling" sign of hand tremor. Voice and speech reflect the same patterns, sometimes appearing as the first obvious symptoms of the disease. Brain surgery is used in an attempt to improve these abnormal body movements, often with good general results, although speech may be little improved or even made worse. Neurologists also are collecting observations on promising drug treatments for Parkinson's disease, such as with L-Dopa.

When a neurologic disease damages the bulbar nuclei (in the brain stem) of the nerves innervating the organs for speech, the effect of bulbar dysarthria is heard. In severe cases, voice may be reduced to a faint grunting, while articulation deteriorates into mumbling or total muteness. Chorea, another neural disorder manifested in sudden jerky movements of the entire body, may be associated with bizarre, explosive disruptions of the speech flow. Cerebellar dysarthria results from disease of the brain part called the cerebellum (which regulates fine motor coordination), leading to various disorganizations of speech including a "drunken" (ataxic) quality.

Mental retardation. Major advances in the science of inheritance (genetics) and in biochemistry have clarified a number of inborn metabolic causes of many types of mental retardation (see BEHAVIOUR, INNATE FACTORS IN HUMAN). Some of these forms of retardation can be avoided through genetic counselling of prospective parents or prevented by prompt treatment following early diagnosis. (In some cases a change in diet is effective.) Improved prenatal care may reduce the size of another group of mentally retarded individuals whose problem stems from brain damage sustained during fetal life before birth. The number of unknown causes in other cases of retardation is still considerable, however.

Management of the mental retardate

The total management of the mentally retarded child concerns a large group of specialists: pediatrician, geneticist, clinical psychologist, audiologist and speech pathologist, and special educators in institutions for such children. Following classification on the basis of a level of educability, the child undergoes a composite training program geared to his capabilities. Intensive training in language usage not only tends to improve his communication skills but also forms a bridge to increased general learning. There has been recent stress on the not infrequent combination of mental retardation with hearing loss; in such cases, the audiologist prescribes a hearing aid and auditory training to improve the receptive aspects of communication.

Language and mental disorder. Expert analysis of the bizarre speech patterns associated with certain psychiatric disturbances is of primary diagnostic significance. If a mute child persists in stereotyped rituals and strange behaviour, a diagnosis of childhood autism is likely to be made. Some experts distinguish this from a similar disorder called childhood schizophrenia, in which previously good general and linguistic development falls apart in association with similarly bizarre behaviour. In adolescence, a sudden change of voice to a shrill falsetto or weird chanting may herald the outbreak of juvenile schizophrenic disease. Infantile lisping, strange distortions of articulation, and various eccentricities in verbal expression are other signs of schizophrasic speech in the adult schizophrenic. Linguistic study may help the psychiatrist in analyzing the patient's ways of thinking and to provide a measure of the sufferer's progress under therapy. Great therapeutic stress is placed on establishing contact with the autistic child by eliciting from him some sort of communication. Language is felt to be one of the best bridges to break open the closed inner world of such children.

Speech of the hard of hearing. Hearing loss that dates from childhood hinders the normal development of language because the most important sensory portal for speech learning remains deficient. Such children learn to say the sounds of speech as they hear them; that is, in a muffled, distorted, or even inaudible fashion. The articulatory disorder (audiogenic dyslalia) usually reflects the measured (audiometric) pattern of hearing loss. If sound waves at high frequencies cannot be heard, speech sounds with formants in that high-frequency region will be affected. The hissing sibilants contain the highest formants and are therefore most typically disturbed by high-frequency hearing loss. The lower frequencies that can still be heard limit the audible formants to this residual range, which transposes the normal formant patterns into the abnormally lowered frequency band. As a result, a sharp hissing S is spoken as a muted Sh, and the light vowels are transformed into their darker counterparts (for example, the word "set" may be pronounced as "shot" or "shöd" as if it were German).

The voice reflects analogous changes. In the case of conductive hearing loss (in which neural structures for hearing are intact), the patient hears himself well through the bones of his skull but cannot hear others. Because his bone conduction remains good, his voice will sound loud to him and he tends to keep it subdued. The opposite occurs with neural (or perceptive) hearing loss in which there is nerve dysfunction. In this case, the patient hears his own voice as poorly as that of others, and he tends to talk in an overloud and screeching voice.

Correction of audiogenic dyslalia may be possible through early fitting of a suitable hearing aid, intensive auditory training, and speech exercises aided by audiovisual playback devices (auditory trainers, tape recorders, visible speech devices, etc.).

Deaf-mutism

Profound or total deafness going back to early childhood without special training inevitably leads to deaf-mutism, the absence of oral language development as a direct result of deafness. Deaf-mute children have traditionally been educated in special schools for the deaf, where the oral method (showing how to shape the oral structures for each speech sound) of teaching speech has competed with the older manual method of allowing the deaf to communicate through their own gestural or finger spelling. Recent advances in training include the liberal use of amplification devices (*e.g.,* group hearing aids) in all school situations as well as the earliest possible fitting of hearing aids following definite diagnosis. This can be accomplished even when the patient cannot communicate that he hears (*e.g.,* in very young babies) through such methods as recording brain-wave patterns in response to measured sound stimulation (EEG response audiometry).

Speech impediments from defective articulators. Dysglossic (from defective oral structures) disorders in articulation have interested mankind for the longest time; the biblical and poetical interchange of the words for "tongue" and "speech" in many languages has kept alive the assumption that speech originates within the fleshy tongue. For the same reason, the popular term tongue-tied still persists to refer to an abnormally immobile tongue and some assumed resulting limitation of linguistic ability. Even the academic designation of the science of languages as "linguistic" is traditionally based on the Latin word *lingua* for tongue.

Tongue-tie. In practice, the condition of a true tongue-tie (ankyloglossia) occurs only rarely and is quite easily corrected through a simple operation. Even when the shortened band beneath the tongue tip is permitted to persist, very little speech disturbance, if any, is audible in such persons. The only limitation of articulation to be expected is the decreased ability to protrude the tongue tip between the teeth for the English Th and the trilling lingual R in southern German, Latin, and Slavic languages. In any event, a true tongue-tie never causes stuttering, lisping, or any other of the major speech disorders.

Loss of tongue. Major defects of the tongue from paralysis, injury, or surgery reduce the articulation of the lingual sounds to the same extent that the tongue's mobility is visibly limited. Spontaneous compensation is usually quite prompt, depending on the patient's general linguistic talent. One exception is complete bilateral (both sides) paralysis of the tongue, which causes a very severe disorder of chewing and swallowing as well as severe limitation of speech intelligibility. The total loss of the tongue (true aglossia) from injury or surgery is often amazingly well compensated. Patients can learn to use residual portions of a tongue stump as well as other oral structures to substitute for the missing tongue; indeed, some persons without a tongue have relearned to speak so well that the listener would not suspect its absence.

Nasal speech. Several types of nasal speech are not easily diagnosed; even specialized physicians are often not fully aware of the differences.

Increased nasal resonance leads to open nasality (hypernasal speech), affecting all oral speech sounds that should not be nasal. Organic causes impair the accuracy of palatal occlusion during emission of the nonnasal sounds. Among these are paralysis, congenital malformation, injury, or defects of the palate. The functional causes of palatal sluggishness include imitation, faulty speech habits, dialectal influences, hearing loss, mental retardation, or psychiatric disorders.

Decreased nasal resonance

Decreased nasal resonance produces closed nasality (hyponasal speech), which muffles the three nasal resonants (M, N, and Ng). The best known organic causes are an acute cold, hay fever, large adenoids, as well as all other nasal diseases that obstruct the airway. Functional causes are less frequent, in the form of a rare, faulty speech habit; occasionally the problem comes from mental retardation or from severe language disability.

Mixed nasality poses a serious problem; it stems from the combination of one cause of open nasality with another of closed nasality (one may be of organic type and the other functional, or both may be organic). A typical combination is the open nasality from paralysis (paresis) of the palate (or its congenital deficiency) combined with closed nasality from obstruction of the nasopharynx by adenoids. The resulting mixed nasality causes the nasal resonants to sound muffled and subdued, while careful testing reveals slight open nasality on all oral sounds.

Treatment of nasal speech is unlikely to be successful without prudent balancing of all factors involved. This responsibility rests primarily with the diagnosing otolaryngologist or phoniatrist. The complaint of "talking through the nose" should never warrant a tonsil and adenoid operation without complete evaluation. If this were done in the example cited just above, removal of the obstructing adenoids would alleviate only the closed nasality, while making the open component more severe with marked deterioration of the patient's speech. This dilemma is often present when adenoids cause chronic middle-ear disease with hearing loss, while the palate is incompetent, as from a slight congenital malformation or paresis. In such case, the patient's general health and his hearing must be weighed against the possibility of making his speech worse.

Cleft palate speech. This type of organic dysglossia has also been named rhinoglossia (Greek *rhin, rhis:* "nose") because it is an organic cause of excessively nasal speech. Clefts of the lip, upper jaw, and hard and soft palate occur in various types and combinations. Cleft palate is a congenital (present at birth) malformation that develops for various reasons during the early weeks of embryonic life. The causes may be grouped as follows: inheritance in some cases; embryonal damage from various environmental causes in others; while still other cases of cleft palate are part of a syndrome of general or multiple malformation, which may again be hereditary, the result of chromosomal aberrations, or of environmental origin. Genetic influences are inferred from evidence that North American Indians (Montana) show a high incidence of cleft palate, but Negroes (as on the island of Jamaica) show an unusually low incidence.

Mechanism of cleft palate disorder

The speech disorder in cleft palate cases is complex. As a direct, mechanical result of the absent velopharyngeal (soft palate-pharynx) closure, voiced sounds assume an abnormal nasal quality from the unusual resonance of the nasal chambers. The influence of nasality on the perceptual and acoustic characteristics of the speech sounds has been discussed earlier. A second component is a mechanical limitation in articulating plosive sounds (*e.g.,* P) because the necessary intra-oral pressure cannot be achieved. For the same reason, the sibilant sounds (*e.g.,* S) are greatly distorted because the articulating air escapes through the nose before it can produce the characteristic hissing noise at one of the places of constriction. The child with an unrepaired cleft palate seems unconsciously to attempt to overcome these mechanical limitations in several ways. He tries to constrict the nostrils through facial grimaces, and he attempts to increase the expiratory air pressure. He also succumbs to the "law of centripetal regression of articulation"; that is, he shifts the articulation of the oral sounds below the point of deficient palatal occlusion, down into the pharynx or even the larynx. It is easy to demonstrate by X-ray fluoroscopy how the larynx becomes constricted during each plosive or sibilant sound in such cases.

These mechanical limitations of articulation in cleft

palate lead to secondary modifications of behaviour. Linguistic ability is retarded through general limitation of speech learning; emotional reactions to the handicap may complicate the clinical picture; a vicious circle is thus established, which in turn impedes the sufferer's general intellectual and special linguistic development.

Other coincidental disorders complicate the pattern of cleft-palate speech. Many cleft-palate patients also suffer from middle-ear infection, and the resulting hearing loss may add the component of audiogenic dyslalia. In other cases, the structural malformation may be complicated by mental retardation. Coincidental genetic factors may aggravate the speech problem when the syndrome of familial (neurally inherited) language disability is superimposed. In such cases, the mechanical speech disorder of rhinoglossia becomes complicated by the additional signs of delayed speech development, articulatory dyspraxia, dysgrammatism, reading and writing disability, etc. This combination is evident in some cases following the successful surgical correction of the palatal deficiency. Although the nasality is promptly alleviated in such cases, the various speech disorders from language disability may persist, since they have nothing directly to do with the previous cleft palate.

Treatment of cleft palate

Management of cleft palate is the task of a well-coordinated team. The plastic surgeon closes the palatal deficiency, the psychologist analyzes the intellectual endowment, the speech pathologist corrects the various components of disordered speech, the audiologist determines coincidental hearing loss, and the otolaryngologist cares for the health of nose and ears. Tonsils and adenoids may be diseased, leading to the frequent complication of middle-ear infection with hearing loss. This condition may require removal of tonsils and adenoids to preserve hearing. A dilemma is then created; removal of tonsils and adenoids is generally contra-indicated in cases of deficient palatal closure because this operation increases the degree of open nasality. The child's welfare then should be carefully considered in order to avoid any harm.

When surgical repair is not feasible, the palatal defect may be covered by a special prosthetic plate (obturator) similar to false dental appliances. This technique has been known for many centuries, and various models of obturators have been constructed in the course of time. Cleft-palate care therefore includes the services of a prosthodontist (who makes false teeth) for the optimal construction of such appliances. If worn by children, obturators should be regularly altered to maintain continuous fit as the patient grows.

Well-organized centres for the management of cleft palate are able to offer excellent care so that the speech impediment can be ideally or almost completely corrected in many cases. The problem of cleft palate thus demonstrates once more that human speech requires complex detailed study of its normal functions and manifold approaches for the correction of its imperfections. (G.E.A./Ed.)

BIBLIOGRAPHY

Phonetics: D. ABERCROMBIE, *Elements of General Phonetics* (1967), a readable survey of selected topics; P. LADEFOGED, *A Course in Phonetics* (1975), a foundation in linguistic phonetics; K.L. PIKE, *Phonetics* (1943), and P. LADEFOGED, *Preliminaries to Linguistic Phonetics* (1971), critical analyses of phonetic theory; R. JAKOBSON, C.G.M. FANT, and M. HALLE, *Preliminaries to Speech Analysis* (1952), the first major account of distinctive feature theory; N. CHOMSKY and M. HALLE, *The Sound Pattern of English* (1968), a comprehensive description of English phonology; P. LADEFOGED, *Elements of Acoustic Phonetics* (1962), an introduction to the physics of speech; I. LEHISTE (comp.), *Readings in Acoustic Phonetics* (1967), a collection of major articles; B. MALMBERG (ed.), *Manual of Phonetics* (1968), authoritative chapters on many aspects of phonetics. Acoustic aspects of speech production are also treated in DENNIS B. FRY, *The Physics of Speech* (1979); J.M. PICKETT, *The Sounds of Speech Communication* (1980); RICHARD M. WARREN, *Auditory Perception* (1982). DAVID CHRYSTAL, *A First Dictionary of Linguistics and Phonetics* (1981), covers main topics in articulatory and acoustic phonetics.

Physiology of speech: V.E. NEGUS, *The Comparative Anatomy and Physiology of the Larynx* (1950), an excellent introduction to the understanding of function and evolution of the voice organ in man and animals; G. FANT, *Acoustic Theory of Speech Production* (1960), a modern, detailed exposition of acoustic phonetics, the science of the acoustic structure of speech sounds and their production; H. FLETCHER, *Speech and Hearing in Communication,* 2nd ed. (1953), a classic work on the physiology of speech and hearing; P.B. DENES and E.N. PINSON, *The Speech Chain* (1963), highly recommended for high school and college level students. See also WILLIAM M. SHEARER, *Illustrated Speech Anatomy* (1979); RODERICK P. SINGH, *Anatomy of Hearing and Speech* (1980); WILLARD R. ZEMLIN, *Speech and Hearing Science: Anatomy and Physiology* (1981); and DAVID ROSS DICKSON and WILMA MAUE-DICKSON, *Anatomical and Physiological Bases of Speech* (1982).

Pathology of speech: R. LUCHSINGER and G.E. ARNOLD, *Handbuch der Stimm- und Sprachheilkunde,* 3rd ed. (1970; Eng. trans., *Voice, Speech, Language,* 2nd ed., 1972), the largest text on disorders of communication with extensive references and international orientation; R. CARHART (ed.), *Human Communication and its Disorders: An Overview* (1969), an important report of the U.S. Department of Health, Education and Welfare on statistics, established facts, and research needs; L.E. TRAVIS (ed.), *Handbook of Speech Pathology* (1957), a fundamental American publication by many leading contributors; C. VAN RIPER, *Speech Correction: Principles and Methods,* 6th ed. (1978), a widely used text for study and references; R.W. WEST and M. ANSBERRY, *The Rehabilitation of Speech,* 4th ed. (1968), another classic in the field of speech pathology. Later monographs include JOHN K. DARBY (ed.), *Speech Evaluation in Medicine* (1981); JOHN E. BERNTHAL and NICHOLAS W. BANKSON, *Articulation Disorders* (1981); BETTY BYERS BROWN, *Speech Therapy* (1981); JOYCE S. TAYLOR, *Speech-Language Pathology: Services in the Schools* (1981); ELIZABETH CARROW-WOOLFOLK and JOAN I. LYNCH, *An Integrative Approach to Language Disorders in Children* (1982); ANDREW SEKEY (ed.), *Electroacoustic Analysis and Enhancement of Alaryngeal Speech* (1982); NORMAN J. LASS *et al.* (eds.), *Speech, Language, and Hearing,* 3 vol. (1982); C. WOODRUFF STARKWEATHER, *Speech and Language: Principles and Procedures of Behavior Change* (1983); and FRANKLIN H. SOLVERMAN, *Legal Aspects of Speech-Language Pathology and Audiology: An Overview of Law for Clinicians, Researchers, and Teachers* (1983).

Speech as an aspect of communication theory is explored in GEORGE A. MILLER, *Language and Speech* (1981); JILL G. DE VILLIERS and PETER A. DE VILLIERS, *Language Acquisition* (1978); ERIC WANNER and LILA R. GLEITMAN (eds.), *Language Acquisition: The State of the Art* (1982); EDMUND B. BOLLES, *So Much to Say: How to Help Your Child Learn to Talk* (1982); LYNNE FEAGANS and DALE CLARK FARRAN (eds.), *The Language of Children Reared in Poverty* (1982); ROY HARRIS (ed.), *Approaches to Language* (1983); WILLIAM E. COOPER and JEANNE PACCIA-COOPER, *Syntax and Speech* (1980); PETER D. EIMAS and JOANNE L. MILLER (eds.), *Perspectives on the Study of Speech* (1981).

See also recent issues of these journals: *American Speech and Hearing Association* (ASHA) *Journal* (monthly); *Journal of Speech and Hearing Disorders* (quarterly); *Journal of Speech and Hearing Research* (quarterly); *Cleft Palate Journal* (quarterly), all U.S.; *Folia Phoniatrica* (bimonthly, Basel); and the *British Journal of Disorders of Communication* (semi-annual, London). Useful reference sources are PAUL H. PTACEK *et al.* (comp.), *Index to Speech, Language, and Hearing: Journal Titles, 1954–78* (1979); and WILLIAM ORR DINGWALL, *Language and the Brain: A Bibliography and Guide,* 2 vol. (1981).

Sponges: Phylum Porifera

The sponges, which constitute the phylum Porifera, are among the most primitive multicellular animals. They number approximately 5,000 described species and inhabit all seas, where they occur attached to surfaces from the intertidal zone to depths of 8,500 metres (29,000 feet) or more. One family, the Spongillidae, is found in fresh water. Adult sponges lack a definite nervous system and do not show conspicuous movements of body parts.

This article is divided into the following sections:

GENERAL FEATURES

Early naturalists regarded the sponges as plants because of their frequent branching form and their lack of obvious movement. The animal nature of sponges, first described in 1755, was confirmed in 1765 after observations of their water currents and the movement of their openings. In structure, function, and development, sponges are distinct from other animals. Many zoologists regard sponges as occupying an isolated position in the animal kingdom and classify them in the subkingdom Parazoa; on the other hand, sponges are sometimes considered relatives of another invertebrate animal group, the coelenterates.

The phylum Porifera may be divided into three classes on the basis of the composition of the skeletal elements—the Calcispongiae and Hyalospongiae include about 20 percent of the known species of sponges; the remainder are placed in the class Demospongiae (see Figure 1).

Importance. The soft elastic skeletal frameworks of certain species of the Demospongiae—*e.g., Spongia officinalis, Hippospongia communis, S. zimocca, S. graminea*—have been familiar household items since ancient times. In ancient Greece and Rome, sponges were used to apply paint, as mops, and by soldiers as substitutes for drinking vessels. During the Middle Ages, burned sponge was reputed to have therapeutic value in the treatment of various diseases. Natural sponges now are used mostly in arts and crafts such as pottery and jewelry making, painting and decorating, and in surgical medicine. Synthetic sponges have largely replaced natural ones for household use.

Commercial value

The living sponge is a mass of cells and fibres, its interior permeated by an intricate system of canals that open as holes of various sizes through the tough dark brown or black skin, which may be hairy from fibre ends that pierce it. Only after it has been completely cleaned of its millions of living cells does a sponge resemble the sponge of commerce; *i.e.,* a soft and elastic spongin skeletal framework. Commercially valuable sponges, which may be found from tidal level to a depth of about 200 feet, usually are harvested by hooking or harpooning in shallow waters, by skin diving or by deepwater fishing. Although the most valuable sponges are found in the eastern Mediterranean area, they also are harvested off the west coast of Florida and the Florida Keys, in the West Indies, off Mexico and Belize, and, to a limited extent, off the Philippines. Because they have the ability to regenerate lost parts, sponges can be cultivated from small fragments.

Sponges are valuable from a scientific point of view because of their unusual cellular organization (the cells do not form tissues such as those found in other animals), their ability to regenerate lost parts, and their biochemical features (they have many compounds not known in other animals). Sponges comprise an important part of the organisms that live in the depths of the sea (benthos) and may be associated with other organisms; *e.g.,* many types of animals live in sponges.

Size range and diversity of structure and colour. Most sponges are a few centimetres in size, but some urn-shaped or shapeless ones are less than a centimetre (0.4 inch); others, shaped like vases, tubes, or branches, may be one to two metres (3.3–6.6 feet) tall, and broad rounded masses may be one to two metres in diameter. Size within a species may vary with age, environmental conditions, and food supply.

The external appearance of sponges is variable. They may appear bushy or treelike and have fingerlike projections. Some, particularly in the class Demospongiae, are shapeless, or amorphous, masses that form thin encrustations on objects or are cushion shaped. A few Demospongiae have well-defined spherical shapes as in *Tethya aurantium,* the sea orange; others may be cup- or fan-shaped. Calcispongiae of the genus *Scypha* are shaped like tubular sacs, with an opening (osculum) at the tip. Members of

From (*Spongia*) T.J. Parker and W.A. Haswell, *A Textbook of Zoology*, St. Martins Press, Inc., Macmillan & Co., Ltd.; (others) G.C. Pimentel, *Natural History*

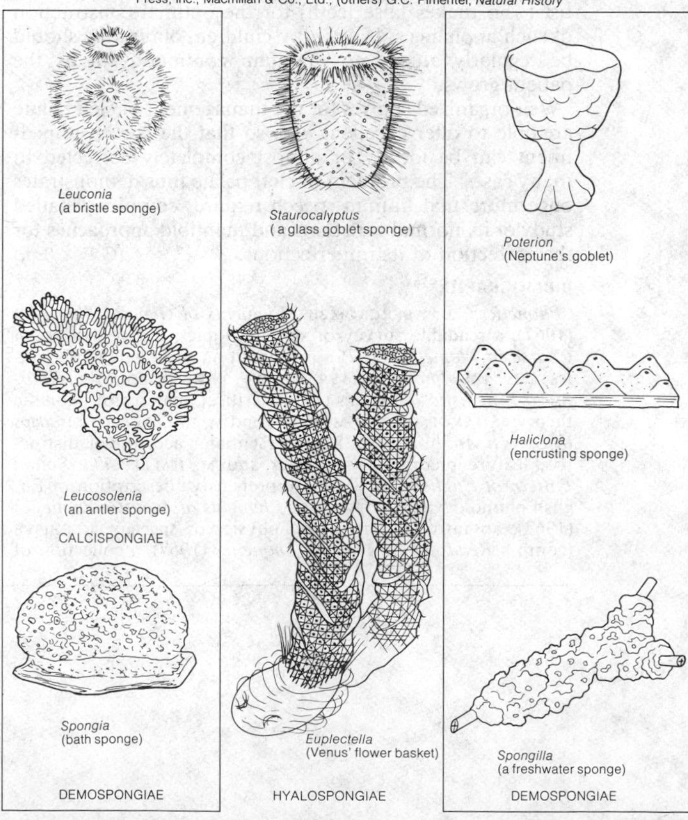

Figure 1: Representative sponges.

the Hyalospongiae are erect or cylindrical, with a stalklike base.

Colour among sponges is variable. Deep-water sponges usually show a neutral colour, drab or brownish; shallow-water sponges, frequently brightly coloured, range from red, yellow, and orange to violet and occasionally black. Most Calcispongiae are white. Some sponges (*e.g.,* the Spongillidae) are often greenish because green algae live in a symbiotic relationship within them; others are violet or pinkish, because they harbour symbiotic blue-green algae. These symbionts endow the sponges with colour as long as light is available; the sponges become white in the dark when no photosynthesis occurs and the algal pigments utilized in photosynthesis are no longer produced. Another variable character in sponges is consistency, which may range from the soft and viscous state of some encrusting species to the hard stonelike quality of the genus *Petrosia.* In addition, the surface of a sponge may be smooth, velvety, rough with protruding skeletal elements called spicules, or conulose (*i.e.,* provided with conical protrusions called conuli).

Effects of symbionts

Distribution and abundance. The Porifera are present at all water depths, from the tidal zone to the deepest regions (abyss). They occur at all latitudes and are particularly abundant in Antarctic waters. Calcispongiae and Demospongiae are found mainly on the rocky bottoms of the continental shelf; the Hyalospongiae are characteristic of the deepest muddy bottoms of oceans and seas. In some environments, sponges are the dominating organisms; sometimes they cover wide areas, especially on rocky overhangs and in the caves of the littoral, or shore, zone. A restricted number of species are adapted to brackish waters; and members of the family Spongillidae (class Demospongiae) populate the fresh waters of rivers and lakes.

NATURAL HISTORY

Life cycle. Most sponges reproduce sexually, although asexual reproduction may occur. Sponges are generally hermaphroditic (male and female germ cells in one animal); sometimes dichogamy, in which male and female germ cells develop at different times in the same animals, occurs.

Sexual reproduction. The fertilization of an egg by a spermatozoan is peculiar in sponges in that a spermatozoan, after its release from a sponge, is carried by the water current until it is captured by a specialized cell called a choanocyte, or collar cell, in another sponge; the choanocyte transforms into an amoeba-shaped cell called a carrier cell, which gives up the spermatozoan to an egg, lying near a chamber formed by choanocytes and containing long lashlike appendages called flagella.

Types of larvae

Development of the embryo may occur in one of several ways characteristic of the different groups; as a result, more than one type of larva is found. The characteristic larva of the Calcispongiae and of some Demospongiae (*e.g., Oscarella*), called an amphiblastula, is oval in shape and has a cavity in the middle; the front half of the larva consists of cylindrical, flagellated cells, the other half of round cells without flagella. The larva swims with the flagellated portion forward. The amphiblastula is preceded by a stage (stomoblastula) in which the central cavity of a hollow mass of cells (blastula) opens outward and is surrounded by round granular cells (macromere), which are distinguished from other cells with flagella (micromere). The most common larval form among the Demospongiae is called a parenchymella; it is solid and compact, with an outer layer of flagellated cells and an inner mass of cells.

A larva swims for a period of time that may vary from a few hours to a few days before it descends to find a surface suitable for attachment. After attachment, the larva undergoes developmental changes (metamorphosis) becoming a young individual called an olynthus in the Calcispongiae, a rhagon in the Demospongiae; the young individual gradually develops into an adult sponge. The metamorphosis following larval attachment involves changes in the relative positions and functions of larval cells. In one larval type (parenchymella), the flagellated outer cells become the collar cells (choanocytes) of the interior of the adult sponge; the interior cells of the larva give rise, in the adult, to the cell layer (pinacoderm) and the different cells (*e.g.,* archaeocytes, collencytes) found in the amorphous substance (mesohyl) that fills the sponge. In the amphiblastula, the choanocytes are derived from the forward flagellated region; the other cells and the mesohyl are derived from the posterior half.

The sexual maturation of sponges is connected with the temperature of the water in which they live. In the temperate regions, maturation occurs mainly from spring to autumn; sometimes two distinct periods of reproduction occur, one in spring, the other in autumn. Some sponges mature at any time of the year; *e.g., Scypha,* formerly called *Sycon.* Tropical sponges also apparently mature any time throughout the year. Sponges for the most part bear living young (*i.e.,* are viviparous); the larvae are released through the canals of the excurrent (outgoing) water system and an opening (osculum) also involved in that system. A few sponges (*e.g., Cliona* and *Tethya*) lay eggs (*i.e.,* are oviparous).

The life-span of sponges is not well known; the small encrusting forms probably live about a year, disappearing during a season unfavourable to their survival; small fragments of an individual, however, may persist and reproduce new individuals in the next season. The large species have a much longer life-span; bath sponges (*Spongia, Hippospongia*), for example, attain a commercially desirable size after seven years and may live as long as 20 years.

Asexual reproduction. Asexual reproduction also occurs in sponges in various ways; the best known method is called gemmulation. Gemmulation begins when aggregates of cells, mostly archaeocytes, which, when they become laden with reserve food granules, are called thesocytes, become isolated at the surface of a sponge and are then called gemmules. These are expelled from the adult sponge and, in some marine species, serve as a normal reproductive process or, sometimes, as a means to carry the sponges over periods of unfavourable conditions when the adults degenerate; *e.g.,* drought, temperature extremes.

Gemmules

The freshwater Spongillidae undergo a slightly different gemmulation. Gemmules consist of aggregates of archaeocytes laden with reserve granules; in addition, however, they are surrounded by protective membranes formed by the archaeocytes. The protective covering is generally reinforced by spicules, which vary in shape according to the species and are useful in classification. Freshwater sponge gemmules allow a species to survive unfavourable conditions in a state in which vital activities are almost completely suspended. In cold regions, gemmulation occurs in winter, and the inactive gemmules are said to hibernate; in warm regions, gemmulation occurs in summer, and the gemmules are said to estivate. In spring or autumn when favourable conditions return, the gemmules germinate, their archaeocytes emerge through an opening (micropyle), the various cellular types differentiate, and a new sponge grows. Other methods of asexual reproduction include formation of stolons (rootlike extensions) and fragmentation of individuals.

Regeneration. The extraordinary capacity of sponges to regenerate is manifested not only by restoration of damaged or lost parts but also by complete regeneration of an adult from fragments or even single cells. Sponge cells may be separated by mechanical methods (*e.g.,* squeezing a piece of sponge through fine silk cloth) or by chemical methods (*e.g.,* elimination of calcium and magnesium from seawater). Dissociated cells settle, migrate, and form active aggregates in which the archaeocytes play an important role. In order for small aggregates of cells to form larger aggregates, the cells must generally become attached to a surface, where they flatten and develop an envelope of special cells (pinacocytes); this is called the diamorph stage. Reconstitution of the choanocyte chambers and of the canal system follow soon afterward, resulting in a young sponge that is functional and able to grow. It is generally believed that the reconstitution process, even if it involves cell division, is not comparable with embryonic development, because the various types of dissociated cells participate in the formation of the new sponge by sorting and rearranging themselves, rather than by differentiating from primitive cell types. Regeneration in sponges is of theoretical interest in connection with certain cell properties; *e.g.,* adhesion, sorting out, and movement.

During unfavourable conditions, sponges are reduced to small fragments that may consist only of masses of archaeocytes covered by layers of pinacocytes. A complete sponge forms from these fragments when favourable conditions return.

Individuality of sponges

The regenerative abilities of sponges, their lack of a central coordinating organ (brain), and the peculiar migratory ability of cells within the organisms combine to make it somewhat difficult to define the individuality of a sponge. Various attempts to establish whether sponges are individuals or colonies have failed to solve the problem, and, thus far, no completely satisfactory criterion for defining a sponge has been found. Zoologists involved in the study of sponges empirically define a sponge individual as a mass that is enveloped by a common ectoderm, *i.e.,* by a common cellular layer.

Ecology. Most Porifera, very sensitive to a wide range of ecological factors, are difficult to raise under laboratory conditions. Few species (*e.g., Hymeniacidon sanguinea*) are able to tolerate long periods of emersion and variations in such physical factors as light, temperature, and salinity.

Habitats. Light is a limiting factor for the survival of most sponges in a given habitat. Littoral-dwelling sponges generally develop in caves, on shadowed walls, or under small shelters such as those provided by crevices. Some species, mainly in the tropics, however, are covered by a metre or less of water and thus are almost completely exposed to irradiation from the sun. Symbiotic relationships between algae and sponges usually occur in strongly illuminated zones; the algae may act as a protective device because they deposit pigments in the superficial cell layers of the sponge. In some sponges (*e.g., Petrosia ficiformis*), colour is related to the number of symbionts; in a cave, for example, sponges gradually change from intensely coloured specimens to light-coloured, sometimes white, ones in the depth of the cave where the number of algae decreases.

Porifera of the family Clionidae (class Demospongiae) live in galleries they excavate in shells of mollusks, in corals, in limestone, and in other calcareous materials. The boring activities of clionids are accomplished by the excavation, possibly involving both chemical and mechanical action, of numerous, small chips of calcium carbonate. Cytoplasmic projections and films put out by sponge cells in contact with a calcareous surface apparently come into intimate contact with the calcium carbonate, resulting in the removal of particles of relatively uniform size. Clionid sponges weaken limestone breakwaters and coral reefs, making them more easily subject to further abrasion by waves. In addition, they weaken oystershells.

Attachment to a surface

Although most sponges settle and grow on hard or rocky surfaces, some anchor to a firm object on soft bottoms, on sand, on mud, or on debris. Unattached sponges are rare. Different species may compete for a surface, and superposition of one species on another sometimes occurs; the presence of a rich population of different species on the same surface may help them to survive by the modifications each contributes to the environmental microclimate surrounding them, thereby providing protection against extreme fluctuations of physical factors such as temperature and light.

Associations with other organisms. The Porifera often grow on or near other organisms, sometimes killing those they cover; the sessile (attached) barnacle *Balanus,* for example, may be killed in this way. In other cases, associations may provide advantages to both organisms, particularly those between sponges and crustaceans. Some crustaceans, mainly crabs, use sponges for camouflage by removing a piece of a living sponge and holding it against their carapace (shell); the best known example of this type of mutualistic association is that of the sponge *Suberites domuncula* and hermit crabs, which live in the shells of gastropod mollusks. The advantage to the sponge is that it is carried by the mollusk; the hermit crab gains protection not only by living in the shell of the mollusk but also through the disagreeable smell and taste of the sponge, which discourages attack by fishes and other enemies.

Various plants and animals may live on the surface of a sponge or inside its canals and cavities. In some cases the associations are specific; *e.g.,* the coral *Parazoanthus axinellae* grows on the sponge *Axinella.* The organisms that live in the cavities of sponges include crustaceans, nematode and polychaete worms, ophiuroid echinoderms (brittle stars), and bivalve mollusks; some inhabit a sponge for occasional shelter or nourishment, others establish more intimate associations as parasites or predators. Young shrimps of the genus *Spongicola* penetrate certain sponges of the class Calcispongiae, live in them in pairs, and presumably are trapped for life in the rigid skeleton of the sponge; the Japanese consider these shrimps a symbol of matrimonial faithfulness. The number of organisms that live within a single sponge may be very high; thousands of organisms of various species, for example, may be found in *Spheciospongia vesparia,* a Caribbean sponge.

Some organisms that live on (called epibionts) and in (called endobionts) sponges act as parasites. Cyclopoid copepods are the most important parasites of marine sponges; in fact, some genera of these crustaceans have become modified as a consequence of their parasitic existence. Freshwater sponges also are attacked by parasites such as rotifers and mites, which lay eggs in them; larvae of the neuropteran insect family Sisyridae (spongillaflies) live in, and feed upon, freshwater sponges. In general, sponges are protected from predators by their disagreeable taste and smell and by their hard skeletal elements (spicules). In some cases, however, sponges are eaten by other organisms; *e.g.,* mollusks—gastropods such as snails and nudibranch slugs, prosobranchs such as *Patella* and *Littorina,* and chitons—some crustaceans, and some fishes (especially on coral reefs).

Algal associations

The most important symbiotic associations of sponges occur with single-celled and multicellular algae. The algae may live in the surface layers of the sponge, inside the cells, or among them. The sponge protects the algae from enemies, from unfavourable environmental conditions, and from their own metabolic waste products; the sponge uses the algae as a source of oxygen, as a mechanism for eliminating its products of metabolism, as a screen against sunlight, and as a food source (consuming both algal waste products and dying algae). Sponges of the freshwater Spongillidae and various species of marine littoral sponges consume dying green and blue-green algae respectively. The algae, which provide the Spongillidae with their characteristic green colour, may be transmitted through the gemmules. In some boring clionid sponges (*Cliona viridis*) of the class Demospongiae, some single-celled brown algae are constantly present. The marine sponges may also harbour multicellular blue-green algae (*e.g., Oscillatoria*), red (Rhodophyceae) and green (Chlorphyceae) algae. Red and green algae sometimes provide skeletal support for certain sponges.

Diseases of sponges. Sponges may be attacked by diseases of epidemic character, the agents of which are not well known. The commercial sponges of the West Indies once were nearly completely destroyed by a fungus-like microorganism; other sponges were not damaged.

FORM AND FUNCTION

The Porifera are unusual animals in that they lack definite organs to carry out their various functions. The most important structure is the system of canals and chambers, called a water-current system, through which water circulates to bring food to the sponge.

Water-current system. The essential elements of the water-current system include the pores, or ostia, through which water enters the sponge (incurrent system); the choanocytes, or collar cells, which are flagellated cells that capture food; and the oscula, openings through which water is expelled (excurrent system). Three types of water-current systems of increasingly complex structure may be distinguished by the arrangement of choanocytes and the development of canals—ascon, sycon, and leucon (Figure 2). The simplest, or ascon, type, found only in certain primitive genera of Calcispongiae (*e.g., Leucosolenia*), is characterized by an arrangement of choanocytes around a central cavity that directly communicates with the os-

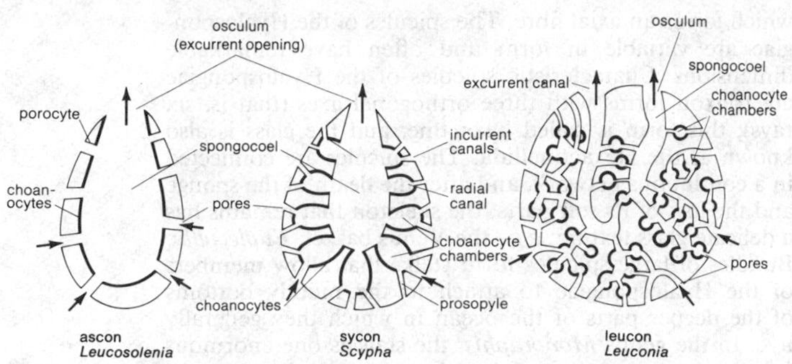

Figure 2: Water current systems in calcareous sponges. Arrows indicate the direction of water flow.

culum. The walls of these sponges are thin, lack canals, and are perforated by pores, which actually are openings through cells (porocytes). The sycon type of water-current system, found also in Calcispongiae is at first characterized by choanocytes that surround fingerlike projections called radial canals of the sponge wall. Water enters the radial canals directly through pores, makes its way into the central cavity, or spongocoel, and leaves by way of an osculum. In most syconoid sponges (*e.g.*, *Scypha*) the radial canals are bordered by incurrent canals through which passes the water entering the pores; other openings (prosopyles) allow water into the choanocytes, from which it passes directly into the internal cavity and out of it through the osculum.

Leucon water-current system

In the leucon type, which is found in the more advanced Calcispongiae and in the other classes (Demospongiae and Hyalospongiae), the radial canals are replaced by numerous small flagellated chambers in which the choanocytes are localized; the chambers, scattered throughout the body of the sponge, have pores through which water passes into a complex system of incurrent canals, then into a spongocoel (internal cavity) by way of excurrent canals. Water enters very small pores found among the cells (pinacocytes), which line the outer surface of the sponge. After passing through a system of incurrent canals and cavities, also lined with pinacocytes, the water reaches the flagellated chambers, enters them through openings (prosopyles), and leaves through other openings (apopyles). The water is expelled through the osculum after passing through a system of excurrent canals and cavities lined with pinacocytes. During the development of many sponges, a simpler water current system (rhagon) precedes the leucon type. The rhagon type is characterized by reduced excurrent canals and by a large central cavity. In some Demospongiae the body is organized in two parts, an external ectosome without choanocytes, and an internal choanosome with choanocytes.

Cell types. The sponges lack a well-defined organization of tissues. Single layers of cells line the outer surface of the body and the internal cavities; other cells, both motile and fixed, and fibres occur in an amorphous substance (mesohyl), gelatinous in nature. It has not been possible thus far to identify with certainty similarities of origin (homologies) between the various types of sponge cells and those of higher animals. Each type of sponge cell performs particular functions; the cells either may gather in certain areas of the sponge or form layers and membranes. They are easily modified, both in form and function, during larval development and during adult life. Furthermore, they have a remarkable ability to migrate and to transform from one cell type to another, although the mechanisms involved are not known. Three principal types of cells may be distinguished—choanocytes, archaeocytes, and pinacocytes–collencytes (Figure 3).

Choanocytes and archaeocytes. The choanocytes are provided with a flagellum, which is surrounded by a collar composed of cytoplasm. The main function of the flagellum apparently is to produce the water current, that of the collar is to capture food particles.

The archaeocytes, which are scattered in the mesohyl, have remarkable potentialities for transformation into various cell types, especially in the Demospongiae. Some persist and reproduce during the life of the sponge without specializing, thus forming an embryonic reserve from which other cellular types may be derived; others become specialized to carry out particular functions. Archaeocytes, often called amoebocytes, are amoeboid cells (*i.e.*, they have the ability to move); their cytoplasm contains large quantities of ribonucleic acid (RNA), and their large nuclei contain small bodies known as nucleoli. Amoebocytes function in regeneration and in transportation of food particles acquired at the choanocytes throughout the body of the sponge. During this distribution process, they carry granules consisting of various substances. Depending on the nature of the substance, amoebocytes may be known by several names; *e.g.*, granulocytes, thesocytes. Amoebocytes laden with various pigments (carotenoids and melanin, sometimes contained in algal symbionts) confer various colours to the sponge.

The archaeocytes may be important in sexual reproduction, if, as is postulated, male and female reproductive cells are derived from them. This role is disputed, however, since in some cases, mainly in the Calcispongiae, reproductive cells, particularly those of the male, are derived from choanocytes.

Pinacocytes, collencytes, and other cell types. Pinacocytes (Figure 3) form the pinacoderm, a single cell layer found on the body surface and lining the canals. Various types of pinacocytes occur—basipinacocytes are in contact with the surface to which the sponge is attached, exopinacocytes are found on the surface of the sponge, and endopinacocytes line the canals. Pinacocytes are flattened cells containing many granules; capable of contracting, pinacocytes may cause a reduction in the volume of the sponge if it is disturbed. In the Calcispongiae, the outer surface of the body also contains flattened granular cells called porocytes because they contain the pores needed to allow water into the sponge. The porocytes can contract, thus closing the pores during unfavourable environmental conditions.

Lophocytes, sclerocytes, and myocytes

The collencytes, found in the mesohyl, secrete fibres and often form a net in the cytoplasm. The mesohyl of sponges contains other types of cells (lophocytes, sclerocytes, myocytes) believed to be derived from archaeocytes. Lophocytes, similar to but larger than collencytes, have long cytoplasmic processes at one end, giving them the appearance of a comet; they apparently secrete fibres (spongin) that form skeletal material. The sclerocytes, or scleroblasts, which also produce skeletal material, are clas-

From R. Buchsbaum, *Animals Without Backbones* (1948); University of Chicago Press

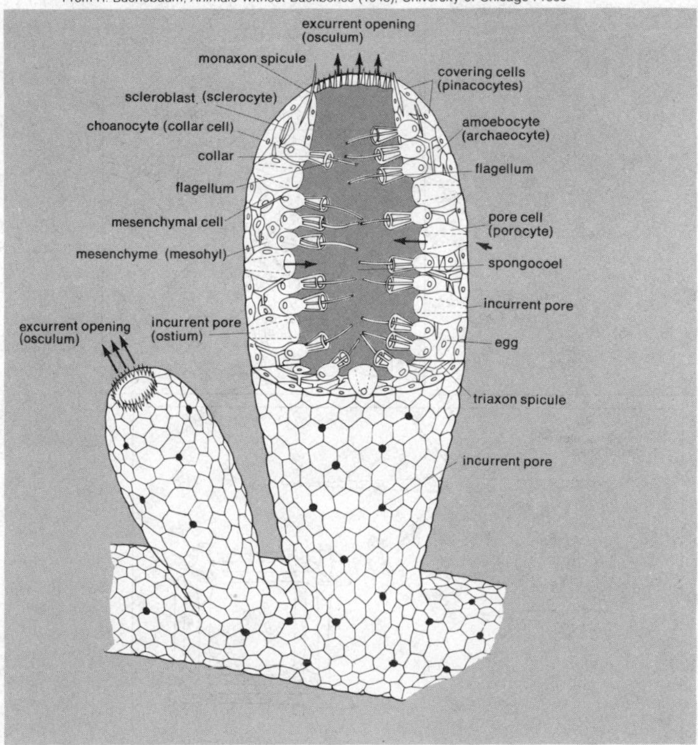

Figure 3: Part of a simple sponge with the upper part cut away to show cell structure.

sified according to the chemical nature of the spicules; calcoblasts secrete calcareous spicules, silicoblasts siliceous (glasslike) ones. The myocytes are elongated, contractile cells, particularly abundant near the oscula, where they control their expansion and contraction. The presence of nerve cells in sponges is a matter of dispute; the general opinion, however, is that none exist, not even in a primitive form.

Skeleton. The skeleton of sponges is of great taxonomic significance. It may be mineral in nature (calcareous or siliceous) or composed of protein and other components (spongin, see Figure 4). The mineral skeleton is formed for the most part by units called spicules, either scattered throughout the sponge or united to form fibres; spicules are classified as megascleres, which function in support, and microscleres, which function in protection and also aid in support.

Spicule types

Mineral skeletons. Calcareous spicules, characteristic of the Calcispongiae, are composed chiefly of calcium carbonate in crystalline forms; *e.g.,* calcite, aragonite. Most calcareous spicules have one axis (monoaxon), which is usually pointed at both ends; these spicules are called oxeas. Triaxons have three rays and are called triacts; tetraxons have four rays and are called tetracts. Figure 4 shows spicule types.

Siliceous spicules, found in the Demospongiae and in the Hyalospongiae, are made essentially of silicic acid; they also contain some water, a small quantity of other compounds containing sodium, potassium, iron, and chlorine, and a small quantity of organic matter, called spiculin, which forms an axial fibre. The spicules of the Hyalospongiae are variable in form and often have remarkable dimensions. Characteristic spicules of the Hyalospongiae are triaxon forms with three orthogonal axes (that is, six rays); this form is called hexactine, and the class is also known as the Hexactinellida. The spicules are connected in a continuous network, and after the death of the sponge and the loss of its soft parts, the skeleton that remains has a delicate glass texture; *e.g.,* the Venus basket, *Euplectella.* Bundles of large spicules form stalks that allow members of the Hyalospongiae to attach to the muddy bottoms of the deeper parts of the ocean in which they generally live. In the genus *Monoraphis,* the stalk is one enormous spicule that may attain a length of two or three metres (6.6–10 feet) and a thickness of approximately one centimetre (0.4 inch).

From (top right, dictyonine framework) R. Buchsbaum, *Animals Without Backbones* (1948), University of Chicago Press; (others) C. Villee *et al., General Zoology*, 3rd ed. (1968), W.B. Saunders Company, Philadelphia

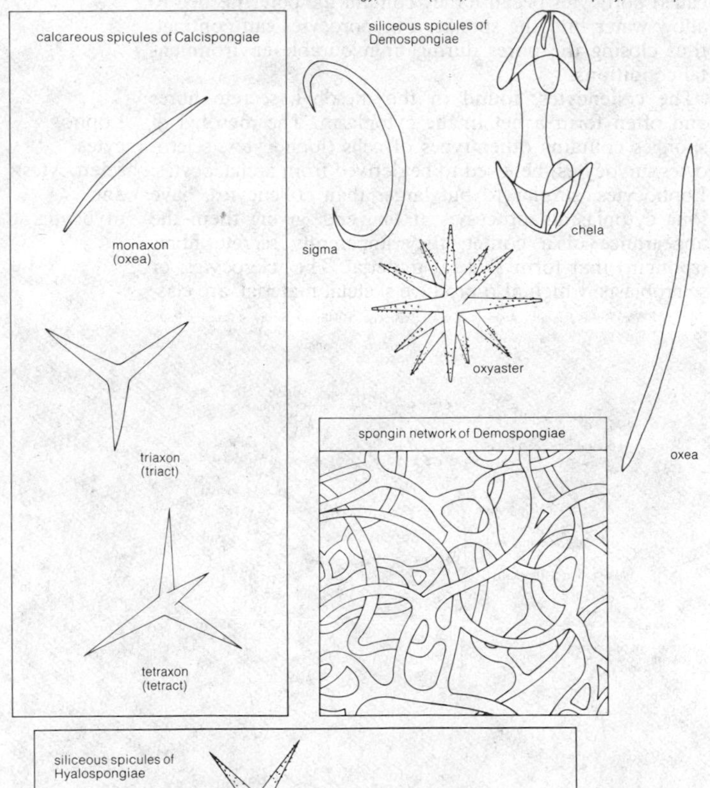

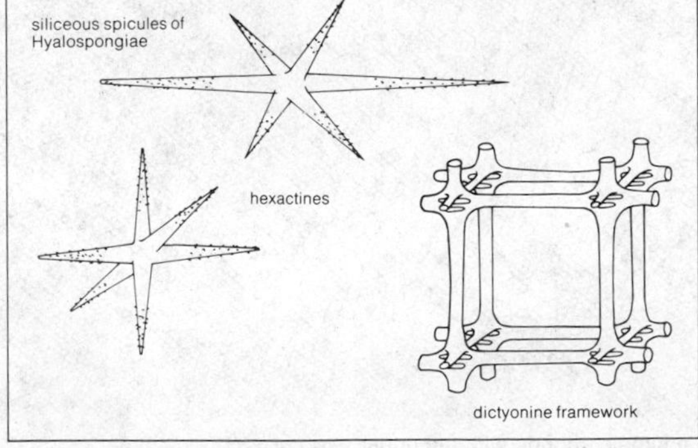

Figure 4: Types of spicules.

The siliceous spicules, consisting of both megascleres and microscleres, of the Demospongiae have an enormous variety of forms. The megascleres may be monaxons with both ends pointed (oxeas), with one end pointed and the other rounded (styles), or with both ends rounded (strongyles). If one end is swollen styles are called tylostyles and strongyles tylostrongyles; the spicules with both ends swollen are called tylotes. If the surface of the spicules is spiny instead of smooth, the spicules are called, respectively, acanthoxeas, acanthostyles, and acanthostrongyles. The megascleres also include triacts with three rays and tetracts, called calthrops, with four rays. Tetracts with one axis (rhabdome) longer than the other three (collectively the cladome) are called protriaenes, plagiotriaenes, anatriaenes, or dichotriaenes, depending on the way the rays of the cladome are directed.

All of the microscleres apparently are derived from a spherical type with many axons (polyaxon); the result is a series of star-shaped spicules, or asters, with various numbers of rays. Spicules with rays missing or reduced (called spheres, sterrasters, and discasters) often form a protective armour around the sponge. More specialized types of microscleres include sigmas, toxas, chelas, and anchoras; the last two have plates or teeth at each end and may be distinguished as isochelas and isanchoras or anisochelas and anisanchoras, depending on whether the ends are equal or unequal.

Other types. A few Demospongiae (*e.g., Oscarella, Halisarca,* and *Chondrosia*) lack skeletons. One group (Ceractinomorpha) has a type of spongin, which, in certain orders (Axinellida, Poecilosclerida, and Haplosclerida), cements the spicules in bundles or meshes, thereby increasing the elastic nature of the skeleton. In another group of Demospongiae (Keratosa), spongin fibres constitute the entire skeleton; the spongin fibres may be branched (order Dendroceratida), netlike (order Dictyoceratida), without inclusions (commercial sponges, which are therefore soft and elastic), or with inclusions (*e.g.,* grains of sand, fragments of spicules). In the genus *Ircinia,* the fibres are accompanied by thin spongin filaments that fill the mesohyl.

Spongin

Specialized types of skeletons in two groups of great paleontological importance are now represented by only a limited number of species, in the Calcispongiae and Demospongiae. Those in the Calcispongiae (Pharetronida) have skeletons formed by an amorphous mass of calcium carbonate, with which few spicules are associated. Those in the Demospongiae (Lithistida) form a heterogeneous group in which irregularly branched spicules (desmas) form a compact skeleton. Some Demospongiae, found mainly on the coral reefs, possess a compact calcareous skeleton, which incorporates both siliceous spicules and organic fibres. (M.Sa.)

Functional features. *Feeding and digestion.* The Porifera are filter feeders, utilizing food particles suspended in the water and captured by the choanocytes. Food particles consist essentially of bacteria, other microorganisms, and particles of organic debris; sponges also probably absorb dissolved organic substances. Experiments with starch grains, bacteria, and particles of carmine pigment show that the particles ingested by the choanocytes are transferred by thesocytes (specialized amoebocytes) throughout the sponge. Intracellular digestion occurs in both choanocytes and thesocytes. A large quantity of food is absorbed by a sponge, and it can use several litres of water a day. The water-current system, therefore, is efficient, in spite of the lack of a nervous coordinating centre. The water flow into and out of the sponge is maintained by continuous movement of the flagella of the choanocytes; flagellar movement pushes water into the choanocyte chambers, creating in them a pressure that extends to the excurrent canals, as water passing into the pores is drawn along the system of incurrent canals. Water flow, which is also regulated by contraction and expansion of the pores and of the oscula, is slow at the pores, fast at the oscula; as a result, water expelled with force through the oscula cannot contaminate water entering the pores. Toxic or irritating substances cause the pores to close.

Oxygen uptake and excretion. Respiratory organs are lacking in sponges; oxygen is supplied by a direct exchange between the tissues and the surrounding water. Consequently, the consumption of oxygen is related to the velocity of the current. Excretion occurs through both the oscula and the surface of the sponge. Special amoebocytes disintegrate in the mesohyl, and their granules are expelled through the canals. The excretory products of the sponges—ammonia and other nitrogen-containing substances—account for their characteristic unpleasant odour. Many sponges (*e.g.,* the tropical sponge *Tedania ignis*) exude large quantities of mucus, and some species produce toxic substances, which may cause inflammation and skin reactions in humans.

Coordination. A sponge usually contracts if it is handled. The oscula close if the sponge is exposed to air, if oxygen is not available, if harmful chemical compounds are present, or if temperatures are extremely high or low. The lack of coordination in the oscula, pores, and choanocytes and the slow reaction of sponges to stimuli confirm the absence of a nervous system. A primitive system of coordination, probably chemical in nature, apparently exists. Contraction of myocytes occurs around the oscula and along the peripheral canals of Demospongiae. Some Calcispongiae of the ascon type reduce their volume through contraction of the superficial layer of pinacocytes.

Biochemical aspects. The sponges produce substances with antibiotic activity (*e.g.,* ectyonin), which may function during the selection of bacteria and other microorganisms on which they feed. The Porifera contain a greater variety of fatty substances (*e.g.,* sterols) than do other animals. Some of these sterols (*e.g.,* clionasterol, poriferasterol) are found only in sponges; others (*e.g.,* cholesterol) are common in other animals. Numerous carotenoid pigments occur in sponges, and melanin, chlorophyll, and phycoerythrin derived from algal symbionts and from the diet also occur. Sponges accumulate silicon, calcium, and considerable quantities of metals. The spongins are iodine or bromine-containing scleroproteins similar to the keratin found in skin, claws, hair, and feathers of other animals. The two types of spongin, known as A and B, differ in composition and structure.

Sterols and pigments

EVOLUTION AND PALEONTOLOGY

Sponges have evolved in a way foreign to that of other animals. They probably arose from a flagellate Protozoa, although it is not certain which group. The choanocytes of sponges resemble the choanoflagellate protozoans. Choanoflagellate protozoan colonies, however, do not develop by way of embryological stages as do the sponges. The primitive structure of the Porifera indicates affinities with certain types of protozoan colonies; both lack integration of parts, mouths, and digestive systems, and both have a type of skeletal formation in which single elements are produced by a single cell or by a small group of cells.

The Porifera appeared in the Early Cambrian Period of the Paleozoic Era (about 550,000,000 years ago). Of the classes known in the Middle Cambrian Period (Hexactinellida or Hyalospongiae, Heteractinellida, and Demospongiae), the Heteractinellida are extinct; the Calcispongiae appear in the Carboniferous Period (about 345,000,000 to 280,000,000 years ago). Living sponges do not differ substantially from many groups in the Paleozoic Era.

Despite the mineral skeleton, the only Porifera well represented as fossils are those with a compact skeleton; *e.g.,* pharetronids (Calcispongiae), lithistids (Demospongiae), and Dictyonina (Hyalospongiae). The oldest sponge fossils, from the Lower Cambrian, are well represented in the Burgess Shale of the Middle Cambrian in western Canada by *Protospongia,* a member of the Hyalospongiae, and by *Eiffelia,* of the extinct Heteractinellida. They resembled a pouch and had very thin walls; their spicules were arranged in a single layer, and their water-current system was probably of an ascon type. Various genera of the order Lyssacina (Hyalospongiae) are known from the Paleozoic from spicules. In the Mesozoic Era (about 225,000,000 to 65,000,000 years ago), the Hyalospongiae gave rise to a group (order Dictyonina) with the compact skeleton commonly found in sediments. Beginning with the Late Cretaceous Period (about 100,000,000 years ago), the species of Hyalospongiae have affinities with recent ones.

Oldest sponge fossils

Calcispongiae appear in the Carboniferous Period (about 345,000,000 to 280,000,000 years ago). The first Pharetronida (Calcispongiae) from the Permian Period (about 280,000,000 to 225,000,000 years ago) have a compact calcareous skeleton and spicules; because calcareous spicules are easily dissolved during fossilization, Calcispongiae lack a compact skeleton and have left few traces.

Demospongiae may have followed a line of evolution originating in Tetractinellida (with four-rayed spicules) and advancing, after reduction of the tetraxon spicules into monoaxons, to Keratosa; in addition, the polyaxon microscleres (asters) evolved into specialized forms (sigmas and chelas), and spongin appeared to cement the spicules, finally developing into a skeleton formed exclusively of horny fibres. Recent opinion, however, suggests that the Demospongiae are a diphyletic class, which is separable into two large groups (Tetractinomorpha and Ceractinomorpha). The Tetractinomorpha have four-rayed megascleres, asters, and no spongin; the Ceractinomorpha have monaxon megascleres, no asters, and spongin. That these morphological differences are accompanied by important embryological differences is supported by the facts that the oldest Demospongiae, from the Cambrian, are monaxonid (with only oxeas) and that the four-rayed spicule originates later, in the Carboniferous Period. Well-represented since the Paleozoic, the Lithistida have a siliceous skeleton of netlike desmas and are considered polyphyletic; the lithistid modification of the skeleton appeared independently in different lines of the Demospongiae. Few lithistid genera are extant. Demospongiae lacking a compact skeleton are poorly represented in sediments.

The phylogenctic relationships among the classes are difficult to ascertain, although common spicular characters may be found among Calcispongiae, Hyalospongiae, and tetractinellid Demospongiae. Noteworthy is the existence of sponges with both calcareous and siliceous elements in their skeleton; these sponges show affinities with both the pharetronid Calcispongiae and the Demospongiae. The extinct Archaeocyatha, with a cup-shaped body fixed on a surface and a skeleton of porous walls, were aberrant forms that lived exclusively in the Cambrian and that are generally considered as a separate phylum, even though they do show some affinities with the Calcispongiae.

CLASSIFICATION

Distinguishing taxonomic features. The general architecture of the skeleton is used to differentiate families, the particular combinations of spicular types to define genera, and the form and dimensions of single spicule types to differentiate species. Other morphological characters include shape, colour, consistency, surface (smooth, rough, or conulose), and distribution and character of the oscula, which often shows remarkable interspecies variation. Cytological and embryological features are used as diagnostic characters in both general classification and species identification of the Demospongiae and Calcispongiae. Ecological and distributional characters are important in distinguishing species, particularly in groups (*e.g.,* haliclonids) in which skeletal and embryological characters are so uniform as to be of little taxonomic value. Although biochemical criteria—for instance, amino acid composition—have been used in some cases to evaluate general phylogenetic problems and separate orders, the results do

Ecological characters

not differ substantially from those obtained with other criteria. (M.Sa./Ed.)

Annotated classification. The classification below, which refers to the three living classes of sponges, is adapted from that of E. Topsent as modified by C. Levi on the basis of embryological data; it is accepted by most experts in the field.

PHYLUM PORIFERA (sponges)

Primitive aquatic invertebrate animals; about 5,000 species in all seas; attach to surfaces from intertidal zone to depths of 8,500 m (29,000 ft) or more; propel water containing food particles through a system of canals in body (filter feeding); composed of many cell types (archaeocytes of various kinds, pinacocytes, collencytes); structure of water-current system variable (ascon, sycon, leucon); skeleton either mineral (calcium carbonate or silicic acid), spongin, sometimes lacking, or of mixed composition; skeletal units (spicules) variable in form; both sexual and asexual reproduction (gemmulation); ability to regenerate lost parts; contain many unique chemical compounds; form symbiotic relationships with many other types of organisms.

Class Calcispongiae

Skeleton of spicules of calcium carbonate; species either vase-shaped compact structures, loose networks of thin tubes, or irregular massive colonies; mostly small in size; inhabit shallow waters of all seas, from intertidal regions to depths of 200 m (660 ft); a few species to 800 m (2,600 ft); about 300 species.

Subclass Calcinea

Larva called parenchymella (solid, compact, with outer layer of flagellated cells, inner mass of cells); flagella of choanocytes (collar cells) arise independently of nucleus; some 3-rayed spicules in most species; water-current system ascon, sycon, or leucon type; includes pharetronid sponges with rigid skeleton of fused spicules or of a calcareous network; genera include *Clathrina, Leucetta, Petrobiona* (a pharetronid).

Subclass Calcaronea

Larva called amphiblastula (oval in shape with front half of flagellated cells, rear half without flagellated cells); flagella of choanocytes arise directly from nucleus; spicules 3-rayed, with one ray characteristically longer than other two; water-current system ascon, sycon, or leucon type; *Leucosolenia, Scypha* (formerly called *Sycon*), *Grantia, Lelapia* (with a rigid skeleton composed of bundles of modified rayed spicules).

Class Hyalospongiae (Hexactinellida)

Skeleton basically of hexactinal (6-rayed) siliceous spicules and lacking in spongin; exclusively marine, in deeper waters of all seas, depths from 25 to 8,500 m (80–29,000 ft); commonly fixed firmly to a hard surface, some species anchored in soft bottom sediments; *Hexactinella, Aphrocallistes, Farrea, Dactylocalyx, Euplectella, Rhabdocalyptus;* about 500 species.

Class Demospongiae

Skeleton of either 1- or 4-rayed siliceous spicules, spongin fibres, or both; skeleton lacking in a few primitive genera; most abundant and widely distributed group of sponges (about 4,200 species); occur from intertidal regions to depths of about 5,500 m (18,000 ft) in seas; Spongillidae the freshwater sponge family; species vary greatly in form and size; range from thin encrustations several cm in diameter to huge cake-shaped species 2 m (6.6 ft) in diameter; many species with desmas (develop as a result of secondary deposits of silica around ordinary spicules); evolution independently among several orders of interlocking of adjacent desmas to form a stony skeleton (lithistid sponges).

Critical appraisal. The living orders of sponges are distributed in the Calcispongiae, Hyalospongiae, and Demospongiae. The Calcispongiae may be separated into two subclasses (Calcinea and Calcaronea), which represent two phyletic series separated mainly by cytological and embryological characters; this classification has replaced the traditional classification of the calcareous sponges into Homocoela and Heterocoela, which was based on the types of the water-current system. The traditional classification of the Hyalospongiae into the orders Lyssacina and Dictyonina is still valid. The separation of the Demospongiae into orders is not well defined, because the phylogeny of the group is not well known. Two groups of orders may be distinguished within the Demospongiae. One, in which spongin is an important skeletal element (Ceratinomorpha), includes Poecilosclerida, Haplosclerida, Dendroceratida, and Dictyocernatida, the latter two derived from another subdivision, the Keratosa. The other group (Tetractinomorpha) includes Homosclerophorida, Tetractinellida, Epipolasida, Hadromerida, and Axinellida; four-rayed spicules are important only in the Homosclerophorida and in the Tetractinellida, but the other orders are clearly related to them. Hadromerida, Axinellida, and Epipolasida are placed in a group called the Clavaxinellida. The Epipolasida, an ill-defined order, are nearest to the Tetractinellida. Many genera of Demospongiae, mainly in the Tetractinomorpha, are transitional, and their actual phylogenetic position is not clear.

Alternative subclassification systems

Other classifications of sponges may concern only differences in detail; *e.g.,* the rank of order or of suborder given to the Dictyoceratida and Dendroceratida, the inclusion of the Homosclerophorida in the Tetractinellida, or the abolition of the order Epipolasida. A classification for the Demospongiae, proposed in 1936, is similar to that stated above in its subdivision into orders but is revolutionary with regard to the placement of families and of genera. It has not been followed in general by the other systematists of the group.

Still another classification of the Porifera places them in a subkingdom of the Parazoa as two phyla (Nuda and Gelatinosa). The Nuda includes a single class and order, the Hexactinellida; the Gelatinosa is divided into two classes (Calcarea and Demospongia). The separation between Nuda and Gelatinosa is based only on the absence or presence of an intercellular matrix of fluids and fibrils around the net of cells. Although the proposal has not yet been evaluated critically, it seems justifiable to keep the Porifera in a single phylum because of the common structural basis regarding their many characters (*e.g.,* anatomy, function, and embryology). Other proposals include establishment of a new order (Pharetronida) separated from the Calcinea and Calcaronea in the Calcispongiae, and the creation of a new class (Sclerospongiae) for the silicocalcareous or coralline sponges.

An important controversy in the systematics of the sponges concerns the value given to species described using traditional criteria. The use of species in classifying sponges is justified by the great variability of diagnostic characters, especially the spicules. Attempts to merge large groups of species into single systematic units have resulted in excessive lumping of species, which has been much criticized. In classifying sponges, therefore, one diagnostic feature is not sufficient; rather, all diagnostic characters should be considered.

BIBLIOGRAPHY

General: P.R. BERGQUIST and C.A. TIZARD, "Sponge Industry," in F.E. FIRTH (ed.), *Encyclopedia of Marine Resources,* pp. 665–670 (1969); W.G. FRY (ed.), "The Biology of the Porifera," *Symp. Zool. Soc. Lond.,* No. 25, (1970), a symposium covering the biology and paleontology of sponges; L.H. HYMAN, *The Invertebrates,* vol. 1, *Protozoa Through Ctenophora,* pp. 284–364 (1940), a thorough treatment of the Porifera; E.A. MINCHIN, "Porifera" in E. RAY LANKESTER, *Treatise on Zoology,* vol. 2 (1900), an ample, classical treatment of the Porifera; MAURICE BURTON, *Sponges* (1974), a British Museum (Natural History) report on sponges of the Indian Ocean; KLAUS RUTZLER, *The Burrowing Sponges of Bermuda* (1974), Smithsonian Contributions to Zoology, No. 165; G.C.J. VOSMAER, *Bibliography of Sponges: 1551–1913* (1928), a complete bibliography to 1913; PATRICIA R. BERGQUIST, *Sponges* (1978), a comprehensive study of sponge biology.

Advanced: M. BURTON, *A Revision of the Classification of the Calcareous Sponges* (1963), a well-illustrated diagnosis and description of the calcareous sponges of the world; M. FLORKIN and B.T. SCHEER (eds.), "Porifera," in *Chemical Zoology,* vol. 2, pp. 1–76 (1968), reviews of various aspects of the biochemistry and physiology of sponges; W.D. HARTMAN, "A Reexamination of Bidder's Classification of the Calcarea," *Syst. Zool.,* 7:97–110 (1958), a critical analysis of the modern classification of Calcispongiae; M.W. DE LAUBENFELS, "Porifera," in *A Treatise on Invertebrate Paleontology,* pt. *E* (1955), a well-documented systematic account of fossil sponges; C. LEVI, "Étude des Halisarca de Roscoff: Embryologie et systématique des Démosponges," *Archs. Zool. Exp. Gén.,* 93:1–181 (1956), a fundamental work, in French, on the embryology of sponges and its connections with systematics; E. TOPSENT, "Spongiaires de l'Atlantique et de la Méditerranée, provenant des croisières du Prince Albert Ier de Monaco," *Résult. Camp. Scient. Prince Albert I,* 75:1–376 (1928), a well-illustrated monumental classic, in French; D.A WEBB, "The Histology, Cytology and Embryology of Sponges," *Q. Jl. Microsc. Sci.,* 78:51–70 (1935), well-documented.

(M.Sa.)

Major Team and Individual Sports

Many animals play, but *homo sapiens* is the only animal to have invented sports. Since sports are an invention, a part of culture rather than an aspect of nature, all definitions of sports are somewhat arbitrary. Whether sports are a human universal found in every known culture or a phenomenon unique to modern society depends upon one's definition of sports. Men and women have always run, jumped, climbed, lifted, thrown, and wrestled, but they have not always performed these physical activities competitively. Although all literate societies seem to have contests of one sort or another in which men, and sometimes women, compete in displays and tests of physical skill and prowess, sports may be strictly defined as physical contests performed for their own sake and not for some ulterior end. By this strict definition, neither Neolithic hunters nor contestants in religious ceremonies such as the ancient Olympic Games were engaged in sports. Insistence on the stipulation that sports must be performed for their own sake means the paradoxical elimination of many activities usually thought of as sports, such as exercises done for the sake of cardiovascular fitness, races run to satisfy a physical education requirement, ball games played to earn a paycheck. Strict definition also means abandonment of the traditional usage in which "sport," derived from Middle English *disporter,* refers to any lighthearted recreational activity. In the minds of some 18th-century aristocrats, a game of backgammon and the seduction of a milkmaid were both considered good sport, but this usage has become archaic.

Strict conceptualization allows the construction of an evolutionary history of sports in which extrinsic political, economic, military, and religious motivations decrease in importance as intrinsic motivations—participation for its own sake—increase. The disadvantage, however, is that the determination that a given activity is truly a sport depends on the answer to a psychological question: What is the motivation of the participants? The question of motivation cannot be answered unambiguously. It is probable that the contestants of the ancient Olympic Games were motivated by the intrinsic pleasure of the contest as well as by the religious imperatives of Greek cult. It is also probable that modern professional athletes are motivated by more than simply economic motives. Thus most scholars assume quietly that popular usage cannot be completely wrong to refer, for instance, to U.S. professional National Football League games as sports.

This article discusses the history of sports and their place in modern society and divides the major competitive sports into two main categories: team and individual. The distinction between the two is rather obvious, the one requiring teamwork among a group of players participating simultaneously, and the other requiring the effort of a single individual unaided by teammates. The particular sports that are covered here are those active ones for which adults in different parts of the world, enjoying them sufficiently in their early forms, have developed uniform codes of rules and specifications and have organized competitive play (*e.g.*, tennis, football, baseball, cricket, and basketball). Not everyone will agree on the selection of sports determined here to be "major." The selection process was based, to a large degree, on popularity, whether that element arose from attendance, participation, media exposure, or any combination thereof. Other criteria were history and tradition. Inevitably, spatial restrictions determined that some sports of obvious major proportions, such as swimming, skiing, and gymnastics, could not be covered in this article.

For coverage of related topics in the *Macropædia* and *Micropædia,* see the *Propædia,* section 513.

For later information on the various team and individual sports, see the *Britannica Book of the Year* section in the BRITANNICA WORLD DATA ANNUAL.

The article is divided into the following sections:

SPORTS IN SOCIETY

History

Origin of sports

No one can say when sports began. Since it is difficult to imagine a time when children did not spontaneously run races or wrestle, it is clear that children have always included sports in their play, but one can only speculate about the emergence of sports as autotelic (played for their own sake) physical contests for adults. Hunters are depicted in prehistoric art, but it cannot be known whether the hunters pursued their prey in a mood of grim necessity or with the joyful abandon of sportsmen. It is certain, however, from the rich literary and iconographic evidence of all ancient civilizations that the hunt soon became an end in itself—at least for royalty and nobility. Archaeological evidence also indicates that ball games were common among the ancient Chinese. If such games were contests rather than ritual performances like the Japanese football game *kemari,* then they were instances of sports in the most rigorously defined sense. That it cannot simply be assumed they were contests is clear from the evidence presented by Greek and Roman antiquity, indicating that ball games seem to have been for the most part playful pastimes like those recommended for health by the 2nd-century AD Greek physician Galen.

SPORTS IN THE ANCIENT WORLD

Egypt. Sports were certainly common in ancient Egypt, where pharaohs demonstrated their fitness to rule by prowess in the hunt and by exhibitions of strength and skill in archery. In such exhibitions, pharaohs such as Amenhotep II (ruled 1450–25 BC) never competed against another person, and there is reason to suspect that their extraordinary achievements were scribal fictions. However, Egyptians with less claim to divinity jumped, wrestled, and engaged in ball games and stick fights of the sort that can still be observed in Egypt.

Crete and Greece. Since Minoan script still baffles scholars, it is uncertain whether Cretan boys and girls who tested their acrobatic skills against bulls were engaged in sports, in religious ritual, or in both.

That the feats of the Cretans may have been both sport and ritual is suggested by evidence from Greece, where sports had a significance unequaled anywhere before the rise of modern sports. Secular and religious motives mingle in history's first extensive "sports report," found in book 23 of Homer's *Iliad* in the form of funeral games for the dead Patroclus. These games were a part of cult and were not, therefore, autotelic, but the contests in the *Odyssey* are essentially secular. Odysseus was challenged by the

Phaeacians to demonstrate his prowess as an athlete. In general, Greek culture included both cultic sports, such as the Olympic Games honouring Zeus, and secular contests.

The Olympic Games

The most famous association of sports and religion was certainly the Olympic Games, which Greek tradition dated from 776 BC but which probably began much earlier. In the course of time, the earth goddess Gaea, originally worshiped at Olympia, was supplanted in importance by the sky god Zeus, in whose honour priestly officials conducted quadrennial athletic contests. Sacred also were the games held at Delphi, in honour of Apollo, and at Corinth and Nemea. These four events were known as the *periodos,* and great athletes, such as Theagenes of Thasos, prided themselves on victories at all four sites. The extraordinary prestige accorded athletic triumphs brought with it not only literary accolades (as in the odes of Pindar) and visual commemoration (in the form of statues of the victors) but also material benefits, contrary to the amateur myth propagated by 19th-century philhellenists. Since the Greeks were devoted to secular sports as well as to sacred games, no polis, or city-state, was considered a proper community if it lacked a gymnasium where, as the word *gymnos* indicates, naked male athletes trained and competed. Except at militaristic Sparta, Greek girls rarely participated in sports of any kind. Women were excluded from the Olympic Games even as spectators (except for the priestess of Demeter). Pausanias, the 2nd-century-AD traveler, wrote of races for girls at Olympia, but these events in honour of Hera were of minor importance.

Rome. Although chariot races were among the most popular sports spectacles of the Roman and Byzantine eras, as they were in Greek times, the Romans of the republic and the early empire were quite selectively enthusiastic about Greek athletic contests. Their emphasis was on physical exercises for military preparedness, an important motive in all ancient civilizations; they preferred boxing, wrestling, and hurling the javelin to running footraces and throwing the discus. The historian Livy tells of Greek athletes appearing in Rome as early as 186 BC, but the contestants' nudity shocked Roman moralists. The emperor Augustus instituted the Actian Games in 27 BC to celebrate his victory over Antony and Cleopatra, and several emperors began similar games, but it was not until the later empire, especially during the reign of Hadrian (AD 117–138), that large numbers of the Roman elite developed an enthusiasm for Greek athletics.

Chariot races in Rome's Circus Maximus were watched by as many as 250,000 spectators, five times the number that crowded into the Colosseum to enjoy gladiatorial combats. Nevertheless, there is some evidence that the latter contests were more popular even than the former. Indeed, the *munera,* which pitted man against man, and the *venationes,* which set men against animals, became popular even in the Eastern Empire, which historians once thought immune from the lust for blood. The greater frequency of chariot races can be explained in part by the fact that they were relatively inexpensive compared to the enormous costs of gladiatorial combats. (The *editor* who staged the games usually rented the gladiators from a *lanista* and was required to reimburse him for losers executed in response to a "thumbs down" sign.) Brutal as these combats were, many of the gladiators were free men who volunteered to fight, an obvious sign of intrinsic motivation. Indeed, imperial edicts were needed to discourage the aristocracy's participation. In AD 63, during the reign of Nero, female gladiators were introduced into the arena.

Roman blood sports

The circus and the hippodrome, a stadium of Greek origin for chariot racing, continued to provide popular sports spectacles long after Christian protests (and heavy economic costs) ended the gladiatorial games, probably early in the 5th century. In many ways, the chariot races were quite modern. The charioteers were divided into bureaucratically organized factions (*e.g.,* the "Blues" and the "Greens"), which excited the loyalties of fans from Britain to Mesopotamia. Charioteers boasted of the number of their victories as modern athletes brag about their "stats," indicating, perhaps, some incipient awareness of what in modern times are called sports records. The gladiatorial games, however, like the Greek games before them, had a powerful religious dimension. The first Roman combats, in 264 BC, were derived from Etruscan funeral games in which mortal combat provided companions for the deceased. It was the idolatry of the games, even more than their brutality, that horrified Christian protestors. The lesser pagan religious association of the chariot races helped them survive late into the post-Constantine period.

SPORTS IN THE MIDDLE AGES

The sports of medieval times were less well-organized. Fairs and seasonal festivals were occasions for men to lift stones or sacks of grain and for women to run smock races (for a smock, not in one). The favourite sport of the peasantry was folk football, a wild sort of no-holds-barred unbounded game that pitted married men against bachelors or one village against another. The violence of the game, which survived in Britain and in France until the late 19th century, was such that Renaissance humanists, such as Sir Thomas Elyot, condemned it as more likely to maim than to benefit the participants.

The nascent bourgeoisie of the Middle Ages and the Renaissance amused itself with archery matches, some of which were arranged months in advance and staged with considerable fanfare. When town met town in a challenge of skill, the companies of crossbowmen and longbowmen marched behind the symbols of St. George, St. Sebastian, and other patrons of the sport. It was not unusual for contests in running, jumping, cudgeling, and wrestling to be offered for the lower classes who attended the match as spectators. Grand feasts were part of the program, and drunkenness commonly added to the revelry. In Germanic areas, a *Pritschenkoenig* was supposed to simultaneously keep order and entertain the crowd with clever verses.

Inter-town archery matches

The burghers of medieval towns were welcome to watch the aristocracy at play, but they were not allowed to participate in tournaments or even, in most parts of Europe, to compete in imitative tournaments of their own. Tournaments were the jealously guarded prerogative of the medieval knight and, along with hunting and hawking, his favourite pastime. At the tilt, in which mounted knights with lances tried to unhorse one another, the knight was practicing the art of war, his raison d'être. He displayed his prowess before lords, ladies, and commoners and profited not only from valuable prizes but also from ransoms exacted from the losers. Between the 12th and the 16th centuries, the dangerously wild free-for-all of the early tournament evolved into dramatic presentations of courtly life in which elaborate pageantry and allegorical display quite overshadowed the frequently inept jousts. Some danger remained even amid the display. At one of the last great tournaments, in 1559, Henry II of France was mortally wounded by a lance blow.

Sports of the medieval aristocracy

Peasant women participated freely in the ball games and footraces of medieval times, and aristocratic ladies hunted and kept falcons, but middle-class women contented themselves with spectatorship. Even so, they were more active than their contemporaries in Heian Japan during the 8th to the 12th century. Encumbered by many-layered robes and sequestered in their homes, the Japanese ladies were unable to do more than peep from behind their screens at the courtiers' mounted archery contests.

SPORTS IN THE RENAISSANCE AND MODERN PERIOD

By the time of the Renaissance, sports had become entirely secular, but in the minds of the Czech educator John Amos Comenius and other humanists, a concern for physical education on what were thought to be classic models overshadowed the competitive aspects of sports. Indeed, 15th- and 16th-century elites perferred dances to sports and delighted in geometric patterns of movement. The ballet developed in France during this period. Horses were trained to graceful movement rather than bred for speed. French and Italian fencers like the famed Girard Thibault, whose *L'Accademie de l'espee* appeared in 1628, thought of their activity more as an art form than as a combat. Northern Europeans emulated them. Humanistically inclined Englishmen and Germans admired the cultivated Florentine game of *calcio* ("kick"), a form of football that stressed the good looks and elegant attire of the players.

Beginnings of organized sports

The development of sports into the forms of the present day began in late 17th-century England when the emphasis gradually shifted from measure, in the sense of balance or proportion, to measurement. During the Restoration and throughout the 18th century, traditional pastimes like stick fighting and bullbaiting, which the Puritans had condemned and driven underground, gave way to organized games, like cricket, which developed under the leadership of the Marylebone Cricket Club (founded 1787). Behind these changes lay a new conception of rationalized competition. Contests that seem odd to the modern mind, like those in which cripples were matched against children, were replaced by horse races in which fleeter steeds were handicapped, a notion of equality that led eventually to age and weight classes (but not height classes) in many modern sports. The traditional sport of boxing flourished throughout the 18th century, guided and regulated by boxer-entrepreneurs like James Figg and his pupil Jack Broughton, and, eventually, by the Marquess of Queensberry, whose 1867 rules replaced Broughton's 1743 attempt to civilize the sport.

In the 18th and 19th centuries, sports became increasingly specialized, and national organizations developed to standardize rules and regulations, to organize sporadic challenge matches into systematic league competition, to certify eligibility, and to register results. England's Football Association was formed in 1863 to propagate that sport (called soccer in the United States), which had developed out of medieval folk football (as, eventually, did rugby and American football). The Amateur Athletic Association followed in 1880. From England and then from the United States, modern sports spread throughout the globe. Sports that originally began elsewhere, such as tennis (which derives from Renaissance France), were modernized and exported as if they too were raw materials imported for British industry to transform and then ship out as finished goods. By the early 20th century, organizations like the International Olympic Committee (founded 1894), the Fédération Internationale de Football Association (1904), and the International Amateur Athletic Federation (1912) had begun to seem inevitable.

Early Asian sports

During the age of imperialism, when Europeans and Americans dominated much of Asia and most of Africa, the colonial powers suppressed traditional sports and introduced their own modern ones. Japan, one of the few non-Western nations where a traditional sport (sumo) rivals a modern one (baseball) in popularity, is also one of the few non-Western nations to contribute a sport (judo) to the modern Olympic Games.

Behind the dramatic transition to modern sports lay the scientific developments that sustained the Industrial Revolution. Technicians sought to perfect equipment. Athletes trained systematically to achieve their physical maximum. New games, like basketball, volleyball, and team handball, were consciously invented to specification as if they were new products for the market. As early as the late 17th century, quantification became an important aspect of sports, and the cultural basis was created for the concept of sports record. The word "record," in the sense of an unsurpassed quantified achievement, appeared, first in English and then in other languages, only in the late 19th century.

The sociological terms used to describe the development of modern sports, such as secularization, rationalization, specialization, bureaucratization, and quantification, all suggest that the formal and structural characteristics specific to 20th-century sports are the characteristics of modern society generally. Although Marxist scholars contend that this development is the result of industrial capitalism, non-Marxists, adapting the sociological theories of the German Max Weber, the Frenchman Émile Durkheim, and the American Talcott Parsons and others, have observed that modern sports antedate industrial capitalism and flourish in societies such as the Soviet Union that have never known a "bourgeois" phase.

Economic analysis demonstrates that the boom in sports participation and in sports spectatorship has depended on the increase of leisure time for the masses. Capitalistic entrepreneurship certainly played a role in the rationalization of sports into a marketable commodity. But the transformation of traditional pastimes into modern sports took place in the schools and universities as well as in business and industry. Modern baseball was formulated by a group of New York City players, but modern soccer was invented in the elite boys' schools of Victorian England, while rowing and track-and-field athletics took their modern forms in English and American colleges and universities. The 19th-century's combination of Christian ethics and rationalized forms is best symbolized by the birth of basketball in 1891 at the YMCA Training School in Springfield, Mass., a stronghold of "muscular Christianity."

Origins of modern sports

While England may be considered the homeland of modern sports, modern physical education can be traced back to German and Scandinavian developments of the late 18th and early 19th centuries. Men like Johann Christoph Friedrich Guts Muths in Germany and Per Henrik Ling in Sweden elaborated systems of exercise that were eventually adopted by British, American, and other schools. These noncompetitive alternatives to modern sports, which also flourished in the form of central European gymnastic displays, did not develop great popularity with schoolchildren or college students. Almost universal in the late 19th century, such gymnastic systems have by and large been replaced by competitive sports—with or without the notion that sports can be a vehicle of ethical instruction. Gymnastic displays can still be witnessed in the disciplined mass formations that accompany major sports competitions, particularly in the countries of eastern Europe. Modern-day individual gymnastics is itself an outgrowth of the earlier European gymnastics form.

While commercial motives encouraged promoters to stage sports events open to all who had the price of admission, class solidarity and exclusiveness led to the invention of the amateur rule, originally formulated in the 1870s to prevent the participation of all those who worked with their hands. The spread of egalitarian ideals and the avarice of individual athletes has had little to do with the demise of amateurism. Rather, barriers to overt professionalization eroded with the realization that the highest levels of physical achievement (and the richest harvest of national and international championships) require expenditures of time and money incompatible with a primary commitment to work or study. Once a university's prestige or a nation's image became dependent upon stellar athletic performances, it was no longer possible to limit the pool of talent to the leisure class. Now that the modern Olympic Games are open to men and women who may earn millions of dollars by their athletic prowess, it is quite improbable that what remains of the Victorian concept of amateur sports as an avocation can endure. The line between amateurism and professionalism has changed through time and will continue to be a point of controversy in sports as long as amateurism, however defined, is a requirement in world competitions.

The controversy over professionalism

Sociological, psychological, and physiological aspects

SOCIOLOGICAL FACTORS

Although the Dutch historian Johan Huizinga called attention to play as an aspect of culture in *Homo Ludens* (1938), his predilection for pageantry and for play tinged with religious ritual forced sociologists to devise alternative paradigms for the relationship of play to other activities. That relationship can be expressed in the form of a diagram:

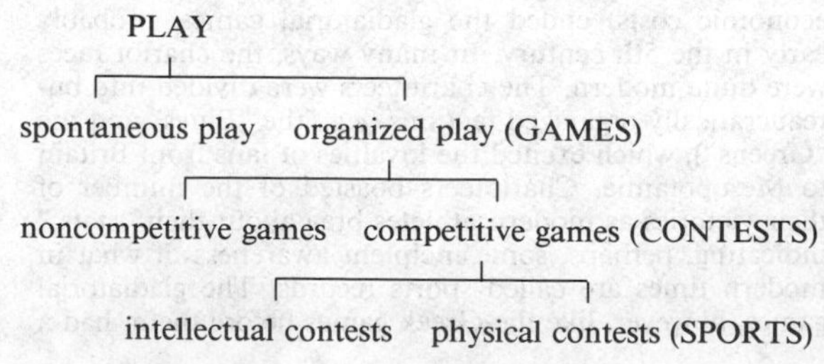

Play can be conceptualized as either spontaneous or regulated. Regulated play—*i.e.*, games—can be contests, like poker, or noncompetitive activities, like leapfrog. Contests can be purely intellectual, like chess, or a combination of physical and intellectual aspects, like rugby.

Competition

Preliterate societies. Competition is such an integral part of Western civilization that some anthropologists and sociologists assume that all games must be contests and are led, therefore, to assert that many preliterate cultures lack games. This assertion is questionable, but many cultures, including some of the most complex, have sought to diminish competition and have favoured noncompetitive games. Such cultures, like those of the Indian subcontinent, have tended to lag behind in the adoption of modern Western forms of sport. There are reasons, however, to suspect that competitiveness may be a universal trait. In Bali, for instance, where Hinduism is the dominant religion, direct social conflict is avoided wherever possible, but the mediated contest of the traditional cockfight indirectly arrays family against family and village against village as the Balinese excitedly bet large sums on the cocks with which they passionately identify.

Most preliterate peoples have sports of one sort or another. As indicated above, these sports are frequently if not invariably associated with cult. The natives of the American Southwest played a stickball game in which the role of the shaman was as important as that of the stick wielders. African youths wrestled one another as part of their rites of passage into manhood. Greek myths like that of swift-footed Atalanta, who said she would marry anyone who could outrun her, testify that footraces as a form of courtship survived into archaic times. The tendency to separate sports from the rest of culture gains strength as the division of labour in society becomes more complex, but the association of sports with the rest of culture has never been lost. An athletic image is almost as useful to the modern politician as it was to Amenhotep II.

Political influence. Politics are in fact an integral aspect of modern sports despite the efforts of some idealists to separate the two. Political decisions determine which sports will be encouraged (traditional or modern), how much public support will be available to promote recreational and elite sports, if differences in gender, race, religion, or ideology will be the basis of discrimination in sports, whether or not athletes will be free to compete in this or that international competition. All of these decisions have prompted bitter controversies, some of which have raged for decades. In nations once colonized by the British, such as Barbados, enthusiasm for cricket is associated with the continued influence of a foreign culture. In the Soviet Union, the Politburo must decide how much money to allocate for national teams of athletes who enhance the system's prestige and how much to devote to facilities to be used by the masses. Women and blacks struggled for decades to achieve integration into the white male preserve of American sports; Jews and Communists were suddenly expelled from German sports clubs in 1933 (on the initiative of the clubs, which anticipated the politics of the Nazi regime). The ostracism of racially segregated South Africa and the use of Olympic boycotts as a means of protest are prime examples of political decisions affecting participation in international sports events.

Barriers to women and minorities

Mass-media influence. That hundreds of millions of people now play sports on a regular basis and equally large numbers watch the Olympic Games and soccer's World Cup on television has enormous economic consequences. Most of the world's governments now have ministries of sport that budget large sums to construct sports facilities and otherwise promote recreational sports for the masses. Such ministries cooperate closely with national sports federations to finance research into "sport science" and to field elite representative teams for international events. Where private enterprise is encouraged, entrepreneurs market equipment, operate commercial sports facilities, and sponsor tournaments. They and other companies purchase sports-related television advertisements that in the late 20th century cost into the hundreds of thousands of dollars per minute.

The development of modern sports has been entwined with the growth of modern mass media. Each depends upon the other. Sports pages and specialized sports journals began to appear in the early 19th century when men such as Pierce Egan in England began to write in the colourfully metaphoric, argot-rich prose now recognized everywhere as typical of sportswriters. Thousands of specialized magazines are published, and sports dailies such as *L'Equipe* (France) or the *Gazzetta dello sport* (Italy) are common in many countries but not in the United States. In the early 20th century U.S. radio and German television pioneered in the development of live sports coverage. In the latter half of the century it became customary for private and public television networks to broadcast 500 or more hours of sports annually. Multiyear contracts for television rights have cost commercial networks as much as $1,000,000,000 or more. Rights to the 1988 Olympics in Seoul and Calgary, Alta., were sold for more than $600,000,000. The popularity of televised sports events guarantees that the networks will continue to budget enormous sums for the right to cover them and that commercial sponsors or governmental agencies will continue to underwrite these costs.

Impact of television

PSYCHOLOGICAL AND PHYSIOLOGICAL FACTORS

Motivational factors. The psychological aspects of sports are more difficult to assess because factors such as motivation are more difficult to measure than the size of an audience or the amount of a contract. The psychological tests that have been administered have produced such a welter of contradictory results that many specialists are ready to abandon the attempt to pinpoint motives. Some generalizations, however, seem tenable. On the whole, physical fitness and the desire for simple relaxation seem to motivate those who shun competitive sports in favour of noncompetitive physical activities such as jogging, hiking, recreational swimming, and aerobics (although the development of aerobics contests testifies to the protean nature of the competitive urge). Important to those who choose sports is the challenge of the contest, the opportunity to test one's physical and mental skills against another person, against nature, or against the abstraction of the sports record. The choice of one sport over another depends on the cultural availability of the sport (few Laotians play baseball), on social group (few truck drivers own polo ponies), on gender (women are not supposed to box), and on individual temperament (some people cannot enjoy golf). There is reason to believe that the distinction between team sports, which emphasize cooperation within the contest, and individual sports, which call for a greater sense of autonomy, is a fundamental one, although an individual may enjoy both.

The challenge of competitive sports

Mental preparation. The will to win is a powerful motive, and individual athletes as well as coaches and administrators have studied such matters as the most efficient type of leadership and the optimal level of pregame stress. Psychologists differ among themselves, but some contend that democratic leadership produces greater individual satisfaction while authoritarian leadership provides "results" (*i.e.*, a higher level of achievement and, consequently, more victories). Many psychological studies have shown that female athletes tend to attribute failure to their lack of effort or skill while male athletes point to external factors such as luck or the strength of the opposition. It has also been established that the ideal level of pregame stress falls between utter relaxation and hypertension and depends in part on the sport; successful archery, for instance, calls for less pre-match aggressiveness than rugby does. Athletes in many sports such as golf, tennis, diving, high jumping, and pole vaulting, where form and timing are crucial, often resort to a different method of pregame "psyching" called imaging or visualizing. This does not so much build aggressiveness as write a visual mental script to be followed in the contest to come.

"Psyching up"

Induced aggressiveness is, of course, a common technique, but "psyched-up" players can be a menace to themselves and others. Injuries are but one consequence. As the desire to win increases in intensity, especially when the players symbolically represent schools, cities, nations, races, religions, or ideologies, considerations of fair play are liable to be lost in the scuffle. In such situations, aggressiveness on the field is often accompanied by violence in the stands, where crowd psychology operates (often in conjunction with alcohol) to reduce normal inhibitions on rowdy behaviour.

Crowd behaviour. Sports-related spectator violence is, however, often more strongly associated with social group than with the specific nature of the sport itself. Roman gladiatorial combats were, for example, history's most violent sport, but the closely supervised spectators, carefully segregated by social class and gender, rarely rioted. In modern times, association football is certainly less violent than rugby, but "soccer hooliganism" is a worldwide phenomenon, while spectator violence associated with the more upper-class but rougher sport of rugby has been minimal. Similarly, crowds at baseball games have been more unruly than the generally more affluent and better-educated fans of American football, although football is unquestionably the rougher sport. Efforts of the police to curb sports-related violence are often counterproductive because the young working-class males responsible for most of the trouble are frequently hostile to the authorities. Media coverage of disturbances can also act to exaggerate their importance and to stimulate the crowd behaviour simultaneously condemned and sensationalized, as is violence on the field. The frequent fights between U.S. National Hockey League players seem to be a consistent feature of sports highlights on television.

Fan violence

Drug usage. Drug abuse must be considered among the other unfortunate aspects of modern sports. The misuse of amphetamines, anabolic steroids, and other drugs has become a central problem of modern sports. One of the touted values of sports is that they better one's health. Pursued in moderation, they certainly do improve muscle tone, increase cardiovascular efficiency, and retard skeletal decalcification. When sports become an obsession, however, they tend ironically to have the opposite effect. The human body is thought of not as a part of the self but as the self's instrument, something to be used and abused. In pursuit of the absolute maximum achievement, 19th-century cyclists began to drug themselves with caffeine and strychnine; some died from the effects of the drugs. Modern chemistry has greatly enlarged the possibilities of artificial stimulation. In the late 20th century came widespread use of amphetamines and anabolic steroids. The former permit athletes to draw upon their physical reserves and continue despite the extremes of exhaustion until they collapse and, occasionally, die. Steroids are thought to increase muscle mass and muscular strength, but the side effects include damage to various organs and, in the case of women, masculinization (*e.g.,* facial hair, deeper voices). Efforts of the International Olympic Committee to limit drug abuse have often been frustrated by national Olympic committees determined upon sports victories at any cost. Efforts to control drug abuse in professional sports and in intercollegiate athletics have frequently been countered by the athletes' concerns regarding personal privacy. Nevertheless, in the United States, codes of varying strictness have been imposed in different sports, part of which includes the requirement of periodic testing for drug use. Olympic athletes now undergo testing prior to participation.

Anabolic steroids

Scientific training. Quite apart from drug abuse, publicly deplored even by some of the abusers, there is the trend to scientific training, which is practiced by most modern countries, and which the German Democratic Republic has developed to a high degree of expertise. While no one questions the instrumental efficiency of such training, there is reason to ask, as have neo-Marxist scholars, whether sports, once conceived as an alternative to work, have not become work's mirror image. The pervasive popularity of modern sports, for children as well as for adults, suggests that the answer must still be negative. Sports continue to be perceived as a domain of freedom unlike what most people experience at work. Almost everyone has experienced the joy of sports. Nevertheless, reflective observers will continue to ponder the pros and cons of the modern drive to instrumentalize the body and to rationalize sports in a quest for the ultimate possible athletic performance. (A.G.)

The quest for perfection

MAJOR TEAM SPORTS

In this article major team sports are considered first. The characteristics of team sports vary from sport to sport, but it is worth noting that some team sports involve the whole team throughout a game more than others. For example, in association football (soccer) and rugby, all players in the game handle the ball. The same is true of basketball and ice hockey. In U.S. and Canadian football, however, most linemen do not handle the ball except in unusual circumstances, such as a fumble, an interception, or a kick allowed to roll free. In baseball, on the defensive team in any given play, the ball may be handled by as few as two players and rarely by as many as four or five; among the offensive team, batters, one by one, and base runners, not exceeding three at a time, are involved.

The team sports discussed here are presented in the following order: first the bat-and-ball games (baseball and cricket), followed by the football games (association football, U.S. football, Canadian football, and rugby), and finally basketball and ice hockey. (Ed.)

Baseball

Baseball is a contest between two teams of nine or 10 players each (depending on whether or not a designated hitter is used) and is played most in the United States, where it is regarded as the national pastime, the game of summer, as cricket is in England. So entwined is baseball in the fabric of American life that many of its terms, originally applicable only to baseball, have come into common idiomatic usage among Americans. When in close combat with American troops during World War II, Japanese soldiers are said to have shouted what they believed to be the ultimate outrage: "To hell with Babe Ruth!"—a reference to the most heroic figure in baseball history.

The president of the United States often throws the ceremonial first pitch in early April to inaugurate the new major-league professional baseball season. As many as 50,000,000 spectators annually watch the best players (a number of whom earn more than $1,000,000 a year) perform with the professional American and National major league teams. The seven-month season is climaxed by the World Series, a best four-out-of-seven competition between the championship teams of the two major leagues. It is an event of enormous nationwide interest and the focus of some international attention; in the late 20th century the U.S. television audience was estimated at more than 100,000,000, with some one-third of the households equipped with television sets watching the series. A World Series income share for players on the winning team grew steadily toward the $100,000 range in response to increasing television revenues.

Popularity of the game

Baseball's appeal is universal, crossing all classes and age groups. It is a game of both individual and collective strengths, including intricate strategic maneuvers, providing a kind of intellectual attraction as well as feats of physical skill and prowess. Of all the major American team sports, it has probably undergone the fewest basic rule changes; to hit for a .300 batting average, the hallmark of outstanding offensive play, is as meaningful today as it was in the 19th century. In addition to its vast literature (the world-champion 1969 New York Mets were the inspiration for nine books), the game is supported by a perpetually growing bank of statistics and records that have been officially kept since 1900 and afford the fan with a constant source of interest.

This historical treasure and scores of traditional yarns and legends have made baseball comparable only to itself. It is, for some, not only a memorable but an almost essential event when a father takes his son to his first game. The heroes of the past have been elevated to a state bordering on mythology, their deeds passed on from generation to generation. The tradition is supported and certified by a hall of fame in Cooperstown, N.Y., a pantheon housing thousands of the game's artifacts.

Baseball is played at a leisurely pace on a field of green—often natural grass, but also lately artificial turf. This setting, unchanged through time except for larger stadiums, provides a nostalgic tie to baseball's pastoral roots. It satisfies, for some, especially older fans, the yearning for what are deemed as the lost values of a kinder age, when most small towns and villages had their "local nine." It is not unusual for fans to retain a lifelong love of the game.

It was the zealotry associated with American baseball fans that led to a long period of confusion over the game's proper roots. A.G. Spalding, a wealthy sporting goods manufacturer, around the turn of the century had felt it demeaning that what had come to be an American institution found its origins in an English game, rounders. Consequently, Spalding in 1904 assembled some like-minded baseball friends and established them, with the aid of a U.S. senator, as an investigative commission. In 1908 the commission issued a report attributing the inventing of the game to Abner Doubleday, a Civil War general, who, it said, devised the game with its name and modern attributes in 1839 at Cooperstown. The ancestor of baseball was said to be a U.S. children's game, old cat, called one-old cat, two-old cat, etc., depending on the number of players. This revisionist interpretation was widely accepted until 1939, when investigations revealed the essentially mythical nature of the theory. Meanwhile, in 1936 the National Baseball Hall of Fame and Museum had already been established at Cooperstown.

The Doubleday myth

HISTORY

Origin. The term baseball (originally base ball) dates from 1744, when a game involving a pitcher who throws a ball to a batter who tries to hit it and then runs to a base and returns to score a run was described in *A Little Pretty Pocket-Book*. Therein an illustration shows a batter holding a bat with a curious flat, fanlike end, a catcher behind him, and a pitcher preparing to throw a small ball underhand. The two bases are marked by posts instead of the modern bags and flat home plate. The book was extremely popular in England and was reprinted in North America in 1762 (New York) and 1787 (Massachusetts).

Many other early references to bat-and-ball games involving bases are known: "playing at base" at the American Army camp at Valley Forge in 1778; the forbidding of students to "play with balls and sticks" on the common of Princeton College in 1787; a note in the memoirs of Thurlow Weed, an upstate New York newspaper editor and politician, of a baseball organized club about 1825; a newspaper report that the Rochester (N.Y.) Baseball Club had about 50 members at practice in the 1820s; and a reminiscence of the elder Oliver Wendell Holmes (Harvard, 1829) that he played a good deal of ball at college.

The Boy's Own Book (1828), a frequently reprinted book on English boys' sports, included in its second edition a chapter on the game of rounders. As described there, rounders had many resemblances to the modern game of baseball: it was played on a diamond-shaped infield with a base at each corner, the fourth being that at which the batter originally stood and to which he had to advance to score a run. When a batter hit a pitched ball through or over the infield, he could run. A ball hit elsewhere was foul, and he could not run. Three missed strikes at the ball and the batter was out. A batted ball caught on the fly put the batter out. One notable difference was that when a ball hit on the ground was fielded, the fielder put the runner out by hitting him with the thrown ball; the same was true with a runner caught off base. Illustrations show flat stones used as bases and a second catcher behind the first, perhaps to catch foul balls. The descent of baseball from rounders seems clear-cut. The first U.S. account of rounders was in *The Book of Sports* (1834) by Robin Carver, who credits *The Boy's Own Book* as his source but calls the game base, or goal, ball.

Rounders

Early years. In 1845 Alexander J. Cartwright, an amateur New York City player, organized a group to formulate rules, many of which still remain. The significant change from rounders was that the runner was put out not by being hit with the thrown ball but by being tagged with it. This change no doubt led to the substitution of the hard ball, which made possible a larger-scale game.

Cartwright's contribution

The adoption of these rules by the Knickerbockers and other amateur club teams in the New York City area led to an increased popularity of the game. The old game with the soft ball continued to be popular in and around Boston; a Philadelphia club that had played the old game since 1833 did not adopt the hard-ball rules until 1860. Until the Civil War, the two versions of the game were called Boston baseball and New York baseball. During the Civil War (1861–65), soldiers from New York and New Jersey taught their game to others, and after the war the New York game became dominant.

In 1854 a revision of the rules specified the weight and size of the ball, dimensions not radically altered later. In 1858 there had been an attempt to organize clubs of the New York City and Philadelphia areas into leagues. In 1859, Washington, D.C., organized a club, and in the next year clubs were formed in Lowell, Mass.; Allegheny, Pa.; and Hartford, Conn. The game continued to spread after the war—to Maine, to Kentucky, and to Portland, Ore. The game was on its way to becoming the national pastime. Baseball was widely played outside the cities, but the big city clubs and their leagues were the dominant force, others being minor, a distinction later perpetuated in organized baseball. In 1865 a convention called to confirm rules and the amateur status of baseball brought together 91 amateur teams from such cities as St. Louis, Mo.; Chattanooga, Tenn.; Louisville, Ky.; Washington, D.C.; Boston; and Philadelphia.

Professional baseball. Professionalism began to appear about 1865–66 as some teams hired skilled players on a per game basis. Amateurs resented the practice and the gambling and bribery that often accompanied it. The first true professional team, the Cincinnati Red Stockings, was organized in 1869; the team toured that year, playing from New York City to San Francisco and winning 56 games and tying one; the team was first defeated in 1870. The desire of many other teams to win led to their becoming professional, though many remained nominally in the amateur National Association of Base Ball Players until the amateurs withdrew in 1870. Thereafter, professional teams largely controlled the development of the sport.

The Cincinnati Red Stockings

The National Association of Professional Base Ball Players was formed in 1871. The teams were the Philadelphia Athletics; the Chicago White Stockings (later the Chicago Cubs, their later city rivals being named the White Sox); the Brooklyn Eckfords; the Cleveland Forest Citys; the Forest Citys of Rockford, Ill.; the Haymakers of Troy, N.Y.; the Kekiongas of Fort Wayne, Ind.; the Olympics of Washington, D.C.; and the Mutuals of New York City. The league disbanded in 1876 with the founding of the rival National League of Professional Baseball Clubs—the change from a players' association to one of clubs being particularly significant. The teams making up the new league represented Philadelphia, Hartford, Boston, Chicago, Cincinnati, Louisville, St. Louis, and New York City. When William Hulbert, president of the league in 1877–82, expelled four players for dishonesty, the reputation of baseball as an institution was established.

League formation. In 1881 the American Association was formed with teams from cities that were not members of or, like Cincinnati, had been expelled from the National League (Cincinnati's team was disciplined in 1880 for playing games on Sunday and allowing liquor on the grounds). After the National League tried to limit players' salaries (a $2,000 maximum for pitchers), the players in 1890 formed a players league, but it quickly failed. The American Association unsuccessfully challenged the National League and late in 1891 merged with it in a 12-team league that constituted a monopoly, an arrangement that prevailed through 1899. By 1900 the National League had shrunk to eight teams: Boston, Brooklyn, Chicago, Cincinnati, New York City, Philadelphia, Pittsburgh, and St.

Louis, the league remaining thus constituted until 1953. The Western League, organized in 1893, had Midwestern members. When in 1900 Charles Comiskey moved his St. Paul (Minn.) team to Chicago as the White Sox, and the Grand Rapids (Mich.) team was shifted to Cleveland, the National League agreed to the moves. When, however, permission was asked to put teams into Baltimore and Washington, D.C., the National League balked, and the "baseball war" was on. The American League, renamed from the Western League, transferred teams from Indianapolis, Ind.; Kansas City; Minneapolis, Minn.; and Buffalo to Baltimore, Washington, D.C., Philadelphia, and Boston. American League teams were also in Detroit and Milwaukee, the latter club moving to St. Louis in 1902. When the Baltimore club moved to New York City in 1903, the league took the form it was to retain until 1953.

The "baseball war"

During the "war," the American League wooed away many of the National League star players. In 1903 the leagues agreed to forbid single ownership of two clubs in the same city and the shifting of franchises from one city to another by either league without permission of the other. They also established rules for transferring players from one league to the other and for moving minor league players into the major leagues. The peace of 1903 resulted in the first World Series, which, after a hiatus in 1904, was held each year thereafter, the winner being the team to win four games out of seven (five out of nine from 1919 to 1921). In the period following the "war," two men arose who contributed greatly to the success of their respective leagues: John J. McGraw, manager of the National League New York Giants (1902–32), and Connie Mack, manager of the American League Philadelphia Athletics (1901–50). The 1903 agreement had included the creation of a three-man National Commission to govern baseball.

The Black Sox scandal

Survival and growth. Baseball suffered a major scandal—subsequently called the Black Sox scandal—when eight members of the Chicago White Sox were accused of accepting bribes to throw the 1919 World Series. The presiding judge for the grand jury that indicted them was Kenesaw Mountain Landis. The players, suspended for the 1921 season by the owner, were found not guilty because of insufficient evidence. Presuming a need to restore baseball's honour, however, Landis banned them from baseball for life after he was named baseball's first commissioner, supplanting the National Commission.

During the 1920s, generally known as a golden age of sports in the United States, the premier hero was George Herman ("Babe") Ruth, who as a New York Yankee rose to fame as a home-run hitter, the "Sultan of Swat." His performance not only assured the success of his team but came to symbolize baseball, which grew steadily in attendance. Even the Great Depression of the 1930s did little to abate the rise in popularity and financial success of the game except at the minor league and Negro league levels (see below *Blacks in baseball* and *The minor leagues*). Night baseball, tried experimentally earlier, began in the major leagues at Cincinnati in 1935. Delayed by World War II, night baseball became almost universal by the 1960s, with all teams but the Chicago Cubs scheduling about half of their home games at night. (The Cubs only acceded to night baseball at home in 1988.) The first night World Series game was played in 1971.

From the 1942 season until the end of World War II, baseball operated under the "green light" order of Commissioner Landis, approved by President Franklin D. Roosevelt. Attendance was off slightly. Many players went into the armed services, most notably Ted Williams, the last man in organized baseball to have a season batting average of more than .400 (.406, 1941; he hit .407 for an incomplete season in 1953), and the quality of play suffered somewhat.

The American Baseball Guild

The postwar period. The 1946 season was marked by the resumption of rising attendance with the return of prominent players from the war. It also was marked by new efforts of players to obtain better pay and conditions of employment. A portent of things to come was the formation in that year of the American Baseball Guild. Although the guild failed in strike attempts and appeals to national and state labour relations boards, its very existence led to reforms before the 1947 season: a minimum major league salary of $5,000; no salary cuts during a season for a major league player moved to the minors; weekly spring-training expense money of $25; a 25 percent limit on annual salary cuts; and establishment of a players' pension fund. Albert B. ("Happy") Chandler, Landis' successor as commissioner (1945–51), in 1950 assured the soundness of the pension fund by signing a six-year contract for broadcasting World Series and All-Star games; the television portion alone amounted to $1,000,000 a year, with a large proportion earmarked for the pension fund. Radio and television rights for season games remained with each club. Later commissioners included Ford C. Frick (1951–65), William D. Eckert (1965–69), Bowie Kuhn (1969–84), and Peter Ueberroth (1984–). A. Bartlett Giamatti was named to succeed Ueberroth in 1989.

Movement and expansion. Continuing financial success, buoyed especially by rising income from television and radio rights led to club movement and league expansion. The National League began the changes. In 1953 the Boston Braves transferred its franchise to Milwaukee (in 1966 it was moved to Atlanta, Ga.). In time for the 1958 season the New York Giants and the Brooklyn Dodgers transferred their franchises to San Francisco and Los Angeles, leaving the New York area temporarily a one-team city. In the American League, the St. Louis Browns' franchise was transferred to Baltimore for the 1954 season. In 1955 the Philadelphia Athletics' franchise was moved to Kansas City (and in 1968 to Oakland). In 1961 the Washington (D.C.) Senators were moved to Minneapolis–St. Paul and renamed the Twins; a new franchise was granted to Washington but lasted only until 1971, when it was transferred to Dallas–Ft. Worth, Texas, and named the Texas Rangers.

American League expansion

Expansion began with the granting of an American League franchise to Los Angeles (later moving to Anaheim as the California Angels) in 1961, thus bringing the American League to 10 teams. In 1962 the National League also expanded to 10 teams with new franchises in New York (the Mets) and Houston (the Astros). In 1968 new franchises to Montreal (the Expos, the first major league franchise outside the United States) and San Diego (the Padres) brought the National League to 12 teams. In the American League in 1969 new franchises to Kansas City (the Royals) and Seattle (the Pilots) brought that league to 12 teams, and both leagues were divided into eastern and western divisions. The 154-game season had been expanded to 162 in 1961. Playoffs between division winners determined the league pennant winners, who then played in the World Series, which was extended into late October. California, which had had no major league baseball prior to 1958, had five teams by 1968. Only the Seattle franchise failed outright and was moved to Milwaukee, where it became the Brewers. A new franchise was granted to Seattle (the Mariners) in 1976. A franchise to Toronto (the Blue Jays) in the same year brought the American League total to 14 teams. The expansion teams were not at first highly competitive, having been stocked from a pool of players supplied by existing teams, which protected their best players. The New York Mets was the first expansion team to win a pennant and a World Series (1969).

The "farm system"

The minor leagues. The minor leagues formed a union in 1901 in order to deal with the confusion resulting from the lack of agreement on contract ownership, salaries, territoriality, and other issues. The current structure was created when the major leagues reached their agreement in 1903, and the minor leagues became a training ground for prospective major league players and a refuge for older players. In 1919 Branch Rickey, then manager of the St. Louis Cardinals, devised what came to be known as the "farm system"; as the price of established players increased, the Cardinals began "growing" their own, signing hundreds of high-school boys at no cost. Other major league clubs followed, developing their own farm clubs. In 1949 the minor leagues were at the height of their popularity: 448 teams in the United States, Canada, Cuba, and Mexico, playing in 59 leagues with an aggregate attendance of nearly 42,000,000, twice that of the 16 major league clubs. The minor leagues, at that time, were divided into six classifications, graded according to the level of playing skills: AAA (triple A), AA (double A), A (single A), B, C, and D. Attendance eroded soon thereafter when the major leagues began broadcasting and televising their games into minor league attendance areas. By the late 1980s, after the American and National leagues had annexed 10 choice minor league territories, the number of minor league teams had been greatly reduced and there remained only 17 leagues divided among four classifications; attendance had dropped, and the minor league clubs generally looked to the major league parent clubs for heavy subsidization. The purpose of the minor leagues had evolved from that of mainly providing local entertainment to that of developing major league talent.

Blacks in baseball. In 1884 two brothers, Welday and Moses Walker, played for Toledo, Ohio, in the American Association, becoming the first black players to compete at the major league level. Black acceptance in organized baseball, however, was short-lived. The first professional black team, the Cuban Giants of Long Island, New York, was organized in 1885. Other black teams were organized and played each other or barnstormed about the country playing against white teams, occasionally including major-leaguers. The Negro National League was formed in 1920 and the Negro Eastern League in 1921, playing in New York City, Chicago, St. Louis, Kansas City, Detroit, and other cities that had absorbed a large influx of blacks from the South during and after World War I. In the 1920s a Negro World Series was begun and was held annually until the leagues failed in the 1930s. A second Negro National League was founded late in that decade, and the Negro American League, formed in 1936, ultimately had eastern and western divisions that in 1952 played a Negro East–West game. Among the most famous players in the various Negro leagues were Josh Gibson, Leroy ("Satchel") Paige, Bill Yancey, John Henry Lloyd, Andrew ("Rube") Foster, and James Thomas ("Cool Papa") Bell. Gibson was credited with hitting 89 home runs in one season. After World War II, attendance at Negro leagues declined due to the loss of outstanding players to formerly all-white teams.

Breaking the colour barrier

In 1947 Jackie Robinson became the first black player in the modern major leagues. He was called to the Brooklyn Dodgers from its Montreal Royals farm club by Dodger president Branch Rickey. Robinson, who helped his team win a pennant in his first year and was named most valuable player in his league after his third year, was followed into the major leagues immediately by Larry Doby, outfielder, and Satchel Paige, pitcher, both of whom played for the American League Cleveland club. Such stars as Willie Mays; Hank Aaron, who set an all-time home-run record; Bob Gibson; Willie McCovey; Ernie Banks; Roberto Clemente; Frank Robinson, who became the first black manager in 1974; Willie Stargell; and Reggie Jackson followed. Negro League players, including Josh Gibson, John Henry Lloyd, and Cool Papa Bell, were later named to the Hall of Fame.

The business of baseball. From the beginning of organized professional baseball, the owners had controlled the game, the players, managers, and umpires. The players had begun to organize as early as 1885, when a group of players with the New York Giants formed the National Brotherhood of Base Ball Players, a benevolent and protective association. Under the leadership of John Montgomery Ward, a lawyer and former major league player, the Brotherhood grew rapidly as a secret organization. It went public in 1886 to challenge the adoption of a $2,000 salary ceiling by the National League. Rebuffed in attempts to negotiate with league owners, the Brotherhood in 1890 formed the short-lived Players' League.

During the National League–American League war of 1900–03, the Protective Association of Professional Baseball Players got National League players to switch to the other league, but with the peace treaty the association died. In 1912 came the Baseball Players' Fraternity, which included most professional players. It was organized after the suspension of Ty Cobb for punching a fan. Later, a threatened strike was settled the day before it was to begin. During World War I the War Department's "play or fight" order ended the fraternity.

Rise of the players. After a 1953 Supreme Court decision reaffirmed a 1922 decision stating that baseball was not a business that was subject to antitrust rules, baseball felt assured that its legal and economic foundation was firm. This foundation is based on the Reserve Rule, or Clause, an agreement among major league teams dating from 1879, whereby the rights of each team to the services of its players are observed by other teams; *i.e.,* a team could designate a certain number of players who were not to be offered jobs by other teams. The original number of five such players was increased to 11 in 1883 and ultimately included a whole team roster.

The Reserve Clause

The recourse the court failed to provide was in substance achieved by the Major League Baseball Players Association, founded in 1953 but largely ineffectual until 1966, when it hired as executive director Marvin Miller, a former labour union official who had also been active in government for labour–management relations. A successful negotiator, he established players' rights and benefits contractually and established grievance procedures with recourse to impartial arbitration. In 1968 the minimum salary was doubled to $10,000, and first-class travel and meal allowances were established in 1970. A threatened players' boycott of spring training was averted in 1969 by a compromise assuring a $20,000 median salary.

In 1970 a new suit was brought in federal court contesting the Reserve Clause. The suit was supported by the players' association, who hired as counsel Arthur Goldberg, a former U.S. Supreme Court justice. The plaintiff was Curt Flood, star outfielder of the St. Louis Cardinals, and the defendants were the commissioner, the two major league presidents, and the major league clubs. Flood claimed that in trading him to the Philadelphia Phillies without his knowledge or approval, the Cardinals had violated the antitrust laws. He refused to report to the Phillies and sat out the season. The court found against Flood, who appealed, and in 1972 the U.S. Supreme Court reaffirmed the 1922 and 1953 decisions exempting baseball from the antitrust laws, but it called on Congress to correct by legislation any inequities. Meanwhile Flood had signed for the 1971 season with Washington on the understanding that he would not be sold or traded without his permission. He quit in midseason, however.

First baseball strike

In 1972 baseball had its first general strike, lasting 13 days and causing the cancellation of 86 regular season games and delaying the divisional play-offs and World Series by 10 days. The players asked for and ultimately got an addition to the pension fund. Another players' strike was averted in 1973, when an agreement was reached that provided compulsory impartial arbitration of salary negotiations and a rule that allowed a player with 10 years of service in the major leagues and the last five with the same club to refuse a trade made without his consent.

These were unprecedented victories for the players, but their greatest triumph came prior to the 1976 season. Pitchers Andy Messersmith of the Los Angeles Dodgers and Dave McNally of the Montreal Expos played the entire 1975 season without signing a contract; their contracts had expired but were automatically renewed by their clubs. Marvin Miller had been waiting for such a test case. The players association filed a grievance on their behalf, contending that a player's contract could not be renewed in perpetuity, a custom first established in 1879. Arbitrator Peter Seitz found for the players. This decision substantively demolished the Reserve Rule.

Stunned, the owners appealed but without success. Negotiations followed, however, and the union agreed to a modification of the Reserve Rule: players with six or more years of major league service could become free agents when their contracts expired and would be eligible to make their own deals. The ruling allowed eligible players who refused to sign their 1976 contracts to choose free agency in 1977.

Free-agency bidding

Twenty-four players took immediate advantage of this new opportunity and went on the open market. Frantic bidding by the clubs followed. Bill Campbell, a relief pitcher with the Minnesota Twins, was the first free agent to make a new connection. He signed a four-year, $1,000,000 contract with the Boston Red Sox, which gave him annually more than 10 times his 1976 salary. As free agency took root, salaries soared. The annual average salary rose from about $41,000 in 1974 to $175,000 in 1981; by the mid-1980s it was in excess of $300,000, with many players making more than $1,000,000 and some of the superstars climbing beyond the $2,000,000 plateau.

The free-agency procedure was the principal issue when the players struck for 50 days at the height of the 1981 season (June 12–July 31), forcing cancellation of 714 games. Once again, the players won. In the settlement it was agreed that clubs losing players to free agency would not receive direct compensation from the free agents' new teams. The union contended this would impede movement, the signing club, in effect, having to pay twice: a huge sum to the player and further compensation to the player's former employer. Under certain conditions relating to the quality of the player, however, the team that lost the free agent could draft a player from among those assigned to a compensation pool by their teams, and it could select an amateur draft choice from the signing team.

The next shutdown, lasting only two days (August 6–7), occurred in 1985, with little disruption to the schedule. It arose from a dispute that eventually centred on the issue of salary arbitration. The owners agreed to increase the minimum salary from $40,000 to $60,000, but the number of major league seasons a player had to serve before qualifying for arbitration was raised from two to three.

As the players' compensation rose, so did the value of the individual franchises. The average price was less than $10,000,000 in the 1960s. In 1984 the Minnesota Twins, operating in the Minneapolis–St. Paul metropolitan area, sold for more than $43,000,000. Fan interest also continued to rise, resulting in record major league attendance levels in the late 1980s. Also, the combined annual revenue for the major league clubs from network television grew from $15,500,000 in 1969 to $90,000,000 in 1984 and to $180,000,000 by the late 1980s.

Records. Records and statistics have long been a prominent feature of baseball, with some of them attaining hallowed status. In 1961, for example, in the first 162-game season, Roger Maris of the New York Yankees broke Babe Ruth's long-standing season home-run record of 60, but since Maris' last two home runs came in the last eight games of the season, Ruth's mark remained in the record book and Maris' was entered with an explanation. In 1974 Henry Aaron broke Ruth's career home-run record.

Babe Ruth and Roger Maris

Some records long held by Ty Cobb of the Detroit Tigers were also toppled. In 1985, Pete Rose of the Cincinnati Reds broke Cobb's lifetime mark of 4,191 hits; Rose played for one more season and then retired with 4,256 hits. Cobb's one-season modern (20th-century) stolen-base record of 96 (1915) fell to Maury Wills of the Los Angeles Dodgers in 1962, when Wills had 104 steals. This was eclipsed in 1974 by the 118 stolen bases of the St. Louis Cardinals' Lou Brock. In 1982, Rickey Henderson, then with the Oakland Athletics, amassed 130 steals. Cobb's lifetime record of 892 steals was surpassed by Brock, who had 938 steals upon retiring in 1979. Not only the lengthened season but the increasing use of fast artificial surfaces in place of grass aided record breaking, especially for hitters. Cobb's career batting average of .367, however, has remained unmatched, as has his record of 12 league batting championships. The highest modern-era single-season average of .424 was set by Rogers Hornsby of the Cardinals in 1924. In pitching, Denton ("Cy") Young set the career mark for wins with 511.

Baseball abroad. Organized baseball was played in Mexico and Cuba from the late 19th century, and in the 1980s four Mexican leagues were in the U.S. minor league system. Cuba, where baseball is the national pastime, was once a U.S. spring-training site and furnished numerous players to U.S. major leagues until the breaking off of diplomatic relations after the Castro revolution of 1958. Organized baseball is also played in Puerto Rico, Venezuela, the Dominican Republic, and frequently in Panama in the winter months. Both native and U.S. major and minor league players make up the rosters.

Baseball was introduced to Japan in the 1870s by missionaries and teachers and became a national sport. It was organized professionally in the 1930s, when U.S. professional teams toured there. Organized baseball bloomed after World War II. In the mid-1950s some U.S. players appeared on Japanese teams, and a limit on the number of U.S. players per team was imposed. Japan had its own Babe Ruth figure, Sadaharu Oh, who in his playing career (1959–80) hit 868 home runs. There are two six-team leagues, the Pacific and the Central, which play a 130-game schedule culminating in the Japan Series. Television contributes greatly to baseball revenue in Japan.

Baseball in Japan

Amateur baseball. After the divorce of amateur from professional baseball in 1870, amateur baseball continued to thrive on vacant lots in towns and cities and on pastures in the country. The first national amateur baseball program was the American Legion Junior League, founded in 1926, later called the American Legion Baseball League, with an upper age limit of 19.

The American Amateur Baseball Congress, founded in 1935, conducts baseball programs for youths from the age of eight to 19 and adults in six divisions. Little League, founded in 1939 and originally for boys eight to 12 years old, accounted for more than 2,500,000 players in the United States by the early 1980s. Two additional divisions for boys up to 18 were later added, and in 1974 girls were admitted to play. Other organized leagues for young players included the Babe Ruth League, founded in 1952, and PONY (Protect Our Nation's Youth) Baseball, Inc.

By the 1980s more than 1,600 colleges fielded baseball teams under the governance of the National Collegiate Athletic Association, which in 1963 led in the forming of the U.S. Baseball Federation, representing all amateur groups. From 1972 it conducted a collegiate world series with teams selected by its Japanese equivalent. Play by military service teams made baseball a minor sport in The Netherlands, Italy, Belgium, England, Spain, Australia, and Tunisia. Baseball was designated an official Olympic sport beginning with the 1992 Games in Spain. (Je.Ho.)

PLAY OF THE GAME

Baseball is a contest between two teams of nine or (if a designated hitter is used) 10 players each. Four bases are laid out at angles of a 90-foot (27.4-metre) square at one end of a broad field of play. Teams alternate as batters ("ins") and fielders ("outs"), exchanging places when three of the batting side are "put out"; both sides having batted constitutes an inning. As the batter, a player stands at the base designated home plate (a distance of 60 feet six inches from the pitcher's plate) and attempts to hit a ball thrown by a pitcher so that it will go out of reach of the fielding side, and then to run from base to base counterclockwise with the intent to return to home base and thus score a run. The side that scores the most runs at the end of nine innings (times at bat) wins, except that if the home team, which always bats last, is ahead after the visitors have completed their ninth turn at bat, the game ends. If the teams are tied at the end of nine innings, the game proceeds until the tie is broken, the home team again always having a last bat.

Scoring

Field of play and equipment. *Grounds.* The only restrictions for the major league playing fields are that the distance to the fence from home plate along the foul lines be 250 feet (75 metres) or more; and that for fields built after 1958 the distance along the foul lines should be at least 325 feet and the distance from home plate on a line through second base to the centre-field fence be at least 400 feet. (See Figure 1.)

The playing field was traditionally covered with grass, except for the pitcher's circle, the base paths, the adjacent infield from first to third base, and the home plate area. Since the introduction of artificial turf, the field has been mostly covered, except for the areas around the pitcher's plate, home plate, and the bases. Canvas bags filled with soft material and attached by metal stakes driven in the ground mark first, second, and third base. Home plate is a flat pentagonal white slab of rubber embedded flush in the ground. The distance to the stands or fence behind home plate should be at least 60 feet but may taper off along the foul lines in the outfield. Coaches' boxes are in foul territory behind first and third base; and next-batter

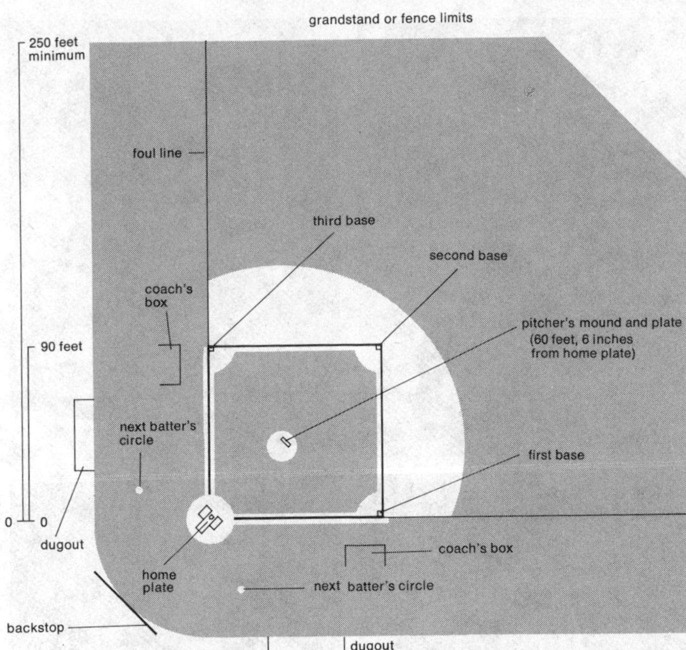

Figure 1: Layout of a representative baseball field.

("on-deck") circles are off to one side and behind the batting boxes.

The ball and bat. The ball has a cork and rubber core, around which yarn is tightly wrapped; the cover is two snugly fitted pieces of white leather sewn together. The circumference is from nine to $9^1/_4$ inches (23 to 23.5 centimetres) and the weight between five and $5^1/_4$ ounces (142 and 149 grams). The bat is a smooth rounded stick of solid or laminated wood, not longer than 42 inches or thicker at the barrel end than $2^3/_4$ inches, tapering to the handle end. There is no weight restriction, but no metal or other reinforcement can be used in construction of the bat. (For beginning players, however, aluminum bats may be used.) The handle may have tape and adhesive material, such as pine tar, applied to it to improve the grip.

Gloves. Baseball was originally played bare-handed. First the catcher, who catches every pitch not hit, and then the first baseman, who takes many throws for putouts from the infielders, and finally all players adopted gloves. All gloves are constructed of leather with some padding. The catcher's glove, or mitt, presents a solid face except for a cleft between the thumb and index finger and is thickly padded except at the centre, where the pitched ball is caught. The glove cannot exceed 38 inches in circumference and $15^1/_2$ inches from top to bottom. The first baseman's glove is thinner and more flexible, a solid expanse of leather for the four fingers with a webbing connecting the thumb and index finger. All other players' gloves are finger gloves with leather straps connecting the thumb and index finger. Batting gloves, designed to improve the batting grip, are now worn by most batters.

Protective gear. The catcher wears a padded metal mask with bars across the front, a solid, padded chest protector, and light metal, padded shin guards. The umpire behind home plate wears similar equipment. At bat, players wear a lightweight plastic batting helmet that flares down over the ears to protect the temples.

Functions of umpires

Conduct of the game. Umpires control the game. One behind home plate calls balls and strikes on the batter, determines whether a batter has been hit by a pitch or has interfered with the catcher, or vice versa, and calls runners safe or out at home plate. He and the other three umpires, stationed near first, second, and third base, may call hit balls foul or fair; the other three call runners safe or out at the first three bases. Any umpire may call an illegal pitching motion, known as a balk. An umpire may ask for help from his fellows if he was out of position to see a play, and the first or third base umpire may be appealed to when it is a question if a batter has taken a full swing or not that may account for a strike.

Principles of play. The bases are called first, second, and third base and home base or plate. All batting is done at home plate. Base running proceeds from home plate along the base lines (the boundaries of the square). A run is scored when a player, having successively touched first, second, and third, reaches home plate.

The fielding team

Seven of the nine players on the fielding team take their positions in the infield and outfield, preparing to catch (field) the ball as soon as possible after it is hit by the batter. The other two, the pitcher and the catcher, form the battery. While awaiting a pitch, the catcher crouches behind and within stepping distance of home plate but not close enough to impede the batter's activities. The pitcher stands near the centre of the infield. He puts the ball in play by throwing it to the catcher. The batter, standing on one side of home plate, gets a chance to hit the ball as it passes him on its way to the catcher.

The pitcher and the batter are the central figures in the game, which is a succession of plays. Each play begins when the pitcher delivers the ball to the batter and lasts until the pitcher holds the ball again, standing with his foot against the pitcher's plate, or rubber, ready to toss the next pitch. If the ball travels past the batter to the catcher and is then tossed directly back to the pitcher, it is a complete play. If the ball is batted, the play goes on until the ball has been fielded, all base running has come to a stop, and the ball has returned to the pitcher.

When the batter hits the ball inside fair territory (the area of the playing field between the foul lines running on a line with first and third bases and extending to the outer limit of the field), he is entitled to start running around the bases. The fielding team's defensive arrangement places its seven movable men within the fair territory. Four of them, the infielders, patrol the ground between first and second and between second and third. The other three,

By courtesy of *The Sporting News*

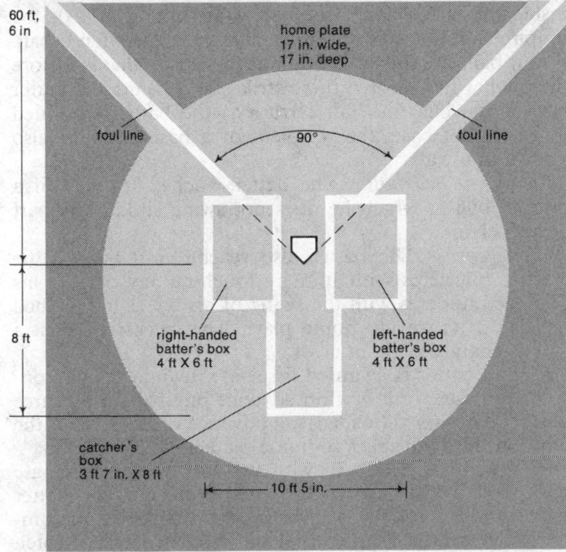

Figure 2: Layout (top) of the pitcher's mound and plate and (bottom) home plate.

the outfielders, play the outfield, the sweep of the field from foul line to foul line beyond the two base lines.

The fielders' playing positions

The outfielders are called right fielder, centre fielder, and left fielder with relation to a man standing on home plate and facing toward second base, but there are no visible boundaries separating the three fields. With the exception of the pitcher and catcher (and in their case only at the moment of putting the ball in play), there is no restriction on the movements of the members of the fielding team. The four infielders are named first baseman, second baseman, shortstop, and third baseman, stationed in that order from first base around the rim of the infield to third.

Offense. The objective of the offense is to score runs by hitting fair balls out of the reach of the defense. Each team strives to advance its players around the bases to score as many runs as possible before the third out ends its half of the inning at bat. The first batter up for each side in the first inning is the first man in the batting order. In succeeding innings, the first batter is the next man in the order after the last batter in the previous inning to complete his turn at bat.

Hitting the ball. The ultimate successful batting feat is to drive a pitched ball inside the foul lines and beyond the confines of the playing field. This constitutes a home run, which entitles the batter to run at any speed around the bases, touching each with his foot, to score a run at home plate. Any and all runners who are on base when the home run is hit precede the home-run hitter to the plate in the order in which they reached base, and register a run each.

Failing such a hit, the batter aims to drive the ball so that it cannot be caught either before touching the ground in fair territory or soon enough after touching ground to be thrown to first or any other base before the batter or any other runner gets there. If he succeeds in getting on base before the ball gets there, he has made a hit. A one-base hit is called a single, a two-base hit, a double, and a three-base hit, a triple. If a batter makes it all the way to home plate on a hit within the confines of the field, it is called an inside-the-park home run; such a feat is quite rare. Driven balls are generally categorized as flies or fly balls (balls hit high into the air) or grounders (balls hit at a downward angle into the ground).

Advancing base runners

With the ball thus hit by the batter into fair territory, any members of his team who are already occupying bases advance as far as possible toward home plate before the ball is returned to the infield. They must avoid being tagged out. A batter may also reach base safely because of an error by the fielder; *i.e.,* failure to catch the ball or an inaccurate throw. Failure to tag a runner with the ball when the fielder has a chance to make a putout in this way also is an error.

Base on balls. A batter may reach first base without having hit the ball. Whenever the batter does not swing at a pitched ball, and the ball does not cross the plate inside the strike zone (see below *Defense: Putouts*), the umpire standing behind the catcher calls the pitch a ball. If four balls are thus called in a turn at bat—that is, before the pitcher has thrown three strikes and before the batter has hit the ball into fair territory—the batter is entitled to go to first base, the recipient of a base on balls, also known as a walk.

Hit by pitched ball. The batter reaches first base if a pitched ball at which he does not swing strikes any part of his person.

Interference. The batter also reaches first base if the catcher interferes with him by touching any part of his body or interferes with the swing of his bat as the pitched ball is on its way to home plate. The catcher in such a case is charged with an error.

When a batter is awarded first base, teammates on consecutive bases from first on advance one base; if all three bases are occupied (loaded), all advance one base; thus the man on third advances to home plate and scores a run.

Missed third strike. If, with two out or with first base unoccupied regardless of how many are out, the batter swings and misses the ball for his third strike, or the umpire calls the third strike, and the catcher does not catch the pitched ball before it touches the ground, the batter is entitled to run for first just as if he had hit the ball in fair

Stages in the famous swing of Boston Red Sox outfielder Ted Williams, who played in 1939–60.

AP/Wide World Photo; by courtesy of the National Baseball Library

territory. The catcher must then get the ball and throw to first ahead of the batter in order to put him out. If such a pitched ball rebounds off the catcher out into the infield, the pitcher or any infielder may make the pickup and throw to first, just as if it were an infield grounder.

The infield fly rule. The infield fly rule applies only if both first and second or first, second, and third bases are occupied, there are fewer than two out, and the batter hits a high fly that in the judgment of the umpire can readily be caught by an infielder or the pitcher or catcher inside fair territory. In such circumstances the umpire immediately declares the batter out, whether or not the ball is actually caught. This law was enacted in 1895 because clever infield players would pretend to catch the fly but at the last moment would let it strike the ground, thus setting up a force play (see below *Infielders*) at both third base and second base, which could then be made a double play with a quick throw to another base. An attempt to bunt (a light tap of the ball rather than a full swing at it; see below *The bunt*) under the conditions noted above, which results in a fair fly, is not regarded as an infield fly.

Stolen bases. The base runner need not wait on a base until a teammate hits the ball. He may advance at his own risk on the bases at any time the ball is in play, his only restraint being the threat of being tagged out; that is, of being touched with the ball in the hand of a member of the fielding team when he is not on a base. When the pitcher delivers the ball to the batter, the runner can match his speed with the strength and accuracy of the catcher's arm. If the runner makes such an attempt and succeeds in reaching the next base without being tagged out, he is said to have stolen a base. A double steal may be attempted with runners at first and third base. When a runner steals a base, the play is usually so close that he elects to slide into base to avoid the tag. Sliding is common on any close play.

The double steal

The bunt. Nearly every time a batter tries to hit a ball

he takes a full swing, aiming to drive it as fast and as far as he can. There are times, however, when he tries to bunt the ball—that is, tries to tap it lightly with the bat—to make it roll slowly along the ground in fair territory but off as much as possible to one side or the other of a straight line from catcher to pitcher. The bunt is usually intended to be a sacrifice; that is, the batter expects to be thrown out at first base, but one or more runners may be able to proceed to their next base while the ball is being fielded and thrown to first base.

The sacrifice

The batting order. Each of the nine players on a team must take his turn at bat, except as noted below. The first two positions usually are assigned to players fast afoot who make frequent contact with the ball and reach base consistently. The best leadoff hitter is also one who can judge whether the pitch will be a strike or a ball if he lets it pass him without swinging. By waiting out the pitcher, letting the bad pitches pass, he draws many a base on balls. A base on balls for the leadoff hitter is just as good as a single. Getting on base is the leadoff's main offensive function. For batter number two the manager selects a good hit-and-run player, a batter who seldom strikes out and also is skilled in driving the ball toward the right side of the field. For this reason, ideally, he should hit left-handed. A first baseman, when his base is occupied, must play close to the base to prevent the base runner from assuming a large leadoff. This leaves a vacancy between first and second base, an inviting and easy target for a good left-handed batter. The number two batter should also be a capable bunter.

Number three is usually the best all-around offensive player on the team, having running speed combined with batting power and skill. Many of the greatest hitters of all time have been, in the main, number three in their team's batting order—Ty Cobb, Babe Ruth, Rogers Hornsby, Eddie Collins, George Sisler, Joe DiMaggio, Ted Williams, Stan Musial, Willie Mays, Roberto Clemente, Al Kaline, Carl Yastrzemski, and Don Mattingly. Sometimes these hitters batted fourth, however, usually when their teams lacked another outstanding power hitter.

Numbers four and five are the long-distance hitters, not likely to hit the ball safely as often as number three, but often with greater distance. The remaining positions in the batting order scale downward to the highly skilled defensive stars, players whose value to the team is their mastery of their fielding position. Number nine is almost invariably the pitcher, except that in the American League from 1973, the pitcher did not bat. He was replaced in the batting order by a designated hitter (the DH), usually batting in one of the more likely run-producing positions. Because a pitcher is called on for duty only about once in four or five days, the hitting ability of pitchers is rarely considered in evaluating the worth of pitchers. In every other position a player's worth always represents his combined batting and fielding skills.

The designated hitter

Substitutions. Substitutions may be made at any point in the game when time has been called by the umpire. A player taken out of the lineup cannot return in the same game. Without making any substitution, the manager may at any time in the game shift his players from one fielding position to another. He may shift all nine positions in fielding, but he cannot change a player from one place to another in the batting order.

The use of a substitute as an offensive tactic most commonly involves sending in a pinch hitter; that is, taking a weaker hitter out of the lineup and substituting another player whose likelihood for driving the ball for a hit or a fly to the deep outfield is greater than that of the player next up in the batting order. Such a pinch hitter must be a player not already in the lineup nor in the batting order at any previous time in the game. Except where there is a designated hitter, the pinch hitter most often substitutes for the usually weak-hitting pitcher.

Defense. To meet the offensive force of the team at bat, the rules provide the fielding team with ways of making putouts. A putout removes the player from offensive play until his next turn at bat. The batting team's inning continues until three putouts are made; then it goes into the field and the rival team comes to bat.

Putouts. Most putouts are made by (1) striking out the batter; (2) catching a fly; (3) throwing the batter out; or (4) tagging out a base runner. The batter is struck out when the pitcher succeeds in preventing him from hitting the ball into fair territory within the limit of three strikes. Strikes are counted on the batter whenever he swings at a pitched ball and misses or when he does not swing at a pitched ball that passes him inside the strike zone. Umpires signal strikes and putouts with an emphatic movement of the right arm.

The strike zone is a prescribed area in front of the batter. Its top is in line with the midpoint between the top of the shoulders and the top of the uniform pants, and the bottom is in line with the top of the knees. Its long sides extend upward from the straight sides of home plate. The strike zone is thus an imaginary rectangular box 17 inches wide, facing toward the pitcher, the length of its vertical sides depending on the height of the batter. When the ball passes through this rectangular box at any point and the batter does not swing, it is called a strike, as if he had swung and missed. A strike also is counted when the batter fouls the ball to the ground or out of the field of play. Fouling the ball means striking it with the bat but not driving it inside fair territory. This foul strike is not counted if the batter has two strikes against him, provided he swings at the ball in fouling it. If, with two strikes, he fouls in an attempt to bunt—that is, merely blocks the ball with his bat—his foul counts as a third strike.

Foul balls and force outs

A batter is put out if a fielder catches a batted ball before it touches the ground, whether it is a fair ball or foul. A foul tip, a pitched ball that the batter merely flicks slightly with his bat, however, counts only as a strike even if it is caught and held by the catcher and does not count as a putout unless it occurs on the third strike.

A member of the offensive team is tagged out if, when running the bases and not in contact with a base, he is touched by the ball in the hand of a member of the fielding team. A member of the batting team is thrown, or forced, out if he bats a ball that touches the ground before being caught (usually by an infielder or the pitcher) and that is then thrown for the putout to the first baseman, who touches first base before the batter reaches the base.

The force play. Only one runner may have title to a base at any given moment. It is therefore possible for a runner to be thrown out at second base, third, or even at home plate without being tagged. The batter becomes a runner entitled to try to reach first base safely the instant he hits a fair ball that strikes the ground. If there is a teammate on first when the ball is hit, that base runner is no longer entitled to first base and must run to second. If runners are on first and second or on all three bases, they are all forced to run when the batter hits a fair ball that strikes the ground. Any base runner forced to run can be put out, or retired, by a fielder having the ball who can touch the base before the runner reaches it.

This method of retiring base runners is called the force play. With first base occupied and the ball driven along the ground to the pitcher or an infielder, the ball can often be first thrown to second base for a force out of the man from first base, then relayed to the first baseman to retire the batter—two outs on one play, a double play. The second-to-first double play is the most common form.

The double play

A runner can also be thrown out without being tagged if he has left his base before a fly ball is caught. With the catching of the fly, the runner must return to the base he just left before being eligible to advance. If the catcher of the fly throws the ball to that base before the runner returns and touches it, he retires the runner. The runner may attempt to reach the next base after the catch, a tag being required there for the putout.

Intentional pass. Occasionally a base on balls is given not because of the pitcher's inaccuracy (see above *Base on balls*) but for tactical reasons. If, for instance, the team at bat has a runner in scoring position (*i.e.,* on second or third base, or both) but none on first, and especially if the man at bat is more likely to make a safe hit than the man who will follow him in the batting order, it is considered sound tactics to give the batter an intentional pass, or base on balls, to first base. The catcher moves from behind the plate to one side after the pitcher delivers the ball, and the pitcher delivers four pitches that the batter cannot reach while standing in the batter's box. The intentional pass sets up a possible force play at any base and the possibility of a double play if the next batter can be induced to hit a ground ball into the infield.

Substitutions. Defensive substitutions are also common in the late innings of a game when a team is protecting a lead. A fleet-footed outfielder, for example, will replace a slower player who is more valued for his hitting. The most frequent defensive substitution, however, is that of one pitcher for another (see below *Pitching*).

Defensive positions. An outstanding team usually has a star player at each middle position—catcher; "the keystone combination," meaning the second baseman and shortstop; and centre fielder.

Outfielders. The three outfielders are positioned in order to be able to catch batted balls driven reasonably high in the air beyond the infield. The outfielder must be able to judge the trajectory of such flies and have enough speed to run to the point where the ball will come down.

Batted or thrown balls that pass beyond the infielders along the ground must be run down and picked up by the outfielders. Strong throwing arms are essential, as is accuracy in throwing the ball to the right point in the infield. An alert outfielder can also add to his value by moving in as a backup of the infield when the ball has been batted to some point other than his own area and is being thrown about by his teammates in an effort to retire runners. The centre fielder is usually chosen for his speed and expert judgment of fly balls. The centre fielder will not only station himself at a strategic point for each batter but will often direct the playing positions of his outfield teammates on either side. Almost invariably the great defensive outfielders of baseball history, such as Tris Speaker, Max Carey, Terry Moore, Joe DiMaggio, and Willie Mays, have been centre fielders.

Role of the centre fielder

Infielders. The infielders form the inner ring of defense. They sometimes catch line drives on the fly, but mainly they pick up grounders skipping along the ground toward the outfield or shooting swiftly across the grass on one or more bounces. When a batted ball strikes the ground, the play becomes a race between the batter running to first and an infielder gaining control of the ball and throwing it.

UPI

A spectacular fly catch made by Willie Mays (New York Giants, now San Francisco Giants) during the All-Star Game, July 12, 1955.

The four infielders shift positions to guard against each batter's individual power, as do the outfielders. They have the additional responsibility of guarding the bases when occupied. When a ball is batted along the ground, only one of them is called upon to gain control of it, but at least one of the others almost always covers a base to take the throw; sometimes two bases must be covered for a possible throw, and sometimes all three. If an attempted bunt is anticipated, the first and third basemen move in from their accustomed positions toward home plate, ready, as are the pitcher and catcher, to rush toward the bunted ball and to throw it to second, third, or home for the force play or to first to retire the runner.

The shortstop

Each position has its special fielding requirements. Shortstop is the most difficult and demanding of the defensive positions, requiring outstanding agility, range, and a strong throwing arm. The throw from the shortstop to first base is the longest and most difficult. The batted ball may be hit to his right or left or straight at him. He may have to come in quickly on a slow "hopper," or catch a line drive or towering pop-up (a usually easily caught fly). Many of the game's greatest fielding players have been shortstops, among them John ("Honus") Wagner, Dave Bancroft, Luke Appling, Lou Boudreau, Harold ("Pee Wee") Reese, Marty Marion, Luis Aparicio, and Ozzie Smith.

The second baseman's function is very much the same as the shortstop's, but on the right side of the infield. His shorter distance from first gives him an extra instant to throw. On a force play at second, whether or not a part of a double play, either the second baseman or the shortstop must cover second to catch the throw, with his foot touching the base, just as the first baseman does on an out at first. The force play is always a potential double play. The second baseman, coming to the base to take the throw, must turn to his left for the throw to first base to complete the double play. Thus, acrobatic skill in pivoting and avoiding the oncoming runner is vital in a second baseman. Among the great second basemen are Nap Lajoie, Charlie Gehringer, Eddie Collins, Billy Herman, Joe Gordon, and Bill Mazeroski.

The third baseman, playing nearer the batter than the shortstop or second baseman, is not called on to cover as much ground, but his reflexes must be exceptional. The grounder aimed his way reaches him or is past him into the outfield sooner than at second or short. On his most difficult play, the fielding of a bunt or a roller between home plate and his position, the third baseman has a throw to first that is shorter than those the second baseman and shortstop ordinarily make, and he often has more time in which to make it. Harold ("Pie") Traynor, Eddie Mathews, Brooks Robinson, and Mike Schmidt have been considered outstanding third basemen.

The first baseman's fielding of grounders is made easier because of his position near the base that the batter is running toward. Often the first baseman is able to touch base with his foot with ample time to spare after picking up the grounder. When there is no time for that, his throw may be a mere underhand toss to the player (usually the pitcher) who moves over to cover first. When the first baseman plays in for a bunt, the second baseman covers first base. First basemen are often left-handers, an advantage in throwing from their position, and are generally among the most powerful hitters in the lineup; they have included stars such as Lou Gehrig, Jimmie Foxx, Willie McCovey, and Hank Greenberg.

The battery. The pitcher and catcher together are known as the battery or as batterymen. As a fielder, the pitcher may function as an emergency first baseman, and he fields bunts or other infield grounders hit his way.

The catcher, as a fielder, is mainly a catcher of high flies, usually fouls. On such flies, ability to perceive the angle at which the ball leaves the bat is necessary to get a quick start in the right direction from home plate.

Skills of the catcher

The "good hands" essential to every player are especially important for the catcher. Throughout the game he must catch the pitched balls not hit by the batter and sometimes pitches that strike the ground near the plate. When the bat flicks the ball slightly in passing, the catcher's good hands are needed most. If the batter has two strikes, the ability of the catcher to catch such a tipped ball and hold it results in a strikeout. If the ball eludes the catcher's grasp, it becomes a mere foul ball.

The catcher sometimes fields a bunt or a half-hit ball just in front of the plate. Agility in pouncing upon the ball and accuracy in throwing to the proper base are then required. The catcher's throwing arm is a valuable element in his team's defense. Base runners will be cautious of straying too far from their bases when the catcher has a quick and strong arm. When a runner attempts to steal a base, the attempt usually becomes a match between the catcher's throwing arm and the runner's speed. A strong throwing arm has been the hallmark of baseball's greatest catchers, including Mickey Cochrane, Leo ("Gabby") Hartnett, Bill Dickey, Yogi Berra, and Johnny Bench.

Important as is his fielding, the catcher functions even more importantly as the counselor of the pitcher, as well as the rest of the team. As the only player in the defensive lineup who has the whole game in front of him at all times, the catcher is best placed for advising teammates when necessary. In general, the catcher directs the pitching strategy. For most pitchers, and particularly for those with less experience, the catcher, squatting behind the plate with his hands together between his knees, signals with the fingers of his bare hand what the next pitch should be. His knowledge of the pitcher's and the batter's abilities and peculiarities guides him. The catcher keeps his partner under constant study, alert to signs of weakening, even in a veteran pitcher. Occasionally, the catcher consults with the manager to replace one pitcher with another.

Pitching. Until a batter hits the ball, the game is a duel between the pitcher (and catcher) and the batter, which is repeated as each batter comes to bat. Each batter that a pitcher strikes out or forces to hit a pop-up (an easily caught fly) or easily fielded grounder is a gain for the defense, preventing runs and bringing the team closer to its turn at bat and a chance to score.

Until about 1870, the pitcher was merely a player assigned to put the ball in play by pitching it to the batter to hit. One man generally did nearly all the pitching for a club all season, with a change pitcher to relieve him of some of the load. This change pitcher was usually an outfielder, and the two would often merely exchange fielding positions without leaving the game. With the start of league baseball in the 1870s, the pitcher became more important in defensive play. His use of speed and control became a deciding element in championship contests.

Of the 24 players on a major league club's normal active roster, usually 10 are pitchers. In a staff of 10 pitchers, the manager usually names his best four or five at any given time as starting pitchers, or the rotation starters. They take their turn every four or five days, resting in between. The remainder of the staff constitutes the bullpen squad or the relief pitchers. When the manager or pitching coach detects signs of weakening on the part of the pitcher in the game, these bullpen pitchers begin warming up by throwing practice pitches. An effective relief pitcher is one who has good control of his pitches. He often enters the game when the offensive team poses a scoring threat with one or more base runners and a dangerous hitter at bat. Since the early 1950s relief pitching has grown in importance, and it has become extremely difficult for a team to win a championship without a strong bullpen.

Pitching rotation

Control. Pitching demands more exact coordination of mental and muscular faculties and more continuous physical exertion than any other position in the game. On each pitch the pitcher is aiming at the strike zone, or a small part of it, 60 feet six inches from the plate on which his foot pivots in the act of pitching the ball. His ability to throw the ball where he aims it is known as his control. Lapses of control become apparent to the catcher with a slowing up of fast pitches and a dulling in the break of the curve. To the spectators, they are seen as increasing bases on balls and safe hits. Less often, as a pitcher begins to tire, his loss of control may result in hit batters and wild pitches. Each base on balls puts a potential run on first base, as does each batter hit with a pitched ball.

The balk. A balk is an infraction the pitcher can commit with a runner or runners on base. It may occur when: (1) in pitching the ball to the batter, the pitcher does not have his pivoting foot in contact with the pitching plate; (2) the pitcher does not hold the ball in both hands in front of him at chest level before starting his delivery, or, once started, does not continue his motion; or (3) the pitcher starts to make a throw to first base when a runner is occupying that base but does not go through with the throw. When a balk is called by the umpire, all runners on base advance one base each.

The pitching repertoire. A pitcher's speed is usually the index of his general ability. Although the curve was developed in the late 1860s and other variations from the straight line of fastball pitching developed in succeeding epochs, the fastball remains the basis of pitching skill. Some pitchers have been capable of throwing the ball 100 miles per hour. Noted fastball pitchers include Walter Johnson, Robert ("Lefty") Grove, Bob Feller, and Nolan Ryan.

The curveball

The fundamental, or regulation, curve is a swerving pitch that breaks away from the straight line, to the left (the catcher's right) if thrown by a right-handed pitcher, to the right if by a left-hander.

Focus on Sports

Tom Seaver displaying excellent pitching form as he hurls in a game for the New York Mets during the 1975 season.

Some pitchers also employ a curving ball that breaks in the opposite way from the regulation curve, a pitch known variously as the fadeaway (Christy Mathewson), the screwball (Carl Hubbell), or some other name applied by the pitcher himself. The effect is to endow the pitcher with a reverse curve. In both curves and reverse curves, the ball reaches the batter at a slower rate of speed than the fast ball, and the deception is almost as much a result of the slower ball's falling away from the bat as of its swerving from a straight trajectory.

A comparatively new pitch, called the slider, was introduced in the 1920s by George Blaeholder, who otherwise had an undistinguished major league career. The slider is a cross between the fast ball and the curve and includes the best features of both. It is thrown with the speed and the pitching motion of the fast ball, but, instead of the wide sweep of the conventional curve, it has a short and mostly lateral break; in effect, it slides away from the hitter.

Relatively few pitchers use the knuckleball, the power of which lies in its lack of axial rotation, making it subject to air currents. No one, including the pitcher, knows exactly how any knuckleball pitch will behave. The ball is wobbly as it approaches the batter and so is harder to hit solidly than a spinning ball. The knuckleball, however, is difficult to catch, and rather often it is missed by the catcher (a passed ball). The knuckler is thrown with an easy, almost lobbing, motion, and, because of the minimal arm strain, knuckleball pitchers may have remarkable longevity.

In the 1970s the premier relief pitcher, Bruce Sutter, introduced the split-finger fast ball, which broke downward at the plate in a motion often compared, with some exaggeration, to a ball rolling off a table. In the early days of organized baseball, artificial aids were allowed the pitcher in throwing what was called the spit ball. Simple saliva, saliva produced by chewing tobacco or sucking on slippery elm, or sweat was applied to the ball. The ball thus treated dropped sharply at the plate. The pitch was outlawed in 1920, though pitchers then using it were allowed the pitch until they retired. Since then, pitchers have from time to time been suspected of using it.

Illegal pitches

Similar effects have been sought by those who illegally scar the surface of the ball with a sharp object like a belt buckle or tack or with an abrasive tool, such as a file or emery board. Some batters, for their part, have looked for illegal advantage by drilling a hole down the barrel of a bat and filling it with cork or rubber balls, which decreases weight and increases bat speed and "liveliness."

(Je.Ho./G.P.L.)

Cricket

Cricket, England's national summer sport, is a game of skill played with bat and ball between two teams of 11 players each on a large field. It is played throughout the world, particularly in the British Isles and the Commonwealth, and matches range from informal, weekend afternoon encounters on village greens to top-level international contests spread over five days and played between leading professional players in grand stadiums.

The teams take turns at batting (an innings) and bowling, changing places at the conclusion of an innings. Teams have one or two innings each depending on the prearranged duration of the match, and the object of the game is for one side to score more runs than the other. The batting side defends its wickets (two sets of three sticks set in the ground 22 yards [20.12 metres] apart at the centre of the field) and attempts to score runs by hitting the ball and running to the far wicket or by hitting the ball to or beyond the marked boundaries of the field. The bowlers, delivering the ball with a straight arm, try to break (hit, so that the bails [see below *Play of the game*] fall) the wicket with the ball, which is one of several ways that the batsman is dismissed, or put out.

HISTORY

Origin. Cricket is believed to have begun as a game in which country boys bowled at a tree stump or at the hurdle gate into a sheep pen. This gate consisted of two uprights and a crossbar resting on the slotted tops; the crossbar was called a bail and the whole gate a wicket. The fact that the bail could be dislodged when the wicket was struck made this preferable to the stump, which name was later applied to the hurdle uprights. Early manuscripts differ about the size of the wicket, which acquired a third stump about 1780, but by 1706 the pitch, the area between the wickets, was 22 yards long.

The ball, once presumably a stone, has remained much the same since the 17th century, weighing between five and six ounces (140 and 170 grams). Its modern weight was laid down in 1774 and its circumference standardized in 1838. The primitive bat was no doubt a shaped branch of a tree, resembling a modern hockey stick but considerably longer and heavier. The change to a straight bat was made to meet the cult of length bowling (see below *Bowling*), which had been evolved by the Hambledon cricketers. The bat was shortened in the handle and straightened and broadened in the blade, which led to forward play, driving, and cutting (see below *Batting*). As few bowlers were able to combine length with break, swerve, and flight, batting dominated bowling through the 18th century.

The early bat

The early years. The earliest reference to an 11-a-side match, played in Sussex for a stake of 50 guineas, dates from 1697. In 1709 Kent met Surrey in the first recorded intercounty match at Dartford, and it is probable that around this time a code of laws (rules) existed for the conduct of the game, although the earliest known version of importance is dated 1744. Sources suggest that cricket was limited to the southern counties of England during the early 18th century, but it was soon discovered by society and transferred to London, notably at the Artillery Ground, Finsbury, which saw a famous match between Kent and All-England in 1744. Heavy betting and disorderly crowds were common at matches.

The Hambledon Club, playing in Hampshire on Broadhalfpenny Down, was the predominant cricket force in the second half of the 18th century before the rise of the Marylebone Cricket Club (MCC) in London. Founded in 1787, the MCC had its home from the outset at Lord's Cricket Ground, which was named after its founder, Thomas Lord, and has become the headquarters of world cricket. In the following year the MCC published a revised code of laws, of which it remains the controlling body for world cricket, although it has ceded authority in England (see below *Reorganization*).

Lord's Cricket Ground and the MCC

In 1836 the first North counties versus South counties match was played, clear evidence of the spread of cricket. In 1846 the All England XI, founded by William Clarke, of Nottingham, began touring the country, and from 1852, when some of the leading professionals seceded to form the United All England XI, these two teams monopolized the best cricket talent until the rise of county cricket (see below *County cricket*). They supplied the players for the first English touring team overseas to Canada and the United States, in 1859.

Sport and General Press Agency

Sir Donald Bradman (Australia) at the finish of a cut. S.C. Griffith (England) is wicketkeeper, and W.J. Edrich is at slip. Bradman established Australian and Test match records between 1928 and 1948.

Technical development. Until early in the 19th century all bowling was underhanded, and most bowlers favoured the high tossed lob. The next bowling development was "the round arm revolution," in which many bowlers began raising the point at which they released the ball. Controversy raged furiously, and in 1835 the MCC rephrased the law to allow the hand to be raised as high as the shoulder. The new style led to a great increase in pace, or bowling speed. Gradually bowlers raised the hand higher and higher in defiance of the law. Matters were brought to a head in 1862 when an England team playing against Surrey left the field at London's Kennington Oval in protest against one of their number's being no-balled (penalized for throwing an unfair pitch) for raising his bowling arm above the shoulder. As a result of the incident, in 1864 the bowler was officially accorded full liberty to bowl overhand. From time to time umpires have had trouble with bowlers who, rather than bowling the ball, illegally "threw" it (*i.e.*, cocked and then, in the release, straightened the arm).

Bowling methods

The batsmen now learned to protect themselves better with pads and tubular rubber batting gloves, and a cane handle increased the resilience of the bat. Only the best batsmen, however, could cope with fast bowling because most pitches were bad. As the grounds improved, the batsmen went over to the offensive.

In the early 20th century so many runs were being scored that a reform of the leg-before-wicket law (introduced in the 1774 laws against a batsman deliberately preventing the ball from hitting his wicket) was debated, and the MCC denounced the overpreparation of pitches. But the heavy scores were due primarily to the performances of several outstanding batsmen. This was cricket's golden age.

The googly and new bowling styles

There now appeared in cricketing vocabulary the googly, a word coined in Australia when B.J.T. Bosanquet, on the 1903–04 MCC tour, first exploited his ability to bowl an offbreak with a leg-break action. Other new bowling styles were also discovered, causing batsmen to adjust their technique.

The reaction of authority to the evolution of cricket in the 20th century was visible in a series of attempts to help the bowler and to quicken the tempo of the game. As early as 1902 the bowling crease had been extended in length; in 1907 the use of a new ball after every 200 runs had been legalized; in 1918–19 the eight-ball over was first used in Australia (it became standard for many years there and in South Africa, New Zealand, and the West Indies); in 1927 a smaller ball was authorized; in 1937 the leg-before-wicket law was extended to cover balls pitching outside the off stump; in 1947 the size of the wicket, increased in 1931, was established at its present size; and in the 1980s daily minimum numbers of overs to be bowled were established in Test and county cricket.

The Bettmann Archive

Probably the most renowned cricketer of all, W.G. Grace (right), of Victorian England, batting in an 1890s match. J.P. Dorman is wicketkeeper.

County cricket. Although the press acclaimed a "champion county" as early as 1827, qualification rules for county cricket were not laid down until 1873, and it was only in 1890 that the format of the county championship was formalized by the counties themselves. Gloucestershire dominated the 1870s, thanks to the legendary W(illiam) G(ilbert) Grace and his brothers E.M. and G.F. Grace. From the 1880s to World War I, Nottinghamshire, Surrey, Yorkshire, Lancashire, Kent, and Middlesex constituted the Big Six that dominated county cricket. After World War I the northern counties, led by Yorkshire and Lancashire, largely professional teams, were the leaders. Surrey, with seven successive championships, dominated in the 1950s and Yorkshire in the 1960s, followed by Kent and Middlesex in the 1970s.

The legendary W.G. Grace

After a postwar boom slow play and lower numbers of runs characterized the 1950s, and this defensive nature of county cricket led to progressively decreased attendance. In the 1960s the MCC and the counties introduced a one-day knockout competition (the Gillette Cup—since 1981 the NatWest Bank Trophy) and a separate Sunday afternoon league, which revived public interest, although most counties remained dependent financially on proceeds from football pools and money received from Test (international) matches and broadcasting fees. The immediate registration of overseas players was permitted, and each county was allowed one such player, who, however, could still play for his national team. While the change worked well for the counties, it also strengthened the national teams for whom those players appeared. In county cricket, bonus points were created to encourage batsmen and bowlers to be more attacking, and in 1988, to help the development of young batsmen and spin bowlers, a limited number of four-day games partially replaced the hitherto traditional three-day format for the county championship.

Other first-class cricket. From 1806 (annually from 1819) to 1962, the Gentlemen versus Players match pitted the best amateurs against the best professionals. The series was ended in 1962 when the MCC and the counties abandoned the distinction between amateurs and professionals. The Oxford versus Cambridge match has been played mainly at Lord's since 1827. University cricket was a kind of nursery for county cricket, and the match became a high point of the summer season in London.

Reorganization: the Cricket Council. A reorganization of the administration of English cricket took place in 1969, resulting in the end of the MCC's long reign as the controlling body of the game, though it still retained responsibility for the laws. With the setting up of the Sports Council (a government agency charged with control of sports in Great Britain) and with the possibility of obtaining government grant aid for cricket, the MCC was asked to create a governing body of the game on the lines generally accepted by other sports in Great Britain. Thus was inaugurated the Cricket Council, comprising the Test and County Cricket Board (TCCB), the National Cricket Association (NCA), and the MCC. The TCCB, which amalgamated the Advisory County Cricket Committee and the Board of Control of Test matches at Home, is responsible for all first-class and minor counties cricket in England and for overseas tours. The NCA consists of representatives from clubs, schools, and armed services cricket, umpires, and the Women's Cricket Association.

End of MCC control

International cricket. The English introduced cricket wherever a ground was available and two teams could be collected. The firmest roots are in those countries that were members of the Imperial Cricket Conference. The conference was founded in 1909 by England, Australia, and South Africa (which ceased to be a member on leaving the Commonwealth in 1961), and they were joined as full members by India, New Zealand, and the West Indies in 1926 and Pakistan in 1952. In 1965 the conference was renamed the International Cricket Conference and brought in as associate members the United States, Sri Lanka, and Fiji, followed by Bermuda, The Netherlands, Denmark, East Africa, Malaysia, Canada, Gibraltar, Hong Kong, Papua New Guinea, Argentina, Israel, Singapore, West Africa, Bangladesh, Kenya, and Zimbabwe. In 1981 Sri Lanka was elevated to full-member status, and from 1984 Italy, Switzerland, The Bahamas, France, and Nepal entered in a subsidiary class of affiliate membership.

Australia. Cricket began in Australia in 1803, introduced by a British ship's crew, and play among cricket clubs began in the mid-1820s. The first interstate match took place in 1856, and the first English touring team was received in 1861–62. In 1892–93 New South Wales, Victoria, and South Australia contested the Sheffield Shield, presented by Lord Sheffield, who had taken an English team to Australia in 1891–92. Queensland joined the competition in 1926–27, Western Australia in 1947–48, and Tasmania in 1977–78. A one-day knockout competition began in 1969–70. Each state has an association of affiliated clubs that controls players and grounds. Clubs are graded and competitions are arranged for each grade. First-grade teams, in which novices play with great cricketers, are the recruiting ground for the state team.

National cups and trophies

New Zealand. Cricket was first played in New Zealand in the 1840s, and the first interprovincial match was played between Auckland and Wellington in 1860. In South Island, the discovery of gold in Otago brought many Australians, who helped to spread the game. An English team first visited the country in 1864.

The New Zealand Cricket Council was formed in 1894. Each province has its own association, made up of delegates from affiliated clubs. The Plunket Shield, donated by a former governor general, has been played for annually since 1906–07 by Auckland, Wellington, Canterbury,

F.S. Trueman bowling for England in a Test match against Australia. Batsman A.K. Davidson and umpire J. Langridge watch the delivery. Trueman took a world-record number of wickets in Test matches in the period 1952–65.

Sport and General Press Agency

Otago, Northern Districts, and Central Districts. It was replaced in 1975–76 by the Shell Series.

West Indies. Cricket began in the West Indies in the early 19th century, but the first intercolonial match took place in 1865 between Barbados and Demerara (now Guyana). In 1891 a triangular tournament was contested between Demerara, Barbados, and Trinidad, and in 1894–95 the first English team visited. In 1927 a board representing all the islands was set up to control competitions and to organize overseas tours. Jamaica joined the other three in a knockout tournament in 1956. In 1965–66 the Windward Islands and the Leeward Islands joined the others in an annual competition for the Shell Shield, succeeded in 1987–88 by the Red Stripe Cup.

India. English settlers introduced cricket in India during the 18th century, and the army helped to popularize it. The first all-Indian club was the Orient Cricket Club, formed in 1848 by the Parsis, a religious sect. In 1877 the Parsis defeated the Europeans in Bombay, and this encouraged the Parsis to send teams to England in 1886 and 1888. The first English side visited India in 1889–90.

The Bombay Pentangular series

In 1892–93 the Parsis met the Europeans in the Presidency Matches, which developed into the Bombay Pentangular series with the additional participation of the Hindus, Muslims, and a team not ethnically connected to the above groups called "The Rest." In 1926–27 the MCC sent a strong side to India, and the princes began to pick their own sides and to employ professional English coaches. A national championship was instituted in 1934–35 for the Ranji Trophy, and the zonal Duleep Trophy was introduced in 1961–62.

Pakistan. After partition in 1947, Pakistan staged its initial first-class match in February 1948. A national championship for the Qā'id-e A'zam (Great Leader) trophy, named for Mohammed Ali Jinnah, one of the creators of Pakistan, was begun in 1953–54 and was later joined by the Patron's Trophy tournament and the Pakistan Automobile Corporation (PACO) tournament.

South Africa. Cricket was taken to South Africa in the early 19th century by British troops, and by the time the first English side visited in 1888–89 the game was established in several centres. The Currie Cup, the main domestic championship, began the following year.

Since the late 1960s race and politics have dominated cricket in South Africa. It was cut off from most of its traditional international competition in 1970 because of its apartheid (racial separation) policies. In 1977, with the fusion of the three existing national bodies into the South African Cricket Union, the game became officially nonracial, but controversy continued, as did the international ban.

Sri Lanka. The first Ceylonese cricket club was formed in Colombo in 1832, and from 1887 until the 1930s the main match of the season was Europeans (locals) against Ceylonese. The first visiting English side came in 1882, and it was England who provided the opposition in Sri Lanka's inaugural Test match 100 years later.

Test matches. The first Test (international) match, played by two national teams of the best players, was between Australia and England in Melbourne in 1877, Australia winning. When Australia again won at the Oval at Kennington, London, in 1882, the *Sporting Times* printed an obituary notice announcing that English cricket would be cremated and the ashes taken to Australia, thus creating the "play for the Ashes." The Ashes, kept in an urn at Lord's irrespective of which country is victorious, are those of a stump or bail burned on the England tour of Australia in 1882–83. For the rest of the 19th century, the two countries met almost yearly. With W.G. Grace, the greatest cricketer of Victorian England, on its side, England was generally too strong, though Australia had the greatest bowler of his era in F.R. Spofforth and the first of the great wicketkeepers in J.McC. Blackham.

The "Ashes"

In 1907 South Africa first played Test matches in England and also took on Australia, whose dominance between the two world wars was symbolized by the prodigious run scoring of D.G. (later Sir Donald) Bradman. This period saw a notable growth in the number of Test-match countries, with the arrival of the West Indies in 1928, New Zealand in 1930, and India in 1932. The visit of the English side to Australia, in 1932–33 severely strained relations between the countries because of the "bodyline" (leg theory) bowling tactics, in which the ball is bowled close to or at the batsman; this scheme was devised by the English captain, D.R. Jardine, to curb Bradman's scoring.

After World War II there were Test matches in England every summer, Australia being the most frequent visitor, and the Test ranks were increased by the addition of Pakistan in 1952. With interest stimulated by radio and television broadcasts and extensive newspaper coverage, there was a steady escalation of tours between the Test-playing countries, to the extent that while the first 500 Test matches were spread over 84 years, the next 500 occupied only 23. Sri Lanka's entry as the eighth Test-playing nation in 1982 came during an era dominated by the West Indies, whose attack was devastatingly founded, for the first time in cricket history, on four fast bowlers.

Test crises of the late 1960s

Test cricket has faced a number of crises since the late 1960s. One of these occurred in 1969–70, causing a South African tour of England to be canceled because of opposition to the South African racial separation policy. Violence, damage, and disruption of play had been

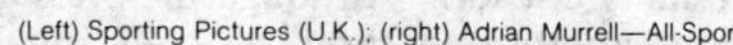

(Left) Sporting Pictures (U.K.); (right) Adrian Murrell—All-Sport

Ian Botham (left) of Great Britain, an outstanding all-around player, bowling. Sunil Gavaskar (right) of India, displaying his exceptional batting skill.

threatened. A further threat to Test cricket was posed by an Australian television network executive, Kerry Packer, who signed many of the world's leading players for a series of private contests between 1977 and 1979. Reprisals were brought against the players but were overruled after court action in England. The players returned to the fold, but commercialism had taken hold of the game. In 1982 the agreement of 12 first-class English players to take part, in breach of official guidelines, in a commercially-sponsored South African tour with fees of up to £50,000 per player led to the players' being banned from Test cricket for three years. Cricketers from Sri Lanka and the West Indies also toured to South Africa and received more stringent sanctions, and the engagement of English professionals as players and coaches in South Africa threatened a serious division between the Test-playing countries.

One-day internationals—answering the complaint that Test matches went on too long—began in 1972. In 1975 England, Australia, the West Indies, New Zealand, India, Pakistan, Sri Lanka, and East Africa contested the first World Cup in England in a series of one-day matches of 60 overs a side. The event was a great success and continued at four-year intervals. It was held outside England, in India and Pakistan, for the first time in 1987. By this stage the one-day international was supplanting the five-day Test match in public appeal.

Women's cricket. Women first played cricket in England in the 18th century. In 1887 the first club, White Heather, was formed, and it survived to 1957. In 1890 two professional teams known collectively as the Original English Lady Cricketers were in action.

In 1926 the Women's Cricket Association was founded and in 1934–35 sent a team to Australia and New Zealand. Australia paid a return visit in 1937, and since World War II tours have increased. The International Women's Cricket Council was formed in 1958 by Australia, England, The Netherlands, New Zealand, and South Africa and later included India, Denmark, and several West Indian islands. A World Cup was instituted in 1973, two years ahead of men's cricket, and England and Australia played in the first women's matches at Lord's in 1976.

The International Women's Cricket Council

PLAY OF THE GAME

Field of play and equipment. *The ground.* Cricket grounds vary in size from great arenas such as Lord's in London ($5\frac{1}{2}$ acres [two hectares]) and Melbourne Cricket Ground that is even larger ($9\frac{1}{4}$ acres) to village greens and small meadows. Level turf of fine texture is the ideal surface, but where this is unavailable, any artificial covered surface, such as coir matting or artificial turf on a firm base, may be used. The limits of the playing area are usually marked by a boundary line or fence (see Figure 3).

Wicket and creases. A wicket consists of three stumps or stakes, each 28 inches (71.1 centimetres) high and of equal thickness (about $1\frac{1}{4}$ inches in diameter), stuck into the ground and so spaced that the ball cannot pass between them. Two pieces of wood called bails, each $4\frac{3}{8}$ inches (11.1 centimetres) long, lie in grooves on the tops of the stumps. The bails do not extend beyond the stumps and do not project more than half an inch above them. The whole wicket is nine inches (22.86 centimetres) in width. There are two of these wickets, which a batsman defends and a bowler attacks, and they are approximately in the centre of the ground, facing one another at each end of the pitch (also sometimes called the wicket), which is an area 22 yards (20.12 metres) long and 10 feet (3.04 metres) wide between the wickets.

Bowling, return, and popping creases

Lines of whitewash demarcate the creases at each wicket: the bowling crease is a line drawn through the base of the stumps and extending four feet four inches (1.32 metres) on either side of the centre stump; the return crease is a line at each end of and at right angles to the bowling crease, extending behind the wicket; and the popping crease is a line parallel with the bowling crease and four feet in front of it. The bowling and return creases mark the area within which the bowler's rear foot must be grounded in delivering the ball; the popping crease, which is 62 feet (18.90 metres) from the opposing bowling crease, demarks the batsman's ground.

Bat and ball. The blade of the paddle-shaped bat is made of willow and must not be broader than $4\frac{1}{4}$ inches (10.8 centimetres). The length of the bat, including the handle, must not exceed 38 inches (96.5 centimetres). The ball, which has a core of cork built up with string, is encased in polished red leather, the halves of which are sewn together with a raised seam. Slightly smaller, harder, and heavier than a baseball, it must weigh between $5\frac{1}{2}$ and $5\frac{3}{4}$ ounces (156 and 163 grams) and be between $8\frac{13}{16}$ and nine inches (22.4 and 22.9 centimetres) in circumference.

Dress. Players usually wear white trousers and shirt, white boots (shoes), a white sweater, often trimmed with club colours, and club caps of kaleidoscopic variety. The batsman wears white pads (leg guards), an abdominal protector, and batting gloves reinforced to protect the fingers; at the top levels of the game batsmen also wear helmets, sometimes with a face guard, and other body protection. The wicketkeeper also wears pads and reinforced gauntlets (the other fielders do not wear gloves).

Rules of the game. One player on each team acts as captain. There are two umpires, one standing behind the bowler's wicket, the other at square leg about 15 yards from the batsman's popping crease (see Figure 3), to control the game according to the laws; two scorers record its progress. The object of the game is for one side to score more runs than the other.

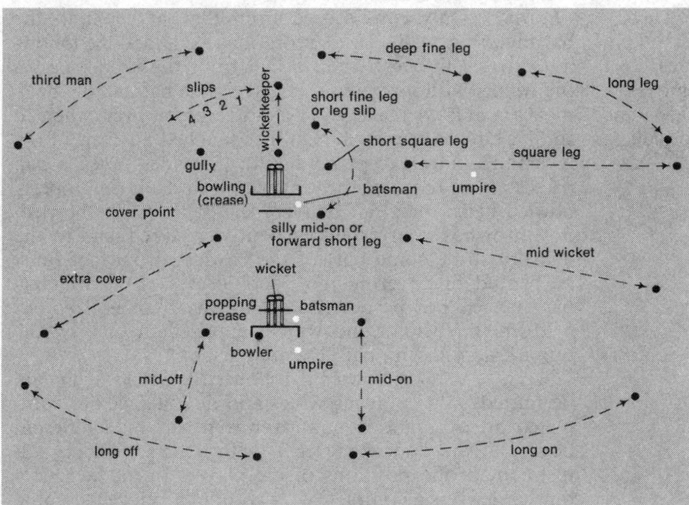

Figure 3: Location of wickets and principal playing positions on cricket field.

At the start of a match, the captain who wins the toss of a coin decides whether his own or the other side shall take first innings (always plural); *i.e.,* proceed successively as batsmen—the first two as a pair together—to the wicket and try to make as many runs as possible against the bowling and fielding of their opponents. An innings is completed when 10 batsmen have been dismissed (the remaining batsman, having no partner, is declared "not out"), when the captain of the batting side declares his innings closed before all 10 men are out, or, in a match of one innings a side, when the allotted number of overs expires. Results are recorded by the margin of runs, or, if the side batting last passes the other side's total before all their batsmen have been dismissed, by the number of their wickets (*i.e.,* batsmen still to be dismissed) outstanding.

Scoring innings and matches

Matches are decided either by the number of runs scored in one innings each (usually one-day matches), or on the aggregate of runs made by each side in two innings. International (Test) matches last five or six days (30 playing hours), other first-class matches from three to four days, and the bulk of club, school, and village matches one day.

The nonbatting side takes up positions in the field. One man is the bowler, another is the wicketkeeper, and the remaining nine are positioned as the captain or the bowler directs (see Figure 3). The first batsman (the striker) guards his wicket by standing with at least one foot behind the popping crease. His partner (the nonstriker) waits behind the popping crease at the bowler's end. The bowler tries to hit the batsman's wicket or to dismiss him in other ways (see below *Methods of dismissal*).

Runs. The batsman tries to keep the bowler from hitting the wicket, while also trying to hit the ball sufficiently hard to score a run; *i.e.,* enable him to run to the other end of the pitch before any fieldsman can pick up the ball and throw it to either wicket to knock off the bails. If the wicket is broken, either by a thrown ball or by the wicketkeeper or bowler with ball in hand, before either batsman is in his ground, the batsman is dismissed. The striker does not have to run after he has hit the ball, nor does it count in any way if he misses the ball or if his body is struck by it. But if he gets a good hit and thinks he can score a run, he races for the opposite wicket and his partner runs toward him. When each has made good his ground by touching his bat beyond the popping crease at the opposite end, one run is recorded to the striker; if there is time, they will run back for a second or more runs, crossing again. If an even number of runs is scored, the striker will receive the next ball; if an odd number, then the nonstriker will be at the wicket opposite the bowler and will face the next ball. Any runs thus made count to the batsman, otherwise they are extras. When a ball from a hit or any of the extras mentioned below goes as far as the boundary, the runners stop and four runs are scored. If the batsman hits the ball full pitch over the boundary (on the fly) he scores six runs.

Extras. Only runs scored from the bat count to the batsman, but to the side's score may be added the following extras: (1) byes (when a ball from the bowler passes the wicket without being touched by the bat and the batsmen are able to make good a run); (2) leg byes (when in similar circumstances the ball has touched any part of the batsman's body except his hand); (3) wides (when a ball passes out of reach of the striker); (4) no balls (improperly bowled balls; for a fair delivery the ball must be bowled, not thrown, the arm neither bent nor jerked, and in the delivery stride some part of the bowler's front foot must be behind or covering the popping crease), off which a batsman cannot be out (except as noted under *Methods of dismissal* below) and which, apprised in time by the umpire's cry of "no ball," he may try to hit.

Byes, leg byes, wides, and no balls

Overs. When a bowler has bowled six balls (eight are permitted), not counting wides and no balls, he has completed an over and a new over is begun by a different bowler at the opposite wicket, with a corresponding adjustment of the positions of the players in the field. If a bowler delivers a complete over without a run being scored from the bat (even though the opponents may have scored extras by means of byes or leg byes), he has achieved a maiden over.

Methods of dismissal. There are 10 ways in which a batsman or striker can be dismissed (put out), the most usual being:

Bowled. The batsman is out bowled if the bowler breaks the wicket; *i.e.,* dislodges a bail with the ball.

Caught. He is out caught if a ball hit by the batsman is caught before it touches the ground.

Stumped. He is out stumped if, in playing a stroke, he is outside the popping crease (out of his ground) and the wicket is broken by the wicketkeeper with ball in hand.

Leg before wicket. Essentially, leg before wicket (lbw) is illegal interference, whether accidental or intentional, with a ball that otherwise, in the opinion of the umpire, would hit the wicket. The batsman is out lbw if he intercepts with any part of his person, except his hand, that is in line between wicket and wicket, a ball that has not first touched his bat or his hand and that has or would have pitched (hit the ground) in a straight line between the wickets or on the off side provided the ball would have hit the wicket. The batsman may also be out lbw if he intercepts the ball outside the off stump having made no genuine attempt to play the ball with his bat.

Run out. Either batsman is out run out if, while the ball is in play, his wicket is broken while he is out of his ground. If the batsmen have passed each other, the one running for the wicket that is broken is out; if they have not crossed, the one running from that wicket is out.

Hit wicket. The batsman is out hit wicket if he breaks his own wicket with his bat or any part of his person while playing the ball or setting off for a run.

Less usual ways of dismissal are:

Handled the ball. Either batsman is out if, with the hand not holding the bat, he willfully touches the ball while it is in play, unless with the consent of the opposing side.

Hitting the ball twice. Batsman is out if he hits the ball, except in defense of his wicket, after it has been struck or stopped by any part of his person.

Obstructing the field. Either batsman is out if he willfully obstructs the opposite side by word or action.

Timed out. An incoming batsman is out if he willfully takes more than two minutes to come in.

Strategy and technique. The disposition of the field will vary widely according to the technique of the bowler or of the batsman, the condition of the pitch, the state of the game, and the tactics determined by the captain. He may place his fieldsmen as he thinks best, and he may alter their positions, if he wishes, after each ball. There are no foul lines in cricket so a hit in any direction is a fair ball. The objectives of the captain of the fielding side are: (1) to place his men in positions where the batsman may give a catch; *i.e.,* hit a drive or a fly ball to a fielder and (2) to save runs; *i.e.,* to block the path of the ball from the batsman's scoring strokes (intercept or trap grounders). The tactical possibilities for a captain in directing his bowlers and fieldsmen and the batsmen are manifold and constitute one of the attractions of the game.

As there are only 11 players on a team and two of them must be the bowler and wicketkeeper, only nine other positions can be occupied at any one time. The field is spoken of as being divided lengthwise into off and on, or leg, sides in relation to the batsmen's stance, depending upon whether he bats right- or left-handed; the off side is the side facing the batsman, and the on, or leg, side is the side behind him as he stands to receive the ball.

Fielding positions

To sum up, the objective of the bowler is primarily to get the batsman out and only secondarily to prevent him from getting runs, though these objectives have tended to become reversed in one-day, limited-overs cricket. The objective of the batsman is to protect his wicket first and then to make runs, for only runs can win a match. The objective of each fielder is, first, to dismiss the batsmen, and, second, to prevent the striker making runs.

Bowling. Bowling can be right- or left-arm. For a fair delivery, the ball must be propelled, usually overhand, without bending the elbow. The bowler may run any desired number of paces as a part of his delivery (with the restriction, of course, that he not cross the popping crease). The ball generally hits the ground (the pitch) before reaching the batsman, although it need not. The first requisite of a good bowler is command of length; *i.e.,* the ability to pitch (bounce) the ball on a desired spot, usually at or slightly in front of the batsman's feet, and varying with the pace of the bowler, the state of the pitch, and the reach and technique of the batsman. The second requisite is command of direction. On this foundation a bowler may elaborate with variations—finger spin, swerve, alteration of pace and flight, the path of the ball, and the manner in which it is propelled—that lend deceptiveness and uncertainty as to exactly where and how it will pitch. A good-length ball is one that causes the batsman to be uncertain whether to move forward to play his stroke or to move back. A half volley is a ball pitched so far up to the batsman that he can drive it fractionally after it has hit the ground without having to move forward. A yorker is a ball pitched on or inside the popping crease. A full pitch is a ball that the batsmen can reach before it hits the ground. A long hop is a ball short of good length.

Length and spin in bowling

The primary purpose of the spin is to bring the ball up from the pitch at an angle that is difficult for the batsman to anticipate. The two swerves are the inswinger, which moves in the air from off to leg, and the away swinger, or outswinger, which swerves from leg to off.

Batting. A batsman may hit right-handed or left-handed. Good batting is based on a straight (*i.e.,* vertical) bat with its full face presented to the ball, although a cross (*i.e.,* horizontal) bat can be used effectively to deal

Batting strokes

with short bowling. The chief strokes are: forward stroke, in which the batsman advances his front leg to the pitch (direction) of the ball and plays it in front of the wicket (if played with aggressive intent, this stroke becomes the drive); back stroke, in which the batsman moves his rear leg back before playing the ball; leg glance (or glide), in which the ball is deflected behind the wicket on the leg side; cut, in which the batsman hits a ball on the uprise (after it has hit the ground on the off side), square with or behind the wicket; and pull or hook, in which the batsman hits a ball on the uprise through the leg side.

Fielding. The ideal fieldsman is a fast runner, with quick reactions and the ability to throw quickly and accurately. He should be able to anticipate the batsman's strokes, to move quickly to cut off the ball in its path, and to judge the flight of the ball in the air to make a safe catch.

Wicketkeeping. The wicketkeeper is a key member of the fielding side. He takes position behind the striker's wicket, 10 to 20 yards back for the fast bowlers or directly behind for those of slower pace. He must concentrate on every ball, being ready to stop a ball that passes the wicket, to stump a batsman if he leaves his ground, or to receive a ball returned to him by a fielder. (M.K.W./R.Al.)

Association football (soccer)

Association football, called soccer in the United States, is usually played outdoors, between two teams of 11 players each with the object of putting a ball by kicking or butting into the opposing team's goal. It is the most widely played ball game in the world and the most popular as a spectator sport. The simplicity of the rules and the ability to play it practically everywhere has contributed to this popularity. It is played on all continents and in well over 150 countries. At the last census by the world governing body, there were 40,000,000 registered players at all levels. In addition, there are many thousands of others in numerous countries involved in pickup games in streets, on parking lots, on school playgrounds, in parks, and even, as in Brazil, on beaches. At the 1984 summer Olympic Games the football matches registered almost 1,500,000 spectators, the highest number for any Olympic sport. The world's largest football stadium, in Rio de Janeiro, holds crowds of up to 200,000 for football matches.

HISTORY

Origins. From antiquity, games existed in which two teams, or sides, attempted to kick, push, or otherwise propel a ball in opposite directions toward the opponents' goal. The ball varied in shape from round to oval as it does today. A football game was played in China as early as 206 BC, and by AD 500 round footballs stuffed with hair were in use. In ancient Greece a game with elements of football, *episkuros,* or *harpaston,* was played, and it had migrated to Rome as *harpastum* by the 2nd century BC. In this game play began with a ball being thrown in the air between two teams, each of which tried to push it beyond the opponents' goal line. Roman legions may have introduced the game throughout Europe and in England during the Roman occupation (AD 43/44–410). One report has the Irish kicking a stuffed ball even earlier.

In 7th-century Japan there was a football game. In the 14th century *calcio* ("kick") was played in Florence; it persists as a festival game. Also in medieval Europe there were mob games, called *mêlées,* or mellays, in which a ball, usually an inflated animal bladder, was advanced by kicking, punching, and carrying. As many as 100 players from two towns or parishes started at a midpoint and used their localities' limits as goals. King Richard II of England banned the game in 1389 because it interfered with archery practice, and later monarchs issued similar proscriptions into the 15th century, to little effect.

The medieval *mêlée*

Shrove Tuesday was a traditional football day in both England and Scotland from the 12th century. At Chester the game was said to be in commemoration of the day in 217 when a mighty flying wedge drove the Romans out. A similar explanation was given for a game celebrating the driving out of the Danes from Kingston-on-Thames in the 8th century. The field in later games came to be from 80 to 100 yards (about 73 to 91 metres) long with a goal at each end formed by driving two sticks in the ground two or three feet (0.6–0.9 metre) apart. The ball was an inflated bladder encased in leather. When one team drove the ball through the opponent's goal, the game ended.

Football in a less violent form was played in England from the 17th century by youths from wealthy and aristocratic families at public (*i.e.,* private) schools, although the authorities frowned on it as too rowdy for young gentlemen. Rules varied from school to school, but all forbade running with the round ball or passing it forward.

The early years. When association football arose in England, it was first played as a winter game between residence houses at public schools such as Winchester, Charterhouse, and Eton but not often between schools, for each school had its own rules, some allowing limited handling of the ball and others not. Public schoolboys who went up to the universities could not play football there except with old schoolmates. An attempt to codify rules and remove differences was made at Cambridge University in 1843, and in 1846 most of the public schools adopted what were called the Cambridge rules, which were also used at that university and later by graduates who formed football clubs. Then in 1862 and 1863 a series of meetings of school and nonschool clubs in the London area and surrounding counties agreed to print the rules and by so doing left the rugby game outside of the newly formed Football Association (FA).

The Cambridge rules

The new rules were not at once universally accepted; many clubs continued to play their own, especially in and around Sheffield, the first provincial club to join the FA. In 1867 the Sheffield Football Association was founded, the forerunner of county associations formed later. Sheffield and London played two matches in 1866, and in 1867 a match pitting Middlesex against Kent and Surrey was played under the revised rules. In 1871 all 15 FA clubs were invited to subscribe for purchase of a trophy cup to be played for by all clubs. By 1877, 43 clubs were competing, and the original dominance of the London area began to diminish. By the end of the 1870s only the Scottish Association rules varied from the FA's. Attendance grew until in 1893 the final Cup game drew 45,000 spectators, in 1897 more than 65,000, and in 1901 more than 100,000.

Professionalism. Professionalism became an issue in 1884, and two clubs were excluded from the FA for using professional players, but professionalism was eventually permitted by the FA, though not all clubs allowed it. The issue of professionalism first arose with "broken time," recompense for time lost at football from players' regular jobs. Ultimately professionalism came to mean full-time employment of players. The teams using professionals were mainly in the midlands and the north. Professionalism led 12 clubs to form the Football League, intended to be national in scope, in 1888. A second division was introduced in 1892, and the total number of teams increased to 28. The Irish formed a league in 1890 and the Scottish in 1891. The Southern League began in 1894.

The Football League

Later national leagues outside Great Britain followed the British model. A league was formed in The Netherlands in 1889, but professionalism was not adopted there until 1954. Germany completed its first national championship season in 1903, but the Bundesliga, a comprehensive national league, did not evolve until 60 years later. In France, where the game was introduced in the 1870s, a professional league did not begin until 1932, shortly after professionalism had been adopted in the South American countries of Argentina and Brazil. The FA, while legalizing professionalism from 1885, was determined to preserve amateurism, as were some of Britain's southern clubs, but ultimately professionalism prevailed, the London FA yielding to it in 1906.

The Football League became more national in 1920, when the Southern League was absorbed as a third division, the midlands and northern clubs maintaining their superiority. Thereafter, though the FA Cup was prestigious, the weekly Football League matches formed the backbone of British football. Seasonal attendance at Football League matches in the years between the two world wars rose to around 28,000,000 by 1938. After World II it peaked at 41,000,000 in 1949. By 1986, however, attendance had slumped to a low of 16,000,000 before reorganization of the four divisions, the introduction of play-offs, and associated cup competitions produced a modest revival.

International competition. British engineers and businessmen first carried the game abroad: to Prague and Graz, Austria, in the 1880s, and to Vienna, where two clubs were formed in the 1890s. In 1887 a textile mill representative introduced the game in Russia. The first football match in Turkey was played in 1895 between British residents and Greek students, who had learned the game from British sailors. Danes formed the Boldspil (ball game) Union in 1889, the same year that The Netherlands federation was formed. In Malmö, Swed., English residents played both rugby and association football and occasionally combinations of the two. Belgian and Swiss associations were formed in the 1890s, and British sailors had introduced the game to Brazil in the late 1870s.

Oddly enough, in comparison with other British sports in the 19th century, association football did not travel first or even very effectively to what later became the Commonwealth countries and to the United States. The game played from the 1870s in Canada and from the 1880s in Australia and New Zealand was rugby, often in the same confusion with soccer that had attended the late and slow establishment of the rules in Great Britain.

Soccer in the United States

After U.S. football emerged early in the 20th century as the most popular football sport in the United States, soccer survived as an intercollegiate sport, first under the aegis of the National Collegiate Athletic Association (NCAA) from 1905, and from 1924 under that of the Intercollegiate Soccer Association of America, which in turn later affiliated with the NCAA. The soccer schools were originally all in the East: Pennsylvania, Cornell, Harvard, Haverford, Princeton, and Yale in the 1920s. Originally a spring game, soccer became a spring and autumn game, and finally an autumn game. Later, where climate allowed, as in California, it was played year round.

Outside the schools, the game was most popular in cities where immigrant groups played it: St. Louis, Mo.; Philadelphia; Chicago; Cincinnati, Ohio; and Cleveland, to which later Hispanic migration added New York City and Los Angeles. The U.S. Soccer Federation was formed in 1913, affiliated with the Fédération Internationale de Football Association (FIFA), and sponsored competitions. The American Football League, a group of Eastern professional teams, began in 1923. Most of the players were imported, the Bethlehem Steel Company team specializing, for example, in Scottish players. Foreign teams toured the United States, at first usually winning all their games, and U.S. teams began to play abroad. U.S. teams have participated in the World Cup from 1930, but traditionally they have not gone far in the competition.

The U.S. professional game became national in 1968 when the new North American Soccer League (NASL) began play. The league did not survive long, however. The game was slow to attract American sports fans, and the mortality rate of teams ran high along with the frequent switching of franchises from one city to another. Competition from such favourite U.S. sports as baseball and football was difficult to overcome. If one player was responsible for popularizing the game as a spectator sport in the United States, it was the Brazilian World Cup player Pelé, signed by the New York Cosmos in 1975. But interest waned after the early 1980s, and the NASL finally collapsed prior to the 1985 season. The demise of the NASL, however, did not result in a total collapse of professional soccer. After experimentation, soccer officially moved indoors in 1978 with the institution of the six-a-side Major Indoor Soccer League, a concept designed to create a faster, higher-scoring game for American tastes. It developed attendance problems nonetheless. At the same time, at grass-roots level, progress was such that in 1987 more than 2,000,000 youngsters were regularly playing in youth leagues throughout the country and filtering talent into high schools and colleges. More universities were fielding soccer teams than squads for U.S. football.

Indoor soccer

International organization. In 1904, when the game had spread across the continent of Europe to the point at which international organization was needed, Belgium, Denmark, France, The Netherlands, Spain, Sweden, and Switzerland founded the FIFA. The English FA had been consulted earlier, but "in a monumental example of British insularity," as the official FA history later put it, had failed to take the lead expected of it, though England voiced agreement with the concept in 1905 and joined the association the following year. The FA had, however, in 1882 set up the International Football Association Board as an international rule-making body, with English, Scottish, Welsh, and Irish representation, and it continued as such. In 1913 the FIFA was given representation on the board, but they were voted out after Britain withdrew from the world governing body in 1920 over the reinstatement of Germany and its World War I allies. The FIFA representation, however, was resumed four years later.

The FA did consult with the FIFA, especially on the question of amateurism, a problem that came to a head with the unofficial inclusion of soccer in the Olympic Games of 1900 and 1904 and its official inclusion thereafter, except in the 1932 Games. The commitment of the International Olympic Committee (IOC) was to pure amateurism; the FIFA allowed its national associations to handle the question independently. Uruguay won in the 1924 and 1928 Games with virtually professional teams. Some nations refused to compete. The IOC wavered; the popularity of the sport worldwide may have discouraged ironhanded enforcement. After winning in 1908 and 1912, Britain withdrew in protest of the professionalism of other national teams in 1920 and did not permanently rejoin the FIFA until 1946, having temporarily returned in the interim. After World War II Communist-bloc countries were almost completely dominant.

The World Cup

World championships. The FIFA organized the World Cup championship series, the first being played at Montevideo in 1930 and won by Uruguay. The World Cup competition was scheduled every four years between the Olympic Games. The European Cup of Champion Clubs play for national league champions began in 1955 among the 33 countries of the Union des Associations Europèene de Football (formed in 1954), which also began the European Cup-Winners' Cup series in 1960. Other cup competitions followed, including the South American Copa Libertadores de América in 1960, which led to an unofficial championship played between the winners of the South American and the European Champions' cups. It was later given FIFA approval. (For winners of these cups, see SPORTING RECORD in the *Micropædia*.) The International Inter-City Industrial Fairs Cup began tentatively in 1955 but by 1971 was firmly established, renamed the UEFA Cup, and with an annual entry of 64 teams had become Europe's largest tournament. For national teams there are established competitions as well: South American Championship (1916), African Nations Cup (1957), and European Football Championship (1960), formerly known as the European Nations Cup.

Spectator problems. The excitement of regional, national, and international rivalries in soccer has provided the game with intensely loyal fans whose enthusiasm at times has turned them to violence. Before the late 1950s, crowd disturbances before, during, and after British matches were rare and confined to a few spontaneous, isolated incidents. In contrast, Latin-American countries had years before fenced off and even dug moats around the fields of play to keep unruly fans at bay. But the 1960s brought frightening increases in violent, sometimes premeditated, activity, which contributed to the decrease in attendance. Soccer became the unwilling catalyst for antisocial behaviour. The problem worsened in the next decade when segregation of rival fans became essential. The trend culminated in the 1985 Heysel Stadium tragedy in Brussels. Thirty-nine spectators, mostly Italian, died and 400 were injured at the European Champions' Cup final when a wall collapsed under pressure from rioting Liverpool supporters charging fans of the Italian Juventus of Turin team. English clubs were then banned from European competition, but the so-called British disease of hooliganism had already been exported to most other European countries.

PLAY OF THE GAME

Equipment and field of play. The object of the game is to propel the ball into the goal, using any part of the body except the hands and arms; the side scoring more goals wins. The ball is a round, leather-covered, inflated rubber bladder 27–28 inches (about 68–71 centimetres) in circumference and 14–16 ounces (397–454 grams) in weight. The players move the ball by hitting it with head or foot from one teammate to another or by dribbling—a series of very short kicks, usually with the instep or side of the foot. Only the goalkeeper of the 11 players is allowed to handle the ball, and he is restricted to the penalty area, a rectangular area in front of the goal, 44 yards (40.2 metres) wide and extending 18 yards (16.5 metres) into the field. The goal is eight yards (7.3 metres) wide and eight feet (2.4 metres) high. The game is of 90 minutes' duration and is divided into halves. The teams change ends after a five-minute half-time interval. FIFA rules prescribe a playing field (pitch) 100 to 130 yards (90 to 120 metres) long and between 50 and 100 yards (45 and 90 metres) wide; however, for international matches, it must be 110–120 yards (100–110 metres) long and 70–80 yards (64–75 metres) wide (see Figure 4). Women and schoolchildren usually play a shorter game on a smaller field. The game is controlled by a referee, who is also the timekeeper, and two linesmen who patrol the touchlines, or sidelines, signaling when the ball goes out of play.

The ball

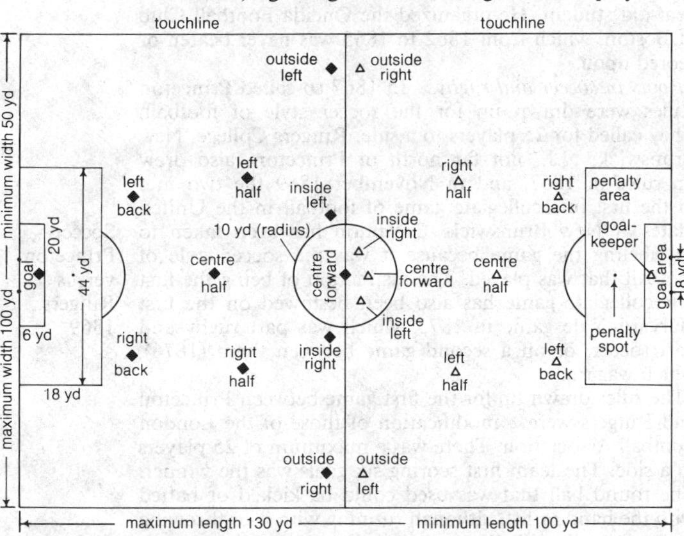

Figure 4: Soccer field and the positions of players at the kickoff.

The biggest changes have been in uniforms and equipment. Clothing has become attenuated, and heavy boots have given way to shoes. Many players have discarded shin guards. Conformity of dress is not essential, provided that the sides can be identified and the goalkeeper is distinguishable. Players may participate barefoot.

Fouls. Free kicks are awarded for fouls or violations of rules; all players of the offending side must be 10 yards (nine metres) from the ball. Free kicks may be either direct, from which a goal may be scored, for more serious fouls such as kicking an opponent, tripping, or handling the ball; or indirect, from which goals cannot be scored until after the ball has touched another player, awarded for lesser violations such as obstruction (interfering with an opponent while not playing the ball). A penalty kick, a direct free kick awarded to the attacking side in the penalty area, is taken from a spot 12 yards (11 metres) from the centre of the goal, with all players other than the defending goalkeeper and the kicker outside the penalty area. Variance in rule interpretations was notable from the 1960s. In South America, for example, shoulder charges, harassment of the goalkeeper, and tackling from behind were not viewed as seriously as they were elsewhere; but interfering with a player not playing the ball was strictly penalized. From 1970 a player guilty of a serious foul was given a warning yellow card, and a second such foul brought a red card and ejection from the game.

The penalty kick

Rules. Considering the tremendous advances in play in the 20th century, it is remarkable that there have been only two major alterations of the rules in the period—those related to "offside" and to player substitution. A man is offside if he receives a forward pass from a colleague in the opponent's half with fewer than two opponents—three before the rule was changed—between himself and the goal line. The interpretation often causes controversy, even though the linesmen generally guide the referee by positioning themselves alongside the foremost attacker on each team. The flagrant use of substitutes in many countries forced the International Board to alter the rule limiting teams to 11 players. At first it was hoped to restrict changes to injured players, but it is now permissible to replace any two at any time in competitive matches. Substitutes were used for the first time in the World Cup in 1970—two from five on the reserve bench—and it proved an invaluable innovation because of the heat and altitude of Mexico City, site of the contest. Substitutions can be made at any time during a match but only after the referee stops play. The exchange must take place at the halfway line. A substitute can only enter the field of play after the player he is replacing is taken off, either as a result of an injury or for tactical reasons. A substituted player may not return to the game.

Use of substitutes

Maneuvers. While solo runs and dribbles are spectacular, association football is essentially a team game, based on accurate passing of the ball among members of the same side. Passing produces the fluid movements and varied patterns that contribute to the game's attractiveness. A distinctive feature is the development of heading (introduced in the 1860s), and many thrilling goals are scored by a forward jumping to hit the ball with his forehead.

Too much can be made of numbers and systems. Basically, the aim is to put a man with time and room to spare in a shooting position near the opponent's goal, and it does not matter whether the man is nominally a forward or a defender. Attitude is an important factor to go along with technical excellence in achieving the aim.

Tactics. Although professionalism and the league system brought benefits, they are partly responsible for the growing blight of defensive football. Herbert Chapman, shrewd manager of England's Arsenal team in the 1930s, pulled back the centre halfback to be a third back and operated with four forwards instead of five. Italy, possibly the most commercialized soccer country, introduced the Catenaccio system (see Figure 5), with an extra man, named the sweeper or libero (free man), behind another four defenders, plugging holes where they developed.

Defensive strategies

Ideally, with both tactics the solid defenses were the springboard for quick counterattacks and, in Scotland's Alex James, Arsenal had the man to organize them. But with most imitators it was solely a case of stopping the other side from scoring. A defensive outlook was also encouraged by the European club tournaments, which were played on a home and away basis, the winning side being that with the greater aggregate of goals. As a result, visiting teams did not go for a win but concentrated on keeping down the opponent's score in the hope of obtaining more goals in the return match.

One of the few attacking ideas to come forward after World War II was the withdrawn centre forward (see Figure 6) of Hungary's Nandor Hidegkuti in the 1950s. He played behind the attack, luring the centre halfback with him, and the inside forwards were the spearhead. The line had an M shape instead of the fashionable W formation.

Teams used to have specialists who stuck to their roles—

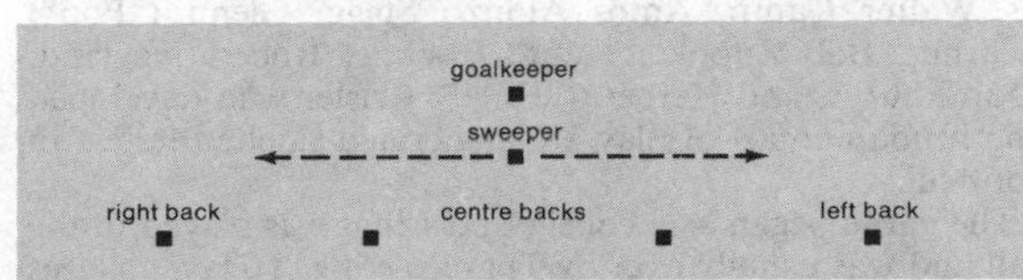

Figure 5: Catenaccio defense, showing the positions of players and the range of the sweeper.

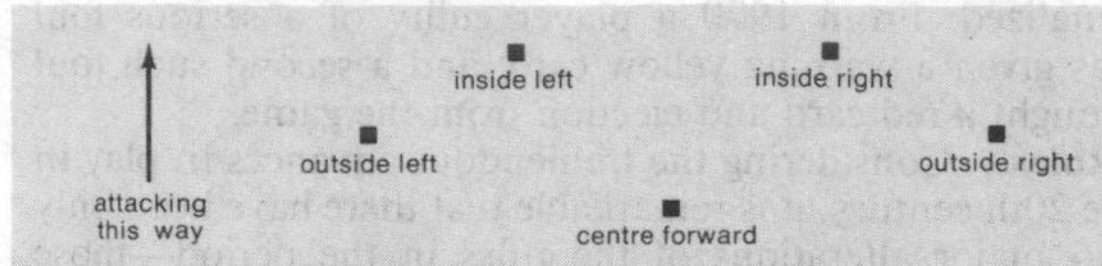

Figure 6: The positions of players for the withdrawn centre forward attack.

wingers out on the touchlines, backs deep in defense, and centre forwards lying upfield. They gradually gave way to all-around players who realized their responsibilities in all departments of the game. Work rate became as important as skill, and method football took over. Brazil grouped its outfield players in a 4–2–4 formation when winning the 1958 World Cup and still gave outlet to its brilliant individualists. England won the World Cup in 1966 playing 4–3–3—without a winger—and four years later often operated 4–4–2, fielding only two strikers up front.

Modern formations

UPI

World-famed soccer star Pelé (Brazil) has characteristically darted past the defender to intercept the ball and take a shot at the goal during the 1970 World Cup final against Italy at Mexico City. Brazil won 4–1 to become world champions for the third time.

In the early 1970s, however, The Netherlands' innovation of "total football," in which positions were largely ignored, enjoyed some success. Every outfield player attacked as well as defended. The quality of the individuals carried the system along, but The Netherlands failed to win the 1974 World Cup. Then in the late 1980s, experiments were made with a variation of 4–4–2 using a packed midfield in a 4–5–1 formation, which was able to saturate the opposition, leaving a solitary striker in attack. Emphasis on defense to avoid defeat continued in the pressurized atmosphere of a highly competitive professional business. (J.D.Ro./B.Jo.)

U.S. football

United States-style football is a body-contact, 11-man team sport of running, kicking, and passing the ball. The gridiron sport, as it is called because of the field's design, is indigenous to the United States and has not been taken up in the rest of the world to the degree that other U.S. sports, such as basketball and baseball, have; it has spread to some other countries, however, and has achieved some international popularity through television viewing.

U.S. football evolved as the product of the imagination of early players and coaches who continuously adapted the game to the equipment, players' skills, and the playing rules in effect during their time. It was coaches such as Walter Camp, Amos Alonzo Stagg, Glenn ("Pop") Warner, Bob Zuppke, Knute Rockne, Robert Neyland, Don Faurot, and Herbert ("Fritz") Crisler who developed the fundamentals of play and generated public interest in football.

The game began as a college sport that was played in the fall and was usually over by Thanksgiving. Today, colleges have a limited practice of about three weeks in the spring, begin their fall schedule in late August, and continue through the New Year holiday with National Collegiate Athletic Association (NCAA) divisional championships and bowl games. The professional teams play exhibition games in July and continue their season through the Super Bowl in the last week of January. High school teams play shorter schedules that often lead to city and state championship tournaments.

HISTORY

Amateur football. Football in its crudest form was known in America virtually from the time British colonists established their first settlements. There is evidence that as early as 1609 teams or groups of men were kicking around an air-filled bladder, as they had in their mother country. More than two centuries were to pass, however, before the game took root in the colleges.

Students at Princeton University in 1820 played a game known as Ballown, in which a ball was batted with the fist. By 1840 an organization had been formed to schedule games and choose sides. Many other colleges developed forms of the game, some of them becoming notoriously violent. There were no established rules at any of the colleges, and sides might be of any number agreed upon. Following the introduction of a round rubber ball in the 1850s, considerable skill was developed in kicking the ball a long distance, dribbling it with the foot, and passing it (by foot) to a teammate; these were the skills of modern association football (soccer).

The first formal football organization in the United States was established in 1862 by Gerritt Smith Miller, a 17-year-old student. He organized the Oneida Football Club of Boston, which from 1862 to 1865 was never beaten or scored upon.

Roots in soccer and rugby. In 1867 so-called Princeton Rules were drawn up for the soccer style of football. They called for 25 players to a side. Rutgers College, New Brunswick, N.J., not far north of Princeton, also drew up rules in 1867, and in November 1869 the two met in the first intercollegiate game of football in the United States at New Brunswick. Exception has been taken to so labeling the game because it was the soccer style of football that was played. The distinction of being the first intercollegiate game has also been bestowed on the first Harvard–Yale game in 1875, which was part rugby and part soccer, or on a second game between them (1876), which was rugby.

Soccer—Princeton versus Rutgers, 1869

The rules drawn up for the first game between Princeton and Rutgers were a modification of those of the London Football Association. There was a maximum of 25 players to a side. The team first scoring six goals was the winner. The round ball that was used could be kicked or batted with the hand or fist, although running with it or throwing it was not allowed. Rutgers won the game, 6 goals to 4. The second game, at Princeton, was won by Princeton, 8 goals to 0. A third scheduled game was barred by the two colleges.

Columbia, Cornell University of Ithaca, N.Y., and Yale were among the schools that took up football in the early 1870s, all adopting the kicking game. Harvard, where football had been banned, revived the game in 1871 and played what was known as the Boston Game, essentially a kicking game with elements of rugby. Representatives from Princeton, Yale, Columbia, and Rutgers met in New York City in 1873 and formulated the first intercollegiate rules in the United States with the code of the London Football Association as their model. In that year Yale lost to Princeton, 3 goals to 0, in the inaugural meeting of what is today intercollegiate football's oldest continuous rivalry. Yale then met a team from England known as the Eton Players in the first international match in the United States and won, 2 goals to 1. The game played was probably soccer. Yale was won over by the Eton Players to 11-man football and thereafter fought for the principle until it was adopted generally in 1880.

First intercollegiate rules

Harvard, because it played a different game, had declined to participate in the 1873 rules convention and looked elsewhere for competition. It found a rival in the football club of McGill University in Montreal. The teams met twice in the spring of 1874 at Cambridge, Mass. McGill played football under the code of the Rugby Football Union of England. Harvard's football was largely soccer. The first of the two games was played under Harvard's rules. The next day the teams met under McGill's rules, using an egg-shaped, rugby-style ball.

Harvard was won over completely to rugby as a result of its matches with McGill. Then came an event that contributed greatly to the shape of the game as it developed in the United States. Harvard challenged Yale to a game under "Concessionary Rules" and thus inaugurated one of the most celebrated of all U.S. football rivalries. The game was played in November 1875 at New Haven, Conn., and was part rugby and part soccer. They played with 15 players on a side instead of 11 as Yale would have preferred, and Harvard won by 4 goals and 4 tries, or touchdowns, to none. Despite its decisive defeat, Yale was so taken with rugby that it became a convert and adopted the rules. Observers from Princeton who saw the game also were won over to rugby, and in 1876 representatives of Princeton, Harvard, Yale, and Columbia organized the Intercollegiate Football Association. They adopted the code of the Rugby Football Union with a change in the scoring rule—instead of a match being decided by a majority of goals alone, it was decided by a majority of touchdowns. The egg-shaped leather ball replaced the round rubber ball of soccer. Rugby thus became the American college football game just as other schools were entering the intercollegiate lists.

Rugby—Harvard versus Yale, 1875

The first game in the Middle West was played in 1879 between the University of Michigan, Ann Arbor, and Racine College of Wisconsin. Though Michigan had organized a team as early as 1873, it had been unable to find an opponent until the Racine game. In 1881 Michigan inaugurated intersectional competition by sending its team east to play Yale, Harvard, and Princeton, losing to all three in the space of five days. In 1887 the University of Notre Dame in South Bend, Ind., made its debut against Michigan and lost 8–0 at South Bend. On the Pacific coast, football was being played between classes at the University of California, Berkeley, as early as 1881, but not until the 1890s did football take hold seriously. The Southwest was a late starter, but in no part of the country did the game become more of a craze. The University of Texas, Austin, was the first to organize, in 1893.

Evolution of American football. In its early years, American game was purely a test of brawn, with dull pileups and entanglements of bodies in marked contrast with rugby's speed and wide-open action over the breadth and length of the field. The man who conceived and designed most of the basic changes and departures from rugby and brought about their acceptance was Walter Camp, now rightly known as the "Father of American Football."

Walter Camp

In 1880 Camp initiated the first of the major changes in the evolution of the American game. This was the substitution of scrimmage for the scrummage, or scrum, of rugby. In scrummage the ball was put between two opposing interlocked packs of rushers, or forwards, who endeavoured to heel the ball backward to their own backs. In the new scrimmage, the ball was given into the orderly possession of one team, one of whose members, the snapback (now the centre), then put it in play without interference by "snapping" it with the foot to another player designated the "quarterback." Thus Camp also initiated the role of the quarterback, which was to become, for many, the most glamorous position in football. In the same year, he finally succeeded in his efforts to have the number of players reduced from the 15 of rugby to the 11 of modern U.S. football. Camp, too, was the one who came up with the standard alignment for 11 men—seven forwards in the line, a quarterback, two halfbacks, and a fullback.

In 1882 Camp introduced a system of downs and yardage to be gained. This followed as a result of the tactics used at the time to keep indefinite possession of the ball. No means had been devised for forcing surrender of the ball, and a team that was unable to score but chose not to let its opponent have the chance to score was able to maintain possession indefinitely. Camp's rule called for a team to surrender the ball if it failed to gain five yards (raised to 10 in 1906) in three downs (raised to four in 1912). The new rule gave rise to the practice of marking the field with horizontal lines five yards apart, giving it the appearance of a gridiron. The rule was the heart of American football. It encouraged the planned running attack, replacing kicking as the predominant element of play.

The following year Camp introduced a scoring system to end disputes over the outcome of games. Point values were given to the various scoring methods—safety (tackling a ball carrier behind his own goal line), 1 point (against team in possession of the ball); touchdown, 2 points; goal after touchdown, 4; and field goal, 5. Over the years the point values changed several times, reflecting especially the diminishing importance of kicking. In 1912 the scoring had evolved as follows: the safety was 2 points, the field goal 3, the touchdown 6, and the conversion after touchdown was 1 point. In 1958 teams were given the option of running or passing for a 2-point conversion.

In 1888 came another change that was to transform the pattern of the game. Tackling up to this time had been permitted only from the waist up—the rule of rugby. An 1888 rule permitted tackling as low as the knees, and along with this came a prohibition against linemen blocking with extended arms, requiring them to keep their arms at their sides. The forward line of players, which had been extended across the field, was therefore forced to contract. The players in the backfield, who also had spread wide for the lateral passing of the ball, as in rugby, also moved close together behind their forwards for protection. In these positions the backs formed the close-order alignment of the T—which became the original, standard formation of American football (see Figure 8).

The T formation

Mass formations. In 1890 the first of many mass formations that were to make the game so hazardous was unveiled. The man who originated it was Amos Alonzo Stagg, famous as a player at Yale from 1885 to 1889 and far more renowned for his 63 years of coaching college teams, 41 of them at the University of Chicago. Stagg devised the "ends back" formation in his first year of coaching at the International YMCA Training School in Springfield, Mass. He moved the ends from their regular positions at each end of the line to positions behind the line, where, along with the back, they became interferers, pushers, and pullers, helping the ball carrier to advance. The resulting impact on the defense was much more forceful than anything previously known. In 1891 Stagg presented a second mass formation known as the "turtleback," a massing of the team into a solid oval directed against the opposing tackle. Harvard used this formation in 1893 and was credited by some with being its originator.

In 1892 the most devastating of the mass plays was introduced—the "flying wedge," a kickoff tactic invented at Harvard. The flying wedge was an extension of the so-called V trick, credited to both Princeton and Lehigh University, Bethlehem, Pa., in which the kicker, instead of kicking off to start a half, nudged the ball with his toe and then picked it up and ran with it as his teammates formed a V-shaped mass around him. In 1892 Harvard added momentum to the mass by starting the wedge in motion before the ball was put in play. The sensational device was adopted immediately, and in 1893 it was in general use. It added to the roughness of the game and, by the end of the season, football was under attack for its violence. The army and navy departments canceled the game between the service academies in 1894, and the Intercollegiate Football Association began to break up.

Flying wedge

In 1894 the University Athletic Club of New York invited Yale, Princeton, Harvard, and Pennsylvania to send representatives to a meeting to form a new rules committee. This group banned the V trick and the flying wedge by a requirement that the kickoff travel at least 10 yards to be in play unless touched by a member of the receiving side. It was also against the rules for more than three men to group more than five yards in back of the line of scrimmage to project a mass play.

The violence of mass plays continued, however. In 1894 Stagg, then at the University of Chicago, introduced a "tackles back" formation and at Pennsylvania, the coach, George Woodruff, originated a "guard back" arrangement that was widely imitated. Harvard declined to give up its flying wedge. Yale and Harvard broke relations after a rough 1894 game. In 1895 Yale and Princeton adopted a separate code. To curb mass play they ruled that the team on offense must have seven players on the line of scrimmage and that only one back might be in forward motion before the snap of the ball.

Also in 1895, colleges in the Middle West, dissatisfied with the divided leadership of the East, asserted their independence. The presidents of Chicago, Illinois, Michigan, Minnesota, Northwestern, Purdue, and Wisconsin universities met and took steps toward organizing what was to become the Western Conference (Big Ten). At a second meeting in 1896 they barred freshmen from varsity teams and set a limit of three years on varsity eligibility. Later they established faculty control of athletics.

In the summer of 1896 the two groups in the East met in an effort to resolve their differences. They set up a permanent rules committee and put a curb on momentum in mass plays by ruling that "no player on the side in possession of the ball shall take more than one step toward his opponent's goal before the ball is in play without coming to a full stop." In 1910 the rules committee required seven men on the line to put an end to mass plays.

Emergence of the modern game. The season of 1905 was one of the ugliest, if not the most critical, U.S. football has ever gone through. According to tabulations of the *Chicago Tribune,* there were 18 deaths and 159 other injuries of consequence resulting from college games. There was a mounting uproar of protest as the season progressed. President Theodore Roosevelt summoned representatives of Harvard, Yale, and Princeton to the White House and requested them to take steps to save the game.

National opposition to violence

At a meeting in New York City late in 1905, representatives of about 60 colleges and universities appointed a football rules committee of seven members and organized the Intercollegiate Athletic Association of the United States with Captain Palmer E. Pierce of West Point as its first president. The American Football Rules Committee (the old committee), under Walter Camp, met with the association's Football Rules Committee in 1906 in New York City. In 1910 the Intercollegiate Athletic Association of the United States became the National Collegiate Athletic Association (NCAA), the governing body of intercollegiate athletics in the United States.

The forward pass

One of the committee's changes was the legalization of the forward pass. One of the men most instrumental in the introduction of the forward pass was John Heisman, for whom college football's most prized individual trophy was later named. In 1895, while a coach at Auburn, he had seen a forward pass thrown in a game between North Carolina and Georgia, 11 years before it was legal to throw the ball forward. The North Carolina player who caught it ran 70 yards for a touchdown. The Georgia coach, Pop Warner, protested the pass as illegal, but the referee stated that he had not seen it and allowed the touchdown.

In 1903 it occurred to Heisman that the forward pass he had seen thrown eight years before could be the salvation of the game by loosening up the strangling mass play. He wrote to Camp suggesting that the forward pass be incorporated into the game, and in 1904 he did so again. Others joined in, and the forward pass was approved in 1906.

In addition to legalizing the forward pass, the 1906 rules changes were: (1) reduction of the length of the game from 70 to 60 minutes, divided into 30-minute halves, (2) establishment of a neutral zone, separating the forward line of teams by the length of the ball, (3) increasing the distance required to be gained in three downs from five to 10 yards, (4) banning of hurdling (jumping over opposing players), (5) prohibiting offensive centres, guards, and tackles from dropping behind the line of scrimmage unless they fell back five yards to replace a back, (6) stipulation that punts striking the ground put all members of the kicking team on side (behind the ball) except the kicker, (7) marking of the field with lengthwise stripes five yards apart, changing it from a gridiron to a checkerboard, (8) addition of a second umpire, and (9) requirement that substitutes report to the referee. A central board of officials, which Camp had advocated in 1905, was established.

In 1910 the rules committee took the final step to end mass plays. Seven men of the offensive team were required on the forward line, while interlocked interference and aiding the runner by pushing or pulling were outlawed. The effect of these changes was so pronounced that the balance of power switched from the offense to the defense. There was a falling off in scoring, and numerous games ended in scoreless ties. To correct the imbalance, the rules committee in 1912 increased the number of downs from three to four. The length of the playing field was reduced from 110 to 100 yards (90 metres) and end zones 10 yards deep were established behind the goal lines, within which forward passes could be completed for touchdowns. The kickoff, formerly made from the centre of the field, was moved back to the kicking side's 40-yard line. Gradually, early restrictions on the forward pass were removed.

Emergence of Notre Dame

The awakening to the immense possibilities of the forward pass came primarily as a result of a sensational exhibition by Notre Dame in defeating Army in the inaugural game of their rivalry in 1913 at West Point. Notre Dame's name in football meant nothing to the East at the time, and Army was heavily favoured. With quarterback Gus Dorais throwing to end Knute Rockne (later the most famous coach in football history) and to back Joe Pliska, Notre Dame caught Army completely unprepared and scored an astonishing 35–13 victory over the cadets and their battering-ram running game. Later that same season Army used the forward pass against Navy and won 22–9.

Actually, Notre Dame was not the only trailblazer of the forward pass. Numerous teams had used the pass since its inception in 1906. Probably the most successful of all in that year was a St. Louis University (Missouri) team, coached by Eddie Cochems, that won every game in its season and used the pass from the very first.

Spread of the game. The early dominance of Harvard, Princeton, and Yale gave way in the 1890s as other teams and regions achieved renown for football prowess. Legendary teams included Pennsylvania in 1894–98, Fielding Yost's "point-a-minute" teams at the University of Michigan in 1901–05, and Stagg's 1905–09 teams at Chicago. The rise of the Carlisle Indian School to fame began in the 1907 season. In 1907, 1911, and 1912 Carlisle was one of the strongest teams in the country and gave the football world the player who is often ranked as the greatest of all time—Jim Thorpe. During the 1912 season Thorpe scored the remarkable total of 25 touchdowns and 198 points.

The Carlisle Indians and Jim Thorpe

Coaching. With the opening up of the game, the coach became more important, as a deviser of systems, plays, pass patterns, and defensive arrangements. Famous coaches of the day, in addition to Camp, Stagg, Heisman, and Yost, included Percy Haughton of Harvard, Gilmour Dobie of the University of Washington, Seattle, and especially Knute Rockne of Notre Dame and Pop Warner.

Rockne achieved a celebrity status that surpassed that of any other coach in history, with the possible exception of Stagg. Rockne created little, but he was the most magnetic of all coaches, one of the smartest and wittiest. Becoming head coach at Notre Dame in 1918, he saw his team (which included George Gipp, who Rockne later said was

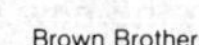
Brown Brothers

Ball carrier for Notre Dame plunges through the Stanford line during the Rose Bowl game, Jan. 1, 1925.

the greatest back Notre Dame ever had) win every game in 1919 and again in 1920. His fame became nationwide when his 1924 team, with its "Four Horsemen" backfield, won the national championship.

Knute Rockne's Notre Dame shift

Rockne credited Stagg as the originator of the shift installed at Notre Dame in 1914, in which the backs moved just before the snap of the ball from their T formation into a box alignment behind the left or right side of the line. A year later the ends also shifted out from the line. The Notre Dame shift lost its effectiveness with successive decrees of the rules committee to eliminate its momentum. In 1924 it was ruled that the team must come to an absolute stop and remain stationary "momentarily." In 1927 a pause of one second was imposed. In 1931 the pause had to be "at least one second," and after Rockne's death that year the shift vogue waned.

Tactical innovations. Contributing to the decline of the Notre Dame system was the rise in popularity of the wingback formations originated by Warner. One of the most creative minds in football and one of the most successful of all coaches in 44 years at Georgia, Cornell, Carlisle, Pittsburgh, Stanford, and Temple University (Philadelphia), Warner devised first a single wingback formation and then a double wingback (see Figure 8).

Football became increasingly complex as coaches devised new formations, plays, and defenses. The modern T formation—employing principles worked out by Stagg, including the stand-up position of the quarterback behind centre, quarterback fakes in which the quarterback pretends to hand the ball to one back and then gives it to another or keeps it himself, and the man in motion—was the creation in the 1930s of George Halas and his Chicago Bears coaching staff of the professional National Football League and Clark Shaughnessy, who had succeeded Stagg at the University of Chicago. The Bears' 73–0 defeat of the Washington Redskins in the NFL championship game of 1940 and the overwhelming success that same year of Stanford University, then coached by Shaughnessy, started the trend toward reviving the formation. The T has not been displaced since then, although many variations have been introduced. In 1941 Don Faurot at the University of

The split T

Missouri introduced the split T, with wider line spacing (splits) and a sliding, ball-carrying quarterback rather than a spinning ball feeder, with options of keeping, pitching out, and passing. Another variation was a so-called wing T, a combination of the T and the single wing.

During the late 1950s and 1960s, the University of Delaware wing T, which had been developed by Dave Nelson and popularized by Forest Evashevski at the University of Iowa, was the dominant offensive formation. The Delaware wing T followed other wing T formations of the post-World War II era. Ray Eliot at Illinois, Lou Little at Columbia, Aldo ("Buff") Donelli at Boston University, Clarence ("Biggie") Munn at Michigan State, and Charles ("Rip") Engle at Pennsylvania State had variations of the wing T formation. The wishbone T, I formation, wing T, veer, "shotgun," and various flanker formations came into vogue thereafter (see below *Strategy and tactics*).

Teams, players, and scandals. Football had become a national mania and large-scale business enterprise in the United States by the 1920s. Highly publicized football heroes such as the Four Horsemen of Notre Dame and Harold ("Red") Grange of Illinois won new football followers the country over. Attendance mounted, and huge crowds became commonplace as new and larger stadiums went up across the land. As money poured in and more and more colleges assumed heavy obligations in expanding their athletic plants, winning teams were needed to draw income to meet mounting budgets. The scramble to obtain the best high-school and preparatory-school talent led to unscrupulous recruiting practices by some schools.

Recruiting practices

Financial inducements were offered in violation of amateur regulations, and educational requirements were let down to get good players into college.

The college football world was rocked in 1929 when a *Carnegie Foundation Bulletin* exposed the extent of unethical practices and named some of the most prestigious universities. Respectable colleges took corrective measures, and for a while it seemed football might be limited to intramural competition. But the intercollegiate game had too strong a hold in society to be downgraded more than temporarily. Despite crackdowns by individual colleges and the NCAA, such practices continued. (D.M.Ne./A.D.)

The money game

The problem grew more critical when college football moved into the multimillion-dollar category during the 1960s and '70s. Attendance for college games increased to more than 35,000,000 in 1980. Huge stadiums were built and big ones were enlarged; Michigan Stadium, for example, seats well over 103,000. But it was television, more than anything else, that turned the big-time sport into a gigantic, million-dollar enterprise. Major colleges budgeted more than $1,000,000 a year for football and took in millions of dollars in television revenue and gate receipts. By the late 1980s television networks were paying more than $46,000,000 a year for rights to college games. The regulation of television rights to college games led to court battles between the NCAA and individual colleges and the NCAA lost control of television rights for its members. Increasing numbers of colleges were punished by the NCAA for recruiting violations, and academic scandals arose as some colleges changed athletes' transcripts to meet eligibility requirements.

All-America teams. In 1889 an all-star college football team was picked, and it has been an annual custom since. Walter Camp's All-America teams appeared annually in *Collier's Weekly* for many years, but it has been established that it was Caspar Whitney who picked the first teams, probably in consultation with Camp. The first All-America team that Camp picked was in 1897. Camp died in 1925, and from that year through 1947 Grantland Rice picked the teams. In 1925 the Associated Press started selecting a team, and the other two major news-gathering agencies, the United Press and the International News Service (which merged in 1958), came out with teams. Other magazines and newspapers have printed their own selections over the years. None has been looked upon as official to the degree that Camp's and Rice's were.

The Rose Bowl

Postseason games. The idea of the postseason, or "bowl," game was launched at Pasadena, Calif., on Jan. 1, 1902, when the Tournament of Roses Committee of that city arranged the first Rose Bowl game between Michigan and Stanford. Michigan's "point-a-minute" team, coached by Fielding Yost, won 49–0. The next Rose Bowl was not played until 1916, but since then it has been held every New Year's Day. In the mid-1930s Miami, New Orleans, Dallas, and El Paso, Texas, started the Orange, Sugar, Cotton, and Sun bowls, respectively. The number of bowl games has continued to grow since that time.

The bowls began contracting with college conferences to have the league champions play against an invited opposing team each year. The Rose Bowl has pitted the Big Ten Conference champion against the Pacific Eight (later the Pacific Ten) Conference champion since 1947. The Sugar Bowl has the Southeastern Conference champion as one of its teams; the Orange Bowl has the Big Eight Conference winner; and the Cotton Bowl is hosted by the Southwest Conference champion.

Professional football. *Early history.* The first professional football game to be officially recognized as such was played in the township of Latrobe, Pa., on Aug. 31, 1895, when a team from Latrobe beat one from Jeannette, 10 miles away, by the score of 12–0. During the next few years other professional teams appeared. In Pittsburgh the Allegheny Athletic Club was created, and its rosters bore the names of the most famous college players of the day. Upper New York state followed Pennsylvania into professional football soon after the start at Latrobe. There were teams in Buffalo, Syracuse, Watertown, Auburn, Corinth, Clayton, Oswego, Alexandria Bay, and Ogdensburg.

In 1902 Connie Mack of baseball fame organized a football team that he named the Philadelphia Athletics. In the lineup was George ("Rube") Waddell, the pitcher of Mack's baseball team. Mack claimed the "championship of the world" after his club vanquished a squad representing Pittsburgh, which had Christy Mathewson, another baseball pitcher, as its fullback.

Zuppke's idea

The combination of World War I, a chance remark by Robert Zuppke, veteran coach of the University of Illinois, and the enthusiasm of George Halas in Chicago for football combined in 1918 to spark the beginning of the modern major league game. Zuppke, at the postseason banquet of his 1917 Illinois team (on which Halas had been an outstanding end), said that it was unfortunate that football players at the time when they were just beginning to learn something about the game were graduated from college and played it no more. A few weeks later, reporting for training at Great Lakes Naval Training Station in Illinois, Halas found several former college stars eager to continue playing.

League organization. Eleven league franchises were sold at $100 each when the American Professional Football Association was officially formed on Sept. 17, 1920. Jim Thorpe was elected president, and George Halas purchased a franchise for the Staley Starch Company of Decatur, Ill., which had recently made him athletic director. The first 11 teams in the league were the Canton (Ohio) Bulldogs (Thorpe's team); Cleveland Indians; Dayton (Ohio) Tigers; Chicago Cardinals; Decatur Staleys, who became the Chicago Bears in 1922; and teams in Akron, Ohio; Massillon, Ohio; Rochester, N.Y.; Rock Island, Ill.; Muncie, Ind.; and Hammond, Ind.

Jeffrey E. Blackman

New York Jets quarterback Ken O'Brien pitches the ball to halfback Johnny Hector in a sweep play during an NFL game with the New Orleans Saints.

The league had a perilous beginning that fall. Few games were played, and there seemed little chance that the league would survive. In April 1921, however, the league elected Joe Carr, an experienced promoter, as its new president. Carr created an immediate realignment of teams. Massillon, Muncie, and Hammond dropped out; Green Bay, Wis.; Buffalo; Detroit; Columbus, Ohio; and Cincinnati, Ohio, came in; and a full schedule was completed, with the Chicago Bears winning more games than any other team. The name was changed to the National Football League in 1922, with Carr continuing as president until his death in 1939. In 1933 the NFL played in two divisions, with an annual championship game.

Red Grange joins the Chicago Bears

The first trend toward prosperity began in 1925, when Red Grange left the University of Illinois to play with the Chicago Bears. Grange was the biggest name in the sports world at that time, and he was the spark that professional football needed. Grange and the Bears then went on a coast-to-coast tour that sowed the seeds of interest in the sport. Grange established himself as one of the all-time stars of the NFL before he retired in 1935.

The modern era. With considerable opposition from NFL owners, a rival league, the All America Football Conference began play in 1946 with eight teams representing Brooklyn (N.Y.), Buffalo, Chicago, Cleveland, Los Angeles, Miami (replaced by Baltimore the following year), New York City, and San Francisco. Under an agreement between the leagues, Baltimore, San Francisco, and Cleveland moved their teams into the NFL in 1950, and the balance of the AAFC players were pooled and drafted by the 13 clubs in the NFL. After one season the NFL was reorganized into 12 clubs: the New York Yanks, Chicago Bears, Chicago Cardinals, Cleveland Browns, Detroit Lions, Green Bay Packers, Los Angeles Rams, New York Giants, Philadelphia Eagles, Pittsburgh Steelers, San Francisco 49ers, and Washington Redskins. In 1952 the Yanks franchise moved to Dallas for one year, after which it was allowed to transfer to Baltimore.

Interest in the game was spurred by the introduction of unlimited substitution of players (1950), which led to specialization in player and coaching roles and a more polished game. There also developed a greater emphasis on passing. The 1958 championship between Baltimore and New York, a nationally televised game and the first to be decided in overtime, is often referred to as the turning point in the popularity of the professional game.

Rozelle succeeds Bell

Bert Bell, veteran player, coach, and owner, was commissioner of the league from 1946 until his death in 1959. Pete Rozelle, general manager of the Los Angeles Rams, was named as Bell's successor in 1960. In that year the Cardinals moved to St. Louis, and a new team, the Dallas Cowboys, was added to the league. The Minnesota Vikings (Minneapolis–St. Paul) were added to the league in 1961, the Atlanta Falcons in 1966, and the New Orleans Saints in 1967.

In 1959 another rival, the American Football League (AFL), was organized, with Lamar Hunt the first president and Joe Foss serving as its first commissioner. Initially, in 1960, the teams were the Boston (later New England) Patriots, Buffalo Bills, Denver Broncos, Houston Oilers, New York Titans (from 1963, Jets), Oakland Raiders, Dallas, and Los Angeles; the Los Angeles franchise was transferred to the San Diego Chargers in 1961, and the Dallas franchise to the Kansas City Chiefs in 1963. The Miami Dolphins were added to the league in 1966.

NFL expansion

A merger of the two leagues was announced in 1966, effective in 1970. By the start of the 1967 season, the two leagues had begun preseason interleague play, and a total of 26 cities from coast to coast were represented. In January 1970 the new National Football League began and consisted of two conferences—the National Conference and the American Conference, each with three divisions. Rozelle remained as commissioner. The league was increased to 28 teams in 1976 with the addition of the Seattle Seahawks and the Tampa Bay Buccaneers. In 1982 the Oakland franchise moved to Los Angeles, in 1984 the Baltimore Colts moved to Indianapolis, Ind., and in 1988 the St. Louis Cardinals moved to Phoenix, Ariz.

The teams were aligned as follows:

National Conference, Eastern Division: Dallas, New York Giants, Philadelphia, Phoenix, Washington, D.C. *Central Division:* Chicago, Detroit, Green Bay, Minnesota, Tampa Bay. *Western Division:* Atlanta, Los Angeles, New Orleans, San Francisco.

American Conference, Eastern Division: Buffalo, Indianapolis, Miami, New England, New York Jets. *Central Division:* Cincinnati, Cleveland, Houston, Pittsburgh. *Western Division:* Denver, Kansas City, Los Angeles, San Diego, Seattle.

The boom period. Interest in the merged leagues was immediate and universal. The Green Bay Packers, under coach Vince Lombardi, were the NFL champions, and they defeated the Kansas City Chiefs, the AFL champions, 35–10 in the first Super Bowl in January 1967 before 63,035 fans in the Los Angeles Coliseum. From then on, the Super Bowl became the biggest annual one-day sports event in the United States. Starting in 1970, when the merger was completed and the two leagues became one, a play-off system was developed in which eight teams played down to the final two for the Super Bowl game and the NFL championship. This was increased to 10 teams in 1978. (For NFL, AFL, and Super Bowl champions, see SPORTING RECORD in the *Micropædia.*)

Rozelle led the league through the days of merger and into the era of great wealth. When he took over as NFL commissioner in 1960, each of the fairly solid 13 franchises in the league was worth an average of $2,000,000. By the early 1980s, largely because of television contracts amounting to billions of dollars, each of the 28 franchises was estimated to be worth $40,000,000 and more.

Rozelle negotiated a contract for television rights in 1961 that was worth $4,650,000, and each of the 13 teams shared equally. In 1982 the NFL signed a five-year television contract for a total value of $2,000,000,000. Each of the 28 teams in the league would then earn an average of $14,000,000 a year before selling a single ticket.

As owners began reaping great profits, players began demanding a greater share of the income. Numerous strike threats came and went, and in the summer of 1970 there was a boycott of training camps by veteran players. This, too, was settled, with added money in the players' pension fund and insurance and other fringe benefits. But when the owners signed the television contract of 1982, the players demanded 55 percent of gross income as their share. The league owners refused, and a strike was called midway in the season of 1982. After eight weeks a settlement was reached. According to the terms of the settlement, each player's salary was increased significantly. The owners, however, won the battle against giving the players a fixed percentage of team income.

The mid-season players' strike

Despite these vicissitudes, fans turned out to fill stadiums across the nation and watched games on television by the millions. Magnificent new arenas were built, including ones with roofs—such as the Superdome in New Orleans, the Astrodome in Houston, the Kingdome in Seattle, and the Silverdome in Pontiac, Mich.—to house NFL teams.

The 1960s saw a greater emphasis on the refinement of defensive tactics against the pass. In the belief that the defenses had become too dominant, rules were amended in the 1970s to increase offensive production. The effect was immediate, and defensive coaches responded in the 1980s by utilizing a 3–4 formation; other formations and specialized players against the pass have continued to develop (see below *Other rule variations*).

Yet another rival of the NFL came into existence in 1982 with the formation of the 12-team United States Football League (USFL). The teams in the USFL were New Jersey, Philadelphia, Boston, and Washington, D.C., in the Atlantic Division; Chicago, Michigan, Tampa Bay, and Birmingham (Ala.) in the Central Division; and Arizona, Oakland, Los Angeles, and Denver in the Pacific Division. The league, in its first season in 1983, played its games in the spring and early summer, contrary to the traditional fall football season, and the owners signed a two-year, $20,000,000 television contract before the league staged its first game. The USFL went out of business after three seasons and sued the NFL for antitrust violations; it won the case but received only one dollar in damages.

USFL–NFL competition

PLAY OF THE GAME

Rules for college, professional, and high school football are fundamentally the same; the most notable differences are pointed out in the following discussion.

Field of play and equipment. U.S. football is played on a field measuring 100 yards (91 metres) in length from goal line to goal line, with an end zone 10 yards in depth behind each goal line, and 160 feet in width (Figure 7). Goalposts 23 feet 4 inches apart—18 feet 6 inches apart in the NFL—are erected on each end line, the limit of the end zone. A connecting crossbar is 10 feet above the ground. Parallel lines the width of the field are marked five yards apart between goal lines. An inbounds line the length of the field is marked 53 feet 4 inches inside each side line—70 feet 9 inches in the NFL.

The ball has the shape of a prolate spheroid. A leather case covers a rubber bladder inflated to the pressure of $12^1/_2$ to $13^1/_2$ pounds (0.78–0.94 kilograms per square centimetre). Its long axis measures $10^7/_8$ to $11^7/_{16}$ inches (27.62 to 29.05 centimetres); its short circumference measures $20^3/_4$ to $21^1/_4$ inches; and its weight is from 14 to 15 ounces (400 to 425 grams). A rubber-covered ball may be used by NCAA and High School Federation teams.

The mandatory equipment for college and high school players includes head protectors, shoulder pads, hip pads, thigh guards, mouthguards, jerseys with numbers, and soft knee pads covered by pants. Other equipment, including shoes, knee braces, gloves, and injury pads, is worn but not required. The NFL has less stringent requirements for much mandatory equipment.

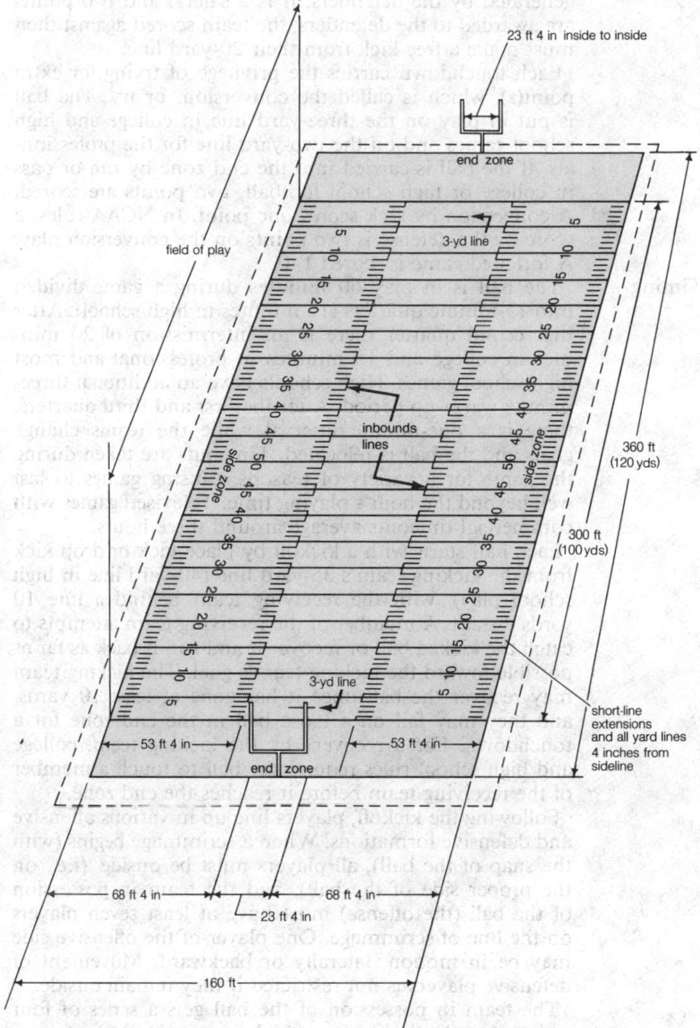

Figure 7: Football field according to NCAA specifications. Professional field varies slightly.

By courtesy of the National Collegiate Athletic Association

Principles of play. The number of players on a team (11) was established by rule in 1880, and until 1941 players were required to play offense and defense and participate in the kicking game. In 1945 the University of Michigan took advantage of the 1941 rule change, permitting unlimited substitution, for the first time and instituted platoon football, one of the game's most important innovations. Free substitution was banned in 1953, but subsequent rule changes allowed its return by 1965. Presently, the offensive, defensive, and kicking teams may each have 11 players, most of whom specialize in a particular position.

The free-substitution rule

Before the start of the game, the referee tosses a coin in the presence of the opposing captains after asking one of them to call heads or tails. The winner of the toss has the choice of goals, or kicking or receiving the first kickoff. The loser of the toss gets the choice at the start of the second half. In college football the winner of the toss may delay his choice until the second half.

Each team's objective is to score more points than its opponent, and the team with the most points at the end of the game is the winner. Points are usually scored by running the ball or receiving it from a pass above, on, or across the opponent's goal line for a touchdown (six points) or by kicking the ball from scrimmage by place kick or drop kick (a virtually obsolete technique) above the crossbar and between the uprights for a field goal (three points). A touchdown may also be scored when a loose ball is recovered in the opponent's end zone. If a play ends with the ball behind the defenders' goal line, and the impetus that caused the ball to cross the goal line was generated by the defenders, it is a safety, and two points are awarded to the defenders; the team scored against then must make a free kick from their 20-yard line.

Each touchdown carries the privilege of trying for extra point(s), which is called the conversion, or try. The ball is put in play on the three-yard line in college and high school games and on the two-yard line for the professionals. If the ball is carried into the end zone by run or pass in college or high school football, two points are scored. A conversion by kick scores one point. In NCAA rules, a score by the defense is two points on the conversion play. A forfeited game is scored 1–0.

Timing

The ball is in play 60 minutes during a game divided into 15-minute quarters (12 minutes in high school). After the second quarter there is an intermission of 20 minutes in college and 15 minutes in professional and most high-school games. High schools have an additional three-minute warm-up period. After the first and third quarters, there is a one-minute interval while the teams change goals and the ball is relocated. Timeouts are taken during the game for a variety of reasons, causing games to last well beyond the hour's playing time. Televised games with commercial timeouts average around three hours.

Each half starts with a kickoff by place kick or drop kick from the kicking team's 35-yard line (40-yard line in high school play), with the receiving team behind a line 10 yards distant. A member of the receiving team attempts to catch the kicked ball or recover it and run it back as far as possible toward the kicking team's goal. The kicking team may recover the ball once it has gone at least 10 yards, and they may fall on a loose ball in the end zone for a touchdown. For a recovery by the kicking team, college and high school rules require the ball to touch a member of the receiving team before it reaches the end zone.

Following the kickoff, players line up in various offensive and defensive formations. When a scrimmage begins (with the snap of the ball), all players must be onside (*i.e.,* on the proper side of the ball), and the team in possession of the ball (the offense) must have at least seven players on the line of scrimmage. One player of the offensive side may be in motion, laterally or backward. Movement of defensive players is not restricted if they remain onside.

The team in possession of the ball gets a series of four scrimmage downs during which it must either advance the ball a minimum of 10 yards or forfeit possession to the defenders. Each down starts with the ball resting on the ground and the teams separated by a neutral zone the width of the ball's length. The centre snaps or passes the ball between his legs to a back who may run with or kick the ball or hand or pass it to a teammate who runs or passes. Opponents try to stop any advance toward their goal line by tackling the runner, batting down or intercepting passes in flight, or legally kicking the ball. Tackling is grasping the runner's body with the arms and putting him to the ground, pushing him out of bounds, knocking him down with a body block, or stopping his forward progress by any legal means. Each down ends when the ball becomes dead—as when the ball carrier is stopped or tackled, when a forward pass is incomplete, when the ball is carried or fumbled out of bounds, or when the opponents gain possession. If the attacking team has advanced the ball 10 yards from where the series started at the end of any down, it gets a new series of four downs with a new scrimmage line from which it must again gain 10 yards or relinquish the ball. If the attacking team has not advanced the ball at least 10 yards at the end of the fourth down, the ball is given to the defenders and they become the attacking team. Scrimmage downs, in successive series for one team or the other, continue until a series ends in a score, the opponents gain possession, or time expires. Another kickoff (free kick) follows a score, and the same pattern (free kick–run back–scrimmage–score–change of possession) is repeated until playing time for the half expires. After a touchdown (and try for extra points), or after a field goal, the former defenders receive the ensuing kickoff.

First down renewal

During any scrimmage down, but usually the fourth and last, the attacking team may surrender the ball to the defenders by kicking it. When this is done, the kicking team may not interfere with a defender's opportunity to catch the ball. A defender may gain added protection by signaling (arm aloft) for a fair catch. If he does so, he must stand fast after a catch, and the kicking team is prohibited from tackling him. A free kick after a fair catch is permitted in the NFL and high school rules.

Three methods of kicking the ball are permitted: the now-rarely-used drop kick, made by dropping the ball from the hands and kicking it as it touches the ground; a place kick, made by kicking the ball while it is resting on the ground or a tee (the ball may be steadied by another member of the team); and a punt, made by dropping the ball from the hands and kicking it before it strikes the ground.

Strategy and tactics. *Offense.* After the change from a scrum to a scrimmage and the establishment of a scrimmage line (1880) and the snapping of the ball with the hand, the T formation with a balanced line became the dominant offensive formation in the game. (See Figure 8 for offensive formations.) In the T formation, three of the backs (left halfback, fullback, and right halfback) line up from four to five yards from the ball and parallel to the line of scrimmage. The fourth back, the quarterback, is positioned directly behind the centre and parallel with the line of scrimmage. In the modern T, the quarterback handles all the snaps. Handing the ball from the snapper to the quarterback went out of style for several decades beginning in 1910 when the quarterback was no longer required by rule to handle the ball before it could be touched by another back, except on a kick. The direct pass from centre entered the game during this period, and the single wing, double wing, and Notre Dame box were in command until the post-World War II era. Rockne's Notre

The backs

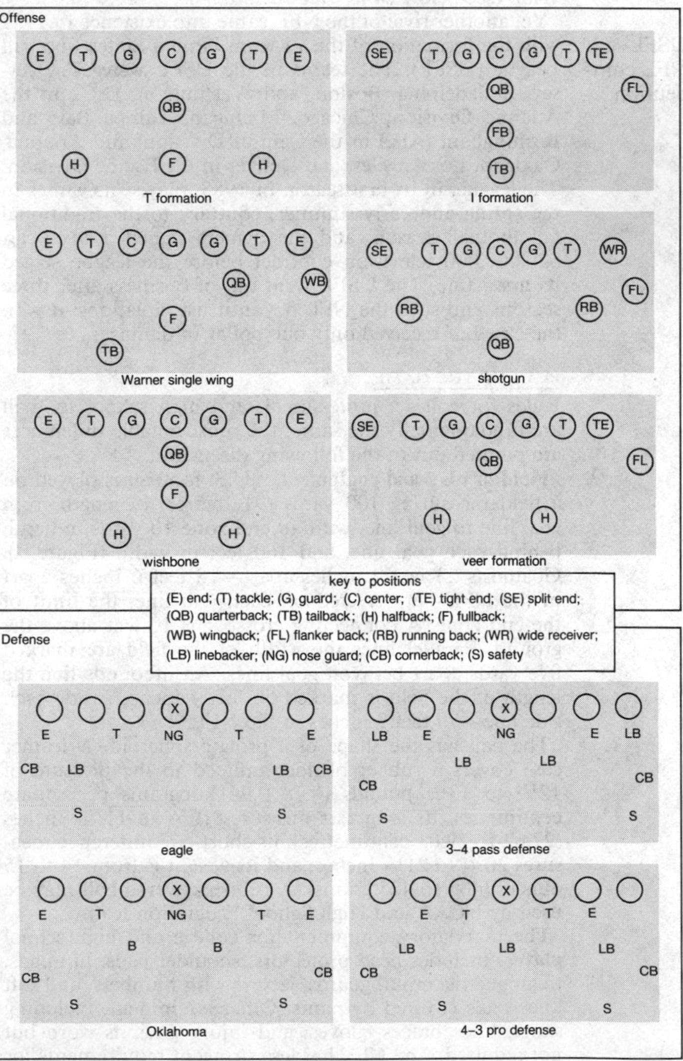

Figure 8: Offensive and defensive formations.

Dame system, employing a balanced line and a backfield shift from the T to the box formation, was widely used in the 1920s and 1930s but was seldom employed after World War II. General Robert Neyland of Tennessee and Henry Russell ("Red") Sanders of UCLA were two of the most successful single-wing coaches in the early 1950s.

In the Notre Dame box the two forward backs (quarterback and wing back) lined up slightly more than one yard behind the line, with the two rear backs (tailback and fullback) about 4½ yards behind it. The ball was always passed to them by a direct pass from the centre.

The direct snap

Warner's single and double wing with a direct pass from centre, developed largely at Pittsburgh and Stanford, operated from an unbalanced line with two linemen on one side of the centre and four on the other and a widely deployed backfield. In the single-wing formation, the forward halfback (wingback) stands one yard behind the line and up to one yard outside the end. The quarterback (blocking back) is placed about a half yard to the rear of the wingback and about two yards inside the wingback position. The fullback (plunging back) is 1½ yards to the rear and one yard inside the quarterback. Single-wing teams shift to the left as well as the right. In the double-wing formation each of the halfbacks (wingbacks) stands one yard behind the line and one yard outside his end. The quarterback (blocking back) stands about two yards behind the strong side guard. The fullback (plunging back) is positioned from 3½ to 4½ yards behind the centre; he handles the ball first on most plays and is a key man in starting the delicately measured reverses. Warner's unbalanced single- and double-wing formations and variations of them remained popular beyond World War II.

The I formation and the wishbone are variations of the T formation. The I began as the invention of Coach C.M. Hollister of Northwestern University around 1900 with all four backs lined up in tandem behind the centre. The quarterback would hand to one of them, diving directly into the line or slightly off tackle. Coaches in recent years took one of the backs out of the tandem lineup behind the centre and placed him as a wide receiver or a wingback or slot-back blocker. This formation change developed the power-sweep toss and off-tackle plays complemented by play-action and drop-back passing attacks.

The wishbone and veer attacks, both triple-option systems featuring running attacks, became highly popular in the 1970s and have continued to have wide usage. The wishbone sets the backs in an inverted Y behind the centre. The quarterback may hand off or pretend to hand off to the fullback, keep the ball and pass or himself run (usually wide around the defensive line), or pitch to a halfback. The veer accomplishes a similar option technique with a split backfield.

The "shotgun"

The "shotgun," a variation of an earlier short-punt formation, has become extremely popular as a passing formation especially on third-down, long-yardage situations. Positioned five to seven yards behind the centre, the passer is able to observe the defensive formation and the type of pass defense. The formation also helps the blockers to protect the passer.

Defense. Defensive objectives vary with the down, distance to gain, score, time, and position of the ball on the field. The main objectives in order of importance by most standards are: (1) prevent a score; (2) acquire the ball by forcing a fumble, intercepting a pass, or stealing the ball; (3) prevent a first down; (4) consume time by giving up yardage but not scores; (5) score by interception, blocked punt, or stolen ball; (6) intimidate by hard tackling; (7) discourage the offense by confusing them; (8) limit the offense to as few plays as possible. Changing defenses from down to down requires a change of personnel. The Nickel Defense, using five defensive backs in obvious passing situations, is the most visible of defensive changes. All defenses are subject to the chess principle of meeting offensive strength with defensive strength, which requires defensive players to oppose an equal number of offensive players. (See Figure 8 for defensive formations.)

Unlike the offense, the defense may have as many or as few players on the line of scrimmage or in the secondary (the defensive backfield) as required to meet the defensive objective. Defensive linemen are players in three- or four-point stances (a low crouch with one or both hands touching the ground) on the line of scrimmage and positioned opposite offensive linemen or in seams between them. Linebackers, in a variety of spacings, stand from one to three yards behind the defensive linemen and outside the offensive formation, their number determined by the number of linemen and players in the secondary. The secondary players are generally positioned behind the linebackers but sometimes are on the line of scrimmage and may rush the passer. Players in the secondary are called safeties and cornerbacks. Each defensive scheme has a number of different pass coverages that are zone (covering a specific defensive area), man-to-man, and combination zone and man-to-man. There are variations of the zone defenses and man-to-man coverages.

Defensive formations

To accomplish their defensive objectives, coaches use a variety of defenses, and there have been 12 basic defenses in football history. Defenses change as rules are altered and the style of play swings through cycles. Before the development of the forward pass in 1906, the 7–3–1 was the common defense, and this was followed by the 7–1–2–1 (7 and a diamond) and 7–2–2 (7 and a box), which were effective until around 1930. The 6–2–2–1 appeared in the 1930s and still had adherents in the 1980s. Since World War II, defenses, called by various names, with seven-man lines, four-deep backs, and a variety of linebackers and pass coverages dominated all levels of football. Both six- and seven-man line defenses have been altered over the years to four- and five-man line defenses to meet particular offensive threats. The 3–4 defense is a popular defense against the pass.

Playing rules. U.S. football celebrated its playing-rules centennial in 1976 by commemorating the first meeting in Springfield, Mass., where eight college students assembled the original 61 rules. Although students started U.S. football, they have no voice on the NCAA rules committees today. Football has always been a sport with a relatively high risk of injury. As the sport developed, safety and injury prevention became the dominant playing-rules priority. All U.S. football was governed by the NCAA playing rules until a rash of serious injuries and fatalities prompted the National Federation of State High School Associations (NFSHSA) to write its own rules in 1932. The NFL followed suit in 1933 and 1934 and, like the high schools, used the NCAA rules as their basis. The NFSHSA and the small-college National Association of Intercollegiate Athletics (NAIA) joined forces in 1958 to form the National Rules Alliance. The alliance dissolved in 1977 and the small colleges adopted NCAA rules. Today there are three separate rules committees and codes: the NCAA, the NFL, and the NFSHSA.

Officials. The game is supervised by seven officials in the NFL, four to seven in the colleges, and as few as three in high school. All officiating crews have a referee with general oversight and control of the game, who is assisted by umpires, linesmen, field judges, back judges, line judges, and side judges. The referee is the sole authority for the score, and his decisions on rules and other matters pertaining to the game are final. The referee declares the ball ready for play and keeps track of the time between plays when it is not assigned to another official. He administers all penalties and, at the snap, is positioned behind and to the side of the offensive backfield. The umpire has jurisdiction over players' equipment and line play on both sides of the neutral zone, including noting any linemen illegally downfield. He is also responsible for the legality of the snap, counting offensive players, and determining the legality of passes and kicks relative to the neutral zone. He is positioned five to seven yards behind the defensive line. The linesman is responsible for the operation of the chain and down indicator outside the sideline and has jurisdiction over the neutral zone and scrimmage formation infractions. He keeps count of the downs and indicates forward progress of the ball on his side of the field. The line judge is responsible for actions in the neutral zone and scrimmage formation infractions. He indicates forward progress on his side of the field and instructs the auxiliary down-indicator operator. The

The referee

back judge counts the number of players on the defensive team, rules on long kicks and passes, and observes eligible receivers leaving the neutral zone. The field judge is responsible for timing the 25-second count and observing kicks, passes, and eligible receivers on his side of the field. He rules on the status of the ball in his area. The side judge observes eligible receivers, kicks, and passes on his side of the field and assists in counting defensive players.

In addition to their primary duties, all officials have a joint responsibility for calling fouls (*i.e.*, infractions of the rules). Each one carries a marker, which he drops when he calls a foul, and a whistle to signal that the ball is dead. At the end of the play, he reports the infraction to the referee, who enforces the prescribed penalty and uses one or more of the 47 hand signals. The officiating crew has assistants on the field and in the press box.

Fouls and penalties. Penalties may be the loss of five, 10, or 15 yards or half the distance to the goal line; loss of down (for a foul committed by the offensive team); automatic first down (against the defense); the award of the ball to the offended team at the spot of the foul; and disqualifications. Distance penalties may be combined with loss of down, automatic first down, and disqualification. The enforcement spot of the penalty depends on whether the foul occurred during a pass, kick, or run. In NCAA rules, violations are fouls without a distance penalty and the offending teams are charged a time out. Violations are charged for improper equipment, crowd noise, and coaches' conference violations.

The most frequent penalties

In the NCAA, NFL, and NFSHSA, offensive illegal procedure, false starts, offensive holding, offside and encroachment, clipping, delay of game, and illegal-motion fouls are the most frequently called penalties. Procedure fouls have been the most-penalized infractions since the inception of the game and constitute about 65 percent of all fouls. Personal fouls—roughing the passer, kicker, or holder, late hits, striking a blow to the head, spearing, ramming, butting, and other contact acts—are automatic first downs when inflicted by the defense. Loss of down, the severest of offensive penalties, also includes a yardage penalty for pass interference, illegally kicking, batting, handing the ball, or illegally throwing or touching a forward pass. Illegally throwing a backward pass out of bounds is also a loss of down and a five-yard penalty. Penalties may not exceed half the distance from the enforcement spot to the offending team's goal line. The most controversial fouls, because of the difficulty of the judgments called for, are defensive pass interference and offensive holding.

Other rule variations. Some of the main differences between the NCAA, NFL, and NFSHSA rules not mentioned above are as follows:

NFL divisional play-offs or championships cannot end in a tie. If the score is tied after the regulation 60 minutes, additional periods of 15 minutes each are played. The first team to score is declared the winner, and the game ends immediately. Only one period of overtime is allowed after regular season games, which may thus eventually end in a tie.

Overtime periods

High schools and NCAA teams may use kicking tees for field-goal attempts.

NCAA defensive players may not advance a recovered fumble or backward pass; an NFL defense may advance a recovered fumble; and high schools allow any player to advance a fumble or backward pass.

The NCAA and NFL permit one forward pass during a down; the high schools, two.

The NCAA and high schools allow a team 25 seconds to put the ball in play after it is declared ready for play; the NFL permits 30 seconds.

The NFL has an official time out two minutes before each half ends.

The NFL has a spot penalty (the ball is advanced to the spot where the foul occurred) for defensive pass interference; the NCAA has a spot penalty if the foul occurs less than 15 yards downfield and a 15-yard penalty from the previous spot if the infraction occurs more than 15 yards downfield. High schools always have the 15-yard penalty, and both NCAA and high schools award an automatic first down.

The NFL and high schools permit a free kick for a field goal after a fair catch.

The NCAA and high schools declare the ball carrier down when any part of the body, other than the hand or foot, touches the ground. In the NFL a ball carrier who falls can get up and run again unless he was first in contact with an opponent.

The NFL declares the ball dead when the quarterback is in the grasp of a tackler (he need not be put to the ground).

The NFL allows a restricted defensive checking of pass receivers.

The NFL requires that a pass receiver touch both feet to the ground inbounds for a pass to be complete; the NCAA and high schools require one foot.

The NFL uses instant videotape replays to determine some questionable calls, and an official's decision on the field may be changed by an official in the press box.

The NFL has fewer restrictions on blocking below the waist than the NCAA, and high schools prohibit it.

(D.M.Ne.)

Canadian football

HISTORY

The early years. Football in the form of rugby was taken to Canada by British immigrants not long after William Webb Ellis' historic run with a soccer ball in 1823 on the playing fields of Rugby School. The first account of rugby football in Canada dates to 1862 when British regiments in Montreal were playing the game on an informal basis, and the formation of the Montreal Football Club in 1868 gave the sport an official Canadian birth date.

In the United States at that time, the schools were still playing according to the Princeton Rules, a game that more closely resembled soccer. Soccer might even have become the great U.S. game if Harvard had not broken away and started playing a rugbylike game under Boston Rules, which isolated them from their Ivy League brethren at Yale, Columbia, Princeton, and Rutgers. Harvard's search for opponents brought them into competition with Montreal's McGill University.

The McGill–Harvard matches

The schools first met in Cambridge, Mass., on May 14 and 15, 1874, for two games that had a profound effect on the development of football on both sides of the border. Because McGill only brought 11 of their usual 15 players, Harvard players decided that they preferred this innovation, and 11 eventually became the standard number of a U.S. football team. The Canadians, however, returned home and reverted to the English-style game with 15 players on a side. Today, a Canadian team has 12 men on a side, a move suggested as early as 1900 but not widely used until 1912.

The colleges did not set the early pace in Canadian football as they did in the United States. Instead it was the clubs, such as the Toronto Argonaut Rowing Club, the Hamilton Amateur Athletic Association, and other groups in Guelph, Stratford, London, and Port Hope, that banded together to form the first league.

In 1882 the Ontario Rugby Football Union was formed, immediately followed by the Quebec Rugby Football Union. These groups and others combined in a loose confederation under the name of the Canadian Rugby Football Union, later shortened to Canadian Rugby Union. The colleges formed the Intercollegiate Rugby Football Union in 1898. In its formative years Canadian football was a player's game with no stadiums, admission charges, or other forms of commercialization. By 1900 railroads were opening the west and the game was played over most of Canada's 3,000-mile expanse. Still, when Governor General Lord Earl Grey offered a cup for the amateur football championship of Canada in 1910, Ontario and Quebec were playing the best football by far, with teams in other regions more or less overlooked. Despite its amateur beginning, competition for the Grey Cup, as Lord Grey's trophy came to be known, has, since 1954, been challenged exclusively by teams that now make up the professional Canadian Football League.

Grey Cup competition

Development of the modern game. As with many Canadian institutions, the game of football felt a strong U.S.

influence. One of the earliest and most prominent came in the person of Frank ("Shag") Shaughnessy, a former Notre Dame player and coach who in 1912 took over as football coach at McGill. He brought motion into the backfield, created the idea of a secondary on defense, and generally kept one step ahead of those who copied his moves. Within 10 years he had completely transformed the Canadian game.

In the 1930s several U.S. college stars went north in search of jobs in cities like Winnipeg, Regina, Calgary, and Edmonton. Among them was Fritz Hanson, a running back from North Dakota State University, who in 1935 teamed with seven other Americans to lead Winnipeg through an undefeated season in the west. Winnipeg fans contributed a then unheard-of $7,500 to send the club east, where they beat a powerful Hamilton team 18–12 and brought the west its first Grey Cup. The eastern teams responded with a rule that only Americans living in town on January 1 could play during that year. When the Regina (now Saskatchewan) Roughriders won the western championship in 1936 without adhering to the rule, they were ruled ineligible for Grey Cup play. Sarnia beat Ottawa 26–20 for the cup that year amid howls of western protest.

After the 1936 controversy, the colleges withdrew from Grey Cup competition altogether. Professionalism had been increasing in the game to that point, and professional–amateur interplay became common. By the 1950s, however, it was obvious that the days of amateur–professional play were numbered, as the professional teams of the Eastern Big Four (Toronto, Hamilton, Ottawa, Montreal) and the Western Interprovincial Football Union (Winnipeg, Saskatchewan, Calgary, Edmonton, Vancouver) dominated competition. (In 1987 Montreal dropped out and Winnipeg moved into the Eastern Division.) In 1956 the two groups joined the Canadian Football Council (later the Canadian Football League) and the amateurs were ruled out of Grey Cup play.

A major impetus in the turn of professionalism was the 1948 Calgary team, a powerhouse built around coach Les Lear, quarterback Keith Spaith, receiver Woody Strode, and Chuck Anderson, all from U.S. professional teams. After the team won in the west, a large proportion of the population of the city boarded special trains for Toronto, where the fans staged a wild two-day celebration and the team won the Grey Cup, beating Ottawa 12–7. After this, every city in the country felt it had to put on a better show than Calgary and hire U.S. players to compete on the football field. The league limit on imports per team was gradually increased from six to 16, with the remaining 20 nonimports. Players in the CFL have, since 1965, been classified as imports or nonimports based on football training rather than place of birth or citizenship.

Use of U.S. players

Canadian teams found themselves competing with U.S. professional teams for top U.S. college players. At one point, in 1951 and 1953, Winnipeg raided the NFL and signed defensive tackle Dick Huffman of Los Angeles and end Harry ("Bud") Grant of Philadelphia, respectively, while in 1954 Calgary signed quarterback Eddie LeBaron of Washington, end Gene Brito of Washington, and defensive end Ed Henke of San Francisco. In 1955 Harry Sonshine did the same type of raiding for Toronto. Dozens of U.S. players joined the Canadian league, which at the time offered higher salaries than the NFL. With the new players came a mercurial rise in status for the Grey Cup competition, which became a week-long festival and the premier sporting event in the country.

The 1960s were sobering years, as the rivalry between the NFL and the AFL priced the Canadians out of the top talent market. Merger of the two U.S. leagues in 1970 restored a degree of normalcy.

PLAY OF THE GAME

Although Canadian football stems from English rugby, modern rules changes have brought it closer and closer to U.S. football. The playing field is larger, being 110 yards (100 metres) long and 65 yards (59.4 metres) wide. The end zones are 20 yards (18.6 metres) deep. The wide field encourages lateral passing, and the deep end zones, forward passing for touchdowns. There are 12 men on a team. The extra man is invariably used in the backfield or as a wide receiver on offense and as a back on defense. The other positions are the same as those in U.S. football and have the same names.

A team has only three downs in which to make a first down in the Canadian game. Teams must try for the big gain, which makes the play more open than in U.S. football. To offset the lack of a down, defensive linemen must be one yard away from the ball when they take their stance. Also, all offensive backs may be in motion before the ball is snapped. Blocking is unlimited on rushing plays and is permitted downfield after a pass has been completed. Blocking above the waist is allowed only on punt returns, and a kicked ball still in bounds must be played; tacklers, however, cannot come within five yards of the safety back fielding the punt until he has touched the ball. One point is scored if the team in possession kicks the ball over the defending team's goal line and the defending team fails to return the ball out of the goal area, 20 yards beyond the goal line, or if the defending team's safety back is tackled or run out of bounds in his own end zone or he chooses to concede the point after receiving a kick.

After scoring a touchdown, the scoring team may choose to kick for a one-point convert (conversion in U.S. football) or, scrimmaging from the five-yard line, to attempt a two-point convert by either running or passing the ball over the goal line. The defending team on all convert plays can score two points if, by blocking a one-point convert attempt and recovering the ball, or intercepting a pass, or recovering a fumbled ball on all convert attempts, it returns the ball over the other team's goal line.

Other scoring is exactly the same as that of the U.S. professional game. Offensive and defensive formations are also similar to those in U.S. football. (D.Gi./J.F.I.)

Rugby

Rugby, also known as rugger, is a football game played with an oval ball by two teams of 15 or 13 players each, its distinctive features being: (1) players may use their hands and catch, throw, or run with the ball in addition to maneuvering it with their feet as in association football (soccer); and (2) the scrum, or scrummage, a method of putting the ball in play from a set formation in which eight men on each team—six in a 13-per-side game—form a closely packed group including two front rows of three men each, the ball being thrown onto the ground between them and each team trying to get possession. Although the ball may be kicked or carried or passed from player to player by hand or foot, it may not be passed forward. Players running with the ball inevitably caused tackling to become a part of the game. A tackle occurs when, depending on the form of rugby being played, a player carrying the ball is held by one or more opponents so that he is brought to the ground or the ball touches the ground, or he is unable to free himself without delay and is unable to continue play. Scoring in the game is achieved by touching the ball down in the opponents' goal area behind their goal line (a try) and by kicking the ball over the crossbar between the opponents' goalposts (a goal).

Running and tackling

There are two principal types of rugby football: Rugby Union, which is the 15-a-side amateur game; and Rugby League, a 13-a-side partly professional game. The chief differences between the two are described under *Rugby League* below.

HISTORY

Rugby Union. *Origins.* According to tradition, rugby began in 1823, when, during a game of football at Rugby School, William Webb Ellis picked up the ball and ran with it. The run was a clear violation of the rules of the game that later came to be called association football, or soccer; but the illegality proved popular and led to the game of rugby, the primarily ball-handling game, as distinct from soccer, the primarily kicking game. More exact historians date the origin of rugby to about 1838–39 and identify the dauntless runner as one Mackie. In the early 1840s it became accepted that a player could "run-in," that is, catch a ball on the rebound and, if none of his teammates was ahead of him, carry the ball across the goal line and touch it down. In 1846 rules of rugby were published at the school. From 1840 to 1860 many varieties of football were played with rules varying from school to school and from club to club, in some cases mixing soccer and rugby. In 1863 the Football Association (FA) was formed in London, and after a futile attempt to reconcile the rules to accommodate the two games, rugby was left outside the FA.

In 1871 the Rugby Football Union (RFU) was formed as the English governing body, and the first match between England and Scotland was played. The Scottish Football Union was founded in 1873 (from 1924 it was called the Scottish Rugby Union). The game in both England and Scotland had developed mainly at the public (private) schools. In Ireland a club had been organized at Trinity College in 1865 and others followed. The Irish Football Union and a rival North of Ireland Football Union were formed in 1874. The two merged as the Irish Rugby Football Union in 1879. The Welsh Rugby Union was formed in 1881, and the organization of what came to be called the home unions was complete.

Rugby abroad. Soldiers, businessmen, engineers, diplomats, and students carried rugby to the countries of the British Empire. The Southern Rugby Football Union (later called the Australian Rugby Football Union) was founded in 1875. In that year rugby was first played in southern Africa at Cape Town. British regiments helped found a club at King William's Town in 1878. The Kimberley diamond discovery spread the game into that region (1883–86), and rugby was being played in the Johannesburg and Pretoria areas by 1888. The Western Province formed a union in 1883; the South African Rugby Football Board was established in 1889. The first match in New Zealand was played at Nelson in 1870, and by 1890 there were about 700 clubs organized in various provincial unions. The New Zealand Football Union was founded in 1892. Australia, South Africa, and New Zealand, particularly the last two, remained strongholds of the game.

Australian rugby

In 1882 unions were formed in Ontario and Quebec that soon affiliated with the Canadian Rugby Union. The original game was played through World War II in the two provinces, but a modified form of it arose and came to be called Canadian football. In the Maritime Provinces and British Columbia the rugby game persisted. Intercollegiate competition began in 1898, although in 1874 McGill University, playing an essentially rugby game, had two matches with Harvard University in the United States, playing an essentially soccer game. This event was important in the development of U.S. football.

Influence in Canada

British businessmen, students, and foreign-service personnel introduced the game to Europe from the 1870s, particularly in the French cities of Le Havre, Nantes, Bordeaux, and Paris. In France the game was governed by the Union des Sociétés Françaises de Sports Athlétiques, a multisports group, from 1887, and from 1920 by the Fédération Française de Rugby, with which 173 clubs were affiliated (increased to 400 in the 1980s). Romanian students at the University of Paris took the game home with them and formed clubs that at first were affiliated with a multisports organization as in France. The Federatia Romana de Rugby was founded in 1931. Just as Australia, South Africa, and New Zealand became rugby strongholds, so did France and, to a lesser extent, Romania.

English engineers introduced the game to Argentina in the 1880s, and the Argentine Rugby Union was founded in 1899. Soldiers took the game to Fiji in the mid-1880s; the Fiji Rugby Union was formed in 1913. A Japanese student who had learned the game at Cambridge University took it home with him in 1899, and by the late 1980s Japan had more than 80,000 players representing schools, universities, and factories.

In the United States and Canada, rugby competed with association football in a situation like that earlier in Great Britain, where clubs played by their own rules and occasionally combined elements of both games. Although U.S. football had largely supplanted both soccer and rugby by late in the 19th century, rugby enjoyed a revival from 1905 on the Pacific coast after U.S. football was banned there in the aftermath of a public furor over violence and player deaths and injuries. Rugby remained popular there after U.S. football had been restored to its preeminent position. West coast players largely made up the teams that won at the 1920 and 1924 Olympic Games, after which rugby was dropped as an Olympic sport. In the late 1920s rugby began to be played in the New York area, and it soon spread to such eastern universities as Yale, Princeton, and Harvard, which formed the Eastern Rugby Union. English teams, notably Cambridge University, visited during the 1930s. During World War II rugby largely disappeared, but it was revived in New York in the early 1950s, as was the collegiate game.

On the centenary of the RFU in 1971, 50 countries sent representatives to the Centenary Congress at Cambridge. At that time, England had 1,600 clubs, with more than 100,000 regular players. Japan had 60,000 players; Fiji, 12,000; and Romania, 6,500. The United States of America Rugby Association was formed in 1975, including the Eastern, Midwestern, Pacific Coast, and Western unions and involving 1,000 clubs and 50,000 players. In Canada, Rugby Union was particularly strong in British Columbia. Across Canada during the 1970s, rugby clubs increased from 100 to nearly 200 and players from 5,000 to 10,000, and they continued to grow thereafter.

Growth in North America

Two significant schisms occurred in the history of rugby. First, in 1895, 22 northern England clubs resigned from the RFU and formed the Rugby League. The dissident clubs had asked for "broken time," compensation for players who lost time from work while playing rugby. Second, allegations of professionalism in French rugby led to a breaking off of competition between the United Kingdom and France (1931–39); play was resumed in 1947.

Development of Rugby League. The Northern Football Union, comprising the teams that had seceded from the RFU in 1895, was called the Rugby Football League from the 1920s, and the breakaway game was thereafter referred to as Rugby League. Rugby League professionals are different from other sports professionals in that they do not devote full time to the game but hold other jobs. They are paid a fee for matches. (Differences in rules and play between Rugby Union and League are discussed below under *Play of the game.*)

Development of game. Although it has been played in other parts of the British Isles, such as southern Wales and the London area, the professional Rugby League game has established a firm foothold in Britain only in the three northern counties of Yorkshire, Lancashire, and Cumbria. An amateur branch of the game has, however, spread throughout Britain since its organization was taken over by the British Amateur Rugby League Association in 1973. At that date there were 150 amateur league clubs; by 1987 there were more than 800 clubs with some 20,000 players. It is played in nearly 40 universities.

The League game has also taken firm root in France, Australia, New Zealand, and Papua New Guinea. Like Rugby Union, the League game in France is largely confined to the southern part of the country, and it has flourished on a strictly competitive basis. In Australia the main centres of the game are Sydney and Brisbane, though it is widely played in cities and towns throughout the country and has a larger following than has Rugby Union. In New Zealand the game is less firmly established than Rugby Union, but it is played in most cities and big towns and is notably strong in Auckland and Wellington.

Rugby League strongholds

As a partly professional game, requiring a steady intake of money from gate receipts, Rugby League has been ahead of Rugby Union in developing along crowd-pleasing lines. The reduction of a team from 15 to 13 players, for instance, left the field less cluttered and so more suitable for attractive open play. Rugby League was also ahead of Rugby Union in introducing laws to curb the stagnation of repeated kicks over the touchline.

Organization and tournaments. *Rugby Union.* That rugby was predominantly a British and Commonwealth game is shown by the fact that the International Rugby Football Board, the rule-making body established in 1886, had only English (six) and Scottish, Irish, and Welsh (two each) members at its founding in 1886. The number of

English members was reduced to four in 1911 and to two in 1948, when New Zealand, South Africa, and Australia were admitted with one member each. In 1958 all were given two members. Although France played its first international matches (against New Zealand and England) in 1906, it was not admitted to the board until the late 1970s. It was not until the mid-1980s that the scope of the board was widened by the creation of associate member countries, which, however, were not accorded voting rights.

Meanwhile in 1934 the Fédération Internationale de Rugby Amateur (FIRA) was founded with Germany, France, The Netherlands, Italy, Portugal, Romania, Sweden, Czechoslovakia, and Catalonia as members. The federation later expanded to include other European and Mediterranean countries. All FIRA matches were to be played under International Board rules. Thus, unlike other sports, Rugby Union has two international bodies.

Play variation among countries

The kinds of competition vary among different rugby countries. From the beginning in England, Scotland, Ireland, and Wales, club competition consisted mainly of friendly matches. County cup competition from the late 1880s involved an elimination (knockout) tournament, not league play. The same was true of university competition. National club competition came only in the 1970s.

Elsewhere club rugby was almost universally based on the league system, often with cup competitions added. Such was the case in New Zealand from the early days, so that interclub leagues came to span a range of 15 grades of players from those for small boys up to the senior clubs. Interprovincial competition began in 1902 with play for the Ranfurly Shield, given by the Earl of Ranfurly, who was then governor general. Play for the shield is by challenge. South Africa, too, has leagues for clubs and a national competition among provincial teams for the Currie Cup, given in 1891 by Sir Donald Currie to the British team about to tour South Africa, for presentation to the best South African team. Ultimately the cup went to the South African Board as a trophy.

The highest level of international competition for Rugby Union teams is the World Cup, played for the William Webb Ellis Trophy. The World Cup was inaugurated in 1987 and hosted jointly by New Zealand and Australia, with the final in Auckland. Sixteen countries took part, by invitation. The eight International Board countries—minus South Africa because of its government's apartheid (racial segregation) policy—were joined by Argentina, Romania, Fiji, Tonga, Japan, the United States, Canada, Italy, and Zimbabwe.

The highest level of international rugby before the staging of the first World Cup was the Test series—two or more games between national teams. Such competition began between New Zealand and Australia in 1894 and continued under firm Test conditions from 1903. South African and British Test matches began in 1891. In 1888 a British team toured New Zealand and Australia, and its successors continued to do so regularly. New Zealand first played in Great Britain in 1888–89 and 1905–06, and South Africa did so in 1906–07 and 1912–13. Such tours continued except in the war years. In the 1920s New Zealand, South Africa, and Australia toured regularly in each other's countries, and by mid-century New Zealand and South African matches were recognized as unofficial world matches. In 1967, however, the South African policy of apartheid led to postponement of a tour by South Africa because the New Zealand team included Maoris. New Zealand, with Maori players, did tour South Africa in 1970. A South African tour in Great Britain in 1969–70 aroused protests against apartheid, but the matches were played. National rugby unions did not ostracize South Africa because of the apartheid policy as did other national sports organizations. In 1973 the New Zealand Rugby Union protested its government's refusal to let South Africa tour there. South Africa did tour New Zealand in 1981.

Political involvement

International competition in France began when New Zealand toured there in the 1905–06 season, and England first met France later in the same season. France played in the home unions competition in 1909–10 but was not truly competitive until after World War II. The French made their first overseas tour in 1958, to South Africa, where they became the first visiting national team to win since a British team did so in 1896. France played Romania regularly from 1924; in their first match after World War II, in 1957 at Bucharest, the crowd numbered 110,000, the largest attendance at any rugby game up to that time.

In the last quarter of the 20th century, touring continued to be popular. South America (usually mostly Argentines) became a new force, even beating South Africa. The troubles of the latter on tour continued, not from national unions or clubs but from segments of the public, with matches in the United States canceled or played clandestinely after a New Zealand tour had been violently protested during play. Romania rose in stature as a touring team. (For records of Rugby Union international competition, see SPORTING RECORD in the *Micropædia.*)

Rugby League. Although Rugby League is played at strength in no more than four countries, the national teams of these four, Great Britain, France, Australia, and New Zealand, played a World Cup tournament from 1954 to 1972 under the governancy of the Rugby International Board (founded 1946). There were regular tours somewhat after the manner of Rugby Union tours, by Australia, for example, in Great Britain and France and by Great Britain in Australia and New Zealand. The French toured Australia and New Zealand, and the New Zealanders toured in Great Britain and France.

In less far-ranging international encounters, Great Britain settled into a pattern of playing France at home and away each season, and Australia had more or less regular matches against New Zealand. Matches between Australia and New Zealand were for the Trans-Tasman Cup, which was retained by the one country until beaten in a Test series by the other. A national team, though less regularly, represented Wales. (For records of Rugby League World Cup competition and Test matches, see SPORTING RECORD in the *Micropædia.*)

In 1975 international Test-match championships involving England, France, Australia, and New Zealand replaced the World Cup competition.

PLAY OF THE GAME

Field of play and equipment. Based on International Board rules, rugby is played on a rectangular field not more than 75.5 yards (69 metres) wide; the maximum distance between the goal lines is 110 yards (100 metres) and beyond each goal line the end zone, called "in goal," extends not more than 24.07 yards (22 metres). At the centre of the goal lines are two goalposts 18 feet six inches (5.6 metres) apart with a crossbar 10 feet (three metres) above the ground. (See Figure 9.)

The inflated ball is oval, less pointed than the U.S. and Canadian football. It is 11 to 11.8 inches (280 to 300 millimetres) long, 22.9 to 24.4 inches (580 to 620 millimetres) in circumference, and weighs 14.5 to 15.5 ounces (400 to 440 grams). The outside casing of the ball is usually of leather or plastic.

Ball dimensions

The players wear jerseys, shorts, stockings, and studded (cleated) boots. Rigid protective equipment is not allowed.

Principles of play. *Rugby Union.* The game is controlled by a referee assisted by two touch judges, and there are normally two periods of 40 minutes each.

From the general free-for-all with hacking (kicking in the shins) and tripping that existed in the early days, the game was gradually refined until it reached its present state. When the first match between England and Scotland was played in 1871, there were 20 men on each team, and it was not agreed to reduce the number to 15 until 1877. Scotland won the 1871 game, scoring the only goal of the match. Scotland and England each achieved a try, but it was not possible to win a match in any other way than by scoring goals. A try, touching the ball down in the goal area behind the opponents' goal line, scored no points but allowed the player's team an unimpeded place kick at goal from a point on the field not farther from the touchline than the try had been scored. In 1875–76 it was agreed that if the number of goals (field goals) kicked by each side

Tries and goals

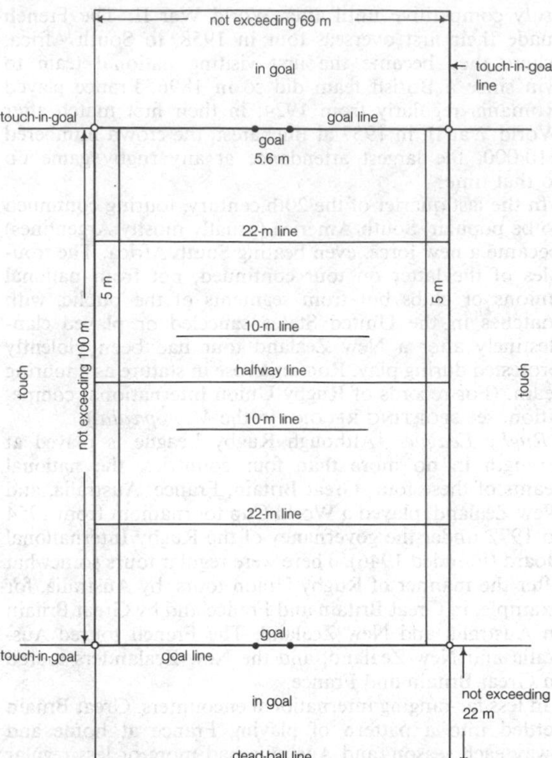

Figure 9: Rugby playing field, showing divisions and goals.

was the same or if no goal was kicked, the result would be decided by the number of tries achieved. Thus was the try (in U.S. and Canadian football, a touchdown), the scoring of which was to become the chief aim of the game, for the first time brought into the reckoning. A further refinement was introduced during the 1886–87 season with the adoption of the Cheltenham College rating, which had been in force at that college for some 20 years, making three tries equal to one goal. A number of changes to the scoring system were made over the next several years, but from 1905 the modern scoring values were essentially established, a try being worth three points, its subsequent conversion into a goal providing an additional two points. Dropped goals, at that stage worth four points, in 1948 were devalued to three, and in 1971 a try was revalued at four points. A dropped goal is scored by a drop kick from the field—*i.e.,* when a player, in play, lets the ball fall from his hands and kicks it at the first rebound as it rises so that it goes between the goal posts and above the crossbar. Three points may also be scored by a successful penalty kick at goal awarded for an infringement of the laws by the opposition.

Scrums and line-outs

The two basic set pieces, or formations, of the game are the scrum and the line-out. A scrum is formed by the eight forwards of each side bending forward, binding one another with their arms, and pushing against the opposing eight forwards similarly bound in three ranks or rows. The ball is put into the tunnel between the two front rows, whose members use their feet to try to procure the ball for their team. A line-out is the method of bringing the ball back into play after it has gone out over the touchline (out-of-bounds). To form a line-out, at least two forwards of each team line up in single files in a line perpendicular to the spot where the ball crossed the touchline. A gap or space is left between the two lines of players, and the ball is thrown in above this gap so that the forwards of both teams may try to grab it or otherwise obtain possession of it for their team.

While the forwards are forming a scrum or a line-out, the other players, normally divided into two halfbacks, four three-quarters (the left- and right-centre backs and left- and right-wing backs), and a fullback, take up position several yards apart in various formations between their forwards and their own goal line. For a line-out the three-quarters stay at least 10 yards back, the idea being that by passing or running or kicking the ball in the open field they may find a way either of scoring a try or of dropping a goal.

Besides the scrum and the line-out there is also the loose maul or ruck. This occurs when, in the open field, the progress of the ball is temporarily checked—by a player dropping it, falling over while carrying it, or being held by an opponent while in possession of it, for instance—and two or more players gather round and struggle to procure the ball for their team. The maul or ruck is an especially profitable source of possession because the opposing defense is unlikely to be as strictly aligned as it is for a scrum or a line-out. Blocking, an integral part of U.S. and Canadian football, is not allowed.

The game settled into the pattern of big forwards struggling for the ball so that their faster and more agile backs could pass it and run with it in the hope of scoring goals. But as players increased in pace through improved fitness, without a corresponding increase in the size of the field, the open spaces became fewer, defenses became more effective, and attacking moves were all too easily stifled. Play began to stagnate and to become dull, both for the player and for the spectator. In order to reverse this trend and to encourage the return of flowing movement to the game, the International Board made several important changes in the laws in 1964. It was ruled that while a line-out (putting the ball back in play after it had gone out-of-bounds) was taking place, each set of three-quarters must remain at least 10 yards nearer their own goal line than the point of the line-out, thus leaving a clear no-man's-land in which attacks could be developed; that backs must not advance beyond the hindmost foot of scrums until the ball was out; that forwards must not advance from a scrum until the ball was out; and that the team throwing in the ball at a line-out had the right to determine the shortness of the line-out, thus preventing opponents from straggling across the field in a defensive screen. Another change, in 1970, made it illegal for a player to kick the ball directly over the touchline or sideline except from within 25 yards of his own goal line.

Rule changes of 1964

One of the charms of the Rugby Union game is the infinite variety of its tactics. In a basic orthodox situation, like a scrum on the right-hand side of the field, the ball may simply be passed rapidly by hand through the halfbacks and the centre three-quarters to the left-wing three-quarter, each man running a few yards before parting with the ball. The wing may then be able to run past his immediate opponent by swerving or sidestepping or simply by using strength and speed; a try will probably be scored. But the attacking team may already have tried an orthodox move of this kind and may have discovered that the opposition is especially strong defensively and also possesses exceptional speed. In this case, the attacking team must depart from the orthodox and try to discover a chink in their opponents' armour elsewhere.

Rugby League. The League variant is played on similar

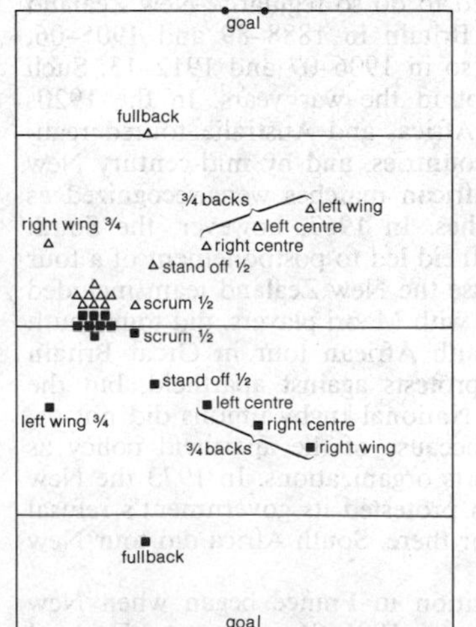

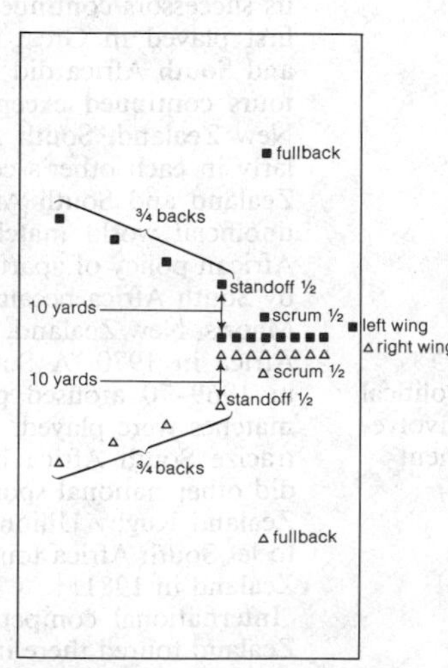

Figure 10: (Left) Players in position for a scrummage. (Right) Positions of players for a line-out.

Forwards engaged in a scrummage (Wales–France Rugby International, Paris, 1970).
Sports Illustrated photograph by Gerry Cranham, © Time Inc.

fields, and the aim, as in Union football, is to score tries and goals. As in Rugby Union, a try in Rugby League is worth four points and a conversion two points, but a penalty kick is two points instead of three and a dropped goal one point rather than the three in Rugby Union.

Scoring variations

There are only 13 men on a Rugby League team instead of 15. The two who have been dispensed with are the two wing forwards, so that a League scrum has three men in the front row, two in the second, and one in the back. There are no line-outs in Rugby League; if the ball goes out of play over the touchline, a scrum is ordered. Nor is the Union game's ruck or maul to be found in Rugby League. When a player is brought down in possession of the ball, he has to be allowed to stand up face-to-face with an opponent and attempt to tap the ball back to his own teammates with his foot. (D.B.J.F.)

Basketball

The only major sport strictly of U.S. origin, basketball was invented by James Naismith (1861–1939) on or about Dec. 1, 1891, at the International Young Men's Christian Association (YMCA) Training School (now Springfield College), Springfield, Mass., where Naismith was an instructor in physical education. Naismith prepared a set of 13 simple rules embodying five principles that still govern today's game:

1. There must be a ball—large, light, and handled with the hands. 2. There shall be no running with the ball. 3. No member of either team shall be restricted from getting the ball at any time it is in play. 4. Both teams are to occupy the same area, yet there is to be no personal contact. 5. The goal shall be horizontal and elevated.

Principles of the game

Naismith used as goals two half-bushel peach baskets, which gave the sport its name. The students were enthusiastic. After much running and shooting, William R. Chase chanced to connect on a mid-court shot and that historic contest ended in a 1–0 score. The Springfield students went home on Christmas vacation and told their friends and the local YMCA people about the newly invented game. Numerous associations wrote Naismith for a copy of the rules, which were published in the Jan. 15, 1892, issue of the *Triangle,* the campus paper.

HISTORY

The early years. In the early years, the number of players on a team varied according to the number in the class and the size of the playing surface. In 1894 teams began to play with five on a side when the playing surface was less than 1,800 square feet (167.2 square metres); the number rose to seven when the gymnasium measured from 1,800 to 3,600 square feet and up to nine when the playing areas exceeded that. In 1895 the number was occasionally set at five by mutual consent and, two years later, the rules stipulated five, and this number has remained.

Since five of Naismith's original players were Canadians, not surprisingly Canada was the first country outside the United States to play the game. Basketball was introduced in France in 1893, in London in 1894, in Australia, China, and India soon thereafter, and in Japan in 1900.

While basketball helped swell the membership of YMCAs because of the availability of their gyms, within five years the game was outlawed by various associations because where the gyms formerly were occupied by classes of 50 or 60 members, the areas were now monopolized by only 10 to 18 players. The banishment of the game induced many members to terminate their YMCA membership and to hire halls to play the game, thus paving the way to the professionalization of the sport.

Early uniforms and equipment

Originally, players wore one of three styles of uniforms: knee-length football trousers; jersey tights, as commonly worn by wrestlers; and short padded pants, forerunners of today's uniforms, plus knee guards. The courts often were of irregular shapes with occasional obstructions such as pillars, stairways, or offices that interfered with play. In 1903 it was ruled that all boundary lines must be straight. In 1893 the Narragansett Machinery Co., of Providence, R.I., marketed a hoop of iron with a hammock style of basket. Originally, a ladder, then a pole, and finally, a chain fastened to the bottom of the net was used to retrieve a ball after a goal had been scored. Nets open at the bottom were adopted in 1912–13. In 1895–96 the points for making a basket (field goal) were reduced from three to two, and for making a free throw (shot uncontested from a line in front of the basket after a foul had been committed) from three to one.

At first, spectators behind the basket leaned over the railings and deflected the ball to favour one side or hinder the other, and in 1895 teams were urged to provide a four-by-six-foot screen for the purpose of eliminating interference. Soon after, wooden backboards proved more suitable. Glass backboards were legalized by the professionals in 1908–09 and by colleges in 1909–10. Fan-shaped backboards were made legal in 1940–41, and transparent backboards, although commonly used in public auditoriums since the mid-1930s, were finally authorized in 1946–47. In 1920–21 the backboards were moved two feet, and in 1939–40 four feet, in from the end lines to reduce frequent stepping out-of-bounds.

A soccer ball was used for the first two years. In 1894 the first basketball was marketed. It was laced, close to 32 inches (81 centimetres) or about four inches larger than the soccer ball in circumference, and weighed less than 20 ounces. By 1948–49 when the laceless molded ball was made official, the size had been set at 30 inches.

Introduction to colleges

The distinction of becoming the first college to play the game belongs to either Geneva College (Beaver Falls, Pa.) or the University of Iowa. C.O. Bemis heard about the new sport at Springfield and tried it out with his stu-

By courtesy of the Basketball Hall of Fame, Springfield, Mass.

Players shooting into a closed-bottom peach basket in an outdoor game of basketball, 1892.

dents at Geneva in 1892. At Iowa, H.F. Kallenberg, who attended Springfield in 1890, wrote Naismith for a copy of the rules and also presented the game to his students. At Springfield, Kallenberg met Amos Alonzo Stagg, who became athletic director at the new University of Chicago in 1892. The first college basketball game with five on a side was played at Iowa City, Iowa, on Jan. 18, 1896. The University of Chicago won, 15–12, with neither team using a substitute. Kallenberg refereed that game, a common practice in that era—and some of the spectators took exception to some of his decisions. (R.G.Lo./W.G.M.)

The colleges formed their own rules committee in 1905, and by 1913 there were at least five sets of rules: the collegiate, YMCA-Amateur Athletic Union, and state militia groups, and two varieties of professional rules. Teams often agreed to play under a different set for each half of a game. To establish some measure of uniformity, the colleges, AAU, and YMCA formed the Joint Rules Committee in 1915. This group was renamed the National Basketball Committee (NBC) of the United States and Canada in 1936 and until 1979 served as the game's sole amateur rule-making body. In that year, however, the colleges broke away to form their own rules committee, and during the same year the National Federation of State High School Associations likewise assumed the task of establishing separate playing rules for the high schools. The NCAA Rules Committee for men is a 12-member board composed of representatives from six Division I schools and three each from Divisions II and III. It has jurisdiction over colleges, junior colleges, the National Association of Intercollegiate Athletics (NAIA), and Armed Forces basketball. There is a similar body for women's play.

Growth of the game. Basketball grew steadily but slowly in popularity and importance in the United States and internationally in the first three decades after World War II. Interest in the game deepened as a result of television exposure, but with the advent of cable television, especially during the 1980s, the game's popularity exploded at all levels. Given a timely mix of spectacular players, such as Earvin ("Magic") Johnson, Julius Erving ("Dr. J"), Larry Bird, and Michael Jordan, and the greatly increased exposure, basketball moved quickly to the forefront of the American sporting scene, alongside such traditional leaders as baseball and football. Four areas of the game developed during this period: U.S. school and college basketball, women's basketball, international basketball, and professional basketball. (For results of the U.S. college tournaments, international men's and women's champions, and U.S. professional champions see SPORTING RECORD in the *Micropædia.*)

U.S. school and college basketball. Basketball at the school and college level developed from a structured, rigid game in the early days to one that is often fast-paced and high-scoring. Individual skills improved markedly, and although basketball continued to be regarded as the ultimate team game, individualistic, one-on-one performers came to be not only accepted but used as an effective means of winning games.

In the early years games were frequently won with point totals of less than 30, and the game, from the spectator's viewpoint, was slow. Once a team acquired a modest lead the popular tactic was to stall the game by passing the ball without trying to score, in an attempt to run out the clock. The NBC, seeing the need to discourage such slow-down tactics, instituted a number of rule changes. In 1932–33 a line was drawn at mid-court and the offensive team was required to advance the ball past it within 10 seconds or lose possession. Five years later, in 1937–38, the centre jump following each field goal or free throw was eliminated. Instead, the defending team was permitted to inbound the ball from the out-of-bounds line underneath the basket. Nearly four decades passed before an alteration of like magnitude was made in the college game. After experimentation the NCAA Rules Committee installed a 45-second shot clock in 1985, restricting the time a team could control the ball before shooting, and one year later implemented a three-point shot rule for baskets made beyond a distance of 19 feet nine inches.

Rule changes to speed up the game

More noticeable alteration in the game came both at the playing and coaching levels. Stanford University's Hank Luisetti was the first to use and popularize the one-hand shot in the late 1930s. Until then the only outside attempts were two-handed push shots. In the 1950s and 1960s a shooting style evolved from Luisetti's push-off one hander to a jump shot, which is released at the top of the jump. West Virginia University guard Jerry West and Purdue University's Rick Mount were two players who demonstrated the devastating effectiveness of this shot.

Coaching strategy changed appreciably over the years. Frank W. Keaney, coach at Rhode Island University from 1921 to 1948, is credited with introducing the concept of "fast breaking" basketball, in which the offensive team rushes the ball upcourt hoping to get a good shot before the defense can get set. Another man who contributed to a quicker pace of play, particularly through the use of the pressure defense, was Adolph Rupp, who became the University of Kentucky's coach in 1931 and turned their program into one of the most storied in basketball history.

Defensive coaching philosophy, similarly, has undergone change. Whereas pioneer coaches such as Oklahoma A&M University's Henry Iba or Long Island University's Clair Bee taught strictly a man-to-man defense, the zone defense, developed by Cam Henderson of Marshall University in West Virginia, later became an integral part of the game (see below *Play of the game*).

Restricting taller players

Over the years one of the rules makers' concerns was to neutralize the advantage of taller players. At six feet five inches Joe Lapchick was considered very tall when he played for the Original Celtics in the 1920s, but as even taller players appeared, rules were changed in response. To prevent tall players from stationing themselves near the basket, a rule was instituted in 1932–33 prohibiting the player with the ball from standing inside the foul lane with his back to the basket for more than three seconds; the three-second rule later applied to any attacking player in the foul lane. In 1937–38 a new rule forbade any player from touching the ball when it was in the basket or on its rim (basket interference), and in 1944–45 it became illegal for any defending player to touch the ball on its downward flight toward the basket (goaltending).

Era of George Mikan

Nevertheless, with each passing decade, the teams with the tallest players tended to dominate. Bob Kurland (seven feet) led Oklahoma A&M to two NCAA championships in the 1940s and led the nation in scoring in 1945–46. In the same era George Mikan (six feet 10 inches) scored more than 550 points in each of his final two seasons at DePaul University before going on to play nine professional seasons in which he scored more than 11,000 points. Mikan was an outstanding player, not only because of his size but his ability to shoot sweeping hook shots with both hands.

In the 1950s Bill Russell (six feet nine inches) led the University of San Francisco to two NCAA championships before going on to become one of the greatest centres in professional basketball history. Wilt Chamberlain (seven feet, $1\frac{1}{16}$ inches) played at the University of Kansas before turning professional in the late 1950s and is regarded as the greatest all-around big man ever to play. It remained, however, for seven-foot $1\frac{3}{8}$-inch Lew Alcindor (later Kareem Abdul-Jabbar) to most influence the rules. After his sophomore (1966–67) year at the University of California at Los Angeles (UCLA), the dunk shot was banned from collegiate basketball, ostensibly because the rules committee felt, again, that the big men had too great an advantage. The rule was rescinded for the 1976–77 season and the dunk shot became an important part of the game, electrifying both fans and players.

Much as the big men were important in the game's development, so too did the small- and medium-sized performers play a vital role. Bob Cousy, playing at Holy Cross College and later for the Boston Celtics, was regarded as one of the game's first great playmakers. He was among the first to use the behind-the-back pass and between-the-legs dribble as effective offensive maneuvers. Later, such smaller players as Providence College's Ernie DiGregorio, the University of North Carolina's Phil Ford, and Indiana's Isiah Thomas, proved the importance of their role. Between those two extremes are players like Louisiana State University's Pete Maravich, who set an all-time collegiate scoring record of 44.5 points per game in the 1969–70 season; Earvin Johnson, the point guard who led Michigan State University to a championship in 1979; Oscar Robertson, a dominating performer for the University of Cincinnati in the late 1950s; and Larry Bird of Indiana State University, who demonstrated versatility.

Effect of television

Nothing influenced the college game's growth, however, more than television. The NCAA championship games were televised nationally from 1963, and by the 1980s all three major television networks were telecasting intersectional college games during the November-to-March season. Rights fees for these games soared from a few million to well over $50,000,000 by the late 1980s. During the regular season more than 200 Division I basketball games were being telecast nationwide by cable networks, generating both revenue and tremendous exposure.

In the evolution of college basketball the darkest hours have been related to gambling scandals, the most serious of which arose in 1951. But in the 1960s, '70s, and '80s the game was again touched by the problem. Also, as the game began to draw more attention and generate more income, the pressure to win intensified, resulting in an outbreak of incidents of rule violations, especially with regard to recruitment of star players.

Postseason tournaments

The most identifiable phase of college basketball in America is the postseason tournament held in March. Interest in the NCAA tournament paralleled the growth of the game. The first basketball tournament was staged by the AAU in 1897 and was won by New York City's 23rd Street YMCA, later to become a traveling professional team known as the New York Wanderers. Although the YMCA was prominently identified with the game in its early years, it did not hold its first national tournament until 1923, and that event took place until 1962. The first national tournament for colleges was held in 1937 and was conducted by an organization in Kansas City, Mo., that later became the National Association of Intercollegiate Athletics.

New York City basketball writers organized the first National Invitation Tournament (NIT) in 1938, but a year later the New York City colleges took control of the event. Until the early 1950s, the NIT was considered the most prestigious U.S. tournament, but with the growth of the college-run NCAA championship, the NIT became a consolation event for teams that failed to make the NCAA selections. Originally all teams in the NIT were invited to New York City and the games were played in Madison Square Garden. From the early 1980s, however, the first three rounds were played at regional or campus sites before the final four teams were brought to New York City.

Manny Millan—SPORTS ILLUSTRATED

A dunk shot by Akeem Abdul Olajuwon of the University of Houston during an NCAA championship game with North Carolina State University.

The first NCAA tournament was played in 1939, and its growth took place in three stages. The first era ran through 1964, when it was essentially a tournament for champions of various conferences. There were just eight teams in the 1939 field, and by 1963 it had been expanded to 25 teams, all champions of their respective conferences, plus several successful independent teams. The most outstanding teams of the 1940s and 1950s participated in both tournaments, but, after the gambling scandals that followed the 1950 NIT championship, a rule was passed prohibiting a team from playing in both. Afterward the NCAA tournament progressively outgrew the NIT.

In 1964 the second era dawned as the UCLA Bruins, coached by John Wooden, began a period of domination over the NCAA field. From that season until 1975 Wooden led his teams to 10 NCAA championships. Only championships by Texas Western in 1966 and North Carolina State in 1974 interrupted UCLA's reign. In the eyes of many, the UCLA dynastic period probably had a regressive effect on the game's growth; a sport with such high predictability lost some of its attractiveness.

The third growth stage came with the end of UCLA's dominance. Champions began to emerge from all sections of the country. From the field of 25 in 1974, the NCAA tournament expanded to 64 participants, including not only conference championship teams but other outstanding teams from the same conferences as well. Three weeks of play culminate with the Final Four weekend, an event now comparable in general public interest and media attention with the Super Bowl and World Series.

Championships at the Division II, Division III, and NAIA levels also continued to grow in interest, reaping some of the fallout from the Division I popularity. The National Junior College Athletic Association tournament, first held in 1945, has been held in Hutchinson, Kan., since 1949. (L.W.D.)

High school basketball

About 17,000 high schools in the United States have basketball teams. Forty-eight of the 50 states annually conduct statewide tournaments in one or as many as five divisions. The other two states, New York and California, which formerly conducted state tournaments, now have district or area championships. Several states, including Arkansas, Georgia, Louisiana, Iowa, Oklahoma, Pennsylvania, Rhode Island, South Carolina, Tennessee, and Texas, conduct annual tournaments for girls. Between 1917 and 1930 the University of Chicago, under Stagg, sponsored a national schoolboy tournament, but the National Federation of State High School Athletic Associations, founded in 1920, opposed its continuance.

The most famous high school team of all time was the Passaic (N.J.) "Wonder Team" between 1919 and 1925, which won 159 consecutive games, until defeated by Hackensack. Another colourful team was Carr Creek, Ky., of 1927–28, consisting of eight players, all related, who owned no uniforms, lost the state tourney finals in four overtime periods, to Ashland High (13–11), then won three contests in the national tournament in Chicago before losing to Vienna, Ga., the national champions.

Basketball for children

While basketball is competitively a winter sport, it is played on a 12-month basis—on summer playgrounds, in church, municipal, and industrial halls, in schoolyards and family driveways, and in summer camps—often on an informal basis between two or more contestants. Many grammar schools, youth groups, municipal recreation programs, churches, and other organizations conduct basketball programs for youngsters of less than high school age. Jay Archer, of Scranton, Pa., introduced "biddy" basketball in 1950 for boys and girls under 12 years of age, the court and equipment being adjusted for size.

U.S. women's basketball. Clara Baer, who introduced basketball at the H. Sophie Newcomb College for Women in New Orleans, influenced the women's style of play with

Pam McGee, centre for the University of Southern California, bringing down a rebound during a game with Rutgers.
By courtesy of the University of Southern California, Los Angeles

her set of women's rules, published in 1895. On receiving a diagram of the court from Naismith, Baer mistook dotted lines, indicating the areas in which players might best execute team play, to be restraining lines, with the result that the forwards, centres, and guards were confined to specified areas. This seemed appropriate because many felt that the men's game was too strenuous for women.

Women's rules

Women's rules over the years frequently have been modified. Until 1971 there were six players on a team, and the court was so divided that the three forwards played in the forecourt and did all the scoring, while the three guards covered the backcourt. Senda Berenson staged the first women's college basketball game in 1893 when her freshman and sophomore Smith College girls played against one another. In April 1895 the girls of the University of California (Berkeley) played Stanford University. Despite a multitude of hindrances (such as being "unladylike"), women's basketball gradually secured a foothold. In 1971, when women's rules were changed to reduce the number on a team from six players to five and women were freed from the limits imposed by the halfcourt game, it quickly raised the level of individual skills and competition.

NCAA jurisdiction

In the early 1980s control of the women's game was shifted from the Association for Intercollegiate Athletics for Women (AIAW) to the NCAA, a move that not only streamlined the operation and made it more efficient but also added to its visibility. The women's NCAA championship tournament runs concurrently with the men's, and its final game is nationally televised. Under NCAA rules the size of the basketball used by women was reduced slightly, creating a higher-scoring game. The Olympics added women's basketball in 1976. The U.S. team lost 112–77 to the Soviet team in the finals that year. Individual women stars have been heavily recruited by colleges, but the Women's Professional Basketball League (WPBL), begun in 1978, lasted only three years. This, however, did not slow the development of stars in the college ranks.

International competition. The success of international basketball was greatly advanced by Forrest C. ("Phog") Allen, a Naismith disciple and a former coach at the University of Kansas, who led the movement for inclusion of basketball in the Olympic Games in 1936 and thereafter. (For Olympic champions, see OLYMPIC GAMES: *Team sports.*) Basketball has also been played in the Pan-American Games since their inauguration in 1951. The international game is governed by the Fédération Internationale de Basketball Amateur (FIBA). World championships began in 1951 for men and in 1953 for women. Under international rules the court differs in that there is no front or back court, and the free-throw lanes form a modified wedge shape (see Figure 11). There are some differences in rules, including those governing substitutions, technical and personal fouls, free throws, intermissions, and time-outs. A team must try for a goal within 30 seconds. Outside the United States there are few places that strictly separate amateur from professional athletes.

International rules

Basketball has caught on particularly well in Italy. There are three levels of amateur competition in Italy, roughly comparable to the NCAA's Divisions I, II, and III. The Superior Division has 12 teams in major cities, including two in Rome. The national team, which represents Italy in world tournaments, is selected from among the best performers on all teams.

Throughout Europe, where much basketball activity is sponsored by corporations, spring tournaments match teams in a two-year cycle. In Soviet-bloc countries most teams are sponsored by the military or by trade unions. Every four years, two years before the Olympics, the world tournament is held, bringing zone qualifiers together in brackets designed to pair teams of near-equal ability.

Professional basketball. The professional game first prospered largely in the Middle Atlantic and New England states. Trenton (N.J.) and the New York Wanderers were the first great professional clubs, followed by the Buffalo Germans, who started out in 1895 as 14-year-old members of the Buffalo (N.Y.) YMCA and, with occasional new members, continued for 44 years, winning 792 out of 878 games.

A group of basketball stylists who never received the acclaim they deserved because they played for various towns

Focus on Sports

Larry Bird of the Boston Celtics releases his classic jump shot in an NBA 1987 play-off game with the Milwaukee Bucks.

in their heyday consisted of Edward and Lew Wachter, Jimmy Williamson, Jack Inglis (a behind-the-back dribbler), and Bill Hardman. They introduced the bounce pass and long pass as offensive weapons and championed the rule (adopted in 1923–24) that made each player, when fouled, shoot his own free throw.

Before World War II, the most widely heralded professional team was the Original Celtics, which started out in 1915 as a group of youngsters from New York City, kept adding better players in the early 1920s, and became so invincible that the team disbanded in 1928, only to regroup in the early 1930s as the New York Celtics. They finally retired in 1936. The Celtics played every night of the week, twice on Sundays, and largely on the road. During the 1922–23 season they won 204 of 215 games.

The Original Celtics, Rens, and others

Another formidable aggregation was the New York Renaissance (the Rens), organized by Robert Douglas in 1923 and regarded as the strongest all-black team of all time. During the 1925–26 campaign they split a six-game series with the Original Celtics. During the 1932–33 season the Rens won 88 consecutive games. In 1939 they trimmed the Harlem Globetrotters and the Oshkosh All Stars for the world championship pro tournament in Chicago. Among the great professional clubs were the New York Nationals; Fond du Lac, Wis.; East Liverpool, Ohio; the Paterson, N.J., Crescents; and the South Philadelphia Hebrew All Stars—better known as the Sphas.

The pro leagues

The first professional league was the National Basketball League (NBL) formed in 1898 to protect the players against unscrupulous promoters and to save the sport from extinction because of rough play. Their game differed from the college rules in that a netting usually separated the players from the spectators and the players bounced off the ropes like prizefighters in a ring; the ball could not go out of bounds; and the players were permitted to resume dribbling after halting. Because of the inequality of the teams or inability of the weaker clubs to meet expenses, leagues did not survive for more than a few seasons, and new circuits invariably arose. As a rule, the same players performed in these leagues, some playing for several cities or clubs within the same seasons.

The Depression of the 1930s hurt professional basketball, and a new NBL was organized in 1938 in and around the upper Middle West. Professional basketball assumed major league status with the organization of the new Basketball Association of America in 1946 under the guidance of Walter A. Brown, president of the Boston Garden. Brown contended that professional basketball would succeed only if there were sufficient financial support to nurse the league over the early lean years, if the game were conducted upon a high standard, and if all players were restricted to contracts with a reserve rule protecting each team from raiding by another club. Following a costly two-year war, the BAA and the NBL merged in 1949 to form the National Basketball Association (NBA).

Formation of the NBA

To help equalize the strength of the teams, the NBA established an annual college draft permitting each club to select a college senior in inverse order to the final standings in the previous year's competition, thus enabling the lower standing clubs to select the more talented collegians. In addition, the game was altered through three radical rules changes in the 1954–55 season: (1) a team must shoot for a basket within 24 seconds after acquiring possession of the ball; (2) a bonus free throw is awarded a player anytime the opposing team commits more than six (later five, now four) personal fouls in a quarter or more than two personal fouls in an overtime period; and (3) two free throws are granted for any backcourt foul.

After a struggle to survive, including some large financial losses and several short-lived franchises, the NBA took its place as the major professional basketball league in the United States. A rival 11-team American Basketball Association (ABA), with George Mikan as commissioner, was launched in the 1967–68 season, and a bitter feud developed with the NBA for the top collegiate talent each season. In 1976 the ABA disbanded, and four of its teams were taken into the NBA.

Like college basketball, the NBA grew increasingly popular through the 1980s. Attendance records were broken in that decade by most of the franchises, a growth pattern stimulated at least in part by the increased coverage by cable television. The NBA grew to a membership of 27 teams in the late 1980s, including expansion teams in Charlotte, N.C.; Miami; Minneapolis, Minn., and Orlando, Fla. The play-offs followed the traditional 81-game schedule, involving 16 teams and beginning in late April. Played as best-of-seven series, the final pairings stretched into late June. Although basketball is traditionally a winter game, the NBA still fills its arenas and attracts a national television audience in late spring. The NBA grew to a point at which the average annual player salary reached around the $500,000 level by the late 1980s. Many superstars earned more than $1,000,000 yearly.

NBA expansion

PLAY OF THE GAME

Court and equipment. The standard basketball court is in the shape of a rectangle 50 feet (15.24 metres) by 94 feet; high school courts may be slightly smaller. There are various markings on the court, including a centre circle, free-throw lanes, and a three-point line, that help regulate play. The international court varies somewhat in its markings. (See Figure 11.) A goal, or basket, 18 inches (45.7 centimetres) in diameter is suspended from a backboard at each end of the court. The metal rim of the basket is 10 feet above the floor. The backboard in professional and college play is a six-foot-wide by 3½- or (in college) four-foot-high rectangle made of a transparent material, usually glass. A fan-shaped board is used in high school games. The spherical inflated ball measures 29 to 30 inches in circumference and weighs 20 to 22 ounces (567 to 624 grams). Its covering is leather or composition.

Rules. The rules governing play of the game are based on Naismith's five principles requiring a large, light ball, handled with the hands; no running with the ball; no player restricted from getting the ball when it is in play; no personal contact; and a horizontal, elevated goal. The rules are spelled out in specific detail by the governing bodies of the several branches of the sport and cover the playing court and equipment, officials, players, scoring and timing, fouls, violations, and other matters. The officials include a referee and two umpires in college play (one umpire in NBA play), two timers, and two scorekeepers. One player on each team acts as a captain and speaks for his team on all matters involving the officials, such as interpretation of rules. Professional and high school games are divided into four periods, college into two.

The officials

Since the 1895–96 season, a field goal has scored two points and a free throw one point. When the ABA was founded in 1967, it allowed three points for shots from outside a boundary line set at a maximum of 25 feet from the basket. With varying distances, the change was

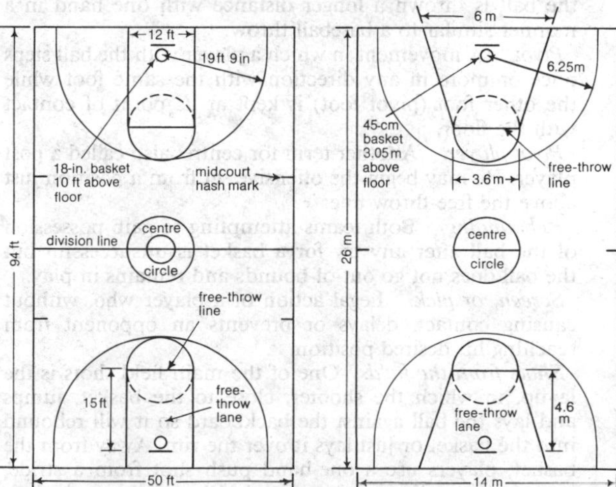

Figure 11: *Basketball courts.*
(Left) U.S. college court. The three-point line for the NBA is 23 feet nine inches from the top of the arch to the centre of the basket. The arch then joins a straight line running parallel to the sidelines, three feet from the sideline (not shown). (Right) International court.

adopted officially by the NBA and, in 1985, by colleges.

Basketball is a noncontact game. A player may pass or bounce (dribble) the ball to a position whereby he or a teammate may make a try for a basket. A foul is committed whenever a player makes such contact with an opponent so as to put him at a disadvantage. It provides the offended player with a free throw, an unhindered throw for a goal from behind the free-throw (foul) line, which is 15 feet from the backboard. If a player is fouled while shooting and the shot is good, the basket counts and he is awarded one free throw; if the shot misses, he gets two free throws. Infractions such as unsportsmanlike conduct or grasping the rim are technical fouls, which award a free throw to the opposition.

Fouls and violations

In other rules changes designed to speed up college games, a team loses possession if it fails to advance the ball within five seconds while being "closely guarded." Other common infractions occur when a player (with the ball) takes an excessive number of steps or slides; causes the ball to go out-of-bounds; steps over the foul line while tossing for a free throw; steps over the end line or sideline while tossing the ball in to a teammate, or fails to pass the ball in within five seconds; runs with, kicks, or strikes the ball with his fist; dribbles a second time after having once concluded his dribble (double dribble); remains more than three seconds in his free-throw lane while he or his team has the ball; causes the ball to go into the backcourt; retains the ball in the backcourt more than 10 seconds (30 seconds for women); or fails to shoot within 45 seconds of the time the ball is put into play (24 seconds in the professional game). Penalty is loss of the ball—opponents throw in the ball from the side.

Common terms used in basketball include the following:

Blocking. Any illegal personal contact that impedes the progress of an opponent who does not have the ball.

Dribble. Ball movement by bouncing the ball. A dribble ends when a player touches the ball with both hands simultaneously or does not continue his dribble.

Held ball. Called when two opponents have one or two hands so firmly upon the ball that neither can gain possession without undue roughness. It also is called when a player in the front court is so closely guarded that he cannot pass or try for a goal or is obviously withholding the ball from play.

Jump ball. A method of putting the ball into play. The referee tosses it up between two opponents who try to tap it to a teammate.

Pass. Throwing, batting, or rolling the ball to another player. The main types are: (1) the chest pass—ball is released from a position in front of the chest; (2) the bounce pass—the ball is bounced on the floor to get it past a defensive opponent; (3) the roll pass on the floor; (4) the hook pass (side or overhead); and (5) the baseball pass—the ball is thrown a longer distance with one hand in a manner similar to a baseball throw.

The bounce pass

Pivot. A movement in which a player with the ball steps once or more in any direction with the same foot while the other foot (pivot foot) is kept at its point of contact with the floor.

Pivot player. Another term for centre; also called a post player. He may begin the offensive set from a position just above the free-throw line.

Rebounding. Both teams attempting to gain possession of the ball after any try for a basket is unsuccessful but the ball does not go out-of-bounds and remains in play.

Screen, or pick. Legal action of a player who, without causing contact, delays or prevents an opponent from reaching his desired position.

Shots from the field. One of the main field shots is the layup, in which the shooter, close to the basket, jumps and lays the ball against the backboard so it will rebound into the basket or just lays it over the rim. Away from the basket, players use a one-hand push shot from a stride, jump, or standing position, and a hook shot, which is overhead. Some players can dunk or slam dunk the ball, jamming the ball down into the basket.

Traveling (running with the ball). Progressing in any direction in excess of the prescribed limits while holding the ball.

Turnover. Loss of possession of the ball by a team before any member has been able to try for a basket.

Other special terms are discussed below.

Principles of play. Each team of five players consists of two forwards, two guards, and a centre, usually the tallest man on the team. At the beginning of the first period of a game the ball is put into play by a jump ball at centre court; *i.e.,* the referee tosses the ball up between the opposing centres, higher than either can jump, and when it descends each tries to tap it to one of his teammates, who must remain outside the centre circle until the ball is tapped. Subsequent periods of professional and college games begin with a throw in from out-of-bounds. Jump balls are also signaled by the officials when opposing players share possession of the ball (held ball), or simultaneously cause it to go out-of-bounds. In U.S. college games the alternate-possession rule is invoked in jump-ball situations, with teams taking turns getting possession. After each successful basket (goal or field goal) the ball is put back in play by the team that is scored on by one player passing the ball in from behind the end line where the score was made. The ball is put in play in the same manner after a successful free throw; if two have been awarded, after the second if it is successful. After non-shooting violations the ball is awarded to the opposing team to be passed inbounds from a point designated by an official.

The jump ball

A player who takes possession of the ball must pass or shoot before taking two steps or must start dribbling before taking his second step. When the dribble stops, the player must stop his movement and pass or shoot the ball. The ball may be tapped or batted with the hands, passed, bounced, or rolled in any direction.

As basketball has progressed, various coaches and players have devised intricate plays and offensive maneuvers. Some systems emphasize speed, deft ball handling, and high scoring; others stress ball control, slower patterned movement, and lower scoring. A strategy based on speed is called the fast break. When fast-break players recover possession of the ball in their backcourt, as by getting the rebound from an opponent's missed shot, they race to beat the defense to its backcourt by a combination of speed and passing and try to make a field goal before the opponents have time to set up a defense.

Systems of offense

Some teams, either following an overall game plan or as an alternative when they do not have the opportunity for a fast break, employ a more deliberate style of offense. The guards carefully bring the ball down the court toward the basket and maintain possession of the ball in the front court by passing and dribbling and by screening opponents in an effort to set up a play that will free a player for an open shot. Set patterns of offense generally use one or two pivot, or post, players who play near the free-throw area at the low post positions (between the free-throw line and the end line) or at high post positions (between the free-throw line and the basket). The pivot players are usually the taller players on the team and are in position to receive passes, pass to teammates, shoot, screen for teammates, and tip in or rebound (recover) missed shots. All of the players on the team are constantly on the move, executing the patterns designed to give one player a favourable shot—and at the same time place one or more teammates in a good position to tip-in or rebound if that player misses.

Systems of defense also have developed over the years. One of the major strategies is known as man-to-man or man-for-man. In this system each player guards a specific opponent, except when "switching" with a teammate when he is screened or in order to guard another player in a more threatening scoring position. Another major strategy is the zone, or five-man, defense. In this system each player has a specific area to guard irrespective of which opponent plays in that area. The zone is designed to keep the offense from driving in to the basket and to force the offense into taking long shots. The zone defense is not permitted in the professional game.

Systems of defense

A great many variations and combinations have been devised to employ the several aspects of both man-to-man and zone defensive strategies. The press, which can be either man-to-man or zone, is used by a team to guard its opponent so thoroughly that the opposition is forced to hurry its movements and especially to commit errors that force turnovers. A full-court press applies this pressure defense from the moment the opposition takes possession of the ball at one end of the court. Well-coached teams are able to modify both their offensive and defensive strategies according to the shifting circumstances of the game and in response to their opponents' particular strengths and weaknesses and styles of play.

(W.G.M./R.G.Lo./L.W.D.)

Ice hockey

Ice hockey requires two teams, each with usually six players who wear ice skates. The object is to propel a vulcanized rubber disk, the puck, past a goal line and into a net guarded by a goalkeeper. With its speed and its frequent physical contact, ice hockey has become one of the most popular of international sports. The game is an Olympic sport, and in the Soviet Union there are more than a million registered players performing regularly in leagues. It is perhaps Canada's most popular game. For good reason ice hockey is called the world's fastest team game. In no other contact sport do the competitors reach speeds of 30 miles (almost 50 kilometres) per hour, and the puck has been clocked at speeds of over 100 miles per hour. (For records, see SPORTING RECORD in the *Micropædia* and the article OLYMPIC GAMES.)

HISTORY

Canadian origin

Origins. Until the mid-1980s it was generally accepted that ice hockey derived from English field hockey and Indian lacrosse and was spread throughout Canada by British soldiers in the mid-1800s. Research then turned up mention of a hockeylike game, played in the early 1800s in Nova Scotia by the Micmac Indians, which appeared to have been heavily influenced by the Irish game of hurling; it included the use of a "hurley" (stick) and a square wooden block instead of a ball. It was probably fundamentally this game that spread throughout Canada via Scottish and Irish immigrants and the British army. The players adopted elements of field hockey, such as the "bully" (later the face-off) and "shinning" (hitting one's opponent on the shins with the stick or playing with the stick on one "shin" or side); this evolved into an informal ice game later known as shinny or shinty. The name hockey—as the organized game came to be known—has been attributed to the French word *hoquet* (shepherd's stick). The term rink, referring to the designated area of play, was originally used in the game of curling in 18th-century Scotland. Early hockey games allowed as many as 30 players a side on the ice, and the goals were two stones, each frozen into one end of the ice. The first use of a puck instead of a ball was recorded at Kingston Harbour, Ont., in 1860.

Early organization. The first recorded public indoor ice hockey game, with rules largely borrowed from field hockey, took place in Montreal's Victoria Skating Rink in 1875, between two teams of McGill University students. Unfortunately, the reputation for violence that the game would later develop was presaged in this early encounter, where, as *The Daily British Whig* of Kingston, Ont., reported, "Shins and heads were battered, benches smashed and the lady spectators fled in confusion." The first organized team, the McGill University Hockey Club, formed in 1877, codified their game's rules and limited the number of players on a side to nine.

By the late 1800s ice hockey competed with lacrosse as Canada's most popular sport. The first national hockey organization, the Amateur Hockey Association (AHA) of Canada (which limited players to seven a side), was formed in Montreal in 1885, and the first league was formed in Kingston during the same year, with four teams: the Kingston Hockey Club, Queen's University, the Kingston Athletics, and the Royal Military College. Queen's University scored a 3–1 victory over the Athletics in the first championship game.

By the opening of the 20th century sticks were being manufactured, shin pads were worn, the goaltender began to wear a chest protector (borrowed from baseball), and arenas (still with natural ice and no heat for spectators) were being constructed throughout eastern Canada. In 1892 national attention was focused on the game when the Canadian governor general, Frederick Arthur, Lord Stanley of Preston, donated a cup to be given annually to the top Canadian team. The three-foot-high silver cup became known as the Stanley Cup and was first played for in 1893–94. The first winner was the Montreal Amateur Athletic Association team; since 1917 it has gone to the winner of the National Hockey League play-offs.

Emergence of professional hockey

In 1899 the Canadian Amateur Hockey League was formed. All hockey in Canada at the time was "amateur," it being "ungentlemanly" to admit to being paid for athletic services. Thus the first acknowledged professional hockey team in the world was formed in the United States, in 1903, in Houghton, Mich. The team, the Portage Lakes, was owned by a dentist named J.L. Gibson, who imported Canadian players. In 1904 Gibson formed the first acknowledged professional league, the International Pro Hockey League. Canada accepted professional hockey in 1908 when the Ontario Professional Hockey League was formed. By that time Canada had become the centre of world hockey.

League rivalries. The National Hockey Association (NHA), the forerunner of the National Hockey League, was organized in 1910 and became the strongest association in North America. Rising interest in the game created problems, however, for there were few artificial-ice rinks. In 1911 the Pacific Coast Hockey Association (PCHA) was formed by Joseph Patrick and his sons, who built two enclosed artificial-ice arenas, beginning a boom in the construction of artificial-ice rinks.

The PCHA became involved in a money and player war with the NHA. Although the NHA ultimately emerged as the stronger league, it was the PCHA that introduced many of the changes that improved the game. The only radical rule change adopted by the NHA was to reduce the number of players on a side to six, and that move was made to save money. The western league retained seven-man hockey, but it allowed the goalie to leap or dive to stop the puck. Under the previous rules, a goalie had had to remain stationary when making a save. The western league also changed the offside rule. Under the old rules a player had been deemed offside if he was ahead of the puck carrier when he received a pass. The PCHA divided the ice into three zones by painting two blue lines across the surface and allowed forward passing in the centre zone between the blue lines. This opened up the game and made it more exciting. Another innovation in the western league was the idea of the assist. Previously, only the goal scorer had been credited with a point. In the PCHA the player or players who set up his goal were credited with an assist. The first numbered uniforms also appeared in their league.

Formation of the NHL

The National Hockey League. Like some of its predecessors the NHA had its dissenters. In a move to eject one of the league members, the NHA decided to disband and form a new league. The result was the creation in 1917 of the National Hockey League (NHL), which became the world's foremost professional hockey league. In 1924 the first U.S. team, the Boston Bruins, joined the NHL. In 1925 the New York Americans and Pittsburgh Pirates were admitted, followed in 1926 by the New York Rangers, the Chicago Black Hawks, and the Detroit Cougars (later called the Red Wings). To stock the new teams, the NHL bought out the Patricks' league in 1926 for $250,000. Among the players who shifted to Boston was Eddie Shore, known as a "rushing" defenseman, whose style helped change the game. He was one of the sport's most ferocious and, many experts say, its most skilled player, a forerunner of such future NHL players as Gordie Howe, who played mostly for the Detroit Red Wings. Pittsburgh and the New York Americans eventually dropped out of the league, and until the expansion of 1967, the NHL was composed of six teams—the Rangers, the Bruins, the Black Hawks, the Red Wings, the Toronto Maple Leafs, and the Montreal Canadiens.

In 1967 the NHL undertook one of the greatest expansions in professional sports history when it doubled in size to 12 teams. A new 12-team league, the World Hockey Association (WHA), was formed in 1972, and the ensuing rivalry caused an escalation in players' salaries. In 1979 the NHL, which had grown to 17 teams, merged with the WHA to become a 21-team league.

International ice hockey

On the international level, amateur hockey remained supreme. League competition among amateurs in England began in 1903. The International Ice Hockey Federation (IIHF) was formed in Europe in 1908. Its five original members were Great Britain, Bohemia, Switzerland, France, and Belgium. The first European championship was held at Avants, Switz., in 1910, with Great Britain the winner. From that time the federation broadened its membership, taking applicants from the world over. Canada captured the first Olympic Games title in 1920 and, concurrently, the first IIHF world championship. Canada also won at the first Winter Olympic Games in 1924, retaining both Olympic and world ice hockey championships until 1936, when Great Britain triumphed. In 1963 the Soviet Union began a long series of victories. Except for the increasing number of teams, there was little change in the organization of European ice hockey.

Play-offs and championships. In the NHL, the ultimate prize is the Stanley Cup. The winner is determined after a series of play-offs. Before 1967 the teams that finished first and third and second and fourth played best-of-seven series to determine which would play for the Stanley Cup. The winners then met in another best-of-seven series for the cup. When the league formed two divisions, each division held a similar play-off series. The finalists from each then met. Beginning in 1980, an expanded play-off system involved 16 of the league's 21 teams.

NHL individual awards are the Vezina Trophy to the goalie voted best at his position by NHL managers; the William M. Jennings Trophy for the goalie or goalies with the team permitting the fewest goals; the Calder Trophy, for the rookie of the year; the Hart Trophy, for the most valuable player; the Norris Trophy, for the outstanding defenseman; the Art Ross Trophy, for the top point scorer; the Lady Byng Trophy, for the player best combining clean play with a high degree of skill; the Conn Smythe Trophy, for the play-offs' outstanding performer; the Frank J. Selke Trophy, for the best defensive forward; the Jack Adams Award, for the coach of the year; the Bill Masterton Memorial Trophy, for the player who best exemplifies perseverance, sportsmanship, and dedication to hockey; and the Lester Patrick Trophy, for outstanding service to hockey in the United States. NHL players receive cash awards if they are voted onto the first or second teams of the all-stars chosen by the Professional Hockey Writers' Association after the completion of each season.

Until the late 1970s only a few non-Canadians had played in the NHL. The growth of collegiate hockey in the United States, however, led to a greater proportion of NHL players born in the United States. The level of hockey in Europe—especially in the Soviet Union, Czechoslovakia, Finland, and Sweden—increased greatly in the years following World War II, and the NHL had many European players by the 1980s. The Soviet Union's national team became one of the strongest in international competition and in 1972 almost beat Team Canada, made up of selected Canadian-born NHL stars.

Amateur hockey

The Amateur Hockey Association of the United States (AHAUS), in conjunction with the U.S. Olympic Committee, chooses players for the Olympics; the AHAUS also chooses the national team for world championships, held annually. Most of its players are collegians. The major college championship in the United States is the National Collegiate Athletic Association (NCAA) tournament. The decline of the Canadian Amateur Hockey Association in international competition has been blamed on the fact that many of its men were turning professional while teenagers. Canadian senior amateur hockey—which has no age limit—has as its top prize the Allan Cup, determined after eliminations. Canadian junior players—up to 20 years of age—meet in a similar series for the Memorial Cup.

To determine which teams meet for the world amateur championship, the IIHF has set up three classes. Six countries are in Class A, eight in Class B, and the rest in Class C. The six teams in Class A automatically are eligible for the world championship and the Olympics. The team that does the worst in that division moves down the next year to Class B. The team with the best record in Class B automatically moves up to Class A. The same procedure is followed in Group C.

PLAY OF THE GAME

Rink and equipment. NHL hockey is played for the most part on a standard-sized rink shaped like a round-cornered rectangle that is 200 feet (61 metres) long and 85 feet wide (see Figure 12). International rinks are usually 184–200 feet by 85–98 feet, and U.S. college rinks, 200 feet by 100 feet. The goal cage is four feet high and six feet wide. Any shot that completely clears the goal line, a two-inch- (five-centimetre-) wide stripe on the ice across the front of the cage, is a goal. In front of the goal is the crease, an area four feet deep and eight feet wide, demarcated by a red line; no attacking player may enter the crease unless the puck is there. The IIHF crease is semicircular. The blue lines that divide the ice into three zones are 60 feet out from the goal line and are painted across the width of the ice. The area between the blue lines is called the neutral zone. This zone is bisected by the red centre line.

The crease

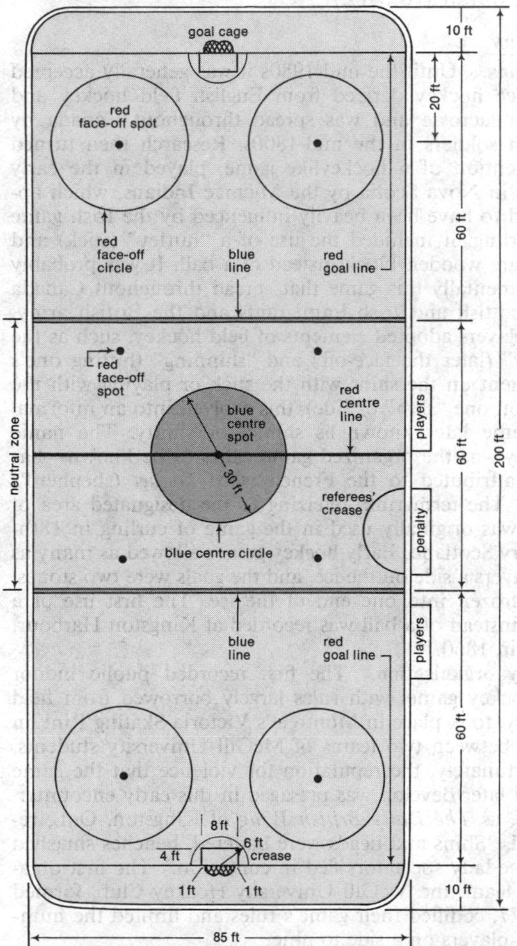

Figure 12: Professional ice hockey rink.

Virtually all equipment—for children, amateurs, or professionals—is the same. Goalies wear face masks. Forwards and defensemen wear the same type of skates, but the goaltender's blades are flatter because they need more balance and are stationary for longer periods. The shoes of goaltenders' skates are fitted with rubber protection for the toes. Under their uniforms goaltenders wear a chest protector, shoulder pads, quilting from wrist to shoulder, and pads to protect the kidneys, thighs, and knees. Except for the chest protector, forwards and defensemen wear the same protective gear under their uniforms. Since 1979–80 all players entering the NHL must wear helmets; helmets and face masks are mandatory in NCAA and IIHF play.

Over his uniform a goalie wears extra equipment. Pads up to 10 inches wide protect him from the tips of his skates to above his knees. They not only afford protection but also aid in blocking shots. On his free hand the goalie wears a glove similar to a first-baseman's baseball mitt, with a wide webbing that enables him to catch the puck. The stick hand is encased in a glove with a wide backing that protects his arm. The goalie's stick has a wider shaft and blade than those of the other players. Fully dressed, goaltenders carry 30 pounds (over 13 kilograms) of equipment, five pounds more than the others.

NHL influence

Rules and principles of play. The modern game on every level—amateur, collegiate, international, and professional—has been influenced largely by the National Hockey League.

Checking—body contact to take an opponent out of the play—is permitted anywhere on the ice. Players may not make or take a pass that has traveled over a red line and a blue line; if this occurs, the play is ruled offside. A face-off, in which an official drops the puck between opposing players, follows the infraction. In hockey competition that has no red line an offside infraction involves a pass that has traveled across the two blue lines. Face-offs are held at the point of the infraction. Players who precede the puck into the attacking zone also are ruled offside, and a face-off is held at a "face-off spot" near the attacking blue line. A face-off also begins each period and is used as well after a goal and after any stoppage of play.

Clif Garboden—Stock, Boston, Inc.

Referee about to drop the puck as players for Harvard and Boston College prepare for a face-off in the neutral zone.

Players

The goalkeeper rarely leaves his goal area. The usual alignments of the other five players are three forwards—the centre, a left wing, and a right wing—and two defensemen—a left defenseman and a right defenseman.

Ideally, the attacking team moves as a unit, led by the forwards. The centre generally is the most adroit stickhandler of the attackers and must be able to get by onrushing defenders. When he cannot, he passes off to one of his wings or drops the puck behind him for one of his defensemen. If he is able to get over the other team's blue line, he attempts to set up his men. He tries to do this by drawing the opposition toward him and then passing to one of his wings or defensemen.

A player may handle the puck as often or as long as he likes, so long as he does not close his glove on the puck. A player may not pass the puck with his open hand. The goalie, however, is generally not subject to either restriction.

The game is divided into three periods of 20 minutes playing time each. Hockey games may end in a tie unless the rules stipulate an overtime period to serve as a tiebreaker. In the case of a tie in college hockey one 10-minute sudden-death overtime period is played in regular season play. NHL teams play a five-minute sudden-death overtime period. During the play-offs college hockey has 10-minute overtime periods until there is a winner, while the NHL has the same system with 20-minute periods. There is no overtime period in international hockey.

In organized ice hockey a victory is worth two points in the standings; a tie is worth one. A goal counts as a point for the team, but individual points may be awarded to as many as three players for one goal. One point goes to the player who scored the goal, and a point each is awarded for an assist to the last two of the scorer's teammates who touched the puck, providing that the opposition did not handle the puck in the interim.

Of the major sports ice hockey is the only one in which substitutions are permitted while the game is in play. The game is so fast and so demanding that forwards generally skate only 90 seconds at a time. This means that there are at least 10 "line changes" a period, and if play were stopped each time a line change is made the tempo would be markedly decreased. Defensemen usually stay on the ice for a slightly longer period of time.

Infractions and penalties

Because of the speed and contact there are many infractions, not all of them having to do with "hitting" penalties. Play is stopped for an offside and for the infraction called icing, which occurs when a team shoots the puck out of its zone past the other team's goal line. Icing is not called against a team when it is shorthanded; if the teams are even-handed, the puck is returned to the defensive zone of the team that iced it for the face-off. No player, however, may delay the game by intentionally shooting the puck out of the rink or by shifting the goalposts.

Minor penalties are most commonly assessed for excessive use of the body or equipment to impede the opposition. For a minor infraction the offending player must remain in the penalty box at the side of the rink for two minutes while his team plays shorthanded. If the opponents score at any time during that penalty period, the penalized player may return to the ice. Penalties incurred by the goalie are served by a teammate. A major penalty for violent play or a misconduct penalty for abusing an official results in the loss of a player for five or 10 minutes or for the remainder of the game. Unless there is deliberate injury, the offender's team makes a substitution and is not shorthanded when play resumes. Violent play in modern professional hockey has drawn much criticism.

There are three common types of shots in hockey. One of these, the slap shot, has been timed at more than 100 miles an hour. Bobby Hull, who played mostly for the Chicago Black Hawks and was the first NHL player to score more than 50 goals in a season, had one of the game's hardest slap shots. The slap shot differs from the wrist shot in that the player brings his stick back so far that it is nearly perpendicular with the ice and then brings

Bruce Curtis

Goalie for the Montreal Canadiens wearing protective equipment.

the stick down in an arc, swatting the puck as he follows through. It is not as accurate as the wrist shot, in which the player puts his stick on the ice near the puck and without a windup snaps his wrist to fire off a shot.

The other most common shot is the backhander, taken when the puck goes to the other side of the stick from which the player normally shoots. If he is a right-handed shooter, for example, he takes the backhander from his left side. It is taken when there is not enough time to shift the puck to his normal shooting position. The backhander generally is not as hard or as accurate as the wrist shot, but it has the advantage of being taken quickly. Many experts agree the hardest backhander in the professional game belonged to Maurice ("The Rocket") Richard of the Montreal Canadiens. A natural left-handed shooter, he played right wing. He was the first in the NHL to score 50 goals in a season.

Offensive and defensive play and strategy

Strategies. Speed is an essential requirement of the game. In the sport's early days a team could get away with having a few slow defensemen. But contests at all levels became so quick that offensive and defensive roles often are reversed, and defensemen may find themselves at the forefront of the action. Slower players must have other attributes to make a team; they must, for example, be able to check well, to prevent the other players from getting past them. But, since everyone on the team handles the puck at some point during a game, a premium is placed on puck-carrying ability. The man with the puck is in control, and the play can go only so fast as he directs it. Centre Wayne Gretzky, while playing for the Edmonton Oilers, was the dominant scorer in the NHL for most of the 1980s due to his outstanding puck handling and his accurate shooting and passing.

If a forward has the puck, the defensemen trail the play. If a defenseman is leading an offensive thrust, called a "rush," one of the forwards backs him up. The opposition, meanwhile, attempts to gain control of the puck or to dislodge it. The most common way is for the defending player to poke his stick at the puck. A defender may also block, check, or hit the player with his body, as long as it falls within the rules defining allowable contact. Ideally, the defending team's defensemen lay back, straddling their blue line, away from the boards. They then can move to the centre to halt a breakthrough or can drive a man into the boards if he attempts to go along the sides. If the attacking players find that they have difficulty in stickhandling past the opposition, they may try a long shot "on goal." They may also shoot the puck into the other team's zone and chase it, two attacking players going after the puck—one to handle the opponent, who is sure to go after it, and the other to try to wrest the puck away. The third forward, meanwhile, takes up a position about 20 feet in front of the goal, in the centre of the ice, in a spot known as the "slot." In the slot he is in position to shoot if he gets the puck. The defensemen on the attacking team take up positions on the blue line to prevent the defending team from getting a breakaway. Often the puck is passed to the defensemen, who shoot from the blue line, 60 feet out, from their position known as the "point." Long shots rarely go in, so defensemen try to keep long shots low, which gives the attackers a chance at a rebound.

Many fans do not see goals scored in hockey because so many go in on rebounds or deflections. While a shot is taken, no attacking player may be in the goalie's crease, a rectangle eight feet across and four feet out from the goal line; but there is much physical contact in front of the net, and the puck may ricochet off a skate, a stick, or any part of the body. Any kind of shot that puts in a goal is allowable, unless the shooter has raised his stick above his elbow; but the puck may not be deliberately kicked in, and it cannot be thrown in with the hand.

One of the most unusual spectacles in hockey occurs when a team that is trailing by one goal takes its goaltender out of the net in the final seconds of the game. The goalie is replaced by a forward in the hope that the extra man on offense will give the team a chance for a tie. Another rare and exciting play is the penalty shot, which is called when a stick is thrown to deflect a shot or when a player with an open path to the goal is pulled down from behind. The team against which the infraction was committed selects a player to skate unopposed to the opponent's goal and take one shot to beat the goalie; this generally results in a score for the shooting team.

The officials

Officiating. All NHL and international games and many collegiate games are under the control of one referee, two linesmen, and various off-ice officials. Referees are responsible for calling penalties and are the final arbiters of whether a goal has been scored. Linesmen call offsides and icing infractions; they may also stop play in order to inform a referee that a team has too many players on the ice. In some NCAA games two referees and no linesmen or two referees and one linesman are used, one of the referees being the final arbiter of disagreements. The IIHF sanctions the two-referee system for games under the jurisdiction of national federations. The goal judges are stationed behind each cage in a raised booth behind the boards. The goal judges' function is to signal a goal when the puck has crossed the goal line. They are not concerned with whether the goal is legal, merely whether it was scored. To indicate a goal, they flip a switch that stops the clock and triggers a red light. The other officials are the penalty timekeeper, who must not let a player out of the penalty box until his penalty time is served or a goal is scored; the game timekeeper, who is in charge of running the official clock and who stops the clock during play stoppages; and the official scorer, who decides who gets credit for the goals and assists and also keeps track of the goalie's saves, or stops. (G.Es./S.I.F./S.W.Fi.)

MAJOR INDIVIDUAL SPORTS

The individual sports are those that require the skill of a single athlete in competition with one or more other athletes. Sometimes the athletes are in a one-on-one competition, as in singles tennis, and sometimes they compete against a field of players, the best score winning, as in golf. Participants in individual sports are sometimes called a "team" when they form a group from a single school or institution that plays other like groups or teams, such as golf teams, tennis teams, or bowling teams. The difference here is that the athlete on an individual sport "team" still performs largely without the aid of teammates, as opposed to such sports as football and basketball, which are heavily dependent on teamwork. All of the major team sports discussed in the first part of this article involve the use of a ball, or as in the case of ice hockey, a puck; some of the individual sports, on the other hand, such as boxing and athletics, do not involve a ball. The individual sports discussed here are the ones that have generally achieved the widest international participation and interest, including tennis, golf, athletics, boxing, and bowling. (Ed.)

Tennis

Reduced to its simplest terms, tennis is a game in which two opposing players (singles) or pairs of players (doubles) use tautly-strung rackets to hit a ball of specified size, weight, and bounce over a net on a rectangular court. Points are awarded to a player or team whenever the opponent fails to correctly return the ball within the prescribed dimensions of the court. Organized tennis is played according to rules sanctioned by the International Tennis Federation (ITF), the world governing body of the sport. Tennis originally was known as lawn tennis, and formally still is in Britain, because it was played on grass courts by Victorian gentlemen and ladies. It is now played throughout the world on a variety of surfaces.

The origins of the game can be traced to a 12th–13th-century French handball game called *jeu de paume* ("game of the palm"), from which was derived a complex indoor racket-and-ball game: real (royal) tennis. This ancient game is still played to a limited degree and is usually called real tennis in Britain, court tennis in the United States, and royal tennis in Australia. The modern game of tennis is played by millions in clubs and on public courts. Its period of most rapid growth as both a participant and a spectator sport began in the late 1960s, when the major championships were opened to professionals as well as amateurs, and continued in the 1970s, when television broadcasts of the expanding professional tournament circuits broadened the appeal of the game.

Modern innovations

A number of major innovations in fashion and equipment fueled and fed the boom. The addition of colour and style to tennis wear created an entirely new subdivision of leisure clothing. Tennis balls, which historically had been white, now came in several hues, with yellow the colour of choice. Racket frames, which had been of a standard size and shape and constructed primarily of laminated wood, were suddenly manufactured in a wide choice of sizes, shapes, and materials, the most significant milestones being the introduction of metal frames beginning in 1967 and the oversized head in 1976.

While tennis can be enjoyed by players of practically any level of skill, top competition is a demanding test of both shot making and stamina, rich in stylistic and strategic variety. From its origins as a garden-party game for ladies in whalebone corsets and starched petticoats and men in long white flannels, it has evolved into a physical chess match in which players attack and defend, exploiting angles and technical weaknesses with strokes of widely diverse pace and spin. Tournaments offer tens of millions of dollars in prize money annually. (For winners of the major men's and women's championships and of the Davis Cup competition, see SPORTING RECORD in the *Micropædia.*)

HISTORY

Origin and early years. There has been much dispute over the invention of modern tennis, but the officially recognized centennial of the game in 1973 commemorated its introduction by Major Walter Clopton Wingfield, of Nantclwyd in north Wales, in 1873. He published the first book of rules that year and took out a patent on his game in 1874, although historians have concluded that similar games were played earlier and that the first tennis club was established by the Englishman Harry Gem and several associates in Leamington in 1872. Wingfield's court was of the hourglass shape that had been adopted by badminton. The publication of his version of "Sphairistiké, or Lawn Tennis," led to a spate of other claims to the invention of the game, most of which involved a rectangular court. At the time, the Marylebone Cricket Club (MCC) was the governing body of real tennis, whose rules it had recently revised. After a distinguished real tennis player, J.M. Heathcote, developed a better tennis ball of rubber covered with white flannel, the MCC in 1875 established a new, standardized set of rules for tennis.

Meanwhile, the game had spread to the United States in the 1870s. Mary Outerbridge of New York has been credited with bringing a set of rackets and balls to her brother, a director of the Staten Island Cricket and Baseball Club. But research has shown that William Appleton of Nahant, Mass., may have owned the first lawn tennis set and that his friends James Dwight and Fred R. Sears popularized the game.

An important milestone in the history of tennis was the decision of the All-England Croquet Club to set aside one of its lawns at Wimbledon for tennis, which soon proved so popular that the club changed its name to the All-England Croquet and Lawn Tennis Club. In 1877 the club decided to hold a tennis championship, and a championship subcommittee of three was appointed. It decided on a rectangular court 78 feet (23.77 metres) long by 27 feet (8.23 metres) wide. They adapted the real tennis method of scoring—15, 30, 40, game—and allowed the server one fault (*i.e.,* two chances to deliver a proper service on each point). These major decisions remain part of the modern rules. Twenty-two entries were received, and the first winner of the Wimbledon Championship was Spencer Gore. In 1878 the Scottish Championships were held, followed in 1879 by the Irish Championships.

The All-England Croquet and Lawn Tennis Club

Spread of the game. There were several alterations in some of the other rules (*e.g.,* governing the height of the net) until 1880, when the All-England Club and the MCC published revised rules that approximate very closely those still in use. The All-England Club was the dominant authority then, the British Lawn Tennis Association (LTA) not being formed until 1888. In 1880 the first U.S. championship was held at the Staten Island Cricket and Baseball Club. The victor was an Englishman, O.E. Woodhouse. The popularity of the game in the United States and frequent doubts about the rules led to the foundation in 1881 of the U.S. National Lawn Tennis Association, later renamed the U.S. Lawn Tennis Association and, in 1975, the U.S. Tennis Association (USTA). Under its auspices, the first official U.S. national championship, played under English rules, was held in 1881 at the Newport Casino, Newport, R.I. The winner, Richard Sears, was U.S. champion for seven consecutive years.

The first official U.S. championship

Tennis had taken firm root in Australia by 1880, and the first Australian championships were played in 1905. The first New Zealand National Championship was held in 1886. In 1904 the Lawn Tennis Association of Australasia (later of Australia) was founded.

The first French National Championships were held at the Stade Français in 1891, but it was an interclub tournament that did not become truly international until 1925; the French Federation of Lawn Tennis was established in 1920. Other national championships were inaugurated in Canada (1890), South Africa (1891), Spain (1910), Denmark (1921), Egypt (1925), Italy (1930), and Sweden (1936). In 1884 a women's championship was introduced at Wimbledon, and women's national championships were held in the United States starting in 1887.

Outstanding players. Tennis in the 1880s was dominated by the remarkable twin brothers William and Ernest Renshaw. William won the Wimbledon singles championship seven times, on three occasions defeating his brother in the final. Ernest was victorious once, and in partnership they won the doubles championship, first played at Oxford in 1879, seven times.

In the 1890s public interest began to wane. The Wimbledon Championships showed a financial loss in 1894 and 1895; the All-England Club committee turned back to croquet to revive its flagging fortunes. The popularity of Wimbledon and tennis were reestablished by two more brothers: Reginald and Laurie Doherty. Reginald won the Wimbledon singles from 1897 to 1900. Laurie won from 1902 to 1906, took the U.S. championship in 1903, and won a gold medal in the Olympic Games in 1900.

Revival by the Doherty brothers

The early 20th century. The first international team competition was the Davis Cup, officially called the International Lawn Tennis Challenge Trophy, which was donated by U.S. doubles champion Dwight Davis in 1900. Only Great Britain challenged the first year and was defeated by the United States, Davis himself playing on the victorious team. There was no challenge in 1901, but in 1902 a strong British team that included the Doherty brothers went to America. The United States retained the trophy, but the following year the Doherty brothers helped Britain win the cup, which it retained the next three years.

The Doherty reign ended in 1906, but tennis was by then firmly established. The new star was Norman Brookes, the first in a long line of Australian champions and the first left-hander to reach the top. He won at Wimbledon in 1907 and again on his next visit, in 1914. He and his doubles partner, Tony Wilding of New Zealand, wrested the Davis Cup from Great Britain in 1907 and held it until 1911, arousing enduring public interest in Australia and New Zealand.

Of the women champions of the early 1900s, Dorothea Douglass (later Mrs. Lambert Chambers) won the Wimbledon Championship seven times, beginning in 1903. In 1905, however, Douglass met her match in the first U.S. women's champion to win at Wimbledon, May Sutton, who again defeated her at Wimbledon in 1907. The outbreak of World War I in 1914 interrupted tennis activities in Britain and Europe, but with the exception of 1917, when a Patriotic Tournament was held, U.S. championships continued to be played.

The dominant champions of the early postwar years were

May Sutton, the first U.S. women's champion to win at Wimbledon, in her match with Dorothea Douglass (U.K.), 1905.
Culver Pictures

W.T. ("Big Bill") Tilden of the United States and Suzanne Lenglen of France. Tilden, the U.S. champion from 1920 through 1925 and again in 1929, won the Wimbledon title in 1920, 1921, and 1930. In the same period Tilden won 15 Davis Cup singles.

Suzanne Lenglen

Lenglen reigned supreme over the ladies' game from 1919 to 1925, and were it not for the war might have started her international career earlier. She won the Wimbledon championship at her first attempt in 1919, from 1920 to 1923, and in 1925, not having competed in 1924 because of illness. She had developed a powerful as well as accurate game by practicing with men, and she needed far more freedom of movement than restrictive ladies' fashion of that time had allowed. Her first appearance at Wimbledon in a calf-length white dress with short sleeves and without petticoat or suspender (garter) belt caused a sensation.

Central Press Photo

Suzanne Lenglen, France, outstanding player between 1919 and 1925, striding forward to complete a forehand return.

France also made its mark on men's tennis with the fabulous "Four Musketeers"—Jean Borotra, Henri Cochet, René Lacoste, and Jacques Brugnon. Among them, they monopolized the Wimbledon singles title from 1924 through 1929, won 10 French and three U.S. singles championships, and won five Wimbledon and 10 French doubles championships. They captured the Davis Cup from the United States in 1927 and held it until 1933.

Helen Wills Moody

A new U.S. woman star, Helen Wills (later Mrs. Moody and then Mrs. Roark), won the first of her seven U.S. singles titles in 1923; she went on to win at Wimbledon eight times between 1927 and 1938 and won the French singles four times between 1928 and 1932. Only once, early in her career, did she play against Lenglen, at Cannes on the French Riviera, where she lost in two straight sets. That historic meeting between the poker-faced Wills, in her trademark white eyeshade, and the flamboyant Lenglen, in her daring dress and silk bandeau, was chronicled in sports and society pages on both sides of the Atlantic. Wills's great rival, however, was another American, Helen Jacobs, Wimbledon champion in Wills's absence in 1936 and U.S. champion from 1932 to 1935.

The Englishman Fred Perry won the Wimbledon singles for three consecutive years (1934–36), the U.S. championship in 1933, 1934, and 1936, the Australian in 1934, and the French in 1935. From the United States came champions that included Sidney Wood, Ellsworth Vines, and Don Budge, who in 1938 became the first man to win all four major titles—the Australian, French, Wimbledon, and U.S.—in one season, a feat that came to be known as the grand slam. Alice Marble, the most aggressive net-rusher the women's game had seen to that time, won the U.S. singles in 1936 and from 1938 to 1940, and in 1939 won the singles, doubles, and mixed doubles at Wimbledon, a "triple" previously accomplished only by Lenglen and Budge.

Alice Marble's triple

The postwar period. The development of the game was interrupted by World War II, but international tennis resumed in 1946 with U.S. players again dominant, led by Jack Kramer, the U.S. champion of 1946–47 and Wimbledon champion of 1947 before he turned professional. He was succeeded by Pancho Gonzales, Bob Falkenburg, Frederick (Ted) Schroeder, J. Edward ("Budge") Patty, and Dick Savitt. American women won every Wimbledon and U.S. singles title from 1946 through 1958, the string of champions including Pauline Betz, Louise Brough, Margaret Osborne DuPont, Doris Hart, Maureen Connolly, Shirley Fry, and Althea Gibson, the first black champion. Connolly, nicknamed "Little Mo," won the three Wimbledon and three U.S. championships that she played between 1951 and 1954 and in 1953 became the first woman to achieve the grand slam.

Australian domination in the 1950s and '60s

Australia ruled men's tennis in the 1950s and '60s, winning the Davis Cup in 15 of 18 years. Among the Wimbledon and U.S. singles champions who played for Harry Hopman, the outstanding nonplaying Australian captain, were Frank Sedgman, Lew Hoad, Ken Rosewall, Mal Anderson, Ashley Cooper, Neale Fraser, Rod Laver, Fred Stolle, Roy Emerson, and John Newcombe.

The broadening international horizons of the game were reflected in the Wimbledon triumphs of players such as Jaroslav Drobny, an expatriate Czech, in 1954 and Alex Olmedo, from Peru, in 1959; and in the victories of Mexican Rafael Osuna in the U.S. championship in 1963; Manuel Santana of Spain in the U.S. championship in 1965 and Wimbledon in 1966; and Brazilian Maria Bueno, the U.S. champion four times and Wimbledon champion three times between 1959 and 1966.

Australian Margaret Smith Court was the second woman to win the grand slam, in 1970, and she set the all-time record for singles, doubles, and mixed-doubles titles in the four major championships; 65 between 1960 and 1975, including three Wimbledon, six U.S., five French, and 11 Australian singles. Billie Jean Moffitt King set a record for career Wimbledon titles, winning six singles, 10 doubles, and four mixed between 1961 and 1979.

Professional and open tennis. As tennis began to establish its popularity, there was need for professionals to coach and to organize, but unlike real tennis, there were no competitions in which professionals could play. This changed in 1926 when Charles C. ("Cash and Carry") Pyle, a successful sports promoter in the United States, offered Suzanne Lenglen $50,000 to go on a professional tour of America playing Mary K. Browne, who had been U.S. singles champion from 1912 to 1914. He also signed four male players. The tour, played in major arenas, drew large crowds and was a financial success. For the next 40 years, pro tennis consisted primarily of barnstorming tours that featured the reigning champion playing a recently signed amateur champion.

Pro barnstorming

Starting in the 1930s, many of the amateur champions became barnstorming professionals. After World War II, Jack Kramer became the pro champion and in the early

1950s took over promotion of the pro tour. He kept raiding the amateur ranks, signing such stars as Frank Sedgman, Tony Trabert, Lew Hoad, and Ken Rosewall. They made money with the one-night stands, but their matches were virtually unreported. Although the traditional tournament circuit was avowedly amateur, leading players were paid substantial guarantees "under the table" in addition to expenses. For more than four decades there was discussion of having "open" competition between amateurs and pros to end the hypocrisy of "shamateurism," but proposals were always defeated by conservative elements within the ILTF. In 1967, however, two new professional groups were formed: the National Tennis League, organized by former U.S. Davis Cup captain George MacCall, and World Championship Tennis (WCT), founded by New Orleans promoter Dave Dixon and funded by Dallas oil and football tycoon Lamar Hunt. Between them, they signed a significant number of the world's top players, professional and amateur.

In 1967 a British proposal for a limited schedule of open tournaments was voted down by the international federation, but the British LTA refused to accept the verdict. In December 1967, despite threat of expulsion from the International Lawn Tennis Federation (ILTF—later the ITF), the LTA voted to abolish the distinction between amateurs and pros in their tournaments. This revolutionary step forced an emergency meeting of the ILTF in March 1968 in which 12 open tournaments were approved. The era of open professionalism in tennis dawned in 1968.

Acceptance of open tournaments

The first open tournament was the British Hard Courts at Bournemouth in April 1968, where the champions were Ken Rosewall and Virginia Wade. The first open Wimbledon was a joyous occasion, as many past champions who had been stripped of membership in the All-England Club when they turned professional were welcomed back. The total prize money was £26,150 ($62,760), of which £2,000 went to men's singles champion Rod Laver and £750 went to women's singles winner Billie Jean King. The singles titles at the first U.S. Open, with a total purse of $100,000, were won by Arthur Ashe, the sport's first black male champion, and Wade. Within two decades the major championships had multimillion-dollar purses, and top players could expect to earn in excess of $1,000,000 a year on the court alone. Laver became the first player to sweep the major titles a second time and the first to do so as a professional.

The transition years from quasi-amateurism to full-fledged professional tennis were rife with political disputes and lawsuits for control of what had become a big-money sport. Both male and female players formed guilds: the men's Association of Tennis Professionals (ATP) and the Women's Tennis Association (WTA), which in 1986 became the Women's International Tennis Association (WITA). Previous player unions had been ineffective, but the ATP showed itself a potent political force when the majority of its members boycotted Wimbledon in 1973 in a dispute over the eligibility of the Yugoslav pro Nikki Pilic. The women's union proved similarly unified. The women had a separate pro tour, apart from the men, except at the major championships, since 1971.

Players' guilds

The first few seasons of open tennis were ruled by players who were products of the old system and reflected its behavioral standards and norms. These included the compact, classical Rosewall, the Australian John Newcombe, and the Americans Arthur Ashe and Stan Smith.

As television, in America and later worldwide, became an increasingly significant force in tennis, a new breed of flamboyant and often flippant, cocky, and quick-tempered player developed. Among them was Ilie Nastase—a dark, handsome, mercurial Romanian noted for his rapid mood swings. While winning the 1972 U.S. Open, the 1973 French Open, and four Masters titles, he created chaos and controversy on the court with colourful, and occasionally off-colour, tantrums and tirades. He was perhaps an influence on Jimmy Connors, a brash American whose aggressive, blood-and-guts, all-court style and feisty temperament captivated audiences whether they loved or loathed him. In 1974 Connors won Wimbledon and the Australian and U.S. opens. In an intensely competitive era that produced short careers, Connors enjoyed extraordinary longevity at the top. He won Wimbledon again in 1982, the U.S. Open four more times, and the WCT Championship in 1977 and 1980.

Nastase and Connors

Jimmy Connors (U.S.), a major player in world tennis during the 1970s and 1980s, serving at Wimbledon.

Sporting Pictures (U.K.)

Following the fiery Connors as the dominant player was the relatively cool Bjorn Borg, who led Sweden to its first triumph in the Davis Cup in 1975. Practically unbeatable on slow clay, he won the French Open six times between 1974 and 1981 and remarkably adapted his game to fast grass, adding a sledgehammer serve and underspin approach shot, to win Wimbledon five years running, 1976–80. No player had done that since the champion had to play through the draw, starting in 1922. The American John McEnroe ended Borg's Wimbledon reign in 1981 and beat him in the 1980–81 U.S. Open finals. Between 1979 and 1984 McEnroe, a torrid-tempered left-hander of exquisite athleticism and racket control, won Wimbledon three times, the U.S. Open four times, the Masters three times, and the WCT Championship four times.

The balance of power in men's tennis shifted back to Europe in the 1980s. Borg inspired a new wave of players in Sweden. A sophisticated junior-development system created a group of Swedish players—led by 1982, 1985, and 1988 French Open champion Mats Wilander. Another European country with a long tennis tradition that reached new heights in the 1980s was Czechoslovakia. One of the foremost players and coaches in Europe in the 1920s and '30s was the Czech Karel Kozeluh. Czechoslovakia produced men's Wimbledon champions Jaroslav Drobny in 1954 and Jan Kodeš in 1973. Among the players to come out of Czechoslovakia's player-development system and become dominant in the 1970s and 1980s were Martina Navratilova, who became a U.S. citizen; Hana Mandlikova, who became an Australian citizen in 1987; and Ivan Lendl, who took up residence in the United States. The European tennis boom of the 1980s also swept West Germany, which produced Boris Becker, who won the Wimbledon singles in 1985 at age 17 (the youngest man and first unseeded player to do so), and Steffi Graf, who in 1987 ended Navratilova's five-year reign as the top-ranked woman in tennis and in 1988 won the grand slam, becoming the first woman to do so since Margaret Court in 1970.

The Czech tradition

Emergence of Steffi Graf

Graf's emergence also ended an extraordinary streak by the American Chris Evert, who had won at least one of the grand slam singles titles for 13 consecutive years, 1974–86, an unprecedented feat. A paragon of back-court consistency and controlled temperament, Evert was the perfect contrast in both style and personality to several net-rushing rivals: the Australian Evonne Goolagong, who won her first Wimbledon in 1971, at age 19, Billie Jean King, and Navratilova, whom Evert played in 13 grand slam finals in one of the game's greatest rivalries. Evert, probably more than anyone, popularized the two-handed backhand, and she made a steady baseline game the prevalent style of a whole generation of women players.

Organization and tournaments. The ITF and the national associations that comprise it govern tennis worldwide; they oversee international competitions such as the Davis Cup and Federation Cup and tennis in the Olympic Games, which was restored to medal-sport status for the 1988 Games—the first time since 1924. The professional circuits were governed from the late 1970s by the Men's and Women's International Professional Tennis councils. These groups, made up of representatives of the ITF, players, and tournaments, oversee the international calendar, the implementation of rules and codes of conduct, and the training and supervision of tour officials. The councils work closely with the ATP and WITA, which supply a number of services and benefits to players and tournaments and maintain rankings that provide the basis for entry into tournaments and seedings.

The major championships. Until 1974, when South Africa won by default over India, only four nations had won the Davis Cup: Australia, Great Britain, France, and the United States. The championships of those four countries are the traditional "major" tournaments that make up the grand slam. Wimbledon in Britain is the oldest, having been played on the lawns of the All-England Club since 1877. The French championships, played at Stade Roland-Garros in Auteuil, on the outskirts of Paris, are recognized as the world's premier clay-court tournaments. The U.S. championships were played on grass from their inception in 1881 through 1974; the next three years they were played on a synthetic clay surface at the West Side Tennis Club in Forest Hills, N.Y., and in 1978, the tournament moved to the rubberized asphalt courts of the USTA National Tennis Center in nearby Flushing Meadow Park. The Australian Championships were played on grass in several cities until 1968, when they moved to Melbourne; in 1988 they moved within that city to the synthetic courts of the new Australian National Tennis Centre.

The championship team events

The principal team events are the Davis Cup, Federation Cup, and Wightman Cup (U.S. versus British women). The Davis Cup series consists of five matches played over three days: two singles, one doubles, then two "reverse" singles. From 1923 through 1965 the Davis Cup draw was played in two zones, and from 1966 through 1980 in four zones. Starting in 1981, the top 16 teams competed in a World Group and all other participating nations in four zones. The Federation Cup, inaugurated in 1963, is contested at one site over a one-week period, each series consisting of three matches: two singles and a doubles. The Wightman Cup alternates between U.S. and British sites and comprises best-of-seven matches: five singles and two doubles.

PLAY OF THE GAME

Court and equipment. The dimensions of the tennis court are 78 by 27 feet (23.77 by 8.23 metres) for singles and 78 by 36 feet (23.77 by 10.97 metres) for doubles. The height of the net at the centre is three feet, and it is supported at each side of the court by posts $3\frac{1}{2}$ feet high at three feet outside the court (see Figure 13). Tennis was originally called "lawn tennis," and grass courts are still in use, but the most common court materials today are clay (called "hard courts" in most places, although in the United States that term refers to any hard surface), cement, and a number of cushioned asphalt derivatives and synthetic surfaces. The latter may be hard surface or artificial grass, materials that have become popular for indoor courts along with the traditional wood. A tennis ball consists of a pressurized rubber core covered with high-quality cloth, usually wool mixed with up to 35 percent nylon. Balls gradually go soft with use, and in tournament play they are changed at regular intervals agreed upon by officials and depending upon such factors as the court surface. Balls must have a uniform outer surface, and, if there are any seams, they must be stitchless. The ITF specifies that the ball must be between $2\frac{1}{2}$ inches (6.35 centimetres) and $2\frac{5}{8}$ inches in diameter, and between two ounces (56.7 grams) and $2\frac{1}{16}$ ounces in weight. The ball must have a bound between 53 inches and 58 inches when dropped 100 inches upon a concrete base.

Court surfaces

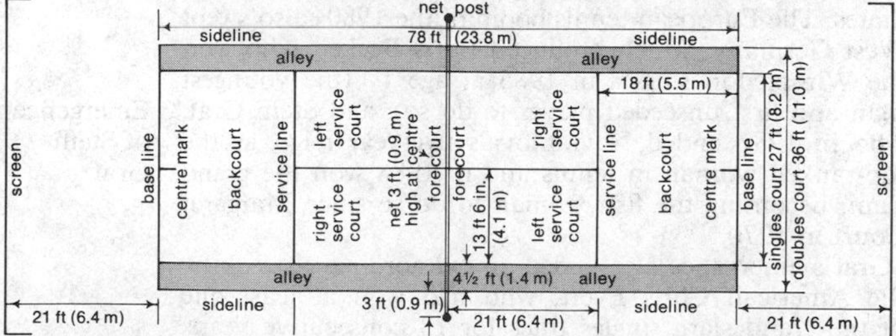

Figure 13: Playing area for lawn tennis (metric dimensions are rounded off). The alleys are used only in doubles play.

Nothing in the rules defined the racket until 1981. After an ITF committee had made studies of the so-called "double-strung" or "spaghetti" racket, introduced in 1977, which had two layers of strings that imparted topspin on the ball, it was banned by the following rule: "A racket shall consist of a frame, which may be of any material, weight, size or shape and stringing. The stringing must be uniform and smooth and may be of any material. The strings must be alternately interlaced or bonded where they cross. The distance between the main and/or cross strings shall not be less than one quarter of an inch nor more than one-half inch. If there are attachments they must be used only to prevent wear and tear and must not alter the flight of the ball."

The ITF racket rule

Principles of play. Opponents spin a racket or toss a coin to decide on side and service. The winner may decide to serve or receive serve first, in which case his opponent chooses the side, or may decide on a choice of side, in which case the opponent may choose to serve or receive service first. The players serve alternate games and change sides after every odd number of games.

Beginning each game from behind his right-hand court, the server has both feet behind the baseline and strikes the ball diagonally across the net and into the opponent's right-hand service court. Should the ball on service strike the top of the net before falling in the correct service court, it is a "let" and is replayed. The server is allowed one miss, or "fault," either into the net or outside the opponent's service court. Failure to deliver a correct service on two attempts constitutes loss of the point.

Return service and volley

To return service, the receiver strikes the ball back before it hits the ground a second time, over the net and within the boundaries of the opponent's court. After the service has been correctly returned, either player may volley the ball (*i.e.,* hit it before it bounces) or hit it after its first bounce, and the point continues until one player fails to make a correct return. This may occur if he fails to hit the ball over the net, if he hits it outside the opponent's boundaries, or if he fails to hit it before it strikes the ground a second time on his side of the net.

To win a game, a player must win four points and have a margin of two. The scoring goes 15, 30, 40, game; this system, derived from real tennis, is medieval in origin. It never has been satisfactorily explained why three points equal 40 rather than 45. Zero is generally referred to as "love," which is thought to be derived from *l'oeuf,* the French word for "egg." The server's score is called first; thus, 30–15 means that the server has two points to one, whereas 15–30 means that the receiver has two points to one. If both players reach 40, the score is said to be "deuce," and the game continues until a player achieves first "advantage" and then the two-point margin for "game." There is no limit to the number of times a game can go to deuce before it is decided, but in some competitions, a so-called "no-ad" system is used, which means that no two-point margin is required and the first player to win four points wins the game. As points make up a game, games make up a set, and sets make up a match. The first player to win six games traditionally wins the set, although again a two-game margin is required; thus, a five-games-all set cannot be won before 7–5.

Since the early 1970s virtually all competitions have come to employ tiebreakers to eliminate marathon sets. Usually played at six games all, the tiebreaker can consist of an odd number of points with no two-point margin required ("sudden death") or an even number of points with a two-point margin required. For example, in a 12-point tiebreaker the first player to reach 7 points with a margin of 2 wins the tiebreaker game and the set, 7–6. Virtually all tournaments now play tiebreakers at six games all. In major tournaments and the Davis Cup and Olympic Games, men generally play best-of-five-set matches and women best-of-three. In most other tournaments, men now also play best-of-three sets; women occasionally play best-of-five for finals.

Doubles play and scoring

The same basic principles of play and scoring apply to doubles. Service alternates between the two opposing teams, but each team must decide at the start of each set which partner shall serve first. Equally, the receiving team must decide at the start of each set which of them shall receive service first, and they then receive service on alternate points for that game and set. Thus, the server will alternate sides of the court on successive points in each game, but the receiver will always receive on the same side of the court during that game (and the set).

Strategy and technique. Although successful strokes and strategy can vary widely on different court surfaces, on all but the slowest courts there has always been a premium on a punishing serve and effective play at the net. The server usually has a considerable advantage for two reasons. With a combination of power and clever angle and spin, he can win points outright with the serve, called an "ace" if the opponent cannot get his racket on the ball and a "service winner" if the opponent reaches it but cannot play it, or the server can force such a weak return that his second shot is an easy "kill." Especially on faster surfaces, the server may also follow his delivery to the net and establish his position. At the net, a player is always vulnerable to a passing shot—one angled cross-court or played down-the-line, beyond reach—but if the serve or approach shot puts the opponent under enough pressure, the server, now at the net, has the upper hand, since a volley is generally easier to put away (play for a point) than a ground stroke (one played on a bounce). An effective first serve is a considerable asset on any surface. The best servers not only deliver the ball hard, but they vary their patterns so that a receiver cannot anticipate where the serve is coming. Equally important is the ability to deliver an effective second service (one made after an initial fault), usually with less power but more spin or "kick."

Volleying technique

For good volleyers, the key to winning is to get to the net, behind either the serve or approach shot. For players whose strength is their ground stroke, the priority is to maneuver the opponent into a vulnerable position for a winning passing shot, placement, or drive that forces an error. All shots after the serve—volley or ground stroke—can be played either on the forehand (where, if the racket were viewed as an extension of the hand, the palm would be striking the ball) or the backhand (where the back of the hand would be striking the ball).

Styles of play at the top level have varied widely with changing court surfaces. When most major tournaments were played on grass, for instance, there was a distinct advantage to a powerful serve-and-volley game and short, controlled, underspin ground strokes that kept the ball low. When slow clay became the predominant surface of the professional game in the mid-1970s, there was more emphasis on solid ground strokes and topspin, which allowed players to loop the ball well over the net and have it bounce high, pinning opponents to the backcourt. Hard-surface courts of medium speed and true bounce favour an all-court game and enable both net rushers and baseliners to play their preferred styles.

Other strokes, besides the serve, volley, and drive, include the lob, overhead smash, half volley, and drop shot. The lob, a soft high-arched loop, can be played either defensively, to try to recover from an awkward, vulnerable position where an attacking stroke is impossible, or offensively, to get the ball over the reach of an opponent at the net and put him on the defensive. The player who makes an offensive lob often follows it to the net, but if a lob is not high enough to get over the opponent, it can be returned with an overhead smash, the most forceful of strokes. The player making the smash often leaps to hit the ball with a stroke similar to the serve from a position approximating the service toss. The half volley is a shot played on a very short bounce, usually a defensive stroke effected when one cannot quite reach an opponent's shot in the air and volley it. The drop shot, which is often hit from the same motion as a drive, attempts to get the ball just over the net with underspin so that it barely bounces, either catching an opponent flat-footed in the backcourt where he cannot reach the ball or forcing him to run in and lunge at the ball, leaving him off balance.

The smash

(A./B.S.Lo.)

Golf

Golf is a cross-country game played by striking a small ball with various clubs from a series of teeing grounds into a like series of holes on a course. The player who holes his ball in the fewest strokes wins. The game originated in Scotland and has spread from obscure antiquity to worldwide popularity. Played in the beginning on seaside links with their crisp turf and natural hazards and afterward on downs, moorland, and parkland courses of various lengths and characteristics, it combines with its open air and exercise an intrinsic fascination. Its players participate at every level, from recreational golf to popular televised professional tournaments. Despite its attractiveness golf is not a game for everyone; it requires a high degree of skill that is honed only with great patience and dedication, and it requires an investment in equipment and fees that persons of average means may not feel worthwhile. The novice is often discouraged by these factors.

HISTORY

Origin and early years. The game's origin has long been a subject of controversy. Broadly, the issue has been whether it originated in Scotland or Holland. Its antiquity in Scotland is beyond question because of documentary proof of its long lineage. The first written reference to the sport was made in 1457, when the Parliament of King James II decreed that both "Fute-ball and Golfe be utterly cryed downe" because they interfered with the practice of archery, which was necessary for the defense of the realm. Similar decrees were also enacted in 1471 and 1491; the latter decree, which was issued during the reign of James IV, indicted them as "unproffitable sportis." One obvious implication of these laws is that golf had become a popular obsession in Scotland even before the mid-15th century.

Controversy over origin of the game

Continental games. Comparisons between ancient continental games and Scottish golf make an interesting study, with the balance of evidence in favour of Scotland. During the Roman domination in Europe, a popular game was *paganica* (from *paganus,* "country-man," or "rustic"), a cross-country pastime played with a bent stick and with, it seems, a leather ball stuffed with feathers, like the early golf balls in Scotland; but it can be disregarded merely as a link between legend and history. Early games in the Netherlands have a more striking similarity to golf, notably the Dutch game of *kolven* or *kolf* because of the name *kolf* for a club and the fact that the clubs seen in early Dutch pictures suggest something like golf. Of the continental games the game of *chole* (*choulla* or *choulle*) had some resemblance to golf. More Belgian (Flemish) than Dutch, it was a cross-country pastime in which each side, whether one player or several, used one ball and played to a prearranged target—a church door, for example—at a considerable distance from the starting point.

The games of *kolven* and *chole*

Scotland. Scotland's King James IV, who had embargoed the game in 1491, later became the first player of whom there is authentic record. The Lord High Treasurer's accounts early in the 16th century include payments for the King's equipment—"golf clubbis and ballis." The

Stuarts gave the game its first woman golfer, too—Mary, Queen of Scots, who was charged with playing in the fields beside Seton only a few days after the murder of her husband, Darnley. James VI was noted for promoting the game. When he succeeded to the English throne as James I, he took his courtiers and his clubs with him.

Development of golfers' associations. *Early British societies.* There is a tradition that James I introduced golf to Blackheath in 1608, which has been given, erroneously according to some authorities, as the foundation year of the historic Royal Blackheath Golf Club. Although King James and his courtiers played their golf somewhere in the vicinity, it is doubtful whether any organized societies then existed, and research has set its date nearly two centuries later. W.E. Hughes, editor of the *Chronicles of Blackheath Golfers,* ascribes the club's foundation to 1787.

The oldest club with documentary proof of its origin is the Company of Gentlemen Golfers, now the Honourable Company of Edinburgh Golfers, whose modern home is at Muirfield in East Lothian. Its genesis was a move by a group of players to hold a competition or tournament. In 1744 "several Gentlemen of Honour skillful in the ancient and healthfull exercise of Golf" petitioned the Edinburgh city council to provide a silver club for annual competition on the links of Leith.

The Society of St. Andrews, now the Royal and Ancient Golf Club of St. Andrews, Scotland, was formed in 1754 by a group of 22 golfers who played there. The rules that the society adopted were almost identical with the Edinburgh Gentlemen Golfers' rules. These two clubs played major roles in the development of the game in Scotland. Eventually, the Royal and Ancient Golf Club (R. and A.) became, by common consent, the oracle on rules. In 1919 it accepted the management of the British Open and Amateur championships. The R. and A. thus became the governing body for golf in the British Isles and throughout most of the Commonwealth.

Early clubs in England

With the birth of the Royal North Devon Club in 1864, the game took a firm foothold in England. It was the first course on seaside links outside Scotland. The Royal Liverpool Club was established in 1869 on a rabbit warren at Hoylake. In its infancy players simply cut holes with their penknives and stuck feathers in them for the guidance of those who were coming behind. The rabbits were the greenkeepers. By 1870 the club was fairly founded, and members played matches against Blackheath, Royal North Devon Club at Westward Ho!, and others. Their influence widened interest in the game. The Royal Liverpool Club hosted Great Britain's first Amateur Championship in 1885 and the first English Amateur Championship in 1925. The first Scotland–England amateur match was organized in 1902, and it was at Hoylake in 1921 that an unofficial contest between British and U.S. players, a curtain raiser to the Amateur Championship, was played and served as the genesis of the Walker Cup series.

The United States and Canada. The following advertisement, which appeared in James Rivington's *Gazette* in New York on April 21, 1779, clearly refers to golf: "To the GOLF PLAYERS: The Season for this pleasant and healthy Exercise now advancing, Gentlemen may be furnished with excellent CLUBS and the veritable Caledonian BALLS, by enquiring at the Printer's." The *South Carolina and Georgia Almanac* of 1793 published, under the heading "Societies Established in Charleston," the following item: "Golf Club Formed 1786." The *Charleston City Gazette and Daily Advertiser* of Sept. 18, 1788, reported: "There is lately erected that pleasing and genteel amusement, the KOLF BAAN." Later notices dated 1791 and 1794 referred to the South Carolina Golf Club, which celebrated an anniversary with a dinner on Harleston's Green in the latter year. Although these fragments constitute the earliest clear evidence of golf clubs in the United States, the clubs appear to have been primarily social organizations that did not survive the War of 1812.

Early records of golf in America

The first permanent golf club in the Western Hemisphere was the Royal Montreal Golf Club, established in 1873. The members played on Fletcher's Fields in the city's central area until urban growth compelled a move of some miles to Dixie, a name derived from a group of Southern refugees who arrived there after the U.S. Civil War. The Royal Quebec Golf Club was founded in 1874; the Toronto and Niagara, Ont., clubs in 1876; and the Brantford, Ont., club in 1879. In the meantime, golf was played experimentally at many places in the United States without taking permanent root until, in 1885, it was played in Foxburg, Pa. The Oakhurst Golf Club in West Virginia, which later became the Greenbrier Club, is said to have been formed in 1884; and the Dorset Field Club in Dorset, Vt., claims to have been organized and to have laid out its course in 1886, although in both instances written records are lacking. The Foxburg Golf Club has provided strong support for the claim that it was organized in 1887 and is the oldest golf club in the United States with a permanent existence. Foxburg also claims the oldest U.S. golf course.

Golf as an organized game in the United States, however, usually is dated from the founding of the St. Andrew's Golf Club at Yonkers, N.Y., in 1888. Its progenitor was John Reid, a Scot from Dunfermline who became known as "the father of American golf." Reid, on learning that fellow Scot Robert Lockhart was returning to the old country on business, asked him to bring back some golf clubs and balls. This done, Reid and his friend John B. Upham tried them out on Feb. 22, 1888, over an improvised three-hole layout. That fall, five men formed the club and in the spring moved to a course in an apple orchard. There, it is said, they hung their coats and a jug of good Scotch whiskey in a convenient apple tree, and they subsequently became known as the "Apple Tree Gang." The club made its final move in 1897 to Mt. Hope in Westchester County, N.Y.

Other early courses included Newport, R.I. (1890); Shinnecock Hills on Long Island (1891); and the Chicago Golf Club (1892) at Wheaton. The Tuxedo Golf Club, New York, founded in 1889, met the Shinnecock men in 1894 in what has been assumed to be the first interclub match in the United States. The Newport club staged an invitation tournament for amateurs in September 1894, and in October the St. Andrew's Club promoted a similar competition. These were announced as championships, but that was questioned because the events were each promoted by a single club and on an invitational basis. It was from the controversy roused by these promotions that the United States Golf Association (USGA) was instituted in 1894. Its aims were to organize the U.S. Amateur and Open championships and to formulate a set of rules for the game. The founding fathers, two from each club, were from St. Andrew's, Shinnecock Hills, Chicago, the Country Club at Brookline, and Newport. The U.S. national championships—the Amateur, the Women's Amateur, and the Open—were inaugurated in 1895.

First championships and the founding of the USGA

Other countries. Before organized clubs had been established in North America, colonies of British settlers, merchants, and civil servants carried golf with them.

India has the oldest club outside of Great Britain; the Royal Calcutta Golf Club was founded in 1829, and the Royal Bombay Golf Club came about 12 years later. The Royal Calcutta initiated an amateur championship for India, and the two clubs paved the way for many in the Far East. The Royal Bangkok Golf Club (1890) was first housed in an ancient temple. Golf came to China when the Shanghai Golf Club was formed in 1896, until which time the game was apparently unknown outside of Hong Kong. The Japanese a few years later constructed a course at Kōbe. The Tokyo Golf Club was founded in 1914. With the boom in the popularity of the game in Japan after World War II, players came to be numbered in the thousands, despite the fact that the shortage of open land made the game enormously expensive to play.

The first club in Australia, the Royal Adelaide Golf Club, was formed in 1870, and it is believed that the game was played in Melbourne in 1847 but went into abeyance for nearly half a century, the gold rush having taken priority over golf for the settlers.

New Zealand origins have been dated from the formation of the Christchurch Golf Club in 1873. South Africa's first course was at the Maritzburg Golf Club, the first in Natal, in 1884, though the Royal Cape Golf Club (1885) has been rated as the country's senior club.

Development of equipment. How the ball is hit and directed is the essence of the game. The result can be fun or frustration, delight or despair. The changing story of the ball's manufacture falls broadly into well-defined phases, beginning with the "feathery," which was used for centuries until it was superseded by gutta-percha.

The feather-ball era. For many years balls were made from wood, but in the early 17th century feather balls were introduced and were hailed as an advance. These balls consisted of boiled feathers that were compressed through a hole left in pieces of stitched leather that composed the cover. For stuffing in the feathers a wooden tool was first used, after which the stuffing iron had to complete the job. When the leather case was crammed beyond increase, the hole was stitched up, the ball hammered and made as round as possible, and then painted white. The whole process was so slow that the maker did well to finish four in a day, so that they cost as much as five shillings each. Although the "feathery" could be hit a long way, it became sodden and disabled in wet weather and was destroyed by hacks from iron clubs, so that the balls were short-lived as well as expensive.

Manufacture of the feather ball

The gutta-percha era. Gutta-percha, the evaporated milky juice or latex of various South American and South Pacific islands trees, is soft and impressible at the temperature of boiling water, but becomes hard and nonbrittle and retains its shape when cooled. It is not affected by water except at boiling temperature. The emergence of the gutta-percha ball about 1848 brought a revolutionary change in the game. The professionals had divided views, however. St. Andrews' Allan Robertson, a leading manufacturer of "featheries," would have nothing to do with it at first; but "Old Tom" Morris, who was then his assistant, wisely foresaw the possibilities of the "gutty," and on this issue the two actually parted company in 1852, Morris going into business on his own. The ball was heartily welcomed by the golf community, not least for its economy—cost, one shilling each—and its coming immediately swelled the golfing ranks. The first examples were smooth and ducked suddenly, a problem corrected when the ball makers learned to mold balls with raised or indented surface patterns so they would fly properly.

The rubber ball. The beginning of the 20th century introduced a new ball and a new era. The U.S. patent of the rubber ball, the invention of Coburn Haskell, a golfer of Cleveland, and Bertram G. Work of the B.F. Goodrich Company, involved a tension-wound rubber thread around a solid rubber core. Its resilience was a great improvement over the "gutty," which was a hard, irresponsive ball that required skill and strength to get into the air after the tee shots. The rubber ball was easier to hit and gave the striker great pleasure and a sense of power. Its impetus created a tidal wave in the game's popularity. Elderly men found it easier to play, and hosts of women and children were drawn into the game. A number of varieties of ball then appeared from manufacturers catering to the golfer's desire to hit the ball farther. Length was the lure, and the trade race upset the design of courses. Championship and other tees had to be sited farther back. Shortly after World War I the Royal and Ancient Club enacted what is called "the 1-62 formula"—that the ball should have a maximum weight of 1.62 ounces (45.93 grams) and a minimum diameter of 1.62 inches (4.11 centimetres). The USGA tried for two years a ball 1.55 ounces (43.94 grams) in weight and 1.68 inches (4.27 centimetres) in diameter, but in 1932 it reverted to a weight of 1.62 ounces while retaining a diameter of 1.68 inches. This larger-sized "American" ball was ruled mandatory by the British Professional Golf Association in 1968 and had replaced the small ball throughout the world by 1980.

Invention of the rubber ball

Early clubs. No golf club from the early 17th century exists; the oldest clubs known were discovered in a house in Hull along with a newspaper carrying a date of 1741. All of these clubs were made of wood, and antiquarian theory is that they were used in the time of the Stuart kings.

In the Royal and Ancient Club's museum there are specimens of ancient clubs including two woods and an especially notable putting cleek—*i.e.,* a putter having an iron head on a wooden shaft—made in the second half of the 18th century by Simon Cossar of Leith, club maker to the Company of Gentlemen Golfers. When Robertson saw that golfing would not be ruined by the gutta-percha ball, he realized the value of iron clubs for approaching and made a cleek for steadier putting. Other developments included "Young Tom" (son of "Old Tom") Morris' idea for the cup-faced niblick for playing the shorter approaches.

Introduction of iron heads

The club makers of outstanding repute in the early 19th century were Hugh Philp at St. Andrews and the McEwan brothers of Musselburgh, notably Douglas, whose clubs were described as models of symmetry and shape. They were artists at a time when clubs were passing from "rude and clumsy bludgeons" to a new and handsome look.

New manufacturing methods. The hickory shafts of the woods—the play club (modern driver), the spoons, and the brassie—had been spliced to heads of apple or beech faced with horn. The harder rubber ball, however, brought about the use of persimmon and, later, laminated club heads. Hard insets appeared in the faces. Increased demand led to the adaptation of shoe-last machine tools for the fashioning of wooden club heads. Sockets were bored in the club heads, and shafts were inserted rather than spliced. Drop-forging completely replaced hand forging in the fashioning of iron clubs, and faces were deepened to accommodate the livelier ball and were machine lined to increase the spin on the ball in flight. Composition materials were developed as an alternative to leather in grips, and the grip foundations were molded in so many ways that they were regulated in 1947. Inventive minds created novel clubs, not only centre-shafted and aluminum putters and the sand wedge but also types that were such radical departures from the traditional form and make that they could not be approved by the USGA or the R. and A. In its revised code of 1908 the R. and A. ruled that it would not sanction any substantial departure from the traditional form and make of golf clubs. This principle has been invoked many times.

Experiments with steel shafts went through several phases. In 1924 the Union Hardware Company of Torrington, Conn., drew a seamless shaft of high-carbon steel that could be heat-treated and tempered. It was approved by the R. and A. in 1929 and substantially replaced hickory in the early 1930s. Later, shafts of fibreglass, aluminum, graphite, and titanium were introduced. By the 1970s the technique of investment casting, a method of casting rather than forging to enhance the perimeter weighting of iron clubs, was commonplace, and a decade later "woods" made of metal were in widespread use, even by many tournament professionals. These and dozens of minor innovations were incorporated into production techniques that were quality controlled by computers and other electronic means. Balls also underwent a major change with the introduction principally of Surlyn, a synthetic material that was difficult to cut and thus could withstand the hacking blows of the game's millions of weekend practitioners.

Steel shafts

Improvement of the shaft was accompanied by the general introduction of numbered, rather than named, clubs and by the merchandising of matched sets rather than individual clubs. Clubs had become more numerous and more finely graduated than the names that traditionally had been applied to them, and shafts could be manufactured to specifications for flexibility and point of flex. Whereas formerly a golfer seeking new clubs went through a rack of mashies until he found one that "felt right" and then tried to find other clubs of similar feel, he later bought a whole set manufactured to impart the same feel. The merchandising opportunities inherent in the numbered and matched sets were carried to an extreme, and in 1938 the USGA limited the number of clubs a player might use in a round to 14. The R. and A. concurred in a similar edict the next year.

Players and tournaments. There is no doubt that the development of golf as an organized sport was distinctly British, and Britain produced the first great players of the game. As the early golfing associations, or clubs, became established in Scotland and then England, there emerged a group of professionals who made golf balls, fashioned and repaired clubs, laid out and maintained courses, and gave lessons. Many of them were outstanding golfers and

The British tradition

would take on all comers in the popular stakes (money) matches of their day. St. Andrews' Robertson, for example, regarded as the greatest golfer of his time, according to legend, was never beaten in a stakes match played on even terms (that is, without giving his opponent a handicap). The British professionals and their amateur counterparts represented the best golf in the world from the second half of the 19th century, when the sport began to gain some world prominence, up to about the 1920s, when U.S. players began to excel. With the tremendous increases in financial rewards to be gained in golf after about 1950, especially on the U.S. professional tour, and with the great mobility provided by jet transportation, golfers from other countries (*e.g.,* Australia, New Zealand, South Africa, Japan, and Argentina) began to appear in the top tournaments.

The premier championships. The most prestigious championships are the Open and Amateur championships of the British Isles and the U.S. Open, Amateur, Professional Golfers Association (PGA), and Masters. The Walker Cup for amateurs and the Ryder Cup for professionals are important team golfing tournaments that have pitted U.S. golfers against those of Great Britain and Ireland. From 1979 a European team (including Britons) replaced Great Britain in Ryder Cup play. (For winners of these championships, see SPORTING RECORD in the *Micropædia.*)

British tournaments and players. The Open Championship of the British Isles, which the British like to call The Open to emphasize the tradition and priority of the event begun in 1860, was the concept of the Prestwick Club in Scotland, whose minutes recorded a proposal that all clubs should contribute to raise a fund for a trophy for professional competition. Their hope, however, was badly disappointed, and the offer of support was so meagre that Prestwick decided to go it alone and spent 30 guineas on the ornamental challenge belt to be awarded to the champion. The early championships were dominated by Willie Park, "Old Tom" Morris, and his son, "Young Tom," who retired the belt by winning it three times in succession, 1868–70. In the absence of a prize, there was no championship in 1871; but the next year a cup, which has been in competition ever since, was put up.

The Open Championship

At the end of the 19th century, England was producing great players. John Henry Taylor and Harry Vardon, together with James Braid, a Scotsman, among them won the Open Championship 16 times between 1894 and 1914. These three supreme golfers were known as "the great triumvirate" and were primarily responsible for the formation of the Professional Golfers Association in 1901. This body is responsible for professional tournaments in Great Britain and for the biennial Ryder Cup match (for professionals) when it is played there.

The British Amateur Championship was started in 1885 after the Royal Liverpool Golf Club at Hoylake had proposed a tournament "open to all amateur golfers." The tournament attracted nearly all the best amateurs of the time, but it was not immediately recognized as the championship. The following year the Royal Liverpool suggested to the R. and A. that the tournament be established as the amateur championship, and 24 clubs joined together to purchase a trophy and manage the event. Among British players who won the amateur championship at least two times before the series was interrupted by World War I were H.G. Hutchinson, John Ball (who won it eight times), J.E. Laidlay, and H.H. Hilton. The interwar years were marked by many outstanding players, including Cyril Tolley, Amateur champion in 1920 and 1929; Roger Wethered, Amateur champion in 1923; and Scots Hector Thomson, Jack McLean, and A.T. Kyle.

The British Amateur Championship

The Ladies' Golf Union in Britain was formed in 1893. The first British Ladies Amateur Championship was held that year on the old St. Anne's course in England. One of the first outstanding woman golfers was Dorothy Campbell, who won the Ladies Amateur Championship in 1909 and 1911 and was runner-up in 1908. She won the U.S. Women's Amateur Championship in 1909, 1910, and 1924 and the Canadian championship in 1910, 1911, and 1912. Among the many notable women who played championship golf between the wars were Joyce Wethered and Cecil Leitch, each of whom won the British Ladies Amateur title four times. (For winners of the U.S. Women's Open, the British and U.S. Amateur Championships, and the Curtis Cup, see SPORTING RECORD in the *Micropædia.*)

Joyce Wethered (left) of Great Britain and Bobby Jones (right) of the United States, two of golf's greatest players, dominated the game in the 1920s.

(Left) AP/Wide World Photo; (right) Brown Brothers

U.S. tournaments and players. The first official U.S. Open, Amateur, and Women's Amateur championships were held in 1895. Walter J. Travis was the first great U.S. golfer. He proved his ability as a golfer by winning the U.S. Amateur (1900–03) and the British Amateur title the only year he entered this event—1904. Jerome D. Travers, the next great American champion, was a player with indomitable courage and nerve that rarely failed him. He won the U.S. Amateur Championship (1907–08, 1912–13) and the U.S. Open title in 1915.

The U.S. championships

After World War I the influence of the many Scottish golfers who had emigrated to the United States became evident. U.S. golfers virtually monopolized the British Open Championship until Henry Cotton won in 1934, a feat he repeated in 1937 and 1948. From the 1920s into the 1980s U.S. teams dominated the Walker Cup and Ryder Cup matches, as U.S. women golfers did the Curtis Cup tournament from its inception in the 1930s.

U.S. golfers had begun to show their prowess in 1913, when Francis Ouimet became a national hero by defeating Vardon and Edward Ray, two of the best British professionals, for the U.S. Open. Also notable was Charles ("Chick") Evans, who was the first golfer to win the U.S. Open and Amateur in the same year (1916). But Bobby Jones has been regarded as the greatest amateur golfer of modern times. His career was brilliant from his debut in national competition in the U.S. Amateur of 1916 until his unparalleled performance in 1930 of winning all four of the world's most difficult titles—the British Amateur, the British Open, the U.S. Amateur, and the U.S. Open.

Early amateur golf champions

The popular appeal of the U.S. Amateur Championship has been seriously weakened by departures to the professional ranks, however, and it has become exceptional for an amateur champion to resist the lure of tournament money. In the late 1930s the professional circuit, underwritten by civic and club organizations throughout the country, began putting up major prize money for the experts. In 1936 aggregate prize money totaled $100,000, but by the late 20th century the PGA circuit was offering several million dollars in prizes annually. The first outstanding golfers were Walter Hagen and Gene Sarazen. After 1940 Byron Nelson, Ben Hogan, and Sam Snead shared the major portion of prize money and were followed by such top competitors as Arnold Palmer, Billy Casper, Lee Trevino, Jack Nicklaus, and Tom Watson. By the 1980s Nicklaus was not only the game's all-time money winner, he had won a remarkable 20 major championships, more than anyone else in golfing history. It was not until 1970 that a British professional made the first serious dent into U.S. supremacy. Tony Jacklin, after playing successfully on the American circuit, became U.S. Open champion by a seven-shot margin. This was the first time a Briton had won America's most important championship since Ted Ray had done so half a century before. U.S. dominance of the men's British Open from 1970 to 1983 was broken only by Gary Player of South Africa in 1974 and Severiano Ballesteros of Spain in 1979.

David Cannon—All-Sport USA

Jack Nicklaus, a dominant U.S. golfer from the 1960s to the 1980s, attempting to sink a putt during a U.S. PGA Championship tournament.

U.S. women golfers

Among the great U.S. women golfers was Glenna Collett Vare, who dominated the game in the 1920s. After World War II, the Ladies' Professional Golf Association (LPGA) was established, thanks in large part to the skill and appeal of Mildred ("Babe") Didrikson Zaharias and Patty Berg. Then came Louise Suggs and Betsy Rawls, who were followed by Mickey Wright, Kathy Whitworth, and JoAnne Carner. The LPGA tour made a leap in popularity in 1978 when Nancy Lopez won nine tournaments in her rookie season, including five in succession.

International competition. *Matches and tournaments.* The first organized series of regular international matches were between Great Britain and the United States. The amateur team match between the two countries for the Walker Cup was inaugurated in 1922 and the professional team match (Ryder Cup) in 1927. The women's amateur team match (Curtis Cup) began in 1932. Although the competition in all of these contests has often been close, the U.S. teams managed to win the cups with great consistency. In an attempt to bring parity to the Ryder Cup the format was changed in 1979 to broaden the British team to include continental European players as well.

Circuits. The coming of jet transport stimulated competition. Ocean hopping became routine, enabling outstanding players from South America, Australia, New Zealand, and South Africa to compete in the premier championships in Great Britain and the United States and on the rich U.S. PGA tour. Among the successful players from the Southern Hemisphere were Bobby Locke (South Africa), a magnificent putter, Peter Thomson and Kel Nagle (Australia), left-hander Bob Charles (New Zealand), and Roberto de Vicenzo (Argentina). Also prominent was South Africa's Gary Player, who was one of only four men (with Sarazen, Hogan, and Nicklaus) to win each of the game's four major professional championships, constituting the grand slam of modern golf.

With more overseas players entering, and sometimes winning, tournaments in the United States and Great Britain, more U.S. and British players began to take part in various circuit itineraries in other parts of the world—in Australia, New Zealand, South Africa, and the Far East. In Japan the game has become an endemic fever.

The emoluments of professional golf

Finance. Professionals with expertise and crowd-pulling attributes have become a new affluent society thanks to the cosponsorship, by the PGA, local promoters, and private companies, of lucrative weekly tournaments with television rights to negotiate. The modern professional also has many sources of peripheral income. The great Harry Vardon received £50 with his medal for winning his record sixth British Open in 1914. By 1971 the winner's prize was £5,500; and in 1972 for the first time all professionals in the championship proper received prize money. Prize money in the United States, however, far exceeded that of any other country. By the mid-1980s the total purse for the U.S. professional tour was $25,000,000. A PGA senior tour was launched at the beginning of the 1980s, and within seven years its total purse was $10,000,000. (Senior golf tournaments, for players age 55 and over, had been organized from the early part of the 20th century.)

PLAY OF THE GAME

Courses. The game consists in playing the ball from a teeing ground into a hole by successive strokes in accordance with the rules. The stipulated round consists of 18 holes, and most golf courses have 18. Standard 18-hole courses measure from 6,500 to 7,000 yards (5,900 to 6,400 metres); individual holes are from 100 to 600 yards (90 to 550 metres). Some courses, however, have only nine holes, and these are played twice in a stipulated round. The clubs are designed for the various positions in which the ball may come to rest and for the various distances to the hole. The objective is to hole the ball in the fewest strokes.

In the early 19th century there was no agreement on the number of holes on a golf course; localities differed widely in the matter. When the popularity of Leith, with its five holes, waned and St. Andrews became the hub, the round of 18 holes was established. Originally the St. Andrews holes filed straight out alongside the shore and were played in reverse for the return journey—11 holes each way. In 1764 the round was modified to 18 holes. The variety of courses gives golf an intrinsic charm.

Equipment. *Golf balls.* Regulation balls have a maximum weight of 1.62 ounces (45.93 grams) and a minimum diameter of 1.68 inches (4.27 centimetres). In U.S. competition the velocity of the ball may not exceed 250 feet (75 metres) per second when measured under prescribed conditions on an apparatus maintained by the USGA, but there is no velocity specification for British play.

Golf clubs. In the average good player's set there are usually either three or four wood clubs and nine or 10 irons (no more than 14 clubs may be carried during a round). No two clubs in a set are the same. There are differences in length and suppleness of shaft, weight, size and shape of head, the angle at which the shaft ends and the head begins (the lie), and the angle of the face of the club from the vertical (the loft).

Club purposes by number

The various clubs are known both by number and by name. The number of a club largely designates its length and the pitch of its head, which translates into the distance and height a club will drive a ball. Generally, the lower the number, the greater the distance potential; distance decreases and pitch (thus height) increases progressively as club numbers go up. The woods are mostly used for driving the longer distances. Sources differ on the name equivalency of the numbered clubs, but the most widely used clubs may be identified as follows: Woods—number 1 (driver), number 2 (brassie), number 3 (spoon), number 4 (baffy), and number 5 (replaces number 3 or 4 iron). Irons—number 1 (driving iron), number 2 (midiron), number 3 (mid-mashie), number 4 (mashie iron), number 5 (mashie), number 6 (spade mashie), number 7 (mashie-niblick), number 8 (pitching niblick), number 9 (niblick), number 10 (wedge), and putter (carries no number).

Rules. The rule-making bodies for golf are the R. and A. and the USGA. They attempt to perpetuate the uniformity in rules by exchanging views on interpretations and on recommendations for revision. The present code makes an amazing contrast with the first rules, 13 in number, that were framed by the Honourable Company. The first of them ordained that the ball had to be teed within a club length of the previous hole and the tee had to be on the ground. Tee and green were one. The ball struck from the tee was not to be changed, and the player could (Rule 5) take his ball out of water or "watery filth" to play it and allow his opponent a stroke. The St. Andrews golfers, in founding the Royal and Ancient Club, adopted almost exactly the Leith rules. There were periodical reforms before the rules committee of the R. and A. was formed in 1897 to become the final authority.

The rules committee has co-opted representatives from the Commonwealth, the European Golf Federation, the United States, and the British Unions Advisory Committee. Britain and America have had separate codes at various times, but a uniform code went into effect in 1967.

The rules of golf define an amateur golfer as "one who plays the game solely as a nonremunerative and nonprofit-making sport." But the elasticity of this definition perturbs the game's legislators for what it does not define. The whole question of status in its various aspects engages the attention jointly of the R. and A. and the USGA. In general, an amateur remains so until and unless he takes specific action toward becoming a professional, even though he might have indicated his intention of becoming a professional in the future.

Driving, playing the fairway, and hazards

Procedure. The starting place for each hole to be played is the teeing ground. The front is indicated by two markers, and the teeing ground is the rectangular space two club lengths in depth directly behind the line indicated by the markers. The player tees his ball anywhere within this space, usually setting it up on a small wooden or plastic peg (called a tee), and strikes it toward the hole. The stroke from the teeing ground is called the drive. For this, the player usually employs a number 1 wood club, or driver, although to avoid a hazard or to attempt to place his ball in a favourable position for his second shot (for example, on a long hole with a sharp bend, or dogleg) he may prefer one of the other woods or an iron. On short, par-three holes most players use an iron.

The preferred line to the hole is generally a clear, mowed route called the fairway. The fairway was historically bordered by unmowed vegetation—heather, grasses, weeds, bushes—called rough. Most modern courses in the United States, however, are not characterized by deep and tangled rough and when inland make effective use of trees. At strategic places along the preferred line to the hole and guarding the putting green are obstacles called bunkers, depressions filled with sand (sand traps). Some holes require the player to cross streams or ponds. Both bunkers and bodies of water are termed "hazards."

Approaching and putting

Middle irons are used until the player has come within close range of the green. Two methods of play are then open for the approach shot: the golfer may pitch the ball all the way and depend on backspin to stop it near the pin, or he may play a chip shot, in which the ball flies part way through the air, as to the edge of the close-clipped surface of the green, and then rolls the remaining distance.

The hole itself measures 4¼ inches in diameter and at least four inches deep, and it is set in an area of turf especially prepared and maintained and closely mowed for putting. When the player putts he uses a straight-faced club and rolls the ball across the putting green toward and eventually into the hole.

Forms of play. *Match and medal play.* There are two distinct forms of play: match play and stroke (medal) play. In match play the player and his opponent are playing together and competing only against each other, while in stroke play each competitor is competing against every other player in the tournament. In match play the game is played by holes, and each hole is won by the player who holes his ball in the fewer strokes. If both players score the same number of strokes, the hole is halved. When a player has won one more hole than his opponents, he is said to be 1 up. The match is won by the player who is leading by a number of holes greater than the number of holes remaining to be played, as, for example, 3 up and 2 to play. In stroke play the competitor who holes the stipulated round or rounds in the fewest total strokes is the winner. Amateur championships once were all at match play and open championships and most professional events at stroke play, covering four 18-hole rounds. Some amateur events have adopted stroke play (the match play U.S. Amateur event was at stroke play from 1965 to 1973), as has the U.S. PGA Championship.

Scoring

Stroke play requires a greater degree of consistency in a player, for one hole where he lapses into a high figure can ruin his total and cost him victory. The same high score on a hole in match play means only the loss of that hole. In both match and stroke play, players can compete as individuals or as partners. When two players compete as partners, each playing his own ball, the better ball on each hole is their score for that hole; this is a four-ball or best ball match. Two players may compete as partners with two others, each pair playing alternate strokes on a single ball; this is a match foursome. The advent of televised championships wrote the death notice for match play in professional golf. By scheduling the leaders together on the final round, exciting finishes are made most probable.

Handicaps. Players of varying abilities compete against each other by using handicaps. A handicap is the number of strokes a player receives to adjust his score to a common level. The better the player, the smaller his handicap, and the best players have handicaps of zero (scratch players). A scratch player whose average score is 70 can have an even match with a player whose average score is 80 by giving him a handicap of 10 strokes. Handicap golf is limited to amateur competitions, and championship tournaments are played without handicaps.

Par golf. Every course has a par, which is defined as the score an expert (*i.e.,* a scratch player) would be expected to make, and many courses also have a bogey, which is defined as the score that a moderately good golfer would be expected to make. Both par and bogey are defined as errorless play without flukes and under ordinary weather conditions, allowing two strokes on the putting green. Par is essentially a U.S. term that came into use in the early 1900s as a base for computing handicaps. Bogey is essentially a British term that came into use in England in 1891 and was derived from a mythical Colonel Bogey, who was described as uniformly steady but never overbrilliant. Colloquially in the United States, "bogey" is used to indicate a score one stroke above par.

The bogey

Variants. *Par-three golf.* Par-three golf courses, on which each hole measures 100 yards more or less and plays at par three, were developed as a result of the shortage of available open land in congested urban areas. Whereas a regulation 18-hole course may stretch to more than 7,000 yards, about four miles, an 18-hole par-three, or short-hole, course can be laid out in about 1,800 yards.

Driving ranges. Driving ranges were developed as commercial establishments at which golfers and aspiring golfers could, for a small fee, practice their swings. They, too, have appealed to golfers in areas in which courses are overcrowded and are especially popular in Japan, where such conditions prevail. (F.Mo./J.R.Go.)

Athletics

Athletics, or track-and-field sports, consist of competitions in running, walking, jumping, and throwing events. Although these contests are called track and field (or simply track) in the United States, they are generally designated as athletics elsewhere. This section covers the history, the organization, and the administration of the sport, the conduct of competitions, and the rules and techniques of the individual events, and some of the sport's most prominent athletes. (For records, see SPORTING RECORD and OLYMPIC GAMES in the *Micropædia*.)

Track-and-field athletics are the oldest forms of organized sport, having developed out of man's most basic activities—running, walking, jumping, and throwing. Athletics has become the most truly international of sports, with nearly every country in the world engaging in some form of competition. Most nations send teams of men and women to the quadrennial Olympic Games and to the official World Championships of track and field. There also are several continental and intercontinental championship meets held, including the European, Commonwealth, African, Pan-American, and Asian.

Within the broad title of athletics come as many as two dozen distinct events. These events, generally held outdoors, make up a meet. The outdoor running events are held on a 400-metre or 440-yard oval track, and field events (jumping and throwing) either inside the track's perimeter or in adjacent areas.

In many parts of the world, notably the United States, Canada, and Europe, the sport moves indoors during the winter; because of limited space, some events are modified and several are eliminated altogether.

Also within the general scope of track-and-field athletics come separate but related competitions that are not contested on the track. Cross-country running competition is carried out on various types of countryside and parkland. Marathons and races of other long distances are run on roads, and the long-distance race walks are contested on measured road courses. The rules followed by all organized competitions are established and enforced by the International Amateur Athletic Federation (IAAF) and its member body from each nation. The IAAF also ratifies all world records.

HISTORY

Origin and early development. There is little in the way of definitive records of athletics' early days as an organized sport. Egyptian and Asian civilizations are known to have encouraged athletics many centuries before the Christian Era. Perhaps as early as 1829 BC, Ireland was the scene of the Lugnasad or Tailteann Games involving various forms of track-and-field activity. The Olympic Games of Greece, traditionally dated from 776 BC, continued through 11 centuries before ending in about AD 393. These ancient Olympics were strictly male affairs. Greek women were reputed to have formed their own Heraea Games, which, like the Olympics, were held every four years.

The Olympic Games

Athletics as practiced today was born and grew to maturity in England. The first mention of the sport in England was recorded in 1154, when practice fields were first established in London. Sport was banned by King Edward III in the 1300s, but revived a century later by Henry VIII, reputed to be an accomplished hammer thrower.

Modern development. The development of the modern sport, however, has come only since the early 19th century. Organized amateur footraces were held in England as early as 1825, but it was from 1860 that athletics enjoyed its biggest surge to that date. In 1861 the West London Rowing Club organized the first meet open to all amateurs, and in 1866 the Amateur Athletic Club (AAC) was founded and conducted the first English championships. The emphasis in all these meets was on competition for "gentlemen amateurs" who received no financial compensation. In 1880 the AAC yielded governing power to the Amateur Athletic Association (AAA).

The first meet in North America was held near Toronto in 1839, but it was the New York Athletic Club, formed in the 1860s, that placed the sport on a solid footing in the United States. The club held the world's first indoor meet and helped promote the formation in 1879 of the National Association of Amateur Athletes of America (NAAAA), to conduct national championships. Nine years later the Amateur Athletic Union (AAU) took over as national governing body, amid reports that the NAAAA was lax in enforcing amateurism.

The Olympic Games revival

Athletics was well established in many countries by the late 1800s, but not until the revival of the Olympic Games in 1896 did the sport become truly international. Although begun modestly, the Olympics provided the inspiration and standardizing influence that was to spread interest in athletics worldwide. In 1912 the International Amateur Athletic Federation (IAAF) was founded, and by the time that organization celebrated its 75th anniversary in 1987 it had more than 170 national members. Its rules applied only to men's competition until 1936, when the IAAF also became the governing body of women's athletics.

Major international competitions before World War II included the Olympics, the British Empire Games, and the European Championships, but after the war athletics experienced its greatest period of growth, taking root especially in the developing countries. By the 1950s African, Asian, and Latin-American nations had begun to produce world-class athletes.

Organization and tournaments. Top-level competition in athletics is still restricted to the amateur athlete, although the definition of "amateur" continues to evolve. The IAAF over time has reduced its definition of an amateur athlete to the simplest possible terms: "An amateur is one who abides by the eligibility rules of the IAAF" is the complete rule, allowing for change whenever the federation alters any of its other rules.

Funding athletes

Until the 1980s the IAAF attempted to keep its athletes from benefiting financially from the sport. This was always a struggle, however, as star athletes and eager meet promoters managed to circumvent the rules. So did entire nations: eastern European countries provided government aid to athletes, other countries encouraged military personnel to concentrate on track and field training, and U.S. athletes received college scholarships in return for their skills.

Financial aid was made acceptable in the 1980s through the use of trust funds. Athletes were permitted to accept payment for appearing in competition, for performing well, for appearing in television commercials, or for other sport-related activities. The money was placed in trust; training expenses could be charged to the fund, with the remaining funds, if any, going to the athlete on retirement from competition. Some athletes were reported to have made several hundred thousand dollars a year under the new system.

The primary functions of the international federation are to maintain a set of rules that are uniform throughout the world, to approve world records for outdoor and indoor competition, and to promote international athletics. While continuing to administer athletics competition in the Olympic Games, the IAAF began its own quadrennial World Championships in 1983, established World Cup competitions, and established walking, cross-country, marathon and other road-races, indoor track-and-field, and junior competitions.

Each IAAF member nation has its own set of rules and maintains its own set of records in line with international guidelines. The amateur athletic federations of individual countries conduct their own national championships.

U.S. governing bodies

In the United States, for example, The Athletic Congress (TAC) alone has the power to select international teams (except for the Olympic team, which is under the jurisdiction of the United States Olympic Committee), to establish rules, and to accept or reject records. It also conducts the national championships and other competitions. Meets in which participation is restricted to college or university athletes usually are governed by the rules of the National Collegiate Athletic Association (NCAA), National Association of Intercollegiate Athletics (NAIA), or one of two junior (two-year) college groups. Most U.S. secondary schools come under the aegis of the National Federation of State High School Athletic Associations.

The details of the conduct of athletics competitions vary with the location and the level and type of meet. To a great degree the basic sport has been standardized by the rules of the IAAF. Outdoor track events take place on the 400-metre (about 440-yard) oval running track. Track compositions differ greatly. Once almost all tracks were of natural materials (dirt, clay, cinders, and crushed brick being the most common), but all major competition tracks now are made of synthetic materials. The synthetic track provides more consistent and faster footing in all weather conditions. Field-event performers also benefit from improved footing; jumpers and javelin throwers perform on the same materials used for synthetic tracks, while the throwers of the shot, discus, and hammer work in circles made of concrete.

Indoor track meets adapt themselves to widely varying and often limiting conditions. Tracks range in size generally from 150 to 200 metres or 160 to 220 yards and have synthetic surfaces over wood. Some tracks have banked curves, other are unbanked. Cross-country running utilizes any terrain that is available—parks, golf courses, farmland. The prescribed IAAF distance in international races for men is approximately 12,000 metres (7.5 miles) and for women 4,000 metres. Road events include walking, marathon, and other road runs of widely varying distances.

MEETS

Equipment. Every event has items of equipment that are essential to the conduct of the event. All athletes, for example, require shoes that give traction and protection with minimum weight. Other items of equipment include the starting blocks used by sprinters and hurdlers, hurdles, vaulting poles, and the implements employed in the various throwing events.

Timing and measurements. Exacting timing and measurement of performances are a vital part of athletics, not only to determine winners at the meet in question but also to provide marks that can be compared for record purposes. Fully automatic timing, using photography, is required for world records and all major competitions. Timing, once done in fifths of a second and then in 10ths, now is done in 100ths of a second. By rule, an aiding wind of more than two metres per second (4.473 miles per hour) nullifies a record time in distances up to 200 metres. Metric measurements are required for both track and field events. even in the United States. The only English-measure distance that remains popular is the one-mile run. With the 1987 inauguration of the World Indoor Championships the IAAF began accepting indoor records. There are, however, no official records for any track event not run or walked entirely on the track, such as the marathon or road races.

Metric measurements

Presentation. Athletics meets differ greatly in presentation. The typical school, university, or club meet is of one-day duration. Conference meets generally last two days, while national championships require three to four days to accommodate large numbers of athletes. The Olympic Games and World Championships are scheduled for eight days of athletics competition.

All track events begin with the firing of a gun. In races of one lap or less the runners remain in their marked lanes for the entire distance. In longer events the runners may ignore the lane markers and run as close to the inside edge of the track as is prudent. The runner whose torso reaches the winning line first is the winner.

Field events

Field events have two types of qualifying competitions. In the smaller meets all participants are allowed three attempts, with the top six to nine athletes getting three more. In the larger meets there is a qualifying round from which about 12 athletes advance to the finals, at which stage the remaining competition proceeds in the same manner as in the smaller meets. The exceptions in field-event competition are the vertical jumps—the high jump and pole vault. Jumpers are given three tries at each height; three consecutive misses cause elimination.

Although athletics is basically an individual sport, team scoring is sometimes important. Dual meets are always scored, but there are no official scores for multi-team international meets, such as the Olympic Games. Conference and national meets among universities also are scored officially. The points allotted to individual events and places vary from meet to meet. A national competition may award 10 points for first place, eight for second, and so on. Similarly, an international dual meet awards five points for first place, three for second, two for third, and one for fourth. The team with the highest point total wins the meet. Cross-country meets always are scored, with the winner getting one point, second place two points, etc., the low score winning.

Runners have a chance to compete the year round. The indoor season lasts from January through March; the outdoor competition lasts until June for schools and colleges, with the higher-level individual competitors participating in track through September. In the United States autumn is given over to cross-country running. International cross country is held in winter.

Conflicts and controversies. Athletics, occupying centre stage at all international games, generates its share of conflicts. Until the IAAF's trust-fund system there was continual concern about athletes earning money by violating rules. From about 1970 the question of drug usage has been a major issue. Athletes are forbidden to use a number of drugs that are said to improve performance. Testing for such use is required at the major meets, and, while the great majority of athletes tested are found to be free of banned drugs, each year a small number of athletes are found guilty of violating the drug rule and are suspended from competition, usually for 18 months. Most frequently the violators have used anabolic steroids in an attempt to increase muscle size and strength.

EVENTS

As many as 25 events may make up a men's meet; women compete in a few less. The men's track events at championship meets generally include the 100-, 200-, 400-, 800-, 1,500-, 5,000-, and 10,000-metre runs; the 3,000-metre steeplechase; the 110- and 400-metre hurdles; and the 400- and 1,500-metre relays. The field events usually include the high jump, pole vault, long jump, and triple jump; and the shot put and the discus, hammer, and javelin throws. The decathlon, combining 10 track and field events, is also included. Women run much the same schedule, with 100-metre instead of 110-metre hurdles. but do not compete in the steeplechase, pole vault, or hammer throw. They compete in the heptathlon rather than the decathlon, and both men and women run the marathon. Women walk up to 10,000 metres and men up to 50,000 metres.

Running. *The sprints.* The relatively short sprint distances, ranging up to 400 metres, require a sustained top speed. Originally all sprinters started from a standing position, but in the 1880s the crouch start was invented, and it became a rule that sprinters must start with both feet and both hands on the track. The introduction of the adjustable starting block aided the quick start, critical in the sprints.

Ken Regan—Camera 5

Carl Lewis, an outstanding U.S. sprinter, coming off the blocks at the start of a 100-metre dash during the 1988 Olympic trials.

"The fastest human"

The current record holder at 100 metres generally is considered to be "the fastest human." Holding that title have been such champions as Eddie Tolan, Jesse Owens, Bobby Morrow, Bob Hayes, and Carl Lewis (all of the United States), Valeriy Borzov (U.S.S.R.), and Ben Johnson (Canada). Johnson set a record-breaking time of 9.83 seconds as he won the 1987 World Championships. Outstanding women sprint champions have included Fanny Blankers-Koen (The Netherlands), who won four gold medals in the 1948 Olympics, Wilma Rudolph (U.S.), who won three in 1960, Marita Koch (East Germany), who was a winner at all three sprint distances, and Florence Griffith Joyner (U.S.), who set world records at 100 and 200 metres in 1988.

The 400 metres is run in lanes all the way; distance is equalized by a staggered start, the sprinters being spaced progressively farther up the track based on the distance their lane is from the inside edge. Outstanding in this event were Lee Evans (U.S.), whose 43.86 mark remained the world record 20 years after he set it in 1968, and Alberto Juantorena (Cuba), whose 44.26-second time in the 1976 Olympics was the fastest without the aid of high altitude. He also won the 800 metres, becoming the first man to win both events in the Olympics. Jarmila Kratochvilova (Czechoslovakia) also won such an unprecedented double victory in the 1983 World Championships for women.

Middle-distance running. The longer the race, the more endurance is needed. The middle-distance events, in this discussion, range from 800 to 2,000 metres. Some authorities regard the 3,000-metre race as a middle-distance.

Middle-distance runners usually are able to perform well at either the shorter or the longer distances. Racing tactics, including pacing, are more important at these than at any other distances. Even though it is no longer a championship event the mile is still a glamour event. The race to be the first to run a mile in less than four minutes captured world attention. It finally was achieved in 1954 by Roger Bannister of England. A "sub-four" is still a notable time, even though it is now accomplished regularly and some runners, such as John Walker (New Zealand) and Steve Scott (U.S.), have run under four minutes more than 100 times. Other great middle-distance runners include Paavo Nurmi (Finland), who won both the 1,500 (the metric "mile") and 5,000 metres on the same day in the 1924 Olympics, and Sebastian Coe (U.K.), who won two Olympic gold medals at 1,500 metres and two silver at 800 metres. Two Soviet women created memorable middle-distance records. Tatyana Kazankina won five world records, while Lyudmila Bragina established eight. Mary Decker Slaney (U.S.) also won consistently at the middle distances.

The four-minute mile

Long-distance running. There is some difference of opinion over the dividing line between middle-distance and long-distance runs. The long-distance events considered here are those ranging from 3,000 metres upward and including the marathon, steeplechase, cross-country, and road runs. The 30,000-metre run is the longest for which the IAAF keeps records. Speed becomes an even less important factor in the longer runs and pace and endurance correspondingly more so. The longer the run the less likely there is to be a "finishing kick," a burst of speed at the end of the race.

Runners may also overlap the long- and middle-distance events. Nurmi, Gunder Hägg (Sweden), and Said Aouita (Morocco) all set world records at both 1,500 and 5,000 metres. Nurmi won at all distances above 1,000 metres except the marathon. Distance runners provide the most prolific record setters, including Nurmi, Ron Clarke (Australia), and Emil Zátopek (Czechoslovakia), the last of whom performed the remarkable feat of winning the marathon and the 5,000- and 10,000-metre races at the 1952 Olympic Games. The longer races for women have been slow to develop, but a number of runners have been able to compete at various distances, including Ingrid Kristiansen (Norway).

The steeplechase combines long-distance running with hurdling, each runner being required to clear seven water jumps and 28 hurdles in a 3,000-metre course. Although hurdling is an important aspect of the event, by far the greatest need is the ability to run the distance. Steeplechase competitors are often specialists, but there are examples of fine distance runners who have successfully overcome more experienced hurdlers. Henry Rono (Kenya), one of the most successful at the steeplechase, also held world records at 3,000, 5,000, and 10,000 metres.

The marathon

The marathon was a key event at the first modern Olympic Games in 1896, and it has become a major attraction of the Olympics and other international contests. The race originally commemorated the feat of a Greek soldier who in 490 BC supposedly ran from Marathon to Athens to bring news of the Greek victory over the Persians. At 26 miles, 385 yards (42,186 metres) the marathon is the longest race of the track meet. Hannes Kolehmainen (Finland) and Zátopek are two of the more memorable marathoners. Records for the marathon are not officially recognized.

Hurdling. The hurdling events combine sprinting with negotiating a series of obstacles called hurdles. Men run the

Jordanka Donkova (centre) of Bulgaria leading Cornelia Oschkenat (left) of East Germany to win the 100-metre hurdles at the 1988 Olympic Games in Seoul.
AFP Photo

110-metre high hurdles over 10 barriers 42 inches (106.7 centimetres) high and 10 yards (9.14 metres) apart. The 400-metre intermediate hurdles also covers 10 hurdles, 36 inches (91.4 centimetres) in height and 35 metres (38.29 yards) apart. Women now run both the 100-metre high and 400-metre hurdles. A hurdler may knock down any number of hurdles but is disqualified if he runs out of his lane or uses his hands to knock over hurdles. The object is to make the hurdling action smooth and rhythmic so as not to disrupt forward progress.

High hurdlers need excellent speed, most champions also being good sprinters. An excellent example is Harrison Dillard (U.S.), who won the 100-metre flat race in the 1948 Olympics and the high hurdles in the 1952 Games. Intermediate hurdlers also combine speed with hurdling ability. Glenn Davis (U.S.), who won both the 1956 and 1960 Olympics, was a world-record breaker on the flat as well as over the hurdles. Edwin Moses (U.S.) virtually revolutionized the event with his unusual 13-stride (between hurdles) technique. He also won two Olympics and achieved a winning streak lasting nearly 10 years.

Relays. The relays involve four runners per team, each member carrying a baton for 25 percent of the total distance before passing it to the next team runner. Two events, the 4 × 100- and 4 × 400-metre relays, are standard. They are included both in low-level dual meets and in the Olympic Games and the IAAF World Championships. Speed is essential in both events, and the ability to pass the baton well is especially crucial in the shorter event, where each runner covers 100 metres. Exchanging the baton while running about 25 miles per hour brings to the event a quality of suspense. Many races have been won or lost by the quality of baton passing. Other relay events—the 4 × 200-, 4 × 800-, and 4 × 1,500-metres—are run much less frequently.

Baton passing

Walking. This event, also called race walking, is relatively minor. Aside from the Olympic and other multination competitions, it is seldom a part of track meets. Olympic competition is over 20,000 and 50,000 metres, while other distances are used in individual competitions. Records are approved only when made on the track.

Jumping. Men compete in four jumping events: the high jump, long jump, triple jump, and pole vault. Women compete in all except the pole vault.

The high jump. There is one basic rule for high jumping: the jumper must leave the ground from one foot, not two. The object is to clear a thin bar perched atop two standards, and as long as the jumper does not have three consecutive misses, he remains in the competition. Jumpers may enter the competition at any height above the minimum height and are allowed to pass any height as the bar is raised to new levels. Inflated or foam-rubber landing pits have replaced dirt and sawdust pits. The modern pits are of value because jumpers often land on the back of the shoulders and neck.

Jumping styles have evolved in the 20th century with techniques called the scissors, eastern cut-off, western roll, and straddle (or belly roll) preceding the universally accepted Fosbury flop. Named for its inventor, Dick Fosbury (U.S.), the 1968 Olympic champion, the flop involves an approach from almost straight ahead, then twisting on takeoff and going over head first with the back to the bar. Charles Dumas (U.S.), a notable example of the straddle jumpers, in 1956 became the first man to clear 7 feet (2.13 metres). Valeriy Brumel (U.S.S.R.) held the high-jump record for 10 years using the straddle jump. A woman jumper, Iolanda Balas (Romania), achieved remarkable feats in the event, establishing 13 world records and a winning streak of 140 meets.

The pole vault. Pole vaulting is conducted along the lines of the high jump; *i.e.,* vaulters attempt to vault over a crossbar placed on uprights, they have three tries at each height, and they land in an inflated or composition pit.

The vaulter runs down a runway for about 45 metres (150 feet) carrying a pole. After planting the end of the pole in a box that is sunk below ground level, the vaulter leaves the ground and pulls himself upward until he is almost doing a handstand on the pole. He twists as he nears the crossbar and arches over it feet first and face down.

Evolution of the pole

The first poles, of solid ash, cedar, or hickory, were heavy and cumbersome. Once the bamboo pole was introduced in 1904 it was quickly adopted. Records set with bamboo lasted until 1957, when records were set with an aluminum pole and a steel pole; these were followed by the fibreglass pole in the 1960s.

The dominant vaulter of all time was Cornelius Warmerdam (U.S.), who scored six world records; he was the first vaulter to go over 15 feet and he set a record of 15 feet 7¾ inches (4.77 metres) that lasted for 15 years. No one came close to him in the bamboo era, but the constant improvement of fibreglass poles helped vaulters such as Sergey Bubka (U.S.S.R.) push the record well over 5.79 metres (19 feet) in the 1980s.

The long jump. Long jumping, formerly called broad jumping, is the least complicated of the field events. Speed is the most essential ingredient for a successful jump. Jumpers make their approach down the runway at nearly top speed, plant a foot on the takeoff board, and leap into the air. A legal jump requires that no part of the forward foot extend beyond the board. The most popular long-jumping style is called the "hitch-kick," in which the runner seemingly walks in air.

Two distinct landmarks stand out in the history of long jumping. The first of these was the achievement of Jesse Owens (U.S.), who on May 25, 1935, jumped 26 feet 8¼ inches (8.13 metres), a record that was to endure for 25 years. The second, believed by many to be the greatest single track-and-field feat ever, was Bob Beamon's (U.S.) leap of 8.90 metres (29 feet 2½ inches), a jump that exceeded the old world record by 55 centimetres (21½ inches). In 33 years the record had gone up less than nine inches and in one day Beamon pushed it up almost two feet.

Notable among the women jumpers are Heike Drechsler (East Germany) and Jackie Joyner-Kersee (U.S.), both of whom leaped over 7 metres (23 feet).

The triple jump. Once known as the hop, step, and jump, the triple jump includes three distinct segments of action. The jumper comes down the runway and bounds off a takeoff board, similar in style to but a little slower than long jumpers. The first segment involves the jumper executing a hop by landing on the same foot from which he took off. Then he takes a step, landing on the other foot, and concludes with a jump into the sand pit.

Outstanding triple jumpers

Among the outstanding competitors, Adhemar da Silva (Brazil) won two Olympics and set five world records; Jozef Schmidt (Poland), also a two-time Olympic Champion, set a record in 1960 of 17.03 metres (55 feet 10½ inches) and was the first to go over the 17-metre barrier; and Viktor Saneyev (U.S.S.R.) had three world records and three Olympic wins and one second place. Women began competing in the triple jump in the mid-1980s.

Throwing. The four standard throwing events—shot put, discus, hammer, and javelin—all involve the use of implements of various weights and shapes that are hurled for distance.

Bob Beamon (U.S.) as he breaks the world record in the long jump at 29 feet 2½ inches (8.9 metres) during the 1968 Olympic Games in Mexico City.
UPI/Bettmann Newsphotos

The shot put. The putting action is best described as shoving the shot since the rules require that the arm may not extend behind the shoulders during the putting action. The spherical shot is made of metal. The men's implement weights 16 pounds (7.256 kilograms) and is about five inches (12.7 centimetres) in diameter. Women put a four-kilogram (eight-pound 13-ounce) shot about 10 centimetres in diameter. The IAAF allows a slight range in specifications.

The putter must launch the shot from within a ring 2.134 metres (seven feet) in diameter and so must gather momentum for the put by a rapid twisting movement. Shot putters are among the largest athletes in track and field, the biggest ranging from 250 to 300 pounds (113 to 136 kilograms). Beginning in the 1950s weight training became a major part of a shot putter's training program. In that same period the O'Brien style of putting was popularized with outstanding results. Developed by Parry O'Brien (U.S.), the style involved a 180-degree turn (rather than the usual 90-degree turn) across the ring, getting more speed and momentum into the action. O'Brien was the best exponent of the style, winning three Olympic medals (two gold) and raising the record from 58 feet 10¾ inches (17.95 metres) to 63 feet four inches (19.30 metres).

Some athletes have turned to a style in which the putter spins one and a half turns before releasing the shot, a technique developed by Brian Oldfield (U.S.).

The discus throw. Discus throwing is considered by many the classic event of athletics, the Greek poet Homer having made references to discus throwing in the 8th century BC. Modern male athletes throw a two kilogram (four-pound 6½-ounce) platter-like implement from a 2½-metre (eight-foot 2½-inch) circle. The discus is launched after the thrower, starting at the back of the circle, has completed one and a half turns. The women's discus weighs one kilogram.

Feats of Al Oerter

Among discus throwers the feats of Al Oerter (U.S.), the first to throw over 200 feet, are legendary. As a 20-year-old he won at the 1956 Olympic Games, and he won at the following three games as well. He also set four world records. A standout among women throwers was Faina Melnik (U.S.S.R.), who set 11 world records.

The hammer throw. The implement used in the hammer throw is not a conventional hammer but a metal ball about 127 millimetres (five inches) in diameter attached to a wire, the whole implement being about 1,200 millimetres in length and weighing a minimum of 7.26 kilograms (16 pounds). The handle at the opposite end of the wire from the ball is gripped by the thrower and released after three or four body turns have developed maximum centrifugal force. The launching area is slightly smaller than that of the discus. Women do not compete in the event.

American athletes of Irish birth or descent totally dominated the event from the 1890s to the 1930s and included John Flanagan, who unofficially set 17 world records and won three Olympic Games (1900, 1904, and 1908). Since the passing of the Irish dynasty the power shifted to the eastern Europeans. Among them was Yury Sedykh (U.S.S.R.), who won the 1976 and 1980 Olympics and raised the record from 80.32 metres to 86.74 metres.

The javelin throw. Javelin throwing involves a spearlike implement that is hurled with an over-the-shoulder motion at the end of an approach run. It is a direct descendant of spear-throwing contests, introduced in the Olympics of 708 BC. The men's javelin weighs about 800 grams (one pound 12 ounces) and must be at least 260 centimetres (8½ feet) long. The women throw a javelin that must weigh at least 600 grams and be at least 220 centimetres long. It is the only throwing event not using a circle. The javelin is not required to stick but must land point first for a valid throw.

Throwers from Finland have historically been a force in the event. Matti Järvinen, a Finn, established 10 world records and improved the record by 6.22 metres, finally reaching 77.23 metres (253 feet 4½ inches) in 1936. As records continued to be broken there was less and less space within the stadium to throw the javelin safely. Terje Pedersen (Norway) broke the 300-foot (91.44-metre) barrier in 1964, and by 1984 Uwe Hohn (East Germany) had thrown a prodigious 104.80 metres, a throw so great that it influenced a change in the design of the javelin to keep it within the safe confines of the field. Beginning in 1985, throwers used a javelin that, at the same weight, was designed to reduce the length of the throw by 9 to 12 metres (30 to 40 feet). The design of the women's javelin was not changed, and successive world records pushed close to 80 metres by the late 1980s.

Modification of the javelin

Decathlon and heptathlon. Both men and women participate in multi-event competitions, the men in the 10-event decathlon and the women in the seven-event heptathlon, which superseded the earlier pentathlon. The events, which require a two-day schedule, are held basically in worldwide competitions and national championships. In the United States they also are scheduled in many college-conference championships.

Each athlete is given points for his performance in each event, with more points awarded for better marks. The athlete with the most total points wins.

Men compete in five events each day, doing consecutively the 100 metres, long jump, shot put, high jump, and 400 metres on the first day and the 110-metre hurdles, discus throw, pole vault, javelin throw, and 1,500-metre run in that order on the second day. Women do, in order, the 100-metre hurdles, high jump, shot put, and 200-metres on the first day, followed by the long jump, javelin, and 800-metres on the second day.

Jim Thorpe, the great all-around American athlete, won the first decathlon, taking the 1912 Olympic Games contest, and for many years it was mostly an American event. Bob Mathias (U.S.) won his first decathlon at age 17 in 1948 and repeated it four years later. Another two-time winner was Daley Thompson of England, victorious in 1980 and 1984. Notable in the heptathlon was Jackie Joyner-Kersee, a record setter and winner of the 1987 World Championships and 1988 Olympics. (B.Ne.)

Boxing

Boxing is the art of attack and defense with the fists in which the two contestants wear padded gloves, box bouts of from three to 15 rounds (each round normally lasting three minutes), and generally observe the code set forth in the Marquess of Queensberry rules (see below *Queensberry rules*). Boxing contestants are matched in weight and ability, each trying to land hard and often with his own fists and, while doing so, attempting to avoid the blows of his opponent.

The terms pugilism and prizefighting in 20th-century usage are practically synonymous with boxing, although the first term indicates the ancient origins of the sport in its derivation from the Latin *pugil,* "a fighter with the cestus [a hand covering]," related to the Latin *pugnus,* "fist," and derived in turn from the Greek *pyx,* "with clenched fist." The term prizefighting emphasizes pursuit of the sport for monetary gain. (For records see SPORTING RECORD and OLYMPIC GAMES in the *Micropædia.*)

HISTORY

Early years. Presumably people used their fists to settle arguments for many centuries before anyone thought of staging such bouts for the entertainment of others. There is evidence that boxing existed by about 1500 BC in ancient Crete. More recent evidence, however, indicates that the sport was being practiced in Africa much earlier, particularly in the region now known as Ethiopia. Hieroglyphic evidence dating to 4000 BC reveals the spread of the newly developed sport throughout the Nile Valley to Egypt, where it was introduced after a series of successful Egyptian campaigns in Ethiopia.

African origins

The spread of boxing followed the expansion of Egyptian civilization through the Mediterranean and the Middle East. By 686 BC boxing had been refined and perfected enough to be included in the Olympic Games. However, the sport bore little resemblance to what is now known as boxing. Matches were held outdoors, with spectators forming the boundaries. The fight continued without pause until one participant was unable to continue. Although the first boxers primarily fought for glory, rewards were abundant for the victors, usually taking the form of gold, livestock, or trophies.

To protect the hands and wrists, fighters wore thongs of soft leather bound around their fists and often around two-thirds of their forearms. By the 4th century BC, the thongs were made of harder leather, transforming them into offensive weapons as well as protective devices. Late in the history of the Roman Empire, the hand covering called the *cestus,* studded with iron or brass nuggets, was developed, and slaves were forced to battle each other to the death for the entertainment of spectators.

The bareknuckle era. With the rise of Christianity and the concurrent decline of the Roman Empire, pugilism as entertainment apparently ceased to exist for some centuries. A formal bout was recorded in Britain as early as 1681, and by 1698 regular pugilistic contests were being held in the Royal Theatre of London. As London grew, prizefighting, as it came to be known, became quite popular there. The fighters performed for whatever purses were agreed upon plus stakes (side bets), and admirers of the combatants wagered on the outcomes. These matches were fought without gloves and, for the most part, without rules. There were no weight divisions; thus there was just one champion. Lighter men were at an obvious disadvantage. Rounds were designated, but a bout was usually fought until one participant could no longer continue. Wrestling was permitted, and it was common to fall on a foe after throwing him to the ground. Until the mid-1700s it was also common to hit a man when he was down.

17th-century prize-fighting

Although boxing was illegal, it became quite popular, and by 1719 the prizefighter James Figg had so captured the public's imagination that he was acclaimed champion of England, a distinction he held for up to 15 years. One of Figg's pupils, Jack Broughton, is credited with taking the first steps leading to boxing's acceptance as a respectable athletic endeavour. Broughton devised the sport's first set of rules in 1743, and those rules, with only minor changes, governed boxing until they were replaced by the more detailed London Prize Ring rules in 1838. Broughton discarded the barroom techniques that his predecessors favoured and relied primarily on his fists. While wrestling holds were still permitted, a boxer could not grab an opponent below the waist. Under Broughton's rules, a round continued until a man went down; after 30 seconds' rest he had to square off a yard from his opponent or be declared beaten. Hitting a downed opponent was also forbidden. Recognized as "The Father of Boxing," Broughton attracted pupils to the sport by introducing "mufflers," the forerunners of modern gloves, to protect one's hands and the opponent's face.

"The Father of Boxing"

After Jack Slack beat Broughton to claim the championship, fixed fights became common and boxing again experienced a period of decline, though pugilists such as Daniel Mendoza and "Gentleman" John Jackson did have success. Mendoza was an English Jew who weighed only 160 pounds and emphasized speed and the left jab. Jackson, who defeated Mendoza for the championship, contributed to the transformation of prizefighting into boxing by gaining friends of distinction for the sport, thus bringing it a degree of respectability.

In 1814 the Pugilistic Society was started in London to try to bring some control to the sport, and by 1838 the London Prize Ring rules had been accepted in both Britain and America. These rules, which were first used in a championship fight in 1839 in which James "Deaf" Burke lost the English title to William Thompson ("Bendigo"), provided for a ring 24 feet (7.32 metres) square and bounded by two ropes. When a fighter went down, the round ended and he was helped to his corner. The next round would begin 30 seconds later, with each boxer required to reach, unaided, a mark in the centre of the ring. If a fighter could not reach that mark by the end of eight additional seconds, he was declared the loser. Kicking, gouging, butting with the head, biting, and low blows were all declared fouls.

Queensberry rules. Though the London Prize Ring rules did much to help boxing, the brawling that distinguished old-time pugilism continued to alienate most of England's upper class, and it became apparent that still more revisions were necessary to attract a better class of patron. John Graham Chambers of the Amateur Athletic Club devised a new set of rules in 1867 which emphasized boxing technique and skill. Chambers sought the patronage of John Sholto Douglas, the 9th marquess of Queensberry, who lent his name to the new guidelines. The Queensberry rules differed from the London rules in four major respects: contestants wore padded gloves; a round consisted of three minutes of fighting followed by a minute of rest; wrestling was illegal; and any fighter who went down had to get up unaided within 10 seconds—if he could not do so, he was declared knocked out, and the fight was over. During this period the introduction of the first weight divisions also took place.

The new rules at first were scorned by professionals, who considered them unmanly, and championship bouts continued to be fought under London Prize Ring rules. But many young pugilists preferred the Queensberry guidelines and fought accordingly. Prominent among these was James ("Jem") Mace, who won the English heavyweight title under the London rules in 1861. Mace's enthusiasm for gloved fighting did much to popularize the Queensberry rules.

John L. Sullivan

It was, however, John L. Sullivan of the United States who made the move that finally aligned professional fighters on the side of the Queensberry rules. Sullivan claimed the world heavyweight championship in 1882 under the London bareknuckle rules. In 1889 Sullivan defended against Jake Kilrain in the last heavyweight championship bareknuckle fight in the United States, despite the London rules by then having been made illegal in every state. The legal complications following the Kilrain match so upset Sullivan that when he agreed to defend his championship against James J. Corbett, he insisted on Queensberry rules.

Economic impetus. By the early 20th century, boxing had become a shortcut to riches and social acceptance for those near the foot of the economic ladder. It was at this time that professional boxing became centred in the United States, with its expanding economy and successive waves of immigrants. Famine had driven thousands of Irish to seek refuge in America, and by 1915 the Irish had become dominant in professional boxing, producing such standouts as Terry McGovern, "Philadelphia" Jack O'Brien, Mike ("Twin") Sullivan and his brother Jack, Packey McFarland, Jimmy Clabby, and Jack Britton, among others. German, Scandinavian, and central European fighters also emerged. Outstanding Jewish fighters such as Joe Choynski, Abe Attell, "Battling" Levinsky, and Harry Lewis were active before 1915 and were followed by a second wave consisting of Barney Ross, Benny Leonard, Sid Terris, Lew Tendler, Al Singer, Maxie Rosenbloom, and Max Baer. Italian-Americans to reach prominence included Tony Canzoneri, Rocky Marciano, Johnny Dundee, and Willie Pep.

Thomas Hearns (U.S.), winner of championships in four different weight divisions, retaining his title in a 1981 WBA welterweight title fight with Pablo Baez.

Steve Sutton—Duomo

Meanwhile, black Americans also turned to boxing to fight their way to the top, and foreign-born black boxers such as Peter Jackson, Sam Langford, Joe Walcott, and George Dixon came to the United States to capitalize on the opportunities offered by boxing. Joe Gans won the world lightweight championship in 1902, and Jack Johnson became the first black heavyweight champion in 1908. Prejudice against black boxers, however, remained great. Sullivan refused to defend against Jackson, and Jack Dempsey, the "Manassa Mauler," would not fight the black boxer Harry Wills. As champion, Johnson was hounded so relentlessly he was forced to leave the United States. Blacks nevertheless continued to pursue fistic careers, particularly during the Great Depression, which began in 1929. When the black boxer Joe Louis won the world heavyweight championship in 1937 and went on to become one of boxing's most popular champions, blacks became more encouraged, and all-time greats such as Henry Armstrong, "Sugar" Ray Robinson, Archie Moore, Ezzard Charles, "Jersey" Joe Wolcott, Floyd Patterson, Sonny Liston, Muhammad Ali, and Joe Frazier went on to win world championships in various weight divisions. By the last quarter of the 20th century blacks dominated boxing, producing stars such as "Sugar" Ray Leonard, "Marvelous" Marvin Hagler, Thomas Hearns, Larry Holmes, Michael Spinks, and Mike Tyson.

Black American domination

Hispanics also became prominent on the boxing scene, giving the sport such legendary names as Carlos Monzón, Pascual Pérez, Roberto Durán, and Alexis Argüello. Pancho Villa of the Philippines was the first Asian to win a world championship, capturing the flyweight crown in 1923. In the late 20th century East Asia was a boxing hotbed, with many Asians fighting for various world titles.

Organization and tournaments. *Development of amateur boxing.* In 1867 the first amateur boxing championships took place under the Marquess of Queensberry rules. In 1880 the Amateur Boxing Association (ABA), the sport's first amateur governing body, was formed in Britain, and in the following year the ABA staged its first official amateur championships.

In 1888 the Amateur Athletic Union (AAU) of the United States was formed, instituting its annual championships in boxing the same year. In 1926 the *Chicago Tribune* started another amateur competition called the Golden Gloves. It grew into a national competition rivaling that of the AAU. In 1978 a law was passed in the United States forbidding the AAU from governing more than one Olympic sport. This led to the formation of the United States of America Amateur Boxing Federation (USA/ABF), which now governs U.S. amateur boxing.

Amateur boxing spread rapidly to other countries and resulted in several major international tournaments taking place annually, every two years, or, as in the case of the Olympic Games, every four years. Important events include the European Games, Commonwealth Games, Pan-American Games, All-African Championships, and the World Military Games. All international matches are controlled by the Association Internationale de Boxe Amateur (AIBA), formed in 1946 with headquarters in London.

Boxing in socialist nations

Because of their political and social policies, the Soviet Union and other Communist countries do not have professional boxers. However, the Soviet Union joined the AIBA in 1950 and entered the Olympic Games in 1952; they emerged as one of the strongest amateur boxing nations in the world, along with other Communist countries such as East Germany, Poland, Hungary, and Cuba. Cuba, which had produced many excellent professional boxers before professional sports were banned there by Fidel Castro's government, became a dominating force in international amateur boxing. The Cuban heavyweight Teofilo Stevenson won Olympic gold medals in 1972, 1976, and 1980. African countries advanced considerably in boxing after acquiring independence in the 1950s and 1960s.

Professional purses. The man who made boxing into big business was George ("Tex") Rickard, the sport's first great promoter. After staging the world's lightweight championship bout between Joe Gans and Oscar ("Battling") Nelson to publicize the mining town of Goldfield, Nev., in 1906, he realized the potential of boxing. Rickard made an art of boxing publicity, playing on the public's prejudices to boost interest and ticket sales. Five of the bouts that he promoted for Jack Dempsey, heavyweight champion from 1919 to 1926, each made more than $1,000,000. In the Great Depression years that followed Dempsey's retirement, receipts from boxing dwindled. Then in 1935 promoter Mike Jacobs signed Joe Louis to a contract, launching a new era of prosperity in boxing. Louis' career purses totaled more than $5,000,000.

Impact of television

After World War II, television took on an increasingly important role in professional boxing. Because of its relatively low production costs as compared to other sports, professional boxing became a regular feature of most network programming throughout much of the 1950s and early 1960s. After a period of decline, boxing enjoyed a television revival when five American boxers won gold medals in the 1976 Olympics and turned professional following those games. The advent of cable television in the United States also benefited professional boxing in the 1980s, replacing, in many ways, the small neighbourhood boxing clubs that had been declining as the training ground for novice professionals.

Television also greatly increased boxing revenues. Million-dollar purses for heavyweight championships became commonplace by the 1960s, and the heavyweight champion Muhammad Ali earned an estimated $69,000,000 during his 20-year professional career. Million-dollar purses are no longer restricted to the heavyweight division. When middleweights "Sugar" Ray Leonard and Marvin Hagler fought on April 6, 1987, they shared a purse estimated at $30,000,000. Aside from television, casino gambling has been the biggest influence on modern professional boxing in the United States and, to a lesser degree, in continental Europe. Casinos, especially those in Las Vegas, Nev., and Atlantic City, N.J., have found boxing to be a highly successful marketing tool for increasing gaming revenues. Major bouts at casinos also receive national and international television exposure.

Professional organizations. World professional boxing has no single controlling body that is universally recognized. This situation had its origins in the United States in 1920 when two organizations were set up: the National Boxing Association, a private body, and the New York State Athletic Commission, a state agency. Divided control led to a situation in which competing organizations sometimes recognized different boxers as world champions at the same time. In Europe the ruling body was the International Boxing Union, which in 1948 became the European Boxing Union. Several attempts were subsequently made to induce all major professional boxing organizations to agree to the formation of one international ruling body, but to little avail. In 1963 the World Boxing Council (WBC) was formed. In the early 1960s the National Boxing Association changed its name to the World Boxing Association (WBA). In 1983 the International Boxing Federation (IBF) was formed, adding to an already convoluted situation. By the 1980s it was common for most weight divisions to have three so-called "world" champions, which has considerably diluted the championship class in boxing.

The schism in boxing authority

Weight divisions. During the 19th and again at the beginning of the 20th century the popularity of boxing brought about the formation of weight divisions other than the heavyweight class to eliminate the handicap of smaller contestants having to concede excessive weight to their opponents. Some of these weight divisions originated in the United States, others in Great Britain.

The eight traditional weight divisions that are universally recognized are delimited as follows: flyweight (not more than 112 pounds [50.8 kilograms]), bantamweight (118 pounds), featherweight (126 pounds), lightweight (135 pounds), welterweight (147 pounds), middleweight (160 pounds), light-heavyweight (175 pounds), and heavyweight (any weight over 175 pounds). In all world and national title fights, the above weight limits must be strictly observed. If a boxer is over the limit, he is normally given a short time in which to make the stipulated weight. If he still fails, the bout usually ceases to be regarded as a championship contest and the champion, if he is at fault, forfeits his title.

Proliferation of weight classes

Two additional divisions, junior-lightweight (130 pounds) and junior-welterweight (140 pounds), were introduced in the United States in the 1920s. (The term "junior" in boxing has nothing to do with age.) These divisions were formed for the benefit of boxers who were unable, or unwilling, to make the stipulated weight in one of the eight original divisions. The proliferation of weight classes continued until some governing bodies recognized a total of 17 weight classes. New weight divisions recognized by the WBC are: cruiserweight (195 pounds), super middleweight (165 pounds), super welterweight (154 pounds), super bantamweight (122 pounds), super flyweight (116 pounds), light-flyweight (110 pounds), and strawweight (105 pounds).

RULES, TECHIQUES, AND STYLES

Ring, rules, and equipment. Because there is no universally accepted world ruling body for professional boxing, each country has its own set of rules, and in the United States there are different rules in different states. Generally bouts take place in a "ring" that is some 18 to 22 feet square (the size may vary slightly) and surrounded by four strands of rope. Professional bouts may be scheduled to last from four to 12 rounds of three minutes' duration, though two-minute rounds are used in some bouts held in Great Britain. Professional championship bouts had traditionally lasted 15 rounds, but by the late 1980s the WBC, WBA, and IBF championships were all being scheduled for 12 rounds.

Scoring

A referee is stationed inside the ring with the boxers and regulates the bout. In some jurisdictions, the referee scores the contest along with two judges outside the ring. In most jurisdictions, however, the referee does not participate in the judging, and three ringside officials score the bout. The officials award points to each boxer for each round, and a boxer must win on two of the three scorecards to earn a decision victory. Padded gloves, ranging from eight to 10 ounces in weight, are worn by the boxers.

A bout ends in a knockout when a boxer is knocked down and cannot get up or is adjudged not ready to resume the contest after the referee has counted to 10. A fight can be stopped (called a technical knockout) when a boxer is deemed by the referee (and sometimes the ringside physician) to be unable to defend himself, when a boxer is deemed to have sustained a serious injury, or when a boxer or his seconds decide he should not continue. A bout may also end in a decision, when the bout has gone the scheduled number of rounds and the scoring officials decide the winner; in a draw when the officials agree that both boxers fought equally well; in a "no contest" when the referee deems that both men are not giving their best; or in disqualification.

The rules governing amateur boxing are similar in the United States, Great Britain, and continental Europe. Amateur rules, however, differ substantially from those governing professional boxing. Amateur bouts are normally three rounds in duration, and the boxers wear protective headgear. The referee only supervises the boxing, while three to five ringside judges score the bout. The rules are also more stringently enforced in amateur boxing, and disqualification is more more common than in professional boxing.

Techniques. No one phase of boxing is more important than another. An effective offense in boxing depends on the ability to land punches fast and hard enough to penetrate the opponent's guard. Defensive tactics include parrying or warding off punches with one's upraised arms and gloves; stepping backward or sideways out of the arc of a punch; and bending or twisting one's head and upper body out of the blow's path. Footwork is important to both offense and defense. The two generally recognized stances are "orthodox" and "southpaw." The former has the left hand and the left foot forward, the latter the right hand and the right foot forward. "Switch-hitting" boxers are those who change from one stance to another during the course of a bout. In either stance, the lead hand is extended forward in front of the body and the other hand is held near the chin for protection, the chin is tucked into the chest, and the shoulders are hunched. There are variations in individual styles, of course.

The basic punches

There are four basic punches: the jab, hook, uppercut, and cross. All other punches are modifications of these basic punches. The jab, whether thrown from an orthodox or southpaw stance, is a straight punch delivered with the lead hand, which moves directly out from the shoulder. The other punches may be thrown with either hand. The hook is a short lateral movement of arm and fist, with elbow bent and wrist twisted inward at the moment of impact. The uppercut is an upward blow delivered from the direction of the toes. The cross is thrown across the body at shoulder level, usually as a follow-up to a lead from the other hand.

Styles. In bareknuckle fighting the emphasis was on the power of the punch, since bouts usually ended only when one contestant could not continue. The hands were held in front of the body in no particular position, and footwork was practically nonexistent. With the advent of padded gloves and contests decided on points, boxing skills and footwork became more important. James J. Corbett was the first modern heavyweight to concentrate on technique. Ten years after Corbett lost the title, heavyweight champion Jack Johnson showed that he too could box as well as punch. The heavyweight champion Jack Dempsey enjoyed tremendous popularity because he was an aggressive fighter who always sought to knock out his opponent. Dempsey fought from a crouch, bobbing and weaving to leave as little of himself exposed as possible. The heavyweight champion Joe Louis perfected the "stalking" style, a method of patiently pursuing his opponent until he came within range to deliver a knockout blow. Mike Tyson, who won the WBA, WBC, and IBF heavyweight titles in the late 1980s, used a similar style.

Muhammad Ali

Until Muhammad Ali, heavyweights were not expected to move quickly. At his peak, however, Ali was probably the fastest and most skillful heavyweight champion of all time. He danced around the ring with his arm sometimes dangling at his side, but always in position to attack or defend at the right time. Although Ali did not possess a devastating punch, he scored many knockouts by delivering a rapid sequence of blows. Though style remains a matter of individual choice, swift lateral movement and combination punching have, to a large degree, become the two most important aspects of modern boxing technique.

(R.O./N.Co.)

Bowling

Bowling, also called tenpin bowling, is a game in which a ball is rolled down a long, narrow lane toward a group of pins, the object being to knock down more pins than an opponent. The game is quite different from the sport of bowls, or lawn bowls, in which the aim is to bring the ball to rest near a stationary ball called a jack. There are many forms of bowling, but tenpins, the most widely played variation, is the principal form of bowling in the United States, Canada, western Europe, the Far East, Australia, New Zealand, and Latin America. Its many variations include duckpins, candlepins, fivepins, skittles, and ninepins, and differences within the framework of each of the games. For records of Fédération Internationale des Quilleurs and American Bowling Congress championships, see SPORTING RECORD in the *Micropædia*.

HISTORY

Origin and early period. Articles found in the tomb of an Egyptian child buried in 5200 BC included nine pieces of stone, to be set up as pins, at which a stone "ball" was rolled, the ball having first to roll through an archway made of three pieces of marble. The modern sport of bowling at pins probably originated in ancient Germany, not as a sport but as a religious ceremony. As early as the 3rd or 4th century AD, in rites held in the cloisters of churches, parishioners may have placed their ever-present club, or *Kegel* (the implement most Germans carried for sport and, certainly, self-protection), at one end of a runway resembling a modern bowling lane. The *Kegel* was said to represent the *Heide* ("heathen"). A stone was rolled at the *Heide,* and those successfully toppling it were believed to have cleansed themselves of sin. Although the peasants' club evolved into pins, the association remained, and even today bowlers are often called keglers.

German roots

The passage of time brought an increase in the size of the stone rolled at pins, and eventually the ball came to be made of wood. Many variations of the game developed, some played with three pins, others with as many as 17. A biographer of the 16th-century cleric Martin Luther has written that Luther built a bowling lane for his children which he occasionally visited, sometimes throwing the first ball.

Among other significant historical references to bowling are an account of a great feast given the citizenry of Frankfurt in 1463, at which the venison dinner was followed by bowling; notations from 1325 in which "gambling on bowling" in Berlin and Cologne was limited to five shillings; and the award of an ox to the winner of a bowling competition in 1518, given by the city of Breslau (now Wrocław, Pol.).

In the 15th, 16th, and 17th centuries, the game spread into the Low Countries and also into Austria and Switzerland. The playing surfaces were usually cinders or clay, specially treated and sun-baked to a hardness resembling concrete. The roofing over of lanes, first done in London for lawn bowls around 1455, was the beginning of bowling as an all-weather, around-the-clock game. When the lanes were covered or put into sheds (called *Kegelbahns* in Germany and Austria and usually attached to village taverns or guest houses), the playing surfaces ranged from wood or hardened clay to, in later years, asphalt.

Bowls and pins in North America. There is confusion about how and when bowling at pins came to North America, arising from the inconsistent use of the terms bowl, bowler, and bowling. The early British settlers brought lawn bowls with them to America because that was the game they knew best. Dutch explorers under Henry Hudson were said to have brought some form of pin bowling.

Early European pin games

Many of the early European pin games involved rolling the ball along a wooden plank, 12 to 18 inches (30 to 46 centimetres) wide and 60 to 90 feet (18 to 27 metres) long, toward a diamond-shaped formation of nine pins.

The plank still can be found in parts of Europe, notably in eastern European countries, where bowling games called bohle, asphalt, and schere are popular. In these, the nine pins are smaller than tenpins, and the duckpin-type ball, without finger holes, is held in the palm of the hand. The Netherlands has a "plank" game in which a large ball, with only a thumbhole, is rolled on the plank toward the nine pins. The earliest known reference to bowling in the United States was made by Washington Irving in his short story "Rip Van Winkle" (1819–1820).

Emergence of the tenpin game. By the mid-1830s, as bowling at pins was flourishing, the scourge that periodically struck the game in Germany, France, England, and other countries—gambling—became a plague on the U.S. bowling scene. To combat the problem, the state legislature of Connecticut in 1841 banned the playing of "Nine-Pins, whether more or less than nine-pins are used." However, a month before the Connecticut legislation, the town of Perry, N.Y., had enacted a law banning tenpins. There are other earlier signs of tenpin bowling, including a painting, traced to 1810, that shows English dandies playing a game with 10 oddly shaped pins set up outside a factory in Ipswich, Eng., an area that was populated by many Dutch immigrants in the 1700s. Regardless of how tenpins came into being, its popularity spread as German immigrants began populating Chicago; Milwaukee; St. Louis, Mo.; Cincinnati, Ohio; Detroit, and other cities. Although intercity bowling events were becoming common, the lack of uniform playing rules and equipment specifications stifled the development of the game. In 1875 delegates from nine bowling clubs in New York City and Brooklyn, N.Y., organized the National Bowling Association. Some of the legislation agreed upon then is still in effect in modified form, but the group lacked national acceptance.

Organization and tournaments. Disagreement over rules continued, principally as an alignment of New York bowlers against everyone else. On Sept. 9, 1895, the American Bowling Congress (ABC) was organized in New York City. Rules and equipment standards were developed, and the game as it finally was organized remained basically unchanged as the sport grew steadily. An early technological development that helped the sport's progress was the introduction of the hard rubber ball in 1904, its predecessor having been made of lignum vitae, a tropical wood that was durable but that often chipped or otherwise lost its shape. The next big advance was the introduction of the automatic pin-setting machine in the early 1950s. Later, balls made of polyester and urethane were developed and in some cases replaced the hard rubber ball.

The American Bowling Congress

In 1901 the ABC started its national tournament. The Women's International Bowling Congress (WIBC) was organized in 1916 and conducted annual national championships from 1917. While the ABC and WIBC are autonomous organizations, each billing itself as the "world's largest" men's or women's sports organization, respectively, they share a number of functions, including equipment testing and research and the joint issuance of credentials to the mixed leagues that made up more than 70 percent of their late 1980s combined membership of approximately 7,000,000. A third membership organization, the Young American Bowling Alliance (YABA; established in 1982), administers to the league and tournament needs of young bowlers through college age.

In the late 20th century it was estimated that more than 60,000,000 persons bowled at least once or twice a year in the United States. The backbone of the sport continued to be its highly organized, competitive league structure. Most men's and women's leagues consist of eight to 12 teams but some have 40 or more, depending on the number of lanes in the bowling centre. League play is conducted under rules laid down by the three major membership organizations, including the handling of prize funds by the adult leagues. The prize funds are developed from the contestants' entry fees and are distributed to the various teams and individuals on a performance basis.

League structure

Professional bowling. The Professional Bowlers Association of America (PBA) was organized in 1958. It quickly developed a star system and a tournament tour fashioned after that of professional golf. PBA members, helped by a booming television industry, were soon playing for more than $1,000,000 in yearly prize money, a figure that had grown to more than $7,000,000 by the late 1980s. Don Carter became the leading winner in the 1950s, succeeded by Dick Weber in the 1960s and Earl Anthony into the 1980s. The Professional Women Bowlers Association (1959; since 1981 called the Ladies Pro Bowlers Tour [LPBT]) began modest tournament play in the early 1960s. A major influence in development of the game was the Bowling Proprietors' Association of America, founded in 1932. In addition to its trade association functions, it is affiliated with a number of tournaments, most notably the All-Star tournament, a match game event begun in 1941 that in 1971 became the U.S. Open and a part of the PBA tour. The National Bowling Council, founded in 1943 by manufacturers, proprietors, and membership groups, concerns itself with national promotional campaigns and other activities.

Tenpins in other countries. The first tenpin lanes in Europe were installed in Sweden in 1909. Attempts to popularize tenpin bowling elsewhere in Europe were unsuccessful over the next several decades, but the game became popular in Great Britain during World War II, when hundreds of lanes were installed on U.S. military bases.

As league bowling in the United States peaked in the mid-1960s, equipment manufacturers began looking elsewhere for new markets. With assistance from the ABC, the British Tenpin Bowling Association was formed in 1961 and was ready for the boom. With the same ABC assistance, Australia followed suit. Mexico, where Emperor Maximilian had installed a skittles alley in Chapultepec Castle a century earlier, joined the tenpin trend, as did other Latin-American countries.

By the early 1970s the bowling boom had spread to Japan. Leading players for the PBA were invited to compete in an annual Japanese tournament. Unlike the United States, where the male professionals dominated television, however, the most popular bowlers on Japanese television were women. Bowling also became popular in other Asian localities, including Hong Kong, Thailand, Singapore, Korea, and Indonesia.

The bowling boom in Japan

International competition. Documents indicate that an international competition was held in Hannover, Ger., as early as 1891. An early bowling proprietor and promoter in New York City was so taken with the idea of international play that he sponsored an event in Union Hill, N.J., in 1900, but the use of the word international was only thinly justified by the appearance of some teams from Canada. Competitions apparently limited to ninepins and other "small ball" games were held in the German cities of Solingen (1904), Dresden (1908), and Berlin (1914). Few other than German bowlers were entered.

In 1923 a group of American bowlers toured Sweden and were roundly defeated by their hosts. The outcome was the same in 1926, at which time teams from Denmark, Finland, Norway, The Netherlands, and Germany joined the Swedes and Americans in forming the International Bowling Association. In 1929 they held what came to be called the Third International tournament, again in Sweden, followed by a Fourth International held in New York City in 1934. Germany hosted the Fifth International in 1936, as a prelude to, but having no connection with, the Olympic Games in Berlin. It was the last international meet of any consequence until the Fédération Internationale des Quilleurs (FIQ) was formed in 1952 to coordinate international amateur competition. Its headquarters is in Helsinki, and it has grown to more than 70 member nations.

The first world tournament of the FIQ was held in Helsinki in 1954, and from 1967 championships were played every four years. Competition is held in three zones—American, European, and Asian. The organization has four sections, the principal one being devoted to tenpins. The other three are the small-ball games, schere, bohle, and asphalt. FIQ competition is for nonprofessionals; and gold, silver, and bronze medals are awarded to champions and runners-up. Bowling was accepted as a demonstration sport in the summer 1988 Olympic Games in Seoul, South Korea.

PLAY OF THE GAME

Lanes and equipment. The U.S. game of tenpins is played according to the rules and specifications of the American Bowling Congress. The game is played indoors on wooden or synthetic lanes with maximum dimensions of 62 feet 10 11/16 inches (19.17 metres) in length and 42 inches (107 centimetres) in width. The surface, coated with lacquer or plastic-type material, must be free of continuous grooves and must be within 40/1,000th inch (one millimetre) of perfect levelness. The distance from the foul line, past which the player may not slide when delivering the ball, to the centre of the spot on which the headpin stands is 60 feet (18.3 metres). The approach to the foul line has a minimum length of 15 feet (4.6 metres).

The bowling lane

The pins are 15 inches (38 centimetres) tall and arranged in a triangle formation with the point or No. 1 pin at the head of the formation facing the bowler. The centres of the pin spots are 12 inches (30.5 centimetres) apart. The pins have a laminated wood core covered by a plastic coating. The weight ranges between 3.5 and 3.7 pounds (1.6 and 1.7 kilograms).

The ball is of nonmetallic composition—either hard rubber, polyester, or urethane—with a circumference of 27 inches (68.6 centimetres) and a weight limit of 16 pounds (7.3 kilograms). There is no minimum weight.

Principles of play. A game of tenpins consists of 10 frames. Two deliveries (rolls of the ball) per frame are allowed, the ideal being to knock down all pins on the first for a strike. If pins are left standing after the first delivery, the fallen or "dead" wood is removed and a second delivery permitted. If all remaining pins are knocked down, a spare is recorded. A split can occur on the first ball when two or more pins are left standing, separated by at least one fallen pin. Stepping over the foul line is a foul and results in loss of all pins knocked down on that delivery. There are depressed troughs on each side of the lane; a ball falling therein is a gutter ball and out of play, with resulting loss of one delivery.

Scoring

Both a strike and a spare count 10 pins plus additional pins scored on the next two (after a strike) or one (after a spare) deliveries. If two strikes in a row are recorded (a double), the player counts 20 pins in the first frame plus the number of pins he knocks down on his first delivery in the third frame. Should he score another strike, he will have 30 pins in his first frame. A perfect game is 300 and consists of 12 strikes in a row, two additional deliveries being permitted in the 10th, or final, frame (one additional following a spare). Competition in league and tournament play includes individuals, as well as teams of up to five players. Two teams are assigned to a pair of lanes, the bowlers alternating lanes for each frame.

(J.B.P.)

BIBLIOGRAPHY

General works: ROBERT J. HIGGS, *Sports: A Reference Guide* (1982), offers analyses of scholarly and popular literature on sports. An overview of sports literature is presented in *Sport Bibliography,* 11 vol. (1981–83), prepared by the Sport Information Resource Centre and continued by annual supplements. JOHN ARLOTT (ed.), *The Oxford Companion to World Sports and Games* (1975); and FRANK G. MENKE, *The Encyclopedia of Sports,* 6th rev. ed., revised by PETE PALMER (1977), provide brief historical descriptions of many sports and games. For information on equipment, dress, facilities, and differences in rules, see the *Official Rules of Sports & Games* (biennial).

History: See RICHARD D. MANDELL, *Sport, a Cultural History* (1984); WOLFGANG DECKER, *Sport und Spiel im Alten Ägypten* (1987); INGOMAR WEILER, *Der Sport bei den Völkern der Alten Welt* (1981); and JACQUES ULMANN, *De la gymnastique aux sports modernes: histoire des doctrines de l'éducation physique,* 3rd rev. ed. (1977). Competitive sports are surveyed historically in WILLIAM J. BAKER, *Sports in the Western World* (1982). Sports history in individual countries is discussed in: (*Italy*): WILLIAM HEYWOOD, *Palio and Ponte: An Account of the Sports of Central Italy from the Age of Dante to the XXth Century* (1904, reprinted 1969); (*France*): RICHARD HOLT, *Sport and Society in Modern France* (1981); (*Britain*): DENNIS BRAILSFORD, *Sport and Society: Elizabeth to Anne* (1969); J.A. MANGAN, *Athleticism in the Victorian and Edwardian Public School: The Emergence and Consolidation of an Educational Ideology* (1981, reissued 1986); and JOHN HARGREAVES, *Sport, Power, and Culture: Social and Historical Analysis of Popular Sports in Britain* (1986); (*Socialist countries*): JAMES RIORDAN, *Sport in Soviet Society: Development of Sport and Physical Education in Russia and the USSR* (1977); and JAMES RIORDAN (ed.), *Sport Under Communism: The U.S.S.R., Czechoslovakia, the G.D.R., China, Cuba,* 2nd rev. ed. (1981); (*Canada*): ALAN METCALFE, *Canada Learns to Play: The Emergence of Organized Sport, 1807–1914* (1987); (*United States*): BENJAMIN G. RADER, *American Sports: From the Age of Folk Games to the Age of Spectators* (1983); and ALLEN GUTTMANN, *A Whole New Ball Game: An Interpretation of American Sports* (1988).

Sports in modern society: ALLEN GUTTMANN, *From Ritual to Record: The Nature of Modern Sports* (1978), is a study of the social context of modern sports. GÜNTHER R.F. LÜSCHEN and GEORGE H. SAGE (eds.), *Handbook of Social Science of Sport* (1981), includes essays on sport as an important social institution. Another collection is DONALD W. BALL and JOHN W. LOY (eds.), *Sport and Social Order: Contributions to the Sociology of Sport* (1975). JOHN W. LOY, BARRY D. MCPHERSON, and GERALD KENYON, *Sport and Social Systems: A Guide to the Analysis, Problems, and Literature* (1978), offers a survey of sociological and psychological views.

Sport as a cultural institution is explored in NORBERT ELIAS and ERIC DUNNING, *Quest for Excitement: Sport and Leisure in the Civilizing Process* (1986), outlining the sociological, psychological, and physical aspects of sports in the sociocultural process. The role of women in sports is the subject of J.A. MANGAN and ROBERTA J. PARK (eds.), *From "Fair Sex" to Feminism: Sport and the Socialization of Women in the Industrial and Post-Industrial Eras* (1987); and K.F. DYER, *Challenging the Men: The Social Biology of Female Sporting Achievement* (1982), which provides a worldwide survey. The political symbolism of athletic achievement is discussed in NEIL MACFARLANE, *Sport and Politics: A World Divided* (1986); and JOHN M. HOBERMAN, *Sport and Political Ideology* (1984). Psychological aspects of sports are studied in DIANE L. GILL, *Psychological Dynamics of Sport* (1986); JAY J. COAKLEY, *Sport in Society: Issues and Controversies,* 3rd ed. (1986); and ALLEN GUTTMANN, *Sports Spectators* (1986). For sports science and medicine, see LEONARD A. LARSON (ed.), *Encyclopedia of Sport Sciences and Medicine* (1971); and RICHARD MANGI, PETER JOKL, and O. WILLIAM DAYTON, *Sports Fitness and Training* (1987).

(A.G.)

Major sports: (*Baseball*): Historical works include LAWRENCE RITTER and DONALD HONIG, *The Image of Their Greatness: An Illustrated History of Baseball from 1900 to the Present,* updated ed. (1984); and LAWRENCE S. RITTER (comp.), *The Glory of Their Times: The Story of the Early Days of Baseball Told by the Men Who Played It,* new ed. (1984). For a history of black players and the Negro leagues, see ROBERT PETERSON, *Only the Ball Was White* (1970, reprinted 1984). DAVID QUENTIN VOIGT, *Baseball, an Illustrated History* (1987), includes such topics as black baseball and intercollegiate sports.

The *Official Baseball Guide,* containing records and a narrative review of the previous season, and the *Official Baseball Register,* giving the career record of each major league player of the previous season, are published annually by *The Sporting News.* The standard reference work covering the records of professional players since 1871 is JOSEPH L. REICHLER (ed.), *The Baseball Encyclopedia,* 7th rev. ed. (1988). Organization and play of the game itself is the basis of JOE BRINKMAN and CHARLIE EUCHNER, *The Umpire's Handbook,* rev. ed. (1987). BILL JAMES and JOHN DEWAN, *Bill James Presents the Great American Baseball Stat Book,* ed. by GEOFF BECKMAN *et al.* (1987), is a massive collection of the game's statistics.

(Je.Ho.)

(*Cricket*): Literature on the sport is listed in E.W. PADWICK (comp.), *A Bibliography of Cricket,* 2nd rev. ed. (1984), citing the sources up to the end of 1979. Informative histories include H.S. ALTHAM and E.W. SWANTON, *A History of Cricket,* 2 vol. (1963); ROWLAND BOWEN, *Cricket: A History of Its Growth and Development Throughout the World* (1970); E.W. SWANTON (gen. ed.), *Barclays World of Cricket: The Game from A–Z,* new ed., rev. by GEORGE PLUMTRE (1986); and JACK POLLARD, *Australian Cricket: The Game and the Players* (1982). For records, scores, and statistics, see *Wisden Cricketers' Almanack* (annual); PHILIP BAILEY, PHILIP THORN, and PETER WYNNE-THOMAS, *Who's Who of Cricketers: A Complete Who's Who of All Cricketers Who Have Played First-Class Cricket in England with Full Career Records* (1984); CHRISTOPHER MARTIN-JENKINS, *The Complete Who's Who of Test Cricketers,* rev. ed. (1987); BILL FRINDALL (comp. and ed.), *The Wisden Book of Cricket Records* (1986), and *The Wisden Book of Test Cricket 1877–1984,* 2nd rev. ed. (1985); and BILL FRINDALL and VICTOR H. ISAACS (comps.), *The Wisden Book of One-Day International Cricket, 1971–1985* (1985). In addition to British sources, almanacs, annuals, and yearbooks are published in Australia, India, New Zealand, Pakistan, and South Africa.

(Ma.W.)

(*Association football:* [*soccer*]): NORMAN BARRETT (ed.), *World Soccer from A to Z* (1973), is a historical survey presented in dictionary form. TONY MASON, *Association Football and English Society, 1863–1915* (1980), offers a history that shows the effect of the professional game on its spectators. BRIAN GLANVILLE, *A Book of Soccer* (1979), is a source of general information, including history. For records, see JACK ROLLIN, *The Guinness Book of Soccer Facts & Feats,* 4th ed. (1981), and *Soccer: The Records, Facts, and Champions,* 2nd ed. (1988). *Rothmans Football Yearbook* (annual) provides a comprehensive record of the English and Scottish game as well as European and international details.

(J.R.)

(*U.S. football*): Authoritative treatments of the early game include ALLISON DANZIG, *The History of American Football: Its Great Teams, Players, and Coaches* (1956), and his *Oh, How They Played the Game* (1971); and FOREST EVASHEVSKI and DAVID M. NELSON, *Scoring Power with the Winged T Offense* (1957). DAVID L. PORTER (ed.), *Biographical Dictionary of American Sports: Football* (1987), contains a wealth of historical information. See also JOHN MCCALLUM and CHARLES H. PEARSON, *College Football U.S.A., 1869–1972: Official Book of the National Football Foundation* (1972); ROBERT BALDWIN, *College Football Records: 1869–1984* (1987); and *NCAA Football Records* (annual). Professional football is informatively presented in HAROLD CLAASSEN, *The History of Professional Football* (1963); BEAU RIFFENBURGH (ed.), *The Official NFL Encyclopedia,* new rev. ed. (1986); ROGER TREAT, *The Encyclopedia of Football,* 16th ed. (1979); DAVID S. NEFT, RICHARD M. COHEN, and JORDAN A. DEUTSCH, *The Sports Encyclopedia: Pro Football: The Modern Era, 1960 to the Present,* rev. ed. (1987); and *The Sporting News National Football Guide* (annual). For the rules and organization of the game, see DAVID M. NELSON, *Football: Principles and Play* (1962), and *Illustrated Football Rules* (1976). The National Collegiate Athletic Association publishes useful annuals, including *NCAA Football,* a general guide, and *NCAA Football Rules and Interpretations.*

(D.M.Ne.)

(*Canadian football*): The history of the game is surveyed in GORDON CURRIE, *100 Years of Canadian Football: The Dramatic History of Football's First Century in Canada, and the Story of the Canadian Football League* (1968); JACK SULLIVAN, *The Grey Cup Story,* rev. ed. (1974); and GORDON WALKER and DOUGLAS MITCHELL, *Grey Cup Tradition* (1987). For current information, see CANADIAN FOOTBALL LEAGUE, *Facts, Figures, and Records* (annual).

(J.I.)

(*Rugby*): U.A. TITLEY and ROSS MCWHIRTER, *Centenary History of the Rugby Football Union* (1970), is an illustrated history of the Rugby Union game in England; and ERIC DUNNING and KENNETH SHEARD, *Barbarians, Gentlemen, and Players: A Sociological Study of the Development of Rugby Football* (1979), examines the game from its origins to the 1970s. A.M.C. THORBURN, *The Scottish Rugby Union: Official History* (1985); and DAVID SMITH and GARETH WILLIAMS, *Fields of Praise: The Official History of the Welsh Rugby Union, 1881–1981* (1980), complete the coverage of Great Britain. GORDON SLATTER, *On the Ball: The Centennial Book of New Zealand Rugby* (1970), is another history. JOHN HUXLEY and DAVID HOWES (comps.), *Encyclopaedia of Rugby League Football,* 2nd ed. (1980), is a comprehensive reference work. For current information, see *The Rugby Football League Official Guide* (annual); and *Rothmans Rugby League Yearbook* (annual).

(D.B.J.F.)

(*Basketball*): Histories of the game of basketball include BERNICE LARSON WEBB, *The Basketball Man: James Naismith* (1973), a comprehensive biography of the game's inventor. LARRY FOX, *Illustrated History of Basketball* (1974), studies the game from Naismith to the Hall of Fame. Other histories include NEIL D. ISAACS, *All the Moves: A History of College Basketball,* rev. ed. (1984); STANLEY COHEN, *The Game They Played* (1977), a view of the gambling scandals that rocked college basketball in the 1950s; and JOE GERGEN, *The Final Four* (1987), a history of the NCAA. Informative reference sources include RONALD L. MENDELL, *Who's Who in Basketball* (1973), a listing of major names and their roles in the development of the game; and ZANDER HOLLANDER (ed.), *The Modern Encyclopedia of Basketball,* 2nd rev. ed. (1979), and his *NBA's Official Encyclopedia of Pro Basketball* (1981), with general information and statistics.

For further records and statistics, see *The Official NBA Guide* (annual), and *NBA Register* (annual), published by *The Sporting News,* which give the records for the preceding year and the career surveys of all players in that year; and *The Official National Collegiate Athletic Association Basketball Guide* (annual), with U.S. college records, schedules, and statistics.

(L.Do.)

(*Ice hockey*): The history of the game is presented in BRIAN MCFARLANE, *60 Years of Hockey: The Intimate Story Behind North America's Fastest, Most Exciting Sport: Complete Statistics and Records* (1976); S. KIP FARRIGTON, JR., *Skates, Sticks, and Men: The Story of Amateur Hockey in the United States* (1971); JAY GREENBERG, FRANK ORR, and GARY RONBERG, *NHL, the World of Professional Ice Hockey* (1981), with profiles of players and discussion of strategy, great games, and the sport's eccentrics; STAN FISCHLER and SHIRLEY FISCHLER, *Everybody's Hockey Book* (1983), analyzing the structure, organization, and rules of every level from NCAA and IIHF through NHL; and J.W. FITSELL, *Hockey's Captains, Colonels, & Kings* (1987), exploring the Canadian origins of the game and including many new research findings. See also NATIONAL HOCKEY LEAGUE, *Official Guide & Record Book* (annual).

(S.I.F./S.W.Fi.)

(*Tennis*): MORYS G.L.B. ABERDARE, *The Story of Tennis* (1959), provides a historical survey; and MAX ROBERTSON, *Wimbledon: Centre Court of the Game: Final Verdict,* 3rd ed. (1987), is a history of tennis championships. See also ANGELA LUMPKIN, *Women's Tennis: A Historical Documentary of the Players and Their Game* (1981). BILL SHANNON (ed.), *United States Tennis Association Official Encyclopedia of Tennis,* new rev. ed. (1981), is an informative reference source, including records and statistics; for rules and techniques in all phases of the game, see UNITED STATES PROFESSIONAL TENNIS ASSOCIATION, *Tennis, a Professional Guide* (1984).

(B.S.Lo.)

(*Golf*): GEOFFREY COUSINS and DON POTTINGER, *An Atlas of Golf* (1974); and PAT WARD-THOMAS and CHARLES PRICE, *The World Atlas of Golf* (1976), review golf courses, the game, and important events in the game's history. Historical surveys include ROBERT H.K. BROWNING, *A History of Golf* (1955); CHARLES PRICE, *The World of Golf: A Panorama of Six Centuries of the Game's History* (1962), with chapters on pioneers, shotmakers, and masters; GEOFFREY COUSINS, *Lords of the Links: The Story of Professional Golf* (1977); and HERBERT WARREN WIND, *The Story of American Golf: Its Champions and Its Championships,* 4th ed. (1986). Championship and tournament results over the years, records, curiosities, brief biographies, and many other features are found in *The Golfer's Handbook* (annual). DONALD STEEL and PETER RYDE (eds.), *The Encyclopedia of Golf* (1975), is a highly regarded reference work.

(J.R.Go.)

(*Athletics*): MEL WATMAN (comp.), *Encyclopedia of Track and Field Athletics,* new ed. (1981), contains comprehensive information on the sport, its rules, records, and athletes. Historical works include ROBERTO QUERCETANI, *A World History of Track and Field Athletics, 1864–1964* (1964), on the early period; and WALLY DONOVAN, *A History of Indoor Track & Field* (1976). For current events, see *Track & Field News* (monthly); and *Athletics Weekly.* The history of records is traced in ROGER GYNN, *Guinness Book of the Marathon* (1984); BERT NELSON (ed.), *Olympic Track & Field: Complete Men's and Women's Olympic Track and Field Results, 1896–1976, Plus a Wealth of Other Olympic Esoterica* (1979), continued with *Olympic Track & Field, Vol. II* (1987), covering the 1980 and 1984 Olympic Games, and the 1983 World Track and Field Championships; DAVID WALLECHINSKY, *The Complete Book of the Olympics,* rev. ed. (1988); and CORDNER NELSON, *Track's Greatest Champions* (1986). For rules governing international track and field, see INTERNATIONAL AMATEUR ATHLETIC FEDERATION, *Official Handbook* (annual).

(B.Ne.)

(*Boxing*): HARRY MULLAN, *The Illustrated History of Boxing* (1987), is a comprehensive history of professional boxing. BOHUN LYNCH, *The Prize Ring: Illustrated by Reproductions of Old Prints, Several Oil Paintings, and of the Famous Byron Screen* (1925), traces the history of the sport from the bareknuckle period; and HARRY CARPENTER, *Boxing: A Pictorial History* (1975, reissued as *Boxing, an Illustrated History,* 1982), focuses mainly on the professional sport. See also NAT FLEISCHER, *The Heavyweight Championship: An Informal History of Heavyweight Boxing from 1719 to the Present Day,* rev. ed. (1961); and JEFFREY T. SAMMONS, *Beyond the Ring: The Role of Boxing in American Society* (1988). For comprehensive statistics, see *The Ring Record Book and Boxing Encyclopedia* (annual); and its British counterpart, *Boxing News Annual.*

(N.Co.)

(*Bowling*): Historical works include HERMAN WEISKOPF, *The Perfect Game: The World of Bowling* (1978); RAY NELSON, *A History of the ABC: American Bowling Congress* (1984); and WOMEN'S INTERNATIONAL BOWLING CONGRESS, *WIBC History: A Story of 50 Years of Progress, 1916/17–1966/67* (1967). For a general survey, see GEORGE ALLEN and DICK RITGER, *The Complete Guide to Bowling Principles,* 2nd ed. (1986).

(J.B.P.)

Sri Lanka

Sri Lanka (known as Ceylon until 1972) is an independent island state in the Indian Ocean lying off the southeast coast of peninsular India. The Republic of Sri Lanka has a parliamentary form of government and is a republic within the Commonwealth. The island is pear-shaped, with a maximum length of about 272 miles (435 kilometres) and a maximum width of about 140 miles; it has an area of 25,332 square miles (65,610 square kilometres). A shallow sea, Palk Strait, separates Sri Lanka from India; Talaimannar, on Sri Lanka's Mannar Island, is only 22 miles away from Dhanushkodi on India's Pāmban Island. A line of shoals called Adams Bridge runs between Sri Lanka and India immediately south of this point. Colombo is the capital of Sri Lanka, but Sri Jayawardenepura, about five miles outside Colombo, became the capital designate in 1982.

Sri Lanka is a country of great beauty, with scenery varying from the palm-fringed beaches of its coasts to the highlands of the interior, where the famous Buddhist Temple of the Tooth is located at Kandy, once the capital of an independent kingdom. Sri Lanka has also been traditionally associated with elephants, but their numbers have decreased substantially in recent years. The name Ceylon is an English word derived from the Sanskrit Siṃhaladvīpa, meaning "Island of the Sinhalese." The Sinhalese and Pāli name for the country is Laṅkā, and the prefix *Śri* is an honorific. The Tamil name is Īlam, or Ilaṅkai.

The article is divided into the following sections:

Physical and human geography

THE LAND

Relief. Like peninsular India, of which it forms a continuation, Sri Lanka is a fragment of an ancient southern continent that geologists call Gondwanaland.

Both peninsular India and Sri Lanka stand on the same continental shelf, the edge of which does not extend beyond 12 miles from Sri Lanka's coastline. This shelf is shallow, lying at a depth of between 30 and 40 feet (nine and 13 metres) in the Palk Strait and attaining a maximum depth of only about 210 feet. Beyond the edge of the continental shelf the depth increases to about 3,000 feet within two miles.

The relief of the island is dominated by a highland massif situated in the southern central part of the island. This is surrounded by an intermediate zone consisting of upland ridges and valleys, which are separated from the massif by well-defined scarps. The intermediate zone, in turn, is surrounded by an outer or lower coastal lowland zone, except in the southwest, where the land abuts directly onto the sea in the form of cliffs. Elsewhere there is a coastal fringe consisting of a series of lagoons, sandbars, peninsulas, dunes, and marshes. Five-sixths of the country lies at an altitude of less than 1,000 feet.

The four physiographic regions

Regions. For convenience Sri Lanka may be divided into four regions—the central highlands, the southwest, the east, and the northern lowlands. The central highlands, which were formed by faulting, have some fine scenery. The highest point is Pidurutalagala, a rounded peak 8,281 feet (2,524 metres) high; more renowned, however, is the pyramidical Adams Peak, 7,360 feet (2,243 metres) high, which lies to the southwest of Pidurutalagala and is a centre for pilgrimages by Buddhists, Hindus, Muslims, and even Christians.

The southern edge of the central massif consists of a rim of steep scarp running east to west and curving southward in the centre; at one point, called the World's End, the scarp wall forms an almost sheer drop of about 5,000 feet. To the north of the central highlands lies Knuckles Mountain, which is separated from the highlands by the valley of the eastward-flowing Mahaweli Ganga, Sri Lanka's largest river.

The southwestern region is also mountainous and includes the Rakwana, or Bulutota, Range, a continuation of the central massif. Its topography consists of elongated ridges, parallel valleys, and a trellis (crisscross) drainage pattern.

The east consists of an undulating plain dotted with isolated hills or inselbergs (steep-sided hills that remained after the landscape had been scoured by erosion). Among these hills are Westminster Abbey (named for its shape), Monaragalla, and Kataragama.

The northern lowlands region consists of rolling countryside intersected by rivers and marked by occasional ridges and isolated hills. In the extreme north, the Jaffna Peninsula, which is made of limestone, is associated with a coral reef. Several offshore islands have the same formation.

Geologic record. Forming part of a very old landmass, Sri Lanka has experienced a long series of geological events, including folding movements as well as uplifting movements that have resulted in the fracturing and faulting of rocks. These movements, in addition to providing differences in rock composition, account for the scarps that separate the different elevation levels. Climate has also exerted an influence upon the sculpturing of the land surface.

Nearly nine-tenths of the island is floored by rocks of Precambrian age (570,000,000 to 4,600,000,000 years old), consisting of schists (rocks changed by heat and pressure at depth and having a banded and foliated structure) and gneisses (imperfectly foliated rocks changed by heat and pressure, with alternating light and dark bands differing in mineral composition, and more coarsely grained than schists), overlain by sediments changed by heat and pressure. Among the sedimentary rocks, only a few outcrops of shale and sandstone of Jurassic age (from 136,000,000 to 190,000,000 years old) are to be found. These occur in the Tabbowa and Andigama areas; some coal has been found in them. The north and northwest areas are floored by sedimentary limestone of Miocene age (from 7,000,000 to 26,000,000 years old). Gravel deposits adjoining this sedimentary limestone belt may have been laid down in periods when the area lay under a shallow sea during the last 2,500,000 years. Sand dunes and alluvium are commonly deposited in coastal areas. Some coral formations occur at Mathagal in the north and in the Madampe-Ambalangoda area in the southwest.

The rivers

Drainage. The rivers of Sri Lanka are noted for their number rather than for their size. They radiate from the central highlands like the spokes of a wheel, except for the upper course of the Mahaweli Ganga, which has developed different characteristics from the fault movements that have shaped the terrain. Most of the rivers, however, tumble down in a series of waterfalls and cascades before reaching the plain. The Mahaweli Ganga is only 206 miles long and Aruvi Aru 104 miles long; the other rivers, of which there are more than 100, are all less than 100 miles in length. The mouths of the rivers are choked with sand.

Climate. Sri Lanka lies between 6° and 10° north of the Equator and consequently might be expected to experience an equatorial type of climate. Its position in relation to the Indian subcontinent and to the neighbouring seas, however, has resulted in modification of the climate, with a regime of monsoons (rain-bearing winds) being superimposed upon the equatorial regime. Further modifications are caused by relief.

Rainfall is the most important element in the climate. Although Sri Lanka is a small island, the distribution of rainfall is not uniform, varying from more than 200 inches (5,000 millimetres) to less than 40 inches a year in different parts. Further climatic variations in different places are the result of the seasonal incidence of rainfall. Because of elevation and aspect, the central and southwestern parts receive the most rain. Some strips along the extreme northwest and southeast coasts are described as arid because they receive less than 50 inches of rainfall a year; while this is a relatively large amount, much of the moisture is lost through evaporation, in addition to which there are several rainless months. Much of the rain is also lost because it runs off the surface. Cultivation in these areas is restricted to the short rainy season, except when irrigation is resorted to.

The southwest monsoon blows from May to October, and from December to March the northeast trade winds—locally known as the northeast monsoon—prevail. The monsoons are often irregular, beginning or ending earlier or later than expected, thus adding to the hazards of agriculture. Between the monsoons—from approximately October to December and again from March to May—normal equatorial conditions prevail.

The five climatic zones

While the north and east of the island are generally drier, and the south and west wetter, five climatic zones may be distinguished in terms of rainfall: the wet lowlands and the wet highlands in the west; the dry lowlands and the dry highlands in the east; and the arid zones, which, as already mentioned, are in the extreme northwest and southeast. At Colombo in the wet lowlands, annual rainfall amounts to 90 inches, and the average annual temperature is 81° F (27° C); at Watawala in the wet highlands, the annual rainfall amounts to 218 inches, and the average temperature is 65° F (18° C); at Trincomalee in the dry lowlands,

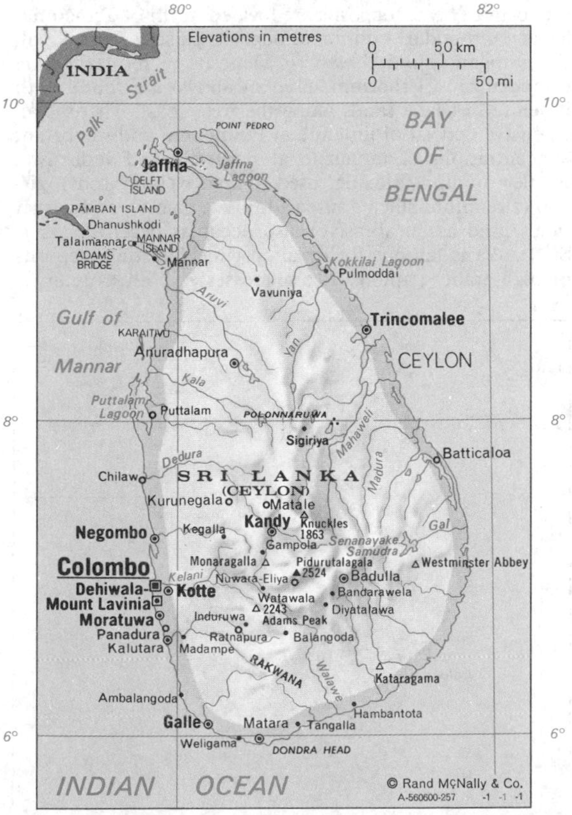

SRI LANKA (CEYLON)

MAP INDEX

Cities and towns

Name	Lat.	Long.
Ambalangoda	6·14n	80·03e
Anuradhapura	8·21n	80·23e
Badulla	6·59n	81·03e
Balangoda	6·39n	80·42e
Bandarawela	6·50n	80·59e
Batticaloa	7·43n	81·42e
Chilaw	7·34n	79·47e
Colombo	6·56n	79·51e
Dehiwala-Mount Lavinia	6·51n	79·52e
Diyatalawa	6·48n	80·57e
Galle	6·02n	80·13e
Gampola	7·10n	80·34e
Hambantota	6·07n	81·07e
Induruwa	6·46n	80·26e
Jaffna	9·40n	80·00e
Kalutara	6·35n	79·58e
Kandy	7·18n	80·38e
Kegalla	7·15n	80·21e
Kotte	6·54n	79·54e
Kurunegala	7·29n	80·22e
Madampe	6·41n	80·02e
Mannar	8·59n	79·54e
Matale	7·28n	80·37e
Matara	5·56n	80·33e
Moratuwa	6·46n	79·53e
Negombo	7·13n	79·50e
Nuwara-Eliya	6·58n	80·46e
Panadura	6·43n	79·54e
Pulmoddai	8·56n	80·59e
Puttalam	8·02n	79·49e
Ratnapura	6·41n	80·24e
Sigiriya	7·57n	80·45e
Talaimannar	9·05n	79·44e
Tangalla	6·01n	80·48e
Trincomalee	8·34n	81·14e
Vavuniya	8·45n	80·30e
Watawala	6·57n	80·32e
Weligama	5·58n	80·25e

Physical features and points of interest

Name	Lat.	Long.
Adams Peak	6·48n	80·30e
Adams Bridge	9·04n	79·37e
Aruvi, *river*	8·49n	79·55e
Bengal, Bay of	9·30n	81·40e
Dedura, *river*	7·36n	79·48e
Delft Island	9·30n	79·42e
Dondra Head *headland*	5·55n	80·35e
Gal, *river*	7·18n	81·46e
Indian Ocean	5·45n	80·40e
Jaffna Lagoon	9·35n	80·15e
Kala, *river*	8·18n	79·50e
Karaitivu, *island*	8·23n	79·47e
Kataragama, *inselberg*	6·23n	81·20e
Kelani, *river*	6·58n	79·52e
Knuckles, *mountain*	7·24n	80·48e
Kokkilai Lagoon	9·00n	80·56e
Maduru, *river*	7·52n	81·31e
Mahaweli, *river*	8·27n	81·13e
Mannar, Gulf of	8·30n	79·30e
Mannar Island	9·03n	79·50e
Monaragalla, *inselberg*	7·06n	80·38e
Palk Bay	9·30n	79·15e
Palk Strait	9·30n	79·30e
Pedro, Point	9·50n	80·14e
Pidurutalagala, *mountain*	7·00n	80·46e
Polonnaruwa, *ruins*	7·56n	81·00e
Puttalam Lagoon	8·07n	79·47e
Rakwana, *mountains*	6·30n	80·35e
Sangamankanda Point	7·01n	81·52e
Senanayake Samudra, *reservoir*	7·11n	81·29e
Walawe, *river*	6·06n	81·01e
Westminster Abbey, *inselberg*	7·02n	81·32e
Yan, *river*	8·55n	81·01e

annual rainfall averages 64 inches, and the temperature 82° F (28° C); at Mannar, on the island of Mannar in the arid zone, rainfall averages 40 inches a year, and the temperature averages 82° F (28° C). Nuwara Eliya in the wet highlands experiences some night frost but no snow. In Sri Lanka in general, temperatures vary little at different seasons; the annual and diurnal (daily) temperature variation does not exceed about 8° F (4° C). Most places in Sri Lanka have a high relative humidity.

Soils. In the wet zone, climate is the dominant factor in the formation and characterization of soils. Lateritic loams (reddish leached iron-bearing soils, composed of a mixture of clay, silt, sand, and organic matter) are the most common. They are generally well drained, friable when dry, but poor. In the dry zones, the same types of rocks result in semilateritic and nonlateritic earths. In the sedimentary limestone areas, thin mantles of red loams, rich in lime, are common. Along the lower courses of the rivers, and on their floodplains, rich rice soils occur. Sandy soils are prevalent on the coastal dunes and sandbars.

Plant and animal life. As Sri Lanka has been occupied by man for many centuries, the natural vegetation cover has been altered by cultivation. The open, rolling grasslands, known as *patanas,* in the eastern highlands of the Uva region are said to have resulted from the destruction of the forests that previously grew there.

Nearly 50 percent of the island, however, is still covered with forest, natural grassland, and wasteland. The best developed evergreen forests are to be found in the wet zone; the larger part of the dry zone forests are of poor composition.

Animal life, once abundant, is now becoming depleted. The elephant population has dwindled to a few hundred. The common forest animals are deer, leopards, bears, jackals, monkeys, wild boars, cheetahs, and wild buffalo.

Settlement patterns. The present-day pattern of population distribution bears little resemblance to that of the period before the advent of the Europeans, which ended with the arrival of the Portuguese in 1505. Earlier Sinhalese and Tamil settlements were confined to the dry lowlands of the north and were focused on Anuradhapura. This environment resembled that of the settlers' original homelands in South India, where rice cultivation was based on irrigation from water tanks. The forested wet zone of southern Sri Lanka remained almost uninhabited until plantation agriculture was introduced by the British in the early 19th century.

Rural settlement. Individual villages are surrounded with cultivated plots and orchards, from which vegetables, fruits, and spices are obtained. Elsewhere, temporary (shifting) cultivation is practiced; after being used for three to five years, the fields are allowed to revert to forest again.

Urban settlement. In the late 20th century about one-fourth of the total population of Sri Lanka was urban, and nearly half of this number lived in towns in the Colombo region alone. The urban population in other districts is relatively small.

THE PEOPLE

Sri Lanka is inhabited by a varied mixture of peoples who have immigrated to the island at intervals since remote times. The population, while consisting of nationals of Sri Lanka, is divided into several groups. The two principal linguistic groups are the Sinhalese, who generally are Buddhists, and the Tamils, who generally are Hindus. (The Sinhalese are divided between the low-country Sinhalese and the up-country, or Kandyan, Sinhalese. The Tamils are divided between the Sri Lanka Tamils and the Tamils of Indian origin.) A major minority are the Muslims (misnamed Moors), who are partly descended from Arab seafarers and speak Tamil. Relations between Sinhalese and Tamils have deteriorated in recent years, more as a result of current economic maladies than for historic reasons. Linguistic and religious groups—as well as the caste groups into which both Sinhalese and Tamils are divided—vie with one another to secure economic and political advantage, using pseudohistoric race myths and concepts in their struggles. Sri Lanka's ethnic and linguistic plurality is reflected in the design of its flag, which shows a yellow lion—symbolizing the legendary origin of the Sinhalese from a lion—on a red background, with a saffron stripe added to represent the Tamils and a green stripe to represent the Muslim minority.

The Sinhalese and Tamil linguistic groups

Other notable groups are the Burghers, who are of mixed Dutch and Eurasian origin; the Eurasians; the Malays; the Europeans who have adopted Sri Lankan nationality; and the Indians. The Veddas, who are believed to be the aboriginal inhabitants of the island, are very few in number and are now practically indistinguishable from other groups, with whom they have intermarried.

THE ECONOMY

Sri Lanka's economy is still precariously dependent upon the exports of its plantation products, which are subject to severe fluctuations in the world market prices as well as to the influence of other factors beyond national control, such as the development of substitutes, changes in people's tastes abroad, changes in manufacturing practices, or the conclusion of multilateral trade pacts. The necessity of diversifying the economy in the agricultural sector by reducing dependence upon imports, especially of food crops, and encouraging the domestic production of substitutes, and achieving a greater degree of industrialization has been partially realized in recent years. The country remains dependent, however, upon imports of rice, sugar, and other foods, as well as of clothing. The diversification of agriculture has been rendered inevitable by falling prices in the world market for tea and rubber—two of the mainstays of the export sector. Tea, rubber, and coconuts together earn most of Sri Lanka's foreign exchange, while tea alone accounts for the largest proportion. The output of rice has been increased through achieving higher yields. Yields in turn are being increased by irrigation, flood control, the use of artificial fertilizers, intensive cultivation, and the use of better seeds.

Resources. Mineral deposits include iron ore, ilmenite (iron titanate, a common black mineral), graphite, and gemstones. Iron ore deposits of high quality, suitable for electrosmelting and found at a shallow depth, have been located in the Ratnapura, Balangoda, Kalutara-Baddegama, Matara-Akuressa, Matale, and Chilaw areas, all in central or southern Sri Lanka. Ilmenite deposits in the form of beach deposits are located north of Trincomalee at Pulmoddai. Additional deposits exist at Turrukovil, Pamunugama, and elsewhere. Deposits of monazite (the principal ore of thorium, used in alloys) are found with ilmenite in beach sands along the west coast. There is an extensive deposit of ilmenite at Pulmoddai and important concentrations of monazite at Beruwela and Induruwa. Rutile (titanium dioxide, used to coat welding rods), zircon (zirconium silicate, used to line furnaces), and garnet sand (used as an abrasive) also occur as beach deposits. Sri Lanka is famous for its almost inexhaustible deposits of high-grade graphite. It also possesses both a quantity

Mineral deposits

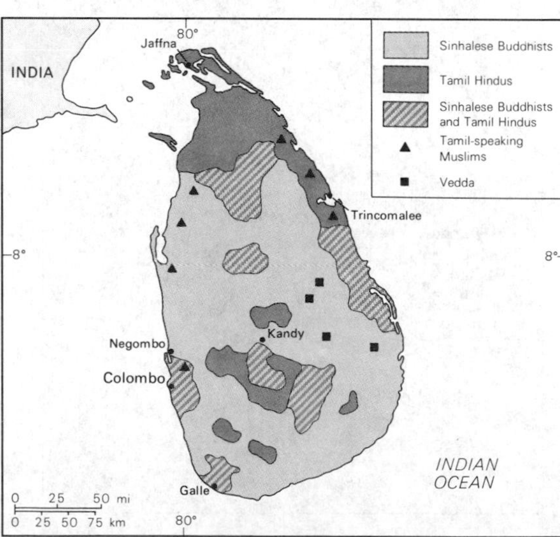

General ethnic composition of Sri Lanka.

and a variety of gemstones, including rubies, sapphires, starstones, and cat's-eyes (gemstones that change in lustre or colour, like the eyes of a cat). Other mineral deposits include large quantities of kaolin (china clay); other clays used for making tiles, bricks, and pottery; an inferior quality of mica; quartz, which is used for glassmaking; and limestone suitable for cement manufacture. Sri Lanka's lagoons and other coastal features are favourable for manufacturing salt from seawater by solar evaporation during the rainless period. Prospecting for oil is in progress, but so far without result.

In addition to the climate and soil, which favour such crops as tea and rubber, the forests constitute a substantial resource, although pure stands of timber are rare. Fish and other edible forms of marine life abound in the seas around the island.

More than 50 waterfalls, some perennial and of considerable size, are found in the hill country; in addition, major irrigation projects, such as those on the Gal Oya, Mahaweli, and Walawe rivers, are also capable of yielding much hydroelectric power.

Agriculture, forestry, and fisheries. As mentioned, tea, rubber, and coconut products are the principal sources of foreign exchange earnings. About one-half of the people in the labour force work in subsistence or plantation agriculture, primarily in rice and tea cultivation; rice is the staple food, although only two-thirds of the country's needs are met by domestic production. Rice is cultivated twice each year with one primary growing season, the *maha* (October–March), and one secondary growing season, the *yala* (April–September). The island's climate allows for almost year-round tea production, and tea is exported each month of the year. Some livestock is raised, including cattle, buffalo, sheep and goats, pigs, and chickens. The government is sponsoring a reafforestation program. Local timber production consists mostly of logs and firewood for domestic consumption.

Livestock

Sea fishing is more important than river fishing. Pearl fishing, once of importance, has been unsuccessful in recent years.

Mining and industry. Graphite is the principal mineral export. Most of the ilmenite produced is exported to Japan. The cement industry is based on the deposits of limestone in the northern part of the country. The production of salt is a government monopoly.

Manufacturing is still of minor importance. Several large-scale industries are engaged in the processing of agricultural produce. Cement, textile, leather, and ceramics industries have been developed. The paper industry uses domestic paddy straw, wastepaper, and imported pulp. Steel-rolling, plywood, and tire manufacturing industries are thriving. Industrial estates are being established to promote light industries. Foreign aid is being used to establish sugar-refining, petroleum-refining, chemical, and textile industries.

In 1978 the government established a free-trade zone on the outskirts of Colombo to attract new industry and foreign investment. Entrepreneurs are allowed to import materials into the zone duty free, provided the imports are used to manufacture products for export. The garment industry dominates the zone, but electronic components and appliances also are manufactured there.

Electricity is generated both by hydroelectric plants and by thermal plants, which are fueled by imported oil. Distribution is confined largely to the cities—Colombo, Nuwara Eliya, Diyatalawa, Norton Bridge, Bandarawela—and some villages.

Finance and trade. The Central Bank administers and regulates Sri Lanka's banking and monetary system and also issues the national currency. Commercial banks include some national banks and branches of foreign banks. Government-sponsored credit institutions include the State Mortgage and Investment Bank, the Agricultural and Industrial Credit Corporation, and the Development Finance Corporation. In 1975 all domestic banks were nationalized.

Sri Lanka's unfavourable balance of trade is exacerbated by its dependence upon agricultural products, which are subject to fluctuations in market value. Imports are largely petroleum products, rice and other foodstuffs, manufactured goods, raw materials, and machinery.

Management of the economy. *The public sector.* The state sponsors a wide variety of industrial corporations, among them a cement works, a chemical factory, an industrial estates corporation that provides ready-made factory units to small industry, a pulp and paper mill, a mineral sands processing plant, an oil refinery, and a steel-rolling mill. The government also sponsors numerous small manufacturing plants as a means of increasing employment. During the 1970s the government sought to improve agricultural productivity through major land reform. A limit was placed on the size of small, privately owned farms, and most of the major tea and rubber plantations were nationalized.

The private sector. Private industrial development is encouraged by such measures as tax exemptions, duty-free raw materials, and tax relief on investment. Foreign investment is also encouraged; it occurs mainly in the manufacture of textiles, electric appliances, transport equipment, metal, and glass. More than one-third of private industry is engaged in the production of food, beverages, and tobacco products.

Taxation. Taxes levied include an income tax on individuals and companies, a tax on wealth, a capital gains tax, and various customs and excise duties. Deficit budgeting has become a permanent feature, due to increased governmental expenditure on welfare services. The deficit is partially made up by market and administrative borrowing and foreign aid in the form of grants and loans.

Trade unions and employer associations. There are numerous trade unions, more than half of which are unions for public servants. Sri Lanka is represented in the International Labour Organisation. Industrial disputes are settled by labour tribunals. Employer associations include those for planters and manufacturers.

Tourism. A Ministry of State for Tourism, Broadcasting, and Information helps to promote tourism from abroad, in cooperation with the private sector and with the participation of international airlines and foreign governments. A number of hotels have been established in Colombo, seaside resorts developed, and additional transport facilities supplied.

Transportation. Sri Lanka has a good road system, although the roads are often uneven in quality. The surfaced roads are in the western lowland, the southern central highlands, and the Jaffna Peninsula in the north. There is also a ferry service from Mannar Island to Pāmban Island, India; it runs parallel to Adams Bridge.

The railways are owned and controlled by the government. They serve the flat, low country, the central hill areas, and the Kelani Valley in the southwest.

Colombo is the principal port. Other ports are Trincomalee on the east coast and Galle on the south coast. Galle handles the overflow of commercial shipping from Colombo. Trincomalee is one of the finest and largest natural harbours in the world. It was formerly a British naval base and now handles some of the island's export trade.

There is an international airport at Colombo. Air Ceylon maintains both international and domestic services.

ADMINISTRATIVE AND SOCIAL CONDITIONS

Government. Sri Lanka is an independent republic within the Commonwealth. The Ceylon Independence Order in Council, issued in 1947, was the basic constitutional document until it was superseded by the constitution of 1972. The former 30-member Senate was abolished in September 1971, and under the terms of the constitution of 1972 the House of Representatives was renamed the National State Assembly. This parliamentary system of government was supplanted by a presidential form of government in the constitution of 1978. The president replaced the prime minister as chief of state, with the power to appoint a prime minister and cabinet. The president is elected directly by the people for a six-year term, although an amendment ratified in 1982 allows the president to seek reelection after serving in office for at least four years. The members of the assembly, however, are elected indirectly by a system of modified proportional representation,

The presidential form of government

according to the number of votes cast for each political party. Assembly members also serve a six-year term. The constitution of 1978 transformed the office of president from a ceremonial position to a position of actual power, not accountable to the assembly.

Sri Lanka is divided into districts, each with an appointed governor and an elected development council. Local authorities consist of municipal councils, town councils, urban councils, and village councils.

Justice. Since independence, the justice system has undergone basic reform in an effort to streamline the colonial judicial and appellate hierarchy and to eliminate some of the judicial vestiges of colonialism. The Administration of Justice Law (1974) simplified the complex system of judicial appeal left from the colonial period; it eliminated the barrister and solicitor system of law practice and instituted in its place the single attorney-at-law practice; and it allowed women to serve as jurors. The system remains elaborate, however, comprising the Supreme Court, the Court of Appeal, the High Court, district courts, magistrate's courts, family courts, and primary courts. The common law of Sri Lanka consists of Roman-Dutch law, but aspects of English law have also been adopted, particularly in commercial matters. Customary law frequently operates in matters concerning the personal status of Kandyans (those living in the former kingdom of Kandy), Tamils, and Muslims. In civil and criminal matters, English procedure generally is followed; the penal code is based on that of India.

The armed forces. The armed services comprise the army, navy, and air force. The army and navy each have a regular force, a regular reserve, a volunteer force, and a volunteer reserve. Service is entirely voluntary; there is no conscription. The navy possesses a frigate, a number of small patrol boats, and smaller craft. The air force possesses a number of aircraft, including jets, light transports, helicopters, and trainers.

Education. Education is free, from kindergarten to university level. Almost all children between the ages of six and 11 attend school, and a high proportion continue until the age of 16 or 18. There are several technical and teacher training schools, colleges, and universities.

Health and welfare. Public health and medical care services are mostly planned and financed by the Ministry of Health, under which is the Department of Health, which is responsible for providing these services. Campaigns are conducted periodically against tuberculosis, cancer, venereal diseases, malaria, and leprosy. In addition to Western medical facilities, Sri Lanka in recent years has revived the practice of traditional medicine, which is conducted under government auspices.

The Ministry of Social Services

The Ministry of Social Services is responsible for public assistance, the relief of distress, the care and welfare of the aged and infirm, the administration of workman's compensation, and the rehabilitation of antisocial persons. Rural development activities include training in the performance of community services and self-help programs. There is a vigorous cooperative movement that is especially active in agriculture, industry, and fisheries.

Wages boards have been established to regulate labour conditions, including conditions of employment, wage rates, industrial safety, and related matters. Wage scales are reviewed periodically in relation to the cost of living index. Unemployment and rising living costs have, nevertheless, caused much labour and student unrest; the increase in the population has been the principal cause of these problems.

CULTURAL LIFE

Sri Lanka has a rich cultural heritage dating from the 3rd century BC. Its artistic tradition centres largely on Buddhist and Hindu religious art and the dance-drama. During the British administration the national arts suffered an eclipse, and since independence there has been a tendency to imitate Indian and Western art forms. The government, however, is aware of the importance of preserving traditional forms.

The national dance-drama

There are three main forms of the national dance-drama. The *kōlam* (a Tamil word for costume) play is a masked dance-drama that is performed annually. The devil dance, an expression of pre-Buddhist beliefs in spirits, is a masked dance performed to alleviate misfortune or illness. Most important is Kandyan dance, the sophisticated national dance. It is performed by elaborately costumed dancers and deals with mythological, historical, and naturalistic themes. It is taught at the National Academy of Dance in Kandy.

Since independence there has been a movement to adapt traditional dramatic forms to the modern stage. Translations of foreign plays are also performed.

Examples of national sculpture, painting, and architecture are seen in the remains of ancient works. These include colossal Buddha images, temples (especially around Kandy), and temple paintings. Other surviving art traditions include ivory carving, metalwork, lacquered woodwork, and basketry.

The Arts Council and the Government College of Fine Arts play an important role in the revival of folk arts and crafts. The national museums contain cultural and artistic collections. The Government Archives are in Colombo. Archaeological reserves, distributed throughout the island, include temples and cities.

The Sri Lanka Broadcasting Corporation provides national, commercial, and educational broadcasting services; it is responsible to the Ministry for Tourism, Broadcasting, and Information. Domestic programs are broadcast in Sinhala, Tamil, and English. There are also broadcasts to Southeast Asia and Europe. (K.Ku.)

For statistical data on the land and people of Sri Lanka, see the *Britannica World Data* section in the BRITANNICA WORLD DATA ANNUAL.

History

Sri Lanka has a continuous record of settled and civilized life for more than two millennia. The content and direction of this civilization has been shaped by that of the Indian subcontinent. The island's two major ethnic groups, the Sinhalese and the Tamils, and its two dominant religious cultures, Buddhist and Hindu, made their way onto the island from India. The various expressions of literate culture parallel those of India, and overall the culture and civilization of Sri Lanka are of the Indic pattern.

Relationship with India

Yet it is also clear that in many respects the island's civilization has achieved an individuality and identity that distinguish it from its neighbour. Cultural traits brought from India have undergone independent growth and change. The Sinhalese language, which grew out of Indo-Aryan dialects, exists only in Sri Lanka and has a distinctive and distinguished literary tradition. Likewise, Buddhism, which has had a continuing existence on the island, has all but disappeared from India after a Hindu revival and persists only in the Himalayan kingdoms. Sinhalese Buddhist art shows similar individuality.

A common experience of European colonial rule and its modernizing influences brought Sri Lanka closer to India and, with the attainment of independence in the mid-20th century, both countries developed similar social institutions and ideologies.

The historic connection between Sri Lanka and India was the result mainly of geographic proximity. Geologically an extension of peninsular India, Sri Lanka's separation from the Indian mainland dates from comparatively recent times. Historically, the island has also been influenced by its location along the east–west sea route. Even before the discovery of the oceanic route from Europe to India in the 15th century, Sri Lanka was a meeting point for Eastern and Western trade. The island was known to Greek and Roman cartographers and sailors and later to Persian, Armenian, and Arab navigators. With the coming of the Europeans, the strategic importance of Sri Lanka increased and Western maritime powers fought to control its shores.

Early Sri Lanka

The island's first human settlers were probably tribes of the proto-Australoid ethnic group, akin to the pre-Dravidian hill tribes of southern India. Remnants of these people were absorbed by the Indo-Aryans who immigrated from India around the 5th century BC and developed into the Sinhalese. The Tamils were probably later immigrants from Dravidian India, their migrations being spread out over a period dating from the early centuries AD to about 1200. The Tamil element was strengthened in the 19th century with the immigration of southern Indians to work on the plantations.

Sri Lanka possesses a continuous historical tradition preserved in written form by Buddhist chroniclers. The core of this tradition—the chronicle called the *Mahāvaṃsa* ("Great Chronicle") and its continuation the *Cūlavaṃsa* ("Little Chronicle")—constitutes a literary record of the establishment and growth of Sinhalese political power and of the Buddhist faith on the island. These works were written at various times by Buddhist monks and are based on other written records and on oral tradition. The *Mahāvaṃsa* accounts, supplemented by commentaries on them and by other historical works in Pāli and Sinhalese, provide a sequential narrative and a chronological framework for the history of the island up to the fall of the Kandyan kingdom in 1815. The excavation of ancient cities and monuments and the deciphering of inscriptions have supplemented and provided a corrective to the evidence from the written records.

PREHISTORIC RECORD

Studies of prehistoric Sri Lanka have not yet achieved a sequence of datable strata. The Stone Age appears to have begun with the Paleolithic, or Old Stone Age (about 1,750,000 years ago), when chert and quartz were abundant because of climatic changes. The earliest Stone Age implements found were made from those materials with a technique similar to that of the Old Stone Age cultures of India, which had identical environmental conditions. The Middle and Upper Paleolithic ages cannot be clearly distinguished because of the difficulty of correlating finds and putting them in a proper sequence. Stone implements of good workmanship, similar to those in India and Europe, have been discovered.

The transformation from food gathering to food producing and some form of settled life marks the transition to the Neolithic Age, or New Stone Age (probably more than 5,000 years ago). The grinding, rubbing, and polishing of stone tools; the use of the ax; and the use of wood, horn, bone, and other materials characterize this period.

The Mesolithic Age, or Middle Stone Age, which preceded the Neolithic Age, has produced rather more artifacts in the island; microliths have been found spread almost throughout, especially among the grasslands in the hill country and the sandy tracts of the coast.

COLONIZATION AND THE SPREAD OF BUDDHISM

According to the earliest Sinhalese tradition, recorded in the *Mahāvaṃsa,* the first Indian colonists on Sri Lanka were Prince Vijaya and his 700 followers, who landed on the west coast near Puttalam (5th century BC). They had been banished for misconduct from the kingdom of Sinhapura by Vijaya's father, King Sinhabāhu, who put them all in a ship and drove them away. According to tradition, when Vijaya's band landed on the island, it was inhabited by *yakṣas* (demons), whom they defeated and chased into the interior. Vijaya married a *yakṣa* princess and had two children by her. Later he drove her and the children away and sent to the Madurai court in India for a Paṇḍu princess and for wives for his 700 followers. Vijaya settled down to reign as king after a ceremonial enthronement and marriage and founded a dynasty. He had no heir to the throne, and toward the end of his reign he sent for his younger brother at Sinhapura. The brother, unwilling to leave his native land, sent his youngest son, Paṇḍuvāsudeva, to Sri Lanka. Paṇḍuvāsudeva landed with 32 followers at Gokaṇṇa (now Trincomalee) on the east coast. He was enthroned at Upatissagama and continued the Vijaya dynasty.

Early settlements

Indo-Aryan settlement. This traditional account contains a kernel of historical fact—the settlement of Sri Lanka by Indo-Aryan tribes from North India. Controversy exists as to the provenance of the early colonists; the legends contain evidence for both the northeastern and the northwestern parts of the Indo-Gangetic Plain. Vijaya's ancestors hailed from Bengal, but his father established himself subsequently in Gujarāt, from where the adventurers were put out to sea. Before arriving in Sri Lanka, their ship called at Supāra on the west coast of India. Their landing in Sri Lanka at Tambapaṇṇi, near Puttalam, would indicate their arrival from western India. Some early tribal names occurring in Sri Lanka also suggest connections with northwestern India and the Indus region.

While considerable evidence points to western India as the home of the first immigrants, it seems probable that a subsequent wave arrived from the east around Bengal and Orissa. One band of settlers landed on the east coast port of Gokaṇṇa, a natural port of disembarkation for vessels arriving from the Bay of Bengal. The traditional accounts of the arrival of Paṇḍuvāsudeva may portray a second wave of migration following the first mentioned in the Vijaya legend. Linguistic affinities between the early Sinhalese and the Prākrits of eastern India strengthen the hypothesis of a migration from this area.

The tradition speaks primarily of colonization by conquest, and tribes of conquerors led by a warrior nobility would have been an important factor in Aryan settlement. But this would have formed only one element of the Aryan migrations. Indo-Aryan traders probably reached Sri Lanka while sailing down the Indian coast; the natural products of Sri Lanka were lucrative items of trade and may have influenced some of these merchants to found settlements. Then there may have been settlements of Buddhist monks, as indicated in the traditional account of Paṇḍuvāsudeva.

The early settlers appear to have encountered a less civilized people, whom they pushed into the interior; some intermarriage probably took place. They also seem to have established contact with the Dravidians of southern India, who helped them in founding the first settlements. This feature is enshrined in the tradition that Vijaya secured a consort for himself and brides for his followers from the Paṇḍu kingdom of Madurai, if this may be presumed to be the Pāṇḍyan Tamil kingdom of southern India.

Indo-Aryan settlements grew in different parts of the island from about the 5th century BC. The settlers came in numerous clans or tribes; the most powerful were the Sinhalas, who eventually gave their name to the descendants of the various groups. The earliest settlers were those on the west-central coast, who pushed inland along the Malwatu Oya and founded a number of riverbank villages. Their seat of government was Upatissagama, where the first kings of the Vijaya dynasty reigned. The settlers of the east coast moved inland along the Mahaweli Ganga. Somewhat later there was perhaps an independent band of immigrants who settled in Ruhuṇa in the southeast, on the mouth of the Walawe Ganga, with Mahāgama as the chief seat of government.

Tradition attributes the founding of the kingdom of Anurādhapura to Paṇḍukkābhaya, the third king of the Vijaya dynasty. With its growth as the strongest Sinhalese kingdom, the city of Anurādhapura and the nearby settlements flourished. Kings built up the city and developed it for urban life; they extended royal control over villages and outlying settlements. The establishment of strong government led to population growth and to extensive colonization of the north-central region. The political system was Brahminic, similar to that of Indo-Aryan kingdoms of the Gangetic Plain.

Conversion to Buddhism. According to Sinhalese tradition, Buddhism was first brought to Sri Lanka by a mission sent out under the patronage of the Mauryan emperor Aśoka (*c.* 269–232 BC) and led by his son, Mahinda. Mahinda and his colleagues were transported by air to the island, in the *Mahāvaṃsa* tradition, and landed on the Mihintalē hill, eight miles from the royal capital. There Mahinda chanced to meet the Sinhalese king Tissa and preached the king a sermon on Buddhism. The king was immediately converted and invited the missionaries to the city. The missionaries were settled in a royal pavilion in the city park of Mahāmegha from where they preached, first to members of the royal family and then to the people. Many embraced the new faith, and some took holy orders and joined the Buddhist *saṅgha* (community of monks). The king donated the Mahāmegha park to the *saṅgha,* and the monastery of Mahāvihāra was established and became the prime centre of Buddhism in Sri Lanka. Mahinda sent for his sister Saṅghamitthā, who arrived with a branch of the Bo tree at Gayā, sacred to Buddhists as the tree under which Buddha attained enlightenment. The sapling was ceremonially planted in the city. Saṅghamitthā founded an order of nuns. A *stūpa* (shrine), the Thūpārāmacetiya, was built by the king for popular worship. Thus, various institutions of Buddhism were founded in the kingdom, and the faith became its established religion.

Though the conversion of King Tissa is of historic importance, the spread of Buddhism among the Sinhalese must have been more gradual, before and after the reign of Tissa. This was the work of many monks, both foreign and local, who went into every village converting people and founding Buddhist institutions among them. By the 2nd century BC the Sinhalese had accepted Buddhism totally, and this faith helped produce a unity and consciousness on which subsequent political and economic strength was founded.

THE CLASSICAL AGE (C. 200 BC–AD 1200)

As Buddhism spread, the Anurādhapura kingdom extended its political control over the rest of Sri Lanka. This age of political centralization began with Duttagāmanī Abhaya (reigned 161–137 BC).

The Anurādhapura period. The Vijaya dynasty of kings continued, with brief interruptions, until AD 65, when Vasabha founded the Lambakaṇṇa dynasty. The Lambakaṇṇas ruled for about four centuries; their most noteworthy king was Mahasena (reigned 276–303), who constructed many major irrigation systems and championed heterodox Buddhist sects.

A Pāṇḍyan invasion from southern India put an end to this dynasty and, briefly, to Sinhalese rule in 432. Dhātusena (reigned 459–477) defeated the Pāṇḍyas and reestablished Sinhalese rule with a line of Moriya kings. His son Kāśyapa I (reigned 477–495) moved the capital from Anurādhapura to the rock fortress of Sigiriya. After Kāśyapa's dethronement the capital was returned to Anurādhapura.

From the 7th century there was an increase in the involvement of South Indian powers in the island's politics and in the presence of Tamil mercenaries in and around the capital. Mānavamma, a Sinhalese royal fugitive, was installed on the throne in 684 with the support of the Pallavas of South India.

Mānavamma founded the second Lambakaṇṇa dynasty, which reigned in Anurādhapura for about 400 years. The dynasty produced a number of distinguished kings who consolidated and extended Sinhalese political power. During this period, Sinhalese involvement with southern India was even closer. Sinhalese kings were drawn into the dynastic battles between the Pāṇḍyas, Pallavas, and Cōḷas. Invasions from South India to Sri Lanka and retaliatory raids were a recurrent phenomenon. The 10th century saw a weakening of political and military power, and the Cōḷas, hostile because of the Sinhalese alliance with Pāṇḍya, attacked and occupied the kingdom in 993 and annexed Rajarata as a province of the Cōḷa empire. The conquest was completed in 1017 when the Cōḷas seized the southern province of Ruhuṇa.

The Polonnaruva period. The Cōḷas occupied Sri Lanka until 1070, when Vijayabāhu liberated the island and reestablished Sinhalese power. He shifted the capital to Polonnaruva (Polonnaruwa), a city that was easier to defend, that controlled the route to Ruhuṇa, and the easterly location of which provided more time to prepare for South Indian attacks. The capital remained there for 150 years. The most colorful king of the Polonnaruva period, and indeed of Sinhalese history, was Parākramabāhu I (reigned 1153–86), under whom the kingdom enjoyed its greatest prosperity. He followed a strong foreign policy, sending a punitive naval expedition to Burma and an army of invasion to the Pāṇḍyan kingdom but achieved no permanent success. After Parākramabāhu, the throne passed to the Kaliṅga dynasty, and the influence of South India increased. Nissaṅkamalla (reigned *c.* 1186–96), a brother of Parākramabāhu's Kaliṅga queen, was the last effective ruler of this period. The last Polonnaruva king was Māgha (reigned 1215–36), an adventurer from South India who seized power and ruled with severity and disrespect for traditional authority.

Government. Kingship was the unifying political institution in the classical period, a symbol of the aims and achievements of the Sinhalese people. The kingship was essentially Brahminic, with strong Buddhist influences. The king's authority was supreme and was elevated by the adoption of Brahminic symbolism. There was a trend toward sanctifying the person of the monarch, with the adoption of extravagant titles and mythical genealogies, and a tendency to style kings as *ḍevas* (gods) and *bodhisattvas* (Buddhas-to-be). Although the absence of a definite law of succession was a weakness leading to many disputes, it had the advantage of ensuring the succession of the ablest candidate; it also gave rise to a strong element of personal despotism, and many kings put the stamp of their personalities on their periods of rule.

Authority of the kings

All of the kings were practicing Buddhists and patrons of Buddhist institutions; the support and blessing of the clergy was essential in a peaceful and continuous reign. This connection between kingship and Buddhism, which continued throughout the period, enabled Buddhism to flourish. Kings built, maintained, and endowed many shrines and monasteries, and intervened to establish order and prevent schism within the Buddhist church. Nobles and commoners too were lavish in their support, and thus Buddhist institutions prospered. Many beautiful temples were built with finely carved sculpture; monasteries throve as centres of learning in the Pāli and Sinhalese languages and in Buddhist philosophy.

The king was supported by an inner administrative hierarchy consisting of members of his family and of influential nobles. A council of state of the highest officers served in a purely advisory capacity. The administration was conducted by various departments whose ministers dealt personally with the king. The *yuvarāja,* the king's chosen heir to the throne, was given responsible office. The army was the major prop of royal absolutism, and the *senāpati,* or commander in chief, was the king's closest counsellor and confidant.

The country was divided into three divisions. Rajarata was the most important, administered under the king's personal control and embracing the most populated, prosperous parts of the country. Ruhuṇa, to the south and southeast, was next in importance and was always ruled by a high officer, often the *yuvarāja;* owing to its remoteness, it sheltered rebels and fugitives and was used by kings under attack to take refuge and organize resistance. Dakkhiṇadesa, to the west, was organized as a province in the mid-Anurādhapura period and was also ruled by a high-ranking viceroy. These divisions were subdivided into cantons (*maṇḍala*) and districts (*rattha*), and they had a descending hierarchy of local officials down to the village headman.

Society was divided into castes, each performing a certain occupation, but the divisions were not as deep as in India. The *govi,* or cultivators, made up the highest caste. Many other castes also engaged in farming. Administrative officials were drawn from the *govi* caste, which was stratified into chiefs, titled men, and peasants. Chiefs were important supporters of royal absolutism and helped administer the government. Nonagricultural people, the *hina,* were considered of lower rank and divided into occupational groups. These caste groups were endogamous; each lived in its own section, along particular streets. Castes were stratified in terms of status, with the lowest on the scale—the *caṇḍālas*—performing the meanest occupation. The nobility owned slaves who worked for them in their fields and also in their homes. Many of the professional castes were self-regulating to a great degree.

Social castes

Irrigation. The Sinhalese civilization was hydraulic, based on the storage and use of water for the regular cultivation of wet fields. The early Indo-Aryan settlers were cultivators of rice, and they settled along river valleys and other suitable lands. They began with simple schemes for damming rivers and storing water below them. Small village works, which stored water in reservoirs by tapping seasonal streams, spread throughout the country and were characteristic of every village; these were probably undertaken communally by the landowners of the village. With the increase in royal power, the attraction of greater revenue through greater production made kings play an active role in the construction of irrigation schemes. Beginning in the reign of King Vasabha (reigned AD *c.* 65–110), large perennial rivers were blocked with massive earthen dams to create colossal reservoirs. From these, water was led through canals to distant fields and through underground channels into the capital city. From this time the technical knowledge of irrigation became more sophisticated.

Further technical progress was achieved in the reign of King Mahāsena; a number of storage tanks and canals are attributed to him, the most outstanding of which is the Minnēriya tank and its feeder canals. Thenceforth the construction and maintenance of large-scale irrigation works became a regular preoccupation of kings. Reservoirs and canals studded the northern and north-central plains, tapping every source of water. Among the most noteworthy was the magnificent Parākrama Samudra in Polonnaruva, the crowning glory of Parākramabāhu's reign, with a storage area of over 5,000 acres for the irrigation of 18,000 acres.

The large works needed a great deal of coordination and central control; they required the mobilization of labour and technical skill at the construction stage and a bureaucratic machinery to operate them and keep them in repair. Regulations to coordinate cultivation of irrigated plots, to control the flow of water, and to collect water dues from the operators had to be administered effectively. These were major functions of the central administration; and in turn they increased the power of the king, to whom accrued the benefits of the resulting increased productivity.

A grain tax, the water dues, and trade in surplus grain were major sources of the king's revenue. They sustained strong political and military power for more than a millennium and enabled the dispatch of expeditions abroad. They also made possible widespread religious building, which culminated in the great age of Parākramabāhu I. His reign also witnessed the high point of Sinhalese creativity in the plastic arts and the greatest strides in irrigation.

DRIFT TO THE SOUTHWEST (1200–1505)

Political changes. After the death of Nissaṅkamalla, the Polonnaruva kingdom was weakened by a succession of ineffective rulers. Non-Sinhalese factions such as the Kaliṅgas and Pāṇḍyas gained power in Sri Lanka as a result of dynastic marriages with South Indian royalty; conflicts between these factions was a common feature. South Indian notables occupied positions of influence under Kaliṅga kings, and their power was buttressed by mercenaries of various races. Māgha's rule was a veritable reign of terror, disregarding traditional authority and established religion. Polonnaruva fell into the hands of non-Sinhalese elements, each vying with the other for power and office.

Rise of non-Sinhalese factions

Central control from Polonnaruva was weakened. Kings of foreign extraction ruling there were unable to exercise political control over outlying provinces. Members of the traditional ruling class gravitated to centres of Sinhalese power located away from the reach of Polonnaruva in strategic terrain relatively inaccessible and defensible from attack; Dakkhiṇadesa, or Māyārata as it was now called, was suitable for this. The first place chosen to reestablish the Sinhalese kingdom was Dambadeṇiya, about 70 miles southwest of Polonnaruva; Vijayabāhu III (reigned 1232–36) and his three successors ruled from there. They made occasional successful raids into Rajarata to attack the Kaliṅga and Tamil rulers but did not attempt to reoccupy Polonnaruva. Under Parākramabāhu II (reigned 1236–70) the Daṁbadeṇiya kingdom achieved great power; it was able to expel the Kaliṅgas from the island with Pāṇḍyan help and to repel an invasion from the Malay Peninsula.

Bhuvanaika Bāhu I (reigned 1272–84) moved the capital northward to Yāpahuva, an isolated rock, which he strengthened with ramparts and trenches. His successors moved the capital southward again to Kurunēgala, and *c.* 1344 to Gampola toward the central highlands. At about the same time, the Alagakōnāra, a powerful Sinhalese family, attained a strong position at Rayigama, near the west coast; the Muslim traveller Ibn Baṭṭūṭah, who visited Sri Lanka in 1344, referred to one of the Alagakōnāras as a sultan named Alkonar. In 1412 the capital was taken by Parākramabāhu VI (reigned 1412–67) to Kōṭṭe, a few miles from present-day Colombo; for a brief period under this king, the Kōṭṭe kingdom expanded and acquired sovereignty over the island.

Generally, the effective control of the Sinhalese kings of the period 1200–1505 did not extend far beyond their capital cities, though they often made extravagant claims. Taking advantage of the collapse of the Polonnaruva kingdom after Māgha's fall and of the drift of Sinhalese political authority to the southwest, a South Indian dynasty called the Ārya Chakaravartis seized power in the north. By the beginning of the 14th century it had founded a Tamil kingdom, its capital at Nallūr in the Jaffna Peninsula. The kingdom of Jaffnapatnam soon expanded southward, initiating a tradition of conflict with the Sinhalese, though Rajarata—by then a largely depopulated country—existed as a buffer between them. Ibn Baṭṭūṭah left a good description of the Jaffna kingdom and its trade.

A politically divided and weakened island was an enticement to foreign invasions in the 13th, 14th, and 15th centuries. The second Pāṇḍyan Empire was constantly interfering in the affairs of Sri Lanka; its forces often supported rival claimants to power and took back considerable sums in payment and booty including, on one occasion, the Tooth Relic—sacred symbol of Sinhalese sovereignty. The Malay ruler Chandrabhānu invaded the island in 1247 and 1258, for reasons not altogether clear. Forces of the Vijayanagar Empire in South India invaded Sri Lanka on a few occasions in the 15th century, and for a brief period the Jaffna kingdom became its tributary. Cheng Ho, the great admiral of the third Ming Emperor of China, led a series of expeditions into the Indian Ocean. In his first expedition (1405–07) Cheng landed in Sri Lanka but withdrew hastily; he returned in 1411, defeated the ruler Vīra Alakeśvara, and took him and his minister captive to China.

Economic changes. The drift of Sinhalese political power to the southwest had drastic social and economic

From E.F.C. Ludowyk, *A Short History of Ceylon*, © 1962 E.F.C. Ludowyk; published by Praeger Publishers, Inc., New York (1967); reprinted by permission of the publishers

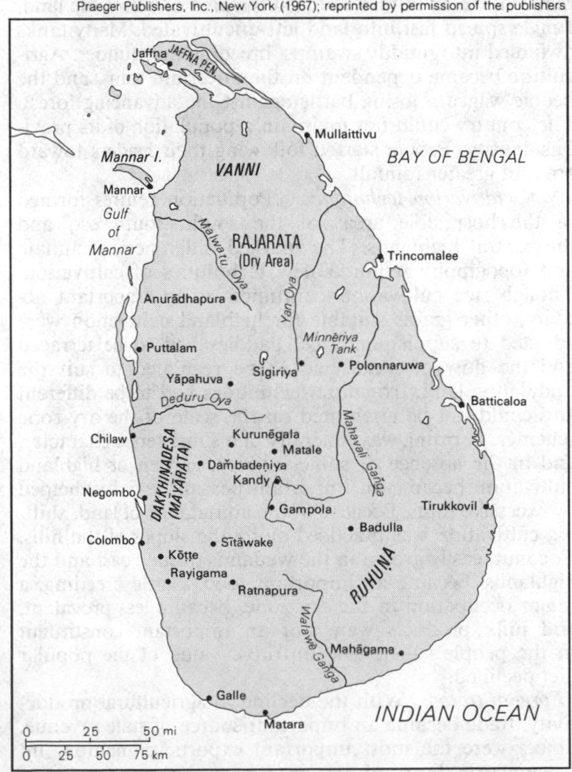

Medieval Ceylon.

Consequences of drift to the southwest

consequences. Population gradually shifted in the direction to which the capital was shifting; this led to the neglect of the interconnected systems of water storage. The once-flourishing Rajarata became a devastated ruin of depopulated villages, overgrown jungle, and dried-up tank beds, and the centres of Sinhalese population soon became the monsoon-wasted lands of the south, southwest, and the central highlands. Consequent changes in agricultural techniques, land use, ownership patterns, and ways of life followed swiftly.

Collapse of the dry-zone civilization. A combination of factors had brought about the collapse of Sri Lanka's dry-zone hydraulic civilization. The pursuit of an active foreign policy under Parākramabāhu I and the many wars it involved was a serious burden on the treasury. The Polonnaruva kings had to maintain a strong standing army and navy. The construction and maintenance of the magnificent Buddhist monuments of the Polonnaruva period must have strained the country's economy. The Polonnaruva state was thus carrying a burden of excessive expenditure that only continuous strong government and high productivity could sustain. The later Polonnaruva kings had neither the ability nor the favourable circumstances to maintain such a high level of revenue and expenditure.

The country's productivity depended on the elaborate system of irrigation, the operation of which was the work of a bureaucracy drawn from the landed gentry, both at the centre and at the village level. When the Kaliṅga dynasty came to power and non-Sinhalese factions rose to high office, the traditional Sinhalese aristocracy was eased out of authority. Mercenary military officers were spread out in the country to control law and order and to assume administrative functions. The Sinhalese noble families withdrew from Rajarata to the courts of Sinhalese leaders who had set themselves up in other parts of the country. Thus the traditional officialdom that had maintained the agricultural and irrigation system disappeared, and traditional methods broke down. The new military administrators had neither the capacity nor the interest to attend to this task. Many of the larger reservoirs breached, and smaller tanks that were fed by excess waters from them also lost their supply. (Some of the destruction was deliberate, caused by rival armies to flood a part of the country.) The amount of water stored for cultivation was reduced, which in turn reduced the area of cultivable land. Jungle spread fast into land left uncultivated. Many tanks dwindled into muddy swamps, breeding mosquitoes. Agriculture became dependent on the uncertain rains, and the people waged a losing battle against the advancing forest. The country could not maintain a population of its previous density. People started following their leaders toward areas of greater rainfall.

Changes in farming techniques

New cultivation techniques. Population centres formed in the hospitable areas of the south, southwest, and the central highlands. The marked difference in climate and topography required new techniques of cultivation. Though rice cultivation continued as an important activity, other grains suitable for highland cultivation were adopted to supplement rice. Paddies had to be terraced and the flow of water had to be regulated to suit the undulating land. Irrigation techniques had to be different and could not be attempted on the scale of the dry-zone schemes. Farming was generally of a subsistence character, and in the absence of sufficient rice, garden or highland cultivation became an important peasant activity, helped by excessive rains. Because of the abundance of land, shifting cultivation was practiced along the slopes of the hills. Coconut, easily grown in the wetlands of the coast and the highlands, became an important food. Cattle breeding, a major occupation in the dry zone, became less prevalent, and milk products were not an important constituent in the people's diet. The nutritive value of the popular diet declined.

The growth of trade

Foreign trade. With the decline in agricultural productivity, trade became an important source of state revenue. Spices were the most important exports: cinnamon, indigenous to the southwestern forests, became an export article in the 14th century; pepper and other spices also increased in export value. These articles were royal monopolies; kings entered into contracts with foreign merchants, fixed prices, and derived the revenue. The people of the land were not involved in any aspect of this trade, nor did they benefit directly from it. Colombo and Galle became prominent ports of external trade; smaller ports in the southwest became centres of coastal and Indian trade. Almost all of the traders were foreigners who settled in colonies in and around these ports.

The major international traders were the Arabs. (Arab interest in the luxury products of Sri Lanka dates from about the 10th century. Arab shipping and trade in the Indian Ocean produced Arab and Indo-Arab colonies in western India and coastal Sri Lanka.) Now Arabs became interested in cinnamon and spices, which began to fetch good prices in Western markets. In 1283 the Sinhalese king Bhuvanaika Bāhu I sent an embassy to the Mamlūk sultan of Egypt to seek a commercial agreement. Arab merchants had friendly contact with royal port officials of Colombo and Galle and helped collect customs and port dues. There is no evidence of seaborne trade by the Sinhalese themselves in this period, and the Sinhalese merchant groups of an earlier era appear to have declined.

Land control. Some significant changes took place in land relations and land control. The grain tax, which had been the pivot of the land revenue system—payable directly to the state in cash or kind—was on its way out during this period. This is partly explained by a breakdown in the administration: kings could not now maintain a specialized machinery for the assessment and collection of the grain tax and other miscellaneous land taxes. These were replaced by a system of service tenure, under which a large proportion of the land was held on the basis of service to the state. This service could be used in a multitude of ways beneficial to the state: to cultivate royal land, to be assigned to various officials as payment, or for the upkeep of public utilities. Tithe-paying lands and service lands were gradually merged. Each plot had a fixed obligatory service attached to it, and anyone who enjoyed that land had to perform that service. These services were extensively assigned to village and regional notables in order to attract their support. The commutation of tax for service also meant a decrease in the circulation of money; copper coins replaced those of gold and silver. This trend was further attentuated by the subsistence character of farming, which curtailed internal trade.

Cities. Capitals were now selected for their military defensibility, and cities were constructed with this in mind—relatively small, located in difficult terrain, somewhat isolated from populated areas. Communications from one place to another were difficult, and excessive mobility was discouraged for military reasons. Cities were not centres of economic life as in the past; they no longer attracted large groups of artisans, merchants, servants, and others dependent on the ruling groups. They were primarily of military importance, with a small cluster of buildings around the palace.

Buddhism and society. The Buddhist church had been a beneficiary of the hydraulic system of the dry zone. Lands, taxes, and water dues were assigned to temples, which also invested in land, had their own tanks excavated, and derived benefits therefrom. Now these sources of revenue had declined. Kings continued their patronage of Buddhism, but their wealth and power had diminished. Nobles and commoners were not rich enough to make substantial benefactions. The great monasteries of Anurādhapura and Polonnaruva were disbanded, and new institutions arose in and around the capitals of Dam̆badeṇiya, Kurunegala, Gampola, Rayigama, and Kotte, but they were not of the size or stature of their predecessors in the dry zone.

Changes in Buddhist institutions

The absence of strong political authority also affected the unity and coherence of the Buddhist church. In this period there was a greater incidence of indiscipline and schism than before. Kings were called upon frequently to purge the *saṅgha* of undesirable elements, and its purification had to be undertaken now and then. Close contacts were maintained, however, with Burma and Siam, and Buddhist missions were exchanged with these countries.

The influence of Hinduism on Buddhist institutions,

theology, and ways of life was more marked during this period. The ruling classes mixed extensively with Tamil royal and noble families, and there was an influx of Brahmins from South India to all parts of the country. *Deva* worship became a marked feature of popular Buddhism. Vedic and post-Vedic gods now assumed importance and were worshipped by kings and commoners in elaborate festivals.

One of the consequences of the drift of the Sinhalese kingdoms to the southwest and the establishment of the Tamil kingdom to the north was the division of the island into two ethnolinguistic areas. Before this division occurred, Tamil settlements were interspersed among the Sinhalese throughout the island. Then the northern and eastern areas became predominantly Tamil; their numbers were strengthened by fresh migrations from South India after the collapse of the Pāṇḍyan kingdom in the 14th century. Jaffna, as the capital of the Tamil kingdom, became the seat of Tamil Hindu culture, with a social organization somewhat akin to that of Tamil Nad. The landowning cultivators, or *vellalas,* were the pivot of the social structure and the holders of political and economic power. A number of lesser castes stood in varying degrees of service relationship to the *vellalas.* Hindu institutions were supported by the kings and the people and were strengthened by the influx of Brahmins. Brahminic temples sprang up in many parts of Jaffna, and rituals and public worship were regularly carried on. The Tamil language struck firm roots in the island and became one of its indigenous languages. Tamil literary culture was fostered by the support of the Jaffna kings and was enriched by the constant contact with South India, yet it developed an individuality of idiom and speech and acquired some linguistic characteristics that distinguished it from its South Indian parent.

Tamil Hindu culture

THE PORTUGUESE IN SRI LANKA (1505–1658)

By 1500 the Portuguese had begun their penetration of the Indian Ocean. In 1505 a Portuguese fleet commanded by Lourenço de Almeida was blown into Colombo by adverse winds. Almeida received a friendly audience from the king of Kōṭṭe, Vīra Parākrama Bāhu, and was favourably impressed with the commercial and strategic value of the island. The Portuguese soon returned and established a regular and formal contact with Kōṭṭe. In 1518 they were permitted to build a fort at Colombo and were given trading concessions.

In 1521 three sons of Vijayabāhu, the reigning king of Kōṭṭe, put their father to death and partitioned the kingdom among themselves. The oldest of the brothers, Bhuvanaika Bāhu, ruled at Kōṭṭe, and the two others set up independent kingdoms at Sītāwake and Rayigama. Māyādunnē, the king of Sītāwake, was an ambitious and able ruler who sought to expand his frontiers at the expense of his brother at Kōṭṭe. Bhuvanaika Bāhu could not resist the temptation of seeking Portuguese assistance. The Portuguese were eager to help the king, and the more he was pressed by Māyādunnē, the greater was his reliance on them. Bhuvanaika Bāhu defended his kingdom against Māyādunnē, who in turn allied himself with the Zamorin of Calicut (in India), an inveterate enemy of the Europeans.

Bhuvanaika Bāhu was succeeded by his grandson Prince Dharmapāla, who was even more dependent on Portuguese support. An agreement (1543) between Bhuvanaika Bāhu and the King of Portugal had guaranteed the protection of the prince on the throne and the defense of the kingdom; in return the Portuguese were to be confirmed in all their privileges and to receive a tribute of cinnamon. The prince was educated by Franciscans; in 1557, when his conversion to Christianity was announced, he became nothing more than a Portuguese protégé. This act undermined the Kōṭṭe dynasty in the eyes of the people. Māyādunnē's wars of aggression were now transformed into a struggle against Portuguese influence and interests in the island, and he annexed a large part of the Kōṭṭe kingdom. After his death, his son Rājasinha continued these wars successfully on land, though like his father he had no way of combating Portuguese seapower.

At the death of Rājasinha in 1593, the Sītāwake kingdom disintegrated for want of a strong successor. The Portuguese captured much of the lands of the Kōṭṭe patrimony and emerged as a strong power in the island. In 1580 Dharmapāla had been persuaded to deed his kingdom to the Portuguese, and, when he died in 1597, they took formal possession of it. Meanwhile a Portuguese expedition to Jaffna in 1560 had no lasting success. A second invasion of 1591, undertaken at the instigation of Christian missionaries, succeeded in installing a Portuguese protégé. Continued unrest and succession disputes made the Portuguese undertake a third expedition, and the kingdom of Jaffna was annexed in 1619.

The Portuguese were now in possession of all Sri Lanka but the central highlands and eastern coast, where an able Sinhalese nobleman, Vimala Dharma Sūrya, had established himself and consolidated his authority. The temptation for the Portuguese to establish hegemony over the entire island was strong, and some attempts were made. These led to protracted warfare and to popular hostility against the foreigners. The Portuguese expanded to the lower reaches of the central highlands and annexed the east coast ports of Trincomalee and Batticaloa.

The Portuguese possessions in Sri Lanka were a part of their *Estado da India;* a captain-general, with his residence at Malwāne, near Colombo, headed the administration and was subordinate to the viceroy at Goa. The most important civil officer was the *vidor da fazenda,* in charge of all revenue matters. An *ouvidor,* or judge, was in charge of all judicial affairs. The administrative structure of the Kōṭṭe kingdom was retained. Sri Lanka was divided into four *dissavanies,* or provinces, each headed by a *dissava.* Other territorial subdivisions were retained. Portuguese held the highest offices, though local officials came from the Sinhalese nobility loyal to the Portuguese.

Portuguese administration

The Sinhalese system of service tenure was retained and used extensively to secure the essential produce of the land such as cinnamon and elephants. The caste system was retained intact and all obligations that had been due to the sovereign now accrued to the Portuguese state. The payment in land to officials was retained and extended to Portuguese officials as well.

The Portuguese lacked a proper understanding of the traditional Sinhalese social and economic structure, and excessive demands put upon it led to hardships and popular hostility. Cinnamon and elephants became articles of monopoly; they provided good profits, as did the trade in pepper and areca nuts (betel nuts). Portuguese officials compiled a *tombo,* or land register, to provide a detailed statement of landholding, crops grown, tax obligations, and nature of ownership.

The period of Portuguese rule was marked by intense Roman Catholic missionary activity. Franciscans established centres in the country from 1543 onward. Jesuits were active in the north. Toward the end of the century Dominicans and Augustinians arrived. With the conversion of Dharmapāla, many members of the Sinhalese nobility followed suit. Dharmapāla endowed missionary orders lavishly, often from the properties of Buddhist and Hindu temples. After the Portuguese secured control of Sri Lanka, they used their extensive powers of patronage and preference in appointments to promote Christianity. Members of the landed aristocracy embraced Christianity and took Portuguese surnames at Baptism. Many coastal communities underwent mass conversion, particularly Jaffna, Mannar, and the fishing communities north of Colombo. Catholic churches with schools attached to them served Catholic communities all over the country. The Portuguese language spread extensively, the upper classes soon gaining proficiency in it.

THE KANDYAN KINGDOM

When Rājasinha I occupied Kandy about 1580, the ruler of that kingdom took refuge with the Portuguese. In 1591 the Portuguese launched an expedition to Kandy to enthrone Dom Philip, an heir of the dispossessed ruler. They were accompanied by an ambitious and distinguished Sinhalese military nobleman, Konnappu Bandāra. Dom Philip was installed as king but died under suspicious circumstances, and Konnappu Bandāra enthroned himself, proclaiming independence from the Portuguese and taking the regnal name of Vimala Dharma Sūrya. The demise of Sītāwake after Rājasinha's death left Kandy the only independent Sinhalese kingdom.

The Portuguese launched another expedition to Kandy in 1594 under Gen. Pedro Lopes de Sousa, planning to enthrone Dona Catherina, a baptized Sinhalese noblewoman. Popular hostility soon built up toward the continued presence of Portuguese troops. Vimala Dharma Sūrya utilized this to his advantage and, making use of guerrilla warfare tactics, routed the Portuguese army in 1594. He captured Dona Catherina, made her his queen, and legitimized and consolidated his rule. He expanded into the old Sītāwaka kingdom and emerged as leader of resistance to the Portuguese. Subsequently, the Portuguese made a few unsuccessful attempts to subjugate Kandy.

Arrival of the Dutch

Vimala Dharma realized that without sea power he could not drive the Portuguese out of Sri Lanka. He saw the arrival of the Dutch as an excellent opportunity to get naval support against his adversaries. The first Dutch envoy, Joris van Spilbergen, met the King in July 1602 and made lavish promises of military assistance. A few months later another Dutch official, Sebald de Weert, arrived with a concrete offer of help and, in view of favourable terms offered by the king, decided to launch a joint attack on the Portuguese. But a misunderstanding between the King and de Weert caused an altercation between the Kandyans and the Dutch, and de Weert and his men were killed.

King Senarat succeeded to the Kandyan throne in 1604 and continued to solicit Dutch support. In 1612 a Dutch envoy, Marcelis Boschouwer, concluded a treaty with Senarat. The King granted the Dutch extensive commercial concessions and a harbour for settlement on the east coast in return for a promise of armed assistance against Portuguese attack. The Dutch were unable to offer adequate assistance, and Senarat turned to the Danes. But by the time a Danish expedition arrived in May 1620, Senarat had concluded peace with the Portuguese. The truce was short-lived, and in 1630 the Kandyans, taking the offensive, invaded Portuguese territory and laid siege to Colombo and Galle. Again the absence of sea power proved a handicap, and another peace was concluded in 1634.

In 1635 Senarat was succeeded by his son Rājasinha II. The Dutch were now firmly established in Batavia in Java and were developing their trade in southern Asia. The King sent emissaries to meet the admiral of the Dutch fleet, Adam Westerwolt, who was then blockading Goa. The fleet came to Sri Lanka and captured Batticaloa from the Portuguese. Westerwolt and Rājasinha concluded a treaty on May 23, 1638, giving the Dutch a monopoly on most of Sri Lanka's cinnamon and a repayment in merchandise for expenses incurred in assisting the King. In May 1639 the Dutch fleet captured Trincomalee and in February 1640 the Dutch and Kandyans combined to take Negombo. But differences arose between the allies over the occupation of captured forts. The Dutch refused to give Trincomalee and Batticaloa to the King until their expenses were paid in full, and Rājasinha realized that the Dutch really wanted to replace the Portuguese as the rulers of the coast.

He nevertheless continued to work with them to expel the Portuguese. In March 1640 Galle was taken, but the progress of the allies was temporarily halted by a truce declared in Europe between the United Provinces and Spain, which at that time ruled Portugal and its overseas possessions. In 1645, the boundaries between Portuguese and Dutch territory in Sri Lanka were demarcated. Jan Thijssen was appointed the first Dutch governor.

The Dutch peace with the Portuguese and occupation of captured territory incensed the King and strained relations between him and the Dutch. In May 1645 war broke out between them. Though Rājasinha could not conquer the occupied lands, he made them worthless to the Dutch, who realized the advantage of coming to terms with the King. In 1649 a revised treaty was signed. The Dutch agreed to hand over some of the lands but again delayed because of the immense debt the King was held to owe them.

The truce with the Portuguese expired in 1652, leaving the Dutch free to resume the war. Kandyans launched attacks on Portuguese positions in the interior provinces of Seven Korles, Four Korles, and Sabaragamuwa, pushing them back to their coastal strongholds, despite fierce Portuguese resistance. Rājasinha was anxious to attack Colombo, but he was put off by the Dutch. He tried to secure guarantees from them for the return of this city after its conquest, and the Dutch made lavish promises. In August 1655 the Dutch were strengthened by the arrival of a large fleet under Gerard Hulft, and they laid siege to Colombo by sea and by land. In May 1656 the Portuguese surrendered the city to the Dutch, who shut the Kandyans out of its gates. Requests for the cession of Colombo met with evasive replies. Highly incensed, Rājasinha destroyed the lands around Colombo, removed its inhabitants, and withdrew to his mountain kingdom.

After a brief respite the Dutch resumed the expulsion of the Portuguese from Sri Lanka. Adm. Ryckloff van Goens arrived with a fleet to continue the attack on Portuguese strongholds in northern Sri Lanka. The Dutch took Mannar in February 1658 and Jaffna in June. They had replaced the Portuguese as masters of coastal Sri Lanka.

DUTCH RULE IN SRI LANKA (1658–1796)

Though the Dutch East India Company first controlled only the coastal lands, the Dutch gradually pushed inland, occupying considerable territory in southern, southwestern, and western Sri Lanka. In 1665 they expanded to the east coast, and thus controlled most of the cinnamon-growing lands and the points of exit and entry in the island.

Dutch administration

Government. The governor, residing in Colombo, was the chief executive; he was assisted by a council of the highest officials. The country was divided into three administrative divisions: Colombo, Galle, and Jaffna. Colombo was ruled by the governor, Galle and Jaffna by commanders. The three divisions were subdivided into dissavanies and districts (*korles*) in the traditional manner. Each dissavani was ruled by a dissava, invariably a Dutch officer; subordinate offices were held by Sinhalese or Tamils loyal to the Dutch.

Economy. Cinnamon, the most lucrative product derived by the Dutch from Sri Lanka, was collected at little or no cost and fetched high prices in European and Asian markets. The peeling of cinnamon was the obligatory duty of the *chalia* caste, which was sent into the woods by Dutch and native officials to obtain the required quantity of the spice. Similarly, another caste was used to supply elephants, also a valuable commodity of trade.

The Dutch continued the Portuguese policy of respecting the traditional land structure and service relationship, but they used it more methodically to further their interests. Officials were remunerated in land, and obligatory services were used for the state. Taxes in kind were collected for the state and used in trade. The Dutch encouraged agricultural production; they tried to increase rice and cash crop cultivation by land grants and tax concessions as well as through state-owned farms cultivated by slave and serf labour.

The Dutch tried to promote trade with neighbouring countries, but under a strictly controlled system. They sought monopolies in the export of cinnamon, elephants, pearls, areca nuts, and other products. This tended to stifle commerce, and thus trade with India declined, leading to a shortage of such essential commodities as rice and textiles. In the early 18th century some relaxation occurred, and private traders from India were admitted into the Sinhalese trade. But control of trade commodities and prices was sought through a system of passes and inspection, and major articles such as cinnamon, elephants, and pearls remained a strict monopoly. Smuggling of contraband goods was encouraged by local traders, Kandyan authorities, and even by Dutch officials. The directors in Holland sent strict instructions to maintain the restrictions, despite the pleas of officials in Sri Lanka for a freer trade, and much effort was spent to curb smuggling.

Law. The Dutch judicial system was well organized. There were three major courts of justice—in Colombo, Galle, and Jaffna; appeals from these courts were heard by the Colombo court. A circuit court, the *Land Raad,* was presided over by the dissava and sat in various districts. Native chiefs were invited to sit on cases involving local custom. The customary law of the land was administered in the courts, unless it clashed violently with Dutch jurisprudence.

Some attempt was made to codify customary law. The *Thesavalamai,* or laws and customs of the Tamils of Jaffna, was codified in 1707. A code of Muslim law was applied with the approval of Muslim headmen. Because of the difficulty in codifying Sinhalese law and custom, Roman-Dutch law was increasingly applied to the Sinhalese of the cities and the sea coast, especially to those who professed Christianity.

Religion. The Netherlands state was ardently Calvinist, and in the early years of Dutch rule an enthusiastic effort was made to spread the reformed faith in Sri Lanka. Catholicism was declared illegal and its priests were banned from the country; Catholic churches were given to the reformed faith, with Calvinist pastors appointed to them. Many Sinhalese and Tamil Catholics nominally embraced Protestantism. But the knowledge of the religion was rudimentary because there were not enough ministers, and very few of them could speak either indigenous language fluently. A body of Christian literature in Sinhalese and Tamil was published (after the establishment of a printing press in 1737). Churches had schools attached to them for elementary education, and there were two seminaries for higher education. Protestantism, however, did not have any substantial impact on the people.

THE BRITISH IN CEYLON (1796–1900)

The British East India Company's conquest of Sri Lanka, which it called Ceylon, occurred during the wars of the French Revolution. When the Netherlands came under French control, the British began to move into Sri Lanka from India. The Dutch, after a half-hearted resistance, surrendered the island in 1796. The British had thought the conquest temporary and administered the island from Madras, but the war with France revealed Sri Lanka's strategic value and persuaded the British to make their hold on the island permanent. In 1802 Ceylon was made a Crown Colony and, by the Treaty of Amiens with France, British possession of maritime Ceylon was confirmed.

Control of Kandy. Upon their arrival in 1796, the British established contact with the king of Kandy and contracted to replace the Dutch as protectors of the kingdom. As they began to organize the administration, the British realized that the continuing independence of Kandy posed problems: the frontier with Kandy had to be guarded at much expense, trade with the highlands was hampered by customs posts and political insecurity, land communications between West and East would be quicker if roads could be built through the centre. The advantages of political unification were obvious, but the Kandyans remained deeply suspicious of all foreigners.

Dissensions within the kingdom gave the British an opportunity to interfere in Kandyan affairs. They failed to reduce the kingdom in 1803 but succeeded in 1815 with the help of Kandyan chiefs whose relations with the king had deteriorated when the kingdom had reached an advanced stage of disintegration. They guaranteed Kandyans their privileges and rights and the preservation of customary laws, institutions, and religion. Though Kandy was administered separately, the trend toward reducing the status of its chiefs and of the Buddhist faith was unmistakable; this led to a popular rebellion against British control in 1818. After its suppression the Kandyan provinces were integrated with the rest of the country.

Though reluctant to upset traditional Sinhalese institutions, the British quickly set a reform process in motion. They abolished slavery, relieved native officials of judicial authority, paid salaries in cash, and relaxed the system of compulsory service tenure. Agriculture was encouraged, and production of cinnamon, pepper, sugarcane, cotton, and coffee flourished. Internal communications were extended. Restrictions on European ownership of land were lifted. There was intensive Christian missionary enterprise in education.

British reforms

The early changes under British rule were systematized by a series of reforms enacted in 1833, which laid the foundation for the subsequent political and economic structure of Ceylon. The British adopted a unitary administrative and judicial system for the whole island. They reduced the autocratic powers of the governor and set up Executive and Legislative councils to share in the task of government; unofficial members (not officials of the government) were gradually appointed to the Legislative Council. English became the language of government and the medium of instruction in schools.

Economic changes. The British eliminated restrictions on the economy. They abolished all state monopolies, did away with compulsory labour service, and promoted the liberation of the economy leading to new economic enterprises. Crown land was sold cheaply to cultivators to encourage plantation agriculture, and capital flowed in. Cultivation of coffee was profitable.

Coffee. From 1830 to the 1870s the phenomenal growth of coffee dominated Ceylon's economic development. Acreage under coffee expanded, and roads were constructed to fill the needs of coffee planters. Because of a labour shortage in the plantations, coolie labour under indenture contracts came from southern India in large numbers beginning in the 1840s.

Tea and rubber. In the 1870s coffee was destroyed by a leaf disease. Experiments with tea as a plantation crop in the 1880s were immediately successful, and tea spread along the upper and lower slopes of the hill country. About the same time, rubber plantations were developed both in the highlands and lowlands, and coconut was cultivated as a plantation crop.

Capital investment poured into tea and rubber, which grew as large-scale industries. These products needed a permanent labour force, and steps were taken to settle Indian labour in the plantations. Ancillary services soon arose. Increasing export trade led to the development of the Colombo Harbour and to railway and road construction. Opportunities were created for the Ceylonese entrepreneur, and employment was plentiful for the English educated.

Capitalist enterprise was restricted, however, to the urban areas and the plantation country. The rest of the country continued with subsistence agriculture, using traditional methods, though the isolation of the village was broken somewhat by roads and railways and the people there were brought into the monetary economy by the increased trade.

CONSTITUTIONALISM AND NATIONALISM (1900–48)

In the 19th century Ceylonese nationalist consciousness expended itself on the social, religious, and educational fronts. Revivalist movements in Buddhism and Hinduism sought to modernize their institutions and to defend themselves against Christian inroads by establishing schools to impart Western education unmixed with Christianity.

Constitutional reforms. Gradually this consciousness spread to the political plane. Regional and communal associations were founded in the educationally advanced parts of the country and began to articulate proposals for constitutional reform. They asked for some Ceylonese participation in the executive, a wider representation in the legislature on a territorial basis, and the adoption of the elective principle in place of nomination. These demands showed a common ideology and approach and revealed a desire to advance within the framework of the colonial constitution.

Because demands were not coordinated or vociferous, the imperial government ignored them. Constitutional reforms passed in 1910 retained the old structure with an appointed executive and a legislature with an appointed majority. There was, however, a limited recognition of the elective principle; an "educated Ceylonese" electorate was established to elect one member to the Legislative Council. Other Ceylonese members were to be nominated on a communal basis.

Growth of nationalist power. During World War I the forces of nationalism in Ceylon gathered momentum. Civil disturbances in 1915 and subsequent political repercussions helped the growth of political consciousness. British arrests of prominent Sinhalese leaders during what was at first a minor communal riot provoked widespread opposition. Leaders of all communities, feeling the need for a common platform to voice a common viewpoint, came together for the first political agitation in the island. In 1919 the Ceylon National Congress was formed, uniting existing Sinhalese and Tamil organizations. The Congress drafted proposals for constitutional reforms, demanding an elected majority in the legislature, control of the budget, and partial control of the executive.

A new constitution was promulgated in 1920 under the governor Sir William Manning and modified in 1924 to satisfy nationalist demands. It provided for an elected majority in the legislature, an increase in the number of territorially elected members, and the election of communal representatives. The country thus attained representative government, but no share was given in the executive, which remained under the governor and the official Executive Council. A finance committee of the legislature was formed, consisting of three unofficial and three official members, which could examine the budget.

The concession of greater power to the nationalists produced the first fissions among them. Sinhalese leaders wanted to do away with communal representation and make territorial representation universal, but minorities desired to retain it to secure power for their communities. Minorities broke away from the Congress to form their own organizations.

Preparation for self-government

A new constitution, framed in 1931, gave Ceylonese leaders opportunities to exercise political power and to gain governmental experience with a view toward eventual self-government. It provided for a State Council with both legislative and executive functions. Besides being a legislative council with an overwhelming majority of territorially elected members, the State Council was divided for executive work into seven committees, each electing its own chairman. These chairmen, or ministers, formed a board of ministers to coordinate their activities and to present an annual budget. The constitution granted universal franchise, thus for the first time bringing all Ceylonese into the political process. It was in operation for more than 15 years and provided the people and their leaders with valuable experience in democracy.

Dominion status. In response to pressure from Ceylonese nationalist leaders, the British in 1945 appointed the Soulbury Constitutional Commission, which drafted a constitution that gave Ceylon internal self-government, retaining some imperial safeguards in defense and external affairs. In 1947 the Ceylon Independence Act conferred dominion status on the colony. (S.Ara.)

SRI LANKA (CEYLON) SINCE INDEPENDENCE

The constitution of independent Ceylon provided for a bicameral legislature with a popularly elected House of Representatives and a Senate partly nominated and partly elected indirectly. A prime minister and his cabinet, chosen from the largest political group in the legislature, held collective responsibility for executive functions. The governor general, as head of state, represented the British monarch. In matters on which the constitution was silent, the conventions of the United Kingdom were observed.

When the first elections were held in 1947, a number of nationalist and communal parties came together to form the United National Party (UNP); it chose Don Stephen Senanayake as prime minister and advocated orderly and conservative progress. The UNP was dominated by the English-educated leaders of the colonial era, who were familiar with the British type of parliamentary democracy that had been established in the island, and it included people from all the ethnolinguistic groups of Ceylon. Its members were bound by the common ideals of Ceylonese nationalism, parliamentary democracy, and gradual economic progress through free enterprise.

Economically, the island's three export products were doing well in world markets and provided 90 percent of foreign exchange earnings. There was a sizeable sterling balance earned during the war. Politically, the coalition government had a substantial majority in Parliament and attracted support as it went. There were, however, some basic weaknesses in the structure. The political consensus that the government represented embraced the upper 7 percent of the population—the English-educated, westernized elite groups that shared in the values on which the structure was founded. To the great mass of Sinhalese-educated or illiterate people, these values appeared irrelevant and incomprehensible. The continued neglect of traditional culture as embodied in religion, language, and art forms created a gulf that divided the ruling elite from the ruled. Inevitably, leaders and movements arose that articulated the voices of traditionalism and revivalism.

Meanwhile, the country began to face economic difficulties. A rapidly increasing population and free import of consumer goods swiftly ate into the country's foreign exchange. The falling price of Ceylon's rubber and tea and the increase in the price of imported food added to the acute foreign exchange problem. Additionally, the expanded school system produced a large number of educated persons who could not find employment.

Sinhala nationalism

These various factors of political and economic discontent converged after 1955, and a new Sinhala nationalism was unleashed. It found a champion in S.W.R.D. Bandaranaike. In the 1956 elections the UNP was swept out of office, and Bandaranaike's Sri Lanka Freedom Party (SLFP) was installed in power at the head of a coalition of like-minded parties—the Mahajana Eksath Peramuna (People's United Front). The new government immediately set about changing the political structure. It made Sinhalese the sole official language and took measures for state support of the Buddhist faith and of Sinhala culture. It wedded the new nationalism to a form of socialism, in which the state was given a positive role in economic development and creation of economic equality.

The period of Sinhala nationalism was also a time of political instability. The language policy alienated the Tamils, who, under the Federal Party, carried on a bitter opposition. Educational policies alienated the small but influential Christian community. Cultural and Buddhist reforms alienated different factions within the Sinhalese.

Bandaranaike was assassinated in September 1959, and the movement suffered a setback and languished for want of a leader. After a period of political instability, his widow, Sirimavo Bandaranaike, was persuaded to gather together the fragments of the SLFP. In 1960 she formed a government that continued to implement the policies of Sinhala nationalism. All private schools were nationalized, and state-subsidized private schools were abolished, in response to a demand the Buddhists had made consistently because of the dominance of Christian missions in the country's educational system. The policy of nationalization of economic enterprise was carried further.

By 1965 the tide of Sinhala nationalism had begun to recede. Language and religion had become less important as political issues. An economic crisis, caused by increasing unemployment, the rising cost of living, an acute shortage of consumer goods, and the failure of state enterprise in industry and trade, made people look back to the UNP. This party gained the support of minorities, and in 1965 it returned to power under Dudley Shelton Senanayake, who, as the son of Don Stephen Senanayake, had served as prime minister (1952–53) after his father's death and briefly in 1960. Senanayake's government enjoyed a five-year term of office, during which it encouraged private enterprise and made an effort to extend agricultural productivity. These measures, while having moderate success, also tended to create inflation and to increase social inequality. The problem of unemployment of the educated could not be solved. The SLFP formed an alliance with Marxist parties and waged a campaign against the government that called for increased state control of the economy. In 1970 this coalition won a landslide victory, and Bandaranaike again became prime minister.

During its period of office (1970–77), the Bandaranaike government enacted reforms that restricted private enterprise and extended nationalization to a number of private industries, a large part of the wholesale and distributive trade, agency houses, and foreign-owned plantations. Measures aimed at reducing social inequality were enacted, and an ambitious program of land reform was put under way. These reforms satisfied the vast majority of underprivileged but did nothing to touch basic economic problems. The Sinhala-educated youth, impatient for radical change, were disillusioned within a year. Their discontent was headed by the Jatika Vimukti Peramuna (National Liberation Front), a group of revolutionary youth who launched an unsuccessful armed rebellion.

In a new constitution proclaimed in 1972, Ceylon became the Republic of Sri Lanka, with a president as the formal head of state but with effective executive power continuing in the hands of a prime minister and cabinet. All existing restraints on the lawmaking powers of the new unicameral legislature were removed. Buddhism was given "the foremost place," and Sinhalese was recognized as the official language.

Constitution of 1972

The continuing economic decline, however, could not be arrested. The acquisition of immense economic power by the state provided the party in power with the opportunity for patronage, nepotism, and corruption. By 1977, unemployment had risen to about 15 percent. The SLFP was left to face the polls on its own in July 1977, and it was defeated by a reorganized UNP under the leadership of J.R. Jayawardene, who became prime minister.

The Jayawardene government arrested the drift toward state control of the economy and took steps to revitalize the private sector and to attract foreign capital. One of its innovations was the creation in 1978 of a free-trade zone north of Colombo, where industries would be geared to an export market. The UNP government set about revising radically the constitution of 1972. In a new constitution promulgated in September 1978, the country was renamed the Democratic Socialist Republic of Sri Lanka and a presidential system, somewhat on the French model, was introduced. The president was head of state as well as head of the executive and of government. Sinhalese and Tamil were recognized as national languages, but Sinhalese was to be the official language. Jayawardene in 1978 became the first president under the new constitution.

Constitution of 1978

Political unrest, however, escalated in the 1980s. The Tamil minority in the country campaigned—with increasingly violent acts of terrorism and rioting—for an autonomous state; there were also instances of bloody anti-Tamil rioting. The unrest was damaging to the economy, and Jayawardene's government repeatedly invoked emergency powers in efforts to curb disorder. (S.Ara./Ed.)

For later developments in the history of Sri Lanka, see the *Britannica Book of the Year* section in the BRITANNICA WORLD DATA ANNUAL.

For coverage of related topics in the *Macropædia* and *Micropædia,* see the *Propædia,* sections 935, 936, 968, and 976.

BIBLIOGRAPHY

General: The administration reports of the various government departments and corporations in Sri Lanka contain much information, as do the publications of the national Association for the Advancement of Science and the Medical Association and such specialized publications as *Tropical Agriculturist, Industrial Ceylon,* and the *Ceylon Journal of Science.* E.K. COOK, *Ceylon,* rev. by K. KULARATNAM (1951), is a good general account, but information on the economy is dated. *A Concise Atlas Geography of Ceylon* (1971), is a helpful adjunct. Relevant chapters by B.H. FARMER in O.H.K. SPATE and A.T.A. LEARMONTH, *India and Pakistan,* 3rd ed. rev. (1967); and by K. KULARATNAM in S.P. CHATTERJEE (ed.), *Developing Countries of the World* (1968), also provide complementary material. H.A.J. HULUGALLE, *Ceylon* (1942), is a delightful general account in concise form. P.G. COORAY, *The Geology of Ceylon* (1969), is a comprehensive work. M.D. RAGHAVAN, *The Karāva of Ceylon* (1961); N.D. WIJESEKERA, *The People of Ceylon,* 2nd ed. (1965); and K. KULARATNAM, *Tamil Place Names in Ceylon Outside the Northern and Eastern Provinces* (1966), throw an objective light on myths and legends about the people and their origins. On the economy, see the INDUSTRIAL DEVELOPMENT BOARD, COLOMBO, *Statistical Guide* (1960) and *Research and Industry* (1970); *Statistical Abstracts of Ceylon 1967–68* (1970); and the *Statistical Pocket Book of Ceylon* (1969). See also TISSA FERNANDO and ROBERT N. KEARNEY (eds.), *Modern Sri Lanka: A Society in Transition* (1979); B.L.C. JOHNSON and M. LE M. SCRIVENOR, *Sri Lanka: Land, People, and Economy* (1981); and HERBERT KEUNEMAN, *Sri Lanka* (1983).

History: See S. ARASARATNAM, *Ceylon* (1964), an interpretative essay of historical development; S.D. BAILEY, *Ceylon* (1952), stronger on the period of Western impact than on early history; H.W. CODRINGTON, *A Short History of Ceylon,* rev. ed. (1947), valuable factual information, though somewhat outdated; B.H. FARMER, *Ceylon: A Divided Nation* (1963), an attempt to explain the contemporary situation in terms of past history; E.F.C. LUDOWYK, *The Story of Ceylon* (1962), a well-presented historical survey, using much recent research; S.A. PAKEMAN, *Ceylon* (1964), a historical survey with much emphasis on British and independent Ceylon; and K.M. DE SILVA (ed.), *Sri Lanka: A Survey* (1977), a collection of essays on political evolution, economy, and society.

Ceylon to 1500: See G.C. MENDIS, *Early History of Ceylon* (1932), first critical treatment of the pre-European period; C.W. NICHOLAS and S. PARANAVITANA, *A Concise History of Ceylon* (1961), the most up-to-date history for this period; *History of Ceylon,* vol. 1, 2 pt. (1959–60), a standard work containing a collection of essays by specialists on different aspects; *The Mahāvaṃsa,* trans. and ed. by W. GEIGER (1912), and *The Cūlavaṃsa,* trans. and ed. by W. GEIGER, pt. 1 and 2 (1929–30), traditional accounts of succeeding royal dynasties that provide an insight into traditional historiography; W. GEIGER, *Culture of Ceylon in Medieval Times* (1960), a remarkable attempt at social history of the Sinhalese from the 5th century BC to the 15th century AD; H.W. CODRINGTON, *Ancient Land Tenure and Revenue in Ceylon* (1938), a description of the traditional system of land tenure and the changes introduced by the European powers; A. LIYANAGAMAGE, *The Decline of Polannaruwa and the Rise of Dambadeniya, circa 1180–1270 A.D.* (1968), an authoritative study of a hitherto neglected period; P.E. PIERIS, *Ceylon: The Portuguese Era,* 2 vol. (1913–14), a detailed survey with emphasis on military and diplomatic history; G.C. MENDIS, *Ceylon Under the British,* 3rd. ed. (1952); L.A. MILLS, *Ceylon Under British Rule 1795–1932* (1933); E.F.C. LUDOWYK, *The Modern History of Ceylon* (1966), a study of the 19th and 20th centuries; T. ABEYASINGHE, *Portuguese Rule in Ceylon, 1594–1612* (1966), an authentic study of a period of Portuguese rule based on Portuguese and Sinhalese sources; C.R. DE SILVA, *The Portuguese in Ceylon 1617–1638* (1972), a detailed study of a period of Portuguese rule based on Portuguese and Sinhalese sources; S. ARASARATNAM, *Dutch Power in Ceylon 1658–1687* (1958), a study of political, economic, and social effects of Dutch rule in Ceylon; L.S. DEWARAJA, *A Study of the Political, Administrative and Social Structure of the Kandyan Kingdom of Ceylon 1707–1760* (1972), a pioneer study of the last independent Sinhalese kingdom; R. PIERIS, *Sinhalese Social Organization: The Kandyan Period* (1956), an analytical study of Kandyan Sinhalese society from the 16th century to the 18th century; K.M. DE SILVA (ed.), *History of Ceylon,* vol. 3, *From the Beginnings of the Nineteenth Century to 1948* (1973), consisting of the results of recent research on British Ceylon brought together in a collection of studies by specialists; W.I. JENNINGS, *The Economy of Ceylon,* 2nd ed. (1951), a survey of Ceylon's economy at the time of its independence, and *The Constitution of Ceylon,* 3rd ed. (1953); W.H. WRIGGINS, *Ceylon: Dilemmas of a New Nation* (1960), an analysis of developments that took place in Ceylon after independence; R.N. KEARNEY, *Communalism and Language in the Politics of Ceylon* (1967); C.A. WOODWARD, *The Growth of a Party System in Ceylon* (1969), a study of politics in Ceylon; A.J. WILSON, *Politics in Sri Lanka 1947–1973* (1974), a comprehensive thematic survey; and J. JUPP, *Sri Lanka: Third World Democracy* (1978), an analysis of the process of establishment of democratic politics in Sri Lanka.

(R.F.Hi./Ed.)

Stalin

During the quarter of a century preceding his death in 1953, the Soviet dictator Joseph Stalin probably exercised greater political power than any other figure in history. Stalin industrialized the Union of Soviet Socialist Republics, forcibly collectivized its agriculture, consolidated his position by intensive police terror, helped to defeat Germany in 1941–45, and extended Soviet controls to include a belt of eastern European states. Chief architect of Soviet totalitarianism and a skilled but phenomenally ruthless organizer, he destroyed the remnants of individual freedom and failed to promote individual prosperity, yet he created a mighty military–industrial complex and led the Soviet Union into the nuclear age.

Stalin's biography was long obscured by a mendacious Soviet-propagated "legend" exaggerating his prowess as a heroic Bolshevik boy-conspirator and faithful follower of Lenin, the founder of the Soviet Union. In his prime, Stalin was hailed as a universal genius, as a "shining sun," or "the staff of life," and also as a "great teacher and friend" (especially of those communities he most savagely persecuted); once he was even publicly invoked as "Our Father" by a metropolitan of the Russian Orthodox Church. Achieving wide visual promotion through busts, statues, and icons of himself, the dictator became the object of a fanatical cult that, in private, he probably regarded with cynicism.

The young revolutionary. Of Georgian—not Russian—origin, Joseph Stalin was born on December 21 (December 9, old style), 1879, as Iosif Vissarionovich Dzhugashvili, son of a poor cobbler in the provincial Georgian town of Gori in the Caucasus, then an imperial Russian colony. The drunken father savagely beat his son. Speaking only Georgian at home, Joseph learned Russian—which he always spoke with a guttural Georgian accent—while attending the church school at Gori (1888–94). He then moved to the Tiflis Theological Seminary, where he secretly read Karl Marx, the chief theoretician of international Communism, and other forbidden texts, being expelled in 1899 for revolutionary activity, according to the "legend"—or leaving because of ill health, according to his doting mother. The mother, a devout washerwoman, had dreamed of her son becoming a priest, but Joseph Dzhugashvili was more ruffianly than clerical in appearance and outlook. He was short, stocky, black-haired, fierce-eyed, with one arm longer than the other, his swarthy face scarred by smallpox contracted in infancy. Physically strong and endowed with prodigious willpower, he early learned to disguise his true feelings and to bide his time; in accordance with the Caucasian blood-feud tradition, he was implacable in plotting long-term revenge against those who offended him.

In December 1899, Dzhugashvili became, briefly, a clerk in the Tiflis Observatory, the only paid employment that he is recorded as having taken outside politics; there is no record of his ever having done manual labour. In 1900 he joined the political underground, fomenting labour demonstrations and strikes in the main industrial centres of the Caucasus; but his excessive zeal in pushing duped workers into bloody clashes with the police antagonized his fellow conspirators. After the Social Democrats (Marxist revolutionaries) of the Russian Empire had split into their two competing wings—Menshevik and Bolshevik—in 1903, Dzhugashvili joined the second, more militant, of these factions and became a disciple of its leader, Lenin. Between April 1902 and March 1913, Dzhugashvili was seven times arrested for revolutionary activity, undergoing repeated imprisonment and exile. The mildness of the sentences and the ease with which the young conspirator effected his frequent escapes lend colour to the unproved speculation that Dzhugashvili was for a time an *agent provocateur* in the pay of the imperial political police.

Work with Lenin

Rise to power. Dzhugashvili made slow progress in the party hierarchy. He attended three policy-making conclaves of the Russian Social Democrats—in Tammerfors (now Tampere, Finland; 1905), Stockholm (1906), and London (1907)—without making much impression. But he was active behind the scenes, helping to plot a spectacular holdup in Tiflis (now Tbilisi) on June 25 (June 12, O.S.), 1907, in order to "expropriate" funds for the party. His first big political promotion came in February (January, O.S.) 1912, when Lenin—now in emigration—co-opted him to serve on the first Central Committee of the Bolshevik Party, which had finally broken with the other Social Democrats. In the following year, Dzhugashvili published, at Lenin's behest, an important article on Marxism and the national question. By now he had adopted the name Stalin, deriving from Russian *stal* ("steel"); he also briefly edited the newly founded Bolshevik newspaper *Pravda* before undergoing his longest period of exile: in Siberia from July 1913 to March 1917.

In about 1904 Stalin had married a pious Georgian girl, Ekaterina Svanidze. She died some three years later and left a son, Jacob, whom his father treated with contempt, calling him a weakling after an unsuccessful suicide attempt in the late 1920s; when Jacob was taken prisoner by the Germans during World War II, Stalin refused a German offer to exchange his son.

Reaching Petrograd from Siberia on March 25 (March 12, O.S.), 1917, Stalin resumed editorship of *Pravda.* He briefly advocated Bolshevik cooperation with the provisional government of middle-class liberals that had succeeded to uneasy power on the last tsar's abdication during the February Revolution. But under Lenin's influence, Stalin soon switched to the more militant policy of armed seizure of power by the Bolsheviks. When their coup d'état occurred in November (October, old style) 1917, he played an important role, but one less prominent than that of his chief rival, Leon Trotsky.

Ministerial posts

Active as a politico-military leader on various fronts during the Civil War of 1918–20, Stalin also held two ministerial posts in the new Bolshevik government, being commissar for nationalities (1917–23) and for state control (or workers' and peasants' inspection; 1919–23). But it was his position as secretary general of the party's Central

Sovfoto

Stalin, 1950.

Committee, from 1922 until his death, that provided the power base for his dictatorship. Besides heading the secretariat, he was also member of the powerful Politburo and of many other interlocking and overlapping committees—an arch-bureaucrat engaged in quietly outmaneuvering brilliant rivals, including Trotsky and Grigory Zinoviev, who despised such mundane organizational work. Because the pockmarked Georgian was so obviously unintellectual, they thought him unintelligent—a gross error, and one literally fatal in their case.

From 1921 onward Stalin flouted the ailing Lenin's wishes, until, a year before his death, Lenin wrote a political "testament," since widely publicized, calling for Stalin's removal from the secretary generalship; coming from Lenin, this document was potentially ruinous to Stalin's career, but his usual luck and skill enabled him to have it discounted during his lifetime.

Lenin's successor. After Lenin's death, in January 1924, Stalin promoted an extravagant, quasi-Byzantine cult of the deceased leader. Archpriest of Leninism, Stalin also promoted his own cult in the following year by having the city of Tsaritsyn renamed Stalingrad (now Volgograd). His main rival, Trotsky (once Lenin's heir apparent), was now in eclipse, having been ousted by the ruling triumvirate of Zinoviev, Lev Kamenev, and Stalin. Soon afterward Stalin joined with the rightist leaders Nikolay Bukharin and Aleksey Rykov in an alliance directed against his former co-triumvirs. Pinning his faith in the ability of the Soviet Union to establish a viable political system without waiting for the support hitherto expected from worldwide revolution, the Secretary General advocated a policy of "Socialism in one country"; this was popular with the hardheaded party managers whom he was promoting to influential positions in the middle hierarchy. His most powerful rivals were all dismissed, Bukharin and Rykov soon following Zinoviev and Kamenev into disgrace and political limbo pending execution. Stalin expelled Trotsky from the Soviet Union in 1929 and had him assassinated in Mexico in 1940.

The policy of "Socialism in one country"

In 1928 Stalin abandoned Lenin's quasi-capitalist New Economic Policy in favour of headlong state-organized industrialization under a succession of five-year plans. This was, in effect, a new Russian revolution more devastating in its effects than those of 1917. The dictator's blows fell most heavily on the peasantry, some 25,000,000 rustic households being compelled to amalgamate in collective or state farms within a few years. Resisting desperately, the reluctant muzhiks were attacked by troops and OGPU (political police) units. Uncooperative peasants, termed kulaks, were arrested en masse, being shot, exiled, or absorbed into the rapidly expanding network of Stalinist concentration camps and worked to death under atrocious conditions. Collectivization also caused a great famine in the Ukraine. Yet Stalin continued to export the grain stocks that a less cruel leader would have rushed to the famine-stricken areas. Some 10,000,000 peasants may have perished through his policies during these years.

Collectivization of agriculture and industrialization

Crash industrialization was less disastrous in its effects, but it, too, numbered its grandiose failures, to which Stalin responded by arraigning industrial managers in a succession of show trials. Intimidated into confessing imaginary crimes, the accused served as self-denounced scapegoats for catastrophes arising from the Secretary General's policies. Yet Stalin was successful in rapidly industrializing a backward country—as was widely acknowledged by enthusiastic contemporary foreign witnesses, including Adolf Hitler and such well-known writers as H.G. Wells and George Bernard Shaw.

Among those who vainly sought to moderate Stalin's policies was his young second wife, Nadezhda Alliluyeva, whom he had married in 1919 and who committed suicide in 1932. They had two children. The son, Vasily, perished as an alcoholic after rising to unmerited high rank in the Soviet Air Force. The daughter, Svetlana, became the object for her father's alternating affection and bad temper. She emigrated after his death and later wrote memoirs that illuminate Stalin's well-camouflaged private life.

The great purges. In late 1934—just when the worst excesses of Stalinism seemed to have spent themselves—the Secretary General launched a new campaign of political terror against the very Communist Party members who had brought him to power; his pretext was the assassination, in Leningrad on December 1, of his leading colleague and potential rival, Sergey Kirov. That Stalin himself had arranged Kirov's murder—as an excuse for the promotion of mass bloodshed—was strongly hinted by Nikita Khrushchev, first secretary of the party, in a speech denouncing Stalin at the 20th Party Congress in 1956.

Stalin used the show trial of leading Communists as a means for expanding the new terror. In August 1936, Zinoviev and Kamenev were paraded in court to repeat fabricated confessions, sentenced to death, and shot; two more major trials followed, in January 1937 and March 1938. In June 1937, Marshal Mikhail Tukhachevsky, at the time the most influential military personality, and other leading generals were reported as court-martialed on charges of treason and executed.

Such were the main publicly acknowledged persecutions that empowered Stalin to tame the Soviet Communist Party and the Soviet elite as a whole. He not only "liquidated" veteran semi-independent Bolsheviks but also many party bosses, military leaders, industrial managers, and high government officials totally subservient to himself. Other victims included foreign Communists on Soviet territory and members of the very political police organization, now called the NKVD. All other sections of the Soviet elite—the arts, the academic world, the legal and diplomatic professions—also lost a high proportion of victims, as did the population at large, to a semi-haphazard, galloping persecution that fed on extorted denunciations and confessions. These implicated even more victims until Stalin himself reduced the terror, though he never abandoned it. Stalin's political victims were numbered in tens of millions. His main motive was, presumably, to maximize his personal power.

Role in World War II. During World War II Stalin emerged, after an unpromising start, as the most successful of the supreme leaders thrown up by the belligerent nations. In August 1939, after first attempting to form an anti-Hitler alliance with the Western powers, he concluded a pact with Hitler, which encouraged the German dictator to attack Poland and begin World War II. Anxious to strengthen his western frontiers while his new but palpably treacherous German ally was still engaged in the West, Stalin annexed eastern Poland, Estonia, Latvia, Lithuania, and parts of Romania; he also attacked Finland and extorted territorial concessions. In May 1941 Stalin recognized the growing danger of German attack on the Soviet Union by appointing himself chairman of the Council of People's Commissars (head of the government); it was his first governmental office since 1923.

Stalin's prewar defensive measures were exposed as incompetent by the German blitzkrieg that surged deep into Soviet territory after Hitler's unprovoked attack on the Soviet Union of June 22, 1941. Khrushchev claimed that Stalin was shocked into temporary inactivity by the onslaught, but, if so, he soon rallied and appointed himself supreme commander in chief. When the Germans menaced Moscow in the winter of 1941, he remained in the threatened capital, helping to organize a great counteroffensive. The battle of Stalingrad (in the following winter) and the Battle of Kursk (in the summer of 1943) were also won by the Soviet Army under Stalin's supreme direction, turning the tide of invasion against the retreating Germans, who capitulated in May 1945. As war leader, Stalin maintained close personal control over the Soviet battlefronts, military reserves, and war economy. At first overinclined to intervene with inept telephoned instructions, as Hitler did, the Soviet generalissimo gradually learned to delegate military decisions.

Role as supreme commander in chief

Stalin participated in high-level Allied meetings, including those of the "Big Three" with Churchill and Roosevelt at Tehrān (1943) and Yalta (1945). A formidable negotiator, he outwitted these foreign statesmen; his superior skill has been acclaimed by Anthony Eden, then British foreign secretary.

Last years. After the war, Stalin imposed on eastern Europe a new kind of colonial control based on native

Postwar foreign policy

Communist regimes nominally independent but in fact subservient to himself. He thus increased the number of his subjects by about a hundred million. But in 1948 the defection of Titoist Yugoslavia from the Soviet camp struck a severe blow to world Communism as a Stalin-dominated monolith. To prevent other client states from following Tito's example, Stalin instigated local show trials, manipulated like those of the Great Purge of the 1930s in Russia, in which satellite Communist leaders confessed to Titoism, many being executed.

Far from continuing his wartime alliance with the United States and Great Britain, Stalin now regarded these countries—and especially the United States—as the arch-enemies that he needed after Hitler's death. At home, the primacy of Marxist ideology was harshly reasserted. Stalin's chief ideological hatchet man, Andrey Zhdanov, a secretary of the Central Committee, began a reign of terror in the Soviet artistic and intellectual world; foreign achievements were derided, and the primacy of Russians as inventors and pioneers in practically every field was asserted. Hopes for domestic relaxation, widely aroused in the Soviet Union during the war, were thus sadly disappointed.

Increasingly suspicious and paranoid in his later years, Stalin ordered the arrest, announced in January 1953, of certain—mostly Jewish—Kremlin doctors on charges of medically murdering various Soviet leaders, including Zhdanov. The dictator was evidently preparing to make this "Doctors' Plot" the pretext for yet another great terror menacing all his senior associates, but he died suddenly on March 5, 1953, according to the official report; so convenient was this death to his entourage that suspicions of foul play were voiced.

Assessment. A politician to the marrow of his bones, Stalin had little private or family life, finding his main relaxation in impromptu buffet suppers, to which he would invite high party officials, generals, visiting foreign potentates, and the like. Drinking little himself on these occasions, the dictator would encourage excessive indulgence in others, thus revealing weak points that he could exploit. He would also tease his guests, jocularity and malice being nicely balanced in his manner; for such bluff banter Stalin's main henchman, Vyacheslav Molotov, the stuttering foreign minister, was often a target. Stalin had a keen, ironical sense of humour, usually devoted to deflating his guests rather than to amusing them.

Stalin's dinner parties

Foremost among Stalin's accomplishments was the industrialization of a country which, when he assumed complete control in 1928, was still notably backward by comparison with the leading industrial nations of the world. By 1937, after less than a decade's rule as totalitarian dictator, he had increased the Soviet Union's total industrial output to the point where it was surpassed only by that of the United States. The extent of this achievement may best be appreciated if one remembers that Russia had held only fifth place for overall industrial output in 1913, and that it thereafter suffered many years of even greater devastation—through world war, civil war, famine, and pestilence—than afflicted any of the world's other chief industrial countries during the same period. Yet more appallingly ravaged during World War II, the Soviet Union was nevertheless able, under Stalin's leadership, to play a major part in defeating Hitler while maintaining its position as the world's second most powerful industrial—and now military—complex after the United States. In 1949 Stalinist Russia signaled its arrival as the world's second nuclear power by exploding an atomic bomb.

Achievements

Against these formidable achievements must be set one major disadvantage. Though a high industrial output was indeed achieved under Stalin, very little of it ever became available to the ordinary Soviet citizen in the form of consumer goods or amenities of life. A considerable proportion of the national wealth—a proportion wholly unparalleled in the history of any peacetime capitalist country—was appropriated by the state to cover military expenditure, the police apparatus, and further industrialization. It is also arguable that a comparable degree of industrialization would have come about in any case—and surely by means less savage—under almost any conceivable regime that might have evolved as an alternative to Stalinism.

Stalin's collectivization of agriculture did not produce—either during his lifetime or during the decades immediately following his death—positive economic results remotely comparable to those attained by Soviet industry. Considered as a means of asserting control over the politically recalcitrant peasantry, however, collectivization triumphantly justified itself and continues to do so, remaining one of the dictator's most durable achievements. Moreover, the process of intensive urbanization, as instituted by Stalin, continued after his death in what still remained a population more predominantly rural than that of any other major industrial country. In 1937, 56 percent of the population was recorded as engaged in agriculture or forestry; by 1958 that proportion had dropped to 42 percent, very largely as a result of Stalin's policies.

The most lasting of all the dictator's achievements may prove to be his elaborately bureaucratized administrative machinery based on the interlinking of the Communist Party, ministries, legislative bodies, trade unions, political police, and armed forces, as also on a host of other meshing control devices. During the two decades following the dictator's death, these continued to supply the essential management levers of Soviet society, often remaining under the control of individuals who had risen to prominence during the years of the Stalinist terror. But the element of total personal dictatorship did not survive Stalin in its most extreme form. One result of his death was the resurgence of the Communist Party as the primary centre of power, after years during which that organization, along with all other Soviet institutions, had been subordinated to a single man's whim. Yet, despite the great power wielded by Stalin's successors as party leaders, they became no more than dominant figures within the framework of a ruling oligarchy. They did not develop into potentates responsible to themselves alone, such as Stalin was during his quarter of a century's virtually unchallenged rule.

That Stalin's system persists, in all its major essentials, after the death of its creator is partly due to the very excess of severity practiced by the great tyrant. Not only did his methods crush initiative among Soviet administrators, physically destroying many, but they also left a legacy of remembered fear so extreme as to render continuing post-Stalin restrictions tolerable to the population; the people would have more bitterly resented—might even, perhaps, have rejected—such rigours, had it not been for their vivid recollection of repressions immeasurably harsher. Just as Hitler's wartime cruelty toward the Soviet population turned Stalin into a genuine national hero—making him the Soviet Union's champion against an alien terror even worse than his own—so too Stalin's successors owed the stability of their system in part to the comparison, still fresh in many minds, with the far worse conditions that obtained during the despot's sway.

Reputation

Stalin has arguably made a greater impact on the lives of more individuals than any other figure in history. But the evaluation of his overall achievement still remains, nearly two decades after his death, a highly controversial matter. Historians have not yet reached any definitive consensus of opinion on the worth of his accomplishments, and it is unlikely that they ever will. To the American scholar George F. Kennan, Stalin is a great man, but one great in his "incredible criminality . . . a criminality effectively without limits," while Robert C. Tucker, an American specialist on Soviet affairs, has described Stalin as a 20th-century Ivan the Terrible. To the British historian E.H. Carr, the Georgian dictator appears as a ruthless, vigorous figure, but one lacking in originality—a comparative nonentity thrust into greatness by the inexorable march of the great revolution that he found himself leading. To the late Isaac Deutscher, the author of biographies of Trotsky and Stalin—who, like Carr, broadly accepts Trotsky's version of Stalin as a somewhat mediocre personage—Stalin represents a lamentably deviant element in the evolution of Marxism. Neither Deutscher nor Carr has found Stalin's truly appalling record sufficiently impressive to raise doubts about the ultimate value of the Russian October Revolution's historic achievements.

To such views, each illuminating a facet of Stalin's personality, may be added the suggestion that Stalin was anything but a plodding mediocrity, being rather a man of superlative, all-transcending talent. His special brilliance was, however, narrowly specialized and confined within the single crucial area of creative political manipulation. Outside the realm of pioneering political maneuver, in which Stalin's flair remains unsurpassed, his qualities appear in no way superhuman, apart perhaps from the dogged persistence with which he was accustomed to pursue to the death both his manifold goals and his innumerable enemies. (R.F.Hi.)

MAJOR WORKS

BOOKS: *Anarkhizm ili sotsializm?* (1949, Russian version of articles published serially in Georgian periodicals, 1906–07; *Anarchism or Socialism?,* 1950); *Natsionalny vopros i marksizm* (1914, based on the article "Natsionalny vopros i sotsial-demokratiya" in the periodical *Prosveshchenie,* 1913, and reissued as *Marksizm i natsionalnokolonialny vopros,* 1934; *Marxism and the National and Colonial Question,* 1935); *Na putyakh k Oktyabryu* (1925; selections translated as *The Road to Power,* 1937); *Voprosy leninizma* (1926, 11th ed., much enlarged, 1939; *Leninism,* 1940, or *Problems of Leninism,* 1940 and 1953), a monumental collection of treatises, articles, reports, and speeches including "Ob osnovakh leninizma" (1924; *Theory and Practice of Leninism,* 1925, and *Foundations of Leninism,* 1932); "K voprosam agrarnoy politiki v SSSR" (1929); "O proyekte konstitutsii Soyuza SSR" (1936; *On the Draft Constitution of the U.S.S.R.,* 1936, and *The New Democracy,* 1937); and "O dialekticheskom i istoricheskom materializme" (1938; *Dialectical and Historical Materialism,* 1941); *Ob oppozitsii* (1928), a massive collection of writings of the period 1921–27; *O pravom uklone v VKP(b)* (speech of 1929 published integrally as a separate book in 1954); *O nedostatkakh partiynoy raboty i merakh likvidatsy Trotskistskikh i inykh dvurushnikov* (1937); *Istoriya Vsesoyuznoy Kommunisticheskoy Partii (Bolshevikov): Kratky kurs* (1938, ostensibly the work of a party committee, but wholly Stalinian in inspiration; *Short History of the Communist Party of the Soviet Union,* 1939); *Iosif Vissarionovich Stalin: Kratkaya biografiya* (1940, 2nd ed. 1947, likewise ostensibly a collective production; *Stalin,* 1943); *O Velikoy Otechestvennoy Voyne Sovetskogo Soyuza* (1942, 5th ed., much enlarged, 1946–52; *The Great Patriotic War of the Soviet Union,* 1945, or *War Speeches, Orders of the Day, and Answers to Foreign Press Correspondents during the Great Patriotic War, July 3, 1941–June 22nd, 1945,* 1946); *Marksizm i voprosy yazykoznaniya* (1950; *Marxism and Linguistics,* 1951); *Ekonomicheskie problemy sotsializma v SSSR* (1952; *Economic Problems of Socialism in the U.S.S.R.,* 1952); *Perepiska Predsedatelya Sovieta Ministrov SSSR s prezidentami SShA i premier-ministrami Velikobritanii vo vremya Velikoy Otechestvennoy Voyny* (1957; *Correspondence with Churchill, Attlee, Roosevelt and Truman, 1941–45,* 2 pt., 1958).

BIBLIOGRAPHY. The standard Soviet edition of Stalin's works in Russian is his *Сочинения,* 13 vol. (1946–51), covering publications up to January 1934. His later works have been issued in Russian in similar format by the Hoover Institution; ROBERT H. MCNEAL (ed.), *Сочинения* 3 vol. (1967), is considered to be the extension, as vol. 14–16, of the standard edition. The standard edition has been translated into English and published in Moscow: IOSIF STALIN, *Works,* 13 vol. (1952); a selection of Stalin's works in English is BRUCE FRANKLIN (ed.), *The Essential Stalin: Major Theoretical Writings, 1905–52* (1972). An annotated bibliography by ROBERT H. MCNEAL, *Stalin's Works* (1967), considers the authenticity of material in Russian attributed to Stalin.

There is no definitive biography of Stalin. The most useful of published studies include ROBERT PAYNE, *Rise and Fall of Stalin* (1965, reissued 1968); ISAAC DEUTSCHER, *Stalin: A Political Biography,* 2nd ed. (1966, reissued 1978), Marxist in its approach; LEON TROTSKY, *Stalin: An Appraisal of the Man and His Influence,* new ed. (1967, reprinted 1970), and *The Stalin School of Falsification,* 3rd ed. (1972; originally published in Russian, 1932), both denunciatory; BORIS SOUVARINE, *Stalin: A Critical Survey of Bolshevism* (1939, reprinted 1972); and BERTRAM D. WOLFE, *Three Who Made a Revolution,* 4th rev. ed. (1964, reprinted 1978). *Stalin,* ed. by THOMAS H. RIGBY (1966), is an excellent short anthology of biographical and critical material. Later studies include ADAM B. ULAM, *Stalin: The Man and His Era* (1973); RONALD HINGLEY, *Joseph Stalin: Man and Legend* (1974); and IAN GREY, *Stalin: Man of History* (1979).

Reliable, detailed firsthand accounts of Stalin's domestic background are few, the only family memoirs not subject to Stalinist censorship being those published by Stalin's daughter, SVETLANA ALLILUYEVA, after emigration: *Twenty Letters to a Friend* (1967; originally published in Russian in the United States, 1967) and *Only One Year* (1969; originally published in Russian in the United States, 1969). For Soviet-censored memoirs by other family members, see *The Alliluyev Memoirs,* trans. and ed. by DAVID TUTAEV (1968).

On Stalin's prerevolutionary career, EDWARD ELLIS SMITH, *The Young Stalin: The Early Years of an Elusive Revolutionary* (1967), attempts to prove that the subject was an agent of the Tsarist political police; LAVRENTY BERIA, *On the History of the Bolshevik Organizations in Transcaucasia* (1949, trans. from the 7th Russian ed.), is the chief classic of Stalinist legend-building. For the historical context, see ROBERT C. TUCKER, *Stalin as Revolutionary, 1879–1929: A Study in History and Personality* (1973).

For the political background of Stalin's mature career, LEONARD SCHAPIRO, *The Communist Party of the Soviet Union,* 2nd ed. (1970), is valuable, as is JOHN A. ARMSTRONG, *The Politics of Totalitarianism* (1961); a more subjective version is ABDURAKHMAN AVTORKHANOV, *Stalin and the Soviet Communist Party: A Study in the Technology of Power* (1959; originally published in Russian in West Germany, 1959). BORIS I. NICOLAEVSKY, *Power and the Soviet Elite* (1965), is a collection of essays bearing on Stalin's activities from 1934 onward. See also KENDALL E. BAILES, *Technology and Society Under Lenin and Stalin: Origins of the Soviet Technical Intelligentsia, 1917–1941* (1978); and EUGÈNE ZALESKI, *Stalinist Planning for Economic Growth, 1933–1953* (1980; trans. from the French).

ROBERT CONQUEST, *The Great Terror: Stalin's Purge of the Thirties,* rev. ed. (1973), is the fullest account of the persecutions of 1937–38, on which ZBIGNIEW K. BRZEZINSKI, *Permanent Purge: Politics in Soviet Totalitarianism* (1956), is also helpful. See further *The Great Purge Trial,* ed. by ROBERT C. TUCKER and STEPHEN F. COHEN (1965), based on the official Soviet translation of the report of court proceedings; JOEL CARMICHAEL, *Stalin's Masterpiece: The Show Trials and Purges of the Thirties—The Consolidation of the Bolshevik Dictatorship* (1976); and ANTON ANTONOV-OVSEYENKO, *The Time of Stalin: Portrait of a Tyranny* (1981; originally published in Russian in the United States, 1980). F. BECK and W. GODIN, *Russian Purge and the Extraction of Confession* (1951, trans. from the German), remains a classic account of Stalin's terror. On this see also WALTER G. KRIVITSKY, *I Was Stalin's Agent* (1939; U.S. title, *In Stalin's Secret Service: An Exposé of Russia's Secret Policies by the Former Chief of the Soviet Intelligence in Western Europe,* 1939, reprinted 1979); and ALEXANDER ORLOV, *The Secret History of Stalin's Crimes* (1953), informative primary sources.

On Stalin's role as wartime leader, SEWERYN BIALER's anthology of Soviet memoir material, *Stalin and His Generals* (1969), is outstandingly useful; so too is HERBERT FEIS, *Churchill, Roosevelt, Stalin: The War They Waged and the Peace They Sought,* 2nd ed. (1967). See further ALEXANDER WERTH, *Russia at War, 1941–1945* (1964, reissued 1970); GEORGII ZHUKOV, *The Memoirs of Marshal Zhukov* (1971; originally published in Russian, 1970); ALBERT SEATON, *Stalin as a Military Commander* (1975), based on the memoirs of Russian generals from 1918 to 1953; H. MONTGOMERY HYDE, *Stalin: The History of a Dictator* (1971, reprinted 1982), especially useful for the coverage of World War II; and JOHN ERICKSON, *The Road to Stalingrad: Stalin's War with Germany* (1975), and *The Road to Berlin: Continuing the History of Stalin's War with Germany* (1983).

On the postwar period, see WILLIAM O. MCCAGG, *Stalin Embattled, 1943–1948* (1978), emphasizing foreign policy; TIMOTHY DUNMORE, *The Stalinist Command Economy: The Soviet State Apparatus and Economic Policy, 1945–53* (1980); and WILLIAM TAUBMAN, *Stalin's American Policy: From Entente to Détente to Cold War* (1982). NIKOLAI TOLSTOY, *Stalin's Secret War* (1981), presents testimony of victims of Stalin's purges. On Stalin's image after his death, see *The Anti-Stalin Campaign and International Communism: A Selection of Documents,* ed. by the COLUMBIA UNIVERSITY RUSSIAN INSTITUTE (1956); BERTRAM D. WOLFE, *Khrushchev and Stalin's Ghost: Text, Background, and Meaning of Khrushchev's Secret Report to the Twentieth Congress on the Night of February 24–25, 1956* (1957, reprinted 1983); and *The Stalin Dictatorship: Khrushchev's "Secret Speech" and Other Documents,* ed. by THOMAS H. RIGBY (1968). Further accounts include GEORGES BORTOLI, *The Death of Stalin* (1975; originally published in French, 1973); ALEC NOVE, *Stalinism and After,* 2nd ed. (1981); ROY A. MEDVEDEV, *Let History Judge: The Origins and Consequences of Stalinism* (1971, trans. from the Russian manuscript), and *On Stalin and Stalinism* (1979, trans. from the Russian). Studies of the effects of Stalinism on the 20th-century Communist movement include ROBERT C. TUCKER (ed.), *Stalinism: Essays in Historical Interpretation* (1977); and ROBERT C. TUCKER, *The Soviet Political Mind: Stalinism and Post-Stalinist Change,* rev. ed. (1971).

(R.F.Hi./Ed.)

Stars and Star Clusters

Stars are massive, self-luminous objects that shine by radiation derived from internal energy sources. Of the trillions of stars comprising the universe, many occur in pairs, multiple systems, and clusters. The members of such stellar groups are physically related through common origin and are bound by mutual gravitational attraction. Somewhat related to star clusters are stellar associations, which consist of loose groups of physically similar stars that have insufficient mass as a group to remain together as an organization.

This article describes the properties and evolution of both individual stars and stellar aggregates. Included in the discussion are the sizes, energetics, temperatures, masses, and chemical compositions of stars, as well as their distances and motions. The myriad other stars are compared to the Sun, strongly implying that "our" star is in no way special.

For coverage of related topics in the *Macropædia* and *Micropædia,* see the *Propædia,* Part One, Division III, especially Section 132.

The article is divided into the following sections:

General considerations

THE SUN AS A POINT OF COMPARISON

Variations in stellar size. With regard to mass, size, and intrinsic brightness, the Sun is a typical star. Its approximate mass is 2×10^{33} grams, its approximate radius 7×10^{10} centimetres, and its approximate luminosity 4×10^{33} ergs per second (or equivalently 4×10^{23} kilowatts of power). Other stars often have their respective quantities measured in terms of those of the Sun.

Table 1 lists data pertaining to the 20 brightest stars, or, more precisely, stellar systems, since some of them are double (binary) or even triple stars. Successive columns give the name of the star, its brightness expressed in units called visual magnitudes and the spectral class or classes (see below *Classification of spectral types*) to which the star or its components belong, the distance in light-years (a light-year being the distance that light waves travel in one Earth year: 9,460,000,000,000 kilometres, or 5,878,000,000,000 miles), and the visual luminosity in terms of that of the Sun (designated by the symbol ☉). All the primary stars (designated as the A component in the Table) are intrinsically as bright as or brighter than the Sun; some of the companion stars are fainter.

Many stars vary in the amount of light they radiate. Stars such as Altair, Alpha Centauri A and B, and Procyon A are called dwarf stars; their dimensions are roughly comparable to those of the Sun. Sirius A and Vega, though much brighter, also are dwarf stars; their higher temperatures yield a larger rate of emission per unit area. Aldebaran A, Arcturus, and Capella A are examples of giant stars, whose dimensions are much larger than those of the Sun. Observations with an interferometer (an instrument that measures the angle subtended by the diameter of a star at the observer's position), combined with parallax measurements (which yield a star's distance; see below *Determining stellar distances*), give sizes of 12 and 22 solar radii for Arcturus and Aldebaran A. Betelgeuse and Antares A are examples of supergiant stars. The latter has a radius some 560 times that of the Sun, whereas the variable star Betelgeuse oscillates between 600 and 900 solar radii. Several of the stellar class of white-dwarf stars, which have low luminosities and high densities, also are listed in Table 1. Sirius B is a prime example, having a size

Dwarf stars

Table 1: The Twenty Brightest Stars

name	visual magnitude* and spectrum		distance in light-years†	visual luminosity ☉	
	A‡	B‡		A‡	B‡
Sirius	−1.50 A1 V	+7.20 dA5	8.6	23.0	0.0080
Canopus	−0.73 F0 Ib		98.0	1,450.0	
Alpha Centauri	+0.10 G2 V	+1.50 K5 V	4.3	1.3	0.3600
Vega	+0.04 A0 V		26.0	52.0	
Arcturus	0.00 K2 III		36.0	110.0	
Capella	+0.05 G III	+10.20 M1 V	45.0	160.0	
Rigel	+0.08 B8 Ia	+6.60 B9	600.0	25,000.0	70.0000
Procyon	+0.34 F5 IV	+10.80 d	11.4	7.6	0.0005
Betelgeuse	+0.41 M2 I (var.)		600.0	21,000.0	
Achernar	+0.47 B5 IV-V		65.0	210.0	
Beta Centauri	+0.61 B1 II	B2(?)	300.0	3,600.0	?
Altair	+0.77 B7 V		16.6	10.0	
Alpha Crucis	+1.58 B1 IV-V	+2.09 B3 V	390.0	2,760.0	1,600.0000
Aldebaran	+0.86 K5 III	+13.00 M2 V	52.0	100.0	0.0013
Spica	+1.12 B1.5 V	+3.10 B3 V	274.0	2,000.0	330.0000
Antares	+0.90 M1 Ib (var.)	+5.10 B4e V	420.0	6,000.0	115.0000
Pollux	+1.15 K0 III		37.0	170.0	
Fomalhaut	+1.18 A3 V	+6.50 K4 V	22.6	13.0	0.1000
Deneb	+1.26 A2 Ia		1,400.0	47,000.0	
Beta Crucis	+1.24 B0.5 V		500.0	5,700.0	

*Negative magnitudes are brightest, and one magnitude difference corresponds to a difference in brightness of 2.5 times; *e.g.*, a star of magnitude −1 is 10 times brighter than one of magnitude +1.5. †One light-year equals about 9.46×10^{12} kilometres (5.88×10^{12} miles). ‡A and B are brighter and fainter components, respectively, of star.
Source: From Peter van de Kamp; C.W. Allen; R. Hanbury Brown; J. Davis, L.R. Allen, and J. Rome; G. Abell.

of 0.01 solar radius, which is comparable to the size of the Earth. Among other notable stars of Table 1, Rigel A is a young supergiant in the constellation Orion and Canopus a bright beacon in the Southern Hemisphere often used for spacecraft navigation.

Stellar activity and mass loss. The Sun's activity is apparently not unique. It has been found that stars of all types are active and have stellar winds. The importance and ubiquity of strong stellar winds became apparent only through advances in space-borne ultraviolet and X-ray astronomy as well as in radio and infrared ground-based astronomy.

Stellar winds

X-ray observations that were made during the early 1980s yielded some rather unexpected findings. They revealed that nearly all types of stars are surrounded by coronas having temperatures of 1,000,000 kelvins (K) or more. Furthermore, all stars seemingly sport active regions, including spots, flares, and prominences much like those of the Sun. Some stars exhibit star spots so large that an entire face of the star is relatively dark, while others display flare activity thousands of times more intense than that on the Sun.

The highly luminous, hot, blue stars have by far the strongest stellar winds. Observations of their ultraviolet spectra with telescopes on rockets and satellites have shown that their wind speeds often reach 3,000 kilometres per second (roughly 2,000 miles per second), while losing mass at rates up to 1,000,000,000 times that of the solar wind. The corresponding mass-loss rates approach and sometimes exceed 10^{-5} solar masses per year, one entire solar mass (perhaps $^1/_{10}$ of the total mass of the star) being carried away into space in a relatively short span of 100,000 years. Accordingly, the most luminous stars are thought to lose substantial fractions of their mass during their lifetimes, as the latter are calculated to be only a few million years.

Ultraviolet observations have proved that to produce such great winds the pressure of hot gases in a corona, which drives the solar wind, is not enough. Instead, the winds of the hot stars must be driven directly by the pressure of the energetic ultraviolet radiation emitted by these stars. Aside from the simple realization that copious quantities of ultraviolet radiation flow from such hot stars, the details of the process are not well understood. Whatever is going on, it is surely complex, for the ultraviolet spectra of the stars tend to vary with time, implying that the wind is not steady. In an effort to understand better the variations in the rate of flow, theorists are investigating possible kinds of instabilities that might be peculiar to luminous hot stars.

Ultraviolet radiation from luminous hot stars

Observations made with radio and infrared telescopes as well as with optical instruments prove that luminous cool stars also have winds whose total mass flow rates are comparable to those of the luminous hot stars, though their velocities are much lower—about 30 kilometres per second. Because luminous red stars are inherently cool objects (having a surface temperature of about 3,000 K, or half that of the Sun), they emit no detectable ultraviolet or X-ray radiation; thus, the mechanism driving the winds must differ from that in luminous hot stars. Winds from luminous cool stars, unlike those from hot stars, are rich in dust grains and molecules. Since nearly all stars more massive than the Sun eventually evolve into such cool stars, their winds, pouring into space from vast numbers of stars, provide a major source of new gas and dust in interstellar space, thereby furnishing a vital link in the cycle of star formation and galactic evolution. As in the case of the hot stars, the specific mechanism that drives the winds of the cool stars is not understood; at this time, investigators can only surmise that gas turbulence and/or magnetic fields in the atmospheres of these stars are somehow responsible.

Strong winds also are found to be associated with objects called protostars, which are huge gas balls that have not yet become full-fledged stars in which energy is provided by nuclear reactions (see below *Star formation and evolution*). Recent radio and infrared observations of deuterium (heavy hydrogen [H_2]) and carbon monoxide (CO) molecules in the Orion Nebula have revealed clouds of gas expanding outward at velocities approaching 100 kilometres per second. Furthermore, high-resolution, very-long-baseline interferometry observations have disclosed expanding knots of natural maser emission of water vapour near the star-forming regions in Orion, thus linking the strong winds to the protostars themselves. The specific causes of these winds remain unknown, but if they generally accompany star formation, astronomers will have to consider the implications for the early solar system. After all, the Sun was presumably once a protostar, too.

Strong winds associated with protostars

DISTANCES TO THE STARS

Determining stellar distances. Distances to stars are basically determined by the technique of trigonometric parallax. When the position of a nearby star is measured from two points on opposite sides of the Earth's orbit (*i.e.*, six months apart), a small angular (artificial) displacement is observed relative to a background of very remote (essentially fixed) stars. Using the radius of the Earth's orbit as the baseline, the distance of the star can be found from the parallactic angle, p. If $p = 1''$ (one second of arc), the distance of the star is 206,265 times the Earth's distance from the Sun—namely, 3.26 light-years. This unit of dis-

Parsec

tance is termed the parsec, defined as the distance of an object whose parallax equals one arc second. Therefore, one parsec equals 3.26 light-years. Since parallax is inversely proportional to distance, a star at 10 parsecs would have a parallax of 0.1″. Stars at greater distances have even smaller parallaxes, and these are more difficult to measure directly. Hence, indirect methods mostly depending on the brightnesses of different classes are used to find the distances for the great majority of stars. The nearest star, Proxima Centauri (a member of the triple system of Alpha Centauri), has a parallax of 0.76″, meaning that its distance is 1/0.76 or 1.32 parsecs, or 4.3 light-years. The parallax of the next closest, Barnard's star, measures 0.55″, so that its distance is nearly six light-years away. Errors of such parallaxes are typically 0.01″, meaning that there is a 50 percent probability that a star whose parallax is 0.065″ lies between 13.3 and 18.2 parsecs (corresponding to parallaxes of 0.075″ and 0.055″, respectively), and an equal chance that it lies outside that range. Thus, measurements of trigonometric parallaxes are useful for only the nearby stars within a few hundred light-years. In fact, of the approximately 100,000,000,000 stars in the Milky Way Galaxy (also simply called the Galaxy), only about 700 are close enough to have their parallaxes measured accurately.

Nearest stars. Table 2 lists information about the 20 nearest known stars. Only Alpha Centauri, Procyon, and Sirius appear in both Tables 1 and 2. Ironically, most of the relatively nearby stars are dimmer than the Sun and are invisible without the aid of a telescope. By contrast, the well-known bright objects often outlining the constellations have parallaxes less than the limiting value of 0.01″ and are therefore well beyond several hundred light-years distance from the Sun. The most luminous stars can be seen at great distances, whereas the intrinsically faint stars can be observed only if they are relatively close to the Earth.

Although Tables 1 and 2 pertain to only a very small number of stars, they nonetheless serve to illustrate some important points. The stars listed fall roughly into three categories: (1) giant and supergiant stars having sizes of tens or even hundreds of solar radii and extremely low average densities—in fact, several orders of magnitude less than that of water (one gram per cubic centimetre); (2) dwarf stars having sizes ranging from 0.1 to five solar radii and masses from 0.1 to about 10 solar masses; and (3) white-dwarf stars having masses comparable to that of the Sun but dimensions appropriate to planets, meaning that their average densities are hundreds of thousands of times greater than that of water.

General categories of stars

These rough groupings of stars correspond to stages in their life histories (see below *Later stages of evolution*). The second category is identified with what is called the main sequence (see below) and includes stars that emit energy mainly by converting hydrogen into helium in their cores. The first category comprises stars that have exhausted the hydrogen in their cores and are burning hydrogen within shells surrounding the core. The white dwarfs represent the final stage in the life of a typical star, embodying that point when most available sources of energy have been exhausted and the star has become relatively dim.

The large number of binary and even multiple systems is notable. These star systems exhibit scales comparable in size to that of the solar system. Some of the nearby single stars have invisible companions detectable only by their gravitational effects on the primary star; this orbital motion of the unseen member causes the visible star to "wobble" or move through space along a wavelike curve rather than following a straight line. The invisible companions do not appear to be self-luminous; some are suspected to have masses on the order of 0.01 solar mass or less, which is in the range of planetary rather than stellar dimensions. Better observations are needed to determine if they are genuine planets or merely extremely dim stars (sometimes called brown dwarfs). Nonetheless, a reasonable inference that can be drawn from these data is that double stars and planetary systems are formed by similar evolutionary processes.

Table 2: The Twenty Nearest Stars

name	visual apparent magnitude and spectrum		distance in light-years	visual luminosity ⊙	
	A*	B*		A*	B*
Alpha Centauri†	0.1 G2 V	1.5 K5 V	4.3	1.30	0.36000
Barnard's star‡	9.5 M5 V		5.9	0.00044	
Wolf 359	13.5 M6e		7.6	0.00002	
Lalande 21185 (BD + 36°2147)‡	7.5 M2 V		8.1	0.0052	
Sirius§	−1.5 A1 V	7.2 dA5	8.6	23	0.00800
Luyten 726–8‖	12.5 M6e V	13.0 M6e	8.9	0.00006	0.00004
Ross 154	10.6 M5e V		9.4	0.0004	
Ross 248	12.2 M6e V		10.3	0.00011	
Epsilon Eridani	3.7 K2 V		10.7	0.30	
Luyten 789–6	12.2 M6 V		10.8	0.00012	
Ross 128	11.1 M5 V		10.8	0.00033	
61 Cygni¶	5.2 K5 V	6.0 K7 V	11.2	0.083	0.04000
Epsilon Indi	4.7 K5 V		11.2	1–87 = 0.13♀	
Procyon♂	0.3 F5I V	10.8 d	11.4	7.6	0.00050
Σ 2398	8.9 M3.5 V	9.7 M4 V	11.5	0.0028	0.00130
Groombridge 34 (BD + 43°44)	8.1 M1 V	11.0 M6 V	11.6	0.0058	0.00040
Lacaille 9352 (CD − 36°15693)	7.4 M2 V		11.7	0.012	
Tau Ceti	3.5 G8 V		11.9	0.44	
BD + 5°1668	9.8 M4 V		12.2	0.0014	
Lacaille 8760	6.7 M1 V		12.5	0.025	

*A and B are brighter and fainter components, respectively, of star. †The two components of Alpha Centauri have masses of $M_1 = 1.0$ and $M_2 = 0.9$ solar mass, respectively. They are separated by 23.1 astronomical units and revolve around one another with a period $P = 79.9$ years. A third component of the system is an 11th magnitude M5 dwarf with a luminosity $L = 0.00006\ L_{Sun}$. ‡These stars have unseen, planet-like companions whose presence is revealed by gravitational attraction on the visible star. §The two components of Sirius are separated by 19.9 astronomical units, $P = 50.1$ years. The bright component has 2.2 solar masses; the faint component is a white dwarf of 0.9 solar mass. ‖The mean separation of these stars is 5.8 astronomical units, $P = 25$ years, but the masses are 0.05 and 0.04 Sun; they probably do not shine by nuclear energy generation but are radiating away gravitational energy. ¶Binary with mean separation $a = 84.2$ astronomical units, $P = 720$ years, $M_1 = 0.58$, $M_2 = 0.57$ solar mass. ♀1–87 = fainter. ♂Binary separation = 15.8 astronomical units, $P = 40.6$ years, $M_1 = 1.8\ M_⊙$, $M_2 = 0.6\ M_⊙$. The fainter component is a white-dwarf star.
Source: From Peter van de Kamp.

STELLAR POSITIONS

Basic measurements. Accurate observations of stellar positions are essential to many problems of astronomy. Positions of the brighter stars can be measured very accurately in the equatorial system (the coordinates of which are called right ascension [α, or RA] and declination [δ, or DEC] and are given for some epoch, for example, 1950.0 or, nowadays, 2000.0). Fainter stars are measured using photographic plates or some other imaging device (*e.g.*, a charge-coupled device, or CCD) with respect to the brighter stars, and finally the entire group is referred to the positions of known external galaxies. These distant galaxies are far enough away to define an essentially fixed, or immovable, system, whereas positions of both the bright and faint stars are affected over relatively short periods of time by galactic rotation and by their own motions through the Galaxy.

Stellar motions. Accurate measurements of position make it possible to determine the movement of a star across the line of sight—its proper motion. The amount of proper motion denoted by μ (in arc seconds per year) divided by the parallax of the star and multiplied by a factor of 4.74 equals the tangential velocity, V_T, in kilometres per second in the plane of the celestial sphere.

Proper motion

The motion along the line of sight, called radial velocity, is obtained directly from spectroscopic observations. If λ is the wavelength of a characteristic spectral line of some atom or ion present in the star, and λ_L the wavelength of the same line on the Earth, then the difference $\Delta\lambda$, or $\lambda - \lambda_L$, divided by λ_L equals the radial velocity, V_R, divided by the velocity of light, c—namely, $\Delta\lambda/\lambda_L = V_R/c$. Shifts of a spectral line toward the red end of the electromagnetic spectrum (*i.e.*, positive V_R) indicate recession, and those toward the blue end (negative V_R) indicate approach. If the parallax is known, measurements of μ and V_R enable a determination of the space motion of the star. Normally, radial velocities are corrected for the Earth's rotation and for its motion around the Sun, so that they refer to the line-of-sight motion of the star with respect to the Sun.

Consider a pertinent example. The proper motion of Alpha Centauri is about 3.5 arc seconds, which, at a distance of 4.3 light-years, means that this star moves 0.00007 light-year in one year. It thus has a projected velocity in the plane of the sky of 22 km/sec. As for motion along the line of sight, Alpha Centauri's spectral lines are slightly blueshifted, implying a velocity of approach of about 20 km/sec. The true space motion, equal to $(22^2 + 20^2)^{1/2}$ or about 30 km/sec, suggests that this star will make its closest approach to the Sun (three light-years) some 280 centuries from now.

Light from the stars

STELLAR MAGNITUDES

Measuring starlight intensity. Stellar brightnesses are usually expressed by means of their magnitudes, a usage inherited from classical times. A star of the first magnitude is about 2.5 times as bright as one of the second magnitude, which in turn is some 2.5 times as bright as one of the third magnitude, and so on. A star of the first magnitude is therefore 2.5^5 or 100 times as bright as one of the sixth magnitude. The magnitude of Sirius, which appears to an observer on Earth as the brightest star in the sky (save the Sun), is −1.5. Canopus, the second brightest, has a magnitude of −0.7, while the faintest star normally seen without the aid of a telescope is of the sixth magnitude. Stars as faint as the 23rd magnitude have been measured with the five-metre (200-inch) telescope at the Palomar Observatory in California, meaning that this instrument can detect stars several million times fainter than can the human eye alone.

Magnitude scales

The scale of magnitudes comprises a geometric progression of brightness. Magnitudes can be converted to light ratios by letting l_n and l_m be the brightnesses of stars of magnitudes n and m; the logarithm of the ratio of the two brightnesses then equals 0.4 times the difference between them—*i.e.*, $\log(l_m/l_n) = 0.4(n - m)$. Magnitudes are actually defined in terms of observed brightness, a quantity that depends on the light-detecting device employed. Visual magnitudes are measured with the eye, and photographic magnitudes are obtained from images on a photographic plate. There also are various types of photoelectric magnitude systems. All magnitude systems must have a reference, or zero, point. In practice, this is fixed arbitrarily and is essentially based on the star catalogs of the ancient Greek astronomers Hipparchus and Ptolemy.

The actually measured brightnesses of stars give apparent magnitudes. These cannot be converted to intrinsic brightnesses until the distances of the objects concerned are known. The absolute magnitude of a star is defined as the magnitude it would have if it were viewed at the standard distance of 10 parsecs. Since the apparent visual magnitude of the Sun is −26.9, its absolute magnitude corresponds to a diminution in brightness by a factor $(2{,}062{,}650)^2$, and is, using logarithms, $-26.9 + 2.5 \times \log(2{,}062{,}650)^2$, or $-26.9 + 31.6 = 4.7$. This is the magnitude that the Sun would have if it were at a distance of 10 parsecs—an object still visible to the naked eye, though not a very conspicuous one and certainly not the brightest in the sky. In a similar manner, the absolute magnitude of the full Moon can be calculated to be +32; to see it 10 parsecs away would require a ground-based telescope with an aperture about 0.4 kilometre wide. The very brightest stars, such as Deneb, Rigel, and Betelgeuse, have absolute magnitudes of −7 to −9, while the faintest known star, the companion to the star with the catalog name BD + 4°4048, has an absolute visual magnitude of +19—about 1,000,000 times fainter than the Sun. Many astronomers suspect that large numbers of such faint stars exist, but most of these objects have so far eluded detection.

Absolute magnitude

Stellar colours. Stars differ in colour. Most of the stars in the constellation Orion visible to the naked eye are blue-white, most notably Rigel (Beta Orionis), but Betelgeuse (Alpha Orionis) is a deep red. In the telescope, Albireo (Beta Cygni) is seen as two stars, one blue and the other orange. One quantitative means of measuring stellar colours involves a comparison of the visual magnitude of the star with a magnitude measured on a photographic plate. Yellow, the colour to which the human eye is most sensitive, contributes most to visual magnitude. The ordinary photographic plate is insensitive to yellow and red light but is sensitive to blue and violet, so that hot blue stars appear bright, and yellow and red stars are recorded as relatively faint. In all magnitude scales, one magnitude step corresponds to a brightness ratio of 2.5. The zero point is chosen so that white stars with surface temperatures of about 10,000 K have the same visual and photographic magnitudes. The conventional colour index is defined as the photographic magnitude, B, minus the visual magnitude, V; the colour index, $B - V$, of the Sun is thus $+5.46 - 4.84 = 0.62$.

Visual magnitudes also can be determined photographically with the aid of orthochromatic or yellow-sensitive plates and yellow filters. Such photovisual magnitudes differ from visual magnitudes less than naked-eye estimates of visual magnitudes by different observers differ among themselves. Actually, basic measurements of stellar magnitudes and colours are now made photoelectrically, although the photographic plate continues to play a central role as an interpolation device when very large numbers of stars are to be measured.

Magnitude systems. It has been found that the older system of stellar magnitudes, normally employed only for photographic and photovisual (or visual) magnitudes, encounters a number of severe difficulties. Problems also arise when only one colour is observed. If, for instance, a star's colour is found to be red, it is impossible without further information to decide whether the star is red because it is cool or whether it is really a hot star whose colour has been reddened by the passage of light through interstellar matter. Astronomers have overcome these difficulties by measuring the magnitudes of the same stars in three or more colours.

Basis of modern magnitude systems

Modern magnitude systems are based on measurements, usually made photoelectrically, of a few standard stars, the measurement accuracy being limited chiefly by the quality of the atmosphere through which the light must pass. Magnitudes that measure light from only parts of the wavelength range are generally named for the colour of the light. Thus, there are blue magnitudes whose range roughly corresponds to that of the (blue) photographic magnitudes; visual magnitudes whose range is centred in the yellow-green part of the spectrum; red magnitudes, and so on.

Observations of stellar infrared light also have assumed considerable importance. In addition, photometric observations of individual stars from space vehicles and rockets have made possible the measurement of stellar colours over a large range of wavelengths. These data are important for hot stars and for assessing the effects of interstellar attenuation.

Bolometric magnitudes. The measured total of all radiation at all wavelengths from a star is called a bolometric magnitude. The corrections required to reduce visual magnitudes to bolometric magnitudes are large for very cool stars and for very hot ones but are relatively small for stars such as the Sun. A determination of the true total luminosity of a star affords a measure of its actual energy output. When the energy radiated by a star is observed at the Earth, only that portion to which the energy detector is sensitive and that can be transmitted through the atmosphere is recorded. Most of the energy of stars like the Sun is emitted in spectral regions that can be observed from the Earth's surface; but a cool dwarf star with a surface temperature of 3,000 K has an energy maximum on a wavelength scale at 10000 angstroms (Å) in the far-infrared, and most of its energy cannot therefore be measured as light. Bright, cool stars can be observed at infrared wavelengths, however, with special instruments that measure the amount of heat radiated by the star. Corrections for the heavy absorption of the infrared waves by water and other molecules in the Earth's air must be made unless an infrared payload has been lofted by balloon or rocket above the atmosphere.

Determining the actual energy output of a star

The hotter stars pose more difficult problems, since the Earth's atmosphere extinguishes all radiation at wavelengths shorter than 2900 Å. A star whose surface temperature is 20,000 K or above radiates most of its energy in the inaccessible ultraviolet part of the electromagnetic spectrum. Measurements made with detectors flown in rockets or orbited in satellites extend the observable wavelength region down to 1000 Å or less, though most radiation of distant stars is extinguished below 912 Å—a region in which absorption by neutral hydrogen atoms in intervening space becomes effective.

To compare the true luminosities of two stars, the appropriate bolometric corrections must first be added to each of their absolute magnitudes. The ratio of the luminosities can then be calculated.

STELLAR SPECTRA

A star's spectrum contains information about its temperature, chemical composition, and intrinsic luminosity. Spectrograms secured with a slit spectrograph consist of a sequence of images of the slit in the light of the star at successive wavelengths. Adequate spectral resolution (or dispersion) might show the star to be a member of a close binary system, in rapid rotation, or to have an extended atmosphere. Quantitative determination of its chemical composition then becomes possible. Inspection of a high-resolution spectrum of the star may reveal evidence of a strong magnetic field.

Production of spectral lines

Line spectrum. Spectral lines are produced by transitions of electrons within atoms or ions. As the electrons move closer to or farther from the nucleus of an atom (or of an ion), energy in the form of light (or other radiation) is emitted or absorbed. The yellow "D" lines of sodium or the "H" and "K" lines of ionized calcium are produced by discrete quantum jumps from the lowest energy levels (ground states) of these atoms. The visible hydrogen lines (the so-called Balmer series), however, are produced by electron transitions within atoms in the second energy level (or first excited state), which lies well above the ground level in energy. Only at high temperatures are sufficient numbers of atoms maintained in this state by collisions, radiations, and so forth to permit an appreciable number of absorptions to occur. At the low surface temperatures of a red dwarf star, few electrons populate the second level of hydrogen, and thus the hydrogen lines are dim. By contrast, at very high temperatures, for instance that of the surface of a blue giant star, the hydrogen atoms are nearly all ionized and therefore cannot absorb or emit any line radiation whatsoever. Consequently, only faint dark hydrogen lines are observed. The characteristic features of ionized metals such as iron are often weak in such hotter stars because the appropriate electron transitions involve higher energy levels that tend to be more sparsely populated than the lower levels. Another factor is that the general "fogginess," or opacity, of the atmospheres of these hotter stars is greatly increased, resulting in fewer atoms in the visible stellar layers capable of producing the observed lines.

The continuous (as distinct from the line) spectrum of the Sun is produced primarily by the photodissociation of negative hydrogen ions—*i.e.,* atoms of hydrogen to which an extra electron is loosely attached. In the Sun's atmosphere, when H^- is subsequently destroyed by photodissociation, it can absorb energy at any of a whole range of wavelengths and thus produce a continuous range of absorption of radiation. The main source of light absorption in the hotter stars is the photoionization of hydrogen atoms, both from ground level and from higher levels.

Spectral analysis. The physical processes behind the formation of stellar spectra are well enough understood to permit determinations of temperatures, densities, and chemical compositions of stellar atmospheres. The star studied most extensively is, of course, the Sun, but others also have been investigated in detail.

Factors that determine the spectral features of stars

The general characteristics of the spectra of stars depend more on temperature variations among the stars than on their chemical differences. Spectral features also depend on the density of the absorbing atmospheric matter, and density in turn is related to a star's surface gravity. Dwarf stars, with great surface gravities, tend to have high atmospheric densities; giants and supergiants, with low surface gravities, have relatively low densities. Hydrogen absorption lines provide a case in point. Normally, an undisturbed atom radiates a very narrow line. If its energy levels are perturbed by charged particles passing nearby, it radiates at a wavelength near its characteristic wavelength. In a hot gas, the range of disturbance of the hydrogen lines is very high, so that the spectral line radiated by the whole mass of gas is spread out considerably; the amount of blurring depends on the density of the gas in a known fashion. Dwarf stars such as Sirius show broad hydrogen features with extensive "wings" where the line fades slowly out into the background, while supergiant stars, with less dense atmospheres, display relatively narrow hydrogen lines.

Classification of spectral types. Most stars are grouped into a small number of spectral classes. The *Henry Draper Catalogue* lists spectral classes from the hottest to the coolest stars (see below *Photometric catalogs*). These types are designated, in order of decreasing temperature, by the letters O, B, A, F, G, K, and M. This group is supplemented by R- and N-type stars (today often referred to as carbon, or C-type, stars) and S-type stars. The R-, N-, and S-type stars differ from the others in chemical composition; also, they are invariably giant or supergiant stars.

The O–M spectral sequence

The spectral sequence O–M represents stars of essentially the same chemical composition but of different temperatures and atmospheric pressures. This simple interpretation, put forward in the 1920s by the Indian astrophysicist Meghnad N. Saha, has provided the physical basis for all subsequent interpretations of stellar spectra. The spectral sequence is also a colour sequence: the O- and B-type stars are intrinsically the bluest and hottest; the M-, R-, N-, and S-type stars are the reddest and coolest.

In the case of cool stars of type M, the spectra indicate the presence of familiar metals, including iron, calcium, magnesium, and also titanium oxide molecules (TiO), particularly in the red and green parts of the spectrum. In the somewhat hotter K-type stars, the TiO features disappear, and the spectrum exhibits a wealth of metallic lines. A few especially stable fragments of molecules such as cyanogen (CN) and the hydroxyl radical (OH) persist in these stars and even in G-type stars such as the Sun. The spectra of G-type stars are dominated by the characteristic lines of metals, particularly those of iron, calcium, sodium, magnesium, and titanium.

The behaviour of calcium illustrates the phenomenon of thermal ionization. At low temperatures a calcium atom retains all of its electrons and radiates a spectrum characteristic of the neutral, or normal, atom; at higher temperatures collisions between atoms and electrons and the absorption of radiation both tend to detach electrons and to produce singly ionized calcium atoms. At the same time, these ions can recombine with electrons to produce neutral calcium atoms. At high temperatures or low electron pressures, or both, most of the atoms are ionized. At low temperatures and high densities the equilibrium favours the neutral state. The concentrations of ions and neutral atoms can be computed from the temperature, the density, and the ionization potential (namely, the energy required to detach an electron from the atom).

The absorption line of neutral calcium at 4227 Å is thus strong in cool M-type dwarf stars, in which the pressure is high and the temperature is low. In the hotter G-type stars, however, the lines of ionized calcium at 3968 and 3933 Å (the "H" and "K" lines) become much stronger than any other feature in the spectrum.

In stars of spectral type F, the lines of neutral atoms are weak relative to those of ionized atoms. The hydrogen lines are stronger, attaining their maximum intensities in A-type stars, in which the surface temperature is about 9,000 K. Thereafter, these absorption lines gradually fade as the hydrogen becomes ionized.

The hot B-type stars, such as Epsilon Orionis, are characterized by lines of helium and of singly ionized oxygen, nitrogen, and neon. In very hot O-type stars, lines of ionized helium appear. Other prominent features include lines of doubly ionized nitrogen, oxygen, and carbon and of trebly ionized silicon, all of which require more energy to produce.

In the more modern system of spectral classification,

MK spectral classification system

called the MK system (after the American astronomers William W. Morgan and Philip C. Keenan who introduced it), luminosity class is assigned to the star along with the Draper spectral class. For example, Alpha Persei is classed as F5 Ia, which means that it falls about halfway between the beginning of type F (*i.e.,* F0) and of type G (*i.e.,* G0). The Ia suffix means that it is a particularly luminous supergiant. The star Pi Cephei, classed as G2 III, is a giant falling between G0 and K0 but much closer to G0. The Sun, a dwarf star of type G2, is classified as G2 V. A star of luminosity class II falls between giants and supergiants; one of class IV is called a subgiant.

BULK STELLAR PROPERTIES

Stellar temperatures. Temperatures of stars can be defined in a number of ways. From the character of the spectrum and the various degrees of ionization and excitation found from its analysis, an ionization or excitation temperature can be determined.

A comparison of the *V* and *B* magnitudes (see above) yields a colour index, $B-V$, which is related to the colour temperature of the star. The colour temperature is therefore a measure of the relative amounts of radiation in two more or less broad wavelength regions, while the ionization and excitation temperatures pertain to the temperatures of strata wherein spectral lines are formed.

Provided that the angular size of a star can be measured (see below *Stellar radii*) and that the total energy flux received at the Earth (corrected for atmospheric extinction) is known, the so-called brightness temperature can be found.

The effective temperature, T_{eff}, of a star is defined in terms of its total energy output and radius. Thus, since σT^4_{eff} is the rate of radiation per unit area for a perfectly radiating sphere and if *L* is the total radiation (*i.e.,* luminosity) of a star considered to be a sphere of radius *R,* such a sphere (called a blackbody) would emit a total amount of energy equal to its surface area, $4\pi R^2$, multiplied by its energy per unit area. In symbols, $L=4\pi R^2\sigma T^4_{eff}$. This relation defines the star's equivalent blackbody or effective temperature.

Since the total energy radiated by a star cannot be directly observed (except in the case of the Sun), the effective temperature is a derived quantity rather than an observed one. Yet, theoretically, it is the fundamental temperature. If the bolometric corrections are known, the effective temperature can be found for any star whose absolute visual magnitude and radius are known.

Stellar masses. Masses of stars can be found only from binary systems and only if the scale of the orbits of the stars around each other is known. Binary stars are divided into three categories, depending on the mode of observation employed: visual binaries, spectroscopic binaries, and eclipsing binaries.

Types of binary stars

Visual binaries. These can be seen as double stars with the telescope. True doubles, as distinguished from apparent doubles caused by line-of-sight effects, move through space together and display a common space motion. Sometimes a common orbital motion can be measured as well. Provided that the parallax, *p,* and therefore the distance are known, such systems permit a determination of stellar masses, m_1 and m_2, of the two members. The angular radius, a'', of the orbit (more accurately, its semimajor axis) can be measured directly, and, with the distance known, the true dimensions of the semimajor axis, *a,* can be found. The period, *P,* of the binary system follows directly. If, in astronomical units, $a=a''/p$, the sum of the masses, m_1+m_2, is, by Kepler's third law, proportional to the cube of the mean distance, *a,* between them and inversely proportional to the square of the period expressed in years. In symbols, $(m_1+m_2)=a^3/P^2$ in units of the Sun's mass. For example, for the binary system 70 Ophiuchi, $P=87.8$ years, $p''=0.20''$, and $a''=4.55''$, so that $a=22.8$ astronomical units (the average distance from the Earth to the Sun, approximately 149,597,870 kilometres), and $m_1+m_2=1.56$ solar masses. From a measurement of the motions of the two members relative to the background stars, the orbit of each star has been determined with respect to their common centre of gravity. The mass ratio, $m_2/(m_1+m_2)$, is 0.42; the individual masses are then 0.90 and 0.66 solar mass.

The star known as 61 Cygni was the first whose distance was measured (via parallax by the German astronomer Friedrich W. Bessel in the mid-19th century) and the first stellar system found to contain a potential planet. Visually, it is a double star separated by 83.2 astronomical units. Its members move around one another with a period of 653 years. The brighter member also seems to have an invisible companion with a mass of about 1 percent that of the Sun; this possible planet (for it would seem too small to ignite nuclear burning on its own) moves about its parent star at a distance of 4,200,000 kilometres, with a period of about 4.8 years.

Though there is currently no clear evidence for Earth-like planets orbiting any other star, minute positional changes in the path of Barnard's star (an M-type dwarf at a distance of some six light-years) do suggest that at least two unseen objects, each having about the mass of Jupiter, accompany it. Careful examination of the motions of a few other stars that are both close to the Sun and of low mass display similar wobbles, but their interpretation is unambiguous. In each case, the wobble could conceivably be caused by a small and dim companion star.

In 1983 an Earth-orbiting infrared satellite observed several nearby stars (including Vega and Fomalhout) around which warm matter was discovered to be spinning in an optically unseen disk. This matter is composed of myriad dust particles mostly a millimetre in size and might be taking part in the first stage of planetary formation. There is now no way, however, to ascertain whether the particles are primordial matter that could develop into planets or are just unpromising bits of interplanetary litter.

Spectroscopic binaries. This type of two-body stellar system is found from radial-velocity observations. At least one member of such a binary has a continuously changing periodic velocity that alters the wavelengths of its spectral lines in a rhythmic way; the velocity curve repeats itself exactly from one cycle to the next, and the motion can be interpreted as orbital motion. In a few cases, rhythmic changes in the lines of both members can be measured. Unlike the case of the visual binaries, the semimajor axes or the individual masses cannot be found for most spectroscopic binaries, since the angle between the orbit plane and the plane of the sky cannot be determined. If spectra from both members are observed, mass ratios can be found. If one spectrum alone is observed, only a quantity called the mass function can be derived, from which is calculated a lower limit to the stellar masses. If a spectroscopic binary is also observed to be an eclipsing system, the inclination of the orbit and often the values of the individual masses can be ascertained.

Rhythmic alteration of wavelengths

Eclipsing binaries. This third category of binaries consists of two close stars moving in an orbit so placed in space in relation to the Earth that the light of one can at times be hidden behind the other. Depending on the orientation of the orbit and sizes of the stars, the eclipses can be total or annular (a ring of one star shows behind the other at the climax of the eclipse) or both eclipses can be partial. The best known example of an eclipsing binary is Algol (Beta Persei), which has a period (interval between eclipses) of 2.9 days. The brighter (B8-type) star contributes about 92 percent of the light of the system, and the eclipsed star provides much less than 8 percent. The system contains a third star that is not eclipsed. Some 20 eclipsing binaries are visible to the naked eye.

Light-curve data

The light curve for an eclipsing binary displays magnitude measurements for the system over a complete light cycle. The light of the variable star is usually compared with that of a nearby (comparison) star thought to be fixed in brightness. Often, a deep, or primary, minimum is produced when a star of higher surface brightness is eclipsed. It represents the total eclipse and is characterized by a flat bottom. A shallower secondary eclipse occurs when the star of higher surface brightness passes in front of the other; it corresponds to an annular eclipse (or transit). In a partial eclipse neither star is ever completely hidden, and the light changes continuously during an eclipse.

The shape of the light curve during an eclipse gives the

ratio of the radii of the two stars and also one radius in terms of the size of the orbit, the ratio of luminosities, and the inclination of the orbital plane to the plane of the sky.

If radial-velocity curves are also available—*i.e.,* if the binary is spectroscopic as well as eclipsing—additional information can be obtained. When both velocity curves are observable, the size of the orbit as well as the sizes, masses, and densities of the stars can be calculated. Furthermore, if the parallax of the system is measurable, the brightness temperatures of the individual stars can be estimated from their luminosities and radii. All of these procedures have been carried out for the faint binary Castor C and for the bright B-type star Mu Scorpii.

Close stars may reflect each other's light noticeably. If a small, high-temperature star is paired with a larger object of low surface brightness and if the distance between the stars is small, the part of the cool star facing the hotter one is substantially brightened by it. Just before (and just after) secondary eclipse, this illuminated hemisphere is pointed toward the observer, and the total light of the system is at a maximum.

The properties of stars derived from eclipsing binary systems are not necessarily applicable to isolated single stars. Systems in which a smaller, hotter star is accompanied by a larger, cooler object are easier to detect than are systems that contain, for example, two main-sequence stars (see below *Hertzsprung–Russell diagram*). In such an unequal system, at least the cooler star has certainly been affected by evolutionary changes and probably so has the brighter one. The evolutionary development of two stars near one another does not exactly parallel that of two well-separated or isolated ones.

Components of eclipsing binaries

Eclipsing binaries include combinations of a variety of stars ranging from white dwarfs to huge supergiants (*e.g.,* VV Cephei), which would engulf Jupiter and all the inner planets of the solar system if placed at the position of the Sun.

Some members of eclipsing binaries are intrinsic variables (see below *Variable stars*). In many such systems, large clouds of ionized gas swirl between the stellar members. In others, such as Castor C, the faint M-type dwarf component might be a flare star, one in which the brightness can unpredictably and suddenly increase to many times its normal value (see below *Peculiar variables*).

The mass of most stars lies within the range of 0.3 to three solar masses. The most massive star determined to date is the O3-type star, HD 93250; this giant contains some 120 solar masses. Though there seems to be no theoretical upper limit on the masses of stars, the physics of instability and fragmentation probably prohibit the formation of stars much more than a couple of orders of magnitude greater than the Sun. On the low mass side, most stars seem to have at least 0.1 solar mass, though, again theoretically, smaller stars could exist. This absolute lower mass limit for a star is about 0.07 solar mass, for below this value an object cannot shine by nuclear energy and simply cools down directly as a black dwarf or even a planet. Jupiter is just such an object. Having 0.001 solar mass, this huge planet was unable to accumulate enough mass to become a star.

Binaries and possible planetary systems. Near the Sun, most stars are members of binaries, and some of the nearest single stars are suspected of having companions. Although some binary members are separated by hundreds of astronomical units while others are contact binaries, binary systems are most frequently built on the same scale as that of the solar system—namely, on the order of 10 astronomical units. The division in mass between two components of a binary seems to be nearly random. A mass ratio of about 1:20 could occur about 5 percent of the time, and under these circumstances a planetary system comparable to the solar system might form.

The formation of double and multiple stars on the one hand and that of planetary systems on the other seem to be different facets of the same process. Planets can presumably be produced as a natural by-product of star formation. Only a small fraction of the original nebula matter is likely to be retained in planets, since much of the mass and angular momentum are swept out of the system. Conceivably, as many as 100,000,000 stars could have bona fide planets in the Milky Way Galaxy.

Stellar radii. Angular sizes of bright red giant and supergiant stars were first measured directly during the 1920s using the principle of interference of light. Only bright stars with large angular size can be measured by this method. Provided the distance to the star is known, the physical radius can be determined.

Eclipsing binaries also provide extensive data on stellar dimensions. The time of eclipse provides the angular size of any occulting object, and so analyzing the light curves of eclipsing binaries can be a useful means of determining the dimensions of either dwarf or giant stars. Members of close binary systems, however, are sometimes subject to evolutionary effects, mass exchange, and other disturbances that change the details of their spectra.

Speckle interferometry

A more recent method, called speckle interferometry, has been developed to reproduce the true disks of red supergiant stars and to resolve spectroscopic binaries such as Capella. The speckle phenomenon is a rapidly changing interference-diffraction effect seen in a highly magnified diffraction image of a star observed with a large telescope.

If the absolute magnitude of a star and its temperature are known, its size can be computed. The temperature determines the rate at which energy is emitted by each unit of area, and the total luminosity gives the total power output. Thus, the surface area of the star and, from it, the radius of the object can be estimated. This is the only way available for estimating the dimensions of white-dwarf stars. The chief uncertainty lies in choosing the temperature that represents the rate of energy emission.

Average stellar values. Table 3 lists surface temperatures, bolometric or total luminosities, and radii in terms of corresponding solar values for main-sequence stars (see below) ranging from very luminous objects to faint M-type dwarf stars. A considerable range exists for each of these quantities. For a given mass (*M,* the fundamental factor), a fair spread in radius (*R*), luminosity (*L*), surface temperature, and spectral class may exist. This spread is produced by stellar evolutionary effects and tends to broaden the main sequence. Masses are obtained from visual and eclipsing binary systems observed spectroscopically. Radii are found from eclipsing binary systems, from direct mea-

Table 3: Temperatures, Luminosities, Masses, and Radii for Main-Sequence Stars

spectral class	temperature (K)	luminosity	mass	radius
O9.5	33,000	30,000.000	18.00	5.90
B0	32,000	16,000.000	16.00	5.70
B2	22,000	8,300.000	10.50	5.10
B3	17,000	2,500.000	8.30	4.80
B5	15,000	750.000	5.40	3.70
B8	12,500	130.000	3.50	2.70
B9	10,800	100.000	2.90	2.50
A0	9,500	63.000	2.60	2.30
A2	9,000	40.000	2.20	2.00
A5	8,700	24.000	1.90	1.80
A7	8,100	11.000	1.80	1.70
F0	7,400	9.000	1.60	1.50
F2	7,100	6.300	1.50	1.30
F5	6,400	4.000	1.35	1.20
F8	6,100	2.500	1.20	1.10
G0	5,900	1.450	1.08	1.05
G2	5,800	1.100	1.00	1.00
G5	5,600	0.700	0.95	0.91
G8	5,300	0.440	0.85	0.87
K0	5,100	0.360	0.83	0.83
K2	4,830	0.280	0.78	0.79
K5	4,370	0.180	0.68	0.74
K8	3,900	0.120	0.58	0.67
M0	3,670	0.075	0.47	0.63
M1	3,500	0.050	0.40	0.56
M2	3,400	0.030	0.33	0.36
M3	3,300	0.014	0.26	0.29
M4	3,200	0.005	0.20	0.21

Source: Compiled from data given by D.M. Popper, D.L. Harris, K. Strand, and C.E. Worley. The temperature scale is based on work of R. Hanbury Brown and his associates, G.J. Peters and E.K.L. Upton, S. Wolff, L.V. Kuhi, and D. Hayes, of D.C. Morton and T.A. Adams, of D.M. Popper, J.E. Stebbins and A.E. Whitford, A. Code, and J.B. Oke.

surements in a few favourable cases, by calculations, and from absolute visual magnitudes and temperatures.

Meaningful average values of R, L, and M can be given only for dwarf stars. Giant and subgiant stars all show large ranges in R for a given mass. Conversely, giant stars of very nearly the same radius, surface temperature, and luminosity can have appreciably different masses.

STELLAR STATISTICS

Some of the most important generalizations concerning the nature and evolution of stars can be derived from correlations between observable properties and from certain statistical results. One of the most important of these correlations concerns temperature and luminosity (or, equivalently, colour and magnitude)..

Hertzsprung–Russell diagram. When the absolute magnitudes of stars (or their intrinsic luminosities on a logarithmic scale) are plotted in a diagram against temperature or, what is equivalent, the spectral types, the stars do not fall at random on the diagram but tend to congregate in certain restricted domains. Figure 1 shows such a plot, usually called a Hertzsprung–Russell diagram for Ejnar Hertzsprung of Denmark and Henry Norris Russell of the United States, who independently discovered the relations shown in it. As illustrated, most of the congregated stars are dwarfs lying closely around a diagonal line called the main sequence. These stars range from hot, O- and B-type, blue objects 10,000 times (or more) brighter than the Sun, down through white A-type stars such as Sirius to orange K-type stars such as Epsilon Eridani, and finally to M-type red dwarfs thousands of times fainter than the Sun. The sequence is continuous, the luminosities fall off smoothly with decreasing surface temperature, the masses and radii decrease but at a much slower rate, and the stellar densities gradually increase.

The main sequence

The second group of stars to be recognized was a group of giants—such objects as Capella, Arcturus, and Aldebaran—which are yellow, orange, or red stars about 100 times as bright as the Sun and have radii on the order of 20,000,000 to 30,000,000 kilometres (or 10 to 20 times as large as the Sun). The giants lie above the main sequence in the upper right portion of the diagram. The category of supergiants includes stars of all spectral classes; they show a large spread in intrinsic brightness, and some even approach absolute magnitudes of −7 or −8. A few red supergiants, such as the variable star VV Cephei, exceed in size the orbit of Jupiter or even that of Saturn, although most of them are smaller. Supergiants are short-lived and rare objects, but they can be seen at great distances because of their tremendous luminosity.

Subgiants are stars that are redder and larger than main-sequence stars of the same luminosity. Many of the best known examples are found in close binary systems where conditions favour their detection.

The white-dwarf domain lies about 10 magnitudes below the main sequence. These stars are in the last stages of their evolution (see below *End states of stars*).

The spectrum–luminosity diagram has numerous gaps. Few stars exist above the white dwarfs and to the left of the main sequence. The giants are separated from the main sequence by a gap named for Hertzsprung, who in 1911 became the first to recognize the difference between main-sequence and giant stars. The actual concentration of stars differs considerably in different parts of the diagram. Highly luminous stars are rare, whereas those of low luminosity are very numerous.

Figure 1 applies to the stars in the galactic spiral arm in the neighbourhood of the Sun and represents what would be obtained if a composite Hertzsprung–Russell diagram were constructed combining data for a large number of the star groups called open (or galactic) clusters, as, for example, the double cluster h and χ Persei, the Pleiades, the Coma cluster, and the Hyades (see below *Star clusters*). It includes very young stars, a few million years old, as well as ancient stars perhaps as old as 10,000,000,000 years.

By contrast, Figure 2 exhibits the type of temperature–luminosity (or colour–magnitude) relation characteristic of globular clusters, the central bulge of the Galaxy, and elliptical external galaxies—namely, of the so-called stellar

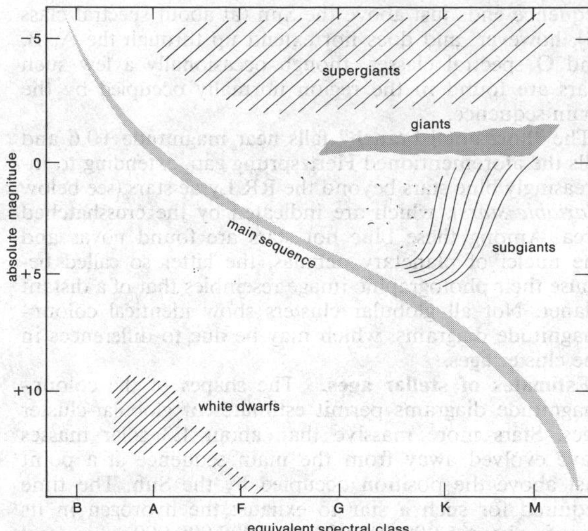

Figure 1: Schematic spectrum–luminosity correlation (Hertzsprung–Russell diagram) of spiral-arm stars in the neighbourhood of the Sun.

From *Astrophysical Journal*, reproduced by permission of the University of Chicago Press

Population II. (In addition to these oldest objects, Population II includes other very old stars that occur between the spiral arms of the Galaxy and at some distance above and below the galactic plane.) Because these systems are very remote from the observer, the stars are faint, and their spectra can be observed only with difficulty. As a consequence, their colours rather than spectra must be measured. Since the colours are closely related to surface temperature and therefore to spectral classes, equivalent spectral classes may be used; but it is stellar colours, not spectral classes, that are observed in this instance.

Population II stars

The difference between the two Hertzsprung–Russell diagrams in Figures 1 and 2 is striking. In Figure 2 there are no supergiants, and, instead of occurring at $M_v = 0$, the giant branch starts at around −3.5 for very red stars and forms a continuous sequence until an absolute magnitude of about 0 is reached. Then there is a band of stars, all about the same colour, that proceeds downward (*i.e.,* to fainter stars) to about $M_v = +3$. The giant branch is connected to the main sequence at about +4 by a narrow band. The main sequence extends to fainter, redder stars in much the same way as in the spiral-arm Population I objects. (Population I is the name given to the stars found within the spiral arms of the Milky Way system and other galaxies of the same type. Containing stars of all ages, from those in the process of formation to defunct white dwarfs, Population I stars are, nonetheless, always associated with the gas and dust of the interstellar medium.) The main

Population I stars

From *Astrophysical Journal*, reproduced by permission of the University of Chicago Press

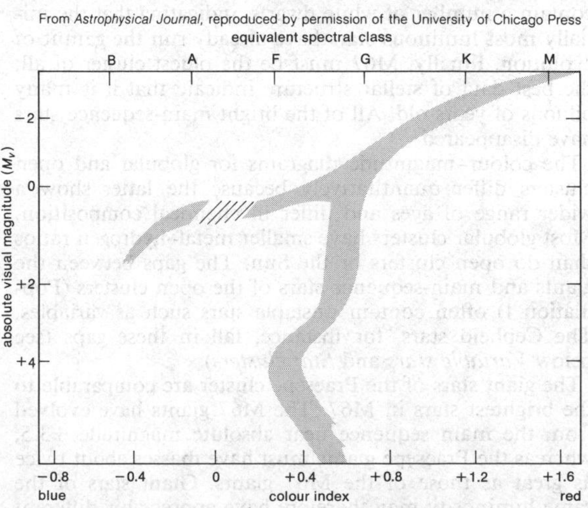

Figure 2: Colour–magnitude array for a typical Population II group of stars in a globular cluster. Absolute magnitude of the RR Lyrae stars (hatched area) is assumed to be 0.6.

sequence ends just above the Sun (at about spectral class G), however, and does not extend up through the A, B, and O spectral classes, though occasionally a few such stars are found in the region normally occupied by the main sequence.

The "horizontal branch" falls near magnitude +0.6 and fills the aforementioned Hertzsprung gap, extending to increasingly blue stars beyond the RR Lyrae stars (see below *Variable stars*), which are indicated by the crosshatched area. Among these blue hot stars are found novas and the nuclei of planetary nebulas, the latter so called because their photographic image resembles that of a distant planet. Not all globular clusters show identical colour-magnitude diagrams, which may be due to differences in the cluster ages.

Estimates of stellar ages. The shapes of the colour-magnitude diagrams permit estimates of globular-cluster ages. Stars more massive than about 1.3 solar masses have evolved away from the main sequence at a point just above the position occupied by the Sun. The time required for such a star to exhaust the hydrogen in its core is about 5,000,000,000 to 6,000,000,000 years, and the cluster must be at least as old. More ancient clusters have been identified. In the Galaxy, globular clusters are all very ancient objects, with ages measured in billions of years. In the Magellanic Clouds, there exist globular clusters such as NGC 1866 that contain numerous blue stars and therefore must be relatively young. Exact ages, however, cannot yet be assigned to globular clusters. The details of the evolutionary tracks depend on hydrogen-metal ratios, helium-hydrogen ratios, and the precise theory of stellar evolution.

Open clusters in the spiral arms of the Galaxy—extreme Population I—tell a somewhat different story. Figure 3 shows a colour-magnitude diagram for several different open clusters, the main feature distinguishing these clusters being their ages. The youngest cluster, the pair *h* and *χ* Persei, which is a few million years old, contains stars ranging widely in luminosity. Some stars have already evolved into the supergiant stage, so that the top of the main sequence is bent over. The stars of luminosity 10,000 times greater than that of the Sun have already largely depleted the hydrogen in their cores and are leaving the main sequence.

The brightest stars of the Pleiades have begun to leave the main sequence and are approaching the critical phase when they will have exhausted all the hydrogen in their cores. There are no giants in the Pleiades. Presumably, the cluster contained no stars as massive as some of those found in *h* and *χ* Persei.

The Beehive, or Praesepe, cluster is older than the Pleiades. All stars much more luminous than the first magnitude have begun to leave the main sequence; there are some giants. The Hyades, about 1,000,000,000 years old, displays a similar colour-magnitude array. These clusters contain a number of white dwarfs, indicating that the initially most luminous stars have already run the gamut of evolution. Finally, M67 must be the oldest cluster of all; the best data of stellar structure indicate that it is many billions of years old. All of the bright main-sequence stars have disappeared.

The colour-magnitude diagrams for globular and open clusters differ quantitatively because the latter show a wider range of ages and differ in chemical composition. Most globular clusters have smaller metal-hydrogen ratios than do open clusters or the Sun. The gaps between the giants and main-sequence stars of the open clusters (Population I) often contain unstable stars such as variables. The Cepheid stars, for instance, fall in these gaps (see below *Variable stars* and *Star clusters*).

The giant stars of the Praesepe cluster are comparable to the brightest stars in M67. The M67 giants have evolved from the main sequence near absolute magnitude +3.5, whereas the Praesepe giants must have masses about twice as great as those of the M67 giants. Giant stars of the same luminosity may therefore have appreciably different masses.

Numbers of stars versus luminosity. Of great statistical interest is the relationship between the luminosities of the stars and their frequency of occurrence. The naked-eye stars are nearly all intrinsically brighter than the Sun, but the opposite is true for the known stars within 20 light-years of the Sun. The bright stars are easily seen at great distances; the faint ones can be detected only if they are close. Only if stars of magnitude +11 were 1,000,000,000 times more abundant than stars of magnitude −4 could they be observed to some fixed limit of apparent brightness. Table 4 lists the relation between the number of stars and their luminosities in the neighbourhood of the Sun. For a sphere of radius 10 parsecs, about seven stars between the fourth and fifth magnitude, 30 stars between the 10th and 11th, and 67 stars between the 14th and 15th could be expected in such a volume. There would be less than one chance in 1,000 of finding a star brighter than magnitude −5. The luminosity function has a maximum near magnitude 15.5.

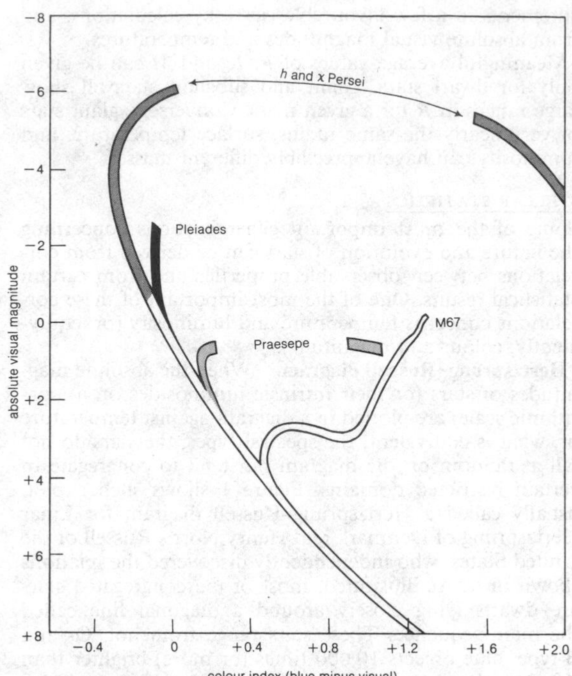

Figure 3: Colour-magnitude arrays for four galactic clusters of different ages.
From *Astrophysical Journal*, reproduced by permission of the University of Chicago Press

Table 4: Relation Between Number of Stars and Their Luminosities

absolute magnitude	number of stars	absolute magnitude	number of stars	absolute magnitude	number of stars
−0.5	0.05	+6.5	12.9	13.5	54
+0.5	0.52	7.5	16.1	14.5	67
+1.5	1.30	8.5	20.0	15.5	80
+2.5	3.20	9.5	24.5	16.5	60
+3.5	4.80	10.5	30.0	17.5	37
+4.5	7.00	11.5	35.0	18.5	23
+5.5	9.50	12.5	42.0	19.5	13

Source: After W.J. Luyten, *Monthly Notices,* Royal Astronomical Society, vol. 139 (1968).

Luminosity function and population type

The luminosity function depends on population type. The luminosity function for pure Population II differs substantially from that for pure Population I. There is a small peak near absolute magnitude +0.6, corresponding to the horizontal branch for Population II, and no stars as bright as absolute magnitude −5. The luminosity function for pure Population I is evaluated best from open star clusters, the stars in such a cluster being at about the same distance. The neighbourhood of the Sun includes examples of both Populations I and II.

Mass-luminosity correlations. A plot of mass against bolometric luminosity for visual binaries for which good parallaxes and masses are available shows that for stars with masses comparable to that of the Sun the luminosity,

L, varies as a power, $3+\beta$, of the mass M. This relation can be expressed as $L=(M)^{3+\beta}$. The power differs for substantially fainter or much brighter stars (see Table 3).

This mass–luminosity correlation applies only to unevolved main-sequence stars. It fails for giants and supergiants and for the subgiant (dimmer) components of eclipsing binaries, all of which have changed considerably during their lifetimes. It does not apply to any stars in a globular cluster not on the main sequence, or to white dwarfs that are abnormally faint for their masses.

The mass–luminosity correlation, predicted theoretically in the early 20th century by the English astronomer Arthur Eddington, is a general relationship that holds for all stars having essentially the same internal density and temperature distributions—*i.e.,* for what are termed the same stellar models.

VARIABLE STARS

Intrinsic variables

Many stars are variable. Some are geometric variables, as in the eclipsing binaries considered earlier. Others are intrinsically variable—*i.e.,* their total energy output fluctuates with time. Such intrinsic variable stars are dealt with in this section.

A fair number of stars are intrinsically variable. Some objects of this type were found by accident, but many were detected as a result of carefully planned searches. Variable stars are important in astronomy for several reasons. They usually appear to be stars at critical or short-lived phases of their evolution; detailed studies of their light and spectral characteristics, spatial distribution, and association with other types of stars may provide valuable clues to the life histories of various classes of stars. Certain kinds of variable stars, such as Cepheids (periodic variables) and novas (explosive variables), are extremely important in that they make it possible to establish the distances of remote stellar systems beyond the Galaxy, as, for example, the Magellanic Clouds and some of the nearer external galaxies. If the intrinsic luminosity of a recognizable variable is known and this kind of variable star can be found in a distant stellar system, the distance of the latter can be estimated from a measurement of apparent and absolute magnitudes, provided the interstellar absorption is also known.

Classification. Variables are often classified as behaving like a prototype star, and the entire class is then named for this star; *e.g.,* RR Lyrae stars are those whose variability follows the pattern of the star RR Lyrae. The most important classes of intrinsically variable stars are the following:

Major types

(1) Pulsating variables—*i.e.,* stars whose variations in light and colour are thought to arise primarily from stellar pulsations. These include Cepheids, RR Lyrae stars, and Delta Scuti stars, all with short regular periods up to a few days; long-period variables; semi-regular variables; irregular red variables; and Beta Canis Majoris stars.

(2) Explosive, or catastrophic, variables—in which the variations are produced by the wrenching away of part of the star, usually the outer layers, in some explosive process. They include SS Cygni or U Geminorum stars; novas; and supernovas (which are usually regarded as representing an enormous explosion involving most of the matter in a star [see below *Later stages of evolution*]).

(3) Miscellaneous and special types of variables—R Coronae Borealis stars; T Tauri stars; flare stars; pulsars (neutron stars); spectrum and magnetic variables; X-ray variable stars; and radio variable stars.

Pulsating stars. An impressive body of evidence indicates that stellar pulsations can account for the variability of Cepheids, long-period variables, semi-regular variables, Beta Canis Majoris stars, and even the irregular red variables. Of this group, the Cepheids have been studied in greatest detail, both theoretically and observationally. These stars are regular in their behaviour; some repeat their light curves with great faithfulness from one cycle to the next over periods of many years.

Much confusion existed in the study of Cepheids until it was recognized that different types of Cepheids are associated with different groups, or population types, of stars.

Classic Cepheids

Cepheids, belonging to the spiral-arm Population I, are characterized by regularity in their behaviour. They show continuous velocity curves indicative of regular pulsation. They exhibit a relation between period and luminosity in the sense that the longer the period of the star, the greater is its intrinsic brightness. This period–luminosity relationship has been used to establish the distances of remote stellar systems.

Cepheids with different properties are found in Population II, away from the Milky Way, in globular clusters. They are bluer than classic Population I Cepheids of the same period, and their light curves have different shapes. Studies of the light and velocity curves indicate that shells of gas are ejected from the stars as discontinuous layers that later fall back toward the surface. These stars exhibit no well-defined relation between period and luminosity; consequently, they are worthless as distance indicators. The distance of a Cepheid in a remote stellar system can be determined only if it is known to be a classic Cepheid.

RR Lyrae stars

Closely associated with Population II Cepheids are the cluster-type, or RR Lyrae, variables. Many of these stars are found in clusters, but some, such as the prototype RR Lyrae, occur far from any cluster or the central galactic bulge. The periods are less than a day, and there is no correlation between period and luminosity. Their absolute magnitudes are about 0.6; *i.e.,* they are about 50 times as bright as the Sun. They are useful for determining the distance of star clusters and some of the nearer external galaxies because their short periods permit them to be detected readily.

Long-period variables also probably owe their variations to pulsations. Here, the situation is complicated by the vast extent of their atmospheres, so that radiation originating at very different depths in the star is observed at the same time. At certain phases of the variations, bright hydrogen lines are observed, overlaid with titanium oxide absorption. The explanation is an outward-moving layer of hot, recombining gas, whose radiation is absorbed by strata of cool gases. These stars are all cool red giants and supergiants of spectral classes M (normal composition), R and N (carbon rich), or S (heavy-metal rich). The range in visual brightness during a pulsation can be a hundredfold, but the range in total energy output is much less, because at very low stellar temperatures (1,500–3,000 K) most of the energy is radiated in the infrared as heat rather than as light.

Unlike the light curves of classic Cepheids, the light curves of these red variables show considerable variations from onc cycle to another. The visual magnitude of Mira Ceti (Omicron Ceti) is normally about nine to 9.5 at minimum light, but at maximum it may lie between five and two. Time intervals between maxima often vary considerably. In such cool objects, a very small change in temperature can produce a huge change in the output of visible radiation. At the low temperatures of the red variables, compounds and probably solid particles are formed copiously, so that the visible light may be profoundly affected by a slight change in physical conditions. Random fluctuations from cycle to cycle, which would produce negligible effects in a hotter star, produce marked light changes in a long-period variable.

Long-period variables appear to fall into two groups: (1) those with periods of roughly 200 days tend to be associated with Population II; (2) those of periods of about a year belong to Population I.

Red semi-regular variables such as the RV Tauri stars show complex light and spectral changes. They do not repeat themselves from one cycle to the next; their behaviour suggests a simultaneous operation of two or more modes of oscillation. Betelgeuse is an example of an irregular red variable. In these stars the free period of oscillation does not coincide with the periodicity of the driving mechanism.

Finally, among the various types of pulsating variable stars, the Beta Canis Majoris variables are high-temperature stars (spectral class B) that often show complicated variations in spectral-line shapes and intensities, velocity curves, and light. In many cases, they have two periods of variation so similar in duration that complex interference or beat phenomena are observed, both in radial velocities and in the shapes of spectral lines.

A large body of evidence suggests that all members of this first class of variable stars owe their variability to pulsation. The pulsation theory was first proposed as a possible explanation as early as 1879, was applied to Cepheids in 1914, and was further developed by Eddington in 1917–18. Eddington found that if stars have roughly the same kind of internal structure, then the period multiplied by the square root of the density equals a constant that depends on the internal structure.

Pulsation theory

The Eddington theory, though a good approximation, encountered some severe difficulties that have been met through modifications. If the entire star pulsated in synchronism, it should be brightest when compressed and smaller while faintest when expanded and at its largest. The velocity should become zeroed at both maximum and minimum light. Observations contradict these predictions. When the star pulsates, all parts of the main body move in synchronism, but the outer observable strata fall out of step or lag behind the pulsation of the inner regions. Running waves are set up within the outer regions (envelope) of the star. Pulsations involve only the outer part of a star; the core, where energy is generated by thermonuclear reactions, is unaffected.

Many years ago, careful measurements of the average magnitudes and colours of RR Lyrae stars in globular cluster M3 showed that all these stars fell within a narrow range of luminosity and colour (or surface temperature) or, what amounts to the same thing, luminosity and radius. Also, every star falling in this narrow range of brightness and size was an RR Lyrae variable. Subsequent work has indicated that similar considerations apply to classic Cepheids. Variability is thus a characteristic of any star whose evolution carries it to a certain size and luminosity.

In the pulsation theory as now developed, the light and velocity changes of Cepheids can be interpreted not only qualitatively but also quantitatively. The complex light curves of Population II Cepheids, for example, have been precisely predicted by the theory. Stellar pulsation, like other rhythmic actions, may give rise to harmonic phenomena wherein beats reinforce or interfere with one another. Beat and interference phenomena then complicate the light and velocity changes. The RR Lyrae stars supply some of the best examples, but semi-regular variables such as the RV Tauri stars, "dwarf" Cepheids such as Delta Scuti, or SX Phoenicis evidently vibrate simultaneously with two or more periods.

Explosive variables. The evolution of a member of a close double-star system can be markedly affected by the presence of its companion. As the stars age, the more massive one swells up more quickly as it moves away from the main sequence. It becomes so large that its outer envelope falls under the gravitational influence of the smaller star. Matter is continuously fed from the more rapidly evolving star to the less massive one, which still remains on the main sequence. U Cephei is a classic example of such a system for which spectroscopic evidence shows streams of gas flowing from the more highly evolved star to the hotter companion, which is now the more massive of the two. Eventually, the latter will also leave the main sequence and become a giant star, only to lose its outer envelope to the companion, which by that time may have reached the white-dwarf stage.

Novas and supernovas

Novas appear to be binary stars that have evolved from contact binaries of the W Ursae Majoris type. One member may have reached the white-dwarf stage. Matter fed to it from its distended companion appears to produce instabilities that result in violent explosions or nova outbursts. The time interval between outbursts can range from a few score years to hundreds of thousands of years.

In ordinary novas the explosion seems to involve only the outer layers, as the star later returns to its former brightness; in supernovas the explosion is catastrophic. Normally, novas are small blue stars much fainter than the Sun, though very much hotter. When an outburst occurs, the star can brighten very rapidly, 10 magnitudes or more in a few hours. Thereafter it fades; the rate of fading is connected with the brightness of the nova. The brightest novas, which reach absolute magnitudes of about −8, fade most rapidly, whereas a typical slow nova, which reaches an absolute magnitude of −5, can take 10 times as long to decline in brightness. The changes in light are accompanied by pronounced spectroscopic changes that can be interpreted as arising from alterations in an ejected shell that dissipates slowly in space. In its earliest phases, the expanding shell is opaque. As its area grows, with a surface temperature near 7,000 K, the nova brightens rapidly. Then, near maximum light, the shell becomes transparent, and its total brightness plummets rapidly, causing the nova to dim.

The mass of the shell is thought to be rather small, comparable with the mass of the Earth. Only the outer layers of the star seem to be affected; the main mass settles down after the outburst into a state much as before until a new outburst occurs. The existence of repeating novas, such as the star T Coronae Borealis, suggests that perhaps all novas repeat at intervals ranging up to thousands or perhaps millions of years; and probably, the larger the explosion, the longer the interval. There is strong evidence that novas are components of close double stars and, in particular, that they have evolved from the most common kind of eclipsing binaries, those of the W Ursae Majoris type, which are pairs of stars apparently similar to the Sun in size but revolving around one another while almost touching.

Stars of the SS Cygni type undergo novalike outbursts but of a much smaller amplitude. The intervals between outbursts are a few months to a year. Such variables are close binaries. The development of this particular type may be possible only in close binary systems.

Eta Carinae

A peculiar object with no known counterpart is Eta Carinae, which appears in the telescope as a fuzzy red "star" slightly less than two arc seconds in diameter. Surrounding it is a roughly elliptical nonuniform shell or halo about 10 arc seconds in diameter. First observed as a star of about the fourth magnitude in 1677, it brightened irregularly, undergoing an outburst in 1843. Unlike an ordinary nova or supernova, it remained bright for several years, fading out of sight to the naked eye about a century ago. Since then, it has shown irregular variations around the seventh magnitude. The first spectrum obtained of the object resembled that of a somewhat abnormal supergiant, but it now shows very complex emission-line structures dominated by radiations of ionized iron. If a star was present, it may have been blown to bits. Eta Carinae was brighter than normal novas, yet it resembles no known supernova; the star proper (excepting its corona) does not appear to be a source of X rays or non-thermal radio-frequency emission.

Probably all variable stars represent more or less ephemeral phases in the evolution of a star. Aside from catastrophic events of the kind that produce a supernova, some phases of stellar variability might be of such brief duration as to permit recognizable changes during an interval of 50 to 100 years. Other stages may require many thousands of years. The period of Delta Cephei, for example, has not changed by a detectable amount since its variability was discovered.

Peculiar variables. R Coronae Borealis variables are giant stars of about the Sun's temperature whose atmospheres are characterized by excessive quantities of carbon. The brightness of such a star remains constant until the star suddenly dims by several magnitudes and then slowly recovers its original brightness. (The star's colour remains the same during the changes in brightness.) The dimmings occur in a random fashion and seem to be due to the huge concentrations of carbon. At times the carbon vapour literally condenses into soot, and the star is hidden until the smog blanket is evaporated. Similar veiling may sometimes occur in other types of low-temperature stars, particularly in long-period variables.

Flare stars

Flare stars are cool dwarfs (spectral class M) that display flares apparently very much like, but much more intense than, those of the Sun. In fact, the flares are sometimes so bright that they overwhelm the normal light of the star. Solar flares are associated with copious emission of radio waves, and simultaneous optical and radio events appear to have been found in UV Ceti, YZ Canis Minoris, and V371 Orionis.

Spectrum and magnetic variables, mostly of spectral class A, show only small amplitudes of light variation but often pronounced spectroscopic changes. Their spectra typically show strong lines of metals such as manganese, titanium, iron, chromium, and the lanthanides (also called rare earths), which vary periodically in intensity. These stars have strong magnetic fields, typically from a few hundred to a few thousand gauss; one star, HD 215441, has a field on the order of 30,000 gauss. Not all magnetic stars are known to be variable in light; these objects also seem to have variable magnetic fields. The best interpretation is that these stars are rotating about an inclined axis. As with the Earth, the magnetic and rotation axes do not coincide. Different ions are concentrated in different areas (*e.g.*, chromium in one area and the lanthanides in another).

The Sun is an emitter of radio waves, but with present techniques it could not be detected—even in its most active phases—at a distance greater than that of the nearest star, about four light-years away. Most discrete radio-frequency sources have turned out to be objects like old supernovas, radio galaxies, and quasars, though well-recognized radio stars also have been recorded on occasion. These probably include flare stars, possibly red supergiants such as Alpha Orionis, the high-temperature dwarf companion to the red supergiant Antares, and the shells ejected from Nova Serpentis 1970 and Nova Delphini. The radio emission from the latter objects is consistent with that expected from an expanding shell of ionized gas that fades away as the gas becomes attenuated. The central star of the Crab Nebula has been detected as a radio (and optical) pulsar.

Measurements from rockets, balloons, and satellites have revealed distinct X-ray sources outside the solar system. The strongest galactic source, Scorpius X-1, appears to be associated with a hot variable star resembling an old nova. Three radio sources have been observed near the X-ray star. One coincides with the star, which shows rapid irregular time variations, as do the optical and radio sources. The other two radio sources lie on opposite sides of the X-ray source and are constant in brightness. X-ray stars may be massive objects near the end of their evolution and may be closely related to pulsars.

Globular clusters are a notable source of cosmic X rays. Some of this X-ray emission appears as intense fluctuations of radiation lasting only a few seconds but changing in strength by as much as 25 times. These X-ray sources have become known as bursters, and several such objects have been discovered outside of globular clusters as well. Some bursters vary on a regular basis, while others seem to turn on and off randomly. The most popular interpretation holds that bursters are the result of binary systems in which one of the objects—a compact neutron star or black hole (see below *End states of stars*)—pulls matter from the companion, a normal star. This matter is violently heated in the process, giving rise to X rays. That the emission is often in the form of a burst is probably caused by something interrupting the flow of matter onto (or into) the compact object or by an eclipsing orbit of the binary system.

Bursters

Stellar structure

STELLAR ATMOSPHERES

To interpret a stellar spectrum quantitatively, knowledge of the variation in temperature and density with depth in the star's atmosphere is needed. Some general theoretical principles are outlined here.

The gradient of temperature in a star's atmosphere depends on the method of energy transport to the surface. One way to move energy from the interior of a star to its surface is via radiation; photons produced in the core are repeatedly absorbed and reemitted by stellar atoms, gradually propagating to the surface. A second way is via convection, which is a non-radiative mechanism involving a physical upwelling of matter much as in a pot of boiling water. For the Sun, at least, a discriminant is possible.

Limb darkening

High-speed photographs of the Sun's disk show that the centre of the disk is brighter than the limb. The difference in brightness depends on the wavelength of the radiation detected; it is large in violet light, small in red light, and nearly vanishes when the Sun is imaged in infrared radiation. This limb darkening arises because the Sun becomes hotter toward its core. At the centre of the disk, radiation is received from deeper and hotter layers (on average) instead of from the limb, and the dependence of temperature on depth can be shown to correspond to the transport of energy by radiation, not by convection, at least in the outer layers of the Sun's atmosphere.

The amount of limb darkening in any star depends on the effective temperature of the star and on the variation in temperature with depth. Limb darkening is occasionally an important factor in the analysis of stellar observations. For example, it must be taken into account to interpret properly the observed light curves of eclipsing binaries, and here again the results suggest transport of energy via radiation.

The layers of a normal star are assumed to be in mechanical, or "hydrostatic," equilibrium. This means that at each point in the atmosphere, the pressure supports the weight of the overlying layers. In this way, a relation between pressure and density can be found for any given depth.

Opacity of a star's atmospheric layers

In addition to the temperature and density gradients, the chemical composition of the atmospheric layers as well as the absorptivity, or opacity, of the material must be known. In the Sun the principal source of opacity is the negative hydrogen ion (H^-), a hydrogen atom with one extra electron loosely bound to it. In the atmospheres of many stars, the extra electrons break loose and recombine with other ions, thereby causing a reemission of energy in the form of light. At visible wavelengths the main contribution to the opacity comes from the destruction of this ion by interaction with a photon (the above-cited process termed photodissociation). In hotter stars, such as Sirius A (temperature = 10,000 K), atomic hydrogen is the main source of opacity, whereas in cooler stars much of the outgoing energy is often absorbed by molecular bands of titanium oxide, water vapour, and carbon monoxide. Additional sources of opacity are absorption by helium atoms and electron scattering in hotter stars, absorption by hydrogen molecules and molecular ions, absorption by certain abundant metals such as magnesium, and Rayleigh scattering (a type of wavelength-dependent scattering of radiation by particles named for the British physicist Lord Rayleigh) in cool supergiant stars.

At considerable depths in the Sun and similar stars, convection sets in. Though most models of stellar atmospheres (particularly the outer layers) assume plane-parallel stratified layers, photographs of the solar granulation belie this simple picture. Realistic models must allow for rising columns of heated gases in some areas and descent of cooler gases in others. The motions of the radiating gases are especially important when the model is to be used to calculate the anticipated line spectrum of the star. Typical velocities are on the order of two kilometres per second in the Sun; in other stars they can be much larger.

Temperature, density, and pressure all increase steadily inward in the Sun's atmosphere. The Sun has no distinct solid surface, so the point from which the depth or height is measured is arbitrary. The temperature of the visible layers ranges from 4,700 to 6,200 K, the density from about 10^{-7} to 4×10^{-7} gram per cubic centimetre, and the gas pressure from 0.002 to 0.14 atmosphere. The visible layers of stars such as the Sun have very low densities and pressures compared with the Earth's atmosphere, even though the temperature is much higher. The strata of the solar atmosphere are very opaque compared with the terrestrial atmosphere.

For stars other than the Sun, the dependence of temperature on depth cannot be directly determined. Calculations must proceed by a process of successive approximations, during which the flux of energy is taken to be constant with depth. Computations have been undertaken for atmospheres of a variety of stars ranging from dwarfs to supergiants, from cool to hot stars. Their validity can be evaluated only by examining how well they predict the observed features of a star's continuous and line spectrum, including the detailed shapes of spectral-line features. Considering the known complexities of stellar atmospheres, the results fit the observations remarkably well.

Severe deviations exist for stars with extended and expanding atmospheres. Matter flowing outward from a star produces a stellar wind analogous to the solar wind, but one that is often much more extensive and violent. In the spectrum of certain very hot O-type stars (*e.g.,* Zeta Puppis), strong, relatively narrow emission lines can be seen; however, in the ultraviolet, observations from rockets and orbiting spacecraft show strong emission lines with distinct absorption components on the shorter wavelength side. These absorption features are produced by rapidly outflowing atoms that absorb the radiation from the underlying stellar surface. The observed shifts in frequency correspond to ejection velocities of about 100 kilometres per second. Much gentler stellar winds are found in cool M-type supergiants.

Effects of rapid stellar rotation

Rapid stellar rotation also can modify the structure of a star's atmosphere. Since effective gravity is much reduced near the equator, the appropriate description of the atmosphere varies with latitude. Should the star be spinning at speeds near the breakup point, rings or shells may be shed from the equator.

Some of the most extreme and interesting cases of rotational effects are found in close binary systems. Interpretations of the light and velocity curves of these objects suggest that the spectroscopic observations cannot be reconciled with simple, orderly rotating stars. Instead, emission and absorption lines sometimes overlap in such a way as to suggest streams of gas moving between the stars. For example, Beta Lyrae (Figure 4), as an eclipsing binary system, has a period of 12.9 days and displays very large orbital-velocity shifts. The brighter member at visible wavelengths is a B9-type star; the other member appears to be a hot, abnormal object whose spectral lines have not been observed. The spectrum of the B9-type component shows the regular velocity changes expected of a binary star but with an absorption (and associated emission) spectrum corresponding to a higher temperature (near spectral class B5) and a blue continuum corresponding to a very high temperature star. The anomalous B5-type spectrum is evidently excited principally by the hotter source; it envelopes the entire system and shows few changes in velocity with time.

Supergiant stars have very extended atmospheres that are probably not even approximately in hydrostatic equilibrium. The atmospheres of M-type supergiant stars appear to be slowly expanding outward. Observations of the eclipsing binary 31 Cygni show that the K-type supergiant component has an extremely inhomogeneous, extended atmosphere composed of numerous blobs and filaments. As the secondary member of this system slowly moves behind the larger star, its light shines through larger masses of the K-type star's atmosphere. If the atmosphere were in orderly layers, the lines of ionized calcium, for example, produced by absorption of the light of the B-type star by the K-type star's atmosphere, would grow stronger uniformly as the eclipse proceeds. They do not, however.

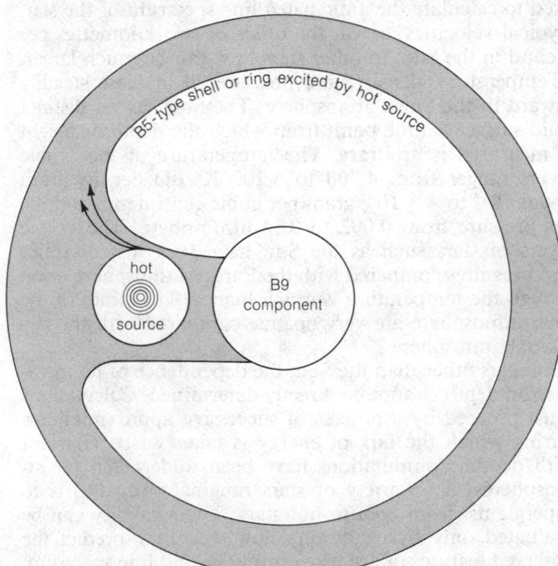

Figure 4: Probable behaviour of gases around "peculiar" double star Beta Lyrae. The nature of the "hot" component is not well understood.

STELLAR INTERIORS

Models of the internal structure of stars—particularly their temperature, density, and pressure gradients below the surface—depend on basic principles explained in this section. It is especially important that model calculations take account of the change in the star's structure with time as its hydrogen supply is gradually converted into helium. Fortunately, given that most stars can be said to be examples of an "ideal gas," there results a basic simplicity of the relations among temperature, density, and pressure. In fact, these quantities can be calculated for main-sequence and white-dwarf stars with greater confidence than can the values for internal temperature and density of the Earth.

Distribution of matter. Several mathematical relations can be derived from basic physical laws, assuming that the gas is "ideal" and that a star has spherical symmetry; both these assumptions are met with a high degree of validity. Another common assumption is that the interior of a star is in hydrostatic equilibrium, a condition whereby the pressure at each point exactly balances the weight of the overlying layers. This balance is often expressed as a simple relation between pressure gradient and density. A second relation expresses the continuity of mass; *i.e.,* if M is the mass of matter within a sphere of radius r, the mass added, ΔM, when encountering an increase in distance Δr through a shell of volume, $4\pi r^2\Delta r$, equals the volume of the shell multiplied by the density, ρ. In symbols this is expressed as $\Delta M = 4\pi r^2\rho\Delta r$.

Hydrostatic equilibrium

A third relation, termed the equation of state, expresses an explicit relation among the temperature, density, and pressure of a star's internal matter. Throughout the star the matter is entirely gaseous, and, except in certain highly evolved objects, it obeys closely the perfect gas law. In such neutral gases the molecular weight is 2 for molecular hydrogen, 4 for helium, 56 for iron, and so on. In the interior of a typical star, however, the high temperatures and densities virtually guarantee that nearly all the matter is completely ionized; the gas is said to be a plasma, the fourth state of matter. Under these conditions the hydrogen molecules are not only dissociated into individual atoms but also the atoms themselves are broken apart (ionized) into their constituent protons and electrons. Hence, the molecular weight of ionized hydrogen is the average mass of a proton and an electron—namely, $1/2$ on the atom-mass scale noted above. By contrast, a completely ionized helium atom contributes a mass of 4 with a helium nucleus (an alpha particle) plus two electrons of negligible mass; hence, its average molecular weight is $4/3$. As another example, a totally ionized nickel atom contributes a nucleus of mass 58.7 plus 28 electrons; its molecular weight is then $58.7/29 = 2.02$. Since stars contain a preponderance of hydrogen and helium that are completely ionized throughout the interior, the average particle mass, μ, is the (unit) mass of a proton, divided by a factor taking into account the concentrations by weight of hydrogen, helium, and heavier ions. Accordingly, the molecular weight depends critically on the star's chemical composition, particularly on the ratio of helium to hydrogen as well as on the total content of heavier matter.

An interior consisting of plasma

If the temperature is sufficiently high, the radiation pressure, P_r, must be taken into account in addition to the perfect gas pressure, P_g. The total equation of state then becomes, $P = P_g + P_r$. Here, P_g depends on temperature, density, and molecular weight, whereas P_r depends on temperature and on the radiation density constant, $a = 7.5 \times 10^{-15}$ ergs per cubic centimetre per degree to the fourth power. With $\mu = 2$ (as an upper limit) and $\rho = 1.4$ grams per cubic centimetre (the mean density of the Sun), the temperature at which the radiation pressure would equal the gas pressure can be calculated. The answer is 28,000,000 K, much hotter than at the core of the Sun. Consequently, radiation pressure may be neglected for the Sun, but it cannot be ignored for hotter, more massive stars. Radiation pressure may then set an upper limit to stellar luminosity.

Certain stars, notably white dwarfs, do not obey the perfect gas law. Instead, the pressure is almost entirely contributed by the electrons, which are said to be particulate members of a degenerate gas (see below *White dwarfs*). If μ' is the average mass per free electron of the totally ionized gas, the pressure, P, and density, ρ, are such that P is proportional to a $^5/_3$ power of the density divided by the average mass per free electron; *i.e.*, $P = 10^{13}(\rho/\mu')^{5/3}$. The temperature does not enter at all. At still higher densities the equation of state becomes more intricate, but it can be shown that even this complicated equation of state is adequate to calculate the internal structure of the white-dwarf stars. As a result, white dwarfs are probably better understood than most other celestial objects.

For normal stars such as the Sun, the energy-transport method for the interior must be known. Except in white dwarfs or in the dense cores of evolved stars, thermal conduction is unimportant because the heat conductivity is very low. One significant mode of transport is an actual flow of radiation outward through the star. Starting as X rays near the core, the radiation is gradually "softened" as it works its way to the surface (typically, in the Sun, over the course of about 1,000,000 years) to emerge as ordinary light and heat. The rate of flow of radiation is proportional to the thermal gradient—namely, the rate of change of temperature with interior distance. Providing yet another relation of stellar structure, this equation uses the following important quantities: a, the radiation constant noted above; c, the velocity of light; ρ, the density; and κ, a measure of the opacity of the matter. The larger the value of κ, the smaller the transparency of the material and the steeper the temperature fall required to push the energy outward at the required rate. The opacity, κ, can be calculated for any temperature, density, and chemical composition and is found to depend in a complex manner largely on the two former quantities.

In the Sun's outermost (though still interior) layers and especially in certain giant stars, energy transport takes place by quite another mechanism: large-scale mass motions of gases, namely convection. Huge volumes of gas deep within the star become heated, rise to higher layers, and mix with their surroundings, thus releasing great quantities of energy. The extraordinarily complex flow patterns cannot be followed in detail, but when convection occurs a relatively simple mathematical relation connects density and pressure. Wherever convection does occur, it is a much more efficient means to move energy than radiative transport.

Source of stellar energy. The most basic property of stars is that their radiant energy must derive from internal sources. Given the great length of time that stars endure (some 10,000,000,000 years in the case of the Sun), it can be shown that neither chemical nor gravitational effects could possibly yield the required energies. Instead, the cause must be nuclear events wherein lighter nuclei are fused to create heavier nuclei, an inevitable by-product being energy.

In the interior of a star, the particles move rapidly in every direction because of the high temperatures present. Every so often a proton moves close enough to a nucleus to be captured, and a nuclear reaction takes place. Only protons of extremely high energy (many times the average energy in a star such as the Sun) are capable of producing nuclear events of this kind. A minimum temperature required for fusion is roughly 10,000,000 K. Since the energies of protons are proportional to temperature, the rate of energy production rises steeply as temperature increases.

For the Sun and other normal main-sequence stars, the source of energy lies in the conversion of hydrogen to helium. The nuclear reaction thought to occur in the Sun is called the proton–proton cycle. In this fusion reaction, two protons (^{1}H) collide to form a deuteron (^{2}H), with the liberation of a positron (the electron's positively charged antimatter counterpart, denoted e^+). Also emitted is a neutral particle of very small (or possibly zero) mass called a neutrino, ν. While the helium ash remains in the core where it was produced, the neutrino escapes from

Proton–proton cycle

the solar interior within seconds. The positron encounters an ordinary negatively charged electron, and the two annihilate each other with much energy being released. This annihilation energy amounts to 1.02 megaelectron volts (MeV), which accords well with the Einsteinian relation, $E = mc^2$ (where m is the mass of the two particles, c the velocity of light, and E the liberated energy).

Next, a proton collides with the deuteron to form the nucleus of a light helium atom of atomic weight 3, ^{3}He. A "hard" X ray (one of higher energy) or gamma ray also is emitted. The most likely event to follow in the chain is a collision of this ^{3}He nucleus with a normal ^{4}He nucleus (or α particle) to form the nucleus of a beryllium atom of weight 7, ^{7}Be, with the emission of another gamma (γ) ray. The ^{7}Be nucleus in turn captures a proton to form a boron nucleus of atomic weight 8, ^{8}B, with the liberation of yet another gamma ray.

Boron-8, however, is very unstable. It almost immediately decays into beryllium of atomic weight 8, ^{8}Be, with the emission of another positron and a neutrino. The nucleus itself thereafter decays into two α particles (the helium nucleus, ^{4}He). These nuclear events can be represented by the following equations:

$$^3\text{He} + {}^4\text{He} \rightarrow {}^7\text{Be} + \gamma \quad \text{(rather slow reaction)}$$
$$^7\text{Be} + {}^1\text{H} \rightarrow {}^8\text{B} + \gamma \quad \text{(rapid reaction)}$$
$$\left.\begin{array}{l} ^8\text{B} \rightarrow {}^8\text{Be} + e^+ + \nu \\ ^8\text{Be} \rightarrow 2\,{}^4\text{He} \end{array}\right\} \quad \text{(instantaneous reactions)}$$

In the course of these reactions, four protons are consumed to form one helium nucleus, while two electrons perish.

The mass of four hydrogen atoms is

$$4 \times 1.00797 = 4.03188 \text{ atomic mass units;}$$

that of a helium atom is 4.0026. Hence, 0.02928 atomic mass units, or 0.7 percent of the original mass, have disappeared. Some of this has been carried away by the elusive neutrinos, but most of it has been converted to radiant energy. In order to keep shining at its present rate, a typical star (*e.g.*, the Sun) needs to convert 674,000,000 tons of hydrogen to 670,000,000 tons of helium every second. According to the formula $E = mc^2$, more than 4,000,000 tons of matter literally disappear into radiation each second.

This theory provides a good understanding of solar-energy generation except for one potential problem. Attempts have been made to detect the neutrino flux from the Sun by means of an intricate experimental apparatus. Fewer neutrinos than expected have been detected so far, and no consensus has been reached regarding this discordance.

Carbon cycle

The main source of energy in hotter stars is the carbon cycle (also called the CNO cycle for carbon, nitrogen, and oxygen), in which hydrogen is transformed into helium, with carbon serving as a catalyst. The reactions proceed as follows: First, a carbon nucleus, ^{12}C, captures a hydrogen nucleus or proton, ^{1}H, to form a nucleus of nitrogen, ^{13}N, a gamma ray being emitted in the process; thus, $^{12}\text{C} + {}^1\text{H} \rightarrow {}^{13}\text{N} + \gamma$. The light ^{13}N nucleus is unstable, however. It emits a positron, e^+, which encounters an ordinary electron, e^-, and the two annihilate one another. A neutrino also is released, and the resulting ^{13}C nucleus is stable. Eventually the ^{13}C nucleus captures another proton, forms ^{14}N, and emits another gamma ray. In symbols the reaction is represented by the equations: $^{13}\text{N} \rightarrow {}^{13}\text{C} + e^+ + \nu$; then $^{13}\text{C} + {}^1\text{H} \rightarrow {}^{14}\text{N} + \gamma$. This ordinary nitrogen, ^{14}N, is stable, but when it captures a proton to form a nucleus of light oxygen-15, ^{15}O, the resulting nucleus is unstable against beta decay. It therefore emits a positron and a neutrino, a sequence of events expressed by the symbols: $^{14}\text{N} + {}^1\text{H} \rightarrow {}^{15}\text{O} + \gamma$; then $^{15}\text{O} \rightarrow {}^{15}\text{N} + e^+ + \nu$. Again, the positron meets an electron and the two annihilate each other while the neutrino escapes. Eventually the ^{15}N nucleus encounters a fast-moving proton, ^{1}H, and captures it, but the formation of an ordinary ^{16}O nucleus by this process occurs only rarely. The most likely effect of this proton capture is a breakdown of ^{15}N and a return to the ^{12}C nucleus, that is: $^{15}\text{N} + {}^1\text{H} \rightarrow {}^{12}\text{C} + {}^4\text{He} + \gamma$. Thus, the original ^{12}C nucleus reappears and the four protons that have been added permit the formation of an alpha particle (or helium nucleus). The same amount of mass has disappeared, though a different fraction of it may have been carried off by the neutrinos.

Only the hottest stars that lie on the main sequence shine with energy produced by the carbon cycle. The faint red dwarfs use the proton–proton cycle exclusively, whereas stars such as the Sun shine mostly by the proton–proton reaction but derive some contribution from the carbon cycle as well.

The aforementioned mathematical relationships permit the problem of stellar structure to be addressed notwithstanding the complexity of the problem. An early assumption that stars have a uniform chemical composition throughout their interiors simplified the calculations considerably, but it had to be abandoned when studies in stellar evolution proved that the compositions of stars change with age (see below *Later stages of evolution*). Computations need to be carried out by a step-by-step process known as numerical integration. They must take into account that the density and pressure of a star vanish at the surface, whereas these quantities and the temperature remain finite at the core. A common procedure is to make the computations from the surface inward and from the centre outward; the two solutions can then be adjusted, giving the same values for the temperature, density, and pressure when they come together.

Resulting models of a star's interior, including the relation among mass, luminosity, and radius, are determined largely by the mode of energy transport. In the Sun and the fainter main-sequence stars, energy is transported throughout the outer layers by convective currents, whereas in the deep interior, energy is transported by radiation. Among the hotter stars of the main sequence, the reverse appears to be true. The deep interiors of the stars that derive their energy primarily from the carbon cycle are in convective equilibrium, whereas in the outer parts the energy is carried by radiation. The observed masses, luminosities, and radii of most main-sequence stars can be reproduced with reasonable and uniform chemical composition.

Chemically homogeneous models of giant and supergiant stars cannot be constructed. If a yellow giant such as Capella is assumed to be built like a main-sequence star, its central temperature turns out to be so low that no known nuclear process can possibly supply the observed energy output. Progress has been made only by assuming that these stars were once main-sequence objects that, in the course of their development, exhausted the hydrogen in their deep interiors. Inert cores consequently formed, composed mainly of the helium ash left from the hydrogen-fusion process. Since no helium nuclear reactions are known to occur at the few tens of millions of kelvins likely to prevail in these interiors, no thermonuclear energy could be released from such depleted cores. Instead, energy is assumed to be generated in a thin shell surrounding the inert core where some fuel remains and is presumably produced by the carbon cycle. Such models are called shell-source models. As a star uses up increasing amounts of its hydrogen supply, its core grows in mass, all the while the outer envelope of the star continues to expand. These shell-source models explain the observed luminosities, masses, and radii of giants and supergiants (see below *Later stages of evolution*).

Shell-source models

The depletion of hydrogen fuel is appreciable even for a dwarf, middle-aged star such as the Sun. The Sun seems to have been shining at its present rate for about the last 20 percent of its current age of 5,000,000,000 years. For its observed luminosity to be maintained, the Sun's central temperature must have increased considerably since the formation of the solar system, largely as a consequence of the depletion of the hydrogen in its interior along with an accompanying increase in molecular weight and temperature. During the past 5,000,000,000 years, the Sun probably brightened by about half a magnitude; in the early Precambrian (about 2,000,000,000 years ago), the solar luminosity must have been some 20 percent less than it is today.

Table 5 gives the results of a typical calculation of the internal structure of the Sun. The carbon and proton–proton cycles as well as evolutionary effects are all accounted

Table 5: Internal Structure of the Sun

r/R	mass within r/R fractional	density (water = 1)	temperature (K)
0.0000	0.0000	149.8000	14,920,000
0.1026	0.0810	86.3000	12,460,000
0.2027	0.3510	35.0900	8,953,000
0.3022	0.5910	14.6300	6,731,000
0.4000	0.8110	3.9200	4,727,000
0.5048	0.9110	1.2030	3,557,000
0.5980	0.9560	0.4470	2,770,000
0.7020	0.9810	0.1550	2,095,000
0.8039	0.9930	0.0608	1,346,000
0.9000	0.9985	0.0197	630,000
0.9540	0.9997	0.0061	290,000
0.9760	0.9999	0.0025	162,000

Source: From J. and N. Bahcall and R.K. Ulrich.

for in this model. Temperature, density, and the fraction of the total mass within a radius r (shown in Table 5 as a fraction of the Sun's radius, R) are listed. Nearly all the matter within the Sun is hotter than 1,000,000 K; the central temperature attains a value of about 15,000,000 K.

Star formation and evolution

Throughout the Milky Way Galaxy (and even near the Sun itself), astronomers have discovered stars that are well evolved or even approaching extinction, or both, as well as occasional stars that must be very young or still in the process of formation. Evolutionary effects on these stars are not negligible, not even for a middle-aged star such as the Sun. More massive stars must display more spectacular effects because the rate of conversion of mass into energy is higher. While the Sun produces energy at the rate of about two ergs per gram per second, a more luminous main-sequence star can release energy at a rate some 1,000 times greater. Consequently, effects that require billions of years to be easily recognized in the Sun might occur within a few million years in highly luminous and massive stars. A supergiant star such as Antares, a bright main-sequence star such as Rigel, or even a more modest star such as Sirius cannot have endured as long as the Sun has endured. These stars must have been formed relatively recently.

Rates of energy production

BIRTH OF STARS AND EVOLUTION TO THE MAIN SEQUENCE

Stars form from the gas and dust of the interstellar medium. The matter between stars is not uniformly distributed in space but is spread in a patchy fashion. Occasionally, a massive cloud will accumulate sufficient matter for its own gravitational attraction to draw it still further together. The details of this process are only beginning to be understood.

As the core of the cloud begins pulling itself together, its internal temperature and density rise until the protostar within reaches incandescence with a faint red glow. At this stage, the protostar is not yet shining by nuclear processes but rather by the energy released via its gravitational contraction. As the internal temperature rises to a few million kelvins, deuterium (heavy hydrogen) is first destroyed. Then lithium, beryllium, and boron are broken down into helium as their nuclei are bombarded by protons moving at increasingly high speeds.

Dwarf stars of the T Tauri type (see below *OB and T associations*) have been observed in the clouds of dark obscuring matter in Taurus as well as in numerous other regions of the Milky Way. These objects might represent stars in the actual process of formation. In fact, several galactic regions in which stars were actually "turned on" may have been observationally identified. Other evidence is provided by colour–magnitude diagrams such as that obtained for the cluster NGC 2264 associated with the star S Monocerotis. In this cluster the brighter part of the main sequence is well defined by stars somewhat more luminous than the Sun. The fainter redder stars whose colours correspond to spectral classes G, K, and M all fall above the main sequence defined by the normal dwarf stars. Presumably, they are contracting toward the main sequence, shining mostly by liberation of gravitational

Sites of possible star formation

energy; however, they might be burning the light helium isotope helium-3 before they reach the main sequence and the proton–proton reaction is ignited.

Many additional sites of possible star formation have been identified in the Milky Way and are being investigated carefully for possible changes. Radio and infrared observations have provided, for example, some sketchy evidence for more advanced pre-stellar objects. The Orion complex, shown in Figure 5, is one such region. Illuminated by several O-type stars, the bright Orion Nebula is partly engulfed by a vast molecular cloud. This dark cloud extends well beyond the few light-years bordered by the photograph and has been studied by means of the radio radiation emitted and absorbed by carbon monoxide and formaldehyde.

The Orion molecular cloud also houses several smaller sites of intense radiation emitted by molecules under very special conditions. Molecules such as hydroxyl (OH) and water vapour (H_2O) have been found by radio techniques to be buried within the core of the cloud fragment. Their extent measures about 10^{10} kilometres, or roughly $^1/_{1,000}$ of a light-year, which is approximately the full diameter of the solar system. While astronomers cannot currently determine whether these regions will eventually form stars more or less like the Sun, it does seem certain that such intensely emitting regions are on the threshold of becoming protostars.

Detailed calculations show that a protostar originally appears on the Hertzsprung–Russell diagram well above the main sequence because it is too bright for its colour. As it continues to contract, it moves downward and to the left toward the main sequence.

By courtesy of Lick Observatory, University of California

Figure 5: The Orion Nebula (NGC 1976, M42), partly engulfed by a vast molecular cloud, various parts of which are probably fragmenting and contracting, with even smaller sites resembling protostars.

SUBSEQUENT DEVELOPMENT ON THE MAIN SEQUENCE

As the central temperature and density continue to rise, the proton–proton and carbon cycles become active, and the development of the (now genuine) star is stabilized. The star then reaches the main sequence where it remains for most of its active life. The time required for the contraction phase depends on the mass of the star. A star of the Sun's mass generally requires tens of millions of years to reach the main sequence, whereas one of much greater mass might take a few hundred thousand years.

By the time the star reaches the main sequence, it is still chemically homogeneous. With additional time, the hydrogen fuel in the core is converted to helium, and the temperature slowly rises. If the star is sufficiently massive to have a convective core, the matter in this region has a chance to be thoroughly mixed, but the outer region does not mix with the core. The Sun, by contrast, has no convective core and the helium-to-hydrogen ratio is maximum at the centre and decreases outward. Throughout the life of the Sun, there has been a steady depletion of hydrogen, so that the concentration of hydrogen at the centre today is probably only about one-third of the original amount. The rest has been transformed into helium. Like the rate of formation of a star, the subsequent rate of evolution on the main sequence is proportional to the mass of the star; the greater the mass, the more rapid the evolution. Whereas the Sun is destined to endure for some 10,000,000,000 years, a star of twice the Sun's mass burns its fuel at such a rate that it lasts about 3,000,000,000 years, and a star of 10 times the Sun's mass has a lifetime measured in tens of millions of years. By contrast, stars having a fraction of the mass of the Sun seem to be able to endure for trillions of years, which is much greater than the current age of the universe.

Relationship between the mass of a star and its rate of evolution

The spread of luminosities and colours of stars within the main sequence can be understood as a consequence of evolution. At the beginning of their lives as hydrogen-burning objects, stars define a nearly unique line in the Hertzsprung–Russell diagram called the zero-age main sequence. Without differences in initial chemical composition or in rotational velocity, all the stars would start exactly from this unique line. As the stars evolve, they adjust to the increase in the helium-to-hydrogen ratio in their cores and gradually move away from the zero-age main sequence. When the core fuel is exhausted, the internal structure of the star changes rapidly; it quickly leaves the main sequence and moves toward the region of giants and supergiants.

As the composition of its interior changes, the star departs the main sequence slowly at first and then more rapidly. When about 10 percent of the star's mass has been converted to helium, the structure of the star changes drastically. All of the hydrogen in the core has been burned out, and this central region is composed almost entirely of inert helium, with trace admixtures of heavier elements. The energy production now occurs in a thin shell where hydrogen is consumed and more helium added to a growing but inert core. The outer parts of the star expand outward because of the increased burning there, and as the star swells up its luminosity gradually increases. The details of the evolutionary process depend on the metal-to-hydrogen ratio, and the course of evolution differs for stars of different population types.

Effects of composition changes

LATER STAGES OF EVOLUTION

The great spread in luminosities and colours of giant, supergiant, and subgiant stars is also understood to result from evolutionary events. When a star leaves the main sequence, its future evolution is precisely determined by its mass, rate of rotation (or angular momentum), chemical composition, and whether or not it is a member of a close binary system. Giants and supergiants of nearly the same radius and surface temperature may have evolved from main-sequence stars of different ages and masses.

Evolution of low-mass stars. Theoretical calculations suggest that, as the star evolves from the main sequence, the hydrogen-helium core gradually increases in mass but shrinks in size as more and more "ash" is fed in through the outer hydrogen-burning shell. Energy is carried outward from the shell by rapid convection currents. The temperature of the shell rises, the star becomes more luminous, and it finally approaches the top of the giant domain. By contrast, the core shrinks by gravitational contraction, becoming hotter and denser until it reaches a central temperature of about 120,000,000 K. At that temperature the previously inert helium is consumed in the production of heavier elements.

Helium burning

When two helium (He) nuclei each of mass 4 atomic units are jammed together, it might be expected that they would form a nucleus of beryllium, Be, of mass 8 atomic units. In symbols, the reaction would be $^4He + ^4He \rightarrow ^8Be$. Actually, however, ^8Be is unstable and breaks down into two helium nuclei. If the temperature and density are high enough, though, the short-lived beryllium nucleus can (before it decays) capture another helium nucleus in what is essentially a three-body collision to form a nucleus of carbon-12—namely, $^8Be + ^4He \rightarrow ^{12}C$.

Provided that the central temperature continues to rise as the core shrinks, increasingly heavy nuclei can be fused. In particular, further reactions can occur by capturing additional helium nuclei, producing in turn oxygen (oxygen-16), neon (neon-20), magnesium (magnesium-24), and so on. (The Sun, being rather small in mass, will probably never reach the core temperature of approximately 600,000,000 K required to fuse carbon and will thus move toward its final state in roughly 5,000,000,000 years, when helium is depleted at its core.) During each of these stages of element production, energy is released, and the star once again establishes hydrostatic equilibrium, at least for a relatively short period of time. Since the energy output of helium fusion (per ton of matter) is much less than for hydrogen burning, the star's lifetime in the helium-burning phase is relatively short; in fact, it is considerably less than 1 percent of the duration of hydrogen fusion.

Ultimately, as the core of the star contracts, the overlying layers expand. The star, aged and severely unbalanced, is on its way to becoming a giant star. The gases making up the interior envelope literally recede away, creating a cooler, distended star called a red giant. These are real stars, and, as noted earlier, such red giants (*e.g.,* Betelgeuse) actually are observed in the sky.

Eventually, the outermost layers reach so far from the source of nuclear burning that they cool to a few thousand kelvins. The result is a weird-looking object having two distinct parts: a well-defined core of mostly carbon ash (a white dwarf; see below) and a swollen spherical shell of cooler and thinner matter spread over a volume roughly the size of the solar system. Such planetary nebulas also are actually observed in large numbers in the sky. Of the nearly 1,000 examples known in the Milky Way Galaxy alone, NGC 7027 is the most intensively studied to date.

Planetary nebulas

Origin of the chemical elements. The relative abundances of the chemical elements provide significant clues regarding their origin. The Earth's crust has been affected severely by erosion, fractionation, and other geologic events, so that its present varied composition offers few clues as to its early stages. The composition of the matter from which the solar system formed is deduced from that of stony meteorites called chondrites and from the composition of the Sun's atmosphere, supplemented by data acquired from spectral observations of hot stars and gaseous nebulas. Table 6, compiled from the efforts of many workers, lists the most abundant chemical (non-terrestrial) elements. This tabulation represents an average pertaining to all cosmic objects in general.

The most obvious feature is that the light elements tend to be more abundant than the heavier ones. That is to say, a plot of abundance against atomic mass, A, shows a decline with increasing A up to about $A = 100$. Thereafter the abundance is more nearly constant. Furthermore, this "curve of cosmic abundances" is not smooth. Among the lighter elements, those of even atomic number tend to be more abundant, and those with atomic numbers divisible by four are especially favoured. The abundance of lithium, beryllium, and boron is very rare compared with carbon, nitrogen, and oxygen. There is a pronounced abundance peak for iron and a relative maximum for lead, the most stable of the heavy elements.

The overwhelming preponderance of hydrogen suggests that all the nuclei were built from this simplest element, a hypothesis first proposed many years ago and widely accepted. It is now agreed, however, that the various elements could not have been formed in the aftermath of the "big bang" that created the universe some 15,000,000,000 years ago. According to this now-defunct idea, all matter was initially compressed into one huge ball of neutrons. As the universe began to expand, its density decreased and the neutrons decayed into protons and electrons. The protons then captured neutrons, one after another, underwent beta decay (ejection of electrons), and synthesized the heavy elements. A major difficulty with this hypothesis, among various other problems, is that atomic masses 5 and 8 are unstable, and there is no known way to build heavier nuclei by successive neutron capture.

Synthesis of heavy elements in massive stars

A large body of evidence supports the idea that the heavy elements have been, and are being, produced in stars. The majority of them, however, are fashioned only in the most massive stars and even for a short period of time after some stars have exploded as supernovas (see below *Evolution of high-mass stars*).

The splitting in the spectral sequence among the cooler stars can be understood in terms of composition differences. The M-type stars appear to have a normal (*i.e.,* solar) makeup, with oxygen more abundant than carbon and the zirconium group of elements much less abundant than the titanium group. The R-type and N-type stars often contain more carbon than oxygen, whereas the S-type stars appear to have an enhanced content of zirconium as compared with titanium. Other abundance anomalies are found in a peculiar class of higher temperature stars, called Wolf-Rayet (or W) stars, in which objects containing predominantly helium, carbon, and oxygen are distinguished from those containing helium and nitrogen, some carbon, and little observed oxygen. Significantly, all these abundance anomalies are found in stars thought to be well advanced in their evolutionary development. No main-sequence dwarfs display such effects.

A most critical observation is the detection of the unstable element technetium, Tc, in the S-type stars. This element has been produced synthetically in nuclear laboratories on Earth, and its longest-lived isotope, technetium-99 is known to have a half-life of 200,000 years. The implication is that this element must have been produced within the past few hundred thousand years in the stars where it has been observed, suggesting furthermore that this nucleosynthetic process is at work at least in some stars today. How the star upwells this heavy element from the core (where it is produced) to the surface (near where it is observed) in such a short time without the star exploding provides an impressive challenge to theoreticians.

During the past few decades, researchers have demon-

Table 6: The Most Abundant Chemical Elements (by numbers)*

element	symbol	abundance	element	symbol	abundance	element	symbol	abundance
Helium	He	6.3 × 10⁷	Magnesium	Mg	45,000	Potassium	K	76
Carbon	C	500,000	Aluminum	Al	2,140	Calcium	Ca	2,300
Nitrogen	N	100,000	Silicon	Si	32,000	Titanium	Ti	35
Oxygen	O	800,000	Phosphorus	P	320	Chromium	Cr	166
Fluorine	F	80	Sulfur	S	16,200	Manganese	Mn	75
Neon	Ne	93,000	Chlorine	Cl	420	Iron	Fe	22,000
Sodium	Na	1,900	Argon	Ar	1,200	Nickel	Ni	500

*Hydrogen = 10^9.

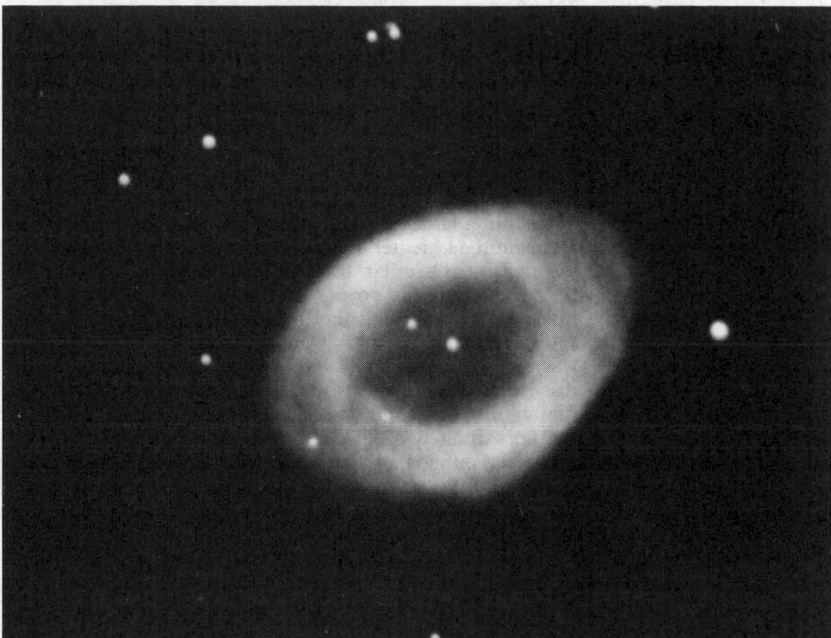

Figure 6: *The Ring Nebula (NGC 6720, M57), a planetary nebula in the constellation Lyra.* A planetary nebula is an object with a small dense core and a large, thin shell (or shells) of matter. The planetary nebula shown here has an angular size that subtends an area of about one-thousandth that of the Moon.
National Optical Astronomy Observatories

strated how elements might be created in stars by nuclear processes occurring at very high temperatures and densities. No one mechanism can account for all the elements; rather, several distinct processes occurring at different epochs during the late evolution of a star have been proposed.

After hydrogen, helium is the most abundant element. Most of it was probably produced in the initial big bang, by which the universe was created. Furthermore, as described earlier, helium is the normal ash of hydrogen consumption, and in the dense cores of highly evolved stars, helium itself is consumed to form, successively, carbon-12, oxygen-16, neon-20, and magnesium-24. By this time in the core of a sufficiently massive star, the temperature has reached some 700,000,000 K. Under these conditions, fragments such as protons, neutrons, and alpha particles also can interact with the newly created nuclei to produce a variety of other elements such as fluorine and sodium. As these "uneven" elements are produced in lesser quantities than those divisible by four, both the peaks and troughs in the curve of cosmic abundances can be explained.

With the core still shrinking and the central temperature and density forced even higher, a fundamental difficulty is soon reached. A temperature of roughly 1,000,000,000 K is sufficient to create silicon (silicon-28) by the usual method of helium capture. This temperature, however, is also high enough to begin to break apart silicon as well as some of the other newly synthesized nuclei. A kind of semi-equilibrium is set up in the star's core—a balance of sorts between the production and destruction (photodisintegration) of silicon. Ironically, though destructive, this situation is also suitable for the production of even heavier nuclei up to and including iron (iron-56) again through the successive capture of helium nuclei.

Evolution of high-mass stars. If the temperature and the density continue to rise, the iron-group nuclei tend to break down into alpha particles, but a large amount of energy is suddenly consumed in the process. The star then suffers a violent implosion, or collapse, after which it soon explodes as a supernova. In the catastrophic events leading to a supernova explosion and for roughly 1,000 seconds thereafter, a great variety of nuclear reactions can take place. And these processes seem to be able to explain the trace abundances of all the known elements heavier than iron.

Supernova explosions as a source of elements heavier than iron

Two situations have been envisioned, and both involve the capture of neutrons. When a nucleus captures a neutron, its mass increases by one atomic unit and its charge remains the same. Such a nucleus is often too heavy for its charge and might emit an electron (or beta ray) to attain a more stable state. It then becomes a nucleus of the next higher element in the periodic table of the elements. In the first such process, called the slow, or *s,* process, the flux of neutrons is low. A nucleus captures a neutron and leisurely emits a beta ray; its nuclear charge then increases by one.

Beta decay is often very slow, and, if the flux of neutrons is high, the nucleus might capture another neutron before there is time for it to undergo decay. In this rapid, or *r,* process, the evolution of a nucleus can be very different from that in a slow process. In supernova explosions, vast quantities of neutrons can be produced, and these could result in the rapid buildup of massive elements. One interesting feature of the synthesis of heavy elements by neutron capture at a high rate in a supernova explosion is that nuclei much heavier than lead or even uranium can be fashioned. These in turn can decay by fission, releasing additional amounts of energy.

The superabundant elements in the S-type stars come from the slow neutron process. Moreover, the observation of technetium-99 is ample evidence that these processes are at work in stars today. Even so, some low-abundance atomic nuclei are proton rich (*i.e.,* neutron deficient) and cannot be produced by either the *s* or *r* process. Presumably, they have been created in relatively rare events—*e.g.,* one in which a quantum of hard radiation, a γ ray, causes a neutron to be ejected.

In addition, no known nuclear process is capable of producing lithium, beryllium, and boron in stellar interiors. These lightweight nuclei are probably produced by the breakdown or "spallation" of heavier elements, such as iron and magnesium, by high-energy particles in stellar atmospheres or in the early stages of star formation. Apparently, these high-energy particles (called cosmic rays) originate by means of electromagnetic disturbances in the neighbourhood of star spots and stellar flares, and they also might arise from supernova explosions themselves. Some of these light-element nuclei also might be produced by cosmic rays shattering atoms of carbon, nitrogen, oxygen, and other elements in the interstellar medium.

Origin of cosmic rays

Finally, the peculiar A-type stars comprise a class of cosmic objects with strange abundance anomalies. These might arise from mechanical effects—selective radiation pressure, photospheric diffusion and element separation, and so on—rather than from nuclear effects. Some stars show enhanced silicon, others enhanced lanthanides. The so-called manganese stars show great overabundances of manganese and gallium, usually accompanied by an excess of mercury. The latter stars exhibit weak helium lines, low rotational velocities, excess amounts of gallium, strontium, yttrium, mercury, and platinum, as well as absences of such elements as aluminum and nickel. When these types of stars are found in binaries, the two members often display differing chemical compositions. It is most difficult to envision plausible nuclear events that can account for the peculiarities of these abundances, particularly the strange isotope ratios of mercury.

END STATES OF STARS

The final stages in the evolution of a star depend on its mass, its angular momentum, and whether it is a member of a close binary.

White dwarfs. All stars seem to evolve through the red-giant phase to their ultimate state along a straightforward path. In most instances, especially among low-mass stars, the distended outer envelope of the star simply drifts off into space, while the core settles down as a white dwarf. Here, the star (really the core) evolves on the horizontal branch to bluer colours and lower luminosities. In other cases, where the star has several solar masses or more, the star may explode as a supernova. Even for these more massive stars, if the residual mass in the core is less than 1.4 solar masses (the Chandrasekhar limit), the stellar remnant will become a white dwarf. The matter in such a dwarf becomes a degenerate gas, wherein the electrons are all stripped from their parent atoms. Gas in this peculiar state is an almost perfect conductor of heat and does not obey the ordinary gas laws. It can be compressed to very high densities, typical values being in the range of 10^7 grams per cubic centimetre. Such a white dwarf no longer has any source of energy and simply cools down forever, becoming in turn a yellow dwarf, a red dwarf, a brown dwarf, and, eventually, perhaps a black dwarf.

Degenerate gas

The energy output of a white dwarf is so small that the object can go on shining mainly by radiating away its stored energy until virtually none is left to emit. How long this might take is unknown, but it would seem to be on the order of trillions of years. The final stage of this kind of low-mass star is typically a ball not much larger than the Earth but with a density perhaps 50,000 times that of water, covered possibly with a thin layer of ice and surrounded by an atmosphere a few metres thick.

The Sun is destined to perish as a white dwarf. But before that happens, it will evolve into a red giant, engulfing Mercury and Venus in the process. At the same time, it will blow away the Earth's atmosphere and boil its oceans, making the planet uninhabitable. None of these events will come to pass locally for several billion years.

The first white dwarf to be recognized was the companion to Sirius. It was originally detected by its gravitational attraction on the larger, brighter star and only later observed visually as a faint object (now called Sirius B), about 10,000 times fainter than Sirius (now called Sirius A) or 500 times fainter than the Sun. Its mass is slightly less than that of the Sun and its size a little less than that of the Earth. Its colour and spectrum correspond roughly to spectral class A, with a surface temperature of 8,000 to 10,000 K. Hence, the energy emission per unit area from the surface must be much greater than that of the Sun. Since Sirius B is so faint, its surface area and thus its volume must be very small, and its average density is on the order of 100,000 times that of water.

Another well-known white dwarf, designated BD + 16°516, is paired with a much cooler K0V dwarf in an eclipsing system. The two stars, whose centres are separated by 2,092,000 km, revolve around each other with a period of 12.5 hours. The white dwarf produces pronounced excitation and heating effects in the K-type star's atmosphere. The white dwarf's mass is about 0.6 that of the Sun, but its diameter is only 16,000 km; hence, its density is about 650,000 times that of water.

Neutron stars. When the mass of the remnant core lies between 1.4 and two solar masses, it apparently becomes a neutron star with a density more than 1,000,000 times greater than even that of a white dwarf. Having so much mass packed within a ball on the order of 50 km in diameter, a neutron star's density can reach that of nuclear values, which is roughly 10^{14} times the average density of solar matter or of water. Such a star is predicted to have a crystalline solid crust, wherein bare atomic nuclei would be held in a lattice of rigidity and strength some 18 orders of magnitude greater than that of steel. Below the crust, the density is similar to that of an atomic nucleus, so the residual atomic cores lose their individuality as their nuclei are jammed together to form a nuclear fluid.

Although neutron stars were predicted in the 1930s, it was not until the late 1960s that observers accidentally discovered a radio source emitting weak pulses, each lasting about 0.3 second with a remarkably constant period of approximately 1.337 seconds. Other examples of such an object, dubbed a pulsar for "pulsating radio star," were soon found. Many of them were detected in the skies of the Southern Hemisphere, where a pulsar was first identified with a supernova remnant.

A large body of evidence now identifies pulsars as rotating neutron stars. All the energy emitted in the pulses derives from a slowing of the star's rotation, but only a small fraction is released in the form of radio-frequency pulses. The rest goes into pulses observed elsewhere in the electromagnetic spectrum and into cosmic rays, with perhaps some into the emission of gravitational energy, or gravity waves. For example, the pulsar at the centre of the Crab Nebula (Figure 7), the most famous of the modern supernovas, has been observed not only at radio frequencies but also at optical and X-ray frequencies, where it emits 100 and 10,000 times, respectively, as much radiation as in the radio spectrum. The slowing of the pulsar's spin also supplies the energy needed to account for the nonthermal, or synchrotron, emission from the Crab Nebula, which ranges from X rays to radio waves.

Pulsars as rotating neutron stars

Pulsar radiation is polarized, both linearly and circularly, and can be understood in terms of a rotating star having a powerful magnetic field of 10^{12} gauss. (By contrast, the Earth's magnetic field is on the order of one gauss.) Various mechanisms have been proposed whereby charged particles can be accelerated to velocities close to that of light itself. Possibly most, if not all, galactic cosmic rays originate from pulsars.

More recently, sudden changes have been observed in the rotation rates of pulsars. The Vela pulsar, for instance, abruptly decreased its spin rate. Such a period change or "glitch" can be explained if the pulsar altered its radius by about one centimetre; this sudden shrinkage of the crust has been called a "star quake" by some researchers. Pulsar phenomena apparently last much longer than the observable supernova remnants in which they were born, since hundreds of pulsars are now cataloged and only a few are associated with well-known remnants. Even so, the statistics of pulsars are likely to be observationally biased, since signals from pulsars at great distances in the Galaxy become distorted by ionized regions of interstellar space.

Black holes. If the core remnant of a supernova exceeds about two solar masses, it continues to contract. The gravitational field of the collapsing star is predicted to be so powerful that neither matter nor light can escape it. The "star" then collapses to what is called a Schwarzschild singularity—or, in popular terms, a black hole. Bodies trapped in its gravity field, or a beam of light directed at such an object, would seemingly just disappear—pulled into a "bottomless pit."

Schwarzschild singularity

Theory aside, astronomers remain unsure if black holes really exist. For further information on the subject, see COSMOS: *Black-hole model for active galactic nuclei.*

(L.H.A./E.J.C.)

Star clusters

GENERAL DESCRIPTION AND CLASSIFICATION

Star clusters fall into two main types: open (or galactic) and globular. Open clusters contain from a dozen to

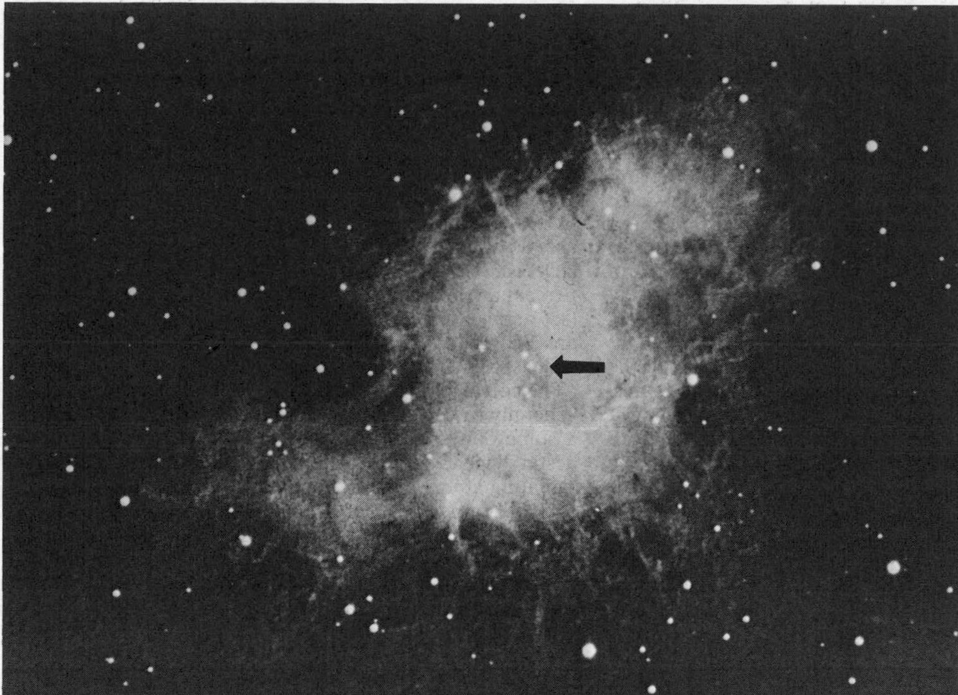

Figure 7: The pulsar (arrow) near the centre of the Crab Nebula (NGC 1952, M1), which is a remnant of a massive star that exploded long ago, spilling its newly created heavy elements into space. The explosion, known as a supernova, was observed by Chinese astronomers in AD 1054.

By courtesy of A. Hewish

many hundreds of stars, usually in an unsymmetrical arrangement. By contrast, globular clusters are old systems containing thousands to hundreds of thousands of stars closely packed in a symmetrical, roughly spherical form. In addition, groups called associations, made up of a few dozen to hundreds of stars of similar type and common origin whose density in space is less than that of the surrounding field, are also recognized.

Stellar associations

Four open clusters have been known from earliest times: the Pleiades and Hyades in the constellation Taurus, Praesepe (the Beehive) in the constellation Cancer, and Coma Berenices. The Pleiades was so important to some early peoples that its rising at sunset determined the start of their year. The appearance of the Coma Berenices cluster to the naked eye led to the naming of its constellation for the hair of Berenice, wife of Ptolemy Euergetes of Egypt (3rd century BC), the only constellation named after a historical figure.

Though several globular clusters, such as Omega Centauri and Messier 13 in the constellation Hercules, are visible to the unaided eye as hazy patches of light, attention was paid to them only after the invention of the telescope. The first record of a globular cluster, in the constellation Sagittarius, dates to 1665 (it was later named Messier 22); the next, Omega Centauri, shown in a modern photograph in Figure 8, was recorded in 1677 by the English astronomer and mathematician Edmund Halley.

Investigations of globular and open clusters greatly aided the understanding of the Milky Way Galaxy. In 1917, from a study of the distances and distributions of globular clusters, the American astronomer Harlow Shapley, then of the Mount Wilson Observatory, California, determined that the galactic centre lies in the Sagittarius region. In 1930, from measurements of angular sizes and distribution of open clusters, Robert J. Trumpler of Lick Observatory, California, showed that light is absorbed as it travels through many parts of space.

The discovery of stellar associations depended on knowledge of the characteristics and motions of individual stars scattered over a substantial area. In the 1920s it was noticed that young, hot blue stars (spectral types O and B) apparently congregated together. In 1949 Victor A. Ambartsumian, a Soviet astronomer, suggested that these stars are members of physical groupings of stars with a common origin and named them O associations (or OB associations, as they are often designated today). He also applied the term T associations to groups of dwarf, irregular T Tauri variable stars, which were first noted at Mount Wilson Observatory by Alfred Joy.

The study of clusters in external galaxies began in 1847, when Sir John Herschel at the Cape Observatory (in what is now South Africa) published lists of such objects in the nearest galaxies, the Magellanic Clouds. During the 20th century the identification of clusters has been extended first to more remote galaxies by the use of large reflectors and other more specialized instruments—Schmidt telescopes.

By courtesy of Eric Lindsay

Figure 8: Globular cluster Omega Centauri (NGC 5139).

The number of open clusters identified, in particular, has in recent years tripled, totaling by the late 1980s an estimated 40,000 such objects in about 1,000 associations.

Distribution within the Milky Way system

Globular clusters. Although globular clusters are widely scattered in galactic latitude (Figure 9), about a third of them are concentrated around the galactic centre, as satellite systems in the rich Sagittarius–Scorpius star fields. Individual cluster masses include up to 1,000,000 suns, and their linear diameters can be several hundred light-years; their apparent diameters range from one degree for Omega Centauri down to knots of one minute of arc. In a cluster such as M3, 90 percent of the light is contained within a diameter of 100 light-years, but star counts and the study of RR Lyrae member stars (whose intrinsic brightness varies regularly within well-known limits) include a larger one of 325 light-years. The clusters differ markedly in the degree to which stars are concentrated at their centres. Most of them appear circular and are probably spherical, but a few (*e.g.,* Omega Centauri) are noticeably elliptical. The most elliptical cluster is M19, its major axis being about double its minor axis.

Globular clusters are composed of Population II objects (*i.e.,* old stars). As noted above, the brightest stars are the red giants, bright red stars with an absolute magnitude of −2, about 600 times the Sun's brightness or luminosity. In only six globular clusters have stars as intrinsically faint as the Sun been photographed, and in no such clusters have the faintest stars yet been recorded. The luminosity function for M3 shows that 90 percent of the visual light comes from stars at least twice as bright as the Sun, but more than 90 percent of the cluster mass is made up of fainter stars. The density near the centres of globular clusters is two stars per cubic light-year, compared with one star per 300 cubic light-years in the solar neighbourhood. Studies of 50 globular clusters showed a difference in spectral properties from stars in the solar neighbourhood—a difference that proved to be due to a deficiency of metals in the clusters, which have been classified on the basis of increasing metal abundance. Globular cluster stars are two to 300 times poorer in metals than stars of the solar neighbourhood. The ratio of metals is higher for clusters near the galactic centre than for those in the halo (the outermost reaches of the Galaxy extending far above and below its plane). The amounts of other elements, such as helium, also differ from cluster to cluster. Radio astronomical studies have set a low upper limit on the amount of neutral hydrogen in globular clusters. Puzzling features in some of these clusters are dark lanes of nebulous matter. Though it is difficult to explain the presence of distinct, separate masses of unformed matter in old systems, the nebulosity cannot be foreground material between the cluster and the observer.

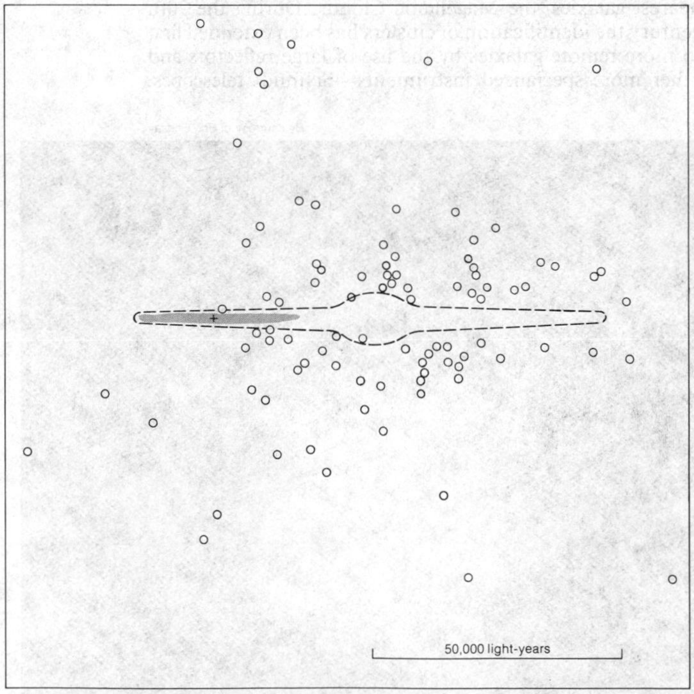

Figure 9: *Distribution of open and globular star clusters in the Galaxy.*
Dotted line indicates probable outline of the Galaxy, a flattened lens-shaped system formed by the stars, as seen edgewise from outside. Eccentric position of the Sun is shown by a cross. Some of the known open star clusters are scattered among the stars in shaded region. Small circles represent globular clusters.

Constituent stars

Nearly 2,000 variable stars are known in the 100 globular clusters that have been examined. Of these, perhaps 90 percent are members of the class called RR Lyrae variables (see above). Other variables that occur in globular clusters are W Virginis, RV Tauri, and U Geminorum stars, as well as Cepheids, Mira stars, eclipsing binaries, and novas.

The colour of a star, as previously noted, has been found generally to correspond to its surface temperature, and in a somewhat similar way the type of spectrum shown by a star depends on the degree of excitation of the light-radiating atoms in it and, therefore, also on the temperature. All stars in a given globular cluster are, within a very small percentage of the total distance, at equal distances from the Earth so that the effect of distance on brightness is common to all. Colour–magnitude and spectrum–magnitude diagrams can thus be plotted for the stars of a cluster, and the position of the stars in the array, except for a factor that is the same for all stars, will be independent of distance.

All such arrays show a major grouping of stars along the main sequence, and the categories range from hot, bright, bluer stars to cool and redder ones. In many cases, a giant branch containing very luminous stars also is present (Figure 10), as are some other minor groupings, but the extent and concentration of the stars in the various parts of the diagram can be quite different from cluster to cluster.

Age of globular clusters

In 1917 a more distinct difference between open and globular clusters was noticed in colour–magnitude diagrams. This was later explained as a result of differences in the courses of evolutionary change that stars with similar compositions but different masses would follow after long intervals of time. The magnitude at which the brighter stars leave the main sequence (the turnoff point or knee) is a measure of the age of the cluster, assuming that most of the stars formed at the same time. RR Lyrae variables, when present, lie in a special region, called the variable gap, near the mean visual magnitude and the blue end of the horizontal (giant) branch of the colour–magnitude diagram. The hydrogen in cluster stars is thought to amount to 70 to 75 percent by mass, helium 25 to 30 percent, and the heavier elements 0.01 to 0.1 percent. Globular clusters prove to be nearly as old as the universe, perhaps 12,000,000,000 to 13,000,000,000 years.

Integrated magnitudes (measurements of the total brightness of the cluster), their diameters, and the mean magnitude of the 25 brightest stars made possible the first distance determinations on the basis of the assumption that the apparent differences were due entirely to distance. The colour–magnitude diagram, or the apparent magnitudes of the variables, if their absolute magnitude is known, however, leads to the best distance estimates. The correction factor for interstellar reddening, due to intervening matter that absorbs and reddens stellar light, is substantial for many globular clusters but small for those in high galactic latitudes away from the plane of the Milky Way, the irregular luminous band of stars and gas clouds for which the Galaxy is named. Distances range from about 8,000 light-years for M71 and NGC 6397 to intergalactic distances of 270,000 light-years for the highly luminous NGC 2419 and 325,000 light-years for the clusters called Palomar 3 and 4.

Velocities and orbits of globular clusters

The radial velocities (the speed at which objects approach or recede from an observer, taken as positive when the distance is increasing) measured by the Doppler effect have been determined from integrated spectra for some 70 globular clusters. The largest negative velocity is −360 km/sec for NGC 6934, while the largest positive velocity is +493 km/sec for NGC 3201. These velocities suggest that the globular clusters are moving around the galac-

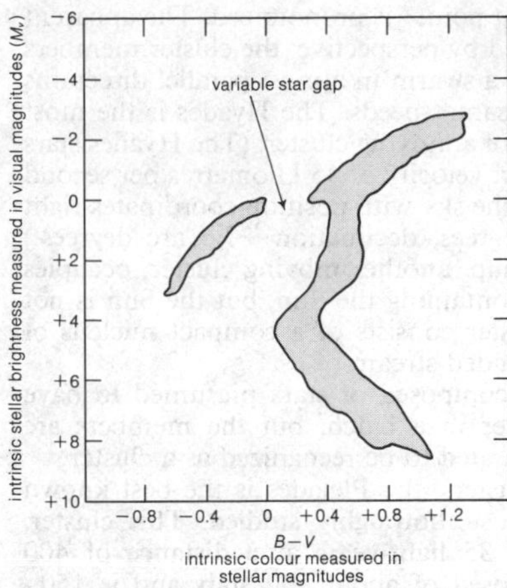

Figure 10: *Colour–magnitude diagram of globular star cluster.*
B and *V* are magnitudes in blue and visual light. Shaded areas indicate regions occupied by globular stars. Variable star gap indicates region in which cluster variables occur.

tic centre in highly elliptical orbits. The globular cluster system as a whole has a rotational velocity of about 140 km/sec relative to the Sun, or 110 km/sec on an absolute basis. For one cluster, Omega Centauri, motions of the individual stars around the massive centre have actually been observed and measured. Though proper motions of the clusters are very small, those for individual stars provide a useful criterion for cluster membership.

The two globular clusters of highest absolute luminosity are in the Southern Hemisphere in the constellations Centaurus and Tucana. Omega Centauri, with an (integrated) absolute blue magnitude of −9.4, is the second richest cluster in variables, with 171. From this large group, three types of RR Lyrae stars were first distinguished in 1902. Omega Centauri is relatively nearby at a distance of 17,000 light-years, and it lacks a sharp nucleus. The cluster designated 47 Tucanae (NGC 104), with an absolute magnitude of −9.5 at a similar distance of 16,000 light-years, has a different appearance with strong central concentration. It is located near the Small Magellanic Cloud but is not connected with it. For an observer situated at the centre of this great cluster, the sky would have the brightness of twilight on the Earth because of the light of the thousands of stars nearby. In the Northern Hemisphere, M13 in the constellation Hercules is the easiest to see and is the best known. At a distance of 20,000 light-years, it has been thoroughly investigated and is relatively poor in variables. M3 in Canes Venatici, 35,000 light-years away, is the cluster richest in variables, with 189 known. Investigation of these variables resulted in the placement of the RR Lyrae stars in a special region of the colour–magnitude diagram.

Open clusters. Open clusters are strongly concentrated toward the Milky Way. They form a flattened disklike system 3,000 light-years thick with a diameter of about 30,000 light-years. The younger clusters serve to trace the spiral arms of the Galaxy, since they are found invariably to lie in them. Very distant clusters are hard to detect against the rich Milky Way background. A classification based on central concentration and richness (Figure 11) is used and has been extended to nearly 1,000 open clusters. Probably about half the known open clusters contain fewer than 100 stars, but the richest have 1,000 or more. The largest have apparent diameters of several degrees, the diameter of the Taurus cluster being 400 arc minutes (nearly seven arc degrees), and that of the Perseus cluster being 240 arc minutes.

Concentration within the Galaxy

The linear diameters range from the largest, 75 light-years, down to five light-years. Increasingly, it has been found that a large halo of actual cluster members surrounds the more noticeable core and extends the diameter severalfold. Cluster membership is established through common motion, common distances, and so on. Tidal forces and stellar encounters lead to the disintegration of open clusters over long periods of time, as stars "evaporate" from the cluster.

Stellar content

Stars of all spectral classes from O to M (high to low temperatures) are found in open clusters, but the frequency of types varies from one cluster to another, as does concentration near the centre. In some (O or OB clusters), the brightest stars are blue, very hot spectral types O or B. In others, they are whitish yellow, cooler spectral type F. High luminosity stars are more common than in the solar neighbourhood, and dwarfs are much more scarce. The brightest stars in some open clusters are 150,000 times as bright as the Sun. The luminosity of the brightest stars at the upper end of the main sequence varies in clusters from about −8 to −2 visual magnitude. (As noted above, visual magnitude is that seen by the eye, as opposed to that registered on ordinary photographs.)

Because of the high luminosity of their brightest stars, some open clusters have a total luminosity as bright as that of some globular clusters (absolute magnitude of −8), which contain thousands of times as many stars. In the centre of rich clusters, the stars may be only one light-year apart. The density can be 100 times that of the solar

By courtesy of Lick Observatory, University of California

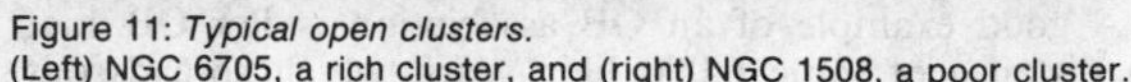

Figure 11: *Typical open clusters.*
(Left) NGC 6705, a rich cluster, and (right) NGC 1508, a poor cluster.

neighbourhood. In some, such as the Pleiades and the Orion clusters, nebulosity is a prominent feature, while others have none. In clusters younger than 25,000,000 years masses of neutral hydrogen extending over three times the optical diameter of the cluster have been detected with radio telescopes. Many of the OB clusters mentioned above contain globules—relatively small, apparently spherical regions of absorbing matter. The most numerous variables connected with open clusters are the T Tauri type (see below) and related stars that occur by the hundreds in some nebulous regions of the sky. Conspicuously absent from open clusters is the type most common in globular clusters, the RR Lyrae stars. Other variables include eclipsing binary stars (both Algol type and contact binaries), Cepheids, flare stars, and spectrum variables, such as Pleione. The last named star, one of the Pleiades, is known to cast off shells of matter from time to time, perhaps as a result of its high rotational speed (up to 322 kilometres per second).

The colour- or spectrum-magnitude diagram derived from the individual stars holds vital information. Colour-magnitude diagrams are available for about 200 clusters on the UBV photometric system, in which colour is measured from the amount of light radiated by the stars in the ultraviolet, blue, and visual (yellow) wavelength regions. In young clusters, stars are found along the luminous bright blue branch, whereas in old clusters, beyond a turnoff only a magnitude or two brighter than the Sun, they are red giants and supergiants (Figure 12).

Distance determinations

Distances can be determined by many methods—geometric, photometric, and spectroscopic—with corrections for interstellar absorption. For the very nearest clusters, direct (trigonometric) parallaxes may be obtained, and these are inversely proportional to the distance. Distances can be derived from proper motions, apparent magnitudes of the brightest stars, and spectroscopically from individual bright stars. Colour-magnitude diagrams, fitted to a standard plot of the main sequence, provide a common and reliable tool for determining distance. The nearest open cluster is the nucleus of the Ursa Major group at a distance of 75 light-years; the farthest clusters are thousands of light-years away.

Motions, including radial velocities and proper motion, have been measured for thousands of cluster stars. The radial velocities of open cluster stars are much smaller than those of globular clusters, averaging tens of kilometres per second, but their proper motions are larger. Open clusters share in the galactic rotation. Used with galactic rotation formulas, the radial velocities provide another means of distance determination.

Moving clusters

A few clusters are known as moving clusters because the convergence of the proper motions of their individual stars toward a "convergent point" is pronounced. The apparent convergence is caused by perspective: the cluster members are really moving as a swarm in almost parallel directions and with about the same speeds. The Hyades is the most prominent example of a moving cluster. (The Hyades stars are converging with a velocity of 45 kilometres per second toward the point in the sky with position coordinates right ascension 94 arc degrees, declination +7.6 arc degrees.) The Ursa Major group, another moving cluster, occupies a volume of space containing the Sun, but the Sun is not a member. The cluster consists of a compact nucleus of 14 stars and an extended stream.

From A. Sandage and O. Eggen, *The Astrophysical Journal* (1969); The University of Chicago Press

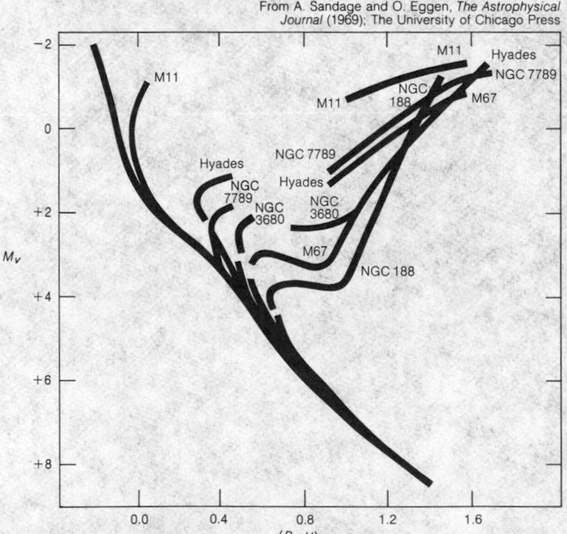

Figure 12: Composite colour-magnitude diagram for six open clusters fitted to the main sequence for very young stars (zero-age). M_v is visual magnitude; $(B-V)_0$ is the colour (blue magnitude minus visual magnitude) for the zero-age stars.

Stellar groups are composed of stars presumed to have been formed together in a batch, but the members are now too widely separated to be recognized as a cluster.

Of all the open clusters, the Pleiades is the best known and perhaps the most thoroughly studied. This cluster, with a diameter of 35 light-years at a distance of 400 light-years, is composed of about 500 stars and is 150,000,000 years old. Near the Pleiades in the sky but not so conspicuous, the Hyades is the second nearest cluster at 130 light-years. Its stars are similar to those in the solar neighbourhood, and it is an older cluster (about 2,000,000,000 years in age). Measurements of the Hyades form a basis for astronomical determinations of distance and age because its thoroughly studied main sequence is used as a standard. Coma Berenices, located 260 light-years away, is an example of a "poor" cluster, containing only about 40 stars. There are some extremely young open clusters. Of these, the one associated with the Orion Nebula, which is some 3,000,000 years old, is the closest at a distance of 1,500 light-years. A still younger cluster is NGC 6611, which formed only about 800,000 years ago. At the other end of the scale, some open clusters have ages approaching those of the globular clusters and seem to be of intermediate type. M67 in the constellation Cancer is 5,500,000,000 years old, and NGC 188 in Cepheus, the oldest known open cluster, is 8,000,000,000 or 9,000,000,000 years of age.

OB and T associations. The chief distinguishing feature of the members of a stellar association is that the large majority of constituent stars have similar physical characteristics. An OB association consists of many hot, blue giant stars, spectral classes O and B, and a relatively small number of other objects. A T association consists of cooler dwarf stars, many of which exhibit irregular variations in brightness. The stars clearly must be relatively close to each other in space, though in some cases they might be widely dispersed in the sky and are less closely placed than in the open clusters.

Distinguishing characteristics

The existence of an OB association is usually established through a study of the space distribution of early O- and B-type stars. It appears as a concentration of points in a three-dimensional plot of galactic longitude and latitude and distance. Approximately 70 have been cataloged and are designated by constellation abbreviation and number (*e.g.,* Per OB 1 in the constellation Perseus). In terms of dimensions, they are larger than open clusters, ranging from 100 to 700 light-years in diameter, and usually contain one or more open clusters as nuclei. They frequently contain a special type of multiple star, the Trapezium (named for its prototype in Orion), as well as supergiants, binaries, gaseous nebulas, and globules. Associations are relatively homogeneous in age. The best distance determinations are from spectroscopic parallaxes of individual stars—*i.e.,* estimates of their absolute magnitudes made from studies of their spectra. Most of those known are closer than 10,000 light-years, with the nearest, named Sco OB 1, at 650 light-years.

Associations appear to be almost spherical, though rapid elongation would be expected from the shearing effect of differential galactic rotation. Expansion, which is on the order of 10 km/sec, may well mask the tendency to elongate, and this is confirmed in some. Tidal forces break up an association in less than 10,000,000 years through differences in the attraction by an outside body on members in different parts of the association.

A good example of an OB association is Per OB 1 at a distance of some 6,000 light-years, which spreads out from the double cluster *h* and χ Persei. A large group of 20 supergiant stars of spectral type M belongs to Per OB 1. Associations with red supergiants may be in a relatively advanced evolutionary stage, almost ready to disintegrate.

T Tauri stars

The T associations (short for T Tauri associations) are formed by groups of T Tauri stars associated with the clouds of interstellar matter (nebulas) in which they occur. About three dozen are recognized. A T Tauri star is characterized by irregular variations of light, low luminosity, and hydrogen line (H-alpha) emission. It is a newly formed star of intermediate mass that is still in the process of contraction from diffuse matter. The small motions of T Tauri stars relative to a given nebula indicate that they are not field stars passing through the nebula. They are found in greatest numbers in regions with bright O- and B-type stars.

T associations occur only in or near regions of galactic nebulosity, either bright or dark, and only in obscured regions showing the presence of dust. Besides T Tauri stars, they include related variables, nonvariable stars, and Herbig-Haro objects, small nebulosities 10,000 astronomical units in diameter, each containing several starlike condensations in configurations similar to the Trapezium, Theta Orionis, in the sword of Orion. These objects are considered to be star groups at the very beginning of life.

The constellation of Cygnus has five T associations, and Orion and Taurus have four each. The richest is Ori T2 with more than 400 members; it has a diameter of 50 by 90 light-years and lies at a distance of 1,300 light-years around the variable star T Ori.

DYNAMICS OF STAR CLUSTERS

Seen from intergalactic space, the Milky Way Galaxy would appear as a giant luminous pinwheel, with more than 100 globular clusters dotted around it. The richest parts of the spiral arms of the pinwheel would be marked by dozens of open clusters. If this panorama could be seen as a time-lapse movie, the great globular clusters would wheel around the galactic centre in elliptical orbits with periods of hundreds of millions of years. The open clusters and stellar associations would be seen to form out of knots of diffuse matter in the spiral arms, gradually disperse, run through their life cycle, and fade away, while the Sun pursued its course around the galactic centre for billions of years.

Young open clusters and associations, occupying the same region of space as clouds of ionized hydrogen (gaseous nebulas), help to define the spiral arms. A concentration of clusters in the bright inner portion of the Milky Way between galactic longitudes 283° and 28° indicates an inner arm in Sagittarius. Similarly, the two spiral arms of Orion and Perseus are defined between 103° and 213°, with a bifurcation of the Orion arm. Associations show the existence of spiral structure in the Sun's vicinity. Older clusters, whose main sequence does not reach to the blue stars, show no correlation with spiral arms because in the intervening years their motions have carried them far from their place of birth.

Origin of galactic O- and B-type stars

All the O- and B-type stars in the Galaxy might have originated in OB associations. The great majority, if not all, of the O-type stars (5,000) were formed and still exist in clusters and associations. Though only 10 percent of the total number of B-type stars are now in OB associations or clusters, it is likely that all formed in them. At the other (fainter) end of the range of stellar luminosities, the number of dwarf variable stars in the nearby T associations is estimated at 12,000. These associations are apparently the main source of low luminosity stars in the neighbourhood of the Sun.

While large numbers of associations have formed and dispersed and provided a population of stars for the spiral arms, the globular clusters have survived relatively unchanged except for the evolutionary differences that time brings. They are too massive to be disrupted by the tidal forces of the Galaxy, though their limiting dimensions are set by these forces when they most closely approach the galactic centre. Impressive as they are individually, their total mass of 10,000,000 suns is small compared to the mass of the Galaxy as a whole—only about 1/10,000. Their substance is that of the Galaxy in a very early stage. The Galaxy probably collapsed from a gaseous cloud composed almost entirely of hydrogen and helium. Between 12,000,000,000 and 13,000,000,000 years ago, before the last stages of the collapse, matter forming the globular clusters may have separated from the rest. The fact that metal-rich clusters are near the galactic nucleus while metal-poor clusters are in the halo or outer fringes may indicate a nonuniform distribution of elements throughout the primordial mass.

In a study of star clusters, a time panorama unfolds—from the oldest objects existing in the Galaxy, the globular clusters, through clusters in existence only half as long, to extremely young open clusters and associations that have come into being since humans first trod the Earth.

CLUSTERS IN EXTERNAL GALAXIES

Clusters have been discovered and studied in at least eight external galaxies, mostly members of the Local Group (a group of about 20 stellar systems to which the Galaxy belongs). At their great distances classification is difficult. Attempts at classification are made from studies of the colours of the light from an entire cluster (integrated colours) or, for a few, from colour–magnitude diagrams. An electronograph (image tube) on a large telescope in the uniquely good observing conditions of Chile has extended studies to cluster stars of apparent magnitude 23, which is a factor of 10^{10} fainter than the bright star Sirius.

Clusters and associations in the Magellanic Clouds

Clusters have been found by the hundreds in some of the nearest galaxies. At the distance of the Magellanic Clouds, a cluster like the Pleiades would appear as a faint 15th magnitude object, subtending 15 seconds of arc instead of several degrees. In the Small Magellanic Cloud, at a distance of 200,000 light-years, about 120 clusters are known. In the Large Magellanic Cloud, at a distance of 180,000 light-years, nearly 1,200 have been cataloged. Most of them are young blue-giant open clusters such as NGC 330 and NGC 1866. The open clusters contain some Cepheid variables and in chemical composition are similar to, but not exactly the same as, those of the Galaxy. The globular clusters fall into two distinct groups. Those of the first group, the red, have a large metal deficiency similar to the globular clusters in the Galaxy, and some are known to contain RR Lyrae variables. The globular clusters of the second group are large and circular in outline, with colours much bluer than normal galactic globular clusters and with ages of about 1,000,000 to 1,000,000,000 years. They are similar to the open clusters of the Magellanic Clouds but are very populous. The observed differences between clusters in the Galaxy and the Magellanic Clouds result from small differences in helium or heavy-element abundances. There are at least 122 associations with a mean diameter of 250 light-years, somewhat richer and larger than in the Galaxy. Sixteen of the associations contain coexistent clusters. Also, 15 star clouds (aggregations of many thousands of stars dispersed over hundreds or even thousands of light-years) are recognized.

Discoveries in the Andromeda Galaxy

In the great Andromeda spiral galaxy (M31) some 2,200,000 light-years away, more than 300 clusters are known, of which perhaps two-thirds are globular. Colour studies of about 50 of these clusters reveal that they have a higher metal content than globular clusters of the Galaxy. Nearly 200 OB associations are known with distances up to 80,000 light-years from the nucleus. The diameters of their dense cores are comparable to those of galactic associations. NGC 206 (OB 78) is the richest star cloud in M31, having a total mass of 200,000 suns and bearing a strong resemblance to the double cluster in Perseus. Some globular clusters have been found around the dwarf elliptical companions to M31, NGC 185, and NGC 205.

M33 in the constellation Triangulum—a spiral galaxy with thick, loose arms (an Sc system in the Hubble classification scheme)—has about 300 known clusters, not many of which have globular characteristics. Of the six dwarf spheroidal galaxies in the Local Group, only the one in the constellation Fornax has clusters. Its five globular clusters are similar to the bluest globular clusters of the Galaxy. No clusters have been discovered in the irregular galaxies NGC 6822 and IC 1613.

Globular clusters in galaxies beyond the Local Group

Beyond the Local Group, at a distance of 45,000,000 light-years, the giant elliptical galaxy M87 in the Virgo cluster of galaxies is surrounded by an estimated 2,000 globular star clusters. Inspection of other elliptical galaxies in Virgo shows that they too have globular clusters whose apparent magnitudes are similar to those in M87, though their stellar population is substantially smaller. It appears that the mean absolute magnitudes of globular clusters are constant and independent of the absolute luminosity of the parent galaxy.

The total number of clusters now known in external galaxies far exceeds the number known in the Milky Way system. For additional information on this and related matters, see GALAXIES: *The external galaxies.*

(H.S.H./E.J.C.)

Astronomical maps

NATURE AND SIGNIFICANCE

The brighter stars and star groupings are easily recognized by a practiced observer. The much more numerous fainter celestial bodies can be located and identified only with the help of astronomical maps, catalogs, and in some cases almanacs.

The first astronomical charts, globes, and drawings, often decorated with fantastic figures, depicted the constellations, recognizable groupings of bright stars known by imaginatively chosen names that have been for many centuries both a delight to man and a dependable aid to navigation. Several royal Egyptian tombs of the 2nd millennium BC include paintings of constellation figures, but these cannot be considered accurate maps. Classical Greek astronomers used maps and globes; unfortunately, no examples survive. Numerous small metal celestial globes from Islāmic makers of the 11th century onward remain. The first printed planispheres (representations of the celestial sphere on a flat surface) were produced in 1515, and printed celestial globes appeared at about the same time.

Use of the telescope in stellar mapping

Telescopic astronomy began in 1609, and by the end of the 17th century the telescope was applied in mapping the stars. In the latter part of the 19th century, photography gave a powerful impetus to precise chart making, culminating in the 1950s in the publication of *National Geographic Society–Palomar Observatory Sky Survey,* a portrayal of the part of the sky visible from Palomar Observatory in California.

Many modern maps used by amateur and professional observers of the sky show stars, dark nebulas of obscuring dust, and bright nebulas (masses of tenuous, glowing matter). Specialized maps show sources of radio radiation, sources of infrared radiation, and quasi-stellar objects having very large redshifts (the spectral lines are displaced toward longer wavelengths) and very small images. Astronomers of the 20th century have divided the entire sky into 88 areas, or constellations; this international system codifies the naming of stars and star patterns that began in prehistoric times. Originally only the brightest stars and most conspicuous patterns were given names, probably based on the actual appearance of the configurations. Beginning in the 16th century, navigators and astronomers have progressively filled in all the areas left undesignated by the ancients.

THE CELESTIAL SPHERE

To any observer, ancient or modern, the night sky appears as a hemisphere resting on the horizon. Consequently, the simplest descriptions of the star patterns and of the motions of heavenly bodies are those presented on the surface of a sphere.

The daily eastward rotation of the Earth on its axis produces an apparent diurnal westward rotation of the starry sphere. Thus, the stars seem to rotate about a northern or southern celestial pole, the projection into space of the Earth's own poles. Equidistant from the two poles is the celestial equator; this great circle is the projection into space of the Earth's Equator.

Figure 13 illustrates the celestial sphere as viewed from some middle northern latitude. Part of the sky adjacent to a celestial pole is always visible (the shaded area in the diagram), and an equal area about the opposite pole is always invisible below the horizon; the rest of the celestial sphere appears to rise and set each day. For any other latitude the particular part of sky visible or invisible will be different and the diagram must be redrawn. An observer situated at the Earth's North Pole could observe only the stars of the northern celestial hemisphere. An observer at the Equator, however, would be able to see the entire celestial sphere as the daily motion of the Earth carried him around.

In addition to their apparent daily motion around the Earth, the Sun, Moon, and planets of the solar system have their own motions with respect to the starry sphere. Since the Sun's brilliance obscures the background stars from view, it took many centuries before observers discovered the precise path of the Sun through the constellations that are now called the signs of the zodiac. The great circle of the zodiac traced out by the Sun on its annual circuit is the ecliptic (so called because eclipses can occur when the Moon crosses it).

The zodiac and the ecliptic

As viewed from space, the Earth slowly revolves about the Sun in a fixed plane, the ecliptic plane. A line perpendicular to this plane defines the ecliptic pole, and it makes no difference whether this line is projected into space from the Earth or from the Sun. All that is important is the direction, because the sky is so far away that the ecliptic pole must fall on a unique point on the celestial sphere (Figure 14).

The principal planets in the solar system revolve about the Sun in nearly the same plane as the Earth's orbit, and their movements will therefore be projected onto the celestial sphere nearly, but seldom exactly, on the ecliptic. The Moon's orbit is tilted by about five degrees from this plane, and hence its position in the sky deviates from the ecliptic more than those of the other planets with the exception of Pluto.

Because the blinding sunlight blocks some stars from view, the particular constellations that can be seen depend on the position of the Earth in its orbit—*i.e.,* on the apparent place of the Sun. The stars visible at midnight will shift westward by about one degree each successive midnight as the Sun progresses in its apparent eastward motion. Stars visible at midnight in September will be concealed by the dazzling noontime Sun 180 days later in March.

Why the ecliptic and celestial equator meet at an angle of 23° 26.6′ is an unexplained mystery originating in the past history of Earth. The angle gradually varies by small amounts as a result of Moon- and planet-caused gravitational perturbations on the Earth. The ecliptic plane is comparatively stable, but the equatorial plane is continually shifting as the Earth's axis of rotation changes its direction in space. The successive positions of the celestial poles trace out large circles on the sky with a period of about 26,000 years. This phenomenon, known as precession of the equinoxes, causes a series of different stars to become pole stars in turn. Polaris, the present pole star, will come nearest to the north celestial pole around

Precession of the equinoxes

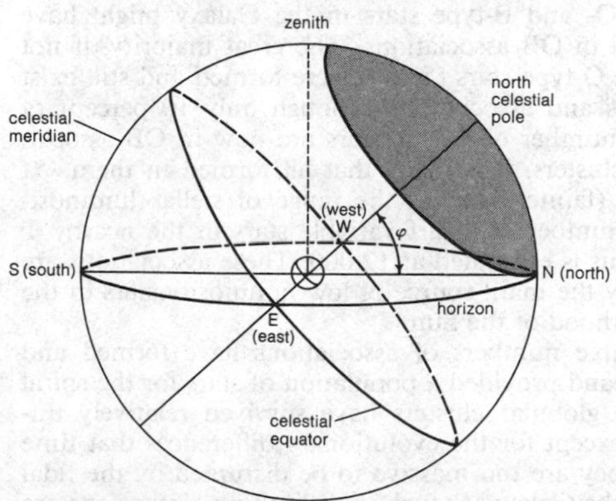

Figure 13: Celestial coordinates seen by an observer in mid-northern latitudes. His celestial meridian is a great circle passing through his zenith and the poles. His astronomical horizon meets the celestial sphere at infinity.

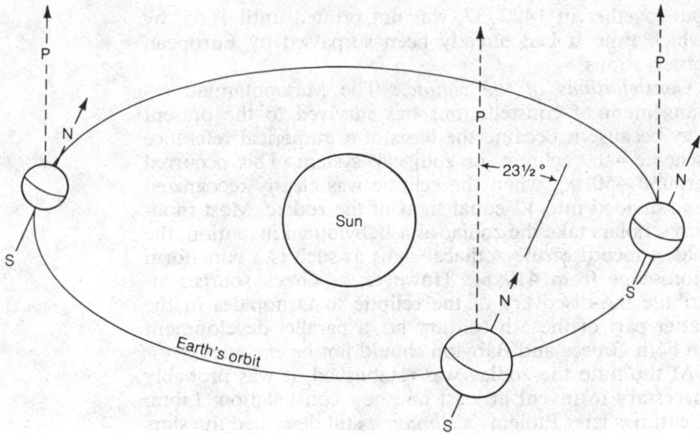

Figure 14: The north celestial (N) and the north ecliptic (P) poles at various positions of the Earth in its annual path around the Sun. Dotted lines are all perpendicular to the plane of Earth's orbit, and all intersect the celestial sphere at the north ecliptic pole. Solid lines drawn through Earth's poles, perpendicular to Earth's Equator, all point to celestial north. The angle of 23½° remains constant.

the year AD 2100. At the time the pyramids were built, Thuban in the constellation Draco served as the pole star, and in about 12,000 years the first-magnitude star Vega will be near the north celestial pole. Precession also makes the coordinate systems on precise star maps applicable only for a specific epoch.

CELESTIAL COORDINATE SYSTEMS

The horizon system. The simple altazimuth system, which depends on a particular place, specifies positions by altitude (the angular elevation from the horizon plane) and azimuth (the angle clockwise around the horizon, usually starting from the north). Lines of equal altitude around the sky are called almucantars. The horizon system is fundamental in navigation, as well as in terrestrial surveying. For mapping the stars, however, coordinates fixed with respect to the celestial sphere itself (such as the ecliptic or equatorial systems) are far more suitable.

The ecliptic system. Celestial longitude and latitude are defined with respect to the ecliptic and ecliptic poles. Celestial longitude is measured eastward from the ascending intersection of the ecliptic with the equator, a position known as the "first point of Aries," and the place of the Sun at the time of the vernal equinox around March 21. The first point of Aries is symbolized by the ram's horns (♈).

Widespread use of the ecliptic system in early Western astronomy

Unlike the celestial equator, the ecliptic is fixed among the stars; however, the ecliptic longitude of a given star increases by 1.396° per century owing to the precessional movement of the equator—similar to the precessional movement of a child's top—which shifts the first point of Aries. The first 30 degrees along the ecliptic is nominally designated as the sign Aries, although this part of the ecliptic has now moved forward into the constellation Pisces. Ecliptic coordinates predominated in Western astronomy until the Renaissance. (In contrast, Chinese astronomers always used an equatorial system.) With the advent of national nautical almanacs, the equatorial system, which is better suited to observation and navigation, gained ascendancy.

The equatorial system. Based on the celestial equator and poles, the equatorial coordinates, right ascension and declination, are directly analogous to terrestrial longitude and latitude (Figure 15). Right ascension, measured eastward from the first point of Aries (see above), is customarily divided into 24 hours rather than 360°, thus emphasizing the clocklike behaviour of the sphere. Precise equatorial positions must be specified for a particular year, since the precessional motion continually changes the measured coordinates.

Galactic coordinates. For problems relating to the structure of the Galaxy, astronomers have introduced the galactic equator, a great circle girdling the sky and centred in the Milky Way. Galactic longitude is measured from a specified location in Sagittarius in the direction of the nucleus of the Galaxy and is taken as positive in a direction obliquely northward in the sky (increasing declination). Galactic latitude is measured from the galactic equator and is positive toward the north galactic pole in Coma Berenices.

THE CONSTELLATIONS AND OTHER SKY DIVISIONS

Ancient references to the constellations

Recognition of the constellations can be traced to early civilization. The oldest astronomical cuneiform texts, from the second half of the 2nd millennium BC, record the Sumerian names of the constellations still known as the lion, the bull, and the scorpion. Drawings of these astronomical animals appear on Babylonian boundary stones of the same period, and the earlier occurrence of these motifs on prehistoric seals, Sumerian vases, and gaming boards suggests that they may have originated as early as 4000 BC. In China a handful of configurations show similarity to those of the West, including the scorpion, lion, hunter (Orion), and northern dipper, suggesting the possibility of a very old common tradition for a few groups, but, otherwise, almost complete independence.

Greek literature reflects the impact of the stars on the life of an agricultural and seafaring people. Homer (*c.* 9th century BC) records several constellations by the names used today, and the first mention of circumpolar stars is in the *Odyssey*. Odysseus is

> Gazing with fixed eye on the Pleiades,
> Boötes setting late and the Great Bear,
> By others called the Wain, which wheeling round,
> Looks ever toward Orion and alone
> Dips not into the waters of the deep.
>
> *Odyssey,* V

In England the Great Bear (Ursa Major), or Big Dipper, was still called Charles's Wain (or Wagon) in Shakespeare's day:

> An't be not four by
> The day I'll be hanged; Charles' Wain is over
> The new chimney and yet our horse not pack'd.
>
> *King Henry IV,* Part I, Act ii, Scene 1

This form derives from Charlemagne, and according to *The Oxford English Dictionary,* apparently from a verbal association of the name of the bright nearby Arcturus with Arturus, or Arthur, and the legendary association of Arthur and Charlemagne.

The earliest systematic account of the constellations is contained in the *Phaenomena* of Aratus, a poet of the 3rd century BC, who described 43 constellations and named five individual stars. Cicero recorded that

> The first Hellenic globe of the sky was made by Thales of Miletus, having fallen into a ditch or well while star-gazing. Afterwards Eudoxos of Cnidus traced on its surface the stars

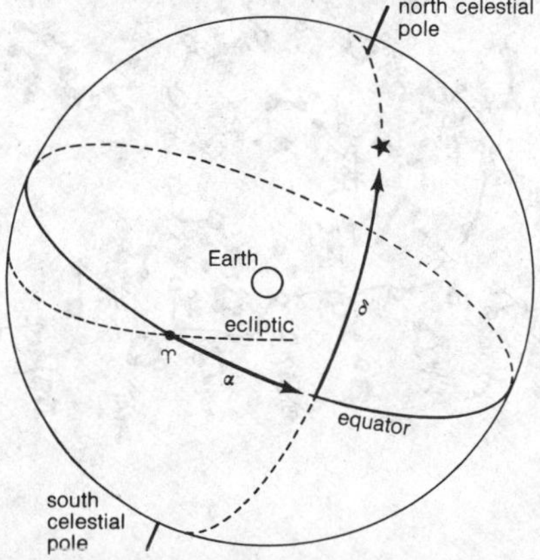

Figure 15: *Equatorial system of coordinates: right ascension (α) and declination (δ) of a star.* Both are angular measurements, though right ascension is usually given in hours rather than degrees of arc and is measured eastward from the "first point of Aries" (♈), where the Sun crosses the celestial equator in March. Declination is considered positive (+) north of the celestial equator and negative (−) south of it.

> that appear in the sky; and . . . many years after, borrowing from Eudoxos this beautiful design and representation, Aratos had illustrated it in his verses, not by any science of astronomy, but by the ornament of poetical description.
>
> *De republica*, I, 14

The *Almagest*

By far the most important list of stars and constellations still extant from antiquity appears in the *Almagest* of Ptolemy (flourished 2nd century AD). It contains ecliptic coordinates and magnitudes (measures of brightness) for 1,022 stars, grouped into 48 constellations. Numerous writers have stated that Ptolemy simply borrowed his material from a now-lost catalog of Hipparchus compiled in 129 BC. A critical analysis of the Hipparchian fragments still extant, including his commentary on the *Phaenomena* of Aratus, indicates that (1) the catalog of Hipparchus did not include more than 850 stars and (2) Ptolemy most likely obtained new coordinates for even those 850 stars. The evidence suggests that Ptolemy, who for over a century has been considered a mere compilator, should be placed among the first-rank astronomical observers of all ages.

Nevertheless, Ptolemy's star list presents a curious puzzle. The southernmost heavens, invisible at the latitude of Alexandria, naturally went unobserved. On one side of the sky near this southern horizon, he tabulated the bright stars of the Southern Cross (although not as a separate constellation) and of Centaurus, but on the opposite side a large area including the first-magnitude star Achernar had been left unrecorded. Because of precession, before 2000 BC this region would have been invisible from Mesopotamia. Perhaps neither Hipparchus nor Ptolemy considered that part of the heavens unnamed by their ancient predecessors. Ptolemy's catalog of 1,022 stars remained authoritative until the Renaissance.

Ptolemy divided his stars into six brightness, or magnitude, classes. He listed 15 bright stars of the first magnitude but comparatively few of the faint, much more numerous but barely visible sixth magnitude at the other limit of his list. Aṣ-Ṣūfī, a 10th-century Islāmic astronomer carried out the principal revision made to these magnitudes during the Middle Ages. Ulugh Beg, grandson of the Mongol conqueror Tamerlane, is the only known Oriental astronomer to reobserve the positions of Ptolemy's stars. His catalog, put together in 1420–37, was not printed until 1665, by which time it had already been surpassed by European observations.

Constellations of the zodiac. The Mesopotamian arrangement of constellations has survived to the present day because it became the basis of a numerical reference scheme—the ecliptic, or zodiacal, system. This occurred around 450 BC, when the ecliptic was clearly recognized and divided into 12 equal signs of the zodiac. Most modern scholars take the zodiac as a Babylonian invention; the oldest record of the zodiacal signs as such is a cuneiform horoscope from 419 BC. However, as Greek sources attribute the discovery of the ecliptic to Oenopides in the latter part of the 5th century BC, a parallel development in both Greece and Babylon should not be excluded.

At the time the zodiac was established, it was probably necessary to invent at least one new constellation, Libra. Centuries later Ptolemy's *Almagest* still described the stars of Libra with respect to the ancient figure of the scorpion.

The decans. Two other astronomical reference systems developed independently in early antiquity, the lunar mansions and the Egyptian decans. The decans are 36 star configurations circling the sky somewhat to the south of the ecliptic. They make their appearance in drawings and texts inside coffin lids of the 10th dynasty (around 2100 BC) and are shown on the tomb ceilings of Seti I (1318–04 BC) and of some of the Rameses in Thebes. The decans appear to have provided the basis for the division of the day into 24 hours.

Besides representing star configurations as decans, the Egyptians marked out about 25 constellations, such as crocodile, hippopotamus, lion, and a falcon-headed god. Their constellations can be divided into northern and southern groups, but the various representations are so discordant that only three constellations have been identified with certainty: Orion (depicted as Osiris), Sirius (a recumbent cow), and Ursa Major (foreleg or front part of a bull). The most famous Egyptian star map is a 1st-century-BC stone chart found in the temple at Dandarah and now in the Louvre. The Zodiac of Dandarah illustrates the Egyptian decans and constellations, but since it incorporates the Babylonian zodiac as well, many stars

By courtesy of the trustees of the British Museum

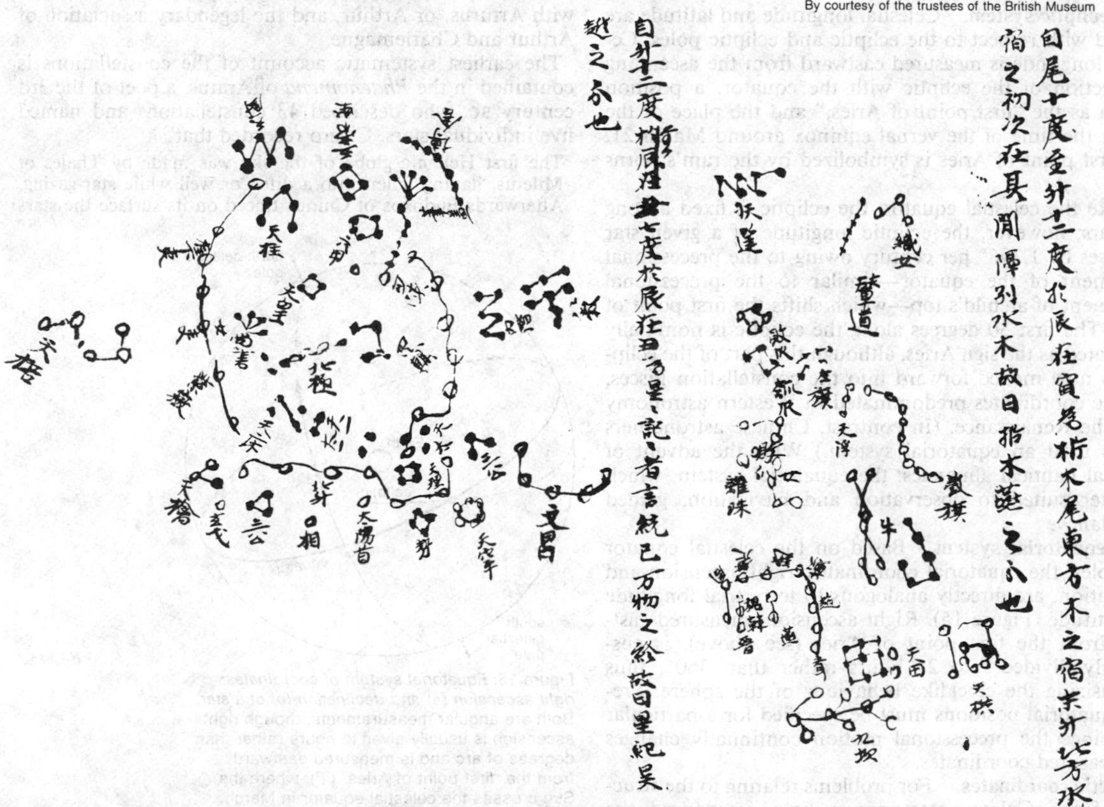

Figure 16: Chinese Tunhuang manuscript, the oldest existing portable star map, excluding astrolabes (*c.* AD 940). In the British Museum (MS. Stein 3326). Actual width of portion shown, about 32 centimetres (12.75 inches).

Table 7: Constellations

name	genitive form	abbre-viation*	meaning	remarks†
Constellations described by Ptolemy: the zodiac				
Aries	*Arietis*	Ari ♈	Ram	
Taurus	*Tauri*	Tau ♉	Bull	*Aldebaran:* Pleiades; M1 (Crab Nebula)
Gemini	*Geminorum*	Gem ♊	Twins	*Castor; Pollux*
Cancer	*Cancri*	Can ♋	Crab	Praesepe (star cluster)
Leo	*Leonis*	Leo ♌	Lion	*Regulus*
Virgo	*Virginis*	Vir ♍	Virgin	*Spica:* Virgo cluster of galaxies
Libra	*Librae*	Lib ♎	Balance	
Scorpius	*Scorpii*	Sco ♏	Scorpion	*Antares:* many star clusters
Sagittarius	*Sagittarii*	Sgr ♐	Archer	Galactic centre; many star clusters
Capricornus	*Capricorni*	Cap ♑	Sea-goat	
Aquarius	*Aquarii*	Aqr ♒	Water-bearer	
Pisces	*Piscium*	Psc ♓	Fishes	
Other Ptolemaic constellations				
Andromeda	*Andromedae*	And	Andromeda (Princess)	M31 (great spiral galaxy)
Aquila	*Aquilae*	Aql	Eagle	*Altair*
Ara	*Arae*	Ara	Altar	
Argo Navis	*Argus Navis*	Arg	Ship Argo	now divided into Carina, Puppis, Pyxis, and Vela
Auriga	*Aurigae*	Aur	Charioteer	*Capella:* M36, M37, M38 (open star clusters)
Boötes	*Boötis*	Boo	Herdsman	*Arcturus*
Canis Major	*Canis Majoris*	CMa	Greater Dog	*Sirius* (brightest star)
Canis Minor	*Canis Minoris*	CMi	Smaller Dog	*Procyon*
Cassiopeia	*Cassiopeiae*	Cas	Cassiopeia (Queen)	Tycho's nova, 1572 (visible in daytime)
Centaurus	*Centauri*	Cen	Centaur	*Alpha* (nearest star to Sun); *Beta*
Cepheus	*Cephei*	Cep	Cepheus (King)	Delta Cephei (prototype for cepheid variables)
Cetus	*Ceti*	Cet	Whale	Mira Ceti (first recognized variable star)
Corona Austrina	*Coronae Austrinae*	CrA	Southern Crown	
Corona Borealis	*Coronae Borealis*	CrB	Northern Crown	
Corvus	*Corvi*	Crv	Raven	
Crater	*Crateris*	Crt	Cup	
Cygnus	*Cygni*	Cyg	Swan	"Northern Cross"; *Deneb*
Delphinus	*Delphini*	Del	Dolphin	"Job's Coffin"
Draco	*Draconis*	Dra	Dragon	Thuban (polestar in 3000 BC)
Equuleus	*Equulei*	Equ	Little Horse	
Eridanus	*Eridani*	Eri	River Eridanus or river god	*Achernar*
Hercules	*Herculis*	Her	Hercules (Greek hero)	M13 (great globular star cluster)
Hydra	*Hydrae*	Hya	Water Snake	
Lepus	*Leporis*	Lep	Hare	
Lupus	*Lupi*	Lup	Wolf	
Lyra	*Lyrae*	Lyr	Lyre	*Vega:* M57 (Ring Nebula)
Ophiuchus	*Ophiuchi*	Oph	Serpent-bearer	
Orion	*Orionis*	Ori	Hunter	*Rigel; Betelgeuse;* M42 (Great Nebula)
Pegasus	*Pegasi*	Peg	Pegasus (winged horse)	Great Square (of Pegasus)
Perseus	*Persei*	Per	Perseus (Greek hero)	Algol (eclipsing star); *h* and *χ* Persei (double cluster)
Piscis Austrinus	*Piscis Austrini*	PsA	Southern Fish	*Fomalhaut*
Sagitta	*Sagittae*	Sge	Arrow	
Serpens	*Serpentis*	Ser	Serpent	
Triangulum	*Trianguli*	Tri	Triangle	M33 (nearby spiral galaxy)
Ursa Major	*Ursae Majoris*	UMa	Great Bear	seven brightest stars are Big Dipper or Plough
Ursa Minor	*Ursae Minoris*	UMi	Lesser Bear	Polaris (the north pole-star)
Southern constellations, added *c.* 1600				
Apus	*Apodis*	Aps	Bird of Paradise	
Chamaeleon	*Chamaeleontis*	Cha	Chameleon	
Dorado	*Doradus*	Dor	Swordfish	Large Magellanic Cloud
Grus	*Gruis*	Gru	Crane	
Hydrus	*Hydri*	Hyi	Water Snake	
Indus	*Indi*	Ind	Indian	
Musca	*Muscae*	Mus	Fly	
Pavo	*Pavonis*	Pav	Peacock	
Phoenix	*Phoenicis*	Phe	Phoenix (mythical bird)	
Triangulum Australe	*Trianguli Australis*	TrA	Southern Triangle	
Tucana	*Tucanae*	Tuc	Toucan	Small Magellanic Cloud
Volans	*Volantis*	Vol	Flying Fish	
Constellations of Bartsch, 1624				
Camelopardalis	*Camelopardalis*	Cam	Giraffe	
Columba	*Columbae*	Col	Dove	constellation formed by Plancius, 1605
Monoceros	*Monocerotis*	Mon	Unicorn	
Constellations of Hevelius, 1687				
Canes Venatici	*Canum Venaticorum*	CVn	Hunting Dogs	M51 (Whirlpool Galaxy)
Lacerta	*Lacertae*	Lac	Lizard	
Leo Minor	*Leonis Minoris*	LMi	Lesser Lion	
Lynx	*Lyncis*	Lyn	Lynx	
Scutum	*Scuti*	Sct	Shield	star cloud in Milky Way
Sextans	*Sextantis*	Sex	Sextant	
Vulpecula	*Vulpeculae*	Vul	Fox	M27 (Dumbbell Nebula)
Ancient asterisms now separate constellations				
Carina	*Carinae*	Car	Keel [of Argo]	*Canopus*
Coma Berenices	*Comae Berenices*	Com	Berenice's Hair	Coma (star cluster); north galactic pole
Crux	*Crucis*	Cru	[Southern] Cross	*Alpha; Beta*
Puppis	*Puppis*	Pup	Stern [of Argo]	
Pyxis	*Pyxidis*	Pyx	Compass [of Argo]	
Vela	*Velorum*	Vel	Sails [of Argo]	
Southern constellations of Lacaille, *c.* 1750				
Antlia	*Antliae*	Ant	Pump	
Caelum	*Caeli*	Cae	[Sculptor's] Chisel	
Circinus	*Circini*	Cir	Drawing Compasses	
Fornax	*Fornacis*	For	[Chemical] Furnace	
Horologium	*Horologii*	Hor	Clock	
Mensa	*Mensae*	Men	Table [Mountain]	
Microscopium	*Microscopii*	Mic	Microscope	
Norma	*Normae*	Nor	Square	
Octans	*Octantis*	Oct	Octant	
Pictor	*Pictoris*	Pic	Painter's [Easel]	
Reticulum	*Reticuli*	Ret	Reticle	
Sculptor	*Sculptoris*	Scl	Sculptor's [Workshop]	south galactic pole
Telescopium	*Telescopii*	Tel	Telescope	

*The 12 constellations of the zodiac are accompanied by their symbols. †First-magnitude stars are given in italics.

must be doubly represented, and the stone can hardly be considered an accurate mapping of the heavens.

Hsiu and nakṣhatra

Lunar mansions. Called *hsiu* in China and *nakṣhatra* in India, the lunar mansions are 28 divisions of the sky presumably selected as approximate "Moon stations" on successive nights. At least four quadrantal *hsiu* that divided the sky into quarters or quadrants were known in China in the 14th century BC, and 23 are mentioned in the *Yüeh Ling,* which may go back to 850 BC. In India a complete list of *nakṣhatra* are found in the Atharvaveda, providing evidence that the system was organized before 800 BC. The system of lunar mansions, however, may have a common origin even earlier in Mesopotamia.

Relationship of the bright stars and their constellations. Ancient peoples sometimes named individual bright stars rather than groups; sometimes the name of the group and its brightest star were synonymous—as in the case of the constellation Aquila and the star Altair (Alpha Aquilae), both names meaning "flying eagles"—or were used interchangeably as in the case of both the star Arcturus (Alpha Boötis, "bear watcher") and the constellation Boötes ("plowman"). In the star list of the *Almagest,* Ptolemy cites only about a dozen stars by name, describing the others by their positions within the constellation figures. Most star names in current use have Arabic forms, but these are usually simply translations of Ptolemy's descriptions; for example, Deneb, the name of the brightest star in the constellation Cygnus (Swan), means literally "tail" of the bird.

The earliest astronomical globes and ancient maps

Ptolemy's placement of the stars within apparently well-known figures indicates the earlier existence of star maps, probably globes. An example survives in the so-called Farnese Globe at Naples, the most famous astronomical artifact of antiquity. This huge marble globe, supported by a statue of Atlas, is generally considered to be a Roman copy of an earlier Greek original. It shows constellation figures but not individual stars, although the stars may have been painted on the stone.

A unique hemispherical celestial map, which furnishes a remarkable connecting link between the classical representation of the constellations and the later Islāmic forms, is painted in the dome of a bath house at Quṣayr ʿAmra, an Arab palace built in Jordan around AD 715. The surviving fragments of the fresco show parts of 37 constellations and about 400 stars.

Circumstantial evidence suggests that a flat representation of the sky, in the form of a planisphere using a stereographic projection, had come into use by the beginning of the present era. This provided the basis for the astrolabe, the earliest remaining examples of which date from the 9th century AD. The open metalwork of the top moving plate (called a spider or rete) of an astrolabe is essentially a star map, and these instruments together with associated manuscript lists provide the basic documentation for Arabic star names.

If astrolabes are excluded, the oldest existing portable star map from any civilization is the Chinese Tunhuang manuscript in the British Museum, dating from about AD 940 (Figure 16). A Latin document of about the same age, also in the British Museum, shows a planisphere to illustrate the *Phainomena* of Aratus, without, however, indicating individual stars. The oldest illuminated Islāmic astronomical manuscript, an AD 1009–10 copy of aṣ-Ṣūfī's book on the fixed stars, shows individual constellations, including stars (Figure 17).

The earliest known western maps of the skies of the Northern and Southern Hemispheres with both stars and constellation figures date from 1440; preserved in Vienna, they may have been based on two now-lost charts from 1425 once owned by the German astronomer and mathematician Regiomontanus. In 1515 the noted German painter Albrecht Dürer drew the first printed star maps, a pair of beautiful planispheres closely patterned on the Vienna manuscripts. Dürer and his collaborators numbered the stars on the charts according to the order in Ptolemy's list, a nomenclature that gained limited currency in the 16th century. The first book of printed star charts, *De le stelle fisse* (1540) of the Italian Alessandro Piccolomini, introduced a lettering system for the stars; although frequently reprinted, application of its nomenclature did not spread.

New constellations: 16th–20th centuries. Star charts contained only the 48 constellations tabulated by Ptolemy until the end of the 16th century. Then Pieter Dircksz Keyser, a navigator who joined the first Dutch expedition to the East Indies in 1595, added 12 new constellations in the southern skies, named in part after exotic birds such as the toucan, peacock, and phoenix.

The southern constellations were introduced in 1601 on

By courtesy of (left) the curators of Bodleian Library, Oxford, (right) Owen Gingerich

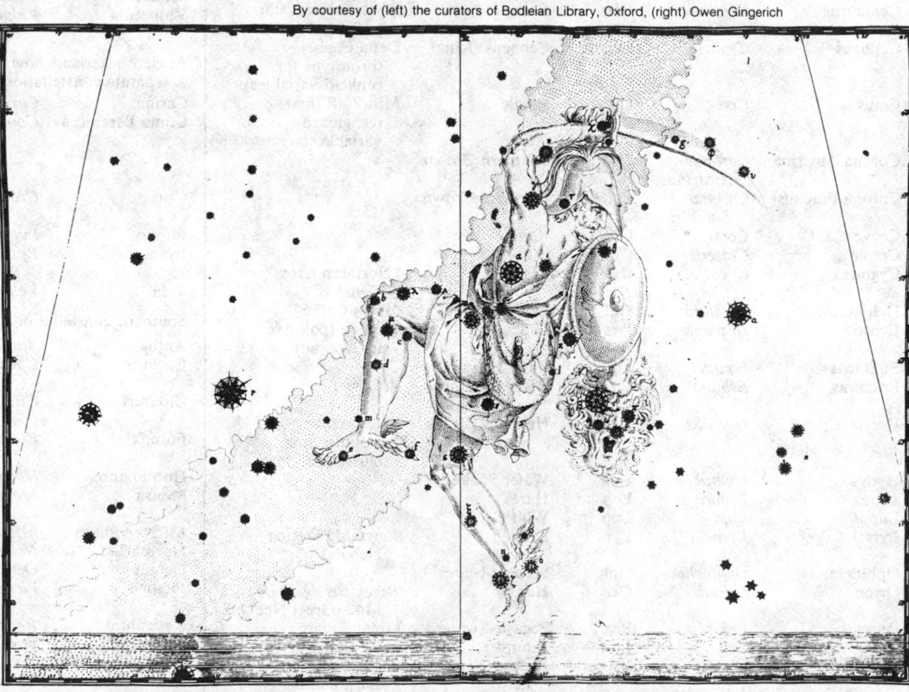

Figure 17: *The constellation of Perseus.*
(Left) From *Ṣuwar al-Kawākib ath-thābitah* ("Book of the Fixed Stars"), executed by ʿAbd ar-Raḥmān ibn ʿUmar aṣ-Ṣūfī, AH 400 (AD 1009–10). In the Bodleian Library, Oxford (MS Marsh 144, p. 111). (Right) From Johann Bayer's *Uranometria,* 1603, a set of maps in which the use of Greek letter notation for bright stars was first introduced. The Milky Way appears as a dotted band through the figure, and the horizontal stripes at bottom indicate the ecliptic band.

Introduction of the southern constellations

a celestial globe by J. Hondius and in 1603 on the globe of Willem Blaeu and on a single plate in the *Uranometria* of Johann Bayer. The *Uranometria,* the first serious star atlas, has a plate for each of the 48 traditional figures (Figure 17). Its scientific integrity rests on Tycho Brahe's newly determined stellar positions and magnitudes (see below).

In his *Uranographia* of 1687, the German astronomer Johannes Hevelius devised seven new constellations visible from mid-northern latitudes that are still accepted, including Sextans (the sextant), named for one of his own astronomical instruments. Fourteen additional southern constellations were formed by Nicolas Louis de Lacaille after his visit to the Cape of Good Hope in 1750. They appeared in the *Memoires* of the Académie Royale des Sciences for 1752 (published in 1756). All other attempts to invent constellations have failed to win acceptance.

The classic atlases of Bayer and Hevelius as well as John Flamsteed's *Atlas Coelestis* (1729) showed only the brighter naked-eye stars. Johann Elert Bode's *Uranographia* of 1801 was the first reasonably complete depiction of the stars visible to the unaided eye. It included an early use of constellation boundaries, a concept accepted and refined by 19th-century cartographers (Figure 18). Friedrich W.A. Argelander's *Uranometria Nova* (1843) and Benjamin A. Gould's *Uranometria Argentina* (1877–79) standardized the list of constellations as they are known today. They divided Ptolemy's largest constellation, Argo Navis (the ship), into four parts: Vela (the sail), Pyxis (the compass), Puppis (the stern), and Carina (the keel).

The list of constellations

The definitive list of 88 constellations was established in 1930 under the authority of the International Astronomical Union. Its rectilinear constellation boundaries preserve the traditional arrangements of the naked-eye stars. The smallest of the constellations, Equuleus ("the Little Horse") and Crux ("the [Southern] Cross"), nestle against constellations that are more than 10 times larger, Pegasus and Centaurus, respectively. The standard boundaries define an unambiguous constellation for each star.

STAR NAMES AND DESIGNATIONS

Of approximately 5,000 stars visible to the unaided eye, only a few hundred have proper names, and less than 60 are commonly used by navigators or astronomers. A few names come almost directly from the Greek, such as Procyon, Canopus, and Antares—the latter derived from "anti-Ares" or "rival of Mars" because of its conspicuous red colour. The stars Sirius ("Scorcher") and Arcturus ("Bear Watcher") are mentioned both by Homer and Hesiod (8th century BC?). Aratus names those two as well as Procyon ("Forerunner of the Dog"), Stachys ("Ear of Corn"?, now Spica), and Protrugater ("Herald of the Vintage," now Latinized to Vindemiatrix).

The *Al* that begins numerous star names indicates their Arabic origin, *al* being the Arabic definite article "the": Aldebaran ("the Follower"), Algenib ("the Side"), Alhague ("the Serpent Bearer"), and Algol ("the Demon"). A conspicuous exception is Albireo in Cygnus, possibly a corruption of the words *ab ireo* in the first Latin edition of the *Almagest* in 1515. Most star names are in fact Arabic and are frequently derived from translations of the Greek descriptions. The stars of Orion illustrate the various derivations: Rigel, from *rijl al-Jawzah,* "Leg of Orion," Mintaka, the "Belt," and Saiph, the "Sword," all follow the Ptolemaic figure; Betelgeuse, from *yad al-Jawzah,* is an alternative non-Ptolemaic description meaning "hand of Orion"; and Bellatrix, meaning "Female Warrior," is either a free Latin translation of an independent Arabic title, *an-najid,* "the conqueror," or is a modification of an alternative name for Orion himself. Only a handful of names have recent origins—for example, Cor Caroli, the brightest star in Canes Venatici, named in 1725 by Edmond Halley.

Arabic names

By courtesy of the Observatories, University of Cambridge

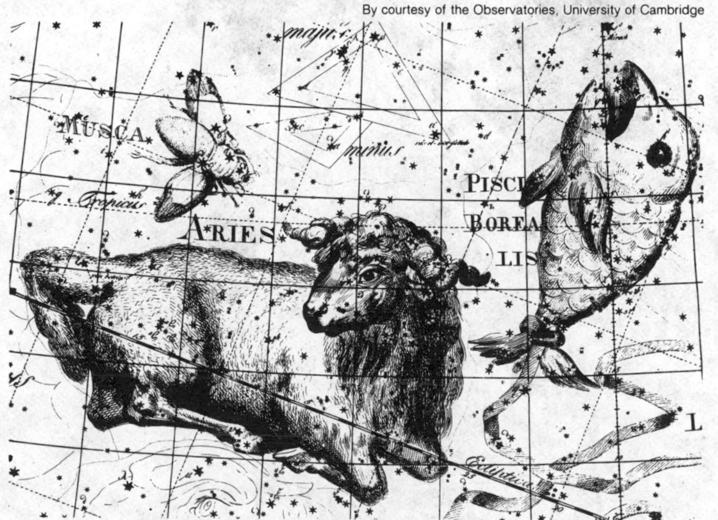

Figure 18: The constellation Aries (the Ram) and others, from Johann E. Bode's *Uranographia,* 1801. The constellation Musca (the Fly) shown here is obsolete: the modern constellation Musca is in the southern skies.

Bayer's *Uranometria* of 1603 introduced a system of Greek letters for designating the principal naked-eye stars. In this scheme, the Greek letter is followed by the genitive form of the constellation name, so that alpha (α) of Canes Venatici is Alpha Canum Venaticorum. Bayer's letters and their extension to newer constellations apply to about 1,300 stars. In *Historia Coelestis Britannica* (published posthumously in 1725), Flamsteed numbered the stars within each of 54 constellations consecutively according to right ascension, and the Flamsteed numbers are customarily used for the fainter naked-eye stars such as 61 Cygni.

Designations of faint and variable stars

An astronomer wishing to specify an even fainter star will usually take recourse to a more extensive or more specialized catalog. Such catalogs generally ignore constellations and list all stars by right ascension. Thus, astronomers learn to recognize that BD +38°3238 refers to a star in the *Bonner Durchmusterung* and that HD 172167 designates one in the *Henry Draper Catalogue* of spectral classifications; in this case, both numbers refer to the same bright star, Vega (Alpha Lyrae). Vega can also be specified as GC 25466, from Benjamin Boss's *General Catalogue of 33,342 Stars* (1937), or as ADS 11510, from Robert Grant Aitken's *New General Catalogue of Double Stars* (1932). These are the most widely used numbering systems. For more obscure names, such as Ross 614 or Lalande 21185, most astronomers would have to consult a bibliographical aid to discover the original listing.

Variable stars have their own nomenclature, which takes precedence over designations from more specialized catalogs. Variable stars are named in order of discovery within each constellation by the letter R to Z (providing they do not already have a Greek letter). After Z the double from RR to RZ, SS to SZ, . . . is used; after ZZ come the letters AA to AZ, BB to BZ, and so on, the letter J being omitted. After the letters QX, QY, and QZ, the names V335, V336, and so on are assigned. Hence, the first lettered variable in Cygnus is R Cygni, and the list reached V1761 by the end of 1981. The names were assigned by the Soviet authors of the *General Catalogue of Variable Stars* (3rd edition, 1969), with the approval of the Commission on Variable Stars of the International Astronomical Union.

The Messier system

Two catalogs are frequently used for designating star clusters, nebulas, or galaxies. The shorter list of these, which includes about 100 of the brighter objects, was compiled in three installments by the French astronomer Charles Messier in the latter part of the 18th century; M1 and M31 are examples of this system, being, respectively, the Crab Nebula and the great galaxy in Andromeda. A much more extensive tabulation in order of right ascension is the *New General Catalogue* (NGC; 1890), followed by the *Index Catalogue* (IC; 1895, 1908); examples are NGC 7009 or IC 1613.

MODERN STAR MAPS AND CATALOGS

Near the end of the 16th century, Tycho Brahe of Denmark resolved to provide an observational basis for the renovation of astronomy. With his large and sturdy (but pre-telescopic) quadrants and sextants, he carefully measured the positions of 777 stars, to which he later added enough hastily observed stars to bring the catalog up to exactly 1,000. A comparable catalog of southern stars was not available until 1678, when the young Edmond Halley published positions of 350 stars measured during a British expedition to St. Helena.

The first Astronomer Royal, John Flamsteed, pioneered the use of telescopic sights for measuring stars' positions. His aforementioned *Historia Coelestis Britannica* listed 3,000 stars, exceeding all former catalogs in number and accuracy. These observations provided the basis for his great *Atlas Coelestis.* Measurements of the third Astronomer Royal, James Bradley, achieved a precision within a few seconds of arc; as reduced by the German astronomer Friedrich W. Bessel in 1818, his positions are the oldest still considered useful in modern astronomy.

Survey and zone maps and catalogs. The German word *Durchmusterung,* literally a "scanning through," was introduced by Argelander, who undertook to list all the stars visible in the eight-centimetre Bonn refractor. Keeping the telescope fixed, he recorded the stars, zone by zone, as the Earth's rotation carried the stars past the field of view. The resulting *Bonner Durchmusterung* (1859–62), or *BD* catalog, contains 324,189 stars to about the ninth magnitude between declinations +90° and −2°. The accompanying charts, published in 1863, far surpassed all former maps in completeness and reliability. These maps are still of great value. The Bonn survey was extended to −23° in 1886, and at Córdoba, Arg., it was carried to the parallel of −62° by 1908, and to the South Pole by 1930. Because observing conditions changed over the many years required, the resulting *Córdoba Durchmusterung,* or *CD,* lacks the homogeneity of its northern counterpart.

The *Bonner Durchmusterung*

In 1867 Argelander proposed to the Astronomische Gesellschaft (German Astronomical Society) a massive project to document stellar positions with far greater precision. Although the observing of selected star positions with meridian circle telescopes had become well established by observers during the 18th and early 19th centuries, the new plan called for meridian observations of all stars down to the ninth magnitude. A score of observatories on four continents, each responsible for a specific zone of declination, cooperated to complete the catalog and its southern supplements. The northern sections, known as the *AGK1,* were published by zones; not until 1912 was the *AGK1* complete to −18°.

Meanwhile, in quite another way, the Dutch astronomer Jacobus Cornelius Kapteyn completed an inventory of the southern sky by the measurement of the positions and magnitudes of about 454,000 stars from a set of photographic plates taken in Cape Town. Known as the *Cape Photographic Durchmusterung* (1896–1900), or *CPD,* the result covers the sky from declination −19° to the South Pole, down to the 11th magnitude.

Astronomische Gesellschaft catalog

Beginning in 1924, the Astronomische Gesellschaft catalog was repeated photographically by the Bonn and Hamburg-Bergedorf observatories; published in 1951–58, the new catalog is called the *AGK2.* Neither the *AGK1* nor the *AGK2* provided information on proper motions (see above). Therefore, another set of photographic plates was obtained in Hamburg during the 1950s in order to obtain the motions; the resulting *AGK3* was distributed on magnetic tape in 1969.

In 1966 the Smithsonian Astrophysical Observatory in Cambridge, Mass., issued a reference star catalog for use in finding artificial satellites from photographs. Although the *SAO Star Catalog* of 258,997 stars contains no new basic data, it does present the information in a particularly useful form. An accompanying computer-plotted atlas (1968), which includes more than 260,000 stars in addition to galaxies and nebulas, achieves an unprecedented accuracy for celestial cartography.

Fundamental catalogs. The measurements of accurate places for vast numbers of stars rests on painstakingly and independently determined positions of a few selected stars. A list of positions and proper motions for such selected stars well distributed over the sky is called a fundamental catalog, and its coordinate system is a close approximation to a fixed frame of reference. When the German astronomers began the *AGK2* in the 1920s, they first required a fundamental reference system that by the following decade was defined in the *Dritter Fundamentalkatalog des Berliner Astronomischen Jahrbuchs,* or *FK3. The Fourth Fundamental Catalogue* (1963), or *FK4,* published by the Astronomisches Rechen-Institut in Heidelberg, contains data for 1,535 stars and has now superseded the *FK3.*

Photometric catalogs. A complete mapping of the sky includes magnitudes (and colours) as well as positions and motions. The great survey catalogs furnished magnitude estimates, but since photometric procedures are

By courtesy of Mount Palomar Observatory; © by the National Geographic Society—Palomar Observatory Sky Survey

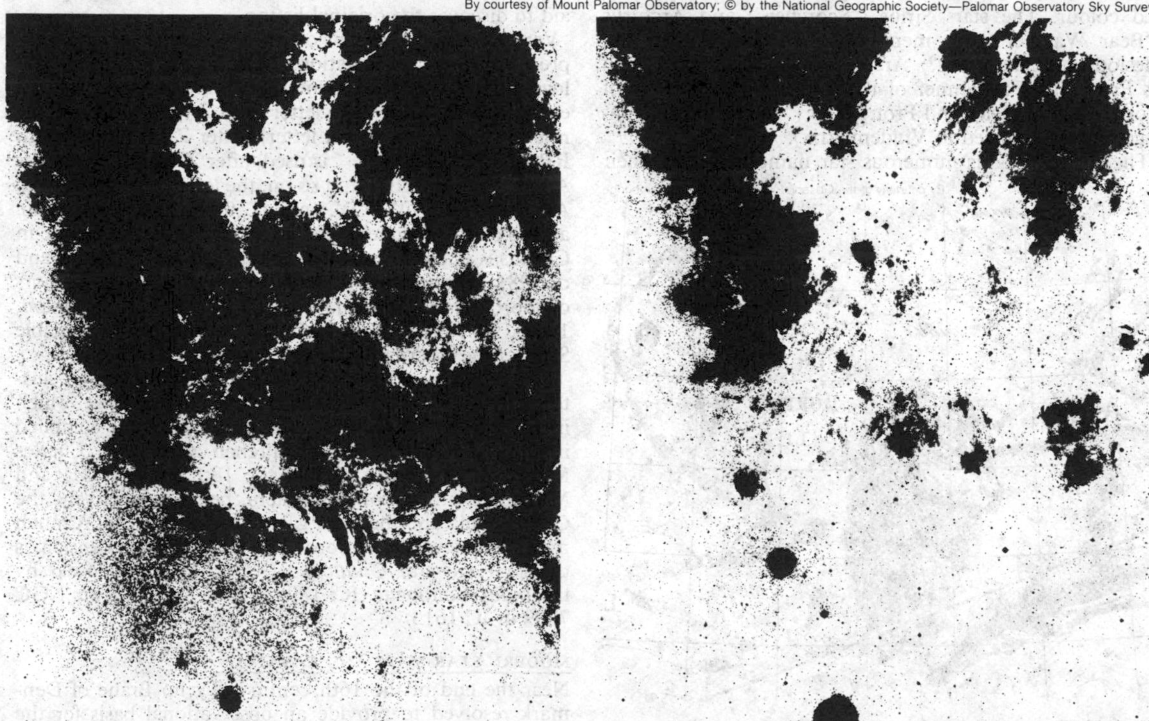

Figure 19: Negative plates showing part of the North America Nebula in (left) red light and (right) blue light. Note the much greater extent of the nebulosity in the dark areas (left).

quite different from astrometric ones, a separate family of photometric catalogs has developed. Visual observations provided the basis for major tabulations published at Oxford, Harvard, and Potsdam around the turn of the century, but these were soon superseded by photographic work. Studies of galactic structure, which required accurate magnitudes for at least some very faint stars as well as the bright ones, led to the establishment of the plan of 206 selected areas. These were well-defined areas of sky with stars of many representative kinds that could be used as standards of comparison, and the *Mount Wilson Catalogue of Photographic Magnitudes in Selected Areas* (1930), made about 20 years later, was for many years a leading reference for celestial photometry. Today, several catalogs of photoelectric measurements in three or more colours set the standards for precision magnitudes.

The *Mount Wilson Catalogue*

Another important quantity that can be measured is a star's spectral type (see above). One of the greatest collections of astronomical data is the *Henry Draper Catalogue* (1918–24), formed at Harvard by Annie Jump Cannon and Edward Charles Pickering. The *HD* lists spectra of 225,300 stars distributed over the entire sky, and the *Henry Draper Extension* (1925–36, 1949) records 133,782 additional spectra.

Photographic star atlases. Astronomical photography was scarcely past its infancy when an international conference in Paris in 1887 all too hastily resolved to construct a photographic atlas of the entire sky down to the 14th magnitude, the so-called *Carte du Ciel,* and an associated *Astrographic Catalogue,* with measured star places down to the 12th magnitude. The original stimulus had come in 1882 with the construction of a 33-cm astrographic objective lens at Paris. For decades the immense *Carte du Ciel* enterprise sapped the energies of observatories around the world, especially in France, and even now is incomplete in the form originally planned. Nowadays such a program could be speedily completed with the use of computerized measuring instruments.

Carte du Ciel

The first photographic atlas of the entire sky (if a set of 55 glass plates offered by Harvard in 1903 be excepted) was initiated by an energetic British amateur. Issued in 1914, the (John) *Franklin-Adams Charts* comprise 206 prints with a limiting magnitude of 15.

The monumental *National Geographic Society–Palomar Observatory Sky Survey,* released in 1954–58, reaches a limiting photographic magnitude of 21, far fainter than any other atlas. (The southernmost band has a slightly brighter limiting magnitude of 20.) Each field was photographed twice with a 124-cm Schmidt telescope at Mount Palomar to produce an atlas consisting of 935 pairs of prints made from the original blue-sensitive and red-sensitive plates, each about 6° square. The atlas proper extends to a declination of −33°, but 100 additional prints from red-sensitive plates now carry the coverage to −45° (Figure 19). Photographic mapping of the southern skies by the United Kingdom's 124-cm Schmidt telescope at Siding Spring Observatory in Australia and by the European Southern Observatory's 100-cm Schmidt at La Silla in Chile has penetrated to stars fainter than magnitude 22.

Atlases for stargazing. Three modern atlases have gained special popularity among amateur and professional observers alike. *Norton's Star Atlas,* perfected through numerous editions, plots all naked-eye stars on eight convenient charts measuring 25 by 43 cm. The *Tirion Sky Atlas 2000.0* (1981) includes some 43,000 stars to magnitude eight and is based primarily on the *SAO Star Catalog.* Its 26 charts, measuring 47 by 33 cm, include bright star names, boundaries of the Milky Way, and about 2,500 star clusters, nebulas, and galaxies. The companion to the *Tirion Atlas—Sky Catalogue 2000.0* (1982, 1985)—summarizes the essential characteristics of 45,269 stars. The second volume of this work catalogs double stars, variable stars, and various kinds of nonstellar objects, including radio and X-ray sources. The German astronomer Hans Vehrenberg's *Photographischer Stern-Atlas* (1962–64), covering the entire sky in 464 sheets, each 12° square, has probably reached wider use than any other photographic atlas because of its quality and comparatively modest cost.

Norton's Star Atlas

There are several handbooks that serve as useful supplements to such atlases. *Burnham's Celestial Handbook* (1978) contains comprehensive descriptions of thousands of astronomical objects. *The Observer's Handbook,* published annually by the Royal Astronomical Society of Canada, lists valuable information for locating and observing a wide range of astronomical phenomena.

(O.G./W.M.Yo.)

BIBLIOGRAPHY

Comprehensive works: GEORGE O. ABELL, *Exploration of the Universe,* 5th ed. (1987), a good introductory account of the properties of stars; LAWRENCE H. ALLER, *Atoms, Stars, and Nebulae,* rev. ed. (1971), a semipopular work emphasizing analyses of starlight, stellar spectroscopy, and evolution, *Astrophysics: The Atmospheres of the Sun and Stars,* 2nd ed. (1963), and *Astrophysics: Nuclear Transformations, Stellar Interiors, and Nebulae* (1954), textbooks intended for senior students, treating ordinary stellar atmospheres, the Sun, variable stars including novas, and stars with extended envelopes; MARTIN SCHWARZSCHILD, *Structure and Evolution of the Stars* (1958, reissued 1965), one of the classic books on the subject, written before the widespread application of modern computers (moderately advanced level); IOSIF S. SHKLOVSKII, *Stars: Their Birth, Life, and Death* (1978; originally published in Russian, 1975), an examination of the achievements of 20th-century astrophysics in the area of star formation and evolution; RUDOLF KIPPENHAHN, *100 Billion Suns: The Birth, Life, and Death of the Stars* (1983; originally published in German, 1980), a readable account of stellar evolution; DONALD A. COOKE, *The Life & Death of Stars* (1985), with excellent illustrations; PAUL MURDIN and LESLEY MURDIN, *Supernovae,* rev. ed. (1978), an excellent nontechnical history; and ALBRECHT UNSÖLD and BODO BASCHEK, *The New Cosmos,* 3rd rev. and enl. ed. (1983; originally published in German, 3rd rev. ed., 1983), a solid, somewhat technical introduction. KENNETH R. LANG and OWEN GINGERICH (eds.), *A Source Book in Astronomy and Astrophysics, 1900–1975* (1979), provides a collection of seminal papers in the field, including much on stellar atmospheres, spectra, evolution and distribution, and variable stars. International reports of research in astronomical and astrophysical sciences, some technical, can be found in the following periodicals: *Astronomical Journal* (monthly) and *Astrophysical Journal* (semimonthly), both published by the American Astronomical Society; *Astronomy and Astrophysics: A European Journal* (semimonthly); *Astrophysics* (quarterly), trans. from Russian; and *Chinese Astronomy and Astrophysics* (quarterly), trans. from Chinese. For less technical articles, see *Astronomy* (monthly); AMERICAN ASSOCIATION OF VARIABLE STAR OBSERVERS, *Journal* (semiannual); ROYAL ASTRONOMICAL SOCIETY, *Quarterly Journal;* and *Sky and Telescope* (monthly).

(L.H.A./E.J.C.)

Clusters and associations: HARLOW SHAPLEY, *Star Clusters* (1930), a dated but classic work; HELEN SAWYER HOGG, "Star Clusters," in *Handbuch der Physik,* vol. 53 (1959), pp. 129–207; G. ALTER, J. RUPRECHT, and V. VANÝSEK, *Catalogue of Star Clusters and Associations,* trans. from Czech, 2nd enl. ed. (1970), and its *Supplement 1,* 3 vol., edited by J. RUPRECHT, B. BALÁZS, and R.E. WHITE (1981); and CECILIA H. PAYNE GAPOSCHKIN, *Stars and Clusters* (1979), an account of modern theory and observational evidence regarding the structure and evolution of stars. Publications of symposia held by the International Astronomical Union are technical but informative; two of particular interest are JAMES E. HESSER (ed.), *Star Clusters* (1980); and JEREMY GOODMAN and PIET HUT (eds.), *Dynamics of Star Clusters* (1985).

(H.S.H./E.J.C.)

Astronomical maps: RICHARD HINCKLEY ALLEN, *Star-Names and Their Meanings* (1899, reprinted as *Star Names: Their Lore and Meaning,* 1963), a classic compendium; for a more trustworthy treatment of Arabic names, see PAUL KUNITZSCH, *Arabische Sternnamen in Europa* (1959). DEBORAH J. WARNER, *The Sky Explored: Celestial Cartography, 1500–1800* (1979), provides a historical overview. JOSEPH NEEDHAM, *Science and Civilisation in China,* vol. 3, *Mathematics and the Sciences of the Heavens and the Earth* (1959); and KNUT LUNDMARK, "Luminosities, Colours, Diameters, Densities, Masses of the Stars," ch. 4 in *Handbuch der Astrophysik,* vol. 5 (1932–33), pp. 210–697 (with a sizable appendix), are both far more germane to astronomical maps than their titles imply. Information on types of star catalogs and classification systems may be found in "Star Catalogues," ch. 6 in IVAN I. MUELLER, *Spherical and Practical Astronomy* (1969). Practical catalogs and atlases include DORRIT HOFFLEIT, *The Bright Star Catalogue,* 4th rev. ed. (1982), with data compiled through 1979 (supplement published in 1983); DONALD H. MENZEL and JAY M. PASACHOFF, *A Field Guide to the Stars and Planets,* 2nd ed., rev. and enl. (1983); and IAN RIDPATH, *Universe Guide to Stars and Planets* (1985).

(O.G./W.M.Yo.)

Statistics

Statistics is the art and science of gathering, analyzing, and making inferences from data. Originally associated with numbers gathered for governments, the subject now includes large bodies of method and theory.

Applied fields have stimulated extensive theoretical and practical work. Trying to improve the accuracy of physical measurements, for example, led the 19th-century German mathematician Carl Friedrich Gauss to develop the method of least squares (a method of analyzing experimental data; see below), which today has evolved to a flexible general theory that is applied and adapted to nearly every quantitative area. This work also contained the seeds of what the 20th-century British statistician Sir Ronald Aylmer Fisher later developed into the design of experiments, a branch of statistics widely used in agriculture for the improvement of crop yield and used to improve the precision of the results obtained in medical, biological, and industrial experimentation.

The ideas of effective design for data gathering are also basic to the construction of sample surveys, a branch of statistics most popularly known for its contributions to public opinion polling, to pre-election forecasting, and to market research. Perhaps even more significant is this branch's service to government through, for example, estimates of amount of unemployment and cost of living, which have become indispensable in attempts to regulate the economy. Sample survey methods have found uses in accounting, inventory control, and other areas.

For modern manufacturing, methods of controlling the quality of manufactured product have been essential. The statistical foundations of sequential analysis were provided by Abraham Wald in 1947 in order to handle problems in quality control. In psychology and education, the statistical theory of tests and measurements has been extensively developed to compare achievement by individuals from diverse places and backgrounds.

The article is divided into the following sections:

THE BASIC PRINCIPLES OF STATISTICAL INFERENCE

Statistical experiments. The basic principles of statistical inference involve the notions of experiment, outcome, sample space, event, and probability. The idea of an experiment includes such examples as tossing a coin, measuring a length, or asking a person which party he or she will vote for at an election. Such experiments have a number of possible outcomes, perhaps infinitely many. When an ordinary die is thrown there are six possible outcomes, corresponding to the numbers 1, 2, 3, 4, 5, and 6. In statistics this collection of all possible outcomes is called a sample space. For the die the sample space can be written as the set {1, 2, 3, 4, 5, 6}. Any single outcome of an experiment, such as the throwing of a 6, is called a point. Certain specified sets of outcomes are called events. The throwing of an even number on a die would be an event, denoted by {2, 4, 6}.

Die throwing and coin tossing

Sets of events are frequently studied. For example, in tossing a coin twice, one possible outcome is "heads first time, tails second time," which is abbreviated to (H, T). Four possible outcomes make up the sample space—(H, T), (H, H), (T, H), and (T, T). If the experimenter asks only whether he gets the same result on both throws, the natural events chosen would be {(H, H), (T, T)} and {(H, T), (T, H)}.

In statistics the results of a large number of experiments form the data used. Sometimes it is assumed that each outcome is independent of any preceding one, as the number thrown on a die is independent of any preceding throws. It is also assumed that there is an underlying probability mechanism determining the nature of the data, as the probability of a coin's coming up heads determines the outcomes of experiments in which a coin is thrown twice. If the underlying probability mechanism is known, then the probability that certain outcomes occur can be calculated. This is the concern of probability theory (see PROBABILITY THEORY).

Statistics is concerned with the application of probability theory to data. If only partial information is available—for example, if the underlying mechanism is one of several—it may be possible to use the data to infer which mechanism generated it and to associate probabilities or degrees of confidence with the various mechanisms. It is possible to perform the experiment a number of times and obtain a sequence of outcomes. Dividing the number of times an outcome of an experiment falls in event A by the number of experiments gives an estimate of the probability of event A. As the number of experiments grows large, the estimate becomes more likely to be close to the true probability $\mathbf{P}(A)$. In mathematical terms, if x_1, x_2, · · · is a sequence of outcomes and A an event, and $N(x_1, x_2, \cdots, x_n; A)$ denotes the number of times the outcome falls in A during the first n experiments, then as n tends to infinity, the chance that $N(x_1, x_2, \cdots, x_n; A)/n$ is close to $\mathbf{P}(A)$ tends to certainty.

Although this fact, known as the law of large numbers, tells the experimenter that he will arrive at the right answer eventually, it does not tell him how close he will be to the right answer after having performed the experiment a certain number of times. This is where statistical methods come in. Under certain conditions statistical methods give an estimate of the error that might possibly be made by performing the experiment a finite number of times.

An experiment is described completely by its sample space S, which is the set of possible outcomes, by a family B of events, and by a probability assignment $\mathbf{P}$ that governs the outcome of the experiment. The independence of two events means that the outcome of one does not imply anything about the outcome of the other. As a practical matter, separation of events in space and time often ensures independence. The concept of statistical or probabilistic independence is intended to extend the common meaning of independence to chance situations in which the occurrence of one event does not change the probability of occurrence of another event.

When events are independent, the probability that they jointly occur is the product of their probabilities: If the events are $A_1, \cdots, A_n$ and the associated probabilities are $\mathbf{P}(A_i)$, $i = 1, \cdots, n$, the probability that all occur is $\mathbf{P}(A_1) \cdots \mathbf{P}(A_n)$.

When a die is tossed twice, for example, the sample space can be written as the set {(1, 1), (1, 2), · · · , (1, 6), (2, 1), · · · , (2, 6), · · · , (6, 6)}; each of the 36 points in this sample space is composed of an outcome on the first toss and an outcome on the second. Thus, (4, 3) denotes a 4 on the first toss and a 3 on the second. The events A_1 and A_2 are independent and the probability of "A_1 and A_2" may be computed as the product of the individual probabilities (see Box, calculation 1), yielding a probability of 1/3.

These ideas of independence apply to statistical investi-

$$(1)\quad \begin{cases} A_1 = \{\text{first toss even}\}, \\ A_2 = \{\text{second toss 4 or less}\} \\ \mathbf{P}(A_1 \cap A_2) = \mathbf{P}(A_1)\mathbf{P}(A_2) = \tfrac{3}{6} \times \tfrac{4}{6} = \tfrac{1}{3} \end{cases}$$

$$(2)\quad \mathbf{P}(X=1) = \mathbf{P}(X=0) = \tfrac{1}{2}$$

$$(3)\quad f(x) = \mathbf{P}(X=x), \quad x \in S$$

$$(4)\quad \mathbf{P}(A) = \sum_{x \in A} f(x)$$

$$(5)\quad f(x) = \frac{n!}{x!(n-x)!} p^x (1-p)^{n-x}, \qquad 0 \leqslant x \leqslant n$$

$$(6)\quad F(x) = \mathbf{P}(X \leqslant x), \qquad -\infty < x < +\infty$$

$$(7)\quad F(b) - F(a) = \mathbf{P}(a < X \leqslant b)$$

$$(8)\quad \int_a^b f(x)\,dx = F(b) - F(a) = \mathbf{P}(a < X \leqslant b)$$

$$(9)\quad \begin{cases} & x \leqslant a & a < x \leqslant b & b < x \\ f(x) & 0 & 1/(b-a) & 0 \\ F(x) & 0 & (x-a)/(b-a) & 1 \end{cases}$$

$$(10)\quad \mu = \int_{-\infty}^{+\infty} x f(x)\,dx$$

$$(11)\quad \nu_r = \int_{-\infty}^{+\infty} x^r f(x)\,dx$$

$$(12)\quad \mu_r = \int_{-\infty}^{+\infty} (x-\mu)^r f(x)\,dx$$

gations in which the data are generated by repetitions of the same elementary operation, each carried out independently of the others.

To develop models for numerical data, a real number or a vector with real components is associated with each outcome in the sample space. The function mapping the outcome to the number or vector is called a random variable. Capital letters are often used to designate the random variable itself and lower-case letters for an unspecified value of a random variable. Thus $\mathbf{P}(X=x)$ represents the probability that the random variable X takes the value x. It is often convenient to forget the functional origin of the idea of random variable and regard the set of values of X as the basic sample space.

Random variables

For example, when a coin is tossed, the outcome may be heads or tails, and heads may be associated with $X=1$ and tails with $X=0$. X, the number of heads, is called a random variable and its values are 0 and 1 with equal probabilities of $1/2$ (see 2).

Using random variables to describe outcomes of experiments gives systematic ways to describe the assignment of probability to sets. In practice, the sample space of the random variable is either a discrete set of values (as in tossing a die) or a continuous set (as in measuring a length). In both cases the sample space consists of a set on the real line. In the discrete case, it may be convenient to give a probability for each point x in the sample space S. Thus for the random variable X a probability mass function f is defined such that its value at x is a probability (see 3). Then the probability of an event A may be computed by summing $f(x)$ for all values of x in A (see 4). For all x, $f(x) \geq 0$ and $\mathbf{P}(S) = 1$.

For example, if p is the probability of success on a single trial, if the outcomes of trials are independent, and if the random variable X is the number of successes in n trials, then (as mentioned in PROBABILITY THEORY) the value of f at x is a term in a binomial expansion (see 5). The probability that the experiment produces all successes or all failures is $p^n + (1-p)^n$. The distribution of probability represented by the values of $f(x)$ is called the binomial distribution. A more complete representation would use $f(x \mid n, p)$ (read "f of x given n and p") rather than $f(x)$ so as to specify the parameters n and p of the distribution.

When probability is smoothly distributed over continuous sample spaces, a difficulty in representing the probabilities is that each point has probability zero, yet the total probability must be one: a line segment consists of points, each of zero length, and yet it has a nonzero length. Developing probability through measures on Borel sets resolves such difficulties (see ANALYSIS: *Real analysis*).

Distribution functions and their properties. For the continuous random variable X with values $x \in S$, a cumulative distribution function F is defined so that its value at x is the probability (see 6) for the random variable to be less than or equal to x. $F(-\infty)$ and $F(+\infty)$ are also defined by: $F(-\infty)=0$ and $F(+\infty)=1$ (the symbol ∞ denotes infinity). The probability in an interval, say $a < x \leq b$, is given by the difference in the values of F evaluated at the endpoints of the interval (see 7).

If F has a derivative $dF(x)/dx = f(x)$ for almost all x, then f is called the probability density function of the random variable X, or more briefly the density function. This brings the integral calculus into play because now, from the fundamental theorem of calculus, the definite integral of f is a probability (see 8). For example, for the uniform distribution on the interval $a < x \leq b$, the density and cumulative are given by specific functions (see 9) that are constant and of constant slope, respectively, over the interval.

The approach via the cumulative distribution function F makes it possible to unify mathematically discrete and continuous distributions as well as mixed ones by employing the Lebesgue-Stieltjes integral.

The problem of finding the value of x such that $F(x) = p$ often arises. Such a value of x is called the pth quantile, or $100p$th percentile, of the distribution; the notation x_p is used. The median of the distribution is $x_{0.5}$, and $x_{0.25}$ and $x_{0.75}$ are the first and third quartiles.

When the random variable X has a distribution with density f, the mean of the distribution, if it exists, is given by the integral (see 10) over the whole real line of the product $xf(x)$. Its value μ is also called the first moment of the distribution. More generally, if it exists, the integral (see 11) of the product $x^r f(x)$ is the rth raw moment of the distribution. Moments about the mean are also used, and the rth moment about the mean is obtained from a similar integral (see 12) involving the rth power of $(x-\mu)$. In the discrete case the integrations are replaced by summations over $x \in S$.

The second moment about the mean is much used in both statistics and probability. It is called the variance of the distribution, or the variance of the random variable X, abbreviated var X, or σ_X^2, or when the name of the random variable is understood, σ^2. Its square root, σ, is the standard deviation.

Variance

In addition to moments defined as average values of the functions X^r and $(X-\mu)^r$, the average values of other functions of random variables frequently arise. If h is a function of X, then when it exists, the expected value of $h(X)$ is defined to be the integral over the whole real line (see 13) of the product of $h(x)$ and the probability density function. Therefore, the mean is $\mathbf{E}(X)$, and $\sigma^2 = \mathbf{E}[(X-\mu)^2]$. It should be noted that $\mathbf{E}$ is an operator, not a notation for a function.

For example, the expected value of the number of successes, X, for the binomial distribution is the product of the number of trials n and the constant probablity p of success in each trial (see 14), derived by evaluating a binomial summation. The variance of X is $(1-p)$ times the mean (see 15).

For the normal distribution (see 16a), upon integration the mean μ of the random variable X is θ_1 (see 17), and the variance σ^2 is θ_2 (see 18). Consequently, the parameters of the normal distribution are said to be μ and σ^2. These results (see 16b) make clear that the normal density decreases exponentially, the exponent being proportional to the square of $(x-\mu)/\sigma$, the distance from x to the mean

(13) $$\mathbf{E}(h(X))=\int_{-\infty}^{+\infty} h(x)f(x)\,dx$$

(14) $$\mu=\mathbf{E}(X)=\sum_{x=0}^{n} xf(x|n,p)=np$$

(15) $$\sigma_X^2=np(1-p)$$

(16) $$\begin{cases} \text{a. } \dfrac{1}{\sqrt{2\pi\theta_2}}\exp\left[-\dfrac{1}{2}\dfrac{(x-\theta_1)^2}{\theta_2}\right]=f(x|\theta_1,\theta_2) \\ \text{b. } \dfrac{1}{\sqrt{2\pi}\sigma}\exp\left[-\dfrac{1}{2}\left(\dfrac{x-\mu}{\sigma}\right)^2\right] \\ \text{c. } \dfrac{1}{\sqrt{2\pi}}\exp\left(-\dfrac{1}{2}y^2\right) \end{cases}$$

(17) $$\mu=\mathbf{E}(X)=\int_{-\infty}^{+\infty} xf(x|\theta_1,\theta_2)\,dx=\theta_1$$

(18) $$\sigma^2=\mathbf{E}[(X-\mu)^2]=\int_{-\infty}^{+\infty}(x-\mu)^2f(x|\theta_1,\theta_2)\,dx=\theta_2$$

(19) $$\mu_Y=a\mu_X+b, \qquad \sigma_Y^2=a^2\sigma_X^2, \qquad \sigma_Y=|a|\sigma_X$$

(20) $$F(x_1,\cdots,x_k)=\mathbf{P}(X_1\leqslant x_1,\cdots,X_k\leqslant x_k)$$

(21) $$F(x_1,\cdots,x_k)=\int_{-\infty}^{x_k}\cdots\int_{-\infty}^{x_1}f(u_1,\cdots,u_k)\,du_1\cdots du_k$$

(22) $$\mathbf{P}(x\in A)=\int_A f(u_1,\cdots,u_k)\prod_{i=1}^{k}du_i$$

(23) $$\mathbf{P}(x\in A)=\int_A dF(u_1,\cdots,u_k)$$

(24) $$F(x_1,\cdots,x_k)=F_1(x_1)\cdots F_k(x_k)$$

(25) $$f(x_1,\cdots,x_k)=f_1(x_1)\cdots f_k(x_k)$$

(26) $$f(x_1,\cdots,x_k)=\prod_{i=1}^{k}f_0(x_i)$$

(27) $$\operatorname{cov}(X,Y)=\int_S(x-\mu_X)(y-\mu_Y)f(x,y)\,dx\,dy$$

(28) $$\mu_Y=\mathbf{E}(Y)=\mathbf{E}\left(\sum_{i=1}^{n}X_i\right)=\sum_{i=1}^{n}\mathbf{E}(X_i)=\sum_{i=1}^{n}\mu_i$$

(29) $$\begin{cases}\operatorname{var}Y=\mathbf{E}[(Y-\mu_Y)^2]=\sigma_1^2+\cdots+\sigma_n^2+2\sigma_{12}+ \\ \quad +2\sigma_{13}+\cdots+2\sigma_{n-1,n} \\ \quad =\displaystyle\sum_{j=1}^{n}\sum_{i=1}^{n}\sigma_{ij}\end{cases}$$

(30) $$\rho_{ij}=\frac{\sigma_{ij}}{\sigma_i\sigma_j}$$

(31) $$\begin{cases}f(x_1,\cdots,x_n|\mu_i,\sigma_i^2,i=1,\cdots,n) \\ \quad =\displaystyle\prod_{i=1}^{n}(2\pi\sigma_i^2)^{-1/2}\exp[-\tfrac{1}{2}(x_i-\mu_i)^2/\sigma_i^2]\end{cases}$$

measured in standard deviation units. The coefficient $1/\sqrt{2\pi}\sigma$ assumes that the total density integrates to unity so that the total probability is 1. [In (16a), (16b), and (16c), π (pi) equals 3.14159 · · ·.]

If $Y=aX+b$, in which a and b are constants and X any random variable with mean μ and variance σ^2, then the mean of Y, written μ_Y, bears the same linear relation to the mean of X that Y bears to X, and the variance of Y is the product of a^2 and the variance of X (see 19).

From any random variable X with mean μ and variance σ^2 a new random variable $Y=(X-\mu)/\sigma$ with mean 0 and variance 1 can be constructed. Such a Y is called a standardized random variable, and, if X is normally distributed, it is said to have the standard normal distribution (see 16c).

To generalize the concept of distribution function to several random variables $X_1, \cdot\cdot\cdot, X_k$ in a k-dimensional Euclidean space, the joint cumulative distribution function F is used. By definition the joint cumulative distribution function (see 20) is the probability of the common occurrence of k events of the type $(x_k \le x_k)$. If any x_i is replaced by $-\infty$, then F takes the value zero. When all x_i are replaced by $+\infty$, $F=1$. If F is differentiable with respect to all the variables, then there is a joint probability density function f such that F is the indefinite multiple integral (see 21) of f. If A is a set in the sample space and $x=(x_1, \cdot\cdot\cdot, x_k)$, then the probability that x belongs to the set A is the multiple integral (see 22) of the density extended over A. Formally the same equality is expressible in terms of a Stieltjes integral (see 23). When integration is performed over all variables but x_i, the cumulative gives $F(+\infty, \cdot\cdot\cdot, +\infty, x_i, +\infty, \cdot\cdot\cdot, +\infty)$, which represents the marginal cumulative distribution of X_i alone. More generally, when exactly r $(1 \le r < n)$ coordinates are set at $+\infty$, the $(k-r)$ th-order marginal distribution of the remaining $k-r$ random variables is obtained.

When the X_i are independent with $F_i(x_i)=\mathrm{P}(X_i \le x_i)$, $i=1, \cdot\cdot\cdot, k$, and have probability density functions $f_i(x_i)$, then the joint cumulative can be represented as the product of the separate distribution functions (see 24), and the joint density as the product of the separate densities (see 25). To represent the distribution of repeated measurements, X_i is allowed to represent the ith measurement, and the f_i is taken to be equal to f_0, so that the products above take a particularly simple form, expressible as a product extended over k index values (see 26) of $f_0(x_i)$.

If two random variables X and Y have a joint density f and if their means are μ_X and μ_Y, the covariance between X and Y (if it exists) is defined as an integral of the product of the differences $(x-\mu_X)$ and $(y-\mu_Y)$, weighted with the joint density (see 27).

Sums of random variables have special interest for statisticians. If X_i has mean μ_i and variance $\sigma_i^2=\sigma_{ii}$ and if $\operatorname{cov}(X_i, X_j)=\sigma_{ij}$, then if $Y=\Sigma X_i$, the mean of Y is the sum of the means of the X_i (see 28) and the variance of Y is the double sum over σ_{ij} (see 29). (In the summation defining Y the sum is from 1 to n.) In other words, the mean of a sum is the sum of the means, and the variance of a sum is the sum of the variances plus twice the covariances. The correlation coefficient between variables X_i and X_j is defined as the ratio of σ_{ij} to the product $\sigma_i\sigma_j$ (see 30).

The correlation coefficient

When all pairs of variables have $\rho_{ij}=0$, then $\sigma_Y^2=\sum_{i=1}^{n}\sigma_i^2$. Independence between all the random variables guarantees $\rho_{ij}=0$, but having all $\rho_{ij}=0$, $i \ne j$, does not guarantee independence.

An important exception is the joint multivariate normal distribution, the only parameters of which are the means, variances, and covariances of the variables. When $\rho_{ij}=0$ for all $i, j, i \ne j$, the joint density can be represented by a product (see 31) of normal densities with typical mean μ_i and variance σ_i^2. For the general joint multivariate normal distribution density is proportional to the exponent of a quadratic form (see 32). If $\|\sigma_{ij}\|$ is the covariance matrix of the n random variables ($\|a_{ij}\|$ denotes the matrix with elements a_{ij}) and σ^{ij} the elements of its inverse, then the quadratic form is expressible (see 33) in terms of the collection $\{\sigma^{ij}\}$, and the constant factor that multiplies the exponential is expressible (see 34) in terms of $|\sigma^{ij}|$, in which $|a_{ij}|$ is the determinant of the matrix with elements a_{ij}. If $\Sigma=\|\sigma_{ij}\|$ and the vector $(x-\mu)$ is defined (see 35), the quadratic form Q can be written more simply in vector and matrix notation, in which T stands for transpose.

$$(32)\quad \begin{cases} f(x_1, \cdots, x_n | \mu_i, \sigma_i^2, \sigma_{ij}, i, j = 1, \cdots, n) \\ = K\exp(-\tfrac{1}{2}Q) \end{cases}$$

$$(33)\quad Q = \sum_i \sum_j \sigma^{ij}(x_i - \mu_i)(x_j - \mu_j)$$

$$(34)\quad K = [|\sigma^{ij}|/(2\pi)^n]^{1/2}$$

$$(35)\quad \begin{cases} (x_1 - \mu_1, \cdots, x_n - \mu_n) = (x - \mu) \\ Q = (x - \mu)^T \Sigma^{-1}(x - \mu) \end{cases}$$

$$(36)\quad Z_n = \frac{Y_n - \mu_n}{\sqrt{\operatorname{var} Y_n}}$$

$$(37)\quad \lim_{n \to \infty} \mathbf{P}(Z_n < z) = \frac{1}{\sqrt{2\pi}} \int_{-\infty}^{z} e^{-\frac{1}{2}x^2}\, dx$$

$$(38)\quad Z_1^2 + \cdots + Z_k^2$$

$$(39)\quad t_k = \frac{Z}{\sqrt{\chi_k^2/k}}$$

$$(40)\quad f(x|\theta) = \theta e^{-\theta x}, \qquad x \geqslant 0, \theta > 0$$

$$(41)\quad \mu = \mathbf{E}(X) = \theta \int_0^\infty x e^{-\theta x}\, dx = 1/\theta$$

$$(42)\quad L(x_1, \cdots, x_n | \theta) = \prod_{i=1}^{n} f(x_i | \theta)$$

Under a variety of conditions, the distribution of sums of random variables tends to a normal distribution as the number of random variables tends to infinity. The statements of conditions leading to these distributions are called central limit theorems. To illustrate, if $X_1, X_2, \cdots$ is a sequence of random variables and $Y_n = X_1 + \cdots + X_n$, and if $\mathbf{E}(Y_n) = \mu_n$ and var Y_n exists, then as n becomes large the sequence of distributions of the standardized random variables Z_n (see 36; each with mean 0 and variance 1) has a limit that is the standard normal distribution (see 37). One set of conditions guaranteeing this limiting distribution is independence of the X_i and identical distributions with finite variances, but other conditions are also available that do not require identical distributions, equal variances, or even independence.

This limiting distribution is also shared by many functions of random variables and is one reason for the importance of the Gaussian or normal distribution in statistical theory. In applications, sums of even a few random variables of the types ordinarily met have distributions the central portions of which can be well approximated by normal distributions.

If $Z_1, \cdots, Z_k$ are independent standard normal random variables, the sum of their squares (see 38) forms a new random variable, χ_k^2; its distribution is called the chi-square distribution with k degrees of freedom.

If Z, a standard normal random variable, and χ_k^2 a chi-square random variable with k degrees of freedom, are independent, then the new random variable, written t_k, which is proportional to Z divided by the square root of the chi-square (see 39), has the distribution known as Student's t distribution with k degrees of freedom. Student was the scientific pseudonym of William Sealy Gosset, the statistician and chemist who discovered the form of the distribution by a combination of mathematical work and empirical work with random numbers, an early application of what is now called the Monte-Carlo method.

The chi-square and t distributions are frequently used in interval estimation and in testing hypotheses.

ESTIMATION

Point estimation. For a random sample with values $x_1 \cdots, x_n$ independently drawn from a distribution F the parameter of which is θ, the problem of estimation is to find a function of the x's, $\hat{\theta}$, that comes close to θ. Here "close" is a vague word that can be given many meanings. If the sample is regarded as composed of random variables $X_1, \cdots, X_n$, and the estimator $\hat{\theta}$ as a function of those random variables, then $\hat{\theta}$ is itself a random variable. Some desirable properties for an estimator $\hat{\theta}$ are (A) that its average error be small: indeed, if the average error vanishes, $\mathbf{E}(\hat{\theta} - \theta) = 0$, and the estimator is said to be unbiassed; (B) that the mean square error $\mathbf{E}(\hat{\theta} - \theta)^2$ be small: this measure combines, in a somewhat arbitrary way, variability of $\hat{\theta}$ with its bias $b = \mathbf{E}(\hat{\theta} - \hat{\theta}$, because $\mathbf{E}(\hat{\theta} - \theta)^2 =$ var $\hat{\theta} + b^2$. (C) Another attractve property is small variance. If, among several unbiassed estimators, one has smallest variance, it is known as the minimum-variance unbiassed estimator. Which of several estimators may be more desirable depends, among other things, upon the costs of errors $(\hat{\theta} - \theta)$ of various sizes. Small variance

Samples contain information about the parameters of a family of distributions, but different families can profitably use different functions to extract this information. Several methods of estimation offer general techniques for finding estimators for parameters. Three techniques are considered here: the method of moments, the method of maximum likelihood, and Bayesian methods.

Method of moments. The moments of a family of distributions are functions of the parameters of the family. If there are only a few parameters, it may be possible to use the first few moments of the distributions together with the sample moments to get estimates of the parameters. If the observed values of the sample moments are equated with the corresponding population moments, expressed as functions of the parameters, the resulting equations for estimates of the parameters may be solved. Thus the estimators choose that member of the family whose moments match the sample moments.

The method of moments may be used, for example, to estimate the parameter θ of an exponential distribution having probability density function proportional to the exponential of $-\theta x$, the values of x being non-negative (see 40). The population mean is calculated (see 41) to be $1/\theta$. The value of the sample mean is $\bar{x} = (x_1 + \cdots + x_n)/n$, and so the method of moments would derive the estimate of θ from $\bar{x} = 1/\hat{\theta}$ and give $\hat{\theta} = 1/\bar{x}$.

The method of maximum likelihood. A widely used method that has attractive large-sample properties is the method of maximum likelihood. For families of discrete distributions, the probability of getting the particular sample that has been observed can be computed, and then those values of the parameters that maximize the probability can be chosen as estimates. If the sample $x_1, \cdots, x_n$ has been independently chosen from a distribution with probabilities $\mathbf{P}(X = x \mid \theta) = f(x \mid \theta)$, in which θ may be a vector, then that probability, called the likelihood, is defined as the product of n probability mass functions, one evaluated at each sample value (see 42).

For continuous distributions the corresponding approach is again to maximize the likelihood function, which is given above (see 42) except that the righthand side is the product of the values, $f(x_i \mid \theta)$, of the density function evaluated at the sample points. Although symbolically the same, the likelihood in the discrete situation is a probability, but in the continuous case it is a measure of the density of probability at the sample point. The one-parameter case is considered. Under broad regularity conditions (dealing with the differentiability of f with respect to θ, and the existence of integrals of functions of f and its derivatives), the estimator θ, the value of θ that maximizes L for the given sample, is the maximum likelihood estimator of θ. Asymptotically (*i.e.*, as n tends to infinity) $\hat{\theta}$ tends to be normally distributed with asymptotic mean θ and asymptotic variance expressed in a simple formula (see 43) in terms of the reciprocal expectation of the second derivative (with respect to θ) of the log of the density.

For example, a sample of size n from the normal distribution with mean 0 and variance θ (or σ^2) has a likelihood

$$(43)\quad \operatorname{var}\hat{\theta}=\frac{1}{-n\mathbf{E}\left[\dfrac{\partial^2 \log f(x|\theta)}{\partial\theta^2}\right]}$$

$$(44)\quad \begin{cases} L(x_1,\cdots,x_n|\theta)=[2\pi\theta]^{-\frac{n}{2}}e^{-\frac{1}{2}\Sigma x_i^2/\theta} \\ \dfrac{\partial \log L}{\partial\theta}=-\dfrac{n}{2\theta}+\dfrac{\Sigma x_i^2}{2\theta^2} \end{cases}$$

$$(45)\quad \hat{\theta}=\sum_{i=1}^{n} x_i^2/n$$

$$(46)\quad \frac{\partial^2 \log f(x|\theta)}{\partial\theta^2}=\frac{1}{2\theta^2}-\frac{x^2}{\theta^3}$$

$$(47)\quad \operatorname{var}\hat{\theta}=\frac{2\theta^2}{n}$$

$$(48)\quad \hat{\sigma}=\sqrt{\hat{\theta}}=\sqrt{\Sigma x_i^2/n}$$

$$(49)\quad L(x_1,\cdots,x_n|\theta)=\prod_{i=1}^{n} f(x_i|\theta)$$

$$(50)\quad B_{pq}=-\mathbf{E}\frac{\partial^2 \log f(x|\theta)}{\partial\theta_p\partial\theta_q},\qquad p,q=1,\cdots,n$$

$$(51)\quad \begin{cases} f(x|\theta_1,\theta_2)=(2\pi\theta_2)^{-1/2}\exp[-(x-\theta_1)^2/2\theta_2] \\ -\infty<x<\infty,\qquad -\infty<\theta_1<\infty,\qquad 0<\theta_2<\infty \end{cases}$$

$$(52)\quad \hat{\theta}_1=\frac{\Sigma x_i}{n}=\bar{x},\qquad \hat{\theta}_2=\frac{\Sigma(x_i-\bar{x})^2}{n}$$

$$(53)\quad \begin{Vmatrix} \dfrac{\theta_2}{n} & 0 \\ 0 & \dfrac{2\theta_2^2}{n} \end{Vmatrix}$$

$$(54)\quad \theta_2/n=\sigma_{\bar{x}}^2/n$$

$$(55)\quad \mu-|z_{\frac{1}{2}\alpha}|\sigma/\sqrt{n}\leqslant \bar{X}\leqslant \mu+|z_{\frac{1}{2}\alpha}|\sigma/\sqrt{n}$$

$$(56)\quad \bar{X}-|z_{\frac{1}{2}\alpha}|\sigma/\sqrt{n}\leqslant \mu\leqslant \bar{X}+|z_{\frac{1}{2}\alpha}|\sigma/\sqrt{n}$$

function and its derivative given by the equations that are exponential and algebraic in form, respectively (see 44). If the derivative is set equal to zero and the equation solved for θ, the maximum likelihood estimate of θ is given by the sum of the squares of the x_i divided by n (see 45). Because the second derivative of the log of the density is a simple expression that is linear in the square of the variable (see 46), and $\mathbf{E}(X^2)=\theta$, the asymptotic variance is proportional to the reciprocal of n (see 47).

Some attractive asymptotic properties of the maximum likelihood estimator when the regularity conditions are met are:

A. That it converges in probability to the true value of θ as $n\rightarrow\infty$. (Estimators that do this are said to be consistent.)

B. That it is asymptotically unbiassed.

C. That among asymptotically unbiassed estimators, no other has smaller asymptotic variance. (Unbiassed estimators having finite variance at least as small as that of any other estimator are said to be efficient.)

D. The maximum likelihood estimator of a function of θ is the same function of the maximum likelihood estimator of θ.

In the example given above the maximum likelihood estimate of θ (or σ^2) was $\Sigma x_i^2/n$. The maximum likelihood estimate of σ is the square root of this expression (see 48).

The extension of this method to vector random variables and vector parameters is straightforward providing further regularity conditions hold. If a sample point consists of the vector $x_i=(x_{1i},\cdot\cdot\cdot,x_{ri})$, and the joint distribution of the r variables has k parameters $\theta=(\theta_1,\cdot\cdot\cdot,\theta_k)$, then one forms the likelihood function that is formally the same as before but now involving vectors (see 49). To find the relative maximum (assumed unique), the partial derivatives with respect to θ_i are taken, they are set equal to zero, and the resulting equations for the maximum likelihood estimates $\hat{\theta}_i$ are solved. Asymptotically the estimators are jointly normally distributed with mean $(\theta_1,\cdot\cdot\cdot,\theta_k)$ and covariance matrix $\| nB_{pq}\|^{-1}$, in which the $\{B_{pq}\}$ are expectations of second partial derivatives of the log of the density (see 50). The vectorial nature of the observations is not central to maximum likelihood estimation, and so the method is illustrated by a one-variable probability distribution with two parameters.

As an example, consider the vector parameter. If the sample is drawn from the normal distribution with mean θ_1 and variance θ_2, so that the normal density is specified (see 51) as before, then it is found that the maximum likelihood estimator of the population mean is the sample mean, and of the population variance is the sample variance (see 52). Furthermore, the covariance matrix is diagonal (see 53), so that asymptotically $\hat{\theta}_1$ and $\hat{\theta}_2$ are independently normally distributed with means (θ_1,θ_2) and variances θ_2/n and $2\theta_2^2/n$, respectively.

For a sample of n independent normally distributed observations, the sample mean $\bar{X}$ is exactly, not just asymptotically, normally distributed with mean θ_1 and variance θ_2 as before (see 54).

Interval estimation. The discussion of estimation has emphasized point estimates for parameters, but it may also be useful to give an interval within which a parameter is likely to lie, together with the chance that the interval includes the parameter. More generally, if the parameter were a vector, a region would be given.

The confidence interval

An important illustration gives the confidence interval, based on a sample size of n, for the unknown mean μ of a normal distribution with known standard deviation σ. The probability is $1-a$ that the sample mean $\bar{X}$ falls (see 55) within a specified distance, $|z_{a2}|\sigma/\sqrt{n}$, of μ, in which $z_{a/2}$ is the $100a/2$ percentage point of the standard normal distribution.

The sample mean $\bar{X}$ is normally distributed with mean μ and standard deviation $\sigma/\sqrt{n}$, so that a rearrangement of the inequalities gives upper and lower bounds for the parameter μ that involve the random variable $\bar{X}$ (see 56). This statement (in 56) is true $100(1-a)$ percent of the time. If the random variable $\bar{X}$ is replaced by the observed sample mean $\bar{x}$, then the statements (in 56) are true or false. They are true in $100(1-a)$ percent of the times this method is used. The limits $\bar{x}\pm|z_{a/2}|\sigma/\sqrt{n}$ are called upper and lower $100(1-a)$ percent confidence limits, and $100(1-a)$ is called the confidence level or confidence coefficient and is expressed either as a percent or a proportion, $1-a$. The interval composed of the points (see 57) between the upper and lower confidence limits is called a confidence interval. A commonly used confidence level is 0.95, and then $|z_{a/2}|=1.96$, or about 2.

If, in general, an upper function $\hat{\theta}_u$ and a lower function $\hat{\theta}_l$ of the sample values can be found—so that the probability for these functions to bound θ is $1-a$ (see 58), then the values of $\hat{\theta}_u$ and $\hat{\theta}_l$ obtained from the sample provide upper and lower $100(1-a)$ confidence limits for θ.

In a sample of size n drawn from a normal distribution with unknown mean μ and unknown variance σ^2, having sample mean $\bar{x}$ and variance $s_{\bar{x}}^2$ of the mean given by $\Sigma(x_i-\bar{x})^2/n(n-1)$, symmetrical $1-a$ confidence limits on μ are given by $\bar{x}\pm|t_{a/2}|s_{\bar{x}}$, in which $t_{a/2}$ is the $a/2$ percentage point of the t distribution with $n-1$ degrees of freedom.

In some investigations, the researcher continues sampling

(57) $(\bar{x}-|z_{\frac{1}{2}\alpha}|\sigma/\sqrt{n}, \bar{x}+|z_{\frac{1}{2}\alpha}|\sigma/\sqrt{n})$

(58) $\mathbf{P}(\hat{\theta}_l \leqslant \theta < \hat{\theta}_u|\theta) = 1-\alpha$

(59) $\operatorname{var} X' = \dfrac{1}{4n[f(x_{0.5})]^2}$

(60) $c(x|\mu,\sigma^2,\gamma) = (1-\gamma)n(x|\mu,1) + \gamma n(x|\mu,\sigma^2)$
$\sigma > 1$

(61) $L(x_1,\cdots,x_n|\theta) = \prod_{i=1}^{n} f(x_i|\theta)$

(62) $h(x_1,\cdots,x_n,\theta) = g(\theta)\prod_{i=1}^{n} f(x_i|\theta)$

(63) $p(\theta|x_1,\cdots,x_n) = kg(\theta)\prod_{i=1}^{n} f(x_i|\theta)$

until his confidence limits have been reduced to a preset size. Finding appropriate stopping rules and setting the limits are problems in sequential estimation.

Interval estimation can be used not only for reporting uncertainty in the value of the parameter, but also for hypothesis testing. If a specific value of the parameter θ, say θ_0, has a reasonable chance of being the true value, and if $1-a$ confidence limits can be set on θ, then if θ_0 is in the confidence region, it can be accepted as possibly being the true value. Otherwise this hypothesis can be rejected.

For example, in a sample of size $n=3$ from a normal distribution, $\bar{x}=2$, $S_{\bar{x}}=0.5$, symmetrical 95 percent confidence limits are set on μ, and a test applied as to whether $\mu=0$ is a reasonable value. This problem has two degrees of freedom, and $t_{0.025}=-4.30$. From the above formulas, the confidence limits are $2\pm4.30(0.5)=-0.15$, $+4.15$, and the hypothetical value 0 is in the interval (though barely). Consequently, 0 is not rejected as the value for μ at the 5 percent level of significance.

Robust estimation. In real data, the appearance of observations that seem not to belong with the rest of the measurements (such as 22.19 in the set 10.01, 10.04, 10.03, 22.19) is so commonplace that systematic methods are required to defend the analyses against them. Setting observations aside has always been a touchy step, especially to those who believe that good work never leads to bad data. One reasonable attitude is that wild observations should be set aside and studied separately so as not to destroy the information in the main body of the data. A few standard methods are applied to afford protection against temptation to make a special analysis to reach a foregone conclusion—and against the criticism that this has been done.

One estimator of location is the sample median, the middle-sized observation if the sample size is odd, or the average of the middle two if it is even. The large-sample distribution of the sample median X' is approximately normal with asymptotic mean $x_{0.5}$, the 50th percentile point of the distribution, and asymptotic variance expressed in terms of the density function evaluated at $x_{0.5}$ (see 59). When f is a normal density function, the population mean and median are both μ. The sample mean $\bar{X}$ is exactly, and the sample median X' approximately, normally distributed. As n grows large, $\operatorname{var}\bar{X} \approx \frac{2}{\pi}\operatorname{var} X'$, and X' is said to have asymptotic efficiency $2/\pi \approx 0.63$ compared with $\bar{X}$. Thus it takes a sample of 100 using the median to get the accuracy of a sample of 63 with the mean. If wild observations contaminate a distribution, however, the efficiency soon favours the median.

For example, a density function c formed as the weighted sum of two normal densities is expressed in terms of a function n and a weighting parameter γ (see 60), in which $n(x \mid \mu,\sigma^2)$ is the ordinate at x of a normal probability density function with mean μ and variance σ^2. For small γ, c is said to be a contaminated distribution, and γ is the fraction of contamination by data having variance σ^2. When $\gamma=0.09$ and $\sigma=3$, X' has a smaller variance than $\bar{X}$, and thus X' would be preferred to $\bar{X}$ as an estimator of μ.

Trimmed means are also resistant to contamination; they are formed by setting aside a fraction a of the largest and smallest measurements, $2a$ in all, and averaging the middle $1-2a$. Empirical studies suggest that, for a large class of distributions, trimming with $a\approx0.25$ seems to be satisfactory for estimating location. For the normal this trimmed mean has asymptotic efficiency of about 0.83 compared with $\bar{X}$ before contamination. For a contaminated distribution c with $\gamma=0.05$ and $\sigma=3$, the mean $\bar{X}$ has efficiency only 0.92 of that of the trimmed mean. With $a=0.25$ and $\gamma=0.10$ this decreases to 0.775.

Trimmed means

Bayesian methods. The methods of estimation described above are often referred to as classical in the sense of standard. The Bayesian approach offers an alternative that gives an especially convenient way of incorporating prior information about the parameters and also of adding further information when it arrives. One disadvantage is that the method apparently cannot proceed without a prior distribution for the parameters. The main device for inference is the posterior distribution of θ, given the data.

For a distribution of the random variable X given parameter θ with probability density function f, the likelihood of a sample of size n is, as before, a product of densities (see 61) each evaluated at sample points. If the prior distribution of θ has density $g(\theta)$, then the joint density of the sample and θ can be represented as the product (see 62) of this density and the likelihood of a sample. The posterior distribution of θ is required, given the sample. It has the density constructed as k times the joint density of the sample and θ (see 63), in which k is a normalizing constant that makes the integral of the function $p(\theta \mid x_1, \cdots, x_n)$ equal to 1, the integral extending over the possible values of θ.

In this present discussion θ is a random variable, whereas in methods of estimation discussed earlier it was regarded as a constant. The interpretation of $p(\theta \mid x)$ is of interest. It tells what the thoughtful observer who provided the prior distribution would believe about the state of the world after he received the data x. If his prior was largely based on personal subjective judgment, then the degree-of-belief interpretation is paramount, and others may prefer different priors and therefore different $p(\theta \mid x)$. When the prior comes from substantial frequency-based observations closely related to the real world, the posterior distribution may well approximate an objective relative frequency distribution. Many practical situations fall between these extremes.

Much of the controversy over Bayesian methods has concentrated on the philosophy of the choice of the prior distribution and the difficulty of attaining agreement or unanimity. After completing a large Bayesian study, the U.S. statisticians Frederick Mosteller and David L. Wallace (1964) concluded that a neglected difficulty in Bayesian inference, as in methods of inference based on likelihood, is the sensitivity of the conclusions to the chosen family of data distributions; that is, to the functional form of f.

For a given $p(\theta \mid x)$, point or interval estimates can be obtained, or $p(\theta \mid x)$ can be used to make decisions. For example, the mean, mode, or median of the posterior distribution might be used as a point estimate for the true value. Alternatively, an interval (u, v) could be set up, like a confidence interval, that includes most of the probability, so that the integral with respect to θ from u to v of $p(\theta \mid x)$ equals $1-a$.

An example is a machine setup in which the proportion of defective parts produced in the initial setting is π and prior data suggest that π is distributed according to a beta distribution $g(\pi)=c\pi^{a-1}(1-\pi)^{b-1}$, in which c is the normalizing constant and $a>0$, $b>0$, $0\leq\pi\leq1$. After a setup, a sample of size n with x defectives has likelihood $f(x \mid \pi)=\pi^x(1-\pi)^{n-x}$. The posterior distribution of π given x defectives in the sample is proportional to

(64) $$p(\pi|x)=k\pi^{a+x-1}(1-\pi)^{b+n-x-1}$$

(65) $$\mu_{post}=\frac{a+x}{a+b+n},\quad \sigma^2_{post}=\frac{\mu_{post}(1-\mu_{post})}{a+b+n+1}$$

(66)

State of Nature	Action a_0 (accept H_0)	a_1 (accept H_1)
θ_0 (H_0 true)	$l(\theta_0, a_0)$	$l(\theta_0, a_1)$
θ_1 (H_1 true)	$l(\theta_1, a_0)$	$l(\theta_1, a_1)$

(67) $$\begin{cases}\text{Risk}(\theta_0)=l(\theta_0,a_0)\,\mathbf{P}(a_0|\theta_0)+l(\theta_0,a_1)\,\mathbf{P}(a_1|\theta_0)\\ \qquad =\mathbf{P}(a_1|\theta_0)=\alpha\end{cases}$$

(68) $$\begin{cases}\text{Risk}(\theta_1)=l(\theta_1,a_0)\,\mathbf{P}(a_0|\theta_1)+l(\theta_1,a_1)\,\mathbf{P}(a_1|\theta_1)\\ \qquad =\mathbf{P}(a_0|\theta_1)=1-\gamma\end{cases}$$

(69) $$\frac{L(x|H_0)}{L(x|H_1)}\leqslant c$$

(70) $$\int_W L(x|H_0)\,dx=\alpha$$

(71) $$f(x)=\frac{1}{\sqrt{2\pi}}e^{-\frac{1}{2}(x-\mu)^2},\qquad -\infty<x<+\infty$$

the product of g and f (see 64). The posterior mean and variance of π are then calculable (see 65).

If both the prior distribution and the data distribution are normal with prior mean and variance μ_0 and $\sigma_0{}^2$, and the data observation and variance are x and σ^2, then the posterior distribution is again normal with mean μ_1 and variance $\sigma_1{}^2$. Their values can be computed from the relations $\mu_1=\dfrac{h_0\mu_o+hx}{h_o+h}$, and $h_1=h_0+h$, in which $h_i=1/\sigma_i{}^2$, $h=1/\sigma^2$, so that $\sigma_1{}^2=1/h_1$.

When little information about θ is available, prior distributions for θ might be diffuse so that in the neighbourhood of any particular value of θ, the distribution is nearly flat. This would give the data greater weight in determining the posterior. Such a distribution is called a gentle prior distribution.

One's prior distribution of the length of a dimly seen and unfamiliar distant object would have a very large standard deviation compared to that of one direct measurement taken with a steel tape. If measurement errors were normally distributed with $\sigma=0.1$ in inches and a gentle prior were used on the true value, the posterior distribution would be approximately normal with mean x and standard deviation 0.1.

HYPOTHESIS TESTING

When the probability model for the mechanism generating the observed data is known, hypotheses about the model can be tested. This involves the question: Could the present set of data reasonably have come from the model if the hypothesis is correct? Usually a decision must be made on the basis of the available data, and some degree of uncertainty is tolerated about the correctness of that decision. These four components (data, model, hypothesis, and decision) are basic to the statistical problems of hypothesis testing.

Use of the null hypothesis

In such problems a null hypothesis is formed (usually denoted H_0) that the assumption to be tested is correct. Then a significance level $\alpha(0<\alpha<1)$ is chosen to indicate how improbable a set of data must be if H_0 is to be rejected. The particular samples to be considered improbable make up the critical region W, a subset of the sample space that has $\mathbf{P}(W \mid H_0)\leq\alpha$. In developing a test of a hypothesis, the central task is to construct the critical region.

When the null hypothesis is rejected, an alternative hypothesis, usually denoted H_1, is accepted in its place. The probability that a sample will lead to this action when the true value of the parameter is in H_1 is called the power, γ, of the test. If testing a hypothesis is viewed as a decision problem, there are two possible actions—"accept H_0" and "accept H_1"—and each has a corresponding loss depending on the true state of nature. (The terms "accept" and "reject" may give a rather unrealistic impression of finality, but they are the ones conventionally used in statistics as standard labels for the two actions; they owe part of their currency to one development of these ideas in the field of quality control, in which manufactured lots of material are accepted or rejected on the basis of samples.)

Many hypotheses concern values of a parameter (θ) in the probability model. In the most basic case both H_0 and H_1 involve a single value of θ (θ_0 and θ_1, respectively) and are said to be simple hypotheses. In this case the loss function may easily be displayed in a table: the two states of nature and the two possible actions determine four distinct values of the loss function (see 66). Here the concepts of decision theory provide a generalization of the classical formulation of hypothesis testing in which the losses are $l(\theta_0, a_0)=l(\theta_1, a_1)=0$ and $l(\theta_0, a_1)=l(\theta_1, a_0)=1$.

Risk is defined as the expected loss, given the state of nature. In that formulation the values of the risk are α at θ_0 (see 67) and $1-\gamma$ at θ_1 (see 68). Thus among all tests with significance level α in a given problem, the one with the greatest power γ has the least risk.

To construct a test of H_0 with maximum power against H_1, a general technique, given in 1933 by the Romanian-born U.S. statistician Jerzy Neyman and the British statistician Egon Sharpe Pearson, may be used. The basis for this technique is the likelihood function $L(x \mid H)$, in which x denotes the sample and H a simple hypothesis. The critical region W for the test is that subset of the sample space for each element of which the ratio of the likelihood function for H_0 to the likelihood function for H_1 is less than or equal to c (see 69), with c chosen to give the desired significance level: the probability of W, assuming H_0 to be true (see 70), is required to be α. The quotient $L(x \mid H_0)/L(x \mid H_1)$ is referred to as the likelihood ratio.

For example, a hypothesis about the value of the mean μ of

(72) $$L(x_1,\cdots,x_n|\mu)=\prod_{i=1}^{n}f(x_i)=(2\pi)^{-n/2}\exp\left[-\tfrac{1}{2}\sum_{i=1}^{n}(x_i-\mu)^2\right]$$

(73) $$\frac{L(x_1,\cdots,x_n|\mu_0)}{L(x_1,\cdots,x_n|\mu_1)}$$

(74) $$-\tfrac{1}{2}\sum_{i=1}^{n}(x_i-\mu_0)^2+\tfrac{1}{2}\sum_{i=1}^{n}(x_i-\mu_1)^2\leqslant\log_e c$$

(75) $$\sum_{i=1}^{n}x_i\leqslant\frac{\log_e c}{\mu_0-\mu_1}+\frac{n}{2}(\mu_0+\mu_1)$$

(76) $$W=\left\{(x_1,\cdots,x_n):\bar{x}\leqslant\frac{z_\alpha}{\sqrt{n}}+\mu_0\right\}$$

(77) $$\begin{cases}\mathbf{P}(W|H_1)=\mathbf{P}\left(\bar{X}\leqslant\dfrac{z_\alpha}{\sqrt{n}}+\mu_0|\mu=\mu_1\right)\\ \quad=\mathbf{P}(\sqrt{n}(\bar{X}-\mu_1)\leqslant z_\alpha+\\ \qquad+\sqrt{n}(\mu_0-\mu_1)|\mu=\mu_1)\\ \quad=\Phi(z_\alpha+\sqrt{n}(\mu_0-\mu_1))\end{cases}$$

(78) $$\lambda(x_1,\cdots x_n;\theta_{01},\cdots,\theta_{0r})=L_0(x_1,\cdots,x_n|\theta)/L_1(x_1,\cdots,x_n|\theta)$$

(79) $$W=\{\lambda:\lambda\leqslant c\}$$

a Gaussian (normal) distribution with variance 1 might be tested (see 71). On the basis of a random sample of n observations $X_1, \cdots, X_n$, the null hypothesis H_0 that $\mu = \mu_0$ is tested against the alternative hypothesis H_1 that $\mu = \mu_1 < \mu_0$. If a prescribed significance level α is used, $\alpha = 0.1$, say, then the appropriate critical region may be constructed. The likelihood function for any value of μ is formed from a product of normal densities each evaluated at sample points (see 72), and the likelihood ratio for the test is a ratio of two such products that differ in the value selected for the parameter μ (see 73). It is more convenient to work with the logarithm of the likelihood ratio, so that $(x_1 \cdots, x_n)$ lies in the critical region when the difference of two sums of squares (namely the quadratics that appear in the exponentials of the normals) yields a value that is less than or equal to $\log_e c$ (see 74). An algebraically equivalent condition is an inequality that sets an upper bound (dependent on c, μ_0, μ_1, and n) on the sum of sample values (see 75). Here c remains unspecified, but that causes no difficulty. In this problem the critical region does not require any distinction between samples that have the same sum. The critical region is described in terms of the sample mean $\bar{x}$: it is composed of the set of n-dimensional points for which the mean is less than or equal to a simple function of z_α (see 76).

As might be expected from the assumption that $\mu_1 < \mu_0$, the critical region is composed of samples with means to the left of μ_0. For this test, the power is calculated (see 77) to be the function Φ evaluated at the sum of z_α and $\sqrt{n}(\mu_0 - \mu_1)$, in which Φ is the standard Gaussian cumulative distribution function. In the Figure power curves are plotted showing how the power depends on the separation between μ_1 and μ_0 and on the sample size n.

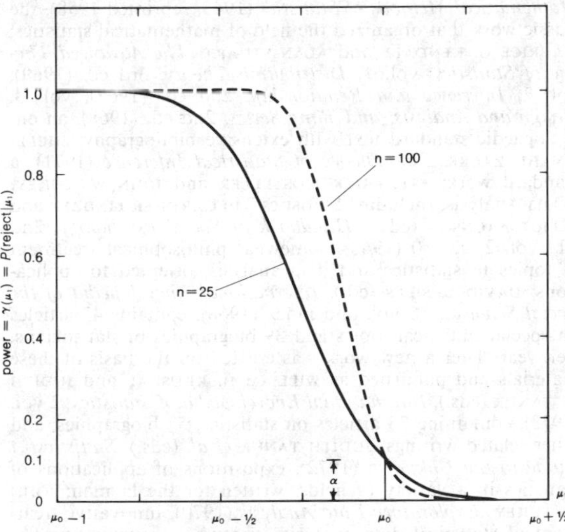

Plot of power curves for the example for $\alpha = 0.10$ and $n = 25$ (solid curve) and 100 (dashed curve; see text).

In the example, the critical region W depends only on having $\mu_1 < \mu_0$. Thus, in this problem the alternative hypothesis H_1 that $\mu < \mu_0$ could be used. Such hypotheses, involving more than one value of the parameter, are called composite. The power γ of the test is now a function of the true value of the parameter within the set of alternatives.

The curves in the Figure represent the power function $\gamma(\mu)$ for the two values of n. In general any attempt to construct a test with maximum power against a composite alternative hypothesis involves the formation of a power function $\gamma(\theta)$ that lies above other possible power functions for all values of θ within H_1. In some problems this is not feasible, and a considerable body of theory has been created to deal with such problems in great generality.

The descriptive level of significance

In practical significance testing, instead of presetting the significance level, the investigator may report the level of significance that would have just rejected the null hypothesis for his data. This level, called the descriptive level of significance or the nominal level of significance, has the advantage of giving a more complete report on the test and allows the reader to set his own significance level.

In more complicated situations a critical region in the original sample space may often be difficult to use because the region is defined by complicated functions of the data. When this happens, a technique that is based directly on a likelihood ratio may be used. The following illustration suggests some of the generality of the technique.

Suppose the parameter is $\theta = (\theta_1, \cdots, \theta_k)$, the null hypothesis is H_0: $(\theta_1, \cdots, \theta_r) = (\theta_{01}, \cdots, \theta_{0r})$ with $r \le k$, and the alternative is H_1: $(\theta_1, \cdots, \theta_r) \ne (\theta_{01}, \cdots, \theta_{0r})$. These hypotheses are not concerned with $\theta_{r+1}, \cdots, \theta_k$. The approach is to determine the maximum value of the likelihood subject to the constraint imposed by H_0 and then use its ratio to the unconstrained maximum as the test statistic. This procedure, known as the likelihood ratio test, plays a role in hypothesis testing analogous to the role of maximum likelihood in estimation. For a random sample of n the test statistic is a function λ that is a ratio of likelihood functions L_0 and L_1 (see 78), in which L_0 is maximized over θ with the constraints that $\theta_i = \theta_{0i}$, $i = 1, \cdots, r$, and L_1 over all θ. From this definition it is clear that $0 \le \lambda \le 1$, and the critical region contains values of λ that are too small for H_0 to be reasonable: it is composed of values of λ that are less than or equal to c (see 79), with c chosen so that $\mathbf{P}(W \mid H_0) \le \alpha$. When the exact distribution of λ is a function of the random sample $X_1, \cdots, X_n$, it is easy to choose c for the desired significance level. Otherwise the distribution of λ must be approximated. Fortunately, a remarkable asymptotic result may be employed: as n becomes large, the distribution of $-2 \log_e \lambda(X_1, \cdots, X_n; \theta_{01}, \cdots, \theta_{0r})$ when H_0 is true approaches a chi-square distribution with r degrees of freedom.

When data can be collected on a continuing basis, the techniques for testing a hypothesis should attempt to reach a decision as soon as the evidence is strong enough. Considered as a decision problem, this situation has three actions: "accept H_0" "accept H_1," and "continue sampling." Such methods are part of the field of sequential analysis.

When hypothesis testing was first mentioned, it was assumed that the probability model underlying the data was known. There is no reason to expect that this will always be the case; the reasonableness of a particular model may be exactly what is to be tested. Alternatively, it may be necessary to test whether the mean of one population is equal to the mean of another, without assuming a particular probability model for either. These are typical of the problems that form the subject of nonparametric hypothesis testing. Ordinarily, nonparametric methods depend less on the detailed shape of the sampling distributions than do methods called parametric. Nonparametric methods when used with measurements typically depend on signs of differences, or on counts, ranks, and permutations, rather than on the specific values.

STRUCTURE IN DATA

Many sets of data arising in actual practice are more complex than the situations and examples that have been described. The data may be collected according to a plan, and its structure must be considered in any analysis. Several properties may be measured for each observation in the sample, and their relationship may be of central importance. A process may be observed over a period of time, and it may be desired to discover or correct for cyclical aspects of its behaviour. These three types of situation are examples, respectively, of experimental design, of regression and correlation analysis, and of timeseries and spectrum analysis. There are almost as many techniques of analysis as kinds of structure in data, but the most widely used are those of linear regression.

Regression analysis

The general setting for regression analysis is as follows. Each observation consists of a value of Y, which is regarded as a response, and a value of each of $X_1, \cdots, X_k$, which are regarded as factors affecting the response. A model that restricts Z to equal a linear combination of $\{U_i\}$ plus ε (see 80) is built, for example, in which Z is some function of Y, the U's are functions of the X's, and ε is random error, attributable to measurement error or natural variation. Z may be regarded as a response; it is often called the dependent variable. The

(80) $$Z=\beta_1 U_1+\cdots+\beta_r U_r+\varepsilon$$

(81) $$\sum_{i=1}^{n}[z_i-(b_1 U_{1i}+\cdots+b_r U_{ri})]^2$$

(82) $$z_i-(b_1 U_{1i}+\cdots+b_r U_{ri})$$

(83) $$\hat{y}=A(b_1 x_1+\cdots+b_k x_k)+B$$

U's, which are called carriers, may depend on the X's in ways prescribed by theory or suggested by preliminary examination of the data; they are often called independent variables, even when they may not be probabilistically or functionally independent. The parameters $\beta_1, \cdots, \beta_r$ in the model are usually called regression coefficients. Such a model is said to be linear because Z depends linearly on the U's.

At an early stage in analyzing data according to this linear or multiple regression model the β's are estimated, whether or not their numerical values are the primary goal of the analysis. One standard method for fitting the model to the data is least squares: given n observations $(y_i, x_{1i}, \cdots, x_{ki})$, estimates ($b$'s) for the β's are chosen that result in the smallest value of the sum of squared deviations from the fitted model (see 81). This sum is differentiated with respect to each of the b's, and the minimization problem is reduced to one of solving a set of r simultaneous linear equations in r unknowns. This can be done without consideration of the probability model for the random error ε, but when that error follows a normal distribution, the least-squares estimates of the b's are the same as the maximum-likelihood estimates.

Ordinarily, it is assumed that the random errors $\varepsilon_1, \cdots, \varepsilon_n$ are independent and have mean 0 and common variance σ^2; it is also assumed that they are the only source of random variation in the data. As a result, the estimated coefficients $b_1, \cdots, b_r$ vary randomly with mean values $\beta_1, \cdots, \beta_r$. When the ε's are normally distributed, the vector $b=(b_1, \cdots, b_r)$ will have a multivariate normal distribution. This fact can be used in setting a confidence region for β or a confidence interval for any single β_j.

Certain hypotheses about the model may be tested: is the carrier U_j necessary (usually posed as H_0: $\beta_j=0$ versus H_1: $\beta_j \neq 0$)? Does the model adequately describe the data? The basis for many such tests is the component of the data that remains when the fitted model is subtracted. For each observation this component is called the residual: it is a typical term (see 82) that appears squared in the sum of squared deviations. The relationship between the residuals and other elements of the model is often examined graphically. Systematic patterns in such plots can show that assuming a common variance σ^2 for the ε's is suspect, that the data have additional structure (to be fitted by adding a carrier to the model), that some U's should have a different form, or that another function of Y is more nearly linear in the U's than the present Z.

While fitting by ordinary least squares, assuming the common variance σ^2 for the ε's, is usually the first step in regression, it is quite sensitive to the presence of contamination or wild observations in the data. Consequently, a different analysis can be undertaken, based on a pattern of unequal variances or fitting the model by minimizing the sum of absolute-value deviations instead of the sum of squares. For these calculations, as well as in graphical examination of the data and the model, the computer has become an indispensable tool.

The discriminant function illustrates one use of linear regression in biology, medicine, the humanities, and the social sciences. When no one property correctly classifies objects into their populations, measures on several properties may improve the process. The linear discriminant function applies multiple regression for this purpose. If $X_1, \cdots, X_k$ are the variables used to aid the classification, $Y=0$ is defined for objects in population Π_0 and $Y=1$ for those in population Π_1. Using data for objects that can be correctly assigned to Π_0 and Π_1, least squares is applied to predicting y from $(x_1, \cdots, x_k)$. The discriminant function is a linear function, with parameters A and B, of a linear combination of the $\{x_i\}$ in which the coefficients are $\{b_i\}$ (see 83). The parameters A and B are arbitrary scaling factors chosen for convenience, and the b_i are the least squares regression coefficients. These b_i, it can be shown, separate the y scores of the populations as widely as possible. To classify new objects, one chooses a cutoff score y_0, and values above it are classified as belonging to Π_1, below it to Π_0.

For example, the rates of use of the words *and, in, of, the,* and *to* by Alexander Hamilton and James Madison in political writing led to the discriminant function

$$\hat{y}=-3.014-0.0195x_1+0.0301x_2+0.0547x_3 \\ -0.0167x_4+0.0420x_5.$$

Here a piece of writing by Hamilton is scored 1 and a piece by Madison 0. The rate of use per 1,000 words of the word numbered i above is x_i. A cut-point, here 0.5, is chosen, and a piece of writing scoring higher is assigned to Hamilton, lower to Madison. Thus a new paper known to be written by one of these two authors having rates $x_1=30$, $x_2=20$, $x_3=60$, $x_4=100$, $x_5=40$ would score $\hat{y}=0.295$ and be classified as by Madison.

BIBLIOGRAPHY. J.L. HODGES, JR., and E.L. LEHMANN, *Elements of Finite Probability,* 2nd ed. (1970); and FREDERICK MOSTELLER, ROBERT E.K. ROURKE, and GEORGE B. THOMAS, JR., *Probability with Statistical Applications,* 2nd ed. (1970), two elementary general texts; PAUL G. HOEL, *Introduction to Mathematical Statistics,* 4th ed. (1971), an elementary calculus-based text; B.W. LINDGREN, *Statistical Theory,* 2nd ed. (1968), an intermediate text; HARALD CRAMER, *Mathematical Methods of Statistics* (1945, reprinted 1958), the classic work that organized the field of mathematical statistics; MAURICE G. KENDALL and ALAN STUART, *The Advanced Theory of Statistics:* vol. 1, *Distribution Theory,* 3rd ed. (1969); vol. 2, *Inference and Relationship,* 2nd ed. (1967); vol. 3, *Design and Analysis, and Time Series,* 2nd ed. (1968), an encyclopaedic standard text with extensive bibliography; SHELEMYAHU ZACKS, *The Theory of Statistical Inference* (1971), a standard work; FREDERICK MOSTELLER and JOHN W. TUKEY, "Data Analysis, Including Statistics," in GARDNER LINDZEY and ELLIOT ARONSON (eds.), *Handbook of Social Psychology,* 2nd ed., vol. 2, ch. 10 (1968), somewhat philosophical treatment of topics in statistics and data analysis, oriented to applications; DAVID L. SILLS (ed.), *International Encyclopedia of the Social Sciences,* 16 vol. and index (1968), contains 47 articles on special statistical topics and 39 biographies of statisticians. Ten years later a new work was created on the basis of these materials and published as WILLIAM H. KRUSKAL and JUDITH M. TANUR (eds.), *International Encyclopedia of Statistics,* 2 vol. (1978), containing 75 articles on statistics, 57 biographies, and other related writings. JUDITH TANUR *et al.* (eds.), *Statistics: A Guide to the Unknown* (1972), expositions of applications of statistics in a variety of fields, written for the layman; JOHN W. TUKEY, *Exploratory Data Analysis* (1970), innovative treatment of statistical data analysis; WALTER A. SHEWHART, *The Economic Control of Quality of Manufactured Product* (1931), a classic work; RONALD A. FISHER, *The Design of Experiments,* 8th ed. (1966), the classic work that established this branch of statistics; NATHAN KEYFITZ, *Introduction to the Mathematics of Population* (1968), the standard work that organized this branch of statistical methods; WILLIAM G. COCHRAN, *Sampling Techniques,* 2nd ed. (1963); and FREDERIC M. LORD and MELVIN R. NOVICK, *Statistical Theories of Mental Test Scores* (1968), two additional standard works. Later comprehensive works on the theory and methodology of statistics, using advanced mathematical methods, include ROBERT D. MASON, DOUGLAS A. LIND, and WILLIAM G. MARCHAL, *Statistics: An Introduction* (1983); JOHN E. FREUND, *Modern Elementary Statistics,* 6th ed. (1984); FRANK H. DIETRICH and THOMAS J. KEARNS, *Basic Statistics: An Inferential Approach* (1983); WILFRID J. DIXON and FRANK J. MASSEY, JR., *Introduction to Statistical Analysis,* 4th ed. (1983); JANE C. MILLER, *Statistics for Advanced Levels* (1983); CALVIN F. SCHMID, *Statistical Graphics: Design Principles and Practices* (1983); JOHN M. CHAMBERS *et al., Graphical Methods for Data Analysis* (1983); RONALD L. IMAN and W.J. CONOVER, *A Modern Approach to Statistics* (1983); JOSEPH NEWMARK, *Statistics and Probability in Modern Life,* 3rd ed. (1983). See also SIR MAURICE G. KENDALL and WILLIAM R. BUCKLAND, *A Dictionary of Statistical Terms,* 4th rev. ed. (1982).

Robust estimation: H.A. DAVID, *Order Statistics* (1970), a standard work with extensive bibliography. Later monographs treating estimation theory include WILLIAM J.J. REY, *Introduction to Robust and Quasi-Robust Statistical Methods* (1983); GEORGE E.P. BOX, TOM LEONARD, and CHIEN-FU WU (eds.), *Scientific Inference, Data Analysis, and Robustness: Proceedings of a Conference* (1983); B.L.S. PRAKASA RAO, *Nonparametric Functional Estimation* (1983); VENKATARAMA KRISHNAN, *Nonlinear Filtering and Smoothing: An Introduction to Martingales, Stochastis Integrals, and Estimation* (1984).

Bayesian methods: D.V. LINDLEY, *Introduction to Probability and Statistics from a Bayesian Viewpoint*, 2 pt. (1965), a standard work; FREDERICK MOSTELLER and DAVID L. WALLACE, *Inference and Disputed Authorship: The Federalist* (1964), large-scale application of Bayesian and other statistical methods to a problem in discrimination; SAMUEL A. SCHMITT, *Measuring Uncertainty: An Elementary Introduction to Bayesian Statistics* (1969), an elementary text; GEORGE E.P. BOX and GEORGE C. TIAO, *Bayesian Inference in Statistical Analysis* (1973), a standard work. See also RICHARD C. JEFFREY, *The Logic of Decision*, 2nd ed. (1983); A.S. HOLEVO, *Investigations in the General Theory of Statistical Decisions* (1978; originally published in Russian, 1976); MADAN M. GUPTA and ELIE SANCHEZ (eds.), *Fuzzy Information and Decision Processes* (1982); Z.W. KMIETOWICZ and A.D. PEARMAN, *Decision Theory and Incomplete Knowledge* (1981).

Hypothesis testing: HERMAN CHERNOFF and LINCOLN E. MOSES, *Elementary Decision Theory* (1959), an elementary text; I.R. SAVAGE, *Bibliography of Nonparametric Statistics* (1962); ABRAHAM WALD, *Statistical Decision Functions*, 2nd ed. (1971), the classic work; E.L. LEHMANN, *Testing Statistical Hypotheses* (1959), a standard work; HOWARD RAIFFA, *Decision Analysis: Introductory Lectures on Choices Under Uncertainty* (1968), an elementary text; HOWARD RAIFFA and ROBERT SCHLAIFER, *Applied Statistical Decision Theory* (1961), a standard work that develops the mathematical tools for Bayesian decision theory.

Structure in data: THEODORE W. ANDERSON, *An Introduction to Multivariate Statistical Analysis* (1958) and *The Statistical Analysis of Time Series* (1971); GEORGE E.P. BOX and GWILYM M. JENKINS, *Time Series Analysis: Forecasting and Control* (1970); GWILYM M. JENKINS and DONALD G. WATTS, *Spectral Analysis and Its Applications* (1968); and OSCAR KEMPTHORNE, *The Design and Analysis of Experiments* (1952), all standard texts; ARTHUR P. DEMPSTER, *Elements of Continuous Multivariate Analysis* (1969), a standard text with a geometric and computational approach; ARTHUR S. GOLDBERGER, *Econometric Theory* (1964), a standard text for multivariate regression methods. Statistical hypothesis testing is discussed also in the following later monographs: STURE HOLM, *Sequential Likelihood Ratio Tests* (1980); WOLF-DIETER HELLER *et al.*, *Schliessende Statistik: Schätzen und Testen* (1980); ERKKI PAHKINEN, *The Method of Support as Statistical Inference Model for Instant Sample* (1981); CLAUDE MOUCHOT, *Statistique et économétrie* (1983).

The following works discuss the use of statistical methods in the social sciences, and other special applications of statistics: JOSEPH F. HEALEY, *Statistics: A Tool for Social Research* (1984); NORMAN R. KURTZ, *Introduction to Social Statistics* (1983); MORRIS HAMBURG, *Statistical Analysis for Decision Making*, 3rd ed.(1983); N.M. DOWNIE and R.W. HEATH, *Basic Statistical Methods*, 5th ed. (1983); GENE M. LUTZ, *Understanding Social Statistics* (1983); RICHARD P. RUNYON and AUDREY HABER, *Fundamentals of Behavioral Statistics*, 5th ed. (1984); MARK L. BERENSON and DAVID M. LEVINE, *Basic Business Statistics: Concepts and Applications* (1983); PAUL NEWBOLD , *Statistics for Business and Economics* (1984); GILBERT GORDON and ISRAEL PRESSMAN, *Quantitative Decision Making for Business*, 2nd ed. (1983); GARY E. MEEK and STEPHEN J. TURNER, *Statistical Analysis for Business Decisions* (1983); YA-LUN CHOU, *Modern Business Statistics: An Applied Approach* (1984); JOHN J. CLARK and MARGARET T. CLARK, *A Statistics Primer for Managers* (1983); CHARLES T. CLARK and LAWRENCE L. SHCKADE, *Statistical Analysis for Administrative Decisions*, 4th ed. (1983); LYMAN OTT and DAVID K. HILDEBRAND, *Statistical Thinking for Managers* (1983); U.K. SRIVASTAYA, G.V. SHENOY, and S.C. SHARMA, *Quantitative Techniques for Managerial Decision Making: Concepts, Illustrations, and Problems* (1983); F.J. RENDALL and L.M. WOLF, *Statistical Sources and Techniques* (1983); VINCENT E. CANGELOSI, PHILLIP H. TAYLOR, and PHILLIP F. RICE, *Basic Statistics: A Real World Approach*, 3rd ed. (1983); RONALD CAULCUTT, *Statistics in Research and Devolopment* (1983); I.B. HOSSACK, J.H. POLLARD, and B. ZEHNWIRTH, *Introductory Statistics with Applications in General Insurance* (1983); ROBERT D. MASON, *Statistics for Managers in Insurance Companies* (1983); WAYNE C. CURTIS, *Statistical Concepts for Attorneys* (1983).

Electronic data processing in statistics is discussed in MARK L. BERENSON, DAVID M. LEVINE, and MATTHEW GOLDSTEIN, *Intermediate Statistical Methods and Applications: A Computer Package Approach* (1983); MARK FINKELSTEIN and GEORGE MCCARTY, *Calculate Basic Statistics* (1982); *SAS User's Guide: Statistics* (1982); DOUGLAS M. KLIEGER, *Computer Usage for Social Scientists* (1984).

Popular works on statistics include JAMES T. MCCLAVE and FRANK H. DITRICH, *A First Course in Statistics* (1983); DOUGLAS DOWNING and JEFF CLARK, *Statistics, the Easy Way* (1983); RICHARD M. JAEGER, *Statistics, a Spectator Sport* (1983); PETER W. ZEHNA and DONALD R. BARR, *Statistics by Calculator* (1982); RONALD E. WALPOLE, *Elementary Statistical Concepts*, 2nd ed. (1983); G. BARRIE WETHERILL, *Elementary Statistical Methods*, 3rd ed. (1983); ARNOLD NAIMAN, ROBERT ROSENFELD, and GENE ZIRKEL, *Understanding Statistics*, 3rd ed. (1983); ROBERT HOOKE, *How to Tell the Liars from the Statisticians* (1983); RICHARD P. RUNYON, *How Numbers Lie: A Consumer's Guide to the Fine Art of Numerical Deception* (1981); SAMUEL KOTZ and DONNA F. STROUP, *Educated Guessing: How to Cope in an Uncertain World* (1983).

Two informative, well-indexed bibliographies are PAUL WASSERMAN (ed.), *Statistics Sources: A Subject Guide to Date on Industrial, Business, Social, Educational, Financial, and Other Topics for the United States and Internationally*, 6th ed. (1980); and JOSEPH ZAREMBA, *Statistics and Econometrics: A Guide to Information Sources* (1980).

(Fr.M./D.C.H./Ed.)

The History of the Eurasian Steppe

The Eurasian Steppe is a belt of grassland that extends some 5,000 miles (8,000 kilometres), from Hungary in the west, through the Ukraine and Central Asia, to Manchuria in the east. Mountain ranges interrupt the steppe, dividing the grassland into distinct segments; but horsemen could cross such barriers easily, so that steppe peoples could and did interact across the entire breadth of the Eurasian grassland throughout most of recorded history. Yet the unity of steppe history is difficult to grasp since the steppe peoples left very little writing behind them for historians to use, and Chinese, Middle Eastern, and European records tell only what happened within a restricted range across their respective steppe frontiers. Archaeology offers real but limited help (grave relics from chieftains' tombs abound but, of course, say little about everyday life and leave political, military, and linguistic alignments to inference). As a result, until about AD 1000, information concerning the rise and fall of steppe empires and the relation between events in the eastern and western portions of the steppe remains fraught with great uncertainty.

The article is divided into the following sections:

PHYSICAL AND HUMAN GEOGRAPHY

Physical features. The lay of the land divides the Eurasian Steppe into two major segments. The first of these may be called the Western Steppe. It extends from the grassy plains at the mouth of the Danube River along the north shore of the Black Sea, across the lower Volga, and eastward as far as the Altai Mountains. The conventional division between Europe and Asia at the Ural Mountains is completely meaningless for steppe history and geography. The grasslands extend continuously south of the Ural Mountains on either side of the Ural River. The Western Steppe therefore constitutes one vast region, some 2,500 miles from east to west and between 200 and 600 miles from north to south. Within its bounds, a vast sea of grass made cross-country movement easy for anyone with a horse to ride. Rivers and streams cut through the grasslands, with trees growing along the banks. Streams flow slowly, trending, for the most part, either north or south and providing an easy mode of transport by river boat in summer and by sleigh in winter. Consequently, animal caravans and river transport made the steppe accessible to commerce even before modern roads and railroads transformed travel conditions.

Hot summers and cold winters divide the year into sharply contrasting seasons. Temperatures are slightly more extreme in the east, but a more critical variable is rainfall, which diminishes as the rain-bearing winds from the Atlantic become increasingly erratic east of the Don. These temperature and precipitation gradients make the Ukraine and adjacent parts of Romania far richer natural pastureland than the land farther east. Peoples of the Western Steppe therefore tended to migrate westward along the steppe, seeking better grass and milder temperatures, whenever political conditions allowed them to do so.

Climate of the steppes

The second major segment of the Eurasian Steppe extends from the Altai Mountains on the west to the Greater Khingan Range on the east, embracing Mongolia and adjacent regions. It is higher, colder, and drier than the Western Steppe, with greater seasonal extremes of temperature than are found anywhere else in the world. Some 1,500 miles from east to west and about 400 to 500 miles from north to south, the Eastern Steppe is in every way a harsher land for human habitation than the Western Steppe. All the same, lower temperatures counteract lower precipitation by reducing evaporation, so that sparse grass does grow, at least seasonally, even where rainfall is only between 10 and 20 inches (250 and 500 millimetres) a year. At higher elevations precipitation increases, and the mountaintops accumulate snow caps from which streams descend into the dry lands below. Irrigated cultivation is possible along such streams. Oasis dwellers, whose skills and goods complemented those of pastoralists, played important roles in steppe history.

Early patterns of migration. These geographical conditions meant that nomads of the Eastern Steppe, living as they did in one of the most severe climates of the Earth, were under constant temptation to move in one of two directions: either southward and eastward toward Manchuria and northern China or westward, passing between the Altai and Tien Shan along the valley of the Ili River and the shores of Lake Balkhash, toward the more inviting grasslands of the Western Steppe. Migrations and conquests funnelling through this Dzungarian Gate, as it is often called, gave the peoples of all the steppe a common history from the onset of horse nomadism. Warfare techniques, life-styles, religious ideas, artistic styles, languages, etc., spread widely across the steppes, never erasing local variations completely but making a single whole of the entire region in a more intimate way than the fragmentary records left by civilized scribes reveal.

The Dzungarian Gate

Manchuria on the east and Hungary on the west are separated from the two main portions of the Eurasian Steppe by the Greater Khingan and Carpathian mountains, respectively, and are also distinguished by relatively benign climates favourable to agriculture. Hence, before modern times, a mixed economy of pastoral and agricultural activities had greater scope in Hungary and Manchuria than in the main areas of the steppe.

The same marginal participation in steppe history prevailed in the interior of Asia Minor, where open grassland, like that of the main portion of the steppe, was contiguous to similar grasslands in northern Syria and on southward into Arabia. On these southern grasslands arose another historically important style of nomad pastoralism that extended across the Red Sea deep into Africa as well. Since bypassing the Caucasus was easy for horsemen, movement from the northern to the southern grasslands occurred repeatedly. As a result, Eurasia's two great pastoral tradi-

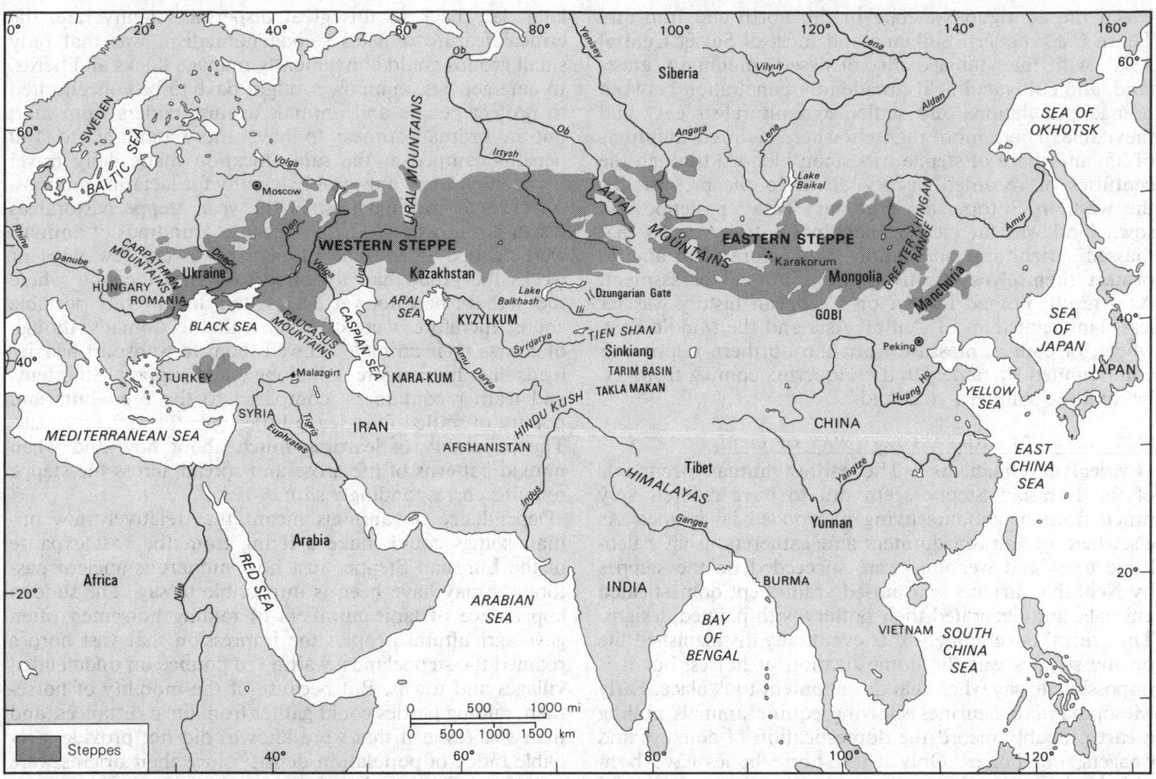

Extent of the Eurasian steppes.

Mingling of northern and southern nomadism

tions—Semitic in the south, Indo-European, Turkish, and Mongol in the north—met and mingled in Asia Minor and on steppe lands south of the Caucasus and therefore shared common traditions. In all likelihood, horses were first domesticated in the north, for example, but came to play important roles in Arabia and even in Africa; while the spread of Islām across the northern steppe attested to the impact of southern nomad ideals upon northerners.

Geography of adjacent regions. Boundaries of the steppe are imprecise. Toward the north the Eurasian grasslands fade into forested landscapes, and because of long winters and short, cool summers, even scant rainfall can sustain scrub growth of spruce and other conifers. The Russian name for such forests is taiga, as steppe is the Russian word for grasslands; and it is convenient to use these terms to describe the two zones of vegetation that set narrow limits on human life in northern Eurasia even today.

The taiga

The taiga was, for the most part, even more forbidding for human beings than the grasslands that lay to the south. In European Russia, a milder climate allowed deciduous forests to grow in some regions. There crops grew better than in the taiga, where agriculture could only be marginally successful, on account of poor soils and short growing seasons. In Asia, where taiga abutted directly on the steppe, hunters and gatherers of the forest were prone to migrate into the open grasslands. There they could establish themselves as nomads, and, being inured to the cold, heat, and hardship of the climate, they were in a good position to compete for a place on even the most forbidding steppe lands of Outer Mongolia. Similar migration from the forested north also occurred sporadically farther west. For example, Goths from southern Sweden penetrated the Ukraine in the early Christian centuries and swiftly adopted the habits and accoutrements of steppe nomads.

Desert areas

To the south the Eurasian Steppe fades into desert; but the deserts of Central Asia are dissected by mountain ranges in far more complicated fashion than the steppe proper. Since rainfall usually increases with elevation, mountains become islands of greenery in otherwise dry landscapes; and streams descending from mountaintops can sustain oasis cultivation in low-lying desert land. Grassland, sometimes merely seasonal, exists in all the mountainous areas of the Central Asian deserts. Complex, locally variable landscapes result. Hence the desert region that extends from the lower Volga and central Iranian plateau eastward through the Kara-Kum and Kyzylkum deserts to the Takla Makan and Gobi in the east is uninhabitable only in some salt-encrusted lowlands. Even in the most barren reaches of unsalted soil, some herbage is occasionally available for animals to pasture on, and oases are often densely populated.

Inhabitants of adjacent regions. Interaction between steppe nomads and the various oasis dwellers of Central Asia was prolonged and intimate. Cities of the oases were often subjected to nomad rule; on the other hand, city dwellers' superior skills regularly captivated unfriendly nomads, and suitably fortified cities could sometimes preserve their independence, even against nomad assault. Looked at from a steppe point of view, China and Europe, together with the cultivable areas of the Middle East, were no more than unusually large oases fed by moisture from adjacent oceans and from the Mediterranean and other inland seas.

Resources available for human life in these favoured regions were obviously more plentiful than in the steppe; and nomadic peoples, even when attached to their own ways of life, were strongly attracted by the wealth and ease that agricultural societies afforded. Movement southward from the steppe into one or another civilized zone was therefore a recurrent feature of Eurasian history. Nomads came as slaves, as traders and transport personnel, or as raiders and rulers. In this latter capacity, they played a politically prominent and often dominant part in Eurasian history. Because of their way of life, steppe peoples found it relatively easy to assemble large, mobile cavalry forces that could probe any weakness in civilized defenses and swiftly exploit whatever gaps they found. The political history of Eurasia consists very largely of nomad raids and conquests and the countervailing efforts by agricultural societies to defend themselves with an appropriate mix of armed force and diplomacy.

The Gobi

Geography did much to shape the pattern of these interactions. In the east the Gobi, dividing Outer Mongolia from China proper, constituted a considerable barrier. Successful raiding across the Gobi required a larger scale organization and more centralized command than was needed further west, where no such geographical obstacles existed. Thus, nomad impact on China was both sporadic and drastic. In Central Asia the complex borderlands between the contiguous steppe in the north and Iran and Turan (*i.e.,* modern Sinkiang and most of Soviet Central Asia), with their tangled mix of desert, mountain, grassland, and cultivated fields, made interpenetration between nomad populations and settled agriculturalists easy and inevitable. There more than elsewhere civilized traditions of life and those of steppe tribesmen blended through the centuries of recorded history down to the present. To the west, in Europe, the boundary between steppe and sown land was far clearer than in Central Asia so that massed agricultural populations were more often able to protect themselves effectively from nomad harassment. As a result, nomad impact on European history was far less significant than in Central Asia and the Middle East, where, of course, pressure from the northern steppe was compounded by raiders and conquerors coming from Tibet and the southern grasslands.

EMERGENCE OF THE PASTORAL WAY OF LIFE

Critical developments. The earliest human occupants of the Eurasian Steppe seem not to have differed very much from neighbours living in wooded landscapes. As elsewhere in Eurasia, hunters and gatherers using Paleolithic tools and weapons were succeeded on the steppes by Neolithic farmers who raised grain, kept domesticated animals, and decorated their pottery with painted designs. The critical development that eventually distinguished life on the steppes was the domestication of horses; but it is impossible to say when that development took place. Early Mesopotamian figurines showing equine animals pulling a cart probably record the domestication of donkeys and onagers, not horses. Only a few horse bones have been identified at early sites, and they may attest to successful hunting rather than domestication. But some time before 2000 BC steppe dwellers learned to keep herds of horses in addition to cattle, sheep, and goats, which were the principal domestic animals in more southerly lands.

Domestication of horses

Maximizing the size of domesticated herds necessitated a migratory way of life because animals kept together for protection and control ate the grass faster than it could grow, especially in the semiarid regions of the steppe. This made it hard to combine grain-growing with herding, as had been customary among Neolithic food producers. Eventually a clear break occurred between peoples who raised crops and animals and others who depended solely on the products of their flocks and herds and moved from pasture to pasture throughout the year.

In all probability nomadism developed into a fully independent way of life only after human beings had learned to live largely on animal milk and milk products, thus tapping a new food source and, in effect, discovering a new ecological niche by displacing male lambs, calves, and colts from their mothers' teats. Lactating animals had to be tamed to allow human beings to milk them by hand, and human populations also had to adjust physiologically by continuing as adults to secrete the enzymes children need to digest their mother's milk. Such adaptations surely took considerable time, but how they proceeded remains unknown.

Adaptation to milk consumption

The great dispersal. Nevertheless, by about 2000 BC these fundamental adjustments had probably been made, since a notable movement of peoples off the steppe and into the forested regions of Europe was underway. Herdsmen and warriors, speakers of Indo-European tongues, carried a distinctive battle-axe and, with the milk of their cattle and other animals, enjoyed a food supply that was clearly superior to those of other peoples. These advantages allowed the newcomers to overrun older farming and fishing populations of the European peninsula, so that their languages and cultures became dominant among later generations of Europeans. Other, related peoples remained on the steppe, occupying the grasslands as far east as the Altai Mountains. Some Indo-European tribes also penetrated the Eastern Steppe, where, however, they presumably shared the landscape with peoples of other tongues. Such remarkable migrations suggest that by around 2000 BC the speakers of Indo-European languages had attained a formidably efficient nomadic way of life.

It is very likely that behaviour patterns observed only later date back to this great dispersal. At any rate, the critical feature of later steppe nomadism was that only small groups could conveniently manage flocks and herds. In emergencies, manpower might have to be concentrated to protect people and animals against raiders from afar; but in ordinary times, to have more than 50 to 100 persons camped at the same location made daily travel between pastures unbearably lengthy for lactating animals. Accordingly, during most of the year, steppe pastoralists dispersed into small kinship groups. Hundreds of animals were tended by dozens of persons. Every few days or weeks the group had to move to a new location where the herbage had not yet been eaten down. Only portable goods, therefore, were of much value to nomads, though of course their animals allowed them to transport heavier loads than human strength alone could support. Still, tents and leather containers, compared to the mud huts and pottery of settled folk, leave little trace for archaeologists. The possibility of learning much about how and when nomad patterns of life arose and spread across the steppe remains correspondingly slim.

Kinship groups

Dependence on animals meant that relatively few human beings could make a living from the vast expanse of the Eurasian Steppe. Just how numerous ancient pastoralists may have been is impossible to say. The sudden appearance of large numbers of raiding horsemen often gave agricultural peoples the impression that vast hordes roamed the steppelands, waiting to pounce on undefended villages and towns. But because of the mobility of horsemen, raiding parties could gather from great distances, and their size (even if that were known) did not provide a reliable index of population density since their origins were unknown. The fact that a very large number of kurgans—*i.e.,* mounds of earth raised atop chieftains' graves—exist in the Western Steppe attests to the availability of relatively abundant manpower in ancient times; but again, such monuments were raised by a chieftain's followers, gathered for the purpose from afar and temporarily. In general, there can be no doubt that nomadic populations always remained far sparser than agricultural populations. Nomad conquerors, however numerous they seemed at the moment of attack, were always far fewer than the settled populations they overran and, partly for that reason, were nearly always absorbed into the conquered society within a few generations.

In historic times, yearly migrations followed a more or less fixed pattern, up and down mountain slopes with the season or north and south across open country for as much as 400–500 miles. When migratory herdsmen lived near cultivators, they often were able to pasture their animals on the stubble left behind after grain had been harvested. Exchanging grain for cheese and other animal products could also be mutually advantageous, even when rents or tribute payments skewed the simple economic symmetry of the relationship.

The rise of confederations. Dispersal across the steppe to maximize milk and meat production could be, and in historic times was, punctuated by occasional assemblages of large numbers of nomads for an annual roundup and slaughter of wild animals, for warlike undertakings against other communities, and for various ceremonial purposes as well. Real or fictitious kinship bonds united adjacent families of herdsmen into tribes; and tribal confederations, built upon ceremonial recognition of the primacy of a high king, were constructed and confirmed at such periodic assemblages.

Prowess in protecting the herds from animal predators had been necessary from the beginning of domestication, but as pastoralism became an established way of life, prowess was redirected toward rival herdsmen. Quarrels over rights to grass and water were perennial, since boundaries between adjacent herding groups were necessarily imprecise and unpoliced. Infringement invited retaliation in the form of raids, and raids provoked counter-raids. Warfare skills were thus inculcated by the nomads' way of life, and their mobility made it possible to concentrate large numbers of experienced warriors wherever a tribal chieftain or high king might decree.

On the other hand, tribes and tribal confederations were

Precarious nature of leadership

always liable to break apart if the constituent groups felt aggrieved or merely distrusted the leader's luck or military skill. Grounds for quarrels over precedence and dignity as well as over grass and water were always present within every steppe polity; and diplomats from civilized states were often able to exploit such weaknesses by pursuing a policy of "divide and rule."

Nomadic customs and institutions thus superimposed fragile political structures on the migratory herding of small kinship groups. The formation of a far-flung war federation around the charismatic figure of a successful captain could occur very quickly. Division came even faster, since the passing of a high kingship from father to son was always precarious. Great men consolidated their power by marrying as many wives as the diversity of their following required, so whenever a great chieftain died, competition to the death among sons of different wives was likely. In effect, tribal confederations had to be reestablished every few generations.

Perhaps not all of these features of nomad life were evident when civilized peoples first experienced the military might that steppe peoples could exert. For example, occupation of the Eastern Steppe by skilled horse nomads had not yet occurred when Indo-European conquerors first arrived in the Middle East, about 1700 BC. Thereafter, scattered texts allow us to infer something about what happened on the Eurasian Steppe, although steppe peoples themselves did not begin to keep records in writing until about 2,300 years later.

MILITARY AND POLITICAL DEVELOPMENTS AMONG THE STEPPE PEOPLES TO 100 BC

The military advantages of nomadism became apparent even before the speed and strength of horses had been harnessed for military purposes. The early conquests of Sargon of Akkad (*c.* 2250 BC) and the Amorite invasions of Mesopotamia before 1800 BC attest to the superior force that nomadic or seminomadic peoples held, even when fighting only on foot. But the full effect of their military strength came with the use of horses, some time around 1700 BC. Military primacy shifted to the northern steppes, where horses were easy to raise. The southern grasslands were less suited to horses, and the nomads of those regions therefore lost the dominance they once had.

Horsepowered warfare. Horses were first used in war to pull light, two-wheeled chariots that carried a two-man crew. A driver held the reins and controlled the team of horses while his companion shot arrows from the chariot's platform. No foot soldiers could stand against this form of attack when it was new. Warriors who had access to horses and chariots therefore enjoyed an easy superiority in battle for nearly five centuries.

The principal beneficiaries were Indo-European tribesmen, speaking languages akin to Sanskrit, who already possessed horses. Along the southern fringe of the Central Asian portion of the steppe, where cultivated lands intermingled with pasture—perhaps in Azerbaijan or farther east in Iran—wheelwrights learned to make spoked wheels that were accurately circular and strong enough to withstand the impact of a human cargo bouncing across natural land surfaces at a gallop. This invention must have occurred about 1700 BC, for soon after that date chariot conquerors overran the entire Middle East. Others invaded India around 1500 BC and extinguished the Indus civilization. Chariots also spread throughout Europe. Even in distant China, by the 14th century BC, rulers of the Shang dynasty (traditional date *c.* 1766–1122 BC) were using chariots and bows very similar to those of the Aryans further west.

Invention of the chariot

Other peoples, of course, soon learned to use chariots in battle. Consequently, the Indo-European incursions of the second millennium BC had only transitory importance in the Middle East. In India, however, the Aryans spread their language and culture throughout most of the Indian subcontinent in subsequent centuries, just as other Indo-European tribesmen had done in Europe some 500 years before.

The specialized artisan skills needed to build light, sturdy chariots were probably lacking among the steppe dwellers. At any rate there is no sign that large numbers of northern nomads ever owned such expensive devices. Chariot warfare, therefore, never affected steppe life profoundly, though it did revolutionize civilized states, inaugurating a militarized, aristocratic Bronze Age that lasted in the Middle East until about 1200 BC.

Then the rise of iron metallurgy cheapened arms and armour sufficiently to allow common foot soldiers to overthrow the chariot aristocracies of the Middle East. But this, too, had no immediate impact upon steppe peoples. Iron arrowheads were not notably better than arrowheads made of flint or obsidian; and the new metal, even if cheaper than bronze, remained too expensive for ordinary herdsmen. Soon after 900 BC, however, another revolution came to ancient patterns of warfare that did affect the steppe profoundly. Men quite simply learned how to ride horseback, thus dispensing with cumbersome, costly chariots and unleashing the full agility and speed of a galloping horse for military purposes.

Assyrians may have pioneered the cavalry revolution. A few wall carvings from the 9th century BC show paired cavalrymen, one of whom holds the reins for both horses while the other bends a bow. This was just the technique charioteers had long been practicing. Riders soon discovered that once their mounts were accustomed to carrying men, it was safe to drop the reins and rely on voice and heel to direct the horse's movements, freeing both hands for shooting with a bow.

Development of cavalry

This extraordinary synergy of man and horse became routine between 900 and 700 BC. As the new art of horsemanship spread, nomads of the northern steppe found themselves in a position to take full advantage of the mobility and striking power a cavalry force could exert. Mounted raiding parties from the steppes became difficult indeed for sedentary peoples to combat, since horsemen could move far faster than foot soldiers and were therefore able to concentrate greater numbers at will and then flee before a superior countervailing force manifested itself. Cavalry was necessary to repel such raids, but raising horses in landscapes where grass did not grow abundantly was very expensive since the grain came directly from stocks that would otherwise feed human beings.

On the steppes, however, nomads could easily increase their supply of horses, if necessary, at the expense of cattle. Mare's milk could be substituted for cow's milk; horseflesh for beef; and horse nomads, who spent most of their waking hours in the saddle, could exploit through enhanced mobility a wider range of pastures from any given encampment. As a result, the primacy early Indo-European peoples had accorded to cattle gave way to a dependence on horses among later steppe peoples. Sheep, goats, camels, and even (in Europe and Manchuria) pigs also had a place in the steppe economy; as did, in favoured locations, the cultivation of grain. But the cavalry revolution of the 9th and 8th centuries BC put horses first because of their usefulness in war.

Scythian successes. The first sign that steppe nomads had learned to fight from horseback was a great raid into Asia Minor launched from the Ukraine about 690 BC by a people whom the Greeks called Cimmerians. Some, though perhaps not all, of the raiders were mounted. Not long thereafter, tribes speaking an Iranian language, whom the Greeks called Scythians, conquered the Cimmerians and in turn became lords of the Ukraine. According to Herodotus, who is the principal source of information on these events, the Scyths (or at least some of them) claimed to have migrated from the Altai Mountains at the eastern extreme of the Western Steppe. This may well be so; and some modern scholars have even surmised that the barbarian invasions of China that brought the Western Chou dynasty to an end in 771 BC may have been connected with a Scythian raid from the Altai a generation or two before Scythian migration westward to the Ukraine.

The Eastern Steppe was, however, too barren and cold for invaders to linger. Consequently, the spread of cavalry skills and of the horse nomads' way of life to Mongolia took several centuries. We know this from Chinese records clearly showing that cavalry raids from the Mongolian steppe became chronic only in the 4th century BC. China was then divided among warring states, and border principalities had to convert to cavalry tactics in order to mount successful defenses. The first state to do so developed its cavalry force only after 325 BC.

Long before then, however, the Scythians had erected a loose confederacy that spanned all of the Western Steppe. The high king of the tribe heading this confederacy presumably had only limited control over the far reaches of the Western Steppe. But on special occasions the Scythians could assemble large numbers of horsemen for long-distance raids, such as the one that helped to bring the Assyrian Empire to an end. After sacking the Assyrian capital of Nineveh in 612 BC, the booty-laden Scyths returned to the Ukrainian steppe, leaving Medes, Babylonians, and Egyptians to dispute the Assyrian heritage. But the threat of renewed raids from the north remained and constituted a standing problem for rulers of the Middle East thereafter.

The sacking of Nineveh

Persian defenses. The Persians, who took over political control of the Middle East in 550 BC, met with little success in punishing steppe incursions. Cyrus the Great, founder of the Persian Empire, was killed in 530 BC while leading a punitive expedition against the Massagetai, who lived north and east of the Caspian; and Darius the Great met with indifferent success in 512 BC when he tried to subdue the Scyths from Europe by crossing the Danube. On the other hand, diplomatic arrangements whereby border tribesmen were paid to guard against raids from deeper in the steppe worked well as long as Persian tax collectors provided a suitable assortment of goods with which to subsidize the friendly borderers. No massive incursions or large-scale infiltrations from the steppe into the Middle East took place, therefore, until after the overthrow of the Persian Empire at the hands of Alexander the Great in 330 BC.

In the next century, however, the collapse of the Persian frontier guard in Central Asia and the consolidation of a new steppe empire based in Mongolia combined to provoke large-scale displacements of peoples westward along the steppe and southward from the steppe onto cultivated ground. For the first time, the natural gradient of the Eurasian Steppe came fully into play when a tribal confederation, called Hsiung-nu by the Chinese, attained an unmatched formidability. This happened at the very end of the 3rd century BC. Neighbours on the steppe, fleeing from the Hsiung-nu, moved south and west, generating in turn a wave of migration that eventually reached from the borders of China as far as northwestern India and the Roman limes along the Danube.

Emergence of the Hsiung-nu

The Hsiung-nu Empire. Just as the Scythian Empire of the Western Steppe was a mirror image of the Persian Empire to the south, the empire of the Hsiung-nu (late 3rd century BC–2nd century AD) mirrored the Chinese empire that had been consolidated in 221 BC by Ch'in Shih Huang Ti and was subsequently stabilized under the Han dynasty (206 BC–AD 221). To judge from Chinese accounts, which are the only ones available, the Hsiung-nu modelled themselves quite closely on Chinese principles, regarding their ruler as the Son of Heaven, just as the Chinese did. Organized warfare across the Gobi alternated with periods of peace, when formalized exchanges of tribute-gifts allowed the rulers on each side to strengthen themselves by acquiring rare and valuable goods to distribute as they saw fit. The Chinese obtained horses for the army and other Imperial uses, while the Hsiung-nu ruler acquired grain, silks, and other luxuries with which to reward his followers.

CLOSURE OF THE IRANIAN BORDERLAND TO STEPPE RAIDERS AND ITS CONSEQUENCES, 100 BC–AD 550

Domination by the Parthians. Initially, the displacements westward that were precipitated by the consolidation of the Hsiung-nu confederacy took the form of a series of migrations into Iran and across the Hindu Kush into India. Various Iranian tribes—Śakas and Kushāns chief among them—were the protagonists of these displacements. Their vacated grazing lands came under the control of Turkish tribes, so that the frontier of Indo-European languages began to shrink back as the Turks advanced.

This pattern of migration altered by the end of the 2nd century BC. At that time the Iranian borderland was again effectually defended by new guardians, the Parthians. They were another Iranian people of the steppe who began to move southward during the 3rd century BC when Alexander's successors, the Seleucids, proved incapable of safeguarding their frontiers against such incursions. Once established on cultivated ground, the Parthians prevented other steppe nomads from following hard on their heels by developing a superior cavalry force and inventing a means for supporting it at relatively little cost.

The key change was the introduction of alfalfa (lucerne) as a cultivated crop. Alfalfa, if planted on fallowed fields, provided a fine fodder for horses, and nitrogen-fixing bacteria that grew on its roots enhanced the fertility of the soil for subsequent grain crops. Moreover, horses stall-fed on alfalfa (with some additional grain) could be bred bigger and stronger than the steppe ponies that had only grass to eat. Big horses in turn could support armoured men on their backs and even carry armour to protect their own bodies. Such armoured cavalrymen, scattered out across the agricultural landscape as lords and local protectors of village communities, could readily assemble a formidable force to oppose nomad raiding parties. Their armour permitted them to withstand enemy arrows while returning shot for shot; and when steppe intruders sought to withdraw, the heavy cavalrymen could pursue farther and faster than ever before, making it hard for a raiding party to find a safe camping ground for the night or a place to graze their horses. In this way cultivated land could support an effective frontier guard against the steppe for the first time since the cavalry revolution had tipped the balance so sharply in favour of steppe dwellers. Even so, big horses and armour were always expensive, and an aristocratic and decentralized (*i.e.,* feudal) political and social system invariably developed with this kind of military establishment.

Introduction of alfalfa

The fame of the Parthian horses soon reached the Chinese Imperial court and led the emperor Han Wu Ti to send an expedition westward as far as Fergana to bring back specimens of the new breed in 101 BC. By that time, enough armoured cavalrymen stood guard over the villages of the Parthian Empire to make further nomad incursions unprofitable. As a result, migration routes along the steppe shifted north of the Caspian. The new balance of forces was registered by the collapse of the Scythian Empire in the 1st century AD. Iranian-speaking Sarmatians took over the lordship of the westernmost regions of the steppe. They presented the Roman army with a new and formidable challenge along the Danube frontier, since at least some of the Sarmatian cavalrymen were armoured in the Parthian fashion. But such warriors were comparatively few in number, and their feudal polity made them unable to organize large-scale raids. As a result, the Roman limes held for another two centuries.

The Sarmatians

Flourishing trade in the east. Relations between the steppe and cultivated lands of Eurasia therefore entered upon a new phase that lasted from approximately 100 BC to about AD 200. Raiding being unprofitable, trading intensified; and nomads found a new or enhanced role as caravan personnel, carrying goods along the Silk Road, which connected China with Syria, after Han Wu Ti's exploratory expedition of 101 BC. North–south caravan routes fed into and supplemented the east–west movement of goods, connecting northern India with Central Asia and Central Asia with the entire expanse of the Eurasian Steppe from Hungary to Manchuria.

The consequences of these intensified communications were considerable. The taste for transparent silk clothing that spread among Roman women of high fashion was less important than the propagation of Buddhism, Judaism, Manichaeism, and Christianity across Asia by missionaries and traders who moved with the caravans. Literary records do not reveal much about the process, but the comparatively abundant information surrounding the birth of Islām in Arabia (AD 610–32) casts much light on the sorts of religious exchanges that must have occurred in caravansaries and around innumerable campfires, where strangers met, telling tales and expounding divergent beliefs.

The spread of religions

About AD 200 this relatively peaceful period of steppe history drew to a close. A new era of upheaval manifested itself at both ends of the Eurasian grassland. In the east, the empire of the Hsiung-nu and the Han dynasty both disintegrated during the first two decades of the 3rd century AD. For three and a half centuries thereafter, political fragmentation on the Eastern Steppe matched the fragmentation of China proper. Barbarian regimes arose in northern China, lasting until the reunification of the country by the Sui dynasty in AD 589.

New barbarian incursions. Throughout this chaotic period in the east, the Iranian borderland with the steppe remained firmly defended. The Sāsānian dynasty (AD 224–651), which supplanted the Parthians after a successful rebellion by a great feudatory, like the previous regime, maintained armoured cavalrymen to guard against steppe marauders. The effect was to funnel all the flights and migrations provoked by the disorders on the Eastern Steppe north of the Caspian and into Europe. This put sporadic strain on the Roman frontier, until, in the 4th century, the limes at the Rhine and Danube collapsed, never to be fully reconstituted.

The Huns

The precipitating factor in this collapse was the arrival of a new people from the east, known in European history as the Huns. They crossed the Don about AD 370 and quickly defeated the Sarmatian and Gothic tribes that were then occupying the westernmost steppe. (The Goths had migrated from the forested north earlier in the 4th century, just as Mongols did far to the east perhaps at nearly the same time.) The Huns incorporated the fighting manpower of their defeated enemies into their expanding confederation by making them subject allies. This new and formidable predatory power provoked the flights and raids that broke through the Roman frontiers in 376, starting a migration of peoples that lasted, on and off, for half a millennium and brought far-reaching changes to Europe's ethnic boundaries.

What, if any, relation may have existed between the Huns of European history and the Hsiung-nu of Chinese records is an unsolved, probably insoluble, conundrum. Even the language spoken by the Huns is in dispute, though most experts believe they were of Turkish speech. For a short time a new empire of the Western Steppe took form under the Huns' most famous ruler, Attila (reigned 434–53); but on his death the subject German tribes revolted, and soon thereafter the Huns as a distinct political or ethnic entity disappeared from Europe. The abrupt rise and fall of Hunnish power, nevertheless, set all the peoples of the Western Steppe in motion; and by the time the flights, migrations, and conquests were over, the Roman Empire in the West had come to an end (AD 476), and Germanic peoples had become rulers of all the Western provinces.

China experienced equally drastic barbarian incursions in the same centuries, submitting to various Turkish, Tungusic, Tibetan, and Mongolian invaders. At the end of the 4th century AD a new confederation, the Juan-juan, arose on the Eastern Steppe; a century later a similar group, the Hephthalites, established their supremacy between the Volga River and the Altai Mountains. After the collapse of the Huns, however, no single confederation arose to dominate the rest of the Western Steppe until a people known as Avars set up headquarters in Hungary in 550 and proceeded to raid far and wide in all directions, exercising hegemony over various Slavic and Germanic tribes until submitting to Charlemagne in 805.

All of these confederations probably embraced more than one language group. Evidence is too scant to tell just how Turkish intermingled with Mongolian, Finno-Ugric, Tungusic, Indo-European, Tibetan, and perhaps still other languages across the length and breadth of the steppe. Linguistic differences were not really of great importance. Life-styles among Eurasian horse nomads had attained a fine adjustment to the grasslands; and with the invention of stirrups in about 500, symbiosis between man and mount achieved a precision that defied further improvement. Accurate shooting on the run became possible for the first time when a rider could stand in his stirrups absorbing in his legs the unsteadiness of his galloping mount. But stirrups also made cavalry lances far more formidable, since a rider, by bracing his feet in the stirrups, could put the momentum of a galloping horse and rider behind the thrust of his spearhead. Thus the enhancement of steppe archery through the use of stirrups was counteracted by a parallel improvement in the effectiveness of the heavy armoured cavalry that guarded Middle Eastern and European farmlands against the steppe nomads.

The invention of stirrups

THE ERA OF TURKISH PREDOMINANCE, 550–1200

A new Turkish confederacy. A new period of steppe history began in 552 when a powerful new Turkish confederacy, headquartered in the Altai Mountains, suddenly developed. Its geographic range was great, extending from the frontiers of China to the Caspian Sea. The new masters of the Asian steppe were skilled in ironwork and used their own runic script, of which a few examples survive. Some of the critical skills of civilization with which steppe peoples had become more familiar through the expanding trade patterns of preceding centuries were thus exploited by a nomad confederacy for the first time. Buddhism and then Islām also penetrated among the Turks, bringing steppe peoples still more closely into touch with other aspects of civilized life.

Nonetheless, the Turkish confederacy remained a tribal nomad polity with both the ferocious formidability and fragility associated with such systems of command. Disputed successions tore it apart more than once before its ultimate dissolution in 734; but prior to that time two principal consequences of the consolidation of Turkish power may be discerned. First, raids and rivalry with the Chinese helped to stimulate China's reunification under the Sui (581–618) and early T'ang (618–907) dynasties, thus renewing the mirror relationship that had previously existed between the Han and Hsiung-nu empires. Second, the rise of an aggressive Turkish power provoked recurrent flights and migrations across the steppe itself. As long as the prowess of Sāsānian barons made the Iranian borderlands impenetrable, refugees from steppe warfare continued to be funnelled north of the Caspian into Europe. Consequently, hordes of Avars, Bulgars, Khazars, Pechenegs, and Magyars—to name only the most successful—followed one another in rapid succession onto the Western Steppe. Each of these peoples established a powerful raiding confederation and exercised domination for varying periods of time over adjacent cultivated lands in the Balkans and central Europe. Two of the tribes were ancestral to the modern states of Bulgaria and Hungary, but the rest, like the Huns before them, dissolved into the general population soon after their military power broke down.

Reunification of China

Shift of attention from Europe to the Middle East. Encroachment by peoples of the steppe onto the cultivated lands of eastern Europe slackened in the 9th century and was reversed by the end of the 10th when more efficient protectors allowed European peasantries to begin moving out into grasslands along the Danube. Armoured cavalrymen on the Parthian model, known to the Byzantines as cataphracts and to the English as knights, reversed the balance between steppe raiders and settled folk in eastern Europe. The gradual rise of knighthood after 732, when Charles Martel first tried the experiment in western Europe, involved a drastic feudal decentralization of political power—decentralization that lasted longer in the east of Europe than in the west and has distracted such marcher states as Hungary and Poland down to modern times.

The rise of knighthood

Yet the rise of knighthood along the European steppe frontier was not the only factor reversing the balance between nomads and settled agriculturalists. Nomad pressure on European cultivators also slackened in the 10th century because the Iranian borderland against the steppe had once again become permeable. Exactly why this happened is unclear. Nothing in military technology seems to explain the fact that Turkish tribesmen as well as detribalized slaves began to arrive within the realm of Islām in such numbers as to be able, after about 900, to exercise decisive military force throughout the Middle East. Perhaps the attractions of city life induced Sāsānian barons to abandon their villages for the easy life of absentee landlords and to allow their military habits to decay. But no one really knows what altered the balance between steppe warriors and Iranian defenders of cultivated lands in such a way as to divert the pattern of steppe migration southward once again. The effect, nonetheless, was to spare eastern Europe from the sort of recurrent invasions it had been experiencing since the 2nd century AD.

The expansion of Islām. Consequences for the Middle East were far-reaching. Islām itself was transformed by the rise of Ṣūfism. How much the Ṣūfis owed to the pagan past of Turkish converts to Islām is unclear, though some practices of dervish orders, which were the main carriers of the Ṣūfi movement, very likely did stem from shamanistic rites and practices of the steppes. In any case, Turkish languages were added to the Arabic and Persian that had previously been the carriers of Middle Eastern high culture; and a proud Turkish consciousness persisted among soldiers and rulers to complicate older ethnic patterns within the heartlands of Islām.

Islām in India

By submitting to Turkish warriors, the realm of Islām acquired a new cutting edge. Rapid expansion at the expense of both Christendom and Hindustan resulted. Raids into India, beginning in the year 1000, led within two centuries to the establishment of Muslim control over the plains of the north. Expansion continued off and on until, by the end of the 17th century, the whole of India had been subjected to Muslim overlordship. On the other flank of Islām, a decisive breakthrough occurred in 1071 when Seljuq tribesmen defeated the Byzantines at Manzikert (modern Malazgirt), thereby confirming their occupation of the grasslands in the interior of Asia Minor. Thus, modern Turkey became Turkish for the first time. This expansion triggered the First Crusade (1095–99), but the crusaders' success only checked, without permanently stemming, the Turkish advance. Instead, toward the end of the 13th century the Ottomans succeeded the Seljuqs as leaders of the struggle against Christendom and continued to advance their frontiers as late as 1683, by which time all of the Balkans and Hungary were under Turkish rule.

Muslim principles deplored strife among the faithful while admiring military success against unbelievers. This belief encouraged newcomers from the steppes to migrate toward the two expanding frontiers of Islām, where they could exercise their military skills, expect rich booty, and win new lands while enjoying the respect and admiration of fellow Muslims. As a result, the mainstream of steppe migration gravitated toward Islām's Christian and Indian frontiers. Arab tribesmen had done the same in the Middle East and North Africa during the first century (632–732) of Muslim history. Thus, after about 900, the military manpower and skills of the northern nomads took over the role that had been played by Bedouins from the south during Islām's first, extraordinary period of expansion.

Developments on the steppe proper. The tribes that remained behind on the Eurasian Steppe were of course affected by this massive Turkish influx into the Middle East. Trade connections with Islāmic lands intensified, and traders from Middle Eastern cities spread Islām far and wide among steppe peoples. To be sure, full compliance with Muslim law was scarcely compatible with pastoral routines of life; but after the 11th century most of the Western Steppe had become, at least superficially, incorporated into the realm of Islām. Along with the religion, heightened familiarity with civilized ways penetrated deep into the steppe. Miniature cities arose at river crossings and at the headquarters of powerful chieftains, where merchants gathered and urban artisan skills began to find limited scope.

Chinese influence

In the Eastern Steppe, Chinese civilization played the same role, although the oasis cities of the Tarim Basin continued to offer steppe peoples alternatives to a purely Chinese pattern of higher culture until long after this period. Collapse of the Turkish Empire in 734, swiftly followed by a drastic weakening of the T'ang dynasty after a massive rebellion in 755, hastened rather than hindered the infiltration of new skills into the Eastern Steppe. The T'ang dynasty recovered control of China only by calling on barbarians for aid, which they received from a newly powerful Uighur confederacy (745–1209) that had started as one of the successor states to the older Turkish Empire of the steppes. But the Uighur horsemen who rescued the T'ang dynasty from its domestic difficulties did so only in return for handsome trade-tribute payments. Once begun, the flow of tribute from China continued as long as Uighur power endured. The Uighurs, of course, consumed some of the goods they carried out of China themselves but traded the rest with neighbours and neighbours' neighbours for grain, slaves, and special goods such as jade, gold, and furs. A far-flung caravan network thus attained greater importance than ever before, binding steppe peoples to oasis cultivators in the south and forest peoples in the north and joining the parallel Muslim trade net of the Western Steppe.

The Uighur confederacy

Such exchanges involved more than simple export and import of goods. Religions continued to travel the caravan routes as they had done for centuries. Buddhism rivalled Islām in the Eastern Steppe, but the Uighurs, interestingly, asserted and maintained their spiritual independence of both of the great civilizations they touched by espousing the Manichaean faith. They also used a Sogdian script, derived from Persian, that supplanted the Turkish runic script and allowed them to create a more thoroughly literate society than earlier steppe peoples had attained.

THE MONGOL EMPIRE, 1200–1368

Emergence of bureaucratic states. The next important transformation of steppe life occurred when nomad peoples began to supplement their age-old tribal organization by borrowing Chinese bureaucratic principles for the management of armed forces. Such experiments first appeared among rising states in northern China after the collapse of the T'ang dynasty in 907. During the next two centuries China's political weakness allowed various barbarian peoples to overrun parts of the north once more while continuing to control ancestral steppe lands. The resulting hybrid states were known to the Chinese as the Khitan (907–1124), Tangut (990–1227), and Juchen (1122–1234) empires. It was natural for them to combine nomad tribal and Chinese bureaucratic principles of management in military and other departments of administration. The Khitan, for example, supplemented their horsemen with foot soldiers and developed combined tactics for using infantry and cavalry together in battle. Even more significant was the way in which their successors in northern China, the Juchen, set up a command structure on bureaucratic principles. The Juchen rulers divided their army into tens, hundreds, and thousands and put appointed officers over each unit. Consequently, among the Juchen, hereditary tribal standing did not necessarily coincide with ascribed military rank. For a brave and lucky man, army service became a career open to talent.

The Chinese had relied on appointed officers to command their soldiers for centuries. By applying the idea to steppe armies, a ruler could at least hope to transcend the fragility previously inherent in tribal confederations. No matter how solemn the binding oaths of blood brotherhood might be, because steppe horsemen had always followed their own tribal leaders to war, any quarrel among chiefs could immediately dissolve a formidable army into its original warring fragments. But in a bureaucratic system, hereditary chieftains no longer had their own tribesmen always at their beck and call. Before a chief contemplating rebellion against central authorities could count on support, he had to overcome his tribesmen's loyalty to appointed commanders. Divided and uncertain loyalties in the ranks therefore made traditional tribal rebellion chancy at best and suicidal if the rebel chieftain's tribesmen failed to follow. Sudden dissolution of steppe confederacies therefore became much less likely.

The decline of the chieftains

The superior stability of steppe polities organized along bureaucratic lines was evident when overthrow resulted not from internal disruption, in the old way, but from conquest at the hands of another bureaucratically organized armed force. The Juchen, for example, supplanted the Khitan only after improving on their rivals' half-hearted efforts to appropriate Chinese patterns of military management; and the Juchen in turn were overthrown by the Mongols under Genghis Khan (1162–1227), whose armies were led by men appointed on the basis of demonstrated

Genghis Khan

efficiency in battle, regardless of birth or hereditary rank.

The triumph of the Mongols. Genghis Khan started his victorious career as a solitary fugitive, and his first followers were men who, like himself, lacked any powerful kindred ties because their clans had met with ill fortune in war. Among such a collection of more or less detribalized warriors, the bureaucratic principle had free rein from the start. Genghis never had to make the compromises with traditional status that would have been necessary if he had not started as a refugee, deprived of the supporting ties so vital to traditional steppe life.

Uninhibited application of the bureaucratic principle endowed Genghis Khan's armies with a remarkable capacity to expand. Instead of simply incorporating tribal war bands into his following, as earlier steppe conquerors had done, Genghis reorganized his defeated foes into tens and hundreds and put his own men in command over each of the units. This practice assured rapid promotion to men of demonstrated ability. A career open to talent allowed an ordinary tribesman to rise to the command of as many as 10,000 men. As in modern armed forces, striving to earn promotion presumably became a way of life for ambitious individuals, whose loyalties were thereby most effectively shifted away from kinship groupings and harnessed to their hope for bureaucratic advancement. By the same token, the Mongol army became capable of indefinite expansion, until literally all of the peoples of the Eurasian Steppe had joined its ranks, from Manchuria in the east to the Ukraine in the west. This remarkable and very rapid military-bureaucratic unification of the steppe was complemented by conquest of most of the civilized lands adjacent to the steppe. Thus, all of China (by 1279), most of the Middle East (by 1260), and all the Russian principalities except Novgorod (by 1241) were brought under the Mongol sway.

Full domination of the steppe

The Mongols, of course, were experienced traders by the time of their conquests. Caravans moved freely throughout their domains, and thousands, perhaps tens of thousands, of persons travelled between Europe and China. Marco Polo's account of his remarkable career in the service of Kublai Khan in China shows how readily the Mongols employed strangers and welcomed merchants from distant lands. Chinese skills were then superior to those of other parts of the world. Consequently, intensified communications under the Mongols allowed the diffusion of certain Chinese skills and tastes to the rest of Eurasia. Gunpowder, the compass, and printing were especially important for Europe. In the Middle East it was Chinese luxuries such as silk, porcelain, and styles of painting that had the most obvious impact.

Mongol religious policy puzzled both Muslim and Christian believers. The early Khans preferred to keep open multiple lines of communication with supernatural powers and therefore encouraged rival faiths—Christian, Muslim, and Buddhist—to coexist at their courts. Eventually a form of Buddhism coming from Tibet won primacy among the Mongols, but this upshot was not finally secured until the 18th century.

Genghis Khan died in 1227, long before the tide of Mongol expansion had reached its height. Down to the end of the century, the Mongol armies remained on the offensive, invading Japan (1281), Annam (modern Vietnam), and Burma (1285–87), and distant Java (1292–93). Throughout this expension, they showed remarkable readiness to exploit new technological possibilities. Even in Genghis Khan's lifetime, the conquest of northern China had required them to master siege techniques; and the conquest of southern China required them to learn to fight from ships as well. They excelled at scouting and logistics and never met a military equal in their extraordinary era of conquest except, perhaps, the Japanese, who turned them back with the help of a typhoon in 1281.

Fragmentation of the empire. The Mongol assault on Europe and the Middle East stopped short of completion due not to military failure but to dissension over the succession—a weakness of steppe empires that Genghis Khan's bureaucratic organization of the armies failed to remedy. A fourfold division among his immediate heirs went along with ceremonial recognition of the primacy of one, who became the great khan, based first at Karakorum in Mongolia and then, after 1267, at Ta-tu (modern Peking) in China.

As time passed, however, cooperation among the separate segments of the Mongol Empire became more and more precarious. With the end of rapid expansion, promotion within army ranks slowed, and the high morale and tight discipline that had been attained in the days of initial success slackened. More important still was the way in which the separate parts of the empire adopted the diverse cultural coloration of their subject peoples. Thus, the Golden Horde in Russia became Muslim and Turkish; the Il-Khans in the Middle East became Persian and Islāmic; and the great khan of China became Sinicized. The steppe way of life survived best in the central region of the empire where the Chagatai khans reigned until 1324. Yet this was the poorest of the four khanates into which Genghis Khan's empire had been partitioned and could not possibly dominate the rest.

Nevertheless, until the end of the 13th century, political unity, at least of a ceremonial kind, was maintained despite sporadic outbreaks of fighting among rival candidates for the supreme power. But after the death of Genghis' grandson Kublai (reigned 1260–94), the separate parts of the empire went their separate ways and soon began to break up internally as subject peoples asserted their independence once again.

DECLINE OF STEPPE POWER

The most important subject people to rise against the Mongol yoke were the Chinese. Rebellions broke out in the south and became so threatening that the remnant of the Mongol army withdrew to the steppe in 1368, intending to reconquer China with help from the distant Golden Horde of Russia. That never happened, but the Mongols did remain a formidable foe for the new Ming dynasty (1368–1644) and in 1449 actually captured a Chinese emperor who had inadvisedly ventured deep into the steppe.

In the Western Steppe, tribal patterns reasserted themselves within the framework of Mongol administration, so hereditary status once again made political confederations precarious. Sometimes a charismatic leader like Timur (died 1405) was able to gather a new confederacy under his banner and terrify the world again; but all such structures were short-lived. More significant were tribal confederations that espoused a special religious faith, such as the followers of Esmāʿīl I, who in 1501 founded a regime that consolidated its power over Iran and part of Iraq in the name of a sectarian version of Shīʿah Islām. The incandescence of Esmāʿīl's faith allowed him to bind nomad tribesmen and believing city folk together into a new and enduring amalgam from which the special character of contemporary Iran descends.

Resurgence under Timur

Yet these and other manifestations of the political-military power that steppe peoples could exert were no more than receding surges of a diminishing tide. In retrospect it is clear that the Mongol Empire constituted the apex of steppe history. The fundamental register of this fact was the slackening of human migration from the steppe—a pattern that had played such a dominating role in Eurasian history since 2000 BC. Recurrent exposure to plague, as a result of the spread of bubonic infection among burrowing rodents of the steppe, may have diminished steppe populations drastically. This is not attested in any known records; all that is sure is that bubonic plague invaded Europe and the Middle East in 1347 via the steppe. Moreover, as late as the 18th century outbreaks of plague in Mediterranean ports continued to occur in connection with the arrival of caravans from the interior. Further indirect evidence of demographic disaster on the steppe in the 14th and 15th centuries is the almost total lack of habitation found on the rich pastures of the Ukraine when settlers from the Russian forestlands began to move southward in the early 16th century. A remnant of the tribesmen who had once pastured their animals in the Ukraine had withdrawn into the Crimean Peninsula, where they retained their political identity as subject-allies of the Ottoman Empire until 1783. Other nomads tended their flocks and herds along the Volga, leaving Eurasia's

The role of the plague

best pasturelands unoccupied. Some catastrophe seems necessary to explain such behaviour; and the fact that rodents in the Ukraine and in Manchuria were discovered to be chronic carriers of bubonic infection in the 20th century suggests what may have happened to steppe populations in the 14th and subsequent centuries.

Whether or not the forays of Mongol horsemen into plague regions of Burma and Yunnan resulted in the transfer of bubonic infection to their native steppe lands at the end of the 13th century, a second by-product of their restless pursuit of military efficiency certainly did contribute in the long run to the overthrow of steppe power. Mongol armies learned about gunpowder from the Chinese and carried it with them for use in sieges wherever they went. Hence after the 14th century both European and Chinese artificers were able to begin elaboration of more and more efficient guns. By about 1650 handguns had become powerful enough to make nomad bows obsolete. Nomads found it hard to acquire guns and harder still to maintain a stock of powder and shot for the guns. Hence their accustomed advantage vis-à-vis infantrymen was undermined when gunfire became decisive on the battlefield, as it did throughout Eurasia by the beginning of the 18th century.

Before nomad military resources suffered this final blow, China experienced another and final conquest from the steppe, when Manchu armies overthrew the Ming dynasty in 1644. The new rulers of China quickly proceeded to extend their power into the Mongolian steppe, where they encountered agents of the Russian tsar. The Russians had begun to overrun the steppe and forest peoples of northern Eurasia after 1480, when the Grand Duke of Moscow formally renounced the suzerainty of the Golden Horde. By 1556 Russian soldiers controlled the length of the Volga. Others crossed the Urals and as early as 1639 had penetrated all the way to the Pacific. Russian and Chinese diplomats therefore had to begin demarcating a border between their respective spheres of influence on the Eastern Steppe as early as 1689; but a definitive border was not achieved until late in the 19th century when Russian soldiers pushed southward in Central Asia to the borders of Afghanistan, while recognizing Chinese authority over adjacent Sinkiang Uighur.

Russian and Chinese advances

Russian and Chinese victories over the steppe nomads and the rulers of Central Asian oases depended on the superiority of firearms wielded by bureaucratically organized armies. The Russian advance also depended on a demographic upsurge that provided a stream of settlers to move out into the steppe lands of the Ukraine and Siberia, beginning about 1550. This agricultural tide continued to advance as recently as the 1950s, when millions of acres in Kazakhstan were put to the plow for the first time, in the hope of increasing Soviet grain harvests.

The Eastern Steppe offered less opportunity for cultivation, except in Manchuria. There, however, the Ch'ing dynasty forbade Chinese settlement until 1912, when the collapse of their rule opened Manchuria to a wave of Chinese settlers. Pioneers from China's crowded hinterland soon brought all of Manchuria's readily cultivable land under crops. As a result, by the 1950s agriculture had reached, or perhaps exceeded, its climatic limits throughout the Eurasian steppe lands, spelling the final eclipse of steppe peoples as a serious factor in world affairs. Some nomadic tribes continue to wrest a hard living from marginal grasslands in Outer Mongolia and other parts of Asia; but the handful who still follow a pastoral mode of existence are no more than a tattered remnant of the steppe peoples who for millennia had played a leading role in Eurasia's political and military history.

BIBLIOGRAPHY. LUC KWANTEN, *Imperial Nomads: A History of Central Asia, 500–1500* (1979), is a compendium of scholarly debate; RENE GROUSSET, *L'Empire des steppes: Attila, Gengis-Khan, Tamerlan* (1939; *The Empire of the Steppes: A History of Central Asia,* 1970), and WILLIAM MCGOVERN, *The Early Settlers of Central Asia* (1939), offer somewhat old-fashioned accounts. OWEN LATTIMORE, *Inner Asian Frontiers of China* (1940), provides a geographically sensitive and firsthand description of that borderland; nothing comparable exists for the rest of the steppe frontier on cultivated lands. For bubonic plague and the decline of the steppe peoples, see W.H. MCNEILL, *Plagues and Peoples* (1976). (W.H.McN.)

Subatomic Particles

Subatomic particles are, literally, particles that are smaller than atoms. The physical study of such particles became possible only during the 20th century, with the development of increasingly sophisticated apparatus to probe matter at scales of 10^{-15} metre and less; yet the basic philosophy of the subject now known as subatomic particle physics dates to at least 500 BC when the Greek philosopher Leucippus and his pupil Democritus put forward the notion that matter consists of invisibly small, indivisible particles, which they called atoms. For more than 2,000 years, however, the idea of atoms lay largely neglected, while the opposing view that matter consists of four elements—earth, fire, air, and water—held sway.

It was in the early years of the 19th century that the atomic theory of matter returned to favour, strengthened in particular by the work of John Dalton, an English chemist, whose studies suggested that each chemical element consists of its own unique kind of atom. As such, Dalton's atoms are still the atoms of modern physics. By the close of the century, however, the first indications began to emerge that atoms are not indivisible, as Leucippus and Democritus had imagined, but that they instead contain smaller subatomic particles.

In 1896 the French physicist Henri Becquerel discovered radioactivity, and in the following year J.J. Thomson, a professor of physics at Cambridge University, England, demonstrated the existence of tiny particles much smaller in mass than hydrogen, the lightest atom. Thomson had discovered the first subatomic particle, the electron. Six years later, Ernest Rutherford and Frederick Soddy, working at McGill University in Montreal, found that radioactivity occurs when atoms of one type transmute into those of another kind. The idea of atoms as immutable, indivisible objects had become completely untenable.

The basic structure of the atom became apparent in 1911, when Rutherford, who had moved to Manchester University, showed that most of the mass of an atom lies concentrated at its centre, in a tiny nucleus. Rutherford postulated that the atom resembled a miniature solar system, with light, negatively charged electrons orbiting around the dense, positively charged nucleus, just as the planets orbit around the Sun. The Danish theorist Niels Bohr soon refined this model by incorporating the new ideas of quantization that had been developed by the German physicist Max Planck at the turn of the century. Planck had theorized that electromagnetic radiation, such as light, occurs in discrete bundles, or "quanta," of energy known as photons. By 1913, Bohr's theory of the atom already incorporated some of the basic elements of modern ideas about subatomic particles.

This article discusses the further development of subatomic particle theory, the various classes of subatomic particles, and current areas of research. See also the articles ATOMS; PHYSICAL PRINCIPLES AND CONCEPTS; MECHANICS; and RADIATION for additional information on the interactions of subatomic particles and on their role in the structure of matter. For specific details on the detection and measurement of subatomic particles, see PARTICLE ACCELERATORS and ANALYSIS AND MEASUREMENT, PHYSICAL AND CHEMICAL.

For coverage of related topics in the *Macropædia* and *Micropædia,* see the *Propædia,* section 112.

The article is divided into the following sections:

BASIC CONCEPTS

Subatomic particles play two vital roles in the structure of matter. They are both the basic building blocks of the universe and the mortar that binds the blocks together. Although the particles that fulfill these different roles are of two distinct types, they do share some common characteristics, foremost of which is size.

Subatomic particles are very small. The particles that inhabit the nucleus, for example, are called nucleons. Nucleons can be either positively charged protons or electrically neutral neutrons. A single nucleon has a diameter of about 10^{-15} metre (a distance known as a fermi in honour of the Italian physicist Enrico Fermi, who did much experimental and theoretical work on understanding the nature of the nucleus and its contents). In comparison an atom is typically 10^{-10} metre across, and the distance across an atomic nucleus of average size is roughly $^{1}/_{10,000}$ the diameter of an atom, or 10^{-14} metre.

The sizes of atoms, nuclei, and nucleons are measured by firing a beam of electrons at an appropriate target. The higher the energy of the electrons, the farther they penetrate before being deflected by the electric charges within the atom. A beam with an energy of a few hundred electron volts (eV), for example, scatters from the electrons in an atom. The way in which the beam is scattered can then be studied to determine the general distribution of the atomic electrons.

At energies of a few hundred megaelectron volts (MeV; 10^6 eV), electrons in the beam are little affected by atomic electrons; they penetrate the atom and are scattered by the positive nucleus. Therefore, if such a beam is fired at liquid hydrogen, whose atoms contain only single protons in their nuclei, the pattern of scattered electrons reveals the size of the proton. At energies greater than a gigaelectron volt (GeV; 10^9 eV), the electrons penetrate within the protons and neutrons, and their scattering patterns indicate an inner structure. Thus, protons and neutrons are no more indivisible than atoms are; instead, they contain still smaller particles, which are called quarks.

Elementary particles. Quarks are as small as or smaller than physicists can measure. In experiments at very high energies, equivalent to accelerating electrons to nearly 1,000 GeV, quarks appear to behave as points in space, with no measurable size; they must therefore be smaller than 10^{-18} metre, or less than one-thousandth the size of the individual nucleons they form. Similar experiments show that electrons, too, are smaller than it is possible to measure.

Electrons and quarks contain no discernible structure; they cannot be reduced or separated into smaller components. It is therefore reasonable to call them "elementary" particles, a name that in the past was mistakenly given to particles such as the proton, which is in fact a complex particle that contains quarks. The term subatomic particle refers both to the true elementary particles, such as quarks and electrons, and to the larger particles that quarks form.

Although both are elementary particles, electrons and quarks differ in some respects. Whereas quarks together form nucleons within the atomic nucleus, the electrons generally circulate toward the periphery of atoms. Indeed, electrons are regarded as distinct from quarks and are classified in a separate group of elementary particles called leptons. There are several types of lepton, just as there are several types of quark (see below). Only two types of quark are contained within protons and neutrons, however, and these together with the electron and one other elementary particle are all the "blocks" that are necessary to build the everyday world. The last block required is an electrically neutral particle called the neutrino.

Neutrinos

Neutrinos do not exist within atoms in the sense that electrons do, but they play a crucial role in certain types of radioactive decay. In the basic process of one type of radioactivity, known as beta decay, a neutron changes into a proton. In making this change, the neutron increases its electric charge by one unit. To keep the overall charge constant, and thereby conform to the fundamental physical law of charge conservation, the neutron must emit a negatively charged electron. In addition, according to the fundamental law of energy conservation, the sum of the energies of the final particles must equal the energy of the initial particle. The combined energy of the electron and proton is less than the energy of the neutron, however, because the neutron emits not only an electron but also a neutrino, which has little or no mass but does have energy. Beta decays are important in the transitions that occur when unstable atomic nuclei change to become more stable, and for this reason neutrinos are a necessary component in establishing the nature of matter.

The neutrino, like the electron, is classified as a lepton. Thus it seems, at first sight, that only four kinds of elementary particles—two quarks and two leptons—should exist. In the 1930s, however, long before the concept of quarks was established, it became clear that matter is more complicated.

Spin. The success of Bohr's model of the atom and its implementation of quantization led during the 1920s to the development of quantum mechanics, which appeared to provide physicists with the correct method of calculating the structure of the atom. In his model, Bohr had taken Planck's ideas of quantization a step further by postulating that the electrons in the atom move only in orbits in which the angular momentum (angular velocity multiplied by mass) has certain fixed values. Each of these allowed values is characterized by a quantum number that can have only integer values. In the full quantum mechanical treatment, developed in the 1920s, three quantum numbers relating to angular momentum arise because there are three independent variable parameters in the equation describing the motion of atomic electrons.

In 1925, however, two Dutch physicists, Samuel Goudsmit and George Uhlenbeck, realized that in order to explain fully the spectra of light emitted by the atoms of alkali metals, such as sodium, which have one outer electron beyond the main "core," there must be a fourth quantum number that can take only two values, $-1/2$ and $+1/2$. Goudsmit and Uhlenbeck proposed that this quantum number refers to an internal angular momentum, or spin, that the electrons possess. This implies that the electrons, in effect, behave like spinning electric charges. Each therefore creates a magnetic field and has its own magnetic moment. The internal magnet of an atomic electron orients itself in one of two directions with respect to the magnetic field due to the rest of the atom. It is either parallel or antiparallel; hence, there are two quantized states—and two possible values of the associated spin quantum number.

Antiparticles. Two years after the work of Goudsmit and Uhlenbeck, the English theorist P.A.M. Dirac provided a sound theoretical background for the concept of electron spin when he introduced the German physicist Albert Einstein's special theory of relativity into quantum mechanics in order to describe the behaviour of an electron in an electromagnetic field. Dirac's relativistic theory showed that the electron must have spin and a magnetic moment, but it also made what seemed a strange prediction. The basic equation describing the allowed energies for an electron would admit two solutions, one positive and one negative. The positive solution apparently described normal electrons. The negative solution was more of a mystery; it seemed to describe electrons with positive, rather than negative, charge.

The positron

The mystery was resolved in 1932, when Carl Anderson, an American physicist, discovered the particle called the positron. Positrons are very much like electrons: they have the same mass and the same spin but opposite electric charge. Positrons, then, are the particles predicted by Dirac's theory, and they were the first example of the so-called antiparticles to be discovered. Dirac's theory, in fact, applies to any subatomic particle with spin $1/2$; therefore all spin-$1/2$ particles should have corresponding antiparticles. Matter cannot be built from both particles and antiparticles, however. When a particle meets an appropriate antiparticle, the two disappear in an act of mutual destruction known as annihilation. Atoms can exist only because there is an excess of electrons and protons in the everyday world, with no corresponding positrons and antiprotons.

Positrons do occur naturally, however, which is how Anderson discovered their existence. High-energy subatomic particles—cosmic rays—rain down on the Earth's atmosphere from outer space, colliding with atomic nuclei to generate showers of particles that cascade toward the ground. In these showers, the enormous energy of the incoming cosmic ray is converted to matter, in accordance with Einstein's special theory of relativity, which states that $E = mc^2$, where E is energy, m is mass, and c is the velocity of light. Among the particles created are pairs of electrons and positrons (see Figure 1). The positrons survive until they come close enough to electrons to annihilate. The total mass of each electron-positron pair is then converted to energy, in the form of a gamma-ray photon.

Using particle accelerators, physicists can mimic the ac-

By courtesy of the Lawrence Berkeley Laboratory

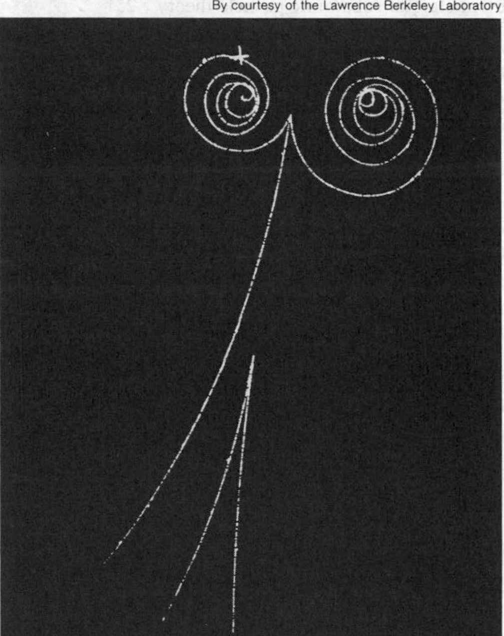

Figure 1: Electrons and positrons produced simultaneously from individual gamma rays curl in opposite directions in the magnetic field of a bubble chamber. In the top example, the gamma ray has lost some energy to an atomic electron, which leaves the long track, curling left. The gamma rays do not leave tracks in the chamber, as they have no electric charge.

tion of cosmic rays, creating collisions at high energy. In 1955 a team led by the Italian scientist Emilio Segrè and the American Owen Chamberlain found the first evidence for the existence of antiprotons in the collisions of high-energy protons produced by the Bevatron, an accelerator at what is now the Lawrence Berkeley Laboratory, in California. Shortly afterward, a different team working on the same accelerator discovered the antineutron.

THE PRESENT STATE OF SUBATOMIC PARTICLE THEORY

Since the 1950s physicists have discovered that protons and neutrons consist of quarks with spin $^1/_2$ and that antiprotons and antineutrons consist of antiquarks. Neutrinos, too, have spin $^1/_2$ and corresponding antineutrinos. Indeed, it is an antineutrino, rather than a neutrino, that emerges when a neutron changes by beta decay into a proton. This reflects a basic law of nature regarding the production and decay of quarks and leptons: in any interaction the total number of quarks and leptons must separately remain constant. Thus, the appearance of a lepton—the electron—in the decay of a neutron must be balanced by the simultaneous appearance of an antilepton, in this case the antineutrino.

Conservation of quarks and leptons

In addition to such familiar particles as the nucleons and the electron, studies have slowly revealed the existence of more than 200 other subatomic particles. These "extra" particles do not appear in the low-energy environment of everyday human experience; they emerge only at the higher energies found in cosmic rays or particle accelerators. Moreover, they soon decay to the more familiar particles after brief lifetimes of only fractions of a second. The variety and behaviour of these extra particles initially bewildered scientists but have since come to be understood in terms of the quarks and leptons. In fact, only six quarks, six leptons, and their corresponding antiparticles seem to be necessary to explain the variety and behaviour of all the subatomic particles, including those that form normal atomic matter.

These quarks and leptons are the building blocks of matter, but they require some sort of mortar to bind themselves together into more complex forms, whether on a nuclear or a universal scale. The particles that provide this mortar are associated with four basic forces.

On the largest scales, the dominant force is gravity, which governs the aggregation of matter to form stars and galaxies and which influences the way that the universe is evolving from its initial big bang. The best understood force, however, is the electromagnetic force, which underlies the related phenomena of electricity and magnetism. The electromagnetic force binds negatively charged electrons to positively charged atomic nuclei and gives rise to the bonding between atoms to form matter in bulk.

Both gravity and electromagnetism are well known at the macroscopic level. The other two forces act only on subatomic scales, indeed on subnuclear scales. The strong nuclear force keeps quarks bound together within protons, neutrons, and other subatomic particles; and rather as the electromagnetic force is ultimately responsible for holding bulk matter together, so the strong nuclear force keeps protons and neutrons together within atomic nuclei. The fourth force is the weak nuclear force. Unlike the strong force, which acts only between quarks, the weak force acts on both quarks and leptons. This is the force that is responsible for the beta decay of a neutron into a proton and for the nuclear reactions that fuel the Sun and other stars.

Since the 1930s physicists have recognized that they can use field theory for all the four basic forces. In mathematical terms, a field describes something that varies continuously through space and time. A familiar example is the field that surrounds a piece of magnetized iron. The magnetic field maps the way that the force varies in strength and direction around the magnet. The appropriate fields for the four basic forces appear to have an important property in common: they all exhibit what is known as gauge symmetry. Put simply, this means that certain changes can be made that do not affect the basic structure of the field. It also implies that the relevant physical laws are the same in different regions of space and time.

At a subatomic, quantum level, these field theories display a significant feature. They describe the action of a force in terms of subatomic particles, called gauge bosons, which in a sense carry the force. These particles differ from the building blocks—the quarks and leptons—by having integer values of the spin quantum number, rather than a value of $^1/_2$. The most familiar gauge boson is the photon, which transmits the electromagnetic force between electrically charged objects, such as the electrons and protons within the atom. The photon acts as a private, invisible messenger between these particles, influencing their behaviour with the information it conveys, rather as a ball influences the actions of children playing catch. Other gauge bosons, with varying properties, are involved with the other basic forces.

Gauge bosons

In developing a gauge theory for the weak nuclear force in the 1960s, physicists discovered that the best theory, which would always yield sensible answers, must also incorporate the electromagnetic force. The result was what is now called electroweak theory. It was the first workable example of a unified theory linking forces that manifest themselves differently in the everyday world. The unified theory reveals the outwardly diverse forces as separate facets of a single underlying force. The search for a unified theory of everything, which incorporates all four fundamental forces, is one of the major goals of particle physics. It is leading theorists to an exciting area of study that involves not only subatomic particle physics but also cosmology and astrophysics.

THE BASIC FORCES AND THEIR MESSENGER PARTICLES

Gravity. The weakest, and yet the most pervasive, of the four basic forces is gravity. It acts on all forms of mass and energy and thus acts on all subatomic particles, including the gauge bosons that carry the forces. The 17th-century English scientist Isaac Newton was the first to develop a quantitative description of the force of gravity. He argued that the force which binds the Moon in orbit around the Earth is the same force which makes apples and other objects fall to the ground, and he proposed a universal law of gravitation.

According to Newton's law, all bodies are attracted to each other by a force that depends directly on the mass of each body and inversely on the square of the distance between them. For a pair of masses, m_1 and m_2, a distance r apart, the strength of the force, F, is given by $F = Gm_1m_2/r^2$. G is called the constant of gravitation and is equal to 6.67×10^{-11} newton-metre^2-kilogram^{-2}.

The constant G gives a measure of the strength of the gravitational force, and its smallness indicates that gravity is weak. Indeed, on the scale of atoms the effects of gravity are negligible compared with the other forces at work. To compare the strengths of the different forces, physicists prefer to use constants that have no dimensions. For gravity, the appropriate pure number is given by the product of G and the square of the mass of the proton, divided by two other fundamental constants of nature, the velocity of light and Planck's constant. The result is about 5×10^{-39}, a very small number that reflects the relative weakness of the gravitational force on the atomic scale.

Although the gravitational force is weak, its effects can be extremely long-ranging. Newton's law shows that at some distance the gravitational force between two bodies becomes negligible but that this distance depends on the masses involved. Thus, the gravitational effects of large, massive objects can be considerable, even at distances far outside the range of the other forces. The gravitational force of the Earth, for example, keeps the Moon in orbit some 384,400 kilometres distant.

The range of the gravitational force

Newton's theory of gravity proves adequate for many applications. In 1915, however, Einstein developed the general theory of relativity, which incorporates the concept of gauge symmetry and yields subtle corrections to Newtonian gravity. Despite its importance, Einstein's general relativity remains a classical theory in the sense that it does not incorporate the ideas of quantum mechanics. In a quantum theory of gravity, the gravitational force must be carried by a suitable messenger particle, or gauge boson. No workable quantum theory of gravity has yet been developed, but general relativity determines some of

Table 1: The Four Basic Forces

name	acts on:	particles of exchange	range	strength	examples: stable systems	examples: reaction induced by force
Gravity	all particles*	proposed graviton, g	long; *i.e.*, $F \propto 1/r^2$	$\sim 10^{-39}$	solar system	object falling
Weak nuclear force	all particles except γ	weak bosons, W and Z	$<10^{-17}$ m	10^{-5}	none	neutron beta decay
Electromagnetism	particles with electric charge	photon, γ	long; *i.e.*, $F \propto 1/r^2$	1/137	atoms, rocks	chemical reactions
Strong nuclear force	quarks and gluons	gluons, g	10^{-15} m	1	hadrons, nuclei	nuclear reactions

*Because all particles have energy or rest mass.

the properties of the graviton, the hypothesized particle of gravity. In particular, it must have a spin quantum number of 2 and no mass, only energy.

Electromagnetism. The first proper understanding of the electromagnetic force dates to the 18th century, when a French physicist, Charles Coulomb, showed that the electrostatic force between electrically charged objects follows a law similar to Newton's law of gravitation. Coulomb found that the force F between one charge q_1 and a second charge q_2 is equal to the product of the charges divided by the square of the distance r between them, or $F = q_1q_2/r^2$. The force can be either attractive or repulsive, because the source of the force, electric charge, exists in two varieties, positive and negative. The force between opposite charges is attractive, whereas bodies with the same kind of charge experience a repulsive force. Coulomb also showed that the force between magnetized bodies varies inversely as the square of the distance between them. Again, the force can be attractive (opposite poles) or repulsive (like poles).

Magnetism and electricity are not separate phenomena; they are the related manifestations of an underlying electromagnetic force. Experiments in the early 19th century by, among others, Hans Ørsted (in Denmark), André-Marie Ampère (in France), and Michael Faraday (in England) revealed the intimate connection between electricity and magnetism and how the one can give rise to the other. The results of these experiments were synthesized in the 1850s by the Scottish physicist James Clerk Maxwell in his electromagnetic theory. Maxwell's theory predicted the existence of electromagnetic waves—undulations in intertwined electric and magnetic fields, traveling with the velocity of light.

Maxwell's electromagnetic theory

Planck's work at the turn of the century, in which he explained the spectrum of radiation from a perfect emitter, led to the concept of quantization and photons. In the quantum picture, electromagnetic radiation has a dual nature, existing both as Maxwell's waves and as streams of particles called photons. The quantum nature of electromagnetic radiation is encapsulated in quantum electrodynamics, the quantum field theory of the electromagnetic force. Both Maxwell's classical theory and the quantized version contain gauge symmetry, which now appears to be a basic feature of the fundamental forces.

The pure number that characterizes the strength of the electromagnetic force is given by $e^2/\hbar c$, where e is the electric charge of the electron (or proton), $\hbar$ is Planck's constant divided by 2π, and c is the velocity of light. The result, known as the fine structure constant because of its relationship to certain effects in atomic spectra, is approximately $^1/_{137}$. It shows that the electromagnetic force is intrinsically much stronger than the gravitational force—some 10^{36} times as strong. At an atomic level the electromagnetic force is almost completely in control; gravity dominates on a large scale only because matter as a whole is electrically neutral.

The gauge boson of electromagnetism is the photon, which has zero mass and a spin quantum number of 1. Photons are exchanged whenever electrically charged subatomic particles interact. The photon has no electric charge, so it does not experience the electromagnetic force itself—in other words, photons cannot interact with one another. Photons do carry energy and momentum, however, and in transmitting these properties between particles they produce the effects known as electromagnetism.

In these processes, energy and momentum are conserved overall (the totals remain the same in accordance with the basic laws of physics); but at the instant one particle emits a photon and another particle absorbs it, energy is not conserved. Quantum mechanics allows this imbalance provided that the photon fulfills the conditions of Heisenberg's uncertainty principle. This rule, described in 1927 by the German scientist Werner Heisenberg, states that it is in principle not possible to know all the details about a particular quantum system. For example, if the exact position of an electron is identified, it is impossible to be certain of the electron's momentum. This fundamental uncertainty allows a discrepancy in energy, ΔE, to exist for a time, Δt, provided that the product of ΔE and Δt is very small—less than the value of Planck's constant (6.6×10^{-34} joule seconds) divided by 2π, or 1.05×10^{-34} joule seconds. The energy of the messenger can thus be thought of as "borrowed," within the limits of the uncertainty principle (*i.e.*, the more energy borrowed, the shorter the time of the loan). Such borrowed photons are called virtual photons to distinguish them from the real photons, which constitute electromagnetic radiation and can in principle exist forever. This concept of virtual particles in processes that fulfill the conditions of the uncertainty principle applies to the exchange of other gauge bosons as well.

Virtual particles

The weak nuclear force. Since the 1930s physicists have been aware of a force within the atomic nucleus that is responsible for certain types of radioactivity which are classed together as beta decay. A typical example of beta decay occurs when a neutron transmutes into a proton. The force that underlies this process is known as the weak nuclear force to distinguish it from the strong nuclear force that binds quarks together (see below).

The correct gauge field theory for the weak nuclear force incorporates the quantum field theory of electromagnetism (quantum electrodynamics) and is called electroweak theory. It treats the weak nuclear and electromagnetic forces on an equal footing by regarding them as different manifestations of a more fundamental electroweak force, rather as electricity and magnetism appear as different aspects of the electromagnetic force.

The electroweak theory requires four gauge bosons. One of these is the photon of electromagnetism; the other three are involved in reactions that occur via the weak force. These weak gauge bosons include two electrically charged versions, called W^+ and W^-, where the signs indicate the type of charge, and a neutral variety called Z^0, where the zero indicates zero charge. Like the photon, the W and Z particles have a spin quantum number of 1; unlike the

Table 2: Gauge Bosons

symbol	spin	mass (GeV)	mean life (s)	typical decays	name
γ	1	0	stable	—	photon
$W^{\pm}$	1	81,800	10^{-25}	$\rightarrow e\nu$,	W
Z^0	1	92,600	10^{-25}	$\rightarrow e^+e^-$	Z
g	1	0	stable	—	gluon
g	2*	0	stable	—	graviton

*Deduced from general relativity; there is no direct evidence for the graviton.

photon, they are very massive. The W particles weigh 81.8 GeV, while the mass of the Z^0 is about 92.6 GeV. By comparison, the mass of the proton is 0.94 GeV, or one-hundredth that of the Z particle.

The charged W particles are responsible for processes, such as beta decay, in which the charge of the participating particles changes hands. For example, when a neutron transmutes into a proton, it emits a W^-; thus the overall charge remains zero before and after the decay process. The W particle involved in this process is a virtual particle. Because its mass is far greater than that of the neutron, the only way that it can be emitted by the lightweight neutron is for its existence to be fleetingly short, within the requirements of the uncertainty principle. Indeed, the W^- immediately transforms into an electron and an antineutrino, the particles that are observed in the laboratory as the products of neutron beta decay. Z particles are exchanged in similar reactions that involve no change in charge.

In the everyday world, the weak nuclear force is weaker than the electromagnetic force but stronger than the gravitational force. Its range, however, is very short. Because of the large amounts of energy needed to create the large masses of the W and Z particles, the uncertainty principle ensures that a weak gauge boson cannot be borrowed for long, which limits the range of the force to distances less than 10^{-17} metre. In terms of a pure number, the weak nuclear force couples to protons with a strength of about $^1/_{100,000}$ or 10^{-5}. As the electroweak theory reveals and as experiments confirm, however, this weak nuclear force becomes slowly stronger as the energies of the participating particles increase. When the energies reach 100 GeV or so—roughly the energy equivalent to the mass of the W and Z particles—the strength of the weak nuclear force becomes comparable to that of the electromagnetic force. This means that reactions that involve the exchange of a Z^0 become as common as those in which a photon is exchanged. It also means that real W and Z particles, as opposed to virtual ones, can be created in high-energy reactions.

Unlike the photon, which is stable and can in principle live forever, the heavy weak gauge bosons decay to lighter particles within an extremely brief lifetime of about 10^{-24} second. This is roughly a million million times shorter than experiments can measure, but physicists can detect the particles into which the W and Z particles decay and so can infer their existence (see Figure 2).

David Parker/Science Photo Library—Photo Researchers

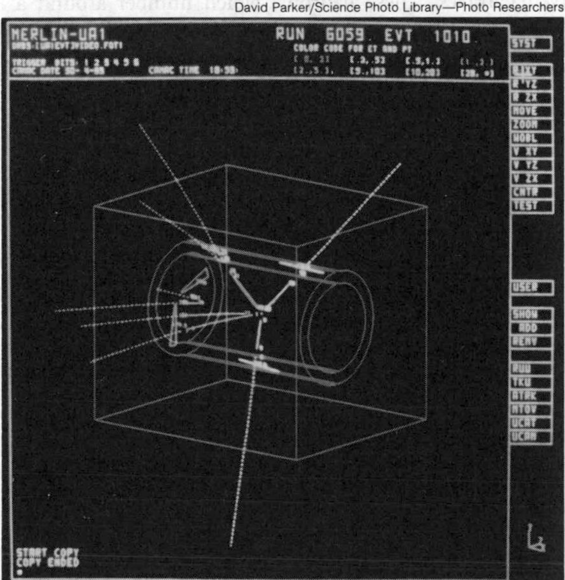

Figure 2: Tracks emerging from a proton-antiproton collision at the centre of the UA1 detector at CERN include those of an energetic electron (straight down) and a positron (upper right). These two particles have come from the decay of a Z^0; when their energies are added together the total is equal to the Z^0's mass.

The strong nuclear force. Although the aptly named strong nuclear force is the strongest of all the fundamental forces, it, like the weak nuclear force, is short-ranged and is ineffective much beyond nuclear distances of 10^{-15} metre or so. Within the nucleus and, more specifically, within the protons and other particles that are built from quarks, however, the strong nuclear force rules supreme; it is typically 100 times stronger than the electromagnetic force, and its strength is characterized by a pure number with the value 1.

Gluons

During the 1970s physicists developed a theory for the strong nuclear force that is similar in structure to quantum electrodynamics. In this theory, quarks are bound together by exchanging gauge bosons called gluons. The quarks carry a property called colour that is analogous to electric charge. Just as electrically charged particles experience the electromagnetic force and exchange photons, so colour-charged, or coloured, particles feel the strong nuclear force and exchange gluons. This property of colour gives rise in part to the name of the theory of the strong nuclear force: quantum chromodynamics.

Gluons are massless and have a spin quantum number of 1. In this respect they are much like photons, but they differ from photons in one crucial way. Whereas photons do not interact among themselves—because they are not electrically charged—gluons do carry colour charge. This means that gluons can interact together, which has an important effect in limiting the range of gluons and in confining quarks within protons and other particles.

The three types of colour charge are called red, green, and blue, although there is no connection between the colour charge of quarks and gluons and colour in the usual sense. Quarks each carry a single colour charge, while gluons carry both a colour and an anticolour charge.

The strong nuclear force acts in such a way that quarks of different colour are attracted to one another; thus, red attracts green, blue attracts red, and so on. Quarks of the same colour, on the other hand, repel each other. The quarks can combine only in ways that give a net colour charge of zero. In particles, such as protons, that contain three quarks, this is achieved by adding red, blue, and green. An alternative, observed in particles called mesons (see below), is for a quark to couple with an antiquark of the same basic colour. In this case, the colour of the quark and the anticolour of the antiquark cancel each other out. These combinations of three quarks (or antiquarks) and quark-antiquark pairs are the only combinations that the strong nuclear force seems to allow.

The constraint that only colourless objects can appear in nature seems to limit attempts to observe single quarks and free gluons. Although a quark can radiate a real gluon just as an electron can radiate a real photon, the gluon never emerges on its own into the surrounding environment. Instead, it somehow creates additional gluons, quarks, and antiquarks from its own energy and materializes as normal particles built from quarks (see Figure 3). Similarly, it appears that the strong nuclear force keeps quarks permanently confined within larger particles. Attempts to knock quarks out of protons by, for example, knocking protons together at high energies only succeed in creating more particles—that is, in releasing new quarks and antiquarks that are bound together and are themselves confined by the strong nuclear force.

LEPTONS AND ANTILEPTONS

The electron is the component of atoms that makes interatomic bonding and chemical reactions—and hence life—possible. Probably the most familiar subatomic particle, the electron was also the first to be discovered. Its negative charge of 1.6×10^{-19} coulomb seems to be the basic unit of electric charge, although theorists have a poor understanding of what determines this particular size.

Physicists classify the electron as a type of lepton. Leptons are a group of subatomic particles that do not experience the strong nuclear force. They do, however, feel the weak nuclear force and the gravitational force; and electrically charged leptons interact via the electromagnetic force.

The electron, with a mass of 0.511 MeV, is the lightest of the charged leptons. The next heaviest charged lepton

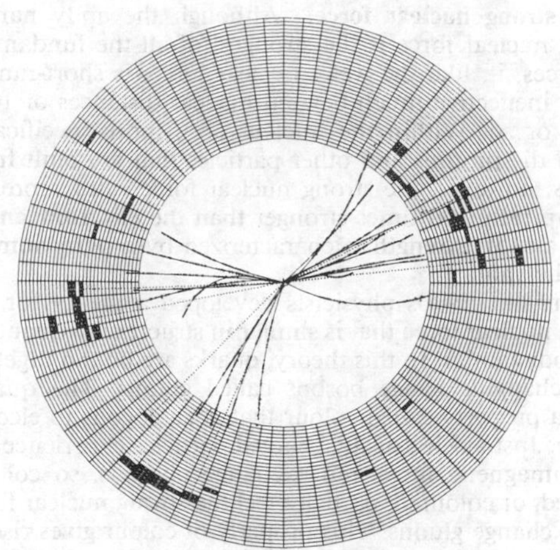

Figure 3: Three "jets" of particles streaming out from an electron-positron collision at the centre of the JADE detector at the DESY laboratory, Hamburg. Two of the jets come from a quark and an antiquark formed in the electron-positron annihilation; the third jet comes from a gluon, radiated by either the quark or the antiquark.
By courtesy of the JADE collaboration

The muon

is the muon. It has a mass of 105 MeV, which is some 200 times greater than the electron's mass but is significantly less than the proton's mass of 938 MeV. Unlike the electron, which appears to be completely stable, the muon decays after an average lifetime of 2.2 microseconds into an electron, a neutrino, and an antineutrino. This process, like the beta decay of a neutron into a proton, an electron, and an antineutrino, occurs via the weak nuclear force. Experiments have shown that the intrinsic strength of the underlying reaction is the same in both kinds of decay, thus revealing that the weak nuclear force acts equally upon leptons (electrons, muons, neutrinos) and quarks (which form neutrons and protons).

Unlike the charged leptons, the neutral neutrinos do not come under the influence of the electromagnetic force. They experience only the weakest two of nature's forces, the weak nuclear force and gravity. For this reason, neutrinos react extremely weakly with matter. They can, for example, pass through the Earth without interacting, which makes it difficult to detect neutrinos and to measure their properties. Thus, even though one experiment has indicated that the neutrino's mass may be around 40 eV, or less than $^1/_{10,000}$ the mass of an electron, the results are questioned by other researchers. Theory does not require the neutrino's mass to be any specific amount, and in the past it was assumed to be zero.

Table 3: Leptons

symbol	spin	mass (MeV)	mean life (s)	typical decays	name
ν_e, ν_μ, ν_τ	½	0?*	stable	—	neutrino
e^-	½	0.5	stable	—	electron
μ^-	½	106	2×10^{-6}	$\rightarrow e\nu_\mu\bar{\nu}_e$	muon
τ^-	½	1,784	3×10^{-13}	$\rightarrow$ hadrons $+ \nu_\tau$	tau

*There is uncertainty as to the precise mass, if any, of the three types of neutrino.

Although electrically neutral, the neutrinos seem to carry an identifying property that associates them specifically with one type of charged lepton. In the example of the muon's decay, the antineutrino produced is not simply the antiparticle of the neutrino. The neutrino carries a muon-type hallmark, while the antineutrino, like the antineutrino emitted when a neutron decays, is always an electron-antineutrino. In interactions with matter, such electron-neutrinos and antineutrinos never produce muons, only electrons. Likewise, muon-neutrinos only give rise to muons, and never to electrons.

The tau

There is a third, heavier type of charged lepton, called the tau. The tau, with a mass of 1,784 MeV, is even heavier than the proton and has a very short lifetime of about 10^{-13} second. Like the electron and the muon, the tau has its associated neutrino.

The tau can decay into a muon, plus a tau-neutrino and a muon-antineutrino; or it can decay directly into an electron, plus a tau-neutrino and an electron-antineutrino. Because the tau is heavy, it can also decay into particles containing quarks. In one example, the tau decays into particles called pi-mesons (see below), which are accompanied by a tau-neutrino.

In summary, there are three types of charged lepton and three types of neutral lepton, together with six related antileptons (see Table 3). In all three cases, the charged lepton has a negative charge while its antiparticle is positively charged. Physicists coined the name lepton from the Greek word for "slender" because, before the discovery of the tau in 1975, it seemed that the leptons were the lightest particles. Although the name is no longer appropriate, it has been retained to describe all spin-½ particles that do not feel the strong nuclear force.

HADRONS

The proton and the neutron are the most common examples of the class of subatomic particles known as hadrons. The name hadron comes from the Greek word for "strong"; it refers to all those particles that are built from quarks and therefore experience the strong nuclear force.

Experiments have revealed a large number of hadrons, of which only the proton appears to be stable. Indeed, even if the proton is not absolutely stable, experiments show that its lifetime is at least in excess of 10^{32} years. In contrast, a single neutron, free from the forces at work within the nucleus, lives an average of 15 minutes before decaying. Within a nucleus, however—even the simple nucleus of deuterium, which consists of one proton and one neutron—the balance of forces is sufficient to prolong the neutron's lifetime so that many nuclei are stable and a large variety of chemical elements exist.

Some hadrons typically exist only 10^{-10} to 10^{-8} second. Fortunately for experimentalists, these particles are usually born in such high-energy collisions that they are moving at velocities close to the speed of light. Their time-scale is therefore "stretched" or "slowed down" so that in the high-speed particle's frame of reference, its lifetime is 10^{-10} second, but in a stationary observer's frame of reference, the particle lives much longer. This effect, known as time dilation in the special theory of relativity, allows stationary particle detectors to record the tracks left by these short-lived particles. These hadrons, which number around a dozen (see Table 4), are usually referred to as stable to distinguish them from still shorter-lived hadrons with lifetimes typically in the region of a mere 10^{-23} second.

Stable hadrons

The stable hadrons usually decay via the weak nuclear force. In some cases they decay by the electromagnetic force, which results in somewhat shorter lifetimes because the electromagnetic force is stronger than the weak nuclear force. The very short-lived hadrons, however, which number 200 or more, decay via the strong nuclear force. This force is so strong that it allows the particles to live only for the amount of time it takes light to cross the particle; the particles decay almost as soon as they are created.

Unstable resonances

These very short-lived particles are called resonances because they are observed as a resonance phenomenon; they are too short-lived to be observed in any other way (see Figure 4). Resonance occurs when a system absorbs more energy than usual because the energy is being supplied at the system's own natural frequency. For example, soldiers break step when they cross a bridge because their rhythmic marching could make the bridge resonate—set it vibrating at its own natural frequency—so that it absorbs enough energy to cause damage.

Subatomic particle resonances occur when the net energy of colliding particles is just sufficient to create the rest mass of the new particle, which the strong nuclear force then breaks apart within 10^{-23} second. The absorption of energy, or its subsequent emission in the form of particles as the resonance decays, is revealed as the energy of the colliding particles is varied.

The hadrons, whether stable or resonant states, fall into

Table 4: Stable Hadrons

symbol	spin	mass (MeV)	mean life (s)	typical decays	name
Mesons (Baryon number $B = 0$)					
$\pi^{\pm}$		140	3×10^{-8}	$\rightarrow \mu^{\pm} \nu_{\mu}$	pion
π^0		135	1×10^{-16}	$\rightarrow \gamma\gamma$	
$K^{\pm}$		494	1×10^{-8}	$\rightarrow \mu^{\pm} \nu_{\mu}$	kaon
K^0		498	$\begin{cases} 1 \times 10^{-10} \\ 5 \times 10^{-8} \end{cases}$	$K_S \rightarrow 2\pi$* $K_L \rightarrow 3\pi$*	
$D^{\pm}$	0	1,869	9×10^{-13}	$\rightarrow K^0 + \ldots$	D
D^0		1,865	4×10^{-13}	$\rightarrow K^0 + \ldots$	
D_S^+		1,971	3×10^{-13}	$\rightarrow \varphi\pi$	D_S
$B^{\pm}$		5,271	1×10^{-12}	$\rightarrow D^0\pi^+$	B
B^0		5,275	1×10^{-12}	$\rightarrow D^0\pi^+\pi^-$	
Baryons (Baryon number $B = 1$)					
p		938	stable†		proton
n		940	1×10^3	$\rightarrow pe^-\bar{\nu}_e$	neutron
Λ		1,116	3×10^{-10}	$\rightarrow p\pi^-$	lambda
Σ^+		1,189	8×10^{-11}	$\rightarrow p\pi^0$	sigma
Σ^0	½	1,193	6×10^{-20}	$\rightarrow \Lambda\gamma$	
Σ^-		1,197	1×10^{-10}	$\rightarrow n\pi^-$	
Ξ^0		1,315	3×10^{-10}	$\rightarrow \Lambda\pi^0$	xi, or cascade
Ξ^-		1,321	2×10^{-10}	$\rightarrow \Lambda\pi^-$	
Ω^-	3/2	1,672	1×10^{-10}	$\rightarrow \Lambda K^-$	omega-minus
Λ_c^+	½	2,281	2×10^{-13}	$\rightarrow \Lambda + \ldots$	lambda-c

*The K^0 and its antiparticle $\bar{K}^0$ mix quantum mechanically to form two physical states, K_L and K_S. †Could be unstable according to grand unified theories, but experiments show that its lifetime is at least 10^{32} years.

two classes: baryons and mesons. Originally the names referred to the relative masses of the two groups of particles. The baryons (from the Greek word for "heavy") included the proton and heavier particles; the mesons (from the Greek word for "between") were particles with masses between that of the electron and the proton. Now, however, the name baryon refers to any particle built from three quarks, such as the proton and the neutron. Mesons, on the other hand, are particles built from a quark combined with an antiquark. As described above, these are the only two combinations of quarks and antiquarks that the strong nuclear force apparently allows.

The baryons are characterized by a baryon number, B, of 1; antibaryons have a baryon number of −1; and the baryon number of the mesons, leptons, and messenger particles is 0. Baryon numbers are additive; thus, an atom containing one proton and one neutron (each with a baryon number of 1) has a baryon number of 2. Quarks therefore must have a baryon number of ⅓, and the antiquarks a baryon number of −⅓, in order to give the correct values of 1 or 0 when they combine to form baryons and mesons.

Conservation of baryon number

The empirical law of baryon conservation states that in any reaction the total number of baryons must remain constant. If any baryons are created then so must be an equal number of antibaryons, which in principle negate the baryons. Conservation of baryon number explains the apparent stability of the proton. The proton does not decay into lighter positive particles, such as the positron or the mesons, because those particles have a baryon number of 0. Neutrons and other heavy baryons can decay into the lighter protons, however, because the total number of baryons present does not change.

At a more detailed level, baryons and mesons are distinguishable in terms of their spin. The basic quarks have a spin of ½ (which may be oriented in either of two directions). When three quarks combine to form a baryon, their spins can only add up to half-integer values; but when quarks and antiquarks combine to form mesons, their spins always add up to integer values. Table 4 lists the stable baryons and mesons and indicates their spins, as well as some of their other properties.

QUARKS AND ANTIQUARKS

The baryons and mesons are complex subatomic particles that are built from more elementary objects, the quarks. To account for all the hadrons that experiments have revealed, at least five and probably six types of quark are necessary, together with their corresponding antiquarks. The six varieties of quark have acquired unusual names: up, down, charm, strange, top, and bottom. (The top quark is the one whose existence is uncertain.) The meaning of these names is not in itself important; they have arisen for a number of reasons. What is more important is the way that the quarks contribute to matter at different levels and the properties that they bear.

The quarks are unusual in that they carry electric charges that are smaller in magnitude than e, the size of the charge of the electron (1.6×10^{-19} coulomb). This is necessary for the quarks to combine together to form, in particular, the proton. Only two types of quark are necessary to build protons and neutrons, the constituents of atomic

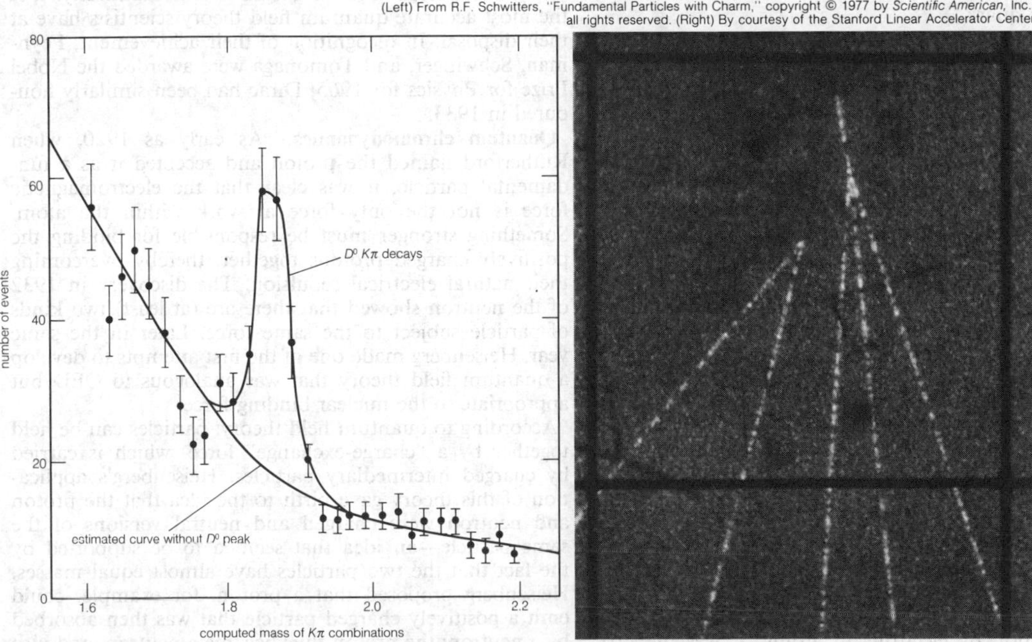

Figure 4: (Left) Graph showing the first clear evidence for the D^0, a neutral charmed meson with a lifetime (4×10^{-13}s) so short that it could at first be detected only as a resonance, here in the total mass-energy of pion-kaon pairs. (Right) The "footprint" of the D^0 in a bubble chamber sensitive enough to reveal its brief life. Because it is neutral, the D^0 leaves no track and is seen as a short gap before it decays into the two charged particles whose tracks form the V on the left.

The up and down quarks

nuclei. These are the up quark, with a charge of $+\frac{2}{3}e$, and the down quark, which has a charge of $-\frac{1}{3}e$. The proton consists of two up quarks and one down quark, giving it a total charge of $+e$. (The positive charge of the proton exactly balances the electron's negative charge, so that matter is neutral overall.) The neutron, on the other hand, is built from one up quark and two down quarks, so that it has a net charge of zero. The other properties of the up and down quarks also add together to give the measured values for the proton and neutron. For example, the quarks have spins of $\frac{1}{2}$. In order to form a proton or a neutron, which also have spin $\frac{1}{2}$, the quarks must align in such a way that two of the three spins cancel each other, leaving a net value of $\frac{1}{2}$.

Up and down quarks can combine to form other particles. For example, the spins of the three quarks can be arranged so that they do not cancel. In this case they form short-lived resonance states, which have been given the name delta, or **Δ**. The deltas have spins of $\frac{3}{2}$, and the up and down quarks combine in four possible configurations—*uuu, uud, udd,* and *ddd*—where *u* and *d* stand for up and down. The charges of these **Δ** states are $+2e$, $+e$, 0, and $-e$, respectively.

The up and down quarks can also combine with their antiquarks to form mesons. The pi-meson, or pion, which is the lightest meson and an important component of cosmic rays, exists in three forms: with charge e (or 1), with charge 0, and with charge $-e$ (or -1). In the positive state, an up quark combines with a down antiquark; a down quark together with an up antiquark compose the negative pion; and the neutral pion is a quantum mechanical mixture of two states—$u\bar{u}$ and $d\bar{d}$, where the bar over the top of the letter indicates the antiquark.

Up and down are the lightest varieties of quarks. Somewhat heavier are a second pair of quarks, charm (*c*) and strange (*s*), with charges of $+\frac{2}{3}$ and $-\frac{1}{3}$, respectively. There also is a still heavier quark, called bottom (or beauty, *b*), with charge $-\frac{1}{3}$. Because the up and down quarks, and the charmed and strange quarks, are pairs, physicists are confident that the bottom quark must also have a partner, with a charge of $+\frac{2}{3}$, and they have named this quark top (or truth, *t*). These heavier quarks and their antiquarks combine with up and down quarks and with each other to produce a range of hadrons, each of which is heavier than the basic proton and pion, which represent the lightest varieties of baryon and meson. There is, however, still no convincing evidence that any hadrons contain a top quark.

THE DEVELOPMENT OF MODERN THEORY

Quantum electrodynamics. The year of the birth of particle physics is often cited as 1932. Near the beginning of that year James Chadwick, working in England at the Cavendish Laboratory in Cambridge, discovered the existence of the neutron. This discovery seemed to complete the picture of atomic structure that had begun with Rutherford's work in 1911. The elementary particles seemed firmly established as the proton, neutron, and electron. By the end of 1932, however, Carl Anderson in the United States had discovered the first antiparticle: the positron, or antielectron. Moreover, Patrick Blackett and Giuseppi Occhialini, working, like Chadwick, at the Cavendish Laboratory, had revealed how positrons and electrons are created in pairs when cosmic rays pass through dense matter. It was becoming apparent that the simple pictures provided by electrons, protons, and neutrons were incomplete and that a new theory was needed to explain fully the phenomena of subatomic particles.

Dirac had provided the foundations for such a theory in 1927 when he wrote his quantum theory of the electromagnetic field. Dirac's theory treated the electromagnetic field as a "gas" of photons (the quanta of light) and it yielded a correct description of the absorption and emission of radiation by electrons in atoms. It was the first quantum field theory.

A year later, Dirac published his relativistic electron theory, which took correct account of Einstein's special theory of relativity. Dirac's theory showed that the electron must have a spin quantum number of $\frac{1}{2}$ and a magnetic moment. It also predicted the existence of the positron, although Dirac did not at first realize that this was a new particle, believing instead that it was a proton. Only with Anderson's discovery of the positron did the picture become clear: radiation—a photon—can produce electrons and positrons in pairs, provided the energy of the photon is greater than about 1 MeV, the total mass-energy of the two particles.

Dirac's quantum field theory was a beginning, but it explained only one aspect of the electromagnetic interactions between radiation and matter. During the following years other theorists began to extend Dirac's ideas to form a comprehensive theory of quantum electrodynamics (QED) that accounts fully for the interactions of charged particles not only with radiation but also with one another. One important step was to describe the electrons in terms of fields, in analogy to the electromagnetic field of the photons. This enabled theorists to describe everything in terms of quantum field theory. It also helped to cast light on Dirac's positrons.

According to QED, the vacuum is filled with electron-positron fields. Real electron-positron pairs are created when photons, represented by the electromagnetic field, interact with these fields. Virtual electron-positron pairs, however, can also exist for minute durations, as dictated by Heisenberg's uncertainty principle, and this at first led to fundamental difficulties with QED.

During the 1930s it became clear that, as it stood, QED gave the wrong answers for quite simple problems. For example, the theory said that the emission and reabsorption of the same photon would occur with an infinite probability. This led in turn to infinities occurring in many situations; even the mass of a single electron was infinite according to QED because, on the time scales of the uncertainty principle, the electron could continuously emit and absorb virtual photons.

It was not until the late 1940s that a number of theorists working independently resolved the problems with QED. Julian Schwinger and Richard Feynman in the United States and Tomonaga Shin'ichirō in Japan proved that they could rid the theory of its embarrassing infinities by a process known as renormalization. Basically, renormalization acknowledges all possible infinities and then allows the positive infinities to cancel the negative ones; the mass and charge of the electron, which are infinite in theory, are then defined to be their measured values.

Renormalization

Once these steps are taken, QED works beautifully. It is the most accurate quantum field theory scientists have at their disposal. In recognition of their achievement, Feynman, Schwinger, and Tomonaga were awarded the Nobel Prize for Physics for 1965; Dirac had been similarly honoured in 1933.

Quantum chromodynamics. As early as 1920, when Rutherford named the proton and accepted it as a fundamental particle, it was clear that the electromagnetic force is not the only force at work within the atom. Something stronger must be responsible for binding the positively charged protons together, thereby overcoming their natural electrical repulsion. The discovery in 1932 of the neutron showed that there are (at least) two kinds of particle subject to the same force. Later in the same year, Heisenberg made one of the first attempts to develop a quantum field theory that was analogous to QED but appropriate to the nuclear binding force.

According to quantum field theory, particles can be held together by a "charge-exchange" force, which is carried by charged intermediary particles. Heisenberg's application of this theory gave birth to the idea that the proton and neutron were charged and neutral versions of the same particle—an idea that seemed to be supported by the fact that the two particles have almost equal masses. Heisenberg proposed that a proton, for example, could emit a positively charged particle that was then absorbed by a neutron; the proton thus became a neutron, and vice versa. The nucleus was no longer viewed as a collection of two kinds of immutable billiard balls but rather as a collection of continuously changing protons and neutrons that were bound together by the exchange particles flitting between them.

Heisenberg believed that the exchange particle involved was an electron (he did not have many particles from which to choose). This electron had to have some rather odd characteristics, however, such as no spin and no magnetic moment, and this made Heisenberg's theory ultimately unacceptable. Quantum field theory did not seem applicable to the nuclear binding force. Then, in 1935, a Japanese theorist, Yukawa Hideki, took a bold step: he invented a new particle as the carrier of the nuclear binding force.

The Yukawa meson

The size of a nucleus shows that the binding force must be short-ranged, confining protons and neutrons within distances of about 10^{-14} metre. Yukawa argued that to give this limited range, the force must involve the exchange of particles with mass, unlike the massless photons of QED. According to the uncertainty principle, exchanging a particle with mass sets a limit on the time allowed for the exchange and therefore restricts the range of the resulting force. Yukawa calculated a mass of about 200 times the electron's mass, or 100 MeV, for the new intermediary. Because the predicted mass of the new particle was between those of the electron and the proton, the particle was named meson.

Yukawa's work was little known outside Japan until 1937, when Carl Anderson and his colleague Seth Neddermeyer announced that, five years after Anderson's discovery of the positron, they had found a second new particle in the cosmic radiation. The new particle seemed to have exactly the mass Yukawa had prescribed and thus was seen as confirmation of Yukawa's theory by the Americans J. Robert Oppenheimer and Robert Serber, who made Yukawa's work more widely known in the West.

In the following years, however, it became clear that there were difficulties in reconciling the properties expected for Yukawa's intermediary particle with those of the new cosmic ray particle. In particular, as a group of Italian physicists succeeded in demonstrating (while hiding from the occupying German forces during World War II), the cosmic ray particles penetrate matter far too easily to be related to the nuclear binding force. To resolve this apparent paradox, theorists both in Japan and in the United States had begun to think that there might be two mesons.

The two-meson theory

The two-meson theory proposed that Yukawa's nuclear meson decays into the penetrating meson observed in the cosmic rays.

In 1947, scientists at Bristol University in England found the first experimental evidence of two mesons in cosmic rays high on the Pic du Midi in France. Using detectors equipped with special photographic emulsion that can record the tracks of charged particles, the physicists at Bristol found the decay of a heavier meson into a lighter one. They called the heavier particle π, and it has since become known as the π-meson or pion. The lighter particle was dubbed μ and is now known simply as the muon. (According to the modern definition of a meson as a particle consisting of a quark bound with an antiquark, the muon is not actually a meson. It is classified as a lepton—a relation of the electron.)

Studies of pions produced in cosmic radiation and in the first particle accelerators showed that the pion behaves precisely as expected for Yukawa's particle. Moreover, experiments confirmed that positive, negative, and neutral varieties of pions exist, as predicted by Nicholas Kemmer in England in 1938. Kemmer regarded the nuclear binding force as symmetric with respect to the charge of the particles involved. He proposed that the nuclear force between protons and protons, or neutrons and neutrons, is the same as the one between protons and neutrons. This symmetry required the existence of a neutral intermediary that did not figure in Yukawa's original theory. It also established the concept of a new "internal" property of subatomic particles, called isospin.

Kemmer's work followed to some extent the trail Heisenberg had begun in 1932. Close similarities between nuclei containing the same total number of protons and neutrons, but in different combinations, suggest that protons can be exchanged for neutrons and vice versa without altering the net effect of the nuclear binding force. In other words, the force recognizes no difference between protons and neutrons—it is symmetrical under the interchange of protons and neutrons, rather as a square is symmetrical under rotations through 90°, 180°, and so on.

To introduce this symmetry into the theory of the nuclear force, it proved useful to adopt the mathematics describing the spin of particles. In this respect, the proton and neutron are seen as different states of a single basic nucleon. These states are differentiated by an internal property that can have two values, $+^1/_2$ and $-^1/_2$, in analogy with the spin of a particle like the electron. This new property is called isotopic spin, or isospin for short, and the nuclear binding force is said to exhibit isospin symmetry.

Isospin

Symmetries are important in physics because they simplify the theories needed to describe a range of observations. For example, as far as physicists can tell, all physical laws exhibit translational symmetry. This means that the results of an experiment performed at one location in space and time can be used to predict correctly the outcome of the same experiment in another part of space and time. This symmetry is reflected in the conservation of momentum—the fact that the total momentum of a system remains constant, unless it is acted upon by an external force.

Isospin symmetry is an important symmetry in particle physics, although it occurs only in the action of the nuclear binding force—or, in modern terminology, the strong nuclear force. The symmetry leads to the conservation of isospin in nuclear interactions that occur via the strong force, thereby determining which reactions can occur.

The discovery of the pion in 1947 seemed to restore order to the study of particle physics, but this order did not last long. Later in the year Clifford Butler and George Rochester, two British physicists studying cosmic rays, discovered the first examples of yet another type of new particle. The new particles were heavier than the pion or muon but lighter than the proton, with a mass of about 800 times the electron's mass. Within the next few years, researchers found copious examples of these particles, as well as other new particles that were heavier than even the proton. The evidence seemed to indicate that these particles were created in strong interactions in nuclear matter, yet the particles lived for a relatively long time without themselves interacting strongly with matter. This strange behaviour in some ways echoed the earlier problem with Yukawa's supposed meson, but the solution for the new "strange" particles proved to be different.

By 1953 at least four different kinds of strange particles had been observed. In an attempt to bring order into this increasing number of subatomic particles, Murray Gell-Mann in the United States and Nishijima Kazuhiko in Japan independently suggested a new conservation law. They argued that the strange particles must possess some new property, called "strangeness," that is conserved in the strong nuclear reactions in which the particles are created. In the decays of the particles, however, a different force is at work, and this weak nuclear force does not conserve strangeness—as with isospin symmetry, which is respected only by the strong nuclear force.

Conservation of strangeness

According to this proposal, particles are assigned a strangeness quantum number, S, which can have only integer values. The pion, proton, and neutron have $S = 0$. Because the strong nuclear force conserves strangeness, it can produce strange particles only in pairs, in which the net value of strangeness is zero. This phenomenon, whose importance was recognized by both Nishijima and the American physicist Abraham Pais in 1952, is known as associated production.

With the introduction of strangeness, physicists had several properties with which they could label the various subatomic particles. In particular, values of mass, electric charge, spin, isospin, and strangeness gave physicists a means of classifying the strongly interacting particles—or hadrons—and of establishing a hierarchy of relationships between them. In 1962 Gell-Mann and Yuval Ne'eman, an Israeli scientist, independently showed that a particular kind of mathematical symmetry provides the kind of grouping of hadrons that is observed in nature. The name of the mathematical symmetry is SU(3), which stands for "special unitary group in three dimensions."

SU(3) symmetry

SU(3) contains subgroups of objects that are related to each other by symmetric transformations, rather as a group describing the rotations of a square through 90° contains the four symmetric positions of the square. Gell-Mann and Ne'eman both realized that the basic subgroups of SU(3) contain either eight or 10 members and that the observed hadrons can be grouped together in eights or 10s in the same way. For example, the proton, neutron, and their relations with spin ½ fall into one group of eight, while the pion and its relations with spin 0 fit into another group of eight (see Figure 5). A group of nine very short-lived resonance particles with spin 3/2 could be seen to fit into a group of 10, although at the time the 10th member of the group, the particle known as the Ω^-, had not yet been observed. Its discovery early in 1964, at the Brookhaven National Laboratory in New York, was confirmation of the validity of the SU(3) symmetry of the hadrons.

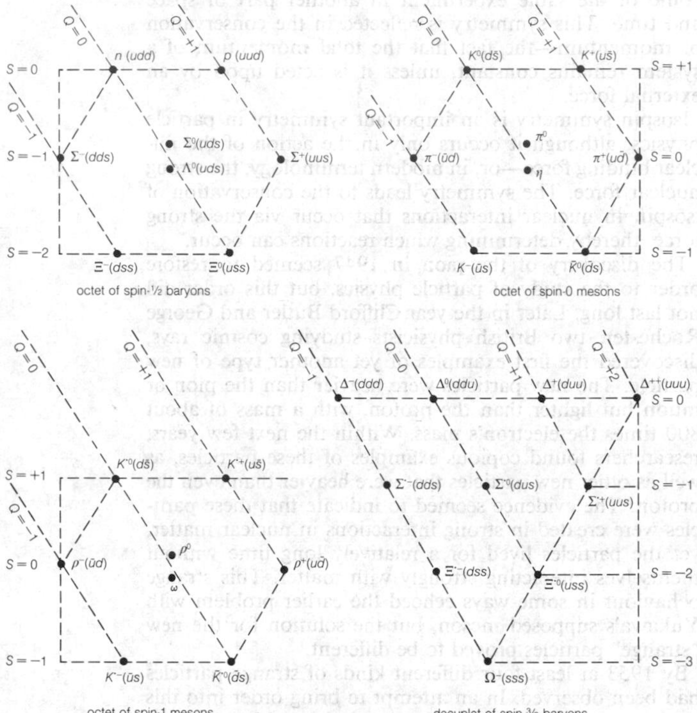

Figure 5: Combinations of the quarks *u*, *d*, and *s* and the corresponding antiquarks to form hadrons. The octets (hexagons) and the decuplet arise when particles are grouped according to strangeness, *S*, and charge, *Q*.

The beauty of the SU(3) symmetry does not, however, explain why it holds true. Gell-Mann and another American physicist, George Zweig, independently decided in 1964 that the answer to that question lies in the fundamental nature of the hadrons. The most basic subgroup of SU(3) contains only three objects, from which the groups of eight and 10 can be built. The two theorists made the bold suggestion that the hadrons observed at the time were not simple structures but were instead built from three basic particles. Gell-Mann called these particles quarks—the name that remains in use today.

By the time Gell-Mann and Zweig put forward their ideas, the list of known subatomic particles had grown from the three of 1932—electron, proton, and neutron—to include most of the "stable" hadrons (see Table 4) and a growing number of short-lived resonances, as well as the muon and two types of neutrino. That the seemingly ever-increasing number of hadrons could be understood in terms of only three basic building blocks was remarkable indeed. For this to be possible, however, those building blocks—the quarks—had to have some unusual properties.

These properties were so odd that for a number of years it was not clear as to whether quarks actually existed or were simply a useful mathematical fiction. For example, quarks must have charges of $+\frac{2}{3}e$ or $-\frac{1}{3}e$, which should be very easy to spot in certain kinds of detectors; but intensive searches, both in cosmic rays and at particle accelerators, have never revealed any convincing evidence for fractional charge of this kind. By the early 1970s, however, 10 years after quarks were first proposed, scientists had compiled a mass of evidence which showed that quarks do exist but are locked within the individual hadrons in such a way that they can never escape one at a time.

This evidence resulted from experiments in which beams of electrons, muons, or neutrinos were fired at the protons and neutrons in such target materials as hydrogen (protons only), deuterium, carbon, and aluminum. The incident particles used were all leptons, particles that do not feel the strong nuclear binding force and that were known, even then, to be much smaller than the nuclei they were probing. The scattering of the beam particles caused by interactions within the target clearly demonstrated that protons and neutrons are complex structures that contain structureless, pointlike objects—the quarks.

Gell-Mann and Zweig required only three quarks to build the particles known in 1964. These quarks are the ones known as up (*u*), down (*d*), and strange (*s*). Since then, experiments have revealed a number of heavy hadrons—both mesons and baryons—which show that there are more than three quarks. Indeed, the SU(3) symmetry is part of a larger mathematical symmetry that incorporates quarks of several "flavours"—the term used to distinguish the different quarks. In addition to the up, down, and strange quarks, there are quarks known as charm and bottom (or beauty), and there is great theoretical prejudice, though scant experimental evidence, for a sixth quark, called top (or truth). These flavours are all conserved during reactions that occur through the strong nuclear force; in other words, charm must be created in association with anticharm, bottom with antibottom, and so on. This implies that the quarks can change from one flavour to another only by way of the weak nuclear force responsible for the decays of particles. Table 5 lists the characteristics of the six quarks.

Conservation of quark flavour

The up and down quarks are distinguished only by their differing electric charges, while the heavier quarks each carry a unique quantum number related to their flavour. The strange quark has strangeness, $S = -1$, the charm quark has charm, $C = +1$, and so on. Thus, three strange quarks together give a particle with an electric charge of $-e$ and a strangeness of -3—just as is required for the Ω^- particle; and the neutral strange particle known as the lambda contains *uds*, giving the correct total charge of zero and strangeness of -1. Using this system, the lambda can be viewed as a neutron with one down quark changed to a strange quark; charge and spin remain the same, but the strange quark makes the lambda heavier than the neutron. Thus the quark model reveals that nature is not arbitrary when it produces particles but is in some sense repeating itself on a more massive scale.

The realization, in the late 1960s, that protons, neutrons, and even Yukawa's pions are all built from quarks changed the direction of thinking about the nuclear binding force. Although at the level of nuclei Yukawa's picture remained valid, at the more minute quark level, it could not satisfactorily explain what held the quarks together within the protons and pions, or what prevented the quarks from escaping one at a time.

The answer to questions like these seems to lie in the

Table 5: Quarks*

quark type	baryon number	charge	strangeness†	charm†	bottom†	top†	mass (MeV)
Down (*d*)	1/3	$-\frac{1}{3}e$	0	0	0	0	7
Up (*u*)	1/3	$+\frac{2}{3}e$	0	0	0	0	5
Strange (*s*)	1/3	$-\frac{1}{3}e$	−1	0	0	0	150
Charm (*c*)	1/3	$+\frac{2}{3}e$	0	1	0	0	1,400
Bottom (*b*)	1/3	$-\frac{1}{3}e$	0	0	−1	0	4,800
Top (*t*)‡	1/3	$+\frac{2}{3}e$	0	0	0	1	?

*Note that antiquarks exist for all flavours of quark and have opposite values for all the quantum numbers listed here. †These are quantum numbers that must be assigned to the quarks to differentiate the various flavours. ‡There is no convincing experimental evidence for the top quark, but its mass must certainly be greater than about 23,000 MeV, otherwise its bound state, toponium, would have been found.

The quark property of colour

property called colour. Colour was originally introduced to solve a problem raised by the exclusion principle that was formulated by the Austrian physicist Wolfgang Pauli in 1925. This rule does not allow particles with spin $1/2$, such as quarks, to occupy the same quantum state; therefore particles containing three quarks of the same flavour, such as the Ω^-, which consists of *sss*, should not exist. The Ω^- can contain one *s* spinning in one direction and a second *s* spinning in the opposite direction, but because there is no third direction, the third *s* should not be allowed.

To resolve this paradox, in 1964–65 Oscar Greenberg in the United States and Yoichiro Nambu and colleagues in Japan proposed the existence of a new property with three possible states. In analogy to the three primary colours of light, the new property became known as colour and the three varieties as red, green, and blue.

The three colour states are comparable to the two possible states of electric charge (positive and negative), and hadrons are analogous to atoms. Just as atoms contain electrically charged constituents whose charges balance overall to give a neutral atom, hadrons consist of coloured quarks that balance to give a particle with no net colour. Moreover, nuclei can be built from colourless protons and neutrons, rather as molecules form from electrically neutral atoms. Even Yukawa's pion exchange can be compared to exchange models of chemical bonding.

This analogy between electric charge and colour led to the idea that colour could be the source of the force between quarks, just as charge is the source of the electromagnetic force between charged particles. The force was seen to be working not between nucleons, as in Yukawa's theory, but between quarks. In the late 1960s and early 1970s, theorists turned to developing a quantum field theory based on coloured quarks. In such a theory, colour would take the role of charge in QED.

It was obvious that the field theory for coloured quarks had to be fundamentally different from QED because there are three kinds of colour as opposed to two kinds of electric charge. To cancel each other and give neutral objects, the two kinds of electric charge must be equal in magnitude but opposite in sign. With colour, three different charges must add together to give zero, so that the colours cannot be equal in the way that electric charges are. In addition, because SU(3) symmetry (the same type of mathematical symmetry that Gell-Mann and Ne'eman used for three flavours) applies to the three colours, quarks of one colour must be able to transform into another colour. This implies that a quark can emit something—the quantum of the field due to colour—that itself carries colour. And if the field quanta are coloured, then they can interact between themselves, unlike the photons of QED, which are electrically neutral.

Despite these differences, the basic framework for a field theory based on colour already existed by the late 1960s, due in large part to the work of theorists, particularly Chen Ning Yang and Robert Mills in the United States, who had studied similar theories in the 1950s. The new theory of the strong nuclear force was called quantum chromodynamics, or QCD, in analogy to quantum electrodynamics, or QED. In QCD the source of the field is the property of colour, and the field quanta are called gluons. Eight gluons are necessary in all to make the changes between the coloured quarks according to the rules of SU(3).

In the early 1970s several theorists working independently discovered that the strong nuclear force between quarks becomes stronger as quarks move apart, preventing the separation of an individual quark, but that it becomes weaker at smaller distances—unlike the behaviour of the electromagnetic force. The quarks have been compared to prisoners on a chain gang. When they are close together, they can move freely and do not notice the chains binding them. If one quark/prisoner tries to move away, however, the strength of the chains is felt and escape is prevented.

Asymptotic freedom

This effect, known as asymptotic freedom, has been attributed to the fact that the virtual gluons that flit between the quarks within a hadron are not neutral but carry mixtures of colour and anticolour (the colour of antiquarks). The farther away a quark moves, the more gluons appear, each contributing to the net force. When the quarks are close together, they exchange fewer gluons and the force is weaker. Only at infinitely close distances are quarks free.

The strong coupling between the quarks and gluons makes QCD a difficult theory to study. Mathematical procedures that work in QED cannot be used in QCD. The theory has nevertheless had a number of successes in describing the observed behaviour of particles in experiments, and theorists are confident that it is the right theory to use for describing the strong nuclear force.

Electroweak theory. The strong force binds particles together: by binding quarks within protons and neutrons, it indirectly binds protons and neutrons together to form nuclei. Nuclei can, however, break apart, or decay, naturally in the process known as radioactivity. One type of radioactivity, called beta decay, in which a nucleus emits an electron, thereby increasing its net positive charge by 1 unit, has been known since the late 1890s; but it was only with the discovery of the neutron in 1932 that physicists could begin to understand correctly what happens in the radioactive process.

The most basic form of beta decay involves the transmutation of a neutron into a proton, accompanied by the emission of an electron to keep the balance of electric charge. In addition, as Pauli realized in 1930, the neutron emits a neutral particle that shares the energy released by the decay. This neutral particle has little or no mass and is known as the neutrino. On its own, a neutron will decay in this way after an average lifetime of 15 minutes; only within the confines of certain nuclei does the balance of forces prevent neutrons from decaying and thereby keep the entire nucleus stable.

The rates of nuclear decay indicate that any force involved in beta decay must be much weaker than the force that binds nuclei together. It may seem counterintuitive to think of a nuclear force that can disrupt the nucleus; however, the transformation of a neutron into a proton that occurs in neutron decay is comparable to the transformations by the exchange of pions that Yukawa suggested to explain the nuclear binding force. Indeed, Yukawa's theory originally tried to explain both kinds of phenomena—weak decays and strong binding—with the exchange of a single type of particle. To give the different strengths, he proposed that the exchange particle couples strongly to the heavy neutrons and protons and weakly to the light electrons and neutrinos.

Yukawa was foreshadowing future developments in unifying the two nuclear forces in this way; however, as is explained below, he had chosen the wrong two forces. He was also bold in incorporating two "new" particles in his theory—the necessary exchange particle and the neutrino predicted by Pauli only five years previously.

Pauli had been hesitant in suggesting that a second particle must be emitted in beta decay, even though that would explain why the electron could leave with a range of energies. Such was the prejudice against the prediction of new particles that theorists as eminent as Bohr in Copenhagen preferred to suggest that the law of conservation of energy might break down at subnuclear distances.

By 1935, however, Pauli's new particle had found a champion in Enrico Fermi. Fermi named the particle the neutrino and incorporated it into his theory for beta decay, published in 1934. Like Yukawa, Fermi drew on an analogy with QED; but Fermi regarded the emission of the neutrino and electron by the neutron as the direct analogue of the emission of a photon by a charged particle, and he did not invoke a new exchange particle.

Fermi's theory, rather than Yukawa's, proved highly successful in describing nuclear beta decay, and it received added support in the late 1940s with the discovery of the pion and its relationship with the muon (see above). In particular, it became clear that the muon decays to an electron and two neutrinos in a process that has exactly the same basic strength as the neutron's decay to a proton. The idea of a "universal" weak interaction that, unlike the strong nuclear force, acts equally upon light and heavy particles (or leptons and hadrons) was born.

The nature of the weak force began to be revealed in 1956, as the result of work by two Chinese-American theorists, Tsung-Dao Lee and Chen Ning Yang. Lee and

Yang were trying to resolve some puzzles in the decays of the strange particles. They discovered that they could solve the mystery, provided that the weak nuclear force does not respect the symmetry known as parity.

The parity operation is like reflecting something in a mirror; it involves changing the coordinates (x, y, z) of each point to the "mirror" coordinates ($-x$, $-y$, $-z$). Physicists had always assumed that such an operation would make no difference to the laws of physics. Lee and Yang, however, proposed that the weak nuclear force is exceptional in this respect, and they suggested ways that parity violation might be observed in weak interactions. Early in 1957, just a few months after Lee and Yang's theory was published, experiments involving the decays of neutrons, pions, and muons showed that the weak nuclear force does indeed violate parity symmetry. Later that year, Lee and Yang were awarded the Nobel Prize for their work.

Parity violation

Parity violation and the concept of a universal form of weak interaction were combined in one theory in 1958 by the American physicists Murray Gell-Mann and Richard Feynman. They established the mathematical structure of the weak interaction in what is known as V-A, or vector minus axial vector, theory. This theory proved highly successful experimentally, at least at the relatively low energies accessible to particle physicists in the 1960s. It was clear that the theory had the correct kind of mathematical structure to account for parity violation and related effects, but there were strong indications that in describing particle interactions at higher energies than experiments could at the time access the theory began to go badly wrong.

The problems with V-A theory were related to a basic requirement of quantum field theory—the existence of a gauge boson, or messenger particle, to carry the force. Yukawa had attempted to describe the weak nuclear force in terms of the same intermediary that is responsible for the strong nuclear binding force, but this approach did not work. A few years after Yukawa had published his theory, a Swedish theorist, Oskar Klein, proposed a slightly different kind of carrier for the weak force.

In contrast to Yukawa's particle, which had spin 0, Klein's intermediary had spin 1 and therefore would give the correct spins for the neutrino and electron emitted in the beta decay of the neutron. Moreover, within the framework of Klein's concept, the known strength of the weak force in beta decay showed that the mass of the particle must be approximately 100 times the proton's mass, although the theory could not predict this value. All attempts to introduce such a particle into V-A theory, however, encountered severe difficulties, similar to those that had beset quantum electrodynamics during the 1930s and early '40s. The theory gave infinite probabilities to various interactions, and it defied the renormalization process that had been the salvation of QED.

Throughout the 1950s, theorists tried to construct field theories for the nuclear forces that would exhibit the same kind of gauge symmetry inherent in Maxwell's theory of electrodynamics and in QED. There were two major problems, which were in fact related. One concerned the infinities and the difficulty in renormalizing these theories; the other concerned the mass of the intermediaries. Straightforward gauge theory requires particles of zero mass as carriers, such as the photon of QED; but Klein had shown that the short-ranged weak nuclear force requires massive carriers.

In short, physicists had to discover the correct mathematical symmetry group for describing the transformations between different subatomic particles and then identify for the known forces the messenger particles required by fields with the chosen symmetry. Early in the 1960s Sheldon Glashow in the United States and Abdus Salam and John Ward in England decided to work with a combination of two symmetry groups, namely, $SU(2) \times U(1)$. Such a symmetry requires four spin-1 messenger particles, two electrically neutral and two charged. One of the neutral particles could be identified with the photon, while the two charged particles could be the messengers responsible for beta decay, in which charge changes hands, as when the neutron decays into a proton. The fourth messenger, a second neutral particle, seemed at the time to have no obvious role: it apparently would permit weak interactions with no change of charge—so-called neutral current interactions—which had not yet been observed.

This theory, however, still required the messengers to be massless, which was all right for the photon but not for the messengers of the weak force. Toward the end of the 1960s, Salam and Steven Weinberg, an American theorist, independently realized how to introduce massive messenger particles into the theory while at the same time preserving its basic gauge symmetry properties. The answer lay in the work of Peter Higgs, an English theorist, who had discovered the concept of symmetry breaking, or, more descriptively, hidden symmetry.

Symmetry breaking

A physical field can be intrinsically symmetrical, although this may not be apparent in the state of the universe in which experiments are conducted. On Earth, for example, gravity seems asymmetrical—it always pulls down. From a distance, however, the symmetry of the gravitational field around the Earth becomes apparent. At a more fundamental level, the fields associated with the electromagnetic and weak nuclear forces are not overtly symmetrical, as is demonstrated by the widely differing strengths of weak and electromagnetic interactions at low energies. Yet, according to Higgs's ideas, these forces can have an underlying symmetry. It is as if the universe lies at the bottom of a wine bottle. The symmetry of the bottle's base is clear from the top of the dimple in the centre, but it is hidden from any point in the valley surrounding the central dimple.

Higgs's mechanism for symmetry breaking provided Salam and Weinberg with a means of explaining the masses of the carriers of the weak force. Their theory, however, also predicted the existence of one or more new "Higgs" particles, which would carry additional fields needed for the symmetry breaking and have zero spin. With this sole proviso, the future of the electroweak theory began to look more promising. In 1971 a young Dutch theorist, Gerard 't Hooft, proved that the theory is renormalizable (in other words, that all the infinities cancel out), and many particle physicists became convinced that the electroweak theory was, at last, an acceptable theory for the weak force.

In addition to the Higgs particle, or particles, electroweak theory also predicts the existence of an electrically neutral carrier for the weak force. This neutral carrier, called the Z^0, should mediate the neutral current interactions, weak interactions in which electric charge is not transferred between particles. The search for evidence of such reactions, and thus further confirmation of the validity of the electroweak theory, began in earnest in the early 1970s.

Search for neutral current interactions

The first signs of neutral currents came in 1973 from experiments at the European Organization for Nuclear Research (CERN) near Geneva. A team of more than 50 physicists from a variety of countries had diligently searched through the photographs taken of tracks produced when a large bubble chamber called Gargamelle was exposed to a beam of muon-antineutrinos. In a neutral current reaction, an antineutrino would simply scatter from an electron in the liquid contents of the bubble chamber. The incoming antineutrino, being neutral, would leave no track; nor would it leave a track as it left the chamber after being scattered off an electron. But the effect of the neutral current—the passage of a virtual Z^0 between the antineutrino and the electron—would set the electron in motion, and, being electrically charged, the electron would leave a track, which would appear as if from nowhere. Examining approximately 1.4 million pictures, the researchers found three examples of such a neutral current reaction. Although the reactions occurred only rarely, there were enough to set hopes high for the validity of electroweak theory.

In 1979 Glashow, Salam, and Weinberg, the theorists who had done much of the work in developing electroweak theory in the 1960s, were awarded the Nobel Prize. By that time enough information on charged and neutral current interactions had been compiled to predict that the masses of the weak messengers required by electroweak theory should be about 80 GeV for the charged W^+ and W^- particles and 90 GeV for the Z^0. There was, however, still no sign of the direct production of the weak messengers, because no accelerator was yet capable of producing collisions energetic enough to create real particles of such large masses (nearly 100 times as massive as the proton).

A scheme to find the *W* and *Z* particles was under way at CERN, however. The plan was to accelerate protons in one direction around CERN's largest proton synchrotron (a circular accelerator) and antiprotons in the opposite direction. At an appropriate energy (initially 270 GeV per beam) the two sets of particles would be made to collide head-on. The total energy of the collision would be far greater than anything that could be achieved by directing a single beam at a stationary target, and physicists hoped it would be sufficient to produce a small but significant number of *W* and *Z* particles.

In 1983 the researchers at CERN, working on two experiments code-named UA1 and UA2, were rewarded with the discovery of the particles they sought. The *W*s and *Z*s that were produced did not live long enough to leave tracks in the detectors, but they decayed to particles that did leave tracks. The total energy of those decay particles, moreover, equaled the energy corresponding to the masses of the transient *W* and *Z* particles, just as predicted by electroweak theory (see Figure 2). It was a triumph both for CERN and for electroweak theory. Hundreds of physicists and engineers were involved in the project, and in 1984 the Italian physicist Carlo Rubbia and Simon van der Meer, a Dutch engineer, received the Nobel Prize for their leading roles in making the discovery of the *W* and *Z* particles possible.

Discovery of *W* and *Z* particles

CURRENT RESEARCH

Experiments. Electroweak theory, which describes the electromagnetic and weak nuclear forces, and quantum chromodynamics, the gauge theory of the strong nuclear force, together give what theorists call the "standard model." Although the model works well, as far as can be measured using present technology, a few points still await experimental verification.

The Higgs particle

Current research is focused on the Higgs particle, the particle associated with the mechanism that allows the symmetry of the electroweak force to be broken, or hidden, at low energies and that requires the *W* and *Z* particles, the carriers of the weak force, to have mass. The particle is necessary to electroweak theory because the Higgs mechanism requires a new field to break the symmetry, and according to quantum field theory all fields have particles associated with them. Researchers know that the Higgs particle must have spin 0, but that is virtually all that can be definitely predicted. Theory provides a poor guide as to the particle's mass or even the number of different varieties of Higgs particles involved.

Good experimental evidence for the top quark is also required. There is strong theoretical prejudice for such a quark because it would complete a set of three pairs of quarks. The quarks are linked together by weak interactions that change one flavour of quark to another, as when a down quark converts into an up quark in the beta decay of the neutron. To change into an up quark, the down quark emits a virtual W^- particle, which materializes as an electron and an electron-antineutrino. In an equivalent reaction, an electron-neutrino and a down quark can interact through the exchange of a W^- particle: the W^- flits from the quark to the lepton, creating an electron and an up quark. It is clear that the weak force, through the agency of the W^-, changes not only the flavour of the quark but also the nature of the lepton. Thus, the electron and its neutrino can be thought of as leptons of different flavour. The charm and strange quarks are similarly related, and the muon and tau pair up with their own brands of neutrino to form leptonic "flavour doublets." There are three lepton doublets, so it seems logical that there should be three quark doublets. Scientists therefore hope to find the sixth flavour of quark, top, which would pair with the bottom quark.

Theory shows that the top quark must be heavier than any of the other quarks but does not provide an estimate for the particle's mass. Experimentalists therefore are not certain at what energies they should look for the top quark. They do know, however, that one of the easiest ways to observe the top quark would be in the production of "toponium," a particle consisting of a top quark bound with a top antiquark. The charm and bottom quarks were discovered in this manner in, respectively, charmonium and bottomonium.

Toponium

In an "onium" state, the quark and antiquark orbit each other until they annihilate either through the strong nuclear force into gluons or through the electromagnetic force into a photon. The strong force, being stronger, dominates, but for technical reasons to do with colour, the decay must involve more than one gluon and the process is slowed down. The quark-antiquark state is thus relatively long-lived, lasting 1,000 times longer than "ordinary" resonance particles, which also decay by the strong nuclear force but live for only 10^{-23} second.

Charmonium and bottomonium are relatively easily produced in the collisions of electrons and positrons. They show up as unusually narrow resonance spikes among the mass of particles produced when the total energy of the electron and positron equals the total energy—or equivalently the mass—of the quark-antiquark state (see Figure 6). Physicists hope to detect toponium in a similar way, using an electron-positron collider. Existing machines have failed to reveal toponium, so it is clear that the particle's mass must be greater than about 45 GeV. There has been speculation that top particles (particles containing a top quark, or antiquark, in combination with a lighter antiquark, or quark, specifically of bottom flavour) have been produced in proton-antiproton collisions at CERN. Certainly, these collisions could produce toponium with a mass of up to 100 GeV or so, but the decay would be extremely difficult to detect amid the debris of the proton-antiproton collisions.

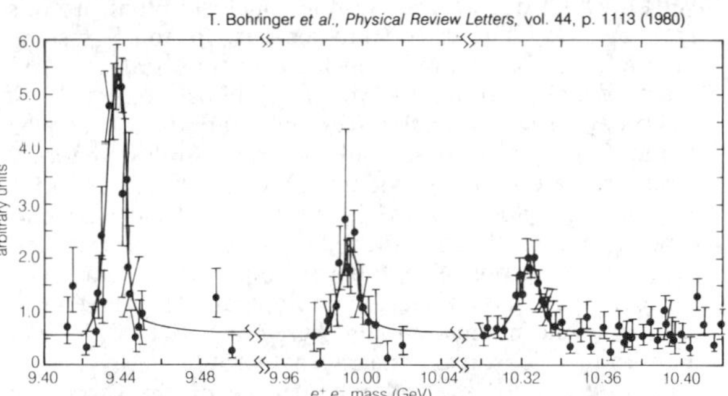

Figure 6: Resonance bumps reveal three members of the bottomonium family, particles built from a bottom quark orbiting a bottom antiquark in different energy states.

Some experimentalists continue to search for signs of free quarks, even though quantum chromodynamics seems to provide an explanation for why quarks appear only in clusters, as baryons and mesons. With an electric charge either $^1/_3$ or $^2/_3$ the size of the standard unit of charge, a single quark would have a distinctive "signature." This is important experimentally because charged particles are detected when they lose energy ionizing, or knocking electrons from, atoms in the material they travel through. The energy lost in this way depends on the square of the charge: a quark with a charge of $^2/_3$ produces $^4/_9$, or just under half, the ionization of an ordinary particle, while a quark with a charge of $^1/_3$ produces only $^1/_9$ the ionization. No convincing evidence for particles with fractions of charge has yet been found, but until it has been proved that single quarks cannot exist, researchers conducting high-energy experiments will continue to keep a close watch to see if quarks are liberated.

Theory. The standard model combining electroweak theory and quantum chromodynamics provides a satisfactory way of understanding most experimental results in particle physics, yet it is far from satisfying as a theory. In addition to the missing Higgs particle and top quark, many problems and gaps in the model have been explained in a rather ad hoc manner. Values for such basic properties as the fractional charges of quarks or the masses of quarks and leptons must be inserted "by hand" into the model; that is, they are determined by experiment and observation rather than by theoretical predictions.

Many theorists working in particle physics are therefore looking beyond the standard model in an attempt to find a more comprehensive theory. One important approach has been the development of grand unified theories, or GUTs, which seek to unify the strong, weak, and electromagnetic forces in the way that electroweak theory does for two of these forces. General arguments indicate that the intrinsic strengths of the electroweak and strong forces become equal at extremely high energies of about 10^{15} GeV, or 10 million million times the energies at which the electromagnetic and weak forces merge into the electroweak force. These energies are far beyond the reach of modern particle accelerators, but GUTs do make predictions that can be tested at more accessible low energies.

Grand unified theories

Any gauge field theory that contains QCD and electroweak theory, in other words, any GUT, must use a mathematical symmetry group that contains the symmetries of both QCD and electroweak theory. There are various possibilities, one of the simplest and among the first to be studied being a theory based on the group SU(5). The idea is that above the grand unification energy of 10^{15} GeV, the larger SU(5) group describes the symmetry of the unified field theory. At lower energies, this grand symmetry breaks down into the symmetries of QCD and electroweak theory.

A theory that links strong and electroweak interactions in this way must link the quarks with the leptons so that the main distinction between the two groups of particles appears only when the grand unification is broken and leptons, which do not feel the strong force, "decouple" from quarks. Indeed, grand unified theories tend to bring the quarks and leptons together into one family. This implies that a quark can convert into a lepton (or vice versa), which in turn leads to the conclusion that protons are not stable but decay into leptons. Protons must be manifestly stable, however, at least on time scales of 10^{17} years, otherwise all matter would be radioactive.

Stability of the proton

The key to resolving this seeming contradiction can be found in the gauge bosons of the grand unified theories. These gauge bosons include not only the photon, Z^0, W^+, W^-, and the gluons of the standard model but also new bosons, named X, that mediate the transitions between quarks and leptons. The X bosons must be very massive; indeed, their masses must be comparable to the energy scale of grand unification and therefore at least 10^{15} GeV. This tremendous mass means that proton decay occurs only rarely, and, in fact, the lifetime of the proton is calculated to be at least 10^{30} years.

It might seem impossible to verify experimentally such a lifetime. Particle lifetimes, or strictly half-lives, are only averages, however. Given a large enough collection of protons, there is a chance that a few may decay within an observable time. This has encouraged physicists to set up a number of proton decay experiments in which large quantities of inexpensive material, usually water, iron, or concrete, are surrounded by detectors that can spot the particles produced if a proton decays. So far, there is no clear evidence that protons decay, and this rules out some of the simplest possible GUTs.

Grand unified theories automatically resolve some of the problems with the standard model. For example, they correctly predict the charges of the quarks and leptons, as well as the relationship between the strengths of the different forces. They are, however, inadequate in many respects. They give no explanation, for example, for the number of pairs of quarks and leptons; they even raise the question of why such an enormous gap exists between the masses of the W and Z bosons of the electroweak force and the X bosons of lepton-quark interactions. Most importantly, they do not include the fourth force, gravity.

The dream of theorists is to find a totally unified theory—a theory of everything, or TOE. Attempts to derive a quantum field theory containing gravity always ran aground, however, until a remarkable development in 1984 first hinted that a quantum theory that includes gravity might be possible. The new development, which is known as superstring theory, contains two important ingredients. First, it regards subatomic particles—quarks, leptons, and bosons—not as points in space, as in conventional field theories, but as extended objects, or "strings." String theories were originally developed in the early 1970s by Yoichiro Nambu at the University of Chicago in an attempt to find a theory for the strong nuclear force. Quantum chromodynamics is now accepted as providing the correct description of strong interactions, but in 1976 the French physicist Joël Scherk and his colleagues found they could rid string theories of certain inconsistencies if they introduced the concept of "supersymmetry."

Supersymmetry provides a means of linking the quarks and leptons, which have spin $1/2$ and are collectively called fermions, with the bosons of the gauge fields, which have spins of 1 or 2 (see Table 2), and the Higgs particle, which has spin 0. Although this has great appeal to many physicists because it helps to unite the otherwise different kinds of particles, it generally leads to a doubling of the number of fundamental particles by introducing photinos, winos, zinos, gluinos, and gravitinos, which have spins of $1/2$ or $3/2$ and are supersymmetric counterparts for the bosons, and sleptons and squarks, fermion counterparts with integer values of spin.

The incorporation of supersymmetry into string theory is known as superstring theory. Its importance was not recognized until an English theorist, Michael Green, and an American, John Schwarz, showed that in two specific cases the superstring theory is entirely self-consistent. All potential problems cancel out, despite the fact that the theory automatically contains a quantum description of gravity. The two cases correspond to superstrings described by two unusually large mathematical symmetry groups—SO(32) and the "exceptional" group $E_8 \times E_8$. The E_8 symmetry group contains the smaller group E_6, one of the symmetry groups favoured by theorists studying possible GUTs. E_6 contains within it the symmetries of QCD and electroweak theory—the theories known to work at low energies. For the first time, a theory, rather than observation, has determined which symmetry group to use and, as far as physicists can tell, has done so accurately.

Superstring theory

The superstring theory seems to operate in a 10-dimensional space—that is, in six dimensions over and above the three dimensions of space and one of time that are perceived in the everyday world. Although this idea seems daunting at first, it does not necessarily pose a problem. Fifty years before the advent of superstrings, the Polish physicist Theodor Kaluza and Oskar Klein considered a unified theory of gravity and electromagnetism based on five dimensions. They argued that the fifth dimension "curls up" to be very small, thus leaving only the four familiar dimensions of space and time. The effects of the fifth dimension would be perceived as electromagnetism when viewed from the restricted perspective of four dimensions. The Kaluza-Klein theory may not have been the ultimate TOE, but it indicated to theorists in the 1980s one possible way to deal with the 10 dimensions of superstrings. The six unwanted dimensions can be considered to be curled up, leaving the physics observed in the low-energy world, where the superstrings, which have miniscule dimensions of 10^{-35} metre, appear as points, with QCD and electroweak theory as workable approximations of the effects of the extra dimensions. It remains to be seen whether superstring theory is the much-desired theory of everything.

BIBLIOGRAPHY. Nonspecialist introductions to particle physics that give a broad outline of the subject include FRANK CLOSE, MICHAEL MARTEN, and CHRISTINE SUTTON, *The Particle Explosion* (1987); YUVAL NE'EMAN and YORAM KIRSH, *The Particle Hunters* (1986; originally published in Hebrew, 1983); PETER WATKINS, *Story of the W and Z* (1986); Y. NAMBU, *Quarks: Frontiers in Elementary Particle Physics* (1985); CHRISTINE SUTTON, *The Particle Connection: The Most Exciting Scientific Chase Since DNA and the Double Helix* (1984, reissued 1985); PAUL DAVIES, *Superforce: The Search for a Grand Unified Theory of Nature* (1984, reprinted 1985); FRANK CLOSE, *The Cosmic Onion: Quarks and the Nature of the Universe* (1983, reissued 1986); HARALD FRITZSCH, *Quarks: The Stuff of Matter* (1983, reissued 1984; originally published in German, 1981); and J.H. MULVEY (ed.), *The Nature of Matter* (1981). More detailed historical accounts can be found in ABRAHAM PAIS, *Inward Bound: Of Matter and Forces in the Physical World* (1986); LAURIE M. BROWN and LILLIAN HODDESON (eds.), *The Birth of Particle*

Physics (1983); and STEVEN WEINBERG, *The Discovery of Subatomic Particles* (1983). More technical introductory texts are DONALD H. PERKINS, *Introduction to High Energy Physics,* 3rd ed. (1987); B.G. DUFF, *Fundamental Particles: An Introduction to Quarks and Leptons* (1986); L.B. OKUN, *Particle Physics: The Quest for the Substance of Substance,* trans. from Russian (1985); IAN J.R. AITCHISON and ANTHONY J.G. HEY, *Gauge Theories in Particle Physics: A Practical Introduction* (1982, reprinted 1984); and GRAHAM G. ROSS, *Grand Unified Theories* (1984). An interesting collection of important papers on electroweak theory is contained in C.H. LAI (ed.), *Selected Papers on Gauge Theory of Weak and Electromagnetic Interactions* (1981). For more recent developments, as well as useful past references, see, for example: SIMON ANTHONY, "Superstrings: A Theory of Everything?" *New Scientist,* 107(1471):34–36 (Aug. 29, 1985); GERARD 'T HOOFT, "Gauge Theories of the Forces Between Elementary Particles," *Scientific American,* 242(6):104–138 (June 1980); P.Q. HUNG and C. QUIGG, "Intermediate Bosons: Weak Interaction Couriers," *Science,* 210(4475):1205–11 (Dec. 12, 1980); and "Anomaly Cancellation Launches Superstring Bandwagon," *Physics Today,* 38(7):17–20 (July 1985). Many of the articles published in *New Scientist* are collected in CHRISTINE SUTTON (ed.), *Building the Universe* (1985).

(Ch.Su.)

Sudan

The Democratic Republic of the Sudan (Jumhūrīyat as-Sūdān ad-Dīmuqrāṭīyah) is the largest African nation in area. It is bounded on the north by Egypt; on the east by the Red Sea and Ethiopia; on the south by Kenya, Uganda, and Zaire; on the west by the Central African Republic and Chad; and on the northwest by Libya. Its total area of 966,757 square miles (2,503,890 square kilometres) represents more than 8 percent of the African continent and almost 2 percent of the world's total land area. Khartoum, the national capital, is located in the northern half of the country at the junction of the Blue and White Nile rivers. The name Sudan derives from the Arabic expression *bilād as-sūdān* ("land of the blacks"), by which medieval Arab geographers referred to the settled African countries that began at the southern edge of the Sahara. (M.e.D.S./J.L.Sp.)

Since ancient times the Sudan has been an arena for interaction between the cultural traditions of Africa and those of the Mediterranean world. In recent centuries Islām and the Arabic language have achieved ascendancy in many northern parts of the country, while older African languages and cultures predominate in the south. Large parts of the country continue to rely upon an agricultural and pastoral subsistence economy, but commercial agriculture—together with more limited mining and industrial development—plays a central role in the northern districts and in the national economy as a whole.

The country has had numerous changes in government since independence in 1956. Successive regimes found it difficult to win general acceptance from the country's diverse political constituencies, a situation symbolized by the lack of a formal constitution until 1973. An early conflict arose between those northern leaders who hoped to impose unity upon the nation through the vigorous extension of Islāmic law and culture to all parts of the country and those who opposed this policy; the latter included the majority of southerners and those northerners who favoured a secular government. From independence until 1972 there prevailed a costly and divisive civil war, fought largely in the south but punctuated by violent incidents in the capital. The Addis Ababa accords of 1972 ended the conflict on terms acceptable to both sides. The appeal of an Islāmic constitution remains strong in some quarters, however, and the comparative lack of economic development in the south has become a new source of regional grievance. Important issues in national life after the civil war have included The Sudan's active role in international politics, ambitious but costly development projects in commercial agriculture, and the problems posed by massive numbers of refugees from troubled lands beyond the country's long borders. (J.L.Sp.)

The article is divided into the following sections:

Physical and human geography

The northern Sudan largely comprises the north central plateau regions on either side of the Nile and includes the narrow ribbon of cultivable land beside the Nile below the Sixth Cataract at Wad Hāmid. The western Sudan includes the entire area of mixed nomadism and peasant agriculture that lies west of the White Nile between Khartoum and Malakāl. This region is subdivided into the four subregions of western Darfur, the Qawz sands, the semidesert, and the Nuba Mountains. The central clay plains area roughly corresponds to the area opposite the western Sudan, to the east of the White Nile between Khartoum and Malakāl.

North of the central clay plains is the eastern Sudan, which is generally devoted to nomadism, but includes the irrigated deltas of the Gash and Barakah rivers. The southern clay plains area includes all of the heavy clay soil subject to flooding in the Upper Nile Basin of southern Sudan. Throughout the region the sources of livelihood are cattle raising, cultivation, and fishing. The Ironstone Plateau and the southern hills region are composed of the area between the Upper Nile Basin and the Nile–Congo watershed, the large hill masses east of the Nile in the southernmost Sudan, and the arid hills and plains of the southeast.

THE LAND

Relief. The Sudan is composed of an immense plain that is bounded on the west by the Nile–Congo watershed and the highlands of Darfur and on the east by the Ethiopian Highlands and the Red Sea Hills (ʿAtbāy). The plain can be divided into the northern area of rock desert of the Sahara; the western Qawz, an area of undulating sand dunes that merges northward into the rock desert; and the central and southern wedge-shaped clay plain, the centre of which is occupied by an enormous swamp known as as-Sudd (the Sudd; also spelled as-Sadd).

Three physical regions

The centre of the clay plain is marked by inselbergs (isolated mountains rising abruptly from the plains), the largest group of which forms the Nuba Mountains (Jibāl an-Nūbah). The volcanic pile of the Jabal Marrah (*jabal,* "mountain" in Arabic) rises out of the Darfur Plateau in the west to altitudes of between 3,000 and 10,000 feet (900 and 3,000 metres) above sea level. The mountains form the Nile–Congo watershed and the western boundary of the central plain.

The western plain is mainly composed of Nubian sandstones, which form a dissected plateau region with flat-topped mesas and buttes. Along the western frontier, the Erdi Plateau stands at 4,760 feet (1,450 metres), the Wādī Howar Plateau at 4,170 feet, and Jabal al-ʿUwaynāt at 2,790 feet.

The Red Sea Hills region is an uplifted escarpment. The scarp slope facing the Red Sea forms rugged hills that are deeply incised by streams. The escarpment overlooks a narrow coastal plain that is 10 to 25 miles (16 to 40 kilometres) wide and festooned with dunes and coral reefs. Further south the eastern uplands constitute the foothills of the Ethiopian highland massif.

In the south there are two contrasting upland areas. The Ironstone Plateau lies between the Nile–Congo watershed and the southern clay plain; the level country is marked with inselbergs. On the Uganda border there are massive ranges with peaks rising to more than 10,000 feet. The Imatong Mountains contain Mt. Kinyeti (10,456 feet), the highest in The Sudan.

Drainage and soils. The drainage pattern of The Sudan may be divided into the four hydrographic regions: the southeastern perennial streams; the central seasonal watercourses; the northern zone of no surface drainage; and the southern clay plain, where—despite heavy and frequent rainfall—the level surface impedes drainage.

All streams and rivers drain either into or toward the Nile. The White Nile enters the country through rapids at Nimule on the Uganda border. It flows northward as the Baḥr al-Jabal until its confluence with the left-bank tributary of the Baḥr al-Ghazāl, after which it is known as the Baḥr al-Abyad. The White Nile receives most of its water from the right-bank Sobat River, which flows from the Ethiopian Highlands to join the Nile near Malakāl. The main stream loses most of its water in as-Sudd as it flows northward to Khartoum.

The Nile River

Most of the Nile system's waters are brought from Ethiopia by the Blue Nile (al-Baḥr al-Azraq), which rises in Lake Tana and flows south and west to enter The Sudan near Guba (Juba), Ethiopia. The river continues northwestward to meet with the White Nile at Khartoum and then flows in a great, curving northward course as the Nile (Nahr an-Nīl).

The surface of the soilless desert is either bare rock, a mantle of bare waste, or sandy expanses of mobile dunes known as ergs. In the semiarid zone, the layer of rock waste is slightly modified to form immature soils; in the Qawz region, soils are brownish red and of low fertility. Alluvial soils occur at the desert deltas of the Gash and Barakah rivers, along the two Niles, and in the alluvial plains of rivers radiating from Jabal Marrah.

The alkaline soils of the central and southern plains are heavy cracking clays. The soil of the Gezira (al-Jazīrah) plain south of Khartoum is deep-cracking, uniform clay that has been deposited during the annual inundations of the Blue Nile, while the clays of as-Sudd were deposited in the area of impeded drainage. The more steeply sloping plain between the Gezira and as-Sudd is an extensive area of cracking clay.

Alkaline soils are also found in the extensive crystalline outcrops of the central plain. The soils of the Ironstone Plateau vary from deep-reddish loams to light soils with a high content of ironstone (a hard rock rich in iron) pebbles. Immature montane soils are found in the Jabal Marrah, the Boma Plateau, and the Imatong Mountains.

Climate. The fundamental climatic factor is the seasonal migration and pulsation of the northern tropical continental air mass and the southern maritime continental air mass, which are divided by the Intertropical Convergence Zone. In winter the north winds of the tropical air mass blow across The Sudan toward the front, which may be as far south as the Tropic of Capricorn. These winds are relatively cool and dry and bring no rain except when they blow across the Red Sea. By April the front begins to move northward across the country, and moist unstable air of the maritime air mass is drawn in from the South Atlantic Ocean. The central and southern Sudan have rainy seasons, the total lengths of which vary according to their latitude.

The Sudan is a hot country, for temperatures are little mitigated by altitude. The central region has the highest mean annual temperatures; at Khartoum temperatures of more than 100° F (38° C) can be recorded during any month of the year. The highest temperatures normally occur just before the rainy season.

Rainfall varies from almost nothing in the north to more than 57 inches (1,450 millimetres) annually in the extreme south. Along the Red Sea the climate is alleviated by sea breezes, and most of the rain falls during winter. Precipitation usually occurs during the summer in showers or thunderstorms in the afternoon or evening. Dust storms are common in the north, while the rainy season lasts for eight to nine months a year in the south.

Rainfall patterns

Plant and animal life. The Sudan has five main vegetational belts that run from east to west, more or less in coincidence with rainfall patterns. The desert region in the north forms about one-fourth of the total area. It is followed southeastward by semidesert, low-rainfall and high-rainfall savanna (grassland) with inland flood plains, and mountain vegetation regions.

Natural vegetation is largely absent because of the effects of centuries of cultivation and because of grass fires that annually may sweep across more than half the country. Further dangers to plant life are the effects of overstocking, soil erosion, the lowering of the water table, and the advance of the desert into the central region.

Wildlife includes the lion, leopard, and cheetah, as well as the elephant, giraffe, zebra, wild ass, rhinoceros, buffalo, hippopotamus, ibex (a type of wild goat), wild sheep, and numerous varieties of antelopes. The chimpanzee, baboon, grivet (a white and green monkey), and colobus monkey are found in the forests. Resident birds include bustards, guinea fowl, several kinds of partridge, geese, cranes, Egyptian vultures, storks, pelicans, plovers, weaverbirds, shrikes, and starlings. Thousands of seabirds, waterfowl, and other birds winter in The Sudan during their migration north. Reptiles include crocodiles and various lizards; snakes are not numerous, but eight varieties found there are poisonous. Insect life is abundant; mosquitoes infest the riverbanks and swamps, seroot flies (large bloodsucking houseflies) are a scourge during the wet months, and scorpions attain eight inches (20 centimetres) in length. The tsetse fly is found south of latitude 12° N whenever suitable conditions occur.

Settlement patterns. Rural settlement is invariably clustered because of problems of water supply, especially during the dry months. Along the northern Nile, villages are often linear and run parallel to the river. In the extreme south, however, dispersed settlement is favoured.

House types vary from north to south. In the north flat-topped roofs and sun-dried bricks daubed with clay prevail, while in the central and southern regions round huts are built with thatched conical roofs made of grass, millet stalks, and wood poles. In the central region compounds of buildings are often surrounded by walls made of millet stalks.

Though towns are few and widely scattered, about one-fifth of The Sudan's population can be considered urban. The southern Sudan was the least urbanized region in 1956, but the southern provinces of Baḥr al-Ghazāl, aʿali an-Nīl (Upper Nile), Gharb al-Istiwāʾīyah (Western Equitoria), and Sharq al-Istiwāʾīyah (Eastern Equatoria) have since experienced a high rate of urban growth. Urbanization has also been relatively rapid in Shamal and Janūb Kurdufān (Northern and Southern Kordofan) and Shamal and Janūb Dārfūr (Northern and Southern Darfur) provinces, where trade is more highly developed. The high urban proportion of the population of an-Nīl (Nile) province is attributable to ʿAṭbarah, the administrative centre that contains the main workshops of Sudan Railways. The high proportion of urban population in al-Baḥr al-Ahmar (Red Sea) province is due to Port Sudan, The Sudan's major outlet to the sea, and the numerous towns in the cotton-growing deltas of the Gash and Barakah rivers. With few exceptions all towns lie along one of the Niles. (M.e.D.S./J.L.Sp.)

The Three Towns

Khartoum, the smallest of the provinces, contains the Three Towns of Khartoum: Khartoum, Omdurman, and Khartoum North. By the early 1980s the population of the Khartoum metropolitan area had grown to about one-twelfth of the country's population. The easily defended site of Khartoum was adopted by the Egyptian-Ottoman government as the colonial capital of the Sudan in about 1830. Today it is firmly established as the centre of power in the country, being the seat of government and higher education and the site of many commercial and industrial undertakings. Omdurman, formerly the capital of the Mahdist state in the Sudan, retains a more traditional atmosphere, while Khartoum North is a new, industrially oriented town.

THE PEOPLE

Arabic is the official language of The Sudan, the most common medium for the conduct of administration, commerce, and urban life throughout the country. It is the native tongue of about half the total population, including both pastoral and agricultural peoples in broad central portions of the country, and it is widely spoken as a second language elsewhere. Although present as a trade language from very early times, Arabic began its rise to prominence in the 14th century with the decline of the Christian kingdoms of medieval Nubia and the subsequent conversion of the northern Sudanese to Islām. Its further success was assured when it was adopted as the language of government by the sultanates of Sennar and Darfur, the Mahdist state, and (with some reservations) by the governments of the Egyptian-Ottoman and Anglo-Egyptian Condominium periods.

Surrounding the central core of Arabic speakers live peoples who have preserved their diverse ancestral languages, which derive from three of the four major language families of the African continent. East of the Nile are the several groups of Hamito-Semitic (Afro-Asiatic) speakers known collectively as the Beja; most speak dialects of Bedawiye, a Northern Cushitic language, but the ʿAbābdah of the far north and Egypt prefer Arabic, and the Amer (Beni Amer) of the far south and Eritrea speak Tigre, a South Semitic language. In the Nuba Mountains live a number of peoples whose languages link them to speakers of the large Congo-Kordofanian language family, most of whom live outside The Sudan to the west and south. The extreme southwestern boundary of The Sudan, however, was drawn in such a way as to include a part of the Azande, a second major Congo-Kordofanian group.

Most of the other African languages spoken in The Sudan belong to the Nilo-Saharan family. Fur, though historically prominent, has only distant linguistic kinsmen, and this can also be said for a number of less important languages spoken in the hilly regions of the west, the Nuba Mountains, and the Ethiopian borderlands. The long Nile corridor from Egypt to Uganda, both north and south of the central Arabic-speaking zone, is dominated by the speakers of two branches of the Eastern Sudanic subfamily. In the north the Nubian cluster includes Nile Nubian and its western relatives such as Midob, Dilling, Birked, and Daju (Dagu). In the south the Nilotic cluster includes the Shilluk, Dinka, Nuer, Bari, and other languages. Also important in The Sudan are English, employed in higher education and in some government and commercial contexts, and the native tongues of the migrant labourers from the west, particularly Hausa. The population is concentrated along the Nile and its tributaries, particularly in al-Jazīrah, Khartoum, and White Nile provinces.

(J.L.Sp.)

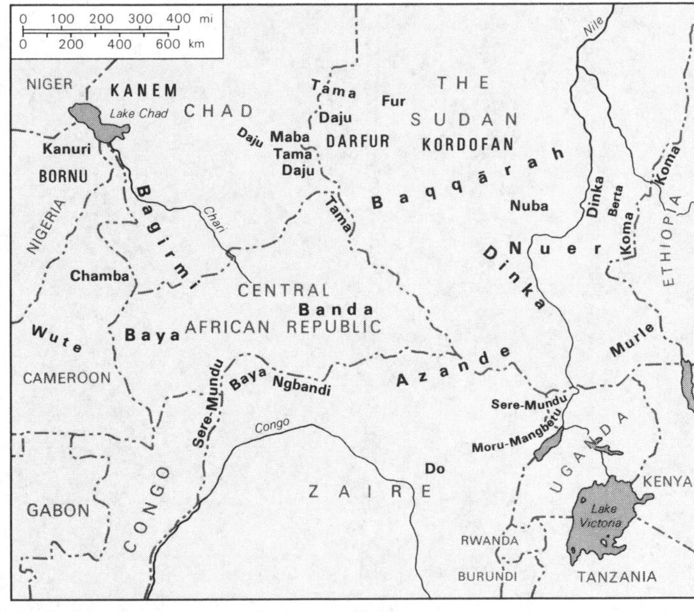

Distribution of the peoples of the eastern Sudan.

TRADITIONAL CULTURES

Because of the great cultural diversity, it is difficult to classify the types of cultures found among the various peoples in the eastern Sudan, which is now shared between the republics of The Sudan, Zaire, Chad, Cameroon, Nigeria, and the Central African Republic. The societies within eastern Sudan portray diverse linguistic, ethnic, social, cultural, and religious characteristics. The selection of cultures that follows merely suggests some rather prominent cultural patterns, illustrative of the wide range present.

The cattle-herding Baqqārah

Peoples and languages. Bedouin Arabs invading southward from Arabia and North Africa reached the area of Lake Chad as early as the 16th century; gradually they intermarried extensively with the Negroid inhabitants, so that many tribes came to exhibit Negroid characteristics. Toward the end of the 18th century, the Baqqārah (nomadic cattlemen), who claim Arab descent, moved eastward to the central regions of what is now the Democratic Republic of The Sudan. This part of the savanna belt is flat and tree covered and suitable to an economy of nomadic cattle husbandry. The majority of the peoples living there have taken not only to raising cattle but also to cultivating millet, sorghum, cotton, and other traditional crops. All are Muslim. Some of the major Baqqārah tribes are the Humr, Messiria, Hawazma, and Rizeigat.

In the Nuba Hills, a rugged, almost mountainous area in a region traditionally known as Kordofan and now a province of the Democratic Republic of The Sudan, there live a Negro people called the Nuba, who, because of the terrain, have tended to be isolated from the peoples migrating about them in the Nile Valley and other areas of the eastern Sudan. The Nuba are subdivided into

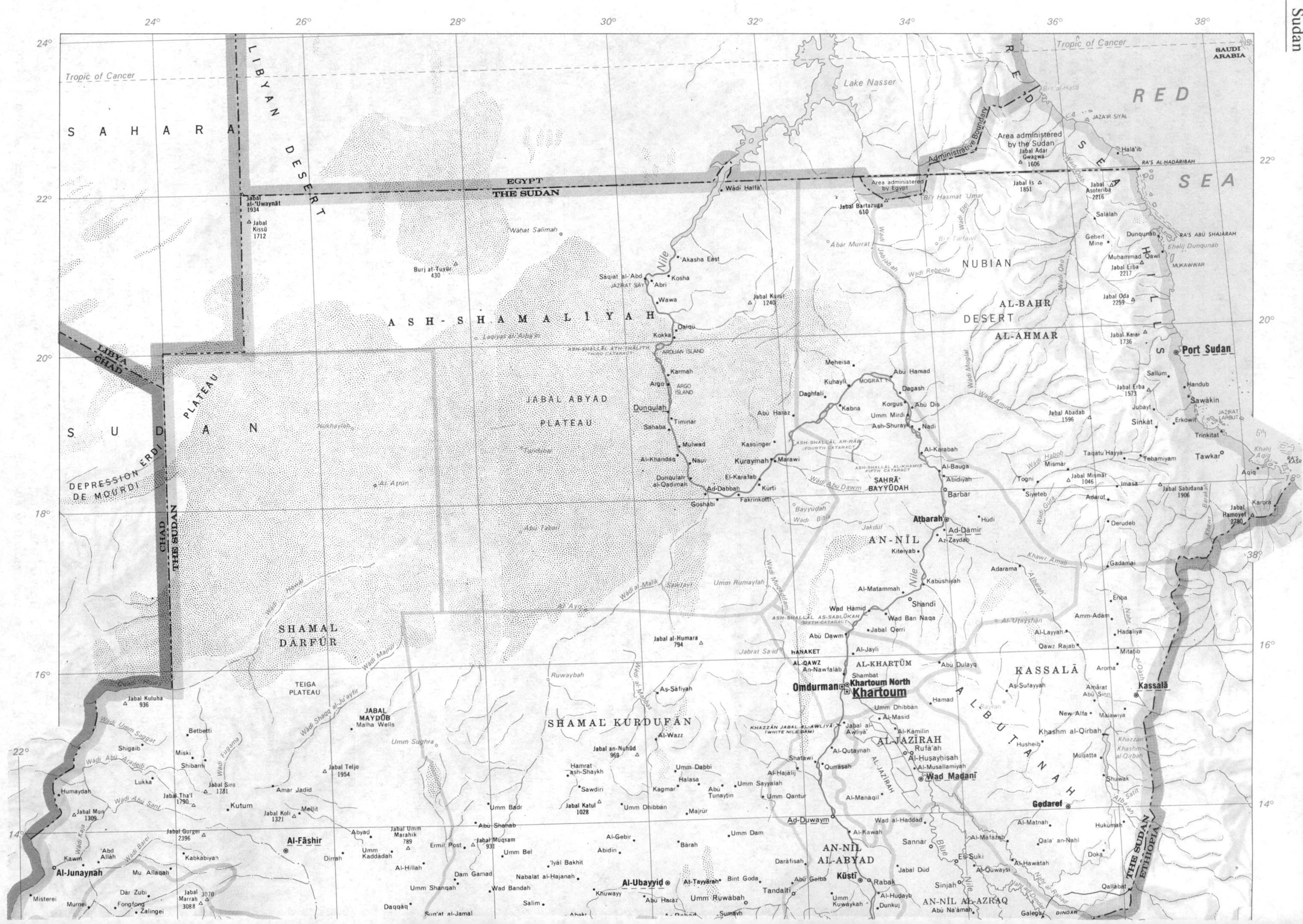
RED SEA
SAUDI ARABIA
Tropic of Cancer
Port Sudan
Sawakin
Hala'ib
Area administered by the Sudan
Area administered by Egypt
Administrative Boundary
NUBIAN DESERT
AL-BAHR AL-AHMAR
Lake Nasser
Wadi Halfa
EGYPT
THE SUDAN
LIBYAN DESERT
SAHARA
ASH-SHAMALIYAH
JABAL ABYAD PLATEAU
Nile
Dunqulah
Marawi
Atbarah
Ad-Damir
Shandi
AN-NIL
SAHRA' BAYYUDAH
Omdurman
Khartoum North
Khartoum
AL-KHARTUM
Kassala
KASSALA
AL BUTANAH
Wad Madani
AL-JAZIRAH
Gedaref
Sannar
AN-NIL AL-AZRAQ
AN-NIL AL-ABYAD
Kusti
Ad-Duwaym
Al-Ubayyid
SHAMAL KURDUFAN
SHAMAL DARFUR
TEIGA PLATEAU
Al-Fashir
Al-Junaynah
ERDI PLATEAU
DEPRESSION DE MOURDI
CHAD
THE SUDAN
LIBYA
CHAD
THE SUDAN
ETHIOPIA
Jabal al-'Uwaynat 1934
Jabal Marrah 3088

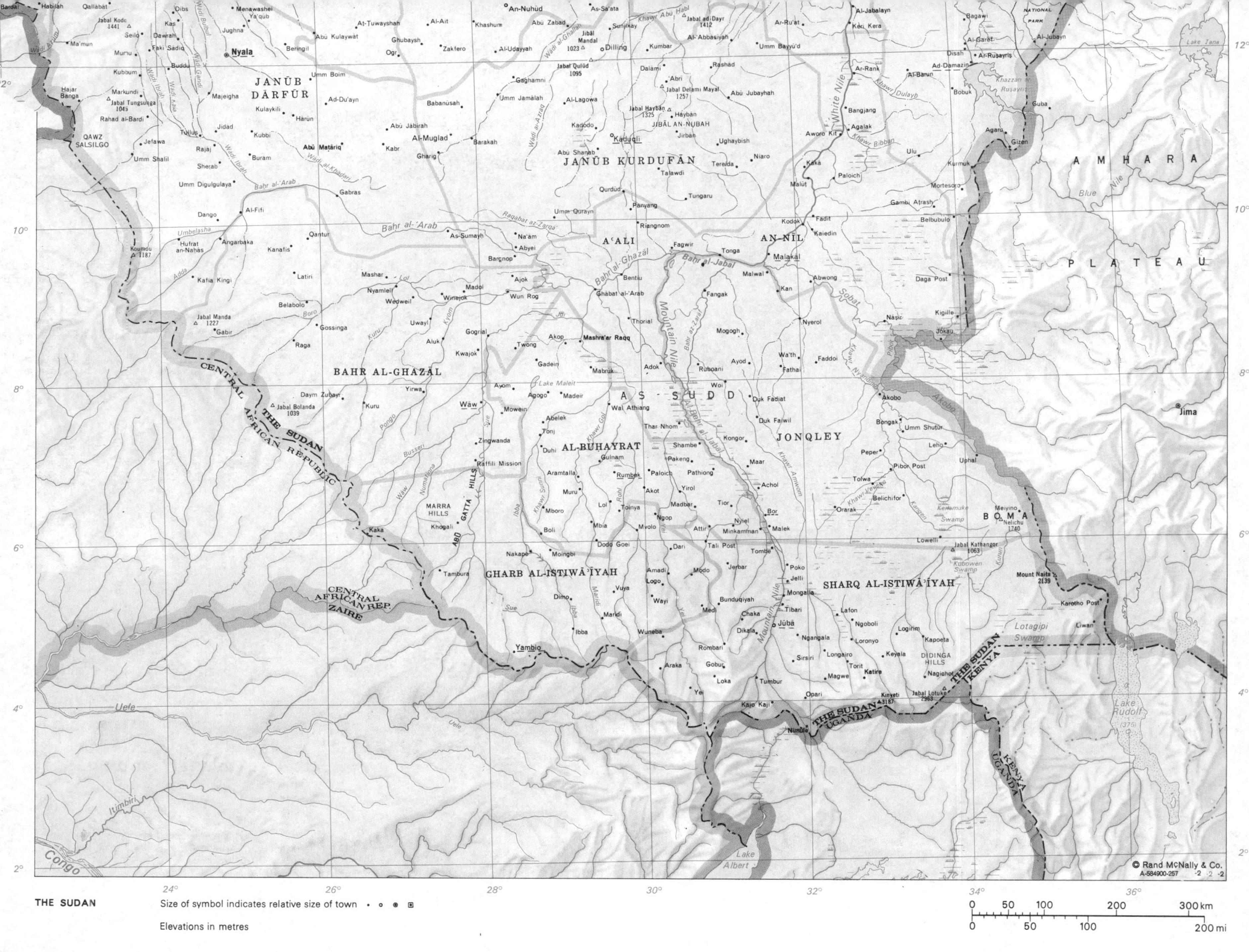
JANŪB DĀRFŪR
JANŪB KURDUFĀN
JIBĀL AN-NUBAH
A'ALI
AN-NĪL
AMHARA
PLATEAU
BAHR AL-GHAZĀL
AS SUDD
AL-BUHAYRAT
JONQLEY
GHARB AL-ISTIWĀ'IYAH
SHARQ AL-ISTIWĀ'IYAH
BOMA
QAWZ SALSILGO
MARRA HILLS
ABŪ GATTA HILLS
DIDINGA HILLS
CENTRAL AFRICAN REPUBLIC
THE SUDAN
CENTRAL AFRICAN REP.
ZAIRE
THE SUDAN UGANDA
THE SUDAN KENYA
KENYA UGANDA
White Nile
Blue Nile
Mountain Nile
Bahr al-Jabal
Bahr al-Ghazāl
Bahr al-'Arab
Sobat
Akobo
Uele
Congo
Lake Albert
Lake Rudolf
Lake Tana
Lotagipi Swamp
Nyala
Dilling
Kadugli
Malakal
Waw
Rumbek
Bor
Jūbā
Yambio
Torit
Jima
Mount Naita 2139
Jabal Kathangor 1063
Jabal Marra
Jabal Bolanda 1039
Jabal Manda 1227
Kinyeti 3187
© Rand McNally & Co.
A-584900-257
THE SUDAN
Size of symbol indicates relative size of town
Elevations in metres
0 50 100 200 300 km
0 50 100 200 mi

MAP INDEX

Political subdivisions

A'ali an-Nīl 9.30n 32.30e
al Baḥr al Ahmar 20.00n 35.30e
al-Buḥayrat 7.00n 29.20e
al-Jazīrah 14.45n 32.20e
al-Kharṭūm 15.55n 32.40e
an-Nīl 18.00n 33.40e
an-Nīl al-Abyaḍ 13.30n 32.20e
an-Nīl al-Azraq 12.20n 34.20e
ash-Shamalīyah 19.00n 30.00e
Baḥr al-Ghazāl 8.20n 26.30e
Gharb al-Istiwā'īyah 4.20n 28.20e
Janūb Dārfūr 11.30n 24.30e
Janūb Kurdufān 11.00n 29.45e
Jonqley 7.40n 32.00e
Kassalā 15.00n 35.30e
Shamal Dārfūr 16.00n 25.40e
Shamal Kurdufān 14.30n 30.00e
Sharq al-Istiwā'īyah 4.50n 32.45e

Cities and towns

'Abd Allāh 13.30n 23.02e
Abekr 12.43n 28.55e
Abelek 7.23n 28.46e
'Ābidīn 13.33n 29.38e
'Abīdīyah 18.14n 33.57e
'Abrī 11.40n 30.28e
'Abrī 20.48n 30.20e
Abū Dawm 16.16n 32.36e
Abū Dīs 19.08n 33.34e
Abu Dulayq 15.54n 33.49e
Abū Gelba 13.11n 31.52e
Abū Ḥamad 19.32n 33.19e
Abū Ḥarāz 12.58n 29.52e
Abū Ḥarāz 19.04n 32.07e
Abū Jābirah 11.04n 26.51e
Abū Jubayhah 11.27n 31.14e
Abū Kulaywāt 12.20n 26.00e
Abū Maṭāriq 10.58n 26.17e
Abū Na'āmah 12.44n 34.08e
Abū Shanab 10.47n 29.32e
Abū Shanab 13.57n 27.47e
Abū Tunayṭin 14.24n 31.01e
Abū Zabad 12.21n 29.15e
Abwong 9.07n 32.12e
Abyaḍ 13.46n 26.28e
Abyei 9.36n 28.26e
Achol 6.34n 31.31e
Adarama 17.05n 34.54e
Adarot 17.50n 36.07e
ad-Dabbah 18.03n 30.57e
ad-Damazin 11.49n 34.23e
ad-Dāmir 17.35n 33.58e
ad-Du'ayn 11.26n 26.09e
ad-Duwaym 14.00n 32.19e
Adok 8.11n 30.19e
Agalak 11.01n 32.42e
Agaru 10.59n 34.44e
Agogo 7.49n 28.52e
Ajok 9.15n 28.27e
'Akasha East 21.05n 30.43e
Akobo 7.47n 33.01e
Akop 8.21n 29.05e
Akot 6.33n 30.03e
al-'Abbāsīyah 12.10n 31.18e
al-Ait 12.22n 27.27e
al-'Atrūn 18.11n 26.36e
al-Barun 11.44n 33.30e
al-Bauga 18.16n 33.55e
al-Fāshir (el-Fasher) 13.38n 25.21e
al-Fifi 10.03n 25.01e
al-Garef 12.03n 34.19e
al-Gebir 13.43n 29.49e
al-Ḥajālīj 14.36n 31.54e
al-Hawātah 13.25n 34.38e
al-Ḥillah 13.27n 27.08e
al-Huḍayb 13.00n 32.50e
al-Ḥuṣayḥiṣah 14.44n 33.18e
al-Jabalayn 12.36n 32.48e
al-Jaylī 16.01n 32.36e
al-Jubayn 12.07n 35.10e
al-Junaynah (Geneina) 13.27n 22.27e
al-Kāmilīn 15.05n 33.11e
al-Karabah 18.33n 33.42e
al-Kawah 13.44n 32.30e
al-Khandaq 18.36n 30.34e
al-Khurtūm, see Khartoum
al-Khurṭūm Baḥrī, see Khartoum North
al-Lagowa 11.24n 29.08e
al-Layyah 16.16n 35.25e
al-Mafāzah 13.36n 34.33e
al-Manāqil 14.15n 32.59e
al-Masīd 15.15n 32.57e
al-Matammah 16.43n 33.22e
al-Matnah 13.47n 35.03e
al-Muglad 11.02n 27.44e
al-Qaḍārif, see Gedaref
al-Quṭaynah 14.52n 32.21e
al-Quwaysī 13.20n 34.05e
al-Ubayyiḍ (el-Obeid) 13.11n 30.13e
al-Uḍayyah 12.03n 28.17e
Aluk 8.26n 27.27e
al-Wazz 15.01n 30.10e
Amadi 5.31n 30.20e
'Amārat Abū Sinn 15.21n 35.45e
'Amm-Adam 16.22n 36.06e
Amar Jadīd 14.28n 25.14e
Angarbaka 9.44n 24.44e
an-Nawfalāb 15.52n 32.32e
an-Nuhūd 12.42n 28.26e
'Aqiq 18.14n 38.12e
Araka 4.20n 30.23e
Aramtalla 6.47n 29.13e
Argo 19.31n 30.25e
Aroma 15.49n 36.08e
ar-Rahad 12.43n 30.39e
ar-Rank 11.45n 32.48e
ar-Ru'at 12.21n 32.17e
ar-Ruṣayriṣ 11.51n 34.23e
ash-Shurayk 18.48n 33.34e
as-Sa'ata 13.37n 29.59e
aṣ-Ṣāfiyah 15.31n 30.07e
aṣ-Ṣufayyah 15.30n 34.42e
as-Sumayḥ 9.49n 27.39e
'Aṭbarah (Atbara) 17.42n 33.59e
Aṭ-Ṭayyārah 13.12n 30.47e
Attir 6.04n 30.50e
aṭ-Ṭuwayshah 12.21n 26.32e
Aworo Kit 10.59n 32.38e
Ayod 8.07n 31.26e
Ayom 7.52n 28.23e
az-Zaydāb 17.26n 33.53e
Babanūsah 11.20n 27.48e
Bagawi 12.19n 34.21e
Bangjang 11.23n 32.42e
Bārah 13.42n 30.22e
Barakah 10.58n 27.59e
Barbar (Berber) 18.01n 33.59e
Bardai 12.43n 22.00e
Bargnop 9.30n 28.28e
Belabolo 8.57n 25.51e
Belbubulo 9.57n 34.04e
Belichifor 6.33n 33.16e
Bentiu 9.14n 29.50e
Berber, see Barbar
Beringil 12.10n 25.41e
Betbetti 15.06n 24.12e
Bint Goda 13.17n 31.33e
Bobuk 11.30n 34.05e
Boli 6.01n 28.43e
Bongak 7.27n 33.14e
Bor 6.12n 31.33e
Buddu 11.54n 24.08e
Bunduqiyah 5.06n 30.53e
Buram 10.49n 25.10e
Būr Sūdān, see Port Sudan
Chaka 4.49n 31.14e
Daga Post 9.12n 33.58e
Dagash 19.22n 33.24e
Daghfalī 19.17n 32.30e
Dalāmī 11.52n 30.28e
Dalqū 20.07n 30.37e
Dam Gamad 13.17n 27.28e
Dango 10.00n 24.45e
Daqqāq 12.56n 26.58e
Darāfisah 13.23n 31.59e
Dari 5.48n 30.21e
Dār Zubi 13.07n 23.40e
Dawrah 12.22n 24.19e
Daym Zubayr 7.43n 26.13e
Derudeb 17.32n 36.06e
Dibs 12.34n 24.14e
Dikala 4.41n 31.23e
Dilling 12.03n 29.39e
Dimo 5.19n 29.10e
Dirrah 13.37n 26.06e
Dīsah 12.02n 34.19e
Dodo Goei 5.57n 27.26e
Doka 13.31n 35.46e
Dongola, see Dunqulah
Duhi 7.07n 28.45e
Duk Fadiat 7.45n 31.25e
Duk Faiwil 7.30n 31.29e
Dunkuj 12.50n 32.49e
Dunqulah (Dongola) 19.10n 30.29e
Dunqulah-al-Qadīmah 18.13n 30.45e
Dunqunāb 21.06n 37.05e
el-Fasher, see al-Fāshir
el-Karafab 18.10n 31.36e
el-Obeid, see al-Ubayyiḍ
Eriba 16.37n 36.04e
Erkowit 18.46n 37.07e
Ermil Post 13.37n 27.36e
es-Suki 13.20n 33.54e
Faddoi 8.07n 32.07e
Fadit 9.58n 32.13e
Fagwir 9.33n 30.25e
Fakī Ṣādiq 12.08n 23.55e
Fakrinkotti 18.01n 31.20e
Fangak 9.04n 30.53e
Fathai 8.05n 31.48e
Fongfong 12.56n 23.14e
Gabir 8.35n 24.40e
Gabras 10.16n 26.14e
Gadamai 17.09n 36.06e
Gadein 8.11n 28.44e
Gaghamni 11.41n 28.19e
Galegu 12.36n 35.02e
Gambi Aṭrash 10.03n 33.47e
Gebeit Mine 21.03n 36.19e
Gedaref (al-Qaḍārif) 14.02n 35.24e
Geneina, see al-Junaynah
Ghābat al-'Arab 9.02n 29.29e
Gharig 10.47n 27.33e
Ghubaysh 12.09n 27.21e
Gizen 10.49n 34.48e
Gobur 4.20n 31.04e
Gogrial 8.32n 28.07e
Goshabi 17.58n 31.06e
Gossinga 8.39n 25.59e
Gulnam 6.55n 29.30e
Habīlah 12.41n 22.33e
Hadalīya 16.10n 36.06e
Ḥajar Banga 11.30n 23.00e
Ḥalasa 14.26n 30.39e
Ḥamad 15.19n 33.43e
Ḥamrat ash-Shaykh 14.35n 27.58e
Handub 19.14n 37.16e
Hārūn 11.20n 25.43e
Haybān 11.13n 30.31e
Hūdī 17.42n 34.17e
Ḥufrat an-Naḥās 9.45n 24.19e
Ḥukūmah 13.52n 36.07e
Humaydah 14.22n 22.31e
Husheib 14.54n 35.07e
Ibba 4.48n 29.06e
Imasa 18.01n 36.12e
'Iyāl Bakhīt 13.25n 28.41e
Jabal al-Awliyā' 15.14n 32.30e
Jabal Dūd 13.25n 33.09e
Jabal Qerri 16.15n 32.48e
Jefawa 10.57n 23.48e
Jelli 5.22n 31.48e
Jerbar 5.39n 31.05e
Jidād 11.05n 24.44e
Jirbān 11.03n 30.36e
Jokau 8.24n 33.49e
Jūbā 4.51n 31.37e
Jubayt 18.57n 36.50e
Jughna 12.24n 25.06e
Kabkābīyah 13.39n 24.05e
Kabna 19.10n 32.41e
Kabr 10.54n 26.50e
Kabūshīyah 16.53n 33.42e
Kadodo 11.04n 29.31e
Kāduqlī 11.01n 29.43e
Kafia Kingi 9.16n 24.25e
Kagmar 14.24n 30.25e
Kaiedin 9.45n 32.11e
Kajo Kaji 3.53n 31.40e
Kākā 10.36n 32.11e
Kan 9.01n 31.47e
Kanafis 9.48n 25.40e
Kapoeta 4.47n 33.35e
Karmah 19.38n 30.25e
Karora 17.42n 38.22e
Karotho Post 5.11n 35.50e
Kas 12.30n 24.17e
Kassalā 15.28n 36.24e
Kassinger 18.45n 31.54e
Katire 4.02n 32.47e
Kawm 13.31n 22.50e
Keri Kera 12.21n 32.46e
Keyala 4.27n 32.52e
Khartoum (al-Khurtūm) 15.36n 32.32e
Khartoum North (al-Khurṭūm Baḥrī) 15.38n 32.33e
Khashm al-Qirbah 14.58n 35.55e
Khashum 12.27n 28.02e
Khogali 6.08n 27.47e
Khuwayy 13.05n 29.14e
Kigille 8.40n 34.02e
Kodok 9.53n 32.07e
Kokka 20.00n 30.35e
Kongor 7.10n 31.21e
Korgus 19.13n 33.29e
Kosha 20.49n 30.32e
Kosti, see Kūstī
Kubbī 11.08n 25.14e
Kubbum 11.47n 23.47e
Kuḥaylī 19.25n 32.50e
Kulaykilī 11.21n 25.36e
Kumbar 12.03n 30.16e
Kuraymah 18.33n 31.51e
Kurmuk 10.33n 34.17e
Kūrtī 18.07n 31.33e
Kuru 7.43n 26.31e
Kūstī (Kosti) 13.10n 32.40e
Kutum 14.12n 24.40e
Kwajok 8.19n 28.00e
Lafon 5.02n 32.27e
Latiri 9.10n 25.43e
Leho 7.07n 33.52e
Liwan 4.54n 35.40e
Logirim 4.43n 33.14e
Logo 5.20n 30.18e
Loka 4.16n 31.01e
Lol 6.26n 29.37e
Longairo 4.30n 32.17e
Loronyo 4.39n 32.38e
Lowelli 5.59n 33.45e
Lukka 14.33n 23.42e
Maar 6.54n 31.33e
Mabrūk 8.07n 29.25e
Madbar 6.19n 30.40e
Madeir 7.50n 29.12e
Madol 9.02n 27.46e
Magwe 4.08n 32.17e
Majeigha 11.33n 24.40e
Majrūr 14.01n 30.27e
Malakāl 9.31n 31.39e
Malawiya 15.16n 36.12e
Malek 6.04n 31.36e
Malha Wells 15.08n 26.12e
Malūṭ 10.26n 32.12e
Malwal 9.19n 31.35e
Ma'mūn 12.15n 22.41e
Mapoi 5.28n 27.40e
Marawi (Merowe) 18.29n 31.49e
Marīdī 4.55n 29.28e
Markundi 11.33n 23.49e
Mashar 9.14n 26.52e
Mashra'ar-Raqq 8.25n 29.16e
Mbia 6.15n 29.19e
Mboro 6.18n 28.45e
Medi 5.04n 30.44e
Meheisa 19.37n 32.57e
Meiyino 6.12n 34.40e
Mellit 14.08n 25.33e
Menawashei 12.40n 24.59e
Merowe, see Marawī
Minkamman 6.03n 31.32e
Miskī 14.51n 24.13e
Mismār 18.13n 35.38e
Misterei 13.07n 22.09e
Mitatib 16.03n 36.11e
Modo 5.29n 30.38e
Mogogh 8.26n 31.19e
Moingbi 5.46n 28.49e
Mongalla 5.12n 31.46e
Mortesoro 10.12n 34.09e
Mowein 7.36n 28.11e
Mu'Allaqah 13.28n 23.57e
Muḥammad Qawl 20.54n 37.05e
Mulwad 18.39n 30.35e
Mumu 12.06n 23.42e
Muqaṭṭa' 14.40n 35.51e
Murnei 12.57n 22.52e
Muru 6.36n 29.15e
Mvolo 6.03n 29.56e
Na'ām 9.42n 28.27e
Nabalat al-Ḥajanah 13.13n 29.02e
Nadi 18.40n 33.42e
Nagichot 4.16n 33.34e
Nakape 5.47n 28.37e
Nāṣir 8.36n 33.04e
Naui 18.28n 30.43e
Ngangala 4.42n 31.55e
Ngoboli 4.57n 32.37e
Ngop 6.16n 30.12e
Niaro 10.38n 31.31e
Nimule 3.36n 32.03e
Nyala 12.03n 24.53e
Nyamlell 9.07n 26.58e
Nyerol 8.41n 32.02e
Nyiel 6.06n 31.13e
Omdurman (Umm Durmān) 15.38n 32.30e
Opari 3.56n 32.03e
Orarak 6.15n 32.23e
Pakeng 6.55n 30.40e
Paloich 6.45n 30.08e
Paloich 10.28n 32.32e
Panyang 10.04n 29.58e
Pathiong 6.46n 30.54e
Peper 7.04n 33.00e
Pibor Post 6.48n 33.08e
Poko 5.38n 31.50e
Port Sudan (Būr Sūdān) 19.37n 37.14e
Qala 'an-Naḥl 13.38n 34.57e
Qallābāt 12.43n 23.26e
Qallābāt 12.58n 36.09e
Qantur 9.45n 25.52e
Qawz Rajab 16.04n 35.34e
Qurdūd 10.17n 29.56e
Qurrāṣah 14.38n 32.12e
Rabak 13.09n 32.44e
Raffili Mission 6.53n 27.58e
Raga 8.28n 25.41e
Rahad al-Baraī 11.18n 23.53e
Rashād 11.51n 31.04e
Rajāj 10.55n 24.43e
Riangnom 9.55n 30.01e
Rombari 4.33n 31.02e
Ruboani 8.06n 30.45e

MAP INDEX (continued)

Rufā'ah 14.46n 33.22e
Rumbek 6.48n 29.41e
Sahaba 18.55n 30.28e
Salālah 21.19n 36.13e
Salim 12.52n 28.40e
Sallūm 19.23n 37.06e
Sannār (Sennar) 13.33n 33.38e
Sāqiat al-'Abd 20.48n 30.19e
Sawākin (Suakin) 19.07n 37.20e
Sawdirī 14.25n 29.05e
Seilo 12.20n 23.50e
Sennar, see Sennār
Shambat 15.40n 32.32e
Shambe 7.07n 30.46e
Shandī 16.42n 33.26e
Shatawī 14.39n 32.06e
Sherab 10.43n 24.47e
Shibarnī 14.50n 24.25e
Shigaib 15.01n 23.36e
Shuwak 14.23n 35.52e
Sinjah 13.09n 33.56e
Sinkāt 18.50n 36.50e
Sirsiri 4.24n 31.53e
Siyeteb 18.00n 35.01e
Suakin, see Sawākin
Sumayḥ 12.43n 30.50e
Sunjikāy 12.20n 29.46e
Suq'at al-Jamal 12.48n 27.42e
Talawdī 10.38n 30.23e
Tali Post 5.54n 30.47e
Tambura 5.36n 27.28e
Tandaltī 13.01n 31.52e
Taqāṭu 'Hayyā 18.20n 36.22e
Tawkar 18.26n 37.44e
Tehamiyam 18.20n 36.32e
Tereida 10.35n 31.17e
Thar Nhom 7.26n 30.29e
Thorial 8.40n 29.56e
Tibari 5.01n 31.43e
Timinar 19.02n 30.29e
Tior 6.23n 31.11e
Togni 18.04n 35.13e
Toinya 6.17n 29.44e
Tolwa 6.38n 32.37e
Tombe 5.49n 31.41e
Tonga 9.28n 31.03e
Tonj 7.17n 28.45e
Torit 4.24n 32.34e
Trinkitat 18.41n 37.43e
Tullus 11.03n 24.33e
Tumbur 4.20n 31.34e
Tungaru 10.14n 30.42e
Twong 8.18n 28.20e
Ughaybish 10.52n 31.05e
Ulu 10.43n 33.29e
Umm Badr 14.14n 27.57e
Umm Bayyū'd 12.05n 31.40e
Umm Bel 13.32n 28.04e
Umm Boim 11.43n 25.57e
Umm Dabbī 14.37n 30.23e
Umm Dam 13.45n 30.59e
Umm Dhibbān 15.26n 32.51e
Umm Digulgulaya 10.29n 24.57e
Umm Durmān, see Omdurman
Umm Jamālah 11.27n 28.12e
Umm Kaddādah 13.36n 26.42e
Umm Kuwaykah 13.00n 32.17e
Umm Mirdi 18.59n 33.32e
Umm Qantur 14.17n 31.22e
Umm Qurayn 9.58n 28.55e
Umm Ruwābah 12.54n 31.13e
Umm Sayyālah 14.25n 31.10e
Umm Shalīl 10.51n 23.42e
Umm Shanqah 13.14n 27.14e
Umm Shuṭūr 7.17n 33.14e
Uphal 6.58n 34.16e
Uwayl 8.46n 27.24e
Vuya 5.21n 29.40e
Wad al-Ḥaddād 13.49n 33.32e
Wad Bandah 13.06n 27.57e
Wad Ban Naqa 16.30n 33.08e
Wad Ḥāmid 16.30n 32.48e
Wādī Ḥalfā' 21.56n 31.20e
Wad Madanī 14.25n 33.28e
Wal Athiang 7.42n 29.40e
Wa'th 8.10n 32.07e
Wāw 7.42n 28.00e
Wawa 20.26n 30.21e
Wayi 5.11n 30.10e
Wedweil 9.00n 27.12e
Winejok 9.01n 27.34e
Woi 7.53n 31.10e
Wuneba 4.50n 30.20e
Wun Rog 9.00n 28.21e
Yambio 4.34n 28.23e
Ya'qūb 12.29n 25.11e
Yei 6.15n 30.13e
Yirol 6.33n 30.30e
Yirwa 7.47n 27.15e
Zakfero 12.10n 27.35e
Zalingei 12.54n 23.29e
Zingwanda 7.10n 27.56e

Physical features and points of interest

Abadab, Jabal, *mountain* 18.53n 35.59e
Abū Aradeib, Wādī, *ravine* 14.12n 23.06e
Abū Dawm, Wādī, *watercourse* 18.28n 31.49e
Abū Gatta Hills 6.06n 27.44e
Abū Ḥabl, Khawr, *watercourse* 12.49n 31.15e
Abū Sanṭ, Wādī, *ravine* 14.11n 23.06e
Abū Shajarah, Ra's, *point* 21.04n 37.14e
Abū Ṭabarī, *well* 17.35n 28.31e
Abyaḍ, al-Baḥr al-, see White Nile
Adda, *river* 9.51n 24.50e
Akobo, *river* 7.48n 33.03e
al-'Ayn, *well* 16.36n 29.19e
al-Gharbiya, Sahara, see Libyan Desert
al-Jazīrah (The Gezira), *physical region* 14.25n 33.00e
Amab, Khawr, *ravine* 17.08n 34.51e
'Amūr, Wādī, *ravine* 18.56n 33.34e
Amwom, Khawr, *watercourse* 7.50n 31.13e
an-Nuhūd, Jabal, *mountain* 14.50n 29.53e
'Aqīq, Khalij, *bay* 18.20n 38.10e
'Arab, Baḥr al, *river* 9.02n 29.28e
Arduan Island 19.55n 30.22e
Argo Island 19.25n 30.27e
ar-Rīḥ, Jazīrat, *peninsula* 18.10n 38.27e
Asoteriba, Jabal, *mountain* 21.51n 36.30e
as-Sudd, *physical region* 8.00n 31.00e
'Aṭbarah, *river* 17.40n 33.56e
Azraq, al-Baḥr al-, see Blue Nile
Azraq, Wādī al-, *watercourse* 10.33n 28.40e
'Azūm, Wādī, *river* 11.33n 20.09e
Barakah, Khawr, *river* 18.13n 37.35e
Barei, Wādī, *ravine* 13.27n 23.57e
Bartazuga, Jabal, *mountain* 21.44n 33.33e
Bayyūḍah, *well* 17.32n 32.07e
Bayyūḍah, Ṣaḥrā', *desert* 18.00n 33.00e
Bibban, Khawr, *watercourse* 11.00n 32.41e
Bitia, Wādī, *watercourse* 17.34n 32.15e
Blue Nile (al-Baḥr al-Azraq), *river* 15.38n 32.31e
Bolanda, Jabal, *mountain* 7.44n 25.28e
Boma, *physical region* 6.10n 34.28e
Boro, *river* 8.52n 26.11e
Bulbul, Wādī, *ravine* 10.59n 24.33e
Busseri, *river* 7.41n 28.03e
Dayr, Jabal ad-, *mountain* 12.27n 30.42e
Delami Mayal, Jabal, *peak* 11.38n 30.23e
Didinga Hills, *mountains* 4.20n 33.35e
Dindar, Nahr ad-, *river* 14.06n 33.40e
Dindar National Park 12.40n 35.20e
Dulayb, Khawr, *watercourse* 11.45n 32.47e
Dunqunāb, Khalij, *bay* 21.05n 37.08e
Elei, Wādī, *ravine* 22.04n 34.27e
Erba, Jabal, *mountain* 20.45n 36.50e
Erba, Jabal, *mountain* 19.04n 36.46e
Erdi Plateau 19.10n 24.00e
Fifth Cataract, see Khamis, ash-Shallal al-
Fourth Cataract, see Rabi', ash-Shallal ar-
Fugama, Wādī, *ravine* 14.43n 24.36e
Gandi, Wādī, *ravine* 11.23n 24.31e
Gash, see Qāsh, Nahr al-
Gezira, The, see al-Jazirah
Ghallah, Wādī al- *watercourse* 10.25n 27.32e
Ghazāl, Baḥr al-, *river* 9.31n 30.25e
Gol, Khawr, *watercourse* 6.55n 30.16e
Gura, Wādī, *ravine* 17.28n 35.10e
Gurgei, Jabal, *mountain* 13.50n 24.19e
Habob, Wādī, *ravine* 18.07n 35.01e
Ḥadāribah, Ra's al-, *cape* 22.04n 36.54e
Hamoyet, Jabal, *mountain* 17.33n 38.02e
Ḥasmat 'Umar Bi'r, *well* 21.46n 34.00e
Haybān, Jabal, *mountain* 11.15n 30.31e
Howar, Wādī, *river* 17.30n 27.08w
Humara, Jabal al-, *mountain* 16.16n 30.59e
Ibba, *river* 7.09n 28.41e
Ibrah, Wādī, *ravine* 10.36n 24.58e
Is, Jabal, *mountain* 21.49n 35.39e
Jabal Abyad Plateau 19.00n 29.00e
Jabal, Bahr al-, *river* 9.30n 30.30e
Jabjabah, Wādī, *watercourse* 22.37n 33.17e
Jabrat Sa'īd, *well* 16.06n 31.50e
Jakdūl, *pond* 17.39n 32.59e
Jur, *river* 8.39n 29.18e
Kaia, Wādī, *ravine* 11.31n 24.15e
Kaiai, Jabal, *peak* 19.54n 36.48e
Kaja, Wādī, *river* 12.02n 22.28e
Kangen, *river* 6.47n 33.09e
Kasr, Ra's, *point* 18.02n 38.35e
Kathangor, Jabal, *mountain* 5.45n 33.59e
Katul, Jabal, *mountain* 14.16n 29.23e
Kenamuke Swamp 5.55n 33.48e
Khadari, Wādī al-, *ravine* 10.29n 26.15e
Khāmis, ash-Shallal al- (Fifth Cataract), *rapids* 18.23n 33.47e
Khashm al-Qirbah, Khazzan, *reservoir* 14.40n 35.55e
Khazzān Jabal al-Awliya, (White Nile Dam), *dam* 15.10n 32.27e
Kinyeti, *peak* 3.57n 32.54e
Kissū, Jabal, *mountain* 21.35n 25.09e
Kobowen Swamp 5.38n 33.54e
Kodo, Jabal, *mountain* 12.26n 23.38e
Koli, Jabal, *mountain* 14.05n 25.31e
Koumou, *mountain* 9.34n 23.38e
Kuluha, Jabal, *mountain* 15.31n 23.25e
Kurun, *river* 5.30n 34.17e
Kuru, *river* 9.08n 26.57e
Kurur, Jabal, *mountain* 20.31n 31.32e
Kyom, *river* 8.58n 28.13e
Laqīyat al-Arba'īn, *oasis* 16.25n 34.30e
Larbut, Jazīrat, *island* 18.47n 37.33e
Libyan Desert (Sahara al-Gharbiya) 22.00n 26.00e
Lol, *river* 9.13n 28.59e
Lotagipi Swamp, *plain* 4.40n 34.50e
Lotuke, Jabal, *mountain* 4.07n 33.48e
Mahbas, Wādī al-, *watercourse* 15.50n 29.45e
Majrūr, Wādl, *watercourse* 15.44n 26.26e
Maleit, Lake 7.55n 28.35e
Malik, Wādl al-, *watercourse* 18.02n 30.58e
Manda, Jabal, *mountain* 8.39n 24.27e
Mandal, Jibal, *hill* 12.09n 29.31e
Maridi, *river* 4.55n 29.28e
Marrah, Jabal, *mountain* 14.04n 24.21e
Marra Hills 6.05n 27.33e
Maydūb, Jabal, *hills* 15.14n 26.30e
Mismār, Jabal, *mountain* 18.06n 35.42e
Moglal, Wādī, *ravine* 19.18n 34.29e
Mountain Nile, *river* 9.30n 30.30e
Mukawwar, *island* 20.48n 37.13e
Mun, Jabal, *mountain* 14.08n 22.42e
Muqaddam, Wādī, *watercourse* 18.04n 31.30e
Muqsam, Jabal, *mountain* 13.38n 27.42e
Murrāt, Ābār, *well* 21.03n 32.55e
Naita, Mount, *mountain* 5.32n 35.19e
Nasser, Lake 21.30n 31.00e
Nelichu, *mountain* 6.08n 34.25e
Nile (Nahr an-Nīl), *river* 21.10n 30.40e
Nūbah, Jibāl an-, *mountains* 12.00n 30.45e
Nubian Desert 20.30n 33.00e
Nukhaylah, *oasis* 19.03n 26.19e
Numatinna, *river* 7.14n 27.37e
Nyanding, Khawr, *watercourse* 8.40n 32.41e
Oda, Jabal, *mountain* 20.21n 36.39e
Odib, Wādī, *ravine* 22.38n 36.06e
Oko, Wādī, *ravine* 21.15n 35.56e
Pibor, *river* 8.26n 33.13e
Pongo, *river* 8.42n 27.40e
Qāsh, Nahr al- (Gash), *river* 16.48n 35.51e
Qawz, Hanakat al-, *dunes* 15.59n 32.01e
Qulūd, Jabal, *hill* 11.41n 29.31e
Rabi', ash-Shallal ar-(Fourth Cataract), *rapids* 18.47n 32.03e
Rahad, Nahr ar-, *river* 14.28n 33.31e
Rayrah, *well* 15.21n 34.41e
Rebeida, Wādī, *ravine* 20.45n 34.06e
Red Sea 23.00n 37.00e
Red Sea Hills, *mountains* 23.00n 35.00e
Rohl, *river* 6.22n 29.46e
Rusayris, Khazzan al-, *reservoir* 11.40n 34.20e
Ruwaybah, *well* 15.39n 28.45e
Sabidana, Jabal, *mountain* 18.04n 36.50e
Sablūkah, Shallāl as- (Sixth Cataract), *rapids* 16.20n 32.42e
Salīmah, Wāḥat, *oasis* 21.22n 29.19e
Salsilgo, Qawz, *dunes* 10.49n 22.54e
Satīt, *river* 14.20n 35.50e
Sawtayr, *well* 17.03n 30.24e
Sāy, Jazirat, *island* 20.42n 30.20e
Shaqq al-Ju'ayfir, Wādī, *ravine* 15.16n 26.00e
Siro, Jabal, *mountain* 14.23n 24.23e
Sixth Cataract, see Sablūkah, Shallāl as-
Sobat, *river* 9.22n 31.33e
Suakin Archipelago, *islands* 18.42n 38.30e
Sunnī, Khawr, *watercourse* 7.09n 28.41e
Sue, *river* 7.41n 28.03e
Tarfawi, Bi'r, *well* 21.04n 34.08e

MAP INDEX (continued)

Name	Lat.	Long.
Teiga Plateau	15.38n	25.40e
Teljo, Jabal, *mountain*	14.42n	25.56e
Tha'l, Jabal, *mountain*	14.13n	24.14e
Thālith, ash-Shallālath- (Third Cataract), *rapids*	19.49n	30.19e
Third Cataract, see Thālith, ash-Shallālath-		
Ṭiwāl, Wādī, *watercourses*	10.25n	23.15e
Tundubai, *well*	18.31n	28.33e
Tungsunga, Jabal, *mountain*	11.29n	23.21e
Tuyūr, Burj aṭ-, *mountain*	20.55n	27.55e
Umbelasha, *river*	9.51n	24.50e
Umm Marahik, Jabal, *hill*	13.40n	26.53e
Umm Rumaylah, *well*	16.55n	31.40e
Umm Saggāt, Wādī, *ravine*	15.15n	23.12e
Umm Sughra, *well*	15.03n	27.12e
'Uwaynāt, Jabal al-, *mountain*	21.54n	24.58e
Veveno, Khawr, *watercourse*	6.40n	32.58e
Wāw, *river*	7.03n	27.13e
White Nile (al-Baḥr al-Abyaḍ), *river*	15.38n	32.31e
White Nile Dam, see Khazzān Jabal al-Awliya		
Yei, *river*	6.15n	30.13e
Zarāf, Baḥr az-, *river*	9.25n	31.10e
Zarqā', Raqabat az-, *watercourse*	9.14n	29.44e

more than 50 different ethnic groups with a multiplicity of languages. Despite their ethnic and linguistic diversity, there exists what has been called a "Nuba culture" based upon some affinities such as clan structure and the regulation of intertribal conflicts. Very little is known about the ancient history of the Nuba tribes, but there are oral traditions that they migrated from the west. The country of the Nuba is well watered, densely wooded, and rich in vegetation. The Otoro is the largest tribe, inhabiting eight hills in the eastern part of Nuba country.

Between Kordofan and Lake Chad, along the northern fringes of the eastern Sudan, there are a number of Negro peoples who were among the first sub-Saharan inhabitants to be strongly influenced by the Arabian commerce and culture penetrating from the north (from about the 11th century onward). Situated on the African frontier of the trans-Saharan caravan routes, these peoples were in a position to develop more diversified cultures and elaborate economies and social structures. Representative of these populations are the groups residing in Darfur, the Republic of The Sudan's westernmost province—the largest resident group being the Fur, after whom the province is named, who occupy the centre. The greater part of the country of the Fur is a plateau—2,000 to 3,000 feet above sea level—with a range of mountains of volcanic origin running north and south and forming the watershed between the basins of the Nile and Lake Chad.

Another important cultural zone inhabited by Negro peoples is the broad band lying just north of the Congolese rain forest, in an area of undulating hills, intersected by many streams and rivers flowing from the divide to either the Nile or the Congo. The zone, lying astride the current boundaries of the Republic of The Sudan, the Central African Republic, and Zaire, is the site of typical Sudanic agriculture—with sorghum and millet usually constituting the staples. Representative of these peoples are the Azande, one of the best known Sudanic-speaking peoples of central Africa; they comprise an agglomeration of invading Sudanic and indigenous tribes differing in origin, language, and culture but thoroughly assimilated and considering themselves all as Azande.

Also numbered among the peoples of the eastern Sudan are the Kanuri, a tall Negro people who inhabit the open savanna country in Borno state, Nigeria.

Major language groups

The major language groups in the eastern Sudan are Congo-Kordofanian, to which the Azande and Nuba languages belong, and Nilo-Saharan, to which the language of the Fur belongs; the term Sudanic languages is applied to these and other languages spoken by peoples from Ethiopia to Nigeria. The Baqqārah tribes are entirely Arabized, and most of the Fur, too, now speak Arabic. Even among the Nuba, Arabic is becoming the lingua franca.

Social organization. *Political and territorial organization.* Broadly speaking, the societies of the eastern Sudan exhibit two types of political organization: the hierarchical systems of the Azande and Fur; and the segmentary systems of the Humr Baqqārah and Otoro. Zandeland, for example, is divided into a number of autonomous chiefdoms. The structure of authority within each chiefdom is pyramidical, with chiefs at the apex of the hierarchy (previously kings), followed by sub-chiefs, deputies, and finally homestead heads. The homestead is the basic political, social, and economic unit. Absolute authority lies with the aristocratic Avongara clan, and commoners can only reach the positions of deputy or homestead head. Local groupings, in which descent is reckoned in the male line, are not associated with clans or sections of clans; they are political and administrative units. Clans have little corporate life, and genealogical links between clansmen are seldom known.

A centralized political and administrative structure also existed among the Fur. There was a sultan at the head of the state, which was divided into four regions in turn divided into districts, subdistricts, and villages. Each village had a council of elders who decided minor cultivation disputes and enforced their decisions by advice and warning. The rights of the village were vested in its inhabitants jointly. Ultimate authority lay with the sultan, who could depose officials beneath him when their power became a threat to his dominance.

In contrast, the Humr Baqqārah have a political system based on a segmentary lineage organization. The tribe is divided into two sections, each of which is divided into a further five sections, each comprising major lineages, camps, and extended families. All these groups have potential leaders. The significant residential and herding unit is the camp, the composition of which changes with the seasons. Within each tribe, and at every level, there is a process of splitting, migration, and resettling that results in a continuous change of alliance among groups and individuals. Blood feuds occur between segments and are settled by payment of blood money. Power among the Humr Baqqārah stems from wealth and strength of personality.

Political organization of the Otoro

The Otoro political system consists of a number of territorial segments that do not coincide with kinship groupings. Clan members are scattered in different localities; the basic political unit is the hill community, whose members share a tract of land and a common code of morality. Feuding between hill communities has been constant, but members of the same hill community must not kill one another. The Otoro have recognized tribal boundaries defined by periodically renewed intertribal treaties. Because of the continual raids and wars between segments, a chieftainship, with the power to use force to maintain peace, has been established.

Family and kinship patterns. In all the societies descent is reckoned in the male line, but the significance of agnatic ties among kin groups differs from one society to another. Among the Azande there are exogamous clans that function primarily as political and administrative units. Clan members are expected to join together to celebrate births, marriages, and funerals. The Azande recognize obligations to the kin of both parents, but greater importance attaches to the paternal connection. Until he is married an Azande has not achieved a man's full status. Marriage is a series of events, each of which is marked by the transfer of goods from one group of kin to the other. Wives of a dead man are inherited by his sons or brothers. Polygyny is also practiced and is regarded as a means of extending affinal relationships and acquiring support. Although divorce is now common, a broken marriage was considered a shameful thing because it destroyed the network of relationships.

The Fur also reckon descent patrilineally, but residence is customarily uxorilocal (with or near the wife's parents). If a husband disagrees with his affines, however, he may take his wife to live with his own group. Cousin marriage, sororate (customary marriage with a deceased wife's sister), levirate (customary marriage to an elder brother's widow), and polygyny are practiced.

Lineage organization of the Humr Baqqārah

Among the Humr Baqqārah, members of the smallest lineage (*surra*), together with their dependents, form a single camp. The organization of a *surra* depends on the number of cattle and the distribution of their ownership among its members. Each *surra* has a leader who is wealthy but who has no administrative functions unless he is already a member of the local government. Whereas members of a camp form the basic unit of cooperation over herding, the household is the main unit of cooperation in agriculture, although some activities connected with agriculture involve a wider group. Preferred marriage within the *surra* is with a parallel cousin. Many first marriages, contracted to conform to the expectation of elders, end in divorce, but in subsequent marriages partners can be freely chosen.

Among the Otoro there are patrilineal clans of various size. With the exception of the Chungur clan, which is the traditional holder of the hereditary chieftainship, all clans are socially of equal order. Clan members intermarry with each other, although clan exogamy was the rule in the past. In the economic and religious spheres the clan does not exercise influence, but it does impose upon its members the collective duty of blood feud in the case of homicide between clans. Patrilineal descent is important in determining the social identity of a person, inheritance, and rights and duties concerning marriage and bridewealth (gifts from the groom and his kinsmen to the father of the bride and his kinsmen). Though the Otoro are patrilineal, matrilineal ties are also important. Polygyny and leviratic marriages are practiced, and bridewealth payments establish wider contact between social groups. Divorce is negotiated and settled by the families concerned. The marriage is dissolved by the total refund of the bridewealth to the former husband.

Social stratification. All the groups have some form of class distinction. The Azande's Avongara clan recognizes rigid distinctions between chiefs and commoners, and generally among the Azande there are distinctions between conquering and conquered groups and slaves. Political, economic, and social status depend on birth, but the politically superior group, the Avongara, must maintain their position by organized political and military means.

The highest political office among the Fur has been that of the sultan, who has been surrounded by a body of councillors dependent on royal patronage. Locally, there has been a descending hierarchy of hereditary fief stewards, village heads, and, lastly, heads of households. Ironworkers have been a despised class not allowed to intermarry with ordinary Fur. Among the Humr Baqqārah, the main distinction is between persons of Arab descent (who hold the positions of power) and non-Arabs. In other respects, a person's wealth and personality determine his successful bid for leadership.

Traditionally, among the Otoro there were no political offices, but only a special hereditary ritual office—that of "chief of the Path," who acted as intermediary in peace negotiations between conflicting parties. Today, however, there are chiefs selected by the local government from among persons of local wealth and importance. In addition there are age-grades; membership in each grade (there are five grades) lasts three years, after which all the members are promoted together to the next higher grade. Promotion is marked with festivities, and members of each age-grade live separately. This system marks the development of a person from an ordinary youth to that of a "big man." Girls also form age-grade groups.

Socialization and education. In all societies under comparison, there are ritual and ceremonial practices marking the stages in the life cycle of the individual—birth, circumcision, puberty, marriage, and death. There is little formal education among the Azande, Otoro, Humr Baqqārah, and Fur.

Circumcision distinguishes boyhood from manhood. It is a recent introduction among the Azande, having spread from the south despite being opposed by the Avongara. Among the Otoro, an individual achieves higher status as he is promoted from one age-grade to another. There is also an association of cicatrization (scarring) with a test of manhood: killing an enemy entitles a person to have a small pattern of scars on his back. Similar patterns are also made on the upper arms of successful hunters. Men take part in wrestling and fighting as part of their training for manhood. Among the Azande and Nuba, there are very few schools at elementary level established by missions. Education has made little headway among the Humr Baqqārah because it comes into conflict with their way of life—people are reluctant to send their children to schools because livestock and cattle herding will suffer. There are a few Qur'ānic schools among the Fur, in which elementary Arabic, arithmetic, and the Qur'ān are taught.

Qur'ānic schools

Economic organization. *Settlement patterns.* The societies exhibit three different patterns of settlement. The Otoro and Azande live in scattered groups. Otoro homesteads are scattered irregularly over hilltops and valleys, a number of homesteads constituting a village, villages combining to form hill communities, a number of which make up the tribe. Similarly, the Azande live in family groups in scattered homesteads separated by strips of bush. Among the Otoro and the Azande, the homesteads are the basic social and economic unit. In contrast, the Fur have more compact settlements. The Fur live in homesteads, a number of which constitute a village. The third type of settlement pattern is that of the Humr Baqqārah, who live in tent camps. Their nomadic existence does not permit the formation of permanent settlements.

Production and technology. The economy of most of the peoples of eastern Sudan is dependent on cultivation, with animal husbandry, and sometimes hunting and fishing, providing an important supplement to agriculture. A wide variety of crops, including grain, sesame, vegetables, sorghum, maize, groundnuts, and cotton, are grown, the latter two sometimes as cash crops. Among the Humr Baqqārah cultivation is a subsidiary occupation. They move in a regular seasonal cycle according to the availability of water and grass. In winter, or at the end of the rains, they move south, and in spring, or during the rains, they move north. Some cultivation of millet and, in recent years, of cotton as a cash crop is undertaken. Throughout their territory the Humr Baqqārah have communal grazing rights, whereas cultivable plots of land are owned individually and handed down from father to son.

The technology of these societies is simple: among the Otoro the making of bedsteads, mat weaving, and pottery are undertaken. The Azande, on the other hand, are prominent as craftsmen and artists. Their superior material culture, particularly their knives, spears, and shields, was one of the factors by which they dominated their neighbours and brought about the spread of their culture. Basketmaking, net weaving, pottery, smelting, metalworking, and ivory and wood carving are also undertaken. There are ironworkers in every Fur village; other Fur crafts include tanning and weaving of cloth and basketry. The Humr Baqqārah produce leather goods and basketry to meet their own needs.

Prominence of Azande arts and crafts

Property and exchange systems. Land among the Otoro, Azande, and Fur is the principal economic asset. Among the Otoro land can be acquired through inheritance, purchase, lease, and by clearing and cultivating new areas. The Otoro and the rest of the Nuba tribes convert nearly their whole agricultural surplus into livestock. Although livestock are used for clan sacrifices, they are not sold for money, and neither are they slaughtered for meat. Among the Nuba tribes, however, people use livestock for certain standardized payments such as bridewealth or gifts to kin relations. Iron, because of its rarity and its use in weapons and tools, became the standard medium of exchange. Handicraft products are purchased with such goods as grain, sesame, hoes, spears, goats, axheads, and, nowadays, with money.

Whereas livestock is a secondary source of wealth to the Otoro, cattle are the primary source of wealth, prestige, and political position for the Humr Baqqārah. Cattle were once the medium of exchange, but during the 20th century cash has become significant.

Before the introduction of cotton and money, wealth among the Azande was primarily in the form of perishable agricultural produce, and it was customary to destroy the property of a man after his death. Only chiefs were able to accumulate wealth, since they received tribute and prisoners of war as perquisites. There was little exchange between households, although iron tools and spears were used in bridewealth payments.

Among the Fur, property consists of houses, domestic articles, rolls of cloth, and cattle kept mainly for resale. Rights over land are held jointly by descent groups and are vested in a titleholder. There are organized marketplaces in which the medium of exchange has been, and still is, money. Previously, cloth may have served as a medium of exchange. Agricultural products are exchanged for tools and utensils, cloth, and other commodities. Labour is exchanged for beer.

Religious practices. The Humr Baqqārah and Fur peoples adhere to Islāmic beliefs and practices, Islām having come to them through Arab influence. Traditional local practices, however, coexist with Islāmic beliefs. Among the Fur, for example, the splashing of sanctuaries with a flour and water paste is carried out to ensure fertility. There are also rain cults thought to have been introduced from farther west. Sacrifices are made at shrines and at ancestral tombs when the rains are likely to fall. The office of rainmaker is hereditary.

Witchcraft of the Otoro and Azande

The Otoro and Azande have their own local beliefs and practices, which are significant as a means of social control, and Islām and Christianity have very little influence. Among the Otoro there is a widespread belief in oracles and witchcraft as a means of punishing offenders and establishing justice. Charms bought from Arab or West African charm sellers, diviners, grain priests, and rainmakers are used to find and punish evildoers. Leprosy, imagined to be caused by supernatural powers, is believed to be connected with offenses such as sexual intercourse in forbidden kinship degrees and homicide. Witchcraft, a magic at the disposal of any individual, is effective only if directed against a person guilty of a crime.

Among the Azande the power of witchcraft is inherited. Diviners, oracles, vengeance magic, and the use of leeches are means of counteracting it. The Avongara clan may not be accused of witchcraft because the chief and his oracle are considered infallible.

Developments in the 20th century. The influence of European contact and of self-government on the societies of the eastern Sudan has varied. Innovations introduced among the Humr Baqqārah have included cotton cultivation, use of cash, wage labour, and improvements in breeding. With the introduction of local government, the traditional power structure was altered, but the traditional agnatic groupings remain as units of administration. The economic and social importance of cattle has not changed.

The Otoro have experienced a number of changes introduced by Europeans and Arabs. Larger tracts of land are being worked, new crops have been introduced, modern chieftainship has been instituted, and a new system of law and order has been introduced. The younger generation of Nuba who work outside their homeland bring back new habits and interests, and the authority of the older generation is thus weakened. Nevertheless, the Nuba still retain their social structure and identity.

Since the incorporation of Darfur into The Sudan at the turn of the 20th century, a new administration has been introduced. The independence of the Fur and other tribes has been modified by the formation of regional local governments, each with its own judicial and financial powers. The basic tribal local government, however, is still founded on the rule of hereditary or traditional headmanship of a tribe or on sultanates.

Attempted resettlement of the Azande

The most noticeable social and economic changes have occurred among the Azande, who since the 1920s have been constantly settled and resettled. In 1945 a resettlement scheme was introduced based upon the manufacture of cloth, cooking oil, and soap from cotton grown by the Azande. It was at first successful, but eventually proved unacceptable to the Azande themselves since it was not in accord with their value system. Sporadic revolt in the area has also delayed development. (A.Al-Sh.)

THE ECONOMY

The Sudan is one of the poorest and least developed countries in the world, with most of its inhabitants dependent on farming and animal husbandry for their livelihoods. Apart from its wide variety of agricultural products, ranging from cotton and gum arabic in the north to timber, tea, and many kinds of fruits and vegetables in the south, there are substantial but largely unexploited reserves of oil and of such minerals as zinc, copper, silver, iron, manganese, and chromium ores, as well as gypsum.

Agriculture, forestry, and fisheries. The main crops of cotton, common millet, *dukhn* (bulrush millet), sorghum, peanuts (groundnuts), sesame, corn (maize), wheat, and castor are raised on land that is either rain fed, irrigated, or subject to flooding. The amount of rain-fed and flooded land varies annually, but irrigation is gradually being extended.

The irrigated areas in the north and east produce the bulk of the commercial crops. They are centred on the Gezira Scheme (al-Jazīrah)—with its Mangil extension—between the Blue and White Niles south of Khartoum and other schemes watered by the Khashm al-Qirbah Dam on the ʿAṭbarah River and ar-Ruṣayriṣ Dam, which provides irrigation water for the Rahad Scheme.

The Sudan's irrigated agriculture is dependent upon abundant supplies of water from the two main branches of the Nile. Future growth of Sudanese agriculture, however, continues to depend on mechanized rain-fed farming in a broad belt running from Kassalā (Kassala) province in the east to Janūb Kurdufān in the west. One of the major disadvantages of this type of agriculture, however, is that rich farmers practice a sophisticated version of traditional shifting cultivation—they farm an area intensively with government-financed equipment for a few years but then move on to more attractive virgin land when yields decline.

Because of the relative anarchy of the mechanized rain-fed sector in agriculture, planners in The Sudan have tended to concentrate their efforts on irrigation schemes, under which cotton is the dominant crop. The bulk of the cotton crop is grown on the Gezira Scheme, situated between the White and Blue Niles south of Khartoum. The scheme, which was begun by the British in 1925 after construction of the Sannār Dam, is farmed by tenant farmers in cooperation with the government and The Sudan Gezira Board, which oversees administration, credit, and marketing. Although The Sudan's total output accounts for only a tiny percentage of world production, its importance in the cotton market results from supplying a large part of the extra-long-staple cotton grown in the world. When synthetic fabrics caused a slump in demand for cotton in the mid-1970s, there was a short-lived experiment to turn the Gezira's production away from cotton into wheat, peanuts, and other cash crops that could be used to satisfy The Sudan's domestic demand for food. In 1978, however, it was decided to halt this venture and return to concentration on cotton production.

There is little development of commercial agriculture in the south. Nevertheless, ambitious projects were identified and, in some cases, begun for the cultivation of tropical crops such as coffee, tea, and tobacco. The south, with its abundant wildlife, might also be used to help spark a tourist industry that has been largely dormant in the country as a whole.

Fruits grown in The Sudan include dates, mangoes, guavas, oranges, and bananas, while onions are the most widespread vegetable. Livestock, primarily cattle, sheep, goats, and camels, is probably The Sudan's most underestimated natural resource.

The Sudan is the world's largest producer of gum arabic, a water-soluble gum obtained from acacia trees and used in the production of adhesives, candy, and pharmaceuticals. The southern forests yield hardwood timber such as mahogany and *sant* (a type of acacia) and softwoods, and there are sawmills near Wāw, Loka, and Katire. The northern woodlands have been deforested by the extraction of wood for fuel and charcoal.

The Nile rivers are the main source of fish, especially Nile perch. Most of the catch is consumed locally, although attempts have been made to export fish to Europe and the Middle East. Significant quantities of fish and shellfish are produced from the Red Sea.

Industry. The manufacturing industry contributes only a small percentage of the gross domestic product. Manufactures include sugar, textiles, cement, leather and footwear, petroleum products, and processed foods.

The Arab Authority for Agricultural Investment and Development (AAAID) in Khartoum has slowly begun to set up agricultural industries. With the opening in 1981 of the Kenana Sugar Scheme, The Sudan was well on the way to achieving self-sufficiency in that commodity. Output at The Sudan's other state-owned sugar factories has been poor. Falling production and poor labour relations elsewhere, particularly in the food-processing and textile industries, have encouraged a breaking off of state-owned sugar factories to private interests. Specific manufacturing industries are being made directly financially accountable and self-sufficient rather than being allowed to depend on protection and subsidies as government corporations.

Development of the oil industry

One area of continuing optimism for the economy as a whole is that of oil. Oil was first discovered in the southwestern Sudan in 1977, and a commercially viable find was made in 1980.

By the early 1980s The Sudan had an installed electrical capacity of about 220,000 kilowatts. The Sannār Dam supplies electricity to the Gezira and to Khartoum, and hydroelectric dams have also been built at Khashm al-Qirbah on the ʿAṭbarah River and ar-Ruṣayriṣ on the Blue Nile.

Finance and trade. All banks operating in The Sudan were nationalized in 1970, but foreign banks were again allowed to operate after 1976. The Bank of Sudan issues all currency and acts as banker to the government. It also holds bilateral trade accounts on behalf of the government and supervises the operations of the seven commercial banks. The Agricultural Bank and the Industrial Bank provide development funds and credit. The banking system is geared primarily to the finance of foreign trade and especially the cotton trade.

The Sudan suffers from an unfavourable balance of trade and a growing national debt. Most foreign exchange is earned from cotton, which accounts for more than half of total exports. Other exports include gum arabic, oilseeds, and livestock products. Imports consist largely of manufactured goods, such as textiles, machinery, vehicles, petroleum products, and iron and steel. The most important trading partners are members of the European Economic Community, Japan, Egypt, and China.

The government's economic role

Administration of the economy. Government control of the economy has been gradually relaxed since the mid-1970s. By 1980–81 this had resulted in liberalization of exchange controls, encouragement of private and foreign investment, payment of market prices to farmers, and a number of other measures designed to make the economy more market, rather than government, regulated.

Since 1978 The Sudan has been operating under an austerity program designed to improve the balance of payments, cut back development spending, consolidate existing projects, and correct cost–price distortions and other constraints that have held back expansion of output and export earnings from cotton and other primary agricultural products. At the same time, negotiations have been undertaken to reschedule debts to external creditors.

Little government revenue is raised by direct taxation, while indirect taxes, such as those on imports and excise and consumption duties, provide more than half the revenue. Other revenue has traditionally been derived from government monopoly profits on sugar, tea, coffee, and salt and proprietary receipts from agricultural and other schemes.

The smallness of the industrial sector and the predominance of rural life have tended to constrain the development of workers' and employers' associations. In 1958 all trade unions were dissolved, but they were permitted to function again in 1961 within limits prescribed by legislation. There are trade unions representing the workers in government ministries, the Sudan Railways, the Central Electricity and Water Administration, and other bodies. Unions normally are affiliated with the three central federations of the Sudanese Workers' Union, the Federation of Workers' Trade Unions in the Private Sector, and the Federation of Workers' Trade Unions of the Public Sector. Political activity by trade unions is discouraged.

Leading businessmen are members of the Sudan Chamber of Commerce. An important pressure group is the Gezira Tenants' Association, which attempts to promote tenants' interests. (E.I.U.)

Transportation. The transport system is underdeveloped and is a serious constraint on economic growth. The country's vast area and the availability of only one major outlet to the sea place a heavy burden on the limited facilities, especially on the government-owned Sudan Railways, which handles almost all foreign trade and employs about one-fifth of all wage earners.

The railway network

The main railway line runs north from al-Ubayyiḍ (el-Obeid) via Khartoum to Lake Nasser and the submerged terminal of Wādī Halfā, with branch lines from Sannār and ʿAṭbarah to Port Sudan and from Sannār to ar-Ruṣayriṣ. There is also a westward extension from al-Ubayyiḍ to Nyala, with a branch line south to Wāw.

Only a small portion of the roads are paved. The remaining roads are generally motorable but unimproved tracks, and they are impassable after rain.

The White Nile and the Baḥr al-Ghazāl are navigable throughout the year. The Jur and Sobat rivers are seasonal. The Blue Nile is not navigable, and the Nile below Khartoum is navigable only in short stretches. The government operates steamer services on the White and the main Nile. Port Sudan, 850 miles south of Suez, Egypt, is the country's main port on the Red Sea. Minor ports include Sawākin, Trinkitat, and ʿAqīq.

The government-owned Sudan Airways operates domestic and international services from the main airport at Khartoum. There are several subsidiary airports, the most important of which are Jūbā and Port Sudan. (M.e.D.S.)

ADMINISTRATIVE AND SOCIAL CONDITIONS

Government. A general reorganization of government followed the military coup d'etat of May 1969. In 1971, legislative, judicial, and executive powers were vested in the president, Maj. Gen. Gaafar al-Nimeiry, who was also commander of the armed forces. The Sudan Socialist Union (SSU) was constituted as the single legal political party. In January 1972 the SSU approved the establishment of the Sudanese People's Assembly of 207 members, of whom 32 members were to be appointed by the president and the remainder elected by popular vote from regional and professional or other constituencies. The first election of members of the Sudanese People's Assembly took place during September–October 1972, and the new government took office in October. Subsequent elections, embodying some changes in the constituencies, took place thereafter at orderly intervals. In 1973 the Sudanese People's Assembly ratified a permanent constitution embodying the principles of agreement reached in the peace settlement of March 1972, and in 1977 a policy of national reconciliation was introduced in the hope of gaining the allegiance of politicians of the era before the coup.

The Southern Region

In 1972 the Southern Region, then comprised of Baḥr al-Ghazāl, al-Istiwāʾīyah, and aʿali an-Nīl provinces, was established with its capital at Jūbā. It was granted limited self-government within the national structure. The People's Regional Assembly was created as the legislative body, its members elected by direct, secret ballot. The High Executive Council, appointed by the president, was formed as the administrative body and was charged with the establishment of a civil service in the south and with other duties. Government in the Southern Region has had a stormy electoral and parliamentary history, and on several occasions the president has exercised his power to dissolve an existing southern regime. In 1983 the Southern Region was redivided into its three original provinces.

Local government

In January 1980 the SSU adopted a recommendation under which the country was to be divided into five regions to encourage increased local self-government. The country's 366-seat National Assembly was dissolved in October 1981. Elections were held in December 1981, and 151 members were chosen for the new Assembly. Regional governments were established for the north, west, midwest, east, and central regions; Khartoum is the seat of the central government. The five regional assemblies oversee local security, health, education, development, transport, and other social matters. In 1983 the Southern was divided into its three original provinces.

All political parties were banned in 1969. Two years later the SSU was established as the country's only party. Its structure is comprised of a National Congress, Executive Committee, and Supreme Political Bureau on the national level (all three chaired by the president); provincial assemblies; and basic units in the villages and towns. Ancillary organizations include the May Youth Corps and the Socialist Sudanese Women's Association. Membership is open to all persons over 18 years of age who are loyal to the government.

Civil justice is administered through the High Court of Justice in Khartoum, province courts, and district judges. There is a body of civil law; where there is no special enactment, cases are decided according to "justice, equity, and good conscience." The criminal code is based upon the Indian Penal Code and is dispensed in major, minor, and magistrate's courts. There are also people's courts that try a substantial proportion of civil and criminal cases in accordance with popular custom. Muslims are subject to the Sharī'ah, the religious law of Islām, in questions of inheritance, marriage, divorce, family relationship, and charitable trusts.

The armed forces have been greatly expanded since 1969, and the military's political role has been defined through the SSU. By the early 1980s the forces consisted of an army, a navy, and an air force. There were also the paramilitary national guard and border police.

Education. In the Muslim areas of the north, boys have long been instructed in religious subjects according to traditional methods. Primary education was begun in the northern Sudan after 1898, and secondary education began in 1913. Postsecondary schools in arts and science, agriculture, veterinary science, engineering, and law were established between 1938 and 1941. In 1947 these schools were brought together within Gordon Memorial College, which was linked in special relationship with the University of London until 1959. Education in medicine began in 1924 with the foundation of the Kitchener School of Medicine, which in 1951 was united with Gordon Memorial College in the University College of Khartoum. In 1956 University College became the University of Khartoum.

Christian missionaries assumed responsibility for formal education in the south prior to independence. Southern education suffered during the civil war; the national authorities curtailed missionary activities, attempted to Arabize the southern schools, and, failing that, closed them in 1962. The southern partisans operated schools in the vernacular languages and English in the areas they controlled, but their resources were extremely limited.

In 1970 the government instituted a four-level educational system. It consists of a six-year primary level; a three-year secondary level; a three-year higher secondary or vocational, technical, or teacher-training level; and three or more years of higher education. In addition, the government has instituted a special program to combat the country's high illiteracy rate. New national universities that emphasize scientific and technical training were opened in 1975 at Wad Madanī in the Gezira and at Jūbā in the Southern Region. The Omdurman Islāmic University offers an advanced curriculum with religious emphasis. The *maʿhad ʿilmī* in the mosque at Omdurman, attended by pupils from Muslim areas, provides theological education and trains religious leaders (*ʿulamāʾ*) and lawyers (*qāḍīs*). The principal centre for the training of intermediate school teachers is the Institute of Education at Bakht ar-Ruda near ad-Duwaym for men and at Omdurman for women. Secondary school teachers are trained at a Higher Institute for Teacher Training at Omdurman. English is the medium of instruction in the university and the secondary schools, but it is being replaced by Arabic in the latter.

Health and welfare. Early in the 20th century the Sudan was reputed to be unhealthy, and epidemics of sleeping sickness, cerebrospinal meningitis, and yellow fever were frequent. The progress of medical and sanitary services under the Sudan Medical Service (later the Ministry of Health), supplemented in many places by missionary institutions, has reduced mortality. Rural areas are served by dispensaries and dressing stations under medical assistants. There are doctors in private practice in the larger towns and a rural midwife service.

Towns are planned so that there are separate first-, second-, and third-class residential areas, as well as commercial and industrial zones. Buildings must conform to regulations such as those governing the materials to be used and the number of stories to be erected. In rural areas where the population is sedentary, housing conforms to local custom, while nomads occupy tents.

The Sudan Police Force, under the authority of the Ministry of the Interior, is responsible for the policing of the entire country. Its duties include internal security, criminal investigation, and the administration of passport migration, nationality, and alien registration. There are also several police reserve companies that are specially trained on quasi-military lines.

Social conditions. In the late 20th century more than three-fourths of the total labour force was engaged in agriculture, forestry, and fishing. Income is higher in urban and semiurban areas than in the larger rural sector. In industry, commerce, and public administration, there is legislation to cover employment exchanges, conditions of employment in factories and in domestic service, and workmen's compensation.

Social and economic divisions

The greatest social and economic divisions—those between the northern and southern regions—have been exacerbated rather than eased over the past century and a half by the policies of the Egyptian-Ottoman, Mahdist, and Anglo-Egyptian Condominium governments. During most of the Condominium period (1899–1955), for example, the British-dominated government banned the entry of northern Sudanese traders, teachers, and missionaries into the south, while allowing European Christian missionaries to proselytize there. Because it was of easier access, the Islāmic north underwent economic and educational advances denied to the south, where the years of civil war further hindered development.

There are other serious problems. One problem has been a loss of trained manpower through emigration to the oil-rich countries of Libya, Saudi Arabia, the United Arab Emirates, and Kuwait. Remittances by Sudanese emigrés form an important source of income for some parts of the country, but the loss of skills has produced chronic personnel crises in a number of programs and projects. In addition, the Sudanese cotton industry has depended upon the availability of large amounts of cheap seasonal labour; a significant portion of this demand has been met by migrants from northern Nigeria, who constitute a large community of severely underemployed yet economically indispensable aliens. During the 1970s The Sudan also became a haven for hundreds of thousands of refugees, particularly from Chad, Uganda, and Ethiopia. Foreign assistance helped to ease the burden of feeding and housing the refugees, but it did not address the deeper problem of their ultimate destiny as foreign communities within The Sudan.

CULTURAL LIFE

The Sudan has chosen a path of mediation and synthesis between the Islāmic and African traditions in its own cultural heritage and between both of these and the intrusive institutions of Western society. This course has not been easy, or flawlessly executed, nor has its final destination yet been achieved. The years of peace and generosity of spirit since the end of the civil war, however, have been a period of much progress, and the vision of tolerance and hope retains its vitality.

The Sudan's highly distinctive and widely admired popular music is its most democratic art form, drawing upon the poetic and melodic wealth of the nation and disseminating it through radio and inexpensive tape cassettes. The airwaves and recording facilities of the Three Towns are accessible to rising talent as well as established masters, and even remote corners of the land share new discoveries and cherished nostalgia. Drama flourishes at the National Theatre and elsewhere in the Three Towns, but performers have hitherto enjoyed only limited opportunities to tour. The popular theatre of Egypt has exerted a strong influence, and a wide variety of European works have also been presented. A rising generation of Sudanese dramatists began to find their own voices during the 1970s, probing contemporary social issues, the meaning of the past, and the possibilities of the human spirit. They have attempted to reach a wider audience through the creation of radio plays, and the highly acclaimed cinematic production of Tayeb Salih's *The Wedding of Zein* has demonstrated the potential of motion pictures.

The Institute of Fine Arts and Technology has served as home to the graphic arts in The Sudan. A number of Sudanese printmakers, calligraphers, and photographers have achieved international recognition. Ibrāhīm al-Ṣalaḥi, who is proficient in all three media, is perhaps the most widely known. Although painting and sculpture have not yet attained similar eminence, gifted artists are active in these media.

Modern Sudanese literature in Arabic has been widely admired since its emergence as a published genre in the 1920s, and the present generation of scholars, centred at the University of Khartoum, has undertaken to place it in a critical perspective. Numerous and promising writers and poets are active in both Arabic and English, and works of Sudanese authorship in the sciences, history, and folklore have also earned critical and popular acclaim.

The Department of Antiquities manages the National Museum, a magnificent Khartoum landmark, and smaller archaeological exhibits in Marawi and al-Ubayyiḍ. The Ethnographical Museum and the Sudan Natural History Museum are affiliated with the University of Khartoum. For statistical data, see the "Britannica World Data" section in the current *Britannica Book of the Year.*

(M.e.D.S./J.L.Sp.)

History

ANCIENT NUBIA

The earliest inhabitants of the Sudan can be traced to Negroid peoples who lived in the vicinity of Khartoum, the Sudan, in Mesolithic (Middle Stone Age) times (30,000–20,000 BC). They were hunters and gatherers who made pottery and (later) objects of ground sandstone. Toward the end of the Neolithic (Late Stone Age; 10,000–3,000 BC) they had domesticated animals. These Negroid peoples were clearly in contact with predynastic civilizations (before *c.* 3100 BC) to the north in Egypt, but the arid uplands separating them from Nubia appear to have discouraged the Egyptians from settling there.

Egyptian influence. At the end of the 4th millennium BC, kings of Egypt's 1st dynasty conquered upper Nubia beyond Aswān, introducing Egyptian cultural influence to a non-Negroid people who were scattered along the riverbank. In subsequent centuries, Nubia was subjected to successive military expeditions from Egypt in search of slaves or building materials for royal tombs, which destroyed much of the Egyptian-Nubian culture that had sprung from the initial conquests of the 1st dynasty. Throughout these five centuries (2800–2300 BC), the descendants of the Nubians continued to eke out an existence on the Nile, an easy prey to Egyptian military expeditions.

Migrations from Libya

Sometime after *c.* 2181, in the period known to Egyptologists as the First Intermediate Period (*c.* 2160–*c.* 2040), a new wave of immigrants entered Nubia from Libya, in the west, where the increasing desiccation of the Sahara drove them to settle along the Nile as cattle farmers. Other branches of these people seem to have gone beyond the Nile to the Red Sea Hills, while still others pushed south and west to Wadai and Darfur. These newcomers were able to settle on the Nile and assimilate the existing Nubians without opposition from Egypt. After the fall of the 6th dynasty (*c.* 2181), Egypt experienced a century and a half of weakness and internal strife, giving the immigrants in Nubia time to develop their own distinct civilization with unique crafts, architecture, and social structure, virtually unhindered by the potentially more dynamic civilization to the north. With the advent of the 11th dynasty (2133), however, Egypt recovered its strength and pressed southward into Nubia, at first sending only sporadic expeditions to exact tribute, but by the 12th dynasty (1991–1786) effectively occupying Nubia as far south as Semna. The Nubians resisted the Egyptian occupation, which was only maintained by a chain of forts erected along the Nile. Egyptian military and trading expeditions, of course, penetrated beyond Semna, and Egyptian fortified trading posts were actually established to the south at Karmah against frequent attacks upon Egyptian trading vessels by Nubian tribesmen beyond the southern frontier.

The Kingdom of Cush. Despite the Egyptian presence in upper Nubia, the indigenous culture of the region continued to flourish, little changed by the proximity of Egyptian garrisons or the imports of luxury articles by Egyptian traders. Indeed, the Egyptianization of Nubia appears to have been enhanced during the decline in Egypt's political control over Nubia in the Second Intermediate Period (*c.* 1786–1567 BC), when Nubians were employed in large numbers as mercenaries against the Asian Hyksos invaders of Egypt. This experience did more to introduce Egyptian culture, which the mercenaries absorbed while fighting in Egyptian armies, than did the preceding centuries of Egyptian military occupation. The defeat of the Hyksos was the result of a national rising of the Egyptians who, once they had expelled the Hyksos from the Nile Valley, turned their energies southward to reestablish the military occupation of Nubia that the Hyksos invasion had disrupted. Under Thutmose I (1525–*c.* 1512 BC) the Egyptian conquest of the Northern Sudan was completed as far as Kurqus, 50 miles south of Abū Ḥamad, and subsequent Egyptian military expeditions penetrated even farther up the Nile. This third Egyptian occupation was the most complete and the most enduring, for despite sporadic rebellions against Egyptian control Nubia was deeply influenced by Egyptian culture. Nubia was divided into two administrative units: Wawat in the north, with its provincial capital at Aswān, and Cush (Kush) in the south, with its headquarters at Napata (Marawī). It was governed by a viceroy, usually a member of the royal entourage, who was responsible to the Egyptian king. Under him were two deputies, one for Wawat and one for Cush, and a hierarchy of lesser officials. The bureaucracy was staffed chiefly by Egyptians, but Egyptianized Nubians were not uncommon. Colonies of Egyptian officials, traders, and priests surrounded the administrative centres, but beyond these outposts the Nubians continued to preserve their own distinct traditions, customs, and crafts. To the Egyptians, Nubia remained a foreign land.

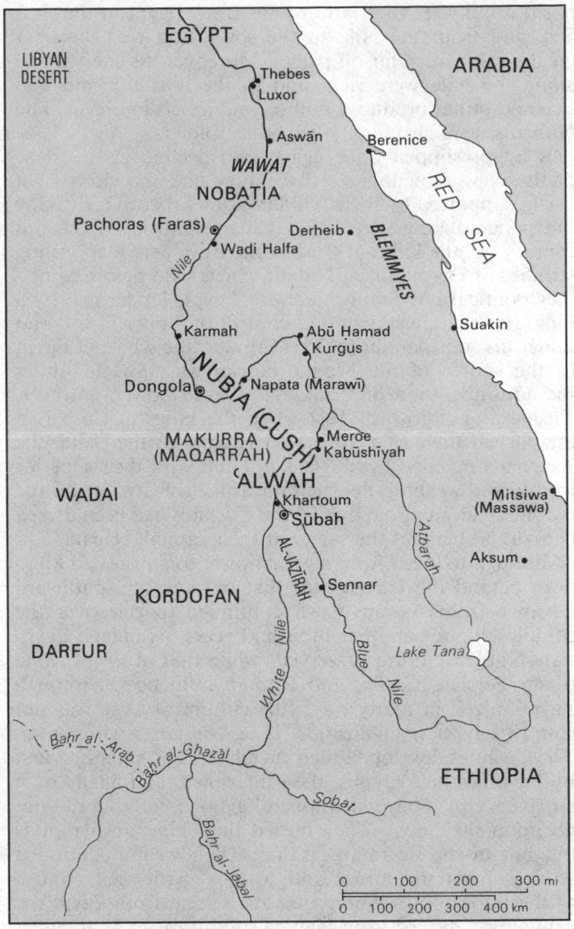

Nubia's wealth

But if it was a foreign land, it was also a rich one. Its

The Nilotic Sudan in ancient and medieval times.

From J. Fage, *An Atlas of African History;* Edward Arnold (Publishers) Ltd.

position athwart the trade routes from Egypt to the Red Sea, and from the Nile to the south and west, brought great wealth from far-off places. Moreover, its cultivations along the Nile were rich, and in the hills the gold and emerald mines produced bullion and jewels for Egypt. The Nubians were also highly valued as soldiers.

As Egypt slipped once again into decline at the close of the New Kingdom (11th century BC), the viceroys of Cush, supported by their Nubian armies, became virtually independent kings, free of Egyptian control. By the 8th century BC, the kings of Cush came from hereditary ruling families of Egyptianized Nubian chiefs who possessed neither political nor family ties with Egypt. Under one such king, Kashta, Cush acquired control of Upper Egypt, and under his son Piankhi (*c.* 751–716 BC), the whole of Egypt to the shores of the Mediterranean was brought under the administration of Cush. As a world power, however, Cush was not to last. Just when the kings of Cush had established their rule from Abū Hamad to the Delta, the Assyrians invaded Egypt (671 BC) and with their superior iron-forged weapons defeated the armies of Cush under the redoubtable Taharqa; by 654 the Cushites had been driven back to Nubia and the safety of their capital, Napata.

Although reduced from a great power to an isolated kingdom behind the barren hills that blocked the southward advance from Aswān, Cush continued to rule over the Middle Nile for another thousand years, its unique Egyptian–Nubian culture preserved, while that of Egypt came under Persian, Greek, and Roman influences. Although Egyptianized in many ways, the culture of Cush was not simply Egyptian civilization in a Nubian environment. The Cushites developed their own language, expressed first by Egyptian hieroglyphs, then their own, and finally by a cursive script. They worshipped Egyptian gods but did not abandon their own. They buried their kings in pyramids but not in the Egyptian fashion. Their wealth continued to flow from the mines and to grow with their control of the trade routes. Soon after the retreat from Egypt the capital was moved from Napata southward to Meroe near Shandī, where the kingdom was increasingly exposed to the Negroid, African cultures farther south at the very time when its ties with Egypt were rapidly disappearing. The subsequent history of Cush is one of gradual decay, ending with inglorious extinction in AD 350 by the king of Aksum, who marched down from the Ethiopian highlands, destroyed Meroe, and sacked the decrepit towns along the river.

CHRISTIAN AND ISLĀMIC INFLUENCE

Medieval Christian kingdoms. The 200 years from the fall of Cush to the middle of the 6th century is an unknown age in the Sudan. Nubia was inhabited by a people called the Nobatae by the ancient geographers and the X-Group by modern archaeologists, who are still at a loss to explain their origins. The X-Group were clearly, however, the heirs of Cush, for their whole cultural life was dominated by Meroitic crafts and customs, and occasionally they even felt themselves sufficiently strong, in alliance with the nomadic Blemmyes (the Beja of the Eastern Sudan), to attack the Romans in Upper Egypt. When this happened, the Romans retaliated, defeating the Nobatae and Blemmyes and driving them into obscurity once again. When the Sudan was once more brought into the orbit of the Mediterranean world by the arrival of Christian missionaries in the 6th century, the Middle Nile was divided into three kingdoms: Nobatia, with its capital at Pachoras (modern Faras); Maqurrah, with its capital at Old Dongola (Dunqulah); and the kingdom of ʿAlwah in the south, with its capital at Sūbah near Khartoum. Between 543 and 575 these three kingdoms were converted to Christianity by the work of Julian, a missionary who proselytized among the Nobatia (543–45), and his successor Longinus, who between 569 and 575 consolidated the work of Julian in Nobatia and even carried Christianity to ʿAlwah in the south. The new religion appears to have been adopted with enthusiasm. Christian churches sprang up along the Nile, and ancient temples were refurbished to accommodate Christian worshippers. After the retirement of Longinus, however, the Sudan once again receded into a period about which little is known, and it did not reemerge into the stream of recorded history until the coming of the Arabs in the middle of the 7th century.

Nobatia, Maqurrah, and ʿAlwah

After the death of the Prophet Muḥammad in AD 632, the Arabs erupted from the desert steppes of Arabia and overran the lands to the east and to the west. Egypt was invaded in 639, and small groups of Arab raiders penetrated up the Nile and pillaged along the frontier of the Kingdom of Maqurrah, which by the 7th century had absorbed the state of Nobatia. Raid and counter-raid between the Arabs and the Nubians followed until a well-equipped Arab expedition under ʿAbd Allāh ibn Saʿd ibn Abī Sarḥ was sent south to punish the Nubians. The Arabs marched as far as Dongola, laid siege to the town, and destroyed the Christian cathedral. They suffered heavy casualties, however, so that when the King of Maqurrah sought an armistice, ʿAbd Allāh ibn Saʿd agreed to peace, happy to extricate his battered forces from a precarious position. Arab–Nubian relations were subsequently regularized by an annual exchange of gifts, trade relations, and the mutual understanding that no Muslims were to settle in Nubia and no Nubians were to take up residence in Egypt. With but few interruptions this peaceful, commercial relationship lasted for nearly six centuries, its very success undoubtedly the result of the mutual advantage that both the Arabs and the Nubians derived from it. The Arabs had a stable frontier; they appear to have had no designs to occupy the Sudan and were probably discouraged from doing so by the arid plains south of Aswān. Peace on the frontier was their object, and this the treaty guaranteed. In return, the Kingdom of Maqurrah gained another 600 years of life.

Islāmic encroachments. When non-Arab Muslims acquired control of the Delta, friction arose in Upper Egypt. In the 9th century the Turkish Ṭūlūnid rulers of Egypt, wishing to rid themselves of the unruly nomadic Arab tribes in their domain, encouraged them to migrate southward. Lured by the prospects of gold in the Nubian Desert, the nomads pressed into Nubia, raiding and pillaging along borders, but the heartland of Maqurrah remained free from direct hostilities until the Mamlūks established their control over Egypt (1250). In the late 13th and early 14th centuries, the Mamlūk sultans sent regular military expeditions against Maqurrah, as much to rid Egypt of uncontrollable Arab Bedouins as to capture Nubia. The Mamlūks never succeeded in actually occupying Maqurrah, but they devastated the country, draining its political and economic vitality and plunging it into chaos and depression. By the 15th century Dongola was no longer strong enough to withstand Arab encroachment, and the country was open to Arab immigration. Once the Arab nomads, particularly the Juhaynah people, learned that the land beyond the Aswān reach could support their herds and that no political authority had the power to turn them back, they began to migrate southward, intermarrying with the Nubians and introducing Arabic Muslim culture to the Christian inhabitants. The Arabs, who inherited through the male line, soon acquired control from the Nubians, who inherited through the female line, intermarriage resulting in Nubian inheritances passing from Nubian women to their half-Arab sons, but the Arabs replaced political authority in Maqurrah only with their own nomadic institutions. From Dongola the Juhaynah and others wandered east and west of the Nile with their herds; in the south, the Kingdom of ʿAlwah stood as the last indigenous Christian barrier to Arab occupation of the Sudan.

The Ṭūlūnids and Mamlūks

ʿAlwah extended from Kabūshīyah as far south as Sennar. Beyond, from the Ethiopian escarpment to the White Nile, lived peoples about which little is known. ʿAlwah appears to have been much more prosperous and stronger than Maqurrah. It preserved the ironworking techniques of Cush, and its capital at Sūbah possessed many impressive buildings, churches, and gardens. Christianity remained the state religion, but its long isolation from the Christian world had probably resulted in bizarre and syncretistic accretions to liturgy and ritual. ʿAlwah was able to maintain its integrity so long as the Arabs failed to combine against it, but the continuous and corrosive raids of the Bedouins throughout the 15th century clearly weakened its power

The fall of ʿAlwah

to resist. Thus, when an Arab confederation led by ʿAbd Allāh Jammāʿ was at last brought together to assault the Christian kingdom, ʿAlwah collapsed (*c.* 1500). Sūbah and the Blue Nile region were abandoned, left to the Funj, who suddenly appeared, seemingly from nowhere, to establish their authority from Sennar to the main Nile.

The Funj. The Funj were a strange and mysterious people. They were neither Arabs nor Muslims, and their homeland was probably on the upper Blue Nile in the borderlands between Ethiopia and the Sudan. Under their leader, ʿAmārah Dunqas, the Funj founded their capital at Sennar and throughout the 16th century struggled for control of the al-Jazīrah region against the Arab tribes who had settled around the confluence of the Blue and the White Niles. The Funj appear to have firmly established their supremacy by 1607–08. By the mid-17th century the Funj dynasty had reached its golden age under one of its greatest kings, Bādī II Abū Daqn (reigned 1644/45–80), who extended Funj authority across the White Nile into Kordofan and reduced the tribal chieftaincies scattered northward along the main Nile to tribute-paying feudatories. But as Bādī expanded Funj power, he also planted the seeds of its decline. During his conquests, slaves were captured and taken to Sennar, where, as they grew in numbers and influence, they formed a military caste. Loyal to the monarch alone, the slaves soon came to compete with the Funj aristocracy for control of the offices of state. Intrigue and hostility between these two rival groups soon led to open rebellion that undermined the position of the traditional ruling class. Under Bādī IV Abū Shulūkh (reigned 1724–62), the ruling aristocracy was finally broken, and the King assumed arbitrary power, supported by his slave troops. So long as Bādī IV could command the loyalty of his army, his position was secure and the kingdom enjoyed respite from internal strife, but at the end of his long reign he could no longer control the army. Under the leadership of his viceroy in Kordofan, Abū Likaylik, the military turned against the King and exiled him to Sūbah. Abū Likaylik probably represented a resurgence of older indigenous elements who had been Arabized and Islāmized but were neither Arab nor Funj. Henceforward, the Funj kings were but puppets of their viziers (chief ministers), whose struggles to win and to keep control precipitated the kingdom into steady decline, interrupted only by infrequent periods of peace and stability established by a strong vizier who was able to overcome his rivals. During its last half century the Funj kingdom was a spent state, kept intact only through want of a rival, but gradually disintegrating through wars, intrigue, and conspiracy, until the Egyptians advanced on Sennar in 1821 and pushed the Funj empire into oblivion.

The spread of Islām. The Funj were originally pagans, but the aristocracy soon adopted Islām and, although they retained many pagan customs, remained nominal Muslims. The conversion was largely the work of a handful of Islāmic missionaries who came to the Sudan from the larger Muslim world. The great success of these missionaries, however, was not among the Funj themselves but among the Arabized Nubian population settled along the Nile. Among these villagers the missionaries instilled a deep devotion to Islām that appears to have been conspicuously absent among the nomadic Arabs who first reached the Sudan after the collapse of the Kingdom of Maqurrah. One early missionary was Ghulām Allāh ibn ʿĀʾid from the Yemen, who settled at Dongola in the 14th century. He was followed in the 15th century by Ḥamad Abū Danana, who appears to have emphasized the way to God through mystical exercises rather than through the more orthodox interpretations of the Qurʾān taught by Ghulām Allāh.

Early missionaries

The spread of Islām was advanced in the 16th century, when the hegemony of the Funj enhanced security. In the 16th and 17th centuries, numerous schools of religious learning were founded along the White Nile and the Shāyqīyah were converted. Many of the more famous Sudanese missionaries who followed them were Ṣūfī holy men, members of influential religious brotherhoods who sought the way to God through mystical contemplation. Although the fervour of Sudanese Islām waned after 1700,

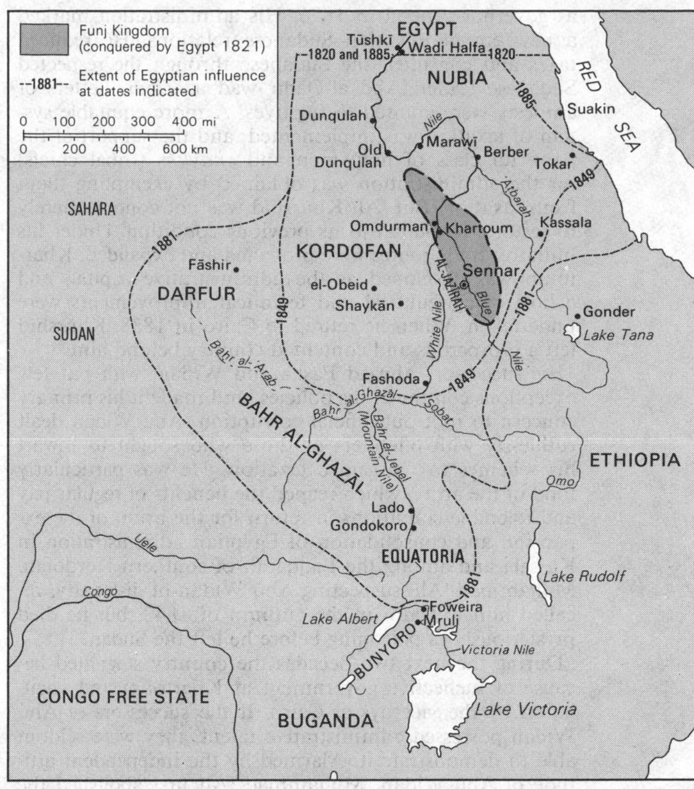

The Nilotic Sudan from the 17th to the 19th century.
From J. Fage, *An Atlas of African History*; Edward Arnold (Publishers) Ltd.

the great reform movements that shook the Muslim world in the late 18th and early 19th centuries produced a revivalist spirit among the Ṣūfī brotherhoods, giving rise to a new order, the Mirghanīyah or Khatmīyah, later one of the strongest in the modern Sudan.

These men, called *fakīs*, attracted a following by their teachings and piety and laid the foundations for a long line of indigenous Sudanese holy men who passed on the way to God taught them by their masters, or who founded their own religious schools, or who, if extraordinarily successful, gathered their own following into a religious order. The *fakīs* held a religious monopoly until the introduction, under Egyptian–Ottoman rule (see below), of an official hierarchy of jurists and scholars, the *ʿulamāʾ*, whose orthodox legalistic conception of Islām was as alien to the Sudanese as were their origins. This disparity between the mystical, traditional *fakīs*, close to the Sudanese, if not of them, and the orthodox, Islāmic jurists, aloof, if not actually part of the government bureaucracy, created a rivalry that in the past produced open hostility in times of trouble and sullen suspicion in times of peace. Recently, this schism has diminished; the *fakī* continues his customary practices unmolested, while the Sudanese have acknowledged the position of the *ʿulamāʾ* in society.

EGYPTIAN–OTTOMAN RULE

Muḥammad ʿAlī and his successors. In July 1820, Muḥammad ʿAlī, viceroy of Egypt under the Ottoman Turks, sent an army under his son Ismāʿīl to conquer the Sudan. Muḥammad ʿAli was interested in the gold and slaves that the Sudan could provide and wished to control the vast hinterland south of Egypt. By 1821 the Funj and the Sultan of Darfur had surrendered to his forces, and the Nilotic Sudan from Nubia to the Ethiopian foothills and from the ʿAṭbarah River to Darfur became part of his expanding empire.

Resistance to Egyptian rule

Collection of taxes under Muḥammad ʿAlīʾs regime amounted to virtual confiscation of gold, livestock, and slaves, and opposition to his rule became intense, eventually erupting into rebellion and the murder of Ismāʿīl and his bodyguard. But the rebels lacked leadership and coordination, and their revolt was brutally suppressed. A sullen hostility in the Sudanese was met by continued repression until the appointment of ʿAlī Khūrshīd Agha as governor general in 1826. His administration marked a new era in Egyptian–Sudanese relations. He reduced taxes and consulted the Sudanese through the respected Sudanese leader ʿAbd al-Qādir wad az-Zayn. Letters of amnesty were granted to fugitives. A more equitable system of taxation was implemented, and the support of the powerful class of holy men and *shaykh*s (tribal chiefs) for the administration was obtained by exempting them from taxation. But ʿAlī Khūrshīd was not content merely to restore the Sudan to its previous condition. Under his initiative trade routes were protected and expanded, Khartoum was developed as the administrative capital, and a host of agricultural and technical improvements were undertaken. When he retired to Cairo in 1838, Khūrshīd left a prosperous and contented country behind him.

His successor, Aḥmad Pasha abū Widān, with but few exceptions continued his policies, and made it his primary concern to root out official corruption. Abū Widān dealt ruthlessly with offenders or those who sought to thwart his schemes to reorganize taxation. He was particularly fond of the army, which reaped the benefits of regular pay and tolerable conditions in return for the brunt of the expansion and consolidation of Egyptian administration in Kassala and among the Baqqārah of southern Kordofan. Muḥammad ʿAlī, suspecting Abū Widān of disloyalty, recalled him to Cairo in the autumn of 1843, but he died mysteriously of poisoning before he left the Sudan.

During the next two decades the country stagnated because of ineffective government at Khartoum and vacillation by the viceroys at Cairo. If the successors of Abū Widān possessed administrative talent, they were seldom able to demonstrate it. Alarmed by the independent attitude of Abū Widān, Muḥammad ʿAlī first abolished the office of governor general and then, just as suddenly, revived it but sought to control its incumbents by limiting their tenure. Thus, no governor general held office long enough to introduce his own plans, let alone carry on those of his predecessor. New schemes were never begun, and old projects were allowed to languish. Without direction the army and the bureaucracy became demoralized and indifferent, while the Sudanese became disgruntled with the government. This state of affairs persisted until the more dynamic viceroy Ismāʿīl took over the guidance of Egyptian and Sudanese affairs in 1862.

Attempts to end the slave trade

During these quiescent decades, however, two ominous developments began that presaged future problems. Reacting to pressure from the Western powers, particularly Great Britain, the governor general of the Sudan was ordered to halt the slave trade. But not even the viceroy himself could overcome established custom with the stroke of a pen and the erection of a few police posts. If the restriction of the slave trade precipitated resistance among the Sudanese, the appointment of Christian officials to the administration and the expansion of the European Christian community caused open resentment. European merchants, mostly of Mediterranean origin, were either ignored or tolerated by the Sudanese and confined their contacts to compatriots within their own community and to the Turko-Egyptian officials whose manners and dress they frequently adopted. They became a powerful and influential group, whose lasting contribution to the Sudan was their lead taken in opening the Southern Sudan to navigation and commerce, thereby bringing the vast Negroid, equatorial regions of the Upper Nile into the orbit of Sudanese history.

Ismāʿīl Pasha and the growth of European influence. In 1863, Ismāʿīl Pasha became viceroy of Egypt. Educated in Egypt, Vienna, and Paris, Ismāʿīl had absorbed the European interest in overseas adventures as well as Muḥammad ʿAlī's desire for imperial expansion and had imaginative schemes for transforming Egypt and the Sudan into a modern state by employing Western technology. First he hoped to acquire the rest of the Nile Basin, including the Southern Sudan and the Bantu states by the great lakes of Central Africa. To finance this vast undertaking, and his projects for the modernization of Egypt itself, Ismāʿīl turned to those capital surplus nations of Europe, where investors were willing to risk their savings at high rates of interest in the cause of Egyptian and African development. But such funds would be attracted only as long as Ismāʿīl demonstrated his interest in reform by intensifying the campaign against the slave trade in the Sudan. Ismāʿīl needed no encouragement. He was genuinely opposed to the slave trade and made sincere efforts to suppress it and to cooperate with the European powers toward that end. Thus, these two major themes of Ismāʿīl's rule of the Nilotic Sudan—imperial expansion and the suppression of the slave trade—became intertwined, culminating in a third major development, the introduction of an ever-increasing number of European Christians to carry out the task of modernization.

Samuel Baker's expedition

In 1869 Ismāʿīl commissioned the Englishman Samuel Baker to lead an expedition up the White Nile to establish Egyptian hegemony over the equatorial regions of Central Africa and to curtail the slave trade on the Upper Nile. Baker remained in Equatorial Africa until 1873, where he established the Equatoria Province as part of Egyptian Sudan. He had extended Egyptian power and curbed the slave traders on the Nile, but he had also alienated certain African tribes and, being a rather tactless Christian, Ismāʿīl's Muslim administrators as well. Moreover, Baker had struck only at the Nilotic slave trade. To the west, on the vast plains of the Baḥr al-Ghazāl (now a province of the Democratic Republic of The Sudan), slave merchants had established enormous empires with stations garrisoned by slave soldiers. From these stations the long lines of human chattels were sent overland through Darfur and Kordofan to the slave markets of the Northern Sudan, Egypt, and Arabia. Not only did the firearms of the Khartoumers (as the traders were called) establish their supremacy over the peoples of the interior but those merchants with the strongest resources gradually swallowed up lesser traders until virtually the whole of the Baḥr al-Ghazāl was controlled by the greatest slaver of them all, az-Zubayr Raḥma Manṣūr, more commonly known as Zobeir Pasha. So powerful had he become that in 1873, the year Baker retired from the Sudan, the viceroy (now called the khedive) appointed az-Zubayr governor of the Baḥr al-Ghazāl. Ismāʿīl's officials had failed to destroy az-Zubayr as Baker had crushed the slavers on the Victoria Nile, and to elevate az-Zubayr to the governorship was the only way to establish at least the nominal sovereignty of Cairo over that enormous province. Thus, the agents of az-Zubayr continued to pillage the Baḥr al-Ghazāl under the Egyptian flag, while officially Egypt extended its dominion to the tropical rain forests of the Congo.

Gordon's administration

Ismāʿīl next offered the governorship of the Equatoria Province to another Englishman, Charles George Gordon, who in China had won fame and the sobriquet Chinese Gordon. Gordon arrived in Equatoria in 1874. His object was the same as Baker's—to consolidate Egyptian authority in Equatoria and to establish Egyptian sovereignty over the kingdoms of the great lakes—but his means were considerably more pacific. He reasserted government control over the stations that had been reoccupied by the slave traders since Baker's departure and stopped the slavers' raids against the local tribes. But Gordon's goal was the lakes, not the river, and he also sought to make the kingdoms of Bunyoro and Buganda (in present Uganda) recognize Egyptian sovereignty. Like Baker, he failed. Although he established stations beyond the Victoria Nile in Bunyoro proper at Foweira and Mruli, his resources were never sufficient to accomplish by force what he could not achieve by peaceful negotiation. When Gordon retired from Equatoria, the lake kingdoms remained stubbornly independent.

In 1877 Ismāʿīl appointed Gordon governor general of the Sudan. Gordon was the first European, Christian governor general of the Sudan. He returned there intending to lead a crusade against the slave trade, and to assist him in this humanitarian enterprise, he surrounded himself with a cadre of European and American Christian officials. In 1877 Ismāʿīl had signed the Anglo-Egyptian Slave Trade Convention, which provided for the termination of the sale and purchase of slaves in the Sudan by 1880. Gordon set out to fulfill the terms of this treaty and in whirlwind tours through the country broke up the markets and imprisoned the traders. His European subordinates did the same in the provinces.

Gordon's crusading zeal blinded him to his invidious position as a Christian in a Muslim land and obscured from him the social and economic effects of arbitrary repression. Not only did his campaign create a crisis in the Sudan's economy but the Sudanese soon came to believe that the crusade, led by European Christians, violated the principles and traditions of Islām. By 1879 a strong current of reaction against Gordon's reforms was running through the country. The powerful slave-trading interests had, of course, turned against the administration, while the ordinary villagers and nomads, who habitually blamed the government for any difficulties, were quick to associate economic depression with Gordon's Christianity. And then suddenly, in the middle of rising discontent in the Sudan, Ismā'īl's financial position collapsed. In difficulties for years, he could now no longer pay the interest on the Egyptian debt, and an international commission was appointed by the European powers to oversee Egyptian finances. After 16 years of glorious spending, Ismā'īl sailed away into exile. Gordon resigned.

The effects of the anti-slavery campaign

Gordon left a perilous situation in the Sudan. The Sudanese were confused and dissatisfied. Many of the ablest senior officials, both European and Egyptian, had been dismissed by Gordon, departed with him, or died in his service. Castigated and ignored by Gordon, the bureaucracy had lapsed into apathy. Moreover, the office of governor general, on which the administration was so dependent, devolved upon Muḥammad Ra'ūf Pasha, a mild man, ill-suited to stem the current of discontent or to shore up the structure of Egyptian rule, particularly when he could no longer count on Egyptian resources. Such then was the Sudan in June of 1881 when Muḥammad Aḥmad declared himself to be the Mahdī ("the divinely guided one").

THE MAHDĪYAH

Muḥammad Aḥmad ibn 'Abd Allāh was the son of a Dongola boatbuilder who claimed descent from the Prophet Muḥammad. Deeply religious from his youth, he was educated in one of the Ṣūfī orders, the Sammānīyah, but he became disgusted with the worldly ways of his teacher and secluded himself on Ābā Island in the White Nile to practice religious asceticism. In 1880 he toured Kordofan, where he learned of the discontent of the people and observed those actions of the government that he could not reconcile with his own religious beliefs. Upon his return to Ābā Island he clearly viewed himself as a *mujaddid,* a renewer of the Muslim faith, his mission to reform Islām and return it to the pristine form practiced by the Prophet. To Muḥammad Aḥmad the orthodox *'ulamā'* who supported the administration were no less infidels than Christians, and when he later lashed out against misgovernment, he was referring as much to the theological heresy as to secular maladministration. Once he had proclaimed himself *mahdī* (a title traditionally used by Islāmic religious reformers) Muḥammad Aḥmad was regarded by the Sudanese as an eschatological figure, one who foreshadows the end of an age of darkness (which happened to coincide with the end of the 13th Muslim century) and heralds the beginnings of a new era of light and righteousness. Thus, as a divinely guided reformer and symbol, Muḥammad Aḥmad fulfilled the requirements of Mahdiship in the eyes of his supporters.

The Mahdī's followers

Surrounding the Mahdī were his followers, the *anṣār,* and foremost among them was 'Abd Allāh ibn Muḥammad, the *khalīfah* ("deputy"), who came from the Ta'āishah tribe of the Baqqārah Arabs and who assumed the leadership of the Mahdist state upon the death of Muḥammad Aḥmad. The holy men, the *faki*s, who for long had lamented the sorry state of religion in the Sudan brought on by the legalistic and unappealing orthodoxy of the Egyptians, looked to the Mahdī to purge the Sudan of the faithless ones. Also in his following, more numerous and powerful than the holy men, were the merchants formerly connected with the slave trade. All had suffered from Gordon's campaign against the trade, and all now hoped to reassert their economic position under the banner of religious war. Neither of these groups, however, could have carried out a revolution by themselves. The third and vital participants were the Baqqārah Arabs, the cattle nomads of Kordofan and Darfur who hated taxes and despised government. They formed the shock troops of the Mahdist revolutionary army, whose enthusiasm and numbers more than made up for its primitive technology. Moreover, the government itself only managed to enhance the prestige of the Mahdī by its fumbling attempts to arrest him and proscribe his movement. By September 1882, the Mahdists controlled all of Kordofan and at Shaykān on November 5, 1883, destroyed an Egyptian army of 10,000 men under the command of a British colonel. After Shaykān, the Sudan was lost, and not even the heroic leadership of Gordon, who was hastily sent to Khartoum, could save the Sudan for Egypt. On January 26, 1885, the Mahdists captured Khartoum and massacred Gordon and the defenders.

The reign of the Khalīfah. Five months after the fall of Khartoum, the Mahdī suddenly died on June 22, 1885. He was succeeded by the Khalīfah 'Abd Allāh. The Khalīfah's first task was to secure his own precarious position among the competing factions in the Mahdist state. He frustrated a conspiracy by the Mahdī's relatives and disarmed the personal retinues of his leading rivals in Omdurman, the Mahdist capital of the Sudan. Having curtailed the threats to his rule, the Khalīfah sought to accomplish the Mahdī's dream of a universal *jihād* (holy war) to reform Islām throughout the Muslim world. With a zeal compounded from a genuine wish to carry out religious reform, a desire for military victory and personal power, and an appalling ignorance of the world beyond the Sudan, the forces of the Khalīfah marched to the four points of the compass to spread Mahdism and extend the domains of the Mahdist state. By 1889 this expansionist drive was spent. In the west the Mahdist armies had achieved only an unstable occupation of Darfur. In the east they had defeated the Ethiopians, but the victory produced no permanent gain. In the Southern Sudan the Mahdists had scored some initial successes but were driven from the Upper Nile in 1897 by the forces of the Congo Free State of Leopold II of Belgium. On the Egyptian frontier in the north the *jihād* met its worst defeat at Tūshkī in August 1889, when an Anglo-Egyptian army under Gen. F.W. (later Baron) Grenfell destroyed a Mahdist army led by 'Abd ar-Raḥmān an-Nujūmī. The Mahdist state had squandered its resources on the *jihād,* and a period of consolidation and contraction followed, necessitated by a sequence of bad harvests resulting in famine, epidemic, and death. Between 1889 and 1892 the Sudan suffered its most devastating and terrible years, as the Sudanese sought to survive on their shrivelled crops and emaciated herds. After 1892 the harvests improved and food was no longer in short supply. Moreover, the autocracy of the Khalīfah had become increasingly acceptable to most Sudanese, and having tempered his own despotism and eliminated the gross defects of his administration he too received the widespread acceptance, if not devotion, that the Sudanese had accorded the Mahdī.

In spite of its many defects, the Khalīfah's administration served the Sudan better than its many detractors would admit. Certainly the Khalīfah's government was autocratic, but while autocracy may be repugnant to European democrats, it was not only understandable to the Sudanese but appealed to their deepest feelings and attitudes formed by tribe, religion, and past experience with the centralized authoritarianism of the Turks. For them, the Khalīfah was equal to the task of governing bequeathed him by the Mahdī. Only when confronted by new forces from the outside world, of which he was ignorant, did 'Abd Allāh's abilities fail him. His belief in Mahdism, his reliance on the superb courage and military skill of the *anṣār,* and his own ability to rally them against an alien invader were simply insufficient to preserve his independent Islāmic state against the overwhelming technological superiority of Great Britain. And as the 19th century drew to a close, the rival imperialisms of the European powers brought the full force of this technological supremacy against the Mahdist state.

The British conquest. British forces invaded and occupied Egypt in 1882 to put down a nationalist revolution hostile to foreign interests and remained there to prevent any further threat to the khedive's government or the possible intervention of another European power. The consequences of this were far-reaching. A permanent British occupation of Egypt required the inviolability of the Nile waters without which Egypt could not survive, not from any African state, who did not possess the technical resources to interfere with them, but from rival European powers who could. Consequently, the British government, by diplomacy and military manoeuvres, negotiated agreements with the Italians and the Germans to keep them out of the Nile Valley. They were less successful with the French, who wanted them to withdraw from Egypt. Once it became apparent that the British were determined to remain, the French cast about for means to force the British from the Nile Valley; in 1893 an elaborate plan was concocted by which a French expedition would march across Africa from the west coast to Fashoda (Kodok) on the Upper Nile, where it was believed a dam could be constructed to obstruct the flow of the Nile waters. After inordinate delays, the French Nile expedition set out for Africa in June 1896, under the command of Capt. Jean-Baptiste Marchand.

British interest in the Nile Valley

As reports reached London during 1896 and 1897 of Marchand's march to Fashoda, Britain's inability to insulate the Nile Valley became embarrassingly exposed. British officials desperately tried one scheme after another to beat the French to Fashoda. They all failed, and by the autumn of 1897 British authorities had come to the reluctant conclusion that the conquest of the Sudan was necessary to protect the Nile waters from French encroachment. In October an Anglo-Egyptian army under the command of General Sir Horatio Herbert Kitchener was ordered to invade the Sudan. Kitchener pushed steadily but cautiously up the Nile. His Anglo-Egyptian forces defeated a large Mahdist army at the ʿAṭbarah River on April 8, 1898. Then, after spending four months preparing for the final advance to Omdurman, Kitchener's army of about 25,000 troops met the massed 60,000-man army of the Khalīfah outside the city on September 2, 1898. By midday the battle was over. The Mahdists were decisively defeated with heavy losses, and the Khalīfah fled, to be killed nearly a year later. Kitchener did not long remain at Omdurman but pressed up the Nile to Fashoda with a small flotilla. Here on September 18, 1898, he met Captain Marchand, who declined to withdraw—the long expected Fashoda crisis had begun. Both the French and British governments prepared for war. Neither the French army nor the navy was in any condition to fight, however, and the French were forced to give way. An Anglo-French agreement of March 1899 stipulated that French expansion eastward in Africa would stop at the Nile watershed.

THE ANGLO-EGYPTIAN CONDOMINIUM

The early years of British rule. Having conquered the Sudan, the British now had to govern it. But the administration of this vast land was complicated by the legal and diplomatic problems that had accompanied the conquest. The Sudan campaigns had been undertaken by the British to protect their imperial position as well as the Nile waters, yet the Egyptian treasury had borne the greater part of the expense, and Egyptian troops had far outnumbered those of Britain in the Anglo-Egyptian Army. The British, however, did not simply want to hand the Sudan over to Egyptian rule; most Englishmen were convinced that the Mahdīyah was the result of 60 years of Egyptian oppression. To resolve this dilemma the Anglo-Egyptian Condominium was declared in 1899 whereby the Sudan was given separate political status in which sovereignty was jointly shared by the khedive and the British crown, and the Egyptian and the British flags were flown side by side. The military and civil government of the Sudan was invested in a governor general appointed by the khedive of Egypt but nominated by the British government. In reality, there was no equal partnership between Britain and Egypt in the Sudan. From the first the British dominated the condominium and set about pacifying the countryside and suppressing local religious uprisings, which created insecurity among British officials but never posed a major threat to their rule. The north was quickly pacified and modern improvements were introduced under the aegis of civilian administrators, who began to replace the military as early as 1900. In the south, resistance to British rule was more prolonged; administration there was confined to keeping the peace rather than making any serious attempts at modernization.

The first governor general was Lord Kitchener himself, but in 1899 his former aide, Sir Reginald Wingate, was appointed to succeed him. Wingate knew the Sudan well, and during his long tenure as governor general (1899–1916) became devoted to its people and their prosperity. His tolerance and trust in the Sudanese resulted in policies that did much to establish confidence in Christian British rule by a devoutly Muslim, Arab-oriented people.

Wingate's administration

Modernization was slow at first. Taxes were purposely kept light, and the government consequently had few funds available for development. In fact, the Sudan remained dependent on Egyptian subsidies for many years. Nevertheless, railways, telegraph, and steamer services were expanded, particularly in al-Jazīrah, in order to launch the great cotton-growing scheme that remains today the backbone of The Sudan's economy. In addition, technical and primary schools were established, including the Gordon Memorial College, which opened in 1902 and soon began to graduate a Western educated elite that was gradually drawn away from the traditional political and social framework. Scorned by the British officials, who preferred the illiterate but contented fathers to the ill-educated, rebellious sons, and adrift from their own customary tribal and religious affiliations, these Sudanese turned for encouragement to Egyptian nationalists; from that association Sudanese nationalism in this century was born.

Its first manifestations occurred in 1921, when ʿAlī ʿAbd al-Laṭīf founded the United Tribes Society and was arrested for nationalist agitation. In 1924 he formed the White Flag League, dedicated to driving the British from the Sudan. Demonstrations followed in Khartoum in June and August and were suppressed. When the governor general, Sir Lee Stack, was assassinated in Cairo on November 19, 1924, the British forced the Egyptians to withdraw from the Sudan and annihilated a Sudanese battalion that mutinied in support of the Egyptians. The Sudanese revolt was ended, and British rule remained unchallenged until after World War II.

The growth of national consciousness. In 1936 Britain and Egypt had reached a partial accord in the Anglo-Egyptian treaty that enabled Egyptian officials to return to the Sudan. Although the traditional Sudanese *shaykh*s and chiefs remained indifferent to the fact that they had not been consulted in the negotiations over this treaty, the educated Sudanese elite were resentful that neither Britain nor Egypt had bothered to solicit their opinions. Thus, they began to express their grievances through the Graduates' General Congress, which had been established as an alumni association of Gordon Memorial College and soon embraced all educated Sudanese. At first the Graduates' General Congress confined its interests to social and educational activities, but with Egyptian support the organization demanded recognition by the British to act as the spokesman for Sudanese nationalism. The Sudan government refused, and the Congress split into two groups: a moderate majority prepared to accept the good faith of the government, and a radical minority, led by Ismāʿīl al-Azharī, which turned to Egypt. By 1943 Azharī and his supporters had won control of the Congress and organized the Ashiqqāʾ (Brothers), the first genuine political party in the Sudan. Seeing the initiative pass to the militants, the moderates formed the Ummah (Nation) Party under the patronage of Sayyid ʿAbd ar-Raḥmān al-Mahdī, the posthumous son of the Mahdī, with the intention of cooperating with the British toward independence. Sayyid ʿAbd ar-Raḥmān had inherited the allegiance of the thousands of Sudanese who had followed his father. He now sought to combine to his own advantage this power and influence with the ideology of the Ummah. His principal rival was Sayyid ʿAlī al-Mirghanī, the leader of the Khatmīyah brotherhood. Although he personally remained aloof from politics, Sayyid ʿAlī threw his support to Azharī. The

The Graduates' General Congress

competition between the Azharī–Khatmīyah faction—remodelled in 1951 as the National Unionist Party (NUP)—and the Ummah–Mahdist group quickly rekindled old suspicions and deep-seated hatreds that soured Sudanese politics for years and eventually strangled parliamentary government.

Although the Sudanese government had crushed the initial hopes of the congress, the British officials were well aware of the pervasive power of nationalism among the elite and sought to introduce new institutions to associate the Sudanese more closely with the task of governing. An Advisory Council was established for the northern Sudan consisting of the governor general and 28 Sudanese, but Sudanese nationalists soon began to agitate to transform the Advisory Council into a legislative one that would include the southern Sudan. The British had facilitated their control of the Sudan by segregating the animist or Christian Africans of the south from the Muslim Arab northerners. The decision to establish a legislative council forced them to abandon this policy; in 1947 they instituted southern participation in the legislative council.

The creation of this council produced a strong reaction on the part of the Egyptian government, which in October 1951 unilaterally abrogated the Anglo-Egyptian agreement of 1936 and proclaimed Egyptian rule over the Sudan. These hasty and ill-considered actions only managed to alienate the Sudanese from Egypt until the Nasser–Naguib revolution in July 1952 placed men with more understanding of Sudanese aspirations in power in Cairo. On February 12, 1953, the Egyptian government signed an agreement with Great Britain granting self-government for the Sudan and self-determination within three years for the Sudanese. Elections for a representative Parliament to rule the Sudan followed in November and December 1953. The Egyptians threw their support behind Ismāʿīl al-Azharī, the leader of the National Unionist Party, who campaigned on the slogan "Unity of the Nile Valley." This position was opposed by the Ummah Party, which had the less vocal but pervasive support of British officials. To the shock of many British officials and to the chagrin of the Ummah, which had enjoyed power in the Legislative Council for nearly six years, Ismāʿīl al-Azharī's NUP won an overwhelming victory. Although al-Azharī had campaigned to unite the Sudan with Egypt, the realities of disturbances in the southern Sudan and the responsibilities of political power and authority ultimately led him to disown his own campaign promises and to declare The Sudan an independent republic with an elected representative Parliament on January 1, 1956.

The end of the condominium

THE REPUBLIC OF THE SUDAN

The triumph of liberal democracy in The Sudan was shortlived. Compared to the strength of tradition, which still shaped the life of the Sudanese, the liberalism imported from the West, disseminated through British education and adopted by the Sudanese intelligentsia, was a weak force. At first parliamentary government had been held in high esteem as the symbol of nationalism and independence. But at best Parliament was a superficial instrument. It had been introduced into The Sudan at precisely the time parliamentary forms were rapidly disappearing from other countries in the Middle East. Political parties were not well-organized groups with distinct objectives, but loose alliances attached opportunistically to personal interests and sectarian loyalties. When the tactics of party management were exhausted, Parliament became debased, benefitting only those politicians who reaped the rewards of power and patronage. Disillusioned with their experiment in liberal democracy, the Sudanese turned once again to authoritarianism.

The Abbud government. On the night of November 16–17, 1958, the commander in chief of the Sudanese army, Gen. Ibrahim Abbud, carried out a bloodless coup d'état, dissolving all political parties, prohibiting assemblies, and temporarily suspending newspapers. A Supreme Council of the Armed Forces, consisting of 12 senior officers, was set up, and army rule brought rapid economic improvements. The Abbud government at once abolished the fixed price on cotton and sold all the Sudanese cotton, rebuilding the nation's foreign reserves. On November 8, 1959, the government concluded an agreement with Egypt on the Nile waters, by which Egypt not only recognized but appeared to be reconciled to an independent Sudan. In the southern Sudan, Abbud's policies were less successful. In the name of national unity the army officers introduced many measures designed to facilitate the spread of Islām and the Arabic language. Important positions in the administration and police were staffed by northern Sudanese. Education was shifted from the English curriculum of the Christian missionaries, who had long been solely responsible for education in the south, to an Arabic, Islāmic orientation. Foreign Christian missionaries were expelled between 1962 and 1964.

Failure in the south

In the southern Sudan itself, the measures of the central government met ever-increasing resistance. In October 1962 a widespread strike in southern schools resulted in antigovernment demonstrations followed by a general flight of students and others over the border. In September 1963 rebellion erupted in eastern al-Istiwāʾīyah and in the Aʿālī an-Nīl province led by the Anya Nya, a southern Sudanese guerrilla organization that believed that only violent resistance would make the government of General Abbud seek a solution acceptable to the southerners. In return the generals in Khartoum increased repression.

Although the northern Sudanese had little sympathy for their countrymen in the south, the intelligentsia was able to use the government's failure there to assail authoritarian rule in the north and to revive demands for democratic government. By 1962, numerous urban elements, including the intelligentsia, the trade unions, and the civil servants, as well as the powerful religious brotherhoods, had become alienated from the military regime. Moreover, the tribal masses and growing proletariat had become increasingly apathetic toward the government. In the end the regime was overwhelmed by boredom and overthrown by the reaction to its lassitude. The means of its overthrow was the southern problem.

In October 1964, students at the University of Khartoum held a meeting, in defiance of a government prohibition, in order to condemn government action in the southern Sudan and to denounce the regime. Demonstrations followed, and, with most of its forces committed in the southern Sudan, the military regime was unable to maintain control. The disorders soon spread, and General Abbud resigned as head of state; a transitional government was appointed to serve under the provisional constitution of 1956.

The Sudan since 1964. Under the leadership of Sir al-Khatim al-Khalifah, the transitional government held elections in April and May 1965 to form a representative government. A coalition government headed by a leading Ummah politician, Muhammad Ahmad Mahjub, was formed in June 1965. As before, parliamentary government was characterized by factional disputes. On the one hand, Mahjub enjoyed the support of the traditionalists within the Ummah Party, represented by the Imam al-Hadi, the spiritual successor to al-Mahdī, while on the other he was challenged by Sayyid Sadiq al-Mahdī, the young great-grandson of al-Mahdī, who led the more progressive forces within the Ummah. Unable to find common objectives, Parliament failed to deal with the economic, social, and constitutional problems in The Sudan. Moreover, the earlier hopes expressed by the transitional government of cooperation with the southerners soon vanished. Conflict continued in the south, with little hope of resolution. A group of young officers led by Col. Gaafar Mohamed el-Nimeiri—tired of having no workable constitution, a stagnant economy, a political system torn by sectarian interests, and a continuing civil conflict in the south—seized the government on May 25, 1969.

Coalition government

The early Nimeiri regime. When Nimeiri and his young officers assumed power they were immediately confronted by threats from Communists on the left and the Ummah on the right. At first Nimeiri and the officers of the Revolutionary Council sought advice from the Communists, who soon became overzealous and tried to eclipse the revolutionary officers, splitting the Sudanese Communist Party. In retaliation Nimeiri disbanded the Sudanese

Communist Party, which immediately went underground.

In March 1970 Nimeiri was threatened again, this time from the right from the Ummah under the Imam al-Hadi. In the subsequent struggle the Imam was killed and his supporters dispersed. Sayyid Sadiq was exiled to Egypt. Nimeiri faced another threat in July 1971 when the resilient Communists launched a military coup against Nimeiri that he narrowly survived. The Communists and their supporters seized control of the government from July 19 to July 22, when the coup collapsed after popular and foreign support held steadfast for the reinstallation of Nimeiri. The abortive coup had a profound effect on Nimeiri. He promised a permanent constitution and National Assembly, established himself as president of the state, and instituted the Sudan Socialist Union (SSU) as the country's only party. It also produced the incentive to press for a resolution to the southern rebellion. (R.O.C.)

The Addis Ababa agreement. In 1971 rebel forces united under Maj. Gen. Joseph Lagu. Thereafter throughout 1971 Lagu maintained a dialogue with the Sudanese government over proposals for regional autonomy and the termination of hostilities, culminating in the Addis Ababa agreement, ratified on March 27, 1972. The agreement ended the 17-year-old southern rebellion against the north and ushered in regional autonomy for The Sudan's southern provinces (al-Istiwā'īyah, Baḥr al-Ghazāl, and A'ālī an-Nīl). Most internal affairs were to be controlled by a legislative body and an executive body headed by a president with the rank of a national vice-president. Special arrangements were also made to integrate the southerners, including a large number from the Anya Nya, into the armed forces serving in the south.

Conflict in the south resurfaced in the 1980s. Nimeiri divided the region into three separate provinces. He was influenced by the growing strength of the fundamentalist Muslim Brotherhood and, in September 1983, modified the nation's laws to be in accord with Islāmic law. These actions encroached on the unity and the autonomy given to the south in the Addis Ababa agreement. In response, guerrilla forces once again united under a blanket organization called The Sudan People's Liberation Movement and established themselves in the south, militarizing the southern provinces. The militarization hampered the distribution of food, which, coupled with diminished harvests due to drought, caused famine to spread throughout the region. After several coup attempts and growing criticism throughout the country and abroad, Nimeiri softened his stance in September 1984 by annulling the state of emergency invoked five months previously, rescinding the tripartite division of the south and suspending the controversial Islāmic courts. These compromises failed to quiet the unrest, which was aggravated by famine and the influx of refugees from neighbouring drought-ridden countries, and Nimeiri was overthrown in a bloodless coup on April 6, 1985, by the newly appointed minister of defense, Gen. 'Abd ar-Rahman Siwar ad-Dahab. The new government had little immediate effect on the north-south conflict; national unification remained illusive.

Foreign relations. A major feature of Sudanese foreign policy under Nimeiri was the attempt to integrate political and diplomatic action and economic development with those of The Sudan's Arab neighbours. Relations with Libya, however, were aggravated by chronic Libyan-backed attempts at a coup. The Sudan and Egypt signed a mutual defense pact in 1976, and in October 1977 the first joint congress of the Egyptian and Sudanese People's Assemblies was held in Cairo. Relations between Libya and The Sudan improved after Nimeiri was overthrown.

Relations with Libya

Nimeiri's early close relations with eastern Europe and the Soviet Union were also modified in the 1970s. In 1972 diplomatic relations were established with the United States and West Germany. In July 1978 Khartoum was the setting for the 15th summit conference of the Organization of African Unity. The appointment of Nimeiri as chairman of that body for 1978–79 was believed to reflect the importance of his ties to both Africa and the Arab nations. Under General Siwar ad-Dahab The Sudan resumed a nonaligned policy, maintaining strong economic ties with Egypt, Saudi Arabia, and the United States.

For later developments in the political history of The Sudan, see the *Britannica Book of the Year* section in the BRITANNICA WORLD DATA ANNUAL. (R.O.C./Ed.)

BIBLIOGRAPHY. The early history of the Sudan is best presented by P.L. SHINNIE in *Meroe: A Civilization of Sudan* (1967); and YUSUF FADL HASAN, *The Arabs and the Sudan* (1967). The age of the Funj is most comprehensively covered by O.G.S. CRAWFORD in *The Fung Kingdom of Sennar* (1951); supported by ANDREW PAUL, *A History of the Beja Tribes of the Sudan* (1954); and R.S. O'FAHEY and J.L. SPAULDING, *Kingdoms of the Sudan* (1974). The best recent history of the Sudan from the Funj sultanate to the present is P.M. HOLT, *A Modern History of the Sudan* (1961). Holt's account may be supplemented by more specialized studies, particularly R.L. HILL, *Egypt in the Sudan, 1820–1881* (1959); and Holt's own study of the Mahdist period, *The Mahdist State in the Sudan, 1881–1898*, 2nd ed. (1970). The reconquest of the Sudan resulted in a great outpouring of historical literature. The campaigns themselves are brilliantly narrated by WINSTON S. CHURCHILL in *The River War: An Account of the Reconquest of the Soudan*, 2 vol. (1899). The formulation of British policy that led to the Anglo-Egyptian reconquest is adequately analyzed by MEKKI SHIBEIKA in *British Policy in the Sudan, 1882–1902* (1952); G.N. SANDERSON, *England, Europe, and the Upper Nile, 1882–1899* (1965); and in the decade immediately following the Fashoda crisis by ROBERT O. COLLINS, *King Leopold, England, and the Upper Nile, 1899–1909* (1968). There is no adequate single history of the Anglo-Egyptian Condominium, although SIR HAROLD A. MACMICHAEL, *The Sudan* (1954); J.S.R. DUNCAN, *The Sudan* (1952) and *The Sudan's Path to Independence* (1957); and GABRIEL WARBURG, *The Sudan Under Wingate* (1971), present a general survey. Thus the student must seek the story of Anglo-Egyptian rule in a host of biographies, memoirs, and personal reminiscences. The transitional period of self-government and the vicissitudes of independence have been narrated by K.D.D. HENDERSON, *Sudan Republic* (1965); and M. OMER BESHIR, *Revolution and Nationalism in the Sudan* (1974). The southern Sudan has its own historical literature, the most useful being RICHARD GRAY, *A History of the Southern Sudan, 1839–1889* (1961); ROBERT O. COLLINS, *The Southern Sudan, 1883–1898* (1962) and *Land Beyond the Rivers: The Southern Sudan, 1898–1918* (1971); JOSEPH ODUHO and WILLIAM DENG, *The Problem of the Southern Sudan* (1963); OLIVER ALBINO, *The Sudan: A Southern Viewpoint* (1970); and M. OMER BESHIR, *The Southern Sudan: Background to Conflict* (1968). DUNSTAN M. WAI, *The African-Arab Conflict in the Sudan* (1981), is an account of the civil war between the northern and southern Sudanese.

M. ABD AL-RAHIM, *Imperialism and Nationalism in the Sudan* (1969), an interpretation of The Sudan's achievement of independence; W.Y. ADAMS, *Nubia: Corridor to Africa* (1977), an eminent archaeologist's introduction to the ancient Sudan; K.M. BARBOUR, *The Republic of the Sudan: A Regional Geography* (1961), a survey of the political and historical background of The Sudan, with chapters on relief, drainage, soils, vegetation, Nile hydrology, and human and economic geography; M.O. BESHIR, *Revolution and Nationalism in the Sudan* (1974), a discussion of the roots of Sudanese national identity; H. DAFALLA, *The Nubian Exodus* (1975), a study of the human cost of development; F.M. DENG, *The Dynamics of Identification: A Basis for National Integration in the Sudan* (1973), a southern perspective on the question of national unity; Y.F. HASAN, *The Arabs and the Sudan* (1967), a study of the Islāmic tradition in The Sudan; A.M. EL-HASSAN (ed.), *An Introduction to the Sudan Economy* (1976), a comprehensive collection of essays, each with a bibliography; P.M. HOLT and M.W. DALY, *A Modern History of the Sudan*, 3rd ed. (1979), an introduction to the modern Sudan; ILO/UNDP EMPLOYMENT MISSION, *Growth, Employment, and Equity: A Comprehensive Strategy for Sudan* (1975), a plan for development, 1976–83; J.K. JACKSON and M.N. HARRISON, "Ecological Classification of the Vegetation of the Sudan," *Khartoum, Forests Department Bulletin*, n.s., no. 2 (1958), a survey of rainfall and soils, followed by a detailed description and classification of the vegetation; J.H.G. LEBON, *Land Use in Sudan* (1965), a regional monograph that contains a series of maps; MINISTRY OF INFORMATION, KHARTOUM, *Sudan Almanac: An Official Handbook* (annual), a valuable source of information supported by reliable statistics; *Sudan Notes and Records* (semi-annual since 1918), the leading journal exclusively devoted to Sudanese studies—particularly significant in the humanities and social sciences; A.J. WHITEMAN, *The Geology of the Sudan Republic* (1971), a comprehensive and systematic account of The Sudan's geology.

On cultures of Sudanese peoples, see E.E. EVANS-PRITCHARD, *Witchcraft, Oracles and Magic Among the Azande* (1937, reprinted 1958) and *The Azande: History and Political Institutions* (1971), the best authoritative accounts; CONRAD C. REINING, *The Zande Scheme* (1966), deals with recent changes among the Azande due to resettlement. P.T.W. BAXTER and AUDREY

BUTT, *The Azande, and Related Peoples of the Anglo-Egyptian Sudan and Belgian Congo* (1953), offers a general ethnographic account. S.F. NADEL, *The Nuba* (1947), is an anthropological study of the Nuba tribes. A.J. ARKELL, "The History of Darfur, 1200–1700 A.D.," *Sudan Notes and Records,* 32:37–70, 207–238 (1951) and 33:129–155, 244–275 (1952); A.C. BEATON, "The Fur," *ibid.,* 29:1–39 (1948); and G.D. LAMPEN, "History of Darfur," *ibid.,* 31:177–209 (1950), are historical accounts. H.G. BALFOUR-PAUL, "A Prehistoric Cult Still Practised in Muslim Darfur," *Jl. R. Anthrop. Inst.,* 86:77–86 (1956); and A.C. BEATON and R.C. COOKE, "Bari and Fur Rain Cults and Ceremonies," *Sudan Notes and Records,* 22:181–203 (1939), are of ethnographic interest. FREDRIK BARTH, "Economic Spheres in Darfur," in RAYMOND FIRTH (ed.), *Themes in Economic Anthropology* (1967), is an interesting analysis of aspects of economic organization among the Fur. IAN G. CUNNISON, *Baggara Arabs* (1966), is a study of lineage organization and politics among the Baqqārah. C.G. and B.Z. SELIGMAN, *Pagan Tribes of the Nilotic Sudan* (1932); and H.A. MACMICHAEL, *A History of the Arabs in The Sudan and Some Account of the People Who Preceded Them and of the Tribes Inhabiting Dárfūr,* 2 vol. (1922, reprinted 1967), and *The Tribes of Northern and Central Kordofán* (1912, reprinted 1967), provide further ethnographic and historical data. J.D. TOTHILL (ed.), *Agriculture in The Sudan* (1948), is a detailed authority on agriculture in The Sudan. C.K. MEEK, *The Northern Tribes of Nigeria,* 2 vol. (1925, reprinted 1969), provides comprehensive data on the cultures of northern Nigeria. A.H.M. KIRK GREEN. "The Linguistic Statistics of Northern Nigeria: A Tentative Presentation," *African Language Review,* 6:75–101 (1967), provides statistics on the languages and population of northern Nigeria. JOSEPH H. GREENBERG, *The Languages of Africa* (1963); and A.N. TUCKER, *The Eastern Sudanic Languages* (1940), provide detailed linguistic classifications and data on the eastern Sudan. Important travel books are HEINRICH BARTH, *Travels and Discoveries in North and Central Africa, . . . 1849–55,* 5 vol. (1857–58; reprinted in 3 vol., 1965); M.O. AL-TUNUSI, *Voyage au Darfour* (1845); IGNAZ PALLME, *Reitebeschreibung von Kordofan* (1843; Eng. trans., *Travels in Kordofan,* 1844); DIXON DENHAM, HUGH CLAPPERTON, and WALTER OUDNEY, *Narrative of Travels and Discoveries in Northern and Central Africa, in the Years 1822, 1823, and 1824* (1826); H.R. PALMER, *Sudanese Memoirs,* 3 vol. (1928); WILHELM JUNKER, *Reisen in Afrika 1875–1886,* 3 vol. (1889–91; Eng. trans., *Travels in Africa During the Years 1875–1886,* 3 vol., 1890–92); JOHN and KATE H. PETHERICK, *Travels in Central Africa, and Explorations of the Western Nile Tributaries,* 2 vol. (1869); and GUSTAV NACHTIGAL, *Sahărâ und Sûdân,* 3 vol. (1879–89). J.S. BIRKS, *Across the Savannas to Mecca* (1979), is a study of the peoples of Darfur province.

(M.e.D.S./J.L.Sp./E.I.U./A.Al-Sh./R.O.C.)

Supportive and Connective Tissues

The skeleton is the supportive framework of an animal body. The skeleton of invertebrates may be either external or internal and is composed of a variety of hard nonbony substances. The more complex skeletal system of vertebrates is internal and is composed of several different types of tissues that are known collectively as connective tissues. This designation includes bone and the various fibrous substances that form the joints, connect bone to bone and bone to muscle, enclose muscle bundles, and attach the internal organs to the supporting structure. (The dermis and blood vessels are also made up of connective tissue. Their composition and development are covered in the articles INTEGUMENTARY SYSTEMS and CIRCULATION AND CIRCULATORY SYSTEMS.)

For a depiction of many supportive and connective tissues of the human body in relation to other parts of the gross anatomy, see the colour Trans-Vision in the *Propædia,* section 421.

For coverage of related topics in the *Macropædia* and *Micropædia,* see the *Propædia,* section 421, and the *Index.*

This article is divided into the following sections:

ANIMAL SKELETAL SYSTEMS

Comparative study of skeletal systems

In addition to its supportive function, the animal skeleton may provide protection, facilitate movement, and aid in certain sensory functions. Support of the body is achieved in many Protozoa by a simple stiff, translucent, nonliving envelope called a pellicle. In nonmoving (sessile) coelenterates, such as coral, whose colonies attain great size, it is achieved by dead structures, both internal and external, which form supporting axes. In the many groups of The pellicle animals that can move it is achieved either by external structures known as exoskeletons or by internal structures known as endoskeletons. Many animals remain erect or in their normal resting positions by means of a hydrostatic skeleton; *i.e.,* fluid pressure in a confined space.

The protective function alone of a skeleton may be provided by structures situated on the body surface; *e.g.,* the lateral sclerites of centipedes and the shell (carapace) of crabs. These structures carry no muscle and form part of a protective surface armour. The scales of fish, the projecting spines of echinoderms (*e.g.,* sea urchins), the minute, needlelike structures (spicules) of sponges, and the tubes of hydroids, raised from the body surface, are similary protective. The bones of the vertebrate skull protect the brain. In the more advanced vertebrates and invertebrates many skeletal structures provide a rigid base for the insertion of muscles as well as providing protection.

The skeleton facilitates movement in a variety of ways, depending on the nature of the animal. The bones of vertebrates and the exoskeletal and endoskeletal units of the cuticle of arthropods (*e.g.,* insects, spiders, crabs) support opposing sets of muscles (*i.e.,* extensors and flexors). In other animal groups the hydrostatic skeleton provides such support.

In a limited number of animals, the hard skeleton transmits vibrations that are sensed by the hearing mechanism. In some forms—*e.g.,* bony fishes and fast-swimming squids—it aids in the formation of buoyancy mechanisms that enable the animal to adjust its specific gravity for travelling at different depths in the sea.

PRINCIPAL TYPES OF SKELETAL ELEMENTS

Certain types of skeleton usually characterize particular animal phyla, but there are a limited number of ways in which an animal can form its skeleton. Similar modes of skeleton formation have been evolved independently by different groups to fulfill similar needs. The cartilaginous braincase of the octopus and squid, which are invertebrates, has a microscopic structure similar to the cartilage of vertebrates. The calcareous (*i.e.,* calcium-containing) internal skeleton of the echinoderms is simply constructed but is essentially not far different from the much more elaborate bones of vertebrates. Skeletal fibres of similar chemical composition occur in unrelated animal groups; for example, coiled shells of roughly similar chemical composition are present in gastropods (*e.g.,* snails), brachiopods (*e.g.,* lamp shells), and cephalopods (*e.g.,* chambered nautilus). The mechanical properties of different skeletal types vary considerably according to the needs of animals of particular size ranges or habits; *e.g.,* aquatic, terrestrial.

Skeletal elements are of six principal types: so-called hard structures, semirigid structures, connective tissue, hydrostatic structures, elastic structures, and buoyancy devices.

Cuticular structures. Hard structures may be either internal or external. They may be composed of bone (calcareous or membranous structures that are rigid), crystals, cuticle, or ossicles (*i.e.,* minute plates, rods, or spicules).

Fish scales

The scales of some fishes (*e.g.,* sturgeon) may be heavy, forming a complete external jointed armour; calcareous deposits make them stiff. They grow at their margins, and their outer surfaces become exposed by disintegration of the covering cell layer, epithelium. Other fish scales—*i.e.,* those of most modern bony fishes—are thin, membranous, and flexible.

Calcareous structures. The external shells of gastropods and bivalve mollusks (*e.g.,* clams, scallops) are calcareous, stiff, and almost detached from the body. The laminated, or layered, shell grows by marginal and surface additions on the inner side. Muscles are inserted on part of the shell, and the body of the animal can be withdrawn into the protection of the shell. Chambered calcareous shells formed by cephalopods and by protozoans of the order Foraminifera become so large and so numerous that the broken remains of the shells may constitute a type of sand covering large areas of tropical beaches; the pieces may also consolidate into rock. Protozoa of the order Radiolaria form skeletons of silica in the form of very complicated bars. The body of the animal flows partly inside and partly outside among the bars.

Coral skeletons are also partly inside and partly outside the animal. Calcareous depositions below a young coral polyp (*i.e.,* an individual member of the animal colony) are secreted by the ectoderm (generally, the outermost of three basic tissue layers), fixed to the surface to which the animal is attached, and thrown up into ridges, which form a cup into which the polyp can contract. A spreading of the base and the formation of more polyps on the base are followed by a central humping up of the soft tissue and further secretion of skeleton. An upright branch is thus formed, and, in time, large branching corals many feet high may arise from the sea floor. Most of the soft tissue is then external to an axial calcareous skeleton, but in rapidly growing corals the skeleton is perforate, and soft tissue lies both inside and outside it. Protection of the animal is provided by the skeletal cups into which each polyp can contract, but usually neither the whole colony nor a single animal has mobility.

The starfishes, brittlestars, and crinoids (Echinodermata) have many types of calcareous ossicles in the mesoderm (generally, the tissue layer between the gut and the outermost layer). These form units that articulate with each other along the arms, spines that project from the body covering and articulate with ossicles, and calcareous jaws (in sea urchins), functioning in complex endoskeletal systems. Less well organized calcareous deposits stiffen the body wall between the arms of the starfish.

Crystals. Crystals form the basis of many skeletons, such as the calcareous triradiate (three-armed) and quadradiate (four-armed) spicules of calcareous sponges. The cellular components of the body of the sponge usually are not rigid and have no fixed continuity; cells from the outer, inner, and middle layers of a sponge are freely mobile. Spicules, which may be of silica, often extend far from the body. They can be shed at times and replaced by new spicules. Skeletal fibres are present in many sponges.

Spicules

Calcareous spicules, large and small, form an important part of the skeleton of many coelenterates. Huge, needlelike spicules, projecting beyond the soft tissue of sea pens (pennatulids), for example, both support the flanges that bear feeding polyps and hinder browsing by predators. Minute internal spicules may be jammed together to form a skeletal axis, as in the red coral. In some corals (Alcyonaria), spicules combine with fibres made of keratin (a protein also found in hair and feathers) or keratins with amorphous calcite (noncrystalline calcium carbonate) to form axial structures of great strength and size, enabling colonies to reach large, bushlike proportions.

Skeletons consisting of cuticle but remote from the body surface give support and protection to other coelenterates, the colonial sedentary hydroids, and form tubes in which pogonophores (small, threadlike aquatic animals) live. Exoskeletons that are superficially similar but quite different from hydroids and pogonophores in both manner of growth and internal support occur in the graptolites, an extinct group, and in the protochordates, *Rhabdopleura* and *Cephalodiscus.* Some graptolites, known only from fossil skeletal remains many millions of years old, had skeletons similar to those of *Rhabdopleura.*

In segmented and in many nonsegmented invertebrates, cuticle is secreted by the ectoderm and remains in contact with it. It is thin in annelid worms (*e.g.,* the earthworm) and thicker in roundworms (nematodes) and arthropods. In many arthropods the cuticle is infolded to form endoskeletal structures of considerable complexity. Rigidity is imposed on parts of the cuticle of arthropods either by sclerotization or tanning, a process involving dehydration (as in crustaceans and insects), by calcification (as in millipedes), or by both, as in many crabs. In most arthropods the body and legs are clearly segmented. On the dorsal (upper) side of each segment is a so-called tergal sclerite of calcified or sclerotized cuticle, usually a ventral (lower) sternite and often lateral pleurites; *i.e.,* side plates. There may be much fusion of sclerites on the same segment. Sometimes fusion occurs between dorsal sclerites of successive segments, to form rigid plates. Leg sclerotizations are usually cylindrical.

Internally, apodemes are hollow rods or flanges derived from the cuticle; they extend inward from the exoskeleton.

Apodemes have a function similar to the bones of vertebrates, for they provide sites for muscle insertion, thereby allowing the leverage that can cause movement of other parts of the skeleton independent of hydrostatic forces. The apodemal system is most fully developed in the larger and more swiftly moving arthropods. The cuticle is a dead secretion and can only increase in thickness. At intervals an arthropod molts the entire cuticle, pulling out the apodemes. The soft body rapidly swells before secreting a new, stiff cuticle. The molting process limits the upper size of cuticle-bearing animals. Arthropods can never achieve the body size of the larger vertebrates, in which the bones grow with the body, because the mechanical difficulties of molting would be too great. The mechanical properties of bone limit terrestrial mammals to about the size of a 12-ton elephant. In water, however, bone can support a heavier animal, such as a blue whale weighing 100 tons. Bone is mechanically unsuited to support an animal as bulky as, for example, a large ship.

Limitation of size by molting

Semirigid structures. Flexible cuticular structures on the surface of unsegmented roundworms and arthropods are just as important in providing support as are the more rigid sclerites. Mobility between the sclerites of body and legs is maintained by regions of flexible cuticle, the arthrodial membranes. Some sclerites are stiffened by closely packed cones of sclerotization at their margins, forming structures that combine rigidity and flexibility.

The so-called mesoglea layer, which lies between the ectoderm and endoderm (the innermost tissue layer) of coelenterates, is thin in small species and massive in large ones. It forms a flexible skeleton associated with supporting muscle fibres on both the ectodermal and endodermal sides. In many branched alcyonarian, or soft corals, the mesoglea is filled with calcareous spicules, which are not tightly packed and thus permit the axis of each coral branch to bend with the swell of the sea. As a result, soft corals, which are sessile and colonial, are very strong and can resist water movements without breaking. In this respect they are unlike the calcareous corals, which break in violent currents of water. The often beautifully coloured, gorgonian corals, or sea fans, are supported by an internal horny axis of keratin. They, too, bend with the water movements, except when very large. In some forms the horny axis may be impregnated with lime. The horny axes are often orientated in complex branches set in one plane, so that the coral forms a feeding net across a prevailing current. Certain chordates also possess a flexible endoskeleton; the rodlike notochord occurs in adult lampreys and in most young fishes. Running just within the dorsal midline, it provides a mechanical basis for their swimming movements. In the higher vertebrates the notochord is surrounded by cartilage and finally replaced by bone. In many protochordates, however, the notochord remains unchanged. Cartilage, too, forms flexible parts of the endoskeletal system of vertebrates, such as between articulating bones and forming sections of ribs.

Connective tissue. Connective tissue forms sheets of varying complexity below the ectoderm of many animals, existing as fine membranes or as complex superficial layers of fibres. Muscles inserted on the fibres form subepithelial complexes in many invertebrates; and vertebrate muscles are often inserted on firm sheets of connective tissue (fascia) deep in the body that are also formed by these fibres. Particular concentrations of collagen fibres, oriented in different directions, occur superficially in the soft-bodied *Peripatus* (a caterpillar-like terrestrial invertebrate). In coelenterates they also occur deep in the body. In many arthropods, collagen fibres form substantial endosternites (*i.e.,* ridges on the inner surface of the exoskeleton in the region of the thorax) that are isolated from other skeletal structures. These fibres are not shed during molting, and the endosternites grow with the body. The fibres do not stretch, but their arrangement provides firm support for muscles and sometimes permits great changes in body shape. (See also *Connective tissues,* below.)

The hydrostatic skeleton. The hydrostatic skeleton is made possible by closed, fluid-filled internal spaces of the body. It is of great importance in a wide variety of animal groups because it permits the antagonistic action of muscles used in locomotion and other movements. The fluid spaces are part of the gastrovascular cavity in the Coelenterata, part of the coelomic cavity (between the gut and the body wall) in the worms, and hemocoelic (*i.e.,* in a type of body cavity consisting of a complex of spaces between tissues and organs) or vascular in mollusks and arthropods. As the exoskeleton becomes more rigid and the apodemal endoskeleton more fully developed in arthropods, the importance of the hemocoele in promoting antagonistic muscle action decreases. In larger and more heavily sclerotized species the hydrostatic skeleton is no longer of locomotory significance; the muscles work directly against the articulated skeleton, as in vertebrates.

Elastic structures. In the larger medusae, or jellyfishes (Coelenterata), the musculature is mainly circular. By contracting its bell-shaped body, the jellyfish narrows, ejecting water from under the bell thus pushing the animal in the opposite direction from that of the water. There are no antagonistic muscles to counteract the contracted circular muscles. A passive, slow return of the bell to its expanded shape is effected largely by the elasticity of the mesoglea layer, which crumples during the propulsive contraction. After the circular muscles relax, the distorted mesoglea fibres pull them out to expand the bell. In many of the larger mammals, elastic fibres are used more extensively. The elephant and whale for example, possess an abundance of elastic tissue in their musculature.

Skeletal structure of jellyfishes

Elasticity of surface cuticle assists recovery movements in roundworms and arthropods, but the stresses and strains that cuticle can withstand are limited. Special sensory devices (chordotonal organs) convey the extent of stress in the cuticle to the animal's nervous system, thus preventing the generation of stresses great enough to damage the structure. There are also elastic units in the base of the wings of some insects. These rather solid elastic structures alternately store and release energy. They have probably been important in the evolution of the extremely rapid wing beat of some insects.

Buoyancy devices. Buoyancy devices are complex structures that involve both hard and soft parts of the animal. In vertebrates they may be closely associated with or form part of the auditory apparatus. A chain of auditory ossicles in mammals transmits vibrations from the tympanic membrane to the internal ear; simpler devices occur in the cold-blooded land vertebrates. In the roach fish, which has sensitive hearing, a chain of four so-called Weberian ossicles connects the anterior, or forward, end of the swim bladder to the auditory organs of the head. Sound vibrations cause changes in volume in the anterior part of the bladder and are transmitted to the nervous system through the ossicles. The swim bladder of other fishes appears to be a buoyancy organ and not skeletal; however, cephalopods capable of swimming rapidly in both deep and shallow water possess air-filled buoyancy organs. The calcareous coiled shell of the bottom-living *Nautilus* is heavy and chambered; the animal lives in the large chamber. The shell behind is coiled and composed of air-filled chambers that maintain the animal in an erect position. When the entire, coiled, lightly constructed shell of *Spirula* sinks into the body, the animal has internal air spaces that can control its buoyancy and also its direction of swimming. In cuttlefish and squids, a shell that was originally chambered has become transformed into a laminated cuttlebone. Secretion and absorption of gases to and from the cuttlebone by the bloodstream provide a hydrostatic buoyancy mechanism enabling the squids to swim with little effort at various depths. This device has probably made it possible for some species to grow to a length of 18 metres (59 feet). Some siphonophores (Coelenterata) have a chambered, gas-filled float, its walls stiffened with a chitin-like structure in *Velella.*

Cuttlebone

VARIETIES OF INVERTEBRATE SKELETONS

Skeleto-musculature of a mobile coelenterate. A sea anemone provides an example of the way in which a hydrostatic skeleton can act as the means by which simple sheets of longitudinal and circular muscle fibres can antagonize each other to produce contrasting movements. The fluid-filled space is the large digestive, or internal, cavity

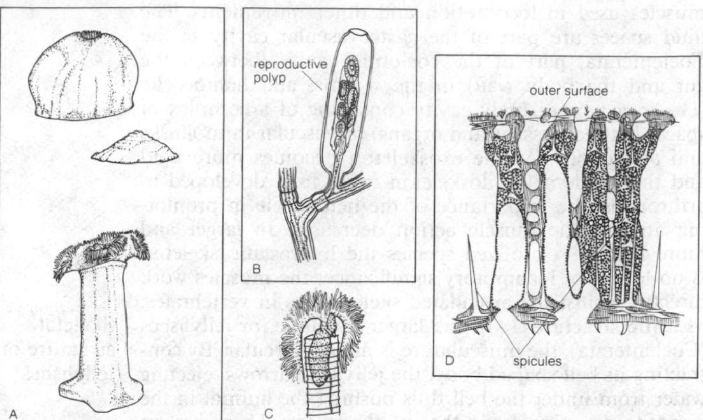

Figure 1: *Skeletal systems of lower invertebrates.* (A) *Metridium* in three conditions; (B) *Obelia;* (C) *Rhabdopleura;* (D) *Grantia.*

From (A) E.J. Batham and C.F.A. Pantin, "Activity in the Sea Anemone Metridium Senile," *Journal of Experimental Biology* (1950), reprinted by permission of Cambridge University Press; (B) T.J. Parker and W.A. Haswell, *Textbook of Zoology*, 2nd ed. (1962), St. Martin's Press, Inc., Macmillan Co., Ltd.; (C) A. Schepotieff, "Die Anatomie von Rhabdopleura," *Zoologische Jahrbucher Abteilung fur Anatomie* (1907), Gustav Fischer Verlag; (D) A. Dendy, "On the Origin, Growth and Arrangement of Sponge Spicules," *Quarterly Journal of Microscopial Sciences*, vol. 1 (1966), Cambridge University Press

of the body. If the mouth is slightly open when both longitudinal and circular muscles of the trunk contract, fluid flows out of the internal space, and the body shrinks. If the mouth is closed, the internal fluid-filled space cannot be compressed; thus, the body volume remains constant, and contraction of the longitudinal muscles of the trunk both shortens and widens the body. Contraction of the circular muscles pulls out relaxed longitudinal muscles, and the body lengthens. Appropriate coordination of muscular action working against the hydrostatic skeleton can produce locomotion movements—such as burrowing in sand or stepping along a hard surface—by billowing out one side of the base of the animal, the other side of the base contracting and forcing fluid into the relaxed, dilated portion. The forward dilated part sticks to the surface, and its muscles contract, pulling the animal forward.

The circular muscles lie outside a substantial layer of skeletal mesoglea fibrils; longitudinal muscles are internal to the layer. The muscle fibres are attached at either end to the mesoglea fibres, which, like vertebrate bones, cannot stretch. Unlike bones, however, the mesoglea sheet is able to change its shape, because its components (fibrils) are set in layers at an angle to each other and to the long axis of the body. Alteration in length and width of the body is accompanied by changes in the angle between two sheets of mesoglea fibrils; thus, support for the muscles can vary greatly in position. The range in change of shape of the sea anemone is implemented by simple muscles and connective tissue mesoglea fibrils. The movements are characteristically slow, often occurring so slowly as to be invisible to the naked eye. Faster movements would engender greater increases in internal pressures, thus placing a needless burden on the musculature. All coelenterates utilize this slow hydrostatic–muscular system, but, as described for the jellyfish, some faster movements are also possible.

Skeleto-musculature of an earthworm. The hydrostatic skeleton of many other animals is provided by the body cavity, or coelom, which is situated outside the alimentary canal and inside the body wall. In an earthworm the body cavity of each segment of the trunk is separated from that of the next by a partition, so that the segmented body possesses a series of more or less isolated coelomic, fluid-filled spaces of fixed volume. The body wall contains circular and longitudinal muscles and some minor muscles. As in the sea anemone, skeletal connective-tissue fibres form the muscle insertions. As a worm crawls or burrows, a group of segments shorten and widen, their total volume remaining the same; contact with the ground is maintained by projection of bristle-like structures from the cuticle (setae). Groups of short, wide segments are formed at intervals along the body; the segments between these groups are longer, narrower, and not in contact with the ground. As the worm crawls, the thickened zones appear to travel backward along the body, because the segments just behind each zone thicken, widen, and cling to the ground, while the segments at the front end of each wide zone free themselves from the ground and become longer and narrower. Thus, the head end of the body intermittently progresses forward over the ground or enters a crevice as the longitudinally extending segments are continuously being lengthened outward from the front end of each thickened zone. It is therefore only the long narrow segments that are moving forward. This mechanism of crawling by the alternate and antagonistic action of the longitudinal and circular muscles is made possible by the hydrostatic action of the incompressible coelomic spaces. The movements of most other annelid worms are also controlled by a hydrostatic skeleton.

Role of the skeleton in crawling

Skeleto-musculature of arthropods. In arthropods the skeleton is formed in part by the cuticle covering the body surface; by internal connective-tissue fibres; and by a hydrostatic skeleton formed by the hemocoele, or enlarged, blood-filled spaces. The cuticle may be flexible or stiff, but

From (A–D) *Zoological Society of the Linnean Society* (1965) and (E) (1958)

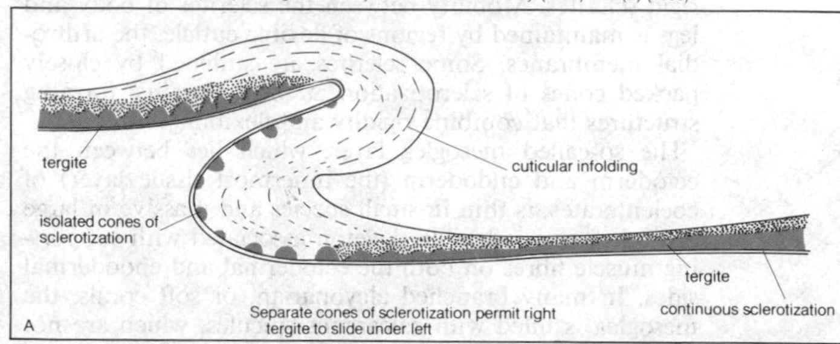

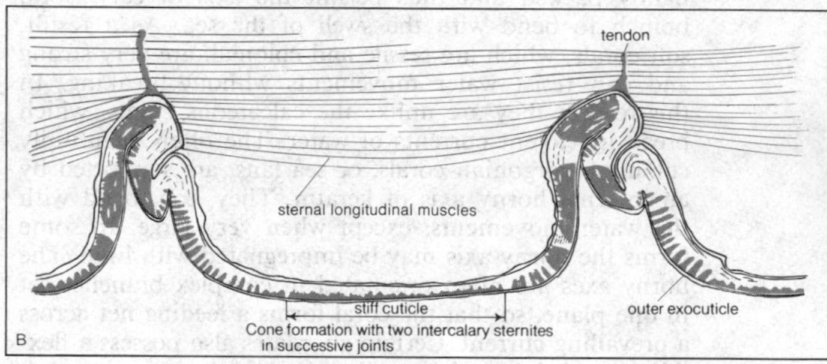

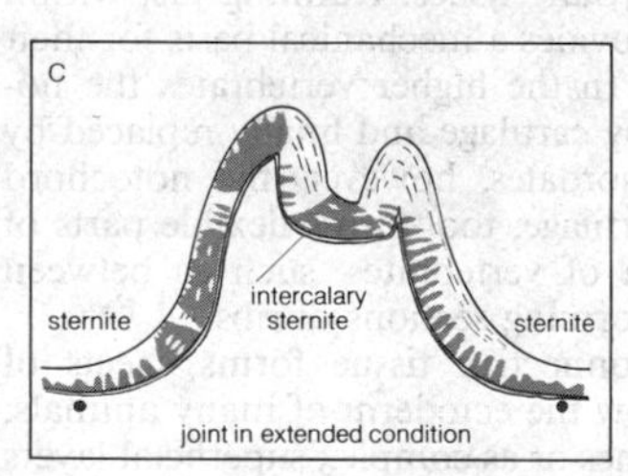

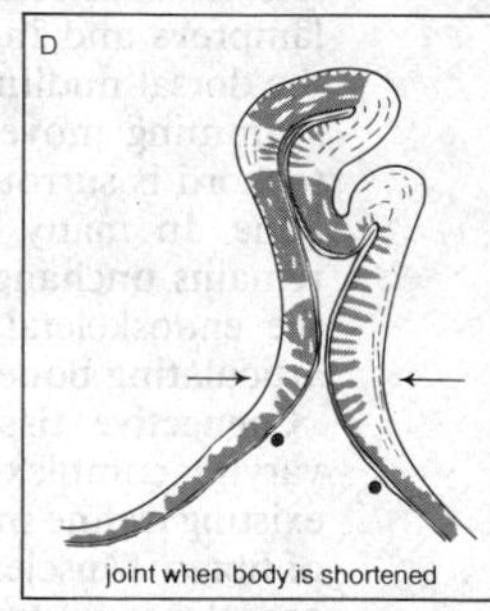

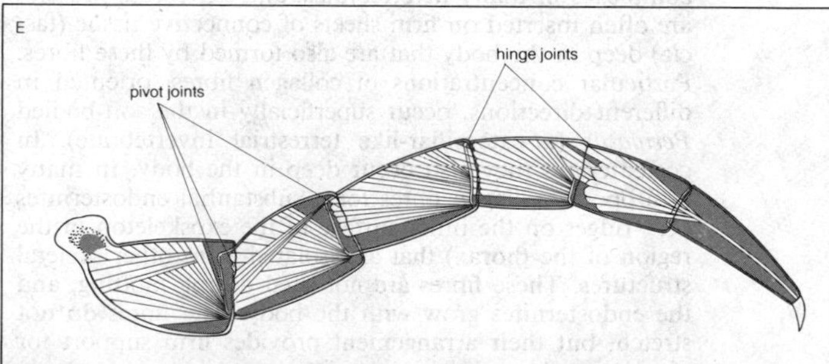

Figure 2: *Skeletal features of a centipede and a millipede.* (A–D) Trunk intersegments of burrowing centipede, *Geophilus*, allow the body to change shape while still presenting a complete external armour of sclerites. (E) The proximal joints in a millipede leg function in a pivotal fashion; the distal joints act as hinges.

it does not stretch. In the Onychophora (*e.g., Peripatus*) the cuticle is thin and much folded, thus allowing great changes in the body shape. The muscular body wall, as in annelids, works against the hydrostatic skeleton in the hemocoele. Each leg moves in a manner similar to the body movement of a sea anemone or *Hydra.* But a unique lateral isolating mechanism allows suitable hydrostatic pressures to be available for each leg. Muscles of a particular leg thus can be used independently, no matter what the other legs may be doing or what influence the body movements may be having on the general hemocoele.

In most adult arthropods the cuticle is less flexible than is that in the Onychophora, localized stiff sclerites being separated by flexible joints between them; as a result, the hydrostatic action of the hemocoele is of less importance. Cuticle, secreted by the ectodermal cells, may be stiffened by deposition of lime or by tanning (sclerotization). Muscle fibres or their connective-tissue supports are connected to the cuticle by tonofibrils within the cytoplasm of ectodermal cells.

The joints between the stiffened sclerites consist of undifferentiated flexible cuticle. Between the distal (*i.e.,* away from the central body axis) leg segments of many arthropods the flexible cuticle at the joint is relatively large ventrally (*i.e.,* on the lower side) and very short dorsally (*i.e.,* on the upper side), thus forming a dorsal hinge. Flexor muscles (for drawing the limb toward the body) span the joint and cause flexure of the distal part of the leg. There are no extensor muscles, however, and straightening of the leg when it is off the ground is effected by hydrostatic pressure of the general hemocoele and by proximal depressor muscles that open the joint indirectly. Between the proximal leg segments (*i.e.,* those closer to the point of insertion of the limb into the body), pivot joints are usually present. They are composed of a pair of imbricating, or overlapping, facets near the edges of the overlapping cylinders that cover the leg segments, one pair on the anterior face of the leg and another on the posterior face. A pair of antagonistic muscles span the leg joint and move the distal segment up or down, without reference to hydrostatic pressure.

Advanced arthropods

The more advanced arthropods—those with the most elaborate sclerites and joints—are no longer dependent upon hydrostatic forces for skeleto-muscular action. Evolution away from the hydrostatic skeleton has made possible faster and stronger movements of one cuticular unit upon another. The type of skeleto-musculature appropriate for fast movements, such as rapid running, jumping, or flying, are quite different from those producing strong movements, such as those used by burrowing arthropods.

The flexible edges of the sclerites of burrowing centipedes (Geophilomorpha) enables them to change their shape in an earthworm-like manner, while preserving a complete armour of surface sclerites at all times. This is made possible by the fact that the marginal zones of the sclerites bear cones of sclerotization that are set in the flexible cuticle, thus permitting flexure in any direction without impairing strength. The surface of the arthropodan cuticle is rendered waterproof, or hydrofuge, by a variety of structures, such as waxy layers, scales, and hairs. These features enable the animals not only to resist desiccation on land but to exist in damp places without uptake of water—a process that could cause swelling of the body and lead to death. The cuticular endoskeleton is formed by an infolding of surface cuticle. Sometimes a large surface sclerite called a carapace covers both head and the thorax, as in crabs and lobsters.

Connective-tissue fibres form substantial endoskeletal units in arthropods. The fibres are not united to the cuticle and are not shed during molting; rather, they grow with the body. A massive and compact endosternite (internal sternite), formed by connective-tissue fibres, frequently lies below the gut and above the nerve cord. In *Limulus,* the horseshoe crab, muscles from the anterior margin of the coxa (the leg segment nearest the body) are inserted on the endosternite, as are other muscles from the posterior margin.

The jointed cuticular skeleton of arthropods enables them to attain considerable size, up to a few metres in length, and to move rapidly. These animals have solved most of the problems presented by life on dry land in a manner unequalled by any other group of invertebrates. They have also evolved efficient flight by means of wings derived from the cuticle. The arthropods can never achieve the body size of the larger vertebrates, although mechanically they perform as well as smaller vertebrates. As mentioned above, the major limiting factor to size increase is the need to molt the exoskeleton.

Skeleton of echinoderms. Among the invertebrates, only the echinoderms possess an extensive mesodermal skeleton that is stiffened by calcification—as in vertebrates—and also grows with the body. The five-rayed symmetry of echinoderms may be likened to the vertebral axis of vertebrates. It is similarly supported; a series of ambulacral ossicles in each ray roughly corresponds with the vertebrae of vertebrates. The ossicles articulate with each other in mobile echinoderms such as starfishes and form the basis of the rapid movements of the arms of crinoids, brittlestars, and similar forms. The ambulacral ossicles and, in many cases, the surface spines provide protection for superficial nerve cords, which extend along the arms and around the mouth. The ossicles also protect the tubes of the water-vascular system, a hydraulic apparatus peculiar to echinoderms. In sea urchins a spherical, rigid body is formed by the five arms coming together dorsally around the anus; the ambulacral ossicles are immobile, and the body wall between the ambulacra is made rigid by a layer of calcareous plates below the ectoderm, which completes the continuous spherical skeleton. Locomotion is carried out by extensible tubefeet, soft structures that are pendant from the water-vascular system. Mobile spines also serve for locomotion in many classes, the base of the spine articulating with a part of some stable ossicle. The fine internal structure of echinoderm sclerites bears no resemblance to that of bone. (S.M.M.)

The vertebrate skeleton

GENERAL CHARACTERISTICS

In vertebrates the adult skeleton is usually formed of bone or cartilage, living substances that grow with the animal, in contrast to the many types of invertebrate skeleton that do not grow or are dead secretions, deposits, or crystals. The internal position of bones and their central position in limbs provide firm support for small and large animals. Muscles can be inserted on all surfaces of the skeleton, in contrast to the limitations of the cuticular skeleton of arthropods, in which muscles occur on only one side. Antagonistic muscles are easily placed upon vertebrate bones to allow contrasting movements at the joints between them.

The component parts of the skeletons of vertebrates, although remarkably uniform in basic plan, are subject to wide superficial differences, which are associated with each class and with adaptations for particular habits or environments. The axial skeleton consists of the skull and the vertebral column. The appendicular skeleton supports the fins in fish and the legs in tetrapods (four-legged animals) and is associated with limb girdles, which become progressively more closely linked with the vertebral column in the higher vertebrates. Superficially there may be an exoskeleton of scales; some scales on the head may be incorporated into the skull.

The fish skeleton in swimming

Swimming of a typical fish occurs by undulations passing along a greater or lesser part of the body. The mechanism for caudal (tail) propulsion involves the vertebral column, the axial musculature, and the lateral surfaces of the body and caudal fin. The vertebral column of the fish can be regarded as a series of rigid units hinged to each other by surfaces that allow the body to bend only sideways. On each side of the vertebral chain lie the great axial muscles of the body; the fibres of this complex group of muscles are more or less parallel to the long axes of the vertebrae. One pair of vertebrae and their associated musculature form the fundamental unit of propulsion. The muscles on the two sides of each vertebral articulation shorten alternately, the surface of the body becoming concave, or bent inward, on the side on which the muscles are shortened and convex, or bent outward, on the side on which they are stretched. The whole tail of the fish is essentially a chain of such units in which the phase of muscular contraction at any one link is slightly ahead of that of the next posterior unit and slightly behind that of the next anterior unit. Each wave of contraction passes tailward along the body, which is thus propelled forward. The greatest thrust against the water is exerted by the tail end. Ribs of various kinds lie between and support the segmental muscles. The fins and their skeletal supports are used as balancing and steering organs. The paired fins are set horizontally in cartilaginous fish, which do not have a swim bladder, and vertically in most bony fishes, in which rapid vibrations or small angular movements provide exact steering. In the air-breathing lungfish, fins are used for stepping on the bottom in a manner that superficially resembles stepping by the legs of a salamander. Indeed, the land vertebrates evolved from extinct fishes that used their fins for stepping; the pentadactyl (*i.e.,* with five digits) skeleton and the form of the forelegs and hindlegs of land vertebrates similarly evolved from the fins of such fishes.

An unjointed elastic notochord is present in the protochordate amphioxus, in the tail of larval ascidians (tunicates), and in the adult cyclostomes (lamprey and hagfish), but there are no vertebrae. Segmental series of muscles are present as in fish, and the resultant swimming movements of these muscles, working with the elastic notochord, are similar to those in fish.

The lateral body undulations caused by the trunk musculature, as seen in fish, are the main propulsive agents in amphibians such as the newt. The feet raise the body from the ground but otherwise serve only to anchor the body while the vertebral musculature allows forward progression by straightening the flank. The same propulsive mechanism serves for locomotion in water and on land. In the reptiles, birds, and mammals a transition of the locomotory force from the body to the limbs occurs. When the vertebral muscles contract isometrically (*i.e.,* against such great pressure that the muscle is unable to shorten), so as to prevent body undulations, the energy for propulsion comes from the limbs. Hands and feet are directed forward, as is the knee; and the elbow is directed backward. The limbs are no longer outstretched laterally but move ventrally below the body. The bones at the heel and elbow are extended to form levers that give origin to powerful extensor muscles of the foot and hand, thus contributing to a locomotory thrust against the ground. The elimination of lateral undulations of the vertebral column as the main propulsive agent is accompanied by the development of dorso-ventral flexibility of the chain of vertebrae; the distance between successive footfalls would be less if the vertebral column remained rigid. Swimming in whales is accomplished by dorso-ventral tail beats, in contrast to that in fish (which beat the tail laterally). The swimming musculature of whales evolved from the nonswimming musculature of terrestrial ancestors. Long antagonistic muscles extend from the whale's skull to the tail and implement the dorso-ventral motion, in contrast to propulsion by means of segmental muscles in fish.

The whale skeleton in swimming

The structure of the vertebrae provides a basis for many movements, including those mentioned above. Mobility sometimes is extreme, as in the necks of certain birds, in which the imbricating, or overlapping, centra (*i.e.,* the main, ventral portion of a vertebra that articulates with that of the adjacent vertebrae) can flex in any direction yet remain firmly interlocked, because the adjacent articular surface of the bony centra are saddled-shaped. The extensive mobility of snakes is mediated by its vertebral structure and its well-developed ribs; in this case, mobility is lost but greater stability achieved by fusion of two or more vertebrae.

The limbs of tetrapods and their limb girdles have become much modified in association with particular habits, such as rapid running, jumping, swimming, and burrowing. The limb bones remain relatively unspecialized in slow-moving animals and in those with climbing ability. Accomplished runners differ from man and the monkeys in that the proximal sector of the leg (humerus in the forelimb, femur in the hindlimb)—*i.e.,* the portion closer to the limb's insertion in the body proper—is short. This sector carries many locomotory muscles but does not project far—if at all—from the trunk. Beyond the short, strong femur and humerus, the limb bones of running animals are elongated, slender, and strong. The distal part of the leg (*i.e.,* that portion further from the trunk) must be narrow and light if it is to move rapidly through a wide angle. The wrist and knee are far from the ground, and in horses and other ungulates (*i.e.,* hoofed animals) the animal stands on its toenails and fingernails (hooves); the whole hand and foot are raised from the ground, thus contributing to leg length.

EMBRYOLOGY OF VERTEBRATE SKELETONS

Development of the notochord

When the early embryo consists of only two tissue layers, ectoderm and endoderm, a longitudinal thickening appears as the result of multiplication of the ectodermal cells. This thickening, the primitive streak, gives rise to the notochord and to the third basic layer, the mesoderm. The longitudinal axis of the embryo is first laid down by the formation of a cylindrical mass of cells, the notochord, proliferated from the primitive (Hensen's) node at the anterior end of the streak. The notochord lies ventral to the developing central nervous system and forms the first supporting structure for the developing embryo.

In fishes such as the shark, cartilaginous vertebrae form around the notochord and to some extent compress it. It persists, nevertheless, as a continuous structure through the length of the vertebral column. In the higher vertebrates, including man, the notochord is a temporary structure, persisting only as a minute canal in the bodies of the vertebrae and in the central part of the so-called nucleus pulposus of the intervertebral disks.

As the notochord is being laid down, cells proliferate from each side of the primitive streak, forming the mesoderm, which spreads out laterally and, as a result of migration and multiplication of cells, soon comes to occupy most of the space between the ectoderm and the endoderm on each side of the notochord. The mesodermal sheets soon become differentiated into (1) a mass lying on each side of the notochord (paraxial mass) that undergoes segmentation into hollow blocks, the mesodermal somites; (2) a lateral plate that becomes separated into an outer layer, the somatopleuric mesoderm, against the future body wall, and an inner layer, the splanchnopleuric mesoderm, against the endoderm of the future gut; and (3) an intermediate mass, the nephrogenic cord, which gives rise mainly to the genitourinary system.

The segmentation of the paraxial mesoderm is a fundamental feature of the development of the vertebrates. The axial skeleton and associated structures develop from part of the mesodermal somite; the appendicular skeleton arises from the somatopleuric mesoderm of the lateral plate. Each somite differentiates into (1) a lateral and superficial plaque, the dermatome, which gives rise to the integumentary tissue; (2) a deeper lateral mass, the myotome, which gives rise to the muscles; and (3) a medial ventral mass, the sclerotome. The sclerotomic cells from each pair of somites migrate until they enclose the notochord, separating it from the neural tube dorsally and from the aorta (the principal blood vessel) ventrally. The sclerotomic tissue retains its original segmentation and condenses to form the forerunner, or blastema, of the centrum of the future vertebra. From each posterolateral half of the condensation, extensions pass backward and eventually meet posteriorly around the neural tube to form the blastema of the neural (dorsal) arch of the vertebra. In the interspaces between adjacent myotomes of each side, an extension from each sclerotomic mass passes laterally and forward to form the costal, or rib, element. It is only in the thoracic (mid-body) region that the costal elements develop into ribs. In the other regions the costal elements remain rudimentary (undeveloped). The mesenchymal blastema of the future vertebra becomes chondrified; *i.e.,* the mesenchymal cells are converted into cartilage cells. In this cartilaginous vertebra, ossification (bone-forming) centres appear, and the cartilage is gradually replaced by bone. The mesenchyme of the embryonic ribs also undergoes chondrification and later ossification. In the thoracic region, in which costal elements are best developed, a cartilaginous sternal bar forms, connecting the anterior, or growing, ends.

Development of appendicular skeleton

The appendicular skeleton begins to develop in the primitive limb bud in the core of mesenchyme that is derived directly from the unsegmented somatopleuric mesoderm. This mesenchyme condenses to form the blastemal masses of the future limb bones. Soon the mesenchyme becomes transformed into the cartilaginous precursors of the individual bones (except in the clavicle). The cartilaginous models determine the general shape and relative size of the bones. There is convincing evidence that the shape of the bones of higher vertebrates is determined by factors inherent in the tissues, and that, once development has begun, extrinsic influences provide the proper conditions for maintaining the normal structure.

The first mesenchymal condensations of the appendicular skeleton are in the region of the future girdles; those for the shoulder girdle appear a little earlier than those for the pelvic girdle. The mesenchymal condensations for the other bones of the limbs appear in order of their proximity to the trunk.

EVOLUTION OF THE VERTEBRATE SKELETON

Vertebral column and thoracic skeleton. The notochord constitutes the earliest structure that stiffens the embryo and appeared in animals before the true vertebral column evolved. A vertebra includes a centrum and a neural arch surrounding the spinal cord.

Lower chordates and fishes. Possession of the notochord distinguishes members of the most advanced phylum, Chordata. In the sea squirts (Urochordata) the notochord is present in the tail region of the larva but disappears after the animal transforms into the adult. In amphioxus (Cephalochordata), the notochord is permanent and extends the whole length of the body. In the cyclostome fishes (Agnatha), the most primitive group within the subphylum Vertebrata, the notochord and its sheath persist throughout life; rudimentary cartilaginous neural arches are found in the adult lamprey. Among the sharks (Selachii), modern representatives possess a vertebral column composed of cartilaginous, partly calcified centra that have their origin within the sheath of the notochord, thus causing its partial absorption. Among the bony fishes (Osteichthyes), the sturgeon has a persistent notochord with a fibrous sheath upon which appear paired cartilaginous arches: dorsally, the neural arches and, ventrally, the hemal arches. The vertebrae of the more advanced bony fishes, such as the salmon and cod, are completely ossified; each centrum develops in the sclerotomic mesoderm outside the notochordal sheath. This is known as perichordal development.

Amphibians and higher vertebrates. In amphibians a vertebra is formed from the sclerotomic tissues of two somites, the tissue from the posterior part of one somite joining that from the anterior part of the somite behind it. In living reptiles the vertebrae are completely ossified. The neural arch has a spinous process and pre- and post-zygapophyses (additional articulating surfaces); at the junction of the arch and centrum is a facet for articulation of the head of a rib. Groups of vertebrae can be distinguished; *e.g.,* the cervical vertebrae are recognizable because the neck is differentiated from the body.

The fibrocartilaginous intervertebral disks uniting the centra of crocodiles have been identified as representing so-called intercentra. Ribs are present in the cervical, thoracic, and lumbar regions of the column.

The sternum may be calcified but is seldom ossified in the reptiles. In the lizards it is a cartilaginous plate articulated with the coracoid processes of the pectoral girdle and with the anterior thoracic ribs. The sternum is absent in the turtles and in the snakes; in the crocodiles it is a wide plate joined by the coracoid processes and by two pairs of ribs.

The skeletons of modern birds show reptilian features with some specialized adaptations to their bipedal locomotion (*i.e.,* by means of one pair of legs) and their power of flight. The neck is very flexible. With its variation in length the number of cervical vertebrae ranges from 25 in the swan to nine in certain small birds. The tendency for the vertebrae to fuse in certain regions is characteristic of birds. The sternum, a very large bone, is positioned like a shield in front of the chest. In flying birds a median keel, the carina, projects ventrally, providing additional surface for the attachment of the pectoral muscles that move the wings. The flightless birds, such as the ostrich, have a keelless, raftlike sternum.

Mammalian vertebrae

In mammals the vertebral centra articulate by means of intervertebral disks of fibrocartilage. Bony disks (epiphyses) formed on the generally flat ends of the centra are characteristic of mammals. Regional differentiation in the mammalian backbone is marked. The number of vertebrae in each group, excepting the caudal vertebrae, is moderately consistent, though there are some exceptions to the group averages. Whereas seven cervical vertebrae are the rule, there are nine or ten in the three-toed sloth and only six in the two-toed sloth and the manatee. The thoracic vertebrae commonly number 13 or 14, although they vary from nine in some whales to 24 in the two-toed sloth. The average number of lumbar vertebrae is about six; but there are two in the duck-billed platypus and 21 in the dolphin. Rib elements are fused to the transverse processes of the cervical vertebrae, and in the lumbar vertebrae they form the so-called transverse processes.

There is an increase in the number of vertebrae that compose the sacrum. In the early developmental stages of the human fetus, the beginnings of the hipbones lie opposite those segments of the spinal column that form the lower lumbar and upper sacral vertebrae. As development proceeds, the sacroiliac joints become established between the hipbones and the upper sacral vertebrae. The sacrum, derived from the 25th to the 29th vertebrae, inclusive, becomes a single bone by their fusion. The whales and sea cows lack a sacrum, although vestiges of a pelvis occur. In some anteaters the posterior sacral vertebrae are fused with the ischium (a bone on each side of the pelvic girdle) through ossification of a connecting ligament. The sacrum of some armadillos consists of 13 vertebrae, caudal vertebrae having become fused with it. The cervical vertebrae of some whales are fused together, because the whale is spindle-shaped for swimming and has no need for a mobile neck such as occurs in most mammals. The centrum of the atlas (first cervical vertebra) of most mammals fuses with that of the axis (second cervical vertebra) and projects from it, but in the duckbilled platypus, as in the reptiles, it is a separate bone.

Spines of vertebrae

The spinous processes of the thoracic vertebrae, excepting the last, point caudally (*i.e.,* toward the tail), and those of the lumbar vertebrae generally point cranially (*i.e.,* toward the head) at the transitional zone between these groups. Spines of one or two thoracic vertebrae are upright; these are known as anticlinal spines. Lying ventral to the intervertebral disks in some mammals (*e.g.,* whale, pangolin) are paired ossicles, the intercentra, which are homologous (of similar origin) with the anterior arch of the atlas. The tail vertebrae vary in number from none in the bat to 49 in the pangolin.

The ribs in mammals correspond in number of pairs to the number of thoracic vertebrae. The ventral ends of the ribs join the costal cartilages, the relations of which follow, with minor variations, the pattern for the human skeleton. Sternal ribs, connecting the more anterior vertebral ribs with the sternum, may be cartilaginous, calcified, or ossified. The mammalian sternum is composed of several pieces: the presternum anteriorly, followed by the mesosternum, made up of a number of segments, and a terminal xiphisternum.

Appendicular skeleton. *General features.* Paired appendages are not found in ancestral vertebrates and are not present in the living cyclostomes (*e.g.,* lampreys, hagfishes). Appendages first appeared during the early evolution of the fishes. Usually two pairs of appendages are present, fins in fish and limbs in land vertebrates. Each appendage includes not only the skeletal elements within the free portion of the limb but also the basal supporting structure, the limb girdle. This portion of the appendage lies partly or wholly within the trunk and forms a stable base for the fin or limb. Each girdle consists of ventral and dorsal masses. In lower fishes these are composed of cartilage; in bony fishes and in land vertebrates they become partly or completely ossified.

The anterior appendages, the pectoral fins or forelimbs, articulate with the pectoral girdle, which is situated just behind the gill region in fish and in a comparable position at the junction of the neck and thorax in land vertebrates.

The posterior appendages, called pelvic fins, or hindlimbs, articulate with the pelvic girdle, which is situated in the trunk region usually just in front of the anus or cloaca (the ventral, posterior body opening in many lower vertebrates). It is by way of the girdles that the weight of the body of land vertebrates is transmitted to the limbs. Because the hindlimb is usually of greater importance in weight bearing, especially in bipedal vertebrates, it articulates with the vertebral column by means of the costal elements of the sacral vertebrae. The vertebrae to which the pelvic girdle are attached usually fuse to form the sacrum. In fishes, however, a sacrum as such does not develop, since the posterior appendages usually do not support the body weight but are used only in locomotion.

Origin of paired fins

The origin of paired fins has been much debated, and many theories have been put forward in explanation. According to the widely accepted fin-fold theory, the paired limbs are derived from the local persistence of parts of a continuous fold that, in ancestral vertebrates, passed along each side of the trunk and fused behind the anus into a single fin. The primitive paired fins were attached to the body by a broad base and carried no weight. Their main function, it would appear, was to act as horizontal stabilizing keels, which tended to prevent rolling movements and possibly also front-to-back pitching movements.

Most authorities agree that the limbs of land vertebrates evolved from the paired fins of fishes. Limbs and fins are thought to have their ancestral counterparts in the fins of certain lobe-finned fishes (Crossopterygii, a nearly extinct group of which the coelacanth is a living example).

Adapted from (A) H.V. Neal and H.W. Rand, *Comparative Anatomy*, Copyright 1950: used with permission of McGraw-Hill Book Company; (B) from D.P. Quiring, *Functional Anatomy of the Vertebrates*, Copyright 1936; used by permission of McGraw-Hill Book Company

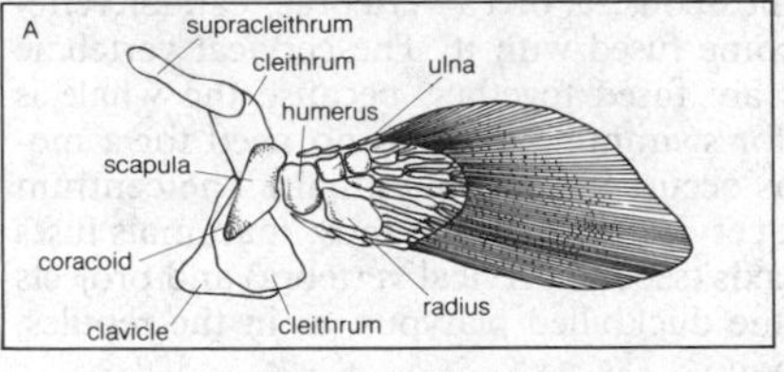

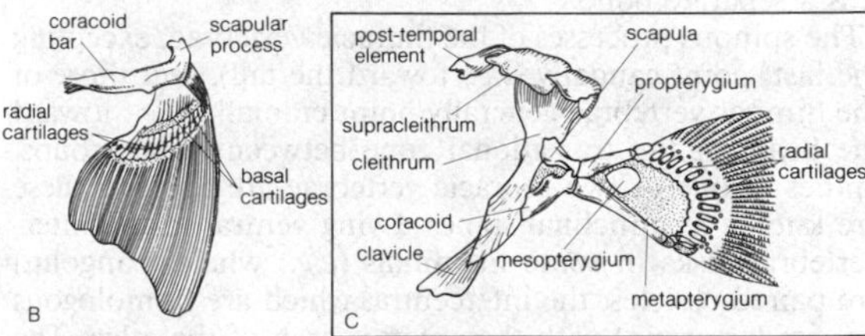

Figure 3: Fins of (A) crossopterygian, (B) cartilaginous, and (C) teleost fish.

The skeleton of the primitive fin consists of a series of endoskeletal rods, each of which undergoes subdivision into a series of three or four pieces. The basal pieces tend to fuse into larger pieces. The most anterior of the basal pieces fuses across the midline with its fellow of the opposite side to form a primitive girdle in the form of a cartilaginous bar. The more distal pieces persist to form the dermal (*i.e.,* on or near the body surface) fin rays.

Pectoral girdle. In a cartilaginous fish such as the dogfish the pectoral girdle consists of a U-shaped endoskeletal, cartilaginous, inverted arch with its ends extending dorsally.

In all other major groups of vertebrates the pectoral girdle is a composite structure. It consists of endoskeletal structures to which secondary dermal components are added as the result of ossification of dermal elements. The components become ossified to form dermal bones. In primitive bony fishes such as the lungfishes, sturgeon, and coelacanths, the main element added is a vertically placed structure, the cleithrum, which supports the scapula. The cleithrum may be joined by a supracleithrum, which in turn is surmounted by a posttemporal element (*i.e.,* at the rear of the skull). The most ventral of the added dermal bones are the clavicles, which unite below the gill chambers with each other or with the sternum. In the holostean fishes (*e.g.,* gar) the clavicle is lost, leaving only the cleithrum.

In tailed amphibians such as newts and salamanders the dermal elements of the pectoral girdle have been completely lost, and only the endoskeletal parts remain, mainly as cartilaginous bars. This retrogression is probably the result of their adaptation chiefly to an aquatic mode of life in which less support is required by the girdles. The ventral part of the girdle forms the coracoid process and the dorsal part the scapula; the latter is the only part that becomes ossified. Only a rudimentary sternum develops.

In most reptiles the primary girdle for the forelimb consists of a scapula and a single coracoid process. The pectoral girdle of the lizard consists of bones formed in cartilage: the scapula and the large coracoid process, forming the glenoid cavity (*i.e.,* the cup-shaped structure in which the humerus articulates), and the dermal bones—the clavicle and interclavicle. The latter is a single T-shaped bone, with the stem in the midline; it is in contact with the sternum. The curved clavicles articulate with each other at their medial ends (*i.e.,* toward the body midline). The cartilaginous suprascapula is present.

The pectoral girdle in birds

In birds the pectoral girdle is essentially similar to that in reptiles. The precoracoid process forms a stout bar that reaches to the sternum. The wishbone, or furcula, which forms from the dermal part of the girdle, consists of two clavicles united in the midline by the interclavicle. Carinate birds (those with a keeled sternum) have a sabre-shaped scapula and a stout coracoid process joined by ligaments at the point at which is found the glenoid cavity for articulation with the humerus. The coracoid process is joined to the sternum; at its dorsal end is the acrocoracoid process. The furcula stands in front of the coracoid processes, its ends connected by ligaments with the acrocoracoid process and with the rudimentary acromion process of the scapula. The girdle of the flightless ratite birds (those with a flat sternum) is little developed, being represented by an ankylosed, or fused, scapula and coracoid process.

Among mammals, the monotremes have two coracoid processes, which articulate medially with the presternum and laterally with the scapula. The coracoids enter into the formation of the glenoid cavity. Also present are an interclavicle (episternum) and an investing clavicle, resembling the bones in reptiles. The clavicle articulates with the acromion process of the scapula. In the opossum the scapula has a spine ending in the acromion, with which the clavicle articulates. A much-reduced coracoid fuses with the scapula and does not meet the sternum. The scapula of placental mammals has a spine ending, generally, in an acromion; the body of the bone is triangular. In mammals that use the forelimb for support in standing, the vertebral margin is the shortest, and the long axis of the scapula runs from it to the glenoid cavity; but in those whose forelimb is used for prehension, or grasping, such as in the primates, or for flight, such as in the bats, the vertebral margin is elongated, and the distance from it to the glenoid cavity is decreased. The long axis is thus parallel with that of the body instead of being transverse. In the placental mammals the coracoid, although developing independently, has dwindled to a beaklike process and fuses with and becomes part of the scapula. It does not articulate with the sternum.

The clavicle is present generally in those placental mammals that have prehensile (capable of grasping) forelimbs (primates, many rodents and marsupials, and others) or whose forelimbs are adapted for flying (bats). In many mammals it is suppressed or reduced, as in cats, or absent, as in whales, sea cows, and hoofed animals.

Pelvic girdle. The pelvic girdle of the elasmobranch fishes (*e.g.,* sharks, skates, and rays) consists of either a curved cartilaginous structure called the puboischial bar or a pair of bars lying transversely in the ventral part of the body anterior to the cloaca; projecting dorsally on each side is a so-called iliac process. Connected with the process is a basal cartilage carrying a series of radialia, the skeleton of the paired pelvic fins. The pelvic girdles of many bony fishes are situated far forward, near the gills.

There are marked variations in the form of the pelvic girdle in the amphibians. In the frog the three parts of the hipbone (ilium, ischium, and pubis) are present. The pubic elements, however, remain wholly cartilaginous. The hipbone is characterized by the great length and forward extension of the ilium. The girdle is connected with the costal element of one vertebra, thus establishing a sacral region of the vertebral column. The acetabulum (the cup-shaped structure in which the femur articulates) is situated at the junction of the three elements.

The pelvic girdle of some reptiles has a loose connection with the spine. In most reptiles the ilium is joined to two sacral vertebrae. Both the pubic and the ischial parts usually meet in the so-called ventral symphysis, from which a cartilage or bone, the hypoischium, projects backward to support the margin of the cloacal orifice, and another, the epipubis, projects forward. A few snakes (*e.g.,* boas) retain vestiges of a pelvic girdle and limb skeleton.

In most birds the ilium extends forward and backward and is fused with the many vertebrae, forming a synsacrum. The slender ischia and pubes do not form symphyses except in the ostrich.

In most mammals the ilium articulates with the sacrum, and the pubes meet in a symphysis anteriorly. A cotyloid bone, formed in the cartilage in the bottom of the acetabulum, is usually found. The symphysis pubis is not present in certain mammals (*e.g.,* moles). In monotremes and marsupials, the marsupial bones that support the pouch have been regarded as part of the epipubis.

Limbs. The pectoral fin of the elasmobranchs has basal cartilages articulating with the pectoral girdle. They carry a number of radial cartilages consisting of varying numbers of short segments; beyond these are delicate fin rays.

The proximal segment of the pelvic fin of sharks is supported by a single basal cartilage and by one or two radialia. In the pectoral fin of the primitive ray-finned fish *Polypterus,* three elements constitute the proximal segment of the fin: two bony rods, the propterygium and the metapterygium, on the margins and an intermediate, partly ossified cartilage, the mesopterygium.

Modifications for an upright position

The adoption of an upright position of the trunk, as seen in certain lemurs and in the great apes, has brought about further modification. In man the lower limbs are used for bipedal locomotion, thus freeing the upper limbs for prehensile use. Many of the great apes have developed the use of the upper limb for an arboreal life; hence, they are sometimes distinguished as brachiators; *i.e.,* animals whose locomotion is by swinging with the arms from branches or other supports.

The skeleton of the free limb of the land vertebrate is divisible into three segments: proximal, medial, distal.

The proximal segment consists of a single bone (the humerus in the forelimb, the femur in the hindlimb). The humerus articulates by its rounded head with the glenoid cavity of the scapula and by condyles with the bones of the forearm. Its shaft is usually twisted and has ridges and tuberosities for the attachment of muscles.

The femur is essentially cylindrical; the ends are expanded. At the proximal end, for articulation with the acetabulum, is the rounded head; near it are usually two elevations (trochanters) for muscle attachment. Three trochanters are characteristic of certain mammals; *e.g.,* horse and rhinoceros. Distally, the femur expands into two condyles for articulation with the tibia. In many types there is an articular facet on the lateral surface for the head of the fibula.

The medial segment of the limb typically contains two bones, the radius and the ulna in the forelimb, the tibia and the fibula in the hindlimb. In the forelimb the radius is anterior, or preaxial (*i.e.,* its position is forward to that of the ulna), in the adjustment of the limb for support and locomotion on land. Mammals in which the radius is fixed in pronation—*i.e.,* in which the forelimb is rotated so that the shaft of the radius crosses in front of that of the ulna—are called pronograde. The radius transmits the weight of the forepart of the body to the forefeet; but it is the ulna that makes the elbow joint with the humerus; into its proximal end are inserted the flexor and extensor muscles of the forelimb.

The tibia and fibula are separate in salamanders and newts, united in frogs and toads. In land reptiles the tibia articulates with both condyles of the femur and with the so-called tritibiale of the ankle. The fibula articulates with the postaxial femoral condyle and with the tritibiale and fibulare. The tibia of birds is long, the fibula reduced. In mammals the fibula is generally reduced and may be fused with the tibia and excluded from the knee joint.

The distal segment of the limb comprises the carpus, metacarpus, and phalanges in the forelimb and the tarsus, metatarsus, and phalanges in the hindlimb. A typical limb has five digits (fingers or toes), which contain the phalanges.

The carpus and tarsus of the higher vertebrates have probably been derived from a primitive structure by the fusion or suppression of certain of its elements. The bones of a generalized carpus (or tarsus) end in three transverse rows: a proximal row of three bones, the radiale (or tibiale), intermedium, and ulnare (or fibulare); a distal row of five carpalia (or tarsalia), numbered one to five from the radial (or tibial) margin; and an intermediate row of one or two centralia.

In many urodele amphibians (*e.g.,* salamanders) the carpus is generalized. In the frogs and toads, however, it is more specialized, only six carpals being present, the third, fourth, and fifth carpalia probably having fused with either or both centralia. In birds the radiale and ulnare are distinct, but the distal bones are fused with the metacarpus to form a carpometacarpus. In mammals various examples of fusion and suppression occur. In man the radiale forms the scaphoid bone; the intermedium forms the lunate bone; the ulnare forms the triquetral. The pisiform bone in man is probably the remains of an extra digit. It may, however, be a sesamoid bone; *i.e.,* an ossification within a tendon. The trapezium and trapezoid are carpalia 1 and 2; the capitate is derived from carpal 3; carpalia 4 and 5 have fused to form the hamate. An os centrale is present in the carpus of many monkeys. In mammals the number of digits varies, but the number of phalanges in each digit present usually corresponds with that of man. In some species, however, the phalanges are more numerous, as when the limb is modified to form a paddle (*e.g.,* in whales).

Fusion and suppression of carpal bones

The tarsus of urodele amphibians has the typical arrange-

From (top) *Zoological Journal of the Linnean Society* (1956)

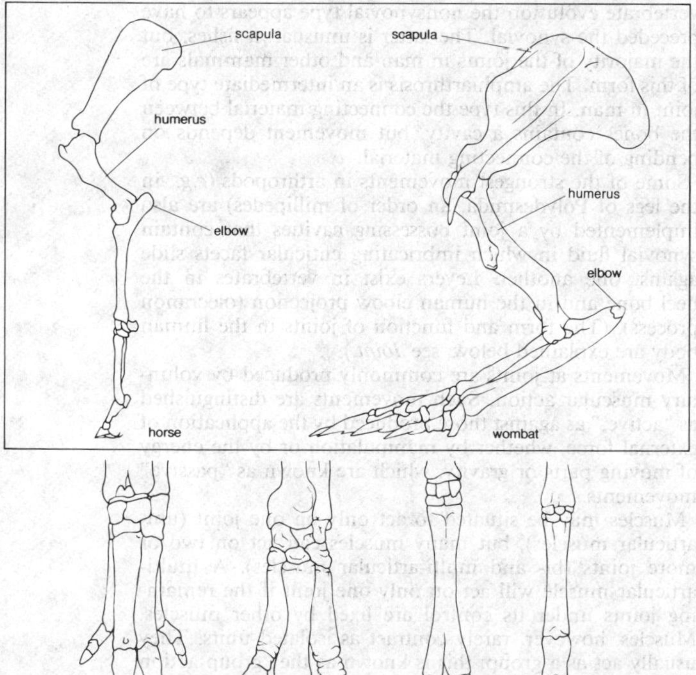

Figure 4: (Top) Left forelimbs of horse and wombat; (bottom) left forefeet of ungulates.

ment of bones. In the frogs and toads the intermedium is absent; two long bones are the tibiale and fibulare. Among the reptiles there is much variation in the composition of the tarsus. Generally, the joint of the ankle is intratarsal, the row of tarsalia being distal to the hinge. In most living reptiles the tibiale and intermedium fuse to form the talus. In birds the ankle hinge is of the reptilian pattern in being intratarsal. The three tarsal cartilages of the embryo fuse to form the talus, which fuses with the tibia to form the tibiotarsus. The tarsalia fuse with the ends of the united metatarsals to make a tarsometatarsus. In the mammalian tarsus the talus is generally composed of the fused tibiale and intermedium, but in some a centrale is included to form a tritibiale. The ankle joint is not intratarsal but is located between the bones of the leg and the first row of tarsal bones, usually the tibia and the talus.

Suppression of digits in hoofed mammals frequently has occurred in the following sequence: the pollex (first digit) is the first to be suppressed, then the minimus (fifth digit), the index (second digit), and finally the annularis (fourth digit). Among the even-toed ungulates (*i.e.,* the artiodactyls; *e.g.,* pig and hippopotamus) the pollex has disappeared, and the other four digits are present, although the second and fifth digits are much reduced. In the camel only the third and fourth digits persist and are of equal importance. Among the odd-toed ungulates (*i.e.,* the perissodactyls; *e.g.,* horse) the right digit is dominant; the others are reduced to rudiments or splints.

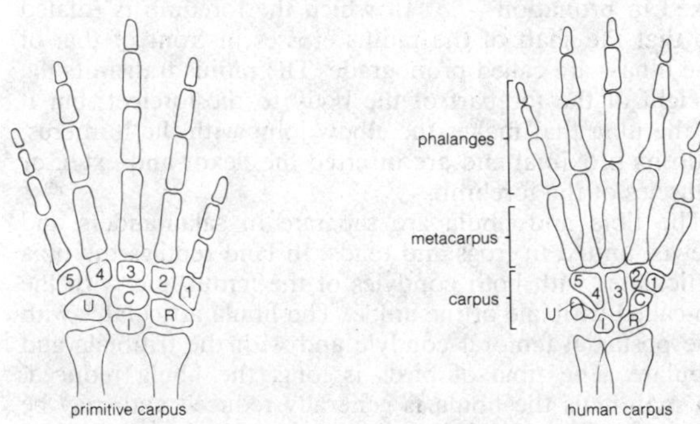

Figure 5: Distal segment of forelimb. (R, radiale; I, intermedium; U, ulnare; C, centrale; 1–5, carpalia)

Joints. The junctions between the bony or cartilaginous units of vertebrate skeletons and between the body-wall ossicles of sea urchins (Echinodermata) are often kept rigid by dovetailed margins. One skeletal unit, however, may move freely on another, as shown by the ambulacral ossicles along the arms of brittlestars, crinoids, and starfishes among the echinoderms and by the leg bones and vertebrae of vertebrates in which joints that permit various types of movement exist.

Joints between the bony or cartilaginous units of vertebrate skeletons are very simple in animals with a cartilaginous skeleton. When bone replaces cartilage, however, stronger and more elaborate joints form. Flat, articulating, cartilaginous surfaces between the vertebral centra of sharks do not permit extensive movement, but it is sufficient for these animals. In sharks, intervertebral cones of notochord persist, with conical ends projecting into the ends of adjacent vertebrae. Joints between bones and cuticular sclerites may permit movement in one plane only, as in most arthropodan joints and the interphalangeal joint in man. Between some bones (*e.g.,* the human femur and pelvis) there is a ball-and-socket device, by which a ball-like articular facet rotates in a concavity, the acetabulum. The femur can thus move in a variety of planes. The bony vertebrae of fishes, amphibians, reptiles, and birds possess centra articulating with one another in a ball-and-socket manner. The terrestrial animals strengthen the ball-and-socket articulation and sometimes restrict its movement by additional imbricating facets (zygapophyses). Snake vertebrae interlock firmly with one another; a hemispherical posterior projection from each articulates with an anterior concavity (*i.e.,* a cup-shaped depression) on the vertebra in front of it. The freely moving joints permit a twisting movement, with extra support being gained by two sets of sliding facets between each pair of consecutive vertebrae. Ball-and-socket joints, common in vertebrates, are easily contrived in animals with an endoskeleton. Among invertebrates are some remarkable parallels. In certain millipedes (Juliformia) heavy circular sclerites encompass each segment and slightly overlap. Rotation of one skeletal ring upon the next, as well as flexion, is possible. The animal can thus curve its hard body in any direction. It can curl up dorso-ventrally with the legs in the middle of a spiral, then walk with the legs on the ground and at right angles to the coiled position. Echinoderms also possess many ball-and-socket joints, such as at the base of spines in sea urchins.

Ball-and-socket joint

Various types of strong hinge joints, easily contrived by an arthropod, also occur in vertebrates. The joint between the skull and the first vertebra in mammals is a strong hinge. A pair of occipital condyles on the skull that articulate against shallow concavities on the anterior face of the vertebra permit a nodding movement of the head. The strongest hinge joints in arthropods also bear a double articulation, as in the leg of the spider and in *Scutigera,* the fastest running centipede. Hinge joints in vertebrates are often composite, being formed or supported by the incorporation of several small bones, as in the human wrist. To facilitate cursorial, or running, habits, flexion is limited to one plane.

A series of small bones at the wrist or ankle can, in contrast, provide, in addition to strength, a marked flexibility in many directions. A leg that can flex in various directions is usually achieved in arthropods by a series of pivot joints. Each joint is set in a different plane along the leg, so that the combined action of the several joints enables the leg to move in any direction. Single endoskeletal joints of vertebrates supply a variety of movements with greater ease; no duplication is necessary.

Synovial and nonsynovial joints

In vertebrates, the joints between bones are constructed in a variety of ways. They fall, however, into two main categories, the synovial joint and the nonsynovial joint. In the former, known also as diarthrosis, a cleft occurs between the free surfaces of two skeletal parts; during movements these surfaces slide on each other. In the nonsynovial type, known also as synarthrosis, the skeletal parts are connected by nonosseous material that permits bending or twisting. The range of movement is greater in the synovial than in the nonsynovial type. In the course of vertebrate evolution the nonsynovial type appears to have preceded the synovial. The latter is unusual in fishes, but the majority of the joints in man and other mammals are of this form. The amphiarthrosis is an intermediate type of joint in man. In this type the connecting material between the bones contains a cavity, but movement depends on bending of the connecting material.

Some of the strongest movements in arthropods (*e.g.,* in the legs of Polydesmida, an order of millipedes) are also implemented by a joint possessing cavities that contain synovial fluid in which imbricating cuticular facets slide against one another. Levers exist in vertebrates in the heel bone and in the human elbow projection (olecranon process). (The form and function of joints in the human body are explained below; see *Joint.*)

Movements at joints are commonly produced by voluntary muscular action. Such movements are distinguished as "active," as against those produced by the application of external force, whether by manipulation or by the energy of moving parts or gravity, which are known as "passive" movements.

Muscles may be situated to act only on one joint (uniarticular muscles), but many muscles can act on two or more joints (bi- and multi-articular muscles). A multiarticular muscle will act on only one joint if the remaining joints under its control are fixed by other muscles. Muscles, however, rarely contract as isolated units. They usually act as a group; this is known as the "group action of muscles." The intricate adjustment and coordination of muscular tensions that are required for posture and movement are under the control of the central nervous system.

Although the general form of the skeleton is hereditary, it is also influenced by mechanical factors, such as pressure on the cartilage at the end of a bone (epiphysis) or stresses applied to the external surface; *e.g.*, from adjacent muscles. The effect of pressure on bone depends on whether the bony surface is covered by periosteum or by cartilage. In the case of the periosteum, which has blood vessels, pressure causes impairment of blood supply and absorption of underlying bone. On the other hand, pressure on cartilage, which has no blood supply, does not cause absorption. Internal strains stimulate bone formation, and when the direction of stress is altered, bony reconstruction takes place.

When a bone is fractured, some bone tissue adjacent to the fracture is absorbed, and a mass of tissue termed callus, at first uncalcified, makes its appearance between and around the broken ends. Cartilage formation commonly takes place in the callus even when the fracture is in a membrane bone; *e.g.*, the parietal bone of the skull. Callus also contains osteoblasts derived from both periosteum and endosteum, the connective tissue within a bone. The formation of callus is greater if there is pressure and movement between the broken ends of the bone and is most pronounced on the concave side when the bony fragments are at an angle. Bony union is effected by calcification and subsequent ossification of the callus. Regeneration of bone is more active in the shafts of long bones, lower jaw, and ribs than in the skull and the spongy ends of long bones. (See below *Bone*, for a complete treatment of bone composition, development, and function.)

(W.J.H./Ed.)

THE HUMAN SKELETAL SYSTEM

Man, as a member of the great group of vertebrates, has an internal skeleton as framework for his body as a whole. This framework consists of many individual bones and cartilages. There are bands of fibrous connective tissue, the ligaments and tendons, in intimate relationship with the parts of the skeleton. Bone, cartilage, ligaments, and tendons are forms of connective tissue, and they are treated in that context in the section *Connective tissue*. This section is concerned primarily with the gross structure and the function of the skeleton of the normal human adult.

Three subdivisions of skeleton

The human skeleton, like that of other vertebrates, consists of three subdivisions, each with origins distinct from the others and each presenting certain individual features. These are (1) the axial, comprising the vertebral column—the spine—and much of the skull; (2) the visceral, comprising the lower jaw, some elements of the upper jaw, and the branchial arches, including the hyoid bone (the branchial arches are barlike ridges and the bones and cartilages that derive from them on either side of the throat and the head of the embryo, corresponding to the bars that support the gills of fish; for the hyoid, see below *The hyoid: example of the anchoring function*); and (3) the appendicular, to which the hip and shoulder girdles and the bones and cartilages of the limbs belong.

When the relation of these three divisions of the skeleton to the soft parts, such as the nervous system, the alimentary respiratory, and circulatory systems, and the voluntary muscles, are considered, it is clear that the functions of the skeleton are of three different types—support, protection, and motion. Of these functions, support is the most primitive and the oldest, just as the axial part of the skeleton was the first to evolve. The vertebral column, corresponding to the notochord in lower organisms, is the main support of the trunk.

The central nervous system lies largely within the axial skeleton, the brain being well protected by the cranium (see below *The cranium: example of the protective function*) and the spinal cord by the vertebral column, by means of the bony neural arches (the arches of bone that encircle the spinal cord) and the intervening ligaments.

A distinctive characteristic of man as compared with other mammals is his erect posture. The human body is, to some extent, like a walking tower that moves on pillars, represented by the legs. Tremendous advantages have been gained from this erect posture, the chief among

From *Cunningham's Textbook of Anatomy*, edited by G.J. Romanes and published by Oxford University Press as an Oxford Medical Publication

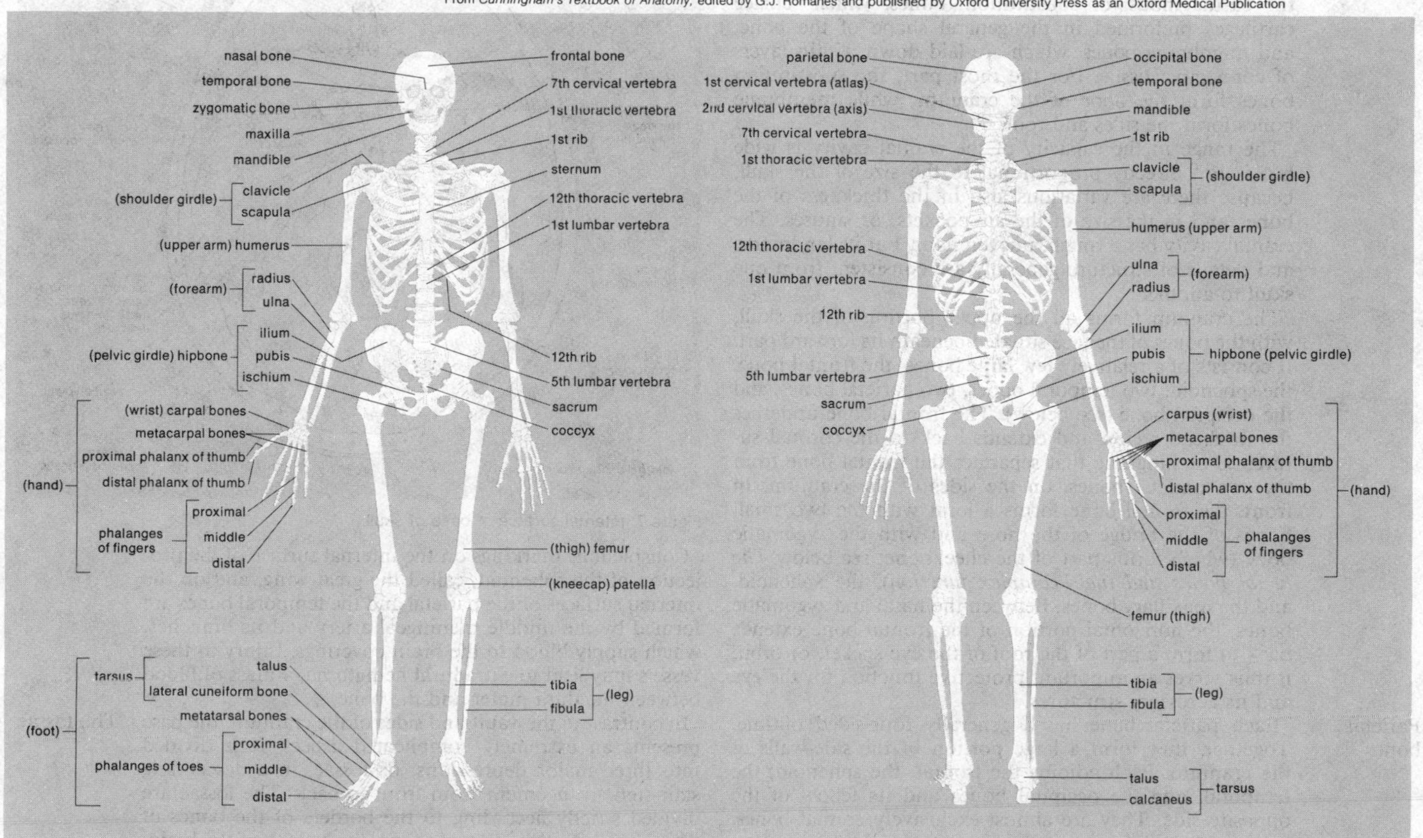

Figure 6: Front and back views of human skeleton.

which has been the freeing of the arms for a great variety of uses. Nevertheless, erect posture has created a number of mechanical problems; in particular, weight bearing. These problems have had to be met by adaptations of the skeletal system.

Protective function of skeleton

Protection of the heart, lungs, and other organs and structures in the chest creates a problem somewhat different from that of the central nervous system. These organs, the function of which involves motion, expansion, and contraction, must have a flexible and elastic protective covering. Such a covering is provided by the bony thoracic basket, or rib cage, which forms the skeleton of the wall of the chest, or thorax. The connection of the ribs to the breastbone—the sternum—is in all cases a secondary one, brought about by the relatively pliable rib (costal) cartilages. The small joints between the ribs and the vertebrae permit a gliding motion of the ribs on the vertebrae during breathing and other activity. The motion is limited by the ligamentous attachments between ribs and vertebrae.

The third general function of the skeleton is that of motion. The great majority of the skeletal muscles are firmly anchored to the skeleton, usually to at least two bones and, in some cases, to many bones. Thus, the motions of the body and its parts, all the way from the lunge of the football fullback to the delicate manipulations of a handicraft artist or of the use of complicated instruments by a scientist, are made possible by separate and individual engineering arrangements between muscle and bone.

In this article, the cranium, the hyoid bone, the rib cage, and other parts of the skeleton are considered in terms of their sharing in these functions.

Bones of the axial and visceral skeleton

THE CRANIUM: EXAMPLE OF THE PROTECTIVE FUNCTION

The cranium—that part of the skull that encloses the brain—is sometimes called the braincase, but its intimate relation to the sense organs for sight, hearing, smelling, and taste and to other structures makes such a designation somewhat misleading.

Development of cranial bones. The cranium is formed of bones of two different types of developmental origin—the cartilaginous, or substitution, bones, which replace cartilages preformed in the general shape of the bone; and membrane bones, which are laid down within layers of connective tissue. For the most part, the substitution bones form the floor of the cranium, while membrane bones form the sides and roof.

The range in the capacity of the cranial cavity is wide but is not directly proportional to the size of the skull, because there are variations also in the thickness of the bones and in the size of the air pockets, or sinuses. The cranial cavity has a rough, uneven floor, but its landmarks and details of structure generally are consistent from one skull to another.

The cranium forms all the upper portion of the skull, with the bones of the face situated beneath its forward part. It consists of a relatively few large bones, the frontal bone, the sphenoid, two temporal bones, two parietal bones, and the occipital bone (see below). The frontal bone underlies the forehead region and extends back to the coronal suture, an arching line that separates the frontal bone from the two parietal bones, on the sides of the cranium. In front, the frontal bone forms a joint with the two small bones of the bridge of the nose and with the zygomatic bone (which forms part of the cheekbone; see below *The facial bones and their complex function*), the sphenoid, and the maxillary bones. Between the nasal and zygomatic bones, the horizontal portion of the frontal bone extends back to form a part of the roof of the eye socket, or orbit; it thus serves an important protective function for the eye and its accessory structures.

Parietal bones

Each parietal bone has a generally four-sided outline. Together, they form a large portion of the side-walls of the cranium. Each adjoins the frontal, the sphenoid, the temporal, and the occipital bones and its fellow of the opposite side. They are almost exclusively cranial bones, having less relation to other structures than the other bones that help to form the cranium.

Important landmarks of the skull, useful not only in measurement but also in specifying the location of injury and of X-ray examination, are found at the four angles of the parietal bone: the upper rear angle is the lambda; the lower rear, the asterion; the upper front angle, the bregma; and the lower front, the pterion. At the lambda, the two parietal bones meet the occipital bone, which forms the back of the cranium. The asterion marks the location, within the cranium, of the lateral venous sinus, a large channel for venous blood that runs between layers of the outermost covering of the brain, the dura mater. The asterion is also the point at which parietal, occipital, and temporal bones meet. The bregma, the upper front corner, lies at the juncture of the parietal bones with the frontal bone. The pterion, the lower front joint, is the region of juncture of frontal, parietal, and sphenoid bones and, in some skulls, is the site of an irregular, isolated bone, called a wormian bone.

Interior of cranium. The interior of the cranium shows a multitude of details, reflecting the shapes of the softer structures that are in contact with the bones.

The internal surface of the vault is relatively uncomplicated. In the midline front to back, along the seam, called the sagittal suture, between the two parietal bones, is a shallow depression—the groove for the superior longitudinal venous sinus, a large channel for venous blood. A number of depressions on either side of it mark the sites of the pacchionian bodies, structures that permit the venous system to absorb cerebrospinal fluid. The large, thin-walled venous sinuses all lie within the cranial cavity. While they are thus protected by the cranium, in many places, they are so close beneath the bones that a fracture or penetrating wound may tear the sinus wall and lead to bleeding. The blood frequently is trapped beneath the outermost and toughest brain covering, the dura mater, in a mass called a subdural hematoma.

From *Cunningham's Textbook of Anatomy* edited by G.J. Romanes and published by Oxford University Press as an Oxford Medical Publication

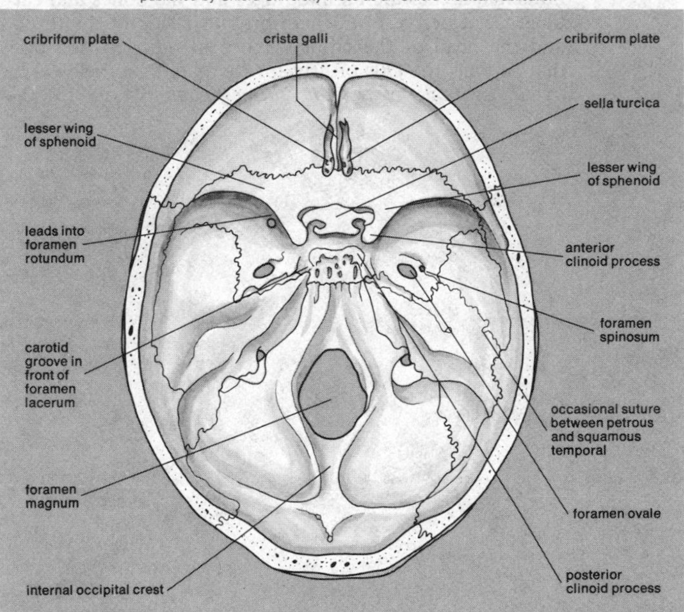

Figure 7: Internal surface of base of skull.

Conspicuous markings on the internal surface of the projection of the sphenoid, called the great wing, and on the internal surfaces of the parietal and the temporal bones are formed by the middle meningeal artery and its branches, which supply blood to the brain coverings. Injury to these vessels may lead to extradural hematoma, a mass of blood between the dura mater and the bone.

The fossae

In contrast to the vault and sides of the cranium, the base presents an extremely complicated aspect. It is divided into three major depressions, or fossae, in a descending stair-step arrangement from front to back. The fossae are divided strictly according to the borders of the bones of the cranium but are related to major portions of the brain. The anterior cranial fossa serves as the bed in which rest the frontal lobes of the cerebrum, the large forward part of the brain. The middle cranial fossa, sharply divided into two lateral halves by a central eminence of bone, contains the temporal lobes of the cerebrum. The posterior cranial fossa serves as a bed for the hemispheres of the cerebellum (a mass of brain tissue back of the brainstem and beneath the rear portion of the cerebrum) and for the forward and middle portion of the brainstem. Major portions of the brain are thus partially enfolded by the bones of the cranial wall.

There are openings in the three fossae for the passage of nerves and blood vessels, and the markings on the internal surface of the bones are from the attachments of the brain coverings—the meninges—and venous sinuses and other blood vessels.

Anterior cranial fossa

The anterior cranial fossa shows a crestlike projection in the midline, the crista galli ("crest of the cock"). This is a place of firm attachment for the important falx cerebri, a subdivision of dura mater that separates the right and left cerebral hemispheres. On either side of the crest is the cribriform (pierced with small holes) plate of the ethmoid, a midline bone important as a part both of the cranium and of the nose. Through the perforations of the plate run many divisions of the olfactory, or first cranial, nerve, coming from the mucous membrane of the nose. At the sides of the plate are the orbital plates of the frontal bone, which form the roofs of the eye sockets. Their inner surfaces are relatively smooth but have a number of sharp irregularities more obvious to the touch than to the sight. These irregularities mark attachments of dura mater to bone.

The rear part of the anterior cranial fossa is formed by those portions of the sphenoid bone called its body and lesser wings. Projections from the lesser wings, the anterior clinoid (bedlike) processes, extend back to a point beside each optic foramen, an opening through which important optic nerves, or tracts, enter into the protection of the cranial cavity after a relatively short course within the eye socket.

Middle cranial fossa

The central eminence of the middle cranial fossa is specialized as a thronelike or saddlelike seat for the pituitary gland. The posterior portion of this seat, or sella turcica ("Turk's saddle"), is actually wall-like and is called the dorsum sellae. The pituitary gland is, thus, situated in almost the centre of the cranial cavity. It is covered over also by the brain coverings and has no connection with the exterior of the cranium except by blood vessels.

The deep, lateral portions of the middle cranial fossa contain the temporal lobes of the cerebrum. In the forward part of the fossa are two important openings: one, the superior orbital fissure, opening into the eye cavity, and the other, the foramen rotundum, for the passage of the maxillary nerve, which serves the upper jaw and adjacent structures. Farther back are the conspicuous foramen ovale, an opening for the mandibular nerve to the lower jaw, and the foramen spinosum, for the middle meningeal artery, which brings blood to the dura mater.

Also in the middle fossa, near the apex of that part of the temporal bone called the petrous (stonelike) temporal bone, is the jagged opening called the foramen lacerum. The lower part of the foramen lacerum is blocked by fibrocartilage, but through its upper part passes the internal carotid artery, surrounded by a network of autonomic nerves, as it makes its way to the interior of the cranial cavity.

The delicate structures of the internal ear are not entrusted to the cranial cavity as such but lie within the petrous portion of the temporal bone in a bony labyrinth into which the thin-walled membranous labyrinth, with its areas of sensory cells, is more or less accurately fitted but with an adequate space for protective fluid, the perilymph, between bone and membrane.

Posterior cranial fossa

The posterior cranial fossa is above the vertebral column and the muscles of the back of the neck. The foramen magnum, the opening through which the brain and spinal cord make connection, is in the lowest part of the fossa. Between its forward margin and the base of the dorsum sellae is a broad, smooth, bony surface called the clivus (Latin for "hill"). The bridgelike pons and the pyramid-like medulla oblongata of the brainstem lie upon the clivus, separated from the bone only by their coverings. Near the foramen magnum are ridges for attachment of folds of the dura mater.

In the sides of the posterior cranial fossa are two transverse grooves, each of which, in part of its course, is separated by extremely thin bone from the mastoid air cells back of the ear. Through other openings, the jugular foramina, pass the large blood channels called the sigmoid sinuses and also the 9th (glossopharyngeal), 10th (vagus), and 11th (spinal accessory) cranial nerves as they leave the cranial cavity.

The vessels, as well as the cranial nerves, are subject to injury at the openings into or from the cranial cavity and in special areas, such as close to the mastoid air cells. In the latter location, mastoiditis may lead to enough breakdown of bone to allow disease-bearing organisms to reach the other structures within the cranial cavity.

THE HYOID: EXAMPLE OF THE ANCHORING FUNCTION

The primary function of the hyoid bone is to serve as an anchoring structure for the tongue. The bone is situated at the root of the tongue in the front of the neck and between the lower jaw and the largest cartilage of the larynx, the voice box. It has no articulation with other bones and has, thus, a purely anchoring function.

The hyoid consists of a body, a pair of larger horns, the greater cornua, and a pair of smaller horns, the lesser cornua. The bone is more or less in the shape of a U, and the body forms the central part, or base, of the letter. In the act of swallowing, the hyoid bone, tongue, and larynx all move upward rapidly.

From *Cunningham's Textbook of Anatomy* edited by G.J. Romanes and published by Oxford University Press as an Oxford Medical Publication

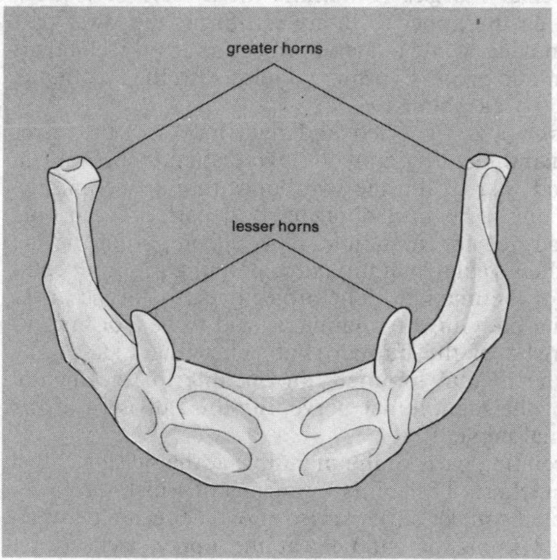

Figure 8: Hyoid bone.

The greater cornua are the limbs of the U. Their outer ends generally are overlapped by the large sternocleidomastoid muscles. The lesser cornua are small projections from the places somewhat arbitrarily called the junctions of the body and the greater cornua. The hyoid bone has certain of the muscles of the tongue attached to it.

Muscles anchored by the hyoid bone

The hyoglossus muscles originate on each side from the whole length of the greater cornua and also from the body of the hyoid. They are inserted into the posterior half or more of the sides of the tongue. The hyoid bone anchors them when they contract to depress the tongue and to widen the oral cavity. The two geniohyoid muscles originate close to the point at which the two halves of the lower jaw meet; the fibres of the muscles extend downward and backward, close to the central line, to be inserted into the body of the hyoid bone. Contraction of the muscles pulls the hyoid bone upward and forward.

Inserting into the middle part of the lower border of the hyoid bone are the sternohyoids, long muscles arising from the breastbone and collarbone and running upward and toward each other in the neck.

Other muscles attached to the hyoid bone are the two mylohyoid muscles, which form a sort of diaphragm for the floor of the mouth; the thyrohyoid, arising from the thyroid (the largest) cartilage of the larynx; and the omohyoid, which originates from the upper margin of the shoulder blade and from a ligament, the suprascapular ligament.

The position of the hyoid bone with relation to the muscles attached to it has been likened to that of a ship steadied as it rides when anchored "fore and aft." Through the muscle attachments, the hyoid plays an important role in mastication, in swallowing, and in voice production.

At the beginning of a swallowing motion, the geniohyoid and mylohyoid muscles elevate the bone and the floor of the mouth simultaneously. These muscles are assisted by the stylohyoid and digastric muscles. The tongue is pressed upward against the palate and the food is forced backwards.

THE FACIAL BONES AND THEIR COMPLEX FUNCTIONS

The maxillae

The upper jaws. The larger part of the skeleton of the face is formed by the maxillae. Though they are called the upper jaws, the extent and functions of the maxillae include much more than serving as complements to the lower jaw, or mandible. They form the middle and lower portion of the eye socket. They have the opening for the nose between them, beneath the lower borders of the small nasal bones. A sharp projection, the anterior nasal spine, is formed by them at the centre of the lower margin of the opening for the nose, the nasal aperture.

The infraorbital foramen, an opening into the floor of the eye socket, is the forward end of a canal through which passes the infraorbital branch of the maxillary nerve, the second division of the great fifth cranial nerve. It lies slightly below the lower margin of the socket.

The alveolar margin, containing the alveoli, or sockets, in which all the upper teeth are set, forms the lower part of each maxilla, while a lateral projection from each forms the zygomatic process, forming a joint with the zygomatic, or malar (cheek), bone.

The lower jaw. The left and right halves of the lower jaw, or mandible, originally are two distinct bones, but in the second year of life the two bones fuse at the midline to form one. The horizontal, central part on each side is the body of the mandible. The upper portion of the body is the alveolar margin, corresponding to the alveolar margins of the maxillae. The projecting chin, at the lower part of the body in the midline, is said to be a distinctive characteristic of the human skull. On either side of the chin is the mental foramen, an opening for the mental branch of the mandibular nerve, the third division of the fifth cranial nerve.

The ascending parts of the mandible at the side are called rami (branches). The joints by means of which the lower jaw is able to make all its varied movements are between a rounded knob, or condyle, at the upper back corner of each ramus and a depression, called a glenoid fossa, in each temporal bone. Another, rather sharp projection at the top of each ramus and in front, called a coronoid process, does not form part of a joint. Attached to it is the temporalis muscle, which serves with other muscles in shutting the jaws.

On the inner side of the ramus of either side is a large, obliquely placed opening into a channel, the mandibular canal, for nerves, arteries, and veins.

The zygomatic arch, forming the cheekbone, consists of portions of three bones: the maxilla, in front; the zygomatic bone, centrally in the arch; and a projection from the temporal bone to form the rear part. The zygomatic arch actually serves as a firm bony origin for the powerful masseter muscle, which descends from it to insert on the outer side of the mandible. The masseter muscle shares with the temporalis and lateral and medial pterygoid muscles the function of elevating the mandible in order to bring the lower against the upper teeth, thus achieving bite.

THE SPINE: ITS ROLE IN PROTECTION, ANCHORING, AND WEIGHT BEARING

In speaking earlier of the three major functions of the skeleton (support, protection, motion), it was indicated that the assumption of the erect posture during the development of the human species has led to a need for adaptation and changes from the arrangements seen in the quadrupeds. The very form of the human vertebral column is due to such adaptations and changes.

The curvature of the spine

The vertebral column. The vertebral column is not actually a column but, rather, a sort of spiral spring in the form of the letter S. The newborn child has a relatively straight backbone. The development of the curvatures occurs as the supporting functions of the vertebral column in man—holding up the trunk, keeping the head erect, serving as an anchor for the extremities—are developed.

The S-curvature makes it possible for the vertebral column to absorb the shocks of walking on hard ground or on pavement; a straight column would conduct the jarring shocks directly from the pelvic girdle to the head. The curvature meets the problem of the weight of the viscera. In an erect animal with a straight column, the column would be pulled forward by the viscera. Additional space for the viscera is provided by the concavities of the thoracic and pelvic regions.

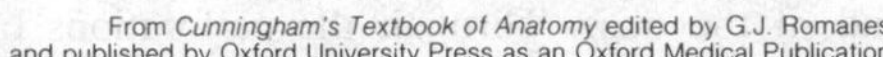
From *Cunningham's Textbook of Anatomy* edited by G.J. Romanes and published by Oxford University Press as an Oxford Medical Publication

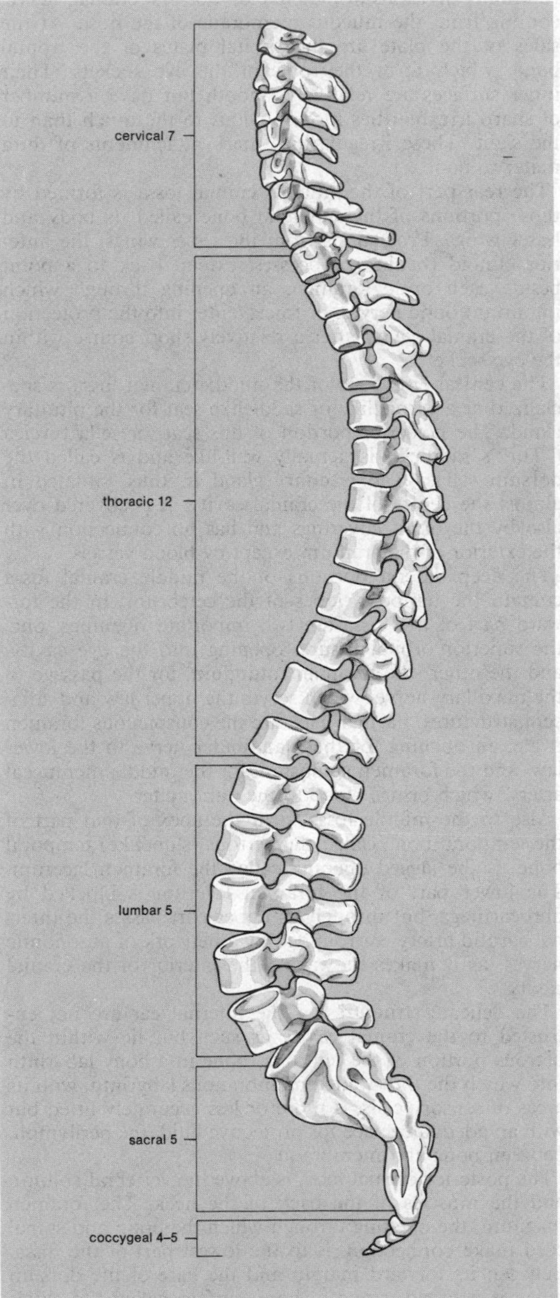

Figure 9: Backbone, from the left side.

Weight distribution of the entire body is also effected by the S-curvature. The upper sector, to a large extent, carries the head; the central sector, the thoracic viscera—the organs and structures in the chest—and the lower sector, the abdominal viscera. If the column were straight, the weight load would increase from the head downward and be relatively great at the base. Lastly, the S-curvature protects the vertebral column from breakage. The doubly bent spring arrangement is far less vulnerable to fracture than would be a straight column.

The protective function of the skeleton is perhaps most conspicuous in relation to the central nervous system, although it is equally important for the heart and lungs and some other organs. A high degree of protection for the nervous system is made possible by the relatively small amount of motion and expansion needed by the component parts of this system and by certain physiological adaptations relating to circulation, to the cerebrospinal fluid, and to the meninges, the coverings of the brain and spinal cord. The brain itself is snugly enclosed within the boxlike cranium. Sharing in the protection afforded by the cranium is the pituitary gland, or hypophysis.

The spinal cord. For the spinal cord, with its tracts of nerve fibres travelling to and from the brain, the placement in relation to the spinal column is somewhat like that of a candle in a lantern. Normally, there is considerable space between the nervous and the bony tissue, space occupied by the meninges, by the cerebrospinal fluid, and by a certain amount of fat and connective tissue. In front are the heavy centrums, or bodies, of the vertebrae and the intervertebral disks—the tough, resilient pads between the vertebral bodies—while in back and on the sides the cord is enclosed and protected by the portion of each vertebra called the neural arch. Between the neural arches are sheets of elastic connective tissue, the interlaminar ligaments, or ligamenta flava. Here some protective function has to be sacrificed for the sake of motion, because a forward bending of part of the column leads to separation between the laminae and between the spines of the neural arches of adjoining vertebrae. It is through the ligamenta flava of the lower lumbar region (the small of the back) that the needle enters the subarachnoid space in the procedure of lumbar puncture.

Anchoring function of the spine

Besides its role in support and protection, the vertebral column is important in the anchoring of muscles. Many of the muscles attached to it are so arranged, in fact, as to move either the column itself or various segments of it. Some are relatively superficial, and others are deep lying. The large and important erector spinae, as the name implies, holds the spine erect. It begins on the sacrum (the large triangular bone at the base of the spinal column) and passes upward, forming a mass of muscle on either side of the spines of the lumbar vertebrae. It then divides into three columns, ascending over the back of the chest. Although slips (narrow strips) of the muscle are inserted into the vertebrae and ribs, it does not terminate thus, for fresh slips arise from these same bones and continue on up into the neck, until one of the divisions, known as the longissimus capitis, finally reaches the skull.

Small muscles run between the transverse processes (projections from the sides of the neural rings) of adjacent vertebrae, between the vertebral spines (projections from the centres of the rings), and also from transverse process to spine, giving great mobility to the segmented bony column.

The anchoring function of the spinal column is of great importance for the muscles that arise on the trunk, in whole or part from the column or from ligaments attached to it, and that are inserted on the bones of the arms and legs. Of these muscles, the most important for the arms are the latissimus dorsi (drawing the arm backward and downward and rotating it inward), the trapezius (rotating the shoulder blade), the rhomboideus, and the levator scapulae (raising and lowering the shoulder blade); for the legs, the psoas (loin) muscles.

THE RIB CAGE

The rib cage, or thoracic basket, consists of the 12 thoracic (chest) vertebrae, the 24 ribs, and the breastbone or sternum. The ribs are curved, compressed bars of bone, each succeeding rib, from the first, or uppermost, becoming more open in curvature. The place of greatest change in curvature of a rib, called its angle, is found several inches from the head of the rib, the end that forms a joint with the vertebrae.

Structure and functions of ribs

The first seven ribs are attached to the breastbone by cartilages called costal cartilages; these ribs are called true ribs. Of the remaining five ribs, which are called false, the first three have their costal cartilages connected to the cartilage above them. The last two, the floating ribs, have their cartilages ending in the muscle in the abdominal wall.

Through the action of a number of muscles, the rib cage, which is semirigid but expansile, increases its size. The pressure of the air in the lungs thus is reduced below that of the outside air, which moves into the lungs quickly to restore equilibrium. These events constitute inspiration (breathing in). Expiration (breathing out) is a result of relaxation of the respiratory muscles and of the elastic recoil of the lungs and of the fibrous ligaments and tendons attached to the skeleton of the thorax. A major respiratory muscle is the diaphragm, which separates the chest and abdomen and has an extensive origin from the rib cage and the vertebral column. The configuration of the lower five ribs gives freedom for the expansion of the lower part of the rib cage and for the movements of the diaphragm.

Bones of the appendicular skeleton

SHOULDER GIRDLE AND PELVIC GIRDLE

The upper and lower extremities of man offer many interesting points of comparison and of contrast. They and their individual components are homologous; *i.e.,* of a common origin and patterned on the same basic plan. A long evolutionary history and profound changes in function of these two pairs of extremities have led, however, to considerable differences between them.

The pelvic girdle

The girdles are those portions of the extremities that are in closest relation to the axis of the body and that serve to connect the free extremity (the arm or the leg) with that axis, either directly, by way of the skeleton, or indirectly, by muscular attachments. The connection of the pelvic girdle to the body axis, or vertebral column, is by means of the sacroiliac joint. On the contiguous surfaces of the ilium—the rear and upper part of the hipbone—and of the sacrum—the part of the vertebral column directly connected with the hipbone—are thin plates of cartilage. The bones are closely fitted together in this way, and there are irregular masses of softer fibrocartilage in places joining the articular cartilages; at the upper and posterior parts of the joint there are fibrous attachments between the bones. In the joint cavity there is a small amount of synovial fluid. Strong ligaments, known as anterior and posterior sacroiliac and interosseous ligaments, bind the pelvic girdle to the vertebral column. These fibrous attachments are the chief factors limiting motion of the joint, but the condition, or tone, of the muscles in this region is important in preventing or correcting the sacroiliac problems that are of common occurrence.

The pelvic girdle consists originally of three bones, which become fused and each of which contributes a part of the acetabulum, the deep cavity into which the head of the thighbone, or femur, is fitted. The flaring upper part of the girdle is the ilium; the lower anterior part, meeting with its fellow at the midline, is the pubis; and the lower posterior part is the ischium. Each ischial bone has a prominence, or tuberosity, and it is upon these tuberosities that the body rests when seated.

The pectoral girdle

The components of the girdle of the upper extremity, the pectoral girdle, are the shoulder blade, or scapula, and the collarbone, or clavicle. The head of the humerus, the long bone of the upper arm, fits into the glenoid cavity, a depression in the scapula. The pectoral girdle is not connected with the vertebral column by ligamentous attachments, nor is there any joint between it and any part of the axis of the body. The connection is by means of muscles only, including the trapezius, rhomboids, and levator scapulae, while the serratus anterior connects the scapula to the rib cage. The range of motion of the pectoral girdle and, in particular, of the scapula is enormously greater than that of the pelvic girdle.

Another contrast, in terms of function, is seen in the shallowness of the glenoid fossa, as contrasted with the depth of the acetabulum. It is true that the receptacle for the head of the humerus is deepened somewhat by a lip of fibrocartilage, the glenoid labrum, which, like the corresponding structure for the acetabulum, aids in grasping the head of the long bone. The range of motion of the free upper extremity is, however, far greater than that of the lower extremity. With this greater facility of motion goes a greater risk of dislocation. For this reason, of all joints of the body, the shoulder is most often the site of dislocation.

LONG BONES OF ARMS AND LEGS

The humerus and the femur are corresponding bones of the arms and legs, respectively. While their parts are similar in general, their structure has been adapted to differing functions. The head of the humerus is almost hemispherical, while that of the femur forms about two-thirds of a sphere. There is a strong ligament passing from the head of the femur to further strengthen and ensure its position in the acetabulum.

The anatomical neck of the humerus is only a slight constriction, while the neck of the femur is a very distinct portion running from the head to meet the shaft at an angle of about 125°. Actually, the femoral neck is developmentally and functionally a part of the shaft. The entire weight of the body is directed through the femoral heads along their necks and to the shaft. The structure of the bone within the head and neck and the upper part of the shaft of the femur would do credit to an engineer who had worked out the weight-bearing problems involved in the maintenance of upright posture.

From *Cunningham's Textbook of Anatomy* edited by G.J. Romanes and published by Oxford University Press as an Oxford Medical Publication

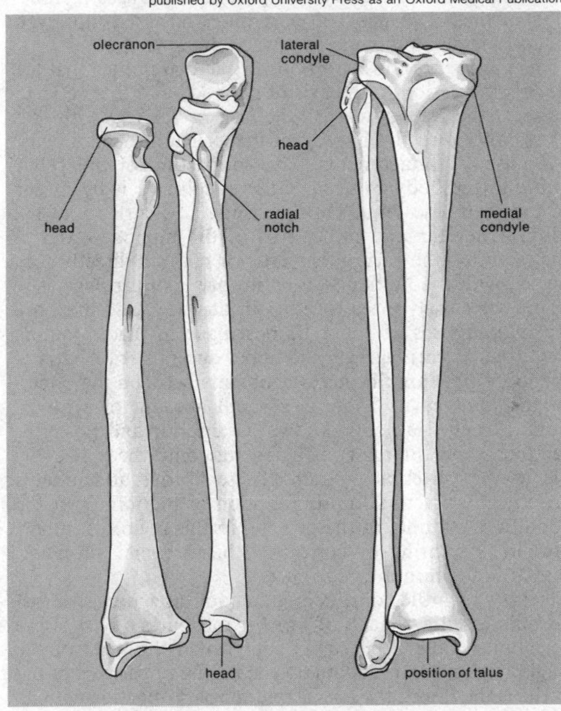

Figure 10: (Left) Forearm, radius and ulna bones. (Right) Lower leg, fibula and tibia bones.

The forearm and the lower leg have two long bones each. In the forearm are the radius—on the thumb side of the forearm—and the ulna; in the lower leg, the tibia (the shinbone) and the fibula. The radius corresponds to the tibia and the ulna to the fibula. The knee joint not only is the largest joint in the body but also is perhaps the most complicated one. The bones involved in it, however, are only the femur and the tibia, although the smaller bone of the leg, the fibula, is carried along in the movements of flexion, extension, and slight rotation that this joint permits. The very thin fibula is at one time in fetal development far thicker relative to the tibia than it is in the adult skeleton.

Radius and ulna

At the elbow, the ulna forms with the humerus a true hinge joint, in which the actions are flexion and extension. In this joint, a large projection of the ulna, the olecranon, fits into the well-defined olecranon fossa, a depression of the humerus.

The radius is shorter than the ulna. Its most distinctive feature is the thick, disk-shaped head, which has a smoothly concave superior surface to articulate with the head, or capitulum, of the humerus. The head of the radius is held against the notch in the side of the ulna by means of a strong annular, or ring-shaped, ligament. Although thus attached to the ulna, the head of the radius is free to rotate. As the head rotates, the shaft and outer end of the radius are swung in an arc. In the position of the arm called supination, the radius and ulna are parallel, the palm of the hand faces forward, and the thumb is away from the body. In the position called pronation, the radius and ulna are crossed, the palm faces to the rear, and the thumb is next to the body. There are no actions of the leg comparable to the supination and pronation of the arm.

HANDS AND FEET

The skeleton of the wrist, or carpus, consists of eight small carpal bones, which are arranged in two rows of four each. The skeleton of the ankle, or tarsus, has seven bones, and, because of the angle of the foot to the leg and the weight-bearing function, they are arranged in a more complicated way. The bone of the heel, directed downward and backward, is the calcaneus, while the "keystone" of the tarsus is the talus, the superior surface of which articulates with the tibia.

In the skeleton of the arms and legs, the outer portion is specialized and consists of elongated portions made up of chains, or linear series, of small bones. In an evolutionary sense, these outer portions appear to have had a complex history and, within man's own mammalian ancestry, to have passed first through a stage when all four would have been "feet," serving as the weight-bearing ends of extremities, as in quadrupeds in general. Second, all four appear to have become adapted for arboreal life, as in the lower primates, the "four-handed folk." Third, and finally, the assumption of an upright posture has brought the distal portions of the hind, now lower, extremities back into the role of feet, while those of the front, now upper, extremities have developed remarkable manipulative powers and are called hands. At what place in the primates a foot becomes a hand is difficult to say, and one might be justified, in fact, in speaking of hands in raccoons, squirrels, and some other nonprimates.

In man, the metatarsal bones, those of the foot proper, are larger than the corresponding bones of the hands, the metacarpal bones. The tarsals and metatarsals form the arches of the foot, which give it strength and enable it to act as a lever. The shape of each bone and its relations to its fellows are such as to adapt it for this function.

Fingers and toes

The phalanges—the toe bones—of the foot have bases relatively large compared to the corresponding bones in the hand, while the shafts are much thinner. The middle and outer phalanges in the foot are short in comparison to those of the fingers. The phalanges of the great toe have special features.

The hand is an instrument for fine and varied movements. In these, the thumb with its skeleton, the first metacarpal bone and the two phalanges, is extremely important. Its free movements include, besides flexion, extension, abduction (ability to draw away from the first finger), and adduction (ability to move forward of the fingers), which are exercised in varying degrees by the great toe also, a unique action, that of opposition, by which it can be brought across, or opposed to, the palm and to the tips of the slightly flexed fingers. This motion forms the basis for the handling of tools, weapons, and instruments. (W.A.)

CONNECTIVE TISSUES

General features of connective tissue

The connective tissues are a heterogeneous group of tissues derived from the mesenchyme, a meshwork of stellate cells that develop in the middle layer of the early embryo. They have the general function of maintaining the structural integrity of organs and providing cohesion and internal support for the body as a whole. The connective tissues include several types of fibrous tissue that vary only in their density and cellularity, as well as more specialized variants ranging from adipose tissue through cartilage to bone. The cells that are responsible for the specific functions of an organ are referred to as its parenchyma, while the delicate fibrous meshwork that binds the cells together into functional units, the fibrous partitions or septa that enclose aggregations of functional units, and the dense fibrous capsule that encloses the whole organ, collectively make up its connective-tissue framework, or stroma. Blood vessels, both large and small, course through connective tissue, which is therefore closely associated with the nourishment of tissues and organs throughout the body. All nutrient materials and waste products exchanged between the organs and the blood must traverse perivascular spaces occupied by connective tissue. One of the important functions of the connective-tissue cells is to maintain conditions in the extracellular spaces that favour this exchange.

Cohesion and support functions

Some organs are suspended from the wall of a body cavity by thin sheets of connective tissue called mesenteries; others are embedded in adipose tissue, a form of connective tissue in which the cells are specialized for the synthesis and storage of energy-rich reserves of fat, or lipid. The entire body is supported from within by a skeleton composed of bone, a type of connective tissue endowed with great resistance to stress owing to its highly ordered, laminated structure and to its hardness, which results from deposition of mineral salts in its fibres and amorphous matrix. The individual bones of the skeleton are held firmly together by ligaments, and muscles are attached to bone by tendons, both of which are examples of dense connective tissue in which many fibre bundles are associated in parallel array to provide great tensile strength. At joints, the articular surfaces of the bones are covered with cartilage, a connective tissue with an abundant intercellular substance that gives it a firm consistency well adapted to permit smooth gliding movements between the apposed surfaces. The synovial membrane, which lines the margins of the joint cavity and lubricates and nourishes the joint surfaces, is also a form of connective tissue. (Bones and joints are treated in detail in the next two sections.)

COMPONENTS OF CONNECTIVE TISSUE

All forms of connective tissue are composed of (1) cells, (2) extracellular fibres, and (3) an amorphous matrix, called ground substance. The proportions of these components vary from one part of the body to another depending on the local structural requirements. In some areas, the connective tissue is loosely organized and highly cellular, in others its fibrous components predominate, and in still others, the ground substance may be its most conspicuous feature. The anatomical classification of the various types of connective tissue is based largely upon the relative abundance and arrangement of these components.

Collagenous and reticular fibres

The fibrous components are of three kinds, collagenous, elastic, and reticular fibres. Most abundant are the fibres composed of the protein collagen. The fibrous components of loose areolar connective tissue when viewed with the light microscope appear as colourless strands of varying diameter running in all directions, and, if not under tension, these have a slightly undulant course (see photo). At high magnification, the larger strands are seen to be made up of bundles of smaller fibres. And the smallest fibres visible with the light microscope can be shown with the electron microscope to be composed of multiple fibrils up to 1000 angstroms (one Å = 1×10^{-7} millimetre) in diameter. These unit fibrils are cross-striated with transverse bands repeating every 640 Å along their length.

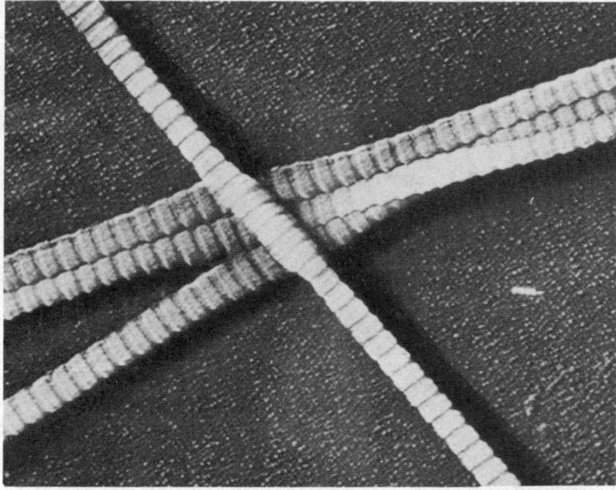

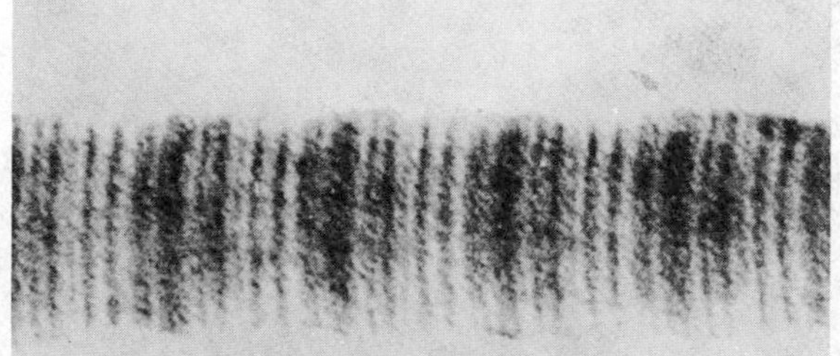

(Top) Electron micrograph of four collagen fibrils shadowed with metal to increase their contrast and reveal their periodic 640-Å cross striation. (Bottom) In a more highly magnified electron micrograph of a collagen fibril stained with phosphotungstate, the cross striation can be resolved into several distinct bands which depend upon the arrangement of the tropocollagen molecules within the fibre.

By courtesy of (top) J. Gross, (bottom) B.R. Olsen

Extracellular fibres. Collagen is of commercial as well as medical interest because leather is the dense collagen of the dermis of animal skins preserved and toughened by the process called tanning. Fresh collagen dissolves in hot water, and the product is gelatin. Under appropriate conditions, collagen can be brought into solution without chemical change. The fundamental units in such solutions are slender tropocollagen molecules about 14 Å wide and 2800 Å long. Collagen appears to be secreted in this form by the connective-tissue cells called fibroblasts, and the tropocollagen molecules assemble extracellularly to form striated collagen fibrils. By an alteration of the physicochemical conditions, tropocollagen in solution can be induced to polymerize with the formation of cross-striated fibrils identical to native collagen, thus simulating in the test tube the process of assembly that is believed to take place during fibrogenesis in the living organism. Analysis of the structure of collagen by X-ray diffraction has shown that the tropocollagen molecule consists of three side-by-side polypeptide chains—linear combinations of a number of amino acids, which are subunits of proteins—each in the form of a left-handed helix. These three left-handed helices are further twisted around one another to form a major right-handed helix. Upon chemical analysis, the amino-acid composition of collagen is found to be unique in its extremely high proline content (22 percent) and in the fact that one-third of the amino acid residues are glycine. It is the only naturally occurring protein known to contain hydroxyproline and hydroxylysine. Two of the three polypeptide chains comprising the tropocollagen molecule are similar in amino acid composition, while the third is distinctly different. In the tissues, the collagen fibrils are believed to be held together by a polysaccharide component that has not been fully characterized.

Reticular fibres are distinguished by their tendency to

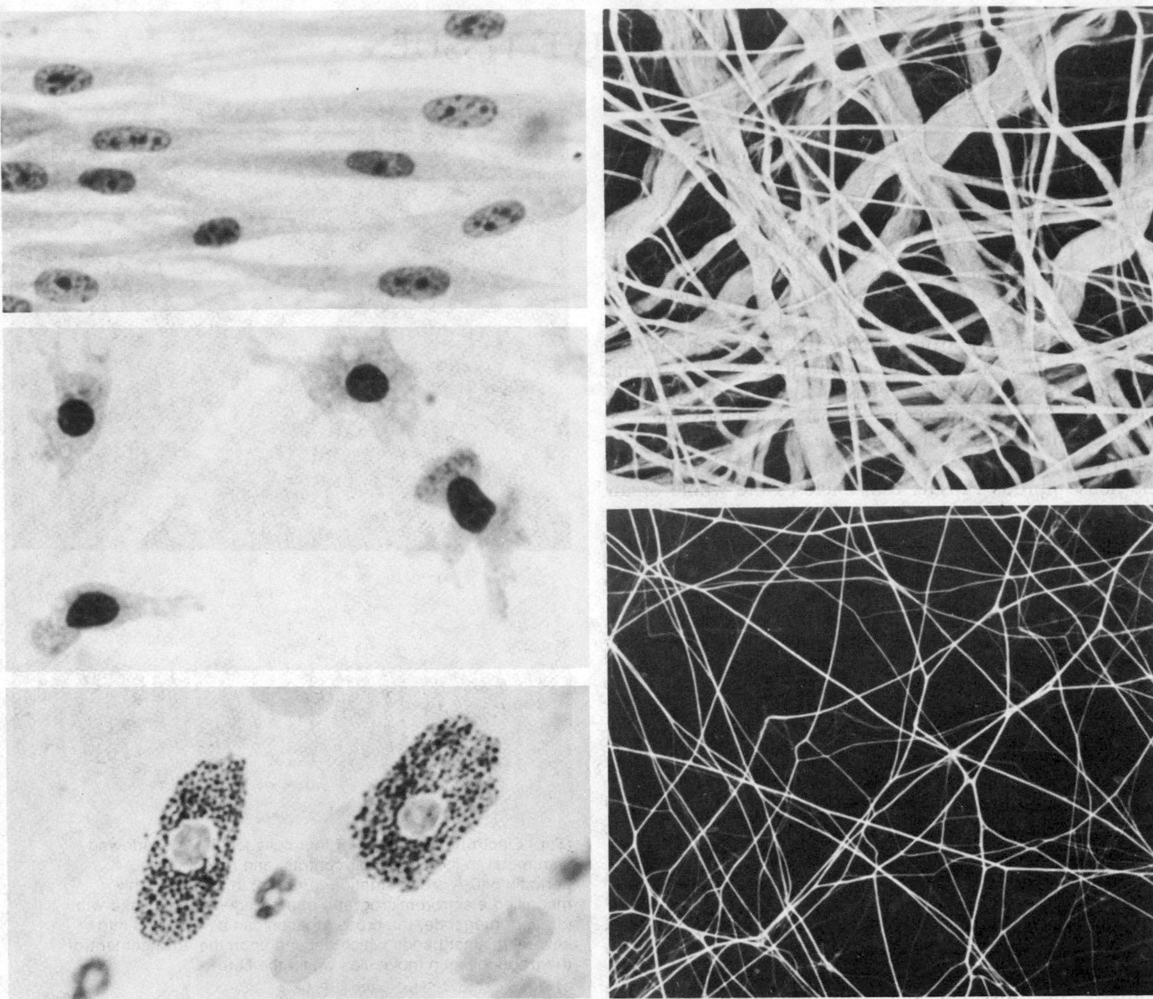

Photomicrographs of connective tissue components.
(Top left) Long fusiform fibroblasts growing in tissue culture (magnified about 520 ×). (Top right) Randomly oriented collagenous fibres of varying size in a thin spread of loose areolar connective tissue (magnified about 370 ×). (Centre left) Four macrophages in cell culture (magnified about 825 ×). Their irregular outline is associated with amoeboid migration. (Bottom left) Metachromatic granules fill the cytoplasm of these mast cells, which have centrally located nuclei (magnified about 750 ×). (Bottom right) Selectively stained network of thin elastic fibres in a thin sheet of areolar connective tissue (magnified about 390 ×).
By courtesy of (top left) W. Bloom and D. Fawcett, *Textbook of Histology*, 9th ed.; W.B. Saunders Company, (top right, centre left, bottom left, bottom right) Don Fawcett

form fine-meshed networks around cells and cell groups, and by virtue of their property of staining black because of adsorption of metallic silver when they are treated with alkaline solutions of reducible silver salts. They were formerly believed to be composed of a distinct protein, reticulin, but electron microscopy has revealed that reticular fibres are small fascicles of typical collagen fibrils interwoven to form a network. It is now apparent that reticular fibres are simply a form of collagen and that their distinctive staining depends upon the mode of association of the fibrils and possibly upon subtle differences in their relation to the polysaccharide material that binds them together.

Elastic fibres

Elastic fibres are composed of the protein elastin and differ from collagenous fibres in dimensions, pattern, and chemical composition. They do not have uniform subunits comparable to the unit fibrils of collagen. They present a variable appearance in electron micrographs; sometimes they appear to have an amorphous core surrounded by minute fibrils, while in other sites they appear to consist exclusively of dense amorphous material. Whether there are in fact two components or whether these are differing forms of the same substance is not yet clear. At the light-microscope level, the fibres vary in diameter and often branch and reunite to form extensive networks in loose connective tissue. When present in high concentration, they impart a yellow colour to the tissue. In elastic ligaments, the fibres are very coarse and are arranged in parallel bundles. In the walls of arteries, elastin is present in the form of sheets or membranes perforated by openings of varying size. Elastic fibres are extremely resistant to hot water, to strong alkali, and even to digestion with the proteolytic enzyme trypsin. They can be digested, however, by a specific enzyme, elastase, present in the pancreas. Upon chemical analysis, elastin, like collagen, is found to be rich in glycine and proline, but it differs in its high content of valine and in the presence of an unusual amino acid, desmosine. As their name implies, elastic fibres are highly distensible and, when broken, recoil like rubber bands. Changes in this property and diminution in their numbers are thought to be, in part, responsible for the loss of elasticity of the skin and of the blood-vessel walls in old age.

Ground substance. The amorphous ground substance of connective tissue is a transparent material with the properties of a viscous solution or a highly hydrated thin gel. Its principal constituents are large carbohydrate molecules or complexes of protein and carbohydrate, often called mucopolysaccharides. One of these carbohydrates is hyaluronic acid, composed of glucuronic acid and an amino sugar, *N*-acetyl glucosamine. Other carbohydrates of the connective tissue are chondroitin-4-sulfate (chondroitin sulfate A) and chondroitin-6-sulfate (chondroitin sulfate C). The sugars of the sulfates are galactosamine and glucuronate. Multiple chains of chondroitin sulfate seem to be bound to protein. These substances in solution are viscous. All substances passing to and from cells must pass through the ground substance. Variations in its composition and its viscosity may therefore have an important influence on the exchange of materials between tissue cells and the blood. Its physical consistency also constitutes a barrier to the spread of particulates introduced into the tissues. It is interesting, in this relation, that some bacteria produce an enzyme, hyaluronidase, which breaks up hyaluronic acid into subunits and alters the viscosity of ground substance. The ability of these bacteria to produce this enzyme is probably responsible for their invasiveness in the tissues.

Stationary and motile cells

Cells of connective tissue. The cells of connective tissue include three types that are relatively stationary, fibroblasts, macrophages, and adipose cells, and several types of motile, migrating cells—mast cells, monocytes, lymphocytes, plasma cells, and eosinophils. The ubiquitous fibroblasts are the principal cells of connective tissue, occurring as long spindle-shaped cells stretched along bundles of collagen fibrils. Their function is to secrete tropocollagen and constituents of the ground substance and to maintain these extracellular tissue components. When organs are injured, the fibroblasts of the stroma are stimulated to proliferate; they migrate into the defect and deposit an abundance of new collagen, which forms a fibrous scar. The macrophages or histiocytes are also important for tissue repair and for defense against bacterial invasion. Like fibroblasts, they are normally fusiform or stellate and are deployed along the collagen fibre bundles, but, if there is tissue damage or bacterial invasion, they withdraw the projections by which they are anchored and migrate by active amoeboid movements into the affected area. They have a great capacity for phagocytosis—the process by which cells engulf cellular debris, bacteria, or other foreign matter, and break them down by intracellular digestion. Thus they represent an important force of mobile scavenger cells.

Adipose cells are connective-tissue cells that are specialized for synthesis and storage of reserve nutrients. They receive glucose and fatty acids from the blood and convert them to lipid, which accumulates in the body of the cell as a large oil droplet. This distends the cell and imposes upon it a spherical form. The nucleus is displaced to the periphery, and other metabolically active constituents of the cell are confined to a thin rim of cytoplasm around the large, central droplet of lipid. Adipose cells may occur in small numbers anywhere in connective tissue, but they tend to develop preferentially along the course of small blood vessels. Where they accumulate in such large numbers that they become the predominant cellular element, they constitute the fat or adipose tissue of the body.

All the cells of connective tissue develop during embryonic life from the mesenchyme, a network of primitive stellate cells that have the potentiality for differentiating along several different lines depending upon local conditions. In addition to the specialized cell types of adult connective tissue described above, it is believed that small numbers of mesenchymal cells persist into postnatal life in the walls of small blood vessels and elsewhere and that these retain the capacity to differentiate into fibroblasts, adipose cells, or histiocytes as the need arises.

Mast cells. In addition to the relatively fixed cell types just described, there are free cells that reside in the interstices of loose connective tissue. These vary in their abundance and are free to migrate through the extracellular spaces. Among these wandering cells are the mast cells; these have a cell body filled with coarse granules that exhibit a characteristic metachromatic staining reaction. The function of these cells is still poorly understood, but they are known to produce and store in their granules two biologically active substances, histamine and heparin. Histamine affects vascular permeability, and heparin, when added to blood, delays or prevents its clotting. Mast cells respond to mechanical or chemical irritation by discharging varying numbers of their granules. Histamine released from them causes fluid to escape from neighbouring capillaries or venules; this results in local swelling, as seen in the welt that appears around an insect bite.

Tissue eosinophils are a type of white blood cell or leukocyte. Some of these migrate through the walls of capillaries and take up residence in the connective tissues. They have polymorphous nuclei and, in the cell substance outside the nuclei, coarse granules that stain with eosin and other acid dyes. In electron micrographs, the granules contain conspicuous crystals. The granules have been isolated and shown to contain a variety of hydrolytic enzymes. Eosinophils are normally widespread in connective tissues of the body, but they are especially abundant in persons suffering from allergic diseases. The cells are believed to phagocytose and break down antigen-antibody complexes.

Eosinophils

Plasma cells, which are present in limited numbers in loose connective tissues and in larger numbers in lymphoid tissue, are essential to the body's immunological defenses. They are specialized for synthesis and release of those specific immune globulins, called antibodies, that combine with and neutralize foreign proteins introduced into the body. Lymphocytes are among the normal cellular elements of the blood, but they may also leave the blood and migrate in the connective tissues. They are small round cells with a thin rim of cytoplasm and only limited synthetic activity. They appear to be able to recognize foreign protein and to respond to its presence by enlargement, proliferation, and transformation into plasma cells. They thus constitute an important reserve of relatively undifferentiated cells capable of sustaining an immunological response. They are the subject of intensive study because of their important role in defense against disease and because they participate in the rejection reaction that often frustrates the surgeon's efforts to transplant organs from one individual to another.

Monocyte and neutrophilic leukocyte

Another of the leukocytes that enter the connective tissues from the blood is the monocyte, a mononuclear cell larger than the lymphocyte and with different potentialities. These migratory cells can divide and, when appropriately stimulated, can transform into highly phagocytic macrophages. Thus at sites of bacterial invasion, when the resident population of fixed macrophages or histiocytes cannot cope with the situation, the monocytes of the connective tissues are reserves that can be mobilized at the focus of infection and can be continually reinforced by emigration of additional monocytes from the blood. This reaction of the blood and connective-tissue cells to injury is called inflammation and is usually accompanied by local heat, swelling, redness, and pain. Under these conditions, the neutrophilic leukocytes (white blood cells called neutrophilic because of their neutral staining characteristics with certain dyes), which are not normally present in connective tissue in significant numbers, may also migrate through the capillary walls in astronomical numbers and join the macrophages in the work of ingesting and destroying bacteria. Voraciously phagocytic, the neutrophils have a short life-span; having accomplished their mission, they die in great numbers. Pus, which may accumulate at sites of acute inflammation, is composed largely of dead and dying neutrophilic leukocytes.

TYPES OF CONNECTIVE TISSUE

The description presented thus far applies to the widely distributed loose areolar connective tissue, which is relatively unspecialized and can therefore be considered prototypic. In the more specialized forms of connective tissues, one component or another may predominate over all the others, depending upon the local structural or metabolic requirements.

Adipose tissue, for example, is a variant of loose areolar tissue in which large numbers of adipose cells make up the bulk of the tissue.

Dense fibrous connective tissue is composed of closely packed bundles of collagen and their associated fibroblasts, but there are relatively few elastic fibres and little ground substance. The term irregular dense fibrous tissue is applied to sites where the collagen bundles are randomly oriented and interwoven, as in the dermis of the skin and the capsules of joints. Regular dense fibrous tissue is the term used to describe tendons, ligaments, and aponeuroses (fibrous sheets that form attachments for muscles), where the collagen fibres are precisely oriented in parallel bundles.

Synovial membrane lining joint capsules is composed of loose vascular connective tissue but has cells specialized

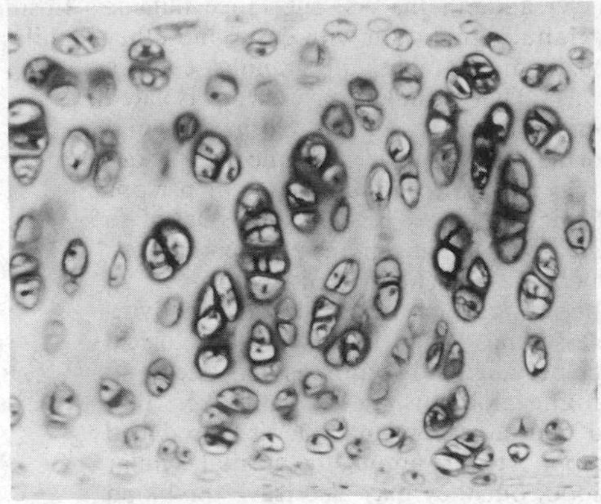

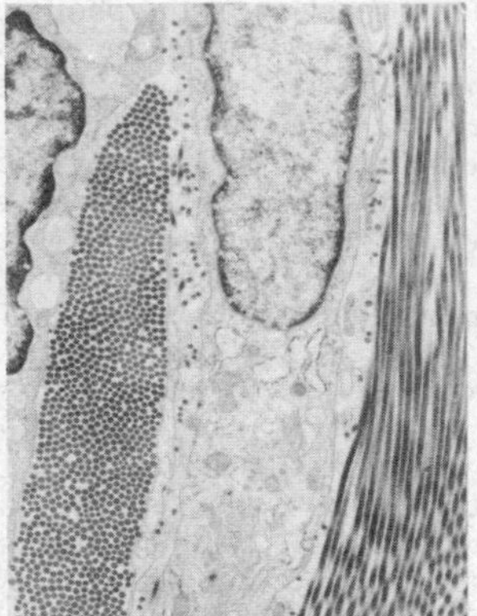

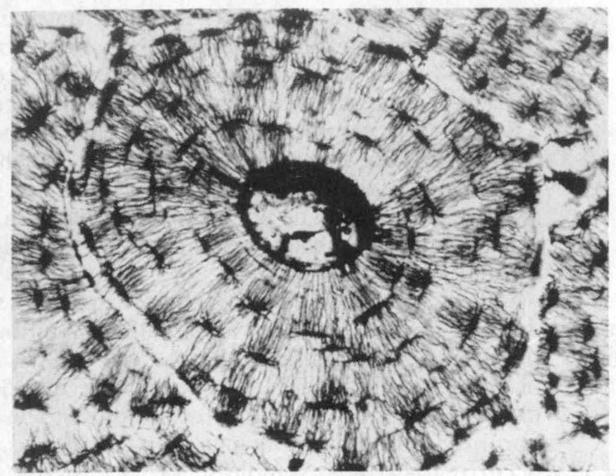

Three types of connective tissue.
(Left) Photomicrograph of hyaline cartilage from the trachea. The chondrocytes are enclosed in lacunae distributed in groups in an abundant matrix (magnified 250 ×). (Centre) Electron micrograph of a small area of connective tissue illustrating the intimate association of cells and fibres. In the centre is a portion of a fibroblast, and on either side are two collagen fibres. The collagen fibre on the left is cut transversely, showing round cross sections of the unit fibrils. The collagen fibre on the right has been cut nearly parallel to its long axis and shows extensive segments of the cross-striated fibrils (magnified about 6,625 ×). (Right) Photomicrograph of a ground section of bone showing a haversian system, or osteon, in cross section, and adjacent interstitial lamellae. The osteocytes occupy flat lacunae, which appear black in this preparation. Slender canaliculi connect neighbouring canaliculi (magnified about 125 ×).

By courtesy of (left) W. Bloom and D. Fawcett, *Textbook of Histology*, 9th ed.; W.B. Saunders Company, (centre, right) Don Fawcett

for secretion of the viscous synovial fluid, which is rich in hyaluronic acid. This fluid serves as a lubricant and nutrient for the avascular joint surfaces. Similar tissue forms sheaths around tendons where they pass over bony prominences.

Cartilage. Cartilage is a form of connective tissue in which the ground substance is abundant and of a firmly gelated consistency that endows this tissue with unusual rigidity and resistance to compression. The cells of cartilage, called chondrocytes, are isolated in small lacunae within the matrix. Although cartilage is avascular, gaseous metabolites and nutrients can diffuse through the aqueous phase of the gel-like matrix to reach the cells. Cartilage is enclosed by the perichondrium, a dense fibrous layer lined by cells that have the capacity to secrete hyaline matrix. Cartilage grows by formation of additional matrix and incorporation of new cells from the inner chondrogenic layer of the perichondrium. In addition, the young chondrocytes retain the capacity to divide even after they become isolated in lacunae within the matrix. The daughter cells of these divisions secrete new matrix between them and move apart in separate lacunae. The capacity of cartilage for both appositional and interstitial growth makes it a favourable material for the skeleton of the rapidly growing embryo. The cartilaginous skeletal elements present in fetal life are subsequently replaced by bone.

Hyaline and elastic cartilage

Hyaline cartilage, the most widely distributed form, has a pearl-gray semitranslucent matrix containing randomly oriented collagen fibrils, but relatively little elastin. In elastic cartilage, on the other hand, the matrix has a pale yellow appearance owing to the abundance of elastic fibres embedded in its substance. This variant of cartilage is more flexible than hyaline cartilage and is found principally in the external ear and in the larynx and epiglottis. The third type, called fibrocartilage, has a large proportion of dense collagen bundles oriented parallel. Its cells occupy lacunae that are often arranged in rows between the coarse bundles of collagen. It is found in intervertebral disks, at sites of attachment of tendons to bone, and in the articular disks of certain joints.

Bone. Like other connective tissues, bone consists of cells, fibres, and ground substance, but, in addition, the extracellular components are impregnated with minute crystals of calcium phosphate in the form of the mineral hydroxyapatite. The mineralization of the matrix is responsible for the hardness of bone. It also provides a large reserve of calcium that can be drawn upon to meet unusual needs for this element elsewhere in the body. The structural organization of bone is admirably adapted to give maximal strength for its weight-bearing function with minimum weight. There are bones strong enough to support the weight of an elephant and others light enough to give internal support and leverage for the wings of birds. (The structure and function of bone are discussed in detail below.) (D.W.F.)

Bone

Bone is a rigid body tissue consisting of cells embedded in an abundant, hard intercellular material. The two principal components of this material, collagen and calcium phosphate, distinguish bone from such other hard tissues as chitin, enamel, and shell.

The functions of bone include (1) structural support for the mechanical action of soft tissues, such as contraction of muscles, expansion of lungs; (2) protection of soft parts, as by the brain case; (3) provision of a protective site for specialized tissues such as the blood-forming system (bone marrow); and (4) a mineral reservoir or sink, whereby endocrine systems regulate the level of calcium and phosphate in the circulating body fluids.

EVOLUTIONARY ORIGIN AND SIGNIFICANCE

Bone is found only in vertebrates, and, among modern vertebrates, only in bony fish and higher classes. Although fossil ancestors of the elasmobranchs and cyclostomes had armoured headcases, serving largely a protective function, which appear to have been true bone, modern cyclostomes have only an endoskeleton, or inner skeleton, of noncalcified cartilage, and elasmobranchs, a skeleton of calcified cartilage. Although a rigid endoskeleton performs obvious body supportive functions for land-living vertebrates, it is doubtful that bone offered any such mechanical advantage to the teleost (bony fish) in which it first appeared, for in a supporting aquatic environment, great structural rigidity is not essential for maintaining body configuration. The sharks and rays are superb examples of mechanical engineering efficiency, and their perseverance from the Devonian attests to the suitability of their nonbony endoskeleton.

Bone and homeostasis

In modern vertebrates true bone is found only in animals also capable of controlling the osmotic and ionic composition of their internal fluid environment.

Marine invertebrates exhibit interstitial fluid compositions essentially the same as that of the surrounding sea water. Early signs of regulability are seen in cyclostomes and elasmobranchs, but only at or above the level of truebone fishes does the composition of the internal body fluids become constant. The mechanisms involved in this regulation are many and complex and include both the kidney and the gills. Fresh and marine waters provide abundant calcium, but only traces of phosphate, and, because relatively high levels of phosphate are characteristic of the body fluids of higher vertebrates, it seems likely that a large, readily available internal phosphate reservoir would confer significant independence of external environment on bony vertebrates. With the emergence of terrestrial forms, the availability of calcium regulation became equally significant. Along with the kidney and the various component glands of the endocrine system, bone has contributed to development of internal fluid homeostasis—the maintenance of a constant chemical composition. This was a necessary step for emergence of land-living vertebrates. Moreover, out of the buoyancy of water, structural rigidity of bone afforded mechanical advantages that are the most obvious features of the modern vertebrate skeleton.

CHEMICAL COMPOSITION AND PHYSICAL PROPERTIES

Depending upon species, age, and type of bone, the bone cells represent 1–15 percent of the volume of bone, but in mature bone in most higher animals usually they represent 1–5 percent. The nonliving intercellular material consists of an organic component, collagen (a fibrous protein arranged in long strands or bundles similar in structure and organization to the collagen of ligaments, tendons, and skin), with small amounts of proteinpolysaccharides, mucopolysaccharides chemically bound to protein and dispersed within and around the collagen fibre bundles, and an inorganic mineral component in the form of innumerable rod-shaped crystals with diameters on the order of 50 Å and lengths from 200 to 2,000 Å. These crystals are arranged parallel with the long axes of collagen bundles and many actually lie in voids within the bundles themselves. Organic material comprises 50 percent of the volume and 30 percent of the dry weight of the intercellular composite, and mineral the remainder. The major minerals are calcium and phosphate, present in proportions ranging from 1.4:1 to 2.1:1. When first deposited, mineral is crystallographically amorphous but with maturation becomes typical of the apatite minerals, the major component being hydroxyapatite, $Ca_{10}(PO_4)_6(OH)_2$. Carbonate is also present, in amounts varying from 4 percent of bone ash in fish and 8 percent in most mammals to more than 13 percent in the turtle, and occurs in two distinct phases, calcium carbonate and a carbonate apatite. Except for that associated with its cellular elements, there is little free water in adult mammalian bone (approximately 8 percent of total volume). As a result, diffusion from surfaces into the interior of the intercellular substance occurs at the slow rates more typical of diffusion from surfaces of solids than within liquids.

Hardness, rigidity, and compressive and tensile strength

The structural role of the skeleton depends on the hardness, strength, and rigidity of bone. The mineral crystals are responsible for hardness, rigidity, and the great compressive strength of bone, but they share with other crystalline materials a great weakness in tension, arising from the tendency for stress to concentrate about defects and for these defects to propagate. On the other hand, the collagen fibrils of bone possess high elasticity, little compressive strength, and considerable intrinsic tensile strength. The tensile strength of bone depends, however, not on collagen alone but on the intimate association of mineral with collagen, which confers on bone many of the general properties exhibited by two-phase materials such as fibre glass and bamboo. In such materials the dispersion of a rigid but brittle material in a matrix of quite different elasticity prevents the propagation of stress failure through the brittle material and hence allows a closer approach to the theoretical limiting strength of single crystals.

The fine structure of bone has thus far frustrated attempts to determine the true strength of the mineral-matrix composite at the "unit" structural level. Compact bone specimens have been found to have tensile strength in the range of 700–1,400 kilograms per square centimetre (10,000–20,000 pounds per square inch), and compressive strengths in the range of 1,400–2,100 kilograms per square centimetre (20,000–30,000 pounds per square inch). These values are of the same general order as for aluminum or mild steel, but bone has an advantage over such materials in that it is considerably lighter. The great strength of bone exists principally along its long axis and hence roughly parallel both to the collagen fibre axis and to the long axis of the mineral crystals.

Elasticity of bone

Although apparently stiff, bones exhibit a considerable degree of elasticity, which is important to the skeleton's ability to withstand impact. Estimates of modulus of elasticity of bone samples are of the order of 420 to 700 kilograms per square centimetre (6,000 to 10,000 pounds per square inch), a value very much less than steel, for example, indicating much greater elasticity of bone. Perfect elasticity exists with loads up to 30 to 40 percent of breaking strength; above this, creep occurs, presumably along natural defects within the bony structure. The modulus of elasticity in bone is strikingly dependent upon the rate at which loads are applied, bones being stiffer during rapid deformation than during slow; this behaviour suggests an element of viscous flow during deformation.

As might be anticipated from consideration of the two-phase composition of bone, variation in the mineral-collagen ratio leads to change in physical properties: less mineral tends ultimately to greater flexibility, and more mineral to increased brittleness. Optimal ratios, as reflected in maximal tensile strength, are observed at an ash content of approximately 66 percent, a value that is characteristic of the weight-bearing bones of mammals.

BONE MORPHOLOGY

Grossly, bone tissue is organized into a variety of shapes and configurations adapted to the function of the bone concerned: broad, flat plates, such as scapula, as anchors for large muscle masses, or hollow, thick-walled tubes, such as femur, radius, ulna, for supporting weight or for use as a lever arm (see above *Human skeletal system*). These different types of bone are distinguished more by their external shape than by their basic structure.

In all bones the basic bone has an exterior layer, termed cortex, that is smooth, dense, continuous, and of varying thickness. In its interior, bony tissue is arranged in a network of intersecting plates and spicules, varying in amount in different bones, enclosing spaces filled with blood vessels and marrow. This honeycombed bone is termed cancellous, and the plates and spicules trabeculae. In mature bone, trabeculae are arranged in an orderly pattern that provides continuous units of bony tissue aligned parallel with the lines of major compressive or tensile force. Trabeculae thus provide a complex series of cross-braced interior struts so arranged as to give maximal rigidity with minimal material.

Bones such as vertebrae, subject to primarily compressive or tensile forces, usually have thin cortices and provide necessary structural rigidity through trabeculae; whereas bones such as the femur, subject to prominent bending, shear, or torsional forces, usually have thick cortices, a tubular configuration, and a continuous cavity running through their centres (medullary cavity). The cortical material of tubular bones is termed compact bone and differs in a number of fine structural details from cancellous bone.

Long bones, distinctive of the body's extremities, exhibit a number of gross structural features in common. The central region of the bone (diaphysis) is the most clearly tubular. At one or commonly both ends the diaphysis flares outward and assumes a predominantly cancellous internal structure. This region (metaphysis) functions to transfer loads from weight-bearing joint surfaces to the diaphysis. Finally, at the end of a long bone is a region known as an epiphysis, which exhibits a cancellous internal structure and which comprises the bony substructure of the joint surface. Prior to full skeletal maturity the epiphysis is separated from the metaphysis by a cartilaginous plate, the growth plate or physis; in bones with complex articulations (such as the humerus at its lower end) or bones with multiple protuberances (such as the femur at its upper end) there may be several separate epiphyses, each with its growth plate.

Four types of cells in bone. Microscopically, bone consists of hard, apparently homogeneous intercellular material, within or upon which can be found four characteristic cell types: osteoblast, osteocyte, osteoclast, and undifferentiated bone mesenchymal cells. The osteoblast is responsible for the synthesis and deposition on bone surfaces of the protein matrix of new intercellular material. The osteocyte is an osteoblast that has been trapped within intercellular material, residing in a cavity (lacuna) and communicating with other osteocytes as well as with free bone surfaces by means of extensive filamentous protoplasmic extensions that occupy long, meandering channels (canaliculi) through the bone substance. With the exception of certain higher orders of modern fish, all bone, including primitive vertebrate fossil bone, exhibits an osteocytic structure. Osteoclasts are usually large, multinucleated cells that, working from bone surfaces, resorb bone by direct chemical and enzymatic attack. Undifferentiated mesenchymal cells of the bone reside in the loose connective tissue between trabeculae, along vascular channels, and in the condensed fibrous tissue covering the outside of the bone (periosteum); they give rise under appropriate stimuli to either osteoblasts or osteoclasts.

Canaliculi networks in bone

Depending on how the protein fibrils and osteocytes of bone are arranged, bone is of two major types: woven, in which collagen bundles and the long axes of the osteocytes are randomly oriented, and lamellar, in which both the fibrils and osteocytes are aligned in clear layers. In lamellar bone the layers alternate every few microns, and the primary direction of the fibrils shifts approximately 90°. In compact bone of many mammalian species lamellar bone is further organized into units known as osteons, or haversian systems, which consist of concentric cylindrical lamellar elements several millimetres long and 0.2–0.3 millimetre (0.008–0.012 inch) in diameter. Osteons exhibit a gently spiral course oriented along the axis of the bone. In their centre is a canal (haversian canal) containing one or more small blood vessels, and at their outer margins is a boundary layer known as a "cement line," which serves both as a means of fixation for new bone deposited on an old surface and as a diffusion barrier. Osteocytic processes do not penetrate the cement line, and hence these barriers constitute the outer envelope of a nutritional unit, osteocytes on opposite sides of a cement line deriving their nutrition from different vascular channels. Cement lines are found in all types of bone, as well as in osteons, and in general they indicate lines at which new bone was deposited on an old surface.

Vascular supply and circulation. In a typical long bone, blood is supplied by three separate systems: nutrient artery, periosteal vessels, and epiphyseal vessels. The diaphysis and metaphysis are nourished primarily by the nutrient artery, which passes through the cortex into the medullary cavity and then ramifies outward through haversian and Volkmann's canals to supply the cortex. Extensive vessels in the periosteum, the membrane surrounding the bone, supply the superficial layers of the cortex and connect with the nutrient-artery system. In the event of obstruction of the nutrient artery, periosteal vessels are capable of meeting the needs of both systems. The epiphyses are supplied by a separate system that consists of a ring of arteries entering the bone along a circular band between the growth plate and the joint capsule. In the adult these vessels become connected to the other two systems at the metaphyseal-epiphyseal junction, but while the growth plate is open there is no such connection, and the epiphyseal vessels are the sole source of nutrition for the growing cartilage; hence they are essential for skeletal growth.

Drainage of blood is by a system of veins that runs parallel with the arterial supply and by veins leaving the cortical periosteum through muscle insertions. Muscle contraction milks blood outward, giving rise to a centrifugal pattern of flow from the axial nutrient artery through the cortex and out through muscle attachments.

REMODELLING, GROWTH, AND DEVELOPMENT

Bone resorption and renewal. Whereas renewal in tissues such as muscle occurs largely at a molecular level, renewal of bone occurs at a tissue level and is similar to the remodelling of buildings in that local removal (resorption) of old bone must precede new bone deposition. Remodelling is most vigorous during the years of active growth, when deposition predominates over resorption. Thereafter remodelling gradually declines, in man until about age 35, after which its rate remains unchanged or increases slightly. From the fourth decade on resorption exceeds formation, resulting in a 5–10 percent loss in bone mass per decade, equivalent to a daily loss of 15–30 milligrams of calcium.

Except for the addition of the ossification mechanisms within cartilage, growth and development involve exactly the same type of remodelling as that in the adult skeleton. Both require continuous, probably irreversible differentiation of osteoclasts and osteoblasts from the undifferentiated bone mesenchyme. Life span of osteoclasts is from a few hours to at most a few days, that of osteoblasts a few days to at most a few weeks.

Bone resorption

Resorption is produced by clusters of osteoclasts that either erode free bone surfaces or form "cutting cones" that tunnel through compact bone and create the cylindrical cavities that may be subsequently filled by osteons. Osteoclastic cells secrete enzymes and hydrogen ions onto the bone surface, dissolving the mineral and digesting the matrix at virtually the same moment. The process is associated with locally augmented blood flow and with a greater surface acidity than elsewhere in bone, despite the fact that the process of dissolving apatite consumes hydrogen ions. Resorption is usually a much more rapid process than formation. Osteoclastic cutting cones have been observed to advance at rates up to 500 microns per day (one macron = 1×10^{-3} millimetre).

Bone formation

Bone is formed on previously resorbed surfaces by deposition of a protein matrix material (osteoid) and its subsequent mineralization. Osteoblasts elaborate matrix as a continuous membrane covering the surface on which they are working at a linear rate that varies with both age and species, but which in large adult mammals is on the order of 1.0 micron per day. The unmineralized matrix constitutes an osteoid seam or border, averaging 6 to 10 microns in thickness during active bone formation. The biochemical and physical sequence of events that prepare matrix for mineralization includes intracellular biosynthesis of collagen by osteoblasts, extrusion of collagen extracellularly in soluble form, maturation or polymerization of collagen into an array of fibrils (in random orientation in rapidly deposited bone, in a highly ordered, regular pattern in slowly formed lamellar bone), binding of calcium to collagen fibrils, and formation of protein-mucopolysaccharide complexes. Mineralization itself depends upon establishment of crystal nuclei within the matrix; this process requires five to ten days and is under the control of the osteoblast, but its exact chemistry is obscure. A suitable nucleating configuration is somehow established, and once nuclei reach a critical size further mineralization proceeds spontaneously in the presence of usual body fluid calcium and phosphorus concentrations. Other collagenous tissues, such as dermis, tendon, and ligament, do not normally calcify, even though bathed by the same body fluids as bone. Although extracellular fluid is a highly supersaturated solution with respect to hydroxylapatite, calcium and phosphorus will not spontaneously precipitate in this crystalline form at normal physiological pH, so that one and the same fluid is indefinitely stable in non-bone-forming regions, yet richly supports mineralization in the presence of suitable crystal nuclei. Mineral movement into new bone is initially rapid and in compact cortical bone is known to reach approximately 70 percent of full mineralization within a few hours after matrix nucleation. This mineral deposition involves replacement of the water that occupied half of the original matrix volume. As water content falls, further mineral diffusion is impeded; and the final mineralization occurs progressively more slowly over a period of many weeks. In normal adult man new bone formation takes up about 400 milligrams of calcium per day, an amount approximately equal to that in the circulating blood.

Osteocyte function

Osteocytes, once thought of as resting cells, are now recognized to be metabolically active and to possess, at least in latent form, the ability to resorb and reform bone on their lacunar walls. Although osteocytes constitute only a small fraction of total bone volume, they are so arranged within bone, and the network of their protoplasmic extensions is so extensive that there is essentially no volume of bony material situated more than a fraction of a micron from a cell or its processes. Of the more than 1,200 square metres (1,435 square yards) of anatomic surface within the skeleton of an adult man, about 99 percent is accounted for by the lacunar and canalicular surfaces. Resorption and deposition on this surface serve both to regulate plasma-calcium concentration and to renew bony material. This renewal may be particularly important because all composite materials change in their physical properties with time. It is not known whether bone properties change sufficiently to have biologic consequence, but to the extent that such change does occur, renewal around osteocytes would provide for the physical maintenance of bone structural material.

Growth and development of bone

Types of bone formation. Bone is formed in the embryo in two general ways. For most bones the general shape is first laid down as a cartilage model, which is then progressively replaced by bone (endochondral bone formation). A few bones (such as clavicle and calvarium) develop within a condensed region of fibrous tissue without a cartilaginous intermediate (membrane bone formation). In long bones a collar of spongy membrane bone is first laid down in the fibrous tissues surrounding the cartilaginous model of the shaft. At the same time the cartilage deep to this collar begins to degenerate and calcify. The bone is then penetrated by blood vessels, which grow into the degenerating model and remove the calcified cartilage enclosed within the collar. Vascular invasion proceeds toward both ends of the model in parallel with continued extension of the bony collar. This leaves a structure consisting of two cartilaginous epiphyses at the ends of a hollow, bony shaft.

Growth from this point on is accomplished in two ways. Radial growth occurs by deposition of new bone on the periosteal surface and roughly equivalent resorption at the endosteal surface. Longitudinal growth involves replacement of cartilage by bone from the shaft side of the growth plate, at a rate closely matched to the production of new cartilage by the plate itself. The growth plate consists of highly ordered rows of cartilage cells; the row farthest removed from the bony shaft is a basal or germinal layer; it is responsible for cell replication and cartilage growth. The complex sequence of longitudinal growth consists of cartilage cell degeneration farthest from the germinal layer, calcification of cartilage in that area, deposition over it of a thin layer of true bone (primary spongiosa), and, finally, osteoclastic resorption to extend the medullary cavity in parallel with longitudinal growth and to reshape the contour of the shaft.

From *Journal of Bone and Joint Surgery* (1952)

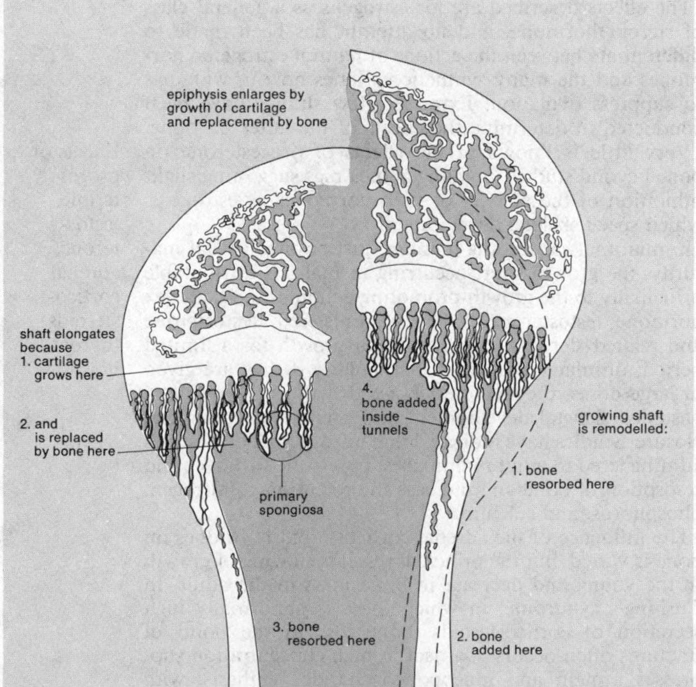

Figure 11: Principal structures involved in (left) growth and (right) remodelling of a typical long bone.

Cartilage growth, degeneration, calcification, and ultimate replacement by bone is responsible for most growth in length in vertebrates. It first begins in the embryo and continues until full skeletal maturity, when in most species the growth plates fuse and disappear.

The appearance of epiphyseal ossification centres and their ultimate fusion, both of which can be detected by ordinary X-rays, normally follows an orderly and predictable sequence that is of great value in the evaluation of disorders of growth and development. Because of the complicated interaction of several tissue elements in the process of endochondral ossification, the metaphyseal region of bones is the seat of, or prominently reflects, many nutritional or metabolic disturbances of growth. Examples of disorders involving this growth mechanism include rickets and achondroplastic dwarfism (see below *Bone diseases and injuries*).

PHYSIOLOGY OF BONE

Calcium and phosphate equilibrium. As important as the structural properties of bone is the role bone plays in the maintenance of the ionic composition of the blood and interstitial fluids of the body. All vertebrates possessing true bone exhibit body-fluid calcium-ion concentrations of approximately 50 milligrams per litre (1.25 millimoles) and phosphorus concentrations in the range of 30–100 milligrams per litre (one to three millimoles). These levels, particularly those of calcium, are extremely important for the maintenance of normal neuromuscular function, interneuronal transmission, cell membrane integrity and permeability, and blood coagulation. The rigid constancy with which calcium levels are maintained, both in the individual and throughout all the higher vertebrate classes, attests to the biological importance of such regulation. Approximately 99 percent of total body calcium and 85 percent of total body phosphorus reside in the mineral deposits of bone, and thus bone is quantitatively in a position to mediate adjustments in concentration of these two ions in the circulating body fluids. Such adjustments are provided by two hormonal control loops (control systems with feedbacks) and by at least two locally acting mechanisms. The hormonal loops involve parathyroid hormone (PTH) and calcitonin (CT) and are concerned exclusively with regulation of calcium-ion concentration.

Calcium and phosphate homeostasis

PTH acts to elevate the ionized calcium level in body fluids and CT (from the ultimobranchial body or C cells of the thyroid) to depress it, and the secretion of each hormone is sensitively controlled by the level of calcium ion in the circulating blood, PTH secretion being inversely related and CT secretion being directly related to calcium ion concentration. At normal calcium concentrations there is a low level of secretion of both hormones.

PTH acts on at least two nonbony effector organs (kidney and intestine) as well as on bone, whereas CT appears to act primarily on bone. The skeletal effects of these hormones are exerted predominantly on the resorptive process. PTH stimulates mesenchymal proliferation and osteoclast induction and accelerates the osteolytic activity of osteocytes. The principal long-term effect of the hormone is a considerable increase in the number of osteoclasts with correspondingly increased resorption. Vitamin D is required for the osseous effects of PTH, and in pharmacological quantities stimulates both osteocytic and osteoclastic resorption in the absence of PTH. Finally, PTH produces acute inhibition of osteoblast function, thus decreasing calcium deposition in new bone in periods of total body-calcium need.

With respect to action on organs other than bone, PTH enhances gastrointestinal absorption of calcium from the diet and, by increasing calcium reabsorption from the fluid within the renal (kidney) tubules, reduces renal excretory losses of calcium. The intestinal effect, like that on bone, requires vitamin D for its expression. Finally, PTH, by interfering with renal tubular phosphate reabsorption, also enhances the renal excretion of phosphate. This mechanism, which serves to lower the level of phosphates in the bloodstream, is significant because high phosphate levels inhibit and low levels enhance osteoclastic resorption. Thus phosphate concentration itself directly modulates the calcium-mediated effects of both parathyroid hormone and the many other agencies that influence bone resorption. Calcium ion itself has similar effects on the osteoclastic process, high levels inhibiting and low levels enhancing the effect of systemically acting agents such as PTH. These local effects constitute the only recognizable control of phosphate, but the PTH loop appears to be the more important regulatory process in calcium-ion homeostasis. At extremely low levels both calcium and phosphate become rate-limiting at the mineralization site as well, reducing both deposition of mineral and osteoblast function.

Calcitonin, acting to offset elevations in calcium ion level, works primarily to inhibit bone resorption, whether by osteoclasts or by osteocytes. It does not appear to have significant effects on tissues other than bone. Calcitonin differs further from PTH in its much more rapid action (minutes as opposed to hours) and in its short duration of action. Its primary function seems to be to offset acute elevations in plasma calcium during feeding.

Physiological and mechanical controls. In the language of control mechanics, remodelling depends upon two control loops with negative feedback: a homeostatic loop involving the effects of PTH and CT on resorption and a mechanical loop that brings about changes in skeletal mass and arrangement to meet changing structural needs. The PTH-CT loop is basically a systemic process, and the mechanical loop is local; the two loops do interact significantly at the level of the cells that act as intermediaries in both processes. A large number of other factors, including minerals in the diet, hormonal balance, disease, and aging, have important effects on the skeleton that interact with the control system.

Controls exerted by mechanical forces

The controls exerted by mechanical forces, recognized for over a century, have been formulated as Wolff's law: "Every change in the function of a bone is followed by certain definite changes in its internal architecture and its external conformation." Of the many theories proposed to explain how mechanical forces communicate with the cells responsible for bone formation and resorption, the most appealing has been postulation of induced local electrical fields that mediate this information exchange. Many crystalline or semicrystalline materials, including both bone collagen and its associated mineral, exhibit piezoelectric properties. Deformation of macroscopic units of bone by mechanical force produces a charge in the millivolt range and current flow on the order of 10^{-15} ampere; both voltage and current flow are proportional to the applied force. Regions under tension act as anode and compressed regions as cathode. Currents of this magnitude are capable of aligning collagen fibrils as they aggregate from the solution phase and are known also to alter the cell-based development of regeneration buds in amphibia. The negative-feedback characteristic of this mechanism lies in the fact that bone accumulates about the cathodal region of this system, hence reducing the electrical effects produced by an applied force. The mechanisms by which the bone mesenchyme responds to mechanical stimuli (whether or not mediated by electrical signals) are uncertain. In general, heavy usage leads to heavy bone, and disuse, as in immobilization associated with injury or severe disease, results in decrease in bone mass and increased excretion of calcium, phosphorus, and nitrogen. The cellular response, however, is discouragingly complex. In broad outline it appears that the local expression of decreased stress is an increase in bone resorption coupled variably with a smaller and secondary increase in bone formation, whereas increased stress appears to be accompanied by a decrease in bone resorption coupled also with a smaller and probably secondary increase in bone formation. The decrease in resorption represents a decreased sensitivity to systemic stimuli, such as PTH, and reflects an interaction between hormonal and physical forces at the cellular level. PTH is the major determinant of all remodelling, structural as well as homeostatic; mechanical forces are the major determinant of where that remodelling occurs.

One of the most arresting features of skeletal remodelling is the tendency for rates of bone resorption and bone formation to change in the same direction. Three mechanisms for this coupling can be identified. The first is homeostatic and rises from the mineral demand created by formation of crystal nuclei in the bone matrix. Unless the calcium demands of increased bone formation can be met from some other source (such as increased diet calcium), they will inevitably lead to increased PTH secretion and bone resorption. Since the level of PTH is a principal determinant of bone resorption, it follows that high levels of formation tend to produce high levels of resorption (and vice versa). A second mechanism is the mechanical force-piezoelectric system discussed earlier. Local bone resorption, by reducing structural volume, concentrates applied forces in the remaining bone; this leads to increased strain and presumably increases the stimulus for local bone repair. A third mechanism is inferred from the observation in adult animals that the induction of specialized bony cells from the mesenchyme proceeds in a predetermined sequence: first osteoclasts and then osteoblasts, so that even on free surfaces resorption usually precedes formation. The ultimate basis of this cellular coupling is not known.

Because of the paramount influences that parathyroid hormone and calcitonin have on bone, their effects have been described in detail in the discussions of calcium and phosphate homeostasis and control of skeletal remodelling.

Estrogens

Hormonal influences. The most striking effects of estrogens are seen in birds, in which during the part of the cycle prior to egg formation a marked increase in osteoblastic activity occurs along the inside surfaces of the long bones, and the medullary cavities become filled with spongy bone. As the egg is formed, this spongy bone is rapidly resorbed, plasma calcium rises dramatically, and calcium is deposited in the shell. In mammals studied prior to skeletal maturity, administration of estrogens produces an accelerated appearance of ossification centres, a slowing in growth of cartilage and bone, and fusion of the epiphyses; the result is an adult skeleton smaller than normal. In older mammals estrogens in certain dosages and schedules of administration may inhibit trabecular bone resorption, and in some species prolonged administration of estrogen may lead to increased bone porosity. In postmenopausal women administration of estrogen suppresses bone resorption and produces a transient decrease in serum calcium and phosphorus and in renal reabsorption of phosphorus, as well as positive calcium balance, effects which help to stabilize the total skeletal bone mass.

The effects described are for estrogens as a general class of steroid hormone, and no attempt has been made to differentiate between the actions of natural estrogenic hormones and the many synthetic varieties now in wide use to suppress ovulation. Extremely few studies have been conducted to determine the effects of the latter on bone.

Effects of progesterone, testosterone, adrenal corticosteroids, thyroid hormone

Very little is known of the effects of progesterone on bone beyond studies in young guinea pigs suggesting slight inhibition of the activity of such hormones as estrogens, which speed skeletal development.

In mammals, including humans, just prior to sexual maturity, the growth spurt occurring in males is attributable principally to the growth-promoting action of the male sex hormone testosterone. When administered, testosterone and related steroids stimulate linear growth for a limited period; ultimately, however, particularly if they are given in large doses, they suppress bone growth as the result of hastened skeletal development and premature epiphyseal closure. Studies have indicated that testosterone derivatives administered to adult mammals suppress the turnover and resorption of bone and increase the retention of nitrogen, phosphorus, and calcium.

The influence of the adrenal corticosteroid hormones on bone is varied, but the principal result is slowing of growth in the young and decrease in bone mass in the adult. In Cushing's syndrome, in which there is abnormally high secretion of corticosteroids, bone loss to the point of fractures often occurs. Cortisol in high concentration suppresses protein and mucopolysaccharide synthesis, with inhibition of bone matrix formation and of incorporation of nucleosides into bone cells.

Lack of the internal secretion of the thyroid gland results in retardation of skeletal growth and development. Action of this hormone to facilitate growth and skeletal maturation is probably indirect, through its general effects on cell metabolism. Thyroid hormone in excess leads in the young to premature appearance of ossification centres and closure of the epiphyses, and in the adult to increased bone-cell metabolism. Commonly in the hyperthyroid adult bone resorption predominates over increased bone formation with resultant loss of bone mass.

Effects of growth hormone and of insulin

The anterior lobe of the pituitary gland secretes a hormone essential for growth and development of the skeleton. This effect of the hormone is indirect and mediated by "sulfation factor," a substance produced in the liver in response to stimulation by the growth hormone. The extent to which growth hormone is involved in skeletal remodelling in the adult is not known, but excessive elaboration of the hormone after maturity leads to distorted enlargement of all bones in the condition known as acromegaly. Excessive elaboration of growth hormone prior to epiphyseal closure leads to gigantism. Studies of the administration of growth hormone to man have indicated marked species specificity; growth in hypopituitary dwarfs is stimulated only by human or primate growth hormone. The principal metabolic effects in man of the hormone are retention of nitrogen and increased turnover of calcium, resulting in increases both in intestinal calcium absorption and in urinary calcium excretion.

Insulin participates in the regulation of bone growth; it may enhance or even be necessary for the effect of growth hormone on bone. Insulin has been found to stimulate growth and epiphyseal widening in rats whose pituitaries have been removed and to promote chondroitin sulfate synthesis in cartilage and bone and the transport of amino acids and nucleosides into bone.

Nutritional influences. The most significant nutritional influence on bone is the availability of calcium. The close relationship between bone and calcium is indicated by the principal processes of calcium metabolism. Bone contains 99 percent of the calcium in the body and can behave as an adequate buffer for maintenance of a constant level of freely moving calcium in soft tissues, extracellular fluid, and blood. The free-calcium concentration in this pool must be kept within fairly narrow limits (50–65 milligrams per litre of extracellular fluid) to maintain the constant internal milieu necessary for neuromuscular irritability, blood clotting, muscle contractility, and cardiac function. Calcium leaves the pool by way of bone formation, by such routes as the urine, feces, and sweat, and periodically by way of lactation and transplacental movement. Calcium enters the pool by the mechanism of bone resorption and by absorption from dietary calcium in the upper intestinal tract.

The significance with respect to bone of adequate availability of calcium to animal or man is that the mechanical strength of bone is proportional to its mineral content. All of the other components of bone, organic and inorganic, are, of course, also essential for bone integrity, but the importance of availability of structural materials is most easily illustrated by consideration of calcium balance (dietary intake versus excretory output). If intake of calcium is limited, maintenance of normal levels of extracellular and soft tissue calcium in the face of mandatory daily losses from this pool by various excretory routes requires that calcium be mined from its storage depot, bone. Abundant mineral intake, then, tends to preserve bone mass, and an increase of positivity of calcium balance has been shown to suppress resorption of bone.

The Recommended Dietary Allowances of the Food and Nutrition Board, National Academy of Sciences–National Research Council (1968) for calcium daily are 800 milligrams for adults and 1.0 to 1.4 grams for adolescents and pregnant and lactating women. The usual daily intake of this element, however, ranges between 500 and 800 milligrams, about 150–250 milligrams from green vegetables and the remainder usually from milk and milk products. Daily urinary excretion of calcium is normally from 50 to 150 or 200 milligrams (the upper limit of normal being uncertain), varying sharply with intake at very low levels but rising only very gradually with increasing intake above 300 to 400 milligrams. Fecal excretion of calcium is much larger than urinary, most of the calcium in the feces being unabsorbed dietary calcium. A man's losses from the skin and in the sweat range from less than 30 milligrams per day to as high as 200 milligrams per day during active sweating. Calcium absorption varies considerably depending on previous and current levels of intake and type of diet. At intakes of 400 milligrams per day, absorption averages 32 percent; at 1,000 milligrams per day, 21 percent.

The other principal mineral constituent of bone, phosphorus, is abundantly available in both milk and in other protein-rich foods, and its daily recommended allowance is the same as for calcium. A prolonged dietary deficiency of phosphate and an extreme deficiency of calcium will result in mineral-poor bone, known as rickets or osteomalacia. The skeleton serves as a storage reservoir for two other cations of considerable physiologic importance, magnesium and sodium. Magnesium ion has a calcium-like effect on parathyroid hormone secretion, and magnesium deficiency has a number of the same effects as calcium deficiency.

Fluoride, an element of proven value and safety in prevention of dental caries when provided in drinking water at concentrations of one part per million, is absorbed into bone lattice structure as well as into enamel and produces a larger crystal more resistant to resorption. Amounts ten or more times that normally taken in fluoridated drinking water have been noted to cause abnormalities of bone collagen synthesis. Extremely large dosages produce in man the more dense but irregularly structured and brittle bone of fluorosis.

Vitamins; proteins

The function of vitamin A remains to be clarified, but it is apparently necessary for proliferation of cartilage and bone growth. Without vitamin A, bone remodelling is also impaired and bones develop in abnormal shapes. Excessive amounts of the vitamin result in thinning of cortical bone and fracture.

Ascorbic acid, or vitamin C, is essential for intracellular formation of collagen and for hydroxylation of proline. In scurvy, a vitamin C deficiency disease, the collagen matrix of bone is either partially or completely unable to calcify (see discussion above on formation of bone).

Vitamin D has several complex physiologic actions that affect the metabolism of bone. The oldest known effect is facilitation of intestinal absorption of calcium and, indirectly, of phosphate. The second target of vitamin D action is the renal tubule. In the child who has rickets administration of the vitamin restores the impaired tubular reabsorption of phosphorus to normal; in the person whose secretion of parathyroid hormone is subnormal, however, the vitamin in large doses has a parathyroid hormone-like effect and reduces the elevated serum phosphorus by suppression of the renal tubular reabsorption of phosphorus. The third site of vitamin D action is the bone cells, in which the vitamin increases citrate production by conversion from pyruvate; the way in which this action is related to the effect of the vitamin on mobilization of bone mineral is at present uncertain. Also at the cellular level both parathyroid hormone and vitamin D stimulate release of calcium from mitochondria, but the hormone cannot do so in the absence of vitamin D, further evidence of the closely coordinated relationship of these important factors. Recent research has shown that to exert its physiologic effects, vitamin D must be converted to 25-hydroxycholecalciferol in the liver and this compound further in the kidney to 1,25-dihydroxycholecalciferol.

Other nutritional factors include protein, which as an essential component of the matrix of bone must be provided by a combination of dietary intake and conversion from other tissues. Changes in acid-base balance also have an influence on the skeleton—acidosis in various clinical disorders and ingestion of acid salts being accompanied by mineral loss. (R.P.He./G.D.W.)

Joint

A joint is a structure that separates two or more adjacent elements of the skeleton. Depending on the type of joint, such separated elements may or may not move on one another. Though this discussion is intended to deal with human joints, its content is applicable as well to those of vertebrates in general and mammals in particular.

The Latin stem word for joint is *art*—(as in articular, articulation); the Greek stem word is *arthro*—(as in arthritis, arthrology). The international vocabulary of arthrology (the science of joints) uses Latin and Greek terms, but the more important of these have well-known English equivalents that will be used here when possible.

SCHEMES OF JOINT CLASSIFICATION

Joints can be classified in two ways: temporally and structurally. Each classification is associated with joint function.

Temporal classification. Joints are either transient or permanent. The bones of a transient joint fuse together sooner or later, but always after birth. All the joints of the skull, for example, are transient, excepting those of the middle ear and those between the lower jaw and the braincase. The bones of a permanent joint do not fuse except as the result of disease or surgery. Such pathological or surgical fusion is called arthrodesis.

All permanent and some transient joints permit movement. Movement of the latter may be temporary, as with the roofbones of an infant's skull during birth, or long-term, as with the joints of the base of the skull during postnatal development.

Structural classification. There are two basic structural types of joint: diarthrosis, in which fluid is present, and synarthrosis, in which there is no fluid. All the diarthroses (commonly called synovial joints) are permanent. Some of the synarthroses are transient; others are permanent.

Types of joint motion

Before proceeding further with joint classification, it is necessary to describe the types of motion made possible by mobile joints. These motions include spinning, swinging, gliding, rolling, and approximation; they can be briefly described as follows: Spin is a movement of a bone around its own long axis denoted by the term rotation in anatomy. Swing, or angular movement, brings about a change in the angle between the long axis of the moving bone and some reference line in the fixed bone. Approximation denotes the movement caused by pressing or pulling one bone directly toward another—*i.e.,* by a "translation" in the physical sense. The reverse of approximation is separation. Gliding and rolling movements occur only within synovial joints and cause a moving bone to swing.

Flexion (bending) and extension (straightening) of the elbow are examples of swing. A swing (to the right or left) of one bone away from another is called abduction; the reverse, adduction. An important example of spin is provided by the radius ("outer" bone) of the forearm; this bone can spin upon the lower end of the humerus (upper arm) in all positions of the elbow. When an individual presses the back of his hand against his mouth, his forearm is pronated, or twisted; when the palm of his hand is pressed against his mouth, his forearm is supinated, or untwisted. Pronation is caused by medial (inward) rotation of the radius, and supination by lateral (outward) rotation. Approximation and separation normally occur only at the symphyses and gomphoses, joints that will be discussed later.

All of the most common movements of bones involve some degree of spin. Pure swings, which are not accompanied by spin, are most often seen in military drill and gymnastic exercises. This topic is dealt with relative to conjunct rotation at synovial joints.

SYNARTHROSES

Classes of synarthroses

Synarthroses are divided into three classes: fibrous, cartilaginous, and fibrocartilaginous; the last class is called symphysis. The tissues that make up these joints are described above (see *Connective tissue*); and the composition of bone, in the section *Bone.*

Fibrous joints. In fibrous joints the articulating parts are separated by white connective tissue (collagen) fibres, which pass from one part to the other. There are two types of fibrous joints: suture and gomphosis.

A suture is formed by the fibrous covering, or periosteum, of two bones passing between them. In the adult, sutures are found only in the roof and sides of the braincase and in the upper part of the face. In the infant, however, the two halves of the frontal bone are separated by a suture (the metopic suture), as are the two halves of the mandible at the chin. Excepting those of the fetus and newborn infant, all sutures are narrow. In the late fetus and newborn child, the sagittal suture, which separates the right and left halves of the roof of the skull, is quite wide and markedly so at its anterior and posterior ends. This

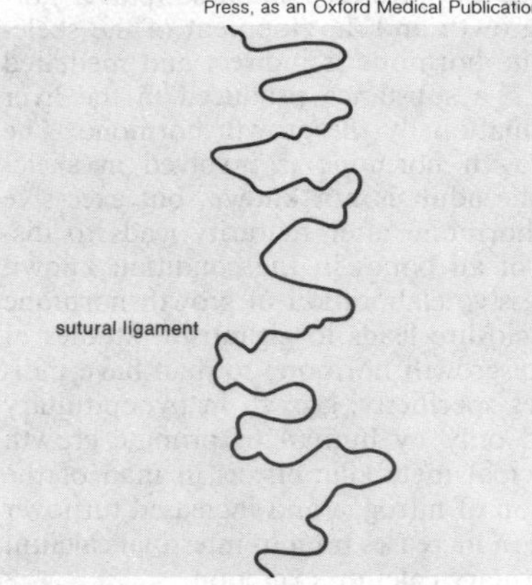

From *Cunningham's Textbook of Anatomy* edited by G.J. Romanes and published by Oxford University Press, as an Oxford Medical Publication

Figure 12: Surface view of portion of sagittal suture.

enables one of the halves to glide over the other during the passage of the child through the mother's pelvis during birth, thus reducing the width of its skull, a process called molding. (The effects of molding usually disappear quickly.) After birth all sutures become immobile joints. The expanded anterior and posterior ends of the sagittal suture are called fontanels; they lie immediately above a large blood channel (superior sagittal sinus). The anterior fontanel provides an easy access for obtaining a blood sample from the very young infant.

Sutures are transient, for they are unossified parts of the skeleton that become fused at various dates from childhood to old age. The fusion is effected by direct conversion of the sutures into bone. Until maturity the sutures are active sites of growth of the bones they separate.

A gomphosis is a fibrous, mobile peg-and-socket joint. The roots of the teeth (the pegs) fit into their sockets in the mandible and maxilla and are the only examples of this type of joint. Bundles of collagen fibres pass from the wall of the socket to the root; they are part of the circumdental, or periodontal, membrane. There is just enough space between the root and its socket to permit the root to be pressed a little further into the socket during biting or chewing. Gomphoses are permanent joints, in the sense that they last as long as do the roots of the teeth involved in them, unless, of course, they are obliterated by disease.

The movement of the root within a gomphosis has a threefold effect. It lessens some of the impact between the upper and lower teeth in biting; it pumps blood and lymph from the periodontal membrane into the dental veins and lymph channels; and it stimulates sensory nerve terminals in that membrane to send signals to the brain centres controlling the muscles of mastication.

Fibrocartilaginous joints; symphysis. A symphysis is a joint in which the body (physis) of one bone meets the body of another. All but two of the symphyses lie in the vertebral (spinal) column, and all but one contain fibrocartilage as a constituent tissue. The short-lived suture between the two halves of the mandible is called the symphysis menti (mentum, meaning chin) and is the only symphysis devoid of fibrocartilage. All the other symphyses are permanent.

The symphysis pubis joins the bodies of the two pubic bones of the pelvis. The adjacent sides of these bodies are covered by cartilage through which collagen fibres run from one pubis to the other. On their way they traverse a plate of cartilage, which, in some instances (especially in the female), may contain a small cavity filled with fluid. Surrounding the joint and attached to the bones is a coat

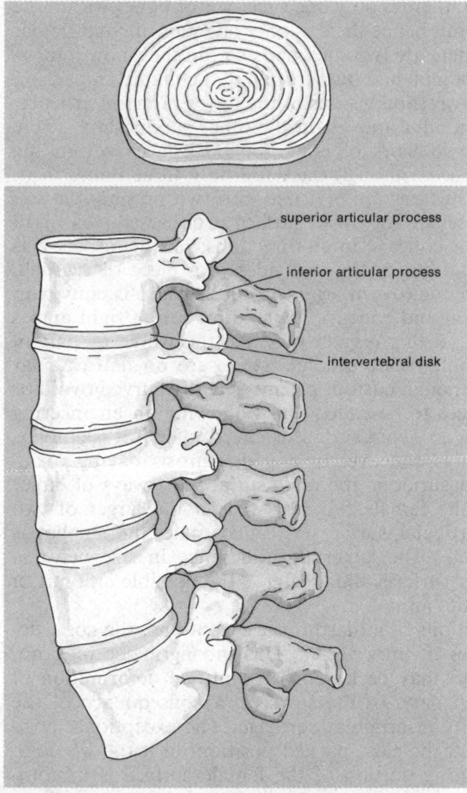

Figure 13: (Top) Cross section of an intervertebral disk. (Bottom) The lumbar vertebrae (left-side view).

Adapted with permission, from *The CIBA Collection of Medical Illustrations* by Frank H. Netter, M.D.

of fibrous tissue, particularly thick below (the subpubic ligament). The joint is flexible enough to act as a hinge that allows each of the two hipbones to swing a little upward and outward, as the ribs do during inspiration of air. This slight movement is increased in a woman during childbirth because of the infiltration of the joint and its fibrous coat by fluid toward the end of pregnancy, the fluid making the joint even more flexible. In both sexes the joint acts as a buffer against the shocks transmitted to the pelvic bones from the legs in running and jumping.

Intervertebral disks

The symphysis between the bodies of two adjacent vertebrae is called an intervertebral disk. It is composed of two parts: a soft centre (nucleus pulposus) and a tough, flexible ring (anulus fibrosus) around it. The centre is a jellylike (mucoid) material containing a few cells derived from the precursor of the spine (notochord) of the embryo. The ring consists of collagen fibres arranged in concentric layers like those of an onion bulb. These fibres reach the adjacent parts of the vertebral bodies and are attached firmly to them. The mass of fibres is embedded in chondrousia—the mixture of ground substances characteristic of cartilage—but yet the ring, although called fibrocartilaginous, is predominantly fibrous, and this fact determines its mechanical properties.

There are 23 intervertebral disks, one found between each pair of vertebrae below the first cervical, or neck (atlas), and above the second sacral (just above the tailbone). The lumbar (lower back) disks are thickest, the thoracic (chest or upper back) thinnest, and the cervical are of intermediate size. These differences are associated with the function of the disks.

In general these disks have two functions: to allow movement between pairs of vertebrae and to act as buffers against the shocks caused by running, jumping, and other stresses applied to the spine. Each of these functions merits separate consideration.

If an intervertebral disk were the only joint between a pair of vertebrae, then one of these could move on the other in any direction; but each pair of vertebrae with an intervertebral disk has also a pair of synovial joints, one on each side of the vertebral (neural) arch. These joints limit the kinds of independent movement possible so that the thoracic vertebrae move in only two directions, and the lumbar in only three; only the cervical vertebrae below the atlas have full freedom of movement.

All intervertebral disks allow approximation and separation of their adjacent vertebrae. This is caused partly by movement brought about by muscle action and partly by the weight of the head and the trunk transmitted to the pelvis when a person is upright. The effect of weight is of special importance. The mucoid substance in the centre of the disk behaves like a fluid. It is acted upon by the person's weight and any other pressure forces transmitted along the spine. Hence the disk flattens from above downward and expands in all other directions. After arising in the morning, and as the day progresses, a person decreases in height because of this compression of the disks. An average decrease of one millimetre in the height of each disk would mean an overall shortening of 2.3 centimetres, or about an inch. The spine lengthens again, of course, during sleep.

Compression of intervertebral disks

In the infant the greater part of the disk consists of the soft centre. Later the fibrous ring becomes relatively thicker in such a way that the soft part is nearer to the back of the disk. As middle age approaches, there is an increase in the fibrous element, the soft centre is reduced in size, and the amount of cartilage is increased. There is a tendency for the posterior part of the fibrous ring to degenerate, so that a sudden violent pressure may rupture the disk and allow the central part to protrude backward against the spinal cord. This condition is commonly referred to as slipped disk.

Cartilaginous joints. These joints, also called synchondroses, are really the unossified masses found between bones or parts of bones that pass through a cartilaginous stage before ossification. Examples are the synchondroses between the occipital and sphenoid bones and the sphenoid and ethmoid bones of the floor of the skull. As already stated, these permit growth of the adjacent bones and act as virtual hinges at which the ethmoid and occipital bones swing upward upon the sphenoid; this allows backward growth of the nose and jaws during postnatal life. The juxta-epiphyseal plates separating the ossifying parts of a bone are also an example. Growth of the whole bone takes place at these plates when they appear, usually after birth. All synchondroses are transient; and all normally have vanished by the age of 25.

DIARTHROSES: SYNOVIAL JOINTS

Structure and elements of synovial joints. The synovial bursas are closed, thin-walled sacs, lined with synovial membrane. Bursas are found between structures that glide upon each other, and all motion at diarthroses entails some gliding, the amount varying from one joint to another. The bursal fluid, exuded by the synovial membrane, is called synovia, whence the common name for this class of

From *Cunningham's Textbook of Anatomy* edited by G.J. Romanes and published by Oxford University Press, as an Oxford Medical Publication

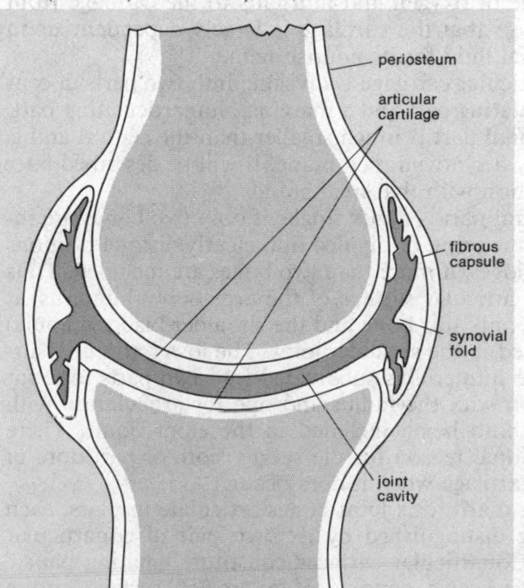

Figure 14: A synovial joint.

joints. Two or more parts of the bursal wall become cartilage (chondrify) during prenatal life. These are the parts of the bursa that are attached to the articulating bones, and they constitute the articular cartilage of the bones.

General structure of synovial joints

A synovial joint consists of a wall enclosing a joint cavity that is wholly filled with synovial fluid. The wall consists of two layers: an outer, complete, fibrous layer and an inner, incomplete, synovial layer (Figure 14). Parts of the outer layer are either chondrified as articular cartilages or partly ossified as sesamoid bones (small, flat bones developed in tendons that move over bony surfaces). Parts of the synovial layer project into the cavity to form fatty pads. In a few diarthroses the fibrous layer also projects inward to become intra-articular disks, or menisci. These various structures will be discussed in connection with the layer to which they belong.

The bones appertaining to a synovial joint are, strictly speaking, outside the joint because it is a complete bursa. Nevertheless, those parts of them that can be seen only after the bursal wall has been opened are usually said to be inside the joint. This custom will be followed here whenever it makes for clarity.

The fibrous layer. The fibrous layer is comprised of two continuous sections—one manifest and one hidden. The manifest part is that which is visible in an unopened joint cavity and is referred to as the investing ligament. At the point where it reaches the articulating bones, it covers their articulating ends as a complete periosteum. This is the hidden part. It is made of white fibrous tissue, composed of collagen fibres along with the cells that produce and maintain them.

Articular cartilage. Where the periosteal part of the fibrous layer covers the articulating part of a bone it becomes permeated with cartilaginous material, and the collagen fibres form a spongework in the meshes of which lie cartilage cells, thus forming articular cartilage. The continuity of the periosteal collagen with that of the articular cartilage can be seen by means of polarized light. Although the articular cartilages of a joint do complete the wall of the articular bursa, they are mechanically and visually distinguishable and merit the separate descriptions they usually receive.

Physical characteristics of articular cartilage

Articular cartilage is of the type called hyaline (glasslike) because thin sections of it are translucent, even transparent, to light. Unlike bone, it is easily cut by a sharp knife. It is deformable but elastic, so that it recovers its shape quickly when the deforming stress is removed. These properties are important for its function.

The surface of articular cartilage is smooth to the finger, like that of a billiard ball, and the cartilage's coefficient of friction is low indeed—0.02 or less. The electron scanning microscope has recently shown, however, that the surface is actually irregular, more like that of a golf ball. The part of the cartilage nearest to the bone is impregnated with calcium salts. This calcified layer appears to be a barrier to the passage of oxygen and nutrients to the cartilage from the bone, so that the cartilage is largely dependent upon the synovial fluid for its nourishment.

Every articular cartilage is divisible into two parts: a central, articulating part and a marginal, nonarticulating part. The marginal part is much smaller than the central and is covered by a synovial membrane. It will be described later in connection with that membrane.

The central part is either single, if only two bones are included in the joint, or divided into clearly distinct portions by sharp ridges, if more than two bones are included. Thus the upper articular surface of the arm bone (humerus) is single, for only this bone and the shoulder blade (scapula) are included in the shoulder joint. The lower articular surface of the humerus is subdivided into two parts, one for articulation with the radius and one for articulation with the ulna, both being included in the elbow joint. There is a functional reason for the subdivision, or partition, of articular cartilage when it does occur.

Within a diarthrosis joint bones articulate in pairs, each pair being distinguished by its own pair of conarticular surfaces. Conarticular surfaces constitute "mating pairs." Each mating pair consists of a "male" surface and a "female" surface, terms explained below. As has just been pointed out, there is only one such pair of bones within the shoulder joint; hence there is only one pair of conarticular surfaces. There are two such pairs within the elbow joint—the humeroradial and humero-ulnar. The radius moves on one of the two subdivisions of the lower humeral articular cartilage, the ulna moves on the other subdivision. There are, then, two pairs of conarticular surfaces within the elbow joint even though there are only three bones in it.

Ovoid and sellar classes of articular surfaces

Articular surfaces are divisible into two primary classes: ovoid and sellar. An ovoid surface is either convex in all directions or concave in all directions; in this respect it is like one or other of the two sides of a piece of eggshell, hence the name (ovum, egg). A sellar surface is convex in one direction and concave in the direction at right angles to the first; in this respect it is like the whole or part of a horse saddle (sella, saddle). There are no flat articular surfaces, although custom permits slightly curved ovoid or sellar surfaces to be called flat. Following an engineering convention, an ovoid surface is called male if it is convex, female if it is concave. In any diarthrosis having ovoid conarticular surfaces, the male surface is always of larger area than the female. For this reason the larger of two sellar conarticular surfaces is called male, the smaller is called female. The larger the difference in size between conarticular surfaces the greater is the possible amount of motion at the joint.

In all positions of a diarthrosis, except one, the conarticular surfaces fit imperfectly. This incongruence may not be great and may be lessened by mutual deformation of the opposed parts of the surfaces, a consequence of the deformability of articular cartilage. The exceptional position is called the close-packed position; in it the whole of the articulating portion of the female surface is in complete contact with the apposed part of the male surface, and the joint functionally is no longer a diarthrosis but synchondrosis. Every joint has its close-packed position brought about by the action of the main ligaments of the joint. A good example is that of the wrist when the hand is fully bent backward (dorsiflexed) on the forearm; another is that of the knee when the thigh and leg are in the military position of attention. It is not assumed constantly because it requires special muscular effort. It is also a dangerous position, for in it two bones in series are converted temporarily into a functionally single, but longer, unit, more likely to be injured by sudden, torsional stresses. Thus a sprained, or even fractured, ankle usually occurs when that joint, when close packed, is suddenly and violently bent.

No articular surface is of uniform curvature; neither is it a "surface of revolution" such as a cylinder is. That part of a male conarticular surface that comes into contact with the female in close pack is both wider and of lesser curvature than is the remainder. Inspection of two articulating bones is enough to establish their position of close pack, flexion, extension, or whatever it may be.

Intra-articular fibrocartilages. Intra-articular fibrocartilages are complete or incomplete plates of fibrocartilage that are attached to the manifest part of the fibrous layer (the investing ligament) and that stretch across the joint cavity between a pair of conarticular surfaces. When complete they are called disks; when incomplete they are called menisci. Disks are found in the temporomandibular joint of the lower jaw, sternoclavicular (breastbone and collarbone), and ulnocarpal (inner forearm bone and wrist) joints. A pair of menisci is found in each knee joint, one between each femoral condyle and its female, tibial counterpart. A small meniscus is found in the upper part of the acromioclavicular joint. These fibrocartilages are really parts of the fibrous layer of the diarthrosis in which they occur and effect a complete or partial division of the articular bursa into two parts, depending upon whether they are disks or menisci, respectively. When the division is complete, there are really two synovial joints—*e.g.,* the sternodiskal and discoclavicular.

A disk or meniscus is a chondrified ingrowth of the fibrous layer, the chondrification being slight and the fibrous element predominating, especially in the part nearest to the investing ligament. Both animal experiment and surgical experience have shown that a meniscus of the knee can be grown again if removed. The growth takes place from the fibrous layer and is wholly fibrous in structure. The function of these intra-articular plates is to assist the gliding movements of the bones at the joints that contain them.

The synovial layer. The inner layer of the articular bursal wall is called the synovial layer (stratum synoviale) because it is in contact with the synovial fluid. Unlike the fibrous layer, it is incomplete and does not extend over the articulating parts of the articular cartilages and the central parts of articular disks and menisci. One can, therefore, designate a "synovial periosteum," covering such parts of the bones as are found within the joint, and a "synovial perichondrium," covering the nonarticulating parts of the articular cartilages.

The layer, commonly called the synovial membrane, is itself divisible into two strata, the intima and the subintima. The intima is smooth, moist, and glistening on its free (synovial) surface. It could be described as an elastic plastic in which cells are embedded. Its elasticity allows it to stretch when one of the articulating bones either spins or swings to the opposite side and to return to its original size when the movement of the bone is reversed. It contains many elastic fibres. These are extremely fine but are easily seen when the membrane is stained by methylene blue. The cells of a synovial membrane can be divided into two classes: synovioblasts and protective cells. The synovioblasts are responsible for the generation and maintenance of the matrix. Their form depends upon their location. They are flattened and rounded at or near the internal surface of the membrane, more elongated and spindle shaped elsewhere. They appear to be quite mobile, able to make their way to the free surface of the membrane and even to enter the synovial fluid. Excepting the regions in which the synovial membrane passes from the investing ligament (fibrous capsule) to the synovial periostea, these cells are scattered and do not form a continuous surface layer as do, for example, the cells lining the inner surface of the gut or of a blood vessel. In this respect they resemble the cells of other connective tissues such as bone and cartilage. Apart from the generation and maintenance of the matrix of the membrane, their function is obscure. They seem to be the only cells capable of secreting hyaluronic acid, the characteristic component of synovial fluid, but direct evidence that they do so is still lacking.

Synovial membrane cells

The protective cells are scattered through the membrane. They are of two kinds, mast cells and phagocytes. The mast cells secrete heparin and play the same part in synovial membrane as they do elsewhere, for example in the skin and the gums. The phagocytes ("swallowing cells") ingest unwanted particles, even such large ones as those of injected India ink; they are, in short, scavengers here as elsewhere. The subintima is the connective tissue base on which the intima lies and may be fibrous, fatty, or areolar (loose). In it are found the blood vessels and nerves that have penetrated the fibrous layer. Both the blood vessels and the nerves form plexuses, to be described later. The areolar subintima forms folds (synovial fringes) or minute, fingerlike projections (villi) that project into the synovial fluid. The villi become more abundant in middle and old age. The fatty parts of the subintima may be quite thin; but in all joints there are places where they project into the bursal cavity as fatty pads (plicae adiposae); these are wedge shaped in section, like a meniscus, the base of the wedge being against the fibrous capsule. The fatty pads are large in the elbow, knee, and ankle joints. In the hip joint a fatty pad is found in the deepest part of the female surface (acetabulum). It is usually, but not always, connected to the male surface (head of femur) and is then called the ligamentum teres.

Functions of the fatty pads

The function of fatty pads depends upon the fact that fat is liquid in a living body and that, therefore, a mass of fat cells is easily deformable. When a joint is moved, the synovial fluid is thrown into motion because it is adhesive to the articular cartilages, the motion of the fluid being in the direction of motion of the moving part. The fatty pads project into those parts of the synovial space in which there would be a likelihood of an eddying (vortical) motion of the fluid if those parts were filled with fluid. In short, the pads contribute to the "internal streamlining" of the joint cavity. Their deformability enables them to do this effectively. Of equal importance is the fact that the fatty pads by their very presence keep the synovial fluid between the immediately neighbouring parts of the male and female surfaces sufficiently thin, with proper elasticity as well as viscosity, to lubricate the joint.

Fatty pads are well provided with elastic fibres that bring about recovery from the deformation caused by pressure across a moving joint and prevent the pads themselves from being squeezed between two conarticular surfaces at rest. Such squeezing can happen, however, as the result of an accident and is very painful because of the large number of pain nerve fibres in these pads.

Three characteristics of the synovial fluid

The synovial fluid. The main features of synovial fluid are: (1) Chemically, it is dialyzate of blood plasma—that is, the portion of the plasma that has "filtered" through a membrane—but contains a larger amount of hyaluronic acid than other plasma dialyzates. (2) Physically, it is a markedly thixotropic fluid; that is, one which is both viscous and elastic. Its viscosity decreases with an increase of the speed of the fluid when it is in motion. Its elasticity, on the other hand, increases with increase of speed of the fluid. Its thixotropy is due to the hyaluronic acid in it. (3) Functionally, it has two parts to play: nutrition and lubrication. It has now been established that it alone, by virtue of its being a blood-plasma dialyzate, can nourish the articulating parts of the articular cartilages. Its thixotropic properties make it suitable for forming what are called elastohydrodynamic lubricant films between the moving and the fixed conarticular surfaces of any mating pair. The motion of the synovial fluid, referred to earlier in connection with the fatty pads, assists its nutritional function by distributing it over the articular surfaces, from which it slowly passes into the interior of the cartilage. The bulk of the fluid comes from the synovial blood capillaries. The source of the hyaluronic acid is not known at present.

Types of synovial joints. Recognition of the bursal nature of synovial joints makes it possible to describe them simply in terms of the bursal wall and to group together a number of types of structures. There are seven types of synovial joints: plane, hinge, pivot, sellar, ellipsoid, spheroidal, and bicondylar (two articulating surfaces). This classification is based on the anatomical form of the articular surfaces.

Plane type or arthrodial. The plane-type or arthrodial joint has mating surfaces slightly curved and may be either ovoid or sellar. Only a small amount of gliding movement is found. Examples are the joints between the metacarpal bones of the hand and those between the cuneiform bones of the foot.

Hinge type or ginglymus. The hinge-type or ginglymus joint is a modified sellar type with each mating surface ovoid on its right and left sides. This modification reduces movement to a backward-forward swing like that allowed by the hinge of a box or a door. The swing of the joint, however, differs from that of a hinge in that it is accompanied by a slight spin of the moving bone around its long axis. This brings the joint either into or out of its close-packed position, which is always that of extension.

The joints between the bones of the fingers (phalanges) and that between the ulna ("inner" bone of the forearm) and the humerus at the elbow are classical examples. When a finger is completely straightened, each of its interphalangeal joints is in close pack, as is the ulnohumeral joint when the arm and forearm are in one line.

Pivot type or trochoid. The pivot-type or trochoid joints are of two forms: in one a pivot rotates (spins) within a ring; in the other a ring moves around a pivot. In each case the ring is composed of fibrous tissue, part of which is converted into cartilage to form a female surface; the remainder may be ossified. Similarly, only part of the pivot is covered by a male articular cartilage. Pivot joints are always of the ovoid class; from a functional aspect, they are the ovoid counterparts of hinge joints.

The atlantoaxial (first and second cervical vertebrae) and the two radio-ulnar joints are examples of pivot joints. In the former, a thick, bony spike projects upward from the axis vertebra to form the pivot. The ring is formed in front by the anterior part of the (ring-shaped) atlas vertebra and completed behind by a transverse band of fibrous tissue that divides the opening of the atlas into two parts; the articulating surfaces are in front. In this joint the ring (atlas) moves around the pivot. It is the chief, though not the only, joint involved when the head is turned from side to side. In the upper radio-ulnar joint, the pivot is formed by the side of the upper end of the radius, and the ring is formed by a female surface on the ulna and a band of fibrous tissue that starts from the ulna behind and returns to it in front. This band lies in the capsule of the elbow joint and is called the radial annular ligament. In the lower radio-ulnar joint, the pivot is formed by the lower end of the ulna, and the ring by anterior and posterior bands of fibrous tissue and a female surface on the ulnar side of the radius. Thus, when the forearm is twisted (pronated) or untwisted (supinated), the limb being free, the pivot moves on the ring in the upper joint, but the ring moves on the pivot at the lower joint.

Movements of sellar joints

Sellar type. The sellar type has already been described in the section dealing with articular surfaces in general. It has two types of movement—both swings—flexion–extension and abduction–adduction. In addition to these it allows movements combining these two; that is, swings accompanied by rotation (spin) of the moving bone.

There are many examples of sellar joints. The best known is the carpometacarpal joint of the thumb, in which the free, first metacarpal moves upon the trapezium. (The carpal bones are those of the wrist, the metacarpals of the hand, and the phalanges of the fingers. The trapezium is a carpal bone.) The articular surface of the latter bone is convex from behind forward and concave from side to side. The thumb can be swung from side to side or from behind forward. But the most frequent movement is that which swings it so that it comes "face to face" with one or another of the fingers, as in grasping a needle or a ball. This movement is called opposition (*i.e.,* of thumb to fingers). The reverse movement is called reposition. During opposition the thumb is rotated around its long axis; it has been said that our civilization depends upon the opposition of the thumb.

Sellar joints are found wherever only two types of movement are required, and a movement of the opposition kind is the habitual one.

Ellipsoid type. The ellipsoid is also a joint having two types of movement but allowing opposition movement only to a small degree. Its surfaces are ovoid and vary in both length and curvature as they are traced from front to back or from side to side, just as the diameter and curvature of an ellipse vary in directions at right angles to each other (hence the name). The joint between the second metacarpal and the first phalanx of the second finger is a good example. The male surface is on the head (finger end) of the metacarpal, at its extremity, and extends, broadening from side to side, on to its palmar aspect. It allows the finger to flex and extend, to swing toward or away from its neighbouring finger, and to swing forward with a slight amount of rotation. Its close-packed position is full flexion. The remaining joints between metcarpals and fingers are of the same type. So also are those between the lower end of the radius and the lunate and scaphoid bones of the wrist (radiocarpal) joint. In this case, however, the close-packed position occurs when the hand is swung backward (dorsiflexed) completely. If a person falls violently on his dorsiflexed hand, fracture of the scaphoid and the lower end of the radius is likely to occur.

From *Cunningham's Textbook of Anatomy* edited by G.J. Romanes and published by Oxford University Press as an Oxford Medical Publication

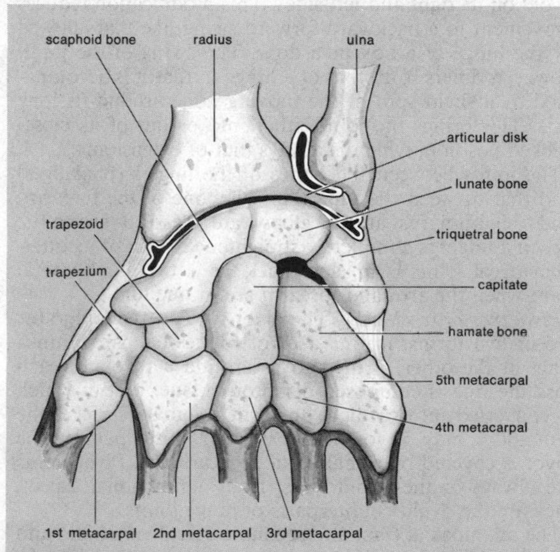

Figure 15: Coronal section through the radiocarpal, carpal, carpometacarpal, and intermetacarpal joints of the wrist.

Spheroidal type. The spheroidal type, also known as a ball-and-socket joint (see Figure 16), is the only one with three types of movement. It is an ovoid joint the male element of which could be described as a portion of a

Adapted from *Cunningham's Textbook of Anatomy* edited by G.J. Romanes and published by Oxford University Press as an Oxford Medical Publication

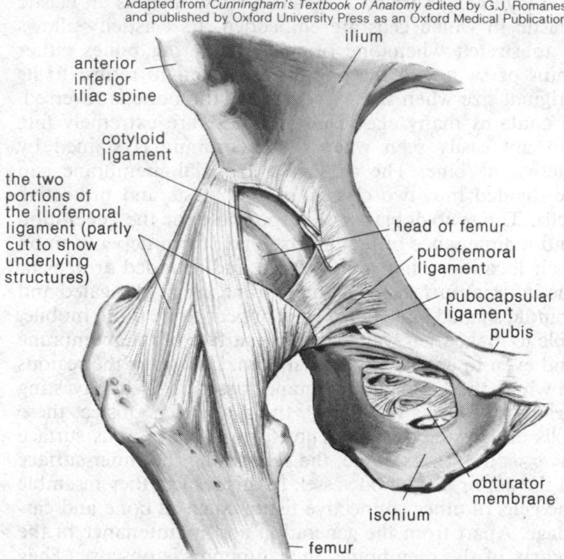

Figure 16: Anterior view of the hip joint, showing attachment of ligaments to femur, ilium, ischium, and pubis.

slightly deformed sphere. It is this fact that allows one of the component bones to swing in various directions and also to spin upon the other bone. The largest spheroidal joints are those at the hip and shoulder. At the shoulder the male surface is on the humerus and faces inward toward the body.

The female surface (glenoid cavity) is at the upper front angle of the scapula and is quite shallow. This allows freedom of movement of the arm upon the body in all directions except backward (extension).

Nevertheless, the utmost amount of swing forward (flexion) or outward (abduction) is 90°; the hand can then be swung further upward by movements of the scapula on the trunk. In accordance with this freedom of movement, the capsule of the joint is long and loose in most positions, and the joint itself is extremely susceptible to dislocation if the surrounding muscles be "off guard." It is in close pack when the arm is fully abducted and outwardly rotated.

The hip joint

At the hip joint the male surface is on the femur and also faces inward; it is larger than that on the humerus. The female surface is on the side of the hipbone. It is contained within a deep, cuplike socket (acetabulum), which permits flexion and extension of about the same amount as at the shoulder but restricts abduction-adduction and rotation of the femur around its long axis. The fibrous capsule is not as loose as that at the shoulder. The hip joint is close packed in the position of fullest extension.

Bicondylar type. Condylar type is better called the bicondylar type, for in it two distinct surfaces on one bone articulate with corresponding distinct surfaces on another bone. The two male surfaces are on one and the same bone and are of the same type (ovoid or sellar). The male surfaces are called male condyles; the female surfaces are female condyles. These joints have two types of movement: one is always a swing; the other is either another swing or a spin.

Bicondylar joints are quite common. The largest is the tibiofemoral joint in which both pairs of mating surfaces are within a single joint. At this joint, flexion and extension are the main movements; but active rotation of the leg on the femur is possible in most people when the leg and thigh are at right angles to each other.

Every vertebra of the cervical, thoracic, and lumbar series is connected to (or separated from) the one below it by a pair of synovial joints as well as by an intervertebral disk. This pair of joints constitutes a bicondylar joint, the shape of whose articular surfaces determines the amount of movement permitted between the vertebra (Figure 13). The atlanto-occipital joint between the skull and the vertebral column is also a bicondylar joint. Finally, the right and left temporomandibular joints, between the lower jaw and the skull, are really two parts of a bicondylar joint, not only by definition—if the base of the skull be considered as a single bone—but also functionally, for one mandibular condyle cannot move without the other moving also.

JOINT LIGAMENTS

Any set of collagen fibres joining one bone of an articulating pair to the other is called a ligament. Thus all the manifest part of the articular bursal wall is a ligament, called either the fibrous capsule or the investing ligament. The former name will be used in the text that follows.

In descriptive medical anatomy, the term ligament is used for special sets of collagen fibres associated with joints. There are two types of these sets: capsular and noncapsular.

Adapted from *Cunningham's Textbook of Anatomy* edited by G.J. Romanes and published by Oxford University Press as an Oxford Medical Publication

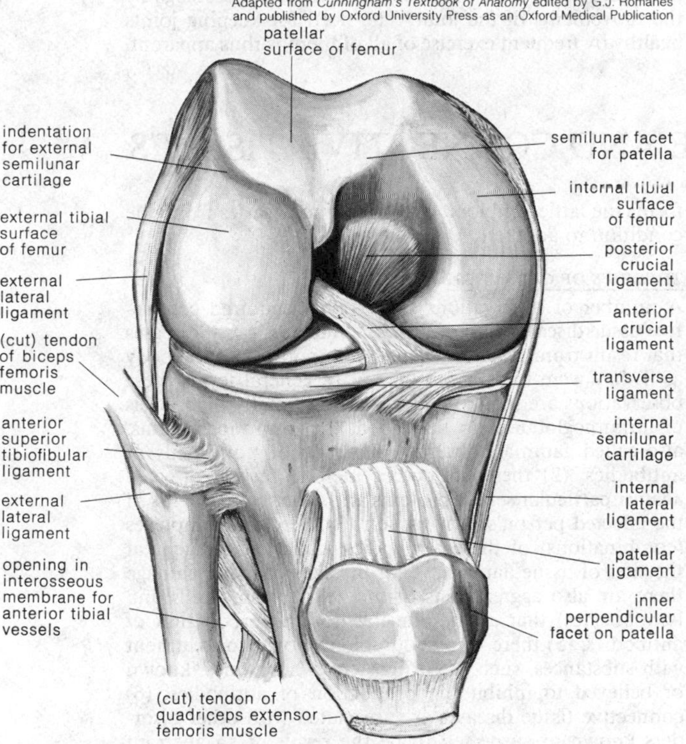

Figure 17: Dissection of knee joint from the front. The patella is thrown down to show the internal semilunar cartilage and transverse ligament.

Capsular ligaments

Capsular ligaments are simply thickenings of the fibrous capsule itself, taking the form of either elongated bands or triangles the fibres of which radiate from a small area of one articulating bone to a line upon its mating fellow. The iliofemoral ligament of the hip joint is an example of a triangular ligament. Capsular ligaments are found on the outer surface of the capsule. There is one exception to this rule: ligaments of the shoulder joint (glenohumeral ligaments) are found on the inner surface.

Noncapsular ligaments are free from the capsule and are of two kinds, internal and external.

The internal type is found in the knee, wrist, and foot. In the knee there are two, both arising from the upper surface of the tibia; each passes to one of the two femoral condyles and lies within the joint cavity surrounded by synovial membrane. They are called cruciate ligaments because they cross each other X-wise. At the wrist most of the articulations of the carpal bones share a common joint cavity, and neighbouring bones are connected sideways by short internal ligaments. The same is true of the tarsal bones that lie in front of the talus and calcaneus.

The external, noncapsular ligaments are of two kinds, proximate and remote. The proximate ligaments pass over at least two joints and are near the capsules of these joints. They are found only on the outer side of the lower limb. Examples are the outer (fibular) ligament of the knee, which passes from the femur to the upper part of the fibula over both the knee and tibiofibular joints, and the middle part of the outer ligament of the ankle joint, which passes from the lowest part of the fibula to the heel bone. These two ligaments, particularly that passing over the ankle, are especially liable to damage (sprain).

The remote ligaments are so called because they are far from, rather than close to, the joint capsule. A notable example is that of the ligaments that pass between the back parts (spines and laminae) of neighbouring vertebrae in the cervical, thoracic, and lumbar parts of the spinal column. These are the chief ligaments of the pairs of synovial joints between the vertebrae of these regions. Unlike most ligaments they contain a high proportion of elastic fibres that assist the spinal column to return to its normal shape after it has been bent forward or sideways.

Functions of the ligaments

Contrary to the opinion of earlier anatomists, ligaments are not normally responsible for holding joint surfaces together. This is because a set of collagen fibres, like a string, can exert a reactive force only if stretched and tightened by some tensile stress. Normally the bones at a joint are pressed together (when at rest) by the action of muscles or gravity. An individual ligament can stop a movement that tightens it. Such a movement will loosen the ligaments that would be tightened by the opposite movement. The one exception to this case is the movement that brings a joint into the close-packed position. This movement is brought about by a combination of a swing with a spin of the moving bone. Experiment shows that the combination of movement screws the articular surfaces firmly together so that they cannot be separated by traction and that the capsule and most of the ligaments are in simultaneous maximal tautness.

NERVE SUPPLY AND BLOOD SUPPLY

The nerve and blood supply of synovial joints follows the general rule for the body: *Ubi nervus ibi arteria*—"Where there is a nerve there also is an artery." Hence the nerve supply will be described first.

Articular nerves. The sources of nerve fibres to a joint conform well to Hilton's law—the nerves to the muscles acting on a joint give branches to that joint as well as to the skin over the area of action of these muscles. Thus the knee joint is supplied by branches from the femoral, sciatic, and obturator nerves that among them supply the various muscles moving the joint. Some of these nerves go to the fibrous capsule and ligaments; others pierce this capsule and reach the synovial membrane. Some of these nerves are sensory; others give both motor and sensory fibres to the arteries that accompany them.

Types of sensory fibres to the fibrous capsule

The sensory fibres to the fibrous capsule are of two kinds: (1) algesic, responsible for painful sensation, particularly when the capsule or other ligaments are overstretched or torn; and (2) proprioceptive, that terminate in various forms of specialized structures and convey information to all parts of the central nervous system, including the cerebellum and the cerebrum. It has been established that this information includes the posture of a resting joint and both the rate and extent of motion at a moving joint. The latter is supplemented by impulses conveyed by the nerves from the muscles acting and the skin affected by the movement.

The sensory fibres to the synovial membrane reach it by piercing the fibrous capsule at various points and form wide-meshed networks in the subsynovial layer. They are mainly algesic in function, stimulation of them giving rise to diffused rather than localized pain (unlike the corresponding fibres to the fibrous capsule). They are found wherever the synovial membrane is, being especially abundant in the fatty pads, and are also present over the peripheral (nonarticulating) parts of the articular cartilage, disks, and menisci. This fact accounts for the great, sickening pain that accompanies injury of these latter structures. The articulating part of the articular cartilage has no nerve supply.

Articular blood and lymph vessels. The arteries in the vicinity of a synovial joint give off subdivisions that join (anastomose) freely on its outer surface. From the network of vessels so formed, branches lead to the fibrous capsule and ligaments and to the synovial membrane. Blood vessels to the synovial membrane are accompanied by nerves, and, when these vessels reach the subsynovial membrane, they proliferate to form another anastomotic network from which capillaries go to all parts of the membrane. These subsynovial arteries also ramify to the fatty pads and the nonarticulating parts of the articular cartilage, disks, and menisci. None, however, go to the articulating part of an articular cartilage, which, therefore, depends for its nourishment upon the synovial fluid. The vessels to the nonarticulating part of the cartilage pass into cartilage canals in its interior. (These canals have a structure resembling that of the haversian canals of bone except that their walls are not ossified; see above *Bone*.) In one form of connective-tissue disease (osteoarthritis), the peripheral parts of the cartilage become ossified and give rise to bony projections. The blood vessels encircling the joint are numerous.

Veins, of course, are found with the arteries. In addition, a joint has a well-developed set of lymphatic vessels the ultimate channels of which join those of the neighbouring parts of the limb or body wall.

JOINT METABOLISM AND NUTRITION

The metabolism and nutrition of the fibrous capsule and ligaments are similar to that of fibrous tissues elsewhere. Their blood supply is relatively small, pointing to a low rate of metabolic changes. Unlike skin, for example, they heal slowly if injured.

The metabolism of articular cartilage, however, is of interest here. It is primarily dependent upon that of its cells (chondrocytes). Carbohydrate metabolism in these cells is similar to that of cells elsewhere and is unaffected by age. The oxygen consumption of the chondrocytes, on the other hand, decreases with age once the cells have matured. All the evidence suggests that the intracellular combustion is of glucose and protein, in that order of preference, rather than of fat. Sulfur passes from the blood to the synovial fluid and from there to the chondrocytes. From these it is transferred to the matrix to help to form chondroitin sulfate and keratosulfate molecules, the main constituents of the cartilaginous material. Chondroitin sulfate could be described as a sulfonated form of hyaluronic acid, the characteristic constituent of synovial fluid. Its presence in the matrix of the cartilage but not in the synovial fluid shows that the chondrocytes are necessary for its formation. After the second decade of life, the proportion of chondroitin sulfate falls and that of keratosulfate rises, as would be expected in view of the corresponding diminution of metabolic activity of the cells.

Formation of chondroitin sulfate

Excepting the articulating parts of the articular cartilages, disks and menisci, all the tissues of synovial joints are nourished directly by the blood vessels. The excepted parts are nourished indirectly by the synovial fluid. This is distributed over the surface of the articulating cartilage by the movements of the joint. The need for keeping joints healthy by frequent exercise of all of them is thus apparent.

(M.A.MacC.)

DISEASES OF THE SUPPORTIVE AND CONNECTIVE TISSUES

Connective tissue diseases

CLASSIFICATION AND GENERAL CHARACTERISTICS

Classification. Diseases of the connective tissue can be divided into (1) a group of relatively uncommon, genetically determined disorders that affect the primary structure of this tissue, and (2) a number of acquired maladies in which the connective tissues constitute the site of several more or less distinctive immunological and inflammatory reactions. The latter conditions formerly were called collagen diseases because the connective tissues, which were found to show similar changes, were once known as the collagen or collagen–vascular system. The term collagen is now restricted to a specific fibrous protein, and there is little or no evidence in the majority of these disorders of any fundamental abnormality in the structure or metabolism of collagen; consequently, the designation collagen disease should be discontinued. The connective tissue diseases are now generally taken to include, besides certain heritable diseases, the following acquired diseases: rheumatoid arthritis, systemic lupus erythematosus, progressive systemic sclerosis (scleroderma), polymyositis (dermatomyositis), necrotizing vasculitides, Sjögren's syndrome (sicca syndrome), rheumatic fever, amyloidosis, thrombotic thrombocytopenic purpura, and relapsing polychondritis.

General characteristics. The above acquired diseases, which will be touched upon in later sections, display certain common clinical features, including inflammation of the joints (polyarthralgia and arthritis), serous (fluid-exuding) membranes (pleurisy, pericarditis), and small blood vessels (vasculitis), and a high frequency of involvement of various internal organs that are particularly rich in connective tissue (*e.g.*, the lungs). The walls of inflamed blood vessels, portions of which may become necrotic (*i.e.*, may die), are often found to contain characteristic deposits of hyaline (translucent) material. This is called fibrinoid because staining with dyes (*e.g.*, eosin) reveals tinctorial properties similar to fibrin (a fibrous protein that forms the lattice of blood clots). Fibrinoid varies from one condition to another.

Features of acquired diseases

THEORIES OF CAUSATION

A number of observations suggest that acquired connective tissue diseases are autoimmune diseases—*i.e.*, diseases that result from reactions against components of the body as if they were foreign substances. In general terms these observations are that: (1) there are abnormally high levels of immunoglobulins in the blood; the immunoglobulins, also called gamma globulins, consist wholly or chiefly of antibodies; (2) these antibodies include several directed against particular serum proteins and other components of the affected person's own tissues; (3) there are complexes (combinations) of these antibodies and their antigens at the sites of tissue damage; (4) at the sites of tissue damage there are also aggregations of the cells (plasma cells and lymphocytes) that are responsible for the production of antibodies; (5) there is a favourable response to treatment with substances, such as corticosteroid hormones, known or believed to inhibit the production of antibodies; (6) connective tissue diseases are associated with other disorders known or suspected to be the result of an aberrant immune reaction.

An account of the effects of the interactions between antibodies and antigens may be found in the *Macropædia* article IMMUNITY. Antibody–antigen interactions may result in the destruction of red or white blood cells or platelets or may inactivate circulating hormones or enzymes. The antibody–antigen complexes may be deposited in the walls of blood vessels and there combine with a substance in the blood called complement, with a variety of injurious effects, including those seen in serum sickness and in rheumatoid arthritis and the kidney damage seen in systemic lupus erythematosus (see below). Last, the interaction may result in cellular immunity, which plays an important role in certain autoimmune disorders that involve solid organs, as well as in transplant rejection and cancer immunity.

Antibody–antigen interactions

HERITABLE DISORDERS OF CONNECTIVE TISSUE

Heritable disorders of connective tissue are a heterogeneous group of generalized, single-gene-determined disorders that affect one or another of the primary elements of the connective tissues (collagen, elastin, or ground substance [mucopolysaccharide]). Many cause skeletal and joint abnormalities that may interfere seriously with normal growth and development. These conditions are rare compared to the acquired connective tissue diseases.

Marfan's syndrome

Also called arachnodactyly (spider fingers), Marfan's syndrome is the least uncommon of the heritable disorders of connective tissue, having an estimated prevalence of about 15 cases per 1,000,000. The main skeletal characteristic is excessive length of the extremities. Weakness of joint capsules, ligaments, tendons, and fasciae is responsible for such manifestations as hyperextensible joints (double-jointedness), recurrent dislocations, spinal deformities, flat feet, hernias, and dislocation of the lens of the eye (ectopia lentis). Cardiovascular abnormalities, which result from degenerative changes in the media (middle coat) of the great vessels, include insufficiency of the aortic valve and aneurysm (weakening of the wall and consequent bulging) of the ascending segment of the aorta.

Marfan's syndrome is inherited as an autosomal dominant trait; in other words, the gene involved is not a sex gene. No more than 15 percent of cases occur as an isolated instance in a family and may be attributable to a new mutation. Death is usually due to heart failure or an aneurysm of the aorta. A normal life span is possible.

Homocystinuria

Homocystinuria, so called because of the presence of homocystine in the urine, may closely resemble Marfan's syndrome. Distinctive from the latter, however, is the frequent occurrence of progressive mental deterioration, a fine skin with a tendency to flushing, osteoporosis (thinning of the bones), which may result in fractures, and thrombosis (blood clotting) of the coronary blood vessels and the peripheral blood vessels of medium size.

Homocystinuria is inherited as an autosomal recessive trait (it is not manifested unless inherited from both parents). Affected persons have a deficiency of an enzyme (cystathionine synthetase) required for the conversion of the amino acid cystathionine to cysteine. Death from vascular occlusion is common during childhood, but persons with the disorder have survived into their 50s.

Ehlers–Danlos syndrome

The Ehlers–Danlos symptom complex is manifested particularly by an abnormal skin elasticity and fragility and by loose-jointedness. The skin, peculiarly stretchable even in early childhood, gradually loses its elasticity. Minor injury can cause lacerations that tend to bleed severely and to extend. Scoliosis (lateral curvature of the spine), recurrent dislocations of joints, and hernias of the abdominal wall or the diaphragm (the muscular partition between the chest and the abdomen) are seen as in the Marfan syndrome, and there may be blue sclerae (the "whites" of the eye).

The underlying defect has not been defined. It is likely that it consists of the abnormal organization of collagen bundles. Some investigators have also detected an excess of elastin fibres. (Collagen and elastin are two of the fibrous proteins in connective tissue.) It is now clear that there are several distinct varieties of the Ehlers–Danlos syndrome. The disease is most commonly inherited as an autosomal dominant trait. Death from rupture of a major blood vessel may occur in childhood, but most affected persons live at least to middle age.

Osteogenesis imperfecta

Osteogenesis imperfecta is a general disorder of connective tissue characterized by thin-walled, extremely fracture-prone bones deficient in osteoblasts (bone-forming cells) as well as by malformed teeth, blue sclerae, and progressive deafness. Two distinct forms of the disease occur: in the early form, the result of a recessive gene, the child at birth suffers from countless fractures, and life expectancy is short; a late, milder, and more common form (osteogenesis imperfecta tarda), the result of a dominant gene, develops in childhood and is typified by single fractures from trivial stress. In both forms, the tendency to fracture lessens at puberty.

The fundamental defect in this disorder appears to involve the collagen fibres. Treatment is limited to surgical fixation of fractures.

Alkaptonuria

Alkaptonuria is a rare, inherited (recessive) disorder in which absence of the enzyme homogentisic acid oxidase results in an abnormal accumulation of homogentisic acid, which is a normal intermediate in the metabolism of the amino acid tyrosine. Some of the homogentisic acid is excreted in the urine, to which, upon alkalinization and oxidation, it imparts a black colour. The remainder is deposited in cartilage and, to a lesser degree, in the skin and sclerae. The resultant darkening of these tissues by this pigment is termed ochronosis and is accompanied by gradual erosion of cartilage and progressive joint disease.

Pseudoxanthoma elasticum

Pseudoxanthoma elasticum, also known as the Grönblad–Strandberg syndrome, has its principal effects on the skin, the eyes, and the blood vessels. The word pseudoxanthoma refers to the yellowish papules (pimplelike protuberances) that occur most commonly in the fold of the skin of the neck, armpits, and groin. The colour results from degenerative changes in the elastic fibres in the deep layers of the skin. Calcium deposition may occur in the skin, and premature arteriosclerosis is common. The characteristic eye lesion is that of angioid streaks of the retina, which are found in at least 80 percent of the cases. Deterioration of vision may occur because of bleeding or degenerative changes. Bleeding in the stomach is also fairly common. The basic lesion appears to be a premature deterioration of elastic fibres of connective tissue.

The mucopolysaccharidoses include six or more separate varieties of a disorder that, in varying degrees, affects the skeleton, brain, eyes, heart, and liver. The varieties have in common the abnormal production, storage, and excessive excretion of one or more mucopolysaccharides (complex, high-molecular-weight carbohydrates that form the chief constituent of the ground substance between the connective tissue cells and fibres).

Hurler's syndrome

Hurler's syndrome, or mucopolysaccharidosis 1, is the least rare and most rapidly fatal. Few children afflicted with it reach the age of 10. Abnormalities begin to appear when the infant is a few months old. Cerebral function deteriorates gradually. Various deformities of the extremities develop, accentuated by stiffness of the joints.

The facial deformities and dwarfed, deformed bodies that occur characteristically in Hurler's syndrome and in mucopolysaccharidosis 2 (Hunter's syndrome) are referred to as gargoylism. Individuals with a mucopolysaccharidosis other than Hurler's syndrome commonly live to adulthood, but a normal life span is unusual.

The mode of inheritance is autosomal recessive in all the types except mucopolysaccharidosis 2, which is sex-linked recessive (only males show the disease).

Myositis ossificans progressiva

In myositis ossificans progressiva, bone develops in tendons, fasciae, and striated (striped or voluntary) muscle. Skeletal growth is normal, although certain abnormalities occur in the majority of cases, particularly shortening of the thumbs or the great toes, or both. Symptoms usually begin in childhood and progress irregularly until the third decade. Lesions may begin abruptly with local tenderness, swelling, and fever, or develop very gradually, with increasing stiffness and firmness as the only symptoms. Death most often results from an infection.

ACQUIRED DISEASES OF CONNECTIVE TISSUE

Rheumatoid arthritis. Rheumatoid arthritis is a chronic disease in which a predominant nonsuppurative inflammation (an inflammation that does not discharge pus) of the peripheral joints often also manifests in ways not directly associated with the joints. These include blood-vessel inflammation in the form of tiny areas of necrosis in the fingertips; chronic leg ulcers and lesions in the peripheral nerves; inflammation of the pericardium and of the sclerae; inflammation and nodule formation in the lungs and pleura (tissue covering the lungs); anemia; enlargement of the lymph nodes; and Sjögren's, or sicca, syndrome (see below). Enlargement of the spleen occurs in approximately 5 percent of affected persons. The disease process within the joints begins as an inflammation of the synovium (joint-lining tissue). In most cases there is an increase, often considerable, in the amount of synovial (joint) fluid. (Rheumatoid arthritis is treated in detail in *Joint diseases and injuries*, below.)

Systemic lupus erythematosus. Systemic lupus erythematosus (SLE) is a chronic inflammatory disease that affects, either singly or in combination, the skin, joints, kidneys, nervous system, serious membranes lining body cavities, and often other organs as well. The disease has a tendency toward remissions and exacerbations and a multitude of immunologic abnormalities, including antibodies that react with components of cell nuclei, as well as antibodies directed against circulating proteins, blood cells, and solid organs. The disease may develop at any period of life but appears with highest frequency during the second to fourth decades. Most affected persons are women. Systemic lupus erythematosus exists in many forms, from the very mild to severe and rapidly fatal. The annual incidence of the disease has been estimated to be at least three to six cases per 100,000 population.

Systemic and discoid lupus erythematosus must be distinguished. The latter is a localized disorder of the skin and is usually confined to a facial rash, which may be similar in appearance to that which occurs in the systemic disease. Only a small minority of persons with discoid lupus erythematosus develop evidence of involvement of organs and structures other than the skin.

Characteristics of systemic lupus erythematosus

The identification of systemic lupus erythematosus is based primarily on certain clinical findings, the most specific and frequent of which include: (1) facial erythema (reddening), which often takes the form of a butterfly-shaped rash over the bridge of the nose and the cheeks, and which occurs in only a minority of adults with the disease; (2) discoid lupus—an erythematous raised patchy eruption that heals with scarring and atrophy of the skin and may be found anywhere on the body; (3) Raynaud's phenomenon (see below); (4) photosensitivity, manifested by unusual skin reaction after exposure to sunlight; (5) nondeforming arthritis; (6) inflammation of the kidneys (glomerulonephritis); (7) inflammation of the chest lining (pleurisy) or the membranous sac enclosing the heart (pericarditis), or both; and (8) central nervous system involvement, in the form of psychosis or convulsions. In addition to specific organ involvement, affected persons also have constitutional symptoms—including fever, weakness, fatigability, and weight loss—that are often the first manifestation of illness.

Some degree of anemia is found in most persons with the disease, often the result of an increased rate of red cell destruction attributable to antibodies that coat the cell and damage its membrane. Low white blood cell counts (leukopenia) and platelet counts (thrombocytopenia) are also characteristic; these, too, can often be traced to the presence of specific autoantibodies. Abnormal bleeding may result from thrombocytopenia or from an antibody that combines with and inactivates certain plasma proteins (clotting factors) involved in blood coagulation. Rheumatoid factor (see the subsection above on rheumatoid arthritis) occurs in about 25 percent of cases. Most important from the standpoint of diagnosis are the antibodies that combine with various components of cell nuclei. One or more of these antinuclear antibodies are present in virtually 100 percent of persons with active disease. The first of these antibodies to be recognized was the lupus erythematosus cell factor, discovery of which permitted detection of previously obscure and unrecognized forms of systemic lupus erythematosus.

The compound thus formed is avidly ingested by certain phagocytic (particle-engulfing) white blood cells called neutrophilic leukocytes, which, distended by the compound of antibody and of lymphocyte-nucleus component, are the characteristic lupus erythematosus cells. Two antibodies fairly characteristic of lupus erythematosus react specifically with deoxyribonucleic acid (DNA) and double-stranded ribonucleic acid (RNA) of cell nuclei. The presence of these two antibodies is associated with an active disease, in particular with inflammation of the kidney and with skin and brain lesions.

Recent evidence strongly suggests the possibility that one or more viruses may be the ultimate source of the antigenic stimulation responsible for the development of these autoantibodies.

The treatment of systemic lupus erythematosus is designed to reduce or control inflammation and to limit the damage done to vital organs. Salicylates (aspirin) are used to relieve pain, particularly when joints are involved, and to reduce fever. In most cases, however, it is necessary to employ corticosteroid hormone to reduce inflammation in acute crises of the disease. Certain antimalarial drugs, such as chloroquine and hydroxychloroquine, have been found to exert an anti-inflammatory effect on skin and joint lesions and are widely used for the treatment of milder forms of the disease.

The course of systemic lupus erythematosus is highly variable. Acute episodes occur, but more commonly the disease gives rise to a subacute or chronic illness that smoulders on for many months or years, subject to spontaneous remissions and exacerbations. There may be long intervals (up to 20 years or more) in which the affected person is entirely free of symptoms, with little or no evidence of the disease aside from serologic abnormalities, which tend to persist indefinitely. In most cases the prospects of survival are determined by the degree of kidney involvement and its responsiveness to treatment with corticosteroids and other measures. Persons with severe and persistent thrombocytopenia (deficiency of blood platelets) and hemolytic anemia or with central-nervous-system disease fare poorly compared to those whose illness mainly involves the joints.

Drug-induced lupus

There are a number of drugs that have been found to be responsible for the induction of a lupuslike disease. Typically, this state is manifested by the appearance of fever, joint pain, pleurisy, deficiency of white blood cells, and the development of various antinuclear antibodies (antibodies that interact with cell nuclei). The clinical features thus resemble closely those of natural lupus, with the exception that evidence of kidney involvement is notably rare, and the symptoms generally disappear upon discontinuation of the offending drug. Drugs that have had this effect include hydralazine, procainamide, various anticonvulsants, isoniazid, the antibiotic penicillin, and penicillamine. In one study, these or other drugs were found to account for 3 to 12 percent of all the cases identified as lupus. Only a small proportion of persons who receive these drugs present evidence of a lupuslike disease.

Progressive systemic sclerosis. Progressive systemic sclerosis, or scleroderma, is a generalized disorder of connective tissue of uncertain causation characterized by inflammatory, fibrotic (increase of fibrous tissue), and degenerative changes in the skin, joints, muscles, and certain internal organs. The term scleroderma refers to the thickening and tightening of skin, by which the disease was first recognized. The disease affects women approximately twice as often as men. The initial symptoms, which usually appear in the third to fifth decade of life, include painless swelling or thickening of the skin of the hands and fingers, pain and stiffness of the joints (polyarthralgia)—often mistaken for rheumatioid arthritis—and paroxysmal blanching and cyanosis (becoming blue) of the fingers induced by exposure to cold (Raynaud's phenomenon). The skin changes may be restricted to the fingers (sclerodactyly) and face but often spread. The disease may remain confined to the skin for many months or years, but in most cases there is insidious involvement of the esophagus (gullet), intestinal tract, heart, and lungs.

Outlook for persons with scleroderma

Although there may be spontaneous improvement in the condition of the skin, those persons with more diffuse scleroderma tend to lose the ability to straighten their fingers. In general, the outlook is poor in cases marked by rapid progression of dermal changes, intestinal malabsorption, or heart failure. In many cases, however, the disease progresses extremely slowly.

Polymyositis. Polymyositis is characterized by inflammation and degeneration of skeletal muscle, in particular, the muscles of the shoulder and pelvic girdles. The muscle disease is manifested primarily by weakness and later by atrophy and contractures. Heart muscle and muscles of the esophagus and larynx may be affected. In at least 15 percent of affected adults, especially those with involvement of the skin, or dermatomyositis, cancers are present.

The diagnosis is supported by an increase in the serum levels of enzymes that are released into the bloodstream when there is active destruction of muscle fibres and is confirmed by microscopic examination of affected muscle.

Necrotizing vasculitides. The symptom complexes included in this category are characterized by inflammation of segments of blood vessels, chiefly small and medium-sized arteries. Clinical manifestations depend upon the site and severity of the arterial involvement.

No single cause or disease mechanism has been identified. In some cases the lesions are similar to those encountered in human serum sickness and in animals given large amounts of foreign protein, in which conditions there is convincing evidence to link the disease to the deposition of immune (antigen–antibody) complexes in the walls of small blood vessels. An antigen (Australia antigen) associated with viral hepatitis (liver inflammation) has recently been found in the serum of several persons with polyarteritis nodosa, raising the possibility that some cases of polyarteritis may result from the deposition in blood vessels of immune complexes of viral antigen and antibody.

In polyarteritis nodosa, formerly known as periarteritis nodosa, inflammation and necrosis of small and medium-calibre arteries leads to local dilation and the formation of small aneurysms. The kidneys are the most frequently involved organs, and the disease is often first manifested by hypertension or other evidence of nephritis (kidney inflammation). Hypersensitivity angiitis tends to involve smaller blood vessels than those affected in polyarteritis nodosa. Frequently, the affected person seems to have experienced hypersensitivity to various drugs, particularly penicillin, sulfonamides, and iodides.

Hypersensitivity angiitis

Wegener's granulomatosis is a disorder marked by the combination of granulomatous lesions of the upper air passages and lower respiratory tract; destructive inflammation of blood vessels, both arteries and veins, especially in the lungs; and localized kidney disease. The disease affects adults of either sex. Corticosteroid therapy is often ineffective, and, in the past, most affected persons succumbed of kidney failure or lung infection within a year. Recently, complete, long-lasting recovery following treatment with various immunosuppressive agents has been reported.

Takayasu's arteritis, with variants called pulseless disease, branchial arteritis, and giant-cell arteritis of the aorta, involves principally the thoracic (chest portion of the) aorta and the adjacent segments of its large branches. Symptoms and signs, including obliteration of the pulses in the arms, are related to narrowing and obstruction of these vessels. Most reported cases have occurred in young Oriental women. The diagnosis and extent of vascular involvement can be established by means of angiography (X-ray observation of the blood vessels). Corticosteroids administered early during the course of illness have a beneficial effect, accompanied on occasion by return of pulses. Anticoagulants may prevent thrombosis (formation of blood clots).

Giant-cell or temporal arteritis occurs chiefly in older people and is manifested by severe temporal or occipital headache (headache in the temples or at the back of the head), mental aberrations, visual difficulties, unexplained fever, anemia, aching pains and weakness in the muscles of shoulder and pelvic girdles (polymyalgia rheumatica), and—in a minority of cases—tenderness and nodularity of the temporal artery. This vessel is the site of an inflammation that is characterized by the presence of numerous giant cells. Treatment with small doses of corticosteroids usually leads to dramatic relief of symptoms.

Sjögren's syndrome. Sjögren's syndrome, or sicca syndrome, is a disease complex characterized by dryness of the eyes (keratoconjunctivitis sicca); dryness of the mouth (xerostomia), often coupled with enlargement of the salivary glands; and rheumatoid arthritis. Sometimes the dryness of the eyes and mouth is associated with other connective tissue diseases, such as systemic lupus erythematosus, polyarteritis nodosa, dermatomyositis, or scleroderma rather than with rheumatoid arthritis. Sjögren's syndrome is a disorder primarily of women past the menopause.

The frequent occurrence of elevated levels of immunoglobulin in the serum and of various antibodies, including antisalivary duct antibody, antinuclear antibody, and antiglobulin antibody (rheumatoid factor) has strengthened suspicion that Sjögren's syndrome is an autoimmune disorder. Treatment is directed toward relief of symptoms.

Rheumatic fever. Rheumatic fever is an inflammatory disease that represents a delayed sequel to infection with the group A hemolytic streptococcus and predominantly affects children between the ages of five and 15 years. Although its name is based upon involvement of the joints, rheumatic fever owes its importance to its tendency to damage the heart. The attack rate of rheumatic fever ranges as high as 3 percent in cases in which streptococcal infection is associated with sore throat and pharyngeal exudate (oozing from the throat surfaces). Persons who have had it are more susceptible to recurrences than the general population is to an initial attack.

Rheumatic fever may be gradual and unnoticed in onset, or it may develop rapidly. Typically, clinical evidence of the disease appears after a symptom-free latent interval of a few days to several weeks after the inciting streptococcal infection. The major indications of its presence in children include inflammation of the heart (especially the valves, manifested by heart murmurs), arthritis, chorea (a nervous disorder involving unceasing, involuntary movements), subcutaneous nodules, and skin rashes, the most characteristic of which is erythema marginatum (reddening of the skin in disk-shaped areas with elevated edges). Fever is common, but not invariably present. Symptoms in adults are usually confined to the heart, the joints, or both. Antibiotics, especially penicillin, are employed during the attack to eradicate the streptococci, whereas aspirin and corticosteroids are used to treat the acute symptoms. Both decrease discomfort but neither shortens the course of illness. Occasionally, death occurs from an overwhelming inflammation of the heart, but, unless there is damage to heart valves, recovery usually is complete. Scarring and deformity of the valves may lead to their narrowing or failure to close properly, and this may eventually lead to the development of heart failure. The prophylactic use of antibiotics (chiefly penicillin) has led to a dramatic reduction in the frequency of streptococcal infections and resultant recurrences of rheumatic fever.

Complications of rheumatic fever

Several antibodies against the streptococcus develop in response to infection. These are directed against various constituents of the microorganism or its products. The mechanisms whereby streptococcal infection initiates the process of rheumatic fever appear to be immunological in nature and to be based in large measure on antigenic cross-reactive relationships between a protein constituent of the streptococcal cell walls and human heart tissue and between other fractions of the streptococcus and a component of joint cartilage. Immunoglobulins produced in response to these bacterial antigens may act as autoantibodies and be responsible for the inflammation of the heart and joints.

Amyloidosis. Amyloidosis is a disorder characterized by the accumulation of amyloid in the connective tissue. Amyloid consists of a filamentous protein that is derived from immunoglobulins. The deposition of this substance may be widespread, with involvement of major organs leading to serious clinical consequences, or it may be limited with little effect on health. Amyloidosis has been separated into a primary form, unrelated to any other disease, and a secondary form, which is associated with chronic infections and inflammatory disorders. It appears that amyloid is related to aging in that deposits are found with increasing frequency in the heart and brain of individuals past the age of 70. Included in the category of primary amyloidosis are a number of heritable forms. As seen by electron microscopy, all the types of amyloid examined consist chiefly of fine fibrils (minute fibres).

Osteoarthritis. Osteoarthritis, also called degenerative joint disease, is a ubiquitous noninflammatory disease of joints; the weight-bearing joints are particularly affected, including the knees and the hips. The disease is characterized by the progressive deterioration of joint cartilage and by the reactive formation of dense bone and of bony projections at the margins of the joint. The term osteoarthritis is actually inaccurate because its suffix, "-itis," implies the existence of a basically inflammatory disorder.

Osteo-arthritis in Neanderthal man

Osteoarthritic changes have been noted in skeletal remains of Neanderthal man (40,000 BC) and in a wide variety of animal species, both large and small. Some erosion of joint cartilage is virtually universal in the elderly and appears to be an inherent part of the aging process. Recent surveys in the United States and Great Britain are the basis of estimates that 40 to 50 percent of the adult population have X-ray-visible changes of osteoarthritis in the hands or feet and that approximately 5,000,000 to 10,000,000 Americans have symptoms as a result of these changes; thus, osteoarthritis is by far the most common form of joint disease. (Osteoarthritis is considered at length in *Joint diseases and injuries*, below.)

Thrombotic thrombocytopenic purpura. Thrombotic thrombocytopenic purpura is a rare disorder that has been included with the connective tissue diseases chiefly because of certain clinical similarities to systemic lupus erythematosus. The main features of this disorder, which usually appears suddenly and intensely in young women, include thrombocytopenic purpura (presence in the skin of red spots from the escape of blood into the tissues as a result of scarcity of blood platelets), hemolytic anemia (anemia resulting from destruction of red cells), changing neurological manifestations, fever, and kidney failure. The principal lesion is that of widespread blockage of small blood vessels—arterioles, venules, and capillaries—by material consisting principally of fibrin, the principal constituent of blood clots. The heart, kidneys, and brain are particularly affected. Corticosteroids remain the principal agent in treatment. Few persons survive longer than a month after onset of the disease.

Relapsing polychondritis. Relapsing polychondritis is an uncommon inflammatory disease that primarily affects cartilages. It begins usually in the fourth or fifth decade and is marked by recurrent periods of inflammation of various cartilages, lasting several weeks to months. The external ear and nose are affected most frequently and are eventually disfigured (cauliflower ear) in a high percentage of cases. Involvement of joint cartilages produces pain and swelling of the joints, and the destruction of these cartilages results in a degenerative joint disease that may be disabling. Most serious is involvement of the trachea (windpipe), which may lead to respiratory obstruction or recurrent pneumonia. The acute manifestations of the disease can usually be suppressed with corticosteroid therapy, but the changes in the cartilages are permanent.

(G.P.R./T.G.B./Ed.)

Bone diseases and injuries

Diseases and injuries of the bone are major causes of abnormalities of the locomotor system. Although physical injury, causing fracture, dominates over disease, fracture is but one of several common causes of hip disease, and bone disease is a common cause of fracture.

Bone diseases and injuries were formerly regarded as conditions that were more mechanical than metabolic. An improved understanding of the dual mechanical and chemical function of bone has permitted a more integrated biological view of bone disease and injuries.

PRINCIPAL TYPES OF DISEASES AND INJURIES

Effects of inactivity and hyper-activity

Abnormal stress on bone. Inactivity has a profound effect on the bone tissue, probably because the mechanical stimulus to bone formation is decreased.

In congenital dislocation of the hip, the socket part of the joint, the acetabulum, loses the mechanical stimulus to normal growth and development because the ball part of the joint, the head of the femur, does not rest in the joint. The acetabulum and a large part of the pelvis develop poorly or not at all, whereas the femoral head, if it makes contact higher up on the pelvis, may stimulate development of a new joint structure. Poliomyelitis affecting the lower extremity in children results in short, thin bones with sometimes severe leg-length discrepancy. In adults, an extremity affected by nerve injury gradually develops osteopenia (a reduced amount of bone tissue), so that it fractures easily. In the elderly, bed rest is regarded as a cause of increased osteopenia with vertebral fractures.

The bone tissue's capacity for remodelling in response to mechanical demand is retained even in the aged. In osteoarthritis, because the weight distribution across the knee or hip joints is uneven, the bone beneath the cartilage hypertrophies on the compression side of the joint and atrophies on the extension side.

Metabolic bone disease. The normal function of bone requires an adequate supply of amino acids (building blocks for proteins) for synthesis of collagen, the chief component for the organic matrix; of calcium and phosphate for mineralization of the organic matrix; and of other organic compounds and mineral elements. Also, growth, repair, and remodelling of the bone tissue require a precisely regulated supply of hormones, vitamins, and enzymes. Skeletal disease, when it is due to inadequacies in the supply or action of the above essentials, associated with abnormalities outside the skeleton, is termed metabolic. Examples of such abnormalities are dietary deficiency and gastrointestinal, liver, kidney, and hormonal diseases. In addition, osteoporosis (age-related loss of bone with tendency to fractures) is traditionally included among the metabolic conditions even though its cause is not known.

Osteopenia and osteo-sclerosis

Changes in bone tissue due to metabolic abnormalities are classified with regard to the amount and composition of the bone tissue. When the amount of bone is lower or higher than normal, the conditions are termed, respectively, osteopenia and osteosclerosis. These terms do not imply any specific disease but simply describe the amount of bone. Osteopenia is common both locally and generally throughout the skeleton. Localized osteopenia is evident in X rays of tumours or infections of bone, in osteonecrosis (death of bony tissue), in fracture, and in conditions of diminished mechanical demand. Osteopenia may thus be associated both with atrophy from disuse and with active remodelling of bone; it occurs when bone resorption occurs faster than bone formation. Generalized osteopenia occurs in osteomalacia, osteoporosis, and osteogenesis imperfecta. Osteosclerosis occurs locally in osteoarthritis, osteonecrosis, and osteomyelitis; it represents an attempt at structural strengthening by thickening of bony trabeculae, but its X-ray appearance may be confused with that of dead bone, retaining its density while adjacent normal bone has become osteopenic. Widespread, but hardly ever truly generalized, osteosclerosis occurs in marble bone disease and in Paget's disease. Except in the latter condition, however, osteopenia and osteosclerosis are not associated with detectable biochemical abnormalities. (These diseases are characterized below.)

When the normal composition of bone tissue is altered by deficient mineralization of the organic matrix, the condition is called rickets if in children and osteomalacia if in adults. The mineralization deficiency is due in part to a lower than normal calcium–phosphate ion product in the body fluids. In rickets the bones become tender, soft, and deformed; X rays show characteristic abnormalities at the growth zones, especially evident at the wrist, knee, and ankle joints. In osteomalacia, bone tenderness and pain accompany the slow development of spontaneous, often symmetric fractures characteristically present in the pelvis and the thigh bones. The X-ray appearance of osteomalacia is rather normal until visible fracture has developed. Biochemical abnormalities usually present in rickets and osteomalacia are increased blood concentration of the enzyme alkaline phosphatase, believed to be important for bone formation or resorption, and decreased blood concentrations of calcium or phosphate or both; the calcium concentration may fall to levels so low that muscle and nerve function are impaired (tetany). Microscopic examination of the bone tissue reveals the deficient mineralization of the organic matrix. The entire skeleton is affected in both rickets and osteomalacia, though abnormalities are more evident in growth centres in children and areas of maximal mechanical load in adults.

Effect of dietary abnor-malities

Insufficient protein, caloric, and vitamin intake interferes with bone formation during growth and remodelling, directly because of an inadequate supply for matrix formation and indirectly because of a deficient production of crucial hormones and enzymes. The effect in the young is stunted growth and in adults is osteopenia.

Deficient intake of calcium or phosphate or both, unassociated with vitamin D deficiency, causes a compensatory action of parathyroid hormone whereby the mineral is mobilized from the skeleton with eventual development of osteopenia. Deficient calcium intake (milk) and excessive phosphate intake (meat) causes osteopenia, fractures, and loss of teeth in dogs, cats, and other animals by excessive compensatory parathyroid hormone action.

Insufficient intake of vitamin D is one of many ways in which rickets may develop. The condition, once universally prevalent, is now rare in countries that ensure adequate supply of vitamin D in fortified milk and healthy living habits including adequate exposure to sunshine. Malabsorption of calcium and vitamin D causes a mixture of osteopenia and osteomalacia and requires high intake of calcium and vitamin D.

Parathyroid hormone is concerned with the maintenance of calcium concentration at the cell membranes. It functions by increasing the passage of calcium through the lining of the intestine, by increasing the resorption of bone tissue, and by increasing the reabsorption of calcium in the renal tubuli. Overactive parathyroid hormone causes osteopenia by excessive resorption of bone; in extreme cases spontaneous fractures may occur. Excessive secretion of parathyroid hormone may be due to a tumour of the parathyroid glands, may be secondary to dietary deficiency or malabsorption of calcium and vitamin D, or may be due to renal osteodystrophy (see below).

Adrenal corticosteroid hormone is associated with skeletal abnormalities, osteopenia, and osteonecrosis. Osteopenia develops because increased levels of corticosteroids, caused by disease (pituitary or adrenal tumour) or by long-term medication (*e.g.,* for asthma), depress the rate of formation of bone tissue. Osteonecrosis is associated with even short-term intake of large doses of high corticosteroid medication.

Effects of kidney disease

The effects of kidney disease on bone reflect the role of the kidney in maintaining calcium and phosphate balance, mediated by parathyroid hormone. The two main units of the kidney, the tubules and the glomerulus, are associated with two groups of bone diseases: the former with a low level of phosphate in the blood (hypophosphatemia) and the latter with renal osteodystrophy (see below), both characterized by rickets and osteomalacia. In addition, kidney transplantation is associated with overactivity of the parathyroid glands and osteonecrosis.

Reabsorption of phosphate by the kidney tubules is deficient in a hereditary disorder, familial hypophosphatemia; the phosphate leak causes low concentration of blood phosphate and, in turn, deficient mineralization of bone tissue, rickets, and osteomalacia. Familial hypophosphatemia is the most common cause of rickets in Europe and the United States. The basic deficiency is treated with high oral doses of phosphate. Advanced forms of the disease still result in stunted growth and skeletal deformity, often necessitating repeated surgery. More complex tubular reabsorption defects are also the cause of bicarbonate, amino acid, and glucose losses; the resulting disease is so severe that the bony abnormalities usually become less important.

Renal glomerular disease with high levels of urea in the blood—uremia—is associated with renal osteodystrophy. The condition leads to severe rickets or osteomalacia associated with compensatory secondary hyperparathyroidism. In children, stunted growth may be the first symptom that leads to detection of the kidney disease; the skeletal abnormality cannot be ascribed solely to an abnormal mineral balance but is probably due also to an adverse effect of uremia on protein metabolism. Growth may resume after successful kidney transplantation, and gross deformity of the extremities may be corrected surgically. Chronic uremia in adults, even when treated by use of the artificial kidney, causes osteoporosis and deposition of calcium apatite in arterial walls and tendon sheaths, probably associated with hyperparathyroidism.

Kidney transplantation is occasionally followed by hyperparathyroidism and osteonecrosis. The overactivity of the parathyroids is ascribed to the fact that, prior to correction of the kidney disease, the glands have had to function at an abnormally high level for such a long time that the mechanisms for shutting them off have become deficient. The cause of osteonecrosis after kidney transplantation is at least partly the high doses of corticosteroid treatment used to prevent rejection of the transplant. Osteonecrosis of the hip or knee joints may cause residual disability after successful kidney transplantation.

Osteoporosis

Generalized osteopenia without evidence of osteomalacia is termed osteoporosis. It may be secondary to metabolic abnormalities discussed above or may be without known cause. Osteoporosis from unknown cause is by far the most common bone disease; it probably occurs in all aged individuals and may sometimes become evident as early as age 30–40. The spine is particularly affected.

Diagnosis of less severe stages of osteoporosis is complicated because the condition is not associated with measurable chemical abnormalities or with observable tissue abnormality other than a decrease in bone mass. It is generally believed that the common fractures in old age, those of the hip, knee, and wrist, are due to osteoporosis. Unlike vertebral fractures in osteoporosis, fractures of the limbs hardly ever occur without a distinct accident, and they are never preceded by bone pain or tenderness. The diminished quantity of bone tissue, the characteristic feature of osteoporosis, is clearly implicated in the diminished resistance of the bones to fracture, but there may also be a change in the quality of the bone tissue.

In women osteoporosis is caused by a change in the hormonal pattern, and hormonal substitution therapy is sometimes used. Except for the occurrence of extremity fractures, the outlook in osteoporosis is on the whole good. Active muscle exercises are advocated both as prevention and as therapy in osteoporosis.

Paget's disease, increasingly common after middle age, is characterized by widespread areas of osteosclerosis; the cause is unknown.

Deficient blood supply to bone. The cells of the bone tissue die if deprived of arterial blood supply for more than a few hours. The condition is called necrosis of bone or osteonecrosis. Osteonecrosis may be caused by injury to blood vessels, associated with dislocation or fracture of bone; by blood clots or gas bubbles in the blood vessels; by invasion of foreign tissue; and by metabolic disease.

Causes and course of osteonecrosis

Osteonecrosis may involve the shaft (diaphysis) or the ends (epiphyses) of the long bones. Sometimes the bone marrow of the diaphysis is primarily involved, and in osteomyelitis it is usually the compact (cortical) bone of the shaft that undergoes necrosis. For mechanical reasons, and because there is a poorer blood supply to cortical bone than to the cancellous bone of the epiphyses, the course of events following osteonecrosis differs in the two types of bone. When cortical bone is involved, the dead bone may prevent healing of osteomyelitis by mechanical irritation. When the cancellous bone of the epiphyses is involved, the lesion is invaded by blood vessels from adjacent bone, and a vigorous repair process ensues, characterized by removal of dead, and the formation of new, bone. The lesion may heal with reconstitution of both structural and mechanical properties, or the process of rebuilding may weaken the bone structure so that it collapses from the mechanical forces across the joint. In these circumstances the joint cartilage is damaged, and osteoarthritis eventually develops. It is for this reason that treatment of osteonecrosis in the early stage consists of protecting the joint from weight bearing; the condition is most often encountered in the hip and the knee.

It has only recently been recognized that osteonecrosis may often develop spontaneously or in association with the use of corticosteroid hormone and in pancreatic disease. In these conditions the immediate cause of impaired blood supply is not clear.

Ionizing radiation injury to bone. Bone tissue and the metaphyseal growth cartilage (the cartilage, between the end of the bone and the shaft, that later becomes bone) may be injured during the course of X-ray treatment of tumours. The risk is well recognized but cannot always be avoided. The most common radiation injury to bone is fracture of the neck of the thigh bone (the femur) following radiation treatment of cancer of the uterus or the bladder. There is pain in the bone before this type of fracture can be seen by X ray; the fracture usually heals without displacement. In children, the X-ray treatment of certain kidney tumours may cause growth abnormalities of the spine with development of lateral curvature (scoliosis); and radium treatment of hemangioma (a tumour made up of blood vessels) of the knee region may cause growth retardation in parts of the metaphyseal cartilages with knock-knee or bowleg deformity. X-ray treatment of certain premalignant bone tumours may make them fully malignant. Intense radiation may cause osteonecrosis, sometimes associated with secondary osteomyelitis.

Infectious diseases of bone. Infection of bone tissue by microorganisms is termed osteomyelitis. Microorganisms may gain access to bone either by spreading in the bloodstream in an infectious lesion elsewhere in the body (hematogenous osteomyelitis) or through a skin wound.

Causes and incidence of osteomyelitis

The incidence of hematogenous osteomyelitis reflects the fact that the body is more susceptible to invasion by microorganisms when nutrition and hygiene are poor. Thus, hematogenous osteomyelitis is common in South America, Asia, and Africa, but in the developed countries the incidence has declined sharply during the last 50 years. In these latter countries hematogenous osteomyelitis is often associated with slum conditions or systemic disease. High-energy fractures, notably motor or missile accidents, and extensive surgery, associated with the direct introduction of microorganisms into bone, however, are increasingly common causes of osteomyelitis worldwide.

Osteomyelitis is commonly caused by pus-forming (pyogenic) microorganisms, usually *Staphylococcus aureus* or *Mycobacterium tuberculosis*. Pyogenic osteomyelitis occurs both by direct routes and by hematogenous spread from an infection of the skin, urogenital tract, lung, or upper respiratory tract. Tuberculosis of the bone is always hematogenous in origin, usually disseminated from lesions in the lungs or the kidneys.

Goran C.H. Bauer

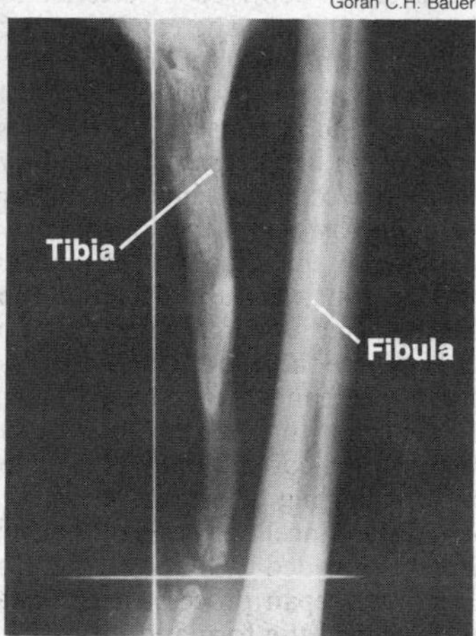

Defect of tibia, caused by septic osteomyelitis in childhood, with compensatory thickening of the fibula (right). The normal bones are shown at left.

Hematogenous osteomyelitis is more common in children than in adults. In children it is usually located in the growing end of the long bones, at the hip, for example. In adults, hematogenous osteomyelitis is commonly located in the vertebrae of the spine (tuberculous or septic spondylitis). Osteomyelitis caused by direct invasion of microorganisms often complicates open fractures and operations for fracture or for degenerative joint disease.

Osteomyelitis is associated with the cardinal symptoms of inflammation: complaints of illness, fever, local redness, swelling, warmth, pain, and tenderness. In the early stages the X-ray appearance may be normal; later, signs of destruction and repair of bone ensue. Untreated, the condition may cause extensive destruction of bone, blocking of the nutrient blood vessels with death of bone tissue, extension to an adjacent joint with development of arthritis, and eventually a break through the skin with the evacuation of pus. It may heal, but occasional flare-ups usually occur, with evacuation of pus and small pieces of dead bone (sequestra) through a persistent communication from skin to bone (a chronic sinus).

The treatment of osteomyelitis is primarily aimed at killing microorganisms with antibiotics and, in later stages, removing pus and sequestra by surgery.

Bone tumour. Primary tumours, more common in children than in adults, are classified as malignant or benign; intermediary forms exist, however, and benign bone tumour may present therapeutic problems because of its location. Primary bone tumours are characterized by their origin in the skeletal tissue elements, for example, bone tissue tumours (the malignant osteogenic sarcoma and the benign osteoma), cartilage tumours (the malignant chondrosarcoma and the benign chondroma), bone marrow tumours (the malignant myeloma and the benign eosinophilic granuloma). Metastatic (secondary) tumours are malignant by definition and are characterized by their site of origin.

Symptoms of bone tumour

Common symptoms of bone tumour are pain, swelling, and fracture that is spontaneous or is caused by only trivial forces. Most bone tumours cause abnormalities observable in X rays—defects in the bone tissue can be seen or bone that has formed in reaction to the tumour or, in some types of tumour, the tumours themselves, which consist of bone. Some bone tumours cause biochemical abnormalities detectable by examination of blood samples: myeloma (production of characteristic protein, a globulin) or metastatic cancer of the prostate (production of the enzyme acid phosphatase). The ultimate identification of bone tumour rests on examination of tissue samples.

Benign tumours may be excised and the defect filled with a bone transplant for structural support. Malignant tumours may be treated by ionizing radiation, chemical agents, or surgery. Treatment of metastatic bone tumour is aimed at suppression of pain and prevention or repair of fracture by external support or, occasionally, by internal fixation. Treatment of malignant primary bone tumour is aimed at destruction of the tumour either by segmental resection of the involved region or by amputation.

FRACTURES

Contributing factors in fractures

A fracture occurs when the bone tissue is subjected to tensile, compressive, or shear forces in excess of its strength. Both the strength of the bone tissue and the nature of the forces acting on bone change from infancy to old age, both normally and as a result of disease. Therefore, the incidence and type of fractures changes with age.

The bone tissue in young adults has high resistance to mechanical deformation. Fractures of cortical bone in adults require tremendous forces, such as those encountered in motor accidents, and are therefore often associated with severe skin injuries and other lesions of soft tissue. Bones in children are springy and resilient, and the membrane enclosing the bones—the periosteum—is thick. Angular deformation of long bones in children therefore often results in incomplete or "greenstick" fractures. In the elderly the bone tissue becomes more brittle, especially the cancellous bone in vertebrae and in shoulder, wrist, hip, and knee joints.

The forces acting on the skeleton of a child normally are defined by body size and weight. Fractures in children are therefore rarely severely displaced or associated with severe soft tissue injury. In adults age 20–50, fractures are often caused by direct, high-energy forces that have an explosive effect on bone and soft tissues and may cause severely displaced open fractures. In the aged, fracture is usually caused by mild forces acting on brittle bone. Such fractures are rarely associated with soft tissue injury and often involve cancellous rather than cortical bone.

Many diseases decrease the strength of the bone tissue, and some expose the body to increased mechanical forces. Osteoporosis, which is prevalent in women over 50, is the major cause of fractures in old age. Less common causes of decreased bone strength are osteogenesis imperfecta, long-term corticosteroid treatment, and osteomalacia. Common causes of locally decreased bone strength are injury of peripheral nerves and tumour.

The existence of a fracture is often deduced from a history of injury and observation of swelling, tenderness,

Diagnosis and classification of fracture

faulty alignment, the sound that the broken ends make, loss of function, and associated injuries. Precise diagnosis is made by X-ray examination.

Most fractures occur without skin injury (closed fractures). The skin wound in open fractures is caused either by severe direct violence or by a sharp bone fragment that pierces the skin from within.

Fracture sometimes develops slowly rather than suddenly. These fatigue, or stress, fractures occur either because the bone tissue is exposed to forces that overwhelm its capacity for structural adaptation or because there is pre-existing disease. Examples of the former are fracture of the thigh bone and fracture of the bones of the foot (march fracture) in soldiers during their initial months of physical training. Bone diseases associated with fatigue fracture are osteomalacia, Paget's disease, and radiation injury to bone. Fatigue fracture usually produces pain even before bone abnormality can be seen in the X rays.

Except when forces act with explosive suddenness, vessels and nerves usually escape injury because of their elasticity and resilience. For anatomic reasons, nerve injury may occur in fracture-dislocation of the hip and in fracture of the long bone of the upper arm (the humerus) through the diaphysis in adults and just above the elbow in children; the latter fracture is associated with compression of the accompanying artery. Fracture and dislocation of the vertebrae caused by severe forces may be associated with spinal cord injury. Certain fractures injure the nutrient blood vessels of the bone tissue with osteonecrosis as a result.

The bone blood vessels rupture when there is fracture. The resultant bleeding causes swelling at the site of fracture (fracture hematoma) and later discoloration of the skin. Occasionally the bleeding is so severe that the circulating blood volume is significantly diminished and shock ensues. The nerve endings of the periosteum are distended by the bleeding caused by fracture, and motion or pressure at the fracture site is painful.

Healing of fracture

A fracture starts to heal at the very moment that it occurs. The fracture hematoma is invaded by cellular elements; these form organic matrix and mineral into bone (callus) that bridges the fracture. Formation of callus is faster in children than in adults and in cancellous bone than in cortical bone. Fracture of the thigh, which may heal in four to six weeks in a toddler, may require as many months in an adult. Similarly, fracture of the cancellous bone of the upper end of the humerus usually requires one-third or less of the time required for healing of a fracture of the cortical shaft of the same bone. Bridging of the fracture is hindered by separation and motion of the bone fragments, poor blood supply, and infection. After the fracture has healed, the region is remodelled by resorption and formation of bone so as to accommodate the microstructure of the bone tissue to precise mechanical demands. This remodelling is most effective in children; in adults gross deformity may exceed the remodelling capacity.

The most severe and most common cause of deficient healing is infection, osteomyelitis, associated with open fractures, which permit direct access for disease-causing organisms. The condition is prevented by treatment of open fractures with antibiotics and closure of the skin. A fracture may also unite slowly or not at all because of deficient blood supply to one or more of the bone fragments, separation of the fragments by distention or interposition of a tendon or ligament, or excessive motion at the fracture site.

The guiding principle in treatment of fractures is restoration of normal length and alignment when necessary and avoidance of motion between the fracture fragments. Some fractures, notably compression fractures of cancellous bone, are inherently stable (remain in normal alignment) and require temporary immobilization by bed rest or a sling only because of pain. Most fractures are stable in acceptable position only after reduction of dislocation and immobilization by fixation, externally by traction or plaster or internally by introduction of metallic screws, plates, nail, or wire (internal fixation).

Nonunion results in a false joint—pseudarthrosis—characterized by pain and motion at the fracture site. Healing may be achieved by immobilization with or without internal fixation and by transplantation of bone to bridge the defect.

Fracture may cause permanent deformity by residual angulation or by shortening because of overlap of cortical bone fragments, compression of cancellous bone, or, in children, arrest of metaphyseal cartilage growth.

Osteoarthritis is a late complication of fracture at a joint when the joint cartilage surfaces are disturbed and the joint is unstable.

DEVELOPMENTAL ABNORMALITIES AND HERITABLE CONDITIONS

Congenital bone diseases. Many important diseases of the locomotor system are congenital in the sense that they become evident at or soon after birth. This does not imply that they all are genetically determined. Most are caused by factors operating during pregnancy, delivery, or early infancy.

Intrauterine and birth injuries

Intrauterine injuries of the locomotor system are dramatically exemplified by the thalidomide catastrophe: children born of some women who received this drug during the initial three months of pregnancy had severe extremity defects (phocomelia). Most intrauterine injuries are probably not caused by drugs, however, but perhaps by viral, hormonal, or mechanical factors. Intrauterine amputations, clubfeet, and congenital dislocation of the hip probably belong to this group. Birth injuries with fracture of the collarbone or humerus occur because of mechanical difficulties during delivery. These fractures heal extremely fast.

Developmental abnormalities

Developmental abnormalities may affect isolated or multiple regions of the skeleton, or they may involve a specific tissue system; the latter are often heritable. Examples of isolated abnormalities are partial or total absence of the collarbone, radius (the long bone on the thumb side of the lower arm), and the thigh bone; congenital false joint in the shin bone (tibia); and absence of a middle segment of a limb (phocomelia; see below). Treatment of these conditions is difficult, often requiring advanced transplantation or orthopedic devices and sometimes necessitating amputation in childhood. Multiple abnormalities are represented by polyostotic fibrous dysplasia, in which affected bone is replaced by connective-tissue matrix of obscure origin. The condition may cause multiple deformities that require surgical correction.

Inherited disorders. Heritable disorders of the skeleton include osteogenesis imperfecta, the Hurler and Marfan syndromes and several disorders of epiphyseal and metaphyseal growth centres. (For a detailed treatment of these heritable disorders, see *Connective tissue diseases*, above.)

Heritable metaphyseal dysplasias, causing bone deformities near the joints, exist in several forms. The primary defect lies in the growth zone of the long bones. One of these conditions (hypophosphatasia) results from a deficiency in the enzyme alkaline phosphatase and is one of the few hereditary generalized disorders of the bony skeleton in which an enzyme defect has been identified. Multiple defects in the growth zones of the skeleton are distinct from familial hypophosphatemia, a condition characterized by low phosphate levels in the blood; it affects the kidney primarily and the skeleton only secondarily. Hemophilia, finally, is a generalized heritable condition that affects the locomotor system only secondarily by bleeding in bones and joints.

THERAPEUTIC AND CORRECTIVE MEASURES

Traction

Traction counteracts muscle pull on the skeleton and is used to reduce and stabilize fractures and to prevent muscle shortening. Traction is applied by ropes and pulleys fastened to the skin by adhesive tape or directly to the skeleton with the aid of metal pins drilled into bone.

Internal fixation (osteosynthesis) of bone is aimed at restoration of continuity and stability during healing of a fracture, arthrodesis, or osteotomy (see below). For this purpose a variety of metal screws, pins, plates, and wires have been developed. The metal used is either stainless steel or a chromium-cobalt-molybdenum alloy that resists the corrosive action of the body fluids.

Arthroplasty, aimed at restoration of normal joint motion, is usually performed because of pain and restricted motion—for example, in rheumatoid arthritis of the elbow or the hip—but occasionally to restrict mobility—for example, in recurrent dislocation of the shoulder. Structural support and smooth gliding surfaces can be obtained by insertion of metallic devices; in the hip, for example, both the ball and the socket of the joint can be replaced. Osteotomy is aimed at correction of bony or articular deformity by cutting through bone and letting the fracture heal in the desired position, usually with the aid of internal fixation.

Arthrodesis is aimed at elimination of motion in a joint (fusion) in order to eliminate pain in osteoarthritis and rheumatoid arthritis, stabilize a joint that is either unstable or lacks useful muscle power, and remove an infectious lesion in arthritis. The operation involves removal of joint cartilage and immobilization; a bone transplant is sometimes used for more rapid restoration of continuity.

Bone resection implies surgical removal of bone and is performed either in the course of an arthroplasty or independently. The operation is performed in certain fractures and for removal of tumour.

Epiphysiodesis (the fixing of the epiphysis to the bone shaft) is aimed at temporary or permanent cessation of growth in a metaphyseal cartilage. The operation is performed at the knee for compensation of growth in the other leg—for example, because of poliomyelitis—or in one of the other growth cartilages in the same knee.

Tendon transfer is aimed at changing the mechanical effect of the corresponding muscle. The operation is performed to restore function lost by paralysis and to correct an abnormality in the motion of a joint.

Transplantation of bone

Transplantation of bone is aimed at stimulation of bone formation and giving structural support until a defect has been bridged by new bone. If the bone cells of the transplant survive, they can continue to form bone and can stimulate adjacent tissue to formation of bone. Without survival, the transplant may function as a scaffold for invasion by tissue from adjacent bone, guided by the microstructure of the dead transplant. Cell-rich cancellous bone stimulates bone formation more effectively than does cortical bone, which gives better structural support.

The fundamental problems in transplantation of bone, as with other tissues, are cell death because of deficient blood supply and a tendency toward rejection. The smaller the transplant, the better are the possibilities that blood vessels will reach the cells in time; this is why many small chips are used for stimulation of bone formation. Another possibility is to transplant bone in continuity with attached vessels in order to preserve the blood supply of the transplant. The immunologic problem is usually circumvented by use of bone from the individual himself (autotransplantation). In children sufficient bone for autotransplantation is often not available; bone from another individual will then be used. An attempt to modify the immunologic reaction to such a transplant is usually made by radiation and by storage in a bone bank.

Common indications for transplantation of bone are nonunion of a fracture, a bone cyst, arthrodesis, and structural defects in cancellous bone caused by compression fracture—for example, the heel bone.

Indications for amputation

Amputation is performed for four reasons: arterial disease, gross injury, tumour, and developmental abnormality, all more common in the legs than in the arms. Arterial disease, arteriosclerosis ("hardening of the arteries"), often associated with diabetes, is common in the aged. Gross injury to nerves, vessels, and soft tissues and primary tumours of bone or other connective tissue usually involve relatively young individuals. Developmental abnormalities—for example, congenital false joint in the tibia—may occasion amputation in childhood. (G.C.H.B./Ed.)

Joint diseases and injuries

Diseases of the joints may be variously short-lived or exceedingly chronic, agonizingly painful or merely nagging and uncomfortable; they may be confined to one joint or may affect many parts of the skeleton. For the purposes of this article two principal categories are distinguished: joint diseases in which inflammation is the principal set of signs or symptoms; and diseases, called noninflammatory in this article, in which inflammation may be present to some degree, as after an injury, but is not the essential feature.

INFLAMMATORY JOINT DISEASES: TYPES OF ARTHRITIS

Arthritis is a generic term for inflammatory joint disease. Inflammation restricted to the lining of a joint (the synovial membrane) is referred to as synovitis. Arthralgias simply are pains in the joints; as ordinarily used, the word implies that there are no other accompanying evidences of arthritis. Rheumatism, which is not synonymous with these, does not necessarily imply an inflammatory state but refers to all manners of discomfort of the articular apparatus including the joints and also the bursas, ligaments, tendons, and tendon sheaths. Inflammation of the spine and its joints is called spondylitis. Regardless of the cause, the inflammation may cause pain, stiffness, swelling, and some redness of the skin about the joint. Effusion of fluid into the joint cavity is common, and examination of this fluid is often a valuable procedure for determining the nature of the disease. The inflammation may be of such a nature and of such severity as to destroy the joint cartilage and underlying bone and bring irreparable deformities. Adhesions between the articulating members are frequent in such cases, and the resulting fusion with loss of mobility is called ankylosis. When apposed joint surfaces are displaced from each other they are said to be dislocated or luxated. Incomplete dislocation is called subluxation.

Bursitis. Inflammation of the bursas is called bursitis (or bursal synovitis). Bursas sometimes are involved along with the joints and tendon sheaths in rheumatoid arthritis and gout. Infectious agents introduced by penetrating wounds or borne by the bloodstream also may result in bursitis, but this is unusual. The prepatellar bursa, located on the lower part of the kneecap, is especially subject to involvement in brucellosis (undulant fever).

Causes of bursitis

The cause of most cases of bursitis appears to be one or another local mechanical irritation. Often the irritation is of occupational origin and occurs in the shoulder region, at the knee, near the hip, and elsewhere. The inflammatory reaction is not a distinctly particularized one and may or may not include deposition of calcium salts. The borderline between bursitis and other painful rheumatic conditions of the soft tissues is indistinct in many instances.

The most common form of bursitis affects the subdeltoid bursa, which lies above the shoulder joint. Bursitis in this circumstance is not the primary abnormality, but results from degeneration and calcification of the adjacent rotator tendon. Direct injury is not usually the cause of calcium deposits and inflammation in the tendon; indeed, heavy labourers are less frequently affected than persons engaged in less strenuous occupations. The bursa proper is affected only when debris from the tendon extends into it, this intrusion being the principal cause of an acutely painful shoulder. The condition occurs most often in middle age and is infrequent among young children. Women are twice as likely to have the condition as men. The onset may be sudden and unprovoked. Pain and tenderness are great and there is difficulty in raising the arm. No single method of dealing with the disorder in all affected persons is known, and response varies widely among individuals. Resting the arm and use of analgesics tend to lessen the discomfort, corticosteroids may reduce inflammation, and carefully graduated exercises may be used to lessen the possibility of lasting stiffness of the shoulder. Many months may pass before complete recovery is attained. Chronic inflammation of the bursa at the side of the hip joint—trochanteric bursitis—has a similar course.

The more clearly traumatic forms of bursitis are exemplified by "beat knee," a bursitis that develops below the kneecap of miners who must kneel over long periods to work narrow coal seams. Bloody fluid distends the bursa and, unless removed early, may cause the walls of the bursa to become thickened permanently. Treatment, which involves protection from further irritation to the extent that this is possible, is otherwise similar to that for subdeltoid bursitis. A fair proportion of these lesions become infected as a consequence of injury to the overlying skin.

Types and routes of infection

Infectious arthritis. Joints may be infected by many types of microorganisms (bacteria, fungi, viruses) and occasionally by animal parasites. There are three routes of infection: by direct contamination, by way of the bloodstream, and by extension from adjacent bony infections (osteomyelitis). Direct contamination usually arises from penetrating wounds but may also come during surgery on joints. Blood-borne infections may enter the joints through the synovial blood vessels. Commonly, however, they first set up foci of osteomyelitis in the long bone near the end of its shaft or next to the joint. The infection then extends into the joint through natural openings or pathological breaches in the outside layer or cortex of the bone. Characteristically hematogenous (blood-borne) infectious arthritis affects one joint (monarthritis) or a very few (oligoarthritis) rather than many of them (polyarthritis), and usually large joints (knee and hip) rather than small ones.

Joint cartilage may be damaged rapidly by formation of pus in infections with such bacteria as staphylococci, hemolytic streptococci, and pneumococci. Tuberculosis of the joint, by contrast, can result in extensive destruction of the adjacent bone and open pathways to the skin without destruction of the cartilage. Tuberculous spondylitis, Pott's disease, is the most common form of this infection. It occurs mostly in young children. Treatment is with the antibiotic streptomycin and the antituberculous drugs isoniazid and para-aminosalicylic acid. A frequent American fungus infection is caused by *Coccidioides immitis,* an organism indigenous to the arid regions of the Southwestern United States. As in the case of tuberculosis, seeding from the lung to the bone usually precedes involvement of a joint. Brucellosis, like tuberculosis, has a particular affinity for the spine. *Brucella suis* is the most likely brucellar organism to cause skeletal disease.

Infections of the joints, like infections elsewhere in the body, often cause fever and other systemic indications of inflammation. Appropriate antibiotics or chemicals are used to eliminate the infection, and early drainage of the exudate is desirable if there is pus.

Among the better recognized virus infections that can cause joint discomforts are rubella (German measles) and serum hepatitis, both of which usually are of short duration and have no permanent effect. Several tropical forms of synovitis have also been reported to be viral. Destructive arthritis sometimes complicates smallpox, but it probably results from supraimposition of a bacterial infection rather than from invasion of the joint by the pox virus proper. Parasitic infestations are unusual, but there have been documented cases of joint involvement by the Guinea worm, *Dracunculus medinensis,* a nematode that affects more than 50,000,000 persons in tropical countries.

Complicating factors in venereal diseases

Infectious arthritis complicates several venereal diseases, including gonorrhea. The gonococcal organism is highly sensitive to penicillin, and early treatment with penicillin usually effects a prompt cure and prevents the marked destruction of the joint that may otherwise ensue. The arthritis of Reiter's disease, which is occasionally confused with gonorrhea and apparently is spread by sexual contact, does not respond to antibiotics but usually improves spontaneously over the course of several months. Characteristically Reiter's disease involves inflammation of the joints, the urethra, and the conjunctiva. Syphilis appears not to infect the joints directly except in the most advanced stage of the disease and in congenital syphilis. The latter frequently causes destructive inflammation in the growing cartilaginous ends of the bones of newborn infants. Untreated it leads to deformity and restriction of growth of the involved part (Parrot's pseudoparalysis), but early treatment with penicillin results in complete recovery. Clutton's joint is another type of congenital syphilitic lesion. It is a true inflammation of the synovial membrane that occurs in youngsters between six and 16 years; although it causes swelling of the knees, it is a relatively benign condition. Lesions characteristic of tertiary syphilis sometimes occur in the joints of children who have congenital syphilis. Yaws, a nonvenereal infection by an organism closely related to that causing syphilis, or identical with it, leads to similar skeletal lesions. The condition has largely been eradicated but only a few years ago affected many millions of persons in tropical areas.

Deformities and destructive changes in the joints in leprosy (Hansen's disease) arise from infection of the nerves by the leprosy bacillus or from infection by some other bacteria.

Infectious arthritis occurs in many animal species and is of considerable economic importance in livestock commerce. A chronic rheumatoid-like arthritis in swine has for many years been a major cause for the condemnation of pork in the United States and other countries. One body of opinion attributes it to infection by *Erysipelothrix insidiosa* (*rhusiopathiae*), another to *Mycoplasma hyorhinis.* Mycoplasma organisms are minute filterable bacteria that lack cell walls. They cause arthritis in many avian and mammalian species. Certain types of these organisms cause pneumonia, but there is no proof that they are responsible for arthritis in humans. The situation with another group of filterable agents, the Bedsonia (*Miyagawanella*), is analogous to this except that rare instances of arthritis occur in the venereal disease lymphogranuloma venereum, which is caused by this organism. *Streptobacillus moniliformis,* an organism commonly found in rats, causes arthritis in other species as well and in humans has been responsible for Haverhill fever, characterized by rash, especially on the arms and legs, and by inflammation of several joints. It usually does not last more than about two weeks and is effectively treated with penicillin.

Rheumatoid arthritis and allied disorders. In several types of arthritis that resemble infectious joint disease no causative agent has been isolated. Principal among these is rheumatoid arthritis. This disorder may appear at any age but is most usual in the fourth and fifth decades. A type that affects children is called Still's disease. Rheumatoid arthritis typically affects the same joints on the two sides of the body. Almost any movable joint can be involved, but the fingers, wrists, and knees are particularly susceptible. The joints are especially stiff when the affected person awakes. Rheumatoid arthritis is not only a disease of the joints. Fatigue and anemia indicate that there is a more generalized systemic involvement. A slight fever may sometimes be present. Lesions also occur in sites outside the joints. Involvement of bursas, tendons, and tendon sheaths is an integral part of the disease. Approximately one of five affected persons has nodules in the subcutaneous tissue at the point of the elbow or elsewhere. Inflammatory changes also are found sometimes in small arteries and the pericardium—the membrane enclosing the heart. The eyes occasionally are involved but not as frequently as in Still's disease or in ankylosing spondylitis (see below).

Signs and course of rheumatoid arthritis

The course of the disease varies greatly from person to person and is characterized by a striking tendency toward spontaneous remission and exacerbation. With continuing inflammation of the joints, there is destruction of the joint cartilage. The degree of articular (joint) disability present in rheumatoid arthritis depends in large measure upon the amount of damage done to this cartilage. If the injury is severe, large areas of bone may be denuded of cartilage, so that adhesions form between the articular surfaces. Subsequent transformation of these adhesions into mature fibrous or bony connective tissue leads to firm union between the bony surfaces (ankylosis), which interferes with motion of the joint and may render it totally immobile. In other instances, the loss of cartilage and bone, coupled with weakening of tendons, ligaments, and other supporting structures, results in instability and partial dislocation of the joint. In a small minority of cases, the disease pursues a rapidly progressive course marked by relentless joint destruction and evidence of diffuse vasculitis (inflammation of blood vessels). Many affected persons are benefited over the course of several months by rest, analgesics, and therapeutic exercises. In approximately one-third of the instances of the disease, it progresses and causes serious incapacity. In the absence of proper physical therapy, the joints may become greatly deformed and ankylosed.

There is now convincing evidence that immunologic reactions play an important role in the causation of the processes just listed. Suspicion of this originated with the

Causation of rheumatoid arthritis

observation that the serum of approximately 80–90 percent of persons with rheumatoid arthritis contains an immunoglobulin (called rheumatoid factor) that behaves as an antibody and reacts with another class of immunoglobulin. This immunoglobulin is produced by cells (plasma cells) that are present in sites of tissue injury. There is evidence to suggest that this agent may be one or more viruses or viral antigens that persist in the joint tissues.

Although there is no cure, basic to the treatment are the conservative methods already noted. Adrenal corticosteroid hormones often induce initial dramatic improvements but do not in any way cure rheumatoid arthritis. Their effectiveness generally diminishes with time, and there are definite disadvantages in their use, such as a greater susceptibility to infection and to peptic ulcers. Intramuscular injections of gold compounds have proven effective in a certain proportion of persons. Surgery is often of value in correcting established deformities. A mild, dry climate seems to be beneficial in some cases, but the improvement is generally not sufficient to justify a move that would disrupt the affected person's life.

There is at times a close association between rheumatoid arthritis and seemingly unrelated disorders. In about one-third of the cases of Sjögren's syndrome there is also rheumatoid arthritis, and high levels of rheumatoid factors are usually present in the bloodstream. In Felty's syndrome, rheumatoid arthritis coexists with enlargement of the spleen and diminution in the number of circulating blood cells, particularly the white blood cells. Removal of the spleen restores the blood to normal but has no effect on the arthritis.

Diseases resembling rheumatoid arthritis

Several other types of polyarthritis resemble rheumatoid arthritis but characteristically lack the rheumatoid factors in the bloodstream. One is associated with the skin disease psoriasis. The frequency of the association, roughly 5 percent, is greater than chance would dictate. Psoriatic arthritis also differs from rheumatoid arthritis insofar as it has a predilection for the outer rather than the inner joints of the fingers and toes; furthermore, it results in more destruction of bone. Another type of arthritis is associated with chronic intestinal diseases—ulcerative colitis, regional enteritis, and Whipple's disease. Ankylosing spondylitis, also known as Marie-Strümpell, or Bechterew's, disease, affects some of the peripheral joints, such as the hip; but its principal location is in the spine and sacroiliac joints. In the spine, the small synovial joints and the margins of the intervertebral disks are both involved. These structures become bridged by bone, and the spine is accordingly rigid. Ankylosing spondylitis is a disease of men, the sex ratio being approximately 8:1 over women. The age of onset is lower than that in rheumatoid arthritis. The general management of the two disorders is much the same, but phenylbutazone is more effective in ankylosing spondylitis than in rheumatoid arthritis.

Collagen diseases. The collagen diseases are so called because in all of them abnormalities develop in the collagen-containing connective tissue. These diseases are primarily generalized or systemic, frequently accompanied by joint complaints. The latter may be trivial in comparison to the systemic problems or may be severe enough to simulate rheumatoid arthritis. One of these diseases, systemic lupus erythematosus (SLE) may affect any structure or organ in the body. Some sort of overlap with rheumatoid arthritis is suggested by the fact that one-quarter of those with SLE have positive serological tests for rheumatoid factor, and perhaps as many patients with rheumatoid arthritis have positive L.E. cell tests. In another collagen disease, generalized scleroderma, the skin becomes thickened and tight. Similar changes occur in other organs, particularly the gastrointestinal tract.

Rheumatic fever

Rheumatic fever often is classified with the collagen diseases. It has certain similarities to rheumatoid arthritis, as the name suggests, but the differences are more impressive. In both conditions, arthritis and subcutaneous nodules occur, and inflammation of the pericardium is frequent. Nevertheless the joint manifestations of rheumatic fever typically are evanescent, while those of rheumatoid arthritis are more persistent. The reverse is true of cardiac involvement in the two disorders. There is no compelling evidence that streptococcal infection is an important causative factor in rheumatoid arthritis, but it appears well established in rheumatic fever.

Arthritis more or less resembling rheumatoid arthritis occurs in roughly one-fourth of youngsters who lack gamma globulins in the blood. In this circumstance there is a deficit in the body's mechanisms for forming antibodies. This has sometimes been cited as an argument against the hypothesis holding that rheumatoid arthritis results from hypersensitivity. (Rheumatic fever and SLE are discussed above; see *Connective tissue diseases.*)

Miscellaneous arthritides. Several types of arthritis appear to be related to an altered state of hypersensitivity. Erythema nodosum is a skin disease characterized by the formation of reddened nodules on the anterior surface of the lower extremities. In the majority of cases pain may arise in various joints and sometimes swelling appears. Lymph nodes at the hilus of the lung (the site of entrance of bronchus, blood vessels, and nerves) are enlarged. The synovitis disappears in the course of several weeks or months. Although this is not always so, many cases are associated with drug hypersensitivity, with evolving infections such as tuberculosis, coccidioidomycosis, and leprosy, and with Boeck's sarcoidosis, a systemic disease in which nodules form in the lymph nodes and in other organs and structures of the body. Synovitis of this sort occurs in 10 to 15 percent of patients with sarcoidosis. Occasionally, sarcoid joint disease becomes chronic and may simulate rheumatoid arthritis.

Palindromic (recurring) rheumatism is an arthritis of unknown cause. There is no fever. Each attack lasts but a day or two and leaves no permanent effects. Nevertheless palindromic rheumatism rarely remits completely and in perhaps one-third of cases eventuates in rheumatoid arthritis. Polymyalgia rheumatica, a relatively frequent although only recently recognized condition occurring in older people, is characterized by aching and stiffness in the muscles in the region of the hips and shoulders, but the joints proper seem not to be involved. There does seem to be some relationship to one type of arterial inflammation, temporal or giant cell arteritis. Polymyalgia rheumatica is not usually accompanied by serious systemic abnormalities and is treated with small doses of corticosteroids.

NONINFLAMMATORY JOINT DISEASES: INJURY AND DEGENERATIVE DISORDERS

Traumatic joint diseases. Blunt injuries to joints vary in severity from mild sprains to overt fractures and dislocations. A sprain is a damage to ligaments, tendons, and muscles that follows a sudden wrench and momentary subluxation of a joint. There is some slight hemorrhage into these tissues and healing usually takes place in several days. More violent stresses may cause tears in ligaments and tendons. Because the ligaments and tendons are so strong they frequently are torn from their bony attachments rather than ripped into segments. Ligamentous, tendinous, and capsular tears are able to heal by fibrous union provided that the edges are not totally separated from each other. Internal derangements of the knee most often arise from tears in the semilunar cartilages (menisci). Usually it is the medial meniscus that is disrupted. These tears are particularly frequent in athletes and develop as the knee is twisted while the foot remains fixed on the ground. Locking of the knee is a characteristic symptom. Because the semilunar cartilages have little capacity for repair, they must be removed surgically. Bleeding into the joint, called hemarthrosis, may also result from injuries. Other things being equal, it is desirable to remove the blood that has leaked from the blood vessels.

Sprains, tears, and dislocations

Most traumatic dislocations are treated by prolonged immobilization to permit the capsular and other tears to heal over. In some instances surgical repairs are required. Fractures of bone in the vicinity of joints may or may not extend into the joint space. Whether they do or not, the normal contour of the joint must be restored or arthritic complications are likely to develop. Other sorts of complication are also seen at times. In Sudeck's atrophy the nearby but unfractured bone becomes porous and is painful. The syndrome is believed to result from neurovascular reflexes originating in the injured tissue. Treatment is therefore directed at interrupting the sympathetic nerve pathways. In Volkmann's contracture, the muscles about the injured joint (most often the elbow) become converted into a shrunken fibrous mass, and the extremity becomes deformed and useless.

Degenerative joint disease. Osteoarthritis is a ubiquitous disorder affecting all adults to a greater or lesser degree by the time they have reached middle age. It is not restricted to humans. The name osteoarthritis is a misnomer insofar as its suffix implies that the condition has an inherently inflammatory nature. For this reason it frequently is called degenerative joint disease or, in Europe, osteoarthrosis or arthrosis deformans. When the spine is involved, the corresponding term is spondylosis. Unlike rheumatoid arthritis, osteoarthritis rarely causes crippling deformities. In the majority of instances, the milder anatomical changes are not accompanied by appreciable symptoms. There are no systemic complaints directly attributable to the joint disease. The changes are characterized by abrasive wearing away of the articular cartilage concurrent with a reshaping of adjacent ends of the bones. As a result, masses of newly proliferated bone (osteophytes) protrude from the margins of the joints.

Osteoarthritis of the hip

The clinical manifestations of osteoarthritis vary with the location and severity of the lesions. The most disabling form occurs in the hip joint, where it is known as malum coxae senilis. Osteoarthritis of the hip, like that of other joints, is classified as primary and secondary. In secondary osteoarthritis, the changes come about as a consequence of some antecedent structural or postural abnormality of the joint. In about half the cases, however, even rigorous examination fails to disclose such an abnormality; in these instances, the osteoarthritis is called primary.

Probably the most frequent cause of osteoarthritis of the hip is congenital dysplasia (dislocation or subluxation of the hip). This term refers to a poor fit of the head of the femur, the long bone of the thigh, with its socket in the pelvis, the acetabulum. There is impressive evidence that many cases arise in infancy as a consequence of swaddling infants or carrying them in headboards, procedures that keep the thighs in an extended position. Before the child is ready for walking, the hip joint has frequently not yet fully developed and the head of the femur is forced out of its normal position by this extension.

Osteoarthritis of the hip occurring in relatively young persons—in their 30s or 40s—frequently follows a progressive course and requires surgical treatment. Two rather different strategies of surgery have been employed: one, an osteotomy, involves reshaping the upper end of the femur so that the load borne by the joint is distributed more efficiently; the other requires removal of the diseased tissue and replacement by an artificial joint.

Aside from the rapidly developing forms, osteoarthritis of the hips also appears frequently in aged persons. Chronologic aging is an important factor in the development of other forms of degenerative joint disease as well, since the lesions increase in frequency and severity as time passes by.

Causes of osteoarthritis

Considerations like these have led to the view that the principal causative factors in degenerative arthritis are faulty mechanical loading and senescent deterioration of joint tissue. Single injuries, unless they leave a joint permanently deformed, rarely result in osteoarthritis. Recurrent small athletic and occupational injuries, such as those arising from heavy pneumatic drill vibrations, apparently are more likely to do so. Lifting heavy weights has been implicated in some studies of spinal involvement.

Aside from surgery of the sort noted in the hip and sometimes the knee, the treatment program is rest and proper exercise, avoidance of injury, the use of analgesics to relieve pain, and several types of physical therapy.

Chondromalacia patellae is a common and distinctive softening of the articular cartilage of the kneecap in young persons, particularly young athletes. It results in "catching" and discomfort in the region of the patella, or kneecap, as the knee is bent and straightened out. Pathologically the changes are indistinguishable from changes that occur early in osteoarthritis. The condition often responds poorly to conservative measures and is treated surgically.

Degeneration of the intervertebral disk is a frequent and in some ways analogous disorder. Often this occurs acutely in young and middle-aged adults, and the pulpy centre of the disk pushes out through tears in the fibrous outer ring (so-called slipped disk). When this takes place in the lumbosacral region, the displaced centre (the nucleus pulposus) impinges on the adjacent nerve roots and causes shooting pains in the distribution of the sciatic nerve—hence the name sciatica. Pain in the small of the back is loosely referred to as lumbago, or lumbosacral sprain. It may be associated not only with degeneration of the intervertebral disk and spondylosis but also with structural anomalies of the region. Principal among these is spondylolisthesis, in which there is an anterior displacement of one lumbosacral vertebral body on another. The episodes respond to bed rest and mechanical support from wearing an abdominal corset or brace. Muscle relaxants may be of value. Recurrences are prevented by avoidance of back strains. Muscle-strengthening exercises are frequently helpful. The protruding tissue is removed by surgery only in cases in which pain and neurological defects are severe and fail to improve after less drastic measures.

CONGENITAL AND HEREDITARY ABNORMALITIES

Clubfoot and other deformities

Congenital abnormalities are not necessarily transmitted from generation to generation but can be acquired during fetal life or soon after delivery. The latter abnormalities usually are structural; the inherited defects may be structural or appear later in life as the consequence of a systemic metabolic defect present from conception. Mention has already been made of congenital dysplasia of the hip. The joint proper may be normal initially in this and in several other congenital disorders; only after other supporting tissues have altered the proper relationships does the contour of the bone and joint become distorted. In arthrogryposis multiplex congenita (multiple congenital crooked joints), many joints are deformed at birth, particularly the hip. The deformities are the consequence of weakness of muscles that, in turn, sometimes results from spinal cord disease. Clubfoot (talipes equinovarus) is a congenital deformity of the foot, which is twisted downward and inward because the ligaments and tendons are too short. Only infrequently are the muscles at fault. Idiopathic scoliosis (lateral curvature of the spine) usually makes its appearance during early adolescence. There is considerable plasticity of the tissues with latitude for correction of these deformities and for preventing their progression. For this reason, the application of splints and other mechanical supports as soon as the condition is recognized is the major part of their management. Surgery is resorted to in cases when other measures have failed.

Structural variations in the lumbosacral spine are common and often harmless. Incompletely ossified interarticular portions of the neural arches of a vertebra constitute a congenital anomaly referred to as spondylolysis; it predisposes to forward slipping of the vertebra later in life and so to the congenital type of spondylolisthesis described above. By contrast, when the failure of bony fusion exists between the right and left halves of the neural arch, the condition is called spina bifida occulta. This does not favour development of conditions that cause backache.

Gout, pseudogout, and ochronotic arthropathy

Several genetically influenced metabolic diseases have important articular manifestations. Gout is the most frequent of these. Chalklike masses of sodium acid urate crystals are deposited in and about the joints. Acute episodes of gouty arthritis are extremely painful. There is a tendency toward involvement of the great toe, a condition known as podagra (see also METABOLISM: *Metabolic diseases*).

Ochronotic arthropathy results from another but rarer inborn error of metabolism. It is characterized by pigmentation and degeneration of hyaline cartilage and by defective breakdown of the amino acids tyrosine and phenylalanine at an intermediate level, causing large amounts of homogentisic acid to accumulate in body fluids and the urine. The urine turns black when exposed to air, a phenomenon called alkaptonuria. After many years severe degenerative changes occur in the peripheral joints and in the spine.

In yet another metabolic disease, chondrocalcinosis, or pseudogout, crystals of calcium pyrophosphate are deposited in joint cartilages. There are several forms of the disease. Sometimes there are no symptoms. In other cases, symptoms are sufficiently severe to cause confusion with rheumatoid arthritis. Some cases run in families.

Other inherited disorders

Joints also are affected by several relatively rare heritable defects in the metabolism of connective tissue matrices. In Hurler's syndrome, for example, the most important manifestations are mental retardation and heart failure, though skeletal growth also is abnormal. Most affected persons do not survive adolescence. Morquio–Brailsford disease, by contrast, is a recessively inherited form of severe dwarfism that is not associated with mental deficiency or cardiac insufficiency. X-ray films of the spine reveal a characteristic misshapen flattened appearance of the vertebral bodies. Premature and severe degenerative changes in the peripheral and spinal joints are usual. Polyepiphyseal dysplasias (abnormal development of a number of epiphyses—the ends or outlying portions of bone, in childhood separated from the main body of the bone by cartilage) are a vaguely similar, though much milder, group of conditions in which precocious osteoarthritis and spondylosis are the first abnormalities to appear. Preexisting changes in the skeleton, resembling a milder form of Morquio–Brailsford disease, may then be discovered by X-ray examination. The hip joint is most severely affected. In some cases the inheritance is dominant, in others recessive. Abnormalities in the fibrous components of connective tissue matrices are exemplified by Marfan's syndrome. Many organs are affected in this condition, and the articular manifestations are less important. The joints are, however, excessively loose, and painful complications develop in about half of these patients.

SECONDARY JOINT DISEASES

Hemorrhagic joint diseases. Hemarthrosis (bleeding into the joints) is a major complication of hemorrhagic disorders. It constitutes, aside from the life-threatening episodes of bleeding, the principal disability arising from the hemophilias.

Most persons with these clotting defects are affected, and usually within the first years of life. Bleeding into the joints is usually precipitated by relatively minor injury but may leave several residual deformities and loss of mobility of the part. Hemarthrosis is not ordinarily present in thrombocytopenic purpura, bleeding associated with a shortage of blood platelets. Recurrent hemorrhage into an isolated joint, in the absence of a systemic tendency to bleed, is a characteristic of pigmented villonodular synovitis, a disease characterized by abnormal thickening and coloration of the synovial membrane. The precise source of this bleeding is not known. This is not a primary inflammatory disease of joints, despite the name, the thickening of the synovial tissue being a response to the hemorrhagic exudation. Large joints, usually of the lower extremity, are affected.

Joint involvement in aseptic necrosis

Aseptic necrosis. Because joint cartilages are without blood vessels, they are more immune to failures in the blood supply than are the underlying bones. Nevertheless, several clinically important joint diseases arise in association with aseptic necrosis—tissue death not caused by infection—of bone next to the joints. The precise nature of the failure of the blood supply is not always known. Fractures are one obvious cause. In caisson disease the obstructive elements are minute gas bubbles formed in the circulating blood from excessively rapid decompression. Decompression syndromes occur principally in divers and tunnel workers. Acute cases take the form of "bends" and frequently are fatal. However, in a large proportion of workers in these occupations, even those who have not experienced bends, extensive infarcts (areas of dead tissue) of bones and secondary osteoarthritis develop after many years. Analogous changes in sickle-cell anemias presumably result from blood clotting related to the abnormality of the red blood cells. There is no entirely persuasive explanation for other types of aseptic necrosis that occur in adults. In each instance, the hip is the joint most affected. Osteochondritis dissecans is a basically similar disorder in which a piece of joint cartilage and of underlying bone breaks off and lodges in the joint cavity. Usually the person affected can remember having injured the joint. The knee is the most frequent site. The condition usually occurs during the second and third decades of life. The displaced fragment causes a creaking sound when the joint is moved and must be removed by surgery.

Two different patterns of aseptic necrosis with joint involvement occur in growing children. One type (so-called slipped epiphysis) is characterized by partial or complete tearing away of an epiphysis, usually as the result of injury. The epiphysis at the upper end of the thighbone is particularly susceptible. Osgood–Schlatter disease is an analogous lesion, but it affects a growth centre (anterior tibial tubercle) at a slight distance from the joint rather than in its immediate vicinity. In the second type of aseptic necrosis in children, the necrosis is not the consequence of mechanical tearing away of the part. The most frequent site is in the head of the thighbone; necrosis at this site is known as Legg–Calvé–Perthes disease. It occurs in youngsters between the ages of three and 13 and is much more frequent in boys than in girls. Persistent pain is the most prominent symptom. Uncorrected severe lesions lead to arrest of growth, deformity, and arthritic changes in the hip joint.

Enlarged joints in acromegaly

Endocrine factors. The only joint lesion clearly related to a malfunctioning of the ductless (endocrine) glands is acromegaly. This disease results from excessive secretion of growth hormone by a tumour of the anterior pituitary gland. The hormone stimulates the proliferation of several skeletal soft tissues including the joint cartilage of the peripheral joints. This causes the enlargement of the fingers that is characteristic of the disease. The enlarged joints are particularly prone to undergo osteoarthritic degeneration. Cretinism, which is related to hypothyroidism, causes dwarfism and abnormally developed bony epiphyses but apparently does not lead to joint disease. Severe diabetes mellitus, however, may result in joint disease arising from the effect of diabetes on the nervous system.

Neurogenic arthropathy. A Charcot joint is a severe degenerative disease that develops when the sensory mechanisms of joints are impaired. The current view is that these joints become excessively strained because the ability to receive stimuli from bodily structures and organs necessary for normal limitation of motion is lacking. As a result the supporting tissues are torn and extreme disintegration of the structure results. Neurogenic arthropathy (joint disease related to nerve lesions) is most often associated with tabes dorsalis, a late form of syphilis affecting the posterior columns of the spinal cord. Other neurological lesions, including those associated with diabetes mellitus, syringomyelia (a disease in which cavities develop in the gray substance of the spinal cord), pernicious anemia, and leprosy, also are sometimes responsible. The disease usually is localized to one joint or one group of joints, depending on the location of the nerve defect. Pain is frequently mild considering the massive distortion of the joint. Treatment is difficult and is based primarily on immobilization and restriction of weight-bearing. Surgical fusion of the joints rarely succeeds.

Hypertrophic osteoarthropathy. In approximately 5 to 10 percent of persons who have primary tumours within the chest, the ends of the bones near the joints become enlarged and painful. New bone is formed in the periosteum and only occasionally do abnormalities develop within the joints themselves. Just how the chest abnormality leads to hypertrophic osteoarthropathy (disease of bones and joints with abnormal growth of bone) is somewhat of a mystery, but there is reason to believe that the vagus nerve is involved, since the condition is usually relieved promptly by cutting the vagus. It is also relieved by removal of the tumour. In this disorder the tips of the fingers become club-shaped, a painless lesion that occurs in many other circumstances, as well.

Shoulder–hand syndrome. The shoulder–hand syndrome, so called because pain in the shoulder is associated with pain, swelling, and stiffness of the hand, only rarely develops in the wake of external injury. Most often it follows a heart attack (myocardial infarction) or is associated with disease in the neck vertebrae; frequently there is no apparent explanation. Most often the syndrome begins with pain and stiffness of a shoulder, followed shortly by pain and swelling of the hand, with vascular (blood vessel) changes in the skin of the hand. Over the course of several months the swelling and vascular changes subside but the skin and soft tissues become tightened. These changes sometimes disappear completely, but in other cases they leave permanent contractures; *i.e.,* flexion and loss of mobility due to the tightening of the fingers. Loss of mineral occurs in the bones of the shoulder, wrist, and fingers. Blocking (interruption of functioning) of sympathetic nerves serving the area, administration of adrenal hormones (corticosteroids), and therapeutic exercises are used in the management of the condition.

Tumours of joints. Tumours of joints are uncommon. In synovial chondromatosis, a benign condition, numerous cartilaginous nodules form in the soft tissues of the joint. The lesion is usually confined to one joint, particularly the knee, and occurs in young or middle-aged adults. It may or may not cause pain or swelling and usually is cured by excision of a portion of the synovial membrane. The tumour rarely becomes malignant. The cartilaginous nodules sometimes also contain islands of bone; in this circumstance the lesion is called synovial osteochondromatosis. Like synovial chondromatosis, synovial osteochondromatosis is often a spontaneous or primary disorder of unknown cause. In many cases, however, it is a development secondary to other diseases of the synovium, such as rheumatoid arthritis and even osteoarthritis.

Synoviomas, malignant tumours of the joints, arise in the tissues around the joints—the capsule, the tendon sheaths, the bursas, the fasciae, and the intermuscular septa or divisions—and only rarely within the joint proper. Although they may occur at any age, they are most frequent in adolescents and young adults. The legs are more often involved than the arms. The tumours spread locally and also to regional lymph nodes and lungs. Synoviomas are not particularly sensitive to X rays, and treatment with drugs has been ineffective. If distant spread has not occurred at the time the condition is identified, radical excision, usually with amputation of the part, is the recommended treatment. (L.S./Ed.)

BIBLIOGRAPHY

Skeletal systems: R.B. CLARK, *Dynamics in Metazoan Evolution* (1964), deals with some aspects of the coelomate condition, hydrostatic skeletons, metamerism, and their evolution. Detailed description of the anatomy of the human skeleton is given in *Cunningham's Textbook of Anatomy,* 12th ed. by G.J. ROMANES (1981); and in PETER L. WILLIAMS and ROGER WARWICK (eds.), *Gray's Anatomy,* 36th ed. (1980). J. GRAY, *Animal Locomotion* (1968), a comprehensive, comparative account of the coordination and mechanisms of vertebrate locomotion, with some chapters on invertebrates (the approach is for the nonspecialist, but the treatment is mathematical and neurological); W.J. HAMILTON (ed.), *Textbook of Human Anatomy* (1956), a concise and readable account of the anatomy of the skeleton of man; A.S. ROMER, *The Vertebrate Body,* 4th ed. (1970), an excellent account of the evolution of the skeleton in vertebrates; J.Z. YOUNG, *The Life of Vertebrates,* 2nd ed. (1962), and *An Introduction to the Study of Man* (1971); KATHY E. GOLDBERG, *The Skeleton* (1982), a popularly written anatomy; and J.E. FRAZER, *Anatomy of the Human Skeleton,* 6th ed. (1965), a classic in the field of osteology. Two works useful for understanding the functional aspects and structural adaptations of bone are G.H. BARNETT, "Joints and Movement" in F. GOLDBY and R.J. HARRISON (eds.), *Recent Advances in Anatomy,* 2nd ed., ch. 12, pp. 404–422 (1962); and M.C. HALL and D.S. KINOSHITA, *Architecture of Bone* (1966).

Connective tissue: Additional information on connective tissues may be found in W. BLOOM and D.W. FAWCETT, *Textbook of Histology,* 9th ed., ch. 10, pp. 131–164, and ch. 12, pp. 347–357 (1968); and in A.W. HAM, *Histology,* 6th ed., pt. 3, ch. 10, pp. 205–227 (1969).

Bone: F.C. MCLEAN and M.R. URIST, *Bone: Fundamentals of the Physiology of Skeletal Tissue,* 3rd ed. (1968), a comprehensive survey of bone structure and metabolic function; H.M. FROST (ed.), *Bone Biodynamics* (1964), a series of authoritative essays on topics of chemistry, structure, function, and disease; W.H. HARRIS and R.P. HEANEY, *Skeletal Renewal and Metabolic Bone Disease* (1970), a review of skeletal remodelling processes, with emphasis on their control mechanisms and on methods of measuring remodelling in the living skeleton; K. RODAHL, J.T. NICHOLSON, and E.M. BROWN (eds.), *Bone as a Tissue* (1960), a series of essays and reviews on topics of bone structure, physiology, and disease; and C.L. COMAR and F. BRONNER (eds.), *Mineral Metabolism,* vol. 1B, 2A, and 3 (1960–69), exhaustive and definitive reviews of the chemistry and metabolism of the principal mineral components of bone. See also MARSHALL R. URIST (ed.), *Fundamental and Clinical Bone Physiology* (1980), which covers bone diseases as well.

Joint: C.H. BARNETT *et al., Synovial Joints: Their Structure and Mechanics* (1961), a text on the general arthrology of synovial joints that contains early advances; M.A. MACCONAILL and J.V. BASMAJIAN, *Muscles and Movements* (1969), which includes a theory of kinematics of muscles and joints and the information about how movements are brought about at individual joints or joint systems as revealed by electromyography; and the *Journal of Bone and Joint Surgery* (8/year), current research in both basic and applied arthrology from all parts of the English-speaking world. DHANJOO N. GHISTA (ed.), *Osteoarthromechanics* (1982), discusses bone physiology, human mechanics, and joint anatomy.

Connective tissue diseases: Detailed accounts of the connective tissue diseases and of the rheumatic disorders in general may be found in W.S.C. COPEMAN (ed.), *Textbook of the Rheumatic Diseases,* 4th ed. (1969); and JAMES A. BOYLE and W. WATSON BUCHANAN, *Clinical Rheumatology* (1971). VICTOR A. MCKUSICK, *Heritable Disorders of Connective Tissue,* 3rd ed. (1966), is an authoritative text dealing with the genetically transmitted connective tissue diseases. IAN R. MACKAY and F. MACFARLANE BURNET, *Autoimmune Diseases* (1963), was one of the first to clearly formulate and champion the role of autoimmunity in the connective tissue diseases and a number of other maladies of obscure etiology. MAX SAMTER (ed.), *Immunological Diseases,* 2nd ed., 2 vol. (1971), describes the mechanisms whereby aberrant immunity leads to tissue damage. Briefer, clinically oriented accounts may be found in MICHAEL MASON and HARRY L.F. CURREY (eds.), *An Introduction to Clinical Rheumatology* (1970), and the *Primer on the Rheumatic Diseases,* 7th ed. (1972). EDMUND L. DUBOIS (ed.), *Lupus Erythematosus* (1966), provides an exhaustive summary of the condition that has been influential in the development of the modern concept of connective tissue disease. See also BERNARD M. WAGNER, RAUL FLEISCHMAJER, and NATHAN KAUFMAN (eds.), *Connective Tissue Diseases* (1983).

Bone diseases and injuries: R.B. SALTER, *Textbook of Disorders and Injuries of the Musculoskeletal System* (1970), a comprehensive modern text dealing with aspects of orthopedics, rheumatology, metabolic bone disease, rehabilitation, and fractures as they relate to joint diseases, including bibliographies in each subsection; W.J.W. SHARRARD, *Paediatric Orthopaedics and Fractures* (1971), a comprehensive textbook written by a specialist in neurological and developmental abnormalities in children; E.E. AEGERTER and J.A. KIRKPATRICK, JR., *Orthopaedic Diseases: Physiology, Pathology, Radiology,* 3rd ed. (1968), a standard text on bone pathology, particularly tumour pathology; L. LICHTENSTEIN, *Diseases of Bones and Joints* (1970), a modern text on nontumorous diseases; and A.H. CRENSHAW (ed.), *Campbell's Operative Orthopaedics,* 5th ed., 2 vol. (1971), a standard text on bone and joint surgery. C.L. BERRY (ed.), *Bone and Joint Diseases* (1982), is a text on the diagnosis of bone disease. For a visual approach, see VICTOR PARSONS and GEORGE STIRLING, *Color Atlas of Bone Disease* (1980).

Joint diseases and injuries: W.S.C. COPEMAN, *A Short History of the Gout and the Rheumatic Diseases* (1964), a scholarly history of arthritis and rheumatism, and (ed.), *Textbook of the Rheumatic Diseases,* 4th ed. (1969); and J.L. HOLLANDER and D.J. MCARTY (eds.), *Arthritis and Allied Conditions,* 8th ed. (1972), two authoritative texts; L. SOKOLOFF, *The Biology of Degenerative Joint Disease* (1969), a systematic consideration of the pathogenesis of osteoarthritis; and J.H. TALBOTT, *Gout,* 3rd ed. (1967).

Suriname

The Republic of Suriname (Republiek Suriname) lies on the northern coast of South America. The country covers 63,251 square miles (163,820 square kilometres), excluding two disputed territories totaling some 6,800 square miles in the southwest and southeast, bordering on Guyana and French Guiana, respectively. Suriname is bordered on the north by the Atlantic Ocean, on the east by French Guiana, on the south by Brazil, and on the west by Guyana. The capital is Paramaribo.

Suriname is one of the smallest countries in South America. Formerly known as Dutch Guiana, it was a plantation colony of The Netherlands. Suriname gained its independence on Nov. 25, 1975.

This article is divided into the following sections:

Physical and human geography

THE LAND

Relief and drainage. The narrow coastal zone, some 226 miles (364 kilometres) long, consists of sandbanks and mudbanks deposited by the southern equatorial currents from the area surrounding the mouth of the Amazon River. South of the mudbanks begins the New Coastal Plain, also formed from sand and clay from the mouth of the Amazon. The region, covering some 6,600 square miles, consists of swampland. The soil of the swamps is clay, in which a great deal of peat has formed. The region is traversed by sandy ridges that run parallel to the coast. Suriname's most fertile soils occur in the inundated lands reclaimed by diking and drainage (polders), which are principally in the New Coastal Plain.

The New Coastal Plain

South of the New Coastal Plain is the Old Coastal Plain, which covers some 1,550 square miles. It consists largely of fine clays and sands and contains a variety of topographies, including old ridges, clay flats, and swamps.

South of the Old Coastal Plain is the Zanderij formation, a 40-mile-wide landscape of rolling hills. This formation rests on bleached sand sediments, rich in quartz. Most of the region is covered by tropical rain forest, but swamps and areas of savanna grassland are also found.

Farther to the south is an area, covering some 80 percent of the country, that consists largely of a central mountain range, its various branches, and scattered hilly areas. The southern four-fifths of the country is almost entirely covered with tropical rain forest. In the southwest near the Brazilian border is the Sipaliwini Plain, another savanna area. The highest summit, at 4,035 feet (1,230 metres), is Juliana Top, in the Wilhelmina Mountains.

Suriname's major rivers flow northward into the Atlantic. They include the Courantyne, which forms part of the boundary with Guyana, the Coppename, the Suriname, and the Maroni, which forms part of the border with French Guiana.

Climate. Suriname has a tropical climate. The populated area in the north has four seasons: a minor rainy season from early December to early February, a minor dry season from early February to late April, a major rainy season from late April to mid-August, and a major dry season from mid-August to early December. Daytime temperatures in Paramaribo range between 73° and 88° F (23° and 31° C), with an annual average temperature of 81° F (27° C). In the interior, diurnal temperature extremes can vary by as much as 18° F (11° C). The range in average temperatures between the warmest month, September, and the coldest, January, is only 3° F (2° C). Rainfall is highest in the central and southeastern parts of the country. Annual rainfall averages 76 inches (1,930 millimetres) in the west and 95 inches in Paramaribo.

Plant and animal life. The flora of the coastal area is better known than that of the interior. It consists of some 4,000 species of ferns and seed plants and a large number of mosses, weeds, and mildews. About 90 percent of Suriname's area is covered with heterogeneous tropical forest consisting of more than 1,000 species of trees. The baboen (*Virola surinamensis*), which grows in the coastal area, is used to make plywood. The kapok (*Ceiba pentandra*) reaches a height of more than 150 feet.

Animal life

There are some 150 species of mammals, including monkeys, wild pigs, deer, manatees, jaguars, ocelots, armadillos, sloths, and anteaters. The tapir is the largest land mammal. Reptiles include caimans, iguanas, and the boa constrictor. The beaches on the eastern part of the coast are breeding grounds for marine turtles, which are protected by law. About 650 species of birds, including hummingbirds, vultures, and parrots, have been identified. Some 350 species of fish occupy coastal and inland waters.

Settlement patterns. Some 80 percent of the total population is concentrated in Paramaribo and the surrounding area. Small urban centres include Nieuw Nickerie, in the northwest near the Guyanese border; Albina, in the northeast on the border with French Guiana; Moengo, in the centre of the bauxite-mining region in northeastern Suriname; and Paranam, in the bauxite-mining and bauxite-processing region on the Suriname River south of Paramaribo. Small settlements of Bush Negroes (descendants of escaped African slaves) and South American Indians make up almost the entire population of the interior. Some Indian villages are located in the coastal area, and nomadic Indian tribes live along the Brazilian border in the south.

THE PEOPLE

The so-called Hindustanis, or East Indians, descendants of contract labourers from India, are the largest ethnic group, with more than a third of the population. The second major ethnic group is the Creoles, people of African or mixed European and African descent, who make up about a third of the population. The descendants of Javanese contract labourers make up about 14 percent of the population. Bush Negroes constitute less than 10 percent of the population, and American Indians make up about 3 percent. Minor ethnic groups include descendants of Chinese, Jewish, Lebanese, Portuguese, and Dutch immigrants; Creoles from the West Indies; and a few North Americans.

Dutch is the official language, but the extent to which

members of the various ethnic groups are able to use the language differs. Most of the population learns Dutch as a second language. English is widely spoken. Additional languages include Sranan (Taki-Taki) and other creole languages; Sarnami, which originated from Hindi and Urdu; Javanese; and a number of American Indian languages.

The principal religion is Christianity, imposed on the population by European colonizers. About a third of the Creoles are Protestant, and another third are Roman Catholic. The East Indians are predominantly Hindu. Most of the Javanese and a small East Indian group are Muslim. Judaism, present in Suriname since the early 16th century, is still practiced, and many of the Chinese are Confucians. African and native Indian religions are still widely practiced.

The population has a relatively high rate of natural increase. Birth and death rates have decreased since the 1960s. About 40 percent of the population is under 15 years of age, and about 75 percent is under 30. After 1973, when it was announced that Suriname would become independent, a large number of people emigrated to The Netherlands. By 1980, according to some estimates, one-third of the population had left the country; many of those who left were professionals and skilled workers.

Refugees

With the rise in 1986 of a guerrilla movement, based in northeastern Suriname and enjoying widespread support among Bush Negroes, the National Army has carried out raids in the Bush Negro villages. The killing and detaining of a large number of Bush Negroes has resulted in the flight of some 10,000 to 12,000 of them to French Guiana.

THE ECONOMY

Suriname has a higher standard of living than many Latin-American countries. During the 1980s the economy experienced a decline, resulting mainly from falling export prices for bauxite and from a reduction in development aid from the United States and The Netherlands. This decline was marked by inflation, a growing budget deficit, and unemployment. Government expenditures account for almost half of total consumption. The civil service employs about 45 percent of the work force.

Agriculture, forestry, and fishing. Less than 1 percent of Suriname's land is arable, and about half of this is cultivated. Most of the farmland is on the New Coastal Plain. In this region drainage is necessary most of the year, owing to a surplus of precipitation. During dry periods evaporation exceeds precipitation, and irrigation is necessary.

More than half of the cultivated land in Suriname is planted with rice, the basic food staple. There are two rice harvests every year, the principal one in the spring and

■ Cities over 10,000
● Cities 5,000 to 10,000
• Cities under 5,000
National capitals
District capitals
PARA District names
International boundaries
International boundaries disputed
District boundaries
Dams
Waterfalls and rapids
Swamps and marshes
National parks
▲ Spot elevations in metres (1 m = 3.28 ft)
Scale 1:5,940,000
1 inch equals approx. 95 miles
Double Transverse Mercator Projection
© Encyclopædia Britannica Inc.

MAP INDEX

Political subdivisions
Brokopondo . . . . 04 20 N 55 20 W
Commewijne . . . . 05 25 N 54 50 W
Coronie . . . . . . 05 50 N 56 20 W
Marowijne . . . . . 04 15 N 54 35 W
Nickerie . . . . . . 04 00 N 57 30 W
Para . . . . 05 30 N 55 15 W
Saramacca . . . . 04 45 N 56 00 W
Suriname . . . . . 05 40 N 54 58 W

Cities and towns
Afobaka . . . . . . 05 00 N 54 59 W
Albina . . . . 05 30 N 54 03 W
Benzdorp . . . . . 03 41 N 54 05 W
Bitagron . . . . . . 05 10 N 56 06 W
Brokopondo . . . . 05 04 N 54 58 W
Brownsweg . . . . 05 01 N 55 10 W
Goddo . . . . 04 01 N 55 28 W
Groningen . . . . . 05 48 N 55 28 W
Mariënburg . . . . 05 53 N 55 03 W
Meerzorg . . . . . 05 49 N 55 09 W
Moengo . . . . . . 05 37 N 54 24 W
Nieuw Amsterdam . . . . 05 53 N 55 05 W
Nieuw Nickerie . . 05 57 N 56 59 W
Onverwacht . . . . 05 36 N 55 12 W
Paramaribo . . . . 05 50 N 55 10 W
Paranam . . . . . . 05 37 N 55 06 W
Totness . . . . . . 05 53 N 56 19 W
Wageningen . . . . 05 46 N 56 41 W
Zanderij . . . . . . 05 27 N 55 12 W

Physical features and points of interest
Atlantic Ocean . . . . . . 06 15 N 56 00 W
Bakhuis Mountains . . . . 04 21 N 56 45 W
Bofroe Rapids . . . 02 59 N 55 52 W
Coeroeni, see Courantyne
Commewijne, river . . . . . . 05 54 N 55 05 W
Coppename, river . . . . . . 05 48 N 55 55 W
Coppename River Mouth Nature Reserve . . 05 59 N 55 35 W
Courantyne (Coeroeni), river . 03 23 N 57 36 W
Eilerts de Haan Mountains . . . . 03 00 N 56 10 W
Eilerts de Haan Nature Reserve . 03 20 N 56 30 W
Gran, river . . . . . 04 01 N 55 31 W
Grandafoetoe Rapids . . . . 03 29 N 55 10 W
Hendrik Top . . . . 04 12 N 56 12 W
Juliana Top . . . . 03 41 N 56 32 W
Kabalebo, river . . 05 02 N 57 21 W
Kayser Mountains. . . . 03 03 N 56 35 W
Lawa, river . . . . . 04 22 N 54 26 W
Lely Mountains . . 04 25 N 54 39 W
Litani, river . . . . . 03 18 N 54 06 W
Lucie, river . . . . . 03 35 N 57 38 W
Maratakka, river . 05 46 N 56 41 W
Maripa Falls . . . . 03 38 N 54 02 W
Maroni (Marowijne), river . . . . 05 45 N 53 58 W
Mount Browns Nature Park . . . . 04 55 N 55 12 W
Mount Tafel Nature Reserve . 03 55 N 56 15 W
Voltz Hill–Raleigh Falls Nature Reserve . . . . . . 04 45 N 56 10 W
Nickerie, river . . . 05 59 N 57 00 W
Oelemari, river . . . 03 13 N 54 09 W
Oranje Mountains . . . . 03 00 N 55 05 W
Paloemeu, river . . 03 21 N 55 26 W
Pikien, river . . . . . 04 01 N 55 28 W
Poeloegoedoe Falls . . . . 04 22 N 54 26 W
Saramacca, river . 05 51 N 55 53 W
Sipaliwini, river . . 02 21 N 56 52 W
Sipaliwini Nature Reserve . . . . . . 02 00 N 56 00 W
Suriname, river . . . 05 55 N 55 10 W
Tapanahoni, river . 04 22 N 54 27 W
Tijger Falls . . . . . 03 56 N 57 56 W
Tumuc-Humac Mountains . . . . 02 20 N 55 00 W
Van Asch van Wijck Mountains . . . . 04 15 N 55 42 W
Wia-Wia Nature Reserve . . . . . . 05 50 N 54 30 W
Wilhelmina Mountains . . . . . 03 45 N 56 30 W
W.J. van Blommestein Lake, reservoir . . 04 45 N 55 00 W
Wonotobo Falls . . 04 22 N 57 58 W

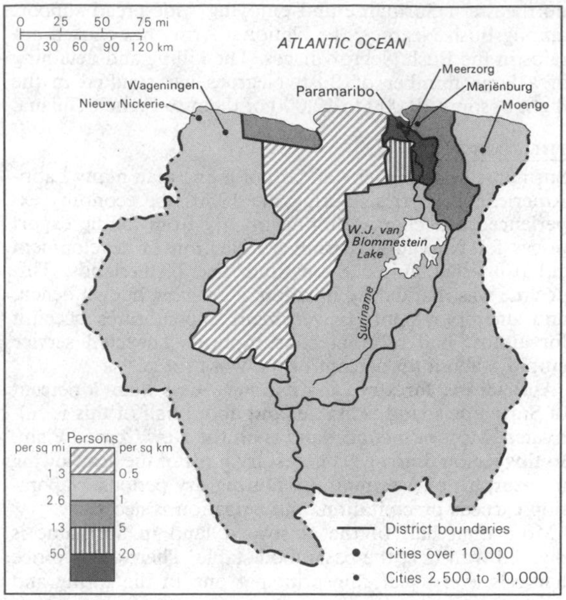

Population density of Suriname.

a second crop in the autumn. Some rice is exported, as are bananas, citrus fruits, coconuts, and palm oil. Sugar, coffee, and cocoa, formerly important export items, are produced mainly for domestic consumption.

Suriname has great timber resources, but they have not been fully exploited. Plywood and timber are exported. There is a small fishing industry, centred in Paramaribo, that exports shrimp to North America.

Industry. The main industry in Suriname is the mining and processing of bauxite. The production of bauxite and its derivatives, aluminum and alumina, is controlled by the Suriname Aluminum Company (Suralco), a subsidiary of the Aluminum Company of America (Alcoa), and Billiton, which is part of Royal Dutch/Shell. Suralco operates mines near Moengo and near Paranam; Billiton has mines near Overdacht. There is an aluminum smelter and an alumina refinery in Paranam.

The Brokopondo Dam and a hydroelectric power plant on the Suriname River produce electricity for the bauxite-refining operations in Paranam. The dam impounds the 600-square-mile W.J. van Blommestein Lake. The Suriname State Oil Company (Staatsolie) produces a limited amount of oil from wells in the Tambaredjo area.

Manufacturing

Apart from the bauxite and wood-processing industries, manufacturing is limited to small import-substitution enterprises. Processed foods, clothing, cigarettes, and construction material are produced for the domestic market.

Finance and trade. Local banks and insurance companies either are subsidiaries of, or cooperate with, foreign companies, mostly from The Netherlands and the United States. Monetary policy is controlled by the minister of finance and the president of the Central Bank of Suriname (established 1957), the bank of issue.

Bauxite, alumina, and aluminum account for almost three-fourths of total exports. Imports consist mostly of fuels, food products, capital goods, industrial products, and industrial raw materials. Suriname's main trade partners are the United States and The Netherlands.

Transportation. Surface transport systems are for the most part limited to the coastal area. The East–West Highway connects Paramaribo with Albina on the eastern border and with Nieuw Nickerie on the western border. There is a road from Paramaribo to Afobaka near the Brokopondo Dam. Only one-fourth of the roads are paved. Rivers and canals are an important means of transport. The lower courses of the larger rivers are accessible to oceangoing vessels. Paramaribo is the chief port. Zanderij, the international airport, began operation in 1934.

ADMINISTRATION AND SOCIAL CONDITIONS

Government. Under the 1987 constitution, legislative power is exercised by an elected 51-member National Assembly, which elects a president and vice president. The president, vice president, and members of the National Assembly serve five-year terms. The president is the chairman of a nonelective, military-influenced Council of State, which ensures that the government's actions conform to the law. It has constitutional powers to annul laws passed by the National Assembly. The judicial system consists of a Court of Justice and three cantonal courts.

Education. Suriname's system of education is modeled on that of The Netherlands, and Dutch is the language of instruction. School attendance is compulsory for children up to age 12, and education at all levels is free. More than 90 percent of the children in the coastal areas attend primary school. Suriname has secondary schools, junior colleges, a teacher's college, and vocational and technical schools. The University of Suriname in Paramaribo, founded in 1968 and renamed the Anton de Kom University in 1980, has faculties of law, medicine, social science and economics, engineering, and natural resources.

Junior and senior education

Health and welfare. Health conditions are relatively good in Suriname. Most tropical diseases are being combated effectively. Medical care in the interior is provided by the Foundation for Medical Mission of the Evangelical Brethren in Suriname, which operates medical centres in the main Bush Negro and American Indian settlements.

Most of the population has health insurance. All collective labour agreements include medical care. Before independence a general health insurance program was introduced for civil servants and registered indigents. The unemployed and workers in the informal sector, however, must obtain a "certificate of poverty" from the government to receive free medical care. Unemployment benefits and other social provisions are almost nonexistent.

CULTURAL LIFE

Suriname is a culturally segmented society. Contact between the ethnic groups is largely limited to the economic sphere. The government has pursued a policy of maintaining traditional cultural values. Fine arts in the more strict definition are primarily middle-class activities that are dominated by Western—primarily Dutch—cultural standards.

Press and broadcasting

There is one government-owned television station, with one channel, and a government-owned radio station, in addition to a number of small commercial radio stations. There are a few government-owned publications and two privately owned daily newspapers.

For statistical data on the land and people of Suriname, see the *Britannica World Data* section in the BRITANNICA WORLD DATA ANNUAL.

History

Christopher Columbus sighted the area that is now Suriname in 1498. A Spanish expedition led by Amerigo Vespucci and Alonso de Ojeda sailed along the coast of Suriname in 1499. The Spanish explorer Vicente Yáñez Pinzón visited the region in 1500. Several attempts at settlement were made by the Spanish, Dutch, British, and French during the first half of the 17th century. The failure of these attempts was partly due to resistance by the native Indian inhabitants.

The first permanent settlement of Europeans in Suriname was established by a group of British planters and their slaves in 1651. The colonists were sent by Francis Willoughby, Lord Willoughby of Parham, the governor of Barbados. In 1667 Suriname was seized by a Dutch fleet, and it was ceded to the Dutch in the same year in exchange for Nieuw Amsterdam (New York). Except for the years between 1799 and 1802 and between 1804 and 1815, when it was under British rule, Suriname remained part of The Netherlands until its independence.

Plantations

Suriname developed into a flourishing plantation colony after Dutch planters, driven out of Brazil from the mid-17th century, settled in the area. Sugar was the main export, and coffee and cacao gained rapidly in importance from the early 18th century. The production of cotton also became more significant during the 18th century, and indigo and wood plantations were established.

Until the mid-19th century Suriname was a typical plantation colony. Most of the population lived on the plantations. The small white population was mainly of Dutch origin; about one-third was Jewish, and the remainder came mostly from France, Germany, and Great Britain. The majority of the population were slaves, mostly from the west coast of Africa.

In 1853, Chinese and Madeiran contract labourers were brought to Suriname to work on the plantations. Many of these workers did not extend their five-year contracts, and they became small-scale merchants. On July 1, 1863, slavery was abolished in Suriname. The former slaves were placed under government supervision for a period of 10 years so that they would be available to perform labour under contract. Contract labourers were brought in to replace the slaves. From 1873 to 1916, East Indians were recruited to work on the plantations. From 1890 to 1939, workers came to Suriname from Java in Indonesia.

Despite efforts to preserve plantation production, Suriname's position as an agricultural supplier continued to decline. By the beginning of the 20th century, bauxite reserves had been found in Suriname. In 1916 Alcoa began operations in the country. Renewed Dutch interest in Suriname, demonstrated by the arrival of the Dutch mining company Billiton in 1939, increased after World War II. The Netherlands began to provide development aid to Suriname in 1948, the year in which the talks concerning the internal political autonomy of the country began.

The bauxite industry

After World War II the issue of universal suffrage served as a catalyst for political mobilization. Political parties were set up, most of them organized along ethnic lines. The light-skinned Creole elite, who opposed universal suffrage, set up the Suriname National Party (NPS). The Progressive Suriname People's Party (PSV) organized the working-class Creoles. At first the East Indians and Indonesians were grouped within one party, but they later split to form the United Hindu Party (VHP; later called the Progressive Reform Party) and the Indonesian Peasants' Party (KTPI). Universal suffrage was instituted in 1948.

In 1954 The Netherlands and its West Indian colonies came to an agreement under which Suriname gained autonomy in its internal affairs. From 1955 to 1975 development aid from The Netherlands increased steadily. From 1964 onward, Suriname, as an associate member of the European Economic Community (EEC), received aid from the EEC's development fund. Despite this aid, Suriname's economic growth was not strong until the 1960s, when, as a result of increases in the production of alumina and aluminum, Suriname had a rate of economic growth that far exceeded levels achieved previously. In the early 1970s economic growth decreased sharply.

The 1958 elections produced a coalition government of the NPS, led by Johan Pengel, and the VHP, led by Jaggernath Lachmon, that lasted until 1967. In 1961 the left-wing Nationalist Republican Party (PNR) was established. Among the East Indian population the Action Front became active.

A split occurred in the NPS–VHP coalition after the 1967 elections. On the basis of an increase in the number of parliamentary seats that they held, the VHP demanded additional political power, but they were refused by the NPS. This led to a coalition of the Action Front and the NPS. The coalition did not last long; in 1969 a Cabinet crisis prompted by strikes in the educational sector led to the fall of the government. A coalition was formed by the VHP and the Progressive National Party (PNP), which was set up by intellectuals who had left the NPS.

The leadership of the NPS passed to Henck Arron after Pengel's death in 1970. Arron made successful overtures toward the PSV, the KTPI, and the PNR. The National Party Alliance, a coalition of these parties—all favouring independence—won the 1973 election. In The Netherlands the ruling socialist party had included Suriname's independence on its policy program. Despite resistance from East Indians, who feared increased Creole domination, Suriname became independent on Nov. 25, 1975.

Economic stagnation

Despite large investments, financed with development aid, the economy stagnated in the late 1970s. Although civil servants made up almost 40 percent of the work force, unemployment remained high, and most of the population had incomes at the minimum subsistence level.

On Feb. 25, 1980, after the government's refusal to sanction trade union activity within the armed forces, a group of army officers seized control of the government. The coup was welcomed by most of the population. The National Military Council (NMR) installed after the coup adopted a cautious position. The leaders of the coup called on the moderate wing of the PNR to form a Cabinet in which civilians would occupy most of the seats. The new Cabinet proclaimed that the country would return to democracy after a transition period of two years and that it would follow a moderate policy. The Dutch government agreed to finance an emergency development program for the first two years of the new regime.

The political shifts toward left-wing radical factions close to the NMR resulted in the publication of the "Manifesto of the Revolution" on May 1, 1981. In August 1981 the formation of the Revolutionary Front was proclaimed, with Lieutenant Colonel Dési Bouterse as chairman. It included the Progressive Workers' and Farm Labourers' Union (PALU), the Revolutionary People's Party (RVP), the PNR, and some of the trade unions. As the military leaders showed few signs of willingness to surrender control, trade unions, business associations, and professional groups began to proclaim their discontent. The conflict reached a climax in December 1982 when 15 prominent civilians, including lawyers, scholars, journalists, and trade union leaders, were executed. The Netherlands and the United States immediately suspended development aid. In February 1983 the PALU and RVP formed a coalition government. A strike in the vital bauxite industry and the threat of a general strike led to the dismissal of this government by the military within one year. Bouterse formed a new Cabinet in which representatives of trade unions and business associations occupied most of the seats.

After the military came to power, government expenditures rose dramatically, owing largely to the growth in defense spending. Government revenues had declined as a result of decreasing revenues from the bauxite sector and the suspension of foreign aid. After 1980, exports declined steadily and international reserves continued to shrink.

The Surinamese Liberation Army

Raids by the Surinamese Liberation Army, a guerrilla group that consisted mainly of Bush Negroes, disrupted bauxite mining and led to the killing of many Bush Negro civilians by the National Army; thousands of Bush Negroes fled to French Guiana.

The deteriorating economic and political situation forced the military to open a dialogue with the leaders of the principal political parties that had operated before the coup. Talks led to an agreement on a constitution limiting the military's political participation to membership in the Council of State and the Security Council.

Elections held on Nov. 25, 1987, resulted in the defeat of the military. The Front for Democracy and Development, a coalition of the VHP, NPS, and KTPI, won 40 of the 51 parliamentary seats. A member of the VHP was elected president, and the NPS obtained the vice presidency.

For later developments in the history of Suriname, see the *Britannica Book of the Year* section in the BRITANNICA WORLD DATA ANNUAL.

For coverage of related topics in the *Macropædia* and *Micropædia*, see the *Propædia*, sections 964, 966, and 974, and the *Index*.

BIBLIOGRAPHY. An overview is provided by HENK E. CHIN and HANS BUDDINGH', *Surinam: Politics, Economics, and Society* (1987). RADJNARAIN MOHANPERSAD NANNAN PANDAY, *Agriculture in Surinam, 1650–1940: An Inquiry into the Causes of Its Decline* (1959), is a succinct analysis. EDWARD DEW, *The Difficult Flowering of Surinam: Ethnicity and Politics in a Plural Society* (1978), examines political history. Essays on Suriname's culture are collected in ALBERT HELMAN (ed.), *Cultureel mozäiek van Suriname* (1977). Historical works include R.A.J. VAN LIER, *Frontier Society: A Social Analysis of the History of Surinam* (1971; originally published in Dutch, 2nd ed., 1971); and CORNELIS CH. GOSLINGA, *A Short History of the Netherlands Antilles and Surinam* (1979). See also GERARD A. NAGELKERKE, *Suriname, a Bibliography, 1940–1980* (1980). (H.E.C.)

Sweden

In area the fourth largest nation of Europe—after the U.S.S.R., France, and Spain—Sweden (Swedish Sverige) lies in the Scandinavian Peninsula bounded by Norway on the west, Finland on the northeast, and the Gulf of Bothnia, the Baltic Sea, and the North Sea on the east, southeast, and southwest, respectively. A narrow sea channel separates it from Denmark to the southwest. Most of the inhabitants live in dense clusters in a relatively small portion of its 173,229 square miles (448,661 square kilometres), but in the years since 1815, during which Sweden has remained at peace, the Swedish people have achieved a remarkably stable and democratic way of life. In form, Sweden's government is a constitutional monarchy, with its seat in Stockholm.

The popular image of Sweden includes such features as the prototype it has provided of the modern welfare state, a "middle way" that is Socialist but non-Communist, and its traditional nonalignment in peace and neutrality in war, which has allowed its people to assume a unique leadership in the world community.

As a country that in many ways has had good luck, including a peripheral but in-between location and vast resources of iron ore and timber, Sweden long ago disavowed the military aggressiveness that once made its armies bulk large during Europe's centuries of dynastic warfare. It chose instead to play a balancing role among the world's conflicting ideological and political systems. It is no coincidence that Swedish statesmen have often been sought out to fill major positions of leadership and mediation within the United Nations.

This article is divided into the following sections:

Physical and human geography

THE LAND

Sweden's four main physical regions are, from the north, the northern mountain and lake region known as Norrland; the lowlands of central Sweden known as Svealand; the relatively low Småland highlands and the small but rich plains of Skåne, the two last areas in Götaland.

Relief, drainage, and soils. From the ancient mountain range with its crest along the Swedish–Norwegian border, the land descends southeast and south. The mountain, or *fjäll,* region has a most dramatic scenery. The highest peaks of Sweden are found in Lappland: Kebnekaise, at 6,926 feet (2,111 metres), and Sarektjåkko, at 6,854 feet (2,090 metres), the latter situated in a national park of great and lonely magnificence. Åreskutan, Helagsfjället and Sylarna peaks lie amid favourite sporting locales in a more southerly location; they are especially popular during the spring and summer.

The four physical regions

The big rivers, or *älvar,* of Norrland flow from the mountains to the sea in the southeast. Many are linked to long, narrow lakes made by dams of moraine, and often they have rapids and falls, many of which have power stations. Several of the larger rivers have huge flows and fall great distances in their course to the sea.

The metallic-ore deposits are found mostly in the lower parts of the highlands, both in the north and farther south. These highlands were not below sea level during the glacial period, and the soil is meagre. Most of the central lowlands were then pressed down below sea level by the glaciers, creating fertile plains of clay, with many lakes. The gravel ridges that are characteristic features of the landscape of the whole region are remains of the last glacial period. In ancient times they were used as highways, but today they serve as gravel and water deposits. Many lakes, big and small, are typical of the central lowlands. Lake Vänern, 2,156 square miles (5,584 square kilometres) in area, is the largest of Sweden's 90,000 lakes and the largest in Scandinavia. The Göta, which drains Lake Vänern into the Kattegatt section of the North Sea at Göteborg, is the only major river of southern Sweden. It is famous for its falls in Trollhättan, located in a region of fertile plains, forests, industries, and numerous small towns.

South of Lake Vättern, which lies east of Lake Vänern, the plains are transformed into a new but lower mountain area, the Småland highlands, seldom over 500 feet (150 metres) above sea level. The soil is stony; the agriculture is small in scale; and the people depend upon small industries that utilize forest products.

The plains of Skåne are the most densely populated agricultural areas of Sweden. The ground consists of rocks from later geological periods, and the soil has been enriched by recent marine deposits. Some clay beds in the northwest contain coal, and the clay itself is used for making fireproof materials.

Typical of Sweden is a rocky coastline with hundreds of small, sometimes wooded islands. Ground by the glacial ice in the same direction, they have a common rounded shape. This type of coast, known as *skärgård,* is found both in the east and west, especially around Stockholm and Göteborg. Other parts of the coast are sandy, and the island of Gotland has limestone rocks.

Climate. The Scandinavian countries profit from the warm Gulf Stream, which allows forests and agriculture farther north than anywhere else on the globe. About 15 percent of the country lies within the Arctic Circle, and the climatic differences between northern and southern Sweden are vast. The temperate west winds of the stream produce a continental climate similar to that of the Soviet Union, which is very cold in winter and very warm in summer. Mean February temperatures range from 7° F (−14° C) at Karesuando in the far north to 27° F (−3° C) in Stockholm and 30° F (−1° C) in Lund in the far south; comparable July figures are 57° F (14° C), 64° F (18° C), and 63° F (17° C).

Interaction of geography and climate

The regions covered by the high mountain range have a more continental climate than the west coast, where the prevailing winds dump heavy rains that diminish as the winds approach the east coast. Also there, precipitation is sufficient for agriculture. Annual precipitation ranges from 15 inches (380 millimetres) in the far north to 22 inches (560 millimetres) in Stockholm and 23 inches (585 millimetres) in Lund.

Snow lies in the mountains of Norrland for eight months, whereas three months is the average length of winter in the highlands of Småland, and one month or less in Skåne. Ice seldom covers the waters of the west coast, but the northern Baltic is usually unnavigable from the end of November to the beginning of May.

The shorter growing period in the north, about three or four months as compared to eight in Skåne, is partly compensated for by the long period of constant daylight. In Karesuando, above the Arctic Circle, the sun remains over the horizon between May 26 and July 18. At the summer solstice on June 21, daylight lasts 23 hours at Haparanda, at the northern end of the Gulf of Bothnia, and in Skåne 17 hours. Long twilight hours are typical of Sweden.

Plant and animal life. Latitude and altitude produce many local variations. In descending order of altitude and latitude, general vegetational zones are alpine regions, birchwoods, a coniferous forest region, and a beech wood region.

The alpine region, down to 1,600 feet (490 metres) in the north and 3,000 feet (915 metres) in the southwest, begins with mosses and lichens at the highest points where growth occurs. Dwarf birches become a more extensive belt of alpine birches in the north, together with rowans, bird cherries, willows, and aspens. The undergrowth is rich in herbs. Lichens, especially reindeer moss, prevail in dry areas.

The coniferous forests that cover 57 percent of Sweden are especially abundant in the north and the Småland highlands. Some farms currently are being converted back to forest. Scotch pines and spruces are often mixed with lowland birches, rowans, and aspens in the north and central parts of Sweden and with oaks, ashes, lindens, maples, and elms in the south. The beech forests are found in Skåne.

The wolf, almost extinct, is protected by law, as are bear and lynx, which are only found in the deep forests of the north. Large domesticated herds of reindeer are common in the northern mountains, while the elk, the most valuable game animal, is common throughout the country. Badgers, foxes, hare, and otters are also hunted, as are the roe deer, which are common in southern and central Sweden.

Birds are numerous, with some migratory species breeding in spring and summer. Songbirds, game birds, and forest birds of prey are found, as are cranes in northern marshy clearings; gulls, terns, and eider ducks are found at the coast. The viper is the only poisonous snake. Salmon, trout, char, pike, and perch are common in rivers and lakes. Both freshwater and marine fisheries are important, especially on the west coast, where shrimp, herring, cod, flatfish, mackerel, and sprat are taken. The crayfish, a favourite among Swedes, is found in many lakes of southern Sweden.

Settlement patterns. Götaland, Svealand, and Norrland are considered the traditional regions of Sweden. The first two take their names from the small, prehistoric clans of Götaland and Svealand who inhabited central Sweden. The Svear and Götar were united into one state about AD 1000. The Götar lived in Västergötland and Östergötland and Småland, the Svear around Lake Mälaren. Certain differences remain in the dialects of these two regions. Skåne and the surrounding regions were taken from the Danish crown in the 17th century, and Skåne is still looked upon as a special region in both language and customs. The food is richer, and the people are said to be warmer and more easygoing than the taciturn northern people.

Variations in cultural character

The vast Norrland was colonized later. It is looked upon as somewhat less important than the old cultural centre of the southern and central regions, and its vast distances are often overlooked. These tendencies have become stronger, with the modern industrial concentration in the southern and central parts.

Rural settlement. Generally, the traditional patterns of villages in the old agricultural areas were broken up in the 19th century to get larger field units and more productive cultivation. In Värmland and Dalecarlia, the traditional red-painted wooden houses still lie side by side in the village centre. In Skåne, a square house with brick and clay applied over a stick frame is the most common form.

Houses built in modern Sweden are basically the same throughout the country. Many small rural holdings have been annexed to neighbouring areas and the empty houses converted to vacation homes. To have homes in both urban and rural surroundings is the dream of many Swedish families, especially those who have had to abandon their rural milieu.

The relatively few castles and manors are found only in southern and central Sweden. The old industrial centres were often concentrated near waterpower and water transportation facilities; the newer ones are situated near railway stations and along the highways.

Urban settlement. The process of urbanization has been rapid during recent decades. About 90 percent of the population lived in the countryside in the mid-19th century, whereas in the late 20th century less than a fifth did so; only a small percentage of the economically active population are farmers.

This shift in concentration has occurred not only in the central cities but also in the areas surrounding them. This is especially true of regions around Stockholm, Göteborg, Malmö, and the cities and towns in the central lowlands. The population has diminished in the interior regions of Norrland, the northwestern portion of Svealand, southeast Götaland, and the isle of Gotland. Often the population shift has been a two-step process, shifting first from the rural areas to small towns and from there to the cities.

THE PEOPLE

The majority of Sweden's population, small in relation to its land area, live in the southern half of the country and most of these in towns or other densely populated areas.

Although different groups of immigrants have influenced Swedish culture through the centuries, the population is unusually homogeneous in language, ethnic stock, and religion. The language, which belongs to the North Germanic (Scandinavian) subgroup of the Germanic languages, is closely related to the Danish, Norwegian, Icelandic, and Faeroese languages. It has been influenced at times by German, but it has also borrowed some words and syntax from French, English, and Finnish. The written language showed the influence of Latin as late as in the early 20th

Homogeneity of the populace

MAP INDEX

Political subdivisions

Älvsborgs Län...58·00n 12·30e
Blekinge Län.....56·20n 15·20e
Gävleborgs Län..61·30n 16·15e
Göteborgs Och Bohus Län......58·30n 11·30e
Gotlands Län....57·30n 18·30e
Hallands Län....56·45n 13·00e
Jämtlands Län...63·00n 14·40e
Jönköpings Län..57·30n 14·30e
Kalmar Län.......57·20n 16·00e
Kopparbergs Län............61·00n 14·30e
Kristianstads Län.............56·15n 14·00e
Kronobergs Län..56·40n 14·40e
Malmöhus Län...55·45n 13·30e
Norrbottens Län..65·30n 21·30e
Örebro Län.......59·30n 15·00e
Östergötlands Län.............58·25n 15·45e
Skaraborgs Län..58·20n 13·30e
Södermanlands Län.............59·15n 16·40e
Stockholms Län..59·30n 18·20e
Uppsala Län.....60·00n 17·45e
Värmlands Län...59·45n 13·15e
Västerbottens Län.............64·00n 17·30e
Västernorrlands Län.............63·00n 17·30e
Västmanlands Län.............59·45n 16·20e

Cities and towns

Abisko..........68·20n 18·51e
Alanäs..........64·10n 15·42e
Alingsås.........57·56n 12·31e
Alunda..........60·04n 18·05e
Älvdalen.........61·14n 14·02e
Älvkarleby.......60·34n 17·27e
Älvsbyn.........65·39n 20·59e
Åmål............59·03n 12·42e
Ammarnäs.......65·56n 16·09e
Ängelholm.......56·15n 12·51e
Ankarsrum.......57·42n 16·19e
Anttis...........67·16n 22·52e
Arboga..........59·24n 15·50e
Åre.............63·24n 13·04e
Årjäng..........59·23n 12·08e
Arjeplog.........66·00n 17·58e
Arvidsjaur.......65·35n 19·07e
Arvika...........59·39n 12·36e
Åsarna..........62·39n 14·21e
Åsele...........64·10n 17·20e
Askersund.......58·53n 14·54e
Åtvidaberg......58·12n 16·00e
Båstad..........56·26n 12·51e
Bastuträsk......64·47n 20·02e
Bengtsfors......59·02n 12·13e
Bergby..........60·56n 17·02e
Bergkvara.......56·23n 16·05e
Bergsjö.........61·59n 17·04e
Bjärnum.........56·17n 13·42e
Björna..........63·34n 18·33e
Bjurholm........63·56n 19·13e
Boden...........65·50n 21·42e
Bollnäs.........61·21n 16·25e
Borås...........57·43n 12·55e
Borgholm........56·53n 16·39e
Borlänge........60·29n 15·25e
Boxholm.........58·12n 15·03e
Bräcke..........62·43n 15·27e
Burgsvik........57·03n 18·16e
Bydalen.........63·06n 13·47e
Byxelkrok.......57·20n 17·00e
Charlottenberg..59·53n 12·17e
Degeberga.......55·50n 14·05e
Degerfors.......59·14n 14·26e
Deje............59·36n 13·28e
Djurås..........60·33n 15·08e
Ed..............58·55n 11·55e
Edsbro..........59·54n 18·29e
Edsbruk.........58·02n 16·28e
Edsbyn..........61·23n 15·49e
Enköping........59·38n 17·04e
Eskilstuna......59·22n 16·30e
Fagersta........60·00n 15·47e
Falkenberg......56·54n 12·28e
Falköping.......58·10n 13·31e
Falun...........60·36n 15·38e
Färjestaden.....56·39n 16·27e
Fårösund........57·52n 19·03e
Finspång........58·43n 15·47e
Fjällåsen.......67·29n 20·10e
Flen............59·04n 16·35e
Fredrika........64·05n 18·24e
Fredriksberg....60·08n 14·23e
Frösön..........63·11n 14·32e
Frövi...........59·28n 15·22e
Furudal.........61·10n 15·08e
Gäddede.........64·30n 14·09e
Gällivare.......67·07n 20·45e
Gamleby.........57·54n 16·24e
Gävle...........60·40n 17·10e
Gislaved........57·18n 13·32e
Glommersträsk..65·16n 19·38e
Gnarp...........62·03n 17·16e
Göteborg (Gothenburg)...57·43n 11·58e
Grangärde.......60·16n 14·59e
Gunnarn.........65·00n 17·40e
Hagfors.........60·02n 13·42e
Hällefors.......59·47n 14·30e
Hällnäs.........64·19n 19·38e
Hallsberg.......59·04n 15·07e
Hallstahammar..59·37n 16·13e
Hallstavik......60·03n 18·36e
Halmstad........56·39n 12·50e
Hälsingborg.....56·03n 12·42e
Hammerdal.......63·36n 15·21e
Haparanda.......65·50n 24·10e
Harmånger.......61·56n 17·13e
Härnösand.......62·38n 17·56e
Hässleholm......56·09n 13·46e
Hede............62·25n 13·30e
Hedemora........60·17n 15·59e
Hemse...........57·14n 18·22e
Hofors..........60·33n 16·17e
Höganäs.........56·12n 12·33e
Högsby..........57·10n 16·02e
Höljes..........60·54n 12·36e
Holmsund........63·42n 20·21e
Hoting..........64·07n 16·10e
Hovmantorp......56·47n 15·08e
Huddinge........59·14n 17·59e
Hudiksvall......61·44n 17·07e
Hultsfred.......57·29n 15·50e
Huskvarna.......57·48n 14·16e
Idre............61·52n 12·43e
Järvsö..........61·43n 16·10e
Jävre...........65·09n 21·59e
Jokkmokk........66·37n 19·50e
Jönköping.......57·47n 14·11e
Jörn............65·04n 20·02e
Junsele.........63·41n 16·54e
Kåbdalis........66·10n 20·00e
Kalmar..........56·40n 16·22e
Kårböle.........61·59n 15·19e
Karesuando......68·25n 22·30e
Karlshamn.......56·10n 14·51e
Karlskoga.......59·20n 14·31e
Karlskrona......56·10n 15·35e
Karlstad........59·22n 13·30e
Karungi.........66·03n 23·57e
Katrineholm.....59·00n 16·12e
Kil.............59·30n 13·19e
Kinna...........57·30n 12·41e
Kiruna..........67·51n 20·16e
Kisa............57·59n 15·37e
Klimpfjäll......65·04n 14·52e
Klintehamn......57·24n 18·12e
Knäred..........56·32n 13·19e
Koskullskulle....67·12n 20·50e
Kramfors........62·56n 17·47e
Krangede........63·09n 16·05e
Kristdala.......57·24n 16·11e
Kristianstad....56·02n 14·08e
Kristinehamn....59·20n 14·07e
Kungälv.........57·52n 11·58e
Kungsbacka......57·29n 12·04e
Kvikkjokk.......66·55n 17·50e
Laholm..........56·31n 13·02e
Laisvall........66·05n 17·10e
Landskrona......55·52n 12·50e
Långban.........59·51n 14·15e
Lärbro..........57·47n 18·47e
Laxå............58·59n 14·37e
Lenhovda........57·00n 15·17e
Lesjöfors.......59·59n 14·11e
Lickershamn.....57·50n 18·31e
Lidköping.......58·30n 13·10e
Lillhärdal......61·51n 14·04e
Limmared........57·32n 13·21e
Lingbo..........61·03n 16·41e
Linköping.......58·25n 15·37e
Lit.............63·19n 14·49e
Ljugarn.........57·19n 18·42e
Ljungaverk......62·29n 16·03e
Ljungby.........56·50n 13·56e
Ljusdal.........61·50n 16·05e
Lövånger........64·22n 21·18e
Lövstabruk......60·24n 17·53e
Luleå...........65·34n 22·10e
Lund............55·42n 13·11e
Luspebryggan....67·01n 19·51e
Lycksele........64·36n 18·40e
Lysekil.........58·16n 11·26e
Malåträsk.......65·11n 18·44e
Malmberget......67·10n 20·40e
Malmö...........55·36n 13·00e
Malung..........60·40n 13·44e
Mariestad.......58·43n 13·51e
Markaryd........56·26n 13·36e
Märsta..........59·37n 17·51e
Mellansel.......63·26n 18·19e
Mellerud........58·42n 12·28e
Mjölby..........58·19n 15·08e
Mölndal.........57·39n 12·01e
Mönsterås.......57·02n 16·26e
Mora............61·00n 14·33e
Motala..........58·33n 15·03e
Näsåker.........63·26n 16·54e
Nässjö..........57·39n 14·41e
Nedre Soppero...68·03n 21·46e
Nordmaling......63·34n 19·30e
Norrköping......58·36n 16·11e
Norrtälje.......59·46n 18·42e
Norsjö..........64·55n 19·29e
Nybro...........56·45n 15·54e
Nyköping........58·45n 17·00e
Nynäshamn.......58·54n 17·57e
Ockelbo.........60·53n 16·43e
Öje.............60·49n 13·51e
Örbyhus.........60·14n 17·42e
Örebro..........59·17n 15·13e
Örkelljunga.....56·17n 13·17e
Örnsköldsvik....63·18n 18·43e
Oskarshamn......57·16n 16·26e
Oskarström......56·48n 12·58e
Östersund.......63·11n 14·39e
Östhammar.......60·16n 18·22e
Ottenby.........56·14n 16·25e
Överkalix.......66·21n 22·56e
Övertorneå......66·23n 23·40e
Oxelösund.......58·40n 17·06e
Pajala..........67·11n 23·29e
Perstorp........56·08n 13·23e
Piteå...........65·20n 21·30e
Polcirkeln......66·33n 21·01e
Ramsele.........63·33n 16·29e
Ramsjö..........62·11n 15·39e
Rätansbyn.......62·29n 14·32e
Rättvik.........60·53n 15·06e
Rensjön.........68·05n 19·49e
Riksgränsen.....68·24n 18·12e
Risbäck.........64·42n 15·32e
Robertsfors.....64·11n 20·51e
Ronneby.........56·12n 15·18e
Roslags Näsby...59·26n 18·04e
Ryd.............56·28n 14·41e
Sädvaluspen.....66·24n 16·51e
Säffle..........59·08n 12·56e
Sala............59·55n 16·36e
Sälen...........61·10n 13·16e
Sandviken.......60·37n 16·46e
Särna...........61·41n 13·08e
Sävsjö..........57·25n 14·40e
Sigtuna.........59·37n 17·43e
Simrishamn......55·33n 14·20e
Skellefteå......64·46n 20·57e
Skelleftehamn...64·41n 21·14e
Skillingaryd....57·26n 14·05e
Skövde..........58·24n 13·50e
Slagnäs.........65·34n 18·05e
Söderhamn.......61·18n 17·03e
Söderköping.....58·29n 16·18e
Södertälje......59·12n 17·37e
Sollefteå.......63·10n 17·16e
Sollentuna......59·28n 17·54e
Sölvesborg......56·03n 14·33e
Sorsele.........65·30n 17·30e
Ställdalen......59·56n 14·56e
Stensele........65·05n 17·09e
Stockholm.......59·20n 18·03e
Stöllet.........60·24n 13·16e
Storlien........63·19n 12·06e
Storuman........65·06n 17·06e
Storvreta.......59·58n 17·42e
Strömstad.......58·56n 11·10e
Strömsund.......63·51n 15·35e
Sundsvall.......62·23n 17·18e
Sunne...........59·50n 13·09e
Svanskog........59·11n 12·33e
Svappavaara.....67·39n 21·04e
Svärdsjö........60·45n 15·55e
Sveg............62·02n 14·21e
Svenljunga......57·30n 13·07e
Tännäs..........62·27n 12·40e
Tärendö.........67·10n 22·38e
Tärna...........65·43n 15·16e
Tierp...........60·20n 17·30e
Tingsryd........56·32n 14·59e
Töcksfors.......59·30n 11·50e
Tomelilla.......55·33n 13·57e
Töre............65·54n 22·39e
Torsby..........60·08n 13·00e
Torup...........56·58n 13·05e
Tranås..........58·03n 14·59e
Trelleborg......55·22n 13·10e
Trollhättan.....58·16n 12·18e
Trosa...........58·54n 17·33e
Uddevalla.......58·21n 11·55e
Ulricehamn......57·47n 13·25e
Umeå............63·50n 20·15e
Umfors..........65·56n 15·00e
Umnäs...........65·24n 16·10e
Uppsala.........59·52n 17·38e
Vålådalen.......63·10n 12·57e
Valdemarsvik....58·12n 16·36e
Valsjöbyn.......64·04n 14·08e
Vänersborg......58·22n 12·19e
Vännäs..........63·55n 19·45e
Vansbro.........60·31n 14·13e
Varberg.........57·06n 12·15e
Värnamo.........57·11n 14·02e
Västerås........59·37n 16·33e
Västervik.......57·45n 16·38e
Växjö...........56·42n 14·49e
Vetlanda........57·26n 15·04e
Vidsel..........65·51n 20·24e
Vilhelmina......64·37n 16·39e
Vimmerby........57·40n 15·51e
Vindeln.........64·12n 19·44e
Virserum........57·19n 15·35e
Visby...........57·38n 18·18e
Vissefjärda.....56·32n 15·35e
Vittangi........67·41n 21·36e
Ystad...........55·25n 13·49e
Ytterhogdal.....62·12n 14·51e

Physical features and points of interest

Amungen, *lake*...61·09n 15·39e
Ångermanälven, *river*..........62·48n 17·56e
Åreskutan, *mountain*.......63·26n 13·06e
Åsnen, *lake*......56·38n 14·42e
Ätran, *river*......56·53n 12·30e
Baltic Sea........56·30n 19·00e
Bolmen, *lake*.....56·55n 13·40e
Bothnia, Gulf of..63·00n 20·30e
Bottenhavet, *gulf*.62·00n 19·30e
Bottenviken, *gulf*.64·30n 23·00e
Dalälven, *river*...60·38n 17·27e
Dalarna (Dalecarlia), *historic region*...61·01n 14·04e
Fårön, *island*.....56·56n 19·08e
Faxälven, *river*...63·13n 17·13e
Götaälv, *river*....57·42n 11·52e
Götaland, *historic region*..........57·30n 15·03e
Gotland, *island*...57·30n 18·33e
Gotska Sandön, *island*..........58·23n 19·16e
Gotska Sandön National Park...58·23n 19·16e
Helagsfjället, *mountain*.......62·55n 12·27e
Hjälmaren, *lake*..59·15n 15·45e
Hornavan, *lake*...66·10n 17·30e
Indalsälven, *river*.62·31n 17·27e
Kalixälven, *river*..65·50n 23·11e
Kalmarsund, *sound*..........56·40n 16·25e
Kattegat, *strait*...57·00n 11·00e
Kebnekaise, *mountain*.......67·53n 18·33e
Könkämäälven, *river*..........68·29n 22·17e
Lainioälven, *river*..........67·22n 23·39e
Lapland, *historic region*...67·30n 21·00e
Ljungan, *river*...62·19n 17·23e
Ljusnan, *river*...61·12n 17·08e
Luleälven, *river*...65·35n 22·03e
Mälaren, *lake*...59·30n 17·12e
Marsfjället, *mountain*.......65·05n 15·28e
Muddus National-park...........67·00n 20·16e
Norra Kvarken, *strait*.........63·36n 20·43e
Norra Storfjället, *mountain*.......65·52n 15·18e
Norrland, *historic region*..........65·00n 18·00e
Öland, *island*....56·45n 16·38e
Padjelanta Nationalpark...67·28n 16·41e
Peljekaise Nationalpark...66·18n 16·58e
Piteälven, *river*...65·14n 21·32e
Sareks National-park.......67·15n 17·30e
Sarjektjåkko, *mountain*.......67·25n 17·46e
Siljan, *lake*......60·50n 14·45e
Skalka, *lake*......66·50n 18·46e
Skåne, *historic region*..........55·59n 13·30e
Skellefteälven, *river*..........64·42n 21·06e
Småland, *historic region*..........57·18n 15·03e
Sommen, *lake*....58·01n 15·15e
Sound, The........55·50n 12·40e
Stora Lulevatten, *lake*..........67·10n 19·16e
Stora Sjöfallet, *waterfall*.......67·29n 18·21e
Stora Sjöfallet Nationalpark...67·44n 18·16e
Storavan, *lake*...65·42n 18·12e
Storuman, *lake*...65·14n 16·54e
Storvindeln, *lake*.65·43n 17·05e
Sulitelma, *mountain*.......67·08n 16·24e
Svealand, *historic region*..........60·30n 15·30e
Sylarna (Sylene), *mountains*.......63·02n 12·13e
Torneträsk, *lake*..68·20n 19·10e
Uddjaur, *lake*....65·55n 17·49e
Umeälven, *river*..63·47n 20·16e
Vänern, *lake*.....58·55n 13·30e
Vättern, *lake*....58·24n 14·36e
Vindelälven, *river*..........63·54n 19·52e

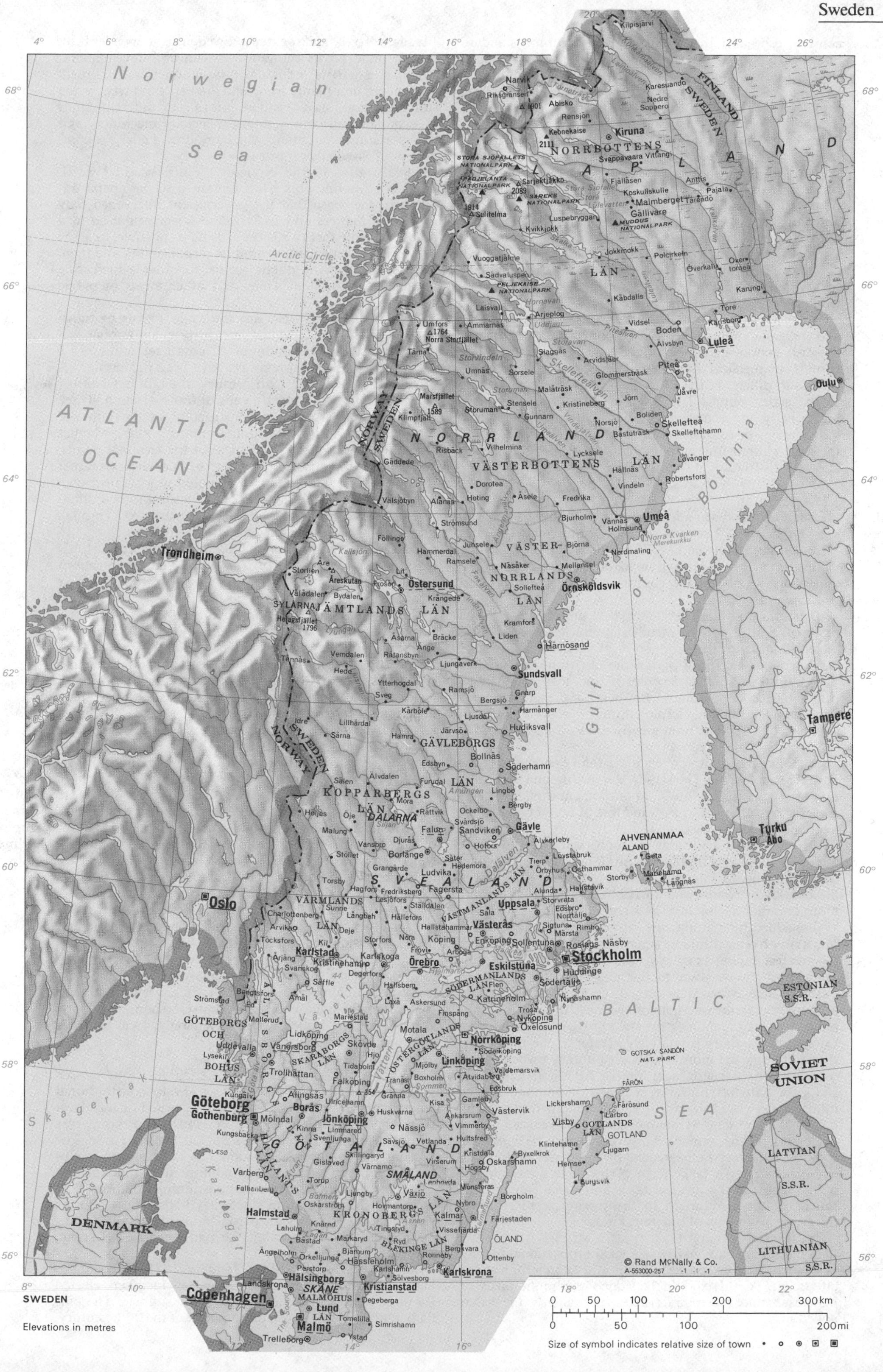
Norwegian Sea
ATLANTIC OCEAN
Arctic Circle
Narvik
Riksgränsen
Abisko
Kilpisjärvi
Karesuando
Nedre Soppero
Rensjön
FINLAND
SWEDEN
Kebnekaise
2111
Kiruna
NORRBOTTENS
LAPLAND
Svappavaara
Vittangi
STORA SJÖFALLETS NATIONALPARK
PADJELANTA NATIONALPARK
Sarjektjåkko
2089
SAREKS NATIONALPARK
Fjällåsen
Koskullskulle
Malmberget
Gällivare
Tärendö
Pajala
Anttis
Sulitelma
1914
Luspebryggan
MUDDUS NATIONALPARK
Kvikkjokk
Jokkmokk
Porjus
Polcirkeln
Övertorneå
Överkalix
Vuoggatjålme
Sadvaluspen
PELJEKAISE NATIONALPARK
LÄN
Kåbdalis
Karungi
Laisvall
Arjeplog
Töre
Karlsborg
Umfors
1764
Norra Storfjället
Ammarnäs
Vidsel
Boden
Älvsbyn
Luleå
Tärna
Slagnäs
Arvidsjaur
Piteå
Storvindeln
Umnäs
Sorsele
Glommersträsk
Jävre
Oulu
Marsfjället
1589
Storuman
Malåträsk
Stensele
Kristineberg
Jörn
Klimpfjäll
Gunnarn
Boliden
Skellefteå
Skelleftehamn
Norsjö
Bastuträsk
NORWAY
SWEDEN
NORRLAND
Vilhelmina
Risbäck
Lycksele
VÄSTERBOTTENS
LÄN
Lövånger
Gäddede
Hällnäs
Robertsfors
Vindeln
Gulf of Bothnia
Dorotea
Valsjöbyn
Alanäs
Hoting
Åsele
Fredrika
Bjurholm
Vännäs
Umeå
Holmsund
Strömsund
Norra Kvarken
Föllinge
Junsele
VÄSTER-NORRLANDS
Björna
Nordmaling
Trondheim
Hammerdal
Ramsele
Kallsjön
Storlien
Åre
Åreskutan
Lit
Östersund
Näsåker
Mellansel
Frösön
Vålådalen
Bydalen
Krångede
Sollefteå
Örnsköldsvik
SYLARNA
JÄMTLANDS LÄN
Helagsfjället
1796
Kramfors
Åsarna
Bräcke
Ånge
Liden
Härnösand
Tännäs
Vemdalen
Rätansbyn
Ljungaverk
Hede
Sundsvall
Ytterhogdal
Sveg
Ramsjö
Gnarp
Bergsjö
Harmånger
Kårböle
Ljusdal
Hudiksvall
Idre
Lillhärdal
Järvsö
Särna
Hamra
GÄVLEBORGS
Bollnäs
Edsbyn
Söderhamn
Sälen
Älvdalen
Furudal
KOPPARBERGS
Amungen
Lingbo
Mora
Rättvik
Bergby
Höljes
Öje
DALARNA
Ockelbo
Siljan
Malung
Falun
Svärdsjö
Sandviken
Gävle
Djurås
Hofors
Vansbro
Borlänge
Älvkarleby
AHVENANMAA ALAND
Turku Åbo
Tampere
Stöllet
Säter
Hedemora
Lövstabruk
Tierp
Geta
Grangärde
Ludvika
SVEALAND
Örbyhus
Östhammar
Mariehamn
Långnäs
Storby
Torsby
Hagfors
Fredriksberg
Fagersta
Alunda
Hallstavik
Oslo
VÄRMLANDS
Lesjöfors
Ställdalen
VÄSTMANLANDS LÄN
Uppsala
Storvreta
Charlottenberg
Sunne
Långban
Hällefors
Sala
Edsbro
Norrtälje
Arvika
Deje
Hallstahammar
Västerås
Sigtuna
Rimbo
Märsta
Töcksfors
Kil
Storfors
Nora
Köping
Enköping
Sollentuna
Roslags Näsby
Karlstad
Karlskoga
Frövi
Arboga
Stockholm
Årjäng
Kristinehamn
Örebro
Hjälmaren
Eskilstuna
Huddinge
Säffle
Degerfors
SÖDERMANLANDS LÄN
Flen
Södertälje
Bengtsfors
Hallsberg
Katrineholm
Nynäshamn
Strömstad
Åmål
Laxå
Askersund
Trosa
ESTONIAN S.S.R.
Mellerud
Vänern
Mariestad
Finspång
Nyköping
Oxelösund
BALTIC SEA
GÖTEBORGS OCH BOHUS LÄN
Lidköping
Motala
Norrköping
Uddevalla
Vänersborg
SKARABORGS LÄN
Skövde
ÖSTERGÖTLANDS LÄN
Söderköping
GOTSKA SANDÖN NAT. PARK
Lysekil
Hjo
Linköping
Tidaholm
Mjölby
Valdemarsvik
SOVIET UNION
Trollhättan
Vättern
Falköping
Tranås
Boxholm
Åtvidaberg
Fårön
Alingsås
Gränna
Edsbruk
Fårösund
Kungälv
Borås
Ulricehamn
354
Kisa
Gamleby
Lickershamn
Göteborg
Gothenburg
Mölndal
Huskvarna
Ankarsrum
Västervik
Lärbro
Jönköping
Vimmerby
Visby
GOTLANDS LÄN
GOTLAND
Kungsbacka
Kinna
Limmared
Nässjö
Hultsfred
Skagerrak
Svenljunga
Sävsjö
Vetlanda
GÖTALAND
Klintehamn
Ljugarn
Kristdala
Byxelkrok
LATVIAN S.S.R.
Läsø
HALLANDS LÄN
Skillingaryd
Gislaved
Värnamo
Virserum
Oskarshamn
Hemse
Högsby
Kattegat
Varberg
SMÅLAND
Torup
Lenhovda
Mönsterås
Burgsvik
Falkenberg
Ljungby
Bolmen
Växjö
Nybro
Borgholm
Oskarström
Hovmantorp
KRONOBERGS LÄN
Kalmar
Halmstad
Åsnen
Färjestaden
DENMARK
Knäred
Laholm
Tingsryd
Vissefjärda
Båstad
Lagan
Markaryd
Ryd
ÖLAND
BLEKINGE LÄN
Bergkvara
Ängelholm
Örkelljunga
Bjärnum
Ronneby
Ottenby
LITHUANIAN S.S.R.
Perstorp
Hässleholm
Karlshamn
Karlskrona
Hälsingborg
Sölvesborg
Landskrona
SKÅNE
Kristianstad
Copenhagen
MALMÖHUS LÄN
Degeberga
Lund
The Sound
Tomelilla
Malmö
Simrishamn
Trelleborg
Ystad
© Rand McNally & Co.
A-553000-257 -1 -1 -1
SWEDEN
Elevations in metres
0 50 100 200 300 km
0 50 100 200 mi
Size of symbol indicates relative size of town

century, especially in formal usage. A common standard language has been in use more than 100 years, though dialectal intonation is often retained. The traditionally varying dialects of the provinces are being homogenized rapidly through the influences of education and the mass media.

The Lapps form a special linguistic group, though they usually understand and speak Swedish as well and are taught both Swedish and the Lappish language at school. From time immemorial, they have inhabited the northern parts of the Nordic countries, retaining their own culture and language, the latter belonging to the Uralic group of languages. Immigration to Sweden after World War II created new language groups, such as Finnish, Serbo-Croatian, Turkish, and Greek. Efforts are being made to make these immigrants and their children learn Swedish, while keeping their mother tongue.

The new immigrants have little diminished the ethnic and religious homogeneity. The great majority of the Swedish people belong to the established Swedish state church, Evangelical Lutheran. Even most of those who profess to different "free churches" in Sweden still belong to the state church. The Swedish state church is organizationally and economically tied to the state, but it is independent in religious matters. Infants are "born into" the state church unless the parents have withdrawn, and later must withdraw if membership is not wanted.

THE ECONOMY

Minerals and forest products

Resources. Sweden's important raw materials are iron ore and lumber. The iron ore now being mined is concentrated largely in the Bergslagen district and in Kiruna-Gällivare-Pajala, an area rich in ore. Kiruna boasts the largest ore deposit in the country and one of the richest in the world.

Of great importance also are the sulfide ores, which often contain important metals. The Skellefteå field completely dominates the production of such metals as gold, silver, copper, and iron pyrite (the last important for the pulp industry). Smaller deposits of zinc, lead, manganese, tungsten, and copper exist elsewhere, and there are large deposits of uranium. Exploitation of coal deposits in southern Sweden has been greatly reduced because of the low quality of the coal.

Productive forest area covers more than one-half of Norrland, Svealand, and Götaland. Harvesting and reforestation are regulated by law. Corporations and other private owners control at least three-quarters of the nation's forest land and timber value.

The forest industry today is concerned not only with the supply of such traditional products as lumber, pulp, paper, and board but also with such products as rayon, plastics, dyes, resins, and turpentine. The latter require more complex technology and consequently pump more "value added by manufacture" into the economy.

Its many rivers with large waterfalls make Sweden one of the greatest exploiters of hydroelectric power.

Industry. In addition to the majority of Swedish industry, which is privately owned, cooperative enterprises account for about one-half of the rest; the remainder is publicly owned, either by the state or by local authorities. Cooperative activity is relatively greater in the retail area. By combining the more important publicly owned industries into one concern, Statsföretag AB (State Enterprise Ltd.), the state has, however, increased its importance and influence in Swedish industry. Mixed enterprises, with half-public and half-private ownership, also exist.

The role of government, however, cannot be measured only by its direct management of industrial or business enterprise: a large percentage of the GNP goes into the public sector in the form of taxes and social charges, and much of this is returned to the private sector through insurance payments of different kinds.

The taxes are charged partly as a strongly progressive national income tax, partly as a local proportional income tax, partly as a tax on net wealth and as inheritance and gift taxes. To this should be added the profit taxes on businesses and the indirect taxes, particularly the value-added tax.

Trade. To a great extent, Sweden is dependent on foreign trade for its economic growth and development. About one-half its industrial production is sold abroad. The once dominant iron and forest products, while still important, have yielded priority to different kinds of manufactured commodities, especially machinery and transportation equipment, which are now the largest component of Sweden's exports.

Administration of the economy. Since World War II, Swedish economic policy has remained in the liberal tradition in the sense that the government intervened only in general matters and has tried to keep regulation to a minimum. The theory has been, as far as possible, to allow companies independent economic responsibility and then, through the growing public sector, to provide increasing resources for social expenses and other forms of public consumption.

Transportation. Trucks are the main means of transporting heavy goods, while the private automobile accounts for about four-fifths of all passenger traffic. As a result, demands for expressways have been increasing.

By the middle of the 19th century, the railways had begun to compete with older means of transportation. Three main principles ruled the construction of the railways: they must not follow existing shipping routes, whether coastal or canal; they should, except for terminal points, be built through sparsely populated or poor districts rather than through rich areas that often could support their own transportation networks; and a connected and coordinating network of railways should be constructed. Through this policy, new towns grew up at the junctions.

The present national traffic policy, dating from 1963, requires that every kind of transport or communications bear its own expenses. This policy has affected the railways in particular: they have suffered from low profits followed by long-term shutdowns and have been able to maintain themselves only by the movement of goods, yet with a reduced share of even this market.

Domestic shipping along the coasts and on lakes and canals has been extremely important throughout Swedish history. Today, intranational shipping has a limited share of all transports. International shipping, on the other hand, is very lively, with a dozen ports engaged in large-scale commerce with foreign nations.

State ownership of airlines and railways

The air services are dominated by the Scandinavian Airline System (SAS), which is owned chiefly by the states of Sweden, Denmark, and Norway. The interests of SAS are concentrated on international aviation, but a few domestic scheduled services are maintained in Sweden. The rest of the domestic traffic is run by Linjeflyg (LIN), half of which is owned by SAS. The most important airports are in Stockholm, Göteborg, and Malmö.

The interests of the state in transportation and communications are wide. The railways are owned and run by the state, which maintains bus traffic on a large scale and has two subsidiaries that dominate the trucking industry.

Local transportation consists mainly of buses, though Stockholm has a subway. Streetcars were abolished in several cities in connection with the switchover to righthand traffic that took place in 1967, but Göteborg and Norrköping retained trolley service. Generally, local traffic is controlled by local authorities.

ADMINISTRATIVE AND SOCIAL CONDITIONS

Government. According to a 1980 constitutional amendment the crown of Sweden is inherited by the eldest royal child, regardless of sex. Previously the crown was inherited in straight lineal descent on the male side. For decades the monarch's position has been almost exclusively symbolic, a status to be confirmed by fundamental law among other far-reaching constitutional reforms that have been in preparation since the 1950s. These reforms already have led, through partial implementation, to important changes concerning the parliament, or Riksdag, and the electoral system.

The national level. Since January 1971, Sweden has had a unicameral parliament with 349 members elected for three-year terms by direct universal suffrage. The parliamentary system, in use during most of the 20th century, is now constitutionally established. The Riksdag can, by a vote of "no confidence" by a majority of the members, force the resignation of the government or dismissal of a Cabinet minister, unless the prime minister appeals to the country within a week for a new election. The terms of office after such an election last only for the remainder of the original parliamentary period.

Interactions of administrative and parliamentary bodies

The government, under the leadership of the prime minister, is administered by 12 departments, each headed by a Cabinet-level minister; there are, in addition, six consultative ministers, or ministers without portfolio. This parliament-appointed government has taken over, in large measure, the former prerogatives of the monarch, though formally they function as his advisers. Although through this arrangement the government often was able to act independently of the Riksdag, the formal prerogatives of the latter have been strengthened by bestowing the right of initiative on the parliamentary committees, which formerly could only discuss propositions from the government. The work of the committees, including constitutional, finance, and 14 other permanent committees, usually is regarded as the most important part of parliamentary activity. The committees are not open to the public, but their reports are published. In many questions, however, the parliamentary-party groups or conferences between party leaders may play an even greater role than the committees.

Certain characteristics of the former dualism between the monarch (the government) and the Riksdag have been kept. The latter alone has the right of taxation.

Power to enact laws is jointly vested in the Riksdag and in the King in Council, which under the contemporary constitutional practice is the Cabinet appointed in observance of parliamentary principles. Power to institute ordinances and regulations in matters concerned with administration and economic policy is reserved by the Instrument of Government for the King in Council alone, which gives it a wide range of independent action. In practice, however, many of the principles for these so-called economic laws are put before the Riksdag, the decision of which is regarded as binding. So the dividing lines are, on the whole, uncertain.

All lawmaking takes place on the national level—local lawmaking does not exist, because Sweden is a unitary and not a federal state. Ordinances and regulations are of a lower power than laws; they are easier to enact and easier to change. Certain ordinances and regulations of a local character—*e.g.,* parking regulations—can be established by local authorities.

Different rules pertain as to how Swedish laws may be changed. Alterations in the constitutional laws—the Instrument of Government (1809), the Act of Succession (1810), the Parliament Act (1866), and the Freedom of the Press Act (1949)—may be instituted only by the approval of two successive parliaments, between which elections must occur. The civil and criminal laws, on the other hand, may be instituted or changed by the combined agreement of government and parliament. The government itself has authority to change ordinances and regulations. If a general law has been instituted in violation of existing fundamental law, the ability of the Swedish courts to test its validity is limited.

County and local government. Implementation of administrative decisions is, in part, the responsibility of the 24 county (*län*) administrations, which represent the national government in regional administration. Each of these is headed by a governor appointed by the government.

Parallel to the county-state administrations are 23 county councils and 284 municipal councils, elected locally to provide local administration. One county, Gotland, comprises a single municipality and thus has a municipal council but no county council. Health and medical care are primarily the responsibility of the county councils, while the local school system and almost all other social services are the responsibility of the municipal councils.

Justice. Swedish law is the result of a long historical development marked by continuity rather than by abrupt changes. As the result of extensive collaboration with the other Nordic countries, a significant degree of legal uniformity exists throughout Scandinavia, especially in the field of civil law. The Swedish judicial system is built upon written law; practice, customary (or common) law, and judicial precedent retain a strong influence, but the following of precedent is not obligatory. The voluminous body of printed matter—generated by the traditionally careful and prolonged lawmaking process—in which reasons and intent of the law are formulated, is an important source of interpretation for courts, authorities, and individual jurists. Judges and high-ranking administrators—as well as prosecutors, senior police officers, and attorneys—have the same academic training. Moreover, the majority of law graduates serve in one of the courts of first instance for two and a half years to gain experience before taking an appointment in the civil service or embracing other careers.

The primary responsibility for the application of legal rules lies upon the courts and the different administrative authorities. The difference between adjudicative and administrative authorities is less in Sweden than in most European countries: their organization and the division of powers between them have both evolved in response to historical trends rather than to deliberate government planning. Administrative authorities are not partisan representatives of those holding political power at any one time; apart from matters of internal organization and procedure, the lower authorities do not take orders from the higher but follow the generally prevailing rules under their own responsibility. Their decisions may be challenged under appeal provisions resembling those in force for the court system, though in most cases, administrative decisions are not subject to review by a regular court.

Three-tiered hierarchy of courts

Sweden has a three-tier hierarchy of courts: the courts of first instance (*tingsrätter*), the intermediate courts of appeal (*hovrätter*), and the Supreme Court (Högsta Domstolen). In addition to the regular courts of justice, there are also a number of special courts and administrative tribunals.

After a reorganization, which merged the former rural and city courts and considerably reduced their number, Sweden now has about 100 courts of first instance. These courts, in addition to their primary concern with civil and criminal cases, perform many duties of an administrative nature related to conveyancing, land development, guardianships, probate, and the like. An unusual feature of courts of first instance is the *nämnd,* or panel of lay assessors, who take part in the main hearings in most criminal and some civil cases. Assessors (*nämndemän*) are elected for six-year terms by local representative councils from among eligible local citizens; often they are reelected for successive terms. The *nämnd,* which has medieval traditions and has constituted a significant element of democracy in Swedish public life, is not to be confused with the Anglo-American and Continental jury. Its members are concerned not only with verdicts but also with such matters as the sentences to be imposed in criminal cases. A qualified majority of the lay assessors prevails over the contrary opinion of the judge.

Of the six courts of appeal, or of second instance, the oldest and largest is the Svea Hovrätt in Stockholm, established in 1614. Besides serving as appellate bodies, these courts also are responsible for the administration of the court system within their respective areas and for the further training of judges. In their adjudicative capacity, courts of appeal operate in divisions. No limits are imposed on the right of appeal, and about 5 percent of the total number of cases tried by lower courts pass on to a higher court.

The Supreme Court, that of third and last instance, has 24 justices (*justitieråd*), but it works in three sections. Because of the great value attached to its decisions as precedents, however, the entire court also can meet in plenary session—if, for example, there is cause to depart from previously applied principles on any point. The Code of Judicial Procedure defines the classes of cases that may be considered by the Supreme Court after their trial in courts of appeal. A separate section of the court, comprising three justices, determines whether to accept a case for review, and about one-seventh of all appellate decisions are reviewed by the Supreme Court. Like the courts of appeal, the Supreme Court need not confine itself to points of law but may also consider new evidence. Its decisions are final.

Among the special courts, the Court of Impeachment (Riksrätten), empowered under the Instrument of Government to try Cabinet ministers, has not been convened since 1854. Of greater importance is the Labour Court (Arbetsdomstolen), established in 1928, which has exclusive competence in controversies concerning the interpretation and application of collective bargaining agreements. Of its seven members, two represent labour and two management. There are also, for example, first instance special water courts (with Svea Court of Appeal and the Supreme Court as appeal instances), special courts for cases relating to land ownership, boundaries and expropriation, a special insurance court, and a court to deal with such matters as undue clauses in standard contracts.

As already noted, the decisions of administrative authorities are not appealable to an ordinary court of justice. Instead, a complainant can take his grievance to the next highest authority or to a specialized tribunal. In theory, a complainant may appeal the decision of a lower administrative authority to the local county administration or to a specialized agency attached to it. From there, two channels are available. In certain cases—of which dissatisfactions with tax assessments are the most numerous—an appeal against the ruling on county level is lodged with one of Sweden's oldest and most notable administrative tribunals, the Fiscal Court of Appeal (Kammarrätten) in Stockholm. The highest instance in the tribunal system is the Supreme Administrative Court (Regeringsrätten). Cases falling within the competence of this court are enumerated by special statute: generally speaking, these are cases in which the legal element prevails, as in taxation or in the institutionalization of the insane, alcoholics, delinquent youth, and the like. The Supreme Administrative Court is also the final court of appeal against the decisions of local representative councils and authorities in those cases in which such decisions are appealable. The second channel, applicable in all other cases, has the King in Council as its highest instance. Like their counterparts in the regular court system, the higher instances in the tribunal system of adjudication are empowered to review questions of both fact and law.

The institution of the ombudsman

The control system—of great importance to guarantee against injustice from either the judiciary or the administrative authorities—is handled to a large extent by the three *justitieombudsmän* appointed by the Riksdag. Their principal task is to oversee the observance of laws and constitutions and to prosecute officials and civil servants who have committed illegal acts. Consequently, the duty of the ombudsman is aimed especially at controlling the ways in which the authorities execute their power and guaranteeing that the rights of the individual are not violated. The Swedish institution of the ombudsman has served as a model for other nations, including the United Kingdom, Denmark, Norway, and Finland, and it has been instituted at various levels of local government throughout the country.

The political process. All Swedish citizens are eligible and may vote at 18 years of age. Sweden's triennial elections result in proportional representation: *i.e.,* each political party receives the same proportion of seats as it receives votes in the general elections. To avoid a proliferation of small parties, however, a party must get either 12 percent of the votes in one constituency or 4 percent of the votes nationwide to be represented in parliament. Of the 349 seats, 310 are elected directly, while the remaining 39 are distributed among the parties so as to achieve proper proportionality.

Proportional representation and citizen participation

Five parties are represented in the Riksdag. With the exception of 100 days in 1936, the Social Democratic Party formed the government continuously from 1932 to 1976. At two periods it formed a coalition with the Centre (formerly the Agrarian) Party, which won the election of 1976, and with the support of the Communist Left Party it formed the government in 1982. The parties receive financial support from the state in proportion to the number of seats they hold.

Education. School attendance is compulsory for nine years, beginning at age seven. The nine-year comprehensive school is divided into three-year stages: lower, middle, and upper. All pupils follow the same curriculum for six years. The first foreign language, English, is introduced in the third year. In upper classes, training in German and French can also be chosen, while in the gymnasium, for example, Russian, Spanish, Finnish, and Italian can be chosen as well. From the seventh year the curriculum is divided into different lines chosen by the pupils themselves from subjects or groups of subjects. Special education is given to all pupils suffering from physical or mental handicaps.

An important guiding principle in Swedish education is that everyone who wants to continue studying after completing comprehensive school shall have the opportunity. Some pupils choose courses that will qualify them for university study. Other, less theoretical curriculums offer a vocational training.

Sweden has 13 universities: Stockholm, Göteborg, and Uppsala each contain two, and Umeå, Lund, Karlstad, Linköping, Örebro, Luleå, and Växjö each contain one. The oldest university, Uppsala Universitet (University of Uppsala), was founded in 1477. Other institutions for higher education offer training, for example, in technology, medicine, art and music, and journalism. A unified educational system was created in 1977 by the integration of these universities and other institutions of higher education that previously had been administered separately. This unified system encompasses traditional university and professional study as well as programs offered by secondary schools.

Adult-education programs

Strong emphasis is given to adult education. Free evening and daytime classes have been sponsored and administered by both local authorities and state government. The instruction follows the same curriculums as the ordinary school, and the adult pupils can either follow classes in separate subjects or choose the entire alternative.

The folk high schools (*folkhögskolorna*) also offer adult education for those 18 years of age and above. Radio and television courses and instruction by correspondence are forms of education with a large geographical range. Study circles arranged by a number of "study societies" cover a large group of subjects from hobbies to purposeful school or university studies.

Health and welfare. Sweden long has been regarded as a leader in social welfare, and, in spite of inequities, the rights of the citizen for social assistance are manifold. Compulsory health-insurance programs reimburse all but small portions of doctors' fees, hospital treatment, and medicines. The national pension system is paid, beginning at 67 years of age, to all citizens and to foreigners resident in Sweden for a certain period. A supplementary pension, introduced in 1960 and based upon average yearly income, is paid in full to all persons born after 1914.

Children's allowances are paid for each child under 16 years of age, and every mother receives a stipend at each childbirth. Unemployment insurance is based on voluntary premiums, but it is subsidized by the state.

The relatively excellent health conditions of the Swedish people can be attributed to the rugged but basically healthy climate and to the many factors that have made it possible to offer free medical care to every citizen. Medical practitioners of all kinds are able to remain in the vanguard of research, and hospital facilities have been kept among the most advanced in Europe. Preventive medicine, in terms of information to the public and early diagnosis, is in an advanced state. Tuberculosis, the disease that once claimed the most lives, is far down on the scale of causes of death. The main causes of death are, today, those of the other advanced nations: circulatory diseases, cancer, and the like. In the more remote areas, health care is provided mainly through a system of smaller hospitals and of provincial doctors, nurses, and midwives employed by the county councils, each covering a specific area.

CULTURAL LIFE

In the pre-industrial period the cultural manifestations of the small upper class were different and separated from the popular ones. The upper classes took their patterns from the European currents and passed them down to ordinary people. In the other direction, inspiration from popular songs, art motifs, and handicraft work enriched the higher culture.

The changing cultural milieu

Today, popular and upper class cultures are no longer separate in this way. The popular political movements of the 20th century advanced the notion that education and the understanding of the arts were the rights of every person, but this idealistic hope has not been met fully. New forms of entertainment—television, weekly magazines, and popular music of the international type—have taken their places. Poetry, avant-garde literature, and classical music still belong to small specialized groups.

The movement for equality between men and women is of long duration in Sweden. Positive results include greater female participation in the labour market, in higher education, and in politics; broader access to the professions (including the clergy); and more equality in wages and salaries.

The state of the arts. The postwar period has been lively: the "Monday group" of composers was inspired by the antiromantic Hilding Rosenberg in the 1920s and drew also upon leading modern composers from abroad. Their repertoire includes orchestral, operatic, and religious works. The vital Swedish folk song has been developed further by a number of musicians, while Swedish jazz became another phenomenon. A number of Swedish opera singers gained renown throughout the West.

Since the 1920s, Harry Martinson has been a favourite poet in Sweden. His motifs range from the romantic Swedish countryside to global and cosmic visions. Among novelists, Vilhelm Moberg is widely known for the epic and dramatic force in his novels of the Swedish emigrants in the United States and of the farmer-soldiers of old Sweden. Younger novelists tend to treat the social and moral aspects of society.

A multifaceted theatre, opera, and ballet life is found in Sweden. Contemporary international plays are staged throughout the country, and the premieres of several of the posthumously performed plays of the American Eugene O'Neill took place in Sweden. Birgit Cullberg has attained international fame as director of the Swedish Royal Ballet in Stockholm. The Swedish stage and film director Ingmar Bergman gained critical acclaim outside Sweden with his film *Wild Strawberries* (1957). Subsequently, his earlier and later films have been shown throughout the world, and he has been hailed as one of the major film makers of all time.

Modern Swedish art was inspired by early 20th-century romantic nationalism, originating with such painters as Carl Larsson, Anders Zorn, and Bruno Liljefors. Carl Milles, who dominated monumental sculpture in the 1920s, is as famous abroad. At the Paris World's Fair in 1925, an important connection was established between Swedish industry and designers who had both academic art education and popular handicraft tradition. Since then, this combination has been vital, and superb results have been achieved in glassware, ceramics, woodwork, textiles, furniture, silver, and stainless steel.

The genuine rural folk traditions are disappearing with settlement in urban areas. Among those remaining in Gotland, Dalarna, and other areas are special national costumes, dances, folk musicians, and the like, and many traditions are found even in urban settlements. Spring is celebrated on the last night of April with big fires across the country. May 1 is the day of workers' demonstrations. The bright Midsummer Night is celebrated with a big cross placed into the ground and laid with flowers and leaves; children dance around it. Some celebrations have a religious background: Advent, Lucia, Christmas, Easter, and Whitsuntide. The Lucia candlelights are a rather new but very popular custom performed on the dark morning of December 13.

Traditional festivals

Cultural institutions. The traditional cultural institutions were initiated and protected by the king. The Drottningholm Theatre; the Swedish Royal Opera; the Royal Dramatic Theatre; the Royal Academy of Music; the Swedish Academy; the Royal Academy of Letters, History, and Antiquities; the Royal Library; and the Royal Swedish Academy of Sciences, all in Stockholm, date from the 18th century. The universities in Lund and Uppsala have traditions from the Middle Ages, when those cities were major European centres of learning.

In modern Sweden organizations and institutions for cultural activities usually can depend upon state and municipal contributions. The state theatre, the state concerts, and the state exhibitions travel around the country. Idealistic organizations collaborate with the labour groups in establishing the 240 *folkets parker* ("peoples' parks"), a type of out-of-doors entertainment hall for dancing, theatre, shows, and concerts in the summer. These organizations and others, for religious or temperance purposes, have educational branches concerned with adult educational programs involving the folk high schools and evening classes. Such activities are partly financed by the government.

The Nobel prizes

Of special note are the Nobel prizes, initiated in 1901 through a bequest by the Swedish millionaire chemist and industrialist Alfred Nobel. Awarded annually in the fields of chemistry, physics, physiology or medicine, literature, peace, and (since 1968) economics to persons throughout the world for specific or general achievements in their fields, they are administered and bestowed by various Swedish academies and institutes. The peace prize is under the aegis of the Norwegian parliament. For statistical data, see the "Britannica World Data" section in the current *Britannica Book of the Year*. (Ed.)

History

EARLIEST SETTLEMENTS

The first migrations into Sweden probably occurred toward the close of the last glacial epoch (*c.* 12000 BC), when tribes of reindeer hunters roamed across the land bridge that joined Sweden with the Continent. From the early postglacial period there are traces of occupation. Finds in the peat mosses of Skåne show a typical food-gathering culture, which later (*c.* 5000–3500 BC) spread throughout southern Sweden. New tribes, practicing agriculture and cattle rearing, made their appearance about 2500 BC, and soon afterward a peasant culture with good continental communications was flourishing in what are now the provinces of Skåne, Halland, Bohuslän, and Västergötland. The so-called Boat-Ax culture (an outlier of the European Battle-Ax cultures) arrived about 2000 BC and spread rapidly. During the Late Neolithic Period, southern and central Sweden displayed the aspects of a homogeneous culture, with central European trade links; in northern Sweden the hunting culture persisted throughout the Stone and Bronze ages.

The Early Bronze Age (from *c.* 1500 BC) was also characterized by strong continental trade links, notably with the Danube Basin. Stone Age burial customs (skeleton sepulture, megalithic monuments) were gradually replaced by cremation. Rock carvings suggest a sun cult and fertility rites. Upheavals on the Continent, combined with Celtic expansion, seem to have interrupted (*c.* 500 BC) bronze imports to Scandinavia, and a striking poverty of finds characterizes the next few centuries. The climate, comparatively mild since the Neolithic Period, deteriorated, necessitating new farming methods. At this time, iron reached the north.

For the Early Iron Age (*c.* 400 BC–*c.* AD 1) the finds are also relatively scanty, showing only sporadic contacts with the La Tène culture, but they become more abundant from the Roman Iron Age (*c.* AD 1–400) onward. The material from this period shows that Sweden had developed a culture of its own, although naturally reflecting external influences.

Trade links between the Roman Empire and Scandinavia gave Rome some knowledge of Sweden. The *Germania* (written AD 98) of Tacitus gives the first description of the Sviones (Swedes), stated to be powerful in men, weapons, and fleets. Other ancient writers who mention Scandinavia are Ptolemy, Jordanes, and Procopius.

THE VIKING AGE

At the beginning of this period a number of independent tribes were settled in what is now Sweden, and their districts are still partly indicated by the present divisions of the country. The Swedes were centred in Uppland, around Uppsala. Farther south the Goths lived in the agricultural lands of Östergötland and Västergötland. The absence of historical sources makes it impossible to trace the long process by which the Swedes gradually subjugated the remaining areas. This historical event is reflected darkly in the Anglo-Saxon epic poem *Beowulf*—which gives the earliest known version of the word *sveorice, svearike, sverige* (Sweden)—and also in the Old Norse epic *Ynglingatal,* contained in the *Heimskringla* of Snorri Sturluson.

As a result of Arab expansion in the Mediterranean area in the 8th and 9th centuries, the trade routes along the Russian rivers to the Baltic Sea acquired enhanced importance. In the second half of the 9th century, Swedish peasant chieftains secured a firm foothold in what is now eastern Russia and ruthlessly exploited the Slav population.

Trade. From strongholds, which included the river towns of Novgorod and Kiev, they controlled the trade routes along the Dnepr to the Black Sea and Constantinople and along the Volga to the Caspian Sea and the East. Trade in slaves and furs was particularly lucrative, as the rich finds of Arab silver coins in Swedish soil demonstrate. Swedish Vikings also controlled trade across the Baltic; and it was for this activity that Birka, generally regarded as Sweden's oldest town, was founded (*c.* 800). Swedish Vikings overran (*c.* 900) the important Danish trading settlement of Hedeby, and they took some part in raids against western Europe. But from the 10th century, control of the Russian market began to slip from Swedish hands into those of Frisian, German, and Gotland merchants. (L.T.N.)

Uppland

Several centuries before the Viking Age, the area of Uppland became the most important in Sweden (*c.* 500). Large grave mounds of local kings were raised near the present city of Uppsala. Political conditions in Sweden before *c.* 1000 are little known, however, and it is only with the reign of Olof Skötkonung (*c.* 994–*c.* 1022) that the political history of Sweden begins.

Christianization. The first attempt to Christianize Sweden was made by the Frankish monk Ansgar in 830. He was allowed to preach and set up a church in Birka, but the Swedes were little interested. A second Frankish missionary was forced to flee. In the 930s another archbishop of Hamburg, Unni, undertook a new mission with as little success. A heathen temple at Uppsala provided a centre for pagan resistance, and it was not until the temple was pulled down at the end of the 11th century that Sweden was successfully Christianized.

The struggle between the old and new religions strongly affected the political life of Sweden in the 11th century. Olof Skötkonung, ruler of all Sweden, was baptized and supported the new religion, as did his sons Anund Jakob (reigned *c.* 1022–*c.* 1050) and Edmund (*c.* 1050–60). The missionaries from Norway, Denmark, and even Russia and France, as well as from Hamburg, won converts, especially in Götaland, the area where the royal dynasty made its home and where early English missionaries had prepared the ground. Many pagans refused to abandon their old faith, however, and civil wars and feuds continued. Claimants vied for the throne until the mid-13th century, when a stable monarchy was finally achieved.

THE 12TH, 13TH, AND 14TH CENTURIES

At the end of the Viking Age, Sweden remained a loose federation of provinces. The old family of kings died out in 1060; after the death in 1066 of Stenkil, son-in-law of the last of these kings, a civil war broke out. Around 1080 Stenkil's sons, Inge and Halsten, ruled, but Inge was overthrown by his pagan brother-in-law Blotsven, who then held the kingship for three years before Inge regained power. Around 1130, Sverker, a member of a magnate family from Östergötland, was acknowledged as king, and this province now became the political centre of Sweden. Sverker sided with the church and established several cloisters staffed by French monks; he was murdered *c.* 1156. During the later years of Sverker's reign, a pretender named Erik Jedvardsson was proclaimed king in Svealand; little is known about Erik, but according to legend he undertook a crusade to Finland, died violently *c.* 1160, and was later canonized as the patron saint of Sweden.

Civil wars. Erik's son Knut killed Sverker's son (1167) and was accepted as king of the entire country. Knut organized the currency system, worked for the organization of the church, and established a fortress on the site of Stockholm. After his death in 1196, members of the families of Erik and Sverker succeeded each other on the throne for half a century. While the families were battling for the throne, the country received its own archbishopric at Uppsala (1164), the country was organized into five bishoprics (Linköping, Skara, Strängnäs, Västerås, and Växjö, joined later by Åbo in Finland), and cloisters were founded. The church received the right to administer justice according to canon law and a separate system of taxation, protected by royal privileges, and the pretenders sought the church's sanction for their candidacies. The first known coronation by the archbishop was that of Erik Knutsson in 1210. The church also gave its sanction to the "crusades" against Finland and the eastern Baltic coast; the action combined an attempt at Christianization with an attempt at conquering the areas.

The reforms of Knut

By the mid-13th century, the civil wars were drawing to an end. The most important figure in Sweden at that time was Birger Jarl, a magnate of the Folkung family. The *jarls* organized the military affairs of the eastern provinces and commanded the expeditions abroad. Birger was appointed *jarl* in 1248 by Erik Eriksson, the last member of the family of St. Erik, to whose sister he was married. Birger's eldest son, Valdemar, was elected king when Erik died (1250). After Birger defeated the rebellious magnates, he assisted his son in the government of the country and gave fiefs to his younger sons. Birger improved the inheritance rights of women, made laws ordering the peace of the home, women, church, and *thing,* and began the building of Stockholm. The Hanse merchants in Sweden received privileges, and the establishment of towns blossomed.

Birger Jarl

Birger died in 1266; in 1275 Valdemar was overthrown by his brother Magnus Ladulås with the help of a Danish army. Two years later, Valdemar agreed to abandon his claims on the crown and in return received parts of Götaland, which he lost in 1279. In 1280 a law was accepted establishing freedom from taxes for magnates who served as members of the king's cavalry, creating a hereditary nobility; the following year, Magnus Ladulås exempted the property of the church from all taxes. Under Magnus' reign, the position of *jarl* disappeared and was replaced by the *drots* (a kind of vice king) and the *marsk* (marshall), together with the established *kansler* (chancellor). The export of silver, copper, and iron from Sweden increased trade relations with Europe, especially with the Hanse cities.

Magnus died in 1290 and was succeeded by his ten-year-old son Birger. The regency was dominated by the magnates, especially by the *marsk,* Torgils Knutsson; even after Birger's coronation in 1302, Torgils retained much of his power. The King's younger brothers Erik and Valdemar, who were made dukes, attempted to establish their own policies and were forced to flee to Norway (1304), where they received support from the Norwegian king; the following year, the three brothers were reconciled. A new political faction was created by the leaders of the church, whom Torgils had repressed, together with a group of nobles and the dukes, and in 1306, the *marsk* was executed. Birger then issued a new letter of privileges for the church, but his brothers captured and imprisoned him. Two years later the kings of Denmark and Norway attacked Sweden on his behalf. Birger was again recognized king of Sweden in 1310, and transferred half of the kingdom to his brothers as fiefs. Erik's territory, together with his earlier acquisitions, then consisted of western Sweden, northern Halland, southern Bohuslän, and the area around Kalmar and stretched across the borders of the three Scandinavian kingdoms. In 1312 the dukes married two Norwegian princesses, increasing their power and dynastic position; but in December of 1317 the dukes were imprisoned by their brother following a family dinner, and they died in prison. The nobility rebelled against Birger, who was forced to flee to Denmark in 1318, and the King's son was executed.

Revolt of the magnates

Code of law. The magnates now seized control of Sweden and reasserted their power to elect a king. They chose Magnus, three-year-old son of Duke Erik, who had shortly before inherited the crown of Norway. In connection with the election, the privileges of the church and the nobility were confirmed, and the king was not to be allowed to raise taxes without the approval of the council and the provincial assemblies. The magnates now revised the laws of Svealand and by the Treaty of Nöteborg (1323) established the Finnish border with Russia. The Danish province of Skåne was bought and put under the Swedish king; by 1335 Magnus ruled over Sweden, Finland, Blekinge, and Norway, to which he soon added Halland. During Magnus' reign, a national law code was established (*c.* 1350), providing for the election of the king, preferably from among the royal sons, and a new town law code was written that gave the German merchants considerable privileges. In 1344 Magnus' elder son Erik was elected heir to the Swedish throne, one year after his younger brother Haakon received the crown of Norway. Erik made common cause with the nobility and his uncle, Albert of Mecklenburg, against his father; and in 1356, Magnus was forced to share the kingdom with his son, who received Finland and Götaland. Two years later, Erik died and the kingdom was again united under Magnus' rule.

In his struggles with the nobles, Magnus received the support of the Danish king, Valdemar Atterdag, and in 1359 Magnus' son Haakon of Norway was engaged to Valdemar's daughter Margaret. The following year, Valdemar attacked Skåne, and Magnus relinquished Skåne, Blekinge, and Halland in return for Valdemar's promise of help against Magnus' Swedish enemies. In 1361 Valdemar attacked Götaland and captured Visby, an important Baltic trading centre. Haakon, who had been made king of Sweden in 1362, and Margaret were married in 1363. Magnus' opponents among the nobility went to Mecklenburg and persuaded Duke Albert's son, also named Albert, to attack Sweden; Magnus was forced to flee to Haakon's territory in western Sweden. In 1364 the Folkung dynasty was replaced by Albert of Mecklenburg. Albert joined in a coalition of Sweden, Mecklenburg, and Holstein against Denmark, and succeeded in forcing Valdemar Atterdag from his throne for several years. Albert was not as weak as the nobles had hoped, and they forced him to sign two royal charters stripping him of his powers (1371, 1383). At the end of the 1380s, Albert had plans to reassert his power, primarily by recalling the royal lands that had been given to the nobles; and in 1388 the Swedish nobles called upon Margaret, now regent of Denmark and Norway, for help. In 1389 her troops defeated and captured Albert, and she was hailed as Sweden's ruler. Albert's allies harried the Baltic and continued to hold out in Stockholm, and it was only in 1398 that Margaret finally won the Swedish capital. In 1396 her great-nephew Erik of Pomerania was hailed as king of Sweden, and in 1397 he was crowned king of Sweden, Denmark, and Norway, marking the beginning of the Kalmar Union.

Albert's attack on Sweden

THE KALMAR UNION

Sweden entered the Kalmar Union on the initiative of the noble opponents of Sweden's German king, Albert of Mecklenburg (1363–89). The nobility, many of whom held estates over the national borders, called on Margaret for help; and after a war with the Germans, Margaret was hailed as the regent of Sweden (1389), with her great-nephew Erik of Pomerania as her successor (1396). The national council announced its willingness to return those royal estates that had been given to its members during Albert's reign, and Margaret succeeded in carrying out the recall of this property. She remained popular with the Swedes throughout her reign, but her successor, Erik, appointed a number of Danes and Germans to administrative posts and interfered in the affairs of the church. His bellicose foreign policy caused him to extract taxes and soldiers from Sweden, arousing the peasants' anger. His war with Holstein resulted in a Hanse blockade of the Scandinavian states in 1426, cutting off the import of salt and other necessities and the export of ore from Sweden, and led to a revolt by Bergslagen peasants and miners in 1434. The leader, Engelbrekt Engelbrektsson, formed a coalition with the national council; in 1435 a national meeting in Arboga named Engelbrekt captain of the realm. Erik agreed to change his policies and was again acknowledged as king of Sweden by the council. Erik's agreement was not fulfilled to the Swedes' satisfaction, however, and in 1436 a new meeting at Arboga renounced allegiance to Erik and made the nobleman Karl Knutsson captain of the realm along with Engelbrekt. Soon after, Engelbrekt was murdered by a nobleman; Karl Knutsson became the Swedish regent, and in 1438 the Danish council deposed Erik, followed in 1439 by the Swedish council.

The Danish council elected Christopher of Bavaria as king in 1440, and Karl Knutsson gave up his regency, receiving, in return, Finland as a fief, whereupon the Swedish council also accepted Christopher. He died in 1448 without heirs, and Karl Knutsson was elected king (Charles VIII) of Sweden. It was hoped that he would be accepted as the union king, but the Danes elected Christian of Oldenburg. The Norwegians chose Charles as king, but a meeting of the Danish and Swedish councils in 1450 agreed to give up Charles's claims on Norway, while the councils agreed that the survivor of Charles and Christian would become the union king or, if this was unacceptable, that a new joint king would be elected when both were dead. Karl refused to accept this compromise, and war broke out between the two countries. In 1457 the noble opposition, led by Archbishop Jöns Bengtsson Oxenstierna, rebelled against Charles, who fled to Danzig. Oxenstierna and Erik Axelsson Tott, a Danish noble, became the regents, and Christian was hailed as king of Sweden. Christian increased taxes, and in 1463 the peasants in Uppland refused to pay and were supported by Oxenstierna, whom Christian then imprisoned. The Bishop of Linköping, a member of the Vasa family, led a rebellion to free the Archbishop, and Christian's army was defeated. Karl Knutsson was recalled from Danzig and again became king, but within six months difficulties between him and the nobles, especially Oxenstierna and Vasa, forced him to leave the kingdom. Oxenstierna served as regent from 1465 to 1466 and was succeeded by Tott; and the battles between the two families led to the recall of Karl Knutsson, who ruled from 1467 to his death, in 1470.

Political conflict. The period of Charles VIII's reigns was marked by the rivalry of two native parties in Sweden: one, led by the Oxenstiernas and Vasas, contained the old landowning class in central Sweden, including the church and the nobility, who preferred the rule of the council to a strong monarch and felt that a distant union monarch was best; the other, led by the Totts and Karl Knutsson and comprising representatives for the growing commercial interests who were interested in uninterrupted trade with Lübeck, saw a national monarchy as the best safeguard for their interests. The new leading family in the 1470s, the Stures, represented the anti-union party.

Party rivalry

After Karl's death, Sten Sture the Elder was elected regent by the council; and his army, including the Totts and their sympathizers, burghers, and men from Bergslagen, defeated Christian's troops in the Battle of Brunkeberg on the outskirts of Stockholm (1471). During Sten's rule, the University of Uppsala was founded (1477). When Christian I died, in 1481, the matter of the union again arose, and in 1483 Hans was accepted as king of Sweden; but Sten managed to delay his coronation until 1497. In 1493 a new element entered Nordic affairs: Hans formed an alliance with the Muscovite Ivan III Vasilyevich directed against Sweden, which led to an unsuccessful Russian attack on Finland in 1495. The council became discontented with Sten's acquisition of power and, in 1497, called on Hans, whose army defeated Sture's. Hans was crowned and Sture returned to Finland. By 1501 Hans's supporters were discontented with his rule, and Sten Sture was recalled as regent. He died in 1503 and Svante Nilsson Sture became regent. In 1506, a new war with Denmark began, in which Lübeck supported the Swedes. Svante died in 1512, and the council now attempted a reconciliation with Denmark under the regency of Erik Trolle, whose family supported the union. Svante's son, Sten Sture the

Younger, led a coup, however, and was elected regent. Peace with Denmark was concluded in 1513.

Last years of the Kalmar Union

The final years of the Kalmar Union were marked in Sweden by the struggle between the archbishop, Gustav Trolle (inaugurated 1516), and Sten Sture the Younger. The Archbishop was head of the council, and he took over the leadership of the pro-union party. A civil war broke out, and in 1517 a meeting of the estates in Stockholm declared Trolle removed from his position. Despite military assistance from Christian II, Trolle was imprisoned. After a defeat by the Swedes, Christian began negotiations and took six noblemen, among them Gustav Vasa, to Denmark as hostages. The Swedish treatment of Trolle brought a papal interdict of Sweden, and Christian could now act as executor. In 1520 the Danish army of mercenaries attacked Sweden, and Sten Sture was mortally wounded in a battle won by the Danes. No leader came forward to replace the regent, and the noblemen and clergy sought a compromise. Christian was acknowledged as king in return for a promise of mercy and constitutional government. The peasants, led by Sten's widow, refused to abandon the war, however, and it was several months before Stockholm capitulated. Christian was then crowned by the Archbishop as hereditary monarch, breaking his promises to the council; and despite promises of amnesty, 82 people, noblemen and clergy who had supported the Stures, were executed for heresy in the Stockholm Bloodbath. The responsibility for this execution has aroused considerable discussion among Swedish and Danish historians; the large part played by Gustav Trolle is now generally accepted.

End of the union. Christian II now appeared to have Sweden under his control, but not all his opponents were dead or in prison. The nephew of Sten's widow, Gustav Vasa, had escaped from his Danish prison and returned to Sweden in 1520. After the Bloodbath, he went to Dalarna, where the Stures had their staunchest support, and soon a rebellion there was underway, followed by others around the country. By the spring of 1521, the army of men from Dalarna had won its first battle with the Danes, and soon noblemen were allying themselves with Gustav, who was chosen regent in August. In 1522 he persuaded Lübeck to aid the Swedish rebels; in 1523 the Danish nobility forced Christian to give up the Danish throne and elected Frederik of Holstein-Gottorp as king. Three months later Gustav Vasa was elected Sweden's king by a meeting of the estates, and the Kalmar Union was dissolved.

The balance of power in Sweden shifted during the union from the monarchy to the nobility, who took over the government of the country while the union kings were resident in the other kingdoms. The monarchs' attempts to control the administration by appointing their own supporters from Denmark aroused protests and rebellion from the Swedes. During the later half of the union, a split developed within the nobility between a pro-union and an anti-union faction. The pro-unionists generally owned estates in Denmark or Norway as well as in Sweden and believed that a union monarch would enable the nobility to exercise greater influence; the anti-union nobles preferred a strong national monarchy supported by a strong national nobility. The king and regents elected in Sweden during the union period came from within the ranks of the anti-union nobility.

An important new class in society was composed of the commercial men and miners from Bergslagen, who were interested in the unimpeded export of Sweden's iron and copper. When the Danish interests conflicted with their own, most notably during the wars with the Germans, these men rebelled and supported a strong national monarchy, as did the burghers, who were also interested in the growth of trade. The church, on the other hand, preferred a weak monarch and supported the union.

The great majority of Swedes continued to be peasants, and cultivation was expanded into areas of Norrland and the Finnish wilderness. The major surplus product was butter; from the mid-14th century, a fourth of Sweden's export consisted of this product. As the lands exempt from taxation owned by the nobility and the clergy increased, the burden of taxation on the peasants grew; from the Engelbrekt rebellion in the 1430s through the remaining decades of the union, the peasants fought on the side of the anti-union forces. (H.En.)

THE 16TH AND 17TH CENTURIES

Separation from Denmark–Norway. Until 1523, Denmark, or the Scandinavian Union, was the only important power in northern Europe. The secession of Sweden started a process of disunion lasting for more than 400 years.

Swedish independence

The events in the 1520s finally weighed the balance toward Swedish independence. After the Bloodbath of Stockholm in 1520, Sweden in 1521 was moved to revolt against Christian. The King went back to Denmark, only to see another revolt there in 1523, upon which he chose to retire to the Netherlands and the protection of his mighty brother-in-law, the Holy Roman emperor Charles V. But there was no hope for Christian to reconquer Sweden. Although the Swedish bishops had as a rule favoured the union, no Swedish bishop after the Bloodbath could possibly dream of an alliance with Christian—the "tyrant" in the propaganda of Gustav I Vasa, who became king in 1523. The victorious independence faction was an alliance between Swedish high nobility, the farmer-miners of the Dalarna region, and Lübeck, the old enemy of a Scandinavian Union. Gustav, in fact, liberated Stockholm in 1523 with the economic and military help of the Hansa. In his next step toward complete independence, however, Gustav convinced the Diet of Västerås in 1527 to transfer the major part of church property to the crown in order to rid Sweden of Hanseatic influence.

Wars between Sweden and Denmark. For more than a century thereafter, an aim of Danish foreign policy was to reestablish the union. The real issue, however, was the competition for mastery of the Baltic Sea (*Dominium Maris Baltici*). In the 16th and 17th centuries the Baltic region was as important as either the Mediterranean or the Atlantic, providing Europe's main source of grain, iron, copper, timber, tar, hemp, and furs. Thus the mastery of the Baltic, in addition to being an internal Scandinavian problem, was vital to the western European powers, which needed free access to the Baltic commodities. These powers, and later Russia, on its ascendancy, wanted a divided but evenly balanced north.

In this perspective, the wars between Denmark and Sweden might be divided into the following periods: (1) the Swedish buildup, 1520–1628; (2) Swedish predominance, 1628–1709; (3) the annihilation of Sweden as a great power (1709–21).

The Swedish buildup. Because of Swedish measures against Lübeck after 1523, which aided the Danes, Denmark had no interest in waging war against dissident Sweden. Further, Denmark had to look to the empire and the Emperor, whose nieces claimed the Danish throne. Thus there was peace in Scandinavia until 1560. Perhaps this was due to the wisdom of the Reformation kings—Christian III of Denmark and Gustav Vasa of Sweden. Russians, from the principality of Moscow, advanced toward the part of the Baltic coast east of Poland in the 1550s. Denmark, since 1360 in possession of Gotland off the eastern coast of Sweden, now also bought the island of Ösel, in the northeastern Baltic. In 1560 Sweden decided on the ominous project of crossing the Gulf of Finland from Finland, hoping to annex the harbour of Reval (now Tallinn) in northern Estonia. This established the Swedish strategy for the following 150 years (*i.e.,* to conquer the important Baltic harbours and to control sufficient parts of the hinterland to dominate and tax the Baltic trade).

Swedish and Danish strategy

Denmark, with Zealand (Sjaelland) and Skåne and the fortifications of Helsingør (Elsinore) and Helsingborg, controlled the Sound; but its offensive strategy was to gain maritime hegemony of the Baltic Sea and to destroy any Swedish harbour in the west. From this point of view, the importance of the Nordic Seven Years' War (1563–70) is that Denmark failed in its aspirations to Baltic hegemony and that the greater part of its navy was sunk off Gotland. Thus Sweden could henceforth transport its armies quite freely in the Baltic area and could not be invaded. This situation remained unchanged until the early 18th century, when Tsar Peter the Great of Russia built Kronstadt, at the eastern end of the Gulf of Finland, and a Baltic fleet.

With its growing mastery of the Baltic area, Sweden needed free access to the Atlantic in order not to depend entirely on the passage through the Sound. Its brief occupation in 1564 of Trondheim, Norway, is an indication of this need, as are Swedish claims to the entire northern half of the Nordic peninsula. These also show that Sweden wanted a harbour in the north, to compete with the Russian harbour of Arkhangelsk. Faced with these pretensions, Denmark decided on a war against Sweden (the Kalmar War, 1611–13), with the ultimate aim of restoring the union. The Danes forced Sweden to accept the occupation of what later became Göteborg harbour until Sweden had paid a huge war tribute, and to give up its pretensions in the north. In four years Sweden had paid the war tribute, chiefly by selling copper on the bourse of Amsterdam. With Dutch support, the harbour of Göteborg grew, thus assuring Swedish access to the Atlantic in case Denmark blocked the Sound.

Swedish predominance. The Thirty Years' War (1618–48) and its aftermath brought a different strategic situation. Denmark tried, not very wisely, to stop the Habsburg advance toward the north in 1625–29. Sweden, suddenly seeing its position in the Baltic threatened by the Emperor, concluded the Truce of Altmark (1629) with Poland, gaining possession of much of Livland. Then Sweden went to war against the Emperor, with the blessing and support of France and of Poland. Denmark was now faced with Swedish armies in the south. Sweden attacked through Jutland in 1645, and at the Peace of Brömsebro Denmark lost the islands of Ösel and Gotland in the Baltic and even the old Norwegian provinces of Jämtland and Herjedalen. For the Danes, worse was to follow. At the Peace of Westphalia (1648), ending the Thirty Years' War, Sweden annexed the bishoprics of Bremen and Verden and established conditions for friendly relations and dynastic alliances with part of the ducal family of the duchies (Holstein-Gottorp). Sweden thus acquired a permanent base south of Denmark.

Swedish gains in the Thirty Years' War

With things seeming to go badly for Swedish armies in Poland, Denmark desperately tried for revenge in 1657. The effort resulted in a catastrophe. Swedish armies repeated the attack of 1645 through Jutland. In the late winter 1658 the Straits froze—an extraordinary occurrence—so that Charles X Gustavus could lead his armies from Jutland over Fyn to Zealand and toward Copenhagen. In the Peace of Roskilde (1658) Denmark lost all its provinces east of the Sound (notably Skåne), and in addition Norway lost Bohuslän and the county of Trondheim. Still the king of Sweden wanted more. He declared another war late in 1658 to take the rest of the kingdom of Denmark–Norway. Perhaps Sweden could have managed, even with heavy resistance, but the Swedish policy was contrary to the interests of the European powers, notably Holland, which went to the aid of Denmark. The county of Trondheim was recaptured, but Sweden retained Skåne and Bohuslän. The Peace of Copenhagen (1660) thus settled the frontiers between Sweden, Denmark, and Norway at their present boundaries.

The annihilation of Sweden as a great power. It suited European powers that Denmark and Sweden should each have its side of the Sound. Denmark got no support when it tried several times to reconquer the very rich province of Skåne. Nor did the Skånians themselves welcome these attempts. In the Great Northern War (1700–21) Sweden was annihilated as a great power. After the defeat of Charles XII any Swedish hope to rule the Baltic Sea was an illusion. Poland was crumbling. Russia had suddenly made its appearance on the Nordic stage, and Prussia was lurking offstage.

The early Vasa kings (1521–1611). In the Bloodbath of Stockholm in November 1520, 82 leading opponents to the Scandinavian Union were put to death or murdered by Christian II and leaders of the Swedish unionist faction. This event became (or was made) a landmark in Swedish history because it compromised the unionist cause beyond recovery. Gustav Eriksson Vasa had lost his father in Stockholm. The next year he began inciting resistance in Dalarna, a mining district north of Lake Mälar. A rising against Christian "the tyrant" spread from Dalarna to all parts of Sweden. Gustav Vasa was elected protector of the realm in the autumn of 1521. With help from Lübeck, Stockholm and Kalmar were liberated from Christian's rule. In 1523 Gustav I Vasa (ruled 1523–60) was elected king of Sweden.

Construction of the Swedish state

Gustav Vasa devoted the major part of his reign to the construction of the Swedish state. He convinced the Diet of Västerås (1527) to seize the properties of the church. This, with other annexations, gave the crown direct possession of about 60 percent of Swedish soil before Gustav Vasa died. He has been compared to a landowner in his behaviour toward the crown properties and the state incomes. He personally took part in developing their administration, and he personally and continuously inspected the crown servants. He nominated county governors himself and reserved the most important charges for members of his own family. Money economy had barely come to Sweden, and many state incomes were therefore paid in kind; some of these were used directly to feed and clothe public servants and soldiers, others were sold to foreign merchants. Gustav took great pleasure in literally filling the treasury, in which condition it was handed over to his son. The nobility was allowed no part in state affairs, and the Diet was convened only for royal propaganda, in which Gustav was a master. The fundamental traits of his reign resemble those of Christian III in Denmark. But Gustav was much rougher than Christian. In the 1530s and 1540s the farmers grumbled over taxes and the clergymen complained about interference in church matters. Gustav met opposition from his former friends —*e.g.,* the farmer-miners of Dalarna—with the same ruthlessness as that from other dissenters. Gustav led a careful foreign policy; nevertheless, a considerable army and a strong navy were created during his reign.

Three of Gustav's sons became kings of Sweden—Erik XIV (ruled 1560–68), John III (1568–92), and Charles IX (1599–1611). Erik XIV was an ambitious and warlike politician. He proposed to Queen Elizabeth of England with much ardour and a portrait of himself, which still exists. In addition to his wars with Denmark and expansion south of the Gulf of Finland, he tried to oust his brothers from their positions. He emptied the royal treasury in a few years and murdered some noblemen. Charged with lunacy (perhaps wrongly) in 1568, he was deposed. It has been demonstrated that his death was due to arsenic.

His brother John acceded to the throne with the help of the high nobility. John married a Polish princess and in-

The Swedish Empire in 1660.

terfered in Polish affairs. Their son Sigismund was elected king of Poland before inheriting the throne of Sweden in 1592. John was a Catholic; this fact was exploited by his uncle Charles, who organized all conceivable Swedish opposition against the recognition of Sigismund. By doing so, Charles made the Diet (and of course the clergy) a political force against the high nobility. The final outcome was the resignation of Sigismund in 1599.

Charles IX was an administrator very much like his father. His foreign policy aimed at dominating the Russian trade routes toward the Kola Peninsula and the White Sea and to grasp as much as possible of the territory (Russian and other) south of the Gulf of Finland. Sweden thus was exposed to Danish attack in 1611; but Charles did not live to experience the defeat in 1613.

The Age of Greatness. The early Vasa kings created the Swedish state. Its chief characteristic was a strong monarchy in a rather rustic and backward economy (with the mining industry as a very noteworthy exception). Its chief weaknesses were opposition from the high nobility and a thirst for revenge from Denmark. In the following decades Sweden relegated Denmark to second place in the north and became a most aggressive great power.

The reign of Gustavus II Adolphus. Gustavus II Adolphus (ruled 1611–32) was only 16 years old when his father, Charles IX, died; so the actual leadership passed to the aristocrat Axel Oxenstierna and the council. After the Kalmar War the King joined in organizing the Swedes for the next war. Civil servants and officers were selected exclusively from among the nobility. A standing army was organized. The infantry was conscripted among the peasants and regularly trained by officers who lived on the King's farms among their soldiers; only the cavalry and the navy were professional. Swedish copper and iron were made into the best firearms of the period. The Swedish field artillery proved especially mobile and effective. The central administration was professionalized and became a model of efficiency; directing it were members of the high nobility, working together in collegiate bodies.

Swedish society under Gustavus II Adolphus

This war potential was not defensive: it could be used only abroad. It was first directed against the Baltic countries, then against the Emperor himself from 1629. The truce with Poland in 1629 gave Sweden the unique chance to keep most of the coast north of Danzig (Gdánsk) and at the same time secure Polish and French support on the German scene. At Breitenfeld, in 1631, a disciplined and mobile Swedish army practically annihilated the imperial army under Graf von Tilly of Bavaria. A year later Gustavus himself fell on the battlefield of Lützen, against imperial forces led by Albrecht von Wallenstein.

Axel Oxenstierna and the Swedish high nobility decided to carry on the war, even though the danger from the Emperor had passed. The enormous cost and debts of the war could be covered only by domination of the Baltic harbours, by French subsidies, and by a continued involvement in Germany. To retire from Germany now would cause the whole Swedish empire to crumble. The tangible results of the peace treaties of the 1640s were Sweden's grip on Denmark and its domination of most of the Baltic harbours.

Reduction of noble possessions. A generation of continuous war had had a profound impact on Swedish society. The Swedish nobility had gained about two-thirds of Swedish and Finnish soil through the transfer of crown property and of royal ground taxes. The nobles wanted to perpetuate this and to introduce the same feudal structure that they had seen and used in their annexations in the Baltic area.

This danger to Swedish and Finnish peasants was not finally averted until the 1680s, when the noble possessions were greatly reduced. The process of reduction had started in the 1650s because of serious financial problems that the peace in Europe brought to Sweden. Comparatively more of the public expenses now had to be met with taxation, but the nobles refused to pay taxes from their enormous possessions. The royalty could then resort to using the non-noble part of the Diet, in which even the peasants had a representation, to obtain consent to reductions. Faced with this threat, the high nobility agreed to pay, and even to minor reductions in their possessions. There then followed, in 1654–60, wars with Poland and with Denmark–Norway and rule by a regency of aristocrats while Charles XI was still a minor during the 1660s. The high nobles were thus able to retain possession of their advantages for yet another generation.

With the reduction of the holdings of the nobility in the 1680s Sweden returned to the political structure of the early Vasa kings. The income of public properties recaptured from the nobility was permanently allotted to public servants, officers, and soldiers. This system, which remained in force throughout the 18th century and far into the 19th, made the crown less dependent on the Diet in matters of finance. The nobles after all made a good deal during the reductions because they were able to rearrange their remaining holdings, thereby creating large contingent domains. The years 1680–1700 were a period of consolidation. It has been called the Carolingian absolutism because it occurred during the reign of Charles XI (ruled 1672–97). But because of the precariousness of the Swedish annexations in the Baltic, the Carolingian absolutism involved a continuous preparation for war.

Sweden's Carolingian absolutism

The successors of Gustavus Adolphus. One of the most fascinating of all the Swedish monarchs was Queen Christina, the daughter of Gustavus Adolphus. Count Oxenstierna and the high nobility governed the realm and made war when she was a child. During her reign (1644–54) the transfer of crown property to the nobility continued on an increasing scale. She proved to have a remarkably independent will. She refused to marry. She used the Diet and threat of reductions to get her proposed husband, Charles Gustavus of the Palatinate, recognized as heir to the throne. Then Christina, daughter of the "saviour of Protestantism," abdicated, converted publicly to Catholicism, and went to Rome.

Charles X Gustav (ruled 1654–60) seems to have pursued the abortive idea of uniting Scandinavia under his scepter. His sudden death permitted another government by the high nobility until 1672, during the minority of his son. Charles XI acceded to the throne in 1672 at the age of 17. The Swedish, or Carolingian, absolutism, named after him, was exploited by his son, the most famous of all Scandinavian kings, Charles XII (ruled 1697–1718).

The reign of Charles XII. Charles XII acceded to the throne at age 15 at a time when, in the hinterland of the Baltic coast, dominated by the Swedes, new states were being formed. Brandenburg and Russia, together with such older states as Denmark and Poland, were natural enemies of Sweden. Denmark, Poland, and Russia made a treaty in 1699, while Prussia preferred to wait and see. War started in 1700, with an overwhelming Swedish victory at Narva. Charles then turned toward Poland (1702–06). In so doing, he gave Peter the Great sufficient time to found St. Petersburg (now Leningrad) and a Baltic fleet and to reorganize the Russian army. Charles XII began his Russian offensive in 1707. The Russians for the first time used a scorched-earth strategy, thus diverting the Swedish armies from Moscow to the Ukraine, where the Swedes suffered a crushing defeat at Poltava in June 1709.

Swedish defeat at Poltava (1709)

Charles spent the next five years in Bender (now Bendery, Moldavian S.S.R.), then under Turkish rule, trying in vain to convince the Turks to attack Russia. The Sultan clearly had no reason to do so, because Peter had turned his attention toward the Baltic. In the years following Poltava, Russia occupied all the Swedish annexations on the Baltic coast and even Finland; Hannover occupied Bremen and Verden; Denmark took Holstein–Gottorp; and Prussia lay waiting for the Swedish part of Pomerania.

Astonishingly, Charles governed Sweden from his residence in Bender during this catastrophe. In 1715 he returned to Sweden (he had left in 1700). He then decided to attack Norway in order to obtain a western alliance against the Baltic powers. On November 30, 1718, during a siege of the fortress of Fredriksten east of the Oslo fjord, Charles was killed by a bullet of either Norwegian or Swedish origin. His death ended the so-called Age of Greatness. By the Peace of Nystad (1721) Sweden formally resigned the Baltic provinces, part of Karelia, and the city of Vyborg (near St. Petersburg) to Russia.

Finland. Under Swedish sovereignty the Finnish tribes gradually developed a sense of unity, which was encouraged by the bishops of Turku. Study in universities brought Finnish scholars into direct touch with the cultural centres of Europe, and Mikael Agricola, the creator of the Finnish literary language, brought the Lutheran faith from Germany. As part of medieval Sweden, Finland had enjoyed, in effect, a semi-independent status, which had been underlined since 1581, when King John III raised the country to the dignity of a grand duchy. In the course of the administrative reforms (1611–32) of Gustavus II Adolphus, Finland became an integral part of the kingdom, and the educated classes thereafter came increasingly to speak Swedish.

On its eastern frontier Finland was harassed by constant warfare, and the danger became more serious when Novgorod, at the end of the medieval period, was succeeded by a more powerful neighbour, the grand duchy of Moscow. In 1595, however, by the Peace of Teusina, the existing de facto boundary, to the Arctic Ocean, was officially recognized by the Russians. By the Peace of Stolbova (1617), Russia ceded Ingermanland and part of Karelia to the Kingdom of Sweden–Finland. The population of the ceded territories was of the Greek Orthodox faith, and when the Swedish government began their forceful conversion to Lutheranism, many fled to Russia and were replaced by Lutheran Finns. Though Finnish conscripts played their part in making Sweden a great power, the role of Finland in the kingdom steadily decreased in importance. As a result of the Great Northern War the Finns lost their faith in Sweden's capacity to defend Finland, and the years of hostile Russian occupation during the war gave them a permanent feeling of insecurity.

Decline of the Scandinavian clergy

The Protestant Reformation. As noted above, the last Scandinavian bishops all had tied their fate to losing causes: the Swedish bishops to a union with Denmark, the Danish bishops to Christian II and the Emperor, the Norwegian bishops to Norwegian sovereignty. Rome could give very little moral or political help, if any. The winning cause, as everywhere else in Europe, was the national monarchies.

In Swedish and Danish towns (though not in Norway) some serious attempts were made by preachers in the 1520s to reform the church. These attempts received royal support. At the Diet of Västerås in Sweden (1527), Gustav Vasa convinced the Estates to surrender most of the church territories or properties to the crown and to support the preaching of the "pure gospel." The monasteries were suppressed, but the organization of the Swedish Church remained intact. Only in the 1540s was the church reorganized by royal intervention. But the Lutheran Confession of Augsburg was not adopted in Sweden until 1593, and then only as a reaction against a dynastic alliance with Poland and attempts to re-Catholicize Sweden. The Swedish clergy remained one of the four estates in the Diet until 1866.

In Denmark and Norway the civil war of 1533–36 offered a unique chance for the King to arrange church affairs as it suited him or the state. The old bishops were arrested and the properties of the church were confiscated. The state took over the religious tasks of the church, and the clergy became a body of civil servants. The clergy had no political power of their own, even though new Lutheran bishops were appointed. After 1536–37 there was no archbishop in Denmark or Norway. A special law, the Church Ordinance of 1537–39, regulated the religious activity and the affairs of the clergy. In retrospect from the 19th century, the system was named a "state church." But because it had no independent institutions of its own, it would be more appropriate from an institutional point of view to call it a confessional state.

Because the Reformation enabled the Scandinavian monarchies to increase their powers enormously, Lutheran orthodoxy became a political necessity in the following centuries. This explains the still existing religious homogeneity in the Scandinavian countries and the existence of "the public religion of the state" (first paragraph of the Norwegian constitution).

Social and economic conditions. As in most of Europe, agriculture was the main preoccupation in the Scandinavian countries in the 16th and 17th centuries. But rising economic activity in these centuries stimulated a more specialized and commercial exploitation of their natural resources.

Because of the growing demand for cereals and meat in western Europe, Denmark underwent the same change as did the countries east of the Elbe—the domanial system was introduced for commercial agriculture and cattle raising. Sweden and Norway had other resources. Their forests were still virgin, thus providing the indispensable raw materials for European shipbuilding and overseas expansion. Because the trees grew slowly, the wood became hard and well suited also for furniture and tools.

The mining industry in Sweden was founded in the 13th century. In the 16th and 17th centuries copper and iron were the most important exports from Sweden. But Sweden also had its own metallurgical industry, producing weapons especially. The mining industry of Norway was less important, but it supplied Denmark with necessary strategical commodities and with silver from the mines of Kongsberg.

The age-old export of western Norway was stockfish, or dried cod. It now had to compete with cod from Newfoundland in North America. All the North Sea countries joined in the herring fisheries.

The Scandinavian countries had very little active foreign trade of their own. Only Dutch and British and to a certain extent German merchants had sufficient capital and foreign relations to organize the export.

The social consequences of these economic changes were profound. In Denmark the free peasant practically disappeared during these centuries. The Danish county population came to consist of serfs and crofters. Correspondingly, the masters of Danish economic and social life were the landlords. But the state was strong enough to assure a public jurisdiction. In contrast to the Swedish nobility, the Danish landlords had more to gain by exploiting their estates than by waging war; the Danish policy of revenge against Sweden was primarily the affair of the crown. Copenhagen was the political and the economic centre of Denmark–Norway; its name means "harbour of merchants," and it was Danish policy to control and profit by the enormous transit through the Sound.

The natural resources of Norway and Sweden gave no economic basis for landlordship. In Norway the peasants remained free. After 1660 most of the crown properties were sold. Although in Denmark they passed over to the landlord class, in Norway the peasants themselves came to buy the farms they used. Characteristic of Norwegian farming was a combination with other activities—farming and fishing along the coast, farming and forestry in the eastern valleys. This latter combination gave rise to a group of most well-to-do farmers, with crofters dependent on them. The naturalization of foreign merchants was also important in these centuries. Thus Norway for the first time in its history got a native bourgeoisie.

The landlordship in Sweden sprang less from economic than from political causes. The Swedish nobility had a vested interest in lifting Sweden from its underdog position of the 16th century. As noted, the nobles acquired strong positions as commanders and administrators in the conquered areas. Thus, in Sweden, they were able to introduce the domanial system on the soil transferred to them during the Age of Greatness. But, in great contrast to Denmark or the conquered areas, serfdom never came to Sweden; the Swedish farmers remained free. Sweden was the only European country in which peasants formed the Fourth Estate in the Diet. Since the Middle Ages royal propaganda had been designed to influence the opinion of the peasants in political matters.

Peasant involvement in Swedish politics

Because Swedish industry was adapted to Sweden's aggressive foreign policy and because exports were in foreign hands, there was little room for an independent bourgeoisie in this period. Social mobility was primarily influenced by the state. Individual careers and personal fortunes could best be made as soldiers, purveyors to the crown, officers, and public servants. In the 16th and 17th centuries the social structure of Sweden also spread to the formerly completely agrarian Finland.

Swedish society had a considerable capacity for assimilation. Although Denmark–Norway did not until 1720 give up hope of recapturing the provinces that had been lost to Sweden around the middle of the 17th century, it could not count on active support from the populations of these provinces.

THE 18TH CENTURY

Charles XII had no successor. In 1718 his sister Ulrika Eleonora had to convene the Diet in order to be elected. In 1720 she abdicated in favour of her husband, Frederick of Hessen (ruled 1720–51).

Growth of parliamentary government. This period saw a transition from absolutism to a parliamentary form of government. The real reason for the change was the complete failure of the policy of "greatness" connected with the Carolingian absolutism. According to the constitutional laws of 1720–23 the power now rested with the estates. The estates met regularly in the Diet, which designated the council. There the king was accorded a double vote but had no right to make decisions. In the Diet, decision making took place in the "Secret Committee," from which the peasants, or the Fourth Estate, were excluded. The public sessions of the estates in the Diet were reserved for speeches and debates. The three upper estates consisted mainly of state servants. Thus the so-called Age of Freedom until 1772 also was an age of bureaucracy.

Adoption of the dual party system in Sweden

During this period, a dual party system evolved; the parties were known by the nicknames "Nightcaps" (or "Caps") and "Hats." Both parties were mercantilist, but the Nightcaps were the more prudent. Up to 1738 the Nightcaps were in power. They led a most careful foreign policy so as not to provoke Russia. From 1738 to 1765 power passed to the Hats, who made treaties with France in order to obtain subsidies and support against Russia. War with Russia in 1741–43 led to a temporary Russian occupation of Finland and to a further loss of Finnish provinces northwest of St. Petersburg. A war with Prussia in 1757–62 was very expensive. The Hats attempted to make Sweden a great economic power; but their economic policy and the war costs led to inflation and financial collapse, and their regime came to an end in 1765.

For some years political confusion reigned in Sweden. The Nightcaps received subsidies from Russia, and their negotiations with Prussia and Denmark intensified party struggle in Sweden. Economic chaos, territorial losses, foreign infiltration, and famine in the countryside undermined the parliamentary system. Historians have sometimes stressed these failures too strongly, however, in glorifying the past Carolingian age and the future Gustavian epoch.

Absolutism of Gustav III. At the death of Adolf Frederick (ruled 1751–71), Gustav III (ruled 1771–92), visiting in Paris, acceded to the throne. Before returning he concluded another treaty with France. In 1772 he used the royal guard and officers of the Finnish army to seize control of the government from the parliament in a bloodless coup d'etat. Gustav tried to exploit the Vasa and Carolingian traditions of personal royal power. He could rely on no class of the Swedish society nor on the political institutions of the 18th century, so he had to make the most of royal propaganda to the public. In this he was not without success; the traditional picture of Gustav is that of "King Charming," the promoter of the arts and sciences.

But Gustav's politics were unstable. Until 1786 he put into effect social reforms that belonged to enlightened despotism, thus enmeshing himself in its traditional dilemma: alienating the "haves" without satisfying the "have nots." Even his solution to the dilemma was a traditional one—war. After Turkey attacked Russia in 1787, Gustav went to war against Russia in 1788 to recapture the Finnish provinces. The Swedish attack failed, partly because of a conspiracy by noble Swedish officers—the Anjala association—who, during the war, sent a letter to Catherine II of Russia, proposing negotiations. Gustav used the treason of the Anjala association to provoke an outburst of genuine patriotism in Sweden, hoping to channel popular opinion through the Diet, which he convened in 1789. This Diet, however, against his will, abolished practically all the privileges of the nobility (*e.g.,* the nobility no longer had special rights to any posts in the administration nor to any category of Swedish land). In March 1792 the King was mortally wounded by a nobleman and former officer of the royal guards. The last years of the King and especially the days between the assassination attempt and his death (March 29) made him a martyr in the minds of his people, perhaps undeservedly.

Conspiracy by the Anjala association

The one notable feat in the Swedish economy during the 18th century was a growth in iron production. With growing competition from Russia, Sweden was a main supplier of iron to the European market. Royal manufactures were a failure, however, and there were no Swedish economic innovations during the century.

In the rural population a social change took place. Most of the peasants during the 18th century came to own their farms. This development coincided with the growth of a large rural proletariat, mainly different types of tenants who served as soldiers or labourers to landlords and peasants. The nobility became less exclusive, and money became more useful for social climbing. But noble birth still helped greatly.

THE NAPOLEONIC WARS AND THE 19TH CENTURY

Royalist reaction. A fear of influences from revolutionary France dominated the Swedish government during the last decade of the 18th century and the first of the 19th. These fears were reflected in major economies in public finances, the legislation of land reforms, and the censoring of French literature. Gustav IV (ruled 1792–1809), unlike his father, Gustav III, was pious and superstitious. He considered events in France to be insults to moral order. A deep aversion toward the revolutionaries and Napoleon characterized his foreign policy. Of decisive importance was his resolution in 1805 to join the coalition against France. When France and Russia signed the Treaty of Tilsit in 1807, Gustav stubbornly accepted war, even with Russia. Denmark, which had sided with France in October 1807, declared war against Sweden in 1808. England, at the moment busy in Spain, could offer little help. Sweden thus became politically isolated, with enemies in the east, south, and west. The Swedish army defended Finland poorly, reaching its nadir when the strong fortress of Sveaborg near Helsingfors was handed over to the Russians by treason. The Russians advanced as far as Umeå in Sweden. Finally, in 1809, a bitter peace was made at Fredrikshamn, in which Sweden surrendered Finland and the Åland Islands (northeast of Stockholm) to Russia.

Surrender of Finland to Russia

In March 1809 Gustav IV was deposed by a group of high officials and officers. More than anything, a widespread longing for a quick and cheap peace brought the men of 1809 to power, but they were unable to save Finland. A new constitution was made, embodying the principle of separation of powers. The division of the Diet in four estates remained. Charles XIII (ruled 1809–18), the uncle of Gustav IV, was elected king. The fact that he was senile and childless opened the question of succession to the throne.

With the consent of Denmark, the commander in chief of the Norwegian army, Christian August (at the moment waging war against Sweden), was elected crown prince, and took the name Charles August. Behind this decision were thoughts of a Scandinavian confederation. This solution was cherished by Denmark and even by Napoleon.

In 1810 Charles August died, and the question of the succession to the throne was reopened. A Swedish lieutenant, Baron Carl Otto Mörner, was sent to Paris to explain the situation to Napoleon. At the same time he worked for his own plans—to pick one of Napoleon's commanders for the throne of Sweden. The choice fell on the prince of Pontecorvo, the marshal Jean-Baptiste Bernadotte. This choice pleased Napoleon, though he may have preferred the Swedish throne to be taken over by his ally King Frederick VI of Denmark–Norway. Meanwhile the French consul in Göteborg and the francophile Swedish foreign minister, Engeström, managed to persuade the Diet to set aside the Danish alternative and to name Bernadotte as crown prince of Sweden in August 1810.

Bernadotte. From his arrival in Sweden in October

1810, Bernadotte, who took the name Charles John, became the real leader of Swedish politics. In designating him for the crown, the Swedes hoped that he would somehow reconquer Finland and the Åland Islands. When Napoleon attacked Russia in 1812, Charles John personally negotiated with Tsar Alexander, offering help against Napoleon if the Tsar would permit Sweden to occupy Finland or even only Åland. The Tsar declined. Quite soon Russia needed no foreign help against Napoleon.

Charles John then turned to the West. In March 1813 he negotiated a treaty with England by which, for participating in the final offensive against Napoleon, Charles John was to obtain Norway. Thus Charles John became commander in chief of the northern allied army, consisting of Prussian, Russian, and Swedish soldiers. He used this army sparingly, especially the Swedish contingent, even at the Battle of Leipzig in October 1813, because he cherished a hope of succeeding Napoleon and also because he needed troops to attack Denmark. After Leipzig, Charles John refused to cross the Rhine; instead he led the northern army against Denmark. The result was the Peace of Kiel, whereby Norway was surrendered.

Charles John's ambitions

By accepting a constitution in Norway, Charles John became heir, peacefully, to his second throne in four years and consequently gained a more independent position in Sweden. He hoped, moreover, to impress favourably liberal circles in France.

The cession of Finland to Russia. In the words of Swedish historian Sten Carlsson, in 1969, "The loss of Finland was the price of the long and still unbroken period of peace that was to begin in 1814." The statement implies that the possession of Finland in the past centuries forcibly brought Sweden in collision with other powers in the Baltic area. When Peter the Great founded the new Russian capital at St. Petersburg and the harbour of Kronshtadt at the bottom of the Gulf of Finland in the first decade of the 18th century, the danger became much more serious. It is significant that Russia acquired wide Finnish areas around St. Petersburg in 1721 and in 1743.

As a part of the Swedish monarchy, Finland had been accorded practically no institutions of its own, but from the middle of the 18th century the majority of officials and intellectuals were of Finnish origin. In those circles there was a growing feeling that Finland had to bear the cost of Swedish extravagances in foreign policy. The feeling was not unfounded. Swedish strategical directives of 1785 implied that in case of Russian attack, Swedish forces should retire from the frontier, leaving Finnish detachments behind, and that under extreme danger the whole of Finland should be evacuated. This strategy was put into effect in 1807–09. Even the treachery of the Anjala association in 1788 was repeated in 1808, when Sveaborg near Helsingfors capitulated to the Russians. The feeling that the Finns could trust nobody other than themselves was born in the end of the 18th century. In 1809 the Finns themselves had to carry the responsibility of coming to terms with Russia. Tsar Alexander offered to recognize constitutional developments in Finland and to give it autonomy as a grand duchy under his throne. When Sweden surrendered Finland in 1809, it even had to give up the Åland Islands northeast of Stockholm. "Russia would not take a trunk (Finland) without the keys." (G.Sa.)

Population, agriculture, and industry. The population of Sweden, which in 1815 was barely 2,500,000, reached 3,500,000 by 1850 and 5,100,000 by 1900. During the period 1815 to 1900, therefore, the country's population had more than doubled, despite a loss of 850,000 emigrants (mainly to North America) during the period 1840 to 1900.

Until the last quarter of the 19th century, Sweden was a predominantly agricultural country. In 1850, 90 percent of the population lived off the land. By 1900 the figure was still as high as 75 percent. At the beginning of the 19th century, rural dwellings were clustered together in the villages, and the fields were cultivated under an old open-field system. The basis for an agricultural modernization was laid down by a statute of 1827 on enclosures (Laga skifte), which stated that when possible the fields of the individual farm should be assembled together in a compact area. Enclosures of lands, which took place throughout the 19th century, changed the face of the countryside. Villages were split up, and scattered farms became the predominant type of dwelling in Sweden. The move away from the village system brought about a widespread reclamation of wasteland and the modernization of agriculture, which accounted in part for the increase in population.

Enclosures

During the first half of the 19th century, trade and industry were still restricted by regulations and guild rules. The middle of the 19th century saw the beginning of industrial organization, primarily in the timber trade, and in the last quarter of the 19th century the industrial revolution began in earnest with the advent of new methods in iron and steel production and the birth of a number of specialized industries, such as those of machines and machine tools. During the greater part of the 19th century, however, Sweden was a poor and overpopulated country.

The conservative era (1815–40). At the conclusion of the Napoleonic Wars, Sweden was hard-hit by an economic slump that lasted until 1830, characterized by abortive attempts to reestablish the value of the currency. After devaluation in 1834, the currency was finally stabilized. Crown Prince Charles John (Carl Johan), who was king under the name of Charles XIV John (ruled 1818–44), pursued a strictly conservative policy. The king's power, invested in him by the constitution, was exploited to the limit; and the ministers were recruited from his henchmen without regard to the wishes of Parliament. In the 1820s the liberal opposition steadily increased its demands for reforms, and 1830 was the year in which liberal opinion made a breakthrough. In Sweden this was indicated by the establishing of a newspaper, *Aftonbladet,* which with Lars Johan Hierta as editor, became the leading journal of the liberal opposition. Simultaneously, the king's one-man-rule, which was exercised through his powerful favourite Magnus Brahe, became even more emphatic. The struggle against the growing liberal opposition, which reached its climax at the end of the 1830s, was characterized by actions against the freedom of the press and indictments of high treason and countered by the liberals with sharp criticism, demonstrations, and street riots.

The growth of the liberal opposition

The liberal reform period. The pressure of the opposition, however, at last forced the king to yield, and the 1840 Parliament, in which the liberal opposition had the majority, forced through the "departmental reform," which meant that the ministers actually became the heads of their own ministries. Another reform of great significance was the introduction in 1842 of compulsory school education. When Charles XIV John died in 1844 and was succeeded by his son Oscar I (ruled 1844–59), the liberal reform period had already gained momentum.

Principal reforms. Among the most important of the reforms was the introduction of free enterprise in 1846, which meant the abolition of the guilds. They were now replaced by free industrial and trade associations. Simultaneously, the monopoly of trade that the towns had held since the Middle Ages was also abolished. Finally, by the introduction of a statute in 1864, complete freedom of enterprise became a reality. The lifting of almost all bans on exports and imports in 1847, together with a reduction in customs duties, was the first step toward free trade. A number of other liberal reforms were introduced: equal rights of inheritance for men and women (1845), unmarried women's rights (1858), a more humane penal code through a number of reforms (1855–64), religious freedom (1860), and local self-government (1862). Another significant step was the decision in 1854 that the state should be responsible for the building and management of main-line railroads.

Parliamentary reform. Oscar I, who took the initiative himself in many of these reforms, became more conservative after the disturbances in Stockholm in 1848. When he was succeeded by his son, Charles XV (ruled 1859–72), the power had in reality gradually passed into the hands of the Privy Council, which, under the leadership of the minister of finance, Baron Johan August Gripenstedt, and the minister of justice, Baron Louis De Geer, completed the reforms. From the beginning of the 19th century the most important of the liberal demands had been for a reform of

Introduction of a two-chamber Riksdag

the system of representation. It was not until 1865–66 that agreement was reached to replace the old Riksdag with its four Estates of nobility, clergy, burghers, and peasantry with a parliament consisting of two chambers with equal rights. The members of the first were chosen by indirect vote and with such a high eligibility qualification that it bore the stamp of an upper chamber representing great landowners and commercial and industrial entrepreneurs. The members of the second were chosen by direct popular vote, which was limited, however, by a property qualification and therefore gave the farmers an advantage.

Political stagnation (1866–1900). The reform of the representative system marks the end of the liberal reform period. During the following 20 years, Swedish politics were dominated by two issues: the demand for an abolition of ground tax, which had been levied from ancient times, and the defense question, where the demand was for an abolition of the military system of *indelningsverket* (that is to say, an army organization in which the soldiers were given small holdings to live on). The defense system was to be modernized by an increase in conscription. The First Chamber's demand for rearmament, however, was impossible in view of the Second Chamber's demand for the abolition of the ground tax. As these issues had been linked together in the 1873 compromise, they were not resolved until 1892, when it was decided to abolish the ground tax and replace the old army organization with a larger and better trained conscripted army. The latter was completed through the defense reform of 1901, which introduced a conscripted army with a 240-day period of service.

The heavily falling prices of corn on the world market in the 1880s gave rise to a serious agricultural crisis. In 1888 a moderate tariff was introduced that was gradually raised in the following years. The Second Chamber, which, since the electoral reform had been dominated by the farmers' party, was at this time split into a protectionist faction and a free-trade faction. With the appearance of the Social Democrats in 1889, the Liberal factions in the Riksdag merging into the Liberal union in 1900, and the Conservative groups forming a united election organization in 1904, there came into being the parties that still dominate Swedish politics today.

Foreign policy. Until the end of the 19th century, foreign policy was still regarded as the monarch's personal province. Already, as crown prince, Charles John had concluded an alliance with Russia against almost unanimous opposition and by so doing initiated the Russia-oriented policy that characterized the whole of his reign. The succession of Oscar I to the throne in 1844 brought no immediate alteration. The only deviation was in his somewhat carefully demonstrated sympathy for the growing Pan-Scandinavian movement. When the German nationals rebelled against the Danish king in 1848, Oscar I aligned himself with Frederick VII and contributed, together with the tsar, to a cease-fire and armistice.

Change in alliance policy. During the negotiations on Schleswig-Holstein, Oscar I was still on the side of Tsar Nicholas I of Russia, aligned more or less against the radical nationalism in Germany. But in reality he endeavoured to extricate Sweden from the conservative Russia-oriented policy that Charles John had initiated in 1812. The opportunity came during the Crimean War (1853–56), when Oscar I adopted a friendly attitude to the Western powers and, among other things, opened Swedish harbours to English and French warships, and tried to induce the Western powers, with the help of Swedish troops, to attack St. Petersburg. With this intention, he signed the November Treaty with the Western powers in 1855. The peace treaty that was concluded in Paris shortly afterward, however, ended the hopes cherished in Sweden of winning Finland, or at least Åland, back again. All that was gained was the Åland Convention, which forbade Russia to build fortifications or have other military installations on Åland.

Pan-Scandinavianism. During the 1840s and 1850s the idea of a united Scandinavia had won great support among students and intellectuals. Crown Prince Charles had spoken out enthusiastically in favour of this ideal, and, after his succession to the throne in 1859, he assured the Danish king of Sweden's solidarity, promising Swedish support to defend the frontier at the Eider—the southern boundary of Schleswig. Encouraged by these promises, Denmark embarked upon the policy that led to the Danish–Prussian War of 1864. In the event, the Swedish government reluctantly refused to honour the king's pledge. Scandinavian unity suffered a decisive defeat and ceased to be the guiding light of Swedish foreign policy.

Promise of cooperation with Denmark

Neutrality and friendship with Germany. In the wars between Prussia and Austria in 1866 and between Germany and France in 1870–71, Sweden was officially neutral, even if in the latter the king's personal sympathies were with France. Oscar II (ruled in Sweden 1872–1907) reoriented the country's foreign policy. The new German Empire under the leadership of Otto von Bismarck excited his admiration. At the same time, connections with Germany became much closer, and from the mid-1870s Swedish politics were influenced by a close friendship with Germany emphasized during the last years of the 19th century by the growing fear of Russia.

The Swedish–Norwegian Union. From the Swedish viewpoint the union with Norway was a disappointment. Instead of an alliance of the two countries, the incompatibilities grew, and the union was actually confined to a joint monarchy and foreign policy. One of the few positive results of the union was an 1825 statute that abolished or greatly reduced tariffs between the countries. The union also had an important influence on Sweden's domestic affairs, and Norway served as a model for Swedish radicals who demanded parliamentary democracy.

The governor-general question

As crown prince in the 1850s, Charles XV had promised the Norwegians that on his succession to the throne he would abolish the post of governor general, which in Norway was regarded as a sign of the country's subordinate position in the union. In reality, this question was relatively unimportant, as the post of governor general had not been occupied by a Swede since 1829 and had been vacant since 1855. When Charles XV succeeded to the throne, however, and tried to honour his pledge to abolish the post, the Swedish Parliament and the government headed by the powerful minister of finance, Baron J.A. Gripenstedt, opposed the resolution. Charles XV was forced to give way. The government, with support from Parliament, had thus strengthened its position over the king. The governor-general question marked the beginning of the struggle for power between king and Parliament that characterized Sweden's internal politics for the latter part of the 19th century. In 1905 the union question again influenced Swedish domestic affairs. With the dissolution of the union, the king's power was usurped, and a government chosen by the majority parties in Parliament and headed by the right-wing leader Christian Lundeberg was appointed to negotiate with Norway. Thus the dissolution of the union led to the first real parliamentary government in Sweden.

THE 20TH CENTURY

The economic expansion that started in the early 19th century laid the foundations for internal developments in Sweden during the 20th century. The turning point came during and immediately after World War I. There was suddenly a worldwide demand for Swedish products such as steel and pulp, matches and ball bearings, telephones and vacuum cleaners. The composition of the population underwent a decisive change, and Sweden was transformed from an agricultural to a modern industrial country.

Political reform. Politically, the economic development meant that a universal and equal franchise was more and more vociferously demanded. The issue was solved in 1907 by a compromise submitted by a Conservative government under the leadership of Arvid Lindman. The motion granted a universal and equal franchise for the Second Chamber, a certain democratization of the First Chamber, and proportional representation for elections to both chambers of the Riksdag. The elections to the Second Chamber in 1911 produced a landslide victory for the Liberal Party (Liberala Samlingspartiet), and Gustav V (ruled 1907–50) was forced to ask Karl Staaff to form a Liberal government.

Defense policy. One of the most important points of Liberal policy in 1911 was a decrease in military expenditure. The realization of this demand led to sharp conflicts between Gustav V and Staaff. As the tension between the great powers grew, a farmers' rally was organized, and 30,000 farmers from all over the country sought out the King and demanded that the country's defenses be strengthened. In his reply (Borggårdstalet, the Courtyard Speech) the King promised to reinforce the military defenses. As he had given this pledge without having consulted the government, it resigned, and the King appointed a civil servant government with Hjalmar Hammarskjöld as prime minister.

The Courtyard Speech

Policy during World War I. During World War I, Sweden attempted to remain neutral and to assert its right to trade with the belligerent countries. For Great Britain, the blockade was an important weapon, and Sweden's demand to import freely favoured Germany exclusively. As a result, the Allies stopped a large percentage of Sweden's trade. This, however, not only affected Sweden's exports to Germany but from 1916 caused a severe shortage of food. The situation was worsened by unrestricted submarine warfare and by the entry of the U.S. into the war in 1917. Hammarskjöld was forced to resign; he was followed by a Conservative government and shortly afterward by a Liberal one, both of which conducted a more diplomatic trading policy with the Allies. In May 1918 an agreement was reached with Great Britain and the U.S. that allowed Sweden again to import produce from the West, on condition that exports to Germany be limited and that a large part of Sweden's merchant fleet be put at the Allies' disposal.

The Social Democrat–Liberal coalition. In the general election of 1917, the left-wing parties (the Social Democrats and Liberals) secured a further increase in their majority in the Second Chamber, and the King was obliged to choose a Liberal–Social Democratic government. Under Nils Edén, the new government, as one of its first measures, amended the constitution. The main issues were woman suffrage and the introduction of a universal and equal franchise for elections to the First Chamber and in local elections.

Domestic policy (1918–45). *Party politics.* From 1920 onward, a line was drawn between the Socialist parties on one side and the Liberals and Conservatives on the other. From 1920 to 1932 the parties held power alternately, but no government had any chance of gaining firm support for its policy in the Riksdag. From a political viewpoint the 1920s were a period of stagnation.

The economic climate. From an economic point of view, however, the picture was quite different. The 1920s were marked by steadily improving trade conditions, and in this boom period Sweden was one of the countries that prospered significantly.

The Great Depression

Like other countries, Sweden suffered severely during the Great Depression of the early 1930s. Unemployment rose, and reductions in wages caused a series of harsh labour conflicts. The election of 1932 brought a considerable advance to the Social Democratic Party, and to some extent to the Farmers' Party as well, and led to a Social Democratic administration under the leadership of Per Albin Hansson. It offered a comprehensive policy to fight the crisis, including extensive public works and a number of moves in support of agriculture. This policy was subjected to scathing criticism by the right-wing parties, but an agreement reached with the Farmers' Party in 1933 made it possible to implement the program. The economic crisis of the '30s was overcome more rapidly in Sweden than in most other countries. As early as 1936, wages had reached their old level, and by the end of the decade unemployment had become insignificant.

From a political point of view, the '30s were a time of preparation, when a series of bills for radical reforms was worked out. The whole program could be summarized in the term *folkhemmet,* in which society is viewed as a "home" for the people, taking care of their needs in unemployment, sickness, and old age, but with the advent of World War II in 1939, reforms were postponed because of rising military expenditure and supply difficulties.

Foreign policy (1918–45). When World War I ended, Russia and Germany were among the defeated nations, and Sweden thus found itself in an unusually good position regarding external security. In 1925 military expenditure was considerably reduced. Problems regarding foreign policy were confined to Sweden's application for membership in the League of Nations, which was granted in 1920, and to its relationship with Finland.

The Åland question

When the Civil War in Finland ended, the problem of Åland reemerged. The inhabitants of the Åland Islands (Finnish Ahvenanmaa) were purely Swedish-speaking, and a plebiscite revealed that almost all were in favour of affiliation to Sweden. The League of Nations, however, decided in 1921 to award Finland the sovereignty of the islands, though with certain conditions pertaining to internal self-government and limiting the right to fortify or otherwise utilize the islands for military purposes.

Hitler's rise to power resulted in a reexamination of Sweden's defense policy, which in 1936 was amended to strengthen the country's defenses. Sweden followed a strictly neutral course, in close collaboration with the other Scandinavian countries and The Netherlands, Belgium, and Switzerland. As a consequence, Hitler's proposal in the spring of 1939 for a nonaggression pact was rejected. Sweden's attempt to form a Nordic defense union or, failing that, a Swedish–Finnish alliance led to nothing, primarily because the Soviet Union objected.

On the outbreak of war in 1939 Sweden declared itself neutral. When the Soviet Union shortly afterward launched an attack on Finland, Sweden gave Finland aid in the form of vast material supplies and a volunteer corps. On the other hand, Sweden, in common with Norway, refused the request made by the Allies to march through Sweden in order to intervene in the war. After the German occupation of Denmark and Norway in 1940, however, Sweden was forced by German military superiority to allow the transit of German troops through Sweden to Norway. Many Norwegians and Danes sought refuge in Sweden, the majority of them with the intention of fleeing to England. When Germany attacked the Soviet Union in June 1941, transit facilities were demanded for a division of German troops from Norway to Finland, and Sweden acquiesced under threat of military reprisals. In 1943 the agreement concerning the transit of German troops was revoked. Toward the end of the war, Norwegian and Danish police were trained and equipped in Sweden. Immediately after the war, Sweden was granted membership in the United Nations, without having relinquished its principally neutral foreign policy.

The welfare state. The coalition government that was formed in 1939 was replaced shortly after the end of the war in 1945 by a Social Democratic government under the leadership of Per Albin Hansson. After his death in 1946, Tage Erlander became prime minister, a post that he held until his resignation in 1969. He was succeeded by Olof Palme, who took over the leadership of the government without any other changes being made in its composition.

The period of social reform. The period 1946 to 1950 may justly be called the great period of reform, during which new, comprehensive laws were adopted concerning old-age pensions, child allowances, health insurance, rent allowances, educational reforms, and the expansion of institutions of higher education and research. Those parts of the Social Democrats' postwar program that aimed at nationalization of industry were not, however, carried through. By tax reorganization the government tried, however, to achieve wider distribution of wealth.

Surprisingly, the years after World War II had been marked by stable trading conditions and a scarcity of labour. During the Korean War, the boom reached its climax, entailing large price rises and rapid inflation. A recession followed at the end of 1951. In Sweden this meant that the upward movement of prices and incomes was interrupted, and for the first time since World War II there was a rise in unemployment. Even though the crisis of 1951–52 was neither serious nor long, it drew attention to the problems of economic stability. The Social Democrats now became primarily preoccupied with securing the advances already achieved. They began to collaborate with the Farmers' Party, and in the autumn of 1951 the Social Democratic government was replaced by a coalition government consisting of Social Democrats and Farmers, which lasted until 1957.

The retirement pension controversy

In the late 1950s the question of a compulsory pension for all employees became a principal political issue. The opposition fought it energetically, mainly because it was feared that control of the pension fund would create a latent risk of complete Socialism; the government finally enacted the bill in 1959.

New constitution. In 1955 a committee to review the constitution of 1809 (the Instrument of Government) was appointed. On its recommendations, the old two-chamber Riksdag was replaced in 1971 by a one-chamber Riksdag composed of 350 members elected by proportional representation. The new Instrument of Government, which entered into force on January 1, 1975, reduced the membership of the Riksdag to 349 (to minimize the risk of evenly divided votes) and the voting age to 18. It also further curtailed the powers and duties of the king, to a point merely ceremonial. King Carl XVI Gustaf, who succeeded Gustav VI Adolf in 1973, was the first king to serve under the new constitution.

Foreign policy. Sweden's foreign policy since 1945 has remained strictly neutral. When the international situation became tense in 1948 during the Berlin blockade, the Swedish government took the initiative in negotiations on a defense alliance between Sweden, Norway, and Denmark. Sweden insisted that the alliance should be truly independent of the great powers, while Norway wanted cooperation with the Western powers; as a result, negotiations came to nothing. In accordance with its policy of neutrality, Sweden has not applied to join the European Economic Community (EEC). Trading policy has been aimed at liberalizing trade, a goal that has been pursued in close connection with the United Kingdom, with which Sweden participated in the establishment of the European Free Trade Association (EFTA) in 1959. Although the Nordic defense alliance was not achieved, Scandinavian collaboration has been intensified by the Nordic Council, which was formally inaugurated in 1952. Among the important results of the council's work were the dropping of passport requirements between the Scandinavian countries, the creation of a free labour market, and the establishment of a far-reaching coordination of economic and social legislation.

Domestic affairs since 1970. In the election of 1970 the Social Democrats lost the absolute majority they had held since 1968. But in spite of this the Social Democratic government of Olof Palme, with the support of the Communists, continued in office until the election of 1976, when the non-Socialist parties won a majority. Palme's resignation brought an end to 44 years of Social Democratic domination. (Jö.We.)

Non-Socialists formed governments from 1976 to 1982, the first coalition being led by Thorbjörn Fälldin (Centerpartiet). His government felt repercussions of the international economic crisis of the 1970s, manifested in unemployment and adverse effects on the standard of living. Political discussion, however, focussed above all on the question of nuclear power. Fälldin, who had campaigned for the cessation of building nuclear power plants, was forced to compromise on this issue. As a result he resigned in October 1978. Ola Ullsten, leader of the Folkpartiet, succeeded him as prime minister, forming a minority government in which one-third of the ministers were women. Following a general election in 1979, the non-Socialist coalition led by Fälldin was returned to office.

The development of nuclear power continued to be a hotly debated issue; in a national referendum in 1980, 58 percent of the voters endorsed the use of not more than 12 nuclear reactors at four plants, which, however, were to be phased out by the year 2010. But in the aftermath of the nuclear reactor disaster at Chernobyl in the Ukrainian S.S.R. in 1986 the government considered a proposal that would abolish these nuclear plants by 1996.

From 1982 the Social Democrats, with the support of the Communists, resumed power. In February 1986 Prime Minister Olof Palme was assassinated by an unidentified gunman, whose motives have remained obscure. Palme was succeeded by Ingvar Carlsson.

For later developments in the political history of Sweden, see the *Britannica Book of the Year* section in the BRITANNICA WORLD DATA ANNUAL.

For coverage of related topics in the *Macropædia* and *Micropædia,* see the *Propædia,* Part Nine, Division II, especially Section 923; Division VI, especially Sections 961 and 963; and Division VII, especially Section 972.

(Ed.)

BIBLIOGRAPHY

Physical and human geography. General materials include fact sheets and booklets on various subjects, published by the Swedish Institute, which are both informative and comprehensive; the NATIONAL CENTRAL BUREAU OF STATISTICS, *Statistical Abstract of Sweden* (annual), a comprehensive statistical reference; and the ROYAL MINISTRY FOR FOREIGN AFFAIRS AND THE SWEDISH INSTITUTE, *Sweden in Europe* (1971), articles on Sweden and on its relation to Europe.

Landscape: AXEL SOMME (ed.), *A Geography of Norden* (1968), an informative introduction to Nordic geography.

The people: EDMUND DAHLSTROM (ed.), *The Changing Roles of Men and Women* (1967), a discussion of a subject of current interest led by a major Swedish sociologist; ROBERT MURRAY, *A Brief History of the Church of Sweden,* 2nd rev. ed. (1969); ISRAEL RUONG, *The Lapps in Sweden* (1967), descriptions of an ethnic minority with interesting traditions and culture.

Economy: MARIE and CHRISTIAN NORGREN, *Industrial Sweden* (1971), a good account; and MARTIN SCHNITZER, *The Economy of Sweden: A Study of the Modern Welfare State* (1970), on the Swedish economy, with American comparisons. See also ELI SCHWARTZ, *Trouble in Eden: A Comparison of the British and Swedish Economies* (1981).

Administration and social conditions: MINISTRY OF EDUCATION AND CULTURAL AFFAIRS, *Adult Education in Sweden* (1970), a brief report on an important issue; NILS ANDREN, *Modern Swedish Government* (1968), a well-known work on the Swedish political system, mainly its formal construction; ALFRED BEXELIUS, *The Swedish Institution of the Justitie-Ombudsman* (1965), coverage of the Swedish ombudsman system; SWEDISH BOARD OF EDUCATION, *The Comprehensive School in Sweden* (1970), a description of the basic educational system; and PIERRE VINDE, *Swedish Government Administration* (1971), a lucid description of how the government works in practice; and JOHN A. FRY (ed.), *Limits of the Welfare State* (1979), a collection of critical reviews on postwar Sweden.

Cultural life and institutions: NIKLAS BRUNIUS, GORAN ERIKSSON, and ROLF REMBE, *Swedish Theatre* (1967), a descriptive review; LEIF FURHAMMAR and BERTIL LAURITZEN, *Film in Sweden* (1966); AKE STAVENOW and AKE H. HULDT, *Design in Sweden* (1961), on the wide range of Swedish design and handicraft; BENGT PLEIJEL (ed.), *Swedish Music: Past and Present* (1967); and ROLF SODERBERG, *Modern Swedish Art* (1963), a good introduction to Swedish 20th-century art.

History. For a good general history of Scandinavia, see PIERRE JEANNIN, *Histoire des pays scandinaves* (1956). The following are general histories of the individual countries: INGVAR ANDERSSON, *Sveriges historia,* 7th ed. (1969; Eng. trans. of 2nd ed., *A History of Sweden,* 1970); ERIK LONNROTH, *Sverige och Kalmarunionen, 1397–1457* (1934), a dissertation dealing with the much-debated Union of Kalmar, mainly concentrated on Swedish aspects but also an interpretation of the document in a Scandinavian concept; S.U.P. PALME, *Kristendomens genombrott i Sverige* (1959), a detailed study of the Christianization of Sweden and the previous pagan cults; LAURITZ WEIBULL, *Kritiska undersökningar i Nordens historia omkring år 1000* (1911), a classic work dealing with Scandinavian legends and myths but also sorting out what little reliable source material there is from the end of the 10th century; GUNNAR T. WESTIN, *Maktkamp i senmedeltidens Sverige* (1971), analytical studies about the power conflict between the church and the crown and Swedish–Danish conflicts in the beginning of the 16th century. RAYMOND E. LINDGREN, *Norway–Sweden* (1959), deals with the Swedish–Norwegian Union from its inception in 1814 to its dissolution in 1905, together with an account of the cooperation between the Scandinavian countries during the 20th century. FRANKLIN D. SCOTT, *Scandinavia* (1975), deals with recent history. STEN CARLSSON, *Svensk historia,* vol. 2, *Tiden efter 1718* (1962), the generally accepted standard work, gives a detailed account of political events; *Den Svenska utrikespolitikens historia,* 10 vol. (1951–59), gives a detailed account of Swedish foreign policy and is written by the country's leading historians. FRANKLIN D. SCOTT, *Sweden: The Nation's History* (1977), covers the country from the Viking Age to the present. MICHAEL ROBERTS, *The Swedish Imperial Experience: 1560–1718* (1979), a review of Sweden's "Age of Greatness."

Switzerland

Landlocked amid the mountains of central Europe, Switzerland is a nation the people of which have no unity of ethnic heritage nor of language or religion and the land of which is splintered by barriers of rock and river; but it is a nation that nonetheless is united and prosperous. Officially known as the Swiss Confederation (French Confédération Suisse, German Schweizerische Eidgenossenschaft, Italian Confederazione Svizzera), Switzerland is a republican federation of 26 cantons, or states, six of which (Appenzell Ausser-Rhoden, Apenzell Inner-Rhoden, Basel-Landschaft, Basel-Stadt, Nidwalden, and Obwalden) are traditionally referred to as demicantons but function as full cantons. It is a *mater fluviorum* ("mother of rivers"), situated at the hydrographic centre of Europe and bordered on the west by France, on the north by West Germany, on the east by Austria and the Principality of Liechtenstein, and on the south by Italy. Two-thirds of its borders follow the natural contours of mountain ridges and crests, lakes, and rivers. Except for minor adjustments, Swiss borders have remained stable since their establishment at the Congress of Vienna in 1815, a stability from which the economy of the nation often has benefitted.

Switzerland's small area of 15,943 square miles (41,293 square kilometres; about one-half the size of Scotland or of Maine) and its modest-sized population give no indication of the country's character or significance on the international scene. Switzerland's geographically imposed role as guardian of Europe's natural trans-Alpine routes has been both a reason for and a basic tenet of its existence—a role expressed in its traditional neutrality in time of war that was sanctioned by the Treaty of Westphalia in 1648 and confirmed in 1815 in Vienna, by the Treaty of Versailles in 1919, and again in 1920, when the Council of the League of Nations acknowledged it as "conditioned by a centuries-old tradition explicitly incorporated in international law." The tradition was upheld even while war raged around Switzerland's borders during 1939–45.

Switzerland owes its existence, however, no less to the will of its inhabitants than to the exigencies of geography. With one-quarter of its area comprising high Alps, lakes, and barren rock and with no seaboard and few natural resources other than waterpower, Switzerland has managed to impose unity on diverse races, religions, and languages: for almost 700 years it has maintained the world's oldest and the European mainland's most virile democracy, achieving an almost unrivalled standard of living. It has become a financial centre and headquarters of more than 300 international institutions, including the International Committee of the Red Cross in Geneva and the Universal Postal Union in Bern.

The article is divided into the following sections:

Physical and human geography

THE LAND

Relief. Switzerland's small area contains an unusual diversity of topographic elements, which are divisible into three distinct regions: the Jura, the Alps, and the plateau area known as the Mittelland.

Diversity of natural relief

The Jura (Celtic: "forest"), a bleak and rolling mountain range in the northwest, occupies about 10 percent of the country. The region was formed under the extended impact of the general Alpine folding, particularly of two phases of that folding. Limestone and marl with rich fossil content are the characteristic rocks. The ridges, covered with meadows and only sparsely forested, receive greater amounts of rainfall than do the valleys, the slopes of which are wooded. Between Val St. Imier and the Doubs, a river that forms part of the border with France, mountains have been reduced by denudation to an undulating plateau, or peneplain. This plateau Jura, which extends into France, is known geographically as the Franches-Montagnes (Free Mountains), a name acquired in 1384 when the Bishop of Basel freed the inhabitants from taxation to encourage settlement of the remote area. The unfolded plateaus of the Jura tableland, atop which mixed agriculture is practiced, rise slightly toward the north and northwest, and their steep edges are forested.

In origin, the Alps were built of large complexes of massed overthrusts of extremely varied rocks. Especially well-known for its scenery is the Valais (a canton), site of the Dufourspitze (15,203 feet [4,634 metres]), the highest point in Switzerland, and the Matterhorn (14,691 feet [4,478 metres]). The northern and southern Swiss Alps are separated by the trough formed by the Rhône and Upper Rhine valleys. The narrowest portion of the trough, the Urseren Valley, lies between two crystalline central massifs, the Gotthard and the Aarmassif.

The Alps' role as the European watershed is most apparent in the central Alpine region of Switzerland, where the

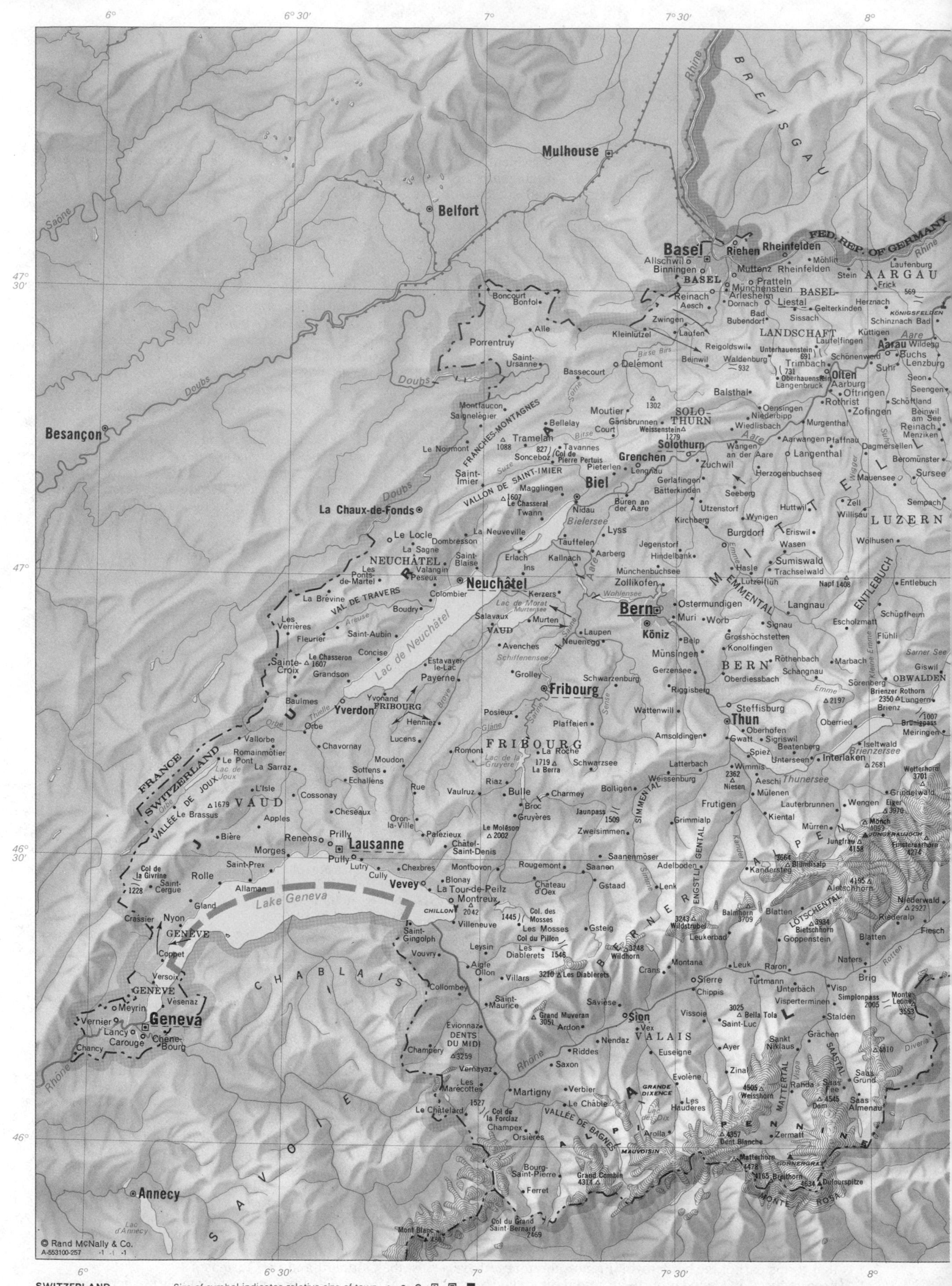

SWITZERLAND

Size of symbol indicates relative size of town • ◦ ⊙ ▣ ▣ ■

Elevations in metres

MAP INDEX

Political subdivisions

Aargau 47·30n 8·10e
Appenzell Ausser-Rhoden 47·27n 9·30e
Appenzell Inner-Rhoden 47·18n 9·21e
Basel-Land 47·32n 7·32e
Basel-Stadt 47·30n 7·50e
Bern 46·45n 7·40e
Fribourg 46·45n 7·05e
Genève 46·15n 6·10e
Glarus 47·00n 9·03e
Graubünden 46·45n 9·30e
Luzern 47·05n 8·05e
Neuchâtel 47·00n 6·55e
Nidwalden 46·35n 8·15e
Obwalden 46·50n 8·25e
Sankt Gallen 47·10n 9·08e
Schaffhausen 47·40n 8·35e
Schwyz 47·05n 8·40e
Solothurn 47·25n 7·35e
Thurgau 47·35n 9·00e
Ticino 46·20n 8·45e
Uri 46·50n 8·40e
Valais 46·10n 7·30e
Vaud 46·40n 6·30e
Zug 47·00n 8·30e
Zürich 47·25n 8·40e

Cities and towns

Aadorf 47·30n 8·54e
Aarau 47·23n 8·03e
Aarberg 47·03n 7·16e
Aarburg 47·19n 7·54e
Aarwangen 47·15n 7·46e
Acquarossa 46·28n 8·57e
Adelboden 46·30n 7·33e
Adliswil 47·19n 8·32e
Aesch 47·28n 7·36e
Aeschi 46·40n 7·42e
Affoltern am Albis 47·17n 8·27e
Agno 46·00n 8·54e
Aigle 46·19n 6·58e
Airolo 46·32n 8·37e
Allaman 46·28n 6·24e
Alle 47·26n 7·08e
Allschwil 47·33n 7·33e
Alpnach-Stad 46·57n 8·17e
Altdorf 46·53n 8·39e
Altstätten 47·23n 9·33e
Alvaneu-Bad 46·40n 9·39e
Amden 47·09n 9·11e
Amriswil 47·33n 9·18e
Amsoldingen 46·43n 7·35e
Amsteg 46·46n 8·41e
Andeer 46·36n 9·26e
Adelfingen 47·36n 8·41e
Andermatt 46·38n 8·36e
Appenzell 47·20n 9·25e
Apples 46·34n 6·25e
Áquila 46·31n 8·57e
Arbedo 46·12n 9·03e
Arbon 47·31n 9·26e
Ardez 46·46n 10·11e
Arlesheim 47·30n 7·37e
Arolla 46·02n 7·29e
Arosa 46·47n 9·41e
Arth 47·04n 8·31e
Ascona 46·09n 8·46e
Ausserferrera 46·33n 9·26e
Avenches 46·53n 7·02e
Ayer 46·11n 7·36e
Baar 47·12n 8·32e
Bad Bubendorf 47·27n 7·44e
Baden 47·29n 8·18e
Bad Pfäfers, see Pfäfers
Bad Ragaz 47·00n 9·30e
Balgach 47·25n 9·35e
Balsthal 47·19n 7·42e
Bargen 47·48n 8·37e
Basel (Bâle) 47·33n 7·35e
Bassecourt 47·20n 7·15e
Bätterkinden 47·08n 7·32e
Baulmes 46·48n 6·32e
Bauma 47·23n 8·53e
Beatenberg 46·42n 7·48e
Beckenried 46·58n 8·29e
Beinwil 47·22n 7·35e
Beinwil am See 47·16n 8·13e
Bellelay 47·16n 7·10e
Bellinzona 46·11n 9·02e
Belp 46·53n 7·30e
Bergün 46·38n 9·45e
Bern (Berne) 46·57n 7·26e
Beromünster 47·12n 8·11e
Biasca 46·22n 8·58e
Biel (Bienne) 47·10n 7·12e
Bière 46·33n 6·20e
Bignasco 46·20n 8·36e
Binningen 47·32n 7·34e
Bischofszell 47·29n 9·15e
Bivio 46·28n 9·38e
Blatten 46·25n 7·50e
Blonay 46·28n 6·54e
Boltigen 46·38n 7·24e
Bonaduz 46·49n 9·25e
Boncourt 47·30n 6·56e
Bonfol 47·29n 7·09e
Boudry 46·57n 6·50e
Bourg-Saint-Pierre 45·57n 7·12e
Braunwald 46·56n 9·00e
Bremgarten 47·21n 8·21e
Breno 46·02n 8·53e
Brienz 46·46n 8·03e
Brig 46·19n 8·00e
Brione 46·18n 8·47e
Brissago 46·07n 8·43e
Broc 46·36n 7·06e
Brugg 47·29n 8·12e
Brunnen 47·00n 8·36e
Brunni 47·03n 8·42e
Brusio 46·14n 10·07e
Buchs 47·10n 9·28e
Buchs 47·23n 8·04e
Bülach 47·31n 8·32e
Bulle 46·37n 7·04e
Buochs 46·58n 8·22e
Büren an der Aare 47·08n 7·23e
Burgdorf 47·04n 7·37e
Bürglen 46·53n 8·40e
Bürglen 47·33n 9·09e
Camedo 46·09n 8·37e
Campo Blenio 46·34n 8·56e
Campocologno 46·13n 10·08e
Capolago 45·55n 8·59e
Carouge 46·11n 6·09e
Cazis 46·43n 9·25e
Celerina 46·31n 9·51e
Cevio 46·19n 8·36e
Cham 47·11n 8·28e
Champéry 46·10n 6·52e
Champex 46·02n 7·07e
Chancy 46·08n 6·00e
Charmey 46·38n 7·10e
Château d'Oex 46·28n 7·08e
Châtel Saint Denis 46·32n 6·54e
Chavornay 46·43n 6·34e
Chêne-Bourg 46·12n 6·12e
Cheseaux 46·35n 6·36e
Chexbres 46·29n 6·47e
Chiasso 45·50n 9·01e
Chippis 46·17n 7·33e
Chur 46·51n 9·32e
Churwalden 46·47n 9·33e
Cimalmotto 46·17n 8·29e
Collombey 46·16n 6·57e
Colombier 46·58n 6·52e
Comologno 46·12n 8·34e
Compatsch 46·58n 10·25e
Concise 46·51n 6·43e
Coppet 46·19n 6·12e
Cossonay 46·37n 6·31e
Court 47·14n 7·20e
Crans 46·19n 7·28e
Crassier 46·22n 6·11e
Cresta 46·28n 9·31e
Cully 46·29n 6·44e
Curaglia 46·41n 8·51e
Dagmersellen 47·13n 7·59e
Davos 46·48n 9·50e
Delémont 47·22n 7·21e
Dielsdorf 47·29n 8·27e
Diessenhofen 47·41n 8·45e
Dietikon 47·24n 8·24e
Disentis 46·43n 8·51e
Domat Ems 46·50n 9·28e
Dombresson 47·04n 6·58e
Dongio 46·27n 8·58e
Dornach 47·29n 7·37e
Döttingen 47·34n 8·16e
Dübendorf 47·25n 8·38e
Dürrenboden 46·57n 8·50e
Dussnang 47·26n 8·58e
Ebnat 47·15n 9·08e
Echallens 46·38n 6·38e
Eglisau 47·34n 8·32e
Egnach 47·33n 9·23e
Einsiedeln 47·08n 8·45e
Elm 46·55n 9·11e
Embrach 47·30n 8·36e
Emmenbrücke 47·04n 8·17e
Engelberg 46·49n 8·25e
Engwilen 47·37n 9·05e
Ennenda 47·01n 9·05e
Entlebuch 47·00n 8·04e
Eriswil 47·05n 7·51e
Erlach 47·03n 7·06e
Ermatingen 47·41n 9·06e
Erstfeld 46·49n 8·39e
Escholzmatt 46·55n 7·56e
Estavayer le Lac 46·51n 6·50e
Euseigne 46·10n 7·25e
Evionnaz 46·11n 7·01e
Evolène 46·07n 7·30e
Faido 46·29n 8·48e
Feldis 46·48n 9·26e
Ferret 45·55n 7·06e
Fiesch 46·20n 8·10e
Filzbach 47·07n 9·08e
Flawil 47·24n 9·12e
Fleurier 46·54n 6·35e
Flims 46·50n 9·17e
Flüelen 46·54n 8·38e
Flühli 46·53n 8·01e
Flums 47·05n 9·20e
Frauenfeld 47·34n 8·54e
Fribourg (Freiburg) 46·48n 7·09e
Frick 47·31n 8·01e
Frutigen 46·35n 7·39e
Fuldera 46·37n 10·22e
Fusio 46·27n 8·40e
Gadmen 46·44n 8·21e
Gais 47·22n 9·27e
Gams 47·12n 9·28e
Gandria 46·01n 9·00e
Gänsbrunnen 47·16n 7·28e
Gelfingen 47·13n 8·16e
Gelterkinden 47·28n 7·51e
Geneva (Genève) 46·12n 6·09e
Gerlafingen 47·10n 7·34e
Gersau 47·00n 8·32e
Gerzensee 46·51n 7·33e
Giornico 46·24n 8·52e
Giswil 46·50n 8·11e
Gland 46·26n 6·16e
Glarus 47·02n 9·04e
Glattfelden 47·33n 8·30e
Gletsch 46·34n 8·22e
Goldau 47·03n 8·33e
Goppenstein 46·22n 7·45e
Gordola 46·11n 8·52e
Göschenen 46·40n 8·35e
Gossau 47·25n 9·15e
Grächen 46·12n 7·50e
Grandson 46·49n 6·38e
Greifensee 47·22n 8·41e
Grenchen 47·11n 7·24e
Grimmialp 46·34n 7·29e
Grindelwald 46·37n 8·02e
Grolley 46·50n 7·05e
Grosshöchstetten 46·55n 7·38e
Gruyères 46·35n 7·05e
Gstaad 46·28n 7·17e
Gsteig 46·23n 7·16e
Guarda 46·47n 10·09e
Guttannen 46·39n 8·18e
Gwatt 46·43n 7·38e
Hallau 47·42n 8·27e
Hasle 47·01n 7·39e
Heiden 47·27n 9·33e
Henniez 46·44n 6·54e
Herisau 47·23n 9·17e
Herznach 47·28n 8·03e
Herzogenbuchsee 47·12n 7·41e
Hindelbank 47·03n 7·32e
Hinterrhein 46·32n 9·12e
Hinwil 47·18n 8·51e
Hochdorf 47·10n 8·17e
Horgen 47·15n 8·36e
Horw 47·01n 8·18e
Hospental 46·37n 8·34e
Hundwil 47·22n 9·19e
Huttwil 47·07n 7·51e
Ilanz 46·46n 9·12e
Il Fuorn 46·40n 10·12e
Indemini 46·06n 8·50e
Innerferrera 46·31n 9·28e
Innerthal 47·06n 8·56e
Innertkirchen 46·42n 8·14e
Ins 47·00n 7·06e
Interlaken 46·41n 7·51e
Intragna 46·10n 8·42e
Iseltwald 46·43n 7·58e
Isone 46·08n 8·59e
Jegenstorf 47·03n 7·30e
Jenaz 46·55n 9·45e
Kallnach 47·01n 7·14e
Kaltbrunn 47·12n 9·02e
Kandersteg 46·30n 7·40e
Kerzers 46·58n 7·12e
Kesswil 47·36n 9·20e
Kiental 46·35n 7·43e
Kilchberg 47·19n 8·33e
Kirchberg 47·05n 7·35e
Kirchberg 47·25n 9·03e
Klausenpass 46·52n 8·51e
Kleinlützel 47·26n 7·25e
Klosters 46·54n 9·53e
Kloten 47·27n 8·35e
Koblenz 47·37n 8·14e
Köniz 46·56n 7·25e
Konolfingen 46·53n 7·38e
Kreuzlingen 47·39n 9·11e
Kriens 47·02n 8·17e
Küblis 46·55n 9·47e
Küssnacht-am-Rigi 47·05n 8·27e
Küttigen 47·25n 8·03e
La Brévine 46·59n 6·36e
La Chaux de Fonds 47·06n 6·50e
Lachen 47·12n 8·51e
Lai, see Lenzerheide
Lancy 46·11n 6·07e
Landquart 46·58n 9·33e
La Neuveville 47·04n 7·06e
Langenbruck 47·21n 7·46e
Langenthal 47·13n 7·47e
Langnau 46·57n 7·47e
Langwies 46·49n 9·43e
Lantsch 46·41n 9·34e
La Punt 46·35n 9·55e
La Roche 46·42n 7·08e
La Sagne 47·03n 6·48e
La Sarraz 46·40n 6·31e
La Tour de Peilz 46·27n 6·49e
Latterbach 46·40n 7·35e
Läufelfingen 47·24n 7·51e
Laufen 47·25n 7·30e
Laufenburg 47·33n 8·04e
Laupen 46·54n 7·14e
Lausanne 46·31n 6·38e
Lauterbrunnen 46·36n 7·55e
Lavin 46·46n 10·06e
Le Brassus 46·35n 6·13e
Le Châble 46·05n 7·12e
Le Châtelard 46·04n 6·58e
Le Locle 47·03n 6·45e
Lengnau 47·11n 7·22e
Lenk 46·28n 7·27e
Le Noirmont 47·13n 6,58e
Lenzburg 47·23n 8·11e
Lenzerheide (Lai) 46·44n 9·33e
Le Pont 46·40n 6·20e
Le Prese 46·18n 10·04e
Les Diablerets 46·21n 7·10e
Les Haudères 46·05n 7·31e
Les Marécottes 46·07n 7·00e
Les Mosses 46·24n 7·07e
Les Ponts de Martel 46·54n 6·41e
Les Verrières 46·54n 6·30e
Leuk 40·19n 7·38e
Leukerbad 46·23n 7·38e
Leysin 46·21n 7·01e
Lichtensteig 47·19n 9·05e
Liestal 47·29n 7·44e
Linthal 46·55n 9·00e
L'Isle 46·37n 6·25e
Littau 47·03n 8·16e
Locarno 46·10n 8·48e
Lucens 46·42n 6·50e
Lugano 46·01n 8·58e
Lungern 46·47n 8·10e
Lumbrein 46·41n 9·08e
Lutry 46·30n 6·41e
Lützelflüh 47·00n 7·41e
Luzern (Lucerne) 47·03n 8·18e
Lyss 47·04n 7·18e
Maggia 46·15n 8·42e
Magglingen 47·09n 7·14e
Maienfeld 47·00n 9·32e
Maloja 46·24n 9·41e
Malvaglia 46·25n 8·59e
Männedorf 47·15n 8·42e
Marbach 46·52n 7·55e
Märstetten 47·36n 9·04e
Martigny 46·06n 7·04e
Martina 46·53n 10·30e
Mauensee 47·10n 8·04e
Meilen 47·16n 8·38e
Meiringen 46·43n 8·12e
Melchtal 46·50n 8·17e
Melide 45·57n 8·57e
Mels 47·03n 9·25e
Mendrisio 45·52n 8·59e
Menziken 47·14n 8·12e
Merishausen 47·45n 8·37e
Mesocco 46·23n 9·14e
Meyrin 46·14n 6·05e
Möhlin 47·34n 7·51e
Mollis 47·05n 9·04e
Montana 46·18n 7·29e
Montbovon 46·29n 7·03e
Montfaucon 47·17n 7·03e
Monthey 46·15n 6·57e
Montreux 46·26n 6·55e
Morcote 45·56n 8·55e
Morges 46·31n 6·30e
Moudon 46·40n 6·48e
Moutier 47·17n 7·23e
Mulegns 46·33n 9·37e
Mülenen 46·38n 7·42e
Münchenbuchsee 47·01n 7·27e
Münchenstein 47·31n 7·37e
Münsingen 46·53n 7·34e
Münster 46·29n 8·16e
Münsterlingen 47·38n 9·14e
Muotathal 46·59n 8·46e
Murgenthal 47·16n 7·50e
Muri 46·56n 7·29e
Muri 47·16n 8·21e
Mürren 46·34n 7·54e
Murten 46·56n 7·07e
Müstair 46·37n 10·27e
Muttenz 47·32n 7·39e
Näfels 47·06n 9·04e
Naters 46·20n 7·59e
Nendaz 46·11n 7·18e
Nesslau 47·13n 9·13e
Netstal 47·03n 9·03e
Neuchâtel 46·59n 6·56e
Neuenegg 46·54n 7·18e

MAP INDEX (continued)

Neuhausen......47·41n 8·37e
Neu Sankt
Johann........47·14n 9·12e
Nidau...........47·07n 7·14e
Niederbipp......47·16n 7·39e
Niederurnen.....47·07n 9·03e
Niederwald......46·26n 8·12e
Niederweningen.47·30n 8·23e
Nyon............46·23n 6·14e
Oberägeri........47·08n 8·37e
Oberdiessbach..46·51n 7·38e
Oberengstringen 47·25n 8·28e
Oberhofen.......46·44n 7·40e
Oberried........46·44n 7·58e
Oberriet.........47·19n 9·33e
Oberuzwil........47·26n 9·08e
Oberwald........46·32n 8·21e
Oensingen.......47·17n 7·44e
Oftringen.......47·19n 7·56e
Olivone.........46·32n 8·57e
Ollon...........46·18n 7·00e
Olten...........47·21n 7·54e
Orbe............46·43n 6·32e
Oron-la-Ville.....46·34n 6·50e
Orsières.........46·02n 7·09e
Osogna..........46·18n 9·00e
Ostermundigen..46·58n 7·29e
Palézieux.......46·33n 6·50e
Parpan..........46·46n 9·33e
Payerne.........46·49n 6·56e
Peseux..........46·59n 6·53e
Pfäfers..........46·59n 9·30e
Pfäffikon.........47·12n 8·46e
Pfäffikon.........47·22n 8·47e
Pfaffnau.........47·14n 7·54e
Pfyn.............47·36n 8·57e
Pieterlen........47·11n 7·20e
Piotta...........46·31n 8·40e
Plaffeien........46·44n 7·17e
Platta...........46·40n 8·51e
Pontresina......46·28n 9·53e
Porrentruy......47·25n 7·05e
Poschiavo.......46·18n 10·04e
Posieux.........46·46n 7·06e
Pratteln.........47·31n 7·42e
Preda...........46·36n 9·46e
Prilly...........46·32n 6·36e
Promontogno....46·21n 9·34e
Pully...........46·31n 6·39e
Rafz............47·37n 8·32e
Ramosch.........46·50n 10·22e
Randa...........46·07n 7·47e
Rapperswil......47·14n 8·50e
Raron...........46·19n 7·48e
Regensberg.....47·29n 8·26e
Regensdorf......47·26n 8·28e
Reichenau.......46·49n 9·24e
Reigoldswil......47·24n 7·41e
Reinach.........47·15n 8·11e
Reinach.........47·30n 7·35e
Reineck.........47·28n 9·34e
Renens..........46·32n 6·35e
Rheinfelden.....47·33n 7·48e
Riaz............46·38n 7·04e
Richisau.........47·02n 8·54e
Richterswil......47·13n 8·42e
Riddes..........46·10n 7·13e
Riederalp.......46·23n 8·01e
Riehen..........47·35n 7·39e
Riggisberg......46·48n 7·29e
Rolle............46·28n 6·20e
Romainmôtier....46·42n 6·29e
Romanshorn.....47·34n 9·22e
Romont..........46·42n 6·55e
Rona............46·34n 9·38e
Ronco...........46·08n 8·44e
Root............47·07n 8·23e
Rorschach......47·29n 9·30e
Rossa...........46·22n 9·08e
Röthenbach.....46·51n 7·45e
Rothrist.........47·19n 7·53e
Rougemont......46·29n 7·12e
Roveredo.......46·14n 9·08e
Rue.............46·37n 6·50e
Rümlang........47·27n 8·32e
Rüti............47·16n 8·51e
Saanen..........46·29n 7·16e
Saanenmöser....47·32n 7·18e
Saas Almenau...46·07n 7·58e
Saas Fee........46·07n 7·55e
Saas Grund......46·08n 7·56e
Sachseln........46·52n 8·15e
Saignelégier.....47·15n 7·00e
Saint-Aubin......46·54n 6·47e
Saint-Blaise......47·01n 6·59e
Saint-Cergue....46·27n 6·09e
Saint-Croix......46·49n 6·31e
Saint-Gingolph...46·24n 6·52e
Saint-Imier.......47·09n 7·00e
Saint-Luc.........46·13n 7·36e
Saint-Maurice....46·13n 7·00e
Saint-Prex.......46·29n 6·28e
Saint-Ursanne...47·22n 7·10e
Salavaux........46·55n 7·02e
Samedan........46·33n 9·52e
Samnaun........46·56n 10·22e
San Bernardino..46·28n 9·12e
San Carlo.......46·25n 8·32e
San Gion........46·38n 8·50e
Sankt Antönien..46·58n 9·49e
Sankt Gallen.....47·25n 9·23e
Sankt
Margrethen.....47·27n 9·36e
Sankt Moritz.....46·30n 9·50e
Sankt Niklaus....46·11n 7·48e
Sankt Peterzell...47·19n 9·11e
Santa Maria......46·36n 10·24e
Sargans.........47·03n 9·26e
Sarnen..........46·54n 8·15e
Sattel...........47·05n 8·42e
Savièse..........46·16n 7·20e
Savognin........40·36n 9·36e
Saxon...........46·09n 7·11e
Schaffhausen....47·42n 8·38e
S-Chanf.........42·36n 9·59e
Schangnau......46·50n 7·52e
Schiers..........46·59n 9·41e
Schinznach Bad.47·27n 8·10e
Schleitheim......47·45n 8·29e
Schlieren........47·24n 8·27e
Schöftland.......47·18n 8·03e
Schöllenen.......46·40n 8·35e
Schuls, see
Scuol
Schönenwerd.....47·22n 8·00e
Schüpfheim.....46·57n 8·01e
Schwanden......47·00n 9·04e
Schwarzenburg..46·49n 7·21e
Schwarzsee......46·40n 7·20e
Schwyz..........47·02n 8·40e
Scuol (Schuls)...46·48n 10·18e
Sedrun..........46·41n 8·46e
Seeberg.........47·09n 7·40e
Seen............47·29n 8·46e
Seengen.........47·19n 8·13e
Seewis..........47·00n 9·32e
Sempach.........47·08n 8·11e
Sennwald........47·16n 9·30e
Seon............47·21n 8·10e
Sertig-Dörfli.....46·44n 9·51e
Suezach........47·32n 8·44e
Sevelen.........47·07n 9·29e
Siebnen.........47·11n 8·54e
Sierre...........46·18n 7·32e
Signau..........46·55n 7·43e
Sigriswil.........46·43n 7·42e
Sils.............46·22n 9·46e
Silvaplana.......46·26n 9·47e
Sins.............47·11n 8·23e
Sion.............46·14n 7·21e
Sirnach.........47·28n 9·00e
Sisikon..........46·57n 8·42e
Sissach.........47·28n 7·49e
Soazza..........46·22n 9·13e
Solothurn.......47·13n 7·32e
Somvix..........46·44n 8·56e
Sonceboz.......47·11n 7·11e
Sonogno........46·21n 8·47e
Sörenberg......46·50n 8·03e
Sottens.........46·39n 6·44e
Speicher........47·24n 9·27e
Spiez...........46·41n 7·39e
Splügen.........46·33n 9·20e
Stäfa...........47·15n 8·44e
Stalden.........46·14n 7·52e
Stammheim......47·38n 8·47e
Stans...........46·57n 8·22e
Stansstad......46·59n 8·20e
Steckborn......47·40n 8·55e
Steffisburg.....46·47n 7·39e
Steg............47·21n 8·56e
Stein............47·33n 7·58e
Stein am Rhein..47·40n 8·51e
Stöckalp........46·48n 8·17e
Suhr............47·22n 8·05e
Sumiswald......47·02n 7·45e
Sursee..........47·10n 8·06e
Susch...........46·46n 10·04e
Tarasp..........46·38n 10·25e
Tavanasa........46·45n 9·04e
Tavannes........47·13n 7·12e
Täuffelen........47·04n 7·12e
Tenigerbad......46·42n 8·57e
Tesserete........46·04n 8·58e
Teufen..........47·23n 9·23e
Thalkirch.......46·38n 9·16e
Thalwil..........47·17n 8·34e
Thayngen.......47·45n 8·42e
Thun............46·45n 7·37e
Thusis..........46·42n 9·26e
Tiefencastel.....46·40n 9·35e
Trachselwald....47·01n 7·45e
Tramelan........47·13n 7·06e
Trasadingen.....47·40n 8·26e
Trimbach........47·22n 7·54e
Trin.............46·50n 9·22e
Trogen..........47·24n 9·28e
Trun............46·45n 8·58e
Tschamut.......46·40n 8·42e
Turbenthal......47·27n 8·51e
Turtmann.......46·18n 7·41e
Twann..........47·06n 7·10e
Unterägeri......47·08n 8·35e
Unterbäch......46·17n 7·48e
Unterschächen..46·52n 8·47e
Unterseen.......46·41n 7·51e
Unterterzen......47·07n 9·15e
Unterwasser.....47·12n 9·19e
Urnäsch.........47·19n 9·17e
Uster...........47·21n 8·43e
Utzenstorf.......47·08n 7·33e
Uznach..........47·14n 9·00e
Valangin........47·01n 6·54e
Vallorbe........46·43n 6·22e
Vals Platz......46·37n 9·11e
Vättis..........46·55n 9·27e
Vaulruz.........46·37n 6·59e
Verbier.........46·06n 7·13e
Vergeletto.......46·14n 8·36e
Vernayaz........46·08n 7·02e
Vernier.........46·13n 6·06e
Versoix.........46·16n 6·10e
Vésenaz........46·14n 6·12e
Vevey...........46·28n 6·51e
Vex.............46·13n 7·24e
Vicosoprano.....46·22n 9·37e
Villars..........46·18n 7·04e
Villeneuve.......46·24n 6·55e
Villmergen......47·21n 8·15e
Vinadi..........46·55n 10·29e
Vira.............46·08n 8·51e
Visperterminen..46·15n 7·54e
Vissoie.........46·13n 7·36e
Vitznau.........47·01n 8·29e
Vouvry..........46·20n 6·53e
Vrin............46·39n 9·06e
Wädenswil.......47·14n 8·40e
Wald............47·17n 8·55e
Waldstatt........47·21n 9·17e
Walenstadt......47·07n 9·19e
Wallisellen......47·25n 8·36e
Wagen an der
Aare............47·14n 7·39e
Wängi...........47·30n 8·57e
Wangs...........47·02n 9·26e
Wasen...........47·03n 7·48e
Wassen..........46·42n 8·36e
Wattenwil.......46·46n 7·30e
Wattwil.........47·18n 9·06e
Weggis..........47·02n 8·26e
Weinfelden......47·34n 9·06e
Weissenburg....46·39n 7·28e
Weisstannen....46·59n 9·21e
Wengen.........46·36n 7·56e
Wettingen.......47·28n 8·19e
Wetzikon........47·19n 8·47e
Wiedlisbach.....47·15n 7·39e
Wiesen..........46·43n 9·43e
Wil.............47·27n 9·03e
Wildegg.........47·25n 8·11e
Wildhaus........47·12n 9·22e
Willisau.........47·07n 8·00e
Windisch........47·29n 8·13e
Winterthur......47·30n 8·43e
Wohlen..........47·21n 8·17e
Wolfenschiessen.46·55n 8·24e
Wolhusen.......47·04n 8·04e
Worb............46·56n 7·34e
Würenlingen.....47·32n 8·16e
Wynigen........47·06n 7·40e
Yverdon.........46·47n 6·39e
Yvonand........46·48n 6·45e
Zell.............47·09n 7·55e
Zermatt.........46·01n 7·45e
Zernez..........46·43n 10·05e
Zillis............46·38n 9·27e
Zizers...........46·56n 9·34e
Zofingen........47·18n 7·57e
Zollikofen.......47·00n 7·28e
Zollikon.........47·20n 8·35e
Zuchwil.........47·12n 7·33e
Zug.............47·10n 8·31e
Zurzach.........47·35n 8·18e
Zuoz............46·35n 9·58e
Zürich..........47·23n 8·32e
Zweisimmen.....46·33n 7·22e
Zwingen.........47·26n 7·32e

Physical features and points of interest

Aare, *river*.....47·37n 8·13e
Aareschlucht,
scenic area......46·44n 8·12e
Adula (Rhein-
waldhorn),
mountain.......46·30n 9·02e
Ägerisee, *lake*....47·07n 8·38e
Albula, *river*......46·42n 9·27e
Albulapass,
pass............46·35n 9·50e
Aletschhorn,
mountain.......46·28n 8·00e
Alps, *mountains*..46·30n 8·30e
Bagnes, Vallée
de, *valley*......46·03n 7·18e
Baldegger See,
lake............47·12n 8·16e
Balmhorn,
mountain.......46·26n 7·41e
Bella Tola,
mountain.......46·15n 7·39e
Berner Alpen,
mountains......46·30n 7·30e
Bernina,
mountains......46·22n 9·50e
Bernina, Passo
del (Bernina-
pass), *pass*......46·24n 10·03e
Bernina, Piz,
peak...........46·21n 9·51e
Berninapass
(Passo del
Bernina), *pass*..46·24n 10·03e
Bieler See, *lake*..47·05n 7·10e
Bietschhorn,
mountain.......46·24n 7·51e
Birse Birs, *river*..47·22n 7·22e
Blanche, Dent,
mountain.......46·03n 7·36e
Blenio, Val,
valley..........46·27n 8·58e
Blinnenhorn,
mountain.......46·26n 8·19e
Blümlisalp,
mountain.......46·30n 7·47e
Bodensee (Lake
Constance; Lake
Konstanz)......47·35n 9·25e
Breithorn,
mountain.......45·56n 7·45e
Brienzer Rothorn,
mountain.......46·48n 8·04e
Brienzer See,
lake............46·43n 7·57e
Broye, *river*.....46·55n 7·02e
Brünigpass, *pass*.46·46n 8·09e
Buin, Piz, *peak*..46·50n 10·08e
Calanca, Val,
valley..........46·22n 9·07e
Campo Tencia,
Pizzo, *peak*......46·26n 8·43e
Ceneri, Monte,
pass............46·08n 8·55e
Chillon, *castle*....46·25n 6·56e
Churfirsten,
mountain.......47·08n 9·17e
Constance, Lake,
see Bodensee
Dammastock,
mountain.......46,39n 8·25e
Dents du Midi,
mountains......46·10n 6·56e
Diveria, *river*.....46·12n 8·09e
Dix, Lac des,
lake............46·03n 7·24e
Dom, *mountain*...46·06n 7·50e
Domleschg,
valley..........46·44n 9·28e
Doubs, *river*.....47·20n 7·03e
Dufourspitze,
peak...........45·55n 7·52e
Eiger, *mountain*..46·35n 8·00e
Emme, *river*......47·13n 7·34e
Emmental, *valley*.46·56n 7·45e
En (Inn), *river*....46·55n 10·28e
Engadin, Ober-,
valley..........46·37n 9·58e
Engadin, Unter-,
valley..........46·50n 10·20e
Engstli Gental,
valley..........46·30n 7·47e
Entlebuch,
valley..........46·58n 8·00e
Finsteraarhorn,
mountain.......46·32n 8·08e
Fluchthorn,
mountain.......46·53n 10·15e
Flüelapass, *pass*..46·45n 9·57e
Forclaz, Col de la,
pass............46·04n 7·00e
Franches-
Montagnes,
mountains......47·15n 7·00e
Fuorn, Passo del
(Ofenpass),
pass............46·37n 10·15e
Furkapass, *pass*..46·34n 8·25e
Geneva, Lake
(Lac Léman)......46·25n 6·30e
Givrine, Col de la,
pass............46·27n 6·05e
Glâne, *river*......46·47n 7·08e
Glarner Alpen,
mountains......46·55n 9·00e
Glärnisch,
mountain.......47·00n 9·00e
Glatt, *river*......47·34n 8·28e
Goms, *valley*.....46·27n 8·15e
Gornergrat,
scenic area......45·49n 7·47e
Gotthard, Massif,
mountains......46·31n 8·31e
Grand Combin,
mountain.......45·56n 7·18e
Grande Dixence,
dam............46·05n 7·28e
Grand Muveran,
mountain.......46·14n 7·08e
Grand Saint-
Bernard, Col du,
pass............45·50n 7·10e
Greifensee, *lake*..47·21n 8·41e
Grimselpass,
pass............46·34n 8·21e

MAP INDEX (continued)

Grimselsee, *lake*..46·34n 8·18e
Gross Windgällen, *mountain*.......46·49n 8·44e
Gruyère, Lac de la, *lake*..........46·38n 7·06e
Hallwiler See, *lake*............47·18n 8·13e
Haslital, *valley*...46·42n 8·10e
Hinterrhein, *river*..............46·49n 9·25e
Inn, see En
Jaunpass, *pass*...46·36n 7·20e
Joux, Lac de, *lake*............46·38n 6·18e
Julierpass, *pass*..46·28n 9·44e
Jungfrau, *mountain*.......46·32n 7·58e
Jungfraujoch, *rail terminal*.....46·33n 7·58e
Jura, *mountains*..46·45n 6·30e
Kander, *river*.....46·43n 7·38e
Kesch, Piz, *peak*.46·38n 9·52e
Kleine Emme, *river*............47·04n 8·17e
Klöntaler See, *lake*............47·02n 8·58e
Königsfelden, *church*..........47·29n 8·14e
Konstanz, Lake, see Bodensee
La Berra, *mountain*.......46·41n 7·11e
Landquart, *river*..46·58n 9·32e
Lauerzer See, *lake*............47·02n 8·36e
Le Chasseral, *mountain*.......47·08n 7·03e
Le Chasseron, *mountain*.......46·51n 6·33e
Léman, Lac, see Geneva, Lake
Le Moléson, *mountain*.......46·33n 7·01e
Leone, Monte, *mountain*.......46·15n 8·06e
Lepontine, Alpi, *mountains*......46·25n 8·50e
Les Diablerets, *mountain*.......46·19n 7·12e
Leventina, Valle, *valley*..........46·25n 9·52e
Limmat, *river*.....47·25n 8·25e
Linth, *river*.......47·07n 9·07e
Linthkanal, *canal*..........47·13n 8·57e
Lorze, *river*......47·15n 8·25e
Lötschental, *valley*..........46·25n 7·50e
Lucerne, Lake, see Vierwald Stätter See
Lucomagno, Passo del (Lukmanïer-pass), *pass*......46·34n 8·48e
Lugano, Lago di, *lake*............45·58n 8·56e
Lukmanïerpass (Passo del Lucomagno), *pass*............46·34n 8·48e
Madonna del Sasso, *monastery*......46·11n 8·33e
Maggia, *river*.....46·09n 8·48e
Maggia, Valle, *valley*..........46·17n 8·40e
Maggiore, Lago, *lake*............45·59n 8·47e
Malojapass, *pass*.46·23n 9·41e
Matterhorn, *mountain*.......45·59n 7·43e
Mattertal, *valley*..46·10n 7·49e
Mauvoisin, *dam*..46·00n 7·25e
Medel, Val, *valley*..........46·37n 8·50e
Mesolcina, Valle, *valley*..........46·20n 9·10e
Mittelland, *physical region*..47·15n 8·00e
Moesa, *river*.....46·13n 9·03e
Mönchsgrat, *mountain*.......46·34n 7·59e
Morat, Lac de (Murtensee), *lake*............46·55n 7·05e
Morteratsch, Piz, *peak*............46·22n 9·51e
Mosses, Col des, *pass*............46·24n 7·06e
Murtensee, see Mora, Lac de
Napf, *mountain*..47·00n 7·56e
Neuchâtel, Lac de, *lake*.........46·52n 6·50e
Niesen, *mountain*.......46·39n 7·39e
Oberalppass, *pass*............46·39n 8·40e
Oberalpstock, *mountain*.......46·40n 8·42e
Oberhauenstein, *pass*............47·21n 7·56e
Obre, *river*.......46·33n 6·09e
Ofenpass (Passo del Fuorn), *pass*............46·37n 10·15e
Pennine, Alpi, *mountains*......46·05n 7·50e
Pfäffikersee, *lake*............47·21n 8·48e
Pierre Pertuis, de, *pass*........47·12n 7·11e
Pilatus, *mountain*.......46·59n 8·15e
Pillon, Col du, *pass*............46·22n 7·13e
Piz Lunghin, *peak*............46·28n 9·35e
Poschiavino, *pass*............46·14n 10·07e
Poschiavino, *river*............46·12n 10·10e
Prättigau, *valley*..46·55n 9·45e
Rabiusa, *river*....46·48n 9·20e
Reuss, *river*......47·28n 8·14e
Rhaetian Alps, *mountains*......46·30n 10·00e
Rhätikon, *mountains*......47·03n 9·40e
Rheinfall, *waterfall*........47·41n 8·38e
Rheinwald, *valley*..........46·32n 9·17e
Rheinwaldhorn (Adula), *mountain*.......46·30n 9·02e
Rhine, *river*......47·37n 7·35e
Rhône, *river*.....46·09n 5·57e
Rickenpass, *pass*............47·14n 9·02e
Rigi, *mountain*.......47·05n 8·30e
Riviera, *valley*....46·15n 8·58e
Rosa, Monte, *mountain*.......45·55n 7·53e
Rotten, *river*......46·17n 7·33e
Saane, *river*......46·59n 7·16e
Saastal, *valley*....46·10n 7·56e
Safiental, *valley*..46·40n 9·18e
Saint-Imier, Vallon de, *valley*..........47·10n 7·00e
Samnaungruppe, *mountains*......47·00n 10·25e
San Bernardino, Passo del, *pass*.46·30n 9·11e
Sankt Gotthard (Passo del San Gottardo), *pass*..46·33n 8·34e
Santa Maria, Giogo di (Wormser Joch), *pass*............46·34n 10·25e
Säntis, *mountain*.47·15n 9·21e
Sardona, Piz, *peak*............46·55n 9·15e
Sarine, *river*......46·54n 7·14e
Sarner See, *lake*..46·52n 8·13e
Schanfigg, *valley*..........46·51n 9·38e
Schiffenensee, *lake*............46·50n 7·10e
Schöllenen Gorge..........46·36n 8·31e
Sempacher See, *lake*............47·09n 8·09e
Sense, *river*......46·54n 7·14e
Sihl, *river*........47·23n 8·32e
Sihlsee, *lake*.....47·07n 8·47e
Siluretta, *mountain*.......46·50n 10·15e
Simme, *river*.....46·41n 7·38e
Simmental, *valley*..........46·37n 7·25e
Simplonpass, *pass*............46·15n 8·02e
Sitter, *river*......47·29n 9·14e
Sorne, *river*......47·22n 7·22e
Spluga, Passo dello, *pass*......46·30n 9·20e
Suhr, *river*.......47·25n 8·04e
Surses, *valley*....46·34n 9·38e
Sustenhorn, *mountain*.......46·42n 8·28e
Sustenpass, *pass*............46·44n 8·27e
Suze, *river*.......47·08n 7·14e
Thielle, *river*.....47·03n 7·05e
Thunersee, *lake*..46·40n 7·45e
Thur, *river*.......47·36n 8·35e
Ticino, *river*......46·11n 8·51e
Titlis, *mountain*..46·47n 8·25e
Tödi, *mountain*...46·49n 8·56e
Toggenburg, *valley*..........47·45n 9·10e
Töss, *river*.......47·33n 8·33e
Travers, Val de, *valley*..........46·57n 6·38e
Tresa, *river*......45·59n 8·47e
Unterhauenstein, *pass*............47·23n 7·52e
Urirotstock, *mountain*.......46·52n 8·33e
Urseren Valley...46·35n 8·32e
Vadret, Piz, *peak*............46·41n 9·57e
Valserrhein, *river*............46·42n 9·10e
Valsertal, *valley*..46·37n 9·10e
Verzasca, *river*...46·09n 8·52e
Via Mala, *gorge*..46·40n 9·26e
Vierwald Stätter See (Lake Lucerne)........47·00n 8·28e
Vorderrhein, *river*............46·49n 9·25e
Wägitaler See, *lake*............47·06n 8·55e
Walensee, *lake*...47·07n 9·12e
Weissenstein, *mountain*.......47·15n 7·31e
Weissfluch, *mountain*.......46·50n 9·48e
Weisshorn, *mountain*.......46·06n 7·42e
Wetterhorn, *mountain*.......46·39n 8·08e
Wigger, *river*.....47·18n 7·53e
Wildhorn, *mountain*.......46·21n 7·22e
Wildstrubel, *mountain*.......46·24n 7·32e
Wohlensee, *lake*..46·58n 7·20e
Wormser Joch (Giogo di Santa Maria), *pass*.....46·34n 10·25e
Zuger See, *lake*..47·08n 8·30e
Zürichsee, *lake*...47·13n 8·45e

different chains meet; from there, the Rhône River flows west, the Rhine River east, the Ticino River south, and the Reuss River north. The fundamental Alpine source point, however, is located in the Upper Engadine at Piz Lunghin, from which streams flow toward the North, the Adriatic, and the Black seas.

In the central Alpine region lies the Gotthard route, the first and shortest north–south passage through the mountains and an important European connection; it was opened around 1225 with the construction of a bridge in the Schöllenen Gorge. The gorge traverses the northern chain, while the southern range is crossed by the St. Gotthard Pass at an altitude of 6,916 feet. The 9.3-mile- (15-kilometre-) long St. Gotthard rail tunnel through the pass was opened in 1882; a twin 10.5-mile road tunnel was opened in 1980.

Between the Jura and the main Alpine ranges lies the hilly Mittelland accounting for 30 percent of the country and enclosed by the two mountain ranges and the two largest lakes, Lake Geneva (Lac Léman) in the west and Lake Constance (Bodensee) in the east. The Mittelland, where the greatest part of the population is concentrated, supports Swiss economic life and guarantees the country's industrial and international importance. As a result, it is becoming highly urbanized, although even in urban Switzerland the feeling of security and rootedness remains alive, symbolized by the mountain peaks that can be seen on the horizon from every point on the plateau.

Climate. The waters may flow away from the Alps in all directions, but the climates of Europe converge upon the Swiss mountains. The Alps are essentially the dividing line between the different climates of central Europe, but Switzerland as a whole combines the four main European climatic types to form a single transitional climate, influenced on the west by the Atlantic climate, which is affected by the Gulf Stream; on the east by that of the eastern European continent; on the south by the Mediterranean climate; and on the north by the middle European cyclonal climate.

Wind systems. Prevailing winds are from the west, but, in the valleys, air currents are channelled into particularly frequent or violent local winds such as the Bise, the northeast wind characteristic of Geneva. The foehn, a brisk south wind that occurs in the large transverse valleys of the northern Alps, makes it possible to grow sweet chestnut, laurel, and tobacco on the northern slopes of the Alps.

Precipitation. Since rainfall tends to increase in direct proportion to altitude, the precipitation map corresponds very closely to the relief map; and, because of the marked variation in reliefs, differences in precipitation within short linear distances are often very great. For example, Sankt Gallen, at 2,180 feet, has an average annual precipitation of 52 inches (1,318 millimetres), while that of the Säntis, 8,200 feet but only 32 miles away, is 114 inches (2,904 millimetres). The average annual precipitation of three-quarters of the country exceeds 40 inches, varying amounts of which fall as snow, which, in turn, characterizes and explains the dense variety of weather phenomena. In the southern town of Lugano (905 feet), which has a Mediterranean climate, only 5 percent of the precipitation is in the form of snow; in Zürich (1,620 feet) 11 percent is snow; and on the Säntis 72 percent is snow. At altitudes above 11,500 feet, all precipitation consists of snow, which becomes impacted into perpetual snowfields and glaciers; the snow line is at about 9,200 feet in the northern Alps and at 10,800 feet in the southern Alps of the Valais.

Dry areas

In the mountains of the interior, distinct dry pockets occur, the most famous being the Rhône Valley in the Valais, closely encircled by the highest (13,000-foot) mountain groups. Precipitation is also slight on the slopes with southern exposure near the cantonal capital of Sion (1,800 feet), but extensive irrigation is possible since the area is surrounded by large snowfields and by glaciers that extend far down into the valleys. The rarefied, germfree, and unexpectedly dry air of such high-altitude towns as Davos (5,121 feet) and Arosa (5,987 feet) permits a more intense, broader spectrum solar irradiation, thus producing a radiant climate long famous in tuberculosis cures. At altitudes of 13,000 feet, precipitation levels rise to 160 inches, and the Mönchsgrat (13,460 feet) in the Jungfrau group has the highest average annual precipitation (163 inches, or 4,141 millimetres) in Switzerland, while Stalden in the encircled Valais has the minimum (21 inches, or 530 millimetres).

Skies and temperatures. The stable high-pressure weather conditions prevailing over central Europe and the Alps during the winter create cold air masses that often are covered by thick, gray layers of fog, a climatic phenomenon with widely varying consequences. The mouths of the northern Alpine valleys, the basins of the Jura Mountains, and the villages and cities of the low areas of the Mittelland are blanketed with fog for days and, often, for weeks on end, while towns located at high altitudes enjoy warm, brilliant, high-pressure conditions and the view of the glistening sea of fog below them. Temperature inversions between mountain and valley locations in close proximity can be quite pronounced, with the higher point having the higher temperature reading. Frequent temperature inversion is a primary reason why high-altitude Swiss sanatoriums remain occupied even during the winter and why, in the present century, the Alpine winter season has gained popularity in Europe for sports as well as for health cures.

Avalanches

With the increase in winter tourism, the study of avalanches has developed as a branch of Alpine climatology, and during threatening weather the research station near Davos publishes daily avalanche bulletins, mainly as a warning for tourists. The Alpine cantons have about 10,000 avalanches annually, more than 8,000 of them in February, March, and April. For centuries, village communes have used *Bannwälder* ("protective forests") on the mountain slopes as protection from these slides, since a 20- to 30-year-old forest can usually stop avalanches. Costly artificial structures protect the villages, highways, and Alpine paths.

Plant and animal life. The vegetation is derived from that of the four European climatic regions converging in Switzerland and from the varied relief. It includes the beeches and oaks of the Atlantic west; hornbeam and larch trees in the more continental east, predominantly in the Engadine and the dry Valais; extensive spruce forests in the northern sub-Alpine region; and chestnut groves in the south. The vegetation boundaries are several hundred metres higher in the south than in the north because of the generally southern exposure.

The Alpine pastures of the Monte Rosa region reach an altitude of 10,800 feet, and until recently the highest Alpine grainfields, which have fallen victim to the decline in Alpine agriculture, lay above Zermatt at an altitude of 6,900 feet. The highest vineyard of central Europe, at an altitude of 3,900 feet, is still located near Visperterminen in the Valais, although the largest vineyards are on the southern-exposed shore of Lake Geneva, on the sunny slope of the Rhône valley, along lakes Neuchâtel and Biel at the foot of the Jura, and in the northern Alpine valley of the Rhine, which is affected by the foehn. On the western Mittelland, a considerable grain-producing area has developed on the sheltered side of the Jura Mountains, an area of scanty rainfall, while in the more humid eastern region, mainly in the cantons of Thurgau and Sankt Gallen, grass cultivation is combined with fruit growing.

Crop cultivation at high altitudes

Swiss animal life is mainly Alpine, but a mixture of species familiar to southern and north central Europe is also found. Animal life is protected, except during a brief annual hunting season. The Alpine tourist may be pleasantly surprised by the sight of the marmot, which lives near the snow line, and the chamois; large herds of the proud ibex, which had died out in the Swiss Alps and has since been carefully re-introduced, have again developed in several areas, especially in the Bernina region of Graubünden (canton). In the forests there are rabbits, foxes, badgers, squirrels, and numerous varieties of birds, while the lake and river trout are especially famous. Snakes and lizards are concentrated in the south, but insects, in profuse variety, are diffused throughout the country.

Settlement patterns. The diversity of geomorphology, climate, and plant distribution in Switzerland provides a wide variety of bases for the formation of settlements, a variety further enhanced by the country's central European location. Switzerland supplies more varied material for the study of the geography of settlements than does any other European country. Even the types of houses vary from one region to another, especially well-known examples being those of the Engadine, the Ticino, the Bernese region, the Jura, and northeastern Switzerland. In atmosphere, too, there are distinct variations: the German-speaking cantons and large cities, such as Bern, Zürich, and Basel, express an earnest and stern efficiency, whereas in the west, especially in Geneva and the canton of Vaud, the Latin influence prevails and life becomes less thrifty and more graceful. In the south, the Ticinese enjoy a more luxuriant climate, and this, too, is perhaps reflected in an easier life-style.

Rural communities. The valleys are the residential areas of Switzerland. Alpine villages extending along the base of slopes are a characteristic sight. Since the extensive river diversions made chiefly during the second half of the 19th century, villages often have expanded into the valley plains, where intensive farming is carried on. The isolation of portions of many valleys, such as those of the Rheinwald, Poschiavino, and Urseren, by barriers of resistant rock or by prehistoric landslides was an impetus to the formation of communes and of the early *Alpgenossenschaften* ("Alpine cooperatives").

The modern network of communes, small but politically important units, stands out in the parallel relief of the Jura and the Alps, since the communes are generally laid out with their boundaries drawn from one mountain crest to the next. Every commune has all the basic living requirements, including pasture, forest, fertile valley bottom, and water. Terraced slopes characterize the sites of villages that serve as bases for "Alpine nomadism," the seasonal moving of livestock to or from the mountains.

Self-sufficiency of the rural communes

Some villages, such as Guarda in the lower Engadine, have a reputation for picturesque beauty, while others, such as Montana in the Valais or Wengen in the Bernese Oberland, have developed into famous resorts and spas. Valley forks, where the traffic from two valleys combines, are attractive sites for settlement, as are places in the Alps such as Amsteg (canton of Uri), Silvaplana (the upper Engadine), and Gordola (near Locarno), where the entrance into an adjacent valley of higher altitude is made gradually. In the Mittelland, with its abundant lakes, delta villages are especially closely related to the environment; in recent decades villages have expanded toward each other and merged, creating population belts all along the lakes. Unfortunately, uncontrolled property speculation has permitted many characteristic, substantial village settlements to spread into the surrounding areas with very little architectural planning. The goals of local environmental protection are clashing with large-scale financial interests, a conflict that is becoming a matter of concern throughout Europe in the important case of Sankt Moritz (Graubünden).

Urban Switzerland. Some Swiss cities originaly developed around monasteries, as did Sankt Gallen, or around Roman settlements, as in the case of Zürich; many developed from villages into market cities. Some, such as Fribourg (1157) and Bern (1191), were founded on a plan; their old sections, located within the protected areas formed by looped river bends, present a fascinating vision with their unified urban architecture. Each city is geographically unique, particularly those lying at the head of a lake, such as Zürich, Geneva, and Luzern, which were essentially harbour towns until the opening of the railroads (a status to some extent regained with the lakes' new importance to the tourist industry). A lake inlet, or the mouth of a river such as the Limmat, Rhône, or Reuss, and moraines and rings of mountains combine with the cities' houses and scenically situated cathedrals and minsters to form composite landscapes of nature and art. Many towns have sprung up around the site of a bridge; as a rule, these have two sections separated by the narrows of a river. Hill towns such as Regensberg and Gruyères, which were medieval fortified settlements with castles and the architecture of which developed through the late Gothic period, have a natural dominance that rather gives them the appearance of scenic ornaments, of crowns gleaming in the distance.

In Switzerland, isolated from Europe by mountainous barriers, location in relation to the traffic pattern has played an important role in urban development. Chur, Martigny, and Bellinzona are keys to a series of Alpine passes. Lugano, which, along with Locarno and Ascona, forms an extensive resort area benefitting from the abundant sunshine of the Mediterranean climate, is a gateway from the south to the Alpine region. Basel's location at the head of Rhine navigation has been of particular significance, since this was the basis of its early prominence as a city of scholars and of its present international importance as an industrial centre. Switzerland's largest cities are Zürich, Basel, Geneva, Bern, Lausanne, Winterthur, Sankt Gallen, and Luzern.

THE PEOPLE

Etruscans, Raetians, Celts, Romans, and Germanic peoples have left their mark on Switzerland in the course of its historical evolution. The present population mainly shows traces of the Alpine, "Nordic," and southern Slav, or Dinaric, peoples. To survive as a cohesive unit, the disparate elements of the Swiss people have had to learn a mutual cooperation to protect the neutrality that has been their safeguard. Their outlook has been shaped largely by economic and political necessity, which has made them realistic, cautious, and prudent in accepting innovation and ingenious in the use of what resources they have. Their lives exhibit acumen, discipline, and thrift and a somewhat Germanic love of order and thoroughness allied with a Latin independence of spirit and an admiration for quality and craftsmanship that makes their products highly valued throughout the world.

Mixed character of the Swiss

One of the distinctive features of the Swiss Confederation is the variety of its languages. About two-thirds of the total population speak German, one-fifth French, one-tenth Italian, and 1 percent Rhaeto-Romanic. Switzerland encompasses the area in which the major cultural regions of western continental Europe—the German, the French, and the Italian—come into contact. Its fourth language, Rhaeto-Romanic, is a linguistic relic preserved amid the mountainous regions between the Gotthard and the East Alps; it is subdivided into even smaller dialect regions. In 1938, a federal popular vote indicative of Swiss sentiment recognized Romansh as a fourth national (though not federally official) language, which was tantamount to a political declaration in favour of national diversity and in opposition to centralized power.

Switzerland also exhibits diversity in the area of religion, although conflicts over faith are rare and there are even churches in which Protestants and Catholics worship together. The great internal population shift caused by industrialization has also resulted in a greater mixture of the religions. The Swiss are divided almost equally into Protestants and Catholics, with a tiny Jewish community.

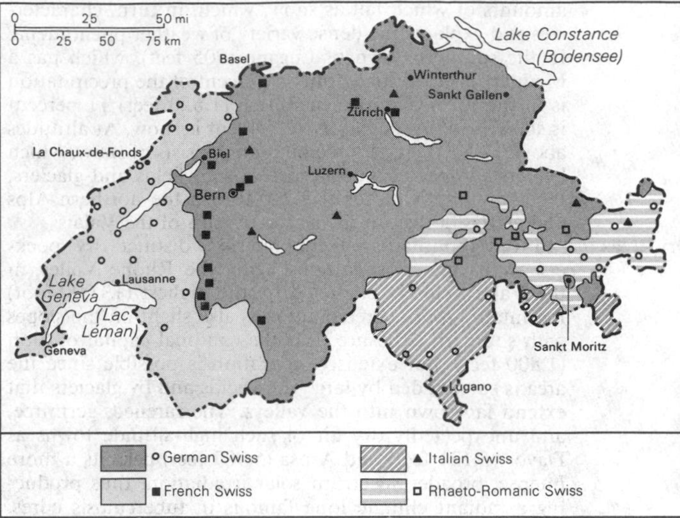

Ethnic composition of Switzerland.

The constitution of 1874 guaranteed full religious liberty but repeated the 1848 constitution's prohibition of settlement by Jesuits (members of the Roman Catholic Society of Jesus) and their affiliated societies in Switzerland. This anti-Jesuit article was repealed in a national referendum in 1973.

THE ECONOMY

The Swiss economy has been molded by several specific factors: a paucity of raw materials; the pressure of urbanization on the limited amount of cultivable land; precipitation, which to a large extent determines the type and size of cultivation; the advantage of being centrally located on international trade routes; scenic beauty; and the inability of the domestic market to absorb the total output of a skilled and efficient population.

Factors shaping the economy

These factors have given rise to industries such as shipping, freighting, banking, and insurance and to export industries requiring skill rather than large imports of raw materials, resulting in high-value, small-bulk industries such as precision-instrument manufacture. An important consequence of the traditional Swiss neutrality has been economic stability even in times of European war.

Agriculture. Agriculture, which employs less than 3 percent of the total population, is characterized by fodder crops and grazing, which occupy three-fifths of the total agricultural area. Grain, occupying only about a sixth of productive land, satisfies barely one-half of the domestic demand. The variation in soil quality within small areas produced by geological conditions and by the relief makes large-scale, single-crop farming impossible; instead, a particularly varied assortment of crops is grown in a limited space. Two-thirds of all farms combine grass and grain cultivation. The Valais, with its abundant sunshine and artificial irrigation, specializes in cultivating fruits, vegetables, and berries. In the southernmost canton of Ticino, a mixed Mediterranean agriculture has been attained, although it is endangered by the disruptions of oversettlement. Viticulture characterizes slopes along many lakes.

The primary agricultural pursuit, however, is cattle raising, for which Switzerland has become important throughout Europe. The income from dairying and cattle raising amounts to about one-half of all agricultural income.

Since the importance of forest to the ecology of large areas was recognized early, an exemplary forestation law forbids reduction of woodlands, which amount to nearly one-quarter of the total area of the country. Forests have become a main feature of the recreational areas located near cities.

Industry. Switzerland's transformation into an industrial state began during the second half of the 19th century; now, most exports consist of manufactured goods and chemicals. Lacking its own mineral and agricultural raw materials, however, Switzerland is forced to import raw materials, foodstuffs, and manufactured goods by costly land routes; raw materials, food, vegetable oils, and fuel account for about a quarter of the imports. Only the outstanding quality of its products, ranging from motors, generators, and turbines to the atomic clock, enables Switzerland to remain competitive. The operations of the first European factory to produce aluminum by electronic methods have remained a model for Europe. The chemical-pharmaceutical industry, centred in Basel, is also a prime competitor in world trade. The chemical industry alone spends great sums on research, and many other industries also collaborate with the country's universities and with the Federal Institutes of Technology at Zürich and Lausanne. Many large firms are merging under the pressure of international competition, although the typical Swiss traits of diversity and division into small units still make it possible for firms in small towns and villages to continue to supply products of worldwide importance.

Hydroelectric power

Although Switzerland lacks mineral power sources to run its industries, the extensive Alpine precipitation, glacial water storage, and the great range of altitudes make hydroelectric power widely available. The electrical industry has become an essential branch of the Swiss economy as a whole, with a few hundred large hydroelectric power plants currently in operation and numerous low-pressure plants situated on the lower courses of the rivers in the Mittelland. Major electrotechnical progress has occurred in the Alps, where large systems of tunnels and subterranean powerhouses have been constructed in suitable valleys. Two of the highest dams in Europe, Mauvoisin (777 feet) and Grande Dixence (932 feet), have been erected in the Valais, where, on the Rhône, the highest rate of hydroelectric power consumption in Europe has been attained. By the late 20th century, 95 percent of the hydroelectric energy worth harnessing for power plants was utilized, and Switzerland had begun to operate thermal power plants. In addition, there are several nuclear power plants.

Trade and finance. Switzerland has trade relations with scores of countries and is outranked only by Belgium-Luxembourg in total per capita imports and exports among the major trading nations of the world. Among its most important trading partners are West Germany, France, Italy, The Netherlands, and Belgium and Luxembourg.

Its central location, political stability, and privacy laws have been vital factors in making Switzerland one of the most important of the world's financial centres, with hundreds of banks on its territory financing the enormous freight stream that flows through the country. In the same context a large industry has grown up, specializing in reinsurance.

Tourism. The deficit in the balance of trade is to a large extent covered by income from tourism. During the Middle Ages, healing spas such as Baden, Bad Pfäfers, Leukerbad, and Rheinfelden flourished, while mountain-pass hospices were the predecessors of Alpine hotels. Since World War II, travel has increased at an explosive rate: hotels, guesthouses, and high-altitude sanatoriums count millions of visitors, as do vacation apartments, youth hostels, and campgrounds. Of the tourists, about 80 percent come from European countries, one-half of these from Switzerland itself. The tourist industry as a whole employs almost as many people as are engaged in farming.

Management of the economy. The long-standing tradition of direct democracy and federalism in Switzerland and the country's heavy dependence on foreign trade have given rise to an equally traditional suspicion of state intervention and to strong and constant support for worldwide free trade. Apart from the post office, telegraph, telephone, and main railway network, all utilities are privately owned or municipal enterprises, in some cases subsidized by cantonal governments. Even the hydroelectric plants are owned by private companies under federal or cantonal grants.

Areas of governmental involvement and restraint

In matters of taxation, federal regulations extend mainly to customs duties and sales and defense taxes. Income taxes are cantonal responsibilities, and rates are fixed by decision of the voters of communal or cantonal parliaments.

Employer–employee relations have generally been good in the late 20th century. The Swiss Federation of Trade Unions has Social Democratic tendencies. Since the Depression of the early 1930s, the unions have gradually denounced the use of strikes as economic and political weapons, and disputes are usually settled by arbitration.

Although the Swiss have tended to reject state intervention in their free market economy, since World War II such intervention has been unavoidable, particularly in relation to the labour market. In the late 20th century, many workers in industry were foreigners. Social tensions became unavoidable, particularly where foreigners threatened to displace the Swiss, and the government was forced to restrict the inflow, thus for the first time breaching the liberal doctrines of Swiss economic policy.

Just as centralized bureaucracy was traditionally distrusted at home, so, in relation to European integration, the Swiss, though acquiring a special arrangement with the European Economic Community in 1972, have preferred the first type of integration offered by the European Free Trade Association.

Transportation. Control of the most important Alpine passes and the ancient routeway through the Mittelland between the Rhône, Rhine, and Danube waterways has given Switzerland a key position in European transit traffic. The main artery of European trans-Alpine traffic, the St. Gotthard route, runs through Swiss territory.

The large-scale technical undertakings of modern highway construction were preceded by those of the railway system, which has thousands of miles of track and includes hundreds of tunnels, among them the 12.3-mile Simplon II Tunnel and the famous winding tunnels of the Gotthard railway, by means of which altitude differences between valley levels are overcome. The entire Swiss railway system has been electrified, thus saving the country from dependence on coal imports. The Swiss Federal Railways, which constitute over half of the system, are operated by the federal government, while the remainder, including the numerous mountain railways, is distributed among over 75 private railroads, partially owned by the cantons and municipalities. The Vitznau-Rigi-Bahn, the first cogwheel railway in the world, was built in 1871 by Nikolaus Riggenbach of Basel and achieved early fame. Automobiles have not displaced rail traffic: in the late 20th century the Swiss Federal Railways still carried passengers and freight on a massive scale.

Since World War II, Switzerland has also maintained its own small "oceangoing fleet" of ships. The popularity of the steamers on Lake Geneva has never flagged since they were inaugurated in 1823. Regular summer services are provided on several lakes by more than 120 vessels, which include a few paddle-wheelers.

Swissair, the national airline, ranks among the world's largest commercial carriers. The largest airports are in Zürich-Kloten and Geneva.

ADMINISTRATIVE AND SOCIAL CONDITIONS

Government. The Swiss Confederation consists of some 3,000 communes, which, like the 26 cantons (including six demicantons, or *Halbkantonen,* which function as full cantons), are largely autonomous and which range in size from Bagnes, with an area of 110 square miles (282 square kilometres), to Rivaz, with an area of 0.1 square mile (0.3 square kilometre). From the multiplicity of small communal republics stems a special quality and, paradoxically, a basis of the inner strength of the entire nation, for each citizen treasures and supports the freedom of the commune, a shared conviction that unites him with the rest of the population in a way that transcends differences of language and of party.

The Swiss Confederation's main body of laws rests upon the Federal Constitution, adopted in 1848 and revised in 1874; its 123 articles established the rights and duties of the citizen and of the governing bodies.

The federal government supervises external and internal security, all transportation affairs, forestry, water conservation, and the like and deals with foreign policy and customs, the postal, telephone, and telegraph systems, the monetary system, and the military organization, as well as with the extensive social insurance programs. It may take steps to adjust the course of the economy and provides for uniform administration of justice in the areas of criminal and civil law.

The organizational units of the federation are the people and the states, or cantons, the Federal Assembly, the Federal Council, and the Federal Supreme Court. Legislative power resides in the bicameral Federal Assembly, comprising the National Council, with 200 deputies elected by a system of proportional representation, and the Council of States, in which each canton is represented by two deputies and each demicanton by one deputy. The administrative Federal Council is a seven-member collegial board, an organization of equals with a rotating presidency, with each councillor presiding over a federal department. Supreme judicial power is vested in the Federal Supreme Court, the seat of which is in Lausanne (Vaud).

The Swiss Civil Code of 1912 has furnished a model for the administration of justice in many countries, and parts have been adopted verbatim. The difficult task of creating and preserving a uniform judicial system within so diverse a national structure has produced a number of great jurists and international law experts in Switzerland. Each canton elects and maintains its own magistracy for ordinary civil and criminal trials. Capital punishment was abolished by the unified federal penal code of 1937, except under circumstances of martial law, general mobilization, or war.

Sovereign power rests with the people, however, who vote on proposed legislation several times a year and elect representatives every four years. The constitution was amended by national referendum in 1971 to grant women the right to vote in federal elections and to hold federal office.

The principal political parties are the Swiss Social Democratic Party, the Radical Democrats, and the Christian Democrats, who in the 1983 election to the National Council won 47, 54, and 42 seats, respectively.

Police and armed forces. Police authority is generally exercised by the cantons, but larger communes also maintain police forces. A small federal police corps enforces special federal laws concerning such crimes as treason and forgery (mainly in collaboration with cantonal police).

In accordance with confederation neutrality, which dates back to the 16th century and in 1815 became international law, the army serves solely to preserve the independence of the country. Defense is based on a system of universal conscription under which every Swiss male is liable for military duty between the ages of 20 to 50 years and, for officers, to 55 years. The training of recruits is followed by eight annual three-week refresher courses and later by shorter supplementary courses. Swiss women may serve as volunteers in the Women's Auxiliary Force. The Swiss is the only soldier in the world who keeps his equipment, including arms and ammunition, at home and who performs his obligatory gunnery duty each year in civilian clothes, a manifestation of the extraordinary degree of trust between citizen and government.

The citizen army

Education. The 1874 constitution stipulates that each canton or half canton is sovereign in education, that elementary education is compulsory and free, and that all public schools must be state directed. The confederation financially assists public elementary schools, vocational training, and the cantonal universities, and, by regulating examinations for the professions, it also influences the curriculum of the secondary schools. The only institutions of higher education maintained by the confederation itself are the Federal Institutes of Technology at Zürich (founded 1855) and Lausanne (federalized 1969). The interior department in Bern administers education, and there is an education department in every canton.

The combination of Alpine scenery and the pedagogic reputation of the country of educational theorists Jean-Jacques Rousseau and J.H. Pestalozzi forms a common attraction, and many thousands of students annually receive their schooling during a sojourn in healthful surroundings, thus combining the useful with the beautiful.

Social welfare. The law stipulates that assistance to the poor is primarily the concern of the family. Public welfare services were developed in a typically federalistic way: first in the communes, then in the cantons, and later in the confederation. Social insurances that were introduced by amendments to the federal constitution already existed in some communities. The most important was compulsory old-age insurance (introduced in 1948), which provides annuities and rent allowances to all men over 65, all women over 62, widows, orphans, and invalids; it is financed by contributions from every worker under 65 and his employer and by smaller contributions from the cantons and the confederation. The old-age subsidy does not cover the cost of living: communes, cantons, and the confederation provide additional support for the destitute out of general revenues. Compensation for loss of earnings due to military service is similarly financed by contributions.

Federal–local interaction in public welfare

Leisure. Surrounded as they are by scenic splendour and always within one-half-hour's journey of mountains, pastures, lakes, and rivers, the Swiss have become extremely sports conscious and have encouraged the growth of skiing, tobogganing, and mountaineering as tourist attractions. Other sports include Swiss-style wrestling, gymnastics, regular Sunday-morning shooting, Hornussen (a kind of Alpine baseball), tennis, golf, ice hockey, soccer, sailing, and swimming. The fishing is good in the lakes and rivers, and when the lakes freeze over, they are used for curling and even horse racing.

CULTURAL LIFE

Although Switzerland may not rank foremost among the centres of European culture, the country can yet boast an impressive list of contributors to the arts and sciences. Perhaps because their country has presented too fine a view with too little challenge, some of Switzerland's creative minds have chosen to live elsewhere. This has been especially true of architects. On the other hand, Switzerland's traditional neutrality and its laws of political asylum have made the country a magnet for many creative persons during times of unrest or war in Europe. The mid-19th century was such a period, as were the 1930s and 1940s, when the rise of Fascism caused a number of German and Austrian and Italian writers such as Thomas Mann, Stefan George, and Ignazio Silone to seek harbour in Switzerland.

If a "Swiss culture" can be spoken of in its broader implications beyond the arts, distinctive French, Italian, and German cultural circles must be recognized, as well as a robust Rhaeto-Romanic culture. In a real sense the four parts of the country represent a definite resistance to levelling or homogenizing influences, political or cultural. In addition, Switzerland's geographical centrality in Europe can be seen reflected in the notion of *Helvetia mediatrix*—Switzerland the mediatress. The Swiss Henri Dunant, founder of the International Red Cross, lives on in the continued sense of many Swiss in a distinct mission of cultural union, a mission revealed not only in the foreign assistance programs toward self-help being carried out in several small and developing nations but also in the unusual number of literary translators within the country.

Folk arts. Folk art in Switzerland is expressed in music, poetry (usually song), dance, wood carving, and embroidery. In the cattle-breeding northern areas, there are many primitive forms of song and music involving, for instance, yodelling, a way of singing marked by rapid switching of the voice to falsetto. There are also trumpet-like instruments made of bark, the perfect form of which is the alphorn. Folk music in mainly pastoral areas has wide-ranging, floating melodies, whereas in the crop-growing regions of the inner and southern Alps, more songlike melodies of limited range are common. The most frequent poetical themes are love and longing for the homeland, as well as historical, patriotic, pastoral, and hunting themes. The vitality of the Alpine folk culture can also be seen in very expressive dances, such as the *Schuhplattler*, with its rapid sequence of jumping and hopping movements.

Wood carving consists partly of chip carving for the decoration of everyday objects, such as milking stools, neckbands for bells, wooden spoons, and distaffs, and partly of figure carving, especially of nativity figures. Decoration of house facades with sayings usually of a religious nature is widespread in Protestant Alpine areas (in Bernese Oberland and parts of the Grisons), but it can also be found to a lesser extent in Catholic regions, such as German-speaking upper Valais.

Embroidery, as a form of folk art, can be seen especially at prominent points of women's clothing, such as cuffs, stomachers, hats, scarves. It has become a home industry in parts of eastern Switzerland.

Architecture. The 12th-century Romanesque style found particularly rich expression in the cathedrals of Geneva, Basel, Lausanne, Sion, and Chur and in the many castles and fortresses; and the Gothic style was expressed in the cathedrals of Zug, Zürich, and Schaffhausen. But in the Renaissance period many architectural masters, especially from the Ticino, gave their talents to Italy: Antonio da Ponte built the Prisons near the Doge's Palace and the Rialto Bridge in Venice; Antonio Contino built Venice's Bridge of Sighs; Domenico Fontana (1543–1607) designed the whole of Lateran Palace, and the facade of St. John Lateran Church, and the Royal Palace in Naples; his nephew Carlo Maderno became architect to Pope Paul V; Francesco Borromini built San Carlino, the gallery of the Spada Palace, and the Filippini Monastery and modified the Falconieri and Barberini palaces; Carlo Fontana built the facade of San Marcello al Corso and the Montecitorio Palace; Baldassare Lenghena, from Maroggia, built the Church of Santa Maria de la Salute, the Rezzonico, Pesaro, and Widmann palaces, the Ospedaletto, and the interior of Scalzi. In a later period, G.B. Gilardi rebuilt the Kremlin in Moscow and his son Domenico the Moscow University and a number of the Soviet capital's palaces. In the 20th century Le Corbusier (Charles-Édouard Jeanneret) was one of the major creative forces behind the International school of architecture that dominated most building trends throughout the West.

Visual arts. The Protestantism of 16th-century Switzerland had a strongly inhibiting effect on Swiss painting and sculpture in general. The peculiar lack of either French or Italian Renaissance influence left Swiss artists in a limbo from which they showed signs of recovery only in modern times. Artists of international renown have included Alberto Giacometti and Paul Klee. The arts are championed by renowned museums not only in cities such as Basel, Zürich, and Geneva but also in small towns such as Winterthur and Schaffhausen, which pride themselves as cultural bastions far beyond the usual provincial standards.

Literature. In the field of literature, Switzerland has produced Jean-Jacques Rousseau, the historian and critic Jacob Burckhardt, Madame de Staël, whose home at Coppet became a centre of European literary life during the 18th century, Gottfried Keller, Conrad Ferdinand Meyer, Jeremias Gotthelf, Charles-Ferdinand Ramus, and the Nobel Prize winners Hermann Hesse and Carl Spitteler. The contemporary dramatists Friedrich Dürrenmatt and Max Frisch have been widely produced outside Switzerland. By the great number of dialects in all the four languages, a living dialect literature is comprehensible. It is an expressive cultural characteristic of nearly each valley.

Music. Although Switzerland is not a leading musical nation, in the 20th century such composers as Arthur Honegger, Othmar Schoeck, and Frank Martin have gained international renown. An annual international music festival is held in Luzern.

Science. Swiss men of science have included Paracelsus (Theophrastus Bombastus von Hohenheim), who in the 16th century brought chemistry into the field of medicine; the Bernoulli family of Basel, who made significant contributions to mathematics over three generations; the innovative mathematician Leonhard Euler; the naturalist and pioneer Alpine scholar Horace Bénédict de Saussure; and the Nobel Prize-winning chemist Alfred Werner. Zürich's Federal Institute of Technology has produced many Nobel Prize winners. For statistical data, see the "Britannica World Data" section in the current *Britannica Book of the Year*. (E.Eg./Ed.)

History

Although the frontiers of Switzerland have remained almost unchanged since 1815, this stability is relatively modern. The history of this area was for centuries that of a small part of the Holy Roman Empire; changes were frequent, and the emergence of a coherent community in the absence of a common race, language, or religion was long in doubt.

SWITZERLAND TO C. 1300

Before the Christian Era there were sporadic settlements of hunters, fishermen, agriculturalists, and armed warriors in caves along the rivers and occasionally on piles beside the lakes, much as elsewhere in the West. A Tène civilization was followed by growing numbers of Celts. By the time of Julius Caesar, Helvetia (as the region was then called) was known as strategically important to Rome, if only because of the Alpine passes. A Roman invading army asserted its superiority at Bibracte in 58 BC, and Roman colonies or garrisons followed at Nyon (Julia Equestris), Augst (Augusta Raurica), Avenches (Aventicum), and near Windisch (Vindonissa), bringing Roman ideas and civilization to the inhabitants.

North of the Rhine were the Germanic "barbarians." In AD 259 the Alemanni began to penetrate the Roman defensive barrier, and during the 5th and 6th centuries they had become permanent residents east of the Aar, with the less numerous Burgundians to the west of it.

These were followed by Ostrogoths, who were in transit only, and by Franks, whose rulers by 639 had secured recognition as kings, thus ensuring permanent connection with the France of the future. All these invaders were pagans; survivors of Roman converts to Christianity had practically disappeared by the 6th century, when missionaries like St. Columban and St. Gall arrived. Five rather inconvenient dioceses were set up—Chur, Sion, Basel, Constance, Lausanne—and Benedictine monasteries, forerunners of many more, were settled and endowed at St. Gall (modern Sankt Gallen), Zürich, Disentis, Romainmôtier, and elsewhere.

Arrival of missionaries

Such political authority as remained was exercised by the counts, who accepted the Frankish monarchs after Clovis as their overlords. Charlemagne crossed this remote corner of his empire more than once, but such unity as his reign implied was broken at the partition of Verdun (843). This left the land west of the Aar in the hands of Lothair, while that to the east was assigned to Louis the German. Thus, these separate influences, along with local devolution, were fused with the Latin traditions of the Roman Church to shape the future.

In the 10th century both Muslim and Magyar marauders reached Swiss territory, but in each case they were too far from their base to have anything more than nuisance value. By 1033 dynastic accident and deliberate policy had brought the whole of what is now Switzerland into the orbit of the Holy Roman emperor Conrad II, and it remained part of the empire until the end of the Middle Ages. With the re-establishment of imperial authority in the 11th century came conflict with the papacy. Switzerland was divided between the supporters of Emperor Henry IV and those of Pope Gregory VII. The Emperor was supported by the counts of Lenzburg, the bishops of Basel and Lausanne, and the abbot of St. Gall, while the Pope could rely on help from the counts of Rheinfelden, Toggenburg, Kyburg, and Zähringen. It was the counts who gained most. Switzerland was by now thoroughly feudalized. The dukes and counts exercised local jurisdiction practically unchecked. From their castles they dominated and also protected the peasants of the countryside, as did the great abbots and bishops also. Only in walled cities such as Basel, Zürich, Solothurn, Bern, and Schaffhausen was there hope of independence.

Its assertion came, however, not from thence but from the peasant communities of inaccessible mountain valleys, the members of which had learned economic cooperation to avert starvation and were determined to secure freedom from forced labour services or feudal payments in cash or kind.

Towns and dynasts. Many towns were deliberately set up by the ruling feudal families as centres of defense, trade, and administration, Bern most obviously so. Fribourg, Thun, Burgdorf, Laupen, and Morat illustrated the power and extent of the Zähringen dynasty, which died out in 1218. The Zähringen authority reverted in part to the emperor, from whom it had derived. The surviving

Foundation of towns

families—Kyburg, Habsburg, and Savoy—pursued much the same policy of territorial aggrandizement. The Kyburgers, with great possessions in Thurgau and Aargau, came to an end in 1264; and after a struggle with the House of Savoy, Rudolf IV (later Rudolf I of Germany) of Habsburg obtained most of the Kyburger territory, thereby becoming the most powerful ruler with whom the Swiss were in contact. Rudolf was already in control of a sizable part of Alsace and of much of the route from the Rhine to Schwyz and Nidwalden, either as protector of the abbeys of Muri and Murbach or as representative of the emperor.

At about the same time, the opening of the St. Gotthard Pass greatly increased the value of the north-south route to Italy and therefore of the communities of Uri, Schwyz, and Unterwalden (Obwalden and Nidwalden). There the peasants had long enjoyed a large measure of freedom from the interference of any feudal overlord and had limited rights to choose their own magistrates, although "high justice" rested with the representative of the feudal lord. In 1231 the men of Uri became directly subject only to the distant Holy Roman emperor, with the right of appointing their own magistrate; and in 1240 Schwyz and Nidwalden obtained a similar privilege from the emperor Frederick II, the validity of which was promptly challenged by the Habsburg overlords. Such uncertainty as there was, however, was largely removed when Rudolf of Habsburg became German king in 1273. The crown meant that he could assert imperial rights in Uri and hereditary family claims in Schwyz and Unterwalden. The heart of Switzerland was at his mercy when he died on July 15, 1291.

The league of 1291. In 1291 Schwyz, Uri, and Nidwalden (Obwalden followed that December) formed the Everlasting League (Ewige Bund), a perpetual alliance for the settlement of disagreements among themselves by arbitration, for the punishment of crime, for resort to law rather than to violence, and for mutual defense. They would accept only natives as judges, and these must not have paid for their office. All this was confirmed by oath and by a sealed document, which marks the traditional inauguration of the Swiss Confederation (an even earlier union is clearly implied, but its exact nature is unknown).

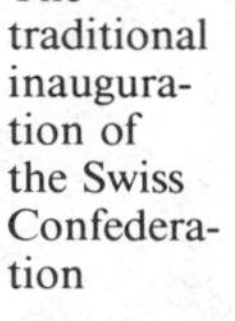
The traditional inauguration of the Swiss Confederation

Rudolf's son, Albert I of Austria, who obtained the German crown in 1298, forced Zürich to abandon its attempt to be comprised within the union. The successive German rulers—Adolf of Nassau (reigned 1292–98), Albert of Austria (reigned 1298–1308), Henry VII of Luxembourg (reigned 1308–13, Holy Roman emperor 1312–13), and Louis IV the Bavarian (reigned 1314–47)—were far too busy elsewhere to intervene in Switzerland, although the Habsburgs relinquished none of their hereditary claims.

THE SWISS CONFEDERATION FROM C. 1300 TO C. 1530

The struggle for independence and subsequent expansion. In 1314 the men of Schwyz attacked the abbey of Einsiedeln, which enjoyed the protection of Frederick III of Austria, who was challenging the claims of Louis the Bavarian to the empire. The Waldstätte (the three forest cantons, Uri, Schwyz, and Unterwalden) supported the latter claimant, and this led to an armed invasion by Leopold, Frederick's brother, in 1315.

Morgarten and the league of 1315. Ships from Luzern attacked Schwyz by water, and Unterwalden was threatened from Entlebuch. Meanwhile a force of mail-clad horsemen advanced toward Lake Egeri (Ägerisee). At Morgarten on November 15, 1315, their passage was blocked at a point where they were unable to charge and were vulnerable to boulders hurled from the mountain slopes, and the attackers were completely defeated. To consolidate their gain, the three allies reaffirmed in a German document (December 9, 1315) their defensive alliance, rejected Habsburg rights, and agreed to make no separate peace. The Habsburgs agreed to a long truce, which lasted, with occasional intermissions, until the end of the century, neither side accepting any permanent renunciation of its claims.

Alliances with Luzern and Zürich

A notable advance was made on November 7, 1332, when Luzern entered into a perpetual alliance with Uri, Schwyz, and Unterwalden, while at the same time maintaining the Habsburg link. It was an alliance and not absorption, but it was advantageous to both sides.

Zürich and Bern. More important was a similar arrangement made with Zürich in 1351. Zürich had secured "immediate" status as a free imperial city in 1218, politically within the Habsburg orbit. It was a flourishing market and manufacturing centre with good defenses, where the nobles were depressed and the artisans were organized into craft guilds. In 1336 an internal revolution enabled the artisans to secure parity with the aristocrats and wealthy merchants; this, in practice, enabled the artisans to exercise supreme power. The dispossessed nobles

Adapted from W. Shepherd, *Historical Atlas*; Barnes & Noble Books, New York

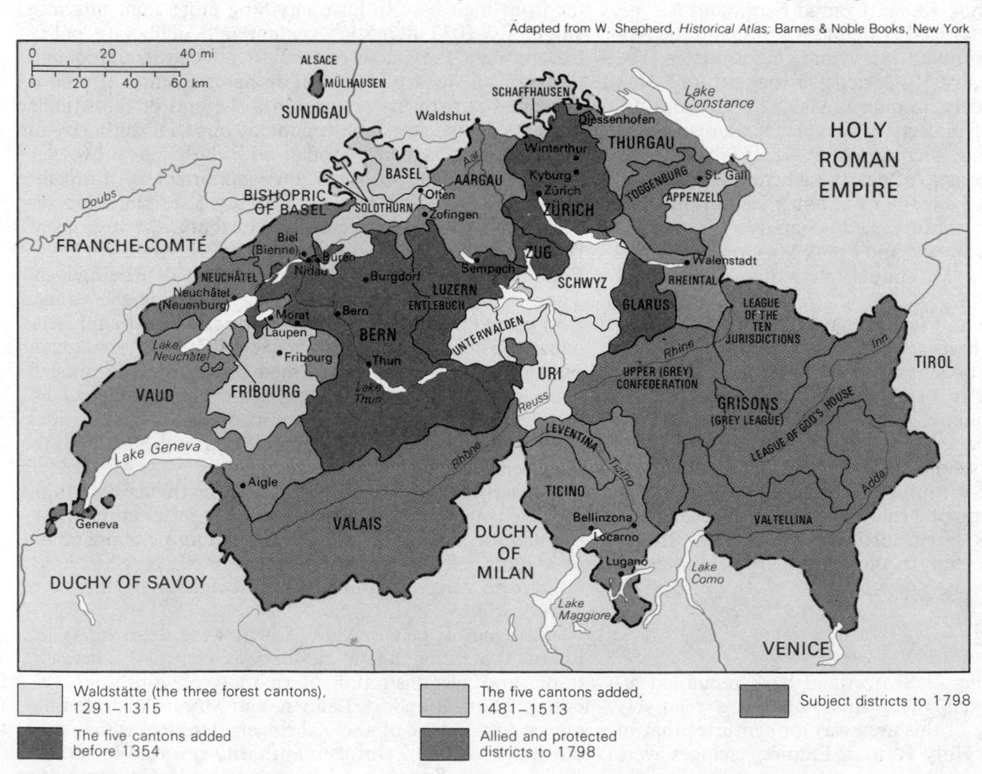

The Swiss Confederation to 1798.

returned to their castles or to neighbouring Rapperswil; they failed to regain power by a coup d'etat in 1350.

The Habsburgs failed to reduce Zürich to submission, and the city's alliance with Luzern and the three interior communities followed as a natural defensive measure (May 1, 1351). Zürich, besieged or threatened by Austria in 1351, 1352, and 1355, resisted at great expense.

Bern escaped Habsburg domination and Savoyard protection, and after 1218 it asserted its freedom as an imperial city and administrative centre. The predominating influence was military and patrician, not artisan, and accident and design enabled its governors to expand steadily over the neighbouring countryside. During the first half of the 14th century, Bern had sometimes been anti-Habsburg without any long-term commitments and had received help from the Waldstätte in successfully defending Laupen against a coalition including Fribourg and Austria in 1339. At other times—in 1342, 1351, 1352, and later—Bern enjoyed Habsburg friendship. For greater security, and to ensure that Unterwalden did not support hostile peasant movements, Bern agreed to a perpetual union with Uri, Schwyz, and Unterwalden in 1353, although this did not prevent Bernese-Habsburg cooperation when it was advantageous to both sides.

Expansion of the confederation. An unsuccessful attack on Solothurn by Rudolf II, count of Kyburg, in 1382 enabled Bern to secure Thun and Burgdorf. This meant direct collision with Leopold III of Tirol, who was opposed by a Swabian League (founded 1377) and by Zürich, Bern, Solothurn, and Zug. At the end of 1385 Luzern suddenly occupied the Habsburg-controlled areas of Rothenburg, Sempach, and the Entlebuch valley. Leopold replied by leading an army of some 4,000 feudal nobles to Sempach; there, on July 9, 1386, he was defeated and killed by a similar force from central Switzerland.

The Habsburgs still remained the lawful overlords of the small district of Glarus, where the inhabitants were anxious to imitate the successful moves toward independence of their immediate neighbours. They had supported Schwyz in 1323 and in 1351 had willingly allowed their land to be used as a base for confederate operations against the Austrian besiegers of Zürich. In June 1352 Glarus was admitted as a somewhat subordinate partner in the Swiss alliance, followed almost immediately by Zug. Both became subject to Austria in 1355; Zug was occupied by Schwyz in 1364 and remained under its protection after the Peace of Torberg in 1368. The men of Glarus occupied Windegg in July 1386; and in April 1388, unsupported by their neighbours, they met the Austrians at Näfels and won their freedom. Thereafter an independent Glarus was a member of the union. Bern characteristically took advantage of the Austrian embarrassment to secure Büren, Nidau, and Olten. After Näfels, the Swiss Confederation was a fact of history; and the eight states—Uri, Schwyz, Unterwalden, Zug, Luzern, Glarus, Bern, and Zürich—had to learn the lessons of cooperation.

The eight-state confederation

In 1370 all these except Glarus and Bern faced the demand from their ecclesiastics for exemption from taxation and military service. This, when war threatened, was unacceptable, and the states agreed by the Priests' Charter (Pfaffenbrief, October 1370) that clergy and laity alike were subject to the same laws; unauthorized commando expeditions were also prohibited, and, in certain cases, the contracting powers agreed to abide by a majority vote. Military success led to an agreement about laws of war in 1393 by eight signatories, including Bern and Solothurn—looting was to be controlled; women, children, and clerical property were protected; and deserters were repudiated by all parties to the agreement.

Switzerland in the 15th and early 16th centuries. With the 15th century came an interval of peace, consolidation, and expansion. Zürich, stronger and wealthier, came to terms with its Habsburg neighbour while adding to its own territory, and Bern expanded to the east and west. The central states recognized that security meant expansion southward as the St. Gotthard route became increasingly used. Glarus opened talks with its southern neighbour, the Upper, or Gray, Confederation. There the bishop of Chur, the abbot of Disentis, and the local barons, Misox and Räzüns, accepted the existence of peasant leagues; thus the Grisons (valley area that included the city of Chur) became almost a Switzerland in miniature on the southern and eastern wings of the confederation.

Around the monastery of St. Gall a flourishing trading city had grown; and as the economic importance of the monastery declined in spite of its wide possessions, tension grew between city and abbot. The citizens found allies in the communities of Appenzell, over which the monastery claimed jurisdiction. The abbot sought help from the Austrians in the Rheintal, to which the Appenzellers replied by an alliance with Schwyz. In 1403 a monastic army was defeated, whereupon the abbot sought and obtained the support of Duke Frederick IV of Austria. Schwyz was bound by treaty to keep clear of such a conflict, but the citizen army of St. Gall beat off one attack and the Appenzellers another in June 1405. After this Appenzell was accepted as an ally by seven confederate states, excluding only Bern.

Alliance with Appenzell

First Italian conquests. In the south the men of Uri were becoming anxious about the security of their communications with northern Italy. The inhabitants of the Leventina (the narrow valley of the upper Ticino River) appealed for help and protection and so, in 1403, became subject to Uri and Obwalden (western Unterwalden); Bellinzona was purchased by Uri but was retaken by Milan in 1422. Uri and Unterwalden appealed for help from their partners. Zürich and Bern took no action, but Luzern and Zug cooperated and Schwyz sent a force toward Domodossola. All these forces joined at Arbedo, where on June 30, 1422, they were surprised and defeated.

The southern expeditions also made contact with Valais, part of which was controlled from Savoy and part ruled by the bishop of Sion. The latter in 1403 made an alliance with Uri, Unterwalden, and Luzern, which only increased internal dissensions.

Conquest of the Aargau and the Old Zürich War. A dispute in 1415 between Duke Frederick IV of Austria and the emperor Sigismund provided the confederates with a pretext to attack the Habsburg possessions south of the Rhine. A Bernese force occupied the Aargau, Zofingen falling in April 1415; a Luzern contingent occupied Sursee and St. Urban; and Zürich made similar gains. Sigismund was forced to pledge part of Aargau to Zürich and Bern—the former taking the portion of the Freiamt east of the Reuss, Bern securing the western half, with pickings left for Luzern. The remainder of the land became a "common lordship" (*gemeine Herrschaft*) of the confederation. This was to cause infinite trouble later, but it was also to prove part of the cement that held the confederation together.

In 1436 Frederick VII, count of Toggenburg and owner of Uznach, Sargans, Gaster, Rheineck, Altstätten, and Feldkirch, died childless. Schwyz and Zürich quarrelled over the partition of the inheritance, and war followed. Unsuccessful, in 1442 Zürich made an alliance with the Habsburg emperor Frederick III and in 1443 was at war with the whole confederation. The city was besieged; its *Bürgermeister* fell in an unsuccessful sortie at St. Jakob an der Sihl (1443) after negotiations for an armistice had broken down and the garrison of Greifensee had been liquidated. In 1444 Frederick III secured support from Charles VII of France, who sent a large force of irregulars to the neighbourhood of Basel. There, at St. Jakob an der Birs, this great army was halted by a Swiss detachment one-tenth its size, which fought until only a few wounded remained (August 26, 1444). The French mercenaries were unprepared for further such encounters, and they left for Alsace (thereafter France sought Swiss friendship rather than face hostility, and the already high reputation of Swiss fighters was enhanced). France made peace at Ensishein (October 1444) with the confederation (minus Zürich, but with Basel and Solothurn added). This implied recognition, and it was followed in June 1446 by the Peace of Constance between Zürich and the confederates on the basis of a return to prewar fromtiers, with Schwyz slightly advantaged and Austria excluded south of the Rhine.

Recognition by France

St. Gall and Thurgau. In August 1451 the abbot of St. Gall entered into a protective agreement with Zürich, Luzern, Schwyz, and Glarus; the city of St. Gall did likewise but added Zug and Bern. Appenzell and Schaffhausen obtained similar support in 1454. Fribourg secured complete independence from Austria in 1452 and assurance of support from Bern. The Swiss seized Thurgau from Sigismund of Tirol, cousin of the Habsburg emperor, in 1460–61. Like Aargau, it became a common lordship. This successful aggression was accompanied by economic advance and a growing degree of comfort and good living, to which the profits of mercenary military service contributed.

Bern gained the leadership that Zürich had sacrificed in its vain attempt to obtain the Toggenburg inheritance, and Bernese hegemony was enhanced by the successful absorption of its feudal nobility into the government.

In 1466, with Bernese influence preponderant in the Aargau, Mülhausen (Alsace) secured its alliance. Support for Mülhausen involved hostility toward the Habsburgs and a general Swiss attack on the Sundgau and Waldshut. By the peace terms of 1468, Mülhausen remained independent and Waldshut was pledged as a guarantee of the payment of a war indemnity of 10,000 gulden by Sigismund of Austria. This was repaid when Charles the Bold of Burgundy lent Sigismund 50,000 gulden and took over Austrian rights in Alsace and the Black Forest as security.

The Burgundian War. Out of these events developed the Burgundian War. Bernese policy was largely shaped by the soldier Adrian von Bubenberg and by his rival, the capitalist politician Niklaus von Diesbach, who was also influential at the court of Louis XI of France. Charles of Burgundy used his rights under the Truce of Saint-Omer to overrun Alsace and threaten Mülhausen in 1470; as a result Louis XI secured a guarantee of Swiss neutrality in the event of a Burgundian attack on France. In 1474 the Swiss were persuaded to extend this neutrality to Sigismund of Austria by the Treaty of Constance, which was followed by Sigismund's denunciation of his concessions to Burgundy.

The execution at Breisach of Charles's representative made a Burgundian threat to the whole of Sigismund's possessions a certainty; the Swiss obtained a promise of financial support from Louis XI and in October 1474 opened hostilities against the Burgundian duke and his ally, Savoy. In March 1476 a Burgundian army was defeated by a Swiss force at Grandson, and rich booty was taken; the Burgundians answered by advancing against Morat. A large Swiss force from every state of the confederation accepted this challenge, relieved Morat, and defeated the enemy in the open field (June 22, 1476). This was the high-water mark of Swiss power; any army in Europe could now be met on at least equal terms. The final demonstration came at Nancy, where Charles the Bold was defeated and slain in January 1477. Had the confederates been able to agree on a common foreign policy, the whole of Franche-Comté could easily have been secured and much of Alsace as well.

High point of Swiss power

Divisions and reconciliation. Instead there was disunion: Zürich refused to support a Bernese "western" expansionist policy; the farmers of Bern, Zürich, and Luzern opposed their own governments; the inner Swiss states resisted any centralization or expansion of the federal union; and everywhere young men willingly sold themselves into service as mercenary soldiers. Civil war was averted by the hermit-saint Niklaus von Flüe (Bruder Klaus); and by the Agreement of Stans (December 1481), Fribourg and Solothurn were admitted to the confederation, now enlarged to ten states. All would help one another to repress any internal opposition.

Diesbach of Bern died in 1475, and his place as the leading Swiss notable was taken unworthily by Hans Waldmann (1436–89), a Zürich millionaire adventurer and dictator, with a policy of civic protection and domination over the agriculturalists, including the central states. Waldmann was deposed and executed in 1489, but the Swiss advance to great power status had been checked at a critical juncture, and the harmony of Bern and Zürich, on which so much depended, had been broken.

In 1499 the emperor Maximilian I, in pursuit of impractical ideals of an efficient and solvent empire, attempted to force imperial jurisdiction and taxation on his Swiss subjects. The result was resistance, leading to the Swabian War; the outcome was a double defeat for the Emperor—at Calven (May 1499) and at Dornach (July 1499). By the Peace of Basel that followed on September 22, the practical independence of the Swiss was assured and Basel (1501) and Schaffhausen (1501) were admitted to the confederation (further evidence that all south of the Rhine repudiated Habsburg overlordship).

The Italian campaigns. With the opening of the 16th century the "Old Confederation," completed by the admission of Appenzell in 1513, faced external conditions that transformed its international position. France had been united under an almost absolute hereditary monarch; the emperor after 1519 was ruler of Spain and much of Italy as well as of the German-Austrian Habsburg territories; the Italian states, which had given intellectual leadership to the West, were no longer able to keep out the "foreigner"; and the papacy, conscious of the danger from the infidel Muslims, could not even eliminate heresy within the Christian Church.

Changes in the Swiss international position

French invasions of Italy, and particularly claims of the French kings Louis XII and Francis I to the Duchy of Milan, affected the Swiss directly. Some 5,000 paid Swiss soldiers helped Louis enter Milan in 1499. Swiss armed men were found both with and against the French at Novara in 1500; their refusal to fight one another led to French control of Milan. Three years later, at Arona, the French reluctantly recognized the fact of Swiss occupation of Bellinzona; but already there was growing opposition to mercenary service and its implications.

The next important paymaster of Swiss troops was the warrior-pope Julius II. In 1510 he brought the confederation, together with Valais, into an agreement to support the Pope (and Maximilian) against Venice. The murder of two Swiss envoys at Lugano was the pretext for sending a Swiss force against the French in northern Italy in 1511, in a raid that reached Milan. In 1512, in conjunction with Venice, a large Swiss army occupied Verona, Pavia, and Milan; the French were again forced to leave, and the Swiss could have been masters of the duchy had political conditions made this feasible. Accepted as allies by Savoy and as "Protector of the freedom of the church" by the Pope, the Swiss had to face yet another French force, again at Novara (June 1513), of which they regained possession.

In 1515 Francis I purchased much Swiss goodwill, and on his invasion of Piedmont in 1515 many of the Swiss soldiers occupying northern Italy agreed to return home. The others, perhaps 20,000 strong, met the invaders at Marignano (September 13–14, 1515) and were driven back decisively after heavy fighting with serious losses. French artillery, and the arrival of Venetian reinforcements, may have been the effective instruments in this (but it meant that the day of Swiss invincible infantry was over, although this was not yet apparent). France also gained a treaty of Perpetual Peace in November 1516, whereby in return for money and economic advantages the Swiss renounced any claims on Milan but retained Bellinzona, Lugano, Locarno, and the Valtellina. Included in the expeditions to Pavia and to Marignano were men from Glarus accompanied by their chaplain, the Catholic priest Huldrych Zwingli (1484–1531).

The Reformation. The condition of the church in Switzerland was no better than elsewhere in western Europe. A poor population supported many privileged clergy, who were often inadequately educated and sometimes negligent in their duties. The many monasteries were wealthy but not popular, and the bishops saw no need for change in the parishes. Religion consisted largely of routine duties, attendance at mass, confession, rituals, and the performance of many external acts of piety. Clerical concubinage was widespread and tolerated by the authorities.

Condition of the church in Switzerland

The popes were paymasters of Swiss soldiers, who formed their bodyguard and served in the papal armies; but enthusiasm waned when payment was lacking or when the service demanded was too strenuous.

Huldrych Zwingli. The impact of the Reformation on Switzerland was felt more in the cities than in the countryside, and it was associated with the names of Erasmus, Zwingli, and Luther. Erasmus had been critical of worldly popes, ignorant friars, complacent monks, and petty abuses, while being careful not to cross the bounds of orthodoxy; he felt that, by the study of the Fathers and of the Bible, the Christian Church could return to the simplicity and excellence of its earliest days. Luther publicly attacked the sale of indulgences in 1517.

Zwingli likewise had turned to Bible study, including Hebrew, and had anticipated Luther in rejection of traditional doctrine where it seemed to conflict with Holy Writ. At the same time, Zwingli was actively concerned, as a patriotic confederate, with the ill effects of mercenary service and the consequential pensions paid to leading politicians by foreign powers. In 1518 he was elected by the canons of the Zürich Great Minster as their stipendiary priest (*Leutpriester*). From 1522 he developed his independent thought into a challenge to the church authorities, first on the question of compulsory abstention from meat eating during Lent, then about clerical marriage—his own marriage was not publicly admitted until 1524—and then to an attack upon the mass as a sacrifice. He defended his views in public debates in Zürich in January and October 1523, which led to making evangelical preaching compulsory and to the rejection of pilgrimages, relics, images, pictures, church organs, and the sale of indulgences.

Zwingli's reforms

The appeal to the Bible as the sole guide to doctrine and observance involved a clash with the Anabaptists, who in 1524 insisted that infant baptism was unbiblical and who called for an independent, locally based church instead of the all-embracing state church of the Zwinglians. They regarded tithes, interest, oaths, military service, and capital punishment as unacceptable and, in turn, were themselves unreasonably feared as antisocial revolutionaries. After a third public debate in Zürich in 1525, they were outlawed.

Other states followed the example of Zürich, the decisive action in every case being the substitution of a commemorative communion service for the Roman mass. Attendance at the Catholic mass was made illegal in Zürich in April 1525, an example followed later by the city of St. Gall and by Schaffhausen, Glarus, Appenzell, Basel, and Bern. Reform was accompanied by the dissolution, often by agreement, of the monasteries, their revenues being used for education and poor relief in some cases, for normal public expenditure in others. The acceptance of the Reformation in Basel was the result of a popular demonstration, itself a protest against the conservatism of a patrician oligarchy, and of the effective preaching, discussion, and writing of John Oecolampadius.

Zwingli's greatest triumph was to secure the adhesion of Bern to his teaching at a well-managed public discussion in January 1528. A Catholic attempt to demonstrate the errors of their opponents at the Baden disputation (1526), at which Zwingli was not present, was followed by efforts to eliminate "heresy" from the confederation. Bern refused to yield to this pressure; there was much sympathy for Zwingli's attack on pensions and mercenary service, and the moral and intellectual condition of the Bernese clergy was deplorable. In 1527 Bern's government accepted married clergy, freedom of evangelical preaching, and control of monastic property, and it finally agreed that the case for and against the older and newer beliefs should be settled by public discussion. At this debate the Zwinglian triumph was both apparent and far-reaching; images and the mass were rejected, and Bern remained exclusively Protestant until the end of the 18th century. There was a minor revolt of the conservative peasants of the Bernese Oberland, which served only to stiffen the determination of the government to maintain religious uniformity.

The spread of the Reformation in the common lordships of Aargau, Thurgau, and neighbouring areas provided a problem of jurisdiction that could only be settled by force. The inner Catholic states—Luzern, Uri, Schwyz, Unterwalden, and Zug—obtained an alliance with Ferdinand II of Austria, brother of the emperor Charles V, which was countered by a Protestant Civic Union that included Constance and Strassburg. When the Catholics made it clear that there would be no freedom for preaching the gospel in lands in which they shared authority, Zürich prepared for war. Zwingli tried unsuccessfully to form a Protestant union, of which Philip of Hesse would be the leading member. Although Philip brought Luther and Zwingli face to face at Marburg (September–October 1529), no full agreement was possible about the presence of Christ in the bread and wine of the Holy Communion.

Problem of jurisdiction over the common lordships

An armed conflict between Zürich and the five inner Catholic states was soon terminated. The Peace of Kappel that followed in June 1529 suggested some toleration in the common lordships, but this was acceptable to neither side in practice. The alliance with Austria was torn up, but this, too, had little practical effect. The prince abbot of St. Gall was refused recognition, and his subjects were encouraged to revolt as well as to apostasy. A threat by a robber baron from the castle of Musso was represented as part of a renewed Catholic plot against the evangelicals; and the failure of Unterwalden to keep promises to Bern enabled Zürich to prevent indispensable supplies of grain and salt from reaching the inner Catholics and then to threaten coercion by force of arms. The second Kappel War brought the defeat and death of Zwingli (October 11, 1531) at Kappel and another defeat, also involving Bern, at Gubel (October 22, 1531).

By the second Peace of Kappel (November 1531), Zürich, Bern, Basel, Schaffhausen, and some other states remained Protestant but unable to advance their cause further; the abbot of St. Gall was restored and imposed his faith on his dominions; and the communities of the common lordships lost their right of future local religious option. Heinrich Bullinger (1504–75) replaced Zwingli as the chief minister of Zürich, but he had none of Zwingli's political influence. Bern turned to defend its southern borders from Savoy and Catholic Valais, which led to its occupation of Vaud (now a canton in southwestern Switzerland) and direct contact with Geneva.

Direct contact between Bern and Geneva

Geneva (Genève), which did not become part of the confederation until 1815, could escape domination by Savoy only by reliance upon Bern, which in turn needed for its security to control the territory, including Lausanne, as far as Lake Geneva. Guillaume Farel (1489–1565) after 1527 evangelized much of Vaud as far as Aigle but met with obstruction in Geneva, which, along with Lausanne, had secured an alliance with Bern and Fribourg. To protect their interests and the achievement of the Reformers, Bernese troops appeared outside Geneva in 1530, forcing the Duke of Savoy to pledge Vaud for security and to allow the gospel to be preached. In 1535 the mass was abolished in Geneva; and in 1536, to prevent a French occupation, a Bernese force easily overran Vaud. The territory on both sides of Lake Geneva was incorporated into the Bernese possessions, and Zwinglian worship was accepted everywhere.

John Calvin. John Calvin (1509–64), already a distinguished French Humanist, had abandoned the Catholic faith and in 1536 issued from Basel his *Institutes of the Christian Religion.* As Calvin passed through Geneva in 1536, Farel, who was finding his pastoral duties there beyond his powers, called on him to stay. Calvin became, even more than Zwingli at Zürich, the dominant influence in Genevan affairs. His political opponents were driven underground; and the freethinker Jacques Gruet and the Unitarian Michael Servetus were put to death. Calvin's system and doctrine were similar, but not identical, to those of Zwingli; but in 1566 they were reconciled by the Second Helvetic Confession. A Presbyterian church with complete local autonomy for the congregations, with ministers, doctors, elders, and deacons, became a model for others to follow. Geneva's application for admission to the confederation was rejected; the danger from Savoy was continued, and as late as 1602 an attack (the "Escalade") was beaten off with difficulty. Thus Geneva was in many ways a besieged fortress, and it submitted to the requirements of a mixed lay and clerical consistory the more willingly for this reason. Its alliance with Bern and the determination of the French that Geneva should not be Savoyard enabled the city to become an intellectual centre and a haven for refugees until the French Revolution.

THE SWISS CONFEDERATION SINCE C. 1530

The Counter-Reformation and the Valtellina. While Calvin was preaching in Geneva, the Catholic Church belatedly set its house in order at the Council of Trent

Reinforcement of the Catholic cause

(1545–63). The reforms were welcomed by the Catholic cantons of Luzern, Uri, Schwyz, Unterwalden, Zug, Fribourg, and Solothurn, while Glarus and Appenzell remained with divided allegiance. The inner cantons insisted on the explusion of the Protestant families from Locarno (1555); many of these found refuge in Zürich, where they contributed valuably to its industrial development, particularly in silk. The Jesuits established a school in Luzern in 1577, and a permanent resident papal nuncio was received there from 1596.

Preachers from Geneva encouraged the French Huguenots to resist, and Catholic Swiss mercenaries fought against them. Numerous French Protestants found refuge in Switzerland after the massacre of St. Bartholomew (August 23–24, 1572). Ludwig Pfyffer of Luzern not only supported the Catholic "Holy League" against Henry of Navarre (later Henry IV) but also united the five inner states with Fribourg in a "Golden League" with Spain (1586), one result of which was the permanent division of Appenzell into two separate half cantons. The accession of Henry IV as king of France (1589) prevented civil war in Switzerland, where 12 cantons (Zürich not included) renewed the league with France in 1602, again allowing French recruitment of soldiers.

A Switzerland of about 1,250,000 inhabitants, divided by religion, laws, language, and economic interests, could no longer play an independent role in 17th-century Europe. Geneva, however, was saved from either Savoyard or French domination; and, even more significantly, the Grisons maintained their position as a valued ally of the confederation. There were three leagues—the League of God's House and the League of the Ten Jurisdictions (both Reformed) and the Grey League (Catholic)—which were threatened by Milan and Venice from the south and by the Habsburgs of Vorarlberg and the Tirol from the east. Internally, much power lay with the great local families, such as the Planta, traditionally pro-Spanish, and the Salis, supported by France and Venice.

An attempt by Venice in 1603 to gain economic advantage and control of the passes leading to the Austrian territories led to a Spanish-Milanese counterattack. The result was internal discord in the Grisons, which continued for a quarter of a century. The leader of the Protestant party in the Grisons, supported by Venice and France, was Georg Jenatsch (1596–1639), who was confronted in 1620 with a massacre of some 500 leading Protestants in the Valtellina. Bern and Zürich offered military aid to Jenatsch, but the inner cantons prevented it from arriving, and the Valtellina was left open to Spanish domination.

Jenatsch, after some preliminary successes, was forced into exile. He returned in 1624 with a French army sent by Cardinal de Richelieu to regain control of the invaded territory but not to restore the Reformed faith there. Jenatsch consequently changed sides and was murdered in January 1639 by conspirators.

The Thirty Years' War. Switzerland's neutrality during the Thirty Years' War was the outcome of its religious and economic divisions rather than of conscious policy; although the value of a Swiss infantry army was diminished by 1618, it was still not negligible. At first the Habsburgs seemed likely to win, which might have had serious implications for eastern Switzerland; but by good management official neutrality was observed, although a number of individuals volunteered for military service with either side, and war needs brought profit to Swiss traders. The threat of invasion made agreement between the 13 Swiss cantons highly desirable, and all the more so because of the need to provide for the administration of the common lordships. The independence of each of the 13, with their allies—the cities of St. Gall, Mülhausen, and Biel (Bienne) and the abbot of St. Gall—was, however, fully recognized.

Swiss neutrality

In 1631–32 Gustavus II Adolphus of Sweden narrowly failed to secure an alliance with the Swiss and insisted upon a stricter observance of neutrality; in September 1632 a Bernese force on its way to help allied Mülhausen was attacked in Solothurn, but further hostilities were avoided by mediation. In September 1633, perhaps because of deliberate negligence by Zürich, Swedish forces entered Stein am Rhein intending to attack the imperialists at Constance but retreated; and again, after much trouble, the situation was adjusted without bloodshed. A parallel episode involving Basel led in 1647 to an agreement for common Swiss defensive measures—the Defensionale of Wyl, which marked a further stage in common Swiss action.

The long negotiations that resulted in the Peace of Westphalia (1648), ending the Thirty Years' War, owed a good deal to the efforts of the representative of Basel—*Bürgermeister* Johann Rudolf Wettstein. In October 1647 he succeeded in obtaining a declaration from the Emperor that the city of Basel and the 13 cantons, with their allies and common lordships, were not subject to imperial jurisdiction. This was written into the final treaty and became part of the public law of Europe.

The Villmergen wars. Difference of religion after 1648 helped the relative stability that characterized 17th-century Switzerland. The Protestant cantons were wealthier and more thickly populated than their Catholic neighbours; but in the Diet they were in a minority, and no agreed alteration in the constitution of the confederation was possible. Internally, power rested in the hands of a relatively small number of patrician families; in Bern, Fribourg, Solothurn, Luzern, Basel, and even Zürich the aristocrats dominated the ruling councils and retained for their members power and the emoluments of office.

The gulf between nobles and peasants

The common people, in general, meekly accepted the religion and the legislation of their superiors. There was, however, a gulf between nobles and peasants; and after 1648 an economic recession helped to intensify the objections of the farmers to paying taxes and dues for the defense and support of the walled towns. Each canton had its own coinage, and in some of them tension was increased by attempts to replace a depreciated currency.

Open trouble started in 1653 with a demand from the Entlebuch farmers for better treatment by Luzern, closer consultation, more legal autonomy, a more satisfactory currency, and relief from a hated salt tax. The government obtained promises of help from neighbouring cantons and made a few concessions, and the trouble died down. But the example, once set, was more widely followed; and a general claim from the peasantry for greater attention led to a gathering at Huttwil (May 1653) and an uprising against Bern, which was easily suppressed, its leaders being punished.

In 1656, after the forcible expulsion of a harmless Protestant community from Arth, fighting took place with the five Catholic cantons against Zürich and Bern. In a battle at Villmergen (January 24, 1656) Bernese forces were defeated; meanwhile, forces from Zürich failed to capture Rapperswil. At the Third Land Peace of Baden, which followed, the right of each canton to enforce religious unity was reasserted. After incidents at Wigoltingen in 1664, Wartau in 1694, and St. Gall in 1697, peace was openly broken in 1712 because the aggressive abbot of St. Gall, Leodegar Bürgisser, had promoted the construction of a highway from Wattwil to Uznach that could be to the disadvantage of the Protestants in the Toggenburg. Bern and Zürich used this as a pretext to occupy most of Aargau, Thurgau, Rheintal, and Toggenburg. Attempts at a compromise failed; there was a serious fight at Villmergen (July 25, 1712), won by Bernese discipline, after which the Peace of Aargau (August 11, 1712) agreed that Protestants and Catholics should enjoy equal rights in the common lordships, repealed the clauses of the second Peace of Kappel (1531), and left the balance of power in the confederation in Protestant hands.

Relations with France

Louis XIV of France did not intervene directly. There had long been a standing agreement allowing Swiss soldiers to serve for pay with the French. This Franco-Swiss alliance had been renewed in September 1663, complete with pensions, arrangements for payments of recruits, and other advantages. But the French occupation of Franche-Comté (1668) and the revocation (1685) of the Edict of Nantes, which had granted religious liberty to the Huguenots, were resented. The Defensionale of Wyl was refurbished in 1668, and in 1674 the Swiss Diet publicly proclaimed its neutrality in continental disputes. French occupation of Strassburg was accepted as inevitable, and

Basel itself was constantly watched by a French garrison in Hüningen. Following diplomatic moves by Bern and Zürich at the French court in 1687, French pressure on Geneva was removed and Swiss soldiers were permitted to serve in British and Dutch regiments if needed (a secret agreement by the Catholics in 1715 to serve France only—the "Trücklibund"—had no binding validity).

The death of the Duchess of Nemours, Princess of Neuchâtel (Neuenburg), in 1707 enabled Bern to arrange for the inheritance to pass to the Protestant King Frederick I of Prussia, but not without objections then and repercussions later.

The 18th century. From 1712 to 1798 Swiss neutrality was fully respected—the 18th century wars passed Switzerland by. The country remained predominantly pastoral and agricultural, poor, and little visited by foreigners for pleasure; it was around the cities of Basel, Zürich, and St. Gall that home industries flourished. Adequate capital and relatively cheap labour were available; weaving in linen, cotton, and silk occupied many hands; and watchmaking and clockmaking began to spread.

There were few exceptions to the general practice of obsequious deference to higher rank and obedience to authority. An attempt to promote a mutiny in the Bernese army in 1723 to secure the freedom of the inhabitants of the Vaud from Bernese oppression ended in failure. The small number of ruling families that controlled everything in Bern took care to stamp out any threat to this monopoly.

In Geneva the aristocratic ruling clique was less successful; fighting in the streets in 1738 ended with a compromise arranged by Bern and Zürich allowing the "citizens," themselves a minority among the inhabitants, a larger voice in affairs. But in 1768 and 1782 attempts to widen the franchise still further were forcibly smothered.

Cantonal separatism and religious exclusiveness were in some measure countered by the formation in 1761–62 of the "Helvetian Society," for all Swiss without distinction of birthplace or confession—and thus a better reflection of the ideas of the Enlightenment than its Catholic parallel, the Helvetische Konkordia Gesellschaft. This did not prevent trouble in Luzern, the most Catholic of Swiss cities, where a struggle between church and state grew out of an attempt to regulate or forbid public dances.

The French Revolution and Napoleon. Close to the surface there was a good deal of vague popular discontent: Fribourg, for example, in 1781 had to deal quite heavily with the peasants of Greyerz (Gruyères) before they submitted to dictation from the centre. The situation was altered by the American Declaration of Independence and by the French Revolution. Swiss residents in Paris formed themselves into a club of patriots in 1790 and were in contact with radicals in Basel and Zürich and with well-wishers in Bern and Brugg. The chief exponents of revolutionary ideas, however, were Peter Ochs, a vain and ambitious artisan leader from Basel, and an idealist from Vaud, Frédéric-César de La Harpe, who acted as tutor to the future tsar Alexander at St. Petersburg. La Harpe returned, determined to secure the independence of Vaud from Bern. There was a rising of inhabitants of Lower Valais against their masters in Upper Valais; the last of the feudal servitudes were removed from the Basel peasantry in 1790; also in 1790 a Swiss battalion in the service of the French king mutinied in Nancy. Even Bern was prepared to offer some carefully guarded concessions. The inhabitants of Vaud, with a new-found watchword "Liberté et Patrie," wanted more.

Popular discontent

The 13 cantons had renewed their military alliance with France in 1777 at Solothurn, but circumstances had altered greatly by the time the King's Swiss Royal Guard was annihilated in Paris by a mob in August 1792. Other Swiss regiments were unreliable and ill-equipped, and a Swiss foreign policy hardly existed. To prevent a Swiss revolution in which equality would end the traditional aristocratic regime, Schultheiss Niklaus Friedrich von Steiger of Bern took the lead; he became head of a party prepared for a possible war with France.

In the autumn of 1792 French military forces entered Savoy and threatened Geneva. Bern and Zürich sent 1,600 men to support the city, but they withdrew on receiving a French assurance that an attack would not take place. A revolution inside Geneva, protected by French arms, followed without incident.

The formation of the First Coalition Against France in 1793 (Great Britain, the Netherlands, Spain, Naples, Austria, and Prussia) was answered by French resistance. The French government demanded the expulsion from Switzerland of dangerous and hostile émigrés, and other opportunities for French intervention in Swiss affairs came easily. The French supported liberal movements in Stäfa and St. Gall; French and Austrian hostile forces crossed Swiss territory near Basel; French agents spread "democratic" propaganda; French generals coveted control of the Swiss passes; the French demanded the expulsion of the British ambassador and called for the annexation by France of part of Valais and the creation of an "independent" republic of Vaud. In 1797 French forces occupied Geneva and Biel; several cantons hurriedly liberalized their constitutions to give wider rights to hitherto disfranchised subjects.

French intervention in Swiss affairs

In January 1798 the French occupied Lausanne and proceeded to liberate Vaud from Bernese oppression; Bern itself was entered on March 5 after little more than token resistance. The remaining cantons, except Schwyz and Nidwalden, hurriedly surrendered, and the French proclaimed on March 28 that they had assumed governmental authority over the "Helvetic Republic."

The Helvetic Republic. Geneva, Neuchâtel, Biel, the territory of the bishop of Basel, Mülhausen, and the Valtellina were excluded from this new Swiss republic of 1798. The republic was to be "one and indivisible," with an elected legislative assembly and a directory. There were 23 cantons, a great council, a senate, and a cabinet, or directory of five, all indirectly elected. There was to be freedom of worship and conscience. Class distinctions were abolished, and all citizens were equal before the law. Justice was centralized; the directors chose the prefects, who, in turn, appointed the subordinate administrative officers, with the commune (*Gemeinde*) as the basic local unit. Large sums of money were paid to France by way of occupation costs, and attempts in central Switzerland to resist the new regime were crushed.

The renewal of war in Europe in 1799 was accompanied by local revolts, a breakaway movement in the Grisons, and an Austrian invasion there. Behind the Austrians came a Russian army, which occupied Zürich in June 1799 and was defeated at the second Battle of Zürich (September 25–26, 1799). For all practical purposes, at the end of 1799 Switzerland was a French-occupied country.

Within the new Swiss state the Republicans found the new democracy meaningless and called for a qualified return to earlier conditions, a suggestion emphatically rejected by the Patriots, defenders of the status quo. A little later the Unionists, who emphasized the coherence and indivisibility of the republic, were opposed by the Federalists, who insisted upon local self-determination and regional differentiation. The Directory was displaced by a committee of the Helvetic Council in January 1800 and this in turn by a controlling assembly of 50 supporting the Republicans. All parties appealed to Napoleon.

The Treaty of Lunéville (February 1801) enabled Napoleon to impose the Constitution of Malmaison in May 1801. This intensified the rivalries of Federalists and Unionists, and the latter produced in 1802 a second highly centralized Helvetic constitution, which was rejected by popular vote. Valais was accepted as an independent republic; there were serious opposition riots demanding a return to the old arrangements. French soldiers reappeared, and in February 1803 Napoleon produced the final text of his Mediation Constitution. A loose unitary state was formed, with 19 cantons, each with its own constitution, a legislature, a president (*Landammann*), and a chancery. The country now formed a free-trade area, with the peasants freed from feudal obligations, torture abolished, education encouraged, many monasteries dissolved, church and state separated, and marriage made a civil contract. Citizenship was widened, there was a federal army, foreign policy, and code of laws. France was permitted to

The loose unitary state of 1803

recruit 16,000 Swiss soldiers, many of whom perished in the ill-fated Moscow campaign of 1812. The Napoleonic "Continental system" pressed hard upon a country that lived by exports and international services; there was a certain amount of smuggling and much unemployment and poverty. There was also, as elsewhere on the continent, a marked upsurge of nationalist feeling; cultural and scientific societies embraced the whole country, for which Johann Rudolf Wyss composed a national anthem, "Rufst Du, mein Vaterland." The Linth Canal (Linthkanal) was a federal enterprise, the first of its kind; Johannes von Müller wrote the first comprehensive history, *Geschichten schweizerischer Eidgenossenschaft* ("History of the Swiss Confederation").

The restoration. There was no Swiss nationalist rising against Napoleonic domination after 1813 as there was in Prussia or Spain. Instead a renewed insistence upon Swiss neutrality, which might protect Napoleon's flank from an invasion, was accepted as public policy but ignored by the allies in their determination to occupy Paris and end the war. In December 1813 the Mediation Constitution was denounced and an attempt made to return to the pre-Revolutionary 13 sovereign cantons. Aargau and Vaud at once protested; the tsar Alexander I supported the protest, and Bern was forced to agree to an enlarged federation. The details were worked out in the "Long Diet" of 1814.

From the Congress of Vienna (1814–15) the Swiss hoped to obtain a recognized frontier, with the provinces annexed by France restored, compensation for damages inflicted by the war, and a recognition of neutrality and independence. The congress decided that the Valtellina, Chiavenna, and Bormio should not return to the confederation and that the Pays de Gex should not come under the control of Geneva. Aargau and Vaud secured recognition, the former territories of the bishop of Basel were divided between Basel and Bern, Neuchâtel remained a Prussian principality within the Swiss confederation, the French annexation of Valais was denounced, and Geneva was admitted with narrowly defined frontiers, north Savoy and the Pays de Gex being accepted as custom-free zones. Swiss neutrality was guaranteed at Paris on November 20, 1815, by France, Austria, Great Britain, Portugal, Prussia, Sweden, and Russia.

Guarantee of Swiss neutrality

A new conservative Swiss constitution (*Der Bundesvertrag*) was signed on August 7, 1815. There were 22 cantons, each with its own constitution and each contributing to a federal army; those with external frontiers were allowed to levy customs duties on imports. Each canton had one vote in the Diet, which alone could (by a two-thirds majority) declare war, conclude peace, and enter into alliances with foreign powers. On all other matters a simple majority was sufficient. Bern, Luzern, Fribourg, and Solothurn retained, with minor modifications, their patrician-ruled status. Zürich, Basel, and Schaffhausen widened their guild organizations. The remaining cantons adopted semidemocratic forms of government.

Switzerland to 1914. Between 1815 and 1830, despite economic difficulties and complaints that political refugees (including Louis-Napoléon Bonaparte) were being given asylum, peace and stability reigned. Communications were greatly improved; commerce, including banking, advanced. New demands were heard for freedom of the press, religious toleration, rights of association, and greater free trade. After the July Revolution in Paris (1830), pressure for a more liberal Swiss constitution grew steadily; objections to the domination of the countryside by the towns were frequently heard, together with demands that popular sovereignty should become a reality. In Neuchâtel voices were raised against Prussian conservatism. In Schwyz the peasants threatened to form a breakaway state; and in Basel this actually took place, Basel-Landschaft separating from Basel-Stadt in 1833. Revisionists called for a representative parliament, a federal postal system, coinage, and a foreign office.

The Sonderbund War. The secularization in January 1841 of the monasteries of Aargau was condemned by the federal diet, which in turn led to numerous protests. When the Jesuits came to Luzern in 1844 there were demands for their exclusion from the confederation. Radical "volunteers" attempted to expel the Jesuits by force. The Catholic and conservative cantons refused to be intimidated and stood by their rights as guaranteed in 1815. In March 1845 volunteers from Bern marched against Luzern to expel the Jesuits and were easily repulsed. The result was that Luzern, Uri, Schwyz, Unterwalden, Zug, Fribourg, and Valais formed a protective union for mutual support—another breach of the Federal Pact. This soon became a *Sonderbund* (a separate federation), which was declared illegal in July 1847, when the diet resolved to inaugurate a new constitution and to drive out the Jesuits. The *Sonderbund* confidently hoped for support from the rulers of Austria, Prussia, and France. Civil war was imminent. In October a federal army under the command of Henri Dufour took the field against the rebels, whose expectation of outside assistance was disappointed. Dufour, with far superior forces, showed his strategic skill. Fribourg capitulated on November 14; Zug on November 21; and after some fighting at Meierskappel, Honau, and Gisikon, Luzern was entered on November 24. Schwyz, Uri, and Valais submitted in quick succession. The revolt was over within a month: the seven insurgent cantons had to meet the cost of the campaign; southern Appenzell and Neuchâtel were fined for failure to contribute to the army; Luzern and Fribourg were obliged to exclude Jesuits; and a revision of the constitution was worked out.

Formation of a separate federation

The new federal state, 1848–60. A government by two chambers was formed—a national council based on numerical representation and a senate, or council of states (Ständerat), consisting of two members from each canton. Together they formed a federal assembly (Bundesversammlung), with a federal council, or cabinet (Bundesrat), chancery (Bundeskanzlei), and supreme court of justice. The president, elected annually, was simply first among equals. Relations with foreign powers were thenceforth the exclusive affair of the federal government; mercenary service and the acceptance of pensions, gifts, tithes, or orders from foreign powers was forbidden. Equality before the law and freedom of the press, of movement, of association, and of religious worship were guaranteed to all. The Jesuits remained excluded, and clergymen could not hold elected offices. Bern was named as the capital, and the Swiss Federal Institute of Technology was opened in Zürich in 1855. Customs ceased to be levied between the cantons, and Switzerland became a unified economic area. The postal system became federal, as did currency, weights, and measures. In August 1847 the opening of the first Swiss railway, between Zürich and Baden, brought new problems—the country lacked coal; there were fierce disputes about capital, contracts, and ownership; and a struggle for control developed. Later the railway system was nationalized.

External affairs. Help to Charles Albert of Sardinia to eliminate the Habsburg regime was refused; even so, the troubles of 1848 in the Grand Duchy of Baden, in northern Italy, and in Neuchâtel nearly involved the confederation in war in defense of political refugees. In Neuchâtel—a canton of the confederation and a principality ruled by the king of Prussia—a republic was proclaimed; but in 1856 a "royalist" reaction gained temporary control and appealed to Frederick William IV of Prussia. The situation was soon reversed, and the royalist leaders were imprisoned, but it required the personal intervention of Napoleon III and the threat of a German-Russian-Austrian invasion to settle the matter. All Prussian rights in Neuchâtel were abandoned (for a consideration), although the monarch retained the empty title of prince.

Proclamation of a republic in Neuchâtel

Swiss neutrality had contributed to the Austrian defeats at Magenta and Solferino (1859). There were Swiss protests at the annexation of Savoy by France in 1860, but again a compromise had to be accepted not altogether to their advantage or satisfaction. Swiss neutrality narrowly escaped infringement during the Franco-Prussian War of 1870–71, when a French army entered Swiss territory, was disarmed and interned, but was allowed to return after peace was restored.

This was followed by renewed railway construction and continued controversy over private ownership, although it was not until 1882 that technical and financial difficulties accompanying the opening of the essential St. Gotthard route were overcome (an indirect consequence was the final abolition of separate cantonal currencies in 1874).

Religion and politics, 1860–1914. The final incorporation of the States of the Church into the kingdom of Italy and the Vatican Council of 1870, followed by the *Kulturkampf*—the conflict between state and church in Germany—had repercussions in Switzerland, where the "old Catholics" were numerous. Obligatory civil marriages were introduced, in spite of opposition from the Catholic bishop of Basel and the papal representative at Geneva. In 1873 diplomatic relations with the Vatican were broken off (and not resumed until 1920). "Popular Initiative" had come in 1867, and the principle of the referendum was now accepted, complete internal free trade was assured, federal control over the army was extended, legal procedure was simplified, and greater economic and educational uniformity were furthered by constitutional revision in 1874.

Rise of working class influences

As elsewhere, 19th-century Switzerland saw the rise of working class influences on the political scene. Home industry was being displaced by factories, where long hours were worked, often by small children. This trend brought about outbreaks of machine smashing by those who feared the loss of both livelihood and independence. Attempts at cooperative unions such as the Grütliverein, formed in 1838, were followed by the formation of trade unions proper. Successful demands for factory legislation were made by the Social Democrats, who emerged as a party of reform between 1870 and 1888.

There were abiding difficulties over education, a sphere in which the cantons, determined to retain controlling influence, resisted federal coordination. In the Ticino local political rivalries almost led to a revolution in 1890 which was prevented by federal intervention. At the same time, the prosecution of German agents or spies sent by Bismarck caused some trouble with Germany, and the traditional Swiss acceptance of political refugees was resented by tsarist Russia. In each case the Swiss government successfully maintained its position.

Switzerland since 1914. Beginning with World War I, Switzerland faced a number of problems and changes during the 20th century.

The War of 1914–18. The advent of World War I in 1914 brought great problems: foreign visitors and workers left the country, which was obligated to defend its neutrality and independence. Tension between the French-speaking minority and the pro-Germans was intensified when evidence was produced of secret information being sent by high-ranking Swiss officers to Germany. Difficulties were created by the considerable number of political refugees (including Lenin) living in Switzerland and by well-meant but ineffective attempts at peace mediation between the combatants. Receipts from Swiss customs dwindled, and an income tax became a necessity as defense costs mounted. Price fixing and rationing were also introduced. Discontent culminated in a general strike in November 1918, inflamed by Marxist elements and accompanied by an influenza epidemic that swept across Europe. Firm government action and the loyalty of the army quickly broke the strike, but political concessions, such as proportional representation, followed. The Soviet embassy was closed.

Peace in Europe brought its own special problems. France demanded, and obtained, full sovereignty over Savoy, reluctantly conceding a free zone. An attempt by the inhabitants of the Vorarlberg to become a 23rd canton of the confederation failed, but Liechtenstein was accepted as an ally and brought within the Swiss postal, customs, and monetary union.

The League of Nations. The League of Nations was formed in May 1920 with its headquarters at Geneva. The Declaration of London (February 1920) recognized the special nature of permanent Swiss neutrality and exempted the Swiss from participation in any future military

Divisions within Switzerland

"sanctions." Switzerland, however, could not be entirely indifferent to or unaffected by Italian Fascism and German National Socialism; there were deep divisions between the French- and German-speaking cantons and between the conservative "bourgeois" elements and the radical socialists. Something of this was reflected in the party disputes between the Catholic-Conservatives, Liberal-Democrats, and Social Democrats. Elections to the Federal Council were hotly disputed, while youthful adherents to a "National Front" rejected traditional democratic procedures in favour of obedience to a leader. Continuous demands for female suffrage from 1884 onward were rejected (until finally met in 1971).

The world depression of the 1930s affected Switzerland less severely than it did the great industrial countries, but the same results on a reduced scale were apparent—bankruptcies, overproduction, and poverty. German claims to rule over all German speakers and German anti-Semitic legislation caused much alarm, as did Communist demonstrations—at one of these in Geneva (November 1932), 16 persons were killed and 60 wounded. Suggestions of a total revision of the constitution were decisively rejected, but agreements favouring industrial peace were readily entered into.

The admission of the Soviet Union to the League of Nations (1934); the Italian invasion of Ethiopia (1935), involving Switzerland in economic sanctions; and the Spanish Civil War (1936), with individual Swiss volunteers serving in the International Brigade, caused disillusionment with the League of Nations. Fascist and Nazi propaganda was countered and military service was made more acceptable. The German occupation of Czechoslovakia in March 1939 intensified defense measures so that the outbreak of war, following Hitler's invasion of Poland at the end of August, saw the Swiss fully prepared.

World War II and after. About 430,000 men were mobilized for the defense of the Swiss frontiers, rationing was introduced, and arrangements were made for adequate payment for soldiers on active service. Disapproval of the Soviet invasion of Finland was evidenced by the collection of 4,000,000 Swiss francs for war sufferers there. The German occupation of Denmark and Norway strengthened determination to resist if attacked, and more men were called to the colours. After the fall of France (when 42,000 men were interned), followed by intensified pro-German propaganda in Switzerland, the army command decided to defend, in case of invasion, only the "*réduit,*" the heartland, including the St. Gotthard and Simplon tunnels.

Determination to resist if attacked

The expected invasion did not take place; instead, amid great economic difficulties and by supplying its neighbours with some equipment (chiefly precision instruments) and by assisting them indirectly in air warfare (and by suffering from mistaken air attacks, as when the Americans bombed Schaffhausen in April 1944), the Swiss rode out the war. At its end there were more than 100,000 refugees or internees within the country. The determination of the Allies that "war criminals" and high Nazi officials should not take refuge with their property in Switzerland caused difficulties, as did the reopening of diplomatic relations with the Soviet Union.

After 1945 Switzerland adopted by plebiscite many of the activities of the welfare state—old age pensions and social insurance of various kinds—and every effort was made to sell Swiss manufactured goods abroad, to attract visitors, and to forward "invisible exports" by banking, insurance, and other services. Without becoming a member of the United Nations, Switzerland participated fully in the Organisation for European Economic Co-operation (OEEC), in the General Agreement on Tariffs and Trade (GATT), and in several of the specialized agencies of the United Nations.

By the late 20th century more and more of the population had moved to or near the largest cities. Women were given the right to vote in federal elections for the first time in 1971, and in 1981 a federal plebiscite approved of measures guaranteeing male and female equality in legal and economic rights. For current political history, see the annual issues of the *Britannica Book of the Year*.

(G.R.P./Ed.)

BIBLIOGRAPHY

General: EMIL EGLI, *Switzerland: A Survey of Its Land and People* (1978), provides a description of landscape, climate, settlement patterns, and economy. JOHN and MOIRA HAWKES, *Switzerland and Liechtenstein* (1970), gives a short introduction, to be supplemented by JOHN GURDON, *Switzerland* (1967). See also the comprehensive ALFRED WALDIS, *Switzerland: The Traveller's Illustrated Guide* (1966); other introductions are provided by *Switzerland* (1982) in the Baedeker series of travel guides; THEO CHOPARD (ed.), *Switzerland Present and Future: A Small Country Re-Examines Itself,* 4th rev. ed. (1963); and JOHN RUSSELL, *Switzerland,* rev. ed. (1962). Specific topography is covered in R.G. COLLOMB, *Bernese Alps West, from the Col du Pillon to the Lötschen Pass* (1970). On the architecture, see ALFRED ALTHERR (ed.), *New Swiss Architecture* (1965). For industrial figures, see the FEDERAL BUREAU OF STATISTICS, *Statistiches Jahrbuch der Schweiz* and the SWISS CREDIT BANK, *The Swiss Economy* (both published annually); the ORGANIZATION FOR ECONOMIC COOPERATION AND DEVELOPMENT, *The Capital Market, International Capital Movements, Restrictions on Capital Operations in Switzerland* (1971); T.R. FEHRENBACH, *The Gnomes of Zurich* (U.S. title, *The Swiss Banks;* 1966), both on banking aspects; MAX WEIBEL, *A Guide to the Minerals of Switzerland* (1966), dealing with a section of the country's raw materials; and the ELECTRONICS INTELLIGENCE DIGEST, *The Electronics Industry and Market in Switzerland* (1965), are illuminating in their various fields. The INTERNATIONAL HOSPITAL FEDERATION, *Hospitals in Switzerland: Report on a Study Tour, September 15–29, 1968* (1970), covers some of the health administration; while G.A. CODDING, *The Federal Government of Switzerland* (1965); E.A. GUTKIND, *Urban Development in the Alpine and Scandinavian Countries* (1965); and CHRISTOPHER HUGHES (ed. and trans.), *The Parliament of Switzerland* (1962) and *The Federal Constitution of Switzerland* (1954), deal with other social conditions. An up-to-date work on transportation is C.W. SEX and B.J. PRIGMORE, *Swiss Motive Power Survey* (1972). See also C.J. ALLEN, *Switzerland: Its Railways and Cableways, Mountain Roads and Lake Steamers* (1967) and *Switzerland's Amazing Railways,* rev. ed. (1965). CAROL L. SCHMID, *Conflict and Consensus in Switzerland* (1981), a study of the relatively harmonious Swiss culture of diverse languages and religions.

History: J. DIERAUER, *Geschichte der schweizerischen Eidgenossenschaft,* 4th ed., 6 vol. (1924–31), standard but superseded by *Handbuch der schweizer Geschichte* (1972–); E. GAGLIARDI, *Geschichte der Schweiz von den Anfängen bis zur Gegenwart,* 3 vol. (1939), detailed; H. NABHOLZ *et al., Geschichte der Schweiz,* 2 vol. (1932–38), scholarly, written by specialists; J.G. GUGGENBUHL, *Geschichte der schweizerischen Eidgenossenschaft,* 2 vol. (1947–48), a reliable narrative; P. DURRENMATT, *Schweizer Geschichte* (1957); W. DRACK (ed.), *Illustrierte Geschichte der Schweiz,* 3 vol. (1958–61), admirable illustrations; E. BONJOUR, *Geschichte der schweizerischen Neutralität,* 2nd ed., 6 vol. (1965–71), an important study; E. BONJOUR, *Geschichte der Schweiz im 19. und 20. Jahrhundert* (1938); E. BONJOUR, H.S. OFFLER, and G.R. POTTER, *A Short History of Switzerland* (1952); M. GODET, H. TURLER, and V. ATTINGER (eds.), *Dictionnaire historique et biographique de la Suisse,* 7 vol. and suppl. (1921–34). The following English-language works are recommended: W. MARTIN, *Histoire de la Suisse, essai sur la formation d'une confédération d'états* (1926; Eng. trans., *A History of Switzerland: An Essay on the Formation of a Confederation of States,* 1931); EDGAR BONJOUR, *Geschichte der schweizerischen Neutralität* (1946; Eng. trans., *Swiss Neutrality: Its History and Meaning,* 1946); and W. OECHSLI, *History of Switzerland, 1499–1914* (1922), rather antiquated.

Sydney

The capital of New South Wales, Sydney is the oldest and the largest city in Australia. Because of its magnificent harbour and strategic position on the southeast coast of Australia, it is also one of the most important ports in the South Pacific. At the beginning of the 19th century when it was still a small convict settlement and the first settlers had barely penetrated the interior, it had already established trade with the Pacific Islands, India, China, South Africa, and the Americas.

The first sight of Sydney, whether from the sea or the air, is always impressive. Built on low hills surrounding a huge harbour with innumerable bays and inlets, the city is dominated by the bulk of the Sydney Harbour Bridge, one of the biggest single-span bridges in the world, and the Opera House, with its glittering white shell-shaped roofs that seem to echo the sails of the many yachts in the harbour. The intricate confusion of water and buildings makes a striking impression either by day or by night.

Because of its history as a great port and its status as the site of the country's main international air terminal, Sydney is perhaps the only city in Australia with a genuinely international atmosphere. Yet it remains a very Australian city, with a nice compromise between the Anglo-Saxon efficiency of its British heritage and the South Seas attractions of its climate and environment.

This article is divided into the following sections:

Physical and human geography

THE LANDSCAPE

Climate. Sydney is situated on latitude 34° S and has an average mean temperature ranging from 72° F (22° C) in January to 54° F (12° C) in July. Its warm, sunny, but temperate climate has encouraged its citizens to develop a pleasure-loving and easygoing attitude to life and to make full use of the opportunities for sailing, swimming, and surfing at their doors. Although the average annual rainfall is 45 inches (1,140 millimetres), much of this falls in short tropical deluges in summer. The humid heat of summer, when the prevailing wind is from the northeast, is tempered from time to time by the arrival of a cold front from the Tasman Sea heralded by a stiff wind from the south known locally as the "Southerly Buster." Sydney is unbearably hot only on a few days each year when a westerly wind brings the hot, dry air from the inland. In winter, however, the westerly wind is cool.

The city layout. The Sydney Statistical Division is spread over an area of 4,790 square miles (12,407 square kilometres) and stretches from the Blue Mountains in the west to the Pacific Ocean in the east and from the southern shore of Lake Macquarie in the north to south of Botany Bay. Only about one-third of this region is classified as urban, but more than 90 percent of the region's population lives in the urban area. A pattern of suburban sprawl, caused partly by the cheapness of land in earlier days and by the ordinary Australian's determination to own his own house and garden, has caused problems for the authorities responsible for sewerage and transport. The sprawl is also in marked contrast to the comparatively small and compact central business district, which is crammed into a narrow rocky peninsula between two arms of the harbour within the five square miles of the City of Sydney proper.

Extent of the Sydney Statistical Division

The same contrast can be seen in the style of buildings. Whereas most of the houses in the suburbs are one-story bungalows built of brick or wood, the high cost of land in the central business district has forced construction of higher buildings. The rapid development initiated in the 1960s has transformed the city centre, which now looks like a smaller Manhattan rising from the shores of the harbour, though in fact the buildings are not high by North

The Opera House and the Sydney Harbour Bridge.
The Photographic Library of Australia

American standards. A rival business centre has sprung up in North Sydney, which is linked to the City of Sydney by the Harbour Bridge.

The standard of architecture is generally mediocre, though there are a few handsome buildings surviving from the 19th century and a few contemporary buildings of distinction, including the brilliantly designed Opera House. Sydney has one magnificent street, Macquarie Street, which leads down from Hyde Park to the Opera House and is lined by all of the important government buildings of the 19th and 20th centuries. Yet the general effect of Sydney is attractive, and the innumerable bays and arms of the harbour, stretching into the land and providing unexpected views from almost every street, make it a most pleasing city.

Sydney is also fortunate in having two magnificent national parks within 25 miles (40 kilometres) of the city centre to the north and south. In these parks the natural Hawkesbury Sandstone bush can be seen at its best and forms a refuge for the wildlife of the area. The mouth of the Hawkesbury River, with its many fingerlike inlets, provides a superb expanse of sheltered water for yachtsmen, while both to the north and south of the city there stretches a string of magnificent sandy beaches, on which the Pacific surf breaks throughout the summer. Other national parks are within 60 miles of the city centre so that Sydney is now almost completely ringed by national parks—a unique distinction for so large a city.

THE PEOPLE

Ethnic origins

Sydney was founded by the British, and the largest proportion of its citizens is still of British stock, if that term is extended to include persons of Irish descent. Since the end of World War II, however, Australia has also taken large numbers of immigrants from other European countries and, since 1960, a number from Asia, including refugees from Lebanon and Vietnam. Many of these immigrants have settled in Sydney. Some of the inner suburbs have a distinctly Greek or Italian character, and almost every suburb has its Greek, Italian, Lebanese, and Vietnamese restaurants. There is also a small Chinatown, and one suburb, Redfern, has a small community of Aborigines living under somewhat depressing conditions.

The two largest Christian denominations are Anglican and Roman Catholic, each with its cathedral, but Sydney now also has Muslim mosques, Jewish synagogues, and Buddhist temples as well as many Christian churches.

THE ECONOMY

Industry and services. About three-quarters of the manufacturing labour force of New South Wales is employed in the Sydney region. Almost half of the total Sydney population is in the work force, and of this about a third is employed in manufacturing (mostly in secondary industry) and the rest in tertiary industry or services. There is no predominant industry in the city itself, though oil refining in the area is important. Sydney has always been essentially a city of government; of local, national, and international commerce; and a shopping and entertainment centre for the state of New South Wales. It rivals Melbourne as a financial centre. Sydney's primary wool market is headquartered at the Wool Centre, which opened in 1975.

Port Jackson (Sydney Harbour) is one of the major ports in Australia. A second port has been developed in Botany Bay, 10 miles to the south, to handle petroleum products.

The role of tourism

Tourism. Sydney has become a centre for international tourists. There are a number of hotels and motels and numerous restaurants, particularly in the neighbourhoods north and east of the central business district. It is possible to find restaurants offering almost every kind of international cooking, though all of them serve Australian wines and Sydney's famous oysters. The city's first modern complex for conventions, popular concerts, indoor sports, and political assemblies opened in 1983.

Transportation. Since 1855 Sydney has had a railway linking the city centre to some of its suburbs. Between World Wars I and II, this radial suburban rail system was electrified, and construction of the city underground railway was begun (the first section was opened in 1926). In 1933, after the completion of the Harbour Bridge, the north shore was linked directly by rail to the city. Both surface and underground railway extensions were completed to the near eastern suburbs in 1979.

Traffic congestion

In spite of development and the existence of an extensive metropolitan bus service, public transport has failed to keep pace with demand. Since World War II, Sydney, like so many other cities, has fallen a victim to the motorcar. The resulting traffic problem is made worse by the geographical layout of Sydney. A high proportion of

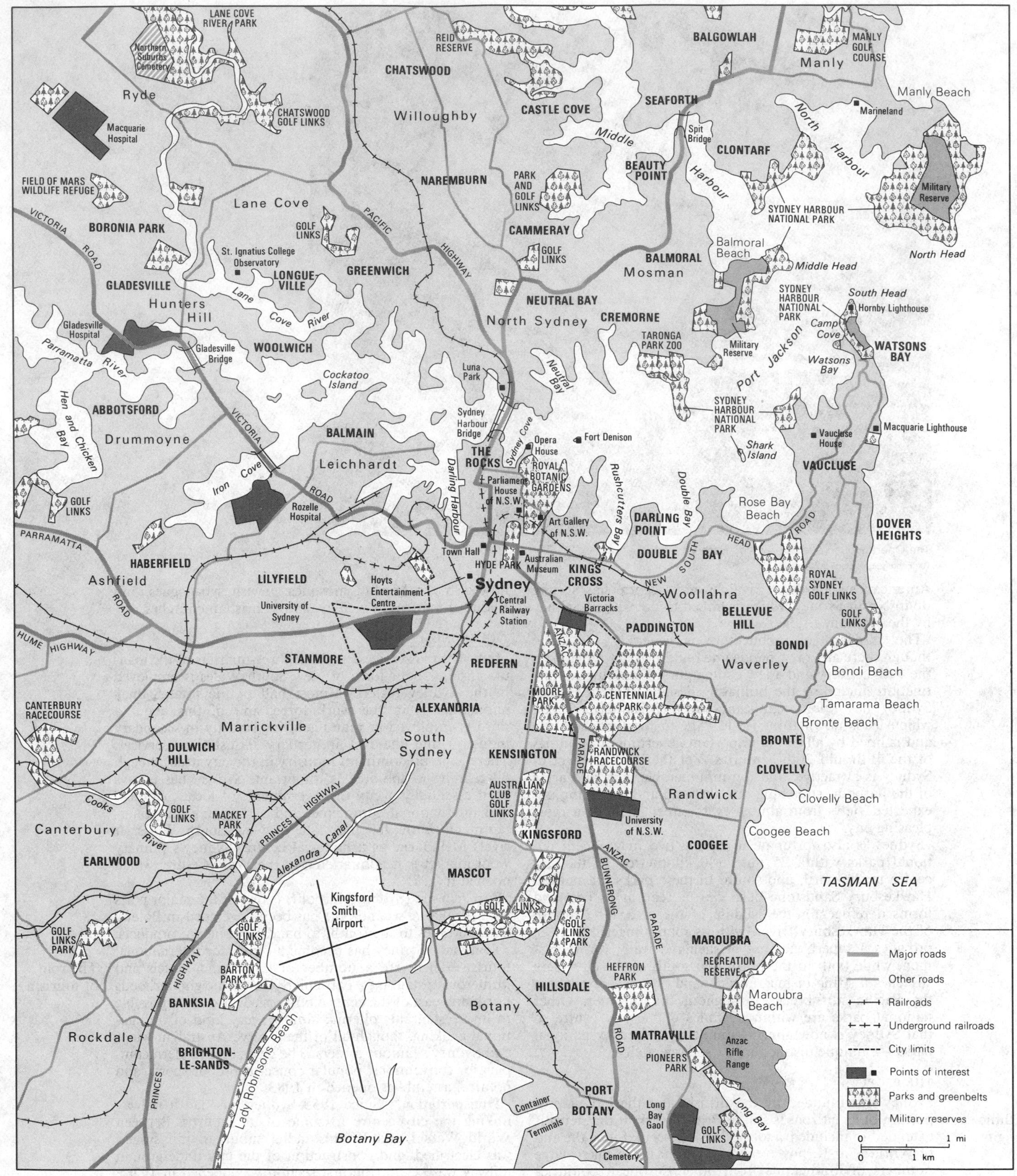

Sydney with its inner suburbs.

those who work in the central business district live in the outer suburbs and must find their way to and from the city by a limited number of routes. All those living on the North Shore, for instance, must cross the harbour by the Harbour Bridge, the only bridge crossing the harbour from north to south. (At the head of the harbour there is a second bridge, at Gladesville, which takes some of the traffic.) It is also difficult for traffic travelling from north to south through the Sydney area to bypass the city. The inevitable consequence is severe traffic congestion aggravated by the narrowness of the streets. Attempts to relieve this by building expressways and thruways have been only partially successful, and Sydney, like other cities, has taken measures to ban all traffic from certain sections of the inner city. To this end, a pedestrian plaza was created in Martin Place, in the centre of the city, in 1971.

A delightful alternative means of transport exists for those who live on the shores of the harbour in the public ferry system, but, for reasons that have always baffled the authorities, this has never been as popular or as profitable as might be expected. The ferryboats nevertheless add a good deal to the attraction and amenity of the city.

The main airport, both for international and internal traffic, is at Mascot, on the shores of Botany Bay, to the south of the city. Access to and from the airport is poor. On the other hand, travellers by sea are fortunate in that passenger liners generally tie up at Circular Quay in the heart of the city, from which they can stroll to the city centre.

ADMINISTRATION

Relations with the state government

Sydney is the capital of New South Wales and the seat of its government and parliament. The state government has delegated matters of local interest to more than 40 local government areas in the Sydney region, including the City Council of Sydney, but has retained direct control of some important matters, such as police and transport. In addition, a number of functions normally exercised by local councils have been transferred to boards, commissions, trusts, and departments established by the state government. The most important of these responsibilities concern water, sewerage and storm drainage, electricity, major roads, fruit and vegetable markets, and many aspects of health and welfare. Furthermore, some land remains under federal control. The result is a somewhat confused and complicated system of government. For historical and political reasons, the boundaries of the City of Sydney have been changed several times. In 1968 the jurisdiction of the City Council was reduced to approximately its original size of about five square miles, so that it is now responsible only for the central business district and the innermost neighbourhoods. The Sydney Statistical Division was established in 1976 to define the territory expected to contain the area's urban development for a period of at least 20 years. The region was delimited by combining the built-up urban area (more than 1,500 square miles) surrounding the central city with the non-urban hinterland (more than 3,200 square miles).

CULTURAL LIFE

Sydney is, above all, a city for physical enjoyment. Few great cities in the world offer such unrivalled opportunities for swimming, surfing, sailing, and other outdoor sports. It is still possible to swim from several beaches in the harbour itself—though pollution is slowly reducing the number of these—and the surf beaches to the north and south of the city are world famous. One of these, Bondi, is a 15-minute drive from the city centre. Some of the beaches to the north of the city, especially those on the Palm Beach peninsula, are very beautiful. The surf is good, though variable, and made comparatively safe by the voluntary lifesaving association, which provides guards and rescue equipment on all beaches throughout the summer months. Sydney is also a city of yachtsmen. On any weekend the harbour is covered with sails of every shape and size, while the Pittwater, an inlet 25 miles to the north, is almost equally popular. There are also many golf courses and excellent facilities for football sports (including soccer and rugby), cricket, and tennis, and the racecourse at Randwick is first class.

Sporting traditions

Australians have been accused of being sports mad, and Sydney-siders, as they call themselves, are certainly no less devoted to sport than their compatriots in other cities. Yet Sydney also has a vigorous cultural and intellectual life. There are three universities in the metropolitan area; the University of Sydney, the University of New South Wales, and Macquarie University. A fine public library, museums (including the Australian Museum, which contains the country's largest natural history collection), and the Art Gallery of New South Wales, as well as a large number of private galleries devoted to contemporary Australian art, add to the cultural attractions. A serious shortage of theatres and concert halls existed in the city, but this was remedied when the Sydney Opera House—in fact a major arts centre—was opened in 1973. This beautiful and costly building was designed by a Danish architect, Jørn Utzon, who won an international competition held for the purpose in 1955. Built on a magnificent site on the harbour, surrounded by water on three sides, it contains a concert hall for the Sydney Symphony Orchestra, a large theatre for opera and ballet, a smaller theatre for plays, a cinema, and rehearsal and recording studios. For opera and ballet Sydney depends chiefly on the Australian national companies, which visit the city for a season each year, but the Sydney Dance Company has also won an international reputation. Sydney has several small theatre groups and a motion-picture industry. A large entertainment centre, seating 5,000, was opened in 1984 to present concerts of popular music and theatrical productions.

Thus, though Sydney has become a large city offering services and amenities comparable with those offered by any major city, there is still no doubt that its most lasting impression and greatest attraction is its physical setting. A high proportion of Sydney's residents can glimpse at least a strip of blue water from their windows, and nearly all can live within an hour of a beach.

History

EARLY SETTLEMENT

When the English explorer Capt. Arthur Phillip arrived off the coast of southeastern Australia with the First Fleet in 1788, he sailed first to Botany Bay, which had been discovered by Capt. James Cook in 1770 and to which he had been directed by the British government. Finding the bay too exposed for safe anchorage and the surrounding country unsuitable for settlement, he looked farther north and soon discovered the entrance to Port Jackson only a few miles away. Phillip's first impressions of Port Jackson, which had been named but not explored by Cook, are recorded in a famous dispatch to Lord Thomas Townshend Sydney, then Home Secretary, dated May 15, 1788.

Discovery of the harbour

> We got into Port Jackson early in the afternoon, and had the satisfaction of finding the finest harbour in the world, in which a thousand sail of the line may ride in the most perfect security. . . .

Captain Phillip immediately decided to move the whole fleet to Port Jackson and to establish the first settlement on a cove, which had a good freshwater spring and in which his ships could anchor close to the shore in deep water. He called it Sydney Cove, after the Home Secretary. Present-day Sydney Cove, where passenger liners tie up at the international terminal, is still the city's heart, though it is more commonly known as Circular Quay. The main commercial port, however, has been moved to Darling Harbour, another bay a little to the west.

The early history of Sydney was grimly dominated by its existence as a British penal colony. Convicts, dumped on this alien shore, found the environment a harsh one. The soil was poor, and the land was rough and had to be cleared by hand. The little settlement was often short of food until the settlers were able to cross the Blue Mountains and find the richer land to the west of the Great Dividing Range. There were also constant troubles between the governors, the free settlers, and the convicts.

With the exploration and settlement of New South Wales, Sydney grew quickly; the British government provided free land, free convict labour, free capital works, and guaranteed markets for the produce of the new colony. Trading links with the rest of the world were quickly established. Under the enlightened governorship of Lachlan Macquarie (1810–21), Sydney developed from a precarious penal settlement into a thriving, respectable town. Macquarie also began a program of public works, including the building of churches, hospitals, barracks, schools, and courthouses, and laid out several parks in and around the city. In this work he was aided by a convict-architect, Francis Greenway, who had been banished for forgery in England. Greenway built several fine buildings in the Regency style, notably the Hyde Park Convict Barracks on Macquarie Street and St. James's Church, which survive today and have been scrupulously restored to their original state.

GROWTH OF THE MODERN CITY

19th-century growth

The most astoundingly rapid growth of Sydney—from 60,000 to 400,000 population—took place in the years between 1850 and 1890, as suburbs of tightly packed terrace houses were built. These houses, with their balconies and decorative cast-iron railings, are now Sydney's most attractive heritage from the past. The first railway, from Sydney to Parramatta, began as early as 1855.

The financial collapse of the 1890s acted as a slight check to Sydney's growth, but population doubled again by 1914 and reached the million mark soon after. Yet during this period Melbourne, the capital of Victoria, was growing still faster, partly as a result of the gold rush in that colony. Temporarily overtaking Sydney in both size and importance, Melbourne became the financial centre of Australia, and it was the capital of the Commonwealth of Australia until the Federal Capital of Canberra was built in 1927 halfway between the two cities. By 1911 Sydney had once again become Australia's largest city, and after World War II it benefitted from a shift in Australia's trade toward North America and Asia and away from Britain. Sydney has remained slightly bigger than Melbourne and is equally important as a centre of finance, commerce, and manufacturing. In its growth it has not escaped the ills that afflict so many other large cities of the world, including pollution, traffic congestion, and crime. Nevertheless, with its population burgeoning past 3,000,000, Sydney has become the most international and most sophisticated of Australian cities.

BIBLIOGRAPHY. General orientation is offered by MICHAEL POULSON and PETER SPEARRITT, *Sydney: A Social and Political Atlas* (1981). The best sources for facts and figures about Sydney are *The Sydney Region Outline Plan, 1970–2000 A.D.*, published by the STATE PLANNING AUTHORITY OF NEW SOUTH WALES (1968); the *City of Sydney Strategic Plan*, published by the COUNCIL OF THE CITY OF SYDNEY (1971), and the COUNCIL'S *1980 City of Sydney Strategic Plan* (1980). A charming portrait of contemporary Sydney, unencumbered by statistics, is GAVIN SOUTER, *Sydney* (1965), with photographs by QUINTON DAVIS. The early history of the convict settlement is graphically told from contemporary documents in JAMES JOHNSTON AUCHMUTY (ed.), *The Voyage of Governor Phillip to Botany Bay* (1970); and JOHN COBLEY, *Sydney Cove, 1788* (1962), *Sydney Cove, 1789–1790* (1963), *Sydney Cove, 1791–1792* (1965), and *Sydney Cove, 1793–1795* (1983). All early histories of Australia necessarily deal with Sydney in part. M.H. ELLIS, *Lachlan Macquarie*, 5th ed. (1978), and *Francis Greenway*, 2nd ed. (1966), are good biographies.

(J.D.Pr.)

Syria

Syria, officially al-Jumhūrīyah al-ʿArabīyah as-Sūrīyah (the Syrian Arab Republic), is a country situated on the east coast of the Mediterranean Sea on the southwestern fringe of the Asian continent. It has an area of approximately 71,500 square miles (185,180 square kilometres). It is bounded by Turkey to the north, by Iraq to the east and southeast, by Jordan to the south, and by Lebanon and Israel to the southwest. The capital is Damascus (Dimashq) on the Baradā River; the city is situated in an oasis at the foot of Jabal (Mount) Qāsiyūn. The present territory does not coincide with ancient Syria, which was the strip of fertile land lying between the eastern Mediterranean coast and the desert of northern Arabia.

The persistent Middle East crisis between the Arab states and Israel has often resulted in political instability in Syria. In the Arab–Israeli War of 1967, Israel occupied the 444 square miles of the Golan Heights in southwestern Syria, and Israel unilaterally annexed the area in 1981. Severe strains are placed on the Syrian economy by the demands of national security and defense, which exhaust much of the national budget, leaving little for development.

This article is divided into the following sections:

Physical and human geography

THE LAND

Relief. *The coast.* Syria has a relatively short coastline, which stretches for about 110 miles (180 kilometres) along the Mediterranean Sea between the nations of Turkey and Lebanon. Sandy bays dent the shore, alternating with rocky headlands and low cliffs. North of Ṭarṭūs, the narrow coastal strip is interrupted by spurs of the Jabal an-Nuṣayrīyah immediately to the east. It then widens into the Sahl ʿAkkār (Plain of ʿAkkār), which continues south across the Lebanon border.

The mountains. The Jabal an-Nuṣayrīyah (Jabal Alawite) range borders the coastal plain and runs from north to south. The mountains have an average width of 20 miles, and their average height declines from 3,000 feet (900 metres) in the north to 2,000 feet in the south. Their highest point, 5,125 feet, occurs east of Latakia. Directly to the east of the mountains is the Ghāb Depression, a 40-mile longitudinal trench that contains the valley of the Orontes River.

The Anti-Lebanon Mountains, or Jabal ash-Sharqī, mark Syria's border with Lebanon. The main ridge rises to a maximum height of 8,625 feet near an-Nabk while the mean height is between 6,000 and 7,000 feet. Mt. Hermon (Jabal ash-Shaykh), a single ridge, is connected farther west to the main range by the Zabadānī Saddle. Syria's highest point, Mt. Hermon rises to 9,232 feet (2,814 metres).

Smaller mountains are scattered about the country. Among these are Jabal ad-Durūz, which rises to 5,905 feet in the extreme south, and the Jabal Abū Rujmayn (the Palmyra Range), which stretches northeastward across the central part of the country.

The Syrian Desert. The undulating plains occupying the rest of the country are known as the Syrian Desert. In general their elevation lies between 980 and 1,640 feet; they are seldom less than 820 feet above sea level. The area is not a sand desert but comprises rock and gravel steppe; a mountainous region in the south central area is known as al-Ḥamād.

Drainage. *Underground water.* Most of the country's drainage flows underground. On the surface, impervious rocks, consisting of clay, marl (clay, sand, or silt), and greensand, cover a relatively small area. Porous rocks cover about half of the country and are mainly sandstone or chalk. Highly porous rocks consist of basalt and limestone. Water penetrates the porous rocks, forming underground springs, rivers, or subterranean water sheets close to the surface. Although the springs are profuse, the water sheets are quickly exhausted and may turn saline in areas of low precipitation.

Principal rivers

Surface water. The Euphrates River is the most important water source and the only navigable river in Syria. It originates in Turkey and flows southeastward across the eastern part of Syria. Construction of a dam on the Euphrates, at Ṭabaqah, Syria, began in 1968. The reservoir behind the dam, Buḥayrat al-Asad (or Lake Assad), began to fill in 1973.

The Orontes is the principal river of the mountainous region. It rises in Lebanon, flows northward through the mountains and the Ghāb Depression, and enters the Mediterranean near Antioch, Turkey. The Yarmūk River, a tributary of the Jordan River, drains the Jabal ad-Durūz and Ḥawrān region and forms part of the border with Jordan in the southwest.

Scattered lakes are found in Syria. The largest is Mamlaḥat (Sabkhat) al-Jabbūl southeast of Aleppo; a seasonal saline lake, it permanently covers a minimum area of about 60 square miles. Other major salt lakes are Jayrūd to the northeast of Damascus and Khātūnīyah to the northeast of al-Ḥasakah. Lake Muzayrīb is a small body of fresh water to the northwest of Darʿā; the larger Buḥayrat Qaṭṭīnah (Buḥayrat Ḥimṣ) is a reservoir to the west of Ḥimṣ (Homs).

Soils. Because of aridity, vegetation plays only a secondary role in soil composition. With the exception of the black soil in the northeastern region of al-Jazīrah, soils are deficient in phosphorus and organic matter.

The most common soils are various clays and loams (mixtures of clay, sand, and silt). Some are calcareous (chalky); others, especially in the area of the Euphrates Valley, contain gypsum. Alluvial soils occur mainly in the valleys of the Euphrates and its tributaries and in the Ghāb Depression. (A.-R.H.)

Climate. *Temperature and precipitation.* The coast and the western mountains have a Mediterranean climate with a long dry season from May to October. In the extreme northwest there is some light summer rain. On the coast, summers are hot, with mean daily maxima of 84° F (29° C), while the mild winters have mean daily minima of 50° F (10° C). Only above 5,000 feet are the summers relatively cool. Inland the climate becomes arid, with colder winters and hotter summers. Damascus and Aleppo have average daily maxima of 91° to 99° F (33° to 37° C) in summer and average daily minima of 34° to 40° F (1° to 4° C) in winter. In the desert, at Tadmur (ancient Palmyra) and Dayr az-Zawr, average daily maxima in summer reach 99° to 104° F (37° to 40° C), with extremes of up to 114° F (46° C). Snow may occur in winter away from the coast, and frosts are common.

The coast and western mountains receive 30 to 40 inches (762 to 1,016 millimetres) of rainfall annually. Rainfall decreases rapidly eastward; the steppe receives 10 to 20 inches a year. Jabal ad-Durūz receives more than eight inches. In the desert area of al-Ḥamād, rainfall decreases to less than five inches a year. Rainfall is variable from year to year, particularly in the spring and autumn months. (C.G.S.)

The winds. In winter the prevailing winds blow from the east, the north, and the west. In summer the prevailing winds are either northerly or westerly. During the summer, the coastal region is subject to westerly winds during the day and easterly at night. Once or twice a year sand-bearing winds, or khamsin, raise a wall of dust almost 5,000 feet high, which darkens the sky.

Plant and animal life. Yew, lime, and fir trees grow on the mountain slopes. The date palm is found in the Euphrates Valley. In both coastal and inland regions, plants include grains, olives, vines, apricot trees, oaks, and poplars. Lemon and orange trees grow along the coast. Garigue, a degenerate Mediterranean scrub, and maquis, a thick scrubby underbrush, cover many slopes.

Forests

Forests are found in the mountains, especially in the Jabal an-Nuṣayrīyah. Glossy-leaved and thorny drought-resistant shrubs such as myrtle, boxwood, turpentine, broom, arbutus, and wild olive abound to the south. Excessive exploitation of the forests for their wood has largely turned them into scrub. Some forests are, however, protected by the government. The steppe is characterized by the absence of natural tree cover, except for some sparsely distributed hawthorns. All other trees—such as those in the orchards of Damascus and Aleppo and along the banks of the Orontes and Euphrates rivers—are cultivated. For a brief period before June the land is covered with a variety of flowering and grassy plants. Under the implacable sun of June, however, the plants soon wither, casting off their seeds onto the dry ground.

Wild animal life is sparse. Wolves, hyenas, foxes, badgers, wild boar, and jackals can still be found in remote areas. Deer, bears, squirrels, and such small carnivores as the marten and the polecat are also found, while desert animals include the gazelle and the jerboa (a nocturnal jumping rodent). Vipers, lizards, and chameleons are common in the desert. Eagles, buzzards, kites, and falcons frequent the mountains. Harmful insects include mosquitoes, sandflies, grasshoppers, and occasionally locusts.

The mule is the beast of burden in the mountains and the camel on the steppe. Other domesticated animals include horses, donkeys, cattle, sheep, goats, and chickens. Bees are also kept.

Traditional regions. There are four traditional regions—the coastal strip, the mountains, the cultivated steppe, and the desert steppe.

The coast. On the coast the fertile alluvial plains are intensively cultivated in both summer and winter. The region is the site of Syria's two principal ports of Latakia (al-Lādhiqīyah) and Ṭarṭūs.

The mountains. Jabal an-Nuṣayrīyah is the only densely forested region. It is the ancient stronghold of the Nuṣayrīs, or ʿAlawites, who form a sect of Shīʿite Islām. The economic resources of the mountains are too meagre to meet the needs of the ever-growing population, and there is a migration to the Ghāb Depression and coastal towns.

The cultivated steppe. This region constitutes the principal wheat zone; agriculture is intensively pursued along the banks of the rivers. Some of Syria's most important cities—Damascus, Aleppo, Ḥimṣ, Ḥamāh, and al-Qāmishlī—are situated there.

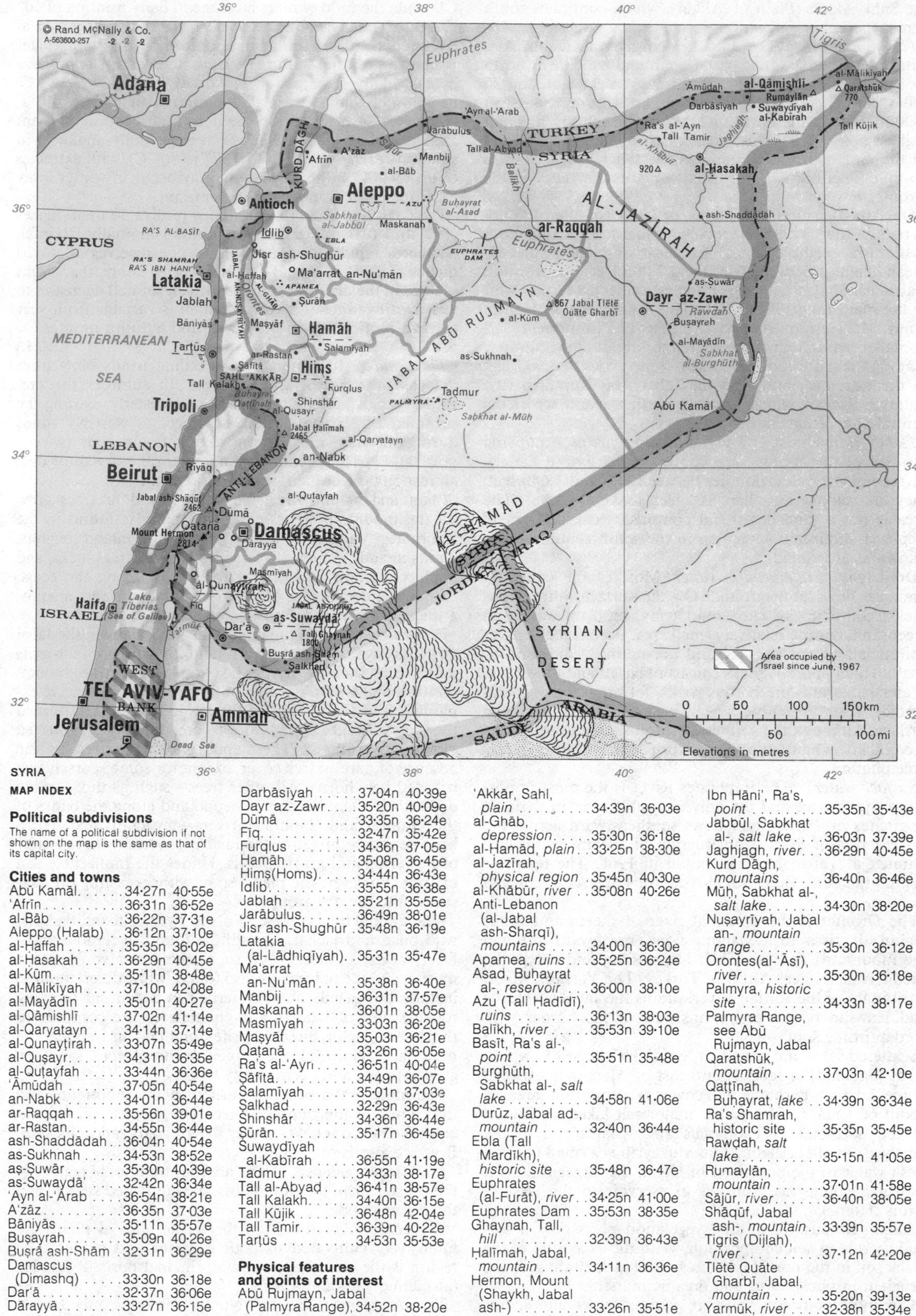

SYRIA

MAP INDEX

Political subdivisions

The name of a political subdivision if not shown on the map is the same as that of its capital city.

Cities and towns

Abū Kamāl 34·27n 40·55e
'Afrīn 36·31n 36·52e
al-Bāb 36·22n 37·31e
Aleppo (Ḥalab) 36·12n 37·10e
al-Ḥaffah 35·35n 36·02e
al-Ḥasakah 36·29n 40·45e
al-Kūm 35·11n 38·48e
al-Mālikīyah 37·10n 42·08e
al-Mayādīn 35·01n 40·27e
al-Qāmishlī 37·02n 41·14e
al-Qaryatayn 34·14n 37·14e
al-Qunayṭirah 33·07n 35·49e
al-Quṣayr 34·31n 36·35e
al-Quṭayfah 33·44n 36·36e
'Āmūdah 37·05n 40·54e
an-Nabk 34·01n 36·44e
ar-Raqqah 35·56n 39·01e
ar-Rastan 34·55n 36·44e
ash-Shaddādah 36·04n 40·54e
as-Sukhnah 34·53n 38·52e
aṣ-Ṣuwār 35·30n 40·39e
as-Suwaydā' 32·42n 36·34e
'Ayn al-'Arab 36·54n 38·21e
A'zāz 36·35n 37·03e
Bāniyās 35·11n 35·57e
Buṣayrah 35·09n 40·26e
Buṣrā ash-Shām 32·31n 36·29e
Damascus (Dimashq) 33·30n 36·18e
Dar'ā 32·37n 36·06e
Dārayyā 33·27n 36·15e
Darbāsīyah 37·04n 40·39e
Dayr az-Zawr 35·20n 40·09e
Dūmā 33·35n 36·24e
Fīq 32·47n 35·42e
Furqlus 34·36n 37·05e
Ḥamāh 35·08n 36·45e
Ḥimṣ (Homs) 34·44n 36·43e
Idlib 35·55n 36·38e
Jablah 35·21n 35·55e
Jarābulus 36·49n 38·01e
Jisr ash-Shughūr 35·48n 36·19e
Latakia (al-Lādhiqīyah) 35·31n 35·47e
Ma'arrat an-Nu'mān 35·38n 36·40e
Manbij 36·31n 37·57e
Maskanah 36·01n 38·05e
Masmīyah 33·03n 36·20e
Maṣyāf 35·03n 36·21e
Qaṭanā 33·26n 36·05e
Ra's al-'Ayn 36·51n 40·04e
Ṣāfītā 34·49n 36·07e
Salamīyah 35·01n 37·03e
Ṣalkhad 32·29n 36·43e
Shinshār 34·36n 36·44e
Ṣūrān 35·17n 36·45e
Suwaydīyah al-Kabīrah 36·55n 41·19e
Tadmur 34·33n 38·17e
Tall al-Abyaḍ 36·41n 38·57e
Tall Kalakh 34·40n 36·15e
Tall Kūjik 36·48n 42·04e
Tall Tamir 36·39n 40·22e
Ṭarṭūs 34·53n 35·53e

Physical features and points of interest

Abū Rujmayn, Jabal (Palmyra Range) 34·52n 38·20e
'Akkār, Sahl, *plain* 34·39n 36·03e
al-Ghāb, *depression* 35·30n 36·18e
al-Ḥamād, *plain* 33·25n 38·30e
al-Jazīrah, *physical region* 35·45n 40·30e
al-Khābūr, *river* 35·08n 40·26e
Anti-Lebanon (al-Jabal ash-Sharqī), *mountains* 34·00n 36·30e
Apamea, *ruins* 35·25n 36·24e
Asad, Buḥayrat al-, *reservoir* 36·00n 38·10e
Azu (Tall Ḥadīdī), *ruins* 36·13n 38·03e
Balīkh, *river* 35·53n 39·10e
Basīt, Ra's al-, *point* 35·51n 35·48e
Burghūth, Sabkhat al-, *salt lake* 34·58n 41·06e
Durūz, Jabal ad-, *mountain* 32·40n 36·44e
Ebla (Tall Mardīkh), *historic site* 35·48n 36·47e
Euphrates (al-Furāt), *river* 34·25n 41·00e
Euphrates Dam 35·53n 38·35e
Ghaynah, Tall, *hill* 32·39n 36·43e
Ḥalīmah, Jabal, *mountain* 34·11n 36·36e
Hermon, Mount (Shaykh, Jabal ash-) 33·26n 35·51e
Ibn Hāni', Ra's, *point* 35·35n 35·43e
Jabbūl, Sabkhat al-, *salt lake* 36·03n 37·39e
Jaghjagh, *river* 36·29n 40·45e
Kurd Dāgh, *mountains* 36·40n 36·46e
Mūḥ, Sabkhat al-, *salt lake* 34·30n 38·20e
Nuṣayrīyah, Jabal an-, *mountain range* 35·30n 36·12e
Orontes (al-'Āṣī), *river* 35·30n 36·18e
Palmyra, *historic site* 34·33n 38·17e
Palmyra Range, see Abū Rujmayn, Jabal
Qaratshūk, *mountain* 37·03n 42·10e
Qaṭṭīnah, Buḥayrat, *lake* 34·39n 36·34e
Ra's Shamrah, historic site 35·35n 35·45e
Rawḍah, *salt lake* 35·15n 41·05e
Rumaylān, *mountain* 37·01n 41·58e
Sājūr, *river* 36·40n 38·05e
Shāqūf, Jabal ash-, *mountain* 33·39n 35·57e
Tigris (Dijlah), *river* 37·12n 42·20e
Tlētē Quāte Gharbī, Jabal, *mountain* 35·20n 39·13e
Yarmūk, *river* 32·38n 35·34e

The nomadic domain

The desert steppe. The arid country is the natural domain of the nomads and seminomads. Sheep graze until the beginning of summer when water becomes scarce, after which the shepherds lead their flocks either westward into the cultivated steppe or to the hills. The area once contained oases that served as caravan towns on the trade route joining Mesopotamia and the Indian Ocean with the countries of the Mediterranean. The most famous of these towns was the ancient Palmyra at the northern edge of the Syrian Desert. The most important feature of the region is the Euphrates River.

Settlement patterns. *Rural settlement.* In traditional rural settlement, the choice of a village site is usually determined by the availability of water. Some of the villages in the Jabal an-Nuṣayrīyah, however, have given priority to the requirements of defense and fortification. Village dwellings stand close together, and village streets are extremely narrow. Usually, there is a small central common overlooked by a minaret (a tall tower attached to a mosque from which the populace is called to prayer). There are usually a few small shops containing articles manufactured in the cities or towns.

Work takes place according to the seasonal rhythm of agriculture. Women generally share in all agricultural labour except plowing. Agricultural machinery, introduced on a large scale after World War II, caused unemployment and drove many villagers to the cities.

Many nomads of the desert steppe have been settled by government programs and as a result of the extension of automobiles and national law into the desert.

Urban settlement. Ten centuries of Greek and Roman rule left an urban mark still to be seen in the towns of Latakia, Palmyra (Tadmur), and Buṣrā ash-Shām. The urban tradition of Islām appears in such cities as Damascus and Aleppo. The continuation of old commercial and religious interests has enabled the cities to maintain their economic and cultural supremacy under the four centuries of Ottoman rule. The great abyss between the rural and urban areas has made economic or social balance difficult to attain. In the late 20th century, however, the cities have been inundated by rural immigrants, creating serious unemployment.

The cities

The national capital of Damascus, situated in the southeast on the banks of the Baradā River, is the largest city in Syria. It is the national headquarters of government and the diplomatic community and is the main centre of education, culture, and industry. It also serves as a marketing centre for mid-Syria and produces traditional handicraft products such as brocades, engraved wood, gold and silver ornaments, and carpets. It is well served by transport facilities and public utilities. The old houses in Damascus are built of soft unbaked bricks, wood, and stone. Contemporary buildings are built of concrete, while hewn stone is reserved for official buildings, mosques, and churches.

Located between the Orontes and Euphrates rivers, Aleppo is a trade and light-industry centre. Its limestone buildings have given the city its name of Halab ash-Shahbā' (Aleppo the White). The city is well served by roads and railroads and is surrounded by an area that specializes in the production of sheep for market in Damascus and other countries. The Mediterranean port of Latakia is surrounded by a rich agricultural region and contains some industry. Because of its seaside location, the city is a major tourist centre.

Ḥimṣ is located in the midst of a fertile plain east of the Orontes River. It is a hub of the country's road and railway systems. Ḥamāh, to the northeast of Ḥimṣ, is bisected by the Orontes River. It contains irrigated orchards and is an agricultural trade centre. There is also some light industry. In 1982 the Syrian armed forces levelled the downtown area while crushing a local rising against the government.

THE PEOPLE

The Syrian people evolved from several origins over a long period of time. The Greek and Roman ethnic influence was negligible in comparison with that of the Semitic peoples of Arabia and Mesopotamia—Aramaeans, Assyrians, Chaldeans, and Canaanites. Later the Turks, like the Greeks and Romans before them, influenced political and economic structures but failed to produce any noticeable change in the dominant Arab character of the Syrian people.

Population groups. *Ethnic groups.* There is a rough correspondence between ethnic and linguistic groupings, although some ethnic groups have been partially assimilated by the Arab majority that includes the Bedouin. Second in number to the Arabs, the Kurds have partially lost their mother tongue. The Armenians may be divided into two groups—the early settlers, who have been more or less Arabized, and the later immigrants, who arrived after World War I and retained their identity and language. The Turkmen intermingle freely with the Kurds and Arabs but have lost none of their ethnic identity in some northern villages. The Assyrians are quickly disappearing as a group because of intermarriage and migration to the cities.

Linguistic groups. The mother tongue of the great majority of the population is Arabic. Listed in descending order according to the extent they are spoken, the other languages are: Kurdish, spoken in the extreme northeast and northwest; Armenian, spoken in Aleppo and other major cities; and Turkish, spoken in villages east of the Euphrates and along the border with Turkey.

Religious groups. Islām, the predominant religion, is practiced by a majority of the population. The Muslims are divided into several sects. The Sunnī sect accounts for about three-quarters of the Muslim population and is in the majority everywhere except in as-Suwaydā' *muḥāfaẓah* (governorate) in the south and the Latakia *muḥāfaẓah* in the north. The 'Alawites (an extreme Shī'ite subsect) are the next largest group, and most live in the Latakia *muḥāfaẓah* or reside mainly in the *muḥāfaẓāt* of Ḥimṣ and Ḥamāh. The Druzes, the third largest group, live in Damascus, Aleppo, and al-Qunayṭirah, with a small proportion in as-Suwaydā' *muḥāfaẓah*.

The Muslim sects

Christians constitute around one-tenth of the Syrian people. They are divided into several churches, which include the Greek Orthodox, Armenian Orthodox, Greek Catholic, Syrian Orthodox, Armenian Catholic, Armenian Apostolic, Syrian Catholic, Maronite, Protestant, Nestorian, Latin, and Chaldean. Jews number a few thousand; most have emigrated to Israel.

Demography. Syria's rate of population increase is out of proportion to the rate of economic expansion. Family planning and birth control are becoming popular among the educated.

Some 80,000 Palestinian Arabs fled to Syria in 1948, and most of the population of the Golan Heights fled to other parts of Syria in 1967 when Israel conquered the region. Increasing numbers of workers and professionals have been leaving the country since the 1950s for other Arab nations, the United States, and western Europe. This movement has caused an alarming drain of Syrian manpower.

Only about half the country's land can support population, and, in addition, around half of the population lives in the cities. The desert steppe, having the lowest density, is populated by Bedouins and oasis inhabitants. In the rest of the country the density, which varies considerably, is highest in the west and northeast and is fairly high along the banks of the major rivers.

THE ECONOMY

Administration of the economy. Socialism became the official economic policy in 1958. Since then, the trend has been toward socialist transformation and industrialization. In commerce, state control is mainly restricted to foreign-exchange operations. Small private businesses and cooperatives are still in operation, and the retail trade is still part of the private sector, despite competition from

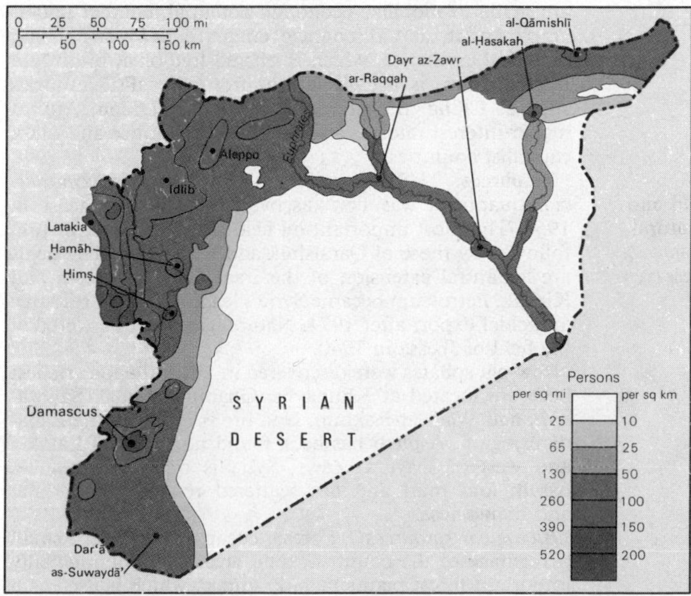

Population density of Syria.

Sheepherder with his flock on the outskirts of a Syrian village near Aleppo.
Shostal Assoc.

consumer cooperatives in the large cities. The government controls the most vital sectors of the country's economy and regulates private business. The state operates the oil refineries, the large electricity plants, the railways, and various manufacturing plants.

Taxation. Indirect taxes, which produce the most tax revenue, are levied on industrial products, customs, exports, and state domains. Direct taxes are levied on wages, circulating capital, livestock, and the transfer of property.

The General Federation of Workers

Trade unions and employer associations. The General Federation of Workers was founded in 1938 and has grown tremendously in power and scope. Composed only of industrial employees, it is represented on industrial boards and is responsible for a wide range of social services. There is also a federation for artisans and vocational workers, and there are associations for the professions and a General Federation of Farmers.

Contemporary economic policies. The government encourages private savings by paying higher rates of interest on deposits and by guaranteeing investment by citizens of other Arab countries. There are severe restrictions on all luxury imports. At the same time strenuous efforts are made to mobilize economic potential, combat underemployment, and discourage emigration. Financial and technical assistance, which is offered free or at minimum interest rates, is usually sought from Socialist countries such as China, Bulgaria, and the Soviet Union. Aid, at higher interest rates, is also sought from France and other capitalist countries.

Oil and natural gas reserves

Resources. *Mineral resources.* Petroleum in commercial quantities was first discovered in the northeast in 1956. The most important oil field is that of Suwaydīyah, followed by those of Qaratshūk and Rumaylān. The fields are a natural extension of the Iraqi fields of Mosul and Kirkūk. Petroleum became Syria's leading natural resource and chief export after 1974. Natural gas was discovered at the field of Jbessa in 1940.

Raw phosphates were discovered in 1962; the four richest beds are located at Khunayfis, Ghadīr al-Jamal, Ṣawwānah, and Wādī ar-Rakhim. Iron ore is found in the Zabadānī region. Asphalt has been found northeast of Latakia and west of Dayr az-Zawr. Syria is rich in limestone, basalt, and marl and has scattered reserves of chrome and manganese.

Biological resources. Forests occupy only a very small percentage of the country's total area. The commercially important forest plants include sumac, which is used as a spice; the wild pistachio, which is important for its oil-rich fruit; laurel, which is used in the production of cosmetics; and the mulberry, whose leaves are fed to silkworms. Pine tree branches are used for smoking tobacco leaves. Other useful plants are winter vegetables such as *khubbayzah,* a kind of spinach; *ʿakkūb,* a flowering plant; and the truffle. Licorice is widely exploited for its root, which is used in the pharmaceutical industry.

Power resources. Local oil supplies constitute a major power resource. With the exception of the Euphrates River, other rivers flowing through Syria produce only small amounts of hydroelectric power. The Euphrates Dam at Ṭabaqah, inaugurated in 1978, has contributed greatly to electrical power generation.

The dominance of agriculture

Agriculture, forestry, and fishing. Agriculture constitutes an important source of income. It provides work for a large segment of the population, including a significant proportion of townspeople. The small number of fishermen use small and medium-sized boats. There are not more than a few hundred forestry workers.

Wheat is the most important food crop, although its production is constantly subject to great fluctuations in rainfall. Barley, corn (maize), and millet are the other important grains. Cotton is the largest and most reliable export crop. Lentils are a major domestic food but are also exported. Other vegetables include onions, potatoes, and sugar beets. Olives, grapes, and apples are grown at high altitudes, while citrus fruits are cultivated along the coast. High-grade tobacco is grown in the area around Latakia.

Livestock raising, including sheep, cattle, camels, and poultry, is important. A reforestation project has been undertaken in the mountains north of Latakia. Most of the nation's timber has to be imported. The annual fish catch includes sardines, tuna, groupers, tunny, and both red and gray mullet.

Industry. *Mining and quarrying.* The principal limestone quarries are located north and west of Damascus, especially near the city of Aleppo, which itself is built of limestone. Basalt, used for road pavement, is quarried in Jabal ad-Durūz and near Ḥimṣ and Aleppo. Marl is used in the cement industry; the main quarries are in the vicinity of Damascus and Aleppo and at ar-Rastān. Sandstone suitable for glass manufacture is mined in the Palmyra mountains. Phosphate ore is mined in Jabal ash-Sharqī, and rock salt is extracted from the mid-Euphrates region. Asphalt and gypsum are also mined, and table salt is produced from the salt lakes.

Manufacturing. Most of the traditional handmade manufactures—damask steel, swords and blades, brass and copper work, wood engravings, gold and silver ornaments, mother-of-pearl inlays, silk brocades—have decreased since the introduction of industrial processing.

Wool, cotton, and nylon textiles are the most important manufactures. The mills are mainly in Aleppo, Damascus, Ḥimṣ, and Ḥamāh. Natural silk is produced at Latakia. Also of importance are the technical engineering industries, most of which are in Damascus. The chemical and industrial engineering products include cement; glass panes, bottles, and utensils; pharmaceuticals; plywood; and batteries. The food-processing industry produces salt, vegetable oils, cotton cake, canned fruit and vegetables, tobacco, and dairy products. Other industries include preparation of superphosphates and urea and refining of oil.

Energy. Muscular energy—both animal and human—is still used for some types of manufacture, for instance in the production of pottery and cooking oil. Modern factories are run by electricity, supplied either by state-owned generating plants or by factory generators. Gas is used on a minor scale in small industries such as goldsmithing, but its supply is limited. Coal is imported and is also used on a limited scale, mainly by blacksmiths.

Electric power

Electricity, largely generated by thermal stations, is used mainly for lighting. There are small hydroelectric stations such as those on the Orontes and Baradā rivers. The major source of electricity is the Euphrates Dam.

Finance. The Central Bank of Syria issues the national currency and exercises control over all other banks that operate in the country. The Commercial Bank of Syria finances trade, markets agricultural products, and carries out foreign-exchange operations. The Real Estate Bank finances the building industry and carries out all ordinary banking operations. An Industrial Development Bank finances the private industrial sector, while an Agricultural Bank extends loans to farmers and agricultural cooperatives. A Popular Bank makes loans to small manufacturers, artisans, and production cooperatives. There is a semiofficial insurance company.

Trade. Syria has an unfavourable merchandise balance of trade. The deficit is offset by revenues from tourism, transit trade returns, foreign aid, and earnings of Syrians overseas.

Imports include industrial and agricultural machinery, motor vehicles and accessories, drugs, food, and fabric. Exports include ginned cotton, petroleum, cotton seeds, barley, lentils, cotton and woollen fabrics, dried fruit, vegetables, skins, and raw wool. Foreign trade is controlled by the state.

Transportation. *Roads.* The road network, which is the chief means of transporting goods and passengers, has continued to expand and improve everywhere. Major roads include the highway between Damascus and Aleppo and the paved road between Damascus and Baghdad, Iraq.

Railways. Syria's railways are well developed. A northern line runs northeastward from Aleppo into Turkey and then east along the border to al-Qāmishlī, where it crosses the northeastern extremity of Syria en route to Baghdad (Iraq). The Hejaz Railway runs from Damascus to Amman (Jordan), and a third runs from Aleppo to Tripoli (Lebanon). Aleppo and Damascus are also linked by rail. Smaller lines run between Ḥimṣ and Rīyāq (Lebanon), and between Beirut (Lebanon) and Damascus. A railway also runs from Latakia to Aleppo, al-Ḥasakah (passing by the Euphrates Dam), and al-Qāmishlī. Another line extends northwest from Aleppo to the Turkish border at Maydān Ikbiz. From Ḥimṣ, a line runs west to the port of Ṭarṭūs, and a line also runs east to the phosphate mines near Tadmur, opening up the desert interior to the Mediterranean.

Ports. The two ports, Latakia and Ṭarṭūs, were built after independence. Latakia has two main jetties, as well as wharves, and warehouses.

Air transport. Syria has international airports at Damascus and Aleppo and domestic airports at al-Qāmishlī, Latakia, Dayr az-Zawr, and Tadmur. The facilities at Damascus and Aleppo can handle jet aircraft. International services connect Syria with Arab, other Asian, and European countries. Domestic services are provided by Syrian Arab Airways.

GOVERNMENT AND SOCIAL CONDITIONS

Government. *Constitutional framework.* The constitution of 1973 declares that Syria constitutes an integral part of the Arab homeland, that all legislative power lies with the people, and that freedom of expression and equality before the law are guaranteed. The enforcement of these principles has not been thorough, however, because of constant political and military tensions.

The regional (Syrian) leadership of the Arab Socialist Ba'th (Renaissance) Party (see below *The political process*) elects the head of state, who must be a Muslim, and appoints the cabinet, which exercises legislative as well as executive powers. Suffrage is universal.

Local government. Syria is divided into *muḥāfaẓāt* (governorates), two province-level cities, *manāṭiq* (districts), and *nawāḥī* (subdistricts). The governors, or *muḥāfiẓīn,* enjoy some power within their administrative divisions, but local government is centralized and is dependent upon the minister of the interior.

The Ba'th Party

The political process. Most authority is wielded by the ruling Arab Socialist Ba'th Party. Since its foundation in 1941 the party has undergone radical internal changes as a result of successive coups d'état and internal power struggles. The party has branch organizations in many Middle Eastern countries, each headed by its own regional leadership. The organs of administration are the National Command, the Regional Command, and the People's Council; the latter operates as a legislature. The supreme national leadership is composed of representatives from each regional branch, who are elected by their own party congresses. The regional leadership for Syria is the highest authority in the country but is subordinate to the national leadership. Actual power resides in the presidency.

All political parties are officially linked together as the National Progressive Front, which is dominated by the Ba'th Party. Participation in the political life of the country is channelled through the particular popular organization to which a citizen may belong. In addition to the unions mentioned above, there is a General Union of Students and a General Federation of Women.

Justice. The principles of Syrian law and equity derive basically from Islāmic jurisprudence, and secondarily from the French civil code. Summary courts try civil, commercial, and penal cases. The headquarters of each administrative district has a First Instance Court for criminal cases. The capital city of each governorate also has a court of appeal. Damascus houses a high court of appeal and a constitutional court, as well as a military tribunal and the *muftī*'s court for the maintenance of Islāmic law. Various non-Muslim sects each have their own courts with jurisdiction over personal status cases.

The armed forces. Military service is compulsory for all adult males; college students receive deferments. Military service provides general and technical—as well as military—education and training. The army is responsible for defense, public works, road construction, and public health. The air force has been equipped with Soviet assistance. There is a small navy. Palestinian Arab guerrilla organizations operate from Syria and have training facilities there.

Education. Schooling is compulsory for all children above eight years of age, and all schoolbooks are free. Schooling is divided into six years of compulsory primary, three years of lower secondary, and three years of upper secondary education. Lower and upper secondary schools provide general (which prepares for university entrance) or vocational curriculums. Secondary schools are open to all elementary students who wish to continue their education. Within this framework, increased attention is being given to technical education. University students attend the universities of Damascus, Aleppo, and Latakia and the Institute of Petroleum at Ḥimṣ. All levels of education have been expanded substantially since 1963, leading to an increase in literacy.

Higher education

Health and welfare. Most endemic diseases in Syria have been eliminated. Health facilities include state and private hospitals and sanatoriums, as well as hospitals and outpatient clinics of the armed forces. There are also a number of public and private outpatient clinics, as well as maternal and child-care, antituberculosis, malaria eradication, and rural health centres.

Child mortality, relatively high, is mostly caused by measles and diseases of the digestive and respiratory systems. Tuberculosis and trachoma are widespread, particularly among the Bedouin, the peasants, and residents of city slums.

Health conditions and sanitation in the cities, towns, and larger villages are generally satisfactory. Running water is supplied to almost all houses, buildings, and public places. Each municipality maintains its streets and collects refuse regularly. Medical services are badly distributed; the majority of the doctors are concentrated in the large cities.

The Ministry of Social Welfare and Labour is empowered to find work for, and distribute cash allowances to, the unemployed. The ministry also encourages such youth activities as athletics, scouting, literacy campaigns, and the organization of cooperatives. The government gives substantial grants to private welfare societies.

The pace of change from an agricultural to an industrial economy, and the accompanying migration to the cities, led to an acute shortage of housing. To aggravate the shortage, young adult males typically break with tradition and leave their parental homes for their own houses. The Ministry of Municipal and Rural Affairs undertakes the construction of blocks of low-income flats in the cities.

Labour legislation establishes minimum wage limits, prohibits child labour, and organizes relations between workers and employers. But economic and social conditions as well as the extent of unemployment make rigorous enforcement impractical. Employees in heavy industry receive the highest industrial wages, textile workers the lowest. State employees have more job security. The major portion of the average salary is generally spent on housing and food, leaving little for clothing, medicine, and recreation.

The upper-income group is composed of senior officials, military officers, the owners of small industrial businesses, and important merchants. The middle-income group comprises the great majority of government officials, shopkeepers, professionals, and farmers. Workers, peasants (farmers who do not own all the land they cultivate), and most employees belong to the lower-income group. Education is the key to social mobility.

The process of socialist transformation has caused much social, political, and economic turmoil and has led to emigration among the wealthy and some religious minorities. The rising birth rate has caused family lands to be broken up into ever smaller lots and has reduced the standard of living of many peasants.

CULTURAL LIFE

The cultural milieu. Long periods of foreign rule contributed little to the development of a national culture. Education was confined to a few, who maintained the country's ancient libraries and manuscripts. After independence in 1946, a new cultural life began to stir, mostly through the medium of a small number of clubs that received some financial assistance from the state.

The Ministry of Culture and National Guidance has been active in directing and promoting the nation's cultural life. An important objective has been the affirmation of the Arab national character in the face of foreign cultural influences.

The state of the arts. Until World War I, the artistic representation of animal or human life was proscribed by Islām. Figurative art was restricted to geometric designs as manifest in the arts of arabesque and calligraphy, which decorate most palaces and mosques.

The fine arts

Following World War I, drawing was taught in the schools and talented artists began to emerge. There is a faculty of fine arts at the University of Damascus. Syrian artists are concerned more with content than with form or style.

Sculpture is mainly confined to decorations hewn in white marble. Damascus is particularly famous for this type of sculpture, and beautiful examples of it can be seen in its palaces and public buildings.

National folk traditions have been emphasized by the state, which has established a museum for national folk traditions in Damascus. The capital also contains the renovated National Museum and separate museums for agriculture and military history. Archaeological museums are located in Aleppo and at major sites. Short-story writing and poetry have flourished, as in the widely read works of Nizār Qabbānī and ʿAlī Aḥmad Saʿīd ("Adonis"). The National Theatre and other theatrical and folk-dance companies give regular performances.

Cultural institutions. The Ministry of Culture has established an Arab institute of music and has made available numerous courses in the figurative and applied arts, as well as centres for teaching the domestic arts. The Arabic Language Academy, founded in 1919, is the oldest such academy in the Arab world. The University of Damascus, however, is the most important of Syria's cultural centres.

Press and broadcasting. Daily, weekly, and fortnightly papers are published. All newspapers are under direct government control, and the magazines and journals are run mostly by official or semiofficial bodies.

Syrian radio broadcasting began in 1947 and has since become the most powerful rival of the local press. The Syrian Broadcasting Service broadcasts mainly in Arabic but also in English, French, Turkish, Hebrew, and German. Radio broadcasts—many of which are devoted to instruction—reach almost every Syrian home.

The Syrian Television Service, which was established in 1960, reaches a large audience throughout the country. Television broadcasting includes educational and cultural programs, drama, music, news, and sports.

For statistical data on the land and people of Syria, see the *Britannica World Data* section in the BRITANNICA WORLD DATA ANNUAL. (A.-R.H./W.L.O.)

History

The earliest prehistoric remains of human habitation found in Syria and Palestine (stone implements, with bones of elephant and horse) are of the Middle Paleolithic Period. In the next stage are remains of rhinoceros and of men who are classified as intermediate between Neanderthal and modern types. The Mesolithic Period is best represented by the Natufian culture, which is spread along, and some distance behind, the coast of the Levant. The Natufians supported life by fishing, hunting, and gathering the grains that, in their wild state, were indigenous to the country. This condition was gradually superseded by the domestication of animals, the cultivation of crops, and the production of pottery. Excavations at Mureybet in Syria have revealed a settlement where the inhabitants made pottery and cultivated einkorn, a single-grained wheat, as early as the 9th millennium BC. Metallurgy, particularly the production of bronze (an alloy of copper and tin), appeared after the mid-4th millennium BC. The first cities emerged shortly thereafter.

EARLY HISTORY

The invention of writing

History begins with the invention of writing, which took place in southern Babylonia perhaps *c.* 3000 BC, the script being an original picture character that developed later into cuneiform. Modern research, however, suggests that clay tokens found at numerous ancient Middle Eastern sites from as early as 8000 BC may have been used as an archaic recording system and ultimately led to the invention of writing.

By the mid-3rd millennium BC, various Semitic peoples had migrated into Syria-Palestine and Babylonia. Knowledge of this period has been enormously enhanced by the excavations at Tall Mardīkh, ancient Ebla, south of Aleppo. The palace has yielded more than 17,000 inscribed clay tablets, dated to about 2600–2500 BC, which detail the social, religious, economic, and political life of this thriving and powerful Syrian kingdom. The language of Ebla has been identified as Northwest Semitic.

In about 2320 BC Lugalzaggisi, the Sumerian ruler of Erech (Uruk), boasted of an empire that stretched to the Mediterranean. It was short-lived; he was defeated by the Semite Sargon I of Akkad, who became the greatest conqueror and most famous name in Babylonian history. Sargon led his armies up the Euphrates to the "cedar mountain" (the Amanus) and beyond. Ebla was destroyed either by Sargon at this time or perhaps by his grandson, Naram-sin (*c.* 2275 BC), and the region of Syria became part of the Akkadian Empire. But the dynasty of Akkad was soon overthrown as its centre and superseded by the dynasties first of Guti and then of Ur.

Nothing certain is known about the authority (if any) that the kings of Ur exercised in Syria, so far away from their capital. The end of their dynasty, however, was brought about chiefly by the pressure of a new Semitic migration from Syria, this time of the Amorites (*i.e.,* the westerners), as they were called in Babylonia. Between about 2000 and 1800 BC they covered both Syria and Mesopotamia with a multitude of small principalities and cities, mostly governed by rulers bearing some name characteristic of the Semitic dialect that the Amorites spoke. The period of Amorite ascendancy is vividly mirrored in the Mari Letters, a great archive of royal correspondence found at the site of Mari, near the modern frontier with Iraq. Among the principal figures mentioned are the celebrated lawgiver Hammurabi of Babylon (himself an Amorite) and a king of Aleppo, part of whose kingdom was the city of Alalakh, on the Orontes near what was later Antioch. Around 1600 BC northern Syria, including the cities of Alalakh, Aleppo, and Ebla in its Amorite phase, suffered destruction at the hands of the aggressive Hittite kings, Hattusilis I or Mursilis I, from central Anatolia.

Earlier, in the 18th century BC, had begun from Syria a movement of people in the opposite direction. This resulted in the Hyksos invasion of Egypt, which was subject to this foreign domination for 108 years. The mixed multitude of the Hyksos certainly included Hurrians, who, not being Aryans themselves, were under the rule and influence of Aryans and learned from them the use of light chariots and horses in warfare, which they introduced into Egypt, Syria, and Mesopotamia. The Hurrians established the kingdom of Mitanni, with its centre east of the Euphrates, and this was for long the dominant power in Syria, reaching its height in the 15th century BC. Documentary evidence for the Mitanni period comes from excavations made in the 1970s at Tall Hadidi (ancient Azu), at the edge of Lake Assad.

The Hurrians

But other nations were growing at the same time, and in the 14th century Syria was the arena in which at least four great competitors contended. The Hurrians were first in possession, and they maintained friendly relations with Egypt, which, after expelling the Hyksos, had established a vast sphere of influence in Palestine and Syria under the kings of the 18th dynasty. Third of the powers disputing Syria in the 14th century were the Hittites, who finally, under their greatest warrior, Suppiluliumas (*c.* 1350 BC), not only defeated the kingdom of Mitanni but established a firm dominion of their own in northern Syria with its principal centres at Aleppo and Carchemish. Fourth was the rising kingdom of Assyria, which became a serious contender in the reign of Ashur-uballit I.

This was the period of the Amarna Letters, which vividly illustrate the decline of Egyptian influence in Syria (especially under Akhenaton), the distress or duplicity of local governors, and the rivalry of the aforesaid powers. Egyptians and Hittites continued their struggle into the 13th century; the Battle of Kadesh (*c.* 1290 BC) led to a treaty maintaining the equal balance. Assyria had already swept away the remains of Mitanni but itself soon fell into decline, and the Hittites were not long afterward driven from their centre in Asia Minor by the migration of "peoples of the sea," western invaders from the isles of the Aegean and from Europe. The dislocation of peoples at this time apparently also led to the migration into northern Syria of a related Indo-European group from Anatolia, the so-called Neo-Hittites. They established a number of principalities, and the area became known as "Hatti-land."

As early as the 14th century various documents mention the Akhlame, who were forerunners of another vast movement of Semitic tribes called, generically, Aramaeans. By the end of the 13th century these had covered with their small and loose principalities the whole of central and northern Syria. The Assyrians, however, were able to guard their homeland from this penetration, and henceforth much of the warfare of Assyrian kings was aimed at the Aramaean states of Syria. At about the same time as the Aramaean invasion, the exodus of Israelite tribes from Egypt was proceeding. As the Israelites toward the end of the 11th century established a kingdom centred upon Jerusalem, the Aramaeans set up their principal kingdom at Damascus, and the wars between kings of Judah or of Israel and kings of Aram make up much of Old Testament history.

The military kings of the Assyrians

But the most formidable enemies of the Aramaeans and often of the Hebrews were the great military kings of the Assyrians. In the 9th and 8th centuries BC the Assyrian Empire was established over the west. At the Battle of Karkar in 853 BC, Shalmaneser III of Assyria was opposed by Bar-Hadad I (Hebrew Ben-hadad; throne name Hadadezer; Akkadian Adad-idri) of Damascus, Ahab of Israel, and 12 vassal monarchs. In 732 Damascus, the Syrian capital, was at length captured by Tiglath-pileser III. But campaigns against the Aramaeans and Neo-Hittites of northern Syria had to be undertaken by the Assyrians until almost the end of the Assyrian Empire. Culturally, the most important achievement of the Aramaeans was the bringing of the alphabet into general use for public and private business.

Before the close of the 8th century BC began a massive southward movement of people, partly of Aryan stock, from the north and west. Pressure of these upon the Assyrian dominions and homeland became ever more severe, and they deeply affected Syria also; and in the 7th century there came the invasion of the Cimmerians, followed by the Scythians. To these, and to the Medes, Assyria finally succumbed with the fall of Nineveh in 612 BC. Nebuchadrezzar, when crown prince of Babylon, finally defeated the attempted rescue of Assyria by Necho II, king of Egypt, and annihilated his army at Carchemish in 605 BC. In 597 he captured Jerusalem and carried its people into exile. Thereafter, Syria was for half a century under the rule of Nebuchadrezzar's successors on the throne of Babylon.

But another and greater power, the Persians, then came to the fore. Under the leadership of Cyrus they extended their conquests into Asia Minor and then came to a final collision with Babylon, which Cyrus occupied in 539 BC. He sent back the exiled Jewish community to Jerusalem, encouraging them to rebuild their Temple. In Darius I's great organization of the Persian dominions, Syria, with Palestine and Cyprus, was the fifth satrapy, bearing the name of "Across the River" (*i.e.*, the Euphrates), with tribute fixed at 350 talents of silver. Damascus and the Phoenician cities were still the chief centres of Syria under the Persians, and in Sidon was the core of the Phoenician revolt against Artaxerxes III, which ended with the destruction of that city in 345 BC. But by this time, the end of the Persian domination was at hand, and the Macedonians under Alexander III the Great were about to bring the whole Middle East under Greek rule and influence.

Alexander invaded Asia Minor in 334 BC, and his victory over the Persians at Issus in 333 was followed by the capture and enslavement of Tyre and Gaza. With the Battle of Gaugamela and the destruction of Persepolis, the downfall of Persia was completed. (C.J.Ga./W.L.O.)

HELLENISTIC AND ROMAN PERIODS

Hellenistic Age. After Alexander's death in 323 BC his marshals contended for control of the country until, after the Battle of Ipsus (301), Seleucus I Nicator gained the northern part and Ptolemy I Soter gained the southern (Coele Syria). This partition between the Seleucids and the Ptolemies was maintained for 100 years. Their administrative methods varied. In the south the Ptolemies respected the existing autonomous cities, imposed a bureaucratic system on the rest of the country, and established no colonies. The Seleucids divided the north into four satrapies and founded many cities and military colonies—among them Antioch, Seleucia Pieria, Apamea, and Laodicea—drawing on European settlers. Republics replaced kings in the Phoenician coastal cities of Tyre (274 BC), Sidon, Byblus, and Aradus. Further political and cultural changes followed.

Partition between the Seleucids and the Ptolemies

In 200 BC (or perhaps as late as 198) Antiochus III the Great defeated Ptolemy V at Panium and secured control of southern Syria, where he introduced the satrapal system. His subsequent defeat by the Romans at Magnesia (December 190 or January 189), however, resulted in the loss of both his territory in Asia Minor and his prestige, thereby fundamentally weakening the Seleucid Empire, which ceased to be a Mediterranean power. Antiochus IV Epiphanes (175–163) stimulated the spread of Greek culture and political ideas in Syria by a policy of urbanization; increased city organization and municipal autonomy involved greater decentralization of his kingdom. His attempted Hellenization of the Jews is well known.

Under the Seleucid kings, with rival claimants to the throne and constant civil war, Syria disintegrated. In the north the Seleucids controlled little more than the areas of Antioch and Damascus. Southern Syria was partitioned by three tribal dynasties: the Ituraeans, the Jews, and the Nabateans. The country was seized later by Tigranes of Armenia (83); he ruled until his defeat by Pompey, who ended years of anarchy by making Syria a Roman province (64–63).

Roman provincial organization. Pompey in the main accepted the status quo, but he reestablished a number of cities and reduced the kingdom of Judaea; 10 cities of the interior formed a league, the Decapolis. The native client kingdoms of Commagene, Ituraea, Judaea, and Nabataea were henceforth subjected to Roman Syria. Parthian invasions were thrown back in 51–50 and 40–39 BC, and Mark Antony's extensive territorial gifts to Cleopatra (Ituraea,

Damascus, Coele Syria, etc.) involved only temporary adjustments.

Under the early empire, Syria, which stretched northeast to the upper Euphrates and, until AD 73, included eastern Cilicia, became one of the most important provinces. Its governor, a consular legate, generally commanded four legions until AD 70. Administrative changes followed, as Rome gradually annexed the client kingdoms. Ituraea was incorporated (*i.e.,* its territories were assigned to neighbouring cities) partly in 24 BC, partly *c.* AD 93. Judaea became a separate province in AD 6, governed by procurators (apart from the short-lived control by Agrippa I, AD 41–44), until the destruction of Jerusalem in 70. Then, the governor was a praetorian legate in command of a legion; next, under Hadrian, he was a consular with two legions, and the province was named Syria Palaestina. Commagene was annexed permanently by Vespasian in 72. The caravan city of Palmyra came under Roman control, possibly during Tiberius' reign. Finally, Nabataea was made the province of Arabia in 105, governed by a praetorian legate with one legion.

Division of Syria

Syria itself was later divided by Septimius Severus into two provinces—Syria Coele in the north with two legions and Syria Phoenice with one. By the beginning of the 5th century it was subdivided into at least five provinces. The frontiers of Syria were guarded by a fortified limes system, which was thoroughly reorganized by Diocletian and his successors (particularly against cavalry attacks) and which endured until the Arab conquest; much knowledge of this system of "defense in depth" has been obtained with the aid of aerial photography.

Economy and culture. Syria's economic prosperity depended on its natural products (*e.g.,* wine, olives, vegetables, fruits, and nuts), on its industries (*e.g.,* purple dyeing, glassmaking at Sidon, linen and wool weaving, and metalwork), and on its control and organization of trade passing by caravan from the East to the Mediterranean through such centres as Palmyra, Damascus, Bostra, and Petra. Syria remained essentially rural. The urban upper and middle classes might be Hellenized, but the lower classes still spoke Aramaic and other Semitic dialects. Roman influences were naturally weaker than Greek, though the army at first helped the spread of Romanization.

The splendour of Syrian culture is seen in the magnificence of the cities (Antioch, ranking among the greatest cities of the empire, was the residence of the governor and later of the *comes Orientis,* who governed the diocese of the East). This splendour is also evident in their schools of rhetoric, law, and medicine; in their art; in their literature and philosophy; and in the variety of their religions, both pagan and Christian.

Byzantine Syria. During the three centuries Syria was administered from Constantinople, its cultural and economic life remained active. Government became more bureaucratic, but it was efficient. In the 4th century, during the campaigns of Constantius and Julian against Persia, Syria had again become a base of operations and at times endured Persian invasion. The Persian menace died down during the 5th century, but it blazed up again in the 6th, when Arabs also added to the danger. The Persian Khosrow I captured Antioch itself (540); and in 573 the Persians were back again. The invasion of Khosrow II, which began in 606, was later rolled back by the victories of Heraclius, but the peace of 628 brought no tranquillity to Syria. (H.H.S./W.L.O.)

MEDIEVAL PERIOD

Islāmic conquest. In the first half of the 7th century, Syria was absorbed into the Muslim caliphate. Arab forces had appeared on the southern border even before the death of the Prophet Muḥammad in 632, but the real invasion took place in 633–634, with Khālid ibn al-Walīd as its most important leader. In 635 Damascus surrendered, its inhabitants being promised security for their lives, property, and churches, on payment of a poll tax. A counterattack by the emperor Heraclius was defeated at the Battle of the Yarmūk River in 636; by 640 the conquest was virtually complete.

Surrender of Damascus

The new rulers divided Syria into four districts (*junds*): Damascus, Ḥimṣ, Jordan, and Palestine (to which a fifth, Kinnasrin, was later added). The Arab garrisons were kept apart in camps, and life went on much as before. Conversion to Islām had scarcely begun, apart from Arab tribes already settled in Syria; except for the tribe of Ghassān, these all became Muslim. Christians and Jews were treated with toleration, and Nestorian and Jacobite Christians had better treatment than they had under Byzantium. The Byzantine form of administration remained, but the new Muslim tax system was introduced. From 639 the governor of Syria was Muʿawiya of the Meccan house of the Umayyads. He used the country as a base for expeditions against the Byzantine Empire, for this purpose building the first Muslim navy in the Mediterranean. When civil war broke out in the Muslim Empire, as a result of the murder of ʿUthmān and the nomination of ʿAlī as caliph, Syria stood firm behind Muʿawiya, who extended his authority over neighbouring provinces and was proclaimed caliph in 660. He was the first of the Umayyad line, which ruled the empire, with Syria as its core and Damascus its capital, for almost a century.

The Umayyads. The early Umayyad period was one of strength and expansion. The army, mainly Arab and largely Syrian, extended the frontiers of Islām. It carried the war against Byzantium into Asia Minor and besieged Constantinople; eastward it penetrated into Khurasan, Turkistan, and northwestern India; and, spreading along the northern coast of Africa, it occupied much of Spain. This vast empire was given a regular administration that gradually acquired an Arab Muslim character. Syrians played an important part in it, and the country profited from the wealth pouring from the rich provinces to the empire's centre. The caliphs built splendid palaces and the first great monuments of Muslim religious architecture: the Dome of the Rock in Jerusalem and the Umayyad Mosque in Damascus. The religious sciences of Islām began to develop, while Christian culture still flourished. Except under ʿUmar II Christians were treated with favour, and there were Christian officials at court.

Development of religious sciences

Under the later Umayyads the strength of the central government declined. There were factions and feuds inside the ruling group: the Arabs of Iraq resented the domination of Syria; the non-Arab converts to Islām (*mawali*) resented the social gap between them and the Arabs; devout Muslims regarded the Umayyads as too worldly in their lives and policies; after the defeat and death of ʿAlī's son Ḥusayn at the Battle of Karbalāʾ in 680, sentiment in favour of the family of ʿAlī was still strong. The later Umayyads could not control these discontents. Their rule was finally overthrown and the family virtually destroyed by the new ʿAbbāsid caliphate in 750.

The ʿAbbāsids. The end of the Umayyad dynasty meant a shift in power from Syria to Iraq. Syria became a dependent province of the caliphate. Its loyalty was suspect, for Umayyad sentiment lingered on, and the last pro-Umayyad revolt was not crushed until 905. The Christian population was treated with less favour; discriminatory legislation was applied to it under some caliphs, and the process of conversion to Islām went on. Closely connected with it was the gradual adoption of Arabic in place of Greek and Aramaic, although the latter survived in a few villages.

From the 9th to the 12th century. As the ʿAbbāsid caliphate disintegrated in its turn, Syria drifted out of the sphere of influence of Baghdad. In 877 it was annexed by the Tūlūnid dynasty of Egypt, and this began a political connection that was to last with intervals for more than six centuries. In northern Syria the Tūlūnids were succeeded by a local Arab dynasty, the Ḥamdānids of Aleppo, founded by Sayf ad-Dawlah (944–967); they engaged in war with Byzantium, in which their early successes were followed by the Greek recovery of Antioch (969). In central and southern Syria another Egyptian dynasty, the Ikshīdids, established themselves (941–969); their successors, the Fāṭimid caliphs of Cairo, later absorbed the whole country.

In spite of political disturbances, the 10th and 11th centuries were a period of flourishing culture. Around the court of the Ḥamdānids lived some of the greatest

Arabic writers: the poets al-Mutanabbi and al-Maʿarrī, the philosopher al-Fārābī, and the anthologist Abū al-Faraj al-Iṣbāhanī. It was a period of ferment in Islāmic thought, when the challenge to Sunnī Islām from Shīʿism and its offshoots reached its height. The Fāṭimids were themselves Shīʿites. At the end of the 10th century Syria was threatened by the Karmatians, adherents of an extreme form of Shīʿism who had established a state in the Persian Gulf. The danger was beaten back, but it returned as an esoteric doctrine spread by the Ismāʿīlīs from their centre at Salamīyah (Selemīya) in northern Syria.

In the second half of the 11th century Syria fell into the hands of the Seljuq Turks, who had established a sultanate in Asia Minor. They occupied Aleppo and then Damascus. But after the death of the sultan Malik-Shāh in 1092 the Seljuq Empire fell to pieces, and between 1098 and 1124 the crusaders occupied Antioch, Jerusalem, al-Karak in Transjordan, and the coast.

The crusaders

The crusaders organized their conquests into four states owing allegiance to the king of Jerusalem. Their situation was precarious. The crusaders were always a minority in their states, and they never penetrated far into the interior. They could maintain their position only so long as the Muslim states surrounding were weak and divided. Zangī, the Turkish ruler of Mosul, occupied Aleppo in 1128 and recovered Edessa from the crusaders in 1144. His son Nureddin united inner Syria and annexed Egypt. After his death, his kingdom was rebuilt and strengthened by his viceroy in Egypt, Saladin, who ended the Fāṭimid caliphate, created a strong kingdom of Egypt and Syria, and defeated the crusaders at the great Battle of Ḥaṭṭīn (1187). He recovered all Palestine and most of the inland strongholds of the crusaders. Soon afterward, however, the Third Crusade recaptured part of the coast.

The Ayyūbids and Mamlūks. After Saladin's death his kingdom was split up among members of his family, the Ayyūbids, who established principalities in Aleppo, Ḥamāh, Ḥimṣ, Damascus, Baʿlabakk, and Transjordan and ruled them until 1260. The period of Nureddin, Saladin, and their successors was of great importance. Thanks largely to the establishment of Italian trading centres on the coast and better security, economic life recovered and Syria reached a level of prosperity such as it had not enjoyed for centuries. The Ayyūbid rulers stimulated culture and architecture. Following the Seljuqs, they created a new land system based on the grant of rights over land in return for military service. They were champions of Islāmic orthodoxy against the sects that had gained ground in the previous era. They built colleges of a new type, the *madrasah,* as centres of learning. Their efforts to stamp out heterodoxy were not completely successful. The Ismāʿīlīs kept their strongholds in the mountains, and their secret organization, the Assassins, had some political importance.

Although strong internally, the state was still in danger from the Bedouin tribes of the desert and from the Mongols, who invaded Syria for the first time in 1260 and sacked Aleppo. They were driven back not by the local rulers but by a new Egyptian military group, the Mamlūks, a self-perpetuating elite of slaves and freedmen, mainly of Turkish and Caucasian origin, who had replaced the Ayyūbids as rulers of Egypt in 1250. In 1260 they defeated the Mongols at the Battle of ʿAyn Jālūt in Palestine; the victorious Mamlūk general, Baybars I, made himself sultan of a reunited kingdom of Syria and Egypt, which he ruled until his death in 1277. This state continued to exist for more than two centuries. In 1291 it won back Acre and other coastal towns from the crusaders, who were expelled; and a few years later it took the last crusading stronghold, the island of Ruad (Arwād). The Mamlūks reorganized the Ayyūbid principalities as six provinces, of which Damascus was the largest and most important. Political power was in the hands of the Mamlūk elite, who held land in virtual ownership in return for military service in the cavalry. But there was a local element in the government, the civil servants being drawn mainly from Syrian Arab families with their tradition of religious learning.

Like the Ayyūbids, the Mamlūks were strictly orthodox in religion. Religious culture flourished and produced a number of great scholars such as the Ḥanbalī jurist Ibn Taymīyah. For religious and political reasons, the Mamlūks dealt severely with the religious minorities living in the coastal mountain ranges: Druze, Maronite Christians, Ismāʿīlīs, and ʿAlawites (or Nusayrīs; adherents of another creed derived from Shīʿism and living in the Jabal an-Nuṣayrīyah). One of the principal reasons for this severity was the fear of the Mamlūks that these minorities might co-operate with the crusaders, should they attempt to return.

Invasion of Timur

In the early Mamlūk period, Syria remained prosperous; the rulers constructed public works, and Venetian merchants carried on their coastal trade. But in 1401 came a blow to economic life: a new Mongol invader, Timur (Tamerlane), sacked Aleppo and Damascus. His empire did not long survive his death in 1405, but the damage had been done. The cities had been burned, a large part of their population killed, and many craftsmen taken away to Central Asia.

OTTOMAN PERIOD

Ottoman government, 16th–17th century. Throughout the 15th century, Mamlūk Syria continued to decline, while a new power was growing to the north, that of the Ottoman Turkish sultanate in Asia Minor. Having occupied Constantinople and the Balkans, it began to look southward. In 1516 Sultan Selim I defeated the Mamlūks in the Battle of Marj Dābiq and occupied the whole of Syria that year and Egypt the next. Although parts of Syria enjoyed some local autonomy, the area as a whole remained for 400 years an integral section of the Ottoman Empire. It was divided into provinces, each under a governor: Damascus, Aleppo, and later Tripoli and Ṣaydā, or Sidon, of which the administrative centre was later moved to Acre. Damascus, the largest, had special importance as the place from which the pilgrimage to Mecca was organized every year. The governor of Damascus led the pilgrimage when possible, and most of the revenues of the province were earmarked for its expenses.

The tax system continued in principle to be that of Muslim law—a land tax, a poll tax on Christians and Jews, and customs duties. But the Ottomans, like their predecessors, gave the right to collect and keep the land tax in return for military service. Later, this system was allowed to decay, and tax collection was turned over to tax farmers (*mültezim*), who became in the course of time nearly a landowning class. The official religious hierarchy of judges, jurisconsults, and preachers served as an intermediary between government and subjects, as did guild masters and the heads of the local mystical orders (*ṣūfīs*).

Within this framework of law, order, and taxation, the local communities were left to regulate their own lives. In the desert, the Bedouin tribes were controlled to some extent by gifts, the encouragement of factions, and occasional military expeditions but otherwise were not interfered with. In the mountains the ʿAlawites and the Ismāʿīlīs of Jabal an-Nuṣayrīyah were watched by the Ottoman governors, but they were not interfered with so long as they paid their taxes. In the Jabal ad-Durūz south of Damascus there grew up a community of Druze farmers under no control and paying no taxes. The authority of the Christian patriarchs over their communities was recognized. In the corps of *ʿulamāʾ* (learned Muslims holding government appointments) most positions except the highest were held by members of local families having a tradition of religious learning. They continued to be, as under the Mamlūks, spokesmen and leaders of the Muslim citizens.

Economic life

The early Ottoman governors paid much attention to agriculture, and their fiscal system was designed to encourage it. In parts of Syria it flourished during the 16th and 17th centuries, and, apart from cereals for local consumption, cotton and silk were produced for export. Aleppo and Damascus not only were important centres of handicrafts but also served as market towns for the desert and countryside and as stages on the desert routes to the Persian Gulf and Persia. Aleppo also was an important centre of trade with Europe; French and English had largely replaced Italian merchants, and there grew up also a class of Syrian Christian and Jewish merchants who developed contacts with Egypt, Italy, and France.

Throughout the 17th and 18th centuries the position of the Christians improved. Catholic missions, protected by France, enlarged the Catholic communities of both Latin and Eastern rites, founded schools, and spread knowledge of European languages. The Oriental colleges in Rome produced an educated priesthood, and the Christian communities in Aleppo and Lebanon brought forth scholars. The traditional Muslim Arab culture could still produce a theologian of some originality in ʿAbd al-Ghanī an-Nābulusī and a systematic jurist in Ibrāhīm al-Ḥalabī.

Decline of Ottoman authority. In spite of widespread unrest in the early 17th century, Ottoman rule was in general stable and effective until the end of that century. After that it declined rapidly, in Syria as elsewhere. Control by the central government weakened; the standard of administration sank; the Janissaries (the elite troops of the sultan) lost their discipline and became a menace to order. The result was a shrinkage of agricultural production, as the villages suffered from the depredations of soldiery and tax collectors and from Bedouin incursions. This was a period of activity in the Syrian desert, and Bedouin tribes, moving northwest from Arabia, extended their control far into the settled land. In the towns there was also a decline. The desert routes were unsafe, and the European merchant colonies were shrinking. But there was still a vigorous commercial life; the standard of craftsmanship was high, and the great tradition of Islāmic architecture was continued.

Ottoman authority did reassert itself to some extent, but in a new form. For most of the 18th century, Damascus was ruled by governors belonging to the ʿAẓm family, loyal to the sultan but with more independence than earlier sultans would have allowed. They controlled the Janissaries, kept back the Bedouin, maintained security, and sometimes extended their authority to other provinces. In the province of Sidon, power was held on similar terms by a ruthless and able Bosnian governor, Aḥmad al-Jazzār (1775–1804), and his group of Mamlūks. Such rulers raised their own armies, but this involved additional taxation and further depressed the condition of the peasants. Agriculture flourished in the hilly districts, which were virtually beyond Ottoman control, free from Bedouin attacks, and ruled by strong local rulers who protected agriculture and made Acre a prosperous centre of trade.

At the beginning of the 19th century Syria had some islands of prosperity: Aleppo and Damascus (each with roughly 100,000 inhabitants), Mt. Lebanon, and certain other secluded districts. In general, however, the country was in decay, the small towns subsisting on local trade, the villagers receding in face of the Bedouin. The Ottoman hold on the country was at its weakest. In Damascus and Aleppo the governors were scarcely able to control the population of city or countryside. The prince of Lebanon, Bashīr II (1788–1840), who had been installed by al-Jazzār and remained quiet while al-Jazzār was alive, gradually extended his control over districts beyond Lebanon. In 1810 the Wahhābīs from central Arabia threatened Damascus.

Egyptian domination. In 1831 the ruler of Egypt, Muḥammad ʿAlī, sent his son Ibrāhīm Pasha at the head of his modern army into Palestine. Helped by Bashīr and other local leaders, Ibrāhīm conquered the country and advanced into Asia Minor. He ruled Syria for almost 10 years. The whole country was controlled from Damascus. There and in the provincial centres the governors were Egyptians, but they were assisted by councils representing the population. In political matters Ibrāhīm relied largely on Bashīr. New taxes were introduced and strictly collected, agriculture was encouraged, and the Bedouin pushed back. After an abortive attempt to introduce trade monopolies, Ibrāhīm encouraged European traders by maintaining better security. The Christian and Jewish populations were treated with consideration.

European intervention in Syria

After a time, Ibrāhīm's rule became unpopular because his taxes were heavy and because he tried to disarm and conscript the population. The European powers (except France) also objected to Egyptian rule in Syria because it was a threat to the Ottoman Empire, the weakness or disintegration of which might cause a European crisis. In 1839 war broke out between Muḥammad ʿAlī and his suzerain, the Sultan. Ibrāhīm defeated the Turkish army, but in 1840 the European powers intervened. After an ultimatum, a British, Ottoman, and Austrian force landed on the Syrian coast; there was a local insurrection encouraged from outside, and the Egyptians were forced to withdraw from Syria, which reverted to the Sultan's government.

Ottoman rule restored. The next 20 years were a period of mounting crises. Lebanon became the scene of a struggle for power between Druzes and Maronites, with undertones of social conflict. In Syria an attempt was made to apply the new Ottoman administrative system. But the new system of taxation and conscription caused unrest. This situation was worsened by the growth of European influence; the Muslim majority became aware of the weakness of the Islāmic community, and the connection of France with the Catholics and of Russia with the Orthodox both encouraged the minorities to hope for a more favourable position and focussed on them the hostility of their Muslim compatriots. There was also economic unrest. European goods flooded the market and replaced some of the products of local craftsmen. This diminished the prosperity of the artisan class, largely Muslim, but increased that of the import merchants, mainly Christians and Jews.

The tension thus generated burst out in 1860 when a civil war of Druzes and Maronites in Lebanon touched off a massacre of Christians by a Muslim mob in Damascus. The Ottoman government sent a special commissioner to punish the guilty and suppress disorder. France sent an expeditionary force, and a European commission discussed the future of the country, coming to the conclusion that Lebanon (the mountain itself but not the coastal towns) should be an autonomous district (*mutaṣarrifīyah*) but that no change should be made in Syria.

From then until the collapse of the Ottoman Empire, Syria continued to be governed as a group of Ottoman provinces. From 1888 there were three: Damascus, Aleppo, and Beirut. The new administrative and legal system was more carefully applied, and a new type of educated official gradually raised its standards. The introduction of railways and telegraphs made possible a stricter control. A French-built railway linked Beirut and Damascus, with a later extension running north to Aleppo, and in 1908 the Hejaz Railway was opened to take pilgrims from Damascus to Medina. Railways and better security encouraged agriculture. Aleppo (population about 200,000) and Damascus (250,000) both had a flourishing trade, but the crafts declined, and the desert routes suffered from the opening of the Suez Canal.

In the cities there was a considerable change in social life. The upper and middle classes adopted the clothes and social customs of western Europe, and Western-style schools flourished. In 1866 the American Protestant Mission opened in Beirut the Syrian Protestant College (later the American University of Beirut), and in 1881 the French Jesuits opened the Université Saint-Joseph in the same town. The Ottoman government opened schools, and young men of the great Arab families of the towns began to attend the higher schools in Constantinople and to go on to civil or military service.

Under Sultan Abdülhamid II (1876–1909) the Muslim Arabs of Syria were reasonably content. His emphasis on Islāmic solidarity frightened the Christians, but the Muslims on the whole still regarded the Ottoman Empire as the political embodiment of Islām. Syrian Arabs played a leading part at the Sultan's court.

Emergence of Arab nationalism

After the Young Turk revolution of 1908, relations between Arabs and Turks grew worse. Power fell into the hands of a Turkish military group whose policy stimulated the growth of opposition. Arab nationalist feeling became more conscious, and political parties, both open and secret, were organized by Syrians in Cairo, Constantinople, and Paris as well as in Syria itself.

World War I. When the Ottoman Empire entered World War I in 1914, Syria became a military base. In 1915 an Ottoman army under German command attacked the British position on the Suez Canal, and from 1916 a British and imperial force based in Egypt, with a French contingent, undertook the invasion of Palestine. By the end of 1917 Gen. Sir Edmund (later Field Marshal Viscount) Allenby had occupied Jerusalem, and by November 1918 his troops had taken Syria. Most Christians and Jews welcomed the occupation; among the Muslims a large proportion had remained loyal to the empire, as being all that was left of the political independence of Islām, but the nationalist societies had made common cause with the ruler of the Hejaz, Sharīf Ḥusayn, forming an alliance with Britain against their Turkish suzerain. An Arab army under the command of Ḥusayn's son Fayṣal was formed in the Hejaz, with Syrian and other Arab officers and British help led by T.E. Lawrence. It took part, under Allenby's general command, in the Syrian campaign helping to capture Damascus.

Allied vacillation over Syria's future

When the war ended, Allenby installed an Arab military administration, under Fayṣal, in Damascus and the interior. The French took over the coast, with Beirut as their centre, and the British took over Palestine. There followed four unsettled years while the fate of Syria was being decided. During the war the British government had made promises, to Ḥusayn and other Arab leaders, that the Arabs would be independent in those countries that they helped to liberate, subject to certain reservations, the precise extent of which has never been clear. Then, in November 1918, Britain and France declared their intention of establishing in Syria and Iraq "national governments drawing their authority from the initiative and free choice of the native populations."

By the Sykes-Picot Agreement of 1916, France was to be free to establish its administration in Lebanon and on the coast and to provide advice and assistance to whatever regime existed in the interior. In March 1920 a Syrian Congress meeting in Damascus elected Fayṣal king of a united Syria including Palestine; but in April the Allied Conference of San Remo decided that both should be placed under the new mandate system and that France should have the mandate for Syria.

MANDATE AND INDEPENDENCE

The French Mandate. In June 1920 a French ultimatum demanding Syrian recognition of the mandate was followed by a French occupation and the expulsion in July of Fayṣal. In July 1922 the League of Nations approved the texts of the French Mandate for Syria and Lebanon. Lebanon had already, in August 1920, been declared a separate state, with the addition of Beirut, Tripoli, and certain other districts, to the prewar autonomous province. Politically, "Syria" henceforth acquired a narrower meaning; it referred to what was left of geographical Syria once Transjordan, Lebanon, and Palestine had been detached from it.

The mandate placed on France the responsibility of creating and controlling an administration, of developing the resources of the country, and of preparing it for self-government. A number of local governments were set up: one for the Jabal Ansariyah, where the majority belonged to the ʿAlawite sect, one for the Jabal ad-Durūz, where most of the inhabitants were Druzes, and eventually one for the rest of Syria with its capital at Damascus.

The French mandatory administration carried out much constructive work. Roads were built; town planning was carried out and urban amenities were improved; land tenure was reformed in some districts; and agriculture was encouraged, particularly in the fertile al-Jazīrah. The University of Damascus was established, with its teaching being mainly in Arabic.

It was more difficult to prepare Syria for self-government because of the difference between French and Syrian conceptions of what was implied. Most French officials and statesmen thought in terms of a long period of control. Further, they did not wish to hand over power to the Muslim majority in a way that might persuade their Christian protégés that they were giving up France's traditional policy of protecting the Christians of the Levant. In Syria, many members of the minorities and a smaller proportion of the majority wanted the French to remain as a help in constructing a modern society and government. The greater part of the urban population, however, and in particular the educated elite, wanted Syria to be independent and to include Lebanon, Palestine, and Transjordan, if possible, and certainly the Druze and ʿAlawite districts.

The first crisis in Franco-Syrian relations came in 1925, when a revolt in Jabal ad-Durūz, sparked by local grievances, led to an alliance between the Druze rebels and the nationalists of Damascus, newly organized in the People's Party. For a time the rebels controlled much of the countryside. In October 1925, bands entered the city of Damascus itself, and this led to a two-day bombardment by the French. The revolt did not subside completely until 1927, but even before the end of 1925 the French had started a policy of conciliation. In 1928, elections were held for a Constituent Assembly. The nationalists won the election and took office in a new government. The assembly drafted a constitution, but their draft was not wholly acceptable to the high commissioner, because it spoke of the unity of geographical Syria and did not explicitly safeguard the French position of control.

In May 1930 the high commissioner dissolved the assembly and enacted the constitution with certain changes. There followed unsuccessful negotiations for a Franco-Syrian treaty, but in 1936 the advent of the Popular Front government in France changed the situation. Negotiations took place with the nationalists, now organized in the National Bloc. A treaty was signed in September 1936. It provided for Syrian independence, Franco-Syrian consultation on foreign policy, French priority in advice and assistance, and the retention by France of two military bases. The Druze and ʿAlawite districts were to be incorporated in Syria but not Lebanon, with which France signed a similar treaty in November. A Parliament was elected; the leader of the Bloc, Hāshim al-ʿAtāsī, was chosen as president of the republic; and a nationalist government took office.

The Syrian government ratified the treaty before the end of 1936, but France never did so. When Turkey put forward claims to Alexandretta, where Turks were the largest element in the mixed population, France found it advisable, for strategic reasons, to yield to its demands. In 1937 the district (later given the Turkish name of Hatay) was granted an autonomous status; in 1939 it was incorporated into Turkey.

By the end of 1938 it was clear that the French government had no intention of ratifying the treaty. In July 1939 the president and government resigned, and the constitution was suspended.

World War II and independence. In June 1940, after the Franco-German armistice, the French in Syria announced that they would cease hostilities against Germany and Italy and recognize the Vichy government. Political uncertainty and the growing scarcity of goods and rising prices caused unrest, which was led by one of the prominent nationalists, Shukri al-Kuwatli. In May 1941 the Vichy government allowed German aircraft to land and refuel en route to Iraq, and in June, British, Commonwealth, and Free French forces invaded Syria. French troops resisted for a month, but Damascus was occupied on June 21 and hostilities ceased at midnight on July 11–12.

From then until 1946, Syria was jointly occupied by British and French forces. At the moment of invasion, the Free French had proclaimed Syrian and Lebanese independence, and this was underwritten by the British government, which recognized French predominance in Syria and Lebanon, provided France carried out its promise of independence. In the interests of its Arab policy, Britain used its position of strength to persuade the Free French to carry out their undertaking. Elections held in 1943 resulted in a nationalist victory, and Shukri al-Kuwatli became president of the republic.

There followed two years of disagreement about the transfer of authority from the French administration to the Syrian and Lebanese governments. A crisis took place in 1945, when the French refusal to transfer control of the local armed forces led to disorders, culminating in a French bombardment of Damascus and British intervention. After long negotiations and discussion in the UN Security Council, agreement was reached on simultaneous British and French withdrawal from Syria and Lebanon. Withdrawal from Syria was completed by April 1946.

Syria had already become a founder member of the United Nations and of the Arab League.

(A.H.Ho./V.E.I./W.L.O.)

SYRIA AFTER INDEPENDENCE

The humiliating failure of the Arab intervention in Palestine against the newly created state of Israel in May 1948 brought serious discredit to the governments of the Arab countries involved, but nowhere more than in Syria.

Syria's heterogeneous population

Fundamental to the Syrian problem was the ethnically, religiously, and socially heterogeneous nature of the emerging republic. The new state united the ʿAlawite and Druze territories, which had formerly enjoyed separate status, with the predominantly Sunnī regions of Damascus, Ḥimṣ, Ḥamāh, and Aleppo. The ʿAlawites and Druzes formed compact communities in their respective regions. Throughout the country, and particularly in the cities, there were large communities of Christians.

In addition to this religious and ethnic heterogeneity, there was an equally important social heterogeneity; the population of Syria was composed of townspeople, peasants, and nomads, three groups with little in common. Economic differences added further complexity; in the cities the ostentatious wealth of the notables contrasted sharply with the poverty of the masses. Those same notables were also the owners of large agricultural estates on which the peasants were practically serfs. It was the Sunnī landowning notables who led the resistance to the French. When Syria achieved independence, they took power and endeavoured to forge a unitary state. They proved unequal to the task.

By 1949 the small but rising middle class, among which new social ideas were developing, and minorities, who resented the growing threat to their particularism, were increasingly opposed to the government. The rulers, having tasted power after so long a struggle for independence, refused those concessions that might have saved them. Moreover, they appeared to be more devoted to achieving pan-Arab goals than to solving the problems closer to home. In the years immediately following World War II, Iraq and Saudi Arabia were making rival bids for pan-Arab leadership. The ruling National Bloc in Syria readily divided into two new parties: a National Party headed by Shukri al-Kuwatli, which represented the business interests of the Damascus notables and supported Saudi Arabia; and a resuscitated People's Party, which represented the interests of the Aleppo notables and supported Iraq. The socialist and secular Arab nationalist Baʿth Party was recruiting followers among students and army officers, winning support particularly among the ʿAlawite and other minorities that were strongly represented among the younger officers of the army.

Military dictatorships in Syria

The colonels. The end of the short-lived civilian order in Syria came in March 1949 when Col. Husni az-Zaim overthrew the Kuwatli government in a bloodless coup. Zaim was himself overthrown in August by Col. Sami al-Hinnawi. A third coup, led by Col. Adib ash-Shishakli, followed in December; in November 1951 Shishakli removed his associates by a fourth coup.

The military dictators of Syria were officers of no particular ideological commitment, and the regimes they led may be described as conservative. All ruled in association with veteran politicians. Among the politically minded army officers at the time, many were pan-Arabist Baʿth Socialists. Opposing the Baʿth officers were officers of a radically different political persuasion, who followed the Syrian Social Nationalist Party (the Parti Populaire Syrien, or PPS), an authoritarian party devoted to the establishment of a pan-Syrian national state.

Shishakli was overthrown in February 1954 by a military coup led by Col. Faisal al-Atasi and Parliament was restored. The PPS forthwith lost its influence in Syrian politics and in the following year was suppressed in the army. From that time the Baʿthists in the army had no serious rival. Changes in agriculture took place in the 1950s, separate from the struggle for control of the state, and they had an important effect on the lives of many people. Capital-intensive cotton production grew rapidly in the newly planted lands of the northeast.

The union with Egypt, 1958–61. The years that followed the overthrow of Shishakli in Syria saw the rise of Pres. Gamal Abdel Nasser of Egypt to leadership of the pan-Arab unity movement. The coalition regime in Syria turned more and more to Egypt for support and also established the first friendly contacts with the Communist countries. In February 1958 Syria, under the leadership of the Baʿth Party, gave up its sovereignty to become, for the next three and one-half years, the "Northern Province" of the United Arab Republic (U.A.R.), of which Nasser was president.

The union of Syria with Egypt proved a bitter disappointment, for the Egyptians tended to treat the Syrians as subordinates. Tensions were heightened when drought damaged Syria's economy. In September 1961 a coup led by Syrian army officers reestablished Syria as an independent state.

(K.S.S./W.R.P./W.L.O.)

The "secessionist" regime, 1961–63. The coup of 1961 paved the way for a return of the old class of notables to power as parliamentary elections were held. The "secessionist" regime, though civilian at the surface, was still under army control, and in the army the Baʿth was powerful. The regime made hardly any concessions to the socialism of the Baʿth and the pro-Nasser pan-Arabists. The secessionist regime set out quickly to undo the socialist measures introduced under the union with Egypt (such as land reforms and the nationalization of large business enterprises), thus playing into the hands of the Baʿth. In March 1963 Baʿthist supporters in the army seized power.

Baʿthist Syria after 1963. The new government was a coalition that included pro-Nasser elements who demanded reunion with Egypt. A month before the Baʿth coup in Syria, the Iraqi branch of the party had seized power in Baghdad. A Baʿthist union between Syria and Iraq seemed imminent, but it was opposed by the pro-Nasser Arab unionists in Damascus and Baghdad. The Baʿth leaders of Iraq and Syria flew to Cairo for unity talks with President Nasser, but Nasser would agree to a union only on his own terms, and the talks failed. The Baʿth regime in Iraq did not outlive the year. In Syria the pro-Nasser Arab unionists were thrown out of power and a Baʿth military dictatorship was established.

The Baʿthists in Syria were soon faced with a serious problem. Although their party was led by Syrians, it was pan-Arab and had branches in Iraq, Lebanon, and Jordan. The continued subordination of the Syrian branch of the party to the central committee gave non-Syrian Baʿthists a considerable say in Syrian affairs. The Syrian branch of the party became independent of the pan-Arab central committee after a coup in February 1966 set up a new military regime in the name of the Syrian Baʿth.

Baʿth split

For some years the Syrian branch of the Baʿth Party, with its ʿAlawite leadership, successfully maintained itself in power. Col. Salah al-Jadid wielded ultimate power until he was deposed in favour of Ḥafiz (Hafez) al-Assad in 1970; Assad was sworn in as president on March 14, 1971. There was popular opposition by the Sunnī majority to the rule of Syria by an ʿAlawite minority.

In a plebiscite vote on February 8, 1978, President Assad was reelected by a large majority to a second seven-year term. Serious internal tension still existed, however. In 1979 an attack against the Aleppo artillery school left 32 ʿAlawite cadets dead. The Muslim Brotherhood, an extremist militant Muslim group, was accused of making the attack, and widespread arrests were made. The Baʿth government increased security to combat the Sunnī resistance; in 1982 government troops suppressed an uprising of the Muslim Brotherhood in the city of Ḥamāh.

External economic aid and diplomatic support were secured by a close alliance of Syria with Libya in September 1980, followed by a treaty of friendship and cooperation signed with the Soviet Union. The Soviet alliance was strained by Syria's support of Iran against Iraq when those nations went to war in 1980. Syrian occupation of much of Lebanon from 1976 dominated Syria's foreign policy; in 1982 many Syrian aircraft and tanks were destroyed in heavy resistance to Israel's invasion of Lebanon.

Economic growth, spurred by the increase in irrigation that had been made possible by completion of the Euphrates Dam and by increasing revenues from oil sales, helped reconcile the Syrian people to the military Ba'th government. Assad continued in office, ruling longer than any previous leader of independent Syria. He was elected to a third seven-year term by plebiscite vote in 1985.

For later developments in the political history of Syria, see the *Britannica Book of the Year* section in the BRITANNICA WORLD DATA ANNUAL.

BIBLIOGRAPHY

Physical and human geography: ANDRÉ RAYMOND (ed.), *La Syrie d'aujourd'hui* (1980); PIERRE BIROT and PIERRE GABERT, *La Méditerranée et la Moyen-Orient,* 2 vol., 2nd rev. ed. (1964); W.B. FISHER, *The Middle East,* 7th ed. (1978); PETER MANSFIELD, *The Middle East: A Political and Economic Survey,* 5th ed. (1980); JACQUES WEULERSSE, *Paysans de Syrie et du Proche-Orient* (1946); EUGEN WIRTH, *Syrien* (1971).

History: Cambridge Ancient History; JACQUES CAUVIN, *Les Premiers villages de Syrie-Palestine du IXème au VIIème millénaire avant J.C.* (1978); PAOLO MATTHIAE, *Ebla: An Empire Rediscovered* (1980, originally published in Italian, 1977); LORENZO VIGANÒ, "Literary Sources for the History of Palestine and Syria: The Ebla Tablets," *Biblical Archaeologist,* 47:6–16 (March 1984); J. PERROT, A. KEMPINSKI, and M. AVI-YOHAN, *Syrie-Palestine,* 2 vol. (1978–80); PHILIP K. HITTI, *History of Syria,* 2nd ed. (1957). G. DOWNEY, *A History of Antioch of Syria: From Seleucus to the Arab Conquest* (1961); M. ROSTOVTZEFF, *The Social and Economic History of the Hellenistic World,* 3 vol. (1941, reprinted 1972), and *The Social and Economic History of the Roman Empire,* 2nd ed. rev. by P.M. FRASER, 2 vol. (1957, reprinted 1979); J.H.W.G. LIEBESCHUETZ, *Antioch* (1972); JEAN-PAUL REY-COQUAIS, "Syrie romaine de Pompée à Dioclétien," *Journal of Roman Studies,* 68:44–73 (1978); HILDEGARD TEMPORINI (ed.), *Aufstieg und Niedergang der romischen Welt,* part 2, vol. 8, pp. 3–294 (1977); A.H.M. JONES, *Cities of the Eastern Roman Provinces,* ch. 10, 2nd ed. (1971); F.M. HEICHELHEIM, "Roman Syria," in TENNEY FRANK (ed.), *An Economic Survey of Ancient Rome,* vol. 4, pp. 121–257 (1938, reprinted 1975). ROBIN FEDDEN, *Syria and Lebanon,* 3rd ed. (1965); CLAUDE CAHEN, *La Syrie du Nord à l'époque des croisades et la principauté franque d'Antioche* (1940); C.F. VOLNEY, *Travels Through Syria and Egypt, in the Years 1783, 1784, and 1785* (1787, reprinted 1972; originally published in French, 1787); J.L. BURCKHARDT, *Travels in Syria and the Holy Land* (1822, reprinted 1983); KARL K. BARBIR, *Ottoman Rule in Damascus, 1708–1758* (1980); A.L. TIBAWI, *A Modern History of Syria, Including Lebanon and Palestine* (1969). ZEINE N. ZEINE, *The Struggle for Arab Independence,* 2nd ed. (1977); STEPHEN H. LONGRIGG, *Syria and Lebanon Under French Mandate* (1958, reissued 1972); GORDON H. TORREY, *Syrian Politics and the Military* (1964); ALBERT H. HOURANI, *Syria and Lebanon* (1946, reprinted 1968); NIKOLAOS VAN DAM, *The Struggle for Power in Syria,* rev. ed. (1981); JOHN F. DEVLIN, *Syria: Modern State in an Ancient Land* (1983).

(W.L.O.)

Taiwan

Taiwan is an island about 100 miles (161 kilometres) off the southeast coast of the China mainland. It is approximately 245 miles long (north–south) and 90 miles across at its widest point; its largest city, Taipei, is the seat of the government of the Republic of China (Nationalist China; Mandarin Chinese Wade–Giles romanization Chung-hua min-kuo). In addition to the main island, the Nationalist government has jurisdiction over 22 islands in the Taiwan group and 64 islands to the west in the Pescadores Archipelago, with a total area of some 13,900 square miles (36,000 square kilometres).

Taiwan is bounded to the north by the East China Sea, which separates it from the Ryukyu Islands, Okinawa, and Japan; to the east by the Pacific Ocean; to the south by the Bashi Channel, which separates it from the Philippines; and to the west by the Taiwan (Formosa) Strait, which separates it from the China mainland. The origin of its Chinese name T'ai-wan (conventionally Taiwan) is not known; it is also called Formosa—meaning "beautiful"—a name given it by Portuguese explorers.

From the mid-1660s to 1895 Taiwan was administered by the Imperial Chinese government, after which (until 1945) the island was ruled by the Japanese as a colony. In 1945 Taiwan reverted to China, and in 1949 it became the last territory controlled by the Nationalist government. The Nationalists have continued to claim jurisdiction over the China mainland, whereas the government of the People's Republic of China on the mainland claims jurisdiction over Taiwan; both governments are in agreement that the island is a province of China. Taipei—since 1949 designated by the Nationalists as the provisional capital of the Republic of China—was the provincial capital until 1967, when the capital was moved to Chung-hsing Hsin-ts'un.

This article is divided into the following sections:

Physical and human geography

THE LAND

Relief. Taiwan is part of the great island system rimming the western Pacific Ocean. The island is formed by a great fault block trending north-northeast to south-southwest and tilted toward the west. The more gently rising western face of the block borders the shallow Taiwan Strait, under which the continental shelf connects the island to the Chinese mainland. The terraced tablelands and alluvial plains along the western face of the block provide the principal areas of dense population and the major cities. The steeply sloping eastern face of the block marks the edge of the continental shelf and the beginning

TAIWAN

of the Pacific Ocean. Aside from one major rift valley, the east coast provides little room for human settlement.

The coastline on the west is simple and straight, bordered with low sand dunes and lagoons. Deepwater ports are situated at Chi-lung (Keelung), at the northern tip of the island, and at Kao-hsiung, on the southwestern coast.

The crest of the Chung-yang Shan-mo (Central Range) lies east of and parallels the island's axis. Scores of peaks rise to about 10,000 feet, the highest being Yü Shan (13,113 feet [3,997 metres]) in the south central part of the island. Around the mountainous area are numerous independent hills, with an average height of 5,000 feet.

Drainage and soils. The rivers, nearly all of which rise in the Chung-yang Shan-mo, are short and subject to extreme seasonal variations in flow. Lacking steady currents, most rivers are unreliable for irrigation or hydroelectric power generation. Late-summer typhoons, however, bring torrential rains that are liable to cause floods, especially in the plains, necessitating an extensive system of dikes. The principal rivers are the Tan-shui Ho in the northwest, the Cho-shui Hsi, in the west, and the Kao-p'ing Hsi in the south. Alluvial soil on the plains and in the valleys covers about one-fourth of the island and is its chief resource. The upland soils, subject to drastic erosion, are leached, acid, and infertile.

The rivers

Climate. Taiwan straddles the tropical and subtropical zones and has warm summers and mild winters. The climate is moderated by the warm waters of the Kuroshio (Japan Current). The summer is long, lasting from April until November (200 days or more). In cold months the mean monthly temperature is about 59° F (about 15° C). Beginning with April, the mean monthly temperature is above 68° F (20° C). The highest mean monthly temperature reaches 86° F (30° C) from June to September. Lowland Taiwan is frost free, while in winter the central mountains are covered with snow.

MAP INDEX

Political subdivisions

Province level
Fu-chien ....24 30 N 120 00 E
Kao-hsiung Municipality ....22 40 N 120 17 E
T'ai-pei Municipality ....25 03 N 121 32 E
T'ai-wan ....24 30 N 120 00 E

County level
Chang-hua .....24 00 N 120 30 E
Chi-lung Municipality ....25 08 N 121 45 E
Chia-i ....23 30 N 120 30 E
Chia-i Municipality ....23 29 N 120 27 E
Hsin-chu ....24 40 N 121 10 E
Hsin-chu Municipality ....24 48 N 120 59 E
Hua-lien ....23 45 N 121 25 E
I-lan ....24 30 N 121 35 E
Kao-hsiung .....23 00 N 120 35 E
Miao-li ....24 30 N 120 55 E
Nan-t'ou ....23 50 N 121 00 E
P'eng-hu ....23 30 N 119 30 E
P'ing-tung ......22 30 N 120 40 E
T'ai-chung ......24 15 N 120 55 E
T'ai-chung Municipality ....24 10 N 120 38 E
T'ai-nan ....23 15 N 120 20 E
T'ai-nan Municipality ....23 00 N 120 11 E
T'ai-pei ....24 50 N 121 35 E
T'ai-tung ....23 00 N 121 00 E
T'ao-yüan ......24 55 N 121 15 E
Yün-lin ....23 40 N 120 20 E

Cities and towns
Chang-hua .....24 05 N 120 32 E
Ch'ang-pin .....23 19 N 121 27 E
Ch'ao-chou .....22 33 N 120 32 E
Ch'e-ch'eng ....22 05 N 120 42 E
Chi-chi ....23 50 N 120 47 E
Chi-lung ....25 08 N 121 44 E
Chia-hsien .....23 05 N 120 35 E
Chia-i ....23 29 N 120 27 E
Ch'ih-shang .....23 07 N 121 12 E
Chin-men ......24 26 N 118 19 E
Chin-shan ......25 13 N 121 38 E
Chu-nan ....24 41 N 120 52 E
Chu-shan ......23 45 N 120 40 E
Chu-tung ....24 44 N 121 05 E
Chung-hsing Hsin-ts'un ....23 57 N 120 41 E
Chung-li ....24 57 N 121 13 E
Erh-lin ....23 54 N 120 22 E
Fang-liao ....22 22 N 120 35 E
Feng-lin ....23 45 N 121 26 E
Feng-shan ......22 38 N 120 21 E
Feng-yüan ......24 15 N 120 43 E
Heng-ch'un .....22 00 N 120 44 E
Hou-lung ....24 37 N 120 47 E
Hsi-hu ....23 58 N 120 28 E
Hsi-lo ....23 48 N 120 27 E
Hsin-ch'eng .....24 08 N 121 39 E
Hsin-chu ....24 48 N 120 58 E
Hsin-ying ....23 18 N 120 19 E
Hsüeh-chia .....23 14 N 120 10 E
Hua-lien ....23 59 N 121 36 E
Hu-hsi ....23 35 N 119 39 E
Hu-wei ....23 43 N 120 26 E
I-lan ....24 46 N 121 45 E
Jen-ai ....24 02 N 121 08 E
Jui-sui ....23 30 N 121 22 E
Kang-shan .....22 48 N 120 17 E
Kao-hsiung .....22 38 N 120 17 E
K'ou-hu ....23 35 N 120 11 E
Kuan-hsi ....24 48 N 121 10 E
Kuan-yin ....25 02 N 121 04 E
Kung-liao ......25 01 N 121 54 E
Lan-yü ....22 02 N 121 33 E
Lang-tao ....22 05 N 121 31 E
Lin-yüan ....22 30 N 120 23 E
Lo-tung ....24 41 N 121 46 E
Lu-kang ....24 03 N 120 25 E
Lü-tao ....22 40 N 121 28 E
Ma-kung ....23 34 N 119 34 E
Ma-tou ....23 11 N 120 14 E
Mai-liao ....23 45 N 120 15 E
Mei-nung ....22 54 N 120 32 E
Miao-li ....24 34 N 120 49 E
Nan-t'ou ....23 55 N 120 41 E
Pan-ch'iao ......25 01 N 121 27 E
Pei-kang ....23 34 N 120 18 E
Pei-nan ....22 47 N 121 07 E
P'ing-tung ......22 40 N 120 29 E
P'o-tzu ....23 28 N 120 14 E
Pu-tai ....23 23 N 120 09 E
San-ch'ung .....25 04 N 121 30 E
Sha-mei ....24 29 N 118 25 E
Shou-feng ......23 52 N 121 30 E
Su-ao ....24 36 N 121 51 E
Ta-chia ....24 21 N 120 37 E
Ta-chien ....24 15 N 121 09 E
Ta-hu ....24 26 N 120 52 E
Ta-wu ....22 22 N 120 54 E
T'ai-chung ......24 09 N 120 41 E
T'ai-ma ....22 37 N 121 00 E
T'ai-nan ....23 00 N 120 12 E
Taipei (T'ai-pei) ....25 03 N 121 30 E
T'ai-tung ....22 45 N 121 09 E
Tan-shui ....25 10 N 121 26 E
T'ao-yüan ......25 00 N 121 18 E
T'ou-ch'eng .....24 52 N 121 49 E
Tou-liu ....23 43 N 120 32 E
T'u-ch'ang ......24 35 N 121 29 E
Tung-ho ....22 58 N 121 18 E
T'ung-hsiao .....24 29 N 120 40 E
Tung-kang ......22 28 N 120 26 E
Tung-shih ......24 15 N 120 49 E
Wu-feng ....24 04 N 120 42 E
Wu-lai ....24 52 N 121 33 E
Yü-li ....23 20 N 121 18 E
Yüan-li ....24 27 N 120 39 E
Yüan-lin ....23 58 N 120 34 E
Yung-k'ang .....23 02 N 120 15 E

Physical features and points of interest
Ch'i-lai chu Shan, *mountain* ......24 05 N 121 19 E
Ch'i-mei Yü, *island* ....23 13 N 119 26 E
Chi-pei Tao, *island* ....23 45 N 119 37 E
Chin-men Tao, see Quemoy
Cho-shui, *river* ...23 50 N 120 15 E
Cho-shui, *river* ...24 43 N 121 50 E
Chung-yang Shan-mo, *mountain range* .23 30 N 121 00 E
Coral Reservoir, see Shan-hu T'an
East China Sea ..26 15 N 121 30 E
Formosa Strait, see Taiwan Strait
Hai-an Shan-mo, *mountain range* .23 25 N 121 25 E
Ho-p'ing, *river* ...24 19 N 121 46 E
Hsi-ch'uan Tao, *island* ....25 59 N 119 56 E
Hsiao-hung-t'ou Yü, *island* .....21 57 N 121 36 E
Hsiu-ku-luan, *river* ....23 28 N 121 30 E
Hsüeh Shan, *mountain* ......24 23 N 121 13 E
Hu-ching Yü, *island* ....23 29 N 119 31 E
Hua-lien, *river* ...23 57 N 121 36 E
Hua Yü, *island* ...23 24 N 119 19 E
Kao-p'ing, *river* ..22 28 N 120 25 E
K'en-ting National Park ...21 58 N 120 48 E
Kuei-shan Tao, *island* ....24 51 N 121 57 E
Lan Yü, *island* ...22 03 N 121 32 E
Liang Tao, *island* 26 20 N 120 13 E
Liu-ch'iu Yü, *island* ....22 21 N 120 22 E
Lü Tao, *island* ...22 40 N 121 29 E
Ma-tsu Tao, *island* ....26 09 N 119 56 E
Mien-hua Yü, *island* ....25 29 N 122 06 E
Nan-hu-ta Shan, *mountain* ......24 22 N 121 26 E
Nan Wan, *bay* ...21 55 N 120 47 E
O-luan Pi, *cape* ..21 54 N 120 51 E
Pa-chao Yü, *island* ....23 22 N 119 29 E
Pacific Ocean ...22 20 N 121 30 E
Pai-sha Tao, *island* ....23 40 N 119 35 E
Pei-kan-t'ang Tao, *island* ....26 13 N 119 59 E
Pei-nan, *river* ...22 46 N 121 10 E
Pei-ta-wu Shan, *mountain* ......22 38 N 120 45 E
P'eng-chia Yü, *island* ....25 38 N 122 04 E
P'eng-hu Ch'ün-tao, see Pescadores
P'eng-hu Shui-tao, see Pescadores Channel
P'eng-hu Tao, *island* ....23 34 N 119 37 E
Penghu, see Pescadores
Pescadores (P'eng-hu Ch'ün-tao), *islands* ....23 30 N 119 30 E
Pescadores Channel (P'eng-hu Shui-tao) ......23 30 N 119 50 E
Philippine Sea ...23 00 N 121 50 E
Quemoy (Chin-men Tao), *island* ....24 27 N 118 23 E
San-tiao Chiao, *cape* ....25 01 N 122 00 E
Shan-hu T'an, *reservoir* ......23 12 N 120 23 E
South China Sea .23 30 N 118 30 E
Ta-an, *river* .....24 24 N 120 36 E
Ta-chia, *river* ....24 20 N 120 33 E
Ta-t'un Shan, *mountain* ......25 11 N 121 31 E
T'ai-lu-ko National Park ...24 10 N 121 25 E
T'ai-lu-ko Hsia, *gorge* ....24 10 N 121 33 E
Taiwan Strait (T'ai-wan Hai-hsia) ......24 00 N 119 00 E
Tan-shui, *river* ...25 11 N 121 25 E
Taroko Gorge, see T'ai-lu-ko Hsia
T'ou-ch'ien, *river* .24 51 N 120 56 E
Tseng-wen, *river* .23 03 N 120 03 E
Tung-chi Yü, *island* ....23 15 N 119 40 E
Tung-ch'üan Tao, *island* ....25 58 N 119 58 E
Tung-ting Tao, *island* ....24 10 N 118 14 E
Tung-yin Tao, *island* ....26 22 N 120 30 E
Wu-ch'iu Yu, *island* ....25 00 N 119 27 E
Yang-ming-shan National Park ...25 09 N 121 33 E
Yü Shan, *mountain* ......23 28 N 120 57 E
Yü-shan National Park ....23 20 N 121 03 E
Yü-weng Tao, *island* ....23 36 N 119 30 E

Mean annual precipitation is 102 inches (2,580 millimetres), although in some years the precipitation in summer alone may exceed 200 inches in some parts of the islands. The upland area receives more rain than the lowlands, and the east receives more than the west. In addition, rainfall is heavier in the north, where winters are drizzly, than in the south, where winters are sunny. Most typhoons and, therefore, most precipitation is concentrated in the months of July, August, and September.

Plant and animal life. There are green plants on the plains all the year round, and more than half of Taiwan is covered by forests. As the climate varies with elevation, so does the natural vegetation. Stands of mixed bamboo, palm, and tropical evergreen grow in the lowlands; subtropical evergreen forests, including camphor laurel, are found from 2,000 to 6,000 feet; broad-leaved evergreen forests of the temperate zone are represented by cedars, cypress, junipers, rhododendrons, maples, and cryptomeria (Japanese cedar) from 6,000 to 8,000 feet; and coniferous forests are found above 7,500 feet.

Animal life, similar to that of the southern Chinese mainland, includes deer, wild boars, bears, monkeys, goats, wildcats, and panthers. Birds include pheasant, geese, flycatchers, kingfishers, larks, and many other species. Fish abound in the coastal areas.

Settlement patterns. The population density of Taiwan has always been highest on the western coastal plains and basins and lowest in the central and eastern mountains. Chinese settlement of Taiwan historically proceeded from south to north along the western coast. Before the introduction of modern transportation, the most convenient access to the interior was along river valleys, and it was up these that the immigrant population expanded.

Urbanization has been the dominant settlement pattern of the 20th century. There has been a noticeable migration from rural areas to towns, especially since mid-century, when the urban population increased from less than half to more than three-fourths of the total population. Three major urban areas have developed: Taipei and its port of Chi-lung in the north and the two port cities of Kao-hsiun in the south and T'ai-chung in the west.

THE PEOPLE

Ethnolinguistic groups. The original inhabitants of Taiwan were Malayo-Polynesian aborigines, who are now organized into quite diverse ethnolinguistic groups. The

T'ai-lu-ko Hsia (Taroko Gorge), a popular tourist spot at the eastern end of the East-West Cross-Island Highway, near the city of Hua-lien, Hua-lien county.

largest of these groups are the Ami, Atayal, and Paiwan. Chinese immigrants largely displaced or assimilated the plains aborigines and carried on a protracted conflict with the mountain aborigines, who were subdued only by the Japanese. The aborigines, nearly all of whom now live in the foothills and highlands, constitute about 2 percent of the population. Although several aboriginal dialects and many tribal customs have been retained, the aborigines have increasingly become assimilated, linguistically and culturally, into modern Taiwanese society.

The great majority of the population—those now called Taiwanese—are descendants of the original immigrants from the Chinese provinces of Fukien and Kwangtung. The Hokkien from southern Fukien constitute the largest of the immigrant groups; their dialect of Chinese is often called the Taiwanese dialect. The Hakka, originally from northern Kwangtung, also have a distinct dialect.

The most recent addition to Taiwan's population are the predominantly Mandarin-speaking Nationalist adherents, who came to Taiwan from all parts of China in the late 1940s. These "mainlanders" still compose about 15 percent of the population. Because of their prominence in the Nationalist government, Mandarin has become the principal language of Taiwan.

Religions. Numerous religions have been introduced into Taiwan from many parts of the world. The Chinese brought their religions, principally Buddhism and Taoism. In 1622 the Dutch introduced Protestant Christianity; two years later the Spanish brought Roman Catholicism to the island. In addition, Confucianism has immensely influenced the Chinese people of Taiwan in ethics, morality, and academic thinking. Religion, however, is not a divisive factor on Taiwan. The Chinese tend to be eclectic about religion, many practicing a little of several kinds.

The principal religions in Taiwan, in addition to the forms of worship of the aborigines, are Taoism and Buddhism. Christians constitute a small but significant percentage of the population; about three-fifths are Protestant and the rest Roman Catholic. There are also a large number of Muslims, most of whom live in the larger cities.

Demography. The population of Taiwan tripled in the first half of the 20th century. From mid-century, however, the rate of growth steadily declined from about 4 percent to less than 2 percent per year. Modern health measures had lowered the death rate, and Nationalist land reform temporarily raised the birthrate by expanding rural opportunities. In response to growing urban opportunities, however, families soon began concentrating more resources on fewer children. In addition, the government actively promoted family planning and birth control.

Family structure. The family has long been the most important organizing unit in traditional Taiwanese society. Based on the Confucian precepts of filial piety and ancestor worship, the patrilineal extended family performs many of the savings, investment, and production functions of Western corporations and provides many of the social services assumed by Western governments. The family owns property, pools its resources, and diversifies the occupations of its members, thus maximizing the returns and spreading the risks across the multiple branches and generations.

THE ECONOMY

During the 20th century Taiwan's economy has been transformed from agricultural to industrial, and the island's postwar economic development has been one of the most spectacular of any developing country. In constant prices, gross national product increased more than 10 times between the mid-1950s and mid-1980s. The major reason was vigorous export promotion in an expanding global economy. Per capita product and personal income quintupled, while a relatively equal distribution of income became more equitable. The major reasons were the initially broad distribution of ownership of land and capital and the high returns to labour, first in agriculture and later in the export industries. The obligation to increase and repay family resources has motivated the individual Chinese and has produced much of the rapid growth of Taiwan's economy. This growth has proceeded in three phases. The first (*c.* 1905–55) was the modernization of agriculture and the development of other primary or extractive industries. The second (*c.* 1935–85) was the development of modern secondary manufacturing industries. The third (since 1965) began the modernization of service industries.

Resources. Although more than 50 kinds of minerals have been found in Taiwan, total mineral resources are modest. In the north, copper, gold, iron, sulfur, and pyrite exist in only token amounts. In the east, limestone, marble, and dolomite are abundant, although their exploitation contributes little to the economy. Coal reserves are rapidly becoming exhausted. Petroleum and natural gas exist in small quantities on shore, but the continental shelf may contain extensive reserves, particularly of natural gas. Forests are most abundant in the high mountains, but their inaccessability makes exploitation uneconomical.

Agriculture. Until the mid-20th century Taiwan's best assets were its fertile soils, tropical climate, and large agricultural labour force. Agriculture provided the logical starting point for economic development after World War II. Since about 1970, however, rising agricultural costs have made agricultural exports uncompetitive, and Taiwan has had to rely increasingly on food imports.

One-quarter of Taiwan's total area is arable, and all available land is fully cultivated, including sloping areas, dry riverbeds, and reclaimed tidal lands. The single most important crop is rice, with which more than one-half of the total cultivated area and most of the irrigated portion is planted. More than two-thirds of the paddy fields are double-cropped. The Japanese introduced improved strains of rice, chemical fertilizers, and modern irrigation methods, and the Nationalists continued to modernize rice production. Rice yields per acre have therefore increased dramatically, although this has created an oversupply.

Rice cultivation

Sugarcane, tea, and fresh bananas, once principal exports, are still important domestically. Other fruits, such as pineapples, litchis, longans, oranges, grapes, and strawberries, abound. Most vegetables—including mushrooms and asparagus, which are canned for export—are produced in the central and southern regions.

Forestry and fisheries. With many mountains, Taiwan has abundant timber. Inaccessibility, low quality, and high costs limit production, however, and have made it necessary to import lumber. In addition, overcutting and inadequate reforestation measures have caused erosion and destructive floods.

With the exception of eels and snails, which are high-value exports, fishery production is mostly for domestic consumption. The warm currents off the east coast provide good deep-sea fishing grounds, especially for tuna.

Mining and quarrying. Petroleum has replaced coal as the major energy source. Domestic natural gas also is produced. The quarrying of marble and dolomite is increasing as rail connections are improved. Salt is produced by solar evaporation along the southwestern coast.

Energy. Taiwan's reserves of coal are small, scattered, and of poor quality. Heavy rainfall and high mountains hold great hydroelectric potential, but most economical sites have been exploited, and hydropower provides a declining proportion of the energy supply. In the 1960s and '70s the principal growth in energy sources came from thermal electric power generation using imported petroleum. Rising oil costs and national defense needs, however, accelerated the development of nuclear electric power. By the 1980s three nuclear plants accounted for one-third of Taiwan's installed capacity and about one-half of actual generation.

Industry. In the 1950s and '60s Taiwan's comparative trade advantage lay in its abundant cheap labour supply. Consequently, labour-intensive light industry predominated, producing such nondurable consumer goods as foodstuffs and textiles, at first largely for domestic consumption but after 1960 increasingly for export. By the 1960s and '70s investment had shifted to more capital-intensive heavy industries turning out consumer durables (appliances, vehicles), producer nondurables (steel, petrochemicals), and producer durables (machinery, ships). Some capital-intensive industries, particularly those run by state firms, have proved unprofitable, but the government maintains them to supply the private sector and to bolster national defense. In the 1970s labour became scarce and wages increased, making Taiwan's labour-intensive exports less competitive. Consequently, both government and private business have accelerated efforts to develop skill-intensive high-technology industries such as those producing specialty chemicals, pharmaceuticals, precision instruments, sophisticated electronics, and information processing systems.

Growth of high technology industries

Trade. Because of Taiwan's limited resources and intermediate technology, its manufactures depend heavily on imported materials, equipment, and technology (particularly from Japan and the United States). Moreover, because of its limited domestic market, Taiwan's manufactures also depend heavily on exports (particularly to the United States). Taiwan therefore balances a chronic trade deficit with Japan against a chronic trade surplus with the United States. In the 1980s Taiwan attempted to diversify its trade with Europe and the Third World.

By the late 20th century manufactured goods accounted for more than 95 percent of all exports, led by electronic products and appliances, articles of clothing, footwear, textile yarns and fabrics, toys and sporting goods, and metal products. Imports were highly diversified, consisting of a variety of consumer goods and raw materials, including petroleum and petroleum products, electronic products, nonelectrical machinery, and chemicals and related products.

Services. Since the mid-1970s there has been an accelerating shift from traditional personal services (small shops and restaurants) to modern personal services (department stores and hotels) and modern commercial services (finance and communications). Commerce and services became internationalized as Taiwan handled a larger proportion of its own trade, imported foreign services such as fast food, and exported services such as construction management and computer programming. Nevertheless, most private businesses remained family firms, most of them small. The cultural importance of the family has made Taiwan's economy lean and flexible, but it also has inhibited an increase in the scale and modernization of accounting, finance, advertising, and trade.

Importance of family

Management of the economy. Government continues to provide about half of the nation's services. Government planners were largely responsible for initiating import-substituting industrial development in the 1950s and for redirecting industrial development toward export promotion in the 1960s.

Economic development has since acquired much momentum of its own. The government continues, however, to run key industries (electricity, steel, petroleum), construct basic infrastructure (railways, highways, waterways), oversee the financial system (both government and private banks), and initiate the development of new sectors by facilitating the transfer of technology and by disseminating market information.

Taxes in Taiwan include income, legacy, commodity, stamp, stock, farm, land, increment on land value, and business taxes. They are levied according to a progressive rate; people with small incomes pay little tax.

The Chinese Federation of Labour (CFL) is a nationwide organization of industrial and craft unions. Other national labour organizations include those for seamen, railway workers, and postal workers. There are local unions in all factories, transportation and public utility units, and occupational and vocational groups.

Transportation. The primary internal transport links are the well-developed highway and railway networks, although domestic air travel is also important. The principal roads consist of a highway running around the perimeter of the island; three east–west highways crossing the island in the northern, middle, and southern regions; and a north–south expressway connecting the major west coast cities. Passenger-bus transportation is provided between large cities and small towns throughout the island. Few people own cars, but many have motorcycles. The railway system of Taiwan consists of a trunk line that roughly parallels the north–south expressway and a smaller line along the east side of the island that extends to the southeastern port of T'ai-tung; the construction of a line in the south will complete the encirclement of the island. The major domestic air routes are between Taipei and the larger cities.

Road networks

External transport links are by sea and air. The international seaports are Chi-lung, Kao-hsiung, T'ai-chung, Su-ao, and Hua-lien. Chi-lung, Kao-hsiung, and T'ai-chung have good facilities for anchoring large ships; Hua-lien has facilities that are somewhat more limited. The Chiang Kai-shek Airport at T'ao-yüan is the facility for international air travel in northern Taiwan. The southern part of the island is served by the international airport at Kao-hsiung.

ADMINISTRATION AND SOCIAL CONDITIONS

Government. For centuries Taiwan has been ruled by outsiders—Imperial Chinese bureaucrats, colonial Japanese administrators, and now Nationalist mainlander refugees. The Nationalist government's claim to rule Taiwan is predicated on its claim to rule all of China, and the institutions governing Taiwan are those designed to govern all of China. Taiwan's status as a nation, however, has become ambiguous since the Communist regime on the mainland achieved general international recognition as the legitimate government of China.

Constitutional structure. The constitution of the Republic of China (adopted in 1947 but effective only in Taiwan since 1949) combines the cabinet and presidential systems of government. The president is the supreme leader of the government and is elected to terms of six years by the National Assembly; the assembly's other major function is to amend the constitution when necessary. The constitution states that assembly members are to be popularly elected to six-year terms. In reality, however, most of the members are aging mainlanders who were elected in 1947 to represent mainland constituencies and have maintained their seats since then. A small but increasing minority of Taiwanese are elected periodically.

The central government also includes five constitutionally mandated councils (*yüans*): legislative, executive, judicial, examination, and control. The legislative *yüan,* the membership structure of which parallels that of the National Assembly, enacts legislation. The executive *yüan,* the Cabinet, is headed by a premier, who is appointed by the president but is nominally answerable to the legislative *yüan.* The judicial *yüan* oversees the court system. The examination *yüan* fulfills the functions of a civil service commission, while the control *yüan* oversees government administration.

The constitution also provides for provincial and local administrative institutions. The island of Taiwan and the cities of Taipei and Kao-hsiung have provincial status. At the local level there are 16 counties (*hsien*) and five municipalities (*shih:* Chi-lung, T'ai-chung, Hsin-chu, Chia-i, and T'ai-nan). According to the constitution, these smaller political units are self-governing, but in reality they have little autonomy from the national government.

Power structure. Since much of Taiwan's central government apparatus is structured as a national government, much of it has become vestigial: legislators from mainland constituencies have no one to represent and are not replaced when they die; governments for mainland provinces are reduced to skeleton size; and many of the functions of government are performed by agencies other than those mandated by the constitution. Political power in Taiwan reflects this situation.

Partisan politics is dominated by the Nationalist Party (Kuomintang; KMT), which was founded in 1894 and has been the ruling party since the establishment of the Republic of China. The KMT apparatus includes the party itself and the electoral, media, and cultural institutions that it supervises. The party provides the ideological rationale for the system as a whole and the arena through which aspiring politicians can legitimize themselves. The chairmanship of the party—the most powerful position in Taiwan—is traditionally held by the president. Only token formal opposition is provided by the Young China Party and the Democratic Socialist Party, although an informal opposition has had some electoral success.

The military and security forces also have considerable power. Manpower mobilization is one of the highest in the world, and military expenditures have long constituted about half of the government's budget. The armed forces include the air force, army, navy, combined service force, military police, and garrison force. Security forces include several agencies coordinated by the National Security Bureau.

Education. Both the Chinese government and the Chinese family have long believed in investing heavily in education, in the postwar period increasingly for girls as well as for boys. In the past, educational opportunities usually were open only to the elite; but in their effort to train loyal citizens and literate workers, the Japanese began to extend primary education to the mass of ordinary Taiwanese. Taiwan now has one of the best educated populations in Asia, second only to that of Japan. The preferred educational route is through liberal arts, looking to a career in government, or through professional training at a prestigious university. As postwar economic development gathered momentum, however, both government and families have also recognized the value of commercial and technical education.

Education is compulsory for 12 years (six years of primary school, three years of middle school, and three years of secondary school); secondary education includes senior high schools and vocational schools. There is also preschool education (kindergarten) and social education, including adult education and special education. There are more than 100 institutions of higher education, more than two-thirds of them private. Among the major public ones are the National Taiwan University (founded 1928) at Taipei, National Chung-hsing University (1961) at T'ai-chung, and National Chung-shan University (also called National Sun Yat-sen University; 1980) at Kao-hsiung.

Health and welfare. Modern health practices were instituted early in the 20th century by the Japanese and were further developed by the Nationalist government. The Japanese eliminated tropical diseases—which until then had been a principal barrier to development in Taiwan—by installing water- and sewage-treatment plants and by training and equipping medical personnel. Taiwan now has a well-developed hospital system and medical profession. Life expectancy and infant-mortality rates are about the same as in most Western countries.

The overall growth in economic prosperity and the Chinese custom of families caring for their elderly and unemployed members generally have kept government welfare expenditures low; but because the birthrate is decreasing at the same time that the number of elderly is increasing, there has been growing concern about the ability of the Chinese family to provide social security in the future. The government has thus been instituting social insurance programs that cover an increasing percentage of the population.

The rapid growth of Taiwan's large urban centres has resulted in housing shortages, which generally have been met by private developers. The government has built some apartments that have then been sold to the public by means of long-term, low-interest loans. In addition, the government has provided free housing for the poor.

CULTURAL LIFE

The people of Taiwan enjoy a rich heritage of traditional Chinese culture and a lively fusion of modern Chinese and Western cultures. The government attempts to preserve and revitalize such traditional arts as painting, calligraphy, ceramics, and music by sponsoring concerts, classes, and competitions. The National Palace Museum in Taipei houses an immense collection of ancient Chinese paintings and books, pottery, porcelain, curios, and sculptures. Elements of traditional popular culture include Chinese opera, Taiwanese opera and puppet theatre, and Chinese and aboriginal folk dances. All major mainland regional cuisines are represented, particularly in Taipei.

In the 1970s and '80s the government gave increasing attention to cultural development, establishing art museums and performance centres in the major cities and libraries and cultural centres in an increasing number of localities. Exhibitions and performances by foreign painters, photographers, musicians, and dancers are frequent. Foreign-trained artists have brought a contemporary touch to their work, while international trends in clothing and life-styles quickly reach Taiwan, which makes many fashionable Western-style consumer goods for export. Domestic television has long carried many foreign programs, and liberalization of import restrictions in the 1980s brought on an invasion of foreign fast food, cosmetics, and other items. Both traditional Chinese exercises and modern Western sports such as baseball are popular. In addition, several national parks have been created in wilderness areas.

The media

There are about 30 daily newspapers and 1,500 periodicals, most of the latter house organs of various organizations. The government sets general guidelines for the political and cultural content of newspapers and periodicals and has powers of confiscation and suspension. There are about 30 radio broadcasting companies with more than 160 stations; one of the three television stations also features educational programs.

For statistical data on the land and people of Taiwan, see the *Britannica World Data* section in the BRITANNICA WORLD DATA ANNUAL. (Y.-c.K./E.A.W.)

History

Taiwan was known to the Chinese as early as the beginning of the 7th century AD, but settlement did not take place until the first quarter of the 17th century after recurrent famines in Fukien Province encouraged the emigration of Fukienese from the Chinese mainland. Before then, the island was a base of operations for Chinese and Japanese pirates. The Portuguese, who first visited the island in 1590 and named it Ilha Formosa ("Beautiful Island"), made several unsuccessful attempts at settlement. The Dutch and Spaniards established more lasting settlements, the Dutch at An-p'ing in southwestern Taiwan (1624), the Spaniards in 1626 at Chi-lung in the north. Until 1646, when the Dutch seized the Spanish settlements, northern Taiwan was under Spanish domination, the south under Dutch control. The Dutch were expelled in 1661 by Cheng Ch'eng-kung, a man of mixed Chinese-Japanese parentage and supporter of the defeated Ming emperors, who

Spanish and Dutch settlements

used the island as a centre of opposition to the Ch'ing (Manchu) regime.

IMPERIAL CHINESE RULE

In 1683, 20 years after Cheng Ch'eng-kung's death, the island fell to the Ch'ing and became part of Fukien Province. Meanwhile, sizable migrations of refugees, Ming supporters, had increased the population to about 200,000. As migrants streamed in from southeastern China, large areas in the north were settled. T'ai-nan (then called T'ai-wan) was the capital. By 1842 the population had risen to an estimated 2,500,000, and both rice and sugar had become important exports to mainland China. In 1858 the Treaty of T'ien-ching (Tientsin) designated two Taiwan ports as treaty ports, T'ai-nan and Tan-shui, the latter a river port, long used as a port of call under the Spanish and Dutch, and downstream from the growing city of Taipei. Tea became an important export crop, and the island's trade centre shifted to the north, particularly to Tan-shui where British and other trading companies established their headquarters.

Japan's continued interest in the island was reflected in a Japanese punitive expedition of 1874 ostensibly to protect the lives of Ryukyu fishermen along the island's coasts. The French blockaded the island during the undeclared Sino-French war of 1884–85 and occupied Chi-lung for a short period. In 1886 Taiwan became a separate province of China with a legal capital at T'ai-chung and a temporary capital at Taipei, which became the legal capital in 1894.

JAPANESE RULE

In 1895, as a result of the Treaty of Shimonoseki after the Sino-Japanese War, China ceded Taiwan and the Pescadores Islands to Japan, and the Japanese occupied Taipei in June of that year over the violent opposition of the Taiwanese population. For several months a Republic of Taiwan was in existence, but it was overcome by Japanese forces. The Japanese also faced the hostility of the aborigines, some of whom remained uncontrolled until the outbreak of the Pacific war. Taiwan was developed as a supplier of rice and sugar for Japan. Irrigation projects, agricultural extension services, and improvements in transportation and power supplies led to rapid increases in Taiwan's gross product. Japanese policy was oriented toward the Japanization of the Taiwanese; Japanese was the language of instruction in a widespread basic educational system, and even after the end of World War II Japanese remained a lingua franca among the various Chinese dialect groups. In the 1930s Japanese economic policy shifted toward the development of industries based on relatively cheap hydroelectric power. Nevertheless, rice and sugar remained the basis of Taiwan's prewar export trade, almost all of which was directed toward Japan. Imports consisted largely of diverse manufactures from Japan. During World War II, Taiwan was a major staging area for Japan's invasion of Southeast Asia.

THE REPUBLIC OF CHINA

Taiwan's history after World War II falls roughly into two periods: one from 1945 to about 1970, when the Nationalist government's position had considerable international support, especially from the United States; and one since 1970, when the major focus of international diplomatic attention shifted to the People's Republic of China.

1945 to c. 1970. As a result of the Cairo agreement of 1943, Taiwan was turned over to the Chinese Nationalist government on Oct. 25, 1945, after the defeat of Japan. Many Taiwanese welcomed liberation from Japanese control; but much to their chagrin, the Nationalists' objectives toward Taiwan were to essentially maintain Japanese colonial institutions—substituting mainlanders for Japanese—and to exploit the island for rebuilding the war-torn mainland. When in early 1947 the Taiwanese urban middle class protested, the mainlanders massacred thousands of them. Thirty years would pass before a new generation of Taiwanese political leaders emerged and mass Taiwanese resentment subsided. (N.S.G./E.A.W.)

In 1949–50, following the victories of the Chinese Communists on the mainland, a stream of Nationalist troops, government officials, and other refugees poured onto the island. Final defeat for Chiang Kai-shek's Nationalists seemed only a matter of time. Little outside assistance was forthcoming; and the United States, among others, appeared determined to allow the civil war to run its course toward the eventual destruction of the KMT and the incorporation of Taiwan into the People's Republic. The People's Liberation Army, however, placed priority on mopping up holdout Nationalist units on the mainland and on subduing Tibet. And because Peking lacked substantial capability to land its forces on Taiwan or even on such lesser remaining Nationalist-held islands as Quemoy and Matsu close by the mainland, there was no immediate prospect of Chiang's final defeat. He survived until the outbreak of the Korean War provided a decisive respite.

U.S. intervention in Korea

When North Korean troops invaded South Korea in June 1950, U.S. Pres. Harry S. Truman, assuming Peking's complicity in the action from the outset, interposed the U.S. 7th Fleet between Taiwan and the mainland; during the conflict the United States increased its economic and military aid to Taipei. In the first of several major crises over Quemoy and Matsu, following the Korean War, the United States incorporated the Republic of China into its Pacific defense system. A mutual defense treaty signed in December 1954 pledged the United States to the defense of Taiwan and the neighbouring Pescadores Islands.

After the Bandung Conference (April 1955) there was substantial hope that Peking might limit its tactics to the "peaceful liberation" of Taiwan. During the initial stages of the post-Bandung talks (begun August 1955) between the United States and China, it seemed that this hope might be formalized in a treaty mutually renouncing the use or threats of force in the Taiwan area. These talks broke down, however, and by 1958 Peking had adopted a more militant approach concerning Taiwan. In August 1958 Peking resumed an artillery bombardment of Quemoy and issued an ultimatum demanding the surrender of the island's Nationalist garrison, an ultimatum broken by the interposition of U.S. naval power and the behind-the-scenes withdrawal of Soviet support.

The extent of U.S. support for Taiwan proved an important factor in the consolidation and rejuvenation of the KMT and its governmental organs. There was a dramatic increase in industrial and commercial construction on Taiwan and a significant improvement in communications and educational facilities. The KMT began incorporating members who were younger, better educated, more widely traveled, and much less likely to have been selected because of political connections alone.

In its first two decades on Taiwan, the KMT began to lose some of its original militancy. Memories of defeat provided the basis for much Nationalist solidarity during the 1950s and early '60s, and most officials, at least publicly, believed that their presence on the island would be temporary. As younger mainlanders and Taiwanese rose to positions of authority, however, and as the pain of defeat faded, Taiwan itself became more the focus of attention.

Yet, the strongest voices associated with Chiang and his son and political heir, Chiang Ching-kuo, continued to insist on the inevitability of reconquest of the mainland. The approved scenario held that this reconquest would originate in an uprising in China, which would be followed by popular demand for a Nationalist return. The certainty of this view waned over the years; but in the mid-1960s the intensification of the Vietnam War and the upheaval on the mainland during the Cultural Revolution revived the hopes of many in the KMT. Thus, economic modernization, despite its success, was never considered as Taipei's main goal. Modernization would provide the necessary basis, it was argued, to build up the power and international prestige of the republic and to assure support from its allies—all required for the eventual counterattack.

U.S. support

The key to external support was the United States, the policy of which was indicated by its position toward the seating question at the United Nations. Until 1970 the United States was able to postpone consideration of resolutions to replace Taipei's representatives with those of Peking. U.S. firmness at the United Nations and other evidence of U.S. fidelity—as well as the reluctance of many independent countries in Africa and Asia to recognize Peking—made Chiang's government confident that its international position was reasonably secure.

During the 1960s this spirit of confidence and lessening of tension was reinforced by an increased American demand for Taiwanese goods, which transformed Taiwan from an aid client of the United States to a trading partner. The economic boom also aided the KMT: the growing Taiwanese interest in collective political demands—including a secret separatist movement that was actively suppressed by the KMT—was transformed into a pursuit of individual economic advancement. Chiang Kai-shek began to turn over the supervision of domestic affairs to his son. The younger Chiang became deputy premier in 1969 and premier in 1972; after his father's death in April 1975 he assumed the chairmanship of the KMT, and from 1978 until his death in 1988 he was president of Taiwan.

Taiwan since 1970. Between 1969 and 1971, U.S. restrictions on trade and travel by Americans to China were eased, and the United States began to explore alternatives to opposing Peking's representation in the United Nations. Meanwhile, a number of countries severed diplomatic relations with Taipei, and in 1971 Taiwan was ousted from the United Nations and the People's Republic seated. U.S. Pres. Richard M. Nixon visited Peking in 1972, and the following year the United States established quasi-diplomatic relations with the People's Republic.

Nixon's visit to Peking

For Taipei, the new U.S.–China diplomacy came as a devastating setback. Nationalist officials began to prepare the island for greater international isolation, but stalemate in relations between China and the United States during the mid-1970s provided a temporary reprieve for the island. That reprieve appeared to be over on Jan. 1, 1979, with U.S. establishment of formal diplomatic relations with the People's Republic of China. In the normalization agreement the United States accepted an end to all official U.S. defense ties with Taiwan and acknowledged the position that there is but one China and that Taiwan is part of China. It thus precluded itself from any future support for an independent Taiwan.

Subsequently, however, the U.S. Congress passed the Taiwan Relations Act, authorizing continued social and economic ties with Taiwan. The United States also unilaterally stated that it would continue to sell defensive arms to Taiwan, a move that complicated U.S.–China talks concerning greater defense cooperation.

Peking added to these complexities in 1979 by adopting a more conciliatory attitude on the island's reunification with China. The Nationalist government, however, has officially refused all offers of contact, trade, or negotiation with the People's Republic, fearing that such transactions would imply acceptance of Communist claims to sovereignty over the island of Taiwan and the rest of China. Unofficially, the Nationalist government allowed increasing indirect visits, trade, and negotiations during the 1980s with the People's Republic, mostly through Hong Kong.

Domestically, the transition in the 1970s from Chiang Kai-shek to Chiang Ching-kuo as president was accompanied by a gradual shift from a more autocratic to a more populist style of authoritarianism. Chiang Ching-kuo's political associates recruited more Taiwanese into higher positions in the KMT and the military, and the President himself made frequent visits to all parts of Taiwan. Gradually an informal political opposition was allowed to emerge. A further indication of the more relaxed political atmosphere was the lifting in 1987 of martial law, which had been in place since 1949. (J.W.Le./E.A.W.)

For coverage of related topics in the *Macropædia* and *Micropædia,* see the *Propædia,* sections 96/10 and 975.

For later developments in the history of Taiwan, see the *Britannica Book of the Year* section in the BRITANNICA WORLD DATA ANNUAL.

BIBLIOGRAPHY. The best general official reference is *Republic of China: A Reference Book,* ed. by HAROLD CHANG (*et al.*), sponsored by Taiwan's Government Information Office. The most comprehensive descriptive geography remains CHENG-SIANG CHEN, *Tai-wan ti chih: A Geography of Taiwan,* 3 vol. (1959–61), in Chinese. An informative overview of postwar economic development is WALTER GALENSON (ed.), *Economic Growth and Structural Change in Taiwan* (1979); and of postwar political history, RALPH N. CLOUGH, *Island China* (1978). On social and cultural background, see EMILY MARTIN AHERN and HILL GATES (eds.), *The Anthropology of Taiwanese Society* (1981). General political history of the Japanese period is found in GEORGE KERR, *Formosa: Licensed Revolution and the Home Rule Movement, 1895–1945* (1974). The most useful study of socioeconomic change in the Japanese period remains GEORGE BARCLAY, *Colonial Development and Population in Taiwan* (1954, reissued 1972). *Free China Journal* (weekly) and *Free China Review* (monthly) provide coverage of current political and cultural events.

(E.A.W.)

Taoism

Taoism, along with Confucianism, is one of the two major indigenous religio-philosophical traditions that have shaped Chinese life for more than 2,000 years.

In the broadest sense, a Taoist attitude toward life can be seen in the accepting and yielding, the joyful and carefree sides of the Chinese character, an attitude that offsets and complements the moral and duty-conscious, austere and purposeful character ascribed to Confucianism. Taoism is also characterized by a positive, active attitude toward the occult and the metaphysical (theories on the nature of reality), whereas the agnostic, pragmatic Confucian tradition considers these issues of only marginal importance, although the reality of such issues is, by most Confucians, not denied.

More strictly defined, Taoism includes: the ideas and attitudes peculiar to the *Lao-tzu* (or *Tao-te Ching;* "Classic of the Way of Power"), the *Chuang-tzu,* the *Lieh-tzu,* and related writings; the Taoist religion, which is concerned with the ritual worship of the Tao; and those who identify themselves as Taoists.

Taoist thought permeates Chinese culture, including many aspects not usually considered Taoist. In Chinese religion, the Taoist tradition—often serving as a link between the Confucian tradition and folk tradition—has generally been more popular and spontaneous than the official (Confucian) state cult and less diffuse and shapeless than folk religion.

Taoist philosophy and religion have found their way into all Asian cultures influenced by China, especially those of Vietnam, Japan, and Korea. Various religious practices reminiscent of Taoism in such areas of Chinese cultural influence indicate early contacts with Chinese travellers and immigrants that have yet to be elucidated.

Both Western Sinologists and Chinese scholars themselves have distinguished—since Han times (206 BC–AD 220)—between a Taoist philosophy of the great mystics and their commentators (Tao-chia) and a later Taoist religion (*Tao-chiao*). This theory—no longer considered valid—was based on the view that the "ancient Taoism" of the mystics antedated the "later Neo-Taoist superstitions" that were misinterpretations of the mystics' metaphorical images. The mystics, however, should be viewed against the background of the religious practices existing in their own times. Their ecstasies, for example, were closely related to the trances and spirit journeys of the early magicians and shamans (religious personages with healing and psychic transformation powers). Not only are the authors of the *Tao-te Ching,* the *Chuang-tzu* (book of "Master Chuang"), and the *Lieh-tzu* (book of "Master Lieh") not the actual and central founders of an earlier "pure" Taoism later degraded into superstitious practices but they can even be considered somewhat on the margin of older Taoist traditions. Therefore, because there has been a nearly continuous mutual influence between Taoists of different social classes—philosophers, ascetics, alchemists, and the priests of popular cults—the distinction between philosophical and religious Taoism in this article is made simply for the sake of descriptive convenience.

There is also a tendency among scholars today to draw a less rigid line between what is called Taoist and what is called Confucian. The two traditions share many of the same ideas about man, society, the ruler, Heaven, and the universe—ideas that were not created by either school but that stem from a tradition prior to either Confucius or Lao-tzu.

Viewed from this common tradition, orthodox Confucianism limited its field of interest to the creation of a moral and political system that fashioned society and the Chinese empire; whereas Taoism, inside the same world view, represented more personal and metaphysical preoccupations.

In the case of Buddhism—a third tradition that influenced China—fundamental concepts such as the nonexistence of the individual ego and the illusory nature of the physical world are diametrically opposed to Taoism. In terms of overt individual and collective practices, however, competition between these two religions for influence among the people—a competition in which Confucianism had no need to participate because it had state patronage—resulted in mutual borrowings, numerous superficial similarities, and essentially Chinese developments inside Buddhism, such as the Ch'an (Japanese Zen) sect. In folk religion, since Sung times (960–1279), Taoist and Buddhist elements have coexisted without clear distinctions in the minds of the worshippers.

This article is divided into the following sections:

General characteristics

THE GREAT SAGES AND THEIR ASSOCIATED TEXTS

Lao-tzu and the Tao-te Ching. Behind all forms of Taoism stands the figure of Lao-tzu, traditionally regarded as the author of the classic text known as the *Lao-tzu,* or the *Tao-te Ching* ("Classic of the Way of Power"). The first mention of Lao-tzu is found in another early classic of Taoist speculation, the *Chuang-tzu* (4th–3rd century BC), so called after the name of its author. In this work Lao-tzu is described as being one of Chuang-tzu's own teachers, and the same book contains many of the Master's (Lao-tzu's) discourses, generally introduced by the questions of a disciple. The *Chuang-tzu* also presents seven versions of a meeting of Lao-tzu and Confucius. Lao-tzu is portrayed as the elder and his Taoist teachings confound his celebrated interlocutor. The *Chuang-tzu* also gives the only account of Lao-tzu's death. Thus in this early source, Lao-tzu appears as a senior contemporary of Confucius (6th–5th century BC) and a renowned Taoist master, a curator of the archives at the court of the Chou dynasty (*c.* 1111–255 BC) and, finally, a mere mortal.

The teachings of Lao-tzu and Chuang-tzu

The first consistent biographical account of Lao-tzu is found in the "Historical Records" (*Shih-chi*)—China's first universal history (2nd century BC)—of Ssu-ma Ch'ien. This concise résumé has served as the classical source on the philosopher's life. Lao-tzu's family name was Li, his given name Erh; and he occupied the post of archivist at the Chou court. He is said to have instructed Confucius on points of ceremony. Observing the decline of the Chou dynasty, Lao-tzu left the court and headed west. At the request of Yin Hsi, the guardian of the frontier pass, he wrote his treatise on the Tao in two scrolls. He then left China behind, and what became of him is not known. The historian quotes variant accounts, including one that attributed to Lao-tzu an exceptional longevity; the narrative terminates with the genealogy of eight generations of Lao-tzu's supposed descendants. With passing references in other early texts, this constitutes the body of information on the life of the sage as of the 2nd century BC; it is presumably legendary (see also LAO-TZU in the *Micropædia*).

Modern scholarship has little to add to the *Shih-chi* account, and the *Tao-te Ching,* regarded by many scholars as a compilation that reached its final form only in the 3rd century BC, rather than the work of a single author, stands alone, with all its attractions and enigmas, as the fundamental text of both philosophical and religious Taoism.

The work's 81 brief sections contain only about 5,000 characters in all, from which fact derives still another of its titles, *Lao Tzu's Five Thousand Words.* The text itself appears in equal measure to express a profound quietism and determined views on government. It is consequently between the extremes of meditative introspection and political application that its many and widely divergent interpreters have veered.

The *Tao-te Ching* as a handbook for rulers

The *Tao-te Ching* was meant as a handbook for the ruler. He should be a sage whose actions pass so unnoticed that his very existence remains unknown. He imposes no restrictions or prohibitions on his subjects; "so long as I love quietude, the people will of themselves go straight. So long as I act only by inactivity, the people will of themselves become prosperous." His simplicity makes the Ten Thousand Beings passionless and still and peace follows naturally. He does not teach them discrimination, virtue, or ambition because "when intellect emerges, the great artifices begin. When discord is rife in families, 'dutiful sons' appear. When the State falls into anarchy, 'loyal subjects' appear." Thus, it is better to banish wisdom, righteousness, and ingenuity, and the people will benefit a hundredfold.

> Therefore the Holy Man rules by emptying their hearts (minds) and filling their bellies, weakening their wills and strengthening their bones, ever striving to make the people knowledgeless and desireless.

The word people in this passage more likely refers not to

the common people but to those nobles and intellectuals who incite the ruler's ambition and aggressiveness.

War is condemned but not entirely excluded: "Arms are ill-omened instruments," and the sage uses them only when he cannot do otherwise. He does not glory in victory; "he that has conquered in battle is received with rites of mourning."

The book shares certain constants of classical Chinese thought but clothes them in an imagery of its own. The sacred aura surrounding kingship is here rationalized and expressed as "inaction" (*wu-wei*), demanding of the sovereign no more than right cosmological orientation at the centre of an obedient universe. Survivals of archaic notions concerning the compelling effect of renunciation—which the Confucians sanctified as ritual "deference" (*jang*)—are echoed in the recommendation to "hold to the role of the female," with an eye to the ultimate mastery that comes of passivity.

The meaning of the Tao

It is more particularly in the function attributed to the Tao, or Way, that this little tract stands apart. The term Tao was employed by all schools of thought. The universe has its Tao; there is a Tao of the sovereign, his royal mode of being, while the Tao of man comprises continuity through procreation. Each of the schools, too, had its own Tao, its way or doctrine. But in the *Tao-te Ching,* the ultimate unity of the universal Tao itself is being proposed as a *social* ideal. It is this idealistic peculiarity that seems to justify later historians and bibliographers in their assignment of the term Taoist to the *Tao-te Ching* and its successors.

From a literary point of view, the *Tao-te Ching* is distinguished for its highly compressed style. Unlike the dialectic or anecdotal composition of other contemporary treatises, it articulates its cryptic subject matter in short, concise statements. More than half of these are in rhyme, and close parallelism recurs throughout the text. No proper name occurs anywhere. Although its historical enigmas are apparently insoluble, there is abundant testimony to the vast influence exercised by the book since the earliest times and in surprisingly varied social contexts. Among the classics of speculative Taoism, it alone holds the distinction of having become a scripture of the esoteric Taoist movements, which developed their own interpretations of its ambiguities and transmitted it as a sacred text.

The interpretation of Chuang-tzu. Pseudohistorical knowledge of the sage Chuang-tzu is even less well defined than that of Lao-tzu. Most of Ssu-ma Ch'ien's brief portrait of the man is transparently drawn from anecdotes in the *Chuang-tzu* itself and as such has no necessary basis in fact. The *Chuang-tzu,* however, is valuable as a monument of Chinese literature and because it contains considerable documentary material, describing numerous speculative trends and spiritual practices of the Warring States period (475–221 BC).

Whereas the *Tao-te Ching* is addressed to the sage-king, the *Chuang-tzu* is the earliest surviving Chinese text to present a philosophy for private life, a wisdom for the individual. Chuang-tzu is said to have preferred the doctrine of Lao-tzu over all others; many of his writings strike the reader as metaphorical illustrations of the terse sayings of the "Old Master."

Whereas Lao-tzu in his book as well as in his life (in legend) was concerned with Taoist rule, Chuang-tzu, some generations later, rejected all participation in society. He compared the servant of state to the well-fed decorated ox being led to sacrifice in the temple and himself to the untended piglet blissfully frolicking in the mire.

Here there is none of the *Tao-te Ching's* studied density. The rambling *Chuang-tzu* opens with a sprightly fable, illustrating the incomprehension of small wildfowl of the majestic splendour of a gigantic bird. Other such parables demonstrate the relativity of all values: the sliding scales of size, utility, beauty, and perfection. There is a colloquy between the Lord of the Yellow River and the God of the Eastern Ocean, in which the complacent self-satisfaction of the lesser spirit is shaken by his unexpected meeting with inconceivable vastness. Humble artisans are depicted, who, through the perfect mastery of their craft, exemplify for their social superiors the art of mastering life. Life and death are equated, and the dying are seen to welcome their approaching transformation as a fusion with the Tao. A succession of acquiescent cripples exclaims in rapture on the strange forms in which it has pleased heaven to shape them. Those involved in state ritual are brought onstage only to be mocked, and the propositions of contemporary logic-choppers are drawn into the unending whirl of paradox, spun out to their conclusions, and so abolished. Such are a few aspects of this wild kaleidoscope of unconventional thought, a landmark in Chinese literature. Its concluding chapter is a systematic account of the preeminent thinkers of the time, and the note of mock despair on which it closes typifies the *Chuang-tzu's* position regarding the more formal, straitlaced ideologies that it parodies.

The Taoist Immortals

Among the strange figures that people the pages of *Chuang-tzu* are a very special class of spiritualized being. Dwelling far apart from the turbulent world of men, dining on air and sipping the dew, they share none of the anxieties of ordinary folk and have the smooth, untroubled faces of children. These "supreme men," or "perfect men," are immune to the effects of the elements, untouched by heat and cold. They possess the power of flight and are described as mounting upward with a fluttering (*hsien*) motion. Their effortless existence was the ultimate in autonomy, the natural spontaneity that *Chuang-tzu* ceaselessly applauds. These striking portraits may have been intended to be allegorical, but whatever their original meaning, these Immortals (*hsien*), as they came to be called, were to become the centre of great interest. Purely literary descriptions of their freedom, their breathtaking mobility, and their agelessness were construed as practical objectives by later generations. By a variety of practices, men attempted to attain these qualities in their own persons, and in time *Chuang-tzu's* unfettered paragons of liberty were to see themselves classified according to kind and degree in a hierarchy of the heavenly hosts (see also CHUANG-TZU in the *Micropædia*).

BASIC CONCEPTS OF TAOISM

Certain concepts of ancient agrarian religion have dominated Chinese thought uninterruptedly from before the formation of the philosophic schools until the first radical break with tradition and the overthrow of dynastic rule at the beginning of the 20th century, and they are thus not specifically Taoist. The most important of these concepts are: the solidarity of nature and man; that is, the interaction between the universe and human society; the cyclical character of time and the universal rhythm and the law of return; and the worship of ancestors, the cult of Heaven, and the divine nature of the sovereign.

Concepts of the universe and natural order. *Cosmology.* What Lao-tzu calls the "permanent Tao" in reality is nameless. The name (*ming*) in ancient Chinese thought implied an evaluation assigning an object its place in a hierarchical universe. The Tao is outside these categories.

Variations on the meaning of Tao

> It is something formlessly fashioned, that existed before Heaven and Earth; . . . Its name (*ming*) we do not know; Tao is the byname that we give it. Were I forced to say to what class of things it belongs I should call it Immense.

Tao is the "imperceptible, indiscernible," about which nothing can be predicated but that latently contains the forms, entities, and forces of all particular phenomena: "It was from the Nameless that Heaven and Earth sprang; the Named is the mother that rears the Ten Thousand Beings, each after its kind." The Nameless (*wu-ming*) and the Named (*yu-ming*), Not-Being (*wu*) and Being (*yu*), are interdependent and "grow out of one another."

Not-Being (*wu*) and Tao are not identical; *wu* and *yu* are two aspects of the permanent Tao: "in its mode of being Unseen, we will see its mysteries; in the mode of the Seen, we will see its boundaries."

Not-Being does not mean Nothingness but rather the absence of perceptible qualities; in Lao-tzu's view it is superior to Being. It is the Void (that is, empty incipience) that harbours in itself all potentialities and without which even Being lacks its efficacy.

Emptiness realized in the mind of the Taoist who has freed himself from all obstructing notions and distracting passions makes the Tao act through him without obstacle.

An essential characteristic that governs the Tao is spontaneity (*tzu-jan*), the what-is-so-of-itself, the self-so, the unconditioned. The Tao, in turn, governs the universe: "The ways of Heaven are conditioned by those of the Tao, and the ways of Tao by the Self-so."

This is the way of the saint who does not intervene but possesses the total power of spontaneous realization that is at work in the universe; of his accomplishments "everyone, throughout the country, says 'It happened of its own accord' (*tzu-jan*)."

The microcosm–macrocosm concept. The conception of the universe common to all Chinese philosophy is neither materialistic nor animistic (a belief system centring on soul substances); it can be called magical or even alchemical. The universe is viewed as a hierarchically organized mechanism in which every part reproduces the whole. Man is a microcosm (small universe) corresponding rigorously to this macrocosm (large universe); his body reproduces the plan of the cosmos. Between man and universe there exists a system of correspondences and participations that the ritualists, philosophers, alchemists, and physicians have described but certainly not invented. This originally magical feeling of the integral unity of mankind and the natural order has always characterized the Chinese mentality, and the Taoists especially have elaborated upon it. The five organs of the body and its orifices and the dispositions, features, and passions of man correspond to the five directions, the five holy mountains, the sections of the sky, the seasons, and the elements (*wu-hsing*), which in China are not material but more like five fundamental phases of any process in space-time. Whoever understands man thus understands the structure of the universe. The physiologist knows that blood circulates because rivers carry water and that the body has 360 articulations because the ritual year has 360 days. In religious Taoism the interior of the body is inhabited by the same gods as those of the macrocosm. An adept often searches for his divine teacher in all the holy mountains of China until he finally discovers him in one of the "palaces" inside his head.

The eternal transformation from Non-Being to Being to Non-Being

Return to the Tao. The law of the Tao as natural order refers to the continuous reversion of everything to its starting point. Anything that develops extreme qualities will invariably revert to the opposite qualities: "Reversion is the movement of the Tao" (*Lao-tzu*). All being issues from the Tao and ineluctably returns to it; Undifferentiated Unity becomes multiplicity in the movement of the Tao. Life and death are contained in this eternal transformation from Non-Being into Being and back to Non-Being, but the underlying primordial unity is never lost.

For society, any reform means a type of return to the remote past; civilization is considered a degradation of the natural order, and the ideal is the return to an original purity. For the individual, wisdom is to conform to the rhythm of the universe. The Taoist mystic, however, not only adapts himself ritually and physiologically to the alternations of nature but creates a void inside himself that permits him to return to nature's origin. Lao-tzu, in trance, "wandered freely in the origin of all beings." Thus, in ecstasy he escaped the rhythm of life and death by contemplating the universal return. "Having attained perfect emptiness, holding fast to stillness, I can watch the return of the ever active Ten Thousand Beings." The number 10,000 symbolizes totality.

By courtesy of the Nelson Gallery-Atkins Museum, Kansas City, Missouri (Nelson Fund)

"Fishing in a Mountain Stream," detail of an ink drawing on silk by Hsü Tao-ning, 11th century. The drawing suggests the Taoist concept of harmony of the universe and man's relative role in the universal order. In the William Rockhill Nelson Gallery and Atkins Museum of Fine Arts, Kansas City, Missouri.

Change and transformation. All parts of the universe are attuned in a rhythmical pulsation. Nothing is static; all beings are subjected to periodical mutations and transformations that represent the Chinese view of creation. Instead of being opposed with a static ideal, change itself is systematized and made intelligible, as in the theory of the five phases (*wu-hsing*) and in the 64 hexagrams of the *I Ching* (*Classic of Changes*), which are basic recurrent constellations in the general flux. An unchanging unity (the permanent Tao) was seen as underlying the kaleidoscopic plurality.

Chuang-tzu's image for creation was that of the activity of the potter and the bronze caster: "to shape and to transform" (*tsao hua*). These are two phases of the same process: the imperceptible Tao shapes the universe continuously out of primordial chaos; the perpetual transformation of the universe by the alternations of Yin and Yang, or complementary energies (seen as night and day or as winter and summer), is nothing but the external aspect of the same Tao. The shaping of the Ten Thousand Beings by the Supreme Unity and their transformation by Yin and Yang are both simultaneous and perpetual. Thus, the saint's ecstatic union is a "moving together with the Tao; dispersing and concentrating, his appearance has no consistency." United with the permanent Tao, the saint's outer aspect becomes one of ungraspable change. Because the gods can become perceptible only by adapting to the mode of this changing world, their apparitions are "transformations" (*pien-hua*); and the magician (*hua-jen*) is believed to be one who transforms rather than one who conjures out of nothing.

Concepts of man and society. *Wu-wei.* The power acquired by the Taoist is *te,* the efficacy of the Tao in the realm of Being, which is translated as "virtue." Lao-tsu viewed it, however, as different from Confucian virtue:

> The man of superior virtue is not virtuous, and that is why he has virtue. The man of inferior [Confucian] virtue never strays from virtue, and that is why he has no virtue.

The "superior virtue" of Taoism is a latent power that never lays claim to its achievements; it is the "mysterious power" (*hsüan te*) of Tao present in the heart of the sage—"the man of superior virtue never acts (*wu-wei*), and yet there is nothing he leaves undone."

Wu-wei is not an ideal of absolute inaction nor a mere "not-overdoing." It is an action so well in accordance with things that its author leaves no trace of himself in his work: "Perfect activity leaves no track behind it; perfect speech is like a jade worker whose tool leaves no mark." It is the Tao that "never acts, yet there is nothing it does not do." There is no true achievement without *wu-wei* because every deliberate intervention in the natural course of things will sooner or later turn into the opposite of what was intended and will result in failure.

The sage who practices *wu-wei* lives out of his original nature before it was tampered with by knowledge and restricted by morality; he has reverted to infancy (that is, the undiminished vitality of the newborn state); he has "returned to the state of the Uncarved Block (*p'u*)." *P'u* is uncut, unpainted wood, simplicity. Society carves this wood into specific shapes for its own use and thus robs the individual piece of its original totality. "Once the uncarved block is carved, it forms utensils (that is, instruments of government); but when the Sage uses it, he would be fit to become Chief of all Ministers. This is why the great craftsman (ruler) does not carve (rule)."

The social ideal of primitivism. Any willful human intervention is believed to be able to ruin the harmony of the natural transformation process. The spontaneous rhythm of the primitive agrarian community and its unself-conscious symbiosis with nature's cycles is thus the Taoist ideal of society.

In the ideal society there are no books; the *Lao-tzu* (*Tao-te Ching*) itself would not have been written but for the entreaty of the guardian of the pass Yin Hsi, who asked the "Old Master" to write down his thoughts. In the Golden Age, past or future, knotted cords are the only form of records. The people of this age are "dull and unwitting, they have no desire; this is called uncarved simplicity. In uncarved simplicity the people attain their true nature."

Chuang-tzu liked to oppose the Heaven-made and the man-made; that is, nature and society. He wanted man to renounce all artificial "cunning contrivances" that facilitate his work but lead to "cunning hearts" and agitated souls in which the Tao will not dwell. Man should equally renounce all concepts of measure, law, and virtue. "Fashion pecks and bushels for people to measure by and they will steal by peck and bushel." He blamed not only the culture heroes and inventors praised by the Confucians but also the sages who shaped the rites and rules of society.

> That the unwrought substance was blighted in order to fashion implements—this was the crime of the artisan. That the Way (Tao) and its Virtue (*te*) were destroyed in order to create benevolence and righteousness—this was the fault of the sage.

Even "coveting knowledge" is condemned because it engenders competition and "fight to the death over profit."

Ideas of knowledge and language. Characteristic of Chuang-tzu are his ideas of knowledge and language developed under the stimulus of his friend and opponent, the philosopher Hui Shih.

Because, in the Taoist view, all beings and everything are fundamentally one, opposing opinions can arise only when people lose sight of the Whole and regard their partial truths as absolute. They are then like the frog at the bottom of the well who takes the bit of brightness he sees for the whole sky. The closed systems—*i.e.,* the passions and prejudices into which petty minds shut themselves—hide the Tao, the "Supreme Master" who resides inside themselves and is superior to all distinctions.

The relativity of moral and epistemological notions

Thus, Chuang-tzu's holy man fully recognizes the relativity of notions like good and evil and true and false. He is neutral and open to the extent that he offers no active resistance to any would-be opponent, whether it be a person or an idea. "When you argue, there are some things you are failing to see. In the greatest Tao nothing is named; in the greatest disputation, nothing is said."

The person who wants to know the Tao is told: "Don't meditate, don't cogitate . . . . Follow no school, follow no way, and then you will attain the Tao"; discard knowledge, forget distinctions, reach no-knowledge. "Forget" indicates that distinctions had to be known first. The original ignorance of the child is distinguished from the no-knowledge of the sage who can "sit in forgetfulness."

The mystic does not speak because declaring unity, by creating the duality of the speaker and the affirmation, destroys it. Those who speak about the Tao (like Chuang-tzu himself) are "wholly wrong. For he who knows does not speak; he who speaks does not know." Chuang-tzu was aware of the fact that, in speaking about it, he could do no more than hint at the way toward the all-embracing and intuitive knowledge.

Identity of life and death. Mystic realization does away with the distinction between the self and the world. This idea also governs Chuang-tzu's attitude toward death. Life and death are but one of the pairs of cyclical phases, such as day and night or summer and winter. "Since life and death are each other's companions, why worry about them? All beings are one." Life and death are not in opposition but merely two aspects of the same reality, arrested moments out of the flux of the universal mutations of everything into everything. Man is no exception; "he goes back into the great weaving machine: thus all beings issue from the Loom and return to the Loom."

Viewed from the single reality experienced in ecstasy, it is just as difficult to distinguish life from death as it is to distinguish the waking Chuang-tzu from the dreaming butterfly. Death is natural, and men ought neither to fear nor to desire it. Chuang-tzu's attitude thus is one of serene acceptance.

Religious goals of the individual. The Confucian saint (*sheng*) is viewed as a ruler of antiquity or a great sage who taught men how to return to the rites of antiquity. The Taoist sainthood, however, is internal (*nei sheng*), although it can become manifest in an external royalty (*wai wang*) that brings the world back to the Way by means of quietism: variously called "non-intervention" (*wu-wei*), "inner cultivation" (*nei yeh*), or "art of the heart and mind" (*hsin-shu*).

Whereas worldly ambitions, riches, and (especially) discursive knowledge scatter the person and drain his energies, the saint "embraces Unity" or "holds fast to the One" (*pao i*); that is, he aspires to union with the Tao in a primordial undivided state underlying consciousness. "Embracing Unity" also means that he maintains the balance of Yin and Yang within himself and the union of his spiritual (*hun*) and vegetative (*p'o*) souls, the dispersion of which spells death; Taoists usually believed there were three *hun* and seven *p'o.* The spiritual soul tends to wander (in dreams), and any passion or desire can result in loss of soul. To retain and harmonize one's souls is important for physical life as well as for the unification of the whole human entity. Cleansed of every distraction, the saint creates inside himself a void that in reality is plenitude. Empty of all impurity, he is full of the original energy (*yüan ch'i*), which is the principle of life that in the ordinary man decays from the moment of birth on.

Proof of sainthood

Because vital energy and spirituality are not clearly distinguished, old age in itself becomes a proof of sainthood. The aged Taoist sage became a saint because he had been able to cultivate himself throughout a long existence; his longevity in itself was the proof of his saintliness and union with the Tao. Externally he had a healthy, flourishing appearance and inside he contained an ever-flowing source of energy that manifested itself in radiance and in a powerful, beneficial influence on his surroundings, which is the charismatic efficacy (*te*) of the Tao.

The mystic insight of Chuang-tzu made him scorn those who strove for longevity and immortality through physiological practices. Nevertheless, physical immortality was a Taoist goal probably long before and alongside the unfolding of Taoist mysticism. The adept of immortality had a choice among many methods that were all intended to restore the pure energies possessed at birth by the infant whose perfect vital force Lao-tzu admired. Through these methods, the adept became an immortal (*hsien*) who lived 1,000 years in this world if he so chose and, once satiated with life, "ascended to heaven in broad daylight." This was the final apotheosis of the Taoist who had transformed his body into pure Yang energy.

The perfect man as pure spirit

Chuang-tzu's descriptions of the indescribable Tao, as well as of those who have attained union with the Tao, are invariably poetic. The perfect man has identified his life rhythm so completely with the rhythm of the forces of nature that he has become indistinguishable from them and shares their immortality and infinity, which is above the cycle of ordinary life and death. He is "pure spirit. He feels neither the heat of the brushlands afire nor the cold of the waters in flood"; nothing can startle or frighten him. Not that he is magically invulnerable (as the adepts of physical immortality would have it), but he is "so cautious in shunning and approaching, that nothing can do him injury."

"A man like this rides the clouds as his carriages and the sun and moon as his steeds." The theme of the spiritual wandering (*yüan yu*), which can be traced back to the shamanistic soul journey, crops up wherever Chuang-tzu speaks of the perfect man.

> Those who let themselves be borne away by the unadulterated energies of Heaven and Earth and can harness the six composite energies to roam through the limitless, whatever need they henceforth depend on?

These wanderings are journeys within oneself; they are roamings through the Infinite in ecstasy. Transcending the ordinary distinctions of things and one with the Tao, "the Perfect Man has no self, the Holy Man has no merit, the

Sage has no fame." He lives inconspicuously among men, and whatever applies to the Tao applies to him.

Symbolism and mythology. Taoists prefer to convey their ecstatic insights in images and parables. The Tao is low and receiving as a valley, soft and life-giving as water, and it is the "mysterious female," the source of all life, the Mother of the Ten Thousand Beings. Man should become weak and yielding as water that overcomes the hard and the strong and always takes the low ground; he should develop his male and female sides but "prefer femininity," "feed on the mother," and find within himself the well that never runs dry. Tao is also the axis, the ridgepole, the pivot, and the empty centre of the hub. The sage is the "useless tree" or the huge gourd too large to be fashioned into implements. A frequent metaphor for the working of the Tao is the incommunicable ability to be skillful at a craft. The skilled artisan does not ponder on his action, but, in union with the Tao of his subject, he does his work reflexively and without conscious intent.

Preservation and transformation of ancient Chinese myths

Much ancient Chinese mythology has been preserved by the Taoists, who drew on it to illustrate their views. A chaos (*hun-tun*) myth is recorded as a metaphor for the undifferentiated primal unity; the mythical emperors (Huang Ti and others) are extolled for wise Taoist rule or blamed for introducing harmful civilization. Dreams of mythical paradises and journeys on clouds and flying dragons are metaphors for the wanderings of the soul, the attainment of the Tao, and the identity of dream and reality.

Taoists have transformed and adapted some ancient myths to their beliefs. Thus, the Queen Mother of the West (Hsi Wang Mu), who was a mountain spirit, pestilence goddess, and tigress, became a high deity—the Fairy Queen of all immortals.

Early eclectic contributions. *The idea of Yin and Yang.* Yin and Yang literally mean "dark side" and "sunny side" of a hill. They are mentioned for the first time in the *Hsi tz'u,* or "Appended Explanations" (*c.* 4th century BC), an appendix to the *I Ching* (*Classic of Changes*): "One [time] Yin, one [time] Yang, this is the Tao." Yin and Yang are two complementary, interdependent principles or phases alternating in space and time; they are emblems evoking the harmonious interplay of all pairs of opposites in the universe.

First conceived by musicians, astronomers, or diviners and then propagated by a school that came to be named after them, Yin and Yang became the common stock of all Chinese philosophy. The Taoist treatise *Huai-nan-tzu* (book of "Master Huai-nan") describes how the one "Primordial Breath" (*yüan ch'i*) split into the light ethereal Yang breath, which formed Heaven; and the heavier, cruder Yin breath, which formed Earth. The diversifications and interactions of Yin and Yang produced the Ten Thousand Beings.

> The warm breath of Yang accumulated to produce fire, the essence of which formed the sun. The cold breath of Yin accumulated to produce water, the essence of which became the moon.

The idea of ch'i. Yin and Yang are often referred to as two "breaths" (*ch'i*). *Ch'i* means air, breath, or vapour—originally the vapour arising from cooking cereals. It also came to mean a cosmic energy. The Primordial Breath is a name of the chaos (state of Unity) in which the original life force is not yet diversified into the phases that the concepts Yin and Yang describe.

Cosmic and active energies

Every man has a portion of this primordial life-force allotted to him at birth, and his task is not to dissipate it through the activity of his senses but to strengthen, control, and increase it in order to live out his full span of life.

The idea of wu-hsing. Another important set of notions associated with the same school of Yin-Yang are the "five agents" or "phases" (*wu-hsing*) or "powers" (*wu-te*): water, fire, wood, metal, earth. They are also "breaths" (*i.e.,* active energies), the idea of which enabled the philosophers to construct a coherent system of correspondences and participations linking all phenomena of the macrocosm and the microcosm. Associated with spatial directions, seasons of the year, colours, musical notes, animals, and other aspects of nature, they also correspond, in the human body, to the five inner organs. The Taoist techniques of longevity are grounded in these correspondences. The idea behind such techniques was that of nourishing the inner organs with the essences corresponding to their respective phases and during the season dominated by the latter.

Yang Chu and the Lieh-tzu. Yang Chu (*c.* 400 BC) is representative of the early pre-Taoist recluses, "those who hid themselves" (*yin-shih*), who, in the *Analects* of Confucius, ridiculed Confucius' zeal to improve society. Yang Chu held that each individual should value his own life above all else, despise wealth and power, and not agree to sacrifice even a single hair of his head to benefit the whole world. The scattered sayings of Yang Chu in pre-Han texts are much less hedonistic than his doctrine as it is presented in the *Lieh-tzu* (book of "Master Lieh").

Lieh-tzu was a legendary Taoist master whom Chuang-tzu described as being able to "ride the wind and go soaring around with cool and breezy skill." In many old legends Lieh-tzu is the paragon of the spiritual traveller. The text named after him (of uncertain date) presents a philosophy that views natural changes and human activities as wholly mechanistic in their operation; neither human effort nor divine destiny can change the course of things.

Kuan-tzu and Huai-nan-tzu. In the several Taoist chapters of the *Kuan-tzu* (book of "Master Kuan"), another text of uncertain date, emphasis is placed on "the art of the heart (mind)"; the heart governs the body as the chief governs the state. If the organs and senses submit to it, the heart can achieve a desirelessness and emptiness that make it a pure receptacle of the "heart inside the heart," a new soul that is the indwelling Tao.

The *Huai-nan-tzu* is a compilation of essays written by different learned magicians (*fang-shih*) at the court of their patron, the Prince of Huai-nan. Although lacking in unity, it is a compendium of the knowledge of the time that had been neglected by the less speculative scholars of the new state Confucianism. The *Huai-nan-tzu* discusses the most elaborate cosmology up to that time, the position of man in the macrocosm, the ordering of society, and the ideal of personal sainthood.

History

TAOISM IN THE CH'IN AND HAN PERIODS (221 BC–AD 220) OF THE CHINESE EMPIRE

Esoteric traditions of eastern China. The textual remains of Taoism during the Warring States period were all presumably produced in connection with official patronage; similarly, developments in Taoist thought and practice during the early Imperial age principally have to be studied from the vantage point of the court. At the Imperial court, representatives of different local traditions met as competitors for official favour, and the court consequently served as the principal meeting place for the exchange of ideas. The historians who recorded the progress of these varying intellectual and religious currents were themselves court officials and often were active participants in the movements they describe. The emperors, anxious to consolidate and expand their power, were a natural focus for wonder-workers and specialists in esoteric arts.

Taoism's influence at the Imperial court

A series of such wonder-workers from the eastern seaboard visited the courts of the Ch'in and early Han. They told of islands in the ocean, peopled by immortal beings—which the *Chuang-tzu* had described—and so convincing were their accounts that sizable expeditions were fitted out and sent in search of them. The easterners brought the cults of their own region to the capital, recommending and supervising the worship of astral divinities who would assure the emperor's health and longevity. One of their number, Li Shao-chün, bestowed on the Han emperor Wu Ti counsels that are a résumé of the spiritual preoccupations of the time. The emperor was to perform sacrifices to the furnace (*tsao*), which would enable him to summon spiritual beings. They in turn would permit him to change cinnabar powder (mercuric sulfide) into gold, from which vessels were to be made, out of which he would eat and drink. This would increase his span of life and permit him to behold the immortals (*hsien*) who dwell on the Isles of P'eng-lai, in the midst of the sea. Here, for the first time, alchemy joins the complex of activities that were supposed to contribute to the prolongation of life.

The Huang–Lao tradition. Also originating in the eastern coastal region (Shantung), alongside these same thaumaturgic (wonder-working) tendencies, was the learned tradition of the Huang-Lao masters, devotees of the legendary "Yellow Emperor" (Huang Ti) and Lao-tzu. The information on the life of Lao-tzu transmitted by Ssu-ma Ch'ien probably derives directly from their teaching. They venerated Lao-tzu as a sage whose instructions, contained in his cryptic book, describe the perfect art of government. The Yellow Emperor, with whose reign Ssu-ma Ch'ien's universal history opens, was depicted as a ruler of the Golden Age who achieved his success because he applied his teachers' precepts to government. The Yellow Emperor also was the patron of technology; and the classic works of many arcane arts, including alchemy, medicine, sexual techniques, cooking, and dietetics, were all placed under his aegis. Unlike Lao-tzu, the Yellow Emperor is always the disciple, an unremitting seeker of knowledge, and the Huang–Lao masters' ideal of the perfect ruler.

From the court of the King of Ch'i (in present-day Shantung Province) where they were already expounding the *Lao-tzu* in the 3rd century BC, the teachings of the Huang–Lao masters soon spread throughout learned and official circles in the capital. Many early Han statesmen became their disciples and attempted to practice government by inaction (*wu-wei*); among them were also scholars who cultivated esoteric arts. Although their doctrine lost its direct political relevance during the reign of the emperor Wu Ti (reigned 141/140–87/86 BC), their ensemble of teachings concerning both ideal government and practices for prolonging life continued to evoke considerable interest and is perhaps the earliest truly Taoist movement of which there is clear historical evidence.

Revolutionary messianism. Among the less welcome visitors at the Han court had been a certain Kan Chung-k'o. At the end of the 1st century BC he presented to the emperor a "Classic of the Great Peace" (*T'ai-p'ing Ching*) that he claimed had been revealed to him by a spirit, who had come to him with the order to renew the Han dynasty. His temerity cost him his life, but the prophetic note of dynastic renewal became stronger during the interregnum of Wang Mang (AD 9–23); and other works—bearing the same title—continued to appear. At this time, promoters of a primitivistic and utopian T'ai-p'ing (Great Peace) ideology continued to support the Imperial Liu (Han) family, claiming that they would be restored to power through the aid of the Li clan. A century and a half later, however, as the power of the Eastern Han dynasty (AD 25–220) declined, the populace no longer hoped for a renewal of Han rule.

T'ai-p'ing messianism

The great Yellow Turban Rebellion broke out in the east in AD 184. Its leader, Chang Chüeh, declared that the "blue heaven" was to be replaced by a "yellow heaven"; and his followers wore yellow turbans in token of this expectation. Worshipping a "Huang-lao Chün," the movement gained a vast number of adherents throughout eastern China. Though they were eventually defeated by the Imperial forces, the tendency towards messianic revolt continued to manifest itself at frequent intervals. A great many charismatic leaders came from the Li family, and certain of them claimed to be the god Lao-tzu returned to earth; a sage of western China, Li Hung, who had actually lived during the 1st century BC, became the favourite recurrent figure of later would-be messiahs. Such revolutionary religious movements, which included Taoist ideological elements, remained a persistent feature of medieval Chinese history. The last recorded Li Hung was executed in 1112. These sporadic popular manifestations of revolutionary messianism, though, did not represent the activities of the formal Taoist organization and must be distinguished from the organized religious Taoism that also appeared at the end of the Later Han period.

DEVELOPMENT OF THE TAOIST RELIGION FROM THE 2ND TO THE 6TH CENTURY

The emergence of a "Taocracy." *The Way of the Celestial Masters.* The protagonist of the *Classic of the Great Peace* is a celestial master. When another important religious movement began in China's far west at about the same time as the group in the northeast arose, in the second half of the 2nd century AD, the same title was given to its founder, Chang Tao-ling. It is with this Way of the Celestial Masters (T'ien-shih Tao) that the history of organized religious Taoism may be said to begin, in that there has been an unbroken continuity from that time down to the present day, as the movement soon spread to all of China.

In AD 142, in the mountains of the province of Szechwan, Chang is said to have received a revelation from T'ai-shang Lao-chün (Lord Lao the Most High). The deified Lao-tzu bestowed on Chang his "orthodox and sole doctrine of the authority of the covenant" (*cheng-i meng-wei fa*), meant as a definitive replacement for the religious practices of the people, which are described as having lapsed into demonism and degeneracy.

The new dispensation at first was probably intended as a substitute for the effete rule of the Han central administration. Chang is said in time to have ascended on high and to have received the title of *t'ien-shih,* and by the latter part of the 2nd century, under the leadership of his descendants, the T'ien-shih Tao constituted an independent religio-political organization with authority throughout the region, a "Taocracy" (rule of Tao), in which temporal and spiritual powers converged. For ceremonial and administrative purposes, the realm was divided into 24 (later 28 and 36) units, or parishes (*chih*). The focal point of each was the oratory, or "chamber of purity" (*ching-shih*), which served as the centre for communication with the powers on high. Here the *chi-chiu* ("libationer"), the priestly functionary of the nuclear community, officiated. Each household contributed a tax of five pecks of rice to the administration, whence came the other common name of the movement, the Way of the Five Pecks of Rice (Wu-tou-mi Tao).

The ritual activities of the libationer seem principally to have been directed towards the cure of disease by prescribed ceremonial means. Believed to be a punishment for evil deeds, whether committed by the sufferer himself or by an ancestor, illness was in fact a sentence pronounced by the San Kuan (Three Officials), judges and custodians of the dead. The sentence was carried out by the spectral hordes of the Six Heavens (Liu T'ien), a posthumous dwelling place of all unhallowed mortals. Against such judicial severity, only formal appeal to higher authority might avail. Using the rising flame and smoke of the incense burner in the centre of the oratory to transmit the message borne by spirits exteriorized from within his own body, the libationer submitted petitions (*chang*) to the appropriate bureau of the three Taoist heavens (*san t'ien*). The Taoist canon contains long lists of the "officials and generals" (*kuan chiang*), each specializing in a different sort of complaint, who would respectively pronounce on the appeal and marshal the celestial forces against the offending demons.

Ritual activities of the libationer

The officiant came to dispose of a large selection of bureaucratic stock drafts: memorials, plaints, and appeals, all of which were modelled on secular administrative usage. Also effective were written talismans (*fu*); drawn by the libationer, these would be burned and the ashes, mixed with water, swallowed by the demons' victim. The libationer also functioned as a moral preceptor, instructing the faithful in the sect's own highly allegorical interpretation of the *Lao-tzu,* which they considered to be the revealed work of Lord Lao the Most High. Their fundamental concern with right actions and good works as being most in the spirit of the Tao and consequently ensuring immunity from disease is also shown by their construction of way stations in which provisions and shelter were placed for the convenience and use of travellers, as well as in the numerous injunctions to charity and forbearance recorded in the written codes of the movement.

Communal ceremonies. Both the nuclear communities and the "Taocratic" realm as a whole were bound together by a ritual cycle, of which only fragmentary indications remain. Among the most important ceremonial occasions were the communal feasts (*ch'u*) offered at certain specific times throughout the year (during the first, seventh, and 10th months) as well as on other important occasions, such as initiation into the hierarchy, advancement in rank or function, or the consecration of an oratory. These feasts were of varying degrees of elaborateness, depending on the circumstances. The common essential element, however, was the sharing of certain foods, in prescribed quantities, among masters and disciples. This was envisaged as a communion with the Tao, at once attesting the close compact with the celestial powers enjoyed by the members of the parish and reinforcing their own sense of cohesion as a group.

The Union of Breaths rite

Much more notorious was the rite known as the Union of Breaths (Ho Ch'i), a communal sexual ritual said to have been celebrated at each new moon. Later Buddhist sources described this as a riotous orgy of outrageous and disgusting license. Several cryptic manuals of instruction for the priest in charge of these proceedings are preserved in the canon; and they depict, however, scenarios of a highly stylized erotic choreography of cosmic significance. Like the communal feasts, these rites might be interpreted as a concentrated and idealized adaptation of older, more diffuse agrarian religious customs. This suggests a pattern of the integration of local practices that has remained characteristic of Taoism throughout its history.

Official recognition of the Taoist organization. In AD 215, the celestial master Chang Lu, grandson of Chang Tao-ling, submitted to the authority of the Han general Ts'ao Ts'ao, who six years later founded the Wei dynasty in the north. This resulted in official recognition of the sect by the dynasty; the celestial masters in turn expressed their spiritual approbation of the Wei's mandate to replace the Han. Under these conditions a formal definition of the relations of organized Taoism to the secular powers developed. In contrast to the popular messianic movements, Lao-tzu's manifestation to Chang Tao-ling was considered to be definitive; the god was not incarnate in them but rather designated Chang and his successors as his representatives on earth. Under a worthy dynasty, which governed by virtue of the Tao, the role of the celestial masters was that of acting as intermediaries for celestial confirmation and support. Only when a responsible ruler was lacking were the celestial masters to take over the temporal guidance of the people and hold the supreme power in trust for a new incumbent. Abetted by this flexible ideology of compromise, the sect made constant progress at the courts of the Wei and Western Chin dynasties until, by the end of the 3rd century, it counted among its adherents many of the most powerful families in North China.

The literature of Taoist esoterism. *The scholiasts.* The most famous of the many commentaries on *Tao-te Ching* was written by Wang Pi (AD 226–249). He is regarded as a founder of the school of Dark Learning (*hsüan-hsüeh*), a highly conservative philosophical movement that enjoyed a certain vogue among the cultured elite of the 3rd and 4th centuries. The *Chuang-tzu* was not long afterward annotated by Kuo Hsiang (died 312), in whose work the fundamental Confucian bias is even more prominent. The writings of these men have in recent years sometimes been called "Neo-Taoism," but nothing could be more misleading. Their primary aim was to harmonize *Tao-te Ching* and *Chuang-tzu* with their own conception of a practical life devoted to affairs of state. As administrators confronted with the challenge of Taoist thought, they preferred not to take its message at face value. Interpretative commentaries continued to be written on the classics of speculative Taoism in which the aid of the most diverse philosophies was called upon, not excluding Buddhism. Like the work of the 3rd and 4th century scholiasts, these represent the ideas of a tiny minority, the members of the scholar-official class. Though excursions into ever more refined scholasticism continued to be a diversion for them, the real creative vitality of Taoism was to be found elsewhere.

Early hagiography of the Immortals

Lives of the Immortals. By the Han period, the careers of those free spirits described in *Chuang-tzu* were the subject of universal interest. The earliest systematic collection of biographical notices on these legendary figures is the *Lives of the Immortals* (*Lieh-hsien chuan*) of the early 2nd century AD. Such collections were a genre of the time. Brief sketches were provided for 72 figures: the same symbolic number as was found in contemporary collections of the "Lives" of the disciples of Confucius, eminent scholar-officials, and famous women. Thus Immortals came to be classified as yet another category in the highly stylized gallery of ancient worthies. Each notice is followed by a short hymn of praise. This was the standard form of inscriptions on stone; its employment in hagiographic literature may have influenced the later development of the chantefable in alternating passages of prose and verse. The text appears to reflect a growing number of local cults dedicated to individual Immortals, while the many plants mentioned suggest the extent of the use of herbal compounds as a means to transcendence.

Inscriptions. These literary notices are supplemented by epigraphic evidence, inscriptions on stone or bronze. The simplest of these are bronze mirrors depicting the plumed figures of airborne Immortals and bearing short rhyming texts of a general nature. Longer and more explicit are the texts of inscriptions on stone: tablets dedicated to the cult of a particular Immortal. They open with their subject's vital statistics, list his latter-day manifestations, and commemorate offerings made in his honour. But all of this is only by way of preface to the core of the inscription, in which his merits are celebrated in verse. Such was the eloquent votive tablet erected in honour of Wang Tzu-ch'iao, a perennial favourite among the Immortals (AD 165). Another, dedicated to Lao-tzu in the same year, describes the supposed author of the *Tao-te Ching* as a god, to whom worship had been paid by the then reigning emperor.

Lao-tzu as a god

Texts on the cult of Lao-tzu. One of the most complex and interesting phenomena in Chinese religious history is Lao-tzu's advancement from sage to god. A scroll found in the walled-up desert library at Tun-huang, the *Book of the Transformations of Lao-tzu* (*Lao-tzu Pien-hua Ching*), shows him in cosmic perspective, omnipresent and omnipotent, the origin of all life. His human manifestations are listed, followed by his successive roles in legendary history, as the sage counsellor of emperors. Next, five of his more recent appearances are mentioned, dated AD 132–155, and localized in west China, where a temple is said to have been dedicated to him in 185. Then the god speaks, to describe his own powers. He recommends to his votaries the recitation of "my book in 5,000 words" (the *Tao-te Ching*) and enjoins a meditation on his own divine attributes as they appear within the adept's body. Finally, he calls upon the faithful to join him, now, when he is about to strike at the tottering rule of the Han dynasty. Evidently the product of a messianic group in west China at the end of the 2nd century, this valuable fragment of only 95 lines is written in a strangely disfigured Chinese, in part a reflection of its popular milieu. But it still shows more clearly than many longer and better preserved texts the essential cohesion of the several aspects of esoteric Taoism: hagiography, recitation of scriptures, and visionary meditation, all of which are here given additional temporal unity by the messianic context.

The Southern tradition. The political partition of China into three parts following the collapse of the Han dynasty in AD 220, the so-called period of the Three Kingdoms, had its spiritual counterpart in certain well-defined regional religious differences. Against the independent dynasties in the north and west stood the empire of Wu, south of the Yangtze River.

Developments in alchemical and other traditions. A region exposed comparatively lately to Chinese influence, this southeastern area had long been famous for its aboriginal sorcerers and dancing mediums. In the course of Chinese colonization, separate learned spiritual traditions developed alongside the ecstatic practices of the populace. To the court of the emperors of Wu came savants and wonder-workers representing a variety of traditions that were to acquire lasting influence.

Among these personages was a certain Ko Hsüan (3rd century AD), who was said to have been initiated into an ancient alchemical tradition. His great-nephew Ko Hung in the next century became one of the most celebrated writers on the various technical means for attaining immortality. In his major work, the *Pao-p'u-tzu* ("He Who Holds to Simplicity"), Ko Hung expounded the alchemical formulas received and transmitted by Ko Hsüan. In so doing, he took care to distinguish the divinely inspired "gold elixir" (*chin-tan*), or "liquefied gold" (*chin-i*)—*i.e.*, preparations of true edible, or potable, gold, the consumption of which leads to immortality (aurifaction)—from the mere counterfeiting of the precious substance, with intention to deceive (aurifiction). These alchemical methods have been designated as belonging to the T'ai ch'ing (Great Purity) tradition, from the name of the heaven of the Immortals to which the elixirs were said to elevate their consumer. The chapters of alchemy in the *Pao-p'u-tzu* are among the earliest documents to describe the art in detail.

The goals and methods of alchemy

Ko Hung enumerated an extensive selection of material substances and practical operations to which he attributed varying degrees of relative efficacy in the prolongation of life. Dietetics (grain and alcohol avoidance), ingestion of solar, lunar, and astral exhalations and their cycling within the body, gymnastics, and conservation of vital fluids through proper sexual techniques were all necessary and fundamental. The usefulness of written talismans and the performance of good works were also not denied. Above all, it was essential that all disease be eliminated from the body before undertaking more positive, specialized practices for achieving immortality. Herbs and plants were useful not only against disease, but in many cases (particularly in that of mushrooms) their use resulted in definite lengthening of life. For a definitive transformation into an immortal (*hsien*), with all the powers and prerogatives that implied, however, an alchemical elixir must be compounded and consumed. Ko Hung admitted, however, that he himself had never succeeded in making one. After a strenuous life in civil and military service, in the course of which he managed to write voluminously on many subjects, this great eclectic scholar is said to have undertaken a long journey to China's colonial dominions in Vietnam in quest of the pure cinnabar found there. He stopped at Lo-fou Shan, near Canton, however, where he died.

The *Pao-p'u-tzu* was nearly finished in 317, when Loyang, capital of the Western Chin dynasty, fell to the Hsiung-nu. This event set off a considerable emigration to the unsubdued region south of the Yangtze River. The Imperial household was followed in its flight by numerous high-ranking dependents and their spiritual ministers. During this period the Way of the Celestial Masters, established at the court of Lo-yang since the early 3rd century, apparently first penetrated in force to the Southeast. While the secular, military menace remained in the North, and factional struggles raged among the emigrants, the Way of the Celestial Masters waged unremitting war against the indigenous sects and cults of demons of the Southeast. Many of the old established families, settled in the region since the end of the Han dynasty, turned away from local traditions to become members of the Taoist faith of their new political superiors. At first these converts were content to entrust the direction of their spiritual lives to the libationers of the movement, though these religious specialists were generally men of lower social standing than themselves. Among the second and third generation of converts from the old aristocracy of Wu, however, new and original impulses, which were to have most profound effects upon the development of Taoism as a whole, began to occur.

The Mao Shan Revelations. The most brilliant synthesis of the Way of the Celestial Masters with the indigenous traditions of the Southeast occurred in the 4th century AD in a family closely related to Ko Hung. Hsü Mi, an official at the Imperial court, and his youngest son, Hsü Hui, were the principal beneficiaries of an extensive new Taoist revelation. A visionary in the Hsüs' service, Yang Hsi, was honoured with the visits of a group of perfected immortals (*chen-jen*) from the heaven of Shang-ch'ing (Supreme Purity), an improvement on the T'ai-ch'ing heaven and the ordinary immortals (*hsien*) that peopled it. In the course of his visions, which lasted from AD 364 to 370, Yang received a whole new scriptural and hagiographic literature, in addition to much practical information from the "perfected" (*chen*) on how it was to be understood and employed. Like the Ko family, the Hsüs belonged to the old aristocracy of Wu, who had been displaced from prominence by the arrival of the great families of the North, to whose Taoist beliefs they had been converted. The perfected assured them that the present unjust order was soon to end and that the rule of men on earth was to be replaced by a universal Taoist imperium. The present (*i.e.*, the 4th century) was a time of trials, given over to the reign of the demonic Six Heavens, and marked by war, disease, and the worship of false gods. The sole mission of the demonic forces, however, was to cleanse the earth of evildoers, a task that would be completed by an overwhelming cataclysm of fire and flood. At that time the Good would take refuge deep in the earth, in the luminous caverns of the perfected beneath such sacred mountains as Mao Shan (in Kiang-su Province), which was the immediate focus of spiritual interest for the Hsüs. There they would complete the study of immortality already begun in their lifetimes, so as to be ready for the descent from heaven of the new universal ruler, Lord Li Hung, the "sage who is to come" (*housheng*). This was prophesied for the year 392. Yang and the Hsüs would get high office in the heaven of Shang ch'ing and rule over a newly constituted earth below, peopled by the elect (*chung-min*).

Synthesis of the Way of Celestial Masters with the Southeast traditions

Yang Hsi's prodigious genius gave great consistency and consummate literary form to his comprehensive synthesis of many spiritual traditions. Popular messianism was adapted to provide an encompassing framework and temporal cogency. Yang and his patrons, however, were also thoroughly familiar with Buddhist thought. In addition to integrating Buddhist concepts into their Taoist system, the perfected also dictated a "Taoicized" version of large portions of an early Buddhist compilation, the *Sūtra in Forty-two Sections* (*Ssu-shih-erh chang Ching*). Buddhist notions of predestination and reincarnation were subtly blended with native Chinese beliefs in hereditary character traits and the clan as a single unit involving mutual responsibility on the part of all its members, living and dead. Furthermore, building upon the Way of the Celestial Masters, the Mao Shan revelations envisaged some reform of the practices of the parent sect. Its sexual rites in particular were stigmatized as inferior practices, more conducive to perdition than to salvation. In place of this, a spiritualized union with a celestial partner was apparently realized by Yang Hsi and promised to his patrons. Other rituals of the Celestial Masters were allowed to continue in use among the Mao Shan adepts but were relegated to a subordinate position. Thus, the movement did not reject but rather incorporated and transcended the older tradition.

Though the perfected inveighed against the popular cults, even elements of these were absorbed and transformed. There is some evidence that, before Yang's inspired writings, Lord Mao himself, the august perfected immortal who gave his name to the mountain, was no more than a local minor god worshipped by an exorcistic priestess in the shadow of Mao Shan. Among the more learned traditions, alchemy received particular attention, being adopted for the first time into the context of organized religious Taoism. The perfected revealed the highly elaborate formulas of several of the elixirs that served them as food and drink. For all their extravagance, they were intended as real chemical preparations and described as being deadly poisonous to mortals. By preparing and ingesting one of them, the younger Hsü probably willingly ended his earthly existence in order to take up the post that had been offered him in the unseen world and to make ready for the coming of the new era.

Absorption of elements from local popular cults

The Ling Pao scriptures and liturgies. Another member of the Ko family was responsible for the second great Taoist scriptural tradition. Ko Ch'ao-fu began composing the *Ling pao Ching* ("Classic of the Sacred Jewel") *c.* AD 397. He claimed that they had been first revealed to his own ancestor, the famous Ko Hsüan, early in the 3rd century. In these works the Tao is personified in a series of "celestial worthies" (*t'ien-tsun*), its primordial and uncreated manifestations. These in turn were worshipped by means of a group of liturgies, which, during the 5th century, became supreme in Taoist practice, completely absorbing the older, simpler rites of the Way of the Celestial Masters. As each celestial worthy represented a different aspect of the Tao, so each ceremony of worship had a particular purpose, which it attempted to realize by distinct means. The rites as a whole were called *chai* ("retreat"), from the preliminary abstinence obligatory on all participants. They lasted a day and a night or for a fixed period of three, five, or seven days; the number of persons taking part was also specified, centring on a sacerdotal unit of six officiants. One's own salvation was inseparable from that of his ancestors; the Huang-lu chai (Retreat of the Yellow Register) was directed towards the salvation of the dead. Chin-lu chai (Retreat of the Golden Register), on the other hand, was intended to promote auspicious influences on the living. The T'u-t'an chai (Mud and Soot Retreat, or Retreat of Misery) was a ceremony of collective contrition, with the purpose of fending off disease, the punishment of sin, by prior confession; in Chinese civil law, confession resulted in an automatic reduction or suspension of sentence. These and other rituals were accomplished for the most part in the open, within a specially delimited sacred area, or altar (*t'an*), the outdoor complement of the oratory. The chanted liturgy, innumerable lamps, and clouds of billowing incense combined to produce in the participants a cathartic experience that assured these ceremonies a central place in all subsequent Taoist practices.

The great Southern masters. Though Taoism never became the exclusive state religion in the South, its most eminent representatives founded powerful organizations that received considerable official support. Lu Hsiu-ching in the 5th century epitomized the Ling Pao tradition, the liturgies of which he codified. His establishment at the great Buddho-Taoist centre, Lu Shan (in Kiangsi Province), carried out ceremonies and provided auspicious portents in favour of the Liu-Sung dynasty (420–479), in whose rulers Taoists complacently agreed to recognize the fulfillment of the old messianic prophesies and the legitimate continuation of the Han dynasty. Lu was frequently invited to the capital (present-day Nanking), where the Ch'ung-hsü Kuan (Abbey) was founded for him and served as the focal point of the Ling Pao movement.

The influence of Lu Hsiu-ching and T'ao Hung-ching

Like Lu, who was a member of the old aristocracy of Wu, T'ao Hung-ching of the 5th and 6th centuries enjoyed even greater renown as the most eminent Taoist master of his time. He spent years in searching out the manuscript legacy of Yang Hsi and the Hsüs, and in 492 retired to Mao Shan, where he edited and annotated the revealed texts and attempted to re-create their practices in their original setting. T'ao's fame as a poet, calligrapher, and natural philosopher has persisted throughout Chinese history; he is perhaps best known as the founder of critical pharmacology. T'ao was an intimate friend of the great Liang emperor Wu Ti (of the 6th century), and his Mao Shan establishment was able to survive the proscription of all other Taoist sects in 504. Though whole Taoist families lived under T'ao's spiritual rule at Mao Shan, he himself stressed the need for celibacy and full-time commitment to the work of the Tao. In his state-sponsored Chu-yang Kuan, T'ao appears to have effected a working synthesis of the public rites of the Ling Pao liturgies with the private and individual practices enjoined in the Mao Shan revelations. This dual practice was to remain a feature of all subsequent Taoist sects. T'ao's primary interest, however, was in the scriptures of the perfected of Shang-ch'ing; and this is reflected in the revelations vouchsafed by these same spiritual agents to a 19-year-old disciple of T'ao's, Chou Tzu-liang, in 515–516. These revelations show a pronounced Buddhist influence, and T'ao was himself reputed to be a master of Buddhist as well as Taoist doctrine. His writings evidence a complete familiarity with Buddhist literature, and it is reported that both Buddhist monks and Taoist priests officiated at his burial rites.

New revelations in the North

State Taoism in the North. Under the foreign rulers of North China, independent developments likewise were in progress. In 415, one K'ou Ch'ien-chih received a revelation from Lao-chün himself. According to this new dispensation, K'ou was designated celestial master and ordered to undertake a total reformation of Taoism. Not only were all popular messianic movements claiming to represent Lao-chün unsparingly condemned but K'ou's mission was particularly aimed at the elimination of abuses from the Way of the Celestial Masters itself. Sexual rites and the taxes contributed to the support of the priesthood were the principal targets of the god's denunciations; "What have such matters to do with the pure Tao?" he irately demanded. The proposed reform was far more radical than that foreseen in the Mao Shan revelations of the Southeast, and K'ou was given concrete temporal power of a sort that the Hsüs had not envisaged. Political and economic factors favoured the acceptance of his message at court; Emperor T'ai Wu Ti (5th century) of the Northern Wei dynasty put K'ou in charge of religious affairs within his dominions and proclaimed Taoism the official religion of the empire. The Emperor considered himself to reign as the terrestrial deputy of the deified Lao-tzu, as is indicated by the name of one of the periods of his reign: T'ai-p'ing Chen-chün (Perfect Lord of the Great Peace). The dominant position of Taoism under the Northern Wei, however, apparently did not long survive K'ou Ch'ien-chih's death in 448.

TAOISM UNDER THE T'ANG, SUNG, AND LATER DYNASTIES

The period of Taoism's greatest success

Taoism under the T'ang dynasty (618–907). China's reunification under the T'ang marked the beginning of Taoism's most spectacular success. The dynasty's founder, Li Yüan, claimed to be descended from the Lao-tzu; as his power increased, even the influential Mao Shan Taoists came to accept him as the long-deferred fulfillment of messianic prophecy. This notion was built into the dynasty's state ideology, and the emperor was commonly referred to as the "sage" (*sheng*). Prospective candidates for the civil service were examined in either the Ling Pao "Classic of Salvation" (*Tu-jen Ching*) or the Mao Shan "Classic of the Yellow Court" (*Huang-t'ing Ching*). Under a series of celebrated patriarchs, the Mao Shan organization dominated the religious life of the age. One of the greatest of the line, Ssu-ma Ch'eng-chen, initiated innumerable government officials and eminent men of letters and served as spiritual master to emperors. The personnel of the Mao Shan revelations even entered into the formal framework of state religion. When Ssu-ma Ch'eng-chen pointed out that the sacred peaks of the Imperial cult were in reality under the superintendence of the perfected of Shang-ch'ing, officially sponsored shrines were erected to them there; and their propitiation was incorporated into the traditional rites.

The wide diffusion of Taoism throughout the vast T'ang empire is reflected by the sizable proportion of Taoist texts discovered in the walled-up caves at Tun-huang (in Kansu Province). This town in the far west of China was the gateway to Central Asia; and here Taoists came into contact not only with Buddhists of many different doctrinal persuasions but also with Nestorian Christians and Manichaeans. Copies of the *Lao-tzu* were sent to the King of Tibet, and the book was translated into Sanskrit at the request of the ruler of Kashmir. It also reached Japan in the 7th century, as did texts of religious Taoism; reports of Taoism's dominance on the continent may still be read in the diaries of Japanese Buddhist pilgrims. The geographic extension of the religion at this time was also represented, in the legendary sphere, by the systematic elaboration of its sacred mountains and the traditions attaching to each of them. They are described by the great hagiographer, Tu Kuang-t'ing, at the end of the T'ang dynasty. In addition to the great "cavern-heavens" (*tung-t'ien*), 10 holy mountains known to the original Mao Shan revelations, he lists 36 lesser cavern heavens and 72 sanctuaries (*fu-ti*). Situated throughout the length and breadth of the empire, they are fitting spiritual guideposts across the dominions of the T'ang, which saw itself as an essentially Taocratic realm.

Taoism under the Sung and Yüan dynasties. *Internal developments.* The Sung (960–1279) and Yüan (1206–1368) periods witnessed a great religious effervescence, stimulated in part, under the Sung, by the menace of foreign invasion and, during the Yüan, by Tantric (esoteric, or occultic) Buddhism that was in vogue among the new Mongol rulers of China. During the preceding centuries the Way of the Celestial Masters, centred at Lung-hu Shan (Dragon-Tiger Mountain, Kiang-si), had been eclipsed by the prestige of Mao Shan. At the end of the Northern Sung period, the 30th celestial master, Chang Chi-hsien, was four times summoned to court by the Sung emperor Hui Tsung, who hoped for spiritual support for his threatened reign. Chang Chi-hsien was credited with a renovation of the ancient sect, thereafter called the Way of Orthodox Unity (Cheng-i Tao), and with the introduction of the influential rites of the "five thunders" (*wu-lei*) into Taoist liturgy.

The founding of new Taoist sects

After the retreat of the Sung government south of the Yangtze River (1126), a number of new Taoist sects were founded in the occupied North and soon attained impressive dimensions. Among them were: the T'ai-i (Supreme Unity) sect, founded *c.* 1140 by Hsiao Pao-chen; the Chen-ta Tao (Perfect and Great Tao) sect of Liu Te-jen (1142); and the Ch'üan-chen (Perfect Realization) sect, founded in 1163 by Wang Ch'ung-yang (Wang Che). This last sect came to the favourable attention of the Mongols, who had taken over in the North, and its second patriarch, Ch'iu Ch'ang-ch'un, was invited into Central Asia to preach to Genghis Khan. The sect enjoyed great popularity, and its establishments of celibate monks continued to be active into the 20th century, with the famous White Cloud Monastery (Po-yün Kuan) at Peking as headquarters. In the South, Mao Shan continued to prosper, while the Ko-tsao sect flourished at the mountain of that name, in Kiangsi Province. This was said to be the spot where the 3rd century immortal, Ko Hsüan, had ascended to heaven; the sect looked to him as its founder, and it transmitted the Ling Pao scriptures, which he was believed to have been the first to receive.

Literary developments. As early as *c.* 570, the need for a comprehensive collection of information on all the schools had resulted in the first great Taoist encyclopaedia. Like other such works in China, it was made up of extracts from sundry books, classified by subject matter. The compilation of similar reference works flourished during the Sung and Yüan periods. The most important is the *Seven Slips from the Bookbag of the Clouds* (*Yün-chi ch'i-ch'ien*) (*c.* 1022), made just after the first printing of the Taoist Canon in about 1016. It is a canon in miniature and contains many important works in their entirety. Hagiography continued to thrive. In addition to many local and sectarian compilations, there were huge general collections, containing the lives of both legendary and historical figures, such as the immense *Comprehensive Mirror of the Immortals* (*Chen-hsien t'ung-chien;* early 12th century). Sectarian historiography also developed; of particular interest are the extensive monographs devoted to the great mountain centres of Taoism. The *Treatise on Mao Shan* (*Mao Shan chih*) (1329) is among the most monumental. It includes lives of the saints and patriarchs, notes on topography and history, and a valuable selection from 1,000 years of literary testimony and inscriptions on the mountain and its Taoism. The new Taoist movements, which took northern China by storm in the 12th and 13th centuries, also furnish their own very copious literature: biographies of their masters and collections of their sayings. Among them is the famous account of the travels (1220–24) of a patriarch of the Ch'üan-chen sect into Central Asia in response to the summons of Genghis Khan. Short moral tracts for missionary purposes were yet another popular genre, and, finally, there are innumerable inscriptions from all periods that provide important data on Taoist establishments and their patrons over the centuries.

Taoist reference works

Alchemical developments. While learned specialists continued to refine alchemical theory, the period witnessed increasing interest in internal alchemy (*nei tan*), in which the language of the laboratory was used to describe operations realized within the body. This, in a sense, was nothing new. Alchemical metaphors had very early been applied to physiology; Ko Hung, for example, called semen the "Yin elixir." By Sung times, however, the systematic interiorization and sublimation of alchemy had become so widespread that all earlier texts of operative, external alchemy (*wai tan*) were henceforth supposed to have really been written about *nei tan,* and the attempt to compound a tangible chemical elixir was thought to have been no more than a hoax. Liturgy also provided its own sublimation of the older art: the *lien-tu* ("salvation by smelting") funeral service was developed at this time, in which an "elixir of immortality" was compounded of written talismans and offered to the deceased.

Syncretism. With such prestigious examples as Ch'an Buddhism (emphasizing intuitive meditation) and Neo-Confucianism (emphasizing knowledge and reason) before them, Taoists did not long delay in constructing interesting syntheses of their own and other beliefs. Confucianism now joined Buddhism as a fertile source of inspiration. The revelations of Hsü Sun, supposed to have lived in the 4th century AD, to one Ho Chen-kung in 1131 inspired the "Pure and Luminous Way of Loyalty and Filial Obedience" (Ching-ming Chung-hsiao Tao). This sect preached the Confucian cardinal virtues as being essential for salvation, and consequently won a considerable following in conservative intellectual and official circles. Another highly popular syncretistic movement of Taoist origin was that of the Three Religions (San Chiao). Its composite moral teachings are represented by popular tracts, the so-called "books on goodness" (*shan-shu*), which have been in extremely wide circulation since the Ming dynasty (1368–1644).

Developments outside the official current. *Communal folk Taoism (shen chiao).* Popular, or folk, religion is not a separate religious tradition but the wholly unorganized undercurrent of Chinese religious culture from the earliest times, shared by all strata of society. The Chinese have no single name for it; it may be called the religion of the gods, or spirits (*shen chiao*). The deities of the popular pantheon come from all traditions. What the deities have in common is that in *shen chiao* they are all gods intimately involved in everyday life as givers of blessings or bringers of calamities. Every object or activity of daily life has its presiding spirit that has to be consulted and feasted or appeased and driven off, especially at all special occasions in the life of the family or the community. The person primarily involved in the practice of *shen chiao* in modern times is the *fa shih* (magician). For the orthodox Taoist priests the *shen chiao* rites are the "little rites"; the *chiao* rituals, the exclusive function of the Taoist priests, are the "great rites." Both kinds of priests—the orthodox and the magicians—operate on different occasions in the same temples and are consulted for the family rites of burial,

Dmitri Kessel, *The World's Great Religions* © Time Inc.

Taoist priest burning incense in honour of two minor deities.

birth, marriage, house construction, and business affairs.

Major exorcism rites (*e.g.*, purification of haunted houses and treatment of the sick or mentally deranged) are performed by the orthodox Taoist priests, who, being ordained into the ranks of the *shen,* have power over the demons with whom they are on an equal footing. The *fa shih* priest's specific function is the manipulation of possessed mediums (specially gifted lay persons). The medium puts himself into a trance in which he becomes the mouthpiece of a deity (or a deceased relative) giving medical, personal, or business advice that is interpreted by the *fa shih.* Professional mediums attached to a temple or a private cult lacerate themselves in trances. This is considered to be a vicarious atonement for the community during the great feasts. A different form of mediumistic communication among lay people is automatic writing, either with a brush on paper or with a stick on sand.

The functions of the folk priest (or magician)

Secret societies. Politically dissident messianic movements have existed and developed separately from the established Taoist church from the very beginning (2nd century AD). Their leaders were priest-shamans, similar to the modern *fa shih* priests of folk Taoism. Their followers were the semiliterate or illiterate classes socially below the tradition of orthodox Taoism, and their organization was similar to that of the syncretistic religions and of modern secret societies. Although the secret societies have had no organizational contact with the Taoist tradition for centuries, their religious beliefs, practices, and symbols contain some Taoist elements, such as initiation rites, worship of Taoist deities, mediumism, and the use of charms and amulets for invulnerability. These influences reached them either directly or through popular religion.

Influence

TAOISM AND CHINESE CULTURE

Taoist contributions to Chinese science. Taoist physiological techniques have, in themselves, no devotional character. They have the same preoccupations as physicians: to preserve health and to prolong physical life. Medicine developed independently from about the 1st century AD, but many Taoist faith healers and hygienists added to medical knowledge.

The earliest surviving medical book, the *Huang Ti nei Ching,* or "The Yellow Emperor's Esoteric Classic" (3rd century BC?), presents itself as the teachings of a legendary Celestial Master addressed to the Yellow Emperor.

Experiments with minerals, plants, and animal substances, inspired to some extent by Taoist dietetics and by the search for the elixir of life, resulted in the 52 chapters of pharmacopoeia called *Pen-ts'ao kang-mu,* or "Great Pharmacopoeia" (16th century).

This interest in science is considered a reflection of the Taoist emphasis on direct observation and experience of the nature of things, as opposed to Confucian reliance on the authority of tradition. Chuang-tzu declared that tradition tells what was good for a bygone age but not what is good for the present.

The Taoist secret of efficacy is to follow the nature of things; this does not imply scientific experimentation but rather a sensitivity and skill obtained by "minute concentration on the Tao running through natural objects of all kinds." This knowledge and skill cannot be handed down but is that which the men of old took with them when they died (*Chuang-tzu*). The image for it is the skill of the artisan admired by the Taoists in their numerous parables on wheelwrights, meatcutters, sword makers, carvers, animal tamers, and musicians.

Though extolling the intuitive comprehension and skillful handling of matter, the Taoists did not observe nature in the Western sense and rejected technology out of their aversion to the artificial. Any new idea or discovery in China was phrased as "what the old masters really meant." This ideology of rediscovery makes it hard to study the evolution of scientific thought. Some progress over the ages (for example, in alchemy) can be seen, but the Taoist contribution to Chinese science might be smaller than it has been assumed.

Taoist imagery. Taoist literature manifests such richness and variety that scholars tend naturally to seek the symbolic modes of expression that served as points of unity within its historical diversity. No image is more fundamental to all phases of Taoism than that of the child. *Tao-te Ching* praises the infant's closeness to the Tao in its freedom from outside impressions, and *Chuang-tzu* describes the spiritual beings nurtured on primal substances, air and dew, as having the faces of children. Thus many of the spirits, both indwelling and celestial, in the esoteric system are described as resembling newborn babes, while the Immortals who appear in visions, though hundreds of years old, are at most adolescent in appearance. Other persistent images are those of mountain and cavern. Present in the older texts, they are carried over, with particular connotations, into the later works. The mountain as a meeting place of heaven and earth, gods and men, and master and disciple (as already in *Chuang-tzu*), takes on a vast downward extension. Beneath the mountains are the great "Cavern-heavens" (*tung-t'ien*) of esoteric Taoism, staffed by a numerous immortal hierarchy. Thus, for example, while Mao Shan is only some 400 metres (1,300 feet) high to the gaze of the profane, the initiate knows that its luminous grottoes plunge thousands of metres into the earth. And *light* is everywhere in Taoist revelation: spirits and paradises alike gleam with brilliance unknown in the world of men.

The image of the child

Influence on secular literature. Already during the Warring States period and the early Han, Taoism had made its appearance in the works of the other schools. Both direct quotations and patent imitations were frequent, and citations from *Tao-te Ching* and *Chuang-tzu* abound throughout later Chinese literature, as do reminiscences of both their style and their content. Esoteric Taoist writings, too, held great fascination for men of letters. Their response might vary from a mere mention of the most celebrated Immortals to whole works inspired directly by specific Taoist texts and practices. Many a poet recorded his search, real or metaphorical, for Immortals or transcendent herbs, or described his attempts at compounding an elixir. A certain number of technical terms became touchstones of poetic diction. The revealed literature of Mao Shan came to have the greatest effect on secular writings. As works of great literary refinement, the *Lives* of the Perfected directly inspired a very famous tale, the *Intimate Life of Emperor Wu of Han* (*Han Wu Ti nei-chuan;* late 6th century), which in highly polished terms describes the visit to the emperor of a goddess, the Queen Mother of the West. This work, in turn, made a decisive contribution to the development of T'ang romantic fiction. Literary accounts of fantastic marvels also drew heavily on the wonders of Mao Shan hagiography and topography. The Mao Shan influence on T'ang poetry was no less important. Precise references to the literature of the sect abound in the poems of the time, while many of the greatest poets, such as Li Po, were formally initiated into the Mao Shan organization. As awareness of these influences increases, scholars are faced with the intriguing question of the possible religious origins of whole genres of Chinese literature (see also EAST ASIAN ARTS).

Influence of Mao Shan literature

Influence on the visual arts. A number of early Chinese books of spiritual interest claim to have been inspired by pictures seen on the walls of local temples. A similar tradition attaches to the *Lives of the Immortals,* which is said to derive from a pictorial work called *Portraits of the Immortals.* As has been noted, the Immortals were depicted on Han mirrors. Other illustrative materials were in close relation to the earliest esoteric Taoist literature. Graphic guides existed from early times to aid in the identification of sacred minerals and plants, particularly mushrooms. A later specimen of such a work is to be found in the Taoist Canon. This practical aspect of Taoist influence resulted in the exceptionally high technical level of botanical and mineralogical drawing that China soon attained. In calligraphy, too, Taoists soon set the highest standard. One of the greatest of all calligraphers, Wang Hsi-chih (303–361), was an adherent of the Way of the Celestial Master, and one of his most renowned works was a transcription of the *Book of the Yellow Court.* The efficacy of talismans, in particular, depended on the precision of the strokes from which they were created. Figure painting was another field in which Taoists excelled. China's celebrated painter Ku K'ai-chih, a practicing Taoist, left an essay containing directions for painting a scene in the life of the first Celestial Master, Chang Tao-ling. Many works on Taoist themes, famous in their time but now lost, have been attributed to other great early masters. Of these, some may have been painted for use in ritual, and religious paintings of the Taoist pantheon are still produced today. The Taoist scriptures, with their instructions for visualization of the spiritual hierarchy, including details of apparel and accoutrements, are ready-made painter's manuals. Finally, the language of speculative Taoism was pressed into service as the basic vocabulary of Chinese aesthetics. Consequently, many secular artists attempted to express their own conceptions of the "natural spontaneity" of *Chuang-tzu* and *Lao-tzu*'s "spirit of the valley." Here Taoism found still wider imaginative extension, and the efforts of these painters are embodied in those magnificent landscapes that have come to be thought of as most characteristically Chinese.

TAOISM AND OTHER RELIGIONS

Confucianism and Buddhism. Confucianism is concerned with human society and the social responsibilities of its members; Taoism emphasizes nature and what is natural and spontaneous in man. The two traditions, "within society" and "beyond society," balance and complement each other. This classic definition is generally correct concerning orthodox Han Confucianism; it neglects some aspects of Confucian thought, such as the speculations on the *I Ching*, that is considered to be among the Confucian Classics and the prophetic occult (*ch'an-wei*) commentaries to the classics. As far as Taoism is concerned, this definition neglects the social thought of the Taoist philosophers and the political aspects of Taoist religion. Chinese Buddhism has been viewed not as a Sinified Indian religion but as flowers on the tree of Chinese religions that blossomed under Indian stimulus and that basically maintained their Chinese character.

Taoist interpretations of Buddhism

The first mention of Buddhism in China (AD 65) occurs in a Taoist context, at the court of a member of the Imperial family known for his devotion to the doctrines of Huang-Lao. The Indian religion was at first regarded as a foreign variety of Taoism; the particular Buddhist texts chosen to be translated during the Han period reveal the Taoist preoccupation of the earliest converts with rules of conduct and techniques of meditation. Early translators employed Taoist expressions as equivalents for Buddhist technical terms. Thus, the Buddha, in achieving enlightenment (*bodhi*) was described as having "obtained the Tao"; the Buddhist saints (*arhat*) become perfected immortals (*chen-jen*); and "non-action" (*wu-wei*) was used to render Nirvāṇa (the Buddhist state of bliss). A joint sacrifice to Lao-tzu and the Buddha was performed by the Han emperor in AD 166. During this period occurred the first reference to the notion that Lao-tzu, after vanishing into the west, became the Buddha. This theory enjoyed a long and varied history. It claimed that Buddhism was a debased form of Taoism, designed by Lao-tzu as a curb on the violent natures and vicious habits of the "western barbarians," and as such was entirely unsuitable for Chinese consumption. A variant theory even suggested that, by imposing celibacy on Buddhist monks, Lao-tzu intended the foreigners' extinction. In approximately AD 300, the Taoist scholar Wang Fou composed a "Classic of the Conversion of the Barbarians" (*Hua hu Ching*), which was altered and expanded in subsequent centuries to encompass new developments in the continuing debate. Although there is no evidence that the earliest Taoist organization, literature, or ceremonies were in any way indebted to Buddhism, by the 4th century there was a distinct Buddhist influence upon the literary form of Taoist scriptures and the philosophical expression of the most eminent Taoist masters.

The process of interaction, however, was a mutual one, Taoism participating in the widening of thought because of the influence of a foreign religion and Buddhism undergoing a partial "Taoicization" as part of its adaptation to Chinese conditions. The Buddhist contribution is particularly noticeable in the developing conceptions of the afterlife; Buddhist ideas of purgatory had a most striking effect not only upon Taoism but especially on Chinese popular religion. On a more profound level the ultimate synthesis of Taoism and Buddhism was realized in the Ch'an (Japanese Zen) tradition (from the 7th century on), into which the paradoxes of the ancient Taoist mystics were integrated. Likewise, the goal of illumination in a single lifetime, rather than at the end of an indefinite succession of future existences, was analogous to the religious Taoist's objective of immortality as the culmination of his present life.

Ch'an Buddhism deeply influenced Neo-Confucianism, the renaissance of Confucian philosophy in Sung times (960–1279), which in Chinese is called "Learning of the Tao" (Tao Hsüeh). In this movement Confucianism acquired a universal dimension beyond a concern for society. Neo-Confucian thought often seems as Taoist as the so-called Neo-Taoist philosophy and literature seem Confucian.

As early as the T'ang dynasty, there are traces of the syncretism of the "Three Religions" (San Chiao), which became a popular movement in Sung and Ming China. A mixture of Confucian ethics, the Taoist system of merits, and the Buddhist concept of reincarnation produced such "books on goodness" (*shan-shu*) as the *Kan ying p'ien* ("Tract on Actions and Retributions"). The school of the "Three Religions" was rejected by most Confucians and Buddhists but received wide support in Taoist circles. Many Taoist masters of those periods transmitted *nei tan* and other techniques of inner cultivation to their disciples while at the same time preaching the moralism of the "Three Religions" to outsiders.

Other Asian religions. The affinities of Taoism with other Asian religions are numerous. If one distinguishes between universal religions of salvation, such as Buddhism and Islām, and the older, more culture-bound, such as Japanese Shintō and Hinduism, Taoism undoubtedly belongs to the second category.

The fact that no record of Shintō antedates the introduction of Chinese script makes it difficult to distinguish between Taoist affinities and influences on Shintō features, such as the cult of holy mountains, the representation of the human soul as a bird, bird dances, the representation of the world of the dead as a paradisiac country of immortality, and the concept of the vital force (*tama*, in objects as well as in man). Like Taoism, Shintō is the religion of the village community.

There was never an attempt to implant a Taoist religion officially in Japan, but a random choice of Taoist beliefs

By courtesy of the Chinese Classic Art Publishing House, Peking

A Confucian (left), a Buddhist (centre), and a Taoist, a painting of a tranquil discussion that exemplifies the peaceful coexistence of the "three ways" in China. The figures show ideal types, each representative of his faith; the Confucian is dressed as a scholar, the Buddhist as a monk, and the Taoist, in his garment of leaves, as a forest ascetic.

and customs have, at various ages, been adopted and transformed at the Japanese court, in the temples, and among the people. Records from the early 7th century contain traces of Taoism, which was appreciated chiefly for its magical claims. The "masters of Yin and Yang" (*ommyō-ji*), a caste of diviners learned in the *I Ching,* Chinese astrology, and occult sciences who assumed importance at court in the Heian period (8th–12th century), probably were responsible for the introduction of Taoist practices, such as the Keng-shen (Japanese Kōshin) vigil and the observance of directional taboos (*katatagae*). In the 8th century, disputations were held at court over Buddhism and the philosophy of Lao-tzu and Chuang-tzu. The *Pao-p'u-tzu* was known, and Kōbō Daishi, the founder of Shingon Buddhism, reported (in 797) on Taoist physiological practices and beliefs in immortals. Buddhist (Shingon and Tendai) ascetics, wandering healers, and mountain hermits known as *yamabushi* probably came closest to Taoism in their techniques for prolonging life (abstinence from grains, etc.) and their magical arts (exorcisms, sword dance) and objects (mirrors, charms), which must have reached them through the Tantric elements in Shingon. Taoist mysticism lives on in that it has influenced the two Chinese Zen schools of Lin-chi (Rinzai) and Ts'ao-tung (Sōtō), introduced in the 12th and 13th centuries and still active in Japan. Popular Taoist moral tracts were printed and widely diffused in the Tokugawa period. Modern Japanese scholarship on Taoism (Dōkyō) ranks very high in the world.

Introduction of Taoist practices to Japan

Western mysticism and religions. The similarity of mysticism in all religions points to the fact that there is only one Inner Way, the experience of which is expressed differently in the respective cultural and religious environments. Lao-tzu's notion of "the One," which is not only primordial unity but the oneness underlying all phenomena, the point in which all contraries are reconciled, was spoken of by such Western mystics as Plotinus, a 3rd-century-AD Greek philosopher, and Nicholas of Cusa, a 15th-century French philosopher.

Similarities between Taoism and Western mystical thought

Taoism, as all other forms of Eastern mysticism, distinguishes itself from Western mysticism by its conscious techniques of mind and body designed to induce trance and to give access to mystical experience. These disciplines of learning to "sit in forgetfulness" are akin to Plotinus' concern to "be deaf to the sounds of the senses and keep the soul's faculty of apprehension one-pointed" and to the 16th-century Spanish mystic Teresa of Avila's state where "the soul is fully awake as regards God, but wholly asleep as regards things of this world and in respect of herself." Lao-tzu's strangely sober and abstract descriptions of ecstatic union with the Tao have been compared to the medieval German mystic Meister Eckeharts' "still desert of the Godhead" and his pupil Heinrich Suso's union of the essence of the soul with "the essence of Nothingness." One instance of Western physiological techniques is the Hesychasts, a sect of Greek Orthodox mystics on Mt. Athos in the 14th century who used respiratory practices and concentration on internal organs to prepare for the mental "Jesus prayer."

TAOISM IN MODERN TIMES

Taoism on Taiwan

The principal refuge of Taoism in the 20th century is on Taiwan. Its establishment on the island is doubtless contemporary with the great emigration from the opposite mainland province of Fukien in the 17th and 18th centuries. The religion, however, has received new impetus since the 63rd celestial master, Chang En-pu, took refuge there in 1949. On Taiwan, Taoism may still be observed in its traditional setting, distinct from the manifestations of popular religion that surround it. Hereditary Taoist priests (Taiwanese *sai-kong*), called "blackheads" (*wu t'ou*) from their headgear, are clearly set off from the exorcists (*fa-shih*) or "redheads" (*hung-t'ou*) of the ecstatic cults. Their lengthy rites are still held, now known under the term *chiao* ("offering"), rather than the medieval *chai* ("retreat"). The liturgy chanted, in expanded Sung form, still embodies elements that can be traced back to Chang Tao-ling's sect. The religion has enjoyed a renaissance since the 1960s, with great activity being carried on in temple building and restoration. The most significant event in the past several centuries of Taoist history, however, probably is the ordination (in 1964) in Taiwan of a Dutch scholar, K.M. Schipper, as a Taoist priest. His systematic, first-hand researches into Taoist practices may very well revolutionize scholarly knowledge of the religion, which will thus acquire an unforeseen historical extension, in the West and into the future. (A.K.Se./M.St./Ed.)

BIBLIOGRAPHY

General works: MAX KALTENMARK, *Lao Tzu and Taoism* (1969; originally published in French, 1965), a good general introduction to Taoist philosophy and religion; HERRLEE G. CREEL, *What Is Taoism?* (1970, reissued 1977), eight essays on Taoist thought; HOLMES WELCH, *The Parting of the Way: Lao Tzu and the Taoist Movement* (1957), a most readable interpretation of the *Tao-te Ching* and first coherent account of the Taoist movement; HENRI MASPERO, *Le Taoïsme et les religions chinoises,* rev. ed. (1971), a classic pioneer work on religious Taoism; MARCEL GRANET, *La Pensée chinoise* (1934, reprinted 1975), the classic work on the basic systems of classification in Chinese thought—difficult but highly enlightening.

Texts: ARTHUR WALEY, *The Way and Its Power* (1934, reissued 1968), a classic translation of the *Tao-te Ching* preceded by a good introduction on its place in Chinese thought; BURTON WATSON, *The Complete Works of Chuang Tzu* (1968), a very readable translation of the most important and most difficult text of Taoist mysticism; ANGUS C. GRAHAM, *The Book of Lieh-tzu* (1961, reissued 1973) a good translation and introduction to Taoist mysticism; MAX KALTENMARK, *Le Lie-sien tchouan* (1953), a translation of the earliest extant Taoist hagiography, with much information on mythology hidden in long notes; KRISTOFER SCHIPPER, *L'Empereur Wou des Han dans la légende taoïste* (1965), a translation of a Taoist hagiographic novel and a study of its ritual background in the Mao Shan sect; JAMES R. WARE, *Alchemy, Medicine and Religion in the China of A.D. 320: The Nei P'ien of Ko Hung* (1966, reissued 1981), an imperfect but complete translation of probably the most important text of religious Taoism; NATHAN SIVIN, *Chinese Alchemy: Preliminary Studies* (1968), an annotated translation of a treatise by a 6th-century alchemist—a most scholarly introduction on the study of Chinese alchemy. The texts of the *Shih-chi* concerning Lao-tzu have been translated and thoroughly discussed in a debate between H.H. DUBS and D. BODDE in the *Journal of the American Oriental Society,* vol. 61, 62, and 64 (1941, 1942, and 1944).

History: (*Taoist speculation and mysticism*): ARTHUR WALEY, *Three Ways of Thought in Ancient China* (1939, reissued 1982), the *Chuang-tzu* studied in relation to the thought of its time; JOSEPH NEEDHAM, *Science and Civilisation in China,* vol. 2, *History of Scientific Ideas* (1956), a highly lucid exposé of early Taoist speculation and later Taoist technology; FUNG YU-LAN, *A History of Chinese Philosophy*, 2nd ed., 2 vol. (Eng. trans. 1952–53, reissued 1973), a standard reference work on the classical period of Chinese thought. On the legends, see HENRI DORÉ, "Lao-tsé et le taoïsme," *Recherches sur les superstitions en Chine,* vol. 18 (1938), not very scientific but giving much information; and ANNA K. SEIDEL, "The Image of the Perfect Ruler in Early Taoist Messianism: Lao-tzu and Li Hung," *History of Religion,* 9:216–247 (1969–70). (*The Taoist religion*): ANNA K. SEIDEL, *La Divinisation de Lao tseu dans le Taoïsme des Han* (1969), an excellent detailed study of the formation of the Taoist system in the early Imperial period; ÉDOUARD CHAVANNES, *Le Jet des dragons* (1916), a classic study and translation of a Taoist liturgy dating from the end of the T'ang dynasty; ARTHUR WALEY, *The Travels of an Alchemist* (1931, reprinted 1963), the account of the Central Asian journey of the second Patriarch of the Ch'üan-chen sect, and *The Poetry and Career of Li Po: 701–762* (1950, reissued 1976), the life of the Taoist poet; J.J.M. DE GROOT, *Les Fêtes annuellement célébrées â Émoui (Amoy)* (1886, reissued 1981), and *The Religious System of China,* vol. 6 (1910, reissued 1976), both valuable pioneering descriptions of the Taoist priesthood and popular exorcists in Fukien at the end of the 19th century; *History of Religions,* vol. 9, no. 2 and 3 (1969–70), issues devoted to the reports from the First International Conference on Taoist Studies, including papers on the conference discussions, on Chuang-tzu, on Neo-Taoism, on Taoist antecedents in Buddhist thought, and on Taoist messianism; HOLMES WELCH and ANNA K. SEIDEL (eds.), *Facets of Taoism: Essays in Chinese Religion* (1979), studies of religious Taoism from the Second International Conference on Taoist Studies; RALPH GUN HOY SIU, *Ch'i: A Neo-Taoist Approach to Life* (1974), a presentation of the Taoist philosophy of time; MICHAEL R. SASO, *The Teachings of Taoist Master Chuang* (1978), a discussion of contemporary liturgical Taoism; and MICHEL SOYMIE, "Bibliographie du Taoïsme—études dans les langues occidentales," in *Études Taoïstes* (*Dôkyô kenkyû*), vol. 3–4 (1968–71), the first comprehensive bibliography of Western-language studies on Taoism and Chinese folk religion.

Taxation

Taxes are levied in almost every country of the world, primarily to raise revenue for government expenditures, although they serve other purposes as well. This article is concerned with taxation in general, its principles, its objectives, and its effects; specifically, the article discusses the nature and purposes of taxation, classes of taxes, the history of taxation, canons and criteria of taxation, shifting and incidence, tax law, tax administration, and the effects of the major types of taxes on economic and social activities. For further discussion of taxation's role in fiscal policy, see GOVERNMENT FINANCE. See also the article INTERNATIONAL TRADE for additional information on tariffs.

For coverage of related topics in the *Macropædia* and *Micropædia,* see the *Propædia,* sections 534 and 552.

This article is divided into the following sections:

The nature of taxation

In modern economies taxes are the most important source of governmental revenue. Taxes differ from other sources of revenue in that they are compulsory levies and are unrequited—*i.e.,* they are not paid in exchange for some specific thing, such as the sale of public property or the issue of public debt. While taxes are presumably collected for the sake of the welfare of taxpayers as a whole, the liability of the individual taxpayer is independent of any benefit received. There are important exceptions to this characterization. Payroll taxes are commonly levied on labour income in order to finance retirement benefits, medical payments, and other social security programs. Because there may be some link between taxes paid and benefits received, payroll taxes are sometimes called "contributions," as in the United States. Nevertheless, the payments are commonly compulsory and the link to benefits is usually quite weak.

PURPOSES OF TAXATION

The various functions of taxation

During the 19th century the prevalent idea was that taxes should serve mainly to finance the government. In earlier times, and again today, governments have utilized taxation for other than merely fiscal purposes. One useful way to view the purpose of taxation, attributable to the American economist Richard A. Musgrave, is to distinguish between objectives of resource allocation, income redistribution, and economic stability. (Economic growth or development and international competitiveness are sometimes listed as separate goals, but they can generally be subsumed under the other three.) In the absence of a strong reason for interference, such as the need to reduce pollution, the resource allocation objective is furthered if tax policy does not interfere with market-determined allocations. The redistributive objective is to lessen inequalities in the distribution of income and wealth to the extent they are considered excessive and unjust. The stabilization objective, which tax policy shares with government expenditure policy (under the rubric of "fiscal policy") and monetary policy, is the maintenance of high employment and price stability.

Because these three functions are interrelated, there are likely to be conflicts among them. Thus the level or composition (or both) of taxes considered necessary for allocative reasons may tend to bear heavily on low-income families. Or taxes that are highly redistributive may conflict with the desired goal of economic neutrality required for an efficient allocation of resources.

CLASSES OF TAXES

Direct and indirect taxes. Taxes are most commonly classified as either direct or indirect, an example of the former type being the income tax and of the latter the sales tax. There is much disagreement among economists as to the criterion for distinguishing between direct and indirect, and it is unclear into which category certain taxes, such as corporate income and property taxes, should be classified. It is usually said that a direct tax is one that cannot be shifted by the taxpayer to someone else.

Types of direct taxes

Direct taxes. Direct taxes are primarily taxes on persons; they are aimed at the individual's ability to pay as measured by his income or his net wealth. The main types of direct taxes are the following.

Individual income taxes are commonly levied on total personal net income in excess of some stipulated minimum. They are also commonly adjusted to take into account the circumstances influencing the ability to pay of the individual, such as family status, number and age of children, and financial burdens resulting from illness. They are often levied at graduated rates, that is, at rates that rise as income rises.

Taxes on net worth are levied on the total net worth of a person—that is, the value of his assets minus his liabilities. As with the income tax, the personal circumstances of the individual can be taken into consideration.

Taxes at death take two forms: the inheritance tax, where the tax object is the bequest received by the person inheriting, and the estate tax, where the object is the total estate left by the deceased. Inheritance taxes usually allow for the personal circumstances of the taxpayer, including his net worth before receiving the bequest and his relation to the donor. Estate taxes are generally graduated according to the size of the estate, and in some countries they make allowance for the number of children involved. In order to prevent the death duties from being circumvented, any rational and efficient tax system has to include a tax on gifts between living persons, particularly those deemed to be made in anticipation of death.

General expenditure or spending taxes are taxes on all income that is not channeled into savings. In contrast to indirect taxes on spending, such as the sales tax, an expenditure tax can be adjusted to an individual's ability to pay by allowing for marital status, age, number of dependents, etc. Although long attractive to theorists, this form of tax has only been used in two countries, India and Ceylon (now Sri Lanka), briefly and unsuccessfully in both cases. Recently an alternative that achieves effects similar to those of the expenditure tax, by exempting most income from capital, has been viewed favourably by tax experts; no country has such a tax.

Types of indirect taxes

Indirect taxes. Indirect taxes are levied on objects and services or transactions. They include general and selective taxes on sales of consumer goods, value-added taxes, taxes on goods in the process of production, taxes on legal transactions, and import or customs duties.

General sales taxes are levies that burden a substantial portion of consumer expenditures. The same tax rate can be applied to all taxed items, or different items can be subject to different rates. Single-stage taxes can be collected at the retail level, as by the U.S. states, or they can be collected at a pre-retail (manufacturing or wholesale) level, as in many developing countries. Multistage taxes are applied at each stage in the production-distribution process. Value-added taxes, one of the most important fiscal innovations of the second half of the 20th century, are commonly collected by allowing the taxpayer to deduct a credit for tax paid on purchases from liability on sales. Such taxes have largely replaced turnover taxes, a defective form of tax in which tax was collected at each stage, with no relief for tax paid at previous stages.

Taxes on specific commodities are called excises, as distinguished from sales taxes and other general consumption levies. Generally applicable sales taxes sometimes exempt necessities in an effort to reduce the burden on low-income households. Excises and customs duties are levied on almost everything, from necessities such as bread, meat, and salt, to nonessentials such as cigarettes, wine, liquor, coffee, and tea, to luxuries such as jewels and furs.

Some excises and customs duties are specific—*i.e.,* they are levied on the basis of weight, length, volume, and other specific characteristics of the tax object. Other taxes are ad valorem—levied on the value of the goods as measured by the price.

Taxes on consumer durables formerly were applied to luxury commodities such as pianos, saddle horses, carriages, and billiard tables. Today the main tax object is the automobile, largely because registration requirements facilitate administration of the tax.

Taxes on intermediate goods and production factors are levied on raw materials, intermediate goods (*e.g.,* mineral oil, alcohol), machines, or labour.

Taxes on legal transactions are levied on the issue of shares, on the sale of houses and land, and on stock exchange transactions. For administrative reasons, they are frequently levied in the form of stamp duties—that is, the legal or commercial document is stamped to denote payment of the tax.

Proportional, progressive, and regressive taxes. Taxes can also be distinguished on the basis of the effect they have on the distribution of income and wealth. A proportional tax is one that imposes the same relative burden on all taxpayers—*i.e.,* where tax liability and income grow in equal proportion. A progressive tax is characterized by a more than proportional rise in the tax liability relative to the increase in income, and a regressive tax is characterized by a less than proportional rise in the relative burden. Thus, progressive taxes reduce the inequality of income distribution and regressive taxes increase it.

Examples of taxes that are generally considered progressive are income taxes and death duties. Income taxes that are nominally progressive may become less so in the upper income categories, however, if it is possible to reduce the tax base by means of deductions or by the exclusion of certain income components from taxable income; on the other hand, in the lower income categories to which a proportional tax rate applies, some progression is introduced through the personal exemptions. Further subtleties are introduced by the fact that income during a given year does not necessarily provide the best measure of taxpaying ability. Transitory increases in income may be saved, and during temporary declines in income consumption may be financed by reducing savings. Thus, the use of "permanent income" as the basis for comparison reveals a pattern of taxation that is less regressive (or more progressive) than the use of annual income.

Sales taxes and excises (except those on luxuries) tend to be regressive, even though they may be nominally proportional, because the share of personal income spent on a specific good declines as the level of personal income rises. Poll taxes, levied as a fixed amount per capita, obviously are regressive.

Because of uncertainty about the shifting of corporate income taxes and property taxes, it is difficult to know whether such taxes are progressive, regressive, or proportionate. This uncertainty is confounded by the fact that determining on whom the burden of such a tax falls depends on whether a national or a state tax is being considered.

In considering both the progressivity and the economic effects of taxation, it is important to distinguish between several concepts of tax rates. The statutory rates are those specified in the law; commonly these are marginal rates, but sometimes they are average rates. Marginal income tax rates indicate the fraction of incremental income that is taken by taxation when income rises by one dollar. Thus if tax liability rises by 45 cents when income rises by one dollar, the marginal tax rate is 45 percent. Income tax statutes commonly contain graduated marginal rates, that is, rates that rise as income rises. Careful analysis of marginal tax rates must consider provisions other than the formal statutory rate structure. If, for example, a particular tax credit (reduction in tax) falls by 20 cents for each one-dollar rise in income, the marginal rate is 20 percentage points higher than indicated by the statutory rates. Since marginal rates indicate how after-tax income changes in response to changes in before-tax income, they are the relevant ones for appraising incentive effects of taxation.

Marginal and average rates of tax

Average income tax rates indicate the fraction of total income that is paid in taxation. The pattern of average rates is the one that is relevant for appraising the distributional equity of taxation. Under a progressive income tax the average income tax rate rises with income. Average income tax rates commonly rise with income, both because personal allowances are provided for the taxpayer and dependents and because marginal tax rates are graduated; on the other hand, preferential treatment of income received predominantly by high-income households may swamp these effects, producing regressivity, as indicated by average tax rates that fall as income rises.

HISTORY OF TAXATION

Effect of ease of administration on taxation

Patterns of taxation throughout history can be explained largely by administrative considerations. Because it is easier to tax imports than to tax domestic output, import duties were among the earliest taxes. Similarly, the simple turnover tax (levied on gross sales) long held precedence over the conceptually preferable value-added tax (which allows credit for tax paid on purchases). As for personal taxes, it is easier to identify, and thus tax, real property than other assets; and a head tax is even easier to implement. It is not surprising, therefore, that the first direct levies were head and land taxes.

Taxes played a relatively minor role in the ancient world. Taxes on consumption were levied in Greece and Rome. Tariffs—taxes on imported goods—were often of considerably more importance than internal excises so far as the production of revenue went. As a means of raising additional funds in time of war, taxes on property would be temporarily imposed. For a long time these taxes were confined to real property, but later they were extended to other assets. Real estate transactions also were taxed. In Greece free citizens had different tax obligations from slaves, and in Rome the tax laws distinguished between nationals and residents of conquered territories.

In Rome, along with consumption taxes and customs duties, there were certain "direct" taxes. The principal of these was the *tributum* paid by citizens and usually levied as a head tax; later, when additional revenue was required, the base of this tax was extended to real estate holdings. In the time of Julius Caesar a 1 percent general sales tax was introduced (*centesima rerum venalium*). The provinces relied for their revenues on head taxes and land taxes; the latter consisted initially of fixed liabilities regardless of the return from the land, as in Persia and Egypt, but later the land tax was modified to achieve a certain correspondence with the fertility of the land, or, alternatively, a 10th of the produce was collected as a tax in kind (the "tithe"). It is noteworthy that at a relatively early time Rome had an inheritance tax of 5 percent, later 10 percent; however, close relatives of the deceased were exempted. For a long time tax collection was left to middlemen or "tax farmers," who contracted to collect the taxes for a share of the proceeds; under Caesar collection was delegated to civil servants.

In the Middle Ages many of these ancient taxes, especially among the direct levies, vanished and gave way to a variety of obligatory services and a system of "aids" (most of which amounted to gifts). The main indirect taxes were transit duties and market fees. In the cities, the concept developed of a tax obligation encompassing all residents: the burden of taxes on certain foods and beverages was intended to be borne partly by consumers and partly by producers and tradesmen. During the latter part of the Middle Ages, some German and Italian cities introduced several direct taxes: head taxes for the poor and net worth or occasionally crude income taxes for the rich. (The income tax was administered through self-assessment and an oath taken before a civic commission.) The use of land taxes and taxes on houses gradually spread.

Taxes as an issue in politics, revolutions, and wars

Taxes have been a major subject of political controversy throughout history, even before they constituted a sizable share of the national income. A famous instance is the rebellion of the American colonies against Great Britain when the colonials refused to pay taxes imposed by a Parliament in which they had no voice; hence the slogan, "No taxation without representation." Another instance is the French Revolution of 1789, in which the inequitable distribution of the tax burden was a major factor.

Wars have influenced taxes much more than taxes have influenced revolutions. Many taxes, notably the income tax (first introduced in England in 1799) and the turnover or purchase tax (Germany, 1918; Great Britain, 1940) began as "temporary" war measures. Similarly, the withholding method of income tax collection began as a wartime innovation in France, the United States, and Britain. World War II converted the income taxes of many nations from upper-class taxes to mass taxes.

It is hardly necessary to mention the role that tax questions play in peacetime politics, where the influence of powerful, well-organized pressure groups is great. Arguments for tax reform, particularly in the area of income taxes, are perennially at issue in the domestic politics of many countries.

Modern trends

The development of taxation in recent times can be summarized by the following general statements, although allowance must be made for considerable national differences: The authority of the sovereign to levy taxes in a more or less arbitrary fashion has been lost, and the power to tax now generally resides in parliamentary bodies. The level of most taxes has risen substantially and so has the ratio of tax revenues to the national income. Taxes today are collected in money, not in goods. Tax farming has been abolished; taxes are assessed and collected by civil servants. There has been a reduction in reliance on customs duties and excises. Many countries increasingly rely on sales taxes and other general consumption taxes. An important late 20th-century development has been the replacement of turnover taxes with value-added taxes. Taxes on the privilege of doing business and on real property have lost ground and are important today mainly as revenue sources for local communities. The absolute and relative weight of direct personal taxation has been growing in most of the developed countries, and increasing attention has been focused on payroll and value-added taxes.

Income taxation, both of individuals and of corporations, payroll taxes, general sales taxes, and (in some countries) property taxes occupy leading positions in modern tax systems. The income tax has ceased to be a rich man's tax; it is now paid by the general populace, and in several countries it is complemented by a tax on net worth. The emphasis on the ability-to-pay principle and on the redistribution of wealth, which led to graduated rates, especially in the case of income taxes, appears to have peaked and been replaced by greater concern for the economic distortions and disincentives caused by high tax rates. A good deal of fiscal centralization has occurred, as reflected in the kinds of taxes levied by central governments. The latter now control the most important taxes (from a revenue-producing point of view): income and corporation taxes, payroll taxes, and value-added taxes. Various ways have been found to allow lower-level governments to share in the tax revenues of central governments.

Although it is difficult to generalize, certain clear patterns can be detected in the relative reliance on various types of taxes by countries at different levels of development. Developed countries usually rely more heavily on individual income taxes than do developing countries but less heavily on corporation income taxes. Among developing countries, reliance on income taxes, especially on corporate income taxes, generally increases as the level of income rises. This pattern may be largely explained by taxes on natural resources; resource-rich countries tend both to be high-income countries and to rely heavily on corporate income taxes to tap their resource wealth. The poorest countries rely more heavily on taxes on international trade (and, to a lesser extent, domestic taxes on consumption), partly because they lack the administrative capacity to implement more sophisticated taxes on income. A relatively high percentage of the total tax revenue of industrialized nations comes from domestic consumption taxes, especially the value-added tax (rather than the simpler turnover tax). Social security taxes—commonly payroll taxes—are much more important in developed countries and the more affluent developing countries than in the poorest countries, reflecting the near lack of social security systems in the latter countries.

Taxes in general represent a much higher percentage of national output in developed countries than in developing countries; similarly, among developing countries, more of national output is channeled to governmental use through taxation in the countries with the highest levels of income. In many respects the tax systems of the developing countries with the highest levels of income resemble those of developed countries more than those of the poorest developing countries.

PRINCIPLES OF TAXATION

The 18th-century philosopher Adam Smith attempted to systematize the rules that should govern a rational system of taxation. In *The Wealth of Nations* (Book V, Chapter II) he set down four general canons:

> I. The subjects of every state ought to contribute towards the support of the government, as nearly as possible, in proportion to their respective abilities; that is, in proportion to the revenue which they respectively enjoy under the protection of the state . . . .
>
> II. The tax which each individual is bound to pay ought to be certain, and not arbitrary. The time of payment, the manner

of payment, the quantity to be paid, ought all to be clear and plain to the contributor, and to every other person....
III. Every tax ought to be levied at the time, or in the manner, in which it is most likely to be convenient for the contributor to pay it....
IV. Every tax ought to be so contrived as both to take out and keep out of the pockets of the people as little as possible over and above what it brings into the public treasury of the state....

Although they need to be reinterpreted from time to time, these principles, especially the first and last, retain remarkable relevance. From the first can be derived both of the leading views of what is fair in the distribution of tax burdens among taxpayers. These are the belief that taxes should be based on the individual's ability to pay, known as the ability-to-pay principle, and the benefit principle, the idea that there should be some equivalence between what the individual pays and the benefits he derives from governmental activities. The fourth of Smith's canons can be interpreted to underlie the emphasis many economists place on a tax system that does not interfere with market decision making, as well as the more obvious need to avoid complexity and corruption.

Horizontal equity

Distribution of tax burdens. The principle of horizontal equity requires that persons in the same or similar positions so far as tax purposes are concerned be subject to the same tax liability. In practice this equality principle is often disregarded, both intentionally and unintentionally. Intentional violations are usually motivated more by politics than by sound economic policy (*e.g.,* the tax advantages granted to farmers, home owners, or members of the middle class in general; the exclusion of interest on government securities). Much of recent debate over tax reform has centred on whether deviations from "equal treatment of equals" are justified.

The ability-to-pay principle. The ability-to-pay principle requires that the total tax burden be distributed among individuals according to their capacity to bear it, taking into account all of the relevant personal characteristics in such a way that the relative loss in economic capacity resulting from the tax is equal. The primary indicator of ability to pay is commonly agreed to be income. There have, however, been important dissents from this view, including those by John Locke and Thomas Hobbes and a number of leading modern tax specialists. The dissenters support their view that equity should be measured by what is taken from the pot (consumption) rather than by what is put in (income) with arguments based on the neutrality of consumption-based taxes toward saving (income taxes discriminate against saving) and the superiority of consumption as a measure of an individual's ability to pay over a lifetime. Some theorists include wealth in the ability-to-pay criterion because its ownership implies some degree of satisfaction (power) and tax capacity even if it generates no tangible income (*e.g.,* collections of art or jewelry). The most suitable taxes from this standpoint are personal levies (income, net worth, expenditure, and inheritance taxes).

The ability-to-pay principle also is commonly interpreted as requiring that direct personal taxes have a progressive rate structure, although there is no way of demonstrating that any particular degree of progression is the right one. Because a considerable part of the population does not pay certain direct taxes, such as income or inheritance taxes, at all, such taxes ordinarily need to be supplemented by direct income transfers such as subsidies or "negative income taxes" if a satisfactory redistribution is to be achieved.

Indirect taxes such as excise, sales, turnover, or value-added taxes can be adapted to the ability-to-pay criterion only to a limited extent—for example, by the taxation of services, the exemption of necessities, or the differentiation of tax rates according to "urgency of need."

Using taxes to redistribute wealth

The prevalent 20th-century view that the distribution of the tax burden among individuals ought to reduce the large disparities of income and net wealth that result from the functioning of the market economy is a complete volte-face from the 19th-century liberal view that the distribution of income ought to be left alone. The argument is that because of differences in talent and other accidents of birth and because of various restrictions and monopoly elements, the market mechanism does not necessarily (even in the long run) distribute income and wealth according to effort and merit; moreover, poverty may result from some work disability or from an unfavourable social or family background. A late 20th-century development has been a partial return to the view that taxes should not be used for redistributive purposes (because of the disincentives and distortions that high tax rates create).

The benefit principle. Under the benefit principle taxes are seen as serving a purpose similar to that of prices in private transactions; that is, they help determine what activities the government undertakes as well as who pays for them. If this principle could be implemented, resource allocation would be directly responsive to the wishes of citizens as consumers of public services, not just as voters. To the extent that the demand for public services does not rise in proportion to income, benefit-related taxes would be regressive.

In fact, it is difficult to implement the benefit principle for most public services because citizens generally have no incentive to pay the tax and reveal their preferences for publicly provided activities, unless they can be excluded from enjoying the benefits of the service if they fail to pay. The benefit principle is utilized primarily in the financing of roads and highways through levies on motor fuels and road user fees. Payroll taxes used to finance social security may also reflect a link between benefits and "contributions," but this link is commonly weak.

The role of tax policy in a market economy

The market economy. The requirement that a tax system be efficient arises from the nature of a market economy. Although there are many examples to the contrary, economists generally believe that markets do a fairly good job in making economic decisions about such factors as consumption, production, and financing. Thus, they feel that tax policy should refrain from pursuing particular ends to the point where it leads to the misallocation of economic resources. In general, so far as the efficient working of a market economy is concerned, taxation should imply a minimum of interference with individual decisions. It should not discriminate in favour of, or against, particular means of production, particular forms of organization, or particular industries. This does not mean, of course, that major social and economic goals may not take precedence over these considerations.

Economists have developed techniques to measure the "excess burden" that results when taxes distort economic decision making. The basic notion is that if goods worth $2 are sacrificed because of tax influences in order to produce goods with a value of only $1.80, there is an excess burden of 20 cents. A more nearly neutral tax system would result in less distortion. Thus an important postwar development in the theory of taxation is that of optimal taxation, the determination of tax policies that will minimize excess burdens. Because it deals with highly stylized mathematical descriptions of economic systems, this theory does not offer easily applied prescriptions for policy, beyond the important insight that distortions do less damage where supply and demand are not highly sensitive to such distortions. Attempts have also been made to incorporate distributional considerations into this theory. They face the difficulty that there is no scientifically correct distribution of income.

Ease of administration and compliance. In discussing the general principles of taxation, one must not lose sight of the fact that taxes have to be administered. This imposes certain limitations on the fiscal process. There are four general requirements for the efficient administration of tax laws: clarity, continuity, cost-effectiveness, and convenience.

Tax laws and regulations must be comprehensible to the taxpayer; they must be as simple as possible, given other goals, as well as unambiguous and certain, both to the taxpayer and to the tax administrator. While the principle of certainty is better adhered to today than in the time of Adam Smith, and arbitrary administration of taxes has been reduced, every country has tax laws that are far from being generally understood by the public. Not only does this result in a considerable amount of error; it also undermines honesty and respect for the law and tends to discriminate against the ignorant and the poor, who cannot take advantage of the various legal tax-saving opportunities that are available to the educated and the affluent. At times, attempts to achieve equity have created complexity, defeating reform purposes.

Tax laws should be changed seldom, and when changes are made they should be carried out in the context of a general and systematic tax reform, with adequate provisions for fair and orderly transition.

The costs of assessing, collecting, and controlling taxes should be kept to the lowest level consistent with other goals of taxation. This principle is of secondary importance; obviously, equity and economic rationality should not be sacrificed to cost considerations. The costs to be minimized include not only government expenses but also those of the taxpayer and of private fiscal agents such as employers who collect taxes for the government through the withholding procedure.

Payment of taxes should cause taxpayers as little inconvenience as possible, subject to the limitations of higher ranking tax principles. Governments often allow the payment of large tax liabilities in installments and set generous time limits for completing returns. Administrative considerations are especially important in developing countries, where illiteracy, lack of commercial markets, absence of books of account, and inadequate administrative resources may hinder both compliance and administration. Under such circumstances the achievement of rough justice may be preferable to infeasible "fine tuning" in the name of equity.

Revenue productivity

Economic goals. The primary goal of a national tax system is to generate revenues to pay the expenditures of government at all levels. Because public expenditures tend to grow at least as fast as the national product, taxes, as the main vehicle of government finance, should produce revenues that grow correspondingly. Income, sales, and value-added taxes generally meet this criterion; property taxes and taxes on nonessential articles of mass consumption such as tobacco products and alcoholic beverages do not.

In addition to producing revenue, tax systems may have other economic goals. Keynesian fiscal policy advocates the use of countercyclical tax policy as a way of promoting overall economic stability. (By comparison, "monetarists" place greater emphasis on monetary policy, and the modern "rational expectations" school questions the efficacy of both.) Countercyclical tax policy distinguishes two kinds of flexibility: automatic flexibility that is tied to changes in the level of economic activity, without intervention by the authorities, and "discretionary" flexibility involving decisions by the authorities to change tax rates or the tax base.

Automatic flexibility implies a tax system that cushions the cyclical fluctuations in prices, employment, and production through variations in tax liabilities (and, consequently, revenues) without changes in the tax laws and without detrimental effects on long-term economic growth. Taxes differ in their cyclical characteristics: Individual and corporation income taxes show the strongest sensitivity to cyclical movements, their returns varying more than the variations in the national product; moreover, since they account for a sizable portion of total tax revenues, their cushioning effect is quite large. Of course, such built-in flexibility requires that the extra revenues received by the government in boom periods be taken out of circulation through a budgetary surplus and not spent, while the decreased revenues received during recessions must register as a budgetary deficit—*i.e.,* the government must not cut back its expenditures during a recession but instead must cover its deficit through additional short-term borrowing.

Discretionary flexibility calls for more active measures, primarily changes in the tax rates themselves, to increase the anticyclical effects of tax receipts. The effectiveness of discretionary changes depends on the speed at which they can be carried out and the time required for the changes to be felt in the economy.

Some economists propose tax policies to promote economic growth. They eschew measures hindering growth and emphasize measures stimulating it. This approach may imply a qualitative restructuring of the tax system (for example, the substitution of indirect taxes for direct taxes to some extent) or special tax advantages to stimulate saving, labour mobility, research and development, etc. Perhaps as important, it implies the need to avoid high marginal tax rates and the tax-induced diversion of resources into relatively unproductive activities.

(F.N./C.E.McL.)

SHIFTING AND INCIDENCE

The incidence of a tax rests on the person(s) whose real net income is reduced by the tax. It is fundamental that the real burden of taxation does not necessarily rest upon the person who is legally responsible for payment of the tax. General sales taxes are paid by business firms, but most of the burden is assumed to rest upon those who buy the goods that are taxed. In other words, the tax is shifted from the business to the consumer. Taxes may be shifted in several directions. Forward shifting takes place if the burden falls entirely on the user, rather than the supplier, of the commodity or service in question—*e.g.,* if an excise tax on luxuries increases their price to the purchaser. Backward shifting occurs when the price of the article taxed remains the same and the cost of the tax is borne by those engaged in producing it—*e.g.,* through lower wages and salaries, lower prices for raw materials, or a lower return on borrowed capital. Finally, a tax may not be shifted at all; for example, a tax on business profits may reduce the net income of the owner of the business.

Forward and backward shifting

Tax capitalization occurs if the burden of the tax is incorporated in the value of long-term assets—*e.g.,* if the price of land declines by an amount that offsets an increase in property taxes. Capitalization can result where there is forward shifting, backward shifting, or no shifting. Thus, an increase in the price of gasoline resulting from higher motor fuel taxes may reduce the value of high-consumption automobiles, a tax on the production of coal that cannot be shifted forward would reduce the value of coal deposits, and a tax that reduces after-tax corporate profits may reduce the value of corporate stock. In all these cases the present owner of the asset takes a capital loss since, when he sells the asset, its price will be lower by the capitalized value of the tax.

It can be difficult to determine the incidence of a tax; indeed, the tax may be partly borne by the taxpayer and partly shifted. In many cases the problem can be adequately resolved by using what economists call partial equilibrium analysis, that is, by focusing on the market for the taxed product and ignoring all other markets. For example, if a small tax were to be imposed on an addictive substance, there is little doubt that it would be borne by the users of the substance, who would pay the tax rather than forgo use of the substance. More generally the incidence of taxation depends on all of the market forces at work. In a market economy the introduction of any tax triggers a whole series of adjustments in consumption, production, the supply of productive factors, and the pattern of foreign trade. These adjustments in turn will have repercussions on the prices of various commodities, productive factors, and assets that may be far removed from the area of the initial impact. In other words, a tax levied on a certain object may affect the prices of nontaxed goods and services that are not even used in the production of the tax object. Thus the initial impact of a tax does not indicate where the ultimate burden will rest unless one knows what repercussions the tax will have throughout the system of interrelated economic variables—*i.e.,* unless recourse is made to what is called general equilibrium theory, a method of analysis that attempts to identify and incorporate the economy-wide repercussions and implications of taxation. In what follows, the attempt will be made to isolate some of the factors involved.

The substitution principle of tax shifting

The direction and extent of tax shifting is determined basically by one principle: The user of a tax object can avoid the tax burden to a greater (lesser) extent the easier (the more difficult) it is for him to find nontaxed or less-taxed alternatives or substitutes for the tax object; the supplier of a production factor that is taxed itself or used in the production of a taxed good can avoid the tax burden to a greater (lesser) extent the easier (the more difficult) it is for him to find equivalent nontaxed or less taxed alternative employment opportunities for this factor. Because the demand for substitute goods will increase, their prices may rise, thus benefiting the producers of such goods and placing part of the tax burden on those individuals who used them before the tax was imposed. Likewise, the productive factors that seek alternative employments to avoid the tax will tend to receive lower returns in those employments, thus placing part of the burden on individuals who supplied the factors in those sectors before the tax was imposed. For example, if wine is taxed while beer is not, these two beverages are regarded as perfect substitutes, and the price of beer does not rise with increased demand, the tax burden will fall on the owners of land used for viticulture and on the workers engaged in it. It will fall mainly on the landowners if the soil is specific to winegrowing and if labour has alternative employment possibilities. If, on the other hand, wine drinkers are determined to drink only wine, they will bear most of the tax burden. If some substitution of beer for wine takes place and the price of beer rises somewhat, both wine and beer drinkers will bear the burden and owners of resources specialized to the production of beer will benefit.

The income effect

In addition to the substitution effect discussed above, one must take into account the income effect. When taxation reduces real income, consumption of certain goods and services (and of leisure) will be reduced. Furthermore, if a tax causes a significant redistribution of real income, and if different income classes have different propensities to save and different patterns of consumption, then the income redistribution will influence the demand for various goods, the supply of labour, and the demand for various resources.

Other considerations affect tax shifting, but they are derived from the basic principle of substitution. The following are most common.

The extent of shifting may vary over time, depending on how long it takes to adjust consumption patterns, reallocate land and capital, retrain labour, etc. Those users and suppliers who have the most difficulty in adjusting will bear the largest burden.

The kind of tax that is imposed affects tax shifting. The broader (narrower) the tax base (*i.e.,* the more [less] inclusive the scope of the tax from the user's point of view), the higher (lower) his tax burden, since the range of nontaxed or less-taxed substitutes at his command is narrower (wider). Thus an excise tax on only a few alcoholic beverages allows partial shifting through a change in the consumption pattern, while a tax on all such beverages does not. In a similar fashion, the returns on capital will be affected less by the taxation of corporation profits alone than by the taxation of both corporation and noncorporation profits.

The smaller the jurisdictional unit imposing the tax, the easier it tends to be for a user to obtain nontaxed or less-taxed substitutes from outside the jurisdiction and for a supplier to find nontaxed or less-taxed outside employment opportunities for his goods and services. Thus a tax levied by a subnational government on the production of a particular good is likely to be borne by suppliers of commodities and productive factors that are immobile. This is particularly relevant to the determination of the incidence of state income taxes and local property taxes, taxes that are often thought to be "exported" to out-of-state consumers. In small communities the only really immobile factors are likely to be real estate, certain local services, and poor families.

The rigidities of imperfect markets are likely to increase the uncertainty of the shifting response. Thus a monopolist may absorb part of a tax in lower profits rather than shift all of the burden to the user of the product. In industries where there are few firms (oligopoly), the price behaviour of a firm is mainly determined by what it expects its competitors to do. It may be especially easy for regulated public utilities to shift taxes forward. Rigid product prices are likely to increase the incidence of taxes on employment, unless monetary policy allows the tax-induced changes in relative prices to take place in the setting of a generally rising price level.

All of these considerations are analytical and theoretical. Efforts have been made to measure the impact of taxation by studying the actual effects of a particular tax on income and employment. These studies reflect the obvious and inherent difficulty that the tax impact cannot be easily isolated from the economic consequences of other events. For example, studies of corporation income tax shifting vary in their results from the conclusion that the tax is not shifted at all to the conclusion that it is shifted by more than 100 percent, depending mainly on the methods used to isolate the tax impact. (M.S.C./C.E.McL.)

TAX LAW

The power to impose taxes is generally recognized as a right of governments. Tax law is the body of rules under which the public authority has a claim on taxpayers requiring them to transfer to the public authority part of their income or their property. The tax law of a nation is usually unique to it, although there are similarities and common elements in the laws of various countries. In general, tax law is concerned only with the legal aspects of taxation, not with its financial, economic, or other aspects. The making of decisions as to the merits of various kinds of taxes, the general level of taxation, and the rates of specific taxes, for example, does not fall into the domain of tax law; it is a political, not a legal, process.

The nature of tax law

Tax law falls within the domain of public law—*i.e.,* the rules that determine and limit the activities and reciprocal interests of the political community and the members composing it—as distinguished from relationships between individuals (the sphere of private law). International tax law is concerned with the problems arising when an individual or corporation is taxed in several countries. Tax law can also be divided into material tax law, which is the analysis of the legal provisions giving rise to the charging of a tax; and formal tax law, which concerns the rules laid down in the law as to assessment, enforcement, procedure, coercive measures, administrative and judicial appeal, and other such matters.

The development of tax law as a comprehensive, general system is a recent phenomenon. One reason for this is that no general system of taxation existed in any country before the middle of the 19th century. In traditional, essentially agrarian, societies, government revenues were drawn either from nontax sources (such as tribute, income from the royal domains, and land rent) or, to a lesser extent, from taxes on various objects (land taxes, tolls, customs, and excises). Levies on income or capital were not considered an ordinary means for financing government. They appeared first as emergency measures. The British system of income taxation, for example, one of the oldest in the world, originated in the act of 1799 as a temporary means for meeting the increasing financial burden of the Napoleonic Wars. Another reason for the relatively recent development of tax law is that the burden of taxation—and the problem of definite limits to the taxing power of public authority—became substantial only with the broadening in the concept of the proper sphere of government that has accompanied the growing intervention of modern states in economic, social, cultural, and other matters.

Predominance of the legislature

The taxing power. The limits to the right of the public authority to impose taxes are set by the power that is qualified to do so under constitutional law. In a democratic system this power is the legislature, not the executive or the judiciary. The constitutions of some countries may allow the executive to impose temporary quasi-legislative measures in time of emergency, however, and under certain circumstances the executive may be given power to alter provisions within limits set by the legislature. The legality of taxation has been asserted by constitutional texts in many countries, including the United States, France, Brazil, and Sweden. In Great Britain, which has no written constitution, taxation is also a prerogative of the legislature.

The historical origins of this principle are identical with those of political liberty and representative government—the right of the citizens to take cognizance, either personally or through their representatives, of the need for the public contributions, to agree to it freely, to follow its use and to determine its proportion, basis, collection and duration

(in the words of the Declaration of the Rights of Man and the Citizen proclaimed in the first days of the French Revolution, August 1789). Other precedents may be found in the English Bill of Rights of 1689 and the rule "no taxation without consent" laid down in the Declaration of Independence of the United States.

Under this principle all that is necessary is that the rights of the tax administration and the corresponding obligations of the taxpayer be specified in the law; that is, in the text adopted by the people's representatives. The implementation of the tax laws is generally regulated by the executive power (the government or the tax bureau).

There have been many encroachments on the principle of the legality of taxation: Sometimes the base or the rate of taxation is determined by government decree rather than by law. The encroachment of the executive power on the territory reserved to the legislature in matters of taxation is generally explained by the need to make tax policy more flexible; urgent amendments may be required by sudden changes in the economic situation, changes so sudden that recourse to relatively slow parliamentary procedure would take too long. A compromise may be reached between the orthodox doctrine of the legality of taxes and the need, under special circumstances, to amend texts on taxation almost immediately, by modifying the text through a decree or an order of the executive (treasury) and ratifying it by the legislative power as soon as possible thereafter.

Limitations on the taxing power. Restraints on the taxing power are generally imposed by tradition, custom, and political considerations; in many countries there are also constitutional limitations. Certain limitations on the taxing power of the legislature are self-evident. As a practical matter, as well as a matter of (constitutional) law, there must be a minimum connection between the subject of taxation and the taxing power. The extent of income-tax jurisdiction, for example, is essentially determined by two main criteria: the residence (or nationality) of the taxpayer and his source of income. (The application of both criteria together in cases where the taxpayer's residence and his source of income are in different countries often results in burdensome double taxation, although the problem can be avoided or restricted by international treaties.) Taxes other than income taxes—such as retail-sales taxes, turnover taxes, death taxes, registration fees, and stamp duties—are imposed by the authority (national or local) on whose territory the goods are delivered or the taxable assets are located.

Jurisdictional limitations

Another self-evident limitation on the taxing power of the public authority is that the same authority cannot impose the same tax twice on the same person on the same ground.

Taxes are generally not levied retroactively, except in special circumstances. One example of retroactive taxation was the taxation of wartime benefits in some European countries by legislation enacted in 1945 when the war and enemy occupation were over.

The requirement of uniformity

A common limitation on the taxing power is the requirement that all citizens be treated alike. This requirement is specified in the U.S. Constitution. A similar provision in other constitutions is that all citizens are equal and that no privileges can be granted in tax matters. The rule is often violated through the influence of pressure groups, however; it is also difficult to enforce and to interpret unambiguously. In countries in which local governments are under the control of the national government, a local tax can be nullified by the central authority on the ground that it violates the national constitution if it transgresses the rule of uniformity and equality of taxpayers.

Aside from the foregoing constitutional, traditional, or political limitations, there is no restraint on the taxing power of the legislative body. Once enacted by the legislature, a tax cannot be judicially restrained. There is no way of mounting a legal attack upon a tax law on the ground that it is arbitrary or unjust, but the application of the law must be correct.

Double taxation. The problem of double and concurrent income taxation by overlapping governmental authorities has become increasingly important, particularly in international law. The growth of international contacts has multiplied the possibility of an individual or corporation being taxed in several countries. Moreover, the expanding financial needs of states have led them to extend their powers of taxation, with the result that cases of double taxation are becoming increasingly frequent and serious.

International tax law

International tax law has two parts. One consists of the provisions of internal tax law whereby national taxes are made applicable to nonresidents and to facts or situations located outside the frontiers. The other part has its source in the growing number of international agreements designed to prevent double taxation, either by defining the field of application of the tax laws of each of the contracting states or, without limiting the field of application, by providing for the granting of credits in each of the contracting states for taxes paid under the legislation of the other.

Nearly all the agreements aimed at preventing international double taxation are bilateral; that is, between two countries. Many bilateral conventions are intended not only to prevent double taxation but also to enable cooperation between the fiscal administrations of the contracting states in combating tax evasion.

Potential problems of internal double taxation exist in federal countries (including the United States, Switzerland, and West Germany). A state legislature may, for example, tax all income arising in the state, whether received by residents or nonresidents, or all income received by residents, even when the source of income is located outside the state borders. Therefore, arrangements for interstate tax coordination may be made, similar to international conventions. Alternatively, a credit for the state tax may be allowed in calculating the federal tax paid on the same object. During the 1980s the "unitary" system used by some U.S. states to tax the whole income of multistate corporations created considerable animosity in other countries. These states employed a formula to apportion between themselves and the rest of the world the entire worldwide income of affiliated firms—one of which did business in the state—that as a group were deemed to be engaged in a unitary business. This system departed radically from standard international practice, which is based on separate accounting for the corporations chartered in each country. Bowing to pressure from foreign governments, the U.S. federal government, and the international business community, most states have abolished or restricted use of this method.

Special tax problems arise when countries are involved in economic integration with each other. When two or more countries form a customs union (free-trade zone), each member state keeps its own system of taxation. The aims of an economic union are more ambitious, entailing far-reaching limitations on the sovereignty of the member states; when countries decide to form an economically integrated area, as have the member countries of the European Communities, they agree to establish a unified economic and financial market. In tax terms, this means the abolition of tax (and other) discriminations and distortions, since they are likely to impede or distort normal movements of goods and capital. To this end the sales and turnover taxes of the European Communities were replaced with value-added taxes, which were "harmonized," as provided in the Rome Treaty of March 1957; all member countries have had to bring their value-added taxes into conformity with a model prescribed by the Community.

Administration of tax laws. Whereas the right to impose taxes and to determine the circumstances under which they will be due is a privilege of the legislative power, administration of the tax law is the responsibility of the executive power. The head of tax administration in a central government is the minister of finance, secretary of the treasury, or chancellor of the exchequer. The actual administration is generally separated into departments because taxes differ so greatly in their bases and methods of collection. In most countries the ministry of finance has three branches charged with the levying of taxes. One collects income taxes; another levies taxes on the transfer of goods and on such legal transactions as stamp fees, inheritance taxes, registration dues, and turnover taxes; a third is responsible for customs and excise duties.

The levying of taxes can be divided into three successive phases: (1) assessment, or the definition of the exact amount subject to taxation under the statute; (2) computation or calculation; and (3) enforcement.

Assessment. The definition of the amount subject to taxation under a particular statute requires an analysis of the taxpayer's situation and of the legal provisions that apply to him. With the income tax (and also some taxes on the transfer of property, such as the inheritance tax), the taxpayer submits a tax return providing information as to his occupation, his real and personal property, his professional expenditures, and other pertinent matters; a corporation supplies, additionally, copies of the balance sheet, profit and loss statement, and minutes of the general meeting that approved these financial reports. The return, with the attached reports and statements, is meant to provide such complete information that the assessing tax official can rely on it to compute the correct tax. In the United States, the income taxpayer's liability is computed by himself subject to review by the taxing authority. Most tax systems also collect information in other ways, in order to inform the authorities as to potential tax liabilities. Records are kept of such matters as the allocation of income by partnerships, trusts, or estates, and the payment of fees, interest, dividends, and other sums exceeding a certain minimum amount. Particularly important are the statements of amounts paid as wages and salaries, which constitute the bulk of the income tax base for individuals in most countries; these are submitted as part of the withholding (pay-as-you-earn) system.

Tax returns

In the case of an annual levy such as the income tax, a return must be filed every year. In many countries, however, individuals who, on the basis of the return previously filed, appear to earn an income below the taxable limit do not have to file a new return annually (this facility is subject to revision at any time). Because it is not easy for some categories of taxpayers to determine the precise amount of their occupational net income, the tax administration frequently reaches an agreement with professional associations, fixing an estimated basis on which the net taxable income of their members will be determined for a period usually exceeding one year; members are then allowed to provide the tax administration with simplified factual information (*e.g.,* for farmers the area of land cultivated, for butchers or bakers the amount of goods sold), instead of filing the standard return.

In many countries a separate assessment procedure has been organized for income from real property; such is the case in the various European countries in which the French system of land register (cadastre) was introduced at the end of the 18th century. The theoretical income of each piece of real property is then determined by the administration of the land register and remains fixed for a relatively long period, except when important changes are made in the property.

In examining tax returns, the basic principle is that a return is assumed to be correct until the assessing official determines otherwise. In countries such as the United States, where the self-assessment method prevails, a minority of returns is selected for audit; most, however, are only checked as to timely arrival, inclusion of all required forms and attachments, and arithmetical accuracy. Except in special circumstances—when, for example, the statute introduces a suspicion of fraud (*e.g.,* if no return has been filed) or creates certain presumptions (as when personal living expenses exceed the reported income)—the administration has no right to shift onto the taxpayer the burden of the proof that he has complied with his liabilities. The golden rule of the tax administrator consists not only in getting as much money as possible for the treasury, but in displaying fairness. The rules of taxation naturally have an authoritarian character, but tax law does not grant the taxing authority a privileged position nor deprive the individual of means of defense against arbitrary taxation.

Tax auditing

Assessing officials have extensive powers in determining the amount subject to taxation. In addition to the routine check, there are numerous sources of information. The return of one taxpayer can be checked against that of another: in some countries whenever an individual or a corporation includes within deductible expenses the interest paid on borrowed money or the fee paid to a professional expert, the return must show the name and address of the payee, and when this information is placed before the appropriate assessing official he can readily determine whether the payee has included the payment in his declared income. Similarly, in countries employing value-added taxes invoices can be cross-checked to be sure that tax claimed as a credit by a business purchaser has actually been remitted by the seller. This ability to cross-check is often said to be a major advantage of value-added tax over other forms of sales taxes, but the advantages are easily overstated, since even with sophisticated computers cross-checking is difficult.

The procedure varies from one country to another and depends largely on the circumstances of the case. An audit may be performed either in the office of the tax agent, by correspondence, or in the taxpayer's office. Tax agents are entitled to examine the books and records kept by the taxpayer, within reasonable limits. They are, within the same limits, entitled to question not only the taxpayer but other persons acquainted with the case. There are, however, legal guarantees, protecting confidential communications and prohibiting disclosures of financial information about the taxpayer. In the United States, for example, federal and common law protect communications between husband and wife or between a client and his attorney acting as such. Under Belgian income-tax law, certain taxpayers, in the course of the assessing official's interrogation, may assert that they are bound by professional secrecy and unable to communicate what they claim to be privileged information; the assessing officer may then consult a special advisory board, composed of the president and two members of the taxpayer's professional or occupational group (lawyers, doctors, notaries, etc.), which will give its opinion as to the taxpayer's probable income.

Bank secrets

Banks in most countries are required to make reports of cash deposits or similar transactions. In most countries, a safe-deposit box in a bank cannot be opened after the death of the client unless a tax official is present. On the other hand, some countries, such as Switzerland, Panama, and various nations in the Caribbean, have turned the guarantee of bank secrecy into a national asset. In such countries banks are legally entitled, or even required, to refuse information to tax agents concerning their clients. Funds from both legal and illegal activities are often channeled through countries with strict bank secrecy laws in order to escape taxation (as well as for other reasons).

Tax authorities do a great deal of intelligence work, using tips from informers such as employees, competitors, and neighbours of the taxpayer. In the United States, informers are encouraged by the payment of fees. But it is a fundamental principle of tax law that information cannot be used against the taxpayer if it has been obtained by unlawful means, and that no evidence or testimony is a valid proof of tax liability unless the taxpayer has had the opportunity to discuss it.

The assessor may find himself in disagreement with the taxpayer, either as to the facts (the amount of income, of deductible expenses, etc.) or as to the manner in which the taxpayer has resolved a question of law or a mixed question of law and fact. The tax agent may use his discretion as to questions of fact, and frequently a compromise is reached on those questions between the taxpayer and the tax agent.

Whenever the tax agent decides questions of law, he is bound by the treasury's position on the particular problem. On unresolved issues, lower taxation officers (field offices) usually request the advice of a higher echelon. Allowing lower-level fiscal authorities discretion in interpreting tax laws runs the risk of encouraging corruption. In some countries, including the United States, written rulings are issued by the administration in advance, thus avoiding disputes at the level of the assessment official. In countries in which this is not done, officials at all levels are free to give informal advice concerning the tax effects of proposed transactions. The taxpayer can file a petition with the competent administrative or judicial authority whenever he believes that the interpretation of the law by the assessing official is wrong.

Computation of the tax. The second phase in levying taxes is the calculation of the amount to be paid. In the American self-assessment method, the liability for income tax is primarily established by the taxpayer himself. Under this method, as a rule, the tax liability reported on the return forms the basis of the assessment record. If the tax administration discovers that additional tax is due, a deficiency statement is issued. Virtually all countries that levy income taxes require withholding on wages and salaries. In some cases the withheld tax discharges the taxpayer's liability and there is no obligation (and sometimes no opportunity) to file a tax return. Many countries provide for prepayment of the withholding tax on dividends and other income from personal property and have set up a "pay-as-you-go" system for professional income. Such provisional payments are calculated by the taxpayer. Advance payment of all or part of the income tax (on a voluntary or compulsory basis) before the return is filed, on the basis of expected income or of the taxable income of the previous year, is also provided for in some countries. In general, however, the final computation of taxes levied on income, on inherited property, or on the transfer of property is made by the tax administration. Sales taxes and value-added taxes are calculated by the taxpayers.

Prepayment of taxes

Enforcement. If the taxpayer fails to pay within the legally prescribed period, or within a very short time afterward, the competent tax office undertakes to collect the amount due. In proceedings against the taxpayer, the tax administration is not in the position of an ordinary creditor suing an ordinary debtor. The law confers a privileged position on the tax administration among the creditors of the taxpayer.

In addition to interest charges on the amount due, various kinds of coercive measures are available to ensure payment. Civil penalties consist generally of a fine added by the collecting agent when the violation is the result of negligence rather than of willful neglect or bad faith. Examples of negligence are the failure to file a required return on time and understatement or underpayment of the tax liability without intent to mislead. Civil penalties are fixed by assessment, so that the procedural remedies of the taxpayer are identical with those provided for the assessment of the tax itself.

Criminal tax fraud is severely punished in some countries; in others failure to fulfill one's fiscal obligations is seen as no different from failure to meet other financial obligations. Certain tax crimes are classed as misdemeanours (such as willful failure to pay certain taxes, to file certain returns, to keep proper records, and to supply proper information); these are punishable by fines or imprisonment or both. Heavier punishment is provided for crimes classed as felonies (such as the making of false statements and, in the United States, tax evasion). In most countries the criminal penalties can be combined with the civil penalties.

Criminal penalties cannot be imposed by the tax administration. Offenses against tax law, whether misdemeanours or felonies, must be tried by courts. The procedure in criminal tax cases is almost identical with that in other criminal cases. The accused is deemed to be innocent until proved guilty; the burden of the proof inevitably rests upon the prosecutor and not upon the taxpayer-defendant.

The judiciary and tax law. The taxpayer has a guarantee against unfairness or error in the application of taxes in the right to appeal to competent, impartial authorities when he disagrees with the determination of the assessing officer.

In some countries disputes between taxpayers and the tax administration are settled by special commissions consisting of high-ranking civil servants (and also of members of various occupational organizations). In others, the decision is the privilege of the judiciary power. In the vast majority of countries, however, a combination of both systems prevails. "Out-of-court" jurisdictions—commissions composed of tax officials and laymen—frequently act as preliminary settlement committees that decide factual questions, leaving the interpretation of the tax law to the courts. In general, when a taxpayer disagrees with the amounts of the tax as calculated by the administration, or thinks he has paid too much, he files a petition with a tribunal, which may be either a specialized court or the ordinary court competent for civil litigation. Even if he must exhaust the administrative processes before he may take a dispute with the tax authorities to court, he can still invoke the jurisdiction of a judicial court to reexamine the case, in respect both of the facts and of the legal arguments.

In almost all countries, the judiciary is headed by a supreme court whose jurisdiction is limited to questions of law. The supreme court is generally competent in tax matters, but an appeal to the court must be based solely on an alleged misapplication of law; should it appear that questions of fact or mixed questions of law and fact are involved, the claim, under most judicial systems, is dismissed. (The U.S. Supreme Court can also decide on the constitutionality of an act of the legislative power.) The judiciary thus has final authority to interpret the tax statute. This interpretation is binding only in the matter submitted to the tribunal. But, in any legal system, reference to interpretative decisions of the courts in comparable cases, especially of the supreme court, is obviously the best argument in a litigation about a disputed point of tax law.

Interpretation of tax laws

When a legal text—in tax law or in other law—requires interpretation because there is a reasonable doubt as to its meaning or scope, the first step is to determine the meaning of the words used, according to the rules of grammar and syntax, not in isolation but in their context and taking into account the subject discussed. As stated by U.S. Treasury tax lawyer Randolph E. Paul, "the meaning of a sentence may be more than that of the separate words, as a melody is more than the notes" (*Taxation in the United States,* 1954). This is the necessary "literal" interpretation of the law: when the current sense of a term is its wide sense, then it must be accepted in its wide sense in a tax law as in any other, unless it can be shown that the legislature used the term in a narrower sense. If the meaning of the text cannot be determined with certainty by the literal method, then the interpreter, in seeking the legislature's intention, will resort to the "historical" method (the study both of the preparatory work and of the place occupied by the text in successive laws on a specific matter) and to the "systematic" or "teleological" interpretation (the position occupied by a legal provision in a legal system as a whole, and the object pursued by the legislature in producing that system).

In addition to these general principles common to the interpretation of all legal texts, some special rules apply to the interpretation of tax laws. One rule is the autonomy of tax law, meaning that tax laws pursue aims that are different from those of other bodies of law. The tax claim is a claim under public law. Its cause lies not in a contractual obligation but in an expression of unilateral will, a decision by the public authority. The function of taxes in the organization of the budget is incompatible with the principles of the law of contracts; such principles apply only to relationships under private law and, therefore, cannot be invoked to interpret provisions of tax law.

Other special rules of interpretation of tax laws derive from the nature of the tax obligation. In a democratic system, a tax can only be imposed by law. Thus the courts or the administration do not have a "creative power" to make things or operations taxable through an analogic interpretation of the text, in cases where it is not proved that the legislature wished them to be taxable. On the other hand, the rule of legality of taxation does not always operate in favour of the taxpayer: the person or body entrusted with the task of applying or interpreting the law cannot introduce any attenuation or relaxation of its effect, even though this might be more than amply justified by circumstances, except in cases where the legislature has authorized the judge or the administration to apply the rules of equity within certain legally prescribed limits.

(J.M.J.v.H./C.E.McL.)

Major types of taxes

PERSONAL INCOME TAX

A personal income tax is a tax that is levied on individuals or family units and that is computed on the basis of income received. It is usually classified as a direct tax because the burden of the tax is presumably on the individuals who pay it. Before World War II, the personal income tax was usually a class tax in the sense that most wage earners, salaried employees, and self-employed individuals were, in effect, exempted from it. Since that time exemptions have been sharply reduced in economically advanced countries. By comparison, in less developed countries the income tax remains a levy on a minority of the population, commonly those employed by the government and in advanced sectors of the economy; for administrative reasons, it is often difficult to extend the tax to the self-employed.

The income tax as an instrument of policy

As an instrument of national policy, the personal income tax has played different roles in different countries at different times. In Great Britain, where the income tax first made its appearance at the close of the 18th century, it was accepted without enthusiasm as a temporary means of raising badly needed revenue in a war emergency. It was revived in 1842 as a peacetime levy to help finance civil expenditures during a period of tariff reform. By 1914 the personal income tax had come to be regarded in a number of countries not only as an important revenue instrument but also as an instrument for achieving social reform through income redistribution. Finally, in most countries it has been used to redirect economic decisions, through preferential treatment of various activities. It also acts as a stabilizer against economic fluctuations because its effect on purchasing power varies inversely with changes in income and employment. In the late 20th century, however, there was somewhat of a movement away from the view that the income tax should be used for these purposes.

The rationale of income taxation. The present widespread acceptance of income taxation as the fairest kind of tax is based on the premise that an individual's income is the best single index of his ability to contribute to the support of government. Moreover, to the extent that a person's ability to pay taxes is affected by other circumstances, such as the number of dependents he supports or extraordinary medical expenses, it is easier to make adjustments for such circumstances by changes in the personal income tax than by changes in sales or property taxes.

Its merits compared with those of other taxes

Another argument for income taxation proceeds from its effects on the national economy. The yield from the personal income tax tends to move up in booms and down in recessions more than do the yields of sales or wealth taxes. This is partly because personal income itself is quite sensitive to changes in the level of economic activity and partly because, under the usual progressive rate structure, when individual incomes rise the additional income received by some taxpayers is taxable at higher bracket rates. Consequently, their tax liabilities fluctuate more than their incomes. Thus the tax serves to offset the effects of expansionary and contractionary forces during business cycles. Indexation of exemptions, deductions, and the measurement of income from capital for inflation—refinements that are necessary for equity and neutrality—reduce this automatic potential for stabilization.

The personal income tax reduces the amount of income individuals have available to spend on consumer goods and services or to save and invest. But this is, of course, what any tax is supposed to do. The question is whether other taxes may achieve the same end more efficiently or with fewer undesirable side effects. It has been argued that an income tax discriminates against saving and is less favourable to economic growth than a direct tax on expenditures because an income tax does, and an expenditure tax does not, fall on income that is saved and made available for investment. On the other hand, an income tax does not have the distorting effect on consumer expenditures that selective excise taxes have (causing buyers to shift from taxed to untaxed items). It does contain distortions and inequities of its own, however.

The extent to which an income tax reduces the incentive to work is difficult to determine. To the extent that the tax reduces total income after taxes, it may lead some persons to work longer in an effort to maintain an established standard of living (the income effect). To the extent that the tax reduces the reward for an extra hour's work, it may make the taxpayer decide to work less and to indulge in more leisure (the substitution effect); presumably, the larger his income and the more steeply progressive the tax, the greater this effect will be. Finally, a progressive income tax is sometimes said to have an adverse effect on investment, especially in the case of risky ventures, but this has been shown to depend on the adequacy of the loss-offset provisions in the tax law.

The meaning of income. Whether or not income is an accurate measure of taxpaying ability depends on how it is defined. The only definition that has been found to be completely consistent and free from anomalies and capricious results is "accrued income," which is the money value of the goods and services consumed by the taxpayer plus or minus any change in his net worth during a given period of time. But this is not a definition that can be applied without important modifications. In the first place, it is generally recognized that changes in net worth resulting from gifts, bequests, and other gratuitous transfers cannot be included in the taxable income of the individual. Second, because of the difficulties of estimation, accretions to wealth are ordinarily not included in an individual's taxable income until they are "realized"; that is, converted into cash or some easily valued form. Finally, and for much the same reason, most countries have chosen not to include in taxable income such forms of imputed income as the rental value of owner-occupied homes.

Distinguishing sources of income

In some countries the personal income tax is imposed on the total income of an individual or family unit, whereas in others income from different sources is taxed under separate rules and often at somewhat different rates. The use of multiple schedules is questionable on grounds of both neutrality and horizontal equity, and countries with schedular taxes frequently supplement them with a progressive rate scale applicable to total income. These schedular income taxes are today found in some South American and African countries. In most industrialized nations, such as Great Britain, personal income has to be reported on one of a number of separate schedules, but assessable income is then lumped and only one tax is imposed. This kind of personal income tax is not usually regarded as a schedular tax. The United States has adopted antishelter provisions that have the effect of converting a nominally global income tax into one having schedular features.

The tests of equity. Before a tax on personal income can be considered to be a completely fair tax, it has to meet the two tests of horizontal and vertical equity. Horizontal equity is achieved when persons with the same income will, under like circumstances, pay the same amount of tax. The important issue here is, of course, what is meant by "like circumstances." Clearly, two families with the same income would not be equally able to pay taxes if one consisted of husband and wife and the other of husband, wife, and four dependent children. But suppose neither family had any children but in one the entire income was earned by the husband whereas in the other both husband and wife worked. Would horizontal equity require that they pay the same or different taxes? Similar questions have been raised concerning families whose equal incomes take the form of wages and salaries in one case and dividends and interest in another or whose income has to be used to pay interest on personal indebtedness or to pay state and local taxes to a greater extent in one case than in the other. In order to compensate for those differences in the sources and uses of income that are thought to affect an individual's ability to pay income tax, most countries allow a wide variety of deductions from statutory personal income before the tax is imposed.

The concept of vertical equity relates to the taxes paid by individuals at different income levels. Clearly, they should not be the same if income is a good index of ability to pay; but how different should they be at different income levels? If a single rate of tax is applied to all personal income in excess of the allowed exclusions, exemptions, and deductions, the tax will be proportionate to taxable income (although it may be progressive when compared to total income). If, however, different tax rates are applicable to different blocks or brackets of income, and if these rates rise as one moves from the lowest bracket to successively higher ones, the tax will be progressive. Those countries that tax total personal income today almost always use graduated or progressive rates; those with schedular income taxes may or may not do so.

Justifying progressive rates

Many attempts have been made to develop a theory that would not only justify the principle of progression but would also result in a mathematically exact scale of equitable taxation. Some theorists, accepting the notion that the taxes a person pays ought to bear some close relation to the benefits he enjoys from the operation of government, have tried to show that, at some levels of income, benefits increase more rapidly than income. But their efforts have served to do little more than reveal the shortcomings of "benefit theory." Others, starting with the premise that an equitable tax is one that imposes equal sacrifices on individuals at different income levels and accepting the view that the utility of any given unit of money becomes less the more money one has, have tried to demonstrate that progression is needed if the sacrifices imposed on the wealthy are not to be less than those imposed on the less well off. But it is debatable whether a dollar has less utility for a very rich person than for a moderately rich one or whether it is scientifically possible to make the sort of interpersonal comparisons that the "sacrifice theories" call for.

Ease of administration. So long as prices are stable and the tax is basically a tax on realized income and does not require an assessment to be made of accrued but unrealized capital gains and losses, the income tax is generally held to be easier to administer than either an expenditure tax or a wealth tax. The difficulty of dealing adequately with inflation and timing issues in the measurement of income raises doubts about this conclusion. A tax on consumer expenditures would require the subtraction of net saving (and possibly capital income) from realized income, and balance sheets would be needed to make certain that saving was correctly reported. The administration of a wealth tax would obviously require a complete accounting for assets and liabilities.

The enforcement of the income tax in many countries, such as the United States, has been made easier by the practice of withholding the tax from wages and salaries. The same approach has not been extended to interest and dividends in the United States, although it has in other countries, such as Colombia. Although compliance is undoubtedly incomplete and complex provisions increase costs for both taxpayers and the fiscal authorities, in general, the income tax raises revenue efficiently and at low out-of-pocket cost to the government.

Types of preferential treatment. A corollary of the proposition that taxes should bear similarly on persons similarly situated is the proposition that when persons are not similarly situated their tax liabilities should differ. To accomplish this, the income tax statutes usually provide for (1) personal allowances or exemptions, which differentiate between large and small family units, and (2) deductions that give preferential treatment to taxpayers reporting expenditures that are thought to justify some lightening of their burden.

Treatment of the family. There are several ways of allowing for differences in family units. One is to give an exemption for each dependent, either on a flat per capita basis or in accordance with a schedule. When income is taxed at graduated rates, exemptions are worth more to high-income than to low-income families. In order to give equal tax allowances for dependents to families of the same size at different income levels, each exemption can be multiplied by the standard or basic rate of tax, and so be converted into a uniform tax credit. Inflation erodes the real value of tax allowances specified in nominal or monetary terms (dollars, pounds, etc.). Historically, this problem has been addressed by periodically adjusting such amounts to higher levels. More recently there has been a trend to "indexing" amounts such as personal exemptions, standard deductions, and bracket limits in the rate structure by linking them to a price index that measures the degree of inflation. Indexing, which need not involve an increase in complexity, increases the equity of the tax system, but it reduces the tax's counter-cyclical influence.

Separate and joint returns

It is not only with respect to the number of dependents that families may differ in taxpaying capacity. In some families only one spouse earns income, whereas in others both husband and wife may work. If, in a family of the latter type, husband and wife are allowed to file separate returns, their combined tax liabilities under a progressive income tax may be less than those of a family similarly situated but with a single income recipient. The two families will pay the same tax if husband and wife are required to file a joint return in which their earnings are pooled, but then the working couple may be taxed at a higher rate than two single people with the same income. The issue between joint and separate returns is further complicated by the fact that if separate returns are permitted, and are subject to the same rate structure as joint returns, families with investment income can reduce their tax liabilities by splitting up their holdings. Depending on how this problem is solved there may be either a penalty or a bonus for marriage.

Various ways of dealing with this problem have been adopted in different countries. In the United States full income splitting has been allowed since 1948, when taxpayers were given the option of filing joint returns using a rate schedule with brackets twice as wide as those in the schedule for married persons electing to file separate returns; *i.e.,* the tax on joint returns is twice the tax that would be imposed if there were only one income receiver and his income were half as large as the joint income. This meant that the tax rate for joint returns did not rise as sharply as that for separate returns, so that a single person was likely to pay more than a married person with the same adjusted gross income but filing a joint return. In 1969 the disadvantage experienced by single persons was reduced by providing a completely separate rate schedule for them. In France, the family is the tax unit; there is only one rate schedule, but relief for family commitments is achieved by what is known as the family-quotient system. This is a form of income splitting in which the single graduated rate schedule is applied to a figure arrived at by dividing total family income by the number of "units" represented, with each child counting as half a unit. The tax, as so determined on a fraction of the family's income, is then multiplied by the number of family "units" to arrive at the family's tax liability. In West Germany, husband and wife are assessed jointly, but income splitting is allowed in the same way that it is in the United States. Sweden also has a dual rate structure, but in that country the difference between the rates applicable to married couples and to single persons varies with the level of income: in the middle income brackets, couples are more heavily taxed; in the high brackets burdens are much the same. Finally, in a number of countries, including India, Japan, Argentina, and Israel, only separate returns are allowed.

Personal deductions. Practice with respect to personal deductions also varies widely. In the United States, for example, such deductions include interest paid on home mortgage debt (but not other personal debt), abnormal medical expenses, philanthropic contributions, and state and local income and property taxes. In Great Britain, on the other hand, virtually no deductions are granted that do not in some measure bear a direct relation to the production of earned income. In South America, where multischedule income taxes are the rule, some countries allow virtually no deductions, whereas in others the latitude permitted in the deduction of personal expenses is very great.

The varied treatment of medical, charitable, and other expenses

In those countries that allow the deduction of extraordinary medical expenses, a stated percentage of the taxpayer's income has to be used for this purpose before any deduction can be taken. In the United States, only those expenses that exceed a small percent of adjusted gross income are deductible, and a similar rule is found in West Germany. On the other hand, in The Netherlands, the whole expense becomes deductible once the minimum is exceeded. The justification for a deduction of this type is that medical expenses are not generally controllable and, when incurred above a certain normal level, reduce an individual's ability to pay taxes relative to others at the same income level.

The justification for deduction of contributions to religious, charitable, educational, and cultural organizations is usually found in the encouragement of socially desirable activities rather than in any allowance for differences in taxable capacity. The contributions that qualify for this deduction vary from country to country, and total contributions are usually limited to some percentage of the taxpayer's income. In Japan, contributions made to government, to local authorities, or to institutions for scientific experiment or research are deductible from taxable income but only to the extent that such payments exceed the lesser of either a certain percentage of income or a specific amount of yen. This, of course, denies any deductions to taxpayers whose contributions amount to only a small fraction of their incomes.

Deductions for personal saving

A third type of deduction—one that serves neither to relieve hardship nor to encourage voluntary support of socially desirable activities—is the deduction that is allowed in some countries for certain kinds and limited amounts of personal saving. These have included: (1) social security contributions and compulsory contributions to private pension funds, for which deductions are allowed in Japan, France, The Netherlands, and Belgium and (2) limited amounts of life insurance premiums, which are deductible in Great Britain, Japan, France, and West Germany. Deductions have also included limited amounts of savings earmarked for the construction of dwellings or placed in savings deposits. One justification for these allowances has been that they encourage low-income taxpayers to seek the protection afforded by life insurance, pension plans, and savings deposits. Another is that they channel the personal savings of such individuals into banks and other financial institutions where they can be used to support capital expansion. Special tax-privileged savings plans were introduced in Japan, West Germany, and Sweden during the late 1950s and early 1960s. In none of these countries, however, were they found to be particularly effective in increasing total personal saving. Such plans may simply redirect a given amount of saving from one form of saving to another.

Another frequently permitted deduction, the justification for which is not entirely clear, is that allowed for interest paid on personal indebtedness. In the case of interest paid on home mortgages, it is generally regarded as one of several special tax concessions granted to home owners. The United States has imposed increasingly strict limits on the deductibility of interest, beginning with denial of any deduction in the case of debt incurred for the purpose of acquiring tax-exempt securities and culminating in 1986 with the denial of deductions for interest on consumer debt and provisions intended to prevent investment interest deductions from sheltering income from other sources. In Canada the interest deduction is denied in the cases of consumer debt and of most home mortgages. Loan interest is deductible in West Germany as a "special expense," as it is in France on monies borrowed from third parties.

Deductions for taxes paid

Still another deduction that does not appear to have much to do with the determination of true income is the deduction for taxes paid. Among the justifications offered for this type of deduction, the most widely accepted is that it contributes to fiscal coordination in a federal system and avoids extremely high rates in the case of overlapping income taxes. In the United States state and local taxes on property and income are deductible. These deductions are tantamount to subsidies from the national to the subnational governments. Foreign taxes on real property and income are also deductible, although most taxpayers elect instead to credit their foreign income taxes against their U.S. tax. Japan and West Germany also allow deductions for local taxes, although Japan specifically excludes the income taxes of prefectural and municipal inhabitants from the exemption allowed for other taxes. Ordinarily, the tax paid with respect to income in one year is not allowed as a deduction in determining the same tax the following year, but an exception to this rule is found in Belgium in the cases of both the multischedule tax on wages and salaries and the progressive surtax on total income.

One way of limiting the use of itemized personal deductions for taxpayers whose total deductions are small is to provide an optional standard deduction. Examples of this practice are found in the United States and West Germany.

Capital gains. The taxation of capital gains and losses presents a special set of problems to which different countries have found different answers. An increase in the value of a capital asset—a share of stock, a corporate or government bond, or perhaps a piece of real estate—increases the net worth of its owner, and thus it can be seen as a form of income. There is a problem, however, of valuing all of the capital assets a taxpayer may own so as to be able to determine how much his net worth has increased or decreased during the taxable year. In practice, this difficulty has usually been avoided by taking into account only those gains and losses that have been realized in the form of cash or its equivalent. Taxing gains only at realization allows taxpayers the benefit of postponing taxation, however. In the United States this problem of deferral is aggravated by allowing gains on assets transferred at death to escape tax permanently. An alternative would be to require that accrued but unrealized gains be taxed, either periodically or at death, as if they had been realized through a sale, a policy known as "constructive" realization.

Determining the value of capital gains

Even realized capital gains may present a problem of valuation. During (or following) an inflationary period an increase in the monetary value of an asset may not mean that there has been an increase in the real (inflation-adjusted) value of the asset. The conceptually correct solution to this problem is to adjust the cost of the asset for inflation, as is done in several Latin-American countries.

Another problem that arises in the taxation of capital gains is that of deciding upon the appropriate rate at which realized gains should be taxed. One answer to this is that they should be treated no differently than other forms of income, an approach followed by the United States in 1986. The difficulty with this answer is that under many circumstances this would be unfair to the taxpayer and might also have undesirable economic effects. If capital gains that have been accruing over a number of years are taxed at regular progressive income tax rates in the year of their realization, the tax on them may be higher than it would have been if the unrealized gains had been taxed annually as they accrued. The knowledge that capital gains are subject to very heavy taxes upon realization can deter individuals subject to high-bracket rates from making investment decisions that are socially desirable. This difficulty is usually handled by taxing such gains at a relatively low rate or by excluding a stated percentage of the gain from taxable income. In either case, this special treatment applies only to long-term gains involving assets that have been held for a minimum length of time.

Some countries, including Canada, France, and West Germany, do not tax capital gains unless they arise out of a business. The line between a business transaction and a personal one is not easy to draw, however. Moreover, the exemption of capital gains provides tremendous pressure to recharacterize ordinary taxable income as exempt capital gains.

Countries that do not, in principle, tax individuals on their capital gains also do not allow capital losses to enter into the determination of taxable income. Those that do tax capital gains ordinarily take capital losses into account only as offsets to capital gains. Even then, deductions of losses are usually limited to prevent abuse.

The negative income tax. The idea of a negative income tax has been considered in the United States as a method of providing very low income families with a stable subsistence level of income in the form of government payments geared into the personal income tax structure. It is viewed as a possible substitute for public assistance or as an alternative to family allowances. The basic elements of this and other so-called transfer-by-taxation plans are (1) a guaranteed minimum level of income adjusted to the size and composition of the family unit, (2) a tax rate to be applied to the difference between the family's income and some specified amount, and (3) a break-even level of income at the point at which the tax liability equals the guaranteed allowance. According to one plan, a negative 50 percent tax rate would be applied to the unused tax exemptions and deductions of families with little or no taxable income. For example, if the family was entitled to total exemptions and deductions of $3,000 and had an adjusted gross income of $1,000, it would receive "negative taxes" amounting to $1,000 (50 percent of $3,000 minus $1,000). In this case the guaranteed minimum—for a family with no adjusted gross income—would be $1,500, and the break-even level would be $3,000. Above the break-even level the family would receive no negative tax. The earned income tax credit in the tax law of the United States amounts to a form of negative income tax, but it is available only to those who are employed and supporting dependent children.

The earned income tax credit

Tax expenditures. It has been shown that preferential treatment can be extended to selected private activities in either of two ways: Tax revenues can be collected and then spent to support the activities as part of the normal budget process, or preferential treatment of the activities can be built into the tax system, as with the deductions allowed for home mortgage interest. In either case the advantages granted can be seen as subsidies provided by the government. This way of viewing the issue leads to the concept of tax expenditures, which can be thought of as the expenditure equivalents of deviations from an ideal tax base. Each year the budget of the U.S. government includes a tax expenditure budget, as well as the traditional budget for appropriations; other countries follow similar practices.

Tax expenditures have the disadvantage that they do not receive the scrutiny accorded appropriations. They are considered by tax-writing committees, rather than by appropriations committees. Once enacted, they take on a life of their own. Moreover, they undermine the perception that the tax system is fair in a way that ordinary expenditures do not.

History of personal income taxation. *Great Britain.* The first country to enact a general income tax was Great Britain, in 1799. To finance the Napoleonic Wars the tax was imposed at a rate of two shillings in the pound (10 percent) on all incomes in excess of £200, with lower rates applying to income between £60 and £200 and income below £60 being exempt. When the war ended in 1815, the tax was allowed to lapse until 1842, when it was revived at seven pence in the pound by the prime minister, Sir Robert Peel. It was again adopted as a temporary measure, this time to enable the government to avoid budget deficits while carrying out major tariff reforms. But succeeding governments, confronted with steadily rising expenditures, were unable to dispense with a tax that was so flexible and elastic, and by the 1880s it was generally accepted as a permanent levy.

The permanent tax

At about this time taxation began to be regarded as a social instrument; but it was not until 1910 that graduated rates were introduced and an abatement was granted of £10 per child to taxpayers whose income did not exceed £500. Then came World War I, during which time the standard rate was raised to six shillings with a supertax on top of that.

Continental Europe. In Europe, a number of German states began experimenting with income taxes in the 1840s. But it was not until the Prussian reforms of 1891 that the income tax became an effective fiscal instrument in any of these states. Thereafter the reform movement spread to other states, and by 1913 the share of the income tax in all state tax collections had risen to about 60 percent. Until 1920, German income taxes were exclusively state taxes; from 1920 to 1945, they were federal taxes. At the close of World War II, they again became state taxes and are now regulated by federal law.

Efforts to enact an income tax in France were begun in the 1870s, but it was not until 1909 that an income tax bill finally passed the Chamber of Deputies only to be held up by opposition in the Senate. The bill was finally enacted as an emergency measure two weeks before war began in 1914, but it was another three years before a permanent income tax system was adopted.

Italy adopted an income tax in 1864 as one of the first products of its unification. The system introduced at that time was one of "objective" taxes that attempted to tax the "productive sources" of income—*i.e.,* land, buildings, and movable wealth. It was not until 1925 that a nationwide tax on total family income was imposed with graduated rates.

Among the Scandinavian countries, Norway introduced an income tax in 1892 and made its rates progressive in 1896; not until 1910 did Sweden adopt a modern income tax on a permanent basis.

The United States. During the Civil War the United States enacted an income tax that remained in effect from 1862 to 1872. The minimum rate in the 1862 law was 3 percent on income above a personal exemption of $600; the maximum rate was 5 percent on income above $10,000. Subsequent amendments raised the maximum rate to 10 percent on incomes over $5,000. An income tax was again enacted in 1894, after President Grover Cleveland had been elected on a platform that promised lower tariffs and other reforms sought by the farmers in the West and South. This law was, however, held to be unconstitutional by the Supreme Court, which forced its backers to seek an amendment to the Constitution that would give Congress the right to impose income taxes without apportionment among the states. In 1913 the Sixteenth Amendment was ratified, and a new personal income tax with rates ranging from 1 to 7 percent on income in excess of $3,000 for a single individual was voted by Congress shortly thereafter. At the end of World War II the minimum rate was 23 percent and the maximum rate was 94 percent; the exemption for a single individual was only $500. Most states also have personal income taxes. To simplify compliance and administration, many states use a definition of taxable income that closely resembles the federal definition.

Later developments. The European and U.S. income tax systems and the recommendations of advisers from those areas have often strongly influenced the systems established by new and developing countries, especially former colonies, as well as systems such as Japan's that have undergone major reform in the 20th century. For example, the quotient system of personal allowances and the shareholder credit system of integrating the corporate and individual income taxes, respectively, have been popular in former French and British colonies, and the income tax of the United States and American advisers have been instrumental in shaping the income taxes of Latin America. Japan's present tax system, developed in the early 1950s, is primarily based upon proposals made by a commission headed by Carl S. Shoup, an American economist.

Additional factors affecting the tax systems of developing countries include experience with inflation and other economic conditions and the particular attitudes and goals of the individual country. Experience with inflation has led some Latin-American countries to introduce inflation adjustment into the measurement of income from business and capital. Reflecting a greater propensity to use governmental intervention to achieve economic objectives, many developing countries employ far-reaching tax incentives in the effort to spur investments conducive to economic development.

International variations in rate structures. Attention has already been called to several types of variations found in the income tax practices of different countries, mainly those having to do with the determination of taxable income. Something should now be said about variations in rate structures. The important variants in these structures are (1) the starting point and levels of first bracket rates, (2) the top bracket or maximum marginal rates, and (3) the income range within which rates rise from the lowest to the highest levels.

Tax brackets

In some countries starting rates are low. The lower the starting rate and the narrower the lowest income brackets, the more progressive an income tax is likely to be at low and medium income levels.

During war emergencies, high marginal tax rates on personal income are viewed as a necessary complement to wage and price controls, but their value in a peacetime tax structure has been questioned. To the extent that they cannot be avoided, such high rates weaken work and risk-taking incentives, and they yield little revenue. There are many people who believe that a better personal income tax would be one with fewer exclusions and deductions, and with generally lower rates. During the 1980s this view prevailed in many countries, and an era of tax reform saw tax rates fall dramatically; for example, in the United States the top marginal rate was reduced from 70 percent in 1980 to 33 percent in 1987. (The rate paid at the very top of the income scale was actually reduced to only 28 percent.) Whereas several decades ago most top-bracket rates would be found ranging between 55 and 75 percent, top rates between 30 and 60 percent are becoming increasingly common. (E.G.K./C.E.McL.)

CORPORATION INCOME TAX

Nearly all countries assess income taxes on corporations as well as on individuals. Corporation income taxes apply to net profits, computed as the excess of receipts over allowable costs, but differ widely in detailed provisions and rates. Since industrialized countries generally have larger corporate sectors than less-developed countries, corporation income taxes tend to be greater in relation to national income and total government revenue in the former than in the latter countries except in major mineral-producing areas. The corporation income tax is an especially productive revenue source in New Zealand, South Africa, the United States, Canada, Australia, and Japan. Less-developed countries such as Kuwait, Iraq, Venezuela, Trinidad and Tobago, Guyana, Chile, and Zambia obtain substantial funds from taxing the net income of oil and other mining corporations.

Relative revenue productivity

In the United States the federal corporation income tax, adopted in 1909, predates the modern individual income tax (authorized by constitutional amendment in 1913). Until World War II the corporation tax usually yielded more revenue than the individual income tax, but with wartime changes the individual tax quickly surpassed the corporation tax and by the 1960s produced more than twice as much revenue. About three-fourths of the states also levy corporation income taxes. The United Kingdom for a long time applied the income tax on corporations (companies) purely as a supplement to the taxation of individuals. Shareholders had to pay tax on dividend income only to the extent that the rate of individual tax applicable to such income exceeded the corporate rate and received refunds if that rate was less than the corporate rate. This system was modified in 1937 and replaced in 1965 by a separate corporation tax. In 1972 the United Kingdom adopted an "imputation system," which resembles in some respects that in effect up to 1965. The earlier British system continues in several Commonwealth countries.

Rationale of the corporation tax. The separate taxation of the incomes of corporations and their shareholders follows the legal principle that they are distinct entities. Some scholars argue that it also accords with economic reality, particularly for large corporations having many shareholders who do not participate actively in controlling the enterprise. They consider a corporation income tax justified as a charge for the privilege of doing business in the corporate form, as a means of covering the costs of public services that especially benefit business, and as a way of capturing part of the profits of large enterprises.

Other scholars maintain that corporations act on behalf of shareholders and should be taxed like a large partnership or, alternatively, only to the extent that their profits are not reached by the individual income tax. Most economists concede that a tax may have to be assessed on corporations to prevent shareholders from escaping current taxation on undistributed profits and, as their shares appreciate in value, converting this income into capital gains, which in most countries either are taxed at lower rates than ordinary income or are free of income tax. A corporation income tax also enables a country or state to tax profits earned within its borders by corporations whose shareholders reside elsewhere.

The problem of rates

Corporation income taxes are mainly flat-rate levies, rather than extensively graduated taxes with rates rising according to income as in the typical individual income tax. An acceptable schedule of progressive rates could hardly be devised for corporations because they differ greatly in scale of operations and numbers of shareholders. Moreover, the stock of a given corporation may be owned either by individuals with high incomes or, as through pension funds, by those with low incomes. A number of industrialized countries have corporation income tax rates on the order of 50 percent, sometimes with reduced rates for small corporations. Where the latter feature exists, safeguards may be instituted to prevent its abuse by enterprises that split into nominally independent corporations without giving up unified control. More spectacular and significant are mergers or acquisitions of corporations motivated or facilitated by the possibility of saving taxes through offsetting the losses of some against the profits of others.

Corporation taxes may be graduated according to the rate of return on invested capital rather than the absolute size of profits. This is accomplished by an excess-profits tax on profits above a certain "normal" rate of return, sometimes further graduated according to the degree to which actual profits exceed the exempt level. The excess-profits tax has been used widely during wars and other national emergencies and to a much lesser extent under other conditions. There are serious difficulties involved in determining accurately the value of invested capital and in selecting an appropriate normal rate of return.

Economic effects. Sharp differences of opinion exist concerning the economic effects of the corporation income tax, partly because it is difficult to determine who actually bears it. The traditional conclusion of economic theory is that the tax is not reflected in prices in the short run and hence must be paid out of profits. If firms try to maximize their profits, the tax will give them no reason to change their prices. The price and output that yield maximum profits before tax will yield maximum profits after tax. Although the tax must be covered by sales receipts, it is not a cost of production in the same sense as, for example, wages but is a share of profits that can be computed only after gross receipts and production costs are known. This reasoning applies equally to competitive and to less-competitive or wholly monopolized industries. Certain qualifications have always been made, but they are fairly minor in nature. More important, the theory relates only to the determination of prices and output given the existing stock of capital. (The technical definition of "short run" in economics is a period of time over which the capital stock does not change.) The theory does not predict what the long-run effects of the tax will be, although it indicates that they will be those of a tax that rests in the first instance on profit recipients rather than on consumers.

Tax shifting

This view of the incidence of the corporation income tax has been increasingly challenged. Its opponents argue that in many industries prices are decisively influenced by the actions of a few leading firms, which have as their objective not maximum profits in the short run but a target rate of return over a period of years. When the rate of corporate income tax is increased, they say, the leading firms will raise their selling prices in order to maintain the target return, and other firms will follow. According to this hypothesis, prices are not competitively determined but are generally at levels lower than those that would yield maximum profits in the short run. Another qualification of the traditional view is that labour unions may share the burden of the tax through lower wage settlements.

The debate among economists and businessmen over the question has not been resolved by empirical research. Studies indicating that in the United States, Canada, and West Germany the corporate income tax is largely shifted forward to consumers by short-run price rises have been vigorously criticized; other studies have supported a contrary conclusion.

If the tax is not shifted forward by increases in prices, it must tend to reduce the return on corporate-equity capital. (Because interest payments are nearly always deductible in determining taxable profits, the return on borrowed capital is not subject to the corporation tax.) The returns on capital in unincorporated enterprises and on bonds and mortgages will tend to fall over time as investors try to avoid the corporate tax by moving to untaxed fields. In this way the corporation income tax may actually burden all capital, rather than only that invested in the corporate sector. A general reduction in rates of return may curtail investment by cutting the reward for success and by reducing the amount of resources available in the form of retained corporate profits and personal savings. This will tend to reduce the rate of growth of national product; however, the effect may not be dramatic. Capital investment is only one factor influencing growth rates, and some analyses indicate that it is less important than influences such as technological innovation and education.

If the corporation income tax falls on the returns on capital, it will be broadly progressive in the aggregate; that is, it will reduce disposable income proportionately more for high-income persons than for low-income persons. This is because the fraction of total income represented by returns from ownership of corporate stock and other capital assets rises with income. This holds, however, only in the aggregate. Some low-income people, including many retired persons, depend heavily on investment income.

On the other hand, to the extent that the tax is shifted through higher prices, it will fall mainly on consumers and, like a sales tax, be regressive with respect to income. A shifted corporation tax will not be especially harmful to investment but it may have an adverse effect on resource allocation and the competitive position of exports in foreign markets.

Policy issues. *Integration.* A major policy issue is whether income taxes on corporations and shareholders should be integrated. Partial integration (or dividend relief) may be attained by lessening or eliminating the so-called double taxation of distributed profits resulting from separate income taxes on corporations and shareholders. Full integration could be achieved only by overlooking the existence of the corporation for income tax purposes and taxing shareholders on undistributed profits as well as on dividends, as if the income had been earned by a partnership. This approach may be suitable for corporations having few shareholders. It is allowed on an optional basis in the United States for certain corporations having only one class of stock and no more than 10 shareholders. Although full integration has generally been conceded to be impracticable for corporations with large numbers of shareholders, the ascendancy of large "master limited partnerships," organizations having many of the characteristics of corporations, including ownership shares that are traded on stock exchanges, calls this view into question.

Reducing double taxation of dividends

One method of partial integration is to apply a reduced rate of corporation tax to the distributed part of profits, as in the split-rate system of West Germany. With a zero rate on distributed profits, the corporate tax would become an undistributed profits tax. Allowing corporations a deduction for dividends paid would have the same effect. The split-rate system offers a tax incentive for distribution of profits and sometimes has been advocated as an instrument for curtailing internal financing of corporations. In support of such a policy, it has been argued that liberal payouts of dividends will strengthen the capital market, improve the allocation of investment funds, and lessen the concentration of industry. Critics have questioned whether these objectives will be attained and have pointed out that larger dividend distributions would tend to reduce savings and investment because shareholders would consume part of the additional income received.

Another approach to integration is to allow shareholders a credit (offset against their individual tax liability) for the corporate tax allocable to dividends received. Such a method functions much like the withholding system on labour income. West Germany combines a credit with its split-rate system to eliminate the added burden of the corporate tax on dividends. The systems employed in the United Kingdom and France provide resident shareholders a credit for about one-half of the corporate tax. A Canadian credit, like a small credit previously granted in the United States, lacked two important refinements present in the French and British systems—the inclusion in dividends of the credit and refunds for shareholders whose individual tax rate is less than the corporate rate. The omission of these features favours high-income shareholders who are subject to high individual tax rates compared with those having lower incomes.

Opinions on the desirability of tax integration differ widely, as do judgments about the economic effects of the corporation tax and the nature of the relationship between corporations and their shareholders. A key question is whether the revenue that is foregone when distributed profits are relieved of so-called double taxation can be replaced by other taxes that are preferable from the standpoint of equity and economic effects. It has been proposed that dividend relief be provided only for dividends paid on newly issued stock. This proposal has the potential for reconciling the need for dividend relief with avoidance of revenue loss and windfall gains for owners of existing shares.

Depreciation allowances

Investment incentives. The adverse effect of the corporate income tax on investment can be lessened by accelerating the rate at which the cost of new machinery and buildings is written off against taxable income through depreciation allowances. Accelerated depreciation may take the form of an additional deduction in the first year—an "initial allowance"—or may be spread over several years. Although the increase in early years in depreciation allowances for any one asset will be matched by a reduction in allowances for this asset in future years—the total being limited to 100 percent of cost—the acceleration is advantageous to the taxpayer. It postpones payment of tax, facilitates financing of investment out of internal funds, saves interest costs, and reduces risk. Another form of incentive, the investment allowance, permits investors to deduct from taxable income a certain percentage of the cost of eligible assets in addition to depreciation allowances. The total deductions thus may exceed the cost of an eligible asset over its lifetime. A related scheme, the tax credit, reduces the income tax payable by a certain percentage of the cost of eligible forms of new investment. Alternatively, an investment grant, in the form of a payment from the government to those making certain kinds of new investment, may be provided. Investment allowances, tax credits, and investment grants reduce the cost of new equipment and plant and thus make investment more attractive.

Many industrialized countries, including the United States, Canada, and the United Kingdom, have used accelerated depreciation and the other special incentives. These incentives reduce tax revenues but may be considered preferable to an outright cut in tax rates, because they are selective, being extended to firms that make new investments but not to other firms. The less-developed countries, in an effort to attract investment by both foreign and domestic companies, sometimes offer accelerated depreciation or investment allowances and more often "tax holidays" that provide full exemption from income tax for new firms for the first several years of operation.

Outlays for research and development, like purchases of plant and equipment, are intended to yield returns over a period of years and are frequently given special tax treatment. In the United States, corporations and individual taxpayers may choose between deducting research and development expenditures in full when made or capitalizing them and writing them off over their useful life—or over five years if the useful life is indeterminable. Canada allows corporations to deduct, immediately, current and capital expenditures for scientific research related to the business and exempts from tax government grants to corporations for research and development.

Accelerated depreciation allowances and current deductions of research and development outlays will result in accounting losses when they exceed net income computed without regard to these deductions. The incentive effects of the provisions can be enhanced (and the discouragement of risky investment resulting from the corporation tax reduced) by permitting net operating losses suffered in one year to be offset against taxable income of other years. Tax laws commonly allow such losses to be carried back against income of prior years (thus giving rise to refunds of income taxes previously paid) or carried forward to future years. If, however, accounting losses that do not reflect economic reality can be "passed through" to the owners of a business, perhaps by the use of a partnership, they can offset income from other sources and therefore provide a tax shelter.

The extent to which investment incentives should be offered is a major policy issue. It is related to the large question of how much emphasis should be placed on present consumption, private and public, rather than future consumption that would result from increased investment. This raises philosophical and political questions as well as technical economic ones. If special investment incentives are offered, should they be varied in order to afford a greater stimulus in recession years than in boom years? This could be a useful means of cyclical stabilization, but there are obvious difficulties in deciding exactly when the changes should be made and, moreover, the variations complicate the planning of private investors.

Depletion allowances

A problem that has attracted much attention in the United States is that of depletion allowances for mineral producers. Depletion allowances are an issue for the individual income tax as well as for the corporation tax. In order to define net income correctly, investors in exhaustible mineral deposits should be allowed deductions from gross income for depletion of these deposits for the same reason that investors in machinery and equipment are granted depreciation allowances. In the United States depletion allowances may be based on "cost depletion" or on "percentage depletion." Cost depletion spreads the cost of acquisition and development of the mineral deposit over its life. Percentage depletion is a stated percentage of annual gross income from mineral extraction (subject to a limit equal to a certain fraction of net income computed without regard to the allowance) and is not restricted to the actual costs incurred in acquiring and developing the minerals. In addition, certain capital costs of development and exploration may be written off immediately when incurred.

Percentage depletion and the deduction of intangible drilling costs have been attacked as an unfair special privilege to mineral producers—particularly the petroleum industry, which accounts for three-fourths of the total allowances. Another criticism is that the provision results in economic inefficiency because it encourages excessive production of minerals by attracting capital and labour that could be more productive in other uses. The defense offered for these tax subsidies is that it is necessary to encourage sufficient exploration and production, considering the especially risky character of these activities and the strategic importance of minerals. This argument is countered by questioning the sense of a policy that stimulates early production of domestic resources, thereby hastening and exacerbating eventual dependence on foreign supplies.

Timing and inflation adjustment. For taxable income to measure economic income accurately it is necessary that recognition of income and deductions for tax purposes closely reflect increases and decreases in net worth, that is, changes in the value of assets and liabilities. If deductions are taken too quickly or if the recognition of income is unduly postponed, the present value of tax liability is reduced. Tax shelters are based on the creation of artificial accounting losses that result from acceleration of deductions and the deferral of recognition of income; such losses arise from partnership investments and are used to offset income from other sources. Depreciation is the most obvious and most important timing issue, but it is not unique. Industries in which timing issues, and therefore the possibility of tax shelters, are especially important include oil and gas, timber, orchards and vineyards, and real estate. The timing rules that are required to prevent the mismeasurement of income can add considerable complexity to the tax system.

Tax shelters

The tax systems of most countries are based on the implicit assumption that prices are stable. If, instead, there is inflation, real (inflation-adjusted) income is mismeasured, and distortions and inequities occur. For example, tax is paid on (or deductions are allowed for) the full amount of interest earned (or paid), even though inflation is eroding the principal. (Part of interest can be seen as merely offsetting this erosion; it is neither income nor an expense.) Tax is also paid on capital gains, with no allowance for inflation; thus fictitious gains are taxed, and tax may even be levied when no real gain occurs. Finally, business is not allowed to recover tax-free its investment in depreciable (and similar) assets and inventories.

Although many developing countries that have experienced high rates of inflation provide for inflation adjustment in the measurement of income, no developed country does so. As long as inflation is expected to be low, the benefits of inflation adjustment are generally thought not to be great enough to justify the increased complexity that would be involved.

Consumption-based direct taxation. One way to avoid the complexities of both timing issues and inflation adjustment is to switch from a tax system based on income to one based on consumption. Under such a system all business purchases would be deducted immediately, or "expensed." Borrowing in excess of investment would be added to income, and lending would be subtracted; the resulting tax base would be consumption. Through the tax saving resulting from expensing, the government, in effect, becomes a partner in all investments; the revenues it subsequently receives are best seen as the return on its investment. A consumption-based tax imposes no burden on income from marginal investments because the private investor keeps all of the income relating to his share of the investment. As a result, such a tax does not favour present consumption over saving for future consumption, as the income tax does. Simplicity—the lack of timing issues and the fact that inflation would have no chance to distort the measurement of consumption—may be even more important than the economic advantages of such a tax.

Advantages of consumption-based taxation

An alternative that is even simpler than consumption-based taxation and that would achieve similar economic effects would be to exempt most capital income from taxation at the individual level; that is, tax only labour income. This proposal, like consumption-based taxation, suffers from the loss of progressivity that results when the tax on most capital income is eliminated. Many advocates of these proposed systems therefore consider the transference of wealth through gifts and bequests to be a form of taxable consumption. Opponents argue that such a gift or bequest would then be taxed twice, first as the consumption of the donor when it is given and second when it is consumed by the recipient. Including gifts and bequests emphasizes the lifetime rather than annual perspective of consumption-based taxes. Taxation of lifetime endowments is not affected by timing or the earning and the spending of income and is therefore viewed by many as a better measure of taxpaying ability than annual income.

Open economy issues. *Determination of income source.* Major corporations commonly operate across state and national boundaries. Because most jurisdictions tax income having its source within their boundaries, a way must be found to determine the source of income of a multi-jurisdictional entity. The states of the United States follow a practice that is quite distinct from that in the international sphere. National governments commonly resort to the convention of "arms-length" prices—the prices that would prevail in a trade between unrelated entities—to determine the split of income resulting from transactions between related parties. The states, by comparison, employ formulas to divide the income of a multistate corporation or a group of related corporations engaged in a "unitary business" between in-state and out-of-state income. Neither of these approaches is totally satisfactory.

International double taxation. Some countries (including the United States) exercise the right to tax the whole income of their nationals even if it is earned abroad. Almost all countries consider it their right to tax income arising within their borders, whether or not the income is earned by individuals or corporations having their residence or exercising their management and control in the country. Increasing attention has therefore been given to the prevention of double taxation between countries, especially as the number of corporations operating in more than one country and the number of stockholders of a corporation residing outside the country in which it operates continue to rise. To illustrate how double taxation may come about, consider a corporation A that has its headquarters in country X and a manufacturing plant in country Y. Country X may tax the profits earned in Y and so may Y. Further complications may arise if some of the shareholders of A live in country Z and are subject to income tax there on dividends received from A, which may also be subject to a withholding tax in X. Relief from double taxation can be provided unilaterally or by treaty. Country X may allow A a foreign tax credit for income tax paid in Y; this is done by, for example, the United States, the United Kingdom, Canada, and West Germany. Alternatively, country X might unilaterally give up its right to tax certain profits earned abroad; this approach is followed by, for example, France and The Netherlands. Countries X and Z might enter into a tax treaty relieving dividends paid by corporations in X to shareholders residing in Z from withholding tax and providing some compensating advantages for X. A network of tax treaties exists among the industrialized countries, but they apply only sketchily to the less-developed countries. There are doubts as to whether the standard provisions found in agreements between rich countries are suitable for agreements between industrialized countries and those at earlier stages of economic development.

Reducing international double taxation

The varying national tax policies can also be used to avoid paying taxes. Many developed countries do not actually tax the majority of investment income (especially interest) that originates within their borders and flows to foreigners. They may thus attract capital from less-developed countries that either do not or cannot tax such income when it is received by their residents, thereby worsening problems of capital shortages. Investment and the related income sometimes are channeled through "tax haven" countries in order to take advantage of tax treaties. To illustrate how this approach can be used to avoid taxes, consider the case of a resident of country R who wishes to invest in country I, with which country R has no tax treaty. If the funds flow through country T, which has a treaty with I, and if income is not reported to R, tax due to I, as well as tax due to R, can be avoided. (It might more properly be said that this involves illegal evasion rather than legal avoidance.) (R.B.G./C.E.McL.)

PAYROLL TAX

Most income taxes include income from both labour and capital in their bases. Taxes on payrolls—wages and salaries only—are seldom used as a source of general revenues (although in some developing countries the income tax base may actually include little beyond wages and salaries, the equivalent of the payroll tax base). Many countries do, however, levy payroll taxes to finance social security benefits, which include retirement and survivors' benefits, disability insurance, and health care. Payroll taxes are often justified by the appearance of a link between the taxes paid (often called contributions) and the benefits received; in fact, this link is commonly quite tenuous.

With the maturity of social security systems around the world, payroll taxes have become an extremely important source of revenue. In the United States, for example, only the individual income tax is more important than the social security taxes, which are far more important than the corporation income tax. Because of international differences in both social security programs and the extent of reliance on general revenues, however, payroll tax systems and rates vary widely among countries.

Payroll taxes are often levied on both the employer and the employee, presumably on the assumption that the ultimate burden will be borne in a similar manner. In fact, the theory of tax incidence suggests that the two components of the levy will have exactly the same incidence in the long run—on labour; it is only in the short run that employers may be adversely affected by their portion of the tax (and even then they might be able to shift the tax onto consumers).

The incidence of payroll taxes

Payroll taxes are virtually always collected through withholding. Unlike income taxes, payroll taxes usually make no allowance for the personal circumstances of the taxpayer, and rather than being levied at graduated rates, payroll taxes often do not apply to income above a ceiling. The tax is thus likely to be regressive, both because of the ceiling on taxable payrolls and because labour income represents a declining fraction of total income as income rises. This effect, however, may be more than offset by the distribution of social security benefits, the majority of which are commonly allocated to the poor. (C.E. McL.)

PROPERTY TAX

A property tax is a tax levied primarily upon land and buildings. In some countries, including the United States, the tax is also levied upon business and farm equipment and inventories. Sometimes the tax extends to automobiles, jewelry, furniture, and even to such intangibles as bonds, mortgages, and shares of stock that represent claims on, or ownership of, tangible wealth. The amount payable is based not on a person's or a company's total net wealth but on gross value without regard to debts.

Levies not ordinarily classified as property taxes are those on transfer of property (by sale, gift, or death), on net wealth, and on capital; special charges for some public service or improvement (such as special assessments in the United States); certain types of agricultural imposts; and portions of income taxes that apply to presumed or actual yield of farm or urban land.

The three principal approaches to the assessment of property are rental value, capital value, and market value. Most Asian countries use annual rental value as the basis of assessment. Under this principle, the tax is based on the average gross-rental income the property is expected to generate under prevailing market conditions. A common approach to the assessment of real property in European countries is that of capital value. The traditional idea is that capital value can be estimated on the basis of rental values, treating them as earnings on capital. Most European countries, however, as well as the United States, endeavour to assess property according to its market value. Some Asian countries employ a fourth, less complex but less fair approach. They simply collect a fixed amount based on a particular unit of land measurement. Laos collects a specific amount per square metre of land. In West Malaysia the annual tax on land is a certain amount per 1,000 square feet.

Determining the value of property

The scope of the tax in different countries varies greatly, depending upon legal factors, administrative realities, tradition, availability of other sources of revenue, the organization of government—especially the relative role of local government, for which this levy is of key significance—and the public services provided. The attempt to extend the tax to other than real property (land and buildings) is almost unique to the United States. There is a strong argument in principle for broad coverage of tangible property, since otherwise the tax discriminates (is not neutral) among types of consumption and investment. Administrative difficulties limit what is possible in practice. Classification of property by different types has served as a basis for varying the effective burdens, sometimes by providing for the exclusion of a fraction of the value of some kinds of property (machinery, forests, mines, securities, furniture, etc.), sometimes by adjusting the rates of tax.

In a simple agrarian economy composed of homogeneous households, property taxation might be thought to provide a fairly good indicator of both ability to pay and benefits from public services. In a complex urban, industrial society this may no longer be true; the practical administrative advantages of taxing immobile real estate may go further than tax principles in explaining the prevalence of this tax.

National differences in taxable property

In most countries, property taxes are used by local or state rather than national governments. Property tax receipts supplied about half of the revenue raised by local governments in the United States. Throughout much of Europe and Latin America and parts of Africa and Asia, one finds taxes that may be broadly classified as property taxes in their functioning and that supply significant proportions of total tax revenue. In several countries the property tax applies in fact primarily to urban real property. The intensity of use varies widely.

In some countries, property tax revenues have lagged far behind the growth of national income because the tax has been based on measures that have not responded to changes in the general level of prices. The original land surveys were designed to serve for long periods, and the taxes were based on surface area or presumed income at rates that might have served moderately well in a world of stable property values. War, inflation, and other forces, however, have made them obsolete; and popular resistance and lack of administrative capacity have generally prevented their modernization.

The tax base

The development of property taxation. One of the most difficult problems in taxing property is to find a reasonable basis of assessment. The problem has grown more difficult as the complexities of economic life have increased. The taxes of the ancient world, of parts of medieval Europe, and of the American colonies were originally land taxes based on area rather than on value. Eventually gross output came to serve as the base. At a later stage, attempts were made to find a measure of what would now be called the individual "ability to pay"; thus, other forms of wealth, such as farmhouses, animals, and implements, were included. At various times, governments have tried to make the tax base one of general property value rather than of specific amounts of different types of particular properties. Yet to reach movable property effectively for taxation has always been difficult; and taxing intangible forms of wealth has proved even harder.

In the United States, the early New England colonies developed taxes that sought to reach all of the "visible estate," real and personal. The "general property tax," applying to all property, was on the statute books of some states by 1800. During the colonial period, the southern and middle colonies made relatively little use of property taxation, but by the middle of the 19th century it had become the principal source of revenue in all the states. The base of the general property tax was defined to include intangible wealth. Yet the value of mortgages and other intangibles consisted largely of claims to rights in real estate and tangible personal property, which were also taxed. The double burden is theoretically indefensible. Because it seemed excessive, and because concealment was easy, enforcement of the tax on intangibles became difficult and ultimately almost impossible. Disintegration of the property tax as a general tax began early and continued into the 20th century as more and more property escaped, legally and nonlegally. Today real estate accounts for the bulk of the property tax base.

The property tax in the United States is the chief source of revenue for local government. State governments once used the tax as an important source of revenue, but few now get more than a small percentage of their revenue from this source. Forty state governments, however, assess some or all of the operating property of railroads and other utilities. For many years, few if any states took serious interest in the way in which local governments administered the tax; but active efforts to improve it expanded after World War II. Some authorities favour a state takeover of the tax, partly because they believe that states would administer it better and partly in order to remove inequalities in taxing capacity among local governments (especially for financing schools).

Administration. Responsibility for the various phases of administration rests almost entirely upon government officials. Administration involves the discovery or identification of the property to be taxed, its valuation, the application of the appropriate tax rate, and collection. Where the amount of tax is measured by income, as in Great Britain and some of the British Commonwealth countries, income rather than capital value must be determined. Self-assessment is seldom applied in this area. Important aspects, especially valuation, are a matter of judgment rather than of fact. The determination of value for tax purposes is not an incidental result, or an automatic by-product, of a transaction entered into for other purposes, such as a wage payment or a retail sale.

Problems of tax administration

Difficult administrative problems arise in determining (1) what actually exists in a physical sense (the location, topography, and area of a piece of land; the size, materials, and condition of buildings; the number and types of machines or items of inventory) and (2) the value of the property. To do this well requires skilled professional personnel, access to information of various types, and appropriate facilities. The quality of most property tax administration is far below satisfactory levels.

Better administration involves a number of things. One is better mapping and the improvement of other means of getting accurate property descriptions. Another is more sources of data about values and more sophisticated approaches to valuation. For some types of properties, such as single-family residences, sales of generally similar properties provide a good basis for valuation. Some properties, such as office and apartment buildings, can be valued on the basis of the income they yield. For unique and highly specialized properties, including factory and other buildings that are integral parts of a business operation, the value for tax purposes must rest on estimates of reproduction cost less depreciation. Business inventories may be valued on the basis of company records and so may machinery and equipment.

Good assessment requires the skills of a permanent professional staff, selected and promoted on a merit basis, working full time at pay comparable to that in private industry and free from political pressures. Such staffs are virtually nonexistent, however. The United States assessor, for example, has typically been a part-time official, usually elected, poorly paid, and without the special training now recognized as essential. Rarely has he had the basic information and other facilities needed. Incompetence has sometimes been compounded by favouritism and corruption. Furthermore, the area under the responsibility of one assessment staff needs to be large enough to permit specialization and the development of expertise. Rarely are staffs large enough to make reasonably current assessments more often than every four or five years. Yet the pace of change and the amount of new construction are so great as to make many assessments significantly obsolete before a new cycle can correct them. Keeping maps and records up-to-date calls for more continuing work than most governments will support, though modern data-processing techniques offer hope of reducing the burden.

Practice in most countries has been to assess at only a small fraction of the full, current market value even when the governing law specifies that assessment shall be at 100 percent. Low valuations mean that tax rates must be higher. Inequities can easily occur in such a system because it may be difficult to prevail in a complaint that an assessment is unfairly high when it is, say, one-fourth of market price even if others are one-fifth or less.

Tax review

Because the tax base, and hence the amount of tax payable, depends upon an official's estimate of value rather than on a free-market test (as with a sales tax) or on the taxpayer's report (as with an income tax), the taxpayer will not have participated in the determination of the assessment. The law usually provides facilities for appeal before the tax becomes final, but these are often of little worth. The taxpayer may be ignorant of procedure, or he may not consider the possible saving worth the trouble.

Tax rates. Because assessments are usually much below market values, nominal tax rates give a misleading impression of the burden.

When government functions were narrow and the property tax the sole source of local revenue, tax rates were determined simply by dividing the figure for estimated expenditure by that for assessed valuation. If spending was to be $400,000 and assessments were $40,000,000, a rate of 1 percent would suffice. Today officials are more likely to estimate the amount that will be available if the existing tax rate is maintained and then try to judge whether taxpayers will consider additional spending to be worth a higher rate of tax. U.S. state governments formerly used the property tax as a flexible element, relying primarily on other taxes. According to whether these were inadequate or in surplus, the state would raise or lower its property tax rate. Many states still have constitutional power to do so. When a strong demand for some particular service appears but officials prefer not to raise their "general fund" rates, the legislature may vote to mandate a "special" rate.

Rate limitations are common, imposed sometimes by the state constitution, often by statute. For each class of government—counties, cities, school districts—a maximum ceiling rate will be set. Sometimes the limit may be changed upon referendum or by special legislative action. It is difficult to judge whether such limitations have been effective in restraining the growth of spending. One result, however, has been the establishment of special districts that have independent taxing power and thus lie outside the limitations.

Theory of property taxation. The property tax illustrates the concepts of tax incidence introduced earlier. The tax on land is likely to be capitalized to the extent it is not offset by benefits of public services. The actual amount a buyer will pay for a plot of land depends upon the net income he can expect from it in relation to the yields available from other investments. If the net income from a plot of land is expected to be $1,200 a year indefinitely, and if the prevailing yield on long-term assets is 6 percent, then the land will be worth $20,000. If a tax of $300 is imposed, then the net yield drops to $900 and the worth of the land falls to $15,000. The tax increase is said to have been capitalized. To the buyer of the land, the tax in effect at the time of purchase will not be a burden thereafter because he has already discounted it in the purchase price. Because land prices generally have gone up over time, the property tax has not so much lowered land prices as retarded their rise.

Shifting and incidence

The extent to which taxes on buildings and other improvements can be shifted involves quite different factors. Moreover, it depends crucially on whether the tax in question is levied by only one small jurisdiction, such as a county, city, or school district, or by all jurisdictions. In the second case, the tax is likely to be borne by owners of capital, except to the extent it results in lower saving and higher prices or lower wages. The first case is more complex and more relevant for policy purposes. The construction of buildings depends upon the willingness of investors to make capital available for them, and taxes affect that willingness. A property tax will be treated as a cost of doing business. It must generally be recovered in higher prices from consumers (or in lower prices paid to suppliers or lower wages paid to workers). Firms that do not succeed in passing the tax on to customers will suffer a lower rate of return on invested capital. Companies in competition with others located where rates are lower may be unable to shift the tax fully to consumers. New investment will go where net earnings after tax are greatest. The supply of capital grows when investment yields are promising; it lags when profits are low. Thus it may be impossible to shift the tax to owners of capital in the long run. The most likely candidates to bear the burden of the tax are owners of local land, labour that cannot (or will not) move in response to the tax, and especially local consumers. As output and prices adjust to changes in tax rates, the taxes will tend to be shifted to consumers. The length of time it takes for a change in a property tax on buildings to be reflected in prices paid by consumers varies from a few months to a number of years. For regulated public utilities, the shifting of a change in tax will usually be more certain, but it requires some time because new rates will have to be authorized by an official agency.

The homeowner cannot shift the tax on his dwelling. The price he paid for the land, of course, will have been adjusted to the tax that was in effect when he purchased the property; this tax is no burden on the owner after his purchase (though few homeowners realize that if the tax had been lower, the price paid for the land would have been higher). The tax on the house closely resembles a tax on other items of consumption, although it tends in the United States to be higher than the burdens on most other consumer goods. Deduction of the tax in computing income for the individual income tax helps reduce the net burden for the homeowner.

Burden of the property tax

The amounts of property tax borne by persons at different levels of income cannot be determined accurately. There is almost no way to take account adequately of the element represented by capitalized land tax in the price of land. Seen as a tax on all income from capital, the property tax on improvements is almost certainly progressive. But if one focuses on the burden of the tax levied by a single jurisdiction, the incidence of the tax is likely to fall on local consumers (and perhaps local workers and landowners). The portion of property tax falling on businesses is presumably shifted to consumers according to their purchases, including those of telephone, electric, and other utility services. Thus, in general, "single jurisdiction" property taxes seem to be either roughly proportional to income or slightly regressive, but, in fact, the total redistributive effect from higher to lower income groups is substantial when account is taken of the degree to which property taxes pay for schools and other services for low-income groups.

There is widespread "horizontal inequity" in property taxes because of unequal assessments upon owners. The tax falls more heavily on some kinds of business (*e.g.,* railroads and other utilities) and some types of consumption (*e.g.,* housing) than on others. In the United States, property taxes on farming as a business tend generally to be low relative to the value of property but high in relation to income. Because property taxation is of such long standing that its many elements have worked themselves into the economy, some portions being capitalized and others variously adjusted to, the inequities have to some extent been reduced.

Exemptions in the United States

The property tax has been increasingly weakened by exemptions. In the United States, for example, exemptions apparently remove roughly one-third of the land area in the average locality. Most land exemptions from tax, however, consist of streets, schools, parks, and other property of local government; therefore, to apply the tax would merely transfer funds from one government account to another. In some localities, state- or federal-government real estate is important, although these bodies sometimes make payments in lieu of local taxes. Property owned and used for religious, educational, charitable, and some other purposes is generally exempt, and in some countries land with a value below a certain minimum is exempt.

Some exemptions are made in order to attract new businesses or to encourage low-income housing. Some localities grant exemptions for part of the value of a "homestead," perhaps with a limitation based on income of the owner-occupant; several give some exemption to persons over age 65 or to veterans. Several authorities also allow income tax credits for residential property taxes.

Economic effects. Property taxation finances local government, not fully but enough to make the independence of local government meaningful. This permits decentralization of government, which may be considered a benefit because it enables a community to exercise a degree of choice.

The property tax may have substantial nonrevenue effects. Where it is heavy enough to bring large revenues, it leads to changes in behaviour, not just because taxpayers have less to spend and save but also because individuals and businesses conduct their affairs differently because of it. Although property tax rates expressed as percentages are usually small, in the United States they apply to capital values and are effectively much higher: if a property that yields 9 percent gross is taxed at 3 percent, the tax is equal to 33 percent of the pretax income—and 50 percent of the 6 percent remaining after tax. A tax of 20 cents for each 80 cents paid for the costs of housing—not as high as actually prevails in many urban areas—is 25 percent when expressed on the same basis as a retail sales tax.

A community with high tax rates on buildings will be at a disadvantage in the national (and international) competition for capital unless it can offer compensatory advantages. The supply of capital for the economy as a whole comes from saving. Whether the property tax affects it materially is not clear. Methods of production requiring relatively large amounts of capital will be discouraged if they are subject to tax.

The effect on new building

The tax on buildings and property other than land distorts resource allocation where older property exists. New, high-quality buildings are taxed more heavily per unit of space than are old ones, including slums. There is no justification for this in the costs that the two types of property and their occupants impose on local government in terms of police, fire protection, etc. Thus the user's payment for the services of local government goes down, relatively, as the building he occupies gets worse, even though public expenses attributable to the property are unchanged or may even increase. Likewise, residents who shift from poorer to better quality housing or business property must pay more toward the costs of government even though they will not ordinarily receive more government services.

Cities that urgently need to replace obsolete buildings paradoxically base much of their financing upon a tax that encourages owners to hold on to deteriorated structures and penalizes owners of new ones. Every increase in the property tax rates on structures (not land) reduces the desirability of putting capital funds into new buildings, creates an incentive against upgrading quality by new construction, and discourages maintenance.

Differences in effective tax rates among localities may have the effect of creating islands of relatively low tax rates. Some communities may have tax bases above average in relation to governmental obligations and can get by with lower tax rates. They attract capital. Some communities, perhaps by the use of zoning, exclude types of property associated with high governmental expense such as high-density housing, which brings many children and requires more schools. Tax rates elsewhere must then be higher. The existence of such enclaves adds to the fiscal imbalance of neighbouring localities and accentuates the difficulties of older areas.

Lower tax rates on the fringes of an urban area encourage suburbanization. Property nearer the centre will be subject to high tax rates, aggravating the troubles of central-city business properties. High taxes on structures also favour horizontal over vertical growth of metropolitan areas.

Where, as in Great Britain, the property tax rests on income, land held idle or far below its best use will yield little revenue. In such cases, the tax incentive for efficient use is notably lacking.

The rates at which timber is cut and minerals extracted can be influenced materially by property taxation. To prevent uneconomical and premature exhaustion of natural resources many states have switched from property taxation of mineral resources to "severance taxes" on the production or extraction of resources.

Taxing the "unearned increment"

Site-value taxation. The use of a land tax as the chief source of revenue has often been proposed. It was favoured by the Physiocrats in 18th-century France. Probably the best-known exponent was a 19th-century American, Henry George. His *Progress and Poverty* (1879) drew upon economic analysis in the tradition of Ricardo and Mill to argue persuasively for a single tax on land and the abolition of other taxes (then predominantly levied on other property). More recently, proposals for heavier taxation of land—site-value taxation—have found increasing support. One argument is that much of what is paid for the use of land reflects socially created demand and is not a payment to bring land into existence. The community can capture in land taxes some of the values it has created—including those resulting from streets, schools, and other facilities. This, it is maintained, would be a more equitable way of financing local government. Another argument is that the revenue from a tax on land would permit a reduction of taxes on buildings, which tend to deter new construction. A third argument is that higher land taxes would make for more efficient use of land.

There is a great deal to be said in favour of increasing taxes on land and thus lowering land prices. Economically, of course, a "high" price for some land is essential in order to encourage the best employment of it. The user of land ought to pay the amount of its worth in its best use; but the owner, facing no cost of production, need not receive all that is paid. Government can reasonably take much of the total paid by the user.

A heavier land tax would change the conditions of ownership. The total collected from users would not change, but private owners of land would retain less, the public treasury getting more. The price system would still allocate land use. Taxes on improvements could then be reduced greatly. The tax relief for deteriorated buildings would be slight, but for those of high quality the reduction could be large in relation to net return on investment. More buildings, new and better ones, would be supplied. Modernization and maintenance of existing buildings would become more profitable.

Over the longer run, landowners would get less of the increments in land values and the public would get more. Socially created values would be channeled into governmental rather than private uses. Taxes could be related more closely to the cost of governmental services.

Problems with site-value taxation

The opponents of site-value taxation point out that the unearned increment in land value has been capitalized and question the fairness of imposing a heavy tax on present land values for which owners have paid in good faith. They doubt the ability of assessors to make fair enough appraisals to support much heavier rates on land. They also doubt whether land alone, excluding buildings, would be an adequate tax base. Moves in the direction of site-value taxation have been made in Australia and New Zealand, South Africa, and parts of western Canada.

(C.L.Ha./C.E.McL.)

SALES AND EXCISE TAXES

Sales taxes are taxes imposed upon the sale of goods and services. A sales tax levied on the manufacture, purchase, sale, or consumption of a specific type of commodity is known as an excise tax. (American terminology in this matter tends to differ from that used in the United Kingdom and former British colonies. In the United States, excises apply to imports as well as to domestic production; in British terminology excises may be applied only to domestic output.) Whereas excises may be based either on quantities of the taxed product (specific excises) or on value, general sales taxes are inherently value-based taxes. Sales taxes are commonly classified according to the levels of business activity at which they are imposed—at the manufacturing or import stage or at the wholesale or retail level. Very often tax rates applied to commodities will vary according to whether the commodities are considered essential or nonessential. Many countries impose excise taxes on such products as gasoline, tobacco, and alcoholic beverages. Although taxes on luxury items are politically popular, luxury consumption is difficult to define for tax purposes, and such taxes raise complex administrative problems while generating little revenue.

Multistage sales taxes, which are imposed at more than one level of production and distribution, without relief for taxes paid at previous stages, are sometimes called turnover taxes. For reasons of administration and simplicity such taxes are based on gross receipts; consequently, the taxable value at each stage includes amounts taxed at the previous stage (as well as the taxes already paid at previous stages). In order to avoid such pyramiding of taxes, an increasing number of governments employ a value-added tax. This is a modified sales tax based on the net value added at each stage rather than on gross receipts. Roughly speaking, an enterprise's net value added within a given period is equal to output minus input, calculated as its total sales minus expenditure on goods and services purchased from other enterprises. Tax liability is not, however, calculated by applying the tax rate to the value added figured in this way. Instead, receipts are used to show the amount of tax at each step; each seller adds the tax to the price and acknowledges this on his bill. Each enterprise's net tax liability is then calculated as the sum of all taxes it collects on goods it sells minus the sum of all the taxes it has paid on goods it has brought. This is sometimes known as the "invoice" or "credit" method of implementing a value-added tax.

Value-added tax

History. Excise taxes were well known in the ancient world. It is said that the Roman emperor Vespasian when asked for the justification of a new excise on public urinals answered, "*Pecunia non olet*" ("Money does not smell"). Excises of various kinds were important sources of public revenue in medieval Europe. In the United States, customs duties were the primary source of federal government revenue before World War I. General sales taxes are a comparatively recent innovation. Multistage turnover taxes were developed during and after World War I in Europe.

The large-scale use of value-added taxation began when France adopted it in 1954; it was subsequently taken up in other European countries, largely as the result of a desire to harmonize tax systems. Its spread to many countries throughout the world is one of the most important fiscal developments of the postwar era.

Sales and excise taxes in various countries. In most countries, excises on automobiles, mineral fuels, tobacco, and alcoholic beverages are among the major excises. A wide variety of other special excises are in use, such as taxes on coffee, sugar, salt, vinegar, matches, and amusements. In the Soviet Union and other Communist countries, general turnover taxes are among the most important sources of revenue. Domestic taxes on goods and services account for about one-fifth of total central government revenues in developing countries with relatively high income levels, one-quarter of revenues in middle-income developing countries, and one-third of revenues in the poorest of the developing countries. Among developed countries, comparable figures for all levels of government range from just over one-sixth in Japan and the United States to one-third or more in Australia, Denmark, and France.

In the United States, single-stage retail sales taxes exist in virtually all the states. Very few states have made use of multistage turnover taxes. Many local governments are also financed by taxes at the retail level. The federal government does not levy a general sales tax; it imposes special excises on liquor, tobacco, motor fuels, automobiles, telecommunications, and other items. In Canada, retail sales taxes are levied in nearly all provinces; the federal government also collects a manufacturer's sales tax.

Most Latin-American countries rely heavily on excises and on sales taxes. Brazil has a manufacturer's tax and a state value-added tax. Excises on tobacco, alcoholic beverages, automobiles, gasoline, and other items are the rule not only in most Latin-American countries but in Africa, Asia, Australia, and New Zealand. The last two also make vigorous use of sales taxes to raise revenue for national government.

In general, excise and turnover taxes have been more important in Latin countries and in the less-developed world than in Scandinavia or in Anglo-Saxon countries. The latter rely comparatively more on direct taxes (income taxes) than do the Latin countries, where resistance to such direct taxation has traditionally been strong. The fact that excise and turnover taxes are easier to administer and enforce may be another reason why they have been preferred in some countries.

The burden of sales and excise taxes. It is generally assumed that sales and excise taxes are borne by the consumer. To facilitate easy collection, most such taxes are levied at the manufacturing, wholesale, or retail level. The tax burden is expected to be shifted to the last buyer in the form of a higher price. Whether the burden is shifted entirely or partly depends on market conditions. If consumers insist on having a commodity, the tax burden can be shifted to them more completely than if they are sensitive to price rises. For goods the prices of which are not much affected by quantities sold, the tax may be added to the price to a greater extent than for goods the prices of which are sensitive to the quantity factor. Usually both the supplier and the consumer share the tax burden in terms of lower profits or higher prices.

Conditions under which tax burden can be shifted

Sales and excise taxes also affect the way in which goods are allocated to different uses. Higher prices resulting from taxation may decrease the quantities produced and sold; manufacturers and sellers may have to reduce production or sales of heavily taxed commodities. In time of war or other stringency, excises and sales taxes can therefore be used as a means of reducing the production and consumption of goods that are not considered essential.

It has been argued that excises interfere with the natural functioning of prices and distribution and therefore have a distorting effect on the economy. More general types of taxes, such as turnover or value-added taxes, are thought to be less distorting in their effects. Single-stage sales taxes, as well as taxes on value added, if applied each at the same rate, are assumed not to affect price relations to any marked degree.

Arguments for and against excise and sales taxes. Certain arguments can be advanced in favour of excise taxes. They can be used to place the burden of taxation on luxuries or nonessential goods rather than on necessities. They can also be allocated in such a way that the tax burden falls on those who receive the benefits of the tax expenditures, as the taxes on motor fuel that are used to build and maintain roads. They can be used to discourage the consumption of certain goods considered undesirable, such as alcoholic beverages and cigarettes, which are often taxed heavily on the grounds of national health (though more often than not this justification has been put forward to conceal a purely fiscal desire for more revenue). To the extent that they are levied on items of consumption that are relatively insensitive to changes in income and prices, their revenues are easy to predict (for the same reasons, revenues may not grow with national output). Finally, they are relatively easy to administer; the costs of collection are low.

Other arguments have been advanced against excise taxes. As mentioned above, they affect the allocation of resources in purely arbitrary ways. Also, the burden they impose is not related to the taxpayer's ability to pay. They discriminate against persons engaged in the consumption or production of the specific goods taxed.

Generally, excises are regressive in that the percentage of income spent on goods liable to taxation is higher among low-income groups. Regressiveness is often increased by the practice of applying the same specific tax to cheaper brands as to more expensive ones.

Sales taxes and excises compared

Some of the disadvantages mentioned in connection with excises do not apply to sales taxes, but some of the advantages do not apply either. Nonselective, single-stage sales taxes do not discriminate between goods if a single flat rate is applied. They can be either more or less regressive than excises. Unlike some excises, they cannot be related to benefits received. Multistage turnover taxes pose more serious disadvantages. Here, the amount of the tax depends on the number of turnover stages at which it is applied. Products that pass through relatively few hands on their way to the market will be taxed less than those that pass through many stages of production or distribution. Thus, the turnover tax provides undesirable incentives for the concentration of economic activity.

This disadvantage of a turnover tax can be avoided by value-added taxation, in which the number of stages of turnover does not matter. The value-added tax affects neither the allocation of resources nor the price structure so long as a single tax rate is applied. It is, however, more difficult to administer. (K.Hä./C.E.McL.)

DEATH AND GIFT TAXES

Death and gift taxes are imposed on gratuitous transfers of property—that is, transfers made without compensation in either money or its equivalent. In this respect they differ from sales taxes imposed on transfers made in exchange for something of value and from property taxes and capital levies that are based on the mere ownership or possession of property and from income taxes levied on earnings.

Death in many countries is considered to be a "taxable event," one that prompts the imposition of a levy by the state. Death taxes are of two kinds: those imposed on the property left at death are known as "estate" taxes and those imposed on the acquisition of property from a person who has died are known as "inheritance" taxes. The two kinds of death taxes are sometimes both used in the same system.

Discrimination on basis of relationship

Inheritance taxes generally discriminate on the basis of relationship: there may, for example, be larger exemptions or lower rates for spouses and children. Inheritance taxes are in the nature of "accessions" taxes, a tax on receiving rather than giving. Even the U.S. estate tax, which is primarily a tax on the estate rather than its acquisition, takes some account of who benefits; anything left to a spouse is tax-free up to one-half of the estate, and anything left to charity is entirely exempt.

Levies on gratuitous transfers between living persons are known as gift taxes. These may be integrated with death taxes to make a single structure of taxation applicable to gratuitous transfers. Death and gift taxes are closely related in France, Germany, and Sweden. A complete "accessions" tax would cumulatively combine both inheritance and gifts received. Japan had such a tax in the 1950–53 period.

Economic importance

Death and gift taxes are of greater symbolic than practical significance. Of all taxes, they are among the least productive of revenue in both absolute and percentage terms, and their relative importance has dwindled with the growth of income, sales, and excise taxes. The tax-rate structure alone is misleading, since the many deductions, exemptions, exclusions, and allowances generally reduce the yield drastically. Moreover, most people have no taxable estate whatever and are never subject to the gift tax. Thus, death and gift taxes are generally imposed not for the purpose of generating revenue but for social reasons. They are meant to reduce inequalities in the distribution of wealth and provide an opportunity to break up large estates. Economic benefits may derive from the resulting reduction in the concentration of economic power. Although death and gift taxes do tend to achieve a more equal distribution of wealth, the magnitude of the effect is small in most countries.

Origin and history. Imposts at death predate general income and sales taxes. Even the Romans imposed a tax on inheritances. Although a death tax was levied in the United Kingdom in 1694, the present structure dates to 1779–80, and the prevailing estate duty was introduced in 1894.

In the United States there were several short-lived death taxes before the present tax was introduced at the federal level in 1916. Many of the states already had death taxes. In an attempt to reduce the lack of uniformity in the inheritance taxes of the various states (and thereby prevent competition between the states) and to protect them from federal incursion, the federal government of the United States gives credit for state inheritance taxes against the estate tax up to a certain point. Death and gift taxes are generally levied by national governments.

The controversy about death and gift taxes. The main argument against large death taxes rests on their possible negative effects on incentives. The argument is that the person building up an estate will be less inclined to do so if he knows a large part of it will never go to his heirs. An economic limit to the usefulness of death taxes may be said to exist when the accumulation of wealth is discouraged to the point of hampering the growth of the economy. Opponents of death taxes also argue that, for the heirs, hardship may result if forced sales must be made to obtain liquid resources with which to pay taxes. In the case of a family business there is a danger that the business will have to be sold quickly below its actual value or that strangers will be brought in to supply funds, with a resulting loss of family control.

The negative arguments may be countered to some degree. It may be that a person who seeks to provide a certain estate for his heirs will have an incentive to work harder, since he will want to leave a large enough estate to absorb the taxes. The problem of cash requirements may be taken care of in various ways, such as provisions allowing the tax to be paid over a period of years. Insurance arrangements may also make liquidation of a business unnecessary.

Economic effects. The economic effects of death taxes are, in a word, unimportant by the usual criteria. There is little reason to believe that a person will alter his consumption patterns because of the prospect of death taxes. Those who might consume more quickly to avoid leaving an estate and paying an estate tax are likely to be offset by those who consume less and save more in order to leave enough to their heirs after taxes. The main effect of death and gift taxes has been to encourage estate planning and the employment of legal devices to minimize taxes rather than to change behaviour.

Effect on business structure and practices

A significant effect that is often overlooked is that on business structure and practices. This stems from two problems that exist in death taxation. One of these is that of setting a valuation on the estate for tax purposes. Another is the problem of liquidity; *i.e.,* getting the cash with which to pay the taxes.

The valuation of an estate suffers from the same problems as the valuation of any property. There may not be an active market in the various assets involved. The assets may be unique in some sense. There may be a problem of "blockage": a large block of stock may actually be worth more than the apparent market value of the individual shares. A family-owned business may be particularly difficult to evaluate. Appraisers may be called in to set a value on the property, but their evaluations may vary widely. These problems introduce an element of uncertainty into estate planning inasmuch as an individual cannot foresee what value will be placed on various assets he might be holding, especially if they are assets for which there is no active market. It is therefore difficult for him to make adequate preparation for the taxes that may have to be paid. To some extent it also complicates the problem of deciding how much to leave to whom.

Even if there were certainty in the valuation of an estate, there remains the problem of paying the taxes. The gravity of this problem depends partly on the nature of the assets in the estate. If they are shares of stock that are traded on a national stock exchange there is relatively little difficulty. If a family-owned business or a major portion of any business is involved, serious losses, including a change of control of the business, may result from attempts to liquidate the ownership interest in order to obtain cash. Thus the problem of liquidity presents a major consideration in estate planning.

In spite of all efforts to mitigate the impact of estate taxes, there is a strong temptation for an owner to convert his assets into a highly marketable, easily evaluated form while he is alive. This may require their sale to another company, either for cash or for nationally traded securities. The result is a merger or absorption of the smaller company and an increase in the concentration of economic power—the opposite of what the taxes are meant to achieve.

Exemptions and rate structure. The exemptions and rate structure that exist in a tax system are an expression of social policy toward (1) institutions that are to be favoured, including marriage, schools, charities, and churches, and (2) redistribution of wealth and income. Exemptions or low rates on gifts and bequests to spouse and children represent a social policy in favour of the family unit. Provisions in tax laws that favour educational, religious, and charitable organizations reflect a desire to encourage private support of these institutions.

Social policy

Tax exemptions and rate structure also serve as an instrument for redistributing wealth and income. But, as in the case of the income tax, the methods of avoidance must be considered before any conclusion is drawn concerning the actual impact of death and gift taxes on the distribution of wealth and income.

Avoidance of death taxes. On the books, death taxes look highly progressive: the rates of taxation approach 100 percent in the highest brackets in some countries. In fact, however, the opportunities for avoidance are so great that death taxes often have little impact on the enjoyment and use of property passing from one generation to the next.

Although most people do not incur any death or gift taxes at all, those who are required to pay are liable to pay substantial taxes if advance plans are not made to prevent it. As a result the avoidance of death taxes has become a major concern, especially since efforts at avoidance have been highly successful and present a serious problem of equity.

Techniques used to avoid the tax

Family bequests provide one of the best ways to reduce death and gift taxes, generally by leaving property to a spouse. Under the prevailing U.S. laws, all that goes to a husband or wife, up to half the total estate, is tax-free; and half of any lifetime gift to a spouse is similarly tax-free. Under inheritance taxes, bequests to a spouse and children are also given preferential treatment.

A common technique of avoiding taxes is to skip a generation by the use of trusts and life estates. Rather than leave everything to one's spouse, the device is to leave the property to children or grandchildren, with the spouse to enjoy the income from the property during his lifetime. The total tax is then generally less than if the estate passed entirely to the spouse and from him to the children.

An obvious way to avoid death taxes is to give one's property away before death. Precisely for this reason, death taxes sometimes take account of "gifts made in contemplation of death" in totaling up the estate for death-tax purposes. Gifts made during life may also be subject to tax at the time they are made.

Exemption of gifts

Gifts to charitable, religious, and educational institutions are generally exempt from death and gift taxes. This fact has made it possible in some instances for a taxpayer to make a tax-free profit through the donation of appreciated property. Sometimes the exemption is used not only to reduce taxes but also to ensure maintenance of family control of a business that would pass to strangers if a large portion of the stock must be sold to pay death taxes. Since charitable contributions are exempt from death and gift taxes, a gift of stock to a charitable foundation can reduce or eliminate the gift or estate tax. The donated stock may be a nonvoting variety, leaving control in the hands of the owners of a small amount of voting stock. The controlling trustees of the foundation may even be members of the family or their agents, hence the family has lost little if anything by this maneuver. It has presumably retained sufficient assets after taxes to yield the income it actually needs; for the rest, it has retained family control of the assets and has ensured perpetuation of family control through trustees. It has lost some of the incidents of ownership, but none that really affect its current standard of living or its economic power.

Integration with other taxes. The death levy has long been regarded as a unique type of impost, to be studied apart from the rest of the tax structure. The current trend is to consider this levy in relation to other taxes, especially those imposed on gifts, income, and capital gains. In this view, any tax that is imposed at death is only one of a series of taxes imposed on the decedent during his life and later to be imposed on the inheritor with respect to the same property.

A persuasive argument can be made for the fuller integration of death and gift taxes. In countries such as the United States where only "gifts made in contemplation of death" are included in the estate for tax purposes, it is necessary to determine what was in the mind of a dead person for a specified period before death. Complete integration of death and gift taxation, whether or not further integrated with income taxation, would eliminate such areas of dispute and litigation. A single schedule applying to all gifts, whether during life or after death, would cover the problem.

Treatment of capital gains at death

Further integration would help mitigate the inequity that results from the separate treatment of capital gains at death. In many countries, including the United States, gains on appreciated property that remains in an estate are forever free of the capital gains tax. The estate does not pay a capital gains tax if it sells the property at the same value it is given for estate tax purposes. Anyone who inherits the property takes it at the appreciated basis for all future capital gains taxes. If the decedent had sold the appreciated property just before he died, he would have had to pay a tax on the gain; the proceeds would then have appeared in his estate and been subject to the estate tax. This appears to represent a pointless inequality of treatment, despite the fact that the full value of the appreciated property will be subject to the estate tax. The large exemptions and deductions in the estate tax may still leave the appreciation free of tax, and the capital gains tax rates are very different from the estate tax rates. Countries that do not have a capital gains tax are not faced with this problem.

One argument against taxing capital gains at death is essentially the one that is used against taxing any capital gains; such gains result from price fluctuations and not from the production of income. Another argument against doing so is that an even greater cash burden would be imposed at death. The introduction of a capital gains tax in Great Britain created new problems for the family company because it forced the company to make provision for postponed tax liabilities in addition to the provision for death duties. A solution to this lies in making allowance for the capital gains tax liability in computing the amount of death tax due.

The gift tax provisions solve a similar problem by requiring the person who receives the gift to take the donor's initial value as his own. Any appreciation that occurs from the time the original donor acquired the property is subject to the capital gains tax when the property is first sold. A similar idea has been proposed as an alternative to the taxation of capital gains at death. This proposal would impose a capital gains tax on the sale (rather than the acquisition) of inherited property.

The complete integration of income, capital gains, death, and gift taxes is sometimes suggested. The accretion in one's economic power (*i.e.,* the increase in the value of one's property, including income) would be evaluated and taxed each year. In the extreme form of this plan, the year of death would just be another year, and the disposition of property would itself have no tax consequences or benefits. But the practical problems of valuation throw doubt on the wisdom of any such approach. (H.M.S./Ed.)

TRADE TAXES

The functions of tariffs

A tariff is a tax levied upon goods as they cross national boundaries, usually by the government of the importing country. The words tariff, duty, and customs are generally used interchangeably. Tariffs may be levied either to raise revenue or to protect domestic industries, but a tariff designed primarily to raise revenue may exercise a strong protective influence and a tariff levied primarily for protection may yield revenue. Gottfried Haberler in his *Theory of International Trade* suggested that the best objective distinction between revenue duties and protective duties (disregarding the motives of the legislators) is to be found in their discriminatory effects as between domestic and foreign producers.

If domestically produced goods bear the same taxation as similar imported goods, or if the goods subject to duty are not produced at home, even after the duty has been levied, and if there can be no home-produced substitutes toward which demand is diverted because of the tariff, then the duty is not protective. A purely protective duty tends to shift production away from the export industries into the protected domestic industries and those industries producing substitutes for which demand is increased. On the other hand, a purely revenue duty will not cause resources to be invested in industries producing the taxed goods or close substitutes for such goods, but it will divert resources from the production of export goods to the production of those goods and services upon which the additional government receipts are spent.

From the purely revenue standpoint, a country can levy an equivalent tax on domestic production, to avoid protecting it, or select a relatively small number of imported articles of general consumption and subject them to low duties so that there will be no tendency to shift resources into industries producing such taxed goods (or substitutes for them). During the period when it was on a free-trade basis, Great Britain followed the latter practice, levying low duties on a few commodities of general consumption such as tea, sugar, tobacco, and coffee. Unintentional protection was not a major issue, because Britain could not have produced these goods domestically. If, on the other hand, a country wishes to protect its home industries its list of protected commodities will be long and the tariff rates high.

Tariffs may be further classified into three groups—transit duties, export duties, and import duties.

Transit duties. This type of duty is levied on commodities that originate in one country, cross another, and are consigned to a third. As the name implies, transit duties are levied by the country through which the goods pass. Such duties are no longer important instruments of commercial policy, but, during the mercantilist period (17th and 18th centuries) and even up to the middle of the 19th century in some countries, they played a role in directing trade and controlling certain of its routes. The development of the German *Zollverein* (customs union) in the first half of

The German *Zollverein*

the 19th century was partly the result of Prussia's exercise of its power to levy transit duties. The most direct and immediate effect of transit duties is to reduce the amount of commodities traded internationally and raise their cost to the importing country. In 1921 the Barcelona Statute on Freedom of Transit abolished all transit duties.

Export duties. Export duties are no longer used to a great extent, except to tax certain mineral and agricultural products. Several resource-rich countries depend upon export duties for much of their revenue. Export duties were common in the past, however, and were significant elements of mercantilist trade policies. Their main function was to safeguard domestic supplies rather than to raise revenue. Export duties were first introduced in England by a statute of 1275 that imposed them on hides and wool. By the middle of the 17th century the list of commodities subject to export duties had increased to include more than 200 articles. With the growth of free trade in the 19th century, export duties became less appealing; they were abolished in England in 1842, in France in 1857, and in Prussia in 1865. At the beginning of the 20th century only a few countries levied export duties: for example, Spain still levied them on coke and textile waste; Bolivia and Malaya on tin; Italy on objects of art; and Romania on hides and forest products. The neo-mercantilist revival in the 1920s and 1930s brought about a limited reappearance of export duties. In the United States, export duties were prohibited by the Constitution, mainly because of pressure from the South, which wanted no restriction on its freedom to export agricultural products.

Export duties are now generally levied by raw-material-producing countries rather than by advanced industrial countries. Differential exchange rates are sometimes used to extract revenues from export sectors. Commonly taxed exports include coffee, rubber, palm oil, and various mineral products. The state-controlled pricing policies of international cartels such as the Organization of Petroleum Exporting Countries have some of the characteristics of export duties.

Export duties may act as a form of protection to domestic industries. As examples, Norwegian and Swedish duties on exports of forest products were levied chiefly to encourage milling, woodworking, and paper manufacturing at home. Similarly, duties on the export from India of untanned hides after World War I were levied to stimulate the Indian tanning industry. In a number of cases, however, duties levied on exports from colonies were designed to protect the industries of the mother country and not those of the colony.

The burden of export duties

If the country imposing the export duty supplies only a small share of the world's exports and if competitive conditions prevail, the burden of an export duty will likely be borne by the domestic producer, who will receive the world price minus the duty and other charges. But if the country produces a significant fraction of the world output and if domestic supply is sensitive to lower net prices, then output will fall and world prices may rise and as a consequence not only domestic producers but also foreign consumers will bear the export tax. How far a country can employ export duties to exploit its monopoly position in supplying certain raw materials depends upon the success other countries have in discovering substitutes or new sources of supply.

Import duties. Import duties are the most important and most common types of custom duties. As noted above, they may be levied either for revenue or protection or both, but tariffs are not a satisfactory means of raising revenue, because they encourage uneconomic domestic production of the dutied item. Even if imports constitute the bulk of the available revenue base, it is better to tax all consumption, rather than only consumption of imports, in order to avoid uneconomical protection.

Import duties are no longer an important source of revenues in developed countries. In the United States, for example, revenues from import duties in 1808 amounted to twice the total of government expenditures, while in 1837 they were less than one-third of such expenditures. Until near the end of the 19th century the customs receipts of the U.S. government made up about half of all its receipts. This share had fallen to about 6 percent of all receipts before the outbreak of World War II and it has since further decreased.

A tariff may be either specific, ad valorem, or compound (*i.e.,* a combination of both). A specific duty is a levy of a given amount of money per unit of the import, such as $1.00 per yard or per pound. An ad valorem duty, on the other hand, is calculated as a percentage of the value of the import. Ad valorem rates furnish a constant degree of protection at all levels of price (if prices change at the same rate at home and abroad), while the real burden of specific rates varies inversely with changes in the prices of the imports. A specific duty, however, penalizes more severely the lower grades of an imported commodity. This difficulty can be partly avoided by an elaborate and detailed classification of imports on the basis of the stage of finishing, but such a procedure makes for extremely long and complicated tariff schedules. Specific duties are easier to administer than ad valorem rates, for the latter often raise difficult administrative issues with respect to the valuation of imported articles.

Tariff schedules

A list of all import duties is usually known as a tariff schedule. A single tariff schedule, such as that of the United States, applies to all imports regardless of the country of origin. This is to say that a single duty is listed in the column opposite the enumerated commodities. A double-columned or multicolumned tariff provides for different rates according to the country of origin, lower rates being granted to commodities coming from countries with which tariff agreements have been negotiated. Most trade agreements are based on the most-favoured-nation clause, which extends to all nations party to the agreement whatever concessions are granted to the most-favoured nation.

Every country has a free list that includes articles admitted without duty. By looking at the free list and the value of the goods imported into the United States under it one might be led to conclude that tariff protection is very limited, for more than half of all imports are exempt from duties. Such a conclusion, however, is not correct, for it ignores the fact that the higher the tariff, the less will be the quantity of dutiable imports. Attempts to measure the height of a tariff wall and make international comparisons of the degree of protection, based upon the ratio of tariff receipts to the total value of imports, are beset by difficulties and have little meaning.

A better method of measuring the height of a tariff wall is to convert all duties into ad valorem figures and then estimate the weighted-average rate. The weight should reflect the relative importance of the different imports; a tariff on foodstuffs, for example, may be far more important than a tariff on luxuries consumed by a small group of people.

A more appropriate measure of protection is that of effective protection. It recognizes that the protection afforded a particular domestic industry depends on the treatment of its productive inputs, as well as its outputs. Suppose, for example, that half of the inputs to an industry are imported and subject to a duty of 100 percent. If the imports with which the industry competes are subject to a duty of less than 50 percent there is no effective protection. Calculating effective protection in a real-world situation requires complex economic analysis.

(A.A.Ps./Ga.S./C.E.McL.)

BIBLIOGRAPHY

Nature and purposes of taxation: Problems of taxation are treated in all textbooks on public finance. Standard sources on government finance include RICHARD A. MUSGRAVE and PEGGY B. MUSGRAVE, *Public Finance in Theory and Practice,* 4th ed. (1984); HARVEY S. ROSEN, *Public Finance,* 2nd ed. (1988); JOSEPH E. STIGLITZ, *Economics of the Public Sector,* 2nd ed. (1988); and ROBIN W. BOADWAY and DAVID E. WILDASIN, *Public Sector Economics,* 2nd ed. (1984). More advanced works include RICHARD A. MUSGRAVE, *The Theory of Public Finance: A Study in Public Economy* (1959), a classic though somewhat dated treatise; CARL S. SHOUP, *Public Finance* (1969); and RICHARD W. TRESCH, *Public Finance: A Normative Theory* (1981). A mathematical treatment of theoretical issues is presented in ANTHONY B. ATKINSON and JOSEPH E. STIGLITZ, *Lectures on Public Economics* (1980). ALAN J. AUERBACH and MARTIN FELDSTEIN (eds.), *Handbook of Public Economics,* 2 vol. (1985–87), surveys issues in government finance.

Useful works on the historical development of fiscal thought include: FRITZ KARL MANN, *Steuerpolitische Ideale: Vergleichende Studien zur Geschichte der ökonomischen und politischen Ideen und ihres Wirkens in der öffentlichen Meinung 1600–1935* (1937, reprinted 1978), a comprehensive history of the ideals, ideologies, and theories of taxation from both the economic and the political-sociological standpoints; RICHARD A. MUSGRAVE and ALAN T. PEACOCK (eds.), *Classics in the Theory of Public Finance* (1958, reprinted 1967); and AMERICAN ECONOMIC ASSOCIATION, *Readings in the Economics of Taxation*, comp. by RICHARD A. MUSGRAVE and CARL S. SHOUP (1959). PETER-CHRISTIAN WITT (ed.), *Wealth and Taxation in Central Europe: The History and Sociology of Public Finance* (1987), is a brief but informative collection of articles. Also see HENRY C. SIMONS, *Personal Income Taxation* (1938, reprinted 1980), a classic discussion of the concepts of personal income as a basis for taxation; WILLIAM VICKREY, *Agenda for Progressive Taxation* (1947, reprinted 1972), an excellent analysis of many of the problems of income taxation; B.E.V. SABINE, *A History of Income Tax* (1966), which surveys the policies in Britain and the United Kingdom from 1799 to the middle of the 20th century; and EDWIN R.A. SELIGMAN, *The Income Tax: A Study of the History, Theory, and Practice of Income Taxation at Home and Abroad*, 2nd rev. ed. (1914, reprinted 1970), which includes in its coverage the United States and its pre-World War I policies.

Current academic thinking about tax policy is reported in economic journals and law reviews. Among economic journals devoted primarily to tax analysis are the *Canadian Tax Journal* (bimonthly); *National Tax Journal* (quarterly); *Public Finance* (three times a year); *Public Finance Quarterly;* and *Finanzarchiv: Zeitschrift für das gesamte Finanzwesen* (three times a year). *Journal of Public Economics* (nine times a year), provides highly mathematical analyses of taxation. Among legal publications specializing in taxation are *The Tax Lawyer* (quarterly); and *Taxes* (monthly). Proposals for tax reform and legislative, judicial, and regulatory developments in the United States are reported in *Tax Notes* (weekly). Excellent analyses of tax policy are offered in the annual *Report of Proceedings of the Tax Conference Convened by the Canadian Tax Foundation.* JOHN EATWELL, MURRAY MILGATE, and PETER NEWMAN (eds.), *The New Palgrave: A Dictionary of Economics*, 4 vol. (1987), includes comprehensive articles on taxation and related topics.

For overviews of tax systems, see JOHN A. KAY and MERVYN A. KING, *The British Tax System*, 4th ed. (1986); JOSEPH A. PECHMAN, *Federal Tax Policy*, 5th ed. (1987), and *Who Paid the Taxes, 1966–85?* (1985); SIJBREN CNOSSEN (ed.), *Tax Coordination in the European Community* (1986); and ORGANISATION FOR ECONOMIC CO-OPERATION AND DEVELOPMENT, *Personal Income Tax Systems Under Changing Economic Conditions* (1986), and *Revenue Statistics of OECD Member Countries, 1965–1985* (1986). UNITED STATES. INTERNAL REVENUE SERVICE, *Statistics of Income: Compendium of Studies of International Income and Taxes* (1985), provides statistical information on tax systems. COUNCIL OF ECONOMIC ADVISERS (U.S.), *Annual Report*, also contains a useful statistical appendix. ADVISORY COMMISSION ON INTERGOVERNMENTAL RELATIONS, *Tax Capacity of the States* (annual), provides information on state and local government finance. Publications of the International Bureau of Fiscal Documentation, such as its *Bulletin* (monthly), *European Taxation* (monthly), or *Corporate Taxation in Latin America* (quarterly), describe developments in tax policy around the world and summarize the important features of many tax systems. CONFEDERATION OF BRITISH INDUSTRY, *Taxation in Western Europe* (annual), provides a comparative study of the modern tax systems of various countries; somewhat dated studies of the tax systems of particular countries may be found in the "World Tax Series," prepared by the International Program in Taxation at the Harvard Law School. On specifics of taxation in developing countries, see HASKELL P. WALD, *Taxation of Agricultural Land in Underdeveloped Economies: A Survey and Guide to Policy* (1959); RICHARD M. BIRD and OLIVER OLDMAN, *Readings on Taxation in Developing Countries*, 3rd ed. (1975); RICHARD GOODE, *Government Finance in Developing Countries* (1984); JOHN F. DUE, *Indirect Taxation in Developing Economies*, rev. ed. (1988); MALCOLM GILLIS (ed.), *Fiscal Reform for Colombia* (1971); and DAVID NEWBERY and NICHOLAS STERN (eds.), *The Theory of Taxation for Developing Countries* (1987), a highly theoretical treatment of the topic.

Types of taxes: On the taxation of income from capital, see MARTIN FELDSTEIN, *Capital Taxation* (1983); ARNOLD C. HARBERGER, *Taxation and Welfare* (1974, reprinted 1988); CHARLES R. HULTEN (ed.), *Depreciation, Inflation, and the Taxation of Income from Capital* (1981); MERVYN A. KING and DON FULLERTON (eds.), *The Taxation of Income from Capital: A Comparative Study of the United States, the United Kingdom, Sweden, and West Germany* (1984); C. EUGENE STEUERLE, *Taxes, Loans, and Inflation: How the Nation's Wealth Becomes Misallocated* (1985); MARTIN FELDSTEIN (ed.), *The Effect of Taxation on Capital Accumulation* (1987); and HANS-WERNER SINN, *Capital Income Taxation and Resource Allocation* (1987; originally published in German, 1985). Effects of taxation are analyzed in HENRY J. AARON and MICHAEL J. BOSKIN (eds.), *The Economics of Taxation* (1980); HENRY J. AARON and JOSEPH A. PECHMAN (eds.), *How Taxes Affect Economic Behavior* (1981); C.V. BROWN, *Taxation and the Incentive to Work*, 2nd ed. (1983); G.A. HUGHES and G.M. HEAL (eds.), *Public Policy and the Tax System* (1980); and LAWRENCE H. SUMMERS (ed.), *Tax Policy and the Economy*, 2 vol. (1987–88).

On the individual income tax, see RICHARD GOODE, *The Individual Income Tax*, rev. ed. (1976); JOSEPH A. PECHMAN (ed.), *Comprehensive Income Taxation* (1977); DAVID F. BRADFORD, *Untangling the Income Tax* (1986); and STANLEY S. SURREY, *Pathways to Tax Reform: The Concept of Tax Expenditures* (1973). Special topics are explored in WALTER J. BLUM and HARRY KALVEN, JR., *The Uneasy Case for Progressive Taxation* (1953, reprinted with additions, 1978); HENRY J. AARON (ed.), *Inflation and the Income Tax* (1976); and STANLEY S. SURREY and PAUL R. MCDANIEL, *Tax Expenditures* (1985). On the corporation income tax, see RICHARD GOODE, *The Corporation Income Tax* (1951); MERVYN A. KING, *Public Policy and the Corporation* (1977); J. GREGORY BALLENTINE, *Equity, Efficiency, and the U.S. Corporation Income Tax* (1980); and CHARLES E. MCLURE, JR., *Must Corporate Income Be Taxed Twice?* (1979). Discussions of the choice between income and consumption as the basis for taxation include NICHOLAS KALDOR, *An Expenditure Tax* (1955, reprinted 1977); JOSEPH A. PECHMAN (ed.), *What Should Be Taxed, Income or Expenditure?* (1980); J.E. MEADE (ed.), *The Structure and Reform of Direct Taxation* (1978); and HENRY J. AARON, HARVEY GALPER, and JOSEPH A. PECHMAN (eds.), *Uneasy Compromise: Problems of a Hybrid Income-Consumption Tax* (1988).

Death and gift taxes are studied in HAROLD M. SOMERS, *Capital Gains, Death, and Gift Taxation* (1965); CARL S. SHOUP, *Federal Estate and Gift Taxes* (1966, reprinted 1980); and GEORGE COOPER, *A Voluntary Tax?: New Perspectives on Sophisticated Estate Tax Avoidance* (1979). On the property tax and other issues of taxation by subnational governments, see DICK NETZER, *Economics of the Property Tax* (1966); HENRY J. AARON, *Who Pays the Property Tax?: A New View* (1975); HARVEY S. ROSEN, *Studies in State and Local Public Finance* (1986); and CHARLES E. MCLURE, JR. (ed.), *The State Corporation Income Tax: Issues in Worldwide Unitary Combination* (1984). On the value-added tax and other indirect taxes, see JOHN F. DUE and JOHN L. MIKESELL, *Sales Taxation: State and Local Structure and Administration* (1983); CLARA K. SULLIVAN, *The Tax on Value Added* (1965); HENRY J. AARON (ed.), *The Value-Added Tax: Lessons from Europe* (1981); and CHARLES E. MCLURE, JR. (ed.), *The Value-Added Tax: Key to Deficit Reduction?* (1987).

Trade taxes are studied in JOSEPH F. KENKEL, *Progressives and Protection: The Search for a Tariff Policy, 1866–1936* (1983), a historical survey; EDMOND MCGOVERN, *International Trade Regulation: GATT, the United States, and the European Community*, 2nd ed. (1986); HARVEY M. APPLEBAUM and GILBERT B. KAPLAN (eds.), *U.S. Trade Law and Policy* (1987); EUGENE T. ROSSIDES, *U.S. Import Trade Regulation* (1986); and MICHAEL DAVENPORT, *Trade Policy, Protectionism, and the Third World* (1986).

Studies of tax reform and contemporary proposals for tax reform include: for the United States, ALBERT ANDO, MARSHALL E. BLUME, and IRWIN FRIEND, *The Structure and Reform of the U.S. Tax System* (1985); ROBERT E. HALL and ALVIN RABUSHKA, *The Flat Tax* (1985); HENRY J. AARON and HARVEY GALPER, *Assessing Tax Reform* (1985); DAVID F. BRADFORD *et al.*, *Blueprints for Basic Tax Reform*, 2nd rev. ed. (1984); and UNITED STATES. DEPARTMENT OF THE TREASURY, *Tax Reform for Fairness, Simplicity, and Economic Growth*, 3 vol. (1984); for Canada, CANADA. DEPARTMENT OF FINANCE, *Tax Reform 1987: Income Tax Reform* (1987), and *Tax Reform 1987: Sales Tax Reform* (1987); for Australia, JOHN G. HEAD (ed.), *Taxation Issues of the 1980s* (1983), and *Changing the Tax Mix* (1986). For a survey of developed countries, see JOSEPH A. PECHMAN (ed.), *World Tax Reform: A Progress Report* (1988).

(C.E.McL.)

Teaching

Measured in terms of its members, teaching is the world's biggest profession. In the late 20th century it was estimated that there were 30,000,000 teachers throughout the world. Though their roles and functions vary from country to country, the variations are generally greater within a country than they are between countries.

Because the nature of the activities that constitute teaching depends more on the age of the persons being taught than on any other one thing, it is useful to recognize three subgroups of teachers: primary-school, or elementary-school, teachers; secondary-school teachers; and university teachers. These three subgroups had, in the late 20th century, an approximate worldwide ratio of 57 percent, 34 percent, and 9 percent, respectively. The proportions differ by country and continents; in North America, for instance, they were 45, 31, and 23; in the Soviet Union, 82, 7, and 11; and in Africa, 75, 21, and 4.

The entire teaching corps, wherever its members may be located, shares most of the criteria of a profession, namely (1) a process of formal training; (2) a body of specialized knowledge; (3) a procedure for certifying, or validating, membership in the profession; and (4) a set of standards of performance—intellectual, practical, and ethical—that are defined and enforced by members of the profession. Teaching young children and even adolescents could hardly have been called a profession anywhere in the world before the 20th century. It was, instead, an art or a craft in which the relatively young and untrained women and men who held most of the teaching positions "kept school" or "heard lessons" because they had been better than average pupils themselves. They had learned the art solely by observing and imitating their own teachers. Only university professors and possibly a few teachers of elite secondary schools would have merited being called members of a profession in the sense that medical doctors, lawyers, or priests were professionals; in some countries even today primary-school teachers may accurately be described as semiprofessionals. The dividing line is unprecise. It is useful, therefore, to consider the following questions: (1) What is the status of the profession? (2) What kinds of work are done? (3) How is the profession organized?

The article is divided into the following sections:

General characteristics of teaching

THE STATUS OF TEACHERS

Teaching enjoys average to high status, depending in part on the amount of study required to prepare for employment. Since this ranges from a relatively brief time to many years, the levels of social and economic status span a wide range.

The economic status. *Salaries.* The salaries of elementary- and secondary-school teachers have generally been relatively low, particularly before 1955, at which time they increased sharply in some countries. In industrialized nations at the beginning of the 20th century, teachers in this group were paid hardly more than semiskilled labourers. In Europe during these years they were relatively better off than they were in the United States, partly because many primary-school teachers in Europe were men, with families to support. In general, primary-school teachers who are women and have relatively little academic training for their jobs tend to receive low salaries. In Brazil in 1957, for instance, the average annual salary of a teacher—usually a woman—in the official state primary-school system was the equivalent of about $850. It was even less, only $231, in the locally financed municipal schools. Teachers may, and generally must, take other jobs or look after their families and homes concurrently. The poorest countries, in any case, still provide relatively low primary-teachers' salaries. In India, for example, poorly trained teachers in village schools are paid only one-tenth as much as teachers in select city schools; and even in commercially prosperous Japan, primary-school teachers are paid only about as much as a bank clerk, an office worker, or a salesperson working in a department store.

When salaries are too low to provide what teachers regard as necessities, they add other jobs. Men are more likely to do this than women. In 1965–66, male municipal schoolteachers in the United States derived 84 percent of their total income from their salaries as teachers; 7 percent from summer employment; and 6 percent from "moonlighting," or working at a second job, during the school year. Working at a second job is much more frequent in countries in which the school day is less than seven hours or the teaching load (for secondary-school teachers) less than about 25 classes a week. In Brazil and other Latin-American countries, for example, where the average teaching load of a secondary-school teacher is about 12 classes a week, many teachers take two full-time teaching jobs, and some are forced to go beyond that to earn a living.

University salaries

The salaries of university teachers and others who teach in postsecondary institutions have traditionally been substantially higher than those of secondary-school teachers. This reflects the fact that university professors generally have spent more years in preparation for their work and are more highly selected. But in recent years university salaries have not increased as much as those of other teachers. Though North American university salaries are among the highest of their kind in the world, they fall below the average incomes of medical doctors, dentists, lawyers, and engineers. Salaries in higher education in the Soviet Union are higher, in relation to other comparable occupations, than U.S. salaries. A teacher in a Soviet pedagogical institute (which trains schoolteachers), for example, is paid slightly more than an engineer who has completed a university course.

Fringe benefits and other advantages. Vacations and leaves of absence give a prized flexibility to teaching careers. One of the attractive things about teaching, for instance, is the long annual vacation, usually in summer, which can be used for recreation, for further study or training, or for earning more money.

Leaves of absence are also more frequent than in other occupations. The sabbatical leave is a widespread practice among universities and is even available in some school systems. Formerly a fully paid leave for study or research every seventh year, it is now often reduced to a fully paid leave for a half year or half-salary for a full year. Maternity leave is generally available to women teachers, and in the United States many teachers are provided with paid maternity leave. Sick leave and short-term leave for personal needs are also often provided—with continuing salary for teachers validly absent for a few days.

Other benefits are becoming quite common; some of them, such as pensions, have been in practice in Europe for many decades. Life and health insurance, another fringe benefit, is usually paid partly or wholly by the school system or the university.

Seniority rights, enjoyed by teachers in many school systems, give them preferential treatment in transfers to other schools and in class assignments within their system.

Social and occupational status. According to a number of sociological surveys, university professors generally rank high in public estimation, comparable to medical doctors, lawyers, owners of large business and industrial establishments, bankers, and officials of national government. On a scale ranging from 1 (high) to 7 (low), a university professor is ranked 1 in most countries and 2 in others. A secondary-school teacher is generally ranked 2 or 3 on the same scale, sharing the level with journalists, clergymen, business managers, accountants, insurance agents, real-estate or land agents, and substantial landowners. A primary-school teacher is generally ranked 3 or 4 on the 7-point scale, on the same level occupied by social workers, office managers, bank clerks, small independent farmers, and foremen.

Occupational status in the teaching profession is generally related to the degree of selection involved in obtaining the teaching post and to the amount of training necessary to qualify for it. In a country with a selective university-preparatory secondary school, such as, for instance, the *lycée* in France, the grammar school in England, and the *Gymnasium* in West Germany, teachers must have the equivalent of a university education and must pass rigorous examinations or selective screening. These teachers have a higher occupational status than teachers in other branches of secondary education, such as industrial or commercial schools, which are less selective and require less training and accept lower examination standards of their teachers. Whenever a secondary-school system is divided into a number of branches or types of schools, the teachers and the public both make status distinctions among them.

Training and selectivity

Throughout the period from about 1850 to 1925, when schooling was becoming universal in the more developed countries, the elementary-school, or primary-school, teacher had lower status than the teachers of the more advanced schools. Still, there was a good deal of variation between countries. In Germany, for example, the primary-school teachers were more frequently men than women, and the male *Volksschullehrer* had relatively high status. If he taught in a rural school, he usually had a comfortable house adjoining the school and was above peasant landowners in social status. If he taught in a city, he could look forward to becoming the head teacher or school director. The German schoolteachers had a series of about seven status positions, from the classroom teacher in the primary school to the department chairman in the *Gymnasium,* or academic secondary school. The four- to six-year primary school was followed by a set of middle schools that were related to the occupational destiny of the student, and the middle schools were followed by a variety of higher secondary schools, some leading to employment and some to the university. Teachers were ranked in this sequence. Many *Gymnasium* teachers—that is, teachers of college-preparatory schools—were scholars of some distinction, almost with the same status as a university teacher. Oswald Spengler, for instance, with his broad-gauged historical writing (*The Decline of the West*), was a history teacher in a Hamburg *Gymnasium* and never a university professor.

In Japan the evolution of the teaching profession has been somewhat similar to that in Germany. Both countries traditionally have had more men than women teaching in elementary schools, and as late as 1964, only 22 percent of Japan's secondary-school teachers were women. Women were not encouraged to become teachers in Japan until after 1874, when the first Women's Normal School was founded. Both countries had several clearly marked status positions within each school level, depending on the amount of training and on seniority. The moral stature of Japanese teachers was regarded as an extremely important part of their qualification.

Status distinctions

Distinctions between primary- and secondary-school teaching die hard. In Europe and South America, for example, adolescent students training in normal schools to become primary-school teachers are generally addressed, referred to, and treated as children, while their counterparts in university preparatory schools are addressed as adults. Prospective primary-school teachers are normally called pupils and not students and are often addressed in the familiar forms of speech (*tu* or *Du* instead of *vous, usted,* or *Sie*) in contrast to university students.

In most modern countries, however, where the goal of universal schooling has been extended to the secondary level, distinctions in status between primary- and secondary-school teachers have moderated. In such situations, secondary-school teaching has become relatively less selective as additional teachers are sought for, at the same time that primary-school teachers have increased their training level and, therefore, their salary and status levels. In a growing number of countries, including West Germany, England, and the United States, primary-school teachers must have as much university-level training as secondary-school teachers, and a single salary scale has been established, based on the amount of training and years of experience. By 1981, for example, the average annual salary of primary-school teachers in U.S. public schools was about 95 percent of that of secondary-school teachers, indicating that the occupational status differential was being eliminated. France, on the other hand, still maintains two different systems of training and has different names for the primary-school teacher (*instituteur*) and the secondary-school teacher (*professeur*).

Whatever the status distinctions may be, the teaching profession in general is an important avenue of upward social mobility. Because teaching does not require capital, property, or family connection, it provides a good opportunity for the economic and social advancement of able and ambitious young people. A study of Chicago public-school teachers in 1964 indicated that approximately half of them had come from families of skilled, semiskilled, or unskilled workers (Robert J. Havighurst, *The Public Schools of Chicago: A Survey Report,* ch. 16, 1964). A study of the social origins of middle-school teachers in Brazil in 1963 showed that approximately half of them had moved up in social class as a result of becoming teachers (Robert J. Havighurst and Aparecida J. Gouveia, *Brazilian Secondary Education and Socio-Economic Development,* ch. 9, 1969).

Within the profession, the degree of status mobility is not great, at least in the primary and secondary schools. A classroom teacher is likely to remain a classroom teacher unless he or she seeks out an administrative post or follows some specialty, such as curriculum work, counselling, or the teaching of handicapped pupils. In university teaching, on the other hand, there is a hierarchy of three or four steps within any institution and of prestige and salary among institutions. Thus a university teaching career in the United States normally leads from the rank of instructor or assistant professor to associate professor and to full professor; in Britain the titles are assistant lecturer, lecturer, senior lecturer or reader, and professor; similar rankings occur in other countries.

Geographical mobility of teachers. The high mobility of university teachers within their country has been noted. They also move from one country to another with relative ease, so that the profession of university teaching has a cosmopolitan character unique among the professions. Most educators at this level belong to international professional organizations and tend to think of themselves as members of a worldwide profession.

For several reasons, there is less geographical mobility among primary- and secondary-school teachers. Because these teachers are licensed (whereas university teachers generally are not) they usually cannot secure a teaching job outside their own country, unless the receiving country has such a severe shortage of teachers that it seeks out immigrant teachers and gives them licenses to teach. Many African nations and India have, for this reason, a relatively large number of North American and European teachers. Language differences also interfere with geographical mobility.

Where there is a national system of state schools, as in France and England, teachers are licensed for the entire system and are able to move from one locality to another more easily than they can in countries in which there are multiple school systems organized on state or provincial lines. In the United States, where each of the 50 states has its own licensing laws and standards, teachers tend to be held within the state (though some states do have "reciprocity" with each other).

The tradition of low regard

Stereotype of the teacher. The aphorism attributed to George Bernard Shaw, "He who can, does; he who cannot, teaches," appears to have wide credence among intellectuals and educated groups. Primary and secondary teaching are often seen as a refuge for mediocre people who are industrious but unimaginative and uncreative. Writing in the *Profession of Teaching* in 1901, a Boston educator, James P. Monroe, said:

> It is, indeed, the exceptional teacher—outside the faculties of colleges—who seriously looks upon himself as a professional man. The ordinary schoolmaster has little of the personal weight, of the sense of professional responsibility, of what may be called the corporate self-respect of the lawyer, the physician, or the engineer. The traditions of the teaching guild do not yet demand a wide education, a slow and laborious preparation, a careful and humble apprenticeship, such as are required for entrance into the really learned professions. A broad education and the poise of mind which follows it are the vital needs of a great majority of the public school teachers of today. They are ceaselessly complaining of a condition of things which is indeed grievous, but which is largely of their own creation. They demand high place without qualifying themselves to hold high place; they rebel at a not uncommon attitude of contempt or of contemptuous toleration on the part of the public, but do not purge themselves of the elements which excite that contempt; they accuse the parents and the public of indifference toward their work, but do little to render that work of such quality as to forbid indifference.

More than 60 years later a professor of education at Utrecht in The Netherlands, Martinus J. Langeveld, taking a rather ambivalent position, quoted the director of a Swiss teacher-training college as saying, "The teaching profession is permeated with individuals who from youth upwards reveal the following characteristics: average drive for power, average ambition, and escapism [*Lebensscheu*]." Langeveld discerned an occupational type, or stereotype, characterized on the one hand by lack of independence or social courage and a limited social horizon, and on the other by industriousness, intellectual interest, achievement motivation, and a love for teaching children.

Whether or not this is to be given credence, it hardly applies to university teachers; and the events of the 1960s seemed to move teachers toward much more social and political action as a group and toward greater personal initiative.

One characteristic that no longer seems to be true is that teaching is a woman's profession. Though most industrialized countries have a preponderance of female teachers at the primary level, there are nearly equal numbers of male and female teachers in the world. The Table shows estimates of the percentage of women teachers in the late 1970s for several countries and areas of the world.

Percentage of Woman Teachers

	elementary level	secondary level	higher education
United States	84	46	24
Soviet Union	71	*	50
Japan	57	26	13
Australia	71	45	*
Western Europe	69	48	37
Brazil	86	54	21†

*Official data not available. †1970 figure.
Sources: UNESCO, *Statistical Yearbook* (1981); U.S. Department of Education, *Digest of Education Statistics* (1981).

There is a good deal of variation in the sex ratio among teachers in European countries. In 1979 the percentage of primary-school teachers who were women in the United Kingdom, France, The Netherlands, and West Germany was 78, 65, 46, and 62, respectively. These percentages reflect the long European tradition of male teachers in the rural village schools.

Building the profession in a new country. Since World War II it has been necessary to create or to rebuild the teaching profession in a new country, under varying conditions. Sometimes it was an old civilization becoming modern, such as in India and China; sometimes it was a tribal society becoming a nation, as in central Africa; and in one case it was a religious society becoming a modern nation, as in Israel. In all such cases, the pattern of schools has been copied from older countries, but the teaching personnel have to be drawn from the human resources available, and thus a wide variety of solutions to the problem of building the profession have been worked out.

Teachers in Israel

In the case of Israel, there were 6,500 teachers in the school system in 1948, 31,700 in 1963, and 54,500 in 1980, while the school enrollment increased from 160,000 to 700,000 and 930,000 during the same years. Since the nation was building a modern economy from a very small beginning, labour was scarce, and especially educated labour. This made it difficult for the state to secure male teachers, since educated men were in high demand for other more prestigious work. Consequently, the great majority of new teachers were women; the military position of Israel after 1967 continued to make recruitment of male teachers difficult. Thus, the proportion of male teachers in the elementary and secondary schools was 49 percent in 1948, 41 percent in 1963, and only about 20 percent in 1980. The government has established a generous scholarship and loan program for prospective teachers and requires students who accept these stipends to teach at least five years. The Teachers' Association is the country's oldest trade union.

The evolution of the teaching profession in Hungary illustrates the problems of the teaching profession and their solution in a society that moves from capitalist to Communist rule after war and revolution. In the period from 1945 to 1950 there was a serious shortage of teachers at all levels, due to wartime loss of life and to flight of teachers and professors to the West. Before World War II most teachers were trained in institutions operated by the

Roman Catholic Church. For the first five years after 1945 there were strenuous attempts to recruit new teachers and to retrain experienced teachers so that they could serve the purposes of the new society. The retraining program consisted of a two-year part-time course of lectures that stressed a "progressive-Marxist" political and economic ideology. There were 10,000 elementary- and secondary-school teachers in this program in 1950.

During the period from 1955 to 1967 there was a systematic upgrading of the training of elementary- and secondary-school teachers in Hungary, similar to what was being done in most countries. More university-level work was required. At the same time, recruiting was aimed at young people from the working class (50 percent of all university students were from peasant or working-class families during the 1950s). Secondary-school entrance became more general during the 1960s and 1970s, and the numbers of students entering secondary schools increased from 54 percent in 1960 to 72 percent in 1970 and 92 percent in 1981, with a corresponding increase of staff. During the period from 1960 to 1980 the number of secondary-school teachers increased from 8,800 to 15,460.

The teaching profession in the Soviet Union. As in all other modern countries, the length of preparation for elementary-school and secondary-school teaching in the Soviet Union has expanded since 1920. Most new teachers have had four years of work in a university or pedagogical institute after completing the basic 10-year school of general education. Competition is intense for places in the universities and pedagogical institutes. About 70 percent of teachers in elementary and secondary schools are women, one of the highest proportions in any major country.

Teachers are paid for a 24-hour week of actual teaching time in elementary schools, and 18 hours in secondary schools. They are paid extra for overtime work, which includes correcting papers in some subjects, holding conferences, and visiting parents. Many teachers earn up to twice the basic salary by extra hours of teaching. In rural areas housing is furnished, including heating and lighting. After the age of 55, teachers may retire on a pension of 40 percent of the last salary received. They may draw the pension and continue to earn a regular salary if they want to continue teaching.

University faculty members have a high status, comparable to that of other professional groups. Their salaries place them among the highest paid workers; they also receive payment for lectures, articles, and books.

FUNCTIONS AND ROLES OF TEACHERS

Broadly speaking, the function of teachers is to help students learn by imparting knowledge to them and by setting up a situation in which students can and will learn effectively. But teachers fill a complex set of roles, which vary from one society to another and from one educational level to another. Some of these roles are performed in the school, some in the community.

Roles in the school or university
- Mediator of learning
- Disciplinarian or controller of student behaviour
- Parent substitute
- Confidant to students
- Judge of achievement
- Organizer of curriculum
- Bureaucrat
- Scholar and research specialist
- Member of teachers' organization

Roles in the community
- Public servant
- Surrogate of middle-class morality
- Expert in some area of knowledge or skills
- Community leader
- Agent of social change

In those areas in which teaching has not yet become a profession, the teacher may fill fewer of these roles. The primary-school teacher in a simple agricultural society, for example, will fill only the first five of the school roles and the first and possibly the second of the community roles.

Some of the roles conflict; that is, the performance of one, that of disciplinarian, for example, tends to conflict with another, such as that of confidant to students, or the role of independent and creative scholar will tend to conflict with that of the bureaucrat. In the community, the role of surrogate of middle-class morality tends to conflict with the role of agent of social change. In the presence of these role conflicts, the teacher must learn to balance, to know when and how vigorously to act in a particular role, and when to shift to another in a flexible way.

Role in curricular design. The family, the government, the church or religious authority, and the economic or business-industrial authority all have an interest in the development of children and youth, and all play a part, therefore, in setting up and controlling formal and many informal means of education. In the more developed societies, they employ teachers to do the work of education, and they work out with the teacher an understanding of what the teacher is expected to do. The more "professional" the teacher is, the more autonomy he demands and is given to teach within the concept of understood and mutually accepted goals and methods.

Teaching of skills, information, and attitudes

The elementary-school teacher must teach the basic mental skills—reading, writing, and arithmetic. Beyond this, the elementary-school teacher must teach facts and attitudes favourable to the nation or the church or any other institution supporting the school. Thus he must teach in a way that is favourable to Communism in the Soviet Union, to a mixed capitalist-socialist economy in Britain or the United States, to the French or Brazilian systems in France or Brazil, and so forth. In a society in which schools are directed by churches or religious groups, as in Spain, he must teach the relevant religious beliefs and attitudes.

In national and state systems of education, the legislature generally requires that certain subjects be taught so as to "improve" the citizenship or the morality or the health of the students. Many systems, for instance, require secondary schools to teach about the pitfalls of alcohol, drugs, and tobacco. A growing number of nations require teaching in favour of conservation of natural resources and protection of the physical environment against air and water pollution. Before World War II a central course required in the Japanese schools was "moral education." After the war, this was abolished by the American occupation forces, on the grounds that it tended to inculcate a kind of authoritarianism and nationalistic ideology. With the ending of the military occupation, however, the Japanese government reintroduced a compulsory course in moral education, which became a source of major controversy between conservatives and progressives within the Japanese educational profession. The French school system also has a compulsory course in "civic morality."

Teaching freedom

Matters of curriculum and choice of textbooks and materials of instruction are determined in some countries with little or no participation of the individual teacher. Thus, in France, with a highly centralized national educational system, the course of instruction in the elementary schools is fixed by the Ministry of Education. In the United States, where each of the 50 states is its own authority, there is much more curricular variation. Some states require statewide adoption of textbooks, whereas others leave such matters to local decision. Many large city school systems have a curriculum department to set policy in such matters, and the individual teacher in a city school system or in certain state systems thus has relatively little power to decide what to teach. There is more flexibility at the secondary-school level than in the primary-school level. As for methods of teaching within the classroom, the individual teacher probably has more autonomy in the United States than in most European school systems.

The university teacher almost anywhere in the world has substantial autonomy in his choice of textbooks, of content to be covered in a particular course, and of methods of teaching. In general the only limits on the university teacher are set by the nature of his teaching assignment. If he is one of a number of teachers who teach a popular course, such as general chemistry or physics or history, which is taken by several hundred students and offered by several different instructors, he may have to use the same textbooks as those used by other instructors, and he may have to prepare his students for common examinations. On the other hand, in those courses that he alone gives, he has wide freedom to choose the content and methods of instruction.

In terms of the professional responsibility of teachers for what they teach, there is a major distinction between the university and elementary-secondary school systems. At the level of higher education, teachers have the power and the responsibility of defining the curriculum—its contents and its methods. This is the essence of academic freedom in higher education. The governing board of the university, whether it be a government or independent university, does not tell teachers what to teach or how to teach. There are, nevertheless, some external requirements operative on the university teacher. If he is preparing his students for examinations not under university control (civil service examinations, state bar and medical examinations, examinations for a certificate as a public accountant, or the like), his autonomy is limited by the necessity that his students be well prepared for these external examinations.

In contrast to the power of the university governing board, the board of an elementary- or secondary-school system has, but generally delegates to the school administration, the power to determine what is taught. The school administration, consisting of the superintendent, school directors, inspectors, and curriculum specialists, has effective power over the curriculum and brings the classroom teacher into the process as much or as little as it chooses. With the growth of teachers' unions and organizations, however, it appears that collective action by teachers is tending to increase the effective autonomy of the classroom teacher. Administrative and legislative prescriptions for the school curriculum are generally resisted in *principle* by the teaching profession; the profession presumes itself better able to decide what to teach and how to teach it.

The doctrine of in loco parentis. When minor children are entrusted by parents to a school, the parents delegate to the school certain responsibilities for their children, and the school has certain liabilities. In effect, the school and the teachers take some of the responsibility and some of the authority of the parents. The exact extent and nature of this responsibility and power vary from one society to another and from one school system to another. This is spelled out to some extent in the law, but much of it is determined by local custom and practice.

There is, of course, a relation between the age of the child on the one hand and the teacher's responsibility and liability for it on the other. The young child *must* obey the teacher, and the teacher may use the methods expected and tolerated in the community to control the child's behaviour. Furthermore, the child's physical safety is entrusted to the school and to the teacher, who thus become legally liable for the child's safety, insofar as negligence can be proved against them.

In the matter of corporal or physical punishment, local attitudes establish a wide range of expected and permissible behaviour on the part of the teacher. In most parts of the world, young children may be punished by a limited infliction of physical pain at the hands of the teacher or school principal, using a wooden ruler or a whip of one kind or another. But there are some systems and cities that explicitly bar a teacher from using corporal punishment. This seems most common in large cities; the teacher in a rural or small-city school is more apt to be expected to use physical measures for controlling pupil behaviour. As students become older, their behaviour is less apt to be controlled by physical measures, and they are more likely to be suspended from classes or expelled from school. This is the common last resort in the upper years of the secondary school and in the university.

Another facet of the doctrine of *in loco parentis* is seen in the relation between parents and teachers with respect to the promotion of pupils and to their counselling or guidance. Parent and teacher may be in conflict about the best procedures to use with a pupil. Shall this pupil be promoted from a fifth to a sixth year class or be "kept back" to repeat the year's work? This decision is generally seen as the responsibility of the school, though the parents may be brought in for consultation. If the parents object to the school's decision, what rights and powers do they have? May they see the school's records on their child? May they examine the pupil's examination papers or other school work? The answers to these questions are more fixed in some countries than in others, but in general, the school's authority is supported in these matters.

Relations between parents and teachers

A more difficult problem is presented by a student, generally an adolescent, who is having serious problems with his school performance or with his school behaviour. He is sent to the school counsellor, who finds him in need of therapeutic counselling and proceeds to counsel him. Must the counsellor secure prior consent from the parents? Must the counsellor disclose to the parents what he learns about or from the student in confidence? Perhaps the counsellor concludes that a part of the student's difficulty is caused by his parents. Must the counsellor tell this to the parents? Is the counsellor intruding on the *privacy* of the parents by asking the student about his relations with them or by listening if the student volunteers such information? This is *terra incognita* for the teaching profession, and has become something of an issue in the places where personal counselling is regarded as part of the school's responsibility.

At the level of higher education, the doctrine of *in loco parentis* does not present as much of a problem for the teacher, since the student, even though he may be legally a minor, is presumed to be a more responsible person. But the university may have a problem in relation to the local police or city government. May university property—including classrooms in which teachers are trying to teach—be regarded as private property, with police and other outside persons barred unless they are explicitly asked for their help? The question (and others like it) has no clear and unequivocal answer.

Extramural activities of teachers. Traditionally, the schoolteacher has been a surrogate of middle-class morality who serves the local community in various clerical or secretarial capacities because he or she can write legibly and spell accurately. Furthermore, the schoolteacher has often been expected to support the local religious group, if there is one, by teaching children, singing in the choir, and so forth. In other words, the teacher is seen as a useful minor civil servant, without deviant political or economic attitudes.

Though this may be true of most teachers in most countries, there are exceptions. In places where the community is polarized along religious or political lines, for instance, teachers generally have to take sides in local politics and cannot easily serve the whole community. Thus, in the small towns of France, the stereotype of schoolteacher is traditionally that of a man with leftist political leanings, always at war with the village priest. In the cities, schoolteachers are needed less to perform local community services and tend as teachers to be politically neutral or invisible.

University teachers are more likely to be leaders in local politics and local civic affairs. Since the university is expected to be a source of ideas as well as of information in controversial areas, university professors may perform this function by taking sides on political and economic issues. Those in the sciences, for example, may become influential advisors on local and state problems of health, water supply, transportation, or the use and conservation of natural resources. When the university teacher does take sides on controversial economic or political issues, he may expect counterpressures to have him discharged, and his institution may or may not support him in the name of academic freedom.

As elementary- and secondary-school teachers have organized themselves for collective action, they have succeeded increasingly in protecting those of their group who do take unpopular positions on political and economic matters. In countries with two-party or multiparty political systems, teachers may now run for elective offices, and they and their organizations are likely to take sides on political issues. Thus the teacher at any educational level is increasingly free to take part in promoting social changes, and at least a few teachers are generally found in leadership roles in local and national politics.

Scholarship and the profession. Within the profession, prestige has traditionally gone to the productive scholar, the one who contributes to the growth of knowledge, literature, or art. Promotion in the university and fame in the world outside the university have gone to the person who does research or scholarly work—and publishes. The university is seen as an institution to discover new knowledge, as well as to pass on what is known, and these two functions are not necessarily tied together. The teacher of adolescents and of university undergraduates does not find that research or scholarly work makes him a better teacher. Only when he is teaching graduate students who themselves are being trained for scholarship does the university professor find himself working at the frontier of knowledge, with his students as apprentices.

Relation between research and teaching

The universities of the world have adapted to this situation in two ways. One is to assign some teachers a teaching role, with a heavy teaching load and recognition when they do a good job of teaching; the other is to give teachers a reduced teaching load and expect them to do research or writing. A second adaptation is to assign some staff members to full-time research with a few graduate students associated with them as apprentices and research assistants. In any case, it is the fact that the universities of the world, which claim the responsibility of advancing knowledge, do continue to judge their teachers more by their research and writing than by their teaching.

University teachers are also much in demand for consultation and advice to industry, business, government, and school systems. The best experts on problems of innovative development and on the conduct of industrial research and development are generally found in universities, and many teachers find as much as a quarter to a half of their time taken with consultation.

THE CAREER OF THE TEACHER

The professionalization of teaching. In the 19th century, systems of public education developed in order to meet the recognized need for universal literacy in an industrializing society. Teaching at this primary level was at first no more than a high-level domestic service, in which the teacher took over some of the child-rearing responsibility of the family. In some parts of the world, a year as a cadet teacher working under a more experienced teacher became the model for teacher training. Frequently, courses were added to the secondary school in the largest town of the county or province, for training classroom teachers. Even today in many countries, notably in Latin America, the training of teachers is still carried on largely in certain types of secondary schools, called "normal schools," which take students (mainly girls) at about age 15 or 16 for a two- or three-year course of study. In Europe and North America, the earlier normal schools or teachers colleges have since moved up to the postsecondary level of higher education. In any event, by the turn of the 20th century some rudiments of a teaching profession had begun to evolve. There was the beginning of a program of formal training; the emergence of a body of specialized knowledge called pedagogy; the imposition of an inchoate system of licensing or certification; and the recognition of a few minimal standards of performance to be defined, expanded, and enforced by the corps of teachers.

The combined efforts of educational reformers and teachers' organizations were required to fashion the beginnings of a profession. Men and women saw themselves becoming committed to a career in teaching and therefore sought to make this career more personally and socially satisfying. The Chicago Teachers' Federation, founded in 1897, for example, comprised a group of female primary-school teachers who were faced by an experimental pension system that was actuarially unsound and by salaries that were very low. Margaret Haley, a dynamic 36-year-old Irish woman, was their leader, and in the 15 years after she helped found the Teachers' Federation, it brought a successful suit against the public utilities, forcing them to pay more taxes; forced the board of education to use the added tax income to increase teachers' salaries; affiliated with the Chicago Federation of Labor; sued the *Chicago Tribune* for revising its lease of school-owned land; and engineered the election of Chicago's woman superintendent of schools to the presidency of the National Education Association. Writing in 1915 in his publication, *The Daybook,* Carl Sandburg referred to her latest victory:

> Margaret Haley wins again!... For fifteen years, this one little woman has flung her clenched fists into the faces of contractors, school land leaseholders, tax dodgers and their politicians, fixers, go-betweens and stool pigeons.... Over the years the *Tribune,* the *News* and the ramified gang of manipulators who hate Margaret Haley have not been able to smutch her in the eyes of the decent men and women of this town who do their own thinking.

Tenure

Gradually, throughout the world, classroom teachers won "tenure" of their positions. In the early days, they were employed by the governing body of the school system on annual contracts; under such a system no teacher was assured of his job for the ensuing school year until he had received formal notice of his reappointment for the year. There then developed the practice of automatic renewal of the contract unless the teacher was notified by a certain date (usually three or four months before the beginning of the school year) that his services would *not* be needed. Finally, as school systems—local, state or provincial, and national—became more stabilized and organized, the rule of life tenure or tenure up to the age of retirement was adopted. Generally, under such a system, after two or three years of satisfactory service, a teacher achieves tenure and cannot be removed from his position except for specific reasons of incompetence or moral turpitude, and, even then, he has the right to a formal hearing on such charges.

This history of public-school teachers, involving a slow upgrading of teacher education combined with a struggle for professional recognition, has not been experienced by university teachers. Because higher education throughout the world has been limited to a selected few, it has correspondingly required relatively few teachers, and they seem to have emerged within the universities and to have been selected by the university authorities themselves. They frequently have constituted an inner circle or closed clique. There have, however, been a few instances of pressure by students and by civil government for improved professional standards. The South American University Reform of 1918, for instance, was started by students at the University of Córdoba in Argentina and was aimed at improving the low professional standards of teachers in Latin American universities.

Organization of university teachers

The status and prestige of the university professor has been relatively high in most countries, and he has needed no politico-economic organization to fight for his professional status. Only in the late 20th century has there been a strong movement organized and led by university teachers to further upgrade or reform their profession. This movement has been particularly apparent in the United States, where the enormous extension of higher education has led to a growing teaching force and a consequent problem of maintaining professional standards. Since the 1950s the American Association of University Professors (AAUP) has pressed for higher salaries, by publishing various studies of salary levels that have singled out universities paying relatively low salaries. At the same time the AAUP has continued an aggressive campaign for academic freedom of the professor, by defining a code of professional ethics for the teacher and a procedure through which an institution must go if it proposes to discharge a professor.

Educational associations and teachers' unions. Professional groups all over the world have organized for collective action to do two quite different things. One objective of a professional organization is to improve the economic status and the working conditions of its members. A second broad objective is to improve the service that the profession performs for society. These two objectives may best be viewed separately, and it is not clear, a priori, to what extent they are mutually conflicting or mutually supportive.

Commencing in the latter half of the 19th century, elementary- and secondary-school teachers banded together to form societies of teachers in the various types of schools and in the various school subjects. Thus Germany and France with their stratified school systems had as many as five teachers' organizations that operated more or less independently of each other. By the middle of the 20th century, however, such organizations in European countries tended to coalesce into strong national organizations.

Professional associations. University teachers have generally organized themselves into associations for the improvement of scholarship and higher education. As a rule they have operated on the assumption that society will support them financially and morally if they do a good job of scholarly research, writing, and teaching. They accept as members scholars who are not actually teaching in higher institutions but are engaged in industrial, artistic, literary, or other work.

Every country has its national learned societies, which hold annual meetings, publish journals, and generally work for the improvement of scholarship. There are national organizations of classicists, foreign-language teachers, biologists, physical scientists, sociologists, psychologists, anthropologists, literature students, historians, and so forth. In addition there are interdisciplinary organizations, such as the Tavistock Institute of Human Relations (Britain) and the Social Science Research Council (U.S.). Selective prestige associations also exist to further the cause of the professions and to honour individual leaders. Some famous examples are the Académie Française, the Royal Academy (Britain), the National Academy of Sciences (U.S.), the Academy of Sciences of the U.S.S.R., and the Nippon Gakushiin (Japan).

International organizations

International associations make the university teaching profession a worldwide force. There are international associations of scholars in chemistry, psychology, sociology, human development, gerontology, and other branches of scholarship. Special attempts have been made in recent years to bridge the gap separating the Communist bloc of nations from the European-North American bloc. International meetings have been held in Yugoslavia, Bulgaria, and Russia, and scholars from the Communist countries have been encouraged to attend conferences in non-Communist countries.

Teachers' unions and teachers' associations. In most countries there is one major teachers' organization to which all or nearly all teachers belong and pay dues. Sometimes membership is obligatory, sometimes voluntary. Thus there is the National Union of Teachers in England, the Japanese Teachers Union, the relatively young Fédération Générale d'Enseignement in France, and the Australian Teachers Union. In the Soviet Union, where much of the political and social life of the people is organized around unions, there are three teachers' unions—for preschool teachers, primary- and secondary-school teachers, and teachers in higher education. These unions in the U.S.S.R. provide pensions, vacation pay, and sick-leave pay and thus touch the welfare of teachers at many points. There are also professional societies for subject-matter specialists within the unions and subordinate to them.

The organizational complex is stable in some countries and changing in others. England, for example, has two different associations for male and female secondary-school teachers, two different associations for male and female headmasters of secondary schools, and a separate Association of Teachers in Technical Institutions. These associations are parallel to the National Union of Teachers, which is open to any qualified teacher from nursery school to university level. The National Union has no political affiliation but is politically powerful in its own right. France, in contrast, has a wide variety of teachers' organizations, with various political leanings, but they do not get on well together and are politically less effective.

In the United States there is a basic rivalry between the National Education Association, which includes teachers of various levels as well as administrators, and the American Federation of Teachers, a trade union that excludes administrators. Since about 1960 the NEA, a loose federation of local, state, and national organizations, has become more militant in working for the economic improvement of teachers and has tolerated strikes. This policy has resulted in a reorganization of the NEA into a looser federation, with classroom teachers operating quite separately from the associations of administrators. It has also brought the NEA into direct competition with the AFT, which is relatively strong in several large cities.

Inter-union rivalry

Although the classroom teachers' organizations began as agents for obtaining better salaries and working conditions, wherever they have succeeded substantially in this effort they have turned to the other activity—setting standards of performance and attempting to improve educational policy and practice. Faced with great difficulties in educating children in the slums and ghettoes of the big cities, the teachers' union in the United States, for instance, has put into its collective-bargaining agreements a statement of interest in, and responsibility for, educational policy and for the development of teaching methods and the training of teachers for those difficult positions.

The various national primary- and secondary-school teachers' associations have moved toward the formation of two loose international federations. One includes the national associations from the Communist bloc of countries—the World Federation of Teachers' Unions. The other, the World Confederation of Organizations of the Teaching Profession, was founded in 1952 and includes most of the national associations from the non-Communist bloc. They both compete for the allegiance of teachers' organizations in the uncommitted countries.

THE TEACHING PROFESSION AND CONTEMPORARY SOCIAL REVOLUTIONS

In almost every country with a free public voice, militants urge professional associations to take sides in political controversies over problems that do not lie in their fields of professional competence. The argument in favour of militancy is that modern societies are engaged in a social revolution that is changing profoundly the nature of contemporary society, that this revolution will have profound effects on the teaching profession, and that teachers should assume responsibility for directing education toward constructive participation in the social revolution.

At the same time, the militants foresee a drastic change in the teaching profession. They see it as: (1) more critical of itself—new members are skeptical of many of the established propositions of pedagogy and of science; (2) impatient for rapid change—the rate of social change of the past few decades is presumed to have been too slow; (3) adopting human welfare—the well-being of all people and especially of the disadvantaged—as the crowning objective of the profession; (4) looking to the student for guidance in the work of the profession—they believe in sharing power with students in the shaping of education; and (5) becoming less concerned with formal professional standards, such as diplomas, licenses, and university degrees, as well as turning more teaching responsibility over to teacher aides, using more pupils as tutors, or admitting students to universities with little or no examination of their formal knowledge. (R.J.H.)

Teacher education

While arrangements of one kind or another for the education of the young have existed at all times and in all societies, it is only recently that schools have emerged as distinctive institutions for this purpose on a mass scale, and teachers as a distinctive occupational category. Parents, elders, priests, and wise men have traditionally seen it as their duty to pass on their knowledge and skills to the next generation. As Aristotle put it, the surest sign of wisdom is a man's ability to teach what he knows. Knowing, doing, teaching, and learning were for many centuries, and in some societies are still today, indistinguishable from one another. For the most part the induction of the young into the ways of acting, feeling, thinking, and believing that are characteristic of their society has been an informal—if serious and important—process, accomplished chiefly by means of personal contact with full-fledged adults, by sharing in common activities, and by acquiring the myths, legends, and folk beliefs of the culture. Formal ceremonies, such as the puberty rite, marked the point at which it was assumed that a certain range of knowledge and skill had been mastered and that the individual could be admitted to full participation in tribal life. (Residual elements of

Unity of knowing and teaching

such ceremonies remain in some modern arrangements; it has been seriously contended that the study of the Latin language in the Renaissance and post-Renaissance school can be interpreted as a form of puberty rite.) Even in the formally established schools of the Greek city-states and of the medieval world there was little separation between, on the one hand, the processes of organizing and setting down knowledge and, on the other, those of teaching this knowledge to others.

This does not mean that prior to the 19th century little attention was given to a training in teaching methods as distinct from "subjects." The great works of medieval scholasticism were essentially textbooks, designed to be used for the purpose of teaching. Today, as in the medieval world, methods of teaching and the organization of knowledge continue to be reciprocally influential. Nor are the problems that today surround the qualifications and certification of teachers wholly new. State, church, and local authorities everywhere have long recognized the importance of the teacher's work in maintaining or establishing particular patterns of social organization and systems of belief, just as radical and reformist politicians and thinkers have looked to the schools to disseminate their particular brands of truth. In medieval and post-Reformation Europe, for example, there was considerable concern with the qualifications and background of teachers, mainly but not entirely with reference to their religious beliefs. In 1559 Queen Elizabeth I of England issued an injunction that prohibited anyone from teaching without a license from his bishop, which was granted only after an examination of the applicant's "learning and dexterity in teaching," "sober and honest conversation," and "right understanding of God's true religion." Thus the certification of teachers and concern for their character and personal qualities are by no means new issues.

What is new for most societies—European, American, African, and Asian—is the attempt to provide a substantial period of formal education for everyone and not just for the small proportion of the population who will become political, social, and religious leaders or for those few who possess surplus time and money for the purpose. Universal literacy, already achieved in most European and American and many Asian societies, has become the goal of all. In an increasing proportion of countries every child now proceeds automatically to secondary education; many remain at school until 16 or 18 years of age, and large numbers go on to some form of postsecondary education and training. The scale and variety of educational provision that all this requires makes the supply, education, training, and certification of an adequate number of teachers a worldwide issue of education policy and practice. In developed and developing countries alike, no factor is of greater importance in relation to the quantity and quality of education; it is significant that a substantial proportion of the budget of the United Nations Educational, Scientific and Cultural Organization (UNESCO) is devoted to the improvement of teacher preparation.

The importance of teacher education

The term "teacher" in this article is used to mean those who work in schools providing education for pupils up to the age of 18. Thus, "teacher education" refers to the structures, institutions, and processes by means of which men and women are prepared for work in elementary and secondary schools. This includes preschool, kindergarten, elementary, and secondary institutions for children from the age of two or three to 18. (The education and training of lecturers and other staff members of technical colleges, polytechnics, universities, and other institutions of postsecondary education, both general and specialized, are treated in EDUCATION, HIGHER.)

THE EVOLUTION OF TEACHER EDUCATION

Teacher education, as it exists today, can be divided into two stages, preservice and in-service. Preservice education includes all the stages of education and training that precede the teacher's entry to paid employment in a school. In-service training is the education and training that the teacher receives after the beginning of his career.

Early development. The earliest formal arrangements for teacher preparation, introduced in some of the German states during the early part of the 18th century, included both preservice and in-service training. A seminary or normal school for "young men who had already passed through an elementary, or even a superior school, and who were preparing to be teachers, by making additional attainments, and acquiring a knowledge of the human mind, and the principles of education as a science, and of its methods as an art" was set up in Halle in 1706. By the end of the century there were 30 such institutions in operation in Germany. Systematic training was linked to an equally systematic process of certification, control of teaching conditions, and in-service study. All public teachers were required to attend a series of meetings to extend their practical knowledge. Parochial conferences took place monthly in the winter, district conferences bimonthly in the summer, a circle conference twice a year, and a departmental conference annually. Each seminary was responsible for maintaining contact with all the teachers working within a six-mile radius, and some established "repetition courses" for experienced teachers who wanted to refresh and add to their knowledge.

The German normal school

Nineteenth-century developments in the United States, Britain, France, Belgium, and Japan owed much to the pattern that had been established in Germany. In Revolutionary France efforts were made to set up a system of normal schools. The École Normale (later the École Normale Supérieure), founded in 1794, closed after a few months; but it was reestablished by Napoleon in 1808 to train teachers for the *lycées.* After 1833 a uniform system of *écoles normales* (initially only for male students) was created, and the normal-school systems of several countries date from the third decade of the century.

During the first 30 years of the 19th century, teacher preparation in the United States, Britain, and elsewhere was dominated by the monitorial methods introduced by Andrew Bell and Joseph Lancaster. In the simplest terms, the method involved a master instructing a number of senior pupils or "monitors," who then passed on their newly acquired knowledge to a larger number of pupils. Such methods were cheap, simple, and, it was widely believed, effective. They required a necessary emphasis upon facts, drill, repetition, mechanical learning, and ease of teaching. By 1820 there were 20 Lancastrian schools in the state of New York, where the system had official status until the middle of the century. With hindsight it is easy to condemn the monitorial system. At the time, when the supply of educated persons available and willing to teach in the elementary schools was severely limited, and when the public funds to employ them were in short supply, the system enabled a large number of children to achieve the minimum level of literacy on which future development could build. Just as the organization of knowledge characteristic of medieval times implied its own pattern of pedagogy, so the Lancastrian system embodied a distinctive approach to the process of teaching; one of the attractions of such systems is that they offer a built-in solution to the problem of reconciling what the teacher needs to know and the methods he should learn.

Lancastrian schools

Among those who were unimpressed by the claims of the Lancastrian system was David Stow, who in 1834 founded the Glasgow Normal Seminary from which "trainers," as his graduates came to be called, went to schools in Scotland and many of the British colonial territories. In the United States, after an uncertain start, the Massachusetts Normal Schools founded by Horace Mann in the 1830s became a model for similar developments in Connecticut, Michigan, Rhode Island, Iowa, New Jersey, and Illinois. In England, churches and voluntary foundations were in process of establishing the first of the teacher training colleges. Australia began the organized preparation of teachers in the early 1850s. At this early stage certain issues were already emerging that were to remain alive for the next hundred years and that are to some extent still relevant today.

The needs of pupils and schools were beginning to advance beyond basic literacy. Human knowledge was becoming more diverse and scientific and was being organized into new disciplinary systems. Secondary education was expanding. The early inclusive pedagogic systems were falling into disfavour. The problem arose of reconciling the teacher's personal need for education with his professional need for classroom technique. There were other than purely pedagogic considerations involved; the inhibitions of class society in England, the demand for practicality in the United States, a fear of liberal agitation in France, the patriotic missionary role of the teacher in Japan—all tended to maintain an emphasis upon the practical techniques of school management and to limit the range and level of the elementary teacher's intellectual accomplishments to mastery of only such subject knowledge as was needed at the school level.

General education versus professional training

Some educators asserted that the curriculum of the normal school should be academic, on the ground that the future teacher needed nothing more than experience of conventional subjects soundly taught. Others argued that training should have a purely professional function, including only such subject knowledge as the teacher would need in his classroom work. Some advocates claimed that the liberal and professional elements could readily be harmonized or integrated. The work of Derwent Coleridge, principal of St. Mark's College, London, who admitted that he took his models not from the pedagogical seminaries of Germany but from the universities of Oxford and Cambridge, exemplified the attempt to introduce a larger element of general education into teacher preparation. Sir James Kay-Shuttleworth, founder of another London college, emphasized basic subject matter; he held that

> not merely the subjects of instruction, but also the methods of teaching the candidates, should be so ordered as to be in itself a preparation for their future vocation as teachers. On this account the oral instruction of classes in a Normal school is greatly to be preferred to any other mode.

In the United States, Horace Mann supported the value of a training in the "common branches" of knowledge, as a means of mental discipline. But the views of Derwent Coleridge, Kay-Shuttleworth, and Horace Mann, in common with those of many other educators of the time, reflected social as well as pedagogical considerations. Mann, it has been suggested, failed to recognize that the Prussian system that so impressed him was one that took lower class pupils and trained them as teachers of the lower classes—a system already under fire from German educators at the time that it was being used as a model for developments abroad.

Between 1870 and 1890, legislation was enacted in a number of countries to systematize and broaden the work of the normal schools. In Japan an ordinance of 1886 established higher normal schools providing a four-year course for boys and girls who had completed eight years of elementary education. A French law of 1879 established a nationwide system of colleges for training women primary teachers (*écoles normales d'institutrices*). In Russia a statute on teachers' seminaries was promulgated in 1870; within five years there were 34 such institutions, with nearly 2,000 students. A further statute in 1872 provided for institutes to train teachers for the new higher grade schools that were beginning to appear in the larger towns. In Scotland, the universities of Edinburgh and St. Andrews established chairs in education in 1876. In the United States a large number of universities had by 1895 set up education departments, and in some of them the preparation of teachers for work in the schools was beginning to be combined with systematic study and research in education processes.

Developments in American universities owed a great deal to the efforts of men such as Henry Barnard, who, as schools commissioner in Rhode Island from 1845 to 1849, stimulated a local interest in education that led to the creation of a department of education at Brown University. Barnard wrote an influential series of books on pedagogy and teacher education and later, as president of Columbia University, inspired Nicholas Murray Butler and others to found Teachers College in 1888. This soon became the foremost university school of education in the United States. It incorporated two schools as teaching laboratories, enrolling children from kindergarten to college age. As its "Announcement" of 1901 made clear, it was not restricted to any one level of professional preparation:

> The purpose of Teachers College is to afford opportunity, both theoretical and practical, for the training of teachers of both sexes for kindergartens and elementary and secondary schools, of principals, supervisors and superintendents of schools, and of specialists in various branches of school work, including normal schools and colleges.

Late 19th- and early 20th-century developments. Until about 1890 the "theoretical" elements in teacher preparation were of two kinds: the study of certain principles of teaching and school management, exemplified in the textbooks written by experienced schoolmen that were published in many countries during the second half of the 19th century; and instruction in "mental and moral philosophy," history of education, psychology, and pedagogics. Some of the most popular and influential works, such as Rosencrantz' *Philosophy of Education,* which was translated into English in the 1870s, made little distinction between philosophical and psychological data. But after 1890 psychology and sociology began to crystallize as more or less distinctive areas of study; students of education had a wider and more clearly structured range of disciplines to draw upon for their data and perspectives and to provide a "scientific" basis for their pedagogic principles.

Evolution of educational theory

In the middle years of the 19th century the ideas of the Swiss educator J.H. Pestalozzi and of the German Friedrich Froebel inspired the use of object teaching, defined in 1878 by Alexander Bain in his widely studied *Education as a Science* as the attempt

> to range over all the utilities of life, and all the processes of nature. It begins upon things familiar to the pupils, and enlarges the conceptions of these, by filling in unnoticed qualities. It proceeds to things that have to be learnt even in their primary aspect by description or diagram; and ends with the more abstruse operations of natural forces.

The work of these pioneers also led to a clearer recognition of the developmental needs and character of childhood. Later contributors to the corpus of ideas that underlie the processes of teacher education continued to provide philosophical, sociological, and psychological justification for particular views of the nature of education and of teaching, and also had a greater or lesser influence on the methods to be employed in classroom and school.

The work of the German philosopher Johann Friedrich Herbart (1776–1841) was of particular importance in this latter respect. Herbart wrote a number of pedagogical works during his teaching career at the universities of Göttingen and Königsberg. In the latter part of the 19th century, the study of education along Herbartian lines became established in every European country, in America, and in Japan. Herbartianism offered a complete system—a philosophical theory, a set of educational aims, a rational psychology, and a pedagogy. Teaching, it held, should build on what the child already knows and should seek to inculcate, by the choice of appropriate materials, the highest moral character. It should be organized in accordance with the "five formal steps" of preparation, presentation, comparison, generalization, and application. The Herbartian doctrine rested as much upon the interpretation of his followers as upon the master's own works, and its influence was of relatively limited duration. Other ideas were coming to the fore, less direct and comprehensive than Herbart's but having greater impact upon the educational consciousness of the next half-century.

The influence of Darwinian evolutionary ideas upon pedagogy was very marked. To the extent that the evolutionary viewpoint emphasized the processes by which individuals become adapted to their environment, as in the teachings of the English philosopher Herbert Spencer, their influence was profoundly conservative. But evolutionary ideas were also embodied within the child development theories of the American psychologist G. Stanley Hall, who argued that the stages of individual growth recapitulated those of social evolution and therefore that the distinctive character and status of childhood must be respected. The American philosopher William James also included evolutionary notions in his psychology. James's emphasis, however, was not so much upon the processes by which individuals adapt as upon those through which they react creatively and positively with their circumstances, helping to shape and change these to meet their needs. James's formulation of associationism, the building up of useful habit systems, had implications for the study of learning that teacher educators were quick to recognize and that were made more significant by the later experiments of the American psychologist Edward L. Thorndike (1874–1949). Thorndike's work with animals stands at the beginning of a tradition that continues to the present day. The laws of learning that he formulated have for long been a staple of teacher training courses in many countries. Thorndike saw psychology as the basis of a genuinely scientific pedagogy, and claimed that "Just as the science and art of agriculture depend upon chemistry and botany, so the art of education depends upon physiology and psychology." He went on to argue, with a degree of confidence that rings strangely today, that

> A complete science of psychology would tell every fact about everyone's intellect and character and behavior, would tell the cause of every change in human nature, would tell the result which every educational force—every act of every person that changed any other or the agent himself—would have.

The greatest influence on teacher-training curricula in the United States and many other countries was exercised not by the experimental psychologists but by the pragmatist philosopher John Dewey. Dewey began with a conception of the nature of scientific method that he generalized into a specific pedagogical approach (popularized by others as the "project" method and, more recently, as inquiry-based learning). This he combined with a consideration of the nature of the child's interests and capacities for learning and life experience, the nature and claims of different types of subject matter, and the importance of democratic values in the social context of the school. Just as James's psychology gave back to the teacher and the school some of the influence on individual development that the interpreters of evolutionary adaptation had seemed to deny, so Dewey's notion of the school as the embodiment of community ideals and the spearhead of social reform lent a new importance to the processes of teacher education.

Conservative and progressive views

It is tempting to categorize these various perspectives as "conservative" or "progressive." The former stress the importance of subject matter and of standard methods of effective instruction: the need for regularity and order in the classroom and for means that will encourage children to apply themselves diligently to learning; the importance of the teacher as a subject-matter expert and as an exemplar of accepted morality; and the existence of objective standards of scholarship and achievement to which teachers and students alike should aspire. The progressives, on the other hand, emphasize a more child-centred approach, designed to build upon the natural interests and curiosity of the child: a flexible pattern of teaching and classroom organization recognizing individual differences in motivation, capacity, and learning style; a conception of the teacher as an organizer of children's learning rather than as an instructor; and the need to integrate the subject matter of different disciplines into topics and projects that have meaning in terms of the pupil's own experience.

Such conservative and progressive ideas have their roots in differing conceptions of the nature of man and society, of knowledge, and of the learning process. The differences are not new. The fortunes of the two perspectives tend to wax and wane in accordance with the times. Thus in the United States, fears of a loss of technological supremacy in the late 1950s encouraged conservative critics to point to the weaknesses of "child-centred" education. In the same way, anxieties about the meaninglessness of the education experienced by the poor, coupled with evidences of widespread alienation among the young, encouraged a revival of interest in progressive ideas in the early 1970s. Many educators, of course, do not fall into either the conservative or the progressive category but draw their ideas from various sources. There has been a tendency in many countries, however, for the curricula of teacher-preparing institutions to be identified with progressive educational ideas.

Many other ideas also influenced the curriculum and organization of teacher preparation during the last decade of the 19th and the first half of the 20th centuries. The dynamic psychology of Sigmund Freud and his early associates, the work of the Gestalt psychologists, the methods of measuring human abilities that were being developed in France, Great Britain, and the United States, the development of religious ideas in the Roman Catholic countries, the imposition of Marxist and Leninist ideologies in the Soviet Union—all of these in varying measure affected the normal schools, teachers' colleges and seminaries, and university departments of education. Such new ideas and systems of thought had their impact at three main levels.

The use of education in promotion of values

First, they influenced the nature of the social commitment that teacher-preparing institutions strove to instill in their students: commitment to the values of democracy and of opportunity in the United States, as exemplified in the writings of Dewey; to a sense of national purpose or patriotism, as in France, Germany, and Japan; to the pursuit of the socialist revolution, as in the post-tsarist Soviet Union; or to a religious outlook as manifested by Catholic doctrine in Italy, Spain, and Latin America.

Second, the philosophers, psychologists, and sociologists helped to redefine the teacher–pupil relationship. Whatever their differences of view, clear continuities are visible among them on such issues as the significance of the child's needs and interests, the weaknesses of the formal academic curriculum, and the nature of individual development.

Third, the new contributions affected the organization of learning through the measurement and assessment of abilities; the diagnosis of special learning problems; the placing of children in homogeneous age and ability groups by means of "tracking" and "streaming"; the emphasis on problem solving; and the project method. These changes, reflected both in the way in which teachers were trained and in the architecture and equipment of schools, transformed education for younger children in many countries during the first half of the 20th century.

Organization of teacher education in the 20th century. The educational doctrines that inspired, conceptualized, and legitimated this transformation themselves reflected other social, political, economic, demographic, and technological changes. Urbanization, the reduction of infant mortality, improvements in child health, the fact that families, individuals, and whole societies could afford longer and better schooling, growth in the size of populations, greater capacity for control by central and local government, the availability of new kinds of educational apparatus and teaching aids—all these did much to shape the progress of teacher education during the decades after 1900.

Levels of teacher preparation

Among the countries of the world the arrangements for the preparation of teachers vary widely. In some countries "monitors" still receive short courses of training as their preparation to teach large classes of young children. In North America, and to an increasing extent in other developed countries, most teachers are university graduates who begin their teacher preparation after completing four to six years of secondary education. Between these extremes many other arrangements exist. At one level, which for present purposes might be called Normal School A, entry is prior to the usual age of completion of secondary education. Training is limited to the achievement of competence in teaching a range of the subjects taught at the primary level and does not last more than five years.

The second level, which may be called Normal School B, also begins prior to the age of completing secondary education, but usually after the "first certificate" at approximately age 16 or at the end of the period of compulsory schooling. This level provides combined courses of education and professional training, the former not necessarily limited to subjects taught at the primary level and extending beyond the usual age of completion of secondary education.

A third level, the college level, requires a full secondary education, usually ending at 18 but not necessarily with the same qualifications as are demanded of university entrants. Two- or three-year concurrent courses of general and professional education lead to the award of a teaching certificate, often valid for work in primary, intermediate, and lower secondary schools.

Finally, there is the university level, in which, after completing a full period of secondary education, the future teacher enters a multipurpose institution of higher education to follow three- to five-year courses of combined general education and professional training, the latter being either concurrent or consecutive, that lead to the award of a university degree and teaching qualification. Such qualification is considered valid for work at primary or secondary levels, or at both, according to the nature of the course followed.

Until the middle 1960s the normal-school pattern applied to students preparing for primary work in many European countries (Austria, Belgium, Spain, France, Italy, Iceland, The Netherlands, Switzerland, and Turkey), in Latin America, and in a number of Asian countries, although in many places there was more than one route to the attainment of qualified teacher status. The education and training of secondary school teachers was complicated by the general growth of secondary education for all. This encouraged the tendency to educate and train both primary and secondary teachers alongside one another in postsecondary colleges or in multipurpose universities. More recently there has been a widespread movement away from the types of training described here as Normal School A and B to the college and university patterns. But the fact that a country has adopted what has been called here the university pattern of training should not be taken to mean that all the institutions in which teachers are prepared are comparable to the pre-existing universities; some are devoted mainly to teacher preparation.

ISSUES AND PROBLEMS IN TEACHER EDUCATION

Elements of teacher education

In nearly all countries, courses of the Normal School B, college, and university categories contain three main elements. The first element is the study of one or more academic, cultural, or aesthetic subjects for the purpose both of continuing the student's own education and of providing him with knowledge to use in his subsequent teaching career. A second element is the study of educational principles, increasingly organized in terms of social science disciplines such as psychology, sociology, philosophy, and history. A third element consists of professional courses and school experience. Primary teachers may also receive instruction in the content and methods of subjects other than their own specialties that figure in the primary curriculum. In normal schools and colleges, and some universities, the three elements run parallel to one another, and the student is professionally committed from the outset of his course. Elsewhere, the study of educational processes and professional work (including school experience) may follow the completion of a period of academic study that the student has begun without any prior commitment to teaching as a career. There are still advanced countries where the possession of a university degree, without any qualification in education as such, is sufficient basis for the award of qualified teacher status. In England and Wales, for example, compulsory training for graduates, generally comprising two terms (six months) of professional and theoretical studies and a further three-month period of school experience, was scheduled to come into effect only in 1973.

General education. The sequencing, balance, content, and organization of general and specialist academic work, courses in education, and professional studies and teaching experience has been a subject of discussion since the earliest days of organized teacher education. The importance of the element of general education has been defended on various grounds. Sometimes such academic work may be highly specialized. Students in many colleges of education in England study only one principal subject, to which they devote about one-third of their total time, and teachers who graduate from universities have often pursued three-year courses for single-subject honours degrees. In the United States and elsewhere the academic element is broader, and the first two years of college or university work may embody a wide range of elective subjects from diverse disciplinary fields. Both patterns have their critics, the first because it produces narrow intellectual specialists, the second because it encourages dilettantism and inadequate depth. Where a pattern of electives is combined with a units/credits system, as in some universities in Japan and the United States, it is claimed that one result is an undesirable fragmentation of study and effort. In his influential *Education of American Teachers* (1963), James B. Conant recommended that half the course requirements of the four-year program of preparation for elementary teachers should be given over to general courses, a further quarter to an "area of concentration," and the remaining quarter to professional studies, including school experience. Prospective secondary teachers would spend still more time on the subjects they were preparing to teach, with less than 10 percent of their time devoted to practice teaching and special methods. Such a subject emphasis for secondary teachers can be found in many countries. In France the École Normale Supérieure still places freedom of study and the nurture of intellectual curiosity above questions of professional teacher training. Generally speaking, wherever there is a stress upon academic excellence and the achievement of high standards of scholarship, there is likely to be skepticism as to the claims of professional training for teaching. Oxford University had still not appointed a professor of education by the beginning of the 1970s.

Skepticism toward professional training

In countries where technical or vocational education forms an important part of secondary school provision, there have sometimes been specialist institutions for the training of teachers for this work. Such teachers tend to have lower status than the secondary school staff who teach academic subjects, and efforts have been made to upgrade the position of the teacher of agricultural and industrial arts, home economics, and handicrafts. Nearly all the universities in England and Wales that now offer the bachelor of education degree for college of education students include technical subjects within their list of approved options.

The element of educational courses in the teacher preparation program has been the object of criticism from academic specialists, defenders of liberal culture, and practical-minded professional educators. The growing range of speculation and empirical data generated by the burgeoning social sciences, philosophy, and history, have provided a rich ore from which those responsible for teacher preparation mined the materials they needed for the construction and legitimation of their pedagogic systems and principles. But such borrowing has done little to establish any very coherent system of educational ideas, or to provide the basis for a systematic theory of teaching adequate to sustain the variety and complexity of teacher preparation programs. In his *Evolution of American Educational Theory* (1964), C.J. Brauner was forced to conclude that

> middleman theorists, inexpert as scholars, had naïvely striven for some impossible synthesis that would be at once faithful to scholarship, useful to the practitioner, intelligible to the populace and thus comprehensive as a discipline, workable as a general method, and defensible as a social institution.

The study of educational principles. There has been much dispute as to whether the study of educational principles is to be seen as part of the liberal element in the course, contributing to the teacher's general education and personal development, or whether it is properly an adjunct to the professional sequence, serving to illuminate and enrich students' method courses and practical work. Where it was well done, the study of the philosophy, sociology, and history of education and of educational psychology clearly served both ends and also provided an introduction to a systematic exploration of human conduct and affairs that was both educationally defensible and important in its own right. But all too often it was not well done. As the field of the social sciences grew, it became increasingly difficult for those employed in teacher-preparing institutions to keep pace. In some places, student teachers could follow courses in psychology, sociology, and so on given by recognized authorities in their respective disciplines, and in all countries there were some prominent social scientists who themselves took a close and direct interest in educational matters. But, given the large number of institutions responsible for teacher preparation and the fact that the majority of their staff were necessarily recruited for their teaching competence rather than for their high academic qualifications, much of the teaching of educational principles tended to become out-of-date and secondhand.

In recent years there has been a revival of interest in the social sciences as an integral feature of teacher-education programs. This is partly a recognition of the popularity of studies of this kind among students, partly a reflection of their relevance in a time of rapid social and educational change, and partly a function of the larger supply of qualified social scientists available to teach them. There is now also becoming available a substantial volume of research material on problems such as the dynamics and correlates of children's learning, language development, differences in individual educability and response to teaching, and social class and educational opportunity. In his 1929 lecture, "The Sources of a Science of Education," John Dewey saw the elements of such a science being drawn out of other natural and social sciences, organized in relation to problems defined by the educational process. These hopes are now closer to realization.

Practical training. Professional and practical studies constitute the third major element in the teacher-preparation program. "Teaching practice" has always been important, initially carried out in the model or demonstration school attached to the normal school or college, later in the schools of the neighbourhood, and more recently in a variety of school, college, and community settings. The model and demonstration school was frequently criticized for the unreality of its teaching settings; some model schools attached to universities tended to become academically oriented and ceased to play an experimental role. But if there are advantages in practicing in more typical schools, there are also difficulties in relating the variety of experience thus attained to the purpose and content of the college course, particularly when there are discrepancies between the methods and approaches taught in the colleges and those that the student encounters in the school. In some countries, experienced teachers view the work of teacher-preparing institutions with a certain amount of disdain. It is sometimes claimed that college and university staff lack the recent, firsthand experience of schools that is needed if training is to be fully effective. Efforts have been made to reduce the separation between school and college; these include the transfer of college staff to periods of classroom teaching and of experienced teachers to college work, dual appointment to a college and to a school where the "teacher-tutor" assumes responsibility for supervision of the student's school-based work, the involvement of teachers' organizations in the determination of national policy on teacher education, the involvement of individual teachers in the government and committee work of teacher-preparing institutions, and the use of periods of school-based teacher education in which a tutor and group of student teachers are attached to a school or a number of schools for an extended period of observation, practical teaching, and theoretical study. Courses are also being devised in which periods of education, training, and paid employment in schools alternate with one another to make up a four- or five-year program.

Model schools

APPOINTMENT PROCEDURES AND PROBATIONARY REQUIREMENTS

Certification

Generally speaking, in federal countries such as the United States, Canada, and Australia, each state or province sets its own requirements for certification, which inevitably do much to shape the content and organization of the teacher-education programs. The variety of such regulations often means that teachers who have received their education and training in one province or state are not qualified to teach in schools elsewhere without satisfying additional requirements. In other countries, such as England and France, requirements are determined on a national basis. Responsibility for recommending the granting of qualified teacher status may, however, be delegated. In England this responsibility is exercised by regional consortia of colleges, local educational authorities, universities, and teacher interests known as area training organizations that were established after 1944.

There are likewise considerable variations among countries in the way in which teachers are appointed to their first posts after graduation from college or university. In a small number of countries, students have a completely free choice among all the schools of the type in which their training qualifies them to teach, and they make their applications directly to the school in which they wish to serve. A more common pattern is that of appointment to the service of a local, state, or provincial authority, which then places the teacher in a school where a suitable vacancy exists. In some places there is a tendency for beginning teachers to be placed in schools in more remote or less desirable areas. In countries that have universal military service, such as Israel, it is sometimes possible for trained teachers to satisfy military requirements by being drafted to a school of the government's choice.

Another aspect of the diversity of certification requirements is the extent to which teachers are permitted to undertake work in subjects other than those they specialized in at college or university. Generally speaking, where national and state rules exist they tend to be interpreted liberally during periods of teacher shortage and more stringently as the supply of teachers improves; it is often possible for a teacher to secure the additional qualifications required to undertake a greater variety of work by taking university summer sessions or other kinds of in-service courses.

IN-SERVICE TRAINING

Training on the job involves more than courses, conferences, and other organized study programs. Such efforts belong to a much broader system of communication whereby all those who are involved in the educational enterprise—teachers, administrators, research workers, curriculum-development specialists, teacher trainers—keep in touch with one another and with developments in their respective fields. One must therefore consider the media that are available for in-service education as well as institutional arrangements by means of which such training is provided.

Printed matter forms the most obvious kind of communication medium among teachers. In all countries there are both general and specialist educational journals and newspapers; educational bodies of various kinds issue their own newsletters, broadsheets, and bulletins. The volume of material published in this form has increased enormously. In some countries books, journal articles, and research reports are systematically abstracted and distributed, and some schools have their own library and information services.

Learning materials

A second group of media for in-service training includes lectures and related types of face-to-face instruction and discussion. Greater use is now being made of seminars, working parties, discussions, and other group activities that require a higher level of individual participation. Alongside these methods, a beginning has been made with the use of case studies and simulation materials. Among the advantages of such techniques are the high degree of personal involvement they encourage, the "realism" of the problems dealt with, a reduction in the didactic element (especially important in work with senior staff), and the opportunities for questions of theory and principle to arise in the discussion of actual teaching and administrative incidents.

Multimedia approaches to in-service studies are encouraged by closed-circuit and broadcast television facilities within individual school systems and local areas. The work that professional and specialist associations have long performed in bringing teachers together for the discussion of issues of mutual concern is now being extended by such developments as the establishment of teachers' centres in Britain. These help to disseminate a wide range of new educational practices and ideas, including those that derive from the teacher-controlled Schools Council for Curriculum and Examinations. In North America, Australia, the United Kingdom, Germany, and some other European countries, credit-bearing courses are now available for teachers through broadcast television, radio, and correspondence tuition.

The use of a wider range of media has diversified the institutional settings in which in-service teacher education is provided. Universities, colleges, teachers' centres, and teachers' homes are now among the places where the teacher can pursue his education and seek to improve his qualifications. Given the larger number of teachers on the staffs of many schools, there is also scope for school-based in-service education. A new idea or principle may find more ready acceptance within a group of like-minded people than when it must make its way against the organizational conservatism of a particular school. Department discussions, staff working parties, and other forms of school-based meetings enable matters of curriculum and organization to be discussed in depth, facilitate the induction of younger members of the profession, and help to limit the isolation of the teacher within the classroom.

Bridging the theory–practice gap

School-based in-service education has the important merit of recognizing that there is a gap between the ideas, techniques, and approaches that teachers acquire as a result of their training and the application of these ideas and approaches within the social system of the school. With the growth of team teaching and interdisciplinary work, and the reinterpretation of the teacher's role as an organizer and manager of learning resources rather than a solo performer on the classroom stage, the importance of bridging this gap will become increasingly important.

FUTURE DEVELOPMENTS IN TEACHER EDUCATION

Coming decades are likely to see continuing development and change in teacher education. Post-secondary and higher education may soon reach between a third and a half of the population in many advanced countries. The teacher must adjust to new developments in educational technology, the growth of human knowledge, and the problem of creating a relevant and appropriate curriculum from the enormous range of material available. There will be new understanding of how children develop and learn. The patterns of authority in society will continue to change, and it is likely that there will be a greater recognition of the importance of moral and personal education in a world of pluralistic values and goals. All these factors will affect the ways in which teachers are educated and trained.

In all countries, whether or not any fundamental institutional changes are contemplated, there are evidences of radical change in the structure of ideas and assumptions that underlie the preparation of teachers. But it is unlikely that coming decades will see the introduction of any comprehensive pedagogical system resembling those of the 19th century. No single theory of learning or teaching is likely to satisfy the diversity of individual needs and societal arrangements. (W.Ta.)

Teaching methods

THE TEACHER AND THE LEARNER

In the act of teaching there are two parties (the teacher and the taught) who work together in some program (the subject matter) designed to modify the learners' behaviour and experience in some way. It is necessary to begin, therefore, with observations about the learner, the teacher, and the subject matter and then to consider the significance of group life and the school. It will then be possible to consider the factors and theories involved in modifying a person's behaviour and understanding. These include theories of learning in education, of school and class organization, and of instructional media.

A child enters school with little if any attainment in written expression and leaves it capable of learning much from human culture. It was thought originally that this progress was just a matter of learning, memorizing, associating, and practicing. The work of psychologists has revealed, however, that the growth of the pupil's intellectual powers must include a large element of development through different phases, beginning with simple sensorimotor coordination; going on to the beginnings of symbolizing, helped by the growth of language and play; and then on to logical thought, provided the material is concrete; and, finally, in midadolescence, on to the power to examine problems comprehensively, to grasp their formal structure, and to evoke explanation. In his emotional life, the child progresses from direct, immediate, uninhibited reactions to more complex, less direct, and more circumspect responses. The physical growth of the child is so obvious as to need no comment. Any attempt to educate the child intellectually and emotionally and for action must take account of these characteristics. Education must pace development, not follow it and not ignore it. The components in the child's overall educational growth are physical and mental maturation, experience, formal teaching through language, and an urge in the learner to resolve discrepancies, anomalies, and dissonances in his experience.

What is required of a teacher is that he enjoy and be capable of sharing work programs with children, designed to modify their behaviour and experience. This means making relevant experience available to the student at the right time. The teacher must be mature, have humour with a sense of status, be firm yet unruffled, and be sympathetic but not overpersonal. With large classes, the teacher becomes a leader of a group, providing stimulating learning situations.

The subject matter taught also has a marked influence on the total teaching situation. It may be conveniently divided into broad headings of languages, humanities, sciences, mathematics, and arts. Although each group of subjects has something in common with others in terms of the demands it makes on the thinker, each area has also something quite specific in its mode of development. Languages call for verbal learning and production based on oral work, particularly during the early phases. The humanities call for an understanding of cause–effect relations of immediate and remote connections between persons and institutions and man in his environment. The sciences call for induction from experience, though deductive processes are required when the laws of science are formalized into mathematical terms. The humanities and sciences both depend on the ability of the learner to hypothesize. Mathematics calls for the ability to abstract, symbolize, and deduce. An interest in the formal and structural properties of the acts of counting and measuring is fundamental. Arts and literature call for a fairly free opportunity to explore and create.

Characteristics of the school community

A large part of the teacher's role is as a group leader, and the group life of the school and the classroom must influence the teaching situation. Group life shows itself in the dynamic structure of the class—including its manner of reaching group decisions, the hierarchy of its members, the existence of cliques and of isolated individuals—and in its morale and overall response to the school and the rest of the staff. The individual pupil also conducts himself under the influence of the group to which he belongs. His achievements and attitudes are subject to evaluation by the group, leading to support or ostracism, and he sets his standards according to these influences.

In many schools, the range of ages in any class is about one year, and the narrow range makes for some uniformity of subject-matter coverage. But in rural one- and two-teacher schools, groups of children may be heterogeneous by age and ability, and the mode of teaching has to cope with a number of smaller subunits moving along at different rates. The teacher's problem is to coordinate the work of these small, dissimilar groups in such a way that all get attention. Creative free activity has to be practiced by one group while another has more formal instruction from the teacher.

The effect of "streaming," or "tracking"—that is, selecting homogeneous groups by both age and intellectual ability—has promoted much inquiry. The practice evokes extreme opinions, ardent support, and vociferous condemnation. The case for uniformity is that putting a pupil with his intellectual peers makes teaching more effective and learning more acceptable. The case against it draws attention to its bad effects on the morale of those children in the lower streams. This view supports the heterogeneous class on the grounds that the strongest are not overforced, and the weakest gain from sharing with their abler fellows. Experimental evidence on the problem is bewilderingly diverse.

The school community is housed in a physical complex, and the conditions of classrooms, assembly places, and play areas and the existence (or nonexistence) of libraries, laboratories, art-and-craft rooms, and workshops all play their part in the effectiveness of the teaching–learning situation. Severe restrictions may be caused by the absence of library and laboratory services.

The social forces immediately outside the school community also influence the teaching situation. These emanate from home, neighbourhood, and wider social groupings. Teaching is a compact among several groups, including teachers, students, and parents, in the first place, with youth organizations and religious and lay groups playing a secondary role. The overall neighbourhood youth subculture also sets standards and attitudes that a teacher has to take into account in his work.

General objectives of teaching. The classification of the general objectives of teaching in terms of school subject matter is not sufficient to explain the ultimate ends of education. These include, essentially, the promotion of a well-integrated person capable of taking a responsible, active role in society. With such a purpose in mind, one may achieve more insight by choosing a psychological analysis of the objectives into the attainment of intellectual abilities and social insights (cognition), the learning of practical active skills (psychomotor learning), and the development of emotions, attitudes, and values (affective learning).

Development of cognitive, affective, and psychomotor learning

Cognitive growth begins at the level of the infant school, with the acquisition of early language and numerical capabilities, and continues increasingly to dominate education to the secondary and higher levels. But the learner is more than an enlarging reservoir of information. With this acquisition goes a growing power to generalize, abstract, infer, interpret, explain, apply, and create. Cognitive training produces a thinker–observer aware of the modes of thought and judgment making up human intellectual activity. In the final stages, the teacher aims at a thinker, critic, organizer, and creator.

In the development of psychomotor learning, the teacher is concerned with the promotion of coordinated skills and their creative use. Instruction begins with the acts of handwriting and plastic art play, characteristic of earlier years of schooling. It includes painting, games, workshop skills, and practical science. It has a high prestige value among the pupils themselves and the wider community.

The permeation of emotional learning throughout the whole educative process is not always obvious, in part because very often it is brought about incidentally. Teachers may be self-conscious and self-critical about the deliberate inculcation of emotional responses, which will provide the energy and a mainspring of social life. The acquisition and application of values and attitudes are most marked by the time of adolescence and dominate the general life of the young individual. Theoretical, aesthetic, social, economic, political, hedonistic, and religious values pervade the school curriculum. Literature, art, the humanities, and religious teaching are all directly involved, and the teaching of science and mathematics can bring about a positive attitude toward cognitive and theoretical values.

A person's emotional structure is the pattern of his values and attitudes. Under the influence of instruction and experience, this structure shows three kinds of change. First, the pupil learns to select those situations and problems to which he will make appropriate emotional responses. Second, in general, an increasing range of situations includes happenings more remote from the learner. At first, emotions are aroused by situations directly affecting the child, but as he becomes more mature he is increasingly involved in affairs and causes far removed from his own personal life. Third, his repertoire of emotional responses gradually becomes less immediate, expressive, and linked with physical activity.

The general design of instruction. The scientific analysis of educative processes has led to a more detailed examination of the total act of teaching, which is intended to make the teacher more aware of all that is involved in a piece of instruction.

Foreknowledge about students and objectives. The complete act of teaching involves more than the presentation and development of lesson material. Before he embarks on a fresh stage of instruction, the teacher must be reasonably clear about two things: (1) the capabilities, achievements, strengths and weaknesses, background, and interests of his learners; and (2) the short- and long-term objectives he hopes to achieve in his lesson and series of lessons. These curricular strategies will have to be put into effect in the light of what is known about the students and will result in the actual tactics of the teaching–learning situation.

Educational psychologists give much attention to diagnosing preinstructional achievements, particularly in the basic subjects of language and number, and to measuring intellectual ability in the form of reasoning power. There has been special emphasis on the idea of the student's readiness at various ages to grasp concepts of concrete and formal thought. Numerous agencies produce test material for these purposes, and in many countries the idea has been widely applied to selection for entry to secondary and higher schools; one of the purposes of so-called leaving examinations is to grade students as to their suitability for further stages of education. The teacher himself, however, can provide the most sensitive diagnoses and analyses of preinstructional capacity, and the existence of so much published material in no way diminishes the effectiveness of his responsibility.

The teaching–learning situation. In the actual instruction, a single lesson is usually a part of a longer sequence covering months or more. Each lesson, however, stands to some extent as a self-contained unit within a sequence. In addition, each lesson itself is a complex of smaller teaching–learning–thinking elements. The progress of a lesson may consist of a cycle of smaller units of shorter duration, each consisting of instruction by the teacher and construction by the learner—that is, alternating phases in which first the activity of the teacher and then that of the learner predominates.

The progress of lessons

The lesson or syllabus proper is thus not to be narrowly conceived of as "chalk and talk" instruction. It is better seen as a succession of periods of varying length of instruction by the teacher and of discovery, construction, and problem solving by the pupil. Although the student's own curiosity, experience, and observation are important, so is the cyclic activity of teacher and learner. The teacher selects, arranges, and partially predigests the material to be learned, and this is what is meant by guiding the learner's discovery and construction activity. It is a role the teacher cannot abrogate, and, even in curricula revised to give the learner greater opportunity to discover for himself, there is concealed a large degree of selecting and decision making by the teacher. This is what teaching is about.

Teachers must face the problem of how to maintain curiosity and interest as the chief motivative forces behind the learning. Sustained interest leads the student to set himself realistic standards of achievement. Vital intrinsic motivation may sometimes be supplemented by extrinsic rewards and standards originating from sources other than the student himself, such as examinations and outside incentives, but these latter are better regarded as props to support the attention of the learner and to augment his interest in the subject matter.

Assessment of results. At the end of the lesson proper or of any other unit or program of instruction, the teacher must assess its results before moving to the next cycle of teaching events. Assuming the occurrence of teaching–learning cycles of instruction-construction activity, it follows that there is a built-in process of frequent assessment during the progress of any period of teaching. The results of the small phases of the learner's problem solving provide at the same time both the assessment of past progress and the readiness for further development.

Progress over longer intervals of learning can be measured by more formal tests or examinations within the school or at local administrative level. Postinstructional assessment may have several purposes: to discover when classes or year groups have reached some minimum level of competence, to produce a measure of individual differences, or to diagnose individual learning–thinking difficulties. A wide variety of assessment can be used for this purpose, including the analysis of work produced in the course of learning, continuous assessments by the teachers, essay-type examinations, creative tasks, and objective tests. The content of the assessment material may also vary widely, ranging from that that asks for reproduction of learned material to that that evokes application, generalization, and transfer to new problem situations.

THE ORGANIZATION OF INSTRUCTION

Educational organization rests to some extent on psychological views about learning, but explicitly it is concerned with the grouping of pupils for educational experience and instruction.

Grading and streaming

Pupils in general are organized by age into what are usually termed grades, classes, or forms. Each school is also usually either comprehensive (containing students pursuing various academic, commercial, and vocational curricula) or based on the so-called dual plan (containing only students pursuing a particular curriculum). In some countries, this dual system is actually tripartite: there may be schools for classical academic study, schools for technical or vocational study, and schools for more generalized, "modern," diversified study. Whether comprehensive or dual-plan, schools frequently have some kind of streaming or multitracking whereby students are grouped according to ability so that there are separate classes for the less able and the more able.

Grading and streaming have recently come in for much criticism. There is a rigidity in the two systems that causes some educators uneasiness, particularly since total education is seen as more than achievement in school subjects. Some countries, notably the United States, have made a start in trying to solve this difficulty by introducing the nongraded school, in which grades are abolished and students are placed individually in "phases" for each subject, through which they progress at their own pace. A similar solution has been to ungrade students for certain basic subjects, such as mathematics and native language, but to have them rejoin their age peers for other school activities. In such systems there is, nevertheless, a kind of grading by intellectual ability, and egalitarians are apt still to be suspicious of them. There is scarcely any clear evidence of the effectiveness of the wholly nongraded system. It would seem probable that the optimum organization may be to combine grading with nongrading. Although this will involve constructing complex timetables, it will also offer the advantages of other, more rigid systems without introducing too many of their disadvantages. For one thing, retaining some grouping by age seems important as a link to extramural activities, in which age peers tend spontaneously to come together.

The modern interest in resources for learning has led to the concepts of general-purpose classrooms, open-plan teaching, and team teaching. The idea of general-purpose classrooms starts from the assumption that the school curriculum can be divided into a few large areas of allied intellectual interests, such as the humanities, languages, and sciences. The total resources available for teaching in each of these areas, including teachers, are then made available in one common teaching space, and ordinary classroom and lesson-period divisions disappear, to be replaced by a real mobility between teachers and learners as they make use of the different resources available, including library and laboratory facilities and various educational hardware (see below *Instructional media*). In the infant and primary schools, similar ideas are introduced in the open-plan system. At both the primary and the secondary levels, however, there is insufficient evidence on the effectiveness of the systems. The attitude and action of the teacher remains the strongest factor, and he may still require some privacy for his teaching.

Team teaching

Team teaching represents an attempt to make better use of every teacher's potential in any subject area, to create a flexible learning situation, and to make nonstreaming more effective. The normal class of 30 pupils with an individual subject teacher is replaced by a larger group of pupils and a team of teachers, who pool their efforts. Although the team plan may take several forms, it generally assumes some variety of the following elements: (1) large-group instruction, in which the total complement of some 50 to 150 students in the program is periodically taught by one teacher (either the same teacher or several teachers in rotation) in a lecture hall; (2) small-group instruction, which alternates with large-group instruction so as to allow small numbers of students and a member of the teaching team to discuss, report, and exchange ideas; (3) independent study, whereby students are given individual projects or library work; and (4) team planning sessions, in which, daily or weekly, the teachers plan, coordinate, report on, and evaluate their programs. The presumed benefits of team teaching are that it makes better use of each teacher's individual interests and strengths; that it avoids unnecessary replication, particularly in such basic subjects as native literature, in which ordinarily several classes led by different teachers cover the same ground; and that teaching in front of one's colleagues is a beneficial practice providing some evaluative feedback. Also, it is said that the less able children do not feel so segregated as in ordinary streamed classes; although they may gain little from the large-group sessions and individual projects, they seem to make real progress in the small seminar groups, without becoming overaware of their more limited capabilities. The reasons for this are obscure. In any event, the most obvious advantage of team teaching is its flexibility, in affording a great variety of possible combinations of student groupings and of educational resources. The major problem is that team teaching cannot be used in all subject areas. Although it may be useful in such areas as the humanities and the social sciences, its provision for lecture-size audiences does not aid the teaching of such subjects as mathematics, in which there are too many individual differences in ability. The same is true of arts and other subjects. Furthermore, without expert leadership, seminars are apt to degenerate into scenes of rather woolly discussions.

The grouping of children by ability, though still practiced, remains a problem. Formal tests are used to separate students according to their ability, and many people feel that separations by such means are neither reliable nor socially desirable. Even with regard to separating the mentally handicapped, there is growing opinion that wherever possible these children should be given basic instruction in special centres and remedial classes in schools for normal children. Handicapped and normal children would thereby share much of their education. Separation of the sexes is also declining in most countries, as the mixing of girls and boys comes to be recognized as healthy and socializing.

INSTRUCTIONAL MEDIA

In general, instructional media are seen by educators as aids rather than substitutions for the teacher. A teacher spends a disproportionate amount of his time in routine chores—in collecting and assigning books and materials and in marking—that could be partly obviated if aids could be so constructed as to free him to concentrate on the central job of promoting understanding, intellectual curiosity, and creative activity in the learner.

Speaking–listening media. In lectures and recordings, the teacher is able to set out his material as he thinks best, but usually the audience reception is weakly passive since there is not much opportunity for a two-way communication of ideas. Furthermore, in lectures, much of the students' energies may be taken up with note writing. This inhibits thinking about the material. Recordings enable one to store lecture material and to use it on occasions when a teacher is not available, but they are rather detached for young learners and seem to evoke better results with older students.

Language laboratories

Language laboratories are study rooms equipped with electronic sound-reproduction devices, enabling students to hear model pronunciations of foreign languages and to record and hear their own voices as they engage in pattern drills. Most laboratories provide a master control board that permits a teacher to listen to and correct any student individually. Many are equipped to use filmstrips or motion pictures simultaneously with the tape recorders. These laboratories are effective modes of operant learning, and, after a minimum vocabulary and syntax have been established, the learning can be converted into a stimulating form of problem solving.

Visual and observational media. Useful visual materials include objects and models, diagrams, charts, graphs, cartoons, and posters; maps, globes, and sand tables for illustrating topographical items; pictures, slides, filmstrips, motion pictures, and television. Facilities include blackboards, bulletin boards, display cases, tables and areas, museums, flannel boards, and electric boards. Such activities as field trips and the use of visiting authorities (usually called resource people) are considered part of visual and observational programs, and even demonstrations, dramatizations, experiments, and creative activities are usually included.

In general, pictures and diagrams, fieldwork, and contrived experiments and observations are all used as concrete leads to the generalizing, abstracting, and explaining that constitutes human learning. To fulfil this function, however, their use must be accompanied by interpretation by an adult mind.

The teacher must offer careful elaboration and discussion, for children's and adolescents' powers to interpret and infer often go astray and thus must be carefully guided. Visual material by itself may even be a hindrance; a scattering of pretty pictures through a history text, for example, does not necessarily produce a better understanding of history. Similar difficulties are inherent in fieldwork—geographical, biological, archaeological, and geological. What is observed rarely gives the whole story and, in the case of archaeological and geological fieldwork, provides an incomplete picture of the past. The teacher must fill in the gaps or somehow lead his students to do so.

Reading–writing media. Reading and writing have formed the staple of traditional education. This assumes sophisticated language attainments and the capacity to think formally and respond to another mind, for a textbook is essentially a mode of communication between a remote teacher and a reader. The material in a textbook is a sample of a subject area, simplified to a level suitable for the reader. Because the sampling in both the text and the exercise might be haphazard, and there can be no feedback to the writer, the teacher has to take on the writer's responsibilities.

Programmed instruction

Programmed learning is a newer form of reading and writing. The most basic form of programmed instruction—called linear programming—analyzes a subject into its component parts and arranges the parts in sequential learning order. At each step in his reading, the student is required to make a response and is told immediately whether or not the response is correct. The program is usually structured so that right answers are apt to be extremely frequent (perhaps 95 percent of the time)—in order, so the theory goes, to encourage the student and give him a feeling of success. In another kind of programmed instruction—called branching programming—the student is given a piece of information, provided with alternative answers to questions, and, on the basis of his decision, detoured, if necessary, to remedial study or sent on to the next section of the program. The two types of program differ fundamentally in their attitudes toward errors and the use of them. The brancher uses them to further the learning; the linearist avoids them. The chief value of programmed instruction in general is that it allows a student to learn at his own pace, without much teacher supervision. Its chief defect is that it can quickly become dull and mechanical for the student.

Computer-based instruction. The large storage and calculating capacities of the computer suggest great potential for its use in the classroom. It can give instructions to the learner, call for responses, feed back the results, and modify his further learning accordingly. The computer can also be used to measure each student's attainments, compare them with past performances, and then advise teachers on what parts of the curriculum they should follow next.

In a fully computer-assisted instruction program, the computer takes over from the teacher in providing the learner with drill, practice, and revision, as well as testing and diagnosis. The form of the teaching may be simply linear or branching, or it can be extended to thinking and problem solving by simulation. The limitations at the moment centre on the learner's responses, which are limited to a prescribed set of multiple choices. Free, creative responses, which one associates with the best of classroom situations, cannot yet be accommodated.

Teaching theories: educational psychology

Traditional theories. *Mental-discipline theories.* The earliest mental-discipline theories of teaching were based on a premise that the main justification for teaching anything is not for itself but for what it trains—intelligence, attitudes, and values. By choosing the right material and by emphasizing rote methods of learning, according to this theory, one disciplines the mind and produces a better intellect.

In classical times, the ideal product of education was held to be a citizen trained in the disciplined study of a restricted number of subjects—grammar, logic, rhetoric, arithmetic, geometry, music and astronomy. The mode of learning was based on imitation and memorizing, and there was heavy emphasis on the intellectual authority of the teacher, as in the socratic method of question and answer. In later centuries, it was further taken for granted that the study of Greco-Roman literature and philosophy would have a liberalizing effect on the student.

In the hands of the Renaissance Dutch philosopher Erasmus and the Jesuit Fathers, this method of instruction took more sensitive account of the psychological characteristics of young learners. Understanding had to precede learning, and, according to the Jesuits, the teacher's first task was careful preparation of the material to be taught (the prelection). But even with this greater awareness of the learner's needs, the concept of mental discipline still underlay the whole process of instruction. Present-day critics of this classical humanistic approach would challenge the alleged power of mental discipline and the rather exclusive value of Greco-Roman thought.

The theory of faculty psychology

The theory of learning involving mental discipline is more commonly associated with Aristotle's "faculty psychology", by which the mind is understood to be composed of a number of faculties, each of which is considered to be relatively independent of the others. The principle had its origin in a theory that classified mental and spiritual life in terms of functions of the soul: knowing, feeling, hungering, reasoning, and doing. From the Middle Ages to the early 19th century, the number of recognized faculties grew and included those of judgment, duty, perception, and conception. Since these were associated with certain parts of the cranium by the phrenologists, it was a natural step to assume that learning would consist of the exercise of these "parts," or mental capabilities (though the education of the senses also had a role, in initiating the rational cognitive processes). Certain school subjects were thought to have particular value as agents for exercising certain faculties. Geometry trained the faculty of reason, and history trained the memory. School subjects came to be valuable as much for what faculties they trained as for their own intrinsic worth. This is the learning theory of formal discipline.

Psychological faculties, used as categories, no doubt influenced the study of so-called mental factors. When different cognitive tests are given and the results compared, similarities are found among all the tests and among smaller groups of them. The bases for the similarities are identified as mental factors, including the ideas of intelligence, reasoning, memory, verbal ability, number capacity, and spatial intelligence. The existence of common mental factors underlying different school subjects would support the idea of formal discipline and would lead to the notion of transfer of training, by which exercise in one school subject leads to improvements in learning of another. The transferred elements could be common facts, learning habits, methods of thinking, attitudes, and values. Though much empirical research has been done on transfer of learning, it has yielded mixed results. Some workers hold that transfer has been possible only insofar as there have been identical elements, and even those who claim a transfer of methods generally insist that transfer has little chance of success unless it is actively explained and applied. Learners have to apply methods consciously to the new field in order to succeed. The opposing view would be that each subject is unique and requires its own mode of thought. A more realistic view may be intermediate—namely, that there is both a common and a specific element in each intellectual field, that mental discipline or transfer of training is to some degree possible but only insofar as the similarities and analogies are utilized, that the process is deliberate, and that a residue of specific subject matter remains in each field. This requires specific learning.

Naturalistic theories. A few educational theorists view the education of the child as an unfolding process. The child develops inevitably as a product of nature, and the main function of the teacher is to provide the optimum conditions for this development. This leads to the theory that the child's experience is the essential thing. A Swiss educator, J.H. Pestalozzi, was a leading theorist in this field, and his practical schemes were designed to provide the most appropriate experience for the child's development. In a sense, the modern revival of the potency of experience is an acknowledgement of the developmental element in learning.

Naturalistic emphasis on creativity

Jean-Jacques Rousseau also started from the assumption that man conforms to nature. Since, more than Pestalozzi, he assumed the certainty of a spontaneous development of powers and faculties, he urged that any form of constraint was to be avoided. Thus it has been held that he saw man as a noble savage growing in isolation in a state of nature. But nature also means a social life. The consequences of Rousseau's basic view have been (1) a reduced emphasis on knowing and greater emphasis on acting and doing, (2) a promotion of positive interests in learning, and (3) an encouragement of the child to depend on his own resources. In their purest form, naturalistic theories are clearly inadequate in the modern world of technology, but their emphasis on spontaneous child activity, as opposed to excessive formal instruction, is a valuable component of the educational process.

Apperception theories. Another theory assumed that human learning consisted essentially of building up associations between different ideas and experiences; the mind, in accordance with the ideas of the 17th-century English philosopher John Locke, was assumed to be at first devoid of ideas. The 19th-century German philosopher Johann Herbart made an important contribution by providing a mental mechanism that determined which ideas would become conscious and which would be left in the subconscious, to be called upon if circumstances warranted it. This was the mechanism of apperception, by which new ideas became associated with existing ideas to form a matrix of association ideas called the apperception mass. New ideas were thus assimilated to the old. A Swiss psychologist, Jean Piaget, argued that such assimilation was not enough, that accommodation of the established ideas to the new experiences was also required.

In any event, ideas such as Herbart's were translated into a sequence of steps presumed to be required to carry out a lesson:

1. Preparation, whereby the teacher starts the lesson with something already known to the class
2. Presentation, introducing new material
3. Association, whereby the new is compared with the old and connected (the stage of apperception)
4. Generalization, whereby the teacher presents other instances of the new idea
5. Application, whereby the ideas are applied to further material, carried out by the child individually (a problem-solving phase)

Though these five steps give the teacher a clear role, they constitute a form of intellectual dominance and could lead to stereotyped lessons restricting the spontaneous creative learning by the pupil. Contemporary curricular revisions, on the contrary, aim at promoting pupil activity.

Conditioning and behaviourist theories. *Classical and operant conditioning.* In the act of classical conditioning, the learner comes to respond to stimuli other than the one originally calling for the response (as when dogs are taught to salivate at the sound of a bell). One says in such a situation that a new stimulus is learned. In the human situation, learning to recognize the name of an object or a foreign word constitutes a simple instance of stimulus learning. Such an event is called sign learning, because, in knowing the sign for something, a person to some extent makes a response to the sign similar to that that he would make to the object itself. Learning new vocabularies, new terms and conventions, or algebraic and chemical symbols all involve some degree of classical conditioning. It is thought probable that one trains the emotions in the same way, for a person may learn to feel pleasure not only when he meets the original situation causing the pleasure but also when he sees some wider context associated with it. This idea is important in school teaching and helps in a general way to explain children's positive and negative feelings toward school, feelings that may have arisen originally from difficulties in learning specific school subjects.

Stimulus learning

Operant, or instrumental, conditioning is so-called because, in making his response, the learner provides the instrument by which a problem is solved. This learning is more important to schoolwork, for teachers are concerned ultimately with drawing forth new responses from their students. Learning is active, and, after the early acquisition of vocabulary, terminology, and rules (by stimulus learning), the learner must use this material in problem-solving responses. By reinforcement (*e.g.*, a reward), both sorts of learning can be combined.

Conditioning theories are not wholly adequate to explain school learning, since the learner is not simply a responder. Intervening between the stimulus and the response is the learner's total conscious structure, made up of the results of experience, previous teaching, attitudes, and his own capacity to comment upon and edit his own response. Simple reinforcement is also inadequate in that the stimulus and the response are not linked in an exclusive one-to-one basis. Several stimuli may evoke a single response, and several responses may be made to a particular stimulus. These form the behavioral bases for the formation of concepts and transfer effects from one topic to another. The two basic modes of stimulus-response learning provide a ground analysis of school learning, but the complexity of academic achievement calls for much elaboration on the simple model.

Cognitive theories. Cognitive theories are appropriate to the school situation, for they are concerned with knowing and thinking. They assume that perceiving and doing, shown in manipulation and play, precede the capacity to symbolize, which in turn prepares for comprehensive understanding. Although the sequence of motor-perceptual experience followed by symbolic representation has been advocated for a long time, Jean Piaget offered the first penetrating account of this kind of intellectual growth. His views have exercised great influence on educators.

Cognitive theories of learning also assume that the complete act of thought follows a fairly common sequence, as follows: arousal of intellectual interest; preliminary exploration of the problem; formulation of ideas, explanations, or hypotheses; selection of appropriate ideas; and verification of their suitability.

The emphasis of optimum sequence and pacing of learning

Teaching based on cognitive theories of learning recognizes, first, the growth in quality of intellectual activity and capitalizes on this knowledge by organizing instruction to anticipate the next stage in development but does not await it; otherwise there would be no instruction; *i.e.*, instruction should pace development but not outstrip it. Second, it seeks to tune the learning situation to the sequences of the complete act of thought and to arrange, simplify, and organize the subject matter accordingly. Some educators emphasize strongly the arousal phase; in many modern science curricula there is, thus, the idea of inquiry training, which tries to arouse in the child a spontaneous rather than a directed interest. Other educators are concerned more with the middle intellectual phases of the thinking sequence—especially the playing with hypotheses or hunches and the working with organizing ideas and concepts.

Once started, the motivation of cognitive learning depends less on notions of reinforcement and more on standards of intellectual achievement generated by the learner himself. Accordingly, the learner may begin to have aspirations and to set himself future standards that are influenced by his past performances and those of his fellows.

Maturation and readiness theories. Readiness theories of learning lean heavily on the concept of maturation in stages of biological and mental development. It is assumed that a child passes through all stages of development in reaching maturity. The teacher finds out what a child is ready for and then devises appropriate materials and methods. Much of the work on reading skills, for instance, makes use of the readiness concept. The Italian educator Maria Montessori claimed that "periods of sensitivity," corresponding to certain ages, exist when a child's interest and mental capacity are best suited to aquiring knowledge of such things as textures and colours, tidiness, and language.

Insofar as Piaget offered a learning theory, it was based on the idea of readiness. But his approach to development does not overemphasize maturation and readiness, for he pointed out that, after the first few months of life, maturation is marginal in its effects, whereas experience is essential. Development through different intellectual phases, he believed, is necessarily coincident with relevant active experience; readiness is actively promoted, not passively entered, and the teacher must endeavour to be a step ahead of any particular level of readiness.

Structural theories. The second half of the 20th century saw a revival of the concept of the structured wholeness of experience, which Gestalt psychologists had first introduced early in the century. The whole of experience, in this view, is more than the sum of its parts. In educational terms, a new experience—such as a new historical text, an exposition in science, or a problem rider in geometry—begins by seeming relatively formless and unstructured. The learner, who does not yet know his way about the material, begins by seizing upon what appear to him to be important features or figures. He then reformulates the experience in these new terms. The insight gradually becomes more and more structured until finally he reaches an understanding or a solution to the problem. It may be that, in all these processes, the learner may try anything he can think of, usually in a haphazard way.

Learning as an act of structuring and relating

Piaget improved upon Gestalt notions by suggesting a thought structure of a more adaptable nature—one that becomes more differentiated and intuitive with experience. He listed three psychological properties of a structure: wholeness, relationship between parts, and the principle of homeostasis, whereby a mental structure adjusts itself to new experience by assimilation and accommodation. This kind of structuralism found quite independent advocates in other fields. In language, for example, an American, Noam Chomsky, believes that there are innate language structures in the young individual, just as Piaget insists that there are thought structures.

A belief in the structural nature of experience would conceive of the teacher as an encourager, example provider, coanalyzer, and cobuilder of mental structures that originate in the learner in a relatively undifferentiated state. The learner is assumed to be active in forming structures and to be making the best he can of the situation he experiences. The teacher's task is to help and moderate this process of the learner's active construction. This notion works easily and well with able children but entails careful selection with less able students.

Others have also stressed the structural nature of advanced cognitive learning. Each area of human knowledge, in this view, is said to have its own unique structure composed of its concepts and their relationships and its own basic modes of progress. It is suggested that teaching a school subject should not lead to too much tampering with the inherent structural order of the subject but should follow the structure and lines of development of the subject itself. Teaching should not be contrived and artificial. Thus, economics should be taught as an economist views it or physics as a physicist views it or language as a linguist views it. Although such ideas are generally attractive, they have not been widely translated with any success into actual school practice. (E.A.P./Ed.)

BIBLIOGRAPHY. General works on teaching include UNESCO, *Statistical Yearbook* (1952–), an annual report including the latest data on teachers throughout the world; A.M. CARR-SAUNDERS and P.A. WILSON, *The Professions* (1933, reissued 1964), a standard work; R.L. EBEL (ed.), *Encyclopedia of Educational Research,* 4th ed. (1969), containing summary articles on teachers in the United States, under various headings; NATIONAL EDUCATION ASSOCIATION, *Today's Education* (bimonthly), a periodical for and about public-school teachers; AMERICAN ASSOCIATION OF UNIVERSITY PROFESSORS, *Academe* (8/yr.), includes reports on salaries and academic freedom of teachers in higher education. Special questions are addressed in MARTHA M. MCCARTHY and NELDA H. CAMBRON, *Public School Law* (1981), discussing constitutional rights of teachers; WAYNE J. URBAN, *Why Teachers Organized* (1982), a history of the teacher union movement; NANCY HOFFMAN, *Woman's "True" Profession: Voices from the History of Teaching* (1971); and LLOYD DUCK, *Teaching with Charisma* (1981), exploring different teaching styles.

A useful recent review of teacher education, on a comparative and international scale, is EDMUND J. KING, *The Education of Teachers* (1970). More detailed comparative perspectives are provided in GEORGE Z.F. BEREDAY and JOSEPH A. LAUWERYS (eds.), *The Education and Training of Teachers, The Yearbook of Education* (1963). J.B. CONANT, *The Education of American Teachers* (1963); and J.D. KOERNER, *The Miseducation of American Teachers* (1963), provide contrasting mid-century perspectives on teacher education in the United States. Similar contrasts for Great Britain may be found in contributions to W. TAYLOR (ed.), *Towards a Policy for the Education of Teachers* (1969). Historical developments for the U.S. are surveyed in W.S. MONROE, *Teaching Learning Theory and Teacher Education, 1890 to 1950* (1952); M.L. BORROWMAN, *The Liberal and the Technical in Teacher Education* (1956); and L.A. CREMIN, *The Transformation of the School: Progressivism in American Education, 1876–1956* (1961); and for England in R.W. RICH, *The Training of Teachers in England and Wales During the Nineteenth Century* (1933); and W. TAYLOR, *Society and the Education of Teachers* (1969). European provision for teacher education is reviewed in J. MAJAULT, *Teacher Training* (1965), in the Council of Europe series "Education in Europe." The Organization for Economic Cooperation and Development (OECD) issued between 1968 and 1970 a series of "Studies on Teachers," which cover all the western European countries, the United States, Canada, and Japan. Recommendations for the reform of teacher education in England and Wales are embodied in the *Report of the Committee of Inquiry on the Training of Teachers* (1972). Teacher education in developing countries is discussed in C. BEEBY, *The Quality of Education in Developing Countries* (1966); and PHILIP H. COOMBES, *The World Educational Crisis* (1967). A.J. ENGEL, *From Clergyman to Don: The Rise of the Academic Profession in Nineteenth-Century Oxford* (1983), is a historical study; FANNIE R. SHAFTEL and GEORGE SHAFTEL, *Role Playing in the Curriculum,* 2nd ed. (1982), explores applications of different techniques in teachers' training.

For teaching methods and theories, see B.S. BLOOM (ed.), *Taxonomy of Educational Objectives: The Classification of Educational Goals,* Handbook 1, *Cognitive Domain* (1956), a comprehensive analysis of the cognitive objectives of education—*i.e.,* those concerned with understanding and interpreting human knowledge; J.S. BRUBACHER, *A History of the Problems of Education,* 2nd ed. (1966), a survey of all aspects of education, particularly valuable for locating information about the theories of education from Greco-Roman times to the present; J.S. BRUNER, *Toward a Theory of Instruction* (1966), Bruner's attempt to translate his ideas about cognitive development into a theory of school instruction, it should be read along with Bruner's earlier *Process of Education* (1960); J.H. FLAVELL, *The Developmental Psychology of Jean Piaget* (1963), a constructive and useful analysis of the entire work, assumptions, methods, and results of the research of Jean Piaget and his coworkers; E.R. HILGARD and G.H. BOWER, *Theories of Learning,* 3rd ed. (1966), a standard work on learning theories, strong not only on behaviourist theories in which the authors deal with every nuance but also on instinct theories and those of the Gestalt, cognitive, and functional schools; R.R. RUSK, *The Doctrines of the Great Educators,* 3rd ed. (1965), a clear account of the contributions to educational theory by leading exponents from early times; L.C. TAYLOR, *Resources for Learning* (1971), a popular discursive comment on the resources for learning, including the role of the teacher, the organization of learning, the educational hardware, and various other modes of learning classes and schools. Methods of theory and practice of training are also discussed in B. ROBERT TABACHNIK, THOMAS S. POPKEWITZ, and BEATRICE BEACH SZEKELY (eds.), *Studying, Teaching, and Learning: Trends in Soviet and American Research* (1981); ALFRED BORK, *Learning with Computers* (1981); D. BOB GOWIN, *Educating* (1981); and MARVA COLLINS and CIVIA TAMARKIN, *Marva Collins' Way* (1982).

The History of Technology

Technology may be defined as the systematic study of techniques for making and doing things. The term itself, a combination of the Greek *technē,* "art, craft," with *logos,* "word, speech," meant in Greece a discourse on the arts, both fine and applied. When it first appeared in English in the 17th century, it was used to mean a discussion of the applied arts only, and gradually these "arts" themselves came to be the object of the designation. By the early 20th century, the term embraced a growing range of means, processes, and ideas in addition to tools and machines. By the second half of the century, technology was defined by such phrases as "the means or activity by which man seeks to change or manipulate his environment." Even such broad definitions have been criticized by observers who point out the increasing difficulty of distinguishing between scientific inquiry and technological activity.

A highly compressed account of the history of technology such as this one must adopt a rigorous methodological pattern if it is to do justice to the subject without grossly distorting it one way or another. The plan followed in the present article is primarily chronological, tracing the development of technology through phases that succeed each other in time. Obviously, the division between phases is to a large extent arbitrary. One factor in the weighting has been the enormous acceleration of Western technological development in recent centuries; Eastern technology is considered in this article in the main only as it relates to the development of modern technology.

Within each chronological phase a standard method has been adopted for surveying the technological experience and innovations. This begins with a brief review of the general social conditions of the period under discussion, and then goes on to consider the dominant materials and sources of power of the period, and their application to food production, manufacturing industry, building construction, transport and communications, military technology, and medical technology. In a final section the sociocultural consequences of technological change in the period are examined. This framework is modified according to the particular requirements of every period—discussions of new materials, for instance, occupy a substantial place in the accounts of earlier phases when new metals were being introduced but are comparatively unimportant in descriptions of some of the later phases—but the general pattern is retained throughout. One key factor that does not fit easily into this pattern is that of the development of tools. It has seemed most convenient to relate these to the study of materials, rather than to any particular application, but it has not been possible to be completely consistent in this treatment. For further discussion of particular areas of technological development, see the articles ELECTRONICS; EXPLORATION; FOOD PROCESSING; INFORMATION PROCESSING AND INFORMATION SYSTEMS; PUBLIC WORKS; TELECOMMUNICATIONS SYSTEMS; TOOLS; TRANSPORTATION.

This article is divided into the following sections:

General considerations

Essentially, techniques are methods of creating new tools and products of tools, and the capacity for constructing such artifacts is a determining characteristic of manlike species. Other species make artifacts: bees build elaborate hives to deposit their honey, birds make nests, and beavers build dams. But these attributes are the result of patterns of instinctive behaviour and cannot be varied to suit rapidly changing circumstances. Man, in contrast with other species, does not possess highly developed instinctive reactions but does have the capacity to think systematically and creatively about techniques. He can thus innovate and consciously modify his environment in a way no other species has achieved. An ape may on occasion use a stick to beat bananas from a tree: a man can fashion the stick into a cutting tool and remove a whole bunch of bananas. Somewhere in the transition between the two, the hominid, or the first manlike species, emerges. By virtue of his nature as a toolmaker, man is therefore a technologist from the beginning, and the history of technology encompasses the whole evolution of man.

In using his rational faculties to devise techniques and modify his environment, man has attacked problems other than those of survival and the production of wealth with which the term technology is usually associated today. The technique of language, for example, involves the manipulation of sounds and symbols in a meaningful way, and similarly the techniques of artistic and ritual creativity represent other aspects of the technological incentive. This article does not deal with these cultural and religious techniques, but it is valuable to establish their relationship at the outset because the history of technology reveals a profound interaction between the incentives and opportunities of technological innovation on the one hand and the sociocultural conditions of the human group within which they occur on the other.

Social involvement in technological advances. An awareness of this interaction is important in surveying the development of technology through successive civilizations. To simplify the relationship as much as possible, there are three points at which there must be some social involvement in technological innovation: social need, social resources, and a sympathetic social ethos. In default of any of these factors it is unlikely that a technological innovation will be widely adopted or be successful.

The sense of social need must be strongly felt, or people will not be prepared to devote resources to a technological innovation. The thing needed may be a more efficient cutting tool, a more powerful lifting device, a laboursaving machine, or a means of utilizing new fuels or a new source of energy. Or, because military needs have always provided a stimulus to technological innovation, it may take the form of a requirement for better weapons. In modern societies, needs have been generated by advertising. Whatever the source of social need, it is essential that enough people be conscious of it to provide a market for an artifact or commodity that can meet the need.

Why some inventions fail

Social resources are similarly an indispensable prerequisite to a successful innovation. Many inventions have foundered because the social resources vital for their realization—the capital, materials, and skilled personnel—were not available. The notebooks of Leonardo da Vinci are full of ideas for helicopters, submarines, and airplanes, but few of these reached even the model stage because resources of one sort or another were lacking. The resource of capital involves the existence of surplus productivity and an organization capable of directing the available wealth into channels in which the inventor can use it. The resource of materials involves the availability of appropriate metallurgical, ceramic, plastic, or textile substances that can perform whatever functions a new invention requires of them. The resource of skilled personnel implies the presence of technicians capable of constructing new artifacts and devising novel processes. A society, in short, has to be well primed with suitable resources in order to sustain technological innovation.

A sympathetic social ethos implies an environment receptive to new ideas, one in which the dominant social groups are prepared to consider innovation seriously. Such receptivity may be limited to specific fields of innovation—for example, improvements in weapons or in navigational techniques—or it may take the form of a more generalized attitude of inquiry, as was the case among the industrial middle classes in Britain during the 18th century, who were willing to cultivate new ideas and inventors, the breeders of such ideas. Whatever the psychological basis of inventive genius, there can be no doubt that the existence of socially important groups willing to encourage inventors and to use their ideas has been a crucial factor in the history of technology.

The rationality of technology

Social conditions are thus of the utmost importance in the development of new techniques, some of which will be considered below in more detail. It is worthwhile, however, to register another explanatory note. This concerns the rationality of technology. It has already been observed that technology involves the application of reason to techniques, and in the 20th century it has come to be regarded as almost axiomatic that technology is a rational activity stemming from the traditions of modern science. Nevertheless, it should be observed that technology, in the sense in which the term is being used here, is much older than science, and also that techniques have tended to ossify over centuries of practice or to become diverted into such para-rational exercises as alchemy. Some techniques became so complex, often depending upon processes of chemical change that were not understood even when they were widely practiced, that technology sometimes became itself a "mystery" or cult into which an apprentice had to be initiated like a priest into holy orders, and in which it was more important to copy an ancient formula than to innovate. The modern philosophy of progress cannot be read back into the history of technology; for most of its long existence technology has been virtually stagnant, mysterious, and even irrational. It is not fanciful to see some lingering fragments of this powerful technological tradition in the modern world, and there is more than an element of irrationality in the contemporary dilemma of a highly technological society contemplating the likelihood that it will use its sophisticated techniques in order to accomplish its own destruction. It is thus necessary to beware of overfacile identification of technology with the "progressive" forces in contemporary civilization.

On the other hand it is impossible to deny that there is a progressive element in technology, as it is clear from the most elementary survey that the acquisition of techniques is a cumulative matter, in which each generation inherits a stock of techniques on which it can build if it chooses and if social conditions permit. Over a long period of time the history of technology inevitably highlights the moments of innovation that show this cumulative quality as some societies advance, stage by stage, from comparatively primitive to more sophisticated techniques. But although this development has occurred and is still going on, it is not intrinsic to the nature of technology that such a process of accumulation should occur, and it has certainly not been an inevitable development. The fact that many societies have remained stagnant for long periods of time, even at quite developed stages of technological evolution, and that some have actually regressed and lost the accumulated techniques passed on to them, demonstrates the ambiguous nature of technology and the critical importance of its relationship with other social factors.

Modes of technological transmission. Another aspect of the cumulative character of technology that will require further investigation is the manner of transmission of technological innovations. This is an elusive problem, and it is necessary to accept the phenomenon of simultaneous or parallel invention in cases in which there is insufficient evidence to show the transmission of ideas in one direction or another. The mechanics of their transmission have been enormously improved in recent centuries by the printing press and other means of communication and also by the increased facility with which travelers visit the sources of innovation and carry ideas back to their own homes. Traditionally, however, the major mode of transmission has been the movement of artifacts and craftsmen. Trade in artifacts has ensured their widespread distribution and encouraged imitation. Even more important, the migration of craftsmen—whether the itinerant metalworkers of early civilizations or the German rocket engineers whose expert knowledge was acquired by both the Soviet Union and the United States after World War II—has promoted the spread of new technologies.

Historical methodology

The evidence for such processes of technological transmission is a reminder that the material for the study of the history of technology comes from a variety of sources. Much of it relies, like any historical examination, on documentary matter, although this is sparse for the early civilizations because of the general lack of interest in technology on the part of scribes and chroniclers. For these societies, therefore, and for the many millennia of earlier unrecorded history in which slow but substantial technological advances were made, it is necessary to rely heavily upon archaeological evidence. Even in connection with the recent past, the historical understanding of the processes of rapid industrialization can be made deeper and more vivid by the study of "industrial archaeology." Much valuable material of this nature has been accumulated in museums, and even more remains in the place of its use for the observation of the field worker. The historian of technology must be prepared to use all these sources, and to call upon the skills of the archaeologist, the engineer, the architect, and other specialists as appropriate.

Technology in the ancient world

THE BEGINNINGS—STONE AGE TECHNOLOGY (TO C. 3000 BC)

Origins of technology

The identification of the history of technology with the history of manlike species does not help in fixing a precise point for its origin, because the estimates of prehistorians and anthropologists concerning the emergence of human species vary so widely. Animals occasionally use natural tools such as sticks or stones, and the creature that became man doubtless did the same for hundreds of millennia before the first giant step of fashioning his own tools. Even then it was an interminable time before he put such toolmaking on a regular basis, and still more aeons passed as he arrived at the successive stages of standardizing his simple stone choppers and pounders and of manufacturing them—that is, providing sites and assigning specialists to the work. A degree of specialization in toolmaking was achieved by the time of Neanderthal man (70,000 BC); more advanced tools, requiring assemblage of head and haft, were produced by Cro-Magnon *Homo sapiens* (perhaps as early as 35,000 BC), while the application of mechanical principles was achieved by pottery-making Neolithic man (6000 BC) and by Metal Age man (about 3000 BC).

Earliest communities. For all except approximately the last 10,000 years, man has lived almost entirely in small nomadic communities, dependent for survival on his skill in gathering food by hunting and fishing and in avoiding predators. It is reasonable to suppose that most of these communities developed in tropical latitudes, especially in Africa, where climatic conditions are most favourable to a creature with such poor bodily protection as man. It is also reasonable to suppose that tribes of men moved out thence into the subtropical regions and eventually into the landmass of Eurasia, although their colonization of this region must have been severely limited by the successive periods of glaciation, which rendered large parts of it inhospitable and even uninhabitable, even though man has shown remarkable versatility in adapting to such unfavourable conditions.

The Neolithic Revolution. Toward the end of the last ice age, some 15,000 to 20,000 years ago, a few of the human communities that were most favoured by geography and climate began to make the transition from the long period of Paleolithic, or Old Stone Age, savagery to a more settled way of life depending on animal husbandry and agriculture. This period of transition, the Neolithic Period, or New Stone Age, led eventually to a marked rise in population, to a growth in the size of communities, and to the beginnings of town life. It is sometimes referred to as the Neolithic Revolution because the speed of technological innovation increased so greatly and the social and political organization of human groups underwent a corresponding increase in complexity. To understand the beginnings of technology it is thus necessary to survey developments from the Old Stone Age through the New Stone Age down to the emergence of the first urban civilizations about 3000 BC.

The earliest tools

Stone. The material that gives its name and a technological unity to these periods of prehistory is stone. Though it may be assumed that primitive man used other materials such as wood, bone, fur, leaves, and grasses before he mastered the use of stone, apart from bone antlers, presumably used as picks in flint mines and elsewhere, and other fragments of bone implements, none of these has survived. The stone tools of early man, on the other hand, have survived in surprising abundance, and over the many millennia of prehistory important advances in technique were made in the use of stone. Stones became tools only when they were shaped deliberately for specific purposes, and, for this to be done efficiently, suitable hard and fine-grained stones had to be found and means devised for shaping them and particularly for putting a cutting edge on them. Flint became a very popular stone for this purpose, although fine sandstones and certain volcanic rocks were also widely used. There is much Paleolithic evidence of skill in flaking and polishing stones to make scraping and cutting tools. These early tools were held in the hand, but gradually ways of protecting the hand from sharp edges on the stone, at first by wrapping one end in fur or grass or setting it in a wooden handle, were devised. Much later, the technique of fixing the stone head to a haft converted these hand tools into more versatile tools and weapons.

With the widening mastery of the material world in the Neolithic Period, other substances were brought into the service of man, such as clay for pottery and brick; and increasing competence in handling textile raw materials led to the creation of the first woven fabrics to take the place of animal skins. About the same time, curiosity about the behaviour of metallic oxides in the presence of

From C. Singer (ed.), *A History of Technology*

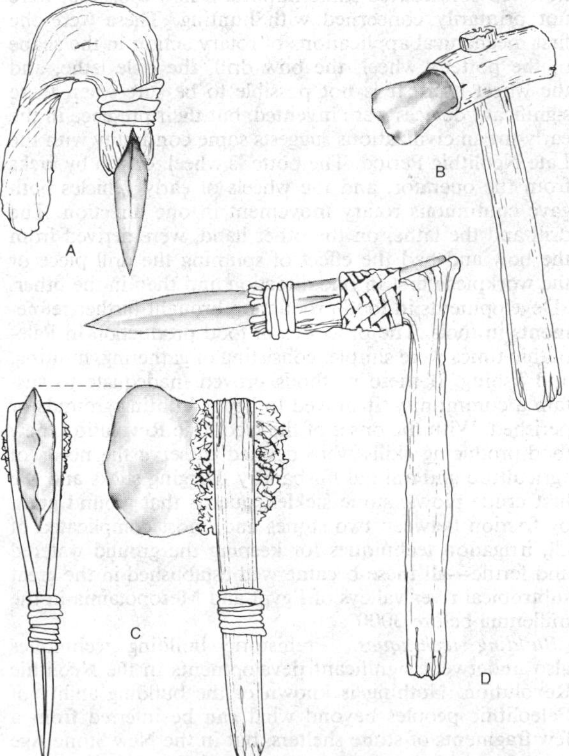

Methods of hafting axes and adzes with stone blades.
(A) Adz with blade bound in split of shouldered haft. (B) Ax with blade inserted in socket of deer antler, which is perforated for the haft. (C) Side and front views of ax with blade gripped in bend of withy, with attachment strengthened with hardened gum and lashing. (D) Adz with blade lashed in wooden sleeve, which is attached to shouldered haft by band of plaited cane.

fire promoted one of the most significant technological innovations of all time and marked the succession from the Stone Age to the Metal Age.

Power. The use of fire was another basic technique mastered at some unknown time in the Old Stone Age. The discovery that fire could be tamed and controlled and the further discovery that a fire could be generated by persistent friction between two dry wooden surfaces were momentous. Fire was the most important contribution of prehistory to power technology, although little power was obtained directly from fire except as defense against wild animals. For the most part, prehistoric communities remained completely dependent upon manpower, but, in making the transition to a more settled pattern of life in the New Stone Age, man began to derive some power from animals that had been domesticated. It also seems likely that by the end of prehistoric times the sail had emerged as a means of harnessing the wind for small boats, beginning a long sequence of developments in marine transport.

Tools and weapons. The basic tools of prehistoric peoples were determined by the materials at their disposal. But once they had acquired the techniques of working stone, they were resourceful in devising tools and weapons with points and barbs. Thus the stone-headed spear, the harpoon, and the arrow all came into widespread use. The spear was given increased impetus by the spear-thrower, a notched pole that gave a sling effect. The bow and arrow were an even more effective combination, the use of which is clearly demonstrated in the earliest "documentary" evidence in the history of technology, the cave paintings of southern France and northern Spain, which depict the bow being used in hunting. The ingenuity of these primitive hunters is shown also in their slings, throwing-sticks (the boomerang of the Australian Aborigines is a remarkable surviving example), blowguns, bird snares, fish and animal traps, and nets. These tools did not evolve uniformly, as each primitive community developed only those instruments that were most suitable for its own specialized purposes, but all were in use by the end of the Stone Age. In addition, the Neolithic Revolution had contributed some important new tools that were not primarily concerned with hunting. These were the first mechanical applications of rotary action in the shape of the potter's wheel, the bow drill, the pole lathe, and the wheel itself. It is not possible to be sure when these significant devices were invented, but their presence in the early urban civilizations suggests some continuity with the Late Neolithic Period. The potter's wheel, driven by kicks from the operator, and the wheels of early vehicles both gave continuous rotary movement in one direction. The drill and the lathe, on the other hand, were derived from the bow and had the effect of spinning the drill piece or the workpiece first in one direction and then in the other.

The bow and arrow

Food production

Developments in food production brought further refinements in tools. The processes of food production in Paleolithic times were simple, consisting of gathering, hunting, and fishing. If these methods proved inadequate to sustain a community, it moved to better hunting grounds or perished. With the onset of the Neolithic Revolution, new food-producing skills were devised to serve the needs of agriculture and animal husbandry. Digging sticks and the first crude plows, stone sickles, querns that ground grain by friction between two stones and, most complicated of all, irrigation techniques for keeping the ground watered and fertile—all these became well established in the great subtropical river valleys of Egypt and Mesopotamia in the millennia before 3000 BC.

Building techniques. Prehistoric building techniques also underwent significant developments in the Neolithic Revolution. Nothing is known of the building ability of Paleolithic peoples beyond what can be inferred from a few fragments of stone shelters, but in the New Stone Age some impressive structures were erected, primarily tombs and burial mounds and other religious edifices, but also, toward the end of the period, domestic housing in which sun-dried brick was first used. In northern Europe, where the Neolithic transformation began later than around the eastern Mediterranean and lasted longer, huge stone monuments, of which Stonehenge in England is the outstanding example, still bear eloquent testimony to the technical skill, not to mention the imagination and mathematical competence, of the later Stone Age societies.

Manufacturing. Manufacturing industry had its origin in the New Stone Age, with the application of techniques for grinding corn, baking clay, spinning and weaving textiles, and also, it seems likely, for dyeing, fermenting, and distilling. Some evidence for all these processes can be derived from archaeological findings, and some of them at least were developing into specialized crafts by the time the first urban civilizations appeared. In the same way, the early metalworkers were beginning to acquire the techniques of extracting and working the softer metals, gold, silver, copper, and tin, that were to make their successors a select class of craftsmen. All these incipient fields of specialization, moreover, implied developing trade between different communities and regions, and again the archaeological evidence of the transfer of manufactured products in the later Stone Age is impressive. Flint arrowheads of particular types, for example, can be found widely dispersed over Europe, and the implication of a common locus of manufacture for each is strong.

Such transmission suggests improving facilities for transport and communication. Paleolithic man presumably depended entirely on his own feet, and this remained the normal mode of transport throughout the Stone Age. Domestication of the ox, the donkey, and the camel undoubtedly brought some help, although difficulties in harnessing the horse long delayed its effective use. The dugout canoe and the birch-bark canoe had demonstrated the potential of water transport, and, again, there is some evidence that the sail had already appeared by the end of the New Stone Age.

Effect of climatic conditions

It is notable that the developments so far described in human prehistory took place over a long period of time, compared with the 5,000 years of recorded history, and that they took place first in very small areas of the Earth's surface and involved populations minute by modern criteria. The Neolithic Revolution occurred first in those parts of the world with an unusual combination of qualities: a warm climate, encouraging rapid crop growth, and an annual cycle of flooding that naturally regenerated the fertility of the land. On the Eurasian-African landmass such conditions occur only in Egypt, Mesopotamia, northern India, and some of the great river valleys of China. It was there, then, that men and women of the New Stone Age were stimulated to develop and apply new techniques of agriculture, animal husbandry, irrigation, and manufacture; and it was there that their enterprise was rewarded by increasing productivity, which encouraged the growth of population and triggered a succession of sociopolitical changes that converted the settled Neolithic communities into the first civilizations. Elsewhere, the stimulus to technological innovation was lacking or was unrewarded, so that these areas had to await the transmission of technical expertise from the more highly favoured areas. Herein is rooted the separation of the great world civilizations, for while the Egyptian and Mesopotamian civilizations spread their influence westward through the Mediterranean and Europe, those of India and China were limited by geographical barriers to their own hinterlands, which, although vast, were largely isolated from the mainstream of Western technological progress.

THE URBAN REVOLUTION (C. 3000–500 BC)

The technological change so far described took place very slowly over a long period of time, in response to only the most basic social needs, the search for food and shelter, and with few social resources available for any activity other than the fulfillment of these needs. About 5,000 years ago, however, a momentous cultural transition began to take place in a few well-favoured geographical situations. It generated new needs and resources and was accompanied by a significant increase in technological innovation. It was the beginning of the invention of the city.

Craftsmen and scientists. The accumulated agricultural skill of the New Stone Age had made possible a growth in population, and the larger population in turn created a need for the products of specialized craftsmen in a wide range of commodities. These craftsmen included a number of metalworkers, first those treating metals that could be easily obtained in metallic form and particularly the soft metals, such as gold and copper, which could be fashioned by beating. Then came the discovery of the possibility of extracting certain metals from the ores in which they generally occur. Probably the first such material to be used was the carbonate of copper known as malachite, then already in use as a cosmetic and easily reduced to copper in a strong fire. It is impossible to be precise about the time and place of this discovery, but its consequences were tremendous. It led to the search for other metallic ores, to the development of metallurgy, to the encouragement of trade in order to secure specific metals, and to the further development of specialist skills. It contributed substantially to the emergence of urban societies, as it relied heavily upon trade and manufacturing industries, and thus to the rise of the first civilizations. The Stone Age gave way to the early Metal Age, and a new epoch in the story of mankind had begun.

Early extraction of metals

By fairly general consent, civilization consists of a large society with a common culture, settled communities, and sophisticated institutions, all of which presuppose a mastery of elementary literacy and numeration. Mastery of the civilized arts was a minority pursuit in the early civilizations, in all probability the carefully guarded possession of a priestly caste. The very existence of these skills, however, even in the hands of a small minority of the population, is significant because they made available a facility for recording and transmitting information that greatly enlarged the scope for innovation and speculative thought.

Hitherto, technology had existed without the benefit of science, but, by the time of the first Sumerian astronomers, who plotted the motion of the heavenly bodies with remarkable accuracy and based calculations about the calendar and irrigation systems upon their observations, the possibility of a creative relationship between science and technology had appeared. The first fruits of this relationship appeared in greatly improved abilities to measure land, weigh, and keep time, all practical techniques, essential to any complex society, and inconceivable without literacy and the beginnings of scientific observation. With the emergence of these skills in the 3rd millennium BC, the first civilizations arose in the valleys of the Nile and of the Tigris–Euphrates.

Copper and bronze. The fact that the era of the early civilizations coincides with the technological classification of the Copper and Bronze ages is a clue to the technological basis of these societies. The softness of copper, gold, and silver made it inevitable that they should be the first to be worked, but archaeologists now seem to agree that there was no true "Copper Age," except perhaps for a short period at the beginning of Egyptian civilization, because the very softness of that metal limited its utility for everything except decoration or coinage. Attention was thus given early to means of hardening copper to make satisfactory tools and weapons. The reduction of mixed metallic ores probably led to the discovery of alloying, whereby copper was fused with other metals to make bronze. Several bronzes were made, including some containing lead, antimony, and arsenic, but by far the most popular and widespread was that of copper and tin in proportions of about 10 to one. This was a hard yellowish metal that could be melted and cast into the shape required. The bronzesmiths took over from the coppersmiths and goldsmiths the technique of heating the metal in a crucible over a strong fire and casting it into simple clay or stone molds to make axheads or spearheads or other solid shapes. For the crafting of hollow vessels or sculpture, they devised the so-called cire perdue technique, in which the shape to be molded is formed in wax and set in clay, the wax then being melted and drained out to leave a cavity into which the molten metal is poured.

Bronze became the most important material of the early civilizations, and elaborate arrangements were made to ensure a continuous supply of it. Metals were scarce in the alluvial river valleys where civilization developed and therefore had to be imported. This need led to complicated trading relationships and mining operations at great distances from the homeland. Tin presented a particularly severe problem, as it was in short supply throughout the Middle East. The Bronze Age civilizations were compelled to search far beyond their own frontiers for sources of the metal, and in the process knowledge of the civilized arts was gradually transmitted westward along the developing Mediterranean trade routes.

In most aspects other than the use of metals, the transition from the technology of the New Stone Age to that of early civilizations was fairly gradual, although there was a general increase in competence as specialized skills became more clearly defined, and in techniques of building there were enormous increases in the scale of enterprises. There were no great innovations in power technology, but important improvements were made in the construction of furnaces and kilns in response to the requirements of the metalworkers and potters and of new artisans such as glassworkers. Also, the sailing ship assumed a definitive shape, progressing from a vessel with a small sail rigged in its bows and suitable only for sailing before the prevailing wind up the Nile River, into the substantial oceangoing ship of the later Egyptian dynasties, with a large rectangular sail rigged amidships. Egyptian and Phoenician ships of this type could sail before the wind and across the wind, but for making headway into the wind they had to resort to manpower. Nevertheless, they accomplished remarkable feats of navigation, sailing the length of the Mediterranean and even passing through the Pillars of Hercules into the Atlantic.

The sailing ship

By courtesy of the Science Museum, London

Drawing of an Egyptian seagoing ship, *c.* 2600 BC, based on vessels depicted in the bas-relief discovered in the pyramid of King Sahure at Abū Sir, Cairo.

Irrigation. Techniques of food production also showed many improvements over Neolithic methods, including one outstanding innovation in the shape of systematic irrigation. The civilizations of Egypt and Mesopotamia depended heavily upon the two great river systems, the Nile and the Tigris–Euphrates, which both watered the ground with their annual floods and rejuvenated it with the rich alluvium they deposited. The Nile flooded with regularity each summer, and the civilizations building in its valley early learned the technique of basin irrigation, ponding back the floodwater for as long as possible after the river had receded, so that enriched soil could bring forth a harvest before the floods of the following season. In the Tigris–Euphrates valley the irrigation problem was more complex, because the floods were less predictable, more fierce, and came earlier than those of the northward-flowing Nile. They also carried more alluvium, which tended to choke irrigation channels. The task of the Sumerian irrigation engineers was that of channeling water from the rivers during the summer months, impounding it, and distributing it to the fields in small installments. The Sumerian system eventually broke down because it led to an accumulation of salt in the soil, with a consequent loss of fertility. Both systems, however, depended on a high degree of social control, requiring skill in measuring and marking out the land and an intricate legal code to ensure justice in the distribution of precious water. Both systems, moreover, depended on intricate engineering in building dikes and embankments, canals and aqueducts (with lengthy stretches underground to prevent loss by evaporation), and the use of water-raising devices such as the shadoof, a balanced beam with a counterweight on one end and a bucket to lift the water on the other.

Urban manufacturing. Manufacturing industry in the early civilizations concentrated on such products as pot-

Egyptian shadoof, "Apuy's House and Garden," tempera reproduction of a wall painting, *c.* 1250 BC, from the tomb of Apuy, Thebes. In the Metropolitan Museum of Art, New York.

By courtesy of the Metropolitan Museum of Art, New York

tery, wines, oils, and cosmetics, which had begun to circulate along the incipient trade routes before the introduction of metals; these became the commodities traded for the metals. In pottery, the potter's wheel became widely used for spinning the clay into the desired shape, but the older technique of building pots by hand from rolls of clay remained in use for some purposes. In the production of wines and oils various forms of press were developed, while the development of cooking, brewing, and preservatives justified the assertion that the science of chemistry began in the kitchen. Cosmetics too were an offshoot of culinary art.

Wheeled vehicles

Pack animals were still the primary means of land transport, the wheeled vehicle developing slowly to meet the divergent needs of agriculture, trade, and war. In the latter category, the chariot appeared as a weapon, even though its use was limited by the continuing difficulty of harnessing a horse. Military technology brought the development of metal plates for armour.

Building. In building technology the major developments concerned the scale of operations rather than any particular innovation. The late Stone Age communities of Mesopotamia had already built extensively in sun-dried brick. Their successors continued the technique but extended its scale to construct the massive square temples called ziggurats. These had a core and facing of bricks, the facing walls sloping slightly inward and broken by regular pilasters built into the brickwork, the whole structure ascending in two or three stages to a temple on the summit. Sumerians were also the first to build columns with brick made from local clay, which also provided the writing material for the scribes.

In Egypt, clay was scarce but good building stone was plentiful, and builders used it in constructing the pyramids and temples that remain today as outstanding monuments of Egyptian civilization. Stones were pulled on rollers and raised up the successive stages of the structure by ramps and by balanced levers adapted from the water-raising shadoof. The stones were shaped by skilled masons, and they were placed in position under the careful supervision of priest-architects who were clearly competent mathematicians and astronomers, as is evident from the precise astronomical alignments. It seems certain that the heavy labour of construction fell upon armies of slaves, which helps to explain both the achievements and limitations of early civilizations. Slaves were usually one of the fruits of military conquest, which presupposes a period of successful territorial expansion, although their status as a subject race could be perpetuated indefinitely. Slave populations provided a competent and cheap labour force for the major constructional works that have been described. On the other hand, the availability of slave labour discouraged technological innovation, a social fact that goes far toward explaining the comparative stagnation of mechanical invention in the ancient world.

Transmitting knowledge. In the ancient world, technological knowledge was transmitted by traders, who went out in search of tin and other commodities, and by craftsmen in metal, stone, leather, and the other mediums, who passed their skills to others by direct instruction or by providing models that challenged other craftsmen to copy them. This transmission through intermediary contact was occurring between the ancient civilizations and their neighbours to the north and west during the 2nd millennium BC. The pace quickened in the subsequent millennium, distinct new civilizations arising in Crete and Mycenae, in Troy and Carthage. Finally, the introduction of the technique of working iron profoundly changed the capabilities and resources of human societies and ushered in the classical civilizations of Greece and Rome.

TECHNOLOGICAL ACHIEVEMENTS OF GREECE AND ROME (500 BC–AD 500)

The contributions of Greece and Rome in philosophy and religion, political and legal institutions, poetry and drama, and in the realm of scientific speculation stand in spectacular contrast with their relatively limited contributions in technology. Their mechanical innovation was not distinguished, and, even in the realms of military and construction engineering, in which they showed great ingenuity and aesthetic sensibility, their work represented more a consummation of earlier lines of development than a dramatic innovation. This apparent paradox of the classical period of the ancient world requires explanation, and the history of technology can provide some clues to the solution of the problem.

The mastery of iron. The outstanding technological factor of the Greco-Roman world was the smelting of iron, a technique—derived from unknown metallurgists, probably in Asia Minor, about 1000 BC—that spread far beyond the provincial frontiers of the Roman Empire. The use of the metal had become general in Greece and the Aegean Islands by the dawn of the classical period about 500 BC, and it appears to have spread quickly westward thereafter. Iron ore, long a familiar material, had defied reduction into metallic form because of the great heat required in the furnace to perform the chemical transformation (about 1,535° C [2,795° F] compared with the 1,083° C [1,981° F] necessary for the reduction of copper ores). To reach this temperature, furnace construction had to be improved and ways devised to maintain the heat for several hours. Throughout the classical period these conditions were achieved only on a small scale, in furnaces burning charcoal and using foot bellows to intensify the heat, and even in these furnaces the heat was not sufficient to reduce the ore completely to molten metal. Instead, a small spongy ball of iron—called a bloom—was produced in the bottom of the furnace. This was extracted by breaking open the furnace, and then it was hammered into bars of wrought iron, which could be shaped as required by further heating and hammering. Apart from its greater abundance, iron for most purposes provided a harder and stronger material than the earlier metals, although the impossibility of casting it into molds like bronze was an inconvenience. At an early date some smiths devised the cementation process for reheating bars of iron between layers of charcoal to carburize the surface of the iron and thus to produce a coat of steel. Such case-hardened iron could be further heated, hammered, and tempered to make knife and sword blades of high quality. The very best steel in Roman times was Seric steel, brought into the Western world from India, where it was produced in blocks a few inches in diameter by a crucible process; *i.e.,* melting the ingredients in an enclosed vessel to achieve purity and consistency in the chemical combination.

Improvements in metal furnaces

Mechanical contrivances. Though slight, the mechanical achievements of the Greco-Roman centuries were not without significance. The world had one of its great mechanical geniuses in Archimedes, who devised remarkable weapons to protect his native Syracuse from Roman invasion and applied his powerful mind to such basic mechanical contrivances as the screw, the pulley, and the lever. Alexandrian engineers, such as Ctesibius and Hero, invented a wealth of ingenious mechanical contrivances including pumps, wind and hydraulic organs, compressed-air engines, and screw-cutting machines. They also devised toys and automata such as the aeolipile, which may be regarded as the first successful steam turbine. Little practical use was found for these inventions, but the Alexandrian school marks an important transition from very simple mechanisms to the more complex devices that properly deserve to be considered "machines." In a sense it provided a starting point for modern mechanical practice.

Introduction of rotary motion

The Romans were responsible, through the application and development of available machines, for an important technological transformation: the widespread introduction of rotary motion. This was exemplified in the use of the treadmill for powering cranes and other heavy lifting operations, the introduction of rotary water-raising devices for irrigation works (a scoop wheel powered by a treadmill), and the development of the waterwheel as a prime mover. The 1st-century-BC Roman engineer Vitruvius gave an account of watermills, and by the end of the Roman era many were in operation.

Agriculture. Iron Age technology was applied to agriculture in the form of the iron (or iron-tipped) plowshare, which opened up the possibility of deeper plowing and of cultivating heavier soils than those normally worked in the Greco-Roman period. The construction of plows improved slowly during these centuries, but the moldboard for turning over the earth did not appear until the 11th century AD, so that the capacity of turning the sod depended more on the wrists of the plowman than on the strength of his draft team; this discouraged tackling heavy ground. The potentialities of the heavy plow were thus not fully exploited in the temperate areas of Europe until after the Roman period. Elsewhere, in the drier climates of North Africa and Spain, the Romans were responsible for extensive irrigation systems, using the Archimedean screw and the noria (an animal- or water-powered scoop wheel) to raise water.

Building. Though many buildings of the Greeks survive as splendid monuments to the civilized communities that built them, as technological monuments they are of little significance. The Greeks adopted a form of column and lintel construction that had been used in Egypt for centuries and was derived from experience of timber construction. In no major sense did Greek building constitute a technological innovation. The Romans copied the Greek style for most ceremonial purposes, but in other respects they were important innovators in building technology. They made extensive use of fired brick and tile as well as stone; they developed a strong cement that would set under water; and they explored the architectural possibilities of the arch, the vault, and the dome. They then applied these techniques in amphitheatres, aqueducts, tunnels, bridges,

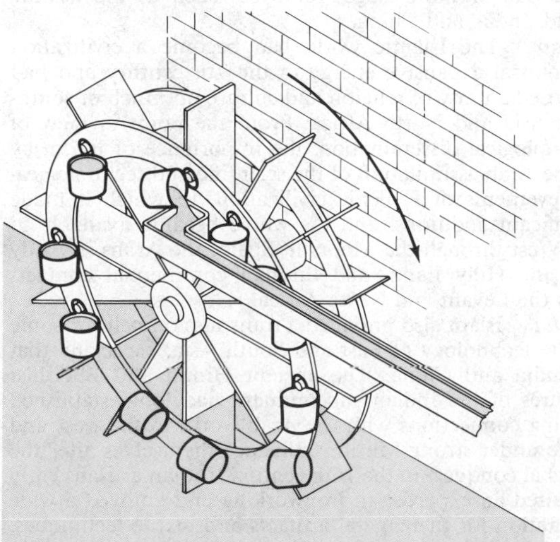

The noria, used to raise water to a higher level. Arrow indicates direction of rotation of the wheel.

A network of Roman aqueducts showing a section undergoing repairs, painting by Michael Zeno Diemer (born 1867). In the Deutsches Museum, Munich.

By courtesy of the Deutsches Museum, Munich

walls, lighthouses, and roads. Taken together, these constructional works may fairly be regarded as the primary technological achievement of the Romans.

Other fields of technology. In manufacturing, transport, and military technology, the achievements of the Greco-Roman period are not remarkable. The major manufacturing crafts—the making of pottery and glass, weaving, leatherworking, fine-metalworking, and so on—followed the lines of previous societies, albeit with important developments in style. Superbly decorated Athenian pottery, for example, was widely dispersed along the trade routes of the Mediterranean, and the Romans made good quality pottery available throughout their empire through the manufacture and trade of the standardized red ware called terra sigillata, which was produced in large quantities at several sites in Italy and Gaul.

Transport. Transport, again, followed earlier precedents, the sailing ship emerging as a seagoing vessel with a carvel-built hull (that is, with planks meeting edge-to-edge rather than overlapping as in clinker-built designs), and a fully developed keel with stempost and sternpost. The Greek sailing ship was equipped with a square or rectangular sail to receive a following wind and one or more banks of oarsmen to propel the ship when the wind was contrary. The Greeks began to develop a specialized fighting ship, provided with a ram in the prow, and the cargo ship, dispensing with oarsmen and relying entirely upon the wind, was also well established by the early years of classical Greece. The Romans took over both forms, but without significant innovation. They gave much more attention to inland transport than to the sea, and they constructed a remarkable network of carefully aligned and well-laid roads, often paved over long stretches, throughout the provinces of the empire. Along these strategic highways the legions marched rapidly to the site of any crisis at which their presence was required. The roads also served for the development of trade, but their primary function was always military, as a vital means of keeping a vast empire in subjection.

Greek sailing ships

Military technology. Roman military technology was inventive on occasion, as in the great siege catapults, depending on both torsion and tension power. But the standard equipment of the legionnaire was simple and conservative, consisting of an iron helmet and breastplate, with a short sword and an iron-tipped spear. As most of their opponents were also equipped with iron weapons and sometimes with superior devices, such as the Celtic chariots, the Roman military achievements depended more on organization and discipline than on technological superiority.

The Greco-Roman era was distinguished for the scientific activity of some of its greatest philosophers. In keeping with Greek speculative thought, however, this tended to be strongly conceptual so that it was in mathematics and other abstract studies that the main scientific achievements are to be found. Some of these had some practical significance, as in the study of perspective effects in build-

Weaving of wool on a vertical loom, detail of a painting on an Athenian scent bottle, *c.* 560 BC. In the Metropolitan Museum of Art, New York.

By courtesy of the Metropolitan Museum of Art, New York, Fletcher Fund, 1931

ing construction. Aristotle in many ways expressed the inquiring empiricism that has caused scientists to seek an explanation for their physical environment. In at least one field, that of medicine and its related subjects, Greek inquiry assumed a highly practical form, Hippocrates and Galen laying the foundations of modern medical science. But this was exceptional, and the normal Hellenic attitude was to pursue scientific enquiry in the realm of ideas without much thought of the possible technological consequences.

From the Middle Ages to 1750

MEDIEVAL ADVANCE (AD 500–1500)

The millennium between the collapse of the Western Roman Empire in the 5th century AD and the beginning of the colonial expansion of western Europe in the late 15th century has been known traditionally as the Middle Ages, and the first half of this period consists of the five centuries of the Dark Ages. We now know that the period was not as socially stagnant as this title suggests. In the first place, many of the institutions of the later empire survived the collapse and profoundly influenced the formation of the new civilization that developed in western Europe. The Christian Church was the outstanding institution of this type, but Roman conceptions of law and administration also continued to exert an influence long after the departure of the legions from the western provinces. Second, and more important, the Teutonic tribes who moved into a large part of western Europe did not come empty-handed, and in some respects their technology was superior to that of the Romans. It has already been observed that they were people of the Iron Age, and although much about the origins of the heavy plow remains obscure these tribes appear to have been the first people with sufficiently strong iron plowshares to undertake the systematic settlement of the forested lowlands of northern and western Europe, the heavy soils of which had frustrated the agricultural techniques of their predecessors.

Effect of the barbarian invasions

The invaders came thus as colonizers. They may have been regarded as "barbarians" by the Romanized inhabitants of western Europe who naturally resented their intrusion, and the effect of their invasion was certainly to disrupt trade, industry, and town life. But the newcomers also provided an element of innovation and vitality. About AD 1000 the conditions of comparative political stability necessary for the reestablishment of a vigorous commercial and urban life had been secured by the success of the kingdoms of the region in either absorbing or keeping out the last of the invaders from the East, and thereafter for 500 years the new civilization grew in strength and began to experiment in all aspects of human endeavour. Much of this process involved recovering the knowledge and achievements of the ancient world. The history of medieval technology is thus largely the story of the preservation, recovery, and modification of earlier achievements. But by the end of the period Western civilization had begun to produce some remarkable technological innovations that were to be of the utmost significance.

Innovation. The word innovation raises a problem of great importance in the history of technology. Strictly, an innovation is something entirely new, but there is no such thing as an unprecedented technological innovation because it is impossible for an inventor to work in a vacuum and, however ingenious his invention, it must arise out of his own previous experience. The task of distinguishing an element of novelty in an invention remains a problem of patent law down to the present day, but the problem is made relatively easy by the possession of full documentary records covering previous inventions in many countries. For the millennium of the Middle Ages, however, few such records exist, and it is frequently difficult to explain how particular innovations were introduced to western Europe. The problem is especially perplexing because it is known that many inventions of the period had been developed independently and previously in other civilizations, and it is sometimes difficult if not impossible to know whether something is spontaneous innovation or an invention that had been transmitted by some as yet undiscovered route from those who had originated it in other societies.

Theory of spontaneous innovation

The problem is important because it generates a conflict of interpretations about the transmission of technology. On the one hand there is the theory of the diffusionists, according to which all innovation has moved westward from the long-established civilizations of the ancient world, with Egypt and Mesopotamia as the two favourite candidates for the ultimate source of the process. On the other hand is the theory of spontaneous innovation, according to which the primary determinant of technological innovation is social need. Scholarship is as yet unable to solve the problem so far as technological advances of the Middle Ages are concerned because much information is missing. But it does seem likely that at least some of the key inventions of the period—the windmill and gunpowder are good examples—were developed spontaneously. It is quite certain, however, that others, such as silk working, were transmitted to the West, and, however original the contribution of Western civilization to technological innovation, there can be no doubt at all that in its early centuries at least it looked to the East for ideas and inspiration.

Byzantium. The immediate eastern neighbour of the new civilization of medieval Europe was Byzantium, the surviving bastion of the Roman Empire based in Constantinople, which endured for 1,000 years after the collapse of the western half of the empire. There the literature and traditions of Hellenic civilization were perpetuated, becoming increasingly available to the curiosity and greed of the West through the traders who arrived from Venice and elsewhere. Apart from the influence on Western architectural style of such Byzantine masterpieces as the great domed structure of Hagia Sophia, the technological contribution of Byzantium itself was probably slight, but it served to mediate between the West and other civilizations one or more stages removed, such as the Islāmic world, India, and China.

Islām. The Islāmic world had become a civilization of colossal expansive energy in the 7th century and had imposed a unity of religion and culture on much of southwest Asia and North Africa. From the point of view of technological dissemination, the importance of Islām lay in the Arab assimilation of the scientific and technological achievements of Hellenic civilization, to which it made significant additions, and the whole became available to the West through the Moors in Spain, the Arabs in Sicily and the Holy Land, and through commercial contacts with the Levant and North Africa.

India. Islām also provided a transmission belt for some of the technology of East and South Asia, especially that of India and China. The ancient Hindu and Buddhist cultures of the Indian subcontinent had long-established trading connections with the Arab world to the west and came under strong Muslim influence themselves after the Mughal conquest in the 16th century. Indian artisans early acquired an expertise in ironworking and enjoyed a wide reputation for their metal artifacts and textile techniques, but there is little evidence that technical innovation figured prominently in Indian history before the foundation of European trading stations in the 16th century.

Reconstruction of the waterpowered mechanical clock built under the direction of Su Sung, AD 1088. By John Christiansen after Joseph Needham, *et al.*

By courtesy of the East Asian History of Science Library, Cambridge, and Cambridge University Press

China. Civilization flourished continuously in China from about 2000 BC, when the first of the historic dynasties emerged. From the beginning, it was a civilization that valued technological skill in the form of hydraulic engineering, for its survival depended on controlling the enriching but destructive floods of the Huang Ho (Yellow River). Other technologies appeared at a remarkably early date, including the casting of iron, the production of porcelain, and the manufacture of brass and paper. As one dynasty followed another, Chinese civilization came under the domination of a bureaucratic elite, the mandarins, who gave continuity and stability to Chinese life but who also became a conservative influence on innovation, resisting the introduction of new techniques unless they provided a clear benefit to the bureaucracy. Such an innovation was the development of the waterpowered mechanical clock, which achieved an ingenious and elaborate form in the machine built under the supervision of Su Sung in 1088. This was driven by a waterwheel that moved regularly, making one part-revolution as each bucket on its rim was filled in turn. The links between China and the West remained tenuous until modern times, but the occasional encounter such as that resulting from the journey of Marco Polo in 1271–95 alerted the West to the superiority of Chinese technology and stimulated a vigorous westward transfer of techniques. Western knowledge of silk working, the magnetic compass, papermaking, and porcelain were all derived from China. In the latter case, Europeans admired the fine porcelain imported from China for several centuries before they were able to produce anything of a similar quality. Having achieved a condition of comparative social stability, however, the Chinese mandarinate did little to encourage innovation or trading contacts with the outside world. Under their influence, no social group emerged in China equivalent to the mercantile class that flourished in the West and did much to promote trade and industry. The result was that China dropped behind the West in technological skills until the political revolutions and social upheavals of the 20th century awakened the Chinese to the importance of these skills to economic prosperity and inspired a determination to acquire them.

Despite the acquisition of many techniques from the East, the Western world of 500–1500 was forced to solve most of its problems on its own initiative. In doing so it transformed an agrarian society based upon a subsistence economy into a dynamic society with increased productivity sustaining trade, industry, and town life on a steadily growing scale. This was primarily a technological achievement, and one of considerable magnitude.

Power sources. The outstanding feature of this achievement was a revolution in the sources of power. With no large slave labour force to draw on, Europe experienced a labour shortage that stimulated a search for alternative sources of power and the introduction of laboursaving machinery. The first instrument of this power revolution was the horse. By the invention of the horseshoe, the padded, rigid horse collar, and the stirrup, all of which first appeared in the West in the centuries of the Dark Ages, the horse was transformed from an ancillary beast of burden useful only for light duties into a highly versatile source of energy in peace and war. Once the horse could be harnessed to the heavy plow by means of the horse collar, it became a more efficient draft animal than the ox, and the introduction of the stirrup made the mounted warrior supreme in medieval warfare and initiated complex social changes to sustain the great expense of the knight, his armour, and his steed, in a society close to the subsistence line.

Water-power and wind power

Even more significant was the success of medieval technology in harnessing water and wind power. The Romans had pioneered the use of waterpower in the later empire, and some of their techniques probably survived. The type of water mill that flourished first in northern Europe, however, appears to have been the Norse mill, using a horizontally mounted waterwheel driving a pair of grindstones directly, without the intervention of gearing. Examples of this simple type of mill survive in Scandinavia and in the Shetlands; it also occurred in southern Europe, where it was known as the Greek mill. It is possible that a proportion of the 5,624 mills recorded in the Domesday Book of England in 1086 were of this type, although it is probable that by that date the vertically mounted undershot wheel had established itself as more appropriate to the gentle landscape of England; the Norse mill requires a good head of water to turn the wheel at an adequate grinding speed without gearing for the upper millstone (the practice of rotating the upper stone above a stationary bed stone became universal at an early date). Most of the Domesday water mills were used for grinding grain, but in the following centuries other important uses were devised in fulling cloth (shrinking and felting woolen fabrics), sawing wood, and crushing vegetable seeds for oil. Overshot wheels also were introduced where there was sufficient head of water, and the competence of the medieval millwrights in building mills and earthworks and in constructing increasingly elaborate trains of gearing grew correspondingly.

Origin of the windmill

The sail had been used to harness wind power from the dawn of civilization, but the windmill was unknown in the West until the end of the 12th century. Present evidence suggests that the windmill developed spontaneously in the West; though there are precedents in Persia and China, the question remains open. What is certain is that the windmill became widely used in Europe in the Middle Ages. Wind power is generally less reliable than waterpower, but where the latter is deficient wind power is an attractive substitute. Such conditions are found in areas that suffer from drought or from a shortage of surface water and also in low-lying areas where rivers offer little energy. Windmills have thus flourished in places such as Spain or the downlands of England on the one hand, and in the fenlands and polders of The Netherlands on the other hand. The first type of windmill to be widely adopted was the post-mill, in which the whole body of the mill pivots on a post and can be turned to face the sails into the wind. By the 15th century, however, many were adopting the tower-mill type of construction, in which the body of the mill remains stationary with only the cap moving to turn the sails into the wind. As with the water mill, the development of the windmill brought not only greater mechanical power but also greater knowledge of mechanical contrivances, which was applied in making clocks and other devices.

Agriculture and crafts. With new sources of power at its disposal, medieval Europe was able greatly to increase productivity. This is abundantly apparent in agriculture,

Post windmill with grinding machinery in mill housing, engraving from Agostino Ramelli's *Li diverse et artificiose macchine,* 1588.
By courtesy of the trustees of the British Museum; photograph, J.R. Freeman & Co. Ltd.

where the replacement of the ox by the faster gaited horse and the introduction of new crops brought about a distinct improvement in the quantity and variety of food, with a consequent improvement in the diet and energy of the population. It was also apparent in the developing industries of the period, especially the woolen cloth industry in which the spinning wheel was introduced, partially mechanizing this important process, and the practice of using waterpower to drive fulling stocks (wooden hammers raised by cams on a driving shaft) had a profound effect on the location of the industry in England in the later centuries of the Middle Ages. The same principle was adapted to the paper industry late in the Middle Ages, the rags from which paper was derived being pulverized by hammers similar to fulling stocks.

Meanwhile, the traditional crafts flourished within the expanding towns, where there was a growing market for the products of the rope makers, barrel makers (coopers), leatherworkers (curriers), and metalworkers (goldsmiths and silversmiths), to mention only a few of the more important crafts. New crafts such as that of the soapmakers developed in the towns. The technique of making soap appears to have been a Teutonic innovation of the Dark Ages, being unknown in the ancient civilizations. The process consists of decomposing animal or vegetable fats by boiling them with a strong alkali. Long before it became popular for personal cleansing, soap was a valuable industrial commodity for scouring textile fabrics. Its manufacture was one of the first industrial processes to make extensive use of coal as a fuel, and the development of the coal industry in northern Europe constitutes another important medieval innovation, no previous civilization having made any systematic attempt to exploit coal. The mining techniques remained unsophisticated as long as coal was obtainable near the surface, but as the search for the mineral led to greater and greater depths the industry copied methods that had already evolved in the metal-mining industries of north and central Europe. The extent of this evolution was brilliantly summarized by Georgius Agricola in his *De re metallica,* published in 1556. This large, abundantly illustrated book shows techniques of shafting, pumping (by treadmill, animal power, and waterpower), and of conveying the ore won from the mines in trucks, which anticipated the development of the railways. It is impossible to date precisely the emergence of these important techniques, but the fact that they were well established when Agricola observed them suggests that they had a long ancestry.

Soap-making

Architecture. Relatively few structures survive from the Dark Ages, but the later centuries of the medieval period were a great age of building. The Romanesque and Gothic architecture that produced the outstanding aesthetic contribution of the Middle Ages embodied significant technological innovations. The architect-engineers, who had clearly studied classical building techniques, showed a readiness to depart from their models and thus to devise a style that was distinctively their own. Their solutions to the problems of constructing very tall masonry buildings while preserving as much natural light as possible were the cross-rib vault, the flying buttress, and the great window panels providing scope for the new craft of the glazier using coloured glass with startling effect.

Military technology. The same period saw the evolution of the fortified stronghold from the Anglo-Saxon motte-and-bailey, a timber tower encircled by a timber and earth wall, to the formidable, fully developed masonry castle that had become an anachronism by the end of the Middle Ages because of the development of artillery. Intrinsic to this innovation were the invention of gunpowder and the development of techniques for casting metals, especially iron. Gunpowder appeared in western Europe in the mid-13th century, although its formula had been known in the Far East long before that date. It consists of a mixture of carbon, sulfur, and saltpetre, of which the first two were available from charcoal and deposits of volcanic sulfur in Europe, whereas saltpetre had to be crystallized by a noxious process of boiling stable sweepings and other decaying refuse. The consolidation of these ingredients into

Gun-powder

The Granger Collection, New York City

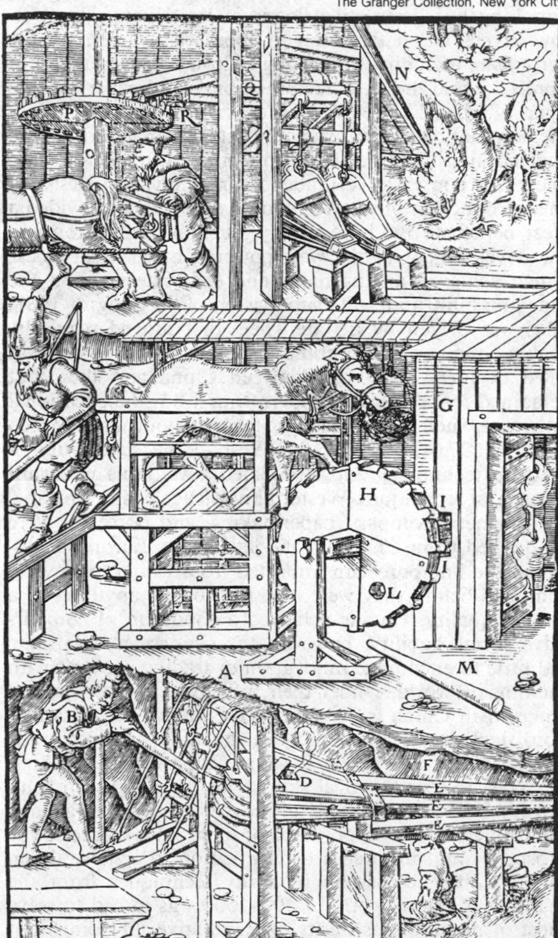

Three methods of ventilating a mine, woodcut from *De re metallica* by Georgius Agricola, published 1556.

an explosive powder had become an established yet hazardous industry by the close of the Middle Ages.

The first effective cannon appear to have been made of wrought-iron bars strapped together, but although barrels continued to be made in this way for some purposes, the practice of casting cannon in bronze became widespread. The technique of casting in bronze had been known for several millennia, but the casting of cannon presented problems of size and reliability. It is likely that the bronzesmiths were able to draw on the experience of techniques devised by the bell founders as an important adjunct to medieval church building, as the casting of a large bell posed similar problems of heating a substantial amount of metal and of pouring it into a suitable mold. Bronze, however, was an expensive metal to manufacture in bulk, so that the widespread use of cannon in war had to depend upon improvements in iron-casting techniques.

The manufacture of cast iron is the great metallurgical innovation of the Middle Ages. It must be remembered that from the beginning of the Iron Age until late in the Middle Ages the iron ore smelted in the available furnaces had not been completely converted to its liquid form. In the 15th century, however, the development of the blast furnace made possible this fusion, with the result that the molten metal could be poured directly into molds ready to receive it. The emergence of the blast furnace was the result of attempts to increase the size of the traditional blooms. Greater size made necessary the provision of a continuous blast of air, usually from bellows driven by a waterwheel, and the combination increased the internal temperature of the furnace so that the iron became molten. At first, the disk of solid iron left in the bottom of the furnace was regarded as undesirable waste by the iron manufacturer; it possessed properties completely unlike those of the more familiar wrought iron, being crystalline and brittle and thus of no use in the traditional iron forge. But it was soon discovered that the new iron could be cast and turned to profit, particularly in the manufacture of cannon.

Transport. Medieval technology made few contributions to inland transport, though there was some experimentation in bridge building and in the construction of canals; lock gates were developed as early as 1180, when they were employed on the canal between Brugge (Bruges; now in Belgium) and the sea. Roads remained indifferent where they existed at all, and vehicles were clumsy throughout the period. Wayfarers like Chaucer's pilgrims traveled on horseback, and this was to remain the best mode of inland transport for centuries to come.

The lateen sail

Sea transport was a different story. Here the Middle Ages produced a decisive technological achievement: the creation of a reliable oceangoing ship depending entirely on wind power instead of a combination of wind and muscle. The vital steps in this evolution were, first, the combination of the traditional square sail, used with little modification from Egyptian times through the Roman Empire to the Viking long boats, with the triangular lateen sail developed in the Arab dhow and adopted in the Mediterranean, which gave it the "lateen" (Latin) association attributed to it by the northern seafarers. This combination allowed ships so equipped to sail close to the wind. Second, the adoption of the sternpost rudder gave greatly increased maneuverability, allowing ships to take full advantage of their improved sail power in tacking into a contrary wind. Third, the introduction of the magnetic compass provided a means of checking navigation on the open seas in any weather. The convergence of these improvements in the ships of the later Middle Ages, together with other improvements in construction and equipment—such as better barrels for carrying water, more reliable ropes, sails, and anchors, the availability of navigational charts (first recorded in use on board ship in 1270), and the astrolabe (for measuring the angle of the Sun or a star above the horizon)—lent confidence to adventurous mariners and thus led directly to the voyages of discovery that marked the end of the Middle Ages and the beginning of the expansion of Europe that has characterized modern times.

Communications. While transport technology was evolving toward these revolutionary developments, techniques of recording and communication were making no less momentous advances. The medieval interest in mechanical contrivances is well illustrated by the development of the mechanical clock, the oldest of which, driven by weights and controlled by a verge, an oscillating arm engaging with a gear wheel, and dated 1386, survives in Salisbury Cathedral, England. Clocks driven by springs had appeared by the mid-15th century, making it possible to construct more compact mechanisms and preparing the way for the portable clock. The problem of overcoming the diminishing power of the spring as it unwound was solved by the simple compensating mechanism of the fusee—a conical drum on the shaft that permitted the spring to exert an increasing moment, or tendency to increase motion, as its power declined. It has been argued that the medieval fascination with clocks reflects an increased sense of the importance of timekeeping in business and elsewhere, but it can be seen with equal justice as representing a new sense of inquiry into the possibilities and practical uses of mechanical devices.

Printing with movable type

Even more significant than the invention of the mechanical clock was the 15th-century invention of printing with movable metal type. The details of this epochal invention are disappointingly obscure, but there is general agreement that the first large-scale printing workshop was that established at Mainz by Johannes Gutenberg, which was producing a sufficient quantity of accurate type to print a Vulgate Bible about 1455. It is clear, however, that this invention drew heavily upon long previous experience with block printing—using a single block to print a design or picture—and on developments in typecasting and ink making. It also made heavy demands on the paper industry, which had been established in Europe since the 12th century but had developed slowly until the invention of printing and the subsequent vogue for the printed word. The printing press itself, vital for securing a firm and even print over the whole page, was an adaptation of the screw press already familiar in the winepress and other applications. The printers found an enormous demand for their product, so that the technique spread rapidly and the printed word became an essential medium of political, social, religious, and scientific communication as well as a convenient means for the dissemination of news and information. By 1500 almost 40,000 recorded editions of books had been printed in 14 European countries, with Germany and Italy accounting for two-thirds. Few single inventions have had such far-reaching consequences.

For all its isolation and intellectual deprivation, the new civilization that took shape in western Europe in the millennium 500 to 1500 achieved some astonishing feats of technological innovation. The intellectual curiosity that led to the foundation of the first universities in the 12th century and applied itself to the recovery of the ancient learning from whatever source it could be obtained was the mainspring also of the technological resourcefulness that encouraged the introduction of the windmill, the improvement and wider application of waterpower, the development of new industrial techniques, the invention of the mechanical clock and gunpowder, the evolution of the sailing ship, and the invention of large-scale printing. Such achievements could not have taken place within a static society. Technological innovation was both the cause and the effect of dynamic development. It is no coincidence that these achievements occurred within the context of a European society that was increasing in population and productivity, stimulating industrial and commercial activity, and expressing itself in the life of new towns and striking cultural activity. Medieval technology mirrored the aspiration of a new and dynamic civilization.

THE EMERGENCE OF WESTERN TECHNOLOGY (1500–1750)

The technological history of the Middle Ages was one of slow but substantial development. In the succeeding period the tempo of change increased markedly and was associated with profound social, political, religious, and intellectual upheavals in western Europe.

The emergence of the nation-state, the cleavage of the Christian Church by the Protestant Reformation, the Renaissance and its accompanying scientific revolution, and the overseas expansion of European states all had interactions with developing technology. This expansion became possible after the advance in naval technology opened up the ocean routes to Western navigators. The conversion of voyages of discovery into imperialism and colonization was made possible by the new firepower. The combination of light, maneuverable ships with the firepower of iron cannon gave European adventurers a decisive advantage, enhanced by other technological assets.

Effect of the Protestant Reformation

The Reformation, not itself a factor of major significance to the history of technology, nevertheless had interactions with it; the capacity of the new printing presses to disseminate all points of view contributed to the religious upheavals, while the intellectual ferment provoked by the Reformation resulted in a rigorous assertion of the vocational character of work and thus stimulated industrial and commercial activity and technological innovation. It is an indication of the nature of this encouragement that so many of the inventors and scientists of the period were Calvinists, Puritans, and, in England, Dissenters.

The Renaissance. The Renaissance had more obviously technological content than the Reformation. The concept of "renaissance" is elusive. Since the scholars of the Middle Ages had already achieved a very full recovery of the literary legacy of the ancient world, as a "rebirth" of knowledge the Renaissance marked rather a point of transition after which the posture of deference to the ancients began to be replaced by a consciously dynamic, progressive attitude. Even while they looked back to classical models, Renaissance men looked for ways of improving upon them. This attitude is outstandingly represented in the genius of Leonardo da Vinci. As an artist of original perception he was recognized by his contemporaries, but some of his most novel work is recorded in his notebooks and was virtually unknown in his own time. This included ingenious designs for submarines, airplanes, and helicopters and drawings of elaborate trains of gears and of the patterns of flow in liquids. The early 16th century was not yet ready for these novelties: they met no specific social need, and the resources necessary for their development were not available.

By courtesy of the Bibliotheque de l'Institut de France, Paris; photograph, The Science Museum, London

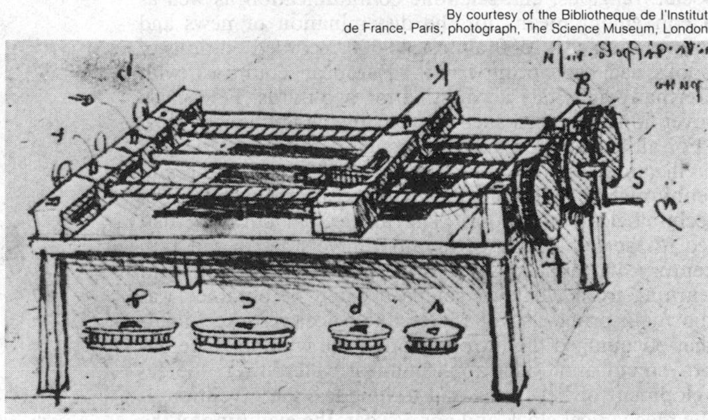

Screw-cutting machine by Leonardo da Vinci, *c.* 1500.
In the Bibliothèque de l'Institut de France, Paris (MS B, folio 70 verso).

An often overlooked aspect of the Renaissance is the scientific revolution that accompanied it. As with the term Renaissance itself, the concept is complex, having to do with intellectual liberation from the ancient world. For centuries the authority of Aristotle in dynamics, of Ptolemy in astronomy, and of Galen in medicine had been taken for granted. Beginning in the 16th century their authority was challenged and overthrown, and scientists set out by observation and experiment to establish new explanatory models of the natural world. One distinctive characteristic of these models was that they were tentative, never receiving the authoritarian prestige long accorded to the ancient masters. Since this fundamental shift of emphasis, science has been committed to a progressive, forward-looking attitude and has come increasingly to seek practical applications for scientific research.

Technology performed a service for science in this revolution by providing it with instruments that greatly enhanced its powers. The use of the telescope by Galileo to observe the moons of Jupiter was a dramatic example of this service, but the telescope was only one of many tools and instruments that proved valuable in navigation, mapmaking, and laboratory experiments. More significant were the services of the new sciences to technology, and the most important of these was the theoretical preparation for the invention of the steam engine.

The steam engine. The researches of a number of scientists, especially those of Robert Boyle of England with atmospheric pressure, of Otto von Guericke of Germany with a vacuum, and of the French Huguenot Denis Papin with pressure vessels, helped to equip practical technologists with the theoretical basis of steam power. Distressingly little is known about the manner in which this knowledge was assimilated by pioneers such as Thomas Savery and Thomas Newcomen, but it is inconceivable that they could have been ignorant of it. Savery took out a patent for a "new Invention for Raiseing of Water and occasioning Motion to all Sorts of Mill Work by the Impellent Force of Fire" in 1698 (No. 356). His apparatus depended on the condensation of steam in a vessel, creating a partial vacuum into which water was forced by atmospheric pressure.

The Newcomen engine

Credit for the first commercially successful steam engine, however, must go to Newcomen, who erected his first machine near Dudley Castle in Staffordshire in 1712. It operated by atmospheric pressure on the top face of a piston in a cylinder, in the lower part of which steam was condensed to create a partial vacuum. The piston was connected to one end of a rocking beam, the other end of which carried the pumping rod in the mine shaft. Newcomen was a tradesman in Dartmouth, Devon, and his engines were robust but unsophisticated. Their heavy fuel consumption made them uneconomical when used where coal was expensive, but in the British coalfields they performed an essential service by keeping deep mines clear of water and were extensively adopted for this purpose. In this way the early steam engines fulfilled one of the most pressing needs of British industry in the 18th century. Although waterpower and wind power remained the basic sources of power for industry, a new prime mover had thus appeared in the shape of the steam engine, with tremendous potential for further development as and when new applications could be found for it.

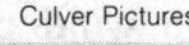

Metallurgy and mining. One cause of the rising demand for coal in Britain was the depletion of the woodland and supplies of charcoal, making manufacturers anxious to find a new source of fuel. Of particular importance were

Culver Pictures

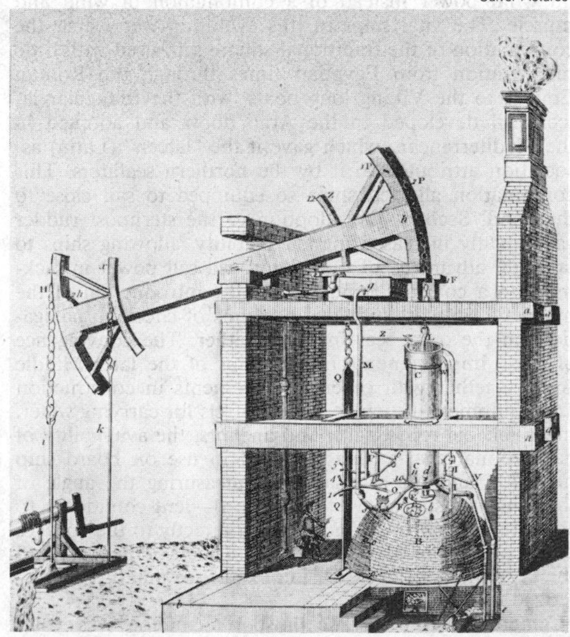

The atmospheric engine of Thomas Newcomen.

experiments of the iron industry in using coal instead of charcoal to smelt iron ore and to process cast iron into wrought iron and steel. The first success in these attempts came in 1709, when Abraham Darby, a Quaker iron-founder in Shropshire, used coke to reduce iron ore in his enlarged and improved blast furnace. Other processes, such as glassmaking, brickmaking, and the manufacture of pottery, had already adopted coal as their staple fuel. Great technical improvements had taken place in all these processes. In ceramics, for instance, the long efforts of European manufacturers to imitate the hard, translucent quality of Chinese porcelain culminated in Meissen at the beginning of the 18th century; the process was subsequently discovered independently in Britain in the middle of the century. Stoneware, requiring a lower firing temperature than porcelain, had achieved great decorative distinction in the 17th century as a result of the Dutch success with opaque white tin glazes at their Delft potteries, and the process had been widely imitated.

The period from 1500 to 1750 witnessed a steady expansion in mining for minerals other than coal and iron. The gold and silver mines of Saxony and Bohemia provided the inspiration for the treatise by Agricola, *De re metallica,* mentioned above, which distilled the cumulative experience of several centuries in mining and metalworking and became, with the help of some brilliant woodcuts and the printing press, a worldwide manual on mining practice. Queen Elizabeth I introduced German miners to England in order to develop the mineral resources of the country, and one result of this was the establishment of brass manufacture. This metal, an alloy of copper and zinc, had been known in the ancient world and in Eastern civilizations but was not developed commercially in western Europe until the 17th century. Metallic zinc had still not been isolated, but brass was made by heating copper with charcoal and calamine, an oxide of zinc mined in England in the Mendip Hills and elsewhere, and was worked up by hammering, annealing (a heating process to soften the material), and wiredrawing into a wide range of household and industrial commodities. Other nonferrous metals such as tin and lead were sought out and exploited with increasing enterprise in this period, but as their ores commonly occurred at some distance from sources of coal, as in the case of the Cornish tin mines, the employment of Newcomen engines to assist in drainage was rarely economical, and this circumstance restricted the extent of the mining operations.

Brass manufacture

New commodities. Following the dramatic expansion of the European nations into the Indian Ocean region and the New World, the commodities of these parts of the world found their way back into Europe in increasing volume. These commodities created new social habits and fashions and called for new techniques of manufacture. Tea became an important trade commodity but was soon surpassed in volume and importance by the products of specially designed plantations, such as sugar, tobacco, cotton, and cocoa. Sugar refining, depending on the crystallization of sugar from the syrupy molasses derived from the cane, became an important industry. So did the processing of tobacco, for smoking in clay pipes (produced in bulk at Delft and elsewhere) or for taking as snuff. Cotton had been known before as an Eastern plant, but its successful transplantation to the New World made much greater quantities available and stimulated the emergence of an important new textile industry.

Historical Pictures Service, Chicago

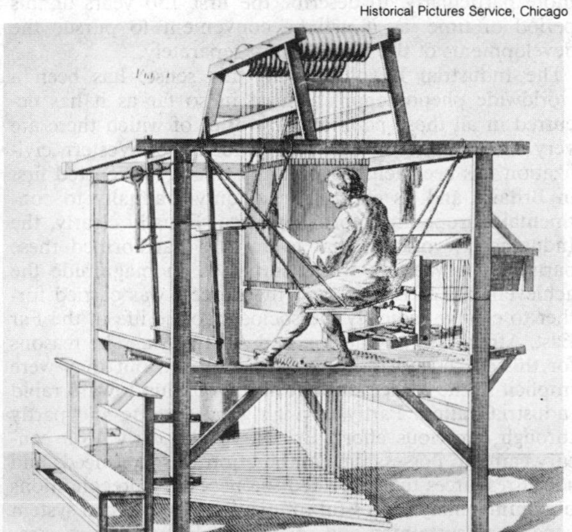

Drawloom, engraving from Diderot's *Encyclopédie,* 18th century.

The woolen cloth industry in Britain provided a model and precedent upon which the new cotton industry could build. Already in the Middle Ages, the processes of cloth manufacture had been partially mechanized upon the introduction of fulling mills and the use of spinning wheels. But in the 18th century the industry remained almost entirely a domestic or cottage one, with most of the processing being performed in the homes of the workers, using comparatively simple tools that could be operated by hand or foot. The most complicated apparatus was the loom, but this could usually be worked by a single weaver, although wider cloths required an assistant. It was a general practice to install the loom in an upstairs room with a long window giving maximum natural light. Weaving was regarded as a man's work, spinning being assigned to the women of the family (hence, "spinsters"). The weaver could use the yarn provided by up to a dozen spinsters, and the balanced division of labour was preserved by the weaver's assuming responsibility for supervising the cloth through the other processes, such as fulling. Pressures to increase the productivity of various operations had already produced some technical innovations by the first half of the 18th century. The first attempts at devising a spinning machine, however, were not successful; and without this, John Kay's technically successful flying shuttle (a device for hitting the shuttle from one side of the loom to the other, dispensing with the need to pass it through by hand) did not fulfill an obvious need. It was not until the rapid rise of the cotton cloth industry that the old, balanced industrial system was seriously upset and that a new, mechanized system, organized on the basis of factory production, began to emerge.

The textile industry

Agriculture. Another major area that began to show signs of profound change in the 18th century was agriculture. Stimulated by greater commercial activity, the rising market for food caused by an increasing population aspiring to a higher standard of living, and by the British aristocratic taste for improving estates to provide affluent and decorative country houses, the traditional agricultural system of Britain was transformed. It is important to note that this was a British development, as it is one of the indications of the increasing pressures of industrialization there even before the Industrial Revolution, while other European countries, with the exception of the Netherlands, from which several of the agricultural innovations in Britain were acquired, did little to encourage agricultural productivity. The nature of the transformation was complex, and it was not completed until well into the 19th century. It consisted partly of a legal reallocation of land ownership, the "enclosure" movement, to make farms more compact and economical to operate. In part also it was brought about by the increased investment in farming improvements, because the landowners felt encouraged to invest money in their estates instead of merely drawing rents from them. Again, it consisted of using this money for technical improvements, taking the form of machinery—such as Jethro Tull's mechanical sower—of better drainage, of scientific methods of breeding to raise the quality of livestock, and of experimenting with new crops and systems of crop rotation. The process has often been described as an agricultural revolution, but it is preferable to regard it as an essential prelude to and part of the Industrial Revolution.

Construction. Construction techniques did not undergo any great change in the period 1500–1750. The practice of building in stone and brick became general, although timber remained an important building material for roofs and floors, and, in areas in which stone was in short supply, the half-timber type of construction retained its popularity into the 17th century. Thereafter, however, the spread of brick and tile manufacturing provided a cheap and readily available substitute, although it suffered an eclipse on aesthetic grounds in the 18th century, when classical styles enjoyed a vogue and brick came to be regarded as inappropriate for facing such buildings. Brickmaking, however, had become an important industry for ordinary domestic building by then and, indeed, entered into the export trade as Dutch and Swedish ships regularly carried brick as ballast to the New World, providing a valuable building material for the early American settlements. Cast iron was coming into use in buildings, but only for decorative purposes. Glass was also beginning to become an important feature of buildings of all sorts, encouraging the development of an industry that still relied largely on ancient skills of fusing sand to make glass and blowing, molding, and cutting it into the shapes required.

Brick and tile manufacture

Land reclamation. More substantial constructional techniques were required in land drainage and military fortification, although again their importance is shown rather in their scale and complexity than in any novel features. The Dutch, wrestling with the sea for centuries, had devised extensive dikes; their techniques were borrowed by English landowners in the 17th century in an attempt to reclaim tracts of fenlands.

Military fortifications. In military fortification, the French strongholds designed by Sébastien de Vauban in the late 17th century demonstrated how warfare had adapted to the new weapons and, in particular, to heavy artillery. With earthen embankments to protect their salients, these star-shaped fortresses were virtually impregnable to the assault weapons of the day. Firearms remained cumbersome, with awkward firing devices and slow reloading. The quality of weapons improved somewhat as gunsmiths became more skillful.

Transport and communications. Like constructional techniques, transport and communications made substantial progress without any great technical innovations. Road building was greatly improved in France, and, with the completion of the Canal du Midi between the Mediterranean and the Bay of Biscay in 1692, large-scale civil engineering achieved an outstanding success. The canal is 150 miles (241 kilometres) long, with a hundred locks, a tunnel, three major aqueducts, many culverts, and a large summit reservoir.

The Canal du Midi

The sea remained the greatest highway of commerce, stimulating innovation in the sailing ship. The Elizabethan galleon with its great maneuverability and firepower, the Dutch herring *busses* and *fluitschips* with their commodious hulls and shallow draft, the versatile East Indiamen of both the Dutch and the British East India companies, and the mighty ships of the line produced for the French and British navies in the 18th century indicate some of the main directions of evolution.

The needs of reliable navigation created a demand for better instruments. The quadrant was improved by conversion to the octant, using mirrors to align the image of a star with the horizon and to measure its angle more accurately: with further refinements the modern sextant evolved. Even more significant was the ingenuity shown by scientists and instrument makers in the construction of a clock that would keep accurate time at sea: such a clock, by showing the time in Greenwich when it was noon aboard ship would show how far east or west of Greenwich the ship lay (longitude). A prize of £20,000 was offered by the British Board of Longitude for this purpose in 1714, but it was not awarded until 1763 when John Harrison's so-called No. 4 chronometer fulfilled all the requirements.

Chemistry. Robert Boyle's contribution to the theory of steam power has been mentioned, but Boyle is more commonly recognized as the "father of chemistry," in which field he was responsible for the recognition of an element as a material that cannot be resolved into other substances. It was not until the end of the 18th and the beginning of the 19th century, however, that the work of Antoine Lavoisier and John Dalton put modern chemical science on a firm theoretical basis. Chemistry was still struggling to free itself from the traditions of alchemy. Even alchemy was not without practical applications, for it promoted experiments with materials and led to the development of specialized laboratory equipment that was used in the manufacture of dyes, cosmetics, and certain pharmaceutical products. For the most part, pharmacy still relied upon recipes based on herbs and other natural products, but the systematic preparation of these eventually led to the discovery of useful new drugs.

The period from 1500 to 1750 witnessed the emergence of Western technology in the sense that the superior techniques of Western civilization enabled the nations that composed it to expand their influence over the whole known world. Yet, with the exception of the steam engine, this period was not marked by outstanding technological innovation. What was, perhaps, more important than any particular innovation was the evolution, however faltering and partial and limited to Britain in the first place, of a technique of innovation, or what has been called "the invention of invention." The creation of a political and social environment conducive to invention, the building up of vast commercial resources to support inventions likely to produce profitable results, the exploitation of mineral, agricultural, and other raw material resources for industrial purposes, and, above all, the recognition of specific needs for invention and an unwillingness to be defeated by difficulties, together produced a society ripe for an industrial revolution based on technological innovation. The technological achievements of the period 1500–1750, therefore, must be judged in part by their substantial contribution to the spectacular innovations of the following period.

Emergence of Western technology

The Industrial Revolution (1750–1900)

The term Industrial Revolution, like similar historical concepts, is more convenient than precise. It is convenient because history requires division into periods for purposes of understanding and instruction and because there were sufficient innovations at the turn of the 18th and 19th centuries to justify the choice of this as one of the periods. The term is imprecise, however, because the Industrial Revolution has no clearly defined beginning or end. Moreover, it is misleading if it carries the implication of a once-for-all change from a "preindustrial" to a "postindustrial" society, because, as has been seen, the events of the traditional Industrial Revolution had been well prepared in a mounting tempo of industrial, commercial, and technological activity from about AD 1000 and led into a continuing acceleration of the processes of industrialization that is still proceeding in our own time. The term Industrial Revolution must thus be employed with some care. It is used below to describe an extraordinary quickening in the rate of growth and change, and more particularly, to describe the first 150 years of this period of time, as it will be convenient to pursue the developments of the 20th century separately.

The Industrial Revolution, in this sense, has been a worldwide phenomenon, at least in so far as it has occurred in all those parts of the world, of which there are very few exceptions, where the influence of Western civilization has been felt. Beyond any doubt it occurred first in Britain, and its effects spread only gradually to continental Europe and North America. Equally clearly, the Industrial Revolution that eventually transformed these parts of the Western world surpassed in magnitude the achievements of Britain, and the process was carried further to change radically the socioeconomic life of the Far East, Africa, Latin America, and Australasia. The reasons for this succession of events are complex, but they were implicit in the earlier account of the buildup toward rapid industrialization. Partly through good fortune and partly through conscious effort, Britain by the early 18th century came to possess the combination of social needs and social resources that provided the necessary preconditions of commercially successful innovation and a social system capable of sustaining and institutionalizing the processes of rapid technological change once they had started. This section will therefore be concerned, in the first place, with

Spread of the Industrial Revolution

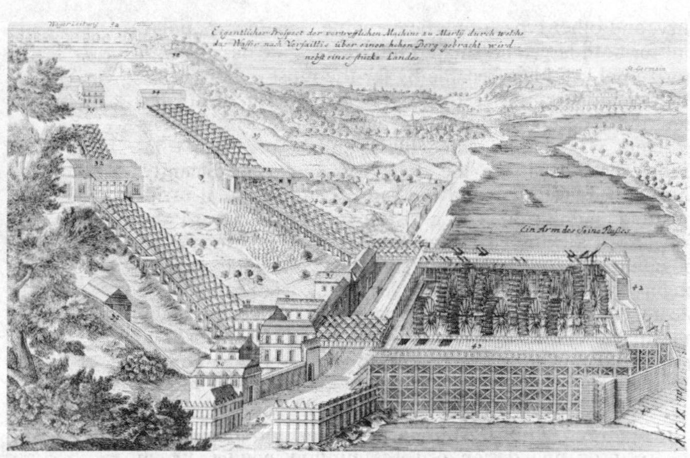

Waterwheels driven by the force of the river current activate a system of pumps to provide an inland water supply. Engraving from Jakob Leupold's *Theatrum Machinarum*, 1724–39.

events in Britain, although in discussing later phases of the period it will be necessary to trace the way in which British technical achievements were diffused and superseded in other parts of the Western world.

POWER TECHNOLOGY

An outstanding feature of the Industrial Revolution has been the advance in power technology. At the beginning of this period, the major sources of power available to industry and any other potential consumer were animate energy and the power of wind and water, the only exception of any significance being the atmospheric steam engines that had been installed for pumping purposes, mainly in coal mines. It is to be emphasized that this use of steam power was exceptional and remained so for most industrial purposes until well into the 19th century. Steam did not simply replace other sources of power: it transformed them. The same sort of scientific inquiry that led to the development of the steam engine was also applied to the traditional sources of inanimate energy, with the result that both waterwheels and windmills were improved in design and efficiency. Numerous engineers contributed to the refinement of waterwheel construction, and by the middle of the 19th century new designs made possible increases in the speed of revolution of the waterwheel and thus prepared the way for the emergence of the water turbine, which is still an extremely efficient device for converting energy.

Windmills. Meanwhile, British windmill construction was improved considerably by the refinements of sails and by the self-correcting device of the fantail, which kept the sails pointed into the wind. Spring sails replaced the traditional canvas rig of the windmill with the equivalent of a modern venetian blind, the shutters of which could be opened or closed, to let the wind pass through or to provide a surface upon which its pressure could be exerted. Sail design was further improved with the "patent" sail in 1807. In mills equipped with these sails, the shutters were controlled on all the sails simultaneously by a lever inside the mill connected by rod linkages through the windshaft with the bar operating the movement of the shutters on each sweep. The control could be made more fully automatic by hanging weights on the lever in the mill to determine the maximum wind pressure beyond which the shutters would open and spill the wind. Conversely, counterweights could be attached to keep the shutters in the open position. With these and other modifications, British windmills adapted to the increasing demands on power technology. But the use of wind power declined sharply in the 19th century with the spread of steam and the increasing scale of power utilization. Windmills that had satisfactorily provided power for small-scale industrial processes were unable to compete with the production of large-scale steam-powered mills.

Steam engines. Although the qualification regarding older sources of power is important, steam became the characteristic and ubiquitous power source of the British Industrial Revolution. Little development took place in the Newcomen atmospheric engine until James Watt patented a separate condenser in 1769, but from that point onward the steam engine underwent almost continuous improvements for more than a century. Watt's separate condenser was the outcome of his work on a model of a Newcomen engine that was being used in a University of Glasgow laboratory. Watt's inspiration was to separate the two actions of heating the cylinder with hot steam and cooling it to condense the steam for every stroke of the engine. By keeping the cylinder permanently hot and the condenser permanently cold, a great economy on energy used could be effected. This brilliantly simple idea could not be immediately incorporated in a full-scale engine because the engineering of such machines had hitherto been crude and defective. The backing of a Birmingham industrialist, Matthew Boulton, with his resources of capital and technical competence, was needed to convert the idea into a commercial success. Between 1775 and 1800, the period over which Watt's patents were extended, the Boulton and Watt partnership produced some 500 engines, which despite their high cost in relation to a Newcomen engine were eagerly acquired by the tin-mining industrialists of Cornwall and other power users who badly needed a more economic and reliable source of energy.

Watt's separate condenser

During the quarter of a century in which Boulton and Watt exercised their virtual monopoly over the manufacture of improved steam engines, they introduced many important refinements. Basically they converted the engine from a single-acting (*i.e.,* applying power only on the downward stroke of the piston) atmospheric pumping machine into a versatile prime mover that was double-acting and could be applied to rotary motion, thus driving the wheels of industry. The rotary action engine was quickly adopted by British textile manufacturer Sir Richard Arkwright for use in a cotton mill, and although the ill-fated Albion Mill, at the southern end of Blackfriars Bridge in London, was burned down in 1791, when it had been in use for only five years and was still incomplete, it demonstrated the feasibility of applying steam power to large-scale grain milling. Many other industries followed in exploring the possibilities of steam power, and it soon became widely used.

Watt's patents had the temporary effect of restricting the development of high-pressure steam, necessary in such major power applications as the locomotive. This development came quickly once these patents lapsed in 1800. The

James Watt's rotative steam engine with sun-and-planet gear, original drawing, 1788. In the Science Museum, London.

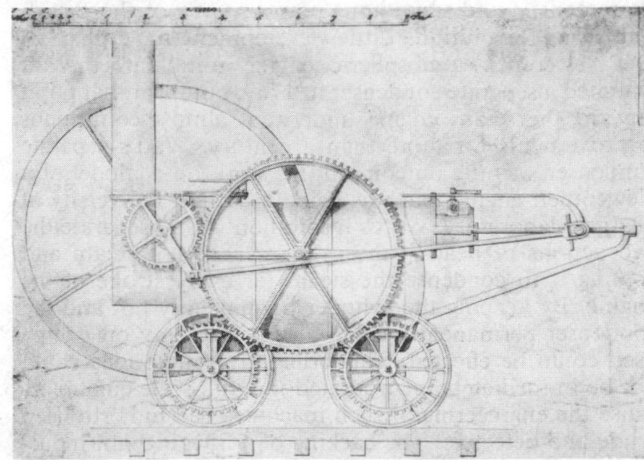

Trevithick steam locomotive, drawing by an unknown artist. In the Science Museum, London.
By courtesy of the Science Museum, London

Cornish engineer Richard Trevithick introduced higher steam pressures, achieving an unprecedented pressure of 145 pounds per square inch (10 kilograms per square centimetre) in 1802 with an experimental engine at Coalbrookdale, which worked safely and efficiently. Almost simultaneously, the versatile American engineer Oliver Evans built the first high-pressure steam engine in the United States, using, like Trevithick, a cylindrical boiler with an internal fire plate and flue. High-pressure steam engines rapidly became popular in America, partly as a result of Evans' initiative and partly because very few Watt-type low-pressure engines crossed the Atlantic. Trevithick quickly applied his engine to a vehicle, making the first successful steam locomotive for the Penydarren tramroad in South Wales in 1804. The success, however, was technological rather than commercial because the locomotive fractured the cast iron track of the tramway: the age of the railroad had to await further development both of the permanent way and of the locomotive.

First steam locomotive

Meanwhile, the stationary steam engine advanced steadily to meet an ever-widening market of industrial requirements. High-pressure steam led to the development of the large beam pumping engines with a complex sequence of valve actions, which became universally known as Cornish engines; their distinctive characteristic was the cutoff of steam injection before the stroke was complete in order to allow the steam to do work by expanding. These engines were used all over the world for heavy pumping duties, often being shipped out and installed by Cornish engineers. Trevithick himself spent many years improving pumping engines in Latin America. Cornish engines, however, were probably most common in Cornwall itself, where they were used in large numbers in the tin and copper mining industries.

Another consequence of high-pressure steam was the practice of compounding, of using the steam twice or more at descending pressures before it was finally condensed or exhausted. The technique was first applied by Arthur Woolf, a Cornish mining engineer, who by 1811 had produced a very satisfactory and efficient compound beam engine with a high-pressure cylinder placed alongside the low-pressure cylinder, with both piston rods attached to the same pin of the parallel motion, which was a parallelogram of rods connecting the piston to the beam, patented by Watt in 1784. In 1845 John McNaught introduced an alternative form of compound beam engine, with the high-pressure cylinder on the opposite end of the beam from the low-pressure cylinder, and working with a shorter stroke. This became a very popular design. Various other methods of compounding steam engines were adopted, and the practice became increasingly widespread; in the second half of the 19th century triple- or quadruple-expansion engines were being used in industry and marine propulsion. By this time also the conventional beam-type vertical engine adopted by Newcomen and retained by Watt began to be replaced by horizontal-cylinder designs. Beam engines remained in use for some purposes until the eclipse of the reciprocating steam engine in the 20th century, and other types of vertical engine remained popular, but for both large and small duties the engine designs with horizontal cylinders became by far the most common.

A demand for power to generate electricity stimulated new thinking about the steam engine in the 1880s. The problem was that of achieving a sufficiently high rotational speed to make the dynamos function efficiently. Such speeds were beyond the range of the normal reciprocating engine (*i.e.,* with a piston moving backward and forward in a cylinder). Designers began to investigate the possibilities of radical modifications to the reciprocating engine to achieve the speeds desired, or of devising a steam engine working on a completely different principle. In the first category, one solution was to enclose the working parts of the engine and force a lubricant around them under pressure. The Willans engine design, for instance, was of this type and was widely adopted in early British power stations. Another important modification in the reciprocating design was the uniflow engine, which increased efficiency by exhausting steam from ports in the centre of the cylinder instead of requiring it to change its direction of flow in the cylinder with every movement of the piston. Full success in achieving a high-speed steam engine, however, depended on the steam turbine, a design of such novelty that it constituted a major technological innovation. This was invented by Sir Charles Parsons in 1884. By passing steam through the blades of a series of rotors of gradually increasing size (to allow for the expansion of the steam) the energy of the steam was converted to very rapid circular motion, which was ideal for generating electricity. Many refinements have since been made in turbine construction and the size of turbines has been vastly increased, but the basic principles remain the same, and this method still provides the main source of electric power except in those areas in which the mountainous terrain permits the economic generation of hydroelectric power by water turbines. Even the most modern nuclear power plants use steam turbines because technology has not yet solved the problem of transforming nuclear energy directly into electricity. In marine propulsion, too, the steam turbine remains an important source of power despite competition from the internal-combustion engine.

Invention of the steam turbine

Electricity. The development of electricity as a source of power preceded this conjunction with steam power late in the 19th century. The pioneering work had been done by an international collection of scientists including Benjamin Franklin of Pennsylvania, Alessandro Volta of the University of Pavia, Italy, and Michael Faraday of Britain. It was the latter who had demonstrated the nature of the elusive relationship between electricity and magnetism in 1831, and his experiments provided the point of departure for both the mechanical generation of electric current, previously available only from chemical reactions within voltaic piles or batteries, and the utilization of such current in electric motors. Both the mechanical generator and the motor depend on the rotation of a continuous coil of conducting wire between the poles of a strong magnet: turning the coil produces a current in it, while passing a current through the coil causes it to turn. Both generators and motors underwent substantial development in the middle decades of the 19th century. In particular, French, German, Belgian, and Swiss engineers evolved the most satisfactory forms of armature (the coil of wire) and produced the dynamo, which made the large-scale generation of electricity commercially feasible.

The next problem was that of finding a market. In Britain, with its now well-established tradition of steam power, coal, and coal gas, such a market was not immediately obvious. But in continental Europe and North America there was more scope for experiment. In the United States Thomas Edison applied his inventive genius to finding fresh uses for electricity, and his development of the carbon-filament lamp showed how this form of energy could rival gas as a domestic illuminant. The problem had been that electricity had been used successfully for large installations such as lighthouses in which arc lamps had been powered by generators on the premises, but no way of subdividing the electric light into many small units had been devised. The principle of the filament lamp was

Development of the electric light

that a thin conductor could be made incandescent by an electric current provided that it was sealed in a vacuum to keep it from burning out. Edison and the English chemist Sir Joseph Swan experimented with various materials for the filament and both chose carbon. The result was a highly successful small lamp, which could be varied in size for any sort of requirement. It is relevant that the success of the carbon-filament lamp did not immediately mean the supersession of gas lighting. Coal gas had first been used for lighting by William Murdock at his home in Redruth, Cornwall, where he was the agent for the Boulton and Watt company, in 1792. When he moved to the headquarters of the firm at Soho in Birmingham in 1798, Matthew Boulton authorized him to experiment in lighting the buildings there by gas, and gas lighting was subsequently adopted by firms and towns all over Britain in the first half of the 19th century. Lighting was normally provided by a fishtail jet of burning gas, but under the stimulus of competition from electric lighting the quality of gas lighting was greatly enhanced by the invention of the gas mantle. Thus improved, gas lighting remained popular for some forms of street lighting until the middle of the 20th century.

Lighting alone could not provide an economical market for electricity because its use was confined to the hours of darkness. Successful commercial generation depended upon the development of other uses for electricity, and particularly on electric traction. The popularity of urban electric tramways and the adoption of electric traction on subway systems such as the London Underground thus coincided with the widespread construction of generating equipment in the late 1880s and 1890s. The subsequent spread of this form of energy is one of the most remarkable technological success stories of the 20th century, but most of the basic techniques of generation, distribution, and utilization had been mastered by the end of the 19th century.

Internal-combustion engine. Electricity does not constitute a prime mover, for however important it may be as a form of energy it has to be derived from a mechanical generator powered by water, steam, or internal combustion. The internal-combustion engine is a prime mover, and it emerged in the 19th century as a result both of greater scientific understanding of the principles of thermodynamics and of a search by engineers for a substitute for steam power in certain circumstances. In an internal-combustion engine the fuel is burned in the engine: the cannon provided an early model of a single-stroke engine; and several persons had experimented with gunpowder as a means of driving a piston in a cylinder. The major problem was that of finding a suitable fuel, and the secondary problem was that of igniting the fuel in an enclosed space to produce an action that could be easily and quickly repeated. The first problem was solved in the mid-19th century by the introduction of town gas supplies, but the second problem proved more intractable as it was difficult to maintain ignition evenly. The first successful gas engine was made by Étienne Lenoir in Paris in 1859. It was modeled closely on a horizontal steam engine, with an explosive mixture of gas and air ignited by an electric spark on alternate sides of the piston when it was in midstroke position. Although technically satisfactory, the engine was expensive to operate, and it was not until the refinement introduced by the German inventor Nikolaus Otto in 1878 that the gas engine became a commercial success. Otto adopted the four-stroke cycle of induction-compression-firing-exhaust that has been known by his name ever since. Gas engines became extensively used for small industrial establishments, which could thus dispense with the upkeep of a boiler necessary in any steam plant, however small.

The Otto cycle

Petroleum. The economic potential for the internal-combustion engine lay in the need for a light locomotive engine. This could not be provided by the gas engine, depending on a piped supply of town gas, any more than by the steam engine, with its need for a cumbersome boiler; but, by using alternative fuels derived from oil, the internal-combustion engine took to wheels, with momentous consequences. Bituminous deposits had been known in Southwest Asia from antiquity and had been worked for building material, illuminants, and medicinal products. The westward expansion of settlement in America, with many homesteads beyond the range of city gas supplies, promoted the exploitation of the easily available sources of crude oil for the manufacture of kerosene (paraffin). In 1859 the oil industry took on new significance when Edwin L. Drake bored successfully through 69 feet (21 metres) of rock to strike oil in Pennsylvania, thus inaugurating the search for and exploitation of the deep oil resources of the world. While world supplies of oil expanded dramatically, the main demand was at first for the kerosene, the middle fraction distilled from the raw material, which was used as the fuel in oil lamps. The most volatile fraction of the oil, gasoline, remained an embarrassing waste product until it was discovered that this could be burned in a light internal-combustion engine; the result was an ideal prime mover for vehicles. The way was prepared for this development by the success of oil engines burning cruder fractions of oil. Kerosene-burning oil engines, modeled closely on existing gas engines, had emerged in the 1870s, and by the late 1880s engines using the vapour of heavy oil in a jet of compressed air and working on the Otto cycle had become an attractive proposition for light duties in places too isolated to use town gas.

The diesel engine

The greatest refinements in the heavy-oil engine are associated with the work of Rudolf Diesel of Germany, who took out his first patents in 1892. Working from thermodynamic principles of minimizing heat losses, Diesel devised an engine in which the very high compression of the air in the cylinder secured the spontaneous ignition of the oil when it was injected in a carefully determined quantity. This ensured high thermal efficiency, but it also made necessary a heavy structure because of the high compression maintained, and also a rather rough performance at low speeds compared with other oil engines. It was therefore not immediately suitable for locomotive purposes, but Diesel went on improving his engine and in the 20th century it became an important form of vehicular propulsion.

Meantime the light high-speed gasoline (petrol) engine predominated. The first applications of the new engine to locomotion were made in Germany, where Gottlieb Daimler and Carl Benz equipped the first motorcycle and the first motorcar respectively with engines of their own design in 1885. Benz's "horseless carriage" became the prototype of the modern automobile, the development and consequences of which can be more conveniently considered in relation to the revolution in transport.

By the end of the 19th century, the internal-combustion engine was challenging the steam engine in many industrial and transport applications. It is notable that, whereas the pioneers of the steam engine had been almost all Britons, most of the innovators in internal combustion were continental Europeans and Americans. The transition, indeed, reflects the general change in international leadership in the Industrial Revolution, with Britain being gradually displaced from its position of unchallenged superiority in industrialization and technological innovation. A similar transition occurred in the theoretical understanding of heat engines: it was the work of the Frenchman Sadi Carnot and other scientific investigators that led to the new science of thermodynamics, rather than that of the British engineers who had most practical experience of the engines on which the science was based.

It should not be concluded, however, that British innovation in prime movers was confined to the steam engine, or even that steam and internal combustion represent the only significant developments in this field during the Industrial Revolution. Rather, the success of these machines stimulated speculation about alternative sources of power, and in at least one case achieved a success the full consequences of which were not completely developed. This was the hot-air engine, for which a Scotsman, Robert Stirling, took out a patent in 1816. The hot-air engine depends for its power on the expansion and displacement of air inside a cylinder, heated by the external and continuous combustion of the fuel. Even before the exposition of the laws of thermodynamics, Stirling had devised a cycle of

The hot-air engine

heat transfer that was ingenious and economical. Various constructional problems limited the size of hot-air engines to very small units, so that although they were widely used for driving fans and similar light duties before the availability of the electric motor, they did not assume great technological significance. But the economy and comparative cleanness of the hot-air engine were making it once more the subject of intensive research in the early 1970s.

The transformation of power technology in the Industrial Revolution had repercussions throughout industry and society. In the first place, the demand for fuel stimulated the coal industry, which had already grown rapidly by the beginning of the 18th century, into continuing expansion and innovation. The steam engine, which enormously increased the need for coal, contributed significantly toward obtaining it by providing more efficient mine pumps and, eventually, improved ventilating equipment. Other inventions such as that of the miners' safety lamp helped to improve working conditions, although the immediate consequence of its introduction in 1816 was to persuade mineowners to work dangerous seams, which had thitherto been regarded as inaccessible. The principle of the lamp was that the flame from the wick of an oil lamp was enclosed within a cylinder of wire gauze, through which insufficient heat passed to ignite the explosive gas (firedamp) outside. It was subsequently improved, but remained a vital source of light in coal mines until the advent of electric battery lamps. With these improvements, together with the simultaneous revolution in the transport system, British coal production increased steadily throughout the 19th century. The other important fuel for the new prime movers was petroleum, and the rapid expansion of its production has already been mentioned. In the hands of John D. Rockefeller and his Standard Oil organization it grew into a vast undertaking in the United States after the end of the Civil War, but the oil-extraction industry was not so well organized elsewhere until the 20th century.

DEVELOPMENT OF INDUSTRIES

Metallurgy. Another industry that interacted closely with the power revolution was that concerned with metallurgy and the metal trades. The development of techniques for working with iron and steel was one of the outstanding British achievements of the Industrial Revolution. The essential characteristic of this achievement was that changing the fuel of the iron and steel industry from charcoal to coal enormously increased the production of these metals. It also provided another incentive to coal production and made available the materials that were indispensable for the construction of steam engines and every other sophisticated form of machine. The transformation that began with a coke-smelting process in 1709 was carried further by the development of crucible steel in about 1740 and by the puddling and rolling process to produce wrought iron in 1784. The first development led to high-quality cast steel by fusion of the ingredients (wrought iron and charcoal, in carefully measured proportions) in sealed ceramic crucibles that could be heated in a coal-fired furnace. The second applied the principle of the reverberatory furnace, whereby the hot gases passed over the surface of the metal being heated rather than through it, thus greatly reducing the risk of contamination by impurities in the coal fuels, and the discovery that by puddling, or stirring, the molten metal and by passing it hot from the furnace to be hammered and rolled, the metal could be consolidated and the conversion of cast iron to wrought iron made completely effective.

Use of coal in the iron and steel industry

Iron and steel. The result of this series of innovations was that the British iron and steel industry was freed from its reliance upon the forests as a source of charcoal and was encouraged to move toward the major coalfields. Abundant cheap iron thus became an outstanding feature of the early stages of the Industrial Revolution in Britain. Cast iron was available for bridge construction, for the framework of fireproof factories, and for other civil-engineering purposes such as Thomas Telford's novel cast-iron aqueducts. Wrought iron was available for all manner of mechanical devices requiring strength and precision. Steel remained a comparatively rare metal until the second half of the 19th century, when the situation was transformed by the Bessemer and Siemens processes for manufacturing steel in bulk. Henry Bessemer took out the patent for his converter in 1856. It consisted of a large vessel charged with molten iron, through which cold air was blown. There was a spectacular reaction resulting from the combination of impurities in the iron with oxygen in the air, and when this subsided it left mild steel in the converter. Bessemer was virtually a professional inventor with little previous knowledge of the iron and steel industry; his process was closely paralleled by that of the American iron manufacturer William Kelly, who was prevented by bankruptcy from taking advantage of his invention. Meanwhile, the Siemens–Martin open-hearth process was introduced in 1864, utilizing the hot waste gases of cheap fuel to heat a regenerative furnace, with the initial heat transferred to the gases circulating round the large hearth in which the reactions within the molten metal could be carefully controlled to produce steel of the quality required. The open-hearth process was gradually refined and by the end of the 19th century had overtaken the Bessemer process in the amount of steel produced. The effect of these two processes was to make steel available in bulk instead of small-scale ingots of cast crucible steel, and thenceforward steel steadily replaced wrought iron as the major commodity of the iron and steel industry.

Manufacture of steel using Bessemer converters, engraving by C. Laplante, 1875.
The Bettmann Archive

The Bessemer converter

Low-grade ores. The transition to cheap steel did not take place without technical problems, one of the most difficult of which was the fact that most of the easily available low-grade iron ores in the world contain a proportion of phosphorus, which proved difficult to eliminate but which ruined any steel produced from them. The problem was solved by the British scientists S.G. Thomas and Percy Gilchrist, who invented the basic slag process, in which the furnace or converter was lined with an alkaline material with which the phosphorus could combine to produce a phosphatic slag; this, in turn, became an important raw material in the nascent artificial-fertilizer industry. The most important effect of this innovation was to make the extensive phosphoric ores of Lorraine and elsewhere available for exploitation. Among other things, therefore, it contributed significantly to the rise of the German heavy iron and steel industry in the Ruhr. Other improvements in British steel production were made in the late 19th century, particularly in the development of alloys for specialized purposes, but these contributed more to the quality than the quantity of steel and did not affect the shift away from Britain to continental Europe and North America of dominance in this industry. British production continued to increase, but by 1900 it had been overtaken by that of the United States and Germany.

Mechanical engineering. Closely linked with the iron and steel industry was the rise of mechanical engineering, brought about by the demand for steam engines and other large machines, and taking shape for the first time in the Soho workshop of Boulton and Watt in Birmingham, where the skills of the precision engineer, developed in manufacturing scientific instruments and small arms, were first applied to the construction of large industrial machinery. The engineering workshops that matured in the 19th century played a vital part in the increasing mechanization of industry and transport. Not only did they deliver the looms, locomotives, and other hardware in steadily growing quantities, but they also transformed the machine tools on which these machines were made. The lathe became an all-metal, power-driven machine with a completely rigid base and a slide rest to hold the cutting tool, capable of more sustained and vastly more accurate work than the hand- or foot-operated wooden-framed lathes that preceded it. Drilling and slotting machines, milling and planing machines, and a steam hammer invented by James Nasmyth (an inverted vertical steam engine with the hammer on the lower end of the piston rod), were among the machines devised or improved from earlier woodworking models by the new mechanical engineering industry. After the middle of the 19th century, specialization within the machinery industry became more pronounced, as some manufacturers concentrated on vehicle production while others devoted themselves to the particular needs of industries such as coal mining, papermaking, and sugar refining. This movement toward greater specialization was accelerated by the establishment of mechanical engineering in the other industrial nations, especially in Germany, where electrical engineering and other new skills made rapid progress, and in the United States, where labour shortages encouraged the development of standardization and mass-production techniques in fields as widely separated as agricultural machinery, small arms, typewriters, and sewing machines. Even before the coming of the bicycle, the automobile, and the airplane, therefore, the pattern of the modern engineering industry had been clearly established. The dramatic increases in engineering precision, represented by the machine designed by British mechanical engineer Sir Joseph Whitworth in 1856 for measuring to an accuracy of 0.000001 inch (even though such refinement was not necessary in everyday workshop practice), and the corresponding increase in the productive capacity of the engineering industry, acted as a continuing encouragement to further mechanical innovation.

Improvements in machine tools

Textiles. The industry that, probably more than any other, gave its character to the British Industrial Revolution was the cotton-textile industry. The traditional dates of the Industrial Revolution bracket the period in which the processes of cotton manufacture in Britain were transformed from those of a small-scale domestic industry scattered over the towns and villages of the South Pennines into those of a large-scale, concentrated, power-driven, mechanized, factory-organized, urban industry. The transformation was undoubtedly dramatic both to contemporaries and to posterity, and there is no doubting its immense significance in the overall pattern of British industrialization. But its importance in the history of technology should not be exaggerated. Certainly there were many interesting mechanical improvements, at least at the beginning of the transformation. The development of the spinning wheel into the spinning jenny, and the use of rollers and moving trolleys to mechanize spinning in the shape of the frame and the mule, respectively, initiated a drastic rise in the productivity of the industry. But these were secondary innovations in the sense that there were precedents for them in the experiments of the previous generation; that in any case the first British textile factory was the Derby silk mill built in 1719; and that the most far-reaching innovation in cotton manufacture was the introduction of steam power to drive carding machines, spinning machines, power looms, and printing machines. This, however, is probably to overstate the case, and the cotton innovators should not be deprived of credit for their enterprise and ingenuity in transforming the British cotton industry and making it the model for subsequent exercises in industrialization. Not only was it copied, belatedly and slowly, by the woolen-cloth industry in Britain, but wherever other nations sought to industrialize they tried to acquire British cotton machinery and the expertise of British cotton industrialists and artisans.

Importance of the British cotton industry

One of the important consequences of the rapid rise of the British cotton industry was the dynamic stimulus it gave to other processes and industries. The rising demand for raw cotton, for example, encouraged the plantation economy of the southern United States and the introduction of the cotton gin, an important contrivance for separating mechanically the cotton fibres from the seeds, husks, and stems of the plant.

Chemicals. In Britain, the growth of the textile industry brought a sudden increase of interest in the chemical industry, because one formidable bottleneck in the production of textiles was the long time that was taken by natural bleaching techniques, relying on sunlight, rain, sour milk, and urine. The modern chemical industry was virtually called into being in order to develop more rapid bleaching techniques for the British cotton industry. Its first success came in the middle of the 18th century, when John Roebuck invented the method of mass producing sulfuric acid in lead chambers. The acid was used directly in bleaching, but it was also used in the production of more effective chlorine bleaches, and in the manufacture of bleaching powder, a process perfected by Charles Tennant at his St. Rollox factory in Glasgow in 1799. This product effectively met the requirements of the cotton-textile industry, and thereafter the chemical industry turned its attention to the needs of other industries, and particularly to the increasing demand for alkali in soap, glass, and a range of other manufacturing processes. The result was the successful establishment of the Leblanc soda process, patented by Nicolas Leblanc in France in 1791, for manufacturing sodium carbonate (soda) on a large scale; this remained the main alkali process used in Britain until the end of the 19th century, even though the Belgian Solvay process, which was considerably more economical, was replacing it elsewhere.

Innovation in the chemical industry shifted, in the middle of the 19th century, from the heavy chemical processes to organic chemistry. The stimulus here was less a specific industrial demand than the pioneering work of a group of German scientists on the nature of coal and its derivatives. Following their work, W.H. Perkin, at the Royal College of Chemistry in London, produced the first artificial dye from aniline in 1856. In the same period, the middle third of the 19th century, work on the qualities of cellulosic materials was leading to the development of high explosives such as nitrocellulose, nitroglycerine, and dynamite, while experiments with the solidification and extrusion of cellulosic liquids were producing the first plastics, such as celluloid, and the first artificial fibres, so-called artificial silk, or rayon. By the end of the century all these processes had become the bases for large chemical industries.

An important by-product of the expanding chemical industry was the manufacture of a widening range of medicinal and pharmaceutical materials as medical knowledge increased and drugs began to play a constructive part in therapy. The period of the Industrial Revolution witnessed the first real progress in medical services since the ancient civilizations. Great advances in the sciences of anatomy and physiology had had remarkably little effect on medical practice. In 18th-century Britain, however, hospital provision increased in quantity although not invariably in quality, while a significant start was made in immunizing people against smallpox culminating in Edward Jenner's vaccination process of 1796, by which protection from the disease was provided by administering a dose of the much less virulent but related disease of cowpox. But it took many decades of use and further smallpox epidemics to secure its widespread adoption and thus to make it effective in controlling the disease. By this time Louis Pasteur and others had established the bacteriological origin of many common diseases and thereby helped to promote movements for better public health and immunization against many virulent diseases such as typhoid fever and diphtheria. Parallel improvements in anesthetics (beginning with Sir Humphry Davy's discovery of nitrous oxide, or "laughing gas," in 1799) and antiseptics were making possible elaborate surgery, and by the end of the century X rays and radiology were placing powerful new tools at the disposal of medical technology, while the use of synthetic

Improvements in control of disease

drugs such as the barbiturates and aspirin (acetylsalicylic acid) had become established.

Agriculture. The agricultural improvements of the 18th century had been promoted by people whose industrial and commercial interests made them willing to experiment with new machines and processes to improve the productivity of their estates. Under the same sort of stimuli, agricultural improvement continued into the 19th century and was extended to food processing in Britain and elsewhere. The steam engine was not readily adapted for agricultural purposes, yet ways were found of harnessing it to threshing machines and even to plowing by means of a cable pulling the plow across a field between powerful traction engines. In the United States mechanization of agriculture began later than in Britain, but because of the comparative labour shortage it proceeded more quickly and more thoroughly. The McCormick reaper and the combine harvester were both developed in the United States, as were barbed wire and the food-packing and canning industries, Chicago becoming the centre for these processes. The introduction of refrigeration techniques in the second half of the 19th century made it possible to convey meat from Australia and Argentina to European markets, and the same markets encouraged the growth of dairy farming and market gardening, with distant producers such as New Zealand able to send their butter in refrigerated ships to wherever in the world it could be sold.

Civil engineering. As far as large civil-engineering works were concerned, the heavy work of moving earth continued to depend throughout this period on human labour organized by building contractors. But the use of gunpowder, dynamite, and steam diggers helped to reduce this dependence toward the end of the 19th century, and the introduction of compressed air and hydraulic tools also contributed to the lightening of drudgery. The latter two inventions were important in other respects, such as in mining engineering and in the operation of lifts, lock gates, and cranes. The use of a tunneling shield, to allow a tunnel to be driven through soft or uncertain rock strata, was pioneered by the French émigré engineer Marc Brunel in the construction of the first tunnel underneath the Thames River in London (1825–42), and the technique was adopted elsewhere. The iron bell or caisson was introduced for working below water level in order to lay foundations for bridges or other structures, and bridge building made great advances with the perfecting of the suspension bridge—by the British engineers Thomas Telford and Isambard Kingdom Brunel and the German-American engineer John Roebling—and the development of the truss bridge, first in timber, then in iron. Wrought iron gradually replaced cast iron as a bridge-building material, although several distinguished cast-iron bridges survive, such as that erected at Ironbridge in Shropshire between 1777 and 1779, which has been fittingly described as the "Stonehenge of the Industrial Revolution." The sections were cast at the Coalbrookdale furnace nearby and assembled by mortising and wedging on the model of a timber construction, without the use of bolts or rivets. The design was quickly superseded in other cast-iron bridges, but the bridge still stands as the first important structural use of cast iron. Cast iron became very important in the framing of large buildings, the elegant Crystal Palace of 1851 being an outstanding example. This was designed by the ingenious gardener-turned-architect Sir Joseph Paxton on the model of a greenhouse that he had built on the Chatsworth estate of the Duke of Devonshire. Its cast-iron beams were manufactured by three different firms and tested for size and strength on the site. By the end of the 19th century, however, steel was beginning to replace cast iron as well as wrought iron, and reinforced concrete was being introduced. In water-supply and sewage-disposal works, civil engineering achieved some monumental successes, especially in the design of dams, which improved considerably in the period, and in long-distance piping and pumping.

Advances in bridge construction

Transport and communications. Transport and communications provide an example of a revolution within the Industrial Revolution, so completely were the modes transformed in the period 1750–1900. The first improvements in Britain came in roads and canals in the second half of the 18th century. Although of great economic importance, these were not of much significance in the history of technology, as good roads and canals had existed in continental Europe for at least a century before their adoption in Britain. A network of hard-surfaced roads was built in France in the 17th and early 18th centuries and copied in Germany. A notable improvement was introduced in road construction by Pierre Trésaguet of France in the later 18th century, in separating the hard-stone wearing surface from the rubble substrata and taking care to provide ample drainage. Nevertheless, by the beginning of the 19th century British engineers were beginning to innovate in both road- and canal-building techniques, with J.L. McAdam's cheap and long-wearing road surface of compacted stones and Thomas Telford's well-engineered canals. The outstanding innovation in transport, however, was the application of steam power, which occurred in three forms.

Steam locomotive. First was the evolution of the railroad: the combination of the steam locomotive and a permanent travel way of metal rails. Experiments in this conjunction in the first quarter of the 19th century culminated in the Stockton & Darlington Railway, opened in 1825, and a further five years of experience with steam locomotives led to the Liverpool and Manchester Railway, which, when it opened in 1830, constituted the first fully timetabled railway service with scheduled freight and passenger traffic relying entirely on the steam locomotive for traction. This railway was designed by George Stephenson, and the locomotives were the work of Stephenson and his son Robert, the first locomotive being the famous *Rocket,* which won a competition held by the proprietors of the railway at Rainhill, outside Liverpool, in 1829. The opening of the Liverpool and Manchester line may fairly be regarded as the inauguration of the Railway Era, which continued until World War I. During this time railways were built across all the countries and continents of the world, opening up vast areas to the markets of industrial society. Locomotives increased rapidly in size and power, but the essential principles remained the same as those established by the Stephensons in the early 1830s: horizontal cylinders mounted beneath a multitubular boiler with a firebox at the rear and a tender carrying supplies of water and fuel. This was the form developed from the *Rocket,* which had diagonal cylinders, being itself a stage in the transition from the vertical cylinders, often encased by the boiler, which had been typical of the earliest locomotives (except Trevithick's Penydarren engine, which had a horizontal cylinder). Meanwhile, the construction of the permanent way underwent a corresponding improvement on that which had been common on the preceding tramroads: wrought-iron, and eventually steel, rails replaced the cast-iron rails, which cracked easily under a steam locomotive, and well-aligned track with easy gradients and substantial supporting civil-engineering works became a commonplace of the railroads of the world.

Beginning of the Railway Era

Road locomotive. The second form in which steam power was applied to transport was that of the road locomotive. There is no technical reason why this should not have enjoyed a success equal to that of the railway engine, but its development was so constricted by the unsuitability of most roads and by the jealousy of other road users that it achieved general utility only for heavy traction work and such duties as road rolling. The steam traction engine, which could be readily adapted from road haulage to power farm machines, was nevertheless a distinguished product of 19th-century steam technology.

Steamboats and ships. The third application was much more important, for it transformed marine transport. The first attempts to use a steam engine to power a boat were made on the Seine in France in 1775, and several experimental steamships were built by William Symington in Britain at the turn of the 19th century. The first commercial success in steam propulsion for a ship, however, was that of the American Robert Fulton, whose paddle steamer *Clermont* plied between New York and Albany in 1807, equipped with a Boulton and Watt engine of the modified beam or side-lever type, with two beams placed

Robert Fulton's *Clermont*

alongside the base of the engine in order to lower the centre of gravity. A similar engine was installed in the Glasgow-built *Comet,* which was put in service on the Clyde in 1812 and was the first successful steamship in Europe. All the early steamships were paddle-driven, and all were small vessels suitable only for ferry and packet duties because it was long thought that the fuel requirements of a steamship would be so large as to preclude long-distance cargo carrying. The further development of the steamship was thus delayed until the 1830s, when I.K. Brunel began to apply his ingenious and innovating mind to the problems of steamship construction. His three great steamships each marked a leap forward in technique. The *Great Western* (launched 1837), the first built specifically for oceanic service in the North Atlantic, demonstrated that the proportion of space required for fuel decreased as the total volume of the ship increased. The *Great Britain* (launched 1843) was the first large iron ship in the world and the first to be screw propelled; its return to the port of Bristol in 1970, after a long working life and abandonment to the elements, is a remarkable testimony to the strength of its construction. The *Great Eastern* (launched 1858), with its total displacement of 18,918 tons, was by far the largest ship built in the 19th century. With a double iron hull and two sets of engines driving both a screw and paddles, this leviathan was never an economic success, but it admirably demonstrated the technical possibilities of the large iron steamship. By the end of the century, steamships were well on the way to displacing the sailing ship on all the main trade routes of the world.

Printing and photography. Communications were equally transformed in the 19th century. The steam engine helped to mechanize and thus to speed up the processes of papermaking and printing. In the latter case the acceleration was achieved by the introduction of the high-speed rotary press and the Linotype machine for casting type and setting it in justified lines (*i.e.,* with even right-hand margins). Printing, indeed, had to undergo a technological revolution comparable to the 15th-century invention of movable type to be able to supply the greatly increasing market for the printed word. Another important process that was to make a vital contribution to modern printing was discovered and developed in the 19th century: photography. The first photograph was taken in 1826 by the French physicist J.-N. Niépce, using a pewter plate coated with a form of bitumen that hardened on exposure. His partner L.-J.-M. Daguerre and the Englishman W.H. Fox Talbot adopted silver compounds to give light sensitivity, and the technique developed rapidly in the middle decades of the century. By the 1890s George Eastman in the United States was manufacturing cameras and celluloid photographic film for a popular market, and the first experiments with the cinema were beginning to attract attention.

Telegraphs and telephones. The great innovations in communications technology, however, derived from electricity. The first was the electric telegraph, invented or at least made into a practical proposition for use on the developing British railway system by two British inventors, Sir William Cooke and Sir Charles Wheatstone, who collaborated on the work and took out a joint patent in 1837. Almost simultaneously, the American inventor Samuel F.B. Morse devised the signaling code that was subsequently adopted all over the world. In the next quarter of a century the continents of the world were linked telegraphically by transoceanic cables, and the main political and commercial centres were brought into instantaneous communication. The telegraph system also played an important part in the opening up of the American West by providing rapid aid in the maintenance of law and order. The electric telegraph was followed by the telephone, invented by Alexander Graham Bell in 1876 and quickly adopted for short-range oral communication in the cities of America, and at a somewhat more leisurely pace by those of Europe. About the same time, theoretical work on the electromagnetic properties of light and other radiation was beginning to produce astonishing experimental results, and the possibilities of wireless telegraphy began to be explored. By the end of the century, Guglielmo Marconi had transmitted messages over many miles in Britain and was preparing the apparatus with which he made the first transatlantic radio communication on Dec. 12, 1901. The world was thus being drawn inexorably into a closer community by the spread of instantaneous communication.

Morse Code

Military technology. One area of technology was not dramatically influenced by the application of steam or electricity by the end of the 19th century: military technology. Although the size of armies increased between 1750 and 1900, there were few major innovations in techniques, except at sea where naval architecture rather reluctantly accepted the advent of the iron steamship and devoted itself to matching ever-increasing firepower with the strength of the armour plating on the hulls. The quality of artillery and of firearms improved with the new high explosives that became available in the middle of the 19th century, but experiments such as the three-wheeled iron gun carriage, invented by the French army engineer Nicolas Cugnot in 1769, which counts as the first steam-powered road vehicle, did not give rise to any confidence that steam could be profitably used in battle. Railroads and the electric telegraph were put to effective military use, but in general it is fair to say that the 19th century put remarkably little of its tremendous and innovative technological effort into devices for war.

In the course of its dynamic development between 1750 and 1900 important things happened to technology itself. In the first place, it became self-conscious. This change is sometimes characterized as one from a craft-based technology to one based on science, but this is an oversimplification. What occurred was rather an increase in the awareness of technology as a socially important function. It is apparent in the growing volume of treatises on technological subjects from the 16th century onward and in the rapid development of patent legislation to protect the interests of technological innovators. It is apparent also in the development of technical education, uneven at first, being confined to the French polytechnics and spreading thence to Germany and North America, but reaching even Britain, which had been most opposed to its formal recognition as part of the structure of education, by the end of the 19th century. Again, it is apparent in the growth of professional associations for engineers and for other specialized groups of technologists.

Increasing awareness of technology

Second, by becoming self-conscious, technology attracted attention in a way it had never done before, and vociferous factions grew up to praise it as the mainspring of social progress and the development of democracy, or to criticize it as the bane of modern man, responsible for the harsh discipline of the "dark Satanic mills" and the tyranny of the machine and the squalor of urban life. It was clear by the end of the 19th century that technology was an important feature in industrial society and that it was likely to become more so. Whatever was to happen in the future, technology had come of age and had to be taken seriously as a formative factor of the utmost significance in the continuing development of civilization.

The 20th century

TECHNOLOGY FROM 1900 TO 1945

Recent history is notoriously difficult to write, because of the mass of material and the problem of distinguishing the significant from the insignificant among events that have virtually the power of contemporary experience. In respect to the recent history of technology, however, one fact stands out clearly: despite the immense achievements of technology by 1900, the following decades witnessed more advance over a wide range of activities than the whole of previously recorded history. The airplane, the rocket and interplanetary probes, electronics, atomic power, antibiotics, insecticides, and a host of new materials have all been invented and developed to create an unparalleled social situation, full of possibilities and dangers, which would have been virtually unimaginable before the present century.

In venturing to interpret the events of the 20th century it will be convenient to separate the years before 1945 from those that followed. The years 1900 to 1945 were dominated by the two world wars, while those since 1945 have been preoccupied by the need to avoid another major war. The dividing point is one of outstanding social and technological significance: the detonation of the first atomic bomb at Alamogordo, N.M., in July 1945.

There have been profound political changes in the 20th century related to technological capacity and leadership. It may be an exaggeration to regard the 20th century as "the American century," but the rise of the United States as a superstate has been sufficiently rapid and dramatic to excuse the hyperbole. It has been a rise based upon tremendous natural resources exploited to secure increased productivity through widespread industrialization, and the success of the United States in achieving this objective has been tested and demonstrated in the two world wars. Technological leadership passed from Britain and the European nations to the United States in the course of these wars. This is not to say that the springs of innovation went dry in Europe: many important inventions of the 20th century originated there. But it has been the United States that has had the capacity to assimilate innovations and to take full advantage from them at times when other nations have been deficient in one or other of the vital social resources without which a brilliant invention cannot be converted into a commercial success. As with Britain in the Industrial Revolution, the technological vitality of the United States in the 20th century has been demonstrated less by any particular innovations than by its ability to adopt new ideas from whatever source they come.

The world wars and their effect

The two world wars were themselves the most important instruments of technological as well as political change in the 20th century. The rapid evolution of the airplane is a striking illustration of this process, while the appearance of the tank in the first conflict and of the atomic bomb in the second show the same signs of response to an urgent military stimulus. It has been said that World War I was a chemists' war, on the basis of the immense importance of high explosives and poison gas. In other respects the two wars hastened the development of technology by extending the institutional apparatus for the encouragement of innovation by both the state and private industry. This process went further in some countries than in others, but no major belligerent nation could resist entirely the need to support and coordinate its scientific-technological effort. The wars were thus responsible for speeding the transformation from "little science," with research still largely restricted to small-scale efforts by a few isolated scientists, to "big science," with the emphasis on large research teams sponsored by governments and corporations, working collectively on the development and application of new techniques. While the extent of this transformation must not be overstated, and recent research has tended to stress the continuing need for the independent inventor at least in the stimulation of innovation, there can be little doubt that the change in the scale of technological enterprises has had far-reaching consequences. It has been one of the most momentous transformations of the 20th century, for it has altered the quality of industrial and social organization. In the process it has assured technology, for the first time in its long history, a position of importance and even honour in social esteem.

Fuel and power. There were no fundamental innovations in fuel and power before the breakthrough of 1945, but there were several significant developments in techniques that had originated in the previous century. An outstanding development of this type was the internal-combustion engine, which was continuously improved to meet the needs of road vehicles and airplanes. The high-compression engine burning heavy-oil fuels, invented by Rudolf Diesel in the 1890s, was developed to serve as a submarine power unit in World War I and was subsequently adapted to heavy road haulage duties and to agricultural tractors. Moreover, the sort of development that had transformed the reciprocating steam engine into the steam turbine occurred with the internal-combustion engine, the gas turbine replacing the reciprocating engine for specialized purposes such as aero-engines, in which a high power-to-weight ratio is important. Admittedly, this adaptation had not proceeded very far by 1945, although the first jet-powered aircraft were in service by the end of the war. The theory of the gas turbine, however, had been understood since the 1920s at least, and in 1929 Sir Frank Whittle, then taking a flying instructor's course with the Royal Air Force, combined it with the principle of jet propulsion in the engine for which he took out a patent in the following year. But the construction of a satisfactory gas-turbine engine was delayed for a decade by the lack of resources, and particularly by the need to develop new metal alloys that could withstand the high temperatures generated in the engine. This problem was solved by the development of a nickel–chromium alloy, and with the gradual solution of the other problems work went on in both Germany and Britain to seize a military advantage by applying the jet engine to combat aircraft.

Developments in engine design

Gas-turbine engine. The principle of the gas turbine is that of compressing and burning air and fuel in a combustion chamber and using the exhaust jet from this process to provide the reaction that propels the engine forward. In its turbopropeller form, which developed only after World War II, the exhaust drives a shaft carrying a normal airscrew (propeller). Compression is achieved in a gas-turbine engine by admitting air through a turbine rotor. In the so-called ramjet engine, intended to operate at high speeds, the momentum of the engine through the air achieves adequate compression. The gas turbine has been the subject of experiments in road, rail, and marine transport, but for all purposes except that of air transport its advantages have not so far been such as to make it a viable rival to traditional reciprocating engines.

Petroleum. As far as fuel is concerned, the gas turbine burns mainly the middle fractions (kerosene, or paraffin) of refined oil, but the general tendency of its widespread application has been to increase still further the dependence of the industrialized nations on the producers of crude oil, which has become a raw material of immense economic value and international political significance. The refining of this material has itself undergone important technological development. Until the 20th century, it consisted of a fairly simple batch process whereby oil was heated until it vaporized, when the various fractions were distilled separately. Apart from improvements in the design of the stills and the introduction of continuous-flow production, the first big advance came in 1913 with the introduction of thermal cracking. This process took the less volatile fractions after distillation and subjected them to heat under pressure, thus cracking the heavy molecules into lighter molecules and so increasing the yield of the most valuable fuel, petrol or gasoline. The discovery of this ability to tailor the products of crude oil to suit the market marks the true beginning of the petrochemical industry. It received a further boost in 1936, with the introduction of catalytic cracking. By the use of various catalysts in the process means were devised for still further manipulating the molecules of the hydrocarbon raw material. The development of modern plastics has followed directly on this (see below *Plastics*). So efficient had the processes of utilization become that by the end of World War II the petrochemical industry had virtually eliminated all waste materials.

Petroleum cracking

Electricity. All the principles of generating electricity had been worked out in the 19th century, but by its end these had only just begun to produce electricity on a large scale. The 20th century has witnessed a colossal expansion of electrical power generation and distribution. The general pattern has been toward ever-larger units of production, using steam from coal- or oil-fired boilers. Economies of scale and the greater physical efficiency achieved as higher steam temperatures and pressures were attained both reinforced this tendency. U.S. experience indicates the trend: in the first decade of the century a generating unit with a capacity of 25,000 kilowatts with pressures up to 200–300 pounds per square inch at 400°–500° F (about 200°–265° C) was considered large, but by 1930 the largest unit was 208,000 kilowatts, with pressures of 1,200 pounds per square inch at a temperature of 725° F, while the amount of fuel necessary to produce a kilowatt-hour of electricity and the price to the consumer had fallen dramatically. As the market for electricity increased, so did the distance over which it was transmitted, and the efficiency of transmission required higher and higher voltages. The small direct-current generators of early urban power systems were abandoned in favour of alternating-current systems, which could be adapted more readily to high voltages. Transmission over a line of 155 miles (250 kilometres) was established in California in 1908 at 110,000 volts; Hoover Dam in the 1930s used a line of 300 miles (480 kilometres) at 287,000 volts. The latter case may serve as a reminder that hydroelectric power, using a fall of water to drive water turbines, has been developed to generate electricity where the climate and topography make it possible to combine production with convenient transmission to a market. Remarkable levels of efficiency have been achieved in modern plants. One important consequence of the ever-expanding consumption of electricity in the industrialized countries has been the linking of local systems to provide vast power grids, or pools, within which power can be shifted easily to meet changing local needs for current.

Alternating current

Atomic power. Until 1945, electricity and the internal-combustion engine were the dominant sources of power for industry and transport in the 20th century, although in some parts of the industrialized world steam power and even older prime movers remained important. Early research in nuclear physics was more scientific than technological, stirring little general interest. In fact, from the work of Ernest Rutherford, Albert Einstein, and others to the first successful experiments in splitting heavy atoms in Germany in 1938, no particular thought was given to engineering potential. The war led to the Manhattan Project to produce the fission bomb that was first exploded at Alamogordo. Only in its final stages did even this program become a matter of technology, when the problems of building large reactors and handling radioactive materials had to be solved; and at this point it also became an economic and political matter, because very heavy capital expenditure was involved. Thus, in this crucial event of the mid-20th century, the convergence of science, technology, economics, and politics finally took place.

Industry and innovation. There have been technological innovations of great significance in many aspects of industrial production during the 20th century. It is worth observing, in the first place, that the basic matter of industrial organization has become one of self-conscious innovation, with organizations setting out to increase their productivity by improved techniques. Methods of work study, first systematically examined in the United States at the end of the 19th century, were widely applied in U.S. and European industrial organizations in the first half of the 20th century, evolving rapidly into scientific management and the modern studies of industrial administration, organization and method, and particular managerial techniques. The object of these exercises has been to make industry more efficient and thus to increase productivity and profits, and there can be no doubt that they have been remarkably successful, if not quite as successful as some of their advocates have maintained. Without this superior industrial organization it would not have been possible to convert the comparatively small workshops of the 19th century into the giant engineering establishments of the 20th with their mass-production and assembly-line techniques. The rationalization of production, so characteristic of industry in the 20th century, may thus be legitimately regarded as the result of the application of new techniques that form part of the history of technology since 1900.

Studies of work and industrial organization

Improvements in iron and steel. Another field of industrial innovation in the 20th century has been the production of new materials. As far as volume of consumption goes, man still lives in the Iron Age, with the utilization of iron exceeding that of any other material. But this dominance of iron has been modified in three ways: by the skill of metallurgists in alloying iron with other metals; by the spread of materials such as glass and concrete in building; and by the appearance and widespread use of entirely new materials, particularly plastics. Alloys had already begun to become important in the iron and steel industry in the 19th century (apart from steel itself, which is an alloy of iron and carbon); self-hardening tungsten steel had been first produced in 1868, and manganese steel, possessing toughness rather than hardness, in 1887. Manganese steel is also nonmagnetic; this fact suggests great possibilities for this steel in the electric-power industry. In the 20th century steel alloys multiplied. Silicon steel was found to be useful because, in contrast to manganese steel, it is highly magnetic. In 1913 the first stainless steels were made in England by alloying steel with chromium, and the Krupp works in Germany produced stainless steel in 1914 with 18 percent chromium and 8 percent nickel. The importance of a nickel–chromium alloy in the development of the gas-turbine engine in the 1930s has already been noted. Many other alloys also came into widespread use for specialized purposes.

Building materials. Methods of producing traditional materials like glass and concrete on a larger scale have also supplied alternatives to iron, especially in building; in the form of reinforced concrete they have supplemented structural iron. Most of the entirely new materials have been nonmetallic, although at least one new metal, aluminum, has reached proportions of large-scale industrial significance in the 20th century. The ores of this metal are among the most abundant in the crust of the Earth, but before the provision of plentiful cheap electricity made it feasible to use an electrolytic process on an industrial scale, the metal was extracted only at great expense. The strength of aluminum, compared weight for weight with steel, has made it a valuable material in aircraft construction, and many other industrial and domestic uses have been found for it. In 1900 world production of aluminum was 3,000 tons, about half of which was made using cheap electric power from Niagara Falls. Production has since risen rapidly.

Importance of aluminum

Electrolytic processes had already been used in the preparation of other metals. At the beginning of the 19th century, Davy had pioneered the process by isolating potassium, sodium, barium, calcium, and strontium, although there was little commercial exploitation of these substances. By the beginning of the 20th century, significant amounts of magnesium were being prepared electrolytically at high temperatures, and the electric furnace made possible the production of calcium carbide by the reaction of calcium oxide (lime) and carbon (coke). In another electric furnace process, calcium carbide reacted with nitrogen to form calcium cyanamide, from which a useful synthetic resin could be made.

Plastics. The quality of plasticity is one that had been used to great effect in the crafts of metallurgy and ceramics. The use of the word plastics as a collective noun, however, refers not so much to the traditional materials employed in these crafts as to new substances produced by chemical reactions and molded or pressed to take a permanent rigid shape. The first such material to be manufactured was Parkesine, developed by the British inventor Alexander Parkes. Parkesine, made from a mixture of chloroform and castor oil, was "a substance hard as horn, but as flexible as leather, capable of being cast or stamped, painted, dyed or carved . . . " The words are from a guide to the International Exhibition of 1862 in London, at which Parkesine won a bronze medal for its inventor. It was soon followed by other plastics, but apart from celluloid, a cellulose nitrate composition using camphor as a solvent and produced in solid form (as imitation horn for billiard balls) and in sheets (for men's collars and photographic film), these had little commercial success until the 20th century.

The early plastics had relied upon the large molecules in cellulose, usually derived from wood pulp. Leo H. Baekeland, a Belgian-U.S. inventor, introduced a new class of large molecules when he took out his patent for Bakelite in 1909. Bakelite is made by the reaction between formaldehyde and phenolic materials at high temperatures; the substance is hard, infusible, and chemically resistant (the type known as thermosetting plastic). As a nonconductor of electricity it proved to be exceptionally useful for all sorts of electrical appliances. The success of Bakelite gave a great impetus to the plastics industry, to the study of coal-tar derivatives and other hydrocarbon compounds, and to the theoretical understanding of the structure of complex molecules. This activity led to new dyestuffs and detergents, but it also led to the successful manipulation of molecules to produce materials with particular qualities such as hardness or flexibility. Techniques were devised, often requiring catalysts and elaborate equipment, to secure these polymers—that is, complex molecules produced by the aggregation of simpler structures. Linear polymers give strong fibres, film-forming polymers have been useful in paints, and mass polymers have formed solid plastics.

Chemical advances in plastics

Synthetic fibres. The possibility of creating artificial fibres was another 19th-century discovery that did not become commercially significant until the 20th century, when such fibres were developed alongside the solid plastics to which they are closely related. The first artificial textiles had been made from rayon, a silklike material produced by extruding a solution of nitrocellulose in acetic acid into a coagulating bath of alcohol, and various other cellulosic materials were used in this way. But later research exploited the polymerization techniques being used in solid plastics, and culminated in the production of nylon just before the outbreak of World War II. Nylon consists of long chains of carbon-based molecules, giving fibres of unprecedented strength and flexibility. It is formed by melting the component materials and extruding them; the strength of the fibre is greatly increased by stretching it when cold. Nylon was developed with the women's stocking market in mind, but the conditions of war gave it an opportunity to demonstrate its versatility and reliability as parachute fabric and towlines. This and other synthetic fibres became generally available only after the war.

Synthetic rubber. The chemical industry in the 20th century has thus put a wide range of new materials at the disposal of society. It has also succeeded in replacing natural sources of some materials: an important example of this has been the manufacture of artificial rubber to meet a world demand far in excess of that which could be met by the existing rubber plantations. This technique was pioneered in Germany during World War I. In this effort, as in the development of other materials such as high explosives and dyestuffs, the consistent German investment in scientific and technical education paid dividends, for advances in all these fields of chemical manufacturing were prepared by careful research in the laboratory.

Pharmaceuticals and medical technology. An even more dramatic result of the growth in chemical knowledge has been the expansion of the modern pharmaceutical industry. The science of pharmacy emerged slowly from the traditional empiricism of the herbalist, but by the end of the 19th century there had been some solid achievements in the analysis of existing drugs and in the preparation of new ones. The discovery in 1856 of the first aniline dye had been occasioned by a vain attempt to synthesize quinine from coal-tar derivatives. Greater success came in the following decades with the production of the first synthetic anti-fever drugs and pain-killing compounds, culminating in 1899 in the conversion of salicylic acid into acetylsalicylic acid (aspirin), which is still the most widely used drug. Progress was being made simultaneously with the sulfonal hypnotics and the barbiturate group of drugs, and early in the 20th century Paul Ehrlich of Germany successfully developed an organic compound containing arsenic (606, denoting how many tests he had made, but better known as Salvarsan), which was effective against syphilis. The significance of this discovery, made in 1910, was that 606 was the first drug devised to overwhelm an invading microorganism without offending the host. In 1935 the discovery that Prontosil, a red dye developed by the German synthetic-dyestuff industry, was an effective drug against streptococcal infections (leading to blood poisoning) introduced the important sulfa drugs. Alexander Fleming's discovery of penicillin in 1928 was not immediately followed up, because it proved very difficult to isolate the drug in a stable form from the mold in which it was formed. But the stimulus of World War II gave a fresh urgency to research in this field, and commercial production of penicillin, the first of the antibiotics, began in 1941. These drugs work by preventing the growth of pathogenic organisms. All these pharmaceutical advances demonstrate an intimate relationship with chemical technology.

Penicillin and antibiotics

Other branches of medical technology made significant progress. Anesthetics and antiseptics had been developed in the 19th century, opening up new possibilities for complex surgery; techniques of blood transfusion, examination by X rays (discovered in 1895), radio therapy (following demonstration of the therapeutic effects of ultraviolet light in 1893), the discovery of radium in 1898, and orthopedic surgery for bone disorders all developed rapidly. The techniques of immunology similarly advanced, with the development of vaccines effective against typhoid and other diseases.

Food and agriculture. The increasing chemical understanding of drugs and microorganisms was applied with outstanding success to the study of food. The analysis of the relationship between certain types of food and human physical performance led to the identification of vitamins in 1911 and to their classification into three types in 1919, with subsequent additions and subdivisions. It was realized that the presence of these materials was necessary for a healthy diet, and eating habits and public-health programs were adjusted accordingly. The importance of trace elements, very minor constituents, was also discovered and investigated, beginning in 1895 with the realization that goitre was caused by a deficiency of iodine.

As well as improving in quality, the quantity of food produced in the 20th century increased rapidly as a result of the intensive application of modern technology. The greater scale and complexity of urban life created a pressure for increased production and a greater variety of foodstuffs, and the resources of the internal-combustion engine, electricity, and chemical technology were called upon to achieve these objectives. The internal-combustion engine was utilized in the tractor, which became the almost universal agent of mobile power on the farm in the industrialized countries. The same engines powered other machines such as combine harvesters, which became common in the United States in the early 20th century, although their use was less widespread in the more labour-intensive farms of Europe, especially before World War II. Synthetic fertilizers, an important product of the chemical industry, became popular in most types of farming, and other chemicals—pesticides and herbicides—appeared toward the end of the period that effected something of an agrarian revolution. Once again, World War II gave a powerful boost to this development. Despite problems of pollution that developed later, the introduction of DDT as a highly effective insecticide in 1944 was a particularly significant achievement of chemical technology. Food processing and packaging also advanced—dehydration techniques such as vacuum-contact drying were introduced in the 1930s—but the 19th-century innovations of canning and refrigeration remained the dominant techniques of preservation.

Farm machinery

Civil engineering. Important development occurred in civil engineering in the first half of the 20th century, although there were few striking innovations. Advancing techniques for large-scale construction produced many spectacular skyscrapers, bridges, and dams all over the world, but especially in the United States. The city of New York acquired its characteristic skyline, built upon the exploitation of steel frames and reinforced concrete. Conventional methods of building in brick and masonry had reached the limits of feasibility in the 1800s in office blocks up to 16-stories high, and the future lay with the skeleton frame or cage construction pioneered in the 1880s in Chicago. The vital ingredients for the new tall buildings or skyscrapers that followed were abundant cheap steel—for columns, beams, and trusses—and efficient passenger elevators. The availability of these developments and the demand for more and more office space in the thriving cities of Chicago and New York caused the boom in skyscraper building that continued until 1931, when the Empire State Building, with its total height of 1,250 feet (381 metres) and 102 stories, achieved a limit not exceeded for 40 years and demonstrated the strength of its structure by sustaining the crash impact of a B-25 bomber in July 1945 with only minor damage to the building. The Depression brought a halt to skyscraper building from 1932 until after World War II.

Skyscraper construction

Concrete, and more especially reinforced concrete (that is, concrete set around a framework or mesh of steel), played an important part in the construction of the later skyscrapers, and this material also led to the introduction of more imaginative structural forms in buildings and to the development of prefabrication techniques. The use of large concrete members in bridges and other structures has been made possible by the technique of prestressing: by casting the concrete around stretched steel wires, allowing it to set, then relaxing the tension in the wires, it is possible to induce compressive stresses in the concrete that offset the tensile stresses imposed by the external loading, and in this way the members can be made stronger and lighter. The technique was particularly applicable in bridge building. The construction of large-span bridges received a setback, however, with the dramatic collapse of the Tacoma Narrows (Washington) Suspension Bridge in the United States in 1940, four months after it was completed. This led to a reassessment of wind effects on the loading of large suspension bridges and to significant improvements in subsequent designs. Use of massed concrete has produced spectacular high arch dams, in which the weight of water is transmitted in part to the abutments by the curve of the concrete wall; such dams need not depend upon the sheer bulk of impervious material as in a conventional gravity or embankment dam.

Transportation. Some of the outstanding achievements of the 20th century are provided by transportation history. In most fields there was a switch from steam power, supreme in the previous century, to internal combustion and electricity. Steam, however, retained its superiority in marine transport: the steam turbine provided power for a new generation of large ocean liners beginning with the *Mauretania,* developing 70,000 horsepower and a speed of 27 knots (27 nautical miles, or 50 kilometres, per hour) in 1906, and continuing throughout the period, culminating in the *Queen Elizabeth,* launched in 1938, with about 200,000 horsepower and a speed of 28.5 knots. Even here, however, there was increasing competition from large diesel-powered motor vessels. Most smaller ships adopted this form of propulsion, and even the steamships accepted the convenience of oil-burning boilers in place of the cumbersome coal burners with their large bunkers.

Advent of the modern ocean liner

On land, steam fought a long rearguard action, but the enormous popularity of the automobile deprived the railways of much of their passenger traffic and forced them to seek economies in conversion to diesel engines or electric traction, although these developments had not spread widely in Europe by the outbreak of World War II. Meanwhile, the automobile stimulated prodigious feats of production. Henry Ford led the way in the adoption of assembly-line mass production; his spectacularly successful Model T, the "Tin Lizzie," was manufactured in this way first in 1913, and by 1923 production had risen to nearly 2,000,000 a year. Despite this and similar successes in other countries, the first half of the 20th century was not a period of great technological innovation in the motorcar, which retained the main design features given to it in the last decade of the 19th century. For all the refinements (for example, the self-starter) and multitudinous varieties, the major fact of the automobile in this period was its quantity.

Unlike the automobile, to which its development was intimately related, the airplane is entirely a product of the 20th century. This is not to say that experiments with flying machines had not taken place earlier. Throughout the 19th century, to go back no further, investigations into aerodynamic effects were carried out by inventors such as Sir George Cayley in England, leading to the successful glider flights of Otto Lilienthal and others. Several designers perceived that the internal-combustion engine promised to provide the light, compact power unit that was a prerequisite of powered flight, and on Dec. 17, 1903, Wilbur and Orville Wright in their *Flyer I* at the Kill Devil Hills in North Carolina achieved sustained, controlled, powered flight, one of the great "firsts" in the history of technology. The *Flyer I* was a propeller-driven adaptation of the biplane gliders that the Wright brothers had built and learned to fly in the previous years. They had devised a system of control through elevator, rudder, and a wing-warping technique that served until the introduction of ailerons. Within a few years the brothers were flying with complete confidence, astonishing the European pioneers of flight when they took their airplane across the Atlantic to give demonstrations in 1908. Within a few months of this revelation, however, the European designers had assimilated the lesson and were pushing ahead the principles of aircraft construction. World War I gave a great impetus to this technological development, transforming small-scale scattered aircraft manufacture into a major industry in all the main belligerent nations, and transforming the airplane itself from a fragile construction in wood and glue into a robust machine capable of startling aerobatic feats.

The Wright brothers' flight

The end of the war brought a setback to this new industry, but the airplane had evolved sufficiently to reveal its potential as a medium of civil transport, and during the interwar years the establishment of transcontinental air routes provided a market for large, comfortable, and safe aircraft. By the outbreak of World War II, metal-framed-and-skinned aircraft had become general, and the cantilevered monoplane structure had replaced the biplane for most purposes. War again provided a powerful stimulus to aircraft designers; engine performance was especially improved, and the gas turbine received its first practical application. Other novel features of these years included the helicopter, deriving lift from its rotating wings, or rotors, and the German V-1 flying bomb, a pilotless aircraft.

The war also stimulated the use of gliders for the transport of troops, the use of parachutes for escape from aircraft and for attack by paratroops, and the use of gas-filled balloons for antiaircraft barrages. The balloon had been used for pioneer aeronautical experiments in the 19th century, but its practical uses had been hampered by the lack of control over its movements. The application of the internal-combustion engine to a rigid-frame balloon airship by Ferdinand von Zeppelin had temporarily made a weapon of war in 1915, although experience soon proved that it could not survive in competition with the airplane. The apparently promising prospects of the dirigible (that is, maneuverable) airship in civil transport between the wars were ended by a series of disasters, the worst of which was the destruction of the *Hindenburg* in New Jersey in 1937. Since then the airplane has been unchallenged in the field of air transport.

Communications. The spectacular transport revolution of the 20th century has been accompanied by a communications revolution quite as dramatic, although technologically springing from different roots. In part, well-established media of communication like printing have participated in this revolution, although most of the significant changes—such as the typewriter, the Linotype, and the high-speed power-driven rotary press—were achievements of the 19th century. Photography was also a proved and familiar technique by the end of the 19th century, but cinematography was new and did not become generally available until after World War I, when it became enormously popular.

The real novelties in communications in the 20th century came in electronics. The scientific examination of the relationship between light waves and electromagnetic waves had already revealed the possibility of transmitting electromagnetic signals between widely separated points, and on Dec. 12, 1901, Guglielmo Marconi succeeded in transmitting the first wireless message across the Atlantic. Early equipment was crude, but within a few years striking progress was made in improving the means of transmitting and receiving coded messages. Particularly important was the development of the thermionic valve, a device for rectifying (that is, converting a high-frequency oscillating signal into a unidirectional current capable of registering as a sound) an electromagnetic wave. This was essentially a development from the carbon-filament electric light bulb. In 1883 Edison had found that in these lamps a current flowed between the filament and a nearby test electrode, called the plate, if the electric potential of the plate was positive with respect to the filament. This current, called the Edison effect, was later identified as a stream of electrons radiated by the hot filament. In 1904, Sir John

The rise of electronics

Ambrose Fleming of Britain discovered that by placing a metal cylinder around the filament in the bulb and by connecting the cylinder (the plate) to a third terminal, a current could be rectified so that it could be detected by a telephone receiver. Fleming's device was known as the diode, and two years later, in 1906, Lee De Forest of the United States made the significant improvement that became known as the triode by introducing a third electrode (the grid) between the filament and the plate. The outstanding feature of this refinement was its ability to amplify a signal. Its application made possible by the 1920s the widespread introduction of live-voice broadcasting in Europe and America, with a consequent boom in the production of radio receivers and other equipment.

This, however, was only one of the results derived from the application of the thermionic valve. The idea of harnessing the flow of electrons was applied in the electron microscope, radar (a detection device depending on the capacity of some radio waves to be reflected by solid objects), the electronic computer, and in the cathode-ray tube of the television set. The first experiments in the transmission of pictures had been greeted with ridicule. Working on his own in Britain, John Logie Baird in the 1920s demonstrated a mechanical scanner able to convert an image into a series of electronic impulses that could then be reassembled on a viewing screen as a pattern of light and shade. Baird's system, however, was rejected in favour of electronic scanning, developed in the United States by Philo Farnsworth and Vladimir Zworykin with the powerful backing of the Radio Corporation of America. Their equipment operated much more rapidly and gave a more satisfactory image. By the outbreak of World War II, television services were being introduced in several nations, although the war suspended their extension for a decade. The emergence of television as a universal medium of mass communication is therefore a phenomenon of the postwar years. But already by 1945 the cinema and the radio had demonstrated their power in communicating news, propaganda, commercial advertisements, and entertainment.

Military technology. It has been necessary to refer repeatedly to the effects of the two world wars in promoting all kinds of innovation. It should be observed also that technological innovations have transformed the character of war itself. One weapon developed during World War II deserves a special mention. The principle of rocket propulsion was well known earlier, and its possibilities as a means of achieving speeds sufficient to escape from the Earth's gravitational pull had been pointed out by such pioneers as the Russian Konstantin Tsiolkovsky and the American Robert H. Goddard. The latter built experimental liquid-fueled rockets in 1926. Simultaneously, a group of German and Romanian pioneers was working along the same lines, and it was this team that was taken over by the German war effort in the 1930s and given the resources to develop a rocket capable of delivering a warhead hundreds of miles away. At the Peenemünde base on the island of Usedom in the Baltic, Wernher von Braun and his team created the V-2. Fully fueled, it weighed 14 tons; it was 40 feet (12 metres) long and was propelled by burning a mixture of alcohol and liquid oxygen. Reaching a height of more than 100 miles (160 kilometres), the V-2 marked the beginning of the space age, and members of its design team were instrumental in both the Soviet and U.S. space programs after the war.

Development of rockets

Camera Press

Test launch of a V-2 rocket.

Technology had a tremendous social impact in the period 1900–45. The automobile and electric power, for instance, radically changed both the scale and the quality of 20th-century life, promoting a process of rapid urbanization and a virtual revolution in living through mass production of household goods and appliances. The rapid development of the airplane, the cinema, and radio made the world seem suddenly smaller and more accessible. In the years following 1945 the constructive and creative opportunities of modern technology could be exploited, although the process has not been without its problems.

SPACE AGE TECHNOLOGY

The years since World War II ended have been spent in the shadow of nuclear weapons, even though they have not been used in war since that time. These weapons have undergone momentous development: the fission bombs of 1945 were superseded by the more powerful fusion bombs in 1950, and before 1960 rockets were shown capable of delivering these weapons at ranges of thousands of miles. This new military technology has had an incalculable effect on international relations, for it has contributed to the polarization of world power blocs while enforcing a caution, if not discipline, in the conduct of international affairs that was absent earlier in the 20th century.

The fact of nuclear power has been by no means the only technological novelty of the post-1945 years. So striking, indeed, have been the advances in engineering, chemical and medical technology, transport, and communications, that some commentators have written, somewhat misleadingly, of the "second Industrial Revolution" in describing the changes in these years. The rapid development of electronic engineering has created a new world of computer technology, remote control, miniaturization, and instant communication. Even more expressive of the character of the period has been the leap over the threshold of extraterrestrial exploration. The techniques of rocketry, first applied in weapons, were developed to provide launch vehicles for satellites and lunar and planetary probes and eventually, in 1969, to set the first men on the Moon and to bring them home safely again. This astonishing achievement was stimulated in part by the international ideological rivalry already mentioned, as only the Soviet Union and the United States had both the resources and the will to support the huge expenditures required. It justifies the description of this period, however, as that of "space age technology."

Power. The great power innovation of this period has been the harnessing of nuclear energy. The first atomic bombs represented only a comparatively crude form of nuclear fission, releasing the energy of the radioactive material immediately and explosively. But it was quickly appreciated that the energy released within a critical atomic pile, a mass of graphite absorbing the neutrons emitted by radioactive material inserted into it, could generate heat, which in turn could create steam to drive turbines and thus convert the nuclear energy into usable electricity. Atomic power stations have been built on this principle in the advanced industrial nations, and the system is still

The harnessing of nuclear energy

undergoing refinement, although so far atomic energy has not vindicated the high hopes placed in it as an economic source of electricity and presents formidable problems of waste disposal and maintenance. Nevertheless, it seems probable that the effort devoted to experiments on more direct ways of controlling nuclear fission will eventually produce results in power engineering. Meanwhile, nuclear physics has been probing the even more promising possibilities of harnessing the power of nuclear fusion, of creating the conditions in which simple atoms of hydrogen combine, with a vast release of energy, to form heavier atoms. This is the process that occurs in the stars, but so far it has only been created artificially by triggering off a fusion reaction with the intense heat generated momentarily by an atomic-fission explosion. This is the mechanism of the hydrogen bomb. So far scientists have devised no way of harnessing this process so that continuous, controlled energy can be obtained from it, although researches into plasma physics, generating a point of intense heat within a stream of electrons imprisoned in a strong magnetic field, hold out some hopes that such means will be discovered in the not-too-distant future.

Alternatives to fossil fuels. It may well become a matter of urgency, before the end of the 20th century, that some means of extracting usable power from nuclear fusion be acquired. At the present rate of consumption, the world's resources of mineral fuels, and of the available radioactive materials used in the present nuclear-power stations, will be exhausted within a period of perhaps a few decades. The most attractive alternative is thus a form of energy derived from a controlled fusion reaction that would use hydrogen from seawater, a virtually limitless source, and that would not create a significant problem of waste disposal. Other sources of energy that may provide alternatives to mineral fuels include various forms of solar cell, deriving power from the Sun by a chemical or physical reaction such as that of photosynthesis. Solar cells of this kind are already in regular use on satellites and space probes, where the flow of energy out from the Sun (the solar wind) can be harnessed without interference from the atmosphere or the rotation of the Earth.

Gas turbine. The gas turbine has undergone substantial development since its first successful operational use at the end of World War II. The high power-to-weight ratio of this type of engine made it ideal for aircraft propulsion, so that in either the pure jet or turboprop form it was generally adopted for all large aircraft, both military and civil, by the 1960s. The immediate effect of the adoption of jet propulsion was a spectacular increase in aircraft speeds, the first piloted airplane exceeding the speed of sound in level flight being the American Bell X-1 in 1947, and by the late 1960s supersonic flight was becoming a practicable, though controversial, proposition for civil-airline users. Ever-larger and more powerful gas turbines have been designed to meet the requirements of airlines and military strategy, and increasing attention has been given to refinements to reduce the noise and increase the efficiency of this type of engine. Meanwhile, the gas turbine has been installed as a power unit in ships, railroad engines, and automobiles, but in none of these uses has it proceeded far beyond the experimental stage.

Use of the gas turbine in aircraft

Materials. The space age has spawned important new materials and uncovered new uses for old materials. For example, a vast range of applications has been found for plastics that have been manufactured in many different forms with widely varied characteristics. Glass fibre has been molded in rigid shapes to provide motorcar bodies and hulls for small ships. Carbon fibre has demonstrated remarkable properties that make it an alternative to metals for high-temperature turbine blades. Research on ceramics has produced materials resistant to high temperatures suitable for heat shields on spacecraft. The demand for iron and its alloys and for the nonferrous metals has remained high. The modern world has found extensive new uses for the latter: copper for electrical conductors, tin for protective plating of less resistant metals, lead as a shield in nuclear-power installations, and silver in photography. In most of these cases the development began before the 20th century, but the continuing increase in demand for these metals is affecting their prices in the world commodity markets.

Automation and the computer. Both old and new materials are used increasingly in the engineering industry, which has been transformed since the end of World War II by the introduction of control engineering, automation, and computerized techniques. The vital piece of equipment has been the computer, and especially the electronic digital computer, a 20th-century invention the theory of which was expounded by the English mathematician and inventor Charles Babbage in the 1830s. The essence of this machine is the use of electronic devices to record electric impulses coded in the very simple binary system, using only two symbols, but other devices such as punched cards and magnetic tape for storing and feeding information have been important supplementary features. By virtue of the very high speeds at which such equipment can operate, even the most complicated calculations can be performed in a very short space of time.

The Mark I digital computer was at work at Harvard University in 1944, and after the war the possibility of using it for a wide range of industrial, administrative, and scientific applications was quickly realized. The early computers, however, were large and expensive machines, and their general application was delayed until the invention of the transistor revolutionized computer technology. The transistor is another of the key inventions of the space age. The product of research on the physics of solids, and particularly of those materials such as germanium and silicon known as semiconductors, the transistor was invented by John Bardeen, Walter H. Brattain, and William B. Shockley at Bell Telephone Laboratories in the United States in 1947. It was discovered that crystals of semiconductors, which have the capacity to conduct electricity in some conditions and not in others, could be made to perform the functions of a thermionic valve but in the form of a device that was much smaller, more reliable, and more versatile. The result has been the replacement of the cumbersome, fragile, and heat-producing vacuum tubes by the small and strong transistor in a wide range of electronic equipment. Most especially, this conversion has made possible the construction of much more powerful computers while making them more compact and less expensive. Indeed, so small can effective transistors be that they have made possible the new skills of miniaturization and microminiaturization, whereby complicated electronic circuits can be created on minute pieces of silicon or other semiconducting materials and incorporated in large numbers in computers. From the late 1950s to the mid-1970s the computer grew from an exotic accessory to an integral element of most commercial enterprises, and computers made for home use became widespread in the '80s.

Semiconductor devices

The potential for adaptation and utilization of the computer seems so great that many commentators have likened it to the human brain, and there is no doubt that human analogies have been important in its development. In Japan, where computer and other electronics technology has made giant strides since the 1950s, fully computerized and automated factories were in operation by the mid-1970s, some of them employing complete work forces of robots in the manufacture of other robots. In the United States the chemical industry provides some of the most striking examples of fully automated, computer-controlled manufacture. The characteristics of continuous production, in contrast to the batch production of most engineering establishments, lend themselves ideally to automatic control from a central computer monitoring the information fed back to it and making adjustments accordingly. Many large petrochemical plants producing fuel and raw materials for manufacturing industries are now run in this way, with the residual human function that of maintaining the machines and of providing the initial instructions. The same sort of influences can be seen even in the old established chemical processes, although not to the same extent: in the ceramics industry, in which continuous firing has replaced the traditional batch-production kilns; in the paper industry, in which mounting demand for paper and board has encouraged the installation of larger and faster machines; and in the glass industry, in which the

Automated chemical production

float-glass process for making large sheets of glass on a surface of molten tin requires close mechanical control.

In medicine and the life sciences the computer has provided a powerful tool of research and supervision. It is now possible to monitor complicated operations and treatment. Surgery has made great advances in the space age. The introduction of transplant techniques has attracted worldwide publicity and interest, but perhaps of greater long-term significance has been the research in biology, with the aid of modern techniques and instruments, that has begun to unlock the mysteries of cell formation and reproduction through the self-replicating properties of the DNA molecules present in all living substances, and thus to explore the nature of life itself.

Food production. Food production has also been subject to technological innovation, such as accelerated freeze-drying and irradiation as methods of preservation, as well as the increasing mechanization of farming throughout the world. The widespread use of new pesticides and herbicides has in some cases reached the point of abuse, causing worldwide concern. Despite such problems, farming has been transformed in response to the demand for more food; scientific farming, with its careful breeding, controlled feeding, and mechanized handling, has become commonplace. New food-producing techniques such as aquaculture and hydroponics, for farming the sea and the seabed and for creating self-contained cycles of food production without soil, respectively, are being explored, either to increase the world supply of food or to devise ways of sustaining closed communities such as may one day venture forth from the Earth on the adventure of interplanetary exploration.

Civil engineering. One industry that has not been deeply influenced by new control-engineering techniques is construction, in which the nature of the tasks involved makes dependence on a large labour force still essential, whether it be in constructing a skyscraper, a new highway, or a tunnel. Nevertheless, some important new techniques have appeared since 1945, notably the use of heavy earth-moving and excavating machines such as the bulldozer and the tower crane. The use of prefabricated parts according to a predetermined system of construction has become widespread. In the construction of housing units, often in large blocks of apartments or flats, such systems are particularly relevant because they make for standardization and economy in plumbing, heating, and kitchen equipment. The revolution in home equipment that had begun before World War II has continued apace since, with a proliferation of electrical equipment.

Prefabricated buildings

Transport and communications. Many of these changes have been facilitated by improvements in transport and communications. The transport developments have, for the most part, continued those well established in the earlier part of the century. The automobile has proceeded in its phenomenal growth in popularity, causing radical changes in many of the patterns of life, although the basic design of the motorcar has remained unchanged. The airplane, benefiting from jet propulsion and a number of lesser technical advances, has made spectacular gains at the expense of both the ocean liner and the railroad. The growing popularity of air transport, however, has brought problems of crowded airspace, noise, and airfield siting.

World War II helped bring about a shift to air transport: direct passenger flights across the Atlantic were initiated immediately after the war. The first generation of transatlantic airliners were the aircraft developed by war experience from the Douglas DC-3 and the pioneering types of the 1930s incorporating all-metal construction with stressed skin, wing flaps and slots, retractable landing gear, and other advances. The coming of the big jet-powered civil airliner in the 1950s kept pace with the rising demand for air services but accentuated the social problems of air transport. The solution to these problems may lie partly in the development of vertical takeoff and landing techniques, a concept successfully pioneered by a British military aircraft, the Hawker Siddeley Harrier. Longer term solutions may be provided by the development of air-cushion vehicles derived from the Hovercraft, in use in the English Channel and elsewhere, and one of the outstanding technological innovations of the period since 1945. The central feature of this machine is a downblast of air, which creates an air cushion on which the craft rides without direct contact with the sea or ground below it. The remarkable versatility of the air-cushion machine is beyond doubt, but it has proved difficult to find very many transportation needs that it can fulfill better than any craft already available. Despite these difficulties, it seems likely that this type of vehicle will have an important future. It should be remembered, however, that all the machines mentioned so far, automobiles, airplanes, and Hovercraft, use oil fuels, and it is possible that the exhaustion of these will turn attention increasingly to alternative sources of power, and particularly to electric traction (electric railroads and autos), in which field there have been promising developments such as the linear-induction motor. Supersonic flight, for nearly 30 years an exclusive capability of military and research aircraft, became a commercial reality in 1975 with the Soviet Tu-144 cargo plane; the Concorde supersonic transport (SST), built jointly by the British and French governments, entered regular passenger service early in 1976.

The Hovercraft

In communications, also, the dominant lines of development continue to be those that were established before or during World War II. In particular, the rapid growth of television services, with their immense influence as media of mass communication, has been built on foundations laid in the 1920s and 1930s, while the universal adoption of radar on ships and airplanes has followed the invention of a device to give early warning of aerial attack. But in certain features the development of communications in the space age has produced important innovations. First, the transistor, so significant for computers and control engineering, has also made a large contribution to communications technology. Second, the establishment of space satellites, considered to be a remote theoretical possibility in the 1940s, had become part of the accepted technological scene in the 1960s, and these have played a dramatic part in telephone and television communication as well as in relaying meteorological pictures and data. Third, the development of magnetic tape as a means of recording sound and, more recently, vision, has provided a highly flexible and useful mode of communication. Fourth, new printing techniques have developed. In phototypesetting, a photographic image is substituted for the conventional metal type. In xerography, a dry copying process, an ink powder is attracted to the image to be copied by static electricity and then fused by heating. Fifth, new optical devices such as zoom lenses have increased the power of cameras and prompted corresponding improvements in the quality of film available to the cinema and television. Sixth, new physical techniques such as those that produced the laser (light amplification by stimulated emission of radiation) are making available an immensely powerful means of communication over long distances, although these are still in their experimental stages. The laser also has acquired significance as an important addition to surgical techniques and as an instrument of space weaponry. The seventh and final communications innovation is the use of electromagnetic waves other than light to explore the structure of the universe by means of the radio telescope and its derivative, the X-ray telescope. This technique was pioneered after World War II and has since become a vital instrument of satellite control and space research. Radio telescopes have also been directed toward the Sun's closest neighbours in space in the hope of detecting electromagnetic signals from other intelligent species in the universe.

Military technology. Military technology in the space age has been concerned with the radical restructuring of strategy caused by the invention of nuclear weapons and the means of delivering them by intercontinental ballistic missiles. Apart from these major features and the elaborate electronic systems intended to give an early warning of missile attack, military reorganization has emphasized high maneuverability through helicopter transport and a variety of armed vehicles. Such forces have been deployed in wars in Korea and Vietnam, and the latter has also seen the widespread use of napalm bombs and chemical defoliants to remove the cover provided by dense forests.

At sea, World War II marked the demise of the heavily armoured battleship. The only large ships to survive in the navies of the world are aircraft carriers. The emphasis now is placed on electronic detection and the support of nuclear-powered submarines equipped with missiles carrying nuclear warheads. The only major use of nuclear power since 1945, other than generating large-scale electric energy, has been the propulsion of ships, particularly the breed of missile-carrying submarines capable of cruising underwater for extended periods.

Space exploration. The rocket, which has played a crucial part in the revolution of military technology since the end of World War II, has acquired a more constructive significance in the space programs of the Soviet Union and the United States. The first spectacular step was Sputnik 1, a sphere with an instrument package weighing 184 pounds (83 kilograms), launched into space by the Soviet Union on Oct. 4, 1957, to become the first artificial satellite. The feat precipitated the so-called space race, in which achievements followed each other in rapid succession. They may be conveniently grouped in four chronological although overlapping stages. The first stage emphasized increasing the thrust of rockets capable of putting satellites into orbit and on exploring the uses of satellites in communications, in weather observation, in monitoring military information, and in topographical and geological surveying. The second stage was that of the manned space program. This began with the successful orbit of the Earth by the Soviet cosmonaut Yury Gagarin on April 12, 1961, in the Vostok 1. This flight demonstrated mastery of the problems of weightlessness and of safe reentry into the Earth's atmosphere. A series of Soviet and U.S. space flights followed in which the techniques of space rendezvous and docking were acquired, flights up to a fortnight were achieved, and men "walked" in space outside their craft.

Manned space flights

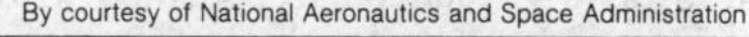
By courtesy of National Aeronautics and Space Administration

U.S. weather satellite orbiting the Earth.

The third stage of space exploration was the lunar program, beginning with approaches to the Moon and going on through automatic surveys of its surface to manned landings. Again, the first achievement was Soviet: Luna 1, launched on Jan. 2, 1959, became the first artificial body to escape the gravitational field of the Earth, fly past the Moon, and enter an orbit around the Sun as an artificial planet. Luna 2 crashed on the Moon on Sept. 13, 1959; it was followed by Luna 3, launched on Oct. 4, 1959, which went around the Moon and sent back the first photographs of the side turned permanently away from the Earth. The first soft landing on the Moon was made by Luna 9 on Feb. 3, 1966; this craft carried cameras that transmitted the first photographs taken on the surface of the Moon. By this time, however, excellent close-range photographs had been secured by the United States Ranger 7, 8, and 9, which crashed into the Moon in the second half of 1964 and the first part of 1965; and between 1966 and 1967 the series of five Lunar Orbiters photographed almost the entire surface of the Moon from a low orbit in a search for suitable landing places. The U.S. spacecraft Surveyor 1 soft-landed on the Moon on June 2, 1966; this and following Surveyors acquired much useful information about the lunar surface. Meanwhile, the size and power of launching rockets climbed steadily, and by the late 1960s the enormous Saturn V rocket, standing 353 feet (108 metres) high and weighing 2,725 tons (92,472,000 kilograms) at lift-off, made possible the U.S. Apollo program, which climaxed on July 20, 1969, when Neil Armstrong and Edwin Aldrin clambered out of the Lunar Module of their Apollo 11 spacecraft onto the surface of the Moon. The manned lunar exploration begun thus continued with a widening range of experiments and achievements for a further five landings before the program was curtailed in 1972.

Space probes

The fourth stage of space exploration has looked out beyond the Earth and its immediate satellite, the Moon, to the possibilities of planetary exploration. The two closest planetary neighbours of the Earth, Venus and Mars, were the first to receive attention. The U.S. space probe Mariner 2 was launched on Aug. 27, 1962, and passed by Venus the following December, relaying back information about that planet indicating that it was hotter and less hospitable than had been expected. These findings were confirmed by the Soviet Venera 3, which crash-landed on the planet on March 1, 1966, and by Venera 4, which made the first soft landing on Oct. 18, 1967. Later probes of the Venera series gathered further atmospheric and surficial data. The U.S. probe Pioneer Venus I orbited the planet for eight months in 1978, and in December of that year four landing probes conducted quantitative and qualitative analyses of the Venusian atmosphere. Surface temperature of approximately 900° F reduced the functional life of such probes to little more than one hour.

Research on Mars was conducted primarily through the U.S. Mariner and Viking probe series. During the late 1960s, photographs from Mariner orbiters demonstrated a close visual resemblance between the surface of Mars and that of the Moon. In July and August 1976, Vikings 1 and 2, respectively, made successful landings on the planet; experiments designed to detect the presence or remains of organic material on the Martian surface met with mechanical difficulty, but results were generally interpreted as negative. Photographs taken during the early 1980s by the U.S. probes Voyagers 1 and 2 permitted unprecedented study of the atmospheres and satellites of Jupiter and Saturn and revealed a previously unknown configuration of rings around Jupiter, analogous to those of Saturn.

In the mid-1980s, the attention of the U.S. space program was focused primarily upon the potentials of the reusable Space Shuttle vehicle for extensive orbital research. The U.S. Space Shuttle *Columbia* completed its first mission in April 1981 and made several successive flights. It was followed by the *Challenger,* which made its first mission in April 1983. Both vehicles were used to conduct myriad scientific experiments and to deploy satellites into orbit. On a mission of the *Challenger* in April 1984, astronauts repaired a malfunctioning orbiting satellite.

At the dawn of the space age it is possible to perceive only dimly its scope and possibilities. But it is relevant to observe that the history of technology has brought the world to a point in time at which man, equipped with unprecedented powers of self-destruction, stands on the threshold of extraterrestrial exploration. Only the gradual accumulation of skills over many millennia, the acceleration in the processes of industrialization in the last 200 years, the diffusion of these processes over the whole Earth, and the vast increase in investment in technology, both in hardware and in social forms of investment such as technical education, could have created the situation the world reached in the 1980s.

Perceptions of technology

SCIENCE AND TECHNOLOGY

Among the insights that arise from this review of the history of technology is the light it throws on the distinction between science and technology. The history of technology is longer than and distinct from the history of science. Technology is the systematic study of techniques for making and doing things; science is the systematic attempt to understand and interpret the world. While technology is concerned with the fabrication and use of artifacts, science is devoted to the more conceptual enterprise of understanding the environment, and it depends upon the comparatively sophisticated skills of literacy and numeracy. Such skills became available only with the emergence of the great world civilizations, so that it is possible to say that science began with those civilizations, some 3,000 years BC, whereas technology, as we have seen, is as old as manlike life. Science and technology developed as different and separate activities, the former being for several millennia a field of fairly abstruse speculation practiced by a class of aristocratic philosophers, while the latter remained a matter of essentially practical concern to craftsmen of many types. There were points of intersection, such as the use of mathematical concepts in building and irrigation work, but for the most part the functions of scientist and technologist (to use these modern terms retrospectively) remained distinct in the ancient cultures.

The situation began to change during the medieval period of development in the West (AD 500–1500), when both technical innovation and scientific understanding interacted with the stimuli of commercial expansion and a flourishing urban culture. The robust growth of technology in these centuries could not fail to attract the interest of educated men. Early in the 17th century, the natural philosopher Francis Bacon had recognized three great technological innovations—the magnetic compass, the printing press, and gunpowder—as the distinguishing achievements of modern man, and he had advocated experimental science as a means of enlarging man's dominion over nature. By emphasizing a practical role for science in this way, Bacon implied a harmonization of science and technology, and he made his intention explicit by urging scientists to study the methods of craftsmen and craftsmen to learn more science. Bacon, with Descartes and other contemporaries, for the first time saw man becoming the master of nature, and a convergence between the traditional pursuits of science and technology was to be the way by which such mastery could be achieved.

Yet the wedding of science and technology proposed by Bacon was not soon consummated. Over the next 200 years, carpenters and mechanics—practical men of long standing—built iron bridges, steam engines, and textile machinery without much reference to scientific principles, while scientists—still amateurs—pursued their investigations in a haphazard manner. But the body of men, inspired by Baconian principles, who formed the Royal Society in London in 1660 represented a determined effort to direct scientific research toward useful ends, first by improving navigation and cartography, and ultimately by stimulating industrial innovation and the search for mineral resources. Similar bodies of scholars developed in other European countries, and by the 19th century scientists were moving toward a professionalism in which many of the goals were clearly the same as those of the technologists. Thus Justus von Liebig of Germany, one of the fathers of organic chemistry and the first proponent of mineral fertilizer, provided the scientific impulse that led to the development of synthetic dyes, high explosives, artificial fibres, and plastics; and Michael Faraday, the brilliant British experimental scientist in the field of electromagnetism, prepared the ground that was exploited by Thomas A. Edison and many others.

The role of Edison is particularly significant in the deepening relationship between science and technology, because the prodigious trial-and-error process by which he selected the carbon filament for his electric light bulb in 1879 resulted in the creation at Menlo Park, N.J., of what may be regarded as the world's first genuine industrial research laboratory. From this achievement the application of scientific principles to technology grew rapidly. It led easily to the engineering rationalism applied by Frederick W. Taylor to the organization of workers in mass production, and to the time-and-motion studies of Frank and Lillian Gilbreth at the beginning of the 20th century. It provided a model that was applied rigorously by Henry Ford in his automobile assembly plant and that was followed by every modern mass-production process. It pointed the way to the development of systems engineering, operations research, simulation studies, mathematical modeling, and technological assessment in industrial processes. This was not just a one-way influence of science on technology, because technology created new tools and machines with which the scientists were able to achieve an ever-increasing insight into the natural world. Taken together, these developments brought technology to its modern highly efficient level of performance.

CRITICISMS OF TECHNOLOGY

Judged entirely on its own traditional grounds of evaluation—that is, in terms of efficiency—the achievement of modern technology has been admirable. Voices from other fields, however, began to raise disturbing questions, grounded in other modes of evaluation, as technology became a dominant influence in society. In the mid-19th century, the non-technologists were almost unanimously enchanted by the wonders of the new man-made environment growing up around them. London's Great Exhibition of 1851, with its arrays of machinery housed in the truly innovative Crystal Palace, seemed to be the culmination of Francis Bacon's prophetic forecast of man's increasing dominion over nature. The new technology seemed to fit the prevailing laissez-faire economics precisely and to guarantee the rapid realization of the Utilitarian philosophers' ideal of "the greatest good for the greatest number." Even Marx and Engels, espousing a radically different political orientation, welcomed technological progress because in their eyes it produced an imperative need for socialist ownership and control of industry. Similarly, early exponents of science fiction such as Jules Verne and H.G. Wells explored with zest the future possibilities opened up to the optimistic imagination by modern technology, and the American utopian Edward Bellamy, in his novel *Looking Backward* (1888), envisioned a planned society in the year 2000 in which technology would play a conspicuously beneficial role. Even such late-Victorian literary figures as Lord Tennyson and Rudyard Kipling acknowledged the fascination of technology in some of their images and rhythms.

Yet even in the midst of this Victorian optimism, a few voices of dissent were heard, such as Ralph Waldo Emerson's ominous warning that "Things are in the saddle and ride mankind." For the first time it began to seem as if "things"—the artifacts made by man in his campaign of conquest over nature—might get out of control and come to dominate him. Samuel Butler, in his satirical novel *Erewhon* (1872), drew the radical conclusion that all machines should be consigned to the scrap heap; and others such as William Morris, with his vision of a reversion to a craft society without modern technology, and Henry James, with his disturbing sensations of being overwhelmed in the presence of modern machinery, began to develop a profound moral critique of the apparent achievements of technologically dominated progress. Even H.G. Wells, despite all the ingenious and prophetic technological gadgetry of his earlier novels, lived to become disillusioned about the progressive character of Western civilization: his last book was entitled *Mind at the End of Its Tether* (1945). Another novelist, Aldous Huxley, expressed disenchantment with technology in a forceful manner in *Brave New World* (1932). Huxley pictured a society of the near future in which technology was firmly enthroned, keeping human beings in bodily comfort without knowledge of want or pain, but also without freedom, beauty, or creativity, and robbed at every turn of a unique personal existence. An echo of the same view found poignant artistic expression in the film *Modern Times* (1936), in which Charlie Chaplin depicted the depersonalizing effect of the mass-production assembly line. Such images were given special potency by the international political and economic conditions of the 1930s, when the Western world was plunged in the Great Depression and seemed to have forfeited the chance to remold the world order shattered by World War I. In these conditions, technology suffered by association with the tarnished idea of inevitable progress.

Paradoxically, the escape from a decade of economic depression and the successful defense of Western democracy in World War II did not bring a return of confident notions about progress and faith in technology. The horrific potentialities of nuclear war were revealed in 1945, and the division of the world into hostile power blocs prevented any such euphoria and served to stimulate criticisms of technological aspirations even more searching than those that have already been mentioned. J. Robert Oppenheimer, who directed the design and assembly of the atomic bombs at Los Alamos, N.M., later opposed the decision to build the thermonuclear (fusion) bomb and described the accelerating pace of technological change with foreboding: "One thing that is new is the prevalence of newness, the changing scale and scope of change itself, so that the world alters as we walk in it, so that the years of man's life measure not some small growth or rearrangement or moderation of what he learned in childhood, but a great upheaval." The theme of technological tyranny over man's individuality and his traditional patterns of life was expressed by Jacques Ellul, of the University of Bordeaux, in his book *The Technological Society* (1964, first published as *La Technique* in 1954). Ellul asserted that technology had become so pervasive that man now lived in a milieu of technology rather than of nature. He characterized this new milieu as artificial, autonomous, self-determining, nihilistic (that is, not directed to ends, though proceeding by cause and effect), and, in fact, with means enjoying primacy over ends. Technology, Ellul held, had become so powerful and ubiquitous that other social phenomena such as politics and economics had become situated *in it* rather than influenced *by it*. The individual, in short, had come to be adapted to the technical milieu rather than the other way round.

While views such as those of Ellul have enjoyed a considerable vogue since World War II, and have spawned a remarkable subculture of "hippies" and others who have sought, in a variety of ways, to reject participation in technological society, it is appropriate to make two observations on them. The first is that these views are, in a sense, a luxury enjoyed only by advanced societies, which have benefited from modern technology. Few voices critical of technology can be heard in developing countries that are hungry for the advantages of greater productivity and the rising standards of living that have been seen to accrue to technological progress in the more fortunate developed countries. Indeed, the antitechnological movement is greeted with complete incomprehension in these parts of the world, so that it is difficult to avoid the conclusion that only when the whole world enjoys the benefits of technology can we expect the more subtle dangers of technology to be appreciated, and by then, of course, it may be too late to do anything about them.

The second observation about the spate of technological pessimism in the advanced countries is that it has not managed to slow the pace of technological advance, which seems, if anything, to have accelerated in the 20th century. The gap between the first powered flight and the first human steps on the Moon was only 66 years, and that between the disclosure of the fission of uranium and the detonation of the first atomic bomb was a mere six and a half years. The advance of the information revolution based on the electronic computer has been exceedingly swift, so that despite the denials of the possibility by elderly and distinguished experts, the sombre spectre of sophisticated computers replicating higher human mental functions and even human individuality should not be relegated too hurriedly to the classification of science fantasy. The biotechnic stage of technological innovation is still in its infancy, and if the recent rate of development is extrapolated forward many seemingly impossible targets could be achieved in the next century. Not that this will be any consolation to the pessimists, as it only indicates the ineffectiveness to date of attempts to slow down technological progress.

THE TECHNOLOGICAL DILEMMA

Whatever the responses to modern technology, there can be no doubt that it presents contemporary society with a number of immediate problems that take the form of a traditional choice of evils, so that it is appropriate to regard them as constituting a "technological dilemma." This is the dilemma between, on the one hand, the overdependence of life in the advanced industrial countries on technology, and, on the other hand, the threat that technology will destroy the quality of life in modern society and even endanger society itself. Technology thus confronts Western civilization with the need to make a decision, or rather, a series of decisions, about how to use the enormous power available to society constructively rather than destructively. The need to control the development of technology, and so to resolve the dilemma, by regulating its application to creative social objectives, makes it ever more necessary to define these objectives while the problems presented by rapid technological growth can still be solved.

These problems, and the social objectives related to them, may be considered under three broad headings. First is the problem of controlling the application of nuclear technology. Second is the population problem, which is twofold: it seems necessary to find ways of controlling the dramatic rise in the number of human beings and, at the same time, to provide food and care for the people already living on the Earth. Third, there is the ecological problem, whereby the products and wastes of technical processes have polluted the environment and disturbed the balance of natural forces of regeneration. When these basic problems have been reviewed it will be possible, finally, to consider the effect of technology on life in town and countryside, and to determine the sort of judgments about technology and society to which a study of the history of technology leads.

Nuclear technology. The solution to the first problem, that of controlling nuclear technology, is primarily political. At its root is the anarchy of national self-government, for as long as the world remains divided into a multiplicity of nation-states, or even into two power blocs, each committed to the defense of its own sovereign power to do what it chooses, nuclear weapons merely replace the older weapons by which such nation-states have maintained their independence in the past. The availability of a nuclear armoury has emphasized the weaknesses of a world political system based upon sovereign nation-states. Here, as elsewhere, technology is a tool that can be used creatively or destructively. But the manner of its use depends entirely on human decisions, and in this matter of nuclear self-control the decisions are those of governments. There are other aspects of the problem of nuclear technology, such as the disposal of radioactive waste and the quest to harness the energy released by fusion, but although these are important issues in their own right, they are subordinate to the problem of the use of nuclear weapons in warfare.

Population explosion. Assuming that the use of nuclear weapons can be averted, world civilization will have to come to grips with the population problem in the next few decades if life is to be tolerable on planet Earth in the 21st century. The problem can be tackled in two ways, both drawing on the resources of modern technology. In the first place, efforts may be made to limit the rate of population increase. Medical technology, which, through new drugs and other techniques, has provided a powerful impulse to the increase of population, also offers means of controlling this increase through contraceptive devices and through painless sterilization procedures. Again, technology is a tool that is neutral in respect to moral issues about its own use, but it would be futile to deny that artificial population control is inhibited by powerful moral constraints and taboos. Some reconciliation of these conflicts is essential, however, if stability in world population is to be satisfactorily achieved. Perhaps the experience of China, already responsible for one-quarter of the world's population, is instructive here: in an attempt to prevent the population growth from exceeding the ability of the country to sustain the existing standards of living, the government imposed a "one-child family" campaign in the 1970s, which is maintained by draconian social controls.

In the second place, even the most optimistic program of population control can hope to achieve only a slight reduction in the rate of increase by the end of the 20th century, so that an alternative approach must be made simultaneously in the shape of an effort to increase the world's production of food. Technology has much to contribute at this point, both in raising the productivity of existing sources of food supply by improved techniques of agriculture and better types of grain and animal stock, and in creating new sources of food by making the deserts fertile and by systematically farming the riches of the oceans. There is enough work here to keep engineers and food technologists busy for many generations.

Ecological balance. The third major problem area of modern technological society is that of preserving a healthy environmental balance. Though man has been damaging his environment for centuries by overcutting trees and farming too intensively, and though some protective measures, such as the establishment of national forests and wildlife sanctuaries, were taken decades ago, great increases in population and in the intensity of industrialization are promoting a worldwide ecological crisis. This includes the dangers involved in destruction of the equatorial rain forests, the careless exploitation of minerals by open-mining techniques, and the pollution of the oceans by radioactive waste and of the atmosphere by combustion products. These include oxides of sulfur and nitrogen, which produce acid rain, and carbon dioxide, which may affect the world's climate through the so-called greenhouse effect. It was the danger of indiscriminate use of pesticides such as DDT after World War II that first alerted opinion in advanced Western countries to the delicate nature of the world's ecological system, presented in a trenchant polemic by the U.S. science writer Rachel Carson in her book *Silent Spring* (1962); this was followed by a spate of warnings about other possibilities of ecological disaster. The great public concern about pollution in the advanced nations is both overdue and welcome. Once more, however, it needs to be said that the fault for this waste-making abuse of technology lies with man himself rather than with the tools he uses. For all his intelligence, man in communities behaves with a lack of respect for his environment that is both short-sighted and potentially suicidal.

TECHNOLOGICAL SOCIETY

Much of the 19th-century optimism about the progress of technology has dispersed, and an increasing awareness of the technological dilemma confronting the world makes it possible to offer a realistic assessment of the role of technology in shaping society at the end of the 20th century.

Interactions between society and technology. In the first place, it can be clearly recognized that the relationship between technology and society is complex. Any technological stimulus can trigger a variety of social responses, depending on such unpredictable variables as differences between human personalities; similarly, no specific social situation can be relied upon to produce a determinable technological response. Any "theory of invention," therefore, must remain extremely tentative, and any notion of a "philosophy" of the history of technology must allow for a wide range of possible interpretations. A major lesson of the history of technology, indeed, is that it has no precise predictive value. It is frequently possible to see in retrospect when one particular artifact or process had reached obsolescence while another promised to be a highly successful innovation, but at the time such historical hindsight is not available and the course of events is indeterminable. In short, the complexity of human society is never capable of resolution into a simple identification of causes and effects driving historical development in one direction rather than another, and any attempt to identify technology as an agent of such a process is unacceptable.

The putative autonomy of technology. Secondly, the definition of technology as the systematic study of techniques for making and doing things establishes technology as a social phenomenon and thus as one that cannot possess complete autonomy, unaffected by the society in which it exists. It is necessary to make what may seem to be such an obvious statement because so much autonomy has been ascribed to technology, and the element of despair in interpretations like that of Jacques Ellul is derived from an exaggerated view of the power of technology to determine its own course apart from any form of social control. Of course it must be admitted that once a technological development, such as the transition from sail to steam power in ships or the introduction of electricity for domestic lighting, is firmly established, it is difficult to stop it before the process is complete. The assembly of resources and the arousal of expectations both create a certain technological momentum that tends to prevent the process from being arrested or deflected. Nevertheless, the decisions about whether to go ahead with a project or to abandon it are undeniably human, and it is a mistake to represent technology as a monster or a juggernaut threatening human existence. In itself, technology is neutral and passive: in the phrase of Lynn White, Jr., "Technology opens doors; it does not compel man to enter." Or, in the words of the traditional adage, it is a poor craftsman who blames his tools, and so just as it was naive for the 19th-century optimists to imagine that technology could bring paradise on Earth, it seems equally simplistic for the 20th-century pessimists to make technology itself a scapegoat for man's shortcomings.

Technology and education. A third theme to emerge from this review of the history of technology is the growing importance of education. In the early millennia of human existence, a craft was acquired in a lengthy and laborious manner by serving with a master who gradually trained the initiate in the arcane mysteries of the skill. Such instruction, set in a matrix of oral tradition and practical experience, was frequently more closely related to religious ritual than to the application of rational scientific principles. Thus the artisan in ceramics or sword making protected the skill while ensuring that it would be perpetuated. Craft training was institutionalized in Western civilization in the form of apprenticeship, which has survived into the 20th century as a framework for instruction in technical skills. Increasingly, however, instruction in new techniques has required access both to general theoretical knowledge and to realms of practical experience that, on account of their novelty, were not available through traditional apprenticeship. Thus the requirement for a significant proportion of academic instruction has become an important feature of most aspects of modern technology. This has accelerated the convergence between science and technology in the 19th and 20th centuries and has created a complex system of educational awards representing the level of accomplishment from simple instruction in schools to advanced research in universities. French and German academies led in the provision of such theoretical instruction, while Britain lagged somewhat in the 19th century, owing to its long and highly successful tradition of apprenticeship in engineering and related skills. But by the 20th century all the advanced industrial countries, including newcomers like Japan, had recognized the crucial role of a theoretical technological education in achieving commercial and industrial competence.

The recognition of the importance of technological education, however, has never been complete in Western civilization, and the continued coexistence of other traditions has caused problems of assimilation and adjustment. The British author C.P. Snow drew attention to one of the most persistent problems in his perceptive essay *The Two Cultures* (1959), in which he identified the dichotomy between scientists and technologists on the one hand and humanists and artists on the other as one between those who did understand the second law of thermodynamics and those who did not, causing a sharp disjunction of comprehension and sympathy. Arthur Koestler put the same point in another way by observing that the traditionally humanities-educated Western man is reluctant to admit that a work of art is beyond his comprehension, but will cheerfully confess that he does not understand how his radio or heating system works. Koestler characterized such a modern man, isolated from a technological environment that he possesses without understanding, as an "urban barbarian." Yet the growing prevalence of "black-box" technology, in which only the rarefied expert is able to understand the enormously complex operations that go on inside the electronic equipment, makes it more and more difficult to avoid becoming such a "barbarian." The most helpful development would seem to be not so much seeking to master the expertise of others in our increasingly specialized society, as encouraging those disciplines that provide bridges between the two cultures, and here there is a valuable role for the history of technology.

The quality of life. A fourth theme, concerned with the quality of life, can be identified in the relationship between technology and society. There can be little doubt that technology has brought a higher standard of living to people in advanced countries, just as it has enabled a rapidly rising population to subsist in the developing countries. It is the prospect of rising living standards that makes the acquisition of technical competence so attractive to these countries. But however desirable the possession of a comfortable sufficiency of material goods, and the possibility of leisure for recreative purposes, the quality of a full life in any human society has other even more important prerequisites, such as the possession of freedom in a law-abiding community and of equality before the law. These are the traditional qualities of democratic societies, and it has to be asked whether technology is an asset or a liability in acquiring them. Certainly, highly illiberal regimes have used technological devices to suppress individual freedom and to secure obedience to the state: the nightmare vision of George Orwell's *Nineteen Eighty-four* (1949), with its telescreens and sophisticated torture, has provided literary demonstration of this reality, should one be needed. But the fact that high technological competence requires, as has been shown, a high level of educational achievement by a significant proportion of the community holds out the hope that a society that is well-educated will not long endure constraints on individual freedom and initiative that are not self-justifying. In other words, the high degree of correlation between technological success and educational accomplishment suggests a fundamental democratic bias about modern technology. It may take time to become effective, but given sufficient time without a major political or social disruption and a consequent resurgence of national assertiveness and human selfishness, there are sound reasons for hoping that technology will bring the people of the world into a closer and more creative community.

Such, at least, must be the hope of anybody who takes a long view of the history of technology as one of the most formative and persistently creative themes in the development of mankind from the Paleolithic cave dwellers of antiquity to the dawn of the space age in the 20th century. Above all other perceptions of technology, the threshold of space exploration on which mankind stands at the end of the 20th century provides the most dynamic and hopeful portent of human potentialities. Even while the threat of technological self-destruction remains ominous, and the problems of population control and ecological imbalance cry out for satisfactory solutions, man has found a clue of his own future in terms of a quest to explore and colonize the depths of an infinitely fascinating universe. As yet, only a few visionaries have appreciated the richness of this possibility, and their projections are too easily dismissed as nothing more than imaginative science fiction. But in the long run, if there is to be a long run for our uniquely technological but willful species, the future depends upon the ability to acquire such a cosmic perspective, so it is important to recognize this now and to begin the arduous mental and physical preparations accordingly. The words of Arthur C. Clarke, one of the most perceptive of contemporary seers, in his *Profiles of the Future* (1962), are worth recalling in this context. Thinking ahead to the countless aeons that could stem from the remarkable human achievement summarized in the history of technology, he surmised that the all-knowing beings who may evolve from these humble beginnings may still regard our own era with wistfulness: "But for all that, they may envy us, basking in the bright afterglow of Creation; for we knew the Universe when it was young."

BIBLIOGRAPHY. The best general work is still CHARLES SINGER *et al.* (eds.), *A History of Technology*, 5 vol. (1954–58, reprinted 1957–65), extended by TREVOR I. WILLIAMS (ed.), with 2 vol. (1978) on the 20th century. The single-volume companion studies, T.K. DERRY and TREVOR I. WILLIAMS, *A Short History of Technology from the Earliest Times to A.D. 1900* (1960, reissued 1970), and TREVOR I. WILLIAMS, *A Short History of Twentieth-Century Technology c. 1900–c. 1950* (1982), are valuable summaries. The French equivalent to these studies is MAURICE DAUMAS (ed.), *Histoire général des techniques*, 5 vol. (1962–79); the first 3 vol. have been translated as *A History of Technology and Invention: Progress Through the Ages* (1969–79). The American counterpart to the British and French works, commendably stronger than both on the social relations of technology, is MELVIN KRANZBERG and CARROLL W. PURSELL, JR. (eds.), *Technology in Western Civilization*, 2 vol. (1967). All these general works concentrate on Western technology; for a different and important perspective, see JOSEPH NEEDHAM, *Science and Civilisation in China* (1954–); 6 vol. in 13 parts have appeared to 1985. Good specialized works include GORDON CHILDE, *What Happened in History*, rev. ed. (1954, reissued 1982), a classic study of man's mastery of the environment before the first civilizations; HENRY HODGES, *Technology in the Ancient World* (1970, reprinted 1977); LYNN WHITE, JR., *Medieval Technology and Social Change* (1962, reissued 1980); ABBOTT PAYSON USHER, *A History of Mechanical Inventions*, rev. ed. (1954, reprinted 1962); and JOHN JEWKES, DAVID SAWERS, and RICHARD STILLERMAN, *The Sources of Invention*, 2nd ed. (1969). FRIEDRICH KLEMM, *A History of Western Technology* (1959, reissued 1964; originally published in German, 1954), is a good selection of documents. The economic and social implications of technological development are explored in W.H.G. ARMYTAGE, *A Social History of Engineering*, 4th ed. (1976); DAVID S. LANDES, *The Unbound Prometheus: Technological Change and Industrial Development in Western Europe from 1750 to the Present* (1969); and S. LILLEY, *Men, Machines and History: A Short History of Tools and Machines in Relation to Social Progress*, rev. ed. (1965). LEWIS MUMFORD, *Technics and Civilization* (1934, reissued 1963), remains a seminal essay. R.J. FORBES, *Man, the Maker: A History of Technology and Engineering* (1950, reissued 1958), is a good outline of the history of technology; as is D.S.L. CARDWELL, *Technology, Science and History: A Short Study of the Major Developments in the History of Western Mechanical Technology and Their Relationships with Science and Other Forms of Knowledge* (1972); R.A. BUCHANAN, *Technology and Social Progress* (1965), may be found useful as an introductory text. Other relevant monographs include: CHARLES SUSSKIND, *Understanding Technology* (1973, reprinted 1975); A. PACEY, *The Maze of Ingenuity: Ideas and Idealism in the Development of Technology* (1974, reissued 1976); BERTRAND GILLE, *The Renaissance Engineers* (1967; originally published in French, 1964); JEAN GIMPEL, *The Medieval Machine: The Industrial Revolution of the Middle Ages* (1976, reissued 1979; originally published in French, 1975); BROOKE HINDLE, *Emulation and Invention* (1981, reissued 1983); and NATHAN ROSENBERG (ed.), *The Economics of Technological Change: Selected Readings* (1971). EUGENE S. FERGUSON, *Bibliography of the History of Technology* (1968), is a comprehensive and thorough study. For more tentative appreciations of modern technology, see JACQUES ELLUL, *The Technological Society* (1964, reissued 1973; originally published in French, 1954); and ARTHUR C. CLARKE, *Profiles of the Future* (1962, reissued 1985). The principal sources of periodical literature are: *Technology and Culture* (quarterly), the journal of the Society for the History of Technology, containing excellent annual bibliographical reviews; and NEWCOMEN SOCIETY FOR THE STUDY OF THE HISTORY OF ENGINEERING AND TECHNOLOGY, *Transactions* (annual).

(R.A.Bu.)

Telecommunications Systems

Telecommunications systems are devices and techniques used for the transmission of information over long distances via wire, radio, or satellite. A wide variety of information is transferred by such systems, including sound, visual images, computer-processed data, and telegraph and teletypewriter signals. This article discusses the principal telecommunications systems and networks, reviews their development, and considers the major problems involved in transmitting large volumes of voice and data communications without damaging loss due to noise and interference. Special attention is given to communication satellite systems and equipment because of their growing importance in long-distance communications. For details about radio and television transmissions, see BROADCASTING. Specifics on computer applications in telecommunications can be found in INFORMATION PROCESSING AND INFORMATION SYSTEMS: *Computers.* (Ed.)

This article is divided into the following sections:

Telegraph

The telegraph was the first and for many years the most important system of telecommunications. In common with other electrical communications media, such as the telephone, the purpose of the telegraph is the instantaneous transfer, by electrical means, of intelligence over distance. Telegraphy differs, however, from other electrical systems because, first, it transmits dispatches or messages as a sequence of codified alphabetic letters, numerals, punctuation, and symbols; and, second, it records them on paper as telegrams at a distant office for delivery to addressees not only as information but for subsequent reference.

The word telegraph was coined in France around 1792 to describe a pioneer optical-relay semaphore system invented by a French physician and inventor, Claude Chappe. Its literal derivation from the Greek *tele,* "far," *graphein,* "to write"—describes present-day teleprinter telegraphy even more accurately than it did any of the systems from Chappe's through the electric telegraphs of the English inventor W.F. Cooke, the English scientist and inventor Sir Charles Wheatstone, and the United States inventor Samuel F.B. Morse. In a typical modern form, a business-office typist, with a few hours' adaptive practice, manipulates a typewriter-like keyboard literally "to write far" in a correspondent's distant office, upon a typewriter-like platen, as though the typing mechanism, platen, and paper were physically present and mechanically linked with the keyboard.

Prior to the general introduction of simple teleprinters in the 1930s, writing far, on the part of senders of messages, was accomplished chiefly through the intermediary of telegraph operators, who had laboriously mastered one of the dot-and-dash codes by which alphanumeric characters were translated into electrical signals that could be transmitted and at the reception point deciphered and written down.

Applications of telegraphy techniques

The techniques of telegraphy are now widely used to measure or transfer measurement data to a distance, either for record purposes or control of machines, weapons, or processes. Another example of increasing utility is the joining together, by means of the telegraph, of geographically separated computers either for storage of information or for processing; *e.g.,* in the control of space-flight vehicles by microwave radiotelegraph.

HISTORY OF TELEGRAPHY

The history of telegraphy embraces four stages: nonliteral or nonalphabetic message transmission—*i.e.,* drums; visual telegraphy or semaphore; wire telegraphy; and wireless telegraphy, or radio. The term telegraph is reserved primarily for the third stage, wire telegraphy, which is emphasized in the following summation.

Pre-electric telegraphy. *Nonalphabetic signalling.* Prehistoric man learned to beat on resonant logs and tree trunks with a stick, then to make more effective drums of stretched membranes, and finally to use the knowledge to extend the range of his voice; rhythms and intonations applied to drum beats could be made to express emotions and ideas. The next step in communicating by means of the drum, the reed pipe, bone whistle, or ram's horn was to prearrange a set of meanings for certain sounds and sequences. The counting of beats led to the development of codes. Smoke signals by day and fires by night were also used by the ancient people of China, Egypt, Assyria, and Greece. Beacon fires, established on line-of-sight locations, brought to Queen Clytemnestra, at her palace at Argos, Greece, the news of the fall of Troy and her husband's imminent homecoming, in 1084 BC. As recounted by the poet Aeschylus, nine relay points on natural prominences covered a total distance of some 500 miles (800 kilometres). Signal fires are also recorded as having been used by the Picts against the Roman invaders of Britain in the 1st century AD and by American Indians in Ohio in early colonial times.

Alphabetic signalling. According to the Greek historian Polybius a method of signalling the 24-letter Greek alphabet was devised by about 300 BC. The code was formed by placing the letters on a grid of five horizontal rows and five vertical columns, so that the first letter, alpha, fell on the first row of the first column and the last, omega, on the fifth row of the fourth column. To signal all 24 positions, 10 vases were held in reserve behind two low walls, in a row, but separated by a few feet. In signalling omega, the sender would place five vases on the left wall and four on the right.

Essentially the same method was used by medieval prisoners to communicate through the wall of adjoining cells. Today's 26-letter Roman alphabet was contained within the five-by-five pattern because I and J were combined as one letter. The numbers were tapped out in series of pairs, 1-1 indicating A. This idea transferred the code from a purely spatial configuration to one involving time. In 1551 an Italian mathematician, Gerolamo Cardano, suggested that five torches on five towers could be used to spell out letters, with all five beacons figuring in the code as "light" or "dark." The invention of the telescope in the 17th century stimulated interest in visual signalling, and several fresh proposals were put forward by such men as the English physicist Robert Hooke, though none was immediately developed.

Visual signalling

Optical telegraphs. Two optical telegraphs, built by and for government, were of particular importance: the semaphore of the First Republic, France, 1794; and the shutter telegraph of the Admiralty, England, 1795.

As to the first, Claude Chappe and his older brother invented in 1791 and applied the name telegraph to their system of two-arm semaphores (from the Greek: "bearing a sign"; see Figure 1A). In 1793 Claude Chappe was given the title "ingénieur-télégraphe." A relay station was a hilltop tower sheltering the operators and equipped with telescopes directed up-line and down-line. At the top of the tower a vertical timber supported a beam (the regulator). At each end of the beam an arm (indicator) could be made to assume seven angular positions 45 degrees apart. The 49 positions accommodated alphabetic letters and symbols.

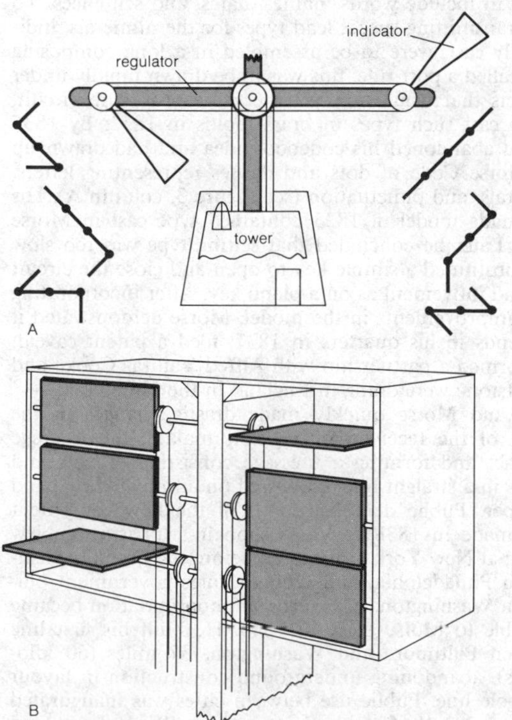

Figure 1: *Optical telegraphs.*
(A) Chappe semaphore. The heavy black lines indicate six of the many possible arm and indicator configurations, representing six hieroglyphs, or coded characters. (B) Murray six-shutter semaphore.

The horizontal beam could be tilted 45 degrees clockwise or counterclockwise, or held in a vertical position. Signals associated with the positions of the beam provided communication in cipher or code. Towers were spaced three to six miles (five to 10 kilometres) apart. At a rate of three signals a minute for each relay under conditions of good visibility, transit time from Toulon to Paris, through 120 towers, was 40 minutes, or, roughly, an hour for a message of 50 signals. This performance was more than 90 times as fast as mounted couriers.

The value of the semaphore telegraph was established when it was used to relay news of French victories over the Austrians at Quesnoy and Condé-sur-Escaut in August 1794. Within the decade, variations of Chappe's semaphore appeared in Russia, Sweden, and Denmark and eventually in Prussia, India, and Egypt.

Only slightly later, in 1795, George Murray, an English bishop credited with many improvements in the telegraph, established for the British Admiralty another successful visual system called a shutter telegraph, consisting of six solid shutters (see Figure 1B), each independently rotatable 90 degrees on a centred horizontal axis, arranged in the three-by-two pattern shown. The code that governed how many and which shutters to open simultaneously was similar to that of Cardano's five light and dark torches except that a larger number of combinations was possible (64 as compared to 32).

The shutter telegraph

Various forms of the Murray shutter rapidly appeared in England and spread to the United States, where a number of vantage points bearing the name Telegraph Hill and Signal Hill still dot maps. A Murray line, used principally by merchants, connected New York and Philadelphia until 1846.

It was while the United States Congress in 1837 was considering a petition to authorize a New York–New Orleans Chappe-semaphore line that Samuel F.B. Morse first argued for government support of his electric telegraph.

Telegraphs using electricity. Prior to the invention of the primary battery in 1800, attempts to communicate alphabetically by electricity had failed as operable systems, usually because conductors of useful lengths could not be insulated against leakage at their points of support. High voltages were impressed on the system at the sending end, but because of losses, the relatively high voltages required to energize the then-known devices for "reading" the signals sent (the attraction or repulsion of pith or cork balls, charged feathers, and bits of paper; or sparks jumping a small gap) were difficult to realize. Despite these obstacles, from 1727 onward investigators kept alive the hope of conveying electric charges away from their source and revealing them at a distance.

Many ingenious proposals were put forward. In 1727 an experimenter in London transmitted an electrical impulse over one-sixth of a mile of thread. Another sent an impulse over two miles of wire, the first wire to be strung through the air for communication. A remarkable letter, signed simply C.M., appearing in a magazine in Scotland in 1753, proposed using 26 separate wires, one for each letter of the alphabet, with a light ball suspended from each at the receiving end; the movement of a ball would signify a letter, which could be written down, creating a written message sent by electric current. A Swiss worker produced an experimental model following C.M.'s suggestion. An Italian physicist, Alessandro Volta, whose voltaic battery finally provided a dependable source of current, in 1777 proposed that an iron-wire signalling line, supported on posts, be strung from Como to Milan, Italy.

Early experiments

Other suggestions did away with the multiplicity of wires by substituting the use of time intervals, in the fashion of the wall tapping by medieval prisoners. Claude Chappe made the important suggestion that identical clockworks at either end of a communication wire could be made to indicate numbers which would be translated into words by a codebook. But Chappe abandoned his electrostatic experiments in favour of his optical semaphore; and in 1816 a synchronized-clock telegraph was produced in Hammersmith, England, with a dial rotated at one revolution per minute to permit reading of letters and numerals through an aperture in a fixed disk hiding the dial. The scheme, which was not pursued, was the precursor of stock tickers and printing telegraphs of a later era.

Electrolytic telegraphs. Other researchers explored another possibility. Noting that when certain liquids were decomposed by an electric current the current could be detected by the formation of bubbles, experimenters in Germany sent current impulses over wires by means of voltaic batteries; the impulses released bubbles in a trough at the receiving end. The scheme proved too slow to be useful.

Needle-telegraph pioneers. The observation of the deflection of a pivoted, magnetized needle by an electric current, reported by Hans Christian Ørsted of Denmark in 1819, pointed the way to the true future telegraph. André-Marie Ampère of France and others predicted the communications applicability of the idea, and as early as 1832 a Russian established a needle-telegraph circuit between the tsar's winter and summer palaces at St. Petersburg.

Carl Friedrich Gauss and Wilhelm Eduard Weber (Göttingen, Germany, 1833) constructed a two-wire telegraph line of copper, carried 1.4 miles (2.3 kilometres) over housetops. The receiver was a heavily constructed bar galvanoscope (a compass-like device for detecting the flow of current) on which was mounted a tiny mirror. A few feet away, a telescope-and-scale arrangement made it possible to observe and record slight movements of the bar. The galvanoscope-mirror device became the forerunner of the mirror galvanometer used on the first transatlantic cables. The code consisted of five successive deflections of the bar, right or left, for each character, again, after the manner of Cardano. It was the forerunner of the modern start-stop teleprinter code. Other researchers developed a two-wire, single-needle telegraph employing a uniform-length, five-unit code and erected a single-wire line nearly six miles (ten kilometres) long, on poles with crossarms, between Munich and Bogenhausen, with an earth (ground) return.

William Fothergill Cooke, an Englishman, devised (at Heidelberg, Germany, in 1836) a three-needle telegraph of six wires and, in 1837, formed a partnership with Charles Wheatstone in London to introduce electric telegraphy as an adjunct to visual signals on railways. Together they

Five-needle telegraph

patented and, in July 1837, demonstrated for railway use a six-wire, five-needle apparatus that could be read visually (see Figure 2). At the receiver, five external pointers were mounted on horizontal shafts that also held the needles of five galvanoscopes mounted behind the scribed panel. The needles moved clockwise or counterclockwise against stops as currents were fed through the respective wires by switches that applied voltage from a sending battery. The sixth wire served as the common return. To send a numeral, only one needle was moved at a time—the receiving operator's eye followed the line of axis of the deflected pointer diagonally toward a selected numeral on the lower edge of the display grid. To send a letter, two switches were moved at the same time; two pointers took diagonal positions and the proper letter was found at the intersection produced by their axes, whether in the upper half or the lower half of the grid. A codebook based on 20 letters and 10 numerals handled the railway's requirements. The system was in use on the railway between Paddington (London) and West Drayton in July 1839 and was extended to Slough (18 miles [29 kilometres]) in 1843. Because six-wire construction was costly, Cooke and Wheatstone, in 1845, patented a successful single-needle instrument, but it required skilled operators. In 1846 several telegraph companies adopted it in England for public use; on the Continent it competed for favour with Morse's register (1844); it employed equal-duration, left and right deflections of a needle to denote characters, in a code resembling Morse.

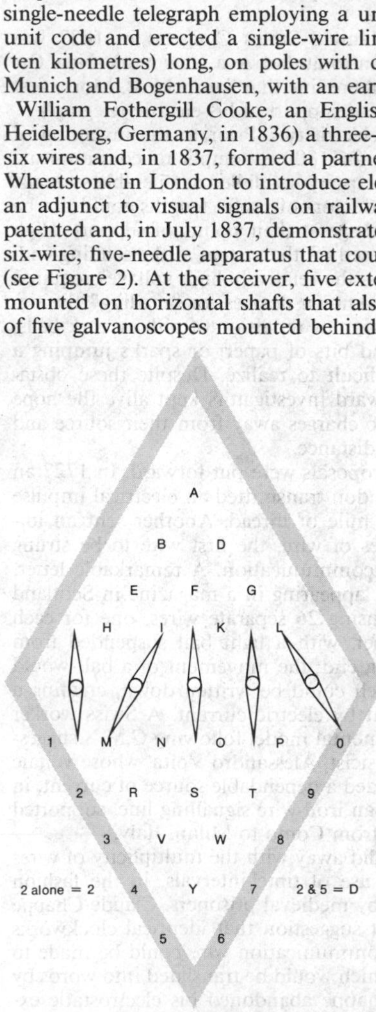

Figure 2: The Cooke and Wheatstone five-needle telegraph (see text).

Electromagnets applied to telegraphy. In 1825, it was learned that it is possible to increase the intensity of magnetic fields many times by introducing soft-iron cores into coils carrying current. The cores were shaped into horseshoe form to attract iron-bar armatures more effectively. Joseph Henry (Albany, New York, 1829) discovered laws governing the design of coils of electromagnets and of applied voltages to produce maximal effects. In 1831 he signalled over a one-mile (1.6-kilometre) circuit by causing a horseshoe electromagnet to swing a pivoted, permanent-magnet armature and strike a bell; he predicted in the same year that his method would be used to communicate other intelligence electrically.

In the United States, Samuel F.B. Morse, in 1832, made sketchbook entries of ideas that involved the electromagnet in telegraphy. In general they called for rows of marks of different lengths on moving tape in response to signals of shorter or longer time duration applied by battery to denote the 10 numerals. Use of a codebook was contemplated to include words, names, dates, and sentences. To gain transmitting speed, lead types for the numerals, individually cast, were to be assembled in a long composing stick called a port-rule; this was to be drawn rapidly under contacts that would apply battery to a two-wire circuit. Morse cast such types in brass molds in 1832. By 1835 he had abandoned his codebook idea and had drawn up the Morse Code of dots and dashes representing letters, numerals, and punctuation (see Figure 3, column A). His handmade model of 1835 contained type cast in Morse Code. Later he concluded that setting type was too slow and substituted a simple key to open and close the circuit by hand movement as on a piano key. After incorporating these improvements in the model, Morse demonstrated it to friends in his quarters in 1837, filed a patent caveat, and formed a partnership with Alfred Vail (as Cooke and Wheatstone were doing in England in the same year).

Development of Morse code

Vail and Morse quickly made drastic changes in the aspect of the receiver, or register, making the leverage compact and forming a message consisting of dots and dashes in a straight line, embossed on an unwinding band of paper. Public demonstrations of the new equipment were made in 1838 at Vail's shop in Morristown, New Jersey; at New York University; before the Franklin Institute in Philadelphia; and United States government officials in Washington. A government appropriation became available to Morse early in 1843. He built his first line between Baltimore and Washington, 37 miles (60 kilometres), abandoning underground construction in favour of a pole line. Public use between cities was inaugurated on May 24, 1844, with the message: "What hath God wrought?" The registers were actuated by terminal relays.

Morse's first line

Early problems of growth. Open-wire pole lines, erected by separate private enterprises under Morse licenses, spread rapidly in the United States and Canada. Because messages had to be transferred between companies for

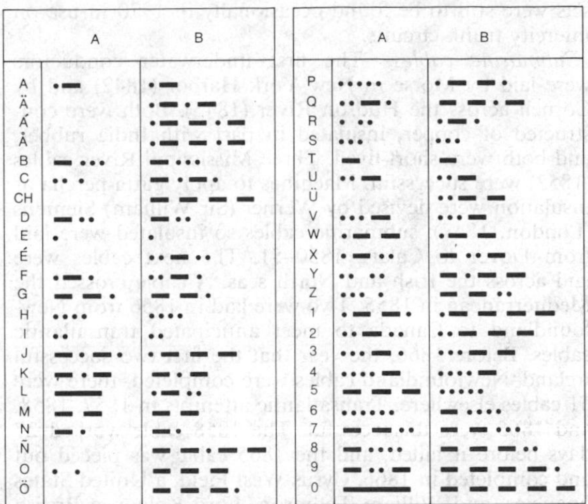

Figure 3: (Column A) American Morse Code. (Column B) Continental, or International, Morse Code.

forward handling, mergers were formed, beginning on a grand scale with the formation in 1851 of the Mississippi Valley Printing Telegraph Company, changed in 1856 to Western Union Telegraph Company. Though Morse was barred from obtaining British patents, he succeeded in introducing his register, as a competitor to Wheatstone's needle, to the various governments of Europe in rapid succession, beginning with France in 1845. Since it lacked letters with diacritical marks, the signalling code drawn up by Morse was not wholly satisfactory for use on the Continent. By agreement, a variant called Continental Morse (Figure 3, column B) was adopted by European countries in 1851. Morse's spaced letters (C, O, etc.) were replaced with unspaced letters. When demonstrated, Morse's 1844 line between Baltimore and Washington was operated as a complete metallic loop, but before being extended to New York and Boston in 1845 the wire loop was replaced by a single wire with current return through the ground. The technical disadvantage of this more economical mode of operation was current leakage from wire to ground at every pole, especially in wet or foggy weather. Morse's register was modified from an embosser to an inker, using inked felt to moisten a tiny recording wheel affixed to the moving armature. The inker, in turn, was replaced by the exceedingly simple sounder (*c.* 1856) after operators (beginning with Vail) had developed the skill to write down what they heard the register "say" as accurately and even more quickly than they could transcribe on a blank what the register "wrote." Operating speed, acquired through practice, was limited by the sender. Normal operating speeds were 20 to 25 words a minute; only exceptional operators maintained speeds of 30 to 35. Railroad operators were often required to transcribe manifold copies by stylus rather than pen. The typewriter was adapted to telegraph office use soon after the introduction in 1878 of key-shift, typebar models.

Operating speeds

Lines and wires. Ezra Cornell, who erected Morse's first line, used glass doorknobs as insulators. Improved insulators of glass and porcelain were soon designed. Initially, wires were of iron; not until about 1900 was strong copper wire available. Lightning arresters and fuses were concomitant developments of the telegraph, anticipating use in power distribution.

Wheatstone and Morse experienced difficulty with insulation in underground installations, but the need was great for such installations. While pole lines were used on railroad rights-of-way in both the United States and Great Britain, practice differed as to city terminations, partly because cities in England were too congested to admit railways above ground. Consequently, underground wires laid in pipe, following gas- and water-mains practice, joined central telegraph offices with pole lines on the outskirts. Electrical failure due to moisture was common; tarred cotton, silk insulation, and gutta-percha proved ineffective. In 1860 aerial cables, consisting of 30 to 100 ground-return copper wires insulated with India rubber and overlaid with narrow tape to prevent abrasion, were being used successfully in construction over housetops in London. When introduced to underground practice, India rubber satisfied requirements.

District telegraphs. Though present-day readers may think of the telegraph in terms of distant-city or global interconnections, for the 35 years from 1845 until telephones became generally available in 1880, the telegraph was the standard metropolitan means of communication. The telegraph ended the isolation of police precincts and fire brigades. District telegraph systems with branch offices and wire networks were established in London (1859), Paris (1864), and in Germany and the United States at about the same time. They consisted of: (1) telegraph offices (in London there were 84), with wires converging at manual-relaying central offices that catered to businesses and the public; (2) a system of instruments and intracity wires offered for lease to business houses that employed their own operators; (3) general messenger services; and (4) burglar-alarm services. Among the messenger services was the pickup and delivery of domestic and foreign intercity messages. The district telegraphs maintained call boxes to summon messengers and for the filing of messages.

A need for a private wire system that required no knowledge of code was met by Wheatstone's direct-reading system, the so-called *A-B-C* system. Similar versions in France were known as Breguet and in Germany as Siemens-Halske. In these systems a step-by-step, ratchet-driven receiving indicator progressed around a clock face displaying all the letters and numerals. A character was read and recorded by the operator each time the pointer stopped. The sending communicator was another dial similarly arranged. When buttons around a circle were depressed they arrested all motion of the communicator and distant indicator. The rotating member inside the communicator was driven by a tiny crank that was turned by the operator. On its shaft was a magnetogenerator that made one-half of a turn per letter traversed, sending to the line one-half cycle of alternating current per letter. Cranking with one hand, the operator could push buttons with the other and continue to crank until inhibited by the depressed character. A speed of eight to 15 words a minute was possible. Wheatstone's magnetogenerator, which was the precursor of both the dynamo and alternator, had avoided the need for a battery.

A-B-C system

The advantages of private wires, otherwise called leased or dedicated circuits, spread from the districts to intercity use in the United States in 1869. Among earliest users were newspaper publishers, quickly followed by stockbrokers.

Telegraphs and the press. In the United States the telegraph and the railroad mail (1834) became catalysts for an evolving journalism. The "penny press," with the aid of the telegraph, was able to feature domestic "spot news" in place of journalism's traditional editorial comments in support of political parties and commentary on intelligence received by mail. After 1866 this transformation carried over into news received by cable.

The concept of a press wire service originated in Europe with the telegraphic activity of such entrepreneurs as Paul Julius Reuter, who supplemented incomplete line construction on the Continent by using pigeons to bridge gaps (1849). In the 1860s he was operating submarine cables wholly or partly owned by Reuters Limited as a news agency. In the United States the first intercity, leased wire service was the Associated Press' New York–Philadelphia–Baltimore–Washington service of 1875. The Associated Press had previously been established (1848) to pool telegraphic expenses.

Increasing the efficiency of wires. Much ingenuity was expended in devising direct-current repeaters so contrived that an operator receiving on line B could interrupt the operator sending on A, and in turn send to him. Also important to the efficient utilization of lines was the so-called duplex, perfected in Germany, which made it possible for one wire to provide separate eastbound and westbound paths for simultaneous transmissions. The schematic wiring of the (later) bridge polar duplex (Figure 4) shows the variable resistances and capacitances used in both artificial lines. These are carefully adjusted to balance

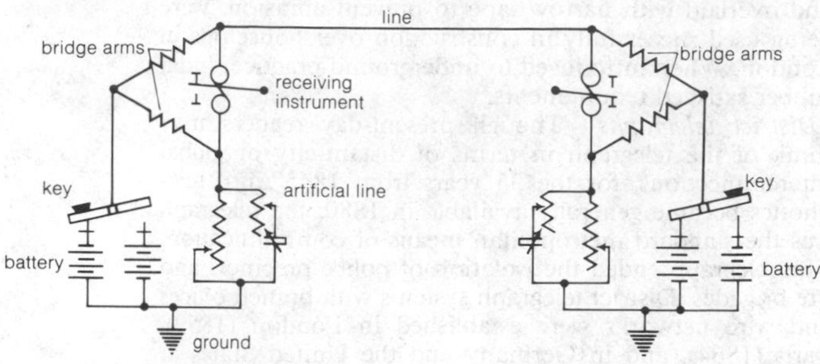

Figure 4: Bridge polar duplex circuit.

(*i.e.,* to match) those of the main line and distant terminal. Balance is achieved when the key at the west terminal, for example, is moved up and down and the west receiving instrument is completely unresponsive to it. The east terminal is balanced similarly. On this facility four operators could handle two telegrams at the same time.

The quadruplex

Thomas A. Edison, in 1874, designed a double duplex, called the quadruplex, requiring the services of eight operators who handled four messages at one time, two in each direction. It filled a need for about 35 years and was confined to hand Morse sending.

A high-speed automatic Morse system (1858), the achievement for which Wheatstone was knighted, was used throughout the world until around 1910 on landlines, and in the early 1980s it was still being used in radiotelegraphy. An inker—a greatly improved Morse register which could run at 70 to 300 words a minute—was the receiver.

The transmitter, first driven by clockwork then by motor, was the first to use holes punched in tape as the control for keying. While sitting in front of a mallet punch, the operator struck anvils with two mallets, one for dots and the other for dashes, with middle feed holes. A third anvil punched feed holes only to separate letters and words. When the tape was passed through the transmitter, sensing pins, called pecker rods, came up through the holes to establish keying contacts. The mechanism was so designed that the contact would lock up on the top hole for the duration of a dash, then be unlatched by the bottom hole following. In time, the slow preparation of tape by mallets was superseded by faster, typewriter-like keyboards.

Using the telephone. During the early days of the telephone, it was found that ground-return circuits on intercity open-wire lines caused intolerable levels of cross talk among telephones. Consequently, two-wire metallic operation was adopted (see below *Development of the telephone*). In the 1880s the simplex circuit was devised (see Figure 5A) in which a ground-return telegraph could be derived from a working metallic telephone pair without interference. Later, a composite set (see Figure 5B) permitted the derivation of two grounded telegraphs. Composite

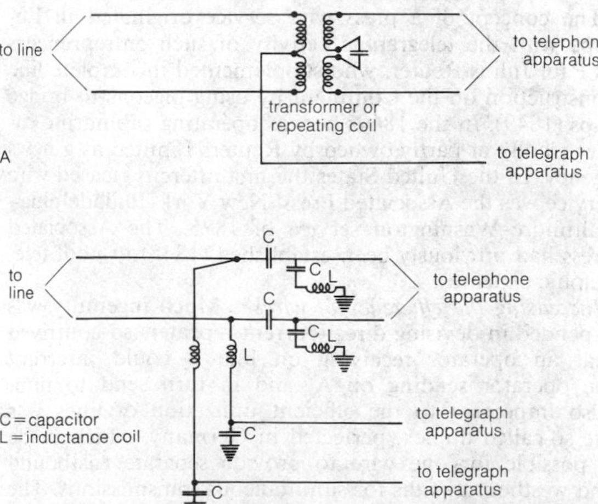

Figure 5: *Telephone-telegraph circuits.*
(A) Simplex circuit; (B) composite circuit.

sets were still to be found occasionally in 1970 in use on intercity trunk circuits.

Submarine cables. The first underwater conductors were laid by Morse in New York Harbor (1842) and by Cornell across the Hudson River (1845). Both were constructed of copper, insulated in part with India rubber, and both were short-lived. Three Mississippi River cables (1853) were successful. Machines to apply gutta-percha as insulation were devised by Werner (Sir William) Siemens (London, 1847); submarine cables so insulated were laid from Dover to Calais, 1850–51. The next cables were laid across the Irish and North seas. A cable crossed the Mediterranean in 1855. Two were laid in 1856 from Newfoundland to Canada to meet anticipated transatlantic cables. Before 1866, the year that the first two successful Ireland–Newfoundland cables were completed, there were 51 cables elsewhere. Transatlantic attempts in 1857, 1858, and 1865 were unsuccessful. The 1858 cable worked 27 days before it failed, and the 1865 cable was pieced out and completed in 1866. Cyrus West Field, a United States financier, and William Thomson, Lord Kelvin, a British physicist and inventor, are famed for their skill and persistence in seeing the transatlantic projects through.

The first transatlantic cable

In 1865 a New York–Paris landline telegraph route was surveyed through British Columbia, Alaska, the Bering Strait, and Siberia. Actual construction began northwestward from British Columbia and eastward from St. Petersburg. Completion of the first two entirely successful transatlantic cables in 1866 ended the project, but public and governmental interest in it was a factor in the purchase of Alaska from Russia by the United States in 1867.

After 1866 nearly a score of transatlantic cables were laid by the British, French, and Americans. Cables laid by Americans in 1924, 1926, and 1928 were inductively loaded with helical tapes of a magnetic alloy (Permalloy or mu-metal) wound around the conductor and under the insulation. By equalizing the arrival time of the high- and low-frequency components of the transmitted signal, the transmitting speed—hence, traffic capacity—of these newer cables was raised. Coupled with the use of vacuum-tube amplifers that were made available in the early 1920s, the fastest of these cables worked in printer-multiplex of eight channels instead of one. By the 1940s, there were 20 transatlantic cables. In the 1950s, some of the cables failed and could not be repaired economically. Telephone cables were laid, beginning in 1956; cable and radio companies alike leased telegraph bands of frequencies in the new cables with the result that the last of the exclusively telegraph transatlantic cables was abandoned in 1966, after a century of cable-system service. In oceans other than the North Atlantic, telegraph cables still operated because alternative facilities obtainable from some telephone cables or satellite-relay services were economically unfeasible.

The original mirror galvanometer (Kelvin, 1858) required two receiving operators, one to watch and call out the signals, the second to transcribe. The method was replaced by Kelvin's delicate ink-siphon recorder (1867), which marked a wavy line on a strip of paper drawn in front of one operator. The dots and dashes of Continental Morse were of equal length, but the dots were transmitted as one polarity and the dashes as the opposite polarity (about 24 volts). The cable was grounded between letters. This was the shortest of all codes used in telegraphy. In the mid-1920s, rotary repeaters and code converters precisely controlled by tuning forks or pendulums made it possible to repeat cable signals on landline or radiotelegraph circuits and vice versa. A submerged vacuum-tube amplifier, powered from shore, was first inserted in an Anglesey–Isle of Man cable in 1943, and in a transatlantic cable for the first time in 1950.

Military uses of the telegraph. The telegraph was first employed militarily by the Allied Army in the Crimean War, at Varna, Bulgaria (1854), where lines were erected to connect command headquarters with troop units. In the same war a submarine cable was laid (1855) across the Black Sea. In the United States a transcontinental telegraph was built in the 1850s. From the Mississippi westward a solitary wire at first ran through a string of forts along the route of the pony express and of ox-drawn

Conestoga wagons. The wire reached the Pacific in 1861, just as the Civil War began.

Use in the U.S. Civil War

The American Civil War made enormous use of the telegraph. Telegraph operators enlisted in large numbers; the president of the merged telegraph companies was made a general and put in charge of all the telegraphs in the North. Lines already installed were placed at the disposal of the army; others were constructed to follow the armies. New techniques suitable for army field use were developed to unreel and reuse wire strung between command posts. Batteries, keys, relays, and sounders became essential war materiel.

In the Spanish–American War (1898), landline and cable telegraphs were geared for the first time to meet the needs of newspaper war correspondents. The war also marked the first time in which cables were cut at sea as an act of belligerency (at Cienfuegos, Cuba, and at Manila), resulting in new provisions in international law to protect such installations. In the Russo-Japanese War (1904–05) radiotelegraphy was used for the first time, both in tactical deployment and in news coverage by civilians.

World War I brought the first use of teleprinter encryption, in which two identically prepared, but meaningless, key tapes are used. One is passed through the transmitter to garble the intelligence tape, while the other, passed through the receiving teleprinter, restores the original message.

The outstanding electric-signalling innovation of World War II was radar, a form of radiotelegraphic direction finder. Radar techniques have been integrated with those of telegraphy to produce some modern forms of the latter.

House's printing telegraph

Printing telegraphs. *Early printing telegraphs.* In 1846, only two years after Morse, Royal E. House of the United States invented a printing telegraph. The transmitter had a keyboard of 28 keys, each assigned a character. Behind the keyboard was a cylinder on the surface of which projected short pegs aligned on a one-turn helix. The cylinder was turned with a crank; its motion was arrested when a peg was blocked by a depressed key. Contacts that closed and opened the line, once for each letter, were positioned at the end of the cylinder. The impulses through an electromagnet stepped a ratchet and printing wheel to corresponding positions at the receiver. When rotation stopped, a miniature press forced a blackened silk ribbon against an endless paper strip, backed by the embossed letter on a wheel, to make a printing impression. Motive power was treadle-compressed air. The system was crude and required two men to send and two men to receive. Its speed was described as "twice as fast as Morse." It lasted only a few years, but is remarkable for its anticipation of the typewriter ribbon, the simplex tape printer of the 1930s, the so-called Hughes printer, and the stock ticker.

David Edward Hughes (Kentucky, 1855) patented a system which became standard in Europe. His chief point of departure from House was to regulate the transmitting cylinder and the receiving typewheel by tuning forks and to keep both rotating without stopping; the only signals sent over the line were one dash per revolution for synchronization and one dot for each letter pressed against paper tape. The tape was gummed and was attached to a blank sheet of paper for delivery. The equipment, antedating electric motors, was driven by weights raised by a treadle and was handled by one operator at each station.

Stock tickers, step-by-step tape printers, operating at 40 words a minute, mounted on pedestals and under bell jars, had a long life (1867–1932). Generically, the piano keyboard, pegged-cylinder transmitter of House and Hughes was combined with the one-alternation-per-character scheme of Wheatstone's *A-B-C.* In the receiver an electrically polarized relay actuated a weight-driven escapement (a ratchet device that permits motion in one direction only and in equal steps) on the printing wheel to move the various letters into position at high speed. Printing was accomplished by impact from an arm actuated by an electromagnet too sluggish to be moved by the rapid reversals of letter-selecting currents but responsive to the steady application of either pole of the battery, applied when the transmitting cylinder's rotation was arrested by a peg-striking key. Two printing wheels, rotating as a unit, were used, one to print letters, the other numbers and fractions. A unison signal brought all tickers on the line into initial register and made the tickers self-winding. By 1933 the market had outgrown step-by-step tickers. They were replaced by 500-characters-per-minute teleprinters. In 1964 these, in turn, were replaced by 900-characters-per-minute, six-level code teleprinters (see below). The use of transparent tape and narrow screens for the projection of quotations for general viewing dates from 1924; the automatic quotation boards for brokerage office data display, from about 1927.

Baudot's system

Time-division multiplex. Jean-Maurice-Émile Baudot (France, 1845–1903), in 1872, invented a time-division multiplex-printing telegraph system containing elements from which modern equipment has evolved. The idea of synchronized rotary motion at both circuit ends (which Chappe had proposed in 1790) led, in 1853, to a proposal that in sweeping a full circle, the first half of the synchronized rotating arms' revolution could put the line at the disposal of one pair of operators, while the second half could be used by a second pair. A further proposal, that a uniform five-unit code be utilized, was made in 1860. Nothing came of either idea at the time. Baudot thought in terms of multiplexing the line, time-dividing its capacity among not two but several pairs of operators. By 1877 the French Administration of Posts and Telegraphs had officially adopted Baudot's working system, the heart of which was a distributor consisting of a stationary faceplate of concentric copper rings swept by brushes mounted on a rotating assembly (see Figure 6). Depending upon traffic-

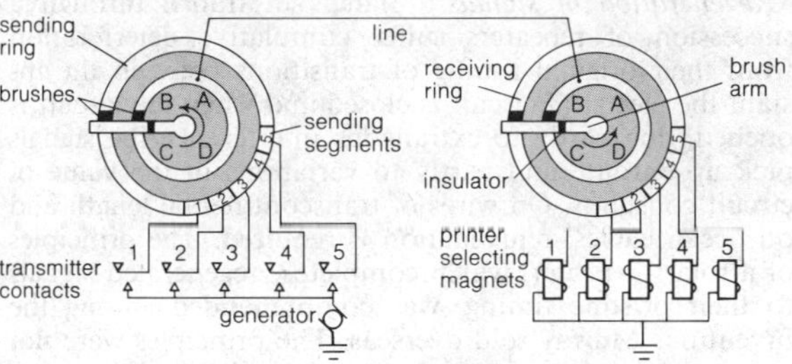

Figure 6: *Baudot time-division multiplex system.*
(Left) Sending ring of one distributor and (right) companion receiving ring (see text).

load capacity and requirements of the line, the faceplate was divided first into sectors: if they were 90° quadrants, as shown, the multiplex became known as a quad; if 120°, a triple; if 180°, a double. A quad would keep four operators busy at each end, interweaving the characters, one at a time, from four telegrams. Each faceplate sector, whatever its arc, was further subdivided into segments representing code pulses of equal length, corresponding to the five levels of the Baudot code. For simplicity Figure 6 shows only the sending ring of one distributor and its companion receiving ring at the far end of the line. There were auxiliary rings, not shown, and brush mounts on the rotating brush arm which paced the transmitting operation and the printing. On the receiving side, each of Baudot's quad printers had the time of three-quarters of a revolution to print and clear out the character that had been set up in its five selecting bars during the initial one-quarter turn. There was therefore no line time lost in separating a character from its follower—a clear gain over Morse Code in any of its forms.

Baudot went further in loading his time-division multiplexed line by duplexing it in the manner described earlier. Baudot adopted the corrected-synchronism method of Hughes but added necessary adaptations to avoid mixing up the channels.

Baudot's inventions of the 1870s were contemporary with the typewriter and although his machines printed on tape some of his patents were used in page-writing typewriters. He was sole originator of the idea of using five sliding, notched, selecting code bars, or disks, as a means of permuting 32 printer controls, as called for by his code. Generically, his method was to block the downward movement of the keys of a typewriter-like mechanism by placing a bundle of thin code bars (numbered one to five) on edge, transversely under the keybars. These bars were then slotted in such a manner that the proper key would be actuated upon receipt of the proper code signal.

The paging function. In the late 1890s attention was directed to transmitting telegrams in page form, dispensing with gumming wheels and similar expedients to affix narrow tape to paper blanks at the receiver.

Murray's time division multiplex system

Donald Murray (England, 1903), taking much from Baudot, devised a time-division multiplex system used by the British Post Office. For receiving, his page printers used cut blanks; for transmitting, he used a typewriterlike keyboard after Rowland (U.S., 1899); but, in five-level configuration, he punched tape with it, like Wheatstone. Murray designed a transmitter to accept such tape and also permuted Baudot's 32 code combinations, assigning those with fewest punched holes scientifically to letters and functions most frequently encountered in telegrams: what is today loosely and not undeservedly called Baudot is in fact Murray's code, revised in minor respects by later American practice and European agreements.

Murray sold his American rights to Western Union and Western Electric in 1912. To American variants of Murray's apparatus was added the auto control—a device like a telephone dial, which was probably the first to interpolate extraneous control signals into language transmission without harm. The auto control dialed control-bell signals, one to five, in the printer's uppercase *J*, printing nothing. Single open wires with ground-return were assigned two, three, or four duplexed channels, each handling 40 to 66 words a minute eastward and westward.

Regeneration of signals. Signals in transit through a succession of repeaters suffer cumulative deterioration from their original timing of transitions between the instant the electrical circuit is closed and when the circuit is opened, due partly to extraneous interference the signals pick up enroute and partly to variations in the value of circuit constants. On wires of transcontinental length and on ocean cables, rejuvenation is required. The principles of a rotary repeater, which completely regenerated signals to their pristine timing, was comprehended among the inventions Murray sold overseas. The principles were not put to work until some returning World War I veterans, who saw telegraph service in Europe, installed a rotary repeater in the United States in 1919. Signal regeneration is of great modern importance in feeding error-free input to computers.

Start–stop printer systems. Though well suited to intercity trunk lines, the multiplex was not adapted to the need for a simple, one-channel, back-and-forth or two-way printer system. To fill the need the simplex printer (later called teleprinter generically, and often, in the United States, by its tradename, Teletype) was developed and applied widely between 1924 and 1928. The simplex at first reverted to the tape-printing method of Baudot and his predecessors for reasons of cost, ruggedness, efficiency, and ease of making paste-over corrections. The tape was manufactured with adhesive on the back and passed through a hand-held wick-moistener before being affixed to the blank and severed, line by line, with a cutting thimble worn on a finger. Since this process was not popular among untrained operators, page-printing machines were furnished for private-wire use.

Simplex printer

The electricity source by that time was being kept so close to 60 hertz (cycles a second) that small synchronous motors in printers could sweep brushes of small distributors over five commutator segments in perfect step. The brushes stopped by being declutched after sweeping the fifth-level pulse in each revolution and then restarted on the next character by a clutching signal received over the line. The start pulse was of the same duration as each of the five signalling pulses; the stop, or rest, pulse was about 1.5 times as long. In modern parlance, the five-level code was transmitted as 7.5 units, pulses, or bits. Start–stop transmission lent itself readily to being repeated by simple forms of start–stop regenerators. Today there is nothing so ubiquitous in telegraphy as the self-synchronizing, start-stop teleprinter, or teletypewriter—in five- to eight-level codes and seven to 11 units.

A 1930 model Teletype was basic to a manually-switched teletypewriter exchange service (TWX), started by American Telephone & Telegraph Company in the United States in 1931. Within 15 years, 65,000 Teletypes had been manufactured, and the name had entered the language through the press in connection with police networks. TWX service in the United States was converted to automatic switching in 1962 and extended to Canada in 1963; at the same time a speed option of 100 words per minute was offered to supplement and possibly to eventually replace the 75 word-per-minute machines. Telex, an automatic-switching service in Europe and elsewhere, originated in Germany and rapidly expanded to other countries after World War II.

Frequency-division multiplex. Though carrier telegraphy (superposition of several telegraph signals on a single carrier) had been anticipated by Bell in his quest for a harmonic telegraph in 1875, practical systems had awaited the development of components such as band-separation filters and vacuum-tube circuitry. Techniques for carrier telephony and telegraphy were perfected at the same time in 1918.

The centres of voice-frequency bands are spaced 4,000 hertz apart for telephony (3,000 hertz on submarine cable). In 1940 frequency-modulated (FM) carrier in preference to amplitude modulation (AM) was adopted in the United States and later became the international standard in Europe.

Facsimile telegraph systems. In 1850 F.C. Bakewell, in London, invented a "copying telegraph," consisting of tinfoil wrapped around a rotating cylinder, upon which writing, added by a pen dipped in varnish, could be scanned by a contact carried by an endless screw. The receiver was similar, except for the substitution of paper wet with a chemical. Successful manipulation of the scanning process in telegraph offices had to wait for the discovery of substances and methods (1934) leading to a dry-process recording paper not affected by long exposures to light. By 1964 over 40,000 simple drum scanner-recorders, known as Desk-Fax, were handling over 50,000,000 messages annually. Operation required no skill, yet insured error-free copy.

"Copying telegraph"

The TelAutograph is a short-line telegraph invented by Elisha Gray of the United States and A.C. Cowper of England about 1895. The transmitter has two rheostats (variable resistors) varied through mechanical linkages by the motion of a stylus held in the hand and moved as in ordinary writing. It leaves a sending record, if desired, by pen on a wide band of paper beneath. Each rheostat is connected to a separate line transmitting a varying current to a coil at the receiving end. The armatures of these coils are correspondingly linked to a recording pen resting on paper. The pen thus reproduces roughly the original stylus writing in facsimile. Refinements were made possible by servomechanisms developed during World War II.

Telegraphic radio-beam circuits. Expansion and improvements have made microwaves a mainstay of telegraphy in many countries. By combining wideband telephone and telegraph dependably on a single telecommunication facility, radio consigned the open-wire plant of the late 1940s to early obsolescence. Telegraph contracts with the railroads were not renewed in the 1950s, and pole lines, except on some multiconductor-cable routes, were abandoned.

Reperforators. A useful means of transmission is to duplicate at the receiver of station B a counterpart of a tape used to transmit at station A. This was done by Murray with five-level code and by F.G. Creed (England, 1902) with three-level cable code. Reperforators and transmitters in the early 1940s were placed in juxtaposition and operated as a unit. For the benefit of switching operators and as an aid in reading the holes in tape, a combined printer reperforator printed a translation either on the edge of a slightly wider tape or directly on the perforations. In the latter the tape was cut chadless; *i.e.,* the holes were not punched all the way through, producing small bits of paper (chads) to be discarded, but were punched as hinged lids. They did not impede penetration by the sensing pins but did permit overtyping.

Beginning in 1934 reperforator offices were installed in

the United States, based on the switching from circuit to circuit of start–stop printer-reperforator transmitters. In the early 1940s the telephone and telegraph companies started to apply similar equipment on a wide scale to large leased teletypewriter networks. This system is described as store and forward. In both applications mentioned there is a momentary storage at the receiving reperforator from line A, cross-office transmission at high speed, and an orderly accumulation of tape at the sending reperforator on line B to queue up with other messages awaiting transmission in turn.

Automatic switching

Two-letter indicators, otherwise called director signals, punched ahead of all other elements of message transmissions automatically to switch messages through reperforators, were in private-wire networks in 1943 and in public-message switching in 1947. Automatic switching may be said to mark the beginning of modern telegraphy.

MODERN TELEGRAPHY

Large business and governmental users of telegraph services began to demand facilities compatible with the computer and its associated machinery, coupled with the need for language and nonlanguage systems on a worldwide basis. As a result wire and radio-telegraph companies broadened their bandwidth offerings, redesigned terminal equipment for greater speed and versatility, and designed switched communication paths through a maze of facilities. New developments include coaxial cables; microwave radio; waveguides; satellite links; and, experimentally, beams of coherent light (laser).

High-speed data transmission. Analogue (continuous) signals can be converted to digital (discrete) signals by pulse-code modulation techniques in which information is transmitted as a series of pulses (see below *Principles and problems of telecommunications*). Digital signals are desirable because they degenerate far less than analogue signals when passed through repeaters enroute to their destination, and because they can be electronically regenerated and freed from noise picked up along the way. Pulse-code modulated signals are equally amenable to complete electronic regeneration at every repeater; so are teleprinter and data signals traversing a pulse-code modulated circuit.

Telegraph and telephone companies in Canada and the U.S., and government telecommunication administrations elsewhere, offer combination telephone-data services under trade names like Datel, Data-Phone, and Broadband Exchange, whereby patrons dial voice-frequency connections as they would long distance. By mutual agreement buttons are then operated, activating apparatus for sending data telegraphically at high speeds. Digital facilities for handling the entire call have been installed on a wide scale.

Like most telegraphic make-and-break contact signals, the wave form of the electrical pulse generated by a dot is square topped, and each transition from the 0-to-1 and the 1-to-0 conditions is abrupt. A curve having such an abrupt rise time becomes sloped and rounded off as it travels along a transmission line. The more sloped the curve, the more it is susceptible to further degradation by the addition of impulse noise picked up enroute from various sources. Devices are installed at various points along the transmission line to counteract some of the adverse effects of the line. These are called equalizers, and they serve to prevent excessive sloping or rounding off of the curve.

Line-of-sight microwave radio is a backbone element in the present-day, high-speed, telegraphic data transmission plant. Traffic capacity of a single microwave circuit may be 1,800 voice-frequency channels. In one application in the late 1960s a 1,200-voice-channel telegraph microwave carried teleprinter pulses, signals for facsimile transmission, broadband (high-speed) data, and special time-division-multiplexed video at rates up to 40,000,000 bits a second. Frequency modulation was used throughout to reduce susceptibility to circuit and extraneous noise. By the mid-1970s, satellite circuits were in daily international broadband telegraph use. Synchronous satellites, maintaining fixed positions 22,300 miles (35,880 kilometres) above the Atlantic, Pacific, and Indian oceans and Earth stations dotting the globe constituted the system (see below *Satellite communications*). Consideration was being given to eventual substitution of digital for analogue transmission, and for expansion of satellite repeaters to provide intra-continental and domestic telegraph and data links.

Satellite transmission

High-frequency bands in the radio spectrum carry major international telegraph loads overseas. Frequency-shift keying shares acceptance with time-division multiplexing of single-sideband systems with subcarriers for high-speed Morse, teleprinter (the prevailing mode), and radiophoto transmissions. Tropospheric (over-the-horizon) circuits are used in special situations. The telegraph frequency-modulated carrier is used extensively for remote control of switching, telemetering, and teleprinter communication over high-voltage power lines. Modern submarine cables, developed primarily for transoceanic telephony, share the overseas-telegraph data-traffic loads with satellites.

Direct-current keyed facilities. The rate at which direct currents are interrupted, or keyed, for signalling purposes is measured in bauds. Steady reversals could be described, for example, as taking place at 50 bauds, 50 bits per second, 25 cycles per second, or at 25 hertz. All mean the same; bauds and hertz are speed terms.

A pair of wires connecting a customer with a telegraph office or a subscriber with a telephone exchange is called a loop; often the loop is divided into sending and receiving legs. Such legs have to operate at the baud or bit rate called for by the service. On–off keying is usually accomplished by closing and opening the circuit, whether the circuit is powered by dc or ac. Circuit loops from the central office to the subscriber and return are usually supplied with a battery voltage or an alternating current (audio frequency) from the central office. If these loops are unusually long and are operated on direct current, the telegraph code may be transmitted by reversing the polarity of the dc power, instead of closing and opening the circuit. Teleprinters and data sets are designed to be versatile in initiating suitable signals on loops. An important condition to be signalled is whether the circuit is idle and, hence, available or busy and not available.

Pulse-code modulation. Pulse-code modulation has been briefly mentioned earlier in the contexts of its digital generation and its adaptability to regeneration and repeater spacing; it is discussed at greater length below in the section *Modulation techniques.* Pulse-code modulation techniques have been adapted to the interweaving of multiple streams of data going directly into data-processing inputs at rates up to 50 kilobits (50,000 bits) a second and bypassing the digital-to-analogue conversion necessary to transmit digits over frequency-division telephone carriers. The growth of pulse-code modulation networks has been rapid in Japan, the United Kingdom, France, and the United States.

Equipment refinements. Most of the elaborate relays and mechanical switches formerly used in direct-current telegraphy were made obsolete by the substitution of ferrite magnetic cores, arranged in arrays, or grids. Magnetization of a core will temporarily store pulses until called upon by a computer control to transfer them to an on-going circuit or logic operation. Such cores or magnetized areas on memory tapes, drums, or disks, with no contacts mounted on parts having mechanical inertia, overcome the drawbacks of the fastest of relays. The techniques and hardware of digital-logic circuit design which evolved in the computer field in the 1960s were applied widely in the telegraph field during the 1970s.

Ferrite magnetic cores

Multichannel carrier facilities. By means of frequency-division multiplex, 4,000-hertz voice-frequency bands can be utilized for teleprinter and data facilities. Guard bands between channels prevent overlap and reduce the usable band to about 3,000 hertz. For 75-words-per-minute printers, where the operating rate is 57 bauds, as many as 26 channels may be spaced 120 cycles apart in a voice band. For 100-words-per-minute eight-level printers operating at 110 bauds, 18 channels may be spaced 170 cycles apart.

Some digital transmissions (for example, high-speed data) need bands in excess of voice-band widths. Broadband facilities are available for such applications in steps from 48 kilohertz to eight megahertz wide. The latter figure has been used for digital signals in missile tracking; the former for frequently-used systems of alternate voice and data.

The terminal–facility interface. Simple relays, contact

rectifiers, or modulators and demodulators (often built as a unit called a modem) are inserted between customers' or branch-office loops and the multiplexed carrier channels. Modems convert binary bits at the telegraph office into a suitable form to modulate the telegraph carrier. The digital-analogue modems designed to couple business machines located on business premises with intercity voice-carrier or broadband facilities are usually called data sets.

Baudot-Code teleprinters. Teleprinter codes have been standardized for circuits that cross international borders. They are adopted by government telegraph administrations or representatives in the International Telecommunications Union headquarters in Geneva, usually upon recommendation of the International Consultative Committee on Telegraphs and Telephones. Its International Alphabet No. 2, as amended, usually called the Baudot Code, permits countries to assign certain code combinations to nationally-used symbols and letters (such as $, £); it merely prohibits their use in international telegrams.

The Baudot Code

Domestic manufacturers produce conforming teleprinters for use domestically, others internationally for sale abroad.

All makers have produced several types. The one selected for brief description here is the 75-words-per-minute Teletype model 28 of 1953 which is still in use today. Its keyboard is shown in Figure 7A and the layout of its printing typebox, viewed from the front of the printer, in Figure 7B. The typebox is a lightweight member moved in steps by a carriage along the line being typed and carrying horizontal, spring-mounted type pallets, in holes arranged as shown. Any one of these, bearing raised type on its end next to the paper platen, may be tapped on the near end by a carriage-borne hammer and driven against the ribbon and paper. In its function of aligning pallets under the hammer, the typebox has two "home" column positions, shown as vertical blank spaces; the typebox is positioned at one or the other by receipt of the figures (FIGS) or letters (LTRS) signals, controlled by keyboard keys so marked. Assuming the LTRS-mode to have been selected, the mechanism that moves the typebox up and down (four positions, from the top) and left and right (four positions left, four right) will take its direction, in order, from the five pulses which arrive in succession to represent any letter transmitted.

The shaded squares represent nonprint code characters. The pallets bear no type; the hammer does no work. In the back of the printer is a function box containing coded levers and contacts, responsive to incoming characters at the same time the typebox is responsive. These levers and contacts do such things as space the typebox carriage between words; bring the carriage back to the beginning of a line (carriage return—C.R.); feed the paper up one line on the platen (line feed—L.F.); and ring a supervisory bell. The function-box mechanism can be arranged at will to carry out the valuable attribute of reading signals—*i.e.*, watching for sequences of two, three, or even more characters and acting upon them. For instance, a FIGS-shift followed by ?/ might constitute a sequence which, upon receipt of the stroke, would throw a switch, starting up tape reperforators to interweave information into the traffic stream. FIGS H is often used to shut down connected teleprinters by switching off their motors. Alternatively, a two-character combination might be selected to disable the machine as a printer but enable it to exercise control and switching functions, thus giving it great versatility in programming the interpolation of constant information stored in tape or devices awaiting release. Examples are telegram serial numbers, place of origin of message, time of day, date. The function box is also a means for controlling printer operations such as tabulating, backspacing for underlining, and automatically measuring paper feedout.

An advantage of typeboxes over the typebars of older teleprinters is that special applications of any code, such as Baudot, can be made simply by changing the typeboxes and key-caps.

From *Technical Review* ®; (top) January 1956 and (bottom) July 1955

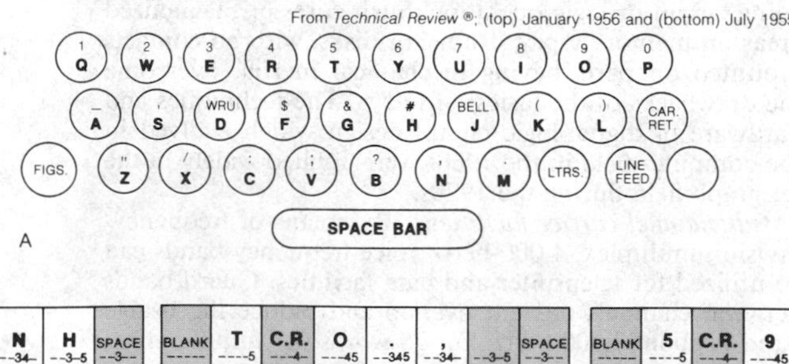

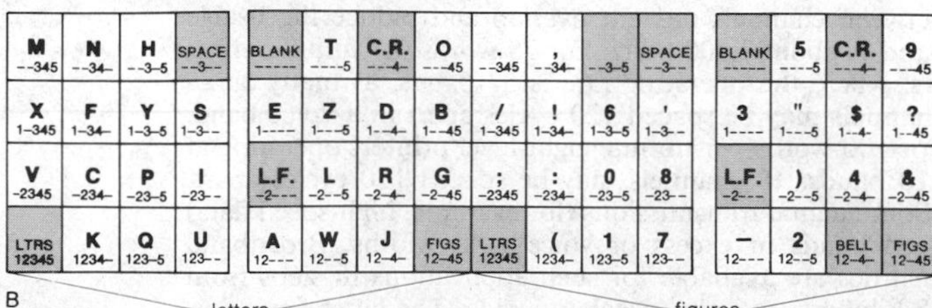

Figure 7: *Baudot-Code teleprinter.*
(A) The five-level, three-row keyboard and (B) the layout of the printing typebox.

ASCII-*type printer systems.* The inadequacy of Baudot five-level code in meeting all practical communicating and switching needs first became apparent when computers achieved a high degree of acceptance in the early 1960s, at which time a competitive effort was made by communication carriers, supported by teleprinter manufacturers, to transmit data economically in the high volumes generated by business machines. Independent system designs found a common denominator in 1966, at least temporarily, in the seven-level American Standard Code for Information Interchange (ASCII). As embodied in the Teletype model 37 of 1968, to which reference will be made, the seven-level code is signalled at 150 words a minute (15 characters a second) from an eight-level tape shown in Figure 8. Circles represent holes punched in the tape by depressing control keys (top line), such as carriage return (CR) and line feed (LF), no holes being punched in levels 6

American Standard Code for Information Interchange

From *Technical Review* ® (November 1967)

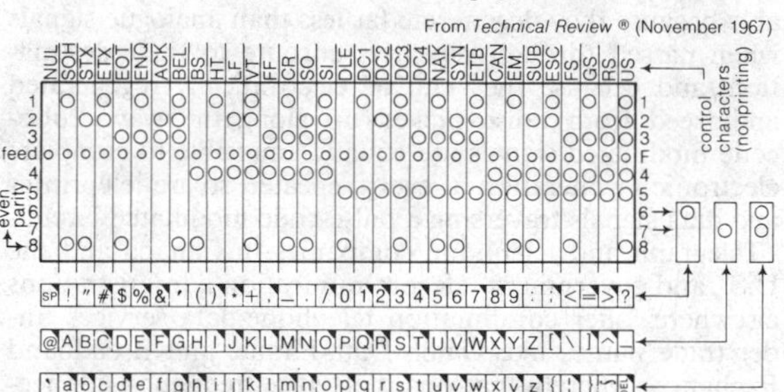

Figure 8: American Standard Code for Information Interchange (see text).

and 7. For alphanumeric symbols (three lines at bottom), depressing a key, with shifts, will punch levels 1 to 5 as shown above it; levels 6 and 7 as indicated at right; and level 8 (parity check for errors) only if needed to make the hole count even. Seven levels accommodate 2^7, or 128, different alphanumeric and control signals. The typist has a four-row keyboard and typebox which print normally lowercase alphabetic letters (new in general telegraphy and shown on the bottom line of the code). A shift to uppercase (capital letters) is made by depressing a shift key and holding it there so long as uppercase is being used, then releasing it to revert to lowercase, the same as on an office typewriter. The number of units, or bits, per eight-level character is ten: seven for intelligence, one for parity check, one for start, and one for stop.

Other modern teleprinters. Several other proprietary codes and systems are in common use over leased telegraph facilities. Computer manufacturers offer telegraphic peripheral units and transceivers that produce readouts at prodigious speeds. Some that print a whole line at a time consist of 80 to 120 wafer-like typewheels—essentially 80 to 120 separate, ganged printers—lined up across the paper band. Each one is independently controlled, not bit after bit, as on a wire, but all bits in each character thrown in at the same instant. In some models the wheels do not stop—a throwback to the Hughes printer of 1855. Outputs are of the order of 1,000 lines a minute, or at the rate of 333 words a second if the lines were filled. Other systems produce copies from cathode-ray tubes, electrostatic, photographic, and electrothermally produced chemical papers, with speeds in the range of 5,000 to 11,000 words a second.

Classes of protection

Error detection and correction. There are two classes of protection: one in which errors in transmission are detected and flagged in some way at the receiver for correction, the other in which errors are detected and automatically corrected before being printed or entering a computer. Complete redundancy in transmission; *i.e.,* sending everything twice and making an automatic check for identity, is simple but would be wasteful of long-distance facilities. Expedients are used to avoid it yet retain the advantages of moderate redundancy. For extreme accuracy (probability being one in 100,000,000 for undetected errors in words of 23 bits each), a code is used that involves a set of several nonprinted characters following each computer word. For many years automatic error-correction has been applied to transoceanic radiotelegraphy in the form of the independently invented J.B. Moore (U.S.) and H.C.A. van Duuren (The Netherlands) uniform codes. The Moore time-division-multiplex printer code consists of seven-level characters, each of which contains three 1s and four 0s. Upon receipt, each character is measured instantaneously for that three to four ratio and rejected by nonprinting if any other ratio is measured. On a fully operative duplex circuit, the receiver at B automatically interpolates an unprinted signal in B's transmission back to A, signifying that a mutilation has occurred; takes over control of A's transmitter; backs A's transmitter a measured number of characters to compensate for the interruption; and triggers resumption of movement of A's tape, beginning with the erroneous character.

Digital computers and peripheral units. What telegraph customers do with data processors is a concern of the telegraph carriers that tailor-make adaptable facilities. Inventories of a branch office may issue punched cards that it is desired to duplicate for record and processing at the concern's head office or warehouse. The telegraph company must be able to cause the stack of cards to be reproduced at a distance quickly and accurately. Plant payrolls, based on names of employees and their time clocked in and out, may be presented to the carrier in bookkeeping-machine form to transmit to an accounting office to be processed, for checks to be written, and for performance to be analyzed. For patrons offering multichannel magnetic tape to be reproduced in a distant office at high speed, data sets that operate on a voice bandwidth are furnished by telegraph carriers. There is a growing field of shared computers and contract processing, both kinds involving occasional interrogation by wire of specialized data banks and obtaining teleprinter responses. An example is stored library-book listings and current-literature abstracts, retrieved by computers upon presentation of descriptors or names of authors.

In addition to these tasks performed for customers, telegraph companies use computers and associated equipment to conduct their own technical functions. In these operations the logic and memory units of computers are employed far more often than the arithmetic unit. To telegraphy, the whole assemblage is less a computer than a complex switch. The control unit, in accordance with stored programs, moves about among the interoffice lines connected with the input, conducting a rollcall to uncover messages bidding for connections; probing the message headers for entitlement to priority service; determining traffic destinations; calling the roll of facility outlets and alternative routes toward destination; assigning, from apparatus held in stock reserve, the necessary interface units; and accomplishing memory storage, access, and transfer. All this complementary equipment may be, as required, independently programmed.

The timing control

A most important component of the control unit of computers, particularly those operating in tandem as in telegraph practice, is the timing control; the techniques for maintaining synchronism between transmitter and receiver are an integral part of this control.

One purpose of installing computers in place of store-and-forward relay systems has been to eliminate that component of total origin-to-destination delay caused by message handling within the office. Computers, by reviewing the status of all messages in storage as frequently as once a second, have cut to one or two seconds cross-office transmissions which formerly took a minute or more.

Carriers and administrations that offer public message service through computers are obligated to provide memory units—random-access magnetic drums, disks, tapes, and matrices—of adequate size to accept all traffic and to guard its integrity. The computer has no control of destination equipment, which may be busy; nor of lines from computer to destination, which may be inadequate at a given moment to handle all loads offered, even though many alternate routes have been engineered into the switching plan. Communication computers are different from others in the comparatively huge amounts of material offered memories for brief retention, from a few seconds to several minutes. For safety, communication computers are often installed as dual-input pairs—one on line, the other for standby protection against catastrophic failure.

Computers used by the several international carriers at the United States gateway connecting points with the land-line telegraph companies have the versatility of computers described later under large private-wire systems. In addition they transform Canadian and United States message formats into others conforming to requirements for delivery in various parts of the world, and vice versa. They act as a buffer against slight speed differences between American and European teleprinters, and they supply serial numbers to messages so that messages may be billed to customers and connecting carriers and taken into account for international settlements in foreign currencies.

Telegraph networks. A description of the public system for the handling of telegrams is best approached through consideration of the simpler private-wire systems, both small and large.

Small private-wire systems. A simple two-way duplexed circuit joining two teleprinters can be extended in usefulness by providing for extra drops or stations en route; each drop can remain silent until activated by local initiative or from a distance. In the case of some press associations more than 200 newspapers are so connected to a duplexed round robin 4,300 miles (6,920 kilometres) long; dispatched from a head office, each newspaper can send in response to query and command and continuously copy all transmissions in both directions around the loop.

Load traffic studies

Within an industrial organization a traffic study is commonly made of loads among all offices; the busy hours and busy half hours during representative days are determined; and costs of alternative patterns of lines and operations are estimated. Out of these studies come least-cost figures for a hierarchy of branch, group, area, and zone offices; their location; an estimation of speed of service to be expected; a circuit layout; and the specification and cost estimates for the rental of lines and equipment. Depending upon all the factors, the types of operation fall into three classes: (1) fully automatic, in which dialed numbers or director letter combinations in message headers set up the paths from points of origin to points of destination; (2) semi-automatic, in which operators at zone offices read destinations by examination of printer-reperforator tape and push buttons to establish connections across the office and onto outgoing circuits; (3) or torn-tape operation, used in compact offices, in which reperforated tape can be torn in message lengths and the lengths inserted in transmitters.

Large private-wire systems. The largest known private network in the world in 1968 was operated by and for the military arm of the United States government on hired facilities. It had nine major computer-controlled centres and 2,700 outstations in the country and ten more zone centres to serve 1,600 transatlantic and transpacific stations. Its compatible and cross-connected civilian counterpart is a fully automatic hybrid network of three zone centres; an average of eight district offices subsidiary to and connected with the zone centres; finally, more than 1,600 subscribers' teleprinters and data sets in 600 cities—a hierarchy of three echelons. It is called hybrid because the zones and districts each carry on simultaneously both alternative functions of private and public networks: (1) a circuit-switching function to join facilities together end to end, point to point, to extend from a dialing subscriber all the way through to his called party, to use ad lib after the connection has been completed; (2) a message-switching function for accepting messages, one at a time, into temporary storage, dismissing the subscriber, then discharging a responsibility to establish a route (thus, store and forward) which the message is to follow to reach its destination.

In sending single, off-network messages, the subscriber dials his zone centre by number. There his equipment is put through to a store-and-forward processing computer, which has many capabilities besides switching calls through. In its memory are stored all alternate routes that messages can take. It makes interconnections with "outside" networks. It can convert one keyboard code, like Baudot or ASCII, to another. It can render compatible the unmatched speeds of teleprinters. It makes message-format conversions. It can provide teleprinter or wideband data channels. It recognizes and appropriately schedules several classes of transmission priorities, and it distinguishes between full-rate and overnight messages. It has a store-and-forward memory. It can accept and switch multiple-address messages; *i.e.,* messages having one text but deliverable to any number of addresses. In its memory it can retrieve lists of such multiple addresses, identified as frequently used groups. It performs message accounting and makes statistical analyses.

Capabilities of the processing computer

The user of this store-and-forward private service must present messages to the computer in a fixed format, subject to the computer's rejection if incorrect. For this reason, off-line preparation of correct tape is preferred over online keyboard manipulation.

In a store-and-forward system it is inevitable that queues of messages should be formed in the computer's memory, each awaiting its turn for transmission to addressees whose teletypewriters are in use. The computer supervises this queue and constantly makes attempts to find the terminal available, following a mathematically determined pattern of intervals between attempts and maintaining an orderly, first-come-first-serve lineup in queue.

Teleprinter-subscribers' exchanges. Intermediate between private-wire leased systems and the public telegram service are the public teletypewriter exchanges, interconnected throughout the world. These systems are much larger than any private-wire system, but basically their operation differs only in detail from circuit switching in the large private-wire systems just described. The exchanges do not incorporate store-and-forward features. In 1969 the largest such system had 43,000 subscribers, using 75-word Baudot and 100-word ASCII-keyboard printers.

In 1970 the Western Union Telegraph Company acquired TWX from the American Telephone & Telegraph Company and amalgamated it with Telex in the continental U.S. The resulting four-echelon hierarchy of switching points consisted of nine zonal junction points, an average of 10 districts per zone and eight subdistricts per district.

Directories supplied to customers differ from the usual telephone directories by embracing continental U.S. and Canada. Busy conditions en route and at the called terminal are fully exposed to the calling subscriber; hence, the number of facilities and pieces of switchable equipment placed for prompt completion of on-demand calls have reached a high mark in telegraphy through Telex and TWX. On the receiving side a Telex will operate unattended. The calling subscriber may ring a bell in the printer to attract attention of anyone present.

Telex and TWX

Characteristic of Telex calls in Europe and America has been the employment of a time-and-zone meter and clock-driven counter that is associated with the subscriber's loop and registers cumulative bulk-charge usage by the month; the clock rate in beats per minute is greater or less in proportion to the mileage zone determined by the number called. Most Telex and TWX connections are half duplex; *i.e.,* they will work alternately, back and forth. Ordinarily the printer associated with a keyboard records faithfully what is sent, but if for some reason the receiving operator wishes to interrupt, he may do so by striking keys at random. This will break up the copy at both ends of the wire to signify an interruption.

Three landline-system telegraph computers went on line in New York, Chicago, and San Francisco in 1969; their versatility was initially applied to Telex calls in the same way that computers had hitherto been applied to large private-wire installations described earlier. A subscriber dials the computer by number for Telex computer communications service beyond that afforded by his ordinary directory calls. If he encounters a busy condition in making a regular call, for instance, and does not wish to wait to redial, the computer, on signal, will store his message immediately and will transmit it to destination as soon as the called party's machine is free. Or the subscriber may offer a collect message; not only will the computer handle it but will bill the addressee also. The computer will relay Telex messages to TWX subscribers. The Telex subscriber may file public telegrams with the computer, addressed to nonnetwork addressees—also multiple-address messages with identical texts, whether for Telex or off-network addressees.

Public telegram service. The acceptance and delivery of regular and overnight telegrams requires the functioning of telegraph offices and agencies connected electromechanically, in one way or another, with reperforator centres—area-relaying offices—so located that each acts as the focal point for traffic originating in or destined to most localities in the area. Each reperforator office is tied in with every other by direct teleprinter channels. With a few exceptions, full duplex operation of 75-words-a-minute Baudot tape printers was characteristic of operation.

In addition to the network of facilities interconnecting area-switching centres, there was a separate network of multiple-trunk duplexed printer channels between pairs of the dozen largest terminal cities and even between a few pairs of city branch offices, like commodity exchanges. The area and terminal networks were mutually supporting as alternate, automatically switchable routes in the event of interruptions to portions of either network.

Gentex and Telex. In telegraphically compact countries like Belgium and The Netherlands, Telex lines and equipment are furnished to each post office so that separate connections may be established from post office of origin to post office of destination for each telegram as it is filed. The service is called Gentex. The economics justifying this is favourable where lines are short and cheap and the facility-utilization factor of no moment.

Operations in large cities. In the early 1980s within a large city there was often a complex of branch offices, and in such cases the hierarchy of facilities appeared on a third level, tributary to the main, or central, office. The central office had pneumatic tubes radiating underground through ducts to the branches for transporting telegrams physically in both directions. Its other ties with a branch were mainly by teleprinters and facsimile-telegram Desk-Fax machines; the telephone was used to a lesser extent. Major business customers of the public message service frequently bypassed the branch offices in one direction or both; some of them manned teleprinter or Desk-Fax tie lines with the main office; some preferred the telephone for sending, others for receiving telegrams. Uniformed messenger boys and call boxes in business offices, once mainstays of message pickup and delivery from main and branch offices, had virtually disappeared.

Desk-Fax

Special arrangements in routing reperforated traffic between main and branch offices were found necessary in large terminal cities. Not only were there complications due to house numbers on one street being assigned to different branches, but many telegrams bore no addresses other than a firm's name. Also the delivery preferences of patrons had to be consulted—whether service was to be by messenger, telephone, Desk-Fax, or teleprinter tie line. The use of facsimile enjoyed popularity among customers until Telex offered advantages as a substitute. The Desk-Fax telegram had merely to be wrapped around a cylinder and in two minutes it could be transmitted or received by a scanning process. In large cities all inbound city tape telegrams were converted to page form: it was done (without computers) by a translator which could count text characters. On the first word space after the 58th character it would automatically insert carriage return and line feed; and so on, from line to line. Additionally, it would count lines from prefix to signature. If there were fewer than 16, it would insert the remainder up to 16 to feed the page blank as a standard-size telegram out of the burster printer. The burster was a device that tore the blank loose from its roll and deposited the completed telegram on a conveyor belt, to be assembled with others for delivery by facsimile or pneumatic tube and messenger. At the same time, punched tape in page mode would be created for semi-automatic switching. An operator, with an explicit route chart to memorize or consult, would push one button in a raster of buttons to transmit the telegram to a branch office by wire, or to a tie-line operator, or telephone delivery department.

Telegraph offices and agencies. Since the mid-1940s, the physical character of telegraph service has changed considerably. Also, individual customers are less frequent users, except for the purpose of sending money. For other services the customer usually makes use of the telephone rather than going to the telegraph office to place his message. (I.S.C./Ed.)

Telephone

The telephone has gradually supplanted the telegraph as the principal system of telecommunications. Not only does the telephone serve as an instrument for reproducing articulate speech and other sounds at a distance through the medium of electric waves but its circuits carry telegraph, telephoto, and television signals and data in a form that can be fed directly into processing devices. In effect, telephone circuits enable computers at remote points to communicate with each other. As a consequence, telephone systems have become an integral part of modern telecommunications systems in general. (Ed.)

DEVELOPMENT OF THE TELEPHONE

The essential elements necessary for the telephone were available at least a third of a century before Alexander Graham Bell's patent was granted in March 1876. The concept of sound as a vibration was understood at the beginning of the 19th century, as was the fact that vibration could be transferred to solid bodies. Michael Faraday in 1831 showed how the vibrations of a piece of iron or steel could be converted into electrical pulses. Though science and technology by that time had reached the point that all that needed to be known for the invention of the telephone was known, more than 40 years were to pass before the telephone was actually to appear.

What was needed was an entrepreneur who could foresee the applications for such a device. Why it took so long for such a person to appear is a question that can be only partially answered by suggesting that it may have been because the social need was not great enough. Though it could be expected that a few persons were experimenting with the idea in the intervening period, in fact there were very few. In the 1820s the English scientist, Charles Wheatstone, demonstrated that musical sounds could be transmitted through metallic and glass rods. By the time he had become involved with the telegraph in the late 1830s, however, he had abandoned the earlier line of investigation and apparently never attempted to connect the two fields. Charles Bourseul of France seems to have been the first to suggest a means for transmitting sounds electrically by means of a diaphragm making and breaking contact with an electrode. There is, however, no evidence that he ever did more than contemplate its possibilities. Other inventors similarly failed to appreciate the potential of instruments they had designed, and Bell, in 1875, appears to have been the first to understand not only that the electrical transmission of voice was possible but that it was commercially practical as well.

Proposed use of a diaphragm

Operating principles. The principles of the telephone are the same today as they were in the 19th century. The voice vibrates the air, which in turn vibrates a diaphragm. The motion of the diaphragm produces a corresponding vibration in an electric current. In the ordinary modern telephone, the diaphragm presses against an assembly of carbon particles and causes their electrical resistance to vary, so that an electric current flowing through the particles is altered and fluctuates in accord with the pressure on the particles. At the receiver, the current flows through an electromagnet. As the power of this magnet fluctuates, so does its attraction for an adjacent steel diaphragm. The diaphragm vibrates, moving the air and producing sound.

Other methods of telephone construction are possible, and several were actually considered in the 19th century.

Work of Philipp Reis

In 1861 Philipp Reis, a German schoolteacher, designed several instruments for the transmission of sound. In them, a contact in an electrical circuit was established between a metal point and a metal strip resting on a membrane in the transmitter (Figure 9). It was Reis's theory that as the membrane vibrated the metal point would

By courtesy of the Smithsonian Institution

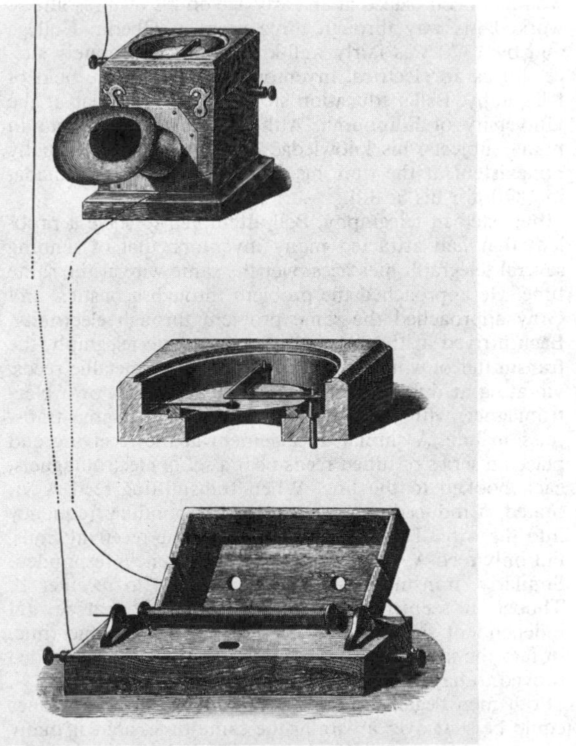

Figure 9: Contemporary sketch of early Philipp Reis telephone transmitter (top) and magnetostriction receiver (bottom). Cut-away view of transmitter in centre shows electrical contact points (see text).

bounce up and down, producing intermittent contact and intermittent current, synchronous with the vibrations, and that, furthermore, the height of the bounce, the force of its return, and the size of the current pulse would vary with the intensity of the sound. Thus, he expected that something of the quality as well as the intensity of the sound would be conveyed. Reis's receiver consisted of an iron needle surrounded by a coil and resting on a sounding box. It was designed to operate on the principle of magnetostriction (a phenomenon in which the length of a metal rod varies as the magnetic field through it varies). It had been known since 1837 that an interrupted current would produce corresponding "ticks" in such a device. Reis believed that simple musical tones could be transmitted by the apparatus—which he called a telephone—and such demonstrations with his instruments were common. In addition, however, there were several reports of successful speech transmission. These reports were subsequently discounted in court cases upholding the Bell patent, largely because it was recognized that speech transmission would be impossible if the instruments operated as Reis believed they did. It is a fact, however, that if the sound entering a Reis transmitter is not too strong, contact between the metal point and the metal strip will not be broken. Instead, the pressure of the former on the latter will fluctuate with the sound, causing fluctuations in the electrical resistance and therefore in the current. Similarly, the receiver will respond to continuously fluctuating as well as to intermittent currents (but not by magnetostriction). The sensitivity, however, is extremely low, so low that it is not unreasonable to question the validity of the limited testimony regarding successful voice transmission in the 1860s.

There is no evidence that Reis himself thought of his devices as more than "philosophical toys," good for lecture demonstrations to illustrate the nature of sound. He authorized their reproduction, and numerous copies were sold for this purpose. No one apparently tried to coax any more out of them.

Early instruments of Gray and Bell. In the period 1872–75 inventors Elisha Gray and Alexander Graham Bell, both working in the United States, developed a number of ideas and instruments that were strikingly similar. Gray, who had been placed at an early age on his own resources, worked his way through three years at Oberlin College and by 1870 was fairly well-known and moderately successful as an electrical inventor, primarily in the field of telegraphy. Bell's education stopped after one year at the University of Edinburgh. Although he was well-read in many subjects, his knowledge of electricity was virtually nonexistent at the time his family emigrated to Canada, in 1870, for his health.

Interested in telegraphy, Bell attempted to solve a problem that had attracted many inventors: that of sending several telegraph messages over the same wire at the same time. He approached the problem through acoustics, and Gray approached the same problem through electricity. Each arrived at the concept of a harmonic telegraph, the transmitter of which consisted of a series of metallic reeds, vibrating at different frequencies, each near its own electromagnet, with the coils all attached to the same transmission line. A similar arrangement at the receiving end placed a series of tuned reeds near a set of electromagnets, each hooked to the line. When transmitting reed A vibrated, it induced a current of a corresponding frequency into the wire. This current went to all the receiving coils, but only reed A, tuned to the same frequency, responded. Similarly, transmitting reed B was tuned to receiver B. Though it seemed theoretically reasonable that several independent signals could be sent out at the same time, in fact the system very quickly broke down and the idea proved to have no commercial value.

Both men began to consider the fact that if a few tones could be sent over a wire at the same time, a great many tones could be transmitted, enough indeed to represent the human voice. Gray understood how he might build a receiver and immediately constructed such a device in the spring of 1874. It consisted of a steel diaphragm in front of an electromagnet, virtually identical with the common modern receiver. But he had no transmitter. Meanwhile, Bell had been considering the possibility of multiple-reed transmitters and receivers (many tuned reeds near a single coil), though he had constructed nothing. In the summer of 1874 he conceived a membrane receiver (similar to Gray's but using a skin membrane with a piece of iron attached to the centre). Having no transmitter, he did not construct the device. In the spring of 1875, however, Bell was led by his telegraph experiments to believe that the inductive force from a piece of iron on a vibrating membrane near a coil might be powerful enough to act as a transmitter, and that his receiver might be sensitive enough to produce the desired effect. In June his assistant, Thomas Watson, constructed two identical instruments, one to be used as a transmitter, one as a receiver. The experiment was performed but failed (it probably would have worked if Bell's surroundings had been quieter). Bell temporarily abandoned the telephone to attend to his financial needs, but he remained convinced he was on the right track. By the end of the year he was writing patent specifications.

That autumn Gray developed a transmitter in which a moving membrane caused one rod to move near another in water to which a small amount of acid had been added to make it electrically conducting (Figure 10). As the distance between the rods changed, so did the electrical

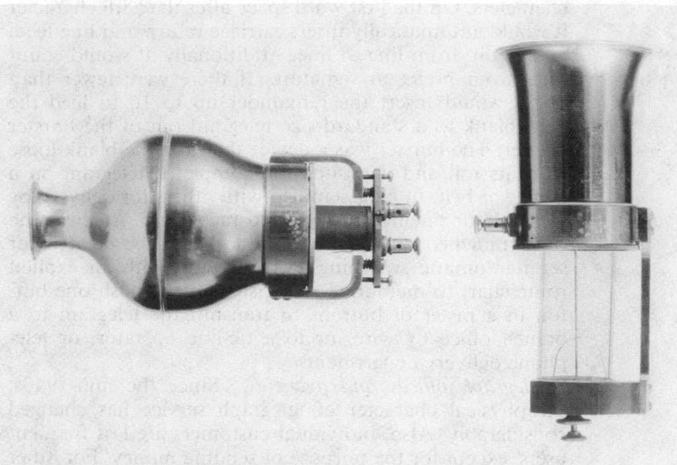

Figure 10: Photograph of Elisha Gray's telephone receiver (left) and transmitter (right). The container for acidulated water and the vertical rod connected to the diaphragm are visible in the transmitter photograph (see text).

By courtesy of the Smithsonian Institution

resistance, and thus the current in the circuit. Apparently Gray did not attempt to test his device. He did prepare a description to be filed at the Patent Office as a caveat, or "notice of invention." The caveat was filed on February 14, 1876. Bell, meanwhile, had completed his specifications and had them notarized in Boston on January 20. They were filed, as a patent application, on February 14.

At this point, neither man had successfully transmitted speech. In some ways Gray was closer to a solution: he used a metal diaphragm that was considerably more efficient than Bell's skin membrane, and he had designed a variable-resistance transmitter. Seemingly as an afterthought Bell had inserted a variable-resistance clause in his patent application; his main emphasis, however, was on the induction device. Gray apparently lost confidence. Perhaps he was convinced that Bell had beaten him; or perhaps he was still unable to see the potential of the idea. In any case, he did virtually nothing to develop his work further in the next critical years.

Bell, on the other hand, clearly felt the goal was at hand. On March 10, 1876 (three days after the patent was issued), he successfully transmitted words using a variable-resistance transmitter formed by a metal rod attached to a membrane, the top of the rod dipped into acidified water. The receiver was a damped reed (damped by holding it against the ear) of one of his telegraphic tuned membranes. Experiments using other variable-resistance transmitters followed, without success. By April he had reverted to his old induction transmitter and found that with some modifications it worked well enough to be demonstrated, most noticeably at the Centennial celebration in Philadelphia in June (Figure 11). The device was still not efficient enough for public use, and it took Bell and Watson the remainder of the year to make it so. The major improvement during that time was substitution of a steel diaphragm for the skin membrane. Commercialization began early in 1877.

Bell's patent claims were granted by the U.S. courts in the broadest possible manner to cover the principle of speech transmission by electricity. Elsewhere they were restricted to the special devices. *Bell's patent claims*

There were, of course, other claimants, such as Elisha Gray. But regardless of the merits of particular claims, it is clear that as an innovator and entrepreneur Bell was virtually alone in recognizing the commercial potential of the telephone.

Immediately after the introduction of the commercial telephone, two things became obvious: that the transmitter was its weakest link and that it would be profitable to develop a better one. Apparently it was also obvious that a variable-resistance device, preferably using some form of carbon, represented the best direction in which to go. Carbon-resistance transmitters were soon developed

Figure 11: An early Bell induction instrument, successfully demonstrated in June 1876. The instrument could be used either as a transmitter or as a receiver. Voice currents flow through the cylindrical coil (centre).
By courtesy of the Smithsonian Institution

by several inventors, with Thomas Edison eventually winning the basic patent rights. By 1878, Edison transmitters, essentially the same as modern devices, were being used commercially.

Other devices and methods. A new type of receiver was invented by Edison in 1878 to avoid interference with the Bell patent in England. In his device a metal stylus rested lightly on a chalk drum, and the transmitted current flowed from stylus to drum as the drum was rotated by hand. Fluctuation in the current caused variations in the frictional resistance between the two components, resulting in corresponding variations in sound that could be heard distinctly. This receiver, in combination with Edison's carbon transmitter, was called his "loud speaking" telephone. Its use was short-lived, however, since the Edison and Bell interests in England soon joined forces, henceforth relying on the Bell induction receiver and the Edison carbon transmitter.

Still another method of transmitting sound electrically was developed in 1878 when A.E. Dolbear, a professor of physics, devised a transmitter in which the diaphragm was one plate of a small battery. When it vibrated, so did the voltage of the battery and the current in the circuit. In a separate arrangement Dolbear designed a receiver with metal plates in the form of a capacitor. The fluctuating current caused one plate to vibrate, producing sound. Dolbear's devices were not competitive as telephone instruments, though the capacitor principle proved valuable in some microphone designs in the 20th century.

Patents. Since the Bell patent, No. 174,465, is often called the most valuable ever issued in the U.S., a brief look at its history is appropriate. In 1877 Bell offered to sell it to Western Union for $100,000; Western Union instead bought the Gray, Edison, and other patents and moved to develop its own telephone network. Suit for infringement was brought by the Bell Company in 1878. In due course Western Union decided to capitulate, obtaining 20 percent of the profit made by the Bell Company on the rental of telephone instruments and relinquishing their own patents. Subsequent court cases in the United States pitted Bell against claims made for several other inventors. A number of these cases were joined together in an appeal to the Supreme Court. In a 4–3 decision in 1893, the Court upheld Bell's claims in the very broad scope mentioned earlier.

Networks. Although to some extent the commercial development of the telegraph could serve as a guide, there were many special problems in the path of the telephone. One of the most formidable arose from the fact that instead of a single terminal in each town, there were many, and each had to be connected to any of the others at a moment's notice. Obviously, the lines had to be brought together at one or more common points where connections could be made. The first commercial telephone switchboard was placed in service in New Haven, Connecticut, in January 1878. It served 21 telephones and consisted of a series of switches so mounted that the various lines could be interconnected. There now existed microphone and receiver, and the wires and switching mechanism necessary to hook them together. There also existed a large number of people who were ready to accept the idea that these new devices were useful to them.

First commercial switchboard

19th-century telephony. Within a very short time after its introduction, telephony was a sophisticated system, capable of connecting moderately large numbers of users over relatively short distances. As a result it is perhaps not surprising that expansion of its uses should have been so rapid, though this is as much a testimony to the energy of the system's promoters as it is to its mechanical and electrical completeness. By March 1880, there were 138 exchanges in operation in the United States, with 30,000 subscribers. By 1887, only a decade after the commercial introduction of the telephone, there were 743 main and 444 branch exchanges connecting over 150,000 subscribers with about 146,000 miles (235,000 kilometres) of wire. Developments in other countries were also rapid, and by 1887 the number of subscribers in Canada was over 12,000, in the United Kingdom 26,000, in Germany 22,000, Sweden 12,000, France 9,000, Italy 9,000, and Russia 7,000.

Some attempts were made to expand the telephone to other uses. Most notable were systems of wired broadcasting, introduced experimentally as early as 1881 and commercially in the 1890s. In the experimental arrangement, microphones were placed on a concert stage in Paris, while in a nearby room receivers (the transmission was stereophonic, consisting of two channels) were provided for listening. Commercially wired broadcasting was most highly developed in Budapest, starting in 1893. By the turn of the century there were 6,500 subscribers in that city. Music, news, stock market reports, and even dramatic presentations were transmitted over the wires on a schedule of up to 14 hours a day. This system continued until supplanted by radio in the 20th century. Similar systems were developed in London and Paris.

LONG-DISTANCE TELEPHONY

As soon as distances of more than local extension were attempted, problems arose and produced a variety of ingenious products and procedures.

Hard-drawn copper wire, the first of these innovations, was stronger than ordinary copper wire and was a better conductor of electricity than the steel wire commonly in use. After a long-distance test between Boston and New York in 1883 proved its worth, hard-drawn copper became the standard material for overhead wire lines.

Development of strong copper wire

Underground cables, important in the cities where mazes of telephone poles and wires were becoming a hazard, were also essential in crossing rivers, lakes, and oceans. Experiments performed in the 1880s led to the widespread use of dry-core cable in the 1890s. The value of the dry core (in which each wire conductor was surrounded by paper and air and the bundle of wires enclosed in a watertight cover) was that it improved the transmission properties of the cable.

It was soon found that reliance on a ground return (having a circuit formed by a wire in one direction and a conducting path through the earth in the other) produced severe problems when two or more wires were routed close to each other. The signals in one wire would get mixed up with the signals in the others in a phenomenon called cross talk. The first public demonstration of an all-metal (two-wire) circuit was made between Boston and Providence in 1881, but general commercial adoption did not take place until the 1890s.

The loading coil. Over the years the length of transmission had increased as various improvements were made. But about 1,200 miles (1,900 kilometres), the distance achieved when Boston and Chicago were connected successfully in 1893, seemed to be a practical maximum. The basic problem was one of distortion introduced into the signal by the electrical characteristics of the circuit. A British theorist, Oliver Heaviside, in 1887 showed the conditions under which distortion could be minimized and suggested that this be done by increasing the inductance of the circuit or line. In 1893 Heaviside suggested further that this might be done by introducing coils along the cable at periodic intervals, but he went no further in calculating precise values or in performing tests. American engineers attempted to apply the theory by using a bimetallic wire of copper and iron to increase the inductance. Work was later shifted to the use of discrete coils located at regular intervals along a line, a technique called loading. The first loaded circuits were opened to public use in May 1900. These applications were completely successful, and the principle was rapidly applied elsewhere. Line lengths doubled; in addition the coil made possible a reduction in the size of wire used on short lines, with consequent valuable savings.

Signal boosters

The repeater. Once the distortion problem was mastered, another need became apparent: that of a means for boosting, or amplifying, the signal. Early efforts attempted to combine the telephone receiver and microphone into something analogous to the telegraph repeater. Though a successful instrument, called a mechanical repeater, was designed in 1904, it was insensitive to low input energy, and the amplification varied somewhat with the frequency of the input signal. It served, however, for a number of years, until replaced by the superior vacuum tube.

Although the three-element vacuum tube was invented by Lee De Forest in 1906, its usefulness as an amplifier in a telephone repeater was not immediately realized; the first commercial demonstrations were made in 1915, when it was shown that three repeaters, or relays, were sufficient to carry voice signals across the United States. De Forest's vacuum tube consisted of a filament (source of electrons), a plate (collector of electrons), and a wire mesh in between for controlling the flow of electrons. A small signal impressed on the grid could result in a greatly amplified signal at the plate.

Getting a signal across the ocean proved more difficult. Repeaters were short-lived, and there was no way to replace them in a submarine cable. Furthermore, many would be needed because of the distortion imposed on the signal. A submarine telegraph cable involves two conductors—one the wire, the other the water—and the effect is to blur the input signal. Commercial transatlantic telephony, therefore, had to rely upon shortwave radio at first; this service was available starting in 1926.

Radio techniques were useful on land also. High-frequency microwave radio links have been commonplace since 1946, when they were first used experimentally. The bandwidth of such a facility is broad enough to handle large numbers of telephone conversations. Even before this, however, the principle of superimposing a number of voice signals on a carrier wave was employed on a coaxial cable, a tubular conductor with another conductor concentric with it. The first commercial messages using the carrier technique were sent in 1937 between New York and Philadelphia.

Transatlantic cable telephony was made possible by the development of a vacuum-tube amplifier with a life expectancy of 20 years, long enough to make the cable laying economical. The development of the plastic polyethylene, which has exceptionally good insulating properties, also contributed to making the project practical.

A coaxial cable with submerged repeaters was laid as a test between Miami and Havana in 1950. When it proved successful, two transatlantic cables were laid in 1956, there were 51 one-way repeaters in each line between Scotland and Newfoundland. Sixteen larger two-way repeaters were used in a single line from Newfoundland to Nova Scotia. The system was capable of handling 60 telephone conversations at a time. Other cables have subsequently been laid in the Atlantic and elsewhere.

Satellite repeaters

Another means of spanning long distances became possible with the advent of satellites. The possibilities were first demonstrated in 1962 by the satellite Telstar, a low-orbit nonsynchronous relay station. Regular commercial service was made possible when the synchronous satellite Syncom II was positioned over the Atlantic in 1963. A synchronous satellite is one whose period of rotation is the same as that of the Earth; if positioned above the equator, it thus appears to be stationary, whereas a nonsynchronous satellite moves with respect to the Earth's surface. Radio signals are sent up to the satellite from one point on Earth, are amplified, and are retransmitted back to another point on Earth. (For a detailed discussion of the use of satellites, see below *Satellite communications.*)

Multiplexing. In view of the fact that the telephone was created out of attempts to develop a multiplex telegraphy system—that is, a system for sending several telegraph messages over the same wire at the same time—it is not surprising that efforts should have been made at an early date to multiplex telephone signals. In 1883 an arrangement was patented that produced what is known as a "phantom" circuit. If one pair of wires carried one conversation and a second pair of wires another, then by proper electrical balancing the two pairs could be used to constitute a third, or "phantom," circuit. Maintaining a balance, however, proved difficult, and it was not until 1910 that a successful practical method was found.

More recently, attention has been paid to utilizing the waste time that occurs in any telephone conversation. One method, called time assignment speech interpolation, was especially well suited to the first two Atlantic cables since they had been laid in pairs, with each cable carrying channels in only one direction. Each cable was only being used, on the average, less than 50 percent of the time. Circuitry installed in 1960 was able to detect the instant that each new speech element commenced and assign it to a vacant channel. The effect was to double the capacity of these cables. Recent improvements in the technique have led to an even larger capacity.

Another method of increasing the capacity of existing channels is by taking only periodic samples of the wave to be transmitted. This technique, which has long been used for multiplex telegraphy, involves a brush rotating rapidly around a segmented disk so as to make successive contact with each of the several segments. In order to convey the more subtle complexities of voice communication, however, the frequency of sampling must be much more rapid and therefore must be done electronically. Experiments in recent years have shown that high quality reproduction can be achieved, with the result that as many as 12 conversations can be carried over a channel formerly reserved for one. The technique, known as pulse code modulation, is discussed in more detail later in this article.

Switching. As the volume of telephone usage has increased, the problems of joining transmitter and receiver have become more complex. By the mid-1880s the switchboard had evolved to a point where hundreds and even thousands of subscribers could be handled. Special switches and flexible cords were devised. Switchboards were produced in multiple units with identical parts so that more than one operator could service the same telephones, and methods were devised whereby each operator could determine which lines were "busy" without listening in.

Originally, individual telephones had been equipped with their own batteries. The first central office with a common battery for talking and signalling was installed in Lexington, Massachusetts, in 1893. Among other things, the development meant that the subscriber could signal the operator merely by lifting the receiver from its hook. Beginning in 1894 this signalling could be done by miniature light bulbs on the switchboard.

Automatic switching systems were contemplated as early as 1881, when an automatic system was shown at the Paris Electrical Exposition. That system proved impractical, but a workable arrangement was patented in 1889. Important modifications were made over the next few years. The essentials of the system consisted of a mechanism that could send out a series of pulses that would first raise, then rotate a shaft through a corresponding number of steps to make the appropriate contact. Thus for the number 295, the shaft would be raised two steps, then revolved through nine large steps, then through five intermediate contact points.

The original patent specifications required the caller to press a different button the required number of times for each number, and separate lines to the central station were

First dial mech-anism

necessary for each button. Improvements eliminated the need for extra lines, and in 1898 a dial mechanism was patented, eliminating the buttons.

The first large test installation of automatic equipment was made in Newark, New Jersey, in 1914; actually the system should be termed semi-automatic, since an operator was still used to accept the incoming calls. The first fully automatic system was installed in Omaha in 1921. (B.S.F.)

Principles and problems of telecommunications

Telecommunications today centres on the problems involved in transmitting large volumes of messages over long distances without damaging loss due to noise and interference. Such problems with short-distance messages are not as severe; the signal travels over two-wire lines as described earlier without additional processing.

Figure 12 shows the basic components of a typical long-distance telecommunications system capable of transmitting voice, teletypewriter, facsimile, data, or television signals. If digital transmission is employed, signals are first processed in a coder that completely transforms their character. Typically the coder includes filtering and coding circuits that convert the signal into digital form; in data transmission this step is bypassed because the signals are already in digital form.

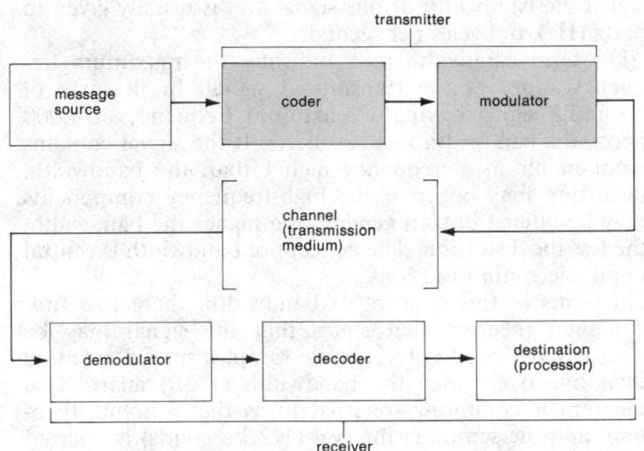

Figure 12: Simplified block diagram of a typical long-distance telecommunications system.

For analogue transmission—that is, transmission of voice and other signals without converting them to digital form—the coding stage may be omitted. Most modern TV and voice communication use the analogue system; data, teletypewriter, and many other forms of telecommunications use digital techniques.

Function of the modulator

After coding, the signal is further processed in a so-called modulator, a device for impressing the intelligence signal onto a radio-frequency signal of the proper frequency for the form of transmission to be used. High-frequency signals are usually used for radio transmission; low-frequency signals are used in coaxial cables and other wire lines (described later). The combination of coder and modulator is called the transmitter.

A receiver picks up the transmitted signal at the destination. A demodulator eliminates the carrier wave, and a decoder transforms the message signal into usable form. In many systems the decoder and demodulator are not physically distinguishable but are simply parts of a subsystem that combines both. In two-way communications systems, with a transmitter and receiver at either end, a modulator-demodulator combination, called modem for short, is employed.

In transmission of speech, music, or picture information, the object is high fidelity—that is, the best possible reproduction of the original message. In some cases, however, other pertinent information may have to be extracted from the received signal. Examples include processing of seismic signals (natural or man-made Earth vibrations) to obtain information about the medium through which they are transmitted and the processing of sonar and radar signals. Signal processing that involves the interpretation of data includes such medical data as electrocardiograms and X-rays and environmental data such as air-pollution measurements.

THE DIGITAL COMMUNICATIONS SYSTEM

Binary system. The basis of relatively noise-free and interference-free telecommunication is the so-called binary signal. The simplest possible signal of any kind that can be employed to transmit messages, the binary signal consists of two states only: the dot-dash of Morse code (see above), an on-off signal in teletype, a 0 or 1 in binary arithmetic, and a punch or no-punch command of computer cards. Practically all voice, picture, instrumentation, and other data can be coded in binary form.

Figure 13 illustrates two kinds of binary signal. Both of these signal sequences carry the same information; *i.e.,* the binary sequence 101,100, or on-off-on-on-off-off. Once a particular pair of signals has been selected, the presence of one or the other is determined by the binary symbol, 1 or 0, that is to be transmitted. These signals are called binary digits, or bits. The transmission rate is described as one bit per time unit. In practice, on-off (Figure 13A) or bipolar (Figure 13B) signals or variations thereof are used.

The simplest form of modulator transmits bursts of a radio-frequency signal when a 1 appears and nothing when the 0 appears. This is the binary version of amplitude modulation, or AM (described later). This binary AM system contains a radio-frequency oscillator, designed to transmit a particular frequency only when a 1 appears and to stop transmitting when the 0 appears.

Frequency-shift keying

Other forms of modulation used for binary signalling include frequency-shift keying, in which a binary 1 or 0 causes the frequency to shift to either one of two predetermined frequencies (representing either 1 or 0); and phase-shift keying, in which the sign, or polarity, of a high-frequency carrier shifts between positive and negative when the binary input shifts from 0 to 1. The first method is the binary version of FM, or frequency modulation (explained later); the second is an example of phase modulation (PM).

Distortion and noise. As a high-frequency radio signal travels through the transmitting path, noise and interference are encountered. Some of this comes from switching circuits and antennas; most is encountered in the atmosphere, or the space between the transmitting and receiving antennas. In addition, the message may be distorted during transmission.

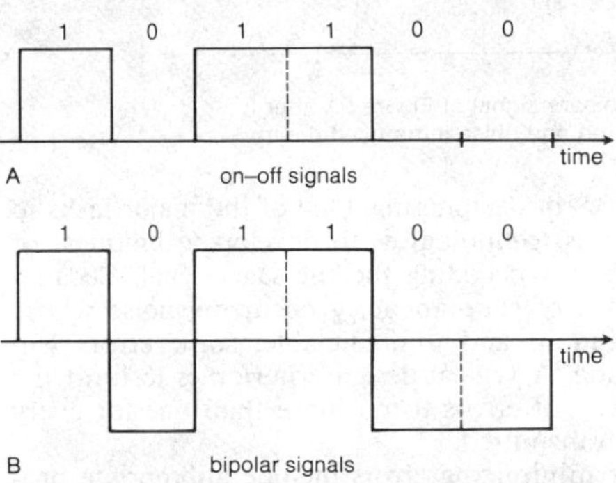

Figure 13: Representation of the binary number (101100) as (A) on-off signals and as (B) bipolar signals.

One common type of distortion is called alternate path propagation, in which a signal traverses two or more different paths, usually because of reflections, and the split signals arrive at the receiver at slightly different times, causing echoes, or in the case of television transmission, ghosts. This is called multipath effect. If the separate paths are of identical length, the individual signals are in effect added together; if the path lengths differ so that they are exactly out of step, they are said to be out of phase with each other, and the result will be to subtract one from the other and reduce the strength of the total received signal. If they are in phase, they add, strengthening the signal, but the overall result of several signal paths, leading to signals that are in phase and out of phase by varying amounts, is fluctuation. Shortwave broadcasts, in which signals are directed into space and reflected back by the Earth's ionosphere, typically show fading characteristics, characterized by fluctuating amplitude.

There are many other sources of signal distortion and attenuation:

Noise added during transmission can include interfering signals in the same frequency range, interference from nearby electrical sources, the effects of electrical storms in the atmosphere, and spurious effects introduced by malfunctioning circuits. The effect of these noise sources often can be minimized or eliminated by appropriate equipment design. In addition to these noise disturbances, there is a type due to "spontaneous fluctuations" that can never be eliminated. The Sun and the Earth's atmosphere continually generate electrical energy at all frequencies. All sources of heat emit so-called thermal noise. Such noise can also arise within the communications system itself.

Thermal noise

Systems design involves predicting the average effects of distortion and noise and providing maximum protection against them. Various modulation and coding schemes have been devised for this purpose, and one of the reasons for using binary signal transmission is in fact to benefit from the improved noise immunity that such transmission offers.

Although signal distortion and noise introduced by the transmission medium are common to all forms of communication, the relative effects differ in various systems. In telephony, signal distortion is a much more serious problem than noise. In space communications, however, in which signals are transmitted over extremely long distances, the desired signal energy received may be only as strong as, or even considerably less than, the noise and it then becomes a major task to sort out the signal from the noise.

Receiving the digital signal. The binary amplitude-modulated signal (explained later) arriving at the receiver (Figure 14) contains whatever noise and distortion was added during transmission. The demodulator portion of the receiver strips away the high-frequency carrier, leaving only a distorted version of the original binary signal sequence and the noise. A typical distorted, noisy signal is shown in Figure 14. Both the distortion and the added noise tend to mask the original signal sequence and thus

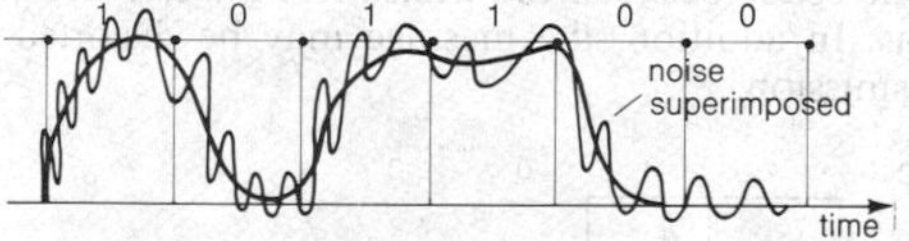

Figure 14: The binary signal of Figure 5A after it has been distorted and noise introduced during transmission.

introduce errors in deciphering. One of the major tasks in communications technology is to develop techniques for reducing errors in decoding the message signal. Because of the presence of spontaneously occurring noise whose effects are random and unpredictable, some errors will always be made. A typical design criterion is to limit the average number of errors to no more than one for every 100,000 bits transmitted.

Methods for minimizing errors include appropriate processing of the signals at the transmitter, coding at the transmitter to make the signals and noise as distinguishable as possible, insertion of filters at the receiver to decrease the noise energy without destroying too much of the signal characteristics, and appropriate signal processing at the receiver. For systems in which fading and multipath predominate, diversity techniques have been developed: several replicas of the signal are transmitted, either in time (time diversity) or using different antennas, receivers, and transmitters (space diversity). By appropriate combination of the separate versions of the received signals, the fading effects may be overcome to some extent.

ANALOGUE-TO-DIGITAL CONVERSION

Thus far the transmission of binary signals has been stressed. If the signal to be transmitted is already binary in form (teletypewriter, computer output), there is no problem. But ordinary voice communications taking place by way of a telephone are not in binary form; neither is the temperature, pressure, solar-flare data, or other information that might be gathered for transmission back to Earth as a part of a space-probe mission. Such forms of data are said to be analogue, or continuously time varying, in contrast to digital (discrete number) data transmission, of which binary transmission is the most important case. In digital communications systems, analogue signals must first be converted to digital form. The process of making this signal conversion is called analogue-to-digital (A/D) conversion.

The sampling process. The basis of the process is sampling, or measuring the analogue wave shape to be transmitted at equally spaced discrete instants of time. The sampled values are further approximated by a specified set of discrete numbers; these numbers are converted to their equivalent binary form and the binary numbers transmitted.

The fact that samples of a continuously varying wave in time (Figure 15A) may be used to represent a wave relies on the assumption that the original wave is constrained in its rate of variation with time. In Figure 15A, for example, the most rapid variation of the analogue signal occurs roughly in the centre. The time between the minimum and maximum excursion is labelled $1/B$ seconds. B is called the bandwidth of this signal and is usually given in hertz (Hz), or cycles per second.

The term bandwidth then indicates the maximum frequency range of the transmitted signal. In the case of an audio signal having a maximum frequency of 4,000 hertz, the bandwidth is 4,000 hertz. If the signal contains components at a frequency higher than the bandwidth, distortion may occur or the high-frequency components may be filtered out. In general, the higher the bandwidth, the less the distortion. The concept of bandwidth is central to all telecommunications.

Concept of bandwidth

In terms of this concept of bandwidth, there is a fundamental theorem that states that the signal may be uniquely represented by discrete samples spaced no more than one over twice the bandwidth ($1/2B$) apart. This theorem is commonly referred to as the sampling theorem, and the sampling interval ($1/2B$ seconds) is referred to as the Nyquist interval (after the American scientist Harry Nyquist).

As an example, in telephone practice the bandwidth is commonly fixed at 3,300 hertz. Filters are actually inserted to prevent higher frequencies from coming through. Samples therefore should be taken every 1/6,600 second. In practice somewhat more samples are used, 8,000 per second, with a spacing or interval of 1/8,000 second (125 microseconds).

Figure 15B shows the sampling process carried out conceptually. The analogue signal is shown being sampled periodically by a switch rotating at least at the Nyquist rate, $2B$ times a second. A mechanical switch is shown for clarity, but in practice high-speed electronic switches are used. The switch essentially allows a small portion of the analogue wave to go through, repeating this process at least $2B$ times each second.

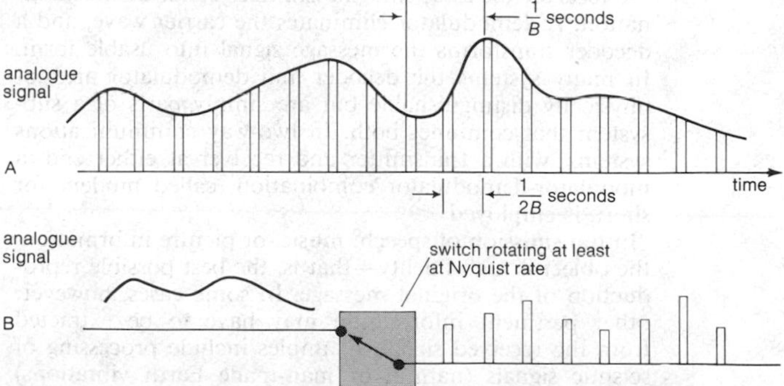

Figure 15: (A) Continuously varying sound wave sampled at intervals of $1/2B$ seconds (B is the bandwidth). (B) Conceptual form of the sampling process (see text).

Conversion to binary form. Not only voice signals but other analogue signals require conversion into binary form for pulse transmission; in each case an arbitrary scale of numbers is chosen to represent varying amplitude. For ease in conversion to binary form, the scale is usually a power of 2; that is, 8, 16, 32, 64, 128, and so on, depending on the degree of precision required. For example, if the problem is transmitting the temperature inside a space vehicle back to an Earth station, the potential variation is only between 9° and 25° C, and since the precision required is not high, a scale of 16 might be used. This would permit using one scale number to represent each degree C between 9° and 25°, and readings would omit fractions. If, on the other hand, in the same circumstances a higher degree of precision were required, a scale of 256 might be employed, permitting the division of the 16 degrees into decimal fractions to record such readings as 15.2° or 21.6°.

Amplitude level requirements

In digital transmission of voice, 128 levels are commonly used because tests have shown that this provides adequate fidelity for the average telephone listener. An unnecessarily large scale is not desirable, because larger scales require more transmitted bits per number. That this is so may be seen from an examination of the encoding process. A portion of an encoding table is shown below:

binary equivalent	decimal number (or signal level)
000	0
001	1
010	2
011	3
100	4
101	5
110	6
111	7

It is apparent that eight levels require three binary digits, or bits; 16 levels require four bits; and 128 levels require seven bits. In general 2^n levels require n bits. A binary encoder performs this conversion.

If 128-level transmission is used, each quantized signal sample must be represented by a sequence of seven bits. All of these bits must be transmitted before the next sample appears. To use more levels, more binary samples would have to be squeezed into the allotted time slot between successive signal samples. The circuitry becomes more costly, and the bandwidth of the system following the binary encoder becomes correspondingly greater, requiring an increased bandwidth for the transmission medium, or channel. Some channels (telephone wires are one example) may not have the bandwidth capability required for the increased number of binary samples and would distort the binary signals. Others are limited by law to a specific bandwidth. Although the accuracy required determines the number of quantization levels used, the resultant binary sequence must still be within the bandwidth tolerance allowed.

An example of a sequence of quantized samples and its binary equivalent is shown in Figure 16A and 16B, respectively. The numbers 7, 6, 5, 6, 5 have been selected arbitrarily. Eight-level (three-bit) samples are shown for simplicity. The entire analogue-digital processing—sampling, quantizing, binary encoding—is shown in block-diagram form in Figure 16C.

The binary signals of Figure 8B provide superior noise immunity to the equivalent quantized sequence of Figure 16A. The receiver has merely to recognize either one of two states in the binary case—the presence or absence of a signal in the on–off sequence shown or a positive or negative signal in a bipolar sequence—an easier task than recognizing one of many possible amplitude levels. More importantly, the maximum signal amplitude that may be used is determined by the transmitter power. In Figure 16A the number 7 uses the maximum power available, while lower numbers use less power. For a given average noise added during transmission, the lower amplitude signals are more readily affected by the noise. In binary signal transmission the signal level is always the same, and all signals are transmitted at the maximum amplitude. The coding into binary form thus provides considerably enhanced noise immunity.

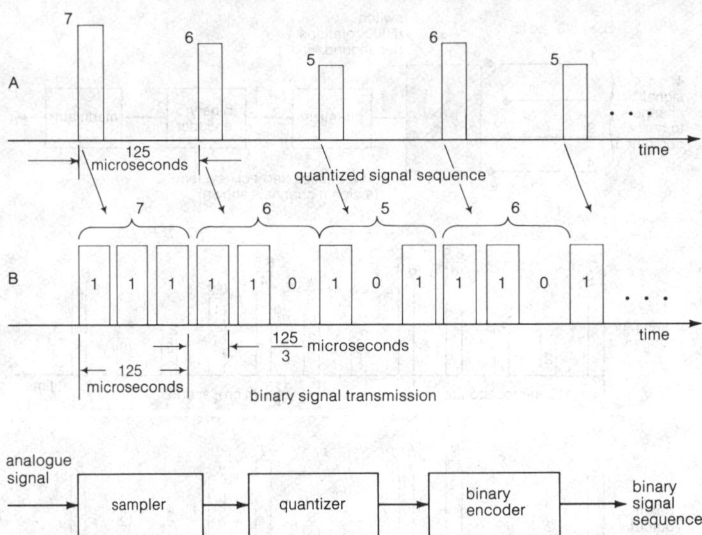

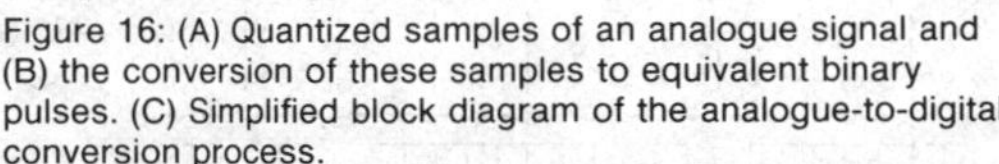

Figure 16: (A) Quantized samples of an analogue signal and (B) the conversion of these samples to equivalent binary pulses. (C) Simplified block diagram of the analogue-to-digital conversion process.

One of the major aims of communications system design has been to find other forms of coded communications signals that provide still better noise immunity. Some of these techniques will be considered later in this article.

MODULATION TECHNIQUES

Pulse-code modulation. Communications systems that use digitized and coded signals are commonly called pulse-code-modulation (PCM) systems. Binary digital systems constitute the most frequently encountered form of PCM systems.

Minimization of noise and interference

The basic characteristic of the PCM system is that it transmits signals in a form that largely overcomes the problems of noise, interference, and other distortion. In addition, the system has other advantages: (1) The signals may be reshaped and strengthened en route, since the information is no longer carried by continuously varying pulse amplitudes but by discrete symbols. The reshaping is carried out by specially designed circuits called repeaters that perform two functions: amplification and reshaping. The signals, having been attenuated (lost power) during transmission, are amplified and reshaped to their original power level and form to combat noise. (2) All-digital circuitry can be used throughout the system. With the advent of integrated circuits this has become economically desirable, and pulse-code-modulation communication of all forms—telephony, telemetering, pure data transmission—is under rapid development throughout the world. (3) Digital signals are in the appropriate form for computer processing. Sophisticated computer techniques may thus be used to carry out signal processing if needed.

A typical pulse-code-modulation system consists of an analogue-digital converter, an appropriate form of modulator at the transmitter to raise the binary signals to the desired frequency range for transmission, and a receiver.

Time multiplexing. An additional process carried out at the transmitter is of utmost importance in the value of pulse code modulation. A multitude of independent signal messages may be sequentially combined for transmission over a common channel. In telephony, for example, a telephone signal (group of pulses) must be sent every 1/8,000 of a second; yet the transmission of the signal takes so little time that a large part of the 1/8,000 of a second is not used. By a process called time multiplexing, a number of signals, representing sequential parts of different telephone messages, can all be sent one after the other and sorted out again at the receiver. The process is diagrammed in Figure 17. Each of the four signal lines shown is successively (sequentially) sampled, the successive samples appearing on the common line following the sampler. In this example each signal line is assumed to be

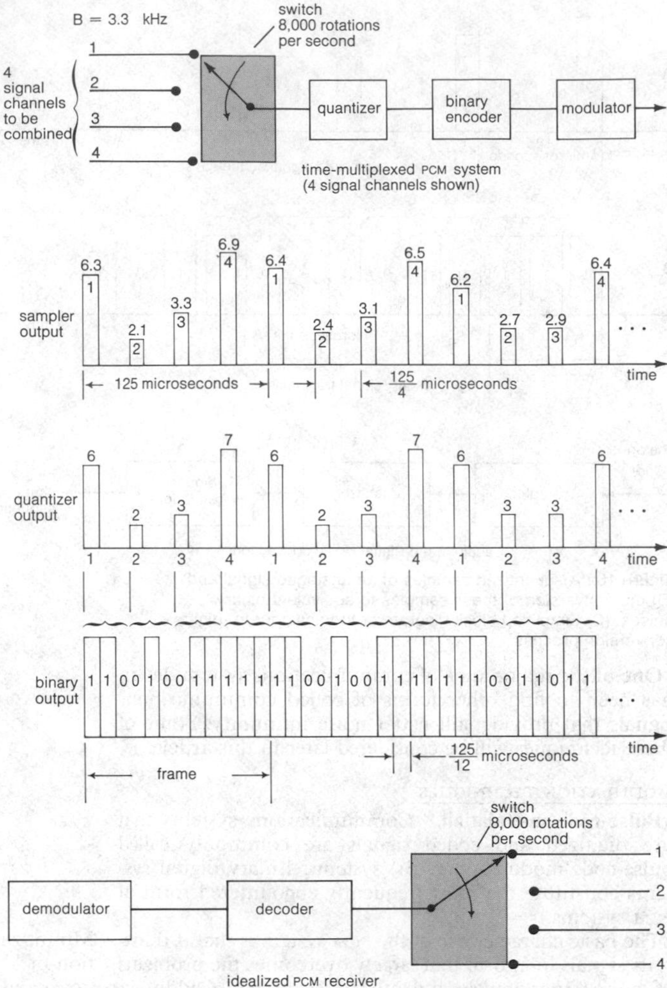

Figure 17: *Elements of a time-multiplexed pulse-code-modulation (PCM) system.*
At the top is a simplified block diagram of the sampler, quantizer, encoder, and modulator for a four-channel system. The analogue signal for each channel is successively sampled, quantized, and then converted to a binary output. At the bottom is a simplified block diagram of an idealized PCM receiver, consisting of a demodulator, decoder, and channel-switching arrangement synchronized with the transmitter sampling switch.

of the same bandwidth, so that the minimum sampling rate required is the same for each.

Versatility of PCM system

A single pulse-code-modulation system may carry several other kinds of signals besides voice. These other signals may not require a sampling frequency of 1/8,000 of a second; some data transmissions may have very slow fluctuations, requiring sampling only once an hour; a great number of such signals can be accommodated along with one or more voice transmissions. In such mixed transmissions, signals with the same bandwidth are first multiplexed into a single stream of samples; different band samples are then interleaved. The sequence of binary signals that represents one sample of each of the signals multiplexed is said to constitute a frame.

The number of signals time multiplexed into one stream varies from application to application. In one telemetering system used aboard a meteorological spacecraft, 544 inputs are multiplexed, of which 32 are sampled once every second, and 512 are sampled once every 16 seconds. Two levels of multiplexing are thus used. In a pulse-code-modulation system used for short-range telephone communication, 24 speech signals are time multiplexed for transmission over the same line. In PCM telegraph systems 660 telegraph channels are multiplexed. In many of these applications seven-bit analogue-to-digital conversion is used; that is, a group of seven bits represents a single sample of the transmitted information.

As more signal channels are multiplexed, the number of bits per second required to represent the composite data stream increases. The bandwidth required of the transmission medium goes up correspondingly, and the high-speed circuitry required to handle the flow ultimately limits the number of channels that may be multiplexed. The circuitry limitation has been changing rapidly, however, due to advances in digital technology. Integrated circuits and smaller electronic components and spacings have been bringing about a revolution in the speed or bandwidth of operation of these circuits.

In one type of telephone system 24 subscribers are time multiplexed into a single circuit. With an eight-kilohertz (thousands of cycles per second) sampling rate and seven-bit binary transmission, 24 × 8,000 × 7 bits of information are transmitted every second. In practice an additional bit time interval is inserted after each seven-bit sequence, so that 1,536,000 (24 × 8,000 × 8) bits per second are actually transmitted. Laboratory demonstrations of systems carrying over 500,000,000 bits per second have been successfully carried out, and such systems may become commercially practicable in the near future. A system of this type could carry hundreds of simultaneous telephone conversations or six simultaneous television broadcasts. Television bandwidths are typically six megahertz (6,000,000 hertz). To sample six signals at twice this rate, using seven-bit analogue-to-digital conversion, would require over 500,000,000 bits per second. The bandwidth required is also of the order of 500 megahertz or more, thus bandwidth considerations play a key role in engineering a system. Coaxial cables, millimetre wave guides, and optical tubes are being considered as transmission media for such high-bandwidth systems.

The reception of time-multiplexed signals requires precise synchronization with the transmitter (Figure 17). After demodulation (removing the carrier frequency), the binary signals are decoded back into quantized signal form. Each signal is then sent to its appropriate destination (in the case of telephony the appropriate telephone line). Electronic switches precisely synchronized with those at the transmitter are used.

Insertion of synchronization processes

The synchronization problem is commonly handled by inserting in every frame a particular symbol or sequence of symbols that is readily recognized at the receiver. The receiver timing information necessary for synchronized switching is then derived from these synchronization pulses.

For telephone communication over short distances of 10 to 50 miles (16 to 80 kilometres), a system has been tested in which a network of 24 telephone subscriber lines are time multiplexed, sampled, and coded into pulse code modulation for carrier transmission. Each voice channel is first filtered to a bandwidth of 4,000 hertz, which determines the signal bandwidth, sampled and multiplexed at the 8,000-per-second rate. Seven-bit quantization and binary encoding are used. The binary pulses occupy half of the 0.65 microsecond's time allocated to them. Each seven-bit signal sequence is followed by an additional eighth time slot, which carries the exchange-area signalling information necessary to connect subscribers. In addition, a framing pulse is added at the end of each frame for synchronization.

Frequency multiplexing. As has been noted, the shift to a specified frequency is accomplished by varying, or modulating, a radio-frequency signal. This signal is called the carrier, and the resultant modulated carrier may be shown to possess frequency components or side bands (described later) in the vicinity of each carrier. If each group of signals modulates a different carrier, the resultant composite group consists of frequencies in the vicinity of each carrier. By spacing the carrier frequencies far enough apart, the signals can be kept distinct. When the group of signals is sent simultaneously from one point to another, the process of combining signals shifted in frequency is called frequency multiplexing. It is sometimes used in place of time multiplexing. More commonly a group of pulse-code-modulation signals, each consisting of a time-multiplexed sequence of signals, is in turn frequency multiplexed. The combination of time and frequency multiplexing thus results in the simultaneous transmission of many individual signals.

The use of frequency multiplexing is particularly common in telephone transmission. Each of the base band signals in a given set, whether time-multiplexed pulse code modulation or the original analogue telephone message, is first raised in frequency to an appropriate carrier, with the carriers spaced apart by at least twice the bandwidth so that the amplitude-modulated signal may be separately recovered. The frequency-multiplexed set, consisting of the sum of all of these signals, may then in turn modulate another, much higher frequency carrier for final transmission over the appropriate transmission medium.

Amplitude modulation. The simplest form of modulation is amplitude modulation (AM), in which the modulating signal slowly varies the amplitude of a carrier. The on–off binary signal sequence switches the carrier on and off.

Carrier and side bands

Physically, an amplitude-modulated signal consists of the carrier frequency plus two side bands separated from the carrier frequency by an amount equal to the frequency of the modulating (voice) signal. Each of these side bands, one above and one below the carrier frequency, carries all of the modulating information. The signal as a whole, therefore, carries with it superfluous information. It is possible to transmit one side band only, eliminating the carrier and the other side band, and still retrieve the modulating information intact.

Systems are in use in which the carrier is taken out before transmission; in systems of this type (suppressed carrier) the carrier is restored at the receiver. Special circuitry and techniques are required at the receiver in such systems. Since the economics involved make it impractical to build such receivers for widespread use, suppressed-carrier transmission is not used for normal radio broadcasting but is reserved for point-to-point communications and other shortwave radio applications, in which it achieves a substantial savings in transmitted power.

Suppressed-carrier systems with both side bands transmitted are commonly called double-side-band AM systems. Systems with one of the two side bands removed (filtered out) are called single-side-band systems and are in common use for all forms of point-to-point communications (radio and wire transmission, data, telephony, telegraphy). Since they too require insertion of a carrier at the receiver, they are not used in conjunction with home receivers. These systems provide still further power reduction and a reduction by one-half in bandwidth.

Frequency-multiplexed single-side-band systems are common in commercial practice. These systems range from those multiplexing simultaneously a few telegraph circuits to those combining many hundreds of telephone circuits.

Frequency modulation. In amplitude modulation, the amplitude of the carrier varies in accordance with the information-bearing, or modulating, signal. In frequency modulation (FM), on the other hand, the frequency of the carrier varies in accordance with the modulating signal. The resultant modulated carrier has a frequency spectrum centred about the unmodulated carrier frequency, again with upper and lower side bands, but the spectrum bears no simple resemblance to the spectrum of the modulating signal.

A simple form of frequency modulation occurs when the modulating signal is a pulse-code-modulation output. In this case the frequency of the carrier shifts between two values, one when a binary pulse is present in the modulating signal and the other when no pulse is present. As an example, in a typical telephone data set using frequency modulation, the two frequencies are 1,200 hertz and 2,200 hertz. At much higher radio frequencies, they could be any pair of frequencies in the desired band. Such a binary FM system is called a frequency-shift-keying (FSK) system. As the spacing between the two frequencies (or frequency deviation) is increased, the FM bandwidth increases accordingly. For small frequency deviations, however, the FM bandwidth corresponds to the AM bandwidth.

Frequency-shift keying

If a continuously varying (analogue) signal rather than the binary data signal is used as the modulating signal, the overall bandwidth of the modulated signal is approximately twice the frequency deviation plus twice the modulating signal frequency. The bandwidth is thus greater than for an AM system. An FM system in which the frequency shift is much greater than the modulating signal frequency is called a wide-band FM system. If the frequency shift is less, it is called a narrow-band FM system.

Even though frequency modulation requires wider bandwidths than the corresponding AM systems, it is employed as a modulation technique because wide-band FM signals are more effective than the equivalent AM signals in combatting noise and interference. The larger the modulation index (and hence the wider the bandwidth required for transmission), the more effectively FM performs.

Communications media

All telecommunications systems in use throughout the world follow some or all of the basic principles outlined above. They differ principally in the specific types of messages handled and the channels or media over which they are transmitted. When digital techniques are employed, once the various types of signals have been encoded into digital form and combined, they cannot be identified as to original source until they are decoded at their destination. The modulation technique (AM, FM) is selected after cost, power, bandwidth requirements, the availability of the proper transmitters and receivers, and the way the particular modulation technique is matched to the channel to introduce a minimum of distortion have been carefully considered. All possible combinations of the various techniques discussed are in fact in use in actual systems.

The three major communications media—wire, radio, and satellite—are discussed below, with examples of systems drawn from each. Wire transmission commonly refers to the transmission of electrical signals over various types of wire lines including open wire, multipair cable (twisted pairs), and coaxial cable. These lines are used to transmit voice frequencies, telegraph, low-speed data, and signalling for carrier systems (combining many voice or data signals by multiplex techniques). Radio transmission commonly refers to the transmission, through the air or space, of electrical signals in relatively narrow frequency bands. Satellite communications involves the use of man-made satellites travelling in Earth orbits to provide communication links between various points on the Earth.

RADIO COMMUNICATIONS

Because radio space is potentially available to any user, international and national regulations have evolved to limit usage, frequency bands available, and geographical limits of transmission. International radio regulations have been developed by the International Telecommunication Union in Geneva.

International Telecommunication Union

Two committees of the International Telecommunication Union are charged with studying technical and operating questions relating to telecommunications and issuing recommendations. These are the International Radio Consultative Committee (CCIR), dealing with radio communications, and the International Telegraph and Telephone Consultative Committee (CCITT), dealing with problems in telegraphy and telephony.

Among the regulations developed by the International Telecommunication Union are those pertaining to radio spectrum utilization, or allocations within particular frequency bands of the radio spectrum. The allocations are generally made on the basis of service type, or usage. The types of services include fixed service, involving radio communication between specified fixed points (point-to-point high-frequency communication and shortwave and microwave links are examples); mobile radio (aeronautical mobile, maritime, land mobile); radio navigation (aeronautical and maritime); broadcasting (AM, FM, and TV broadcasting intended for general public usage); amateur radio; space communications (telemetry, tracking, Earth-space communications as in satellite communications, and communications between space stations); radio astronomy; and standard frequency (radio transmission of specified frequencies of high precision for scientific and technical purposes).

These services are in general distributed in specific bands throughout the radio spectrum, from a few kilohertz to 40 gigahertz (40,000 megahertz). Each service in turn uses several of the modulation techniques mentioned.

In the U.S., for example, AM broadcasting is allocated the 535–1,605 kilohertz band, FM is allocated the 88–108 megahertz band, and television broadcasting is allotted four bands, 54–72 megahertz, 76–88 megahertz, 174–216 megahertz, and 470–890 megahertz (the ultrahigh frequency [UHF] band).

International point-to-point communications

Fixed, point-to-point communication, commonly used for international radiotelegraphy and radiotelephony, is allotted about 60 percent of the spectrum in the so-called HF (high-frequency) band from three to 30 megahertz. Transmission in this range depends on reflection from the ionosphere, a series of ionized layers of the atmosphere ranging in height from 30 to 200 miles (50 to 300 kilometres) above the Earth. Ionization is caused primarily by radiation from the Sun and so varies with height and in time. Transmission conditions thus change with time, resulting in received signals that fluctuate in amplitude. Special procedures are required for shifting frequencies within the high-frequency band as certain frequencies become unusable due to the changing conditions of the ionosphere. Diversity techniques (multiple frequencies, multiple transmitters and receivers, and multiple antennas) are used to combat fading.

High-frequency radiotelegraph systems commonly use either frequency-shift keying or single-side-band transmission with subcarriers. The data transmitted includes Morse, teletypewriter, and other signals. The international standard of signal transmission is 50 signal intervals per second (or 50 baud). With binary data transmission one baud is one bit per second. If one of four possible signals is transmitted every interval, as would be the case with four-frequency FSK, one baud would correspond to two bits in that interval. Automatic error-correction equipment keeps the number of errors in data transmission to less than one in 10,000 bits. Time-division multiplexing is extensively used, with either two or four 50-baud signals being multiplexed to form 100- or 200-baud channels respectively.

Single-side band systems

Single-side-band systems are employed for high-frequency radiotelephony. These systems use from three- to 12-kilohertz bandwidths, accommodating one to four voice channels respectively. In the four-voice-channel system, two channels are transmitted above and two below the carrier frequency. These voice channels can be used alternately to accommodate a group of frequency-division-multiplexed telegraph channels. In one technique, three single-side-band telegraph subcarriers (channels), each carrying 200 baud and requiring 340 hertz bandwidths, are spaced 340 hertz apart to cover a portion of the voice 2,465 hertz band. Each telegraph channel is in turn capable of accommodating four 50-baud teleprinter channels in time-multiplexed form. Facsimile and radiophoto transmission is also carried out with highfrequency communications channels (see above *High-speed data transmission*).

WIRE TRANSMISSION

Major wire lines. Wire lines transmit communications signals ranging from relatively narrow bandwidth telegraph and telephone (voice and data) to wide bandwidth, multiplexed signals and television. The major wire lines employed are open wire (bare-line conductors mounted on poles), multipair cables (aerial cables on poles, cables buried in the ground, underground cables in conduits, and submarine cables for water crossings), and coaxial cables. Each type provides progressively greater bandwidth and hence allows more signal channels to be transmitted (multiplexed).

A single open-wire pair may be used for carrier telephony up to a frequency of 150 kilohertz. In one typical carrier system, 12 voice channels, each requiring nominally four kilohertz, are frequency multiplexed using single-side-band techniques. Transmission in one direction is by means of the 40–88 kilohertz range, while transmission in the other direction uses the 100–148 kilohertz range.

Cable systems provide wider bandwidths than the open-wire systems (up to 500 kilohertz) and hence can accommodate more voice or telegraph channels. In one typical case, 24 voice channels are combined to form a composite single-side-band signal covering the range 40–140 kilohertz. Transmission in the reverse direction in this case is handled by using another pair of wires in the 164–264 kilohertz range.

Coaxial cables allow considerably more bandwidth, ranging into the megahertz range. As many as 600 voice channels may be combined by successive multiplexing to attain a final composite single-side-band signal with the 600 channels stacked side by side in frequency.

Accommodating telegraph channels. Any voice channel or group of channels could be used to accommodate a group of narrower bandwidth telegraph channels. Up to 24 telegraph channels may be multiplexed into one voice channel. Generally this is accomplished by frequency-shift-keying techniques. The spacing between signals in the final multiplexed group is 120 hertz for 60-word-per-minute telegraphy systems and 170 hertz for 100-word-per-minute systems. (M.Sch./Ed.)

SATELLITE COMMUNICATIONS

Communication satellites permit the exchange of live television programs between nations and continents. International telephone and data services are provided through Earth stations located in more than 100 countries, and a number of other satellite systems provide regional and domestic service, as well as communication with ships. The technique basically involves transmitting signals from an Earth station to an orbiting satellite. The equipment aboard the satellite receives these signals, amplifies them, and transmits them to a region of the Earth. Any station within this region can pick up the signals, thus providing a communication link.

The International Telecommunications Satellite Organization, usually referred to as Intelsat, is responsible for all international nonmilitary satellite communication outside the Soviet bloc. Intelsat also provides domestic service in a number of countries. A government-regulated private corporation known as the Communications Satellite Corporation (Comsat) is the U.S. member of Intelsat. An organization called Intersputnik manages satellite communication within the Soviet bloc.

Communication circuits via microwaves

Satellites provide communication circuits between widely separated locations via microwaves. To transmit television and telephone signals between population centres requires high-capacity circuits. As noted above, over land such circuits can be provided in many ways, including pairs of wires, coaxial cables, waveguides, optical fibres, and microwave radio relay systems. Improved submarine cables can carry thousands of telephone signals across oceans, but satellites can provide even greater capacity, in many cases at less cost per channel. Moreover, a satellite system can be put into service quickly, for it does not require the laying of wires or cables from one point to another or, as does a ground microwave system, the construction of intermediate relay or repeater stations. Once a satellite has been launched, communication between two points can be established merely by constructing two Earth stations, and one satellite can serve many stations.

Microwaves are launched from and received by parabolic (bowl-shaped) antennas. The waves diverge along straight lines in narrow beams; microwave repeaters or amplifiers, therefore, must be located within line of sight of one another. On land this can be achieved by using towers and hilltop locations, but transoceanic microwave systems were impossible until the stationing of satellites in the sky.

The width of a beam of microwaves is proportional to the ratio of the wavelength of the microwaves to the diameter of the antenna. Thus, a small antenna on a satellite will receive from or transmit to the part of the Earth that is visible from the satellite, nearly a complete hemisphere, while a larger antenna will receive from and transmit to a more limited region of the Earth's surface. Similarly, a large antenna at an Earth station will transmit to and receive from only the satellite to which it is pointed and not from other nearby satellites.

Development of satellite communications. Rockets were first seriously considered as a means for sending humans through space by the Russian scientist Konstantin E. Tsiolkovsky and the U.S. scientist Robert H. Goddard early in the 20th century. The use of unmanned space vehicles has been appreciated only since World War II, when German V-2 rockets were used in air assaults on London. Although early proposals envisioned manned satellites, the great success of satellite communication has been achieved by the use of highly reliable unmanned satellites.

The theoretical stage. The idea of radio transmission through space is at least as old as the space novel *Ralph 124C41+* (1911), by the U.S. science fiction pioneer Hugo Gernsback. Yet the idea of a radio repeater located in space was slow to develop. In October 1942 the U.S. science fiction writer George O. Smith published the story "QRM Interplanetary" in the magazine *Astounding Science-Fiction.* Smith's "Venus Equilateral" radio repeater, in a position equidistant from Venus and the Sun, was used to relay signals between Venus and the Earth.

Early plan for a manned space station

In 1945 the British author-scientist Arthur C. Clarke proposed the use of an Earth satellite for radio communication between, and radio broadcast to, points widely removed on the surface of the Earth. Clarke assumed a manned space station with living quarters for a crew, built of materials flown up by rockets. The station would be positioned at an altitude of about 22,300 miles (35,900 kilometres) so that its period of revolution about the Earth would be the same as the period of the Earth's rotation. This synchronous satellite, which would always appear in the same place in the sky, would be provided with receiving and transmitting equipment and directional antennas to beam signals to all or parts of the visible portion of the Earth. Clarke suggested the use of solar power, either a steam engine operated by solar heat or photoelectric devices. Three such space stations would provide broadcast to or communication among all locations on Earth except for the most remote regions of the Arctic.

In a paper published in April 1955 the U.S. engineer-scientist J.R. Pierce analyzed various types of unmanned communication satellites. These included passive devices, such as metallized balloons and plane and corner reflectors, that would merely reflect back to Earth part of the energy directed to them. Active satellites, incorporating radio receivers and transmitters, were also considered. Pierce discussed satellites at synchronous altitudes, satellites at lower altitudes, and the use of the Earth's gravity to control the attitude or orientation of a satellite.

These two early papers by Clarke and Pierce showed that very modest powers would suffice for transoceanic communication.

Project SCORE

Early satellites. The first satellite communication experiment was the U.S. government's Project SCORE (Signal Communication by Orbiting Relay Equipment), which launched a satellite on December 18, 1958. This satellite circled the Earth in an elliptical orbit, with a 112-mile (180-kilometre) perigee, its closest point to Earth, and an apogee, its greatest distance from Earth, of 926 miles (1,490 kilometres). The satellite operated in a real-time (immediate) and a delayed-repeater mode, in which messages were recorded on magnetic tape and retransmitted. SCORE functioned for 13 days, until its batteries ran down. It reentered the atmosphere and was destroyed on January 21, 1959.

The U.S. Army Signal Corps's Courier project was a further development of the SCORE approach. Courier 1B was designed primarily to handle teletypewriter data and secondarily to handle voice and facsimile (photographs and drawings) messages. It was launched on October 4, 1960, into an orbit with a 602-mile (968-kilometre) perigee and a 1,215-kilometre apogee. It operated for 17 days.

Echo 1

Echo 1, a balloon 100 feet (30 metres) in diameter, made of a plastic called Mylar and coated with a thin layer of aluminum, was launched on August 12, 1960. The satellite was placed in an almost exactly circular orbit at an altitude of 995 miles (1,600 kilometres) and an inclination of 47.3°. The satellite stemmed from two sources: the construction of such a balloon by the U.S. engineer William J. O'Sullivan as a means for measuring the atmospheric density in a 995-mile orbit and from Pierce's proposal for a passive satellite in his 1955 article.

Communications tests carried out by reflecting radio signals from Echo 1's surface were completely successful. The first transmissions were made between terminals built on the East and West coasts of the United States. Bell Telephone Laboratories built a terminal in New Jersey, the U.S. National Aeronautics and Space Administration (NASA) paying for its use. A terminal on the West Coast was built at Goldstone, California, by NASA's Jet Propulsion Laboratory. Echo 1 was used for experimental telephone, data, and facsimile transmission. Signals from Echo 1 were detected in Europe, but no messages were transmitted across the ocean. Echo 1 remained in orbit for almost eight years and was a conspicuous object in the night sky. Echo 2, launched in 1964, remained in orbit for five years.

Telstar

Echo 1 stimulated a great deal of interest in the development of active satellite communication and led American Telephone and Telegraph Company (AT&T) to build Telstar, launched on July 10, 1962. Telstar was an active satellite with a microwave receiver and transmitter. It was the first satellite to transmit live television and telephone conversations across the Atlantic, which it did on an experimental basis. Telstar was turned off on February 21, 1963. A second Telstar satellite was launched on May 7, 1963 and operated for about two years.

NASA's Relay 1 satellite, built by the Radio Corporation of America (RCA), was launched into an elliptical orbit on December 13, 1962. This active satellite was successfully employed in a number of communication experiments. In September 1963 it was used, with the Syncom 2 satellite, to make a brief transmission between the United States, Brazil, and Nigeria.

First synchronous satellite

Syncom 2, the first synchronous communication satellite, was launched on July 26, 1963. This simple but effective satellite was conceived by Harold A. Rosen of Hughes Aircraft Company. The satellite weighed only 86 pounds (39 kilograms); its light weight made insertion into a synchronous orbit possible with the small boosters available at the time. The satellite performed well.

Syncom 3, launched on August 19, 1964, relayed the first sustained transpacific television picture from the opening ceremonies of the Olympic Games in Tokyo. The first commercial communication satellite, Intelsat 1 (Early Bird), launched on April 6, 1965, was a modified version of Syncom.

Other early experiments. In the early days of satellite communication it was not clear what techniques would prove to be practical or useful, and many were proposed and tested. The very earliest communication by means of a satellite made use of signals reflected from the Moon. As early as 1954 the U.S. Naval Research Laboratory transmitted voice messages in this way, and a naval communications link was established between Washington, D.C., and Hawaii in 1960. The goal of the West Ford project, which originated in 1958, was communication by reflection from a cloud of wires that had been launched into orbit; 44 pounds (20 kilograms) of wires were put into a 1,865-mile (3,000-kilometre) orbit in May 1963. Measurements were made of microwave signals reflected from them, but there was little further development of the project.

The success of Echo decided the issue in favour of man-made satellites, and the success of Telstar in favour of active satellites. The success of Syncom led to the universal use of active synchronous satellites for communication.

Satellite capability

Satellite as a radio repeater. A typical communication satellite has a number of transponders, or repeaters, each providing a channel of information. Each transponder consists of a receiver tuned to a channel, or range, of frequencies lying in the uplink (receive) band of frequencies; a frequency shifter to lower the received microwaves to a downlink (transmit) range of frequencies; and a power amplifier to produce an adequate microwave output power. The number of transponders, or channels, indicates the communication capacity of a satellite. Typically, one channel (a half-circuit) can carry a colour television signal or 1,200 telephone voice signals in one direction.

Propagation. As shown in Figure 18, electromagnetic waves are attenuated (*i.e.,* lose power) in passing through

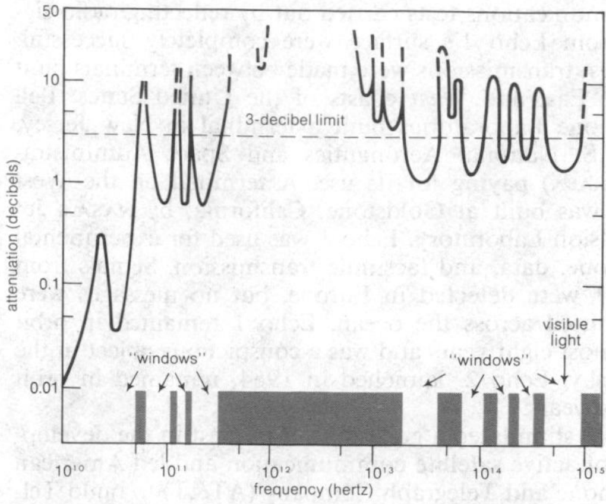

Figure 18: The attenuation of radio waves by the Earth's atmosphere as a function of frequency for an Earth-to-space signal. The chart assumes that the waves originate in clear weather at a high and dry location on the Earth and are directed upward toward space within 45° of vertical (see text).

the ionosphere and the lower atmosphere. In general, an atmospheric attenuation greater than three decibels (dB), corresponding to a loss of half of the transmitted power, is considered excessive. Deliberate attenuation, made by using high microwave frequencies for which atmospheric absorption is great, may be used in communication between military satellites in order to avoid interception of such signals on the ground. For satellite communication with Earth stations, however, only low microwave frequencies are suitable.

Rain also attenuates microwaves. In dealing with rain attenuation, it is useful to consider the attenuation in decibels that is exceeded 0.01 percent of the time, or 52.5 minutes a year. In a region that is neither very dry nor very rainy, the attenuation for this period of time exceeds 43 decibels at 28 gigahertz, 22 decibels at 19 gigahertz, nine decibels at 14 gigahertz, and only one decibel at four gigahertz. In regions where rain attenuation is a serious problem, two Earth stations can be used to communicate with one satellite (diversity), since it is less likely that rainfall will be heavy at both stations simultaneously. Diversity may be desirable at 12 gigahertz in some areas of the world. Except in very dry regions, diversity is necessary for reliable commercial service at 20 gigahertz.

Major frequency bands

Frequency allocations. Through international agreement, three major frequency bands have been assigned for nonmilitary satellite communication. Each band consists of an uplink (Earth station to satellite) and a downlink (satellite to Earth station) at a somewhat lower frequency. The lower frequency band is chosen for the more difficult downlink because rain and atmospheric attenuation are less at lower frequencies. Bands in service include the C band, which uses frequencies from 5.925 to 6.425 gigahertz for the uplink and frequencies from 3.7 to 4.2 for the downlink, and the K band, which uses frequencies from 14 to 14.5 gigahertz for the uplink and from 11.7 to 12.2 gigahertz for the downlink. There also is an assignment, with an uplink from 12.75 to 13.25 gigahertz and from 14 to 14.5 gigahertz and a downlink of from 10.7 to 11.7 gigahertz, that within the United States can be used only for international service. Another assignment has an uplink of 27.5–30 gigahertz and a downlink of 17.7–20.2 gigahertz. The 20-gigahertz downlink is vulnerable to rain and is no longer used commercially.

Characteristics of channels. The bandwidth of a transponder is commonly 36 megahertz (MHz). Such a channel will transmit about 1,200 telephone signals, each with a bandwidth of 4,000 hertz, or one television signal. The total bandwidth of 1,200 telephone signals is only 4.8 megahertz, and the 36-megahertz channel that is used to transmit these signals has seven and a half times this bandwidth. Either wide-deviation frequency modulation is used in satellite communication, or the telephone signals are transmitted as binary pulses by pulse-code modulation. In either case, the use of a broad band of radio frequencies reduces the transmitter power necessary to attain an adequate signal-to-noise ratio in the overall system.

Path loss and power requirements. The power necessary for satisfactory transmission between a satellite and the Earth depends on the total received power necessary at the input of the Earth-based receiver and on the fraction of the power transmitted from the satellite that is picked up by the Earth station antenna. This fraction is the ratio of the area of the receiving antenna on Earth to the area covered by the microwave beam on the Earth. A standard Earth station antenna, for example, has a diameter of about 30 metres. If the antenna beam from the satellite just covers the Earth, the 30-metre antenna receives about $^{4}/_{1,000,000,000,000}$ (4×10^{-12}) of the transmitted power, and the received signal is 114 decibels weaker than the transmitted signal. If the antenna beam of the satellite just covers the continental United States, the received power is about 103 decibels weaker than the transmitted power, or about 11 decibels (14 times) stronger than the power received from a satellite whose antenna beam covers the entire Earth. Because the path loss for transmitting between a pair of antennas is the same in either direction, it is also advantageous to use a narrow receiving beam on a satellite. Thus, it can be advantageous to use a satellite with narrow transmitting and receiving beams, pointed only toward those regions with which communication is desired. Advanced satellites, such as Intelsat 5, have global coverage beams for communicating with nations that have small amounts of traffic, as well as hemispheric and spot beams for areas of heavy traffic.

Types of beams

In order to get a narrow antenna beam, the antenna on the satellite must have a considerable area. The minimum beam width, measured in radians, that can be attained with an antenna of a given diameter is roughly equal to the wavelength divided by the diameter of the antenna. Thus, for a given beam width the diameter of the antenna must be greater at lower frequencies (longer wavelengths) than at higher frequencies. In order for the antenna beam to cover a limited area on Earth, the antenna on the satellite must be quite large (about 2.5 metres in width in Intelsat 5), and the feed, which directs the transmitted power toward the antenna dish or collects the received power from it, must consist of an array of microwave sources such as feed horns. The relative phases and amplitudes of the signals going to the feed horns determine the area of the Earth covered by the antenna beam. This area can be shifted by changing the phases of the signals to the feed horns, either mechanically or electronically. If the phases are shifted electronically, the beam can be made to scan, or hop, from one point to another. By dividing signals among the feed horns it is possible to produce several simultaneous beams aimed at different spots on the Earth. Figure 19 indicates the general configuration of some microwave antennas used for Earth stations and satellites.

The power that must be received at an Earth station for satisfactory operation of a communication satellite channel is proportional to the required ratio of the carrier (received power) to the noise. In normal operation the carrier-to-noise ratio is about 13 to 20 decibels. Signals can be received with some degradation in quality with a carrier-to-noise ratio as low as six or seven decibels, so the design carrier-to-noise ratio provides some protection against rain attenuation or other loss of signal strength.

Thermal noise

Some noise in the receiver can be Johnson, or thermal, noise from rain; thermal noise from space is negligible unless the antenna is pointed at the Sun. Part of the noise comes from the receiver itself. Because Johnson noise is proportional to temperature in kelvins (K; −273.15° C), the noisiness of a receiver is specified by a noise temperature T, such that Johnson noise for temperature T added at the input of the receiver doubles the observed output noise. Thus, in the absence of rain noise power is proportional to the receiver noise temperature T. It is also proportional to the bandwidth, which for a satellite channel is about 36 megahertz (the noise power is $N = kTB$ watts, where B is the bandwidth in hertz and k is the Boltzmann constant [$k = 1.38062 \times 10^{-23}$ joule per degree]). The received power per channel is typically about 126 decibels less than a watt (2.5×10^{-13} watt).

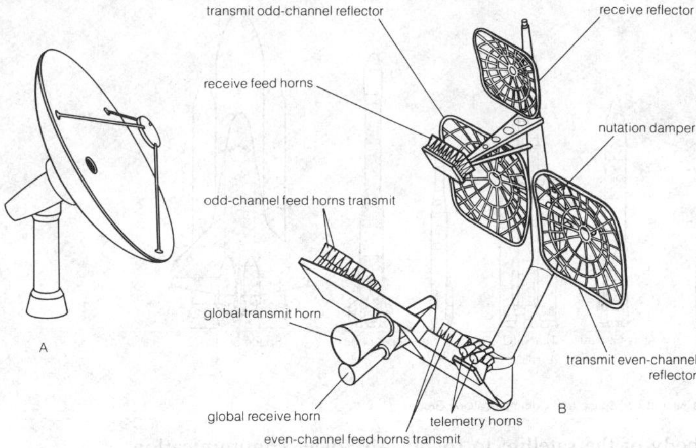

Figure 19: *Antennas.*
(A) Cassegrain Earth station antenna. The parabolic dish directs received microwaves to the convex secondary reflector, which in turn reflects the microwaves in a beam through a hole in the centre on the dish, where they are collected and sent to the receiver. (B) Antennas of the Intelsat 4A satellite. The large reflectors are illuminated by complex arrays of small horns so that the microwave beam covers only a portion of the Earth's surface.
By courtesy of Hughes Aircraft Co. Space and Communications Group

The power received at an Earth station depends on the power transmitted by the satellite (usually from five to 10 watts per transponder), on the area of the Earth's surface covered by the satellite's transmitting beam, and on the area of the Earth station antenna. The gain G of an antenna is related to its area, being proportional to the area divided by the square of the wavelength. The "figure of merit" of an Earth station receiving system is defined as the ratio G/T, the ratio of antenna gain to receiver noise temperature. This ratio may be expressed in decibels. A typical Earth receiver noise temperature is 50 kelvins, and a typical antenna gain is 60 decibels, giving a figure of merit of 20,000, or 43 decibels.

The transmitter power on a satellite is limited by considerations of weight and life; it is important, therefore, that Earth stations have antennas with large areas and that they have low-noise receivers. It is of little use to provide the receiver on a satellite with low-noise receivers because noise at between 200 and 300 kelvins is received from the Earth. Large Earth station antennas can be used for transmitting to satellites as well as receiving from them, and high powers can be used in transmitting (about three kilowatts [kW] for all channels combined).

Limitations. The maximum amount of communication available from satellites is limited by the number and bandwidth of frequency assignments and by other considerations. For a given bandwidth the amount of communication can be increased several ways. Sending independent signals on two polarizations doubles the communication capacity. The first use of two polarizations was on the domestic satellites Satcom, launched on December 12, 1975, and Comstar, launched on May 13, 1976. In addition, using narrow beams from satellites to various regions of the Earth allows reuse of the same frequencies.

The more satellites that can be used simultaneously in synchronous orbit, the greater the total communication capacity. Larger, and hence more directive, Earth station antennas allow the simultaneous use of more satellites. Some Intelsat satellites are spaced as closely as 3° from other satellites. Satellites spaced as far as 14° apart can interfere, however, if small Earth station antennas and correspondingly high powers are used. The U.S. Federal Communications Commission (FCC) has proposed that domestic satellites be spaced 2° apart, even though this spacing is considered too close by some experts.

Satellite technology. Communication satellites are put into orbit by means of rocket launch vehicles, or boosters. During insertion into orbit control is maintained partly by inertial guidance, using gyroscopes and accelerometers, and partly by microwave radar observations, by means of which the position and velocity of the vehicle is determined and commands are given for correcting the orbit.

Launch sequence. Satellites are put into synchronous orbits in the plane of the Equator from sites that do not lie on the Equator. This requires adjusting the plane of the orbit during or after the initial launch phase. The first, or boost, stage lifts the satellite out of the atmosphere and gives it considerable velocity. When this stage burns out, it is separated from the satellite and other stages, falls to Earth, and is destroyed as it passes through the atmosphere. The fairing, which protects the payload (the satellite and associated final stages) as it passes through the atmosphere, is jettisoned. The second stage is then fired, putting the satellite into an intermediate orbit. After the second stage is jettisoned, it remains in orbit for some time. The perigee stage is then fired and ejected; this puts the satellite in an inclined elliptical orbit, an orbit whose apogee is at synchronous altitude (22,310 miles [35,900 kilometres] above the surface of the Earth). While the satellite is in this transfer orbit, tests are performed, and the satellite is positioned for the firing of the apogee motor, which is commonly built into the body of the satellite. (The Titan IIIC transtage can eject into synchronous orbit, so that no apogee motor is needed.) At the apogee of the transfer orbit, the apogee motor is fired, which puts the satellite in a circular synchronous orbit. Satellite antennas and the solar panels can then be extended and the satellite put into its final physical configuration.

Control of attitude and station

The orbit at this point will not be exactly right, nor will the satellite have the correct attitude (point in the right direction). Throughout the life of the satellite the attitude must be controlled and the station kept (the orbit adjusted), because irregularities in the gravitational fields of the Earth, Sun, and Moon—as well as the pressures of light from the Sun and of the solar wind—tend to change the attitude and station.

Launch vehicles. Advances in satellite communication have been made possible by the development of powerful boosters that can launch heavier satellites. In the early 1960s Syncom was launched by a Delta vehicle, which at that time was just able to insert the 86-pound (39-kilogram) satellite into a synchronous orbit. By the 1980s the Delta vehicle could launch a satellite such as the 1,210-pound (550-kilogram) SBS (Satellite Business System). Heavier satellites, such as Intelsat 5, which weighs almost 4,410 pounds (2,000 kilograms), can be launched with the Atlas-Centaur. Military satellites have been launched with these vehicles, and several at a time have been launched with the more powerful Titan IIIC.

Figure 20 shows the relative sizes of various launch vehicles. All of the launch vehicles used through the early 1980s—the Delta, Atlas-Centaur, and Titan—have been refinements and developments of military ballistic missiles—the Thor, Atlas, and Titan, respectively. The Japanese N launch, in some ways similar to the U.S. Delta, is a civilian vehicle. The French Ariane, which has made several successful flights, is a civilian vehicle with capabilities somewhat greater than the Delta or Atlas-Centaur; in its most powerful configuration it should be capable of launching two communication satellites, and a number of commitments have been made to use the Ariane to launch commercial satellites. The U.S. STS (Space Transportation System), or space shuttle, is a manned vehicle; the manned portion is recoverable through a gliding landing on an airfield, and the solid rocket shells through descent into the ocean by parachute. The space shuttle itself can put a payload consisting of several satellites into a low Earth orbit. Propulsion such as the Inertial Upper Stage (IUS) or propulsion incorporated in the satellite itself is necessary for insertion into synchronous orbit.

The reusable U.S. space shuttle

The space shuttle is designed to put up to about 66,150 pounds (30,000 kilograms) into a low orbit. Manned space shuttle flights might make it possible to assemble or to repair large communication satellites in low Earth orbit. Assembly in orbit would be extremely expensive, however, and does not appear to be necessary. Space shuttle plans provide no means for sending astronauts into synchronous orbit, where they would have to go in order to repair communication satellites. In addition, communication satellites have proved to be very long-lived; they tend

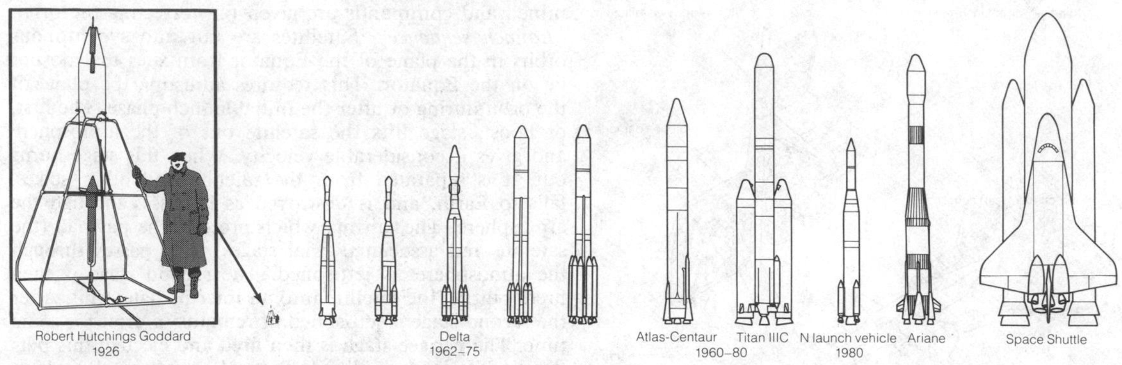

Figure 20: Relative sizes of launch vehicles.

From Harold A. Rosen, *Hughes Aircraft Space Telecommunication;* used with permission from Hughes Aircraft Co. Space and Communications Group

to become obsolete before they wear out. Repair costs may greatly exceed the cost of launching a new satellite. (See also EXPLORATION: *Space exploration.*)

Attitude control and station keeping. In the Syncom and Intelsat 1 satellites, the entire satellite, including the antenna, spun stably around the axis of maximum moment of inertia. Adjustments in axis of spin, or attitude, in rate of spin, and in orbit, or station keeping, were made by an ingenious scheme in which either of two jets were pulsed on briefly. One jet had an off-centre axial thrust and could be used to control both the axis of spin and the plane of the orbit. The other jet had a radial thrust and could be used to alter orbital speed and hence to adjust the period and the eccentricity of the orbit. This scheme of pulsed jet control, which was invented by Harold A. Rosen and Donald Williams, has been used in most later satellites in which the body of the satellite spins in order to attain a stable attitude. Two sets of pulsed jets are provided to guard against failure.

Attitude control by pulsed jets

Intelsat 3, launched in 1968, and all subsequent spinning satellites have had motor-driven, despun platforms at one end, so that antennas can be pointed stably at some point on Earth. Pointing is usually achieved by means of an optical or infrared Earth sensor, which provides a reference for pointing at the Earth. In Intelsat 4, 4A, and 5 and in Comstar a Sun sensor and a clock are used as well. Pointing also can be done by ground command. Pointing is attained by attitude control and by regulating the rate of the motor that drives the despun platform.

Early spinning satellites had a serious disadvantage. A spinning body is stable only if it spins about its axis of maximum moment of inertia; a lossy damper (such as sloshing fluid) will then diminish any periodic nutation, or nodding, of the axis. If the spin is not about the axis of maximum moment of inertia, the damper will cause the nutation to increase rather than diminish, and the satellite will tumble. This arrangement suggested that spinning satellites had to be short along the axis of spin and that only a small satellite could be fitted into a fairing of practical diameter. Anthony Iorillo found theoretically that, if the damping were put in the despun platform rather than in the body of the satellite, the satellite could spin stably around an axis that was not the axis of maximum moment of inertia; his discovery made longer, narrower spinning satellites possible. This feature was first incorporated in a military satellite, Tacsat (tactical communication satellite), launched in 1969, and has been used in most subsequent spinning satellites.

The alternative to attitude control by spinning the body of the satellite and despinning the antenna platform is to control the attitude of the body of the satellite with respect to the Earth (body stabilization). If all three axes of the body are stable with respect to the Earth, as is necessary in pointing an antenna at a particular point on Earth, the satellite must have three-axis stabilization. Three-axis stabilization has been used in many types of space vehicles. A satellite with such stabilization must use jets for station keeping and for gross corrections of attitude. Routine maintenance and corrections of attitude are made by means of spinning inertia wheels. These have a stabilizing effect, and small changes in the rate of spin can cause the body of the satellite to rotate. All Soviet communication satellites, starting with the first Molniya satellite in 1965, have been body-stabilized. The first U.S. operational satellites to use three-axis stabilization were RCA's Satcom, launched in 1975; the LES (Lincoln Experimental Satellite) 8 and 9, launched in 1976; FLTSATCOM (Fleet Satellite Communications), a military satellite launched in 1978; and Intelsat 5, launched in 1980.

Three-axis stabilization

In spinning satellites the solar cells that provide electric power cover the outer cylindrical surface. As the satellite spins, half of the cells are shadowed from the Sun, and most do not face the Sun directly. In a three-axis stabilized satellite the solar cells are placed on panels that can be rotated so that they directly face the Sun. Erecting the solar panels and the antenna arrays on a three-axis stabilized satellite, however, are more complicated operations than deploying the antennas on a spinning satellite. During the 1980s, of U.S.-made satellites, more spinning satellites were in operation and under construction than three-axis stabilized satellites. Further, Intelsat 6, unlike Intelsat 5, was designed to be a spinning satellite.

Electronic technology. Solar cells are the universal source of electric power in operational communication satellites, although some experimental satellites have used thermoelectric generators heated by radioisotopes. A synchronous satellite, which is eclipsed by the Earth during two 44-day seasons each year, for times as long as 70 minutes, carries secondary batteries to provide power during the eclipse. The power necessary for the operation of a communication satellite is considerable; the solar cells of Intelsat 4A, for example, provide 600 watts.

The most common source of microwave power for transmitting signals from communication satellites is the traveling-wave tube. Transistors have been used in some transmitters, but they are not as efficient for microwave frequencies as are traveling-wave tubes. Linearity is another consideration when signals from Earth stations must be transmitted through the same transponder. As improvements are made, the transistor or some other solid-state amplifier may eventually replace the traveling-wave tube, the last vacuum tube used in communication satellites.

As was noted, it is important to have a low-noise receiver at an Earth station in order to reduce the signal power that must be transmitted from the satellite. In some early satellite experiments a very low-noise microwave amplifier, called a maser, was used. The maser is expensive, for it must operate at the temperature of liquid helium, only slightly above absolute zero. The signal received from a satellite is weakest during a rainstorm. Unfortunately, during a rainstorm a considerable amount of Johnson noise is received, corresponding to a temperature of more than 200 kelvins. For this reason there is little advantage in using a receiver with a noise temperature below the 50 kelvins that can be attained with a parametric amplifier. Thus, parametric amplifiers rather than masers are used even in large and costly Earth stations.

Almost all electronic functions in satellites are carried out by means of solid-state devices, especially transistors, which are used to generate and amplify signals and to operate various control functions. LSI and VLSI (large-scale integration and very large-scale integration) circuits, in which many complex on–off or digital functions are performed by a silicon chip about 1/16 square inch (0.4 square centimetre) in size, have come to play an increasingly important part in satellite communication.

Echo suppressors

An important advance has been the production, by Western Electric, of an LSI chip that can be used to cancel echoes. Telephone calls that are transmitted by satellite reach a home or an office over a single pair of wires that transmits the voice to and from the telephone. A speaker can often hear a faint echo of his own voice. If this is much delayed, talking becomes difficult. For this reason, in circuits longer than 1,490 miles (2,400 kilometres), echo suppressors are used to prevent or reduce an incoming signal while a speaker is talking. In satellite communication it takes a signal almost 0.3 second to reach the satellite and return to Earth, and echoes of one's voice are heard about 0.6 second after speaking. When echo suppressors are used in a circuit with so great a time delay, they sometimes cause a speaker to miss remarks of the other party. Tests show that satellite circuits with echo suppressors are rated by users as considerably inferior to usual telephone circuits. The echo-cancelling chip can detect the presence of echoes by comparing the incoming signal with the outgoing signal and can add artificial echoes that cancel those present in the communication circuit. This arrangement makes satellite circuits comparable in quality to ordinary telephone circuits. The idea of cancelling echoes is an old one, but it became economically feasible only through LSI.

Although satellites use both wide-deviation frequency modulation (FM) and digital transmission of voice by pulse-code modulation in order to conserve power and reduce interference, the trend is toward digital transmission. In part this is a general trend in all voice communication, in switching as well as in transmission. Digital transmission also is more efficient than FM when more than one Earth station uses the same satellite repeater. If several FM signals are sent through one repeater, the transponder must operate at a reduced power level in order to reduce nonlinearities that cause one signal to interfere with the others. In digital transmissions Earth stations can be assigned different, short repetitive time intervals for their transmissions (time-division multiplex), and the repeater can operate at full power.

Time-division multiplex requires that Earth stations operate synchronously and send out bursts of data at specific times, so as not to interfere with one another. Besides being more efficient, time-division multiplex makes it easy to switch between channels groups of data that occur in particular time intervals. Time-division switching makes the use of satellite communication much more flexible, and it is becoming a standard feature of satellites. This function, of course, requires complex digital operations, for which LSI and VLSI are ideally suited.

LSI and VLSI also can be useful in controlling the antenna beam position in satellites. The beam direction can be changed by shifting the phases of the microwave signals sent to various feed horns that illuminate the antenna dish, or reflector. For use in satellites all solid-state devices, including LSI and VLSI, must be highly reliable, and they should not be harmed by the low-level but penetrating radiation that is found at synchronous altitudes.

Satellite systems. Several satellites of the same or of different designs used in communicating among a group of Earth stations form a satellite communication system. A system may provide international communication, as does the Intelsat system, or both international and domestic communication; the Soviet Intersputnik organization provides communication within the Soviet Union and among countries of the Soviet bloc. Other satellite systems provide regional or domestic communication. Some systems, such as the Marisat and Marecs and a number of military satellites, provide mobile communication, primarily to ships. Other satellites serve military uses only. Several experimental satellites have been launched, and there are some satellites reserved for use by amateur radio operators.

Intelsat. The first use of communication satellites was to provide international communication. When the U.S. Congress passed the Communications Satellite Act in 1962, creating Comsat and giving it a U.S. monopoly on international satellite communication, no clear provision was made for supplying other forms of satellite service.

Intelsat

International satellite communication required the participation of other nations. Intelsat originated as a joint venture in August 1964, when 11 countries signed agreements to form a global communication system. It has become an international legal entity in which about 100 countries hold investment shares. Comsat is the designated U.S. participant in Intelsat, which is responsible for the design, development, and maintenance of the space segment of the global telecommunication system. Earth stations used for international communication are owned and operated by entities in the countries in which they are located.

Nations that are not members of Intelsat, including those that cannot join because they are not recognized by the United Nations, can obtain satellite communication through Comsat General, a domestic subsidiary of Comsat. An example is Taiwan, which has a large international telecommunications traffic.

By the 1980s the Intelsat system included about 400 Earth stations with some 500 antennas, located in approximately 150 countries. By the mid-1980s Intelsat was providing about 20,000 two-way telephone circuits that were leased full time and a great deal of television and other transmission.

The advance in satellite communication has been outstanding. For example, Intelsat 1, launched in 1965, has one transponder, which provides 240 two-way telephone circuits or one television channel. Intelsat 5, launched in 1980, provides 12,000 telephone circuits and two television channels. Intelsat 1 operates in the 6/4-gigahertz band only. In Intelsat 5 the 6/4-gigahertz frequencies are used four times, and the 14/11-gigahertz frequencies are used twice. Intelsat 5 also has six communication antennas: two global-coverage beams, two hemispheric beams, and two steerable spot beams. The specifications for additional Intelsat satellites provide for even greater capabilities.

Soviet satellites. There are two major types of Soviet satellites. The Molniya satellites, first launched in 1965, are placed in elliptical orbits with a 65° inclination. At this angle the perigee moves very slowly, and the apogee remains in the Northern Hemisphere. Under suitable conditions, the angular velocity near apogee roughly matches the angular velocity of the Earth, and the satellite appears almost stationary in the sky. The satellite is positioned over the Soviet Union every other revolution for about eight hours. Due to its inclination, the Molniya satellite is visible in the most northerly regions of the Soviet Union, where a synchronous satellite would be below the horizon. The second type of Soviet communication satellite is the Statsionar. It is a synchronous satellite and was first launched in 1975.

Molniya satellites

By the end of 1979, 75 Molniya satellites had been launched, of which 28 were known to be out of service. Only one of the 14 synchronous satellites launched was no longer operating. Technical details of Soviet satellites are known only in part. Their communication capacity appears to be less than that of Intelsat satellites.

Domestic systems. Some domestic satellite systems have been established because the communication they provide would be difficult to obtain in any other way. Canada's Telesat system provides communication to the sparsely populated regions of the Northwest Territories as well as to the nation's urban areas. Indonesia's Palapa system provides communication among many islands that would be hard to link otherwise.

Domestic satellite systems in the United States add communication capacity to a range of other communication channels. Such satellite service has several advantages. In the distribution of programs for cable television the same signal must be sent simultaneously to stations in many parts of the country. The transmission of plates from which newspapers and magazines can be printed simultaneously in many locations is a similar application. Satellites can provide many additional long-distance circuits more quickly than laying cables or building ground microwave systems. Once in place, a satellite system can be used to supplement other long-haul facilities when they become overloaded because of regional changes in traffic or because of disasters. The SBS, for example, provides large industries with private networks in which the Earth station is on company premises, thus avoiding the use of cables or ground microwave systems to link the networks to communication facilities.

Canada

Canada's Telesat system uses satellites, called Anik, built by U.S. companies. Three Anik A satellites were in service by the early 1980s; the first was launched in 1972. They have antennas with beams that cover Canada and have 12 transponders. One Anik B satellite, launched in 1978, has 12 transponders in the 6/4-gigahertz band that cover all of Canada and six transponders in the 14/12-gigahertz band that serve a fourth of the nation. Advanced Anik satellites have been designed.

Indonesia

The first two satellites of Palapa A, Indonesia's satellite system, were launched in 1976 and 1977. They are of the Anik A type, and the antenna beams cover some 3,000 islands. The larger and more powerful Palapa B system is designed to use both polarizations and to have 24 transponders.

United States

The United States has the greatest number of domestic satellites. Western Union launched two Westar satellites in 1974 and one in 1979. These operate in the 6/4-gigahertz band and have 12 transponders. The antennas cover the conterminous United States and, with less power, Alaska and Hawaii.

RCA launched Satcom satellites in 1975, 1976, and 1981. These operate in the 6/4-gigahertz band, use both polarizations, and have 24 transponders. Half of the transponders are used in conjunction with separate antennas so that they cover Hawaii as well as the rest of the United States; the other transponders cannot be used for traffic with Hawaii.

Four Comstar satellites were in service by the early 1980s; the first was launched in 1976. They are Comsat General satellites, but their entire communication capacity is leased by AT&T. The satellites operate in the 6/4-gigahertz band and use both polarizations to provide 24 transponders. Communication is provided within all of the United States, including Alaska, Hawaii, and Puerto Rico. In 1981 AT&T ordered three advanced communication satellites, called Telstar 3, which can operate in a higher frequency and have an increased life expectancy of 10 years, instead of the average seven years.

SBS is a joint venture of Comsat General, Aetna Life and Casualty, and IBM (International Business Machines). It launched its first satellite in 1980 and its second in 1981. SBS satellites operate with small ground terminals that use antennas with diameters of 5.5 and 7.7 metres. They provide high-speed networks for large organizations that have multiple, dispersed locations, and they supply data, telephone, teleconferencing and other communication services. The organization using the service owns the Earth station and the rest of the ground-based communication equipment. Service to smaller enterprises is under way. The SBS satellites operate in the 14/12-gigahertz range. The antenna beams cover the United States and the lower part of Canada.

Maritime communication. In general, mobile satellite communication is difficult because of the problem of placing microwave antennas on vehicles. Some narrow-band communication can be provided by ultrahigh frequency (UHF) using essentially nondirectional antennas, but the amount is limited. In contrast to automobiles and airplanes, ships are suitable platforms for microwave antennas of moderate size; the first commercial mobile service was to ships.

Marisat system

The Marisat system, developed by Comsat General, began serving both the U.S. Navy and commercial shipping in 1976. Three satellites were launched, operating in three frequency ranges. The UHF capability, in the 300/250-megahertz band, was leased by the U.S. Navy for five years. Commercial maritime traffic is carried in the 1.6/1.5-gigahertz range. The 6/4-gigahertz range is used for commercial communication links between satellites and Earth stations on both coasts of the United States. Each satellite provides 16 voice and 88 telex channels in the high-power mode (60 watts transmitter power), eight voice and 44 telex channels in the medium-power mode (27 watts), and one voice and 44 telex channels in the low-power mode (seven watts). By 1980 ships flying the flags of more than 35 nations were using Marisat, and more than 460 shipboard terminals had been commissioned for operation with the satellites.

Inmarisat (International Maritime Satellite Organization) was established in July 1979; Comsat was designated the U.S. participant. Marecs, the first Inmarisat satellite, was launched in 1981 from French Guiana, using an Ariane vehicle. Marecs are designed to communicate between shore and satellite in the 6/4-gigahertz band and between ship and satellite in the 1.6/1.5-gigahertz band. By 1982 Marecs had become the primary satellite for Atlantic communication and with Comsat's Marisat was used for the primary Indian and Pacific coverage; Inmarisat provided worldwide maritime service to about 1,200 ships.

Military satellites. In 1960 ARPA (Advanced Research Projects Agency of the U.S. Department of Defense) proposed an elaborate military communication satellite called Advent. The satellite proved far beyond the state of the art and was abandoned in 1962. In June 1965 the Department of Defense directed the U.S. Air Force to launch simple near-synchronous satellites in equatorial orbits. Some 26 of these IDCSP (Initial Defense Communication Satellite Program, later renamed Initial Defense Satellite Communication System [IDSCS]) satellites were launched from 1966 to 1968, usually eight at a time, using the Titan IIIC vehicle. Although these satellites provided useful communication, they were soon outdated.

Tacsat, a large and elaborate communication satellite, was launched for the U.S. Air Force early in 1969 but failed at the end of 1972.

By the early 1980s the major U.S. military communication satellites were the DSCS 2 and FLTSATCOM satellites. The DSCS 2 satellite, of which 10 had been successfully launched by 1981, is a spinning satellite with both global coverage and spot beam antennas. It has a capacity of 1,300 two-way voice circuits. The uplink frequency band ranges from 7.9 to 8.4 gigahertz; the downlink varies from 7.25 to 7.75 gigahertz. The FLTSATCOM satellite began operation in 1978, and by 1981 five had been launched. Each satellite provides high-frequency communication between military forces through more than 20 channels.

Eight LES satellites of various types were launched from 1965 through 1976. These were used to explore various frequencies and to conduct experiments with steerable antenna beams and in nulling against jamming.

The initial requirement of U.S. military satellites was that they provide adequate and reliable communication. The armed forces have become more and more dependent on satellite communication for both strategic and tactical use, but it had become increasingly apparent by the 1980s that existing military satellites would be vulnerable in a number of ways during a war: to jamming by high-power ground-based jammers; to destruction of ground facilities that are used in connection with satellite station keeping and internal operation; to high-altitude nuclear explosions, whose electromagnetic fields and radiation could destroy or cause errors in the operation of satellite electronic equipment; and, finally, to enemy antisatellite weapons. In the future military communication satellite systems will diverge increasingly from commercial systems in several respects.

IDSCP satellites were used to provide early communication for the North Atlantic Treaty Organization (NATO). Two NATO satellites were launched in 1971 and 1972, and three NATO 3 satellites were launched in 1976, 1977, and 1978. The NATO 2 satellites are spinning satellites, with an antenna coverage optimized for NATO use. The up-band is 7.976–8.005 gigahertz, and the down-band is 7.257–7.286 gigahertz. The NATO 3 satellite has one global beam antenna and one spot beam antenna for Europe; it operates in about the same frequency band as NATO 2. Skynet 1 and 2 are British satellites. They were launched in 1969 and 1974 and are similar to DSCS 2.

Amateur satellites. From 1961 to 1978 the United States successfully launched eight OSCAR (Orbiting Satellite

Carrying Amateur Radio) satellites for the use of amateur radio operators; by 1980 five remained. OSCAR 7 has two channels: a 145.85–145.95-megahertz uplink with a 29.40–29.50-megahertz downlink and a 432.125–432.175-megahertz uplink with a 145.925–145.975-megahertz downlink. In 1978 the Soviet Union launched two RS satellites for amateur use.

Experimental satellites. In addition to early experimental satellites such as Echo, Telstar, and Syncom, a large number of other experimental satellites have been launched. NASA launched a series of ATS's (Applications Technology Satellite) that were used mainly to explore various technological features and to gather data on microwave propagation. The last satellite in the series, ATS 6, was used in an experiment in India for direct broadcasting of educational programs to receiving equipment in numerous villages.

Direct television broadcasts

There were several joint ventures in the mid-1970s. Two French–German Symphonie satellites were launched in 1974 and 1975. These three-axis stabilized satellites have global and spot beams in the 6/4-gigahertz band and four transponders. The CTS (Communications Technology Satellite), or Hermis, a U.S.–Canadian experimental satellite launched in 1976, operates in the 14/11-gigahertz band. It has a high-power (200 watts) transmitter for use with small Earth stations, as well as a transmitter of moderate power. Among other options, it can transmit FM television with up to three simultaneous channels.

Other programs include the Italian Sirio, launched in 1977, with beams that cover Europe. The European Space Agency's OTS (Orbital Test Satellite), a three-axis satellite, was launched in 1978. It operates in the 14/12-gigahertz band, uses dual polarization, two European spot beams, and six repeaters of various bandwidth.

Japan had two major experimental programs by the late 1970s. The CS, or Sakura satellite, launched in 1977, has six repeaters in the 30/20-gigahertz band and two repeaters in the 20/18-gigahertz band. The BSE (Medium-Scale Broadcasting Satellite for Experimental Purposes), or Yuri satellite, was launched in 1978 and operates in the 14/12-gigahertz range. It can transmit two FM high-power (100 watts) colour television signals to Japan for experimental broadcasting to homes.

Disadvantages and prospects. Satellites cannot provide separate circuits to individual homes and offices, as can telephone wires, cables, and optical fibres. Although the SBS can link various corporate locations, wires, cables, or fibres must connect individual users to the Earth station. Thus cables compete successfully with satellites between Europe and the United States, and cables with optical fibres are expected to perform even more successfully. The amount of communication that satellites can provide is limited further by the number of orbital positions and the frequencies available.

Limitations

Although it was suggested early in the history of satellite communication, the advantages of direct broadcasting of television signals from satellites to individual users has been questioned. The U.S. experimental Intelsat 4 (1974) was used for a time by India to broadcast educational programs to villages. The joint U.S.-Canadian CTS satellite (1976) had a transmitter powerful enough to transmit television signals to small Earth stations. The Japanese Yuri satellite (1978) was capable of transmitting television signals to small rooftop antennas, but part of the motivation for doing this was a law that required television service to all parts of Japan, a country with regions where cable is uneconomical and reception from Earth-based transmitters impractical. In the United States, by the early 1980s, a number of people had erected antennas to pick up cable and network television programs relayed by satellite. One satellite alone relayed 24 channels, but tens of channels were available from other satellites. (J.R.P./Ed.)

Telecommunications networks

Where communication between a large number of information sources is desired, the sources must be organized into some form of network, as direct connections between any two among a large number would obviously be uneconomical and technically difficult. Generally there are two aspects to the problem of network organization in a geographically distributed communications system. Since most sources (such as an individual telephone subscriber) are idle a good portion of the time, it is possible first to combine or concentrate communications traffic in a localized area. Interconnections are then provided between the various concentration points to effect the appropriate distribution of the signals. Network organization involves the design of systems to carry out the concentration and distribution of traffic in an economical manner, with a minimum of time delay.

The time-multiplexing and frequency-multiplexing techniques discussed earlier are schemes for combining signals from various sources. There is no concentration involved, however, since a channel (whether in time or in frequency) is always allotted to each source.

Telephone and telegraph networks are prime examples of well-established communications networks. They consist of both public and private systems. There exist as well many other types of data-gathering and distribution networks—telemetry networks used in the remote control and operation of geographically distributed industrial processes, communications networks for railroads, and automobile traffic control in large cities. Time-shared computer systems and computerized airline reservation and bank transaction systems, along with cable television (CATV), also are forms of modern data-gathering and distribution networks.

Types of networks

A multitude of data-concentration techniques and various types of network distribution systems are in existence or in the process of being developed. Two major classes, the telephone network and message (digital-data) networks, are described here.

TELEPHONE NETWORKS

A telephone subscriber is usually connected by way of a loop (two- or four-wire line) to a local telephone exchange or end (central) office. End offices are in turn interconnected via a hierarchy of switching centres. The connection medium between centres is called a trunk, which consists physically of cable, coaxial cable, or microwave-radio links.

A typical incoming telephone call is routed at its end office into an appropriate outgoing trunk. With the message destination known, various alternative routes are available. Under the modern direct-distance-dialing system, five classes of switching centres (see Figure 21) come into play. The class 5, or end, offices are the lowest in the hierarchy. They interconnect customers' lines directly and are connected to other end offices and, by trunk, to

Hierarchy of switching centres

From *Transmission Systems for Communications;* Bell Telephone Labs

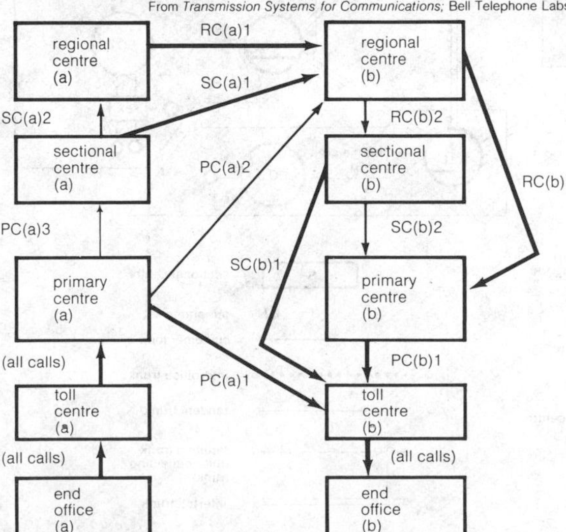

Figure 21: Simplified block diagram of a typical telephone circuit with five classes of switching centres, showing possible alternate routings of a call from end office (a) to end office (b). The order of preference for routing from a given office is indicated by number (see text).

a higher office in the hierarchy. Class 4 switching centres, called toll centres, lead to the higher centres.

A typical set of possibilities for routing a call between an end office in one city and the destination end office in another city is shown in Figure 21. The order of choice in leaving a particular centre is indicated by number. Thus, primary centre 1 is connected directly, via a high-usage trunk, to toll centre 2, which in turn connects to the destination end office. This would be the first choice in routing to end office 2. If this trunk is fully occupied, the route via regional centre 2 is used. If this in turn is unavailable, the route via sectional centre 1 is used. In practice a maximum of seven different links may be allowed.

Automatic switching

Automatic switching using alternate routes provides large economies in connection. High-usage groups are provided between any two offices that carry a sufficiently high mutual traffic.

Figure 22 is an example of a simplified telephone system connecting a group of cities. Various types of channels are used for the interconnecting trunks: coaxial cable, microwave radio, multipair cable, and open-wire line. Each of these carrier systems in turn uses various types of frequency-division-multiplexed schemes to combine many message channels. In the figure, PCM indicates pulse code modulation and PBX a private branch exchange.

Various hierarchies of frequency-division multiplexing, combining individual message channels into groups, then further into mastergroups and supergroups, have been developed following recommendations of the International Telegraph and Telephone Consultative Committee and other organizations.

Microwave-radio communications account for about one-half the trunk mileage in the U.S. In these systems the groups of frequency-multiplexed messages treated earlier

From *Transmission Systems for Communications;* Bell Telephone Labs

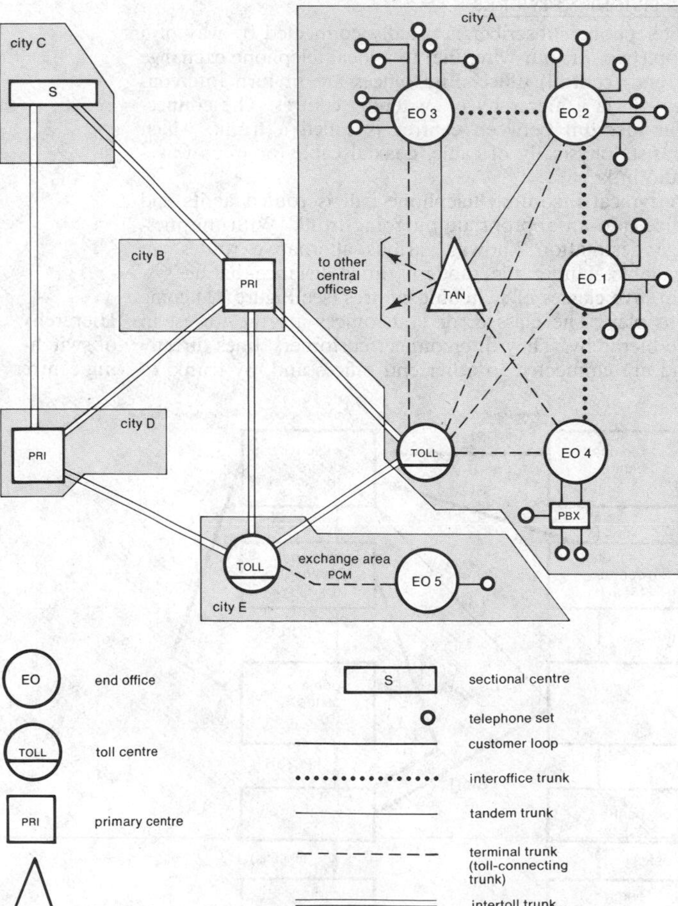

Figure 22: Simplified telephone system for interconnecting a block of cities. The intertoll trunks may be microwave radio, coaxial cable, multipair cable, or open-wire lines and may utilize various types of multiplexing. The exchange area trunk may utilize a pulse-code-modulation (PCM) system.

are most commonly used to frequency modulate carriers in the microwave range. The most common carrier frequencies used are 6,000 and 11,000 megahertz for short-haul transmission (up to 250 miles [400 kilometres]) and 4,000 and 6,000 megahertz for long-haul transmission (up to 4,000 miles [6,400 kilometres]). Overall bandwidths available in these bands are 500 megahertz for the four- and six-gigahertz bands (one gigahertz equals 1,000 megahertz) and 1,000 megahertz for the 11-gigahertz band. Only a fraction of this bandwidth is actually used. For a microwave system, three mastergroups and one supergroup, with a total of 1,860 message channels, are combined to form the modulating signals. The bandwidth of this overall group is on the order of eight megahertz.

Common carrier frequencies

The extremely high frequencies used in microwave transmission enable relatively small antennas to be employed for focussing the energy. Signals are transmitted line of sight between relay stations located 20–30 miles (30–50 kilometres) apart. These repeaters serve to repower the signal periodically. In long-distance transmission the receiver at a relay station converts the microwave FM signal to 70 megahertz. It is then amplified, as much as possible of the noise and interference are removed, and the signal is converted back to the desired microwave frequency for retransmission. Four antennas are commonly used at any one station: two for reception (one for each direction) and two for retransmission.

Switching and dialling. The procedure that enables telephone messages to be placed into a system and switched into a trunk is called switching. As noted earlier, a loop commonly connects the subscriber to a telephone exchange (end office). This loop (using two-wire transmission) provides a path for the two-way speech signals as well as the signals used for ringing, switching, and supervisory functions. The telephone set on the customer's premises consists of a transmitter for converting voice energy into electrical energy, a receiver for performing the reverse process, and appropriate circuitry for carrying out the necessary additional functions.

The conversion from acoustic to electrical energy is accomplished by varying the resistance of carbon granules held between a cup and a diaphragm. Lifting the telephone headset off its hook connects a battery current from the central office to the subscriber's set. This current, flowing through the granules, is varied, or modulated, in accordance with varying pressure on the diaphragm. The telephone receiver is similar in function to a loudspeaker: the varying portion of the loop current passes through a winding on a permanent magnet, causing the magnetic field to vary accordingly, and this in turn changes the force on a diaphragm, causing it to vibrate in accordance with the current fluctuations. The diaphragm moves the air in front and the vibrations are picked up by the ear as a sound wave.

The local exchange office to which a telephone is connected must make the connection between the telephone and an appropriate outgoing trunk. The connection is made by a switching system located at the exchange office. Switching systems have been classified according to the type of switches used (stepping switches, rotary, panel, crossbar); or whether they are electromechanical, electronic, or combinations. A connection must be made at the intersection of an incoming wire and an appropriate outgoing wire.

Since the number of trunks is typically much smaller than the number of subscriber lines, there is a great deal of line concentration, which in turn is possible because an individual customer uses his phone only a small portion of the time.

The appropriate connection is obtained from the number dialled in by the subscriber. A typical seven-digit code allocates four digits (for a maximum of 10,000 possibilities) to a subscriber loop in any one exchange. The exchange itself is identified by the first three digits. The seven numbers are transmitted to the exchange via the subscriber loop by appropriate dialling. In the common dial system each digit dialed sends a different number of pulses to the office. These address digits either control the settings of switches or, in more modern systems, are stored and then

Push-button dialling

used to set up a circuit. In push-button dialling now being introduced, as each button is pushed a two-frequency tone is generated and sent to the central office. The resultant train of tones is interpreted as equivalent dial pulses at the central office and used to set the appropriate switches.

The seven digits allow 9,000,000 telephone numbers to be assigned. Where needed, additional "area code" digits can be assigned; at present three such additional digits are in use in the United States and Canada and two in the U.K.; for international dialling, two international code digits precede the country number and an additional digit to show the language of the party calling.

Typical automatic switching systems in operation include the step-by-step system, used throughout the world for local exchanges and private branch exchanges, accommodating up to 10,000 lines; various crossbar systems for local offices, with up to 30,000 lines; and a computer-controlled electronic switching system capable of handling up to 60,000 lines, employed for both local and toll service exchanges.

Video-telephone service. Early in the 1970s the Bell System introduced video-telephone service. The equipment consists of a 12-button push-button telephone; a display unit with picture (viewing) tube, camera tube, and loudspeaker; a control unit with a microphone; and associated circuitry. The picture signal consists of 250 lines, displayed 30 times per second on a 5.5-inch by 5-inch (14-centimetre by 13-centimetre) screen. The bandwidth required to transmit the signal is one megahertz. The voice-only portion of the telephone call and the voice portion of the video service use normal two-wire subscriber loops. Two more pairs of wires are needed in a telephone cable, however, for the picture signals, one pair for each direction of transmission. Picture (video) signals are switched separately at the central office to which they are connected. Because of this additional switching requirement, not all switching systems can accommodate the system.

For transmission beyond six miles (9.7 kilometres), the picture, voice, and interoffice information are all encoded at a local office into a 6.3-megabit-per-second digital pulse-code-modulation signal. To accomplish this the signal is sampled some 2,000,000 times per second. Three binary digits per sample are then used to produce a six-megabit rate. Voice and data signals of much lower bandwidth are also digitized and then intermixed with the video bits.

Three bits per sample provide representation of the signal by eight amplitude levels, resulting in a coarse and grainy picture. A modified form of pulse code modulation called differential PCM is used to improve picture quality. In this system, the difference between successive amplitude samples is encoded and sent. If the signal is changing slowly, as is normally the case in a picture signal, the encoder signal is often close to zero. More of the eight quantization levels can thus be allocated to this region and fewer to the higher amplitude region, which occurs less often and only when rapid motion is taking place on the screen.

Most 6.3-megabit-per-second encoded video-phone signals are transmitted over microwave radio or coaxial cable trunks. With microwave, up to three such digital signals plus necessary synchronizing signals are sent over one channel. For this purpose, the three signals plus synchronizing signals are sequentially time multiplexed (interleaved), providing a multiplexed bit rate of 20.2 megabits per second. This binary digital stream is then further encoded into a four-level digital stream of 10.1 megabits per second. Each successive pair of binary digits is combined to form one of four possible levels. The encoding results in one-half the bandwidth requirement but reduces signal immunity to noise and distortion. The four-level pulse train is then used to frequency modulate a carrier for transmission over a microwave system.

Encoding for coaxial transmission

Encoding for coaxial transmission is somewhat different. The noise level is less than for microwaves, and there is no signal fading as there is in radio transmission. Eight-level digital transmission can be used to reduce the required bandwidth.

DATA-MESSAGE NETWORKS

Telegraph networks have traditionally provided the capability for data transmission in the form of written messages (see above *Telegraph*). The 1960s, however, saw an explosive growth in data generation and transmission, brought on by the widespread use of high-speed computers. Stock market and bank transactions are rapidly consummated via data-transmission facilities, airline reservations are routinely processed via geographically widespread data networks, and large companies carry out business and bookkeeping transactions via high-speed data networks.

Techniques for efficiently processing, transmitting, and routing these data messages are still undergoing refinement. Much of the data is currently transmitted over the public telephone networks or private, leased voice-quality lines. More engineering effort, however, is going into the development of high-speed data-transmission and switching facilities.

Data-transmission facilities can be conveniently classified into categories of public switched networks or private (leased) lines or networks.

Regular public telephone systems may be used for the transmission and routing of data. Teletypewriters and other low-data-rate (so-called sub-voice-grade) equipment transmitting at up to 150 bits per second can be connected to a teletypewriter exchange service (TWX). Each subscriber has his own dial-up number and is listed in a national directory. Several TWX channels plus telephone circuits can be sent over one voice channel on the telephone network after combining at the local telephone exchange to which they are connected.

Voice-grade signals

Higher data rate signals, at 1,200 bits per second and 2,400 bits per second (voice-grade signals), representing computer or other data-source outputs, may be transmitted by converting the signals into a form suitable for transmission over the telephone network. One device for this purpose uses both frequency-shift-keying (FSK) and phase-shift-keying (PSK) techniques.

The use of voice-grade telephone lines limits the rate of transmission of digital data. Distortion introduced by these lines may be readily corrected in voice signals since the ear is relatively insensitive to distortion of voice signals over a wide range. This distortion is harmful to rapidly varying digital signals, however, introducing many errors at the receiver if not corrected. The problem arises because a connection between two distant points may be routed differently at various times. The transmission characteristics and hence distortion introduced vary with different routing and require different amounts of equalization (correction).

With a voice signal, random variation in distortion is tolerable as long as some average equalization is introduced, but this is not the case with digital signals. Adaptive equalizers—*i.e.,* correction networks introduced at the destination to compensate automatically for deleterious transmission characteristics—are employed to correct the problem. With these equalizers, transmission rates as high as 9,600 bits per second may be possible over the telephone network. The higher transmission rates are accomplished by combining several successive binary digits in a binary data stream and transmitting one of a multiple set of amplitudes or phases of a pulsed carrier. This reduces the required bandwidth, enabling the signal to be transmitted over a three-kilohertz bandwidth line.

Worldwide public teletypewriter service is available through Telex. Telex was introduced in Canada in 1956 and in the U.S. in 1957 and is now combined with the Bell System TWX. The system operates at 66 words per minute (50 baud, or 50 bits per second). Each subscriber has his own number and may dial any other number in his own country, just as with the telephone system.

Private-line data communications

Private-line systems for data communications have come into widespread use in the past decade. These may provide point-to-point communications or, in the case of large systems, network switching as well. They provide an advantage over public systems in that they are assigned (dedicated) to a specific purpose or customer and hence may be specially conditioned to provide superior performance. Voice-grade private lines transmit 2,400 and 4,800 bits per second with conditioning, and adaptive equalization features allowing up to 9,600 bits per second are available.

Private wide-band data channels allowing 500,000-bits-per-second transmission or higher are also currently available.

When many message sources are to be interconnected in one common private network, switching and routing techniques must be incorporated. Unlike telephone (voice) data, different message sources to be interconnected may have vastly different data rates, data statistics, and data-transmission requirements. The data sources to be switched into the same network may include a telemetry signal that is transmitted continuously at a few bits per second, a teletypewriter producing 50 bits per second intermittently, and a satellite computer communicating at a high data rate with a master computer. Unlike the telephone network, in which direct transmission is required and a busy signal is given when the destination or trunks are all occupied, many data messages may be stored until transmission becomes possible. Priority classifications may be set up, with certain messages allowed to go through and others temporarily held up. Some sources may be regularly queried as to whether immediate transmission is required or can come through as facilities become available.

The strategies of combining or concentrating sources with different data rates, of temporarily storing certain messages, and of determining how to connect the sources and how to route them can all be accomplished by computer, and the trend is in the direction of completely automatic computer-message switching.

Several methods are available for connecting many data terminals to one central point or computer. The methods include connection of the terminals to a computer in a time-shared mode or to a local exchange before retransmission elsewhere. In the so-called roll-call polling technique, a computer successively asks, or polls, each terminal in prearranged order whether a message is to be transmitted. If the answer is yes, polling stops and the message is transmitted. Polling then continues with the next terminal. If the answer is no, the computer goes on to the next terminal. Some terminals may be interrogated more than once in a particular sequence, and priorities are often introduced. In the hub polling technique, the terminals are all connected in a line. The first terminal is polled by the computer. If it has nothing to send, the polling message is forwarded down the line to the next terminal. The computer resumes control only when a particular terminal down the line has something to transmit. At the end of the transmission, the computer resumes the polling at the next terminal, which in turn forwards the message down the line. In the contention, or asynchronous, technique, an individual terminal requests transmission when needed. If a transmission channel is available, transmission proceeds. If not, the channel waits its turn in line.

Roll-call polling

In these techniques, as in the method of concentrating low-speed data for retransmission at a higher rate, data storage becomes significant. Devices, called buffers, used to provide this function include magnetic tape, disc, and other kinds of memory devices. Paper tape has long played the same role in teletypewriter systems.

Error control. It has been noted that errors occur in data transmission. More specifically, in binary transmission a 1 may be received as a 0 or vice versa or two adjacent levels may be confused in multilevel phase or amplitude pulse transmission, because of noise added during transmission or on reception of a pulse signal, signal distortion during transmission, signal fading during transmission, and other effects. Much of modern communications research involves the search for new communications systems and techniques that will provide improved error performance. Appropriate signal design and encoding at the transmitter and unique modulation techniques all play a role. Different receiver configurations and processing techniques are also compared on the basis of their error performance.

If noise is the predominant perturbing effect of the transmission medium, frequency modulation provides improvement over amplitude modulation. If fading plays a significant role, single-side-band transmission is usually preferred. Errors may occur in fading when the signal level drops to a level comparable to that of the noise. At this point an FM system deteriorates rapidly compared to an AM system. The FM improvement is possible only when the signal level is high compared to the noise. If noise is the limiting factor in systems performance, the receiver incorporates a matched filter, whose frequency response is just that of the binary signal pulses received.

Noise appearing at the receiver antenna is the predominant deteriorating effect in space communications. In telephone data transmission, however, it is the signal distortion introduced during transmission that plays the major role. Particular types of pulse shapes at the transmitter are used to minimize the distortion. Repeaters spaced at relatively short distances along the transmission path prevent distortion from building up. Equalizers, both of the fixed type and the adaptive type mentioned earlier, reduce the distortion as well.

Signal distortion

With all of these improved techniques, errors still occur, and error-detection and correction techniques are necessary. By appropriately coding a binary pulse-code-modulation sequence, for example, it is possible to detect errors and even to correct them. In such a scheme additional binary digits (redundant bits) are added at the transmitter to the binary message stream in a controlled manner. There are many techniques for adding the redundant bits and determining the optimum number to use, and significant improvements in performance can be realized by their use.

It is possible, by inserting a large number of redundant bits, actually to locate the error in question and correct it. With still more redundant bits two or more errors may be corrected. The disadvantage is that as more redundant bits are added the transmission rate is reduced accordingly. Thus if five redundant bits are added to 10 message bits, there is a one-third reduction in the data rate.

Coded binary transmission has been used in recent space probes. At the large distances involved, the signal power returned is so small compared to the noise received at the Earth receiving-station antennas that the binary pulses must be stretched out over a relatively long time to provide enough signal energy to overcome the noise. The use of coded transmission reduces the errors or allows a faster rate of transmission for the same error rate.

As an example, the signal received from a space vehicle 1,000,000 miles (1,610,000 kilometres) out in space may be on the order of 10^{-16} watt. If the distance is increased by 10,000,000 miles (16,100,000 kilometres), the received power is about 10^{-18} watt. To keep the average number of errors to less than one in 100,000 binary digits—a common design figure—the maximum data rate is 1,000 bits per second. At 1,000,000 miles each bit must last at least 0.001 second to ensure enough signal energy. If the distance is increased to 10,000,000 miles, the maximum data rate is only ten bits per second. Thus, normal voice communication with existing techniques is not possible at these distances.

Increasing data rate. A theorem from information theory, developed in 1948 by U.S. scientist Claude Shannon, is invoked to increase the data rate. Shannon proved that for a communications channel with white noise added (random noise the intensity of which is constant at all frequencies), there exists an upper limit to the information rate in bits per second that may be transmitted over the channel. This he called the capacity of the channel. Packing more bits per second into the channel than this theorem allows increases the probability of an error being introduced. By using a data rate less than the allowed upper limit of capacity, however, the error rate can be made to approach zero with appropriate encoding. The theorem does not tell how this encoding may be carried out, and much of the error-correction encoding effort has gone into this question of finding good codes.

The capacity of the channel depends on three parameters: the bandwidth of the channel (the maximum frequency component it can transmit), the signal power received, and the noise power measured at the same point as the signal. In particular, as the bandwidth gets larger, the capacity increases to a maximum value directly proportional to the ratio of signal power to noise intensity.

Such considerations may be applied to the three-kilohertz voice channel used with the public telephone network. In this case, unlike in space communications, distortion plays a greater role than noise. A channel capacity, however, can be found for it. Typically, it is on the order of 20,000 bits per second or higher. In data networks of the future, with the individual links especially devised for data rather than voice, the rate may be expected to increase considerably. Coding techniques have been investigated for a different type of noise than that which appears in space channels. In the telephone channel, noise bursts tend to occur because of faulty switches in exchanges and lightning bursts. These bursts may last for many bits, wiping out all signal pulses while they last. Various error-control techniques and codes have been developed to handle the problem.

(M.Sch./Ed.)

BIBLIOGRAPHY. MISCHA SCHWARTZ, *Information Transmission, Modulation, and Noise,* 2nd ed. (1970), a basic undergraduate textbook in telecommunications; JAMES MARTIN, *Telecommunications and the Computer* (1969), and *Teleprocessing Network Organization* (1970), two books for a person with some technical background but with no particular experience in telecommunication; DONALD H. HAMSHER (ed.), *Communication System Engineering Handbook* (1967), a highly technical encyclopaedic volume; *Reference Data for Radio Engineers,* 5th ed. (1968), a handbook for practice electronic engineers; *Computer Processing in Communications,* vol. 19 (1970), proceedings of a symposium at Polytechnic Institute of Brooklyn emphasizing the impact of computers and digital processing in the communications field. Some useful periodicals on telecommunications are *Bell Laboratories Record* (monthly); *Bell System Technical Journal* (10/yr); *Telecommunications* (monthly); the IEEE *Transactions on Communication Technology;* and the IEEE *Transactions.* A general history of radio communication is provided by STANLEY LEINWOLL, *From Spark to Satellite* (1979).

Historical and technical treatments of telegraphy include E. HIGHTON, *The Electric Telegraph* (1852); G.B. PRESCOTT, *History, Theory, and Practice of the Electric Telegraph* (1860); R. SABINE, *The Electric Telegraph* (1867); G. SAUER, *The Telegraph in Europe* (1869); J.D. REID, *Telegraph in America* (1879); H.M. FIELD, *Story of the Atlantic Telegraph* (1893); H.G. SELLERS, *A Brief Chronology of Telegraphs, Telephones, and Posts* (1927); R. APPLEYARD, *Pioneers of Electrical Communication* (1930); A.F. HARLOW, *Old Wires and New Waves* (1936); J.M. HERRING and G.C. GROSS, *Telecommunications* (1936); I.S. COGGESHALL (ed.), *American Telegraphy After 100 Years* (1944); A. STILL, *Communication Through the Ages* (1946); R.L. THOMPSON, *Wiring a Continent* (1947); B. DIBNER, *The Atlantic Cable* (1959); INTERNATIONAL TELECOMMUNICATION UNION, GENEVA (ed.), *From Semaphore to Satellite* (1965); H.W. PENDRY, *Baudôt Printing Telegraph System,* 2nd ed. (1920); H.H. HARRISON, *Printing Telegraph System and Mechanisms* (1923); J.A. FLEMING, *Propagation of Electric Currents in Telephone and Telegraph Conductors,* 4th ed. (1927); F.J. BROWN, *Cable and Wireless Communications of the World,* 2nd ed. (1930); T.E. HERBERT, *Telegraphy,* 5th ed. (1930); W.T. PERKINS, *Modern Telegraph Systems and Equipment* (1946); J.W. FREEBODY, *Telegraph* (1959); and N.N. BISWAS, *Principles of Telegraphy* (1964). BROOKE HINDLE, *Emulation and Invention* (1981), includes a study of the invention of the telegraph.

Works that focus on telephony and its key aspects are FREDERICK L. RHODES, *Beginnings of Telephony* (1929), a good general account from a Bell System point of view with excerpts from several of Bell's patent cases; J.E. KINGSBURY, *The Telephone and Telephone Exchanges* (1915), the best account available of the development of telephone apparatus in the early period; A.G. BELL, *The Bell Telephone: The Deposition of Alexander Graham Bell in the Suit Brought by the United States to Annul the Bell Patents* (1908), a prime source for Bell's own account of his work that must be used critically since it was given as court testimony in a case involving large amounts of money and prestige. Other useful references include H.W. MALCOLM, *Theory of the Submarine Telegraph and Telephone Cable* (1917); U.S. NAVY, Navpers 10088, *Digital Computer Basics* (1969); and E.H. JOLLEY, *Introduction to Telephony and Telegraphy* (1970).

Coverage of communication satellite systems and equipment is provided in J.R. PIERCE, *The Beginnings of Satellite Communications* (1968); MARTIN P. BROWN, JR. (ed.), *Compendium of Communication and Broadcast Satellites 1958 to 1980* (1981); COMMUNICATION SATELLITE CORPORATION, *Report to the President and Congress* (annual), and *COMSAT Guide to the Intelsat, Marisat, and Comstar Satellite Systems* (1981).

(M.Sch./B.S.F./I.S.C./J.R.P./Ed.)

The Art of the Theatre

Although a wide range of entertainment is presented in arenas called theatres, the art of theatre is concerned almost exclusively with live performances in which the action is precisely planned to create a coherent and significant sense of drama. Though the word theatre is derived from the Greek *theaomai,* "to see," the performance itself may appeal either to the ear or to the eye, as is suggested by the interchangeability of the terms spectator (which derives from words meaning "to view") and audience (which derives from words meaning "to hear"). Sometimes the appeal is strongly intellectual, as in Shakespeare's *Hamlet,* but the intellectual element in itself is no assurance of good theatre. A good performance of *Hamlet,* for example, is extremely difficult to achieve, and a poor one is much less rewarding than a brilliant presentation of a farce. Moreover, a good *Hamlet* makes demands on the spectator that may be greater than he is prepared to put forward, while the farce may be enjoyed in a condition of comparative relaxation. The full participation of the spectator is a vital element in theatre.

There is a widespread misconception that the art of theatre can be discussed solely in terms of the intellectual content of the script. Theatre is not essentially a literary art, though it has been so taught in some universities and schools. For many years the works of the Greek dramatists, Shakespeare, and other significant writers such as Schiller were more likely to be studied than performed in their entirety. The literary side of a theatrical production works most effectively when it is subordinated to the histrionic. The strongest impact on the audience is made by acting, singing, and dancing, followed by spectacle—the background against which those activities take place. Later, on reflection, the spectator may find that the meaning of the text has made the more enduring impression, but more often the literary merit of the script, or its "message," is a comparatively minor element.

Yet it is often assumed that the theatrical experience can be assimilated by reading the text of a play. In part, this is a result of the influence of theatrical critics, who, as writers, tend to have a literary orientation. Their influence is magnified by the fact that serious theatre cannot be made widely available; for each person who sees an important production, thousands of others will know it only through the notices of critics. While reviewers in the popular papers may give greater credence to such elements as acting and dancing, critics in the more serious journals may be more interested in textual and thematic values. Such influences vary from country to country, of course. In New York City a critic for one newspaper, *The New York Times,* may determine the fate and historical record of a production, assuring it a successful run or forcing it to close overnight. In London, audiences have notoriously resisted the will of the critics, and in some cities, such as Moscow, reviews may take many weeks to appear.

This is not to say that the contribution of the author to the theatrical experience is unimportant. The script of a play is the basic element of theatrical performance. In the case of many masterpieces it is the most important element. But even these dramatic masterpieces demand the creative cooperation of artists other than the author. The dramatic script, like an operatic score or the scenario of a ballet, is no more than the raw material from which the performance is created. The actors, rather than merely reflecting a creation that has already been fully expressed in the script, give body, voice, and imagination to what was only a shadowy indication in the text. The text of a play is as vague and incomplete in relation to a fully realized performance as is a musical score to a concert. The Hamlets of two great actors probably differ more than two virtuoso renditions of Bach's *Goldberg Variations* possibly can. In general, the truly memorable theatrical experience is one in which the various elements of performance are brought into a purposeful harmony. It is a performance in which the text has revealed its meanings and intentions through skillful acting in an environment designed with the appropriate measure of beauty or visual drama.

This article contains a treatment of the art of theatre in the most general terms, an attempt to illuminate what it is and why it has been regarded as a fundamental human activity throughout history. It also deals with the roles of the director and the actor in producing the desired aesthetics. The theatrical traditions of the various cultures of the world are considered at length in articles such as THEATRE, THE HISTORY OF WESTERN; AFRICAN ARTS; EAST ASIAN ARTS; SOUTHEAST ASIAN ARTS; and in articles on the literatures of various nations—*e.g.,* ENGLISH LITERATURE, RUSSIAN LITERATURE. A more extensive treatment of the elements of theatre can be found in THEATRICAL PRODUCTION. The genres of dramatic literature are discussed in LITERATURE, THE ART OF: *Drama.*

For coverage of related topics in the *Macropædia* and *Micropædia,* see the *Propædia,* Part Six, Division II, Sections 622 and 613.

The article is divided into the following sections:

The art of theatre

Roots of Western theatre in Athenian drama

Exactly how the theatre came into being is not known. While it is indisputable that the traditions born in ancient Athens have dominated Western theatre and the theories of Western drama up to the present, it is impossible to state with certainty what the theatre was like even a few years before the appearance of Aeschylus' earliest extant play, *Persians* (472 BC). Legend attributes the invention of the dithyramb, the lyrical ancestor of tragedy, to the poet Arion of Lesbos in the 7th or 6th century BC, but it was not until the creation of the Great (or City) Dionysia in Athens in 534 that tragic drama established itself. The Dionysiac festivals were held in honour of Dionysus, a god concerned with fertility, wine, and prophecy. Dionysiac celebrations, held in the spring, were traditionally occasions for frenzy, sexual license, and ecstatic behaviour welcoming the return of fertility to the land after the winter (reflected dramatically in the *Bacchants* by Euripides). The Great Dionysia was a more formal affair, with its competition in tragedy, but its religious purpose is often cited as a pointer to the origin of drama itself.

Origins in religious rites

In the theories that see drama as a development from primitive religious rites, the dramatist is often described as a descendant of the priest. Theatrical representation could have arisen first from the substitution of an animal for a human sacrifice, say a goat for a virgin or a young warrior. In time, the formula of the sacrifice might have been enacted ritualistically without the actual sacrifice of the animal. (The word tragedy is descended from the Greek *tragōidia,* meaning "song of the goats.")

Considered in such a way, the most famous of Greek tragedies, *Oedipus the King* by Sophocles, can be seen as a formalistic representation of human sacrifice. Oedipus becomes a dramatic embodiment of guilt; his blinding and agony are necessary for the good of all Thebes, because it was by killing his father and marrying his mother that he first brought the gods' curse upon his people. Aristotle felt that the representation on stage of Oedipus' suffering was a means of vicarious purgation, or cleansing, for the spectators.

But other explanations for the origin of drama have been offered. Mimesis, the artistic representation or imitation of an event, has been discerned in such primitive rituals as war dances, which are intended to frighten the enemy and put courage into the hearts of the participants. These dances may imitate the battle itself, or at least the way in which the participants hope to see the battle develop.

The origins of drama have also been attributed to simple storytelling, as when the storyteller adopts a false voice or adds characterization through movement and costume. In such terms, the art of theatre could be described at its most fundamental as the presence of an actor before an audience.

Whatever the primary motivation, the first systematic elaboration of theatre can be seen through the work of the Greek playwrights of 5th-century-BC Athens. Aeschylus apparently inherited a form that consisted of a single actor responding to or leading a chorus. His innovation is generally considered to have been the use of a second actor, and it was either Aeschylus or Sophocles who added a third actor as they competed each year for prizes in the Great Dionysia. Once a third actor had appeared, the chorus gradually declined, and it was the multiplying individual characters who assumed importance. In this way, classical Greece left to posterity a measure of specialization among theatrical performers.

Drama reflecting the rise and decline of civilizations

Beyond these formal elements, however, classical drama offers a pattern of development that has been reenacted continually in other cultures throughout history. The rapid rise and decline of drama in ancient Athens paralleled the rise and decline of the Athenian civilization itself. Great periods of achievement in theatre have tended to coincide with periods of national achievement, when man's breadth of vision expands to encompass the cosmos, as in Elizabethan England. Conversely, periods of excessive materialism, such as those of the decay of ancient Greece or ancient Rome, tend to produce theatre in which ostentation, spectacle, and vulgarity predominate.

Probably more than in other arts, each theatrical style represents an amalgamation of diverse heritages. Although the Greek theatre has long had the most direct influence on Western culture, many later innovations have been borrowed from previously remote cultures such as India, Bali, and Japan. A fundamental difference between borrowings from Greek theatre and borrowings of a more recent and exotic nature is that the techniques of Greek performance have not been handed down with the texts. Most of what is known about the actual performance of Greek plays is the result of scholarly and archaeological research. Information about the nature of the music and of choral dances, for example, is very skimpy.

Influence of Oriental theatre

In the Oriental theatre, on the other hand, techniques as well as texts have survived. For example, the Nō theatre of Japan has been handed down through families of performers with little change for 600 years. In addition to the instructions for performers contained in India's *Nāṭya-śāstra,* there is a major descriptive treatise on music, giving guidance on musical techniques. The *Nāṭya-śāstra,* which may be as old as Aristotle's *Poetics* (4th century BC), is a book with very specific injunctions to performers, including dancers. Some of its techniques may be found in surviving theatre forms such as the kathakali dance in Kerala, India. In turn, some of these techniques have been assimilated by such Western directors as Jerzy Grotowski and Peter Brook. With other writers and directors consciously exploiting techniques and traditions from such forms as Kabuki and Nō, new relationships are inevitable.

There is little doubt that the Greek theatre, with its literary emphasis, has provided Western theatre with a sense of continuity in stories, themes, and formal styles. The plays themselves are regularly revived, with discernible references to specifically modern concerns. It is also notable that the Greek theatre has served as a model for such great writers as Racine and Corneille in France and Eugene O'Neill in the United States. When Arthur Miller's *Death of a Salesman* (1949) touched its audiences with awe and pity in the manner of Aristotle's prescriptions, critics debated whether the play could be genuinely tragic in the Greek sense, given that it had no nobler a protagonist than the salesman Willy Loman.

Implicit in all developments since Athenian drama reached its peak in the 5th century BC has been the measure of the greatness of the Greeks. That the heights which they achieved have never been equaled stands as a powerful argument against an easy belief in the constant progress of mankind.

THEATRE AS EXPRESSION

Mimesis in theatre. The art of the theatre is essentially one of make-believe, or mimesis. In this respect it differs from music, which seldom attempts to imitate "real" sounds—except in so-called program music, such as Tchaikovsky's *1812 Overture,* which suggests the sounds of a battle. In this respect, the art of narrative in literature is much closer to that of the theatre. In a story, considerable attention must be paid to plausibility. Even if the story is not intended to be believed as having actually happened, plausibility is essential if the story is to hold the auditor's attention. The principal factor in plausibility is not precise correspondence with known facts but inner consistency in the story itself.

Importance of maintaining plausibility

Drama also requires plausibility, but in drama it must be conveyed not by a narrator but by the actors' ability to make the audience "believe in" their speech, movement, thoughts, and feelings. This plausibility is based on the connection between the impression made by the actors and the preconceptions of the auditors. If the character Hamlet is to be plausible, the actor must make his audience believe that Hamlet could conceivably be as he is presented. This does not mean that the actor must make his audience believe that he literally is Hamlet, merely that he is plausibly and consistently making-believe to be Hamlet. The aim of a performance is not to persuade spectators that a palpable fiction is fact, that they are "really" there, out on those bitterly cold battlements of Hamlet's castle at Elsinore. Indeed, they are far freer to appreciate the play and to think about it if they are not "really" present. Knowing all the time that it is a figment, they are willing to enter into the make-believe, to be transported, if it is sufficiently convincing. Yet they know that, however thrilling or pleasurable the rapture, it may be shattered at any moment by some ineptitude or mistake on the stage or by a coughing neighbour in the audience.

That is the basic rule, or convention, of the make-believe of the theatre. The actor breaks the basic rule of the game if he forgets his words, or laughs at private jokes, or is simply incompetent, or is unsuited to his part. No audience can accept a vulgar, lumpish, elderly Hamlet, because Hamlet is a young prince whose lines are consistently thoughtful and witty. Yet it is not necessary that the actor playing Hamlet should "really" be all these things; he need only give the impression of being princely, witty, elegant, and young enough to sustain the credulity of the people sharing the make-believe. That credulity can extend a considerable way; several times in her old age the actress Sarah Bernhardt played Hamlet.

Degrees of realism in performance

Thus, in every performance there must be realism in some degree. At certain epochs and in certain kinds of plays the aim has been to be as realistic as possible. But even the most realistic production (*e.g.,* Anton Chekhov's play *The Cherry Orchard* in Konstantin Stanislavsky's production at Moscow) made immense concessions to theatrical artifice. Conversation in real life often leads nowhere; it is full of inconclusive, meaningless, boring passages. It does not necessarily attempt, as every word in Chekhov's play must, to fit into a story, to be part of the expression of a theme, or to introduce and reveal a group of characters.

Though most commercial, light comedies continue to be written and acted as realistically as possible, realistic theatre fell out of fashion in the first half of the 20th century in response to the advent of motion pictures. Just as realistic painting declined when photographs began to achieve similar effects mechanically, so did staging that attempted to reproduce the actual world in every detail decline when such effects became commonplace in films.

Even before the introduction of motion pictures, the theatre was moving toward extravagantly nonrealistic theatrical effects, from the puppet-inspired theatre of Alfred Jarry, author of *Ubu roi* (1896), to the Symbolist dramas of Maurice Maeterlinck, Edward Gordon Craig's concept of the *Übermarionette* ("Superior Puppet") and theatrical surrealism. The most unrealistic productions, however, inevitably retained certain quite realistic features; the actors still had to be recognizably human, no matter how fantastic the script and settings might be.

Theatre as social expression. In different contexts, different aspects of humanity have seemed important and have therefore been stressed in theatrical representation. Renaissance drama, for instance, emphasized the individuality of each character, while in 17th-century theatre, which was much more restricted in its philosophy and in its setting, man was presented not as a creature proclaiming his unique importance in the universe but rather as one adapted to the quite limited environment of 17th-century society. The greatness of the Elizabethan theatre was the universality of its outlook and the breadth of its appeal; these have never been regained. Since the latter part of the 17th century the art of the theatre has been concerned with smaller themes and has aimed at a smaller section of society.

Upper-class audience of 17th–19th-century drama

From the 17th to the 19th century, the theatre's leading characters were persons of breeding and position; the "lower classes" appeared as servants and dependents, mostly presented in low comedy. Rustics were almost automatically ridiculous, although sometimes their simplicity might be endearing or pathetic. The 17th-century plays of Molière are a good deal more egalitarian than English plays of similar date, or even of a century later; but even Molière never allowed the audience to forget that his plays were about, and for, persons of high station. A very clear line is drawn between employers and employed, and the latter, though often more intelligent, never seem to belong to quite the same species.

By the middle of the 19th century European theatre had become at least as much a middle-class as an aristocratic entertainment. Nevertheless, it was still thought important, especially in London, that the actors suggest gentility. George Bernard Shaw, in *Our Theatres in the Nineties* (1932), remarked that to be employed in a good production it was far less important that a young actor be talented than that he speak "well" and be beautifully dressed. The plays that succeeded throughout Europe were plays about men and women of good social position, and the plots were concerned with some infringement, usually sexual, of the genteel code of behaviour; *The Second Mrs. Tanqueray* (1893) by Arthur Wing Pinero is an example.

After the Russian Revolution of 1917 the Soviet theatre broke with gentility. The heroes and heroines of Soviet theatre were splendid, muscular, idealistic workers. In western Europe, however, gentility continued in the 1920s and '30s to be the dominant aim of the fashionable theatre. In New York City it received a setback at the time of the Great Depression of the 1930s. At a famous series of productions at the New York Group Theatre, the director Harold Clurman was in conscious revolt against the oppressive bourgeois gentility of the day. The theatre was not spectacularly successful, however, and it stayed in existence for no more than a few years.

In Europe it was not until after World War II that the theatre made efforts to reflect and to interest a wider section of society. By that time, however, audiences at all levels had lost the habit of theatregoing and were fast losing the habit of moviegoing, as television was becoming the popular medium of drama—indeed, of all entertainment. Theatre began to be directed not to any one class in society or to any one income group, but rather toward anyone who was prepared for the energetic collaboration in the creative act that the art demands.

ELEMENTS OF THEATRE

The theatrical hierarchy. Theatrical art demands the collaboration of the actors with one another, with a director, with the various technical workers upon whom they depend for costumes, scenery, and lighting, and with the business people who finance, organize, advertise, and sell the product.

Collaboration among so many types of personnel presupposes a hierarchy. In the commercial theatre the most powerful person is usually the producer (until recently known as the manager in the British theatre, which has now adopted the American usage). He is responsible for acquiring the investment that finances the production. The rehearsal of the play is conducted by the director (formerly known in Britain as the producer), who is responsible for interpreting the script, for casting, and for scenery and costumes. Under his general direction a stage manager, possibly with several assistants, looks after the organization of rehearsal and the technical side of the performance—light and curtain cues, properties, sound effects, and so on.

Producers, directors, and stage managers

Naturally, the hierarchy varies somewhat in different circumstances. In the state-subsidized National Theatre of Great Britain, for example, the apex of the pyramid is an artistic director, who is more concerned with guiding the policy of the theatre than with details of administration or the preparation of any single production—though he may, of course, also assume responsibility for the preparation of a number of productions.

The dominant expression so far as the audience can tell is nearly always that of the actor with the most important part. It may, therefore, be wondered why theatres are no longer dominated by actor-managers, as they were in 19th-century London, where Sir Henry Irving managed the Lyceum for 21 years (1878–99) as its artistic director, administrator, producer-director, and leading actor. Since Irving's day theatrical business has become infinitely more costly and complicated. Budgets in Irving's time were only a fraction of what they became a century later. A single Broadway musical can now cost in excess of $5,000,000, while the running costs of organizations such as the Royal Shakespeare Company rise to many millions of pounds each year. In addition, there are complicated negotiations with trade unions.

Although the leading actor seems completely to dominate the performance, he is often only a mouthpiece: the words he speaks so splendidly were written by somebody else; the tailor and wigmaker must take some credit for his appearance; that he should play the part at all was usually not his own idea but that of a producer or director.

Even before the actors assemble for the first rehearsal, the producer, director, designer, and—if he is available—the author have conferred on many important decisions, such as the casting and the design of scenery and clothes. In the commercial theatre, the capacity of the theatre that is selected determines the budget and therefore the scale of the production. (Different considerations affect the planning of programs in the subsidized theatre, including responsibility to new writing, to the national heritage, and to a balanced repertoire.) Certainly the most lively part of the work still lies in the period of rehearsal, but much of it has been determined before it begins.

Although it might be supposed that the author would be the best person to direct a play, he usually is not, for several reasons. First, authors are apt to love their brainchildren not wisely but too well; and, like most parents, they are not usually the most impartial judges of their plays' character and quality. Also, authors rarely combine a knowledge of their own craft with a good working knowledge of the quite different craft of direction.

The role of the audience. It is partly because it is a collaborative art, involving so much compromise, that the theatre seems often to lag behind other arts, expressing dated views in a dated manner. There is another reason too: the theatre depends more than most arts upon audience response. If the house is not full, not only does the performance lose money, but it loses force. It is unusual for new ideas, even for new ways of expressing old ideas, to be popular. With few exceptions, people apparently do not go to the theatre to receive new ideas; they want the thrilling, amusing, or moving expression of old ones.

Spectators' lack of response to new ideas

If a performance is going well, the members of its audience tend to subordinate their separate identities to that of the crowd. This phenomenon can be observed not only at the theatre but also at concerts, bullfights, and prizefights. The crowd personality is never as intelligent as the sum of its members' intelligence, and it is much more emotional. Intelligent members of an audience lose, to an extraordinary degree, their powers of independent, rational thought; instead, unexpected reserves of passion come into play. Laughter becomes infectious; grave and solid citizens, as members of an audience, can be rendered helpless with mirth by jests that would leave them unmoved if they were alone.

This being the case, theatre audiences are virtually incapable of an intellectual consideration of the ideas presented to them unless those ideas are already familiar. Familiar ideas can be received effortlessly while the emotional or thrilling or amusing aspects of the presentation are enjoyed. This is why the effectiveness of a theatrical performance never depends solely upon the excellence of a text. Laurence Olivier's performance as Shakespeare's *Richard III* was more exciting than his performances in many superior works of Shakespeare. Theatrical art succeeds to the degree that excitement is engendered in the audience, a factor that is unrelated to the intellectual merits of the text.

The effect of theatre structure. From the 17th to the 20th century few dreamed of building a theatre in other than the now traditional proscenium style. This style consists of a horseshoe auditorium in several tiers facing the stage, from which it is divided by an arch—the proscenium—which supports the curtain. Behind the curtain, the backstage machinery facilitates quick changes of illusionistic scenery. This type of theatre was developed for Italian opera in the 17th century. From the proscenium theatre's introduction, productions of plays of all themes have tended to exploit the audience's pleasure in its dollhouse realism.

The dominance of the proscenium

The proscenium theatre separates the audience from the performers. In the theatres of Elizabethan England, the actors performed in the very midst of their audience. Their theatre had evolved from the courtyards of inns, in which a raised platform was erected for a stage. Some members of the audience stood around it while others watched from windows and galleries surrounding the inn yard.

In the early years of the 20th century, the English actor-manager William Poel suggested that Shakespeare should be staged so as to relate the performers and the audience as they had been on the Elizabethan stage. His ideas slowly gained in influence, and in 1953 just such an "open" stage, with no curtain and with the audience sitting on three sides of it, was built for the Stratford Shakespearean Festival in Ontario. A considerable success, it had a strong influence on subsequent theatre design.

Advantages of the "open" stage

The open stage proved suitable not only for Elizabethan plays but also for a wide repertoire. Probably it will never completely replace the proscenium, which remains more suitable for the countless plays that were written with such a stage in mind, such as the comedies of Molière or the highly artificial comedies of Richard Brinsley Sheridan and Oscar Wilde. On the other hand, the more realistic plays of Ibsen, Shaw, and Chekhov, all written for the proscenium theatre, lend themselves well to the open stage.

There are three solid reasons for preferring the open stage. First, more people can be accommodated in a given cubic space if arranged around the stage instead of just in front of it. This is important not merely for the economic advantage of a larger capacity but also for artistic reasons—the closely packed audience generates more concentration and excitement.

A second reason for preferring the open stage is that the actors are nearer to more of their audience and can therefore be better heard and seen. This point is contested by adherents of the proscenium stage, who claim that the actor at any given moment must have his back turned to a large part of the house and, as a result, must be more difficult to see and hear. If the open stage is used efficiently, however, the actor's back will never be turned to anyone for more than a few seconds at a time.

The third reason is that members of an audience seated all around the stage are far more aware of the presence of the others than is the case in an opera house. The performance thereby is appreciated more as an event jointly shared and created by the audience and the actors.

Since the arguments for the open stage were first made, theatres such as the Arena Stage in Washington, D.C., have been designed "in the round" so that the audience completely surrounds the stage. Other theatres have followed the example of Grotowski's Polish Laboratory Theatre by taking as the starting point an "empty room," in which a different environment may be constructed for each production, radically altering the relationship between actors and audience for each play.

The proscenium has come to be associated so closely with creating "illusion" that it has led to a misconception about the function of drama and to a misdirection of the energies of dramatists, players, and audiences. The single-minded attempt by the actors to create, or by the audience to undergo, illusion reduces drama to a form of deception.

The art of the theatre is concerned with something more significant than creating the illusion that a series of quite obviously contrived events are "really" happening. *King Lear* is far more complex and interesting than that. Art is concerned not with deception but with enlightenment. The painter's art helps its audience to see and the musician's art helps it to hear in a more enlightened way: Rembrandt and Bach are trying not to deceive their audiences but to express and to share their deepest thoughts and feelings. Similarly, the art of the theatre is concerned with expressing the most profound thoughts and feelings of the performers about the story they are enacting, so that the audience may partake in the ritual event.

Art as enlightenment

The influence of writing and scholarship. Like the other arts, the theatre has been the subject of a great deal of theoretical and philosophical writing, as well as criticism, both of a journalistic and of a less ephemeral character. Members of the theatrical profession have probably been influenced by the work of scholars and theorists more than they realize. Scholarship has made Shakespeare's work, for example, far more intelligible and coherent. On the other hand, many of the scholarly debates over small points seem irrelevant in the theatre.

A commendable example of scholarship is the emendation of Mrs. Quickly's description of Falstaff's death in Shakespeare's *Henry V* (Act II, Scene 3), from "a table of green fields," which, in the context, seems unintelligible, to "a [*i.e.,* he] babbled of green fields," which is not only comprehensible but touching. But it scarcely alters the way in which an actress will speak this phrase. It is one descriptive phrase among five or six others relating his fumbling with the sheets, playing with flowers, and smiling at his fingers' ends. It may be the greatest description of the moment of death in all literature; in the course of performance, however, an audience does not follow even so great a passage as this word by word.

A compelling actor playing Hamlet can ask whether 'tis nobler in the mind to suffer the "eggs and bacon" of outrageous fortune and few will be aware that he has not said "slings and arrows." And if Mrs. Quickly says "a table of green fields" with good accent and discretion, the musical flow and emotional effect of this marvelous speech will hardly be diminished.

Until recently, scholars and professionals in the English-language theatre lived almost completely segregated from one another. The tradition is rather different in continental Europe, where for many years the dramaturge has been a vital part of the state theatre companies. A dramaturge is usually a writer, critic, or scholar who advises the theatre on literary points, editing classic texts and perhaps translating foreign plays. With the establishment of the National Theatre of Great Britain in 1962, the idea of a dramaturge was transplanted to Britain, the critic Kenneth Tynan becoming part of the theatre management in 1963. Other British theatres, such as the Royal Shakespeare Company and the Glasgow Citizens' Theatre, have fruitfully married scholarship, in the form of a dramaturge, to their planning of productions.

Fruitful marriage of scholarship and production

Much journalistic criticism is marred by a reviewer or critic who wants to be just without being dull. Justice demands reason and moderation, but such qualities are often less interesting to read than high-coloured opinion. Shaw was perhaps the greatest theatrical and musical critic in English, but he again and again strayed, in the pursuit of readership, into exaggeration, prejudiced partisanship, and facile jokes at the expense of actors, as in his *Our Theatres in the Nineties.*

THE PLACE OF THEATRE IN CONTEMPORARY LIFE

Work, leisure, and theatre. In general, mankind has regarded as serious the activities that help him to survive and to propagate the species. At all levels of sophistication, however, mankind's serious pursuits offer opportunities for entertainment. The ablest members of the human species have never made a clear-cut distinction between work and play. The best workers enjoy their work, be it surgery, carpentry, housework, or fieldwork. They engage themselves in work that permits, even demands, an expression of their invention and ingenuity. Indeed, the most valuable workers are not the most strenuous but rather the most ingenious and resourceful; and as their tasks increase in complexity and responsibility, the need for intelligence and imagination increases. These qualities are also expressed in the play of such people.

Combining work and self-expression

In the times and places in which theatre has become frivolous or vulgar or merely dull, intelligent and imaginative people have stayed away from it. This was the case in London during the first half of the 19th century. A similar movement away from the theatre by the intelligentsia occurred in New York City in the middle of the 20th century, as fewer and fewer serious productions were undertaken. While Broadway became primarily devoted to musicals or star vehicles, interest in serious theatre developed in the smaller and more specialized Off-Broadway and Off-Off-Broadway theatres.

Of the many theories and philosophies propounded about the purposes of theatrical art, from the *Poetics* of Aristotle onward, most presuppose that the theatre is directed toward an elite consisting of the wealthier, more leisured, and better educated members of a community. In these theories, popular theatre is assumed to be noisily cheerful and egregiously sentimental, with easy tunes, obvious jokes, and plenty of knockabout "business." In the 20th century, however, the distinctions between social classes have become progressively more blurred. Egalitarian manners became fashionable, indeed obligatory, and the theories that gave serious art a role exclusively for the upper classes lost much of their force.

Paradoxically, while more people are enjoying more leisure than ever before, there has not been a proportional increase in theatrical attendance. Those engaged in the professions or employed in a managerial capacity, unlike the aristocrats of earlier times, generally allow themselves little leisure time. Of those engaged in industry, whose leisure time has increased, the enormous majority are engaged in dull and repetitive tasks that leave them tired and apathetic at the end of the day. Comparatively few make imaginative, intelligent, and decisive use of their leisure.

The decline in theatrical attendance

The theatre's efforts to appeal to the whole community generally have been futile. There exists an ever-widening gulf: on one side, a small, enthusiastic, and highly vocal minority clamours for art galleries, symphony concerts, and drama; on the other, the vast majority is apathetic to such serious art.

The role of subsidy. A serious theatre, with or without massive public attendance, must be sustained by other financial support. Public funds have been used for this purpose throughout Europe and in much of Asia. The assumption behind such a subsidy is the realistic one that a serious theatre is now too costly to pay its way.

In Great Britain in 1940, under the threat of imminent invasion in World War II, the government took the first steps toward subsidizing theatre by guaranteeing a tour of the Old Vic Theatre against loss. Subsequently, with the establishment of the Arts Council of Great Britain in 1946, its support of theatre increased continually. By the last quarter of the 20th century many millions of pounds were committed each year to supporting a network of regional theatres, small touring groups, so-called fringe theatres, and the "centres of excellence," meaning the National Theatre, Royal Shakespeare Company, English National Opera, and opera at Covent Garden. Subsidy in Britain was the means by which the British theatre industry became the strongest in the world, both as a significant export and as a chief tourist attraction.

Until the middle of the 20th century, private patronage was still the sole support of legitimate theatre in the United States, but eventually charitable support was encouraged by a structure of tax allowances and by philanthropic organizations such as the Ford Foundation. With few exceptions, however, professional theatre in the United States remained strictly a commercial business. Nonprofit regional theatres gradually created an alternative to Broadway, but while the regional theatres have established faithful and discerning audiences, the record of the commercial theatre has been blotted by numerous instances of greed and irresponsibility and an absence of a longer view than immediate personal advantage. Unions have sometimes pressed demands that have made professional theatrical production economically difficult.

Academic theatre. A significant factor for some years has been the theatrical activity conducted by the universities with departments of drama. Their theatres, often handsomer and better equipped than professional houses, present plays of all sorts. Millions of people attend performances in university theatres each year, and in serious planning and choice of programs the academic theatre's standards are far superior to professional theatre, since the aim is educational. Unfortunately, many leading parts, whether in classics or in potboilers, call for assured and authoritative actors, between 35 and 50 years of age. Academic theatre, therefore, is handicapped at the outset by the immaturity of most of its student-actors, though professional actors are sometimes hired for special productions or to become actors-in-residence.

Problems of academic theatre

A more serious drawback is that the direction of drama departments and of university theatres is often entrusted to academics, chosen in most instances for scholarly rather than theatrical distinction. Furthermore, most college theatres operate on extremely low budgets, and, while money without taste and intelligence cannot create good theatre, taste and intelligence without money can seldom do so either. The highest standards can, in certain instances, be achieved by sheer ingenuity, but, in general, shoestring budgets result in that desperate air of "making do"—almost a trademark of academic theatre.

It is a common error in universities to suppose that the mere production of a masterpiece must amount to an educational experience for players and audience alike. It is not so. Incompetent acting and direction can reduce the greatest masterpiece to suffocating, excruciating tedium. Moreover, in many schools, the theatre must be economically self-supporting, and each season one of the successful Broadway musicals of yesteryear is put on to redeem the losses incurred by Shakespeare, Molière, and O'Neill.

In Britain, the universities still, with few exceptions, have been slow to find a place for theatrical art in the curriculum. They frequently continue to take the view that if university students want to act, they must join a club and act in their spare time. But in the 1960s British universities began to come together for annual festivals of student theatre, and many are the professional careers that began with a university group at the Edinburgh Festival.

The search for an audience. In Great Britain, government subsidy has been applied in varying fashion to attract wider audiences to the theatre. Theatre-in-education companies have been formed to tour schools, with both classical and new or improvised plays. (Although rarer, similar companies can be found in the United States and Canada, such as the Living Stage in Washington, D.C., an offshoot of Arena Stage.) Probably the most significant investment has been in the regional theatres, where the intention has been to provide audiences with not only a wide-ranging repertoire but also the opportunity to develop regional voices. The Royal Shakespeare Company and the National Theatre have also made regional tours a significant part of their planning, but London is still the theatre centre of Britain and the audience remains a minority.

In the Soviet Union the statistics of popular interest in art and literature are impressive, but the level of creative work is kept low by censorship. Artistic creation is compelled to conform to party policy, and the political machinery often manipulates popular opinion. In the theatre, success can sometimes be assured to productions that are politically acceptable, denied to those that are not.

In both the East and the West tremendous efforts are being made toward more fruitful use of the leisure time that technology has made available. But by the second half of the 20th century, theatre had become a regular leisure-time activity of only a small minority. Although the civilized world generally regarded a serious theatre as an essential activity, deserving of public support, the mere existence of an intelligent and imaginative theatre does not ensure such support. This can probably be achieved only by profound changes of belief concerning the purpose not merely of theatre but of human existence.

Live theatre has demonstrated an unexpected tenacity in the face of competition from film, television, video, and other popular entertainments such as rock concerts. At one time theatre lovers feared that a new generation of actors, directors, and technicians without professional experience of the theatre would precipitate a decline in theatrical art; on the contrary, many people most identified with movies have taken large risks to perform on the stage, so that actors such as Dustin Hoffman, Martin Sheen, and Lauren Bacall have brought to the theatre precisely those qualities of risk and commitment that make live performance so challenging.

Endurance of theatre in the age of technology

Other factors that contribute to the perpetuation of theatre include the theatrical classics themselves, the classic dramas of different epochs and different cultures such as Molière's *Tartuffe* (1664), Racine's *Phèdre* (1677), Ibsen's *Peer Gynt* (published 1867), Shaw's *Saint Joan* (1923), Brecht's *Mother Courage and Her Children* (1939)—the instances could be multiplied countless times without exhausting the great works of the human spirit. Such works were written for the stage and can only be given full expression by stage representation.

Adaptations for the screen or television of material that was conceived in terms of the stage remain merely adaptations. If the original is a work of genius, the adaptation must seem presumptuously inadequate. Although Laurence Olivier's film adaptations of Shakespeare's *Henry V*, *Hamlet*, *Richard III*, or *Othello* were justified in that thousands of people who would not otherwise have had the opportunity saw the adapted plays magnificently performed, those who saw both the stage and the film versions can testify to the superiority of the theatrical experience. The texts were necessarily garbled and hashed, and the acting and direction were adapted to suit a medium for which the originals were not conceived. Some part of the public will always believe that it is as important to see fine performances of theatrical masterworks as to see the originals of great achievements in painting, sculpture, and architecture, rather than mere photographic reproductions. As long as this is the case, there is a good reason for the continued existence of a live theatre.

Inadequacy of screen adaptations

Another reason for believing in the survival of theatre is that the live theatre can achieve a sense of occasion impossible for canned events. This sense of occasion is a heightening of everyday people and occurrences into a new vividness and significance: not just the heightening of characters and events of the drama but also a heightening of the people who take part, spectators as much as performers. This can occur more effectively if the occasion is a great one, if the house is large and full, if the audience appears to be distinguished, and if celebrated performers are taking part. But the sense of occasion can be achieved more simply, more subtly, and less expensively. What matters is that, when the performance begins, the audience should be excited, receptive, and ready. Yet the heart of the occasion lies not in the auditorium, however bedizened with celebrity, but on the stage. There, a troupe is about to create either a new work or a new interpretation of a classic. The sense of occasion is at its strongest when the cast is distinguished, but even unknown players in obscure performances can create it.

The participating audience

Activity is required of the theatre audience if the performance is to succeed; the audience is required to share with the performer, to assist him in the act of creation. In films and in television, mistakes can be eliminated, unsuccessful scenes can be reshot, even rewritten, and the whole work can be manipulated, edited, titivated, and set before the public with every detail in place. The product has been prefabricated without the cooperation of its audience, which is therefore reduced to the status of a mere consumer. In the theatre, on the other hand, every audience helps to create or to destroy the performance. To some extent, audiences get the performance they deserve.

Moreover, in every live performance is the imminence of disaster. An actor must be skillful and an audience must be imaginative if Macbeth, seeing a phantom dagger in the air, or Othello, falling down in an epileptic seizure, is to be moving and impressive instead of merely ludicrous. Yet it is precisely this hairbreadth division between the sublime and the ridiculous that creates the sense of occasion.

Some dozens of immortally great expressions of the human spirit have been written for performance by live actors for live audiences and cannot be adequately experienced in any other medium. This is why, in spite of economic difficulties, in spite of far smaller technical resources and far greater distributive problems, the live theatre must survive. (T.G./N.Ch.)

Directing

The craft of controlling the evolution of a performance out of material composed or assembled by an author is called directing. The performance may be live, as in a theatre and in some broadcasts, or it may be recorded, as in motion pictures and the majority of broadcast material. The term is also used in film, television, video, and radio to describe the shaping of material that may not involve actors and may be no more than a collection of visual or aural images.

In the theatre there was for a time a confusion of terminology between British usage and that of the United States. The director (as distinct from an old-time actor organizing rehearsals of a play in which he himself appears) emerged during the 19th century, and, like his actors, he worked for an employer who engaged both on contract. The employer, in Britain, came to be known as the manager, while the person directing the action was known as the producer. In the United States the producer has always been the one who engages the actors and finances the production, while the artist who directs the actors and shapes the performance is known as the director. With the advent of films these terms were applied to the new industry, and the American usage eventually found its way into the London theatre. It has since been absorbed by British broadcasting and British regional theatres as well and is now applied generally, although the original British usage is found in many earlier books.

Role of the director

The role of the director varies a great deal, not only according to the medium in which he works but also according to whether or not he works with actors. There is always common ground between directors of drama, whatever the medium, because their success depends not only upon knowledge of the specialized form but also upon understanding of acting and human nature. Traditionally the director is responsible to the play in the same way a symphony conductor is responsible to the score. In some experimental theatres that responsibility expands to include "devising" not only the performance but also the text of a play, partly through improvisations with the actors, with or without the collaboration of an author. In all directing there is a tension between content and form. Because there are many opportunities for jugglery with technical tricks, directors can be tempted toward virtuosity at the expense of meaning. In the musical theatre, for example, directors may attempt to compensate for a weak script by dazzling the audience with mechanically sophisticated sets and elaborate lighting designs. The justification for such measures is highly debatable; in any event, the value of immediate effect must be balanced against that of enduring significance, for the two are often mutually exclusive.

The non-Western context

Outside the Western world, the development of the director's power originally followed the Western pattern only in the performance of Western or Western-type plays, but, more recently, non-Western directors have come to have an influence on traditional non-Western forms. Indigenous Oriental theatre, as typified by the classical theatre of China and the Nō and Kabuki theatres of Japan, is rooted in tradition; its aim is not discovery but rather the perfect presentation of what was discovered long ago. In China's Peking opera before the Communist revolution, techniques were handed down from father to son for generations. In the Nō theatre, and to a lesser extent in the Kabuki, the positions of the performers on their acting platforms and the precise timing of their stylized gestures and vocalizations have all been fixed for centuries. In such traditions a director in the Western sense would be superfluous. But the incorporation of modern lighting and film techniques has strengthened the director's influence generally, as can be seen in the Kabuki theatre, where such widely traveled artists as Ichikawa Ennosuke III have been controversial in Japan for their use of innovative techniques.

19TH-CENTURY DIRECTING

The director as a dominant force began to be recognized in the late decades of the 19th century. His function of guiding the actors, however, was probably being regularly practiced as early as the 4th century BC, when the Greek political orator Demosthenes is said to have been given lessons in speech by an actor named Polus. It is a reasonable assumption that, from the beginning of the existence of an acting profession, it became customary for the most experienced performers to give advice and instruction to their less experienced colleagues: actors are seldom as confident as their performances can suggest, and they need repeated confirmation that their abilities approach their self-imposed standards. Such confirmation is likely to be sought from the most respected member of the company. There is a limit, however, to the value of the help given by a fellow actor; the perspective needed to see all the possibilities of performance is usually attainable only from a viewpoint outside the cast. The importance of this perspective is well illustrated in Hamlet's advice to the players, yet it was well over 200 years after Shakespeare's death before acting companies officially ceased to direct themselves from within.

As Hamlet's advice might indicate, however, directorial control has existed in some form in most theatre productions. The German practice of appointing an *Intendant* to run a theatre company is an early example of the function now referred to in the British theatre as artistic director, combining practical and artistic control over the work of a dramatic company. Goethe, for example, was appointed *Intendant* of the court theatre at Weimar in 1791; his prime concern was a formal balance of production elements, with emphasis on clarity of diction. So strong was his directorial style that the playwright Heinrich von Kleist blamed him entirely for the disastrous first production of his now classic comedy *Der zerbrochene Krug* (*The Broken Jug*) in 1808. It was not until the end of the 19th century that the Goethe-inspired formality of speech made way for greater realism.

In England the first professional director to coordinate the acting, decor, sound effects, and lighting of a production without also performing in it was probably Madame Vestris, who in 1830 controlled the Olympic Theatre in London. At her injunction, the company abandoned certain restrictive traditions of dress that had encouraged staginess and artificiality by inhibiting individuality of characterization. At the same time, she introduced varying degrees of realism into her productions, such as interior settings with real doors and windows (instead of painted ones) and sophisticated stage machinery.

Early directors in the United States

By the 1870s Augustin Daly, although a leading actor in the United States, was also achieving fame for the very personal direction he was giving his company in New York City. Daly's even more famous successor, David Belasco, started his career as an actor and concentrated on directing and play doctoring after the 1880s. He had a flair for vivid staging and is probably the best known director in American theatre history, but he had little or no influence on acting and left behind him no tradition. It was left to an eccentric amateur in Germany to establish an acting company that was eventually to lead to profound changes in theatrical methods throughout the Western world. The Duke of Saxe-Meiningen's actors aimed to achieve a psychological depth of characterization that was quite new for playgoers, and the company also paid meticulous attention to detail in their settings and in the way they managed crowd scenes. In their second tour of Russia in 1890 they had a great influence on Konstantin Stanislavsky, who was beginning to think along the same lines. A few years later, Stanislavsky and V.I. Nemirovich-Danchenko, who had by then established the Moscow Art Theatre, learned further from Anton Chekhov, a playwright so concerned with conveying the inner realities of human nature that his works could not be acted successfully except through entirely new directorial methods.

Meanwhile, in Scandinavia, France, England, and Germany there appeared realistic writers whose plays also called for deeper and subtler acting; thus, a "theatre of significance" grew up alongside the "theatre of entertainment" in those countries, leading to the emergence of original and creative directors. Prominent among these were Harley Granville-Barker in England and André Antoine in France. By the turn of the century nearly all professional productions presented in Europe and America were directed by professional directors—though another two decades were to pass before directors were universally acknowledged in theatre programs.

20TH-CENTURY DIRECTING

Diversity and complexity of modern directing

The craft of the theatre director has become a matter of considerable diversity and complexity in the 20th century. The responsibilities include the style of acting in particular productions, the interpretation of the play, the guidance of the actors in exploring their parts, and sometimes, though controversially, a complete control over their performances. The director also exercises overlordship in matters of decor, costuming, and lighting (sometimes he functions himself in these three areas, but union restrictions in certain countries, notably in the United States, prevent this in commercial productions, even though they allow him the final word). Incidental music, if any, and choreography in a musical play are also under his control, as are visual and sound effects.

These, the director's theatrical instruments, are more numerous and sophisticated than they were in the 19th century. Moreover, the actor is now much more aware of the techniques of voice and speech, so that the director needs at least a theoretical knowledge of how a performer achieves the fully expressive tonal octave of which he should be capable. He must also be sensitive to the rhythms and dynamics of speech and how these are affected by emotion and situation; through the contrasts resulting from these, he can create in performance a pattern that appeals both to the mind and to the senses. A great deal depends, too, upon the composition of his stage pictures, which must never remain static for long, and on how and when his actors move. The function of a modern director might be summed up like this: he creates a succession of focal points that must irresistibly attract the attention of the audience; then, through the quality of the acting, he tries to ensure that these focal points are as relevant as he can possibly make them.

Directorial styles. The backgrounds of individual directors—some have been actors, some stage managers, some have entered the theatre from other professions—have shaped their styles. Yet style in a director is difficult to gauge. It is much affected by material, and the director may be labeled by facile critics according to the kind of production with which he has been most obviously associated. Max Reinhardt was famous in two continents largely because of *The Miracle* (premiered 1911), a play of no great distinction that owed much of its success to his spectacular treatment. His less publicized interpretation of Luigi Pirandello's *Six Characters in Search of an Author,* a psychological play requiring no scenery, was, however, at least as typical of this distinguished Viennese director. The name of Stanislavsky is inextricably linked with that of Chekhov, and he is commonly believed to have been the perfect interpreter of the great Russian playwright. The belief is due less to a full understanding of Chekhov on the part of Stanislavsky than to the fact that Stanislavsky wrote repeatedly and at length about the kind of acting that Chekhov's plays needed. We know from the former's prompt script of *The Seagull* and from Chekhov's letters that the two men differed over some fundamental questions of artistic judgment. Chekhov's letters and Nemirovich-Danchenko's last production of *The Three Sisters* (1938), which continued to be performed for more than 20 years, suggest that the Russian playwright was far better served by Stanislavsky's more reticent partner.

Difficulty of gauging directorial style

The success with which a director has carried out his task is not easily assessed by either playgoer or critic. Both can be deceived by exciting scenery or bold theatrical effects into overvaluing these tools of the trade and forgetting their purpose, which is to ensure an imaginative interpretation of what the author has written. Louis Jouvet, the distinguished 20th-century French director, once wrote:

> There are two kinds of director: the one who expects everything from the play, for whom the play itself is essential; and the one who expects nothing except from himself.

There is much truth in this statement, provided the extremes are not taken too seriously.

Peter Brook of the Royal Shakespeare Company seemed to expect little from the author when he did an outstanding production of *Titus Andronicus* in 1955. If he had put greater faith in Shakespeare and had not eked out the script with a multitude of happy theatrical inventions, the public would have been the poorer. On the other hand, Brook's treatments of Shakespeare's great plays have not invariably been happy; these do not need eking out and rather seem to ask that director and actors build a testament to Shakespeare's poetry and grandeur.

Possibly the best directors cannot be made to fit into categories. Tyrone Guthrie (1900–71), in 45 years of directing every kind of play, progressed from an almost perverse disregard of authors to an ungrudging respect for them. His work ranged from Shakespeare to Aeschylus and took in Gilbert and Sullivan on the way. In viewing the totality of Guthrie's work, what emerges most strongly is an irrepressible comedic originality. The ability to discern comedy inevitably lurking behind the obvious sorrows of existence is evidence of more than maturity; it also demonstrates the director's knowledge of dramatic ways and means, for the face behind the mask is in the best writers always discernible, and in the less good it is still there, to be forcibly exposed. The discovery of the comedy that is latent gives a highlight to good dialogue and the impression at least of an extra dimension to any writing that might otherwise seem featureless.

The need for diversity

Diversity is demanded of a director working in the traditional repertoire of the European classical theatre. Trevor Nunn of the Royal Shakespeare Company may have achieved his most memorable Shakespearean production with his intense, small-scale *Macbeth* (1976), a production designed for fewer than 200 spectators, but he was no less successful in 1980 in staging an epic dramatization of Charles Dickens' novel *Nicholas Nickleby,* which unfolded its story for more than eight hours. It was after demonstrating his mastery of classical theatre—including a production in 1978 of Chekhov's *Three Sisters,* notable for its precise observation of detail and its melancholy humour—that Nunn went on to direct major commercial productions in the musical theatre, including Andrew Lloyd Webber's *Cats* (1981) and the roller-skating spectacle *Starlight Express* (1984). Laurence Olivier, the first director of the National Theatre of Great Britain, became known for his command of a wide range of theatrical styles and was particularly remarkable for his capacity to direct a play in which he also acted the leading part. This is a rare talent. It is extremely difficult for the actor-director to maintain creative objectivity while becoming immersed at the same time in his own personal creation.

Ingmar Bergman, though best known internationally for his work in film, has had considerable impact in Europe with his stage productions, not only in his native Sweden but also in Germany. He is a master of the art of drama in a multitude of forms and techniques and among the most profound directors of modern times. His emendations to the classic plays of Europe and of his fellow Scandinavians are respectfully regarded even by those who do not agree with them. Part of the success of Bergman's productions is due to his handling of actors and the admiration that he inspires in them. Consequently, the best performers throughout the world have regarded an invitation to work for him as an accolade.

Conditions in the American theatre have not encouraged such diversity, and the best known stage directors in the United States have tended to be closely associated with particular writers or kinds of writing. Thus, Elia Kazan remains identified with the early great successes of Tennessee Williams and Arthur Miller; Mike Nichols with sophisticated comedy; José Quintero with productions of Eugene O'Neill; and Harold Prince with Broadway musicals.

International influences

In the second half of the 20th century the chief development in the art of directing has been a strengthening of international influences. Ariane Mnouchkine, for example, directing her own company in Paris, did not hesitate to present plays by Shakespeare as Oriental spectacles, borrowing most successfully from the Kabuki theatre. Where research into the art of acting has been a major interest of directors, there have been surprising convergences from very different traditions, so that when Suzuki Tadashi's Waseda company from Tokyo arrived in Europe in 1972, it found itself being compared in its intense physicality to Jerzy Grotowski's Polish Laboratory Theatre from Wrocław in Poland, though the two companies had been founded independently in the early 1960s.

Although aware of the more exotic techniques available to a theatre director in the late 20th century, Peter Stein in West Berlin concentrated in the 1970s and '80s on some particularly fruitful European conventions, including elaborating the traditions of historical research established by the Duke of Saxe-Meiningen's company and Stanislavsky in Russia. Stein's work with West Berlin's Schaubühne company included group visits to Greece for research on Greek tragedy and to England to prepare for productions of Shakespeare; on those occasions the research itself was dramatized by Stein and the company into complementary performances aimed at helping to illuminate the respective plays. Their work represents perhaps the most thorough synthesis of the directorial ideas of such diverse theorists as Bertolt Brecht—advocating a cool rationality in the theatre—and Antonin Artaud—proposing a visceral "theatre of cruelty."

Inhibitors to imaginative directing

National conditions affect directorial vitality. The vast size of the United States and its hesitation to accept the cultural asset of professional drama, except in a very few cities, polarized the American theatre in the post-World War II period. At one extreme Broadway dominated—highly professionalized but dependent upon the limited vision of speculative investors and demanding little of imaginative directors. Its intellectual sterility encouraged the opposite extreme of Off Broadway and Off-Off-Broadway, where there was both experiment and imagination but also unfortunately much professional incompetence.

A promising development was the establishment of regional theatres in and around the bigger centres of population. Pioneering theatres such as the Arena Stage in Washington, D.C., and the Alley Theatre in Houston, Texas, provided forums not only for a wide repertoire of world theatre but also for new playwrights and directors. As Broadway continued its decline, the regional theatres continued to grow in importance; "schools" of acting, directing, and playwriting emerged in Chicago, San Francisco, Los Angeles, and other cities.

The scarcity of good directors poses the question as to why modern dramatists should not direct their own plays, as Racine and Molière did in the 17th century. Contemporary writers seem more introverted and tend to lack both the stagecraft and the desire to inspire a company of actors. The contemporary English playwright Harold Pinter is a notable exception. An actor himself, he is as good a director as he is a playwright. In Italy, Pirandello established himself as a director uniquely able to realize his own advanced ideas of drama, rather as Brecht later did with the Berliner Ensemble. Dario Fo followed in that tradition, bringing to his own political comedies such as *Accidental Death of an Anarchist* (1970) the fruits of his studies of the traditional Italian commedia dell'arte. Other modern exceptions have included Harley Granville-Barker and George Bernard Shaw, who saw to it that their plays were performed as they wished them to be. Moreover, they both had a marked effect on English acting and laid the foundations for its 20th-century preeminence in the English-speaking world. Shaw, in particular, inspired many a young performer with the understanding of stress, cadence, and rhythm, and even today his stage directions (with most dramatists these are no more than generalized indications and are useless for practical purposes) are models of instructive lucidity from which a director departs only at his peril.

The director's relation to the actor. A proper comprehension of and respect for the actor is indispensable to direction of the highest quality, since the acting in the theatre greatly outweighs such elements as settings, lighting effects, and visual ideas. On this point Jouvet and Shaw both have written aptly. The former said: "The profession of director suffers from the disease of immodesty." And the latter, hardly famous for underestimating his own abilities, advised in *The Art of Rehearsal:*

> Do not forget that though at the first rehearsal you will know more about the parts than the actors, at the last rehearsal they ought to know more about them than you, and therefore have something to teach you about them.

If a director has antagonized his actors and has not, on the contrary, stimulated their imagination so that they have become confidently creative, then failure for him is almost inevitable.

The task is difficult. To communicate with any particular group of actors requires the most balanced judgment. Unlike the orchestral conductor, to whose aims the theatrical director's are closely analogous, he cannot control actual performance. Neither can he, except rarely, tell his actors precisely and in every detail exactly what he wants of them. The minutiae are solely their concern, just as in a concerto they are the concern of the soloist (all actors, basically, are soloists, and their creative powers generally are inhibited by drill sergeant methods). Actors need at least the illusion that their own imaginations have full freedom. To direct by guile is therefore most often the key to success.

Time limitations

The rehearsal process. The director's efforts are naturally affected by the length of time given to rehearsals. These vary according to economic pressures, national customs, and union rules. In some countries, notably the United States, the actors' union has used its powers to escalate salaries and limit working hours. The American director is consequently hard put to find enough time to achieve the depth and polish to which he aspires. His limit may stretch to four weeks on Broadway and to a mere one or two weeks outside New York City. In many parts of Europe, subsidized theatre has been long established, and where this is so conditions are better. Rehearsals can last five or six weeks and may even extend into months. Despite unionization, the length of the rehearsal day for serious drama in Great Britain is left up to the artists themselves. The working day is long and four weeks is usually considered enough time, but it is not uncommon for productions at the National Theatre or the Royal Shakespeare Company to begin through workshops months before the opening performance.

Directorial capacities for patience and self-control usually are put to the test in the last few days of rehearsal. For weeks the company has worked together, and it should have at last reached a result that seems very close to fruitful consummation. The actors may have rehearsed, as in many European countries, on the very stage on which they are to perform. If they are working in Great Britain or the United States, they may have worked in nothing better than a room. In either case, a time must come when scenery, probably incomplete, appears and almost inevitably looks unlike what was expected. The actors have scarcely adjusted themselves to this when the lighting has to be set and cues established. Suddenly, the marvelous magic world that the artists have built and come to inhabit as their own is shattered: the technicians have arrived. There is retrogression and despondency as door handles come off in the actors' hands and complicated speeches written to be spoken to the dying rays of a setting sun are repeated over and over again while the sun obstinately refuses to set. At this point the entire production must be reborn and all its disparate components brought together in rhythm and harmony. The best served artists are those in countries where subsidy permits extended technical rehearsals. In West Germany, eastern Europe, and Scandinavia, artists and technicians may be given a week or more in which they can work together onstage before the first dress rehearsal. The allotted time in the United States may be less than 24 hours.

Casting. There is a crucial responsibility at the other end of the production schedule, before rehearsals even begin. It is the casting process, which is often regarded as an art in itself. An error in casting can be fatal, no matter how much imagination, hard work, and money have been invested in the production. The responsibility should always be the director's, but it is often usurped by the producer in theatres oriented toward the box office, and it has become a frequent habit with the latter to seek either the "right type" for the part or a well-publicized "name," irrespective of the ability to act. The wisest casting often works by opposites, so that a hot-blooded character is best played by an actor whose own personality is cool and objective. Then, as a director of the Royal Academy of Dramatic Art in London observed:

> Two contrary elements fuse harmonically to create a character in depth [who] becomes "real" precisely because he is made up of opposite elements in the same way as people are in life.

Casting, the planning of schedules, and the coordination of differing streams of creativity become more complex in production outside the field of straight drama. The rehearsal period in musicals, for example, is longer, and the strain is greater not so much on the director's artistic resources (for he has a great many helpers) but on his powers of leadership. The presence of a choreographer, with a conductor and an orchestra, the cost of which in Britain and the United States prohibits the use of musicians before the dress rehearsal, in addition to a heightened emphasis on lighting and visual effects, all contribute to creating a vast potential for discord. The director must resolve these and even turn them to advantage. All large-scale entertainments, including most modern musicals, reach the ears of the audience by means of electronic amplification. This introduces the alien element of the sound engineer, who is likely to be more technocrat than artist and may require tactful handling.

Clearly, the director of live entertainment needs to be a person of many qualities, some of which are in conflict with one another. Of all the necessary characteristics, patience perhaps is one of the most important. Unlike directors in other media, the theatre director is both artist and maintenance supervisor: in a long run it is his duty to watch the show at least every two or three weeks, thus ensuring that all that happens on the stage continues to be true to the original intentions. Such recurring watchfulness calls for critical balance and powers of endurance not easily found. (J.B.F./N.Ch.)

Acting

Acting is generally agreed to be a matter less of mimicry, exhibitionism, or imitation than of the ability to react to imaginary stimuli. Its essential elements remain the twin requisites enunciated by the French actor François-Joseph Talma in his tribute to the actor Lekain (1825): "an extreme sensibility and a profound intelligence." For Talma it is sensibility that allows an actor to mark his face with the emotions of the character he is playing and to convey the intentions of the playwright, the implications of the text, and the movements of the "soul" of the character. Intelligence—the understanding of the workings of the human personality—is the faculty that orders these impressions for an audience.

The essential problems in acting—those of whether the actor actually "feels" or merely imitates, of whether he should speak naturally or rhetorically, and of what actually constitutes being natural—are as old as theatre itself. They are concerned not merely with "realistic" acting, which arose in the theatre of the 19th century, but with the nature of the acting process itself.

The ephemeral nature of acting has left it without many practical foundations and only a few theoretical traditions. In the middle of the 18th century the German critic and dramatist Gotthold Ephraim Lessing drew attention to this difficulty: "We have actors but no art of acting." In an artistic field where the measures of greatness are traditionally the subjective reports of witnesses or critics, the understanding of the art has naturally remained in dispute. It remains as true today as when stated by George Henry Lewes in his *On Actors and the Art of Acting* (1875):

> I have heard those for whose opinions in other directions my respect is great, utter judgments on this subject which proved that they had not even a suspicion of what the art of acting really is.

Difficulty of definition

Efforts to define the nature of an art or craft usually are based upon the masterpieces of that field. Without that necessary reference point, vague speculations and generalizations—without proof of validity—are likely. In the visual, musical, and literary arts, this foundation exists; the work of the great masters of the past and the present serves not only to elucidate the art but also to create standards to emulate. It is difficult to imagine what the present state of comprehension of music would be if only the music of today were available, and the achievements of Monteverdi, Bach, Beethoven, and Mozart had to be known only by hearsay. Yet, this is precisely the situation that exists in acting. The actor, in the words of the 19th-century American actor Lawrence Barrett, "is forever carving a statue of snow." That is why the understanding of acting has not equaled the appreciation of it and why the actor's creative process has defied comprehension.

THEORIES OF TRADITIONS

The actor as creative artist and interpreter

Throughout the history of theatre, debate has continued over the question of whether the actor is a creative artist or simply an interpreter. Since the actor's performance is usually based on the play, and the dramatist is conceded to be a creative artist, it is sometimes concluded that the actor must be only an interpretive artist. Some modern exponents of the actor's creativity have indirectly accepted this view and have turned, therefore, to nonverbal theatre. But others deny that this recourse to primitivism is necessary in order to make acting a creative art. When composers like Schubert or Schumann created musical settings for the poems of Heine or Goethe, their music did not lose its essentially creative nature. Verdi used Shakespeare's Othello and Falstaff for his great operas, but his music is no less creative for that. When an artist merely imitates the work of another artist in the same medium, that may properly be called noncreative; the original artist has already solved the basic problems of execution, and his pattern is simply followed by the imitator. Such a work can be considered merely an exercise in skill (or in execution). An artist in one medium who uses an art work of another medium as subject matter, however, must solve the problems posed by his own medium—a creative achievement. It is therefore quite proper to speak of a character as if he were the actor's creation—of John Gielgud's "Hamlet," for example, or John Barrymore's or Jonathan Pryce's. Because a medium offers the potential for creativity, of course, it does not follow that all its practitioners are necessarily creative: there are imitative artists in every medium. But acting can only be understood after it is first recognized as a creative medium demanding a creative act. In "The Art of Acting" the American drama teacher Brander Matthews remarked,

> The actor needs to have under control not only his gestures and his tones, but all other means of stimulating sensibility and these should be ready for use at all times, wholly independent of the words of the text.

In the same work he quoted with approval the words of the great 19th-century Italian tragedian Ernesto Rossi that a "great actor is independent of the poet, because the supreme essence of feeling does not reside in prose or in verse, but in the accent with which it is delivered." And even Denis Diderot, the French philosopher of the 18th century whose famous *Paradox of Acting* (written 1773–78; published 1830) is dealt with below and who was himself a dramatist, stated:

> even with the clearest, the most precise, the most forceful of writers, words are no more, and never can be more, than symbols, indicating a thought, a feeling or an idea; symbols which need action, gesture, intonation, and a whole context of circumstances, to give them full significance.

If the art of acting is regarded as merely interpretive, the external elements of the actor's skill tend to be emphasized, but, when acting is recognized as a creative art, it leads inevitably to a search for the deeper resources that stimulate the actor's imagination and sensitivity. This search presents difficult problems. The actor must learn to train and to control the most sensitive material available to any craftsman: the living organism of a human being in all of its manifestations—mental, physical, and emotional. The actor is at once the piano and the pianist.

Acting should not be confused with pantomime, which is a form of external movements and gestures that describes an object or an event but not its symbolic significance. Similarly, the actor is not to be mistaken for an imitator. Many of the best imitators are unable to act in their own person or to create a character that is an extension of themselves rather than an imitation of someone else. Neither is acting mere exhibitionism; the capacity for "showing off" or entertaining at parties is quite different from the talent demanded of the actor—the ability to put oneself into another character, to create through performance a nonexistent event and bring it to its logical fulfillment, and to repeat this performance not only when one is in a favourable mood but also at specified times and places, regardless of one's own feelings on each occasion.

Genuine and feigned emotion. The most famous instance of supposed acting in ancient Greece was that of the actor Polus performing in the *Electra* of Sophocles, at Athens in the 4th century BC. The plot requires Electra to carry an urn supposed to contain the ashes of Orestes and to lament and bewail the fate she believed had overtaken him. Accordingly, Polus, clad in the mourning garb of Electra, took from the tomb the ashes and urn of his own son (who had recently died), embraced them as if they were those of Orestes, and rendered not the appearance or imitation of sorrow but genuine grief and unfeigned lamentation. Rather than mere acting, this was in fact real grief being expressed.

Rival traditions of acting

From antiquity, rival traditions of acting can be discerned—one stressing the externals of voice, speech, and gesture and the other looking to the actual emotional processes of the actor. Aristotle defined acting as "the right management of the voice to express the various emotions," and this primacy of the voice as the actor's outstanding medium has been widely accepted. "Dramatic ability," he said further, "is a natural gift, and can hardly be taught. The principles of good diction can be so taught." Aristotle did not fall into the common mistake of thinking that acting is only good diction; rather, he simply recognized that diction, unlike acting, can be taught. He was well aware of something more than diction in acting but he knew no way of training it. Aristotle saw good acting resulting either from a great natural quickness of parts or an enthusiasm allied to madness. "By the first of these, we mold ourselves with facility to the imitation of every form; by the other, transported out of ourselves, we become what we imagine."

The dichotomy noted in ancient Greece persisted through ancient Roman theatre and into modern times. On the one hand, there was a recognition of the need for the actor to be affected by the sensations he wishes to arouse in others; on the other hand, a need was also seen for a precise system of expression—the peculiar look, tone, and gesture appropriate to every emotion of the mind.

Beginning of modern acting

Modern European acting began with the Italian commedia dell'arte, the earliest mention of which is in 1545. Until then, the actor was limited to illustrating the text by means of a narrow scheme of gesture and rhetorical speech. But in the commedia dell'arte the actor used only an outline, a plot; he improvised the play, giving free rein to the actor's art, developing his own characters or masks that he repeated in each play. Each character became an extension of the actor's own personality but elastic enough to respond to innumerable dramatic situations; thus, actors began to develop the distinctive stage character of the theatre, whereas previously the emphasis had been on its literary aspects. Since this demanded high skill, the actors joined into companies—in which, incidentally, women began to take major roles for the first time, female characters having traditionally been portrayed by men. The actors became professional, and, by doing so, they stimulated the development of modern drama.

The essential requisite for the drama is its performance. The dramatist's creation finds its fulfillment not in the writer's study but on the stage. This fulfillment can best be achieved through the contribution of the professional actor. Nonetheless, after the formation of acting companies, actors continued to learn by doing. Their schools were professional companies; their classroom, the stage; their teachers, the audience and their fellow players. Schools of dramatic art, isolated from theatres or companies, are a relative innovation in Europe and the Americas.

In contrast, ancient traditions of actors' training have continued unbroken for many centuries in India and Japan, where particular types of theatrical experience are prescribed. India's textbook for actors, the *Nāṭya-śāstra,* has provided specifications for the representation of emotions down to the smallest gesture for nearly 2,000 years, and its influence is still visible in such dramatic forms as *kūḍyāṭṭam,* which has carried on the traditions of Sanskrit drama for about a thousand years, and in the kathakali dance drama, a relative newcomer that emerged contemporaneously with Shakespeare. The Nō theatre of Japan, presently divided into five distinct schools, is directly descended from the theatre of Zeami Motokiyo (1363/64–1443), an actor and author of Nō plays who codified the form in 21 treatises, the most influential of which is the *Fūshi kaden* (1400–18; "Appearance of Flower Transmission"), also known as the *Kaden sho.* Zeami's teachings, originally intended for his descendants in the Kanze school of Nō, are both philosophical and practical regarding actors' training, and his concerns for constant training and discipline anticipate many modern approaches to acting.

Diderot's "Paradox of Acting." The most significant statement on acting is Diderot's *Paradox of Acting.* Because of its polemic brilliance, it remains the most widely known essay on the subject. In the 20th century it provided the guiding precepts for the influential work of the French director and actor Louis Jouvet. Outside France it has found little acceptance within the profession, though its famous paradox—that in order to move the audience the actor must himself remain unmoved—is still highly regarded.

However disputable the solutions it proposes, Diderot's essay contains an excellent description of the actor's problem. What bothered Diderot was the unsolved problem of how the actor, if he were full, really full, of feeling, could play the same part twice running with the same spirit and success and yet be worn out and cold as marble at the third performance. Diderot confirmed this phenomenon by noting "the unequal acting of players who play from the heart. Their playing is alternately strong and feeble, fiery and cold, dull and sublime." This was the case with an actress who in her day was the outstanding example of emotional acting. "She comes on the stage without knowing what she is going to say; half the time she does not know what she is saying; but she has one sublime moment." Diderot knew that actors do feel and experience; but he also knew that some actors refused to recognize the need for craft, for training.

Diderot asked how the actor, if he is himself while he is playing, is to stop being himself: how he is to catch just the point at which he is to stay his hand? Diderot demanded unity in a performance; he demanded respect for the author's concept, and he understood the difficulty of repeating a performance. He demanded a definite course to the passion—a beginning, a middle, and an end. In Diderot's day, however, the problem of developing a technique for creating inspiration in the actor remained unsolved.

The difficulty of solving the problem is illustrated by the work of the 19th-century French teacher François Delsarte, whose influence was widespread not only in France but also in the United States. Delsarte became dissatisfied with routine acting techniques. He observed their mechanical and stultifying character and realized that under the stress of natural instinct or emotion, the body assumes appropriate attitudes and gestures quite different from those described by his teachers. But when he attempted to formulate laws of speech and gesture, on the basis of years of diligent observation and study, he created a series of elaborate pictorial descriptions that were just as mechanical as those he had originally criticized. Knowledge of affective behaviour had not advanced far enough to serve as an aid in solving the problem of the actor: there was still too little understanding of human behaviour, of the relation between the conscious and unconscious, and of the role of the senses.

Delsarte's laws of speech and gesture

Stanislavsky's contribution. It is in this context that the enormous contribution in the early 20th century of the great Russian actor and theorist Konstantin Stanislavsky can be appreciated. Stanislavsky was not an aesthetician but was primarily concerned with the problem of developing a workable technique. He applied himself to the very problems that Diderot and others had believed insoluble: the recapture and repetition of moments of spontaneity or inspiration, which could not be controlled and repeated at will even by many of the greatest actors. In his work as director of the Moscow Art Theatre, he often experienced those flashes of intuition or inspiration that stimulate the imagination and turn something that one understands with the mind into an emotional reality and experience. Stanislavsky described such a moment occurring at a low point in the rehearsals for Chekhov's *Three Sisters,* when "the actors stopped in the middle of the play, ceased to act, seeing no sense in their work." Suddenly something incomprehensible happened: an accidental sound, of someone nervously scratching his fingernails on the bench on which he sat, reminded Stanislavsky of a scratching mouse, setting off an entire sequence of previously unconscious memories that put the work at hand into a new spiritual context.

Later, in examining parts he had played, Stanislavsky became aware of how much his characterizations had been based unconsciously on his memories. With the passing of time, however, the memories and the feelings aroused by them were lost, and he began to repeat mechanically the fixed appurtenances of the role—the movements of the muscles, the mimetics of the face, eyes, arms, and body, and the physical signs of absent emotion. This led him to the perception that creativeness on stage demands a condition that he called "the creative mood." To the genius on stage, this condition almost always comes of itself, and less talented people receive it less often. Although everyone on stage received the creative mood sometimes, none seemed able to control it with his own will.

The role of the creative mood

Stanislavsky's description of the problem thus far had reached the point at which all previous examinations had stopped. By going further and inquiring into technical means for controlling the creative mood, Stanislavsky laid the foundation for the modern approach to the actor's problem. Stanislavsky had no intention of creating inspiration by artificial means; rather, he wanted to learn how to create favourable conditions for the appearance of inspiration by means of the will. He emphasized that other artists may create whenever they are of a mind or feel inspired, but that "the artist of the stage must be the master of his own inspiration and must know how to call it forth when it is announced on the poster of the theatre." If he is unable to find a conscious path to unconscious creativeness, the actor is forced to rely on the superficial aspects of scenic craft and theatrical cliches.

Stanislavsky believed that the problem could be solved through advanced psychology, especially the concept of "affective memory" described by the French psychologist Théodule Ribot in the 1890s. Although there has been confusion and misunderstanding about it, and its very existence has been questioned, the concept of affective memory is of prime importance for the understanding of how spontaneous and emotional experiences occur and can be repeated on the stage.

Affective memory is the reliving of a past experience—with the accompanying positive or negative response—triggered by an analogous experience in the present. Something that has brought pain is anticipated with displeasure the second time. This displeasure, which is felt immediately, rather than remembered, is like a residue of previous appraisals. Affective memory may be linked directly to the memory of a traumatic experience, as the same situation or a similar one recurs, or to an experience that bears little apparent relation to the original, if the memory has been repressed. Of course, affective memories may stem from pleasant experiences as well as unpleasant ones. The concept of affective memory has found a place in several schools of psychology, including the Freudian and the Pavlovian, though different explanations have been offered.

The concept of affective memory is essential to an understanding of how the actor functions and the faculties that have to be trained to develop his talent. It is his unusually sensitive affective memory that enables the actor to respond to events that must be imagined on the stage and to repeat performances. This point was stressed by Stanislavsky's great pupil Yevgeny Vakhtangov, who emphasized that literal emotion—emotion that derives from the presence of an object that actually stimulates it—cannot be controlled and cannot be relied upon to provide the level of response that is required in every performance.

The use of affective memory is not limited only to acting. Wordsworth defined poetry as originating from "emotion recollected in tranquility." Marcel Proust, in a long passage in *Swann's Way,* brilliantly described the working of affective memory and illustrated precisely the way in which it can be recalled. Instances of its presence can be multiplied from all the arts—literary, visual, or musical. But, though in the other arts it can function unconsciously, the actor must learn to use it consciously to satisfy the unique conditions under which he must create.

Stanislavsky's "Method"

The "Method" is the name by which the totality of Stanislavsky's ideas have become most widely known in the United States, where they were chiefly promulgated by the director, actor, and teacher Lee Strasberg, first through the Group Theatre, established in the 1930s, and later through the Actors Studio in New York City. The Method represents a development of Stanislavsky's procedures based not only on his writings but also on his actual achievement in his major productions. It includes the work of Vakhtangov, who demonstrated that Stanislavsky's ideas apply to the essential problems of the actor in any style and not only to the realistic style most often associated with them. The Method became widely known in the mid-20th century largely through the work in films of actors such as Marlon Brando, Rod Steiger, and Geraldine Page, who had studied at the Actors Studio. These actors made a powerful impression and showed a remarkable ability to bridge the gap between stage, screen, and television to an extent that aroused excitement and interest in the rest of the world. So strong was the fusion of performer and role that many of the traits of the character were confused with those of the actor, which led to serious misunderstanding. But at mid-20th century an American style of acting was being born.

Critics who feel that the Method was only one of Stanislavsky's continually developing theories now generally refer to the more complete tradition of Stanislavsky's thought and work as the "System." While the term Method can apply to Stanislavsky's work up to the early 1920s, it largely ignores his later developments—in particular, his embrace of the "method of physical action" in the 1930s. This was a technique that put greater emphasis on the body, with the reasoning that there is a physical aspect to thought and a mental aspect to action; by concentrating on the physical requirements of a part, an actor would become aware of a character's reasoning. In regard to rehearsal, Stanislavsky described his intentions thusly: "Start bravely, not to reason but to act. As soon as you begin to act you will immediately become aware of the necessity of justifying your actions."

The lesson of the Method seemed to be that a character could best be built from the inside out, using, among other techniques, affective memory, which would allow the actor consciously to draw upon genuine emotions from the past. In practice, however, the development of the "method of physical action" arose from Stanislavsky's continued questioning of his own research and was founded on the various discoveries of his own career. The System as it evolved is far from its popular image as a simple technique for introspective character development dependent for success on the personality of the actor; it is rather a process designed for the constant renewal of the actor through the renewal of the Method itself.

Later developments. Stanislavsky was fully aware of alternative ideas regarding the work of the actor; he encouraged, for example, the early work of such a resolute experimentalist as Vsevolod Meyerhold. Meyerhold set out, in rebellion against Stanislavsky's naturalism, to train actors for the production of highly stylized plays, such as the Symbolist dramas of Maurice Maeterlinck. His synthesis of styles gave rise to a training system known as "biomechanics." Borrowing from the commedia dell'arte, as well as such alien influences as Japanese Kabuki, Meyerhold sought to create an actor of athletic accomplishment who could be used by the director as a formal element in the production of a play.

The theatre since World War II has been influenced chiefly by the ideas of Antonin Artaud, Bertolt Brecht, and Jerzy Grotowski. Artaud, a French avant-gardist director, actor, and playwright, exerted an enormous posthumous influence on contemporary theatre through his writings. There he proclaimed the "theatre of cruelty," which is based on the extreme development of gesture and sensory responses by the actors so that they can communicate with the audience at a more profound psychological level than is possible through words. Artaud's ideas achieved international attention in the 1960s through the productions of Peter Brook and the Royal Shakespeare Company, especially *The Persecution and Assassination of Jean-Paul Marat as Performed by the Inmates of the Asylum of Charenton Under the Direction of the Marquis de Sade,* which called for emotional states verging on hysteria from most of the cast during each performance.

The ideas of Artaud, Brecht, and Grotowski

Contrary to the opinion of many, Artaud thought of the theatre not as a psychological but as a plastic and physical domain and of the actor as an "athlete of the heart." For every feeling, every mental action, and every leap of human emotion, there is a corresponding breath that is appropriate to it. Grotowski has pointed out that, if Artaud's principles are analyzed in a practical way, they lead to "stereotyped gestures, one for each emotion." Questionable as some of Artaud's specifications might be, his achievement was to remind actors and directors that in addition to an internal truth, which the early work of Stanislavsky emphasized, there was such a thing as an external truth: what the audience sees is what it believes and feels.

Through his plays and the remarkable productions of the Berliner Ensemble in East Berlin in the 1950s, which represent the most important contribution to theatre of the post-Stanislavsky period, Bertolt Brecht generated ideas about acting that have received wide prominence and have usually been counterposed to those of Stanislavsky. Whereas in Stanislavsky-inspired productions the actors often seem to be exaggerating their individuality, Brecht's characters struck many observers as existing primarily as representatives of a class—in some cases showing self-effacement to the point of dehumanization. Brecht himself, however, denied that his ideas were opposed to those of Stanislavsky. Calling his approach epic realism, he stressed that the stage of a realistic theatre must be peopled by live, three-dimensional, self-contradictory people, with all their passions, unconsidered utterances, and actions. Brecht mentioned some of Stanislavsky's procedures to which he felt indebted—the creation of the given circumstances that motivate the beginning of an event, the emphasis on creating the activity of the day that helps to define the actor's behaviour, and the individualizing of the characters that make up a mass.

Brecht's epic realism

Brecht's most significant contribution to concepts of acting was his theory of the *Verfremdungseffekt,* usually translated into English as "alienation effect," though it has also been translated as "distanciation." The aim of the technique, as Brecht described it, was to "make the spectator adopt an attitude of inquiry and criticism in his approach to the [incidents portrayed]. . . . The actor does not allow himself to become transformed on stage into the character he is portraying. He is not Lear, Harpagon, Schweik; he shows them."

Through maintaining a distance between the actor and the character, it should become possible for actors to comment implicitly upon the characters they are playing, even to address the audience directly about the character. By abandoning the concept of total transformation, the actor can speak his part "like a quotation," though "at the same time he obviously has to render all the quotation's overtones, the remark's full human and concrete shape; similarly the gesture he makes must have the full substance of a human gesture even though it now represents a copy." A Brechtian actor must not only have the ability to assume in a convincing manner the character he is portraying, but he must also be able to step aside from the character, providing commentary as necessary while sustaining the believability of the situation.

Following Brecht and Artaud, the Polish director Jerzy Grotowski made the most thorough effort to rediscover the elements of the actor's art. From the early 1960s to the mid-1970s it was Grotowski's work with the Polish Laboratory Theatre that most stimulated and excited theatre professionals, though not all were in sympathy with the stripped-away concept of staging that he called "poor theatre." He rejected the idea that theatre should attempt to match the spectacle and effects of film and television and declared that the primary element of theatre is the relationship between actor and spectator. The theatre can exist without makeup and without a separate stage; it can exist without lighting and sound effects; but "it cannot exist without the actor-spectator relationship of perceptual, direct, 'live' communion."

Grotowski's "poor theatre"

Although he credited Stanislavsky with having posed the most important questions, Grotowski was not satisfied either with Stanislavsky, who let natural impulses dominate, or with Brecht, who was too much concerned, Grotowski felt, with the construction of the role. To Grotowski, the actor is an individual who works in public with his body, offering it publicly. The work with the actor's instrument consists of physical, plastic, and vocal training to guide him toward the right kind of concentration, to commit himself totally, and to achieve a state of "trance." The actors concentrate on the search for "signs," which express through sound and movement those impulses that waver on the borderline between dream and reality. By means of such signs, the actor's own psychoanalytic language of sounds and gestures is constructed, in the same way as a great poet creates his own language.

In his search for the basic elements of acting, Grotowski turned to the French actor Charles Dullin's rhythm exercises, Stanislavsky's "method of physical action," and Meyerhold's biomechanics and to the training techniques of the Peking opera, India's kathakali dance, and the Japanese Nō theatre. He emphasized, however, that he and his company were not merely accruing techniques but were using physical and mental exercises to free the actor from blocks, eliminating obstacles between the inner impulse and the outer reactions.

THE ACTOR'S QUALIFICATIONS AND TRAINING

In view of the diversity of approaches to the actor's problems, it may seem difficult to arrive at any useful generalizations that are valid for all of them. Even among theatre groups that approach the production of a play from a fixed style or a fixed scale of expression, as in Kabuki and classic Oriental theatre generally, the same basic concerns are apparent. The following is an attempt to set down an approach that has proved successful in a variety of professional procedures.

The qualifications of the actor are generally thought to be a good physique, a retentive memory, an alert brain, a clear, resonant voice with good articulation, and controlled breathing. While looks and the even more important element of personality are undoubtedly factors, their characteristics are difficult to determine; they are usually recognized after the actor has become successful rather than before. Many actors do not possess them offstage but seem to ignite them as soon as they begin to perform. The central element of the actor's talent, as differentiated from his means, is a special sensibility ("fire," "enthusiasm," "spirit," in the words of 18th-century theoreticians), an ability to respond to imaginary stimuli and situations, which makes it possible for him to enter into the experience and emotions of the character he is to represent. These elements have always been recognized as distinguishing the great actor but were assumed to be beyond the reach of the ordinary actor; they were regarded as elements "born in him" and not susceptible to training. This is precisely the area of the modern training of the actor.

Looks and personality

The first stage in the training of the actor's control of his physical, mental, and psychical resources is the ability to relax. Because this ability seems to have little to do with the final achievements in acting, it is often disregarded, but it is basic to any expenditure of will and energy on his part. In a state of physical or mental tension, or both, the actor cannot think, the commands he gives himself are not transmitted, sensation is stifled, and expression is inhibited. The process of relaxation serves to clear the actor of the unnecessary pressures that he has accumulated before the moment of acting begins, to free him of blocks or interferences that may inhibit sensory responses. Physical and mental energies are comparatively easy to train, but sensory control is much more difficult. Relaxation is not a static state or effort. Often in the initial stages of training the actor is subject to strong eruptions of unconscious impulses. He must learn to continue the relaxation, to force his will to maintain his effort on the action of the nerves and the muscles.

The role of concentration

The converse of relaxation is concentration. Everything the actor does demands concentration. His training proceeds by work with imaginary objects: working with real objects often leads to pantomimic or to physical imitation, but the actor may begin with them in order to learn how to respond with his entire organism and to apply such responses to his work with imaginary objects—the real medium of the stage—as he would to real ones. This capacity to respond to stimuli that come not from outward reality but from the promptings of one's own imagination may be seen to some extent in every human being; something akin to it is found in psychology in the study of conditioned reflexes, of automatic and spontaneous reactions, and of behaviour patterns. In heightening the sensory awareness and stimulating the senses to respond more strongly in life, the actor acquires the ability to recreate any object, sensation, or experience in the imagination.

In strengthening his concentration, the actor uses not only will but also a process of self-awareness by which he trains the instrument that is his body and voice to respond to his commands. The very process of concentration and of commitment and involvement must include awareness. The more the actor learns to master concentration, the more aware he becomes.

The actor's sense of truth

An additional factor is the development of the actor's sense of truth—a faculty particularly stressed by Stanislavsky and by followers of his System. The growth of self-awareness is useless if it is not accompanied by a correct evaluation of what is true and what is false. If the actor must rely on outside judgment and remain dependent on it, he may become insecure and lose his spontaneity and responsiveness. His mastery of inner relaxation and concentration helps him achieve a combination of spontaneity, commitment, and awareness. Thus, the actor's involvement and his awareness, rather than being in opposition to each other, are in accord.

The actor's sense of truth is also involved in another major area of the actor's training—his work with actions (the way he behaves physically on the stage), sometimes called the "business" of the actor. Some idea must supply an incentive or intention to pull together what could otherwise be a series of disconnected and unrelated physical deeds. Some purpose, some aim must motivate the actor's will and energy. Any performance thus may be seen as a series of actions—as the score of the play—which must be carried out not simply physically but logically and truthfully. They must accomplish their purpose anew each night at every performance rather than merely repeating the external movements.

To develop spontaneity, to train himself to behave logically and truthfully, and to listen and respond to his partner, the actor practices improvisation—dramatizing contrived situations without a script. Improvisation is of enormous importance in the process of training and also of performance. It teaches the actor to speak rather than to read his lines, and it breaks his unconscious adherence to conventional theatrical patterns of behaviour. It forces him to use his senses and often to discover not only the logic but also the significance of a scene. It compels the actor to work creatively and prevents him from reverting to skillful but mechanical repetition.

By means of exercises that may be remote from the actual roles he plays—such as the "song and dance" (in which a song is rendered syllable by syllable unrelated to the way in which it would usually be sung, thus helping to break the unconscious habits of the actor that affect his performance) or, conversely, the spoken "inner monologue" (in which the actor speaks out what is happening to him at the moment, unrelated to the play), or others—the actor not only intensifies his capacity for experience, but also frees his blocked, or inhibited, impulses. He is enabled to deal with his own subjection to automatic habitual forms of behaviour and mannerisms and to acquire new means of expression, corresponding to the true nature and strength of his impulse.

The basic means of the actor, which have traditionally served as the primary area of his training, are voice and body gesture. The actor's voice must be flexible and expressive of all situations and experiences. It must be able to deliver a "poor" voice or a vulgar, rough, angry, or harsh voice. It must vary as much as the events to be created. His attitudes must be those of the character—of a human who may be ill at ease, slovenly, awkward, debilitated, or natural—giving no indication that it is being accomplished by a skilled craftsman. The methods used to train these tools of the actor derive from other fields, such as from the training of the singer's voice and of some forms of dance and pantomime. These contain many useful exercises for the strengthening of the respective muscles of the voice and body. But while the technical accomplishment in the singer and in the dancer may represent a large part of what is appreciated in their performances, in the actor the very fact of the accomplishment must remain hidden. Technical accomplishment should go unnoticed by the audience.

Voice and body training

THE ACTOR'S APPROACH TO HIS ROLE

Stanislavsky suggested that the actor, in approaching his work on a scene, ask himself four questions: (1) who he is (character), (2) where he is (place), (3) what he is doing there (action and intention), and (4) what happened before he came there (given circumstances). The answers to these questions provide the actor with the necessary background for his performance, helping him to create the scene. In approaching the play in its entirety, the actor must subject his role to more intense analysis: he must search for the spine, or the kernel, of the play as well as its division into separate sections or units of actions. He must discern the beats of the play (*i.e.,* the smallest units of dramatic action into which each role can be divided) as well as the rhythms of the play as a whole, and he must determine what adjustments must be made in his performance for each of the other characters. For some plays an additional element is necessary: the overall mood, or pervading texture, that surrounds the play or out of which the play stems. The attempt to determine it, however, may lead to an excess of verbal and mental gymnastics that are of little actual value, unless the actors have been trained in the proper procedures. The actors must act out the elements involved in the analysis in order to receive any concrete benefit from it; otherwise it may remain superficial or merely intellectual.

Collaboration with the director

Another area deserving attention is the rehearsal process. This is primarily the time in which the director's conception of the play must be harmonized with those of the actors; it is of immense importance that the actor approach the rehearsal in a creative frame of mind, ready to enlarge both his own and his colleagues' interpretations. Without a logical sequence of rehearsals, the actor's creativity cannot be properly stimulated. Without an understanding of the psychology of the rehearsal procedure, much of the work of the actor and the director may be defeated in production. There are, for example, significant possibilities in the reading rehearsal, in which the actors, usually seated in a circle, read aloud from the script and discuss its meanings as they proceed through it. There is enormous value in improvisation, when it is understood and used correctly. The relation between the individual actor and the ensemble is welded during the rehearsals, and it is during rehearsals that the director "blocks" the scenes and the actors memorize their lines.

Styles of performance. In an effort to bring new life to plays of the past and present and to advance the imaginative possibilities of theatre, there has been a rediscovery of "style" in the 20th century. Style is the attribute of any complete achievement; it is not merely the manners and customs of a particular period. Such manners may be more strikingly elegant compared with those of the present, but they remain only manners. The Elizabethan form of theatre had conflicting styles within it, judging from a description of them in *Hamlet,* and so did the Greek and the French classical theatre. Even in Kabuki and Nō theatre there have been conflicts of styles like those in Western theatre.

Style is not, as is sometimes assumed, the opposite of realism. Neither is it necessarily characterized by an expansiveness or broadness in acting. Style is the angle from which reality is observed. It is an attribute of all creative activity—not just of period or classic plays. The search for the specific content and reality of a play leads to style. The search for style in itself or in the traditions of the past often leads to empty forms.

Just as style should not be identified with a particular period, neither should it be associated with specific playwrights. Such terms as Shakespearean style or Chekhovian style actually refer to the theatrical conventions traditionally associated with those dramas—a rhetorical and "larger than life" manner in the first and a static "mood" in the latter. These elements are little related to style; otherwise great Shakespearean and Chekhovian productions could be re-created generation after generation in precisely the same way. The fact is that those dramas must be continually re-created from the new views of each emerging generation.

The term style is often used incorrectly in reference to the theatrical conditions that simulate the original concept, structure, and dynamics of a play. The rediscovery in the 20th century of the Shakespearean stage, for example, led to a new quickness and fluidity, a nearly cinematic technique, in presenting Shakespeare's plays, but these techniques should not be interpreted as the original and therefore correct style of production. Shakespeare continues to be presented in a vast range of styles, even by the Royal Shakespeare Company, which has offered *A Midsummer Night's Dream* as a circus and *The Merry Wives of Windsor* as a 1950s suburban morality play.

Practice has shown that the use of methods traditionally associated with particular types of theatre may bring a fresh understanding to totally unrelated theatrical forms. Ariane Mnouchkine's use of Oriental styles in her Paris productions of Shakespeare, for example, was particularly successful in transmitting the ideas of Shakespeare to a French audience notoriously dubious of Shakespeare's charms.

Techniques of performance. The fundamentals of the actor's art remain the same no matter how bizarre the dramatic context: the actors may portray abstractions, for example, as in Stanislavsky's 1908 production of Maurice Maeterlinck's allegorical fantasy *The Bluebird;* they may play a band of actors producing a play, which they then proceed to perform in a vivid theatrical fashion, as in Yevgeny Vakhtangov's production of *Turandot,* a play by the 18th-century Italian Carlo Gozzi; they may invade the stage as people who demand that their story be told to an audience, as in Pirandello's *Six Characters in Search of an Author;* or they may assume the distorted attitudes appropriate to an expressionist world, as in the classic horror film *The Cabinet of Dr. Caligari* (1919).

Acting in motion pictures and television

The growth of motion pictures, especially the rise of the "talkies," beginning in 1927, greatly affected acting, as theatre talent was diverted from the stage. The requirements of acting in motion pictures, television, theatre, and opera are basically the same, although some of the techniques are different. It is possible to put strips of film together and create a performance that never was actually given. The performance is created by the director rather than by the actor. There have been performers in motion pictures who were thus completely products of the camera and contributed little from an acting point of view, depending rather on their physical charms and personality. Others, however, have been authentic actors, who developed a style perfectly suited to the medium; Charlie Chaplin, for example, ranks as one of the greatest actors of all time in any medium.

Despite the technical demands that are unique to each medium, the properly trained actor moves easily from one medium to another without any diminution of his talent. In the past, those who were trained in the rhetorical and theatrical gesture approach sometimes found difficulty in making the transition to films. The theatre can diminish the impact of action and voice, requiring a heightened intensity to project emotion and meaning to the audience. The camera, however, exaggerates action and emotion. Some actors find it difficult to perform scenes out of sequence, as is usually done in films, and for other actors the close-up can be intimidating. But the fact is that actors training for films usually use the same exercises as theatrical actors—working with imaginary objects and partners, performing appropriate physical and psychological tasks, and others. Moreover, most of the preeminent actors of the 20th century, such as Laurence Olivier, John Gielgud, Louis Jouvet, Katharine Hepburn, Dustin Hoffman, and Al Pacino, have been outstanding in both film and theatre.

The contemporary theatre is characterized by many plays that demand more dynamic and more imaginative physical actions of the actors than previously and that utilize a diversity of audiovisual effects and multimedia devices, particularly in musicals. Under the need to fulfill these demands, acting could easily revert to its old-fashioned externalized forms. In addition, the development of repertory theatres in North America, Britain, and elsewhere, with their eclectic repertoires and their combinations of contemporary and classic plays, could lead to a search for meretricious "style" rather than for genuine content. These pitfalls may be avoided, however, in much the same way as those that faced the actor in previous epochs, by understanding the true fundamentals of the art of acting.

(Le.S./N.Ch.)

BIBLIOGRAPHY

Art of theatre: Few works deal extensively with the aesthetics of theatre as a body of knowledge or theory unrelated to particular productions, schools of playwriting, or historical periods. Notable modern exceptions are ANTONIN ARTAUD, *The Theatre and Its Double* (1958; originally published in French, 1938), which considers theatre in its broadest implications and has had enormous influence on avant-garde theatre since World War II; and JERZY GROTOWSKI, *Towards a Poor Theatre* (1968, reissued 1975), an elucidation of personal artistic values by the director-teacher whose Polish Laboratory Theatre has been among the most controversial and innovative theatres of the century. The ideas of one of the 20th century's most important playwrights and directors emerge in *Brecht on Theatre: The Development of an Aesthetic,* edited and translated by JOHN WILLETT (1964, reissued 1978). A tendentious view of the shaping of 20th-century theatre by an influential director emerges in ERWIN PISCATOR, *The Political Theatre,* translated and edited by HUGH RORRISON (1978; originally published in German, 1929).

Perceptive analyses of aesthetic points of view represented in theatrical production include MORDECAI GORELIK, *New Theatres for Old* (1940, reprinted 1975), a classic work on staging and design that covers the late 19th century and first four decades of the 20th; BERNARD SHAW, *Our Theatres in the Nineties,* 3 vol. (1932, reprinted 1954), an incisive contemporary view of drama in the 1890s; and the writings of such major 20th-century critics as Harley Granville-Barker, Stark Young, George Jean Nathan, and Kenneth Tynan. Personal histories by leading theoreticians and practitioners, including KONSTANTIN STANISLAVSKY, *My Life in Art,* translated from the Russian (1924, reissued 1980); and HAROLD CLURMAN, *The Fervent Years: The Story of the Group Theatre and the Thirties* (1957, reissued 1983), carry implicit commentaries on the art of theatre. KONSTANTIN STANISLAVSKY, *An Actor Prepares,* translated from the Russian (1936, reissued 1980); and TOBY COLE (comp.), *Acting: A Handbook of the Stanislavski Method,* rev. ed. (1955, reprinted 1971), though specialized, develop aesthetic points of view that have underlain much of the theatrical production in the West during the 20th century. A classic study of the aesthetic intentions of theatre is contained in FRANCIS FERGUSSON, *The Idea of a Theatre* (1949, reprinted 1972); while PETER BROOK, *The Empty Space* (1968, reprinted 1981), is a brilliant analysis of theatrical values as manifested in such diverse areas as commercialized drama, the popular, or "rough," theatre, and the dedicated avant-garde, or "holy," theatre. A detailed examination of the development of experimental theatre in the 20th century can be found in CHRISTOPHER INNES, *Holy Theatre: Ritual and the Avant Garde* (1981).

An overview—outdated but still singular—of the many different forms and aesthetic conditions of Oriental theatre is contained in FAUBION BOWERS, *Theatre in the East* (1956, reprinted 1980). Discussions of the conditions under which theatrical forms have emerged appear in many works, including SIR JAMES FRAZER, *The Golden Bough,* 3rd ed., 12 vol. (1907–15), available also in numerous later editions, both complete and abridged, and those of Margaret Mead and other anthropologists. Finally, such periodicals as *Drama Review* (quarterly; formerly, *Tulane Drama Review*), *Theatre Arts* (1939–64), and *Theatre Quarterly* (1971–81), contain important reportorial, critical, and philosophical writing on theatre as both an artistic and a social expression.

(N.Ch./Ed.)

Directing: Many of the most useful guides to directing are biographical in nature, or they document productions of individual directors. A good, if partial, overview of the development of directing from the time of the Meiningen Players is EDWARD BRAUN, *The Director and the Stage: From Naturalism to Grotowski* (1982). *Peter Hall's Diaries: The Story of a Dramatic Battle,* edited by JOHN GOODWIN (1983), presents an intensely personal picture of the role of the artistic director of the National Theatre of Great Britain; HAROLD CLURMAN, *On Directing* (1972), is a personal testament to the practical details of the discipline by one of America's most important directors; and *A Casebook on Harold Pinter's The Homecoming,* edited by JOHN LAHR and ANTHEA LAHR (1971), documents the direction, design, intention, and reception of one of Pinter's most important plays. JIM HILEY, *Theatre at Work: The Story of the National Theatre's Production of Brecht's Galileo* (1981), is a complete documentation of a production by John Dexter. HARLEY GRANVILLE-BARKER, *Prefaces to Shakespeare* (1930; also available in later multivolume editions), is an analysis of the theatrical, as well as the obvious poetic, values to be discovered by anyone staging Shakespeare's plays. An important statement extending the Stanislavsky tradition to more experimental strains of the Soviet theatre and placing them in historical context is EDWARD BRAUN, *The Theatre of Meyerhold: Revolution and the Modern Stage* (1979, reissued 1986). JOHN WILLETT, *Brecht in Context: Comparative Approaches* (1984), is a thoughtful bringing together of the elements that shaped Brecht's ideas of theatre, from music and design to politics; RICHARD SCHECHNER, *Environmental Theater* (1973), is a fundamental statement by a radical American director and theorist; and *Twentieth Century Polish Theatre,* edited by BOHDAN DROZDOWSKI (1979), examines the work of several influential avant-gardists.

JOHN FERNALD, *Sense of Direction: The Director and His Actors* (1968), is a detailed examination of the way a director works with actors, including analyses of scenes from classic plays, showing how to approach them as a director; ELSIE FOGERTY, *Speech Craft: A Manual of Practice in English Speech* (1930), is a guide to what actors should be able to do and the mistakes they can make; TYRONE GUTHRIE, *A Life in the Theatre* (1959, reprinted 1985), presents personal revelations about directing and the theatre; G. WILSON KNIGHT, *Shakespearean Production,* new ed. (1963, reprinted 1981), is a first-class complement to Granville-Barker's *Prefaces;* RICHARD L. STERNE, *John Gielgud Directs Richard Burton in Hamlet* (1967), shows how a great Shakespearean directed this play over a period of four weeks' rehearsal. Other works include JOANN GREEN, *The Small Theatre Handbook: A Guide to Management and Production* (1981); ANDREW MCCALLUM, *Fun with Stagecraft* (1981); and ANN PASTERNAK SLATER, *Shakespeare, the Director* (1982).

(J.B.F./N.Ch.)

Acting: Although the literature on actors and acting is overwhelming, most of it is of little informational value. The best anthology, with useful notes and bibliography, is TOBY COLE and HELEN KRICH CHINOY (eds.), *Actors on Acting: The Theories, Techniques, and Practices of the Great Actors of All Times as Told in Their Own Words,* rev. ed. (1970). The most valuable individual statements are those of Luigi Riccoboni, F.J. Talma, and William Gillette; some of these are reprinted completely in *Papers on Acting,* edited by BRANDER MATTHEWS (1958), which also includes the polemic between Henry Irving and C. Coquelin. A useful introduction to the literature is EDWIN DUERR, *The Length and Depth of Acting* (1962), though flawed by the inability to relate theory to practice.

Basic to modern understanding are the above-mentioned works of Stanislavsky, as well as his *Building a Character* (1949, reissued 1979), and *Creating a Role* (1961, reissued 1981), English trans. edited and abridged by ELIZABETH REYNOLDS HAPGOOD. *Stanislavski's Legacy: A Collection of Comments on a Variety of Aspects of an Actor's Art and Life,* rev. and expanded ed., edited and translated by ELIZABETH REYNOLDS HAPGOOD (1968, reissued 1971), collects further fragments of his thoughts on acting and its critics, as well as his memories of Anton Chekhov. Also useful are ROBERT LEWIS, *Method or Madness?* (1958); LEE STRASBERG, "Acting and the Training of the Actor," in JOHN GASSNER, *Producing the Play,* rev. ed. (1953); ROBERT HETHMON (ed.), *Strasberg at the Actors Studio* (1965); RICHARD BOLESLAVSKI, *Acting: The First Six Lessons* (1933, reprinted 1980); and JEAN BENEDETTI, *Stanislavski, an Introduction* (1982). For a proper appreciation of Stanislavsky's approach, the work of his pupil Yevgeny Vakhtangov is essential, a brilliant description of which is in NIKOLAI GORCHAKOV, *The Vakhtangov School of Stage Art* (1959?; originally published in Russian, 1957). Contributions on acting that add dimensions to the study of the art come from JOSEPH CHAIKIN, *The Presence of the Actor* (1972, reprinted 1980); CHARLES MAROWITZ, *The Act of Being* (1978); MICHEL SAINT-DENIS, *Theatre: The Rediscovery of Style* (1960); VIOLA SPOLIN, *Improvisation for the Theater* (1963, reissued 1983); JOHN HODGSON and ERNEST RICHARDS, *Improvisation,* new rev. ed. (1974, reprinted 1979); and MICHAEL CHEKHOV, *To the Actor: On the Technique of Acting* (1953, reissued 1985).

Essential texts on Oriental theatre include J. THOMAS RIMER and MASAKAZU YAMAZAKI (trans.), *On the Art of the No Drama: The Major Treatises of Zeami* (1984); and JISHO HACHIMONJIYA, *The Actors' Analects,* edited and translated by CHARLES J. DUNN and BUNZO TORIGOE (1969), a collection of "advice and notes" by Kabuki actors of the 17th century. Modern Japanese ideas are explored in SUZUKI TADASHI, *The Way of Acting,* trans. from Japanese (1986). British acting tradition is analyzed in ANTONY SHER, *Year of the King: An Actor's Diary and Sketchbook* (1985), a revealing memoir of his creation of the role of Richard III for the Royal Shakespeare Company; SIMON CALLOW, *Being an Actor* (1984); and LAURENCE OLIVIER, *On Acting* (1986), a book on craft.

No history of acting can be written without a knowledge of what acting consists of and the creative processes involved. German students have in specialized studies and dissertations tried to formulate methods for studying the actor's work by examining critical descriptions, stage directions, and iconographical material. A bibliography is available in HANS KNUDSEN, *Methodik der Theaterwissenschaft* (1971).

(Le.S./N.Ch.)

The History of Western Theatre

Western theatre encompasses a vast range of styles, genres, themes, and functions. It also includes diverse methods of acting, directing, and production. This article reviews the origins and development of the various traditions of the Western theatre, with attention given to each of these elements. The significant theatrical traditions of non-Western cultures are covered in AFRICAN ARTS: *Performing arts;* EAST ASIAN ARTS: *Dance and theatre;* SOUTH ASIAN ARTS: *Dance and theatre;* and SOUTHEAST ASIAN ARTS: *The performing arts.*

For a discussion of drama as a literary form, see LITERATURE, THE ART OF: *Drama,* and the articles on individual national literatures. For detailed information on the arts of theatrical performance and stagecraft, see THEATRE, THE ART OF THE and THEATRICAL PRODUCTION. (Ed.)

The article is divided into the following sections:

The origins of Western theatre

PRECLASSICAL ANTIQUITY

Ritual beginnings. Notwithstanding its great diversity of styles, forms, themes, and functions, the theatre of today has its roots in a basic need to give meaning to the workings of the universe. This suggests that theatre is a social art based on doubt and questioning. From earliest times, man has sought to understand the cycle of nature, the progression from birth to death, and the forces that drive him. Indeed, this understanding has been necessary to man's survival on Earth, particularly when his environment has become hostile or he has had to face natural cataclysms.

The lack of documentary evidence makes it impossible to determine exactly how theatre began, though it is generally believed to have evolved from religious rituals. But it is difficult to decide at which point ritual became theatre. Important clues as to the nature of theatre in prehistoric times can, however, be found by examining the many patterns of drama and ritual that exist throughout the world today, especially in primitive societies.

Nature worship. The most widely held theory about the origins of theatre is that it evolved from rituals created symbolically to act out natural events, thereby bringing them down to human scale and making the unknown more easily accessible. Individuals would express themselves through rhythmic movement using some kind of adornment to depersonalize the body. The earliest known evidence of this is in the cave paintings and engravings at Les Trois Frères in southern France. Dating from the Late Paleolithic Period (about 40,000–10,000 BC), these ancient manifestations of art depict half-human, half-animal figures in animated poses. The figures appear to be dancers wearing the heads and skins of animals, suggesting the early use of mask and costume. Certainly the mask has been one of the most potent means of transcending one's own being or of representing other planes of existence, and in many parts of the world it holds great power and fascination to this day.

The natural elements were given personalities, which were in turn abstracted as spirits and gods. By wearing masks and moving in certain patterns, individuals could impersonate these deities. Sacred dances were performed to influence the course of nature—to bring rain, to facilitate a good harvest or a hunt, and to drive out evil. But one of the most important patterns was the enactment of the cycle of the seasons, dramatized by a battle in which winter gave way to spring. A year-king figure was ritually killed and supplanted by a new king. At first this was probably a human sacrifice of propitiation; later the killing was mimed. In a further development of this theme, the two kings were reduced to a single figure who underwent a process of repeated death and resurrection. This interpretation is used to explain the mock battles in such continuing folk traditions as the European mummers plays or the multiple deaths and rebirths of such figures as the Padstow Horse in Cornwall, England.

Shamanism. A second theory proposes that theatre evolved from shamanistic rituals that manifested to the audience a supernatural presence, as opposed to giving a symbolic representation of it. In this case the shaman, as actor/priest, was able to put himself into a trance and become a medium with the other world. He was believed to travel in the spirit world or be actually possessed by spirits. One of the main activities of shamanism, which is still practiced today, is the exorcism of evil spirits, and this can often involve trance dances in which the shaman performs acrobatics, juggling, or vigorous dancing for long periods, demanding a facility and stamina that would not normally be possible. Fire-walking, fire-eating, and other acts of apparent self-torture, performed while in a trance, are taken as further demonstrations of the supernatural. They represent the opposite pole from illusionism, in which such acts are achieved by trickery. Sometimes puppets are used by shamans as manifestations of supernatural forces in the giving of divinations or oracles. Masks also are an important part of shamanism: it is believed that by putting on a mask the dancer becomes possessed by the spirit represented and takes on the functions of that spirit. The use of body paint and elaborate costumes helps further in the personification of the spirit or demon.

The demon play

These ritual elements gave rise to an archetypal genre known as the demon play, a primitive dance drama in which the force of good exorcises the force of evil. The demon play is still performed in various guises in parts of Asia. An interesting component, which also occurs in later Western theatre, is the use of clowns—often deformed—to parody the more serious figures.

The residue of both functions—impersonator of natural forces and medium with the other world—can be detected in the role of the Western actor today. Shamanism emphasizes the special skills that actors have traditionally developed and that set them apart from the rest of society. It also shows the way the actor's techniques can help to transport imaginatively the audience beyond the actual space where the performance takes place. The "nature worship" theory expresses the idea that disguise is one of the fundamental aspects of the actor's art. Indeed, when an individual addressing a gathering modifies his manner, voice, or appearance, the event becomes theatrical rather than actual. This also conforms to Aristotle's definition of theatre as "an imitation of an action"; *i.e.,* not the action itself. Shamanism, on the other hand, is not an imitation but a direct manifestation.

In cultures where the ritual elements of theatre have remained intact—in South India and Bali, for example—the performances of plays and dance dramas have acquired an aura of deep respect and almost awesome power over their audience. However, where the ritual has continued in empty form long after the full significance of its content has been lost, as in modern performances of mummers plays or the Padstow Horse, it becomes little more than a quaint entertainment. The development of Western theatre lies between these two extremes and polarizes into its two primary types of experience—tragedy and comedy.

ANCIENT EGYPT

In ancient Egypt, religious ritual moved toward a more explicitly theatrical enactment. The pantheon of animal-headed gods and the stories of the soul's journey after death into the other world provided rich material for ceremonies and rituals in which priests were thought to have impersonated the deities by wearing stylized masks and reciting hymns and prayers. Carvings depicting masked dancers, dated at 3500 BC, have been found in Egypt.

The so-called Pyramid Texts have been assembled from fragments of prayers found carved on the walls of royal tombs of the Old Kingdom (from *c.* 2686–*c.* 2160 BC). The most important of these involved the god Osiris. He was the subject of what was known as the Abydos passion play, a yearly ritual performed during the period of the Old Kingdom and until about AD 400. The Abydos passion play depicts the slaying of Osiris and his followers by his brother Seth, the enactment of which apparently resulted in many real deaths. The figure of Osiris, symbolically represented in the play, is then torn to pieces by Seth, after which his remains are gathered by his wife Isis and son Horus, who subsequently restore him to life. The play thus follows the pattern of birth, death, and resurrection, and it also echoes the cycle of the seasons.

The Abydos passion play

Ritual dramas like this were performed to ensure the fertility of women, cattle, and crops and to invest the spirit of the community and its leaders with vitality for the new year. Myths relating to Osiris and Horus were especially important because the pharaoh, while alive, was believed to be an incarnation of Horus, and, after his death, he was believed to be Osiris. By the time the Greek historian Herodotus saw the Abydos passion play on a visit to Egypt in 450 BC, he could record that there was also a tradition of popular drama that used comic elements (*e.g.,* Horus, born as a baby but growing to enormous size and developing a voracious appetite), though it still confined itself to religious themes.

Investigators have discovered another text preserved on papyrus scrolls. Known as the Book of the Dead (from about 1800 BC), it reads very much like an oratorio. Although there is no evidence that it was actually performed, the ritual is full of theatrical elements. It describes the journey of the soul, brought after death by the jackal-headed god Anubis into the Hall of Truth, where the dead man's heart is weighed against a feather. If the heart, made light by goodness, does not outweigh the feather, then the soul is brought before Osiris and granted immortality.

ANCIENT GREECE

Dramatic genres. The first time theatre truly freed itself from religious ritual to become an art form was in Greece in the 6th century BC when the dithyramb was developed. This was a form of choral song chanted at festivals in honour of Dionysus, the god of wine, fruitfulness, and vegetation. Originally, it celebrated his rejuvenation of the earth; later, it drew on Homeric legends for its subject matter. According to Greek tradition, the actor and playwright Thespis invented the drama when he augmented the chorus of the dithyramb with a single actor who wore masks to portray several different characters. With the possibility of dialogue between the actor and the chorus, more complex themes and modes of storytelling could be developed. In 534 BC, at Athens' first dramatic festival, one of Thespis' tragedies won the prize. (Derived from the Greek *tragos,* meaning "goat," the term *tragedy* may have referred to a goat as the prize or as an animal sacrifice made at the festival.) Thereafter, tragedies were performed annually as part of the festival of Dionysus.

The tragedies of Aeschylus

The earliest surviving texts of plays are seven tragedies by Aeschylus dating from the first half of the 5th century BC. Adding a second actor and reducing the chorus from 50 to 12, Aeschylus laid the foundation for an aesthetics of drama that was to influence subsequent plays for well over 2,000 years. Tragedy, it was considered, should deal with illustrious figures and significant events. The plays, which were based on legends or remote history (though given the appearance of truth), were interpreted so as to convey some religious, moral, or political meaning. The entire cosmos was depicted in the drama, represented on a vertical structure: above was the seat of the gods, below was the place of exile and punishment, and in the middle was the flat circle of the Earth, represented by the circular stage, where the action unfolded.

The universal scale of Greek drama was reflected in one of its most characteristic features, the interaction between chorus and protagonist. The function of the chorus was to generalize the particular events by observing and interpreting the action of the play as a kind of ideal spectator.

It provided, as it were, the social background, which in turn gave resonance to the actions of the main characters. Sometimes the chorus would have a particular point of view (as in *Bacchae,* where it represents the followers of Bacchus), while at other times it could be the mouthpiece of the poet. Long speeches and songs made up much of the plays, though these were made more dramatic by the dancing of the chorus. The visual aspect of Greek tragedy was very important, a fact that is easily forgotten as only the words survive.

Sophocles and Euripides

The conventions Aeschylus developed were refined by Sophocles, who brought the chorus up to 15 and added a third actor, thereby making possible a much larger number of characters. Euripides, in his turn, brought greater realism to characterization and strengthened dramatic action by reducing the role of the chorus. The dramatic unities of time, place, and action were usually observed in Greek tragedy by attempting to make the action complete in itself, without superfluities, within a single circuit of the Sun, and in one location. The lack of scene change and the limited number of actors available meant that much of the action, particularly murders and other deaths, took place offstage.

In time, the masks worn by the actors and chorus became more expressive, and their conventionalized representation of character types (old king, young king, old nurse, etc.) meant that each character was instantly recognizable when he entered. The masks also helped to make the portrayal of female characters by male actors more plausible, as well as to make the facial features clearly discernible by the large audience.

The principle occasion for drama was the Great Dionysia (or City Dionysia), a spring festival devoted mainly to tragedy. The *archon,* a city official, chose the poets who were allowed to compete, and for each of them there was a *choregos,* a wealthy man who as part of his civic duties would pay for and organize the production. The actors were paid by the state. Each poet was required to offer three tragedies and a satyr play (a bawdy comic comment on the main theme of the tragedies). The tragedies could be separate plays on a linked theme or a trilogy on one theme. The only surviving complete trilogy is Aeschylus' *Oresteia.* The poet directed his plays, composed the music, and arranged the dances. In the early tragedies, he was also the main actor.

Comedy (from Greek *kōmos,* meaning "revel") was presented competitively in Athens from 486 BC at the Lenaea winter festival, though it fused much earlier traditions of popular entertainment, mime, phallic rites, and revelry in honour of Dionysus. Ancient shamanistic ceremonies also may have influenced its development.

Old Comedy

Old Comedy, of which Aristophanes was the chief exponent, was highly satirical. It was characterized by wildly imaginative material (in which the chorus might represent birds, frogs, wasps, or clouds) that was blended with a grotesque, vulgar, and witty tone, which could still accommodate poetry of great lyrical beauty. The bawdiness of the plays was emphasized by the actors' costumes, which featured jerkins with padded stomachs and large phalli. As in tragedy, masks were worn, though exaggerated for comic effect.

With the decline of tragedy after Euripides' death in 406 BC and the defeat of Athens in 404 BC, comedy increased in popularity.

New Comedy

It began to evolve through the transitional Middle Comedy to the style known as New Comedy, established about 320 BC during the time of Alexander the Great. Only fragments by one writer, Menander, survive from this period, but they indicate a swing away from mythological subjects toward a comedy of manners, concentrating as they do on the erotic adventures of young Athenians and centring on urban family life. Gone were the boisterousness, the religious influence, and the long choruses of the earlier drama. The new, gentler style was reflected in the use of more realistic costumes and masks and in the increasing use of scenery.

The theatre. The outdoor setting for performances of Greek drama traditionally comprised three areas: a large circular dancing floor (*orchēstra* in Greek) on which the action took place and in the centre of which was an altar to Dionysus; behind this, a scene-building and dressing room (*skēne* in Greek, whence "scene"), a low architectural facade to which painted scenery could be fitted, sometimes on revolving panels (*periaktoi*); and around the *orchēstra,* a semicircular auditorium cut into a hillside and fitted initially with wooden benches and later with stone or marble seats. The steep rake and layout of the auditorium enabled audiences of from 10,000 to 20,000 to sit in reasonable proximity to the players. They also enhanced the acoustics. An important stage device used in tragedy during the 5th century BC was the crane (*mēchanē*), which served to fly in the gods (*deus ex machina*) at the end of the play.

ROME

If the quality of theatre is reflected in the values of the civilization out of which it grows, then this is vividly illustrated by the fate of theatre in Roman times. Suffering from vulgarized public taste and a complete lack of originality, nearly all of the Roman plays were imitations or loose translations of Greek dramas, even to the extent of their being performed in Greek costume. Eventually, after 400 years of competing with chariot races, gladiatorial fights to the death, and the spectacle of criminals and Christians being torn apart by wild animals, theatre came to an apparent end.

Several factors must be taken into account in explaining why this happened, but perhaps the main reason lay in the political cynicism with which Roman authorities used circuses and public games, at which theatrical performances took place, to divert the public from economic and political dissatisfaction. The number of official festivals proliferated. In 240 BC, when drama was first included, the games lasted less than a week. By the 1st century AD there were 60 days of games throughout the year, and 300 years after that, 175 days were devoted to games, with plays being performed on 100 of them. Most of these festivals were secular, and theatre soon lost its close ties with religious ritual, degenerating into theatricality and crude spectacle for its own sake.

Native traditions. In spite of the lack of originality shown by dramatists, there were in Italy a number of native comic traditions that helped to shape the style of Roman comedy. The Fescennine verses (*fescennia locatio*) were bawdy, improvised exchanges sung by clowns at local harvest festivals and marriage ceremonies. These are thought to have combined with a tradition of performances by masked dancers and musicians from Etruria to form *saturae,* medleys consisting of jests, slapstick, and songs. The historian Livy says that in 364 BC these Etruscan players were summoned to Rome at a time of pestilence to appease the gods with their dancing and music.

Phlyax plays

From the areas of southern Italy and Sicily settled by the Greeks came the *phlyax* plays in the 4th century BC. Named for the Phlyakes (literally "Gossip Players"), these were burlesques and travesties of mythology and daily life and probably improvised. They were performed on a raised wooden stage with an upper gallery, and the actors wore grotesque costumes and masks similar to those of the Greek Old Comedy. Acrobatics and farcical scenes were a major ingredient of the *phlyax.* The Oscan inhabitants of Campania, in the Neapolitan region of Italy, also had a long tradition of farces, parodies, and political satires influenced by Greek models, which became popular in Rome during the 3rd century BC. This genre was known as *fabula Atellana* ("Atellan play," Atella being the name of a Campanian town). The significance of the *fabula Atellana* is that it introduced a set of stock characters, such as Maccus and Bucco, which were thought to be the direct ancestors of many of the Italian commedia dell'arte characters. The actors wore masks, improvised their dialogue, and worked slapstick routines and other buffoonery into the plots.

Imitation of Greek models. In the literary theatre, plot invention and characters were largely taken from Greek plays. Livius Andronicus, a Greek living in Rome, was the first to adapt Greek plays (in 240 BC), and his example was followed in 235 BC by the poet Gnaeus Naevius, a native of Campania. Naevius can be regarded as the first native Italian playwright, and the genre of comedies he founded was called *fabula palliata* ("play in Greek dress"). His less successful tragedies on Roman history were known as *fabulae praetextae* ("plays in the Roman toga"). Naevius' attempts at satire were audacious enough to land him in prison, which is probably why the noted poet Quintus Ennius, who followed him as a dramatist, limited himself to safe adaptations of Greek tragedies, mostly those of Euripides.

In the 2nd century BC, the two most important comic writers of the Roman theatre, Plautus and Terence (who came from lower class backgrounds), were both influenced by the New Comedy of the Greeks, and their plays retained the Greek setting and costume. Plautus, who had few literary pretensions but a sharp sense of wit and wordplay, blended the comic style of Menander with the *fabula Atellana* to produce vigorous farces about mistaken identities, sexual intrigues, and the mischief of household servants. His 21 surviving plays (of a total of about 130) were in turn to inspire playwrights for centuries to come, including Shakespeare. The braggart soldier, Miles Gloriosus, became one of Plautus' most imitated characters. Terence, who closely followed the style of Menander, aimed at a more discerning audience. His comedies are noted for their grace and delicacy, and they avoided the buffoonery that attracted Plautus.

The works of Plautus and Terence

Seeds of decay. The audience that followed Terence's plays was a small and exclusive one. From the start Roman theatre was dependent on popular taste in a way that had never been known in Greece. If a play failed to please, the manager of the festival was obliged to return part of the subsidy from public funds. Thus, even in Republican times, there was some anxiety to give the public what it wanted, and this proved to be the sensational, the spectacular, and the crude. Huge amphitheatres such as the Colosseum in Rome were built throughout the empire as evidence of the power and grandeur of Rome, but not of its artistic life and energy. The general public preferred boxers, beasts, and mock sea battles to drama. Actors and dramatists were tempted to adapt their style of presentation accordingly. Where it had once been subtle, the acting became coarse and declamatory. The actors took to wearing built-up shoes (*cothurni*) and bigger masks in order to make themselves appear larger than life. Some of the small number of tragedies that were staged were filled out with long processions of animals, gaudy costumes, and elaborate effects, all emphasizing the hollowness of both theatre and audience.

Theatre buildings themselves became grander in the 1st century BC. Erected on flat ground, the raked semicircular auditorium was a freestanding structure of great engineering complexity. With the elimination of the chorus from plays, the *orchēstra* was no longer needed other than as a space for important guests to sit, and the action took place on a wide, raised stage backed by an imposing architectural facade, the *scaenae frons,* which was often two or three stories high. A drop curtain at the front of the stage facilitated scene changes, and the audience could be protected from harsh sunlight by a huge awning. The comfort was unrivaled, but it came too late; what took place on these stages had become trivial and degrading. It is not surprising that serious people avoided the theatres and writers were alienated from them.

One reaction against the excesses of the theatre was the custom of reading tragedies aloud to select gatherings of intellectuals. It is thought that this was the purpose behind the tragedies of Seneca, a Stoic philosopher and statesman under the emperor Nero in the 1st century AD, for there is no record of any of his works having been produced. While his plays lack the craftsmanship of the Greeks, Seneca's importance lies in the fact that he was the principal medium through which Renaissance writers became acquainted with Greek tragedy. His division of the plays into five acts, his exaggeration of the melodramatic and violent aspects of the originals, his emphasis on rhetoric, and his preoccupation with the conflict between passion and reason helped to shape the Elizabethan drama and French Neoclassical tragedy that followed more than a millennium later.

The tragedies of Seneca

Mime and pantomime. After Seneca, serious dramatic literature in Rome virtually ceased, and the newly erected stone theatres were taken over by mime (Latin *mimus*) and pantomime (*pantomimus*) as the level of public taste steadily fell. Pantomime grew out of the wreckage of tragedy as a kind of burlesque ballet in which a chorus chanted the story to musical accompaniment, while a solo actor used mime, gesture, and dance to portray the various characters in a succession of masks. Particular emphasis was placed on the erotic elements of the story.

Of more interest is the mime, which was derived from the Greek mime traditions and the *fabula Atellana.* By the 2nd century BC, it had a large following in Rome. Mime was characterized by great diversity: sometimes the shows were tragicomic dramas, but most often they were indecent burlesques on the gods in which female performers also took part. They featured acrobatics, songs, and slapstick routines. Companies ranged from itinerant groups of six players to the troupe of 60 actors recorded in AD 169. Although the performers were highly skilled (some of them achieved widespread fame), mime contented itself with easy targets, pandering to the taste of the emperor. By the time of the Christian persecutions under Nero and Domitian, mimes were used to ridicule the Christian faith on stage. In *Centunculus,* for example, a clown was baptized and martyred, being grotesquely crucified in a way calculated to burlesque his faith. Sometimes the shows were spiced with sexual acts and real executions on stage. At the end of the Roman era, mime actors were performing throughout the empire, but after the triumph of Christianity the theatre of the day was abominated by the Church Fathers as an art so debased as to have lost any relevance to the general good of society. In the 5th century all performers of mime were excommunicated, and in the following century the theatres were closed.

Diversity of mime performances

The old Roman Empire was Christianized and became divided in two: one based in Rome, the other in Constantinople (modern Istanbul). There being no other outlet for the expression of the supernatural and the cycle of the seasons, semitheatrical religious festivals, magnificent rituals, and processions became once more the principal means of community celebration. These were particularly elaborate in the Byzantine Church, centred in Constantinople. Meanwhile the mimes dispersed. Though the church did its best to prohibit them through the Middle Ages, they managed to carry on their intriguing art illicitly, finding audiences wherever they could. Mime, therefore, preserves the only dramatic continuity between the classical world and modern Europe. The texts and theoretical treatises of the classical world were all to lie largely unused for more than 900 years. The failure of the Roman theatre was that it had lost its seriousness of purpose; the surviving plays were comparatively tired and unimaginative imitations that did not carry the dramatic forms forward to create an important theatrical movement. Yet, in what survived, sufficient elements were present to stimulate a new and powerful theatre during the Renaissance.

Medieval theatre

POPULAR TRADITIONS AND SECULAR THEATRE

During the Middle Ages, theatre began a new cycle of development that strangely paralleled the emergence of the theatre from ritual activity in the early Greek period. Whereas the Greek theatre had grown out of Dionysian worship, the medieval theatre originated as an expression of the Christian religion. The two cycles would eventually merge during the Renaissance, but for centuries before that the theatre was left to grope its way blindly through the Dark Ages. It meant a completely fresh start. The decadence of what remained of the Roman theatre had so offended the upright barbarian invaders, who had no sophisticated culture of their own with which to replace it, that their reaction was to try to prohibit it. Their efforts, however, were not wholly successful.

Between the classical and the medieval periods, theatre was kept alive by the slenderest of threads—the popular entertainers who had dispersed to wander, alone or in small groups, throughout Europe. These were the mimes, acrobats, dancers, animal trainers, jugglers, wrestlers, minstrels, and storytellers who preserved vital skills that survive in the theatre today. They also brought a duality to theatre that still exists: popular theatre and the literary theatre were to grow side by side, feeding off and nourishing each other. During the late Middle Ages these popular entertainers found a more secure place at royal courts and in the households of the nobility, where they acted, sang, and played music at their masters' festivities. The written texts that they developed for performance were, especially in France, literate and often sharply satirical.

Folk play

A further, though minor, influence on the development of theatre was the folk play. This dramatic form had two main sources. One was the symbolic ritual dramas of the seasons such as the Plow Monday play (English Midlands), in which a plow was decorated and pulled around the village (thought to have originally been a fertility god carried around the fields on a plow), or the European folk drama of the Wild Man of the Woods, in which a figure covered with leaves, representing winter, was ritually hunted and "killed." The other source was the mimetic elements in dances held at village feasts. The Morris dance (probably Moorish in origin; from Spanish *morisco*), famed in England but also performed in medieval continental Europe, was strongly mimetic and had dramatic elements in its use of the fool or clown character. It can also be linked with ancient trance dances in its occasional use of the hobbyhorse. The various forms of sword dance found in Europe are another example.

Both ritual and mimetic dance came together in the mummers plays that emerged during the late Middle Ages. The essential elements were some kind of fight in which one of the combatants was killed and the revival of the fighter by a healer or doctor. This pattern also reflects the cycle of death and rebirth, which suggests that the origin of the plays may be much older. Later versions of the mummers plays used the figure of St. George fighting a dragon, and they employed more dialogue to balance the action.

When Christianity spread through Europe, missionaries had great difficulty discouraging the wealth of local folk traditions that flourished in rural communities. Eventually, the reforming bishops decided that it was better to regulate than to prohibit them, so the Roman Catholic Church began incorporating pagan festivals into its own liturgical calendar and remythologizing local rituals. The spring cycle of festivities centring on fertility rituals and the rebirth of summer was adapted to the Christian version of death and resurrection, while Christmas absorbed celebrations around the winter solstice such as the Saturnalia and the Yule Fest, the Teutonic New Year celebration. Christian churches were built on the sites of pagan temples, and folk plays were even organized as part of the village church activities.

Typical of this tolerance was the Feast of Fools, first recorded in France at the end of the 12th century, in which the lower clergy took over the church building, wearing grotesque masks, dressing as women or minstrels, electing a mock bishop, censing with stinking smoke by burning the soles of old shoes, and generally burlesquing the mass. The inversion of status that took place in the Feast of Fools was characteristic of the folk festivals held at the time of carnival (just before the fasting of Lent) and the New Year's Saturnalia. Most of these centred on a mock king, or Lord of Misrule, who guided the follies.

Folk theatre was not a literary genre; its prime concern was to fulfill a communal function in the village. However, its significance in the development of theatre was that, being a style with which everyone was familiar, it could provide a rich stimulus for the more serious theatre that supplanted it. Many farcical scenes from folk dramas were included as interludes in the later religious plays, making them more vigorous and balancing entertainment with didacticism. Divorced from their validating mythology by the domination of Christian myths, the pagan celebrations soon began to lose their primary function, and eventually their true meaning was forgotten.

A consequence of the Roman Catholic Church's choice of Latin as the language of the liturgy was that classical texts continued to be read, and Terence, whose moral tone made him the least offensive of the Roman dramatists, acquired new popularity among a small scholarly elite.

The plays of Hrosvitha of Gandersheim

During the 10th century, at a convent in Gandersheim, Ger., a nun called Hrosvitha wrote six short plays modeled on Terence's style but in modified and Christianized form so as not to corrupt the sisters. Terence's bawds, slaves, and foolish old men were replaced by chaste Christian maids, honest men, and constant Christian martyrs. The plays were never publicly performed, though they may have been privately staged in the convent.

LITURGICAL DRAMA

The tradition of medieval religious theatre stems directly from the mass itself, a complex ritual containing many theatrical elements in its function as a visible reflection of the invisible world. Because it was believed that harmony expressed religious values, an attempt was made from the 9th century to increase the musical effectiveness of the plainsong of the Roman Catholic Church by developing antiphonal singing in which the choir was divided into two parts. From this came the trope, a musical addition or embellishment to certain parts of the liturgy, as, for example, to the final syllable of the Alleluia.

It was in the trope of the Easter mass, recorded in a 10th-century manuscript from the Monastery of St. Gall in Switzerland, that the union of action, impersonation, and dialogue originated. Taken from various sources in the Bible, it dramatizes the visit of the three Marys to the tomb where Christ's body had been buried. They find the sepulchre empty and an angel guarding it. One section of the choir, representing the angel, asks, "Quem quaeritis?" ("Whom do you seek?"), to which the other half responds, and a short dialogue follows. In later versions the angel was represented by the priest in white robes and the Marys by three choirboys. Directions were added, dictating particular actions and precisely how the performers should move. In turn, a spice merchant (the first secular character, who was strikingly similar to the doctor figure of mummers plays and folk dramas) was added to haggle with the three Marys about the price of the ointment. The *Quem quaeritis?* soon spread throughout Europe (more than 400 versions survive), and by the end of the 10th century it had become a self-contained liturgical drama.

During the 11th and 12th centuries, the Nativity, along with other biblical themes, received similar treatment. To accommodate these dramas, the playing areas were extended from the altar to various locations throughout the church. Sometimes scenes were suggested by raised platforms, and machinery was developed to facilitate effects, such as angels descending. The clergy's intention of making the key episodes of the liturgy as vivid and accessible as possible to uneducated congregations was so successfully realized that by the end of the 12th century the plays incorporated spoken dialogue, partly in the vernacular, and were moved outside in front of the church to be performed independently of the liturgical service. One of the first such plays was *Adam,* performed before a French cathedral about 1170.

MYSTERY CYCLES

Use of the vernacular

Once the theatre had been moved outside the church, production of the plays was gradually taken over by the laity, and performances were given entirely in the vernacular. (Liturgical dramas, however, continued to be presented inside the church until the 16th century.) The number of short plays proliferated until they were organized into great cycles covering the whole biblical story from the creation to the Last Judgment, though centring on the Passion and designed to express the humanity as well as the divinity of Christ. In France they become known as *mystères* (from Latin *ministerium,* "service"), in Italy as *sacre rappresentazioni,* in Spain as *autos sacramentales,* in Germany as *Mysterienspielen,* and in England as mystery plays (later mystery cycles). Comprising up to 50 short plays, these cycles were sometimes performed over two or three days. In England the cycles of York, Wakefield, Coventry, and Chester survive, but on the Continent there are many more. As the presentation of these plays grew more elaborate, they became a civic affair, and special organizations took over their staging; *e.g.,* in France it was the *confréries,* while in England, the trade guilds.

Each guild would take responsibility for a particular play, usually related to its work: the building of Noah's ark, for example, would be staged by the shipwrights. Church vestments were replaced by appropriate contemporary costumes, and, because many of the plays called for complex and realistic effects—*e.g.,* scenes of torture and execution or appearances from Hell's mouth—sophisticated properties and machinery were devised to achieve them.

Initially, in the 12th century, the cycles were presented on a series of decorated platforms known as houses or mansions, following the type of layout established in the liturgical drama, with each representing a particular location. These mansions were usually arranged in a straight line or a semicircle with the audience in front. In Italy stages were placed around a city square with the spectators in the centre. An alternative presentation, used in England from the 14th century (and later in Spain), was processional staging on pageant wagons. This is thought to have grown out of the elaborate Corpus Christi processions (from 1311), in which decorated carts displaying religious tableaux were used. The tradition of tournaments and the pageantry set up for royal entries also had an influence. Each play was mounted on a "pageant," or cart, often built and decorated to suggest the scene depicted. These mobile stages were paraded around the town, stopping at various stations where the actors repeated their performance in front of a group of spectators, who then waited for the next cart to appear.

Although both audience and players were united by a common faith strong enough for the actors to rehearse months in advance and for the spectators to stand all day watching the plays, the factor of entertainment became increasingly important. This was, the religious theme notwithstanding, secular theatre. It was the comic characters, especially the devils, who were most popular, and it was here that there may have been an element of professionalism, with the minstrels and jongleurs adding their own skills and brand of humour. Furthermore, once the mystery cycles had abandoned the uniformity of Latin, national differences became accentuated when local customs, idioms, and folk traditions were incorporated into the plays. In England the juxtaposition of solemnity and humour helped to flavour the spirit of the great Elizabethan theatre that was to follow.

MORALITY PLAYS

After the earthy humour and simple devotion of the mystery cycles, the morality plays that appeared during the 15th century show theatre taking what at first seems to be a step backward. These plays, however, reflect the darker worldview of a people that had experienced recurrent plagues and had begun to regard human destiny as "worm's meat," where the skeleton figure of death was a potent emblem constantly alluded to in sermons. Morality plays were virtually sermons dramatized through allegory. They portrayed the span of human life in abstract terms, with Mankind or Humanum Genus setting out on a pilgrimage in which he encountered a whole range of vices and virtues such as Ignorance, Humility, and the Seven Deadly Sins who contended for possession of his soul. The principal themes were the choice between good and evil, the transitory nature of life, and the immediacy of death, all of which reflect a medieval preoccupation with the conflict between the spirit and the flesh. Such concerns were particularly relevant at a time when trade and finance were rapidly expanding, offering merchants the prospect of great personal wealth and a life of material luxury.

The use of allegory

Morality plays probably originated in England, the earliest known text being *The Castell of Perseverance* (*c.* 1405–25). However, one of the best of the genre, *Everyman,* began in the Netherlands, and moralities were frequently performed in France. Performances initially took place in churches, then on simple outdoor stages, though without the visual extravagance that the mystery cycles demanded. Although the plots were stereotyped and the abstract characters allowed little scope for development, morality plays achieved considerable sophistication—they were intended for an educated, middle-class audience—and moved a long way toward secularization, thus forming a significant link between the medieval and the modern theatres. Nevertheless, in the 16th century, at the height of their aesthetic achievement, morality plays were suppressed in England, primarily because religious drama was beginning to become an instrument of politico-religious propaganda under successive Roman Catholic and Protestant governments.

INTERLUDES

As a development of the morality play that drew on the legacy of the minstrel, interludes (from Latin *interludium*) were performed in Europe by small companies of professional actors during the 15th and 16th centuries. The term covers a wide range of entertainment, from simple farces performed on small stages in public places to dramatic sketches performed at banquets in the halls of the nobility. In both cases the plays were purely secular and more concerned with ideas than with morals. They were called *Fastnachtsspiele* in Germany and *kluchtspelen* in the Netherlands; they were also performed in Italy and Spain, but most interludes came from France, where they were known as *soties,* and from England. These pieces usually dealt with the antics of foolish or cunning peasants, exploring the relationship between master and servant or husband and wife. In England the move toward professionalism was accelerated by a law that subjected "all players of farces, minstrels and other entertainers" to be whipped if they did not belong to a member of the nobility.

Secular character of the interludes

The Renaissance

CLASSICAL REVIVAL

By the early 15th century, artists in Italy were becoming increasingly aware that, while Rome had once been the centre of the Western world, its power and prestige had steadily declined since the invading Germanic tribes broke up the empire. The belief that art, science, and scholarship had flourished during the classical period stimulated the desire for a revival of the values of that period. Both architecture and painting found new inspiration in Greek and Roman models, and the discovery of perspective added new possibilities, which in turn were to have a profound effect on stage scenery. At the same time classical literature was reexamined: new texts were found and old ones edited. The capture of Constantinople by the Turks in 1453 resulted in an exodus of Greek scholars to Italy, and they brought with them their knowledge of Greek literature.

The invention in Europe of the printing press made the new learning more widely accessible and revolutionized the whole educational system. Increased commerce encouraged exploration, and the discovery of the Americas by Columbus in 1492 brought about a new outlook on the world. Whereas learning had traditionally been sought in the seclusion of monasteries, the new learning of the Renaissance was more widespread and dynamic. Scholars were not satisfied with merely understanding the ideals of antiquity; they wanted to re-create them. This also gave man new dignity and confidence. The world was regarded not as something to be overcome in order to have a life in the next world, but as something to be enjoyed. The spirit of the Renaissance was epitomized in the words of the Greek philosopher Protagoras: "Man is the measure of all things." Even though this humanist view sometimes clashed with Christian doctrines, the papacy reached, if somewhat reluctantly, a modus vivendi with the new learning. Indeed, the Vatican Library amassed works of classical culture from all over the Christian world. The popes and the wealthy families of Italy became patrons of the arts, gathering scholars and artists in their courts.

THE RENAISSANCE STAGE

The printed Latin texts of Terence, Plautus, and Seneca were widely read. By the end of the 15th century attempts were made to stage their works, first in Rome, sponsored by Pomponius Laetus, and then in Ferrara. At first the stages resembled classicized versions of the mansions used for mystery plays, though compressed onto a single raised stage with curtained entrances between pillars to represent various houses. Later efforts concentrated on re-creating the form of the classical stage inside large halls.

One of the greatest influences on the development of theatre buildings in the Renaissance was the discovery in 1414 of *De architectura* of Vitruvius, a Roman architect of the 1st century. This 10-volume treatise contained valuable information on the scenery used for classical tragedy, comedy, and satyr plays, along with detailed descriptions of the Roman theatre with its auditorium, orchestra, and stage backed by the *scaenae frons*. Vitruvius' work, translated and published all over Europe, was provided with woodcuts showing ground plans and front elevations of classical stages. Various reconstructions of the Roman theatre were built, culminating in the beautiful Teatro Olimpico at Vicenza, designed by the Venetian architect Andrea Palladio and completed in 1585 by Vincenzo Scamozzi. It is Europe's oldest surviving indoor theatre. Palladio had created a magnificent *scaenae frons,* but Scamozzi added three-dimensional perspective vistas of street scenes behind the archways. It was this preoccupation with perspective that characterized future developments of the Renaissance stage and indeed the modern theatre, though the effects were usually achieved through painted backdrops and wings. Sebastiano Serlio's influential *Second livre de la perspective* (1545; *The Second Book of Architecture*), generally referred to as "Architettura," outlined three basic stage settings, suggesting an impressive arrangement of palaces and temples for tragedy, complex street scenes for comedy, and idealized landscapes with trees and cottages for pastoral plays.

The impact of Vitruvius' work

MAJOR THEATRICAL STYLES, TENDENCIES, AND FORMS

Italian Neoclassicism. Ironically, while all the innovations seemed to originate in Italy and then spread through Europe, the plays that were first performed on the new stages were extremely dull. Far from liberating the creative mind, the classical ideals had only constricted it. Partly to blame was the adoption of the so-called Aristotelian unities of time, place, and action, which became, in the hands of theorists, a set of rules so rigid that they strangled drama by forcing it into a framework where the action had to take place in a single location in the space of a single day. At a time of expansion and change, such rules only created a disharmony between form and content and between the stage and the play. A further reason was that this theatre took place inside the palaces of isolated and parochial cities in the presence of a privileged elite. Cut off from the public, lifeless tragedies and limp comedies resorted to philosophical discourse as a substitute for the passion that was meanwhile animating the theatre in England and Spain.

Significantly, the bawdy comedies of Plautus provided inspiration for two of the most interesting dramatists of the Italian Renaissance in the early 16th century. Ludovico Ariosto, a poet at the court of Ferrara, was the first to break away from the strict imitation of classical models and produce a truly Italian flavour in his work. The second figure was Ruzzante (the stage name of Angelo Beolco), who acted in his own farces about rustic life written in the Paduan dialect. Through his use of everyday situations and distinctly Italian character types, Ruzzante introduced a more natural style of acting, drawn from life and observation of people.

The intermezzi

As a relief from the severity of classical plays, intermezzi were introduced between the acts as lighthearted and spectacular diversions, usually dealing with mythological subjects. These rapidly became more popular than the plays themselves and were often performed as independent entertainments at weddings and banquets in the courts of Italian princes. As the scenic aspects of the intermezzi grew more elaborate, changeable scenery was developed, as was complicated machinery with which to mobilize clouds, waves, and sea monsters. Five basic settings were established: heaven, hell, the countryside, the sea, and a city street or square.

Courtly entertainments. During the 15th and 16th centuries, some of Italy's finest painters and musicians were employed to organize entertainments at court. Leonardo da Vinci, who designed a revolving stage in 1490 (it was never built, however), arranged the settings, masks, and costumes of *Festa del Paradiso,* an entertainment given during the wedding celebrations for Lodovico Sforza, duke of Milan. Raphael also painted much admired stage settings. Equestrian ballets and triumphal processions were a spectacular feature requiring careful preparation, and they became the highlight of these displays of power and wealth. Princes, dukes, and monarchs were invited to such festivals and rode on horseback or in ornate carriages in processions of allegorical floats. Sometimes their entrances were choreographed as they passed under specially constructed triumphal arches or towers and open stages with *tableaux vivants.* In France the *entrées solennelles*—entrance processions of great pomposity—were developed to a peak of elaborate ceremonial display. Aquatic pageantry also became popular in the 17th century, with the monarch surrounded by a collection of ornate barges, sea monsters, scallop shells, and ships.

A popular new genre among the Italian nobility in the latter half of the 16th century was the pastoral. It was a sophisticated form of entertainment dramatizing classical themes in the romantic but highly artificial setting of an Arcadian landscape peopled with gentle nymphs, shepherds, magicians, and satyrs.

Opera. One of the most enduring products of the Renaissance theatre was the opera. It grew out of experiments by the Florentine Camerata at the end of the 16th century to revive Greek tragedy. The men who formed the Florentine Camerata believed that the Greeks had originally recited or chanted their plays to music, and in setting out to recreate these conditions, the Camerata used music to heighten the poetic qualities of the dialogue. Heavily influenced by the intermezzi that were currently in fashion, the first attempts were on mythological subjects (Daphne, Orpheus, etc.). The opera was an immediate success. The novelty impact of the music meant that the libretto diminished in importance. By 1607 Claudio Monteverdi had composed his masterpiece, *Orfeo,* which placed the emphasis squarely on music and established the basic form that European opera was to take for the next 300 years.

The Florentine Camerata

At first, opera was performed on special occasions intended to display the patron's status and wealth; thus it was politically important. Great care was lavished on the visual aspects of the opera, and the librettos gave ample opportunities for scene painters and stage engineers to exploit their new mastery of perspective. As the scenery became more opulent, so the shape of the theatre was altered to accommodate it. The proscenium arch was developed to frame the setting and facilitate changes of scenery, while the auditorium was extended to a horseshoe shape. The earliest example of this type of theatre was the Teatro Farnese in Parma (1618–28), the prototype of the modern opera house. From its exclusive beginnings, the appeal of opera broadened, and in 1637 the first opera house was opened to the general public in Venice. By this time, the form had also caught on in Vienna.

Commedia dell'arte. Around the mid-16th century, there emerged in Italy a lively tradition of popular theatre that fused many disparate elements into a vigorous style, which profoundly influenced the development of European theatre. This was the legendary commedia dell'arte ("theatre of the professionals"), a nonliterary tradition that centred on the actor, as distinguished from the commedia erudita, where the writer was preeminent. Although the precise origins of the commedia dell'arte are difficult to establish, its many similarities with the skills of the medieval jongleurs, who were themselves descendants of the Roman mimes, suggest that it may have been a reawakening of the *fabula Atellana,* stimulated and coloured by social conditions in Italy during the Renaissance.

In spite of its outwardly anarchic spirit, the commedia dell'arte was a highly disciplined art requiring both virtuosity and a strong sense of ensemble playing. Its special quality came from improvisation. Working from a scenario that outlined the plot, the actors would improvise their own dialogue, striving for a balance of words and actions. Acrobatics and singing were also used, as well as the *lazzi* (special rehearsed routines that could be inserted into

Importance of improvisation

the plays at convenient points to heighten the comedy). Because the actors stayed together in permanent companies and specialized in playing the same role for most of their professional lives, they achieved a degree of mastery that had been hitherto unknown on the Italian stage and that must have made the rest of the theatre seem all the more artificial. Another reason for the impact of the commedia dell'arte was that it heralded the first appearance in Italy of professional actresses (the best known being Isabella Andreini), though the female characters were never as sharply developed as their male counterparts. Most of the characters were defined by the leather half-masks they wore (another link with the theatre of antiquity), which made them instantly recognizable. They also spoke in the dialect of their different provinces. Characters such as Pantalone, the miserly Venetian merchant; Dottore Gratiano, the pedant from Bologna; or Arlecchino, the mischievous servant from Bergamo, began as satires on Italian "types" and became the archetypes of many of the favourite characters of 17th- and 18th-century European theatre.

From humble beginnings, setting up their stages in city squares, the better troupes—notably Gelosi, Confidenti, and Fedeli—performed in palaces and became internationally famous once they traveled abroad. The commedia dell'arte swept through Europe. It was particularly popular in France, where resident Italian troupes were established before the end of the 16th century. Local variations on the characters appeared in the 17th century. The cheeky servant Pedrolino became the melancholy Pierrot in France, while Pulcinella became Punch in England. By the 18th century the commedia dell'arte was a lost art, though its spirit lived on through the work of the dramatists it inspired, among whom were Molière (stage name of Jean-Baptiste Poquelin), Carlo Goldoni, and William Shakespeare.

Jesuit theatre and school drama. A reflection of the humanist tradition in Europe was the emergence of the school drama in the second half of the 16th century. This was an amateur movement in which Latin plays were performed as part of the curriculum. Soon after the Society of Jesus was founded in 1540 to combat the heresies of the Reformation, it was realized that theatre could be an excellent means of glorifying the Roman Catholic Church and showing the evils of free thought. Consequently, the school play became an important activity in the Jesuit colleges that were established all over the Continent. While retaining both the language and techniques of the classical writers, the Jesuit dramatists turned to biblical themes and the lives of the saints and martyrs for their subject matter. Since part of the educational purpose of this type of drama was to teach pupils how to behave and express themselves in accordance with the requirements of the upper classes, tragedies were preferred to comedies, because the latter were considered unsuitable in their levity and crudeness. In spite of its severity of tone, the Jesuit theatre flourished in the 16th and 17th centuries by adapting to local customs and turning the latest theatrical innovations to its own use. Thus music and singing were incorporated in the plays, which were eventually expanded to include some of the elaborate scenic effects used in contemporary opera. The Jesuit theatre produced no plays of lasting consequence, yet princes took part in its college performances and Roman Catholic emperors attended them. Also, some of the most important dramatists of the European theatre, including Pierre Corneille, Molière, and Goldoni, were educated in Jesuit schools and may have been influenced by their theatrical activities.

Subject matter of the school drama

Although the movement did not reach England for politico-religious reasons, school plays accounted for the first secular comedies in English during the first half of the 16th century—namely, *Ralph Roister Doister* and *Gammer Gurton's Needle.* And, in 1560, Elizabeth I decreed that the scholars of Westminster School should perform a Latin play every Christmas. This practice has endured until the present day, making it perhaps the longest continuous acting tradition in Europe.

Spain's Golden Age. Because the Reformation, which divided Europe in the early 16th century, had not affected Spain, the long tradition of religious drama continued there throughout the Renaissance in the form of *autos sacramentales.* Usually one-act allegories, these plays were performed as part of the Corpus Christi celebrations in which the king participated. As the prudent Spanish clergy had purged religious drama of those elements that laid it open to ridicule in other European countries, *autos* became a serious art form cultivated by some of the finest poets of the Spanish Golden Age.

Autos sacramentales

The vigour of the secular theatre was offset by a lack of permanent playhouses. In the early 16th century, the first professional companies, like that of Lope de Rueda, had to travel about as strolling players, carrying their own equipment with them. They were so poor that, in the words of Cervantes, "their whole baggage would go into a single sack." Lope de Rueda was noted for the lively use of colloquial speech in his short comic sketches known as *pasos.* These were performed between the acts of more serious dramas. Plays were sometimes presented in palace halls, but most often they were performed in *corrales,* where an improvised stage was set up at one end of the square formed by the walls of adjoining houses.

When the first permanent theatres were built, they were not patterned on the Italian model, but rather they incorporated features of the *corrale.* The audience stood in a rectangular courtyard (*patio*) or sat in galleries, with the women having to sit apart in a special gallery of their own. The stage stretched across one end of the square with an inner stage at the back. Very little scenery was used, though there were trapdoors in the floor and machinery above for "flying" people or objects. The theatre was open to the sky, but an awning could be drawn over the audience to provide protection against sunlight and rain. It was a stage well adapted for rhetoric and poetry, where the imagination of the audience could be stimulated. Furthermore, it was a theatre for all social classes. By the end of the 16th century, permanent theatres were established in Seville, Valencia, and Madrid, where two of the first were the Corral de la Cruz (1579) and the Corral del Príncipe (1582). In addition to the main play, programs included short comic sketches, musical interludes, ballads, and dances.

The strength of the Spanish theatre of the Golden Age was that, while embracing some of the Italian innovations in staging and acting (commedia dell'arte troupes exerted a strong influence in Spain from 1574), it was never restrained by the rules of Classicism. Instead, it developed a robust national style that was passionate, romantic, and lyrical and that could weave together comedy and tragedy in a way that was never possible in Italy or France. This style found rich expression in the work of Lope de Vega. His prodigious output of more than 1,000 plays, about 400 of which survive, gives an idea of the audience's insatiable demand for new works. Drawing on a wide variety of materials for tragedies, comedies, pastorals, histories, and the distinctly Spanish genre of *comedias de capa y espada* (cloak-and-dagger plays), Lope portrayed a rigid society divided into three estates: the king, the nobles, and the common people. Entertainment was his first concern, and his depiction of peasant characters, both comic and tragic, was particularly vivid.

The dramas of Lope de Vega and Calderón de la Barca

In the first half of the 17th century the Baroque style of theatre, with its elaborate scenery and stage machinery, was used to great advantage by Pedro Calderón de la Barca. Attached to the Spanish court, he was not under as much pressure as Lope to be prolifically inventive, yet he wrote nearly 200 plays. While lacking the sheer vigour of Lope's works, Calderón's plays are more refined and philosophical, even though many of his characters appear to be rigidly bound by the idea of the *pundonor* ("point of honour"). In later life, Calderón wrote many fine *autos sacramentales* and other plays on religious themes. The idea that "all the world is a stage" was expressed in *El gran teatro del mundo* (c. 1635; *The Great Theatre of the World*) through the hierarchical concept that every man plays his part before God. This theme was also reflected in Calderón's finest play, *La vida es sueño* (1635; *Life Is a Dream*).

Elizabethan and Jacobean theatre. In England the influence of the Italian Renaissance was weaker, but the theatre of the Elizabethan Age was all the stronger for it. Apart from the rediscovery of classical culture, the 16th century in England was a time for developing a new sense of national identity, necessitated by the establishment of a national church. Furthermore, because the English were more suspicious of Rome and the Latin tradition, there was less imitation of classical dramatic forms and an almost complete disregard for the rules that bound the theatre in France and Italy. England built on its own foundations by adapting the strong native tradition of medieval religious drama to serve a more secular purpose. When some of the continental innovations were blended with this cruder indigenous strain, a rich synthesis was produced. Consequently, the theatre that emerged was resonant, varied, and in touch with all segments of society. It included the high seriousness of morality plays, the sweep of chronicle histories, the fantasy of romantic comedies, and the irreverent fun of the interludes.

Basic characteristics

At the same time, the theatre had to contend with severe restrictions. The suppression of the festival of Corpus Christi in 1548 as a means of reinforcing the Protestant Church marked the rapid decline of morality plays and mystery cycles. Their forced descent into satirical propaganda mocking the Catholic faith polarized the audience and led to riots. By 1590, playwrights were prohibited from dramatizing religious issues and had to resort to history, mythology, allegory, or allusion in order to say anything about contemporary society. Flouting these restrictions meant imprisonment. Nevertheless, playwrights managed to argue highly explosive political topics. In Shakespeare's histories, for instance, the subject of kingship is thoroughly examined in all its implications: both the rightful but incompetent sovereign and the usurping but strong monarch are scrutinized—a most daring undertaking during the reign of Elizabeth I (1558–1603). The situation for actors was not helped by the hostile attitude of the City of London authorities, who regarded theatre as an immoral pastime to be discouraged rather than tolerated. Professional companies, however, were invited to perform at court from the beginning of the 16th century (though on a smaller scale than on the Continent), and public performances took place wherever a suitable space could be found—in large rooms of inns, in halls, or in quiet innyards enclosed on all sides with a temporary platform stage around which spectators could gather while others looked out from the windows above. But such makeshift conditions only retarded the development of the drama and kept it on an amateurish level.

The Elizabethan theatre. These conditions were considerably improved during Elizabeth's reign by the legitimizing in 1574 of regular weekday performances and the building of the first playhouse in 1576 by James Burbage. Called simply the Theatre, it was erected in London immediately outside the City boundary. Others followed, including the Curtain, the Rose, the Swan, and the Globe, where most of Shakespeare's plays were first staged. Just as the Spanish playhouse reproduced the features of the *corrale* it had grown out of, so the Elizabethan playhouse followed the pattern of the improvised innyard theatre. It was an enclosed circular structure containing two or three galleries with benches or stools and had an unroofed space in the middle where spectators could stand on three sides of the raised platform stage. Behind the stage was a wall with curtained doors and, above this, an actors' and musicians' gallery. Large numbers of people could be accommodated, and the price was kept low at between one penny and sixpence. This type of stage allowed for fluid movement and considerable intimacy between actors and audience, while its lack of scenery placed the emphasis firmly on the actor interpreting the playwright's words. Such sheer simplicity presented a superb challenge for the writer: the quality of both language and acting had to be good enough to hold the attention of the spectators and make them use their imaginations.

This challenge was quickly taken up by a generation of playwrights who could carry forward the established dramatic forms and test the possibilities of the new stage. Christopher Marlowe was the major innovator, developing a vigorous style of tragedy that was refined by his contemporary, William Shakespeare, who began writing for the theatre about 1590. At this time, professional companies operated under the patronage of a member of the nobility. In Shakespeare's company, the Chamberlain's Men (later renamed the King's Men), the actors owned their playhouse, prompt books, costumes, and properties, and they shared in the profits. Other companies paid rent to the patron and received salaries from him. There were very few rehearsals for a new play, and because the texts were not immediately printed (to avoid pirating by rival companies) each actor was usually given only his own lines, with the relevant cues, in manuscript form. No women appeared on the Elizabethan stage; female roles were taken either by boy actors or, in the case of older women, by adult male comedians. As in Italy, all the actors had to be able to sing and dance and often to make their own music. The great actors of the day were Richard Burbage, who worked in Shakespeare's company, and Edward Alleyn, who was mainly associated with Ben Jonson. In spite of the fact that theatres such as the Globe played to a cross section of London's populace, audiences seem to have been attentive and well behaved.

Professional companies

An alternative to the outdoor public playhouse was the private indoor theatre. The first of these was an abandoned monastery near St. Paul's Cathedral, converted in 1576 by Richard Farrant and renamed the Blackfriars Theatre. Others included the Cockpit, the Salisbury Court, and the Whitefriars. Initially these theatres were closer to the Spanish model, with the bare stage across one end, an inner stage at the back, benches in front for the audience, and galleries all around. Later, they made use of more elaborate scenery and featured the Italian-style proscenium arch. Because of the reduced size of the audience, higher prices had to be charged, which excluded all but the more wealthy and learned segment of the public. This in turn affected the style of writing; these private theatres were mostly used by boy companies that presented a more refined and artificial type of drama. One of their chief dramatists was John Lyly, though Ben Jonson wrote many of his plays for them. Growing rivalry between the boy and adult companies, exacerbated by hostility from the increasingly powerful Puritan movement, resulted in James I imposing even tighter controls and exercising heavy censorship on the theatre when he came to the throne in 1603.

Jacobean theatre. Although the Italian influence gradually became stronger in the early part of the 17th century, the English theatre was by then established and confident enough to take over foreign ideas without losing any of its individuality. Jonson became increasingly preoccupied with the dramatic unities, while other writers of the Jacobean period such as John Webster, Thomas Middleton, and John Ford favoured a more definite separation of comedy and tragedy than had been the case in Elizabethan drama. They were given to sensationalism in their revenge plays, finding inspiration in the darker moods of Seneca and often setting them in Italy.

New trends

Meanwhile, at court the pastoral was finding new popularity, partly because it provided opportunities for spectacular scenery, and with it came the revival of the masque—a sumptuous allegorical entertainment combining poetry, music, dance, scenery, and extravagant costumes. As court poet, Ben Jonson collaborated with the architect and designer Inigo Jones to produce some of the finest examples of the masque. Having spent a few years in Italy, Jones was greatly influenced by the Italian painted scenery and its use of machinery. On his return to England he did much to bring scenic design up to date, introducing many innovations. Members of the court had thorough training in dancing, fencing, singing, instrumental music, and courtly ceremonial. They were therefore well prepared to perform in the masques, even to take solo parts and to appear in the chorus. Masques became even more elaborate under Charles I, but in 1634 Jonson angrily withdrew his contribution when he saw that the visual elements were completely overtaking the dramatic content. When the Civil War broke out in 1642, the Puritans closed all the theatres and forbade dramatic performances of any kind. This created an almost complete break in the acting tradition for 18 years until the Restoration of Charles II, after which the theatre flourished once more, though on quite different lines.

German theatre. While England and Spain were developing their own national styles of theatre, the German-speaking countries lagged well behind, embroiled in constant warfare and religious upheaval and lacking a unifying capital city as a cultural focal point. Classical plays had little more than academic interest, and the tradition remained indigenous albeit crudely medieval. The most notable writer was the Meistersinger Hans Sachs, who transformed the bawdy *Fastnachtsspiele* into more acceptable farces with which to entertain Shrovetide carnival crowds. He also established Germany's first theatre building inside a church in Nürnberg in 1550, though there were no truly professional companies to fill it.

Traveling troupes in Germany

An unexpected stimulus came from touring English troupes that had firmly established themselves in Germany by the end of the 16th century. Although there was a good deal of cross-fertilization between England and the Continent, many English actors chose exile as an escape from monopolies, suppression, and the withdrawal of playing licenses at home. They gave public performances in towns or at rural fairs and private ones in the halls of nobles. Robert Browne's company was the first, arriving in Frankfurt in 1592. In a country where local theatre was weighed down by excessive moralizing, these actors made an immediate impact through their robustness and vivid professionalism. Their repertoire consisted mainly of pirated versions of Elizabethan tragedies and comedies, performed in English, though heavily cut and padded with enough music, dancing, acrobatics, and dumb show to overcome the language barrier. In between the acts a clown figure, combining the English fool and the German *Narr* (from the *Fastnachtsspiel*), took over with improvised antics in pidgin English sprinkled with Dutch and German phrases. Thomas Sackville created one of the first of such clown figures in the character Jan Bouschet. Similar English creations were Hans Stockfisch and Pickelherring—prototypes of the totally German character Hanswurst, who found his way into all the improvised comedies of the day. As the proportion of German actors in the English companies increased, a more indigenous drama developed known as *Haupt-und-Staatsaktionen.* As this term implies, such plays dealt with the intrigues of high characters in high places and abounded with blustering rhetoric and gory sensationalism. The last English troupes left Germany in 1659, by which time the Italian style of staging, with its perspective scenery, had become the fashion in spectacular court operas and the elaborate productions of Jesuit school plays (see above).

Dutch strolling players also visited Germany, performing *vertoonige* ("living tableaux") and contemporary plays, Spanish drama being much favoured. Italian traveling players presented puppet theatre in Austria and southern Germany as an offshoot of the commedia dell'arte, which itself was widely imitated, particularly in Austria. While the strolling players did little to elevate German theatre to the level of the highest art, they did at least establish vital links with neighbouring European cultures, helping to inject new ideas into backward traditions and precipitating the emergence of the professional actor.

French Neoclassicism. Theatre companies in France in the early 16th century were playing a mixed fare of moralities, miracle plays, farces, and soties. The most important company was an amateur guild called the Confrérie de la Passion, which held a monopoly on acting in Paris. In 1548 it opened its own theatre, the Hôtel de Bourgogne, a long narrow room with the stage filling one end, a pit for standing spectators, and two galleries around the walls. Both auditorium and stage were lit by candles. Soon after the theatre opened, the Confrérie was forbidden by decree to perform religious plays for fear that they could be used to debase Roman Catholicism. The feeble traditions of indigenous secular drama in its repertoire were soon overpowered by the Renaissance influence, and dramatists began looking to classical antiquity for inspiration. Civil war, however, halted the appearance of any truly great drama until well into the 17th century. The new plays that appeared in Paris—mainly pastorals and tragicomedies—were written by classical scholars as imitations of the Italian commedia erudita, but the French love of order resulted in the intensification of the dramatic unities of time, place, and action. The first fully professional company, which included women, was that of Valleran-Lecomte; it took over the Hôtel de Bourgogne toward the end of the century, performing its plays on the medieval-style multiple setting stage. The acting in these Neoclassical plays was not given to realism: each actor stood at the front of the stage to declaim his lines and then stepped back to allow the next actor to speak.

National unity came in the early 17th century under Louis XIII and his brilliant adviser, the cardinal de Richelieu, and with unity came the desire (similar to that in Tudor England) to create a strong national culture. Theatre companies were active in the provinces, but Paris, the centre of cultural life, was the goal for which they all aimed. In 1634 the Théâtre du Marais was opened in an indoor tennis court, and in 1641 Richelieu built his own Italian-style theatre (complete with all the latest machinery), which after his death became the Théâtre du Palais-Royal. Richelieu, who took an active interest in theatre, had also tried to purify comedy and tragedy by discouraging what he considered the formless tragicomedy. His efforts, however, were thrown into confusion by the arrival of the first French play of any real worth, Pierre Corneille's *Le Cid* (1637), a tragicomedy that ignored the revered unities. Working smoothly within the rules, Corneille's rival, Jean Racine, took French Neoclassical drama to its greatest heights with his nine tragedies, of which *Phèdre* (1677) is regarded as the pinnacle.

The art of Molière

Both Racine and Corneille were overshadowed by Molière, who is considered the world's greatest comic dramatist. After 13 years of touring France with his company, the Illustre-Théâtre, Molière was accepted at the court of Louis XIV in 1658 and began to elevate the crude farce to the level of sophisticated social comedy, placing it on a par with tragedy. For several years he shared the Petit-Bourbon theatre with a troupe of commedia dell'arte actors led by Tiberio Fiorillo and was much influenced by their realistic style of playing. Later he moved to the Palais-Royal. Far from imitating foreign plays, Molière created distinctly French characters based on an acute observation of social manners. After Molière's death, Louis XIV amalgamated the Illustre-Théâtre with two other companies in 1680 to form Europe's first national theatre, the Comédie-Française, which continues to further the cultural aims of France to the present day.

Spread of national theatres. In the course of the succeeding centuries, national theatres were established in many other European countries but not necessarily for the same reasons. German national theatres fought to shake off the infiltration of French culture and to develop native traditions. It was the aim of the Austrian emperor Joseph II to institute national theatres for all the peoples of his empire so that they might become acquainted with the works of world literature in their own tongue. After establishing a national theatre for the German-speaking population of Austria, Joseph II then supported the Czechs and Slovaks in their efforts toward their own national theatre. Later, one was founded in Budapest for the Hungarians. Gustav II created the Swedish national theatre. Catherine the Great of Russia also set out to introduce her people to the dramatic works of world literature performed in the Russian language.

There was no court theatre in the Netherlands. The performances of plays and the organization of theatre festivals had, since the 15th century, been in the hands of the *Rederijkerskamers*—societies of amateur enthusiasts similar to the French *confréries.* The plays—both serious religious pieces and farces—were usually presented outdoors on a raised platform with a curtained facade. The curtain could be closed for scene changes, though the settings themselves were very simple. In 1617 the first Dutch Academy was opened, and one of its priorities was to foster a higher standard of theatre developing at the time under a strong French influence. This eventually led to the construction of the first indoor theatre in Amsterdam, the Schouwburg.

It opened with *Gysbrecht van Aemstel* (1638), a patriotic play in the classical tradition by the Netherlands' major dramatist, Joost van den Vondel. The Schouwburg, which had a semipermanent setting, was remodeled in 1665 along Italian lines, though this did nothing to stem the general decline in Dutch drama.

Ballet and opera-ballet. If there was a lack of great theatre in France before Corneille, it was well compensated for by extravagant court ceremonials in which dance featured prominently. These reached a high level of sophistication in the later 16th century, stimulated by the presence of Italian dancing masters invited to the French court by Catherine de Médicis. A product of this collaboration was the *ballet comique*, a courtly dance entertainment with words. Another Italian import was changeable-perspective scenery, which was brought to Paris in 1645 by the designer Giacomo Torelli, who completely refurbished the Petit-Bourbon. The staging of court ballets was accordingly adapted to show off the possibilities of the new machinery. Louis XIV often took part in these and earned the title Le Roi Soleil (The Sun King) when he performed as the Sun in *Le Ballet de la nuit* in 1653. Molière was called upon to provide texts for elaborate court festivities at Versailles involving ballets, plays, fireworks displays, and theatrical banquets.

Louis XIV also organized the teaching and presentation of music and dance by setting up academies. The Académie Royal de Musique (1669) was officially given the exclusive right to present operas, which led to a new genre, the opera-ballet, initiated by the composer Jean-Baptiste Lully, which combined vocal scenes with danced interludes. Following the developments in Italian opera, composers made new demands on singers, who had to study for years in order to be able to meet them successfully. After the mid-17th century, singers exerted considerable influence on the structure of new works because they demanded showpiece arias at certain places in the text. The dramatic technique of Baroque opera followed set rules: arias were to be sung at the front of the stage, facing the audience; the chorus was directed as a static body; and the ornate setting was an elaborate decoration with which to please the eye rather than a functional definition of the acting area. One effect of the academies was to transfer dance activities from the court to the professional stage, and in 1681 the first professional dancers appeared in *Le Triomphe de l'amour* (*The Triumph of Love*), choreographed by Charles-Louis Beauchamp to Lully's music.

The opera-ballet of Jean-Baptiste Lully

Restoration theatre. One of the first gestures of Charles II upon his Restoration in 1660 was to reverse Puritan sobriety by encouraging the kind of entertainment and theatrical activities that he had seen during his years of exile at the French court. Within months of his return to London he granted royal patents to Thomas Killigrew and Sir William Davenant to establish two theatre companies, the King's Players and the Duke's Players, respectively. Significantly, they chose to follow the French example and convert two indoor tennis courts as temporary premises rather than take over one of the surviving Elizabethan playhouses. In 1671 Sir Christopher Wren built the Duke's Theatre, Dorset Garden, for Davenant, and three years later he built the first Theatre Royal, Drury Lane, for Killigrew. These theatres combined continental innovations with some of the features of the Elizabethan stage. A curved "apron" stage extended beyond the proscenium arch from which entrance doors opened, indicating that most of the action was played toward the front of the stage with the scenery as a mere background. Stock sets of changeable flats were used, and lighting was provided by candles. The greatest impact, however, came from the introduction of actresses to the English stage, the most famous being Nell Gwyn.

The first productions were reworkings of Elizabethan and Jacobean plays, tailored to suit the tastes of the new aristocratic audience composed almost exclusively of courtiers and their attendants. (The majority of the populace, still under the influence of Puritanism, stayed away and probably could not have afforded it anyway.) Values had changed since Shakespeare's day: the new audience consisted of fashionable young cynics and dilettantes, self-indulgent rakes and wits who prized glittering conversation and were interested only in seeing themselves on stage, however satirical the portrait. Thus came about the bawdy comedy of manners, heavily influenced by Molière but chilled with the dry wit of the London aristocracy. Romance and feeling gave way to intellect in sophisticated plays about cuckoldry, gossip, intrigue, and sexual license, yet tempered with a strong sense of decorum. Although most dramatists of the time did not consider themselves professional writers, George Etherege and William Wycherley developed an elegant style of prose drama that was refined by Sir John Vanbrugh and later William Congreve, whose *Way of the World* (1700) is the finest example of Restoration comedy. At the beginning of the 18th century there was a softening of cynicism in the comedies of George Farquhar, which brought the period to a close.

Comedy of manners

As the late 17th century was not a heroic age, tragedy fared less well in England. The poet John Dryden tried unsuccessfully to combine the merits of Racine and Shakespeare in a genre of rhymed heroic tragedy. His blank-verse tragedy *All for Love* (1677) was more lasting. The weakness of Restoration theatre was that, by concentrating on its aristocratic audience, it excluded most of the populace and was therefore not representative of the various levels of English society. Not surprisingly, the theatre was always struggling to survive, and after the 1670s audiences dwindled. In 1682 the King's Players and the Duke's Players merged to form the United Company, and for 13 years London supported only one theatre.

The rise of a middle-class theatre

THE 18TH CENTURY

A general decline in the level of playwriting during the 18th century was offset in large part by the emergence of some excellent actors and the building of hundreds of theatres throughout Europe. A new audience also emerged at this time. Inflation and the studied carelessness of the aristocracy had left many noble families impoverished, while middle-class merchants and financiers prospered. Intermarriage became a necessity for the nobility and a means of increasing social status for the middle class, whose members constituted the greater part of the new theatregoing public. Eager to enjoy its hard-won privileges but at the same time unable to cultivate the same tastes as the nobility, the middle class demanded something less artificial and formal than the theatre of the late 17th century—something more realistic and genteel. This audience was not prepared to labour over aesthetic subtleties; it wanted sensation.

Middle-class drama. In France, there was no one to carry forward the genius of Racine, and Neoclassical tragedy gave way to the *drame bourgeois* of Denis Diderot, whose moralizing domestic plays made a heavy appeal to the emotions. Voltaire, however, managed to sustain the form of Racine while widening the content to include historical subjects, sometimes exploiting the exoticism of Eastern settings in plays such as *Zaïre* (1732). Voltaire was fortunate to have some of the greatest actors of the period appear in his plays, among them Henri-Louis Lekain. In England George Lillo made tragedy more domestic by using middle-class characters in *The London Merchant* (1731). His example was followed in Germany by Gotthold Ephraim Lessing in *Miss Sara Sampson* (1755), an attempt to shake off French Neoclassical influence and produce a truly German genre—the *bürgerliches Trauerspiel* ("middle-class tragedy"). A similar attempt to be rid of the delicacy of Racine came from the Italian dramatist Count Vittorio Alfieri. In plays such as *Oreste* (1778), he went back to the Greeks for inspiration, filling the old stories with strong passions.

The domestic tragedies of Lillo and Lessing

A more accessible genre for conveying high tragic sentiment was the opera. Kings and princes in nearly every European country built court theatres to house it, and when the composition of the audience widened, huge opera houses were constructed. Milan's Teatro alla Scala (1778), for example, seated more than 2,000 people. Notwithstanding national variations—Henry Purcell and George Frideric Handel in England, Christoph Gluck and

Wolfgang Amadeus Mozart in the Germanic countries—opera remained essentially Italian. The Bibiena family of Bologna reigned as the supreme masters of scenic design, exerting influence throughout Europe. The family's most famous innovation was the *scena per angola,* in which the lines of perspective seem to move to vanishing points on either side of the scene rather than in the centre of the scene. The comic side of opera was expressed in the French *opéra-comique* and the Italian *opera buffa,* in which there was more balance between the music and the libretto. This was particularly the case in the popular English ballad opera, which was more like a play with songs. The best known example of English ballad opera is John Gay's *Beggar's Opera* (1728).

Smaller playhouses also abounded to accommodate the growing number of plays. At the beginning of the century, Paris had three theatres, but by 1791 there were 51. The growth of playhouses in London was discouraged by the Licensing Act of 1737, which gave the lord chamberlain extensive powers to censor all plays and to uphold the monopoly of the two patent theatres in London. Theatre managers, however, found a way around this by filling out their programs with musical items. (Similar laws in Paris were evaded by unlicensed actors who played in *forains,* the illegal theatres of the fairgrounds.) Outside London, the spread of theatres royal in provincial towns gave new importance to the touring circuits, which became valuable training grounds for young actors. It was in this way that the century's greatest actor, David Garrick, gained his early experience. In both tragedy and comedy, Garrick developed a more natural style of acting that became widely influential. As manager of the Drury Lane Theatre, he introduced concealed stage lighting and stopped the practice of spectators sitting on the stage. (Voltaire did the same in France.) It is interesting to note that at a time when Garrick was buried in Westminster Abbey, French actors, under penalty of excommunication, still had to be buried in unconsecrated ground.

Some of the most important dramatic contributions in the 18th century were in the field of comedy. Dominated at first by the tearful comedies of Colley Cibber and Sir Richard Steele in England and the *comédie larmoyante* of Nivelle de La Chaussée in France, the form spluttered to life as a reaction against sentimental drama. Oliver Goldsmith evoked the Elizabethan mood and signaled a return to hearty laughter in *She Stoops to Conquer* (1773); Richard Brinsley Sheridan tried to revive the comedy of manners in *The School for Scandal* (1777).

Goldoni and Gozzi

In France and Italy, the most interesting developments were literary applications of the commedia dell'arte. Banished by Louis XIV, the Italian actors were back in 1716 under the name Comédie-Italienne. This time they softened their style to suit prevailing taste and found a sympathetic writer in Pierre Marivaux, who developed a more refined expression of the commedia dell'arte spirit. In Italy, where the commedia dell'arte was already becoming lifeless, two rival playwrights, Carlo Goldoni and Carlo Gozzi, tried to reform it in different ways. Goldoni replaced the improvised dialogue with fully written texts, and, although he achieved popularity with *Il servitore di due padrone* (*c.* 1745; *The Servant of Two Masters*), he faced bitter opposition from the profession. Gozzi, on the other hand, allowed his actors plenty of opportunity for improvisation. He mixed fairy-tale fantasy and realism in a type of play he called *fiabe,* the best known example being *L'amore delle tre melarance* (1761; *The Love for Three Oranges*). Comedy reached an exuberant peak in two plays by the French dramatist Pierre-Augustin Caron de Beaumarchais: *Le Barbier de Séville* (1775; *The Barber of Seville*) and *Le Mariage de Figaro* (1784; *The Marriage of Figaro*).

A curious offshoot of the commedia dell'arte in England was introduced in 1717 by the actor John Rich. Under the stage name of Lun, he played Harlequin in a new form he called pantomime. The entertainment began with a familiar story or classical legend in verse, then the characters were transformed into commedia dell'arte figures for the harlequinade in which their tricks and adventures were mimed to music. Rich produced a pantomime annually until 1760. The form continued after him and became even more popular in the 19th century.

First theatres in British colonial America

Beginnings of American theatre. The strongly Puritan sentiments of settlers in North America prohibited the development of theatre until the early 18th century when a number of English actors arrived in the South and began staging plays in temporary venues. The first theatres were built in Williamsburg, Va. (*c.* 1716), and Charleston, S.C. (1730). By the mid-1730s a number of theatres had opened in New York, and the first visiting company from London performed in Williamsburg in 1752. In the absence of any local dramatists, the repertoire in America consisted mainly of successes from the London stage. After independence (1782), several of the new states tried to prohibit theatrical performances on moral grounds. To combat this, one touring company announced its presentation of Shakespeare's *Othello* as "a moral dialogue in five acts." By the end of the century, however, professional theatre was well established and such groups as the American Company were giving regular seasons.

THE ROMANTIC THEATRE

The last decades of the 18th century were characterized by a breakaway from the cool reason of Neoclassicism and an urge to reassert freedom and national consciousness. The French and American revolutions were the most notable consequences of this, but there were stirrings throughout Europe. The theatre became an important means of arousing patriotic fervour, a function that was to continue well into the 19th century. At the same time, the doors were opened to the lower classes, who swelled the audience and imposed their own tastes on the theatre. More and more playhouses were built to accommodate the demand.

A spirit of Romanticism swept through all the arts. In the theatre, formalized rules were cast aside to allow for much more individualistic and passionate expression. The emphasis on detail, as opposed to the Neoclassical preoccupation with the general and representative, led toward naturalism on the one hand and a drama of the subjective imagination on the other. Almost every major poet turned his hand to writing plays. The source of inspiration for them all was Shakespeare, who enjoyed a new wave of appreciation in numerous translations and productions all over Europe.

The Sturm und Drang

The English poets, among them Lord Byron, John Keats and Percy Bysshe Shelley, failed in their attempts to create a drama that suited prevailing tastes, partly because they were not prepared to descend to a level that they considered vulgar and partly because they were overshadowed by the weight of their own dramatic heritage, having very little to add to it. By contrast, the influence of Shakespeare in Germany proved liberating. The breakaway from French Neoclassical drama, which had been heralded by Lessing in the 1760s, found full expression in the Sturm und Drang (Storm and Stress) movement that began with Johann Wolfgang von Goethe's tempestuous first play, *Götz von Berlichingen* (1773; Eng. trans., *Götz von Berlichingen*). Its medieval theme led to a wave of historical writing and "gothicism" (a preoccupation with an idealized and melodramatic past that later became especially popular in England) and with it a new interest in the visual aspects of theatre production. The greatest exponent of the genre was Friedrich von Schiller, whose first play, *Die Räuber* (1781; *The Robbers*), left audiences stunned. Goethe and Schiller were both involved with the court theatre at Weimar. When Goethe, as director of the theatre, saw that the Sturm und Drang movement was leading to excess and absurdity, he reverted to a more Classical style of theatre. Heinrich von Kleist, best known for his play *Prinz Friedrich von Homburg* (1821; *The Prince of Homburg*), is considered by some the only dramatist of real merit at the time.

Influence of Kotzebue and Pixérécourt

Melodrama. The reduction of Schiller's poetic style of Romanticism to a level of popular entertainment for unsophisticated audiences resulted in the melodrama that, in spite of its lack of literary merit, became one of the most popular forms of the 19th century. For example, August von Kotzebue, whose work Goethe was reluctantly forced to stage at Weimar, wrote more than 200 melodramas and exerted an enormous influence in England and France. The French dramatist Guilbert de Pixérécourt also enjoyed wide popularity. His play *Coelina, ou l'enfant du mystère* (1800) was translated into English (without acknowledgement) by Thomas Holcroft as *A Tale of Mystery* and became in 1802 the very first melodrama to be seen in England.

Both Kotzebue and Pixérécourt used a great variety of subjects with historical and exotic locations. They took every opportunity to incorporate sensational or terrifying effects, such as floods, fires, and earthquakes, and made use of live animals on stage. In their works, characters tended to be stock types and words became secondary to lively action. Much of the dialogue was accompanied by incidental music in an effort to heighten emotional impact. Even the best actors of the day, including John Philip Kemble and his sister Sarah Siddons, were compelled to appear in melodramas as an alternative to Shakespeare.

The early 19th century. While Shakespearean tragedy remained the main inspiration for serious Romantic drama in Russia, Poland, Hungary, and the Scandinavian countries during the early 19th century, little of true merit was produced. After the French Revolution had settled, Napoleon reconstituted the Comédie-Française in 1799 under the actor François-Joseph Talma, who introduced many reforms and encouraged a less declamatory style of speech. In England, after a triumphant debut at Drury Lane in 1814 as Shylock in Shakespeare's *Merchant of Venice,* Edmund Kean went on to become the greatest actor of the age, specializing in classic villain roles.

The most influential contributions, however, were in the field of popular theatre. Joseph Grimaldi created the much loved clown character in the harlequinade section of the English pantomime, appearing annually at Covent Garden until his retirement in 1823. At about this time, Jean-Gaspard Deburau rekindled interest in the art of mime through his portrayals of the white-faced Pierrot at the Théâtre des Funambules in Paris. Both men became living legends.

A strain of fantastic comedy, influenced by Gozzi in its juxtaposition of the fairy-tale world and reality, was developed in Germany and Austria in the plays of Johann Nestroy and Ferdinand Raimund. In England this found expression in the extravaganza (similar in spirit to the pantomime) mainly through the fairy plays of J.R. Planché. His example was followed later in the century by Sir W.S. Gilbert, who became famous for the satirical operettas he wrote with Sir Arthur Sullivan, notable among which was *Iolanthe* (1882). The English burlesque (a more satirical version of the extravaganza) and the *burletta* (a farce with songs) were also popular forms of the time, as was their French counterpart, the vaudeville, which paved the way for the operetta.

Rise in the number of theatres. A sharp increase in the number of theatre buildings matched the rapid growth in urban development. During the London winter season of 1807, for example, only 10 theatres were operating; by 1870 there were 30. Drury Lane was rebuilt on a huge scale in 1794, designed to seat 3,600 people. This made audiences difficult for actors to control, and naturalistic acting became almost impossible. Most of the new theatres, however, were much smaller.

In 1803 London's Lyceum Theatre substituted gas for candles and oil lamps as a source of illumination, and other theatres were quick to follow suit. This meant that the brightness of light on stage could be controlled to a degree never before known. The disadvantages, however, were an appalling smell and a greatly increased danger of fire from the naked jets of flame. Faced with the prospect of a much wider theatregoing public, theatres became more specialized, catering to particular classes and their corresponding tastes. For middle-class audiences, changes in the auditoriums of European public theatres brought about greater comfort and respectability, with the result that spectators became quieter during the performance. In England, for example, soft seats were installed in the pit by the late 1820s. Galleries with their open boxes were divided into closed boxes near the proscenium arch, allowing for privacy, with the rest of the gallery open and known as the "dress circle." For the poorer sections of the English populace, there were the small "penny theatres" (of which more than 80 existed in London during the 1830s), where patrons paid a penny to see short, crudely mounted productions. Some individuals began to exploit their special talents as singers, dancers, mimics, and jugglers, giving solo performances in ale houses and taverns. These forms of entertainment became so popular that a great chain of provincial and metropolitan theatres sprang up from the music room annex of the public saloon during the second half of the 19th century. In England these forms came to be known as music hall and in the United States as vaudeville.

Romantic realism. The visit to Paris of an English Shakespearean company in 1827 had an immediate effect on French drama and acting techniques, inspiring Victor Hugo to write *Hernani* (1830), which signaled the beginning of a more distinctly literary Romanticism in France. Although this play eventually put an end to Neoclassicism, its first performance caused riots in the Comédie-Française. Historical dramas with a strong nationalist spirit began appearing in nearly every country, finding particularly stirring expression in the opera. In Germany Richard Wagner worked to create a more unified presentation of poetry, music, dance, and scenery in historical and mythic operas such as *Die Meistersinger von Nürnberg* (1868; *The Mastersingers of Nuremburg*), culminating in the first full production of the mighty *Ring des Nibelungen* (1869–76; *The Ring of the Nibelungen*) in the specially constructed Bayreuth Festspielhaus. This theatre, which departed from the Baroque opera house, set a pattern of theatre production that is still followed today: its fan-shaped auditorium was the first to be darkened during the performance to encourage the sharpest concentration on what was happening on stage. Opera of a different style reached a peak in Italy through the works of Guiseppe Verdi.

Popularity of historical dramas and historical operas

The main trend in Europe around the middle of the century was toward Romantic realism and the development of a theatre of ideas. It was at this time that the Russian theatre began to take on new life in Nikolay Gogol's biting satire *Revizor* (1836; *The Inspector General*) and with more delicate comic realism in the plays of Aleksandr Nikolayevich Ostrovsky and Ivan Turgenev. Edward George Bulwer-Lytton wrote one of the first English plays on a contemporary theme (*Money* [1840]), and the Irish writer and actor Dion Boucicault, best known for *London Assurance* (1841), had great success in both London and New York City with his melodramas. It was Boucicault who helped to establish author's copyright in the United States (1856) after he became the first dramatist in Britain to receive a royalty payment for his plays. Lord Lytton gave his name to the Act of 1833, which established author's performance copyright in England.

Eugène Scribe dominated the French stage with his 400 "well-made plays" through which he developed a formula for creating highly commercial theatre wherein plot rather than character was the main concern. Eugène Labiche carried such techniques into farce, and another Scribe disciple, Victorien Sardou, became the leading French dramatist of the second half of the century. In spite of the shallowness of his plays, Sardou provided some memorable roles for the great French actress Sarah Bernhardt. A more serious type of drama, developed by Alexandre Dumas *fils,* was the thesis play (also called problem play), in which social problems were debated.

The French "well-made play"

The actor-manager. If contemporary plays were of a poor standard, the deficiency was partly hidden by flamboyant productions and bravura performances by star actors, many of whom managed their own companies. The 19th century was the heyday of the actor-manager. Star, licensee of the theatre, and arranger of the performance, he dominated the forestage while his fellow actors were relegated to the background as a sort of mobile dressing.

Although the actor-managers chose plays for good acting parts rather than for their dramatic value, they introduced many reforms. In England William Charles Macready, one of the great tragedians of the century, was among the first to introduce full rehearsals for his company. After the monopoly of the patent theatres was removed in 1843,

Samuel Phelps staged nearly all of Shakespeare's plays at Sadler's Wells, including many of the lesser known ones. The greatest actor-manager was Henry Irving, who first made his name in a melodrama by Leopold Lewis called *The Bells* (1871). Although he devoted much time to touring, the Lyceum became London's principal theatre under his management. Irving also helped to raise the status of actors, becoming in 1895 the first English actor to be knighted.

Because of the technical difficulties of manipulating complicated scenic effects (*e.g.,* storms, forest fires, and earthquakes), the star actor was eventually obliged to hand over artistic control to a neutral observer, the stage manager, who could coordinate all aspects of the production. Thus the stage manager's function became increasingly important until he was eventually elevated to the status of *régisseur,* or director.

Movement toward realism. The Romantic movement at the beginning of the 19th century had stimulated an interest in historical plays, which in turn gave rise to an almost obsessive preoccupation with authentic settings and costumes. In England Charles Kean's productions of Shakespeare crowded so much archaeological detail onto the stage that new scenes were often invented to make full use of the designer's research. In Kean's production of *Hamlet* in 1858, for instance, the recurring stage direction "a room in the castle" was represented by at least four different settings. Needless to say, this did incalculable damage to both the pace and fluidity of the play. In such impressive surroundings crowd scenes reached new peaks of popularity and spectacle. Large numbers of exotic animals were also used whenever an excuse could be found. One of the most sensational effects, however, was the "racing drama" in which live horses galloped on moving belts set into the stage floor. In this way, the chariot race of William Young's *Ben Hur* could be staged in New York City in 1899. Realism found its way into domestic dramas, too, one of the earliest innovations being the box set that replaced the perspective backcloth and wings depiction of a room with three solid walls and a ceiling. This feature was introduced to the English stage in 1832 by the actress and singer Madame Vestris at the Olympic Theatre.

Emphasis on scenic realism

A move toward ensemble acting was perhaps the logical continuation of efforts to achieve scenic realism. Madame Vestris demanded a more natural style of playing from her actors, and her example was followed by Charles Kean in his handling of crowd scenes: the extras were divided into small groups, each led by an experienced actor. But the most decisive move toward ensemble playing under the guidance of a modern theatre director was made by George II, duke of Saxe-Meiningen. The Duke was influenced by the stagings of Kean, which he had seen on visits to London. Assisted by the actor Ludwig Chronegk, he assumed control of his state theatre company as director and designer in 1866 and achieved an unrivaled harmony and discipline of playing. The company's extensive European tours between 1874 and 1890 had a considerable impact on actors and actor-managers. On the level of domestic drama, an attempt at contemporary realism was made by the English dramatist T.W. Robertson in the 1860s in both the writing and production of his plays. The style came to be known as "cup-and-saucer" drama because of the meals that were eaten on stage.

The introduction of electricity in theatres allowed for much brighter lighting on stage, providing yet another reason for eliminating exaggerated acting. The first experiments with electric stage lighting were at the Paris Opéra in 1846, but full systems were not installed until about 1880. In England the first use of electric stage lighting was in 1881 at the Savoy Theatre.

The advances in stage production eventually helped to stimulate a higher level of drama. The tradition of the French "well-made play" was carried forward in England on a more serious note in Arthur Wing Pinero's *Second Mrs. Tanqueray* (1893) and with a brilliance of wit that evoked the Restoration comedy of manners in Oscar Wilde's *Importance of Being Earnest* (1895).

The full impact of realist drama in the final decades of the 19th century came from northern Europe, first in the plays of the Norwegian dramatist Henrik Ibsen and later in the work of the Russian playwright Anton Chekhov. Together, though in different ways, they exerted a strong influence on the course of acting and writing that has lasted to the present day. Ibsen achieved international recognition through his verse dramas, *Brand* (1865; Eng. trans., *Brand*) and *Peer Gynt* (1867; Eng. trans., *Peer Gynt*), though his reputation rests mainly on the realistic contemporary plays that set out to expose social evils. *Samfundets støtter* (1877; *Pillars of Society*), *Et dukkehjem* (1879; *A Doll's House*), and *Hedda Gabler* (1890; Eng. trans., *Hedda Gabler*) are among the best known of such works.

Naturalism. As early as 1867, the French novelist Émile Zola had called for a rejection of all artifice in the theatrical arts, as in the novel, demanding that plays be faithful records of behaviour—namely, scientific analyses of life. *Thérèse Raquin,* an 1873 dramatization of his own novel (written in 1867), represents the first consciously Naturalistic drama.

Zola's "slice-of-life" technique found fuller expression in Sweden in August Strindberg's *Fröken Julie* (1888; *Miss Julie*), which heralded a new generation of writers whose plays dealt with themes centring on real contemporary society, treated in action and dialogue that looked and sounded like everyday behaviour and speech. These writers included Gerhart Hauptmann in Germany, Henry Becque in France, and Maxim Gorky in Russia. Partly because their plays often dealt with the gloomier side of life, audiences were at first small. In spite of the lack of commercial success, sympathetic productions were made possible by a number of independent "free" theatres that appeared throughout Europe.

The "slice-of-life" technique in drama

Théâtre-Libre. In 1887 André Antoine, an enthusiastic amateur actor, formed a small company in Paris, which he called Théâtre-Libre. His intention was to provide a showcase theatre for young playwrights of the new Naturalistic drama, from both France and abroad, who could find no other opportunity of bringing their work before the public. Antoine's first production was a group of one-act plays that attracted the attention of leading avant-garde theatre intellectuals such as Zola and Becque. The following year, Leo Tolstoy's *Vlast tmy* (1888; *The Power of Darkness*) was presented, and Théâtre-Libre took on an international significance. Apart from the work of such French writers as Becque and Eugène Brieux, Théâtre-Libre also introduced the plays of Ibsen, Strindberg, Hauptmann, and the Norwegian Bjørnstjerne Bjørnson. Because of financial difficulties the theatre closed in 1896, but by then it had already exerted an enormous influence on playwriting, direction, and acting and had helped to liberate French theatre from the artificiality in which it had been steeped. Antoine encouraged his actors to behave as if they were unaware of the presence of the audience, while his settings aimed to achieve in meticulous detail the impression of real life. He became famous for hanging real carcasses of meat in the stage setting of a butcher's shop.

Major contributions

Freie Bühne. Disturbed by the stagnation of theatre in Germany during the 1880s, young intellectuals tried to promote the revolutionary Naturalistic drama by opening the Deutsches Theater in Berlin, but they soon ran into trouble with the censors. In 1889, a group of writers headed by the theatre critic Otto Brahm formed a private theatre club called the Freie Bühne after Antoine's Théâtre-Libre. Its earliest productions were of Ibsen's *Gengangere* (1885; *Ghosts*) and Hauptmann's first play, *Vor Sonnenaufgang* (1889; *Before Dawn*), and it also staged the latter's better-known *Weber* (1892; *The Weavers*). When Brahm became director of the Deutsches Theater in 1894, the Freie Bühne was attached to it as an experimental division, though by this time the new drama was being accepted throughout Germany in similar theatres dedicated to bringing serious plays to the working class at reasonable prices. Other so-called free theatres in Berlin were the Freie Volksbühne ("Free People's Theatre") and the Schiller Theater.

The independent theatre. Dissatisfaction with established systems of theatre, including the all-powerful actor-manager and the indulgence in scenic spectacle, also existed in England. Critics had long deplored the lack of worthwhile modern English drama, and toward the end of the century William Archer was one of many writers who called for an equivalent of the Théâtre-Libre that would bring the "theatre of ideas" to England. Inspired by Antoine's example, Jacob Grein, a Dutchman living in England, organized the Independent Theatre Club. The theatre opened in 1891 with Archer's translation of Ibsen's *Gengangere,* provoking a storm of moral fury. One champion of the new group and its policies was the theatre critic George Bernard Shaw; his first play, *Widower's House* (1892), which dealt with the subject of slum landlordism, was produced there the following year. The theatre was supported by a small group of subscribers, many of them distinguished writers. Although it ceased activity in 1897, the Independent Theatre Club prepared the way for the Stage Society, founded in 1899. For the next 40 years the society arranged private Sunday performances of experimental plays at the Royal Court Theatre in London.

Moscow Art Theatre. The movement toward Naturalism that was sweeping Europe reached its highest artistic peak in Russia in 1898 with the formation of the Moscow Art Theatre (later called the Moscow Academy Art Theatre). Its name became synonymous with that of Anton Chekhov, whose plays about the day-to-day life of the landed gentry achieved a delicate poetic realism that was years ahead of its time. Konstantin Stanislavsky, its director, became the 20th century's most influential theorist on acting. In the early 19th century Russian theatre had been one of the most backward in Europe, content to play a repertoire of stock theatrical pieces, mainly French comedies and farces, or Russian imitations of them. Little time was spent on rehearsal; the plays were so similar that the same performances and sets could be used time and again. However, the Meiningen Company, which had visited Russia during the late 1880s, had pointed the way to reform with its exemplary discipline.

During a 17-hour conversation in a Moscow restaurant, Stanislavsky, an amateur actor of considerable experience, and Vladimir Nemirovich-Danchenko, a playwright, teacher, and drama critic, talked over their vision of an ideal theatre company, its artistic policy, and its production methods. On the basis of their discussion, they formed a group they called the Moscow Art Theatre Company. No great stir was made until, later that year, they revived Chekhov's *Chayka* (1896; *The Seagull*), which had failed badly in its incompetent first production in St. Petersburg. An instant success, the new production established the reputation of both Chekhov and Stanislavsky. The intimacy and truthfulness of the acting were something entirely new. Through his stagings of several of Chekhov's other plays, *Dyadya Vanya* (1897; *Uncle Vanya*), *Tri sestry* (1901; *Three Sisters*), and *Vishnyovy sad* (1904; *The Cherry Orchard*), Stanislavsky developed a style of infinitely detailed production, the result of long and methodical rehearsals, to achieve an almost perfect surface naturalism.

Stanislavsky's innovations

The American theatre. Although there was no lack of enthusiasm in developing an indigenous American theatre at the end of the 18th century, the plays that appeared proved lifeless and derivative, often little more than adaptations of English successes. It was not until the early 20th century that actors had a chance to portray American characters in well-written roles that were comparable to those of the European theatre. The first play by a native American was Thomas Godfrey's Neoclassical tragedy *The Prince of Parthia* (1767), but recognizable American characters did not appear on stage until Royall Tyler's comedy *The Contrast* (1787). This work introduced a favourite theme of early American drama: the triumph of native honesty and worth over foreign sham and affectation.

The growth of American theatre owed more to its actors than to its dramatists. In the early decades of the 19th century, the finest English actors, notably Edmund Kean, William Charles Macready, and Charles Kemble, visited the United States and provided a stimulus for the local actors they worked with. Before long, the gesture was returned when such American actors as Edwin Booth, Edwin Forrest, and Charlotte Cushman appeared with some success on the London stage. Forrest, whose acting was characterized by muscular strength and great vocal power, was perhaps the first to popularize the virile outdoor image cultivated by many American actors ever since. His most famous role, Spartacus in Robert Bird's *Gladiator* (1831), was specially written for him. The Booths were an eminent acting family: Junius Brutus Booth had acted with Edmund Kean, and his son Edwin with Irving, but they achieved notoriety when another son, John Wilkes Booth, assassinated Abraham Lincoln in 1865.

Eminent American actors

By the middle of the 19th century, the number of theatres in the United States had multiplied. Many of them were based on English models and offered a high standard of comfort and luxury. Detailed historical accuracy in setting and costume first attracted attention in Charles Kean's visiting production of Shakespeare's *King John* (1846), and the new box settings (three solid walls to suggest a room instead of the traditional side wings and backcloth arrangement) began to be used in Edwin Booth's theatre from 1869, after which realistic staging became increasingly popular. This trend was stimulated by the introduction of gas lighting about 1825 and of electric lighting about 1885.

Styles of acting also leaned increasingly toward realism as the century advanced. Joseph Jefferson, whose career spanned 71 years, was the leading comic actor of his day, best remembered in the title role of Dion Boucicault's version of *Rip Van Winkle* in the 1860s. One of the great actress-managers was Mrs. John Drew, who was famed for her frequently revived portrayal of Mrs. Malaprop in Sheridan's *Rivals.* Black American actors were rarely seen on the 19th-century stage; Negro roles were usually played by white actors with black makeup, giving rise to shallow and stereotyped portrayals. One of the first playwrights to treat the American Negro seriously was Boucicault in *The Octoroon* (1859). After a surfeit of melodrama, a more distinctly American style of drama began to evolve through the work of Bronson Howard, whose first play, *Saratoga* (1870), helped to make him the first to earn his living solely by playwriting.

As the population spread westward and southward, spurred by the gold rush and the expansion of the railways, so the demand for theatre became more widespread. In the South showboats on the Mississippi and Ohio rivers provided floating entertainment, mostly melodramas. Most of the leading actors of the time made visits to California, where the first theatres were built in the 1850s. Initially, star actors would work with local resident companies, but the majority of these were eventually overtaken by full touring productions that originated in New York City. By the 1870s, these companies were providing entertainment throughout the country. Booking agencies were formed to liaise between companies and theatres, and from this activity a group of theatre owners, producers, and agents formed the first Theatrical Syndicate in 1896. Although its original aim was to streamline the organization of entertainment and prevent exploitation, it soon gained a monopoly on theatre by controlling bookings in New York City and in key cities on the touring circuits. Because its blatant commercialism discouraged high artistic standards, the monopoly was fiercely resisted by the more innovative producer-directors such as David Belasco, who helped to introduce to the American stage the European fashion for scenic naturalism. Making use of the latest stage machinery, he devised many spectacular effects and used a real flock of sheep on stage in one production of a Passion play.

Popular entertainment. Alongside the developments in "legitimate" theatre, the last decades of the 19th century saw the rise of several forms of popular entertainment that often reached much larger audiences and created a new range of star performers. In these traditions lay the seeds of the 20th century's most popular theatrical genre, the musical comedy.

One of the greatest showmen of the time was P.T. Barnum. Founder of the American legend of "show business," he promoted melodrama, exhibited the midget Tom Thumb in the United States and England, and finally merged with James A. Bailey in 1881 to form "The Greatest Show on Earth," a three-ring circus, which was taken over in England by the Ringling Brothers after Barnum's death. The American brand of spectacular entertainment achieved international fame through Buffalo Bill Cody's Wild West shows, which featured a large cast of cowboys, Indians, and animals, as well as the famous sharp-shooter Annie Oakley. Another form that enjoyed enormous popularity in the United States and England throughout most of the century was the minstrel show, inspired by Thomas Darthmouth Rice. The performers were at first white men with black makeup, though later Negroes appeared in the shows. Sitting in a semicircle and playing banjos, tambourines, bones, and fiddles, they sang comic songs and sentimental ballads interspersed with soft-shoe dances and snatches of cross-fire dialogue.

By the 1880s, the music hall was at the height of its popularity in England, with a proliferation of newly constructed halls all over London and in the main cities. As the audience widened from predominantly male working-class spectators to include middle-class men and women, the layout of the auditoriums changed. The old-style intimate halls with their drinking facilities and tables gave way to larger, more theatrelike buildings, one of the most luxurious of which was the London Pavilion. An evening's bill could feature more than 20 different acts, including jugglers, acrobats, conjurers, ventriloquists, dancers, slapstick comedians, and singers ranging from vulgar to light classical. Two of the most famous performers of the 1880s were Marie Lloyd, who specialized in risqué songs, and the comedian Dan Leno, who, like many music-hall stars, made annual appearances in pantomime as well. Vesta Tilley, the male impersonator, created the character Burlington Bertie; Sir Harry Lauder was the finest Scottish comedian; Little Tich was famed for his short stature and elongated boots; Jules Léotard and Charles Blondin achieved international fame as acrobats; and Grock (original name Charles Adrian Wettach), the greatest clown after Grimaldi, played 20 instruments and delighted London audiences from 1903 until 1924. By then, the music hall was in decline, unable to compete with the new forms of mass entertainment into which many of its performers were drifting—revue, musical comedy, cinema, radio, and, later, television. There was a similar form of entertainment in France, while in the United States vaudeville retained many of the features and acts of the English music hall. It was first presented in New York City in 1881 as an attempt to provide "clean" entertainment for respectable family audiences.

On a more sophisticated level, light opera was developing in Europe out of the German *Singspiel* and the French *opéra-comique.* Early examples were Jacques Offenbach's classical burlesque, *Orphée aux enfers* (1858; *Orpheus in the Underworld*), Johann Strauss's *Fledermaus* (1874; *The Bat*), and the satirical operas of Gilbert and Sullivan. These led to the romantic operettas of Victor Herbert in the United States and Franz Lehár in Austria. But it was Jerome Kern who in the early 20th century first developed a genuinely American sound from ballad and ragtime musical forms that helped to forge the particular identity of the American musical comedy.

Jerome Kern and the American musical comedy

20th-century theatre

The achievements of Realism at the end of the 19th century have continued to the present day, but the most influential innovations in early 20th-century theatre came from a vigorous reaction against Realism. Just as the visual arts exploded into a chaos of experiment and revolt, generating numerous styles and "isms," so the theatre seized upon anything that came to hand in an effort to express the contradictions of the new age. Inspiration was sought in machines and technology, in Oriental theatre, Cubism, Dada, the psychoanalysis of Freud, and the shock of a world war that spawned widespread disillusionment and alienation. The results of this eclecticism were often anarchic and exhilarating: designers and directors were as influential as playwrights, though relatively little theatre of lasting value was produced. Nevertheless, such early experiments set the tone and widened the theatrical vocabulary for all the innovations that have followed.

The beginnings of the revolt against Realism were already hinted at before the 19th century was over, sometimes in the works of the Realist writers themselves. Ibsen, for example, turned increasingly toward Symbolism in his later plays such as *Bygmester Solness* (1892; *The Master Builder*) and *Naar vi døde vaagner* (1899; *When We Dead Awaken*), though still in the Realist mold. Frank Wedekind's *Frühlings Erwachen* (1891; *Spring Awakening*) began its study of adolescent love in the slice-of-life Naturalistic mode and ended in the realm of ghosts and dreams, foreshadowing Expressionism, which was to preoccupy other German dramatists during the 1920s. Strindberg also is regarded as one of the fathers of Expressionism by virtue of his later works such as *Ett Drömspel* (1902; *A Dream Play*) and *Spöksonaten* (1907; *The Spook [Ghost] Sonata*). In France the marionette play *Ubu roi* ("King Ubu"), written in 1888 by Alfred Jarry at the age of 15, created a scandal when it was later performed with live actors in 1896. Its use of puppet techniques, masks, placards, and stylized scenery was to be taken up decades later in French avant-garde theatre.

Wedekind and Strindberg as pioneers of Expressionism

BEYOND REALISM

The new stagecraft. Since Naturalistic scenery had led to an excessive clutter of archaeologically authentic detail on stage, the reaction against it favoured simplicity, even austerity, but with a heightened expressiveness that could convey the true spirit of a play rather than provide merely superficial dressing. One of the first advocates of this view was the Swiss designer Adolphe Appia, who used the latest technology and exploited the possibilities of electric lighting to suggest a completely new direction in stage design. Appia believed that the setting should serve to focus attention on the actor, not drown him in two-dimensional pictorial detail. The imaginative use of light on a few well-chosen forms—simple platforms, flights of steps, and the like—was sufficient to convey the changing mood of a play.

Because his views were so radical, Appia had few opportunities to realize his theories. They were, however, carried forward at the beginning of the century by the English designer and director Edward Gordon Craig, who used strong lighting effects on more abstract forms. He felt that a suggestion of reality could create in the imagination of the audience a physical reality: a single Gothic pillar, for instance, designed to stand alone and carefully lit, can suggest a church more effectively than a cardboard and canvas replica faithful to the last detail. But, like Appia, Craig became better known as a theorist than a practitioner. In his book *The Art of the Theatre* (1905) he outlined his concept of a "total theatre" in which the stage director alone would be responsible for harmonizing every aspect of the production—acting, music, colour, movement, design, makeup, and lighting—so that it might achieve its most unified effect. More controversial were Craig's ideas on the depersonalization of the actor into what he called the *Übermarionette* ("super-marionette"), based on a new symbolic form of movement and gesture (not unlike that of the Oriental actor) in which the actor's ego would not obtrude on the symbolic design. While they may not have found a practical way of achieving their visions, both Appia and Craig exerted an enormous influence on the next generation of directors and stage designers, particularly in their principle of painting with light.

The Austrian director Max Reinhardt came close to achieving many of Craig's ideals, especially in the power he exerted over every aspect of theatrical production. Beginning as an actor in Otto Brahm's company at the Deutsches Theater in Berlin, Reinhardt won acclaim for his inventive staging of Shakespeare's *Midsummer Night's Dream* in 1905 and thereafter devoted himself entirely to directing: he dominated the theatre of central Europe for 25 years. His flair for bold theatricality made him many enemies among the Realists, but it also returned a sense of colour and richness to the theatre of the time. Reinhardt was pragmatic in his approach to acting: rejecting the idea of "one style," he demanded for modern plays a style realistic in feeling but avoiding the drab exactness of Realism. In productions of the classics, he demanded lively, supple speaking in place of the slow, ponderous

The work of Max Reinhardt

delivery of the traditionalists. He always made his actors think afresh about their characters instead of assuming ready-made characterizations.

In his endeavours to break down the separation of stage and auditorium, Reinhardt often took his actors out of the theatre to play in unconventional settings. He produced Sophocles' *Oedipus Rex* in a circus arena in Berlin, and for his production of Karl Gustav Vollmöller's *Mirakel* (performed in 1911 and published in 1912; *The Miracle*), he transformed the huge Olympia exhibition hall in London into a cathedral with the audience as part of the congregation. In 1920 he helped to found the Salzburg Festival and directed Hugo von Hofmannsthal's morality play *Jedermann* (1911; *Everyman*) in the cathedral square. Although he was a master of spectacle, his versatility was such that he directed subtle and intimate plays in small theatres with equal skill.

Russia. At the beginning of the century, Russia was surging toward revolution, which makes it less surprising that some of the first attacks on Naturalistic theatre should have originated there. While continuing in the Realistic vein of his productions of Chekhov's plays and Gorky's *Na dne* (1902; *The Lower Depths*) at the Moscow Art Theatre, Stanislavsky also recognized the need to find new artistic paths. In 1905 he set up a studio for experimental theatre and appointed one of his former actors, Vsevolod Meyerhold, as its director. Influenced by Craig, Meyerhold immediately began to implement his own ideas involving the total supremacy of the director, so that his actors became little more than puppets. So much did this contradict everything the Moscow Art Theatre stood for that Stanislavsky closed the studio and thought further about the function of the actor. Determined that the actor should not in future be subordinated to the director's will, he began to train his company in an approach based on "emotional memory." This emphasized the self-expression of the actor who, in collaboration with the director, should achieve a unified interpretation of the play. After the Revolution in 1917, Stanislavsky allowed himself to become involved in the new plans for the arts that the revolutionary government had conceived, but he refused to allow his theatre to become a platform for spreading propaganda. He believed that his mission was to maintain a high standard of acting that other theatres might emulate when the initial excesses of the Revolution abated. He did, however, achieve a much bolder style in nonrealistic plays such as Maurice Maeterlinck's *Oiseau bleu* (1908; *The Blue Bird*) and in some of the productions toward the end of his career.

Curiously, it was the avant-garde that Lenin's government entrusted to guide the Russian theatre into the new revolutionary era. Meyerhold was back in vogue, declaring that the principles of propagandist theatre conformed with those of Marxism because they attempted to underline the "unindividuality" of man. In 1918 he stage the first Soviet play, *Misteriya-buff* (1921; *Mystery-Bouffe*) by Vladimir Vladimirovich Mayakovsky. With Aleksandr Tairov, director of the Kamerny Theatre, Meyerhold developed the Formalist style, in which representative types replaced individual characters amid Constructivist settings of gaunt scaffolding supporting bare platforms, with every strut and bolt exposed to view. The aggressive functionalism of this type of setting was regarded as having considerable propaganda value when the Soviets were being taught to revere the machine as part of their training to become a great industrial nation. Meyerhold sought to eliminate the actor's personality even further through a system he called "bio-mechanics." Placing emphasis on the physical and athletic aspects of the actor's body, Meyerhold's system drew on a variety of influences, including commedia dell'arte, Kabuki theatre, and the ideas of Craig and the physiologist Ivan Petrovich Pavlov.

Meyerhold's Formalist style

As director of one of the studios of the Moscow Art Theatre from 1920, the more moderate Yevgeny Vakhtangov tried to bridge the gap between Realism and the avant-garde. In place of Stanislavsky's inner realism, he wanted what he called "outer technique." While preserving a deep respect for the actor's art—something he learned from Stanislavsky—he brought bold gesture and vivid colour to his productions, the best of which were a Yiddish performance of *Der Dybbuk* (1920; *The Dybbuk*) by S. Ansky (pseudonym of Solomon Zanvel Rappoport) and *Turandot* (1762; Eng. trans., *Turandot*) by Carlo Gozzi, both staged just before his death in 1922.

Socialist Realism

The experimentation of the 1920s came to an abrupt halt under Stalinist rule with the imposition of Socialist Realism on the arts in 1932. It was decreed that all theatre should be adjusted to the level of the worker-audience with the aim of educating the public in the ideals of the Communist revolution. In practice, this resulted in a wave of simplistic and old-fashioned propaganda plays in which theatrical artistry was sacrificed to party dogma. Theatre virtually ceased to progress, since any originality was condemned as decadent. Scenery became more and more laboriously realistic, for a setting that was in any way impressionistic was condemned as belonging to "abstract art." One of the most successful directors of the time was Nikolay Pavlovich Okhlopov, who was put in charge of the Realistic Theatre (formerly one of the Moscow Art Theatre studios) in 1932. There, he tried to find new ways of presenting plays by using multiple stages and generally breaking away from the constrictions of the proscenium-arch format. In 1938, however, the Realistic Theatre was closed on grounds that its work appealed too exclusively to intellectuals. As part of the reaction against Formalism, Meyerhold was dismissed in 1934, and Tairov, rebuked for being out of touch with his audience, was relieved of his directorship of the Kamerny Theatre and forced to work under a committee.

Italy. As in Russia, the new technology provided a stimulus for the revolt against *verismo* ("realism") in the Italian theatre at the beginning of the century. The most important movement was Futurism. Initiated by Filippo Tommaso Marinetti in 1909, it embraced painting, sculpture, and poetry, as well as theatre, and it prefigured most of the non-Realistic approaches to the theatre that were to follow: Dada, Surrealism, Constructivism, the Theatre of the Absurd, and even the "happenings" of the 1960s.

The Futurist movement

In theatres and art galleries the Futurists devised performances that celebrated the ecstasy of speed, explored states of madness, depicted man as a machine, and had performers moving among the spectators to provoke the audience in a general smashing down of the "fourth wall" and, with it, the illusionary power of theatre.

In 1921 Anton Giulio Bragaglia founded the Teatro Sperimentale degli Indipendenti, which borrowed from the Futurists but subordinated mechanics and technology to the play itself. He aimed to restore theatricality to the drama, using light, multidimensional space, masks, and costumes to Surrealistic effect. He also wished his actors to master the acrobatic aspects of the commedia dell'arte as an antidote to cerebral acting. Another movement was the Teatro Grottesco, which explored the contradictions between outward appearance and inner reality. This became a central theme in the work of the dramatist Luigi Pirandello, whose plays questioned the very basis of realism on a stage that was itself artifice. After his best known play, *Sei personaggi in cerca d'autore* (1921; *Six Characters in Search of an Author*) brought him international fame, he founded in 1925 his own company, the Teatro Odeschalchi, in Rome. After the rise of Mussolini, much of the avant-garde theatre of the late 1920s became aligned with Fascism. Until the 1930s, there was no state support for the theatre, and even then those writers and directors opposed to Fascism were excluded.

Expressionism in Germany. The term Expressionism was coined at the beginning of the 20th century to describe a style of painting that reacted violently against late 19th-century Naturalism and Impressionism. Applied to the theatre, it represented a protest against the existing social order. Initially it was concerned with spirit rather than with matter, and typically sought to get to the essence of the subject by grossly distorting outward appearance or external reality. This "subjective" first phase of Expressionism began in Germany about 1910, though its forerunners had appeared earlier in the plays of Wedekind and in Strindberg's *Ett Drömspel,* which put Realistic drama onto a supernatural plane. The leading exponent of early Expressionism in Germany was Georg Kaiser, whose themes centred on the struggle of the individual to fulfill himself in a hostile civilization. After World War I, the movement gained momentum from the social and political upheaval into which Germany was plunged. This later "activist" phase became more directly political and was represented by the plays of Ernst Toller, which called for a socialist revolution. *Die Maschinenstürmer* (1922; *The Machine Wreckers*) is Toller's best known play.

Characteristics of Expressionist drama

The language of Expressionist drama was stark and exclamatory, often overthrowing the conventions of grammar. Short scenes took the place of longer acts. Shafts of light picked out figures on a darkened stage, and scenery was limited to one or two symbolic forms. Characters were symbols instead of people. All this called for highly stylized acting, and directors looked for inspiration to the world of dance: German cabaret dancers, the eurythmy of Rudolf Steiner, and Rudolf von Laban's system of eukinetics were all important influences. The most notable director of the German Expressionist theatre was Erwin Piscator. Later in the 1920s, when steel, timber, and other materials once again became plentiful, Piscator directed a series of productions using elaborate and expensive machinery. The front of his stage was constructed on a conveyer-belt principle so that the actors appeared to walk from one location to the next. In the centre, a cantilever bridge moved up and down, while slides and films were projected onto different surfaces. Above the proscenium, slogans blazed in lights, and the gigantic shadows of pulsating machines were thrown onto gauzes.

Another director, Leopold Jessner, also made full use of building materials once postwar restrictions on their use had been lifted. His favourite setting was a vast flight of steps extending the entire width of the stage, rising steeply to a platform at the back. Like so many directors of the time, Jessner was greatly influenced by the new stagecraft of Craig and by the work of the Soviet directors of the postrevolutionary Constructivist theatre. Partly because of its abstract nature, Expressionist theatre was exciting but rarely artistically successful. By 1925 the movement was over, giving way to the epic theatre developed and cultivated by Piscator and Bertolt Brecht (see below). Further experiment in the German theatre was cut short by the accession to power by the Nazis in 1933.

Avant-garde in France. At the beginning of the 20th century, France was the international centre for innovation in the visual arts, but such was not the case with the theatre. In Paris theatres were dominated by wealthy patrons eager for the farces of Georges Feydeau and the boulevard tradition of well-made plays about sexual adventure and adultery. However, when the reaction against Realism did come, it had more lasting results than Constructivism, Futurism, or Expressionism, possibly because in France it centred on efforts to dignify the art of the actor rather than to exploit or devalue it. The reaction was initiated by the literary critic Jacques Copeau, who in 1913 set up his own company, the Théâtre du Vieux-Colombier. Although Copeau was influenced by the Naturalistic acting style that Antoine had demanded, he disliked Realistic theatre; yet, he also had an aversion to artificiality. Like Reinhardt, he sought to break down the barrier between the actor and the audience. His stage did away with the front curtain (for the first time on the modern French stage), and it extended out from the proscenium arch to surround the audience on three sides. Decor was used sparingly; the atmosphere for each play was created almost entirely by lighting. The intimate scale (Copeau's theatre seated only 200) allowed for natural delivery and movement, though even in contemporary plays gesture was used selectively to give every action particular significance. Copeau staged plays by a few new authors, but the main thrust of his work was in classics. His productions of Shakespeare and Molière were notable for their lightness, grace, and gaiety, as well as for their strong sense of ensemble playing. In 1921 Copeau opened a theatre school at the Vieux-Colombier that recognized the importance of body movement and vocal expression. One of his pupils, Étienne Decroux, continued this work to become the father of modern mime. Both company and school closed in 1924.

The work of Jacques Copeau

In 1927 the "Cartel" was formed to revitalize French avant-garde theatre and offer a viable alternative to boulevard plays. It comprised four directors, each with his own style: Louis Jouvet and Charles Dullin (both former actors with the Vieux-Colombier) and Georges Pitoëff and Gaston Baty. Jouvet's productions of Molière were his most important contribution; he freed the plays from the weight of tradition that was stifling them. Dullin's productions, which were less subjugated to the text, revealed a flair for movement, music, and bright colours. They stood in sharp contrast to the ascetic productions of Pitoëff, who believed that the director's primary aim should be to focus attention on a play's central idea, eliminating all details of decor and acting that might obscure it. Pitoëff's great contribution was the number of foreign dramatists he introduced to Parisian audiences. Baty, who had served his apprenticeship under Reinhardt, possessed a strong pictorial sense: his groupings and movement were beautifully composed, but they often existed for themselves rather than for the play.

Copeau's nephew, Michel Saint-Denis, formed the Compagnie des Quinze in 1930 with members of the defunct Vieux-Colombier and produced several of André Obey's plays, including *Noé* (1931; *Noah*). By the time the Compagnie des Quinze disbanded in 1934, it had become internationally famous for its lively productions. In the same year, Jouvet, Dullin, Baty, and Copeau were appointed as directors of the Comédie-Française in an effort to revive its flagging morale and declining artistic standards. In place of indulgent star performances, they introduced a more unified approach to production that clarified the text; thus they restored the theatre's high reputation.

Ireland. The establishment of an Irish national theatre during the early years of the 20th century was not a reaction against existing forms of theatre. Rather, it was a nationalist movement to establish an indigenous theatre, independent of European fashion, which could displace the sentimental and imitative plays that dominated the Irish stage. The first step was taken in 1898, when the poet William Butler Yeats and the playwright Augusta, Lady Gregory, founded the Irish Literary Theatre to encourage poetic drama. They soon developed a recognizable company style, and after performances in London Annie Horniman (pioneer of the British repertory movement) provided them with a permanent home in 1904 at the rebuilt Abbey Theatre in Dublin. The brilliant work of the group became world famous; it included the performances of many fine native actors as well as the contributions of outstanding dramatists, most notably J.M. Synge and Sean O'Casey. Several of these writers became interested in innovative techniques and forms. O'Casey, for one, was attracted to the Expressionist theatre and incorporated some of its techniques in *The Silver Tassie* (1929). During the 1920s, Yeats too tried his hand at experimentation, composing poetic dance plays based on the Japanese Nō theatre.

The Irish Literary Theatre

Great Britain. British theatre paid very little attention to the anti-Realistic movements that characterized experimental theatre in the rest of Europe. The domination of the actor-manager was effectively challenged by Harley Granville-Barker and John E. Vedrenne at London's Royal Court Theatre; between 1904 and 1907 they staged numerous new plays by British and continental writers. The major dramatist at the Royal Court—indeed the most important British dramatist of the century—was George Bernard Shaw. With plays such as *Man and Superman* (1903), he made theatre a lively platform for the discussion of social and philosophical issues, usually through the medium of laughter. Shaw availed himself of a wide variety of styles and models, including mythology in *Pygmalion* (1916) and history in *Saint Joan* (1924), but he always transformed his models to make them relevant to his own age.

George Bernard Shaw

The staging of Shakespeare's plays was revolutionized by Granville-Barker's productions at the Savoy Theatre, which were admired for their simplicity, fluidity, and speed. Equally significant for the British theatre was the founding of the first provincial repertory theatre in 1908 by Horniman at the Gaiety, Manchester. It not only provided opportunities for promising British playwrights but also presented works by important continental dramatists. Other repertory theatres followed: Liverpool in 1911 and Birmingham in 1913. For years the repertory movement continued with distinction, but after World War II it was regarded largely as a training ground where actors gained experience before making an assault on London—an attitude that was not rectified until the 1960s.

In London a repertory-style theatre was established by Lilian Baylis at the Old Vic in 1914, but it became most famous as a home for Shakespeare's plays, all of which were staged there over the following nine years. In 1931 Baylis reopened Sadler's Wells Theatre as a centre for opera and ballet. This theatre eventually became the base for the Royal Ballet and the English National Opera. After World War I, production costs and theatre rents rose so sharply that many West End theatres could not afford to remain open. They were taken over by commercially minded impressarios who favoured musical comedy, farce, and melodrama. Because of this situation, serious plays were left to the small theatre clubs.

During the 1930s, experimentation that went beyond straightforward Naturalism increased. Noël Coward revived the comedy of manners in *Private Lives* (1930); J.B. Priestley explored the cyclic concept of time in *Time and the Conways* (1937); and T.S. Eliot found a modern idiom for the poetic drama in his verse play *Murder in the Cathedral* (1935), originally performed in Canterbury cathedral. British acting and directing were stimulated by Theodore Komisarjevsky, who in 1919 emigrated to Britain from the Soviet Union, where he had been director of the Russian imperial and state theatres. His direction of plays by Chekhov and other Russian writers set new standards in English theatre, but his Shakespearean productions at Stratford-upon-Avon in the 1930s often infuriated audiences accustomed to conventional productions. His renderings were full of invention, sometimes brilliant, amusing, and illuminating, sometimes merely wayward. Equally influential was the French director Michel Saint-Denis. After his Compagnie des Quinze disbanded, he settled in England, where he directed several classical productions. Moreover, in 1935, he opened the London Theatre Studio to train young actors in the tradition that Copeau had begun in Paris.

United States. American theatre at the beginning of the 20th century was so heavily dominated by commercialism that some kind of revolt was to be expected. An attempt to establish a European-style art theatre in New York City was made in 1909 with the opening of the New Theatre, but the building was so cavernous and unsuited for experimental work that the venture collapsed after two seasons. Visits by the Abbey Theatre group in 1911, Reinhardt's *Sumurūm* in 1912, Granville-Barker's company in 1915, and Copeau's Vieux-Colombier in 1917 provided exciting glimpses of the work of Europe's art theatres and stimulated a large number of "little theatres" in provincial cities. Dedicated to producing the best of European and classical drama and to fostering new American plays, these groups were staunchly amateur, with their memberships organized by subscription, so that true experiment could be conducted without commercial pressure. One of the first such companies in New York City was the Washington Square Players. From a similar group, the Provincetown Players, emerged the first American dramatist of international stature: Eugene O'Neill. His first full-length play, *Beyond the Horizon,* was successfully produced in 1920. Most of O'Neill's subsequent work represented a restless search for theatrical style: he tried Expressionism in *The Emperor Jones* (1920) and *The Hairy Ape* (1922), masks in *The Great God Brown* (1926), and allegory in his updating of Aeschylus' *Oresteia* trilogy, *Mourning Becomes Electra* (1931), before he found a suitable idiom for modern tragedy in his autobiographical play *Long Day's Journey into Night* (1941; produced 1956).

O'Neill's experimentation with theatrical style

Art theatre was established on a commercially successful basis by New York City's Theatre Guild in 1918. During the next two decades it became the most important platform for American drama, encouraging such playwrights as Robert Sherwood, Maxwell Anderson, and Elmer Rice, in addition to O'Neill and European writers. The Theatre Guild's success quickly spurred independent Broadway producers to follow its example. The artistic challenge was also taken up by various designers, including Lee Simonson, Norman Bel Geddes, and Jo Mielziner, who provided distinguished settings that were realistic, symbolic, or expressionistic as required. The psychological depth of the new drama called for refinements in acting styles: Alfred Lunt, Lynn Fontanne, Helen Hayes, John Barrymore, Katherine Cornell, and Tallulah Bankhead were among the finest actors of the period, combining virtuosity with truthfulness. When the Moscow Art Theatre company visited New York City in 1923, two of its members were so impressed as to stay on and form the American Laboratory Theatre through which to teach the techniques of Stanislavsky. In 1927 *Show Boat* by Oscar Hammerstein II and Jerome Kern set new standards in the musical theatre, and in spite of competition from the expanding motion-picture industry, the number of productions on Broadway grew from 150 in the 1920–21 season to 280 in 1927–28.

The stock market crash of 1929 heralded the end of the unparalleled prosperity of both the theatre and the nation. The nation recovered from the ensuing economic depression, but the theatre, under increasing competition from motion pictures, radio, and television, did not. During the next 30 years, traveling companies all but disappeared, and productions on Broadway shrank to 60 in 1949–50, thereafter averaging between 50 and 60 a year. No new theatres were constructed. Nevertheless, live theatre continued to attract talented writers. From the social protest movement of the 1930s came Clifford Odets, Sidney Kingsley, Lillian Hellman, Thornton Wilder, and William Saroyan. So far, little attention had been paid to actor training, but in 1931 Harold Clurman, Cheryl Crawford, and Lee Strasberg formed the Group Theatre (an offshoot of the Theatre Guild) to develop new writers and evolve a style of acting, influenced by Stanislavsky's system, that sprang from a fresh observation of life rather than from the repetition of familiar clichés. From 1935 to 1939 the WPA Federal Theatre Project, established and funded by the Works Project Administration of the U.S. government to provide employment for out-of-work actors, presented hundreds of productions of all sorts throughout the country and showed that a large untapped audience existed for live theatre at low prices.

The Group Theatre

THEATRE SINCE WORLD WAR II

Efforts to rebuild the cultural fabric of civilization after the devastation of World War II led to a rethinking of the role of theatre in the new society. Competing with the technical refinements of motion pictures, radio, and television (all of which were offering drama), the live theatre had to rediscover what it could give to the community that the mass media could not. In one direction, this led to a search for a "popular" theatre that would embrace the whole community, just as the Greek theatre and the Elizabethan theatre had done. In another, it brought to fruition a new wave of experiments that had started before the war and was not to subside until the early 1970s—experiments that sought more radically than ever to challenge the audience, breaking down the barriers between spectators and performers.

Epic theatre of Brecht. Although Bertolt Brecht's first plays were written in Germany during the 1920s, he was not widely known until much later. Eventually his theories of stage presentation exerted more influence on the course of mid-century theatre in the West than did those of any other individual. This was largely because he proposed the major alternative to the Stanislavsky-oriented realism that dominated acting and the "well-made play" construction that dominated playwriting.

Brecht's earliest work was heavily influenced by German Expressionism, but it was his preoccupation with Marxism and the idea that man and society could be intellectually analyzed that led him to develop his theory of "epic theatre." Brecht believed that theatre should appeal not to the spectator's feelings but to his reason. While still providing entertainment, it should be strongly didactic and capable of provoking social change. In the Realistic theatre of illusion, he argued, the spectator tended to identify with the characters on stage and become emotionally involved with them rather than being stirred to think about his own life. To encourage the audience to adopt a more critical attitude to what was happening on stage, Brecht developed his *Verfremdungs-effekt* ("alienation effect")—*i.e.,* the use of anti-illusive techniques to remind the spectators that they are in a theatre watching an enactment of reality instead of reality itself. Such techniques included flooding the stage with harsh white light, regardless of where the action was taking place, and leaving the stage lamps in full view of the audience; making use of minimal props and "indicative" scenery; intentionally interrupting the action at key junctures with songs in order to drive home an important point or message; and projecting explanatory captions onto a screen or employing placards. From his actors Brecht demanded not realism and identification with the role but an objective style of playing, to become in a sense detached observers.

Brecht's *Verfrem-dungs-effekt*

Brecht's most important plays, which included *Leben des Galilei* (*The Life of Galileo*), *Mutter Courage und ihre Kinder* (*Mother Courage and Her Children*), and *Der gute Mensch von Sezuan* (*The Good Person of Szechwan,* or *The Good Woman of Setzwan*), were written between 1937 and 1945 when he was in exile from the Nazi regime, first in Scandinavia and then in the United States. At the invitation of the newly formed East German government, he returned to found the Berliner Ensemble in 1949 with his wife, Helene Weigel, as leading actress. It was only at this point, through his own productions of his plays, that Brecht earned his reputation as one of the most important figures of 20th-century theatre.

Certainly Brecht's attack on the illusive theatre influenced, directly or indirectly, the theatre of every Western country. In Britain the effect became evident in the work of such playwrights as John Arden and Edward Bond and in some of the bare-stage productions by the Royal Shakespeare Company. Western theatre in the 20th century, however, has proved to be a cross-fertilization of many styles (Brecht himself acknowledged a debt to traditional Oriental theatre), and by the 1950s other approaches were gaining influence.

Theatre of Fact. A more uncompromising method of bringing social issues to the stage has been Documentary Theatre, or the Theatre of Fact. In this case, the presentation of factual information usually takes precedence over aesthetic considerations. Out of the social protest movement that arose during the years of depression in the 1930s, a unit of the WPA Federal Theatre Project in the United States (see above) adopted what it called a Living Newspaper technique, taking inspiration from motion pictures (especially in the use of short scenes) to present highlighted versions of contemporary problems. The technique has since had varying degrees of success on stage. Real events are reconstructed and interpreted, either through fictional revisions or through the use of authentic documentary materials (*e.g.,* transcripts of trials, official reports, and lists of statistics). The form became popular in the 1960s through works such as Rolf Hochhuth's *Stellvertreter* (1963; *The Representative*), Peter Weiss's *Ermittlung* (1965; *The Investigation*), Heinar Kipphardt's *In der Sache J.R. Oppenheimer* (1964; *In the Matter of J. Robert Oppenheimer*), and in the Royal Shakespeare Company's *US* (1967). It has been used in Scotland in the 1980s by John McGrath's group called 7:84.

The Living Newspaper technique

Theatre of the Absurd. The postwar mood of disillusionment and skepticism was expressed in bizarre terms by a number of foreign playwrights living in Paris. Although they did not consider themselves as belonging to a formal movement, they shared a belief that human life was essentially without meaning or purpose and that valid communication was no longer possible. The human condition, they felt, had sunk to a state of absurdity (the term was coined by the French Existentialist novelist and philosopher Albert Camus). Some of the first plays of the Theatre of the Absurd, as the school came to be called, were concerned with the devaluation of language: Eugène Ionesco's *Cantatrice chauve* (*The Bald Soprano*, or *The Bald Prima Donna*) and Arthur Adamov's *Invasion* (*The Invasion*), both produced in 1950, and Samuel Beckett's *Waiting for Godot,* first produced in French as *En attendant Godot* in 1953. The spirit of Absurdism, however, can be traced back to Alfred Jarry's anarchic *Ubu roi,* produced in 1896. Logical construction and rationalism were abandoned in the Absurd school to create a world of uncertainty, where chairs could multiply for no apparent reason or humans turn inexplicably into rhinoceroses. Later Absurdist writers included Harold Pinter of Great Britain and Edward Albee of the United States, though by the 1960s the movement had nearly burned itself out.

Theatre of Cruelty. During the early 1930s, the French dramatist and actor Antonin Artaud put forth a theory for a Surrealist theatre called the Theatre of Cruelty. Based on ritual and fantasy, this form of theatre launches an attack on the spectators' subconscious in an attempt to release deep-rooted fears and anxieties that are normally suppressed, forcing people to view themselves and their natures without the shield of civilization. In order to shock the audience and thus evoke the necessary response, the extremes of human nature (often madness and perversion) are graphically portrayed on stage. Essentially an anti-literary revolt, the Theatre of Cruelty usually minimizes the text by emphasizing screams, inarticulate cries, and symbolic gestures. Artaud tried to achieve these ideals in his production of *Les Cenci* (1935), but his real influence lay in his theoretical writings, notably *Le Théâtre et son double* (1938; *The Theatre and Its Double*). Only after World War II did the Theatre of Cruelty achieve a more tangible form, first in the French director Jean-Louis Barrault's adaptation of Franz Kafka's *Prozess* (*The Trial*), produced in 1947, and later through the plays of Jean Genet and Fernando Arrabal. The movement was particularly popular during the 1960s, in part due to the success of Peter Brook's 1964 production of Peter Weiss's *Marat/Sade* for the Royal Shakespeare Company.

Surrealist theatre

Poor theatre. In terms of furthering the actor's technique, the Polish director Jerzy Grotowski, together with Stanislavsky and Brecht (see above), are the key figures of the 20th century. Grotowski first became internationally known when his Laboratory Theatre, established in Opole, Pol., in 1959, triumphantly toured Europe and the United States during the mid-1960s. His influence was further enhanced by the publication of his theoretical pronouncements in *Towards a Poor Theatre* (1968). Grotowski shared many ideas with Artaud (though the connection was initially coincidental), especially in the conception of the performer as a "holy actor" and the theatre as a "secular religion." Theatre was to go beyond mere entertainment or illustration; it was to be an intense confrontation with the audience (usually limited to fewer than 60). The actors sought spontaneity within a rigid discipline achieved through the most rigorous physical training. Rejecting the paraphernalia of the "rich theatre," Grotowski stripped away all nonessential scenery, costumes, and props to create the so-called poor theatre, where the only focus was the unadorned actor. His productions included adaptations of Calderón's *Príncipe constante* (1629; *The Constant Prince*) and the Polish writer Stanisław Wyspiański's *Akropolis* (1904; *Acropolis*).

Jerzy Grotowski's influence on acting

The poor theatre became a worldwide fashion during the late 1960s and early 1970s, even though most groups who attempted it produced only self-indulgent imitations that tended to exclude the audience. Significantly, this sense of reduction was evident in Grotowski's own work: from 1976 he excluded the audience altogether, preferring to work behind closed doors. The spirit of poor theatre has been more theatrically conveyed by Peter Brook. After leaving England in 1968 to establish the International Centre of Theatre Research in Paris, Brook created a series of vivid productions that included *Ubu roi* (1977), a scaled-down version of Georges Bizet's opera *Carmen* (1982), and *Le Mahabharata* (1985), a nine-hour version of the Hindu epic *Mahābhārata.*

United States. By the beginning of the 1950s the vitality of American theatre was acknowledged around the world. The international reputation of Eugene O'Neill was complemented by two potent young dramatists: Arthur

Miller, who turned the ordinary man into a figure of tragic stature in *Death of a Salesman* (1949) and *The Crucible* (1953), and Tennessee Williams, who created a world festering with passion and sensuality in plays such as *A Streetcar Named Desire* (1947). At the same time, the director Lee Strasberg, together with Elia Kazan, was codifying the teachings of Stanislavsky into "the Method," which generated both controversy and misunderstanding. Although the Actors Studio, founded by Kazan in 1947, produced many fine actors, including Marlon Brando, Geraldine Page, and Paul Newman, the Method proved inadequate as an approach to acting in classical plays; it was best suited to the realism of the new American plays and films.

Off-Broadway. This phenomenon developed as a reaction to the commercialism of New York theatre. More experimental plays could be presented in smaller buildings outside the main theatre district. The artistic success of many of these productions meant that some writers (Edward Albee, for example), could graduate to Broadway. Off-Broadway also enabled black playwrights such as James Baldwin and Leroi Jones (Imamu Amiri Baraka) to dramatize racial issues with a frankness that had not previously been seen on the American stage.

"Off-Off-Broadway"

During the 1960s, a strong avant-garde theatre movement known as "Off-Off-Broadway" emerged. Among the most influential groups were Joseph Chaikin's Open Theatre, Richard Schechner's Performance Group, Julian Beck's and Judith Malina's Living Theatre, and Peter Schumann's Bread and Puppet Theatre. These groups sought to smash the barriers between the actor and the audience, exploring ritual, sexuality, nudity, and primitivism. They also signaled, however, a movement away from literary values: coherent speech and concise dialogue were in most cases replaced by improvisations, grunts, and shrieks. As with the British "fringe theatre," this movement generated great excitement and vitality, but at its worst it produced gratuitous violence, self-indulgence, and ultimately the alienation of the very audience that it set out to embrace. The political wing of the avant-garde was street theatre, or "guerrilla theatre," where short agitprop ("agitational propaganda") plays were performed on city streets or in parks. In this manner, the San Francisco Mime Troupe combined political protest with the techniques of the commedia dell'arte to reach a non-theatregoing public. By the late 1970s, the wild experiments had dissolved into conventional playwriting, mostly of mediocre quality; Sam Shepard and David Rabe were exceptions. Even by the mid-1980s, very little had emerged to replace the exuberance of that period when theatre seemed to have found a new immediacy and a fresh way of involving all segments of the community.

Government subsidy. In spite of state aid from organizations such as the New York State Council on the Arts, created in 1960, and the National Endowment for the Arts (1965), the running of American theatre has remained strongly commercial. The most consistently successful American playwright from the 1960s to the 1980s has been Neil Simon, whose comedies such as *The Odd Couple* (1965) and *Plaza Suite* (1968) have fared very well. On Broadway theatre management, because of economic factors, has been reluctant to stage serious new plays unless they have been proven successes in London. A notable exception to this situation has been the New York Shakespeare Festival, founded by Joseph Papp in 1954 under the name Shakespeare Workshop. From 1962 it has occupied a permanent site—the outdoor Delacorte Theatre in Central Park—where it offers free entertainment. Since 1981, it has received a regular subsidy from New York City. Outside New York City, regional theatre has continued to expand with resident professional companies being established in many cities—the Guthrie Theatre in Minneapolis, Minn., for example. Such companies offer both commercial and experimental theatre as an alternative to touring Broadway hits.

Revitalization of the musical comedy

The musical comedy. After Rodgers and Hammerstein breathed new life into the musical comedy with *Oklahoma!* (1943), the form acquired more sophistication with such Broadway successes as *Guys and Dolls* (1950) and *My Fair Lady* (1956), and it broke new ground in *West Side Story* (1957), which conveyed much of the plot through dance. The range of subjects widened: hippie culture was introduced in *Hair* (1967); religion was popularized in *Godspell* (1971) and *Jesus Christ Superstar* (1971); and dance became the central element in shows such as *A Chorus Line* (1975) and *Dancin'* (1978). By the 1980s, Stephen Sondheim had become the most innovative force in the musical theatre, combining the roles of lyricist and composer in such works of immense technical sophistication as *Company* (1970), *A Little Night Music* (1973), and *Sunday in the Park with George* (1984).

University theatre. Another major source of theatre in the United States is supplied by the drama departments of colleges and universities. The American Educational Theatre Association (AETA) was established in 1936 with 80 members, but by the 1980s, as the American Theatre Association (ATA), it included about 1,600 U.S. college and university drama departments. All of these have their own theatre; some are as well equipped as Broadway and regional theatres. In addition to promoting work by local student groups, many university theatres from time to time employ professional actors and directors for summer stock productions.

Great Britain. World War II had left British theatre in a precarious state. In London's West End, about a fifth of the theatres were destroyed or damaged by bombing. Furthermore, production costs multiplied, an entertainment tax of 10 percent of gross receipts was imposed by the government, and theatre managements—many of them controlled by a monopoly known as The Group—tended to choose thrillers, light comedies, revues, and Broadway musicals over more demanding plays. In the early 1950s the star system dominated the theatre, and one of the most prominent dramatists was Terence Rattigan. The classics, however, were kept robustly alive by the last of the actor-managers: Sir Donald Wolfit, Sir Laurence Olivier (later Lord Olivier), and Sir John Gielgud. Olivier and Gielgud were supported by a generation of outstanding actors, many of whom had begun their careers in the 1930s and were able to adapt to changes in the theatrical climate (as well as to the growth of motion pictures and television) through to the 1980s. These actors included Sir Ralph Richardson, Sir Michael Redgrave, and Dame Peggy Ashcroft.

By the mid-1950s, the influence of Brecht was becoming apparent. The director Joan Littlewood was one of the first to use his techniques; in 1953 she moved her company, the Theatre Workshop (formed in 1945 in Manchester for working-class audiences), to the Theatre Royal, Stratford, in the East End of London. There she encouraged young writers and evolved a series of highly successful collective productions, many of them (*e.g., Oh, What a Lovely War!* [1963]) developed through improvisation. After observing the Berliner Ensemble at work in Germany, George Devine set up the English Stage Company at the Royal Court Theatre in 1956 to encourage new playwrights and promote foreign drama. That year marked a turning point in British theatre, with Samuel Beckett's *Waiting for Godot* (in his own translation) introducing the Theatre of the Absurd and John Osborne's *Look Back in Anger* initiating a new wave of antiheroic, "kitchen-sink" dramas. Other young writers at the Royal Court were Arnold Wesker and John Arden. The wider distribution of higher education grants after World War II meant that by the mid-1950s a new breed of actors was coming out of drama schools to perform these new plays. The rise of actors such as Peter O'Toole, Albert Finney, Tom Courtenay, Joan Plowright, and Alan Bates brought fresh energy to the theatre and marked a transition away from the elegant actors of the late 1940s who exuded upper-class sophistication.

Proliferation of "fringe" theatres

Alternative theatre. A vigorous reaction against the mainstream of theatre erupted in the late 1960s, stimulated by a wave of political protest around the world, visits by French and American avant-garde companies, an upsurge of "alternative culture," and an abolition of the lord chamberlain's powers of censorship (1968). Following the example of the Traverse Theatre in Edinburgh, a profusion of "fringe" theatres sprang up in converted cellars, warehouses, and the back rooms of pubs. Rock music, Dada, and Artaud were inspiration for groups such as The People Show, Pip Simmons Theatre Group, and Ken Campbell's Road Show. Other companies—Foco Novo, Portable Theatre, 7:84, Belt & Braces, and CAST—were more politically motivated. From these came several major dramatists, including Howard Brenton, David Hare, Trevor Griffiths, and David Edgar, all of whom had been assimilated into mainstream theatre by the end of the 1970s. Although most fringe plays quickly disappear without a trace, several have successfully transferred to the West End. Indeed, the fringe continues to provide an important stimulus for the British theatre.

National theatres. Since the early 1960s, Britain's theatrical reputation had rested mainly on the work produced by its two national companies. Peter Hall formed the Royal Shakespeare Company in 1961 as a reorganization of the Shakespeare Memorial Theatre at Stratford-upon-Avon. The following year, he was supported by two codirectors, Peter Brook and Michel Saint-Denis, and the company opened a permanent London base at the Aldwych Theatre to explore modern and classical plays while concentrating on Shakespeare at Stratford. During this period, Brook established himself as one of the finest directors of the century, two of his most memorable productions being *King Lear* (1962) and *A Midsummer Night's Dream* (1970). In 1982, under the artistic directorship of Trevor Nunn and Terry Hands, the company left the Aldwych and moved into the newly built Barbican arts complex in the City of London, while retaining the Stratford theatre.

The first attempts to set up a permanent national theatre in London were made in the 19th century, though it was not until 1962 that Sir Laurence Olivier formed the National Theatre company, which was temporarily housed in the Old Vic. After delays by successive governments, work began in 1969 on the National Theatre building (housing three separate theatres), situated on the south bank of the Thames not far from the site of Shakespeare's Globe Theatre. It finally opened in 1976 under the directorship of Peter Hall (later knighted).

The importance of these two companies is that, apart from providing lavish reassessments of classical plays featuring the best actors of the day, they have been able to commission large-scale works that no one else could have afforded: John Whiting's *Devils* (1961) and Peter Shaffer's *Royal Hunt of the Sun* (1964) both broke away from the "well-made play" construction, leaning toward the Epic Theatre of Brecht; and David Edgar's 8½-hour dramatization of Dickens' *Nicholas Nickleby* (1980) proved a huge success in London and in New York City. Notwithstanding the emphasis on classical work, both companies have retained a strong commitment to contemporary drama and have nurtured Britain's leading dramatists of the 1970s and 1980s, including Harold Pinter, Edward Bond, Tom Stoppard, Alan Ayckbourn, David Hare, and Howard Brenton.

Government subsidy. One of the major changes in British theatre since World War II has been that state subsidy plays an increasingly vital role in its development and survival. While the subsidy has helped to shield the theatre from commercial pressures, it has left the theatre vulnerable and overdependent on continuing grants.

State aid began with the formation of the Council for the Encouragement of Music and the Arts (CEMA) in 1940. From this developed the Arts Council of Great Britain in 1946 with the aim of providing "State support for the arts, without State control." It has encouraged new writing and supported fringe, touring, community, and repertory theatres, including the two national companies, besides subsidizing Regional Arts Associations and other artistic ventures. By keeping ticket prices artificially low, the Arts Council has helped to make serious drama accessible to most of the population and thereby provides a widespread alternative to commercial theatre.

From the early 1960s, the sums given to the Arts Council by the government increased substantially. By the end of the 1970s, however, the rate of expansion had outstripped the supply of money, and most subsidized theatre companies were facing serious cutbacks, some actually closing. As a consequence, in the 1980s the government and the Arts Council adopted a policy of encouraging theatres to seek additional sponsorship from industry.

Regional theatre. In the provinces theatre is divided into touring, repertory, and amateur companies. Large theatres in the main cities are visited by touring companies, and at Christmastime most of them stage an elaborate pantomime that often runs for three or four months. After a lean period in the 1950s when it competed with television, repertory theatre (now also known as regional theatre) found new life in the 1960s with the building of many fine civic playhouses, some even equipped with additional studio theatres for experimental work. Improved conditions, longer runs, and increased subsidies resulted in higher artistic standards. The repertory theatres remain a valuable testing ground for actors, directors, and dramatists, often supplying new plays and productions for the West End. The vast amateur-theatre movement in Britain (there were about 17,000 groups by the mid-1980s) is coordinated by the British Theatre Association, formerly called the British Drama League. The association also runs many training courses throughout the country. Although there is little movement from amateur to professional status, the National Youth Theatre has given many prominent actors their first experience in theatre. Most professionals graduate from drama schools, some of the most reputable being the Royal Academy of Dramatic Art (RADA), the Central School of Speech and Drama, and the Guildhall School of Music and Drama.

Importance of repertory theatres

Australia, New Zealand, and Canada. From the early 1970s, a characteristic style of theatre emerged in Australia, spawned mainly by smaller companies. Typical examples of such companies are the Australian Performing Group in Melbourne and the Nimrod Theatre in Sydney, both of which are dedicated to promoting the work of new writers. New Zealand has witnessed similar efforts. Most of the plays have been produced in Auckland's Mercury Theatre and Wellington's Downstage, with very few being performed outside New Zealand. Canadian drama has been equally slow to reach the international stage in spite of vigorous efforts to encourage new plays. More prestigious is the annual Shakespeare Festival at Stratford, Ont. Founded in 1953 by Tyrone Guthrie, it has produced a consistently high standard of work and has attracted some of the finest Canadian and British actors.

France. Although France has produced a number of outstanding dramatists since World War II, including Jean Anouilh, Jean-Paul Sartre, Samuel Beckett, Jean Genet, and Marguerite Duras, the development of the theatre has been dominated by directors. A leading force, and one of the greatest actors of the century, has been Jean-Louis Barrault, who excelled in both classical and modern plays. As a mime (trained by Decroux), he achieved international fame for his re-creation of the pantomimes of Deburau in the film *Les Enfants du paradis* (1945; "The Children of the Gods"), and as a director he became the foremost exponent of the poetic dramas of Paul Claudel. In 1946 he left the Comédie-Française with his wife, the actress Madeleine Renaud, to form the Compagnie Renaud-Barrault, which has remained one of France's finest and most innovative companies.

The achievements of Jean-Louis Barrault

Mime found another champion in Marcel Marceau. He developed the character Bip in 1946 and has since toured the world many times with his solo performances.

An attempt to widen the appeal of theatre was made in 1951, when Jean Vilar was appointed director of the Théâtre National Populaire (TNP). At the huge Palais de Chaillot in Paris (seating nearly 3,000), Vilar brought together new audiences by presenting a repertoire of mainly classical plays at ticket prices that students and workers could afford. As part of a policy to decentralize French theatre by setting up provincial companies, the TNP was moved to Villeurbanne in 1972 under the directorship of Roger Planchon. A move toward collective creation in the late 1960s precipitated a wave of vigorous avant-garde companies such as Ariane Mnouchkine's Théâtre du Soleil and Jérôme Savary's Grand Magic Circus. By the mid-1980s, however, the absence of gifted new writers shifted the emphasis in French theatre to reassessments of classical plays, particularly those of Molière. Two of the most prominent directors have been Antoine Vitez at the Théâtre National de Chaillot and Patrice Chéreau at the Théâtre des Amandiers at Nanterre.

Germany. Few dramatists of distinction appeared in Germany after World War II in spite of the stimulus created by the return of Brecht, the rebuilding of theatres, and the large amounts of money poured into the theatrical arts by both the East and West German governments. Consequently, German classics and foreign plays dominated the stage. The two notable German-speaking dramatists of the 1950s, Max Frisch and Friedrich Dürrenmatt, were both Swiss. Outstanding work, however, was achieved by the Austrian-born actor, Fritz Kortner, who returned to West Germany from the United States in 1947 to direct a series of productions imbued with meticulous realism. Throughout the 1960s, there was more sense of experiment in plays by Peter Weiss (living in Sweden), Peter Handke, and Günter Grass. Peter Stein, director of the Schaubühne in Berlin from 1970 to 1985, earned international acclaim through his innovative interpretations of foreign plays, especially Gorky's *Dachniki* (1905; *Summerfolk*) in 1974 and Aeschylus' *Oresteia* in 1981. In East Germany, where the theatre has been heavily controlled by the state and geared toward educating the workers on farms and in factories, Socialist Realism has proved a deadening influence.

Soviet Union. After Stalin's death in 1953, the heavy restrictions on Soviet theatre began to loosen, signaling a slow and cautious return to experiment. The influence of Meyerhold (rehabilitated in 1955) was discernible in productions by the veteran Nicolay Okhlopkov, who remained the most original and stimulating director of his day. The scale of the Soviet theatre was gigantic: companies played in more than 50 languages; there were vast numbers of theatres, many with huge and superbly equipped stages; companies of 100 actors or more were not unusual, and they maintained extensive repertoires. Yet, the security derived from enormous state subsidies, combined with the vast output of work, tended to give rise to mediocre standards.

So large was the theatregoing public that the professional theatre could not satisfy the demand for dramatic entertainment, and every encouragement was given to the amateur movement. Most companies accepted responsibility for at least one amateur group, the members of the company giving much time to advising and training it. Amateur companies of outstanding merit were given the title "people's theatre." The close relations between amateurs and professionals were mutually beneficial, for professionals found that the contact infused freshness and reality into their work.

Shift in emphasis

In the 1960s, the theatre gradually began to free itself from ideology, placing more emphasis on entertainment value. Socialist heroes gave way to ordinary citizens on the stage; farce and vaudeville were revived; and absurd, grotesque, and fantastic elements reappeared in new plays. By the late 1970s, one or two of the experimental companies could once more take their place alongside the best in Europe. The Rustavelli Company from Georgia was acclaimed during its visits to Britain in 1979 and 1980. Yury Lyubimov, director of the prestigious Taganka Theatre, successfully reproduced his adaptation of Dostoyevsky's *Prestupleniye i nakazaniye* (1866; *Crime and Punishment*) in London in 1983 with English actors. In search of even more artistic freedom, he defected to the West the following year.

Other European countries. Of all the eastern European countries, Poland has produced the most exciting theatre, but because of heavy censorship this has come from directors rather than from writers. Experiment has long been encouraged within the state-subsidized system, and in the 1960s several Polish dramatists of the pre-World War II period, including Stanisław Wyspiański, Stanisław Ignacy Witkiewicz, and Witold Gombrowicz, were rediscovered in powerful productions that commented on contemporary issues. Apart from Jerzy Grotowski, prominent directors included Andrzej Wajda, Józef Szajna, and Tadeusz Kantor. The latter was the founder of the Cricot 2 theatre group, and his production in 1975 of *Umarla klasa* (*The Dead Class*), mixing puppets and actors, recalled Gordon Craig's concept of the *Übermarionette*. A strong mime company was led by Henryk Tomaszewski. In Czechoslovakia mime had another gifted exponent in Ladislav Fialka, and at the National Theatre in Prague during the 1950s Josef Svoboda was widely regarded as the world's leading stage designer.

In Italy theatre was stimulated by the establishment of permanent regional companies (*teatri stabili*) immediately after World War II. The first of these, the Piccolo Teatro di Milano, was controlled by Giorgio Strehler, Italy's finest director. His production of Carlo Goldoni's aforementioned play *Servitore di due padrone,* frequently revived since 1947, became world famous. The abolition of censorship in 1962 opened the way for more adventurous experimental theatre, though once again directors overshadowed playwrights. The exception has been Dario Fo, a brilliant actor, mime, director, and dramatist, whose political farces evoked the spirit of the commedia dell'arte. One of his most widely translated plays is *Morte accidentale di un anarchico* (1970; *Accidental Death of an Anarchist*).

BIBLIOGRAPHY

Reference works: Among the most informative general references are JOHN GASSNER and EDWARD QUINN (eds.), *The Reader's Encyclopedia of World Drama* (1969); PHYLLIS HARTNOLL (ed.), *The Oxford Companion to the Theatre,* 4th ed. (1983); and GERALD BORDMAN, *The Oxford Companion to American Theatre* (1984). Comprehensive bibliographies include BLANCH M. BAKER, *Theatre and Allied Arts* (1952, reprinted 1967); DAVID CHESHIRE, *Theatre* (1967); and FREDERIC M. LITTO, *American Dissertations on the Drama and the Theatre* (1969). Journals treating all aspects of theatre include *Drama Review* (quarterly); *Drama* (quarterly); and *New Theatre Quarterly* (formerly *Theatre Quarterly*). Some other useful periodicals are *Theatrephile* (quarterly), which is devoted to research in popular theatre; and *Essays in Theatre* (semiannual), an international scholarly publication.

General historical works: CLIFFORD LEECH and T.W. CRAIK (eds.), *The Revels History of Drama in English,* 8 vol. (1976–83), a detailed and well-illustrated guide to British and American theatre from medieval to modern; ALLARDYCE NICOLL, *World Drama from Aeschylus to Anouilh,* 2nd rev. ed. (1976), a comprehensive one-volume analysis of the development of drama; GEORGE ALTMAN *et al., Theater Pictorial* (1953); GEORGE FREEDLEY and JOHN A. REEVES, *A History of the Theatre,* 3rd rev. ed. (1968); BAMBER GASCOIGNE, *World Theatre* (1968); PHYLLIS HARTNOLL, *A Concise History of the Theatre* (1968, reprinted 1973); RICHARD SOUTHERN, *The Seven Ages of the Theatre,* 2nd ed. (1968); RICHARD LEACROFT and HELEN LEACROFT, *Theatre and Playhouse: An Illustrated Survey of Theatre Building from Ancient Greece to the Present Day* (1984).

National and special studies: E.T. KIRBY, *Ur-Drama: The Origins of Theatre* (1975); ALLARDYCE NICOLL, *Masks, Mimes and Miracles: Studies in the Popular Theatre* (1931, reissued 1963); MARGARETE BIEBER, *The History of the Greek and Roman Theatre,* 2nd rev. ed. (1961); H.D.F. KITTO, *Greek Tragedy: A Literary Study* (1939, reprinted 1976); OLIVER TAPLIN, *Greek Tragedy in Action* (1978); J. MICHAEL WALTON, *The Greek Sense of Theatre: Tragedy Reviewed* (1984); E.K. CHAMBERS, *The Medieval Stage,* 2 vol. (1903, reprinted 1978); GLYNNE WICKHAM, *Early English Stages, 1300–1660,* 3 vol., 2nd ed. (1980–81); ALLARDYCE NICOLL, *A History of English Drama, 1660–1900,* 6 vol. (1952–59, reprinted 1961–65); M.C. BRADBROOK, *A History of Elizabethan Drama,* 6 vol. (1960–79); E.K. CHAMBERS, *The Elizabethan Stage,* 4 vol. (1923, rev. ed. 1951); ALAN C. DESSEN, *Elizabethan Stage Conventions and Modern Interpreters* (1984); GERALD EADES BENTLEY, *The Profession of Dramatist in Shakespeare's Time, 1590–1642* (1971), and *The Profession of Player in Shakespeare's Time, 1590–1642* (1984); A.M. NAGLER, *Theatre Festivals of the Medici, 1539–1637,* trans. from the German (1964, reprinted 1976); ALLARDYCE NICOLL, *Stuart Masques and the Renaissance Stage* (1937, reprinted 1980); N.D. SHERGOLD, *A History of the Spanish Stage: From Medieval Times Until the End of the Seventeenth Century* (1967); JOSEPH SPENCER KENNARD, *The Italian Theatre,* 2 vol. (1932, reprinted 1964); GIACOMO OREGLIA, *The Commedia dell'Arte* (1968, reprinted 1982; originally published in Italian, 1961); J.L. STYAN, *Drama, Stage, and Audience* (1975); FREDERICK W. HAWKINS, *Annals of the French Stage from Its Origins to the Death of Racine,* 2 vol. (1884, reprinted 1970), and *The French Stage in the Eighteenth Century,* 2 vol. (1888, reprinted 1969); JOHN LOUGH, *Paris Theatre Audiences in the Seventeenth and Eighteenth Centuries* (1957, reprinted 1972); HAROLD HOBSON, *French Theatre Since 1830* (1979); W.H. BRU-

FORD, *Theatre, Drama, and Audience in Goethe's Germany* (1950, reprinted 1974); RAYMOND MANDER and JOE MITCHENSON, *British Music Hall,* rev. ed. (1974); GEORGE ROWELL, *The Victorian Theatre, 1792–1914,* 2nd ed. (1978); MARK SLONIM, *Russian Theater, from the Empire to the Soviets* (1961); HAROLD B. SEGEL, *Twentieth-Century Russian Drama* (1979); BOHDAN DROZDOWSKI and CATHERINE ITZEN (eds.), *Twentieth Century Polish Theatre* (1979); BROOKS ATKINSON, *Broadway,* rev. ed. (1974); BARNARD W. HEWITT, *Theatre U.S.A. 1668–1957* (1959); BENJAMIN MCARTHUR, *Actors and American Culture, 1880–1920* (1984); MARTIN ESSLIN, *The Theatre of the Absurd,* 3rd rev. ed. (1980); JOHN ELSOM, *Post-War British Theatre,* rev. ed. (1979), and JOHN ELSOM (ed.), *Post-War British Theatre Criticism* (1981); RONALD HAYMAN, *British Theatre Since 1955* (1979); JOHN RUSSELL TAYLOR, *Anger and After: A Guide to the New British Drama,* 2nd rev. ed. (1969, reprinted 1977), and *The Second Wave: British Drama of the Sixties* (1978).

(K.G.R.)

Theatrical Production

Theatrical production comprises all aspects of planning, rehearsing, and presenting a work to an audience at a particular time and place by living performers using either themselves or inanimate figures such as puppets as the medium of presentation. A theatrical production can be either dramatic or nondramatic, depending upon the activity presented. While dramatic productions frequently conform to a written text, it is not the use of such a text but rather the fictional mimetic (from Greek *mimēsis,* "imitation," "representation") nature of the performer's behaviour that makes a work dramatic. A person walking a tightrope is performing an acrobatic act, whereas a person who pretends to be an acrobat walking a tightrope is performing a dramatic act. Both performers are engaged in theatrical presentation, but only the latter is involved in the creation of dramatic illusion. Though a dramatic performance may include dancing, singing, juggling, acrobatics, or other nondramatic elements, it is concerned mainly with the representation of actual or imagined life.

In nondramatic theatrical productions there is no imitation of "another existence" but simply the entertainment or excitation of the audience by the performer. Whether acrobatic or musical, gestural or vocal, such activity is theatrical because it is presented by a living performer to an audience, but it remains nondramatic so long as it has a purely presentational quality rather than a representational one.

In any single theatrical production, one or another type of activity may so prevail that there is little difficulty in determining the aesthetic nature of the final work. A play by the 19th-century Norwegian dramatist Henrik Ibsen, with its depiction of middle-class behaviour, minimizes nondramatic activity; the recital of a song by the 19th-century Romantic composer Franz Schubert, by contrast, with its emphasis upon musical values, may ignore dramatic elements and, to a great extent, even the act of presentation itself. Between these extremes, however, there are many types of theatrical production in which the aesthetic nature of the form is less simple. Opera, for example, employs both drama and music, in shifting patterns of emphasis.

In the 20th century in Europe and the United States several forms arose that combine dramatic and nondramatic material. Vaudeville, or music hall, for instance, employs a succession of fictional sketches, musical and dance numbers, feats of dexterity, and other acts, some of which are representational, others not. In the musical theatre, song and dance serve both to further the narrative and to provide a break from purely dramatic presentation. This variety also characterizes much of Oriental theatre, in which dramatic moments are elaborated in dancelike exhibitions. In light of these examples, the definition of what constitutes theatrical production must remain elastic.

The present article examines the chief elements of theatrical production and the development of theatres and staging and concludes with a survey of scenic design, stage lighting, stage machinery, costumes, and makeup. For a general discussion of theatre as an art form, with specific treatment of the crafts of acting and directing, see THEATRE, THE ART OF THE. Drama as a literary genre is treated in LITERATURE, THE ART OF. The history of dramatic literature is covered in THEATRE, THE HISTORY OF WESTERN; and with that of the other genres according to language—*e.g.,* AMERICAN LITERATURE; FRENCH LITERATURE. For coverage of related topics in the *Macropædia* and *Micropædia,* see the *Propædia,* Part Six, Division II, especially Section 622.

The article is divided into the following sections:

Elements of theatrical production

According to the British director Peter Brook, theatre occurs whenever someone crosses neutral space and is watched by another person. This definition raises some problems, such as the difficulty of determining neutral space, but it is useful in its firm commitment to demystifying theatrical production. In former times the idea of the actor as motivated by a desire to create astonishment and wonder was sometimes seen as the basis of all theatre. Certainly there are types of performance that entail ritual and magic, but theatre is far more frequently rooted in attempts to structure emotion and experience.

Generally speaking, all theatrical productions have certain elements in common: the performer or performers, their acting in space (usually some sort of stage) and time (some limited duration of performance), and a producing process and organization.

THE PERFORMER

Skills and attributes. The work of the actor falls into five main areas: (1) the exhibition of particular physical, including vocal, skills; (2) the exhibition of mimetic skills, in which physical states and activities are simulated; (3) the imaginative exploration of fictitious situations; (4) the exhibition of patterns of human behaviour that are not natural to the actor; and (5) interaction, while engaging in these activities, with other actor-characters and with members of the audience.

At certain times in the history of Western theatre, the highest degree of physical skill has been associated with nondramatic performance. In Oriental theatre, however, such distinctions do not apply. Chinese opera and Japanese drama require the actor to play one type of role for his entire professional life. The actor must play this role in a manner strictly determined by tradition, reproducing specific patterns of movement and speech that can only be mastered by first gaining control of complex physical skills. Later, if especially gifted, an actor may bring to a role certain refinements of the tradition, which may be handed down to a succeeding generation.

Western drama, however, does not usually provide the actor with quite so defined a repertoire of movements and utterances. It is true that actors in the Italian commedia dell'arte of the 16th to the 18th century specialized in one role and transmitted to their successors a body of situations, speeches, and *lazzi* (stage sketches, or routines). Nevertheless, they seem to have had more leeway than their Oriental counterparts in exercising invention and personal expression. Great rhetorical skill has been demanded of the Western actor, however, for the intricate metrical patterns of Greek, Latin, French, English, and Spanish drama have been part of the glory of their respective theatres.

Naturalistic theatre, which flowered in the late 19th century, made rhetoric obsolete, requiring the actor to hide virtuoso performing skills by creating the illusion of everyday behaviour. This meant that more weight was given to the actor's personal attributes. The magnetism of a performance derived no longer from stylized behaviour but from intense personal revelation. This requires a marked ability to focus energies, to concentrate intently either upon the audience directly or upon a fellow actor and, thereby, indirectly upon the audience. All good actors can project a concentrated force, or "presence," which has become increasingly important to the actor in performance as set patterns of playing have disappeared. Presence is not a fixed, definable quality but rather a process of continuous growth and change that takes place before the eyes of the audience.

Relation to the audience. In nondramatic theatre the performer generally acknowledges the presence of the audience and may play directly to it. In dramatic theatre the actor may or may not do so. In Greek Old Comedy, an actor speaking for the author might cajole, advise, or challenge the spectators. By contrast, the naturalistic actor plays as though a "fourth wall" closes off the room of the stage. Between these two extremes fall a variety of relationships. In some instances, although direct contact is made, the audience is itself assumed to be playing a role, as in trial plays in which the audience is treated as a jury or as spectators in the court of justice. In other instances, the actor may address the audience one moment and play as though there were a fourth wall the next.

The quality of the contact between performer and audience is subtly modified by the nature of the performer's place and role in society. In the broadest terms, the performer may be seen as a celebrant, servant, or critic of society. As a celebrant, the actor performs an almost priestly function, and in certain types of production the actor may in fact be a priest. In such instances, the actor mediates between the audience and the divine or spiritual dimension. In Greek tragedy, Japanese Nō theatre, and medieval mystery plays the actions of the performers have a religious as well as dramatic significance, but this is by no means always the case.

More often the actor has been a servant, akin to the household retainer or court jester. In classical Rome actors were slaves or lowly freedmen. In Elizabethan England the actor was nominally the protégé of a powerful courtly patron or, if he lacked patronage, was considered a rogue and vagabond. Such performers, as servants or inferiors, necessarily approached their audiences in supplicatory terms. With the growth of the commedia dell'arte companies, which were established on a commercial basis, the relationship between actor and audience changed into one of producer and consumer.

In the 19th century, with the flourishing of the Romantic movement and the rise of nationalist consciousness throughout Europe, the actor as rebel began to appear.

The role of the theatre was then a powerful one; actors learned to utilize the material of the play, even of classic works, to make political statements. Later, in the 20th century, the traditional boundaries between actors and spectators were broken down, and the performer became in some cases a virtual assailant of the audience. The Living Theatre, formed in 1947 in New York City by Julian Beck and Judith Malina, engaged the audience in direct personal and physical contact. In the 1970s, Augusto Boal of Brazil developed the theatre of the oppressed, in which performance was intended to serve the triple function of entertainment, education, and consciousness-raising. Similar techniques found wide use in the 1970s and '80s in such special-interest movements as feminist theatre, homosexual theatre, black theatre, prison theatre, theatre of the deaf, theatre of the handicapped, and theatre of the aged.

The actor as character. Another aspect of the dramatic performer's work has to do with the portrayal of characters, both as individuals and as types. In portraying an individual character, the performer adopts a fictional framework and acts according to the text's demands. When playing Macbeth, for instance, he behaves "as if" he sees the phantom dagger referred to in the text. In many roles, however, the actor must work within established categories of stock types. Roman comedy, for instance, utilized a limited number of stock characters, such as the cunning slave, the passionate young lover, and the suspicious old father. The king, the wise counselor, the raging tyrant are examples derived from historical and biblical sources; the leading man, the juvenile, the ingenue, and the villain are examples from theatrical tradition itself.

Stock characters

While stock types stress those features of personality common to all human beings, naturalistic, or "slice-of-life," drama seeks to individualize each role. This requires that the actor as well as the author draw from personal observation and experience. With the rise of dramatic Naturalism in the late 19th and early 20th centuries, there arose corresponding theories of acting, notably those of Konstantin Stanislavsky, director of the Moscow Art Theatre. While an actor of this period might start with a generalized "type" (a country doctor, for example), efforts during rehearsal were bent on differentiating this doctor from any other. This style of acting demanded extensive preparation, with rehearsal periods of up to a year.

Naturalistic acting raises questions about the relation between the actor and the role performed: Does the actor merely simulate behaviour, or does he in some sense actually experience the passions and thoughts of the character? Central to the actor's art though this question is, it has never been satisfactorily answered.

SPACE AND TIME

The distinction between actor as performer and actor as character is matched by a distinction between the presentational and representational nature of space and time in theatrical production.

The playhouse area. Performer and audience exist together in a common area, within which there is a clearly delineated performing space (ring, stage platform, pit) and an audience space, the two structurally related. Some of the more common patterns of relationship are (1) an amphitheatre, with a bank of spectators half surrounding a playing area; (2) a circle of spectators standing or sitting around a ring in which the performance takes place; and (3) rows of seated spectators facing a raised platform. Theatre space is often associated with a special building, but this has not always been the case, nor is it always the case in modern times. Often theatre space has embraced a town square or even an entire town so that performers and audience are able to mingle. Modern attempts to create a space within which the distinction between performer and audience is blurred (called environmental theatre) echo earlier examples from the popular theatre.

Performance space and audience space

Isolation of the performer. Almost all productions (the so-called happenings of the 1960s are notable exceptions) endeavour to achieve two basic aims. First, every production seeks to impart a special quality to the theatrical area. Use of a theatrical building may in itself provide a heightened sense of locale. Otherwise, special decoration of familiar locales (town, market square) may transform them into ceremonial or festive spaces. Next, every production tries to make the performer visible and audible to the audience. On flat ground the circle or ring has often proved best. In hilly country the amphitheatre is the readiest solution. When a playing area is to be permanent, some means of raising the performer above the level of the crowd is often introduced, such as boards laid over trestles. The degree to which the performer is to be isolated depends partly on how complete and detailed a view of the presentation the audience expects.

The isolation of the performer has, however, another property. Marking out a playing area was in early antiquity an activity connected with religion. In classical Greece, for instance, the altar of the god Dionysus was surrounded by a circle for dancing. This was the origin of the performance space. Even when the direct religious tie was broken, stepping into the ring or onto the stage was still regarded as a passage into another world. This is equally true of the sawdust ring of the circus and the bare boards of the trestle stage. Some traditional theatres, especially those of the Orient, still regard the act of preparing to go on stage (putting on makeup, for instance) as sacred. Because of this, the isolation of the actor is spiritual almost as much as physical.

Symbolic aspects

Illusion of place. In dramatic production the magical property with which a performing area is invested is augmented by the fictional action of the drama. The stage becomes another locale by an act of imagination undertaken by both actors and audience. The illusion of place may be created simply by speech: at the opening of a scene in Shakespeare's *Twelfth Night,* for instance, one of the characters asks, "What country, friends, is this?" and is told, "This is Illyria, lady." It may be created visually, by the designer's ingenuity; the audience sees a room or a garden, and its attention is fixed on this imaginary setting, while its consciousness of the stage as a performing space becomes secondary.

In some productions, especially those inspired by the antinaturalistic theories of the Russian director Vsevolod Meyerhold, the audience is constantly reminded that it is in a theatre. Naturalistic productions, in contrast, following the principles of Stanislavsky, encourage a clear distinction between performing area and viewing area. On the other hand, the theatre has often reconciled the contradictory elements of dramatic space. The ancient Greek theatre combined the actor's platform with a more public dancing circle, to which there was ready access from the seats. The 18th-century English stage moved out from a recessed picture of a representational locale to a projecting apron that merged with the auditorium. In both examples, the theatre found a physical convention for mediating between actor and audience.

Real versus illusory time. Time likewise has a dual character in drama. The performer and audience exist together in chronological time. But the actor as character exists in dramatic time. Neoclassical drama of the 17th century, especially in France, endeavoured to make the duration of the performance coincide with that of the play's action. But, as a rule, drama has achieved its effects by accentuating the discrepancy between "real" and "illusory" time.

On one hand, the performer projects a sequence of activity upon which the audience concentrates intensely. Because it is difficult to maintain full attention over very long periods, it must be modulated; that is, stimulated, relaxed, and stimulated again. These contrasts and suspense make the real time spent at a performance absorbing and deeply felt. This experience is heightened by the illusion that another time scheme is also operating, that of the fictional event. Some drama gains its effects by suggesting that chronological and dramatic time differ between, but not within, scenes; that is, months may pass between Act I and Act II of *Three Sisters* by the Russian playwright Anton Chekhov, but within any act the dramatic time scale is the same as the chronological one. Shakespeare, however, presents a scene in *Othello* (Act II, scene 2) that takes about 25 minutes to play, yet during this scene an

Modulation of attention

entire night supposedly passes. One of the most extensive temporal schemes in drama is to be found in the medieval cycles of miracle plays, which unfolded over a period of two to four days and which covered the history of the universe from a time before Genesis to the Day of Judgment yet to come.

In contrast to this ambitious inclusion of all time is the handling of time in Japanese Nō theatre, in which real time, with its inevitable passage, is retarded to create a sensation of timelessness. The deliberate pace of the performer, the reiteration of the drum, and the unchanging facade of the stage add to this impression. The American Robert Wilson has devised performances that may last through the night. In these circumstances, the tension that results from expectation and that directs the mind to anticipate events and outcomes is dissipated, the spectator tires, and the mind fluctuates between waking and half-sleeping states in which the events on the stage mingle with mental fantasies to produce a new mode of consciousness.

THE PIECE AND ITS PERFORMANCE

Planning and rehearsal

Preparation of content. Traditionally the dramatic piece has been planned in advance and rehearsed, although there are degrees of advance planning and rehearsal. Even the supposedly impromptu performances of the commedia dell'arte players could not take place without detailed preparation beforehand. In much dramatic theatre advance planning involves the preparation of a written script, sometimes prepared by a dramatist and sometimes created by the actors themselves in collaboration with each other or with a writer. The script thus may be either a tentative scenario or a finished blueprint of the final presentation (a playtext).

Whether scenario or playtext, a piece consists of segments of activity arranged in a meaningful sequence. More often than not this is a narrative sequence, and thus each segment of activity presents a step in the unfolding of a story. But the sequence may also be based on a common motif or recurrent characters. The segments of activity, usually termed episodes or scenes, can include many kinds of behaviour—*e.g.,* persuasion of one person by another, delivery of a speech, singing of a song, hand-to-hand combat.

Theatrical tradition and social practice largely determine the scope of the material to be presented. In ancient Greece, for example, myths often provided the material for tragedy, with debate, lamentation, prophecy, and choral comment constituting the main activities. In other traditions, storytelling, singing, acrobatics, and speeches are the ingredients. The dramatist, manager, and actor all operate within the context of performing routines and production conditions. Material drawn from other arts and from personal experiences may also be used.

Performing the piece. The occasion affects the manner in which the actor addresses the audience or represents a character; it also influences his physical appearance. In Japanese Nō theatre and ancient Greek drama, the actor is often transformed by costume into a superhuman figure. Raised headdresses, painted or masked faces, enveloping robes all contribute to the creation of a figure endowed with symbolic significance. In some societies, the actor is viewed not as a hero or demigod but as the epitome of contemporary society.

Although the actor is the focus of attention while performing, the preparatory and rehearsal phases tend to be organized by others. While in the Renaissance the actors themselves were in control of all phases of production, at other times they have been under the control of theatre managers and stage directors. A significant part of the alternative theatre movement in the mid-20th century was an attempt on the part of actors to establish a collective organization and to reclaim a share of power in the process of making theatre.

The importance of stage scenery is determined by the degree to which either the auditorium or playing area needs to be transformed for a performance. Four possibilities exist: little or no change is introduced into either area (as in the Elizabethan public theatre); the playing area remains unaltered while the audience area is changed (as in erecting banks of seating in a town square); the playing area is changed while the audience area remains fixed (as in proscenium theatre, in which a frame or arch separates the stage from the auditorium); or both areas are transformed (as in Renaissance court theatre or some contemporary theatrical productions).

The fixed playing space often has emblematic significance. In Japan, the Nō stage has three pine trees symbolizing heaven, Earth, and man, and on the Kabuki stage the right-hand side is more eminent than the left. The Elizabethan playhouse used trap doors to signify transit from Earth to heaven or hell. The practice of changing the visual and physical arrangement of the playing area became widespread in Europe during the Renaissance. At first, designers devised generalized scenery to be used for tragic, comic, and pastoral dramas. Later they created a setting unique to a particular play. With the emergence of designed space and changeable scenery, there arose an entire profession of scenic architects and mechanics whose work at times overshadowed that of the actors in importance. By the 20th century the designer's task had become so complex that it was usually divided among scenic, costume, and lighting personnel and involved technicians, electricians, stagehands, prop masters, wardrobe mistresses, and many others working together.

The emergence of set design

No single pattern for production exists, since there are too many social and personal variables at work. Certain broad observations can be made, however. First, any production is normally part of a more continuous enterprise. The continuity may be provided by the civic or religious life of the community, the stable associations of an acting troupe, or the permanence of a producer's office.

Patterns of theatrical production

Next, the production process tends to be either cooperative or hierarchical. The company for which Shakespeare wrote and to which he belonged seems to have been a collective. It remained for more than 25 years a community of professional associates and friends. More usual is the hierarchical organization, in which a single individual controls a production. In most instances, the professional specialty of that leader is dictated by the conditions of the particular theatre in which he works. In 17th-century France, for instance, the leader virtually had to be an actor (Molière was an actor turned actor-manager-dramatist). In the commercial theatre of the 20th-century United States he virtually has to be an impresario.

Finally, the mode of planning and rehearsing a production may be influenced by the artistic concept of an individual or a group. As long as theatre was part of a continuing tradition, its mode of production varied little, being conditioned partly by the social role of theatre and partly by the type of material the actor performed. Thus, the actor who played one type of role for an entire professional life concentrated on perfecting recurrent stage routines, while the actor who handled many different roles within a brief season had to be more adaptable.

During the 19th century there evolved new theories of production that affected both styles of performance and methods of rehearsal. Gradually, the idea of ensemble arose, stressing harmony of ideal and craft among what was usually a small group of actors in order to achieve a unity of effect. These ideas necessitated the careful orchestration of all elements of production. In the 18th and early 19th centuries, the dominant element was the star actor; it then became the star ensemble (the Moscow Art Theatre, for instance) and, through the ensemble, the director.

Aspects of theatrical production

The development of international communications has had its effect on the theatre. The advent of railway and steamship travel in the 19th century led to an increase in international touring by theatre companies, and performers such as the French actress Sarah Bernhardt and the Italian operatic tenor Enrico Caruso became as well known in North and South America as in Europe. In the 20th century the cinema, radio, and television and video recording extended even further the range of potential audiences for theatrical performances. In the 1960s The Living Theatre inspired a whole generation of performers throughout the world, and Jerzy Grotowski's Polish

Laboratory Theatre influenced performers who had never been to Europe or seen him work firsthand. International theatre festivals that bring together performers from many varied traditions have become regular occurrences.

TYPES OF PRODUCTION

Numerous forms of spectacle, such as dramatic and nondramatic pageants, the circus, son et lumière, and gymnastic presentations, are closely allied with theatre and indeed are considered by some classifications to be theatrical. Some of these types of production are treated more fully in the article PAGEANTRY AND SPECTACLE.

Pageantry. Nondramatic pageantry includes civic processions, such as parades, as well as static displays, such as gymnastic demonstrations. The appeal of nondramatic pageantry lies in overwhelming visual spectacle. The performer is presented as a member of the collective, and, even where one individual may stand out, such as the parade "royalty," he is essentially passive and wins attention merely as the focal point of a number of performers. In certain religious pageants the focal figure is not a living person at all but the icon or statue of a god or saint.

Dramatic pageantry has much in common with the nondramatic: both have communal involvement, stress on visual display, processional or static masses, and a fictional character. Segments of the pageant may illustrate a historical or legendary incident, or the pageant as a whole may have a historical, mythical, or allegorical theme. Performers in the United States reenacting the dumping of tea into Boston Harbor exemplify historical pageantry; in England the assault on the Castle of Beauty by Knights of the Mount of Love, a pageant celebrating the marriage of Prince Arthur to Catherine of Aragon in 1501, exemplifies the allegorical type common at Renaissance courts. Pageantry of both the dramatic and nondramatic sort continues to play a significant role in the legitimization of political actions and the assertion of social prestige.

Nondramatic theatre. Nondramatic productions include diverse oral and musical presentations, circus and vaudeville acts, gymnastic displays, and ceremonial occasions such as the coronation of a monarch. There is no narrative line in such productions, but the technical virtuosity of the performers or the ritual significance of the event becomes the focus of audience attention. As a form of presentation, the circus encompasses a wide range of different types of performance, including feats of daring, illusion, and skill. The type of circus performance that comes closest to dramatic theatre is that of clowns. The clown engages in simplified and circumscribed dramatic activity, sometimes a ludicrous parody of other forms of performance, but one that follows established conventions of dress, gesture, and behaviour.

The clown

In the latter part of the 20th century, boundaries between types of theatrical production have been increasingly eroded. As circuses have declined in popularity, circus techniques have been incorporated into other forms of theatre. So-called third theatre companies often use circus training techniques, and actors employ juggling and acrobatic skills in their dramatic performances. The British Footsbarn company, which travels the world in a manner reminiscent of the medieval and Renaissance players, uses circus imagery and techniques in its productions of Shakespeare. Samuel Beckett used the image of the clown in *Waiting for Godot* to create a parable on the absurdity of the human predicament.

Cabaret and vaudeville

Cabaret and vaudeville shows also bring together different types of performance, such as music and dancing, dramatic sketches, feats of daring, and illusion. These productions can take place in any kind of theatre or in nightclubs and restaurants, since staging requirements are usually minimal. It is possible to see this kind of performance as deriving directly from the street entertainers of folk culture and from the entertainments that took place between courses during medieval court banquets.

Dramatic theatre. The most common form of dramatic theatre is the presentation of a scripted play in which the actions of the performers depict a narrative. Typically, performers of such works consist of actors portraying characters, although Sicilian Paladin puppets, Javanese *wayang* shadow puppets, and Japanese *bunraku* puppets are examples of nonliving representations of characters, manipulated by living performers.

In some forms of dramatic production, music and dance may provide or supplement the narrative content. Opera inhabits a special region between drama and music and has prompted much discussion as to the relative importance of literary and musical elements in advancing opera's dramatic aspects. The musical development of opera predominated in the 17th and 18th centuries, whereas new works and productions since Richard Wagner in the late 19th century have increasingly emphasized dramatic features. Operetta and musical comedy are often seen as more closely allied to the theatre than to opera (see MUSICAL FORMS AND GENRES).

The musical, which has developed out of the operetta and musical comedy as an indigenous American theatrical genre, has become a powerful art form in its own right. Beginning with Oscar Hammerstein and Jerome Kern's *Show Boat* in 1927 and proceeding by way of the Rogers and Hammerstein musicals to the work of Leonard Bernstein and Stephen Sondheim, the musical has exhibited a growing sophistication and maturity in both themes and techniques. The modern musical integrates singing, dancing, and acting to a degree that no other Western theatre form attempts.

Dance theatre. While dance usually is recognized as an art in its own right, it sometimes shares so many features with the theatre that it is difficult to distinguish the two. Dance figured strongly in the early development of drama in the West and remains an essential feature of Asian drama.

Dance theatre, combining elements of dramatic presentation and dance, may be considered a separate art form. Originally this type of performance was predominantly American, though the term Dance Theatre was adopted by an independent theatre founded in Wuppertal, W.Ger., in the mid-1970s by Pina Bausch. Bausch, who sought to break down the traditional boundaries between theatrical forms, was one of the most innovative performers in European theatre in the 1980s.

Mime. Mime remains closely connected to drama, being merely a highly specialized form of enactment. Relying on movement without words, it enjoyed an immense vogue in imperial Rome, contributed to the style of commedia dell'arte, and underwent a revival in the latter half of the 20th century at the hands of such French performers as Jean-Louis Barrault and Marcel Marceau (see DANCE, THE ART OF).

SYSTEMS OF PRODUCTION

Since planning, rehearsal, and performance are common to all theatrical productions, the various systems of organizing and conducting these activities provide a useful set of production classifications.

The single performance. Single or limited performance of a presentation, as part of institutional or communal life, has been fairly common throughout the history of the theatre. The Greek city-state (polis), the medieval town, the Japanese temple, and the American high school are but a few of the bodies that have typically sponsored such dramatic performances. The Greek city-state and the medieval town organized their productions in a strikingly similar way, with the municipality exercising control. Until at least the 4th century BC, however, the Athenians presented new plays every year, whereas the medieval townspeople annually reenacted the same plays or variations of them. Yet in both systems many aspects of production were the same from year to year so that, single performance notwithstanding, each individual offering relied upon an established tradition.

The Renaissance court masque

This was less true of the Renaissance court masque (an allegorical dramatic performance featuring music and especially dancing), which was also presented only once. Although each production belonged to a tradition of courtly entertainment, masques of the 16th and 17th centuries became increasingly lavish and novel. A court official was responsible for the overall piece, much in the manner of the later theatre manager or entrepreneur. It was he who recommended a dramatic poet to provide the text, hired the actors, made arrangements for stage scenery, and approved the results before offering them to the sovereign. The most fundamental distinction between this kind of production and earlier institutional types is that the masque was devised to the taste and at the will of one person, the monarch.

The permanent company. The development of a production system depending on a permanent company introduced a new element into theatre—professional virtuosity. The emergence of professional theatre companies was a feature of Renaissance urbanization. Various courts had maintained performers throughout the medieval period, but these were usually musicians or single performers. With the emergence of the town, the theatre company began to appear throughout Italy, France, Germany, England, and Spain, usually consisting of between five and 16 actors who devoted their lives to their craft.

The repertory troupe. Initially, the company was obliged to tour, since neither court nor city could employ full-time professionals. As a result, the actors became accustomed to performing in all kinds of places: halls, outdoor platforms, chapels, and village greens. To compensate for the lack of scenery, the actors used a rich array of costumes—some traditional for recurrent characters or situations, some opulent for their own sake. At all times the actors kept a number of plays in their repertoire so that they could either mount a new play at each performance during an extended stay in one place or repeat plays on request. When a troupe finally settled in one city, it continued this mode of presentation, and thus the modern repertory system was born.

Some permanent troupes performed pieces in which each actor portrayed a stock figure. Italian commedia dell'arte and Japanese Kabuki theatre both utilized such types. Molière, though as a dramatist far less rigid in portraying stock types, led a company each of whose members specialized. English and Spanish troupes, however, because of the demands of the plays, used actors who were much more flexible. The English and Spanish playwrights used a much wider range of characters in their episodic plays, and actors were required to play more than one role in productions. Otherwise, the companies had a great deal in common. Actors bought plays from writers, hired any supporting personnel they needed, and took the profits. Usually, the performers worked on a share system, dividing the proceeds among themselves.

Commercial management. The repertory troupe eventually came to be managed by an individual; the actor-manager was in his heyday from the late 18th to the early 20th century. As an employer, he was concerned less with the welfare of the actor and more with the profit he could extract from the public. Gradually, out of this change emerged the stock company and the single-show association. The stock company was an acting troupe usually managed and organized for a limited season to give a number of plays. Sometimes the manager would take the leading roles and engage others in support; otherwise, he would hire all the performers. The major shift in mode of production came when the stock companies stopped presenting plays in repertory and extended the run of a single play. This happened when city populations grew large enough to keep one play running for an indefinite time. At the end of the 17th century, a London play that ran for eight performances was deemed a success. In 1728, however, a production of John Gay's *Beggar's Opera* made theatrical history by running for 62 performances. By the mid-20th century, successful productions might run for several years. In London *The Mousetrap,* a dramatization of a thriller by Agatha Christie, has run for more than 30 years.

The stock company

With the extended run there was little need to maintain a company of actors, even for a season. Instead, single-show contracts were negotiated for actors, stage managers, scenic artists, a host of associates, and a theatre. Since a play was to be repeated indefinitely, it was feasible to invest more money in the accoutrements. Out of this system developed the need for an overall supervisor. At first, the manager or actor-manager undertook this task. Later, individuals specializing in this work appeared. As the play acquired commercial importance, the role of the dramatist changed so that by the 20th century the name of the dramatist had become a significant factor in selling a production.

The modern repertory company. During the rise of the stock company and single-show system, there continued to exist highly refined examples of the repertory ensemble. The Comédie Française, originally an amalgamation of two Parisian troupes, has existed since 1680. In opera the repertory system remains fundamentally unchanged. Toward the end of the 19th century, however, a widespread transformation of the acting ensemble and the repertory system it supported occurred throughout Europe. New theatres, devoted to naturalistic staging, were successfully established, and these, in time, became national theatres supported by the state.

Particularly famous among repertory companies are the Moscow Art Theatre and the Berliner Ensemble; others include the Abbey Theatre of Ireland, the Royal Shakespeare Company of the United Kingdom, and the Théâtre National Populaire of France. In Japan, the traditional Kabuki and Nō theatres have been declared national treasures. All of these theatres, because of government subsidy, maintain large staffs of actors, directors, designers, and other artists and craftsmen. Production is continuous. New plays or, more often, revivals of old plays enter the repertoire, while former productions are dropped. The works of major national authors receive regular performance, thus establishing the main lines of tradition for the company. Sometimes these repertory troupes conduct schools for training young people who might then enter the company.

Other systems. Besides these systems of production there are several forms known collectively as alternative theatre and later as third theatre. The impulses for the alternative theatre arose in the mid-1960s from a sense of dissatisfaction with traditional theatre, in terms of both its repertoire and its production methods and hierarchical structures. Known variously as underground, experimental, guerrilla, Off-Broadway, or fringe theatre, these nontraditional forms became widespread in the general climate of youthful political involvement throughout the Western world. In the United States, the Civil Rights Movement of the early 1960s and the peace campaigns of the Vietnam War era resulted in the formation of a large number of innovative companies. Notable among these groups were the San Francisco Mime Troupe, Bread and Puppet Theatre, and El Teatro Campesino. The San Francisco Mime Troupe revived commedia dell'arte techniques in their politically motivated street performances. El Teatro Campesino invented the *acto* in an attempt to create a specifically Chicano (Mexican-American) theatre. Many of their early performances took place on the picket lines during the California agricultural workers' strikes in the 1960s. Later, El Teatro Campesino explored Chicano mythology and history, inventing the *mito,* a form of ritualized exchange between performers. The debt of the alternative theatre groups to the earlier agitprop groups is immense (see below, *Developments in Russia and the Soviet Union: The propagandist theatre*).

As political ferment diminished in the early 1970s, many of the groups began to explore new directions. Members of The Living Theatre in the United States and the Polish Laboratory Theatre, as well as the Nordisk Theaterlaboratorium in Holstebro, Den., and other groups in North America and Europe, live cooperatively, share a common view of life, and seek to reflect that view in their productions. This shared life is superficially reminiscent of the touring troupe, but the endeavour to achieve a company ethos is closer to the religious motive of an earlier day.

MEANS OF ARTISTIC CONTROL

While communal theatres exercise collective control of production, artistic control has traditionally rested with a single member of the production company.

Actor domination. Perhaps the supreme example of the actor-dominated production can be found in the commedia dell'arte tradition. Not only did the actor have financial and administrative control over production, but the very quality of performance was woven almost wholly out of the actor's art. At first, in the 16th century, the commedia troupe consisted of traveling actors; by the 17th century many of them had found permanent residence at the courts of Italy and elsewhere in Europe. Each actor had a special role (Arlecchino, Pantalone, Brighella, and the inamorato, or lover, among others) with its attendant set speeches and traditional business. The young would learn the tradition appropriate to a role and, if talented, embroider upon that tradition. Thus prepared, the actors would improvise a presentation on the thread of a story selected by the troupe leader. Scenarios of commedia dell'arte plays did exist, but they were only pale shadows of the production itself, which came to life only in performance.

Other actor-dominated theatres include the Elizabethan theatre, Chinese opera, and Kabuki. In these instances, however, the blending of administrative control and artistic preeminence did not go so far as in the commedia dell'arte. The Elizabethan professional company, for example, had a production system that was based upon actor control of the repertory, but the artistic character of the work was determined by the plays that were presented. However fine the actor's art, the dramatist's contribution was paramount.

Dramatist and director domination. During certain periods the work of the dramatist, regardless of his subsequent involvement, determined the creative process in production. In ancient Greece the selection of a play was the first step in production. In the 19th and 20th centuries the acquisition of a script was also the preliminary step in establishing the single-show association. Only occasionally, as in the court theatre at Weimar, of which Johann Wolfgang von Goethe took charge during the late 18th century, did the dramatist take responsibility for establishing and conducting the theatrical enterprise. Rarely has the dramatist dominated a production system, unless, as occurred with Molière, he was also an actor. A notable exception was the German playwright Bertolt Brecht.

In imperial Rome, the *dominus gregis* (manager of the festivals at which theatrical performances were given) controlled the lives and probably the art of the Roman comedians. During the 18th century the theatrical actor-manager came into prominence. But it was in the 19th century, with the rise of the stage director, that artistic and, in large measure, administrative control passed into the hands of a nonperformer.

The stage director was responsible for modulating the acting, correlating the animate and inanimate aspects of production, and creating a single effect that inevitably became the expression of his own genius. At the beginning of the 20th century, the British actor and director Edward Gordon Craig carried the ideal of unity even further by recommending the merger of director and scenic designer and advocating the reduction of actors to automatons completely responsive to the director-designer's vision.

The designer's rise to special importance had begun during the Renaissance. In the first half of the 17th century, the architect and designer Inigo Jones was the driving force behind the elaborate productions of the English court masque, while the stage machinery of Nicola Sabbatini and the designs of Giacomo Torelli exerted considerable influence in Italy and France.

Puppetry

A special theatrical form in which one person typically functions as manager, designer, and director is the puppet show. A puppet is any inanimate figure manipulated by a human being. The figure may be a three-dimensional hand-operated or body-operated puppet, either miniature or approaching life size; a two-dimensional shadow puppet manipulated by means of sticks; or a string-operated three-dimensional puppet, called a marionette. All types share a common aesthetic principle whereby their movement in a highly restricted space creates the illusion of lifelikeness. In some cultures, such as the Javanese and the Turkish, the puppet show has been a major theatrical form. In Japan the *bunraku* doll theatre commands a respect and a following comparable to those accorded the traditional live-actor theatres. In fact, many plays of the prominent writer Chikamatsu Monzaemon were written originally for the puppet theatre (see POPULAR ARTS: *Puppetry*).

AIMS AND FUNCTIONS

Religious. Most historians agree that drama emerged from religious ritual. At what precise point ritual became drama is uncertain, but formal drama is first known from ancient Greece.

Certainly, religious festivals gave rise to dramatic expression by reenacting the passion and trials of the god or man-god on whom the religion centred. In Christian Europe, biblical plays became attached to particular festivities, notably the Feast of Corpus Christi. Similarly, the story of the assassination of the 7th-century Shīʿite hero al-Ḥusayn ibn ʿAlī, grandson of the Prophet Muḥammad, was enacted at the Muslim festival of *taʿziyah.* As in ancient Greece, these festivals extended over many days and involved the whole community. In the 20th century, as popes and other religious leaders have traveled around the world to address the faithful, huge outdoor ceremonies have been conducted, often with the use of staging and lighting effects borrowed from the commercial theatre.

Educational and developmental. Initially, any educational aims of theatre were subsumed under its religious aims. But with the growth of educational institutions came student performances. A play might be enacted to cultivate appreciation of its literary qualities, to celebrate a graduation, or to commemorate a national holiday. At first these productions were communal in character and occasional in presentation. Then, for brief periods in Elizabethan and Jacobean England, school and choral masters endeavoured to turn this communal activity into a commercial operation by utilizing boys as professional actors.

Early in the 20th century, the educational philosophy of the dancer Isadora Duncan inspired a new emphasis on education in the theatre. Duncan, drawing inspiration from ancient Greece, sought to free dance from the strictures of classical ballet. Her work in teaching, along with that of Émile Jaques-Dalcroze, the Swiss founder of eurythmics, provided the cornerstone for educational dance. Children were given dance classes to develop both physical ability and self-expression.

The practice of producing school plays goes back at least to the Elizabethan period in England, when it was used to train pupils in rhetorical skills. In the 20th century a range of alternative activities have been explored under the heading of "drama in education." These classes have no direct performance aim and do not make a distinction between performer and audience. Classes can pursue a variety of aims: physical development, self-dramatization and self-expression, the dynamics of group relationships, role-playing, decision-making, and fantasy-exploration to develop the imagination. Some work has been done to bring drama into the centre of the school curriculum and to use its flexible methods as a medium for teaching other subjects, such as language skills.

Drama has also been used to enable psychiatric patients to reveal and objectify their mental traumas. Drama therapy, or psychodrama, employs theatre to promote healing rather than to analyze.

Theatre for development

Since 1950 many dramatic techniques have been utilized in an entirely new area called theatre for development. Theatre has been used, primarily in what is called the Third World, to foster literacy programs, population planning campaigns, and agricultural development programs. In Indonesia, for example, *wayang* shadow puppets have been used, with the content of traditional plays altered to include family planning messages. In some projects, theatre programs are prepared using villagers as consultants regarding content effectiveness.

Commercial. Theatre as a purely economic enterprise can be traced to the Renaissance, when there developed a professional theatre of the marketplace. Productions were offered in large population centres or were taken to villages and towns where a potential audience already existed. With a shift from theatre devised for an independently existing occasion to speculative theatre, seeking to create its own occasion, there is a shift from a communal to a cosmopolitan audience. Instead of presenting plays at times that inherently hold sacred or civic meaning and, therefore, draw together the entire populace, commercial companies present plays with some frequency in order to attract a public large enough to support them. Instead of fulfilling a preordained social purpose, the commercial theatre has to justify itself and persuade people to attend by providing novelty and entertainment. (See above, *Commercial management.*) (B.Be./C.Ba.)

History of theatres and staging

ORIGINS OF THEATRE SPACE

The English word theatre derives from the Greek *theatron,* literally, "a place for seeing"; in its most common usage, it has come to signify a building or place so arranged that people can see and hear a performance given by others.

Forerunners of formal theatre

The civilizations of the Mediterranean basin in general, the Far East, northern Europe, and the Western Hemisphere before the voyages of Christopher Columbus in the second half of the 15th century have all left evidence of constructions whose association with religious ritual activity relates them to the theatre. Studies in anthropology suggest that their forerunners were the campfire circles around which members of a primitive community would gather to participate in tribal rites. Karnak in ancient Egypt, Persepolis in Persia, and Knossos in Crete all offer examples of architectural structures, purposely ceremonial in design, of a size and configuration suitable for large audiences. They were used as places of assembly at which a priestly caste would attempt to communicate with supernatural forces. The transition from ritual involving mass participation to something approaching drama, in which a clear distinction is made between active participants and passive onlookers, is incompletely understood. Eventually, however, the priestly caste and the performer became physically set apart from the spectators. Thus, theatre as place emerged.

DEVELOPMENTS IN ANCIENT GREECE

Visual and spatial aspects. During the earliest period of theatre in ancient Greece, when the poet Thespis—who is credited both with inventing tragedy and with being the first actor—came to Athens in 534 BC with his troupe on wagons, the performances were given in the agora (*i.e.,* the marketplace), with wooden stands for audience seating; in 498, the stands collapsed and killed several spectators. Detailed literary accounts of theatre and scenery in ancient Greece can be found in *De architectura libri decem,* by the 1st-century-BC Roman writer Vitruvius, and in the *Onomasticon,* of the 2nd century AD, by the Greek scholar Julius Pollux. As these treatises appeared several hundred years after classical theatre, however, the accuracy of their descriptions is questionable.

Theatre of Dionysus

Little survives of the theatres in which the earliest plays were performed, but essential details have been reconstructed from the architectural evidence of the Theatre of Dionysus in Athens, which has been remodeled several times since its construction in stone by the politician Lycurgus on the south slope of the Acropolis in about 330 BC. The centre of the theatre was the original dancing place, a flat, circular space containing the altar of Dionysus, called the orchestra. In the centre stood a platform with steps (*bemata*) leading to the altar (thymele). Nearby was the temple out of which the holy image would be carried on festival days so that the god could be present at the plays.

Theatrical representations, not yet wholly free of a religious element, directed their appeal toward the whole community, and attendance was virtually compulsory. Thus the first concern of theatre builders of the day was to provide sufficient space for large audiences. In the beginning, admission was free; later, when a charge was levied, poor citizens were given entrance money. It seems reasonable to assume, from the size of the theatres, that the actors performed on a raised platform (probably called the *logeion,* or "speaking place") in order to be more visible and audible, while the chorus remained in the orchestra. In later times there was a high stage, with a marble frieze below and a short flight of steps up from the orchestra. The great Hellenistic theatre at Epidaurus (Figure 2) had what is believed to have been a high, two-level stagehouse.

The earliest productions did not have a background building. The actors dressed in the *skēnē* (from which the word "scene" is derived), which was then a small tent, and the chorus and actors entered together from the main approach, the *parodos.* The earliest properties, such as altars and rocks, could be set up at the edge of the terrace. The first extant drama for which a large building was necessary was Aeschylus' trilogy the *Oresteia,* first produced in 458 BC. There has been controversy among historians as to whether the *skēnē* was set up inside a segment of the orchestra or outside the edge of the orchestra. The *skēnē* in its later development was probably a long, simple building at the left of the orchestra terrace.

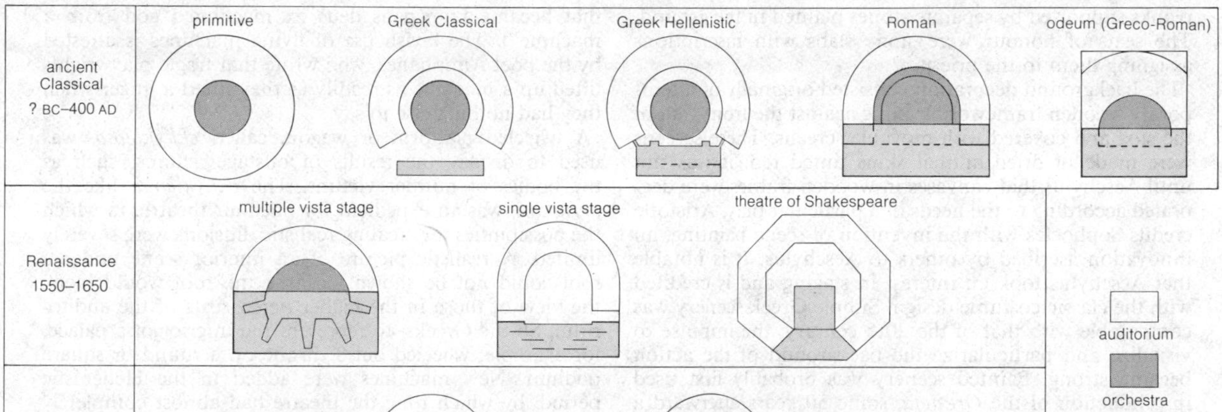

Figure 1: Form outline plans of Western theatres.

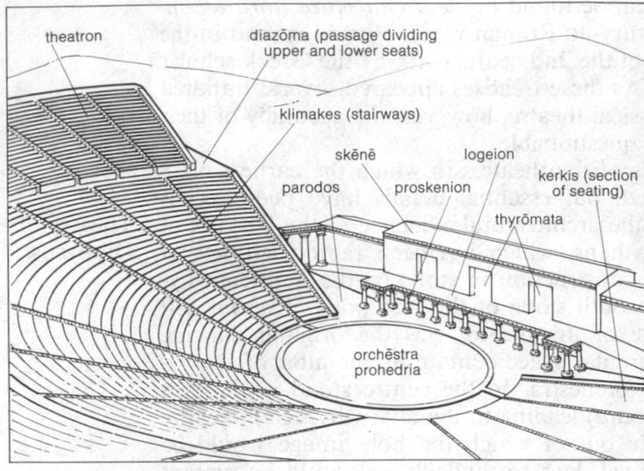

Figure 2: *Hellenistic theatre at Epidaurus, Greece. (Left) Reconstruction. (Right) Ruins of the theatre.*
From (left) H. and R. Leacroft, *The Theatre;* Roy Publishers Inc. and Methuen & Co. Ltd., and (right) Ewing Galloway

The chorus

In the first period of Greek drama, the principal element of the production was the chorus, the size of which appears to have varied considerably. In Aeschylus' *Suppliants,* there were 50 members of the chorus, but in his other plays there were only 12, and Sophocles called for 15. The size of the chorus became smaller in the 5th century, as the ritual element of drama diminished. Since the number of actors increased as the chorus shrank, and the plots of the dramas became more complex, doubling of roles became necessary. On a completely open stage such substitutions were delayed, and the suspense of the drama was dissipated. Dramatic plausibility was also vitiated by the fact that gods and mortals, enemies and friends, always entered from the same direction. The addition of a scenic facade, with three doors, more than doubled the number of entrances and gave the playwright more freedom to develop dramatic tension. About 425 BC a firm stone basis was laid for an elaborate building, called a stoa, consisting of a long front wall interrupted at the sides by projecting wings, or *paraskēnia.* The spectators sat on wooden benches arranged in a fan shape divided by radiating aisles. The upper rows were benches of movable planks supported by separate stones planted in the ground. The seats of honour were stone slabs with inscriptions assigning them to the priests.

The background decoration consisted originally of a temporary wooden framework leaning against the front wall of the stoa and covered with movable screens. These screens were made of dried animal skins tinted red; it was not until Aeschylus that canvases in wooden frames were decorated according to the needs of a particular play. Aristotle credits Sophocles with the invention of scene painting, an innovation ascribed by others to Aeschylus. It is notable that Aeschylus took an interest in staging and is credited with the classic costume design. Simple Greek scenery was comparable with that of the 20th century; the impulse to visualize and particularize the background of the action became strong. Painted scenery was probably first used in production of the *Oresteia;* some 50 years afterward a second story was added to the wooden scene structure. A wooden colonnade, or portico, the *proskēnion,* was placed in front of the lower story of the building. This colonnade, which was long and low, suggested the exterior of either a house, a palace, or a temple. Painted screens set between the columns of the *proskēnion* suggested the locale.

The invention of scene painting

In the beginning, scenery was probably altered slightly during the intermissions that separated the plays of a trilogy or a tetralogy or during the night between two festival days. By the latter part of the 5th century, scene changes were accomplished by means of movable painted screens. Several of these screens could be put up behind one another so that, when the first one was removed, the one immediately behind appeared.

Soon after the introduction of the facade, plays were uniformly set before a temple or a palace. To indicate a change of scene, the *periaktoi* were introduced. These were upright three-sided prisms—each side painted to represent a different locality—set flush with the palace or temple wall on either side of the stage. Several conventions were observed with regard to scenery; one was that if only the right *periaktos* was turned, it indicated a different locality in the same town. According to another convention, actors entering from the right were understood to be coming from the city or harbour and those from the left to be coming from the country.

The "flying machine"

The permanent facade was also used to hide the stage properties and the machinery. Evidence for the use of the so-called flying machine, the *mēchanē* (Latin *machina*), in the 5th century is given in the comedies of Aristophanes; a character in his play *Peace* ascends to heaven on a dung beetle and appeals to the scene shifter not to let him fall. The *mēchanē* consisted of a derrick and a crane. In the time of Euripides it was used conventionally for the epilogue, at which point a god descended from heaven to sort out the complications in the plot, a convention that became known as deus ex machina ("god from a machine"). The lavish use of flying machines is attested by the poet Antiphanes, who wrote that tragic playwrights lifted up a machine as readily as they lifted a finger when they had nothing else to say.

A wheeled platform or wagon, called *ekkyklēma,* was used to display the results of offstage actions, such as the bodies of murder victims. The *ekkyklēma,* like the *periaktoi,* was an expedient for open-air theatre, in which the possibilities for creating realistic illusions were severely limited. A realistic picture of an interior scene under a roof could not be shown, because the roof would block the view of those in the higher tiered seats of the auditorium. So the Greeks, to represent the interior of a palace, for example, wheeled out a throne on a round or square podium. New machines were added in the Hellenistic period, by which time the theatre had almost completely lost its religious basis. Among these new machines was the *hemikyklion,* a semicircle of canvas depicting a distant city, and a *stropheion,* a revolving machine, used to show heroes in heaven or battles at sea.

(Ho.B./C.Ba./G.C.I.)

Acoustics. Much recent study has centred on the problem of acoustics in the ancient theatre. The difficulty in achieving audibility to an audience of thousands, disposed around three-fifths to two-thirds of a full circular orchestra in the open air, seems to have been insoluble so long as the performer remained in the orchestra. A more direct path between speaker and audience was therefore essential if the unaided voice was to reach a majority of spectators in the auditorium. Some contend that the acoustical problems were to a degree alleviated when the actor was moved behind and above the orchestra onto the raised platform, with more of the audience thus being placed in direct line of sight and sound with him. By this time, the actors' masks had reached considerable dimensions, and there are grounds for believing that their mouth orifices were of help in concentrating vocal power—much as cupped hands or a rudimentary megaphone would be.

Increased architectural and engineering sophistication in the Hellenistic Age encouraged further innovations. The theatres of mainland Greece, the Aegean islands, and southern Italy had been constructed in hillsides whenever possible, so that excavation and filling were kept to a minimum; or, lacking a suitable slope, earth was dug out and piled up to form an embankment upon which stone seats were placed. By contrast, the cities of Asia Minor, which flourished during the Hellenistic Age, did not rely on a convenient slope on which to locate their theatres. The principles of arch construction were understood by this time, and theatres were built using vaulting as the structural support for banked seating. Archaeological remains and restoration of theatres at Perga, Side, Miletus, and other sites in what is now Turkey exhibit this type of construction. By a third method, auditoriums were hewed out of rock. Of some six such Greek theatres extant, two excellent examples (both extensively remodeled in Roman times) are the great theatre at Syracuse in Sicily and that at Argos in the Peloponnese. The best preserved of all Greek theatres, also in the Peloponnese and now partially restored, is the magnificent theatre at Epidaurus. This theatre provided seats for some 12,000 people, and its circular orchestra is backed by a stagehouse and surrounded on three sides by a stone, hillside-supported bank of seats. Both chorus and actors performed in the orchestra, but only the actors used the two levels of the stagehouse as well. Theatre construction flourished during the Hellenistic Age as never before in classical times, and no city of any size or reputation was without its theatre. (G.C.I.)

Vaulted seating construction

DEVELOPMENTS IN ANCIENT ROME

The development of the theatre, following that of dramatic literature, was slower in Rome than in Athens. The essential distinction between Roman and Greek stage performances was that the Roman theatre expressed no deep religious convictions. Despite the fact that the spectacles were technically connected with the festivals in honour of the gods, the Roman audience went to the theatre for entertainment. The circus was the first permanent public building for spectacles, which included chariot races and gladiatorial fights. When Etruscan dancers and musicians were introduced in 364 BC, they performed in either the circus, the forum, or the sanctuaries in front of the temples. The players brought temporary wooden stands for the spectators. These stands developed into the Roman auditorium, built up entirely from the level ground.

Theatre as entertainment

Stage design. The most important feature of the Roman theatre as distinct from the Greek theatre was the raised stage. As every seat had to have a view of the stage, the area occupied by the seating (*cavea*) was limited to a semicircle. As in Greek theatre, the scene building behind the stage, the *scaenae frons,* was used both as the back scene and as the actors' dressing room. It was no longer painted in the Greek manner but tended to have architectural decorations combined with luxurious ornamentation (Figure 3). The audience sat on tiers of wooden benches, *spectacula,* supported by scaffolding. There was no curtain; the back scene, with its three doors, faced the audience.

When the popular comedies or farces of southern Italy were introduced to Rome, they came with their own distinctive type of stage—the *phlyakes* stage. Comedies in Italy were mimes, usually parodies of well-known tragedies, and the actors were called *phlyakes,* or jesters. They used temporary stage buildings of three main forms. One was the primitive low stage, a rough platform with a wooden floor on three or four rectangular posts. The second was a stage supported by low posts, covered with drapery or tablets; sometimes steps led up to a platform and a door was indicated. The third type was a higher stage supported by columns, without steps but usually with a back wall. The stages often had a short flight of five to seven steps in the centre, leading to the podium. The forewall, covered with drapery, was often decorated, and the background wall usually had objects hanging from it. The rear wall sometimes had other columns, besides the ones set at the corners, as well as doors and, in several cases, windows to indicate an upper floor. The door was usually behind a heavily decorated porch, with a sloping or gabled roof supported by beams and cross struts. Among the furnishings there were usually trees, altars, chairs, thrones, a dining table, a money chest, and a tripod of Apollo (*i.e.,* an oracular seat). The stage was set up in the marketplace in the smaller towns and in the orchestras of Greek theatres in the larger cities.

Coincident with the development of the *phlyakes* stages,

By courtesy of the Deutsches Archaeologisches Institut, Rome; photograph, Art Reference Bureau

Figure 3: Roman stage, or *scaenae frons,* with the presentation of a mime; drawing by G. von Cube, 1905, of a fresco in the Caseggiato dei Gladiatori, Pompeii.

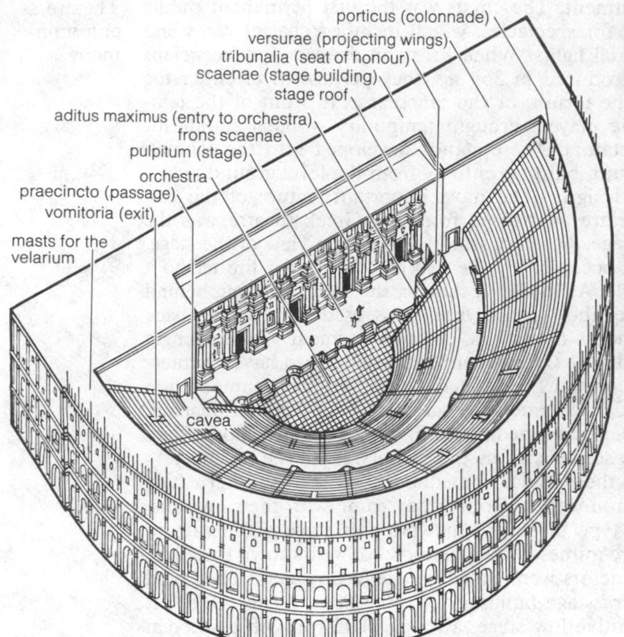

Figure 4: *Roman theatre.*
(Left) Reconstruction of a typical Roman theatre. (Right) Remains of the theatre at Şabrāth, Libya, 2nd century AD.
From (left) H. and R. Leacroft, *The Theatre;* Roy Publishers Inc. and Methuen & Co. Ltd., and (right) UPI

Roman stone theatres

and under the inspiration of Hellenistic colonists, the Romans began to build stone theatre buildings. Beginning by remodeling Greek and Hellenistic theatres, they eventually succeeded in uniting architecturally their own concept of the auditorium with a single-level, raised stage. This they did by limiting the orchestra to a half circle and joining it to the auditorium, thereby improving on the acoustics of Greek and Hellenistic theatres. They also brought to perfection the principles of barrel and cross vaulting, penetrating the seat bank at regular intervals with *vomitoria* (exit corridors). The raised stage was at a single, much lower level than in the Hellenistic theatre. It was roofed, and entrances to it were increased to five: three, as before, in the wall at the rear of the stage and one at each side (Figure 4). The Romans' love of ostentatious architecture led them to adorn the permanent background with profuse sculptures. In some theatres a drop curtain was used to signal the beginning and end of performance. In some cases, a canvas roof was hoisted onto rope rigging in order to shade the audience from the sunlight. (Ho.B./C.Ba.)

The Roman stage

In Roman theatres the stage alone was used by the actors, who entered the playing space from one of the house doors or the side entrances in the wings. The side entrance on the audience's right signified the near distance and the one on the audience's left the farther distance. If a scene took place in a town, for instance, an actor exiting audience right was understood to be going to the forum; if he exited audience left, he might be going to the country or the harbour. *Periaktoi* at the side entrances indicated the scenery in the immediate neighbourhood. If the play required a character to move from one house to another without bringing him on the stage, which represented the street, the actor was supposed to use the back door and the *angiportum* (*i.e.,* an imaginary street running behind the houses). Since interior scenes could not be represented easily, all action took place in front of the houses shown in the background. If a banquet was to be depicted, the table and chairs would be brought on stage and removed at the end of the scene. Costumes were formalized, but real spears, torches, chariots, and horses were used.

The orchestra became part of the auditorium in Rome, reserved by law for those of privileged rank, who seated themselves there on a variety of portable chairs and litters. The orchestra was no longer needed as part of the performance area because the chorus had long since ceased to be an integral part of drama. The tragedies of Seneca, in the 1st century AD, included a chorus because they were patterned after Greek models. But they never achieved the popularity of earlier comedies, especially those of Plautus and Terence. These works had at first been performed on temporary wooden stages that had been erected on a convenient hillside and sometimes surrounded by temporary wooden seating.

Until the late republic, a puritanical Senate had banned all permanent theatre building within the city of Rome itself as decadent. Thus, theatres there were temporary structures, set up in the Campus Martius for the duration of public games. In 55 BC, however, the triumvir Pompey the Great built Rome's first permanent stone theatre. Another public stone theatre was built in Rome in 13 BC and named after Marcellus, son-in-law of the emperor Augustus. Both were used for the *scaenae ludi* ("scenic games"), which were part of religious festivities or celebrations of victory in war and which were paid for by triumphant generals and emperors. During the Roman Empire civic pride demanded that all important cities have theatres, amphitheatres, and, in many instances, a small, permanently roofed theatre (*theatrum tectum,* an odeum, or music hall) as well. In fact, it is from outlying cities of the empire such as Arausio (Orange), Thamagadi (Timgad), Leptis Magna, Şabrāth, and Aspendus that archaeological evidence provides most of the firsthand knowledge of Roman theatre building. The best preserved Roman theatre, dating from about AD 170, is at Aspendus in modern Turkey.

Vitruvius' treatise on architecture. Literature is another source for knowledge of Roman theatre. *De architectura libri decem* ("Ten Books on Architecture"), by the Roman architect Vitruvius (1st century BC), devotes three books to Greek and Roman theatre design and construction. The author gives general rules for siting an open-air theatre and for designing the stage, orchestra, and auditorium. These rules are based on principles of Euclidian geometry in matters of layout and proportion. His dicta on the provision of good sight lines from auditorium to stage are generally sound. Apart from that, however, his treatise is not very helpful. He mentions changeable scenery but is vague about what was involved. Vitruvius' notion of acoustics, which he claims is based on theory as well as practice, appears to be vaguely associated with Greek ideas of musical theory but has since been proved to have no scientific or mathematical basis. Indeed, his views on this important matter were to cause problems for almost 2,000 years.

The odeum. Vitruvius has nothing to say about the roofed odeum (or odeon, "singing place"), which, according to some authorities, represents the high point of theatre building in the ancient world. Theatre history has, unfortunately, largely overlooked these buildings. Excavation work has revealed more than 30 of them, in a wide range of building materials. Odea were apparently first built in Athens under Pericles (5th century BC). They continued to be built throughout the Hellenistic Age and also in the Roman Empire up to the time of Emperor Severus Alexander (3rd century AD). They range in size from one with a seating capacity of 300–400 to one of 1,200–1,400. Experts disagree as to their specific purpose and use but claim they exhibited a refinement of detail and architectural sophistication found in no other Greco-Roman buildings devoted to the performing arts. They are most often found in Greek cities dating from Hellenistic times, on the grounds of private villas built by Roman emperors from Augustus to Hadrian, and in major cities of the empire, usually dedicated to the emperors. One of the most imposing, which also boasts the greatest span for a wooden trussed roof in the ancient world, was the Odeon of Agrippa, named after the emperor Augustus' civil administrator. This Roman building in the Athenian agora, dating from about 15 BC, is beautifully detailed, with an open southern exposure and a truncated curvilinear bank of seating. It achieves an atmosphere of great dignity and repose, despite the vast size of the room. In the last years of the Roman Empire the odeum was, it is claimed, the only remaining home of the performing arts, because by this time open-air theatres had long been given over to sensational and crude popular entertainments.

Odeon of Agrippa

Greek and Roman theatre building influenced virtually all later theatre design in the Western world, the theatres of the Spanish Golden Age, the English Elizabethan period, and the 20th-century avant-garde, with its experiments in primitive theatre-in-the-round techniques, being exceptions to this pattern. The architectural writings of Vitruvius became the model for the theatre building of the later Renaissance and early Baroque periods.

(G.C.I./C.Ba.)

DEVELOPMENTS IN ASIA

Although the emergence of Asian theatre was not simultaneous with that of ancient Greece and Rome, it merits discussion here rather than as an appendage to the history of Western drama.

India. Indian theatre is often considered the oldest in Asia, having developed its dance and drama by the 8th century BC. According to Hindu holy books, the gods fought the demons before the world was created, and the god Brahmā asked the gods to reenact the battle among themselves for their own entertainment. Once again the demons were defeated, this time by being beaten with a flagstaff by one of the gods. To protect theatre from demons in the future, a pavilion was built, and in many places in India today a flagstaff next to the stage marks the location of performances.

According to myth, Brahmā ordered that dance and drama be combined; certainly the words for "dance" and "drama" are the same in all Indian dialects. Early in Indian drama, however, dance began to dominate the theatre. By the beginning of the 20th century there were few performances of plays, though there were myriad dance recitals. It was not until political independence in 1947 that India started to redevelop the dramatic theatre.

In the 4th century a codification was written of the *śāstra,* or the staging conventions of the dance. It lists not only the costumes, makeup, gestures, and body positions but also any plots considered unsuitable, and it is the most complete document of stagecraft ever compiled. There is no scenery in Indian dance, although there are usually a few properties, such as a three-foot-high brass lamp. A curtain is used, however, by troupes that dance *kathākali,* an ancient danced drama of southwestern India. The curtain itself is a cloth rectangle that is held between the stage and a large lamp by two stagehands.

The dancers perform a group of preliminary dances behind the curtain until they make an important entrance called "peering over the curtain." In this, a character fans the lamp by pulling the curtain in and out until the flames are spectacularly high. The dancer, still hiding his face, displays his hands and legs at the borders of the curtain. At the climactic moment the dancer pulls the curtain aside, displaying his awesome makeup, and stagehands remove the curtain until the next dramatic entrance.

Classical Indian drama had as its elements poetry, music, and dance, with the sound of the words assuming more importance than the action or the narrative; therefore, staging was basically the enactment of poetry. The reason that the productions, in which scenes apparently follow an arbitrary order, seem formless to Westerners is that playwrights use much simile and metaphor. Because of the importance of the poetic line, a significant character is the storyteller or narrator, who is still found in most Asian drama. In Sanskrit drama the narrator was the *sūtra-dhāra,* "the string holder," who set the scene and interpreted the actors' moods. Another function was performed by the narrator in regions in which the aristocratic vocabulary and syntax used by the main characters, the gods and the nobles, was not understood by the majority of the audience. The narrator operated first through the use of pantomime and later through comedy.

The narrator's role

A new Indian theatre that began about 1800 was a direct result of British colonization. With the addition of dance interludes and other Indian aesthetic features, modern India has developed a national drama. Two examples of "new" theatre staging are the Prithvi Theatre and the Indian National Theatre. The Prithvi Theatre, a Hindi touring company founded in 1943, utilizes dance sequences, incidental music, frequent set changes, and extravagant movement and colour. The Indian National Theatre, founded in Bombay in the 1950s, performs for audiences throughout India, in factories and on farms. Its themes usually involve a national problem, such as the lack of food, and the troupe's style is a mixture of pantomime and simple dialogue. It uses a truck to haul properties, costumes, and actors; there is no scenery.

China. The most noticeable contrast between China and other Asian countries is that traditionally China has produced virtually no dance. The classic theatre of the Chinese is called "opera" because the dialogue is punctuated with arias and recitatives. Of the amazingly detailed written record of Chinese theatre, the first reference to opera was during the T'ang dynasty (618–907). The development of the opera style popular today took place during the Manchu rule of the 19th century. The Empress Dowager, the last hereditary ruler of China, was so enamoured of opera that she had a triple-deck stage (representing heaven, hell, and earth) constructed in the summer palace at Peking. The most important individual in Chinese theatre of the 20th century, Mei Lan-fang, an actor and producer, was the first to apply scholarship in reviving ancient masterpieces and opera forms.

In general, Chinese theatrical performances start in the early evening and conclude after midnight. The performance itself consists of several plays and scenes from the best known dramas. The audience drinks tea, eats, and talks, and there are no intermissions. The stage itself has a curved apron, covered only by a square rug. On one side is a box for the orchestra, which plays throughout the evening. There is neither a curtain nor any setting to speak of other than a simple, painted backdrop. The virtual absence of scenery accentuates the elaborate and colourful costumes and makeup of the actors.

The Chinese theatrical performance

During a typical performance, the members of a Chinese theatre audience stop talking to each other only at climactic moments. The actors are concerned with their movements only when they are at the centre of the stage; when they stand at the sides they drink tea and adjust their costumes in full view of the audience. An interpretation of this behaviour was the view of the 20th-century German dramatist Bertolt Brecht that a Chinese actor, in contrast to a Western actor, constantly keeps a distance between himself, his character, and the spectator; his performance is mechanistic rather than empathic.

Property men walk around on stage setting up properties for the next play before the preceding one is finished. There are usually very few properties, only a table and a few chairs. A chair may act as a throne, a bench, a tower if an actor stands on it, a barrier if he stands behind it, and so on. A curtain suspended in front of two chairs represents a bed. Doors and stairs are always suggested: an actor mimes opening a door and taking a high step when he "enters" a room.

There are a number of stage conventions; all entrances, for instance, are from a door stage left, and all exits through a door stage right. After a fight scene, the man who is defeated exits first. Wind is symbolized by a man rushing across the stage carrying a small black flag. Clouds painted on boards are shown to the audience to represent either the outdoors or summer. Fire, however, is always represented realistically, either by the use of gunpowder or by pyres of incense. The Chinese feel that Western dramatic realism atrophies the imagination.

Japan. Japan is unique in Asia in having a living theatre that retains traditional forms. When an attempt is made in the West to recreate the original production of a Greek tragedy or even a play by Shakespeare, its historical accuracy can only be approximated. In Japan the traditions of stagecraft and costumes for both drama and dance have remained unaltered. Japanese staging developed far earlier than did that of the West; by the time of Shakespeare, for instance, the Japanese had already invented a revolving stage, trapdoors, and complex lighting effects.

Nō theatre

Although there are many kinds of theatre in Japan, the best known are the Nō and the Kabuki. Nō was developed by the late 14th century and was first seen by Westerners in the 1850s. It developed from the *dengaku,* a rice planting and harvesting ritual that was transformed into a courtly dance by the 14th century, and from the *sarugaku,* a popular entertainment involving acrobatics, mime, juggling, and music, which was later performed at religious festivals.

Two performers and adherents of Zen Buddhism in the late 14th century, Kan'ami and his son Zeami Motokiyo, combined the *sarugaku* elements with *kuse-mai,* a story dance that uses both movements and words. Soon *dengaku* elements were added, and the distinctive Nō style slowly emerged. Like the Zen ways of tea ceremony, ink drawing, and other arts, Nō suggests the essence of an event or an experience within a carefully structured set of rules. There are scores of Nō theatres in Japan today, even though the design of a Nō theatre is so stylized that it is not usable for other types of performances. The Nō stage is a platform completely covered by a curving temple roof. The audience sits on three sides of the stage and is separated from it by a garden of gravel, plants, and pine trees.

Masks are used, though they are restricted to the principal dancer and his companions. The male characters are costumed in brilliant stiff brocades and damasks well suited to the grandiose posturing of the actors. The female roles are played in bright flowered brocades. The outer robes of both sexes are of a fine-woven gauze, light and suitable for the gliding dances when sleeves and fans float in the air. Mask carving is an important art in Japan, and Nō masks add considerable beauty to the traditional robes. Most costumes are based on the classic court hunting dress of the Heian (794–857) and Kamakura (1192–1333) periods.

Kabuki staging techniques

Kabuki troupes, originally composed only of women, developed in the early 17th century. By the 1680s Kabuki had become an established art form, and curtains and scenery were introduced. Kabuki was first seen in western Europe during the latter part of the 19th century, but it was not until the 1920s that it was accepted there as something more than quaint. The work of the Russian film director Sergey Eisenstein was influenced by the Kabuki troupe that toured the Soviet Union in 1928, and Kabuki staging devices were tried out in theatres in the Soviet Union, France, and Germany; one Kabuki actor, in turn, brought back Russian techniques that influenced the Japanese theatre.

A Kabuki theatre in Tokyo is one of the largest legitimate theatres in the world, with a 91-foot- (28-metre-) wide stage and seating for 2,599 people. Running through the audience and connecting the stage with the rear of the auditorium is the platform runway, called the *hanamichi.* It is utilized for significant entrances and exits, processions, and dance sequences. Its purpose is to unite the actor and audience by moving the actor out of the decorative background. Originally there were two runways, with a connecting bridge at the rear of the auditorium. Because of economic pressure to seat more people and the influence of Western architecture, the second *hanamichi* was removed in the early 20th century.

The scenery for Kabuki may be as elaborate and complex as that found anywhere; the stage, for instance, may be a house, a forest, and a river simultaneously. Some settings are triple-level palaces, with the actors using all levels at once; others have only a simple backdrop.

Kabuki costumes are of the Edo period (1603–1868), when Kabuki is considered to have been at its height. Wigs and makeup carefully conform to classical tradition, enabling habitual playgoers to recognize the type of play and characters at a glance. Many of the costumes are much exaggerated; all are designed to accentuate dramatic movement. Courtesans and heroes, for instance, wear stilts that raise them several inches off the ground.

Bali. Balinese theatre is included here as representative of theatre in the smaller nations of Asia, such as Thailand, Kampuchea (Cambodia), Laos, Malaysia, the Philippines, and Vietnam, in all of which drama consists almost exclusively of dance. Balinese dancing may take place anywhere; usually it is executed in front of a temple or a pavilion used for community meetings. The audience sits on three sides of the performers or, occasionally, in the round. The musicians, called the gamelan, sit on one side of the stage area.

Balinese scenic "devices"

There are neither settings nor visible indications of scene changes; location is suggested by the dialogue or the facial expressions and gestures of the actors. A scenic "device" is employed at the beginning of each section of the dance; for instance, the dancer makes a gesture called "opening the curtain." The hands, palms out, are in front of the face; they separate on a diagonal line to reveal the figure, stopping only when the full, formal posture of Balinese dance is reached. (Ho.B./C.Ba.)

THE MIDDLE AGES IN EUROPE

In terms of performances and theatres, Roman drama reached its height in the 4th century AD, but it had already encountered opposition that was to lead to its demise. From about AD 300 on, the church tried to dissuade Christians from going to the theatre, and in 401 the fifth Council of Carthage decreed excommunication for anyone who attended performances on holy days. Actors were forbidden the sacraments unless they gave up their profession, a decree not rescinded in many places until the 18th century. An edict of Charlemagne (*c.* 814) stated that no actor could put on a priest's robe; the penalty could be banishment. This suggests that drama, most probably mime, had ridiculed the church or that it had tried to accommodate religious sensibilities by performance of "godly" plays.

The invasions of the barbarians from the north and east accelerated the decline of Roman theatre. Although by 476 Rome had been sacked twice, some of the theatres were rebuilt. The last definite record of a performance in Rome was in 533. Archaeological evidence suggests that the theatre did not survive the Lombard invasion of 568, after which state recognition and support of the theatre was abandoned. Theatre did continue for a while in the Eastern Roman Empire, the capital of which was Constantinople, but by 692 the Quinisext Council of the church passed a resolution forbidding all mimes, theatres, and other spectacles. Although the effectiveness of the decree has been questioned, historians until recently used it to signify the end of thc ancient theatre.

The assumption now is that although official recognition and support of performances were withdrawn and theatres were not used, some remnants of at least the mime tradition were carried on throughout the Middle Ages. Christian writings suggest that performers were familiar figures. For instance, two popular sayings were "It is better to please God than the actors" and "It is better to feed paupers at your table than actors." Apart from the mime tradition, one Roman playwright, Terence, retained his reputation through the early Middle Ages, probably because of his literary style. (Ho.B.)

Women performers

Women performers were widespread during the period as jugglers, acrobats, dancers, singers, and musicians. There were women troubadours and jongleurs, and many of the

French chansons are written from the point of view of female narrators, notably the *chansons de mal mariée,* or complaints by unhappily married women. Generations of ecclesiastical authorities protested against the great choruses of women who poured into churches and monasteries on feast days, singing obscene songs and ballads. Complaints are recorded from the 6th century AD to the 14th about women taking part in licentious public performances on festive occasions. Women were also active participants in the later mumming plays; the *London Mumming* of *c.* 1427 was presented by an all-female cast, while in the Christmas *Mumming at Hertford,* the young king Henry VI saw a performance consisting of "a disguysing of the rude upplandisshe people compleynynge on hir wyves, with the boystous aunswere of hir wyves."

Church theatre. Medieval religious drama arose from the church's desire to educate its largely illiterate flock, using dramatizations of the New Testament as a dynamic teaching method. It is doubtful whether there is any connection between the drama of classical times and the new rudimentary dramatizations that slowly grew into the miracle and mystery cycles of plays in the Middle Ages. As early as the 10th century in Switzerland, France, England, and Germany, short and simple dramatic renderings of parts of the Easter and Christmas liturgy of the mass were being performed. As these short scenes grew in number, small scenic structures, called mansions, *sedum, loci,* or *domi* (the Latin words for seats, places, and homes, respectively), were placed at the sides of the church nave. At these were acted stories of the Nativity, Passion, or Resurrection, depending upon the particular season of the Christian calendar. At the conclusion of each scene the congregation turned its attention to the next mansion, so following a succession of scenes set out at intervals around the nave. Gradually, the performance of liturgical drama passed out of the hands of the clergy and into those of the laity, probably via the trade guilds of craftsmen, which were also religious fraternities. More and more secular interludes crept into the dramas—to such an extent that the dramas moved out of the church building into the public square. The individual plays became linked in cycles, often beginning with the story of the creation and ending with that of the Last Judgment. Each play within the cycle was performed by a different trade guild. Many of the plays from different cycles have survived and can still be seen in parts of England. (G.C.I./C.Ba.)

Play cycles

Staging conventions. A number of staging conventions that evolved in the church were to continue throughout the Middle Ages. Apart from the mansions there was a general acting area, called a *platea, playne,* or *place.* The methods of staging from these first liturgical dramas to the 16th-century interludes can be divided into six main types. The first involved the use of the church building as a theatre. In the beginning, for Easter tropes (embellishments of the liturgy), a tomb was set up in the north aisle. As dialogue was added, the entire nave was used, and within this space different localities were indicated by mansions. A few mansions housed numerous elaborate properties, particularly those for the Last Supper. Some mansions had curtains so that characters or objects might be revealed at a particular moment or concealed at the end of an episode. Sometimes the choir loft was used to represent heaven and the crypt to represent hell.

The second type of staging evolved by the 12th century, as drama began to outgrow the capacity of the church to contain it. As long as the action was confined to the central theme, it could be played in an arrangement of mansions down the length of the nave. But as the subject matter extended to include both Old and New Testament history, the action was transferred to a stage outside the west door of the church. In 1227 Pope Gregory IX decreed the removal of what had become a show from holy ground to the marketplace or an open field. During the same period the language of the plays began to change from Latin to the vernacular. When drama was first taken outdoors, the crucifix was placed at one end, no doubt where it would have appeared above the altar in the church. Mansions were placed alongside each other, usually in sequences reflecting earlier church performances.

Stationary setting

A third type of staging was the so-called stationary setting, found outside of England, which involved placing the mansions in a wider range of locales. Here the audience accepted three conventions. One was the symbolic representation of localities by the mansions; the second was the placing of the mansions near each other; and the third was the use for acting purposes of such actual ground as was enclosed by or in front of each mansion (Figure 5). The mansions were placed in either a straight or a slightly curved line, and all of the scenery was visible simultaneously. Because of their scope, many of the plays were divided into parts separated by intermissions ranging from one to 24 hours. During the intermissions, mansions were changed. Also, some mansions might represent more than one location; the identity of the mansions was announced before each segment of a play. It is difficult to know exactly how many mansions were used; in a play at Lucerne, Switz., in 1583, for instance, 70 different locations were indicated, though only about 32 mansions were actually used.

The mansions of heaven and hell

The two mansions almost always present were those representing heaven and hell, set at opposite ends of the playing area. The earthly scenes were set in the middle, and the two opposing mansions were supposed to represent man's dual nature and the choices that faced him. In the 15th and 16th centuries, heaven was usually raised above the level of the other mansions. Sometimes heaven had a series of intricate turning spheres, from which emanated the golden light of concealed torches. The hell mansion was designed to be the complete opposite of that of heaven; some portions of it, for instance, were below stage level. Sometimes hell was made to look like a fortified town, an especially effective image when Jesus Christ forced open the gates to free the captive souls. The entrance to hell was usually shaped like a monster's head and was called Hell's Mouth, emitting fire, smoke, and the cries of the damned.

The fourth type of staging was in the round. In France

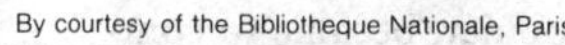
By courtesy of the Bibliotheque Nationale, Paris

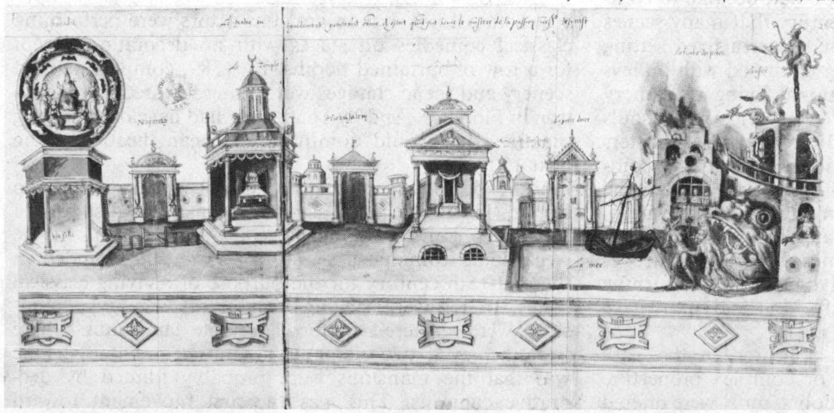

Figure 5: The setting for the Valenciennes mystery play, miniature by Hubert Cailleau, 1547. In the Bibliothèque Nationale, Paris.

Figure 6: *Staging techniques originating in the Middle Ages.*
(Left) Staged processional with pageant carts, or *carros*, honouring Cardinal Archduke Albert's entry into Brussels, 1596; etching, 16th-century German school. In the Metropolitan Museum of Art, New York. (Right) Use of the curtained platform stage shown in "Market Theatre, Brussels" by F. van der Maulen (1632–90). In Schloss Vaduz, Liechtenstein.

By courtesy of (left) the Metropolitan Museum of Art, New York, Harris Brisbane Dick Fund, 1917; (right) Sammlungen des Regierenden Fursten von Liechtenstein; photograph, (right) Kunstverlag Wolfrum, Vienna

and England particularly, surviving Roman playhouses were used for drama, and the mansions were probably placed in a circle. The play *Castle of Perseverance* from this period was intended to be performed within a moated round. Within the moat was an earthen bank on which the mansions were placed. Within the bank was a circle of flat earth with a tower structure in the centre. Members of the audience perambulated in the centre from mansion to mansion. The actors dressed in a small tent outside the round. Entry to the circle was over one bridge. The remains of several of these rounds still exist, the principle one being Piram Round in Cornwall.

Processional staging

The fifth type of staging employed movable settings. Processional staging was particularly popular in Spain. The wagons, called *carros,* on which the scenery was mounted were positioned next to platforms that had been erected in every town (Figure 6). Developments were somewhat different in England and the Netherlands. There, the mansions themselves became portable, being called pageant wagons in England and *wagonseel* in the Netherlands. Beneath the raised platform was a curtained space with room for the actors. Although the number of settings available was the same as for the mansion presentation, only one wagon was visible at a time; the audience remained stationary, and the successive pageants were wheeled into place before it. Sometimes the pageant wagons were quite elaborate structures: a realistic ark, stocked with animals and possibly floated on water, might be constructed for the story of Noah and the Flood; or an ingenious model of a whale, able to contain an actor within its belly, might be used for the story of Jonah.

Special effects, which were very popular, became so complex and numerous by the 15th century that many scenes were added to show them off. For flying, a fixed setting was often placed against a building equipped with pulleys and windlasses on its roof. Additional flying machinery was also hidden inside the heaven mansion. Angels, souls released from limbo, devils, and fire-spitting monsters could be shown flying. The machinery became so complex that 17 people were needed simply to operate the hell scenes at a theatre at Mons, in what is now Belgium. Trapdoors were used for sudden appearances, disappearances, and substitutions of dummies for actors in scenes of violence. In a production involving Barnabas' burning at the stake, bones and entrails stuffed in the dummy gave off a realistic smell.

Morality plays

The morality plays, which first appeared in the 14th century, made use of no scenery or complex properties. Although some were performed indoors, most were offered outside on a stage that anticipated the English Elizabethan public theatre. A fixed facade was built at the rear of a large platform, and there were three openings at stage level that could be used to show interior scenes. A second level included similar openings, and a third level had a throne for the figure being honoured by the morality.

The last type of staging, and the one about which least is known, was the curtained platform (see Figure 6). Toward the end of the Middle Ages itinerant professional actors who performed interludes required only a curtain behind them for staging. (Ho.B./C.Ba.)

Courtly diversions. Another kind of theatre flourished in the courts—more or less impromptu entertainments, deriving from the medieval love of tournament. Essentially secular diversions, they were most sumptuously costumed and caparisoned, with the emphasis on spectacle. This type of theatrical entertainment grew in popularity throughout Europe, culminating during the 16th century.

Another manifestation of courtly theatrical display took place on the triumphant entry into a city of a prince and his entourage after victory in war or on the occasion of a neighbouring ruler's visit. Public participation was usually invited, and sometimes mandated, to help augment the sense of occasion. Such entertainment was followed by private festivities held at court. On occasion, a group of strolling players would also be invited to perform in the great hall or courtyard of the palace.

The theatre of the Middle Ages was essentially one of participation, and throughout its development it never lost an intimacy between actors and audience. It was a theatre that combined realism with considerable symbolism. (G.C.I./C.Ba.)

DEVELOPMENTS OF THE RENAISSANCE

Just before 1500, Italian amateur actors were performing classical comedies on stages with no decoration except for a row of curtained booths. By 1589, complex painted scenery and scene changes were being featured in production in Florence. And by 1650, Italy had developed staging practices that would dominate European theatre for the next 150 years.

In the beginning of the Renaissance, there were two distinct kinds of theatrical productions. The first was of the type presented by the humanist Julius Laetus at the Accademia Romana, a semisecret society he founded in the mid-15th century for the purpose of reviving classical ideals. In terms of staging, several medieval-type mansions were clustered to form a single large unit. There were, however, two elements not found previously. One was that the mansions were probably framed by decorative columns. This was the first movement toward the framework that would develop into the proscenium arch—the arch that encloses the curtain and frames the stage from the viewpoint of the audience. (The first permanent proscenium was built in the Teatro Farnese at Parma, Italy, in 1618–19, a temporary one having been constructed by Francesco Salviati 50 years earlier.) The second innovation was that the mansions, by being linked, were treated as components of a general city street. In 1508 at Ferrara a background painted according to the rules of perspective was substituted for the mansions; the scene included houses, churches, towers, and gardens.

The revival of theatre building in Italy. The revival of theatre building, first sponsored by 16th-century ducal courts and academies in northern Italy, was part of the general renewal of interest in the classical heritage of Greece and Rome. The ruins of classical theatres were studied as models, along with Vitruvius' treatise on classical architecture. There were, however, new conditions that fundamentally affected design. First of all, the theatre's move indoors gave rise to problems of lighting and acoustics. Second, the newly formulated laws of perspective in painting, when applied to stage and scenic design, brought about a profound change in the effect of a stage on an audience. The first Renaissance theatres, like those of early antiquity, were temporary wooden constructions in gardens, ballrooms, and assembly halls. Sometimes they were hastily erected affairs, put up to celebrate the births and weddings of ducal offspring or to commemorate victories in war. The theatrical performances given were mostly of allegorical pageantry, but the scenic spectacle was calculated to dazzle the eye and often succeeded. One court vied with another for the services of painters, sculptors, architects, and innovators in stagecraft. Such artists as Leonardo da Vinci, Michelangelo, Vasari, Bramante, Raphael, and a host of other Italian painters, sculptors, and architects, as well as poets, such as Tasso, and musicians, such as Monteverdi, strove to please and exalt the reputations, real or imaginary, of their princely patrons.

Elaborate spectacle

A more sober attempt to revive the classical theatre was made by the academies, organized by upper-class gentlemen who assembled to read and, on occasion, to participate in and to support financially productions of classical drama. The plays were generally of three kinds: contemporary poetic dramas based on ancient texts; Latinized versions of Greek dramas; and the works of Seneca, Terence, and Plautus in the original. Toward the middle of the 15th century, scholars discovered the manuscripts of the Roman writer Vitruvius; one of these scholars, the architect and humanist Leon Battista Alberti, wrote *De re aedificatoria* (1452; first printed in 1485), which stimulated the desire to build in the style of the classical stage. In 1545, Sebastiano Serlio published his *Trattato de architettura,* a work that concentrated entirely on the practical stage of the early 16th century.

The treatise of Serlio

Serlio's treatise on the theatre had three especially significant items. The first was a plan for an auditorium and stage that assumed a rectangular hall, with spectators arranged in the same pattern as in the Roman *cavea* (*i.e.,* the tiered semicircular seating area of a Roman theatre), the difference being that the semicircle of the audience was cut short by the sidewalls. Second, his three types of stage designs—tragic, comic, and satiric—were the same as Vitruvius' classifications. Third, for the stage, he started with a Roman acting platform, but instead of the *scaenae frons,* he introduced a raked platform, slanted upward toward the rear, on which the perspective setting of a street was made up of painted canvases and three-dimensional houses. Since the perspective required that the houses rapidly diminish in size with distance, the actors were able to use only the front houses. Serlio used three types of scenes, all with the same basic floor plan. Each required four sets of wings (*i.e.,* the pieces of scenery at the side of the stage), the first three angled and the fourth flat, and a perspective backdrop.

Palladio's Teatro Olimpico

The Accademia Olimpica in the little town of Vicenza, near Venice, commissioned a famous late Renaissance architect, Andrea Palladio, to design a theatre. This, the Teatro Olimpico, was the first permanent modern indoor theatre, and it has survived intact (Figure 7). Palladio thoroughly researched his subject (the outdoor classical theatre of Rome) and without knowing it designed something now considered very close to a Roman odeum. It is a scaled-down version of an outdoor Roman theatre, with shallow open stage and a heavily sculptured, pedimented, permanent background. A colonnade of heroic proportions, surmounted by sculptured figures, surrounds a steeply stepped bank of seating. Overhead is a painted sky. To promote an intimate stage–auditorium relationship, he used a flattened ellipse in planning the seating, rather than the classic half circle. The interior was to be lit by tallow candles mounted in wall sconces. Palladio died before the building was finished, and his follower Vincenzo Scamozzi completed the work in 1585. Behind the five stage entrances (attributed to Scamozzi) are static, three-dimensional vistas of streets receding to their separate vanishing points; it is not certain whether this was the intent of the original design. In performance, the theatre is efficient if the auditorium is full, and speech carries quite well because of the small volume, flat ceiling, modulated sidewalls, excellent vertical sight lines, and direct hearing lines from all seats to the stage. The exterior is an ungainly, masonry-walled structure with a wood-trussed, tiled roof.

In 1588–89 Scamozzi designed the Teatro all'Antica, a small court theatre for the Gonzaga family at Sabbioneta.

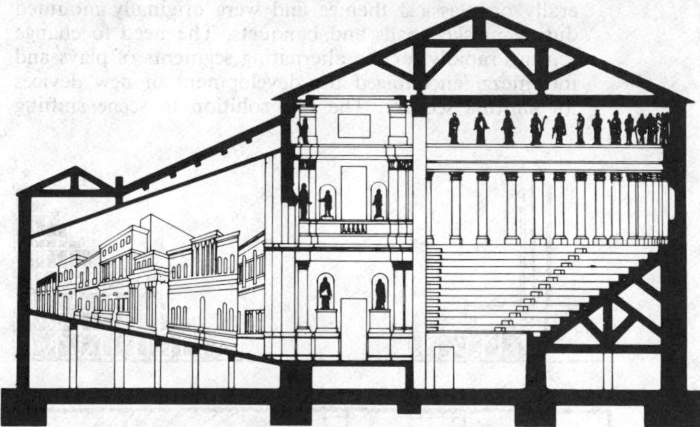

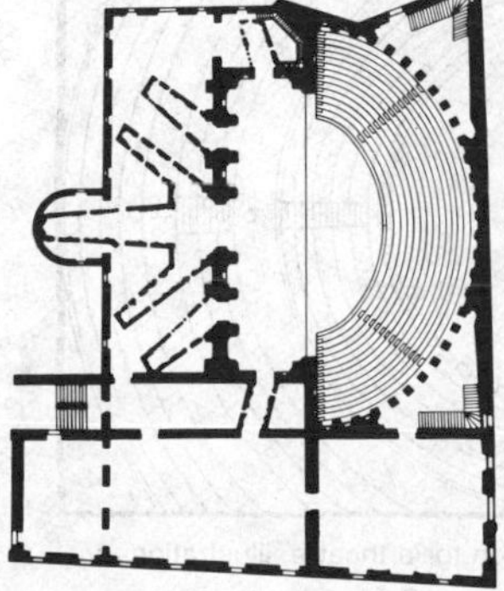

Figure 7: *The first permanent indoor theatre.* Teatro Olimpico, Vicenza, Italy, designed by Andrea Palladio and completed by Vincenzo Scamozzi, 1585. (Top) View of stage and auditorium. (Centre) Section. (Bottom) Plan.

By courtesy of (centre, bottom) George C. Izenour; photograph, (top) Foto Tapparo e Trentin, Vicenza

Unlike the Teatro Olimpico the stage here is a single architectural vista behind a shallow-raked open platform, after the manner of the stage illustrated by Sebastiano Serlio (Figure 8). At Sabbioneta a divided horsehoe-shaped bank of seating leaves an empty arena, at floor level, in front of the stage. This space, backed by the permanent bank of seating, can be used for additional seating, but it also accommodates other uses and paves the way for the most famous and influential of all Renaissance theatre buildings, the Teatro Farnese.

Teatro Farnese

The Teatro Farnese lies about 12 miles west of Sabbioneta at Parma, in a palace of the Farnese family. The theatre, designed by Giovanni Battista Aleotti and built in 1618 (but not used until 1628, to celebrate the marriage of a Medici daughter to a Farnese son), was the first proscenium theatre to be designed for movable scenery (Figure 9) and is the earliest large-scale indoor theatrical facility to have survived. It was severely damaged by fire bombing in World War II but has since been restored to its former glory. There has also survived an extensive catalog giving details of events held there, including some contemporary comment on performances. The catalog describes the variety of uses to which the theatre was put: drama, opera, and ballet were performed on stage; equestrian acts and sumptuous balls were held in the spacious arena between stage and seating, which could also be flooded to a depth of two feet and used for mock naval battles; and, in addition, the theatre accommodated such court ceremonies as ambassadorial receptions, proclamations of state, and princely extravaganzas. The Teatro Farnese has windows (as did the Teatro Olimpico and the Teatro all'Antica at Sabbioneta before it) behind and above the banked seating, which helped to illuminate the space during daytime use; tallow candles or animal-fat lamps, in wall and overhead fixtures, were the only source of nighttime illumination for this and all interior theatres until the introduction of gas lighting in the 19th century. The Teatro Farnese set the style for stage and auditorium design over the next 250 years, with the exception of the courtyard-patio (*corrales*) theatre in Spain and the Elizabethan and Jacobean theatre of England. (G.C.I./Ho.B./C.Ba.)

Developments in staging. In the latter half of the 16th century, intermezzi became a popular element of theatrical production. These entertainments, inserted between the acts of a play and totally unrelated to it, were generally on classical themes and were originally mounted during masked balls and banquets. The need to change settings rapidly for the alternating segments of plays and intermezzi encouraged the development of new devices for shifting scenery. The first solution to scene shifting

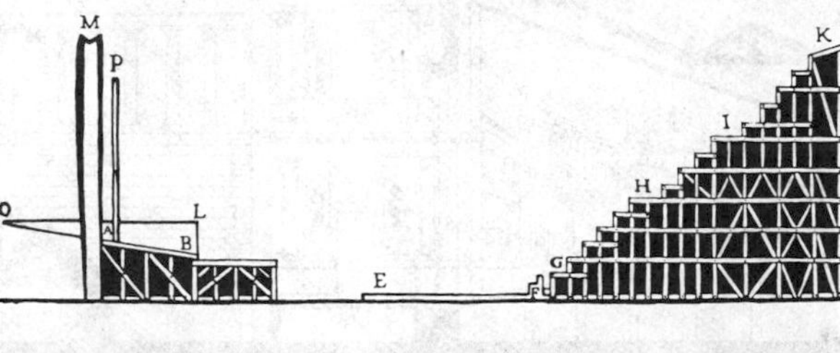

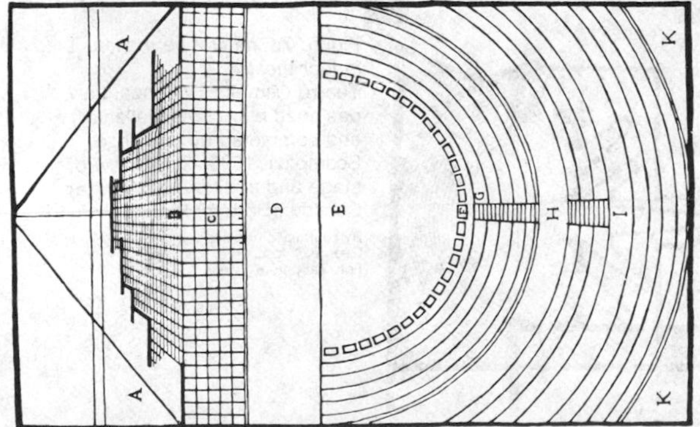

Figure 8: Sebastiano Serlio's design for a theatre, illustration from his *Architettura*.

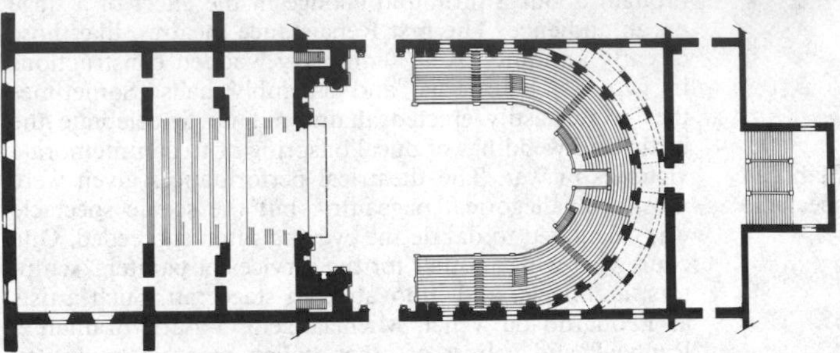

Figure 9: *The first proscenium theatre designed for movable scenery.*
Teatro Farnese, Parma, Italy, designed by Giovanni Battista Aleotti, 1618. (Top) View looking toward the stage. (Bottom) Plan.

By courtesy of (top) the Soprintendenza di Parma, (bottom) George C. Izenour; photograph, (top) Comm. Luigi Vagni, Parma

adopted for intermezzi was derived from discussions of *periaktoi* found in Vitruvius. Nicola Sabbatini's "Manual for Constructing Theatrical Scenes and Machines," published in 1638, listed three main methods of changing scenery: one used *periaktoi;* the second maneuvered new wings around those already there; and the third pulled painted canvas around the wings to conceal the previously visible surfaces. In addition, the author explains how to change the flat wings near the back of the stage by sliding them in grooves or turning them like pages in a book. All of Sabbatini's devices indicate a considerable simplification of Serlio's wings (*e.g.,* the substitution of painted details for three-dimensional ones).

The demands of scene changing required that flat wings replace the angled ones. The problem of transferring a perspective picture successfully to a series of flat wings was not solved until 1600. By 1650 angled wings were completely outmoded; at each wing position as many flats were set up, one behind the other, as there were settings. Scenery was changed by removing the visible wings to reveal the set behind. Grooves were made in the stage floor to support the flats and facilitate their movement. The background was painted on two flats, called shutters, which met at the centre of the stage; and cloths that could be rolled up were occasionally used.

The chariot-and-pole system

The final step in scene-shifting was introduced by Giacomo Torelli in 1641, when he perfected the chariot-and-pole system. According to this system, slots were cut in the stage floor to support uprights, on which flats were mounted. These poles were attached below the stage to chariots mounted on casters that ran in tracks parallel to the front of the stage. As the chariots rolled to the centre of the stage, they carried the flats into view. An elaborate system of winches, ropes, and pulleys made it possible to change every part of a setting by turning a single winch. This invention, adopted by every European country except England and Holland, was the standard method of shifting scenery until the end of the 19th century.

The Italians were particularly taken with special effects and delighted in elaborating on medieval practices. Most of the special effects were associated with the intermezzi and involved the replacement of biblical characters of the Middle Ages by pagan deities. Machines capable of flying up to 50 characters might be used. According to Serlio, moving mechanical figures representing men, animals, and objects were cut out of pasteboard and drawn across a scene by invisible wires. In many productions clouds that engulfed the stage would hide the activity of lowering painted cloths and flats (Figure 10). The front curtain was used to conceal the scenery and increase amazement at the beginning of a performance. At first the curtain was dropped, but, as this was hazardous, the roll curtain was soon adopted.

By courtesy of the Harvard Theatre Collection

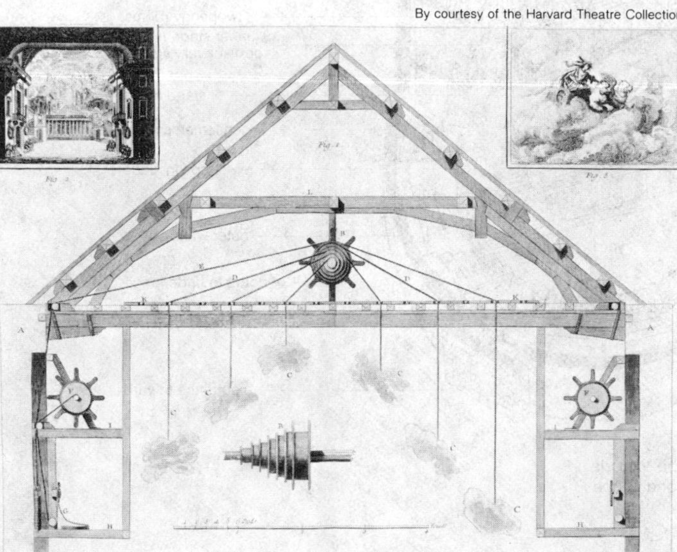

Figure 10: Stage grids and clouds used in Renaissance and Baroque theatre. Cross-section diagram from *Dictionnaire des Sciences* shows method of operation, and insets illustrate the effect created.

Commedia dell'arte

Alongside the theatre of the aristocracy existed the enormously popular commedia dell'arte. The term commedia dell'arte only began to be used in the mid-18th century, though it has since come to denote the traveling companies of actors whose masked, improvised farces enjoyed a period of great popularity in Italy and throughout Europe in the 16th and early 17th centuries. The origins of the commedia are questionable, though it seems most likely that it derived from an ancient tradition of popular dancing and buffoonery, combined with stock characters from Roman comedy. Popular legend associates commedia performances with improvised acting in the open air, but evidence suggests that the commedia was not infrequently performed in enclosed spaces, since its emergence in the early 16th century proves it to be quite clearly a commercial theatre. The development of the commercial theatre, perceived by Vasari in the 16th century as an extraordinary innovation, parallels the emergence of the commedia companies, known for at least a century and a half as performers of *commedia mercenaria* (mercenary commedia), *commedia all'improvviso* (improvised commedia), *commedia delle maschere* (mask commedia), and, in France, as the *comédie italienne.* The basis of the commedia companies was continuity; roles and plots were transmitted orally, often from generation to generation. The companies traveled constantly and performed in hired indoor spaces, only occasionally on outdoor stages, making use of perspective scenery when they could but relying primarily on the skills of individual actors. Particularly famous were Francesco Andreini and his wife, Isabella, who was a playwright and poet in her own right, besides being a successful actress, Tiberio Fiorillo, and Vicenza Armani, whose arrival in many cities was accompanied by ceremonial cannon fire.

The commedia dell'arte is best remembered as a theatre of stock types that later degenerated into pantomime clowns but that caught and held the imagination of audiences across the centuries. In fact, the greatest significance of the commedia has often remained hidden; its emergence as a specific form of theatre in the 16th century marks a fundamental change in the history of Western theatre as a whole. In the precommercial theatre, performance was characterized by the mutual participation of actors and audience. In the commercial theatre, where actors have to sell themselves to the audience, the emphasis shifts away from the role of the audience onto the skills of the actors. So the commedia dell'arte began as a festive people's theatre of the medieval world and became an actors' theatre. Its rise to fame and popularity marks the precise moment of the start of the theatre industry.

The birth of the theatre industry

The 16th and 17th centuries in France. In 16th-century France most theatrical activity was associated with the Confrérie de la Passion, a Parisian organization set up for the performance of mystery cycles. In 1402 the company was granted permission to stage any mystery play, but by 1548 it had been forbidden to produce sacred mysteries, this satirical forum for the lower clergy having proved to be too much for the ecclesiastical authorities. The company was granted, instead, complete control over secular drama, and they converted the Hôtel de Bourgogne into a theatre. The sets consisted of paintings of houses, unusual for the variety of localities represented within the same stage area.

Despite the number of critics seeking to hold to the classical "unities"—*i.e.,* the notion that a play should concern a single course of action set in one day, in one place—popular sentiment inspired plays with numerous settings. Such a play could be presented by the use of curtains, by changing scenery, or by a third method, the *décor simultané,* which was utilized by Laurent and Mahelot, the designers for the Confrérie. In this scheme, several localities were represented on the stage at the same time—each on a different portion of the stage—using angled mansions of wooden frames covered with canvas. When a play needed more mansions than could be fitted onstage at once, units were converted by removing the canvas coverings or by opening curtains to show an interior scene. Molière inherited a permanent town square set when he moved into the Petit-Bourbon in 1658.

The Elizabethan stage. During the early part of the 16th century, there were two distinct types of theatre in England. One was represented by small groups of professional actors who performed in halls, inns, or marketplaces. The location of a play was established by the words and gestures of the actors. As in the commedia dell'arte, these localities had little significance. The second type of theatre, found in the London area, was made up of amateurs, usually university students, performing for the royal court and assorted gentry. The audience and the actors were educated, acquainted with the classics, and knowledgeable about theatre in other countries, particularly France. The stage was probably set with buildings made of laths, covered with painted canvas, with cloud borders masking the upper part of the acting area.

The significant achievement of the Elizabethan stage was connected with the theatres of professional acting groups, not the court theatre. During the second half of the 16th century, as they became successful, the troupes no longer needed to remain itinerant. In 1576 the first permanent public theatre, called simply the Theatre, was erected by the actor James Burbage. The building boom continued until the end of the century; the Globe, where Shakespeare's plays were first performed, was built in 1599 with lumber from the demolished Theatre.

The rise of permanent public theatres

The typical Elizabethan stage was a platform, as large as 40 feet square (more than 12 metres on each side), sticking out into the middle of the yard so that the spectators nearly surrounded it (Figure 11). It was raised four to six feet and was sheltered by a roof, called "the shadow" or "the heavens." In most theatres the stage roof, supported by two pillars set midway at the sides of the stage, concealed an upper area from which objects could be raised or lowered. At the rear of the stage was a multileveled facade with two large doors at stage level. There was also a space for "discoveries" of hidden characters, in order to advance the plot; this was probably located between the doors. Some scenes took place in a playing area on the

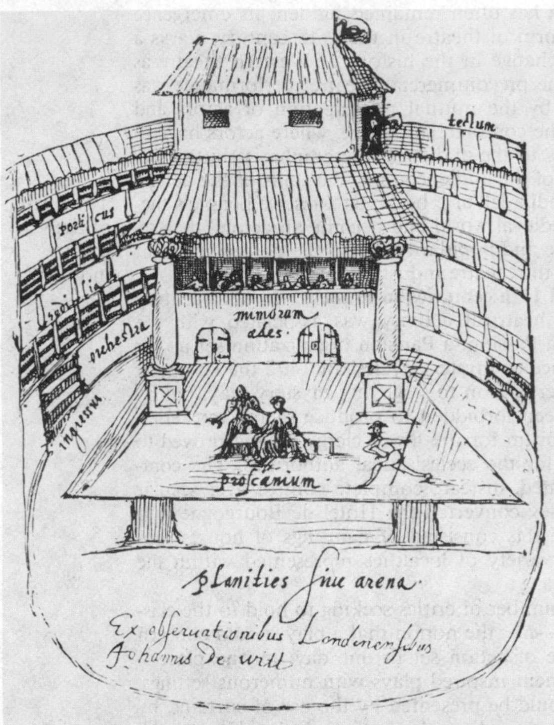

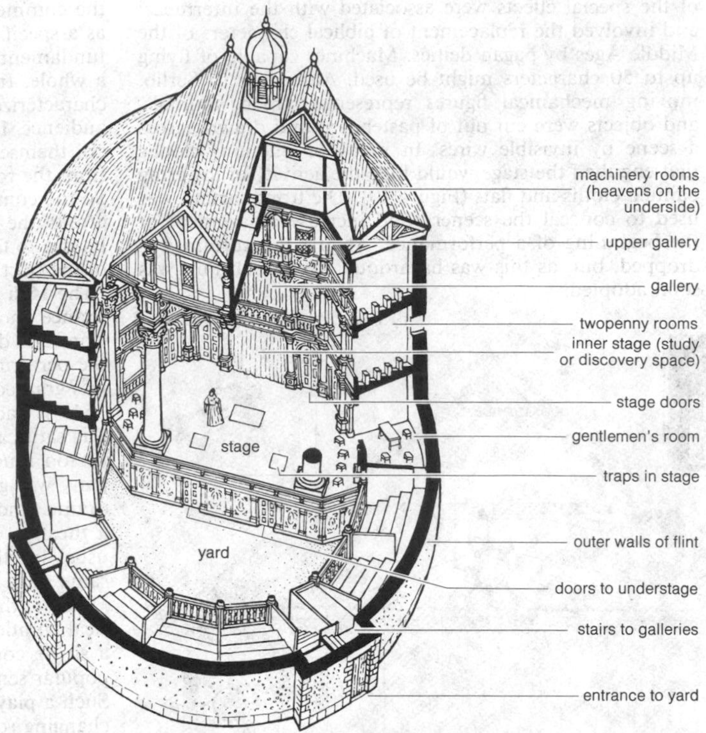

Figure 11: *Elizabethan theatres.*
(Left) The Swan Theatre, London, drawing by Johann DeWitt, *c.* 1596. In the Victoria and Albert Museum, London. (Right) Conjectural reconstruction of the second Globe Theatre, London, 1614.
By courtesy of (left) the Victoria and Albert Museum, London; (right) from H. and R. Leacroft, *The Theatre*

second level of the facade, but, again, historians disagree as to which scenes they were.

Properties were occasionally carried onto the platform stage, but from extant lists it is obvious that they were few in number. Some properties were so cumbersome that they remained onstage throughout a performance. Smaller properties were probably revealed in the discovery space, and servants carried some properties on and off. It appears that the audience was not concerned by the scenic inconsistencies.

All of the theatre buildings were round, square, or octagonal, with thatched roofs covering the structure surrounding an open courtyard. Spectators, depending on how much money they had, could either stand in the yard, which may have sloped toward the stage, sit on benches in the galleries that went around the greater part of the walls, sit in one of the private boxes, or sit on a stool on the stage proper.

The importance of this type of theatre was its flexibility. In some ways it was similar to earlier attempts to reconstruct the *scaenae frons* of the Romans; it had the facade and the entrance doors. The Elizabethan theatre differed in that it had a main platform, an inner stage, and an upper stage level that made movement possible in all directions instead of simply along the length of a narrow stage.

Spain's Golden Age. Religious drama developed in Spain during the Middle Ages only in the northeast because the Moors occupied the remainder of the peninsula. During the 16th century, as Spain became the most powerful country in Europe, it started to develop a sophisticated theatre. Following a period of interest in classical drama and the introduction of printing, in the late 15th century there appeared Juan del Encina, the founder of modern Spanish drama. Although the origin of professional status among players is obscure, it is known that actors in Spain were being paid as early as 1454. The popularity of the theatre mushroomed in the 1570s, and among the playwrights of this era were such masters as Lope de Vega, Cervantes, and Calderón de la Barca.

During this Golden Age in Spain, the theatre assumed a form more flexible than that of the Italian or French stages. The model was that of the *corrales*—courtyards enclosed by the backs of several houses—in which the earliest troupes had performed. The staging arrangements were almost identical to those in contemporary London. The stage itself was a raised platform, without a front curtain or a proscenium arch but with a permanent facade at the back. Stages were about 28 feet long and 23 to 30 feet deep. The open platform was usually backed by a facade of two levels, with pillars dividing the lower level into three openings. The second level, basically a gallery, usually represented towers, city walls, or hills.

Spanish staging conventions, like those of the Elizabethan theatre, tended to be simple. To denote a change of location, an actor merely exited and reentered. Occasionally, a curtain might have been used to augment the scenic effect, being drawn aside to permit upstage action. As with Shakespeare, however, locale was suggested by poetic discourse rather than by visual symbolism. The stage probably derived directly from the medieval wagon platform that had been used in the public square. Backstage were the actors' dressing rooms and stage property rooms. A shallow roof, supported by the primary backstage structure, extended partway over the platform, though probably not far enough to require any additional support. Three kinds of scenic background were utilized: the facade; the curtains concealing the facade, which were used when the location was not particularly important; and medieval-type mansions, which were sometimes erected on the main stage. As spectacle increased after 1650, painted flats with doors and windows were set into the facade in place of curtains. After a period of time, awnings were rigged over the seating, and, eventually, the addition of a permanent roof made it an indoor theatre. Seville at one time boasted seven permanent theatres; the most important in Madrid was the Corral de la Cruz, opened in 1579. The *corrales* themselves, enclosing a square or rectangular courtyard, were unroofed until the 18th century; when roofs were added, a row of windows was added under the eaves. Seating consisted of benches on the ground level and balconies set in the containing walls for wealthier patrons. A special boxlike gallery, called the *cazuela,* the "stewpot," was assigned to women spectators. Above the *cazuela* were galleries for members of the city government, the clergy, and the aristocracy.

Figure 12: The court theatre in the palace of Versailles, France, designed by Jacques-Ange Gabriel in 1769 and restored in 1957.
Robert Doisneau—Rapho/Photo Researchers

BAROQUE THEATRES AND STAGING

The combination of two artistic innovations—the formulation of the laws of perspective in the 15th century and the production of the first opera in 1597—provided the foundation for the Baroque theatre, which was to last until the 19th century. During this era all countries were brought into the same orbit, although Italy remained the primary inspiration. The classically inspired drama of the 16th century gave way to a variety of entertainments—intermezzi, ballet, masques, and opera. The invention of new means of presenting spectacular visual effects encouraged the installation of more and more elaborate machinery in theatre buildings. The result was that spectacle dominated all other aspects of production. (Ho.B./C.Ba.)

Court theatres. The Baroque architectural style, beginning in Italy and spreading across Europe, dominated theatre building between about 1650 and 1790. Its chief characteristics are refinement in detail of the proscenium stage and of the Renaissance horseshoe-shaped auditorium and seating plan. The innovations of the period were introduced in the private court theatres. As many as five shallow balconies were stacked vertically in the auditorium. For the first time there appeared an orchestra pit in front of the stage, sunk below ground level. The stage floor, which previously had extended only a few yards back from the proscenium arch, was now deepened to accommodate scenery, equipment, and dancing.

The rise of grand opera and ballet

With the rise of grand opera and ballet, inventors and designers were called upon to provide increasingly elaborate, portable, perspective scenery and complicated stage machinery, both above and below stage, to effect scene changes (nearly always carried out in full sight of the audience). Famous names of this period include the Italians Giacomo Torelli and the Bibiena family, whose ingenious settings were unrivaled for originality. A rigid court etiquette dictated that the lines of perspective should provide a perfect stage picture from the point of view of the royal box, which directly faced the stage. Since, moreover, the building of theatres was controlled by the ducal or imperial purse, a rigid architectural formalism, varying only in detail, became the fashion, not to be broken until late in the 19th century. The auditorium was planned in tiers, a vertical stratification that reflected the ordering of society by class. A good example is the French court theatre at Versailles (1769), designed by King Louis XV's architect, Jacques-Ange Gabriel (Figure 12). For a court theatre, its stage is exceptionally well equipped, mechanized in the manner of the Bibiena family, with an overhead pulley system for flying drops and borders, while the flat wings and shutters making up the elaborate scene were mounted on frames attached to carriages that ran on rails beneath the stage and so could easily be changed. Engravings of the time indicate that the court theatres were used for balls, concerts, and the like, as well as for stage performance. Though small, these costly court theatres witnessed the first productions of many operas by composers such as Haydn and Mozart, and they also played an important part in fostering the development of classical ballet.

Public theatres. *The opera house.* There were two kinds of public theatre in the 18th century. One was a logical development of the earlier private court theatres, reflecting a sophisticated, urban, aristocratic demand for theatre as entertainment. The Teatro alla Scala (1776–78) in Milan is a good example of the numerous theatres erected by 18th-century nobility in the capitals of Europe. Public theatres such as La Scala differ from private court theatres only in the size of the auditorium and stage. Whereas Versailles had seated fewer than 700 in the auditorium, La Scala could accommodate more than 2,000. Opera, generally including a ballet, was by this time the most popular form of entertainment, especially in Italy.

La Scala

The Restoration playhouse. The other kind of public theatre, peculiar to England, was the Restoration playhouse. The Baroque horseshoe-shaped auditorium, with its deep stage and orchestra pit, was generally in favour all over western Europe, fixing the design and style of opera houses in particular. In it the actor played in front of elaborately painted scenery and behind the proscenium arch. The Restoration playhouse, however, while borrowing the fully rigged stage of the Baroque theatre, provided, in addition, a deep apron stage thrusting out from the proscenium, upon which most of the action took place. Thus, the actor played, as it were, in the auditorium and away from the scenic backing; the English, with their Shakespearean tradition, were loath to abandon the intimate contact between actor and audience that the Elizabethan theatre had allowed. At either side of the forestage were doors by which actors entered; above these doors were additional boxes, for spectators, stacked one above the other in the Baroque manner.

Influence of technical achievements. Theatre lighting in this period was provided by wick-fed illuminants concealed behind the wings and proscenium arch and at the edge of the stage apron. In the auditorium either a large, single, central fixture, as at La Scala, or a number of smaller ceiling fixtures, as at Versailles, was the custom. All were kept burning during performance, and the habit of lighting the auditorium persisted until late in the 19th century. (G.C.I.)

The court masques served to introduce Italian staging to England. The masques were allegories designed to honour a particular person or occasion by comparing them favourably with mythological characters or situations. Inigo Jones, the foremost English architect of his time, produced masques and other entertainments at the English court from 1605 to 1640. He had visited Italy between 1596 and 1604 and was the individual most responsible for acceptance of Italian stage design in England. From his sketches it is known that Jones went through several phases in his designs, starting in 1604 with the *décor simultané,* mentioned above, in which different localities were represented on different portions of the stage. In 1605 he introduced simple perspective settings—two painted representations of houses with a painted back shutter. The same year he experimented with *periaktoi,* creating a globe, with no visible axle, that revolved to reveal eight dancers sitting inside.

Influence of Inigo Jones

His masques all had painted proscenium arches, into which he set a falling curtain. By 1635 Jones designed a setting that utilized four angled wings, like Serlio's, and four shutters at the rear, three of which could be drawn to the sides in two parts (Figure 13). Jones' design for

Figure 13: Stage designed by Inigo Jones in the Italian manner for a production of *Florimène*, 1635. In the Devonshire Collection, Chatsworth, England.

a masque in 1640 is considered the first design of the Baroque theatre in England. Four sets of side wings were placed on each side of the stage, each wing consisting of two flats. There were four shutters at the rear, with each dividing into two parts for easy removal. Each wing had either a header (*i.e.,* a horizontal unit that joins two upright wings, to form a flat arch) or a sky border (a horizontal piece of scenery, designed to look like the sky, which masks the space above the set). To give the illusion of distance, the side wings were made in exaggerated perspective, with each succeeding wing in significantly smaller scale than the one preceding. The disadvantage of using smaller sized flats toward the back of the stage was that if the actors stood too close to them the illusion would be destroyed. The actors were therefore restricted to the front of the stage. In successive decades, attempts were made to give the stage area greater depth by multiplying the number of flats on each side. In sum, with the exception of the chariot-and-pole system of scene changing, Jones introduced all of the major Italian developments into England.

After Inigo Jones, English scenery practices and stage conventions were similar to those of Italy. Sets were changed by sliding them in grooves in the stage floor and overhead. Since the curtain was raised after the prologue and remained up throughout the performance, all scene shifting was in view of the audience. It was not until 1750 that an "act drop" was used; previously, even intermezzi were performed in front of a full stage setting.

As interest in spectacle increased, the scene painter became more important, and by the late 18th century each theatre had two or more permanent scene painters. The best known designer around the end of the 18th century was Philip James de Loutherbourg, a painter; from 1771 he worked for the actor-manager David Garrick as scenic designer at the Drury Lane Theatre in London, and he is credited with changing the orientation of design from the architectural to the landscape era, thus marking the end of the Baroque in England. He was one of the pioneers of the cut cloth, a double back cloth in which there was an opening in the one nearer the audience that revealed a vista painted on the back one. He also utilized transparent scenery; in one production he cut the moon out of the canvas back cloth, replaced it with gauze, and lit it from behind. The importance that Loutherbourg's landscape painting of the back cloth assumed is shown by the fact that the Drury Lane pantomime of 1779 was specially written for the scenery he had designed while on a trip to Derbyshire. His depiction of actual places in England started a vogue for "local colour." Loutherbourg's single most important contribution, however, was that he achieved a unity of design because he directed both the scenery and the lighting and effects of a single production.

Loutherbourg's contributions

Scenic design. Significant changes in scenic design were made by Italy's Bibiena family, of whom the best known members were Ferdinando, Francesco, Giuseppe, Antonio, and Carlo. Around 1703, at Bologna, Ferdinando introduced angled perspective. Previously, stage design was based on one-point perspective using a single vanishing point, in which all lines appear to recede with distance toward one point at the centre of the background. Bibiena, however, used perspective with two vanishing points; if this technique were used to render a large, flat building as seen from one corner of it, for example, the base and roof lines of one side extended into the distance would appear to meet at some point off to the right and those of the other side at another point off to the left. Furthermore, by locating these points quite low, Bibiena gave the structures the effect of immense size. Buildings, walls, or courtyards were placed in the centre of the set and vistas at the sides, and the scale of settings, which had previously been designed to make the scenery an extension of the auditorium, was altered. The front wings were painted as though they were only the lower part of a building. The result of these innovations was that Bibiena's sets seemed so large that they created a feeling of fantasy (Figure 14). Despite its apparent size, though, an angled-perspective setting required less stage space than one with a central alley. Many of the settings divided the stage into a foreground, for the actors, and a background, for distant objects. A drop, designed to resemble a series of arches or columns, often marked the rear of the acting area.

Angled perspective designs

Another designer who developed the angled scene independently of Bibiena was Filippo Juvarra, a major Italian architect of the early 18th century, who began his work, as did many artists of the period, with the decoration of court entertainments. Some of his most intriguing scenic designs, in terms of architectural fantasy, were executed for a marionette theatre owned by his patron. These designs are of particular interest to theatre historians because Juvarra usually included plans of the stage settings showing exactly how the wings were placed. Juvarra's sets were basically curvilinear, leading the audience's eye to the foreground instead of the sides. In several sketches he designed a permanent set with a large archway opening up to a series of vistas, which varied from a landscape to a perspective corridor. His designs foreshadowed the interest in landscape that was not to find its complete development until almost a century later.

In the second half of the 18th century, several new

Figure 14: Drawing for an interior setting by Giuseppe Bibiena. In the Victoria and Albert Museum, London.

By courtesy of the Victoria and Albert Museum, London

Late 18th-century developments

directions in thinking led to stylistic changes in scenery. One was the increased interest in history, spurred by the rediscovery of Pompeii in 1748. Scenery of classical ruins overgrown with vines became popular. Plays based on folk literature were produced with Gothic architectural settings. The most important new direction was that scenic designers introduced "mood"; they started to emphasize light and shadow to create an atmosphere. The best known artist of this period was the Italian engraver Giambattista Piranesi, who executed more than 1,000 engravings of Roman ruins and prisons. He did not particularly apply himself to the theatre, yet his designs were inspired by contemporary stage settings and were in turn themselves an inspiration for other designers.

Developments in France and Spain. Although Italian-style scenery was introduced to the French court before, it was not popular until after 1640. The first theatre in France with a permanent proscenium arch and a stage designed for flat wings was constructed in 1641 for Cardinal de Richelieu. In 1645 an Italian designer, Giacomo Torelli, popularly called "the great sorcerer," was imported by Richelieu's successor, Jules Cardinal Mazarin, to design for the new theatre, the Palais-Royal. In 1646–47 Torelli remodeled the Palais-Royal to accommodate his invention of the chariot-and-pole system of scene shifting. Pierre Corneille, the founder of French classical tragedy, was commissioned to write *Andromède* for the remodeled theatre (Figure 15). Although the play progressed through spoken episodes, each act provided an excuse for Torelli to introduce elaborate machinery, including the revolving stage. Until Torelli, the changing of scenery had marked a structural break in the dramatic presentation. Torelli put aside all previous methods, which were so distracting to the audience, and introduced set changes within, rather than at the ends of, the scenes. The audience was mesmerized by the scenery mysteriously changing while the action of an opera or ballet proceeded without interruption.

For the wedding of Louis XIV, in 1660, Gaspare Vigarani went to France from Italy to build the Salle des Machines, the largest theatre in Europe. It was 226 feet long, only 94 feet of which was occupied by the auditorium. Its stage, 132 feet deep, had a proscenium arch only 32 feet wide. One of Vigarani's machines, 60 feet deep itself, was used to fly the entire royal family and their attendants on stage for the finale. Vigarani was succeeded by his son, who was in turn followed by the Jean Berains, father and son.

By courtesy of the Metropolitan Museum of Art, New York, Elisha Whittelsey Fund, 1951

Figure 15: Set design by Giacomo Torelli for Act II of Corneille's *Andromède*, as performed in the Palais-Royal theatre, Paris, 1650; engraving by F. Chauveau. In the Metropolitan Museum of Art, New York.

Designs of the Jean Berains

The Berains established a distinctly French style of design, emphasizing heavy lines, curves, and encrusted ornamentation. They usually designed only one set for each act but used many machines and special effects. This combination of static scenery and dynamic machinery was to remain in vogue in French opera through the 18th century. After 1682 the influence of the court on public theatre declined. After 1690 the King became so puritanical that plays were no longer encouraged.

In contrast to court opulence was the Comédie-Française, for which a theatre was built in 1689 from a converted tennis court. The stage was equipped for flat wings and shutters, but since scene changes were few, the machinery was minimal. The typical background for tragedies was the *palais à volonté* (literally "palace to order"), a neutral setting without particularized details. For comedy the typical scene was *chambre à quatre portes* ("room with four doors"), an informal interior. By 1700 Paris had two types of theatres, epitomized by the Opéra, with its Baroque scenery and machines, and the Comédie-Française, which did not rely on spectacle.

The first true spectacle in a public theatre was the 1755 production of Voltaire's *Orphelin de la Chine* (*Orphan of China*), with its supposedly accurate Chinese scenery and costumes. Subsequently the Comédie-Italienne, permanently performing in Paris, introduced local colour and increased the use of spectacle. Giovanni Nicolò Servandoni, originally a Florentine who lived in Paris from 1724 to 1746, translated Italian styles to French taste. His use of perspective gave the illusion of space without falling back on the obvious geometry that characterized the High Baroque. He took over as director of the Salle de Machines, where his work in its turn influenced the designers of Italy and Germany. At the Opéra, as opposed to public theatres, spectacle was used throughout the 18th century. Its best known designers included the painter François Boucher. And although many famous painters designed settings, there is still no comparison with the works of the Italians of this period. The financial problems of the theatres did much to prevent a forward thrust in French design. Ironically, the most sumptuous spectacle of the latter part of the 18th century occurred in France in 1794, after the Revolution: the National Convention decreed "The Festival of the Supreme Being," designed by the painter Jacques-Louis David and conducted by the revolutionary government leader Robespierre—Neoclassicism in the service of the Republic.

After the 1760s, theatres were built in the Italian style, with ovoid auditoriums and enlarged stages. By the 1780s, when the standing pit fell into disuse, all of the spectators were finally seated, off the stage. The seated pit was not to become accepted in France until the 19th century.

In Spain during this period, theatre began to decline. Although Italian-style scenery was used occasionally, it was not common until brought from Florence in 1626 by Cosimo Lotti, who staged many outdoor productions on the grounds of the Buen Retiro palace in Madrid. For one, he built a floating stage on a lake, and the special effects included a shipwreck, a water chariot drawn by dolphins, and the destruction of Circé's palace. This production was lit by 3,000 lanterns, and the spectators watched from gondolas. In 1640 Lotti built a permanent theatre in Madrid, the Coliseo, which probably had the first proscenium arch in Spain. The next decade saw a decline in both court and public theatres. By 1650 the Coliseo was reopened, but its popularity had diminished by 1700. By the late 1600s Spain had lost most of its economic and political power, and its theatre through most of the Baroque was a watered-down version of Italian concepts.

Developments in northern Europe. One country outside the Italian influence during this period exhibited an interesting theatre plan. In 1638 Jacob van Campen, an architect, designed a theatre in Amsterdam that had no counterpart elsewhere in Europe. The auditorium was elliptical, with two tiers of boxes on one side opposite a stage facade with open balconies over the sides. The facade itself consisted primarily of pillars with cornices above them, and painted panels, representing different localities rather than a unified setting, were set between the pillars. The whole concept of the panels was probably directly derived from the simultaneous stage of the Middle Ages.

The constantly shifting politics of northern Europe, and particularly of Germany, in the 16th and 17th centuries was the primary cause for the late development of professional theatre in this region. Theatre in Germany owes its impetus to the English troupes that started touring the country in the early 17th century. At first, the English performed in courts, and by 1650 they were traveling across the country regularly. To attract the non-English-speaking audience, the troupes gradually inserted German phrases, speeches, and then whole scenes. As early as 1626, German actors were joining the troupes, and by 1680 English actors had been completely displaced. Because Germany was politically divided and there were no large cities, the troupes had to travel constantly to find new audiences. To attract the disparate spectators, a company might have as many as 100 plays in its repertoire. These conditions combined to make it impossible to rehearse and mount plays with any great professionalism.

First Viennese opera house

Between the mid-17th and the late 18th century the aristocracy ignored public theatre in favour of opera. The first Viennese opera house was built in 1652 by Giovanni Burnacini and is similar to the courtyards of Italian Renaissance palaces in the two levels of its auditorium, framed by a double arcade of rounded arches. Italians played an important part in every aspect of theatre at the imperial court until the late 18th century. The first performance at the Viennese opera house was of an Italian opera.

In the public theatre, the work of the manager Johann Friedrich Schönemann led to the establishment in 1767 of the Hamburg National Theatre, the first noncommercial public theatre, subsidized by a group of rich citizens. This marked the beginning of a movement that gained force during the next decade and can be found even today in East German theatre. The prevailing attitude was that theatre is a cultural institution that, like museums, should be available to all citizens.

This movement toward permanence greatly influenced the evolution of staging in the 18th century. As audiences grew larger, and as cities developed, a troupe was able to reduce the number of plays in a repertoire, and this in turn led to better productions. And as the theatre building grew in size and substance, the chariot-and-pole system of scene shifting was introduced. Interest in historical accuracy of sets and costumes was stimulated by the chivalric plays popular in the 1770s. During the next two decades dramatists were writing plays that relied on complex set pieces, including bridges and walls. Doors and windows were set up between the wings, marking the first development toward the box set—a set representing three walls of a room, the fourth being the plane of the proscenium.

Early Russian staging. Russian theatre can be traced back to the pagan rituals of the ancient Slavs, the later Christian festivals, and, in the Middle Ages, the mixed rituals of these two influences. As early as the 10th century there were mummers, called *skomorokhi,* probably itinerant comedians who performed in small towns and villages. Suffering the same fate as the actors of western Europe during the early Middle Ages, the mummers were the victims of measures taken by the princes as well as the church. Their specialties were trained-animal acts, usually with bears, and puppet shows. The Greek Orthodox Church introduced some morality plays in Russia, but they were limited in scope and number. Since the mass was celebrated in the vernacular, the church did not need the aid of morality plays for the dissemination of its message. At the beginning of the 17th century, the only theatre using a literary text and a trained company was the drama brought from Poland to the Ukraine.

The Tsar's theatre

In 1672 the first public performance of a play was offered in Moscow. A special theatre was built in the Tsar's residence; there seems to have been no scenery outside a fir tree on either side of the stage, although there was a sliding curtain. The Tsar (Alexis), who was so excited that he sat in the theatre for 10 hours on the day of the first performance, paid for the founding of a theatrical school. The problem with the theatre during the next 80 years was precisely that it had been founded on the Tsar's order: it was attached to the court and subsidized by the aristocracy (who chose German directors); it assumed political overtones and aimed at pleasing only the monarchy.

The beginning of change came in 1730, when an Italian group brought the commedia dell'arte, elaborate sets, and machinery to Moscow. During the next 10 years, Italian opera and ballet were also introduced to Russia. Despite the success of foreign companies, the significant event was the birth of the national theatre in 1749. This enterprise was open to the public, and, although it was popular, lack of funds made it a weak rival to court theatre. Its impact lay in the fact that it introduced the concept of theatre to a large audience.

By the end of the 18th century, companies were touring the major cities, and privately owned theatres were being opened. In general, only the aristocracy patronized the theatre, and nobles established their own serf troupes. One prince, who owned 21,000 serfs, established his own ballet, opera, and dramatic companies. Owners occasionally rented their troupes for public performances, until the abolition of serfdom in 1861. Little is known of the staging of their productions beyond the fact that it was imitative of French and Italian theatre.

DEVELOPMENTS IN THE 19TH CENTURY

Theatre in France after the Revolution. Under Napoleon, French theatre was little different from that of the 1780s, specializing in Neoclassical drama. Popular drama, as performed by what were known as "boulevard theatres," introduced melodrama, a form that was to dominate theatre in the 19th century. Melodrama, in turn, by popularizing departures from Neoclassicism and capturing the interest of large audiences, paved the way for Romantic drama.

The dramatic debut of Romanticism is dated at 1830, when public pressure forced the Comédie-Française to produce Victor Hugo's *Hernani.* After a spirited opening at which Hugo's Bohemian claque overwhelmed the staid regular theatregoers, Romanticism was victorious and ruled the Parisian stage for 50 years. The grandiose bombast of Romanticism did not overturn the Baroque, it merely diluted it; the formal artificial structure was broken into sentimental, melodramatic episodes depicting the distraught hero buffeted by an unfeeling world and the awesome elements. The melodramas introduced natural disasters that were significant to the plot, so that emphasis could be placed on special effects and spectacle. Dramatists also deliberately included exotic locales or examples of local colour, so that a variety of historical periods and fantastic sets would hold the attention of the audience. Throughout the 19th century, architectural perspective was replaced by neo-Gothic sentimentalization of nature. Painted Romantic scenery, in the style of Loutherbourg, was the rage in France.

Staging of Romantic drama

The two important designers of this period were Jacques Daguerre, who was also the inventor of the daguerreotype, an early photographic technique, and Pierre-Luc-Charles Ciceri, the most important designer of this period. The panorama, a major scenic innovation, was invented in 1787 and first used on the London stage in 1792. The panorama was set up in a circular building in which the audience, sitting on a central platform, was totally surrounded by a continuous painting. Daguerre started his career as one of the first panorama painters. He went on to invent the diorama, in which the audience sat on a platform that revolved to show paintings on proscenium-like stages. Although the scenery remained stationary, Daguerre created the illusion of constant change by controlling the light on the semitransparent sets. The panorama was more popular than the diorama because it did not depend on the ability to alter stage lighting. Its shape, though, was altered to resemble the diorama. The next development in spectacle was the moving panorama, in which a continuous scene was painted on a long cloth, hung from an overhead track, and attached at both ends to spools. When the spools were turned, the cloth moved across the stage so that the actors with their carriages and other props could move from one location to another without changing wings and drops. The sky borders were dispensed with, and flats of architectural units or natural objects forming an arch were placed at the front of the stage, through which was seen a distant view painted on a curved panorama stretching across the back and sides of the stage.

Ciceri's contributions to staging

Ciceri's importance arose from his abilities to depict local colour, ruins, and historical backgrounds. He founded the first scenic studio in Paris independent of a theatre, with specialists in various types of design. After the opening of the new Opéra in 1822, interest in spectacle was so great that promptbooks were published, describing scenery and special effects and how they could be adapted for theatres with less equipment.

By the end of the 19th century, the process of scenic design and construction had become standardized. The director gave the requirements to the scenic designer, who made cardboard models. The scenery was constructed by the theatre's carpenters and then sent to a scenic studio for painting. (Ho.B.)

German Romanticism and Naturalism. The 19th century in Germany was a study in contrasts. The beginning decades saw the rise of Romanticism, which, 50 years later, was still strong, primarily in the figure of the composer Richard Wagner. The century's middle decades of political and economic disillusionment before the unification of Germany were conducive to the emerging Naturalist school, the philosophy of which was first embodied in the Meiningen Players, organized in 1866 by George II, duke of Saxe-Meiningen.

By the middle 1820s, after the defeat of Napoleon, the political turbulence in Germany led to municipal control over the theatre and strict censorship. Repertoires consisted of "safe" classics and insipid new plays, resulting in competent but uninspired theatre. This competence was reflected in the staging. One of the few important designers of this period was Karl Friedrich Schinkel, who had been trained in both Italy and Germany. He introduced the diorama in Berlin in 1827.

One true innovator during the first half of the 19th century was Ludwig Tieck, who advocated realistic acting on a platform stage. With the help of an architect, he tried to reconstruct an Elizabethan public stage. He also championed the open stage in the belief that pictorial realism destroys the true illusion of the theatre. Invited by William IV of Prussia to stage *Antigone* at the court theatre in Potsdam in 1841, Tieck extended the apron in a semicircle over the orchestra pit and built a *skēnē* as the only background for the drama. In 1843 he adopted Elizabethan conventions to the proscenium theatre for a production of *A Midsummer Night's Dream.* Using the front part of the stage as a large open space, he built a unit in the rear consisting of two stairs leading to an acting area eight feet above stage level. The stairs framed an inner stage below the platform. He then hung tapestries at right angles to the proscenium, thus masking the sides of the stage. Although Tieck was universally respected, it was not until the 1870s that his innovations received widespread support. The works of Wagner and Saxe-Meiningen were responsible for this change in the public's attitude.

Wagner's impact

Wagner's works were the dramatic culmination of Romanticism and the contribution it was destined to make to modern theatre practices. German Romanticism was in great part a protest movement against the dominance of French Neoclassicism. Instead of structuring dramatic action according to fixed patterns of logical progression, the Romantics wanted dramatic structures born of human experience. This stress on what was to be called "organic form" was a protest against the received tradition of dramatic theory and staging practices. German Romanticism, also known as Sturm und Drang ("Storm and Stress"), a movement generally attributed to the influence of the young Goethe at the end of the 18th century, turned to a revival of the Gothic style of the Middle Ages to escape Neoclassicism. The new middle-class audiences identified with the lonely soul against the world—a sentimental world of windswept mountain crags and gloomy, mouldering castles.

Romanticism later broke into two camps. The first of these, called historical Romanticism, held that history is continuous, and that once its import has been grasped, the present can be recognized to be as "historical" as anything that occurred in the past. The second Romantic group, with which Wagner was associated, was concerned only with the use of history to reach absolute truths. Wagner believed that the study of history leads ultimately to prehistory and thus to transhistorical mythology, the realm of absolute truths. What is particularly interesting is that the first type, historical Romanticism, eventually found its home in the theatre in the realist school. Wagner's myth-Romanticism faded by the late 1800s, although Romantic contributions to staging exerted their influence well into the 20th century.

Wagner wanted to use myth to reunite modern man with the passion from which rationalism, the industrial process, and capitalism had separated him. For him, the theatrical manifestation of the myth was the music drama, and he hoped to combine music, acting, stage space, design, and lighting to establish the primeval mood of myth (Figure 16). To house his music drama, Wagner designed the Festspielhaus in Bayreuth, which opened in 1876, marking a rejection of the Baroque stratified auditorium and a return to classical, democratic principles of theatre design. The seating is fan-shaped, a belated acknowledgment of the fact that good lateral sight lines are essential for the enjoyment of performances on a proscenium stage. Wagner did away with the box seats, from which the wealthier theatregoers had watched each other instead of the stage for hundreds of years. Another striking feature is the absence of any radial or parallel aisles. Side aisles and two vomitory exits provide the only access to seating, thus further concentrating and compressing the main body of seats in front of the proscenium. Wagner had the orchestra lowered into a pit (the "mystic gulf"), so that it became the hidden source of an enveloping sound.

The stage itself was raked upward toward the rear, and the scenery was shifted by using the chariot-and-pole system. Wagner introduced a system of steam vents to make a steam curtain to hide scene changes. For him the theatre could no longer be the aggregate of the parts contributed by various hands. The ideal was the *Gesamtkunstwerk* ("total work of art"), in which all the elements of performance would be integrated. Nothing could be left to chance; all must be directed toward the same end.

By courtesy of (top) Theatermuseum, Munich, (bottom) Bibliotheque de l'Arsenal, Paris, Collection Rondel; photograph, (bottom) Marc Garanger

Figure 16: *Wagner's staging techniques.*
(Top) *Das Rheingold*, painting by J. Hoffmann of the 1876 production in Bayreuth. In the Theatermuseum, Munich. (Bottom) Print by Bergen showing a backstage view of the same production. In the Bibliothèque de l'Arsenal, Paris.

The Meiningen Players

At the time Wagner was introducing his music drama, George II, duke of Saxe-Meiningen, began to take an interest in the theatre of his court. The theatre itself, built by his father in classical-revival style in 1831, had a facade decorated with pillars crowned by a Greek pediment. The building contained not only the auditorium and stage house but also an assembly hall for balls, banquets, and other nontheatrical festivities. Saxe-Meiningen tried to create the illusion of reality with accurate spectacle and lifelike acting. He studied the distinctions between nations within the same historical period; the result was unprecedented historical accuracy (Figure 17). Saxe-Meiningen also insisted on using authentic period furniture, and the success of his troupe led to the opening of theatrical supply houses. The Duke designed all scenery, properties, and costumes for his troupe. Costumes were made of authentic materials. Characters appearing in chain mail wore chain mail and not some lighter substitute. Swords were of authentic weight. In this way, it was reasoned, the actor's physical sensation of wearing the costumes induced empathetic feelings for the character, and these feelings formed the basis of "lifelike" acting. Saxe-Meiningen viewed scene design as similar to architectural design in that it shapes whatever activity it shelters. He insisted on the continuous and direct relation between the design of a set and the actors' movements within it. Among his innovations is the abandonment of the practice of using only pastel colours for scenery; instead of sky borders as overhead masking, he used richly coloured banners, foliage, and other devices. Saxe-Meiningen was one of the first designers to break the surface of the stage floor into different levels.

From 1866 to 1874 the troupe performed only in Meiningen; for the following 16 years it toured 38 cities in nine countries. It had enormous impact on the history of the theatre, as it achieved complete illusion in every facet of its productions. Saxe-Meiningen is considered the single most important influence on the directors who inaugurated 20th-century stagecraft; he introduced the pictorial massing of crowds. He coordinated and controlled the work of his actors and established the ensemble as the basis for creative work in the theatre. There were no stars in the Meiningen Players. Casting policy required that actors play leading roles in some productions, subordinate roles in others. The supernumeraries were subjected to the same discipline, and the crowd was sectionalized under the leadership of actors. Actors were required to learn practical skills appropriate to their roles. The Saxe-Meiningen movement toward unified productions influenced other major figures such as André Antoine in France and Konstantin Stanislavsky in Russia, great apostles of realism and the founders of modern theatre.

Influence on others

However disparate the aims of Saxe-Meiningen and Wagner were, they had a great deal in common. Between them they established the principle that a production should be subordinated to the will of one individual who directs and integrates all aspects of the preparation. The profession of theatre director came into being with their vision of theatre.

Russian imperial theatre. Russian drama in the 19th century also got off to a slow start because of strict government censorship, particularly after 1825. This atmosphere was conducive, as in Germany, to the flowering

Figure 17: Scene from *Miss Sara Sampson* by Gotthold Ephraim Lessing, designed about 1884 by George II, duke of Saxe-Meiningen. In the Staatliche Museen, Meiningen, East Germany.

By courtesy of the Staatliche Museen, Meiningen, East Germany

of Romanticism, especially as manifest in patriotic spectacles. Melodrama, Shakespeare, and musical plays were the backbone of Russian repertory until the 1830s. The best known plays of the new realistic school were those of Aleksandr Ostrovsky, Nikolay Gogol, and Ivan Turgenev.

Until 1883 the imperial theatres, under strict government controls, had a monopoly on productions in Russia's two major cities, Moscow and St. Petersburg. It was not until the monopolies were rescinded that public theatre was able to expand, although the state troupes, such as the Bolshoi in Moscow, continued to offer the most professional productions.

Through the 1850s each theatre had its own few stock settings. The box set had been introduced in the 1830s, but it was to take several decades to become popular. Realism began to dominate scenic design by the 1850s, particularly at the Maly Theatre in Moscow. Historically accurate settings began to appear in the 1860s, when one theatre hired a historian to help the designer of Aleksey Tolstoy's *Death of Ivan the Terrible.* Previously, settings had followed the neutral style of the German designer Alfred Roller, whose pupils were the major designers for the state theatres. The unified production techniques of Meiningen were not seen in Russia until the Moscow Art Theatre flourished at the beginning of the 20th century.

Historical accuracy

British theatre and stage design. In 19th-century Britain the audiences shaped both the theatres and the dramas played within them. The upper class favoured opera, while the working class, whose population in London alone tripled between 1810 and 1850, wanted broadly acted theatre with scenic wonders and machinery. And as the audience grew in number, the Georgian theatre building, which was small and intimate, began to disappear.

In the early 19th century an important designer was William Capon, who utilized pieces set at various raked angles and elaborate back cloths as an alternative to flats and wings. His sets were also large enough not to be overpowered by the larger theatres. One of Capon's sets, depicting a 14th-century cathedral, was 56 feet wide and 52 feet deep. His sets were historically accurate even though the practice of having several designers work independently on the same production was still in effect.

The productions of John Philip Kemble, the manager of first the Drury Lane and then the Covent Garden, marked the shift from Neoclassicism to Romanticism in English stage design. He valued theatricality over historical accuracy, as the audience demanded an increased use of spectacle with each passing year. As melodrama became more popular, the effects multiplied until, in an 1820 production of *King Lear,* the storm noises were so realistic that Lear could not be heard. In 1823 Kemble began to reverse this trend and started to use accurate sets and costumes for Shakespeare, and within 15 years historical accuracy was dominant.

Rise of Romanticism

Another important contributor to the history of staging was Lucia Vestris, an actress and manager at the Olympic Theatre. She controlled all the elements of a production and combined them into a single, integrated unit. She also was enamoured of spectacle and is credited with introducing the box set on the London stage in 1832, although there is some evidence pointing to its use as early as 1794. In this new set, the sidewalls of rooms were built solidly from front to back so that the actors, instead of entering as usual between side wings set parallel to the footlights, came in through doors set on hinges. She treated the box set realistically, attaching knobs to doors, for example.

Introduction of the box set

By the 1840s, because of political conditions, many theatres were bankrupt. The next 20 years saw a gradual recovery, with few dramatic innovations in design. One important manager of this era was Charles Kean, a pictorial realist, whose first major attempt to ensure accuracy in every production detail was made in 1852 with *King John.* In the following year, Kean gave the audience a printed list of authorities consulted with regard to the authenticity of each production. In mounting Shakespeare as lavishly as possible while at the same time emphasizing historical accuracy, Kean practically buried his actors in historical costume, settings, and pageantry.

In the second half of the 19th century, burlesque, extravaganza, and musical drama held the largest audience appeal. The music hall also came into prominence, as incidental entertainment was separated from drama. In the period from 1860 to 1880, the theatre continued to expand, and the number of buildings alone increased 50 percent in the first 10 years. The first manager of significance was Charles Fechter, who revived interest in the box set. He also discontinued entrances from the wings, heretofore a standard practice of actors even when the wings represented solid walls. Fechter also used a stage that sank by hydraulic mechanism, later perfected by the Germans, which allowed scenery to be shifted in the basement (see below *Development of stage equipment*).

Influential managers

The most important management team was that of Sir Squire Bancroft and his wife, Marie Wilton, at the Prince of Wales Theatre. Producing plays by Thomas W. Robertson, they succeeded in melding character and stage business. Spectacle was no longer embellishment but an emphasizing of realistic visual details. The Bancrofts' productions also finally won general acceptance for the box set; they were as accurate in modern plays as in Shakespeare; and they firmly anchored the acting behind the proscenium arch. Theatre boxes had been replaced by open balconies, which no longer extended to the proscenium wall. This made it possible for the Bancrofts and others to lower the proscenium arch. In 1880 they even extended the arch downward on either side and across the floor of the stage to emphasize the analogy of the picture frame. Modern, realistic interior settings were constantly used, and the acting was keyed to the settings. Although Fechter had employed realistic stage business as early as 1860, the Bancrofts were the first to standardize it and make it a tradition.

The greatest of the actor-managers was Sir Henry Irving, the manager of the Lyceum Theatre from 1878 to 1901. The best known designers of the period, Hawes Craven and Joseph Harker, worked for Irving. He hired historians to advise on the accuracy of productions and enlisted easel painters such as Sir Lawrence Alma-Tadema to design scenery for *Cymbeline* and *Coriolanus* and Sir Edward Burne-Jones for *King Arthur.* After Irving saw the Meiningen performances in London in 1881, he modeled his Shakespearean productions on what he had seen. Irving was also the first manager to use the front curtain to hide major scene changes, and he completely darkened the auditorium during performance, as Wagner had done.

The widespread changes in staging methods during the 19th century were possible because of changes in architecture and the development of machinery. The complex scenery of the Victorian theatre required increased flying around the stage, with a complicated counterweight system, and this in turn fostered one of the most popular features of the staging of this period—the flying of actors as well as scenery.

During this period the arrangement of the stage floor also changed to fit the requirements of spectacle. After 1850 the stage floor was usually constructed so that floorboards could be removed for raising and lowering machinery between the joists. Sometimes a vertical panorama would run from overhead through a groove in the floor. The changes in stage floors made possible new scenic effects to meet the audience demand. The traps of the Elizabethan and Georgian eras, for instance, were greatly elaborated. The most famous trap was a "ghost glide," a sort of dumbwaiter that made actors appear to rise from the earth and glide through space.

As stage lighting improved with the introduction of gaslight (see below *Stage lighting*), the deficiencies of two-dimensional scenery in terms of realism became increasingly apparent. The taste for verisimilitude led Edward Godwin, the father of Edward Gordon Craig, frequently to commission three-dimensional scenic elements for his productions. Since the groove system of scene-changing was unsuitable for such pieces, he dispensed with it and hired a crew of 135 stage hands. The new trend also rendered the naked stage obsolete, for reasons of gravity. Irving, who was instrumental in accepting new developments in lighting, also introduced black masking pieces at the front of the stage to prevent light spill. Irving's importance to theatre is comparable to that of Saxe-Meiningen. His emphasis on pictorial realism marks the high point of British theatre before World War I.

Theatre and stage design in America. The first recorded performance of a play written by an American was in 1690 at Harvard College. The first permanent American theatre was built in Philadelphia in 1766; it was made of brick and imitated English buildings in arrangement and general architecture. In 1752 Lewis Hallam, a member of a distinguished theatrical family, arrived with a troupe from England, thus marking the beginning of professional theatre in America. The theatre in America for the next 40 years was similar to British provincial theatre, with simple sets for easy traveling; few cities could yet afford theatre buildings. By the 1790s, however, troupes were based in Boston, New York City, Philadelphia, and Charleston, S.C., and many permanent theatres were being erected.

The first decades of the 19th century brought not only multiplication of playhouses in the larger Eastern cities but also the extension of theatre to interior regions. The frontier spirit was embodied by Samuel Drake, who took the first company west (to Kentucky) in 1815. Drake designed an adjustable proscenium that could be set up in any large room. The front curtain was a roll drop (lowered from behind the proscenium arch), and three sets of wings (one each for exteriors, ornate interiors, and simple interiors) and six roll drops (including a garden, a street, and a wood) completed his scenic repertoire.

Theatre on the frontier

After 1825, New York City had higher standards of theatrical production and more theatre buildings than any other city in America. Although decoration and furnishings created an impression of luxury, the early urban theatres were in fact filthy and rat-infested. They had little or no fire protection, and between 1820 and 1845, no fewer than 25 theatre buildings burned down. Although most productions used stock sets and props, occasionally an elaborate or specific set was added. Interest in historical accuracy was not a major production concern until 1830, when Charles Kean visited with his Shakespeare troupe from England.

During the latter third of the 19th century, the general scenic trend was toward greater naturalism, with particular emphasis on local colour. The major design innovations came from the managers of troupes permanently based at a theatre. One such manager was Edwin Booth, whose new theatre, opened in 1869, introduced several new concepts in the United States. The most important innovation was that the stage floor was flat and had no grooves; elevators raised set pieces from the 50 feet of working space below the stage, and flying machines moved other pieces into the 76 feet of overhead space. In Booth's new theatre he abandoned the apron and used box sets almost exclusively.

Innovations of Edwin Booth

Another important manager was Augustin Daly, who furthered the trend of realism. While the members of his troupe changed considerably during its three-decade history, it was the best example of the permanent stock company in the history of the American theatre. Daly stressed the unity of every production and controlled each element himself. His first success, *Saratoga,* by Bronson Howard, in 1870, was the first play to give a realistic picture of American life of the day.

Steele MacKaye, also active during this period, holds a unique place in theatre as an actor, manager, playwright, inventor, and designer. In an age of mechanical inventions, producers were seeking a means of effecting scene changes that would not require an intermission. In 1879, MacKaye filed a patent for a "double stage," a feature he subsequently introduced in the Madison Square Theatre in New York City. He built an elevator platform on which one scene might be set while an earlier scene was being played below. The new scene was then merely lowered, with its own stage floor, to the appropriate level, while the previous scene rolled back behind it.

Among MacKaye's other mechanical innovations were a folding theatre chair with coatrack attached, a sliding stage, a theatre ventilation system, the first installation of an electric lighting system in a theatre (1885), devices to produce cloud, ocean wave, and rainbow effects, the substitution of overhead lighting for footlights (which had been in use since the early Baroque period), and a process for fireproofing scenery. For financial reasons, some of his more grandiose schemes were never executed. For the World's Columbian Exposition in Chicago in 1893, for example, he designed a "Spectatorium" for musico-spectacle-dramas; it called for a sky dome that encircled the stage, a curtain made of light, a sliding stage for scene changes, and an auditorium seating 10,000 people.

In 1896 six men formed the Theatrical Syndicate, which acquired almost complete control over American theatre. They were interested only in commercially profitable works, such as productions featuring performers with large followings. The major opposition to the syndicate came from David Belasco, a producer and playwright. Belasco's aim as a producer was to bring complete realism to the stage, and it is difficult today to appreciate how spectacularly far he carried this pursuit (Figure 18). In 1879, in his production of *The Passion Play,* the story of Jesus Christ from birth to Resurrection, he arranged for a live flock of sheep to be herded onstage. When the actor James O'Neill (father of playwright Eugene O'Neill), who played Christ, was dragged before Pontius Pilate and crowned with thorns, members of the audience fainted. And after

The Theatrical Syndicate

By courtesy of the Theatre Collection, New York Public Library at Lincoln Center, Astor, Lenox and Tilden Foundations

Figure 18: David Belasco's realistic setting for the New York production of "Tiger Rose," 1917.

the performance, when O'Neill walked around the city, people sank to their knees and prayed to him. The play aroused such religious frenzy that Jews were assaulted on the street outside the theatre, and a court injunction forbade further performances.

The power of the Theatrical Syndicate was so great that in 1904 Belasco was forced to rent Convention Hall, a leaky building in New York City, for his productions. During the first performance there was a violent rainstorm, and the audience had to sit through the last act holding umbrellas. Belasco's productions became so popular that the syndicate was finally forced to compromise with him, thus breaking their stranglehold on the American theatre.

(Ho.B./G.C.I./C.Ba.)

THE EVOLUTION OF MODERN THEATRICAL PRODUCTION

Underlying the theatrical developments of the 19th century, and in many cases inspiring them, were the social upheavals that followed the French Revolution. Throughout Europe the middle class took over the theatres and effected changes in repertoire, style, and decorum. In those countries that experienced revolutionary change or failure, national theatres were founded to give expression to the views and values of the middle class, whose aspirations in these cases coincided with a more general movement of national liberation. In western Europe a different pattern of development emerged, varying considerably in each country but having the unified features of a demand for "realism" on the stage, which meant a faithful reflection of the life-style and domestic surroundings of the rising class in both its tragic and its comic aspects; an adjunct to this development was the demand for increased decorum and cleanliness in the auditorium.

In England, where the Industrial Revolution was more advanced than in the other European countries, the middle class had to struggle for its own theatres against the entrenched power of the two patent houses (licensed by the Crown), Drury Lane and Covent Garden, which had enjoyed an almost total monopoly of dramatic theatre since 1660. As early as 1789, attempts were made to evade the legal restrictions on building new theatres. The Reform Bill of 1832, which enfranchised the propertied middle class and established its political power, led to the Theatres Act of 1843, which gave London a "free theatre." The expected flood of new theatre buildings did not occur, and no major building took place for 16 years. This is probably because there were already sufficient illegal theatres in operation when the act was passed. The boulevard theatres of Paris experienced less trouble in establishing themselves. The rise of the middle-class theatres caused the decline of both the patent houses in London and the Comédie-Française—the national theatre of France. After much political struggle, centring particularly around censorship, the Comédie-Française, unable to compete with the boulevard theatres, capitulated and presented the plays of the new school for the new audiences.

Theatres Act of 1843

As the new class came into the theatres, the theatres were cleaned up. Samuel Phelps at The Sadler's Wells Theatre instituted audience controls that drove out the old audience and paved the way for respectability. The Bancrofts, as representative as any of the new movement, took over the run-down Prince of Wales' Theatre, cleaned up the auditorium, and placed antimacassars on the seats. They also dropped the melodrama and attracted a wide audience with the social comedies of Tom Robertson, making a considerable fortune in the process.

Throughout the 19th century, cities throughout Europe and North America exploded in size, and industrial centres attracted labour to their factories and mills. The working-class suburbs of cities and the industrial towns created their own demand for entertainment, which led to the construction of large theatres.

Accelerating this change was the growth of the railways. The pattern of theatre was disrupted in England as productions were mounted in London and sent on tour. The old provincial stock companies folded and theatres became touring venues rather than producing houses. A breed of managers arose who made money from the possession of the bricks and mortar property rather than by presenting their own productions. In the United States the Theatrical Syndicate established great fortunes from the New York theatres and the almost unlimited touring circuit that the railways opened up. The change in status from enterprise to industry gave rise to the commercial theatre systems of the West End in London and Broadway in New York City. Improvement in travel in general made it possible to increase the links between the two systems early in the 20th century, and the exchange of productions further extended the possibilities of profitable exploitation.

The impact of the railroad

Modern theatre began around 1885 with the revolt of the younger generation against the material injustices of society. Those in revolt founded so-called independent theatres to present a more critical or scientific view of the workings of society or so-called art theatres to rise above vulgar materialism with the establishment of aesthetic standards. The independent theatres took the Meiningen Players as their starting point. The art theatres looked to Wagner for inspiration.

The new Naturalism. The first of the independent theatres was the Théâtre-Libre ("Free Theatre") founded in 1887 by André Antoine, who made his living as a clerk for the Paris Gas Company. The Théâtre-Libre was an amateur theatre with no home of its own. It hired rooms or theatres where they were available and sold tickets for its performances to a closed membership. In this way it avoided censorship. Antoine's original intention was to present plays that had been rejected by the Comédie-Française, and thus the repertoire was eclectic. The major impact the group made was with a number of naturalistic plays. The theatre was at this time lagging behind literature, and, although Émile Zola had written an essay entitled "Naturalism in the Theatre" in 1881 and had produced what is seen as the first Naturalist play, *Thérèse Raquin,* in 1873, no theatre devoted itself to a Naturalist policy until Antoine founded the Théâtre-Libre.

Following on the scientific developments and the philosophical skepticism of the 19th century, the social reformers of the last two decades of the century probed into the causes of human behaviour and postulated that the meaning of human character was to be found in its interaction with the physical, social, and economic environment. The new theatre demanded "truthfulness" not only in the writing but also in the acting and stage setting. The actors were expected to ignore the audience and to behave and speak as though they were at home. Antoine is normally credited with being the first to require an actor to turn his back on the audience; from this style of acting arose the concept of the "fourth wall" separating the stage from the audience. Behind this "wall"—invisible to the audience, opaque to the actors—the environment portrayed was to be as authentic as possible. Antoine himself designed rooms and then decided which wall would be "removed." In *The Butchers,* he hung animal carcasses on the stage.

The "fourth wall"

It is possible, however, to overestimate Antoine's commitment to Naturalism, since a great deal of his repertoire was not naturalistic and the descriptions of several of the Théâtre-Libre presentations show an imaginative experimentation with lighting effects that goes well beyond creating realistic temporal and atmospheric conditions. The first production of the Théâtre-Libre had no scenery at all but only a few pieces of furniture borrowed from Antoine's mother, yet it was this production that set the Naturalist style. Zola, the philosopher of the movement, had deplored the fact that the Naturalist theatre began by creating an external representation of the world instead of concentrating on the inner state of the characters. Strindberg showed that a few carefully selected properties could suggest an entire room. With the ideas of Antoine and Strindberg, the days of flapping canvas doors and kitchen shelves painted on the walls of the set came to be numbered. The more natural and detailed the acting became, the more it clashed with a painted background.

Antoine's innovations did much to establish the principle that each play requires its own distinct setting. In 1906, as director of the state-subsidized Théâtre de l'Odéon, he produced classical plays in which he strove for realism not by means of period decor and costume but by re-creating theatrical conventions of the 1600s.

The new pattern of theatre set in France was imitated in Germany during the same period. Otto Brahm modeled his theatrical society, the Freie Bühne, founded in Berlin in 1889, after Antoine's Théâtre-Libre. Its first production was Ibsen's *Ghosts.* On the basis of this and other examples, it could be said that Ibsen pioneered the repertoire, Saxe-Meiningen the staging methods, and Antoine the organizational form for a range of small, independent theatres springing up throughout Europe.

The Freie Volksbühne

With both ideological aims and theatrical tastes in mind, members of the German middle-class theatre audience formed an organization called the Freie Volksbühne in 1890 for the purpose of buying blocks of tickets and commissioning performances and even productions for its membership, which included a large working-class element. Early in its history the organization split between the Freie Volksbühne, who were attempting to make theatre available to a wider audience, and the Neue Freie Volksbühne, who had specific Socialist attachments and policies. Eventually the two arms recombined and were able not only to subsidize performances but also to build their own theatre and mount their own productions.

During the 1890s in France, a similar program of democratization was attempted. One of the prime movers in this was Romain Rolland, whose book *The People's Theatre* (*Le Théâtre du peuple,* 1903), inspired similar movements in other countries.

In England the works of Ibsen aroused great interest and attracted the attention of the censors. The first English independent theatre was organized by Jack Thomas Grein, and its first production in 1891 was Ibsen's *Ghosts.* Grein's intention of finding British writers of the new drama was frustrated until the arrival of George Bernard Shaw, the most famous Ibsenite of them all, in 1892, with his first play, *Widowers' Houses.* Shaw remained the mainstay of the independent theatre movement in Britain. His pre-eminence in the independent theatre in England coupled with the success of Arthur Wing Pinero in the commercial realist theatre led to a major innovation in staging in England. Both playwrights participated in the casting of their plays, which in Pinero's case led to a break away from the old stock company casting and the institution of casting to type. Shaw was able to impose his own interpretation and stage direction on the production of his plays.

Russia also followed the pattern of the independent theatre movement that developed in France, Germany, and England (see below *Developments in Russia and the Soviet Union*).

Reactions to Naturalism. The Théâtre-Libre had scarcely been established when the reaction against Naturalism got under way. Symbolism developed out of a total opposition to the philosophy that lay behind Naturalism. It sought an intuitive and spiritual form of knowledge, regarded by its proponents as higher than that which science could provide. If Naturalism attacked the materialist values of society from a critical and reformist standpoint, Symbolism rejected them altogether. In their manifesto of 1886 the Symbolists suggested that subjectivity, spirituality, and mysterious internal forces represented a higher form of truth than the objective observation of appearances. The Belgian Maurice Maeterlinck, the most successful Symbolist playwright, gave as his opinion that an old man sitting at his table, surrounded by silence, was more dramatic and true-to-life than the lover who strangles his mistress in a tirade of jealousy. The Symbolists drew for example and inspiration on Wagner and on the later plays of Ibsen. They were influenced by the poets Mallarmé and Baudelaire, and the latter's poem *Correspondences,* which finds comparative values in colours and musical notes, is often seen as the first manifesto of the movement. The expressive paintings of Gauguin were also influential.

The Symbolist theatre

The first of the Symbolist theatres was the Théâtre d'Art started by the French poet Paul Fort in 1890. Fort was principally concerned with the power of the poetic text but nevertheless made some ingenious contributions to staging. In his production of the Frenchman Pierre Quillard's play *The Girl with the Cut-off Hands* (1891), the actors intoned their lines behind a gauze curtain, backed by a gold cloth framed with red hangings. In front of the gauze, a girl in a long blue tunic repeated the actors' lines and commented on their feelings. This is the first instance in which the setting of a play derives entirely from the ideas of the director and the designer rather than from tradition or from direct evidence in the text of the play itself. The setting for *The Girl with the Cut-off Hands* is a visual image, suggested by the play but not dictated by it. It is a poetic vision and does not place the play in a specific context.

In 1893, Aurélien Lugné-Poë founded the Théâtre de l'Oeuvre. Guided by the belief that the spoken word creates the scenery, Lugné-Poë attempted unity of style instead of illusion of place and employed such painters as Henri de Toulouse-Lautrec, Maurice Denis, Odilon Redon, Édouard Vuillard, and Pierre Bonnard. Lugné-Poë's production of Maeterlinck's play *Pelléas and Mélisande* typified his technique—no furniture or props were used; the stage was lit from overhead, most of the time to a level of semidarkness; a gauze curtain created the illusion of mist; and backdrops painted in gray tones conveyed a general air of mystery. The one production of the Théâtre de l'Oeuvre that has had the greatest historical significance was not seen as anything more than a scandalous, schoolboy joke in its own time. Alfred Jarry's *Ubu roi* ("King Ubu") was produced in 1896, with nonrealistic settings and costumes. All the scene settings were displayed simultaneously on a backdrop, and the costumes and makeup were deliberately grotesque, as was the acting style, an amalgam of buffoonery, the horror of Grand Guignol, and extravagant mock-tragedy.

Production of *Ubu roi*

Far from posing an alternative to the materialist values of the bourgeois audience, the first line of *Ubu roi* attacked the audience's values head on. When Firmin Gémier, in the title role, advanced to face the audience, looked directly into their eyes, and uttered the first scandalous word of the text, "*merdre*" ("excrement"), a pattern was set that has been followed by many avant-garde theatre companies throughout the 20th century. The dialectics of conflict had shifted from being contained within the stage area to being opened between the stage and the auditorium. If an attack on the audience were to be mounted effectively, however, the separation of stage and auditorium had to be diminished. Various attempts were subsequently made either to contain stage and auditorium in a single unified spatial area or to adapt existing spaces in order to break through the barrier imposed by the proscenium arch.

The influence of Appia and Craig. The two most important theoreticians and designers of the non-illusionist movement were the Swiss Adolphe Appia and the Englishman Edward Gordon Craig. Appia began with the assumption posited by Wagner that the fundamental goal of a theatrical production was artistic unity. Appia felt, however, that the incongruity of placing three-dimensional actors in front of two-dimensional settings, which many of the stage reformers rejected, was intensified by the mythic, symbolic nature of the Wagner operas. He concluded that there were three conflicting elements in production—the moving three-dimensional actor, the stationary vertical scenery, and the horizontal floor. He categorized stage lighting under three headings: a general or acting light, which gave diffused illumination; formative light, which cast shadows; and imitated lighting effects painted on the scenery. He saw the illusionist theatre as employing only the first and last of these types. Appia proposed replacing illusory scene painting with three-dimensional structures that could be altered in appearance by varying the colour, intensity, and direction of lighting. The solid structures, according to Appia, would serve to create a bond between the horizontal floor and the vertical scenery and enhance the actor's movements, which were rhythmically controlled by the music of the score. The lights, too, would change in response to the musical score, thus reflecting or eliciting changes in emotion, mood, and action. In creating a scene, Appia conceived of light as visual music with an equal range of expression and intensity.

Appia elaborated his theory through a series of proposed designs and mise-en-scènes (complete production plans) for Wagner's operas. He was brutally rebuffed by Wagner's widow, who considered his projects the work of a madman. Intensely shy, he created only a few designs and realized even fewer productions. His influence spread largely through his three books on staging and lighting design published from 1899 onward, one exemplary performance in a private theatre in Paris in 1905, and his collaboration with Émile Jaques-Dalcroze. Jaques-Dalcroze was a fellow Swiss who developed, and published in 1906, a system of physical exercises that he called eurythmics, intended to inculcate in the student a sense of rhythm and control over it. The exercises made liberal use of space and grew into an expressive dance movement. For Appia, eurythmics became a part of his integrated system of production. In 1912, at Hellerau on the outskirts of Dresden, as part of one of the first garden city developments in Europe, a large hall was built to the design of Appia and Jaques-Dalcroze. Stage and auditorium were united as a single rectangular hall without proscenium or separate lighting. The walls and ceiling were hung with translucent silk through which beams of light filtered. The lighting equipment comprised 10,000 lamps, all controlled by a gigantic console capable of fine gradations of intensity. Appia designed an abstract scenic architecture of platforms and steps that could be arranged in a variety of combinations. Every trace of illusionistic scenery was dispensed with, and the setting served only as a structural foundation for the rhythmic, gymnastic movements of the players. The few performances, which were interrupted by the outbreak of World War I, were attended by many of the leading innovative directors in Europe at that time.

Eurythmics

The use of diffuse light solved one of the most vexatious problems of electric lighting—how to blend the individual beams. This problem was equally trying in the illusionist theatre, where the consciousness of separate lightbeams coming from distinct mechanical sources ruined the naturalistic effect. The backdrop remained as a large, finite, painted expanse that any reasonable amount of light revealed to be of a different order than the three-dimensional pieces in front of it. It also necessitated, because of the critical rising sight lines from the stall seats, a series of hanging borders to mask the top limits of the cloth. As lanterns began to be hung on bars above the stage, the number of borders increased. The Austrian producer Max Reinhardt is credited with the frustrated cry, "Will no one rid me of this dirty washing?"

To address this problem the lighting designer Mariano Fortuny y Madrazo constructed a dome that backed the stage area with a gentle curve and overhung the stage. At first he covered the dome with white translucent cloth, an extension of an earlier experiment in which he hung strips of cloth from the ceiling of the stage and diffused light through them. Later the dome had a plaster surface and the lights were diffused by reflection, playing on its inside surface. Instead of a flat, restricted backdrop there was now a spacious vault that created an impression of indeterminate distance. The dome was expensive and very cumbersome to maneuver and was soon replaced by a cyclorama (horizon or sky-cloth), which is still used today. This consists of a cloth stretched over a semicircular framework to mask the rear wall and corners of the stage. Some modern theatres have been built with a permanent plaster cyclorama.

The Fortuny dome and cyclorama

The Fortuny dome and the cyclorama became essential tools of the scenic illusionists, but their invention served the anti-illusionists equally well, as they gave a sense of space beyond the finite limits of the stage, gave solidity to the stylized decor, and silhouetted the rhythmic action of the players against a background of diffused light. Edward Gordon Craig, the son of the designer Edward Godwin and the actress Ellen Terry, began his career as an actor in Irving's company and became a designer at the turn of the century, just before the publication of the first of his many books on the theatre. Craig and Appia met in 1914 and shared a deep admiration for each other's work and a great deal of agreement on conceptual matters. There were, however, certain crucial differences. The most fundamental of these arose out of their differing backgrounds. Appia began his work with Wagner, and for him the music dominated and controlled the work. Craig was an actor before becoming a designer and director, and for him all the elements of production were of equal value. Appia had no apparent interest in theatre history, whereas Craig had an abiding interest in it. Appia was a retiring, contemplative thinker; Craig was a polemicist.

Whereas Appia's work followed a continuous developing line, Craig's was characterized by a restless experimentation. His early productions of Purcell and Handel operas at the start of the century explored the use of the "frieze" or "relief" stage—a wide, shallow stage surrounded by drapes, structures in geometric shapes, and a lighting system that dispensed entirely with footlights and side lighting and used only overhead sources. In order to facilitate this and make colour changes possible, Craig devised an overhead bridge accessible from both sides. Although Craig's designs stressed vertical planes as against Appia's horizontal ones, in the operas he utilized a series of levels for the action. His designs for Purcell's *Dido and Aeneas* used no wings or borders. The back drape ascended to the flies (space over the stage from which scenery and lights can be hung), and the proscenium was very low in contrast to the great width of the stage. The sides of the setting were enclosed by curtains hung at right angles to the proscenium arch. What impressed many of those who were present was the use of colour symbolism in the costumes, settings, and lighting and the extraordinary consistency with which Craig manipulated all of the elements of the mise-en-scène.

Craig's operatic productions

One of Craig's most interesting scenic innovations was a flexible structure made of hinged screens, which permitted a fluid readjustment of space during performance. He experimented with movable proscenium arches for adjusting the stage opening to suit the play or scene. His experiments with all sorts of materials and the effects of coloured light upon them greatly increased the resources of the stage. He proposed placing the lighting control booth at the rear of the auditorium, which is the current practice, to allow the lighting engineer to coordinate the lighting to the actors' movements.

Perhaps Craig's main contributions to the development of staging were his advocacy of the need for one artist to control the production and his insistence upon the study of theatre history. The controlling artist for Craig, unlike Wagner and Appia, was to be the director. If the theatre was ever to become a mature art form in its own right, rather than a haphazard conglomeration of bits and pieces of other art forms, it needed a controlling genius to discipline and coordinate the interaction. Craig's own productions bear out his ability to realize this scheme, and he encouraged the work of a group of gifted directors who followed him.

In the process of working out his thesis, Craig addressed himself to the question of the actor. The actors of Craig's day (like the theatres and their machinery) were ill-equipped for carrying out his production schemes. For the Purcell productions, he used a high percentage of amateurs who could be taught to carry out his instructions. The professional actors of the conventional late-19th-century theatres were not very sophisticated in their technique. Craig was not alone in complaining of the inadequacy of the established actors in light of the new theatre. The French Symbolists debated whether the actor would have to be banished from the stage before any serious theatre could be created. Even Eleonora Duse, the great Italian actress, declared that for the theatre to be saved all actors would have to die of the plague. Craig's writings were virulent in his scorn for the actor whose idiosyncrasies constantly imposed themselves between the work and the audience, whose wayward, fickle emotions and feelings constantly sentimentalized and diminished the theatrical effect. He was not opposed in principle to all actors; his admiration of Irving, his mother Ellen Terry, and Duse was profound, and he considered Isadora Duncan a supreme artist, but he did promote the concept that he called the *Übermarionette* ("Superpuppet"). Craig's intention is not fully clear—whether he envisioned mechanical figures that would defy the physical restrictions of the human body or, as seems more likely, puppets that would be controlled from inside by human beings, children, or dwarfs. Nevertheless, he joined a growing chorus of people calling

The problem of the actor

for the elimination of individual actors' idiosyncrasies and the "dematerializing" of the stage and propelled these demands into public debate.

Although the *Übermarionetten* were never realized, the principle was accepted. Later directors such as Meyerhold, Reinhardt, and Copeau recognized the necessity of a studio-school attached to their theatres and of regular training for the actors in advanced techniques, if they were to be able to realize their concepts on stage and eliminate the interference of actors' own egos and emotions. From this flows the present acceptance in the West of a long and intense period of training as necessary for all actors entering the profession. The Eastern theatre, which Craig and those following him have continually returned to study, has always understood this necessity.

Importance of study of theatre history

Craig's understanding of theatre history was linked to a revival throughout Europe of the study of theatre history. Craig's opinion was that it would be impossible to create a new theatre without making a serious study of previous theatres. He ascribed the short life of some innovative theatres to the fact that they had not adequately studied their predecessors. The study of theatre history spread widely enough to embrace the long-established Oriental theatre forms. Craig's own productions drew on Japanese theatre, the Greeks, and the Baroque and Romantic periods. The most important effect of this research and use of theatre history was to liberate stage production from the narrow confines of contemporary style and fashion. If the past could be incorporated into the present, an almost limitless range of production possibilities was opened up. This liberation, in turn, increased the demands made upon the actors.

Other developments in the study of movement. The Frenchman François Delsarte laid stress on a connection between mental attitude and physical posture and discovered that one's emotional state is communicated through one's physical appearance. Eventually Delsarte codified his observations in a chart of gestures, which was used as a guide for expression and characterization by many amateur theatre companies in the middle years of the 20th century. The further elaborated discipline of reflexology, which seeks to analyze mind–body interaction, was developed by a variety of philosophers and psychologists and was very influential in the early years of the Soviet Union (see below *Developments in Russia and the Soviet Union*).

The work of Isadora Duncan

Another theorist of movement, the American-born dancer Isadora Duncan, was the daughter of a disciple of Delsarte, and reflexology was at the heart of Duncan's dancing. It is not surprising that, in addition to Dalcroze's eurythmics, Duncan should have inspired the development of educational dance. Reflexology is also the root from which spring the contemporary areas of drama therapy and the use of games and improvisation in actor training.

Duncan rejected the narrow and inhibiting classicism of the Russian ballet and returned to the Greeks for inspiration. Her dances were realizations of "soul-states," which she regarded as emanating from the solar plexus. By using her feelings and physical responses to the music as the impulse for movement, she removed dance from the domain of the highly trained ballet dancer and demonstrated its wider potential.

Duncan's work was important to those searching for answers to the problems posed for the actor by non-Naturalist theatre, since it showed a way to gain direct access to deep feelings without resorting to psychological analysis. Unfortunately, though, Duncan offered no systematic prescription for accomplishing this. Duncan herself was a sufficiently disciplined artist to impress Edward Gordon Craig as a solo performer. What her approach lacked, however, was a disciplined framework by which other performers could be trained and an extension of the movement vocabulary that might widen the range of theatrical purposes to which it could be put.

Impact of electricity

Development of stage equipment. From a technical point of view, the harnessing of electric power exerted a greater influence on stage design and production techniques than any other single invention. Stage lighting, as opposed to mere stage illumination, became raised to the status of an art form and revolutionized stage decoration, stage design, and stage form in that order. For the first time since the theatre moved indoors during the Renaissance, adequate and safe illumination became possible. But beyond mere function and safety there was inherent in the medium a flexibility and subtlety that has allowed it to become an integral part of scenic effect and to heighten visual expression for artistic purposes (see below *Stage lighting*).

Beyond the development of stage lighting and the theories and techniques pioneered by Appia and Craig, electricity provided the solution to many of the problems that were arising with respect to scene changing. The demand for rapid changes of cumbersome naturalistic sets coincided with demands for a dematerialized stage that could flow smoothly from one symbolic vision to another. In addition, those seeking to "retheatricalize the theatre" wanted an open stage on which scene changes could be accomplished simply and rapidly. New inventions and instrumentation made practical many of the theoretician's ideas, and these were adapted by designers, directors, and stage engineers on both sides of the Atlantic, with the greatest centre of innovation being Germany.

In 1896 Karl Lautenschläger introduced a revolving stage at the Residenz Theater in Munich. Elevator stages permitted new settings to be assembled below stage and then lifted to the height of the stage as the existing setting was withdrawn to the rear and dropped to below-stage level. Slip stages allowed large trucks to be stored in the wings or rear stage and then slid into view. New systems for flying were developed. Hydraulic stages made it possible to raise sections of the stage, tilt them or even rock them to simulate, for example, the motion of a ship. All of these mechanisms required larger backstage facilities, higher flying towers, greater depth and width of stages, and increased understage space.

German theatres began as early as 1890 to incorporate mechanized orchestra pit apron lifts, which provided a means for altering the point of contact between stage and auditorium (actor and spectator). Confrontations between actor and audience were the prime concern of Georg Fuchs, who founded the Künstler Theatre in Munich in 1907. He held that, in order to be relevant, the theatre must reject the picture-frame stage and the Italianate auditorium. He proposed an indoor amphitheatre in which, on a projecting stage, the action could be thrown forward into the audience space. According to Fuchs, the stage designer should not try to produce an illusion of depth since depth is part of the theatre architecture and cannot be added by scenery. Fuchs's view was the culmination of the search for three-dimensionality that had passed through five essential stages since the 18th century. At first, an illusion of depth was achieved by painting perspective scenery on canvas; then the ground plan of the set was rearranged to envelop the actor with the set. The third phase was the introduction of objects for the actor to touch. With Appia and Craig there came the realization that an actor's movement manifests itself in contrast to inanimate objects, such as platforms and other masses. Fuchs introduced the final phase joining the playing space to the area in which the audience is situated. In Fuchs's theatre, designed by Max Littman, the acting area could be extended forward by covering the orchestra pit, and the size of the stage opening could be changed by adjusting the inner proscenium, which had a door at stage level and a balcony above. The floor of the stage was divided into sections, each of which was mounted on an elevator so that it could easily become a platform. Four cycloramas, surrounding the stage, could be changed electrically.

Evolution of three-dimensionality

The influence of Reinhardt. The director who was best placed to utilize the freedom afforded by the study of theatre history and the new mechanization was Max Reinhardt. Reinhardt began as an actor at the Deutsches Theater in Berlin, as part of the Naturalist Freie Bühne company, in 1893. In 1900 he joined a small cabaret theatre and began introducing plays into the entertainment. Later, he returned to control the Deutsches Theater, to which he added the smaller Kammerspiele next door. In these theatres and elsewhere he initiated a series of productions that made Berlin one of the outstanding theatrical centres of Europe. Not only did Reinhardt feel at home in two theatres—one small and intimate, the other a medium-size house—he actually preferred the alternation of size and styles. In 1910 he staged *Oedipus Rex* in the Zirkus Schumann, an amphitheatre, in an attempt to recapture the union of actors and audience that had existed in classical Greek theatre. From 1915 to 1918 Reinhardt directed the Volksbühne, and in 1919 he opened his own theatre, the Grosses Schauspielhaus, which had an open stage and the full complement of stage machinery (Figure 19). This theatre was obviously derived from the Dionysian theatre at Athens, and he hoped that it would embody modern life as the arena had embodied the Greek community.

The Grosses Schauspielhaus

Reinhardt was not a traditionalist, however (he showed a completely different approach when he converted a ballroom in Vienna into a formally designed intimate theatre); rather, he was a true eclectic whose more than 500 productions represented virtually every style. He believed that theatre, which had become shackled to literature, must be offered instead for its own sake. He reexamined the physical layout of the theatre building and the spatial relationship between the actors and the audience. Believing that the director must control every facet of a production, Reinhardt worked closely with his designers, Ernest Stern, Alfred Roller, Oscar Strnad, Emil Orlik, and the Norwegian Expressionist painter Edvard Munch. His productions usually featured a particular motif or the staging conventions of a historical period. After beginning with a three-dimensional, drab naturalism, he adapted the abstract solids that Appia had inspired and later applied surface decoration derived from contemporary art movements such as Art Nouveau, the Vienna Sezession, and Munch's Expressionism. He used unit settings with detachable parts ("plugs") and revolving stages that revealed different facets of the same construction; he adapted the conventions of Oriental theatre; and he mounted open-air productions of the medieval *Everyman* in the square outside the cathedral in Salzburg. Reinhardt exerted a strong influence on the designers of the German Expressionist cinema as well as on stage artists. In fact, the first productions of Expressionist plays were mounted under his management. His eclecticism helped to reconcile the differences between conflicting movements by romanticizing the realistic and fleshing out the idealistic with solid structures.

Reinhardt made one further great contribution to the development of stage production. Although he exerted considerable power and was the controlling genius behind several theatres, his way of working was significantly different from that envisaged by either Craig or Appia. Craig saw the director as the despot exercising rigid control over all aspects of the production, whereas for Appia (and Wagner before him) the poet was the initiator of the production and the figure whose word was law. Reinhardt diplomatically combined the talents of a team of collaborators. He was careful to gather around him gifted colleagues, designers, dramaturges, and engineers. Bertolt Brecht served early in his career as a member of the Reinhardt collective. This process of cooperation rather than direction produced one significant feature that is still the strength of the German theatre on both sides of the border. In order to control the complexity of his productions, to incorporate his research into the rehearsals and later performance, and to coordinate the work of all collaborators into the production plan, Reinhardt's productions required a *Regie-buch* that went much further than all previous promptbooks. The *Regie-buch* became a plan for the production, incorporating interpretive ideas as well as staging concepts. This concept was later utilized by Brecht and developed into the *Modellbuch* ("model book"), a full record of the production that could be used as a pattern for succeeding productions.

The *Regie-buch*

British innovations. While most English productions during this period were in the realistic tradition, several steps were being taken toward nonillusionistic staging. One director, Sir Frank Benson, began by mounting plays in the realistic style of Sir Henry Irving but by 1900 had started to simplify his staging. He produced Shakespeare's plays with only a few stock sets, focusing primary attention on the actors. William Poel, also producing Shakespeare, attempted to re-create an Elizabethan theatre. Throughout Europe at this time there was a considerable revival of interest in seeing Shakespeare's plays performed with something approaching the original effect. The various social and theatrical pressures that had resulted in the truncating, rearranging, and rewriting of the plays throughout the 18th and 19th centuries had dissipated. Unfortunately the plays were also in danger of disappearing under the weight of the settings of both the historical Romantic style and the new theatre machinery.

Between 1912 and 1914 the actor-manager Harley Granville-Barker staged Shakespeare in such a way that the action could be continuous, an approach influenced by his having worked with Poel. He remodeled the Savoy Theatre by adding an apron, or extension of the stage, and doors in front of the proscenium. He divided the stage into three parts—the apron, a main acting area, and a raised inner stage with curtains. This permitted a continuous flow of action and eliminated the rearrangement of scripts that had previously been necessary for nonillusion-

By courtesy of Morris Gest

Figure 19: The Grosses Schauspielhaus, Berlin, designed by Hans Poelzig, 1919.

istic staging. Norman Wilkinson and Albert Rutherston, artists with reputations outside the theatre, were his principal designers, and their settings typically consisted of brightly painted, draped curtains. Granville-Barker's style and particularly the use of drapes in the settings reflect clearly the influence of Craig's early work for the Purcell Operatic Society.

Influence of the fine arts. The development of the modern theatre and its staging techniques took place during a period when even more radical changes were taking place within the fine arts. In fact, it would be true to say that many of the developments in staging arose primarily out of innovations in painting. Much of Craig's work is influenced heavily by the work of William Blake and the Pre-Raphaelites. The Symbolist theatres in Paris enlisted many of the innovative painters of the time, such as Denis, Vuillard, Bonnard, Sérusier, and Toulouse-Lautrec.

Painters in the theatre

Concurrently with developments in the arts, and often underlying them, innovations in technology were radically altering human perception of the world. The advent of photography, and subsequently motion pictures, created new ways of seeing and new perceptions of movement and time. These perceptions were also being altered by the development of motorized transport, through the coming of the railways, the automobile, and the airplane. In a related context, the growth of colonial empires and improvements in transportation brought Europe into contact with many disparate cultures and their aesthetic traditions. Developments in psychology led in the first decades of the 20th century to increased understanding of the communicative power of design and thus to the principles of modern advertising.

For the theatre, these developments had several profound effects. The first was the new scenography of the Symbolists, of Appia, Craig, and others. Scenic art ceased to depict natural settings or specific locales and became more suggestive, seeking to arouse the imagination and the emotions. Along with the experiments in painting that emphasized the sensory, affective properties of the art over its imitative functions, it followed that artists in the theatre would investigate its affective potential.

The innovations of Kandinsky

The Russian-born artist Wassily Kandinsky, who is credited with producing the first purely abstract painting, created several theatre pieces on his way to full abstraction. These productions employed sound (even an offstage choir), light, moving structures, and human action, but this latter was purely functional and had no narrative or interactive significance. Kandinsky revised the Wagnerian concept of the integrated work of art, pointing out that it was based on the assumption that all the various elements of theatre brought together simultaneously in concert would produce an effect that was greater than the sum of the parts. Kandinsky's thesis was that this was a superficial conglomeration in which, no matter what the theoretical position might be, the elements alternated in supremacy. Appia had criticized Wagner for keeping conventional representational sets, and Craig had criticized Appia for being under the thrall first of the music and then of the dance. Kandinsky went further than even Craig and proposed that the theatre of the future would comprise three elements: musical movement, colour movement, and dance movement—*i.e.,* sound, colour, and mobile forms. All of these elements were of equal value. In his longer essay "Concerning the Spiritual in Art" (1914), Kandinsky set out in complex intellectual terms how this new theatre, based on spirituality rather than materiality, could be constructed.

Bauhaus experiments

Certain aspects of Kandinsky's theories were capable of rigorous testing. The Bauhaus, a German school of design founded in Weimar by Walter Gropius in 1919, where Kandinsky was a teacher and Oskar Schlemmer was head of the theatre section, conducted a series of experiments on actors' movements in space. Schlemmer and his colleagues devised elaborate costumes that transformed the actor-dancers into "moving architecture." By treating the stage as a black box, the researchers created a laboratory in which to examine the perception of a wide range of movements. Craig's concept of the *Übermarionette* became the subject of a series of experiments regarding the geometry of the human figure, the possible limits of the articulation of limbs, the extensions of movements into three-dimensional space, the restrictions placed on human movement by the force of gravity, and the ways in which dancers' movements work against gravity and cooperate with it. A range of dances were conceived and performed under the title of *The Triadic Ballet.* This work was a fantasy in which the dancers' costumes transformed them into "metaphysical anatomy." The ballet achieved the dematerialization of the stage as contrasting shapes in contrasting colours appeared to propel themselves along a variety of paths in three-dimensional space. Experiments were also made in rhythmic movement, mechanical theatre, light theatre, and projection. The Bauhaus group laid down no prescriptive plans as to what direction theatre should take but opened up a variety of possibilities, which were then offered for other artists to follow.

When the Bauhaus was closed at the start of the Nazi period, several members of the staff moved to the United States. Out of seminars and teaching laboratories, a line of work developed, largely instigated by John Cage and Merce Cunningham, that explored the use of chance in creating works of theatre and broke free from the concept of an integral composition. Cunningham created a range of dance works that favoured the occurrence of chance (or aleatoric) correspondences between the elements of the dance over the orchestration of effects by the choreographer. The U.S. choreographer and designer Alwin Nikolais also carried on work derived from the principles of the Bauhaus with his dance company.

During all this work, in its movement away from the depiction of nature, the position of the artist changed. In the anti-illusionist theatre, the artist became not only the means of putting across a message but to some extent the originator of it. At the heart of the Symbolist theatre was the old romantic concept of the artist as a creative genius with heightened perception and powers. Once this was linked to the idea of the work of art as a vehicle through which the artist could proselytize his views, the result was Expressionism.

Production aspects of Expressionist theatre. Expressionism in the theatre arose out of the same impulse to rebel against the materialist values of the older middle-class generation that gave rise to both the reformist Naturalist theatre and the aestheticist Symbolist theatre. This opposition was clearly expressed through the themes and often the titles of such plays as *Vatermord* ("Patricide"). The forerunners of Expressionism are generally accepted to be the German actor and playwright Frank Wedekind, who criticized the reformist Ibsenite movement for failing to attack the morality of bourgeois society, and Strindberg. Wedekind sought in his plays to expose what lay beneath the surface of gentility and decorum; in the process, he often introduced roles that served more as emblems than as realistic characters.

Strindberg's early plays are usually included in the Naturalist repertoire. After a period of personal crisis between 1894 and 1897, the form of Strindberg's plays disintegrated into dream visions or confessional monodramas in which everything is seen through the eyes of the single protagonist. The single focus of these plays was taken over by the Expressionists, as was the use of stereotyped characters—the Son, the Stranger, etc.

In addition to Wedekind and Strindberg, the Austrian painter and writer Oskar Kokoschka must be mentioned; in fact, some authorities would date Kokoschka's plays as the first truly Expressionist drama. His early plays, *Murder Hope of Women* (1909), *Sphinx and Strawman* (1911), and *The Burning Bush* (1913), seem to take Strindberg's painful depictions of the destructive relationships between the sexes and liberate them from any dependence on articulate speech. The plays are episodic and have no clear narrative. They are constructed out of violent visual images. Kokoschka is not remotely concerned with giving any sign or resemblance of surface reality whatsoever. In his view, the theatre, like painting, should communicate through "a language of images, visible or tangible signs, graspable reflections of experience and knowing . . . ." In this, Kokoschka was the first to break completely with the literary tradition and to assert that the theatre communicates ultimately through a visual language.

Effects of World War I

The Expressionist period spanned the period of World War I, which changed the nature of the movement. Before the war Expressionism was largely concerned with screaming protests against rampant materialism and the loss of spirituality. In this period the coming war was seen as a necessary agent of purification for society. Many of the Expressionist dramatists died in the slaughter on the Western Front. Those who survived were transformed, and Expressionism took on a more overtly political complexion. The change from private protest to political argument was what made it possible to develop the techniques of the Expressionist theatre, and to extend them for wider use.

The major Expressionist theatre was Der Tribune, in Berlin. The Expressionist stage neither simulated reality nor suggested unreality. It existed in its own right as the platform from which direct statements could be made. Settings therefore tended to be abstract or, when specific, highly subjective. Techniques of distortion and incongruous juxtaposition expressed either the ideological position of the director or dramatist or the state of mind of the protagonist, or both. In Expressionist plays the walls of houses might lean at sharp angles, threatening to crush the protagonist; windows might light up like eyes spying on the secret and intimate; trees might take on the shape of the skeleton signifying Death. In this way, instead of simply forming the milieu for the action, the setting became a dramatic force. This aspect of Expressionism has been appropriated to great effect by the cinema, in which camera angles and special lenses can render the ordinary expressive. Leopold Jessner in his stage production of *Richard III* (1920) placed Richard at the height of his power at the top of a flight of steps. The steps below Richard were crowded with soldiers in red cloaks with white helmets. The effect when they knelt was of Richard sitting on top of a mound of skulls with a river of blood flowing through them.

The action of many Expressionist plays was fragmented into a series of small scenes or episodes. This style of theatre was called *Stationendrama* ("station drama") and was clearly derived from the principles of the medieval mystery plays. This led to a consideration of the scene in the theatre as being self-contained. Significance and meaning derived from the juxtaposition or accumulation of scenes rather than from a continuous narrative progression from scene to scene, and from this it followed that there need be no consistency of setting. In Ernst Toller's *Man and the Masses* (1920) the scenes alternated between reality and dream throughout the play.

Characterization in Expressionist drama

The characters in Expressionist drama were often impersonal or nameless. Very often they served to illustrate some aspect of the protagonist's thought or feelings or expressed aspects of the world and society. In Toller's *Transfiguration* (1918) the soldiers on the battlefield had skeletons painted on their costumes. Characters were frequently presented as fragments of a unified consciousness. Crowds were often not differentiated but were used in mass to express or underline the power of the protagonist's position. Expressionist roles often required actors to express aspects of character through the use of isolated parts of the body. The character of Dr. Strangelove in Stanley Kubrick's film of that name, whose right arm must be restrained from giving the Nazi salute of its own volition, makes comic use of an Expressionist technique.

Two further developments can be attributed to the Expressionist movement. The director Leopold Jessner capitalized on the earlier innovations in stage design. His use of steps and multiple levels earned his stage the name *Treppenbühne* ("stepped stage"). He utilized screens in the manner advocated by Craig, and his productions illustrated a plastic concept of stage setting, which allowed the action to flow freely with minimum hindrance. Some of Jessner's productions relied heavily on steps and levels for this plasticity, but in others he used solid three-dimensional setting features standing in three-dimensional space. Jessner reclaimed and utilized the full space of the stage. In his 1921 production of *Othello,* a central rostrum served a variety of spatial functions. Upon his arrival in Cyprus, Othello and the accompanying crowd flooded out of a trapdoor at the rear of the rostrum and poured over the top of it onto the front stage; Othello, moving no further than the top of the rostrum, appeared to rise from a sea of people, towering above them. In a later scene, this same rostrum supported Desdemona's bed, with drapes towering into the flies, surrounded by space. The isolated solid unit within the total stage space has become a distinctive feature of contemporary set design and staging.

Expressionist use of stage space

The second contribution of the Expressionist movement was to bring the mask back into common usage. Initially, the mask signified typical or depersonalized characters; later, it became a device for distancing the audience from the characters altogether, as it was used by Brecht in *The Caucasian Chalk Circle* (1948) and other plays.

Expressionism was relatively short-lived, although there was a brief revival of the theatrical mode in the 1960s when casts of actors dressed in black jeans and sweaters sat on boxes on black-curtained stages and intoned their lines as the ego, id, and libido of someone's psychological crisis. Nevertheless, Expressionism contributed to the modern stage a range of techniques that have become the stock in trade of most directors and designers; though in most contemporary cases the influence of Expressionism has been mediated through Brecht (see below *The influence of Brecht*).

The influence of Piscator. The great German theatrical director Erwin Piscator trained as an actor and began his professional career during World War I, running an entertainment theatre for fellow soldiers in Belgium. After the war Piscator set out to create a theatre that had a clear place and function in a world that also contained machine guns and artillery shells. His first such efforts brought him into association with the Dadaists.

The Dadaist movement

Dada began as an oppositional movement in Zürich in 1916 at the Cabaret Voltaire. In neutral Switzerland a group of artists that included Hugo Ball, Emmy Hennings, Tristan Tzara, and Jean Arp took on the mantle of Alfred Jarry. Whereas Jarry had assaulted the audience through an unusual play, the Dadaists began the disintegration of form entirely. Songs were written with only sounds for lyrics. Ball wrote verses without words. Tzara shredded manuscripts and recited from pieces reassembled randomly. Nonsensical sketches were performed in outlandish cardboard costumes. The painter Marcel Janko constructed masks that, according to Ball, inspired "passionate gesture, bordering on madness." For some, Dada was anti-art; for others, it was a new direction in art. Dada was an extension of the Expressionist movement although what was expressed was not passion or the search for spirituality but derision and withering contempt.

Dada's contribution to staging lay in destroying all accepted notions of what the stage should be and should express and in attacking the cultural values of the audience in particular and society in general. This precedent later gave a powerful lead to many antiestablishment groups and artists after 1968 whose objectives have been described as "offending the audience" or "disrupting the spectacle." Dada left Zürich and spread through Germany in the postwar period of the 1920s. One art form engendered by Dada was that of photomontage, in which graphics and edited photographic images were combined to convey propagandist images. The principal artist in this field was John Heartfield, who had changed his German name of Helmut Herzfelde during World War I as a gesture of protest, and who contributed many designs for Piscator. In one of his montages, the vapour trails of five airplanes soaring over the ruins of the Spanish town of Guernica were altered to resemble the fingers of a skeletal hand. The principle of montage became important in Piscator's work.

Photomontage

Piscator later commented that Dada had shown the way forward but was not enough. A more overtly political and direct form of theatre was needed, and this theatre, unlike any of the concepts of the Volksbühne movement, should be allied to the political struggle of the proletariat.

The proletarian theatre, consisting of both amateurs and professionals, played in workers' halls and established the principle of free admission for the unemployed, which freed the theatre from its bourgeois status as an economic commodity. Piscator further eroded traditional relationships with a number of innovations in staging. In *Russlands Tag* ("Russia's Day"; 1920) the setting was a map, which established the political, geographical, and economic context for the play. In *Konjunctur* ("Conjunction"; 1928) this principle was extended to a larger stage. The play dealt with oil speculation, and the setting was a series of oil derricks. As the play progressed, the number and size of the derricks grew. The setting became part of the action and an environment for it, and the growth of the setting became a comment on the action of the play. In the *Rote Rummel Revue* ("Red Riot Review"; 1924), produced for the German Communist Party, Piscator began the action with a fight in the auditorium. The protagonists came out of the audience to argue their points of view and commented on the action of the various scenes. In *Tai Yang Erwacht* ("Tai Yang Awakes"; 1931) the setting, designed by John Heartfield, extended from the stage along the walls of the auditorium. A conspicuous feature of Piscator's propagandist productions was the climactic singing of "L'Internationale," the Socialist and Communist anthem, by both actors and audience.

Political theatre

Piscator established the political relevance of his work in a number of ways. In a revolutionary production of Schiller's *Die Räuber* (*The Robbers*) performed at Jessner's Staatstheater in Berlin, Piscator costumed and made up the minor character Spielberg, a noble character driven by society to crime, to resemble Trotsky. The German theatre in particular has since that time tended to interpret classic plays in a contemporary light. In Piscator's production of *Sturm über Gottland* ("Storm over Gothland"; 1927), which is set in the 14th century, a filmed prologue showed the major actors moving toward the camera, metamorphosing in the process from historically costumed characters to representations of modern historical figures; the protagonist, for example, turned into Lenin. In *Paragraph 218* (1929), which was about abortion reform, a tour was organized that used the performances to initiate discussion. Such associated discussions have since been a strong part of women's theatre and other political forms.

In several productions, Piscator dramatized or inserted verbatim political documents, news reports, or direct quotations from public figures. In one instance, an injunction was taken out by supporters of the former kaiser to prevent such a use of a direct quote in a 1927 production of Aleksey Tolstoy's *Rasputin.* Piscator offered the former kaiser a contract to appear in person. When this was rejected, the performance was stopped at the point in the show at which the quote would have been delivered and an actor explained the censorship ban. Direct comment of this kind was used frequently by Joan Littlewood and the Theatre Workshop company in Britain in the 1950s and '60s to comment on political actions and to establish common cause with the audience.

Piscator's use of film in theatre

The most important and advanced scenic device used by Piscator was projected film. In *Trotz Alledem* ("In Spite of Everything"; 1924) the second of his revues for the Communist Party, Piscator acquired through a contact a large quantity of war newsreel footage, which had never been shown because the censor considered that it would adversely affect war morale among the civilian population. The screening of the film as part of the whole stage montage lent an added authenticity to the documentary material presented in front of it and created a sensation. In this instance it established a principle, which has been built on by other political and documentary playwrights and directors, that one function of the political stage should be to make manifest what is concealed in politics.

Piscator established three distinct uses of film in his productions. What he called didactive film presented objective information and up-to-the-minute facts as well as historical ones; it gave the spectator facts about the subject of the production. Dramatic film contributed to the development of the action and served as a "substitute" for the live scene; where live scenes wasted time with explanations, dialogues, and action, film could illuminate a situation in the play with a few quick shots. Film commentary accompanied the action in the manner of a chorus. It addressed the audience, drew attention to important developments in the action, leveled criticism, made accusations, and provided important facts. Piscator should also be credited with the innovation of the jotter screen, a small, auxiliary screen onto which facts, figures, titles, dates, and other bits of information can be projected.

Piscator's work veered from the austere proletarian theatre productions to a lavish use of modern machinery in other productions. In Toller's *Hoppla, wir leben!* (*Hurrah! We're Alive;* 1927), a multiroomed house structure allowed projection onto a variety of screens in juxtaposition with live action. In *The Good Soldier Schweik* (1928) the actors performed among cutout caricatures drawn by George Grosz. In this production, Schweik on his travels marched against the direction of a moving treadmill at the front of the stage. Brecht later employed this idea with considerable success in *Mutter Courage und ihre Kinder* (1941) as Courage and her children pulled her wagon against the direction of the revolving stage.

There are two other innovations that Piscator added to the repertoire of staging devices. He conceived that the postwar world was too complex in its political and economic operations for any one playwright to comprehend it totally. He took the concept of the dramaturgic collective from Reinhardt and extended it to make it the basis of his production method. Writers, dramaturges, economists, politicos, and statisticians worked together to produce a script. Existing play scripts were subjected to analysis and restructuring by the collective. The second invention was the "stage of destiny." A great deal of Piscator's life was spent trying to realize a project for staging Tolstoy's novel *War and Peace.* When he finally accomplished this ambition, the judgments of history were incorporated into the narrative.

The style of theatre that Piscator propounded, using montage and juxtaposition of short independent scenes to create dialectical and often contradictory effects, he called epic theatre. Brecht, who had served in Reinhardt's dramaturgic collective and played an even greater part in Piscator's, appropriated this term for his own theatre. He also adapted and advanced many of the ideas and methods of Piscator's work.

Futurism in Italy. Although it produced one major dramatist, Luigi Pirandello, in the period between the two world wars, the Italian theatre contributed very little to staging or theatre production. What was important was the work of the Futurists led by Marinetti. This movement predated the Dadaists, but its politics were oppositional only with respect to the liberal democrats. Far from attacking war, the Italian Futurists welcomed it. They embraced and glorified the machine culture of the 20th century. Their theatre presentations were scandalous. On one occasion they smeared the seats with glue so that the audience would stick to them; they sold the same ticket to more than one person and provoked fights in the audience. The content and shape of their presentations were similarly designed to shock, provoke, and antagonize the bourgeois audience. With the accession to power of Mussolini's Fascists, whom they supported, their aggression diminished and they became absorbed into the establishment.

Borrowings from music hall and variety shows

The Futurists built their performances upon an examination of the techniques and forms of music hall and variety shows. The variety stage clearly held an audience's attention without the use of such stable theatrical elements as plot, characterization, and even dialogue. The Futurists went further, using variety forms and techniques without motivating reason or logical content, and created abstract theatre. Later the Dadaists took over many of their ideas in a different cause. What unified Futurist performances, however, was the concept of attractions. An attraction was whatever element in a particular act held the audience's attention. Variety bills were constructed to produce an effective and contrasting variation of types of acts—acrobats opened the show, a solo juggler concentrated the attention, a singer or whistler capitalized on this concentration, a musical act expanded it further, a chorus line of girls kicked in unison, and a climactic situation raised anticipation for the entry of the solo star comedian. The Italian Futurists never really exploited the full possibilities of this concept, which was taken much further in Russia.

Developments in Russia and the Soviet Union. *The great directors.* Until 1883 there were only five state theatres in Russia. When the embargo on non-state theatres was lifted, private initiatives followed. The most important of these was the Moscow Art Theatre (after 1939 the Moscow Academic Art Theatre), formed in 1898 by Konstantin Stanislavsky and Vladimir Nemirovich-Danchenko. The repertoire of the Moscow Art Theatre was less contentious than those of the other independent theatres, and it was the first of these theatres to emphasize theatrical production rather than censored or neglected plays. Stanislavsky had been deeply impressed by the work of the Meiningen Company and particularly by the discipline imposed on rehearsals by the Duke's stage manager, Ludwig Chronegk. In order to produce theatre in which all the elements were fully integrated, Stanislavsky decided that an autocratic, if not despotic, director was necessary.

The Moscow Art Theatre

His first production, Aleksey Tolstoy's *Fyodor Ivanovich,* which Stanislavsky had rehearsed on a country estate and designed on the basis of detailed research into costumes and historical settings, caused a sensation. Later Stanislavsky came to the opinion that the Meiningen approach was successful in creating an external unity of effect but deficient in transforming the internal techniques of the actors. The actors merely imitated the outward behaviour of the characters. With plays increasingly calling for a deeper understanding of psychological motivation, Stanislavsky saw the necessity for a more complex and subtle technique for transforming the thought processes and emotions of the actor into those of the character. The role of the director was thus transformed from that of despot to a combination of coach, teacher, and psychologist. Stanislavsky devoted the rest of his career to perfecting his famous "method," by which actors assumed the "identity" of their characters; it must be stressed that his was a method and not a style—each production was created in its own specific style. His early stage settings were overwhelmingly naturalistic, impressively detailed and accompanied by a vast array of sound effects. Fortunately, at the outset of the Moscow Art Theatre work, the plays of Chekhov formed a major part of the repertoire, and Chekhov argued successfully for a more selective style of setting and against the drowning of his plays by choruses of birds and frogs. Stanislavsky is credited with being the first person to produce a systematic study of the actor's craft. His influence and that of his Moscow Art Theatre are still to be seen in much of the theatre produced on the world's stages.

Stanislavsky's "method"

The early work of Meyerhold

Vsevolod Meyerhold was one of the actors in the original Moscow Art Theatre, playing among other roles Konstantin in *The Seagull* and Tussenbach in *Three Sisters.* In 1905 Stanislavsky, sensing the difficulties of approaching nonrealistic theatre through the acting methods of the Moscow Art Theatre, asked Meyerhold to open a studio to investigate nonrealistic approaches to acting. Meyerhold's work in the studio appears to have been more imaginative than disciplined, involving painters, poets, musicians, and actors in a series of multimedia experiments. Prior to the Revolution he was director of the imperial theatres in Leningrad. After the Revolution he became head of the Soviet theatre organization. In both these areas, Meyerhold carried on the experimental work begun in the Moscow Art Theatre.

Meyerhold's early experimental work followed the patterns laid down by Craig, Appia, and Fuchs, committing him to a "theatricalized" theatre and anti-illusionism. In his production of Blok's *Fairground Booth* (1906) and his subsequent writings on this work, Meyerhold explored the concept of a theatre of the grotesque. A disjointed rather than a uniform style—the contrasting of the comic and the tragic rather than their reconciliation in the tragicomic, the dispelling of illusion by blatant theatrical devices, the use of distorted perspectives—seemed to him the most appropriate style for 20th-century theatre. Other writers, directors, and artists were also concerned with the development of the grotesque at that time, but Meyerhold's productions of the Blok play and of Andreyev's *Life of Man* (1906) were high points, representative of a line of theatrical work that utilizes mixed forms in the theatre to express the contradictions and inconsistencies of life. The Theatre of the Absurd of the 1950s and early 1960s took this technique further to demonstrate that life is not merely inconsistent but fundamentally absurd.

Meyerhold's staging of Molière's *Dom Juan* (1910) was a key production in the process of "retheatricalizing" the theatre. Meyerhold used his historical research to reproduce many of the features of the early Baroque theatre. He built over the orchestra pit and extended the stage area forward by about 20 feet. He abolished the curtain, so necessary to the theatre of illusion, and conducted set changes in full view of the audience. The stage was lit with hundreds of candles and the auditorium remained lighted during the performance. The intention was to extend the experience of theatregoing beyond the mere watching of a play. The disposition of the auditorium and the circumstances under which people arrived at the theatre were to be part of the experience. Meyerhold believed that bright light inspired a festive mood in the spectators when they arrived at the theatre and that this disposed the actors to respond with equal enjoyment.

The Russian preoccupation with the physical aspects of performance not unnaturally led to a decline in respect for the written text, which became only one subservient means the theatre had at its disposal for creating enjoyable experiences. Of much greater importance to the Russians, since the text could be cut and reshaped and rewritten at will, was the physical technique of the actor. Throughout his studio period before the Revolution, Meyerhold

By courtesy of Society for Cultural Relations with the U.S.S.R.

Figure 20: Anti-illusionist stage of Vsevolod Meyerhold designed for his production of *Revizor* (*The Government Inspector*) by Gogol, Moscow, 1926.

was exploring circus movements, commedia dell'arte, and Japanese theatre in order to devise a new system of training actors. Both he and his younger contemporary Yevgeny Vakhtangov in their productions placed great emphasis on the rhythmic control of stage action and the physical agility of the actors. After the Revolution the demand for a popular theatre of ideology intensified this research and increased the numbers searching.

Meyerhold's "biomechanics"

Meyerhold codified his study of movement in a system known as biomechanics. The two roots of this term, in suggesting a living machine, also demonstrate the aim of the system. Meyerhold acknowledges a great debt to Frederick W. Taylor's work in all his writings on the subject.

Meyerhold constructed a set of 16 études as the basis of biomechanics. These études were chosen from an eclectic range of sources, including the circus, Chinese and Japanese theatre, and sport, and they formed the basis of his extended movement vocabulary. The études were sequences of precise muscular movements intended to evoke particular emotions in the performer. This process attempted to systematize the kinesthetic relationship between outer movement and inner feeling, to enable actors to experience this relationship, and to train them to control it.

Even after so short a time, it is not easy to reconstruct Meyerhold's biomechanics from the remaining evidence because of his fall from favour under Stalin. But, if the exact form of biomechanics has not survived, many of the underlying principles of Meyerhold's movement studies have, and the example of his training program is embodied in the work of many of the present-day advanced theatre groups. Less well known is the work of Vakhtangov, which is important because of the ways in which he combined the inner techniques of Stanislavsky with the external expressive techniques of Meyerhold. An investigation of the work of Jerzy Grotowski shows the continuation of this process and many of the specific techniques (see below *The influence of Grotowski and the Polish Laboratory Theatre*).

Later experiments

Like Piscator, Meyerhold experimented with the use of film, projected images, and graphics in his productions, and there has been some largely irrelevant controversy as to who copied whom. The period after the Revolution saw many of the Constructivist ideas used in architecture and design taken over into the theatre. The settings from Meyerhold's Constructivist period featured complicated stage machinery. All attempts at illusion were stripped away to reveal skeletal frameworks with moving parts. The abstract platforms and steps of Craig, Appia, and Jessner had entered the machine age. The sets, whatever their other origins, are the logical outcome of Meyerhold's study of movement and his efforts to reveal the mechanics of the actors' articulation. But Meyerhold and his designers were not content to provide a neutral acting area. The Constructivist settings were incorporated into the action, and the actors' movement was coordinated with the shape, dimensions, functions, and movements of the setting.

This emphasis on the rhythms of performance led Meyerhold to conceive of a theatre, designed but never built, in which all the dressing rooms opened directly onto the stage so that the actors could remain constantly aware of the stage proceedings. It has been said of Meyerhold that his rehearsals looked like performances and his performances looked like rehearsals. Against the prevailing approach of Stanislavsky, epitomized in the "building" of a character, Meyerhold instituted a holistic approach whereby the actors did not "mark" the actions but gave prototypical performances in rehearsal. Each rehearsal then produced a more complex prototype, and the process continued into the public performances. This approach is the one accepted now by many advanced theatre groups.

What unites Meyerhold and Piscator is their concept of an infinitely variable theatre within an oval shell, which would provide the total means to construct the environment and stage–audience relationship best suited for each production. Piscator commissioned plans for such a theatre from Walter Gropius, director of the Bauhaus. The project was called *Totaltheatre.* A remarkably similar building was designed for Meyerhold. Neither were ever built.

Other Russian directors

The Russian theatre during these years produced many other talented and innovative directors. Three who deserve mention are Nikolay Evreinov, Aleksandr Tairov, and Nikolay Okhlopkov.

Like Craig in England and Meyerhold in his own country, Nikolay Evreinov looked to the history of theatre as the true basis for freedom and innovation. In 1907–08 he mounted a cycle of medieval plays through which he wished to capture the artistic essence of each kind of stage, unconfined by pedantic reconstruction. A cycle of plays from the Spanish Golden Age was presented in a large hall—each play given an original setting to re-create the atmosphere of the original performances. One play was set on boards and trestles in an innyard, another given a court setting with the full effects of the Baroque theatre.

Evreinov also began to explore the relationship between theatre and life, particularly how the processes of acting in the theatre related to social strategies. His work has had a considerable influence on the development of psychodrama and the therapeutic process of acting out concealed traumas. He also anticipated the sociological school of theatre analysts and acting coaches of the 1960s and '70s.

Aleksandr Tairov used abstract settings of Cubist design and took the training of his actors so far as to posit the idea of the actor-dancer. The European tours of his Kamerny Theatre in the 1920s aroused special interest in France and sparked off a run of emulators.

Nikolay Okhlopkov, claimed Meyerhold, was the ideal biomechanical actor. His later work as director of the Moscow Realistic Theatre was innovative in the manner in which he planned the shape and relationship of both stage and audience for each individual production. His centre-stage production of Gorky's *Mother* had subordinate stages and a walkway behind the audience. He experimented with stages in front of, behind, within, and above the audience. His intention was to revive the festival spirit and incorporate the audience into the spectacle, and his methods were not restricted to the spatial. In *The Iron Flood,* a play about guerrillas in the Russian Civil War, the audience was kept outside the theatre until the Red Army arrived to break open the doors and the audience flooded into the auditorium. The stage in this production was obliterated and replaced by an embankment running along one side of the room with small promontories jutting out into the audience, breaking up any fixed focus in order to make the audience follow the fluid action. The theatre laboratories of Grotowski and Odin Theatre follow the Okhlopkov tradition in their handling of space.

Russian Futurism—Suprematism. The Russian Futurists, or Suprematists, declared their lineage from Jarry and their affiliation with the Italian Futurists in their first manifesto "A Slap in the Face of Public Taste" (1912). They differed from the Italians in that they were internationalist rather than nationalist in their politics and that their performances developed beyond the early antibourgeois, anti-art cabaret and variety shows that characterized both Italian Futurists and the Dadaists. The early Russian Futurist activities consisted of provocative street actions and cabaret performances, but with *Victory over the Sun,* an "opera" created in 1913 by the writer Alexey Kruchenykh, the composer Mikhail Matyuchin, and the painter Kazimir Malevich, they produced a work that expressed modern machine culture. The piece had affinities with Kandinsky's Expressionist pieces in that the setting consisted of geometric forms, pieces of machinery, and fragments of typography. The text consisted of nonsense syllables and words without syntax. The costumes and masks were designed to eliminate the human element by transforming the actors into machines. An offstage accompaniment of battle noises, cries, and discordant choral and solo singing provided the score. The whole work optimistically predicted a new age when man's mechanical inventions would supplant the Sun as the source of power. Later generations were to be more concerned with the dangers inherent in the realization of that proposition.

According to the composer Matyuchin, *Victory over the Sun* represented the first occurrence on a stage of the disintegration of traditional text, staging, and musical harmony. In retrospect, this production and the other Futurist works, including the early works of the poet Vladimir Mayakovsky, appear as extreme examples of a feverish experimentation concerned with separating analytically the various components of theatrical performance and resynthesizing these elements into new relationships. This analytical investigation and experimentation characterized the work of Kandinsky, Oscar Schlemmer, and the Bauhaus group as well; the work of the Expressionists, Piscator, and later Brecht began the resynthesis.

Theatrical manifestos

The theatre since the advent of Naturalism had been prone to producing manifestos of various kinds. As time went by, these declarations became less concerned with what theatre should be doing and more concerned with defining what theatre was. From Appia, Craig, and Fuchs onward there was a consistent body of theatre theory that had little to do with dramatic theory. The play and the playwright diminished in importance. The old dramatic criticism based on playtexts and how these were interpreted by actors lost relevance in the new world. The concept of genres such as tragedy, comedy, and farce collapsed as more and more theatre productions attempted to cope with experiences that could not be categorized so neatly.

Film, declared Lenin, was the most important of the media. The availability of resources for films that had an educational purpose rather than a commercial one stimulated filmmaking and the study of film as an art form. The director Dziga Vertov's manifesto for Soviet film sets out to free film from intrusive elements such as music, literature, and theatre. The "theatre" that Vertov disclaimed was equally rejected by the theatre makers around him who derived inspiration from the developments in film. Sergey Eisenstein, who worked in theatre and film, developed further the Italian Futurist concept of the montage of attractions. The implementation of this theory would eliminate all the random, haphazard nature of theatre, which Craig saw as destructive to any concept of the theatre as art. Whereas Craig put his trust in the intuitive genius of an individual director, the Russians tried to find a generally applicable theory. The artist-genius was replaced by the artist-theorist.

The propagandist theatre. Political theatre in postrevolutionary Russia combined agitation (the use of catchphrases and half-truths to exploit popular grievances) with propaganda (the use of historical and scientific arguments for purposes of indoctrination) in a form that came to be called agitprop. This form of theatre is explicitly intended to arouse the audience to action and to propagate the views and values of the sponsoring organization. In practice, the term agitprop is usually reserved for left-wing political theatre, though the form itself does not imply any particular ideology, nor is it restricted to politics. In fact, one of the greatest uses of agitprop techniques today occurs in commercial advertising. The reputation of political agitprop for poor aesthetic quality probably reflects the fact that many of the groups using it have viewed the political message as the raison d'être for the work and any aesthetic considerations have been deeply distrusted as interfering with its political purity.

Agitprop

Immediately after the Revolution the various arts were enlisted to further the propagandist aims of the Bolsheviks. Ships and trains were decked out with a variety of communicative devices ranging from poster art to poets reading their work. In a country where few could read the newspapers, actors acted out the news stories in a Living Newspaper. In 1921 a group of Moscow actors formed the Blue Blouses, a company named for the workers' overalls its members wore as their basic costume. This group inspired the formation of other professional and amateur factory groups throughout the Soviet Union. Their work and methods set the standard for political theatre groups in other countries between 1921 and 1939.

Blue Blouse performances

The performances of the Blue Blouses were typically around an hour and a half long and began with a parade in which the actors presented themselves to the audience. The aim of this and similar groups was to be able to perform anywhere, and staging demands were extremely simple. The performances were montages comprising dramatic monologues, sketches, dialogues, mass declamations, and movement derived from dance and gymnastics. They frequently made use of animated posters for rapid cartoon characterization—similar to the photographers' dummy boards with cutout faces that permit tourists to be photographed as cowboys or bathing beauties. Music was a prominent element, including instrumental numbers and folk and popular songs, often with satiric lyrics. Film was rarely used, but the Blue Blouses made a specialty of using flickering light on slowly moving actors to create the illusion of silent film. The dance and gymnastic routines seem to have been the most conventional and apolitical forms, but they were in practice the Blue Blouses' greatest strength. In the process of moving scenic pieces, the actors could acrobatically combine to compose pictures, diagrams, and structures. One report of a sketch entitled "Industrialization" describes actors in costumes representing factories and power stations finally coming together to represent the government program for industrialization.

The Blue Blouses constructed their programs cleverly, juxtaposing the more overtly political pieces with the more entertaining pieces. The organization of a bill in this way was not new, since music hall and variety theatres had used this sort of planning for many years. What was new was the use of these skills for an ideological purpose, rather than simply to extract applause from an audience.

Ironically, the Blue Blouse movement was suppressed by Stalin in 1928. The reason seems to have been that the Blue Blouses saw satire as a legitimate part of their repertoire and proceeded to attack the inequities that followed the Revolution and the survival of prerevolutionary thought and class distinctions. In 1928 such a program was held to be counterproductive, and a more agreeable line of thought was called for. The doctrine that followed was called Socialist Realism, a political derivative of Naturalism that sought to present typical figures in a typical landscape. With state direction these were always liable to turn into idealized figures in an idealized landscape.

Influence abroad

Just before their disbanding, the original Blue Blouse group made a tour of Germany in 1927 to celebrate 10 years of the Revolution. The visit coincided with the presence in Germany at a Communist-backed congress of representatives from many other countries. As a result, there arose an international movement of workers' theatre groups performing, with varying degrees of skill, agitprop in the Blue Blouse mode. Whereas the Blue Blouses in their heyday could expect official support for their minimal required facilities, the groups in nonsocialist countries could not, and a new resourcefulness resulted. One of the many German groups formed had a furniture pantechnicon in which it toured the working-class tenement courtyards, lowering a side of the van to reveal a ready-made stage that could quickly be folded up and driven away in advance of a police raid. Groups elsewhere took their theatre to public gathering places, often symbolic sites. Groups performed in the streets, on the backs of flat motor trucks, at mass meetings in city squares, as well as on the steps of employment exchanges and government offices. The Korean resistance to the Japanese invasion was aided by agitprop groups that stayed one step ahead of the Japanese troops. Troupes of this kind were used later by the North Vietnamese during the Vietnam War. Agitprop has remained a consistent part of the Chinese government's education program in rural areas. The techniques of the Blue Blouses and other agitprop groups were emulated by the Teatro Campesino, the first of the Chicano theatres in the United States, which was founded in California as part of the farmworkers' union campaign for recognition in the mid-1960s.

Political festivals. In the years immediately following the Russian Revolution, mass spectacles were mounted in many Soviet cities. The subjects of these spectacles were drawn from events in the Revolution and the subsequent Civil War. They were a conscious attempt to create a new form of social ritual out of the celebratory reenactment of revolutionary events. They also represent an attempt to create a new proletarian art form, and in this they arose naturally from the broader movement to utilize art for social purposes. The former Futurists and Suprematists painted the fronts of buildings and exploited the bustling atmosphere of street markets for their performances. The ideological point of such actions was that the theatres, concert halls, and art galleries had been the preserve of the privileged; proletarian artists proclaimed their allegiance by creating it in the streets.

It seemed only reasonable that Leningrad, which had seen so much of the high drama of the Revolution, should be the city that presented the most memorable mass spectacles. In 1920, five of these were presented, climaxing in *The Storming of the Winter Palace,* directed by Evreinov, with the help of the directors of the other spectacles. The performers numbered more than 8,000, and the spectators have been estimated at 100,000. A 500-piece orchestra provided accompaniment. The spectacle reenacted the events leading up to the October Revolution in Leningrad, on the site at which they actually happened.

Mass spectacle

The spectacles corresponded directly with the proposal by Rousseau and Diderot in 18th-century France that the theatre be made the church of the secular state. These productions were almost certainly influenced by the arguments of Romain Rolland for a people's theatre at the beginning of the century and were the most vivid examples of the large-scale revival of pageant theatre that was very strong in many European countries and North America between the two world wars. A change of Soviet policy in 1921 phased out the mass spectacles, though they have not disappeared entirely. The Bicentennial celebrations in the United States in 1976 included reenactments of the Battle of Lexington, among others. During the opening ceremonies of the Los Angeles Olympic Games in 1984, performers presented a "condensed" history of the settling of the United States. In the socialist countries the tradition is continued in more disciplined and less imaginative forms in military parades and the large athletic Spartakiades.

Influence in the West

As Soviet society settled into a more dogmatic and defensive period after 1921 and particularly after 1928, the unrestrained release of emotion sparked by the mass spectacles, the critical satire of the Blue Blouses, and the highly imaginative and often idiosyncratic experimental work of the directors came increasingly to be seen as dangerous to the state. In direct opposition to the direction in which 20th-century art was moving—*i.e.,* away from representation toward abstraction—the Soviet aesthetics branded any tendency toward abstraction as Formalist and established Socialist Realism, which was in effect a reduction of the older forms of Naturalism and psychological realism, as the official mode.

Developments in France. At the turn of the century, the preeminence of Paris as the centre of avant-garde theatre had declined and the lead had passed to Berlin and later Moscow. The revival in the French theatre produced a theory diametrically opposed to that of Meyerhold and Tairov. Jacques Copeau founded the Théâtre du Vieux-Colombier in 1913, arguing that the director's job was to translate faithfully a play into a "poetry of the theatre." Believing the actor to be the only important element in a production, he advocated the return to a bare stage. In the Vieux-Colombier he removed the proscenium arch to create a raised open platform. At the rear of the stage he placed an alcove with a balcony, a structure similar to that of the Elizabethan theatre. In a succession of productions and with great ingenuity this permanent setting could be transformed with minor alterations and adaptations to suit a whole season of varied plays.

Jacques Copeau

Copeau's reasoning was based on an assessment that the modern theatre had initiated a mass of new staging techniques but had singularly failed to find the new dramatists to maintain the literary standard of the theatre. He founded his theatre in hopes of attracting those new dramatists. This effort largely failed, and Copeau's contribution to the history of the theatre consists almost entirely in his approach to staging. The restriction of scenic means on the bare stage placed great stress upon the actor's ability to play in a variety of styles. In the school attached to the theatre, Copeau pursued a program of actor training very much in line with that of Meyerhold, encompassing exercises drawn from commedia dell'arte, folk theatre, masked theatre, Oriental theatre, and Dalcroze eurythmics. His actors trained with the Fratellini family, the great Italian family of circus clowns and acrobats. Copeau's aim was to equip his actors with a wide cultural understanding and a full range of physical and vocal skills. Rehearsals were improvisational. The discipline and self-denial inherent in Copeau's program provided an example for others to follow not only artistically and administratively but also morally. The line of influence from Copeau, his colleagues Charles Dullin and Louis Jouvet, and their students extends throughout the European theatre. The example of the Théâtre du Vieux-Colombier can be followed through many of the leading postwar European theatres, such as Giorgio Strehler's Piccolo Teatro of Milan and the Old Vic and the Royal Court theatres of London.

Developments in the United States. The currents of innovative stagecraft eventually reached the United States. The first migration was represented by the Viennese Joseph Urban, who when he went to the Boston Opera before World War I took with him an entire atelier of draftsmen and scenic artists. Urban moved into musical comedy and eliminated the acreage of painted vistas and box sets manufactured by the stock scenic studios.

The next change grew out of marginal experimental groups, such as the Provincetown Playhouse on Cape Cod in Massachusetts and the Neighborhood Playhouse in New York City, which fostered designers such as Robert Edmond Jones, Cleon Throckmorton, and Aline Bernstein (Figure 21). By the middle 1920s, their simple, tasteful romanticism had invaded Broadway as the groups had become commercial and as the more artistic theatre managers extended commissions to the free-lance designers. The industrial designer Norman Bel Geddes entered the growing ranks of theatre artists and devised grandiose projects and engineering marvels (Figure 22). With the impetus provided by ecstatic reports from Europe on the work of Reinhardt, Copeau, Meyerhold, and Tairov, American directors such as Arthur Hopkins and Philip Moeller attempted to synthesize the elements of production into a persuasive whole. The imaginative poetry of Robert Edmond Jones was balanced by the sensible craftsmanship of Lee Simonson for the Theatre Guild. Simonson as the exponent of "selective realism" was more attuned to the practicalities of the earthbound psychological problems that provided the staple fare of Broadway's "serious" drama.

Broadway staging

By courtesy of Theatre Collection, New York Public Library at Lincoln Center, Astor, Lenox and Tilden foundations

Figure 21: A simultaneous setting by Robert Edmond Jones for O'Neill's *Desire Under the Elms,* Provincetown, 1924.

By the 1930s, scenery consisted of solid carpentry and tasteful furnishings that were tailored to the mood, atmosphere, and mechanical requirements of the individual play. The Urban style in musical comedy design was replaced by that of Albert Johnson—a style characterized by loose colour and calligraphic line that went well with the sharp revues that prevailed until World War II. In

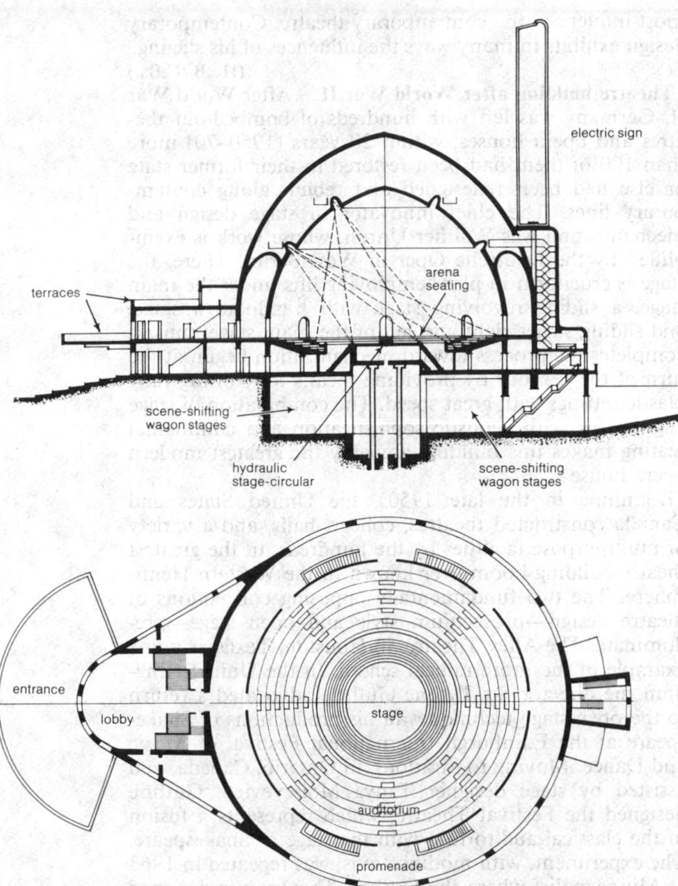

Figure 22: The project Theatre #14 designed by Norman Bel Geddes in 1922 for a theatre proposed for the Century of Progress Exposition, Chicago (1933–34). (Top) Section. (Bottom) Plan.

By courtesy of Edith Lutyens Bel Geddes (Mrs. Norman Bel Geddes) for the Norman Bel Geddes Estate

staging musicals, a peculiar division persisted between the direction of the plot and comedy segments and that of the production numbers—the sumptuous song-and-dance displays under the separate supervision of a "stager" who was noted for his taste. Director-producer George Abbott surmounted this artificial departmentalization in an important step forward in the development of the rhythmic, lively musical show that became America's contribution to world theatre.

The Living Newspaper

The importation of Blue Blouse techniques, through direct exposure to German groups or through political theatre groups formed by ethnic immigrants, led to one sensational development in the United States. The Living Newspaper had been a relatively crude form of propaganda elsewhere. Under the Federal Theatre Project (1935) several Living Newspapers were produced, of which *Triple-A Ploughed Under* (1936) and *One Third of a Nation* (1938) are probably the best known examples. These productions were articulate documentaries of great sophistication. So impressive were they that the model was reexported into Europe as the basis for many documentary theatre productions. Another refinement of these techniques married to the skill of Broadway-experienced professionals produced the political revue *Pins and Needles* (1937), which was put on to aid a strike and which ran on Broadway for 1,108 performances.

The influence of Brecht. By 1936 a wide range of experimentation and innovation had established the parameters of the contemporary theatre. The training of actors in the Western theatre has since become more organized to take in concepts and programs from the earlier innovators. There are few schools today that do not acknowledge the work of Stanislavsky in their training. Less obvious but equally pervasive is the influence of Reinhardt and Copeau, largely by way of their pupils in teaching. And towering above all others (save perhaps Stanislavsky) is the figure of Brecht. It is reasonable to argue that Brecht absorbed, and in turn perpetuated, more influences than any other individual in the modern theatre.

Of central importance in establishing this argument is Brecht's essay "On Experimental Theatre" (1940), in which he reviews the work of Vakhtangov, Meyerhold, Antoine, Reinhardt, Okhlopkov, Stanislavsky, Jessner, and other Expressionists. Brecht traces through the modern theatre the two lines running from Naturalism and Expressionism. Naturalism he sees as the "assimilation of art to science," which gave the Naturalistic theatre great social influence, but at the expense of its capacity to arouse aesthetic pleasure. Expressionism (and by implication the other anti-illusionist theatres), he acknowledges, "vastly enriched the theatre's means of expression and brought aesthetic gains that still remain to be exploited." But it proved incapable of shedding any light on the world as an object of human activity, and the theatre's educational value collapsed. Brecht recognized the great achievements of Piscator's work, in which he himself played a significant role, but proposed a further advance in the development of so-called epic theatre.

Brecht's epic theatre

Brecht's Marxist political convictions led him to propose an alternative direction for the theatre that would fuse the two functions of instruction and entertainment. In this way the theatre could project a picture of the world by artistic means and offer models of life that could help the spectators to understand their social environment and to master it both rationally and emotionally. The main concept of Brecht's program was that of *Verfremdungseffekt* ("alienation"). In order to induce a critical frame of mind in the spectator, Brecht considered it necessary to dispense with the empathetic involvement with the stage that the illusionary theatre sought to induce. Generally, this has been understood as a deadening coldness in the productions, but such an interpretation proceeds from a general ignorance of Brecht's own writings on the subject. Rather, he insisted, as Appia, Craig, and the Symbolists did before him, that the audience must be reminded that it is watching a play.

Brecht's ideas can be approached through the image presented by the theatre he chose to work in on his return to East Germany in 1947. The auditorium of the Theater am Schiffbauerdamm is lavish to the point of fantasy, decorated with ornate plaster figures. The stage, by complete contrast, is a vast mechanized scenic space in which everything is clearly exposed to view as theatrical and man-made. In the contrast between the comfort of the auditorium and the science of the stage lies the condition of Brecht's theatre. The audience was there to be entertained but also to think scientifically.

Many of the techniques of Brecht's staging were developments of earlier work. The use of three-dimensional set pieces in a large volume of space clearly derived from Jessner. His delight in the use of machinery and in particular the revolving stage came from Piscator. The insistence on the actors' demonstrating through the physical disposition of the body their *gestus* ("attitude") toward what is happening derived from Meyerhold, though with Brecht the *gestus* was always socially based. The clearest of his alienation devices, the projection of captions preceding the scene so that the audience knows in advance what will happen and therefore can concentrate on how it happens, derived from Piscator's jotter screens and film captions.

Brecht acknowledged in his work the need for the actor to undergo a process of identification with the part, and he paid tribute to Stanislavsky as the first person to produce a systematic account of the actor's technique. Brecht required his actors to go beyond Stanislavsky and to incorporate a social attitude or judgment into their portrayal. Characterization without a critical judgment was in Brecht's view seductive artifice; conversely, social judgment without the characterization of a rounded human being was arid dogmatism. The theatre of mixed styles and means that Meyerhold and others constructed to cope with the grotesque experience of modern living was transformed by Brecht into a political principle. He used mixed means and styles to expose the contradictions, inconsistencies, and dialectics of situations and characters. Brecht's strongest theatrical effects were created through the juxtaposition of inconsistent attitudes in a character. Although the settings in Brecht's productions were clearly theatrical, the costumes and properties were not. Great care was taken to make each property and its use authentic for the period or character (Figure 23). In Brecht's theatre, if a chicken were to be plucked the actor did not mime or roughly approximate the action—the chicken was plucked. Costumes had to make clear the social class of the persons wearing them. This places Brecht directly in the line with the Meiningen Players, though again the *gestus* is particularly social rather than historical.

Rehearsal methods

Brecht's methods of rehearsal were especially innovative. The methods worked out in his own company, the Berliner Ensemble, established a directing collective well advanced beyond those of Reinhardt and Piscator. In Brecht's theatre, the director, dramaturge, designer, and composer had equal authority in the production. The designer had a special function; in addition to designing the sets and costumes, he also produced, for early rehearsal purposes, a series of sketches of key moments in the action. The rehearsals became a process of testing hypotheses about the play and its production. What held the collective together and made the method workable was the story, or fable. All the elements of production were synthesized for telling this story in public. At some points the music conveyed the meaning, at other times the setting, or the actors, or the words did. Brecht often invited observers to the rehearsals in order to test the clarity of the story. The process of testing could continue into the performance period. When the company was satisfied that the staging was correct, the production was photographed and a *Modellbuch* was prepared with photographs set against the text to show the disposition of the stage at all times and to mark significant changes of position on the part of the actors. The *Modellbuch* was then available (in a more advanced form than the designer's sketches) as the basis for any subsequent productions.

The *Modellbuch* has aroused resentment on the part of directors who prefer to respond freely to the text. Brecht's intention was not to limit but to provide a document as scientific evidence of an experiment that could be used in further research. Since the finished text was, in any case, only one facet of the fable, the model book gave evidence of other aspects of the story and its telling.

Brecht's influence on the contemporary theatre has been both considerable and problematic. His Marxist views have proved a real stumbling block to his assimilation in the West, and his use of formalist techniques in the service of entertainment has presented difficulties in the socialist countries. There is no doubt that the settings and costumes of his productions are the features that have most influenced the contemporary theatre. Contemporary design exhibits in many ways the influences of his staging. (Ho.B./C.Ba.)

From the Mordecai Gorelik Collection

Figure 23: Setting for a scene in *Mutter Courage und ihre Kinder*, staged by Bertolt Brecht for the 1949 production by the Berliner Ensemble.

Theatre building after World War II. After World War II, Germany was left with hundreds of bombed-out theatres and opera houses; within 20 years (1950–70) more than 100 of them had been restored to their former state or else had been redesigned and rebuilt along contemporary lines. The chief innovator in stage design and mechanization was Walther Unruh, whose work is exemplified by the Deutsche Oper in West Berlin. There, the stage is cruciform in plan, employing lifts under the main stage, a sliding revolving stage with trapdoors upstage, and sliding stages right and left of the main stage; thus, it completes the process toward mechanization begun at the turn of the century by providing means for shifting fully plastic settings with great speed. The combination of stage engineering with acoustic sophistication and continental seating makes this building arguably the greatest modern opera house.

Beginning in the late 1950s, the United States and Canada constructed theatres, concert halls, and a variety of multipurpose facilities by the hundreds, in the greatest theatre-building boom ever known in the Western Hemisphere. The two fundamentally opposing conceptions of theatre design—proscenium style and open stage—predominate. The Alley Theatre, in Houston, Texas, is a fine example of the more radical school. In the United Kingdom the director Sir Tyrone Guthrie advocated a return to the open-stage techniques in his productions of Shakespeare at the Edinburgh International Festival of Music and Dance. Moving to Stratford, in Ontario, Canada, and assisted by stage designer Tanya Moiseyevich, Guthrie designed the Festival Theatre, which represents a fusion of the classical auditorium with the stage of Shakespeare. The experiment, with modifications, was repeated in 1963 at Minneapolis, where the Guthrie Theater was designed to Guthrie's specifications. The Guthrie Theater, while it is reminiscent of his earlier theatre at Stratford, exhibits a studied asymmetry in plan and section in contrast to the older theatre's ordered symmetry. A number of new British theatre buildings have been built in emulation of this design. (G.C.I./C.Ba.)

Internationalism in the theatre today has erased national and local styles in decor and staging. The great leap in facilities for travel and the network of international festivals throughout the world has greatly facilitated the cross-fertilization of styles and influences. It is not surprising that the resulting eclecticism of taste has imposed certain imperatives on theatre design. This has also been affected by an interaction of economic factors. Theatres occupy prime sites in city centres. In the post-World War II building boom, these sites became targets for property speculators seeking to exploit them for more profitable purposes. The return on investment and capital costs in theatres is very low in comparison with other fields of investment. In Britain a vast number of theatres disappeared completely in the decade following 1945.

Economic factors

The keynote in the postwar rebuilding of theatres has been flexibility. Eclecticism in style has led to demand for flexible auditoriums. In response to directorial demand, a number of theatres were built in Scandinavia in which the size and relationship of stage and auditorium can be adjusted by mechanical means.

It has become customary for many contemporary theatres to have a studio theatre attached to a main-house theatre. These studios are usually well-equipped "black boxes" with adaptable seating that allows a limited variety of forms of presentation—usually end-on, half-thrust, full-thrust, and arena staging. The National Theatre in London has three auditoriums of different types. The Royal Shakespeare Company has three auditoriums in Stratford and also uses some improvised areas; the company has two auditoriums in London. This variety of facilities lends flexibility to production planning. Less commercial productions can also be mounted in the studio theatres when the risk is too high to give them main-house runs.

The rise of alternative theatre spaces. The search for flexibility in designing a multipurpose hall that could be used for theatre, music, exhibitions, and sporting events has rarely been successful. The acoustic needs of theatre and music are widely different, and acoustic shields (suspended or freestanding panels used to alter the acoustic properties of a space) are at best corrective devices. Nevertheless, economic factors have frequently dictated that this is the only possible way in which smaller communities can be provided with performance spaces, and the design of such spaces is becoming more sophisticated and efficient.

The adverse economics of Broadway has severely restricted the range of productions that can be presented in those theatres. Investment is high and the risk of losing all has led to a policy that favours mass-appeal productions such as the musical, which can at least produce a high box-office return. Experimental productions stand little chance of finding a backer. Since the 1950s the sterility of Broadway has been countered by a growth of small Off-Broadway theatres, and, in turn, so-called Off-Off-Broadway. Nontheatre buildings have been pressed into use—cafés, garages, fire stations, churches, lofts, and shops. The example of the converted theatres in New York City spread to other countries. In many cases these theatres have been the home of innovative companies for many years. Otherwise they have formed the basis of a new touring circuit for small companies. The growth of the study and practice of theatre in educational institutions, starting in the United States in the 1930s and spreading to Europe after World War II, led to the formation of many small experimental and radical theatre groups in the 1960s and '70s. These groups formed the nucleus of the companies adapting and playing the informal theatres.

One further reason for the development of adaptable, flexible, and multipurpose theatre spaces has been the pattern of decentralization followed by many Western governments since World War II. In France, in particular, there has been a government policy of subsidizing theatre away from Paris through the founding of *maisons de la culture* ("houses of culture") and *centres dramatiques* ("dramatic centres"). The dual policy has been to create the facilities for a range of cultural activities in the towns and cities of the provinces and to establish theatre companies touring in specific areas from a home base. The development of lightweight electronic equipment, particularly lighting control, has greatly facilitated touring.

The influence of Grotowski and the Polish Laboratory Theatre. The other major tendency in today's theatre arises from an investigation of the sources of the theatre's uniqueness and strength. The prophet of this search was the French dramatist and poet Antonin Artaud, with his vision of a total, visceral theatre with the potency and terror of primitive myths. As was the case with Craig and Appia, his actual performances were few, but his writings inspired many directors, such as Peter Brook in England, Gerald Savory in France, and Jerzy Grotowski, whose Polish Laboratory Theatre, a fiercely dedicated acting ensemble, sought to cut through the bonds of the polite literary tradition to rediscover basic human drives and conflicts. The actors in the Laboratory Theatre undergo exhaustive exercises designed to break down the layers of superficial technique and repressions. Each production is conceived as a unique entity, requiring its own playing space and actor–audience relationship; the rectangular hall-theatre is rearranged according to the dictates of each production. Grotowski relies on his own dramaturgical skills in freely molding the texts and on his architect-designer for the carving of the space in which the ritual takes place.

Poor theatre

Grotowski's form of theatre is often called poor theatre on account of the simple circumstances in which it takes place. This characteristic recalls Copeau's idea of "the greatest possible effect from the least possible means." The internationalism of the theatre is now such that groups modeled on Grotowski's have appeared throughout the world. Eugenio Barba, of Odin Theater in Holstebro, Den., a pupil of Grotowski, has formulated the ideological position of these theatres under the term third theatre. His book *The Floating Islands* (1979) examines a theatre existing independently that creates from whatever material resources are at hand. Barba has sought to return to theatre as a way of life, seeing this pattern in the origins of the commedia dell'arte, the wandering players, and in Molière's company. The third theatre groups give performances, but they insist that the relationships engendered by their work, inside and outside the company, are the criteria by which they judge it. The members of the Odin Theatre have established a form of bartering in which they exchange their work for some cultural offering from the people of the regions they visit.

Because the third theatre is a way of life, the actors' "work" is a full-time activity. Actors have their own daily training regimen. The actors' work is enriched by the acquisition of other skills, particularly the techniques of Oriental theatre.

Because of the crippling expense of mainstream Western theatre and the development of these experimental groups, the theatre in the late 20th century has become highly polarized. On the one hand, there are "rich" commercial productions that rely heavily on technological spectacle; on the other hand are the small "poor" experimental groups exclusively centred on the art of the actor. Consequently, the traditional centres of theatre are losing their potency, except in their power to divert. The sources of real theatrical advance and interest are now dispersed throughout the world, and one is as likely to find exciting work in New Guinea as in New York City and London.

The component crafts of theatrical production

SCENIC DESIGN

Historical development. The execution of scenic effects passed from the guilds in the late Middle Ages to artists, with their apprentices and assistants, during the Renaissance and the Baroque and to commercial scene-painting studios from the mid-19th century until today. Each tiny Baroque state maintained a court painter and staff to embellish the court revels, masques, and operatic presentations. Large permanent companies such as the Paris Opéra, La Scala in Milan, Covent Garden in London, and the Vienna State Opera employed their own artists and shops. The independent actor-managers, stock companies, and traveling troupes and acts of the late 1800s ordered stock settings from firms that were prepared to turn out acres of mountain crags, sumptuous temples and palaces, picturesque hovels, and town squares. Historical research was crammed into every meticulously painted border, side wing, and backdrop, but no thought was given to the particular requirements of the individual scripts.

Stock settings

The major firms printed illustrated catalogs so that single hangings or complete backgrounds could be ordered by number through the mail. Leading managers, such as Sir Henry Irving in England and Max Reinhardt on the Continent, and the French art theatres commissioned painters who either did the painting themselves or supervised its execution from their sketches. In the United States, even on Broadway, the standard procedure well into the 1920s was for the actor-producer-director to dispatch a ground plan to the scenic shop, which made up a coloured model based on research and, after approval of the design, made the finished setting. The scenic artists who made such settings were highly skilled artisans, with thorough art schooling; though they frequented art galleries and museums, they seldom attended the legitimate theatre. As a result, free-lance designers with a better understanding of theatre began to play a greater role on the New York stage, and studios arose that catered to their new, personal styles. Bergman Studios, for example, executed works by Robert Edmond Jones, Lee Simonson, Norman Bel Geddes, Donald Oenslager, and Jo Mielziner, and Triangle Studios, an outgrowth of the Urban migration from Vienna and Munich, concentrated on musical comedies. Generally, carpentry, painting, property, and drapery shops were separate businesses. Not until the 1950s would all branches of scenery making in New York City be found under one roof. With the decline of theatrical activity, the all-in-one studio became an economic necessity. In London, the shops remain separate. Major theatres in Europe and most resident theatres in the United States maintain their own shops. The support facilities of the major West German theatres resemble small industrial concerns.

Contemporary procedures. Design procedures are fairly similar throughout the world. First, the script is studied closely and notes are made of mandatory action and mechanical requirements. Next, there is a consultation with the director on a production scheme. Thumbnail sketches are expanded into colour renderings or a model, if the structure is complex or the setting is primarily plastic, usually on a scale of one-half inch to one foot. Extensive research is undertaken and incorporated into the designs. Upon approval, the sketches are translated into working drawings. The execution shops are sent a ground plan, a section to determine masking and light placement, elevations of all units, and all details that require larger scale. The designer does not break down the elements into construction pieces or into actual framing or building details; this is done by the layout man in the scenic form. Usually there is a great deal of questioning and discussion between the artist and the technicians over the mechanics and the use of materials before the final drawings are consigned to the shops.

The modern scenic shop

In spite of the marginal financial status of the legitimate theatre, the physical layout of a modern scenic shop is extensive; vast amounts of space and equipment are required for the wide variety of designs to be translated into solid items, especially in the rush of preparations for the theatre season. Templates for flats, which once occupied the major amount of floor space, have been supplanted by three-dimensional fabrication, with scene-shifting wagons and overall stage decks. More recently, a blacksmith shop has been a requirement, since metal has replaced lumber in the scaffolding and in delicate open-tracery sets. The power tools, both for lumber and for metal, and all the workbenches are mounted on casters for mobility; essentials such as traveler tracks, winch motors, and the material stock for immediate use are stored around the edges. The paint shop also has required a larger space since looser, wetter techniques were adopted and bulk objects replaced flats and drops, which could be painted on upright frames. The drapery department produces soft maskings, drapes, upholstery, and any other special scenery covering. Vacuum form machines turn out ornaments wholesale and also make sizable, lightweight plastic objects that could not be carved in Styrofoam or wood. The drafting layout room is where mechanical problems are solved, the work is distributed, and models are translated into working drawings. Working models have come back into use to represent the sculptured units on the open stages that have replaced traditional flat scenery of the peephole tradition. If there is room, an acting company may practice on an elaborate structure for a few days before it is moved to the theatre. Ideally, the electrical shop is incorporated into the scenic complex to service the units that onstage will come within the province of the production electrician.

Properties, once produced in quaint workshops, are now a part of the scenic firms' mundane output. Celastic casting (the production of plastic props) has taken over from wood turning and whittling. The procurement of ready-made props, furniture, and dressing is handled by the property master, but the artistic choice resides with the designer. On today's open stages the primacy of properties demands the absolute rightness of every object in the visual ensemble. The theatre has sheltered the last remaining medieval craftsmen, the scenic painters and the blacksmiths; the production property master is the last all-around handyman.

The work of the stage staff is now much more demanding in skill, and the heads of departments need a wider range of knowledge and experience than in the days of box sets and flatting. Special businesses, employing the cream of the available theatre technicians, have been established to bridge the technical gap (particularly in the field of engineering) between the designer's demands for a particular production and the resident technicians' range of skills. These firms also fulfill a research function in pioneering new technical solutions to problems.

Increasing specialization

Theatre design has become an extremely specialized field. Stock sets have almost completely disappeared, each production having its own specifically designed setting. There are still possibilities for artists from other branches of the fine arts to design sets—David Hockney, the painter, has contributed designs of great distinction. The collaboration between the choreographer Merce Cunningham and the visual artist Robert Rauschenberg, both of the United States, has had a long and successful history. Most designers, however, now go through a formal training and are considered to have entered a profession. Many designers specialize in either set or costume design, and since 1950 there has arisen the new profession of lighting design (see below). Prior to this time, directors frequently arranged their own lighting with or without the cooperation of the set designer. The complexity of modern lighting equipment has created the need for a specialist. In spite of this trend, there remain some artists—Franco Zefferelli, for one—who almost singlehandedly design their own productions.

The development of design has come to be closely tied to economic developments. It is split between large lavish spectacles able to compete with film and television and a minimalist theatre that seeks to survive by stressing those elements that clearly distinguish theatre from film and television. The former clearly favours the development of more spectacular ingenuity, particularly in the field of engineering. The latter tends more subtly to create innovative designs in constrained circumstances. There have been signs in many theatres of a return to the principle on which the Elizabethan theatre was built—simple settings and lavish costumes (with the addition of dramatic lighting effects).

The work of the designer is being made much easier by the development of computer graphics. Three-dimensional pictures can be constructed on a screen, and these can incorporate specific sightlines from critical seats in the auditorium. Designs are drawn up on the basis of ground plans and elevation drawings and then demonstrated by a model. (Ho.B./C.Ba.)

STAGE LIGHTING

Historical development. The classic Greek *theatron* was built in the open air, usually on a hillside, and placed so that the afternoon sunlight came from behind the audience and flooded the performing area with light. The larger Roman theatres were also outdoors, but the added luxury of coloured awning stretched over the spectators softened the glare of the sun. Later, in the Middle Ages, the miracle and mystery plays were performed outdoors on the front steps of the church and the adjoining square. In England, the pageant wagon, complete with actors and properties, was drawn through the main street of a town. Until the 16th century, the theatre continued to be basically an outdoor institution.

Beginnings of artificial lighting

Under the patronage of the aristocracy in Italy, private performances, pageants, and tableaux began to be given indoors. Serlio, the Italian architect, gave considerable attention to theatre design and in a treatise written in 1545 discussed theatre construction and the creation of lighting effects. He recommended placing candles and torches behind flasks filled with amber- and blue-coloured water. Palladio's indoor theatre, also in Italy, used the common everyday light sources: torches, pine knots, open wick lamps, and tallow candles. In England at the end of the 16th century, the Globe Theatre was used for summer performances of Shakespeare's plays, but in winter performances were given in the completely enclosed Blackfriars Theatre. Artificial light, mainly candles, was used in several indoor theatres to light the stage and the auditorium.

In the early 17th century, Inigo Jones introduced several innovations in lighting and stagecraft, using reflectors to intensify the light sources and making use of colour on stage. The earliest known definite description of stage lighting may be found in *Sciena d'Comoedia* (1628) by Joseph Furtenbach. He describes the use of oil lamps and candles set in a row along the front edge of the stage but out of sight of the audience as well as vertical rows of lamps behind each wing at the sides of the stage. The common method of lighting the stage and auditorium was by means of tallow candles. As seen in old prints, these candles were mounted in crude hoops or chandeliers, which were hoisted aloft on pulleys to hang in dripping splendour. Gold decorations applied to the interior of the auditorium caught the many reflections. The inconvenience of the lighting system was that candles were expensive and hard to control. The twisted wicks had to be constantly trimmed during the performance, and this was the duty of the snuff boy. A transformation from light to darkness was effected by the agile skill of the candle snuffers.

When David Garrick used footlights at the Drury Lane Theatre in 1765, he masked the candles with metal screens. By 1784, when Richard Brinsley Sheridan managed the Drury Lane, all lights used to illuminate the stage were out of sight, hidden by the now familiar wings and borders.

A floating oil wick lamp was replaced after 1783 by the Argand oil lamp, in which the cylindrical wick was enclosed in a glass chimney to steady the flame and provide a brighter, whiter, and cleaner light source. And so the chimneyed oil lamp replaced the candle, but it was still hung in clusters above and bracketed to the walls. At the Haymarket Theatre in London, the oil lamps had chimneys of white and green glass that were controlled by levers, so that raising or lowering the chimneys could effect light changes. Actually, the result merely made the actors and scenery visible. Stage design and stagecraft had now advanced as far as was technically possible under the limitations of low-intensity stage lighting.

Introduction of gas lighting

The first major advance in several centuries was the introduction of gas lighting. A Scottish engineer, William Murdock, developed a practical method to distill gas from coal for illumination. The first successful adaptation of gas lighting for the stage was demonstrated in the Lyceum Theatre, London, in 1803 by a German, Frederick Winsor. The Chestnut Street Opera House in Philadelphia installed a gas lighting system in 1816 and supplied its own gas by installing a gas generator on the premises. (Gas stations and city mains did not come into use before 1850.) The advantages of gas lighting were immediately realized and exploited, despite the initial cost. No new methods of lighting, however, were devised for stage lighting. The conventions remained the same: footlights (*i.e.,* a row of lights across the front of the stage floor); borderlights (a long horizontal row of lights used for the general lighting of the stage from above); and striplights (a row of lights, usually mounted in a trough reflector and placed in the wings to illuminate specific portions of the stage or setting).

Even without a chimney, an open gas jet flame was brighter than oil lamps or candles. The additional advantage was control; by varying the control valves from a central point, a smooth increase or decrease of light could be effected, and at variable speeds. For the first time, to add to the realism of the play, the auditorium lights could be darkened. Elaborate central control systems were devised, with a main regulator, branch mains, more and more regulators, branch mains, and valves. This growing array of valves and pipes was organized into circuits and displayed on the "gas table"—the forerunner of the modern switchboard.

But there were also disadvantages to gas: namely, heat, offensive vapours, and the serious fire hazard of the open flame. A protective code was established to provide guards, screens, and glass chimneys and was made compulsory. In 1890, after the introduction of electric lighting, the incandescent gas mantle was developed. Although the mantle greatly improved the quality of light—brighter and whiter—the hazards of fire still remained.

Introduction of the limelight

Although Thomas Drummond, a British engineer, invented the limelight in 1816, it did not come into general use until some 30 years later. Limelight is produced by directing a sharp point of oxyhydrogen flame against a cylindrical block of lime. The tiny area of lime becomes incandescent and emits a brilliant white light that is soft and mellow. As the lime is slowly consumed by burning, the block of lime has to be slowly and constantly turned by an operator to supply the flame with a fresh surface. Since the brilliant area was very small, the addition of a mirrored reflector was necessary to give accurate control.

The intensity of the limelight permitted it to be directed onto the stage from the auditorium. Since it offered control as well as intensity, the limelight was quickly adapted to follow individual performers around the stage. The sharpness produced by the small point source made possible the creation of realistic effects, such as sunlight and moonlight, and moving effects, such as clouds, water, and fire.

Electrification. An advance of great importance was the introduction of the electric carbon arc, which was exhibited in experimental form in 1808 by Sir Humphry Davy. The Paris Opéra developed the earliest electric arc effect—a beam of sunlight—as early as 1846. By 1860 the Paris Opéra had also developed a lightning machine, a rainbow projector, and a luminous fountain. Most important, the company made the earliest spotlight, a carbon arc and reflector housed in a hood, which included a lens and a shutter.

Development of incandescent light

The next great advance in lighting was the development of the incandescent electric lamp, in which light is produced by a filament electrically heated to incandescence. The invention of a practical electric lamp by Thomas Edison in 1879 marked the beginning of the modern era of stage lighting. Gas was quickly discarded; within one year the progressive Paris Opéra introduced the new system. Two years later, at the Electrotechnical Exposition in Munich, a small theatre was erected that used electric lighting exclusively for both stage and auditorium. The success of the experiment received worldwide acclaim. In London the Savoy Theatre was the first to install the new lights; while in Boston the Bijou Theatre followed the new trend in 1882. The following year, 1883, the Landestheatre in Stuttgart, the Residenztheatre in Munich, and the Staatsoper in Vienna were the first completely electrified theatres.

At the turn of the century, incandescent lamps were in almost universal use for stage lighting, but no new methods or techniques of lighting appeared. The conventional footlights, borderlights, and striplights were merely electrified, and the arc light was used for concentrated light sources. Gradually, new improvements provided brighter lamps that were both more durable mechanically and available in larger wattages. Metallic filaments replaced carbon, and, finally, drawn tungsten filament lamps appeared in 1911. The use of inert gas in place of a vacuum produced lamps of even higher efficiency and larger sizes. The introduction of concentrated coil filaments made practical the development of the incandescent spotlight. And the refinement of the incandescent spotlight added an exciting new tool for the advance of stage lighting and the further development of stagecraft. Gradually the arc spotlight was replaced by the new incandescent spotlight, which provided all the advantages of flexibility and control.

In his music dramas, Wagner suggested new possibilities for the use of light and design in a unified production—a lyrical synthesis. Adolphe Appia and Gordon Craig gave tremendous impetus to the new plastic stagecraft. Their conception of the stage was a cubic volume of space bathed in a continuous play of functioning light. All the vast optical effects of Baroque design previously obtained with paint were now possible by means of light.

About 1902, in Germany, Mariano Fortuny y Madrazo developed an elaborate system of soft reflected light using arc lights bounced off coloured silk fabrics. The simulation of natural lighting was remarkable, but the entire mechanism was too bulky and intricate and required the construction of a special theatre. In the course of his experiments, Fortuny evolved a dome-shaped cyclorama, a rear wall surfaced in plaster. Flooded with light, it gave the illusion of infinite space and was the perfect means of simulating spectacular sky and background effects. Because it was dome-shaped, however, it occupied a large amount of stage space and tended to distort optical projections. In modified form, as a curved, hanging cyclorama, it became an indispensable tool of the new stagecraft. Earlier, Sir Henry Irving had used transparent coloured lacquers to coat lamps to produce colour effects, using separate circuits for each colour. Irving was also the first producer to introduce organized light rehearsals in his productions. David Belasco, with his electrician Louis Hartman, developed a standard of realism in stage lighting that anticipated the motion picture and that remains in effect in today's theatre. In their lighting laboratory, Belasco and Hartman developed and refined many new lighting instruments.

Individual sources were developed and used to light the acting areas from above the proscenium as well as from the auditorium.

The first dimmer boards

The earliest types of electrical dimmer board—a centralized control of the intensity of all of the lights—followed the conventions of the gaslight era. Groups of resistance-type dimmers were permanently wired to particular circuits in the footlights or borderlights. The only open or flexible dimmer circuits were the floor pockets (*i.e.,* electrical outlet boxes set in the floor of the stage) used to accommodate a wide variety of floodlights and special effects. Like the pipes and rubber tubing of the gas mains, all electrical circuits were wired solid. The location of the large banks of resistance dimmers in permanent installations of this kind was backstage in the wings and in close communication with the stage manager, who could see what was happening on stage. Later, however, even in large Broadway musicals, the array of portable switchboards may be (and is sometimes) relegated to the cellar or some other place with a scant view of the action on stage.

With the inception of individual spotlights for controlled-area illumination, in contrast to the earlier banks of footlights and borderlights, there arose a need for a flexible patch panel, in which temporary connections of such lights could be easily made and controlled. A group of spotlights could now be placed for the most effective direction, colour, and overall intensity. It became possible, for example, to place several spotlights together to achieve the realistic effect of an actor lighting an oil lamp, upstage right, without flooding the entire set with light.

The first electricity that was commercially available was direct current. For arc lights and resistance dimmers, today or 50 years ago, direct current presents no problems, and many theatres still draw their main supply of electricity from direct current. Most up-to-date theatres have the benefit of alternating current, which allows the use of more advanced dimmers.

Use of colour in stage lighting

The use of colour in stage lighting adds immeasurably to the realistic and atmospheric mood of a setting. Through the use of contrasting colours, the power of light to reinforce plastic qualities may be enhanced, and accents of appropriate intensity may be obtained. Coloured glass is the oldest medium of coloured light still in use in the theatre. As glass does not fade and comes in a variety of pure colours as well as some tints, it may be used in permanent installations for footlights or borderlights. Glass is available in cast roundels or in sheets; in sheet form, it is cut into narrow strips and mounted in holders to protect it as it expands and contracts with changes in heat. On the negative side, glass is heavy, fragile, and expensive, and its colour range is limited.

Gelatin is an expendable colour medium made of purified animal matter that is dyed and dried in sheets. It comes in a wide range of colours, it is cheap, and its light-transmission properties are excellent. Gelatin, however, is affected by moisture, and it deteriorates rapidly under heat. Plastic colour mediums are now available in the same range of colours as gelatin and have the advantages of durability, resistance to water, and strength. Although plastic costs more than gelatin, it lasts about five times longer. Later plastic colour mediums have been made of Mylar, which is virtually indestructible and more resistant to heat than sheet glass, which is much more expensive.

Light sources. The earliest incandescent spotlight used a rather heavy plano-convex lens. The socket assembly with attached reflector moved forward and backward in the housing in relation to the lens and widened or narrowed the spread of the beam of light. As higher wattage lamps appeared, larger diameter lenses were required, and soon they grew too bulky. Larger and more practical spotlights were made possible by the adaptation of the Fresnel, or stepped, lens, a type of lens invented in the 1820s, consisting of thin concentric sections that allow much more efficient use of a light source and, therefore, much smaller lamps. A slightly pebbled effect on the rear of the lens helped give an even, soft light with soft edges. Fresnel spotlights became available in wattages as low as 50 or, with a 24-inch lens, as high as 10,000.

Illumination sources. The refinement of the coiled filament made possible the development of the tubular lamp, which in turn made possible a second type of spotlight, the ellipsoidal reflector spotlight. This type of spotlight uses an ellipsoidal reflector to gather the light at the focal point of the reflector. In front of the reflector, the beam of light is shaped by means of adaptable shutters, an iris, or a predetermined pattern. One or two lenses are used as an objective to project the image. The field of the beam is of even intensity, and a hard or soft edge can be obtained by focus adjustment. The focal lengths of the lenses can be changed if necessary to compensate for the length of throw or to widen or narrow the field. Special wide-angle lenses are useful in projecting patterns, such as leaves, at close distance. Available in a range from 250 to 3,000 watts, the ellipsoidal spotlight is a highly efficient and versatile light source. The larger ellipsoidal spotlight can also be fitted with coloured quartz patterns of any design, from realistic clouds to abstract rotating patterns. Used in combinations at different intensities, a cyclorama can be flooded with light in either bold or subtle patterns.

The ellipsoidal reflector spotlight

Borderlights and striplights are available with wiring for control in three circuits. Older types had reflectors that produced a soft, even blend; later versions use a range of highly efficient sealed-beam lamps, such as the quartz halogen sealed-beam lamps, which are available in a variety of wattages and reflectors—from flood to narrow spot. Mounted in striplights, the sealed-beam lamps have become a versatile and effective source, either for lighting large surfaces or as a strong backlight wash. Television and motion-picture lighting has rapidly developed such sources, which were initiated in the theatre.

Use of floodlights

A floodlight is a refined version of the old bunchlight—a half dozen old filament lamps grouped into a square housing, usually painted white on the inside to serve as a reflector. Later, a single large-wattage lamp replaced such multiple lamps. Floodlights today are usually ellipsoidal reflectors in a wide or narrow beam. The reflectors are mat-finished, accommodate a variety of lamp sizes, and do not require a lens. The quality of light is soft and diffused; it is ideal for a wash of light over a drop or a cyclorama. Usually, more than one circuit is used to achieve a variety of colour changes. Large banks of fluorescent lamps with colour filters are effective in lighting a large and very high cyclorama, but the difficulty in dimming fluorescent sources has limited their use.

The parabolic "beam" projector was developed for outdoor lighting and slightly modified for stage lighting. The familiar carbon arc searchlight, which throws an intense narrow beam of light several miles into the night sky, is a simple parabolic unit without a lens. Such a searchlight consists of a strong pinpoint source (the arc) and a large parabolic reflector of silvered glass. The same simple optical principles were adapted to incandescent lamps for floodlighting the exteriors of buildings. The output is highly efficient, but to reinforce it and control it a lens can be added in front of the source. Used in a phalanx as far offstage as possible, beam projectors can serve as a strong source to give the effect of long rays of sunlight streaking across the stage. A most significant advance was made by hanging beam projectors so that they provided backlighting; this resulted, for the first time, in the actors' being strongly separated from the background, creating an illusion of depth and a haze.

Projections and special effects. A significant amount of lighting equipment has been developed for "special effects." Standard effects include moving clouds, water ripple, fire effects, rain or snow, painted rainbows, and fireworks. For practicality, most special effects are built around a standard spotlight housing. The effect head, containing a painted or photographic transparent disk and the mechanism for revolving it, is placed in front of the spotlight housing. An additional objective lens is used to magnify and focus the image.

The oldest effect projector, dating from the World War I era, is the Linnebach lantern, often called a "scene" projector. It is simple both in principle and in construction. A concentrated light source is placed in a deep black box, and a painted slide is placed on the side of the box left open; since light travels in straight lines, the design painted on the glass is thus projected against a drop onstage, greatly enlarged, at a relatively short distance. Since no lens is used in a Linnebach lantern, the light source must be powerful and concentrated. The design must be simple and bold, for any line narrower than the point source itself will be lost. The overall effect is stylized and borders on the abstract. Rear projection with at least two projectors is required for any ambitious production. Large incandescent lights replaced the original carbon arcs in the Linnebach lantern.

About mid-20th century there was renewed interest in the use of projections. Fortunately, the development of new projection equipment provided a powerful instrument to produce effects not possible before. In the post-World War II years at the music festivals at Bayreuth, Ger., Richard Wagner's grandson Wieland reduced three-dimensional scenic elements to the barest essentials and then flooded the stage with multiple, overlapping projected patterns. In later years more scenic elements were added to give variety of texture and depth to the flow of light and pattern. Still later at the Festspielhaus in Salzburg, Austria, the productions of Wagner's music dramas designed by Gunther Schneider-Siemssen elaborated this concept to achieve even more dramatic and sumptuous productions; he filled the vast, extra-wide stage with patterns of light in depth, softened with scrims (loosely woven meshes that diffuse the light) and translucent drops (backdrops with sections dyed to transmit some light). The Czechoslovakian designer Josef Svoboda did more than any other contemporary designer with "visions in space." For some productions, Svoboda used a direct, journalistic approach, massing three-dimensional screens to create a montage effect with slides and film. Polyvision, a production conceived and executed by Svoboda for the Czech pavilion at the 1967 international exhibition at Montreal, was a brilliant multimedia experience. In his other productions, which were equally stylized but more indirect and abstract, he used alternating surfaces of scrim and scenic elements to catch the patterned light, cast complex shadows, and float in depth before a seemingly infinite background.

Svoboda's productions

Innovative contributions to lighting and the use of projections were also made in dance. The American Alwin Nikolais made very original use of dancers, costumes, light, and projections to form moving geometric and abstract designs. At times, the moving bodies of the dancers become the screen for the projections. The Robert Joffrey Ballet, which is also based in New York City, in its production *Astarte,* created a unique combination of film and slides on a moving, pulsating screen.

Lighting controls. The dream of a practical system of remote control of lighting has always tantalized designers. Relays for remote switching have been commonplace for years. Motor-driven dimmers have proved practical for controlling auditorium lighting but for stage lighting are too cumbersome, expensive, and limited in speed control and are unpredictable in responding to changes. Banks of resistance and transformer switchboards were too bulky to be installed in a light booth at the rear of the auditorium with a clear view of the stage.

The first primitive but successful remote-controlled dimmer was used in 1890 but not perfected until later; it used a reactor coil operating on a relatively small amount of direct current to control a huge amount of alternating current.

Remote control became a reality largely as the result of the development by George Izenour of Yale University in 1948 of a dimmer using the thyratron, a type of electron tube. His concept brought continuous and instantaneous control to remote systems for the first time. In addition to its simplicity of operation, the development gave the lighting designer the facility for an "infinite" combination of preset cues. It also became practicable to install the control console at a vantage point in the auditorium from which the lighting designer (or operator) could see every nuance of lighting on stage.

Meanwhile, transformer manufacturers achieved a major breakthrough in design with the development of new magnetic alloys. The result was a reactor with great efficiency and speed. This new reactor, combined with the silicon rectifier, another post-World War II development, resulted in a device called a magnetic amplifier, which has no moving parts or tubes and can control large amounts of alternating current with no time lag.

Tube manufacturers, meanwhile, were furthering the development of the transistor, namely, the silicon-controlled rectifier, or SCR, a transistor-like device that can handle heavy currents and perform in the same manner as the thyratron tube but with the advantage that it is compact, lightweight, inexpensive, efficient, and long-lasting. Control consoles using all three types of dimmers are in current use.

The design of lighting control boards is no longer a matter only of electrical engineering, in which the only concerns are engineering requirements or code specifications. Previously, the lighting designer had to make the most of whatever the engineers had given him. Now the remote lighting-control console gives the lighting designer a flexible, artistic tool. Freed from the limitations of the mechanical controls and of the personnel who would operate them, the lighting artist can concentrate on the execution of his concept. No longer is there any reason for the mechanical limitations to interfere with the lighting.

Figure 24: Stage design by Josef Svoboda for the 1958 production of *August Sunday* by the National Theatre, Prague, showing his use of patterned lighting to achieve special designs.

Advances in stage lighting

The biggest advance in stage lighting control in recent years has been the ability to record instantly and recall on cue the entire contents of a stage picture. A video display unit can present the information on the lighting state for any cue in an easily readable form. The present systems work on a principle of one dimmer for each light in order to eliminate cross patching of circuits. In the previous generation of preset boards, each lantern was equipped with a number of dimmers and several cues could be preset. On cue the board cut from one set of dimmers to another to effect the change. The memory system board is much more flexible and is probably capable of even further development and sophistication. The development of memory system boards and new lighter weight dimmer packs are a material help to touring.

Lighting design. In the era of painted wings and drops, the standard illumination was an even, flat wash from footlights and borderlights. Architecture and furniture, including tables and chairs, were painted into the background with heavy shadows and exaggerated perspective. The actors had to resort to grotesquely heavy makeup to convey any facial expression, while their very presence (and every movement) was visually in conflict with the forced perspective of the painted scenery. By contrast, the impressive effects of modern lighting made it seem almost limitless in its possibilities. Borrowing effects from Rembrandt and other painters, the theatre designer began to "paint with light"—putting light where he wanted it and taking it away from where he did not want it. Thus, romantic effects were born, such as that of the lone figure in a shaft of searing light, isolated by darkness. The first requisite of stage lighting, however, is visibility. Good illumination provides plasticity and modeling of the actors and of the inanimate objects. Superior lighting is orchestrated to underline the development of the drama.

Many plays permit no approach other than realism, which must be achieved by suggestion. Nature provides the model. On a cloudy day, the overcast sky diffuses the direct sunlight and produces a soft, shadowless light of low intensity and cool colour. Intense "sunlight" on stage and the attendant light of the bright sky together produce reflected light that diffuses or fills in shadows, while the ambient light of the stage "Moon" reflected from sky, trees, and buildings is too weak to wash out the shadows. So, by means of the direction, diffusion, and intensity of light, as well as its colour, it is possible to suggest time, place, and season.

The means of suggesting natural lighting indoors are more arbitrary. The simulated sky or sunlight seen through a door or window—a scenic element provided by the dramatist and the designer—is essential to indicate the time of day or night. To render the feeling of bright daylight flooding a room, the strong motivating light (*i.e.,* light that suggests the direction of its source) must be supplemented with additional light from other directions for adequate illumination. If only a sliver of sunlight creeps through a parted curtain in a dark room as the scene begins, the mood may be retained as the scene progresses as the illumination of important areas is slowly increased. Artificial light indoors is easier to suggest because it more closely approaches the normal quality of stage lighting. Actual light fixtures are used on stage to suggest the sources of the light, and opaque shades can be used on some of these fixtures so that they cast actual patches of light against walls and furniture. The exteriors seen through doors and windows are darkened and different in colour from their appearance in a brightly sunlit scene. The walls fall off in shadow even though the general illumination is more diffused and even than in daylight. Light serves as a unifying medium for the stage composition. It is a mobile and changing accent that reinforces the action, sustains the mood, and focuses the attention of the audience. Light and shade, brightness and contrast, define the size and shape of objects, but it is colour that creates emotional response, mood, and atmosphere.

Use of back-lighting

The dynamic potential of lighting is best realized when the changes of light underscore and propel the development of the drama. The first real attempt at creating space and a real haze on stage (in a depth of 30 feet) came into being with the use of backlighting—light emanating from the rear of the stage rather than the front—which made the actors appear to be pulled away from the background (Figure 25). At first, parabolic beam projectors were used to achieve this effect, then ellipsoidal spotlights, and later, in some instances, sealed-beam parabolic reflector lamps. The ellipsoidal reflector spotlights afford the best control and the least spill. The beam projector may be deployed in a battery offstage to create the illusion of paths of sunlight or moonlight or a strong sidelight or crosslight. For strong crosslight, clusters of low-wattage units were supplanted by powerful ellipsoidal spotlights, hung low. With the addition of lamps attached to the auditorium's boxes, or box booms, besides the lamps already on the balcony rail or ceiling coves, modern lighting began to take shape. The open stage of the musical and dance furthered the development of effective lighting.

The square pattern of modern lighting

In bold outline, modern lighting can be described in terms of a square consisting of a lucid pattern of strong

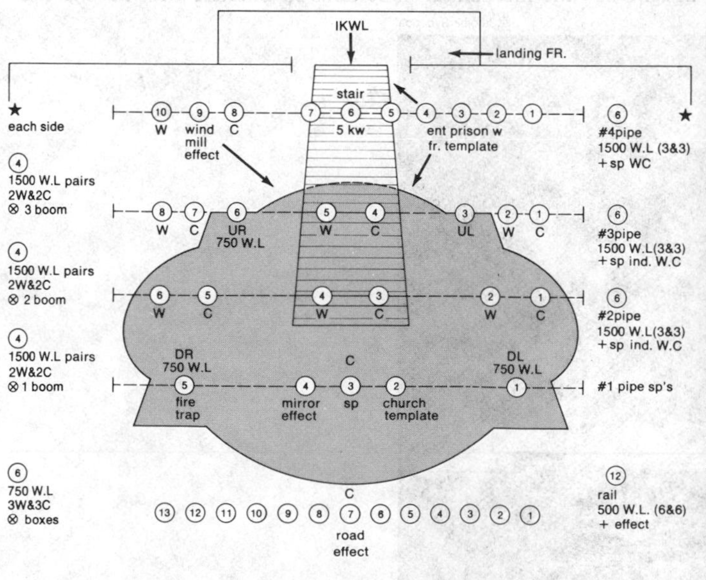

(Right) Alfred DeSio

Figure 25: *Modern lighting.*
(Left) Light plan for *Man of La Mancha.* (Right) Scene in the New York production showing the use of backlighting.

backlight, paths of strong crosslight, and the necessary fill light from the front from the boxes and first pipe (*i.e.,* lights hanging from a horizontal pipe just inside the proscenium) on stage, plus special lights as needed. Richer colours are used in the backlighting and crosslighting. Lights creating warm and cool effects are wired to circuits that allow them to be controlled right, centre, and left stage. The crosslighting coming from offstage and from the box booms is usually less saturated in colour. The lights on the balcony rail give a pale wash—passive illumination to produce visibility without destroying the sharp modeling of the backlighting and sidelighting. Special lights, in colour or clear, cut through particular areas from the box booms and the pipes on stage.

When box sets began to go out of style, and suggestive sets, skeletal fragments without ceiling and walls, were introduced, the necessary lighting technique was already within reach in the layouts for musicals. There was need for more special lights, different circuiting, softer colours, more pattern projections, and more intricate, overlapping changes of light. The pattern of back, sides, and front, however, still holds; it is a clear-cut, three-dimensional approach, with distinct functions meshing into a controlled pattern.

For the most part, ellipsoidal reflector spotlights are used to cover acting areas from all locations. Fresnel spotlights are used for area washes or to accent plastic scenery elements. The appearance of scenery as it is illuminated by the lighting intended for the acting areas is totally unpredictable; it is necessary to provide separate blending or accent lighting for most plastic scenery. Patterned projections, such as leaves or abstract patterns, may be used in wide-angle, ellipsoidal spotlights to project on scenery that is solid or even made of gauze.

The three-dimensional approach to lighting developed within the confines of the proscenium stage; it is also valid for the thrust stage or arena theatre. For theatre in the round, the predominant angles for lighting tend to be sharper and also to be steeper, to avoid spill into the audience area that would disturb the spectators. The ellipsoidal reflector spotlight is used for all acting areas, and an added high hat (a hollow tube that extends six to 12 inches) will confine unwanted spill as well as hide the lens and colour frame.

In simple language, lighting is a matter of hanging the right instrument in the right place and focusing on the right target. Stage lighting cannot be mastered except through the observation and experience that are necessary to learn the practical and aesthetic functions of light. It is essential to know the physical characteristics of different light sources and how and when to use them to best advantage. It is also mandatory to learn the complexities of control and how to build lighting changes. Stage lighting must be more than good illumination. Light must be used as a subtle flux, exerting a subconscious influence that unifies all the media of the theatre.

The creative concept formed for lighting a production requires that the essential qualities of the play be understood and absorbed. The theme or main line of the script may suggest an overriding motif: enervating heat, damp clamminess, dappled sunlight, cold penetrating north light, a feeling of being in limbo or underwater. The final choice must satisfy the particular qualities of the production and the concepts of the playwright, director, and actors, as well as the designer. Attending run-throughs in the final period of rehearsals reinforces previous impressions and suggests refinements in the rhythmic changes of light required. The actors' performances suggest lighting changes that can enhance the emotional range of the total performance.

(Ra.Ho.)

STAGE MACHINERY

In the modern theatre, a variety of mechanisms are used to erect, position, and manipulate scenery. These devices fall into three categories: hoists, lifts, and horizontal drives.

Use of hoists

Hoists are used for flying (*i.e.,* raising or lowering) scenery up to or down from the stage penthouse; lifts are used to bring up scenic elements from beneath the stage floor; and horizontal drives are used to slide platforms, flats, and large properties from the wings onto the visible part of the stage or from one area of the stage to another.

Hoists are the most common type of mechanism in the theatre, and there are three types: counterbalance, electrical, and fluid drive. The simplest method of hoisting is by counterbalancing, and there are two types: the hemp system and the iron-counterweight system. In the hemp system, sandbags and iron ingots are used as a counterbalance. Four to six lines are attached to a batten; each line passes over its associated "loft block" and then goes to the master headblock sheave. The iron-counterweight system is similar except that the lines are made of wire rope and the operating rope is not directly attached to the hoisting line. Instead, it is a fixed system, held between the master headblock sheave and a fixed-tension sheave. For counterweighting, there is an arbor or carriage in which the iron weights are placed. Finally, there is a lock–rail combination to ensure the safe use of the counterweights.

In an electrically powered stage hoist system, electricity may provide only the pulling power while still requiring counterbalancing (electrical counterweight-assisted hoists), or it may provide the lifting ability and the force needed to counterbalance (pure-power hoists). There are two types of electrical counterweight-assisted hoists, traction drive and linkage drive. In the traction-drive system, the hoisting line-counterweight system is not directly coupled to the electric motor drive, and slippage may occur during acceleration and deceleration of the payload. It varies according to velocity and the weight of the payload. Consequently, traction-drive hoists are utilized only when a relatively constant weight is lifted at a constant velocity, such as the asbestos curtains, light bridges, and orchestra shells. The linkage drive is similar to the traction-drive hoist, except that the hoisting lines are attached directly to the motor.

The second category of electric hoist is the pure-power type, in contrast to the counterweight-assisted type. It consists of a motor (usually placed on a gridiron), a brake, a gear reducer, and a drum around which several hoisting lines wind. At the Metropolitan Opera House in New York City, there are 110 motors linked into a single console that can be run by a single operator.

The third type is the fluid-drive system, in which an electric power unit is used to run a fluid piston, which in turn moves the hoisting lines. Advantages to this system are that the electric generator does not have to be physically near the fluid drive, so the system is virtually noiseless, and that the operator may divide the power between any number of pistons, a feat not possible with an electric motor alone.

Use of lifts

Lifts are used in the theatre to move platforms, actors, scenery, and other production elements above or below the stage floor. In contrast to the hoist, which is supported by the over-stage structure, the lift is supported and guided by the stage floor or the cellar floor below the stage. The two general types of lifts are the architecturally integrated and the temporary production apparatus.

Architecturally integrated lifts must be designed in accordance with local building-safety codes: in New York City, for instance, only two types can be built into a theatre. One of these, the direct-plunger lift, is hydraulically driven, using a piston attached to a portion of the stage floor. The piston operates under hydraulic pressure (like the pure-power hoist) and is expanded and collapsed to elevate the associated platform. The other type, the screw-actuated lift, is either electrically or hydraulically driven and coupled to a vertical screw through a nut in which the upper end of the screw is connected to a portion of the stage floor.

The layout and installation of permanent architecturally integrated lifts must be carefully determined; the frequency of use and the type of events to be accommodated must be envisioned, along with the attendant inflexibility of the permanent mechanization of the stage floor. In general, architecturally integrated lifts are successfully employed where they are designed to meet the specific production needs of a permanent resident company.

Use of horizontal drives

Horizontal drives are used to rotate, propel, and project scenery, actors, properties, etc., from offstage areas onto the acting area. To meet audience demand for rapidly changing scenery, designers often utilize a system of horizontally moving platforms. Although the articulation of horizontal motion on the stage is unlimited, there are several established configurations that are easily identifiable. These include the wagon, in which scenery is built on a low platform mounted on casters so that it can be quickly rolled onstage and offstage; the jackknife stage, similar to the wagon except that it is anchored at one corner from which it pivots onstage and offstage; and the revolve or turntable, in which several settings are built on a huge circular platform, or turntable, which is revolved so that only the appropriate setting may be seen through the proscenium. In each of these, the scenery may be changed when the unit is offstage and then rolled back on. Treadmills and revolving segments are also used. (W.Cr./C.Ba.)

COSTUME DESIGN

Theatrical costumes are neither historical nor contemporary; they elaborate a style and convention of their own. Their success in any production depends in large measure on the designer's ability to understand and interpret the director's production concept. The spirit of the production and the director's aims may call for special emphasis on certain characteristics in clothing. Designs may be copies of period costumes or may attempt only to evoke a period.

Museums and other repositories of the decorative and literary arts are rich sources of inspiration. Since the subject of theatrical costume design is so closely related to the art and history of dress, the reader's attention is called to the article DRESS AND ADORNMENT, in which these topics are treated comprehensively.

Historical development. *Classical theatrical costume.* Theatrical costumes were an innovation of Thespis, in Greece in the 6th century BC, and theatrical costumes are still called "the robes of Thespis." Athenians spent lavishly on the production and costumes at the annual drama contests since each poet was given a wealthy citizen, the *chorēgos,* who, encouraged by the honour of a separate state impresario's prize, tended to make the event a demonstration of his spending power.

The earliest tragedies were played in long, rich robes similar to those worn by the priests of Dionysus. To increase the height and importance of the principal actors, Aeschylus introduced the buskin, Asiatic elevated boots, called *kothornoi* in Greek, which became one of the chief characteristics of the Greek tragic actor. The soles increased in thickness according to the status of the wearer. To balance his height, padding often was used to add bulk to the actor's stature. Members of the chorus did not wear these boots so that they could dance with ease. The performers were clad in stage tunics, chitons, which were long-sleeved, high-girdled, and elaborately embellished, as were their long and short cloaks (himations and chlamyses). Aeschylus was renowned for the brilliant mounting and costuming of his tragedies, and by the time of his death, in 456 BC, a traditional tragic costume had evolved. Each costume was in a symbolic colour.

By courtesy of the Hermitage, Leningrad

Figure 26: Scene from a burlesque showing Heracles tempting Apollo. Actors wear short tunics and tubular pants of Greek Old Comedy. Detail from a phlyax vase in the Hermitage, Leningrad.

Greek masks

The most important feature of the Greek costume was the mask, which indicated the character's age, sex, station, and customary mood. The masks were made of linen, cork, or wood and were skillfully carved and painted. Their funnel-shaped mouths are thought to have acted as megaphones to amplify the voice. In his *Onomasticon,* Julius Pollux, a Greek writer of the 2nd century AD, gives a detailed account of the special features accorded to each character. He enumerates 30 masks used in tragedy and lists the characteristics of the comedy series, which are particularly exaggerated and grotesque. The *onkos,* a high ornate headdress, crowned some masks, adding height and thus importance to the wearer.

In the Doric mimes and Old Comedies, the upper class characters wore stage chitons and cloaks, and the lower classes and slaves wore short tunics, revealing pendant phalli. These character tunics were often worn under light-fitting vests and over grotesque padding of torso and buttocks (Figure 26).

Mimic horses, satyrs, bird figures, and other animal imitations were much in evidence. Aristophanes, in *The Wasps, The Birds,* and *The Frogs,* calls for all manner of such figures and clothing. Actors performed in skins and wore horses' heads, birdlike visors, and mock wings.

In the later comedy of Menander, the phallus and mythological elements were abandoned, for his intention was to represent urban life, and the costumes worn reflected this intention. Masks became more stereotyped; they were used over and over again for character parts in different plays. Colour symbolism still held great importance.

Roman drama had its indigenous roots in the Etruscan mimetic dances. Mime without masks, together with acrobatic dancing, became a favourite part of the day's entertainment at the games or circuses. Plays, too, were among the diversions; to satisfy the crowd's taste for realism and sensation, legions of spectacularly dressed soldiers were introduced to the tragedies. Costumes for tragedy were modeled on Greek styles; by Roman times the name *cothurnus* (from *kothornoi*) had come to designate the tragic genre itself. Kings and queens in tragedies wore appropriate padding, tall wigs, and sleeved *syrma* (the robe corresponding to the chiton). Bands of bright hues decorated the costumes of happy characters, and gray, green, or blue those of fugitives. Gods and goddesses were distinguished by their insignia; seers were clad in woolen garments over a shorter, less full *syrma;* and huntsmen rolled a purple shawl around their left arms. Slaves wore leather jackets and light breeches or braids indicating their barbarian origin. In the *fabula palliata,* Roman comedies on Greek subjects and based on Greek models, actors wore chitons and the pallium, a cloak resembling the himation. In tales of Rome based on Greek models, and *fabula togata,* actors were costumed in the mantle and toga. The heroes of plays dealing with Roman history, called *fabulae praetextatae,* wore togas with the *praetexta* decoration indicating magistrates.

The *fabula Atellana,* rustic plays originating in southern Italy, were given both public and private performances. In the homes of patricians, young noblemen often took the parts of the standard characters—the bragging, greedy Maccus, the stupid Bucco, the foolish miser Pappus—wearing masks to disguise their identities. Their masks, known as *personae,* were decorated with hair; they were not worn by professional actors until introduced by the actor Quintus Roscius in the 1st century BC. Before their introduction, wigs (*galeri*) were worn. Also, Italian comedians wore a flat slipper called the *succus.*

Roman mime costume

The garment peculiar to mime productions was a gay coloured patchwork jacket called *centunculus,* and this name became applied to mime actors in general. At Corneto, a tomb painting depicts Stupidus (the fool of the mimes) wearing another coat covered with coloured patches, a tall pointed cap decorated with a tassel, and a square, short cloak known as a *ricinium.* Because of this garment, the mime players were also known as *riciniati.* The producers of the mimes also provided their performers with gigantic phalli. "The mimes," it was said, "pulled down the gods and heroes from on high and provided them with phalli."

As drama in Rome declined, the mimes introduced plays on the theme of the oldish cuckold and the frail and plotting lover, which became most bawdy and obscene during the 6th century AD, as did the pantomimes featuring lavish licentious entertainments. Such entertainment continued to be presented until the fall of the Roman Empire later in that century. Through the Early Middle Ages, jugglers, fools, and small mime troupes roamed through Europe, but a record of organized drama has yet to be found.

Medieval costume. Originally, mystery plays were performed before the altar, with the actors, priests, and clerics wearing church vestments. The miracle plays, which retold incidents in the lives of saints, were also originally played by clerics and actors. Inventories were kept of garments made and bought, and these lists indicate that Adam and Eve were clad in close-fitting white leather, God in bishop's robes, and Jesus in a simple white robe. Cain, Abel, Joseph, Lazarus, and other biblical characters would appear in contemporary clothes, hoods, pourpoints or doublets, or loose gowns. A female character was indicated by the simple addition of a kerchief on the head. During the 12th century, when the performances moved outside the church, priestly vestments were still the main costumes.

When European craft guilds became responsible for the mounting and dressing of these productions, their scenic plans became ornate and ambitious, and the early simplicity was lost. The exotic robes, angels with gilded limbs, halos, and ornate wings may be seen in the paintings of the 15th-century Flemish masters Lucas van Leyden, Memling, and Van Eyck. Satan and his devils enjoyed great popularity with the large audiences. Their grotesque masks, lashing tails, fangs, and snouts in lurid blacks, reds, and blues are well recorded by artists of the period. There is a large collection of devil masks preserved at the Tiroler Landesmuseum Ferdinandeum in Innsbruck, Austria.

In the morality plays, concerned with allegorical subjects, that became popular toward the end of the 14th century, costumes personified the virtues and vices, life and death, and similar abstractions. The Bible stories and morality dramas were also taken through the streets on two-story pageant carts; these processions of gorgeously dressed groups and tableaux can be seen in 15th-century paintings such as Piero di Cosimo's "Triumph of Theseus and Ariadne" and Botticelli's "Triumph of Chastity."

Renaissance costume. From the early 14th century, in addition to religious performances, secular theatre also developed in the form of popular celebrations, spectacles, royal and ambassadorial entries, weddings, and other lavish entertainments that surround the royal courts. A monarch entering a town or dominion would do so with a large entourage in full pomp and heraldic dress. These entrances included a series of stops at stages placed at various intervals en route. *Tableaux vivant* and mimes were performed in costumes similar to those worn in the mystery and morality plays. With the gradual decline of church power and the revival of classic ideas, Renaissance designers found their inspiration in the myths and legends of Greece and Rome.

Costumes of royal celebrations

Countries and designers competed in the sumptuousness of their displays. The progresses in England, *entrées* in France, *trionfi* in Italy were based on the triumphal processions of the ancient world. The monarch or emperor was glorified as the hero, and his entourage and vassals appeared in semiclassical grandeur. There were floats of allegorical figures and legions of splendour such as Caesar had never dreamed.

The Italian designers, who included artists as eminent as Leonardo da Vinci, led the field. Costume plates of specific festivals indicate the awe-inspiring splendour of these occasions.

At court, the tragic, comic, and satiric dramas of classical theatre were revived, with the addition of entertaining entr'actes. From these descended the intermezzi—pantomimes that included song and dance. Again, the designers wished to appeal to the eye of the Renaissance public. The designer in charge of theatrical productions for the court of Mantua in the mid-16th century explained in his treatise on stagecraft that the Italian object was to captivate and charm the audience:

> I tell you especially that I make efforts to dress the actors always in as noble a fashion as is possible for me, but in such a manner that there is a sense of proportion among them, in view of the fact that the rich costume . . . particularly in these times when pomp is at its highest peak, adds much reputation and beauty to comedies, and even more to tragedies. I would not hesitate to dress a servant in velvet or colored satin, as long as his master's costume were embroidered or decorated with gold, so rich that there would be maintained the proper proportion between them. . . . I do my utmost to dress the actors very differently from one another, and this is of great help, both in adding beauty and in facilitating the understanding of the plot.

In 1589 the sophisticated Florentine court produced an intermezzo called "Harmony of the Spheres," a spectacular type of masque, with music, that was the immediate forerunner of opera. Etchings of the Grand Ducal fetes in Florence of 1606, 1608, 1615, and 1616 show groups of dancers in towering plumed classical helmets, Roman costume, and cuirass (body armour) worn over doublets, with Roman labels hung from the cuirass, over breeches and hose, to cover the thighs. The Renaissance developed these labels into an exaggerated ornate skirt and named it the *tonneler.* Each item of costume was decorated with a profusion of curved ornaments, flowers, vines, and animal and human forms, suggestive of Baroque design.

Strongly influenced by these Florentine specialists during a visit to Italy, Inigo Jones transformed English court masques and entertainments in the early part of the 17th century. The Duke of Devonshire's archives at Chatsworth preserve his designs. Through him, English designs followed the Italian pattern: breastplates molded to the body, plumes, helmets, and various Roman kilts mixed with modified elements of contemporary dress. Ladies' costumes followed the dress of the period more closely but strove for a looseness and for the transparency of fabric typical of classical dress. Decolletage and low-cut bodices were much in evidence, with bosoms often veiled with gauze. The cost of these costumes was borne by the wearers, the lords and ladies of the court. There seemed at times no limit to their embroidered, bejeweled luxury and fine headpieces.

Early English costumes

Little pictorial evidence of the first public theatres in England survives. It is known, however, that the best part of the actors' wardrobes were gifts from wealthy patrons. One drawing of Shakespeare's *Titus Andronicus* dated 1595 shows contemporary costume mixed with *costume à la romaine* similar in design to the courtly work of Inigo Jones. Mixtures of styles and periods were accepted by the audiences. Certain famous characters such as Shakespeare's Sir John Falstaff became identified with a particular type of dress; a sketch that Inigo Jones made of Sir William Davenant in *The Temple of Love,* produced in 1635, was inscribed: "a roabe of russet Girt low w[t] a great belley . . . the sleeues shorte . . . buskines to shew a great swolen legge . . . a great head and balde. Like a S[r] Jon fall staff."

In Italy, the commedia dell'arte presented a multiplicity of character and types. Their fine costumes evolved from garments representing different Italian provinces and rustic personalities and gradually became stylized, subject to the dictates of changing taste. To make the costumes decorative or funny there were exaggerations in form and colour. The characters of the lovers appeared in contemporary street clothes, and comic personages in curious or grotesque garb with leather half-masks (Figure 27). They were ideal theatre clothes for they identified the characters, allowed complete freedom for movement and acrobatic dancing, and charmed the spectator with their amusing devices, patterns, and colour motifs. A typical character, Arlecchino, originally dressed in shreds and patches, emerged by the 17th century in a suit of red, blue, and green triangles arranged symmetrically and joined together with yellow braid. One hundred years later, the triangles became diamonds, and his soft cap was exchanged for a pointed one. Now as Harlequin he still appears as a central character in English pantomime, carrying his original

Figure 27: Typical costume worn by players in commedia dell'arte. Anonymous German engraving of Arlecchino, early 18th century. In the Victoria and Albert Museum, London.

By courtesy of the Victoria and Albert Museum, London

wooden sword and wearing his black mask. A fine pictorial record of the commedia characters may be seen in the works of the 17th-century French artists Jacques Callot and Antoine Watteau.

The commedia dell'arte performed throughout Europe and was especially popular at the French court. Molière's company also toured France in improvised farces based on the style of the commedia. Actors in his comedies played in contemporary dress, but they also performed with the King and court in brilliantly dressed spectaculars at Versailles. Texts were by Molière, music by Jean-Baptiste Lully, and costumes and decor by Jean Berain.

The Restoration of the English monarchy in 1660 led to the opening of theatres again, and the great innovation was the introduction of actresses. Talented, confident, and flamboyant ladies replaced the Elizabethan boy actors. Records indicate that "splendidly clothed" persons lent costumes, and wardrobe keepers now aided players in selecting from available stock. The ladies chose the gown most becoming and elaborate. No attempt was made at character dressing or historical accuracy.

The introduction of actresses

Costume in Baroque opera and ballet. A galaxy of specialists joined the courts of Louis XIII and Louis XIV, with Giacomo Torelli, the chief originator of Baroque theatre, arriving from Venice. This monumental scenic style included magnificent colonnades, temples, palaces, and scenes so lavish that only the great ruling houses could afford them. Designers such as Torelli brought great prestige to their patrons. An outburst of Baroque opulence bore witness to the power and splendour of the Sun King. In France in the early 17th century, the designer Daniel Rabel worked inventively, producing many witty and droll effects and costumes of grotesque conception. Burlesque costume had found its way to amuse the court.

Henri Gissey and the great Jean Berain were attached to the Royal Cabinet of Louis XIV. Gissey is most famous for his celebrated Carrousel (1662), a horse spectacular never since surpassed in its magnificence—500 noblemen in plumed regalia escorted by a greater number of elaborately dressed attendants. Costumes represented different nations, each having a particular colour scheme: the Romans were in red and gold led by the King; the Turks in black and yellow; the Indians in white and gold; the Americans in green and gold. The marvelous scene played in front of the Louvre was indeed the grandest fantasy in costuming, with both horses and riders decorated in full Baroque trappings.

Chroniclers record gorgeous costumes appearing in ballet, opera, and dramatic offerings; gold brocades covered with lace, diamonds, emeralds, ribbons, and immense trains graced the stages of France. The French surpassed the Italians in their opera costumes, which were richer than any elsewhere. In the designs of Jean Berain there is a homogeneity of style that is the mark of a great master. In 1680 women first appeared on the operatic stage. Berain's costumes for them were serious and noble in style, based on contemporary court dress. Their tight bodices and flared basque shirts had decorative overskirts with trains; they followed an almost uniform silhouette. The headdress, also carefully designed, was a formal arrangement of feathers or lace. Male garments were in the Roman style, the tunic fitting tightly to the chest, worn with *tonneler* (short skirt), high boots, and cape. To avoid monotony, Berain devised an amazing variety of ingenious trimmings—embroideries, fringes, slashings, puffs and paddings, inlaid ornamental motifs, pastes, and semiprecious stones to punctuate every small decorative panel and part (Figure 28). Scaly bodies, bejeweled ones, serrated leaves—every elegant or fantastic theatrical device was used to create a sophisticated ensemble. Berain coordinated all aspects of scenic decor in an equally in-

Berain's costumes

By courtesy of (left) Victoria and Albert Museum, London, (right) Bibliotheque de l'Arsenal, Paris

Figure 28: (Left) Jean Berain's design for the costume of a female dancer with castanets, 1685. In the Victoria and Albert Museum, London. (Right) Costume design for a French peasant girl by Jean-Baptiste Martin, early 18th century. In the Bibliothèque de l'Arsenal, Paris.

dustrious way and as a decorative artist dominated French and European taste and costume design.

After Berain died in 1711, the sumptuous Baroque of the early years of Louis XIV declined. Berain's son Jean succeeded his father as court designer and carefully documented his father's drawings, which are now kept at the Musée de L'Opéra and at the Victoria and Albert Museum in London.

By 1721 Claude Gillot's designs for the ballet *Les Éléments* showed a great change in taste. Heavy fabrics and embroideries used by Berain were replaced by lighter, more delicate weights and appliqués. Ladies' costume, following the caprices of the contemporary modes, included a panier. Peasant and rustic characters began to appear and were most popular with the court, in beribboned garments of pastel satins and silks. Extensive records of these costumes exist in the form of engravings.

Costume of the 18th and 19th centuries. Jean-Baptiste Martin, who was appointed designer for the Paris Opéra in 1748, devised decorative and amusing Rococo variations for the male dancer's traditional costume. Incas, Africans, Chinese, and Mexicans graced his ballets, and under his direction the *tonneler* took on an elliptical shape.

All the elegance and sophistication seen in Rococo court circles of Louis XV were brought to the stage by Martin's successor, Louis-René Boquet. His designs were theatricalized versions of the new fashionable silhouette. Boquet clothes were delicate, artificial, and pale in tone, trimmed with garlands and Rococo finery. All Europe imitated the French ideas, the English and German facsimiles without Boquet's innate good taste.

Denis Diderot wrote in 1758 of the current fashions in the French theatre:

> Ostentation spoils everything.... Wealth has too many caprices: it can dazzle the eye, but not touch the heart. Beneath the garment that is overloaded with gilding, I never see more than a rich man, and it is a *man* I look for....
>
> Comedy ought to be played in informal dress. On the stage it is not necessary to be either more or less dressed up than one is at home....
>
> The more serious the play, the more austerity there must be in costume....
>
> What expense were not our actors put to for the production of *l'Orphelin de la Chine*? How much has it not cost them to rob this work of part of its effect?

Historical authenticity of 18th-century French costumes

In 1755 the great French actors Henri-Louis Lekain and Mlle Clairon, who were also bent on more simplicity and historical accuracy, dressed Voltaire's play *L'Orphelin de la Chine* without the hoops or overskirts of currently fashionable dress, while the men appeared dressed as Tartars and Chinamen. In 1789 the French tragedian François-Joseph Talma provoked a scandal by appearing in Voltaire's *Brutus* in a severely simple toga appropriate to the ancient Roman setting of the play.

In England David Garrick abandoned heroic Roman garments in favour of realistic, contemporary dress, which he designed himself to insure the simplicity he desired (Figure 29). The Irish actor Charles Macklin was first to play Shakespeare in authentic "ancient dress" when he appeared on the stage in 1773 as Macbeth in a Highland military habit.

By courtesy of the trustees of the British Museum; photograph, J.R. Freeman & Co. Ltd.

Figure 29: David Garrick costumed for the role of Richard III; engraving by William Hogarth, 1746. In the British Museum.

Public knowledge of historical costume was increasing, though some critics disapproved, believing it weakened the plot. The thirst for historical accuracy won the day, in part because of the efforts of its major champion, the 19th-century playwright and antiquary James Robinson Planché. A playbill of a Planché production of 1824 read:

> Shakespeare's Tragedy of King John with an attention to Costume never equalled on the English Stage. Every Character will appear in the precise HABIT OF THE PERIOD, the whole of the Dresses and Decorations being executed from indisputable Authorities.... King John's Effigy in Worcester Cathedral... Queen Elinor's Effigy in the Abbey of Fontevraud.... Illuminated Mss in the British Museum, Bodleian and Bennet College Libraries... &c.

Planché's success amply reimbursed the management for the enormous expenditures required to make even the meanest extra's garments authentic. Correct costumes became the order of the day. The actor-manager Charles Kean splendidly mounted a series of Shakespearean productions in London in the 1850s. In Germany, August Wilhelm Iffland's productions closely followed the same reforms, and costume designers were urged to emulate the past.

Dance costume

Dancers, too, wished to be liberated from the pannier and *tonneler.* In *Pygmalion,* a ballet of her own composition, Marie Sallé danced in London in 1734 dressed only in a muslin robe like that of a Greek statue; she wore no panniers, petticoat, or bodice, and her hair was loose and without ornament. The French ballet master Jean-Georges Noverre had advocated drastic reform in dance dress as early as 1760. He proposed to put his dancers in simple draperies of contrasting colours, worn in such a manner to reveal the figure in movement. Both male and female dancers became increasingly impatient with the hampering Rococo conventions; and as dancing technique grew even more intricate, designers prepared innovations that anticipated the general development in fashion. By the end of the 18th century, every woman had abandoned her panniers and was "dressed only in a single muslin robe."

Civil codes at the start of the 19th century greatly aided those who would reform theatrical costume. The fashion for classic robes and tunics modeled on Greek and Roman patterns took to the streets; the high-heeled shoe was replaced by a flat slipper.

Leading French ballet designers of the 19th century were Auguste Garneray and Hippolyte Lecomte. The former's work shows ingenuity in adapting contemporary dress to suggest different lands and other periods. The latter was originally a painter of historical episodes; accuracy rather than imagination is the distinguishing quality of his designs. In 1832 the influence of the Romantic period was first seen in ballet with a production of *La Sylphide.* Eugène Lami designed for Marie Taglioni, the greatest dancer of her day, a muslin dress, an ethereal costume that became the new uniform of the classical dancer. This design is still worn today.

Opera and dramatic productions followed Planché's regard for period and regional detail. Unfortunately, the elaborate stage settings and the costumes were seldom coordinated successfully. This led the Duke of Saxe-Meiningen to design his own productions, as he wished to achieve an integrated style. He was the first of the directors who controlled all aspects of production. His example has been followed by the most prominent directors of the 20th century.

Amid spectacular scenery, large ensembles danced and mimed in fanciful versions of contemporary and historical dress in the ballet-extravaganzas of the 1880s (forerunners of the Folies-Bergères revues of Paris) that played at La Scala in Milan and the London Alhambra. The ingenious designer C. Wilhelm (original name C. Pitcher) translated insects, flowers, birds, and reptiles into dance costumes. The main interest, however, lay in framing the female figure, and most of the costumes were designed to reveal as much as the law permitted.

20th-century costume. At the turn of the century, the theories of Appia and Craig called for symbolism and voiced a strong reaction against the naturalism of Meiningen and the Moscow Art Theatre. Appia advocated that stage costume should evoke and suggest, but never copy historical lines.

A painters' theatre arose after Diaghilev's presentation of the Ballet Russe in 1909 in Paris. The brilliant palettes and well-coordinated decors (of Bakst, Benois, and Roerich) were praised. Nathalie Goncharova's design for *Le Coq d'or* in 1914 was unprecedented in its use of vivid colours, chiefly shades of red, yellow, and orange, with other colours for discordant emphasis. The forms of the costumes and their decorations were based on Russian folk dress (of fairly recent times, though transformed and made uniquely of their epoch by the jagged influence of Cubism). Avant-garde artists of many of the flourishing movements of modern art—Cubists, Constructivists, Surrealists—brought about an acceleration of innovation in design concepts, which in previous centuries had evolved gradually throughout Europe.

Expressionist theatre costumes

Appia, Craig, and Diaghilev led others to experiment. Meyerhold's 1907 production of Leonid Andreyev's play *The Life of Man*, with expressionistic costumes designed by Theodore Komisarjevsky, was purely mechanical in its design. The German advocates reasoned that since the actor man is enclosed in the space of the stage, either the stage must be arranged according to the illusion of reality so as to fit the natural man or the natural man must be transformed to match the cubist and abstract space of the stage.

As modern dance evolved, its rapid rhythms and pace offered the costume designer new challenges and scope for original work. The productions of Merce Cunningham and Alwin Nikolais in New York City presented unique shapes that attempted to express the exploration of time and space. Nikolais made his costumes part of a total stage design, a theatrical abstraction of the way he saw man—as part of a socioeconomic mechanism, an agreeable but not a central part. Accused of dehumanizing the dancers, he maintained they are rather an expression of a greater state of being for man, of the experience of living in a world of motion, sound, colour, and action, which strongly affects them and is affected by them.

The rise of the American musical owes much to the close collaboration of the composers, writers, and choreographers with the designers. In a musical the costume designer's task is manifold. The designs must capture the spirit of the music and lyrics, interpret the period, heighten the characterization of the actors, and help the dancers in their varied, often athletic routines. The costumes for *My Fair Lady* (1956) and *West Side Story* (1957) were especially successful in these respects.

New concepts in 20th-century costume

The radical creative talents of Brecht created new production concepts and styles; the clothes worn conveyed to the audience in a satirical fashion not only a characterization of the wearer but also his social status. Another compelling force in contemporary experimental theatre, Jerzy Grotowski, conceived his production *Akropolis* at the Polish Laboratory Theatre as a poetic paraphrase of an extermination camp. There is no hero and no individuality among the characters. The costumes were bags full of holes covering naked bodies, and the holes were lined with material suggesting torn flesh; wooden shoes covered the feet, and anonymous berets the heads.

A form of 20th-century pageantry can be seen in the designs of Tanya Moiseyevich for the simple thrust stage of the Tyrone Guthrie Theater, Minneapolis, Minn., and the Festival Theatre, Ontario, Canada. For the brilliant productions of these theatres, with their deft handling of large crowd scenes, highly skilled costumers are engaged each season. The costumes and props that they make enhance the productions' limited scenic elements, recalling the style of the Greek classic theatre and that of Japan. The growth of such regional theatres in Europe and the United States has afforded many opportunities for costume designers. Most of the opera and repertory companies that operate in larger cities have their own well-established costume workshops.

Contemporary design. Coordination of costume sketches with the scenic and lighting designers' schemes is essential from the start. The line, shape, and colour of the entire company's costumes must be viewed in relation to the set and the production's lighting plot. Rough preliminary sketches are made and discussed, revised, and redrawn. A thorough and creative meeting of minds at this stage is invaluable. It may be necessary to call many production meetings before the final rough sketches are approved by the director.

The costume designer

The costume designer can now search for the appropriate fabrics. Fabric buying is a time-consuming and arduous task, conditioned by the size of the production budget. Costumes can be made from an enormous variety of materials; often what is needed can be located only with ingenuity and imagination in some unusual place. The correct weight and weave must be selected if the cutter and draper are to translate the sketches into fact. The fabrics must be suitable for shaping and molding the silhouettes and styles as indicated by the designer, and they must hold up for as long as the production runs. Heavy-textured wools, fine cottons, upholstery fabrics, industrial felts and rubbers, natural fibres, and man-made stiffeners help to create costumes for varied stage characters. When they are finally selected, small samples of the fabrics are stapled to the rough sketches.

Once the cast list is made known, final costume renderings can be completed. Many designers sketch details of all millinery, wig work, and accessories. Hand props, such as snuff boxes, are also often considered the costume designer's responsibility. Spectacles, parasols, and walking sticks also fall in this category.

The costume maker

The management submits approved final designs to costume makers and invites bids. The costumers estimate prices according to the number of man-hours required for manufacture and the price of the materials to be used. The designer often confers with the producer regarding the figures submitted by the costume makers. The designer may recommend a particular firm because it has the craftsmanship and skills required for a particular style of work. Contracts are finally drawn up and construction begins.

A costume house is staffed with experienced and creative craftsmen, who translate all items of the costume sketch into shapes fashioned in the chosen fabrics. Millinery, jewelry, armour making, and dyeing can often be supervised by the designer under one roof. The construction of costumes starts with the appropriate underwear and necessary padding. Corsets, hooped skirts, panniers, bustles, and petticoats form the base on which period silhouettes are fashioned; they are fitted on the actors before the basic muslin pattern of the overgarments. On the skills of the cutter, draper, and fitting hands rests the ultimate success of the finished garment. All fittings are crucial, and the designer normally is present to supervise.

At the second fitting, shoes, wigs, and headwear must be tried on; and at the third and final fittings, the complete outfit is presented for approval of the designer and cutter. The dress parade follows, usually held onstage before the appropriate setting. This parade, ideally, is held at least 10 days before the dress rehearsal to allow for revisions by the director. Despite the long continuing collaboration, the designer still may find himself spraying, re-dyeing, and artificially aging garments to make the stage picture perfect in every detail. Last-minute adjustments can be most satisfying. When the costumes are completed, the production's own wardrobe staff takes over responsibility from the costume house. Supplied with inventories and wardrobe plots, the staff takes care of all items during the run of the production. (M.H./C.Ba.)

THEATRICAL MAKEUP

Theatrical makeup is the practice of painting, enhancing, or altering the face, hair, and body of the actor with cosmetics, plastic materials, and other substances; it is also the collective term for the materials used in making up. Actors have used makeup in the theatre for a long time, not only to look their best and to transform their appearance but also to ensure that they will be seen and recognized by the entire audience. How well an actor is seen depends upon the distance between him and the farthest spectator and the amount of available light. Distances blur the features and make recognition of the actors extremely difficult for the spectators.

Historical development. It is impossible to say when the first actor daubed paint on his face in an attempt to make his performance more effective. Some maintain that Thespis, the first actor to step out of the chorus in Greek theatre in the 6th century BC, smeared his face with white lead and red cinnabar. He may have done so, but the very large size of some of the Greek theatres (containing up to 15,000 spectators) made the use of the masks a more practical solution. Not only did masks enable the actor to play more than one role but their larger-than-life size and exaggerated features enabled the audience to identify the actor's role from a distance.

Use of masks

The Roman theatre borrowed and continued the use of the mask. Evidently some actors thought that their own faces would be more effective, however, since there are contemporary descriptions of certain mimic actors with painted faces. Like the Roman mimes, the traveling actor-comedians of the commedia dell'arte in the 16th century developed a set of stock characters using masks. There may have been some continuity of tradition, for there are resemblances between the comedians' leather masks and those of the Roman farces.

As actors in the 17th century began to perform in permanent theatres, in which they were separated from the audience by the proscenium arch, they had to deal with the problem of making the face look distinctive in illumination from candles and oil lamps. It is probable that the actors adapted the cosmetics of fashionable ladies to their own use.

The use of cosmetics increased greatly during the 18th century. Women, and men to a lesser extent, painted their faces with lead oxide for a pale complexion and cinnabar (mercuric sulfide) for rouge. Both were poisonous compounds. With the widespread use of cosmetics it was noticed that the paler faces were easier to see in dim light. By the 1770s the use of white paint was general upon the stage even though it tended to conceal the expressive motion of the muscles.

The impact of artificial light

The introduction of limelight in 1816, of gaslight in 1817, and of arc lights in 1846 created the necessity for a more subtle use of cosmetics on the stage. The actor's palette consisted at this time of white chalk, carpenters' blue chalk, papers impregnated with red colouring, and India ink. Some actors were known to make up their faces with whitewash rubbed off the walls, dust scraped from red bricks, and black from a burned match, paper, or cork. Credit for the invention of greasepaint belongs to Carl Baudin of the Leipziger Stadt Theatre. Wishing to conceal the join between the front edge of his wig and the forehead, he mixed a flesh-coloured paste of zinc white, yellow ochre, vermillion, and lard. By 1890 theatrical greasepaints were available commercially in many colours, and other items of makeup also began to be manufactured for use in the theatre.

Contemporary practices. The practice of makeup in the theatre has changed greatly with the wave of vitality that swept over the theatre after World War II. As the stage was thrust into the auditorium and the audience was arranged experimentally on all sides of the acting area, the actor was brought closer to the spectator, making close scrutiny possible. Poorly executed and heavy makeup looked obvious, and several time-honoured practices had to be abandoned. Red dots in the corners of the eyes and the use of bright eyeshadow (which had first been used to counteract the effects of footlights) appeared ridiculous. Actors began to reject greasepaint in favour of a makeup that had been developed for the motion-picture industry, a water-soluble cake makeup capable of being spread in a thin wash of colour, making a completely natural look possible. The desire for naturalism in appearance became very important.

Many improvements in makeup techniques were developed primarily for films and television and rapidly adopted by the theatre. There has been a great change in theatrical wigs, for example, which once had a band of silk that was blended with colour into the forehead. This type of wig was not successful for film work since the join was obvious to the camera. A new type of wig was developed, and now most wigs for films and theatre are made with an edge of plastic lace into which hairs are knotted. When the lace is glued to the forehead the hairs seem to grow from the skin, resulting in a natural-looking hairline.

Film and television makeup artists have perfected the use of foam rubber and plastic facial appliances to the point that a young actor can be transformed into a very old man and yet withstand the scrutiny of a camera close-up. This process frequently takes a makeup artist and an assistant four or more hours to complete. Audiences accustomed to these miracles of transformation have come to expect the same verisimilitude in the theatre. But this kind of makeup requires more time than is generally practical in the theatre, and the cost can be prohibitive. Theatres cannot hope to compete with the motion-picture industry; one film budgeted $1,500,000 to transform a large cast of actors into realistic-looking apes.

There is a growing trend in the theatre to include makeup in the total production design. What was once considered the prerogative and responsibility of the individual actor is now being influenced by designers, directors, and, in some instances, by makeup artists. In most German opera houses, for example, singers are not allowed to do their own makeup. A staff of makeup artists assures that each makeup is executed as designed and that the style is consistent. This expert supervision has hitherto been considered possible only in the motion-picture industry or in commercial television because of costs, but government subsidy of theatres and television in England and other European countries has enabled the hiring of such specialists. Rubber latex makeup can be used on the stage to give the skin the textured look of extreme old age, to make bald caps, and to make realistic-looking false noses, jowls, and other forms of sagging flesh.

The ideology of many alternative theatre groups has led to a rejection of makeup. In these theatre companies the actor does not seek to hide behind a character but is present as himself in public, relating directly with the audience. The Living Theatre was one such company. Even when named roles were assigned, as in *Frankenstein,* the actor was clearly visible beneath the role. In theatre such as this, the use of makeup is anathema in its illusionistic sense but can be used in a ritualistic sense. Experiments in ritual theatre have resulted in the use of masks and highly decorative or symbolic makeup, as is found in the Chinese Opera or the Kabuki theatre. Laboratory theatre companies have concentrated on the actor's control of the processes of transformation. Grotowski encouraged the actor to try to transform himself without the help of makeup. If makeup were used only after all the other possible changes of character had been explored, then its use would be much more expressive. The growth of the alternative theatre circuit in Britain, which has brought performances to small intimate rooms, has similarly pushed the actor to try all other means of characterization without the use of makeup, which would appear grotesque at close range. The result is that many younger British actors do not use makeup at all, even on main stages. (S.D./C.Ba.)

BIBLIOGRAPHY

Directing and performing: JOHN GASSNER, *Producing the Play,* rev. ed. (1953), descriptions of standard practices in major aspects of theatrical production until the middle of the 20th century; and TOBY COLE and HELEN KRICH CHINOY (eds.), *Actors on Acting,* new rev. ed. (1970), and *Directors on Directing,* 2nd rev. ed. (1963, reprinted 1976), collections of essays by actors and directors, respectively. The insights of prominent persons in the field, with coverage of their working methods, are found in EUGENIO BARBA, *The Floating Islands: Reflections with Odin Teatret,* trans. from Danish, Italian, and Norwegian (1979); JERZY GROTOWSKI, *Towards a Poor Theatre* (1968, reissued 1975); and ERWIN PISCATOR, *The Political Theatre* (1978; originally published in German, 1929). Studies of directing include EDWARD BRAUN, *The Director and the Stage: From Naturalism to Grotowski* (1982).

Historical developments of the theatre: PHYLLIS HARTNOLL (ed.), *The Oxford Companion to the Theatre,* 4th ed. (1983), is a reference source. For further research, the following bibliographies are recommended: DAVID F. CHESHIRE, *Theatre: History, Criticism, and Reference* (1967), a guide to theatre books in English, with emphasis on the British stage; and CLAUDIA JEAN BAILEY, *A Guide to Reference and Bibliography for Theatre Research,* 2nd rev. ed. (1983). Studies of theatrical history and philosophy include OSCAR G. BROCKETT, *History of the Theatre,* 4th ed. (1982); ALLARDYCE NICOLL, *The Development of the Theatre: A Study of Theatrical Art from the Beginnings to the Present Day,* 5th rev. ed. (1966); BARRETT H. CLARK, *European Theories of the Drama; with a Supplement on American Drama: An Anthology of Dramatic Theory and Criticism from Aristotle to the Present Day,* rev. ed., edited by HENRY POPKIN (1965); GEORGE FREEDLEY and JOHN A. REEVES, *A History of the Theatre,* 3rd rev. ed. (1968); A.M. NAGLER, *Sources of Theatrical History* (1952, reissued 1959); and KEIR ELAM, *The Semiotics of Theatre and Drama* (1980). Specific periods and areas are examined in MARGARETE BIEBER, *The History of the Greek and Roman Theater,* 2nd rev. ed. (1961); E.K. CHAMBERS, *The Medieval Stage,* 2 vol. (1903, reprinted 1978); A.M. NAGLER, *Theatre Festivals of the Medici, 1539–1637* (1964, reprinted 1976); A.M. NAGLER, *Shakespeare's Stage,* enlarged ed., trans. from the German (1981); MICHAEL HATTAWAY, *Elizabethan Popular Theatre* (1982); GIULIANA RICCI, *Teatri d'Italia: Dalla Magna Grecia all'Ottocento* (1971); MARGARETE BAUR-HEINHOLD, *The Baroque Theatre: A Cultural History of the 17th and 18th Centuries* (1967; originally published in German, 1966); LESLIE HOTSON, *The Commonwealth and Restoration Stage* (1928, reissued 1962); MICHAEL R. BOOTH, *Victorian Spectacular Theatre, 1850–1910* (1981); HOWARD GOORNEY, *The Theatre Workshop Story* (1981); GERALD M. BERKOWITZ, *New Broadways: Theatre Across America, 1950–1980* (1982); FAUBION BOWERS, *Theatre in the East* (1956, reprinted 1980); A.C. SCOTT, *An Introduction to the Chinese Theatre* (1958); and BALWANT GARGI, *Theatre in India* (1962).

Theatre buildings and design: Historical developments are studied in the following works: WILLIAM TYDEMAN, *The Theatre in the Middle Ages: Western European Stage Conditions, c. 800–1576* (1978); GEORGE R. KERNODLE, *From Art to Theatre: Form and Convention in the Renaissance* (1944); BARNARD HEWITT, *The Renaissance Stage: Documents of Serlio, Sabbattini, and Furttenbach* (1958); ALAN C. DESSEN, *Elizabethan Stage Conventions and Modern Interpreters* (1984); ANDREW CURR, *The Shakespearean Stage, 1574–1642,* 2nd ed. (1980); ASHLEY HORACE THORNDIKE, *Shakespeare's Theater* (1916, reprinted 1968); C. WALTER HODGES, *The Globe Restored* (1953, reprinted 1977); ALLARDYCE NICOLL, *Stuart Masques and the Renaissance Stage* (1938, reprinted 1980); and PER BJURSTRÖM, *Giacomo Torelli and Baroque Stage Design* (1961).

Architecture and construction of theatres are examined in DONALD C. MULLIN, *The Development of the Playhouse: A Survey of Theatre Architecture from the Renaissance to the Present* (1970); ROBERTO ALOI, *Architetture per lo spettacolo* (1958); MAXWELL SILVERMAN, *Contemporary Theatre Architecture: An Illustrated Survey* (1965); JO MIELZINER, *The Shapes of Our Theatre* (1970); HAROLD BURRIS-MEYER and EDWARD C. COLE, *Theatres and Auditoriums,* 2nd ed. (1964, reprinted 1975); OSKAR SCHLEMMER, LASZLO MOHOLY-NAGY, and FARKAS MOLNÁR, *The Theater of the Bauhaus* (1961, reissued 1979; originally published in German, 1925); GERHARD GRAUBNER, *Theaterbau: Aufgabe und Planung* (1968); GEORGE C. IZENOUR, *Theater Design* (1977); and EDWIN O. SACHS and ERNEST A.E. WOODROW, *Modern Opera Houses and Theatres,* 3 vol. (1896–98, reprinted 1981). Of special interest is WALTHER UNRUH, *Theatertechnik: Fachkunde und Vorschriftensammlung* (1969), a study of theatre machinery by a master of stage engineering. Aspects of stage setting and scenery are explored in LEE SIMONSON, *The Stage Is Set* (1964); LÉON MOUSSINAC, *The New Movement in the Theatre* (1931, reissued 1967); MORDECAI GORELIK, *New Theatres for Old* (1940, reprinted 1975); WALTER RENÉ FUERST and SAMUEL J. HUME, *Twentieth-Century Stage Decoration,* 2 vol. (1929, reissued 1967); RENÉ HAINAUX (ed.), *Stage Design Throughout the World Since 1935* (1956), *Stage Design Throughout the World Since 1950* (1964), *Stage Design Throughout the World Since 1960* (1973), and *Stage Design Throughout the World, 1970–75* (1976), chiefly illustrative material collected by the International Theatre Institute; DENIS BABLET, *Edward Gordon Craig* (1966, reissued in 1981 as *The Theatre of Edward Gordon Craig;* originally published in French, 1962); JARKA BURIAN, *The Scenography of Josef Svoboda* (1971, reprinted 1977); and ANDREW MCCALLUM, *Fun with Stagecraft* (1981).

Light, colour, costume, and makeup, and their interrelation on the stage are the subjects of THEODORE FUCHS, *Stage Lighting* (1929, reissued 1963); WILLARD F. BELLMAN, *Lighting the Stage: Art and Practice,* 2nd ed. (1974); RICHARD PILBROW, *Stage Lighting,* rev. ed. (1979); GÖSTA M. BERGMAN, *Lighting in the Theatre* (1977); THEODORE KOMISARJEVSKY, *The Costume of the Theatre* (1932, reprinted 1968); JAMES LAVER, *Drama, Its Costume & Décor* (1951); JACK CASSIN-SCOTT, *Costumes and Settings for Staging Historical Plays,* 4 vol. (1979; U.K. title, *Costumes and Settings for Historical Plays*); JOHN T. WILLIAMS, *Costumes and Settings for Shakespeare's Plays* (1982); MILLIA DAVENPORT, *The Book of Costume,* 2 vol. (1948, reissued in 1 vol., 1979); HILAIRE HILER and MEYER HILER, *Bibliography of Costume: A Dictionary Catalog of About Eight Thousand Books and Periodicals* (1939, reissued 1967); ISABEL MONRO and DOROTHY E. COOK (eds.), *Costume Index: A Subject Index to Plates and to Illustrated Text* (1937), with a *Costume Index Supplement,* ed. by ISABEL MONRO and KATE M. MONRO (1957); IWAO KONGOW, *Nō-isho: Japanese Nō-Play Costume,* 2 vol. (1934); RUTH M. SHAVER, *Kabuki Costume* (1966); MAX TILKE, *Oriental Costumes: Their Designs and Colors* (1923; originally published in German, 1923); and RICHARD CORSON, *Stage Makeup,* 7th ed. (1986), and *Fashions in Hair: The First Five Thousand Years,* rev. ed. (1980).

(B.Be./G.C.I./Ho.B./Ra.Ho./
M.H./S.D./C.Ba.)

Theology

Theology, meaning literally the study of God, is a discipline of religious thought that is restricted in its narrower sense, because of origination and format, to Christianity, but in its broader sense, because of its themes, to other religions. The themes of theology are God, man, the world, salvation, and eschatology (or the study of last times).

The article is divided into the following sections:

Nature of theology. The concept of theology that is applicable as a science in all religions and that is therefore neutral is difficult to distill and determine. The problem lies in the fact that theology as a concept had its origins in the tradition of the Greeks but that it obtained its content and method only within Christianity. Thus, theology, because of its peculiarly Christian profile, is not readily transferable in its narrow sense to any other religion. In its broader thematic concerns, theology as a subject matter is germane to other religions.

The terminological problem

The Greek philosopher Plato (*c.* 428–348/347 BC), with whom the concept emerges for the first time, associated with the term theology a polemical intention—as did his pupil Aristotle. For Plato theology described the mythical, which he allowed may have a temporary pedagogical significance that is beneficial to the state but is to be cleansed from all offensive and abstruse elements with the help of political legislation. This identification of theology and mythology also remained customary in the later Greek thought. In distinction to philosophers, "theologians" (as, for example, the poets of myth—*e.g.,* the 8th-century-BC Greeks Hesiod and Homer—or the cultic servants of the oracle at Delphi [Greece] and the rhetors of the Roman cult of emperor worship) testified to and proclaimed that which they viewed as divine. Theology thus became significant as the means of proclaiming the gods, of confessing to them, and of teaching and "preaching" this confession. In this practice of "theology" by the Greeks lies the prefiguration of what later would be known as theology in the history of Christianity. In spite of all the contradictions and nuances that were to emerge in the understanding of this concept in various Christian confessions and schools of thought, a formal criterion remains constant: theology is the attempt of adherents of a faith to represent their statements of belief consistently, to explicate them out of the basis (or fundamentals) of their faith, and to assign to such statements their specific place within the context of all other worldly relations (*e.g.,* nature and history) and spiritual processes (*e.g.,* reason and logic).

Limitations

Here, then, the above indicated difficulty becomes apparent. In the first place, theology is a spiritual or religious attempt of "believers" to explicate their faith. In this sense it is not neutral and is not attempted from the perspective of removed observation—in distinction to a general history of religions. The implication derived from the religious approach is that it does not provide a formal and indifferent scheme devoid of presuppositions within which all religions could be subsumed. In the second place, theology is influenced by its origins in the Greek and Christian traditions, with the implication that the transmutation of this concept to other religions is endangered by the very circumstances of origination. If one attempts, nevertheless, such a transmutation—and if one then speaks of a theology of primitive religions and of a theology of Buddhism—one must be aware of the fact that the concept "theology," which is uncustomary and also inadequate in those spheres, is applicable only to a very limited extent and in a very modified form. This is because some Eastern religions have atheistic qualities and provide no access to the *theos* ("god") of theology. If one nonetheless speaks of theology in religions other than Christianity or Greek religion, he implies—in formal analogy to what has been observed above—the way in which representatives of other religions understand themselves.

Relationship of theology to the history of religions and philosophy. *Relationship to the history of religions.* If theology explicates the way in which the believer understands his faith—or, if faith is not a dominating quality, the way in which a religion's practitioners understand their religion—this implies that it claims to be normative, even if the claim does not, as in Hinduism and Buddhism, culminate in the pretention to be absolutely authoritative. The normative element in these religions arises simply out of the authority of a divine teacher, or a revelation (*e.g.,* a vision or auditory revelation), or of any other kind of spiritual encounter over against which one feels committed. The newly evolving discipline of the history of religions, which encompasses also religious psychology, religious sociology, and religious phenomenology as well as philosophy of religion, has emancipated itself from the normative aspect in favour of a purely empirical analysis. This empirical aspect, which corresponds to the modern conception of science, can be applied only if it functions on the basis of objectifiable (empirically verifiable) entities. Revelation of the kind of event that would have to be characterized as transcendent, however, can never be understood as such an objectifiable entity. Only those forms of religious life that are positive and arise out of experience can be objectified. Wherever such forms are given, the religious man is taken as the source of the religious phenomena that are to be interpreted. Understood in this manner, the history of religions represents a necessary step in the process of secularization. Nevertheless, it cannot be said that theology and the history of religions only contradict one another. The "theologies"—for want of a better term—of the various religions are concerned with religious phenomena, and the adherents of the religions of the more advanced cultures are themselves constrained—especially at a time of increasing cultural interdependency—to take cognizance of and to interpret theologically the fact that besides their own religion there are many others. In this regard, then, there are not only analytical but also theological statements concerning religious phenomena, particularly in regard to the manner in which such statements are encountered in specific primitive or high religions. Thus, the objects of the history of religions and those of theology cannot be clearly separated. They are merely approached with different categories and criteria. If the history of religions does not surrender its neutrality, since such a surrender would thereby reduce the discipline to anthropology in an ideological sense (*e.g.,* religion understood as mere projection of the psyche or of societal conditions), theology will recognize the history of religions as a science providing valuable material and as one of the sciences in the universe of sciences.

Contributions of the history of religions to theology

Relationship to philosophy. The relationship of theology to philosophy is much more difficult to determine, because it is much more complicated. The problems can here only be mentioned. If one does not adhere to the narrow concept of philosophy that reduces it positivistically to logic or epistemology (theory of knowledge) but rather understands philosophy as the discipline that attempts to explicate the totality of being, the difference between this latter interpretation of philosophy in relation to theology becomes apparent. If theology is responsible to an authority that initiates its thinking, speaking, and witnessing—*e.g.,* a document containing revealed truth, as well as the spiritual testimony related to it—philosophy bases its arguments on the ground of timeless evidence, an evidence with which autonomous reason understands itself to be confronted. Since, on the other hand, theology also uses reason and systematically develops its tenets—however much its critical reflections are based on religious convictions—there are many common areas that have partly complementary significance but that partly also lead to polemical tensions.

The significance of theology. *The religious significance of theology.* Just as in the case of religions themselves, so also their theological reflections are not limited to a special religious sphere, separated from common life. Whoever speaks of God and the gods speaks at the same time of man and of the meaning of existence. He makes therewith statements about the world, its conditions of being created, its estrangement from the purpose of creation (*e.g.,* sin), and its determined goal (eschatology or view of the last times). Out of these statements result normative directives for life in the world, not only for the purpose of gaining access to salvation but also for concrete ethical behaviour in the context of the I–Thou (or person to person) relationship, of the clan, of the nation, and of society. In ancient times, all aspects of life (*e.g.,* relationship between the sexes, hygiene, work, and other aspects) were determined religiously and permeated by cultic forms and practices. In this regard, every religion contains the totality of being that its "theology" intends to express—if one also includes certain rudiments of reflection in primitive religion in the concept "theology."

The scope of theological reflections

In primitive religions the tribe represents the pivot around which all world relations turn. The primeval (or mythical) time to which the tribe traces its own origins is also the time of salvation and fulfillment. Therefore, primitive religions primarily concern themselves with the ancestral cult. Involved in tribal concerns in the realm of religious thought are conceptions of mana (spiritual power, or force); *i.e.,* the teaching that tribal heads, medicine men, and sorcerers are subjects of special charisma (spiritual power or influence) and more potent powers of life. In Eastern religions, as in Western religions, this understanding is infinitely refined, developed, and theologically reflected. In regard to the relationship of man to the world, many Eastern religions (especially Hinduism) have a definite skeptically tinged negative view of all reality, which is especially pronounced in contrast to the Christian doctrine of creation. Though this doctrine points to a "happy event" in Christianity, the call to life and reality is understood in Eastern thought in the opposite manner:

Man and the world

> To be man implies being cut off from all true reality. Creation should have never happened, and its faults should be eliminated as soon as possible. . . . The illusion that I am is a calamity. Not death is to be explained, but rather birth. (Stephen Neill).

The cultural importance of theology. Since theology does not remain restricted to transcendent statements and to an esoteric and sacred realm, and since it rather encompasses all worldly dimensions (cosmology, anthropology, historiology, and other areas), it has always had important significance for cultural evolution and general intellectual life. Western historians hardly need to be reminded of the fact that the Old Testament prophetic theology of history (*e.g.*, the 8th-century-BC Hebrew prophets Amos and Isaiah) has decisively influenced the origins of the concept *history* and, indeed, has made this concept possible in the first place. On Old Testament theology of history is based the understanding of history as a linear process, as directed to a goal (*i.e.*, the Kingdom of God), and as qualified by the characteristic of singularity. This view of history contrasts with a cyclical understanding of successive events; *i.e.*, the view that history repeats itself. The fact that university and school were originally initiated by the church (as is still very often the case in mission fields) is based on the fact that theology has thematized in its various subjects the various dimensions of life (nature, history, ethics, and other disciplinary areas). Also, much of modern philosophy has emerged out of theological themes and categories—in such modern thinkers as the existential philosophers Martin Heidegger and Jean-Paul Sartre and even in the Communist thinker Karl Marx remnants of this fact are still observable. Modern philosophy has, by and large, only gradually emancipated itself from this theological origin, but this emancipation also has taken place in a manner that has retained the dialectical relationship of theology and philosophy. That theological questions in the modern age of secularism are less openly posed than in the time of the Middle Ages does not reduce their lasting significance. They always reemerge, often in disguised form, such as in the quest for the meaning of life and existence or in the nihilistic resignation over against that quest; furthermore, they reemerge in the quest for the dignity of human existence, the inviolability of life, the determination of human rights, and many other such questions. A theologian such as the German-American thinker Paul Tillich has investigated specifically the secular realm in view of the relevance of these latent theological questions that are posed by modern man in his relationship to a constantly changing world.

The emergence of theological questions in a secular age

Theological themes. The themes discussed by theology are of universal dimensions. They encompass the doctrine of God, of man, and of the world. Even when no "doctrine of God" exists in the strict sense of the term, as in the case of what are sometimes called "atheistic" religions (*e.g.*, certain forms of Hinduism and Buddhism), man and the world are understood in the context of finality and therefore have religious aspects. The inclusion of the world in theological discussion also implies that behaviour in the world—that is, ethics—is included in theology; in some areas (*e.g.*, Confucianism) this aspect gains a dominating position. Ethical conceptions—derived from theological concepts in the broad meaning of theology—are developed in contradictory forms: they can lead to ascetic world denial but also to a definite world affirmation. The first form is realized in Buddhism and Hinduism, the second in Confucianism. In Christianity both forms are represented. The theological theme of the relation of man and the world has been described by the 17th-century French scientist and thinker Blaise Pascal as the doctrine of the "dignity and poverty of man"—*i.e.*, the doctrine of creation and fall—and, related to this, the proclamation of salvation and the presentation of a path to salvation. This path leads, in the various religions, into greatly diverging directions. It can be placed under the exclusive direction of divine grace (as in Amida Buddhism and in Protestant Christianity); it can be left to the activity and initiative of man (as in Confucianism); or it can be characterized by a combination of the two principles (as in Zen Buddhism and in the Roman Catholic combination of grace and merit). Finally, theology also includes among its various themes statements concerning the process and goal of history (eschatology), especially concerning the relation of secular history and history of salvation.

Functions of theology. The vastness of theological interests and aspects implies that theology can master the material with which it is confronted only within a broad spectrum of partial disciplines. Since theology is based on authority (revelation), and since this authority is documented in the Holy Scriptures (especially in Christianity), it is constrained to engage in philological and historical studies of these sources and, related to these studies, also with hermeneutical (critical interpretive) questions. This historical task broadens into a concern with the history and tradition of the religion that a particular theology represents. In this concern many difficult and controversial questions arise, including whether and to what extent the canon (scriptural standard) of the sources of revelation is glossed over and modified by tradition and what normative value the modifying tradition has or should have. These problems play an important part in the relationship between Protestantism and Catholicism, even though the problems are also treated independently by each confession.

Controversial questions in theology

The question of truth posed by theology requires the constitution of a discipline that specifically concerns itself with fundamental questions (systematic theology). Its task can be determined in the following manner: (1) It has to develop the totality of religious teachings (dogmatics, or the doctrine of faith). (2) It has to interpret man's existence in the world and, related to this, to determine the norms (ethics derived from faith) for action in the world—*e.g.*, for the disposition toward one's fellow man and toward societal and political structures and institutions. (3) It further has to represent its claim to truth in the context of confrontation with other claims to truth and with other criteria of verification (apologetics, polemics). As part of this concern, theology's task is to explain reasonably, in view of historical relativism, the absolute claim of the truth that it represents. Related to this is the modern-day task of coordinating its doctrine of creation or its doctrine of the revelation of the transcendent (*e.g.*, the Christ event in Christianity) with the world view of modern natural science and its thesis of the immanency of being—*i.e.*, of being that is self-contained. Another aspect of this task is the confrontation with other religions' claim to truth, which can lead to vastly different results: either—this is noted only as an example—it can lead to the thesis of the complementary positions of individual religions and therefore to tolerance (as for example in Hinduism as well as in some schools in the West) or to one's own religion's claim to be absolute (as in Christianity, at least among the most important of its representatives). But also, in the last mentioned situation, such a claim is widely modified. It can manifest itself by a total rejection of other religions as "devil's work," but it can also be expressed in an interpretation of other religions as first steps to and as seeds of a religious development, the completion of which it knows itself to be.

The vast dimension of theological themes implies that theology is, with its many disciplines, a microcosmic image of the university. Even though it is a science in which the believers or the adherents of a particular religion explicate and critically analyze the truth that is represented by them, it nevertheless has to remain free within the framework of this commitment, and it has to fulfill the responsibility of its scientific task on the basis of its own autonomy. The opposite of this freedom would arise when an institution (*e.g.*, the church) restricted the range of theological inquiry with normative claims, forcing the discipline therewith to assume ideological functions. The struggle concerning the freedom and limitations of theology—*i.e.*, concerning responsible criticism and authority—is a struggle that has accompanied the history of theology from the very beginnings to the present.

BIBLIOGRAPHY. FRIEDRICH SCHLEIERMACHER, *Brief Outline on the Study of Theology* (1850, reissued 1977; originally published in German, 1811, 2nd ed., 1830), is still the best picture of theology as a whole and all its parts. KARL RAHNER and HERBERT VORGRIMLER, *Theological Dictionary* (1965; originally published in German, 1961); and JOHN MACQUARRIE, *Twentieth-Century Religious Thought*, 2nd rev. ed. (1981), together cover a vast range of topics and themes of theology, past and present. GERHARD VON RAD, *Old Testament Theology*, 2 vol. (1962–65; originally published in German, 1957–60); and RUDOLF BULTMANN, *Theology of the New Testament*, 2 vol. (1951–55, reissued in 1 vol., 1965; originally published in German, 1948–53), are the most important texts dealing with Holy Scripture in modern times. MIRCEA ELIADE, *The Myth of the Eternal Return* (1954, reissued 1974; originally published in French, 1949); and OSCAR CULLMANN, *Christ and Time*, 3rd rev. ed. (1962; originally published in German, 1946), deal with Christianity as a historical religion in contrast to nonhistorical interpretations of religion. ADOLF VON HARNACK, *History of Dogma,* 7 vol. (1895–1900, reissued 1976; 3rd German ed., 1894–97), is the classic study of the history of Christian theology in relation to Greek thought. The new disciplines of religious study, namely, the history and the phenomenology of religions, are introduced and illustrated by RUDOLF OTTO, *The Idea of the Holy,* 2nd ed. (1957, reissued 1980; 9th German ed., 1922); and *The History of Religions: Essays in Methodology,* ed. by MIRCEA ELIADE and JOSEPH KITAGAWA (1959). Modern theology, from the 18th century to the present, is treated in contrasting new ways by KARL BARTH, *Protestant Thought from Rousseau to Ritschl* (1959, reissued 1971; originally published in German, 1947), and *Church Dogmatics,* 4 vol. (1936–61; originally published in German, 1932–59); and PAUL TILLICH, *Perspectives on 19th and 20th Century Protestant Theology* (1967), and *Systematic Theology,* 3 vol. (1951–63, reissued 1975), are exhaustive treatments of the most fully developed theologies in Catholic and Protestant churches.

(H.Th.)

Principles of Thermodynamics

Thermodynamics is that part of physical science that is concerned with the conditions that material systems may assume and the changes in conditions that may occur either spontaneously or as a result of interactions between systems, including interactions such as heat, which cannot be described in terms of mechanics. It is basic to the distinction between mechanics and thermodynamics that according to mechanics all the energy of a system in any state is convertible to work, whereas according to thermodynamics only a fraction of the energy of a system in most states is convertible to work without other effects. The scope of thermodynamics has been steadily broadening since early in the 19th century as a result of a better understanding that has grown up of its underlying principles.

The word thermodynamics was derived from the Greek words *thermē* ("heat") and *dynamis* ("force"). The beginnings of the study of thermodynamics are found in the early 19th century in the study of the motive power of heat; that is, the capability of hot bodies to produce mechanical work. These early studies revealed several underlying principles, the most important of which are the first and second laws of thermodynamics. The discovery and clear enunciation in 1850 of the two laws by Rudolf Julius Clausius, a German mathematician and physicist, broadened greatly the scope of the subject. Throughout the rest of the 19th century it developed into a science, now known as classical thermodynamics, concerned primarily with physical systems in or passing through stable equilibrium states (the terms system and state are defined below). More recently thermodynamics has been extended to include physical systems in nonequilibrium states.

Although the development of thermodynamics, in contrast to other aspects of the study of physics, has progressed without regard to the details of the microscopic structures of physical systems, many scientists, beginning with Ludwig Eduard Boltzmann, an Austrian physicist, have felt that the laws of thermodynamics might be justified and explained by means of detailed microscopic descriptions of matter and the laws of mechanics (classical or quantum) and statistics. Work in this direction has resulted in the development of the branch of thermodynamics known as statistical thermodynamics, which, though it plays an important role in the evaluation of properties of systems, has not achieved one of its original goals, namely, the derivation of the laws of thermodynamics from the laws of mechanics. In particular, it now appears that the second law of thermodynamics is an independent law of nature. This particular point will be clarified below.

This article is divided into two parts. In the first part, the general principles of thermodynamics that apply to any physical system in any state—and the corollaries of these principles—are presented without reference to the detailed microscopic structure of matter. The presentation, therefore, encompasses both classical and nonequilibrium thermodynamics. In the second part, the detailed microscopic structures of physical systems are considered, and the states of such systems are discussed in the light of the laws of both quantum mechanics and thermodynamics. Quantum mechanics and thermodynamics are shown to be complementary parts of physical science, and they are neither separable nor are they derivable one from the other.

The article is divided into the following sections:

Historical overview of classical thermodynamics

Temperature is probably the earliest thermodynamic concept to attain operational status. Early in the 17th century Galileo, an Italian astronomer and physicist, devised a thermoscope that was a rudimentary thermometer. Soon thereafter a liquid-expansion thermometer with bulb and stem, open at the top, was devised in France by Jean Ray. In 1640 the grand duke Ferdinand II of Tuscany, one of the founders of the Florentine Academy of Experiment, invented the sealed-stem alcohol thermometer. Such devices were put to clinical (determining degrees of fever), agricultural (incubation), and meteorological uses.

Early attempts to measure temperature

The purpose of these instruments was to measure a quantity, that had as yet been undefined, that was more objective in nature than the physiological sensations of hotness and coldness. An equilibrium concept was probably involved; namely, that all bodies exposed to the same atmosphere would ultimately attain the same degree of hotness or coldness, despite any contrary evidence of the senses. An associated concept of the equilibrium concept was that temperature is a driving potential that causes some influence to pass from one body to another of unequal hotness or coldness. Thus, when a body is taken from a warm room to the cold outdoors, its length begins immediately to decrease.

What was it that passed from one body to another at different temperatures? Was it temperature itself that was transmitted? The English philosopher and scientist Francis Bacon as early as 1620, and the Florentine Academy a few years later, began to make this distinction between this influence and temperature; but it was more than a century before Joseph Black, a chemist at the University of Glasgow, in 1770 made the distinction sharply. He showed by mixing equal masses of pairs of liquids of different temperatures that the temperatures of the two substances often changed by radically different amounts. Indeed, a large change in temperature of a solid body produced no change at all in the temperature of a mixture of ice and water or of water and steam. Temperature was not necessarily conserved or even transmitted in the process.

Black established the science of calorimetry, which led to the establishment of the caloric theory, based upon the following postulates: (1) Caloric is an all-pervading elastic fluid, the particles of which repel one another strongly. (2) Particles of caloric are attracted by particles of matter. (3) Caloric is conserved. (4) Caloric is either sensible (*i.e.,* change in caloric is associated with change in temperature) or latent. (5) Caloric has weight. These postulates were intended to account for expansion and contraction upon heating and cooling, variations in heat capacity, calorimetry, latent heat, and gain in weight of certain metals when heated in air (calcined). Frictional heating was subsequently accounted for by postulating that friction reduced the attraction between caloric and matter.

Toward the end of the 18th century, Count Rumford (Benjamin Thompson), an expatriate American colonial engineer and physicist, attacked the validity of the caloric theory on the basis of experiments intended to show that caloric could be created and, therefore, was not conserved. More refined measurements on the generation of heat by frictional work were made nearly a half century later by an English physicist, James Prescott Joule.

Carnot's heat engine

In 1824 Sadi Carnot, a French military engineer, introduced the concept of the heat-engine cycle, a concept that permitted a sharp distinction to be made between interactions of systems and changes in their states. Carnot then proved from conservation of caloric and the impossibility of the production of work without compensating changes in the environment that (1) a reversible cyclic engine is the most efficient possible means of producing work from heat, and (2) all reversible cyclic engines operating between the same pair of heat reservoirs must have the same efficiency. Although the proof, as it turned out, was invalid, Clausius asserted in 1850 that Carnot's principle is itself a basic postulate and is, in effect, what came to be known as the second law of thermodynamics.

In the decade of the 1840s Joule laid the foundations of the first law of thermodynamics by showing that the amount of work required to bring about a given change of state is independent of the kind of work (whether mechanical, electric, or magnetic), the rate of doing work, or the method of delivering it. Joule concluded that work can be converted into heat, with a fixed ratio of one to the other, and that heat can be converted into work. In 1844 Julius Robert von Mayer, a German physician and physicist, postulated that in a work-producing cycle the heat introduced must exceed the heat rejected by an amount proportional to the work. He deduced the value of the proportionality constant from calculation of cycles in a gaseous system.

In 1849 Lord Kelvin (William Thomson), an engineer of Glasgow, pointed out the conflict between the caloric basis of Carnot's arguments and the conclusions reached by Joule. In 1850 Clausius resolved the difficulty by stating explicitly the first and second laws of thermodynamics. Within a few years Clausius defined and named the property entropy that is conserved in all reversible processes, and derived from the second law the principle of increase of entropy.

The first law was stated by Clausius as follows: In all cases in which work is produced by the agency of heat, a quantity of heat is consumed that is proportional to the work done; and, conversely, by the expenditure of an equal quantity of work, an equal quantity of heat is produced. He applied this statement to a cyclic process in a system (a concept with which he credits Carnot) in order to obtain a statement of the first law in terms of work and heat without reference to alteration in the state of the system. This led naturally to a definition of the property energy—called mechanical energy by Kelvin and contracted to energy by J. Willard Gibbs, an American mathematician and physicist. Clausius stated the second law in the following terms: A passage of heat from a colder to a hotter body cannot take place without compensation.

Clausius' paper of 1850 marked the birth of the science of thermodynamics. Immediately thereafter, Kelvin, who had previously displayed an interest in the theory of temperature, proposed and discussed various definitions for thermodynamic temperature scales, including the one that now bears his name. James Clerk Maxwell, a physicist of Edinburgh and Cambridge, averred that two bodies each equal in temperature to a third body are equal in temperature to each other. This statement, which is sometimes called the zeroth law of thermodynamics, is an incomplete version of a condition for equilibrium, subsequently derived by Gibbs and others. Maxwell also devised a number of mathematical relations that now bear his name. Kelvin and Max Planck, a German physicist, later restated the second law, so as to avoid the undefined term compensation used by Clausius, in terms of the impossibility of a perpetual-motion machine of the second kind (see below).

In the years 1873–78 Gibbs published three papers that proved to be definitive as regards the conditions for equilibrium. These papers provided a mathematical method so orderly and systematic that they have served as the foundations of physical chemistry and many subsequent applications of classical thermodynamics.

At the turn of the century, the French mathematician Henri Poincaré addressed the problem of definition of temperature and heat and the statement of the first and second laws. In 1909 Constantin Carathéodory, a Greek mathematician teaching in Germany, presented an alternative logical structure in which he shunned use of the term heat. It is closest in method and spirit to that used here. He states the two laws as follows: First, an extensive property exists the increment in which is the work received by the system while surrounded by an adiabatic wall (an adiabatic wall being one that permits only work interactions between the system and its surroundings). Second, in the neighbourhood of any prescribed initial state are states that cannot be reached by an adiabatic process.

In 1918 Walther Nernst, a Nobel-Prize-winning chemist of Germany, stated the Nernst heat theorem, treated below, which is essentially the third law of thermodynamics, which rounds out the exposition of classical thermodynamics by providing a common base for values of entropy for all atoms or molecules that can be formed from simpler species.

Basic concepts and laws of thermodynamics

SYSTEMS, STATES, AND PROPERTIES

The description of physical phenomena is based on the concept of state of a system and the changes of state that occur either spontaneously or because of interactions with other systems. Knowledge of the states of a system is equivalent to knowledge of the outcomes of all possible observations on the system; namely, observations of all its properties.

The term system means any identifiable collection of matter that can be separated from everything else by a well-defined surface so that changes in everything else need not affect the condition of the collection. Examples of systems are a number of water molecules confined within a watertight container, a thermonuclear plasma (a special collection of charged particles) confined by a suitably designed magnetic field, and the vapour of a solid within a cavity in the solid.

The particles of a system may have a finite rest mass, as do molecules, atoms, or electrons, or zero rest mass, as do photons. The number of particles of a system can be large, as in a cubic centimetre of tungsten, or small, as in a hydrogen atom.

At any instant of time a system is in a condition called a state, which encompasses all that can be said about the results of any measurements or observations that can be performed on the system at that time. The state at a given instant of time determines the properties of the system. A property is any quantity the value of which depends upon the state but not the history of the system. For a given state the value of a property can be determined by some type of measurement (some physical operation or test). When the values of all properties of two states are identical, the two states are identical; otherwise they are different.

Measurements and values compared

Because of unavoidable quantum mechanical considerations, a simple measurement, no matter how nearly perfect, will not yield the precise value for a property. In general, a very large number of measurements of the same kind is required to yield the precise value, each measurement performed on a duplicate of the system in the given state or on the same system reprepared in the same state and each yielding a different result. The value of a property is defined, therefore, as the sum of all the results of the measurements of the property divided by the number of measurements (in other words, the arithmetic average or expectation value of all the results of the measurements of the property). It will be shown below that a state can be described by a set of weighting factors, or probabilities, that enter into the evaluation of all properties.

Although an indefinite number of properties can be associated with a state, the values of these properties are not all independent of each other. The number of independent properties is either small or large, depending on the type of state in question; that is, on whether or not it is a stable equilibrium state. The meaning of the terms that define the various types of states will be given below.

WORK AND NONWORK

An interaction between two systems such that whatever happens in each of the interacting systems could have been brought about while the sole effect external to each system was the change in level of a mass in a gravity field will be defined as work; that is, work is an interaction that must satisfy a test: each of the interacting systems is separately required to experience the same changes as in the actual interaction, but, through alteration of circumstances external to that system, the effect outside of it is solely the rise or fall of a mass. If this test can be satisfied by both systems, then the original interaction is work.

It can be shown from experimental evidence that the following interactions conform to the definition just cited and are, therefore, work interactions: (1) the displacement of a point on the boundary of a system at which point a force is exerted in the direction of the displacement by another system (this is essentially the definition of work in mechanics, which is less general than the one given here, which covers interactions other than those considered in mechanics; the present definition implies that the force applied on a body by a stationary force field, such as gravity or an electrostatic field, results in no work, even though the body is in motion—for example, freely falling); (2) the electromagnetic interactions between primary and secondary coils of a transformer; and (3) the exchange of radiation emitted by lasers. Such radiation consists of wave particles, which are in order relative to each other as contrasted with those, for example, from an incandescent lamp, which are randomly arranged. On the other hand, it can be shown by virtue of the laws of thermodynamics that the exchange of radiation between a hot system and a cold system (such as blackbody radiation) does not conform to the requirement stated in the definition of work and is not, therefore, a work interaction.

Work is one of several distinguishable types of interaction that can occur between two systems. Any interaction that is not work will be hereinafter called nonwork. A special type of nonwork interaction that will be treated below in detail is a heat interaction. In general, an interaction is fully specified if the exact sequence of states, called the path, of each of the interacting systems is specified. In turn, the path of one of the systems and the interactions that occur specify the process experienced by the system. In an interaction that satisfies the definition of work, each system is said to be experiencing an adiabatic process.

The state and, therefore, the values of the properties of a system can change either spontaneously or as a result of interactions with other systems. During changes of state the values of certain properties are subject to limitations imposed by the laws of physics. The limitations imposed by thermodynamics are consequences of the first and second laws, which will be stated here in an unusually general way.

FIRST LAW

The first law is a statement of existence of a property called energy. It is based on the concept of work and can be stated as follows: For any process involving no effects external to the system except displacement of a mass between specified levels in a gravity field, the magnitude of that mass is fixed by the end states of the system and is independent of the details of the process. This law has many implications or corollaries, some of which are as follows.

Consequences of the first law

1. *Uniqueness of work values.* By virtue of the first law a unique number can be assigned to a work interaction between two systems. This number is n when n arbitrarily selected units of mass are displaced between two arbitrarily specified levels in a gravity field. The sign of work is selected positive when work is done by a system—that is, when the sole external effect would be the rise of a weight.

2. *Definition of energy.* By virtue of the first law, the work in an adiabatic process depends on the initial and final, or end, states only. It follows that a property of a system can be defined, called energy, such that its change of value between states A_1 and A_2 is equal to the work W^a_{12} involved in an adiabatic process that has A_1 and A_2 as end states. In terms of symbols, if E_1 and E_2 denote the energies of states A_1 and A_2, respectively, and W^a_{12} the work done in any adiabatic process connecting A_1 and A_2, the difference $E_2 - E_1$ is equal to the negative of W^a_{12}; *i.e.,*

$$E_2 - E_1 = - W^a_{12}. \qquad (1)$$

Energy is only partially defined by equation (1) because the difference between E_1 and E_2 does not specify the values of E_1 and E_2. An arbitrary value such as zero, however, can be assigned to E_0 of some reference state A_0, so that the energies of all other states are fixed by equation (1).

It will be shown below that by virtue of the laws of thermodynamics certain interactions that cause change of energy cannot be described as work. The corresponding process is, by definition, a nonadiabatic process. Because energy is a property, the energy change associated with any nonadiabatic process will equal numerically the work in any adiabatic process between the same end states.

It can be readily verified that energy is an additive or extensive property; that is, the energy of a whole is equal to the sum of the energies of its parts.

3. *Conservation of energy.* The magnitude of the work in an adiabatic process can be positive, negative, or zero, depending on the end states of the process, but zero adiabatic work does not necessarily imply identical end states. An adiabatic zero-work change of state may occur spontaneously in a system, as, for example, when an electrical capacitor discharges through an internal resistor. During such a process, equation (1) requires that the energy of the system remain invariant. This is the so-called law of conservation of energy, which is a consequence of the first law of thermodynamics. The first law, on the other hand, cannot be deduced from the law of conservation of energy.

A system that experiences an adiabatic, zero-work process is said to be isolated from all other systems in the environment.

4. *Impossibility of perpetual-motion machine of the first kind.* A perpetual-motion machine of the first kind (PMM1)

is any system that undergoes a cycle and has no external effect except the rise of a weight. The term cycle (or cyclic process) is defined as a process in which the initial and final states of the system are identical.

By virtue of the first law, the work of an adiabatic cycle must be equal to zero and, therefore, a PMM1 is impossible.

5. *The first law and relativity.* According to the general theory of relativity, the energy E of a system is equal to the product of its mass m and the square of the speed of light c in a vacuum, namely,

$$E = mc^2. \tag{2}$$

By virtue of the first law, the energy E of an isolated system is conserved. Therefore, equation (2) requires that the mass m of the system is also conserved, regardless of the processes occurring within the system (such as chemical reactions, nuclear reactions, and creation and annihilation of particles). Moreover, if the energy of a system is altered by virtue of an adiabatic or nonadiabatic interaction, the mass of the system must also be altered in accordance with equation (2). In most applications the energy transferred to or from a system is so much smaller than the total energy mc^2 of the system that the change in mass is negligible.

Conservation of mass

SECOND LAW

The second law is a statement of existence of stable equilibrium states. More than the first law, the second law distinguishes thermodynamics from other parts of physics. Because it has far-reaching implications concerning the properties and behaviour of matter, it is frequently invoked in discussions of philosophy as well as in discussions of physics.

Of the many statements of the second law, those of Clausius, Planck, and Carathéodory are the most notable. All of these statements imply the existence of a stable equilibrium state for given values of energy, the number of particles, and the constraints (see below)—an implication that is here taken to be the essential element of the second law.

The term equilibrium state means a state that does not change with time while the system is isolated from all other systems in the environment. Equilibrium state is sometimes confused with steady state: a steady state does not change with time even though the system, rather than being isolated, is interacting with other systems.

If a system is in an equilibrium state, a finite change of state may be caused by interactions with the environment, including those that leave no finite net effects in the environment. Several types of equilibrium states can be distinguished. Among these is the stable equilibrium state for which a finite change of state cannot occur, regardless of interactions that leave no net effects in the environment.

Consistent with its nature, a system might assume any one of a set of possible states, but some of the possible states may be prohibited by restrictions imposed by the environment. These restrictions are called constraints. For example, a given amount of gas may assume any of a large number of states. The same amount of gas, however, confined in a gas-tight container of fixed volume is restricted to states with volumes smaller than or equal to the volume inside the container. The possible states of the system that are consistent with the constraints will be called allowed states.

Constraints on systems and allowed states

The second law can now be stated as follows: Among all the allowed states of a system with given values of energy, numbers of particles, and constraints, one and only one is a stable equilibrium state.

The second law cannot be derived from the laws of mechanics (either classical or quantum). The second law asserts that a stable equilibrium state exists for each value of the energy, whereas in mechanics the only stable state is that of minimum energy, what is known as the ground state.

Some corollaries of the second law are as follows.

1. *State principle.* By virtue of the second law, stable equilibrium states exist, and a unique stable equilibrium state corresponds to each set of values of energy, numbers of particles, and constraints. The uniqueness implies the following corollary: the value of any property of a system in a stable equilibrium state may be expressed as a function of the values of the energy, numbers of particles, and constraints only. This corollary is known as the state principle.

2. *Reversible and irreversible processes.* A process is reversible if the system and its environment can be restored to their initial states, except for differences of smaller order of magnitude than the maximum changes that occur during the process.

If a system starts from any allowed state and reaches the corresponding stable equilibrium state with no net effect on the environment, then the process would not be reversible. For if it were, the system, starting from the stable equilibrium state, could undergo a process that ends at another state with no net effect on the environment. This conclusion, however, violates the definition of a stable equilibrium state. A process that is not reversible is called irreversible.

3. *Impossibility of perpetual-motion machine of the second kind.* It can be shown from the definition of a stable equilibrium state that a system in such a state can receive but cannot produce work. The plausibility of this corollary will be evident from the observation that work can always be used to change from any state to a nonequilibrium state by creating relative velocity of parts or compression to a smaller volume. If a system in a stable equilibrium state were to produce work, that work could be used to cause the system itself to end in a nonequilibrium state with no net effects on the environment—contrary to the definition of its initial state.

This corollary applies strictly only to systems of which the energy can be increased indefinitely, such as any system with particles free to move from one place to another or any system with translational degrees of freedom. Most practical systems satisfy this requirement. The generalization to systems that do not satisfy the requirement, such as a nuclear-spin system, is discussed below under *Negative temperature.*

A perpetual-motion machine of the second kind (PMM2) is any device that would deliver net work—*e.g.,* raise an external weight—while undergoing a cycle and interacting with a single system in a stable equilibrium state. A perpetual-motion machine of the second kind is a device that permits a system to violate the corollary stated above and is, therefore, impossible.

Prior to the discussion of the fourth corollary, it is necessary to define the terms mutual stable equilibrium and reservoir. Two systems A and B are said to be in mutual stable equilibrium if the combined system AB is in a stable equilibrium state. It can be readily verified that, if two systems are in mutual stable equilibrium, each system must be in a stable equilibrium state. Moreover, if the two systems are brought into communication so that interactions are not prohibited, no interactions will occur.

Reservoirs as systems

A reservoir R is a special kind of a system that provides useful reference states for applications of the laws of thermodynamics and satisfies the following conditions: (1) it is closed to the transfer of rest mass—*i.e.,* its boundaries cannot be crossed by material particles; (2) its constraints are invariant with time—for example, its volume has the same value at all times; (3) it passes through stable equilibrium states only; and (4) in the course of finite interactions it remains in mutual stable equilibrium with a duplicate of itself that experiences no such interactions. An example of a reservoir is a mixture of solid, liquid, and vapour water in mutual stable equilibrium while enclosed in a container.

4. *Work done by a system in combination with a reservoir.* A system A in combination with a reservoir R can experience a work interaction with other systems either directly or through an intermediate device X, or both, while X is undergoing a cyclic process (Figure 1). During this work interaction no rest mass is exchanged between A and R while the state of A changes from A_1 to A_2. The work done is denoted by W_{12}^R for processes in general and by $(W_{12}^R)_{rev}$ for processes that meet reversibility criteria.

By virtue of the first and second laws it can be shown

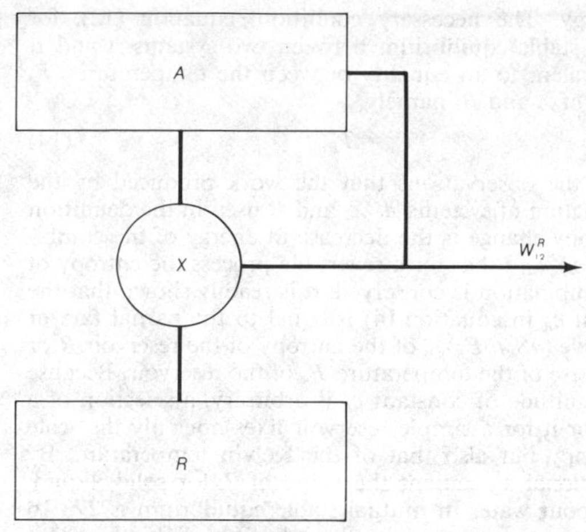

Figure 1: Production of work by a system A interacting with a reservoir R through an intermediate device X (see text).

that for a given change of state from A_1 to A_2, the work $(W^R_{12})_{rev}$ is the same for all reversible processes and for all reservoirs in mutual stable equilibrium with each other; that is, $(W^R_{12})_{rev}$ is fixed by the end states A_1 and A_2. Moreover, W^R_{12} cannot exceed $(W^R_{12})_{rev}$ when both correspond to the same change of state from A_1 to A_2.

ENTROPY

The two laws of thermodynamics imply the existence of a property called entropy that is conserved in all reversible processes. Its definition is based on another property called available work.

Available work. Because for a given system and reservoir $(W^R_{12})_{rev}$ depends on the end states of the system only, a property can be defined called available work (symbolized Ω, omega), such that its change of value between states A_1 and A_2 is equal to the work $(W^R_{12})_{rev}$: that is (using the symbol ≡ to imply definition),

$$\Omega_2 - \Omega_1 \equiv -(W^R_{12})_{rev}. \tag{3}$$

It can be easily verified that available work is an additive or extensive property.

Definition of entropy. Because both energy and available work are extensive properties, the difference between them is also an extensive property. Entropy will be defined as the extensive property S the change of which, DS, in a change of state is equal to a positive constant c_R times the difference between the corresponding changes of energy DE and available work $D\Omega$ evaluated with respect to a standard reservoir. This definition can be written in the form of an equation; *i.e.*,

$$DS \equiv c_R\,(DE - D\,\Omega). \tag{4}$$

The symbol D denotes a change, finite or infinitesimal, in magnitude of the property the symbol of which it precedes.

The standard reservoir may be chosen to be a mixture of solid, liquid, and vapour water in mutual stable equilibrium, and an arbitrary value, as explained below, may be assigned to the constant c_R. Subject to subsequent considerations, an arbitrary value may be assigned to the entropy of an arbitrarily selected reference state of the system. Thereafter, by means of equation (4), a value may be found for any state, equilibrium or nonequilibrium, once values for E and Ω have been determined by appropriate measurements.

Entropy changes in adiabatic processes. If the process from state A_1 to state A_2 in system A is adiabatic—that is, system A experiences only work interactions—then the work done by A must, by equation (1), equal the decrease in the energy of A. For a reversible adiabatic process the work done must, by equation (3), also equal the decrease in available work, so that the difference between the decrease in energy and the decrease in available work must be equal to zero. It follows from equation (4) that for a reversible adiabatic process the entropy change of the system is equal to zero; that is, the entropy is invariant. Moreover, because the fourth corollary states that the work for any adiabatic process cannot exceed that for the reversible adiabatic process, it follows that for an adiabatic process in general the entropy change must be greater than or at least equal to zero. In terms of symbols these conclusions can be written as

$$(DS)^a_{rev} = 0, \text{ for reversible adiabatic processes,} \tag{5}$$

and

$$(DS)^a \geq 0, \text{ for adiabatic processes} \tag{6}$$

(the symbol > means "greater than," and ≥ means "greater than or equal to").

Principle of increase of entropy. When equation (6) is applied to any process in an isolated system—*i.e.*, to an adiabatic process for which the work is zero—it becomes

$$DS\text{ (isolated)} \geq 0. \tag{7}$$

Thus, the entropy of an isolated system may remain constant or may increase, but a decrease of entropy in an isolated system is impossible. Because any process in any system may be conceptually changed to a process in an isolated system by including in the isolated system all systems with which the original system interacts, the conclusion represented by equation (7) is of great generality. Equation (7) is known as the principle of increase of entropy, although it may be more strictly said to be the principle of the impossibility of a decrease of entropy. According to this principle, whenever any process occurs in nature, the total entropy of all systems involved in the process must either increase or, if the process is reversible, remain constant.

STABLE EQUILIBRIUM

Criterion for stable equilibrium. Changes of state in an isolated system can occur only until the system reaches the unique stable equilibrium state consistent with the given values of energy, numbers of particles, and constraints. It follows from equation (7) that the entropy of the stable equilibrium state must be larger than that of any equilibrium or nonequilibrium state with the same values of energy, numbers of different particles, and constraints. By the same token, a criterion for stable equilibrium is that the entropy of the system should be at its maximum value for fixed values of energy, numbers of particles, and constraints.

Equations relating properties for stable equilibrium states. By virtue of the state principle, the simplest illustrations of the laws of thermodynamics are provided by applications to systems in or passing through stable equilibrium states. For the properties and the relations between properties of systems in such states can be expressed by means of relatively simple mathematical forms.

Composition of systems in stable equilibrium states

The term numbers of particles, as used in the state principle, implies certain species of particles. The set of species selected must be a minimum set in terms of which the composition of all allowed states may be described. Such a minimum set of species, which will be unique in the number of members for a given system regardless of the choice of species to make up the set, is called a set of components.

For a system A with given fixed values E of energy, n_1, $n_2, \ldots, n_k$ of the numbers of particles of components 1, $2, \ldots, k$ of the set of k components, and $\beta_1, \beta_2, \ldots, \beta_s$ of constraints $1, 2, \ldots, s$ of the set of s constraints, the uniqueness of the corresponding stable equilibrium state implies that the value of any property of A in that state must be fully and uniquely determined by the given fixed values. Moreover, for all stable equilibrium states, the values of a property F may be expressed as a mathematical function having a single value for each single set of values $E, n_1, n_2, \ldots, n_k, \beta_1, \beta_2, \ldots, \beta_s$; that is,

$$F = F(E, n_1, n_2, \ldots, n_k, \beta_1, \beta_2, \ldots, \beta_s). \tag{8}$$

Several relations like equation (8) for several properties may be manipulated mathematically to express the values of any property as a function of the values of any set of independent properties of stable equilibrium states. A set of independent properties is such that the value of each property in the set can be varied without affecting the values of the remaining properties in the set.

Expressions for entropy and energy

Two functions of interest to subsequent considerations are those that relate the values of entropy S to the values of $E, n_1, n_2, \ldots, n_k, \beta_1, \beta_2, \ldots, \beta_s$, and the values of energy E to the values of $S, n_1, n_2, \ldots, n_k, \beta_1, \beta_2, \ldots, \beta_s$. These functions are denoted as

$$S = S(E, n_1, n_2, \ldots, n_k, \beta_1, \beta_2, \ldots, \beta_s) \tag{9}$$

and

$$E = E(S, n_1, n_2, \ldots, n_k, \beta_1, \beta_2, \ldots, \beta_s). \tag{10}$$

In general, the change of entropy per unit change of energy, or of any of the numbers of particles, or of any of the constraints can be evaluated with the help of equation (9). The same remark applies to energy and equation (10). Such changes are called partial derivatives and are used to define a number of useful properties that have meaning for stable equilibrium states only.

Mutual stable equilibrium of closed systems. If two systems A and B that are closed to the transfer of rest mass taken together constitute a system in a stable equilibrium state, then the entropy of that system must be at a maximum for the value of its energy. One of the consequences of this requirement will be seen from a possible variation—a conceptual alteration of state consistent with the description of the system and the constraints imposed on it and its parts A and B by the environment—in which the energy of A is increased by a small amount denoted by dE_A, and that of B is decreased by the same amount, while both A and B pass through stable equilibrium states without changes of values of their constraints. The entropy of part A is correspondingly altered by the amount dS_A. This amount can be expressed as

$$dS_A = \left(\frac{\partial S_A}{\partial E_A}\right)_{n,\beta} dE_A,$$

in which $(\partial S_A/\partial E_A)_{n,\beta}$ denotes the rate of change of S_A per unit change of E_A as A passes through stable equilibrium states while its numbers of particles (n) and its constraints (β) are held constant, namely, the partial derivative of S_A with respect to E_A. A similar expression can be written for the entropy change dS_B of B, so that the alteration dS of combined system AB is given by the expression

$$dS = \left(\frac{\partial S_A}{\partial E_A}\right)_{n,\beta} dE_A + \left(\frac{\partial S_B}{\partial E_B}\right)_{n,\beta} dE_B. \tag{11}$$

It can be shown that if the entropy S is to be at a maximum for the given fixed value of energy $E_A + E_B$ of the combined system AB and for both positive and negative variations dE_A, then it is necessary that the two partial derivatives $(\partial S_A/\partial E_A)_{n,\beta}$ and $(\partial S_B/\partial E_B)_{n,\beta}$ be equal to each other, namely,

$$\left(\frac{\partial S_A}{\partial E_A}\right)_{n,\beta} = \left(\frac{\partial S_B}{\partial E_B}\right)_{n,\beta}. \tag{12}$$

The quantity $(\partial S/\partial E)_{n,\beta}$ of a system may be thought of as a potential that governs the tendency of energy to pass from one system to another. It can be shown that it is a "capturing tendency" in that if

$$\left(\frac{\partial S_A}{\partial E_A}\right)_{n,\beta} > \left(\frac{\partial S_B}{\partial E_B}\right)_{n,\beta},$$

"Capturing" and "escaping" tendencies

then dE_A may be greater than zero (energy may pass from system B to system A) in an actual process but not less than zero (because less than zero would be contrary to the principle of increase of entropy). Conversely, the reciprocal quantity $(\partial E/\partial S)_{n,\beta}$ may be thought of as an "escaping tendency."

Temperature. The potential that governs the flow of energy is called temperature. A scale of temperature may be defined in terms of any function of $(\partial S/\partial E)_{n,\beta}$ or $(\partial E/\partial S)_{n,\beta}$ that continuously increases or decreases with either. The scale commonly used in thermodynamics is the Kelvin scale of temperature. It is denoted by T and defined as

$$T \equiv \left(\frac{\partial E}{\partial S}\right)_{n,\beta}, \tag{13}$$

so that T becomes a measure of the escaping tendency of energy. The necessary condition, equation (12), for mutual stable equilibrium between two systems A and B is equivalent to an equality between the temperatures T_A and T_B of A and B, namely,

$$T_A = T_B. \tag{14}$$

From the observations that the work produced by the combination of systems A, X, and R used in the definition of entropy change is the decrease in energy of the combination AR and that for a reversible process the entropy of that combination is conserved, it is readily shown that the constant c_R in equation (4) is equal to the partial rate or derivative $(\partial S_R/\partial E_R)_{n,\beta}$ of the entropy of the reservoir R or the inverse of the temperature T_R of the reservoir. Because the magnitude of constant c_R is arbitrary, a selection of a value for it for a simple reservoir fixes not only the scale of entropy but also that of the Kelvin temperature. By international agreement the value of T for solid, liquid, and vapour water in mutual stable equilibrium is 273.16 K. Among the reasons for the selection of this five-digit figure is that it causes the temperature interval between the freezing and boiling points of water under a pressure of one atmosphere to be almost exactly 100 degrees. If any other reservoir R' is used with X and A, the change in entropy found from equation (4) for a change in state of system A from A_1 to A_2 will be the same as that found using R if constant c_R' is taken equal to the inverse temperature of the reservoir R'.

Entropy constant

When the number 273.15 is subtracted from the value of any given Kelvin temperature T, the result will be the Celsius temperature t, or t (degrees Celsius) $\equiv T - 273.15$.

Heat. An argument will now be outlined to prove that certain nonwork interactions are entirely distinguishable from work in that no fraction of any one such interaction will satisfy the definition of work.

If two systems A and B are in stable equilibrium states and each is under constant constraints, but they are not in mutual stable equilibrium, then an interaction could occur between them. By virtue of the third corollary of the second law, any such interaction must be a nonwork interaction; that is, its effects on at least one system, say A, could not have been produced while the sole external effect was the rise of a weight. In general, however, the effects on A could be produced while weights external to A are raised and, in addition, a change of state of B takes place. It can be shown that maximum work will be delivered to the weights if the process is carried out reversibly and each system passes through stable equilibrium states. A reversible cyclic device X (Figure 2) interposed between systems A and B will permit these conditions to be fulfilled. The device X may produce work, but the reversible interactions experienced by A with X and X with B cannot be work by virtue of corollary 3 of the second law.

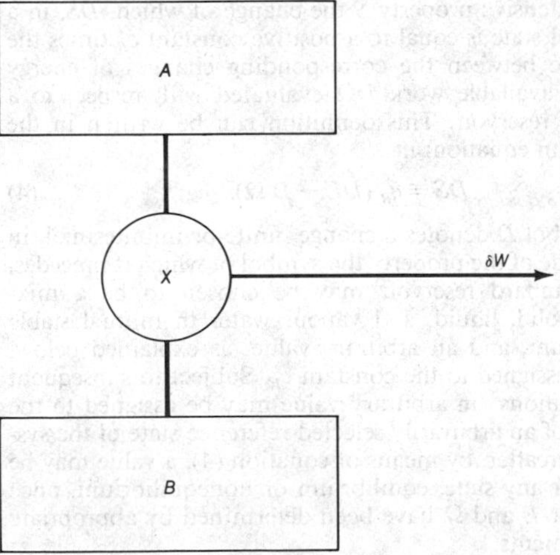

Figure 2: Production of work by a reversible cyclic device X that undergoes reversible nonwork interactions with systems A and B (see text).

For the reversible process just described it can be shown

from the functions that relate energy to entropy and other independent properties that the work δW that will be delivered to the weights is equal to the negative of the energy change dE_A of system A times the ratio $(T_A - T_B)/T_A$. This conclusion can be written as an equation; *i.e.*,

$$\delta W = -\frac{T_A - T_B}{T_A} dE_A. \quad (15)$$

In equation (15), the symbol d denotes an infinitesimal change of the value of a property, whereas δ denotes an infinitesimal amount of a quantity that is not a property or state function. Work is not a property of any system, and therefore δW is the appropriate way to indicate an infinitesimal amount of W.

Because dE_A is a measure of the magnitude of the interaction experienced by A with X, equation (15) expresses the work produced as a fraction of the magnitude of that interaction. As systems A and B approach mutual stable equilibrium, temperatures T_A and T_B approach equality, a necessary condition, and the fraction that represents the ratio of δW over dE_A approaches zero; that is, the work that can be obtained from the interaction between A and B through X becomes a vanishingly small fraction of the magnitude of the interaction. Moreover, it can be shown that then the interactions between A and X and between X and B are exactly equal, and each may be expressed as a product of temperature and entropy change $T_A dS_A$ and $T_B dS_B$.

In the limit, therefore, as T_A approaches T_B, the cyclic device X is no longer required, and the nature of the interaction approaches something completely distinguishable from work. It is this special kind of interaction that is called heat and denoted by the symbol Q. Moreover, for any process for which a system passes only through stable equilibrium states of fixed constraints and for a change of state corresponding to changes dS in entropy and dE in energy, the infinitesimal amount of heat $(\delta Q)_{rev}$ received by the system is given by the relations

$$(\delta Q)_{rev} = TdS = dE. \quad (16)$$

If the interacting systems pass only through stable equilibrium states, then the process will be reversible.

Heat is not a property of a system. Accordingly, the symbol δQ is used to denote an infinitesimal amount of heat but not the change in value of a property. Nor is heat contained within a system.

Meaning of heat

The term heat is used here in a special sense that is quite foreign to the popular conception of its meaning. A different term might have been used were it not for the historical association of the word heat with thermodynamics. It will be observed from the context that the word heat is reserved here for a very special kind of interaction between systems, which only by virtue of the laws of thermodynamics is entirely distinguishable from all other kinds of interactions, including the special kind called work. If a less restrictive definition had been used, then some of the relations between heat and entropy given here would not always hold.

Heat and flow of entropy. When a heat interaction occurs between two systems A and B that pass through stable equilibrium states, the process is reversible. For the combined system AB the process may be considered an adiabatic process for which the work is zero, so that, in accordance with equations (5) and (7) expressed in terms of subsystems A and B, $DS_A + DS_B = 0$. Because, from equation (16), DS_A is equal to $(\delta Q_A/T)_{rev}$ and different from zero, the heat interaction is associated with a flow of entropy from A to B if heat flows from A to B and conversely. By way of contrast, work in a reversible process leaves the entropies of the interacting systems unaltered.

To system B may be added a part that is not in a stable equilibrium state and that may experience an irreversible process without affecting the state of the other part or the interaction between A and B. Although the process as a whole is no longer reversible, the interaction is the same as before and could appropriately be called heat. A flow of entropy from A to B is still associated with the flow of heat from A to B, but the increase of entropy in B exceeds the amount that has flowed from A; that is, the statement $dS > \delta Q/T$ may be written for the irreversible process, and

$$dS \geq \frac{\delta Q}{T} \quad (17)$$

for processes in general.

For an adiabatic process equation (17) reduces to equation (6). For other processes equation (17) will apply provided that the only nonwork interactions are heat; that is, at least locally where the interaction occurs, the behaviour on each side of the boundary is the same as if both systems were passing through stable equilibrium states, with identifiable temperatures, and the process was reversible. It can readily be shown that certain nonwork interactions when used in place of δQ will not satisfy equation (17).

Inequality of Clausius. An inequality that was first stated by Clausius bears his name. It is as follows: For an irreversible cycle the sum of ratios, each of which is a heat δQ received by the system divided by the temperature T at which the heat is received, is always less than zero. When each amount of heat δQ is very small, the sum of the ratios $\delta Q/T$ can be represented by a cyclic integral, and the inequality of Clausius may be expressed by the relation

$$\left(\oint \frac{\delta Q}{T}\right)_{irrev} < 0. \quad (18)$$

(The symbol $\oint$ means to integrate over a closed path, the complete cycle.) The inequality of Clausius follows directly when the inequality of equation (17) is applied to each step of an irreversible cycle and summed up for all the steps, because dS, being the change in a property, sums up to zero. Application of the inequality of Clausius is restricted, of course, to processes for which all nonwork interactions are heat.

Work, heat, and change of energy. If work and heat interactions occur successively, then the total energy change dE will be the sum of the work effect $(-\delta W)$ and the heat effect δQ; or, by equations (1) and (16),

$$dE = \delta Q - \delta W, \quad (19)$$

the minus sign resulting from the conventions regarding the signs for heat and work.

Expression (19) for change of energy is applicable, of course, only to those processes for which the interactions are identifiable as heat and work. Because heat and work are limiting cases of actual processes, equation (19) is strictly applicable only where all interactions have been carried to these limits.

Reversible cyclic engine. By reference to the definition of heat, it will be observed that the reversible interactions between A and X and between X and B in Figure 2 are heat interactions in which one part of X is in equilibrium with A and another part with B, whether or not A and B are close to mutual stable equilibrium. Because the process for the combined system AXB is adiabatic, it can be shown that the heat δQ_B received by B is equal to the heat δQ_A received by A times the negative of the ratio of the temperatures of B and A; namely,

$$\delta Q_B = -\frac{T_B}{T_A} \delta Q_A. \quad (20)$$

The work produced by cyclic device X is, by equation (19), equal to the negative of the sum $\delta Q_A + \delta Q_B$, and, because of equation (20),

$$\delta W = -\delta Q_A - \delta Q_B = \frac{T_A - T_B}{T_A}(-\delta Q_A). \quad (21)$$

It is seen from equation (21) that X will produce positive work if $T_A > T_B$ and $\delta Q_A < 0$; that is, if heat flows from the hotter system to X and from X to the cooler system. The fraction η of the heat received from the hotter system that X converts to work is

$$\eta = \frac{T_A - T_B}{T_A} \quad (22)$$

Reversible cyclic engines

This quantity is called the Carnot efficiency after Carnot, who, before the discovery of the first and second laws of thermodynamics, made the following statements concerning the efficiency of engines working between reservoirs at specified levels of temperature: The efficiency of a reversible engine has a fixed value that is the same for all reversible engines and is greater than that of any irreversible engine.

An example of a reversible cycle in which a system receives all heat at one temperature and rejects all heat at another with reversible adiabatic changes between the two temperatures is the Carnot cycle, devised by Carnot. Its efficiency is given by equation (22).

Work-producing systems and devices. A problem of economic and social importance in heat engineering is the production of work to be used for practical purposes such as lifting weights, driving electric generators, propelling vehicles, or operating cutting tools. Work can be obtained from any system that is not in a stable equilibrium state as it changes toward a stable equilibrium state without changes in constraints. For example, work may be obtained by lowering a weight inside a closed system while causing—through appropriate levers, belts, and pulleys—a weight to rise outside. The production of work need not end until the internal weight has reached the lowest position in the gravity field that the configuration of the system permits. Similarly, an electric storage battery may produce work until it is completely discharged. The maximum work that can be produced by the system adiabatically will be obtained if the process is executed reversibly—that is, at constant entropy. The maximum work is only a fraction of the energy of the system. This fraction is larger the farther the system is initially from stable equilibrium; *i.e.,* the larger the difference between the maximum entropy corresponding to the initial energy and the entropy of the initial nonstable state. The fraction is equal to zero when the difference in entropy just described is equal to zero—namely, when the system is initially in a stable equilibrium state.

On the other hand, a system in any state, including a stable equilibrium state, can produce work when combined with a system in the environment that passes through stable equilibrium states but is not in mutual stable equilibrium with the first. The maximum work that can be obtained is the maximum possible decrease in the available work when the system in the environment acts as a reservoir, or it is the maximum possible decrease of one of the other availability functions discussed below when other conditions are imposed by the environment. In order to obtain this maximum, the work-producing process must be completely reversible. For example, if the system with the elevated weight described in the preceding paragraph is at a higher or lower temperature than the atmosphere, then further work may be obtained by interposing a Carnot heat engine between the system and the atmosphere, so that the system is gradually cooled or heated to the temperature of the atmosphere as heat flows to the engine and produces work. If the whole process is executed reversibly, then the maximum possible work will be produced.

The greatest sources of work are fuels found in nature that are either not themselves in stable equilibrium states—for example, uranium in a reactor—or are not in mutual stable equilibrium with the atmosphere from which they have been isolated in the course of geologic history—for example, the fossil fuels coal and petroleum. In either case, the maximum work can be obtained only by a reversible approach to stable equilibrium or mutual stable equilibrium.

In the case of uranium, a reversible nuclear reaction is required; for the fossil fuels, a reversible chemical reaction. A close approximation to a reversible chemical reaction is found in lead storage batteries used in automobiles for starting and for lighting. No close approximation to a reversible nuclear reaction has yet been realized in practice, although in principle such a reaction is possible.

Because the cost of work includes not only fuel costs but also capital costs that usually increase as irreversibility in the process is reduced, the economical means of producing work may in some respects depart radically from the reversible means. For example, in fossil-fueled central power stations, fuel and oxygen in the air enter into an irreversible chemical reaction that raises the temperature of the resulting products by about 2,000 degrees on the Kelvin scale and reduces the work available by about one quarter. Energy from these hot products is then transferred irreversibly across a large temperature difference to appear as heat added to liquid and vapour water that is the working fluid of a heat engine. The loss in work available is again about one quarter of that of the original fuel and air. Irreversibility in the heat-engine cycle accounts for another 10 percent, so that about 40 percent is actually realized as work delivered to the electrical distribution system.

Economical production of work

A Carnot cycle is an obvious but usually impractical means to produce work from heat interactions with hot products of chemical or nuclear reactions. Most commonly used is the Rankine cycle, in which heat is used to generate vapour from a liquid; the vapour is expanded through a work-producing engine, condensed to liquid as it rejects heat to the environment, and pumped back into the vapour generator. The Stirling cycle, which has had only limited application, passes through gaseous states only.

Simple systems

STABLE EQUILIBRIUM STATES

A closed simple system is one in which the numbers of particles of the various components are fixed and the only constraint provided by the environment is an upper value for the volume of the system. By virtue of the state principle, volume (regardless of shape) and energy become sufficient to determine a stable equilibrium state, and the number of independent properties is two. A system that is not influenced by capillarity and external force fields is a simple system. These conditions may be satisfied despite capillarity and gravity fields if homogeneous parts of the system are large, so as to have small surface-to-volume ratio, yet shallow in the vertical direction of the gravity field and free of electric and magnetic fields created by external bodies.

Definition of a simple system

For stable equilibrium states of a closed simple system, entropy S or any other property can be regarded as fixed by the two independent properties volume V and energy U; therefore, S can be expressed as a function of V and U of the form

$$S = S(V,U). \tag{23}$$

For a number of reasons the energy E of a simple system is denoted by a different symbol U and is called the internal energy. Alternatively, equation (23) may be solved for U in terms of S and V to give

$$U = U(S,V). \tag{24}$$

The energy change dU between two neighbouring stable equilibrium states can be expressed in terms of the corresponding entropy and volume changes, dS and dV, respectively, by means of the relation

$$dU = \left(\frac{\partial U}{\partial S}\right)_V dS + \left(\frac{\partial U}{\partial V}\right)_S dV. \tag{25}$$

The first partial differential coefficient has already been identified (by equation 13) as the Kelvin temperature. The second is the rate of energy change with change in volume in reversible adiabatic compression or expansion. It can be shown to be the negative of the pressure p that the system exerts on constraining walls. Substitution of the temperature T and the pressure p in equation (25) results in the equation

$$dU = TdS - pdV, \tag{26}$$

in which the first term in the right-hand member represents the heat and the second the work of a reversible process. It may be observed, however, that equation (26) holds for any change between neighbouring stable equilibrium states regardless of the nature of the process, because it is a relation between properties and changes in values of properties. But for the general process, the terms (TdS) and ($-pdV$) are not in general equal to the respective heat and work that may be involved in the process.

By means of the criterion of stable equilibrium and equation (26), it can be shown that not only the temperature but also the pressure must be uniform throughout a simple system in a stable equilibrium state.

Representation of states on diagrams. Because a stable equilibrium state in a simple system is determined by two independent properties, all such states may be represented by points on a surface in a space in which two of the three coordinates represent independent properties and the third the dependent property. Alternatively, the traces of planes of constant value of one property may be shown on a two-dimensional chart in which the coordinates represent the other two properties. Two common choices of the latter class are pressure–volume (p–V) and temperature–entropy (T–S) charts. An example of the former is shown in Figure 3 (left), with traces of planes of constant temperature from the pressure–volume–temperature space and of planes of constant entropy from the pressure–volume–entropy space. On the p–V chart the area under a curve of states represents the work done on a slowly moving piston that confines the fluid in a cylinder. On the T–S chart (Figure 3 [right]) the area under the curve represents the heat received by the system in a reversible process passing through the states represented by the curve. Because the

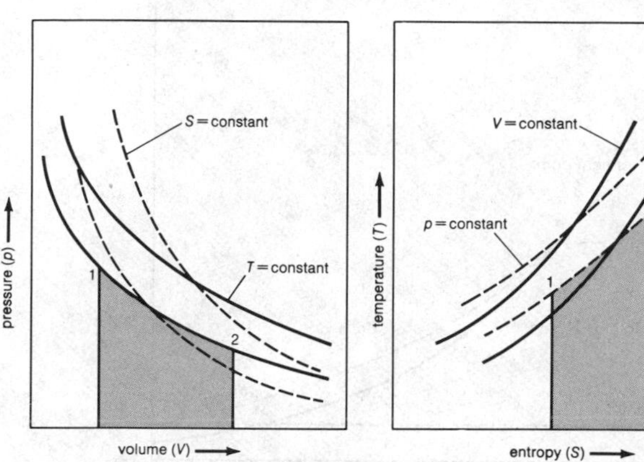

Figure 3: *Relationships between thermodynamic properties of systems.*
(Left) Relationships of pressure and volume of systems maintained at fixed temperature (T) or at fixed entropy (S).
(Right) Relationships between temperature and entropy of systems maintained at fixed pressure (p) or at fixed volume (V).

change of energy of a system undergoing a cycle is equal to zero, it is seen from equation (19) that the cyclic integral $\oint \delta Q$ must be equal to the cyclic integral $\oint \delta W$. For a reversible cycle, TdS may be substituted for δQ and pdV for δW so that

$$\oint TdS = \oint pdV. \tag{27}$$

For any cycle, therefore, the area enclosed by the representation on the T–S chart is equal to that on the p–V chart; for example, the areas enclosed by the representations of the Carnot cycle in the p–V and T–S charts (Figure 4 [left] and 4 [right]) are equal.

Reversible constant-pressure process. The reversible process at constant pressure, because of its practical importance, warrants special consideration. Because for constant pressure the change in the product pV is also p times the change in V, pdV, it can be shown that the expression for the heat $(\delta Q)_p$ received by the system is equal to the change of an extensive property called enthalpy, which is defined by the relation $H \equiv U + pV$; that is,

Enthalpy

$$(\delta Q)_p = dH. \tag{28}$$

Thus, in any heating of a simple system in such a way (for example, under a piston loaded by a weight) that its boundary expands slowly as it maintains constant pressure, the enthalpy of the system increases by the amount of heat added.

MAXWELL RELATIONS

For a closed simple system that assumes only stable equilibrium states, it follows from equation (26) that the partial derivative $(\partial T/\partial V)_S$ is equal to the negative of the partial derivative $(\partial p/\partial S)_V$. This equality is one of the Maxwell

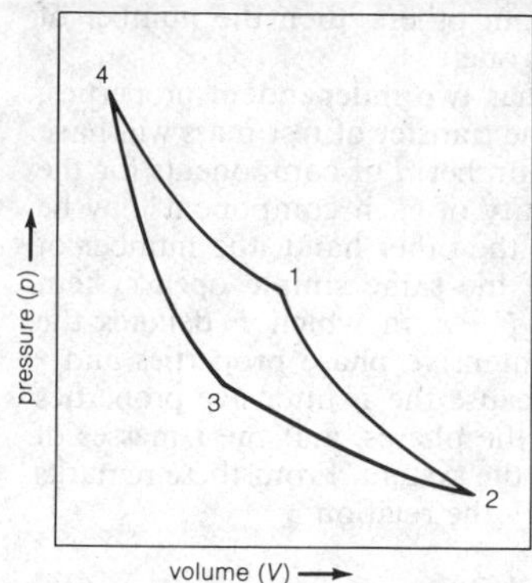

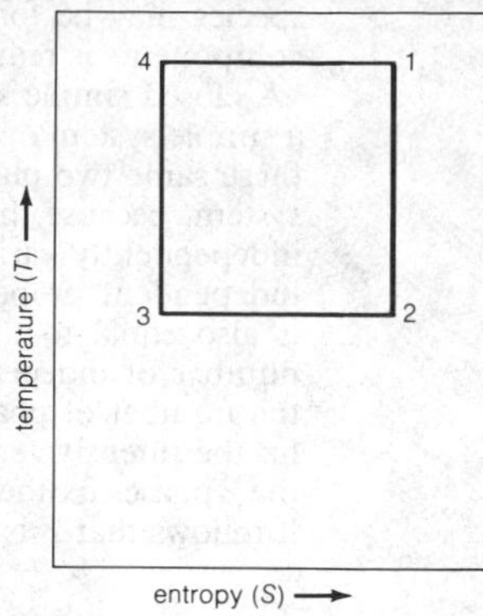

Figure 4: *Relationship between work done and heat received by a fluid undergoing a Carnot cycle.*
The lines from state 1 to state 2 represent reversible and adiabatic expansion of the fluid; from 2 to 3, reversible compression at fixed temperature accompanied by heat rejection; from 3 to 4, reversible and adiabatic compression; from 4 to 1, reversible expansion at fixed temperature accompanied by heat reception. The enclosed area (left) represents the net work done by the fluid during the complete cycle; it is exactly equal to the enclosed area (right) that represents the net heat flow to the fluid.

relations, named (as mentioned above) for the man who first stated them. The other Maxwell relations may be derived from the definitions of the thermodynamic properties enthalpy H, Helmholtz free energy Ψ, and Gibbs free energy Z (zeta); these definitions, respectively are:

$$H \equiv U + pV, \tag{29}$$
$$\Psi \equiv U - TS, \tag{30}$$
$$Z \equiv H - TS. \tag{31}$$

The Maxwell relations resulting from equations (26), (29), (30), and (31), are the following:

$$\left(\frac{\partial T}{\partial V}\right)_S = -\left(\frac{\partial p}{\partial S}\right)_V, \tag{32}$$
$$\left(\frac{\partial T}{\partial p}\right)_S = \left(\frac{\partial V}{\partial S}\right)_p, \tag{33}$$
$$\left(\frac{\partial S}{\partial V}\right)_T = \left(\frac{\partial p}{\partial T}\right)_V, \tag{34}$$
$$\left(\frac{\partial S}{\partial p}\right)_T = -\left(\frac{\partial V}{\partial T}\right)_p. \tag{35}$$

These four equations relate the entropy, a property whose value cannot be measured directly, to the properties pressure, volume, and temperature, all of which can be directly evaluated.

PHASE RULE

An intensive property of system A is defined as a property of which the value at a spatial point in a part of A approaches a limit independent of the size of the part as the size is reduced until it can no longer be identified as a system. As a system is subdivided into smaller and smaller parts, at some point a part becomes so small as compared with the extent of force fields between the parts that it is no longer isolatable and may not, therefore, be considered a system.

For certain stable equilibrium states of a simple system, parts of the system may assume different values of intensive properties; for example, liquid and vapour water may coexist in mutual stable equilibrium for which liquid and vapour parts have the same pressure and temperature but radically different densities. Each such part is called a phase. More generally, a phase of a system is the collection of all homogeneous parts open to the transfer of rest mass and having identical values of their intensive properties.

In the absence of chemical reactions and membranes that are permeable to one substance and not to another, the number of components of a phase of a multiphase system will be identical with the number of molecular species present in the whole system. As soon, however, as a chemical reaction is permitted in which some of these species may be formed from others, then the number of components is reduced by one.

A closed simple system has two independent properties; a simple system open to the transfer of rest mass will have these same two plus the number n of components for the system, because the quantity of each component may be independently varied. On the other hand, the number of independent properties of the same simple open system is also equal to the sum $F+r$, in which F denotes the number of independent intensive phase properties and r the number of phases, because the F intensive properties fix the intensive states of the phases, and the r masses of the r phases fix the size of the system. From these remarks it follows that F is given by the relation

$$F=n+2-r. \tag{36}$$

The Gibbs phase rule

This is the phase rule of Gibbs. It reveals, for example, that for a single-component open system, such as water, the number of independent intensive properties may be 2, 1, or 0 if the number of phases present is 1, 2, or 3, respectively. Thus, for water vapour, temperature and pressure are independent properties; *i.e.,* after the value of one is arbitrarily selected, the value of the other may be arbitrarily selected. For coexisting liquid and vapour, either pressure or temperature may be considered the independent property; for coexisting solid, liquid, and vapour (the triple point), the values of all intensive phase properties are fixed by the nature of the substance, and the value of none may be arbitrarily selected. The triple-point temperature of water has been chosen as a fundamental point in defining the Kelvin temperature scale.

SIMPLE ONE-COMPONENT SYSTEMS

Phases. All systems that consist of a single pure molecular species, such as argon, oxygen, or water, exhibit largely common patterns of coexisting phases. A closed system of this kind, being a simple system, has two independent properties and the relationships between properties for stable equilibrium states may therefore be shown as a surface in three-dimensional space. The projection of one such surface onto the pressure–temperature plane is shown in Figure 5 (top) and onto a pressure–volume plane in Figure 5 (bottom). It will be evident from these figures that the solid may be heated under constant pressure until some liquid appears. Further heating increases the proportion of liquid present at constant temperature until the solid vanishes, leaving only liquid. Further heating increases the temperature of the liquid until vaporization begins, provided that the pressure is less than the critical pressure. Continued heating increases the proportion of vapour present at constant temperature until the liquid vanishes, leaving only vapour. The vapour may then be raised in temperature indefinitely or until chemical dissociation destroys the assumed purity of the molecular species.

At the critical pressure the coexisting liquid and vapour states are identical, and the vaporization process contracts to an infinitesimal process. At higher pressures no vaporization occurs. It becomes clear, then, that liquid and vapour states differ in degree rather than in kind, because any liquid state can be transformed to any vapour state by a process for which the system remains in a single-phase condition throughout. The same cannot be said of the transition from solid states to either liquid or vapour states.

Processes at constant volume and at constant pressure. When a simple system is heated at constant volume, no work occurs at the boundaries, so that the heat, according to equation (23), is equal to the increase in energy as well as to the product of temperature and increase in entropy:

Heat capacities

$$(\delta Q)_V = dU = TdS.$$

The heat of a constant-volume process is therefore equal to the area under the curve on a temperature–entropy chart. The constant-volume heat capacity is defined in terms of the partial derivatives of energy and entropy as follows:

$$C_V \equiv \left(\frac{\partial U}{\partial T}\right)_V = T\left(\frac{\partial S}{\partial T}\right)_V; \tag{37}$$

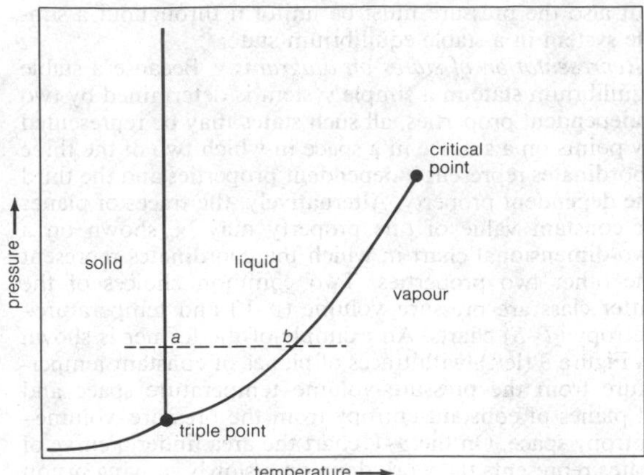

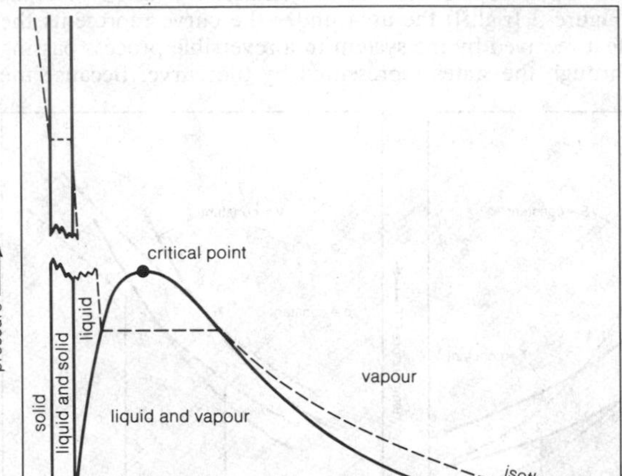

Figure 5: *Relationships between phases of a pure substance.* (Top) The horizontal broken line through *a* and *b* represents the effects of absorption of heat by a substance at a constant pressure. (Bottom) The broken line from lower right to upper left represents the effects of compressing a substance, initially entirely vaporous, while keeping the temperature fixed (an isothermal process).

and the constant-volume specific heat is defined similarly as

$$c_v \equiv \left(\frac{\partial u}{\partial T}\right)_v = T\left(\frac{\partial s}{\partial T}\right)_v, \tag{38}$$

in which lowercase letters denote values per unit of mass or per mole. By reference to equation (28) it will be seen by analogy that the corresponding definitions of heat capacity and specific heat at constant pressure are as follows:

$$C_p \equiv \left(\frac{\partial H}{\partial T}\right)_p = T\left(\frac{\partial S}{\partial T}\right)_p \tag{39}$$

and

$$c_p \equiv \left(\frac{\partial h}{\partial T}\right)_p = T\left(\frac{\partial s}{\partial T}\right)_p. \tag{40}$$

By means of Maxwell relations it can be shown that the difference between the two heat capacities is given by the product of two partial derivatives, both of which are fixed entirely by the relation between p, V, and T:

$$C_p - C_V = T\left(\frac{\partial p}{\partial T}\right)_V\left(\frac{\partial V}{\partial T}\right)_p. \tag{41}$$

When a phase change occurs during constant-pressure heating or cooling, the temperature is unchanged by the heating or cooling as long as both phases are present. The heat required in such a process to change a unit mass from one phase to the other is equal, according to equation (28), to an increase in enthalpy. It is called the latent heat of that phase change. Thus, a latent heat of fusion

h_{jl}, a latent heat of vaporization h_{fg}, and a latent heat of sublimation h_{ik} can be defined by means of the relations

$$h_{jl} = h_l - h_j = T(s_l - s_j), \quad (42)$$

$$h_{fg} = h_g - h_f = T(s_g - s_f), \quad (43)$$

$$h_{ik} = h_k - h_i = T(s_k - s_i), \quad (44)$$

in which subscripts j, l, f, g, i, and k refer, respectively, to solid in equilibrium with liquid, liquid in equilibrium with solid, liquid in equilibrium with vapour, vapour in equilibrium with liquid, solid in equilibrium with vapour, and vapour in equilibrium with solid.

In a two-phase region the change in any extensive property is directly proportional to the corresponding change in any other for a fixed value of temperature, and the pressure is a function of temperature only. From these observations and Maxwell relations (33) or (34), it follows that the rate of change of pressure with temperature change for a two-phase mixture is equal to the ratio of the entropy change to the volume change when a fixed quantity of the substance is changed from one phase to the other—*e.g.*, from liquid state to vapour state. Alternatively, the ratio of enthalpy change to volume change gives the rate of change of pressure with change in the natural logarithm (ln) of temperature:

The Clapeyron relation

$$\frac{dp}{dT} = \frac{s_2 - s_1}{v_2 - v_1} \quad (45)$$

$$\frac{dp}{d(\ln T)} = T\frac{dp}{dT} = \frac{h_2 - h_1}{v_2 - v_1}. \quad (46)$$

These equations are used to express the Clapeyron relation.

Equation of state. The mathematical relation between the pressure, volume, and temperature for stable equilibrium states of a closed simple system is called its equation of state. Although it will be subsequently shown to be a relation that does not completely specify the nature of the system, the mathematical relation is an important one because the three properties it relates are relatively easily measured.

Experimentally it is found that the relation between the pressure, volume, and temperature of a system is extremely complicated. No explicit mathematical expression has ever been devised that represents all the stable equilibrium states of any one simple system. Instead, equations have been proposed, each of which represents some limited range of states of a particular system. The complexity of equations of state ranges from that for a perfect gas with a single constant to those for liquid and vapour states, of which that for water is an example. Many equations in this category have between 10 and 100 constants, the values of which must be determined so as to fit experimental data.

For the range of liquid and vapour states of a pure molecular species, the general pattern of the p-v-T relation is best shown by drawing a graph of the quantity pv/RT versus the ratio of pressure to critical pressure. If v is taken to be the specific volume (the volume per unit mass) and R is chosen so that pv/RT becomes unity at zero pressure and infinite specific volume for any temperature, then a coincidence occurs: pv/RT is unity for every temperature for that substance, provided only that the specific volume is infinitely large. The constant R is called the gas constant of the molecular species.

The molecular weight of oxygen is 32 and the molecular weight M for any species is inversely proportional to the gas constant R of the molecular species. Thus, the molecular weight M of any species can be defined as 32 times the ratio of the gas constant of oxygen and the gas constant of the species:

$$M \equiv 32\,\frac{R\ (\text{for } O_2)}{R}. \quad (47)$$

It follows that the volume occupied by a molecular weight of a gas at very low pressure is the same for all gases for any selected pair of values of p and T. Moreover it is directly proportional to T and inversely proportional to p.

The universal gas constant

The product of molecular weight M and gas constant R is the same for all gases and is called the universal gas constant (denoted by $\boldsymbol{R}$). The result is an equation, called the perfect-gas equation of state, that appears frequently in the literature of thermodynamics; that is,

$$pv/\boldsymbol{R}T = 1, \quad (48)$$

in which v is the volume occupied by one molecular weight, or one mole, of gas.

The equation of state (48) applies, therefore, to any pure molecular species in states for which the specific volume is extremely large and the pressure, at finite temperature, is therefore extremely small. It holds within 2 percent for water vapour at a pressure of one atmosphere and with correspondingly better precision as the pressure is lowered. A gas that conforms to equation (48) is called a semiperfect gas.

By means of Maxwell relations and equation (23) it can be shown in the case of a semiperfect gas that internal energy, enthalpy, and both heat capacities are functions of temperature only and are independent of the effects of volume or pressure. Moreover, the difference $c_p - c_v$ between the specific heats is equal to the gas constant R when all three quantities are defined in terms of unit mass or, alternatively, in terms of molecular weight.

When quantum effects are not important, an approximate expression for the specific heat may be obtained from statistical thermodynamics. It is

$$c_v = \frac{f}{2}R, \quad (49)$$

in which f denotes the number of active degrees of freedom of the molecule (the number of independent ways in which the space configuration of the molecule may change). For a mass concentrated in a point, f would be three (corresponding to the three directions of translation), and c_v would be $3R/2$. With spatial distribution of the mass, additional degrees of freedom appear by virtue of rotation and vibration of the molecule. The number of such degrees of freedom active in a molecule depends, in accordance with quantum theory, on the temperature. In Table 1 are shown the molal heats of several gases at room temperature along with the corresponding number of degrees of freedom $c_v/(^1/_2R)$. For a monatomic gas this number of degrees of freedom proves to be three almost exactly; for diatomic gases it is nearly five (corresponding to two degrees of rotational freedom); and for more complex molecules, a number in excess of five, which

Table 1: Molal Specific Heats of Gases at Room Temperature

	c_V	c_p	$c_V/(\frac{1}{2}R)$	$c_p/(\frac{1}{2}R)$	$k = c_p/c_V$
He*	2.979	4.965	3.000	5.000	1.667
H_2	4.88	6.87	4.92	6.91	1.406
O_2	5.02	7.00	5.05	7.04	1.406
N_2	4.97	6.96	5.01	7.00	1.400
CO	4.97	6.96	5.01	7.00	1.400
H_2O	6.02	8.01	6.07	8.06	1.330
CO_2	6.81	8.80	6.86	8.85	1.292

*And all other monatomic gases.

implies vibrational degrees of freedom. For all except the monatomic molecule, the value of c_v increases with temperature as new degrees of freedom become active.

The expressions for energy, enthalpy, and entropy of a semiperfect gas are as follows:

$$u = \int_{T_0}^{T} c_v dT + u(T_0), \quad (50)$$

$$h = \int_{T_0}^{T} c_p dT + u(T_0) + RT_0, \quad (51)$$

$$s = \int_{T_0}^{T} c_v \frac{dT}{T} + R\ln\frac{v}{v_0} + s(T_0, v_0)$$

$$= \int_{T_0}^{T} c_p \frac{dT}{T} - R\ln\frac{p}{p_0} + s(T_0, p_0); \quad (52)$$

in these equations the subscript 0 refers to an arbitrarily selected state.

Perfect gas

The perfect gas is a special case of the semiperfect gas—namely, that for which the internal energy and the enthalpy both depend upon temperature but the heat capacities are independent of temperature. The integrals of the previous expressions can now be resolved to give the following:

$$u = c_v(T - T_0), \tag{53}$$

$$h = c_pT - c_vT_0, \tag{54}$$

$$s = c_v \ln\frac{T}{T_0} + R\ln\frac{v}{v_0} + s_0,$$

$$= c_p \ln\frac{T}{T_0} - R\ln\frac{p}{p_0} + s_0, \tag{55}$$

in which s_0 denotes the arbitrary value of s at T_0 (for which u is zero) and at p_0.

For a reversible adiabatic process in a perfect gas, the following relations hold: pv^k = constant, Tv^{k-1} = constant, and $pT^{-k/(k-1)}$ = constant; in these relations, k is the ratio c_p/c_v.

In 1873 the Dutch physicist Johannes van der Waals proposed the following equation, which in a qualitative way describes both the liquid and the vapour states of a pure species:

$$p = \frac{RT}{v - b} - \frac{a}{v^2}. \tag{56}$$

Van der Waal's equation

In this equation a and b are constants for any one species. Not only does this equation approach that of the semiperfect gas as v goes to infinity, but the equation also provides for a region of coexisting states that is capped by a critical state, as in actual substances. Below the temperature T_c (equal to $8a/27Rb$), three values of v correspond to each value of p. Pairs of high-volume and low-volume states, such as P and R (Figure 6), may be found at each pressure–temperature combination. The one pair for which the areas $PQbP$ and $QaRQ$ are equal can be shown to be the pair that can coexist in mutual stable equilibrium.

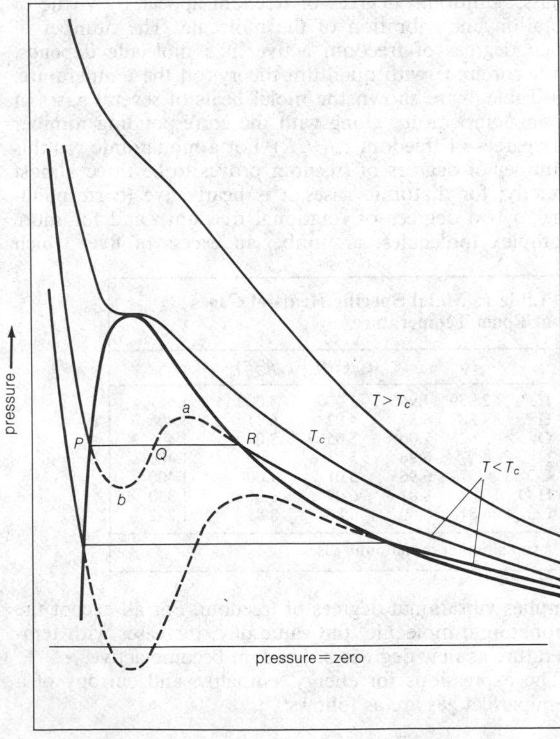

Figure 6: Relations between pressure (p) and volume (v) of liquid and vapour states of a pure molecular species at different temperatures according to the van der Waals equation (see text).

An approximate justification of the van der Waals equation can be made based in part on the Newtonian equation of motion for a collection of particles having the following characteristics: (1) the particles are uniform rigid spheres; (2) their diameters are appreciable fractions of the mean distances between them, except at infinite specific volume; and (3) they exert finite attractive forces, which vary with the distance between them, as well as infinite repulsive forces upon contact.

Equations of state, by proper assignment of values of constants, can be made to represent quantitatively (as contrasted with qualitatively for the van der Waals equation) the properties of many molecular species with fair precision. An equation has been developed that represents the properties of water within the precision of virtually all experimental measurements on the liquid and vapour phases of water.

Virial equations of state

A general type of equation of state, which can be made to fit almost any range of gaseous states at the expense of indefinite increase in the number of constants, is the virial form. It may be written as

$$\frac{pv}{RT} = 1 + B\rho + C\rho^2 + D\rho^3 + \ldots, \tag{57}$$

in which ρ denotes the density, and the coefficients B, C, D, . . . , called the second, third, fourth, . . . virial coefficients, are functions of temperature only. Substantial progress has been made in determining the forms of the functions B and C for the simpler molecular structures by means of models of the structure and force fields between them.

Critical point. The relationships between the various properties of a pure molecular species at and near the critical point have been the subject of many studies. It appears from these that certain mathematical singularities occur at the critical point, including an infinite value for the heat capacity at constant volume, which indicate that no continuous equation relating pressure, volume, and temperature can represent the actual variation in these properties for states closer than a few degrees in temperature to the critical point. A so-called scaling law has been devised to cope with the complications in the mathematical description of this region.

Fundamental equations. As was implied above by the development of the equation of state for a semiperfect gas, such an equation alone is not adequate to yield the values of energy u, enthalpy h, and entropy s. It must be supplemented by a knowledge of the variation of heat capacity with temperature.

A type of equation for which any of the properties p, T, u, v, s (or any algebraic combination of these) not explicit in it are found by differentiation is called a fundamental equation, and the corresponding function has been called a characteristic function. For a simple system, the four characteristic functions—specific energy u, specific enthalpy h, specific Helmholtz free energy ψ, and specific Gibbs free energy ζ—are expressed in terms of fundamental equations as follows:

$$u = u(v,s),\ T = \left(\frac{\partial u}{\partial s}\right)_v,\ p = -\left(\frac{\partial u}{\partial v}\right)_s, \tag{58}$$

$$h = h(p,s),\ T = \left(\frac{\partial h}{\partial s}\right)_p,\ v = \left(\frac{\partial h}{\partial p}\right)_s, \tag{59}$$

$$\psi = \psi(v,T),\ p = \left(\frac{\partial \psi}{\partial v}\right)_T,\ s = -\left(\frac{\partial \psi}{\partial T}\right)_v, \tag{60}$$

$$\zeta = \zeta(p,T),\ v = \left(\frac{\partial \zeta}{\partial p}\right)_T,\ s = -\left(\frac{\partial \zeta}{\partial T}\right)_p, \tag{61}$$

where the specific Helmholtz free energy ψ and the specific Gibbs free energy ζ are defined by

$$\psi \equiv u - Ts \text{ and } \zeta \equiv h - Ts. \tag{62}$$

SIMPLE MULTICOMPONENT SYSTEMS

Gibbs equation. The change of entropy dS between neighbouring stable equilibrium states of a simple system open to the transfer of rest mass can be expressed in terms of the corresponding change of energy dU, volume dV, and number of particles dn_i ($i = 1, 2, \ldots, k$) of the k components in the system. By use of equation (9) it can be shown that the expression for dS involves partial derivatives as coefficients that multiply the changes in the independent properties U, V, n_1, n_2, . . . , n_k:

$$dS = \left(\frac{\partial S}{\partial U}\right)_{V,n} dU + \left(\frac{\partial S}{\partial V}\right)_{U,n} dV + \left(\frac{\partial S}{\partial n_1}\right)_{U,V,n} dn_1 + \ldots + \left(\frac{\partial S}{\partial n_k}\right)_{U,V,n} dn_k, \quad (63)$$

in which subscript n denotes all of $n_1, n_2, \ldots, n_k$ that can be held constant. Upon identifying, as in equation (23), the first two partial derivatives in terms of pressure p and temperature T and introducing a new quality μ_i to be defined shortly, equation (63) becomes what is called the Gibbs equation:

$$dS = \frac{1}{T} dU + \frac{p}{T} dV - \frac{\mu_1}{T} dn_1 - \ldots - \frac{\mu_k}{T} dn_k. \quad (64)$$

Chemical potential

The quantity μ_i, which is called the chemical potential of component i in the system, is defined as follows:

$$\mu_i \equiv -T\left(\frac{\partial S}{\partial n_i}\right)_{U,V,n} \text{ for } i = 1,2, \ldots k. \quad (65)$$

Mutual stable equilibrium. Upon seeking the conditions that must be satisfied in order that two or more phases should be in mutual stable equilibrium while open to transfer of rest mass between them, it is unnecessary to consider any states for which any one phase would be in a nonequilibrium state if it were suddenly isolated. It is unnecessary because any change of state that could occur spontaneously while the phase was isolated would be one of many allowed changes of state when it was not isolated and would, therefore, serve as an indication that at least one spontaneous change is possible and that equilibrium does not exist.

It is sufficient, therefore, to consider only those states for which the individual phases are in stable equilibrium states when isolated. The Gibbs equation provides a general statement of the change of entropy of a simple phase that may exchange component substances with neighbouring phases as it passes through stable equilibrium states. If the formation of any new part unlike the existing parts is prohibited by the definition of the phase, then a set of stable equilibrium states is prescribed for which the Gibbs equation expresses changes in entropy between states in the set.

A heterogeneous system may be considered to be made up of several homogeneous phases, within each of which the formation of a new part is prohibited as proposed above. The states that these phases may assume consistent with mutual stable equilibrium may now be found by seeking out the state of maximum entropy of the whole system for a given volume and energy. This kind of procedure was used above to show that the phases of such a system must have equal temperatures. By similar reasoning it can now be shown that the phases must have equal pressures and equal values of the chemical potential μ_i of each component i present in all the phases. That is, among the necessary conditions for stable equilibrium of a multiphase simple system (*i.e.,* in the absence of force fields and capillarity) is uniformity throughout the multiphase system of temperature, pressure, and chemical potential of each component present in all the phases.

Of these conditions the one most open to exception is equality of pressure. In order for it to apply, an encroachment of the volume of each phase upon every other, for constant energy and composition of each phase, must be an allowed variation in state of the system. Wherever phases are separated by a rigid boundary, which may be permeable to one or more components, then equality of pressure between such phases is not necessary to mutual stable equilibrium.

If two phases are separated by a wall that is permeable to some components but not permeable to others, then equality of chemical potential of those other components across the wall is not necessary. An exception can be made as regards the potentials T, p, and μ_i in cases in which a transfer of energy, volume, and component i can occur at stable equilibrium in one direction but not in the other direction. Then a condition for mutual stable equilibrium becomes, because entropy is to be maximized, that the temperature in the phase that can receive energy but cannot supply it may be greater than or equal to the temperature in phases that can both receive and supply energy. Similar statements can be made in regard to pressure and the transfer of volume and in regard to chemical potential of component i and the transfer of that component.

These statements imply that potentials T, p, and μ_i are escaping tendencies for energy, volume, and component i, respectively. For equilibrium each escaping tendency must be balanced as between phases, unless the escape of one flux has reached its upper limit for a phase so that no further escape is possible. For such a phase it is necessary for equilibrium that the escaping tendency be not less than that in other phases, but it may be more. This consideration is relevant for certain quantum effects at low temperature, for two phases separated by a movable solid boundary that has come up against a stop and behind which the pressure may be greater than the pressure in front (but not less), and for exhaustion of a phase as regards one component.

From the definitions of enthalpy H (29), Helmholtz free energy Ψ (30), and Gibbs free energy Z (31), it is readily shown that the chemical potential can be expressed in alternative forms; that is,

$$\mu_i = \left(\frac{\partial U}{\partial n_i}\right)_{V,S,n} = \left(\frac{\partial H}{\partial n_i}\right)_{p,S,n} = \left(\frac{\partial \Psi}{\partial n_i}\right)_{V,T,n} = \left(\frac{\partial Z}{\partial n_i}\right)_{p,T,n}. \quad (66)$$

The last of these is known as the partial Gibbs free energy ζ_i of component i in the phase. In view of the definition of Z, μ_i may also be expressed in terms of the partial enthalpy h_i and the partial entropy s_i; thus,

$$\mu_i = \left(\frac{\partial Z}{\partial n_i}\right)_{p,T,n} = \left(\frac{\partial H}{\partial n_i}\right)_{p,T,n} - T\left(\frac{\partial S}{\partial n_i}\right)_{p,T,n} = \zeta_i = h_i - Ts_i. \quad (67)$$

In general, lowercase symbols with subscript i denote the partial property. For a phase of pure component i, any partial property is identical with the corresponding specific property—that is, the value of the property per unit mass, which is here taken to be the mole. The chemical potential of a component i in a mixture containing i is equal to the specific Gibbs free energy of i in a phase of pure i in equilibrium with the mixture through a membrane permeable to i alone.

A semipermeable membrane such as the one just proposed is one across which the pressure need not be balanced in order to maintain equilibrium. By definition of the membrane, encroachment of the mixture phase into the volume of the pure phase cannot occur, but the reverse encroachment can occur. The membrane must, of course, have sufficient structural strength to support the pressure difference.

The expression for the chemical potential of a semiperfect gas in terms of temperature and pressure is found from equations (67), (51), and (52). It proves to be the sum of a simple function of pressure p and temperature T plus a relatively complicated function $f_i(T)$ of temperature as follows:

$$\mu_i = RT \ln p + f_i(T), \quad (68)$$

in which the function $f_i(T)$ is different for different semiperfect gases i. For a given temperature, however, equation (68) indicates that the chemical potential increases with increase in pressure. That is, temperature being fixed, the escaping tendency increases as the pressure increases.

Three equations will be recorded here but not derived.

1. The Gibbs equation as an expression for the change in Gibbs free energy of a phase between neighbouring stable equilibrium states:

$$dZ = Vdp - SdT + \sum_i \mu_i \, dn_i. \quad (69)$$

In the equation the short notation $\sum_i \mu_i \, dn_i$ has been used to denote $\mu_1 dn_1 + \mu_2 dn_2 + \ldots + \mu_k dn_k$, in which subscript $i = 1, 2, \ldots, k$ denotes a component substance.

2. The Gibbs free energy as a summation of products of chemical potentials and numbers of moles of component substances i of a phase:

$$Z = \sum_i \mu_i n_i. \qquad (70)$$

Gibbs–Duhem equation

3. The Gibbs–Duhem equation, which relates for a phase the changes between stable equilibrium states in temperature, pressure, and numbers of moles of components:

$$SdT - Vdp + \sum_i n_i d\mu_i = 0. \qquad (71)$$

Mixtures of gases. *Gibbs–Dalton rule for mixtures.* Gibbs revised the earlier rule of the 18th- and 19th-century English physicist John Dalton for determining the properties of a mixture of gases from the properties of the pure components. Two equivalent statements of the Gibbs–Dalton rule for mixtures are as follows: (1) The pressure in a mixture of different gases is equal to the sum of the pressures of the different gases as existing each by itself at the temperature of the mixture and with the same value of the chemical potential as it has in the mixture. (2) The pressure of a mixture of different gases is equal to the sum of the pressures of the pure components each existing as a phase in equilibrium with the mixture through a membrane permeable to the component.

Using single subscripts to refer to components in the mixture and double subscripts to refer to pure component phases, the Gibbs–Dalton rule takes the form

$$p = p_{11} + p_{22} + p_{33} + \ldots \qquad (72)$$

for

$$T = T_{11} = T_{22} = \ldots, \qquad (73)$$

and

$$\mu_1 = \mu_{11},\ \mu_2 = \mu_{22}, \ldots. \qquad (74)$$

In this notation p_1 would have no "operational" meaning because no instrument has been devised that can measure the pressure of component 1 when it is part of a mixture.

It can now be shown from the Gibbs–Dalton rule and the Gibbs–Duhem equation that the number c_i of mass units of component i in unit volume of the mixture (the concentration c_i of i in the mixture) is equal to the density ρ_{ii} or the inverse of the specific volume v_{ii} of i in the pure phase in mutual stable equilibrium with the mixture. The concentration c_i denotes the ratio of mass n_i of i in the mixture to the volume v of the mixture. It follows immediately that the density ρ (or $1/v$) of the mixture is the sum of the densities ρ_{ii} (or $1/v_{ii}$) of the pure phases.

Further application of the Gibbs–Duhem equation yields the following expressions for extensive properties:

$$U = nu = \sum_i n_i u_{ii},$$

$$H = nh = \sum_i n_i h_{ii},$$

$$S = ns = \sum_i n_i s_{ii},$$

$$\Psi = n\psi = \sum_i n_i \psi_{ii}, \text{ and}$$

$$Z = n\zeta = \sum_i n_i \zeta_{ii} = \sum_i n_i \mu_{ii} = \sum_i n_i \mu_i. \qquad (75)$$

In these equations the mass n_i of component i in the mixture will be identical with n_{ii} the mass of i in the pure phase if the volume of the pure phase ii that is in mutual stable equilibrium with the mixture is made equal to the volume of the mixture. The result is in accord with Dalton's concept that each component behaves as if it were present alone.

A further conclusion that can be reached is that a Gibbs–Dalton mixture of semiperfect gases is itself a semiperfect gas. That is, for the mixture the ratio pv/RT is equal to unity if v is the volume per mole of all components and R the universal gas constant. If a specific gas constant is used and v is the volume per unit mass, then the mixture behaves as a semiperfect gas with a molecular weight M that is the mass m of the mixture divided by the total number n of moles of all components. It is also the average of the molecular weights M_i of the components, each weighted proportionately to the mole fraction y_i of that component in the mixture:

$$M = \frac{m}{n} = \sum_i y_i M_i.$$

Mixing gases. Some further results of the Gibbs–Dalton rule will be given here without proof. If a number of pure species are confined by thin partitions in separate parts of an insulated volume V in such quantities that their pressures are equal when their temperatures are equal, then when the partitions are removed (or destroyed), the gases will mix irreversibly without change in temperature, pressure, energy, or enthalpy. The change of entropy ΔS is greater than zero, as is appropriate for an adiabatic irreversible process. It is given by the negative of the product of the number n of moles of all components multiplied by the gas constant R and a mean logarithmic mole fraction:

$$\Delta S = -nR \sum_i y_i \ln y_i, \qquad (76)$$

in which y_i denotes the mole fraction of the species i in the final mixture. Both the Helmholtz free energy and the Gibbs free energy decrease in the mixing process.

The Gibbs–Dalton rule holds in regions of state in which the pressure is low relative to the critical pressure of every component. Outside these regions an equation of state for a mixture may be devised from the equations of state of its components, with varying degrees of precision, by means of certain combining rules. One of these rules, proposed by the 19th- and 20th-century French physicist Émile Amagat, states that the volume of a mixture is the sum of the volumes of the pure components—each at the pressure and temperature of the mixture. A 20th-century U.S. chemist, James Alexander Beattie, later proposed a rule of more general application that prescribes how the coefficients in the Beattie–Bridgman equations for the pure components may be combined in order to obtain the corresponding coefficients for the mixture.

Vapour pressures of pure liquids. The vapour of a pure species may be in mutual stable equilibrium with its liquid at a flat interface at the normal or saturation vapour pressure corresponding to its temperature. The vapour may also, however, be in mutual stable equilibrium at a nonwetting porous wall that is permeable to vapour but not to liquid or at a curved interface, either of which can support a pressure difference between liquid and vapour. The effect of change in pressure of the liquid on the corresponding vapour pressure is called the Poynting effect. It is found by equating chemical potentials of liquid and vapour. For an incompressible liquid and a semiperfect vapour, the Poynting effect proves to be approximately proportional to the change in pressure on the liquid. For water at 40° C (104° F) the equilibrium pressure of the vapour increases by 1 percent when the pressure on the liquid is increased by a factor of 200.

The Poynting effect

Ideal solutions. When a solute is added to a volatile solvent, the volatility of the solvent is reduced. The effect is to reduce the pressure of solvent vapour that is in equilibrium with the liquid in proportion to the reduction in the mole fraction of solvent in the solution. Thus the effect on the volatility is the same for equal numbers of moles of different solutes in solution, the mole being measured as described by equation (47). This observation, which holds only for dilute or ideal solutions, is expressed in Raoult's rule. The rule states that at given pressure p and temperature T the pressure p_1^v of pure solvent vapour in equilibrium with the solution is equal to the product of the mole fraction x_1 of solvent in the solution and the vapour pressure p_1° of pure liquid solvent at the pressure and temperature of the solution. By ignoring the small Poynting effect on the vapour pressure of the solvent, the rule of boiling-point raising may be derived from Raoult's rule by mathematical deduction. It is that the rate of change of boiling temperature T with mole fraction x_2 of solute 2, as solute is added to a dilute solution,

Raoult's rule

is equal to the rate of change of boiling temperature of pure solvent 1 with the logarithm of the pressure p_1° on the pure solvent. The mathematical statement of the rule of boiling-point raising is given by the relation

$$\left(\frac{\partial T}{\partial x_2}\right)_{x_2\to 0} = \left[\frac{dT}{d(\ln p_1^{\circ})}\right]_{x_2=0}. \qquad (77)$$

For water at 25° C (77° F) the value of $(\partial T/\partial x_2)$ is about 17° C (31° F) or, more practically, 0.17° C for each mole percent of solute regardless of the nature of the solute.

Figure 7 depicts a container in which volatile solvent liq-

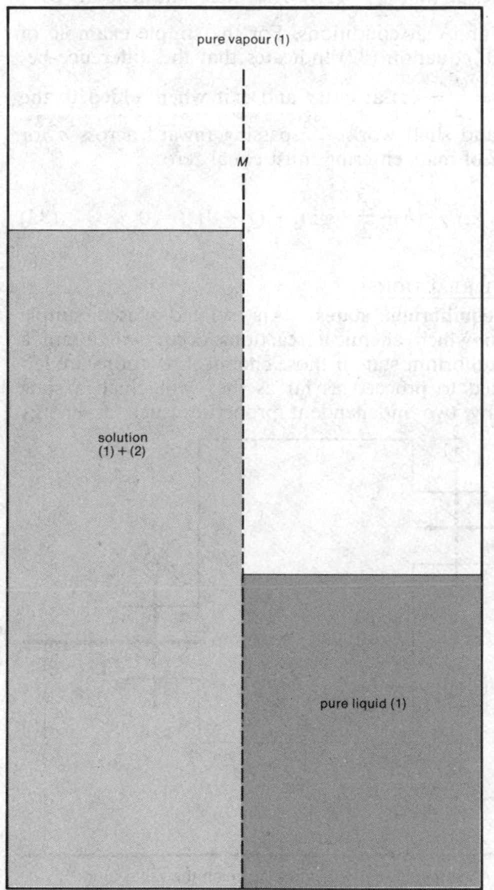

Figure 7: Equilibrium between a pure volatile liquid (1), a solution of nonvolatile substance (2) in liquid (1), and the vapour of substance (1). Substance (1) can pass through the membrane (M), but substance (2) cannot. The difference in the vapour pressures of solvent and solution causes the liquid levels to be unequal. The difference in pressure between pure liquid and solution is called the osmotic pressure (see text).

uid 1 is separated from a solution containing nonvolatile solute 2 by a wall M permeable to 1 only. The wall extends only part way to the top, leaving a vapour space with free access of vapour 1 from one liquid surface to the other. Because the pressure of vapour in mutual stable equilibrium with the solution is less, by Raoult's rule, than that in equilibrium with the pure solvent, the height of the solution surface must be greater than that of the pure liquid by enough to provide the appropriate hydrostatic head of vapour between them. The corresponding hydrostatic head of liquid, of course, is much greater and accounts, except for the head of vapour, for a substantial difference between the pressure of the solution and the pressure of the solvent with which it is in equilibrium through the semipermeable wall. This difference in pressure, which is required to prevent migration of solvent into the solution, is called osmotic pressure. With the usual approximations for a dilute solution and a perfect vapour, it can be shown by equating chemical potentials of solvent across the wall that the osmotic pressure P is approximately equal to the product of gas constant R,

Osmotic pressure

temperature T, and number of moles c_2 of solute per unit volume of solution.

By means of the Gibbs–Duhem equation (71) and the assumption of perfect vapours for the two components of a binary solution, it can be shown that Raoult's rule requires that the pressure p_2^{v} of solute vapour in equilibrium with a solution is proportional to the mole fraction x_2 of solute in the solution; that is, p_2^{v} is equal to k_2x_2, k_2 being a constant of proportionality. This relation is known as Henry's rule. Unlike Raoult's rule, in which the coefficient of x_1 is the vapour pressure of the pure solvent, the proportionality constant k_2 bears no simple relation to the properties of the components. Of course, if Raoult's and Henry's rules were to hold over the whole range of x_2 from 0 to 1, then k_2 would be the vapour pressure of pure solute. In general, however, the laws hold only for dilute solutions; that is, for x_2 nearly zero. An example of the variation of vapour pressures of a binary mixture of two completely miscible volatile species is shown in Figure 8, in which the distinction between Henry's rule constant k_2 and the vapour pressure p_2° of pure solute is made evident.

Henry's rule

Equation (68) for the chemical potential of a semiperfect gas can be used in combination with Raoult's and Henry's rules to show that any change in chemical potential of solvent in a solution between two states at the same temperature is proportional to the change in $RT \ln x_1$. Similarly, the change in chemical potential of solute is proportional to change in $RT \ln x_2$. Expressions for the chemical potentials, therefore, are

$$\mu_1 = RT \ln x_1 + \mu_1^{\circ} \qquad (78)$$

$$\mu_2 = RT \ln x_2 + \mu_2^{\circ}, \qquad (79)$$

in which μ_1° is the chemical potential of pure solvent ($x_1 = 1$) at the pressure and temperature of the solution. The quantity μ_2° is the chemical potential of pure solute in a hypothetical ideal-solution state for which x_2 is unity. Equations (78) and (79) indicate that the logarithm of the mole fraction of a component is the measure of the escaping tendency of that component.

When to an ideal solution at a given pressure and temperature is added some pure solvent starting from the same pressure and temperature, it can be shown that the total volume occupied by solution and solvent remains unchanged by the process of dissolving. Similar statements may be made concerning the total energy and total enthalpy. One consequence is that no heat flows to or from the fluids during this process of solution; thus, the heat of solution is zero, and the process is adiabatic. The total entropy, on the other hand, increases during the process of solution, as would be expected from equation (6) for an irreversible adiabatic process. In general, a similar addition of pure solute to an ideal solution will result in change in total volume, energy, and enthalpy, and the

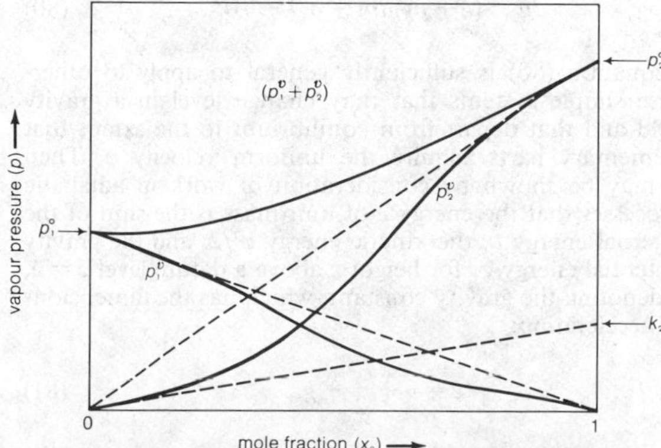

Figure 8: Variation of vapour pressure above solutions of two completely miscible volatile substances, 1 and 2, from pure 1 ($x_2 = 0$, $P_1^{v} = p_1^{\circ}$) to pure substance 2 ($x_2 = 1$, $P_2^{v} = p_2^{\circ}$). The Henry's rule constant, k_2, is shown as the tangent to the graph of p_2^{v} at $x_2 = 0$.

heat of solution will not be zero. The change in volume, energy, and enthalpy per unit of solute added will be independent of the composition of the solution over the range of ideality.

BULK FLOW

A kind of transfer of matter in which each elementary piece of the flowing fluid can be considered to be a closed and separable system bounded by a prescribed surface is called bulk flow. Contrasting with this definition is transfer of material by molecular diffusion, in which the flowing molecules cannot be considered to be closed and separable systems.

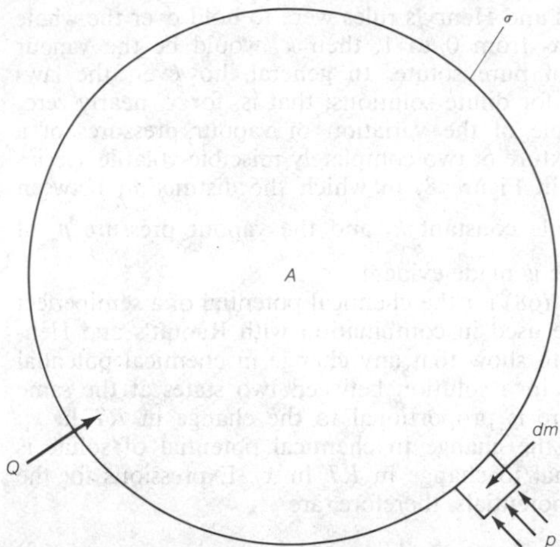

Figure 9: Schematic calculation of the change in energy of system resulting from the introduction of additional mass (see text).

Figure 9 shows a system A enclosed within a fixed boundary σ and an infinitesimal adjacent mass dm separated from A by a part of σ that is penetrable by A. The mass dm may be pushed across σ to join the larger mass inside. The work done by the surroundings on the combined system comprising A and dm will be equal to the product $pvdm$—namely, the pressure p multiplied by the specific volume v and the mass dm. This statement must be qualified by limiting it to slow motion of the boundary of dm and to zero shear effects in the fluid.

It can now be shown from equation (19) that the change in energy found within the boundary σ is the initial value of $E + pV$ for the mass dm, or $(e + pv)\ dm$, e denoting energy per unit mass. To this must be added any heat δQ that crosses the boundary of the combined system, and from it must be subtracted any work δW_x, called shaft work, that crosses boundary σ by virtue of torque in a rotating shaft or the equivalent. The corresponding statement for the energy change dE within σ when an infinitesimal mass of fluid dm crosses σ is

$$dE = (e + pv)dm + \delta Q - \delta W_x. \qquad (80)$$

Equation (80) is sufficiently general to apply to otherwise simple systems that may change level in a gravity field and that depart from equilibrium to the extent that elementary parts acquire the uniform velocity φ. Then it may be shown by consideration of work in adiabatic processes that the energy e of unit mass is the sum of the internal energy u, the kinetic energy $\varphi^2/2$, and the gravity potential energy gz for height z above a datum level $z = 0$, g denoting the gravity constant, which has the dimensions of acceleration:

$$e = u + \frac{\varphi^2}{2} + gz. \qquad (81)$$

Equation (80) may now be repeated after substituting the enthalpy symbol h for $u + pv$:

$$dE = (h + \frac{\varphi^2}{2} + gz)\ dm + \delta Q - \delta W_x. \qquad (82)$$

A special case of the problem of bulk flow is one for which inward flow and outward flow occur, each in one or more channels, and the state of the fluid within the control volume is the same at all times. The state of the control volume for which this assumption holds is called a steady state, and the flow condition is called steady flow. A simple example with single entry and single exit is shown in Figure 10. It would apply to a boiler, for which W_x is zero, and to a steam turbine, for which Q is nearly zero, as well as to many other engineering devices. Steady flow

The condition of steady state requires that dE be zero. The value of $(h + \frac{\varphi^2}{2} + gz)dm$ is then summed up over all entry and exit conditions. For the simple example of Figure 10, equation (82) indicates that the difference between $(h + \frac{\varphi^2}{2} + gz)$ at entry and exit when added to the heat Q' and shaft work W_x' passing inward across σ for each unit of mass entering must equal zero:

$$(h + \frac{\varphi^2}{2} + gz)_1 - (h + \frac{\varphi^2}{2} + gz)_2 + Q' - W_x' = 0. \qquad (83)$$

CHEMICAL REACTIONS

Stable equilibrium states. An isolated closed simple system in which chemical reactions occur will attain a stable equilibrium state if those chemical reactions are left uninhibited to proceed as far as they will. Such a state is fixed by two independent properties such as energy

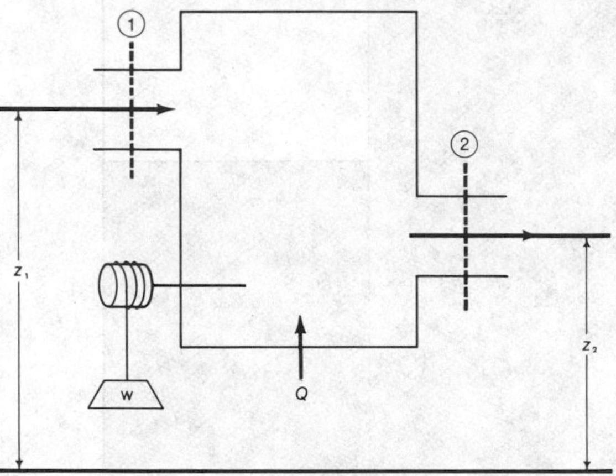

Figure 10: A system in a steady state in which the state of the fluid between boundaries 1 and 2 is the same at all times. The net mass flux across the entire boundary of the system must be zero. The heights of boundaries 1 and 2 above a datum are denoted z_1 and z_2 (see text).

and volume or temperature and volume, and it is called a state of chemical equilibrium. Among the properties of the chemical equilibrium state fixed by the two independent properties are the proportions of the molecular species present.

When a chemical reaction proceeds at such a rate that chemical equilibrium is not achieved, each state passed through may be considered, for the purposes of analysis, to be a stable equilibrium state for which an anticatalyst has prevented chemical reaction. Between these states the system may experience chemical reaction in such degree as to produce a certain chemical aggregation in a second state different from that in the first. These states may be considered to have been achieved by successively removing and replacing an agent, such as an anticatalyst, that prohibits a chemical reaction. In the presence of such an agent each stable equilibrium state would correspond to a different set of proportions of species that would constitute a system with its own set of allowed states. To identify the state, therefore, it is necessary to add to the two independent properties required by the state principle an additional property that identifies the system. For example, for a mixture of molecules of nitrogen (N_2), hydrogen (H_2), and ammonia (NH_3) and the chemical reaction of formation of ammonia from the elements N_2 and H_2,

$$\frac{1}{2}N_2 + \frac{3}{2}H_2 \rightleftarrows NH_3,$$

the energy, volume, and some measure of the degree to which this reaction has proceeded in one direction or the other would be required to identify the system and its stable equilibrium state.

Heat in chemical reactions. For any chemical reaction in a simple system, for which heat Q and work W are the only interactions, the energy change ΔE is given, according to equation (19), by the difference between heat and work: $\Delta E = Q - W$. For a chemical reaction in a system held at constant volume, the heat $(Q)_V$, in the absence of other interactions, is given by the increment in energy:

$$(Q)_V = \Delta E. \qquad (84)$$

For a chemical reaction in a system held at constant pressure, the heat $(Q)_p$ is given by the increment in enthalpy:

$$(Q)_p = \Delta H. \qquad (85)$$

For steady flow between entry section 1 and exit section 2, the heat interaction, in view of equation (83), is the increase in enthalpy $H_2 - H_1$ between the two sections plus any shaft work W_x:

$$Q = H_2 - H_1 + W_x.$$

For a chemical reaction at constant volume in an isolated system, no change in energy occurs despite the large change in temperature that is usually observed, as may be seen from equation (84) in which $(Q)_V$ (and therefore ΔE) is equal to zero for an isolated system.

When values are sought in the literature for the properties E and H for use in the preceding equations or for S and Z for use in other equations, it is found that for different molecular species they are not available on a common base—that is, an arbitrarily selected zero state is used for each separate species independently of that for any other. It is necessary, therefore, to supplement data for the molecular species with data on change in values of properties when each species is formed from the chemical elements without change in pressure or temperature.

Equilibrium between chemically reacting species. Included in the description of a system is the set of possible states that the system may assume. The choice of this set is often arbitrary and may be made to suit convenience in approximating a real system and its behaviour. For example, a system consisting of a mixture of hydrogen and oxygen gases may or may not have included among its possible states those in which water has been formed by chemical reaction.

The description of a multicomponent system may or may not permit a certain chemical reaction in which some species are formed from others. Whenever a reaction is permitted that was not permitted before, the number of components, each of which must be independently variable, decreases by one. Moreover, one new kind of change of state is introduced—namely, a variation in which certain species leave phases in which they are actual components to form other species in phases in which these others are actual components.

For a reaction such that a moles of A combine with b moles of B, etc., to form k moles of K plus l moles of L, etc., the stoichiometric (chemical-reaction) statement is

$$aA + bB + \ldots \rightleftarrows kK + lL + \ldots. \qquad (86)$$

This statement implies that the change Δn_A in number of moles of species A resulting from the reaction, when divided by the coefficient a, is numerically identical with similar quotients for the other species; *i.e.*,

$$\frac{\Delta n_A}{a} = \frac{\Delta n_B}{b} = \ldots = -\frac{\Delta n_K}{k} = -\frac{\Delta n_L}{l} = \ldots = -\Delta\xi. \qquad (87)$$

The common value of the ratios, sometimes called the degree of reaction, is denoted by $\Delta\xi$. The stable equilibrium state in a system for which reaction (86) is allowed must be the state for which the entropy is at a maximum for all the states having given values of energy and volume of each phase. By reference to the Gibbs equation (64), it can be shown that this maximum is attained when the chemical potentials μ_A, μ_B, ..., μ_K, μ_L, ... of species A, B, ... K, L, ... are related as in the following equation, which is called the equation of chemical equilibrium:

$$a\mu_A + b\mu_B + \ldots - k\mu_K - l\mu_L - \ldots = 0. \qquad (88)$$

Because for each component of a Gibbs–Dalton mixture of semiperfect gases the chemical potential may be simply expressed, as in equation (68), in terms of the logarithm of the partial pressure of the species in the mixture, the condition for stable equilibrium becomes such that a product of powers of the partial pressures p_A, p_B, ..., p_K, p_L, ... is the same for a given temperature regardless of the proportions of the components that make up the mixture. This product is called the equilibrium constant in terms of pressure. For reaction (86) it is given by

$$\frac{p_K^k \, p_L^l \cdots}{p_A^a \, p_B^b \cdots} = K_p(T). \qquad (89)$$

The variation of K_p with variation in temperature for a number of familiar reactions is shown in Figure 11.

From O.A. Hougen, K.M. Watson, and R.A. Ragatz, *Chemical Process Principles*, 2nd ed. (1957), used with permission of John Wiley and Sons, Inc.

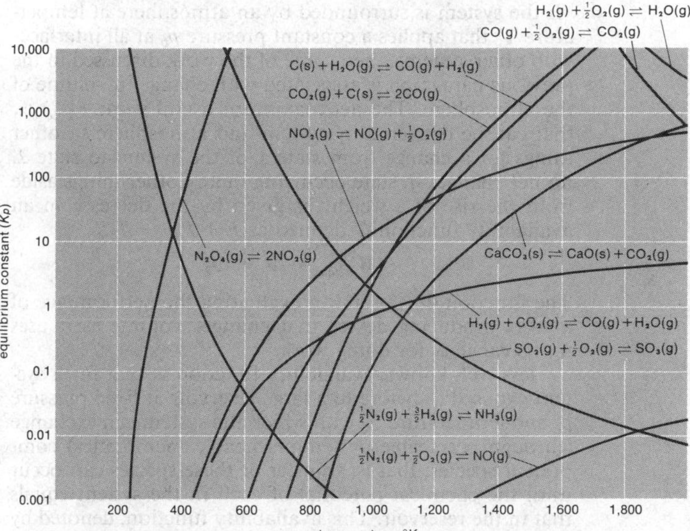

Figure 11: Variation in equilibrium constant, K_p, with variation in temperature for several chemical reactions (see text).

For a chemical reaction among the components of an ideal solution, a similar equilibrium constant is found for which the mole fraction x_I of component I is substituted in equation (89) for the partial pressure of component I:

$$\frac{x_K^k \, x_L^l \cdots}{x_A^a \, x_B^b \cdots} = K_x(T). \qquad (90)$$

Equilibrium constants

When a gas mixture is not a Gibbs–Dalton mixture or a solution is not ideal, then a property called the fugacity takes the place of pressure in equation (89), and one called activity takes the place of mole fraction in (90). (For the definitions of these properties, see MATTER: *Solutions and solubility*.)

Because each of these so-called equilibrium constants changes with change in temperature, some knowledge of the rate of change of the value of K with temperature is of great value. This rate is expressed most simply as the rate of change of ln K with temperature, and it proves to be equal to the quotient of the change in enthalpy when the reaction occurs at constant pressure and temperature and the product RT^2. In non-ideal mixtures (or solutions) the change in enthalpy must be measured between a reactants state for which the fugacity (or activity) of each reactant species is unity and a product state for which the fugacity (or activity) of each product is unity:

$$[d(\ln K_a)/dT]_p = \frac{\Delta H^\circ}{RT^2}. \qquad (91)$$

AVAILABILITY FUNCTIONS

The economic and engineering importance of a system in a given state is often determined by its available work Ω_R with reference to ambient systems as a reservoir. The function Ω_R, which was used above to introduce and define entropy, proves to be one of a number of availability functions (all of which were stated or implied by Gibbs in his papers of 1873 and 1877–78).

The decrease in Ω_R between two states of a system is the maximum work that can be obtained from the system and a reservoir at T_0, no net changes of state occurring in any other systems aside from, for example, the rise of an external weight. The maximum work is also the value of the work produced by system and reservoir in a reversible process and is a value common to all reversible processes joining the two prescribed states of the system. In view of equation (4) and the definition of the entropy constant c_R, the decrease in available work Ω_R may now be identified as the decrease in the quantity $(E - T_0S)$, in which the subscript 0 is introduced to refer to the reservoir. The value of Ω_R itself may be taken to be the maximum possible decrease in $(E - T_0S)$, which is also the decrease when the system changes to a state of mutual stable equilibrium with the reservoir.

If the system is surrounded by an atmosphere at temperature T_0 that applies a constant pressure p_0 at all interfaces with other systems, then some of the work discussed in the previous paragraph is associated with change in volume of the atmosphere. The net maximum useful work, $(W_u)_{max}$, that can be delivered by system and atmosphere to other things for a change from state 1 of the system to state 2, no net changes in state occurring in any other things aside from the rise of a weight, is given by the decrease in an availability function Φ defined as $E + P_0V - T_0S$:

$$(W_u)_{max} = \Phi_1 - \Phi_2.$$

The function Φ is useful in evaluating the performance of a work-producing device that changes volume as it uses up its capacity for doing work.

A less well-known availability function is that for a system exposed as before to a large reservoir at fixed pressure p_0 and temperature T_0 with which the system can exchange (through permeable or semipermeable membranes) component species; that is, transfer of these species can occur until the chemical potential of each in the system equals that in the reservoir. This availability function, denoted by Ξ, has a minimum value of zero. It is given by the relation

$$\Xi \equiv E + p_0V - T_0S - \sum_i \mu_{i0}n_i, \tag{92}$$

μ_{i0} denoting the chemical potential of component i in the reservoir.

NEGATIVE TEMPERATURE

In the interest of simplicity, the third corollary of the second law was stated above as follows: A system in a stable equilibrium state can receive work but cannot produce it. Although this statement is satisfactory with regard to all ordinary systems, which are also called normal systems, recent developments in the theory of nuclear spins—the spinning of neutrons and protons of the atomic nucleus that contributes to both the angular momentum and the magnetic moment of the atom—have shown that some systems, which will be called special systems, in stable equilibrium states can produce work but cannot receive work.

Characteristics of special systems

A special system requires the following characteristics: (1) the energy of its allowed states has a finite upper limit; and (2) it must be coextensive in space with another system that shields it from work interactions that would change its volume or the velocity of its parts. For example, a lithium fluoride crystal may be considered to contain two distinct systems occupying the same space. The first, a special system, consists of the nuclear spins of the atoms of the crystal and has the energy of these spins. The second, a normal system, consists of the same atoms in the crystal, but its energy does not include that of the nuclear spins of the atoms. The stable equilibrium states of the two coextensive systems can be identified and distinguished because each comes to equilibrium in itself much more rapidly than they together approach mutual stable equilibrium.

It can be shown by reference to the second law of thermodynamics that for a closed special system the entropy–energy diagram is as shown in Figure 12. The curve ABC represents stable equilibrium states as well as the upper boundary for the region of all allowed states for given

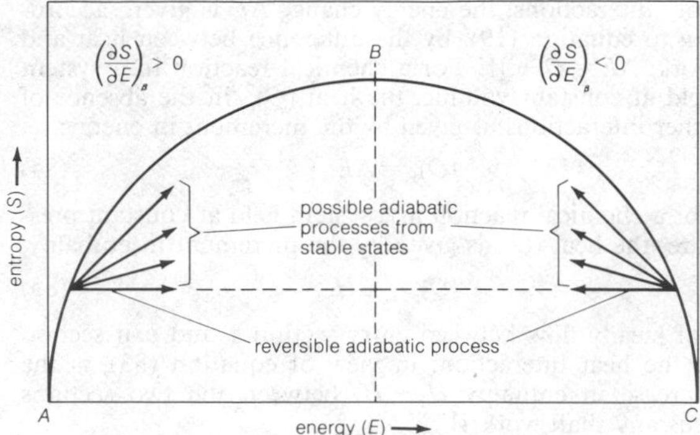

Figure 12: Entropy–energy diagram for a closed special system, for which negative absolute temperatures exist (see text).

values of constraints β. Normal stable equilibrium states, which a special system may assume, are those on the AB part of the curve. Special stable equilibrium states are those on the BC part of the curve, and for these special equilibrium states the energy decreases with increase of entropy. In view of the definition of temperature (equation [13]), the temperature is therefore represented by a negative number.

The significance of negative temperatures on the scale of hotness and coldness can best be described in terms of the reciprocal Kelvin scale τ, in which $\tau \equiv 1/T$. The possible range of values of τ is from minus infinity to plus infinity, with the hottest temperature possible at minus infinity and the coldest temperature possible at plus infinity. Thus, negative temperatures correspond to hotter levels (the direction of heat flow being from hot to cold) than plus infinity on the Kelvin scale. The so-called absolute zero on the Kelvin scale becomes plus infinity on the τ scale of temperature.

THIRD LAW

Valid calorimetric experiments at temperatures near zero on the Kelvin scale invariably are in accord with the following postulate, which is the third law of classical thermodynamics: The entropy of any finite system approaches a noninfinite value as the temperature on the Kelvin scale approaches zero.

States to which the third law is applied

The third law applies only to stable equilibrium states and implies that the heat capacity at constant constraints must go to zero at zero temperature. It follows that a substance cannot be treated as a perfect gas at temperatures near zero, because for a perfect gas the specific heat capacity at constant volume is constant, and the entropy, as given by equation (55), approaches minus infinity. For crystalline substances near zero temperature, the variation of heat capacity is often found to be proportional to T^n, n being greater than unity.

From the third law in combination with the second law, it can be shown that for any finite system all paths of stable equilibrium states for fixed values of constraints β_i must converge on a single value of entropy as they approach zero temperature, as shown in Figure 13.

From the curve of stable equilibrium states for constant values β_{il} of constraints β_i, a branching may occur, as shown by Pn of Figure 13, but the states along Pn cannot be stable equilibrium states. They may be metastable or unstable, and the constant-entropy process nk from one of these states to the corresponding stable equilibrium state can be neither reversible nor adiabatic. Moreover, the change at zero temperature from n to m may be a spontaneous irreversible change to a stable equilibrium

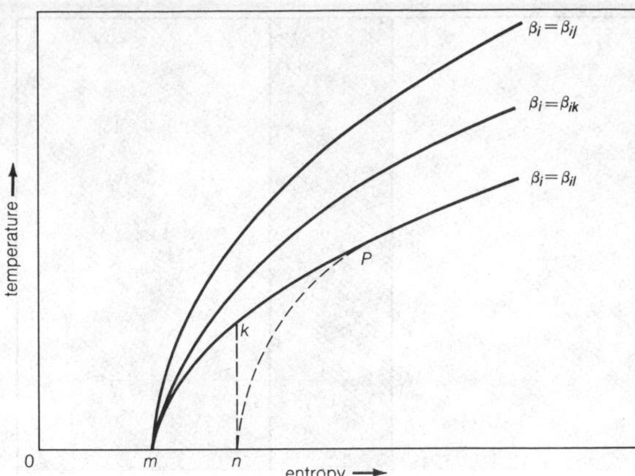

Figure 13: Convergence of values of entropy of stable equilibrium states of a system upon a single value at very low temperatures, as postulated by the third law of thermodynamics. For a given value β_{il} of constraint β_i, *Pm* represents stable equilibrium states and *Pn* metastable states (see text).

state. It follows that, as the temperature approaches zero, the magnitude of the entropy change in any isothermal reversible process approaches zero. This is the Nernst heat theorem, named for the Nobel-Prize-winning German chemist, which is a corollary of the third law as stated above. An equivalent statement is that, as the temperature approaches zero, the magnitude of the entropy change between any pair of stable equilibrium states at the same temperature approaches zero.

Nernst heat theorem

Because the change between stable equilibrium states may involve a change in value of a constraint, such as the volume, all states that can coexist in stable equilibrium at zero temperature must have the same minimum value of the entropy for the same mass. Moreover, if a system consisting of chemically reacting species can be brought into a stable equilibrium state by imposing appropriate electrostatic forces in an electrolytic cell, then the system must have the same minimum value of entropy whether in the reactants state or the products state.

It is appropriate now to assign the value zero to the minimum value of the entropy for a given system. The energy at any finite temperature for given values of constraints β may be found from the experimentally determined relation between the heat capacity C_β and temperature by integrating the product $C_\beta\, dT$ from temperature zero to temperature T:

$$[E - E_{(T=0)}]_\beta = \int_{T=0}^{T=T} C_\beta\, dT.$$

Similarly, the entropy at any finite temperature may be found by integrating the product $(C_\beta/T)dT$:

$$S_\beta = \int_{T=0}^{T=T} \frac{C_\beta}{T}\, dT.$$

It is possible, therefore, to determine the values of Gibbs free energy $(E + pV - TS)$ for chemically reacting species at some standard pressure and temperature and, from these values, the conditions for chemical equilibrium, including the equilibrium constants—all without experimental values for the chemical reaction as such between the species.

Force fields

NONRELATIVISTIC EFFECTS

When to the conditions for a simple system, gravitational, electrical, and magnetic constraints in the form of applied force fields are added, an additional term appears in the Gibbs equation for each additional constraint. Each added term is a product similar to the product pdV in that it represents the work done in a reversible process in which the value of a constraint is varied.

When a gravity field is applied to a system of mass small enough so that the field is affected by it only negligibly, a gravity potential γ may be defined as the increase in energy per unit mass of an elementary system as it is moved from a reference level $(\gamma = 0)$ to the given level while entropy, number of particles, and volume constraint are held constant. The Gibbs equation (64) for a system of mass m then becomes

$$dS = \frac{1}{T}\,[dE + pdV - \sum_i \mu_i dn_i - md\gamma]. \tag{93}$$

A simple and familiar condition for stable equilibrium that can be deduced from the Gibbs equation in form (93) is that for an otherwise simple fluid system in a gravity field, the rate of change of pressure with vertical distance is proportional to the density of the fluid. The proportionality factor proves to be g, the so-called acceleration of gravity.

A modification of the Gibbs equation similar to but more complicated than that given above for a gravity field has been devised to apply to a dielectric material, a material of which the electrically charged component species cannot move from one position in the material to another as it changes between neighbouring stable equilibrium states in an electric field between the plates of a capacitor. Another has been devised for a magnetic material in a magnetic field. (They will not be given here.)

RELATIVISTIC EFFECTS IN A GRAVITY FIELD

In an extremely intense gravity field, relativistic effects cannot be ignored. By combining the Einstein relation between energy and mass $(E = mc^2)$ with the first and second laws, the following two conclusions are reached: (1) For stable equilibrium in a vertical column, it is necessary, as in nonrelativistic systems, that the temperature, $(\partial E/\partial S)_{n\beta}$, be uniform. (2) If a system is held at constant volume and lifted reversibly and adiabatically—that is, at constant entropy S—the pressure and temperature of the system both increase. More specifically, the increase in the natural logarithm of the pressure when the system is lifted from the level at which the gravity potential γ is arbitrarily assigned the value zero to a level at which it has the value γ is equal to the quotient of γ and the square of the speed of light c. A similar statement holds for temperature. Since the square of the speed of light c is a very large number, the effect on pressure and temperature will be small except in very intense gravitational fields.

The relation between temperature and gravity potential may be derived by consideration of a cycle in which a pure molecular species in a triple-point state (for example, solid, liquid, and vapour in mutual stable equilibrium) is lifted reversibly, adiabatically, and at constant volume from the reference level $\gamma = 0$ to the level γ, heated reversibly at constant temperature, lowered reversibly and adiabatically to $\gamma = 0$, and cooled to the original state. Because of the increase in mass in the heating process, the work of descent will exceed the work of ascent. The efficiency of this cycle may then be equated to that of a Carnot cycle in terms of temperature, as in equation (22), to obtain the desired relation.

Steady rate processes

Many applications of thermodynamics involve interactions between systems some or all of which are passing through nonequilibrium states. For example, chemical and nuclear reactions and flow of energy and matter are processes occurring in systems passing through nonequilibrium states.

The analysis of nonequilibrium states is more difficult, both conceptually and numerically, than that of stable equilibrium states. For example, because the number of properties required for the description of nonequilibrium states is larger than that for stable equilibrium states, the mathematical relations between properties are correspondingly more complicated.

Problems of analysis of nonequilibrium states

In the interest of simplicity, the following applications are restricted to systems in steady states having fixed time rates of change of extensive properties. These applications will be called steady rate processes.

APPROACH TO MUTUAL STABLE EQUILIBRIUM

If two systems I and II are each in a stable equilibrium state but not in mutual stable equilibrium, a process in which they change toward mutual stable equilibrium will occur if they are connected by an intermediate system *M*. Depending upon the nature of the three systems and their states, the process that occurs may be caused by the transfer through *M* of energy alone or of matter with energy. The rate at which such transfer occurs will depend upon the initial departure from mutual stable equilibrium of systems *I* and *II*. By means of the first and second laws of thermodynamics and one additional postulate to them, a number of useful relationships between rates and potential differences or gradients may be determined for a large variety of rate processes, most of which are irreversible.

Generally it is possible to conceive of the process in *M* as being caused by two systems *I* and *II*, each of which would immediately assume a stable equilibrium state if the communication with *M* were suddenly stopped. To meet this requirement, the conductivity of matter or energy in *I* and *II* must be very great, so that whatever the influence on *I* of interaction through *M* with *II*, that influence will be felt uniformly through *I* and similarly with *II*. If the region is fluid, this result could be attained by minimal stirring of the fluid.

Under these circumstances, values of properties may be assigned to systems *I* and *II*. Region *M*, on the other hand, is in a nonequilibrium state. Nevertheless, values of intensive properties such as temperature and chemical potential of component *i* can be assigned to a point *A* in the region *M* by the method known as local isolation. This method consists of isolating a region comprising point *A* and measuring the intensive property for this region when it reaches a stable equilibrium state. The value of the property in the limit as the size of the region is reduced to the smallest consistent with isolation may be taken to be the value at point *A*.

Region *M* will be assumed to be in a steady state; that is, the rate of change of any intensive property of *I*, *II*, or *M* is negligible. Extensive properties of *I* and *II*, on the other hand, may change at a finite rate, and any such rate is called a flux. Thus, an energy flux J_u is defined as the negative of the change of energy of *I* per unit time and, because of steady state in *M*, the change of energy of *II* per unit time:

Fluxes of extensive properties

$$J_u \equiv -\frac{dU_I}{dt} = \frac{dU_{II}}{dt}. \quad (94)$$

Similarly a flux of component *i* is denoted by J_i and is given by

$$J_i \equiv -\frac{dn_{iI}}{dt} = \frac{dn_{iII}}{dt}. \quad (95)$$

Under the steady-state conditions assumed and with *I* and *II* each held at constant volume, any one flux must depend upon those differences in intensive properties between *I* and *II* that measure the departure from stable equilibrium. Among these may be differences in temperature, pressure, mole fraction of component *i*, potential of component *i*, etc. The choice of differences that is made is governed by the postulate to be employed. It is made by expressing the rate of entropy generation in the process in terms of the Gibbs equation and using the resulting expression to define conjugate pairs of fluxes and forces. Each flux is then expressed in terms of all the forces so defined.

The region *M* between *I* and *II* may be subdivided into vertical laminas *dM*, over any face of which, for interaction in one direction only, the values of all intensive properties are uniform. For any one lamina, therefore, constant-volume stable equilibrium regions *I* and *II* may be substituted for material adjoining *M* without altering the process in the lamina (Figure 14).

For steady state in *dM* the rate of entropy generation in the process will be wholly accounted for by changes of entropy in *I* and *II*. Because the Gibbs equation (64) states the entropy change of a phase such as *I* or *II* in terms of the temperature, chemical potentials of components, change in energy, and change in masses of components, it will yield an expression for the rate of entropy change in terms of temperature, chemical potentials, and rates of change of energy and masses. These rates of change

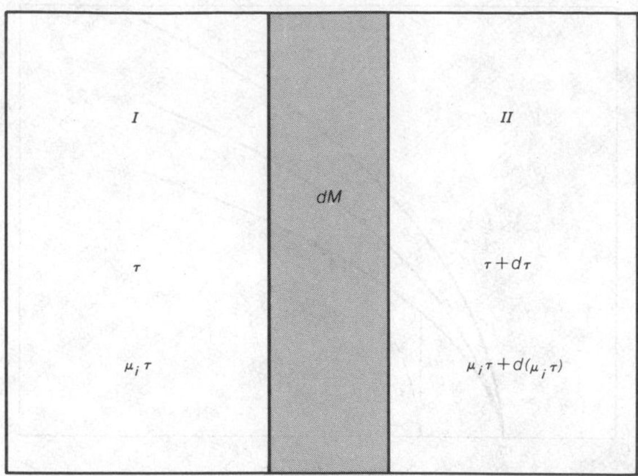

Figure 14: Two systems, *I* and *II*, each in stable equilibrium but not in mutual stable equilibrium, interacting through a thin intermediate system *dM*, which is in a nonequilibrium state. The symbol τ represents the quantity $1/T$, the reciprocal of the absolute temperature (see text).

are the fluxes, J_u and J_i, of energy and of component *i*, as indicated above. Because of the steady-state condition these fluxes may prove to be identical for regions *I* and *II*, but they will differ at most only infinitesimally for an infinitesimal thickness of the lamina *dM*.

The rate of entropy generation in the whole process is found by summing for regions *I* and *II* the rates of entropy change, one of which will be negative and the other positive, to get an infinitesimal difference between two finite rates. This rate of entropy generation will then be the sum of products of fluxes and differences between *I* and *II* of potentials. These products are $J_u d(1/T)$ and $J_i d(-\mu_i/T)$, symbol *d* denoting the difference between the value in *II* and the value in *I* of the potential in parentheses. Thus the expression for the rate of entropy generation $d\dot{S}$ is

$$d\dot{S} = J_u d\left(\frac{1}{T}\right) + \sum_i J_i\, d\left(-\frac{\mu_i}{T}\right), \quad (96)$$

in which $\sum_i$ denotes summation over all component substances $i = 1, 2, \ldots k$.

This last expression serves the purpose of identifying conjugate fluxes and forces; that is, for energy flux J_u the difference $d(1/T)$ is the conjugate force, etc.

Conjugate fluxes and forces

Each flux J_u, J_i of equation (96) is a function of the state of one of the stable equilibrium regions *I* or *II* and of the forces $d(1/T)$, $d(-\mu_i/T)$, with the further condition that, whatever the state, the flux will be zero when all forces are zero—that is, for mutual stable equilibrium. Purely mathematical considerations indicate that the functional relation between a flux such as J_u and the forces $d(1/T)$, $d(-\mu_i/T)$ is a very simple one, provided that the fluxes are small; *i.e.*, provided that the departure from mutual stable equilibrium is small. This functional relation is that the flux is equal to the sum of terms each consisting of a force multiplied by a coefficient *L*. From thermodynamic considerations it can be shown that the magnitudes of the coefficients *L* are fixed once the nature and states of regions *I* and *M* are fixed. They are independent of the magnitudes of the forces $d(1/T)$ and $d(-\mu_i/T)$. The functional relation is thus given by

$$J_u = L_{uu} d\left(\frac{1}{T}\right) + \sum_j L_{uj}\, d\left(-\frac{\mu_j}{T}\right) \quad (97)$$

$$J_i = L_{iu} d\left(\frac{1}{T}\right) + \sum_j L_{ij}\, d\left(-\frac{\mu_j}{T}\right), \quad (98)$$

in which the first subscript on an *L* refers to the flux and the second to the force term in which it appears. Although exceptions to them may doubtless be found, these equations are of general application to rate processes and become increasingly valid the more nearly all the fluxes approach zero. They are known as phenomenological equations, and the coefficients *L* are known as conductivities.

The Onsager reciprocal relation, the additional postulate

The Onsager reciprocal relation

referred to above, is as follows: The matrix of coefficients L of a set of equations such as (97) and (98), in which conjugate pairs of fluxes and forces are identified through expression (96) for the rate of entropy production, is symmetrical; that is,

$$L_{ij} = L_{ji} \text{ for } i, j = u, 1, 2 \ldots . \quad (99)$$

Lars Onsager, a Norwegian–American theoretical chemist, stated this new law in 1931 in an argument based on a principle of statistical mechanics called the principle of microscopic reversibility and a postulate that is closely related to the second law of thermodynamics. The new law was subsequently shown to be of general application in irreversible processes and was extended to a wide variety of phenomena.

Phenomenological equations

The phenomenological equations reduce to special forms for various special systems and force conditions and are known under different names. For example, Fourier's law of heat conduction (for the 19th-century French mathematician and physicist Jean-Baptiste Fourier), Ohm's law of electric current flow (for the 19th-century German physicist Georg Simon Ohm), Fick's law of neutral particle diffusion (for the 19th-century German physiologist Adolf Eugen Fick), and the law of ambipolar diffusion of positive and negative charges are all special cases of the linear phenomenological equations. The constants appearing in the laws just cited, such as electric resistance in Ohm's law, may be expressed easily in terms of the conductivities L of the phenomenological equations.

FLOW OF A SUBSTANCE THROUGH A BARRIER

A relatively simple application of the thermodynamics of rate processes is to the flow of a single-component substance through a barrier M under conditions such that the phenomenological equations (97) and (98) are valid. An example would be the flow of helium through a rubber membrane between two stable equilibrium regions I and II. The Onsager reciprocal relation is simply that $L_{u1} = L_{1u}$, subscript 1 referring to helium.

The two forces are the differences across the membrane $d(1/T)$ and $d(\mu_1/T)$. When the flux of helium is zero, then the difference $d(1/T)$ causes its conjugate energy to flow downgrade in temperature and upgrade in $1/T$. When the temperature difference and $d(1/T)$ are zero, then its conjugate helium will flow downgrade in chemical potential and in μ_1/T. Each of these forces, however, tends to cause its nonconjugate flux, as well as its conjugate flux, in one or the other direction. This behaviour is called coupling. In the absence of coupling, the coefficients L_{u1} and L_{1u} would both be zero.

By virtue of coupling, the two forces may be set in relation to each other so as to stop the flow of helium because of a balance between the opposing influences of the two forces. Such a steady state will be attained spontaneously if a temperature difference is maintained between I and II for a long enough period of time while the volumes of I and II are held constant. The flow of helium will eventually cease—or at least approach zero as a limit as time proceeds. A flow of energy will persist, however, in the steady-state condition by virtue of the temperature difference.

It can be seen from the second phenomenological equation (98) that the ratio L_{1u}/L_{11} is equal to the ratio of forces $d(\mu_1/T)/d(1/T)$ when J_1 is zero. From the two equations (97) and (98) taken together it can be seen that the ratio L_{u1}/L_{11} is equal to the ratio of fluxes J_u/J_1 when $d(1/T)$ is zero. Because the Onsager reciprocal relation requires that L_{1u} be equal to L_{u1}, it follows that the ratio of forces when J_1 is zero must equal the ratio of fluxes when the temperatures of I and II are equal.

By means of a simple thermodynamic analysis, the ratio of forces $d(\mu_1/T)/d(1/T)$ may be expressed in terms of the ratio of pressure difference to temperature difference dp/dT, which then proves to be proportional to the excess of J_u/J_1 for dT equal to zero over the enthalpy h_1 of helium in region I. The actual relation is

$$\left(\frac{dp}{dT}\right)_{J_1=0} = -\frac{1}{v_1 T}\left[\left(\frac{J_u}{J_1}\right)_{dT=0} - h_1\right]. \quad (100)$$

This relation gives the ratio of the pressure gradient to the temperature gradient for which the particle flow is stopped. Because it can be shown that for simple bulk flow J_u/J_1 is h_1 for fluid crossing any section in which the temperature is uniform in the direction of flow, it follows from equation (100) that bulk flow may be stopped even in a temperature gradient by zero pressure gradient. Whenever the energy flux per unit particle flux differs from h_1 in constant-temperature flow, then a pressure gradient is necessary to stop flow in a temperature gradient.

The Knudsen effect

Application of equation (100) to the flow of a perfect gas may be made for a porous plug with pore sizes very small compared with the mean distance travelled by gas molecules between collisions or compared to flow between emitting and receiving surfaces separated by a distance that is very small compared with the mean distance between collisions. For both of these the result is the same and can be shown to be

$$\left(\frac{dp}{dT}\right)_{J_1=0} = \frac{1}{2}\frac{p}{T} \quad (101)$$

or, for a finite length,

$$\left[\frac{p^I}{p^{II}} = \sqrt{\frac{T^I}{T^{II}}}\right]_{J_1=0}. \quad (102)$$

These relations describe what is known as the Knudsen effect.

The excess over the enthalpy flux of the energy flux across the barrier per unit of matter flowing when dT is zero is called the heat of transport and is denoted by q_1^*:

$$q_1^* \equiv \left(\frac{J_u}{J_1}\right)_{dT=0} - h_1. \quad (103)$$

It is the direct heat interaction that must be provided between regions II and I (Figure 14) when one unit of mass flows from I to II through M if the temperatures of I and II are to be maintained equal. Its magnitude can be found, in accordance with (100), by a measurement of the ratio dp/dT that corresponds to a flux J_1 of zero. The value found in this way for the heat of transport through a rubber membrane for nitrogen is −260 calories per gram mole and for hydrogen +100.

Statistical thermodynamics

Early mechanical theories of heat

The mechanical theory of heat was developed concurrently with thermodynamics. It relates heat to changes in the motion of the atoms and molecules of matter. The history of the theory can be traced back to the Greek philosophers Democritus (*c.* 400 BC) and Epicurus (*c.* 300 BC). The French philosopher Pierre Gassendi developed in the 17th century a theory in which all material phenomena are attributable to the indestructible motion of atoms. Although the English philosopher Robert Hooke, the German philosopher and mathematician Gottfried Wilhelm Leibniz, and the Swiss mathematician and physicist Daniel Bernoulli improved upon it in the 17th and 18th centuries, the theory was not firmly established until Joule demonstrated experimentally in the 19th century that a quantitative relation exists between heat and work when they produce identical effects.

After Joule's demonstration the theory developed rapidly into a science of major importance that became known as statistical mechanics or statistical thermodynamics. Its subject is the relation between the laws of thermodynamics and the details of the structure of matter. The development of this science, which can be traced through Hermann Ludwig Ferdinand von Helmholtz, a German physicist and anatomist; Clausius; Maxwell; and Boltzmann, culminated in the work of Gibbs, who in 1901 presented an exposition of statistical thermodynamics that excels in completeness, rigour, and generality. Although the exposition of Gibbs is stated in terms of classical mechanics, it is better adapted to quantum mechanics, which in some ways it anticipates.

Perhaps because Gibbs's contribution was not fully understood, a less general and less rigorous molecular statistics prevailed in the literature, with few exceptions, until after World War II.

GIBBSIAN STATISTICS

According to classical mechanics, the state of a system having N degrees of freedom (that is, independent ways in which the space configuration of the system may change) is fully specified by the values of N position coordinates $q_1, q_2, \ldots, q_N$, and N momentum coordinates $p_1, p_2, \ldots, p_N$. For example, the state of a system consisting of n point particles (particles without internal structure and therefore without internal degrees of freedom) is specified if the position coordinates along three Cartesian axes x, y, and z and the corresponding momentum coordinates along these same axes for each of the particles are specified. For such a system the number N of the degrees of freedom is equal to three times the number n of the particles of the system.

The position of a particle in space may be represented geometrically by a point in three-dimensional space having coordinates x, y, and z. The state of the particle involves not only the values of the coordinates x, y, and z but also the values of momentum component (which fixes the velocity component) p_x in the x direction, p_y in the y direction, and p_z in the z direction. These considerations suggest a mental extension of the concept of space to six dimensions, having coordinates x, y, z, p_x, p_y, and p_z. The state of the particle could then be completely described by a point in the six-dimensional space for which the values of x, y, z, p_x, p_y, and p_z are appropriately fixed.

The particle just discussed is said to have three degrees of freedom, and its state can be represented by a point in a six-dimensional space. A collection of two such particles might have six degrees of freedom, and the representation of its state would call for a 12-dimensional space. The number of degrees of freedom of a more complex system is the number of independent kinds of displacement to which the system is subject. The state of such a system having N degrees of freedom may be represented geometrically in classical mechanics by a point in $2N$-dimensional space having as coordinates $q_1, q_2, \ldots, q_N$, $p_1, p_2, \ldots, p_N$. This $2N$-dimensional space was called by Gibbs phase space.

Phase space

According to Gibbs, the term thermodynamic state of a system with N degrees of freedom does not necessarily correspond to a unique point in phase space, but to a set of probabilities of the system being in any one of the allowed points consistent with the constraints imposed on the system. Because any set of allowed states in classical mechanics forms a continuum, Gibbs introduced a probability density or distribution P, which he called the coefficient of probability, such that the product $Pdq_1dq_2 \ldots dq_Ndp_1dp_2 \ldots dp_N$ is equal to the probability of the system being in states having values of coordinates between q_1 and $q_1 + dq_1$, q_2 and $q_2 + dq_2, \ldots, q_N$ and $q_N + dq_N$ and values of momenta between p_1 and $p_1 + dp_1$, p_2 and $p_2 + dp_2, \ldots$, and p_N and $p_N + dp_N$. For a given thermodynamic state, the distribution P will be a corresponding function of q's and p's. Furthermore, because a system must be at some one of the allowed states, the sum of all the probabilities must always be equal to unity or, by the same token, the integral of the distribution P over all q's and p's must be always equal to unity.

Various types of thermodynamic states correspond to particular mathematical forms of the distribution P. For example, Gibbs assumed without proof that, for the stable equilibrium states of a system with N degrees of freedom, the coefficient of probability P corresponding to the state $q_1, q_2, \ldots, q_N, p_1, p_2, \ldots, p_N$ of energy ε is equal to the number 2.718282 (the base of natural logarithms) raised to the $(\Psi - \varepsilon)/\Theta$ power, in which Ψ and Θ are constants; in other words, P is given by the exponential relation

$$P = \exp\left(\frac{\Psi - \varepsilon}{\Theta}\right). \tag{104}$$

He called this distribution of probabilities a canonical distribution. Further discussion of Gibbsian statistics will be omitted because the quantum thermodynamics discussed below, though based on Gibbsian ideas, is more complete.

QUANTUM THERMODYNAMICS

Definition of state. In contrast to classical mechanics, a fundamental premise of quantum mechanics is that at a given time the most that can be said about results of measurements on a system is the probability of finding particular values of properties, such as coordinates and momenta, rather than the particular values that will be observed. This premise reflects the principle of indeterminacy first introduced by the German physicist Werner Heisenberg. It requires a description of the state of a system in terms of probabilities.

The principles of quantum mechanics may be stated by means of a number of mathematical formulations. Among these, the best known are the wave formulation by the German physicist Erwin Schrödinger, the vector formulation by the English physicist P.A.M. Dirac, and the matrix formulation by Heisenberg. The matrix formulation is especially suited to the exposition of quantum thermodynamics and is adopted below (for a discussion of matrices in general, see the article ALGEBRA).

Any property of a system that in classical mechanics may be expressed as a function of position and momentum coordinates is expressed in quantum mechanics by a matrix. For example, the Hamiltonian function of classical mechanics, which is the energy of the system, is represented by the Hamiltonian matrix. Matrix representations are used also for properties (such as spin) that have no classical analogue. The method of calculation of elements of matrices is specified by the principles of quantum mechanics.

Matrices and eigenvalues

Each matrix possesses eigenvalues; that is, a set of numbers that can be found by solving the characteristic equation of the matrix. The eigenvalues of the matrix of a property are real, as distinguished from complex, in the mathematical sense. Each one corresponds to a possible outcome of a measurement of the property performed on the system. For example, a measurement of the energy of a system in a given condition will yield any one of the real eigenvalues of the Hamiltonian matrix of the system. The number of eigenvalues of a property may be either finite, as with spin, or infinite, as with energy for most systems.

According to quantum mechanics, it is impossible to predict from knowledge of the condition of a system which eigenvalue a measurement will yield. Instead, the most that can be said at any instant of time is the probability that a measurement will yield a given eigenvalue.

The state of a system is defined as the set of all probabilities for the outcomes of all measurements that may be performed at a given instant of time. That is, the state of a system is represented by Table 2, in which $\overline{F}, \overline{G}, \overline{H}, \ldots$

Table 2: State of a System

property	$\overline{F}$	$\overline{G}$	$\overline{H}$	
Probabilities	$W(F_1)$	$W(G_1)$	$W(H_1)$	…
	$W(F_2)$	$W(G_2)$	$W(H_2)$	…
	•	•	•	
	•	•	•	
	•	•	•	

denote observable properties and in which $W(F_1)$ denotes the probability that any one measurement of property $\overline{F}$ will yield the eigenvalue $F_1, \ldots, W(G_1)$ denotes the probability that any one measurement of property $\overline{G}$ will yield the eigenvalue $G_1, \ldots$, and so forth. It can be shown that these probabilities can be combined to form a matrix $[\rho]$, called the density matrix. Conversely, a systematic procedure exists for determining from a given density matrix $[\rho]$ the probability $W(E_n)$ that a measurement of energy corresponding to the Hamiltonian matrix $[E]$ will yield the energy eigenvalue E_n of $[E]$. Again, the procedure yields the probability $W(F_m)$ that a measurement of property $\overline{F}$ corresponding to matrix $[F]$ will yield the eigenvalue F_m of $[F]$.

Values of properties. Because measurements of a property $\bar{F}$ of a system in a given state yield different eigenvalues F_m, each with a probability $W(F_m)$ specified by the density matrix $[\rho]$ that represents the state, an expectation value or simply a value of the property corresponding to the given state is defined as the weighted average of the various possible eigenvalues, each eigenvalue being weighted by the probability that it will be observed. Symbolically, the value F of a property $\bar{F}$ may be represented as a sum over many terms, each of which is the product of a probability $W(F_m)$ and the eigenvalue F_m; that is,

$$F=\sum_m W(F_m)F_m, \quad (105)$$

in which the symbol $\sum_m$ denotes summation over all eigenvalues, and each eigenvalue is represented by a different symbol (different value of the subscript m) even when two or more eigenvalues have the same value. (For some matrices several distinct eigenvalues may have identical numerical values. The eigenvalues are then called degenerate.)

Reversible equation of motion. Quantum mechanics provides an equation, called the equation of motion, from which can be found the rate of change of the density matrix $[\rho]$ with time for some reversible and adiabatic processes. The equation will not be given here.

Conditions for equilibrium are found from the equation of motion. If the eigenvalues of the density matrix $[\rho]$ for an equilibrium state are denoted by $x_1, x_2, \ldots, x_m, \ldots$ and the eigenvalues of the Hamiltonian matrix $[E]$ by $E_1, E_2, \ldots, E_m, \ldots$, it can be shown that a necessary and sufficient condition for equilibrium is that the first eigenvalue x_1 be equal to the probability $W(E_1)$, that a measurement of the energy will yield the first eigenvalue E_1, the second eigenvalue x_2 be equal to $W(E_2)$, etc. Moreover, for equilibrium states the value of the energy E can be expressed as a sum of terms each of which is the product of x_m and E_m; that is,

$$E=\sum_m x_m E_m. \quad (106)$$

General expression for entropy. According to the first and second laws of thermodynamics, entropy is a state function of a system. Moreover, it must be invariant in any reversible adiabatic process. From these two conditions and the requirement that it be an extensive state function, the value S of entropy can be shown to be proportional to a mean of the natural logarithms of the eigenvalues of the density matrix. When $y_1, y_2, \ldots, y_m, \ldots$ denote the eigenvalues of the density matrix $[\rho]$ (corresponding to an arbitrary state, which is not necessarily equilibrium or stable equilibrium), the mean is calculated by weighting each $\ln y_m$ with the value y_m. In mathematical form this statement is expressed

$$S=-k\sum_m y_m \ln y_m, \quad (107)$$

in which k is a universal constant that proves to be the Boltzmann constant.

Pure states. A pure state is defined as one for which the eigenvalues of the density matrix $[\rho]$ are all equal to zero, except for one that is equal to unity. It follows from equation (107) that the entropy of a pure state is equal to zero.

It can be shown that any pure state may be described also by means of a wave function of quantum mechanics; and, conversely, states that can be described by wave functions correspond to zero entropy. In general, however, the entropy of a system is not equal to zero, and the state of the system cannot in general, therefore, be described by a wave function.

Stable equilibrium states. In the language of quantum thermodynamics, the criterion for stable equilibrium (see above *Stable equilibrium*) implies that the density matrix for a stable equilibrium state be such that the entropy (equation [107]) is at its maximum for given values of energy and numbers of particles. When this criterion is applied to a system of which the numbers of particles are known without uncertainty (the probability of the value for the number of particles of a given kind that is found by a measurement is unity), it yields the eigenvalues $x_1^\circ, x_2^\circ, \ldots, x_m^\circ, \ldots$ for the stable equilibrium states as functions of the energy eigenvalues $E_1, E_2, \ldots, E_m, \ldots$ of the Hamiltonian matrix of the system and the temperature of the stable equilibrium state in question. The various mathematical functions are as follows:

$$x_1^\circ=\frac{\exp(-E_1/kT)}{\sum_m \exp(-E_m/kT)};\ x_2^\circ=\frac{\exp(-E_2/kT)}{\sum_m \exp(-E_m/kT)};\ldots \quad (108)$$

$$T\equiv\left(\frac{\partial E}{\partial S}\right)_\beta, \quad (109)$$

$$E=\sum_m x_m^\circ E_m=\frac{\sum_m E_m \exp(-E_m/kT)}{\sum_m \exp(-E_m/kT)}, \quad (110)$$

and

$$S=-k\sum_m x_m^\circ \ln x_m^\circ$$
$$=k\ln\left[\sum_m \exp(-E_m/kT)\right]+\frac{E}{T}. \quad (111)$$

Because the eigenvalues $x_1, x_2, \ldots, x_m, \ldots$ of the density matrix for any equilibrium state and, therefore, the eigenvalues $x_1^\circ, x_2^\circ, \ldots, x_m^\circ, \ldots$ of the density matrix for any stable equilibrium state represent probabilities that measurements of energy will yield eigenvalues $E_1, E_2, \ldots, E_m, \ldots$, respectively, equation (108) can be thought of as analogous to the canonical distribution postulated by Gibbs, provided that the two constants Θ and Ψ in equation (104) are expressed in terms of the temperature T and the energy eigenvalues $E_1, E_2, \ldots, E_m, \ldots$. It can be shown that Θ and Ψ are given by the relations

$$\Theta=kT \quad (112)$$

and

$$\Psi=kT\ln\left[\sum_m \exp(-E_m/kT)\right] \quad (113)$$

It can be readily verified from equations (111) and (113) that the function Ψ is equal to the Helmholtz free energy of the system; *i.e.*, equal to $E-TS$. Moreover, because the energy eigenvalues $E_1, E_2, \ldots, E_m, \ldots$ are in general functions of the values of the constraints, the Helmholtz free energy Ψ is a function of temperature and the constraints and, therefore, a characteristic function. This means that in quantum thermodynamics the problem of evaluating the properties of any system with numbers of particles that are known without uncertainty and in a stable equilibrium state reduces to the problem of evaluating the energy eigenvalues as functions of the constraints. The evaluation of the energy eigenvalues is a difficult mathematical task that has been carried out for only a very few systems. The difficulty, however, is in the calculation rather than in the conception of the evaluation.

The canonical partition function

The quantity Q_c, called the canonical partition function, is defined as the sum of $\exp(-E_1/kT)$, $\exp(-E_2/kT)$, $\exp(-E_3/kT)$, etc. It appears in the expressions for many properties of systems in stable equilibrium states. For example, because

$$Q_c\equiv\sum_m \exp(-E_m/kT), \quad (114)$$

it follows that the probability x_m° of observing an energy eigenvalue E_m is the quotient of $\exp(-E_m/kT)$ and Q_c, that the Helmholtz free energy per mole is the product of (kT) and the logarithm of Q_c, and that the entropy is the sum of the product $k\ln Q_c$ of k and logarithm of Q_c and the quotient E/T of the value of the energy and the temperature:

$$x_m^\circ=\frac{\exp(-E_m/kT)}{Q_c};$$

$$\Psi=kT\ln Q_c;$$

and

$$S=k\ln Q_c+\frac{E}{T}.$$

GRAND SYSTEMS

Stable equilibrium states. In many systems the numbers of particles may be uncertain either because the system is open to the transfer of rest mass or because particles can be created and annihilated within the system. The terminology of Gibbs suggests that such systems be called grand systems.

Uncertainty in the numbers of particles means that measurements of these numbers for a grand system in a given state yield different particle-number eigenvalues. This uncertainty is analogous to that associated in general with the energy. It follows that an expectation value rather than a dispersion-free value (that is, rather than a unique value that is observed as a result of every measurement) is assigned to the number of particles of each component of a state of a grand system. Without discussion of the matrix formalism for grand systems, some results applicable to stable equilibrium states will be given.

A stable equilibrium state of a grand system is fully described by the set of eigenvalues $x_1^\circ, x_2^\circ, \ldots, x_m^\circ, \ldots$ of the density matrix that maximizes the entropy of the system at given values of energy, numbers of particles of the components, and constraints. The mth eigenvalue x_m° is equal to the probability that a suitable measurement will yield the mth energy eigenvalue E_m and the mth number-of-particle eigenvalues $n_{1m}, n_{2m}, \ldots, n_{km}$ for the set of k components of the system. It can be expressed as a function of the energy eigenvalues $E_1, E_2, \ldots, E_m, \ldots$ of the Hamiltonian matrix of the system, the eigenvalues $n_{11}, n_{12}, \ldots, n_{1m}, \ldots$ of the number of particles of component number one, the eigenvalues $n_{21}, n_{22}, \ldots, n_{2m}, \ldots$ of the number of particles of component number two, ..., the total potentials $\mu_1, \mu_2, \ldots, \mu_k$ of the k components 1, 2, ... k, and the temperature T of the stable equilibrium state in question. It is given by the relation

$$x_m^\circ = \frac{\exp[(n_{1m}\mu_1 + n_{2m}\mu_2 + \ldots + n_{km}\mu_k - E_m)/kT]}{\sum_m \exp[(n_{1m}\mu_1 + n_{2m}\mu_2 + \ldots + n_{km}\mu_k - E_m)/kT]}. \quad (115)$$

The sum in the denominator of (115) is called the grand partition function Q_g; *i.e.*

$$Q_g \equiv \sum_m \exp[(n_{1m}\mu_1 + n_{2m}\mu_2 + \ldots + n_{km}\mu_k - E_m)/kT]. \quad (116)$$

The grand partition function

It appears in many relations between properties for grand systems in stable equilibrium states. For example, for a grand system with volume V as the only independent constraint, the equation of state is given by the relation

$$pV/kT = \ln Q_g. \quad (117)$$

Equation (117) applies to grand systems in gaseous, liquid, or solid forms.

The one-particle approximation for one-component systems. The energy eigenvalues of most systems can be computed only approximately. A class of approximations that consists in expressing each energy eigenvalue of the system as a sum of energy eigenvalues of suitably defined subsystems, each having one particle only, is called the one-particle approximation. It is valid for some crystals and for dilute gases at such low densities that short-range interparticle forces (forces that act between particles in close proximity) can be neglected, and long-range forces on each particle are independent of the positions of other particles. Some results of the analysis applicable to dilute gases will be given below.

In the context of the one-particle approximation, each of the energy eigenvalues $E_1, E_2, \ldots, E_m, \ldots$ of a dilute gas having one component only (namely, consisting of a number of particles of a single type) is expressed as a sum of terms such that each term is a positive integer multiplied by an energy eigenvalue of a system that has one particle only and for which the eigenvalues can be evaluated. For example, if $\nu_{m1}, \nu_{m2}, \ldots, \nu_{mj}, \ldots$ denote the positive integers that appear in the sum for the mth eigenvalue E_m and $\varepsilon_1, \varepsilon_2, \ldots, \varepsilon_j, \ldots$, the energy eigenvalues of the system with the one particle, then E_m is given by the relation

$$\begin{aligned} E_m &= \nu_{m1}\varepsilon_1 + \nu_{m2}\varepsilon_2 + \ldots + \nu_{mj}\varepsilon_j + \ldots \\ &= \sum_j \nu_{mj}\varepsilon_j \text{ for all values of } m. \end{aligned} \quad (118)$$

Equation (118) is interpreted as meaning that of the n_m particles associated with the energy eigenvalue E_m, ν_{m1} have energy ε_1, ν_{m2} have energy $\varepsilon_2, \ldots, \nu_{mj}$ have energy $\varepsilon_j, \ldots$. From this interpretation it follows that the sum of all the positive integers $\nu_{m1}, \nu_{m2}, \ldots, \nu_{mj}, \ldots$ must be equal to n_m; *i.e.*,

$$\nu_{m1} + \nu_{m2} + \ldots + \nu_{mj} + \ldots = \sum_j \nu_{mj} = n_m. \quad (119)$$

The values that each integer ν_{mj} can assume are restricted by the nature of the particles in question. For certain particles, called fermions, each ν_{mj} may be either zero or unity for all values of the subscripts m and j; *i.e.*, for any energy eigenvalue E_m of the overall system and any energy eigenvalue ε_j of the auxiliary one-particle system. For example, because electrons are fermions a grand system consisting of electrons has, for a state with an energy eigenvalue E_m, at most one electron of one-particle energy eigenvalue ε_j. (This restriction is equivalent to the so-called exclusion principle of atomic physics, announced in 1925 by the Austrian physicist Wolfgang Pauli.) On the other hand, for certain particles called bosons, each of the integers ν_{mj} may have any positive integral value as well as the value zero. In a grand system consisting of photons—which are bosons—in a state with energy eigenvalue E_m, any number of photons from zero to n_m may have a particular energy ε_j.

Fermions and bosons

When the allowed numerical values of the integers ν_{mj} are considered, the properties of a dilute gas in a stable equilibrium state can be expressed as functions of the one-particle energy eigenvalues $\varepsilon_1, \varepsilon_2, \ldots, \varepsilon_j, \ldots$ rather than the eigenvalues $E_1, E_2, \ldots, E_m, \ldots$ of the overall system. For example, the expectation or average value ν_j of the number of particles that can be thought of as having one-particle energy ε_j—namely, the expectation value ν_j of the integers $\nu_{1j}, \nu_{2j}, \ldots, \nu_{mj}, \ldots$—is defined as the sum of terms each being an integer ν_{mj} multiplied by the probability x_m° that a suitable measurement will yield the energy eigenvalue E_m.

It can be shown that, if μ denotes the total potential of the single component of the grand system, then ν_j is given by the relations

$$\nu_j = \sum_m x_m^\circ \nu_{jm} = \frac{1}{\exp[(\varepsilon_j - \mu)/kT] + 1} \text{ for fermions} \quad (120)$$

and

$$\nu_j = \sum_m x_m^\circ \nu_{jm} = \frac{1}{\exp[(\varepsilon_j - \mu)/kT] - 1} \text{ for bosons.} \quad (121)$$

Relation (120) is called the Fermi–Dirac factor, and the corresponding dilute gas is said to obey Fermi–Dirac statistics, formulated for this class of particles in 1926–27 by the physicists Enrico Fermi, then working in Italy, and Paul A.M. Dirac in England. Relation (121) is called the Bose–Einstein factor, and the corresponding dilute gas is said to obey Bose–Einstein statistics, introduced in 1924 by the Indian physicist Satyendra Nath Bose and subsequently extended by Einstein.

Again, for a system with volume V as the only constraint, it can be shown that the equation of state, (117), and the value n of the number of particles are given by the relations

$$\frac{pV}{kT} = \sum_j \ln\{1 \pm \exp[(\mu - \varepsilon_j)/kT]\}^{\pm 1} \quad (122)$$

and

$$n = \sum_j \{[\exp(\varepsilon_j - \mu)/kT] \pm 1\}^{-1}, \quad (123)$$

in which the plus sign in $\pm$ applies to fermions and the minus sign to bosons.

Fundamental equation for one-component simple systems. For a system for which both sets of eigenvalues $E_1, E_2, \ldots, E_m, \ldots$ and $\varepsilon_1, \varepsilon_2, \ldots, \varepsilon_j, \ldots$ are functions of volume V only, equations (122) and (123) indicate that p and n are functions of volume V, temperature T, and potential μ only. In principle, the p and n functions can be combined so as to eliminate volume V and obtain a fundamental equation that gives the total potential as a function of n, p, and T. But because equations (122) and (123) are transcendental, the derivation of such a fundamental equation is a difficult mathematical task. Under certain conditions it can be done with the aid of some approximations that are additional to the one-particle approximation.

For example, for a dilute gas in which the molecules have three translational degrees of freedom and of which the temperature is sufficiently high and pressure sufficiently low, it can be shown that the potential μ can be approximated by the expression

$$\mu = kT\ln p - \frac{5}{2}kT\ln T - kT\ln q_s - kT\ln\frac{k(2\pi mk)^{3/2}}{\hbar^3}, \quad (124)$$

in which m denotes the mass of each particle of the system; $\hbar$, Planck's constant divided by 2π; and q_s, the partition function associated with the energy eigenvalues for the internal structure of each molecule:

$$q_s = \sum_i \exp(-\bar{\varepsilon}_i/kT).$$

Such a gas is called a semiperfect gas. Consistent with the relations found for a semiperfect gas above without reference to the detailed structure of the molecules of the system, its fundamental equation is independent of n. This result reflects conformity with the definition of a simple system, which excludes capillarity. In contrast with equation (68), equation (124) gives the chemical potential per particle instead of per mole. It includes, therefore, the Boltzmann constant k, which is related to a single molecule and which is equal to the universal gas constant R divided by the number of molecules contained in a mole.

Boltzmann constant

As indicated earlier, the heat capacities of a semiperfect gas are functions of temperature. From equation (124) may be found the following expressions for specific heats per molecule:

$$c_p = \frac{5}{2}k + 2kT\frac{\partial \ln q_s}{\partial T} + kT^2\frac{\partial^2 \ln q_s}{\partial T^2}$$

and

$$c_v = \frac{3}{2}k + 2kT\frac{\partial \ln q_s}{\partial T} + kT^2\frac{\partial^2 \ln q_s}{\partial T^2},$$

in which $\partial^2 \ln q_s/\partial T^2$ denotes the partial derivative of $\partial \ln q_s/\partial T$ with respect to T. Because q_s is a function of T, both specific heats are functions of T.

A particular semiperfect gas is one for which the heat capacities c_p and c_v are independent of temperature. As stated above, such a gas is called a perfect gas. A gas behaves as a perfect gas either when the molecules have no internal structure, so that q_s is unity, or when q_s can be approximated by the product $g\exp(-\bar{\varepsilon}_0/kT)$, in which g and $\bar{\varepsilon}_0$ are constants.

Electronegativity of atoms and molecules. An atom or a molecule may be regarded as a grand system with electrons as its only component particles because it can exchange energy and electrons while reacting chemically with other atoms and molecules.

An atom A of atomic number z contains z units of positive electric charge in addition to its electrons. It has all the energy eigenvalues of the neutral atom and of each of the multiply (positively) charged ionized atoms. In addition, it can be negatively charged. In this section, consideration will be limited to atoms having energy eigenvalues corresponding to a singly charged negative ion; *i.e.*, an ion with $z+1$ electrons.

The eigenvalues n_i of the number of electrons in atom A are such that

$$n_i = i = 0, 1, 2, \ldots, z, z+1;$$

that is, the atom can be fully ionized ($i = 0$), partially ionized ($i < z$), neutral ($i = z$), or singly negatively charged ($i = z+1$).

For each n_i, one energy eigenvalue ($g_{i0} = 1$) will have the minimum numerical value E_{i0}. Each eigenvalue E_{i0} represents the energy of the so-called ground state of A with exactly n_i electrons. Moreover, an infinite number of energy eigenvalues E_{ij} ($j = 1, 2, \ldots$), each with a multiplicity or degeneracy g_{ij}, correspond to the excited states for each n_i.

For a stable equilibrium state at temperature T, the value n of the number of electrons of the atom is given in terms of the above notation by the relation

$$n = \frac{\sum_{i,j} n_i g_{ij}\exp[(n_i\mu - E_{ij})/kT]}{\sum_{i,j} g_{ij}\exp[(n_i\mu - E_{ij})/kT]}, \quad (125)$$

in which the symbol $\sum_{i,j}$ denotes a double summation, one over all values of i from zero to $z+1$ and the other over all values of j from zero to infinity. The number n may assume any value between 0 and $z+1$, although n_i can assume only integral values.

For given n and T values equation (125) can be solved for the value of the potential μ. Although the solution is numerically difficult, some general results are readily established: (1) For a fully ionized atom (that is, for the minimum value $n = 0$) μ is minus infinity, and for a singly charged negative ion (that is, for the maximum value $n = z+1$) μ is plus infinity, both for all values of T. Such extreme values of μ are always obtained when the value of the number of particles of the grand system is either minimum or maximum. They are consistent with the interpretation of the potential μ as an escaping tendency. (2) For values of n in the range between z and $z+1$, the potential μ is positive. For all other values the potential μ is negative. (3) For a neutral atom (that is, for $n = z$), in the limit as T approaches zero, μ is equal to one-half the difference between the energy eigenvalues of the ground states of the singly charged negative ion and the singly charged positive ion. It can also be written in the form

$$\mu = -\frac{I_1 + A_1}{2}, \quad (126)$$

in which I_1 and A_1 are, respectively, the first ionization energy and the electron affinity of the atom. For example, for the hydrogen atom the first (and only) ionization energy is equal to 13.6, the electron affinity is 0.7, and, therefore, the potential μ is -7.15, all in electron-volt units.

Since μ is a measure of the escaping tendency of a species, $-\mu$ is a measure of a capturing tendency or power to attract. The power of an atom to attract electrons is called the electronegativity of the atom. The preceding analysis indicates that electronegativity can be identified with the potential $-\mu$ of electrons in an atom, and its value can be computed by means of quantum thermodynamics. Similar results can be obtained for molecules and for solid surfaces.

Summary

The concepts of a system and states of a system adopted throughout this article are more general than are usually adopted in the science of thermodynamics. In the first part of the article, in which the microscopic structure of the particles that constitute the system is ignored, the many relations for systems in stable equilibrium states that are well known to classical thermodynamics are derived. The method, however, lends itself well to the treatment of states other than stable equilibrium inasmuch as the values of entropy may be found for such states.

In the second part, the microscopic structure is brought into consideration but without loss of the concept of an unambiguous stable equilibrium state. This result is achieved through the quantum-mechanical interpretation of measurement as an operation that yields definite eigenvalues with certain probabilities. The results are, first, many relations familiar to statistical mechanics that permit evaluation of properties of a system from the known structure of the particles and, second, a means of applying the laws of thermodynamics to systems that are large or small, simple or complicated. The limitation of thermodynamics, frequently applied in the past, to macroscopic systems no longer applies. To illustrate this generality, thermodynamic ideas are applied above to a single atom in order to discover the meaning of the previously recognized quantity electronegativity.

BIBLIOGRAPHY. E. MENDOZA (ed.), *Reflections on the Motive Power of Fire, by Sadi Carnot; and Other Papers on the Second Law of Thermodynamics, by É. Clapeyron and R. Clausius* (1960, reissued 1977), on the original theoretical development of the first and second laws; ROBERT BRUCE LINDSAY (ed.), *Julius Robert Mayer, Prophet of Energy* (1973), a carefully edited and translated selection of works of the 19th-century scientist who made perhaps the first attempt to demonstrate the conversion of heat into work; *The Scientific Papers of James Prescott Joule,* vol. 1 (1884, reprinted 1963), on the experimental foundations of the first law; W.D. NIVEN (ed.), *The Scientific Papers of James Clerk Maxwell,* 2 vol. (1890; reissued in 1 vol., 1965), includes the development of the Maxwell relations; *The Collected Works of J. Willard Gibbs,* 2 vol. (1928, reprinted 1957), the definitive treatment of equilibrium statistical mechanics in terms of classical mechanics; MAX PLANCK, *Treatise on Thermodynamics,* 3rd ed. (1927, reissued 1945; trans. from the 7th German ed. of 1922), on the connection between the second law and the concept of reversibility and statement of impossibility of perpetual motion of the second kind; HENRI POINCARE, *Thermodynamique* (1892), definitions of temperature and heat and statements of the first and second law; C. CARATHEODORY, "Untersuchungen über die Grundlagen der Thermodynamik," *Math. Annln.,* 67:355–386 (1909), a rigorous mathematical exposition.

GILBERT NEWTON LEWIS and MERLE RANDALL, *Thermodynamics,* 2nd ed. rev. by KENNETH PITZER and LEO BREWER (1961), extensive application of the Gibbsian conditions of equilibrium to heterogeneous systems; W.M. LATIMER, *The Oxidation States of the Elements and Their Potentials in Aqueous Solutions,* 2nd ed. (1952), experimental data on chemical reactions; NORMAN F. RAMSEY, "Thermodynamics and Statistical Mechanics at Negative Absolute Temperatures," *Phys. Rev.,* 103:20–28 (1956), on special systems that can assume negative temperatures on the Kelvin scale; A.B. PIPPARD, *The Elements of Classical Thermodynamics for Advanced Students of Physics* (1957, reprinted 1966), a concise and consistent application of principles to systems in equilibrium; GEORGE N. HATSOPOULOS and JOSEPH H. KEENAN, *Principles of General Thermodynamics* (1965, reprinted 1981), a broad, rigorous, and logically complete exposition of classical thermodynamics, including the application of entropy to nonequilibrium systems, the combination of the postulates of thermodynamics, and of statistical mechanics through the use of information theory; S.R. DE GROOT, *Thermodynamics of Irreversible Processes* (1951, reprinted 1963), general and extensive application of the Onsager reciprocal relations and the theory of rate processes; RICHARD C. TOLMAN, *The Principles of Statistical Mechanics* (1938, reprinted 1979), a scholarly exposition of classical and quantum statistical mechanics, including the density matrix; R.H. FOWLER, *Statistical Mechanics,* 2nd ed. (1936, reprinted 1965), written from the viewpoint of molecular statistics, and, with E.A. GUGGENHEIM, *Statistical Thermodynamics* (1939, reprinted 1956), extensive applications to terrestrial physics and chemistry. See also GEORGE N. HATSOPOULOS and ELIAS P. GYFTOPOULOS, "A Unified Quantum Theory of Mechanics and Thermodynamics," *Found. of Physics,* 6:15–31, 127–141, 439–455, 461–570 (1976).

(J.H.K./G.N.Ha./E.P.G.)

Thomas Aquinas and Thomism

St. Thomas Aquinas (Italian San Tommaso d'Aquino) was a Christian philosopher who developed his own conclusions from Aristotelian premises, notably in the metaphysics of personality, creation, and Providence; a theologian responsible in his two masterpieces, the *Summa theologiae* and the *Summa contra gentiles,* for the classical systematization of Latin theology; and a poet who wrote some of the most gravely beautiful eucharistic hymns in the church's liturgy. Although many modern Roman Catholic theologians do not find him altogether congenial, he is recognized by the Roman Catholic Church as its foremost Western philosopher and theologian.

Thomism refers both to the doctrinal system of St. Thomas Aquinas and to the explanations and developments made by his followers. The main phases in the philosophical and theological tradition of the Thomistic school are the personal synthesis of St. Thomas, the work of the great commentators, and the modern revival.

This article is divided into the following sections:

LIFE AND WORKS

Early years. Thomas was born in 1224 or 1225, at Roccasecca, near Aquino, on the road from Rome to Naples, where his parents were in possession of a modest feudal domain on a boundary constantly disputed by the emperor and the pope. His father was of Lombard origin; his mother was of the later invading Norman strain. His people were distinguished in the service of Emperor Frederick II during the civil strife in southern Italy between the papal and imperial forces. Thomas was placed in the monastery of Monte Cassino near his home as an oblate (*i.e.,* offered as a prospective monk) when he was still a young boy; his family doubtless hoped that he would someday become abbot to their advantage. In 1239, after nine years in this sanctuary of spiritual and cultural life, young Thomas was forced to return to his family when the Emperor expelled the monks because they were too obedient to the Pope. He was then sent to the University of Naples, recently founded by the Emperor, where he first encountered the scientific and philosophical works that were being translated from the Greek and the Arabic. In this setting Thomas decided to join the Friars Preachers, or Dominicans, a new religious order founded 30 years earlier, which departed from the traditional paternalistic form of government for monks to the more democratic form of the mendicant friars (*i.e.,* religious orders whose corporate as well as personal poverty made it necessary for them to beg alms) and from the monastic life of prayer and manual labour to a more active life of preaching and teaching. By this move he took a liberating step beyond the feudal world into which he was born and the monastic spirituality in which he was reared. A dramatic episode marked the full significance of his decision. His parents had him abducted on the road to Paris, where his shrewd superiors had immediately assigned him so that he would be out of the reach of his family but also so that he could pursue his studies in the most prestigious and turbulent university of the time.

Entry into the Dominican order

Studies in Paris. Thomas held out stubbornly against his family despite a year of captivity. He was finally liberated and in the autumn of 1245 went to Paris to the convent of Saint-Jacques, the great university centre of the Dominicans; there he studied under Albertus Magnus, a tremendous scholar with a wide range of intellectual interests.

Escape from the feudal world, rapid commitment to the University of Paris, and religious vocation to one of the new mendicant orders all meant a great deal in a world in which faith in the traditional institutional and conceptual structure was being attacked. The encounter between the gospel and the culture of his time formed the nerve centre of Thomas' position and directed its development. Normally, his work is presented as the integration into Christian thought of the recently discovered Aristotelian philosophy, in competition with the integration of Pla-

"Apotheosis of St. Thomas Aquinas," altarpiece by Francesco Traini, 1363. In the Sta. Caterina, Pisa.
Alinari—Art Resource

tonic thought effected by the Fathers of the Church during the first 12 centuries of the Christian Era. This view is essentially correct; more radically, however, it should also be asserted that Thomas' work accomplished an evangelical awakening to the need for a cultural and spiritual renewal not only in the lives of individual men but also throughout the church. Thomas must be understood in his context as a mendicant religious, influenced both by the evangelism of St. Francis of Assisi, founder of the Franciscan order, and by the devotion to scholarship of St. Dominic, founder of the Dominican order.

Study of Aristotle's works

When Thomas Aquinas arrived at the University of Paris, the influx of Arabian–Aristotelian science was arousing a sharp reaction among believers; and several times the church authorities tried to block the naturalism and rationalism that were emanating from this philosophy and, according to many ecclesiastics, seducing the younger generations. Thomas did not fear these new ideas, but, like his master Albertus Magnus (and Roger Bacon, also lecturing at Paris), he studied the works of Aristotle and eventually lectured publicly on them.

For the first time in history, Christian believers and theologians were confronted with the rigorous demands of scientific rationalism. At the same time, technical progress was requiring men to move from the rudimentary economy of an agrarian society to an urban society with production organized in trade guilds, with a market economy, and with a profound feeling of community. New generations of men and women, including clerics, were reacting against the traditional notion of contempt for the world and were striving for mastery over the forces of nature through the use of their reason. The structure of Aristotle's philosophy emphasized the primacy of the intelligence. Technology itself became a means of access to truth; mechanical arts were powers for humanizing the cosmos. Thus, the dispute over the reality of universals—*i.e.*, the question about the relation between general words such as "red" and particulars such as "this red object"—which had dominated early Scholastic philosophy, was left behind; and a coherent metaphysics of knowledge and of the world was being developed.

During the summer of 1248, Aquinas left Paris with Albertus, who was to assume direction of the new faculty established by the Dominicans at the convent in Cologne. He remained there until 1252, when he returned to Paris to prepare for the degree of master of theology. After taking his bachelor's degree, he received the *licentia docendi* ("license to teach") at the beginning of 1256 and shortly afterward finished the training necessary for the title and privileges of master. Thus, in the year 1256 he began teaching theology in one of the two Dominican schools incorporated in the University of Paris.

Years at the papal Curia and return to Paris. In 1259 Thomas was appointed theological adviser and lecturer to the papal Curia, then the centre of Western humanism. He returned to Italy, where he spent two years at Anagni at the end of the reign of Alexander IV and four years at Orvieto with Urban IV. From 1265 to 1267 he taught at the convent of Santa Sabina in Rome and then, at the request of Clement IV, went to the papal Curia in Viterbo. Suddenly, in November 1268, he was sent to Paris, where he became involved in a sharp doctrinal polemic that had just been triggered off.

Opposition to the Averroists

The works of Averroës, the outstanding representative of Arabic philosophy in Spain, who was known as the great commentator and interpreter of Aristotle, were just becoming known to the Parisian masters. There seems to be no doubt about the Islāmic faith of the Cordovan philosopher; nevertheless, he asserted that the structure of religious knowledge was entirely heterogeneous to rational knowledge: two truths—one of faith, the other of reason—can, in the final analysis, be contradictory. This dualism was denied by Muslim orthodoxy and was still less acceptable to Christians. With the appearance of Siger of Brabant, however, and from 1266 on, the quality of Averroës' exegesis and the wholly rational bent of his thought began to attract disciples in the faculty of arts at the University of Paris. Thomas Aquinas rose in protest against his colleagues; nevertheless, the parties retained a mutual esteem. As soon as he returned from Italy, Thomas began to dispute with Siger, who, he claimed, was compromising not only orthodoxy but also the Christian interpretation of Aristotle. Aquinas found himself wedged in between the Augustinian tradition of thought, now more emphatic than ever in its criticism of Aristotle, and the Averroists. Radical Averroism was condemned in 1270, but at the same time Thomas, who sanctioned the autonomy of reason under faith, was discredited.

In the course of this dispute, the very method of theology was called into question. According to Aquinas, reason is able to operate within faith and yet according to its own laws. The mystery of God is expressed and incarnate in human language; it is thus able to become the object of an active, conscious, and organized elaboration in which the rules and structures of rational activity are integrated in the light of faith. In the Aristotelian sense of the word, then (although not in the modern sense), theology is a "science"; it is knowledge that is rationally derived from propositions that are accepted as certain because they are revealed by God. The theologian accepts authority and faith as his starting point and then proceeds to conclusions using reason; the philosopher, on the other hand, relies solely on the natural light of reason. Thomas was the first to view theology expressly in this way or at least to present it systematically, and in doing so he raised a storm of opposition in various quarters. Even today this opposition endures, especially among religious enthusiasts for whom reason remains an intruder in the realm of mystical communion, contemplation, and the sudden ecstasy of evangelical fervour.

Literary form of his works

The literary form of Aquinas' works must be appreciated in the context of his methodology. He organized his teaching in the form of "questions," in which critical research is presented by pro and con arguments, according to the pedagogical system then in use in the universities. Forms varied from simple commentaries on official texts to written accounts of the public disputations, which were significant events in medieval university life. Thomas' works are divided into three categories: 1) commentaries on such works as the Old and New Testaments, the *Sentences* of Peter Lombard (the official manual of theology in the universities), and the writings of Aristotle; 2) disputed questions, accounts of his teaching as a master in the disputations; 3) two *summae* or personal syntheses, the *Summa contra gentiles* and the *Summa theologiae,* which were presented as integral introductions for the use of beginners. Numerous *opuscula* ("little works"), which have great interest because of the particular circumstances that provoked them, must also be noted.

The logic of Aquinas' position regarding faith and reason required that the fundamental consistency of the realities of nature be recognized. A *physis* ("nature") has necessary laws; recognition of this fact permits the construction of a science according to a *logos* ("rational structure"). Thomas thus avoided the temptation to sacralize the forces of nature through a naïve recourse to the miraculous or the Providence of God. For him, a whole "supernatural" world that cast its shadow over things and men, in Romanesque art as in social customs, had blurred men's imaginations. Nature, discovered in its profane reality, should assume its proper religious value and lead to God by more rational ways, yet not simply as a shadow of the supernatural. This understanding is exemplified in the way that Francis of Assisi admired the birds, the plants, and the Sun.

The inclusion of Aristotle's *Physics* in university programs was not, therefore, just a matter of academic curiosity. Naturalism, however, as opposed to a sacral vision of the world, was penetrating all realms: spirituality, social customs, and political conduct. About 1270, Jean de Meun, a French poet of the new cities and Thomas' neighbour in the Rue Saint-Jacques in Paris, gave expression in his *Roman de la Rose* to the coarsest realism, not only in examining the physical universe but also in describing and judging the laws of procreation. Innumerable manuscripts of the Roman poet Ovid's *Ars amatoria* ("Art of Love") were in circulation; André le Chapelain, in his *De Deo amoris* ("On the God of Love") adapted a more refined version for the public. Courtly love in its more seductive forms became a more prevalent element in the culture of the 13th century.

At the same time, Roman law was undergoing a revival at the University of Bologna; this involved a rigorous analysis of the natural law and provided the jurists of Frederick II with a weapon against ecclesiastical theocracy. The traditional presentations of the role and duties of princes, in which biblical symbolism was used to outline beautiful pious images, were replaced by treatises that described experimental and rational attempts at government. Thomas had composed such a treatise—*De regimine principum* ("On the Government of Princes")—for the King of Cyprus in 1266. In the administration of justice, juridical investigations and procedures replaced fanatical recourse to ordeals and to judgments of God.

Resistance of traditional theologians

In the face of this movement, there was a fear on the part of many that the authentic values of nature would not be properly distinguished from the disorderly inclinations of mind and heart. Theologians of a traditional bent firmly resisted any form of a determinist philosophy which, they believed, would atrophy liberty, dissolve personal responsibility, destroy faith in Providence, and deny the notion of a gratuitous act of creation. Imbued with Augustine's doctrines, they asserted the necessity and power of grace for a nature torn asunder by sin. The optimism of the new theology concerning the religious value of nature scandalized them.

Although he was an Aristotelian, Thomas Aquinas was certain that he could defend himself against a heterodox interpretation of "the Philosopher," as Aristotle was known. Thomas held that human liberty could be defended as a rational thesis while admitting that determinations are found in nature. In his theology of Providence, he taught a continuous creation, in which the dependence of the created on the creative wisdom guarantees the reality of the order of nature. God moves sovereignly all that he creates; but the supreme government that he exercises over the universe is conformed to the laws of a creative Providence that wills each being to act according to its proper nature. This autonomy finds its highest realization in the rational creature: man is literally self-moving in his intellectual, volitional, and physical existence. Man's freedom, far from being destroyed by his relationship to God, finds its foundation in this very relationship. "To take something away from the perfection of the creature is to abstract from the perfection of the creative power itself." This metaphysical axiom, which is also a mystical principle, is the key to St. Thomas' spirituality.

Last years at Naples. At Easter time in 1272, Thomas returned to Italy to establish a Dominican house of studies at the University of Naples. This move was undoubtedly made in answer to a request made by King Charles of Anjou, who was anxious to revive the university. After participating in a general chapter, or meeting, of the Dominicans held in Florence during Pentecost week and, having settled some family affairs, Thomas resumed his university teaching at Naples in October and continued it until the end of the following year.

Although Thomas' argument with the Averroists had for years been matched by a controversy with the Christian masters who followed the traditional Augustinian conception of man as fallen, this latter dispute now became more pronounced. In a series of university conferences in 1273, Bonaventure, a Franciscan friar and a friendly colleague of Thomas at Paris, renewed his criticism of the Aristotelian current of thought, including the teachings of Thomas. He criticized the thesis that philosophy is distinct from theology, as well as the notion of a physical nature that has determined laws; he was especially critical of the theory that the soul is bound up with the body as the two necessary principles that make up the nature of man and also reacted strongly to the Aristotelians' denial of the Platonic–Augustinian theory of knowledge based upon exemplary Ideas or Forms.

The disagreement was profound. Certainly, all Christian philosophers taught the distinction between matter and spirit. This distinction, however, could be intelligently held only if the internal relationship between matter and spirit in individual human beings was sought. It was in the process of this explanation that differences of opinion arose—not only intellectual differences between idealist and realist philosophers but also emotional differences. Some viewed the material world merely as a physical and biological reality, a stage on which the history of spiritual persons is acted out, their culture developed, and their salvation or damnation determined. This stage itself remains detached from the spiritual event, and the history of nature is only by chance the setting for the spiritual history. The history of nature follows its own path imperturbably; in this history, man is a foreigner, playing a brief role only to escape as quickly as possible from the world into the realm of pure spirit, the realm of God.

Relationship of matter and spirit for Thomas

Thomas, on the contrary, noted the inclusion of the history of nature in the history of the spirit and at the same time noted the importance of the history of spirit for the history of nature. Man is situated ontologically (*i.e.,* by his very existence) at the juncture of two universes, "like a horizon of the corporeal and of the spiritual." In man there is not only a distinction between spirit and nature but there is also an intrinsic homogeneity of the two. Aristotle furnished Aquinas with the categories necessary for the expression of this concept: the soul is the "form" of the body. For Aristotle, form is that which makes a thing to be what it is; form and matter—that out of which a thing is made—are the two intrinsic causes that constitute every material thing. For Thomas, then, the body is the matter and the soul is the form of man. The objection was raised that he was not sufficiently safeguarding the transcendence of the spirit, the doctrine that the soul survives after the death of the body.

In January 1274 Thomas Aquinas was personally summoned by Gregory X to the second Council of Lyons, which was an attempt to repair the schism between the Latin and Greek churches. On his way he was stricken by illness; he stopped at the Cistercian abbey of Fossanova, where he died on March 7, 1274. In 1277 the masters of Paris, the highest theological jurisdiction in the church, condemned a series of 219 propositions; 12 of these propositions were theses of Thomas. This was the most serious condemnation possible in the Middle Ages; its repercussions were felt in the development of ideas. It produced for several centuries a certain unhealthy spiritualism that resisted the cosmic and anthropological realism of Aquinas.

Importance of the university environment

Assessment. The biography of Thomas Aquinas is one of extreme simplicity; it chronicles little but some modest travel during a career devoted entirely to university life: at Paris, the Roman Curia, Paris again, and Naples. It would be a mistake, however, to judge that his life was merely the quiet life of a professional teacher untouched by the social and political affairs of his day. The drama that went on in his mind and in his religious life found its causes and produced its effects in the university. In the young universities all the ingredients of a rapidly developing civilization were massed together, and to these universities the Christian Church had deliberately and authoritatively committed its doctrine and its spirit. In this environment, Thomas found the technical conditions for elaborating his work—not only the polemic occasions for turning it out but also the enveloping and penetrating spiritual milieu needed for it. It is within the homogeneous contexts supplied by this environment that it is possible today to discover the historical intelligibility of his work, just as they supplied the climate for its fruitfulness at the time of its birth.

Thomas Aquinas was canonized a saint in 1323, officially named doctor of the church in 1567, and proclaimed the protagonist of orthodoxy during the modernist crisis at the end of the 19th century. This continuous commendation, however, cannot obliterate the historical difficulties in which he was embroiled in the 13th century during a radical theological renewal—a renewal that was contested at the time and yet was brought about by the social, cultural, and religious evolution of the West. Thomas was at the heart of the doctrinal crisis that confronted Christendom when the discovery of Greek science, culture, and thought seemed about to crush it. William of Tocco, Aquinas' first biographer, who had known him and was able to give evidence of the impression produced by his master's teaching, says:

> Brother Thomas raised new problems in his teaching, invented a new method, used new systems of proof. To hear him teach a new doctrine, with new arguments, one could not doubt that God, by the irradiation of this new light and by the novelty of this inspiration, gave him the power to teach, by the spoken and written word, new opinions and new knowledge.

(M.-D.Ch.)

THOMISM

Aquinas' position. Although making respectful use of Aristotle and the Platonists, Augustine and the Fathers, Thomas Aquinas developed a distinctive position. His originality was shown in treating existence (*esse*) as the supreme act or perfection of being in God as well as in created things, in reserving the creative act to God alone, in denying the presence of matter in angels, and thus in distinguishing between God and creatures by a real composition of existence and essence as principles in all created beings. Also characteristic was his teaching that the human soul is a unique subsistent form, substantially united with matter to constitute human nature. Aquinas maintained that the immortality of the human soul can be strictly demonstrated, that there is a real distinction of principles between the soul and its powers of knowing and willing, and that human knowledge is based upon sense experience leading to the mind's reflective activity. He held that both man and lower creatures have a natural tendency or love toward God, that supernatural grace perfects and elevates our natural abilities, and that blessedness consists formally in knowing God Himself, a knowledge accompanied by our full love of God.

This coherent but complex body of Thomistic doctrines was critically explained and developed during subsequent centuries. Views of St. Thomas on individuation and the localization of angels, man's nature and the unity of the world, appeared among the theses condemned in 1277 by Bishop Étienne Tempier at Paris and by Archbishop Robert Kilwardby at Oxford. At stake were the manner and extent of using Aristotle and his Arabian commentators in explaining Christian theology. The later 13th century was crowded with "correctorial" literature—treatises attacking and defending basic positions of St. Thomas, especially on the unicity of the human substantial form and the distinction of essence and existence. His precise meaning was lost even by some Thomists, who treated essence and existence as distinct things and overlooked the unifying relation between the substantial form and existence.

"Correctorial" literature

Commentators. Encouragement toward consulting Aquinas' own writings came with the adoption of his doctrine by the Dominican Order (1278, 1279, 1286), his canonization by Pope John XXII (1323), and the special place accorded to his works at the Council of Trent. The scientific task of analyzing his thought was executed by a line of devoted commentators during the period 1400–1650. The first was the Dominican Jean Capréolus (*c.* 1380–1444), called the Prince of the Thomists, who recognized the need to make a direct integral study of the texts of St. Thomas. In his *Four Books of Defenses of the Theology of St. Thomas Aquinas,* Capréolus made a systematic use of the sources against the Scotists and Ockhamists. Another major Dominican commentator was Tomaso de Vio, Cardinal Cajetan, who made elaborate expositions of St. Thomas' *Summa theologiae* and *On Being and Essence.* He made his own restatement of the Thomistic arguments and drew upon many other writings of St. Thomas. Cajetan's independence was displayed in his work *On the Analogy of Names,* where he proposed the influential division of kinds of analogy into inequality, attribution, and proportionality, as well as in his opinion that the human soul's immortality can be supported only by probable reasons.

The classical commentary on St. Thomas' *Summa contra gentiles* was done by the Dominican Francesco Sylvestri of Ferrara (*c.* 1474–1528), who showed the importance of this work for the relation of faith and philosophy, the meaning of person, and the desire of God. After the mid-16th century, the Thomistic commentators became involved in the intricate theological controversies on grace and premotion. Highly systematized presentations of opposing views were introduced into the commentaries on the *Summa theologiae* made by the Spanish Dominican theologian Domingo Bañez and the Spanish Jesuit authors Francis Toletus and Gabriel Vázquez. But the new Renaissance tendency to give separate treatment to philosophical and theological issues, as well as the pressures of seminary education, undermined the usefulness of the commentary form of approach to St. Thomas. A new trend is present in the Dominican John of St. Thomas (1589–1644), who issued a separate *Cursus Philosophicus* ("Course in Philosophy") and then a *Cursus Theologicus* ("Course in Theology") in Thomistic thought. Using the framework of logic, philosophy of nature, and metaphysics, John assembled the philosophical teachings of St. Thomas under these systematic headings and reformulated the material for students who would then study theology. There were original features in his logic, including the distinction between formal and objective concepts and the stress on intentional signs.

Studies by John of St. Thomas

Modern Thomism. Throughout the 17th and 18th centuries, Thomism continued to be presented in philosophy and theology courses or manuals, especially in the Dominican Order. Most Thomistic manuals of this period were watered with the opinions of other Schoolmen and remained remote from modern problems. In most Catholic seminaries and universities of the early 19th century, eclecticism was the rule and more attention was paid to Descartes, Locke, and Wolff than to Aquinas. The modern revival of authentic Thomism began at this time in Italy. Vincent Buzzetti (1777–1824) and the Jesuit teacher Serafino Sordi (1793–1865) were instrumental in urging a direct study of the text of Aristotle and Aquinas. The revolutions of 1848 had a decisive influence upon both the Holy See and the Society of Jesus toward finding sound principles on God, man, and society in the works of St. Thomas. In editions of their philosophy manuals appearing after 1850, this renewal of Thomistic thought was advocated by three influential Jesuit writers in Italy and Germany: Luigi Taparelli d'Azeglio, Matteo Liberatore, and Joseph Kleutgen. Their own positions in epistemology, metaphysics, and social theory remained eclectic, but they did give impetus to the work of studying St. Thomas and the other Schoolmen in the light of modern intellectual and social issues.

Decisive support for this movement came with Pope Leo XIII's encyclical *Aeterni Patris* (1879). It noted the importance of sound doctrine for meeting today's problems and called for a restoration of the Christian philosophy of the Fathers and medieval Doctors, augmented where necessary by the reliable advances of modern research. Leo asked especially for a recovery of the wisdom of St. Thomas, whom he hailed as "the special bulwark and glory of the Catholic Faith." This program required an accurate historical study of St. Thomas himself and his major commentators, combined with a readiness to use the evidences and resources of modern learning and science. St. Thomas was declared the universal patron of Catholic schools, and a canon (1366, par. 2) in the new Code of Canon Law (1917) required philosophy and theology teachers to adhere to the method, doctrine, and principles of St. Thomas. This established the special authority of the Common Doctor in the church's teaching institutions, without impairing the recovery of all the other sources of Christian thought, the careful discussion of commonly recognized difficulties, and the effort to evaluate modern teachings.

Thomism in the 20th century

Thomists of the 20th century concentrated upon two major tasks: a historical investigation of St. Thomas' doctrine in its medieval context and a rethinking of that doctrine in reference to contemporary problems. Pioneer historians were Pierre Mandonnet and Martin Grabmann, who investigated the life of Aquinas, the canon of his writings, and his historical relationships. The setting of Thomistic doctrine in the wider medieval intellectual currents was described by Maurice de Wulf and Étienne Gilson. The latter also brought out the basic role of existence in Thomistic metaphysics, which he contrasted with other historical forms of metaphysics. Some general presentations of Thomistic thought were made by showing the development of the principles of act and potency in the major areas of philosophy. The Dominican R. Garrigou-Lagrange stressed the problem of God and providence; A. Sertillanges, another Dominican, made the act of creation central to his exposition; the Jesuit Martin D'Arcy brought out the dynamic and effective aspects in the mind of Aquinas.

At the University of Louvain, Désiré-Joseph Cardinal Mercier and his associates concentrated on the challenge of modern thought for Thomism. They treated the epistemological issue at the outset of philosophy, so that metaphysics might have the support of a well-founded realism. The aim of Joseph Maréchal was to reformulate the major thinkers, especially St. Thomas, in terms of the mind's dynamic affirmation of being and ultimate reference to the reality of God. Francesco Olgiati used a metaphysical realism of substance to establish the critical relevance of Thomism to Cartesian and empiricist thinkers. How to unite the various kinds of methods and knowledges in a human order was the main concern of Jacques Maritain, but he also applied the Thomistic concept of person and community to the problem of democracy.

After World War II, Thomists faced three major tasks: to develop an adequate philosophy of science, to take account of the phenomenological and psychiatric findings on man, and to evaluate the ontologies of existentialism and naturalism. (J.D.Co.)

MAJOR WORKS

THEOLOGICAL TREATISES: *Scriptum super IV libros Sententiarum* (1254–56); *De veritate* (1256–59); *Summa contra gentiles* (*c.* 1258–64; *On the Truth of the Catholic Faith,* 1955); *Summa theologiae* (1265 or 1266–73; incomplete); *De potentia Dei* (1259–68; *On the Power of God,* 1932–34); *De malo* (undated; *On Free Choice*); *De spiritualibus creaturis* (undated; *On Spiritual Creatures,* 1949); *De anima* (undated; *The Soul,* 1949); *De unione Verbi incarnati* (undated); *De virtutibus* (1269–72; *On the Virtues in General,* 1951).

BIBLICAL COMMENTARIES: *Expositio in Evangelium S. Matthaei* (1269–72); *Expositio in Job ad litteram* (1261–64); *Expositio in Evangelium Joannis* (1269–72); *Exposition in S. Pauli Apostoli epistolas* (undated; incomplete); *In psalmos Davidis expositio* (1272–73).

COMMENTARIES ON ARISTOTLE: *In octo libros Physicorum expositio* (1268–71; *Commentary on Aristotle's Physics,* 1963); *In tres libros De anima* (undated; *The Commentary of St. Thomas Aquinas on Aristotle's Treatise on the Soul,* 1946); *In librum De sensu et sensato expositio* (1270–71); *In decem libros Ethicorum expositio* (1271–72; *Commentary on the Nicomachean Ethics,* 1964); *In duodecim libros Metaphysicorum expositio* (*c.* 1272; *Commentary on the Metaphysics of Aristotle,* 1961); *In libros De caelo et mundo expositio* (1272–73); *In libros Posteriorum analyticorum expositio* (undated; probably late).

OTHER WORKS: (PHILOSOPHICAL TREATISES): *De ente et essentia* (before 1256; *On Being and Essence,* 1949); *Contra impugnantes Dei cultum et religionem* (1256; *An Apology for the Religious Orders,* 1902); *De regno (De regimine principum) ad regem Cypri* (1266; *On Kingship,* 1949); *De perfectione vitae spiritualis* (1269–70); *De unitate intellectus contra Averroistas* (1270; *The Unicity of the Intellect,* 1946); *De aeternitate mundi contra murmurantes* (1270–72); *De substantiis separatis, seu de angelorum natura* (undated; *Treatise on Separate Substances,* 1959). (HYMNS AND LITURGICAL COMPOSITIONS): "Pange, lingua, gloriosi" (1264); "Verbum supernum prodiens" (1264; "The Word of God Proceeding Forth"); office for the Feast of Corpus Christi (*c.* 1264), including the sequence "Lauda Sion Salvatorem" ("Praise, O Zion, thy Salvation").

BIBLIOGRAPHY. St. Thomas' first biography was that of his disciple, WILLIAM OF TOCCO, published in *Acta Sanctorum,* vol. 1, pp. 656–686 (March 1865); new ed., with other biographies, *Fontes vitae S. Thomas Aquinatis,* 6 fasc. (1912–37). See also ANGELUS M. WALZ, *Saint Thomas Aquinas: A Biographical Study* (1951; originally published in Italian, 1945).

Latin editions of the Opera omnia: Rome, 17 vol. (1570), called *Piana* because they were published under Pius V; new and rev. ed., 25 vol., Parma (1852–73, reprinted 1948–50); then in Paris, Vivès ed., 34 vol., (1871–80); and a critical edition, called *Leonina* because it was requested by Leo XIII, which began publication in 1882. Of all his works, the *Summa theologiae* has been the most frequently reedited. An excellent edition was published by the Institute of Medieval Studies in Montreal, 5 vol. (1941–45).

English translations: The two *Summae,* by the English Dominicans, 22 vol.(1911–34); selections, by THOMAS GILBY, *Philosophical Texts* (1951, reissued 1982), and *Theological Texts* (1955); and ANTON C. PEGIS, *Basic Writings of St. Thomas Aquinas,* 2 vol. (1945). TERRY L. MIETHE and VERNON J. BOURKE (eds.), *Thomistic Bibliography: 1940–1978* (1980), lists more than 4,000 books and articles by and about St. Thomas in European languages. It continues VERNON J. BOURKE, *Thomistic Bibliography: 1920–1940* (1945); and PIERRE MANDONNET and JEAN DESTREZ, *Bibliographie Thomiste,* 2nd rev. ed. (1960), covering items up to 1920.

Studies: ÉTIENNE GILSON, *The Philosophy of St. Thomas Aquinas* (1924; rev. ed., *The Christian Philosophy of St. Thomas Aquinas,* 1956; originally published in French, 1922); MARIE D. CHENU, *Toward Understanding St. Thomas* (1964; originally published in French, 1950); and M.C. D'ARCY, *St. Thomas Aquinas* (1953). On historical and doctrinal contexts, see PIERRE MANDONNET, *Siger de Brabant et l'averroïsme latin au XIIIe siècle,* 2nd ed. (1908); ÉTIENNE GILSON, *The Spirit of Medieval Philosophy* (1936; originally published in French, 1932), *The Spirit of Thomism* (1964), and *History of Christian Philosophy in the Middle Ages* (1955); M.D. CHENU, *Nature, Man and Society in the Twelfth Century* (1968; originally published in French, 1957); and FERNAND VAN STEENBERGHEN, *La Philosophie au XIIIe siècle* (1966). See also ARMAND A. MAURER (ed.), *St. Thomas Aquinas, 1274–1974: Commemorative Studies,* 2 vol. (1974), 35 essays by neo-scholastic scholars; DAVID B. BURRELL, *Aquinas: God and Action* (1979), an advanced linguistic discussion of St. Thomas' *Summa theologica*; and FERNAND VAN STEENBERGHEN, *Thomas Aquinas and Radical Aristotelianism* (1980), a study of major aspects of St. Thomas' thought.

Thought and Thought Processes

In everyday language the word thinking covers several distinct psychological activities. It is sometimes a synonym for "tending to believe," especially with less than full confidence. ("I think that it will rain, but I am not sure.") At other times it denotes attentiveness ("I did it without thinking"); or it denotes whatever is in consciousness, especially if it refers to something outside the immediate environment. ("It made me think of my old grandmother.") In the sense on which psychologists have concentrated, thinking is intellectual exertion aimed at finding an answer to a question or a means of achieving a desirable practical goal.

The psychology of thought processes concerns itself with activities similar to those usually attributed to the inventor, the mathematician, or the chess player; but psychologists have not reached agreement on any definition or characterization of thinking. For some it is a matter of modifying "cognitive structures" (*i.e.,* perceptual representations of the world or parts of the world). Others view thinking as internal problem-solving behaviour.

Perhaps the most satisfactory provisional conception of thinking is one that applies the term to any sequence of covert symbolic responses (*i.e.,* occurrences within the human organism that can serve to represent absent events). If such a sequence is aimed at the solution of a specific problem and fulfills the criteria for reasoning, it is called directed thinking. Reasoning, of which rudimentary forms can be inferred to occur in infrahuman mammals, is a process of piecing together the results of two or more distinct previous learning experiences to produce a new pattern of behaviour. Directed thinking contrasts with other symbolic sequences that have different functions; *e.g.,* the simple recall (mnemonic thinking) of a chain of past events.

In the past, psychologists and laymen often identified thinking with conscious experiences. But as the scientific study of behaviour came to be recognized generally as the task of psychology, the limitations of introspection as a source of data have become widely apparent. It thus has become more usual to treat thought processes as intervening variables or constructs with properties that must be inferred from relations between two sets of observable events. These empirically available events are inputs (stimuli, present and past) and outputs (responses, including bodily movements and speech). For many psychologists such intervening variables are of interest as aids in dealing with and in making sense of the immensely complicated network of associations between stimulus conditions and responses, the analysis of which otherwise would be prohibitively cumbersome. Others are concerned, rather, with identifying cognitive (or mental) structures that are held to underlie a human being's observable behaviour without his necessarily being aware of them.

This article is divided into the following sections:

General considerations

ELEMENTS OF THOUGHT

The prominent use of words in thinking ("silent speech") has encouraged the belief, especially among behaviourist and neobehaviourist psychologists, that to think is to string together linguistic elements subvocally. Early experiments (largely in the 1930s) by E. Jacobson and L.W. Max revealed that evidence of thinking commonly is accompanied by electrical activity in the muscles of the thinker's organs of articulation. This work later was extended with the help of more sophisticated electromyographic equipment, notably by A.N. Sokolov. It became apparent, however, that the muscular phenomena are not the actual vehicles of thinking but represent rather a means of facilitating the appropriate activities in the brain when an intellectual task is particularly exacting. The identification of thinking with speech was assailed by L.S. Vygotski and by J. Piaget, both of whom saw the origins of human reasoning in the ability of children to assemble nonverbal acts into effective and flexible combinations. These theorists insisted that thinking and speaking arise independently, although they acknowledged the profound interdependence of these functions, once they have reached fruition.

Following different approaches, a 19th-century Russian physiologist (I.M. Sechenov), the U.S. founder of the behaviourist school of psychology (J.B. Watson), and a 20th-century Swiss developmental psychologist (Piaget) all arrived at the conclusion that the activities that serve as elements of thinking are internalized or fractional versions of motor responses; that is, the elements are considered to be attenuated or curtailed variants of neuromuscular processes that, if they were not subjected to partial inhibition, would give rise to visible bodily movements.

Sensitive instruments can indeed detect faint activity in various parts of the body other than the organs of speech; *e.g.,* in a person's limbs when the movement is thought of or imagined without actually taking place. Such findings have prompted statements to the effect that we think with the whole body and not only with the brain, or that "thought is simply *behaviour*—verbal or nonverbal, covert or overt" (B.F. Skinner). The logical outcome of these and similar statements was the peripheralist view (Watson, C.L. Hull) that thinking depends on events in the musculature, feeding proprioceptive impulses back to influence subsequent events in the central nervous system, ultimately to interact with external stimuli in determining the selection of a course of overt action. There is, however, evidence that thinking is not precluded by administering drugs that suppress all muscular activity. Furthermore, it has been pointed out (*e.g.,* by K.S. Lashley) that thinking, like other more-or-less skilled activities, often proceeds so quickly that there is simply not enough time for impulses to be transmitted from the central nervous system to a peripheral organ and back again between consecutive steps. So the centralist view that thinking consists of events confined to the brain (though often accompanied by widespread activity in the rest of the body) was gaining ground in the third quarter of the 20th century. Nevertheless, each of these neural events can be regarded both as a response (to an external stimulus or to an earlier neurally mediated thought or combination of thoughts) and as a stimulus (evoking a subsequent thought or a motor response).

Thinking as a brain function

The elements of thinking are classifiable as "symbols" in accordance with the conception of the sign process ("semiotic") that has grown out of the work of some philosophers (*e.g.,* C.S. Peirce, C.K. Ogden, I.A. Richards, and C.R. Morris) and of psychologists specializing in learning (*e.g.,* C.L. Hull, N.E. Miller, O.H. Mowrer, and C.E. Osgood). The gist of this conception is that a stimulus event

x can be regarded as a sign representing (or "standing for") another event y if x evokes some part, but not all, of the behaviour (external and internal) that would have been evoked by y if it had been present. When a stimulus that qualifies as a sign results from the behaviour of an organism for which it acts as a sign, it is called a "symbol." The "stimulus-producing responses" that are said to make up thought processes (as when one thinks of something to eat) are prime examples.

This treatment, favoured by psychologists of the stimulus-response (S-R) or neo-associationist current, contrasts with that of the various cognitivist or neorationalist theories. Rather than regarding the components of thinking as derivatives of verbal or nonverbal motor acts (and thus subject to laws of learning and performance that apply to learned behaviour in general), adherents of such theories see them as unique central processes, governed by principles that are peculiar to them. These theorists attach overriding importance to the so-called structures in which "cognitive" elements are organized. Unlike the S-R theorists who feel compunction about invoking unobservable intermediaries between stimulus and response (except where there is clearly no other alternative), the cognitivists tend to see inferences, applications of rules, representations of external reality, and other ingredients of thinking at work in even the simplest forms of learned behaviour.

The Gestalt school of psychologists held the constituents of thinking to be of essentially the same nature as the perceptual patterns that the nervous system constructs out of sensory excitations. After mid-20th century, analogies with computer operations acquired great currency; in consequence, thinking frequently is described in terms of storage, retrieval, and transmission of items of information. The information in question is held to be freely translatable from one "coding" to another without impairing its functions. The physical clothing it assumes is regarded as being of minor importance. What matters in this approach is how events are combined and what other combinations might have occurred instead.

THE PROCESS OF THOUGHT

Laws of association: contiguity, similarity

According to the classical empiricist-associationist view, the succession of ideas or images in a train of thought is determined by the laws of association. Although additional associative laws were proposed from time to time, two invariably were recognized. The law of association by contiguity states that the sensation or idea of a particular object tends to evoke the idea of something that has often been encountered together with it. The law of association by similarity states that the sensation or idea of a particular object tends to evoke the idea of something that is similar to it. The early behaviourists, beginning with Watson, espoused essentially the same formulation but with some important modifications. The elements of the process were conceived not as conscious ideas but as fractional or incipient motor responses, each producing its proprioceptive stimulus. Association by contiguity and similarity were identified by these behaviourists with the Pavlovian principles of conditioning and generalization.

The Würzburg school, under the leadership of Külpe, saw the prototype of directed thinking in the "constrained-association" experiment, in which the subject has to supply a word bearing a specified relation to a stimulus word that is presented to him (*e.g.,* an opposite to an adjective, or the capital of a country). Their introspective researches led them to conclude that the emergence of the required element depends jointly on the immediately preceding element and on some kind of "determining tendency" such as *Aufgabe* ("awareness of task") or "representation of the goal." These latter factors were held to impart a direction to the thought process and to restrict its content to relevant material. Their role was analogous to that of motivational factors—"drive stimuli," "fractional anticipatory goal responses"—in the later neobehaviouristic accounts of reasoning (and of behaviour in general) produced by C.L. Hull and his followers.

Külpe, Hull, and Selz

Hull's theory resembled G.E. Müller's earlier "constellation theory" of constrained association. Hull held that one particular response will occur and overcome its competitors because it is associated both with the cue stimulus (which may be the immediately preceding thought process or an external event) and with the motivational condition (task, drive stimulus) and is thus evoked with more strength than are elements associated only with the one or the other. O. Selz pointed out that in many situations this kind of theory would imply the occurrence of errors as often as correct answers to questions. It thus was untenable. Selz contended that response selection depends rather on a process of "complex completion" that is set in motion by an "anticipatory schema," which includes a representation of both the cue stimulus and the relation that the element to be supplied must bear to the cue stimulus. The correct answer is associated with the schema as a whole and not with its components separately. Selz's complex completion resembles the "eduction of correlates" that C.E. Spearman saw as a primary constituent of intellectual functioning, its complement being "eduction of relations," that is, recognition of a relation when two elements are presented.

The determination of each thought element by the whole configuration of factors in the situation and by the network of relations linking them was stressed still more strongly in the 1920s and 1930s by the Gestalt psychologists on the basis of W. Köhler's experiments on "insightful" problem solving by chimpanzees, and on the basis of later experiments by M. Wertheimer and of K. Duncker on human thinking. They pointed out that the solution to a problem commonly requires an unprecedented response or pattern of responses that hardly could be attributed to simple associative reproduction of past behaviour or experiences. For them, the essence of thinking lay in sudden perceptual restructuring or reorganization, akin to the abrupt changes in appearance of an ambiguous visual figure.

Thinking as perceptual reorganization

The Gestalt theory has had a deep and far-reaching impact, especially in drawing attention to the ability of the thinker to discover creative, innovative ways of coping with situations that differ from any that have been encountered before. This theory, however, has been criticized for underestimating the contribution of prior learning and for not going beyond rudimentary attempts to classify and analyze the structures that it deems so important. Later discussions of the systems in which items of information and intellectual operations are organized have made fuller use of the resources of logic and mathematics. Merely to name them, they include the "psychologic" of Piaget, the simulation of human thinking with the help of computer programs using list-processing languages and tree structures (H.A. Simon and A. Newell), and extensions of Hull's notion of the "habit-family hierarchy" (I. Maltzman, D.E. Berlyne).

A further development of consequence is a growing recognition that the essential components of the thought process, the events that keep it moving in fruitful directions, are not words, images, or other symbols representing stimulus situations; rather, they are the operations that cause each of these representations to be succeeded by the next, in conformity with restrictions imposed by the problem or aim of the moment. In other words, directed thinking can reach a solution only by going through a properly ordered succession of "legitimate steps." These steps might be representations of realizable physicochemical changes, modifications of logical or mathematical formulas that are permitted by rules of inference, or legal moves in a game of chess. This conception of the train of thinking as a sequence of rigorously controlled transformations is buttressed by the theoretical arguments of Sechenov and of Piaget, the results of the Würzburg experiments, and the lessons of computer simulation.

Implicit trial and error

Early in the 20th century both E. Claparède and John Dewey suggested that directed thinking proceeds by "implicit trial-and-error." That is to say, it resembles the process whereby laboratory animals confronted with a novel problem situation try out one response after another until they sooner or later hit upon a response that leads to success. In thinking, however, the trials were said to take the form of internal responses (imagined or conceptualized courses of action, directions of symbolic search); once attained, a train of thinking that constitutes a solution often can be recognized as such without the necessity of implementation through action, followed by sampling of external consequences. This kind of theory, popular among behaviourists and neobehaviourists, was stoutly opposed by the Gestalt school whose insight theory stressed discovery of a solution as a whole and in a flash.

The divergence between these theories appears, however, to represent a false dichotomy. The protocols of Köhler's chimpanzee experiments and of the rather similar experiments performed later under Pavlov's auspices show that insight typically is preceded by a period of groping and of misguided attempts at solution that soon are abandoned. On the other hand, even the trial-and-error behaviour of an animal in a simple selective-learning situation does not consist of a completely blind and random sampling of the behaviour of which the learner is capable. Rather, it consists of responses that very well might have succeeded if the circumstances had been slightly different.

Heuristic (probabilistic) thinking; computer simulation

A. Newell, J.C. Shaw, and H.A. Simon pointed out the indispensability in creative human thinking, as in its computer simulations, of what they call "heuristics." A large number of possibilities may have to be examined, but the search is organized heuristically in such a way that the directions most likely to lead to success are explored first. Means of ensuring that a solution will occur within a reasonable time, certainly much faster than by random hunting, include adoption of successive subgoals and working backward from the final goal (the formula to be proved, the state of affairs to be brought about).

MOTIVATIONAL ASPECTS OF THINKING

The problem to be taken up and the point at which the search for a solution will begin are customarily prescribed by the investigator for a subject participating in an experiment on thinking (or by the programmer for a computer). Thus, prevailing techniques of inquiry in the psychology of thinking have invited neglect of the motivational aspects of thinking. The conditions that determine when the person will begin to think in preference to some other activity, what he will think about, what direction his thinking will take, and when he will regard his search for a solution as successfully terminated (or abandon it as not worth pursuing further) barely are beginning to attract investigation. Although much thinking is aimed at practical ends, special motivational problems are raised by "disinterested" thinking, in which the discovery of an answer to a question is a source of satisfaction in itself.

In the views of the Gestalt school and of F.C. Bartlett, the initiation and direction of thinking are governed by recognition of a "disequilibrium" or "gap" in an intellectual structure. Similarly, Piaget's notion of "equilibration" as a process impelling advance from less equilibrated structures, fraught with uncertainty and inconsistency, toward better equilibrated structures that overcome these imperfections, was introduced to explain the child's progressive intellectual development in general. Piaget's approach may also be applicable to specific episodes of thinking. For computer specialists, the detection of a mismatch between the formula that the program so far has produced and some formula or set of requirements that define a solution is what impels continuation of the search and determines the direction it will follow.

Neobehaviourists (like psychoanalysts) have made much of secondary reward value and stimulus generalization; *i.e.*, the tendency of a stimulus pattern to become a source of satisfaction if it resembles or has frequently accompanied some form of biological gratification. The insufficiency of this kind of explanation becomes apparent, however, when the importance of novelty, surprise, complexity, incongruity, ambiguity, and uncertainty is considered. Inconsistency between beliefs, between items of incoming sensory information, or between one's belief and an item of sensory information evidently can be a source of discomfort impelling a search for resolution through reorganization of belief systems or through selective acquisition of new information.

Novelty, incongruity, uncertainty

The motivational effects of such factors have been receiving more attention since the middle of the 20th century, mainly because of the pervasive role they have been found to play in exploratory behaviour, play, and aesthetics. But their role in all forms of thinking also began to be appreciated and studied in relation to curiosity, conflict, and uncertainty. As evidence accumulates about the brain processes that underlie fluctuations in motivational state, and as psychophysiological equipment with which such fluctuations can be monitored comes in for increasing use, future advances in the theory of thinking are likely to correct the present imbalance and give due prominence to motivational questions. (D.E.B.)

Types of thinking

Expressive and disciplined thinking

The spectrum or range of thinking reflects the relative intensity of intrinsic and extrinsic influences. When intrinsic processes operate strongly and are relatively free of environmental constraints, a person thinks expressively: he imagines, fantasizes, dreams, hallucinates, or has delusions. As his thinking becomes dominated by external stimuli, he tends to become more logical, directed, disciplined; the process then is identified by such terms as judging, conceptualizing, and problem solving.

Sigmund Freud recognized this distinction between expressive and disciplined function in contrasting what he called primary and secondary process thinking. Freud held that one's impulses and wishes arise from unconscious sources and determine primary process thinking, while the pursuit of exterior objects and goals determines secondary process thinking, which he associated with planning, rational control, and continuous organization. These two aspects of thinking also can be called, respectively, autistic (determined by subjective emotional-motivational activities) and realistic (oriented toward the external environment). The terms are not mutually exclusive but rather correspond to relative degrees of influence of different conditions that enter into thinking.

In a broad sense, then, activities called thinking are internally adaptive responses to intrinsic and extrinsic stimuli; not only do they express inner impulses but they also serve to generate environmentally effective, goal-seeking behaviour.

REALISTIC THINKING

Convergent thought processes. It has been proposed that certain forms of thinking call on one's abilities to assemble and organize information. The result of such thinking satisfies a defined goal in the achievement of an effective solution to a problem. These forms are called convergent thinking and become apparent when situations arise in which one's ability to cope with a task demands resources beyond the explicit stimuli presented; *i.e.*, converges the components of one's past and present experience in organizing or directing one's response.

Experimental approaches. In studying thinking experimentally, investigators often use standardized tasks that have measurable outcomes; for example, a human subject (say, a young child) may be shown three levers—one black, the other two white. Initially, the standard task may be for the child to discover that for pulling the black lever he will receive some reward (perhaps something good to eat) but that for pulling either white lever he will get no reward at all. Orderly procedures are established under which experimental changes can be introduced to observe their effects on the thinker's performance. The results are compared with those obtained under a standard control condition without the changes.

Among the variables that can be manipulated are the amount of information available to the individual (*e.g.*, the black lever may also be illuminated); the kind or degree of incentives under which he works (*e.g.*, a larger or better tasting reward); the order or arrangement of objects (*e.g.*, black lever in the middle or on the right); the instructions provided; the subject's familiarity or degree of prior experience with the task; and the stress under which he functions, such as punishment for mistakes or the threat of failure. The thinker's personality characteristics provide another set of variables for study; for example, subjects who typically exhibit high levels of anxiety can be compared in their task performance with those who ordinarily show little anxiety; or the performance of a person who shows a compelling need to achieve success can be compared with that of a person who exhibits strong fears of failure.

Conditions that affect realistic thinking

Research results indicate that any condition that increases the complexity of a task requiring convergent thinking tends to make the solution more difficult and time-consuming. The more multiple choices (*e.g.,* ten levers instead of three) a thinker is offered, the more difficult the solution of the task is likely to be. Irrelevant items of information, such as the illumination of all levers, may complicate a problem; and as irrelevant data become more numerous or as relevant information becomes less accessible to or discoverable by the thinker, the solution becomes more difficult.

Finding a solution is helped by providing the thinker with cues, guidelines, rules, or other appropriate ways of orienting himself toward the problem (*e.g.,* he may be pointed toward the right lever). Performance is uncertain to the degree that the individual must discover these directions by his own efforts. When separate cues must be combined (*e.g.,* the colour of the lever and the presence or absence of illumination), the more suitable they are for the required relationship, the more efficient the process of solution tends to be.

Individual traits and factors. Conditions that increase the thinker's motivation, such as incentives and special instructions, tend to improve performance. A person's response to these conditions, however, depends on his personality characteristics; very anxious people typically show particularly impaired performance when the task is difficult or stressful. An important consideration is the set (or expectation) of the person; a person's tendency toward rigidity—inability to adapt readily to changing conditions of the task—is likely to have adverse effects on his performance. Instruction or special training that aids one in overcoming his prior sets fosters his ability to achieve correct solution.

Realistic thinking may be aided or hindered by the individual's strategies and cognitive or perceptual style. Such characteristics include the way a person attends to and uses sensory information; he may, for example, focus on inessentials, may fail to observe details accurately, or may be disturbed by complexities in the task stimuli. Also important to convergent thinking are the individual's abilities to analyze and to synthesize sensory information.

Realistic thinking tends to be elicited when the individual perceives no obvious or immediate path to a desired goal. It is likely to begin with his recognition of a problem—otherwise, his behaviour would simply indicate the operation of habits or the automatic production of responses. Realistic thinking continues with one's consideration of alternatives, each marked by some uncertainty or risk. He next begins processing information (including pertinent past experience) by analyzing, combining, and organizing available and potential resources for reaching his goal. In the final phase of the process he produces a response; it may be a wrong solution, a partial solution, or a correct solution. Recycling of these phases (recognition, considering alternatives, processing data, and responding) may continue in a complex way until the goal finally is reached or until the process ends in failure.

Phases of realistic thinking

The explicitness of these phases varies with the complexity of the task, as well as with the problem-solving skills of the individual. In this connection, the individual may show evidence of "learning how to learn"; that is, he may exhibit a progressive increase in skill as he encounters a series of similar problems.

Judgment. A simple form of realistic thinking that lends itself well to controlled experimentation is inferred from one's ability to discriminate discrete objects or items of information (*e.g.,* distinguishing a lion from a tiger). The outcome is a judgment, and the process may be called decision making. The availability of information, the rate at which it is presented, the set (expectancy) of the judge, and the number of alternatives available to him influence the efficiency of his judgment. Redundancy (or surplus) of information facilitates judgment; for example, the lion may be discriminated on the basis of a number of different sensory cues: he is tan or brown, he lacks stripes, he has a mane, and so on. Within what is called the general theory of adaptation level, the decision-making response is considered to be a weighted average of various stimuli: focal (the specific sensory properties of the lion and tiger), contextual (the background in which they are observed), and residual (such intrinsic or experiential factors as memory for other brown or striped objects). Variations in one or more of these three types of stimuli shift the judge's decision in one direction or another in relation to his immediately preceding judgment.

Concept attainment. A more complex form of realistic thinking is inferred when an individual is asked to identify or use a *class* of items, as in selecting several different kinds of triangle from an array of other geometric figures. The individual may proceed to link together in his thinking a newly experienced group of objects according to one or more of their common properties. He thus may be able to give them a general name, as in first learning the meaning of the term triangle, or he may determine whether a newly given object fits a category he already knows. Physical objects are multidimensional; that is, they may vary in shape, size, colour, their location in relation to other objects, their emotional significance, or their connotative meaning. How a person identifies such dimensions, develops hypotheses (or tentative conclusions) about which of the specific dimensions define a class, arrives at the rules of class membership, and how he tests various hypotheses all reflect his ability to grasp concepts. Successful performance in all these processes leads to his formulation of pertinent rules based on his ability to classify specific items (see LEARNING AND COGNITION: *Concept formation*).

Linking by common properties

Problem solving. Still more complex forms of realistic thinking seem to occur when tasks are presented in which the goal is impossible (or very difficult) to achieve directly. In such situations, people commonly appear to pass through intermediate stages of exploring and organizing their resources; indeed, one may first need to exert himself in understanding the problem itself before he can begin to seek possible directions toward a solution. Familiar examples of problem-solving tasks include anagrams (*e.g.,* rearrange "lpepa" to spell "apple"); mathematical problems; mechanical puzzles; verbal "brain teasers" (*e.g.,* Is it legal for a man to marry his widow's sister?); and, in a more practical sense, design and construction problems. Also of interest are issues of human relations, games, and questions pertinent to economics and politics.

Trial and error. Problem-solving activity falls broadly into two categories: one emphasizes simple trial and error; the other requires some degree of insight. In trial and error, the individual proceeds mainly by exploring and manipulating elements of the problem situation in an effort to sort out possibilities and to run across steps that might carry him closer to the goal. This behaviour is most likely to be observed when the problem solver lacks advance knowledge about the character of the solution, or when no single rule seems to underlie the solution. Trial-and-error activity is not necessarily overt (as in one's observable attempts to fit together the pieces of a mechanical puzzle); it may be implicit or vicarious as well, the individual reflecting on the task and symbolically testing possibilities by thinking about them.

Solutions through insight. In striving toward insight, a person tends to exhibit a strong orientation toward understanding *principles* that might bear on the solution sought. The person actively considers what is required by the problem, noting how its elements seem to be interrelated, and seeks some rule that might lead directly to the goal. The insightful thinker is likely to centre on the problem to understand what is needed, to take the time to organize his resources, and to recentre on the problem (reinterpret the situation) in applying any principle that seems to hold promise.

Understanding, organizing, and applying principle

Direction and flexibility characterize insightful problem solving. The thinker directs or guides his steps toward solution according to some plan; he exhibits flexibility in his ability to modify or to adapt procedures as required by his plan and in altering the plan itself. Both characteristics are influenced by the thinker's attitudes and by environmental conditions. If, for example, the task is to empty a length of glass tubing of water (without breaking it) by removing wax plugs about a half-inch up the tube from each end, and the only potential tools are a few objects ordinarily found on a desk top, the usual appearance and functions of such common objects may make it difficult for the problem solver to see how they can be adapted to fit task requirements. If a paper clip is perceived as holding a sheaf of papers in the usual way, such perception would tend to interfere with the individual's ability to employ the principle that the clip's shape could be changed: straightened out for use in poking a hole in the wax.

Formal, logical processes. A special form of problem solving employs formal, systematic, logical thinking. The thinker develops a series of propositions, often as postulates; *e.g.,* the shortest distance between two points is a straight line. He builds a structure of arguments in which statements are consistent with each other in reaching some goal, such as defining the area of a triangle. This kind of logical, mathematical reasoning applies formal rules in supporting the validity of successive propositions.

Inductive and deductive thinking

Both inductive and deductive processes may be used by a problem solver. In inductive thinking one considers a number of particular or specific items of information to develop more inclusive (or general) conceptions. After aspirin was synthesized, for example, some people who swallowed the substance reported that it relieved their *particular* headaches. Through induction, the reports of these *specific* individuals were the basis for developing a more inclusive notion: aspirin may be helpful in relieving headaches in general.

Deduction is reasoning from general propositions—or hypotheses—to more specific instances or statements. Thus, after the general hypothesis about the effectiveness of aspirin had been put forward, physicians began to apply it to specific, newly encountered headache cases. The deduction was that, if aspirin is *generally* useful in managing pains in the head, it might also be helpful in easing pains elsewhere in the body. Although a person may deliberately choose to use induction or deduction, people typically shift from one to the other, depending on the exigencies of the reasoning process.

Students of problem solving almost invariably have endorsed some variety of mediation theory in their efforts to understand realistic thinking. The assumptions in that kind of theory are that implicit (internal) representations of experience are stored in and elicited from memory and are linked together during the period between the presentation of a stimulus and the implementation of a response. Those theorists who prefer to avoid the use of unobservable "entities" (*e.g.,* "mind") increasingly have been invoking the nervous system (particularly the brain) as the structure that mediates such functions.

Creative thinking. Divergent (or creative) thinking has been defined as an activity that leads to new information, or previously undiscovered solutions, rather than to a predetermined, correct solution (as in convergent thinking). Some tasks call for flexibility, originality, fluency, and inventiveness, especially for problems in which the individual must supply his own, unique solution. The "problem" might be a personal, emotional difficulty that needs resolution or expression.

Four progressive stages. A number of processes or phases have been identified as typical of creative thinking. In what logically would be the first phase (*i.e.,* preparation), the thinker assembles and explores his resources and perhaps makes preliminary decisions about their value in solving the problem at hand. Incubation represents the next period, in which he mulls over possibilities and shifts about from one to another relatively free of any rigid rational or logical preconceptions and constraints. Incubation seems to be at least partly unconscious, proceeding without the individual's full awareness. Illumination occurs when resources fall into place, and a definite decision is reached about the result or solution. Verification (refinement or polishing), the process of making relatively minor modifications in committing ideas to final form, follows. Often enough, objective standards for judging creative activity (*e.g.,* musical composition) are lacking; an important criterion is the emotional satisfaction of the creator.

Preparation, incubation, illumination, verification

Although the four phases have been ordered in a logical sequence, they often vary widely and proceed in different orders from one person to the next. Many creative people attain their goals by special strategies that are not neatly describable.

The phases of preparation, incubation, illumination, and verification are characteristic of creative thinkers generally but do not guarantee that a worthwhile product will ensue. Results also depend on whether an individual has the necessary personality characteristics and abilities; in addition, the quality of creative thinking stems from the training of the creator. The artist who produces oil paintings needs to learn the brushing techniques basic to the task; the scientist who creates a new theory does so against a background of previous learning. Further, creativity intimately blends realistic (objective) and autistic (subjective) processes; the successful creator learns how to release and to express his feelings and insights.

Creative thinking is a matter of using intrinsic resources to produce tangible results. This process is markedly influenced by early experience and training. School situations, for example, that encourage individual expression and that tolerate idiosyncratic or unorthodox thinking seem to foster the development of creativity.

Artistic versus scientific creativity. While the processes of creative thinking in artistic and scientific pursuits have much in common, there are also distinctive differences. The artist places more importance on feeling and individual expression, often going to extremes to divorce himself from environmental constraints. The scientist relies more on disciplined, logical thinking to lead him in new directions. Artistic endeavour is dominantly expressive (although clearly oriented toward a goal), while scientific inventiveness is dominantly disciplined (although flexibly receptive to feelings and to imaginative experiences).

Thinking in groups. It might be supposed that greater efficiency should be achieved if several people collaborate to solve a problem than if only one individual works on it. Such results are by no means invariable.

Although groups often may increase the motivation of their members to deal with problems, there is a counterbalancing need to contend with conflicts arising among members of a group and with efforts to give it coherent direction. Problem solving is facilitated by the presence of an effective leader who not only provides direction but permits the orderly, constructive expression of a variety of opinions; much of the leader's effort may be devoted to resolving differences. Success in problem solving also depends on the distribution of ability within a group. Solutions simply may reflect the presence of an outstanding individual who might perform even better by himself.

Although groups may reach a greater number of correct solutions, or may require less time to discover an answer, their net man-hour efficiency is typically lower than that achieved by skilled individuals working alone.

Brainstorming for new solutions

A process called brainstorming has been offered as a method of facilitating the production of new solutions to problems. In brainstorming, a problem is presented to a group of people who then proceed to offer whatever they can think of, regardless of quality and with as few inhibitions as can be managed. Theoretically these unrestricted suggestions increase the probability that at least some superior solutions will emerge. Nevertheless, studies show that when individuals work alone under similar conditions, performance tends to proceed more efficiently than it does in groups.

Under special circumstances, however, a group may solve problems more effectively than does a reasonably competent individual. Group members may contribute different (and essential) resources to a solution that no individual can readily achieve alone; such pooling of information and skills can make group achievements superior in dealing with selected problems. Sometimes social demands may require group agreement on a single alternative, as in formulating national economic or military policies under democratic governments. When only one among several alternative solutions is correct, even if a group requires more time, it has a higher probability of identifying the right one than does an individual alone.

One difference between problem solving by a group and by an individual is the relative importance of covert or vicarious processes. The group depends heavily on verbal communication, while the individual, in considerable degree, attacks the problem through implicit, subjective, silent activity.

AUTISTIC THINKING

When the intensity of extrinsic (or environmental) influence is greatly reduced and intrinsic (or internal) influences dominate, thought processes tend to become autistic, or especially responsive to emotional and motivational impulses; autistic thought processes include so-called free association, fantasy (and reverie), dreaming, and pathological thinking. Often seeming to arise from wishes or needs, autistic thinking may represent an activity through which the individual symbolically gains gratification that the environment does not provide. For instance, one's wishes may be fulfilled only in dreaming. According to Freud, autistic thinking is especially influenced by unconscious tendencies that otherwise might find no expression.

Free association. A person freely associates by responding verbally when the usual constraints of logic, goal orientation, or controlled sequence of thinking are removed or reduced. His responses are likely to reflect aroused emotional activity or impulses; for example, during free association, ordinarily forgotten and repressed past experiences seem to be more readily remembered. What is actually produced in free association (as in other forms of autistic thinking) may not always seem to be particularly coherent or meaningful. Some theorists suggest that such responses are likely to symbolize rather than to state an impulse directly. Thus a psychoanalytic theorist might imagine that a young woman's verbal associations about being run over by a beer truck symbolically disguise a socially unacceptable wish to be seduced in some illicit romantic encounter.

One technique that is claimed to be helpful in uncovering an individual's latent or repressed tendencies is the word-association test, devised by Carl Jung, a Swiss psychiatrist. The test taker is presented with a list of words, to each of which he is supposed to respond by saying whatever he thinks of first. It is theorized that especially significant responses may be identified by such clues as the person's delay in responding, by his use of words that indicate strong emotion, or by unusual or bizarre responses. The word chair for example, prompts many people to say table; the analyst is likely to be alerted if the response is *criminal* or *blood.*

Fantasy. Fantasizing is definable as comparatively well organized sequences of thinking in which sensory imagery prevails. When a person who is otherwise awake tends to lose contact with the environment and his thinking proceeds with little or no concern for logical considerations, conditions become favourable for fantasizing. The activity may also take on a problem-solving character, especially when the thinker periodically monitors the process to evaluate the degree to which he may have progressed toward a solution. Fantasy tends to be highly egocentric, dramatic, pleasurable, and free flowing; it may range from vaguely conscious reverie to vivid, almost hallucinatory visual, auditory, or tactual daydreams.

Psychologists have tried to infer the details of such covert processes by asking people to respond to ambiguous stimuli in whatever way they wish, and by so doing to project their inner experiences. Well-known projective methods include the Rorschach Test, in which inkblots in black and white and colour are used as stimuli; and the so-called Thematic Apperception Test (TAT), in which pictures (of people, for example) are shown, about which the subject is asked to make up stories. The Rorschach Test is believed by some to provide evidence of a person's originality, of the balance he maintains between emotional and logical thinking, and of typical ways in which he perceives the environment; some psychologists assert that the TAT may yield clues to a person's motivational characteristics, his inner conflicts, and his attitudes toward other people.

Rorschach and other projective tests

Others hold that those projective methods are most untrustworthy and that their use can lead to dangerously misleading conclusions (as in mistakenly committing people to psychiatric hospitals).

Certain marginal states of consciousness seem especially favourable for autistic thinking. An example is the drowsy (hypnagogic) period experienced just before falling asleep; at such times, images and apparently random thinking may well up and "float" freely. Similar (hypnopompic) experiences that emerge on awakening also have been reported. Roughly equivalent activities may occur even when one seems fully awake, but when autistic processes hover between full fantasy and conscious orientation to the environment.

Drugs may induce a variety of alterations in thinking; there may be heightened sensitivity to sensory stimuli and responsiveness to inner states through enhanced imagery and unusual ideational activity. Dosed with some drugs, people seem completely to withdraw from the environment and may show evidence of hallucinatory and delusional experiences.

Dreaming. Autistic thinking during sleep is called dreaming. Reduction in external stimulation while one is asleep permits intrinsic activities to exert a strong influence on thought processes. Some psychoanalytic theorists interpret dreaming as a mechanism for maintaining sleep and fulfilling wishes. Freud held that impulses may be expressed in disguised form when one dreams, particularly if their frank expression would be in conflict with the dreamer's moral and social standards. Freud wrote that the original wish that prompts dreaming corresponds to the dream's latent content. Such latent content is to be inferred from the dream as it is directly experienced (the manifest content). The meaning of any dream, according to Freud, lies in its latent content; to the extent that the latent wish is unacceptable to or threatens the dreamer, he is said to employ mechanisms of symbolic imagery, condensation, displacement, and secondary elaboration to disguise it. Condensation refers to the combining of elements; by itself, a knife may suggest a hostile weapon, but dreamed of in combination with other eating utensils it appears innocuous. In displacement the dreamer shifts an impulse from one object to another; he may dream of slicing a melon (manifest) rather than an enemy (latent). Secondary elaboration is the process of imposing structure to increase the coherence and logic of the dream.

Freud's theories of dreams

Other theorists suggest that in many instances dreams do not hold the latent or hidden significance that Freud assigned them. These critics indicate that dreams may simply be the result of random remembering or of imagery that wells up during sleep. In such dreaming, the sequence of dream elements would represent little more than transient associations (see SLEEP AND DREAMS).

In their efforts to study dreaming in terms of more objective evidence, some investigators record electrical activity generated by the brains of sleeping people. People are most likely to say they have been dreaming if they are awakened during a period of so-called rapid eye movement, at which times distinctive changes in brain activity are observable. When people are chronically wakened whenever such signs of dreaming appear, they tend to develop symptoms of psychological disturbance (*e.g.,* hallucinatory activity) during daylight hours. When later permitted to sleep without interruption, they give evidence of dreaming intensively, as if to compensate for previous deprivation. It would appear that dreaming may meet some fundamental physiological need.

Physiological studies of dreaming

Although dreaming largely seems to express intrinsic activity, it can be influenced by external stimuli and is likely to include experiences that symbolize such stimuli. A light tap on the foot of a sleeper, for example, might prompt him to dream of buying a new pair of shoes.

Pathological thinking. One popular system for classifying disturbances in personality is based on general patterns or categories of activity called behaviour disorder, neurosis, and psychosis.

Behaviour disorders. Individuals who are judged to show difficulty in self-control, in ability to withstand stress, or who hold unorthodox moral and social standards are likely to be labelled as exhibiting behaviour disorders. The thinking of such people appears to be essentially "normal" in that they show efficient awareness of the environment. Behaviour disorder is displayed mainly in antisocial acts, stemming from what many observers consider to be the individual's deviant evaluation of what is "right" or "wrong," or of what is socially acceptable.

Neurosis. According to some theories, persons classified as neurotic are thought to suffer deep-lying conflicts, controlled in varying degrees by repression. Their tensions are held to produce feelings of anxiety and guilt and to lead to emotion-laden thinking (or worrying). Such theories also posit the operation of so-called ego-defense mechanisms, or activities believed to allow the individual to keep his distressing, repressed impulses from his own awareness. Thus his reasoning may be altered, as in dreaming. Defense mechanisms include rationalization, which justifies actions on a false basis, as when a soldier who enjoys killing feels he does so through patriotism; projection, which attributes to others one's own impulses, as when a hater feels hated; denial, or refusal to admit unacceptable or embarrassing aspects of experience; reaction formation, in which one acts contrary to his repressed impulses, as when he drowns his lecherous tendencies in excessive piety; and rigidity, or excessively careful, fixed thinking (see also MENTAL DISORDERS: *Psychoneuroses*).

Psychosis. When one's thinking seems grossly disturbed over an appreciable period, he is usually classified by psychiatrists as psychotic. Severe personality disorders of this sort may result from environmental stress, bodily disease, chemical or toxic factors, or any number of experiential influences (*e.g.,* combat experiences, loss of loved ones). The relation between thinking and environmental constraints seems grossly distorted in some forms of psychosis; the effect may be disorientation in time, in space, or in personal identity. In significant degree, the psychotic's emotional and cognitive processes appear to the observer to be independent of what is happening in the surrounding environment.

Bizarre symptoms of psychosis

Some ideational symptoms observed among psychotics are bizarre hallucinatory activities such as those reflected in vivid visual or auditory experiences (*e.g.,* hearing "voices") perceived by the individual as coming from the environment; delusions, ostensibly false beliefs that dominate thinking, such as notions of being persecuted or of having a special identity or a mission (as of being appointed to destroy the world); stereotyped, repetitive ideation or actions, such as the incessant recurrence of silly, emotionless "laughter" or detailed rituals resembling peculiar kinds of calisthenics.

Psychotic persons also may show signs of amnesia, inability to understand what others are saying, failures of attention, disorganization of thinking as expressed in meaningless or incoherent speaking or writing. Among psychotics who are likely to be identified as schizophrenics, speech tends to become odd, fragmented, and difficult to follow rationally; their idiosyncratic use of words is common, along with apparently meaningless phrases and sometimes disregard for sentence structure. Instances of what some claim to be "second sight," divine inspiration, possession by spirits, or extreme detachment from ordinary concerns all are likely, in psychiatric settings, to be interpreted as temporary psychotic episodes.

Thought processes cover a remarkably wide range of types; many are poorly understood or may not even be known to professional psychologists. It seems clear, however, that any kind of thinking mediates between intrinsic (bodily) activities and extrinsic (external) sources of stimulation, each type of thought process representing a resultant of autistic and environmental influences. (W.E.V.)

BIBLIOGRAPHY. R. THOMSON, *The Psychology of Thinking* (1959), a readable summary account of experimental approaches to thinking; P.C. WASON and P.N. JOHNSON-LAIRD (eds.), *Thinking and Reasoning* (1968), a collection of reprinted readings by many of the leading contributors to the field; G. HUMPHREY, *Thinking: An Introduction to its Experimental Psychology* (1951), a scholarly and thorough critical review of theoretical treatments. The most influential directions in 20th-century theorizing may be found in M. WERTHEIMER, *Productive Thinking,* ed. by S.E. ASCH *et al.* (1945), on Gestalt theory; O.H. MOWRER, *Learning Theory and the Symbolic Processes* (1960), on S-R or neo-associationist behaviour theory; A. NEWELL and H.A. SIMON, *Human Problem Solving* (1971), on computer simulation; JEAN PIAGET, *La Psychologie de l'intelligence* (1947; Eng. trans. 1950), a compressed account of the first 20 years of this author's work; F.C. BARTLETT, *Thinking* (1958), the treatment of thinking as a form of skill, sometimes known as the "information-processing" approach; and L.S. VYGOTSKI, *Thought and Language* (1962; orig. pub. in Russian, 1934), the fountainhead of most Soviet research on the topic. D.E. BERLYNE, *Structure and Direction in Thinking* (1965), reviews experimental findings, discusses crucial problems, and attempts a synthesis that draws on S-R behaviour theory, Piaget's ideas, and modern Soviet research, among other developments. See also GILBERT RYLE, *On Thinking* (1979), eight essays by an important theorist; and CHARLES HAMPDEN-TURNER, *Maps of the Mind* (1981), a survey of concepts of the mind held by many theorists throughout history.

Tientsin

Tientsin (Wade-Giles romanization T'ien-ching, Pinyin romanization Tianjin), the third largest municipality of the People's Republic of China after Shanghai and Peking, is located to the east of Hopeh Province at the northeastern extremity of the North China Plain. Central Tientsin (the municipality's urban core) lies about 60 miles (96 kilometres) southeast of central Peking and about 35 miles inland from the Po Hai (Po Gulf), a shallow inlet of the Yellow Sea. Tientsin Municipality, like Peking and Shanghai, is under direct control of the State Council and covers an area of about 4,365 square miles (11,305 square kilometres). Tientsin (meaning literally Heavenly Ford) has been an important transport and trading centre since the Yüan (Mongol) dynasty (1206–1368). It is China's second largest manufacturing centre after Shanghai and the leading port in North China.

Tientsin was famous as a cosmopolitan centre long before the arrival of the European trading community in the 19th century. Its maritime orientation and its role as the commercial gateway to Peking fostered the growth of an ethnically diverse and commercially innovative population. The city is noted for its woven handicraft products, terra-cotta figurines, hand-painted woodblock prints, and extensive seafood cuisine.

This article is divided into the following sections:

Physical and human geography

THE LANDSCAPE

The city site. Central Tientsin is located at the point where the Tzu-ya and the Hsin-k'ai rivers, and the north and south sections of the Grand Canal (Pei Yün-ho and Nan Yün-ho, respectively) converge before merging into the Hai Ho (Hai River), which then flows eastward into the Po Hai. The city stands at an elevation of less than 15 feet (five metres) above sea level on a level alluvial plain. Some low-lying areas east of the city are only about six feet above sea level, and the majority of the built-up area is below 12 feet.

The municipality borders on the Po Hai to the east, Peking Municipality to the northwest, and Hopeh Province to the north, west, and south. Between 1955 and 1967 Tientsin was a subprovince-level city, which served as the capital of Hopeh Province. Its jurisdiction extended over the built-up urban core and eastward along the Hai Ho to include the port at T'ang-ku. At that time, Tientsin city was administratively separate from the Tientsin Special District, which had its seat at Yang-liu-ch'ing, southwest of central Tientsin.

In 1967 Tientsin Municipality was made a first-order, province-level administrative unit, and the area under its immediate control was expanded to include counties (*hsien*) formerly under the special district. The city simultaneously became the special district seat but lost its position as provincial capital. In the early 1980s Tientsin Municipality was composed of 13 urban and suburban districts (*ch'u*) and five rural counties. The municipality was under direct jurisdiction of the central government in Peking.

Climate. Despite Tientsin's proximity to the sea, it has a distinctly continental climate with sharp daily and seasonal temperature fluctuations. It is subject to the full effects of the cool, dry Siberian high-pressure system during the winter (October to April), while in the summer (May to September), the high pressure system over the North Pacific Ocean brings hot and rainy weather. Winter precipitation is minimal, and the air is dry, with relative humidity averaging 50 percent. In summer, moist, rain-bearing southerly winds prevail, and the average relative humidity exceeds 70 percent. The average annual temperature is 56° F (13° C), with a January average of 39° F (4° C) and a July average of 84° F (29° C). Severe winter storms are common, but typhoons seldom occur.

Flood-control measures

Drainage. The Hai Ho was long subject to frequent flooding. As the main outlet for the rivers of the North China Plain, it frequently became heavily silted during the spring and summer months; during the winter season its water level was often too low for navigation. Extensive water conservation began in 1897. The river was straightened to facilitate tidal action and to shorten the distance to the sea. Locks were constructed to regulate the flow of water from the river into its many canals, the river and the sand bars at its mouth were dredged, and silt-laden water was diverted into settling basins.

Since 1949 multipurpose flood-control, irrigation, and navigation improvements have been made. Construction of the Kuang-ting Reservoir on the Yung-ting Ho near Peking has helped alleviate flood damage within metropolitan Tientsin. New diversion channels have also been built to control the floodwaters of the Ta-ch'ing and Tzu-ya rivers to the southwest.

Plant and animal life. The marshy lakes and floodplains around Tientsin abound with numerous varieties of reeds, bulrushes, and shrubs, such as tamarisk. Closer to the seashore, Russian thistle, glasswort, and artemisia can be found. Freshwater fish (including silver and golden carp) are raised in ponds and marshy depressions.

The central district

The city layout. The urban core of Tientsin extends for about seven miles from east to west and about nine miles from north to south. Ho-p'ing, the central district, is located on the west bank of the Hai Ho, just below the large bend of the Hai Ho. It is the main commercial and financial centre, and its two main streets of Ho-p'ing Lu (Ho-p'ing Road) and Chieh-fang Lu have several large department stores, restaurants, and hotels.

The old "Chinese" city is situated immediately to the northwest of Ho-p'ing Lu. It is bounded by the four wide boulevards of Tung, Hsi, Pei, and Nan Ma-lu that follow the course of the old rectangular wall. The street pattern in the old city is winding and irregular, in contrast to the more regular gridded pattern in the foreign-developed zones to the south and west. The old city is subdivided into four smaller sections, each of which in traditional times had special marketing and commercial functions.

North and west of the old city and continuing across the Nan Yün-ho is the mixed residential and industrial Hung-ch'iao District. It extends to the confluence of the Tzu-ya Ho, Pei Yün-ho, and Hai Ho. The northern outskirts

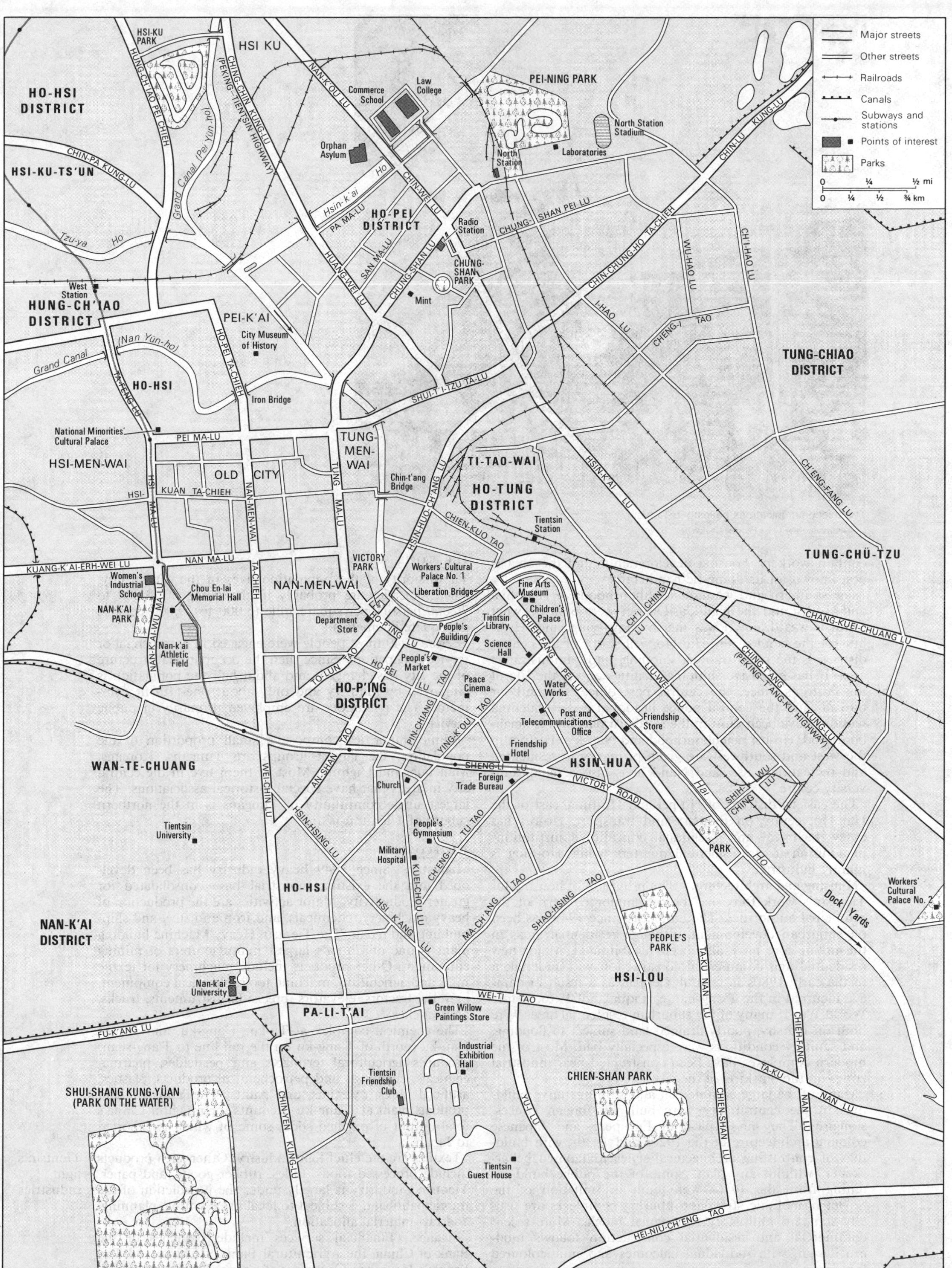

The city of Tientsin.

The telecommunications building in Tientsin.
Li Changyuan—New China Pictures Co./Eastfoto

contain workers' housing developments, and the area is best known for its domestic handicrafts.

The southern and western neighbourhoods of Hsin-hua and Ho-hsi and the Nan-k'ai District were built on what (until it was drained) was marshy, low-lying land. Hsin-hua, at the bend of the Hai Ho well south of the central district, is the main trading, shipping, and administrative area. It has extensive shipping facilities and is the site of the customs office, the central post office, the harbour bureau, and the central police headquarters. Residential sections have been built in the southern part of this neighbourhood. Ho-hsi neighbourhood and Nan-k'ai District in the west and southwest are given primarily to residential and recreational use, and Nan-k'ai is also a major university centre.

The eastern districts of Ho-pei and Ho-tung, east of the Hai Ho, centre on industry and transport. Ho-pei has a few technical and vocational educational institutions in addition to its residential quarters, while Ho-tung is mainly industrial.

Housing and architecture. The provision of housing for Tientsin's work force has been a major concern of the municipal authorities. The emphasis since 1949 has been on suburban development, although residential areas in the urban core have also been rehabilitated. Major new residential and commercial construction was undertaken in the early 1980s in central Tientsin as a result of damage incurred in the T'angshan earthquake of 1976. Before World War II many of the suburban residential areas were built on marshy, poorly drained land subject to flooding, and sanitary conditions were especially bad. Most of the modern complexes have been constructed near industrial zones on the outskirts of the city.

Many of the large commercial and administrative buildings in the central city were built by foreign concessionaires. They are typical of European and Japanese colonial architecture of the 1920s and 1930s, with buildings of contrasting architectural styles juxtaposed helter-skelter, without any plan. Some of the public buildings dating from the 1950s were built in imitation of the Soviet monolithic style, and housing complexes are usually standard multistory rectangular blocks. More recent commercial and residential construction follows modern design, with individual balconies and multicoloured facades.

THE PEOPLE

The majority of the population lives in the central city, where densities are probably in the range of 15,000 to 75,000 persons per square mile (6,000 to 29,000 persons per square kilometre).

Before 1949 most people were engaged in commercial or service occupations. Since then the occupational structure of the city has changed, and about half the population is employed by industry and only about one-fifth in commerce. The remainder are employed primarily in public services.

Ethnic minorities compose a small proportion of the population; the largest groups are Tungans, Koreans, Manchus, and Uighurs. Most of them live in the central city in areas that have special historical associations. The largest single community of Tungans is in the northern suburb of T'ien-mu-ts'un.

THE ECONOMY

Industry. Since 1949 heavy industry has been developed and the existing industrial base consolidated for greater productivity. Major activities are the production of heavy machinery, chemicals, and iron and steel and shipbuilding and repair. The Tientsin Heavy Machine-building plant is one of China's largest manufacturers of mining equipment. Other products include machinery for textile mills and agriculture, machine tools, electrical equipment, bicycles, tractors, elevators, precision instruments, trucks, and watches.

The chemical complex at Ta-ku, T'ang-ku, and also at Han-ku (north of T'ang-ku on the rail line to T'ang-shan) produces agricultural fertilizers and pesticides, pharmaceuticals, chemicals and petrochemical products, plastics, artificial fibres, dyestuffs, and paints. The Yung-li alkali products plant at T'ang-ku accounts for much of China's total output of purified soda, some of which is exported to Japan.

Tientsin's light industries

Textiles are the chief light industry. Other such products include processed foods, hides, rubber goods, and paper. Tientsin's industry is largely under the jurisdiction of the municipality and is subject to local price setting, planning, and raw-material allocation.

Finance. Financial services include branches of the Bank of China, the Agricultural Bank of China, and The People's Insurance Company of China. Retail and wholesale trade is managed by commerce bureaus that are responsible to municipal and provincial authorities. Pricing and personnel matters are managed locally, while the distribution of commodities, long-range planning, and high-level financial management are handled by provincial-level bureaus responsible to Peking. A municipality-run General Trade Corporation formed in the early 1980s helps coordinate and improve the efficiency of domestic and foreign trade by assuming functions previously performed by central government agencies.

Transportation. Tientsin is North China's leading transport centre. The Ching-p'u railway runs south from Tientsin to Shanghai via Chi-nan, Shantung Province, and Süchow, Kiangsu Province. The Ching-shan railway runs north from Peking through Tientsin and Shan-hai-kuan on the Hopeh–Liaoning border to Shenyang, Liaoning Province. The lines are served in Tientsin by three railway stations, classification yards, and extensive maintenance and repair facilities.

Railway services

Heavily traversed inland waterways radiate to the south and southwest along the Grand Canal and Tzu-ya and Ta-ch'ing rivers; they connect the city with Pao-ting, Ts'ang-chou, and Heng-shui in southern Hopeh Province. The Ching-T'ang Kung-lu highway from Peking through Tientsin to T'ang-ku is the main all-weather freight road to the sea. Other main roads extend southward along the Ching-p'u railway into Shantung Province, westward to Shansi Province, and northward to Ch'in-huang-tao, northeastern Hopeh, and the Northeast (formerly Manchuria).

Intraurban and suburban transport is extensive. Several dozen intraurban trolley, electric-trolleybus, and motor bus routes connect the city's railway stations and serve the near suburban districts. The first 7.5 miles (12 kilometres) of Central Tientsin's subway line was in operation by mid-1983. In addition, about two dozen long-distance motor bus routes connect the urban core with more distant rural areas.

Tientsin is the main collection point and transshipment centre in North China for goods manufactured for export and is the chief port of entry for heavy machinery and other capital-intensive imports. Much of China's total foreign trade by value is handled through Tientsin's outport and fishing port of T'ang-ku.

ADMINISTRATIVE AND SOCIAL CONDITIONS

Government. The Tientsin People's Congress is the city's chief administrative body. It's predecessor, the Municipal Revolutionary Committee, was established in 1967 during the political disruption of the Great Proletarian Cultural Revolution (1966–69). Prior to 1967 responsibility for the management of the city's affairs was shared by a number of bureaus under both party and governmental control.

The People's Congress

The Tientsin Municipal Planning Commission plays a key role in managing industry and commerce. It controls the supply and distribution of industrial raw materials, sets production levels, allocates funds for capital investments, determines manpower needs, supervises product research and development, and coordinates transportation, public works, and environmental policy.

Public utilities. Major public works projects since 1949 have helped alleviate chronic flood damage and have improved the city's water supply and sewage disposal systems. Marshy, low-lying lands have been drained and converted to agricultural and recreational use, new roads have been constructed, and streetlights have been installed.

The supply of fresh water has always been a problem because of the city's location near the sea at low elevation. Severe water shortages developed in the early 1980s because of industrialization, population growth, and drought that cut off the water supply from Miyun Reservoir northeast of Peking. These shortages were temporarily alleviated by diverting water from the Huang Ho, to the south, but construction was also undertaken to divert water from the Luan Ho, to the northeast. The project began in late 1981, and its initial stage was completed in late 1983. Swampy lowlands to the southwest have been drained; one of the most extensive was converted into the large recreational area of the Shui-shang Kung-yüan (Park on the Water).

The city's water supply

Electricity is generated by thermal power plants (fuelled with coal), and the city is connected by a power grid with Peking and T'ang-shan, Hopeh.

Health. Tientsin has many Western-style and Chinese hospitals, with separate facilities for children, workers, and members of ethnic minorities. After the Cultural Revolution,Tientsin also developed one of China's earliest and most effective urban planned birth programs. In 1973 an Office of Planned Births was established by the municipality and was granted status and authority equal to the Department of Public Health.

Education. Before the Cultural Revolution about one-sixth of Tientsin's population was enrolled in educational institutions. During the late 1960s and early 1970s, enrollments fell. By the late 1970s, to support China's modernization program, considerable investments had been made to improve and expand scientific and technical institutions, especially those supportive of petrochemical, iron and steel, and marine services and engineering industries. The general universities of Nan-k'ai and Tientsin are located in Nan-k'ai District, on the southwestern periphery of the city. Other higher educational institutions include the Polytechnic Institute, the Central Conservatory of art and music, a medical school, and a teacher training school. Work-study schools attached to factories supplement formal educational programs.

CULTURAL LIFE

The city has several museums and a major library. The Fine Arts Museum is noted for its collection of Yüan, Ming, and Ch'ing dynasty paintings, while the City Museum of History and the Tientsin Science Hall have more contemporary displays. The Tientsin Library is the municipality's largest library.

Special exhibits are held at the Industrial Exhibition Hall and the National Minorities' Cultural Palace, and the People's Festival Hall is used for operas, plays, and concerts. The largest movie house is the Peace Cinema. There is also an astronomical observatory.

There are several dozen parks and recreation centres. Victory Park and the Children's Park are in the centre of the city, and the Hsi-ku, Nan-k'ai, People's, Chien-shan, Shui-shang, and Pei-ning parks are in the urbanized area. Recreational clubs have also been built for industrial workers, and there are four stadiums.

Recreational facilities

History

EVOLUTION OF THE CITY

The marshy, poorly drained area surrounding contemporary Tientsin was sparsely populated until the Sung dynasty (960–1126), when the settlement of San Ch'a K'ou was built on the west bank of the Hai Ho. The original settlement was later joined by the larger town of Chih-ku, built on high ground at the confluence of the Tzu-ya and Hai rivers. Chih-ku grew rapidly as a port and commercial centre, and it became the chief storage, transfer, and distribution point for grain and other foodstuffs from central and southern China.

Origins of the city

In recognition of the importance of Chih-ku (then called Hai-chin) as a shipping centre, the Yüan (Mongol) government (1206–1368) established offices for the regulation of navigation and customs and expanded the town's warehouse and harbour facilities. The city also became a major salt producer when salterns were constructed along the Hai Ho.

The development of modern Tientsin began during the Ming dynasty (1368–1644), when the national capital was shifted from Nanking to Peking. In 1368 the settlement became a garrison town and was named T'ien-chin-wei (Defense of the Heavenly Ford). A large military base was built and a rectangular wall constructed in 1425. The town prospered as it became the main gateway to Peking, and its population was swelled by immigrants from Shantung, Kiangsu, and Fukien provinces.

By the beginning of the Ch'ing (Manchu) dynasty (1644–1911/12), Tientsin had become the leading economic centre of North China because of its location at the northern terminus of the Grand Canal (Ta Yün-ho). As better inland waterway connections were established, there was a steady increase in the city's volume of trade. Members of the first Dutch diplomatic mission to China in the mid-17th century commented favourably on the well-constructed 25-foot- (7.6-metre-) high wall surrounding the city and noted the many temples and the large commercial and marketing area.

The period of foreign control

Economic prosperity declined temporarily during the mid-19th century when the European nations trading with China unremittingly pressed their demands for commercial and diplomatic privileges. The treaties of Tientsin, during the second Opium War (1856–60) against China, were signed by the British, French, and Chinese in 1858. Among their provisions, they authorized the establishment of British and French concessions in Tientsin. Between 1895 and 1902 concessions were given to Japan, Germany, Russia, Austria-Hungary, Italy, and Belgium. Hostilities were resumed in Tientsin in 1860, and the city was shelled by the British and French; the Convention of Peking then declared Tientsin an open trading port. Ten years later, a violent expression of Chinese antiforeign feeling erupted in the city when the French Catholic orphanage and cathedral were attacked. In 1900 renewed anti-foreign demonstrations led to the shelling and occupation of the city by Allied (Western) forces and the destruction of the old city wall.

By the end of the 19th century, Tientsin had grown to more than 200,000 people, with about half the population residing within the old "Chinese" city. Living conditions for the Chinese were in sharp contrast to those in the spacious, well-tended European quarters that were distributed to the southeast and along the riverbanks.

Tientsin became an important ocean shipping centre by 1900. The Huang Ho shifted its course, and the Grand Canal became silted up in the early 1850s, thereby restricting inland waterway traffic through the city, and shipping operations were shifted eastward along the banks of the Hai Ho. Facilities were also built at Ta-ku and T'ang-ku at the mouth of the Hai Ho.

THE 20TH CENTURY

The Chinese Republic period

Under the Republic of China (1911–49), Tientsin became a special municipality (*shih*) under the direct administration of the National government. In 1935 the Japanese attempted to extend their control over North China by establishing an autonomous area in eastern Hopeh Province, which was to be administered by Japanese military authorities in Tientsin. One year later, the Japanese presented demands to the Chinese authorities that were designed to weaken Chinese control over the area. With the opening of the Sino-Japanese War (1937–45), Tientsin was occupied by the Japanese, and in 1939 the Japanese blockaded the British and French concessions in response to anti-Japanese demonstrations.

During the Communist Revolution (1945–49), Tientsin remained under Nationalist control until mid-January 1949, when the city was captured by the Communists. Since then, Tientsin's growth as a trading and manufacturing centre has been responsive to internal development needs. Despite its proximity to Peking, the city retains a distinctive character, attributable to its functional and utilitarian origins.

BIBLIOGRAPHY. KENNETH G. LIEBERTHAL, *Revolution and Tradition in Tientsin, 1949–52* (1980), examines interrelations among economic development, administrative organization, and mass mobilization strategies during the early years of Communist control. KATHERINE CH'U LYLE, "Report from China, Planned Birth in Tianjin," *China Quarterly,* 85:551–67 (1980), documents family planning programs in the late 1970s.

(B.Bo.)

Time

One facet of human consciousness is the awareness of time. Humans feel the passage of time in their personal experience and observe it in their environment. Time, as experienced, is a one-way flow at a pace that is slow enough to be perceptible. (Actually, only material fluids flow; but, like psychic experiences in general, that of time can be described only in the language of material phenomena.) People feel, think, and act in the time flow. (A.J.T.)

This article is divided into the following sections:

Time and its role in the history of thought and action

NATURE AND DEFINITION OF TIME

Time appears to be more puzzling than space because it seems to flow or pass or else people seem to advance through it. But the passage or advance seems to be unintelligible. The question of how many seconds per second time flows (or one advances through it) is obviously an absurd one, for it suggests that the flow or advance comprises a rate of change with respect to something else—to a sort of hypertime. But if this hypertime itself flows, then a hyper-hypertime is required, and so on, ad infinitum.

Again, if the world is thought of as spread out in space-time, it might be asked whether human consciousness advances up a timelike direction of this world and, if so, how fast; whether future events pop into existence as the "now" reaches them or are there all along; and how such changes in space-time can be represented, since time is already within the picture. (Ordinary change can, of course, be represented in a space-time picture: for example, a particle at rest is represented by a straight line and an oscillating particle by a wavy line.)

Process philosophers versus philosophers of the manifold

In the face of these difficulties, philosophers tend to divide into two sorts: the "process philosophers" and the "philosophers of the manifold," respectively. Process philosophers—such as Alfred North Whitehead, an Anglo-American metaphysician who died in 1947—hold that the flow of time (or human advance through it) is an important metaphysical fact. Like the French intuitionist Henri Bergson, they may hold that this flow can be grasped only by nonrational intuition. Bergson even held that the scientific concept of time as a dimension actually misrepresents reality.

Philosophers of the manifold hold that the flow of time or human advance through time is an illusion. They argue, for example, that words such as past, future, and now, as well as the tenses of verbs, are indexical expressions that refer to the act of their own utterance. Hence, the alleged change of an event from being future to being past is an illusion. To say that the event is future is to assert that it is later than this utterance; then later yet, when one says that it is in the past, he or she asserts that it is earlier than that other utterance. *Past* and *future* are not real predicates of events in this view; and change in respect of them is not a genuine change.

Again, although process philosophers think of the future as somehow open or indeterminate, whereas the past is unchangeable, fixed, determinate, philosophers of the manifold hold that it is as much nonsense to talk of changing the future as it is to talk of changing the past. If a person decides to point left rather than to point right, then pointing left *is* what the future was. Moreover, this thesis of the determinateness of the future, they argue, must not be confused with determinism, the theory that there are laws whereby later states of the universe may be deduced from earlier states (or vice versa). The philosophy of the manifold is neutral about this issue. Future events may well exist and yet not be connected in a sufficiently lawlike way with earlier ones.

One of the features of time that puzzled the Platonist Augustine, in the 5th century AD, was the difficulty of defining it. In contemporary philosophy of language, however (influenced by Ludwig Wittgenstein, a Cambridge philosopher), no mystery is seen in this task. Learning to handle the word *time* involves a multiplicity of verbal skills, including the ability to handle such connected words as *earlier, later, now, second,* and *hour.* These verbal skills have to be picked up in very complex ways (partly by ostension), and it is not surprising that the meaning of the word *time* cannot be distilled into a neat verbal definition. (It is not, for example, an abbreviating word like *bachelor.*)

The philosophy of time bears powerfully on human emotions. Not only do individuals regret the past, they also fear the future, not least because the alleged flow of time seems to be sweeping them toward their deaths, as swimmers are swept toward a waterfall. (J.J.C.S.)

PRESCIENTIFIC CONCEPTIONS OF TIME AND THEIR INFLUENCE

Temporal existence, death, and survival

The individual's experience and observation of time. The irreversibility and inexorability of the passage of time is borne in on human beings by the fact of death. Unlike other living creatures, they know that their lives may be cut short at any moment and that, even if they attain the full expectation of human life, their growth is bound to be followed by eventual decay and, in due time, death (see also PERCEPTION, HUMAN: *Time perception*).

Although there is no generally accepted evidence that death is not the conclusive end of life, it is a tenet of some religions (*e.g.,* of Zoroastrianism, Judaism, Christianity, and Islām) that death is followed by everlasting life elsewhere—in *sheol,* hell, or heaven—and that eventually there will be a universal physical resurrection. Others (*e.g.,* Buddhists, Orphics, Pythagoreans, and Plato) have held that people are reborn in the time flow of life on Earth and that the notion that a human being has only one life on Earth is the illusion of a lost memory. The Buddha claimed to recollect all of his previous lives. The Greek philosophers Pythagoras and Empedocles, of the 6th and early 5th centuries BC, whose lives probably overlapped that of the Buddha, likewise claimed to recollect some of their previous lives. Such rebirths, they held, would continue to recur any number of times unless a person should succeed in breaking the vicious circle (releasing himself from the "sorrowful wheel") by strenuous ascetic performances.

The belief that a person's life in time on Earth is repetitive may have been an inference from the observed repetitiveness of phenomena in the environment. The day-and-night cycle and the annual cycle of the seasons dominated the conduct of human life until the recent harnessing of inanimate physical forces in the Industrial Revolution made it possible for work to be carried on for 24 hours a day throughout the year—under cover, by artificial light, and at a controlled temperature. There is also the generation cycle, which the Industrial Revolution has not suppressed: the generations still replace each other, in spite of the lengthening of life expectancies. In some societies it has been customary to give a man's son a different name but to give his grandson the same name. To name father and son differently is an admission that generations change; but to name grandfather and grandson the same is perhaps an intimation that the grandson is the grandfather reincarnate.

Thus, though every human being has the experience of irreversible change in his own life, he also observes cyclic change in his environment; hence the adherents of some religions and philosophies have inferred that, despite appearances, time flows cyclically for the individual human being, too.

Interpretations of time in different ages and lands

The human experience and observation of time has been variously interpreted. Parmenides, an Italiote Greek (Eleatic) philosopher (6th–5th century BC) and Zeno, his fellow townsman and disciple, held that change is logically inconceivable and that logic is a surer indicator of reality than experience; thus, despite appearances, reality is unitary and motionless. In this view, time is an illusion. The illusoriness of the world that "flows" in time is also to be found in some Indian philosophy. The Buddha and, among the Greeks, Plato and Plotinus, all held that life in the time flow, though not wholly illusory, is at best a low-grade condition by comparison, respectively, with the Buddhist Nirvāṇa (in which desires are extinguished) and with the Platonic world of Ideas; *i.e.,* of incorporeal timeless exemplars, of which phenomena in the time flow are imperfect and ephemeral copies.

It has been held, however—*e.g.,* by disciples of the Greek philosopher Heracleitus—that the time flow is of the essence of reality. Others have held that life in the time flow, though it may be wretched, is nevertheless momentous; for it is here that a person decides his destiny. In the Buddhist view, a person's conduct in any one of his successive lives on Earth will increase or diminish his prospects of eventually breaking out of the cycle of recurrent births. For those who believe in only one earthly life, however, the momentousness of life in the time flow is still greater because this life will be followed by an everlasting life at a destination decided by conduct in this brief and painful testing time. The view that life in time on Earth is a probation for weal or woe in an everlasting future has often been associated—as it was by the Iranian prophet Zoroaster (*c.* 600 BC)—with a belief in a general judgment of all who have ever lived to be held on a common judgment day, which will be the end of time. The belief in an immediate individual judgment was also held in pharaonic Egypt. Both of these beliefs have been adopted by Jews, Christians, and Muslims.

Cyclic view of time in the philosophy of history. The foregoing diverse interpretations of the nature and significance of the individual human being's experience and observation of time differ sharply from each other, and they have led to equally sharp differences in views of human history and of ultimate reality and in prescriptions for the conduct, both collective and individual, of human life. Thinkers have been divided between holders of the cyclic view and holders of the one-way view of time and between believers in the different prescriptions for the conduct of life that these differing views have suggested. Variations in the two basic views of time and in the corresponding codes of conduct have been among the salient characteristics distinguishing the principal civilizations and philosophies and higher religions that have appeared in history to date.

Environmental recurrences and religion. The cyclic theory of time has been held in regard to the three fields of religion, of history (both human and cosmic), and of personal life. That this view arose from the observation of recurrences in the environment is most conspicuously seen in the field of religion. The observation of the generation cycle has been reflected in the cult of ancestors, important in Chinese religion and also in older civilizations and in precivilizational societies. The observation of the annual cycle of the seasons and its crucial effect on agriculture is reflected in a ceremony in which the emperor of China used to plow the first furrow of the current year; in the ceremonial opening of a breach in the dike of the Nile to let the annual floodwaters irrigate the land; and in the annual "sacred marriage," performed by a priest and priestess representing a god and goddess, which was deemed to ensure the continuing fertility of Babylonia. A cycle longer than that of the seasons is represented by the recurrent *avatāras* (epiphanies, incarnate, on Earth) of the Hindu god Vishnu (Viṣṇu) and in the corresponding series of buddhas and *bodhisattvas* (potential buddhas). Although the only historical Buddha was Siddhārtha Gautama (6th–5th century BC), in the mythology of the northern school of Buddhism (the Mahāyāna), the identity of the historical Buddha has been almost effaced by a long vista of putative buddhas extending through previous and future times.

Seasons, generations, eons

In contrast to northern Buddhism and to Vaiṣṇava Hinduism, Christianity holds that the incarnation of God in Jesus was a unique event; yet the rite of the Eucharist, in which Christ's self-sacrifice is held by Catholic and Eastern Orthodox Christians to be reperformed, is celebrated every day by thousands of priests, and the nature of this rite has suggested to some scholars that it originated in an annual festival at the culmination of the agricultural year. In this interpretation, the bread that is Christ's body and the wine that is his blood associate him with the annually dying gods Adonis, Osiris, and Attis—the divinities, inherent in the vital and vitalizing power of the crops, who die in order that people may eat and drink and live. "Unless a grain of wheat falls into the earth and dies, it remains alone; but, if it dies, it bears much fruit" (John 12:24).

The cyclic view in various cultures. The cyclic view of history, both cosmic and human, has been prevalent among the Hindus and the pre-Christian Greeks, the Chinese, and the Aztecs; and it has reappeared in modern Western society, although this civilization was originally Christian—that is, was nurtured on a religion that sees time as a one-way flow and not as a cyclic one.

Yin-Yang, Love-Strife, kalpas

The Chinese, Hindus, and Greeks saw cosmic time as moving in an alternating rhythm, classically expressed in the Chinese concept of the alternation between Yin, the passive female principle, and Yang, the dynamic male principle. When either Yin or Yang goes to extremes, it overlaps the other principle, which is its correlative and complement in consequence of being its opposite. In the philosophy of Empedocles, an early Greek thinker, the equivalents of Yin and Yang were Love and Strife. Empedocles revolted against the denial of the reality of motion and plurality that was made by his Eleatic predecessors on the strength of mere logic. He broke up the Eleatics' motionless, and therefore timeless, unitary reality into a movement of four elements that were alternately harmonized by Love and set at variance by Strife. Empedocles' Love and Strife, like Yin and Yang, each overlapped the other when they had gone to extremes.

Plato translated Empedocles' concept from psychological into theistic terms. At the outset, in his view, the gods guide the cosmos, and they then leave it to its own devices. But when the cosmos, thus left to itself, has brought itself to the brink of disaster, the gods resume control at the 11th hour—and these two phases of its condition alternate with each other endlessly. The recurrence of alternating phases in which, at the darkest hour, catastrophe is averted by divine intervention is similarly an article of Vaiṣṇava Hindu faith. In guessing the lengths of the recurrent eons (kalpas), the Hindus arrived, intuitively, at figures of the magnitude of those reached by modern astronomers through meticulous observations and calculations. Similarly, the Aztecs of Meso-America rivaled modern Westerners and the Hindus in the scale on which they envisaged the flow of time, and they kept an astonishingly accurate time count by inventing a set of interlocking cycles of different wavelengths.

Plato and Aristotle took it for granted that human society, as well as the cosmos, has been, and will continue to be, wrecked and rehabilitated any number of times. This rhythm can be discerned, as a matter of historical fact, in the histories of the pharaonic Egyptian and of the Chinese civilizations during the three millennia that elapsed, in each of them, between its first political unification and its final disintegration. The prosperity that had been conferred on a peasant society by political unity and peace turned into adversity when the cost of large-scale administration and defense became too heavy for an unmechanized economy to bear. In each instance, the unified state then broke up—only to be reunited for the starting of another similar cycle. The Muslim historian Ibn Khaldūn, writing in the 14th century AD, observed the same cyclic rhythm in the histories of the successive conquests of sedentary populations by pastoral nomads.

Cultural morphology in Vico and Spengler

In the modern West, an Italian philosopher of history, Giambattista Vico, observed that the phases through which Western civilization had passed had counterparts in the history of the antecedent Greco-Roman civilization. Thanks to a subsequent increase in the number of civilizations known to Western students of cultural morphology, Oswald Spengler, a German philosopher of history, was able, in the early 20th century, to make a comparative study of civilizations over a much broader spectrum than that of Vico. The comparison of different civilizations or of successive periods of order and disorder in Chinese or in pharaonic Egyptian history implied, of course, that, in human affairs, recurrence is a reality.

The application of the cyclic view to the life of a human being in the hypothesis of rebirth was mentioned earlier. This hypothesis relaxes the anxiety about being annihilated through death by replacing it with a no less agonizing anxiety about being condemned to a potentially endless series of rebirths. The strength of the reincarnationists' anxiety can be gauged by the severity of the self-mortification to which they resort to liberate themselves from the "sorrowful wheel." Among the peoples who have not believed in rebirth, the pharaonic Egyptians have taken the offensive against death and decay with the greatest determination: they embalmed corpses; they built colossal tombs; and, in the Book of the Dead, they provided instructions and spells for ensuring for that portion of the soul that did not hover around the sarcophagus an acquittal in the postmortem judgment and an entry into a blissful life in another world. No other human society has succeeded in achieving this degree of indestructibility despite the ravages of time.

One-way view of time in the philosophy of history. When the flow of time is held to be not recurrent but one-way, it can be conceived of as having a beginning and perhaps an end. Some thinkers have felt that such limits can be imagined only if there is some timeless power that has set time going and intends or is set to stop it. A god who creates and then annihilates time, if he is held to be omnipotent, is often credited with having done this with a benevolent purpose that is being carried out according to plan. The omnipotent god's plan, in this view, governs the time flow and is made manifest to humans in progressive revelations through the prophets—from Abraham, by way of Moses, Isaiah, and Jesus, to the Prophet Muḥammad (as Muslims believe).

Salvation history and the "axis age"

This belief in *Heilsgeschichte* (salvational history) has been derived by Islām and Christianity from Judaism and Zoroastrianism. Late in the 12th century, the Christian seer Joachim of Fiore saw this divinely ordained spiritual progress in the time flow as unfolding in a series of three ages—those of the Father, the Son, and the Spirit. Karl Jaspers, a 20th-century Western philosopher, has discerned an "axis age"—*i.e.,* a turning point in human history—in the 6th century BC, when Confucius, the Buddha, Zoroaster, Deutero-Isaiah, and Pythagoras were alive contemporaneously. If the "axis age" is extended backward in time to the original Isaiah's generation and forward to Muḥammad's, it may perhaps be recognized as the age in which humans first sought to make direct contact with the ultimate spiritual reality behind phenomena instead of making such communication only indirectly through their nonhuman and social environments.

The belief in an omnipotent creator god, however, has been challenged. The creation of time, or of anything else, out of nothing is difficult to imagine; and, if God is not a creator but is merely a shaper, his power is limited by the intractability of the independent material with which he has had to work. Plato, in the *Timaeus,* conceived of God as being a nonomnipotent shaper and thus accounted for the manifest element of evil in phenomena. Marcion, a 2nd-century Christian heretic, inferred from the evil in phenomena that the creator was bad and held that a "stranger god" had come to redeem the bad creator's work at the benevolent stranger's cost. Zoroaster saw the phenomenal world as a battlefield between a bad god and a good one and saw time as the duration of this battle. Though he held that the good god was destined to be the victor, a god who needs to fight and win is not omnipotent. In an attenuated form, this evil adversary appears in the three Judaic religions as Satan.

Evolutionary and dialectical views

Observation of historical phenomena suggests that, in spite of the manifestness of evil, there has been progress in the history of life on this planet, culminating in the emergence of humans who know themselves to be sinners yet feel themselves to be something better than inanimate matter. Charles Darwin, in his theory of the selection of mutations by the environment, sought to vindicate apparent progress in the organic realm without recourse to an extraneous god. In the history of Greek thought, the counterpart of such mutations was the swerving of atoms. After Empedocles had broken up the indivisible, motionless, and timeless reality of Parmenides and Zeno into four elements played upon alternately by Love and Strife, it was a short step for the Atomists of the 5th century BC, Leucippus and Democritus, to break up reality still further into an innumerable host of minute atoms moving in time through a vacuum. Granting that one single atom had once made a single slight swerve, the build-up of observed phenomena could be accounted for on Darwinian lines. Democritus' account of evolution survives in the fifth book of *De rerum natura,* written by a 1st-century-BC Roman poet, Lucretius. The credibility of both Democritus' and Darwin's accounts of evolution depends on the assumption that time is real and that its flow has been extraordinarily long.

Heracleitus had seen in phenomena a harmony of opposites in tension with each other and had concluded that War (*i.e.,* Empedocles' Strife and the Chinese Yang) "is father of all and king of all." This vision of Strife as being the dominant and creative force is grimmer than that of Strife alternating on equal terms with Love and Yang with Yin. In the 19th-century West, Heracleitus' vision has been revived in the view of G.W.F. Hegel, a German Idealist, that progress occurs through a synthesis resulting from an encounter between a thesis and an antithesis. In political terms, Heracleitus' vision has reappeared in Karl Marx's concept of an encounter between the bourgeoisie and the proletariat and the emergence of a classless society without a government.

Apocalyptic views

In the Zoroastrian and Jewish-Christian-Islāmic vision of the time flow, time is destined to be consummated—as depicted luridly in the Revelation to John—in a terrifying climax. It has become apparent that history has been accelerating, and accumulated knowledge of the past has revealed, in retrospect, that the acceleration began about 30,000 years ago, with the transition from the Lower to the Upper Paleolithic Period, and that it has taken successive "great leaps forward" with the invention of agriculture, with the dawn of civilization, and with the progressive harnessing—within the last two centuries—of the titanic physical forces of inanimate nature. The approach of the climax foreseen intuitively by the prophets is being felt, and feared, as a coming event. Its imminence is, today, not an article of faith but a datum of observation and experience. (A.J.T.)

EARLY MODERN AND 19TH-CENTURY SCIENTIFIC PHILOSOPHIES OF TIME

Isaac Newton distinguished absolute time from "relative, apparent, and common time" as measured by the apparent motions of the fixed stars, as well as by terrestrial clocks. His absolute time was an ideal scale of time that made the laws of mechanics simpler, and its discrepancy with apparent time was attributed to such things as irregularities in the motion of the Earth. Insofar as these motions were explained by Newton's mechanics (or at least could not be shown to be inexplicable), the procedure was vindicated. Similarly, in his notion of absolute space, Newton was really getting at the concept of an inertial system. Nevertheless, the notion of space and time as absolute metaphysical entities was encouraged by Newton's views and formed an important part of the philosophy of Immanuel Kant, a German critical philosopher, for whom space and time were "phenomenally real" (part of the world as described by science) but "noumenally unreal" (not a part of the unknowable world of things in themselves). Kant argued for the noumenal unreality of space and time on the basis of certain antinomies that he claimed to find in these notions—that the universe had a beginning, for example, and yet (by another argument) could not have had a beginning. In a letter dated 1798, he wrote that the antinomies had been instrumental in arousing him from his "dogmatic slumber" (pre-critical philosophy). Modern advances in logic and mathematics, however, have convinced most philosophers that the antinomies contain fallacies.

Static versus dynamic systems

Newtonian mechanics, as studied in the 18th century, was mostly concerned with periodic systems that, on a large scale, remain constant throughout time. Particularly notable was the proof of the stability of the solar system that was formulated by Pierre-Simon, marquis de Laplace, a mathematical astronomer. Interest in systems that develop through time came about in the 19th century as a result of the theories of the British geologist Sir Charles Lyell, and others, and the Darwinian theory of evolution. These theories led to a number of biologically inspired metaphysical systems, which were often—as with Henri Bergson and Alfred North Whitehead—rather romantic and contrary to the essentially mechanistic spirit of Darwin himself (and also of present-day molecular biology).

Contemporary philosophies of time

TIME IN 20TH-CENTURY PHILOSOPHY OF PHYSICS

Minkowski space–time and Lorentz transformations

Time in the special theory of relativity. Since the classic interpretation of Einstein's special theory of relativity by Hermann Minkowski, a Lithuanian-German mathematician, it has been clear that physics has to do not with two entities, space and time, taken separately, but with a unitary entity space–time, in which, however, timelike and spacelike directions can be distinguished. The Lorentz transformations, which in special relativity define shifts in velocity perspectives, were shown by Minkowski to be simply rotations of space–time axes. The Lorentz contraction of moving rods and the time dilatation of moving clocks turns out to be analogous to the fact that different-sized slices of a sausage are obtained by altering the direction of the slice: just as there is still the objective (absolute) sausage, so also Minkowski restores the absolute to relativity in the form of the invariant four-dimensional object, and the invariance (under the Lorentz transformation) of the space–time interval and of certain fundamental physical quantities such as action (which has the dimensions of energy times time, even though neither energy nor time is separately invariant).

Possible fifth-dimensional hypertime

Process philosophers charge the Minkowski universe with being a static one. The philosopher of the manifold denies this charge, saying that a static universe would be one in which all temporal cross sections were exactly similar to one another and in which all particles (considered as four-dimensional objects) lay along parallel lines. The actual universe is not like this, and that it is not static is shown in the Minkowski picture by the dissimilarity of temporal cross sections and the nonparallelism of the world lines of particles. The process philosopher may say that change, as thus portrayed in the Minkowski picture (*e.g.,* with the world lines of particles at varying distances from one another), is not true Bergsonian change, so that something has been left out. But if time advances up the manifold, this would seem to be an advance with respect to a hypertime, perhaps a new time direction orthogonal to the old one. Perhaps it could be a fifth dimension, as has been used in describing the de Sitter universe as a four-dimensional hypersurface in a five-dimensional space. The question may be asked, however, what advantage such a hypertime could have for the process philosopher and whether there is process through hypertime. If there is, one would seem to need a hyper-hypertime, and so on to infinity. (The infinity of hypertimes was indeed postulated by John William Dunne, a British inventor and philosopher, but the remedy seems to be a desperate one.) And if no such regress into hypertimes is postulated, it may be asked whether the process philosopher would not find the five-dimensional universe as static as the four-dimensional one. The process philosopher may therefore adopt the expedient of Henri Bergson, saying that temporal process (the extra something that makes the difference between a static and a dynamic universe) just cannot be pictured spatially (whether one supposes four, five, or more dimensions). According to Bergson, it is something that just has to be intuited and cannot be grasped by discursive reason. The philosopher of the manifold will find this unintelligible and will in any case deny that anything dynamic *has* been left out of his world picture. This sort of impasse between process philosophers and philosophers of the manifold seems to be characteristic of the present-day state of philosophy.

The theory of relativity implies that simultaneity is relative to a frame of axes. If one frame of axes is moving relative to another, then events that are simultaneous relative to the first are not simultaneous relative to the second, and vice versa. This paradox leads to another difficulty for process philosophy over and above those noted earlier. Those who think that there is a continual coming into existence of events (as the present rushes onward into the future) can be asked "Which present?" It therefore seems difficult to make a distinction between a real present (and perhaps past) as against an as-yet-unreal future. Philosophers of the manifold also urge that to talk of events becoming (coming into existence) is not easily intelligible. Enduring things and processes, in this view, can come into existence; but this simply means that as four-dimensional solids they have an earliest temporal cross section or time slice.

When talking in the fashion of Minkowski, it is advisable, according to philosophers of the manifold, to use tenseless verbs (such as the "equals" in "2 + 2 equals 4"). One can say that all parts of the four-dimensional world exist (in this tenseless sense). This is not, therefore, to say that they all exist *now,* nor does it mean that Minkowski events are "timeless." The tenseless verb merely refrains from dating events in relation to its own utterance.

The clock paradox

The power of the Minkowski representation is illustrated by its manner in dealing with the so-called clock paradox, which deals with two twins, Peter and Paul. Peter remains on Earth (regarded as at rest in an inertial system) while Paul is shot off in a rocket at half the velocity of light, rapidly decelerated at Alpha Centauri (about four light-years away), and shot back to Earth again at the same speed. Assuming that the period of turnabout is negligible compared with those of uniform velocity, Paul, as a four-dimensional object, lies along the sides AC and CB of a space–time triangle, in which A and B are the points of his departure and return and C that of his turnaround. Peter, as a four-dimensional object, lies along AB. Now, special relativity implies that on his return Paul will be rather more than two years younger than Peter. This is a matter of two sides of a triangle not being equal to the third side: AC + CB < AB. The "less than"—symbolized <—arises from the semi-Euclidean character of Minkowski space–time, which calls for minus signs in its metric (or expression for the interval between two events, which is

$$ds = \sqrt{c^2dt^2 - dx^2 - dy^2 - dz^2}\ ).$$

The paradox has been held to result from the fact that, from Paul's point of view, it is Peter who has gone off and returned; and so the situation is symmetrical, and Peter and Paul should each be younger than the other—which is impossible. This is to forget, however, the asymmetry reflected in the fact that Peter has been in only one inertial system throughout, and Paul has not; Paul lies along a bent line, Peter along a straight one.

Time in general relativity and cosmology. In general relativity, which, though less firmly established than the special theory, is intended to explain gravitational phenomena, a more complicated metric of variable curvature is employed, which approximates to the Minkowski metric in empty space far from material bodies. Cosmologists who have based their theories on general relativity have sometimes postulated a finite but unbounded space–time (analogous, in four dimensions, to the surface of a sphere) as far as spacelike directions are concerned, but practically all cosmologists have assumed that space–time is infinite in its timelike directions. Kurt Gödel, a contemporary mathematical logician, however, has proposed solutions to the equations of general relativity whereby timelike world lines can bend back on themselves. Unless one accepts a process philosophy and thinks of the flow of time as going around and around such closed timelike world lines, it is not necessary to think that Gödel's idea implies eternal recurrence. Events can be arranged in a circle and still occur only once.

Dilatation of time in gravitational fields and black holes

The general theory of relativity predicts a time dilatation in a gravitational field, so that, relative to someone outside of the field, clocks (or atomic processes) go slowly. This retardation is a consequence of the curvature of space–time with which the theory identifies the gravitational field. As a very rough analogy, a road may be considered that, after crossing a plain, goes over a mountain. Clearly, one mile as measured on the humpbacked surface of the mountain is less than one mile as measured horizontally. Similarly—if "less" is replaced by "more" because of the negative signs in the expression for the metric of space–time—one second as measured in the curved region of space–time is more than one second as measured in a flat region. Strange things can happen if the gravitational field is very intense. It has been deduced that so-called black holes in space may occur in places where extraordinarily massive or dense aggregates of matter exist, as in the gravitational collapse of a star. Nothing, not even radiation, can emerge from such a black hole. A critical point is the so-called Schwarzschild radius measured outward from the centre of the collapsed star—a distance, perhaps, of the order of 10 kilometres. Something falling into the hole would take an infinite time to reach this critical radius, according to the space–time frame of reference of a distant observer, but only a finite time in the frame of reference of the falling body itself. From the outside standpoint thc fall has become frozen. But from the point of view of the frame of the falling object, the fall continues to zero radius in a very short time indeed—of the order of only 10 or 100 microseconds. Within the black hole spacelike and timelike directions change over, so that to escape again from the black hole is impossible for reasons analogous to those that, in ordinary space–time, make it impossible to travel faster than light. (To travel faster than light a body would have to lie—as a four-dimensional object—in a spacelike direction instead of a timelike one.)

Time beyond infinite time

As a rough analogy two country roads may be considered, both of which go at first in a northerly direction. But road A bends round asymptotically toward the east;

i.e., it approaches ever closer to a line of latitude. Soon road B crosses this latitude and is thus to the north of all parts of road A. Disregarding the Earth's curvature, it takes infinite space for road A to get as far north as that latitude on road B; *i.e.,* near that latitude an infinite number of "road A northerly units" (say, miles) correspond to a finite number of road B units. Soon road B gets "beyond infinity" in road A units, though it need be only a finite road.

Rather similarly, if a body should fall into a black hole, it would fall for only a finite time, even though it were "beyond infinite" time by external standards. This analogy does not do justice, however, to the real situation in the black hole—the fact that the curvature becomes infinite as the star collapses toward a point. It should, however, help to alleviate the mystery of how a finite time in one reference frame can go "beyond infinity" in another frame.

Expanding universe; creation; τ time

Most cosmological theories imply that the universe is expanding, with the galaxies receding from one another (as is made plausible by observations of the red shifts of their spectra), and that the universe as it is known originated in a primeval explosion at a date of the order of 15×10^9 years ago. Though this date is often loosely called "the creation of the universe," there is no reason to deny that the universe (in the philosophical sense of "everything that there is") existed at an earlier time, even though it may be impossible to know anything of what happened then. (There have been cosmologies, however, that suggest an oscillating universe, with explosion, expansion, contraction, explosion, etc., ad infinitum.) And *a fortiori,* there is no need to say—as Augustine did in his *Confessions* as early as the 5th century AD—that time itself was created along with the creation of the universe, though it should not too hastily be assumed that this would lead to absurdity, because common sense could well be misleading at this point.

A British cosmologist, E.A. Milne, however, proposed a theory according to which time in a sense could not extend backward beyond the creation time. According to him there are two scales of time, "τ time" and "t time." The former is a time scale within which the laws of mechanics and gravitation are invariant, and the latter is a scale within which those of electromagnetic and atomic phenomena are invariant. According to Milne τ is proportional to the logarithm of t (taking the zero of t to be the creation time); thus, by τ time the creation is infinitely far in the past. The logarithmic relationship implies that the constant of gravitation G would increase throughout cosmic history. (This increase might have been expected to show up in certain geological data, but apparently the evidence is against it.)

Time in microphysics. Special problems arise in considering time in quantum mechanics and in particle interactions.

Quantum-mechanical aspects of time. In quantum mechanics it is usual to represent measurable quantities by operators in an abstract many-dimensional (often infinite-dimensional) so-called Hilbert space. Nevertheless, this space is an abstract mathematical tool for calculating the evolution in time of the energy levels of systems—and this evolution occurs in ordinary space–time. For example, in the formula $AH - HA = i\hbar(dA/dt)$, in which i is $\sqrt{-1}$ and $\hbar$ is $1/2\pi$ times Planck's constant, h, the A and H are operators, but the t is a perfectly ordinary time variable. There may be something unusual, however, about the concept of the time at which quantum-mechanical events occur, because according to the Copenhagen interpretation of quantum mechanics the state of a microsystem is relative to an experimental arrangement. Thus energy and time are conjugate: no experimental arrangement can determine both simultaneously, for the energy is relative to one experimental arrangement, and the time is relative to another. (Thus, a more relational sense of "time" is suggested.) The states of the experimental arrangement cannot be merely relative to other experimental arrangements, on pain of infinite regress; and so these have to be described by classical physics. (This parasitism on classical physics is a possible weakness in quantum mechanics over which there is much controversy.)

Conjugate relation of energy and time

The relation between time uncertainty and energy uncertainty, in which their product is equal to or greater than $h/4\pi$, $\Delta E \Delta t \geqslant h/4\pi$, has led to estimates of the theoretical minimum measurable span of time, which comes to something of the order of 10^{-24} second and hence to speculations that time may be made up of discrete intervals (chronons). These suggestions are open to a very serious objection, viz., that the mathematics of quantum mechanics makes use of continuous space and time (for example, it contains differential equations). It is not easy to see how it could possibly be recast so as to postulate only a discrete space–time (or even a merely dense one). For a set of instants to be dense, there must be an instant between any two instants. For it to be a continuum, however, something more is required, viz., that every set of instants earlier (later) than any given one should have an upper (lower) bound. It is continuity that enables modern mathematics to surmount the paradox of extension framed by the Pre-Socratic Eleatic Zeno—a paradox comprising the question of how a finite interval can be made up of dimensionless points or instants.

Time in particle interactions. Until recently it was thought that the fundamental laws of nature are time symmetrical. It is true that the second law of thermodynamics, according to which randomness always increases, is time asymmetrical; but this law is not strictly true (for example, the phenomenon of Brownian motion contravenes it), and it is now regarded as a statistical derivative of the fundamental laws together with certain boundary conditions. The fundamental laws of physics were long thought also to be charge symmetrical (for example, an antiproton together with a positron behave like a proton and electron) and to be symmetrical with respect to parity (reflection in space, as in a mirror). The experimental evidence now suggests that all three symmetries are not quite exact but that the laws of nature are symmetrical if all three reflections are combined: charge, parity, and time reflections forming what can be called (after the initials of the three parameters) a CPT mirror. The time asymmetry was shown in certain abstruse experiments concerning the decay of K mesons that have a short time decay into two pions and a long time decay into three pions.

Charge–parity–time symmetry

Time in molar physics. The above-mentioned violations of temporal symmetry in the fundamental laws of nature are such out-of-the-way ones, however, that it seems unlikely that they are responsible for the gross violations of temporal symmetry that are apparent in the visible world. An obvious asymmetry is that there are traces of the past (footprints, fossils, tape recordings, memories) and not of the future. There are mixing processes but no comparable unmixing process: milk and tea easily combine to give a whitish brown liquid, but it requires ingenuity and energy and complicated apparatus to separate the two liquids. A cold saucepan of water on a hot brick will soon become a tepid saucepan on a tepid brick; but the heat energy of the tepid saucepan never goes into the tepid brick to produce a cold saucepan and a hot brick. Even though the laws of nature are assumed to be time symmetrical, it is possible to explain these asymmetries by means of suitable assumptions about boundary conditions. Much discussion of this problem has stemmed from the work of Ludwig Boltzmann, an Austrian physicist, who showed that the concept of the thermodynamic quantity entropy could be reduced to that of randomness or disorder. Among 20th-century philosophers in this tradition may be mentioned Hans Reichenbach, a German-U.S. Positivist, Adolf Grünbaum, a U.S. philosopher, and Olivier Costa de Beauregard, a French philosopher-physicist. There have also been many relevant papers of high mathematical sophistication scattered through the literature of mathematical physics. Reichenbach (and Grünbaum, who improved on Reichenbach in some respects) explained a trace as being a branch system; *i.e.,* a relatively isolated system, the entropy of which is less than would be expected if one compared it with that of the surrounding region. For example, a footprint on the beach has sand particles compressed together below a volume containing air only, instead of being quite evenly (randomly) spread over the volume occupied by the compressed and empty parts.

Statistics, causality, and the molar clock

Another striking temporal asymmetry on the macro level, viz., that spherical waves are often observed being emitted from a source but never contracting to a sink, has been stressed by Sir Karl Popper, a 20th-century Austrian and British philosopher of science. By considering radiation as having a particle aspect (*i.e.*, as consisting of photons), Costa de Beauregard has argued that this "principle of retarded waves" can be reduced to the statistical Boltzmann principle of increasing entropy and so is not really different from the previously discussed asymmetry. These considerations also provide some justification for the common-sense idea that the cause–effect relation is a temporally unidirectional one, even though the laws of nature themselves allow for retrodiction no less than for prediction.

A third striking asymmetry on the macro level is that of the apparent mutual recession of the galaxies, which can plausibly be deduced from the red shifts observed in their spectra. It is still not clear whether or how far this asymmetry can be reduced to the two asymmetries already discussed, though interesting suggestions have been made.

The statistical considerations that explain temporal asymmetry apply only to large assemblages of particles. Hence, any device that records time intervals will have to be macroscopic and to make use somewhere of statistically irreversible processes. Even if one were to count the swings of a frictionless pendulum, this counting would require memory traces in the brain, which would function as a temporally irreversible recording device.

TIME IN 20TH-CENTURY PHILOSOPHY OF BIOLOGY AND PHILOSOPHY OF MIND

Organisms often have some sort of internal clock that regulates their behaviour. There is a tendency, for example, for leaves of leguminous plants to alter their position so that they lie in one position by day and in another position by night. This tendency persists if the plant is in artificial light that is kept constant, though it can be modified to other periodicities (*e.g.*, to a six-hour instead of a 24-hour rhythm) by suitably regulating the periods of artificial light and darkness. In animals, similar daily rhythms are usually acquired, but in experimental conditions animals nevertheless tend to adapt better to a 24-hour rhythm than to any other. Sea anemones expand and contract to the rhythm of the tides, and this periodic behaviour will persist for some time even when the sea anemone is placed in a tank. Bees can be trained to come for food at fixed periods (*e.g.*, every 21 hours), and this demonstrates that they possess some sort of internal clock. Similarly, humans themselves have some power to estimate time in the absence of clocks and other sensory cues. This fact refutes the contention of the 17th-century English philosopher John Locke (and of other philosophers in the Empiricist tradition) that time is perceived only as a relation between successive sensations. The U.S. mathematician Norbert Wiener has speculated on the possibility that the human time sense depends on the α-rhythm of electrical oscillation in the brain.

Biological rhythms

Temporal rhythms in both plants and animals (including humans) are dependent on temperature, and experiments on human subjects have shown that, if their temperature is raised, they underestimate the time between events.

Despite these facts, the Lockean notion that the estimation of time depends on the succession of sensations is still to some degree true. People who take the drugs hashish and mescaline, for example, may feel their sensations following one another much more rapidly. Because there are so many more sensations than normal in a given interval of time, time seems to drag, so that a minute may feel like an hour. Similar illusions about the spans of time occur in dreams.

It is unclear whether most discussions of so-called biological and psychological time have much significance for metaphysics. As far as the distorted experiences of time that arise through drugs (and in schizophrenia) are concerned, it can be argued that there is nothing surprising in the fact that pathological states can make people misestimate periods of time, and so it can be claimed that facts of this sort do not shed any more light on the philosophy of time than facts about mountains looking near after rainstorms and looking far after duststorms shed on the philosophy of space.

The idea that psychological studies of temporal experience are philosophically important is probably connected with the sort of Empiricism that was characteristic of Locke and still more of the Empiricists George Berkeley and David Hume and their successors. The idea of time had somehow to be constructed out of the primitive experience of ideas succeeding one another. Nowadays, concept formation is thought of as more of a social phenomenon involved in the "picking up" of a language; thus, contemporary philosophers have tended to see the problem differently: humans do not have to construct their concepts from their own immediate sensations. Even so, the learning of temporal concepts surely does at least involve an immediate apprehension of the relation of "earlier" and "later." A mere succession of sensations, however, will go no way toward yielding the idea of time: if one sensation has vanished entirely before the other is in consciousness, one cannot be immediately aware of the succession of sensations. What Empiricism needs, therefore, as a basis for constructing the idea of time is an experience of succession as opposed to a succession of experiences. Hence, two or more ideas that are related by "earlier than" must be experienced in one single act of awareness. William James, a U.S. Pragmatist philosopher and also a pioneer psychologist, popularized the term *specious present* for the span of time covered by a single act of awareness. His idea was that at a given moment of time a person is aware of events a short time before that time. (Sometimes he spoke of the specious present as a saddleback looking slightly into the future as well as slightly into the past, but this was inconsistent with his idea that the specious present depended on lingering short-term memory processes in the brain.) He referred to experiments by the German psychologist Wilhelm Wundt that showed that the longest group of arbitrary sounds that a person could identify without error lasted about six seconds. Other criteria perhaps involving other sense modalities might lead to slightly different spans of time, but the interesting point is that, if there is such a specious present, it cannot be explained solely by ordinary memory traces: if one hears a "ticktock" of a clock, the "tick" is not remembered in the way in which a "ticktock" 10 minutes ago is remembered. The specious present is perhaps not really specious: the idea that it was specious depended on an idea that the real (nonspecious) present had to be instantaneous. If perception is considered as a certain reliable way of being caused to have true beliefs about the environment by sensory stimulation, there is no need to suppose that these true beliefs have to be about an instantaneous state of the world. It can therefore be questioned whether the term *specious* is a happy one.

Time-consciousness

Two matters discussed earlier in connection with the philosophy of physics have implications for the philosophy of mind: (1) the integration of space and time in the theory of relativity makes it harder to conceive of immaterial minds that exist in time but are not even localizable in space; (2) the statistical explanation of temporal asymmetry explains why the brain has memory traces of the past but not of the future and, hence, helps to explain the unidirectional nature of temporal consciousness. It also gives reasons for skepticism about the claims of parapsychologists to have experimental evidence for precognition; or it shows, at least, that if these phenomena do exist they are not able to be fitted into a cosmology based on physics as it exists today. (J.J.C.S.)

Time as systematized in modern scientific society

TIME MEASUREMENT: GENERAL CONCEPTS

Accuracy in specifying time is needed for civil, industrial, and scientific purposes. Although defining time presents difficulties, measuring it does not; it is the most accurately measured physical quantity. A time measurement assigns a unique number to either an epoch, which specifies the moment when an instantaneous event occurs, in the sense of time of day, or a time interval, which is the duration of a continued event. The progress of any phenomenon that undergoes regular changes may be used to measure time. Such phenomena make up much of the subject matter of astronomy, physics, chemistry, geology, and biology. The following sections of this article treat time measurements based on manifestations of gravitation, electromagnetism, rotational inertia, and radioactivity.

Series of events can be referred to a time scale, which is an ordered set of times derived from observations of some phenomenon. Two independent, fundamental time scales are those called dynamical—based on the regularity of the motions of celestial bodies fixed in their orbits by gravitation—and atomic—based on the characteristic frequency of electromagnetic radiation emitted or absorbed in quantum transitions between internal energy states of atoms or molecules.

Fundamental time scales

Two time scales that have no relative secular acceleration are called equivalent. That is, a clock displaying the time according to one of these scales would not—over an extended interval—show a change in its rate relative to that of a clock displaying time according to the other scale. It is not certain whether the dynamical and atomic scales are equivalent, but present definitions treat them as being so.

The Earth's daily rotation about its own axis provides a time scale, but one that is not equivalent to the fundamental scales because tidal friction inexorably decreases the Earth's rotational speed (symbolized by the Greek letter omega, ω). There are also other sources of variation. Rotational time is needed for civil purposes, celestial navigation, and tracking of space vehicles.

The decay of radioactive elements is a random, rather than a repetitive, process, but the statistical reliability of the time required for the disappearance of any given fraction of a particular element can be used for measuring long time intervals.

Principal scales. Numerous time scales have been formed; several important ones are described in detail in subsequent sections of this article. The abbreviations given here are derived from English or French terms. Universal Time (UT; the mean solar time of the meridian of Greenwich, England), Coordinated Universal Time (UTC; the basis of legal, civil time), and leap seconds are treated under the heading *Rotational time.* Ephemeris Time (ET; the first correct dynamical time scale) is treated in the section *Dynamical time,* as are Barycentric Dynamical Time (TDB) and Terrestrial Dynamical Time (TDT), which are more accurate than Ephemeris Time because they take relativity into account. International Atomic Time (TAI; introduced in 1955) is covered in the section *Atomic time.*

Relativistic effects. Accuracies of atomic clocks and modern observational techniques are so high that the small differences between classical mechanics (as developed by Newton in the 17th century) and relativistic mechanics (according to the special and general theories of relativity proposed by Einstein in the early 20th century) must be taken into account. The equations of motion that define TDB include relativistic terms. The atomic clocks that form TAI, however, are corrected only for height above sea level, not for periodic relativistic variations, because all fixed terrestrial clocks are affected identically. TAI and TDT differ from TDB by calculable periodic variations.

Apparent positions of celestial objects, as tabulated in ephemerides, are corrected for the Sun's gravitational deflection of light rays.

Clocks. The atomic clock is the only object that both generates a precise time scale and tells time. It has made possible new, highly accurate techniques for measuring time and distance. These techniques, involving radar, lasers, spacecraft, radio telescopes, and pulsars, have been applied to the study of problems in celestial mechanics, astrophysics, relativity, and cosmogony.

Atomic clocks serve as the basis of scientific and legal clock times. A single clock, atomic or quartz-crystal, synchronized with either TAI or UTC provides the SI second (that is, the second as defined in the International System of Units), TAI, UTC, and TDT immediately with high accuracy.

Time units and calendar divisions. The familiar subdivision of the day into 24 hours, the hour into 60 minutes, and the minute into 60 seconds is of ancient origins but has come into general use since about AD 1600. When the increasing accuracy of clocks led to the adoption of the mean solar day, which contained 86,400 seconds, this mean solar second became the basic unit of time. The adoption of the SI second, defined on the basis of atomic phenomena, as the fundamental time unit has necessitated some changes in the definitions of other terms.

In this article, unless otherwise indicated, second (symbolized s) means the SI second; a minute (m or min) is 60 s; an hour (h) is 60 m or 3,600 s. An astronomical day (d) equals 86,400 s. An ordinary calendar day equals 86,400 s, and a leap-second calendar day equals 86,401 s. A common year contains 365 calendar days and a leap year, 366.

The system of consecutively numbering the years of the Christian Era was devised by Dionysius Exiguus in about 525; it included the reckoning of dates as either AD or BC (the year before AD 1 was 1 BC). The Julian calendar, introduced by Julius Caesar in the 1st century BC, was then in use, and any year whose number was exactly divisible by four was designated a leap year. In the Gregorian calendar, introduced in 1582 and now in general use, the centurial years are common years unless their numbers are exactly divisible by 400; thus, 1600 was a leap year, but 1700 was not.

Leap years

Lengths of years and months. The tropical year, whose period is that of the seasons, is the interval between successive passages of the Sun through the vernal equinox. Because the Earth's motion is perturbed by the gravitational attraction of the other planets and because of an acceleration in precession, the tropical year decreases slowly, as shown by comparing its length at the end of the 19th century (365.242196 d) with that at the end of the 20th (365.242190 d). The accuracy of the Gregorian calendar results from the close agreement between the length of its average year, 365.2425 calendar days, and that of the tropical year.

A calendar month may contain 28 to 31 calendar days; the average is 30.437. The synodic month, the interval from New Moon to New Moon, averages 29.531 d.

Astronomical years and dates. In the Julian calendar, a year contains either 365 or 366 days, and the average is 365.25 calendar days. Astronomers have adopted the term *Julian year* to denote an interval of 365.25 d, or 31,557,600 s. The corresponding Julian century equals 36,525 d. For convenience in specifying events separated by long intervals, astronomers use *Julian dates* (JD) in accordance with a system proposed in 1583 by the French classical scholar Joseph Scaliger and named in honour of his father, Julius Caesar Scaliger. In this system days are numbered consecutively from 0.0, which is identified as Greenwich mean noon of the day assigned the date Jan. 1, 4713 BC, by reckoning back according to the Julian calendar. The *modified Julian date* (MJD), defined by the equation MJD = JD − 2,400,000.5, begins at midnight rather than noon and, for the 20th and 21st centuries, is expressed by a number with fewer digits. For example, Greenwich mean noon of Nov. 14, 1981 (Gregorian calendar date), corresponds to JD 2,444,923.0; the preceding midnight occurred at JD 2,444,922.5 and MJD 44,922.0.

Historical details of the week, month, year, and various calendars are treated in the article CALENDAR.

ROTATIONAL TIME

The Earth's rotation causes the stars and the Sun to appear to rise each day in the east and set in the west. The apparent solar day is measured by the interval of time between two successive passages of the Sun across the observer's celestial meridian, the visible half of the great circle that passes through the zenith and the celestial poles. One sidereal day (very nearly) is measured by the interval of time between two similar passages of a star. Fuller treatments of astronomical reference points and planes are given in the articles STARS AND STAR CLUSTERS: *Astronomical maps;* and MECHANICS: *Celestial mechanics.*

The plane in which the Earth revolves about the Sun is called the ecliptic. As seen from the Earth, the Sun moves eastward on the ecliptic 360° per year, almost one degree per day. As a result, an apparent solar day is nearly four minutes longer, on the average, than a sidereal day. The difference varies, however, from 3 minutes 35 seconds to 4 minutes 26 seconds during the year because of the ellipticity of the Earth's orbit, in which at different times of the year it moves at slightly different rates, and because of the 23½° inclination of the ecliptic to the Equator. In consequence, apparent solar time is nonuniform with respect to dynamical time. A sundial indicates apparent solar time.

The introduction of clocks and watches during the 17th century made apparent solar time unsuitable for civil use. Therefore, mean solar time was introduced; it is defined below. The difference between apparent solar time and mean solar time, called the equation of time, varies from zero to about 16 minutes.

The measures of sidereal, apparent solar, and mean solar time are defined by the hour angles of certain points, real or fictitious, in the sky. Hour angle is the angle, taken to be positive to the west, measured along the celestial equator between an observer's meridian and the hour circle (a great circle passing through the poles) on which some celestial point or object lies. Hour angles are measured from zero through 24 hours.

Sidereal time is the hour angle of the vernal equinox, a reference point that is one of the two intersections of the celestial equator and the ecliptic. Because of a small periodic oscillation, or wobble, of the Earth's axis, called nutation, there is a distinction between the true and mean equinoxes. The difference between true and mean sidereal times, defined by the two equinoxes, varies from zero to about one second.

Mean solar time

Apparent solar time is the hour angle of the centre of the true Sun plus 12 hours. Mean solar time is 12 hours plus the hour angle of the centre of the fictitious mean Sun. This is a point that moves along the celestial equator with constant speed and that coincides with the true Sun on the average. In practice, mean solar time is not obtained from observations of the Sun. Instead, sidereal time is determined from observations of the transit across the meridian of stars, and the result is transformed by means of a quadratic formula to obtain mean solar time.

Standard time. Local mean solar time depends upon longitude; it is advanced by four minutes per degree eastward. In 1869 Charles F. Dowd, principal of a school in Saratoga Springs, N.Y., proposed the use of time zones, within which all localities would keep the same time. Others, including Sir Sandford Fleming, a Canadian civil engineer, strongly advocated this idea. Time zones were adopted by U.S. and Canadian railroads in 1883.

In October 1884 an international conference held in Washington, D.C., adopted the meridian of the transit instrument at the Royal Observatory, Greenwich, as the prime, or zero, meridian. This led to the adoption of 24 standard time zones; the boundaries are determined by local authorities and in many places deviate considerably from the 15° intervals of longitude implicit in the original idea. The times in different zones differ by an integral number of hours; minutes and seconds are the same.

The International Date Line is a zigzag line in the mid-Pacific Ocean near 180° longitude. When one travels across it westward a calendar day is added; one day is dropped in passing eastward.

During World War I, daylight-saving time was adopted in various countries; clocks were advanced one hour to save fuel by reducing the need for artificial light in evening hours. During World War II, all clocks in the United States were kept one hour ahead of standard time for the interval Feb. 9, 1942–Sept. 30, 1945, with no changes made in summer. Beginning in 1967, by act of Congress, the United States has observed daylight-saving time in summer, though state legislatures retain the power to pass exempting laws, and a few have done so.

Reckoning of days and hours. The day begins at midnight and runs through 24 hours. In the 24-hour system of reckoning, used in Europe and by military agencies of the United States, the hours and minutes are given as a four-digit number. Thus 0028 means 28 minutes past midnight, and 1240 means 40 minutes past noon. Also, 2400 of May 15 is the same as 0000 of May 16. This system allows no uncertainty as to the epoch designated.

In the 12-hour system there are two sets of 12 hours; those from midnight to noon are designated AM (ante meridiem, "before noon"), and those from noon to midnight are designated PM (post meridiem, "after noon"). The use of AM and PM to designate either noon or midnight can cause ambiguity. To designate noon, either the word noon or 1200 or 12 M should be used. To designate midnight without causing ambiguity, the two dates between which it falls should be given unless the 24-hour notation is used. Thus, midnight may be written: May 15–16 or 2400 May 15 or 0000 May 16.

Universal Time. Until 1928 the standard time of the zero meridian was called Greenwich Mean Time (GMT), and in accord with astronomical tradition the epoch 0000 GMT occurred at noon. In 1925 the numbering system was changed so that the day began at midnight, as does the civil day. To alleviate the resulting confusion, in 1928 the International Astronomical Union (IAU) adopted the term Universal Time (UT).

In 1955 the IAU defined several kinds of UT. The initial values of Universal Time obtained at various observatories, denoted UT0, differ slightly because of polar motion. A correction is added for each observatory to convert UT0 into UT1. An empirical correction to take account of annual changes in the speed of rotation is then added to convert UT1 to UT2. UT2 has since been superseded by atomic time.

Precise values of UT1, which give the Earth's rotational position in space, are derived by the Bureau International de l'Heure (BIH) from values determined at about 75 observatories.

Variations in the Earth's rotation rate. The Earth does not rotate with perfect uniformity, and the variations have been classified as (1) secular, resulting from tidal friction, (2) irregular, ascribed to motions of the Earth's core, and (3) periodic, caused by seasonal meteorological phenomena.

Separating the first two categories is very difficult. Observations made since 1621, after the introduction of the telescope, show irregular fluctuations about a decade in duration and a long one that began about 1650 and is not yet complete. The large amplitude of this effect makes it impossible to determine the secular variation from data accumulated during an interval of only about four centuries. The record is supplemented, however, by reports—not always reliable—of eclipses that occurred tens of centuries ago. From this extended set of information it is found that, relative to dynamical time, the length of the mean solar day increases secularly about 1.6 milliseconds per century, the rate of the Earth's rotation decreases about one part per million in 5,000 years, and rotational time loses about 30 seconds per century squared.

Changing length of the day

The annual seasonal term, nearly periodic, has a coefficient of about 25 milliseconds.

Coordinated Universal Time; leap seconds. The time and frequency broadcasts of the United Kingdom and the United States were coordinated (synchronized) in 1960. As required, adjustments were made in frequency, relative to atomic time, and in epoch to keep the broadcast signals close to the UT scale. This program expanded in 1964 under the auspices of the IAU into a worldwide system called Coordinated Universal Time (UTC).

Since Jan. 1, 1972, the UTC frequency has been the TAI frequency, the difference between TAI and UTC has been kept at some integral number of seconds, and the difference between UT1 and UTC has been kept within 0.9 second by inserting a leap second into UTC as needed. This is done by making the last minute of a month, preferably June or December, contain 61 seconds.

About one leap second per year has been inserted since 1972. Estimates of the loss per year of UT1 relative to TAI due to tidal friction range from 0.7 second in 1900 to 1.3 seconds in 2000. Irregular fluctuations cause unpredictable gains or losses; these have not exceeded 0.3 second per year.

Time determination. The classical, astrometric methods of obtaining UT0 are, in essence, determinations of the instant at which a star crosses the local celestial meridian. Instruments used include the transit, the photographic zenith tube, and the prismatic astrolabe.

The transit is a small telescope that can be moved only in the plane of the meridian. The observer generates a signal at the instant that the image of the star is seen to cross a very thin cross hair aligned in the meridian plane. The signal is recorded on a chronograph that simultaneously displays the readings of the clock that is being checked.

The photographic zenith tube (PZT) is a telescope permanently mounted in a precisely vertical position. The light from a star passing almost directly overhead is refracted by the lens, reflected from the perfectly horizontal surface of a pool of mercury, and brought to a focus just beneath the lens. A photographic plate records the images of the star at clock times close to that at which it crosses the meridian. The vertical alignment of the PZT minimizes the effects of atmospheric refraction. From the positions of the images on the plate, the time at which the star transits the meridian can be accurately compared with the clock time. The distance of the star from the zenith (north or south) also can be ascertained. This distance varies slightly from year to year and is a measure of the latitude variation caused by the slight movement of the Earth's axis of rotation relative to its crust.

The prismatic astrolabe is a refinement of the instrument used since antiquity for measuring the altitude of a star above the horizon. The modern device consists of a horizontal telescope into which the light from the star is reflected from two surfaces of a prism that has three faces at 60° angles. The light reaches one of these faces directly from the star; it reaches the other after reflection from the surface of a pool of mercury. The light traversing the separate paths is focused to form two images of the star that coincide when the star reaches the altitude of 60°. This instant is automatically recorded and compared with the reading of a clock. Like the PZT, the prismatic astrolabe detects the variation in the latitude of the observatory.

DYNAMICAL TIME

Dynamical time is defined descriptively as the independent variable, T, in the differential equations of motion of celestial bodies. The gravitational ephemeris of a planet tabulates its orbital position for values of T. Observation of the position of the planet makes it possible to consult the ephemeris and find the corresponding dynamical time.

The Moon as a time-keeper

The most sensitive index of dynamical time is the position of the Moon because of the rapid motion of that body across the sky. The equations that would exactly describe the motion of the Moon in the absence of tidal friction, however, must be slightly modified to account for the deceleration that this friction produces. The correction is made by adding an empirical term, aT^2, to the longitude, λ, given by gravitational theory. The need for this adjustment was not recognized for a long time.

The U.S. astronomer Simon Newcomb noted in 1878 that fluctuations in λ that he had found could be due to fluctuations in rotational time; he compiled a table of Δt, its difference from the time scale based on uniform rotation of the Earth. Realizing that nonuniform rotation of the Earth should also cause apparent fluctuations in the motion of Mercury, Newcomb searched for these in 1882 and 1896, but the observational errors were so large that he could not confirm his theory.

A large fluctuation in the Earth's rotational speed, ω, began about 1896, and its effects on the apparent motions of both the Moon and Mercury were described by the Scottish-born astronomer Robert T.A. Innes in 1925. Innes proposed a time scale based on the motion of the Moon, and his scale of Δt from 1677 to 1924, based on observations of Mercury, was the first true dynamical scale, later called Ephemeris Time.

Ephemeris Time. Further studies by the Dutch astronomer Willem de Sitter in 1927 and by Harold Spencer Jones (later Sir Harold, Astronomer Royal of England) in 1939 confirmed that ω had secular and irregular variations. Using their results, the U.S. astronomer Gerald M. Clemence in 1948 derived the equations needed to define a dynamical scale numerically and to convert measurements of the Moon's position into time values. The fundamental definition was based on the Earth's orbital motion as given by Newcomb's tables of the Sun of 1898. The IAU adopted the dynamical scale in 1952 and called it Ephemeris Time (ET). Clemence's equations were used to revise the lunar ephemeris published in 1919 by the U.S. mathematician Ernest W. Brown to form the *Improved Lunar Ephemeris* (ILE) of 1954.

Ephemeris second. The IAU in 1958 defined the second of Ephemeris Time as 1/31,556,925.9747 of the tropical year that began at the instant specified, in astronomers' terms, as 1900 January 0^d 12^h, "the instant, near the beginning of the calendar year AD 1900, when the geocentric mean longitude of the Sun was 279° 41′ 48″.04," that is, Greenwich noon on Dec. 31, 1899. In 1960 the General Conference of Weights and Measures (CGPM) adopted the same definition for the SI second.

Definition of the second

Since, however, 1900 was past, this definition could not be used to obtain the ET or SI second. It was obtained in practice from lunar observations and the ILE and was the basis of the redefinition, in 1967, of the SI second on the atomic time scale. The present SI second thus depends directly on the ILE.

The ET second defined by the ILE is based in a complex manner on observations made up to 1938 of the Sun, the Moon, Mercury, and Venus, referred to the variable, mean solar time. Observations show that the ET second equals the average mean solar second from 1750 to 1903.

TDB and TDT. In 1976 the IAU defined two scales for dynamical theories and ephemerides to be used in almanacs beginning in 1984.

Barycentric Dynamical Time (TDB) is the independent variable in the equations, including terms for relativity, of motion of the celestial bodies. The solution of these equations gives the rectangular coordinates of those bodies relative to the barycentre (centre of mass) of the solar system. (The barycentre does not coincide with the centre of the Sun but is displaced to a point near its surface in the direction of Jupiter.) Which theory of general relativity to use was not specified, so a family of TDB scales could be formed, but the differences in coordinates would be small.

Terrestrial Dynamical Time (TDT) is an auxiliary scale defined by the equation TDT = TAI + 32.184 s. Its unit is the SI second. The constant difference between TDT and TAI makes TDT continuous with ET for periods before TAI was defined (mid-1955). TDT is the time entry in apparent geocentric ephemerides.

The definitions adopted require that TDT = TDB − R, where R is the sum of the periodic, relativistic terms not included in TAI. Both the above equations for TDT can be valid only if dynamical and atomic times are equivalent (see below *Atomic time: SI second*).

Almanacs

For use in almanacs the barycentric coordinates of the Earth and a body at epoch TDB are transformed into the coordinates of the body as viewed from the centre of the Earth at the epoch TDT when a light ray from the body would arrive there. Almanacs tabulate these geocentric coordinates for equal intervals of TDT; since TDT is available immediately from TAI, comparisons between computed and observed positions are readily made.

Since Jan. 1, 1984, the principal ephemerides in *The Astronomical Almanac,* published jointly by the Royal Greenwich Observatory and the U.S. Naval Observatory, have been based on a highly accurate ephemeris compiled by the Jet Propulsion Laboratory, Pasadena, Calif., in cooperation with the Naval Observatory. This task involved the simultaneous numerical integration of the equations of motion of the Sun, the Moon, and the planets. The coordinates and velocities at a known time were based on very accurate distance measurements (made with the aid of radar, laser beams, and spacecraft), optical angular observations, and atomic clocks.

ATOMIC TIME

Basic principles. The German physicist Max Planck postulated in 1900 that the energy of an atomic oscillator is quantized; that is, it equals $h\nu$, where h is a constant (now called Planck's constant) and ν is the frequency. Einstein extended this concept in 1905, stating that electromagnetic radiation is localized in packets, later called photons, of frequency ν and energy $E = h\nu$. Niels Bohr of Denmark postulated in 1913 that atoms exist in states of discrete energy and that a transition between two states differing in energy by the amount ΔE is accompanied by absorption or emission of a photon that has a frequency $\nu = \Delta E/h$. For detailed information concerning the phenomena on which atomic time is based, see ELECTROMAGNETIC RADIATION; ATOMS: *Major ideas and discoveries;* MECHANICS: *Quantum mechanics.*

Atomic transitions

In an unperturbed atom, not affected by neighbouring atoms or external fields, the energies of the various states depend only upon intrinsic features of atomic structure, which are postulated not to vary. A transition between a pair of these states involves absorption or emission of a photon with a frequency ν_0, designated the fundamental frequency associated with that particular transition.

Atomic clocks. Transitions in many atoms and molecules involve sharply defined frequencies in the vicinity of 10^{10} hertz, and, after dependable methods of generating such frequencies were developed during World War II for microwave radar, they were applied to problems of timekeeping. In 1946 principles of the use of atomic and molecular transitions for regulating the frequency of electronic oscillators were described, and in 1947 an oscillator controlled by a quantum transition of the ammonia molecule was constructed. An ammonia-controlled clock was built in 1949 at the National Bureau of Standards, Washington, D.C.; in this clock the frequency did not vary by more than one part in 10^8. In 1954 an ammonia-regulated oscillator of even higher precision—the first maser—was constructed.

Cesium clocks. In 1938 the so-called resonance technique of manipulating a beam of atoms or molecules was introduced. This technique was adopted in several attempts to construct a cesium-beam atomic clock, and in 1955 the first such clock was placed in operation at the National Physical Laboratory, Teddington, Eng.

In practice, the most accurate control of frequency is achieved by detecting the interaction of radiation with atoms that can undergo some selected transition. From a beam of cesium vapour, a magnetic field first isolates a stream of atoms that can absorb microwaves of the fundamental frequency ν_0. Upon traversing the microwave field, some—not all—of these atoms do absorb energy, and a second magnetic field isolates these and steers them to a detector. The number of atoms reaching the detector is greatest when the microwave frequency exactly matches ν_0, and the detector response is used to regulate the microwave frequency. The frequency of the cesium clock is $\nu_t = \nu_0 + \Delta\nu$, where $\Delta\nu$ is the frequency shift caused by slight instrumental perturbations of the energy levels. This frequency shift can be determined accurately, and the circuitry of the clock is arranged so that ν_t is corrected to generate an operational frequency $\nu_0 + \varepsilon$, where ε is the error in the correction. The measure of the accuracy of the frequency-control system is the fractional error ε/ν_0, which is symbolized γ. Small, commercially built cesium clocks attain values of γ of ± 1 or 2×10^{-12}; in a large, laboratory-constructed clock, whose operation can be varied to allow experiments on factors that can affect the frequency, γ can be reduced to $\pm 5 \times 10^{-14}$.

Accuracy of atomic clocks

Between 1955 and 1958 the National Physical Laboratory and the U.S. Naval Observatory conducted a joint experiment to determine the frequency maintained by the cesium-beam clock at Teddington in terms of the ephemeris second, as established by precise observations of the Moon from Washington, D.C. The radiation associated with the particular transition of the cesium-133 atom was found to have the fundamental frequency ν_0 of 9,192,631,770 cycles per second of Ephemeris Time.

The merits of the cesium-beam atomic clock are that (1) the fundamental frequency that governs its operation is invariant; (2) its fractional error is extremely small; and (3) it is convenient to use. Several thousand commercially built cesium clocks, weighing about 70 pounds (32 kilograms) each, have been placed in operation. A few laboratories have built large cesium-beam oscillators and clocks to serve as primary standards of frequency.

Other atomic clocks. Clocks regulated by hydrogen masers have been developed at Harvard University. The frequency of some masers has been kept stable within about one part in 10^{14} for intervals of a few hours. The uncertainty in the fundamental frequency, however, is greater than the stability of the clock; this frequency is approximately 1,420,405,751.77 Hz. Atomic-beam clocks controlled by a transition of the rubidium atom have been developed, but the operational frequency depends on details of the structure of the clock, so that it does not have the absolute precision of the cesium-beam clock.

SI second. The CGPM redefined the second in 1967 to equal 9,192,631,770 periods of the radiation emitted or absorbed in the hyperfine transition of the cesium-133 atom; that is, the transition selected for control of the cesium-beam clock developed at the National Physical Laboratory. The definition implies that the atom should be in the unperturbed state at sea level. It makes the SI second equal to the ET second, determined from measurements of the position of the Moon, within the errors of observation. The definition will not be changed by any additional astronomical determinations.

Atomic time scales. An atomic time scale designated A.1, based on the cesium frequency discussed above, had been formed in 1958 at the U.S. Naval Observatory. Other local scales were formed, and about 1960 the BIH formed a scale based on these. In 1971 the CGPM designated the BIH scale as International Atomic Time (TAI).

The long-term frequency of TAI is based on about six cesium standards, operated continuously or periodically. About 175 commercially made cesium clocks are used also to form the day-to-day TAI scale. These clocks and standards are located at about 30 laboratories and observatories. It is estimated that the second of TAI reproduces the SI second, as defined, within about one part in 10^{13}. Two clocks that differ in rate by this amount would change in epoch by three milliseconds in 1,000 years.

Time and frequency dissemination. Precise time and frequency are broadcast by radio in many countries. Transmissions of time signals began as an aid to navigation in 1904; they are now widely used for many scientific and technical purposes. The seconds pulses are emitted on Coordinated Universal Time, and the frequency of the carrier wave is maintained at some known multiple of the cesium frequency.

Radio time signals

The accuracy of the signals varies from about one millisecond for high-frequency broadcasts to one microsecond for the precisely timed pulses transmitted by the stations of the navigation system loran-C. Trigger pulses of television broadcasts provide accurate synchronization for some areas. When precise synchronization is available a quartz-crystal clock suffices to maintain TAI accurately.

Cesium clocks carried aboard aircraft are used to synchronize clocks around the world within about 0.5 microsecond. Since 1962 artificial satellites have been used similarly for widely separated clocks.

Relativistic effects. A clock displaying TAI on Earth will have periodic, relativistic deviations from the dynamical scale TDB and from a pulsar time scale PS (see below *Pulsar time*). These variations, denoted R above, were demonstrated in 1982–84 by measurements of the pulsar PSR 1937+21.

The main contributions to R result from the continuous changes in the Earth's speed and distance from the Sun. These cause variations in the transverse Doppler effect and in the red shift due to the Sun's gravitational potential. The frequency of TAI is higher at aphelion (about July 3) than at perihelion (about January 4) by about 6.6 parts in 10^{10}, and TAI is more advanced in epoch by about 3.3 milliseconds on October 1 than on April 1.

By Einstein's theory of general relativity a photon produced near the Earth's surface should be higher in frequency by 1.09 parts in 10^{16} for each metre above sea level. In 1960 the U.S. physicists Robert V. Pound and Glen A. Rebka measured the difference between the frequencies of photons produced at different elevations and found that it agreed very closely with what was predicted. The primary standards used to form the frequency of TAI are corrected for height above sea level.

Two-way, round-the-world flights of atomic clocks in 1971 produced changes in clock epochs that agreed well with the predictions of special and general relativity. The results have been cited as proof that the gravitational red shift in the frequency of a photon is produced when the photon is formed, as predicted by Einstein, and not later, as the photon moves in a gravitational field. In effect, gravitational potential is a perturbation that lowers the energy of a quantum state.

PULSAR TIME

A pulsar is believed to be a rapidly rotating neutron star whose magnetic and rotational axes do not coincide. Such bodies emit sharp pulses of radiation, at a short period P, detectable by radio telescopes. The emission of radiation and energetic subatomic particles causes the spin rate to decrease and the period to increase. $\dot{P}$, the rate of increase in P, is essentially constant, but sudden changes in the period of some pulsars have been observed.

Although pulsars are sometimes called clocks, they do not tell time. The times at which their pulses reach a radio telescope are measured relative to TAI, and values of P and $\dot{P}$ are derived from these times. A time scale formed directly from the arrival times would have a secular deceleration with respect to TAI, but if P for an initial TAI and $\dot{P}$ (assumed constant) are obtained from a set of observations, then a pulsar time scale, PS, can be formed such that δ, the difference between TAI and PS, contains only periodic and irregular variations. PS remains valid as long as no sudden change in P occurs.

It is the variations in δ, allowing comparisons of time scales based on very different processes at widely separated locations, that make pulsars extremely valuable. The chief variations are periodic, caused by motions of the Earth. These motions bring about (1) relativistic variations in TAI and (2) variations in distance, and therefore pulse travel time, from pulsar to telescope. Observations of the pulsar PSR 1937+21, corrected for the second effect, confirmed the existence of the first. Residuals (unexplained variations) in δ averaged one microsecond for 30 minutes of observation. This pulsar has the highest rotational speed of any known pulsar, 642 rotations per second. Its period P is 1.55 milliseconds, increasing at the rate $\dot{P}$ of 3.3×10^{-12} second per year; the speed decreases by one part per million in 500 years.

Continued observations of such fast pulsars should make it possible to determine the orbital position of the Earth more accurately. These results would provide more accurate data concerning the perturbations of the Earth's motion by the major planets; these in turn would permit closer estimates of the masses of those planets. Residual periodic variations in δ, not due to the sources already mentioned, might indicate gravitational waves. Irregular variations could provide data on starquakes and inhomogeneities in the interstellar medium.

RADIOMETRIC TIME

Atomic nuclei of a radioactive element decay spontaneously, producing other elements and isotopes until a stable species is formed. The life span of a single atom may have any value, but a statistical quantity, the half-life of a macroscopic sample, can be measured; this is the time in which one-half of the sample disintegrates. The age of a rock, for example, can be determined by measuring ratios of the parent element and its decay products.

Half-life

The decay of uranium to lead was first used to measure long intervals, but the decays of potassium to argon and of rubidium to strontium are more frequently used now. Ages of the oldest rocks found on the Earth are about 3.5×10^9 years. Those of lunar rocks and meteorites are about 4.5×10^9 years, a value believed to be near the age of the Earth.

Radiocarbon dating provides ages of formerly living matter within a range of 500 to 50,000 years. While an organism is living, its body contains about one atom of radioactive carbon-14, formed in the atmosphere by the action of cosmic rays, for every 10^{12} atoms of stable carbon-12. When the organism dies, it stops exchanging carbon with the atmosphere, and the ratio of carbon-14 to carbon-12 begins to decrease with the half-life of 5,730 years. Measurement of this ratio determines the age of the specimen.

For an extended discussion of the principles of radiometric dating, including sources of error, see GEOCHRONOLOGY: *Relative and absolute dating.*

PROBLEMS OF COSMOLOGY AND UNIFORM TIME

It has been suggested—by the English scientists E.A. Milne, Paul A.M. Dirac, and others—that the coefficient G in Newton's equation for the gravitational force might not be constant. Searches for a secular change in G have been made by studying accelerations of the Moon and reflections of radar signals from Mercury, Venus, and Mars. The effects sought are small compared to observational errors, however, and it is not certain whether G is changing or whether dynamical and atomic times have a relative secular acceleration.

A goal in timekeeping has been to obtain a scale of uniform time, but forming one presents problems. If, for example, dynamical and atomic time should have a relative secular acceleration, then which one (if either) could be considered uniform?

By postulates, atomic time is the uniform time of electromagnetism. Leaving aside relativistic and operational effects, are SI seconds formed at different times truly equal? This question cannot be answered without an invariable time standard for reference, but none exists. The conclusion is that no time scale can be proved to be uniform by measurement. This is of no practical consequence, however, because tests have shown that the atomic clock provides a time scale of very high accuracy. (W.Ma.)

BIBLIOGRAPHY

Time in the history of thought and action: (*Eastern*): CHARLES ELIOT, *Hinduism and Buddhism,* 3 vol. (1921, reissued 1971); FUNG YU-LAN, *A History of Chinese Philosophy,* 2nd ed., 2 vol. (Eng. trans. 1952–53, reprinted 1983); R.C. ZAEHNER, *The Dawn and Twilight of Zoroastrianism* (1961). (*Pre-Socratic*): HENRI FRANKFORT *et al., The Intellectual Adventure of Ancient Man* (1946, reissued 1977); JOHN BURNET, *Greek Philosophy, Thales to Plato* (1914, reissued 1968). (*Classical Greek*): W.K.C. GUTHRIE, *A History of Greek Philosophy,* 6 vol. (1962–81); JACQUELINE DE ROMILLY, *Time in Greek Tragedy* (1968); NORMAN W. DE WITT, *Epicurus and His Philosophy* (1954, reprinted 1976). (*Christian and Muslim*): JAMES BARR, *Biblical Words for Time* (1962); OSCAR CULLMANN, *Christ and Time,* rev. ed. (1962; 3rd rev. German ed., 1962); SAINT AUGUSTINE, *Confessions* (many English translations), the most important work of Greco-Roman thought on the problems of experienced time and the difficulty of grappling with them; IBN KHALDŪN, *al-Muqaddimah* (written in the early 14th century; Eng. trans., *The Muqaddimah: An Introduction to History,* 3 vol., 1958, reissued 1974), undoubtedly the greatest work of its kind. (*18th and 19th centuries*): GIAMBATTISTA VICO, *The New Science,* trans. by THOMAS G. BERGIN and MAX H. FISCH (1948, reissued 1984; 3rd Italian ed., 1744), a seminal work on the ontal significance of history; G.W.F. HEGEL, *The Logic of World and Idea,* trans. by H.S. MACRAN (1929), and *Science of Logic,* trans. by W.H. JOHNSTON and L.G. STRUTHERS (1929); KARL MARX, *Selected Works of Marx and Engels,* by C.P. DUTT, 2 vol. (1942); CHARLES DARWIN, *On the Origin of Species by Means of Natural Selection* (1859, many later editions). (*20th-century studies*): OSWALD SPENGLER, *The Decline of the West,* 2 vol. (1926–28, reissued 1981–83; originally published in German, 1919–22); the symposium volume, *History and the Concept of Time* (1966); S.G.F. BRANDON, *History, Time, and Deity* (1965); STEPHEN TOULMIN and JUNE GOODFIELD, *The Discovery of Time* (1965, reprinted 1983), history of the changing attitude toward time that arose from the geology and biology of the 19th century; MIRCEA ELIADE, *The Myth of the Eternal Return* (1955, reissued 1974; originally published in French, 1949); FRANCIS C. HABER, *The Age of the World: Moses to Darwin* (1959, reprinted 1978).

Contemporary pure studies of time: Two reference works in the study of time are G.J. WHITROW, *The Natural Philosophy of Time,* 2nd ed. (1980); and J.T. FRASER (ed.), *The Voices of Time,* 2nd ed. (1981). Both contain extensive references and the latter extensive bibliographies. See also numerous issues of the journal *Studium Generale* (monthly, 1955–71); G.J. WHITROW, *The Nature of Time* (1973; U.K. title, *What Is Time?,* 1972); P.C.W. DAVIES, *The Physics of Time Asymmetry* (1974), and *Space and Time in the Modern Universe* (1977); D.H. MELLOR, *Real Time* (1981); W. NEWTON-SMITH, *The Structure of Time* (1980); and GEORGE N. SCHLESINGER, *Aspects of Time*

(1980). (*Multidisciplinary symposia*): J.T. FRASER *et al.* (eds.), *The Study of Time: Proceedings of the First Conference of the International Society for the Study of Time* (1972); ROLAND FISCHER (ed.), *Interdisciplinary Perspectives of Time* (1967); RUDOLF W. MEYER (ed.), *Das Zeitproblem in 20. Jahrhundert* (1964); JOSEPH CAMPBELL (ed.), *Man and Time* (1957). (*Emphasis on philosophy*): Two books of readings with extensive bibliographies are RICHARD M. GALE (ed.), *The Philosophy of Time* (1967, reissued 1978); and J.J.C. SMART (ed.), *Problems of Space and Time* (1964). See also the UNIVERSITY OF CALIFORNIA, BERKELEY PHILOSOPHICAL UNION, *The Problem of Time* (1935, reprinted 1969), and individual philosophers mentioned in the text. (*Literature and the arts*): GEORGE KUBLER, *The Shape of Time* (1962); ERWIN PANOFSKY, *Studies in Iconology* (1962, reissued 1972); GEORGES POULET, *Studies in Human Time* (1956, reprinted 1979; originally published in French, 1950); HANS MEYERHOFF, *Time in Literature* (1960, reissued 1974). (*Psychology*): JEAN PIAGET, *The Child's Conception of Time* (1969; originally published in French, 1946); JOHN E. ORME, *Time, Experience and Behaviour* (1969); PAUL FRAISSE, *The Psychology of Time* (1963, reprinted 1975; originally published in French, 1957); NORMAN O. BROWN, *Life Against Death: The Psychoanalytical Meaning of History* (1959, reissued 1972); JOHN COHEN, *Psychological Time in Health and Disease* (1967). (*Biology and medicine*): GAY G. LUCE, *Biological Rhythms in Psychiatry and Medicine* (1970, reprinted 1978); CURT P. RICHTER, *Biological Clocks in Medicine and Psychiatry* (1965, reissued 1979); ERWIN BÜNNING, *The Physiological Clock*, rev. 3rd ed. (1973); J.L. CLOUDSLEY-THOMPSON, *Rhythmic Activity in Animal Physiology and Behaviour* (1961); *Biological Clocks*, the Cold Spring Harbor Symposia on Quantitative Biology, vol. 25 (1960). (*Physics*): ADOLF GRUENBAUM, *Philosophical Problems of Space and Time*, 2nd. ed. (1973), discusses many important issues including that of temporal asymmetry; his *Modern Science and Zeno's Paradoxes* (1967) provides a discussion of problems concerned with the continuity of time. See also OLIVIER COSTA DE BEAUREGARD, *Le Second Principe de la science du temps* (1963); RICHARD SCHLEGEL, *Time and the Physical World* (1961); and THOMAS GOLD (ed.), *The Nature of Time* (1967). For process philosophy, see MILIC CAPEK, *The Philosophical Impact of Contemporary Physics* (1961).

Time as systematized in modern scientific society: Definitions, formulas, and tables concerning time, ephemerides, and calendars are given in joint publications of the Nautical Almanac Offices of the United Kingdom and United States, including *The Astronomical Almanac* (annual) and the *Explanatory Supplement to the Astronomical Ephemeris and the American Ephemeris and Nautical Almanac* (1961, reissued 1977). The 1984 *Almanac* contains a supplement concerning the IAU astronomical constants, time scales, and reference frame introduced that year. The *Annual Report* of the BUREAU INTERNATIONAL DE L'HEURE provides results on rotational time, including new techniques, atomic time, and Earth rotation. *Spherical Astronomy* (1966), by EDGAR W. WOOLARD and GERALD M. CLEMENCE, is a mathematical treatment of fundamental positional astronomy. IVAN I. MUELLER, *Spherical and Practical Astronomy* (1969), concerns practical usages for geodesy, including polar motion; GERALD P. KUIPER and BARBARA M. MIDDLEHURST (eds.), *Telescopes* (1960, reprinted 1977), describes astrometric instruments; ROBERT R. NEWTON, *Ancient Astronomical Observations and the Accelerations of the Earth and Moon* (1970, reissued 1976), discusses ancient eclipse reports critically. Articles in journals include: W. MARKOWITZ, R.G. HALL, L. ESSEN, and J.V.L. PARRY, *Physical Review Letters*, 1:105–106 (1958), on the cesium frequency; T.C. VAN FLANDERN, *Astrophysical Journal*, 248:813–816 (1981), on a possible change in *G;* and DONALD BACKER, *Journal of Astrophysics and Astronomy*, 5:187–207 (1984), on time from pulsar PSR 1937+21.

(A.J.T./J.J.C.S./W.Ma.)

Tissue Culture

Tissue culture involves removing fragments of cell-containing material from a plant or animal and placing them in an artificial environment in which they can continue to function biologically. A tissue in culture may consist of a single cell, a population of cells, or, as in organ culture, all or part of an organ, in which different cell types interact in specific ways. The complex plants and animals contain many different kinds of specialized cells whose activities are interdependent and coordinated. Cells in culture may multiply; they may exhibit specialized activity (*i.e.*, locomotion); they may change size, form, and state of differentiation (*i.e.*, the kinds of different structures and functions they display); and they may interact in other complex ways. Thus, cultures of heart cells may display typical rhythmical beating, cells from the pancreas may produce the hormone insulin, and cells from the plant known as the deadly nightshade (*Atropa belladonna*) may produce the alkaloid compound atropine.

This article is divided into the following sections:

Uses of tissue culture

Cultures of cells and organs have been used to study cell composition and form; cellular, genetic, biochemical, and reproductive activity; the nature of specialized cell functions (*i.e.*, differentiation); the effects of physical, chemical, and biological agents—for example, drugs, hormones, or viruses; and structural and behavioral differences between abnormal cells, such as cancers, and their normal counterparts.

One of the traditional uses of tissue culture has been as an aid in the diagnosis of disease. A physician may, for example, culture a tissue sample to identify a simple bacterial or parasitic infection. Other diagnostic applications of tissue culture include the classification of brain tumours, identification of enzyme deficiencies in metabolic diseases, and identification of chromosomal abnormalities. Tissue culture is also used in the formulation and testing of new drugs and vaccines. The demonstration in 1949 that the causative virus of poliomyelitis would grow in cultures of human cells resulted in the preparation of vaccines that provide immunity against several viral diseases, including influenza, measles, and mumps.

The results of experiments in cell growth and differentiation have also added considerably to the body of scientific knowledge about basic biological and biochemical processes. Cell and organ culture techniques made possible an understanding of the nutrition and metabolism of many kinds of cells.

Most recently, however, the use of tissue culture methodology in the discipline of somatic cell genetics has opened new areas of investigation in the study of mammalian, and particularly human, genetics. One great advantage of tissue culture as a research tool is that it permits control of the cellular environment in a fashion and to a degree not possible inside the body, allowing the behaviour of cells to be both explored and manipulated. Some applications of somatic cell genetics are discussed below.

GENERAL BACKGROUND AND DEFINITIONS

The cell consists of a central nucleus, the cytoplasm, which surrounds the nucleus and contains the bulk of the cellular chemical machinery, and the cell membrane, which mediates all interaction between the cell and its environment. Within the nucleus are the chromosomes, bodies on which the genes are carried in linear order. The totality of a cell's genes and chromosomes is called its genome.

Genes are molecules of deoxyribonucleic acid, or DNA, each of which specifies the structure of a particular protein. The proteins constitute the basic chemically mediating molecules of the cell (enzymes) and also form important parts of its structure. All cells may be classified as either germ cells or somatic cells. Germ cells consist of sperm and egg cells whose mating constitutes the act of conception and leads to reproduction of a new individual. Somatic cells are body cells not connected with this reproductive process.

A tissue is a structural and functional aggregation of similar cells and their associated materials; *e.g.*, connective and vascular tissues in animals and sclerenchyma and xylem in plants are tissues that perform similar functions, namely those of support and internal transport. An organ such as the lung, liver, or brain is a complex structural unit composed of several tissues. A clone is a population of cells derived from a single cell by asexual reproduction; it represents the most uniform possible biological population. The nutrient medium is the material in which tissue culture cells are placed and from which the cells derive the molecules necessary for their reproduction and other functions.

ORIGINS AND METHODS OF TISSUE CULTURE

Tissue culture is a relatively recent development. The first attempt to grow cells from higher plants and animals in nutrient media was made at the turn of the 20th century. In 1907 the U.S. zoologist Ross G. Harrison successfully demonstrated the growth of frog nerve cell processes in a medium of clotted lymph. Thereafter a number of experimenters succeeded in cultivating animal cells, using as culture media a variety of biological fluids, such as lymph, blood serum, plasma, and tissue extracts to support cell growth and functions that could not be maintained in synthetically processed media.

Cells in culture can be examined directly by light microscopy or by the techniques of photomicrography and cinephotomicrography; in the latter, time-lapse motion pictures are taken through the microscope, permitting visualization of the movements of cells and their component parts. Cells in culture can also be fixed, *i.e.*, treated with agents that kill the cells but preserve many of their structural features. The cells can then be studied by selective staining of specific structures, or they can be sliced into very thin sections, allowing otherwise hidden structural details to be revealed by the light microscope or the electron microscope. Finally, cells in culture can be examined by the techniques of biochemistry and immunology, such as analysis of protein composition, enzyme activity, and antigenic reactivity.

Techniques for examining cells

Cells can be cultivated in many ways—as layers or sheets, on glass or plastic surfaces, or as suspensions in liquid or semisolid media. In general, only cancer cells multiply readily in suspension. While some kinds of cells, including many cancer cells, apparently can be perpetuated forever in tissue culture, most normal somatic cells can be cultivated only for approximately 50 or 100 generations, after which time their rate of multiplication slows markedly. The cause of this "aging" is not yet understood, but the phenomenon itself does not impose severe limitations on the culture of normal cells since even before the growth process begins to decline, many billions of cell progeny can be produced in the test tube, furnishing an enormous supply of cells for experimental studies. Furthermore, cells can be stored in viable condition at extremely low temperatures and can be reinitiated into active growth after many years without apparent change in structure or behaviour. Mixtures of synthetic materials supplemented with small amounts of blood serum or its macromolecular components are now readily available for use as nutrient media in which cells can be grown at rapid rates for long periods of time. It is necessary, of course, to maintain sterile conditions so as to prevent contamination of either cells or culture media by microorganisms such as bacteria and fungi. A typical photomicrograph of a cell culture growing as a sheet one cell thick is shown in Figure 1.

Cultures may be initiated from tiny samples of an extremely large variety of tissues. The tissue may be minced with scissors or dispersed by means of an appropriate enzyme, which digests the intercellular cementing substances, leaving single cells or small clumps. This material, called the inoculum, is then deposited in dishes containing nutrient medium. The cells usually attach to the dish and grow out from the initial inoculum. In order to maintain a suspension culture, the liquid medium may be continuously agitated, or its viscosity may be increased by the addition of materials such as agar. Cultures generally are incubated at a temperature close to that of the normal environment in which the cells originated.

TISSUE CULTURE AND SOMATIC CELL GENETICS

The limitations of classical genetics. One of the most important applications of modern tissue culture has been in the area of genetics and molecular biology of humans and other complex organisms. Classical genetics of humans and other higher organisms involves the mating of many pairs of selected individuals and the subsequent study of the distribution of particular characteristics among the offspring. The germ, or sex, cells carry out the reproduction process and eventually yield a complete new organism. Systematic study of characteristics passed down through such matings was initiated in the 19th century by the Austrian monk Gregor Mendel, who experimented with plant breeding. It was Mendel who founded the discipline known as classical genetics, which has yielded important information about hereditary processes in plants, insects such as the fruit fly (*Drosophila*), and, somewhat less ef-

Study of heredity

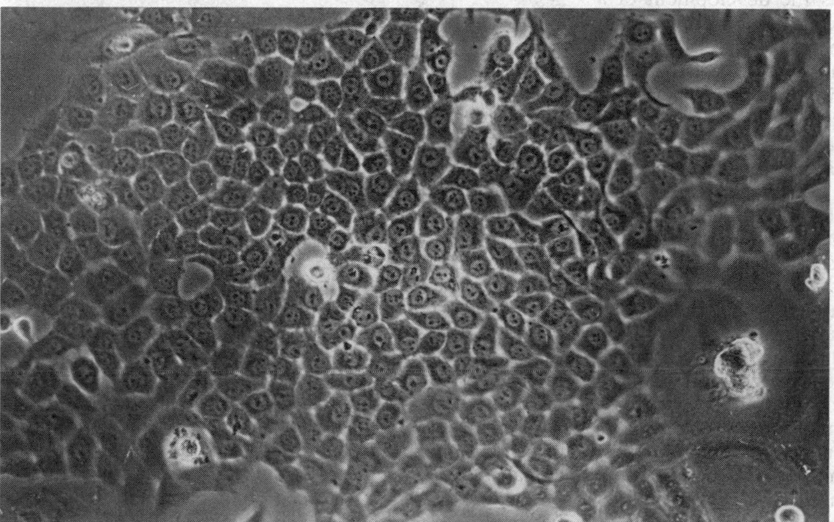

Figure 1: Photomicrograph of a culture of human cells growing as a sheet one cell thick.

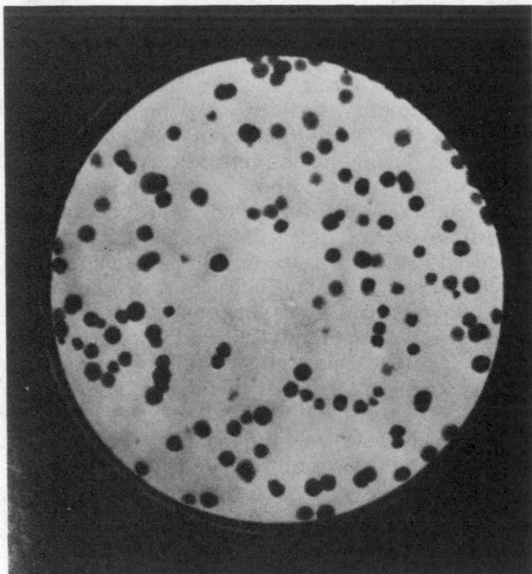

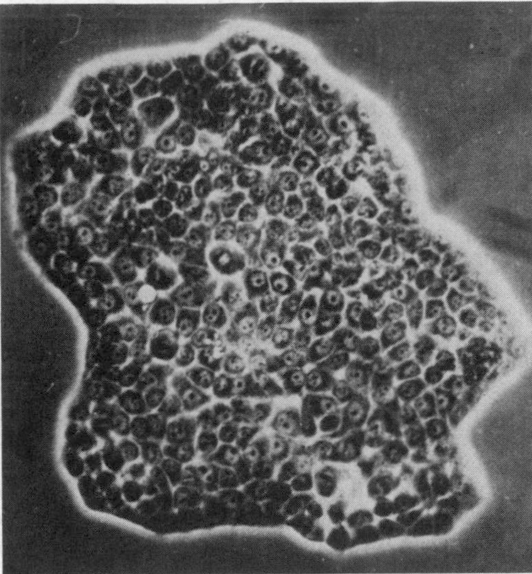

Figure 2: (Left) Demonstration of the single-cell plating procedure in which discrete colonies develop from single cells placed in a nutrient medium. (Right) Photomicrograph of a typical colony.

fectively, certain mammals, such as the mouse and the guinea pig. This experimental approach, however, has been far less successful in human research for two reasons. First, the time required for normal human reproduction is much greater than that required for, to cite a common example, the fruit fly, in which thousands of new offspring can be produced in a matter of days. Further, it is not possible to use human subjects to carry out the particular matings that would answer specific genetic questions. Consequently, as late as 1956, human genetics was still a primitive and incomplete discipline.

Origins of somatic cell genetics. Tissue culture made possible a new approach to the genetics of man and other complex organisms. The concept of somatic cell genetics, developed by Theodore T. Puck and his co-workers at the Eleanor Roosevelt Institute for Cancer Research and the Florence R. Sabin Laboratories of the University of Colorado School of Medicine, Denver, involves study of the genetics of the mammalian somatic, or body, cells rather than of the germ cells. Since each somatic cell contains a nucleus and its component chromosomes and genes, it appeared to these researchers that the necessity for human mating could be bypassed, and the much shorter reproductive cycle of cells substituted for the long time period necessary for reproduction of the entire organism.

This concept required adaptation and application of the basic methodologies of bacteriology to genetic and genetic biochemical analysis of the somatic cells of complex organisms. It also necessitated a series of new laboratory techniques. The first of these was the development of a simple, reliable procedure for taking tissue samples from any individual and culturing the resulting cells for long periods under conditions such that integrity of the chromosomal structure could be maintained. Also necessary was a technique whereby single cells could be grown into discrete colonies, visible to the unaided eye, in a simple operation applicable to thousands of cells simultaneously and under conditions such that every viable cell would produce a colony. It had been shown earlier by Katherine Sanford and her colleagues at the National Institutes of Health (NIH) that occasional single cells, when sealed in capillary tubes under stringently controlled conditions, could be made to grow into large populations. Subsequently, the single-cell plating technique was developed by which a similar result could be achieved for many thousands of single cells simultaneously in a simple, quantitative, reproducible, and routine operation (see Figure 2).

Next, means were devised by which mutant colonies can be recognized and cultured in new populations. These populations can then be used in genetic experiments in which a particular mutation is used as a genetic marker to trace the operation of hereditary mechanisms. Finally, it became necessary to identify each of the human chromosomes and to be able to analyze the chromosomal constitution of any cell culture. The first complete identification of each of the human chromosomes was carried out in Denver, and in 1959 the first human chromosome study group assembled there and devised the classification presently in use for the human chromosomes (see Figure 3). By the 1960s all of the essential elements for the new discipline of somatic cell genetics had been achieved, and a new means for study of the genetics of man and other mammals, based on cell growth in tissue culture, became available.

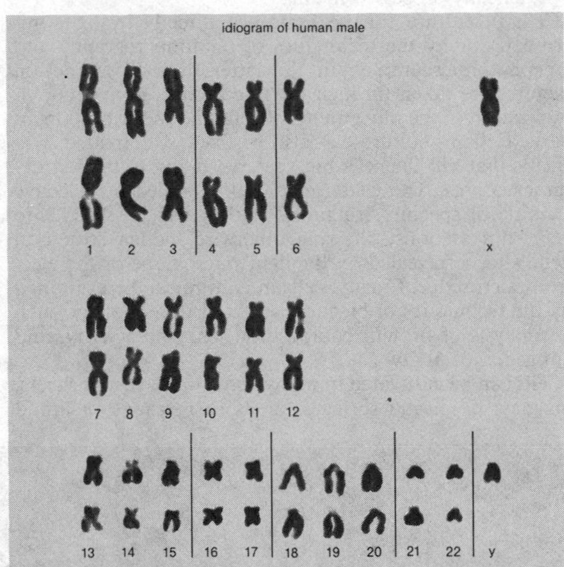

Figure 3: Classification of the normal human male chromosomes according to the internationally accepted system established in 1959.

APPLICATIONS OF TISSUE CULTURE

These developments in somatic cell genetics have made possible enormous gains in the understanding of genetic processes and structures in man and other higher organisms and have permitted application of the techniques of molecular biology to higher organisms in a fashion not previously possible. Clonal cell cultures can now be readily prepared from any individual, and single-gene mutants of cell cultures can be produced and developed into new clonal stocks. The effects of mutagens on mammalian and other kinds of cells has been studied; mutation analysis has made possible the delineation of the genetic–biochemical pathways underlying various metabolic processes; and an impressive number of previously enigmatic human diseases have now been identified as being caused by changes in the number or structure of the chromosomes. Finally, prenatal diagnosis of such chromosomal diseases, as well as of a number of diseases due to single-gene mutations, is now possible.

Production of hybrid cells. Using tissue culture, researchers have developed a simple and convenient method for causing coalescence or fusion of cells, so that chromosomes from one cell can be added to those of another. This important technique made possible the creation of many kinds of hybrid cells. The process of introducing chromosomes from one cell into another constitutes a new kind of cell mating and has enabled the production of large numbers of different cell hybrids. Classical genetics permits mating and production of hybrids only between members of the same species. Hybridization in tissue culture permits hybrid formation between individual cells of widely different species and growth of large cultures of these new interspecies hybrids. Thus, one of the great barriers that sharply restricted the scope of classical genetic science has been eliminated. In one very important series of hybrid cells, single human chromosomes were incorporated into Chinese hamster (*Cricetulus griseus*) cells, allowing the functions of individual human chromosomes to be separately studied and defined (see Figure 4).

Hybrid cells

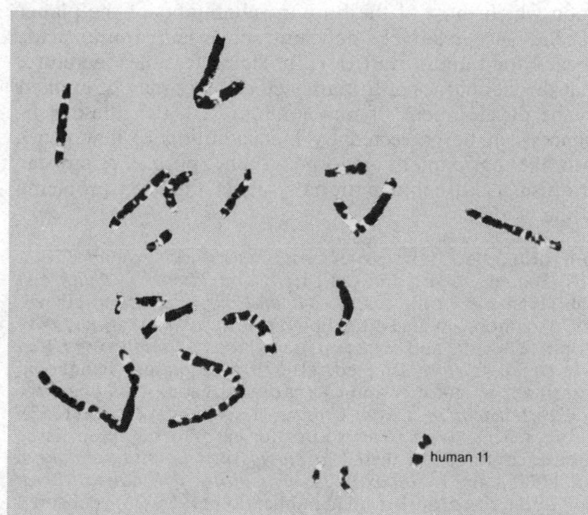

Figure 4: Chromosomes of a hybrid cell obtained by fusion of a Chinese hamster (*Cricetulus griseus*) ovary cell with a human cell to produce a new cell containing all of the chromosomes of the former and the single human chromosome 11.

Translating the genetic code. By means of somatic cell genetic studies in tissue culture great advances have been made in identifying specific human genes; examining their biochemical actions in normal and diseased developmental processes; determining their association with particular chromosomes; and mapping their positions on the chromosome with great precision. Such studies are making it possible for researchers to isolate particular human DNA fragments that carry the genetic code for specific proteins and to introduce these fragments into bacteria. In this way large numbers of such particular DNA fragments can be produced. The DNA segments are radioactively labelled and used as probes to diagnose the presence of genetic diseases, study gene regulatory phenomena, and facilitate identification of new protein molecules important to human health. Moreover, such proteins can then be synthesized cheaply and on a large scale by bacteria into whose genomes the critical DNA regions have been inserted. A new industry for fermentative synthesis of important biological molecules has been created as a result of these activities.

Tissue culture studies have also shown the existence of a considerable amount of DNA in the mammalian genome consisting of highly repetitive sequences that do not code for protein and whose function is unknown. Moreover, it has been demonstrated that the coding sequences in the mammalian cell are interrupted by noncoding DNA intervals, called introns, whose function remains to be elucidated. Studies in tissue culture have demonstrated the critical role of cell surface receptors, which act as targets in specific cells for different hormones, drugs, and other active molecules. These receptors mediate the characteristic actions of these all-important molecules on cell chemistry. Studies of cells in culture have revealed the specific molecular requirements for growth and other functions and demonstrated that different states of cellular differentiation have characteristic nutritional requirements. Specific cell membrane structures have been defined, and detailed biochemical and immunological properties of cell membrane elements have been demonstrated.

Research into cell structure, mutations, and cancer. Tissue culture studies have demonstrated the existence within mammalian cells of a universal cellular structure called the cytoskeleton; it consists of an integrated network of different kinds of fibres, some of which are rigid and some of which are contractile. This cytoskeletal system, which corresponds in some degree to the skeletal and muscular system of the body, gives the cells of each tissue their characteristic shape and is of critical importance in cell locomotion and ingestion of particles from surrounding fluid. In addition, however, the cytoskeleton regulates a variety of the cell's biochemical activities, including aspects of growth control that differentiate normal cells from some kinds of cancer.

The cytoskeletal system

In addition to the examination of normal cells, tissue culture has been used to study a variety of cell mutants produced artificially or obtained from patients with various genetic diseases; the nature of specific mutations responsible for particular diseases has thus been elucidated. Furthermore, methods for detection of environmental mutagens and carcinogens and for identification of cell mechanisms that repair genetic damage have been developed. These investigations promise important contributions to preventive medicine: identification of substances that may result in cancer and genetic disease is a necessary step in preventing exposure to such hazards.

Knowledge of the molecular biology of mammalian viruses has made major advances through the techniques of tissue culture. A crucial discovery has been the identification of a set of viral genes that play a critical role in cancer. Such genes, called oncogenes, are also present in normal cells but usually in inactive form; they can be activated under certain circumstances to produce cancer. In addition, specific chromosomal aberrations have been identified as being associated with various human cancers, among them a specific deletion in the short arm of chromosome 3 accompanying small-cell carcinoma of the lung, a deletion in chromosome 11 that is a frequent concomitant of Wilms' tumour of the kidney, and a deletion in chromosome 13 associated with a cancer of the retina. These examples illustrate how developments in tissue culture are uncovering basic phenomena at the cellular and molecular levels that promise dramatic advances in the understanding of body functions in health and disease.

Oncogenes

Contributions to immunological research. In the field of immunology, tissue culture studies have illuminated the extremely complex ways in which the two different subpopulations of the white cells of the blood, the so-called T cells and B cells, interact with foreign molecules and with each other. These cells produce the soluble antibodies responsible for protection against such infectious agents as viruses and bacteria and form the phagocytic cells that normally rid the body of pathologic cells. Production and identification of monoclonal antibodies; *i.e.*, antibodies consisting of a single molecular species that interact with a single molecular grouping, has been one of the great triumphs of tissue culture and somatic cell genetic methodologies. Another crucial insight into the immunological response resulting from the techniques for manipulating DNA is an explanation of how the body is able to produce a sufficient diversity of antibodies to confer protection against almost any kind of foreign protein (antigen). Experiments have demonstrated that genes specifying the code for that part of the antibody molecule that combines specifically with different antigens have huge potential for genetic recombination. Thus millions of different gene combinations are possible, each of which can code for a different antibody. Each antibody is then capable of combining structurally with a different antigenic substance.

Use of single-cell survival curves. The development of single-cell survival curves, used to measure the doses of physical, chemical, or biological agents required to kill or alter mammalian cells, is another application of modern tissue culture techniques. The procedure involves placing measured numbers of single cells into a series of dishes in the same nutrient medium and exposing each dish to a different graded dose of the agent under investigation. The dishes are incubated at 99° F (37° C) and removed from the incubator after several days, and the number of colonies that have developed from each cell are counted. When the number of surviving colonies is plotted against the dose, as shown in Figure 5, a highly reproducible curve is obtained for each agent, from which the mean

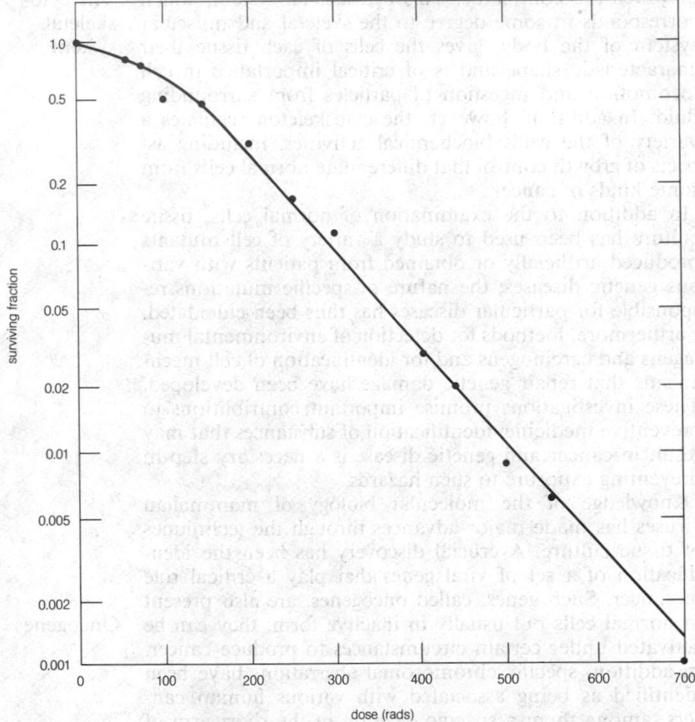

Figure 5: Single-cell survival curve showing the fraction of cells that retain the ability to form colonies after various doses of X-radiation. Survival curves of this kind offer a simple and reliable means for measuring the action of physical, chemical, and biological agents on the reproduction of mammalian cells.

lethal dose of the agent for that particular cell can be determined. This method made possible the first accurate measurements of lethal doses of different agents at the cellular level. Figure 5 represents the survival curve for human cells treated with X-radiation in tissue culture; this curve revealed that the previously accepted value for the cellular lethal dose of X-rays was more than 500 times too high. The development of these standards of measurement ushered in the era of quantitative mammalian cell radiobiology and made possible much more effective use of radiotherapy in medicine. Similiar curves have been plotted to demonstrate and analyze radiation repair processes at the cellular level; to establish mechanisms of action of chemicals, drugs, viruses, and antibodies; and to study cellular defenses against such toxins.

One noteworthy medical application of survival curves has been developed by Sidney Salmon at the University of Arizona (Tucson). In the treatment of cancer the physician often faces the dilemma of choosing the most effective chemotherapeutic agent for a particular patient. When single cells derived from a small sample of the tumour are grown in tissue culture, varying concentrations of different chemotherapeutic agents can be added to the cultured populations, and single-cell survival curves can be constructed for each agent under consideration. The physician can then select the therapeutic agent that produces the best specific response.

Future experimentation. A significant aspect of modern tissue culture developments is the possibility that these may resolve at least some of the ethical problems connected with the question of human experimentation in medicine. The availability of large numbers of new drugs and treatments and the necessity of monitoring toxic environmental agents make it mandatory that careful tests be devised for definitive evaluation of benefits and risks to man. The use of animal models is far from adequate in assessing human conditions. It now appears possible that animal testing for toxicity of biological agents and for other biological modes of action can be supplemented with tissue culture studies on human cells to produce far more definitive results with less human cost.

Application to plant cells

While tissue culture has been practiced for more than 50 years, the concepts and methods of somatic cell genetics—first developed in connection with mammalian cells—are now being vigorously applied to plant cells. Specifically, the concepts of new gene and chromosome insertions are being studied in an effort to improve nutritional properties of crops and to confer greater resistance to deleterious agents. Cereal crops, particularly rice and corn—upon which most of the human inhabitants of the planet depend—are relatively deficient in certain amino acids needed for human nutrition. It seems feasible, therefore, that the techniques of somatic cell genetics may be applied to the development of new strains, in which these deficiences can be corrected by incorporation of new genes into the basic plant genome. Such approaches appear promising and could materially affect the food problems of the world.

BIBLIOGRAPHY. EDWARD N. WILLMER, *Cytology and Evolution*, 2nd ed. (1970), and (ed.) *Cells and Tissues in Culture*, 3 vol. (1965–67); JOHN PAUL, *Cell and Tissue Culture*, 5th ed. (1975), a more advanced textbook; DONALD J. MERCHANT, RAYMOND H. KAHN, and WILLIAM H. MURPHY, *Handbook of Cell and Organ Culture*, 2nd ed. (1967), a laboratory handbook; MARGARET R. MURRAY and GERTRUDE KOPECH, *A Bibliography of the Research in Tissue Culture, 1884–1950*, 2 vol. (1953), a comprehensive reference source for early literature on tissue culture, continued by their *Current Tissue Culture Literature*, 5 vol. (1965); and by *Index of Tissue Culture: A Guide to Literature in the Field*, an irregular publication (1966–76) sponsored by the Tissue Culture Association and the National Library of Medicine; C.V. RAMAKRISHNAN (ed.), *Tissue Culture* (1965); CHARITY WAYMOUTH (ed.), *Advances in Tissue Culture* (1970); and DENIS A.T. NEW, *The Culture of Vertebrate Embryos* (1966), reviews on specialized topics; and VINCENT J. CRISTOFALO and GEORGE H. ROTHBLAT (eds.), *Nutrition and Metabolism of Cultured Cells* (1971), an advanced book concerned with the entire field of tissue culture and its theories and implications. For plant tissue culture see D.S. INGRAM and J.P. HELGESON (eds.), *Tissue Culture Methods for Plant Pathologists* (1980); TREVOR A. THORPE (ed.), *Plant Tissue Culture: Methods and Applications in Agriculture* (1981); JOHN H. DODDS and LORIN W. ROBERTS, *Experiments in Plant Tissue Culture* (1982); and J.M. BONGA and D.J. DURZAN, *Tissue Culture in Forestry* (1982). See also KARL MARAMOROSCH and HIROYUKI HIRUMI (eds.), *Practical Tissue Culture Applications* (1979); EZIO GIACOBINI, ANTONIA VERNADAKIS, and ABRAHAM SHAMAR (eds.), *Tissue Culture in Neurobiology* (1980); RENATO BASERGA (ed.), *Tissue Growth Factor* (1981); and PHILLIP G. NELSON and MELVYN LIEBERMAN (eds.), *Excitable Cells in Tissue Culture* (1981).

Reference sources for specialized applications to somatic cell genetics include T.C. HSU, *Human and Mammalian Cytogenetics: An Historical Perspective* (1979); HENRY HARRIS, *Cell Fusion* (1970); BORIS EPHRUSSI, *Hybridization of Somatic Cells* (1972); LEROY HOOD *et al.*, *Molecular Biology of Eucaryotic Cells* (1975); THEODORE T. PUCK, *The Mammalian Cell as a Microorganism* (1972); DAVID M. PRESCOTT (ed.), *Methods in Cell Biology*, (irregular; formerly METHODS IN CELL PHYSIOLOGY); THEODORE T. PUCK and F.T. KAO, "Somatic Cell Genetics and Its Application to Medicine," *Annual Review of Genetics*, 16: 225–271 (1982).

(T.T.P./Ed.)

Tissues and Fluids

By definition, a tissue is a collection of cells having similar structures and performing special, as well as similar, functions. Those tissues, such as muscle, that consist almost entirely of cells devoted to a single purpose are known as simple tissues. Other tissues, such as those lining the alimentary canal (digestive tract) of higher animals, may serve a variety of functions; therefore, they are called composite tissues. Within the tissues and within their cellular components, circulating body fluids maintain the homeostasis of the organism. This article treats the nature, formation, and function of tissues and fluids in both animal and plant bodies. For a depiction of some of the tissues of the human body, shown in relation to each other, see the colour Trans-Vision in the *Propædia*: Part Four, Section 421.

The article is divided into the following sections:

THE TISSUES AND FLUIDS OF ANIMALS

Very early in the evolution of animals, different tissues tended to become aggregated into organs, and the organs themselves divided into specialized parts. The simple pouchlike outgrowth of glandular cells from the side of the alimentary canal of amphioxus, a primitive chordate animal, for example, is now represented in complex vertebrates by a separate liver, pancreas, and gallbladder. Thus, an animal can be considered as a collection of tissues that are often, but not always, united into organs and organ systems. The fluids that are produced by tissues and in which they are bathed usually are considered as tissues only when they have a definite and continuing cell content.

Classification of tissues

Anatomical classification. The classification of tissues has always been determined by the methods available for their study. Hence, because early investigators were accustomed to dividing an animal body into its organ systems, tissues were first classified anatomically according to the organ system from which they came—*i.e.,* nervous tissues, digestive tissues, reproductive tissues, and so on. This system proved inadequate, however, when it became obvious that there were more tissues than could be accounted for by the few types that were peculiar to a specific organ system. This realization led to an attempt to classify tissues according to the cell types of which they are composed: tissues composed of epithelial cells covered the outside of organs; those composed of endothelial cells lined the inside of organs; and those consisting of stroma cells were thought to serve as a functionless matrix in which other functional cells were embedded. Tissues that did not have an obvious function were collectively called connective tissue because it was thought that their sole purpose was to connect one type of cell to another. This category included the elastic tissue of tendons, the cartilage of joints, the main skeletal elements, and even blood, although there appears to be no logical connection in structure or function between blood and bone. Despite such seeming inconsistencies, however, this method of classification was useful in drawing attention to the similarities that occur throughout the animal body. A particular type of epithelial cell, for example, may be found in many different locations and in many kinds of organs.

Inadequacies of classification systems

Embryological classification. The great surge in structural embryology (the study of the formation and development of the embryo in plants and animals) that occurred when tissues were being classified according to cell types led to a system of tissue classification based on embryological origin. In the course of embryological development in most animals, it is fairly easy to recognize those cells that originate on the outside of the embryo (ectodermal cells), those that originate on the inside of the embryo (endodermal cells), and those that lie between the inside and outside of the embryo (mesodermal cells). This classification, although valuable for the information it reveals concerning evolution, is of far less value when applied to specific tissues. The epidermal and mesodermal elements of skin, for example, are confused; how far back the mouth ectoderm goes by infolding before true endoderm starts has been the subject of endless semantic arguments.

Functional classification. The most useful of all systems is to classify tissues according to the functions that they perform. On this basis tissues can be divided into three distinctive classes and a miscellaneous class. One of the distinctive classes contains those tissues that are used for assimilation, storage, transport, and excretion of food or waste products—*i.e.,* those tissues that serve an animal's needs for growth, repair, and energy. Involved in assimilation are the alimentary tissues, which not only break down food products to derive energy but also transform energy into utilizable sources that can be stored and released as required (see DIGESTION AND DIGESTIVE SYSTEMS). In any but the smallest animals the products secured by the alimentary tissues or liberated from the storage tissues are transported to other areas of the body, a function that is performed by blood and lymph. The role of tissues such as those in the lung and kidney is to excrete waste products from the body.

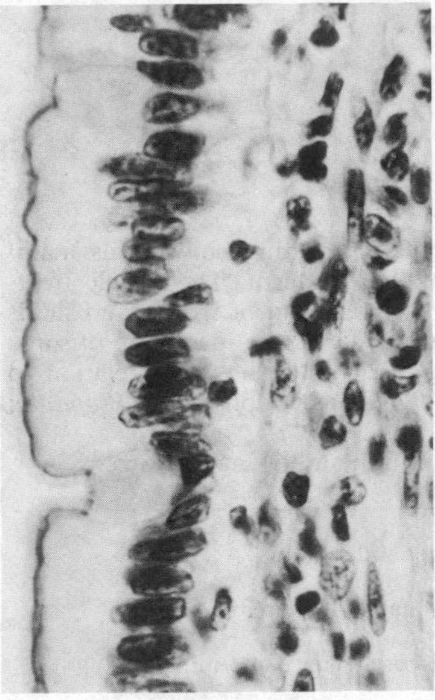
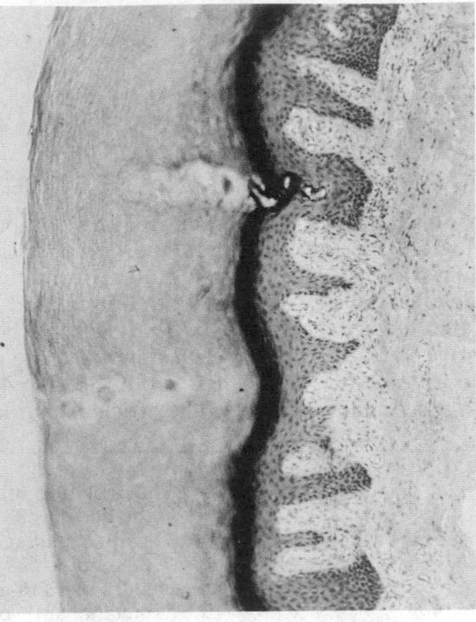
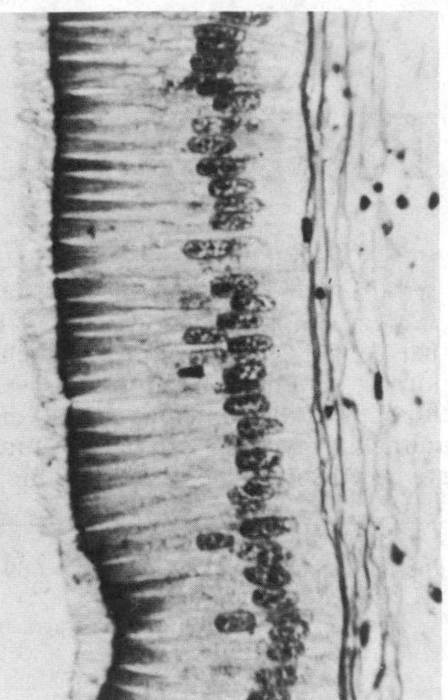

Figure 1: Photomicrographs of epithelial cells.
(Left) Simple columnar epithelium of small intestine showing striated (grooved) border. (Centre) Stratified squamous epithelium of the skin of the fingertip. (Right) Ciliated epithelium from the alimentary tract of a mussel.
Don W. Fawcett, M.D.

Another group of tissues classified according to function contains those used for coordination. This group includes those tissues that coordinate the organism in relation to its external environment as well as those that coordinate the parts of the organism internally. External coordination is performed by the central nervous system (brain and spinal cord) and its associated sense organs; internal coordination, though aided by the sense organs, is largely the responsibility of the chemical secretions (hormones) of specialized endocrine glands.

The third distinctive group of tissues according to the functional classification contains those required for support and movement, the skeletal and muscular tissues. The fourth group includes tissues used for reproduction; the hemopoietic tissues, which are concerned with the production of blood cells; and tissue fluids.

TISSUES FOR ASSIMILATION, STORAGE, TRANSPORT, AND EXCRETION

Alimentary tissues. The principal tissues involved in assimilation lie along the alimentary canal, the anterior end of which is the mouth. Lining the mouth is a simple form of covering tissue, or epithelium, known as squamous (scaly) epithelium because it consists of flattened, overlapping cells. It is also called stratified epithelium because there are several layers of cells. In such an arrangement, which is necessary in an area of rough usage like the mouth, cells that are detached from the surface can be replaced quickly by those underneath. Because they are in direct contact with the air, these tissues must be kept moist. Interspersed among the epithelial cells, therefore, are numerous cells that secrete a slimy fluid called mucus. In many animals these cells are aggregated into small glands. Surface tissues (epithelia) containing mucous cells are called mucous membranes; irrespective of the type of epithelium involved, such membranes line the entire alimentary canal.

Tongue and salivary glands

The mouth of terrestrial animals also contains the tongue, which is the main food-gathering organ of many amphibians, some reptiles, and even a few mammals. Regardless of the organism, the interior of the tongue invariably consists of a mass of well-vascularized (blood-filled), interlacing muscle fibres; the tissues covering the surface of the tongue, on the other hand, differ from one group of animals to another. The squamous epithelium on the upper surface of most, if not all, animals is cornified epithelium; it is capable of producing keratin, the tough material that comprises horns, hooves, and nails. The surface of the mammalian tongue contains pits that extend down to the underlying mucus-producing tissues, from which arise pillars of various shapes. With this arrangement, sensory nerve endings in the pits can be kept constantly moist; yet, the organ itself is so tough on the surface that it can be used for scraping or rasping.

Mammals require such large quantities of mucus to moisten food and to protect oral membranes that they have developed specialized glands, the salivary glands, with ducts leading into the mouth. Anatomically, these glands are botryoidal; physiologically, they are merocrine; and biochemically, they are mixed. These terms also apply to many other glands. A botryoidal gland is one with many branching ducts, each of which finally terminates in a hollow spherical gland, thus giving the appearance of a bunch of grapes. A merocrine gland is one in which no part of the cytoplasm (the part of a cell exclusive of the nucleus) of the secreting cell is lost; all the granules of the secreted product pass through the cell membrane and into the lumen (cavity) of a duct, in which they are dissolved and distributed. A mixed gland is one that produces a number of products; thus, the salivary glands yield a serous fluid called mucus, which is a dispersion of a protein in water, and small quantities of the digestive enzymes ptyalin and maltase. (Enzymes are proteins that control chemical reactions in living matter.) The total of all these secretions is saliva, the importance of which is indicated by the fact that its daily output in man exceeds that of urine.

Esophagus and stomach

After leaving the mouth, food passes down the esophagus, a muscular tube that histologically—*i.e.*, in terms of its tissue structure—is little more than an extension of the mouth. Internally, the esophagus is lined with a thick coat of the same type of stratified squamous epithelium as is found in the mouth. There is a longitudinal layer of striated muscle (muscle in which the bands, or striations, represent areas of different composition), the contractions of which control swallowing, and a thin circular layer of nonstriated muscle that is separated from the epithelium-lined lumen by a cushion of connective tissues. The esophagus enters the stomach, an organ of variable tissue construction in different animals; it is primarily a sack, or a series of sacks, that holds, churns, and partially digests the contents. In the human stomach the entire inner surface is covered with a simple columnar-shaped epithelium from which thousands of pits, or gastric glands, descend into the underlying layer of connective tissue. In the stomachs of some animals the glands are confined to small areas, and much of the inner stomach wall is composed of stratified squamous, and even occasionally keratinized, epithelium. The outer stomach wall consists of three layers of nonstriated muscle fibres that run longitudinally, circularly, and diagonally.

Interesting tissues in the stomach are the gastric glands, which are simple in structure but complex in cellular makeup and function. In most organisms the glands are S-shaped tubular structures, but sometimes they are branched. The cells forming the glands are of four types. In the gastric pit, the part of the gland that opens into the stomach, the cells resemble the general epithelial lining and are active secretors of mucus. Just below the pit is the isthmus, a section of the gland containing a few mucus-producing cells and many hydrochloric-acid-secreting ones; the acid is necessary in the digestive process. Between the isthmus and the base of the gland is the neck, which contains additional mucus cells and a few that produce hydrochloric acid. The base of the gland consists mostly of cells that secrete an enzyme that catalyzes the breakdown of proteins in the stomach; the base also includes several of another type of cell, the exact function of which is still in doubt.

Small intestine

After partial digestion in the stomach, from which only a very few simple substances are absorbed, the food passes to the small intestine. In higher vertebrates all the tissues and structures of the small intestine are modified for the sole purpose of absorption, which is a direct function of surface area. The inner wall of the small intestine consists of a series of connecting ridges. Arising from the ridges are millions of finger-like projections called villi, the centre of each of which contains blood vessels that remove absorbed materials. The tightly packed epithelial cells covering the villi are themselves covered with even smaller projections (microvilli). This combination of villi and microvilli results in a total absorptive surface of the small intestine that is approximately 10,000 times greater than that of a smooth tube. The tissues of the remaining length of the alimentary canal are primarily devoted to the recycling of water. They do not have villi and are usually covered with a simple epithelium containing numerous mucus-secreting cells.

In lower vertebrates the glands that produce the enzymes necessary to convert food substances into absorbable molecules are found along the entire length of the small intestine. In all higher forms, however, the larger surface area creates a greater demand for enzymes. As a result, the glands are located in a completely separate organ, the pancreas, which, in tissue structure and secretory function, closely resembles a salivary gland.

Fatty tissue

Digested food materials of all types, as well as undigested droplets of fat, are picked up by the blood from the small intestine and transported to other parts of the body either for storage or for immediate use. Fat is stored in fat cells, which develop from undifferentiated cells in connective tissue. At an early stage of their development, the undifferentiated cells become filled with small fat droplets; later, these coalesce into a large single fat droplet. In some lower vertebrates, particularly amphibians, fat cells are localized, forming fat bodies that are distinct from the surrounding tissue. In most higher forms, however, fatty (adipose) tissue is dispersed throughout the body, although fat cells do tend to aggregate into fat masses in certain areas, particularly in the layers beneath the surface of the skin.

Liver tissues. The bulk of nutrient-bearing blood goes to the liver, which is probably the most important single tissue in the maintenance of the mammalian body. The evolutionary mechanism by which the liver reached this important function is not entirely clear. Many invertebrates and such lower vertebrates as amphioxus have outgrowths from the anterior region of the alimentary canal, apparently for the purpose of increasing the secretory area. In the cyclostomes (*e.g.,* lamprey, hagfish) the lumen of a much-branched outgrowth remains open; hence, the liver in these animals is a series of intercoiled tubes. In higher forms, however, there is no lumen; instead, the liver consists essentially of many-sided (polygonal) cells so closely pressed together that all trace of a tubular origin is lost. The cells cluster about much-branched blood vessels, from which phagocytes (cells that ingest and destroy foreign materials) migrate and become interspersed among the liver cells. There is also a network of branching ducts, originating as intercellular spaces, that collect bile (a fluid secreted by the liver that aids in digestion) and form the bile duct, which leads to the gallbladder. Despite the fact that they perform a multiplicity of functions, all liver cells appear to be of the same type.

When blood reaches the liver from the small intestine, its carbohydrate content is adjusted either by the removal of excess sugars and their conversion to glycogen particles that are stored in the liver or by the addition of sugar through the breakdown of previously stored glycogen. Poisonous substances carried by the blood are either detoxified, if possible, or removed from the blood and stored. Partially broken down erythrocytes (red blood cells), arriving from the spleen at the rate of about 3,000,000 per second, are picked up by the phagocytes and broken down further; the breakdown products are either recycled or, as in the case of excess pigments, excreted through the bile. Liver cells also control the synthesis and distribution of fat in the form of large molecules composed of both lipid and protein (lipoprotein); the synthesis of all proteins in blood plasma; and the synthesis of urea, a nitrogenous waste that is subsequently excreted by the kidney.

Blood and lymph. To refer to blood as a tissue is a semantic, not a scholarly, definition, because in some invertebrates (*e.g.,* annelids) the blood is almost acellular (lacking in cells), and in the great majority of invertebrates it contains at the most only a few leukocytes (white blood cells). Only at the vertebrate level do the oxygen-carrying pigments of the blood become localized in specific blood cells, and only at the mammalian level do they lose their nuclei. The acellular portion of blood is called plasma when it is in a blood vessel and lymph when it passes out through the walls of capillaries (tiny blood vessels) to bathe the cells in surrounding tissues (see below *Blood and lymph*).

Respiratory pigments

The most important function of blood is to carry oxygen, which is transported by a respiratory pigment; the best known pigments are the hemoglobins. These compounds, which contain iron, are found in all vertebrates and also in many annelids, insects, and a few mollusks. Other respiratory pigments include the hemocyanins, which contain copper, and the hemovanadins, which contain vanadium. All of these pigments function in much the same manner: they pick up oxygen from the air and transport it to the cells, where it is released. The blood of most animals also contains leukocytes of various forms and functions.

Blood plasma contains approximately 7 percent dissolved proteins, including the globulin fraction, which is of great immunological importance; other constituents include nutrients and hormones. The most important function of plasma is to maintain a proper fluid balance among the various tissues of the body. The lymph that passes through the walls of capillaries and bathes the tissues collects in lymph vessels and is recycled back into the bloodstream.

Kidney tissues. The original function of the vertebrate kidney was to remove water from the body cavity (coelom) of aquatic animals. The primitive kidney consisted of little more than a longitudinal duct opening at its posterior end into the cloaca (a passage into which waste products are discharged) and contained at its anterior end a series of funnels with cilia (lashing hairlike projections) to remove the excess fluid. This type of kidney is found in the larvae (*e.g.,* tadpoles) of many vertebrate animals. Early in the evolutionary history of aquatic vertebrates a tissue was developed that permitted excess blood fluids to be removed by a similar mechanism: a small, tangled mass of capillaries (the glomerulus) entered a pouch in the side of the longitudinal coelomic duct. With the adaptation of early vertebrates to terrestrial life, however, it was necessary that water be conserved; the coelomic funnel disappeared, and the glomerulus with its pouch (Bowman's capsule) no longer led directly into the excretory duct but into a highly complex series of tubules designed to concentrate and recycle water while permitting the removal of some water-soluble wastes.

Adult vertebrates known as the anamniota (fishes and amphibians) have a kidney structure very much like that of the embryo; the adult kidney of amniotes (reptiles, birds, and mammals), however, is derived from the posterior end of the embryonic kidney (see EXCRETION AND EXCRETORY SYSTEMS). In the anamniotic kidney, venous blood goes directly into a large sinus (a cavity or hollow space within a structure of the body). Located in this sinus are branched, tangled tubules, each of which terminates in a Bowman's capsule containing arterial blood that comes directly from the heart through a series of branches of the main artery in the body. After its passage through the glomerulus, the arterial blood empties into the sinus, which, at its anterior end, drains into a large vein.

Embryonic amniotes have a very similar structure, but a pouched outgrowth from the posterior end of the collecting tubule develops completely new units around it. This outgrowth becomes the ureter (the duct that carries urine from the kidney to the urinary bladder), and the pouch becomes the renal pelvis (a saclike cavity at which the ureter is attached to the kidney). The excretory units (nephrons), each of which consists of a Bowman's capsule, glomerulus, and tubule, then develop in the surrounding tissue and become attached through one or more branches to the renal pelvis. Arterial blood enters the kidney through the renal artery directly from the dorsal aorta (the main posterior artery from the heart). It then passes through arterioles (tiny arteries) to the glomerulus in the Bowman's capsule; a great deal of water and all but the largest molecules in the blood are forced through the walls of the glomerulus by the high pressure of the blood. (The human kidney excretes about 7.5 litres [two gallons] of water an hour through the glomeruli; of course, most of this is subsequently reabsorbed.) Blood leaves the glomerulus through another set of arterioles that form a network of capillaries around the coils of the kidney tubules; it then returns to the heart through the venous system.

Nephrons

Histologically, the kidney tubule is divided into three parts: a thick proximal section that is adjacent to the Bowman's capsule and consists of columnar or cubical epithelial cells with large numbers of microvilli on their surface; a distal portion of very similar structure that leads to the collecting duct; and, between the two, a long, but variable, length of thin-walled tubule. The proximal portion of the tubule has the dual function of reabsorbing materials to be recycled—*e.g.,* water, glucose, amino acids, ascorbic acid, sodium, chlorides, and bicarbonates—and of removing from the blood in the arterioles surrounding the tubule those substances that do not pass through the walls of the glomerulus. The thin-walled portion of the tubule further concentrates the urine, and in the final convoluted section the water, sodium, and phosphate contents of the urine are adjusted to the requirements of the body.

Apart from the capillaries and tubule cells described, there are a few specialized tissues in the kidney. Located around the neck of each arteriole, where it enters the glomerulus, is a cuff of juxtaglomerular cells; these are thought both to control the flow of blood into the glomerulus and to secrete an enzyme. Another interesting cellular adaptation is the presence of podocytes in the walls of the Bowman's capsule. As the name podocytes indicates, these are "footed" cells that protrude from the wall of the capsule and press against the glomerulus, thereby improving fluid flow by maintaining a clear space between the blood vessels of the glomerulus and the wall of the capsule.

Lung tissues. Animal tissues to secure oxygen and excrete carbon dioxide are extremely variable (see RESPIRATION AND RESPIRATORY SYSTEMS). In many small invertebrates, gas exchange takes place directly through the body wall or through external gills, which are thin, often tufted extensions of the body wall through which the blood circulates. The protected gill first appears in the pelecypod mollusks (*e.g.,* clam, oyster, scallop); it is a folded sheet of parallel anastomosing (connecting) blood vessels that are covered first by the mantle (the tissue covering the soft body organs of a mollusk) and then the shell. Adaptation for life on land, however, required the development of the lung, an internal sac with a heavily vascularized wall into which air could be drawn and from which waste gases could be expelled by the expansion and contraction of adjacent structures. The first such organ appears in the gastropod mollusks (*e.g.,* snail, slug, whelk); an analogous structure, in the form of an outgrowth from the anterior end of the alimentary canal, was developed by the lungfish and persists in most adult amphibians, in which the walls of the sac begin to show folding. The increased demand for oxygen occasioned by rapid movement on land resulted in the evolution of multilobed, heavily vascularized lungs in reptiles, birds, and mammals. Gases were inhaled and exhaled first by the simple contraction of the thoracic (chest) walls and later with the assistance of the diaphragm (a muscular partition that separates the thoracic cavity from the abdominal cavity).

Respiratory structures in animals

Two other mechanisms for gas exchange were developed by the arthropods (*e.g.,* insects, spiders, crustaceans). In scorpions the interior surface of a series of four pairs of ventral pouches is folded into a number of lamellae (thin plates). Because of the pagelike appearance of this arrangement, it is called a book lung. In insects and a few other groups (*e.g.,* onycophorans and centipedes), thin-walled ducts, supported by rings of chitin (a horny substance), conduct atmospheric gases to small pouches that are in direct contact with tissues. That this system is extremely efficient in small animals is indicated by its ability to meet the extraordinary oxygen demands of, for example, the flight muscles of many insects. But because it cannot be adapted to large organisms, terrestrial arthropods that use this system have never reached the sizes attained by those animals that have lungs.

TISSUES FOR COORDINATION

None of the tissues so far described would be able to function satisfactorily were they not coordinated in relation to both the external and the internal environment of the animal. Coordinating tissues are broadly classified into those that are physical (nervous and sensory tissues) and those that are chemical (endocrine tissues).

Physical coordinators. It may be stated as a broad generalization that both physical and chemical coordination in invertebrates are performed by the same tissues, because the nervous tissues of many invertebrates also serve as hormone sources. (Hormones, chemical substances secreted into the bloodstream by endocrine glands, have specific effects on other organs.) In vertebrates most endocrine functions are isolated in specialized glands, several of which, such as the pineal and hypophysis in the brain, are derived from nervous tissue. The basic unit of all nervous tissue is the neuron, which, with few exceptions, consists of a cell body from which protrude numerous branching cytoplasmic processes (dendrites) and one long fibre (the axon). The dendritic fibres act as interconnections between neurons; the axon either transmits impulses to an organ (efferent axon) or collects impulses from sensory organs (afferent axon; see NERVES AND NERVOUS SYSTEMS). Internally, the cell body of the neuron contains considerable quantities of what were once called Nissl bodies, which consist of stacks of rough-surfaced endoplasmic reticulum (a convoluted membranous network in cells) with large numbers of ribosomes (granular structures consisting of protein and ribonucleic acid—RNA) sandwiched between them. The presence and structure of the Nissl bodies indicate that RNA plays a major role in the functioning of the nerve cell and is probably responsible for the storage of information (memory). Aggregations of neurons are known as ganglia.

The neuron

In addition to neurons, and also associated with the central nervous system, ganglia, and the axon itself is a tissue that may be either in the form of glia cells or Schwann cells. The former, which are also known as neuroglia cells, constitute a special type of connective tissue that is interspersed among nerve cells and fibres. The Schwann cells are large, flattened cells that are wrapped in such a tight spiral around the axon that most of their cytoplasm has been squeezed out through their membrane. In effect, the axon is wrapped in many layers of membrane with only a little cytoplasm on the inner and outer surfaces. Membranes have a central lipid (fatty) layer; the nerve, therefore, is covered by an insulating layer of lipids that is commonly known as the myelin sheath.

There are three principal types of neuroglia cells: astrocytes, which, as the name indicates, are star-shaped cells with numerous branches at their ends; oligoglia (also

Types of neuroglia cells

called oligodendroglia or oligodendrocytes), which have fewer but thicker branches than astrocytes and are generally smaller; and microglia, which are the smallest of the three. It was once thought that these cells serve merely as connective tissue to support neurons. Evidence is accumulating, however, that they may play a more active role not only in transmitting nutrients and forming enzymes but also in the conduction of neural impulses. Because the short ends of some oligoglia are wrapped tightly around the capillaries in the brain, they could form a direct conducting path for hormones. The astrocytes become active principally when there is neural damage, at which time they assume a phagocytic function.

A slice across the brain or spinal cord shows it to be divided into two regions, descriptively called gray matter and white matter. The former, which is on the outside of the brain and on the inside of the spinal cord, contains the neurons; the white matter owes its appearance to the lipid content of the myelin sheaths around the nerves of which it is largely composed. A typical neuron has about 100 dendritic branches; these may form junctions (synapses) either with dendritic branches from other cells (axodendritic synapses) or with the surface of another neuron (axosomatic synapses). Impulses originating in one neuron may or may not be transmitted through the synapses to other neurons; the mechanism of such selective transmission, on which depend thought, reason, and memory, is not at present fully understood.

A neuron not only receives and transmits impulses to other dendrites but it may also receive an impulse from a sense organ in an outlying part of the body or transmit an impulse to an outlying muscle. The bundles of axons through which these impulses are carried are called nerves. At the terminal end of a transmitting axon in, for example, a muscle, there is a short spray of branches known as axonal telodendria, each of which terminates in a structure called a bouton. When an impulse reaches the boutons, they secrete the chemical acetylcholine, which, because the boutons are in molecular contact with the membrane of the muscle, causes the muscle to contract. Although the nerves leading to the abdominal muscles of the viscera are structurally similar, they operate by a different method. Because visceral muscles are not anchored to joints or bones, they are in a constant state of partial contraction, and movement is produced either by increasing (exciting) or decreasing (depressing) this state. The excitatory nerves mediate their action through the release of acetylcholine; the depressant nerves, through the release of adrenaline or noradrenaline.

There are a few specialized types of neurons in the central nervous system. In many invertebrates and vertebrate larvae, giant neurons carry impulses directly across areas at which they would otherwise be interrupted. Another highly specialized type of giant neuron, the Purkinje cell, lies at the junction of the cerebral cortex and the medulla of the cerebellum, an area in the brain that coordinates locomotor functions and is most highly developed in birds and mammals. Each Purkinje cell has many dendritic branches that ramify through the whole of the outer (molecular) layer of the cerebral cortex. The only afferent nerves leaving the cerebral cortex are those that are made up of the axons of Purkinje cells. In the inner (granule) layer of the cerebellar cortex are large numbers of small granular cells, the dendritic branches of which receive impulses from the axons of incoming (afferent) nerves. Each granular cell has a single axon that rises vertically through the molecular layer and then divides into two branches that run in opposite directions and synapse with the dendrites of some of the Purkinje cells. The union of all the Purkinje cells with the granular cells, which has been likened to a telephone distribution system, is the mechanism for the transmission of the extremely complex nervous impulses required for the locomotor responses of mammals and birds.

Afferent nerves (those that conduct impulses toward the brain and spinal cord) reaching other areas of the central nervous system come from sense organs (receptors) that receive either internal or external stimuli. For higher animals the most important of these are the photoreceptors, the light-sensitive nerve endings located in the rods and cones of the retina of the eye (see SENSORY RECEPTION: *Photoreception*). Chemoreceptors, or taste buds, usually consist of two types of cell pressed together into a small, pear-shaped Y. The receptor cells, which are elongated into an apical process that is in contact with the medium to be tasted, are heavily innervated by terminal buds of the afferent nerves; they are separated from each other by the sustentacular (supporting) cells that lie beneath the surface and are not innervated. There is considerable argument as to whether the human perception of sweet, sour, salty, metallic, and bitter are sensed by the same nerve endings or by different ones; there is still more argument as to which of these senses are present in lower vertebrates. Catfish have "taste buds" in slender projections on their lips, called barbels, and insects have very similar structures both in their antennae and, in the case of butterflies, in their feet (see SENSORY RECEPTION: *Chemoreception*).

Chemoreceptors

The vibroreceptors (those sensitive to mechanical vibrations) apparently are present in relatively few animals. Except for the ear, the most developed of such organs are located in the fish, in which they extend in lines along the length of the body (see SENSORY RECEPTION: *Mechanoreception*). Although the function of sensory structures in animals other than man is difficult to determine, it appears that most organisms possess heat and cold receptors, which are different organs; each apparently consists of a single cell permeated by a terminal treelike branching of a nerve. Pressure sensors, on the other hand, usually consist of a fluid-filled cavity and several cells bunched around the end of a nerve. In man these receptors, called Pacinian corpuscles, are very large (up to four millimetres, or 0.2 inch); they are found in the deeper layers of the skin and throughout the body, at points at which pressure sensation is necessary—*e.g.*, joints, tendons, ligaments.

Chemical coordinators. In many invertebrates chemical stimulators are secreted by the neurons themselves and then move to their place of action along the axon. Such is the case with the hormone in crustaceans that controls the lightening or darkening of the body in response to the environment. The hormonal activities of neurons, however, are nowhere better shown than in the insects, the principal endocrine glands of which are the corpora allata (wing-shaped bodies) and the corpora cardiaca (heart-shaped bodies) that lie alongside the brain. Neurons in the brain secrete large colloidal (jellylike) granules that pass beyond the axon to the heart-shaped bodies and then to the wing-shaped bodies. Some evidence indicates that these colloid granules are also liberated directly into the hemolymph (the fluid in invertebrate tissues and body cavities).

The principal endocrine tissues of the higher vertebrates are the thyroid gland, parathyroid glands, endocrine constituents of the pancreas, interrenal chromaffin tissues of the adrenal gland, and the pituitary gland (see ENDOCRINE SYSTEMS). Of these the thyroid gland presents the clearest evolutionary and histological picture. In mammals this gland secretes not only the hormone thyroxine (tetraiodothyronine) but also smaller quantities of another hormone, triiodothyronine; both have a powerful effect on both rate of maturation and general metabolism. A similar product (monoiodotyrosine) is synthesized by many algae, and both monoiodotyrosine and diiodotyrosine are found in all invertebrates, in many of which the synthesis is apparently centred in the pharyngeal region (the portion of the digestive tract lying between the mouth and the esophagus and forming the respiratory organs of aquatic vertebrates). In the most primitive vertebrates (the cyclostomes) there appears, as an outgrowth of the pharyngeal region, an exocrine gland (one that secretes through a duct, as for example, the digestive glands) that is not unlike a salivary gland in structure. In all higher forms, embryological development of the thyroid gland begins with a duct connected to the pharynx, just as in the lower vertebrates. Ultimately, however, it becomes a ductless (endocrine) gland that is divided into lobes and lobules, which are small, spherical collecting pouches surrounded by cells that secrete the hormone into the lumen of the pouch. Blood vessels in the organ pick up the thyroxine and transport it around the body. The thyroid

Endocrine glands

is chemically linked to the pituitary gland by a system of negative feedback; that is, as the secretory activity of one increases, that of the other decreases.

The parathyroids are also pharyngeal derivatives that are represented in most teleost (bony) fishes by structures called ultimobranchial bodies and in higher forms by four small endocrine glands imbedded in the back part of the thyroid, two on each side. These glands, which have completely lost their lobular structure, consist of a tangled mass of cellular cords, the secretory products of which pass directly to capillaries. The secretions appear to have their principal effect on the calcium–phosphorus ratio in blood.

The endocrine portions of the pancreas (a large gland located behind the stomach that secretes digestive enzymes as well as hormones) are called the islets of Langerhans. In some lower vertebrates, however, the islets are individual glands, completely separated from the pancreas. Like the parathyroids, the islets also consist of tangled cords; they contain four kinds of cells that are designated by the first four letters of the Greek alphabet—alpha, beta, gamma, and delta. The alpha cells are filled with dense masses of granules that yield the hormone glucagon, which, because it is antagonistic to the hormone insulin, prevents the synthesis of glycogen, protein, and fat. The beta cells, which are the most numerous cells in the islets, also consist of large masses of granules that produce insulin, a hormone that controls the sugar (glucose) content of the blood. The function of the gamma and delta cells is not yet known.

Although in mammals interrenal and chromaffin cells are combined into the adrenal gland, the former being the cortex (outside) and the latter the medulla (inside), both tissues are quite distinct. (There are two adrenal glands in mammals, one associated with each kidney.) The interrenal tissues, which exist as separate glands in all vertebrates except birds and mammals, secrete hormones, of which cortisone is a typical example. The cells of these tissues are usually distinguished by the presence in their cytoplasm of large vesicular mitochondria (granular or rodlike bodies, which, in this case, contain fluid-filled cavities). Chromaffin cells, which occur in most animals as scattered clumps, secrete the hormones adrenaline and noradrenaline. The cells are large and ovoid, resembling neurons in all but their lack of axons and dendrites.

The pituitary, which has a dual origin and a dual function, is the most important endocrine gland of the body. It originates from two separate locations: one part, the adenohypophysis, develops as an upgrowth from the roof of the mouth; the other part, the neurohypophysis, develops as a downgrowth from the floor of the brain. The adenohypophysis is divided into three regions, the anterior lobe, the intermediate lobe, and a third lobe that connects to the neurohypophysis. Like most endocrine glands, the anterior lobe consists of tangled masses of cords with numerous types of secreting cells. The hormones secreted by this region mostly interact with the secretions from other endocrine glands to control the internal environment of the body. The neurohypophysis not only has direct axonic connections with the brain but also contains numerous neurosecretory cells (neurons that produce one or more hormones). The products of these cells pass directly to the anterior lobe, the activities of which they control. Thus, through the neurohypophysis the brain can control the secretions of the anterior lobe and thereby adjust the internal environment to the external environment, conditions of which are communicated to the brain by the sense organs. A typical example of such control is found in birds. When the brain becomes aware of increasing day length through impulses from the eye, it stimulates the neurohypophysis to secrete neurohormones. These, in turn, stimulate the anterior lobe to release hormones that cause the rapid development of the gonads, thus assuring that the bird will be in condition to breed in the spring.

Neurohormones

TISSUES FOR SUPPORT AND MOVEMENT

Connective tissues. Connective tissues hold the body together. Most such tissue is of the white fibrous type, which is divided into two kinds, loose and dense, although the two actually grade imperceptibly into each other. White fibrous connective tissue has several roles—it envelops and often penetrates organs to hold them together, encloses muscles, and forms a considerable proportion of the spongy layers of the skin. It is composed of a loose meshwork of a relatively inelastic fibrous protein (collagen), the fibres of which are interspersed in a gelatinous matrix that contains numerous leukocytes derived from the blood. When glandular organs contain considerable quantities of connective tissue—as do, for example, the spleen and thymus—the leukocytes increase in number and become star-shaped cells, the terminal processes of which anastomose to form a loose three-dimensional network. This is best seen in such invertebrates as flatworms, in which a stellate reticulum (a network of star-shaped cells) fills all the space not occupied by discrete internal organs. Mucoid connective tissue, which contains much more gelatinous substance than connective tissue, is found in all embryos as the initial stage in the development of connective tissue; and though rare in adult animals, it does form in the main bulk of such outgrowths as cockscombs and turkey wattles.

Connective tissue of great structural strength consists of almost pure collagen fibres arranged in parallel layers, as in tendons. In ligaments, fibres of elastin, a fibrous protein that is brownish in colour, are mixed with collagen fibres, in which case the tissue is often called yellow elastic connective tissue.

Cartilage. Although usually classified as connective tissues, cartilage and bone are better regarded as supportive in function. Cartilage is the product of cells known as chondrocytes, which secrete around themselves a clear, jellylike mass of a sugar-like substance containing sulfur (chondroitin sulfate). Cartilage of this type, which is found in the adult skeletons of cyclostomes as well as in small sharks and rays, is called hyaline cartilage. In larger sharks the deposition of calcium salts modifies the hyaline cartilage into calcified cartilage, which, because it resembles bone in composition but not in structure, must be clearly differentiated from bone. Another modified form of cartilage is fibrous cartilage, which grades almost imperceptibly into fibrous connective tissue at, for example, the junction of tendons with bone or cartilaginous joints. Elastic cartilage (Figure 2) contains yellow elastic fibres; one of the places at which this type of cartilage appears as a supporting structure is in the outer ears of mammals.

Chondrocytes

Cartilage is also found in some invertebrates, such as in the cranial capsule (head covering) of cephalod mollusks (*e.g.,* squid, octopus), but the principal skeletal substance of invertebrates is chitin—a hard, waterproof, inelastic nitrogenous polysaccharide. Among the animals in which it is found are cnidarians (*e.g.,* hydroids, corals, sea anemones), mollusks, bryozoans ("moss animals"), nematodes (roundworms), and acanthocephalians (spiny-headed worms) as well as the better known arthropods (see SUPPORTIVE AND CONNECTIVE TISSUES: *Varieties of invertebrate skeletons*).

Chitin

Bone. Bone is derived from cells called osteoblasts, which lay down crystals of calcium phosphate known as apatite, in bone. When calcium phosphate is deposited in connective tissue, the resulting structure is called direct bone; when it is deposited as a replacement for cartilage, the resulting structure is called indirect bone. Because the osteoblasts move into a thick, fibrous sheet of white connective tissue during direct bone formation, the somewhat misleading term of membrane bone is often used. At the beginning of direct bone formation, the osteoblasts produce columnar structures (trabeculae) arranged so as to provide the maximum support for the bone that forms on both sides. The space between the trabeculae is filled with red bone marrow. As the osteoblasts become encased in bone, they turn into stellate cells known as osteocytes, which maintain contact with each other through long, branching surface projections. Because the osteocytes cluster around blood vessels, a cross section through a bone appears as a series of concentric rings with a small opening in the centre, called the haversian canal; this opening is actually the space occupied by the blood vessel. Membrane bones, such as those of the growing skull, frequently change their shape with the aid of cells known as osteoclasts. Osteoclasts break down the existing bone

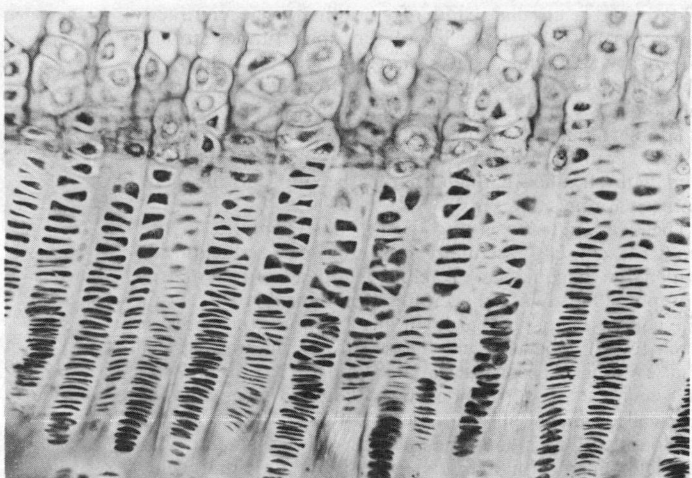

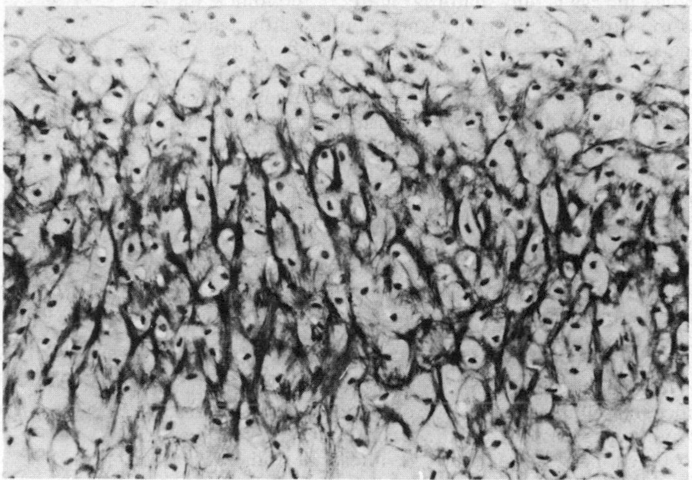

Figure 2: *Photomicrographs of cartilage.*
(Top) Hyaline cartilage of the epiphyseal plate (rabbit tibia).
(Bottom) Elastic cartilage.
Don W. Fawcett, M.D.

into material that can be redistributed to new positions by osteoblasts.

Indirect bone formation, in which bone replaces cartilage (Figure 2), occurs in the shaft bones (those of the arms and legs) of all animals and in the jawbones of most of them. A cell known as chondroclast dissolves the chondroitin sulfate, leaving a soft mucus-like material into which the osteoblasts move. As in the case of direct bone formation, the osteoblasts first build internal trabeculae and then encase them with solid bone. On the shank of bones (the long portion between the ends) there is always a lamellar layer of bony plates wrapped around the outside.

Muscle. Muscle, a relatively simple tissue of complex function, has primarily two kinds of cells. One cell type, found in smooth muscle, contains one nucleus; it is controlled by the autonomic nervous system (the nerves outside the central nervous system that control involuntary body functions, such as breathing and digestion) and is concerned with the maintenance of the body's interior environment. The other cell type makes up striated (striped) muscle, which is also known as skeletal muscle; it is a multinucleate cell (cell with many nuclei) innervated by the central nervous system. Because the latter is under voluntary control, it can coordinate the organism with its external environment. Although cardiac (heart) muscle consists of striated cells (fibres) that are branched and interlocking, this type of muscle is under autonomic nervous control and has a unique system for the conduction of nerve impulses (see MUSCLES AND MUSCLE SYSTEMS).

Smooth muscle tissue generally occurs in simple sheets that are wrapped around, or run along, internal organs. At points at which the cell membranes are fused, the individual cells are interconnected by projections (called nexuses) that run from one cell into the other. Only a relatively few cells contain nerve endings, the impulses being transmitted from cell to cell through the nexuses. This arrangement can readily result in such rhythmic movements as the peristalsis (wavelike muscle contractions) of the intestine.

The striated cells that make up skeletal muscles are very different from those of smooth muscle cells. Each cell consists of numerous long, minute, threadlike structures (myofibrils) that are of two kinds: large fibrils composed of the protein myosin give rise to dark-banded striations; thin fibrils composed of the protein actin give rise to light-banded striations. The myosin bands are designated as the A bands and the actin bands as the I bands after the manner in which they refract (bend) light. When a muscle cell contracts, the thin actin fibres slip in between or coil around the thick myosin fibres; even when fully stretched, the actin fibres still slightly overlap the myosin fibres. This system permits a large degree of extension and contraction without breaking cytoplasmic continuity.

Myofibrils

Because striated muscle cells have several nuclei, it is customary to refer to them as muscle fibres rather than cells. These fibres are grouped together into strands, each surrounded by a thin layer of connective tissue. The strands, in turn, are gathered into bundles that are connected by a thicker layer of connective tissue, and the bundles are held together as a muscle. At each end of a muscle the tissue is infiltrated by white fibrous connective tissue, which itself becomes a ligament for attachment. Unlike smooth muscle, in which only a few cells contain nerve endings, each fibre of a striated muscle is in contact with the terminal of an afferent nerve.

The muscles of the heart were, until very recently, regarded as a single large syncytium (a multinucleate mass of cytoplasm resulting from a fusion of cells). It now appears, however, that fine divisions do exist between the fibres. The muscle fibres in this organ branch and are interlaced; they continue to contract rhythmically long after all connections to the nervous system have been severed.

OTHER TISSUES AND TISSUE FLUIDS

Reproductive tissues. The most important of the reproductive tissues, the gonads (ovaries and testes), produce the gametes (eggs and sperm, respectively). These organs are simplest in the teleost fishes, in which each gonad consists of a simple closed sac, the anterior wall of which carries the spermatogonia (the precursors of mature sperm) in the male and the oogonia (the precursors of mature eggs) in the female. These gamete-producing cells are inactive except during the breeding season, when they proliferate so rapidly that the distended sac often occupies 60 percent of the total body space.

Male reproductive tissues

In all other vertebrates the testes develop as an independent body of tubules surrounding a lumen. The distal end of the tubules contains spermatogonia, and the resulting sperm accumulate in many different forms in a central area in the testes. The network of tubules leads to a duct that may, in some forms, have both a spermatheca (a small bulbous sac) for the accumulation of sperm and an ejaculatory pouch for the expulsion of seminal fluid (the sperm and the liquid secretions in which they are carried). In addition to the seminiferous tubules (those in which the sperm are formed), the testes of vertebrates contain interstitial cells (undifferentiated connective tissue cells lying between the testicular tubules) that secrete male hormones (Figure 3). In vertebrates the sperm duct (vas deferens) joins with the kidney duct (ureter) just before leaving the body. In some invertebrates, notably flatworms, the testes are diffuse structures, actually clumps of spermatogonia scattered throughout the body with ducts leading to a short vas deferens. Although many annelids (*e.g.*, earthworms) contain two or more pairs of segmentally arranged tests, the sperm still leaves the organism by a single duct.

The principal features of the male reproductive system—testes and sperm duct—are common throughout the animal kingdom, but in all groups there are many accessory sexual glands, some of unknown function. In mammals the main accessory glands are the prostate and Cowper's gland. In the former, which is a mass of branched tubules embedded in a matrix of fibrous connective tissue, the secreting tubules open by numerous ducts into the urethra

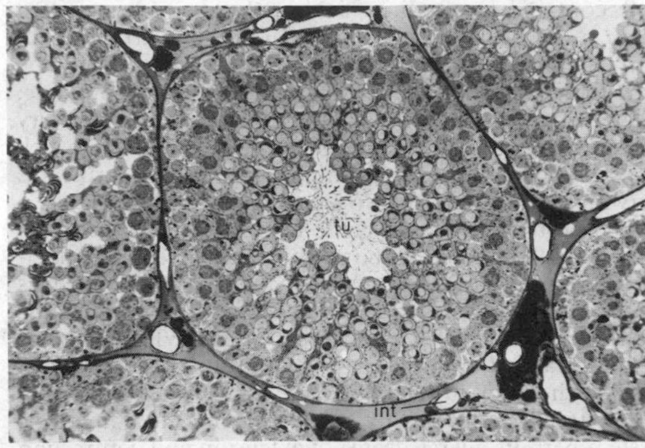

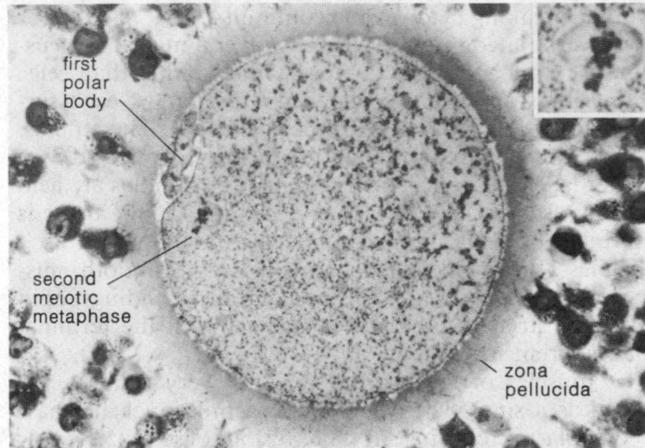

Figure 3: *Photomicrographs of reproductive tissues.*
(Top) Testicular tissue showing the seminiferous tubules (tu) and interstitial cells (int). (Bottom) A recently ovulated human egg with its first polar body.
(Top) Don W. Fawcett, M.D., (bottom) L. Zamboni

(the duct that conducts urine from the urinary bladder to the exterior); it is the excretion of the prostate that forms the main mass of seminal fluid. Cowper's glands also lead into the urethra; they consist of branched tubules that secrete a thick, viscous substance for which no useful function has yet been found in most mammals. In rodents, however, the substance forms a vaginal plug that apparently helps to keep the sperm in the vagina of the female.

Female reproductive tissues

In many animals in which fertilization occurs outside the body, the female reproductive system consists of an egg-producing gland (the ovary) and a tube (the oviduct) to convey the eggs to the exterior. In all vertebrates except bony fishes, no direct connection exists between the ovary and the oviduct; the latter terminates internally as an open funnel that is pressed against the ovary only at the time of ovulation (release of the egg from the ovary). In both oviparous and viviparous forms, the tissues of the oviducts are divided into specific areas for specific functions. In oviparous vertebrates (those that lay eggs) the upper portion of the duct is lined with a mucous epithelium containing simple tubular glands that secrete a dense albuminous fluid, a protein that constitutes egg white. As the egg twists in its passage through this region, each of the ends of the thick albumin is twisted into a chalaza, one of the two spiral cords for holding the egg in the centre of the shell. The next region of the oviduct contains two types of tubular glands that are sometimes branched. One set of these glands secretes additional albumin; the other set of glands secretes a substance that constitutes the liquid portion of the egg white. The next oviduct region lays down a coat of keratin as the base over which the next section deposits the calcareous shell.

In viviparous mammals (those who bear live young) the term oviduct is usually applied only to the region that lies between the internal funnel and the uterus (the organ in which the embryo and fetus develop). The tissues of this oviduct are quite simple, consisting of ciliated epithelium, with a few mucus-secreting cells, thrown into longitudinal folds that fill most of the lumen. At the time of ovulation the blood vessels in the oviduct become engorged with blood, and a circular band of smooth muscle contracts rhythmically so that the lip of the open funnel strokes the ovary and thus secures the egg. The epithelium of the uterus is also deeply folded and contains numerous blood vessels and mucus-secreting glands. The vagina is a simple tubular structure that, in virgins, is coated with ciliated epithelium; ultimately, this is replaced at its distal end with stratified epithelium that becomes cornified in some mammals.

The ovarian tissue is one of the most complex in the body. It consists essentially of a surface epithelium in which the oogonia are developed and a central matrix composed largely of collagen fibres and fibroblasts (cells in the connective tissue that form and maintain the fibres in such tissue). Oocytes (cells derived from mature oogonia that eventually become eggs) are budded into the matrix, in which each is surrounded by a flattened layer of what are called nurse cells. As the egg matures, it becomes surrounded by a membrane and lies within a small cavity (follicle) filled with a fluid secreted by the nurse cells. When the egg is fully mature (Figure 3), the follicle moves to the surface of the ovary and ruptures, after which the egg is taken up by the oviduct. The cleft in the follicle then closes, and because it becomes filled with yellow pigmented cells, it is known as the corpus luteum, or yellow body. The luteal cells secrete a hormone that both inhibits further egg production and assists in preparing the uterus for implantation of the egg. In such animals as the frog, in which large quantities of eggs are produced at the same time, no corpora lutea are formed; instead, the remnants of the ovary survive as a shrivelled body that does not commence egg production again until the next breeding season. In forms having heavily yolked eggs, such as birds, a dense mesh of blood vessels surrounds the follicle; yolk is transferred to the egg through the nurse cells, which remain in contact with the outer surface of the egg.

Hemopoietic tissues. Hemopoietic tissues, which produce the cellular components of blood, have an interesting evolutionary history. In the cyclostomes they appear in scattered masses throughout the intestinal wall, but by the time the level of lungfish is reached, the tissues have become aggregated into a rather well-defined mass in the wall of the stomach. In amphibians and reptiles the hemopoietic tissues are segregated as a distinct organ, the spleen; it is filled with a red pulp consisting primarily of large cells (hemocytoblasts) from which are differentiated all the various types of blood cells. The spleen in these organisms is permeated by arteries that divide into extremely thin-walled arterioles through which the white cells enter the blood; there is still some argument, however, concerning the manner in which the red cells get into the blood.

Production and destruction of blood cells

In mammals the spleen has lost entirely its hemopoietic function; its sole concern is to sort out and destroy erythrocytes that are no longer useful. The production of the cellular constituents of blood has been transferred to the red bone marrow, which fills the spaces in trabecular, or spongy, bone. Here are produced large cells called myeloblasts, which, as the need develops, differentiate into three types of leukocytes; into erythroblasts, from which the erythrocytes are formed; or into multinucleate megakaryocytes, which ultimately produce the blood platelets (minute granular bodies that function in blood clotting). In a normal human, erythrocytes are produced at the rate of about 3,000,000 per second, a figure that may double following serious injury and blood loss. Simultaneous with production, 3,000,000 erythrocytes per second are broken up in the spleen and the pieces passed to the liver, where they are broken down further. Excess pigments are excreted as bile pigments; the remainder are recycled.

Tissue fluids. The most important tissue fluid is lymph, which, as mentioned previously, is a colourless substance derived from blood that filters through the walls of capillaries to bathe the cells in all the tissues of the body (for a detailed discussion, see below *Blood and lymph*).

Another blood fluid of great importance but of little-known function is cerebrospinal fluid. This colourless watery substance, which fills the cavities of the brain and spinal cord, is, to all intents and purposes, identical with the aqueous fluid that fills the eye. Cerebrospinal fluid is a specialized form of lymph; as such, it contains a few lymphocytes, a type of white blood cell that is formed in lymphoid tissues found in such organs as the spleen, tonsils, and lymph nodes. The fluid reaches the cavities of the central nervous system through a complex of tangled capillaries known as the choroid plexus, which is located in the roof of one of the brain cavities (for a detailed discussion, see below *Cerebrospinal fluid*).

Milk

A third body fluid of immense importance is that secreted by the milk-producing glands located in the breasts of female mammals. These are actually greatly enlarged sebaceous glands (saclike structures, usually opening into hair follicles, which secrete an oily fluid that lubricates the skin and hair); it is the large fat drops secreted by these glands into the fluid of the breasts that produces the familiar white emulsion known as milk. In most mammals the glands are activated by a hormone contained in the placenta (the vascular organ that connects the fetus with the maternal uterus), which is eaten by the mother shortly after the birth of its young. Hormones from the corpus luteum of the ovary also enter into the mechanism for initiating milk production. In primitive mammals, such as the duck-billed platypus, milk is not elaborated; instead, the secretion of slightly enlarged sebaceous glands is licked from the surface of the skin by the newborn, which, unlike other mammals, are hatched from eggs. Some birds also produce "milk," so called because of its opaque white appearance; female pigeons, for example, grind grain in the gizzard (a muscular enlargement of the alimentary canal), predigest it to a milky substance, and then regurgitate it for the young. (Pe.G.)

Blood and lymph

Blood is a cell-containing fluid that transports oxygen, water, carbon dioxide, products of metabolism, and internal secretions (*e.g.,* hormones). Blood is also defined as a tissue, constantly circulating throughout animals; it is a means by which the constancy of the internal environment is maintained, and it is also the route by which the defenses against injury and disease may be quickly mobilized. Lymph is a fluid that is derived from the tissues of animal bodies and conveyed to the blood stream by lymphatic vessels. The circulatory system, which contains blood and lymph, is an important connecting pathway; it permits a continuous integration among various tissues and organs of animals and facilitates contact with the environment outside the body.

This section compares blood and lymph in a number of living systems. For more specific information about human blood, see BLOOD. The human lymphatic system is treated in the article CIRCULATION AND CIRCULATORY SYSTEMS.

DEFINITIONS AND ORIGIN

Definitions. Blood in mammals may be defined as the red fluid that is pumped by the heart into arteries and returns to the heart in veins, following a complex but completely closed circular path. The red colour of mammalian blood is caused by hemoglobin, an oxygen-carrying protein in red cells (erythrocytes). Mature red blood cells of mammals, which contain no nuclear component, are disk shaped and float in a nearly colourless liquid called plasma. Plasma also contains white cells (leukocytes) and tiny bodies called platelets, which seal wounds. The grainy cytoplasmic component of one type of white cell, called granulocytes, constantly changes shape, engulfing and destroying unwanted particles. A nongranular type of white cell (lymphocytes) originates in mammalian lymphoid tissue (*e.g.,* spleen, lymph nodes) and has important immunological functions. Lymph, a rather colourless, sometimes milky liquid, drains from the tissues into lymph vessels, which converge into a thoracic duct, which empties into the blood. The above definitions of blood and lymph also apply (with modifications) to vertebrates other than mammals; *i.e.,* the red cells of other vertebrates contain nuclei but are red, except in the icefish, which has colourless blood. White cells vary in shape not only among vertebrates but even among mammals. The platelets of mammals resemble tiny disks of cytoplasm, but those of other vertebrates have nuclei.

Invertebrate animals have a great variety of liquids, cells, and modes of circulation. In insects, a heart pumps fluid, called hemolymph, through an open system to the tissues. In some worm species the fluid contains pigmented cells, but the fluid, called coelomatous fluid, does not circulate; in others the fluid circulates, but the cells may contain no pigment.

Perhaps blood should be defined by its functions, rather than by its appearance—when passing through skin, gills, or lungs, blood picks up oxygen from outside the body and loses carbon dioxide that was picked up in the metabolizing tissues; when passing through tissues, blood does the reverse and also picks up metabolized food, which maintains the cells of the body, and passes poisonous molecules and excess water to the kidneys for excretion.

Origin. How did the need for blood and lymph arise? Life probably originated in the oceans from molecules that accidentally developed an ability to reproduce, to form cells, and to evolve by reproducing many of the accidental changes (mutations) that occurred in their hereditary material. Most of the early cells must have developed certain deficiencies, and many survived only if they also developed the ability to depend on other cells, either as food sources or for transporting food, oxygen, and waste products.

Eventually, aggregations of specialized cells became organized into bodies whose inner cells lost contact with the outer world and with each other. An electronic system (the nervous system) and liquid systems of blood and lymph developed to provide communication among specialized body regions. In addition, as organs became complicated, both structurally and functionally, they developed a mechanism (hormones) for transmitting, receiving, and integrating information. A hormone is formed in one organ and transported in the blood to another site, where its major effect is exerted. An increase in blood sugar, for example, causes an increase in synthesis (in the pancreas) of the hormone insulin, which causes a decrease in blood sugar; an increase in the activity of the pituitary gland, in the brain, causes an increase in the activity of the adrenal glands, near the kidneys; and adrenal secretions in turn cause a decrease in pituitary activity. Mechanisms such as those provided by hormones enable a multicellular organism to outlive the individual cells comprising it; the removal of dead cells and of other particles too large to be transported by the blood to the kidneys for excretion is carried out by white cells.

Hormones

The blood has a mechanism that prevents its being emptied through wounds. Platelets in mammals and cells called thrombocytes in other vertebrates aggregate at a wound site, and, in the plasma near them, a clot, composed of a protein called fibrin, forms. Invertebrates may rely on the motion of cells to plug their wounds.

In the brief discussion of blood and lymph that follows, it may seem as if in species most alien to man the least sophisticated fluids exist; *i.e.,* fewer and less specialized proteins occur, as well as more primitive, all-purpose cells, but this may reflect limitations of knowledge.

PLASMA

Small molecules and the regulation of water content. Water molecules, which are the main component of body fluids, probably form clusters that break up rapidly except at water-repellent surfaces (*e.g.,* as provided by fats), where the clusters are more stable and icelike. The complex mixture of fatty and nonfatty structures in cell membranes, therefore, profoundly affects the behaviour of water and the substances dissolved in it. Although water itself and certain small molecules and ions (charged particles) pass through the membranes of all active cells, certain other molecules cannot; urea, an organic compound larger than most ions, however, apparently passes into cells by disrupting water clusters.

When two solutions containing different quantities of a substance are separated by a membrane that allows only water to pass (a semipermeable membrane), water flows through the membrane to the solution containing the most substance, in an attempt to equalize the concentrations on both sides of the membrane. When a cell is placed in water, therefore, it swells, because water passes into the cell through the membrane in response to the dissolved molecules and ions inside the cell; these particles are said to exert an internal pressure, called osmotic pressure, which may cause the cell to burst, or lyse (or, in the case of blood cells, hemolyse). If a cell is placed in a solution containing a higher concentration of a substance than that found in the cell, water leaves the cell through the membrane, and the cell assumes a wrinkled, or crenated, appearance. Living cells, including the blood cells in plasma, must expend metabolic energy to maintain an osmotic equilibrium.

Cell lysis

The salt concentrations in present-day seas are higher than those within cells. Invertebrate animals capable of regulating the water content of their circulating body fluids usually lower it to about two-thirds that of the surrounding ocean; aquatic mammals also are able to perform this physiological regulation. Other animals apparently need no such regulation. The body fluids of echinoderms, for example, resemble seawater; among crustaceans, the shore crab (*Carcinus*) regulates its water content, but the spider crab (*Maia*) does not. *Rhithropanopeus* is able to swell when it must molt; its eyestalks produce a hormone that prevents water inflow at other times. Animals that cannot regulate their water content and thus tolerate only a narrow range of salt concentrations (stenohaline animals) probably are restricted to oceanic life; animals that are able to regulate their water content (euryhaline animals) are free of this restriction. Mechanisms other than those involving a circulating body fluid, however, enable certain animals to regulate their water content; *e.g.,* some coelenterates and flatworms (Platyhelminthes), which live in freshwater, utilize a diffusely branched system to remove water.

Some cyclostomes (hagfish and lampreys), among the most primitive fishes, live in the ocean, are permeable to water, and regulate their osmotic pressure. Elasmobranch fishes (sharks and rays) maintain a blood osmotic pressure above that of seawater by retaining urea, which is excreted rapidly in other vertebrates by the kidneys. The advantages to marine animals of maintaining specific osmotic pressures are not well known. Saltwater fishes lose some regulatory ability in the cold; as a result, the concentration of salts in the plasma increases, so that it acts as an "antifreeze." Fishes in freshwater also may be affected by cold, but their plasma loses ions, which means that it freezes more easily.

The ability of an animal to retain salts when moving to freshwater may have been a prerequisite to the evolution of animals capable of retaining both salts and water on land. The urine of freshwater fishes contains a low concentration of salts. Amphibians and many crabs return to water when some as yet unknown mechanism senses the need for water to dilute body fluids. A specific region in the brain of amphibians produces a hormone similar to the antidiuretic hormone of man, which regulates water retention. Among reptiles, the evolutionary success of crocodiles over dinosaurs may be attributable to the development in crocodiles of a skin more impermeable to water; certain crocodiles, however, when dehydrated, return to the water, taking in more water through the skin than by drinking.

Although a sense of thirst is necessary in all animals living on land, the composition of their internal fluids may vary. Most of the osmotic pressure in the plasma of water-dwelling crustaceans, for example, is provided by salts; half of that in land-dwelling insects is provided by organic compounds called amino acids.

Regulation of ion content in man

The regulation of the content of ions in the plasma of vertebrates, especially mammals, appears increasingly complex at higher evolutionary levels; but perhaps man seems most complex because he has been studied most. The plasma concentrations of ions such as sodium, potassium, and calcium are regulated by hormones; but human emotional stress increases the activity of the adrenal glands, whose secretions affect the transport of sodium and potassium ions across cell membranes.

Glucose has relatively little effect on the osmotic pressure of plasma, but it is an important source of energy in cells; it must be available at all times, therefore, within controlled levels. Blood-glucose levels in vertebrates are regulated by two hormones formed in the pancreas, insulin and glucagon. Insulin, synthesized when plasma-glucose concentration increases, stimulates the liver to convert excess glucose into a storage compound, glycogen. Glucagon acts in the opposite way; *i.e.,* it increases abnormally low levels of plasma glucose. Among vertebrates, either hormone may dominate in maintaining the proper levels of plasma glucose, whose concentration is profoundly affected by feeding and by stress.

Because fatlike substances do not dissolve in water and force a specific arrangement of water molecules around them, they usually circulate surrounded by protein molecules, so that their water-hating (hydrophobic) areas do not come in contact with water in the plasma.

Proteins and their various roles. There are about 20 kinds of amino acids that link together in a specific order to form protein molecules. Each amino-acid sequence is determined by heredity; in turn, the sequence of amino acids determines the shape of each protein. A mosaic-like arrangement of amino acids with positive and negative charges may comprise most of the exposed parts of a protein molecule; other amino acids, which are hydrophobic, are found inside the coil-shaped molecule and thus do not come in contact with water surrounding it. The function of a protein molecule depends on its shape.

During evolution, a chance mutation may result in the replacement of one amino acid in a specific protein molecule by another. If the newly inserted amino acid destroys the function of the protein, an organism may die; on the other hand, the loss of a protein function by mutation may be compensated for by another mutation, either in the protein molecule itself or in some other one. If an animal survives a partial loss of function, the loss may be discovered if the animal becomes ill. Many proteins function as enzymes (biological catalysts); some enzymes (*e.g.,* several blood-clotting factors) have been shown to exist only because people born without them develop specific symptoms. Mutations that do not affect function can be discovered only by analyzing proteins whose sequences of amino acids have been established. The insulin of vertebrates, whose amino-acid sequence has been established, functions only if the two functional chains comprising the molecule are not altered; a mutation in the nonfunctional section that connects the chains does not inactivate the molecule.

Since an enzyme catalyzes a reaction involving a specific compound, it can be identified. An enzyme whose shape must change before it becomes active or a protein involved in the structure of an organism usually can be distinguished only by crude tests. Many active enzymes function efficiently only with molecules prepared from the same species. Although others (*e.g.,* insulin, blood-clotting Factor VIII) derived from one mammalian species will function if injected into another species, they act as antigens; *i.e.,* they stimulate formation of proteins called antibodies in the injected species. These enzymes, therefore, are recognized in the injected animal as foreign in composition, if not in function. The specificity of proteins for their own hosts has limited the understanding of their functions in species remote from man. Crude separation of plasma proteins carried out in mammals other than man show that proteins such as albumin and alpha, beta, and gamma globulins occur in them.

Species-specific enzymes

Albumin, a rather small protein that dissolves in water, comprises more than half the total proteins found in mammalian plasma, contributes to the blood osmotic pressure, and transports certain ions and fatty acids. Yet, humans born without it appear normal. The second most abundant protein in mammalian blood is a long, large molecule called fibrinogen. When blood clots, a series of enzyme interactions converts an inactive plasma enzyme (prothrombin) into an active enzyme (thrombin) that removes two pairs of amino-acid groups from each fibrinogen molecule to convert it into a molecule called a fibrin monomer. Molecules of the fibrin monomer then link together to form strands of fibrin, the visible clot. The remaining liquid, plasma lacking fibrinogen, is called serum. Fibrinogen, prothrombin, and many other proteins are formed in the liver. In animals other than mammals, some clotting enzymes, as well as the events that trigger their interactions, may be restricted to the cytoplasmic component of specific sensitive cells (see below *Thrombocytes and platelets*).

Gamma globulins are produced by plasma cells and lymphocytes that probably occur only in vertebrates. Some other globulins carry specific metal ions, which colour them—*e.g.,* mammalian transferrin, which carries iron, is brown, and ceruloplasmin, which carries copper, is blue.

Hemoglobin

The most deeply coloured globulins have a specific slot in which they carry a flat molecule (heme) containing iron. In vertebrates, four globulin-heme moieties form one hemoglobin molecule in the red cells, where it remains until the cells die. Many polychaete worms have developed a similar protein; slight difference in the structure of its heme, however, makes it green in colour. A variety of polychaete blood proteins exists. The noncirculating coelomic fluid of some polychaetes contains hemoglobin; other polychaetes have two hemoglobins—one in the plasma and another in coelomic cells. Hemoglobin predominates in young *Serpula* polychaetes, green pigment (chlorocruorin) in older ones, and another polychaete, *Arenicola,* has a very large hemoglobin molecule. Hemocyanin, a large protein molecule that contains copper and turns blue when it takes up oxygen, occurs in many mollusks, where it may be the main plasma protein. All the pigment types mentioned pick up oxygen molecules easily and release them where they are needed. A change of shape in each hemoglobin subunit accompanies oxygen uptake or release and is transmitted to the other units in a way that facilitates the process (see COLORATION).

FORMED ELEMENTS

Red cells (erythrocytes). The hemoglobin in the plasma of some worms allows them to carry about ten times more oxygen than can an equal volume of seawater. The localization of hemoglobin in red cells increases this capacity another four times. The evolution of cells with such a singular function is traceable by arranging species in order of the increasing oxygen-carrying efficiency of their red cells. The mature red cells of mammals lack nuclei. Not only does a nucleus take space; it also requires oxygen; mammals, therefore, have the most efficient red cells, at least so far as oxygen-carrying ability is concerned. It thus is tempting to presume that, if no further evolutionary progress occurs, even though mutations continue, a maximum efficiency has been attained. Indeed, one can say that in the following aspects, evolution of red cells apparently stopped long ago: the total volume of red cells in proportion to the total volume of blood varies relatively little among mammalian species; in addition, all normal red cells have about the same high concentration of hemoglobin, above which the molecules would soon interfere with each other or even form crystals. On the other hand, the diameter of red cells varies greatly, ranging from less than 3 to more than 9 micrometres, or microns (1 micrometre is 0.001 millimetre). Both Indian and African elephants have large red cells (9.2 micrometres in diameter), but no clear relationship between red-cell size and total body size exists among other species.

Evolution and red-cell size

Red cells apparently became smaller as life on land developed or evolution in general progressed, but the relationship between red-cell size and evolutionary advancement is not clear. The supposedly primitive hagfish, for example, has red cells 26.4 micrometres long; those of the related lamprey are only 14.3 micrometres. The red cells of many sharks, about as large as those of some amphibians, are larger than those of many other fishes.

The disk-shaped mature erythrocytes of most mammals have thick, rounded edges and lack nuclei. When such a cell is cut in half, both halves may assume a disk shape and resemble small red cells. Certain membrane components in the smallest red cells (two to four micrometres in diameter), which occur in ruminants such as cows, occur in a proportion different from that in other mammalian red cells. The fact that red cells are thin in the centre may increase their efficiency in gas transport. The efficiency of gas exchange and transport may be increased also by the fact that the shape of red cells can be distorted into cones, clubs, and dumbbells as they pass through the extremely narrow blood capillaries.

Perhaps red and white blood cells originate in the same cells in bone marrow. The need for red cells is conveyed in mammals by a protein (erythropoietin). The protein is formed by the action of a substance (erythrogenin), synthesized by the kidneys when they lack oxygen, on another molecule (erythropoietinogen), which is synthesized in the liver. A severe loss of red cells and the subsequent decrease in available oxygen is normally followed by a flood of young red cells, which still have nuclear material. The mature red cells of mammals contain many enzymes important for their maintenance and partly responsible for their death when they fail; the oldest cells, therefore, should die first, and they do in some mammals (*e.g.,* mouse, dog, and man); in other species, however, red-cell death may occur at any age in an apparently random manner. Although it has been suggested that red cells must pump out sodium ions and retain potassium ions to survive, dogs and some other mammals have about the same proportions of sodium and potassium ions in both red cells and surrounding plasma; yet their cells live no longer than do those of man. On the other hand, the less heat a vertebrate species produces, the longer its red cells live: turtle erythrocytes, for example, live longer than those of man; red cells of birds and mice have a shorter existence.

Extreme differences between sodium- and potassium-ion concentrations in erythrocytes exist in various species (see Table 1) and even within breeds in one species.

Table 1: Concentration of Potassium and Sodium Ions in Plasma and Red Cells of Certain Vertebrates

	potassium ions*		sodium ions*		percentage of red cells replaced per day
	red cells	plasma	red cells	plasma	
Man	95	4	19	138	1
Dog	8	4	97	143	1
Chicken	119	6	18	154	3

*Milli-equivalents per 1,000 millilitres.

White cells. All poorly pigmented cells normally found floating in blood, hemolymph, or coelomic fluid may be called leukocytes, although those in the hemolymph and coelomic fluid of invertebrates are often called hemocytes and coelomocytes, respectively. White cells in hemolymph and coelomic fluid include cells that eat (phagocytize) foreign particles, as do the granulocytes of mammals; cells that recognize and chemically attack only specific foreign matter, as do the lymphocytes and plasma cells of mammals; and cells that clump together when disturbed, as do the thrombocytes. The distinctions among functions and blood-cell types of animals other than man, however, have not yet been clearly established.

A superficial resemblance exists among some mammalian blood cells and those of other animals. Some white cells of sea cucumbers (Holothuroidea), for example, resemble mammalian white blood cells called basophils; gastropod mollusks have cells that resemble lymphocytes and granular amoebocytes that resemble certain granulocytes of man (eosinophils); crustaceans have coelomocytes that clump around foreign cells and eat them; and insects have a multitude of hemocytes some of which resemble human white cells while others do not. The evolution of insects and other arthopods diverged from that of man and other chordates so long ago that the blood cells of these two animal groups do not provide any evidence of a common ancestry.

Plasmatocytes

The most active white cells in insects, called plasmatocytes, can spread either over surfaces of parasites forming membranous capsules or over foreign particles; often they become granular. Hemocytes, most abundant in the last immature stage (larval instar) of insects, decrease in numbers during the nonfeeding stage called pupation, after which, in certain insects, new cells are formed. When a pupa is injured, hemocytes appear to seal the wound; actual clotting in insects, however, is initiated by cells called cystocytes (coagulocytes). When hemolymph flows from a wound, cystocytes enlarge, break down, and either turn the plasma around them cloudy or form threads around which the plasma jells. Other insect hemocytes show no identifiable activity.

Echinoderms and worms also contain blood cells very different from those of man. Echinoderm groups differ in their types of blood cells; all, however, have phagocytes to eat foreign particles, and other hemocytes to repair damage and to seal wounds. Echinoderm blood cells probably form from stem cells (so-called lymphocytes); active movement of cells within the heartless hemal system may transport food throughout the body. Hemoglobin-containing cells occur in some burrowing echinoderms. The variety of cells in hemal and coelomic fluids among echinoderms and even within various areas of one individual possibly reflects a range of requirements totally different from those of man, so that there are no blood kinships between man and echinoderms. Among vertebrates, relationships are clearer; *e.g.*, fishes and amphibians have granulocytes, lymphocytes, and, probably, a type of white cell present in human blood and referred to as a monocyte.

Thrombocytes and platelets. The thrombocytes of fishes, amphibians, reptiles, and birds resemble the cells that aggregate at wounds in invertebrates; in vertebrates, however, the plasma apparently has more responsibility in the clotting process. Since no thrombin (an enzyme involved in clotting) forms when thrombocytes are removed from the plasma of fishes, these cells, which break down on contact with a wound, must liberate substances that convert plasma prothrombin (an enzyme precursor) to thrombin, which then converts plasma fibrinogen into fibrin strands (a clot). In contrast to other vertebrates, the plasma of mammals contains an inactive enzyme, Factor XII, also called the Hageman factor. Mammalian Factor XII, upon contact with some hard foreign substance, becomes an active enzyme that initiates clotting. The contact-sensitive thrombocytes of other vertebrates are analogous to small disks of cytoplasm (platelets) in mammals. Platelets are derived from large bone-marrow cells (megakaryocytes). Although platelets aggregate in plasma under a variety of conditions, which also cause the aggregation of thrombocytes, and their clumping, or sticking, is accompanied by the liberation of several important substances, they contribute to the clotting of plasma only by making available a chemical component of their membranes (phospholipids). Platelets, however, are essential for sealing wounds in mammals.

Factor XII

Lymphocytes and lymph. Animals must recognize their own cells, so that they do not eat them. The system by which vertebrates protect themselves (*i.e.*, development of specific immunities), however, has not yet been found in the invertebrates. Hagfish appear to be the most primitive animals to have lymphocytes, form antibodies, and reject tissue grafts. From the higher fishes to man, lymphocytes and plasma cells become progressively more abundant, antibodies more specific, and tissue grafts less successful.

As blood flows through the capillaries, dissolved substances pass between the blood and the surrounding tissues. Most of these substances pass readily through the capillary walls, but a small amount of protein, once forced from the plasma, cannot return because the protein molecules are too large. This protein and waste fluids pass from the cells into the lymph vessels, which have much more permeable walls and within which the pressure is much lower than that in the capillaries. The fluids are pushed through the vessels by the motion of organs and muscles, their flow directed by valves along the way; in fishes, amphibians, reptiles, and some birds, a heartlike organ (the lymph heart) helps the circulation. As it flows, the lymph passes through many glandlike masses of tissue, called lymph nodes, and through the thymus, a glandular body present in all vertebrates. Birds have an extra lymphatic organ, the bursa of Fabricius. In all vertebrates, the lymph vessels combine, finally reaching a duct (*e.g.*, the thoracic duct in mammals) from which the lymph enters the venous bloodstream.

In very young animals, lymphocytes are formed in the thymus; later they form from cells in the bone marrow and are transported, and deposited at, certain nodes or organs. The fate of each lymphocyte depends on the information or stimulation it receives at its point of deposition. The lymphocytes in gut-associated lymph tissues or those in the bursa of birds, for example, are apparently prepared to form antibodies if they are needed. In mammals, a lymphocyte at a lymph gland may be stimulated by a molecule (antigen) to form a specific antibody. Certain lymphocytes first form a globulin known as immunoglobulin M (IgM); then the lymphocytes divide, and each daughter cell receives some IgM. If stimulated again by more antigen molecules, the lymphocytes again divide, liberating their IgM and transforming into plasma cells that form a smaller globulin (IgG). Some antigen molecules probably remain with certain cells in the lymph node and eventually stimulate new lymphocytes passing the lymph node. Speed, intensity, and complexity of these reactions apparently increase from cyclostomes through elasmobranchs to bony fishes. Most of their globulins of fishes probably resemble human IgM. Amphibians, however, may be more advanced; bullfrogs may form IgM, then IgG, or IgG first, depending on the type of antigen molecule injected. The antibodies formed by a bullfrog injected with serum of one mammalian species react with the serums of other mammals; the antibodies of mammals, however, are more specific. The serum of a rabbit immunized to serum of one fish species, for example, reacts less with serums of other fishes; in fact, the extent of interaction of the serums serves as a measure of evolutionary relationships among species.

Fate of lymphocytes

The vertebrate thymus plays a role in determining which lymphocytes survive, apparently stimulating their division and then destroying undesired ones. Lymphocytes may spend only a few hours at a time in the blood and many months elsewhere. The variety of lymphatic systems among vertebrate species probably has some relationship to the immunological functions required for each. The ability of man's immunological system to distinguish differences in blood-group substances means that there are many blood incompatibilities; *i.e.*, few humans, unless they are twins, have completely identical sets of blood groups. Perhaps the thymus destroys cells that know too much; *i.e.*, cells that would form antibodies against substances or tissues that are useful (see IMMUNITY). (L.V.)

Cerebrospinal fluid

In the vertebrate embryo the central nervous system is formed as a hollow tube with a canal extending its entire length. In later life the canal remains open in the brain stem but narrows considerably in the spinal cord. In each of the two cerebral hemispheres of the brain the canal widens into cavities called ventricles. The cerebrospinal fluid (CSF) fills these ventricles and the canal within the brainstem. It also surrounds and bathes the spinal cord and the brain, acting as a lubricant and a mechanical barrier against shock. The fluid flows slowly from the ventricles, the principal site of formation; down through the canal of the brainstem; and ultimately out into the tissue spaces surrounding the central nervous system.

Distribution

It is a clear and colourless liquid of low specific gravity. Like the blood it is slightly alkaline in reaction, having a pH of 7.3–7.4. It is about 99 percent water and has an average freezing point of 0.57° C (33°F). The fluid normally has less than five leukocytes (mononuclears or possibly lymphocytes) per cubic millimetre and no red blood cells. The relationship of the various chemical constituents of the cerebrospinal fluid to that of blood plasma is shown (Table 2).

FUNCTIONS OF CEREBROSPINAL FLUID

The cerebrospinal fluid's many functions are chiefly mechanical. It bathes brain and spinal cord and helps to bear the weight of the brain. It lubricates the surfaces between the meninges covering the brain and spinal cord, on the one hand, and those covering the bones that encase them, on the other. The fluid is a buffer that distributes the force of a blow on the head. It helps to keep intracranial

Table 2: Comparison of Normal Cerebrospinal Fluid and Blood Plasma Average Values

	cerebrospinal fluid	blood plasma
Calcium	2.4 mEq/1	5.2 mEq/1
Carbon dioxide tension	46 mm Hg	40 mm Hg
Chloride	124 mEq/1	100 mEq/1
Bicarbonate	22 mEq/1	22 mEq/1
Glucose	50–80 mg/100 ml	70–110 mg/100 ml
Lactate	1.7 mEq/1	1.7 mEq/1
Lipids, total	1.25 mg/100 ml	876 mg/100 ml
Cholesterol	0.4 mg/100 ml	180 mg/100 ml
Cholesterol esters	0.3 mg/100 ml	126 mg/100 ml
Magnesium	2.6 mEq/1	1.8 mEq/1
Nonprotein nitrogen	19 mg/100 ml	27 mg/100 ml
Ammonia	6 μg/100 ml	56 μg/100 ml
Creatinine	1.1 mg/100 ml	1.6 mg/100 ml
Urea	14 mg/100 ml	14 mg/100 ml
Uric acid	0.24 mg/100 ml	4 mg/100 ml
Phosphorus	1.6 mg/100 ml	4 mg/100 ml
Potassium	3 mEq/1	4.5 mEq/1
Protein, total	15–45 mg/100 ml	7,000 mg/100 ml
Prealbumin	5%	0 (?)
Albumin	50%	56%
Globulin, total	45%	44%
Alpha globulin	15%	14.5%
Beta globulin	19%	12%
Gamma globulin	11%	17.5%
Sodium	142 mEq/1	137 mEq/1

pressures relatively constant; its volume decreases to compensate for increased arterial pulsations or greater volume of blood or brain tissue and increases to compensate for a decrease in these factors, as in degeneration or atrophy of the brain. By means of the cerebrospinal fluid, substances are removed from the tissues of brain and spinal cord and carried into the blood stream, and the fluid may possibly act also in the reverse direction. Materials carried away by the fluid include metabolic waste products, antibodies, abnormal chemical constituents, and pathologic products of disease. It helps to circulate drugs administered in therapy. It does not carry enough nutritional substances to be of much help in the normal metabolism of nervous tissue.

During certain diseases that affect the meninges or the central nervous system or both, the cerebrospinal fluid may change significantly in physical characteristics, cytological constituents, and chemical contents; and there may be microbiologic and serologic alterations in the fluid. Careful examination of the cerebrospinal fluid in such a situation may be very useful in differential diagnosis. Table 3 illustrates the changes in the profile of the cerebrospinal fluid in the differentiation of certain diseases of the meninges and the central nervous system.

FORMATION, REABSORPTION, AND FLOW

Mechanisms of formation

Although there are still differing views concerning the mechanisms of the formation of cerebrospinal fluid, the general belief is that the fluid originates largely by filtration across the membranes that line the spaces containing the fluid (the ependyma of both the choroid plexuses and the ventricles, as well as the arachnoid) but also by active secretion of substances such as protein and sodium.

From the cerebrospinal spaces the fluid enters into the venous system. It was formerly held that the greater part of the fluid is absorbed through the arachnoid villi or pacchionian granulations and passes into the dural sinuses and thence into the venous blood. Probably, however, much of the fluid is absorbed into the veins from the spaces around the spinal roots and cranial nerves and from the perivenous spaces. Some may also be absorbed

Table 3: Cerebrospinal Fluid in Differential Diagnosis

condition or disease	initial pressure (mm CSF)	spinal subarachnoid block	appearance	cells (per mm³)	protein (mg/100 ml)	glucose (mg/100 ml)	chlorides as NaCl (mg/100 ml)	colloidal gold curve	comments
Normal	70–150	absent	clear colourless	0–5 mononuclear	15–45	50–80	700–750	00000000	
Infections on the central nervous system and meninges									
Acute purulent meningitis	200–600	absent	cloudy to purulent	500–20,000 mainly polymorphonuclear	100–1,000	10–20 mg or less	575–700	variable	organisms may be found by direct stain or culture
Tuberculous meningitis	200–500	absent	opalescent to faint yellow	100–500 mainly lymphocytes	60–700	15 mg or less	525–675	variable	tubercle bacilli may be found by stain or guinea pig inoculation
Cryptococcus meningitis	200–400	absent	slightly opalescent	100–500 mainly lymphocytes	50–300	30–40 mg or less	normal or slightly decreased	variable	yeasts may be found with India ink stain or special culture
Syphilitic meningitis	150–300	absent	clear to slightly opalescent	300–2,000 mononuclear	50–400	normal or slightly decreased	normal or slightly decreased	first or midzone	serologic tests usually positive
Parenchymatous central nervous system syphilis	normal	absent	clear	10–50 mononuclear	50–100	normal	normal	first or midzone	serologic tests usually positive except in late treated tabes
Viral meningitis and encephalitis	100–250	absent	clear	25–250 polymorphonuclear early; later lymphocytes	40–80	normal (occasionally more)	normal	normal or non-specific	occasionally virus may be found
Acute anterior poliomyelitis	normal	absent	clear	50–250 mainly mononuclear	40–100	normal	650–750	variable	polymorphonuclear cells may be found in preparalytic stage; gradual rise in protein
Brain abscess	200–800	absent	clear colourless	30–100 mainly mononuclear	40–200	normal	normal	variable	polymorphonuclear cells present early, before encapsulation
Miscellaneous meningeal and nervous system diseases									
Carcinomatous meningitis	150–400	absent	clear to opalescent	100–500 mainly mononuclear	40–200	moderately decreased	normal	variable	cancer cells may be found in stained sediment
Brain tumour	150–500	absent	clear to yellow	usually normal, may be up to 50–100	20–150	normal	normal	variable	pleocytosis usually indicates tumour near ventricles or meninges
Spinal cord tumour	normal or decreased	partial or complete	clear to yellow	usually normal	50–5,000	normal	normal	first or midzone	with complete block may be marked increase in protein
"Guillain-Barre syndrome"	normal	absent	clear to yellow	normal	50–1,000	normal	normal	variable	often marked increase in protein without associated pleocytosis
Subarachnoid or ventricular hemorrhage	150–400	absent	bloody yellow	crenated red blood cells	50–500	normal	normal	variable	fluid grossly bloody; supernatant yellow
Multiple sclerosis	normal	absent	clear colourless	5-50 mononuclear	40–70	normal	normal	first zone in 20%; variable in 40%	

through the ventricular ependyma and, in a reverse direction, through the choroid plexus and some, by osmosis, directly into the pial veins on the brain surface and into the capillaries of the pia arachnoid.

Unlike the blood, the cerebrospinal fluid is not given energy for circulation by an organ like the heart; but there is a definite movement of the fluid from the lateral ventricles down into the third and fourth ventricles, the basal cisterns, and the subarachnoid space; and there is constant circulation in the sense that the fluid is being continuously secreted and absorbed. There is clinical evidence that obstruction of one opening, the foramen of Monro, between one lateral ventricle and the third ventricle will cause hydrocephalus on one side, with enlargement of that ventricle, and that obstruction of the Sylvian aqueduct will cause hydrocephalus on both sides, involving the third and both lateral ventricles. The forces that bring about the flow of the cerebrospinal fluid and affect its rate include the arterial pulsations within the choroid plexus, respiration, the increase in venous pressure brought about by thoracic and abdominal movements, movements of the head and body and changes in their position, and filtration and secretion pressures.

The normal adult has from about 100 to 150 millilitres of cerebrospinal fluid. This fluid is replaced every six to eight hours or three or four times a day. Abnormally large volume is caused either by excessive formation or deficient absorption.

USE IN DIAGNOSIS: LUMBAR PUNCTURE

In lumbar puncture a needle is inserted into the subarachnoid space in the lumbar region, and a little cerebrospinal fluid is withdrawn for use in diagnosis. In most cases the cerebrospinal fluid pressure is also measured and the flow of the fluid investigated. The interspace between the third and fourth lumbar vertebrae is chosen for the site of the puncture because at this level the spinous processes are farthest apart and because, in the adult, this point is below the level of the lower end of the spinal cord.

After clear fluid has been obtained, the pressure is determined, ordinarily by means of the Ayer water manometer. Pressures from 70 to 150 millimetres (of cerebrospinal fluid) are normal. If the pressure is within the normal range and there is no other contra-indication, such as suspected intracranial disease, the Queckenstedt test is done. This is a test of the response of spinal fluid pressure to constriction of the jugular veins in the neck and release of the constriction. Normally the pressure rises rapidly and falls with equal rapidity. A slow, incomplete rise and fall or no response whatever is a positive Queckenstedt reaction and indicates a partial or complete spinal subarachnoid block. The Ayala index, computed by dividing the final pressure by the initial pressure and multiplying by the amount of fluid removed (at least ten millilitres must be removed if the test is to be reliable), helps in differentiating between an expanding intracranial lesion and other causes of pressure within the cranium. A quotient of 5.5 to 6.5 is normal. A swift drop in pressure and a quotient of less than 5 are indications of a small fluid reservoir and point to the possible presence of brain tumour or abscess, obstructive hydrocephalus, or a spinal subarachnoid block. A large reservoir is indicated by a value of more than 7, and nonobstructive hydrocephalus or cerebral atrophy is suspected.

Contra-indications against lumbar puncture

Lumbar puncture is contra-indicated by infections in or near the puncture site, by systemic infections (except when meningitis is suspected), and by symptoms or signs of increased intracranial pressure (unless diagnostic gains outweigh potential dangers). If the contra-indications mentioned are taken into account aftereffects of lumbar puncture are usually negligible. Postpuncture headache, the most frequent sequel, occurs in 15–30 percent of patients. It usually is mild and lasts only a day or two. The occasional severe headache may incapacitate for a week or longer; it is often accompanied by neck stiffness, is aggravated by movement, and is lessened or relieved by lying down. Current studies tend to indicate that postpuncture headache may occur less frequently if a needle of very narrow gauge is used.

(R.N.DeJ.)

Fluid and electrolyte balance

The chemical events by which body tissues are built and maintained and by which energy is provided for bodily activity can take place only in a watery solution in which the hydrogen ions and electrolytes are kept within relatively narrow limits. Disturbances of water, electrolyte, and acid–base balance impair the functioning of many organs, especially those concerned with contractility and nerve conduction.

THE NORMAL FUNCTION OF WATER AND ELECTROLYTES IN THE BODY

The fluids and electrolytes of the body are the water that pervades it and the ions formed from the acids, alkalis, and salts that are dissolved in it. Ions are atoms or groups of atoms that bear positive or negative electrical charges. Those bearing positive charges are called cations; those bearing negative charges are anions. The ions are called electrolytes because the solution that contains them is able to transmit an electrical current.

The fluids in the body may be classified into two main divisions: the fluid within the cells and the fluid outside (extracellular fluid). The extracellular fluid can be further divided into the fluid within blood vessels (intravascular fluid) and the fluid around the tissues.

Electrolytes. The electrolytes and their concentrations are shown in Table 4. They are not dispersed evenly throughout the fluids of the body. Sodium and chloride

Table 4: Normal Distribution of Ions in Intracellular (Muscle) and Extracellular Fluids in Man

	intracellular (mEq/kg) H_2O	extracellular (mEq/kg) H_2O
Cations		
Sodium (Na^+)	10	145
Potassium (K^+)	150	5
Calcium (Ca^{++})	2	3
Magnesium (Mg^{++})	15	2
Total	177	155
Anions		
Chloride (Cl^-)	5	105
Bicarbonate (HCO_3^-)	10	25
Organic acids	120	6
Phosphate ($PO_4^{\equiv}$)		2
Proteins	42	17
Total	177	155

Source: J.R. Robinson, "Water and Life," *World Review of Nutrition and Dietetics.*

are confined mainly to the extracellular fluids; potassium, magnesium, phosphate, and organic acids are present in highest concentration inside the cells. Bicarbonate is found in the extracellular fluid at a little more than twice its concentration in the tissue cells, while the concentration of free hydrogen ions is twice as great within the cells as outside them. This difference with respect to hydrogen ions means that most tissue cells are slightly more acidic than the fluid that bathes them.

Because of the permeability of the walls of the capillaries (the smallest of the blood vessels), the concentrations of electrolytes in the plasma (the blood apart from its cells) and in the extracellular fluid outside the blood vessels is similar. Interchange between these two extracellular compartments is limited, however, in respect to protein molecules, the concentrations of which, except in the fluid bathing the cells in the liver, is much greater in the plasma.

Hydrostatic and osmotic pressures

Thus, the plasma volume is largely the result of two opposing forces—the hydrostatic pressure, which tends to force water outward, and the osmotic pressure of the plasma proteins, which attracts water into the network of vessels. In spite of the differences in the pattern of ions in the cells and in the extracellular fluid, their osmotic pressure under normal conditions is identical. Hydrostatic pressure, in this context, is the pressure in the body fluids as a result of the mechanical forces exerted upon them. These forces include that resulting from the contractions of the heart. Osmotic pressure comes into play when two solutions of differing concentrations are separated by a semipermeable membrane. The solvent—*e.g.,* water—tends to move through the membrane into the more concentrated solution.

Hydrogen-ion concentration. Life is possible only if the blood is kept within a narrow range of alkalinity. The normal range, in terms of hydrogen-ion concentration (pH), is from 7.35 to 7.45. This range is close to neutrality, represented by a pH of 7; a pH of less than 7 represents acidity.

The blood contains the bases bicarbonate, proteins, and phosphate, and the weak acid, carbonic acid. The degree of alkalinity of the blood depends principally on the ratio of the concentrations of carbonic acid (H_2CO_3) and of the base bicarbonate (HCO_3^-).

In the pulmonary alveoli—the small air-filled spaces in the lungs from which oxygen is removed and into which carbon dioxide from the blood diffuses—the partial pressure of carbon dioxide is about 40 millimetres of mercury; in a mixture of gases the partial pressure of each gas is the proportion of the total gaseous pressure contributed by that particular gas. This alveolar carbon dioxide pressure gives rise to a concentration of carbonic acid in the blood plasma of about one milliequivalent per litre. (A milliequivalent [mEq] is the number of grams of a substance dissolved in one millilitre of normal solution.) The alveolar pressure of carbon dioxide is kept steady by the equal rate at which carbon dioxide is produced by the tissues and eliminated by respiratory ventilation.

Bicarbonate concentration, on the other hand, is regulated in the kidneys by the tubules. These are the long, fine tubes of the kidney's functional units, the nephrons. In health the bicarbonate concentration is kept at about 22 to 24 milliequivalents per litre of plasma. When the plasma bicarbonate falls below 24 milliequivalents, the amount filtered out of the blood in the kidneys is entirely reabsorbed by the tubules until the concentration is raised to this level; when the concentration rises above 24 mEq per litre, all the bicarbonate filtered out is excreted in the urine.

Water. The body of a normal man weighing 65 kilograms (about 145 pounds) contains approximately 40 litres (about 42 quarts) of water; of this about 28 litres (30 quarts) are inside the cells of the body and 12 litres are outside. Of the 12 extracellular litres, about 2–3 litres are in the blood plasma—and the rest are around the tissues outside the blood vessels.

Water passes rapidly through almost all cell membranes and readily enters and leaves almost all the bodily spaces normally containing fluid. Its final distribution is determined by osmotic and hydrostatic pressures.

The volume of bodily water normally remains constant because the amounts ingested and eliminated are equal. Physiologically, thirst and satiety are influenced by a group of nerve cells in the hypothalamus, at the base of the brain.

Imperceptible loss of water

At rest, and in temperate climates, there is an imperceptible loss of water from the surface of the body and in the air breathed out. This loss amounts to about 800 millilitres in 24 hours. It is increased when the surrounding temperature is elevated or when atmospheric humidity is low. Losses in this range become perceptible in other circumstances and form the cloud of moisture in one's breath on a winter day or the moisture that condenses on the inner side of a waterproof garment. Greater losses of water occur, of course, during vigorous exercise in the heat, and the losses from the bodily surfaces are then perceptible as sweat. The amount of water lost in the urine amounts to from one to two litres in 24 hours.

THE DEPLETION OF WATER AND SALTS IN THE BODY

Sodium depletion. In health the equality between the amount of sodium excreted and the amount ingested depends largely on normal kidney function. In temperate climates negligible amounts of sodium are lost in the stools and from the skin, and the power of the normal kidneys to conserve sodium in the face of reduced intake is virtually absolute. Salt depletion is usually the result of excessive loss of salt through faulty kidney function, rather than of inadequate intake.

Loss of sodium is usually accompanied by a reduction in body water. Pure sodium depletion unaccompanied by water loss, although uncommon, may arise when the response to abnormal losses of salt and water is unrestricted water intake, as, for example, when excessive sweating occurs in unfavourable environments and when the fluid loss is replenished by salt-free liquids. In these circumstances, the change in total body water may be negligible, in spite of considerable salt deficiency.

Causes. Failure of the kidney to conserve salt may occur because of kidney disease or because of inadequate hormonal control. Thus, a chronic infection of the urinary tract, acute ischemic renal failure (failure of the kidney to function normally because of inadequate blood supply), or insufficient adrenocortical hormones—hormones from the outer substance of the adrenal gland—may be responsible. Excessive loss of salt and water in the urine also occurs during the excessive secretion of urine that is induced by high levels of blood sugar in the disease diabetes mellitus. If the diabetes causes acidosis, which is a decreased alkalinity of the blood and tissue fluids, the process by which sodium is returned to the blood from the tubular filtrate in return for hydrogen ions is upset. Salt depletion may also be induced by the excessive or prolonged use of diuretics, substances that induce increased excretion of urine. Salt depletion also results from diarrhea, vomiting, and other situations involving external loss of salt-containing fluids.

Sodium loss during diabetes

Consequences. Because sodium is predominantly extracellular, salt depletion leads quickly to a fall in the volume of extracellular fluid. Water tends to be excreted to balance intracellular and extracellular osmotic pressures. This volume decrease is responsible for such effects as loss of elasticity of the skin, diminution of the pressure within the eyeballs, and dryness of the tongue. Thirst may be prominent, but tends to be less severe when the sodium levels in the blood are low. The fall in blood volume causes fainting, low blood pressure, a reduced rate of glomerular filtration in the kidney, and a reduced volume of urine. (The glomeruli are clusters of minute blood vessels, capillaries, through the walls of which fluid is filtered from the blood into the nephrons, in the first stage of the production of urine.) The capacity of the body to rid itself of wastes decreases, and kidney failure develops. The pulse rate rises. Constriction of blood vessels diminishes the circulation through the skin so that the skin and the hands and feet become cold.

Treatment. Persons with mild degrees of sodium depletion, whose blood pressure is normal, usually need merely to drink salted water to recover a normal sodium level. In more severe cases, or when there is vomiting, the physician injects isotonic salt solution into a vein. (An isotonic salt solution is of the same osmotic pressure as the plasma; it contains about 0.9 percent sodium chloride.) When there is severe sodium depletion there often are losses of other electrolytes, which must also be restored.

Water depletion. The reduced water intake that is most often responsible for water depletion may result either from difficulties in drinking, as when there are sores in the mouth and throat, or from circumstances that cut off access to fresh water—for example, shipwreck, or becoming lost in the desert.

Excessive loss of water in the urine because of disease that interferes with the kidney's ability to concentrate the urine is a less common cause of water depletion.

As water is lost from the blood, the plasma concentration of sodium rises. Water is drawn from the cells, and intracellular dehydration occurs. The body loss of water is thus shared both by the extracellular and the intracellular fluids. For this reason, the clinical features of dehydration are not as obvious as those of salt depletion. Thirst, the result of stimulation of a thirst centre in the hypothalamus, is usual unless the person is senile, confused, or unconscious. The migration of water from the intracellular fluid to the extracellular helps to maintain the volume of the latter for a time, so that the blood pressure remains unaltered until considerable water depletion has occurred. The affected person then often shows mental confusion or complains of dizziness and difficulty in swallowing. Ultimately, flow of blood to the kidneys is reduced, and blood levels of urea and other wastes become abnormally high. The water depletion is treated by giving liquids; these should be salt-free unless salt loss is also present.

Potassium depletion. Potassium depletion occurs in a wide variety of disorders. The healthy person eliminates about one-quarter of his daily intake of potassium in the stools and three-quarters in the urine. The bulk of urinary potassium is delivered into the channel of the nephron tubule by the cells lining the far end of the tubule (the distal tubule); these cells excrete potassium or sodium ions and, in exchange, take sodium ions from the liquid filtered out of the blood and into the tubule from the glomerulus.

Two types of potassium loss

Causes. Potassium depletion results from excessive loss of potassium from the intestinal tract or in the urine. Gastrointestinal losses are caused by severe acute or chronic diarrhea and by loss of intestinal fluid from vomiting, drainage through a gap in the intestinal wall (a fistula), or by aspiration—withdrawal of intestinal contents by suction in the course of medical treatment.

Loss of potassium in the urine is more subtle in its development. It occurs when the excretion of potassium ions in exchange for sodium ions is increased in the renal tubules. This increased excretion may result from administration of large amounts of sodium-containing fluids or from the use of diuretics, or it may occur as one feature of disorders such as Cushing's syndrome (a symptom complex resulting from overproduction of adrenocorticotropic hormone by the pituitary) or aldosteronism (the overproduction of the hormone aldosterone by the adrenals).

Excessive loss of potassium also results from diseases or drugs that suppress tubular secretion of hydrogen ions; with fewer hydrogen ions to exchange for sodium, more potassium will be lost in the exchange process.

Conditions that interfere with the activity of the cells in the maintenance of their concentration of potassium and in excluding or eliminating sodium (the process called the sodium pump) also lead to potassium depletion and increased loss of potassium in the urine. These conditions include a deficiency of oxygen; impaired carbohydrate metabolism, as seen in starvation or diabetes; dehydration; and acidosis.

Consequences and treatment. Because most of the body's potassium is inside the cells, severe depletion of potassium may occur without alteration in the potassium level of the plasma, and identification of the disorder is made difficult by the inaccessibility of the intracellular fluid to analysis.

Effects of potassium deficiency

A person whose potassium is depleted tends to be apathetic and physically weak; he is mentally confused, and his abdomen is distended. Potassium deficiency, sufficiently severe to cause a fall in plasma-potassium levels, is characterized by generalized muscular weakness with some degree of paralysis. Sensations of pins and needles in the skin are common. The electrocardiogram—tracings reflecting heart activity—shows characteristic changes. Severe potassium depletion may lead to death if it remains uncorrected.

The condition is treated by administration of potassium salts orally or by injection into a vein. Oral administration is more commonly used and is less dangerous.

THE ABNORMAL ACCUMULATION OF WATER AND SALTS IN THE BODY

Potassium intoxication. A rise in plasma-potassium levels above normal usually occurs only when the kidney fails to function normally and there is a resultant reduction in the amount of urine excreted.

Persons with this disorder are dull, lethargic, and confused. The condition of weakness and paralysis of muscles is indistinguishable from that seen in persons with low blood levels of potassium. The pulse becomes irregular, and some degree of heart block develops. (In heart block, the upper and lower chambers of the heart tend to beat independently, which interferes with the heart's efficiency as a pump.) If the plasma-potassium level rises above eight milliequivalents per litre, there is danger that the heart will stop beating.

Measures taken to correct the high plasma levels of potassium include avoidance of fruits and fruit juices that are rich in potassium, avoidance of protein, and taking of substances such as sodium- or calcium-ion-exchange resins, which absorb potassium from the blood and from the intestinal secretions.

Magnesium deficiency and intoxication. The adult body contains about 25 grams (0.9 ounce) of magnesium, 60 percent of which is in the bones. The most frequent cause of deficiency of magnesium is replacement of fluids lost during prolonged diarrhea or vomiting with fluids containing electrolytes, but without magnesium supplements. Depletion also may result from prolonged use of diuretics, chronic diarrhea, severe malnutrition, and alcoholism. In addition, excessive secretion of the hormone aldosterone or of parathyroid hormone may lead to magnesium deficiency. Magnesium chloride and magnesium hydroxide are given to correct the condition.

Magnesium intoxication occurs in kidney failure and causes symptoms related to the central nervous system. When the kidney recovers normal function, the abnormal levels of magnesium disappear without special treatment.

Water intoxication. When healthy persons drink large volumes of water, they can respond to this with corresponding increases in the amounts of urine excreted. The capacity of the body to excrete water depends upon many factors, which include the rate of glomerular filtration and the power of the distal tubules of the kidneys to produce a dilute urine; this ability in turn depends upon the presence of sodium in the distal renal tubules and the capacity of the nephron to reabsorb the sodium without reabsorbing water. (Each distal tubule is that portion of the nephron tubule that is furthest from the portion of the nephron that encloses the glomerulus.) Many persons who are ill have a restricted ability to dilute the urine when given large amounts of water, including persons suffering from acute and chronic kidney disease, severe heart failure, disease of the adrenal glands, and cirrhosis of the liver (a disease involving destruction of liver cells and formation of scar tissue). Occasionally, tumours of the ovaries or lungs secrete a substance with antidiuretic properties that lead to water intoxication. After surgery some people may be incapable of diluting the urine because of the liberation of vasopressin by the stress of the operation. Vasopressin is a hormone released by the hypothalamus; its many functions include contraction of small blood vessels and suppression of urine excretion.

Effects of vasopressin

In all the circumstances mentioned, even a modest water intake reduces the level of sodium ions in the plasma and may produce disordered cerebral function, dizziness, headache, nausea, mental confusion, convulsions, coma, and death.

Treatment consists of restricting water intake. In severe cases salt solution is injected into a vein.

Water and salt retention (edema). Abnormal accumulation of water and salt in the body has fascinated physiologists and clinicians for several centuries, and before the discovery of modern diuretic drugs gross edema was a common complication of a variety of diseases, the victim being drowned, as it were, in the high tide of his own body fluids. Death from edema was well known to the ancients, who often made a series of superficial cuts in the limbs in an attempt to release the fluid from the distended tissues as a remedy of the last resort.

Causes. The fundamental cause of edema is a fault in the physiological mechanisms that control the volume of the extracellular fluids. Figure 4 illustrates how a healthy individual undergoes slight fluctuations in the water and salt content even when consuming a diet fixed in calories, nitrogen, water, and salt. These natural ripples on the surface of the body fluids, which ebb and flow over periods of several days, are due to the operation of a hunting, or servo-feedback, mechanism for the control of body fluid volume. Such a mechanism must involve (1) a detector that identifies lack of stability in the system, (2) an integrator that analyzes the information, and (3) an effector organ that adjusts the rate of excretion of water and salt according to need. Whatever its clinical cause, edema represents a vast tidal wave upon the extracellular sea and arises from a breakdown in the system responsible for volume control. Little is known about the first two components of the volume-control system, but the kidney

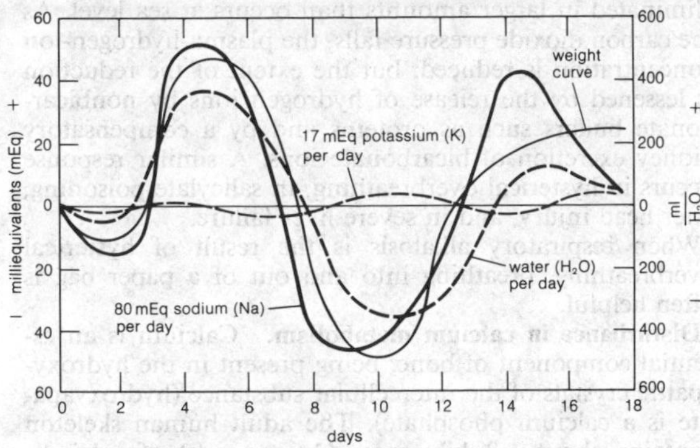

Figure 4: Cumulative sodium (Na^+), potassium (K^+), and water (H_2O) balance in subject on a constant diet at rest.

is certainly the effector organ, and edema arises when the kidney fails to meet its biological commitment.

The common primary event responsible for all types of generalized edema is an inadequate blood volume induced either by loss of plasma proteins or by inadequate cardiac output. The first condition may arise because of excessive loss of protein in the urine or from the gastrointestinal tract, failure of protein synthesis by the liver, or as a result of gastrointestinal malabsorption or of malnutrition; inadequate filling of the arterial circulation occurs in heart failure.

A fall in the concentration of plasma proteins disturbs the balance of factors that influences the exchange of fluid between the vascular and extravascular compartments. As a result, fluid moves from the blood into the tissues, where it accumulates. The resulting fall in blood volume activates the volume-control system and stimulates the kidney to conserve water and salt in an attempt to repair the deficit; as a result, the accumulation of edema fluid is merely aggravated. The physiological link between low blood volume and reduced arterial-filling pressure, on the one hand, and renal water and salt retention by the kidney, on the other, is far from clear, but probably includes the operation of pressure-sensitive areas in the thyrocarotid and renal arteries, the atria (upper chambers) of the heart, the juxtaglomerular apparatus in the kidney, and the adrenal cortex (Figure 5). The thyrocarotid pressure-sensitive area is also called the carotid sinus; it is located at the point where the common carotid arteries, the principal arteries to the head, divide to form the internal and external carotids. The renal arteries, the arteries to the kidneys, are branches of the abdominal portion of the aorta. The juxtaglomerular apparatus is made up of specialized cells in the middle coat of the arterioles (small arteries) that bring blood to the glomeruli. As a consequence, both the rate of secretion of aldosterone and vasopressin (ADH) is increased, and water and salt conservation is promoted. In addition, hemodynamic effects on the renal circulation and the influence of other hormonal agents (as yet inadquately defined), which may act principally on the reabsorption of sodium in the proximal convoluted tubule of the kidney, may contribute.

Pressure-sensitive areas

Consequences. The effects of generalized edema vary with its severity and with the part of the body predominantly affected. All tissues are involved to some extent, but swelling of the legs is almost universal and is partly the result of the hydrostatic effect of the upright posture. In the nephrotic syndrome, in which the urinary loss of protein is caused by glomerular disease, the edema is generalized; in heart failure it tends to accumulate either in the pulmonary circulation (pulmonary edema) or in the systemic circulation—*i.e.,* in the legs and the abdominal cavity; in liver disease caused by local factors within the liver and disturbance in the portal circulation, the peritoneal cavity (the space that in disease develops between the membrane lining the abdomen and the membrane covering the abdominal organs) is the most commonly involved. Edema in this region is called ascites. Localized edema may arise in a limb or other single part from venous or lymphatic obstruction; even localized edema activates the volume-control system, since the edema fluid is derived from the body fluids as a whole. The detector mechanism is stimulated, and water and salt retention encouraged. When the water and salt content of the rest of the body then remains within normal limits, the swelling of the affected part continues.

Treatment. The treatment of edema is the correction of the underlying cause of the disturbance; this correction involves appropriate therapy for kidney, heart, and liver disease, and measures aimed at ameliorating absolute and conditional undernutrition. If, as is often the case, this is not possible, the kidneys may be induced to excrete water and salt by the administration of diuretics that specifically inhibit sodium transport somewhere in the nephron; a large number of these agents are available and are remarkably successful.

DISTURBANCES IN ACID–BASE BALANCE AND MINERAL METABOLISM

Disturbances in acid–base balance. Fluctuations in hydrogen-ion concentration arise in many circumstances in health and disease. Four primary types of disorder are recognized: metabolic acidosis and alkalosis, and respiratory acidosis and alkalosis. The first two of these involve increased or decreased alkalinity of the blood plasma because of some change in the metabolic process; the second two arise from disorders in the carbon dioxide exchange in the lungs.

Metabolic acidosis. Metabolic acidosis arises from three main causes: (1) there may be an increased formation of acids during the metabolic process, as occurs, for example, in diabetes or starvation, during exercise, or as a result of reduced levels of oxygen in the tissues (acetoacetic and lactic acids are especially important in these contexts); (2) there may be diminished excretion of hydrogen ions, as occurs in several situations, including kidney failure; (3) there may be increased loss of base such as bicarbonate ions, as occurs in diarrhea and as a result of fistulas (openings) in the walls of the intestines.

The increased concentration of hydrogen ions in the plasma interferes with the reversible process by which carbon dioxide combines with water to form carbonic acid, and by which carbonic acid in turn becomes ionized into hydrogen ions and bicarbonate ions. Because of the high hydrogen-ion concentration, the production of bicarbonate falls and carbonic-acid levels rise.

The increase in hydrogen ions also stimulates the respira-

From R. Passmore and J.S. Robson (eds.), *Companion to Medical Studies*

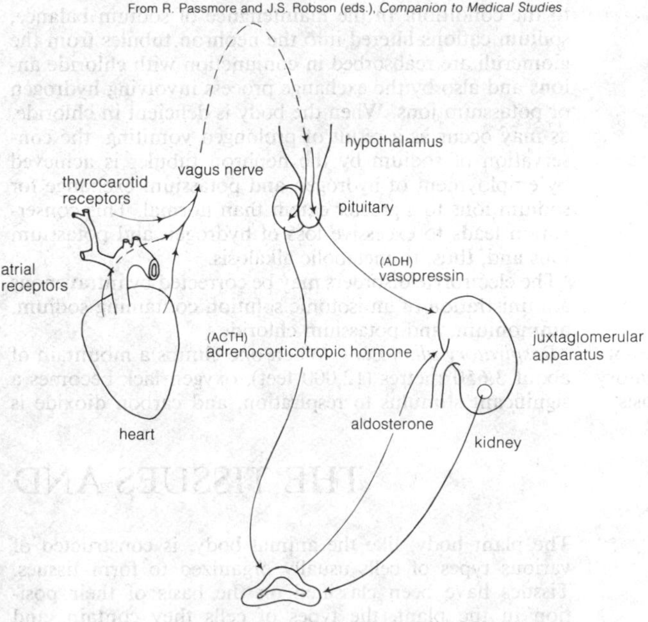

Figure 5: *Volume-control system.*
Low blood volume leads to increased secretion of vasopressin (also called antidiuretic hormone, ADH), adrenocorticotropic hormone (ACTH), and aldosterone, leading to conservation of salt and water and consequent increase in the volume of the blood.

tory centres in the brain to increase the rate and depth of breathing. Increased amounts of carbon dioxide are, thus, eliminated by the lungs, and the carbon dioxide pressure in the blood plasma falls below normal levels. This decrease reduces the formation of carbonic acid and lessens the tendency of the blood to become less alkaline.

Recovery of the normal alkalinity depends on the regeneration of bicarbonate by the cells of the kidney tubules during the process of hydrogen-ion excretion in exchange for sodium ions. In severe cases, this process is assisted by administration of sodium bicarbonate.

Causes of respiratory acidosis

Respiratory acidosis. If the ability of the lungs to expel carbon dioxide is impaired—for example, by depression of the respiratory centre, as occurs in barbiturate or morphine poisoning, or because of paralysis of respiratory muscles, as in poliomyelitis—carbon dioxide is retained in the body and the plasma-carbon dioxide pressure rises above its normal value of 40 millimetres of mercury. As a result, levels of carbonic acid and of hydrogen ions rise in the tissues and blood. This situation is mitigated by the acceptance of hydrogen ions by substances such as proteins, with the resultant generation of bicarbonate ions. The kidneys also respond to the elevated carbon dioxide pressure by reabsorbing bicarbonate ions and forming new bicarbonate ions.

Respiratory acidosis is dealt with by treatment of the underlying disease. Occasionally assisted or artificial respiration is needed.

Metabolic alkalosis. During digestion of a large meal the secretion of hydrochloric acid (HCl) by the stomach involves the withdrawal of hydrogen ions from the blood. If vomiting occurs, the hydrogen ions are lost from the body along with chloride ions, and the blood-hydrogen-ion concentration falls, increasing the alkalinity of the blood plasma. At the same time, the plasma levels of bicarbonate ions rise.

The fall in hydrogen-ion concentration reduces the stimulus to respiration. Carbon dioxide elimination by the lungs is reduced, and the pressure of carbon dioxide in the plasma rises, causing increased formation of carbonic acid and reducing the excess alkalinity.

Chronic metabolic alkalosis, induced by the taking of large amounts of sodium bicarbonate over long periods, especially when there is a high intake of calcium in the diet, may lead to deposition of calcium in the kidneys.

Severe potassium depletion also causes metabolic alkalosis, and depletion of chloride ions sometimes contributes to the condition. In the maintenance of sodium balance, sodium cations filtered into the nephron tubules from the glomeruli are reabsorbed in conjunction with chloride anions and also by the exchange process involving hydrogen or potassium ions. When the body is deficient in chloride, as may occur as a result of prolonged vomiting, the conservation of sodium by the nephron tubules is achieved by employment of hydrogen and potassium exchange for sodium ions to a greater extent than normal. This conservation leads to excessive loss of hydrogen and potassium ions and, thus, to metabolic alkalosis.

The electrolyte disorders may be corrected by intravenous administration of an isotonic solution containing sodium, ammonium, and potassium chloride.

Causes of respiratory alkalosis

Respiratory alkalosis. When one climbs a mountain of about 3,650 metres (12,000 feet), oxygen lack becomes a significant stimulus to respiration, and carbon dioxide is eliminated in larger amounts than occurs at sea level. As the carbon dioxide pressure falls, the plasma-hydrogen-ion concentration is reduced; but the extent of the reduction is lessened by the release of hydrogen ions by nonbicarbonate buffers such as proteins and by a compensatory kidney excretion of bicarbonate ions. A similar response occurs in hysterical overbreathing, in salicylate poisoning, after head injury, and in severe liver failure.

When respiratory alkalosis is the result of hysterical overbreathing, breathing into and out of a paper bag is often helpful.

Disturbance in calcium metabolism. Calcium is an essential component of bone, being present in the hydroxyapatite crystals of the intercellular substance (hydroxyapatite is a calcium phosphate). The adult human skeleton contains about 1.2 kilograms (2.6 pounds) of calcium. Because the skeleton takes about 20 years to be formed, the growing child must retain from his diet an average of 160 milligrams (0.005 ounce) of calcium a day. There is a continuing turnover of skeletal calcium, about 500 milligrams (0.02 ounce) being reabsorbed from the bone and replaced daily. The surfaces of the hydroxyapatite crystals have a layer of ions and water, and it is around this layer that exchange of calcium and other ions takes place.

Among the many factors that affect calcium-plasma levels are the two hormones thyrocalcitonin and parathyroid hormone, vitamin D levels, and the hydrogen-ion concentration of the plasma.

High levels of parathyroid hormone tend to raise plasma levels of calcium, and vitamin D causes absorption of calcium from the intestine. Thyrocalcitonin depresses the plasma-calcium levels.

Common causes of calcium disorders

Disorders of calcium metabolism are most commonly the result of endocrine abnormalities or of nutritional deficiency. Thus oversecretion and undersecretion of parathyroid hormone cause elevated and depressed levels of calcium in the plasma, respectively. Increased secretion of thyrocalcitonin is extremely rare, but may result from a tumour of the thyroid cells that secrete the hormone.

In kidney failure, high levels of urea in the blood appear to increase resistance to the action of parathyroid hormone and of vitamin D: this increased resistance causes a depressed level of calcium in the plasma, which, in turn, leads to secondary enlargement of the parathyroid glands.

Low levels of plasma calcium are also found in rickets and osteomalacia. These two related diseases, occurring in children and adults, respectively, involve inadequate deposition of calcium and phosphorus in the bones; a principal cause is insufficient intake of vitamin D. In another disease, osteoporosis, characterized by light, brittle bones, the plasma levels of calcium are normal or only slightly reduced, and no benefit is derived from taking increased amounts of vitamin D.

Disturbances in phosphorus metabolism. The human body contains about 700 grams (1.5 pounds) of phosphorus; of this about 80 percent is in the bones. Phosphorus deficiency is known to occur in cattle that graze on poor land and has been held responsible for stunting of growth and weakness. The existence of a primary phosphate deficiency in man is not yet established. It may occur in persons who take large doses of nonabsorbable antacids such as aluminum and magnesium hydroxide, which interfere with the intestinal absorption of phosphate.

(J.S.Ro.)

THE TISSUES AND FLUIDS OF PLANTS

The plant body, like the animal body, is constructed of various types of cells usually organized to form tissues. Tissues have been classified on the basis of their position in the plant, the types of cells they contain, and the function of these cells. No single criterion, however, adequately expresses the complex interaction of cells and their association in the form of specific tissues.

Tissues with cells that continuously divide to produce new cells are termed meristematic tissues. They give rise to the mature tissue systems of the plant of which three can be distinguished: (1) the dermal tissue system, which makes up the outer layers or protective tissue of the plant; (2) the vascular tissue system, which includes the water- and food-conducting tissues, xylem and phloem, respectively; and (3) the fundamental or ground tissue system, which includes all other tissues exclusive of dermal and vascular. Although mature tissues may consist of one cell type (simple tissues), they more often are made up of a variety of cell types (complex tissues).

Classification of plant tissues

MERISTEMATIC TISSUES

All tissues of the plant are derived from cell-producing tissues called primary tissue meristems, which begin to form early in embryonic development. The primary tissue meristems are designated protoderm, procambium, and ground meristem. Protoderm functions to produce the dermal or "skin" tissue system of the plant; procambium gives rise to the vascular or conducting tissue system; and ground meristem is the precursor of the fundamental or ground tissue system.

As the young embryo develops, protoderm tissue, which forms from the peripheral cells, is clearly delimited from the other tissues as the embryo elongates and becomes bilaterally symmetrical—that is, with mirror-image halves. At this stage procambium is also evident. The ground meristem originates from the embryonic tissue situated between protoderm and procambium.

Root and shoot systems

The cotyledons or first leaves (seed leaves) are the first organs formed. Soon after they begin to develop, the shoot apical meristem forms between them. At the end of the embryo opposite the cotyledons, the root apical meristem forms. The root and shoot apical meristems continuously contribute cells to the primary tissue meristems, which, following differentiation and maturation, give rise to the primary tissues and the primary plant body. The primary tissues include primary xylem, primary phloem, cortex, pith, and epidermis. In young stems the arrangement of tissues as seen in cross section is as follows: outermost tissue, the epidermis; cortex; primary phloem; and primary xylem. The pith occupies the centre of the stem (see Figure 6).

In many plants vegetative development is essentially complete when the primary tissues have matured. This is true in many lower vascular plants such as club mosses, horsetails, and some ferns; in monocotyledons (flowering plants with parallel-veined leaves, such as grasses, orchids, and palms); and in some nonwoody dicotyledons (flowering plants with net-veined leaves, such as violets and poppies). In other herbaceous dicotyledons, however, and in woody plants, formation of new tissues continues after primary growth is complete. The production of these tissues and the continuation of growth in such plants are attributable to the lateral meristems, regions of cell division that contribute to growth in stem thickness. These meristems, called the vascular cambium and the cork cambium, are responsible for producing the secondary tissues—secondary xylem, secondary phloem, and periderm—that form the secondary plant body (see Figure 6). The vascular cambium is chiefly responsible for increasing the diameter of the plant.

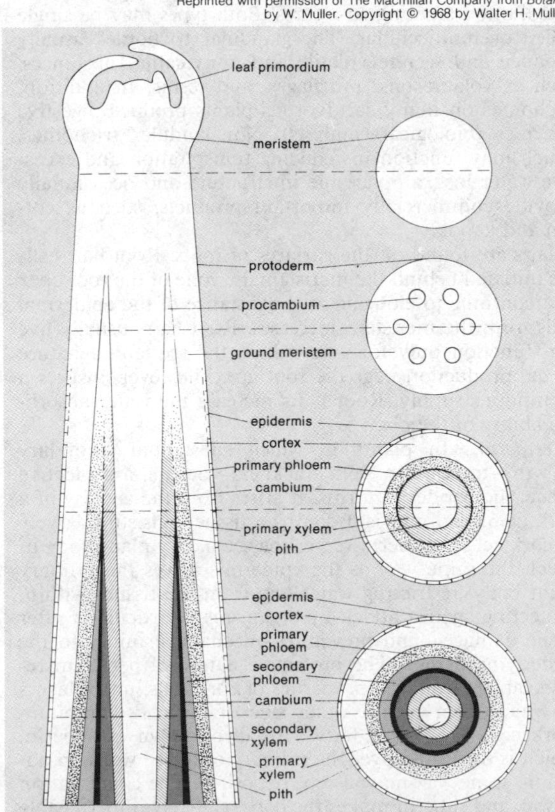

Figure 6: *Tissue organization in a stem tip.* (Left) Longitudinal section. (Right) Cross section at different levels.

Lateral meristems

Apical meristems. The cells of the shoot and root apical meristem are organized in precise patterns that are characteristic of various plant groups. Knowledge of the arrangement and organization of cells at the apex is useful for descriptive purposes and for making structural comparisons between plants. Apical organization, however, is known to vary during normal development and is often influenced by seasonal changes.

Various regions of the apex can be distinguished from each other by examination of such features as cell and nucleus size, frequency and planes of cell division, and wall thickness. At the summit of the shoot apex a group of meristematic cells constitutes a so-called initiation zone, which gives rise to cells of the surface layer and a region below, the zone of central mother cells, which divide infrequently. Surrounding the latter zone is the peripheral zone, within which most of the apical activity takes place—cell divisions are frequent and leaf primordia and procambium cells are initiated. Below the central mother cell zone lies a zone termed the rib meristem, whose cells are arranged in radial, regular, longitudinal rows and divide transversely; much of the fundamental tissue system is derived from the rib meristem. Various kinds of mature tissues are produced in the plant body because the cells of the shoot apex divide at different rates and in different planes. Although in some plants, apical meristems lack distinguishable zones, the cells of the shoot apex retain the ability to divide at different rates and in different planes.

Function of apical meristems

Despite the structural differences in apical meristems of various groups of plants, they function in similar ways. All apical meristems (1) produce cells that differentiate into primary-tissue meristems, which in turn produce the primary tissues of the plant; (2) initiate organs, primarily leaves and branches, in a coordinated manner and in a genetically determined pattern; and (3) contribute to the increase in length of the plant.

Lateral meristems. The vascular cambium, which produces xylem and phloem cells, originates from procambium that has not completely differentiated during the formation of primary xylem and primary phloem. The cambium is thought to be a single row of cells that produces new cells: externally, the secondary phloem, and internally, the secondary xylem. Because it is not possible to distinguish the cambium from its immediate cellular derivatives, which also divide and contribute to the formation of secondary tissues, the cambium and its immediate derivatives are usually referred to as the cambial zone.

Unlike the apical meristems, which consist of a population of similar cells, the cambium consists of two different cell types; the fusiform initials and the ray initials (see Figure 7). The fusiform initials are elongated tapering cells that give rise to all cells of the vertical system of the secondary phloem and xylem. The ray initials are isodiametric cells—about equal in all dimensions—and they produce the vascular rays, which constitute the horizontal system of secondary tissues. The fusiform and ray initials of the cambium divide in a tangential plane (*i.e.*, parallel to the stem surface) generating xylem mother cells toward the inside and phloem mother cells toward the outside. These cells in turn continue to divide tangentially, producing new cells that add to the xylem and to the phloem. Divisions of the cambium cells and xylem and phloem mother cells do not result in the production of equal amounts of secondary xylem and secondary phloem; because the cambium produces more cells internally than externally, more secondary xylem is produced than secondary phloem. Because divisions in the fusiform and ray

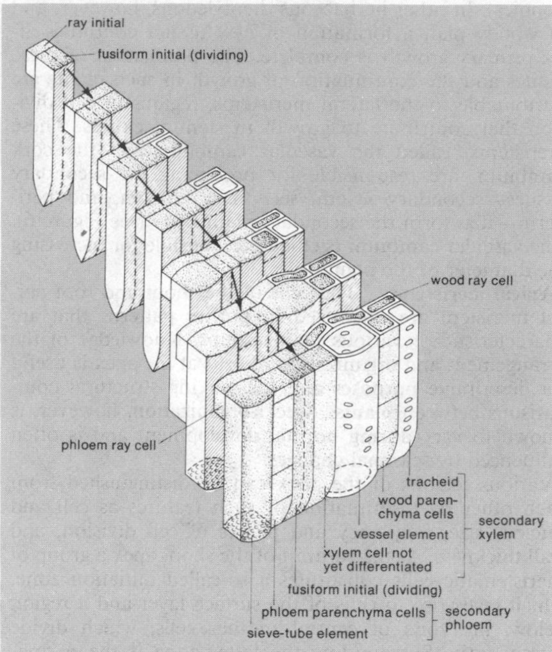

Figure 7: Production of secondary xylem and phloem cells by cambial initials.

initials are primarily tangential, new cells are regularly arranged in well-defined radial rows, a characteristic pattern for secondary vascular tissues.

Divisions in the cambium not only produce secondary vascular tissues but also increase the circumference of the cambium. As new cells are continuously added to the inside of the cambium, the cambium increases laterally (in circumference) to keep pace with the growth of the stem. In some plants this is accomplished simply by radial division of the fusiform and ray initials. In other plants, the mechanism for increasing cambial diameter or increasing the number of cambial cells is more complex. If cambial activity is extensive, the primary tissues lying outside the cambium, such as primary phloem, cortex, and epidermis, may be crushed by the pressure of new secondary tissue growth or become torn and obliterated because they cannot accommodate to the rapidly increasing diameter of the plant.

As growth proceeds the cork cambium forms in living cells of the epidermis, cortex, or, in some plants, phloem and produces a secondary protective tissue, the periderm. The cork cambium is, like the vascular cambium, a lateral meristem that produces cells internally and externally by tangential divisions. Unlike the cambium, the cork cambium consists of one cell type.

Intercalary meristems. Another type of meristem active in certain plants, especially horsetails and grasses, is the intercalary meristem. These cells possess the ability to divide and produce new cells, as do apical and lateral meristems. They differ, however, in being situated between regions of mature tissue, such as at the base of grass leaves, which are themselves located on mature stem tissue. In many instances intercalary meristems function for only a short time and eventually completely differentiate into mature tissues. Intercalary meristems are usually located at positions on the stem where leaves have emerged (nodes) and are largely responsible for elongation in grass shoots and leaves.

MATURE TISSUES

Dermal (protective) tissues. *Epidermis.* The epidermis, or surface cell layer, which covers all organs of the plant including stem and root, leaf, flower, fruit, and seed, functions in a variety of ways. It limits transpiration—evaporation of water from the surface of the plant, especially the leaf. Specialized cells facilitate gaseous exchange between the outside air and internal tissues. The epidermis also serves as a protective barrier, restricting insect and bacterial invasion of the underlying cells. In view of the many functions of this tissue, it is not surprising that it is also structurally variable. The epidermis may consist of either one cell layer or several.

Function of epidermis

The epidermis forms from protoderm, one of the primary tissue meristems. In addition to cellulose, the main carbohydrate component of wood, epidermal cells produce a fatty substance, cutin, which permeates the cell wall, eventually forming an outer layer, the cuticle. Although a cuticle covers the epidermis of all higher plants, the extent to which it develops depends on the plant species and the environment in which it grows. The cuticle is responsible for the protective functions of the epidermis. In some plants wax is also deposited on the cuticle and within the matrix of the cell wall. Waxy deposits may occur as thin layers or as thick layers such as those seen on leaves of the Brazilian wax palm, *Copernicia cerifera,* from which the commercially important carnauba wax is collected. The wax covering further serves to control water loss. Other substances, such as lignin, crystals, and mucilage, occur in epidermal cell walls of certain plants.

The epidermis is not continuous over the surface of the plant but is interrupted by pores that serve as channels to the interior tissues. The pores are bordered by specialized, often kidney-shaped epidermal cells, called guard cells. The combination of pore and guard cells is referred to as the stoma. Two to several epidermal cells, called accessory cells, may be adjacent to the guard cells and participate in stomatal opening and closing. The accessory cells and the stoma constitute the stomatal apparatus. There is considerable variation in the development, structure, and distribution of the stomatal apparatus in plant species. The size, shape, and wall thickenings of the guard cells are important in stomatal function and gaseous exchange.

Another important group of structurally modified epidermal cells includes hairs (trichomes) which occur as outgrowths of epidermal cells and, when present, are usually characteristic of the particular plant. Trichomes may be either glandular, consisting of a stalk terminating in a globular head, or nonglandular, consisting simply of elongated, often tapering structures. Both types may be single celled or multicellular. The glandular trichomes usually produce and secrete volatile and nonvolatile substances, such as volatile oils, mucilages, and resins. In addition, trichomes on many carnivorous plants produce digestive enzymes (biological catalysts). Nonglandular trichomes, which may function in reducing transpiration and excessive water loss, are variable in structure and occasionally provide commercially important products, such as cotton and kapok.

Root hairs

Hairs are found on the surfaces of roots. Root hair cells are initiated behind the meristematic zone of the root apex and continue to elongate as the distance of the epidermal cells from the meristem increases. Root hairs usually live and function only for a few days; the sequential nature of the production near the root apex, however, insures a continuous supply. Root hairs increase the water absorbing ability of the plant.

Periderm. In plants in which substantial secondary growth—increase in stem thickness—occurs, a protective tissue, the periderm, forms. It arises from the activity of a cork cambium and is a complex tissue consisting largely of cork cells. Periderm serves the secondary plant body in much the same way as the epidermis serves the primary plant body, restricting water loss from the tissues within, protecting against attack by organisms—particularly after tissue damage—and preventing mechanical injury to the underlying tissues. The protective nature of periderm results largely from the properties of cork cells, many layers of which form on the outer side of the cork cambium. Cork cells produce a fatty substance known as suberin, which is deposited over the primary cellulose walls; in addition, some wax may also be deposited. The combination of wax and suberin makes the cork relatively impermeable to the passage of water and gases. In certain plants some cork cells remain thin walled and alternate with thick-walled cells. Neither cell type is alive when mature. At maturity all cork cells become filled with air or, in some instances, with resins or tannins that produce the dark pigmentation characteristic of certain types of cork and may have a protective function.

As secondary growth continues, the outer periderm layers crack and peel, and new layers of periderm form in tissues underlying the older periderm. In certain parts of the periderm, loosely arranged groups of cells often project above the other cells, forming prominent markings on the outer surface of the plant. These groups of cells, called lenticels, are similar to stomata in that they provide for passage of air to the interior tissues. The term bark is a nontechnical one usually referring to all tissues outside the vascular cambium. It may include parts of the phloem, cortex, and epidermis as well as periderm.

Vascular (conducting) tissues. All vascular plants, such as ferns, gymnosperms, and angiosperms, possess a well-developed vascular system that conducts water and food materials through the plant axis to the various organs; it usually also functions in support. The vascular system consists basically of two complex tissues, the xylem and phloem. The two tissues are distinctive, each being made up of several different cell types and each functioning in its own way. Movement of water and dissolved salts from the root system to other parts of the plant takes place through the xylem. Transfer of food materials produced in photosynthetic tissue or accumulated in storage organs occurs through the phloem (The structure and function of these tissues is described in detail below.)

Xylem and phloem

Fundamental (ground) tissues. The axis of most plants is composed of relatively large amounts of fundamental, or ground, tissues. The most common are parenchyma, collenchyma, and sclerenchyma (see Figure 8). These are simple tissues, but parenchyma and sclerenchyma are often found as components of complex tissues.

Parenchyma. Parenchyma is made up of thin-walled, commonly polyhedral (many-sided) living cells. The most common tissue in vascular plants and perhaps the most primitive, parenchyma is the chief constituent of the cortex and pith, the photosynthetic tissue of leaves, the pulp of fruits, and the endosperm (starchy nutrient tissue for the developing embryo) of many seeds. It is also found associated with the primary and secondary xylem and phloem. Although structurally simple, parenchyma cells may be highly specialized in a physiological sense. Some cells, especially those of the leaf and cortex, contain chloroplasts, which are small membrane-enclosed pigment bodies active in photosynthesis. Parenchyma containing chloroplasts is known as chlorenchyma. Other parenchyma cells may function in the production and storage of food substances necessary for maintenance of the plant. Parenchyma cells containing starch, lipid (fats), or protein are common in fruits, seeds, and especially in storage organs, such as rhizomes (creeping horizontal stem structures), bulbs, and tubers (underground storage stems, such as potatoes). Some parenchyma cells synthesize and accumulate other products such as crystals of calcium oxalate, tannins, mucilages, and resins. In addition, water, pigments, and soluble salts are found within parenchyma cells. Parenchyma tissue is therefore of primary importance to the plant.

Collenchyma. Collenchyma is basically a supporting tissue that provides structural rigidity for many plant organs. It is found chiefly in the cortex of stems and in leaves. For many herbaceous plants it is the chief supporting tissue, especially during early stages of development. In plants in which secondary growth occurs, the collenchyma tissue is only temporarily functional and becomes crushed as woody tissue develops. Collenchyma is located along the periphery of stems beneath the epidermal tissue. It may form a complete cylinder or occur as discrete strands that constitute the ridges and angles of stems and other supporting structures of the plant.

Collenchyma cells, polygonal in cross section, are much longer than parenchyma cells. The strength of the tissue results from the unevenly thickened cell walls and the longitudinal overlapping and interlocking of the cells. The cells have protoplasts, often containing chloroplasts, and they produce a thick cellulose wall. The wall is not uniformly thick in all cells, and thickening may occur predominately in longitudinal strips at the corners of the cell, on the tangential (*i.e.,* outer, toward the stem exterior) surface of the cell, or around the spaces between adjacent cells. Pits are present in the cell wall and provide a mechanism for intercellular communication. An important feature of collenchyma is that it is extremely plastic—the cells can extend and thus adjust to increase in growth of the organ.

Location of collenchyma wall thickenings

Sclerenchyma. The major function of sclerenchyma is support. Unlike collenchyma, mature cells of this tissue are generally nonliving and have heavily thickened walls containing lignin. The size, shape, and structure of sclerenchyma cells are not uniform. Two distinct types of cells occur: those that are greatly elongated are termed sclerenchyma fibres; those that are essentially uniform in diameter are called sclereids (see Figure 8). The division is arbitrary, and intermediate and overlapping types of sclerenchyma cells commonly occur, even within one plant organ.

Fibres may occur singly or in groups of few to many cells with their long, tapering ends interlocked, thus providing maximum support. They may be found almost anywhere

From T. Weier, C. Stocking, and M. Barbour, *Botany* (1970); John Wiley & Sons

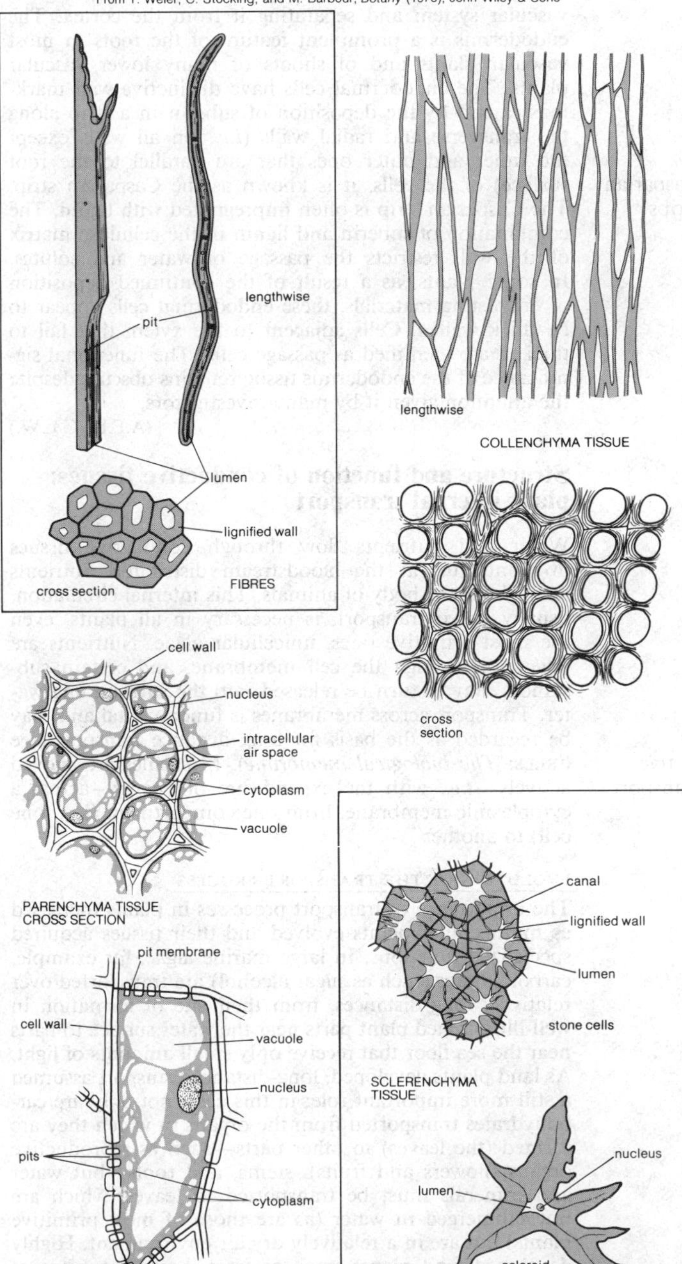

Figure 8: Cell types and tissues.

in the plant body and are classified according to position. Cortical fibres and phloem fibres are characteristic of the stems and roots of many plants. Fibres also partially or completely surround vascular bundles in leaves and in the plant axis. Most fibres have extremely thick cell walls containing pits, and the cell lumen is very narrow or completely obscured.

Sclereids occur singly or in groups and are present in various tissues of the plant such as periderm, cortex, pith, xylem, and phloem. They also occur in leaves and fruits and constitute the hard shell of nuts and the outer hard coat of many seeds. Sclereid walls are commonly pitted, and the pits may be extensively branched. Sclereids are extremely variable in form and are classified according to shape. Brachysclereids or stone cells are isodiametric; macrosclereids are rod shaped; osteosclereids are bone shaped; that is, elongated with enlarged ends; and asterosclereids are star shaped or otherwise branched. The utility of this classification is limited by the occurrence of sclereids that do not fit into any of the categories.

Casparian strips

Endodermis. The endodermis, another kind of ground tissue, usually consists of a layer of cells surrounding the vascular system and separating it from the cortex. The endodermis is a prominent feature of the roots in most vascular plants and of shoots of many lower vascular plants. The endodermal cells have distinctive wall markings caused by the deposition of suberin in a strip along the transverse and radial walls (*i.e.,* on all walls except the inner and outer ones that are parallel to the root surface) of the cells; it is known as the Casparian strip. The Casparian strip is often impregnated with lignin. The combination of suberin and lignin in the cellulose matrix of the wall restricts the passage of water and solutes. In some plants, as a result of the continued deposition of encrusting materials, these endodermal cells appear to be thick walled. Cells adjacent to the xylem that fail to thicken are identified as passage cells. The functional significance of the endodermis tissue remains obscure despite the attention given it by many investigators.

(A.E.D./C.L.W.)

Structure and function of conductive tissues: plant internal transport

Active transport

Water and nutrients flow through conductive tissues in plants just as the bloodstream distributes nutrients throughout the body of animals. This internal circulation, usually called transport, is necessary in all plants, even the most primitive ones, unicellular algae. Nutrients are taken up through the cell membrane, and certain substances may in turn be released into the surrounding water. Transport across membranes is fundamental and may be regarded as the basis for long distance transport (see CELLS: *The biological membrane*). Molecules are moved actively—*i.e.,* with the expenditure of energy—across a cytoplasmic membrane, from one compartment (*e.g.,* one cell) to another.

EVOLUTION OF THE TRANSPORT PROCESS

Xylem and phloem

The importance of transport processes in plants increased as multicellular plants evolved and their tissues acquired specialized functions. In large marine algae, for example, carbohydrates (such as sugar alcohol) are transported over relatively long distances, from their site of formation in well-illuminated plant parts near the water surface to parts near the sea floor that receive only small amounts of light. As land plants developed, long-distance transport assumed a still more important role; in this case, not only are carbohydrates transported from the organs in which they are formed (the leaves) to other parts—such as reproductive organs (flowers and fruits), stems, and roots—but water and minerals must be transported to leaves, which are not submerged in water (as are those of most primitive plants) but are in a relatively dry air environment. Highly developed land plants, such as trees, have two types of tissues specialized for long-distance transport: the xylem and the phloem. Water and dissolved mineral nutrients ascend in the xylem (the wood of a tree, such as an oak or a pine) and products of photosynthesis, mostly sugars, move from leaves to other plant parts in the phloem (the inner bark of a plant).

Evolving land plants faced not only the problem of transport but also the problem of supporting their weight. Aquatic plants are supported by their buoyancy in water. Even large seaweed do not need a rigid stem; flotation devices such as gas-filled bladders hold them upright and enable them to grow toward the water surface and obtain sufficient sunlight for photosynthesis. On land, a rigid, self-supporting structure is necessary for plants; this structure, the xylem, consists of tiny rigid tubes through which water and dissolved mineral nutrients can move. The rigidity of the tubes within a stem is sufficient to make it self-supporting.

Land plants take up water from the soil through the roots; the few rare exceptions, such as some plants of the Peruvian desert that grow in dry soil, rely on adaptations that enable them to obtain water from the air. In most plants, then, water ascends through the xylem, the tiny capillaries of the woody stem tissue, into all plant parts but primarily into the leaves, from which it is transpired (evaporated) into the air. In this way, the mineral nutrients are transferred from the soil to all above-ground plant parts.

Plants living in humid habitats, such as the small and primitive mosses and liverworts, do not have a well-developed xylem. Similarly, water plants that have returned from land to an aquatic habitat during evolution have a reduced xylem; such plants, which have readapted to an aquatic environment, are not woody, because they need neither water-conducting tissues nor a self-supporting structure. On the other hand, tall land plants such as trees and vines (lianas) have the most highly developed long-distance transport systems. Vines differ from trees in that their xylem serves primarily for water conduction; they depend, for the most part, on other plants for support. Certain vines are of great length (a few hundred metres) and have extremely highly developed tissues for transporting water and nutrients.

Most of the material that comprises a plant's dry weight is a consequence of photosynthesis, in which light energy is converted into chemical energy used to synthesize organic substances. Carbon dioxide from the air and water, which the plant takes from the soil, are utilized during photosynthesis, which occurs mostly in green plant parts—especially the leaves (see PHOTOSYNTHESIS). Since plants shed their leaves either continuously or periodically but still increase in size, it is clear that many photosynthetic products must be transported out of the leaves and carried to all other plant parts; this process takes place primarily in the phloem.

Girdling experiments

The discovery of the functions of xylem and phloem (wood and bark) was made following that of the circulation of blood in the 17th century. By the early 19th century, it had been established that water ascends from roots into leaves through xylem and that photosynthetic products descend through phloem. Experiments now called girdling experiments were performed, in which a ring of bark is removed from a woody plant. Girdling or ringing does not immediately interfere with upward movement of water in the xylem, but it does interrupt phloem movement. In some plants surgical removal of phloem is difficult; in this case phloem may be killed by using steam (steam girdling). Xylem conduction is normally not affected by such treatment, and movement in the two transport tissues can thus easily be distinguished. Girdling experiments, however, are not entirely foolproof. The question as to whether or not mineral nutrients can ascend in the phloem illustrates the kinds of difficulties that may be encountered. Much smaller amounts of mineral nutrients reach the leaves in girdled plants than in ungirdled ones. From this observation it might be concluded that some nutrients ascend in the phloem of ungirdled trees; girdling, however, interrupts the flow of sugars into roots. Roots are thereby starved and take up fewer mineral nutrients; the reduced flow of mineral nutrients to the leaves of girdled plants can thus be explained as a secondary effect.

It was once widely believed that flogging a fruit tree increases the crop. The rational explanation of this is simple: flogging a tree damages the phloem; *i.e.,* it girdles the tree, perhaps partially. Girdling increases the sugar concentration of the leaves by restricting downward transport to the roots and may thus directly or indirectly stimulate flowering or, if done after fruit-set, may increase fruit size.

STRUCTURAL BASIS OF TRANSPORT

Cell-to-cell transport. Two features of plant cells differ conspicuously from those of animal cells. In plant cells the protoplast, or living material of the cell, contains one or more vacuoles, which are vesicles containing aqueous cell sap. Plant cells are also surrounded by a relatively tough but elastic wall. Water entering the vacuole by osmosis (*i.e.,* movement of water across a membrane into regions of lower water concentration, such as cell interiors, which normally contain dissolved substances) expands the protoplast and consequently the cell wall until the internal pressure is balanced by the elastic counterpressure of the wall. Spaces between and within cell walls are sufficiently large to permit water to flow around all cells. The space available for free water flow is called apoplast. Water in apoplast originates from the roots and contains nutrients taken up by them. Nutrients enter a cell by crossing the outer cytoplasmic membrane.

Entry into the protoplast

Because mature cell walls are dead structures, metabolic activities—the chemical reactions of living systems—occur within protoplasts. Substances can enter a protoplast by cytoplasmic connections between neighbouring cells (plasmodesmata) or by active transport mechanisms requiring energy and a group of enzymes called permeases. Plasmodesmata penetrate neighbouring cell walls at areas called pits. Some substances pass out of cells into the apoplast and are transported by energy-requiring processes into the protoplast of another cell.

Structure of xylem and phloem. *The xylem.* Cell-to-cell transport takes place in all multicellular plants, but it is a slow process; the higher plants evolved the specialized tissues, xylem and phloem, for rapid long-distance transport. The woody tissue, xylem, contains highly specialized cells for water conduction. The cells are long and reinforced by strong, woody walls; their protoplast breaks down and dissolves after wall growth is completed, so that the entire inside of the cell becomes available for rapid water conduction. In other words, the water-conducting cells of xylem are dead when functional. In the more primitive conifers the xylem consists largely of spindle-shaped cells called tracheids, which have a diameter around 0.04 millimetres (0.0016 inch) and a length of about three millimetres (0.12 inch). Flowering plants have a more highly specialized xylem, in which the mechanical function and the water conduction function have been separated during evolution. Tracheids, the primitive conducting cells, have evolved to form fibres for mechanical strength and vessels for water conduction. Vessel elements are barrel-like cells with widths of up to 0.5 millimetre (0.02 inch) in some plants. Vessel elements are arranged end-to-end; their end walls are partly or wholly dissolved, and rows of such cells thus form long capillaries (tubes), up to several metres in length. These tubes are the vessels.

Function of the pits

Conducting units—tracheids in conifers and vessels in flowering plants—have overlapping ends that are laterally connected by means of numerous pits. Pits are "windows" in the walls consisting of a thin wall membrane through which water but not an air–water interface (a bubble) can easily pass from one conducting unit to the next. Numerous vessels of limited length thus provide a certain protection against injury: that is, since water pressures in the xylem are often well below zero (*i.e.,* the water is under tension), air will be sucked into any injured xylem vessel and spread immediately throughout it but cannot pass through the wet pit membranes into the uninjured units. Damage is thus confined to the units that are injured and cannot easily spread; in addition, the smaller the conducting unit, the more confined is the damage. Plants with large, highly efficient vessels are much more vulnerable to injury, as is evident, for example, from the vulnerability of the elm, which has large vessels, to the Dutch elm disease, in which the water-conduction vessels are injured by beetle activity and fungal growth. In general, both the less efficient but safer coniferous wood and the more highly efficient but more vulnerable wood of flowering plants have been successful during evolution. Very tall trees occur in both groups; *e.g., Sequoia* among the conifers and *Eucalyptus* among the flowering plants.

The phloem. The conducting elements of the phloem underwent evolutionary changes somewhat similar to those of the xylem. The conducting elements of conifers, called sieve cells, are similar in shape and dimensions to tracheids. They do not have a woody wall, however, and they are alive at functional maturity even though their cytoplasm may be highly specialized and the cells have usually lost their nucleus during development. In flowering plants the conducting elements in the phloem, called sieve elements, are arranged end-to-end to form sieve tubes, a name derived from the sievelike end walls through which passage of food from one cell to the next occurs. Sieve cells and sieve elements are almost invariably accompanied by special companion cells believed to control, to a certain extent, the metabolism of the nucleus-free conducting cells.

Sieve elements

Vascular tissue. In primary tissues, such as leaves, strands of phloem and xylem run parallel, forming conducting bundles. These form a network of veins that can be seen when a leaf is held against a light. Xylem sap from the stem enters a leaf through the petiole (leaf stalk) and spreads throughout the leaf blade in the xylem part of the conducting bundles, or veins. Photosynthetic products enter the phloem tissues of the veins, and they are transported from the leaf through the phloem of the petiole.

Throughout most of the plant, xylem and phloem channels run more or less in an axial, or longitudinal, direction, although this path may not be precisely parallel with the stem axis. In most stems of monocotyledonous plants—flowering plants with one seed leaf, such as lilies, grasses, palms—the tissue is primary; *i.e.,* it is formed entirely by the growing shoot tip. Because such plants have no cambium tissue in their stems, they have no secondary growth and thus show relatively little increase in stem diameter. The conducting tissue consists of narrow strands, containing both xylem and phloem, distributed throughout the plant. A single crosswise section through the stem of a coconut palm may contain 20,000 vascular bundles, which are connected into a complex network by numerous cross connections; if the stem is injured, alternate pathways of transport are available.

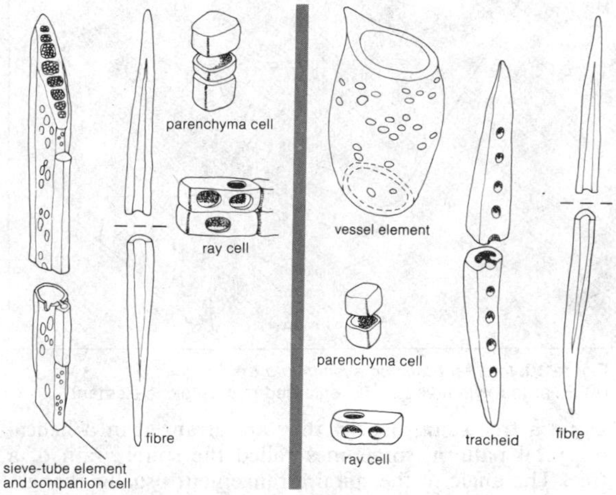

Figure 9: Cells of the (left) phloem and (right) xylem.

Tree stems of both conifers and dicotyledonous plants (flowering plants with two seed leaves, such as oaks, maples, elms) contain a cell layer called the vascular cambium that gives rise to secondary xylem and phloem. With each season's secondary growth, the stems increase in diameter. Xylem is formed as a woody cylinder on the inner side of the cambium layer near the centre of the stem. The vessels are deposited by the cambium as a complex network in such a way that an injury to the stem interrupts the local flow of water, but water continues to flow around the injury. Phloem is formed toward the outside of the stem from the cambium layer, forming the inner, conducting bark. The conducting phloem layer remains very thin, less than 0.5 millimetre (0.02 inch), and is renewed each year. Older phloem serves only for food storage. Conducting and storing phloem comprise the living bark.

Both xylem and phloem have limited longevity. The oldest phloem layers are the outermost—the dead bark of the stem surface. The yearly amounts of xylem visible in cross sections of stems as distinct rings are known as annual rings. The oldest xylem layers (*i.e.,* the oldest annual rings) are in the dead central core, or heartwood, of the woody stem, which can often be recognized by its darker coloration. The lighter coloured sapwood is living and functions as storage tissue and, especially in the outermost sapwood, as conducting tissue; the younger annual rings comprise the sapwood. In some highly specialized tree species with large vessels (such as some oaks, ashes, and others) only the very outermost growth ring functions in water conduction. Conducting tissues seldom run straight

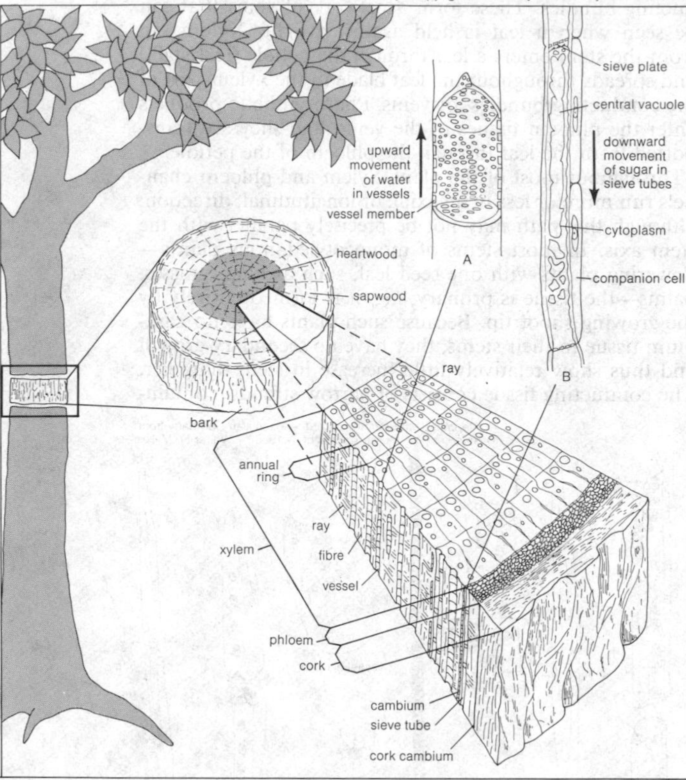

Figure 10: *Internal transport system in a tree.* (A) Enlarged xylem vessel; (B) enlarged mature sieve element.

along a tree stem; usually they are arranged in a helical or spiral pattern, sometimes called the spiral grain of a tree. The angle of the spiral arrangement usually changes from year to year; the path of water up a tree stem may therefore be very complicated if more than one growth layer acts as a conducting tissue. Functionally, the effect of the variable spiral grain is to distribute water to all parts of the tree from any root.

Ray tissue

An important tissue in the stems of conifers and dicotyledonous trees is the ray tissue. Rays, small strands of radially running tissue, are continuous from the stem centre through the xylem and phloem and serve for radial conduction and storage of starch. No rays are present in monocotyledonous stems, however; more or less radially running bundles that originally connected the stem with leaves, which have fallen from lower stem parts, serve the same purpose.

Gas exchange and transport in leaves. Although some transpiration (evaporation) of water occurs from the surfaces of all leaf cells, most of it takes place through special structures called stomata; these structures are pores whose openings are controlled by a flexible pair of cells called guard cells. The movement of guard cells is controlled so that they open during daylight hours and close at night or under conditions of excessive water stress. The stomatal opening not only permits the escape of water vapour but also allows carbon dioxide to enter leaves for photosynthesis. Photosynthesis ceases as night falls, and excessive water loss is prevented by stomatal closure.

Most water, which is taken up by roots and ascends into leaves, is lost by transpiration. Transpiration is necessary for two reasons. One is the necessity of keeping stomata open throughout the daylight hours for the entry of carbon dioxide. The second is the fact that xylem sap is very dilute; *i.e.,* it contains much water. In order for sufficient quantities of soil nutrients to be accumulated in leaf cells, large amounts of water must be transpired.

Stomata are very efficient in transpiring water. Water molecules that emerge from such a small pore can escape without interference in all radial directions. (From an open surface water molecules can escape only in a straight line because of mutual interference of neighbouring molecules.) Thus, water can evaporate through a multiperforate membrane (with many pores) almost as efficiently as from an open water surface of equal size even though the total area of all the pores is extremely small. The advantage of the multiperforate membrane is that the size of the pore opening can be controlled.

Xylem sap entering leaves from the stem spreads out into the xylem tissues of all veins and from vein ends into the walls of other leaf cells. Thus surrounded by xylem sap, leaf cells live in an environment not unlike that of algal cells in water. Solutes—dissolved nutrients—brought up from roots can be taken up from the xylem sap into the cell interior. Any solute not actually used by the leaf cells can either be transported to the leaf surface or transferred into the phloem to be returned to the plant body for use in other plant parts; certain substances of no value to the plant are deposited in the form of crystals, sometimes in special crystal cells along the phloem path.

Movement of gases in leaves

Leaf tissue is very spongy—*i.e.,* the cells are surrounded by an abundance of communicating gas spaces. Water evaporates from cell walls into the gas space, diffuses into the stomatal cavity, and then moves into the air through the stomatal pore between the guard cells. Within the gas spaces of the leaf, gases presumably move by diffusion and perhaps, as leaves are moved about by wind, by convection.

The bark of the stem also contains stomata when young and secondary structures of similar function—openings in the bark called lenticels—when older. Very young stems are usually green and function somewhat like leaves; *i.e.,* they photosynthesize and transpire. Photosynthesis in older stems is negligible although transpiration continues. Transpiration through lenticels takes place in the summer, but closure of lenticels largely prevents transpiration in the winter.

Uptake of water and mineral nutrients from the soil. Water uptake from the soil by root cells is passive, in that water may be pulled into the root by low xylem pressure and also follows osmotic gradients caused by the mineral nutrients, which are taken up actively (*i.e.,* with the expenditure of metabolic energy) across root cell membranes. As the mineral nutrients—the ions (charged components) of inorganic salts—are taken up, they are largely incorporated into organic molecules. Thus, the solutes in xylem sap are mostly complex organic substances, sometimes of a specific nature; for example, nicotine synthesis takes place in the roots of tobacco plants, where nitrogen is incorporated into compounds that have moved to the roots through the phloem as sugars. If a tomato shoot is grafted onto a tobacco rootstock, nicotine-containing tomato leaves are formed. On the other hand, a tobacco shoot grafted onto a tomato rootstock results in a plant with nicotine-free tobacco leaves. Many other specific nitrogen-containing substances originate in the roots; in most plants, however, nitrogen is transported to the leaves from the roots in the form of compounds known as amino acids and amides.

The major chemical elements needed by a plant are: carbon, hydrogen, oxygen, phosphorus, potassium, nitrogen, calcium, iron, and magnesium; in addition, many others are required in very small amounts. A lack of any element may result in deficiency diseases. A few elements taken up by plants are of no nutritive value and usually are eliminated (*e.g.,* sodium chloride) or crystallized (*e.g.,* silica), sometimes by deposition in special cells.

Casparian strips

The plant is able to control to some extent the substances that enter. If equal amounts of sodium and potassium are available to roots of plants, and the amount of the two elements inside the plant is analyzed, less sodium is likely to be found than potassium, which is a vital nutrient. The structural basis for the control of uptake of substances into roots is the so-called Casparian strip, a conspicuously thickened wall area of one cell layer around primary roots; it prevents excess soil solution from being pulled directly into the central part of the root where the xylem is located. As a result, the soil solution has to pass through a cell barrier in which uptake can metabolically be controlled. After nutrients are inside living root cells and have been converted to appropriate compounds, the latter are released into the xylem and move to above-ground parts.

PROCESS OF XYLEM TRANSPORT

Quantitative aspects. The sum of the cross-sectional areas of all the branches of a tree approximately equals that of the stem; this means that the total amount of conducting tissue remains about the same from roots to leaves. In terms of water movement, the velocity of movement might be expected to be uniform throughout the entire axial system of stem, branches, and twigs. Because some trees (*e.g.,* oaks) have thick twigs, however, the velocity of water movement is greater in the stem than in the twigs at any time. Similarly, in tree species with slender branches (such as birches), the reverse is true. Normally the proportion of xylem to leaves supplied by that xylem is greater in plants growing in dry habitats than in plants found in wet ones and may be as much as 700 times greater in certain desert plants than in aquatic plants and herbs of relatively humid forest floors. The leaves of dry-habitat plants thus are more richly supplied with water-conducting xylem tissue than are those of moist habitats.

The velocity of sap movement in trees varies throughout a 24-hour period. During the night, especially a rainy night, sap flow may stop; velocity increases with daylight, peak rates being found in the early afternoon. Peak velocities correlate with vessel size; the rate of sap flow in trees with small vessels is about two metres (seven feet) per hour; that in trees with large vessels, about 50 metres (160 feet) per hour. The energy required to lift water in both cases is comparable; in large-porous trees water simply moves faster through fewer and larger vessels.

Mechanism of sap ascent. It was demonstrated about 1900 that living cells of the stem are not responsible for water movement. It is now generally recognized that water in the xylem moves passively along a gradient of decreasing pressures. Under certain special conditions water is pushed up the stem by root pressure. This may be the case with herbaceous (nonwoody) plants in the greenhouse under conditions of ample water supply and little transpiration. In nature, these conditions may be met in early spring before the leaves emerge, when the soil is wet and transpiration is low. Under such conditions, water movement is caused by active uptake of ions (charged particles) and by the entry of water from the soil into the roots. Most of the time, however, water is pulled into the leaves by transpiration. A gradient of decreasing pressures from the base to the top of a tree can be measured, even though pressures are low.

The cohesion theory of sap ascent

A vacuum pump cannot pull water to a height of more than 10 metres (about 33 feet). Since many trees are far taller than 10 metres, the mechanism by which they move water to their crowns has been sought. Is it possible for trees to pull water into their crowns along a decreasing pressure gradient or do they employ some other mechanism? If trees pull water, that in the xylem would have to be held on the tracheid and vessel walls by adhesion, and water molecules would have to hold together by cohesion. The hypothesis that water is pulled upward along a pressure gradient during transpiration has been called the cohesion theory. Two critical requirements of the cohesion mechanism of sap ascent are: (1) sufficient cohesive strength of water and (2) existence of tensions (*i.e.,* pressures below zero) and tension gradients in stems of transpiring trees.

Although the tensile strength of water is very high, an excessive pull exerted on a water column will break it. The tallest trees are about 100 metres (330 feet) high. A nonmoving water column at an atmospheric pressure of one atmosphere at the base of the tree is exposed to a pressure of minus nine atmospheres (*i.e.,* a tension of nine atmospheres) at the top. Calculations show that, under conditions of peak flow at midday, this gradient increases by about 50 percent; in other words, a transpiring sequoia would have a pressure in the xylem of minus 14 atmospheres at the top if the basal pressure is one atmosphere. If the pressure at the base is minus ten atmospheres because of dry soil, however, the pressure at the top drops to minus 25 atmospheres.

It has now been shown that negative pressures and gradients of negative pressures do exist in trees with an ingeniously simple device called the pressure bomb. A small twig is inserted in a container (the pressure bomb), its cut stump emerging from a tightly sealed hole. As pressure is applied to the container and gradually increased, water from the xylem emerges from the cut end as soon as the pressure being applied is equal to the xylem tension that existed when the twig was cut. This method has been used to measure gradients of negative pressures in trees; the cohesion theory thus would seem to explain the sap-ascent mechanism.

PROCESS OF PHLOEM TRANSPORT

Quantitative aspects. Products of photosynthesis, primarily sugars, move through phloem from leaves to growing tissues and storage organs. The rate at which these substances are transported can be measured in various ways; *e.g.,* as velocities in distance traveled per unit time or as mass transfer in (dry) weight transported per unit time. Velocities appear to be graded—*i.e.,* some molecules move faster than others within the same channel. Peak velocities of molecules usually are of the order of 100 to 300 centimetres (40 to 120 inches) per hour. Average velocities, more difficult to measure but significant in mass-transfer considerations, are lower.

Velocity of phloem transport

Mass transfer can be measured by weighing a storage organ, such as a potato tuber or a fruit, at given time intervals during its growth. Mass transfer per cross-sectional area of conducting tissue is referred to as specific mass transfer and is expressed as grams per hour per square centimetre of phloem or sieve tubes. With a given specific mass transfer, the velocity with which a liquid of a certain concentration flows can be calculated; in dicotyledonous stems, for example, specific mass transfer is between ten and 25 grams per hour per square centimetre of sieve tube tissue at times of peak performance. In certain tree species the sieve tubes can be tapped to obtain an exudate. The concentration of this exudate, multiplied by the measured average velocity, is of the same order of magnitude as specific mass transfer, indicating that liquid movement through sieve tubes could account for transport.

Much of the experimental work on phloem transport now is done with the aid of radioactive substances; radioactive carbon dioxide administered to an illuminated leaf is incorporated into sugar during photosynthesis and carried from the leaf. The velocity of this movement can be measured by determining the arrival of radioactivity at given points along the stem. Whole plants, as long as they are reasonably small, can be pressed against photographic film after the conclusion of a similar experiment, and the photographic image will indicate the portions to which radioactive sugar has moved.

Mechanism of phloem transport. The mechanism of phloem transport has been studied by plant physiologists for many years. A number of hypotheses have been put forth over the past years, but none is entirely satisfactory. One fundamental question is whether sugars and other solutes move en masse as a flowing solution or whether transport takes place independently of the solvent water.

The phenomenon of exudation from injured sieve tubes supports the first possibility, which has been further supported by a discovery involving aphids (phloem-feeding insects); when aphids are cut away from plants while feeding, their mouthparts remain embedded in the phloem. Exudate continues to flow through the mouthparts; the magnitude of the rate of this exudation indicates that transport within the sieve tube to the mouthparts occurs as a flow of solution.

Evidence against solution flow is the movement of substances in opposite directions through a section of phloem at any one given time. This, however, has never been convincingly demonstrated in just one sieve tube. On the other hand, attempts to find simultaneous movement of sugars and water along a phloem path, in order to demonstrate solution flow, have been only partially successful.

Mass flow

Mass-flow hypotheses include the pressure-flow hypothesis, which states that flow into sieve tubes at source regions (places of photosynthesis or mobilization of storage products) raises the osmotic pressure in the sieve tube; removal of sugars from sieve tubes in sink regions—*i.e.,* those in which sugars are removed for growth and storage—lowers it. Thus a pressure gradient from source to sink is established in sieve tubes that would allow solution flow. The electroosmotic hypothesis postulates that solution is moved across all sieve plates (areas at which individual sieve elements end) by an electrical potential that is maintained by a circulation of cations (positively charged chemical ions), such as potassium. Transport hypotheses postulating solute movement independent of solvent water include the spreading of solute molecules between two liquid phases and the active movement of molecules by a type of cytoplasmic movement that is often referred to as cytoplasmic streaming.

TRANSPORT AND PLANT GROWTH

Storage and circulation. It is important to realize that the plant, with its two transport systems, xylem and phloem, is able to move any substance to virtually any part of its body; the direction of transport is usually opposite in the two systems, and transfer from one system to the other takes place easily. An exception is transport into flowers and certain fruits, in which flow in each system is unidirectional.

Numerous substances move from roots to mature leaves through xylem and are transferred from the leaves, together with sugars, through the phloem to other plant parts. In the autumn months in temperate regions, plants store most of the products resulting from photosynthesis during the summer months in structures such as stems, bulbs, and tubers and mobilize it in the spring when new growth begins. A few plants, such as some tropical monocotyledons (certain palms, for example), store food for many years for use at the time of flowering and fruit-set at the end of their life-span.

Transport of growth-regulating substances. Plant hormones, or growth regulators, are effective in very small amounts; they induce or enhance specific growth phenomena. Because the site of hormone synthesis is different from its place of action, hormones must be transported before they can exert their effects. There are several groups of plant hormones; each has different effects on plant growth. The best known plant hormones are the auxins, the most common of which is called indole acetic acid. Auxins are formed in young, growing organs, such as opening buds, and are transported away from tips of shoots toward the base of the plant, where they stimulate the cells to elongate and sometimes to divide. Responses to gravity and light are also under auxin control. Auxin moves to the lower side of a leaning stem; cells on the lower side then elongate and cause the stem to bend back to a vertical position. Response to gravity in many roots is the opposite of that in shoots; the same mechanism of auxin distribution is responsible, but roots react to different quantities of the hormone than do shoots. Similar auxin distributions are responsible for phototropic responses—*i.e.,* the growth of plant parts such as shoot tips and leaves toward light. In certain cases auxin may be destroyed on the illuminated side.

Auxin transport

Auxin is not normally transported through vascular tissue; moreover, transport is polar—*i.e.,* it takes place along the stem from tip to base, regardless of the stem's position. Velocities of transport are of the order of five to 10 millimetres (0.2 to 0.4 inch) per hour, and transport requires the expenditure of metabolic energy. There is evidence that most growth hormones can be transported through xylem or phloem, but, at least in the case of auxin, the transport mechanism is specific.

Hormone transport is also involved in the stimulation of flowering. In some plants, flowering is triggered by short or long days. The receptor of this stimulus is in the leaves. A chemical substance, probably a flowering hormone of as yet unknown nature, then moves to the shoot apex and causes a transformation of the vegetative growing point into a flowering shoot.

Many growth-correlating phenomena are effected by transported hormonal stimuli. A vigorously growing terminal (topmost) shoot may inhibit lateral buds lower down from growing out and may force later branches to bend down. If the terminal shoot is removed, laterals grow out and topmost lateral branches bend upward. In leaning trees with secondary tissue (wood), the cambium produces compression wood on the lower side (in conifers) or tension wood on the upper side (in dicotyledons) in response to a hormone; the stem responds by pushing (in conifers) or pulling (in dicotyledons) itself upright. Transport of growth-regulating substances is thus largely responsible for the characteristic shape of each plant species (see also BIOCHEMICAL COMPONENTS OF ORGANISMS: *Hormone*).

(M.H.Z.)

BIBLIOGRAPHY

The tissues and fluids of animals: WILLIAM BLOOM and DON W. FAWCETT, *A Textbook of Histology,* 10th ed. (1975); and WILFRED M. COPENHAVER, *Bailey's Textbook of Histology,* 17th ed. (1978), standard textbooks that emphasize human tissues; DONALD I. and GAIL R. PATT, *Comparative Vertebrate Histology* (1969), one of the few works covering other vertebrates in addition to man; ANNA-MARY CARPENTER, *Human Histology* (1968), a very fine colour atlas; W. PENFIELD (ed.), *Cytology and Cellular Pathology of the Nervous System* (1932), a standard work in this field; but ALF BRODAL, *Nevro-anatomi i relasjon til klinisk nevrologi* (1943; Eng. trans., *Neurological Anatomy in Relation to Clinical Medicine,* 2nd ed., 1969), deals with the topic more broadly; JACK H. PRINCE *et al., Anatomy and Histology of the Eye and Orbit in Domestic Animals* (1960), a comprehensive reference work, but the same author's *Comparative Anatomy of the Eye* (1956) is easier for the general reader to understand; HANS S. HELLER, *Neurohypophysis* (1957), for those with a special interest in the pituitary gland; G. FORTEZA BOVER and R.B. CANDELA, *Atlas de citología sanguínea* (1963; Eng. trans., *Atlas of Blood Cytology: Cytomorphology, Cytochemistry, and Cytogenetics,* 1964), the most comprehensive work on blood; GARTH CHAPMAN, *Body Fluids and Their Functions,* 2nd ed. (1980), a good treatment of body fluids; JEAN OLIVER, *Nephrons and Kidneys* (1968), for comparative kidney structure.

Blood and lymph: E.C. ALBRITTON (ed.), *Standard Values in Blood* (1952), with comprehensive tables; F.M. BURNET, *Cellular Immunology,* 2 vol. (1969), an essential work; O.F. KAMPMEIER, *Evolution and Comparative Morphology of the Lymphatic System* (1969), a classic, but almost exclusively morphological; R.G. MACFARLANE and A.H.T. ROBB-SMITH (eds.), *Functions of the Blood* (1961), a unique, somewhat outdated collection of comparative physiological studies; L. VROMAN, *Blood* (1967), a readable account.

Cerebrospinal fluid: D. BOWSHER, *Cerebrospinal Fluid Dynamics in Health and Disease* (1960), a detailed study of the pressure relationships and hydrodynamics of cerebrospinal fluid in both normal and diseased states; H. DAVSON, *Physiology of Ocular and Cerebrospinal Fluids* (1956), a review of the functions and biochemistry of cerebrospinal fluid as well as of ocular fluids; R.N. DEJONG, *The Neurologic Examination,* 4th ed. (1979), a textbook dealing with the anatomic and physiologic basis of the neurologic examination with separate chapters on cerebrospinal fluid circulation and syndromes, spinal puncture, examination of the cerebrospinal fluid, and related examinations and procedures; R.A. FISHMAN, "Cerebrospinal Fluid," in A.B. BAKER (ed.), *Clinical Neurology,* 2nd ed., vol. 1 (1962), an authoritative discussion on the physiology and composition of spinal fluid and various spinal fluid syndromes; S. LUPS and A.M.F.H. HAAN, *The Cerebrospinal Fluid* (1954), a well-recognized textbook by Dutch investigators on the functions and anatomy of cerebrospinal fluid; H.H.

MERRITT and F. FREMONT-SMITH, *Cerebrospinal Fluid* (1937), although now somewhat out-of-date, remains the classic reference book; J.W. MILLEN and D.H.M. WOOLLAM, *The Anatomy of the Cerebrospinal Fluid* (1962), a comprehensive discussion of the morphologic aspects of cerebrospinal fluid by current British investigators; W.W. TOURTELLOTTE *et al., Post-Lumbar Puncture Headaches* (1964), a detailed critical analysis of the various theories regarding post lumbar puncture headache and methods for prevention and treatment.

Fluid and electrolyte balance: D.A.K. BLACK, *Essentials of Fluid Balance,* 4th ed. (1967), a good introductory account of fluid and electrolyte disorders; C.L. COMAR and F. BRONNER (eds.), *Mineral Metabolism,* 3 vol. (1960–69), a modern comprehensive review of mineral metabolism with an extensive bibliography; E.B. FLINK, "Therapy of Magnesium Deficiency," *Ann. N.Y. Acad. Sci.,* 162:901–905 (1969), a useful summary of modern research in all aspects of magnesium metabolism; J.L. GAMBLE, *Chemical Anatomy, Physiology and Pathology of Extracellular Fluid,* 3rd ed. (1954), a classic, historically valuable work on fluid and electrolyte balance; L.J. HENDERSON, *Blood* (1928), a classic work on acid–base balance in the blood; H.L. MARRIOTT, *Water and Salt Depletion* (1950), a classic, simple account of problems of water and salt balance; G.G. NAHAS, "Current Concepts of Acid–Base Measurement," *Ann. N.Y. Acad. Sci.,* 133:3–4 (1966), a good summary of modern research and thought on problems of acid–base balance; P.B. OLIVA, "Lactic Acidosis," *Amer. J. Med.,* 48:209–225 (1970), a good, well-documented review of lactic-acid acidosis; J.P. PETERS and D.D. VAN SLYKE, *Quantitative Clinical Chemistry,* 2 vol., 2nd ed. (1946), a classic introduction to problems of acid–base control in man; J.R. ROBINSON, *Fundamentals of Acid–Base Regulation,* 4th ed. (1973), a modern, simple introduction to problems of acid–base control in man; J.S. ROBSON, J.M. BONE, and A.T. LAMBIE, "Intracellular pH," vol. 11:213–277, *Advances in Clinical Chemistry* (1968), a modern, well-documented review of the concepts and measurement of intracellular pH; O. SIGGAARD-ANDERSEN, *The Acid–Base Status of the Blood,* 3rd ed. (Eng. trans. 1965), a modern account of acid–base control in the blood and in man; J.M. VAUGHAN, *The Physiology of Bone,* 3rd ed. (1981), a modern, short, well-documented review of calcium and bone metabolism.

The tissues and fluids of plants: College-level textbooks on this subject include: A.J. EAMES and L.H. MACDANIELS, *An Introduction to Plant Anatomy,* 2nd ed. (1947, reprinted 1977); K. ESAU, *Plant Anatomy,* 2nd ed. (1965); A. FAHN, *Plant Anatomy* (1967; orig. pub. in Hebrew, 1962); and W.H. MULLER, *Botany,* 4th ed. (1979). A comprehensive review for the specialist is K. ESAU, "The Phloem," in the *Encyclopedia of Plant Anatomy* (1969); P.M. RAY, *The Living Plant* (1963), is an introductory treatment in paperback.

Conductive tissues: plant internal transport: The following three books contain extensive bibliographies through which the reader will find his way into every aspect of the literature: K. ESAU, *Plant Anatomy,* 2nd. ed. (1965), an excellent college-level textbook on anatomy, with chapters on xylem, phloem, leaves, and roots; M.B. WILKINS (ed.), *The Physiology of Plant Growth and Development* (1969), a graduate-level book, containing chapters on transport of nutrients, growth regulators, mineral uptake, photosynthesis, and movement of stomata; M.H. ZIMMERMANN and C.L. BROWN, *Trees: Structure and Function* (1971), a profusely illustrated college-level tree physiology textbook, discussing xylem and phloem transport as well as growth correlations in trees. For continuing reviews, the reader is also referred to the *Annual Review of Plant Physiology* and to supplement volumes to the *Encyclopedia of Plant Physiology,* new series.

(Pe.G./L.V./R.N.DeJ./J.S.Ro./A.E.D./C.L.W./M.H.Z.)

Titian

Titian was recognized early in his own lifetime as a supremely great painter, and his reputation has never suffered a decline in the intervening centuries. The art theorist Giovanni Lomazzo in 1590 declared him "the sun amidst small stars not only among the Italians but all the painters of the world." The universality of Titian's genius is not questioned today, for he was surpassingly great in all aspects of the painter's art. In his portraits he searched and penetrated human character and recorded it in canvases of pictorial brilliance. His religious compositions cover the full range of emotion from the charm of his youthful Madonnas to the tragic depths of the late "Crucifixion" and the "Entombment." In his mythological pictures he captured the gaiety and abandon of the pagan world of antiquity, and in his paintings of the nude Venus ("Venus and Adonis") and the Danae ("Danae with Nursemaid") he set a standard for physical beauty and often sumptuous eroticism that has never been surpassed. Other great masters—Rubens and Nicolas Poussin, for example—paid him the compliment of imitation.

EARLY LIFE AND WORKS

The traditional date of Titian's birth was long given as 1477, but today most critics favour a later date of birth—1488/90. Titian (in Italian Tiziano Vecellio), son of a modest official, Gregorio di Conte dei Vecelli, and his wife, Lucia, was born in the small village of Pieve di Cadore, located high amid mountain peaks of the Alps, straight north of Venice and not far from the Austrian Tyrol. At the age of nine he set out for Venice with his brother, Francesco, to live there with an uncle and to become an apprentice to Sebastiano Zuccato, a master of mosaics. The boy soon passed to the workshop of the Bellini, where his true teacher became Giovanni Bellini, the greatest Venetian painter of the day. Titian's early works are richly evident of his schooling and also of his association as a young man with another follower of the elderly Giovanni Bellini, namely, Giorgione of Castelfranco (1477–1510). Their collaboration in 1508 on the frescoes of the Fondaco dei Tedeschi (the German Exchange) is the point of departure for Titian's career, and it explains why it is difficult to distinguish between the two artists in the early years of the 16th century. Only ruined outlines of the frescoes survive, the "Allegory of Justice" being the chief scene assigned to Titian. The etchings (1760) of the frescoes by Antonio Maria Zanetti, already in a much faded condition, give a better notion of the idealism and the sense of physical beauty that characterize both artists' work. The problem of distinguishing between the paintings of Giorgione and the young Titian is virtually insuperable, for there is little solid evidence and even less agreement among critics about the attri-

Influence of Giorgione

By courtesy of the Staatliche Museen Preussischer Kulturbesitz Gemaldegalerie Berlin (West)

"Self Portrait," by Titian, *c.* 1550. In the Staatliche Museen Preussischer Kulturbesitz, West Berlin.

bution of several works. The present tendency among Italian writers is to assign far too much to Titian in his youth.

It is certain that Titian's first independent commission was for the frescoes of three miracles of St. Anthony of Padua. The finest in composition is the "Miracle of the Speaking Infant"; another, the "Miracle of the Irascible Son," has a very beautiful landscape background that demonstrates how similar in topography and mood were Titian's and Giorgione's works at this time. In fact, after Giorgione's death in 1510, Titian assumed the task of adding the landscape background to Giorgione's unfinished "Sleeping Venus" (Gemäldegalerie, Dresden), a fact recorded by a contemporary writer, Marcantonio Michiel. Still Giorgionesque is the somewhat more lush setting of Titian's "Baptism of Christ" (*c.* 1515, Capitoline Museum, Rome), in which the donor, Giovanni Ram, appears at the lower right.

The authorship of individual portraits is the most difficult of all to establish, but the "Gentleman in Blue" (so-called "Ariosto") is certainly Titian's because it is signed with the initials T.V. (Tiziano Vecellio). The volume and the interest in texture in the quilted sleeve seem to identify Titian's own style. On the other hand, "The Concert" has been one of the most debated portraits, because since the 17th century it was thought to be most typical of Giorgione. The pronounced psychological content as well as the notable clarity of modelling in the central figure has led 20th-century critics to favour Titian. Technique and the clear intelligence of the young Venetian aristocrat in the "Young Man with Cap and Gloves" has led modern critics to attribute this and similar portraits to Titian.

The earliest compositions on mythological or allegorical themes show the young artist still under the spell of Giorgione in his creation of a poetic Arcadian world where nothing commonplace or sordid exists. The inspiration lies in the idyllic world of the love lyrics of the 16th-century Italian poets Jacopo Sannazzaro and Pietro Bembo. "The Three Ages of Man," where the erotic relationship of the young couple is discreetly muted and a mood of tenderness and sadness prevails, is one of the most exquisite of these. The contemporary "Sacred and Profane Love" is likewise set in a landscape of extraordinary beauty, but here the allegory is less easily understood. The most generally accepted interpretation holds that the two women are the twin Venuses, according to Neoplatonic theory and symbolism. The terrestrial Venus, on the left, stands for the generative forces of nature, both physical and intellectual, while the nude Venus, on the right, represents eternal and divine love. Essentially an ideally beautiful young woman rather than a cruel biblical antiheroine is the lovely "Salome."

MATURE LIFE AND WORKS

Marriage

Sometime in the early 1520s Titian brought to his house in Venice a young woman from Cadore whose name was Cecilia. Two sons were born in 1524 and 1525, first Pomponio, who became a priest, and second Orazio, later a painter and Titian's chief assistant. During Cecilia's grave illness in 1525, Titian married her. She recovered and later gave birth to two daughters, Lavinia (born 1529/30) and another who died in infancy. On Cecilia's death in 1530, the artist was disconsolate and he never remarried.

Mythological paintings. Titian's fame had spread abroad, and Alfonso I d'Este sought him as one of the chief masters in a cycle of mythological compositions for his newly rebuilt rooms called the Alabaster Chambers in the castle at Ferrara. Two of the canvases are now in the Prado at Madrid: the "Worship of Venus" and "The Andrians"; one of the most spectacular, the "Bacchus and Ariadne," is in the London National Gallery. The gaiety of mood, the spirit of pagan abandon, and the exquisite sense of humour in this interpretation of an idyllic world of antiquity make it one of the miracles of Renaissance art. Warmth and richness of colour help to balance the intentionally asymmetrical grouping of the figures, placed in richly verdant landscape that is also an integral part of the design. At this time Titian partially repainted the background of Giovanni Bellini's "Feast of the Gods" (National Gallery of Art, Washington, D.C.), so that the picture would better fit the series in the same room at Ferrara.

The standard for the reclining nude female obliquely placed in the picture space was established by Giorgione in the "Sleeping Venus." In Titian's "Venus of Urbino" the ideal rendering of the body and the position remain virtually unchanged, except that the goddess is awake and reclines upon a couch within the spacious room of a palace. For sheer beauty of form these two works were never surpassed. Despite the inherent eroticism of the subject, Titian managed it with restraint and good taste. Variations on the theme recur throughout his career.

The "Assumption"

Religious paintings. Among the religious paintings Titian produced between 1516 and 1538 is one of his most revolutionary masterpieces, the "Assumption" (1516–18). This large and at the same time monumental composition occupies the high altar of Sta. Maria dei Frari in Venice, a position that fully justifies the spectacular nature of the Virgin's triumph as she ascends heavenward, accompanied by a large semicircular array of angels, while the startled Apostles gesticulate in astonishment at the miracle. When the painting was unveiled it was quickly recognized as the work of a very great genius.

The posture of the Madonna in the "Assumption" and the composition of Titian's "Madonna and Child with SS. Francis and Alvise and Alvise Gozzi as Donor" reveal the influence of Titian's contemporary Raphael; and the pose of St. Sebastian in the "Resurrection Altarpiece," the influence of Michelangelo. These influences, however, are of secondary importance since the landscapes, the physical types, and the colour are totally Titian's own.

In the "Pesaro Madonna" (1519–26) Titian created a new type of composition, in which the Madonna and Saints with the male members of the Pesaro family are placed within a monumental columnar portico of a church. The picture is flooded with sunlight and shadows. This work established a formula that was widely followed by later Venetian Renaissance painters and served as an inspiration for some Baroque masters, including Rubens and Van Dyck.

Such a quantity of masterpieces by Titian followed that only a few can be mentioned. The poetic charm of the artist's pictures with landscape continues in the "Madonna and Child with St. Catherine and a Rabbit" and the "Madonna and Child with SS. John the Baptist and Catherine of Alexandria" (*c.* 1530). The "Entombment" is his first tragic masterpiece, where in a twilight setting the irrevocable finality of death and the despair of Christ's followers are memorably evoked. The stately "Presentation of the Virgin in the Temple," a very large canvas, reflects the splendour of Venetian Renaissance society in the great architectural setting, partly in the latest style of the contemporary architects Serlio and Jacopo Sansovino. The pageantry of the scene also belongs to well-established tradition in Venetian art, but the organization, with its emphasis on verticals and horizontals, constitutes Titian's interpretation of the High Renaissance style.

Titian and Charles V

Portraits. One of Titian's great triumphs came when he answered the call to Bologna in 1530 at the time of Charles V's coronation as Holy Roman emperor. In 1531, in keeping with his social state, he moved to a Venetian palace known as the Casa Grande, which survives as a 20th-century slum. Titian returned to Bologna to portray Charles V again on the occasion of the second meeting of Charles V and Pope Clement VII in the winter of 1532–33. The portrait of "Charles V in Armour" (1530) and another painted in January 1533 are lost, while only a less important work, "Charles V with Hound" (1532–33; Prado, Madrid), a copy of a portrait by Jakob Seisenegger, survives. Charles was so pleased with Titian's work that in May 1533 he bestowed upon the artist the most extraordinary honour of knighthood. Thereafter, the Austrian-Spanish Habsburgs remained Titian's most important patrons. Charles attempted to induce Titian to go to Spain in 1534 to prepare a portrait of the Empress, but the artist wisely refrained from undertaking the arduous journey.

Titian's other portraits in the 1520s and 1530s provide a gallery of the leading aristocrats of Italy. A splendid example is "Alfonso d'Avalos, Marques del Vasto" (1533), brilliantly rendered in gleaming armour ornamented with gold. He is accompanied by a small page whose head reaches his waist. The introduction of a secondary figure to give scale is a device frequently adopted by Titian. Another refulgent portrait in armour, but without the secondary figure, is that of "Francesco Maria della Rovere, Duke of Urbino" (1536–38). Emphasis here is given to the Duke's military career, not only by the armour but also by the baton in hand and the three others in the background. These works are essentially idealized state portraits, although the heads are very convincingly rendered. "Doge Andrea Gritti" is to a greater extent a symbol of the office—that is, that of ruler of Venice. The gigantic body in a canvas of large size is sweeping in design and commanding in presence. In later works, too, Titian very effectively managed the scaling of a figure to appear massive by filling the space of the canvas—in his portraits of Pietro Aretino, for example, where he gives his subject a leonine bulkiness. Allowing more space around the figure in "The Young Englishman," he projected a personality of cultivated elegance and human warmth.

LATE LIFE AND WORKS

Travels and commissions. *Portraits.* The large number of masterpieces in portraiture that Titian continued to create throughout the rest of his life is astounding. Pope Paul III and his grandson, Cardinal Alessandro Farnese, began to compete with Emperor Charles V for Titian's services. At the request of the Pope, the painter travelled to Bologna in May 1543 and there prepared the celebrated official portrait of "Pope Paul III Without Cap." Although a state symbol of the Pontiff, the characterization of the crafty statesman, bent with age, comes through.

Titian's next major association with the Farnese came in 1545–46, when he made his only visit to Rome, lodged in the Belvedere Palace of the Vatican. For the first time Titian was able to see the archaeological remains of ancient Rome and also the Renaissance masterpieces of Michelangelo, Raphael, Sebastiano del Piombo, and others. The effect upon the master's own style was relatively slight, understandably enough, since he was already a mature and famous artist.

"Paul III and His Grandsons"

Of portraits of the Farnese family carried out at this time, few remain. The most celebrated of all is "Paul III and His Grandsons Ottavio and Cardinal Alessandro Farnese" (1546; Museo e Gallerie Nazionali di Capodimonte, Naples). A painting of a family group, it is most searching in psychological revelation. The feeble Pope, then aged 78, appears to turn suddenly in his chair toward Ottavio Farnese, his 22-year-old grandson. Ottavio's overly obsequious bow and his shrewd Machiavellian profile demonstrate Titian's sheer genius in understanding and recording character. As a foil, the great churchman Cardinal Alessandro Farnese stands quietly by. It is no wonder that the portrait is not completely finished, for Paul III must have found it too revealing of the feud within the Farnese family.

If one were forced to name Titian's two greatest portraits, the choice might fall upon the Farnese group and upon another, "The Vendramin Family." Here the situation is quite different, for the two heads of the clan kneel in adoration of a reliquary of the Holy Cross, accompanied by seven sons ranging in age from about eight to 20. This portrait group is a tour de force in technical brilliance, richly beautiful in colour, running the emotional gamut from gravity to the innocence of childhood.

On his departure from Rome, in June 1546, Titian's association with the Farnese ended. He received no payment for his pictures, and his hopes for recompense in the form of a benefice for his son Pomponio were never realized. Titian decided to throw in his lot with the Habsburgs. Consenting to undertake the arduous journey to Augsburg, he set out in the depths of winter in January 1548 to cross the Alps to reach the Emperor's court. There he carried out one of his most memorable works, the equestrian "Emperor Charles V at Mühlberg," designed to commemorate the Emperor's victory over the Protestants the year before. It is the great state portrait par excellence, intended to show the Emperor as a Christian knight, as he wished posterity to remember him. Titian minimized the disfiguring lantern jaw and gave great dignity of bearing to his subject. In sheer mastery of the painter's art, the picture is unsurpassed. The handsome armour, with its gleaming highlights and reflected colour, the rose sash across the chest (a symbol of the Catholic party and the Holy Roman Empire), and the superb sunset landscape all contribute to make it one of the masterpieces of all time.

In December 1548 Charles instructed Titian to proceed to Milan to prepare likenesses of Prince Philip on his first trip outside of Spain. Once again, in the fall of 1550, Charles obliged Titian to travel to Augsburg to remain until May 1551, when he executed one of his greatest state portraits, the "Philip II" in full length. In this portrait of Philip, when still a prince aged 23, Titian achieved another tour de force in sheer beauty of painting, and he treated gently the surly face of the arrogant young man.

Religious paintings. Like some of Titian's earlier religious paintings, "Christ Before Pilate" is a work in which Titian managed a large crowd in a processional manner leading to the focal point, the figure of Christ at the left. Here the people are in a state of turmoil as they demand Christ's crucifixion. The composition, however, marks a new phase in Titian's development, far removed from the Renaissance serenity of the "Presentation," which is not explainable by the subject alone. The compact massing of figures, the oblique position of the steps and the wall at the left, and the general effect of excitement are indicative of the mid-16th-century style known as Mannerism. Titian assimilated and recreated, however, to produce a masterpiece far surpassing anything of which the Mannerist artists were capable.

"Christ Before Pilate"

Titian's religious compositions after his visit to Rome in 1545–46 reveal to some degree his contact with ancient art and the works of Michelangelo. In "Christ Crowned with Thorns" the burly muscular figures are thus explained, as perhaps is the violence of the whole interpretation.

Last years in Venice. On his return to Venice in 1551, Titian remained there for the rest of his life except for summer visits to his native city of Pieve di Cadore. In his last 25 years his productivity was undiminished in quantity and in creative ideas.

Portraits. Among his portraits is the full-length, dashingly rendered figure of the Duke of Atri, who is dressed in red velvet. One of the latest and most dramatic was "Jacopo Strada," in which this brilliant antiquarian, writer, and art collector is shown presenting to the spectator a small statue, a Roman copy of an Aphrodite of Praxiteles. Here again, the scope and variety of Titian's invention is astonishing in this new composition, so notable for lively action, psychological perception, and pictorial beauty. One must not forget Titian's "Self Portrait," in which he presents himself with great dignity, wearing the golden chain of knighthood. The intelligent, tired face is fully rendered, while the costume is sketched in lightly with a free brush. One of the most remarkable late works is the "Triple Portrait Mask" or "Allegory of Prudence," in which Titian, gray-bearded and wearing a rose-coloured cap, represents old age, his son Orazio, maturity, and presumably Marco Vecellio stands for youth.

"Self Portrait"

Religious paintings. The "Trinity" (or "La Gloria"), painted for Charles V's personal devotion, reflects central Italian art to a lesser degree than the earlier "Christ Crowned with Thorns." The glowing richness of colour predominates in this adoration of the Trinity in which Charles V and his family appear among the elect. The "Martyrdom of St. Lawrence" marks a further step in new compositional directions that culminate in Baroque form in the following century. St. Lawrence upon his gridiron is placed obliquely in space, and the steps reverse the direction to the right. Although dramatic power invests the main action in the foreground, the night scene with the tall flares and mysterious light suggests the supernatural. In his late religious pictures Titian veils the human forms in shadowy light and so increases the dominant mood of spirituality. One sees this effect in the late "Entombment," in which muted colour prevails, and in the awesome tragedy of the "Crucifixion." The "Christ Crowned with

Thorns," employing essentially the same composition as in the earlier version, is now seen through a veil of darkness, and the colour is broken into tiny spots and areas. All is miraculous in the "Annunciation," in which Gabriel rushes in and an assembly of angels in glory hovers about the Virgin. Titian's final word and last testament is the "Pietà," intended for his own burial chapel but left unfinished and completed by Palma il Giovane. The master and his son, Orazio, appear as tiny donors on the small plaque to the right. The monumentality of the composition is established by the great architectural niche flanked by Moses and the Hellespontic sibyl, while the figures are grouped in a long diagonal. The subdued colour befits the all-prevailing sorrow and the immutability of death in this, one of the artist's most profound achievements.

"Pietà"

Mythological paintings. The "Venus and Cupid with an Organist" and the "Venus and the Lute Player" are variations on the theme of the earlier "Venus of Urbino." Aside from the emphasis on the idealized beauty of the nude goddess, it is generally believed that symbolism is involved in these pictures, although the precise meanings have been variously interpreted. Beauty of sound (music) and beauty of vision are common to both. In the first example, a Renaissance garden with fountain and trees in perspective completes the background, which is separated from the figures by a dark red velvet curtain. More symbolism of an erotic nature is present in the embracing couple, a stag, and the satyr on the fountain. In the second picture, the background consists of a broad river valley and the distant Alpine peaks so dear to Titian's heart. This late landscape, painted in the artist's free illusionistic style, is extraordinarily beautiful.

The "Venus with a Mirror" (National Gallery of Art, Washington, D.C.), the one original among several versions, is a natural theme for the goddess of love and beauty. Yet Titian is the first artist to show her with a mirror held by Cupid. Her form is somewhat more heroic than hitherto, and her head to a limited degree is inspired by ancient sculpture. The superb quality of the flesh tones is enhanced by the cloak of dark red velvet, trimmed with fur.

A group of several important pictures of mythological themes was created by the master in 1554–62 for Charles's successor, Philip II of Spain, who never bothered to remunerate Titian for any of them. From the letters of the artist to the King, it is clear that he planned the paintings in pairs, but otherwise they do not constitute a comprehensive iconographic program. The first pair (still in Madrid) consists of the "Danae with Nursemaid" and the "Venus and Adonis." The magnificent nude Danae lies upon her couch, knees raised, as Jupiter descends to her in the form of golden rain, and her nursemaid rather amusingly attempts to catch the coins in her apron. This work (of which there exist numerous replicas and copies) is undoubtedly the most voluptuous in Titian's entire repertory. In colour and technique, as well, the "Danae" is one of Titian's greatest achievements; one is tempted to say that no other artist ever equalled him in imagination and in the depiction of sheer beauty of this work. In the "Venus and Adonis," the goddess, depicted from the back, attempts to restrain her muscular young lover as he is about to depart for the hunt, his dogs straining at the leash. The rose of his costume and the red velvet cushion beneath Venus are foils in the colour composition to the flesh tones and the sunlit landscape.

The "Perseus and Andromeda" was intended to be a companion to "Medea and Jason," according to Titian's letter, but for some reason the second picture was never carried out. Andromeda, bound to the rock at the left, awaits deliverance as Perseus descends from the sky to slay the monster. Her powerful physique reflects Titian's familiarity with the work of Michelangelo, yet Andromeda's body is more feminine and graceful than any of the Florentine's masculine-looking women. Titian's sensitivity to female beauty is unfailing.

"The Rape of Europa"

"The Rape of Europa" is surely one of the gayest of Titian's "poesies," as he called them. Taken by surprise, Europa is carried off, arms and legs flying, on the back of Jupiter in the form of a garlanded white bull. A putto (chubby, naked little boy) on the back of a dolphin appears to be mimicking her, and cupids in the sky follow the merry scene. Titian's fondness for oblique compositions is most successfully applied here, for it contributes to the sense of movement, and it allows for the extensive seascape and the mountainous shore. The sheer wizardry of Titian's technique is nowhere more fully demonstrated than in the misty distances shot through with blues and sunset rose and in the expanse of sea with its iridescent lights.

In "The Rape of Europa" Titian reached the climax of his powers, and by good fortune the picture has survived in almost perfect condition. On the contrary, two other great "poesies" done for Philip II are sadly abused by time and restorers, particularly the "Diana and Callisto," and less so the "Diana and Actaeon." The assembly of female nudes in a variety of poses, befitting the action, illustrates two episodes of the Diana legend as told by Ovid in his *Metamorphoses,* books II and III. "Diana and Actaeon" depicts Actaeon, the youthful hunter of heroic body, just as he unwittingly happens upon Diana and her nymphs as they are bathing (and before Diana punishes him by transforming him into a stag). Behind him is a great rose-coloured curtain. A landscape of extraordinary beauty and a vaulted passage form the setting within which the maidens are gathered. The organization of the rather complex design once more presages Baroque compositional methods. In the companion picture, the goddess discovers that Callisto, one of her maidens who had taken the vow of chastity, is pregnant. Though she was deceived by Jupiter's trickery, she is, nevertheless, banished and later, according to the legend, transformed into a bear. A standing and rather fulsome nude rips the drapery from the reclining Callisto. The golden canopy in the trees above Diana is the cloth of honour referring to her divinity. The glorious deep blue sky with golden clouds and the green branches of the tree supply the backdrop for the nude bodies. Diana, tall and imperious, is magnificent, despite the surface damage that has destroyed much of the paint. Subtleties abound in every movement and every gesture.

"Tarquin and Lucretia"

The latest of these compositions carried out for Philip II was the "Tarquin and Lucretia," a dramatic work of great vigour that proves that the aged master had lost none of his creative powers. Rather than Lucretia's suicide because of her rape by Tarquin, which is the more common subject, Titian chose to represent Tarquin's violent attack upon her. Again the rich colour is equally as important as the action. Against the green curtain and white sheets the rose velvet breeches of Tarquin and his green and gold doublet stand out in rich brilliancy.

The end came on August 27, 1576, when the great master died of old age, while a plague was raging in Venice. He was interred in the church of Sta. Maria dei Frari, where two of his most famous works may still be seen.

Through his long life Titian was highly successful in all branches of the painter's art. In his interpretation of Christian iconography he was infused in his youth with the poetic styles of the elderly Giovanni Bellini and his contemporary Giorgione. Titian created new compositions such as the "Assumption" and the "Pesaro Madonna" and later in his life the "Martyrdom of St. Lawrence," and he carried out a never-ending succession of new conceptions as his career matured. He gained international fame as a portraitist, beginning as a Giorgionesque painter and developing into a major creator of the state portrait for the glorification of rulers. The revival of the culture of the ancient world lies at the root of Renaissance culture in the arts and in literature; inspired by the ancient poets such as Ovid, Catullus, and Theocritus, Titian recreated pictorially the legends of Greece and Rome in a series of incomparable masterpieces.

MAJOR WORKS

RELIGIOUS PAINTINGS: Frescoes of three miracles of St. Anthony of Padua (1510–11; Scuola del Santo, Padua); "Gipsy Madonna" (*c.* 1510; Kunsthistorisches Museum, Vienna); "Salome" (*c.* 1515; Galleria Doria-Pamphili, Rome); "Assumption" (1516–18; Sta. Maria dei Frari, Venice); "Madonna and Child with SS. Francis and Alvise and Alvise Gozzi As Donor" (signed 1520; Pinacoteca, Ancona); "Resurrection Altarpiece" (signed 1522; SS. Nazaro e Celso, Brescia); "Pesaro Madonna" (1519–26; Sta. Maria dei Frari, Venice); "Entombment" (1526–32; Louvre, Paris); "Madonna and Child with St. Catherine and a Rabbit" (*c.* 1530; Louvre, Paris); "Madonna and Child with SS. John the Baptist and Catherine of Alexandria" (*c.* 1530; National Gallery, London); "The Presentation of the Virgin in the Temple" (1534–38; Accademia, Venice); "Christ Before Pilate" (signed 1543; Kunsthistorisches Museum, Vienna); three Old Testament subjects (1543–44; Sta. Maria della Salute, ceiling of the sacristy, Venice); "Christ Crowned with Thorns" (1546–50; Louvre, Paris); "Martyrdom of St. Lawrence" (1548–57; Gesuiti, Venice); "Trinity" ("La Gloria") (1554; Prado, Madrid); "Crucifixion" (1558; S. Domenico, Ancona); "Entombment" (1559; Prado, Madrid); "Magdalen" (*c.* 1560; Hermitage, Leningrad); "Annunciation" (1560–65; S. Salvatore, Venice); "Madonna and Child in Evening Landscape," (1562–65; Alte Pinakothek, Munich); "Christ Crowned with Thorns" (1570–76; Alte Pinakothek, Munich); "St. Jerome" (1575; Nuevos Museos, Escorial); "Pietà" (1576; Accademia, Venice).

MYTHOLOGICAL PAINTINGS: "Sacred and Profane Love" (1512–15; Borghese Gallery, Rome); "Flora" (*c.* 1515; Uffizi, Florence); "The Three Ages of Man" (*c.* 1515; National Gallery of Scotland, Edinburgh, lent by the Duke of Sutherland); "Bacchus and Ariadne" ("Ferrara Bacchanals," 1520–23, National Gallery, London); "Worship of Venus" (1518–19) and "The Andrians" (1523–24; both in Prado, Madrid); "Venus Anadyomene" (*c.* 1525; National Gallery of Scotland, Edinburgh, lent by the Duke of Sutherland; "Venus of Urbino" (1538; Uffizi, Florence); "Jupiter and Antiope," so-called "Venus of El Pardo" (*c.* 1540, perhaps finished *c.* 1560; Louvre, Paris); "Venus and Cupid with an Organist" (signed *c.* 1550; Prado, Madrid); "Venus with a Mirror" (1550–55; National Gallery of Art, Washington, D.C.); "Danae with Nursemaid" (1553–54; Prado, Madrid); "Venus and Adonis" (1553–54; Prado, Madrid); "Perseus and Andromeda" (1554–56; Wallace Collection, London); "Diana and Actaeon" and "Diana and Callisto" (1559; National Gallery of Scotland, Edinburgh, lent by the Duke of Sutherland); "The Rape of Europa" (*c.* 1559–62; Isabella Stewart Gardner Museum, Fenway Court, Boston); "Venus and the Lute Player" (*c.* 1560; Metropolitan Museum of Art, New York); "Nymph and Shepherd" (*c.* 1570; Kunsthistorisches Museum, Vienna); "Tarquin and Lucretia" (1571; Fitzwilliam Museum, Cambridge); "The Flaying of Marsyas" (*c.* 1570–76; Uměleckohistorické Muzeum, Kroměříž, Czech.).

PORTRAITS: "The Concert" (1510–12; Pitti Palace, Florence); "Gentleman in Blue," so-called "Ariosto" (signed *c.* 1512; National Gallery, London); "Young Man with Cap and Gloves" (1512–15; Earl of Halifax Collection, Garrowby Hall, London); "Man with a Glove" (1520–22; Louvre, Paris); "Federico II Gonzaga, Duke of Mantua" (*c.* 1523; Prado, Madrid); "Alfonso d'Avalos, Marques del Vasto" (1533; Marquis de Ganay Collection, Paris); "Francesco Maria della Rovere, Duke of Urbino" (1536–38; Uffizi, Florence); "Doge Andrea Gritti" (1535–38; National Gallery of Art, Washington, D.C.); "The Young Englishman," so-called (1540–45; Pitti Palace, Florence); "Pietro Aretino" (*c.* 1545; Pitti Palace, Florence); "Clarice Strozzi" (1542; Staatliche Museen Preussischer Kulturbesitz, Berlin); "Pope Paul III Without Cap" (1543; Museo e Gallerie Nazionali di Capodimonte, Naples); "The Vendramin Family" (1543–47; National Gallery, London); "Paul III and His Grandsons Ottavio and Cardinal Alessandro Farnese" (1546; Museo e Gallerie Nazionali di Capodimonte, Naples); "The Emperor Charles V at Mühlberg" (1548; Prado, Madrid); "Giovanni Battista Castaldo" (1548; Becker Collection, Dortmund); "Self Portrait" (*c.* 1550; Staatliche Museen Preussischer Kulturbesitz, Berlin); "Philip II" (1550–51; Prado, Madrid); "Giovanni Francesco Acquaviva, Duke of Atri" (1552; Staatliche Kunstsammlungen, Kassel); "Lavinia with Fan," so-called (1555–60; Gemäldegalerie, Dresden); "Jacopo Strada" (1567–68; Kunsthistorisches Museum, Vienna); "Triple Portrait Mask," "Allegory of Prudence" (*c.* 1570; National Gallery, London).

BIBLIOGRAPHY. SIR JOSEPH A. CROWE and GIOVANNI B. CAVALCASELLE, *Titian: His Life and Times* (1877, reprinted 1978), the first major monograph on the artist; ADOLFO VENTURI, *Storia dell' arte italiana,* vol. 9, pt. 3, pp. 93–386 (1928, reprinted 1968), with summary of documents; HANS TIETZE, *Tizian: Leben und Werk,* 2 vol. (1936; shorter editions in English in 1 vol., 1937 and 1950); BERNARD BERENSON, *Italian Pictures of the Renaissance, Venetian School,* vol. 1, pp. 183–192 (1957), a list of authentic works, and illustrations; RODOLFO PALLUCCHINI, *Tiziano,* 2 vol. (1969), fully illustrated; ERWIN PANOFSKY, *Problems in Titian, Mostly Iconographic* (1969); HAROLD E. WETHEY, *The Paintings of Titian,* vol. 1, *The Religious Paintings* (1969), vol. 2, *The Portraits* (1971), vol. 3, *Mythological and Historical Paintings* (1975), a complete corpus with catalogue raisonné. *Tiziano nelle Gallerie Fiorentine* (1978), a comprehensive survey of works attributed to Titian in the collections of the Pitti and Uffizi Galleries, Florence; DAVID ROSAND, *Titian* (1978), an introductory text; CHARLES HOPE, *Titian* (1980), a work that contradicts much established opinion.

(H.E.W.)

Tokyo–Yokohama Metropolitan Area

The Tokyo–Yokohama metropolitan area is an urban agglomeration on the Pacific coast of central Japan, including the capital city of Tokyo (Tōkyō), the port city of Yokohama, and the manufacturing centre of Kawasaki. Tokyo means eastern capital, the name given the city when the capital of Japan was moved eastward in 1868 from Kyōto, meaning capital. Yokohama derives from the fact that the original fishing village was situated on a lateral (*yoko*) beach (*hama*) of Tōkyō-wan (Tokyo Bay).

The centre of the Tokyo–Yokohama metropolitan area is Tokyo, part of the metropolitan prefecture (*to*) of Tokyo—comprising Tokyo, neighbouring industrial and residential cities, and rural districts, including the Bonin Islands (Ogasawara-guntō) in the Pacific. Tōkyō-to lies within the Tokyo–Yokohama metropolitan area, which also includes the prefectures of Saitama (Saitama-ken), Chiba (Chiba-ken), and Kanagawa (Kanagawa-ken). The cities of Yokohama and Kawasaki are in Kanagawa prefecture.

This article is divided into the following sections:

Physical and human geography

THE LANDSCAPE

Site. The Tokyo–Yokohama metropolitan area extends inland from the western coast of Tōkyō-wan. The city of Tokyo lies at the mouth of the Sumida-gawa (Sumida River). To its east, around the northern end of Tōkyō-wan, are suburbs comprising the prefecture of Chiba, which is separated from Tokyo by the Edo-gawa (Edo River). To the north of Tokyo city are the suburbs of Saitama Prefecture (Saitama-ken). South of Tokyo, separated from it by the Tama-gawa (Tama River), is the great industrial centre of Kawasaki. The port of Yokohama (Yokohama-kō) lies southwest of Kawasaki. Still farther south, on Miura-hantō (Miura Peninsula) and around Sagami-wan (Sagami Bay), are other municipalities that are part of the Tokyo–Yokohama metropolitan area. The metropolitan boundary in the southwest is roughly delimited by Kanagawa prefecture's border with Shizuoka and Yamanashi prefectures.

Terrain

The original terrain consisted mostly of river deltas, upland hills, and sand dunes. The present coastline is lined with warehouses, docks, and industrial sites. South of Yokohama is the rocky coast of Miura-hantō, with the naval harbour of Yokosuka (Yokosuka-kō). Farther south, on Sagami-wan, are the historic town of Kamakura and other resorts that are crowded with vacationers in summer.

Soil. The east side of the Sumida-gawa consists of alluvial soil that has settled as much as 13 feet in some places as the groundwater has been drawn off for industrial purposes. Efforts have been made to contain this process by regulation. Higher land in the metropolitan area consists of layers of volcanic origin on top of sand and gravel, sloping gently upward toward the mountains in the west.

To the south of Tokyo lies a hilly section, varying in height from 164 to 656 feet that has been developed as a residential area. Farther south and west, these plains and hills end in the steep Okutama and Chichibu mountains, consisting of old geologic formations cut by the Tama-gawa and its tributary valleys. The steeper slopes are wooded, and the foothills are terraced with cultivated fields; the river supplies water to Tokyo. The mountains form part of the Chichibu-Tama National Park.

Climate. The climate of Tokyo is generally mild, although the summers are hot and humid. The annual mean temperature is 58.5° F (14.7° C). The January mean is 40.5° F (4.7° C), and the August mean is 79.5° F (26.4° C). Japan's climate is controlled by the summer and winter monsoons: in summer, masses of warm, humid air from the Pacific; in winter, a flow of cold, dry air from Siberia. There are two rainy seasons: June–July and September–October. Tokyo usually has two or three typhoons a year during the autumn rainy season. The average annual rainfall is about 57 inches (1,460 millimetres).

In midwinter, temperatures may fall below freezing in the mornings. From January to March there are several snowfalls. The plum and camelia bloom in January on the southern coast of the metropolitan area, and Tokyo's spring reaches its climax in March and April with cherry blossoms and many varieties of flowers. The iris and azalea blossom in May, followed by the gloomy monsoon month of June. In the summer months the blue and purple hydrangea appear. After the autumnal rains, the trees begin to turn—the maples red, the ginkgo yellow. This is the season when chrysanthemum shows are held.

Animal life. Wild animals are rare except in the mountains, where wild boars, foxes, and monkeys are found. Trout live in the mountain streams; in the lowlands the streams are polluted, but this situation is improving because of strict enforcement of antipollution laws. Birds are relatively abundant in the residential areas, particularly doves, sparrows, crows, and gulls. The Imperial Palace moats are visited by several kinds of waterfowl from northern regions. Other seasonal visitors include the Japanese bush warbler, great tit, dusky thrush, bull-headed shrike, grey starling, and swallows; in the suburbs one can see the white egret and hear the song of the skylark.

Industrialization, motorization, and population growth have brought water and air pollution. Fuji-san (Mt. Fuji), about 55 miles (90 kilometres) away, once visible on clear days in winter from the centre of Tokyo, now can be seen only when the factories are shut down for the January holidays or when wind blows away the smog. The prefectural and municipal governments have established environmental protection offices in an effort to combat pollution.

Plan of the old city

Layout. The inner part of Tokyo was the old town of Edo. The town was once dominated by the castle of Edo, which was burned during the Meiji period; the emperor now lives in the Imperial Palace, within the grounds of the former castle. The castle and the adjacent area where the high feudal lords had their dwellings was encircled by two moats, the *uchibori* ("inner moat") and *sotobori* ("outer moat"). Unlike European medieval cities, Japanese castle towns had no walls. The warriors and lords lived between and outside the moats, forming the *yashiki machi* ("resi-

The Tokyo–Yokohama metropolitan area.

dential town"). Along the roads and in the town area were merchants' shops and the houses of nonwarriors, comprising the *machiya* ("town house") section. Shintō shrines and Buddhist temples formed *tera machi* ("temple town") on the urban fringes.

The castle and the residences of the feudal lords had beautiful gardens, some of which have been preserved and are now open to the public. The town area was divided into rectangular blocks named after various occupational groups, such as *gofuku-chō* ("silk-goods town"), *sakana-machi* ("fish town"), and *kaji-chō* ("blacksmith town"). The residential areas of the lower samurai class also had their functional names: *okachi-machi* ("infantry town") and *takasho-machi* ("hunters with hawk"). There were also landscape names: *ta-machi* ("paddy town"), *hayashi-chō* ("wood town"), *komagome* ("horse grazing"), and *fujimi-chō* ("town from which Fuji-san can be seen").

The centre of trade was Nihombashi (Japan Bridge), from which five main highways began and which is still the zero-mile mark of the national-highway system. Nihombashi and its vicinity was a busy wholesale marketplace and also a retail and financial area. The banks of the rivers and canals were crowded with boats coming from Ōsaka and other coastal regions of Japan. On the highways there were post towns every few miles. The first post towns from Edo were Shinagawa, Shinjuku, Itabashi, and Senju, all now part of Tokyo city.

The marshy downtown area had to be drained with

The Imperial Palace with the Nijū-bashi (Double Bridge), used only on formal state occasions and on national holidays, in the foreground.
Shinichiro Morimoto—Orion Press

canals, and the Tone and Ara rivers had to be prevented from flooding. As Edo grew, water for human consumption was brought in by aqueduct and distributed through wooden pipes; this system became the basis of modern Tokyo's water supply.

The early houses were made of wood, and Edo was so repeatedly in flames that fires were called the flowers of Edo. A great fire in 1657 damaged large parts of Edo, destroyed the main tower of the castle, and killed 100,000 inhabitants. After the earthquake and fire of 1923, the downtown area was largely rebuilt, and it was rebuilt again after World War II.

The main shopping street is Ginza Street, running northeast to southwest and lighted brightly at night. A stroll on the Ginza is popularly known as Ginbura. The northern extension of Ginza is Nihombashi Street, a busy central shopping area that includes the best department stores. It passes through Tokyo's financial district. From Ginza a street leads westward to Hibiya Park and the Imperial Palace. Nearby are the government-office district and the Yūrakuchō amusement centre.

The Marunouchi district

To the east of the Imperial Palace, separated from it by broad gardens and a moat, lies the Marunouchi business district, the heart of Japanese business activity, with offices and banks, the Chamber of Commerce, the central railroad station, the Central Post Office, and the International Telephone and Telegraph Corporation building.

Tokyo's Metropolitan Government Offices are situated at the southern end of the Marunouchi district. To the north, across the outer moat, is the Kanda area, with many universities, bookstores, publishers, and hospitals. Other important areas are Taitō-ku, in the north, and Shiba, in the south—commercial and residential areas of high population density. To the east of the Sumida-gawa is Kōtō-ku, a low-lying marshy area drained by canals that create a checkerboard effect, which is an industrial and working-class district.

In the western part of Tokyo, roughly within the loop of the Yamanote Line, is the uplands residential area. This quiet, tree-shaded section contains most of the foreign embassies as well as Tokyo University, Waseda University, Keiō University, and other universities and research institutes. Farther west and southwest of the Yamanote loop are middle-class residential neighbourhoods, the growth of which began after the earthquake of 1923 when city dwellers moved outward into the upland fields. In these areas the houses are generally frame, with some multistoried apartment houses. With the improvement of commuting facilities, Tokyo's eastern and northeastern suburbs have also grown as middle-class residential areas.

Yokohama

The growth pattern of Yokohama and Kawasaki has been similar to that of Tokyo. The whole area within 20 to 30 miles of Tokyo's central railway station has become a commuting area. Older towns have become suburbs of Tokyo. Yokohama's business district is concentrated around its port. At the northern end of the business district, near Sakuragicho Station, is the central shopping street of Isezaki. South of the business district is the hilly Yamate residential area, separated by Motomachi Street where there are many interesting shops. The northern coast of Yokohama is an industrial area. Just south of the port, industrial and port facilities have been established along the coast at Honmoku and Negishi.

Tokyo and Yokohama are divided into wards (*ku*), composed of towns (*machi*) having several tens of thousands of inhabitants each; some *machi* are further divided into smaller blocks known as *chōme.* Originally these blocks were neighbourhood units, but they now function only as postal addresses and for purposes of registration. The older *machi* each have a tutelary deity (*ujigami*) with a shrine. Residents of a *machi* visit the shrine on festival days to pray for safety and prosperity. These festivals are full of colour: stalls are set up, and there is music and dancing. Among the more famous shrines are the Asakusa, Hie (Sannō), Kanda Myōjin, Nezu, and Fukagawa, dating from the Edo period. The Meiji Shrine in Tokyo, dedicated to the Meiji emperor and his consort, is a kind of national monument and centre of worship for the whole country.

Building styles. The dwellings in metropolitan Tokyo vary from the tiny wooden house of two or three stories sandwiched between high office buildings to the large suburban homes of affluent citizens. Some people live over their shops or behind them. As part of social and economic reforms instituted after World War II, the large estates in the Yamanote loop, once the site of feudal residences in the Edo period, were subdivided into small lots or adapted to such other uses as schools or public gardens. This residential area, however, is becoming increasingly commercial, with offices, hotels, and apartment buildings for the upper class. The uplands have been invaded by office buildings and apartment houses. Throughout the metropolitan area there are many housing developments, ranging in size from several hundred homes to more than 10,000. Construction is carried on by the Japan Housing Corporation, municipalities, prefectures, and private companies.

About 30 percent of the dwellings in Tokyo Urban Prefecture are wooden apartment units, although the number of fireproof ferroconcrete buildings is increasing. Building

Yokohama harbour.
Takanori Ishii—Bon

styles are a mixture of Eastern and Western. While few purely Japanese buildings remain, even a modern apartment will have one or two rooms with a tatami (reed-mat) floor and sliding doors. Kawagoe, an old castle town about 23 miles from Tokyo, has traditional merchant houses with heavy tile roofs and plaster walls.

The central business districts of Tokyo, Yokohama, and other cities consist mainly of ferroconcrete buildings. Their maximum height was formerly limited to about 100 feet to prevent earthquake damage, but since the late 1960s numerous taller buildings that can withstand earthquakes have been constructed. Outside of the central business district, buildings tend to be small in area because of the high price of land.

Central Tokyo. In the governmental district of Kasumigaseki, southwest of the Imperial Palace, one can study building styles by eras. The Sakuradamon (Sakurada Gate), formerly one of the entrances to the castle of the shoguns, leads across the moat to the Imperial Palace Plaza. The entrance passage is crooked for reasons of defense. To the south is the tall Police Department building and the older Ministry of Justice building of reddish brick, put up in the 19th century. Nearby is the Ministry of Foreign Affairs, a postwar modern building. The Prime Minister's Mansion, of an older (1930s) style, is at the core of the governmental district. The National Diet Building beyond is made of granite from the islands of the Inland Sea (Seto-naikai). Overlooking these governmental buildings is the Kasumigaseki Building, rising 482 feet (147 metres).

Government buildings

The Marunouchi district to the east of the Imperial Palace was developed as a business centre on vacant land formerly owned by the government. Marunouchi means inside castle; in this district is the outer-moat zone of the Edo castle, where the feudal lords had their mansions. A commercial centre, consisting of red-brick buildings of three or four stories, was built there around the turn of the 20th century. These gave way in the 1920s and 1930s and after World War II to ferroconcrete buildings that are resistant to fire and earthquake. The Dai-Ichi Life Insurance Building is in Renaissance style. The postwar buildings are of lighter and taller construction, an example being the Tokyo Metropolitan Government Office. The former Imperial Hotel, designed by Frank Lloyd Wright in 1916, withstood the earthquake of 1923; it was torn down in 1967 and replaced by a plainer, taller structure in 1970.

The uptown area to the south has changed much less; many older buildings are still preserved. The old lecture hall of Keiō University, of wooden construction with black-and-white-checkerboard walls, belongs to the early Meiji period. To the west, the Akasaka Detached Palace, completed in 1909, is now used for national guests.

To the north, near the Kanda-gawa (Kanda River), one finds a contrast of building styles and civilizations in the Yushima Seidō (a Confucian shrine rebuilt in 1935), the Kanda Myojin Shrine (a Shintō shrine rebuilt in 1934), and the Nikolai-dō (Eastern Orthodox Cathedral, dating from 1884).

Contemporary features. Modern buildings include the Palace-side Building adjacent to the northern moat, occupied by the Mainichi Press; the Tokyo Cathedral, with a sky-piercing tower; the National Theatre, the World Trade Centre Building, and the International Trade Centre on Harumi Pier. One of the highest structures in the world is a 1,092-foot television tower, erected in 1958 and modelled on the Eiffel Tower in Paris; it dominates the Tokyo skyline. The Shinjuku Railway Station on the western Yamanote line has been developed as a civic centre. The complex includes the station, two department stores, and other buildings with offices and shops. Nearby is another commercial district containing the Keiō Plaza Hotel. Similar complexes have been developed elsewhere in the metropolitan area—for example, at the Shimbashi Station in the central business district and at Yokohama Station. Department stores have decentralized by locating at railway stations throughout Tokyo—Shinjuku, Shibuya, Ikebukuro, Ueno, and Asakusa—where they compete with the stores of the central business district of Ginza–Nihombashi.

The Shinjuku development

THE PEOPLE

The population of the metropolitan area is growing, partly through migration from other parts of Japan and partly from natural increase. The western part of Tokyo and the uplands are chiefly middle-class and upper-class residential areas. Blue-collar workers live east of the Sumida-gawa and in the industrial areas of Kawasaki and Yokohama. Tokyo is a melting pot for all Japan, and in the downtown area one can hear the Kansai (Ōsaka-Kyōto) accent and the Tōhoku (northeastern region) dialect. Most of the many foreigners in the metropolis do not live in national enclaves. Exceptions are the Chinese in Yokohama and Koreans in several areas.

THE ECONOMY

The Tokyo metropolitan area is the largest commercial centre of Japan, and its port of Yokohama is the country's largest. Most important businesses and banks have their head offices in the central business district, as do foreign

The Kasumigaseki Building, overlooking the Shinkansen express train, which runs through downtown Tokyo.
Toichi Sakakibara

companies and banks. Before World War II, Tokyo was Japan's second industrial city after Ōsaka, but since the war Ōsaka has declined in comparison to Tokyo.

Industry. The Tokyo–Kawasaki–Yokohama manufacturing region, called the Keihin Industrial Zone (Keihin Kōgyō Chitai), is one of the four major industrial agglomerations in Japan. In the late 19th century, manufacturing developed within the cities of Tokyo, Kawasaki, and Yokohama. It later expanded into the suburbs: along the Tōkaidō Line (railway) to the southwest; westward to Sagamiōno, and along the Chūō Line to Tachikawa, Hino, and Hachiōji; along the Ara-kawa to the northwest; along the Keihin-Tōhoku Line to the north; along the Jōban Line to the northeast; and on the Sōbu Line around the northeastern coast of Tōkyō-wan into Chiba Prefecture.

Tokyo itself has much light manufacturing, including textiles, toiletries, and printing and publishing. It is a centre of cultural activity and information. It also produces goods requiring an abundant labour force, such as electrical products, cameras, and automobiles. A large proportion of the establishments are family-size or are relatively small shops with fewer than 30 workers, most of them subcontracting to larger concerns. The Yokohama–Kawasaki district is an area of heavy industry specializing in chemicals, machinery, metallurgy, petroleum refining, ships, motor cars, and fabricated metal products. A centre for iron and steel, petroleum refining, petrochemicals, electric power, and other heavy industries is also located on the Chiba–Ichihara coast at the northeast end of Tōkyō-wan. Another heavy-industrial centre is at Kashima about 60 miles northeast of Tokyo on the Pacific coast. The machinery and light industries have been decentralizing inland from Tokyo in the area 30 to 60 miles from the city, where a number of industrial parks have been established.

Commerce. Tokyo is a centre of wholesaling, drawing goods from all over the country and abroad and distributing them into the surrounding area. It is also Japan's financial centre. The banks, insurance companies, stockbrokers, and similar establishments are concentrated in the central business district.

Transportation. Tokyo is the national traffic centre; it is also an important international nodal point of the western Pacific and the Far East. The metropolitan area is spanned with a dense network of electric railways and subways, bus lines, and motor highways. Tokyo Station is not only the central railroad station of the metropolis but also central for all Japan. Trains to Ōsaka and beyond start from Tokyo Station. Another important Tokyo terminal is Ueno Station, from which lines run to various parts of northern Japan. Shinjuku Station is the terminus of trains from central Honshu and some trains from the east. Interurban service in the Tokyo area is by the Japan National Railways and various privately owned electric lines. Tokyo and Yokohama formerly had trams, almost all of which have been replaced by buses and subway lines.

Tokyo's system of automobile expressways consists of a loop around the central business district and several radial lines connecting with the national expressways.

The airport at Narita, more than 40 miles east of the city, handles most international traffic; the Haneda airport, about eight miles southwest of Tokyo, serves mainly domestic air passengers and cargo. Atsugi Air Field, west of Yokohama, is reserved for use by the U.S. Navy.

Tōkyō-wan has four major ports. Yokohama is the largest, followed by the industrial ports of Kawasaki and Chiba and the port of Tokyo. Ferryboats carrying cars have several lines across Tōkyō-wan.

ADMINISTRATIVE AND SOCIAL CONDITIONS

Government. Tokyo is not only the national capital but also the centre of the Kantō region, which comprises the prefectures of Ibaraki, Tochigi, Gumma, Saitama, Chiba, and Kanagawa. It houses all the institutions of the national and regional governments, as well as the offices of the local government and of government corporations, such as the telephone and telegraph corporation. Most of these are located near the Imperial Palace. Foreign embassies and international institutions have their offices in the central business district and in the western part of the city. The metropolis of Tokyo is administered by a governor and a metropolitan assembly of 126 members; all are elected to office.

Because Tokyo is the place of political decision, nearly all of Japan's prefectures have offices there. Major cities and towns have their Tokyo offices. Federations of local government, such as the Mayors' Association, are located in Tokyo, as are the headquarters of political parties and many other semigovernmental institutions.

Efforts to break up and decentralize this massive agglomeration of power have never succeeded. The migration of governmental offices out of Tokyo will apparently be limited to research sections.

Public utilities. The water used in Tokyo, Yokohama, Kawasaki, and other parts of the metropolitan area is supplied by aqueduct systems. Local waterworks and private industrial and residential systems supplement the supply. Tokyo draws its water principally from the Tama and Tone-Edo rivers and from three reservoirs—at Murayama (Lake Tama), at Yamaguchi (Lake Sayama), and at Ogōchi on the upper Tama (Lake Okutama). To meet increasing demand, additional dams have been built on the upper Ara and Tone rivers, which are connected by a canal with the Murayama–Yamaguchi reservoirs. Yokohama, Kawasaki, Yokosuka, and neighbouring towns get their water from the Sagami-gawa, which is dammed at two points. Most of the metropolitan area is supplied with gas by the Tokyo Gas Company. Gas plants are located mainly on the coast, where domestic and imported coal, petroleum, liquid gas, and natural gas are brought in by ship. Petroleum and bottled propane gas are also widely used for heating and cooking.

The Ginza district, a principal shopping area located in central Tokyo.
Harald Sund

The city's electric supply

The Tokyo Electric Company serves the entire Kantō region, as well as Yamanashi Prefecture and the eastern half of Shizuoka Prefecture. About 15 percent of the power comes from hydroelectric stations on the Tone and Kinu rivers in Kantō; the rivers Shinano and Azusa in central Honshu; and Inawashiro-ko (Lake Inawashiro) in the Tohoku region of northern Honshu. The bulk of Tokyo's power comes from thermal stations located on Tōkyō-wan and at Kashima to the northeast. Electricity is also generated by atomic power stations, including one at Tokai, 65 miles northeast, and another on the Fukushima coast, 120 miles northeast, of Tokyo.

Health and security. The Tokyo–Yokohama metropolitan area shares the problems of other large urban areas with respect to pollution, noise, and lack of air and sunlight. Its residents nevertheless live better than people in small cities and towns because they have superior medical care and social services.

The medical school of Tokyo University, founded in the latter part of the 19th century, is known for its Institute of Medical Science. The medical school of Keiō University is another research hospital. A number of university hospitals in Tokyo are open to the public, but most hospitals are run by the national, prefectural, and municipal governments or public organizations such as the Red Cross. In addition, there are special hospitals for children, the aged, and patients suffering from cancer, tuberculosis, or heart disease.

Colleges and universities

Education. In Tokyo, as in other large cities, more than 90 percent of the ninth-year graduates go on to high school. Almost half of Japan's university and college students are to be found in Tokyo Metropolitan Prefecture and Kanagawa Prefecture. Tokyo University has several faculties and many research institutes. Other leading universities are Tokyo Institute of Technology, Hitotsubashi University (trade and commerce), and Tokyo University of Arts. There are also national universities for industry and agriculture, languages, medicine, dentistry, the merchant marine, and other fields. Tokyo Metropolitan University and Yokohama City University are public municipal institutions. Among private universities, Waseda and Keiō are the oldest and most highly regarded, especially in the fields of literature, politics, and business. The largest university is Nihon.

CULTURAL LIFE

Tokyo is at the centre of national cultural activity. It is also the home of various institutions for national and international cultural communication. Modern Japan has been strongly influenced by the West, to which Tokyo and Yokohama have been gateways; Western technology and life-styles first took root in those cities.

Museums

If Tokyo has been less a centre of Japanese traditions than have Kyōto, Ōsaka, and Nara, it has, nevertheless, many valuable cultural properties from the past. The Imperial Household Agency Library and the Tōyō Bunka Kenkyūjo (Institute of Oriental Culture; part of Tokyo University) hold collections of classical books. There are the National Archives and the National Diet Library. The Tokyo National Museum in Ueno Park concentrates on the art and history of Japan and Asia. The Kokuritsu Kagaku Hakubutsukan (National Science Museum), the Zoological Garden, and the National Museum of Western Art are also located in Ueno Park, as is the Tokyo Metropolitan Art Museum. Elsewhere in Tokyo there are numerous smaller collections and galleries. Near the Imperial Palace are the National Museum of Modern Art and the Technical and Engineering Museum. Tokyo and Yokohama also have their own local historical records and exhibits, such as a museum of folkways, in the city of Musashino, and a museum of old houses, in Kawasaki.

A wide range of theatre is available, from the traditional Kabuki to modern drama. Symphonic works, operas, and various other kinds of Western music and dance are performed.

Parks

Tokyo's parks are not as large as those of European and American cities, but they are numerous. Among the better known are the East Garden of the Imperial Palace, Hibiya Park, Ueno Park (with its zoo), and the Meiji Shrine's Outer Garden (with its baseball stadium and other playing fields). The latter, along with Komazawa Olympic Park and Yoyogi Sports Centre, was one of the main centres of the Olympic Games in 1964. In the western part of Tokyo are the smaller natural parks of Inokashira, Zenpukuji, and Shakujii, with lakes. Some of the larger private gardens of the Edo period are now open to visitors. The most impressive of these is the Inner Garden of the Meiji Shrine with its irises and water lilies, a favourite spot of the Meiji emperor. There are also several botanical gardens.

In Yokohama, the best parks are Nogeyama and Yamate,

Komazawa Olympic Park, Tokyo.
Shinichiro Morimoto—Orion Press

on hills overlooking the harbour, and Yamashita Park on the coast. Sankei-en (Sankei Garden), formerly a private estate, contains a collection of historic buildings brought from other parts of the country.

Suburban recreation areas include the Tama Zoological Park, where visitors can ride by bus through the lion section, and near it the *kodomo no kuni* ("children's country"). Places of excursion from Tokyo and Yokohama include the Okutama and Sagami valleys, the Chichibu and Tanzawa mountains, the Fuji-Hakone-Izu and the Nikko national parks, the Izu-hantō (Izu Peninsula) with its many hot springs, the active volcanic islands of Ō-shima and Miyake-jima, the Miura-hantō, and many others. There are also amusement parks with roller coasters and similar rides, such as Kōrakuen, Tamagawaen, Toshimaen, and Yomiuriland. Japan's first Disneyland (amusement park), which opened in 1983, is also located in Tokyo.

The most popular team sport in Japan is baseball. Tokyo has four professional teams; Kawasaki and Yokohama each have one team. There are also university teams, and the Waseda–Keiō games are followed intently. A number of golf courses are located in the suburbs.

History

The eastern part of the present central city of Tokyo was originally called Edo ("estuary"), because it stood at the point where the Sumida-gawa enters Tokyō-wan. A castle was built overlooking the marshy lowland of the river in 1457. The river separated the ancient provinces of Musashi in the west and Shimofusa in the east, and the castle occupied an important strategic position.

The area had been inhabited in prehistoric times by peoples of the Jōmon (2500–250 BC) and the Yayoi (250 BC–AD 250) cultures. The Yayoi lived on uplands and cultivated rice on marshy deltas and in valley bottoms. With the consolidation of a Japanese empire in the 6th century, the area became part of Musashi Province. Musashi and its surrounding regions were peripheral because the central government was located farther west. They rose in importance when Tokugawa Ieyasu established the shogunate (military government) in Edo in 1603. During the 17th century the old castle was rebuilt and enlarged, and the town was laid out, becoming the residence of the whole Tokugawa hierarchy. By the mid-19th century Edo had become a metropolis with a population of 1,200,000. After the fall of the Tokugawa shoguns and the reestablishment of the authority of the emperor, the capital of Japan was moved from Kyōto to Edo in 1868; the city was then renamed Tokyo.

Growth of Tokyo area

The municipal area of Tokyo city at the end of the 19th century consisted of 15 wards (*ku*). Together with the surrounding counties, it formed Tokyo Urban Prefecture. It had become not only the political but the commercial and financial centre of the country. Its growth was checked by the great earthquake and fire of September 1, 1923, which severely damaged the downtown areas of Tokyo and Yokohama. During Tokyo's reconstruction the streets were widened, and many ferroconcrete buildings were put up. At the same time, the suburbs began to grow. At the beginning of the 1930s Tokyo city had 2,000,000 people and the suburban municipalities 3,000,000. In 1932, 20 new wards were added. During World War II, metropolitan Tokyo was established by amalgamating the city and its surrounding suburbs and counties. Large parts of Tokyo and Yokohama were destroyed by U.S. air raids in 1944 and 1945. After the war, starting in the 1950s, the Tokyo area grew enormously with the expansion of the Japanese economy.

The port of Kanagawa (later incorporated into Yokohama), which was opened in 1859, expanded along with Japan's export trade. The city was completely new and Western in its characteristics. In 1872 it was connected to Tokyo by railroad. Along with Tokyo it was largely destroyed in the great earthquake and fire of 1923 and severely damaged by U.S. air raids in 1945. By the late 20th century Yokohama was the second largest city in Japan, after Tokyo.

Kawasaki, situated between Tokyo and Yokohama, was formerly a post town on the Tōkaidō (the ancient highway between Tokyo and Kyōto). The Tokyo–Yokohama railway had a station there, and it became a centre of industrial development. The city expanded rapidly during the 1930s, was almost completely destroyed in World War II, and was subsequently rebuilt. The coastal area is the centre of heavy industry, including iron and steel, petroleum refining, chemicals, and thermoelectric power. Electrical machinery, food, and other light industries are in the centre of the city. Kawasaki is now a leading industrial city of Japan; its inland area has become a residential suburb of Tokyo.

BIBLIOGRAPHY. A dated but comprehensive source, in English, is the INTERNATIONAL GEOGRAPHICAL UNION, REGIONAL CONFERENCE, *Geography of Tokyo and Its Planning* (1957). The ASSOCIATION OF JAPANESE GEOGRAPHERS, *Japanese Cities* (1970), contains many useful studies of Tokyo. A German-language discussion is S. KIUCHI, "Tokio als Weltstadt," in J.H. SCHULTZE (ed.), *Zum Problem der Weltstadt* (1959). The TOKYO METROPOLITAN GOVERNMENT has published an atlas, *Regional and City Planning for Tokyo* (1964). H. AONO and S. BIRUKAWA, *Tōkyō-to* (1967), is an academically written study of the Tokyo region (in Japanese). EDWARD G. SEIDENSTICKER, *Low City, High City: Tokyo from Edo to the Earthquake, 1867–1923* (1983), is an analytical study of the city at a critical period in its modern development. S. KIUCHI, *Tokyo* (1968) and *Kanagawa, Saitama, Chiba* (1969), contain colour photographs and maps. K. KODAMA and H. SUGIYAMA, *Tōkyō-to no rekishi* (1969), is a history (in Japanese). Statistical data may be found in the *Statistical Yearbook of Japan*, by the national government, the *Yearbook of the City of Tokyo*, published by the TOKYO METROPOLITAN GOVERNMENT and *Japan Municipal Yearbook*, by the MAYOR'S ASSOCIATION.

(S.K.)

Tolstoy

The enduring fame of Leo Tolstoy, Russian author, reformer, and moral thinker, rests mainly on two novels, *War and Peace* and *Anna Karenina.* A deeply contradictory man, Tolstoy was an individualistic aristocrat who in his later years tried unsuccessfully to lead the life of a poor peasant, a sensualist who ended up as an intransigent puritan, a man of singular vitality who feared death at almost every step. This extraordinary duality of character led him in middle life to abandon his career of a mere writer of fiction to become a radical Christian; in a stream of essays, pamphlets, and largely didactic short stories and plays, he propagated his belief in a life of love and faith and his rejection of property and such man-made institutions as governments and churches.

Early years and marriage. Lev Nikolayevich, Graf (Count) Tolstoy (also spelled Tolstoi), was born on September 9 (August 28, old style), 1828, on his family's estate at Yasnaya Polyana, about 100 miles (160 kilometres) south of Moscow, in Tula Province. Tolstoy's parents died when he was a child, and he was raised by relatives. Private tutors had charge of his early education. At 16 he entered the Kazan University (now Kazan [V.I. Lenin] State University), but, disappointed with the formal instruction there, he returned to Yasnaya Polyana in 1847 to manage his estate and conduct his own education. In neither did he achieve much success, preferring the social whirl of Moscow and St. Petersburg to life in the country. In his diary, he recorded his moral transgressions. In his youthful entries there is already evidence of an unusual analytical talent in his realistic probing into the suppressed motives of his own behaviour.

Disgusted with this shiftless existence, Tolstoy in 1851 joined his soldier brother Nikolay in the Caucasus. In the following year he also entered the army and acted with bravery in several engagements against the hill tribes. Much of his leisure he spent in writing, completing his first published work, *Detstvo* (*Childhood*), which appeared in the magazine *Sovremennik* ("The Contemporary"). The material of *Childhood* is treated with conventional realism, except for digressive lyrical passages in the manner of the English novelist Laurence Sterne, whose *Sentimental Journey* Tolstoy partially translated at this time. He is autobiographical in this and in later works, but what captivates readers of *Childhood* is its fresh and precise choice of significant detail and the amazing reliving of forgotten common experiences of childhood that, once recalled, exert a nostalgic charm. Sequels to *Childhood*—*Otrochestvo* (*Boyhood*) and *Yunost* (*Youth*)—lack this special charm, perhaps because an analysis of the moral failings of youngsters tends to dominate these two works. Tolstoy's experiences in the Caucasus are reflected in "Nabeg" ("The Raid") and "Rubka lesa" ("The Woodfelling"), his first short stories dealing with war. The theme is treated in a youthful spirit, but the exacting realistic analysis of military activity is tinged with that critical awareness of false heroics that became a central feature of his *Sevastopolskiye rasskazy* (1855–56; *Sevastopol*).

Sketches of military life

Transferred to the Danube front in 1854, Tolstoy participated in the siege of Sevastopol during the Crimean War. He described these experiences in his *Sevastopol* sketches, in which he contrasted the simple heroism of the common soldier with the false heroics of military leaders. At the end of the fighting in 1856, he left the army and went to St. Petersburg, where he became the idol of competing literary groups that sought his support of their social and aesthetic views. A pronounced individualist, he rebuffed the coteries and left for Yasnaya Polyana.

Early short stories

He went abroad in 1857, to France, Switzerland, and Germany. The criticism of stories based on his travels (*e.g.,* "Lyutsern" ["Lucern"]) caused him to lose interest in literature. Yet he continued to write. Between 1855 and 1863 he wrote a series of short stories—including "Zapiski markera" ("The Memoirs of a Billiard-Marker"), "Dva gusara" ("Two Hussars"), "Albert," "Tri smerti" ("Three Deaths"), "Semeynoye schastye" ("Family Happiness"), "Polikushka," and "Kholstomer" (not published until 1886)—in which he concentrated mainly on moral problems. These stories anticipate his later concern with the harm a materialistic society inflicts on the natural, unspoiled man but represented no artistic advance on his earlier writing. In fact, the subjective moralistic emphasis is a defect, although many passages are persuasively argued. Only in the "Two Hussars" did Tolstoy avoid this pervasive subjectivism. There, the evil influences of society on one of the characters are artistically suggested rather than didactically argued. "Kholstomer," a satire on human beings from the point of view of a horse, is also

The Bettmann Archive

Tolstoy.

something of an exception, for by his art Tolstoy somehow convinces the reader that the noble horse's natural life is superior to man's absurd, unnatural existence. The contrast between the natural man and the spoiled product of sophisticated society deeply interested Tolstoy, and he treated the theme with brilliant artistry in *Kazaki* (*The Cossacks*). The highly civilized protagonist suffers in comparison with the freedom-loving uninhibited Cossacks of the village in which he lives. Several of them are among Tolstoy's most memorable characterizations.

In the late 1850s Tolstoy became concerned with the poor state of education among the peasantry, and, on returning from his travels, he started a school for peasant children at Yasnaya Polyana. The success of his original teaching methods, which anticipated modern progressive education, drew him deeper into pedagogical studies. He journeyed to Europe again in 1860–61, visiting Germany, France, Italy, England, and Belgium and investigating educational theory and practice. Absorbed by this interest, he published an educational magazine, in which he developed his pedagogical theories, and compiled textbooks that won wide acceptance because of their simplicity and attractive approach.

In 1862 Tolstoy married Sonya (Sofya) Andreyevna Bers, a girl from a middle class family with wide intellectual interests. He dropped his educational activities and for the next 15 years devoted himself with all his ardent nature to married life. For the most part it was an intense but happy existence, and 13 children were born. He now managed his estate with much success and resumed writing, creating his two greatest masterpieces, *Voyna i mir* (*War and Peace*) and *Anna Karenina.*

The great novels. It took Tolstoy almost seven years to write his vast epic *War and Peace,* generally regarded as one of the two or three greatest novels in world literature. In this supreme effort he went far beyond his previous writings both in scope and treatment. In it, all the stuff of life is woven in enormous tapestry, and the rich material and numerous characters are handled with unsurpassed objectivity. Perhaps in no other novel does the mastery of realistic detail and the amazing subtlety and variety of psychological analysis so successfully create the total impression of life being lived completely and naturally.

The scheme of *War and Peace*

War and Peace, covering the period 1805–14, is primarily concerned with the histories of five aristocratic families, the members of which are portrayed against a vivid background of Russian social life and the titanic struggle of clashing armies during Napoleon's invasion of Russia. In this huge panorama appear the aristocracy and the peasantry, officers and privates of the army, the Russian and French emperors, diplomats and courtiers, town life and country life, and realistic pictures of war. The theme of war, however, is subordinated to the story of family existence, which at that time involved Tolstoy's optimistic belief in the life-asserting pattern of the natural stages of man—birth, childhood, maturity, love, marriage, birth again, and death. As models for two of the families, Tolstoy drew upon members of his own family, and the unforgettable heroine Natasha is modelled on his sister-in-law Tanya Bers. One has only to read her published diary, however, to realize how the witchery of his art has transformed her into the vital, poetic, "natural" woman of the novel. The moral conflict between two of the main protagonists (bumbling, questing Pierre and polished, intellectually proud Andrey) is also Tolstoy's—Andrey's conviction that one should live for the sake of doing good for oneself being opposed to Pierre's ultimate belief that one should live for the sake of serving others. Tolstoy varied his realistic method of individualizing characters in accordance with the human types portrayed: it may be brilliant externalization, as in the case of a shallow society beauty; or psychological analysis in depth, as in that of an emotionally complex woman supposedly patterned after Tolstoy's mother; or acute symbolism, as in the creation of the peasant Platon Karatayev, who exists as a personification of the simplicity and truth living in the gray masses of Russia.

The sections of the novel that critics have frequently objected to are those in which Tolstoy set forth his philosophy of history and theorized about war and its architects. He anticipated these objections, and in 1868 he published an article explaining his views on these matters. There are two kinds of actions, he declared: those that do, and those that do not, depend upon individual will. In the historical process, he wrote, there is a minimum of freedom; the actions of so-called makers of history and leaders of war depend on the actions of countless other people and to this extent are predetermined. What troubled him was the historians' practice of fixing responsibility for what occurs in life upon individuals whom they call "great men" and endow with heroic virtues and vices. On the contrary, Tolstoy argued, natural law—the principles of right or justice regarded by many thinkers as common to all mankind and thus independent of formal law—determines the lives of human beings no less than the processes of nature itself. There is no free choice; all is ruled by an inexorable historical determinism. But it can hardly be denied that his labouring of such subjects interferes with the unity of *War and Peace* and represents an artistic lapse.

Though it is similar to *War and Peace* at least in narrative method and style, *Anna Karenina* has more artistic unity. Tolstoy's philosophy of life was in the process of changing between the writing of the two books. *War and Peace* is a life-loving, optimistic novel, and its main characters are morally robust and masters of their inner conflicts; *Anna Karenina,* which deals with Russian society in the 1860s, is pessimistic, and the inner conflicts of its characters, often unresolved, sometimes bring about human disaster. There is an inevitability about the tragic fate that hangs over the adulterous love of Anna and Vronsky. "Vengeance is mine, I will repay" is the epigraph of the novel and the leitmotiv of the whole story. Anna pays not so much because she transgresses the moral code but because she refuses to observe the proprieties customarily exacted in such liaisons by the hypocritical high society to which she belongs. Her love for Vronsky is a deep and lasting passion, and, unable to play the hypocrite, she unhesitatingly confronts high society with the sincerity of her love. Society's smug condemnation assures the tragic consequences of the affair. The sinful romance of Anna and Vronsky is effectively contrasted with the happy love and marriage of Kitty and Levin, which appears to have been inspired by Tolstoy's own experiences in marriage. Further, Levin's anguished doubts about the meaning of life, his haunting thoughts of suicide, and his desire to sympathize with the peasants are clear echoes of Tolstoy's own struggle at this time.

The moral basis of *Anna Karenina*

Last years as Christian reformer. Though happily married, famous as a novelist, and enjoying a large income, Tolstoy had become dissatisfied with himself by the time he finished *Anna Karenina.* An incessant probing into the purpose of life, which had troubled him since his youth, drove him to a state of spiritual crisis. In *Ispoved* (*A Confession*) he poignantly relates the moral and spiritual suffering he endured in his search for an answer to the meaning of life. The crisis came to a head in 1879. At one point he contemplated suicide. He found little help in the writings of philosophers, theologians, and scientists that he systematically examined, but the peasants, for whom he felt a deep sympathy, gave him a clue. One must serve God, they told him, and not live for oneself.

Ultimately Tolstoy became convinced that the teachings of Christ, as revealed in the New Testament, contained the answer to his question about the meaning of life. There is a power in each of us, he declared, that enables us to discern what is good, and we are in touch with that power. Our reason and conscience flow from it, and the purpose of our conscious life is to do its will; that is, to do good. From what he believed to be Christ's real utterances, corrected as he felt they should be if they were to retain their original substance, he formulated five commandments to guide him: do not be angry; do not lust; do not bind yourself by oaths; resist not him that is evil; and be good to the just and the unjust. These commandments, with some modifications, became the basis for his future activities and teachings.

Conversion to Christian anarchism

Tolstoy's new convictions took a form of Christian anarchism that led him to disavow immortality and reject the authority of the church, which in turn was to excommunicate him in 1901. Further, he opposed organized government because it maintained itself through coercion, and he condemned private property because he believed that ownership was secured by force. He would have preferred to divest himself of his own property, but, bowing to the wishes of members of his family, he legally transferred his estate to them.

Following his spiritual crisis, Tolstoy devoted much time after 1880 to writing books, pamphlets, and articles on various aspects of his religious, social, moral, and artistic views. Though they lack the absorbing interest of the personal experience he related in *A Confession,* they are written in the same clear prose and often reveal his remarkable gift for logical and persuasive argumentation. The most important of these many discursive writings are *Kritika dogmaticheskogo bogoslaviya* (*An Examination of Dogmatic Theology*), a powerful attack on the Russian Orthodox Church; *V chyom moya vera* (*What I Believe*), an attempt to systematize his views on religion; *Tak chto zhe nam delat?* (*What Then Must We Do?*), a vivid account of his experiences in the slums of Moscow and an analysis of the causes of poverty; and *Tsarstvo bozhiye vnutri vas* (*The Kingdom of God Is Within You*), the fullest statement of his Christian anarchism, in which he developed his belief in nonresistance to evil and reached the conclusion that governments exist largely for the sake of the rich and powerful and by their use of force persecute the masses of mankind and murder them in the violence of war. Some essays attack specific social and governmental practices, such as the use of intoxicants and tobacco in "Dlya chego lyudi odurmanivayutsya?" ("Why Do Men Stupefy Themselves?") and the execution of revolutionists in "Ne mogu molchat!" ("I Cannot Be Silent!"). Others call for reforms, advocating, for instance, the land tax proposed by the American economist Henry George (*Pisma o genre dzhorzhe* [*Letters on Henry George*]).

Religious and social essays

In 1897 Tolstoy completed *Chto takoye iskusstvo?* (*What Is Art?*), an attempt to develop an aesthetic system in terms of his religious, moral, and social views. He maintained that a work is art only when it "infects" the reader, hearer, or viewer with the condition of the artist's soul. If there is no union between the artist and his audience through "infection"—that is, if a communication of sympathetic feelings is not conveyed—then the work has failed as art. Among the several degrees of art that Tolstoy recognized, the highest is "religious art"—that which infects people with feelings "flowing from the love of God and man." On this basis, he rejected as art some of the works of, for example, Shakespeare and Wagner. With that maddening consistency that is as much the hallmark of pride as of humility, he relegated his own great works of fiction up to this point to the category of "bad art," because they did not conform to the moral purpose of his new theory.

After his spiritual crisis Tolstoy, apart from his voluminous nonfiction, wrote several tales with a moral purpose, in a bare style devoid of the abundant details of his previous fiction. "Chem lyudi zhivy" ("What Men Live By"), "Dva starika" ("Two Old Men"), "Vrazhye lepko, a bozhye krepko" ("Evil Allures, but Good Endures"), "Mnogo li cheloveku zemli nuzhno?" ("How Much Land Does a Man Need?"), and "Tri voprosa" ("Three Questions") are cast in this new manner. These little masterpieces of construction, which focus on peasant life, belong to his category of "good universal art." Though a moral is present, it is never allowed to obtrude on the artistic unity of the story. Another series of tales, different in manner because they are intended to appeal to educated readers, are closer to the style of his earlier fiction. The finest are the unfinished "Zapiski sumasshedshego" ("Notes of a Madman"), a mystical treatment of man's despair in the face of life's defeats, and "Smert Ivana Ilicha" ("The Death of Ivan Ilich"), in which the hero, a symbolic Everyman, discovers the inner light of faith and love only when confronted by death. The problem of sex, which deeply concerned Tolstoy in his new belief that man's moral health depended on his ability to approach closer to the ideal of chastity, becomes the central theme of "Kreytserova Sonata" ("The Kreutzer Sonata"), a convincing artistic study of jealousy and ill-tempered polemic against society's sexual education of young men and women. Sex is also the main concern of "Dyavol" ("The Devil"), a story inspired by an episode in Tolstoy's life: a man, deeply in love with his young wife, cannot overcome his lust for a pretty peasant girl. The husband's despairing struggle with carnal desire is told with all Tolstoy's psychological mastery.

Sexual themes

A full-length novel, *Voskreseniye* (*Resurrection*), written when he was 71, was Tolstoy's major artistic effort after his "conversion." It is the story of a nobleman who seduces a young girl. She becomes a prostitute and is convicted of a crime that she did not commit, and the conscience-stricken hero, determined to marry her, follows her to Siberia. Though his love redeems her, in the end she refuses to marry him. There are many fine things, especially in the first part, where the account is cast in a bewitching poetic atmosphere. And the trial scene is a brilliant piece of realistic narrative. But *Resurrection* represents a marked falling off, artistically, from *War and Peace* and *Anna Karenina.* It bears evidence of haste, and the moral preaching and sharp attacks on the judicial and penal systems—however deserved—and on the religious services of the church are in the spirit of Tolstoy the polemicist rather than the literary artist.

After his "conversion" Tolstoy strove, by no means with complete success, to bring his daily existence into conformity with his altered views. He abandoned smoking and drinking, became a vegetarian, and often dressed in simple peasant clothes. Since he now believed that no one should depend upon the labour of others, he became as self-sufficient as possible, cleaning his own room, working in the fields, and making his own boots. In the hope of approaching closer to his ideal of chastity, he tried to conquer fleshly desires in his relations with his wife. He also engaged in philanthropic activities, such as the organization of famine relief. The eloquence of Tolstoy's moral and religious writings, his fame, and his vital personality attracted many adherents. Disciples organized colonies in which they endeavoured to live together according to his precepts. Tolstoy distrusted such organized efforts. The truth that brings happiness cannot be preached, he declared; it can be achieved only by individuals who honestly look within themselves. As his own reputation increased and knowledge of his views spread throughout Russia and abroad, hundreds of people from all over the world made their way to Yasnaya Polyana to see and talk with him.

But the older sons, and his wife especially, had little sympathy for Tolstoy's views and his altered way of life. Endless visits of "converts"—the "dark people," his wife called them—and the interference of one of them, V.G. Chertkov, in family affairs caused frequent quarrels between husband and wife. Contrary to his hopes, she refused to surrender her possessions and join him in a life of comparative asceticism. In fact, to secure the family's comfortable existence, she obtained, much against his will, the copyrights of his works printed before 1880, and these writings provided considerable income from editions that she herself published.

During the last part of his life Tolstoy withheld from publication various works, either because he was dissatisfied with them or because he wished to avoid quarrelling with his wife over copyright ownership. In 1911, a year after his death, several of them appeared; they are among his best creations. One is a short novel, *Khadzhi-Murat,* the story of a brave Caucasian warrior who deserts to the Russians and is killed attempting to see his son in secret. The vivid narrative method and psychological revelation of mutual misunderstandings entitle it to a place among the most superb examples of his art. Equally effective, though shorter, are "Otets Sergy" ("Father Sergius"), the story of an aristocrat who conquers his lust and spiritual pride and becomes a hermit-monk; "Falshivy kupon" ("The False Coupon"), a study in fictional form of how the example of goodness, in contrast with the evil-begetting power of evil, inspires good deeds; and "Alyosha Gorshok," a perfect short story of a peasant youth who finds contentment with his lot through submission to all adversities.

Posthumous stories and plays

Several plays were included in the first posthumous collection of his works. Tolstoy believed that drama was "probably the most influential province of art," and at various periods he devoted much effort to writing plays. But he lacked certain of the qualifications necessary to the dramatist, and, though in some instances he succeeded, his plays are inferior, artistically, to his fiction.

Vlast tmy (*The Power of Darkness*), Tolstoy's highest achievement in drama, was first performed in 1888. It is a realistic tragedy of peasant life conceived as an illustration of one of his favourite later themes, suggested by the subtitle, "If a Claw Is Caught, the Whole Bird Is Lost." The initial evil action of the protagonist—his seduction of another man's wife—leads him to commit further sins, including the final sin of murder. A striking contrast is *Plody prosveshcheniya* (*The Fruits of Enlightenment*), a comedy that genially satirizes the foibles of aristocratic society. Tolstoy never finished *I svet vo tme svetit* (*The Light Shines in Darkness*), though it had a special autobiographical importance, for it concerns the hero's failure to convince his family of the wisdom of his beliefs. *Zhivoy trup* (written 1902; *The Living Corpse*) deals with the tragedy of a drunkard. Conscience-stricken over the harm he has caused his wife, he pretends to have died so that she may marry the man she loves. When the police reveal that he is actually alive, he kills himself. The moralizing that appears in Tolstoy's writing in his old age is absent from his play, which is filled with kindness and sympathetic understanding of the erring ways of mankind.

The aging Tolstoy felt keenly the painful contradiction between the life of ease that the family lived and the life he wanted to live—the simple existence of a religious hermit, free of worldly goods and dedicated to service to others. He realized that his position made a mockery of his professed faith. Finally, the worsening domestic situation forced him to leave home stealthily one night, accompanied by his doctor and youngest daughter, Aleksandra, in search of, he hoped, a refuge where he could live quietly and closer to God. A few days later, on November 20 (November 7, O.S.), 1910, he died of pneumonia at the remote railway junction of Astapovo, in Ryazan Province.

Assessment. Tolstoy's eminence as a literary artist has never been seriously questioned by critics; he is universally accepted as one of the greatest writers of fiction in the world. Although never dependent on preceding Russian authors, he may have been influenced by foreign writers, such as Jean-Jacques Rousseau, Sterne, Stendhal, and later, William Thackeray. But there has never been unanimity about his reputation as a thinker. The dualism of Tolstoy's moral and intellectual development, however, has come to be more thoroughly understood by modern students of his thought. In his tireless search for truth he sought for absolutes in a world of incomplete knowledge and imperfect men. As a consequence, his unwillingness to compromise, his compulsive need to achieve the ultimate rational explanation, often led him to push theory to the limits of absurdity, which many believe he came very close to doing in his views on history, nonviolence, education, and art. But any systematic study of his thought reveals its relation to the concepts of 19th-century liberalism. He believed that the whole history of the last 2,000 years had been shaped essentially by the moral development of individuals and the demoralization of governments. Tolstoy placed his faith in the moral development of the people as a final answer to what he regarded as the universal oppression of the many by the few. For him, the progressive movement toward a classless and stateless condition of mankind depended, contrary to the economic determinism and violent class struggle of Marxism, upon the growing moral perfection of each individual through observance of the supreme law of love and the consequent repudiation of every form of violence. Despite the extreme to which he carried his rationalism, Tolstoy is today generally considered to be one of the most influential moralists of the 19th century. (E.J.Si.)

MAJOR WORKS

NOVELS: *Voyna i mir* (1865–69; *War and Peace,* trans. by Louise and Aylmer Maude in "Great Books of the Western World," vol. 51, 1952; trans. by Constance Garnett, 1961); *Anna Karenina* (1875–77; trans. by R.S. Townsend, 2 vol., 1958); *Voskreseniye* (1899; *Resurrection,* trans. by Louise Maude, 1957).

STORIES: *Detstvo* (1852; *Childhood* in *Childhood, Boyhood, Youth,* trans. by R. Edmonds, 1964); "Nabeg" (1853; "The Raid," trans. by Constance Garnett in *Tolstoy Tales,* 1947); *Otrochestvo* (1854; *Boyhood*); "Rubka lesa" (1855; "The Woodfelling" in complete works: *Tolstoy Centenary Edition,* trans. by Louise and Aylmer Maude, 1928–37); "Dva gusara" (1856; "Two Hussars" in complete works); *Yunost* (1857; *Youth*); "Kholstomer" (written 1863, first published 1886; in complete works); *Kazaki* (1863; *The Cossacks,* in *The Cossacks; The Death of Ivan Ilyich; Happy Ever After,* trans., by R. Edmonds, 1960); "Chem lyudi zhivy" (1881; "What Men Live By" in *Tolstoy Tales,* trans. by Louise and Aylmer Maude, 1947); "Dva starika" (1885; "Two Old Men"); "Mnogo li cheloveku zemli nuzhno?" (1886; "How Much Land Does a Man Need?"); and "Tri voprosa" (1903; "Three Questions")—all in translation in complete works; "Zapiski Sumasshedshego" (1884; "Notes of a Madman" in *Notes of a Madman and Other Stories,* trans. by S.S. Koteliansky, 1943); "Smert Ivana Ilicha" (1886; "The Death of Ivan Ilich" in complete works); "Kreytserova sonata" (1891; "The Kreutzer Sonata" in *The Kreutzer Sonata, The Devil, and Other Tales,* trans. by Aylmer Maude, 1940) "Dyavol" (1889; "The Devil" in *The Kreutzer Sonata*); "Otets Sergy" (written 1898, first published 1911; "Father Sergius" in complete works); *Khadzi-Murat* (written 1904, first published 1911; trans. in complete works); "Falshivy kupon" (written 1904, first published 1911; "The False Coupon" in complete works); "Alyosha Gorshok" (written 1905, first published 1911; "Alyosha the Pot").

PHILOSOPHICAL AND SOCIAL WRITINGS: *Ispoved* (written 1878–79, first published 1882; *How I Came to Believe—"My Confession,"* trans. 1921); *Kritika dogmaticheskoga bogosloviya* (written 1880, first published 1891; *An Examination of Dogmatic Theology*); *V chyom moya vera* (written 1883, banned 1884; *What I Believe,* trans. by Aylmer Maude, 1940); *Tak chto zhe nam delat?* (finished 1886, first published 1902; *What Then Must We Do?); Tsarstvo bozhiye vnutri vas* (1894, *The Kingdom of God Is Within You*); "Dlya chego lyudi odurmanivayutsya" (1890; "Why Do Men Stupefy Themselves?"); "Ne mogu molchat!" (1908; "I Cannot Be Silent!"); *Pisma o Genri Dzorzhe* (1897; *Letters on Henry George*); and *Chto takoye iskusstvo?* (1898; *What Is Art?*)—all translations in complete works.

BIBLIOGRAPHY

Editions, selections, letters, and diaries: ЛЕВ НИКОЛАЕВИЧ ТОЛСТОЙ, *Полное собрание сочинений,* 90 vol., ed. by ВЛАДИМИР Г. ЧЕРТКОВ (1928–58), is the most complete Russian edition of Tolstoy's works, the so-called Jubilee Edition, including his letters, notebooks, and diaries. Another major Russian edition is ЛЕВ НИКОЛАЕВИЧ ТОЛСТОЙ, *Собрание сочинений,* 20 vol. (1960–65). Of editions in English translation none is complete; the most useful are *The Complete Works of Count Tolstoy,* trans. by LEO WIENER, 24 vol. (1904–05, reprinted 1968); and *Tolstoy Centenary Edition,* trans. by LOUISE and AYLMER MAUDE, 21 vol. (1928–37). Translations of single fictional works are also available in the Everyman's Library and in Penguin Classics. Selections in English of nonfictional works include AYLMER MAUDE (ed.), *Tolstoy on Art* (1924, reprinted 1973); *Tolstoy's Writings on Civil Disobedience and Non-Violence* (1967); ALAN PINCH and MICHAEL ARMSTRONG (eds.), *Tolstoy on Education* (1982). See also *The Journal of Leo Tolstoi, 1895–1899,* trans. by ROSE STRUNSKY (1917); *The Diaries of Leo Tolstoy,* 3 vol., trans. by C.J. HOGARTH and A. SIRNIS (1917); *Last Diaries,* ed. by LEON STILMAN (1960, reprinted 1979); PAUL BIRYUKOV (ed.), *Tolstoi's Love Letters: With a Study on the Autobiographical Elements in Tolstoy's Work,* trans. by SAMUEL S. KOTELIANSKY and VIRGINIA WOOLF (1923); *The Private Diary of Leo Tolstoy, 1853–1857,* trans. by LOUISE and AYLMER MAUDE, 2nd ed. (1927, reprinted 1972); *The Letters of Tolstoy and His Cousin Countess Alexandra Tolstoy, 1857–1903,* trans. by LEO ISLAVIN (1929); *Tolstoy's Letters,* 2 vol., selected, ed., and trans. by REGINALD F. CHRISTIAN (1978).

Recollections of Tolstoy: SERGEI A. BERS, *Recollections of Count Leo Tolstoy,* trans. by CHARLES E. TURNER (1893); ILYA TOLSTOY, *Tolstoy, My Father,* trans. from the rev. Russian ed. by ANN DUNNIGAN (1971; originally published in Russian, 1914, rev. ed., 1969); MAXIM GORKY, *Reminiscences of Leo Nicolayevitch Tolstoi,* trans. by SAMUEL S. KOTELIANSKY and LEONARD WOOLF (1920, reprinted 1978; originally published in Russian, 1919); SOFIIA A. TOLSTAIA, *The Autobiography of Countess Sophie Tolstoi,* trans. by S.S. KOTELIANSKY and LEONARD WOOLF (1922); ALEKSANDR B. GOLDENVEIZER, *Talks with Tolstoi,* trans. by S.S. KOTELIANSKY and VIRGINIA WOOLF (1923, reprinted 1969); COUNT LEON L. TOLSTOI, *The Truth About My Father* (1924); AYLMER MAUDE (ed.), *Family Views of Tolstoy* (1926); SOFIIA A. TOLSTAIA, *The Diary of Tolstoy's Wife, 1860–1891,* trans. by ALEXANDER WERTH (1928), and *The Final Struggle: Being Countess Tolstoy's Diary for 1910,* trans. by AYLMER MAUDE (1936, reprinted 1980; originally published in Russian, 1932); TATIANA A. KUZMINSKAYA, *Tolstoy As I Knew Him,* trans. by NORA SIGERIST *et al.* (1948), recollections by a sister of Tolstoy's wife; TATIANA TOLSTOY, *The Tolstoy Home: Diaries of Tatiana Sukhotin-Tolstoy,* trans. by ALEC BROWN (1951, reprinted 1966), and *Tolstoy Remembered* (1977; originally published in French, 1975), recollections by Tolstoy's daughter; SERGEI TOLSTOY, *Tolstoy Remembered by His Son,* trans. by MOURA BUDBERG (1961, originally published in Russian, 1949); VALENTIN BULGAKOV, *The Last Year of Leo Tolstoy,* trans. and abridged by ANN DUNNIGAN (1971; originally published in Russian, 2nd ed., 1918), recollections of Tolstoy's secretary.

Biographies: PETR A. SERGEENKO, *How Count L.N. Tolstoy Lives and Works* (1899; originally published in Russian, 1898); AYLMER MAUDE, *The Life of Tolstoy,* 2 vol. (1908–10; rev. ed. 1930), one of the best accounts of Tolstoy's post-confessional years; PAUL I. BIRYUKOV (comp.), *Leo Tolstoy: His Life and Work* (1911); VLADIMIR G. CHERTKOV, *The Last Days of Tolstoy,* trans. by NATHALIE A. DUDDINGTON (1922, reprinted 1973), a valuable account of the family struggle of the last years; ALEXANDER I. NAZAROFF, *Tolstoy: The Inconstant Genius* (1929, reprinted 1971); EMILE J. DILLON, *Count Leo Tolstoy: A New Portrait* (1934, reprinted 1972); DERRICK LEON, *Tolstoy: His Life and Work* (1944); ERNEST J. SIMMONS, *Leo Tolstoy* (1946, reissued in 2 vol., 1960); ALEXANDRA TOLSTOY, *Tolstoy: A Life of My Father,* trans. by ELIZABETH R. HAPGOOD (1953, reprinted 1973), and *Out of the Past* (1981); HENRI TROYAT, *Tolstoy* (1967, reprinted 1980; originally published in French, 1965), an excellent work on Tolstoy's life. On Countess Tolstoy, see CYNTHIA ASQUITH, *Married to Tolstoy* (1960, reprinted 1969); and ANNE EDWARDS, *Sonya: The Life of Countess Tolstoy* (1981). Works on Tolstoy as a literary figure include EDWARD CRANKSHAW, *Tolstoy: The Making of a Novelist* (1974); MARTIN GREEN, *The Challenge of the Mahatmas* (1978), *Dreams of Adventure, Deeds of Empire* (1979), and *Tolstoy and Gandhi, Men of Peace: A Biography* (1983), comprising the trilogy *The Lust for Power,* which explores the impact of great personalities on literature; WALTER KERR, *The Shabunin Affair: An Episode in the Life of Leo Tolstoy* (1982); BORIS EIKHENBAUM, *Tolstoi in the Sixties,* trans. by DUFFIELD WHITE (1982; originally published in Russian, 1931), and *Tolstoi in the Seventies,* trans. by ALBERT KASPIN (1982; originally published in Russian, 1960), the work of a renowned Russian historian of literature, exploring Tolstoy's period of maturity.

Criticism and interpretation: CHARLES E. TURNER, *Count Tolstoi As Novelist and Thinker* (1888, reprinted 1974); AYLMER MAUDE, *Tolstoy and His Problems,* 2nd ed. (1902, reprinted 1974); DMITRI S. MEREZHKOVSKI, *Tolstoi As Man and Artist* (1902, reprinted 1970), a classic interpretation that has exercised great influence; ALEXANDER H.G. CRAUFURD, *The Religion and Ethics of Tolstoy* (1912); GEORGE R. NOYES, *Tolstoy* (1918, reprinted 1968); JANKO LAVRIN, *Tolstoy: A Psycho-Critical Study* (1924; rev. as *Tolstoy: An Approach,* 1944, reprinted 1968); HELEN E. DAVIS, *Tolstoy and Nietzsche* (1929, reprinted 1971); DERK BODDE, *Tolstoy and China* (1950, reprinted 1967); ISAIAH BERLIN, *The Hedgehog and the Fox: An Essay on Tolstoy's View of History* (1953, reprinted 1967), one of the best books on Tolstoy's world view; GEORGE STEINER, *Tolstoy or Dostoevsky: An Essay in the Old Criticism* (1959, reprinted 1971), a vivid account of the man and his work; THEODORE REDPATH, *Tolstoy,* 2nd ed. (1969), including a note on modern Russian work on Tolstoy; REGINALD F. CHRISTIAN, *Tolstoy's "War and Peace"* (1962), a valuable source study, and *Tolstoy: A Critical Introduction* (1969), examining Tolstoy's lesser known works. See also THOMAS MANN, *Goethe und Tolstoi* (1932); К. ЛОМУНОВ, *Драматургия Л.Н. Толстого* (1956); НИКОЛАЙ К. ГУДЗИ, *Лев Толстой,* 3rd rev. ed. (1960); АНДРЕЙ А. САБУРОВ, *"Война и мир" Л.Н. Толстого: проблематика и поэтика* (1959), a representative Soviet study; RUTH G. BENSON, *Women in Tolstoy: The Ideal and the Erotic* (1973); THOMAS G.S. CAIN, *Tolstoy* (1977), an analysis of the major fiction; EDWARD B. GREENWOOD, *Tolstoy: The Comprehensive Vision* (1975); EDWARD WASIOLEK, *Tolstoy's Major Fiction* (1978), with a good bibliography; MALCOLM JONES (ed.), *New Essays on Tolstoy* (1978), including a valuable survey of Tolstoy studies. Comparative studies of Tolstoy's literary relationships include LOGAN SPEIRS, Tolstoy and Chekhov (1971); JOHN BAYLEY, *Tolstoy and the Novel* (1966); LEV SHESTOV, *Dostoyevsky, Tolstoy and Nietzsche* (1969); BORIS SOROKIN, *Tolstoy in Prerevolutionary Russian Criticism* (1979). Tolstoy's philosophical and political views are discussed in GORDON W. SPENCE, *Tolstoy the Ascetic* (1967); and RONALD V. SAMPSON, *The Discovery of Peace* (1973; U.K. title, *Tolstoy: The Discovery of Peace*). DAVID R. EGAN and MELINDA A. EGAN, *Leo Tolstoy: An Annotated Bibliography of English-Language Sources to 1978* (1979), includes more than 2,000 items.

Tools

A tool is an implement or device used directly upon a piece of material to shape it into a desired form. The date of the earliest tools is extremely remote. Tools found in northern Kenya in 1969 have been estimated to be about 2,600,000 years old, and their state of development suggests that even older tools may remain to be discovered.

The present array of tools has as common ancestors the sharpened stones that were the keys to early human survival. Rudely fractured stones, first found and later "made" by hunters who needed a general-purpose tool, were a "knife" of sorts that could also be used to hack, to pound, and to grub. In the course of a vast interval of time, a variety of single-purpose tools came into being. With the twin developments of agriculture and animal domestication, roughly 10,000 years ago, the many demands of a settled way of life led to a higher degree of tool specialization; the identities of the ax, adz, chisel, and saw were clearly established more than 4,000 years ago.

The common denominator of these tools is removal of material from a workpiece, usually by some form of cutting. The presence of a cutting edge is therefore characteristic of most tools, and the principal concern of toolmakers has been the pursuit and creation of improved cutting edges. Tool effectiveness was enhanced enormously by hafting—the fitting of a handle to a piece of sharp stone, which endowed the tool with better control, more energy, or both.

It is helpful to draw the distinction between hand and machine tools. Hand tools are those used by craftsmen in manual operations, such as chopping, chiseling, sawing, filing, or forging. Complementary tools, often needed as auxiliaries to the shaping tools, include such implements as the hammer for nailing and the vise for holding. A craftsman may also use instruments that facilitate accurate measurements: the rule, divider, square, and others. Power tools—usually hand-held, motor-powered implements such as the electric drill or electric saw—perform many of the old manual operations and as such may be considered hand tools. Machine tools are analogous to hand tools in their function as shaping implements, but they require stationary mounting and mechanical drive for the working of strong materials, primarily metal, and the mass processing of precision parts.

For information on the development of agricultural implements, see the article AGRICULTURE, THE HISTORY OF.

This article is divided into the following sections:

Early history of hand tools

GEOLOGICAL AND ARCHAEOLOGICAL ASPECTS

The oldest known tools date from 2,600,000 years ago; geologically, this is close to the end of the Pliocene Epoch, which had extended over 4,500,000 years and was the last of five epochs constituting the Tertiary Period (the 65,000,000 years of which had seen the rise of mammals). The Pliocene was succeeded by the Pleistocene Epoch, which began about 2,500,000 years ago and was terminated only recently, perhaps 10,000 years ago, with the recession of the last glaciers, when it was supplanted by the Holocene (Recent) Epoch. Pleistocene and Stone Age are in rough correspondence, for, until the first use of metal, about 5,000 years ago, stone was the principal material of tools and implements.

At first, humans were casual tool users, employing convenient sticks or stones to achieve a purpose and then discarding them. Although humans may have shared this characteristic with some other animals, their differentiation from other animals may have begun with the deliberate making of tools to a plan and for a purpose. A cutting instrument was especially valuable, for, of all carnivorous animals, humans are the only ones not equipped with tearing claws or canine teeth long enough to pierce and rend skin: humans need sharp tools to get through the skin to the meat. Naturally fractured pieces of stone with sharp edges that could cut were the first tools; they were followed by intentionally chipped stones. For archaeologists, the finding of primitive, intentionally made cutting tools indicates and confirms the early presence of humans at a site. Once understood, fire helped shape wooden implements before adequate stone tools were available for the purpose.

Fire was also the basis of metallurgy. When in historic time the powers of water and wind were applied to the daily tasks of grinding grain and raising water, the way to industrialization was opened.

The idea of relating human history to the material from which tools were made dates from 1836 when Christian Jürgensen Thomsen, a Danish archaeologist, was faced with the task of exhibiting an undocumented collection of clearly ancient tools and implements. Thomsen used three categories of materials—stone, bronze, and iron—to represent what he felt had been the ordered succession of technological development. The idea has since been formalized in the designation of a Stone Age, Bronze Age, and Iron Age.

Thomsen and the three-age system

The three-age system does not apply to the Americas, many Pacific Islands, or Australia, places in which no Bronze Age existed before the native inhabitants were introduced to the products of the Iron Age by European explorers. The Stone Age is still quite real in some remote regions of Australia and South America, and it existed in the New World at the time of Columbus' first visit. Despite these qualifications, the Stone–Bronze–Iron sequence is of value as a concept in the early history of tools.

The Stone Age was of great duration, having occupied practically all of the Pleistocene Epoch. Copper and bronze appeared more than 5,000 years ago; iron followed in the next millennium or so and as an age includes the present.

The apparently abrupt transition from stone to bronze tends to mask the critical discovery of native metals and their utilitarian use and fails to indicate the significant discoveries of melting and casting. From bronze one can infer the crucial discovery of smelting, the process by which most of the common metals can be recovered from their ores. Smelted copper necessarily preceded bronze, a mixture of copper and tin, the first alloy. Iron came later, when technique, experience, and equipment were able to provide higher temperatures and cope with problems involved with its use.

STONE AS A MATERIAL

The Stone Age is divided into two contrasting periods: the Old Stone Age, a long era of stagnation; and the New Stone Age, a brief period of swift progress.

The Paleolithic Period, or Old Stone Age, endured until about 10,000 years ago and was characterized by tools of chipped stone, cutting tools with rough and pock-marked surfaces and generally serrated cutting edges. The later Paleolithic was also an era of wood, horn (antler), and bone. These three materials, all softer than stone but nevertheless intractable, could not be worked successfully without the aid of harder stone tools, such as serrated blades and gravers, or burins, small scrapers with either pointed or narrow, chisel-like ends. Bone was a particularly useful material, for its toughness made feasible barbed fishhooks, eyed needles, and small leatherworking awls.

The term Neolithic Period, or New Stone Age, defines the second period, at the beginning of which ground and usually polished stone tools, notably axes, came into widespread use after the adoption of a new technique of stoneworking. The beginning of the Neolithic, the retreat of the last glaciers, and the invention of food crops, involving agriculture and animal domestication, were more or less contemporary events. The period terminated with the discovery of metals.

The revolutionary art that created the definitive ground and polished tools of Neolithic man was essentially a finishing operation that slicked a chipped tool by rubbing it on or with an abrasive stone to remove the scars of the chipping process that had produced the rough tool. Not only was the edge keener than ever before, but the smooth sides of the edge also promoted deeper penetration and, hence, greater effectiveness, with the added advantage of easier tool extraction from a deep and wedging cut.

Stones for toolmaking

As a tool material, the term stone covers a wide variety of rocks, ranging from the dense and grainless flint and obsidian to coarse-grained granite and quartzite. Each kind of stone has certain unique properties that are further influenced by temperature and humidity. Stone of any kind is difficult to manipulate. It has been noted, for example, that the Australian Aborigines reject as unsuitable a great many of the flints they have worked on, sometimes in the ratio of 300 rejects to one accepted tool. This high discard rate may help explain the thousands upon thousands of stone artifacts that have been found.

Flint, homogeneous and isotropic (having equal properties in all directions), is the stone of first choice for toolmaking. Reasonably well distributed over much of the world, it is an impure quartz, a form of silica, usually opaque and commonly of gray or smoky-brown colour. It is harder than most steels, having no cleavage planes, but displaying the conchoidal, or shell-like, fracture of a brittle material that leaves a sharp edge when flakes are detached. (Glass, which may be considered an artificial quartz, also exhibits the conchoidal fracture.) Obsidian, a volcanic glass of rather limited distribution, is usually black or very dark and, because of its conchoidal fracture, was used like flint. Most edged stone tools, however, were of flint. Flint was once an object of trade, and flint mines were in Neolithic time what iron mines became at a later age.

Types of stone tools. Three principal types of tools appeared in the long Paleolithic Period, with substantial variations occurring within each type. The types are distinguished principally by workmanship but also vary in size and appearance and are known as core, flake, and blade tools. The core tools are the largest; the earliest and most primitive were made by working on a fist-sized piece of stone (core) with a similar stone (hammerstone) and knocking off several large flakes on one side to produce a jagged but sharp crest. This was a general-purpose implement for the roughest work, such as hacking, pounding, or cutting. The angle of the cutting edge was rather large because of the sphericity of the stone. In time, thinner, sharper, and more versatile core tools were developed.

Although large flakes with sharp edges of small angle were a by-product of core-tool manufacture and were well suited for slitting and scraping, they were not flake tools in the proper sense. True flake tools derived from an advanced technique practiced more than 2,000,000 years later that sought the flake and discarded the core from which it had been detached; flake tools were made deliberately to serve a certain function and were not the casual spin-off of another operation. Finally, there were blade tools, longish slivers of stone with keen unserrated edges, directly useful as knives or as stock from which other pieces might be skillfully broken to serve numerous purposes. While flake and blade tools were developing, core tools were refined by overall chipping to create thinner and more efficient forms.

Techniques for making stone tools. Archaeologists have noted three different techniques for working stone to successive stages of refinement in the Paleolithic Period. The first and always basic method employed the hammerstone to fashion either a large and rude core tool such as the chopper, whose form persisted for perhaps 2,000,000 years, or to rough out (block in) large tool blanks that would be brought to final form by removing small flakes. The hammerstone technique produced short and deep flake scars. A variation employed the anvil stone, a large stationary stone against which the workpiece was swung to batter off large flakes.

Soft-hammer technique

The second method was the soft-hammer, or baton, technique, based on a discovery of perhaps 500,000 years ago that hard stone (flint in particular) could be chipped by striking it with a softer material. The baton was a light "hammer," an almost foot-long piece of bone, antler, or even wood, whose gentler blows detached only quite small flakes that left smooth, shallow scars. Such small flakes, when removed from the large scars left by the hammerstone, reduced the coarse and jagged edge to many small serrations, giving a straighter and more uniform cutting edge whose angle was also more acute than formerly and, hence, sharper.

Pressure flaking was the third technique. In this, a short, pointed instrument of bone, antler, or wood was used to pry, not strike, off tiny flakes in order to leave the smallest scars. As the least violent and most advanced of the methods of working stone, it gave the craftsman the ultimate in control for the removal of materials in the shaping of an implement.

To judge from the few remaining hand-tool-making societies, it is likely that every early man was adept at making new tools quickly and easily and on the spot, as fast as the old ones were blunted or broken. The earliest simple tools, made by taking convenient hand-sized stones and giving them sharp crests by a few well-placed blows, were evidently discarded after use, for their widespread dispersal suggests that they were made at the place of use and abandoned after serving their purpose. Tens of thousands of prehistoric stone tools survive, compared with only very few bits and pieces of the skeletal remains of the makers. Stone, of course, is imperishable, whereas bone is not, and one individual might have made several hundred tools.

Limitations of stone tools. The possibilities in the design of stone tools were limited by the inflexibility and brittleness of the material. The design effort was constrained to the sizing of the tool to the intended task and the development of sharper, longer, and more usefully shaped cutting edges that always required backing to support them. In use, the bending and twisting of long knifelike tools had to be avoided lest the action destroy them; this would also have been true of chisels and gouges. Similarly, even the much later heavier tools, such as the ax and adz, required care in use.

The effectiveness of stone tools has been demonstrated from time to time by both archaeologists and modern workers unaccustomed to such tools. An experienced operator using a stone knife can skin a small animal about as quickly and deftly as he can using steel. When the stone tool is subjected to substantial forces, however, the worker must use caution, intelligence, and control. Care is required to avoid twisting or prying with a stone blade (knife or ax); a thin blade may snap, and a thick one may collect local nicks.

PALEOLITHIC TOOLS

Classifying early tools

Early tools are classified by their industry, or type of workmanship. Such tool traditions are identified by a name derived from the site at which the type first drew archaeological attention. For example, the primitive chopping tools that persisted for nearly 2,000,000 years, first identified in Olduvai Gorge, east of Lake Victoria, Tanzania, constitute the so-called Oldowan industry, regardless of the part of the world in which implements of similar workmanship happen to be found.

The sequence of traditions shows growth and development; it does not imply abrupt transitions at certain times or the disappearance of an old industry with the advent of another. A new technique simply meant that something better or different could be accomplished, from the refinement of the cutting edge or the upgrading of old tool forms to the manufacture of a completely new tool. Innovation sometimes was possible only by drawing upon previously unworkable materials.

An overview of the products of the successive toolmaking industries shows that much effort went into cutting edges in the longitudinal direction of the pieces of flint. Knifelike instruments predominated and, thus, defined the nature of the fundamental need, namely, that of a cutting tool which could slit and sever.

With the passage of time and the acquisition of skills, the average size of the tool decreased; there was more cutting edge per pound of material, an important factor when flint had to be imported to a region. This trend was reversed in the Neolithic Period, when the heavy woodsman's ax and adz became essential elements for clearing forests for agriculture and timber. The world was then changing from an economy based on gathering and hunting food to a way of life founded on raising food.

Archaeologists have named the early tools by guessing at their presumed use, often in the light of other known facts about the culture in which the tradition appeared. As the tools move closer to the present, and specialized forms are seen in the creation of a wider variety of products, the descriptive name is on firmer ground.

Eoliths. The first act of the drama of tools is hazy. There are what have been called eoliths, "tools from the dawn of the Stone Age." Such stones with sharp fractures, found in great quantities in layers from the geological epochs before the Pleistocene, were once assumed to be tokens of human presence in the preceding Pliocene and even earlier Miocene epochs. These rocks, fractured by glacier pressure, wave action, or temperature change, are no longer taken as indexes of humans, although primitive peoples undoubtedly used them as ready-made objects before they deliberately started to fracture similar rocks in the late Pliocene. There are detailed criteria by which human-flaked and nature-flaked stones can be distinguished almost unerringly. Human origin is also evidenced by association with detached flakes and the stones that served as hammers.

The oldest known tool

The tools found in 1969 at the Koobi Fora site, near Lake Rudolph in northern Kenya, consisted of five choppers, a number of flakes, and a couple of battered stones. The tools lay on the surface; the flakes were found three feet below them in tuff (volcanic rock) datable to about 2,600,000 years ago. The oldest previously known tools had been from Olduvai Gorge, Tanzania. These Oldowan tools, as well as the jaw and teeth of a man who may have been the toolmaker, were found in the 1950s under tuff having a potassium–argon date of about 1,800,000 years, a lower Pleistocene age.

All of these tools are of a single type, a general-purpose implement that changed little in form during the next 2,000,000 years. It is variously known as a pebble tool, pebble chopper, chopping tool, or simply as a chopper (see Figure 1A). Waterworn and hence rounded, up to about the size of a fist, the pebble, preferably flattish rather than spherical, was given a few violent but skillfully applied blows by a hammerstone. Several large flakes or chips were knocked off the stone to create on it a sharp and roughly serrated crest, or ridge, yielding an implement that was edged at one end and could be gripped at the opposite end. Rudimentary, yet versatile, the chopper could be used to hack, mash, cut, grub roots, scrape, and break bones for their marrow.

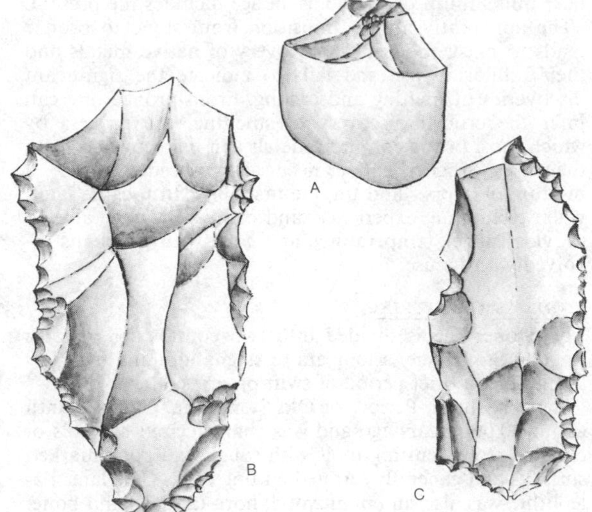

Figure 1: *Paleolithic tools.*
(A) Oldowan chopper, the oldest manufactured tool.
(B) Acheulian hand ax, or flat hatchet, a superior chopper.
(C) Scraper, a flake tool.

Although the large, sharp-edged flakes struck from the pebble were themselves useful for light cutting and scraping, it was not until perhaps 40,000 years ago that there was a development of flake-tool industries in which preshaped flakes were purposefully detached from a core that was then discarded. But the Oldowan chopper and the struck-off flakes—the earliest generalized primitive tools—between them solved the problems of how to get through the skin of a slain animal, dismember it, and divide the meat.

The Acheulian industry. As the Pleistocene Epoch progressed, humans slowly developed the primitive chopper into a better instrument. About half a million years ago a superior implement finally appeared after nearly 2,000,000 years of effort. The industry, or style, is known as the Acheulian, and the typical implement was the flint hand ax (sometimes called a fist hatchet [Figure 1B]). Throughout the ages the plump chopper and its bluntly angled crest had been streamlined by starting with a longer piece of stone and flaking the entire surface to produce an almond-shaped (amygdaloid) implement eight to 10 inches (20 to 25 centimetres) long. This stone, much thinner than the chopper, was also sharper and more effective because the cutting edges were formed from the intersection of two curved and flaked surfaces (bifacial working).

The Acheulian hand ax

This Acheulian hand ax was the product of evolution; certain of the intermediate stages, clearly leading to the typical and standardized form, have been identified as Chellean and Abbevillian. Despite the term ax, the tool was not hafted but was simply held in the hand. One end was tapered, the other rounded. The tapered end might be rather pointed or have a small straight edge. The tool was sharp for most of its periphery and seems to have been primarily a hunter's knife but probably very useful, too, for other purposes, such as chopping, scraping, grubbing, and even piercing. Sharp, thin and symmetrical, light and elegant, it was quite different from the heavy chopper, with its rather blunt edge.

Another biface, the Acheulian cleaver, assumed prominence about 250,000 years later. A variant of the hand ax, it had a wide cutting edge across the end instead of a point and was better suited than the hand ax for hunting or hacking wood.

The Neanderthal tool kit

Neanderthal man, an excellent hunter and toolmaker, appeared on the scene about 110,000 years ago, just ahead of the last glaciation but well within the Acheulian. His tool kit was impressive for the wide variety of hand axes, borers, knives, and choppers it contained. The kit was novel for its scrapers and heavily serrated blades having a sawlike appearance, implements that were essential to the working of wood, bone, and horn into tools and weapons. The Neanderthals regularly used fire, and it is presumed that they could make it, although the direct evidence is missing. Fire was useful in tool manufacture, for charring the end of a stick not only helped shape the point by making it easier to scrape but also hardened it, as for a spear point. This fire hardening was probably the first man-made modification of a natural property. Thoroughly wet wood, bent to shape and brought to dryness over the heat of a fire, would retain its bent form, a most useful property.

The Mousterian flake tools. The Mousterian and related flake industries followed the Acheulian. A refinement of the prepared-core technique, termed Levallois, was developed during the middle to upper Acheulian. In this method, a core was craftily trimmed in such a manner that a skillfully applied last blow would detach a large, preshaped flake directly usable as an implement; the core was discarded. Such a flake tool, with one flat surface, is known as a unifacial tool because a single bevel forms the working edge. There are two principal kinds of flakes, points and scrapers. The former are roughly triangular, with two trimmed or sharp edges meeting in a point, the base or butt of the triangle being thick and blunt. The side scrapers have a sharp edge in the long direction of the flake, with an opposite, thicker butt section (Figure 1C). The scraper could function as a knife, although it is speculated that it was used for working wood and skins, a supposition leading to the idea that skins were being used for clothing.

Late Paleolithic toolmaking. The fourth phase of Paleolithic toolmaking was introduced perhaps 40,000 years ago by the Aurignacian industry, a forerunner of the last and most brilliant achievements of the Old Stone Age. Extraordinary inventiveness was characteristic of the Aurignacian tradition and its several short-term successors. They can be lumped into a unit of development that spans the next 25,000 years.

Fully modern man—whose first representative is the Cro-Magnon—emerged within this period, perhaps 35,000 years ago, during the time of the development and elaboration of stone technology, which, by providing a variety of specialized tools, mostly of the flake and blade types, at last brought materials other than stone into extensive use. It was also a time when the great plains in northern and eastern Europe carried such a heavy reindeer population, in addition to wild horses and mammoths, that it has been called the Reindeer Age. This produced a hunting economy providing food and great quantities of bone, horn, skin, sinews, and, while the mammoth lasted, ivory; with it grew new technologies exploiting the unique properties of materials hitherto unworkable because of their hardness. This technological diversification was made possible by new techniques and stone tools, whose specialization and complexity fit them to the fresh tasks. The most significant tool was the burin, or graver, a stout, narrow-bladed flint able to scrape narrow grooves in bone; two parallel grooves, for example, would allow a sliver of bone to be detached as stock for a needle, pin, awl, or other small object. Larger pieces of bone were worked into hooks with one or more barbs or points. Sections of antler were carved into splitting wedges to work out long pieces of bone to form the dartlike projectiles of the spear-thrower. Sandstone polishers were added to the tool kit to sharpen and shape tips, needles, and other articles.

The stone burin

A spectacular item that developed by the end of the Paleolithic was the spear-thrower, a hand-held stick, of wood or antler, notched at one end. Functioning as an extension of the arm, it added considerable kinetic energy, and therefore range, to a short spear tipped with flint or bone. The tipped projectile represented still another innovation, for it was the first hafted implement.

Hafting, or the fitting of a handle to a cutting edge, was a momentous and far-reaching invention of about 35,000 years ago. It was a critical step toward the creation of new tools and improved models of old ones. In its simplest form, the haft may have been no more than a grass or leaf bundle whose limited function was to protect the hand when a fractured stone was used as a knife. Mechanically, the handle became a force-transmitting intermediary between the source of the force and the toolhead. An extension of the arms, the handle provided an increased radius of swing. This moved the toolhead faster to give it more kinetic energy for a harder and more telling blow than the arms alone could provide. A man using a hand-held axhead could cut only small trees, whereas with a hafted ax he could fell a tree of almost any size.

The prepared-core technique that provided preshaped flakes was refined and extended to provide preshaped blades, long, slender pieces of flint of trapezoidal cross section, each corner having a straight cutting edge without the serrations of a chipped tool. This is known as the blade-tool industry, a final complement to the core- and flake-tool technologies. Such blades made thin and splendid knives of great variety; many of these knives were backed; that is, the back of the blade was blunted for safer handling. Thin blades were further reduced to smaller pieces, often having a geometric form such as triangular, square, or trapezoidal, called microliths. These small bits of sharp flint were cemented (using resin) into a groove in a piece of wood to form a tool with a cutting edge longer than it was feasible to produce in a single piece of brittle flint; examples are a spear with a long cutting edge or the farmer's sickle of later date.

The first bows

The second major mechanical invention of the Upper Paleolithic was the bow, a device even more effective than the spear-thrower for increasing the distance between the hunter and the hunted. It is difficult to date precisely, for the only evidence of its use is found in cave paintings. Mere finds of stone points without bows prove nothing because such tips were used on the projectiles of spear-throwers. The earliest representations of the bow come from North Africa from 30,000 to 15,000 BC. Once the bow had been devised, it spread with astonishing rapidity, its effectiveness making it the weapon par excellence. When the bow was pulled, it stored the gradually expended energy of the archer's muscles; this energy was suddenly released to give the projectile a "muzzle velocity" far higher than that possible from a spear-thrower and of superior accuracy. It was a principal weapon through the 15th century AD and was ousted then only by gunpowder.

NEOLITHIC TOOLS

The Neolithic Period, or New Stone Age, the age of the ground tool, is defined by the advent around 7000 BC of ground and polished celts (ax and adz heads) as well as similarly treated chisels and gouges, often made of such stones as jadeite, diorite, or schist, all harder than flint. A ground tool is one that was chipped to rough shape in the old manner and then rubbed on or with a coarse abrasive stone to remove the chip scars either from the entire surface or around the working edge (see Figure 2A). Polishing was a last step, a final grinding with fine abrasive. That such a tool is pleasing to the eye is incidental; the real worth of the smoothing lay in the even cutting edge, superior strength, and better handling. The new ax would sink deeper for a given blow while delivering a clean and broad cut; its smooth bit, more shock resistant than the former flaked edge, had less tendency to wedge in a cut.

Although the polished stone tool is the index to the Neolithic Period, it may be noted that the ice sheets were receding and climatic conditions were assisting the conversion of hunters into herdsmen. The new, relatively sedentary life spawned further inventions, such as pottery. From the standpoint of tools, the potter's kiln and art were necessary steps to metals, for a modification of the kiln probably provided the high temperatures and equip-

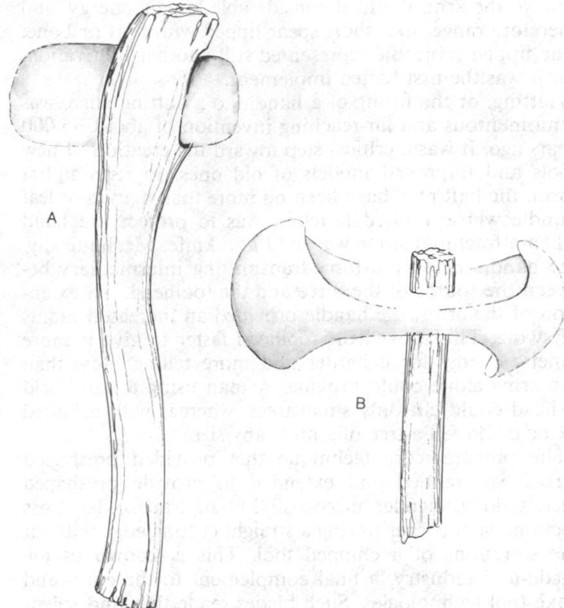

Figure 2: *Neolithic tools.*
(A) Stone ax, a ground tool, made by chipping to rough shape, then rubbing to give a nonserrated edge. (B) Stone ax made by pecking, a technique involving light, rapid blows followed by grinding.

ment needed for metalworking, first for melting native metals and later for the smelting process that gave rise to a wealth of metals, several of which proved to be superior materials for tools.

The ax in land clearance

The polished Neolithic ax, a heavy implement, was in sharp contrast to the delicate small-stone work of the last stages of the Paleolithic Period and was a reversal of the traditions of products that had yielded ever more lineal feet of cutting edge per pound of stone. The ax and its companion adz met the need to clear land as agriculture developed. An efficient tree-cutting tool was indispensable for the slash-and-burn agriculture then devised. Trees were either cut down or killed by ringing them with an ax; the debris was burned over, with the ashes conferring a slight enrichment of the stump-filled field. The earth was next scarified with sticks or stone-headed hoes resembling the adz to prepare it for seeding among the stumps. Without manuring or other treatment, the land was exhausted after a few years, necessitating a repetition of the clearing process elsewhere. The consequence was a shifting settlement pattern, with a good ax needed not only for felling trees but also for working timber for settlement.

Wood began its broad role in human life with the ground and polished tools of the Neolithic. Home and fire, furniture and utensils, cradle and coffin were products of the ax, adz, and chisel, which could fashion wood intricately and with precision. This kit of tools turned wood into an almost universal building material, for a host of new things was now possible, such as dugout canoes of oak, paddles and framing for hide-covered boats, sledges, skis, wooden platters and ladles, as well as other household gear. Mortise and tenon joints were invented for the structural framing of substantial habitations. Some of the gabled houses were up to 100 feet (30 metres) long and 20 wide and are believed to have served as both granaries and living quarters for perhaps 20 people comprising several families.

In a revealing experiment, 4,000-year-old polished stone axes, furnished by the Danish National Museum and carrying the sharpness left after their last use 4,000 years ago, were fitted with ash handles modeled after that of a Neolithic hafted ax preserved in a bog, giving the ax an overall length of nearly 25 inches (63 centimetres). (A modern steel felling ax has a 36-inch handle.) When these were used in a Danish forest, it was soon found that the violent action of the modern technique of swinging a steel ax and putting shoulder and weight behind the blade to give long and powerful blows was disastrous, either ruining the edge or breaking the blade. Proper handling meant short, quick strokes that chipped at the tree, the body action being constrained to mainly elbow and wrist motion. After getting into form, the men found it possible to fell an oak tree of more than one foot (0.3 metre) in diameter in half an hour or a pine, two feet in diameter, in less than 20 minutes. Six hundred square yards (one-eighth acre, or 0.05 hectare) of silver birch forest were cleared by three men in four hours. One axhead cut down more than 100 trees on its original (old) sharpening. It was concluded that Neolithic men and their ground flint axes had no great difficulties in making large clearings in the forest for the purposes of cultivation. It may also be remarked that it was less trouble to clear the forest than to break the age-old and tough sod of the plains.

Flint mining

The Neolithic farmer of northern Europe, with his practice of deforestation for agriculture, was completely dependent upon polished axes. This created a heavy demand for good stone that depleted local sources and resulted in flint mining in well-endowed locations in what are now England, Belgium, The Netherlands, France, Denmark, Sweden, Poland, Portugal, Sicily, and Egypt. Often more than just mining, these operations were ax factories where flints were shaped into rough form by chipping at the pithead and then traded. Grinding and polishing were done by the consumer.

An idea of the magnitude of such a mining enterprise is offered by the well-explored workings known as Grimes Graves, about 80 miles (130 kilometres) northeast of London. The site covers about 34 acres (14 hectares) and includes both opencast workings and 40-feet-deep shafts with radiating galleries that exploited the flint deposit laid down as a floor under chalk beds. Excavation was probably by wooden shovel (a product of the polished ax and chisel) or possibly the shoulder blades of oxen. It is estimated that 50,000 picks made of red-deer antler were used during the 600 years of activity in the mine, which began about 2300 BC.

A last innovation of the Neolithic was the augmentation of the two older techniques of working stone, chipping (or flaking) and grinding, by a third, the pecking, or crumbling, method (Figure 2B). In this procedure a point of the stone being worked was bruised by a hard hammerstone, the struck points crumbling into powder under relatively light but rapidly delivered blows. This technique allowed the manufacture of tools from numerous varieties of appropriate but nonflaking stone and the production of hollow ware, such as querns for grinding grain, mortars, and bowls. It also could be applied to flakable stone; such a stone, after having been roughed out by flaking, was pecked to level the ridges between flake scars before grinding and polishing.

Stone tools maintained themselves during the Metal Age, yielding only slowly to the new material, which was expensive and the product of special skills. The copper and bronze tools and weapons for hunting, warfare, husbandry, and domestic use that constitute impressive displays in museums were rare luxuries. Even the much more abundant iron, which overtook and replaced copper and bronze articles, was available only sparingly for many centuries.

EARLY METALS AND SMELTING

The discovery that certain heavy "stones" did not respond to hammerblows by flaking or fracturing but were instead soft and remained intact as their shapes changed marked the end of the long Stone Age. Of the pure, or native, metals, gold and silver seem to have attracted attention at an early date, but both were too soft for tools. The first metals of value for toolmaking were natural copper and meteoric iron. Although they were scarce, they were tough and potentially versatile materials that were suited for new purposes, as well as many of the old. They also introduced a new problem, corrosion.

Metalworking. Copper occurs in native state in many parts of the world, sometimes in nuggets or lumps of convenient size. It is malleable; that is, it can be shaped by hammering while cold. This also hardens copper and allows it to carry a sharp edge, the hammered edge being capable of further improvement on an abrasive stone. After a certain amount of hammering (cold-working), copper becomes brittle, a condition that can be removed as often as necessary by heating the material and plunging it into cold water (quenching). The softening operation is known as annealing, and repeated annealings are necessary if much hammering is required for shaping.

Among early toolmakers, nuggets of copper were hammered into sheets, divided into strips, and then separated into pieces to be worked into arrowheads, knives, awls, choppers, and the like. Copper was also shaped by beating pieces of the soft metal into appropriately shaped stone cavities (molds).

Use of meteoric iron

Meteoric iron, widely distributed but not in heavy deposits, was a highly prized material more difficult to fabricate than the softer copper. Its celestial origin was recognized by the ancients, for the Egyptians called it black copper from heaven, and the Sumerians denoted it by two characters representing heaven and fire.

Like copper, iron hardens under the hammer and will then take a superior edge. Iron can be annealed, but the process is quite different from that of copper because, with iron, slow cooling from a high temperature is necessary. Meteoric iron is practically carbonless and, hence, cannot be hardened in the manner of steel; a high nickel content of about 8 percent makes it relatively corrosion resistant.

For early toolmakers, small meteorites were the most convenient sources of iron, but larger bodies were hacked at with copper and stone tools to yield tool-sized pieces for knives, spear points, arrowpoints, axheads, and other implements. Meteoric iron was beaten into tools in much the same way as copper, although it could not be forced into a mold in the manner of the softer metal. Much rarer than copper, meteoric iron also was often used for jewelry, attested to by burial finds of necklaces of iron and gold beads, iron rings along with gold rings, and ornaments in sheet form.

Casting. In casting, a liquid metal is poured into a cavity or a mold, where it takes the shape of the mold when it congeals; casting shapes the metal to essentially final form once a proper cavity has been prepared. Some touch-up work may be needed; for an edged copper tool, such as an ax or knife for example, hammering the cutting side gives a keen edge.

A great step forward was made with the discovery that gold, silver, and copper could be melted and cast with many advantages. Casting meant that the size of the tool was no longer dependent on the size of a chunk of available copper. Old tools could be added to a melt instead of being thrown out. This reuse of old metal accounts in part for the scarcity of virgin-copper implements.

To make the procedures of melting and casting possible, several innovations were required. Pottery making, already well established, provided the knowledge of heat-based processes. Clay vessels were essential to working with fluid metal, for, in all but the most primitive operations, it was necessary to convey the melt from furnace to mold. Aside from providing crucibles, pottery making taught how to restructure a fire with a deep bed of prepared charcoal to provide a heat superior to that of a simple campfire. Tongs of some sort had to be devised to carry the hot crucible; it is surmised that green branches were bent around the pot and replaced as needed.

Molds

A number of forms of molds were developed. The most primitive was simply an impression of a stone tool in clay or sand to give a cavity of the desired form. A more durable mold resulted when the cavity was worked into stone. Cavities of uniform depth allowed flat but profiled pieces to be cast. For example, some ax blade castings were roughly T-shaped, the arms of the T being afterward bent around to clasp a handle of some sort, with the bottom of the T becoming the cutting edge. A one-piece mold, prepared for a dagger, could have a groove for most of the length of the cavity to provide a stiffening rib on one side. With experience, closed but longitudinally split and, hence, two-piece molds were devised, each side having a groove down the middle to furnish a strengthening rib on both sides of the blade.

Split molds for copper were not desirable because pure copper is a poor metal for casting. It contracts a good deal on cooling and has a tendency to absorb gases and thereby become porous, blistered, and weak. Also, molten copper exposed to atmospheric oxygen contains embrittling cuprous oxide.

Smelting. Perhaps 1,000 years after humans learned about melting virgin copper, they found that still another stone, a brittle one directly useless for tools, would produce liquid copper if sufficiently heated while in contact with charcoal. This step was epoch making, for it was the discovery of smelting, or the separation of a metal from a chemical compound called ore. Smelting, as differentiated from melting, was the first metallurgical operation and is still the principal method of gaining metals from their ores. Copper was the first metal to be smelted; it was another 1,000 years before iron was reduced from its ores.

As mined, raw ore is a nonchemical mixture of ore proper (heavy) and earthy matter, or gangue (light); the two may be largely separated by crushing the raw ore and washing away the lighter gangue. The ore proper is a chemical compound of oxides, sulfides, carbonates, hydrates, silicates, and small amounts of impurities such as arsenic and other elements. Smelting frees the metal from the various combinations with which it is bound into the compound form. A preparatory step is to heat the washed ore (roasting, or dressing) not only to dry it but also to burn off sulfides and organic matter. Early practice involved heating the ore in intimate contact with charcoal to provide the essential reducing atmosphere, producing a metallic sponge made up of metal and slag. For chemical as well as practical reasons, the iron of tools, wrought iron, continued to be worked out of the spongy mass until the Middle Ages.

Originally copper smelting was terminated at the spongy stage. Early smelters soon discovered that better results were obtained when the metallic sponge was left in the furnace and subjected to draft-induced high temperatures. The metal became liquid and seeped down to the hearth, as did the slag, which, being lighter than the metal, floated over it, permitting recovery of the copper.

At some time during the copper period, a new kind of "copper" happened to be made by smelting together two separate ores, one bearing copper, the other tin. The resulting metal was recognized as being far more useful than copper alone, and the short period of copper tools came to an end. The new metal, a copper–tin alloy of mostly copper, was bronze. It was produced in the fluid state at a temperature less than that needed for copper, could be formed economically by casting, and could be hammer-hardened more than copper. The tin noticeably increased the liquidity of the melt, checked the absorption of oxygen and other gases, and suppressed the formation of cuprous oxide, all features that facilitated the casting operation. A two-piece, or split, mold, impracticable for copper, worked very well with bronze. Furthermore, it was found that bronze expanded just a bit before solidifying and thus picked up the detail of a mold before it contracted in cooling.

Dawn of the Bronze Age

The earliest bronzes were of uneven composition. Later, the tin content was controlled at about 10 percent, a little less for hammered goods, a little more for ornamental castings. The edges of hammered bronze tools of this composition were more than twice as hard as those obtained from copper.

The Bronze Age of tools and implements began about 3000 BC. In the course of the following 2,000 years the much more abundant iron supplanted bronze for tools, but bronze continued to be used in the arts.

All of the early metals were expensive commodities in antiquity and were monopolized by kings, priests, and officials. Most metal was diverted to the manufacture of weapons for professional soldiers. Industrial use was severely limited. The metal chisel was used on stone for buildings of state or for fashioning furniture for the wealthy; the common man living in a mud or reed hut had no reason to own such a tool.

Generally speaking, molds for copper and bronze were of baked clay, although soft stone was sometimes carved; metal molds are known from about 1000 BC. Sectional molds of three and four pieces, permitting more complex castings, are known from about 2600 BC. The earliest metal tools and implements were simply copies of existing stone models. It was only slowly that the plasticity of the new medium and especially the possibilities inherent in casting were appreciated. The stone dagger, for example, was necessarily short because of its extreme brittleness. With copper and then bronze, it became longer and was adapted to slashing as well as to stabbing. Casting allowed forms that were impossible to execute in flaked stone, such as deeply concave surfaces. Holes could be cast in, rather than worked out of, the solid.

Pottery imitations of bronze

Sometimes the process was reversed. There were, for example, pottery imitations of bronze vessels for the poorer classes, with such necessary adjustments as a heavier lip for the pottery jug. The lines of bronze daggers have been noted in stone daggers of a later date, despite the difficulty of imitating a metal object in stone. Bronze axheads were copied in stone, even to the shaft hole, which was difficult to produce and impractical for a stone tool; it is possible that some of the stone replicas of bronze daggers and axes were used for ceremonial rather than utilitarian purposes.

Malleable metal had several advantages over a brittle material, such as stone or bone or antler. It could be severely deformed without breaking and, if badly bent, could probably be returned to service after straightening. It was shock resistant and chip-proof, good qualities for use in the ax, adz, and chisel, and the edges could be kept keen by hammering or abrasion; its sharpness was, however, inferior to that of good stone. In particular, metal allowed the fashioning of many small items, articles of a size awkward to make of bone or horn, such as pins, fishhooks, and awls. Copper pins were stronger, tidier, and more attractive than the fish bones and thorns they replaced for securing clothing; even in the 3rd century BC there were shapes resembling the modern safety pin. Tweezers were invented, but whether for depilatory or surgical purpose is unknown; there are artifacts presumed to be scalpels. Plates, nails, and rivets also developed early.

The most common tools were awls and pointed instruments suitable only for wood and leather. Woodworking was facilitated by the invention of the toothed copper saw, made of smelted metal and cast to shape. Edged tools—the ax, adz, and chisel, at first similar to stone models—became predominant, and, although not nearly as sharp as the tools they replaced, they had the advantage of toughness and could easily be resharpened. In particular, the chisel made it possible to use cut stone for construction purposes, principally in temples and monuments. Abrasive sand under metal "saw blades" allowed stone to be cut neatly, just as the sand under tubes (made from rolled-up strips) that were turned provided a boring device for larger holes.

IRON AND STEEL TOOLS

Iron technology was derived from the known art of reducing copper and bronze. The principal requirement was a furnace capable of maintaining a reducing atmosphere—*i.e.,* one in which a high temperature could be maintained from a good draft of air. The furnace had to be tall enough to allow the iron to drop from the smelting zone and form a slaggy lump, usually called a bloom.

After aluminum, iron is the most abundant metal, constituting about 5 percent of the Earth's crust. Copper is in short supply, having a presence of only 0.01 percent. Iron ore suitable for simple smelting was widely distributed in the form of surface deposits that could be scraped up without elaborate mining procedures.

The limitations imposed by the dearth of metals in the Bronze Age were now lifted; new tools and implements became possible, and their numbers could increase until even the poorer classes would have access to metal tools. The iron of antiquity was wrought iron, a malleable and weldable material whose toughness was enhanced by forging. Brittle cast iron, versatile and widely used in modern industry, was unknown to the ancients, and it would have been of no value for their edged tools and implements. The earliest history of smelted iron is obscure, with the first scanty evidence of man-made iron dating from about 2500 BC in the Middle East. A thousand years later, the abundance of ores led to the displacement of copper and bronze by iron in the Hittite Empire.

During most of its history, iron was not recovered in a molten state but was reduced to a spongy aggregate of iron and slag formed at a temperature well below the melting point of pure iron (1,535° C, or 2,795° F). This plastic metallic sponge was consolidated by hammering to squeeze out slag and weld the iron particles into a compact and ductile mass; thus it was called wrought iron, essentially pure iron with remnants of unexpelled slag coating the iron particles. Wrought iron contains so little carbon that it does not harden usefully when cooled rapidly (quenched). When iron containing 0.4 to 1.25 percent carbon is heated to 950° C, or 1,740° F, and then plunged into water or oil, it is hardened.

Iron importance in the Middle East

By about 1200 BC, when iron had become important in the Middle East, humans had learned how to create on wrought iron a steel surface, or case, that could be hardened by heating and quenching. This case was produced by the prolonged heating of wrought iron packed in a deep bed of glowing charcoal. The procedure worked because a surface of red-hot carbonless iron readily absorbs carbon from the carbon monoxide generated in the enveloping charcoal fire.

Knowledge of casting gathered from working with smelted copper and bronze did not apply to a metal whose shape could be changed only by hammering. Moreover, the malleability of iron is less than that of copper for the same temperatures, which means that the smith has to work harder to change the shape of the metal. Stone hammers gave way to hafted bronze hammers, iron itself coming into use later. The first anvils—for copper and bronze—were convenient flat stones; they were followed by increasingly larger cast-bronze models that in turn were superseded by rudimentary forms of the modern type, in which several pieces of iron are welded together. The earliest iron artifacts are of ruder appearance than the bronze articles that came before them.

A valuable property of wrought iron is the ease with which two or more pieces may be united by hammering while the metal is at a high temperature. Even at the production stage, small pieces of spongy iron were united into larger blooms. Hammer welding had been practiced before by goldsmiths and, in spite of the difficulties due to gassing, was even used for joining copper to make, for example, tape by welding together strips cut from plate. Welding became an essential production procedure. When iron tools had reached the end of a useful life, they could be reused by welding the scrap into a blank and starting over, a process akin to the melting of copper and bronze scrap to cast new tools.

Iron compared to bronze

Iron ordinarily has twice the flexibility of bronze and is much tougher, for a bar of iron can be bent back upon itself without fracturing, whereas a bronze bar (such as a sword blade) breaks after only a light bend (bronze blades repaired by casting new metals into the fractured sections are known). Bronze, in other words, is brittle when compared to iron, although copper is not. As the tin content of bronze rises, hardness increases, but ductility is lost. Most of the malleability is missing from cold bronze with 5 percent tin, and ductility becomes practically nil at a 20 percent tin content. The cutting edge of a hammered bronze tool is superior to that of a similarly treated iron tool, and it is corrosion resistant.

In the Early Iron Age, when the metal was still in scarce supply, local armament makers were the chief consumers of the new metal. Agricultural tools, needed for clearing forests and for cultivation, were the next iron tools to develop. Axes, picks, and hoes also were needed. Iron was smelted in the Middle East before 2500 BC, but the Iron Age proper was 1,000 or more years in maturing. Its full development came with the discovery of hardening by carburization (addition of carbon) and heat treating, which led to superior edged tools of great toughness.

Later development of hand tools

During the evolution of tools over more than 2,000,000 years, using as principal materials, successively, stone, bronze, and iron, humans developed a number of particular tools. Taken together, these specialized tools form an inverted pyramid resting upon the first general-purpose tool, the nearly formless chopper. With the discovery of metals and the support of numerous inventions allowing their exploitation, the first approximations to the modern forms of the basic tools of the craftsman established themselves, with the main thrust of further development directed at improving the cutting edges.

The need for specialized tools

The earliest tools were multipurpose; specialized tools were latecomers. A multipurpose tool, although able to do a number of things, does none of them as well as a tool designed or proportioned for one job and one material. The way in which a tool is hafted provides the primary distinction between the knife, ax, saw, and plane. An application or craft is best served by a further specialization or form within a category: the knives of the butcher, woodcarver, and barber reflect their particular tasks. When confronted with the unusual, a skilled craftsman develops a special tool to cope with the situation. In the early 19th century, for example, a joiner had dozens of planes in his kit to deal with the many moldings, rabbets, and jointings he had to produce before the day of machine-made stock and mill-planed lumber.

PERCUSSIVE TOOLS

Several tools involve a violent propulsion to deliver a telling blow. These have been named percussive tools, and their principal representatives are the ax and hammer. Under these two names are found an immense number of variations. The percussive group may also be called dynamic because of the swift motion and the large, short-term forces they develop. This means that mass and velocity and, hence, kinetic energy and momentum are factors related to the force generated or transmitted. The distribution of weight between the head and handle and the mechanical properties of the head (*i.e.,* its suitability for a cutting edge or its lack of elasticity) must also be recognized in the design of a percussive tool. Obviously, these various influences were not formally considered during the agelong trial-and-error evolution of a now successful tool, but recognition of them aids in identifying the evolutionary stages of the tool.

Percussive tools generally have handles that allow them to be swung; that is, their rapid motion endows them with kinetic energy. The attainable energy of a blow depends upon a number of factors, including the weight of the toolhead, the angle through which it is swung while gaining speed, the radius of the swing (handle length plus part or all of the arm length), and the muscle behind it all. There is a permissible energy level for a given task and tool, set by either the nature of the task or the material of the tool. Thus, a blacksmith flattening a one-inch iron bar needs a heavy, fairly long-handled hammer, whereas a light and short-handled hammer, used with wrist action, is appropriate for forging a small, soft gold wire. A hafted flint ax is an effective tool, but it may be destroyed if swung too hard or if twisted while in the cut. Bronze and steel axes can, and do, take longer handles than the stone ax and, being of tougher material, will not break under use that would fracture a stone head.

The physics of percussive tools takes into consideration the centre of gravity and what is technically called the centre of percussion—*i.e.,* a unique point associated with a rotation, in this case the arc through which the tool is swung before delivering its blow and coming to rest. The tool's centre of gravity is readily found because it is the balance point, or location along the handle at which the tool can be picked up loosely and still remain in the horizontal position. The centre of percussion is the ideal point at which striking should occur on the toolhead to minimize the sting of the handle in the operator's hand as well as to deliver a blow with maximum force; this point is farther out than the centre of gravity and should be as close to the centre of the head as possible. This last condition is best met with a light handle and heavy toolhead, which places the centre of gravity close to the head and the centre of percussion in an optimum location in the cutting edge.

Centre of percussion

It is apparent that the sheer weight of the head is of paramount importance in promoting a proper balance, or hang, to the tool. On this basis alone, the shift from stone axheads to metal was a step in the proper direction because metal heads of the same size as those of stone are about three times as heavy. With the heavier head, the centre of gravity of the hafted tool is closer to the head, and the centre of percussion is more likely to be properly located.

With the mallet and chisel still other interrelations are involved. When working stone, a brittle material that responds to a sharp tool point by breaking into small chips, the sculptor strikes many light blows to remove material. As a consequence, mallets have short handles and the amplitude of swing is small, allowing a succession of rapid blows without undue fatigue. To provide energy and momentum, the mallet head is heavy. Being of wood, it does not rebound in the manner of a metal head but stays on the chisel, which transmits the blow to the cutting edge and focuses it into a small area of stone to be spalled off. The net effect of the proper combination of all elements—the properties of wood, chisel, and stone, the weight of the head (perhaps even heightened by a lead-filled cavity), and the short handle—is to waste the least energy. The wooden head is of course expendable, particularly if it is of a one-piece clublike construction, for it becomes badly battered from contact with the metal chisel. A more refined mallet consists of a separate head and handle, the head having a working face of end-grain wood.

Working metal with a chisel requires that heavy blows be struck to enable the chisel to dig into the metal and lift out a chip. A steel hammer with a hardened face is used, and in this operation it is the soft end of the chisel that is battered and needs periodic dressing.

Hammers and hammer-like tools. "Hammer" is used here in a general sense to cover the wide variety of striking tools distinguished by other names, such as pounder, beetle, mallet, maul, pestle, sledge, and others. The best known of the tools that go by the name hammer is the carpenter's claw type, but there are many others, such as riveting, boilermaker's, bricklayer's, blacksmith's, machinist's ball peen and cross peen, stone (or spalling), prospecting, and tack hammers. Each has a particular reason for its form. Such specialization was evident under the Romans, and a craftsman of the Middle Ages wrote in AD 1100 of hammers having "large, medium and small" weight, with further variations of "long and slender" being coupled with a variety of faces.

Since a pounder, or hammerstone, was the first tool to be used, it may also have been the first to be fitted with a handle to increase the blow. Although some craftsmen of the soft metals still favoured the hand-held stone, presumably for its better "feel," hafting was an enormous technological advance. Yet it created a problem of major proportions that still persists—the joint between the handle and the head must carry shock loads of high intensity, a situation even more complicated with the ax than the hammer because the ax may be subjected to twisting on becoming wedged in a cut. The most satisfactory solution for metal heads is to create a shaft hole in the toolhead; it is a poor solution for a stone tool because it weakens the head, although it was tried, especially in stone imitations of bronze axheads.

The hafting problem in percussive tools

In hammer hafting, it is possible to distinguish between long handles that allow tools to be swung to give them speed and those simpler handles by which a tool such as a pavement tamper may be picked up so that it can be dropped. A long handle, even if not needed for dynamic effect (as in a tool used only for light blows), makes the tool easier to control and generally reduces operator fatigue.

The oldest form of hafted hammer, probably the miner's maul of Neolithic date, had a conical or ovoid stone head with a circumferential groove at midheight; many such rilled stones have been found in flint, copper, and salt mines and elsewhere, though very few handles have survived. Such a stone could be bound to a short section of sapling with a branch coming off at an angle, twisted fibres or sinew serving as the ties (Figure 3A). With such a side-mounted head it is likely that the handle's principal

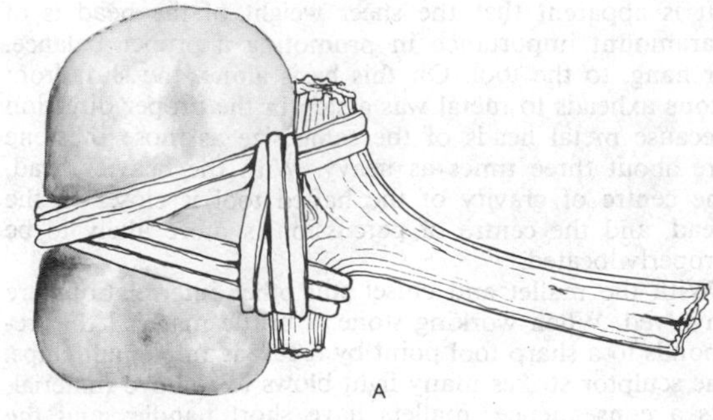

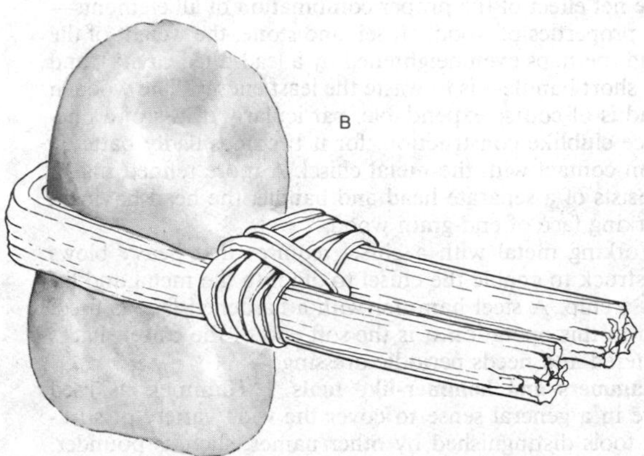

Figure 3: *Hafted hammers.*
(A) Hammer of rilled stone bound onto a knee-shaft handle, a device that was most satisfactory when merely lifted and dropped. (B) Hammer bound into a bent branch; used when the work required a heavier swing.

function was to lift and guide the head so that it might do its work by simply dropping, the binding being too weak to carry much of the extra shock produced by swinging the tool. Better shock resistance could be attained by bending a long flexible branch around the groove in the stone and securing it with lashings (Figure 3B).

Hammers and pounders of material other than stone were widely used; essentially clublike, they may be called self-handled. Clubs of hardwood might have one end thinned for grasping, or a mallet-like tool could be made from a short section of log with a projecting branch to serve as a handle. Similar mallets were made by piercing a short piece of wood and fitting a handle to it; this also gave an end-grain strike and made it more durable than a simple club. Antlers modified by trimming off tines are known from the Paleolithic Period. Such "soft" hammers were used for striking chisels of stone to prevent the destruction of the more valuable tool. Such tools, especially the wooden mallet, were used on metal chisels as well, particularly by stonecutters, because a very heavy blow on a light tool does not necessarily remove more stone than a moderate blow. There is a good deal of evidence that bone, antler, and flint wedges were used to split wood; here the use of a soft hammer would have been imperative.

The hammer as it is best known today—*i.e.,* as a tool for nailing, riveting, and smithing—originated in the Metal Age with the inventions of nails, rivets, and jewelry. For beating lumps of metal into strips and sheet, heavy and compact hammers with flat faces were needed. These, in lighter form, were suited to riveting and driving nails and wooden pegs.

In the beginning, hafting of metal hammers followed the stone-tool tradition. The first step away from lashing came with casting a socket opposite the head into which the short end of an L-shaped wooden handle was fitted and further supported by lashings. Such a tool was necessarily light. Ultimately the idea of piercing the head with a shaft hole for a handle occurred to the Europeans in the Iron Age. This was several hundred years after it had become common practice among the bronze workers of the Middle East. The shaft hole, although posing fastening problems that still exist, allowed heavy hammers—mauls and sledges—to be made for smithing iron.

Shaft holes for handles

The familiar claw hammer that can pull bent nails dates from Roman times in a well-proportioned form, for the expensive handmade nails of square or rectangular cross section did not drive easily. Aside from the claw hammer, other special forms of the peen—the end opposite the flat face—were developed. Hemispherical, round-edged, and wedgelike shapes helped the metalworker stretch and bend metal or the mason to chip or break stone or bricks. An especially important hammer was the filemaker's; equipped with two chisel-like heads, it was used to score flat pieces of iron (file blanks) that were subsequently hardened by heating and quenching.

Ax and adz. The ax and adz are similar enough to be considered together. This is especially the case with ancient tools that were small and ineffective because they were made of brittle stone or had unsatisfactory hafting. The difference between the tools lies in the relation of the cutting edge to the handle. In the ax the cutting edge and handle are parallel, whereas in the adz they stand at right angles. The ax and some adzes chop diagonally across the grain of the wood, but the developed adz, with its long handle, cuts with the grain, and the nature of the chips is quite different. The ax is used for felling or cutting through, whereas the adz is used for smoothing and leveling, although some forms were developed to scoop out gutters or to dig out logs to make canoes. The adz was often shorter handled than the ax and, because of this, was essentially a chipping tool rather than the shaving tool it became when the handle was lengthened. The great problem of both tools is satisfactory hafting; the shock impact between the toolhead and handle threatens any type of connection, however ingenious.

The celt, a smooth chisel-shaped toolhead that formed either an ax or adz, dates from the invention of agriculture and the domestication of animals. The earliest true axheads, made of fine-grained rock with ground edges, are of Swedish provenance and date from about 6000 BC. Even earlier, self-handled axes, made of reindeer antler, were used. The brow tine, an antler branch running nearly at right angles to the main stem (beam), was sharpened, giving a small ax (Figure 4A) with a haft of about eight inches (20 centimetres). By sharpening the tine the other way, a tiny adz was created. Some of these small bone implements have survived as the Lyngby tools, named from a Danish site of perhaps 8000 BC.

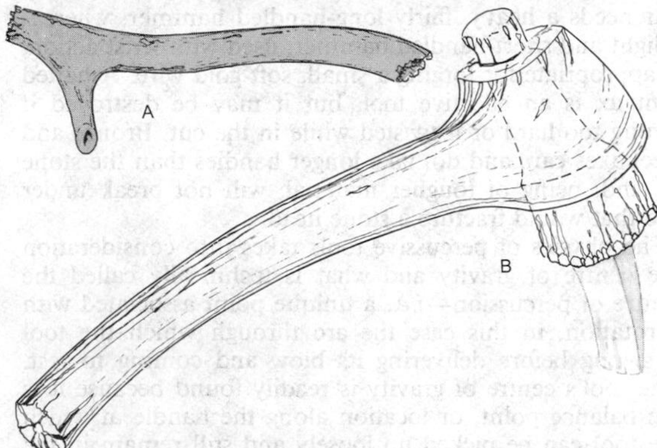

Figure 4: *Ax and adz.*
(A) Lyngby ax, a self-handled ax made from a reindeer antler. (B) Stone adz head with a socket of antler inserted in a wooden haft.

A subsequent design socketed a stone blade in a short length of antler that was perforated for a handle (Figure 4B). This Maglemosian style, from a Danish site of about 6000 BC, was a popular model for several thousand years despite its narrow cutting edge and length of about 20 inches.

The desire for a better feel or a longer cutting edge, or perhaps the shortage of antlers, led to a great variety of haftings. A common arrangement involved lashing heavy celts to knee-shaft handles made from branched tree sections (see Figure 3A). To permit the use of larger celts, the stone was sometimes fitted into a wooden handle, but this created the danger that the handle would fail due to the weakening hole. Heavy, clublike handles with ample strength at the hole gave the tool an unfavourable balance.

Surviving examples of celts of soft stone are believed to have been restricted to nonwoodworking axes, used for killing game or perhaps for certain ritual purposes. Hardstone axes with shaft holes, often obvious imitations of bronze axes, are associated with the Bronze Age. They are among the supreme examples of stoneworking and are products of the pecking technique. From their delicacy it may be inferred that these axes were not for the working of wood.

An Egyptian relief of about 2500 BC, the time at which the pyramids were being built, shows a metal ax (copper or bronze) of curious shape, almost semicircular, lashed to a wooden handle along its diameter. The same picture shows a knee-shaft adz whose metal blade makes an angle of about 30° with the handle. If the number of pictures and artifacts of the adz is a guide, the adz was more widely used than the ax. Generally speaking, the adz had a short handle, with angles of the order of 60° between blade and handle. Although the Egyptians became skilled metalworkers, this was not reflected in their tools, the designs of which hardly changed over 2,000 years.

On the other hand, bronze axes and adzes from Mesopotamia of even the period 2700 BC are shaft-hole types, the hole for the handle being formed in the mold. Aside from eliminating the nuisance of lashing the blades, these castings permitted a heavier head than the thin-bladed Egyptian models and had better dynamic characteristics.

Shaft-hole axes and adzes were also being cast in Crete in about 2000 BC. At the same time, a new tool was created there. The double-bit (two-bladed) ax, classically associated with the Minoans, was first known in 2500 BC as a votive ax, a piece of tomb furniture made of riveted bronze plates. It became a working tool when it was cast in bronze with a shaft hole about 500 years later. Double-bit adzes also date from this time, as do ax–adz combinations. The succeeding Mycenaean, Greek, and Roman civilizations carried these designs forward. According to Homer, Ulysses used a double-bit ax of a type that disappeared with the use of bronze. Illustrations or artifacts from the Middle Ages reveal only iron single-bit types, although in a bewildering variety of profiles. By mid-19th century the double-bit was again in use, principally in the United States as a lumberman's ax. The ax was also used in Canada and Australia, where it is still marketed.

The ax of Ulysses

In western Europe the advent of metal was about 500 years later than in the Middle East. In making the transition from stone to metal, Europeans continued the tradition of the knee-shaft handle. Another type of metal head was given a wide slot, by either forging or casting, into which a cleft knee-shaft was fitted and lashed. This was the palstave. To minimize splitting of the shaft, a stop was later cast at the bottom of the slot. Subsequently, one or two eyes, or loops, were furnished in the casting to allow firmer lashing.

The socketed head, perhaps carried over from the spearhead, was an improvement because the knee-shaft stub sat in a socket with greater security, although it still required lashing. Like its predecessors, this tool was small, almost toylike; the cutting edges of about 1½ inches and short handles suggested a one-handed operation. Adzes were similarly proportioned, as were hammers.

The Bronze Age smiths of Europe were slow in inventing the shaft hole that those of the Middle East had developed in an earlier millennium. The knee-shaft tradition, with its socketed head, entered even the Iron Age before shaft-hole tools appeared in Europe. To forge a socket is a difficult enough operation with even modern equipment. A shaft hole, however, is fairly simple to make, but such tools appeared in northern Europe well after the Iron Age was under way, perhaps after 500 BC. By this time, expensive bronze had been supplanted by plentiful iron for use in tools.

Bronze tools had been relatively delicate in design; their iron successors soon gained size and developed in character and effectiveness to display specialized forms. Of these, two are especially important. First, there was the felling ax of the woodcutter, the blade beveled on both sides for symmetry and often fitted with a flat end suited to driving splitting wedges. There were numerous variations of this form as the tool evolved toward its finely balanced modern conformation.

The iron ax had little advantage over its bronze forerunners until smiths discovered carburization and could produce a temperable steel along the cutting edge. This must have occurred early, for repeated heatings of the edge in forging would draw in small quantities of carbon from the charcoal of the fire. A number of Roman axes subjected to analysis have been found to contain steel.

Steeling the axhead

Steeling, or the welding of strips of steel to the iron head, was invented in the Middle Ages. The head was first rough-forged by bending a properly shaped piece of flat iron stock around an iron handle pattern to form the eye. Steeling could take one of two forms. In the first, a strip of steel was inserted between the overlapping ends and the whole welded into a unit (inserted steeling). For the second, the overlapping ends were welded together and drawn to a V-shape over which a V-shaped piece of steel was then welded (overcoat, or overlaid, steeling). Inserted steeling was regarded as superior because it furnished about three times as much steel to resist loss of metal by repeated grinding and sharpening. The manufacture of steeled, or two-piece, axes ended in the early 20th century. Thereafter heads were made of a single piece of high-carbon steel whose properly tempered edge was backed by a tough body.

To convert felled timber into squared timber, special tools were required. As the log lay on the ground or on low blocking, vertical sides were produced by using a broadax, or side ax. Somewhat shorter handled than the felling ax, it had a flat face, the single bevel being on the opposite or right side; it sliced diagonally downward as the carpenter moved backward along the log. The head was heavy, about twice that of a felling ax, and, although it was a two-handed tool, the broadax was never swung in the manner of a felling ax but, instead, was raised to waist height and allowed to fall with minimum added pressure. The handle was bent, or offset to the right, to give finger clearance when "hewing to the line" on a debarked log. A felling ax was used to score a line, after which the broadax was used to split off the wood along the score line. Hewn timber found in old buildings often carries the faint marks of the scoring.

If the timber was to be presented to view it was smoothed by an adz that removed the last of the score marks and left a type of ripple finish. For this purpose a long-handled adz was used, the radius of its gentle swing originating in the carpenter's shoulder. The blade was beveled on the inside and removed material in the same manner as does a plane.

The adz was once an indispensable tool of general utility. In addition to surfacing, it was particularly useful for trueing and otherwise leveling framework such as posts, beams, and rafters, in setting up the frames of wooden ships, and in dressing ships' planking. For special purposes the blade was round instead of flat, allowing the adz to cut hollows such as gutters. Dugout canoes, log coffins, and stock watering troughs, all cut from a whole log, were products of the adz. Short-handled adzes were used by coopers and makers of wooden bowls.

CUTTING, DRILLING, AND ABRADING TOOLS

Knife. The same jagged crest on the Paleolithic chopper that developed into the ax also developed into another broad tool category, the knife, which combined a uniquely shaped sharp blade with a handle that optimized the position of the cutting edge. In contrast to the blades of the ax, adz, chisel, or plane, the motion of a knife is a slicing action made in the direction of its edge.

The first hafting of stone knives may have taken the form of a protective pad of leaves or grass. Next, pieces of flint were set into grooves of wooden handles and cemented with resin or bitumen to leave the sharp cutting edges exposed. The Metal Age produced a longer and tougher blade that could be set into a handle, or riveted to a hand-grip. Some knives, such as surgical knives and razors, were cast with a handle (self-handled). Copper, bronze, and iron blades were hammered to produce a locally hard edge.

The knife handle

Aside from the utilitarian use of the knife in the field, kitchen, and workshop, variations giving it the status of a weapon appeared in the form of daggers and short and long swords. The stabbing dagger probably had its origin in the Neolithic Period, although an effectively thin and adequately strong blade did not appear until the Iron Age.

Hunting knives, equally useful as fighting knives, developed an overall style, proportion, and balance that changed little over the centuries after the introduction of iron. The first known folding knife is a Roman model of the 1st century AD. Beginning in the late Middle Ages many improvements in detail were introduced. These included fancy handles and springs and locks for the blade.

As individual crafts emerged, an impressive number of convenient but single-purpose knives were fashioned to suit the specialized tasks of various craftsmen, including goldbeaters, farriers, shoemakers, and farmers.

Drilling and boring tools. A varied terminology is related to making holes with revolving tools. A hole may be drilled or bored; awls, gimlets, and augers also produce holes. An awl is the simplest hole maker, for, like a needle, it simply pushes material to one side without removing it. Drills, gimlets, and augers, however, have cutting edges that detach material to leave a hole. A drilled hole is ordinarily small and usually made in metal; a bored hole is large and in wood or, if in metal, is usually made by enlarging a small hole. Drilling usually requires high speed and low torque (turning force), with little material being removed during each revolution of the tool. Low speed but high torque are characteristic of boring because the boring tool has a larger radius than a drill.

The Upper Paleolithic Period furnished the first perforated objects of shell, ivory, antler, bone, and tooth, although softer, perishable materials, such as leather and wood, were undoubtedly given holes by the use of bone or antler splinters. How holes were made in harder materials is subject to speculation; it has been suggested that flint blades were trimmed to sharp points by bilateral flaking and that these points were turned by hand, a very slow process. Another scheme involved the use of an abrasive sand under the end of a stick that was twirled back and forth between the palms. At some unknown time, more efficient rotation was attained by wrapping a thong around the stick or shaft and pulling on the ends of the thong. Such a strap, or thong, drill could be applied to drilling either with an abrasive or with a tool point hafted onto the end of the stick. The upper end of the shaft required a pad or socket (drill pad) in which it could rotate freely.

Invention of the bow drill

After the invention of the bow, sometime in the Upper Paleolithic Period, the ends of the thong were fastened to a bow, or a slack bowstring was wrapped around the shaft to create the bow drill. Because of its simplicity, it maintained itself in Europe in small shops until the 20th century and is still used in other parts of the world. Abrasive drilling in stone was well suited to the high-speed bow drill. For larger holes the amount of material that had to be reduced to powder led to the idea of using a tube, such as a rolled copper strip, instead of a solid cylinder. This is called a core drill because the abrasive trapped between rotating tube and stone grinds out a ring containing a core that can be removed.

A new and more complicated tool, the pump drill, was developed in Roman times. A crosspiece that could slide up and down the spindle was attached by cords that wound and unwound about it. Thus, a downward push on the crosspiece imparted a rotation to the spindle. A flywheel on the spindle kept the motion going, so that the cords rewound in reverse to raise the crosspiece as the drill slowed, and the next downward push brought the spindle into rotation in the opposite direction.

The earliest (perhaps Bronze Age) drill points had sharp edges that ultimately developed into arrow shapes with two distinct cutting edges. This shape was effective, especially when made of iron or steel, and remained popular until the end of the 19th century, when factory-made, spiral-fluted drills became available at reasonable cost to displace the blacksmith-made articles.

The basic auger originated in the Iron Age as a tool for enlarging existing holes. It had a crossbar so that it might be turned with two hands, and it resembled a pipe split lengthwise. The auger was sharpened in several ways: on the inside of the semicircular end, along the length, or on both. The end might be forged into a spoon shape and the edges sharpened so that cutting could take place at the bottom of the hole in addition to the sides. To clear the hole of parings it was necessary to pull the auger from its hole and turn the workpiece over. Augers with spiral or helical stems that brought the shavings or chips to the surface were an invention of the Middle Ages, although one example dates from Roman Britain.

The brace and breast swivel

The familiar and common brace, a crank with a breast swivel at one end and a drill point at the other, is first seen in a painting of about 1425 that shows the biblical Joseph at his bench. This brace and other early examples are shown fitted with a bit of small diameter. It has been suggested that the function of the new tool was to make a small, or pilot, hole for the larger auger bit. This is a reasonable assumption, for the crank, fashioned from a wide board, had insufficient strength (because of its cross grain) to drive a large bit (see Figure 5A). This weakness was later counteracted by reinforcing the two weak sections with metal plates, a practice that continued until about 1900 despite the commercial introduction of iron sweeps (cranks) in about 1860 (Figure 5B). This invention permitted the boring of holes of up to one inch in diameter with one-handed operation; larger holes still required two-handed augers. An iron sweep is noted in a German manuscript of 1505, and an English book of 1683 has a metal brace as part of a blacksmith's kit.

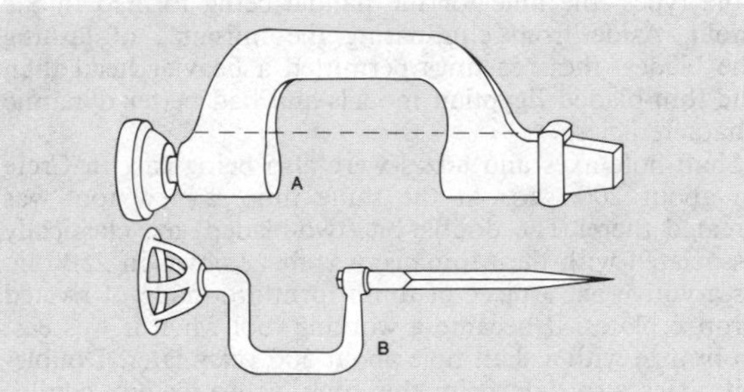

Figure 5: *Braces.*
(A) Early one-piece wooden brace showing weak sections (dotted lines). (B) All-metal blacksmith's "wimble" of late 17th century; the metal crank was not generally applied to the woodworker's brace until two centuries later.

Early wooden braces were equipped with a large socket into which bits with appropriate shanks could be fitted interchangeably. When the sweep came to be made of iron, bits were given square shanks that fit into simple split chucks (holders) and were secured with a thumbscrew. Soon the screwed shell chuck and ratchet was devised to set the standard for the modern tool. By 1900 the swivel turned on ball bearings instead of a leather washer, and the metal parts were nickel-plated.

The bow and pump drills, suitable only to small work, required two hands, one to steady the tool, the other to operate it. One-hand drills began to appear in about 1825. Their essential elements were a steeply pitched screw and a nut that mated with it; when the latter was pushed down, the screw and attached bit turned. Many variations of the principle were offered before the modern push drill assumed its present, convenient form. It is still suitable for only light work in wood.

Both the bow and pump drills remained the metal-worker's prime tool for drilling small holes until the first geared hand drill was invented in 1805. Like every other tool, it underwent many improvements before acquiring its present rugged simplicity. Its great advantage lies in its unidirectional motion and the gearing that rotates the drill faster than the rate at which the crank is turned. The one-directional motion allowed better drills to be designed, and, with their greater efficiency in chip production, it was not long (1822) before drills with spiral flutes were proposed. A manufacturing problem—the flutes had to be hand filed—was not solved until the 1860s when the invention of a milling machine made possible the now universal twist drills.

Augers were used for boring both across the grain of wood and along the grain. The latter operation produced wooden pipes and pump casings or wheel hubs; special bits of many forms were designed for these purposes. The more common use of the auger or bit was in the cross-grain direction to make holes for wooden pins (treenails, or trunnels) or bolts for connections. The modern auger bit has a screw ahead of the cutting edges that pulls the auger into the workpiece. This screw provides an automatic feed and relieves the worker of the necessity of pushing the tool. Although the idea appeared in the mid-16th century, application of the principle was limited until the advent of screw-making machinery in the mid-19th century.

The modern auger

Saw. The chipped flint knife, with its irregular edge, was not a saw in the proper sense, for though it could sever wood fibres and gash bone or horn, it could not remove small pieces of material in the manner of a saw. Furthermore, the necessarily broad V-shaped profile of the flint saw severely limited its penetration into the workpiece; the nature of its cut was limited to making an encircling groove on a branch or a notch on something flat.

The true saw, a blade with teeth, one of the first great innovations of the Metal Age, was a completely new tool, able to cut through wood instead of merely gashing the surface. It developed with smelted copper, from which a blade could be cast. Many of the early copper saws have the general appearance of large meat-carving knives, with bone or wooden handles riveted to a tang at one end. Egyptian illustrations from about 1500 BC onward show the saw being used to rip boards, the timber being lashed to a vertical post set into the ground.

The use of relatively narrow, thin, and not quite flat blades made of a metal having a tendency to buckle, coupled with poorly shaped teeth that created high friction, required that the cutting take place on the pull stroke. In this stroke the sawyer could exert the most force without peril of buckling the saw. Furthermore, a pull saw could be thinner than a push saw and would waste less of the material being sawed.

The familiar modern handsaw, with its thin but wide steel blade, cuts on the push stroke; this permits downhand sawing on wood laid across the knee or on a stool, and the sawing pressure helps to hold the wood still. Operator control is superior, and, because the line being sawed is not obscured by the fuzz of undetached wood fibres or sawdust, greater accuracy is possible. Some tree-pruning saws have teeth raked to cut on the pull stroke to draw the branch toward the operator. Blades that are thin and narrow, as in the coping saw (fretsaw or scroll saw), are pulled through the workpiece by a frame holding the blade. Electric reciprocating and sabre saws, which have narrow blades that are supported at only one end, pull the blade when cutting to prevent buckling. The carpenter's pull saw for wood requires the craftsman to sit on the floor and use his feet to stabilize the wood he is sawing. Long forgotten by the Western world, it has been kept alive in China and Japan, where some craftsmen still favour it.

Although there is no positive evidence of either the type of saw or the method used, the Egyptians were able to saw hard stone with copper and bronze implements. The blade, probably toothless, rode on an abrasive material such as moistened quartz sand. The 7½-foot (two-metre) granite coffer still in the Great Pyramid carries saw marks.

During the Bronze Age the use of saws for woodworking was greatly extended, and the modern form began to evolve. Some saws with narrow blades looked very much like hacksaw blades, even to the holes at either end. They might have been held in a frame or pinned into a springy bow of wood.

Iron saws resembling those of copper or bronze date from the middle of the 7th century BC. A major contribution to saw design was noted in the 1st century AD by Pliny the Elder, whose works are one of the major sources on the technology of the ancients. Pliny observed that setting the teeth—that is, bending the teeth slightly away from the plane of the blade alternately to one side and the other, so creating a kerf, or saw slot, wider than the thickness of the blade—helps discharge the sawdust. He seems to have missed the more practical point that the saw also runs with less friction in the now wider slot. The Romans, always ingenious mechanics, added numerous improvements to both simply handled saws and frame saws but did not make push saws despite the advantage of the kerf that made the saw easier to work with and less liable to buckle. Roman saw sets and files have been found in substantial numbers. The small handsaws were sometimes backed with a stiffening rib to prevent the buckling of thin blades; today's backsaw still carries the rib. Frame saws, in which a narrow blade is held in tension by a wooden frame (see Figure 6), were exploited in many sizes, from the small carpenter's saws to two-man crosscut saws and ripsaws used for making boards.

Roman improvements in saws

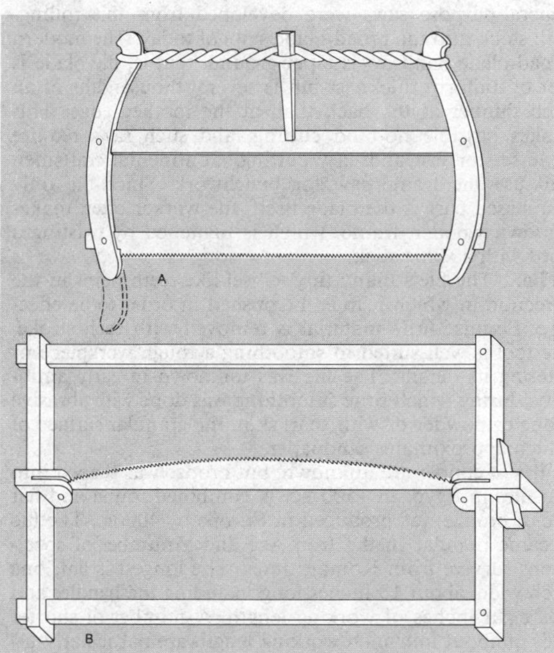

Figure 6: Framed saws in which a thin blade is put under tension (A) by a cord and twisting stick and (B) by a wedge.

The time and provenance of the push saw are uncertain, although it appears that it may date from the end of Roman times, well before the Middle Ages. Nevertheless, after the decline of the Roman Empire in the West, the use of the saw seems to have declined as well. The ax again became the principal tool on the return to the more primitive state of technology. Saw artifacts are very few in number, and even the Bayeux Tapestry of about 1100 shows no saw in the fairly detailed panels dealing with the construction of William the Conqueror's invasion fleet; only ax, adz, hammer, and breast auger are among the woodworking tools.

With the Middle Ages came the search for a nonclogging tooth to be used when crosscutting green and wet wood. The new saws were long, with handles at both ends, so that two men might each pull, adjacent teeth being raked in opposite directions. To provide space for the cuttings, M-shaped teeth with gaps (gullets) between them were developed; this tooth conformation, first noted in the mid-15th century, is still used in modern crosscut saws manufactured for coarse work and for cutting heavy timber.

Perhaps even more important than crosscutting was the need to rip a log lengthwise to produce boards. Saws for this purpose were generally called pit saws because they were operated in the vertical plane by two men, one of whom, the pitman, sometimes stood in a pit below the timber or under a trestle supporting the timber being sawed. His mate stood on the timber above, pulling the saw up; the pitman and gravity did the work of cutting on the downstroke, for which the teeth were raked. A pit saw occasionally was nothing more than a long blade with two handles (a whipsaw), but more often it was constructed as a frame saw, which used less steel and put the blade under tension.

The fretsaw was a mid-16th century invention that resulted from innovations in spring-driven clocks. It consisted of a U-shaped metal frame, on which was stretched a narrow blade made from a clock spring, the best and most uniform steel available, for it was not forged but rolled in small, hand-powered mills. These relatively thin blades had fine teeth that were well suited to cutting veneer stock from decorative wood for furniture of all kinds.

Water-powered rolling mill products

By the middle of the 17th century, large waterpowered rolling mills in England and some parts of the Continent were able to furnish broad strips of steel from which wide saws could be fashioned in many varieties. In particular, the awkwardly framed pit saw was largely replaced by a long, two-handled blade of increased stiffness. Smaller general-purpose saws were developed from this rolling-mill stock into the broad-blade saws of today. The modern broad-blade handsaw is taper ground, that is, the blade is not of uniform thickness but is several thousandths of an inch thinner at the back than at the toothed edge. This makes possible no-bind cutting, and such saws require little set for fast and easy cutting. Continental craftsmen still use the frame saw for benchwork. Since the only purchased part is the blade itself, the worker often makes his own wooden frame, which is tightened by twisting a cord with a short stick.

File. The file's many tiny, chisel-like teeth point in the direction in which it must be pushed in order to be effective. Because little material is removed with each stroke, the tool is well suited to smoothing a rough workpiece or altering its details. The file was unknown in early antiquity, during which time smoothing was done with abrasive stone or powder or with sharkskin, the granular surface of which approximates sandpaper.

Files of copper are unknown, but bronze was shaped into flat files in Egypt in 1500 BC. A combined round and flat file of bronze was produced in Europe by 400 BC. The file became popular in the Iron Age and a number of specimens survive from Roman times. The longest is flat, one inch wide, about 15 inches long including the handle, and has eight inches of working length. A number of shorter files of about four-inch working length are particularly interesting because of the notch they carry near the handle. The V-shaped cross section (called knife-shaped today) indicates that these files were intended for dressing saw-teeth. The notch enabled the workman to set the teeth—*i.e.,* bend successive teeth to alternate sides to gain a free-running saw. These files had straight-across and coarse toothing, but the advantages of obliquely cut teeth and of double-cut (intersecting) teeth were appreciated early.

A treatise written in AD 1100 mentions files of square, round, triangular, and other shapes. At this time files were made of carburized steel that was hardened after the files were cut by either a sharp, chisel-like hammer or a chisel and hammer. An illustrated manuscript of 1405 that was copied by a succession of later authors shows a polygonal file; the screeching of the filing operation is commented upon, too, with the curious suggestion that files be made hollow and filled with lead to eliminate the noise. In 1578 a writer asserted that the only way in which threads could be cut in screws was with the file.

Although Leonardo da Vinci had sketched a file-making machine, the first working machine was not produced until 1750, and it was a century later before machine-cut files substantially replaced those cut by hand. Power-driven, hand-cut rotary files are still used on dense metals because hand-formed, discontinuous teeth dissipate the heat well.

The ordinary file, in terms of its material and cut, is primarily used on cast iron and soft steel. Other materials—various nonferrous alloys, stainless steels, and plastics—are better accommodated with files of special composition and tooth formation (cut). A wide selection is manufactured.

Rasps, or, more correctly, rasp-cut files, have a series of individual teeth produced by a sharp, narrow, punchlike chisel. Their very rough cut is suited to the fast removal of material from soft substances, such as wood, hooves, leather, aluminum, and lead.

Chisel. The remote origin of the chisel may lie with the stone hand ax, the almond-shaped tool that was sharp at one end. Although long, rectangular chisel-shaped flints appeared in about 8000 BC, the later Neolithic Period evinced a more workmanlike version that was finished by grinding. With care, flint and obsidian chisels can be used on soft stone, as shown by intricate sculptures in pre-Columbian South and Central America. Gouges—*i.e.,* chisels with concave instead of flat sections, able to scoop hollows or form holes with curved instead of flat walls—were also used during this period. Chisels and gouges of very hard stone were used to rough out both the exteriors and interiors of bowls of softer stone such as alabaster, gypsum, soapstone, and volcanic rock. The final finish was produced by abrasion and polishing.

Copper chisels

The earliest copper chisels were long, in the manner of their flint forebears. Such so-called solid chisels of copper (and later of bronze) were used not only for working wood but soft rock as well, as many magnificent Egyptian monuments of limestone and sandstone testify.

By using bronze, a better casting metal than copper, and molds, it was possible to economize on metal by hafting a short chisel to a wooden handle. This also resulted in less damage to the mallet. The round handle was either impaled on a tang with a cast-on stop (tanged) or set into a socket (socketed); both forms of hafting presaged modern forms. The Egyptians used the chisel and clublike mallet with great skill and imagination to make joints in the construction of small drawers, paneled boxes, furniture, caskets, and chests.

The use of iron meant that tools had to be forged; no longer were the flowing lines and easily made cavities of casting available to the toolmaker. Consequently, early iron chisels were rude and solid. Tanged chisels were easier to make than socketed chisels, for which the socket had to be bent from a T-shaped forging. Hardened steel edges (first developed by accident) were created by repeatedly placing the iron in contact with carbon from the charcoal of the forge fire.

Chisels and gouges were made in great variety in later centuries as generally increasing wealth created a demand for more decoration and luxury in both religious and secular trappings and furniture. The rough and heavy tools of the carpenter were refined into more delicate models suited to woodcarvers, to joiners who did wall paneling and made stairs, doors, and windows, and to cabinetmakers. In the 18th century a woodcarver's kit may have contained more than 70 chisels and gouges.

Plane. The plane is a cleverly hafted cutting edge, the function of which is to skin or shave the surface of wood (see Figure 7). Used to finish and true a surface by removing the marks of a previous tool (adz, ax, or saw), a plane leaves the surface smooth, flat, and straight. The plane and the related spokeshave are unique tools because both depend upon a constant depth of cut that is given by the slight projection of the blade beyond the sole, or base, of the instrument.

The plane is an anomaly for which no line of descent has been identified. Pliny the Elder ascribes its invention to Daedalus, the mythical Greek representative of all handiwork.

Origins of the plane

It has been suggested that the Paleolithic unifacial (flat) scraper is the remote ancestor of the plane. While it is true that localized planing of a very poor sort, such as removing high spots, can be done with such a scraper, the difference in design and action between the two is too great to proclaim the scraper the forerunner of the plane. The adz seems a more likely progenitor. Early adzes were beveled (sloped) on the outside, although later, with better hafting and longer handles, the bevel was moved to the inside. The blade and handle of an outside-beveled adz could be used in a plane-like fashion to lift a shaving; however, the control of the blade projection, or depth of cut

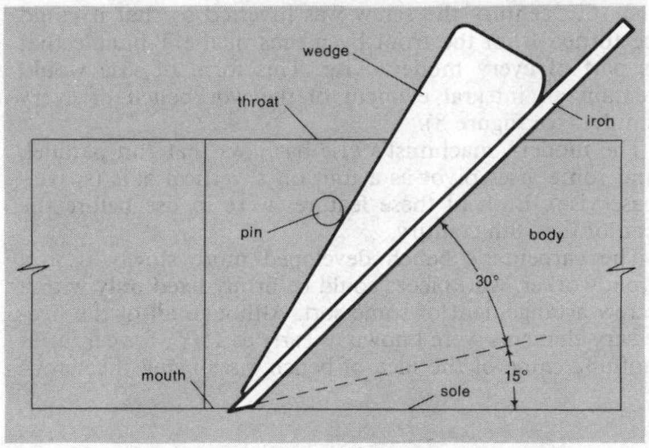

Figure 7: *Essential features of a plane.*
The body is pierced by a wide throat with a narrow slit (mouth) on the bottom, or sole. In this case, the iron (blade) is held in place by a wedge and pin, an arrangement common from Roman times to the 16th century. The cutting edge makes a 15° angle with the horizontal.

(or thickness of shaving), is critical to the concept of the plane and is met in only one other tool, the spokeshave.

The earliest illustrations of wood finishing, the surfacing of pieces of furniture, are Egyptian and show the surfaces being scrubbed with flat objects that appear to be abrasive stones or blocks riding on abrasive sand. Presumably the surfaces had been dressed by an adz, and the marks of this tool needed to be erased. Stone scrapers are not in evidence, and, although the adz is shown, it is being used as an adz, not as an improvised plane.

The Romans were the first known users of the plane, the earliest examples coming from Pompeii. In a manner of speaking, these planes are full-blown, without a prehistory and without even vague antecedents. The modern plane differs in details but not in principle or in general appearance.

These Pompeian planes were of comfortable size, being about eight inches long and 2¼ inches wide. The blade was relatively narrow, about 1½ inches as opposed to the modern width of about two inches. The sole was made of iron, one-quarter-inch thick, that was bent to form a shallow box filled with a wooden core; it was cut away at the back to form a handgrip, while the mouth was cut out about one-third of the way from the front. The cutting blade, or plane iron, was held in position by a wooden wedge tapped under an iron bar placed across the mouth. Frontier posts in Great Britain and Germany have yielded nearly a dozen Roman planes, ranging in length from 13 to 17 inches. Three constructions are represented: iron sole with a wooden core, all wood, and wood reinforced with iron plates at the sides of the mouth.

Planes can be divided into two main categories: the first, typified by the common bench plane, consists of a straight iron and a flat sole and is used for working flat surfaces; the second includes a variety of planes defined by the profile of the iron and sole. If the iron has a concavity, a projection or molding is created in the workpiece; if the iron has a projection, a groove is dug. Generally speaking, planes with profiled irons and correspondingly fluted soles are molding planes. Some of the Roman planes had irons for cutting rectangular grooves.

After the decline of the Roman Empire, the plane apparently fell into disuse. Practically no planes, and only a few other tools, have survived from the period of AD 800–1600. Secondary sources, such as illuminated manuscripts, legal documents, carvings, and stained-glass windows, do provide some information, but they lack details.

Categories of planes

By the late 17th century the plane was firmly reestablished in the craftsman's tool kit. Bench planes, or common planes, were used for surfacing panels or for creating straight edges on boards so that two or more might be joined into a wide panel. Boards were sawed or split (riven) from the log and were, consequently, quite rough. The first planing operation was done with the roughing, or fore, plane, which was of medium length, possibly 16–18 inches. This fore plane had a slightly convex iron that removed saw and adz marks but left hollows that needed to be leveled by straight-iron planing. If the workpiece was long, a long-bodied trying, or jointing, plane, having a length of about 30 inches, was needed to remove large curves in the wood. Short planes—a common length was about nine inches—were called smoothing planes for the final finish they produced.

Planes with straight irons and flat soles could easily be made by the craftsman himself. Taste and fashion in 17th-century wood carving, however, prized decorative features such as moldings and beadings, which led to a proliferation of plane types and established plane making as an industry.

The indispensable common (straight iron) plane was improved in a number of details throughout the years. In Roman planes the wedge holding the iron was jammed against a cross bar in the mouth of the plane. This feature, awkward because it impaired the free escape of the shaving, was eliminated in the 16th century by seating the wedge in tapered grooves.

The top iron

Another improvement was the invention of the top iron, apparently an English innovation of the late 18th century. This top iron, or chip breaker, used an inverted plane iron placed over the cutting iron to limit the thickness of the shaving and help it to curl out of the mouth. Now called the double iron, it is a feature of all but the smallest of modern planes.

As advanced metallurgy and machine tools allowed good castings to be accurately mass produced, wooden planes were gradually displaced in Britain and the United States by cast-iron bodies with wooden handles.

The 19th century saw much effort in Britain and the United States aimed at eliminating the wedge, which required the use of a hammer to adjust the iron. Various methods for the easy removal and accurate setting of the iron culminated in the screw and lever adjustor for the iron and the cam-actuated cap. This final evolution was completed about 1890, and changes since that time have been trivial. Despite their advantages, continental Europe has not been partial to iron-bodied planes with screw and lever adjustments, and such tools cost much more than the still common wooden plane with wedge and hammer adjustment.

The spokeshave, which may be likened to a short-bodied plane with a handle on either side allowing the tool to be pulled toward the operator, has left little in the way of a record. The term was first used about 400 years ago, but the earliest known example seems to be only half as old. Both the English word and the German *Speichenhobel* suggest that it was originally the specialized tool of a wheelwright that became generalized for use on convex surfaces. As with the plane, the cutting blade (iron) projects only slightly from the short sole to regulate the depth of cut.

The drawknife is a handled blade that is pulled toward the operator. It is a rather questionable relative of the plane, for, though it lifts shavings in a similar manner, it lacks the positive thickness control of the plane. The tangs at the ends of the modern knife are bent at right angles in the plane of the blade. While it is used in much the manner of a spokeshave, the drawknife is actually a roughing tool for the quick removal of stock. Skill is required in its use because the depth of cut is regulated by the tilt of the blade, and the grain of the wood tends to assert itself. The drawknife appears to be an older tool than the spokeshave and has undergone a change since the Viking times when it was first used. Under the Viking craftsmen the handles were bent at right angles to the plane of the blade, and the tool seems to have been used for smoothing axed or adzed timber in medieval Scandinavia, Russia, and elsewhere.

TOOL AUXILIARIES

Workbench and vise. The workbench and vise form an organic unit, for the vise is a fixture that is either part of the carpenter's bench or is attached to the machinist's bench.

Neither a bench nor a mechanical fixture would have offered an advantage in the early chipping or flaking of stone. On the contrary, complete freedom in the positioning of the workpiece and hammer was essential to permit the many small, yet discretely placed and directed, blows that were the crux of fashioning stone tools. When large and unidirectional forces needed to be applied, as in woodworking, many phases of metalworking, or even in the manipulation of bone and horn, the advantage of a bench or a fixed rest became apparent.

Wood assumed its important role in structures, furniture, and fittings with the development of polished stone tools (ax and chisel) in the Neolithic Period and was skillfully exploited for finer work with the advent of copper and bronze tools. Most of the furniture of ancient times no longer exists, but much visual evidence, provided largely by sculptures, representations on vases, mosaics, and wall frescoes, depicts all manner of furniture, such as thrones, stools, benches, footstools, couches, cupboards, tables, chests, and beds.

Evidences of ancient furniture

Oddly enough, a stout table or workbench is missing from the renderings of busy Egyptian shops. The workpieces are on the floor, and the craftsman is kneeling or bending over his work or sitting on a low stool, even in those scenes in which tables are being finished. Perhaps the craftsman used his feet to position the work on the floor while using a chisel and mallet to effect joinery work, a practice still known in some areas.

Evidence in Europe suggests that the woodworker made use of a table or workbench as long ago as the Neolithic Period. The simplest form of table bench was a short length of heavy board split from a trunk and supported on four legs made of saplings set into bored holes. This style of bench, with its four legs somewhat splayed for greater stability, became common in Roman times. As the first users of the plane, the Romans found that a stout workbench was a necessity; truing a surface without a bench on which to lay and secure the wood was nearly impossible.

Two early methods, still in use, were devised for holding the workpiece. The simplest procedure was to use wooden pegs set into holes in the bench top; the other was to use what are variously known as bench stops, holdfasts, or dogs. The stems of these T-shaped iron fittings were set into holes in the workbench, and a sharp end of the horizontal part of the T was turned to engage the wood.

Other arrangements came into use, including trestles for supporting wood to be sawed and specialized benches—horses—on which the leatherworker or coppersmith sat while facing a raised workpiece. A small workpiece was often held by a strap that was tightened when the craftsman placed his foot in a loop that formed the free end and dangled beneath the table. Such horses proliferated from medieval times onward as new specialties developed.

The anvil and horn

A frequent accessory of the metalworker's bench was the anvil, which is still informally present on many machinist's vises in a rudimentary form suited to light work. Aside from making castings, metalworking was largely concerned with forging. The earliest anvils were convenient flat stones, usable for only the simplest kind of flat work. Anvils with the characteristic overhang, or horn, were first cast in bronze and, later, welded from short lengths of iron. Bench anvils were necessarily small, and the large free-standing specimens of the smith had to await the development of cast iron. Only then were larger masses of metal conveniently available.

The medieval carpenter's bench was still very much like the Roman's, with pegs serving as end fixtures. The metalworker, especially the craftsman using a file to shape and clean small forgings and castings (harness gear, buckles, and so on), used a simple rest, essentially a notched post driven into the ground in front of his bench, to support his workpiece.

Within a century, according to the pictorial record, the metalworkers' rest was replaced by a screw vise, at first quite small. This vise was like a hinge; one leaf or jaw was fastened to the bench, and the other was pulled up to clamp the workpiece and was tightened by the use of a nut and bolt passing through the middle of the hinge. Portable clamp-on vises that can be attached to a plank, tabletop, or bench top date from 1570.

Closing the vise by turning the tightening nut with a wrench was a slow and awkward process. At the end of the 16th century the screw was inverted so that it could be turned from the front by means of the T-handle that is part of every modern vise. This form of vise would remain an integral element of the workbench of every smithy (see Figure 8).

The modern machinist's vise has jaws that run parallel, and some vises pivot as a unit on a vertical axis (swivel-base vise). Both of these features were in use before the end of the 18th century.

The carpenter's bench developed more slowly. For a woodworker, workpieces could be firmly fixed only with a screw arrangement of some sort. Although all of the necessary elements were known as early as 1505, for centuries nothing came of the idea of bench vises using the screw.

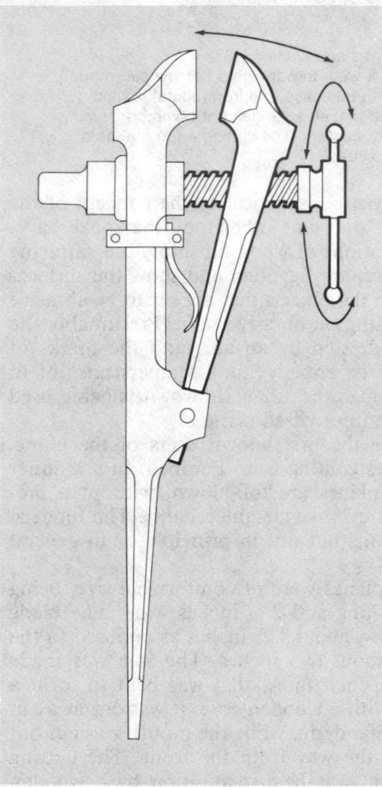

Figure 8: Blacksmith's vise, with long spikelike foot for extra support.

The woodworker needs two types of vises. One holds (clamps) the board into place so that its long edges may be trued and planed; custom places this vise at the left front of the bench, a convenient location for the right-handed workman. The second vise is at the right side of the table; its moving jaw has an adjustable bench stop that permits long pieces of wood to be held between it and a fixed stop in the bench top. Both types of vise were developed and made part of the same bench by the early 19th century.

Tongs, pincers, and pliers. Tongs, pincers, tweezers, and pliers have the common task of holding or gripping objects so that they may be handled more easily. The early use of fire created a new problem, that of handling hot coals. Two sticks probably served as the first uncertain holders, but bronze bars may have replaced wooden tongs as early as 3000 BC. An Egyptian wall painting of about 1450 BC shows a crucible supported between two bow-shaped metal bars. The same painting shows a craftsman with a blowpipe in his mouth holding a small object over a fire with a tweezer-like instrument about eight to 10 inches long. Bronze loops capable of handling large and heavy crucibles also appeared at this time.

Handling hot coals

Spring-back, or tweezer-like, tongs were the model used by the early ironsmith. The change to the mechanically more effective hinged tongs was slow, and it was not until 500 BC that they became common in the Greek blacksmith's kit. Pivoted tongs, with short jaws and a long handle, have quite a mechanical advantage over tweezer-like tongs. A pair of 20-inch pivoted tongs is capable of exerting a gripping force of nearly 300 pounds (135 kilograms) with only a 40-pound squeeze from the smith's hand. Such tongs were constructed with one handle slightly shorter than the other so that an oval ring could be slipped over the two to help secure the grip.

Small tongs, often called pliers or forceps, were particularly valuable to the early craftsman, who put them to many and varied uses. The Romans sharpened the jaws of tongs to create cutters and pincers. The pincers were useful for pulling bent nails because of the leverage they were capable of exerting. Although they were originally a carpenter's tool, pincers became a principal tool of the farrier because old nails had to be pulled from horses' hooves before new shoes could be fitted and nailed on.

SCREW-BASED TOOLS

Invention of the screw. Although Archimedes is credited with inventing the screw in the 3rd century BC, his screw was not today's fastener but actually two other screw-type devices. One was a kind of water pump; still used today for large-volume, low-lift, industrial applications, the device is now called the inclined screw conveyor. The second was the "endless screw," actually the worm of a worm and gear set, one of the ancients' five devices for raising heavy weights. With the state of the mechanical arts as it was then, Archimedes' concept of the screw was actually as a motion-transforming device and was more hypothetical than practical.

By the 1st century BC, heavy wooden screws had become elements of presses for making wine and olive oil and for pressing clothes. The character of the screw took on a new dimension, for these screws were used to exert pressure; their modern counterparts are called power screws. These press screws were turned by means of hand spikes thrust into radial holes in the cylindrical end. The problem of making the internal thread of the nut prevented the use of small threaded fasteners in metal construction. The external thread, however, was readily, if tediously, made by filing.

Problem of the nut

Metal screws and nuts appeared in the 15th century. The square or hexagonal head or nut was turned with an appropriate box wrench; a T-handled socket wrench was developed in the 16th century. Some screws used in 16th-century armour have slots (nicks) in which a screwdriver may have been used, although this tool is not shown. Deep notches on the circumferences of the heads of other armour screws suggest that some type of pronged device was used to turn them. Slotted, roundheaded screws were used in the 16th century, but few screw-and-nut-fastened clocks are in evidence earlier than the 17th century. Metal screws were called machine, or machinery, screws since they were made of metal and mated with threaded holes.

The wood screw differs from the machine screw in that the wood into which it is turned is deformed into a nut. It must, however, be started in a hole made by awl or drill. Aside from a few and sometimes doubtful artifacts from Roman times, the wood screw is not mentioned until the mid-16th century, when it appears in a mining treatise. Here a screw tapered to a point, carrying a slotted head and looking very familiar except for its left-handed thread, is described so casually as to suggest that it was a common article. It is remarked that the screw is superior to the nail, which is also shown being driven by a claw hammer. There is no mention of a screwdriver.

Screwdrivers and wrenches. The simple screwdriver was preceded by a flat-bladed bit for the carpenter's brace (1744). The handled screwdriver is shown on the woodworker's bench after 1800 and appears in inventories of tool kits from that date. Screwdrivers did not become common tools until 1850 when automatic screw machines began the mass production of tapered, gimlet-pointed wood screws. In its early form, the screwdriver was made from flat stock; its sometimes scalloped edges contributed nothing to function. Being flat, the blade was easy to haft but weak when improperly used for prying. The present form of the screwdriver, round and flattened only at the end, was devised to strengthen the shaft and make use of readily available round-wire stock.

Origin of the screwdriver

Early box and socket wrenches fit only a particular nut or screw with flat surfaces on the head. The open-end wrench may have rectangular slots on one or both ends. In their earliest forms, such wrenches, with straight, angled, or S-shaped handles, were made of wrought iron. Cast iron came into use around 1800. Modern wrenches are drop forgings and come in many formats.

The limitations of fixed-opening wrenches were addressed in the early 19th century when sliding-jaw types were developed to accommodate a range of flats. In these, the end of an L-shaped handle provided the fixed jaw, and the parallel jaw was arranged to slide along the handle until it engaged the flats. In the first models, in the 1830s, the sliding jaw was fixed into position by a wedge that was hammered into place. By 1835 patents for screw wrenches began to proliferate; in these, the sliding jaw was positioned and held by means of a screw whose axis was parallel to the handle. The most common example is the monkey wrench, whose name first appeared in about 1858. A convenient variation of this type of wrench is the thin and angled Crescent wrench, a modern innovation.

The plumber's pipe wrench is a serrated-jaw variation of the monkey wrench, whose additional feature of a pivotable movable jaw enables it to engage round objects, such as rods and pipes.

MEASURING AND DEFINING TOOLS

Plumb line, level, and square. A plumb line is a light line with a weight (plumb bob) at one end that, when suspended next to a workpiece, defines a vertical line. "Plumb" comes from the Latin *plumbum,* or "lead," the material that replaced stone as the weight for the bob or plummet.

While an end-weighted string defines the vertical, its direct use for plumbing walls (making them vertical) is awkward. The Egyptians devised a tool resembling the letter E, from which a plumb line was suspended from the upper outboard part of the E. When the tool was placed against a wall, the wall was determined to be vertical when the string just touched the lower outboard part of the E. Oddly, this useful tool was apparently forgotten for many centuries and has reappeared only in modern times.

The tool for determining horizontal direction is called a level. The Egyptians used an A-frame, on which a plumb line was suspended from the vertex of the A. When the feet of the A were set on the surface to be checked, if the plumb line bisected the crossbar of the A, the surface was horizontal. The A-frame level was used in Europe until the middle of the 19th century. Sometimes a variation is shown in which the frame is an inverted T with a plumb line suspended from the top of the vertical stem.

The hose level

Because the surface of a body of water is always horizontal, a trough or channel filled with water can serve as a reference in some situations. The hose level, first described in 1629, consisted of a length of hose fitted with a glass tube at each end. Water was added until it rose in both vertically held tubes; when the surfaces of the water in each tube were at the same height, the object was level. This idea was impractical with only leather hose, but the development of vulcanized rubber hose in 1831 led to a resurgence of the device in 1849. Because the hose could be carried through holes in the wall, around partitions, and so on, the instrument enabled levels to be established in awkward circumstances.

The spirit, or bubble, level, a sealed glass tube containing alcohol and an air bubble, was invented in 1661. It was first used on telescopes and later on surveying instruments, but it did not become a carpenter's tool until the factory-made models were introduced in the mid-19th century. The circular level, in which a bubble floated under a circular glass to indicate level in all directions, was invented in 1777. It lacked the sensitivity of the conventional level.

The square appeared in the ancient Egyptian world as two perpendicular legs of wood braced with a diagonal member. In the following centuries many variations were designed for specific purposes, including a square with shoulders that allowed it also to cast a mitre of 45 degrees. Iron squares were rarely used before 1800, and factory-made metal squares did not appear until 1835. The adjustable, or bevel, square was used for angles other than 90 degrees beginning in the 17th century. In the earliest examples, the thin blade moved stiffly because it was riveted into a slot in the thick blade. Later models of the 19th century, however, were equipped with a thumbscrew that permitted the thin blade to be adjusted with respect to the thicker blade.

Compass, divider, and caliper. Compass, divider, and caliper are basically instruments that have two legs pivoted to each other at the top and are concerned with small-distance measurement or transfer. The compass and divider have straight legs; the caliper has curved legs.

The terms compass and divider are often interchanged, for each instrument can be used to draw circles, mark divisions (divide a given distance), or simply mark a distance. Technically, a compass is a drafting instrument that has one pen or pencil point and one sharp point that is positioned at the centre of the circle to be described; a divider, on the other hand, has two sharp points, one for the centre, the other for scribing or marking. Caliper is a corruption of "calibre," the diameter of a hole (as in a firearm) or of a cylindrical or spherical body. The outside caliper has inwardly curved legs that measure the diameters of solids created by rotating tools, such as lathe-turned objects; the inside caliper has outwardly curved legs for measuring bores.

Dividers and calipers were known to both the Greeks and Romans, though the caliper was uncommon. A divider with a circular sector, or wing, connecting the two legs was sketched in 1245; its modern counterpart is the wing divider with a thumbscrew clamp and screw for fine adjustment. The caliper is mentioned in the Middle Ages, but the divider was the principal tool of the architect working on full-scale layouts of stonework, such as in the construction of a cathedral. Such dividers were large, often half as tall as a man. The divider underwent refinements that made it an important drafting instrument for Albrecht Dürer and Leonardo da Vinci; Leonardo suggested improvements that included the knuckle-joint hinge (to

Proportional dividers

increase rigidity) and the adjustable proportional divider (Roman proportional dividers had a fixed pivot that gave only one ratio). Leonardo's notes also show the beam compass with a screw adjustment for large radii, as well as a compass that had interchangeable points, in which one leg had a clamp for different drawing media, such as graphite or chalk.

Chalk line. "Snapping a line," a technique familiar in ancient Egypt, is employed in modern building construction. The procedure uses a taut, chalk-covered cord that is stretched between two points; the cord deposits a straight line of chalk when it is plucked and snapped onto the surface. After 5,000 years the only change in this technique is that, whereas the Egyptians used wet red or yellow ochre, the modern craftsman follows the method of Greek masons who employed white and red chalks in addition to wet ochre.

Rules. The unit of linear measure in the ancient world, the cubit, was simply the length from the elbow to the extremity of the middle finger. Although the cubit gave an order of magnitude, it was hardly a standard, and it varied widely in different times and places.

One of many royal Egyptian cubits had a length of $20^{64}/_{100}$ inches. It was divided into seven palms (measured across the fingers, not the knuckles), making a palm almost three inches. Each palm was, in turn, divided into four digits of about three-quarters of an inch apiece. Thus, 1 cubit = 7 palms = 28 digits. On occasion, digits were subdivided into 10ths, 14ths, or 16ths.

The common rule of Egyptian masons and carpenters was made of wood, had a narrow cross section, and had one beveled edge, with the two left-hand palms carrying the smaller divisions of digits. Some Egyptian rods were made of stone and used digits divided into 16ths. These may have been ceremonial rods or, perhaps, master gauges for calibration and comparison; their brittleness would make them unsuitable for the rough handling received by mason's tools.

The Romans introduced folding rules of bronze in 12- and six-inch sizes. These were probably "pocket" instruments for officials, too expensive to be used by ordinary craftsmen who probably used plain strip rules.

Only scanty evidence exists that graduated rules were used in the Middle Ages and the Renaissance; plain straightedges seem to have predominated. In 1683 an English writer described foot rules as having $^1/_8$-inch subdivisions. The folding rule, now made of wood, reappeared at the end of the 17th century.

Measurement was long characterized by great national and regional differences. Because every large city in Europe and most towns had a different, but locally standard, "foot," rules with four different graduations (one on each face) were made.

POWER TOOLS

A power tool is technically a power-driven hand tool or portable power tool; these names distinguish it from the stationary power tool such as the drill press. While power tools are generally driven by electricity, the category also includes small pneumatic tools driven by compressed air, such as air impact wrenches and hammers. Gasoline-engine-driven tools (chain saws, gas-powered drills, and so on) are not included.

The two most popular power tools

The most popular power tools are the electric drill and the electric circular saw. Like its manual counterpart, the electric drill rotates a tool bit, but the circular saw has no manual prototype. Jigsaws, sabre, and reciprocating saws have familiar blades, as do electric screwdrivers, but many power tools are contemporary creations built around the ubiquitous electric motor. Among modern power tools are polishers, several kinds of sanders (circular, belt, oscillating, and reciprocating), shears, and nibblers. Power tools, in limited commercial and industrial use before World War II, are now produced by the millions, largely for the home workshop. (R.S.H./Ed.)

Machine tools in industry

Machine tools are stationary power-driven machines that shape or form parts made of metal or other materials. The shaping is accomplished in four general ways: (1) by cutting excess material in the form of chips from the part; (2) by shearing the material; (3) by squeezing metallic parts to the desired shape; and (4) by applying electricity, ultrasound, or corrosive chemicals to the material. The fourth category covers modern machine tools and processes for machining ultrahard metals not machinable by older methods.

Machine tools that form parts by removing metal chips from a workpiece include lathes, shapers and planers, drilling machines, milling machines, grinders, and power saws. The cold forming of metal parts, such as cooking utensils, automobile bodies, and similar items, is done on punch presses, while the hot forming of white-hot blanks into appropriately shaped dies is done on forging presses.

Tolerances

Modern machine tools cut or form parts to tolerances of plus or minus one ten-thousandth of an inch (0.0025 millimetre). In special applications, precision lapping machines can produce parts that are within plus or minus two millionths of an inch (0.00005 millimetre). Because of the precise dimensional requirements of the parts and the heavy cutting forces exerted on the cutting tool, machine tools combine weight and rigidity with delicate accuracy.

HISTORY

Before the Industrial Revolution of the 18th century, hand tools were used to cut and shape materials for the production of goods such as cooking utensils, wagons, ships, furniture, and other products. After the advent of the steam engine, material goods were produced by power-driven machines that could only be manufactured by machine tools. Machine tools (capable of producing dimensionally accurate parts in large quantities) and jigs and fixtures (for holding the work and guiding the tool) were the indispensable innovations that made mass production and interchangeable parts realities in the 19th century.

The earliest steam engines suffered from the imprecision of early machine tools, and the large cast cylinders of the engines often were bored inaccurately by machines powered by waterwheels and originally designed to bore cannon. Within 50 years of the first steam engines, the basic machine tools, with all the fundamental features required for machining heavy metal parts, were designed and developed. Some of them were adaptations of earlier woodworking machines; the metal lathe derived from woodcutting lathes used in France as early as the 16th century. In 1775 John Wilkinson of England built a precision machine for boring engine cylinders. In 1797 Henry Maudslay, also of England and one of the great inventive geniuses of his day, designed and built a screw-cutting engine lathe. The outstanding feature of Maudslay's lathe was a lead screw for driving the carriage. Geared to the spindle of the lathe, the lead screw advanced the tool at a constant rate of speed and guaranteed accurate screw threads. By 1800 Maudslay had equipped his lathe with 28 change gears that cut threads of various pitches by controlling the ratio of the lead-screw speed to the spindle speed.

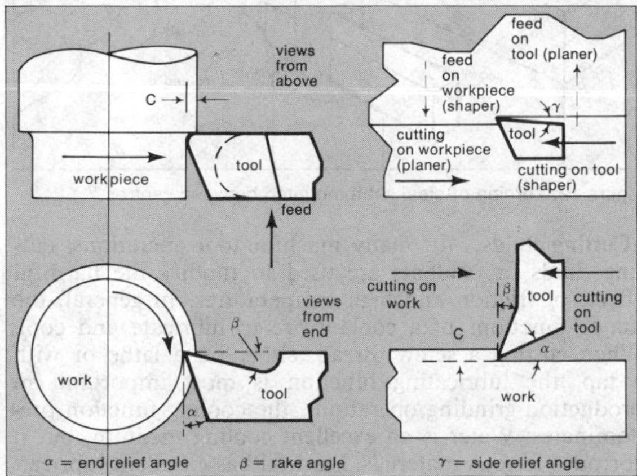

Figure 9: *Single-point cutting tools.*
(Left) Lathe tool; (right) planer and shaper tool.
Depth of cut is indicated by C.

The shaper was invented by James Nasmyth, who had worked in Henry Maudslay's shop in London. In Nasmyth's machine, a workpiece could be clamped horizontally to a table and worked by a cutter using a reciprocating motion to plane small surfaces, cut keyways, or machine other straight-line surfaces. A few years later, in 1839, Nasmyth invented the steam hammer for forging heavy pieces. Another disciple of Maudslay, Joseph Whitworth, invented or improved a great number of machine tools and came to dominate the field; at the International Exhibition of 1862, his firm's exhibits took up a quarter of all the space devoted to machine tools.

Invention of the steam hammer

Britain tried to keep its lead in machine-tool development by prohibiting exports, but the attempt was foredoomed by industrial development elsewhere. British tools were exported to continental Europe and to the United States despite the prohibition, and new tools were developed outside Britain. Notable among these was the milling machine invented by Eli Whitney, produced in the United States in 1818, and used by Simeon North to manufacture firearms. The first fully universal milling machine was built in 1862 by J.R. Brown of the United States and was used to cut helical flutes in twist drills. The turret lathe, also developed in the United States in the middle of the 19th century, was fully automatic in some operations, such as making screws, and it presaged the momentous developments of the 20th century. Various gear-cutting machines reached their full development in 1896 when F.W. Fellows, an American, designed a gear shaper that could rapidly turn out almost any type of gear.

The production of artificial abrasives in the late 19th century opened up a new field of machine tools, that of grinding machines. C.H. Norton of Massachusetts dramatically illustrated the potential of the grinding machine by making one that could grind an automobile crankshaft in 15 minutes, a process that previously had required five hours.

By the end of the 19th century a complete revolution had taken place in the working and shaping of metals that created the basis for mass production and an industrialized society. The 20th century has witnessed the introduction of numerous refinements of machine tools, such as multiple-point cutters for milling machines, the development of automated operations governed by electronic and fluid-control systems, and nonconventional techniques, such as electrochemical and ultrasonic machining. Yet even today the basic machine tools remain largely the legacy of the 19th century.

MACHINE-TOOL CHARACTERISTICS

All machine tools must provide work-holding and tool-holding devices and means for accurately controlling the depth of the cut. The relative motion between the cutting edge of the tool and the work is called the cutting speed; the speed in which uncut material is brought into contact with the tool is called the feed motion. Means must be provided for varying both.

Because an overheated tool may lose its cutting ability, temperatures must be controlled. The amount of heat that is generated depends on the shearing force and the cutting speed. Because the shearing force varies with the material being cut and the tool material varies in its tolerance for high temperatures, the optimum cutting speed depends both on the material being cut and the cutting-tool material. It is also influenced by the rigidity of the machine, the shape of the workpiece, and the depth of the cut.

Optimum cutting speed

CUTTING TOOLS

Metal-cutting tools are classified as single point or multiple point. A single-point cutting tool is shown in Figure 9 (left) performing a turning operation on a rotating cylindrical workpiece. Such tools are also used for increasing the size of holes, or boring. Turning and boring are performed on lathes and boring mills. Multiple-point cutting tools have two or more cutting edges and include milling cutters, drills, and broaches (Figure 10).

Figure 9 (right) represents two types of operation; either the tool is moving on a straight path against the stationary

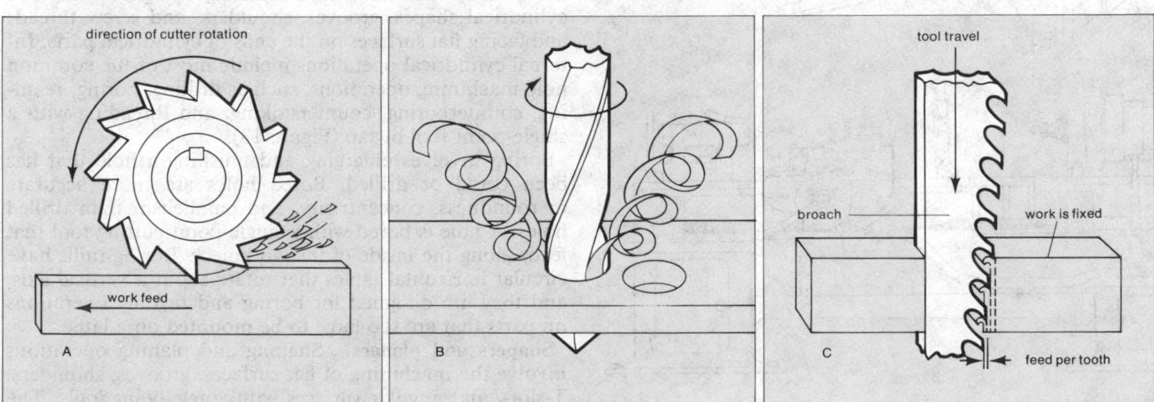

Figure 10: *Multiple-point cutting tools.*
(A) Milling with plain milling cutter. (B) Machining with twist drill. (C) Action of broaching tool.

workpiece, as on a shaper, or the workpiece is moving against the stationary tool, as on a planer. Relief or clearance angles (designated by the symbol a in Figure 9) must be provided to prevent the tool surface below the cutting edge from rubbing against the workpiece. Rake angles (symbol β in Figure 9) are often provided on cutting tools to cause a wedging action in the formation of chips and to reduce friction and heat.

Tool materials. In order to remove chips from a workpiece, a cutting tool must be harder than the workpiece and must maintain a cutting edge at the temperature produced by the friction of the cutting action.

Carbon steel. Steel with a carbon content ranging from 1 to 1.2 percent was the earliest material used in machine tools. Tools made of this carbon steel are comparatively inexpensive but tend to lose cutting ability at temperatures at about 400° F (205° C).

High-speed steel. In 1900 the introduction of high-speed steel permitted the operation of tools at twice or three times the speeds allowable with carbon steel, thus doubling or trebling the capacities of the world's machine shops. One of the most common types of high-speed steel contains 18 percent tungsten, 4 percent chromium, 1 percent vanadium, and only 0.5 to 0.8 percent carbon.

Cutting at red heat

Cast alloys. A number of cast-alloy cutting-tool materials have been developed; these nonferrous alloys contain cobalt, chromium, and tungsten and are particularly effective in penetrating the hard skin on cast iron and retaining their cutting ability even when red hot.

Cemented tungsten carbide. This material was first used for metal cutting in Germany in 1926. Its principal ingredient is finely divided tungsten carbide held in a binder of cobalt; its hardness approaches that of a diamond. Tungsten carbide tools can be operated at cutting speeds many times higher than those used with high-speed steel.

Oxides. Ceramic, or oxide, tool tips are one of the newest developments in cutting-tool materials. They consist primarily of fine aluminum oxide grains, which are bonded together.

Diamonds. Diamonds have been used for many years for truing grinding wheels, in wire-drawing dies, and as cutting tools. For cutting applications they are used largely for taking light finishing cuts at high speed on hard or abrasive materials and for finish-boring bronze and babbitt-metal bearings.

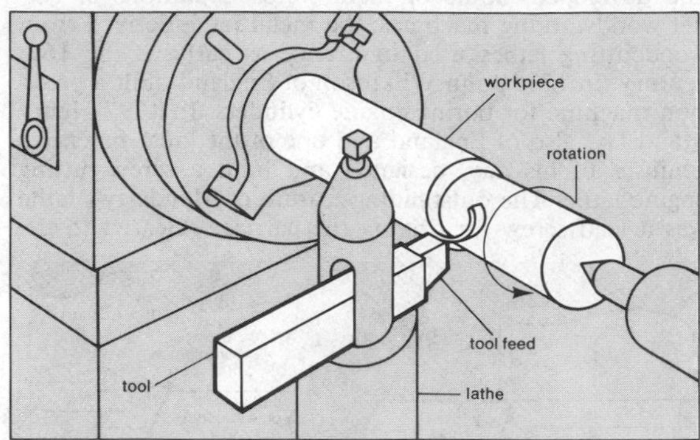

Figure 12: Turning of steel shaft mounted between centres.

Cutting fluids. In many machine-tool operations, cutting fluids or coolants are used to modify the harmful effects of friction and high temperatures. In general, the major functions of a coolant are to lubricate and cool. When cutting a screw thread, either on a lathe or with a tap, the lubricating function is most important; in production-grinding operations, the cooling function predominates. Water is an excellent cooling medium, but it corrodes ferrous materials. Lard oil has excellent lubricating qualities, but it tends to become rancid. Sulfurized mineral oil is one of the most popular coolants. The sulfur tends to prevent chips from the work from welding to the tip of the tool. For sawing and grinding operations, soluble oil, which is an oily emulsion freely miscible in water, is commonly used.

BASIC MACHINE TOOLS

Hundreds of varieties of metal machine tools, ranging in size from small machines mounted on workbenches to huge production machines weighing several hundred tons, are used in modern industry. They retain the basic characteristics of their 19th- and early 20th-century ancestors and are still classed as one of the following: (1) turning machines (lathes and boring mills), (2) shapers and planers, (3) drilling machines, (4) milling machines, (5) grinding machines, (6) power saws, and (7) presses.

The engine lathe

Turning machines. The engine lathe, as the horizontal metal-turning machine is commonly called, is the most important of all the machine tools (Figure 11). It is usually considered the father of all other machine tools because many of its fundamental mechanical elements are incorporated into the design of other machine tools.

The engine lathe is a basic machine tool that can be used for a variety of turning, facing, and drilling operations. It uses a single-point cutting tool for turning and boring (Figure 12). Turning operations involve cutting excess metal, in the form of chips, from the external diameter of a workpiece and include turning straight or tapered cylindrical shapes, grooves, shoulders, and screw threads and facing flat surfaces on the ends of cylindrical parts. Internal cylindrical operations include most of the common hole-machining operations, such as drilling, boring, reaming, counterboring, countersinking, and threading with a single-point tool or tap (Figure 13).

Boring involves enlarging and finishing a hole that has been cored or drilled. Bored holes are more accurate in roundness, concentricity, and parallelism than drilled holes. A hole is bored with a single-point cutting tool that feeds along the inside of the workpiece. Boring mills have circular horizontal tables that rotate about a vertical axis, and they are designed for boring and turning operations on parts that are too large to be mounted on a lathe.

Shapers and planers. Shaping and planing operations involve the machining of flat surfaces, grooves, shoulders, T-slots, and angular surfaces with single-point tools. The largest shapers have a 36-inch cutting stroke and can machine parts up to 36 inches long. The cutting tool on the

(Top) From John Jacob Holtzapffel, *Hand or Simple Turning* (1976), Dover Publications, Inc., N.Y.

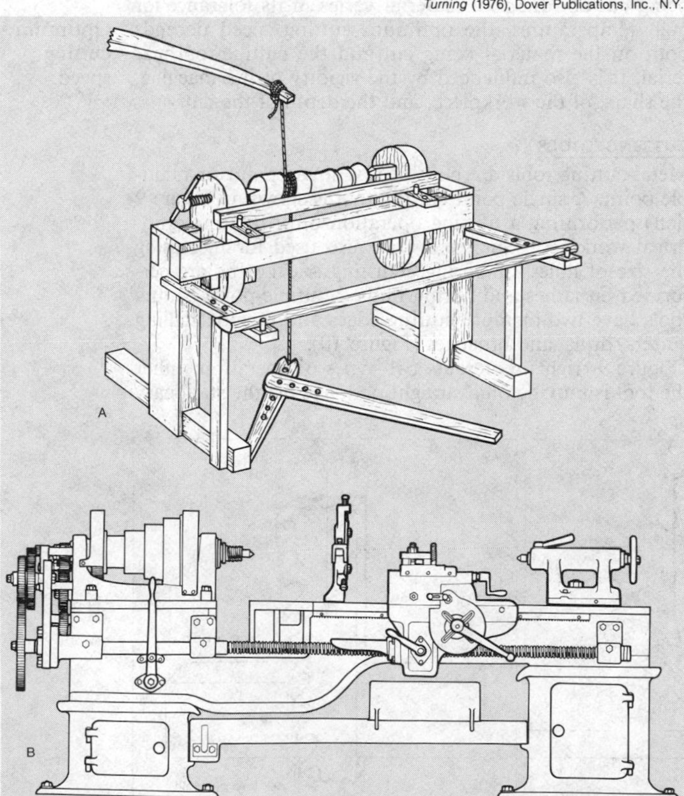

Figure 11: *Lathes.*
(A) Pole lathe, 17th century. (B) Self-acting lathe with lead-screw and change gears, 19th century.

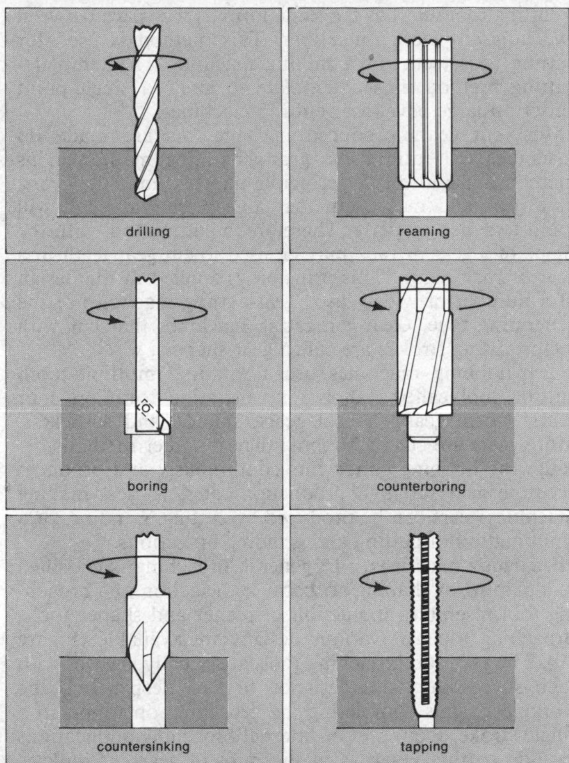

Figure 13: Common hole-machining operations.
Adapted from W.J. McCarthy and R.E. Smith, *Machine Tool Technology*

shaper oscillates, cutting on the forward stroke, with the workpiece feeding automatically toward the tool during each return stroke.

Planing machines perform the same operations as shapers but can machine longer workpieces. Some planers can machine parts up to 50 feet long. The workpiece is mounted on a reciprocating table that moves the workpiece beneath a cutting tool. This tool, which remains stationary during the cutting stroke, automatically feeds into the workpiece after each cutting stroke.

Drilling machines. Drilling machines, also called drill presses, cut holes in metal with a twist drill (Figure 10). They also use a variety of other cutting tools to perform the following basic hole-machining operations: (1) reaming, (2) boring, (3) counterboring, (4) countersinking, and (5) tapping internal threads with the use of a tapping attachment (Figure 13).

Tapping

Milling machines. A milling machine cuts metal as the workpiece is fed against a rotating cutting tool called a milling cutter (Figure 10). Cutters of many shapes and sizes are available for a wide variety of milling operations. Milling machines cut flat surfaces, grooves, shoulders, inclined surfaces, dovetails, and T-slots. Various form-tooth cutters are used for cutting concave forms and convex grooves, for rounding corners, and for cutting gear teeth.

Milling machines are available in a variety of designs that can be classified as the following: (1) standard knee-and-column machines, including the horizontal and the vertical types; (2) bed-type or manufacturing machines; and (3) machines designed for special milling jobs.

Grinding machines. Grinding machines remove small chips from metal parts that are brought into contact with a rotating abrasive wheel called a grinding wheel or an abrasive belt. Grinding is the most accurate of all of the basic machining processes. Modern grinding machines grind hard or soft parts to tolerances of plus or minus 0.0001 inch (0.0025 millimetre).

The common types of grinding machines include the following: (1) plain cylindrical, (2) internal cylindrical, (3) centreless (Figure 14), (4) surface (Figure 12), (5) off-hand, (6) special, and (7) abrasive-belt.

Power saws. Metal-cutting power saws are of three basic types: (1) power hacksaws, (2) band saws, and (3) circular disk saws. Vertical band saws are used for cutting shapes in metal plate, for internal and external contours, and for angular cuts.

Presses. This large class of machines includes equipment used for forming metal parts by applying the following processes: shearing, blanking, forming, drawing, bending, forging, coining, upsetting, flanging, squeezing, and hammering. All of these processes require presses with a movable ram that can be pressed against an anvil or base. The movable ram may be powered by gravity, mechanical linkages, or hydraulic or pneumatic systems. Appropriate die sets, with one part mounted on the movable ram and the matching part mounted on the fixed bed or platen, are an integral part of the machine. Punch presses stamp out metal parts from sheet metal and form the parts to the desired shape. Dies with cavities having a variety of shapes are used on forging presses that form white-hot metal blanks to the desired shapes. Power presses are also used for shearing, bending, flanging, and shaping sheet metal parts of all sizes. Power presses are made in various sizes, ranging from small presses that can be mounted on a workbench to machines weighing more than 1,000,000 pounds (450,000 kilograms).

Dies

MODIFICATIONS OF BASIC MACHINES

Certain machine tools have been designed to speed up production. Although these tools include features of the basic machine tools and perform the same operations, they incorporate design modifications that permit them to perform complex or repetitive operational sequences more rapidly. Furthermore, after the production machine has been set up by a skilled worker or machinist, a less skilled operator also can produce parts accurately and rapidly. The following are examples of production machine tools that are modifications of basic machine tools: (1) turret lathes, including screw machines; (2) multiple-station machines; (3) gang drills; and (4) production milling machines.

Turret lathes. Horizontal turret lathes have two features that distinguish them from engine lathes. The first is a multiple-sided main turret, which takes the place of the tailstock on the engine lathe (Figure 15). A variety of turning, drilling, boring, reaming, and thread-cutting tools can be fastened to the main turret, which can be rotated intermittently about its vertical axis with a hand wheel. Either a hand wheel or a power feed can be used to move the turret longitudinally against the workpiece mounted on the machine spindle.

The second distinguishing feature of the turret lathe is the square turret mounted on the cross slide. This turret also can be rotated about its vertical axis and permits the use of a variety of turning tools. A tool post, or tool block, can be clamped to the rear of the cross slide for mounting

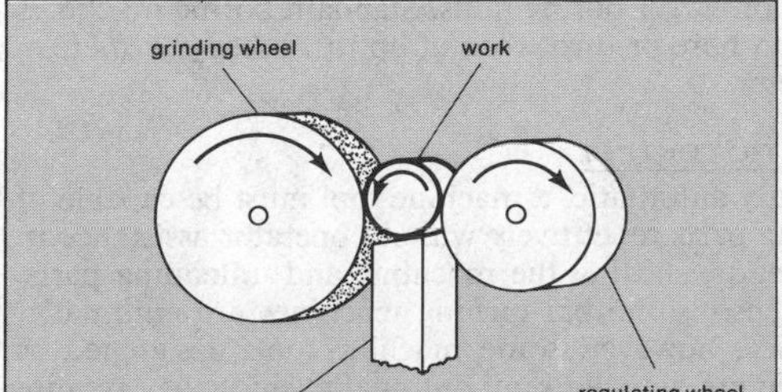

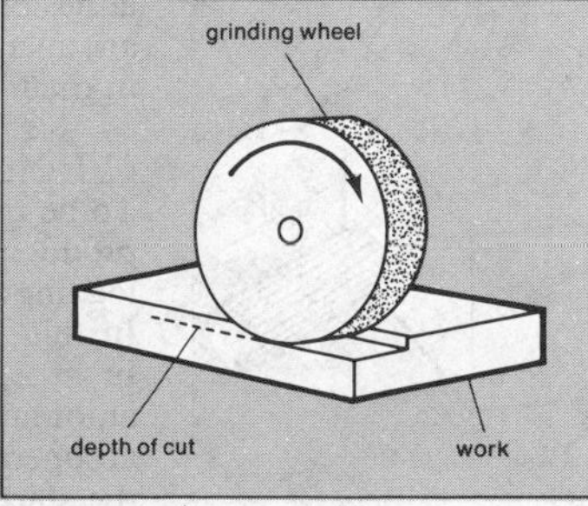

Figure 14: (Left) Centreless grinding operation. (Right) Surface grinding operation.

additional tools. The cross slide can be actuated either by hand or by power.

Turret lathes may be classified as either bar machines or chucking machines. Bar machines formerly were called screw machines, and they may be either hand controlled or automatic. A bar machine is designed for machining small threaded parts, bushings, and other small parts that can be created from bar stock fed through the machine spindle. Automatic bar machines produce parts continuously by automatically replacing of bar stock into the machine spindle. A chucking machine is designed primarily for machining larger parts, such as castings, forgings, or blanks of stock that usually must be mounted in the chuck manually.

The chucking machine

Multiple-station machines. Several types of multiple-station vertical lathes have been developed. These machines are essentially chucking-type turret lathes for machining threaded cylindrical parts. The machine has 12 spindles, each equipped with a chuck. Directly above each spindle, except one, tooling is mounted on a ram. Parts are mounted in each chuck and indexed for up to 11 machining operations. The finished part is removed at the 12th station.

Gang drills. A gang-drilling machine consists of several individual columns, drilling heads, and spindles mounted on a single base and utilizing a common table. Various numbers of spindles may be used, but four or six are common. These machines are designed for machining parts requiring several hole-machining operations, such as drilling, countersinking, counterboring, or tapping. The workpiece is moved from one drilling spindle to the next, where sequential machining operations are performed by one or more operators.

Production millers. Milling machines used for repetitive-production milling operations generally are classified as bed-type milling machines because of their design. The sliding table is mounted directly onto the massive bed of the machine and cannot be raised or moved transversely; table movement is longitudinal only. The spindle head may be adjusted vertically to establish the depth of cut. Some machines are equipped with automatic controls that require only a semiskilled operator to load parts in fixtures at each end of the table and start the machine. One part can be unloaded and replaced while the other is being machined.

SPECIAL-PURPOSE MACHINES

Special-purpose machine tools are designed to perform special machining operations, usually for production purposes. Examples include gear-cutting and gear-grinding machines, broaching machines, lapping and honing machines, and boring machines.

Gear-cutting machines. Three basic cutting methods are used for machining gears: (1) form cutting, (2) template cutting, and (3) generating. The form-cutting method uses a cutting tool that has the same form as the space between two adjacent teeth on a gear. This method is used for cutting gear teeth on a milling machine. The template-cutting method uses a template to guide a single-point cutter on large bevel-gear cutting machines.

Most cut gears produced in large lots are made on machines that utilize the gear-generating method. This method is based on the principle that two involute gears, or a gear and rack, with the same diametral pitch will mesh together properly. Therefore, a cutting tool with the shape of a gear or rack may be used to cut gear teeth in a gear or rack blank. This principle is applied in the design of a number of widely used gear-cutting machines of the generating type. Gear-generating machines that cut with reciprocating strokes are called gear shapers.

Hobbing

Gear-hobbing machines use a rotating, multiple-tooth cutting tool called a hob for generating teeth on spur gears, worm gears, helical gears, splines, and sprockets. More gears are cut by hobbing than by other methods because the hobbing cutter cuts continuously and produces accurate gears at high production rates. In gear-making machines gears can be produced by cutting, grinding, or a combination of cutting and grinding operations.

Broaching machines. In general, broaching is classified as a planing or shaping art because the action of a broaching tool resembles the action of planer and shaper tools. Broaching tools of various designs are available (Figure 10). The teeth on broaching tools are equally spaced, with each successive tooth designed to feed deeper into the workpiece, thus completing the broaching operation in a single stroke. Examples of internal broaching applications include cutting keyways in the hubs of gears or pulleys, cutting square or hexagonal holes, and cutting gear teeth. External grooves can be cut in a shaft with an external broaching tool. Some broaching machines pull or push broaching tools through or over the workpiece.

Lapping and honing machines. Lapping and honing operations are classified under the basic art of grinding. Lapping is a process in which a soft cloth impregnated with abrasive pastes or compounds is rubbed against the surface of a workpiece. Lapping is used to produce a high-quality surface finish or to finish a workpiece within close size limits. Dimensional tolerances of two millionths of an inch (0.00005 millimetre) can be achieved in the hand or machine lapping of precision parts such as gauges or gauge blocks.

Honing is a low-speed surface finishing process used for removing scratches, machine marks, or small amounts of metal, usually less than 0.0005 inch (0.0125 millimetre), from ground or machined surfaces. Honing is done with bonded abrasive sticks or stones that are mounted in a honing head. In a typical honing operation, such as honing automotive engine cylinder walls, a honing machine with one or more spindles is used. The honing head rotates slowly with an oscillating motion, holding the abrasive sticks against the work surface under controlled light pressure.

Abrasive sticks

Boring machines. Boring can be done on any type of machine that is equipped to hold a boring tool and a workpiece and that is also equipped to rotate either the tool or the workpiece in the proper relationship (Figure 13). Special boring machines of various designs are used for boring workpieces that are too large to be mounted on a lathe, drill press, or milling machine. Boring and turning operations are also performed on large vertical turret lathes or on larger boring mills. Standard boring machines are able to bore or turn work of up to 12 feet (3.6 metres) in diameter.

AUTOMATIC CONTROL

To be truly automatic, a machine tool must be capable of producing parts repetitively without operator assistance in loading parts, starting the machine, and unloading parts. In this sense, some bar-turning machines are automatic. In practice, however, some machine tools designated as automatic are actually semi-automatic, since they require an operator to load the workpiece into the machine, press the start button, and unload the part when the operation is completed.

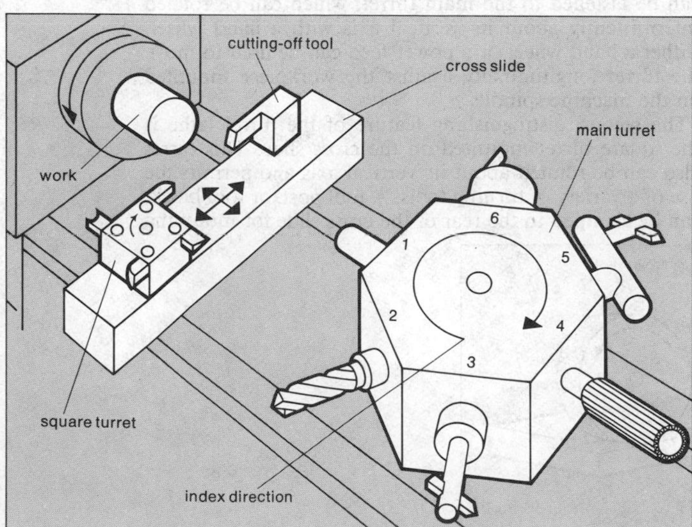

Figure 15: Horizontal turret lathe.

The tooling for automatic machines is more complex than for hand-controlled machines and usually requires a skilled worker to make the setup. After the setup, however, a less skilled operator can operate one or more machines simultaneously. Tracer lathes and numerically controlled machine tools are examples of machines that use varying degrees of automatic and semi-automatic control.

Tracer techniques. The tool slide on a tracer lathe is guided by a sensitive, hydraulically actuated stylus that follows an accurate template. The template may be an accurate profile on a thin plate or a finish-turned part. Although tracing mechanisms generally are accessory units attached to engine lathes, some lathes are especially designed as automatic tracing lathes. Optional accessories for use on tracing lathes include automatic-indexing toolheads and one or more cross slides for operations such as facing, grooving, and chamfering.

Tracing lathes can machine all common cylindrical shapes, straight and tapered shoulders, and irregular curves. Accessory tools permit facing, grooving, and chamfering operations. An unlimited combination of cutting speeds, feeds, and types of cuts may be used, including roughing cuts and finishing cuts. On machines equipped for automatic operation, changes in speed, feed, and cutting tools are automatic. (W.J.McC./Ed.)

Numerical control (NC). Many types of machine tools and other industrial processes are equipped for numerical control, commonly called NC. The earliest forms of NC were developed in the 1950s when the movements of the axes of machine tools were assigned numerical values to facilitate the replacement of handwheels and dials by control logic. NC requires accurate product design values; early systems were limited by the lack of detailed analyses for the geometrical drawings of the components to be manufactured. Later in the decade, this problem was overcome when computers were developed that could describe geometric tool movements as functions of a part-programming language. One of the best known of these early languages of tool instructions was APT (Automatically Programmed Tools).

A significant development of the early 1960s was a system known as Sketchpad, which enabled engineers to draw designs on a cathode-ray tube by using a light pen and a keyboard. When this system was connected to a computer, it enabled designers to study drawings interactively and facilitated the modification of their designs.

An NC system or device is one that controls the actions of a machine or process by the direct insertion of numerical data at some point; the system also must automatically interpret at least some portion of the data. Various kinds of numerical control systems use data coded in the form of numbers, letters, symbols, words, or a combination of these forms.

The instructions necessary for machining a part by NC are derived from the part drawing and are written in coded form on a program manuscript. The following kinds of data may be included on the manuscript: (1) sequence of operations, (2) kind of operation, (3) depth of cut, (4) coordinate dimensions for the centre of the cutting tool, (5) feed rate, (6) spindle speed, (7) tool number, and (8) other miscellaneous operations.

The coded information is punched into a ribbon of one-inch-wide machine-control tape with a tape-punching machine similar to a typewriter. The tape, usually made of paper or plastic, is inserted into the NC system, which is connected to the machine tool. The NC system interprets the information on the tape, thus activating relays and electrical circuits that cause the machine's servomechanisms and other controls to perform a sequence of operations automatically. On some NC systems, the coded information is inserted into the machines on punched cards or magnetic tape instead of punched tape. The tape can be stored for future use on the same machine or on others like it at any location. NC machines can produce parts accurately to tolerances of 0.001 or 0.0001 inch (0.025 or 0.0025 millimetre) depending on the design of the machine, the NC system, and other factors, such as environmental temperature.

NC systems on machine tools can be classified into two basic types: (1) point-to-point and (2) continuous-path. Point-to-point systems, commonly used on machines that perform hole-machining and straight-line milling operations, are relatively simple to program and do not require the aid of a computer.

Continuous-path NC systems are commonly used on machines that perform contouring operations, such as milling machines, lathes, flame-cutting machines, and drafting machines. Program preparation for continuous-path machines is more complex and usually requires the aid of a computer.

COMPUTER-AIDED MACHINING

Computer numerical control (CNC). Altering the operating procedures of early NC systems required changing the hardware of the machine tool itself. In the 1970s CNC systems (Figure 16), controlled by dedicated mini- or microcomputers, were developed to enable machine tools to be readily adapted to different jobs by altering the control program, or software. Consequently, CNC machine tools are easier to operate and more versatile than their NC counterparts, and their programming is simpler and can be rapidly tested. Since they have less control hardware, they are cheaper to maintain and are generally more accurate. CNC systems can be used with a wide range of machine tools such as milling machines and lathes. Many are equipped with graphic displays that plot the shapes of the components being machined. Some simulate tool movements, while others produce three-dimensional views of components.

From D. Gibbs, *An Introduction to CNC Machining* (1984), Cassell Computing

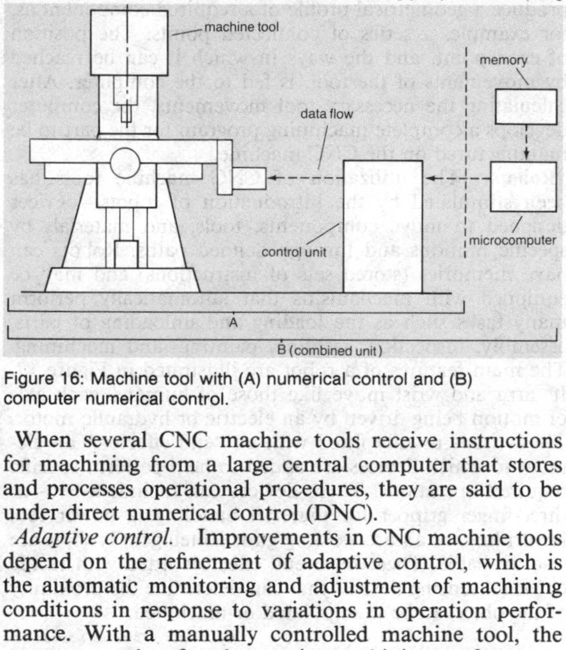

Figure 16: Machine tool with (A) numerical control and (B) computer numerical control.

When several CNC machine tools receive instructions for machining from a large central computer that stores and processes operational procedures, they are said to be under direct numerical control (DNC).

Adaptive control. Improvements in CNC machine tools depend on the refinement of adaptive control, which is the automatic monitoring and adjustment of machining conditions in response to variations in operation performance. With a manually controlled machine tool, the operator watches for changes in machining performance (caused, for example, by a dull tool or a harder workpiece) and makes the necessary mechanical adjustments. An essential element of NC and CNC machining, adaptive control is needed to protect the tool, the workpiece, and the machine from damage caused by malfunctions or by unexpected changes in machine behaviour. Adaptive control is also a significant factor in developing unmanned machining techniques.

One example of adaptive control is the monitoring of torque to a machine tool's spindle and servomotors. The control unit of the machine tool is programmed with data defining the minimum and maximum values of torque allowed for the machining operation. If, for example, a blunt tool causes the maximum torque, a signal is sent to the control unit, which corrects the situation by reducing the feed rate or altering the spindle speed.

Machining centres. A further development in the automation of machine tools is the "machining centre," usually a vertical milling machine fitted with automatic tool-changing facilities and capable of several axes of control. The tools, of which there can be more than 100, are generally housed in a rotary magazine and may be changed by commands from the machine tool program. Thus, different faces of a workpiece can be machined by a combination of operations without moving it to another machine tool. Machining centres are particularly suitable for the batch production of large and complex components requiring a high degree of accuracy.

Computer-aided design and computer-aided manufacturing (CAD/CAM). The technology of CNC machine tools has been enhanced by parallel advances in CAD/CAM. In the first NC systems, CAD and CAM were regarded as separate functions. Gradually they have come to be treated as an integrated operation, with manufacturing processes being considered at the product design stage.

CAD enables designers to use computers to analyze and manipulate design data. Using a graphics workstation or computer terminal to display three-dimensional figures, the designer can examine a proposed design from different angles, in various cross sections, and in many sizes. Details of the completed design are transferred to a second terminal on which a set of engineering drawings can be produced. All aspects of the design are closely scrutinized at this stage, and, after final changes are made, the finished, fully dimensioned design is drawn on a specialized computer printer called a plotter.

CAD/CAM systems also allow design data to be stored in numerical (digitized) form, from which machine-control tapes and disks may be prepared directly. The CAD and CAM systems may then be linked by computer-assisted part programming. With this technique a CAD system can produce a geometrical profile of a required component as, for example, a series of connected points. The position of each point, and the ways in which it can be reached by movements of the tool, is fed to the computer. After calculating the necessary tool movements, the computer develops a complete machining program for the part to be manufactured on the CNC machine.

Robots. The utilization of CNC machine tools has been stimulated by the introduction of robots—devices designed to move components, tools, and materials by specific motions and through defined paths. Robots can have memories (stored sets of instructions) and may be equipped with mechanisms that automatically perform many tasks such as the loading and unloading of parts, assembly, inspection, welding, painting, and machining. The main features of a robot are illustrated in Figure 17. Its arm and wrist move like those of humans, each axis of motion being driven by an electric or hydraulic motor. The wrist is usually fitted with an "end effector," an element to which devices are added to help perform specific required operations. These devices can include a two- or three-finger gripper for material handling, a power tool for drilling, or an arc-welding gun. "Intelligent" robots are also available. These have end effectors fitted with tactile or visual sensing devices that can determine the proximity of the object to be manipulated or machined.

By courtesy of Cincinnati Milacron, Inc.

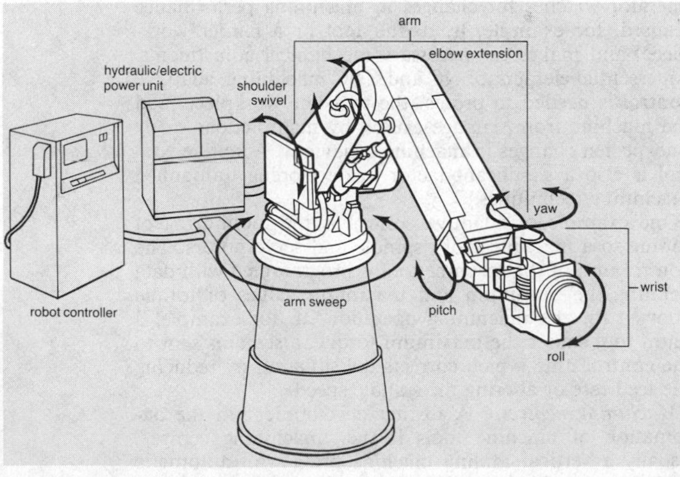

Figure 17: Industrial robot.

Flexible manufacturing system (FMS). A group of manufacturing cells linked by an automatic material handling system and a central computer is called a flexible manufacturing system. The computerized coordination of FMS enables components to be produced at very low costs, even when only small quantities are to be made. The main feature of FMS is its ability to switch from the machining of one component to another (or between separate manufacturing processes) without undue interruption. Each machine control unit stores many part-producing programs in its computer memory. The FMS master computer uses direct numerical control (DNC) to select and activate these programs as they are needed during the manufacturing process. As the master computer governs the supply of workpieces to the machine, the part program controls individual tooling. If a variety of machining operations are needed, a large number of tools may have to be carried: some milling operations, for example, require 60 to 100 tools.

Computer-integrated manufacturing. Computers have come to be used in all stages of manufacture: design, scheduling, management, manufacturing, and testing. The integration of these phases of computer involvement is called computer-integrated manufacturing. For further information about robots, see the articles AUTOMATION and COMPUTERS.

NONCONVENTIONAL METHODS OF MACHINING

Traditional machining processes work on the principle that the tool is harder than the workpiece. Some materials, however, are too hard or too brittle to be machined by conventional methods. The use of very hard nickel-based and titanium alloys by the aircraft engine industry, for example, has stimulated nonconventional machining methods, especially "electrical methods."

Electrical methods of machining. Some machining methods rely on electrical phenomena—rather than mechanical means—for cutting and machining workpieces.

Electron-beam machining (EBM). The EBM technique is used for cutting fine holes and slots in any material. In a vacuum chamber, a beam of high-velocity electrons is focused on a workpiece. The kinetic energy of the electrons, upon striking the workpiece, changes to heat, which vaporizes minute amounts of the material. The vacuum prevents the electrons from scattering, due to collisions with gas molecules. EBM is used for cutting holes as small as 0.001 inch (0.025 millimetre) in diameter or slots as narrow as 0.001 inch in materials up to 0.250 inch (6.25 millimetres) in thickness. EBM is also used as an alternative to light optics manufacturing methods in the semiconductor industry. Because electrons have a shorter wavelength than light and can be easily focused, electron-beam methods are particularly useful for high-resolution lithography and for the manufacture of complex integrated circuits. Welding can also be done with an electron beam, notably in the manufacture of aircraft engine parts.

Electrical-discharge machining (EDM). EDM involves the direction of high-frequency electrical spark discharges from a graphite or soft metal tool, which serves as an electrode, to disintegrate electrically conductive materials such as hardened steel or carbide. The electrode and workpiece are immersed in a dielectric liquid, and a feed mechanism maintains a spark gap of from 0.0005 to 0.020 inch (0.013 to 0.5 millimetre) between the electrode and the workpiece. As spark discharges melt or vaporize small particles of the workpiece, the particles are flushed away, and the electrode advances. The process is accurate, but slow, and is used for machining dies, molds, holes, slots, and cavities of almost any desired shape. In CNC wire machining, a thin copper wire is used as the tool for cutting out two- and three-dimensional fretwork profiles.

Electrochemical machining (ECM). ECM resembles electroplating in reverse. In this process metal is dissolved from a workpiece with direct current at a controlled rate in an electrolytic cell. The workpiece serves as the anode and is separated by a gap of 0.001 to 0.030 inch (0.025 to 0.75 millimetre) from the tool, which serves as the cathode. The electrolyte, usually an aqueous salt solution, is pumped under pressure through the inter-electrode gap,

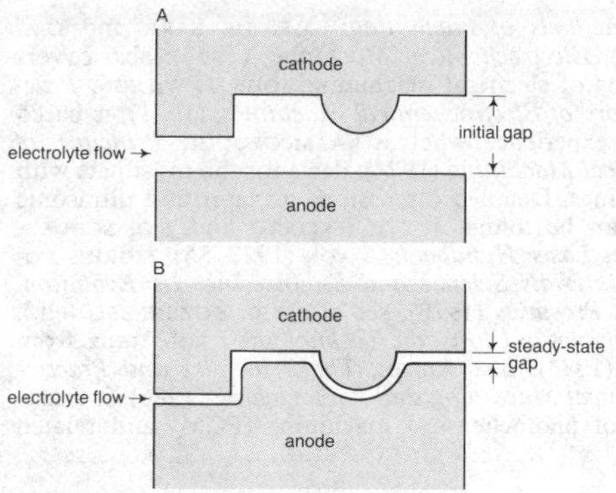

Figure 18: *Electrochemical machining (ECM).* (A) Initial electrode configuration and (B) final electrode configuration.

From J.A. McGeough, *Principles of Electrochemical Machining* (1971), Chapman and Hall, London

thus flushing away metal dissolved from the workpiece. As one electrode moves toward the other to maintain a constant gap, the anode workpiece is machined into a complementary shape (see Figure 18). The advantages of ECM are lack of tool wear and the fact that a softer cathode tool can be used to machine a harder workpiece. Applications of ECM can be found in the aircraft engine and automobile industries, where the process is used for deburring, drilling small holes, and machining extremely hard turbine blades.

Other versions of ECM include electrolytic grinding, which includes about 90 percent ECM with 10 percent mechanical action; electrochemical arc machining (ECAM), in which controlled arcs in an aqueous electrolyte remove material at a fast rate; and capillary drilling, in which acid electrolytes are used to machine very fine holes.

Ion beam machining (IBM). In IBM a stream of charged atoms (ions) of an inert gas, such as argon, is accelerated in a vacuum by high energies and directed toward a solid workpiece. The beam removes atoms from the workpiece by transferring energy and momentum to atoms on the surface of the object. When an atom strikes a cluster of atoms on the workpiece, it dislodges between 0.1 and 10 atoms from the workpiece material. IBM permits the accurate machining of virtually any material and is used in the semiconductor industry and in the manufacture of aspheric lenses. The technique is also used for texturing surfaces to enhance bonding, for producing atomically clean surfaces on devices such as laser mirrors, and for modifying the thickness of thin films and membranes.

Laser machining (LM). LM is a method of cutting metal or refractory materials by melting and vaporizing the material with an intense beam of light from a laser. Drilling by laser, although costly in energy since material must be melted and vaporized to be removed, is used to cut small holes (0.005 to 0.05 inch [0.13 to 1.3 millimetres]) in materials that are too difficult to machine by traditional methods. A common application is the laser drilling of diamonds to be used as dies for drawing wire. Lasers also are used to drill and cut ceramics and substrates for integrated circuits; the aircraft industry uses CNC-controlled lasers to cut profiles and to drill holes in engine parts.

Plasma arc machining (PAM). PAM is a method of cutting metal with a plasma-arc, or tungsten inert-gas-arc, torch. The torch produces a high-velocity jet of high-temperature ionized gas (plasma) that cuts by melting and displacing material from the workpiece. Temperatures obtainable in the plasma zone range from 20,000° to 50,000° F (11,000° to 28,000° C). The process may be used for cutting most metals, including those that cannot be cut efficiently with an oxyacetylene torch. With heavy-duty torches, aluminum alloys up to six inches (15 centimetres) thick and stainless steel up to four inches (10 centimetres) thick have been cut by the PAM process. The process is used for the profile cutting of flat plate, for cutting grooves in stainless steel, and, on lathes, for turning large, hardened steel rolls.

Other methods of machining. *Ultrasonic machining (USM).* In USM, material is removed from a workpiece with particles of abrasive that vibrate at high frequency in a water slurry circulating through a narrow gap between a vibrating tool and the workpiece. The tool, shaped like the cavity to be produced, oscillates at an amplitude of about 0.0005 to 0.0025 inch (0.013 to 0.062 millimetre) at 19,000 to 40,000 hertz (cycles per second). The tool vibrates the abrasive grains against the surface of the workpiece, thus removing material. Ultrasonic machining is used primarily for cutting hard, brittle materials that may be conductors of electricity or insulators. Other common applications of USM include cutting semiconductor materials (such as germanium), engraving, drilling fine holes in glass, and machining ceramics and precious stones.

A modified version of the process is ultrasonic twist drilling, in which an ultrasonic tool is rotated against a workpiece without an abrasive slurry. Holes as small as 80 micrometres have been drilled by this type of USM.

Chemical machining (CHM). This nonelectrical process removes metal from selected or overall areas by controlled chemical action. Masking tape can be used to protect areas not to be removed. The method is related to the process used for making metal printing and engraving plates. Two types of chemical machining processes include chemical blanking, which is used for cutting blanks of thin metal parts, and chemical milling, which is used for removing metal from selected or overall areas of metal parts.

Photochemical machining (PCM). PCM is an extension of CHM that uses a series of photographic and chemical etching techniques to produce components and devices in a wide range of metals, especially stainless steel.

Water-jet machining. In the water-jet machining process, water is forced through tiny nozzles under very high pressures to cut through materials such as polymers, brick, and paper. Water-jet machining has several advantages over other methods: it generates no heat, the workpiece does not deform during machining, the process can be initiated anywhere on the workpiece, no premachining preparation is needed, and few burrs form during the process. An abrasive is occasionally added to the water to improve the rate of material removal, especially in finishing work. The offshore industry uses seawater as the working fluid when applying this technique.

(W.J.McC./J.A.McG.)

BIBLIOGRAPHY

Hand tools: The literature on hand tools is generally fragmented and without a single comprehensive treatment. Archaeological and anthropological information concerning the earliest tools may be found in: CHESTER S. CHARD, *Man in Prehistory,* 2nd ed. (1974); ROBERT J. BRAIDWOOD, *Prehistoric Men,* 8th ed. (1975); KENNETH P. OAKLEY, *Man the Tool-Maker,* 6th ed. rev. (1972); and F. CLARK HOWELL, *Early Man* (1973). Specific treatments are given in FRANÇOIS BORDES, *The Old Stone Age* (1968; orginally published in French, 1961); and JACQUES BORDAZ, *Tools of the Old and New Stone Age* (1970). The rise of metal tools is found in LESLIE AITCHISON, *A History of Metals,* 2 vol. (1960); and THOMAS A. RICKARD, *Man and Metals,* 2 vol. (1932, reprinted in 1 vol. 1974). From Roman times onward, WILLIAM L. GOODMAN, *The History of Woodworking Tools* (1964, reissued 1976), is definitive. R.A. SALAMAN, *Dictionary of Tools Used in the Woodworking and Allied Trades, c. 1700–1970* (1975), is a comprehensive and very well-illustrated account. HENRY C. MERCER, *Ancient Carpenters' Tools: Together with Lumbermen's, Joiners', and Cabinet Makers' Tools in Use in the Eighteenth Century,* 5th ed. (1975), should not be missed; and PETER C. WELSH, *Woodworking Tools, 1600–1900* (1966), PAUL B. KEBABIAN and WILLIAM C. LIPKE (eds.), *Tools and Technologies: America's Wooden Age* (1979), and ALDREN A. WATSON, *Hand Tools: Their Ways and Workings* (1982), include a wealth of illustrations. CHARLES SINGER *et al.* (eds.), *A History of Technology,* 8 vol. (1954–84); and MAURICE DAUMAS (ed.), *Histoire générale des techniques,* 5 vol. (1962–79), give wide but unconnected treatments. The first three volumes of Daumas's work cover the history of technology to the middle of the 19th century and have been published in English as *A History of Technology & Invention: Progress Through the Ages,* 3 vol. (1969–79). Illustrated by original drawings, ERIC SLOANE, *A Museum of Early American Tools* (1964); and EDWIN TUNIS, *Colonial Craftsmen and the Beginnings of American Industry* (1965), are highly informative because techniques and products of their period are shown in addition to tools. Relevant articles also may be found in serial publications such as *Technikgeschichte* (quarterly); NEWCOMEN SOCIETY FOR THE STUDY OF THE HISTORY OF ENGINEERING AND TECHNOLOGY, *Transactions* (annual); and *Technology and Culture* (quarterly). The EARLY AMERICAN INDUSTRIES ASSOCIATION, *Chronicle* (quarterly), frequently contains articles on the history of hand tools. Many 19th-century books give detailed accounts of tools as well as of processes. Examples are CHARLES HOLTZAPFFEL and JOHN JACOB HOLTZAPFFEL, *Turning and Mechanical Manipulation,* 5 vol. (1843–52). See also the article entitled "Tool" by JOSEPH G. HORNER in the 11th edition of the *Encyclopædia Britannica,* vol. 27, pp. 14–47, which contains a well-illustrated account of 19th-century developments in both hand and machine tools.

Machine tools: Good sources of general information on the subject are VICTOR E. REPP and WILLARD J. MCCARTHY, *Machine Tool Technology,* 5th ed. (1984); and E. PAUL DEGARMO, J. TEMPLE BLACK, and RONALD A. KOHSER, *Materials and Processes in Manufacturing,* 6th ed. (1984). The most authoritative, although highly technical, source for all phases of machine tools is the AMERICAN SOCIETY FOR METALS, *Machining,* ed. by TAYLOR LYMAN (1967). A useful source on the history of machine tools is L.T.C. ROLT, *A Short History of Machine Tools* (1965). VICTOR E. REPP, O.A. LUDWIG, and WILLARD J. MCCARTHY, *Metalwork: Technology and Practice,* 7th ed. (1982), is a good text for the secondary school level. A comprehensive source of technical data on machine tools is ERIC OBERG, FRANKLIN D. JONES, and HOLBROOK L. HORTON, *Machinery's Handbook,* 22nd ed. (1984).

Electrical methods of machining: A.E. DE BARR and D.A. OLIVER (eds.), *Electrochemical Machining* (1968), also covers other methods of electrical machining; JOHN F. WILSON, *Practice and Theory of Electrochemical Machining* (1971), is based on industrial experience, whereas J.A. MCGEOUGH, *Principles of Electrochemical Machining* (1974), deals for the most part with research findings. Detailed discussions on laser and ultrasonic machining can be found in F.T. ARECCHI and E.O. SCHULZ-DUBOIS (eds.), *Laser Handbook,* 5 vol. (1972–85); MORRIS COHEN (ed.), *Materials Science and Engineering: Its Evolution, Practice, and Prospects* (1978); see also L.D. ROZENBERG (ed.), *Physical Principles of Ultrasonic Technology,* 2 vol., trans. from the Russian (1973). D.M. ALLEN, *The Principles and Practice of Photochemical Machining and Photoetching* (1986), is a useful account of photochemical machining (PCM) and related techniques.

Computer-aided machining: SEROPE KALPAKJIAN, *Manufacturing Processes for Engineering Materials* (1984); and GEOFFREY BOOTHROYD, *Fundamentals of Metal Machining and Machine Tools* (1975), are both very informative sources on computer-aided machining as they relate to machine tool technology. For a more technical work, see RAYMOND SHAH, *NC Guide: Numerical Control Handbook,* 2nd ed. (1979). Two useful introductory texts are MIKELL P. GROOVER and EMORY W. ZIMMERS, JR., *CAD/CAM: Computer-Aided Design and Manufacturing* (1984); and DAVID GIBBS, *An Introduction to CNC Machining* (1984).

(R.S.H./W.J.McC./J.A.McG.)

Toronto

Toronto is situated on the northern shore of Lake Ontario; it is Canada's most populous metropolitan area, the seat of government of the Canadian province of Ontario, and the financial and commercial heart of Canada. It is little more than an hour's flying time from both New York City and Chicago. Since the 1950s Toronto has grown phenomenally from a rather sedate provincial town—"Toronto the Good"—to a lively, thriving, cosmopolitan metropolitan area.

The article is divided into the following sections:

Physical and human geography

THE LANDSCAPE

The city layout. The site of the city is almost uniformly flat, although three to four miles (five to six kilometres) inland there is a fairly sharp rise of some 40 feet (12 metres)—the shoreline elevation of the former glacial Lake Iroquois. Streets are laid out in a grid, although the pattern is modified to some extent by diagonal roads roughly following the shoreline. The central business areas are located around Bloor and Yonge streets and Yonge and Queen streets. The central financial district, with its numerous insurance and banking offices and the Toronto Stock Exchange, is in the vicinity of King and Bay streets, south of the old City Hall (1899).

The city skyline is dominated by the CN Tower (1,815 feet), and the Toronto–Dominion Centre, Commerce Court, and First Canadian Place, each of which is more than 50 stories high. Other notable buildings include the new City Hall (1958), Eaton Centre, the Metropolitan Toronto Library, the Ontario Science Centre, and Roy Thomson Hall, noted for its excellent acoustics. Extensive new housing and mixed-use projects, together with the restoration and rehabilitation of heritage buildings, have brought extraordinary vitality to the urban core.

Toronto is a Great Lakes port and, through the St. Lawrence Seaway, an ocean port as well. It handles more than 2,500,000 tons of freight annually. The lakefront is separated from the downtown area by railway tracks and an expressway. Ferry service connects the dock area to the Toronto Islands, about half a mile offshore, which have yacht clubs, a small airport, recreational facilities, and a residential community.

North of the central business district is the fashionable Yorkville–Cumberland boutique shopping area, to the south of which are Queen's Park, the Ontario Parliament Buildings, and the University of Toronto. Large expanses of grass and tall shade trees make this a pleasant area, complementing the ravines that form so important an element in the metropolitan parks system. One of the most attractive residential areas in Toronto is Rosedale, an older neighbourhood of dignified houses and winding, tree-lined streets quite close to the downtown centre, which itself contains many attractive streets of modest, well-designed houses.

Climate. Toronto's geographical situation on Lake Ontario modifies the climate somewhat, although winter temperatures may frequently drop below zero. Heavy snowfall, however, is rare even in January and February, the coldest months. July and August are humid, with temperatures in the 90s (°F; 30° C).

THE PEOPLE

During part of the 1950s and 1960s Toronto became one of the fastest growing urban areas in North America. The influx of European immigrants transformed the character of the city: traditionally Protestant and largely of British origin, by 1961 less than half the inhabitants of the central

Ontario Place in Toronto, designed by Eberhard Zeidler and completed in 1971.

city were of British extraction. During the 1970s and early 1980s European immigrants were augmented by large numbers from the West Indies and Asia.

THE ECONOMY

Industry and trade. Toronto enjoys the economic benefits of its position on the Great Lakes and of its development as a rail and trucking centre. It is readily accessible to major industrial centres in the United States and to oceangoing shipping. As the capital of Canada's richest and most populous province, the city has a widely diversified economy. Ontario produces more than half of Canada's manufactured goods and most of its manufactured exports; it has immense resources of raw materials—minerals, timber, water, agricultural products, and hydroelectric power. The Toronto Stock Exchange is, in value of trading, one of the largest stock exchanges in North America.

Transportation. Policy for public transportation is coordinated by the Metropolitan Toronto Transit Commission (TTC). The modern, efficient subway has two major lines, one running north–south and the other east–west. Additional lines operate during rush hours. Seventeen miles west of the centre of the city is Toronto International Airport, Canada's busiest air terminal.

ADMINISTRATIVE CONDITIONS

The Municipality of Metropolitan Toronto is governed by the Metropolitan Council. Each council member serves a three-year term and is also a member of a city or borough council. The responsibilities of the council include housing, finance, police protection, education, water supply, sewage disposal, and health and welfare provisions. Additional services for the city of Toronto itself are provided by a mayor and a city council.

CULTURAL LIFE

The city is an important cultural centre. The Toronto Symphony Orchestra and other musical groups have an international reputation. There are three major theatres, together with many small experimental theatres. The Art Gallery of Ontario and the Royal Ontario Museum have excellent collections, and there are numerous privately owned galleries. Other attractions include the Ontario Science Centre, with its imaginative working exhibits, and Ontario Place, a large complex of recreational facilities on man-made islands that are an extension to the permanent Canadian National Exhibition. The city has several institutions of higher learning—the University of Toronto with its colleges, Erindale and Scarborough, York University with Glendon College, and Ryerson Polytechnical Institute. The Ontario College of Art offers a wide diversity of excellent programs. A new zoo, opened in 1975; dozens of excellent restaurants, boutiques, and movie theatres; and the Toronto Maple Leafs (ice hockey), the Argonauts (football), and the Blue Jays (baseball) all add to the colour and vitality of this vigorous community.

There is an active winter season of cultural activities, with a rich fare of concerts, theatre, opera, ballet, and films. Lectures, seminars, evening classes, and meetings of all kinds cover a multitude of subjects, and the religious life of the community is sustained by a variety of churches, synagogues, mosques, temples, and other meeting places. Many ethnic groups organize traditional festivals, balls, entertainments, and social activities.

In 1967 the Metropolitan Toronto Corporation assumed responsibility for the Canadian National Exhibition—reputed to be the world's largest annual exhibition—which was first launched in 1879 as the Toronto Industrial Exhibition. An international air show; agricultural, animal, and flower displays; theatrical and musical events; and a fairground attract millions of visitors in the late summer each year. The permanent buildings are used for trade shows and other special events between seasons.

The Metropolitan Toronto Parks Department administers approximately 7,000 acres (2,800 hectares) of parkland, and ambitious plans have been made for the development of Toronto's waterfront. The Metropolitan Toronto and Region Conservation Authority is an important joint provincial-municipal agency concerned with the development of recreational areas, flood control, and the conservation of existing woodlands and waterways. It is responsible for the implementation of a large part of Toronto's regional waterfront-development plan. The authority also offers assistance and technical advice to rural landowners.

Local recreational areas

Toronto is the main regional tourist centre serving the Muskoka Lakes, the Haliburton Highlands, and Georgian Bay, all magnificent lakeland and forest areas with fine hunting, fishing, and camping facilities. There has been a remarkable increase in winter sports, and although Ontario's highest point is only 2,183 feet (665 metres), good skiing facilities are available within easy reach of the city. Algonquin Provincial Park is some 163 miles to the north, Niagara Falls is 80 miles south, and the city is surrounded by beautiful rolling farmland, with well-marked sites of historical and architectural interest. Camping, cottaging, boating, and fishing in summer and skiing, ice hockey, and curling in winter are the most popular forms of outdoor recreation.

History

EARLY SETTLEMENT

The first known settlement in the Toronto area, Teiaiagon, inhabited first by the Seneca and later by the Mississauga

Indians, was on the east bank of the Humber River. In the 17th century it became a trading post, strategically situated at the crossing of ancient Indian trails going west to the Mississippi and north to Lake Simcoe and beyond into vast wilderness areas. These land and water routes were followed by explorers, fur traders, missionaries, and others intent upon opening up and exploiting the resources of the Great Lakes region.

By the mid-18th century the name Toronto had come to be commonly used for one of three tiny forts built (1720–50) in the area by the French to defend their trade with the Indians against English and other European competitors. The French were defeated in 1759 and the forts were subsequently destroyed, but the settlement survived as a trading post.

At the end of the Seven Years' War with France (1763), Canada came under British sovereignty; during and after the U.S. War of Independence it was a haven for those American colonists who preferred British rule to that of the new Republic. Some 40,000 United Empire loyalists are said to have settled in the Great Lakes and St. Lawrence areas at this time, and during the 19th century large numbers of immigrants came from Great Britain.

In 1787 Lord Dorchester, governor in chief of Canada, opened negotiations with three Indian chiefs for the purchase of a site for the future capital of Ontario; about 250,000 acres (100,000 hectares) fronting the lake were acquired in exchange for £1,700, bales of cloth, axes, and other trading goods.

Ontario's first parliament met in 1792 at Niagara, but in 1793 Col. John Simcoe, lieutenant governor of Upper Canada, selected the present site of Toronto for his capital because of its fine harbour, strategic location for defense and trade, and the rich potential of its wilderness hinterland. He changed its name from Toronto to York; two years later (1795) Ontario's capital consisted of only 12 cottages and a small military establishment on the edge of the wilderness.

Occupation by U.S. forces in 1813

While the British were engaged with France in Europe, the United States declared war on Britain; and York, with a population of 700, was practically defenseless. It was taken in April 1813 and was pillaged and occupied by U.S. forces for 11 days before being retaken by the British. The Speaker's Mace was carried off but was returned in 1934; the Royal Standard is still in the U.S. Naval Academy, Annapolis, Maryland.

Economic depression in Great Britain following the Napoleonic Wars drove many overseas, and York's population increased from 720 (1816) to about 9,000 in 1834, when the city was incorporated and the old name of Toronto restored. In 1849 there was a disastrous fire that destroyed some 15 acres of the downtown area, including St. James' Cathedral, St. Lawrence Market, and many offices, stores, and warehouses, but the city soon recovered.

EVOLUTION OF THE MODERN CITY

Rapid development followed the coming of the Grand Trunk and Great Western railways in the 1850s, and for a decade prosperity was enhanced by a treaty with the United States (1854) that gave certain of Canada's products free entry to markets south of the border. The timber resources of the province were exploited, and large areas of land were converted to farming. Thus, Toronto grew rapidly as an industrial, trading, and distributing centre; its population was 45,000 in 1861, 208,000 in 1901, and 522,000 in 1921.

Prosperity and security were reflected in civic improvement, great building activity, and cultural progress. Between the city's incorporation (1834) and Canada's national confederation under the British North America Act of 1867, many of Toronto's buildings of historical and architectural importance were constructed, including the new St. James' Cathedral, St. Lawrence Hall, and University College (now part of the University of Toronto), all of which are still extant. The Grand Opera House (since demolished) was opened in 1874, a stolid successor to the numerous small theatres of midcentury that were mostly converted barns. King's College (founded 1827), later to become the University of Toronto, was constructed in 1843 on the site of the present Ontario Parliament Buildings (1886).

During the 50 years from 1834 to 1883, the city maintained its boundaries virtually unchanged. Some reclamation near the lake improved lakeshore properties and docking facilities. Largely by the annexation of adjacent villages and towns, the area of the city was doubled by 1900 and doubled again by 1920. In 1930 the metropolitan area included the central city, four towns (Leaside, Mimico, New Toronto, and Weston), three villages (Forest Hill, Long Branch, and Swansea), and five townships (Etobicoke, East York, North York, Scarborough, and York).

The Great Depression of the 1930s caused severe financial problems for suburban Toronto. Capital debt payments could not be met, and expenditure on public services—sewage and piped water supply in places remote from the lake, for example—had to be postponed. A rapid increase in population after World War II added to the municipal burden, and many solutions were investigated. In 1953 the Ontario Municipal Board recommended for the 13 municipalities the establishment of a federated form of government unique in North America. The Municipality of Metropolitan Toronto Act was passed, and a 25-member Council of Metropolitan Toronto met for the first time on January 1, 1954. One of the first tasks of the council was to find ways and means of dealing with common major problems by united action, while also permitting local matters to be handled independently. Since the joint credit of the combined municipalities was much greater than the sum of their credits as individual authorities, financing was greatly simplified. A common level of assessment and tax rate on property—the main source of revenue—was agreed upon by each municipality. A most significant feature of the system was that members of the Metropolitan Council were appointed by virtue of their election to office either as mayors, aldermen, or controllers of a particular municipality, thus ensuring a high degree of coordination and good communication between the central body and the local municipalities.

Uniting of the metropolitan area

The Metropolitan Council worked well: it resolved many of the difficult sewage and water problems; it greatly improved transportation by constructing expressways and roads, a new airport terminal building (1962), and an excellent subway; it authorized the construction of new schools and the renovation of old ones; and it introduced a regional parks system in an attempt to control future development.

Administrative reorganization

In 1967 the Corporation of Metropolitan Toronto was reorganized. The 13 municipalities were reduced to six, and the council was increased to 33 members. Later legislation gave the boroughs the option to rename themselves cities. The council considerably extended its responsibilities in education and the social services, adding, for example, urban renewal, waste disposal, and ambulance and library services. In 1975 and 1980 the council was again increased in size, and it added to its jurisdiction such problems as the control of urban development and housing for the elderly.

BIBLIOGRAPHY. The Municipality of Metropolitan Toronto publishes documents and statistical reports about constituent departments, and the City of Toronto Planning Board produces studies on developments as, for example, *The Central Waterfront Information Base Study, Uses* (1977). Other references are: ERIC R. ARTHUR, *Toronto: No Mean City,* 2nd ed. (1974), and *From Front Street to Queen's Park: The Story of Ontario's Parliament Buildings* (1979); RICHARD P. BAINE and A. LYNN MCMURRAY, *Toronto: An Urban Study,* rev. ed. (1977); LARRY S. BOURNE *et al.* (eds.), *Urban Futures for Central Canada: Perspectives in Forecasting Urban Growth and Form* (1974); WILLIAM DENDY, *Lost Toronto* (1978); LEONARD O. GERTLER and RONALD W. CROWLEY, *Changing Canadian Cities: The Next 25 Years* (1977); PETER G. GOHEEN, *Victorian Toronto, 1850 to 1900: Pattern and Process of Growth* (1970); THOMAS HOWARTH *et al., Two Cultures, Two Cities: Milano, Toronto: Symposium Proceedings* (1977); HAROLD KAPLAN, *Urban Political Systems: A Functional Analysis of Metro Toronto* (1967); DONALD B. KIRKUP, *Metropolitan Toronto: Past and Present* (1974), containing aerial photographs; ROBERT A. MURDIE, *Fac-*

torial Ecology of Metropolitan Toronto, 1951–1961: An Essay on the Social Geography of the City (1969); GEORGE A. NADER, *Cities of Canada,* 2 vol. (1975–76); ALBERT ROSE, *Governing Metropolitan Toronto: A Social and Political Analysis, 1953–1971* (1972); JACOB SPELT, *Toronto* (1973); MIKE FILEY, *A Toronto Album: Glimpses of the City That Was* (1970), and *Toronto: The Way We Were: Photos & Stories About North America's Greatest City* (1974); EDITH G. FIRTH, *The Town of York: A Collection of Documents of Early Toronto,* 2 vol. (1962–66); EDWIN C. GUILLET, *Toronto from Trading Post to Great City* (1934); WILLIAM E. MANN, *The Underside of Toronto* (1970); DONALD C. MASTERS, *The Rise of Toronto, 1850–1890* (1947, reprinted 1972); JESSE E. MIDDLETON, *The Municipality of Toronto: A History,* 3 vol. (1923); and G. PELHAM MULVANY, *Toronto: Past and Present* (1884, reprinted 1970). TIMOTHY J. COLTON, *Big Daddy* (1980), is a life of the founder of metropolitan Toronto.

(Th.Ho.)

Torts

Tort is a legal term used by common-law jurisdictions to cover a variety of harmful behaviour, from physical attack on one's person to interference with one's goods or use and enjoyment of one's land, economic interests, and honour, reputation, and privacy. Other legal systems use different terms for this wide and amorphous area of the law. The Germans talk of unlawful acts; the French-inspired systems use interchangeably the terms *délits* (and *quasi-délits*) and civil responsibility. Despite differences of terminology, however, this area of the law is primarily concerned with liability for behaviour that the legal order regards as socially unacceptable, typically warranting the award of damages to the injured party. It is broadly true to say that most western European and common-law systems tend to regard as actionable the same factual situations. But if the results are often quite similar, the arrangement of the law and the methodology often differ significantly. The German Civil Code has a strong tendency to abstraction and systematization, displaying its university origins and contrasting sharply with the more casuistic (here, law deriving from authority based on cases considered one-by-one as opposed to law deriving from a general principle) and judge-made law of the common-law systems. In between there are the 19th-century codifications, which are the products of the natural school of law and which have adopted manifesto-like provisions in their codes. Typical of this approach is the French Civil Code of 1804; much contemporary French law results from interplay between judicial activity and doctrinal writing.

Tort law, until recently the junior partner to contract law in the law of civil obligations, has since World War II expanded everywhere, though especially in continental Europe. At the same time, criticism of it has led to its replacement either partially by specialized schemes or, in rare cases, by complete systems of accident compensation. Criticism has also provoked serious discussion about the impact of the welfare state, modern insurance practices, and the importance of economic analysis in the proper development of the law.

For coverage of related topics in the *Macropædia* and *Micropædia,* see the *Propædia,* Part Five, Division Five, especially Section 553.

This article is divided into the following sections:

FUNCTIONS OF TORT

Throughout its long history tort has pursued different aims: punishment, appeasement, deterrence, compensation, and efficient loss spreading of the cost of accidents. None offers a complete justification; all are important, though at different stages one may have been more prominent than the rest.

Punishment and appeasement. Originally tort and criminal law were indistinguishable, and even when the two branches began to acquire independent identities the former remained for a very long time in the shadow of the latter. Offenses against the community and the king's interests increasingly became the subject of criminal law, whereas wrongs against the individual came to be dealt with by the emerging (or, in the case of continental Europe, reemerging Roman-inspired) law of torts. Early tort law, however, was concerned only with the most serious kinds of wrongs—bodily injury, damage to goods, trespass to land—and not until the 19th century did it cover such conduct as intentional infliction of economic loss and, in modern times, negligently inflicted economic loss or other violations of subtler interests. This independent growth resulted from the need to buy off private vengeance and to strengthen law and order during the Middle Ages. Punishment and appeasement are no longer major aims. Nevertheless, some common-law jurisdictions—notably in the United States—retain the element of punishment for certain types of tortious conduct. These punitive or exemplary damages, as they are sometimes called, are in England limited to three rather narrow instances, of which perhaps the most difficult is the case of an activity calculated by the defendant to make a profit (a term not confined to moneymaking in the strict sense). In these instances it is felt that "it is necessary to teach the wrongdoer that tort does not pay" by making him not only "compensate" the plaintiff for the latter's "loss" but also disgorge any gain he may have made from his conduct. That this is right few would doubt. Less defensible, however, is the resulting windfall for the plaintiff and the loss of important procedural safeguards for the defendant where "punishment" is meted out by an unpredictable and unguided jury. Civil-law systems have, by contrast, taken a hostile attitude toward penal damages in civil actions, though there are limited instances in the German law of tort (privacy) and French law of contract (*astreinte*) in which a penal element is allowed to creep into the civil award.

Limited instances of punitive damages

Deterrence. In its modern, economic sense, deterrence aims at reducing the number of accidents by imposing a heavy financial cost on unsafe conduct and promoting economic efficiency. A distinction is necessary between specific and general deterrence. The former depends largely on the admonitory effect of tort law. This, however, is limited where insurance cushions the defendant from the economic consequences of an adverse judgment (though insurance premiums may subsequently be increased); and it almost completely evaporates in instances such as road traffic accidents where harm is statistically inevitable and in most cases results from momentary inattention, the occurrence of which no tort award can ever prevent. Tort law is, therefore, in some cases a second-best means for preventing accidents.

Calabresi's theory of general deterrence

Very different is the theory of general deterrence principally argued by the U.S. legal scholar Guido Calabresi in *The Cost of Accidents* (1970). In Calabresi's words, general deterrence involves deciding

> what the accident costs of activities are and letting the market determine the degree to which, and the ways in which, activities are desired given such costs. Similarly it involves giving people freedom to choose whether they would rather engage in the activity and pay the costs of doing so, including accident costs, or, given the accident costs, engage in safer activities that might otherwise have seemed less desirable.

Calabresi's approach reflects the belief that the market mechanism not only achieves the optimum allocation of resources but also ensures that most of society's decisions vis-à-vis accident-causing activities are left to the cumulative choice of individuals rather than to imposition by government.

But is it possible to rely on the degree of rationality in human behaviour seemingly presupposed by economic theories? And is it always possible to identify the activity that causes the accident? For example, a tool defectively manufactured by A injures one of B's employees who has been supplied with it by B. Whose activity has caused this injury? And in accidents involving automobiles and pedestrians can such an economic choice be made? Calabresi treats the motorist as the best cost avoider on the grounds that he has both better information and the means of reducing such accidents, but are such assumptions truly tenable? Finally, general deterrence so conceived cannot provide all the answers, as Calabresi is well aware. Wider considerations of fairness and justice also obtain, and it would be a mistake to assert that certain antisocial activities can and will be allowed so long as those taking part in them are prepared to pay for them. Moreover, collective judgments are often reached, and an infinite number of calculated risks determined, according to political criteria rather than cost-benefit equations.

Compensation as the most important function of tort law

Compensation. Compensation is the most important function of tort law, and modern insurance practice has made it easier to satisfy the injured without financially crushing the injurer. The welfare state, however, is now the main source of accident compensation. But even where tort law plays a major compensatory role—for example, in the most serious cases of injury—it does not function with great efficiency. For though tort lawyers often regard tort as the compensation system that caters best to the particular victim on the basis of the pre-accident situation and prognosis of his future, it nonetheless remains expensive, capricious, and dilatory. The Royal Commission on Civil Liability and Compensation for Personal Injury (1978) in England estimated that it cost 85 pence to award £1 of net benefits to the victim. (The administrative cost of the New Zealand Scheme is apparently less than 10 percent.) The tort system is capricious in that compensation may depend on finding a tort-feasor (wrongdoer) and credible witnesses, not to mention a good lawyer. Delay can also produce injustice, especially since it tends to benefit wealthy defendants (usually insurance companies) who can sometimes delay payments in the hope that such delay will wear down a plaintiff so that he accepts a low settlement. Difficulties of this kind have led some authors to refer to the tort law as a "forensic lottery" and have given rise to remedial legislation in areas particularly affected, such as automobile accidents. Most importantly, they have led many jurists to reconsider the utility of modern tort law.

Loss spreading. Compensation in its crudest form meant that the cost of an accident was shifted from the victim to the tort-feasor. For a long time the only plausible excuse for such a shift was deemed to be the tort-feasor's fault. Certainly it seemed right to make wrongdoers pay. The corollary, that he who is not at fault need not pay, also appealed to 19th-century judges and jurists, who were often more concerned with shielding nascent industries from the crushing costs of litigation than with compensating the growing number of such industries' victims. Though the first argument still has its appeal, the second has lost cogency given the modern insurance system. This has revolutionized tort reasoning, for victims can now be compensated without tort-feasors' being ruined financially. It thus helps erode the requirement of fault, while strict liability correspondingly proliferates (see below *Liability without fault*). Finally, where liability without fault has not been introduced in an open manner, such notions as fault, foreseeability, and causation become stretched in an attempt to do justice to the victim while allegedly remaining faithful to a fault-based law of torts. It is only in recent times that Anglo-American courts have tended to refer openly to such considerations, and they have been active not only in shifting the loss but also in trying to pin it on the person who is in the best position to spread it.

COMPARATIVE CLASSIFICATION

Although the common law of torts is in many ways wider than the modern European law of delict, it offers similar solutions. For example, in English common law tort serves such modern problems as product liability or liability for negligent statements, whereas French and German law have frequently relied on contractual solutions. In contrast, the German Civil Code has a basic provision excluding compensation for negligently inflicted pure economic loss that, along with a narrow rule of vicarious liability, has encouraged the expansion of the law of contract. Defamation also is regarded primarily as a tort in the common law but as a crime in civil-law systems, although in the latter it is now seen as a potentially important heading of civil liability. A third difference exists between what the common law describes as trespass to land and the tort of nuisance and what civil lawyers have seen primarily as part of the law of immovable property.

PROTECTION OF LIFE, LIMB, AND FREEDOM OF MOVEMENT

Intentional interference. All legal systems offer protection to life, health, and physical integrity, to which they attach great importance. For example, they regard offenses leading to personal injury, such as assault (an act producing in the plaintiff/victim a reasonable expectation of immediate, unlawful force) and battery (the intentional application of unlawful force), as both torts and crimes capable of attracting serious criminal sanctions. The same is true of the complete restriction of the plaintiff's freedom of movement without lawful excuse, which can be actionable both as a tort and as a crime. Complicated rules—usually contained in specific criminal statutes—may, however, remove the unlawful element in some cases (*e.g.,* lawful arrest by a police officer and, in limited instances, by a private citizen). Consent by the victim/plaintiff may also make an otherwise unlawful interference lawful. Consent to the infliction of grievous bodily harm, however, is generally regarded as unacceptable, and consent in the context of negligent medical malpractice suits tends to raise complicated issues to which there exist various legal responses.

Some offenses as both torts and crimes

The importance attached by the modern law to human life and limb is also obvious from the appearance (mainly in the 1960s) of a number of statutory schemes intended to afford redress to victims of crimes of violence (*e.g.,* the English Criminal Injuries Compensation scheme). This is particularly useful in cases where the assailant is not known or not considered worth suing. Compensation comes through funds specifically allotted by Parliament, and the amounts are usually calculated in approximate accordance with normal tort rules.

Most tort rules covering intentionally inflicted personal injury, though important, are nowadays handled by the criminal courts (sometimes with the plaintiff also appearing as a civil party and claiming damages, as in France). Tort law's main contribution is accordingly found in the numerically more significant negligent interferences with life and physical integrity.

Negligence. The conceptual approaches of the common-law, French, and German-inspired systems are quite different. In practice, however, where personal injury is concerned, there must be conduct that (a) is intentional or, more frequently, careless; (b) is not justifiable; and (c) leads to ("causes" in a legal sense) harm. Regarding (a), the common-law systems for various reasons have been slower than the civil-law systems in imposing liability for inaction. Nonetheless there is a marked tendency—especially in some jurisdictions in the United States—to relax this individualistic rule, with courts and statutes increasingly imposing liability, especially in the context of rendering assistance to victims of traffic accidents. This change typically imposes a duty to come to the aid of another person. More frequently, however, by-standers are encouraged to act as good samaritans by ensuring that the standard of care they have to display is lowered, thereby shielding them against subsequent actions by ungrateful victims. French law by contrast has since 1945 recognized a general duty to aid a person in physical danger if that can be done without risk to the rescuer.

Good samaritans

The conduct must be culpable—*i.e.,* intentional or, more typically, careless. Modern legal systems resort to objective criteria to determine the requisite standard of care: the defendant must behave as the *bonus pater familias* or, as common lawyers put it, the reasonable man. Both definitions are essentially the anthropomorphic conception of justice enabling courts to adjust the requisite standard according to factors such as the magnitude of the injury, the cost of avoiding it, and the likelihood of its being realized. Nowadays courts tend to treat as carelessness errors that even a reasonable man would make. Here the legal and ordinary meanings of negligence diverge, and this transformation commonly occurs where insurance is obligatory and the courts know that by characterizing the defendant's conduct as negligent they are actually compensating the victim without ruining the defendant.

Finally, the conduct must have caused the plaintiff's hurt. The problem of causation is widely discussed, though the solutions tend to be similar. The approach in Germany (and, at times, in the United States) is more theoretical than in France and England. Both in Germany and in France the test of causation is the "adequate cause," and, though differently understood by these systems, this tends to produce results analogous to those reached by the common-law test of "foreseeability."

Gray areas. Despite every system's concern for human life and health, interference with these interests is not automatically compensated. In some cases the manner of infliction of the harm determines whether compensation is decreed, as with physical injury resulting from some failure to act. In others the nature and timing of the interference influence the extent of tort compensation. Compensation for nervous shock is affected by the former consideration, injury to a fetus by the second.

Legal systems approach these problems differently. The concepts they use to achieve the desired aim of controlled compensation also differ. The German-inspired systems have long behaved as if the solution depended on a proper application of causative theories. Common law has also tended to disguise the real policy issues, judges often giving the impression that the answer depends on foreseeability or the presence or absence of a "duty of care." Actually, the policy reasons for such hesitation are common to all; and the modern tendency—evidenced both by judicial decisions and by doctrinal writing—is to admit this. For example, it is widely recognized that nervous shock can lead to multiplicity of actions—some no doubt based on faked claims. Equally important, however, must be the realization that claims of nervous shock have a low priority in a world of limited resources, a world unable to cope adequately or even at all with many kinds of serious accidents, illness, or disease. Though the present trend both in the United States and in England is to play down the validity of these administrative objections, most systems seem to rely on an impressive variety of rules of thumb in an attempt to limit the number of successful plaintiffs. One such rule depends on the distinction between nervous shock accompanied by physical or psychological manifestations and mere anguish, pain, or grief—the latter remaining uncompensated. Though widely accepted by both common-law and civil-law systems, this rule has been challenged in some U.S. jurisdictions. Another device is to limit compensation to a person within the danger zone; another and more liberal approach allows even those not within the danger zone to recover damages so long as their shock results from seeing or hearing the accident with their own unaided senses. But even here exceptions are being made in the case of "meritorious" plaintiffs. In England a mother who suffered shock through seeing her injured husband and children in the hospital soon after the accident (at which she was not present) was allowed to recover damages (*McLoughlin* v. *O'Brian,* [1983]).

Administrative barriers to compensation

Problems also arise when injury is inflicted to a fetus or when harm is suffered by a female prior to conception. Initially both common-law and civil-law systems were reluctant to sanction damages for prenatal injuries, due to evidentiary reasons—the difficulty of establishing a causal link between accident and fetal injury—and conceptual difficulties connected with the foreseeability of the victim/fetus. The precise legal status of the fetus has also troubled experts in criminal and property law. Damages were first awarded to a fetus in the United States in 1946, in Australia in 1972, in Canada in 1973, and in 1976 in England by the Congenital Disabilities (Civil Liability) Act. Differences remain as to details (*e.g.,* is it enough that the fetus was viable at the time of the injury or must it also be born alive?).

A more recent and even more troublesome development has been the so-called wrongful life and wrongful birth actions, appearing first in the United States (from about the early 1970s) and later in Europe. The harmful event is typically negligence on the part of a doctor who either fails to carry out effectively a sterilization operation, with the result that an "unwanted" child is born (whether impaired in health or otherwise), or fails to diagnose an illness in the mother—*e.g.,* rubella in the early stages of pregnancy—with the result that the opportunity for an abortion is lost and a child is born with impaired health. The child's action (for wrongful life) consists mainly of a claim that but for the doctor's negligence it would not exist at all; the parents' claim (for wrongful birth) is for pain and suffering and, most importantly, the extra costs of rearing the "unwanted" child. The first claim has been rejected by courts of all systems on grounds ranging from the most technical (how does one assess damages?) to the most philosophical (should the court be allowed to decide issues of the value and quality of life?). In reality, however, these and other arguments are excuses for the courts' refusal to come to grips with a serious problem on which there is no general consensus. Though courts have been slow to recognize such claims to children, they are, nonetheless, increasingly willing to grant them special damages connected with their handicap, and judges also are more generously inclined when compensating parents who bring wrongful birth actions.

Courts increasingly favouring special damages

PROTECTION OF PROPERTY

Land and its enjoyment. In modern civil-law systems protection is given by provisions found in both the property and tort sections of the codes. Common-law systems give property owners equivalent protection, but through the law of torts. Thus, direct physical intrusion on the property of another falls within the province of the old tort of trespass. This succeeds without any proof of special damage and is defeated only by rather narrowly defined pleas such as that of imminent necessity (to protect the intruder or his property) or inevitable accident.

Other interests in land, however, receive a more qualified protection and must yield to the test of reasonableness. A miscellany of wrongs, ranging from encroachment of branches or roots to falling tiles or slates from nearby roofs, are covered by the amorphous tort of private nuisance, which also covers such interferences as excessive vibrations, noise, smells, and other, more modern, instances of pollution. The emphasis is not on the unreasonableness of the defendant's conduct, as in the tort of negligence, but on the unreasonableness of the interference with the plaintiff's use and enjoyment of his land. The unifying element is the type of harm, and the law's overall aim is to protect an individual's right to enjoy the amenities of his land within the general framework of give and take necessary in an increasingly crowded world.

Balancing competing interests is, therefore, the key feature, and numerous judgments make it a difficult area of law. Its particular interest lies in the fact that along with other branches of the law (*e.g.,* administrative law, criminal law) it can help perform zoning functions in the use of land; however, attempts to utilize it in protecting the environment have not, on the whole, been very successful. In short this is an old tort that has been deployed to cope with modern developments, especially by North American systems.

The gravity of any interference with the plaintiff's land is a major consideration. Older English decisions distinguish between sensible material damage to the land and mere interference with its use and enjoyment. The distinction—not found in any rigid form in civil-law systems—is, however, often unworkable; and to the extent that it reflects a past valuing of tangible forms of property over intangible ones it may be inadequate. The duration of the interference may also be crucial, temporary annoyances being, on the whole, more tolerable. The nature of the locality has also been taken into account. This has a mixed effect, however. It has certainly helped preserve rural and residential areas against intruding noxious trades; but it has also permitted increased industrial pollution.

The more important the purpose of the activity complained about, the greater the tendency to grant effective authorization of the nuisance by legislative fiat. But the effect of the nuisance—typically an oil refinery or airport—on its victims can be catastrophic, often amounting to indirect expropriation of their land. Hence there exist special compensation acts or constitutional clauses providing for compensation.

Chattels. The law affords wide protection to proprietary interests over chattels. Again, this can involve using a proprietary remedy to reclaim goods removed from their rightful owner or to claim damages for chattels affected by a tort-feasor's intentional or negligent conduct. Intentional interference with goods is unusual and therefore receives specialized treatment by some systems. Most cases arise in connection with damaged movables, and here the more modern tort of negligence often applies, the problem usually being the extent of compensation. For example, if an automobile is damaged in a collision its owner will be able to claim from the wrongdoer the cost of repairs. But can such cost be claimed if it exceeds that of purchasing a similar vehicle? And what of extra transportation costs incurred during the period of repair or the expense of hiring an equivalent substitute? Even more controversial are recent claims for such injuries as a lost or ruined holiday following damage to the vehicle. Though the latter claim tends to be regarded as extravagant (and beyond the competence of tort law at least), the others tend to be satisfied, subject to the rules of remoteness and the pervading test of reasonableness (*e.g.,* the victim cannot hire a luxury automobile to replace a damaged economy car). In other instances, however, theoretical doubts may arise as to whether there is interference with property or mere economic loss. For example, if a canal leading to a millpond collapses, trapping but not damaging a vessel, has the owner of the vessel suffered property damage or mere economic loss? Or if a fire forces the police to cordon off an area, depriving its residents of access to their automobiles, have they suffered a property interference? Sometimes courts focus on the duration of the interference and treat prolonged deprivation as equivalent to property damage. In other cases, however, they treat these instances as cases of pure economic loss and reject any claim for compensation.

Majority of cases connected with damaged movables

Negligently inflicted pure economic loss. Economic loss can arise in numerous ways: an employer deprived of the services of a key employee; a child deprived of the financial support of its father; negligent advice given by A to B and relied upon by C; a defective will that deprives someone of a legacy; or road works that damage A's electricity cable, depriving many nearby factories of electrical power.

Common-law and German-inspired systems have here faced enormous difficulties, partly because the courts' reasoning seems to be motivated by administrative considerations: if one such claim is accepted many others will follow. Another difficulty stems from the fact that many of these cases sit uncomfortably on the traditional divide between contract and tort. Yet a third problem arises from the particular structural deficiencies of each system. For example, the narrow rule of vicarious liability found in the German Civil Code, along with its express exclusion of negligently inflicted pure economic loss from the protection of the main tort provision, has led German lawyers to expand their law of contract to provide a remedy in some of the above-mentioned situations. In contrast, a rigid law of contract, especially in the English common law, has led to an expansion—often farfetched and ill-considered—of the law of tort. On the whole, however, German law and common law have come up with fairly similar solutions proclaiming, unlike French law, a general though increasingly ill-defined hostility toward compensating pure economic loss.

PROTECTION OF HONOUR, REPUTATION, AND PRIVACY

The protection of individuals' honour, reputation, and privacy in Western systems is, on the whole, adequate, though varied. One factor is the difficulty of balancing proper protection and free speech. Another is the historical preference of civil-law systems for bringing many instances of defamation under criminal law. Finally, the constitutional environment has had a great impact on this part of tort law. In the United States the tendency since the mid-1960s has been to sacrifice the tort of defamation and human reputation to the First Amendment and free speech. Thus, American law does not allow an action (at any rate where media defendants are involved) unless the plaintiff/victim can prove that the allegation was made with "actual malice"—that is, with knowledge that it was false or with reckless disregard of whether it was false or not. In the United States the plaintiff must also prove that the defendant's statement is false, with the result that many of the traditional common-law defenses are bypassed. The idea behind this is that any contrary decision restricts the constitutional right to free speech.

Importance of constitutional environment

English law by contrast is much more jealous of reputation, though numerous complicated defenses also make sure that free speech is not totally throttled. But in the main the English law of defamation is complex and archaic. The old distinction between libel and slander (defamatory matter in permanent and in transient form, respectively) is preserved; the plaintiff is not entitled to legal aid (with the practical consequence that only wealthy people can afford to sue); the action can succeed without any proof of special damage (giving an unwarranted advantage to corporations, since they thus acquire the benefit of rules designed for human beings); the cause of action does not survive the death of either party; and, finally, juries are often used and are entitled (in one of the rare instances of English law) to award punitive damages. No summary can do justice to this peculiar but important tort; but, according to Tony Weir in *A Casebook on Tort,* it may well be that its defects arise "because it uses a single remedy, the action for damages, in order to perform three distinct purposes: (a) to permit people to clear their reputation from unfounded allegations; (b) to allow people to claim compensation for harm they suffer because others have abused freedom of speech; and (c) to repress gratuitous vituperation, scurrilous disparagement and malignant calumny." Weir goes on to say that "only for (b) are damages the appropriate remedy. For (a) we need a procedure for retraction or correction, and for (c) we need the public stocks."

Protecting the various aspects of the human personality and privacy is also a growing concern of Western legal systems, though again they set about achieving this aim in different ways. The need for such a protection was first stressed by German and U.S. academics toward the end of the 19th century, but their arguments were rejected on both sides of the Atlantic because of fears that it would lead to increased litigation and inhibit free speech. By the beginning of the 20th century, however, the first attempts at protection were made in Germany and the United States. Many of these dealt with the unauthorized use of a person's likeness. Others concerned unauthorized use of names or publication of private correspondence. With litigation, a patchy but growing protection began to emerge. The Constitution of Bonn of 1949 reacted against the utter disregard for human dignity prevalent during the Third Reich and for the first time inserted into German law general provisions protecting human personality. Protection of this sort was transferred to the field of civil law in the early and middle 1950s, when a series of important decisions gradually shaped a general right of personality for the violation of which damages could be awarded under the general law of delict. The process was complicated and protracted, and what exists now is a casuistic, judge-made right. But in general the protection afforded to human privacy is extensive, with German judges attempting the difficult feat of balancing the competing interests with great courage and effectiveness.

Conflict between protecting human privacy and free speech

American law meanwhile was classifying and refining the many headings of actionable privacy created by statute or wide-ranging judicial pronouncements (appropriation of likeness; unreasonable intrusion; false light cases, *i.e.,* those in which the plaintiff claims to have been placed in a false light by the defendant; and public disclosure of private facts on a matter that would be highly offensive and objectionable to a reasonable person of ordinary sensibilities). The overall protection thus achieved was extensive and not dissimilar to that of German law, though once again the concern to protect First Amendment rights has seriously stunted certain headings of actionable privacy.

The protection of privacy acquired a new urgency in the 1960s and 1970s as increased technological ability to collect, collate, and disseminate information made it possible to interfere with human personality, solitude, and privacy to an unprecedented extent. In some countries, such as France, new articles were introduced in the civil code to deal with the matter, while others passed special legislation dealing with a modern and dangerous form of invasion connected with data banks and the linking-up of information contained within them. To this tendency even English law has not been immune, though the protection afforded remains patchy and casuistic. The creation of a general right of privacy was rejected in the early 1970s, partly on the grounds that it was difficult to define but also possibly because of sustained opposition from the press. Thus, although English law does not recognize a general right of privacy similar to that embodied in the French Civil Code or created by the German courts, it often achieves comparable results through the ingenious use of existing torts (defamation, trespass, nuisance, passing off) or the law of contract, criminal law, or restitution.

LIABILITY WITHOUT FAULT

The growing dissatisfaction with fault. Whatever the original foundations of tortious liability, by the 19th century it had come to rest firmly upon the notion of fault. The principle that a human being should make good the harm caused by his fault seemed eminently reasonable. But the converse of this principle, namely that there can be no liability where there is no fault, offered an additional attraction to an era that was concerned with not making nascent industries liable; in this sense fault could help retain the boundaries of liability within manageable proportions. To this coincidence of morality and economic expediency the notion of fault doubtless owes much of its aura of soundness and inevitability. Consequently, when the first serious challenge to the notion started to materialize toward the end of the 19th century, it invariably had to be disguised.

19th-century view of fault

Fault, as understood in the 19th century, presupposed free will and, further, that an agent could choose between performing an action in a perceptibly dangerous way and performing it in some safer way. Thus, legal negligence involved something of personal moral shortcoming; the person who was held liable had been guilty of ethical as well as legal wrong. And since fault involved a more or less informed choice, it was possible to see how the prospect of liability could influence a choice for the better—a concept embodying the principle of social utility, for it theoretically edified potential defendants by encouraging them to behave more carefully.

With the growing mechanization and industrialization of the second half of the 19th century and the resulting multiplication of accidents this kind of approach came under more and more scrutiny. Consequently both the moral and the purely educative aspects of the fault system were increasingly questioned, especially as insurance companies were now meeting the cost of accidents; in addition, the idea of leaving victims uncompensated became politically unattractive as the extended franchise made politicians more sensitive to voters' grievances. This change of attitude, however, could not alone have altered the legal system if economic changes had not also favoured reappraisal of the problems of civil liability. From the turn of the century, industry, with the help of insurance, became increasingly sturdy and less in need of protection. The shift toward the plaintiff's point of view manifested itself in three main ways: greater use of the doctrine of vicarious liability; increased objectivization of the notion of carelessness, coupled with the use of presumptions of carelessness; and, finally, the open introduction of strict liability.

Vicarious liability. Vicarious liability is liability imposed on the master of a servant for the tort of that servant when committed in the course of his employment. This is a form of strict liability since the "innocent" master is made liable for the fault of his servant.

Many reasons have been advanced to justify this departure from the fault principle. The doctrine seems to have developed more in response to the demands of social convenience and rough justice than as a consequence of clear, consistent legal planning.

Most systems have opted for true vicarious liability—*i.e.,* liability that makes the master liable for the servant's wrongs. However, German law and, in varying degrees, other German-inspired systems have opted for what is sometimes called the "master's tort" theory. This theory probably results from a misreading of Roman texts as well as the desire to protect small industrial concerns at the end of the 19th century. It makes the master liable only if he is personally at fault in selecting or supervising his servant or failing to supply him with proper equipment. It is enshrined in the German Civil Code, and in practice it has proved so unacceptable as to lead first, to the ingenious expansion of the law of contract (aided by a number of codal provisions) in order to rectify the shortcomings of the law of tort and, later, to the discovery of what common lawyers would call personal nondelegable duties, allowing the imposition of primary liability on the employer under the German code.

The "master's tort" theory

This peculiarity apart, all systems agree that vicarious liability will be imposed only if there is a master–servant relationship and the wrong is committed in the course of employment. Where simpler operations have been involved, the control test has been crucial for determining whether this relationship or that between employer and independent contractor is the one involved. (In the latter the employer bears no responsibility for the wrongdoing of the contractor.) But in more complicated situations all systems resort to a variety of tests that include, for example, how remuneration (wage or lump sum) is paid, to what extent a worker is integrated into the employer's business, who supplies the capital or equipment, and, more generally, all the surrounding circumstances and the other terms of the contract. By far the most troublesome problem, however, is whether the wrong was committed in the course of employment. Its solution tends to be impressionistic, depending on the skillful use of numerous and often contradictory decisions, which can be used only as helpful guidelines and not as rigid principles. There appears to be a tendency to interpret this requirement more strictly in German than in French law and its derivatives, with the common law standing somewhere in between.

Presumptions of fault and responsibility. The trend away from identifying negligence with moral blameworthiness, coupled with a tendency to put the onus of proof of non-fault on the defendant, often resulted in liability that was in all but name strict liability. The most forthright developments occurred in France, where the courts transformed the code to accommodate problems arising in an industrial society.

This change came in the late 19th century when the French courts, faced with an inactive legislature and growing social pressures to compensate victims of industrial accidents, boldly created a new rule of liability out of the seemingly unpromising first paragraph of article 1384 of the code. The article in question, which proclaims generally that one is responsible not only for one's own acts but also for damage done by things in one's control, was originally conceived as a stylistically desirable linking sentence between the first two delict provisions, which enunciated the rule of fault liability, and the last two provisions, which dealt with some narrow instances of risk liability (*e.g.,* animals, collapsing buildings). But in 1896 the Cour de Cassation (the highest court of civil and criminal matters in France) felt that the time had come to give these words an independent significance, thereby enabling the widow of a victim of a boiler explosion to recover damages without having to prove the fault of the victim's employer. Within a year of this decision the French Chamber passed a workman's compensation act, in effect removing accidents at work from the province of tort law. This piece of legislation constituted a temporary delay in the development of the new rule. The appearance of the automobile, however, gave the rule fresh life, and after some hesitation, the Cour de Cassation finally accepted in the Jand'heur decision (1930) that article 1384 established a presumption of responsibility against the guardian of a thing; this responsibility could not be rebutted by evidence of no fault or lack of explanation of the cause of the damage but only by clear positive evidence that the damage was due to an event unforeseeable and external both to the guardian and to the thing that made the accident unavoidable. In the years that followed much refinement took place of the elements of liability (the meaning of "thing," causation, definition of guard, etc.), but the trend has been to expand liability, especially in the context of traffic accidents. This expansion, largely the result of increased insurance protection, received a boost in 1968 when the Cour de Cassation decided that the rule of article 1384 could be used in favour of nonpaying car passengers and, more recently, in 1982 when in the Desmares decision the defense of contributory fault of the victim was seriously restricted by the second chamber of the court. This decision represented a bold step toward protecting nonmotorists, but its precise ambit was unspecified, raising fears of increased insurance premiums and provoking considerable judicial uncertainty. Perhaps the most beneficial effect of this decision, however, was to hasten enactment of a strict liability road traffic act.

Strict liability road traffic act

Strict liability statutes. The French Road Traffic Act of July 5, 1985, a long and stylistically complicated enactment, has gone a long way toward improving the position of victims of traffic accidents, though not as far as some would have wished. For example, although any contributory negligence on the part of some victims (children under the age of 16 and adults over 70 [article 3]) is completely ignored, that on the part of others, notably the drivers themselves, may be taken into account (article 4), their negligence reducing or in appropriate circumstances even extinguishing their damages. It was only compromises such as this, however, that ensured the passing of the act. Be that as it may, the act is indicative of a modern trend to introduce strict liability through specialized statutes rather than to elaborate the already overworked article 1384 of the Civil Code.

Strict liability statutes are proliferating the world over and survive alongside judge-made rules such as that enunciated by the English decision of *Rylands* v. *Fletcher,* [1868], which held that anyone who in the course of "non-natural" use of his land accumulates thereon for his own purposes anything likely to do mischief if it escapes is answerable for all direct damage thereby caused. The German statutes, however, deserve special attention. First, in Germany strict liability has been introduced only by specific enactments, while the Civil Code, minor exceptions apart, remains faithful to the fault principle. Moreover, such is the monopoly of the legislator in this area that the courts have even restrained themselves from extending analogous strict liability statutes to similar situations (though other German-inspired systems—*e.g.,* the Austrian—have not followed this route). Second, the vast majority of German strict liability statutes contain similar clauses on the monetary limits of liability per damage-inflicting incident. Likewise, defenses such as contributory negligence appear in most statutes. Finally, the compensation under the statutes does not cover damages for pain and suffering, so that if such items are to be claimed, or the monetary limits are inadequate, recourse to the ordinary rules of tort is permissible. In other systems, however (*e.g.,* the Swiss), where the strict liability statutes do not contain the above-mentioned type of limitations, application of the ordinary law is excluded.

TORT LAW AND ALTERNATIVE METHODS OF COMPENSATION

Compensation for personal injury and damage to property is a major aim of tort law. The objective is full compensation wherever possible and in this respect tort compensation differs from funds received from the welfare state system in that the latter often tend to be calculated on a flat-rate basis.

Compensation for physical injury includes consideration of past and future economic losses as well as monetary satisfaction for a variety of nonfinancial items of damage, such as pain and suffering or loss of amenities, which are not amenable to precise mathematical calculation. The various headings of damage do not have exact parallels in all systems, but similar factors tend to be taken into account when calculating the final award. In some systems, such as the French, where the actual calculation of damages is treated as a question of fact and is left to the judge of first instance, regional variations in the size of awards occur. In England, by contrast, since the abolition of civil juries in personal injury cases there has been a greater standardization for certain headings of damages. Common-law systems prefer lump sum awards, whereas in civil-law systems periodic payments are favoured. In many instances the difference appears to be one of theory rather than of practice. Thus, even where periodic payments are preferred, courts often order or facilitate the award of damages in a lump sum, partly because victims tend to prefer this method and partly because any future complications are avoided. A third and perhaps equally important reason is that lawyers can more easily exact their fees from lump sums than from relatively small installments, however regular.

Lump sum awards

If the victim dies all systems tend to allow his estate to claim whatever he could have claimed had he been alive. The conditions for bringing this action, however, vary (German law, for example, is more restrictive than English law). Right to action is also given to the dependents of the deceased. In the common-law systems this is expressly created by statute (the so-called fatal accidents or wrongful death statutes); in German law the action is authorized by the Civil Code, while in French law and its derivatives it is based on the general provision of article 1382. Systems also tend to differ over the question of who should be allowed to sue under this heading. Common-law statutes specifically designate the list of dependents, insisting additionally that they are actually supported by the deceased at the time of his death or, at the very least, have a reasonable probability of an imminent dependency. In contrast, German law limits claims to persons having a legal right to maintenance. French law appears to be open-ended, insisting only on actual dependency at the time of the death. The difference with the other two major systems is, however, more apparent than real, the courts often excluding claims by non-relatives through various causative devices.

Alongside tort social welfare systems proliferate, operating through a tangle of complicated rules, often with little or no attempt to relate the two systems. The full picture of compensation for accidents depends on close study of parallel but limited schemes—*e.g.,* for accidents at work, for road traffic accidents, or for victims of crime—which in some systems coexist along with tort but in others tend to displace it. This unhappy coexistence is one of immense complexity and, no doubt, waste, both of which most commentators have criticized. Despite such criticisms, few countries have attempted the kind of wholesale reform of the all-embracing no-fault system of compensation that New Zealand introduced in the early 1970s, a system that is financed out of general taxation, contributions from employers and employees, and a levy on motor vehicles. There are several reasons for this but cost is, no doubt, an important factor, even though critics of the tort system maintain that one should also weigh the extra cost of automatic compensation against the savings brought by the abolition of the tort system. But further difficulties exist. Should such automatic compensation be linked to accidents or should it also cover disease and illness? Should compensation be determined by the victim's circumstances prevailing before the accident or should it be based on flat rates? And should the emphasis be on compensating the victim's economic loss with, perhaps, token sums being awarded for non-pecuniary loss (as with the New Zealand scheme); or should non-pecuniary loss receive more generous treatment (as under tort law)? The debate on all these points is continuing and, no doubt, adds to the theoretical and practical interest of this subject, even though there is little sign of the New Zealand system being adopted in any major Western country.

TORT AT THE CROSSROADS

Tort law is, on the one hand, increasingly attacked as complicated, slow, and costly; on the other hand, its province expands daily and awards made under it are often huge. The extent to which rules intended for a relatively primitive society have been adapted to meet new ends is impressive. The convergence attained by the various Western systems is also noteworthy, although that convergence was long concealed by different historical approaches and legal conservatism.

BIBLIOGRAPHY. (*American law*): The best treatise is *Prosser and Keeton on the Law of Torts,* edited by W. PAGE KEETON, 5th ed. (1984). MARK A. FRANKLIN and ROBERT L. RABIN, *Cases and Materials on Tort Law and Alternatives,* 3rd ed. (1983), is one of the most stimulating casebooks. (*English law*): The standard authority for English law is *Clerk & Lindsell on Torts,* 15th ed., edited by R.W.M. DIAS (1982). JOHN G. FLEMING, *The Law of Torts,* 6th ed. (1983), offers the most modern treatment. R.W.M. DIAS and B.S. MARKESINIS, *Tort Law* (1984), adopts a policy-oriented presentation of the law. P.S. ATIYAH, *Accidents, Compensation, and the Law,* 3rd ed. (1980), provides a thought-provoking account of the workings of various systems of compensation.

(*French law*): HENRY MAZEAUD *et al., Traité théorique et pratique de la responsabilité civile délictuelle et contractuelle,* 6th ed., 3 vol. in 4 (1965–83), is the classic exposition of the law. An excellent modern presentation is GENEVIÈVE VINEY, *Les Obligations; la responsabilité: conditions,* vol. 4 in *Traité de droit civil,* edited by JACQUES GHESTIN, 4 vol. (1977–82). (*German law*): KARL LARENZ, *Lehrbuch des Schuldrechts,* vol. 1, 13th ed. (1982), and vol. 2, 12th ed. (1981); and HEIN KÖTZ, *Deliktsrecht,* 3rd ed. (1983), are highly respected treatises.

(*Comparative law*): H.L.A. HART and TONY HONORÉ, *Causation in the Law,* 2nd ed. (1985), is the classic monograph on causation. Other comparative discussions include ANDRÉ TUNC, *La Responsabilité civile* (1981); KONRAD ZWEIGERT and HEIN KÖTZ, *Einfürung in die Rechtsvergleichung auf dem Gebiete des Privatrechts,* 2nd rev. ed., 2 vol. (1984), the first edition of which is also available in English as *An Introduction to Comparative Law* (1977); and F.H. LAWSON and B.S. MARKESINIS, *Tortious Liability for Unintentional Harm in the Common Law and the Civil Law,* 2 vol. (1982).

(B.S.M.)

Organ and Tissue Transplants

A transplant, in the context of this article, refers to a section of tissue or to a complete organ that is removed from its original natural site and transferred to a new position in the same person or in a separate individual. The term, like its synonym, graft, was borrowed by surgeons from horticulture. Both words imply that success will result in a healthy and flourishing graft or transplant, which will gain its nourishment from its new environment.

This article is divided into the following sections:

TRANSPLANTS AND GRAFTS

Transplants of animal tissue have figured prominently in mythology since the legend of the creation of Eve from one of Adam's ribs. Historical accounts of surgical tissue grafting as part of the cure of patients date back to the early Hindu surgeons who, about the beginning of the 6th century BC, developed techniques for reconstructing noses from skin flaps taken from the patient's arm. This method was introduced into Western medicine by the great Italian surgeon Gaspare Tagliacozzo in the 16th century. The flap was left attached to the arm for two to three weeks until new blood vessels had grown into it from the nose remnant. The flap was then severed and the arm freed from the reconstructed nose.

It was found that extremely thin pieces of skin could be cut free and would obtain enough nourishment from the serum in the graft bed to stay alive while new blood vessels were being formed. This free grafting of skin, together with the flap techniques already mentioned, have constituted the main therapeutic devices of the plastic surgeon in the correction of various types of defects. Skilled manipulations of such grafts can produce surprising improvements in the appearance of those born with malformed faces and in the disfigurements resulting from severe burns. Cornea, which structurally is a modified form of transparent skin, can also be free grafted, and corneal grafts have restored sight to countless blind eyes.

Blood transfusion can be regarded as a form of tissue graft. The blood-forming tissues—bone-marrow cells—can also be transplanted. If these cells are injected into the bloodstream, they home to the marrow cavities and can become established as a vital lifesaving graft in patients suffering from defective marrow.

Organ and limb grafts

The chief distinguishing feature of organ and limb grafts is that the tissues of the organ or limb can only survive if blood vessels are rapidly joined (anastomosed) to blood vessels of the recipient. This provides the graft with a blood supply before it dies from lack of oxygen and nourishment and from the accumulation of poisonous waste products.

As can be seen from the examples cited, living-tissue grafts may be performed for a variety of reasons. Skin grafts can save life in severe burns, can improve function by correcting deformity, or can improve appearances in a cosmetic sense, with valuable psychological benefits. Organ grafts can supply a missing function and save life in cases of fatal disease of vital organs, such as the kidney.

A tissue removed from one part of the body and transplanted to another site in the same individual is called an autograft. Autografts cannot be rejected. Similarly, grafts between identical twins or highly inbred animals—isografts—are accepted by the recipients indefinitely. Grafts from a donor to a recipient of the same species—allografts or homografts—are usually rejected unless special efforts are made to prevent this. Grafts between individuals of different species—xenografts or heterografts—are usually destroyed very quickly by the recipient. (The methods used to prevent rejection are discussed in full, below.)

Tissue or organ grafts may be transplanted to their normal situation in the recipient and are then known as orthotopic—for example, skin to the surface of the body. Alternatively, they may be transplanted to an abnormal situation and are then called heterotopic—for example, kidneys are usually grafted into the lower part of the abdomen instead of into the loin (the back between the ribs and the pelvis), as this is more convenient. If an extra organ is grafted, it is called auxiliary, or accessory—for example, a heterotopic liver graft may be inserted without removal of the recipient's own liver.

Grafts are usually performed for long-term effects. Occasionally, the limited acceptance of a skin allograft may be lifesaving, by preventing loss of fluid and protein from extensive burned surface in severely ill patients. The graft also provides a bacteria-proof covering, so that infection cannot occur. When the allograft is removed or rejected, the patient may be sufficiently recovered to receive permanent autografts (see BURNS).

Certain tissues, including bone, cartilage, tendons, fascia, arteries, and heart valves, can be implanted even if their cells are dead at the time of implantation or will be rejected shortly thereafter. These are structural implants rather than true grafts or transplants. They are more akin to the stick to which a rose is attached for support—although their support is essential, their function does not depend on biological processes. In fact, xenografts or inert manufactured devices may often be equally suitable substitutes.

TISSUE TRANSPLANTS

Skin. Most skin grafting is with autografts; the special indication for skin allografts in severely burned patients has been mentioned. Skin allografts seem to be rejected more aggressively than any other tissue, and there are many experimental situations in which skin grafts between two inbred strains of animal fail, although kidney grafts between the same strains survive indefinitely. There can be no doubt that if rejection could be predictably and safely overcome, there would suddenly be a whole new field of surgery. With autografts, the donor skin is limited to what the patient has available, and sometimes in extensive burn cases this becomes a matter of robbing Peter to pay Paul. If allografts were not rejected, skin from cadavers could be used for coverage of burned areas without the need for subsequent autografting, and many lives would be saved.

Flap grafts. Flap grafts as used by Tagliacozzo are particularly valuable if fat as well as skin has been lost. The procedure of raising a flap and keeping the donor site adjacent to the recipient bed can be complicated and uncomfortable for the patient. The cosmetic results are good, and the fat under the skin contained in the flap can be used to cover exposed bone or to allow movement in a contracted joint or to fashion a new nose.

Full-thickness free-skin grafts. Full-thickness free-skin grafts are the maximum thickness that can survive without a blood supply, and they are therefore in some danger of failure to survive. These grafts produce good cosmetic appearances and are especially useful on the face. The main defect of a full-thickness free-skin graft is that, unless it is very small, the donor site from which it comes becomes a defect that needs to be closed in its own right and may itself need skin grafting.

Split or partial-thickness skin grafts. Split, or partial-thickness, skin grafts are by far the most commonly used grafts in plastic surgery. Superficial slices of skin the thickness of tissue paper are cut with a hand or mechanical razor. The graft, which contains living cells, is so thin that it usually gains adequate nourishment directly from the raw surface to which it is applied, and the risk of failure to take (that is, to survive in the new location) is therefore much less than with full-thickness grafts. Another major advantage is that the donor site is not badly damaged. It is tender for only two or three weeks, and it resembles a superficial graze both in appearance and in the fact that healing takes place from the deep layer of the skin left behind. Split skin grafts can be taken quickly from large areas to cover big defects. They tend to have an abnormal shiny reddish appearance that is not as satisfactory cosmetically as the other types of skin graft.

Cornea, blood vessel, and heart valves

Other tissue transplants. *Cornea.* There are certain forms of blindness in which the eye is entirely normal apart from opacity of the front window, or cornea. The opacity may be the result of disease or injury, but, if the clouded cornea is removed and replaced by a corneal transplant, normal vision can result. Since cells of the cornea remain viable for some 12 hours after death, a cornea can be grafted if it is removed within that period. Cooling will slow the process of deterioration, although the sooner the section of cornea is transplanted the better. The graft bed to which a cornea is transplanted has no blood supply. Nourishment comes directly by diffusion from the tissues. Because most rejection factors are carried in the bloodstream, the lack of blood vessels permits most corneal allografts to survive indefinitely without rejection. Rejection can occur if, as sometimes happens, blood vessels grow into the graft.

Blood vessels. By far the most satisfactory blood-vessel transplant is an autograft, similar in principle to skin autografts. Blood-vessel grafts are frequently used to bypass arteries that have become blocked or dangerously narrowed by fatty deposits, a condition caused by degenerative atherosclerosis (hardening of the arteries). Such atherosclerotic deposits in the coronary and carotid arteries are responsible, respectively, for most heart attacks and strokes. If atherosclerosis affects the main artery of the leg, the result is, first, pain in the calves, and then gangrene of the foot, necessitating amputation of the leg. If dealt with early, the effects of the arterial blockage can often be overcome by removing a nonessential superficial vein from the leg, reversing it so that the valves will not obstruct blood flow, and then joining this graft to the affected artery above and below the block—thus bypassing the obstruction. Coronary-artery-bypass grafting has become one of the most common surgical operations in developed countries.

Vein or arterial allografts are far less successful. In time the walls tend to degenerate, and the vessels either dilate, with the danger of bursting, or become obstructed.

Heart valves. Valvular diseases of the heart can be dangerous, since both a blocked valve and a valve that allows blood to leak backward create a strain on the heart that can lead to heart failure. If the valve is seriously damaged it can be replaced with a xenograft valve or a manufactured mechanical valve. Neither is ideal. Xenograft valves have a normal central blood flow, but after a few years they may become rigid and cease to function. Plastic valves—usually of the ball-valve or trapdoor types—force blood to flow around the surface of the ball or trapdoor flap, and this tends to damage red blood cells and cause anemia.

Bone. When fractures fail to unite, autografts of bone can be extremely valuable in helping the bone to heal. Bone allografts can be used for similar purposes, but they are not as satisfactory, since the bone cells are either dead when grafted or are rejected. Thus, the graft is merely a structural scaffold that, although useful as such, cannot partake actively in healing.

Fascia. Fascia, sheets of strong connective tissue that surround muscle bundles, may be used as autografts to repair hernias. The principle of use is like that for skin.

Nerves. Nerves outside the brain and spinal cord can regenerate if damaged. If the delicate sheaths containing the nerves are cut, however, as must happen if a nerve is partially or completely severed, regeneration may not be possible. Even if regeneration occurs it is unlikely to be complete, since most nerves are mixed motor and sensory paths and there is no control ensuring that regenerating fibres take the correct path. Thus, there will always be some fibres that end in the wrong destination and are therefore unable to function. Defective nerve regeneration is the main reason why limb grafts usually are unsatisfactory. A mechanical artificial limb is likely to be of more value to the patient.

Transfusions

Blood. Blood transfusion has been one of the most important factors in the development of modern surgery. There are many lifesaving surgical procedures that are possible only because the blood loss inevitable in the operation can be made up by transfusion. Blood transfusion is of value in saving life following major injury, bleeding ulcers, childbirth, and many other conditions involving dangerous loss of blood. Purified blood components can be transfused to treat specific defects; for example, platelets are used to correct a low platelet count, and clotting factor VIII is given to counteract the clotting defect in classic hemophilia.

Bone marrow. Diseases in which the bone marrow is defective, such as aplastic anemia, may be treated by marrow grafting. Some forms of leukemia can be cured by destroying the patient's bone marrow—the site of the cancerous cells—with drugs and irradiation. Marrow grafting is then necessary to rescue the patient. There is a tendency for the patient to reject the allografted marrow, and there is an additional hazard because immune-system cells in a marrow graft can react against the patient's tissues, causing serious and sometimes fatal graft-versus-host disease. To avoid these complications, special immunosuppressive treatment is given. The use of monoclonal antibodies (see below *Monoclonal antibodies*) to selectively remove harmful lymphocytes from the donor marrow has produced encouraging results in preventing graft-versus-host disease.

ORGAN TRANSPLANTS

Organ transplants are, for a variety of reasons, more difficult to perform successfully than are most other grafts. Despite these difficulties, kidney transplant has now become a routine operation in most developed countries. Heart and liver grafting have also become established, and promising results have been obtained with pancreas and combined heart–lung grafts.

The kidney. The surgery of kidney transplantation is straightforward, and the patient can be kept fit by dialysis with an artificial kidney before and after the operation. The kidney was the first organ to be transplanted successfully in humans, and experience is now considerable. Effective methods of preventing graft rejection have been available since the 1960s.

Effects of kidney disease

Fatal kidney disease is relatively common in young people. When there is deterioration of kidney function, eventually, despite all conventional treatment, the patient becomes extremely weak and anemic. Fluid collects in the tissues, producing swelling, known as dropsy or edema, because the kidneys cannot remove excess water. Fluid in the lungs may cause difficulty in breathing and puts an excessive strain on the heart, which may already be suffering from the effects of high blood pressure as a result of kidney failure.

Waste products that cannot be removed from the body can cause inflammation of the coverings of the heart and the linings of the stomach and colon. As a result, there may be pain in the chest, inflammation of the stomach leading to distressing vomiting, and diarrhea from the colitis. The nerves running to the limbs may be damaged, resulting in paralysis. Treatment with the artificial kidney followed by kidney grafting can eliminate all these symptoms and has a good chance of permitting the dying person to return to a normal existence. Unfortunately, in most countries only a minority of patients receive this treatment because of a shortage of donor kidneys.

Artificial kidney treatment for about 12 hours, two to three times a week, removes all the features of kidney failure in one to two months. The patient then is able to leave the hospital and can be assessed as to suitability for a transplant. As has been mentioned, the kidney graft is heterotopic. The diseased kidneys are left in place, unless their continued presence is likely to impair the patient's health after a successful graft.

Transplantation and postoperative care. The patient may receive a kidney from a live donor or a dead one. Cadaver kidneys may not function immediately after transplantation, and further treatment with the artificial kidney may be required for two to three weeks while damage in the transplanted kidney is repaired. The patient is given drugs that depress immune responses and prevent the graft from being rejected. Immediately after the operation, for the first week or two, every effort is made to keep the patient from contact with bacteria that might cause infection. The patient is usually nursed in a separate room, and doctors and nurses entering the room take care to wear masks and wash their hands before touching him. The air of the room is purified by filtration. Close relatives are allowed to visit the patient, but they are required to take the same precautions. When stitches have been removed the patient is encouraged to get up as much as possible and to be active, but, in the first four months after the operation, careful surveillance is necessary to make sure that the patient is not rejecting the graft or developing an infection. He may be discharged from the hospital within a few weeks of the operation, but frequent return visits are necessary for medical examination and biochemical estimations of the blood constituents, to determine the state of function of the graft, and to make sure that the drugs are not causing side effects. Each patient requires a carefully adjusted dose of the immunosuppressive drugs that prevent transplant rejection.

Maintenance of health after transplantation

Once the dosage of immunosuppressive drugs is stabilized, patients are encouraged to go back to a normal existence and return to work. The only restrictions are that they must continue to take their drugs and make frequent visits to the outpatient department for surveillance. Patients can return even to heavy work, such as driving a bulldozer, but more often a relatively light job is preferable. Women can bear children after a transplant, and men can become fathers. The course of events is not always so happy, unfortunately. If the patient rejects the kidney or develops a serious infection, it may be necessary to remove the graft and stop administration of the immunosuppressive drugs. The patient must then return to regular maintenance treatment with an artificial kidney but may receive a second or even a third graft.

Data on kidney transplant results. In kidney grafts involving identical twins, in which case rejection is not a problem, recipients have survived more than 25 years. A number of patients who have received kidneys from unrelated cadaver donors have survived more than 20 years, demonstrating that in some patients rejection can be controlled with standard immunosuppressive drugs. There has been a gradual improvement in the overall results of kidney transplants. The patient mortality has declined to around 10 percent per year, death usually being due to infection associated with immunosuppressive treatment; to complications of dialysis in patients whose kidneys have failed; or to other facets of kidney disease, such as high blood pressure and coronary artery disease. Recipients also face an increased risk of malignant growths, particularly lymphomata (growths of the lymphoid system that are probably due to virus infections). Kidney-graft survival has improved since the introduction of the immunosuppressive agent cyclosporine (also called cyclosporin A; see below), and many centres have achieved a one-year survival rate of 80 percent and a two-year rate of 70 percent for patients with a functioning kidney graft from an unrelated cadaver donor. One-year survival rates of 80 to 90 percent have been attained for kidney grafts between parent and child and more than 90 percent for grafts from well-matched sibling donors. As these statistics indicate, the patient who develops permanent kidney failure now has a reasonable chance of good treatment from a combination of dialysis and kidney transplantation. Those fortunate enough to receive a well-functioning kidney can expect complete rehabilitation.

The heart. The heart is a pump with a built-in power supply; it has a delicate regulatory mechanism that permits it to perform efficiently under a wide range of demands. During moments of fear, passion, or violent exercise, the heart rate increases greatly, and the contractions become more forceful, so that the pumping of the blood intrudes on the consciousness; this is experienced by the individual as palpitations. Cessation of the heartbeat has also been, throughout the ages, the cardinal sign of death. Thus, it is perhaps not so surprising that there was an intense public interest when the first attempts were made at transplanting a human heart. The objectives of heart transplantation, nevertheless, are the same as those of other organ grafts.

Appropriate circumstances for a heart transplant

One of the most important advances in surgery since World War II has been in direct operations on the heart. Heart valves are repaired or replaced with artificial valves, and techniques have been developed so that the heart can be stopped and its function taken over temporarily by an electrical pump. If, however, the muscle of the heart is destroyed, as occurs in certain diseases, the only operation that can cure the patient is to replace the heart with a graft or possibly an artificial heart. Blockage of the coronary arteries and certain other heart-muscle diseases can kill the patient because the muscle of the heart cannot contract properly. A patient with one of these diseases who is close to dying is, therefore, a possible recipient for a heart transplant.

A group of American investigators perfected the technique of heart transplantation in the late 1950s. They showed that a transplanted dog's heart could provide the animal with a normal circulation until the heart was rejected. The features of rejection of the heart are similar to those of the kidney. The cells that produce immune reactions, the lymphocytes, migrate into the muscle cells of the heart, damage it, and also block the coronary arteries, depriving the heart of its own circulation. In most experiments it was more difficult to prevent rejection of the heart than of the kidney. Despite this, rejection was prevented for long periods in animals. Based on this experimental work, the next logical step was to transplant a human heart into a patient dying of incurable heart disease. This step was taken in 1967 by a surgical team in Cape Town, South Africa.

In the years immediately following the first transplant, numerous heart allografts were performed at medical centres throughout the world. Unfortunately, many recipients succumbed to rejection of the transplanted organ. Furthermore, the heart is more sensitive to lack of blood than the kidneys are; it must be removed from the donor more quickly and can be preserved without damage for only a short period of time. Because of these difficulties—particularly the problem of rejection—the number of heart transplants performed worldwide dropped considerably after the initial excitement abated. Steady advances in detecting and treating rejection were made throughout the 1970s, however; and the introduction of the immunosuppressant cyclosporine in the 1980s brought even further improvements in the long-term survival rates for heart-graft recipients. Interest in the procedure revived, and many hundreds of heart transplants have now been performed. A number of patients have lived five or more years after the operation, and heart grafting has become an accepted therapy for otherwise incurable heart disease. Experimental artificial hearts have also been implanted, but these require a cumbersome external power supply and long-term survival rates are not known.

The liver. Many of the functions of the liver are not known. It is a complicated organ that produces the clotting factors and many other vital substances in the blood and that removes many wastes and poisons from the circulation. It is, in effect, a chemical factory. The two categories of fatal liver disease that may be treated by liver grafting are nonmalignant destructive diseases of the liver cells—for example, cirrhosis—and primary cancer of the liver affecting either the main liver cells or the bile ducts. The liver is extremely sensitive to lack of blood supply and must be cooled within 15 minutes of the death of the donor. The operation can be difficult, since the liver is rather large and of complex structure. Both its removal from the cadaver and its grafting into the recipient are major surgical operations. The operation is more difficult in humans than in animals; particularly, the removal of the diseased liver from the recipient. This may be much enlarged and adherent to surrounding structures so that its removal may result in serious bleeding. Once transplanted, the liver must function immediately or the patient will die. There is no treatment available that is comparable to the use of the artificial kidney for kidney disease. If the liver functions well immediately after transplantation, the rest of the management is similar to that followed in kidney operations, and the same drugs are given. Many early liver transplantation operations failed, but an increasing number have successfully restored dying patients to normal existence. Children do especially well following liver transplantation. The commonest fatal liver disease in childhood is a congenital deficiency of bile ducts called biliary atresia. Several centres have obtained a 90 percent one-year survival in children after liver grafting, although up to 25 percent of these patients may require retransplantation due to failure of the first graft.

The lung. Chronic fatal disease of the lung is common, but the progress of the disease is usually slow, and the patient may be ill for a long time. When the lung eventually fails, the patient is likely to be unfit for a general anesthetic and an operation. The function of the lung is to allow exchange of gases between the blood and the air. The gas passes through an extremely fine membrane lining the air spaces. This exposure to air makes the lungs susceptible to infection, more so than any other organs that have been grafted. Lung infection is one of the commonest causes of death after the grafting of other organs, and it is consequently not surprising that infection has caused failure of many lung transplants. Even a mild rejection reaction can severely damage the gas-exchange membrane, and the patient may die before the rejection is reversed. The actual ventilation of the lungs by rhythmic breathing is a complicated movement controlled by nerves connecting the brain to the lungs and to the muscles that produce the breathing. Cutting the nerves can interfere with the rhythmicity of breathing, and this may be an important cause of the difficulties of successfully transplanting both lungs. Nevertheless, these difficulties have been overcome. If only one lung is transplanted, however, the patient's own diseased lung may interfere with the function of the graft by robbing it of air and directing too much blood into the graft. Further progress may depend on a safer, more perfect control of rejection. Currently, grafting both lungs with the heart is the best method of achieving a satisfactory lung graft.

Failure of lung transplants from infection

The heart and lungs. The technique of transplanting the heart and both lungs as a functioning unit was developed in animal experiments at Stanford Medical Center in California. Despite the technical feasibility of the operation, rejection could not be controlled by conventional immunosuppression. With the availability of cyclosporine researchers were able to obtain long-term survivors with combined heart–lung transplants in primate species. Applications to human patients have been remarkably successful. Two-thirds of the patients who received transplants at Stanford are surviving, and other centres have adopted this treatment for patients with severe lung fibrosis and failure of the right side of the heart, which pumps blood into the lungs. Unfortunately, many organ donors have been maintained on ventilators, a process that frequently leads to lung infections; as a consequence, the availability of donor heart–lung units is limited. Furthermore, the lungs are vulnerable to damage from lack of blood, and so transplantation must be performed expeditiously.

The pancreas. The pancreas consists of two kinds of tissues: endocrine and exocrine. The latter produces pancreatic juice, a combination of digestive enzymes that empty via a duct into the small intestine. The endocrine tissue of the pancreas—the islets of Langerhans—secrete the hormones insulin and glucagon into the bloodstream. These hormones are vital to the regulation of carbohydrate metabolism and exert wide-ranging effects on the growth and maintenance of body tissues. Insufficient insulin production results in type I diabetes mellitus, a disease that is fatal without daily injections of insulin. Even with insulin therapy, many diabetics suffer kidney failure and blindness due to the disease's effects on the small blood vessels. There are reasons to believe that a normally functioning pancreas graft will prevent the progression of these complications.

Much effort has been devoted to removing the islets of Langerhans from the pancreas with a view to grafting the separated islets or even the isolated insulin-producing beta cells. Unfortunately, it is very difficult to obtain sufficient islets from the fibrotic human pancreas, and it appears that isolated islets are highly susceptible to rejection. A number of clinical attempts at islet grafting have been made without long-term success. Transplanting the vascularized pancreas has, however, been more encouraging. It is customary to graft the body and tail of the pancreas; that is, half the pancreas is transplanted, using the splenic artery and vein for vascular anastomosis. One of the difficulties with this procedure has been dealing with the digestive juice produced by the transplanted pancreas. A further complicating factor has been the fact that corticosteroids—frequently used for immunosuppression in transplant patients—aggravate diabetes. The availability of cyclosporine has permitted the avoidance of corticosteroids and has prompted renewed interest in pancreas grafting. The procedure is particularly attractive when a patient with diabetic kidney failure can receive a kidney and pancreas graft from the same donor. A technique with encouraging early results has been to insert the pancreas graft very close to the patient's own pancreas in the so-called paratopic position. This allows drainage of insulin directly into the liver, while the pancreatic juice is diverted into the stomach, where the digestive enzymes are inhibited by stomach acid. It is certainly most gratifying to patients who have been undergoing regular dialysis and taking insulin to be free from both these onerous treatments and to be permitted to eat and drink without restriction. The one-year functional survival rate for pancreatic grafts has reached 30 percent; further advances in surgical technique will be needed before the rate matches the results obtained in kidney grafts. It is of interest that the vascularized pancreas probably is less susceptible to rejection than the kidney.

SPECIAL LEGAL AND ETHICAL PROBLEMS

Legal aspects. In most countries, the law on organ transplantation is poorly defined, as legislation has not yet been created to cope with this advance in surgery. The existing framework relating to physical assault and care of the dead has no provision for organ transplantation. It is customary to ask the permission of the relatives, but, because organ removal must take place immediately after death, it may be impossible to reach the relatives in time. It has been suggested that there should be a widespread campaign to encourage persons to provide in their wills that their organs be used for transplantation. An alternative is to provide by law that permission is assumed unless removal has been forbidden by the individual in his lifetime. Such laws have been passed in Denmark, France, Sweden, Austria, and Israel. Compulsory postmortem examination, a far more extensive procedure than organ removal for grafting, is required in most countries after unexpected death, and this compulsion is not a matter of public concern and debate.

There would seem to be no reason why organ removal for transplantation purposes should not also be acceptable to public opinion, provided there is a mechanism by which individuals in their lifetime can refuse this permission. This, of course, requires an efficient register of those who indicate their refusal; the register would be consulted before any organs would be removed. It is important that there be public reassurance that considerations of transplantation would not impair normal resuscitative efforts of the potential donor.

Ethical considerations. *Defining death.* Transplantation has obviously raised important ethical considerations concerning the diagnosis of death of potential donors, and, particularly, how far resuscitation should be continued. Every effort must be made to restore the heartbeat to someone who has had a sudden cardiac arrest or breathing to someone who cannot breathe. Artificial respiration and massage of the heart, the standard methods of resuscitation, are continued until it is clear that the brain is dead. Most physicians consider that beyond this point efforts at resuscitation are useless.

In many countries, the question of how to diagnose brain death—that is, irreversible destruction of the brain—has been debated by neurologists and other medical specialists. Most of these experts agree that when the brain stem is destroyed there can be no recovery. The brain stem controls the vital function of breathing and the reflexes of the eyes and ears, and it transmits all information between the brain and the rest of the body. Most countries have established strict guidelines for how brain-stem death is to be diagnosed and what cases are to be excluded—for example, patients who have been poisoned, have been given drugs, or have developed hypothermia. The neurological signs of brain-stem death must be elicited by a trained clinician who is not concerned directly with the transplant operation. These signs are reverified after an interval, and, if there is the slightest doubt, further reverifications are made until the criteria are unequivocally met. The guidelines are not seriously disputed, and there has never been a recovery in a case that fulfilled the criteria of brain-stem death.

Determination of brain death

Shortage of donors. Another area of ethical concern is the dilemma posed by the shortage of donor organs. Advances in immunosuppressive therapy have put increasing pressure on the supply of donor organs, and medical personnel sometimes find themselves having to determine who among the potential recipients should receive a lifesaving graft. Furthermore, there is a danger of commercial interests becoming involved with people willing to sell their organs for personal gain, and there is definite risk that organized crime might procure organs for rich and unscrupulous people.

REJECTION

Human beings possess complex defense mechanisms against bacteria, viruses, and other foreign materials that enter the body. These mechanisms, which collectively make up the immune system, cannot, unfortunately, differentiate between disease-causing microorganisms and the cells of a lifesaving transplant. Both are perceived as foreign, and both are subject to attack by the immune system. This immune reaction leads to rejection, the greatest problem in successful tissue and organ grafting.

Immune responses. In order to understand why rejection occurs and how it may be prevented, it is necessary to know something of the operations of the immune system. The key cells of the immune system are the white blood cells known as lymphocytes. These are of two basic types: T lymphocytes and B lymphocytes. These cells have the capacity to distinguish "self" substances from such "nonself" substances as microorganisms and foreign tissue cells. Substances that provoke an immune reaction are recognized by the presence of certain molecules, called antigens, on their surface.

T lymphocytes are responsible for what is called cell-mediated immunity, so named because the T cells themselves latch onto the antigens of the invader and then initiate reactions that lead to the destruction of the nonself matter. B lymphocytes, on the other hand, do not directly attack invaders. Rather, they produce antibodies, proteins that are capable of initiating reactions that weaken or destroy the foreign substance. The overall immune reaction is exceedingly complex, with T lymphocytes, B lymphocytes, macrophages (scavenger cells), and various circulating chemicals waging a coordinated assault on the invader.

The mechanisms of rejection

Transplant rejection is generally caused by cell-mediated responses. The process usually occurs over days or months, as the T lymphocytes stimulate the infiltration and destruction of the graft. The transplant may be saved if the cell-mediated reactions can be suppressed. Antibody attack of transplanted tissues is most apparent when the recipient has preexisting antibodies against the antigens of the donor. This situation can arise if the recipient has been previously exposed to foreign antigens as the result of pregnancy (during which the mother is exposed to fetal antigens contributed by the father), blood transfusions, or prior transplants. Unlike a cell-mediated reaction, antibody-mediated rejection is rapid, occurring within minutes or hours, and cannot be reversed.

Selection of donor and tissue matching. The factors that provoke graft rejection are called transplantation, or histocompatibility, antigens. If donor and recipient have the same antigens, as do identical twins, there can be no rejection. All cells in the body have transplantation antigens except the red blood cells, which carry their own system of blood-group (ABO) antigens. The main human transplantation antigens—called the major histocompatibility complex, or the HLA (human leukocyte group A) system—are governed by genes on the sixth chromosome. HLA antigens are divided into two groups; class I antigens, which are the target of an effector rejection response; and class II antigens, which are the initiators of the rejection reaction. Class II antigens are not found in all tissues, although class I antigens are. Certain macrophage-like tissue cells—called dendritic cells because of their finger-like processes—have a high expression of class II antigens. There has been much interest in trying to remove such cells from an organ graft, so that the rejection reaction will not be initiated. There has been some experimental success with this approach, although it has not yet been applied clinically.

Histocompatibility antigens

Tissue typing involves the identification of an individual's HLA antigens. Lymphocytes are used for typing. It is important also that the red blood cells be grouped, since red-cell-group antigens are present in other tissues and can cause graft rejection. Although transplantation antigens are numerous and complicated, the principles of tissue typing are the same as for red-cell grouping. The lymphocytes being typed are mixed with a typing reagent, a serum that contains antibodies to certain HLA antigens. If the lymphocytes carry HLA antigens for which the reagent has antibodies, the lymphocytes agglutinate (clump together) or die. Typing serums are obtained from the blood of persons who have rejected grafts or have had multiple blood transfusions or multiple pregnancies; as previously stated, such persons may develop antibodies to transplantation antigens.

Tissue typing

If the lymphocytes of both the recipient and the potential donor are killed by a given serum, then, as far as that typing serum is concerned, the individuals have antigens in common. If neither donor nor recipient lymphocytes are affected, then donor and recipient lack antigens in common. If the donor lymphocytes are killed but not those of the recipient, then an antigen is present in the donor and is missing from the recipient. Thus, by testing their lymphocytes against a spectrum of typing sera, it is possible to determine how closely the recipient and donor match in HLA antigens. As a final precaution before grafting, a direct crossmatch is performed between the recipient's serum and donor lymphocytes. A positive crossmatch usually contraindicates the donor–recipient transplant under consideration.

There is now considerable knowledge concerning the inheritance of transplantation antigens, but, even so, tissue typing is not sufficiently advanced to give an accurate prediction of the outcome of a graft in an individual case, particularly when the donor and recipient are not related to one another. In accordance with Mendelian laws of inheritance, a person obtains one of a pair of chromosomes from each parent. Therefore, a parent-to-child transplant will always be half-matched for transplantation antigens. Siblings have a one-in-four chance of a complete match of the HLA antigens, a one-in-four chance of no match, and a one-in-two chance of a half-match.

The blood-transfusion effect. Since following a blood transfusion some patients become sensitized to the transplantation antigens of the donor, it was expected that prior blood transfusion could only harm the recipient's prospects for a successful organ graft. Careful analysis of results, however, showed the contrary. Specifically, the results of kidney grafting in patients who had received previous blood transfusions without regard to HLA matching were much better than in patients who had never received a blood transfusion. Although a great deal of effort has been expended to determine the mechanisms involved, researchers still do not know how the immune system is modified by prior blood transfusions. Most centres now give blood transfusions before transplantation, though some patients do develop HLA antibodies against a wide spectrum of the population and therefore become very difficult to transplant. This pool of highly sensitized patients is getting larger throughout the world, not only from blood transfusions, but also from patients who have rejected kidney grafts and are back on dialysis, and from women who have had multiple pregnancies.

A special application of the blood-transfusion effect involves repeated small blood transfusions from a potential donor who is a close relative of the patient. If sensitization does not occur, subsequent kidney-graft results are excellent. Some patients, however, develop a positive crossmatch to donor lymphocytes and cannot receive a graft from that donor.

Donor-specific blood transfusions

Immunosuppression. The aim of transplantation research is to allow the recipient to accept the graft permanently with no unpleasant side effects. With current drugs that are used for this purpose, after some months the dosage can often be reduced and sometimes even stopped without the graft's being rejected. In such a case, the patient is no longer susceptible to infections. There would appear to be adaptation of the recipient toward the graft and the graft toward the recipient. The adaptation is probably akin to desensitization, a process used sometimes to cure patients suffering from asthma by giving them repeated injections of small doses of the pollen to which they are sensitive.

Azathioprine. Azathioprine is one of the most widely used immunosuppressive agents; it also has been used to treat leukemia. It can be given by mouth, but the dose must be carefully adjusted so that the blood-cell-forming tissues in the bone marrow are not damaged, which could lead to infections and bleeding. The white-blood-cell and platelet counts need to be determined frequently to make sure that azathioprine is not being given in too large a dose. It is an extremely valuable drug and has been the basis of most immunosuppressive regimens in patients with organ grafts. At first, high doses are given, but eventually the doses may be reduced. Even years after transplantation, small doses of azathioprine may still be needed to maintain coexistence between graft and host.

Corticosteroids. Cortisone and its relatives, prednisone and prednisolone, are very useful in patients with organ grafts. They can be given by mouth, but although not damaging to the blood-forming cells, they do predispose the body to infection, cause stunted growth in children, and have other injurious effects. Persons receiving these substances may develop bloated complexions with swollen faces, may tend to gain weight and become diabetic, and their bones may become brittle. Few recipients of organ transplants, however, can do without corticosteroids, particularly during an active rejection crisis.

Antilymphocyte serum. If rabbits receive repeated injections of mouse lymphocytes, they become immunized and develop antibodies against the mouse cells. The serum from the rabbits' blood can be injected into mice and will often prevent them from rejecting grafts, both from other mice and even, sometimes, from other species. Such antilymphocyte serums can be produced between a variety of species, but in higher mammals, particularly humans, it has been difficult to obtain a powerful immunosuppressive serum without side effects of toxicity.

The activity of the serum lies in its gamma globulin, which contains the antibody proteins. Antilymphocyte globulin is used in humans but contains many proteins that are ineffective and may be harmful. It can be added to standard azathioprine and cortisone treatment without adding to the toxicity of these agents, and it is extremely useful in treating rejection crisis in kidney-graft recipients who have not responded to corticosteroids. Unfortunately, it has been difficult to obtain a consistently effective product, and there are not good methods of assaying the potency of one serum compared with another. Even when they are prepared by exactly the same methods from the same species, one batch may differ greatly from another. The horse has usually been used to produce antilymphocyte serum for the treatment of human patients, but some persons are sensitive to horse proteins and become extremely ill when treated with horse serum. Such patients may, however, be successfully treated with rabbit antilymphocyte globulin.

Monoclonal antibodies. An important development in antibody production followed the discovery that an antibody-forming lymphocyte can be fused with a cancerous bone-marrow cell. The resulting hybrid cell produces the antibody specified by its lymphocyte progenitor, while from the cancer cell it obtains the characteristic of multiplying indefinitely in laboratory cultures. The culturing of the hybrid yields a clone of cells that produce one specific antibody—a "monoclonal" antibody. Such agents are exclusively specific in action and there is no theoretical limit to the number of antibodies that can be produced by different hybrid cell lines. Monoclonal antibodies can be regarded as highly specific antilymphocyte globulin without many of the unwanted materials that are present in the ordinary, polyclonal antilymphocyte serum described above. Some monoclonal antibodies have been produced that appear to be effective as immunosuppressive agents in humans. Further advances in this area are expected.

Cyclosporine. A new type of immunosuppressive agent was found as a natural product of an earth fungus by the Sandoz Laboratories. This material, called cyclosporine, is a stable, cyclic peptide with powerful immunosuppressive activity affecting especially the T lymphocytes. Cyclosporine was found to prevent organ graft rejection in a number of animal species, and when the drug was used in humans the expected immunosuppressive effect was again observed. It has been used in recipients of all types of organ grafts with improved immunosuppressive results. Unfortunately, cyclosporine is toxic to the human kidney, and there is fear that prolonged use of the agent could lead to permanent renal damage. Cyclosporine also increases the growth of hair on the face and body, which can be distressing to female patients. It is a difficult drug to use because, being fat soluble, its absorption is variable and each patient needs to be individually studied to ensure that the dosage is adequate but not excessive.

It is clear that none of the agents so far used to prevent rejection is ideal. No one would use such dangerous agents except as a last resort in a desperate situation. This, unfortunately, is the exact plight of a person in need of a vital organ transplant. Immunosuppression is, however, much more effective and less dangerous than it used to be, and we can expect advances with new chemical derivatives, in particular monoclonal antibodies and nontoxic analogues of cyclosporine.

ORGAN AND TISSUE BANKS

Without a blood supply organs deteriorate rapidly. Cooling can slow down the process but cannot stop it. Organs differ in their susceptibility to damage. At body temperature, irreversible destruction of the brain occurs after more than three to five minutes; of the heart, liver, pancreas, and lung, after 10 to 30 minutes; of the kidney, after 50 to 100 minutes; and of the skin and cornea, after six to 12 hours. Although the shorter the time the organ is deprived of its blood supply the better, the cornea can be removed for grafting at relative leisure, but every minute is of vital importance for a liver transplant. When a kidney is removed from a living donor, it is not necessary to use elaborate preservation techniques. The operations on the donor and recipient are performed at the same time, and the recipient is prepared to receive the graft by the time that the donor organ is removed. Cadaver kidneys are removed as soon as possible after the donor's death, preferably within an hour. Cool solutions are infused into the blood vessels of the kidney, which is then kept at 4° C (39° F) in a refrigerator or surrounded by ice in a vacuum flask. At the same time, the recipient is prepared for operation. Kidneys can be conserved in this simple way for 24 to 48 hours with little deterioration, and during this time they can be moved for long distances. For a kidney to be preserved from 48 to 72 hours, a complicated machine is required to provide artificial circulation. Cool, oxygenated, physiological solutions, with the same osmotic pressure as blood, are passed through the blood vessels of the kidney. The imperfections of the machinery mean that there is a slow deterioration of the organ that does not occur normally in the body. To keep a kidney undamaged for longer than 72 hours is difficult. Blood cells, spermatozoa, and certain other dissociated tissue cells can be frozen to subzero temperatures and kept alive indefinitely. Special preserving fluids will prevent cell destruction by ice crystals, but these fluids have damaging effects if introduced into whole organs such as the kidney.

Preservation of kidneys for transplantation

Long-term storage and banking of organs seem unlikely in the near future. Preservation techniques for the heart, lung, liver, and pancreas have not been so extensively studied as the kidney. The principles are the same, although these other organs will not tolerate such long periods without a blood supply. Grafting is performed as quickly as possible, preferably within eight hours for the liver and pancreas, four hours for the heart, and two hours for the combined heart-and-lung graft. Much research will be necessary before it is possible to keep organs banked in the way that blood can be stored.

BIBLIOGRAPHY. FRANCIS D. MOORE, *Give and Take* (1964), an account of the history of organ transplantation; *Ethics in Medical Progress*, ed. by G.E.W. WOLSTENHOLME and MAEVE O'CONNOR (1966), proceedings of a symposium sponsored by the Ciba Foundation, discussing the ethical aspects of transplantation; ROY Y. CALNE, *Renal Transplantation*, 2nd ed. (1967), a technical account of kidney grafting with a discussion of immunological aspects; his *A Gift of Life* (1970), a book for the nonspecialist, covering the immunological and clinical aspects and the ethics of organ grafting; RUSSELL SCOTT, *The Body As Property* (1981), a comprehensive examination of the ethical and legal aspects of organ transplantation. THOMAS E. STARZL, *Experience in Hepatic Transplantation* (1969), the first full account of the pioneer work on liver grafting; *Liver Transplantation: The Cambridge-King's College Hospital Experience*, ed. by ROY Y. CALNE (1983), a later source on liver grafting; CHRISTOPHER PALLIS, *ABC of Brain Stem Death* (1983), a collection of articles from the *British Medical Journal*, with a description of brain-stem destruction and how it is recognized; PETER J. MORRIS (ed.), *Kidney Transplantation: Principles and Practice*, 2nd ed. (1984), a work on theory and methods; ROBERTA G. SIMMONS, SUSAN D. KLEIN, and RICHARD L. SIMMONS, *Gift of Life: The Social and Psychological Impact of Organ Transplantation* (1977), a work based on exhaustive studies.

(R.Y.C.)

Transportation

From earliest times the conditions in which man lives have been powerfully influenced by the ease and speed with which he has been able to move himself and his materials from point to point on the Earth's surface. By harnessing nature directly and indirectly, man has been able to explore and exploit the Earth's resources. The chief landmarks in the history of transportation—the wheel, the sail, the steam engine, the internal-combustion engine, the electric motor, and the great technological breakthrough of flight—promise, as the 21st century approaches, to be capped by the rocket engine, which frees man from dependence on Earth's atmosphere and permits him to visualize travelling to other planets. (E.A.J.D.)

The article is divided into the following sections:

PRE-INDUSTRIAL TRANSPORTATION

Primitive transportation

EARLY LAND TRANSPORT

Early man was a wanderer—of necessity rather than choice. Food was scarce; enemies abounded. Techniques were invented for carrying loads, on the end of a stick on one shoulder, on the single yoke, or on both ends of a pole carried across the shoulders, the double yoke. A slain deer or buffalo could be carried on a pole borne by two men; a 5,000-year-old alabaster relief from Sumer shows a large vessel carried thus between two bearers.

The travois. The earliest agricultural workers probably shifted hay on the forked branch of a tree. From this developed the Y-shaped sledge, or travois, used in more recent times by North American Indians. The travois was two poles tied together, with the inverted V resting on the back of a man or animal. Between the poles was slung a wooden or net frame. The Y-sledge was widely used in northern Europe and in the cattle regions of Africa.

The slide car. Whereas the travois can be put together and taken apart as necessary, the slide car is permanent. In the slide car, two shafts are harnessed to a horse or other draft animal; their ends drag along the ground and the shafts are kept apart by crossbars. The very wide geographical distribution of the slide car is proof of its antiquity, and it held its own in some mountainous districts of Europe until recent times.

Sledges and skis. By 5000 BC the sledge was in common use in northern Europe, North America, Egypt, Assyria, and the Middle East. Originally a simple rectangular platform that could be either hauled or pushed, it was soon improved by the addition of runners. Sledges can travel well over snow, marsh, clay, or grass, and to this day are used in Lapland, northern Asia, and British Columbia.

Use of sledges for hauling

The Egyptians and Assyrians used them to move the materials required for their pyramids, obelisks, and huge river statues, and they constructed some of the earliest known roads to enhance the capabilities of the sledge. The use of runners in the form of skis is also very old. A carving on a rock-face in northern Norway dating to about 2000 BC is clearly identifiable as a man on skis.

Animal transport. The ass, native to northeastern Africa, was almost certainly the first draft animal and was in common use in northeast Africa, upper Egypt, the Mediterranean Basin, and the Near and Far East well before 3000 BC. By that date pack animals were in regular service on the caravan routes stretching from eastern Europe and North Africa to India and China. A graphic presentation of convoys of pack asses regularly crossing the Syrian Desert and the Taurus Mountains (Turkey) is obtained from the surviving business letters of a group of Assyrian merchants established in central Asia Minor about 2000 BC. An Egyptian relief from Bari Hasan, dated around 1900 BC, shows the arrival of the Canaanites with their pack asses laden with children and tribute. The ox, the reindeer, the elephant, the yak, the buffalo, and the llama were also used in earlier times.

The camel, both the one-hump (Arabian) and the two-hump (Bactrian) varieties, was uniquely fitted by nature for long overland journeys through desert regions, thanks to its extraordinary capacity to store food and water and its ability to walk on soft sand. The camel could carry up to 600 pounds (270 kilograms) in weight. The most important draft animal for the future, the horse, was a relative latecomer. When or where horses were first domesticated is not known; they were introduced to Egypt by the Hyksos about 1675 BC.

EARLY WATER TRANSPORT

Rafts. Before ships and even boats, man must have had a wide variety of rafts and similar craft. The type varied according to environment; in Egypt, where the Nile was flanked by papyrus and timber was scarce, the first floats consisted of bundles of rushes tied together. While the small models that have survived are not sufficiently detailed to indicate their mode of construction, a close parallel can be seen in modern Peru, where coastal fishermen use reed rafts, known as caballitos. Basically, the caballito consists of two or three conical bunches of reeds, cut off square at their bases and lashed side by side, with the pointed end turned up to form a prow. Caballitos have a considerable history; a pottery vase in the form of such a boat is dated around 1200 BC.

Boats of inflated skins

Inflated skins. In Mesopotamia and the eastern Mediterranean development proceeded on different lines. On the Tigris and Euphrates, where papyrus was lacking, an early skin float inflated with air provided a vehicle on which a man could lie and kick or paddle himself across a river. From the single or double float there evolved the wooden raft to which were attached a number of inflated skin floats, producing a platform capable of supporting a substantial load. One of the earliest pictorial records of these rafts comes from Nineveh. At destination, after disposal of the cargo, the timbers of the raft were sold and the skins deflated and transported by pack animal back to their place of origin for future use. Similar craft were used until recently on downstream journeys on the Tigris.

Closely allied to the skin float, which is kept buoyant by air pressure, is the skin boat, which consists of a flexible leather cover stretched around an internal frame. Such craft survive today in the kayaks of the Eskimo, the curraghs of the west coast of Ireland, the coracles of Wales, the modern canvas canoe, and other counterparts scattered widely over Asia and America. There is strong evidence that the coracle type was first developed in Asia. Coracles were in common use for carrying cargo on the Tigris and Euphrates as early as the 9th century BC.

The dugout. As Neolithic man acquired better tools, dugouts superseded bark canoes. Dugouts are found wherever there are suitable forests, the limiting factor being the tree diameter. Dugouts constructed in North Africa often had beams of no more than 18 inches (46 centimetres). The ancient British canoe of the Bronze Age was 35 feet (11 metres) long with a depth of two feet (0.6 metre) and a beam of nearly five feet (1.5 metres).

The development of larger craft from the primitive dugout involved more complex construction. From the remains of two boats, probably of the Iron Age, found in the river Humber in England, one possible line of advance can be deduced. The hull was roughly pontoon-shaped, with five thick floor planks bevelled and grooved to fit each other and sewn together with withies (willows). A more promising line of development may be inferred from various types of canoe hulls in the Pacific. In the Maori type of canoe, the tree trunk was hollowed out, and additional freeboard was provided by lashing beams to either side, thus providing bulwarks, which did not quite reach stem or stern. Where the available timber did not have a diameter large enough to provide sufficient stability, outrigger floats were fitted. To secure the necessary freeboard for any carrying capacity required, additional planks were fitted at each side, as in the canoes of the Marshall Islands today. As time went on and the craft became more and more complex, the dugout part of the hull made a smaller and smaller contribution to buoyancy and in the end survived only as the keel. Although the most primitive of the earliest forms of water transportation, the dugout led to the cargo ships and passenger liners of today. (D.O'N.)

The wheel and the road

The wheeled vehicle was one of man's most important technological developments, fundamental to trade and travel. Evidence indicates it was invented only once—in the Tigris-Euphrates Valley by the Sumerians about 3500 BC. Not surprisingly, this discovery occurred in this earliest urban civilization where farmers produced a surplus to support city dwellers and needed transportation for crops. The invention of wheeled vehicles necessarily followed the taming of draft animals and the development of metallurgy for making saws and axles. The earliest evidence for a wheeled vehicle is a pictograph on a late Uruk tablet from Erech (Warka) in Mesopotamia representing a roofed, boxlike sledge mounted on four solid wheels.

WHEELED VEHICLES IN ANCIENT TIMES

The earliest wheeled vehicles were furnished with a single pole and solid wheels. Wheels ordinarily were made of two or three segments fastened with transverse struts and strengthened with a swelling around the hub. The very careful construction of these wheels casts doubt upon theories that wheels evolved from logs turning under wagon beds. Actual wheels have survived from ancient times; pictures and toy vehicles supply additional details. The rims of the earliest wheels were studded with copper nails; specimens fitted with bronze tires (*c.* 2000 BC) have been unearthed. Circular axle holes and the use of linchpins to secure the wheels indicate that the wheels turned on the axletree, though this was not the only arrangement. A copper model from Tall Ajrab had wheels rigidly fastened to an axle that revolved in metal loops, which were fastened to the bottom of the car.

Early wheels

Little evidence survives to indicate the exact nature of the chassis of the four-wheeled wagon, despite the custom of burying the royal hearse with the corpse. Several models show wheels directly attached to the wagon bed. There is no evidence of pivoted front axles to facilitate turning. Four-wheeled military wagons on the Sumerian "Standard" of Ur show the body resting on the axles.

Oxen probably served as some of the earliest draft animals. Harnessed on either side of a pole as though drawing a plow, they pulled the vehicle with a yoke that rested on their shoulders and was fastened to the pole tongue. The earliest war chariots were drawn by the fast-moving onager (*Equus hemionus onager*), a wild ass native to western India and Baluchistan. Evidence for the manoeuvrable onager-drawn two-wheeled war chariot comes first from the Diyala region, nearer than Sumer to the native land of these animals. A copper model from Tall Ajrab (*c.* 2800 BC) shows a chariot with tripartite disk wheels studded with nails. The driver stands on a small platform over the axle and holds reins passing through nose rings of four onagers. (Bridles were unknown in the 3rd millennium.) The chariot has a single pole with two animals on either side; the two outside onagers pull on their neighbours' collars. The animals are shown with the ox harness, which was unsuitable for them. A breast band, essential to supplement the yoke, pushed on the onager's windpipe, significantly decreasing his tractive power. Perhaps for this reason, or because of the diminutive size of the onagers, pictures show four of them abreast pulling these vehicles.

Wheeled vehicles spread from Sumer through Asia and Europe. There were wheeled vehicles in the Indus Valley and the Central Asia steppes by 2500 BC, in northern Syria in the Khābūr and upper Euphrates by about 2200 BC, on the Orontes by 2000 BC, in China by 1500 BC, and in Sweden by 1300 BC.

By about 2000 BC two important developments had greatly increased the use of two-wheeled vehicles. One was the domestication of the horse and the other the invention of spoked wheels. Together they revolutionized warfare by producing the light two-wheeled military chariot. A two-wheeled chariot with spoked wheels is depicted on a seal from Hissar in northeastern Iran *c.* 2000 BC. Technologically, chariots were triumphs of invention. They also were expensive. Since only kings, chieftains, or wealthy men could afford them, warfare acquired an aristocratic cast for hundreds of years. This new invention, the military chariot, enabled barbarians to burst into what is now the Middle East and overrun the civilized areas: the Hyksos conquered Egypt about 1700 BC, and the Kassites took Babylon about 1525 BC. About 1550 BC the war chariot reached Crete and was sculptured on a royal grave stela at Mycenae, the earliest European representation of a chariot. In the war chariot of the 2nd millennium, horses were yoked on either side of a pole and controlled by a snaffle bit; *i.e.,* a bit made of two links of metal. The pole was heat-bent to run under the platform up to the correct height for the yoke. The body of the chariot was very light, consisting of a high dashboard, perhaps of wickerwork, with a floor of planks or woven leather thongs resting on the axle. The wheels were demountable and fastened with linchpins. In Egyptian and Assyrian chariots the number of spokes varied from four to six or eight. Surviving chariots from Egyptian tombs are skillfully made from various woods. The Assyrians reintroduced the four-horse team.

The military chariot

Greece and Rome. Though the chariot, as an instrument of war, lost favour in classical Greece and Rome, it continued in use for circus races, frequently with a four-horse team. The Greeks used farm carts and the Romans both two- and four-wheeled baggage vehicles. Roman passenger vehicles were of varied types: two-wheeled (the *carpentum* and *cisium*) and four-wheeled (the *carruca* and *raeda*). Roman passenger vehicles evidently were not suspended, for the *arcera,* built especially for the ill, disappeared in favour of the litter, which was more comfortable. The Romans seem to have had the pivoted front axle; reliefs and mosaics show the wagons raised a considerable distance above the axles, thus implying an undercarriage. For this reason the Romans used four-wheeled conveyances for long and rapid journeys, even though two-wheeled vehicles were readily available.

The Romans made an important innovation by substituting two shafts for the pole that the Mesopotamians had used for pulling vehicles. This enabled the vehicle to be drawn by one instead of two animals. The first break with the pole-drawn vehicle is shown in a wall painting preserved at Pompeii, which was destroyed in AD 79. This painting depicts a goat, harnessed between shafts, drawing a two-wheeled chariot. His collar resembles that in the modern harness.

Scandinavia. Before the end of the 2nd millennium BC the wheeled vehicle had spread to Sweden, as shown by a rock carving at Kivik, where the outline of a four-wheeled wagon resembles one formed by coupling two carts. Much evidence of barbarian wagons comes from graves. Along with the pole and yoke form of traction, barbarians had taken over the idea of burying the hearse with the royal corpse. Wagons in Hallstatt burials are mostly four-wheeled with heat-bent rims and iron tires; the wheels turn on axles and are held in place by linchpins. The

Barbarian wagons

Figure 1: Dejbjerg wagon, made in a Celtic workshop in south Germany or northeast France, 1st century BC. In the Nationalmuseet, Copenhagen.

By courtesy of the Nationalmuseet, Copenhagen

Dejbjerg wagon, from Denmark, a sophisticated product of the wheelwright's art, dates from the 1st century BC. It had wheels with grooves for turning sticks to act as roller bearings. The Dejbjerg wagon has been reconstructed with a pivoted front axle (Figure 1). At Bell there is evidence for a movable front axle. Excavations uncovered three iron rods lying in such a position as to form a Y, with the arms attached to the rear axle and the point to the front axle, in the same manner as indicated on the rocks at Kivik. The most recent of these buried hearses is the four-wheeled wagon in the 9th-century Oseberg ship burial; with the coming of Christianity the custom disappeared. The Oseberg wagon has a curious clinker-built body; its construction is so impractical it can never have been used except for ceremonial purposes. Though the Oseberg wagon has also been reconstructed with a pivoted front axle, some maintain such a restoration is a mistake, that the Celts never knew the movable front axle. This theory ignores the evidence from Kivik and from Bell, the obvious expertise of barbarian craftsmen, and the fact that the Romans took over from the Celts their *raeda,* a four-wheeled wagon that was used for long distance travel.

Asian innovations spread west. From the point of view of internal security, trade and communications, literature, and education, the late classical and early medieval period in western Europe was one of decline, but with respect to technology the era was one of progress. A number of improvements in horse harness appeared in the West, brought from the East where they had been invented long before. A Chinese work of the 4th century BC describes wheels with 30 spokes; and such wheels, dating from the 4th or 3rd century BC, have been excavated. By this time the Chinese had already known the chariot for more than 1,000 years and had introduced a number of refinements into its construction. For example, they built dished wheels (for greater strength, a concave construction, the spokes inclining to the nave), and by the 4th century BC they were employing the shaft chariot.

Chinese chariots

When the West began using the breast and collar harness is uncertain. Linguistic evidence shows the Slavs had a word for breast strap before the 6th century AD; the term for shoulder collar was employed in Europe in the 8th and 9th centuries. Illustrations show the shoulder collar by AD 800 (perhaps at Pompeii in the 1st century), but it is difficult to tell how widely it was employed, because artists before the 14th and 15th centuries were little interested in realism. Other medieval improvements included the nailed horseshoe (early 9th century), whiffletree, dished wheel, harnessing in tandem, and suspended vehicles.

(M.N.B.)

THE ROADS OF THE ANCIENT WORLD

In the central and eastern Mediterranean areas, and particularly in Greece and Asia Minor, wheeled vehicles were in more common use than elsewhere, and some progress was made in primitive road construction. The deliberately made rut, characteristic of the central and eastern Mediterranean, makes its first and most prominent appearance in

Malta, in association with a society in the Late Neolithic and Early Bronze ages. These ruts were more or less uniform in their depth (three to six inches, or eight to 15 centimetres), width (eight inches, or 20 centimetres), and gauge (44–57 inches, or 112–145 centimetres). That they were deliberately constructed is shown by the fact that in some cases ruts occupy the centres of specially hollowed stone blocks placed in paved roads. Though they are of course a different type of construction, these roads foreshadowed the wooden and stone railways used in the mining industries of central Europe and Great Britain before the Industrial Revolution. Their likeness to modern railways is emphasized by the provision of sidings and passing places.

The roads of China. China developed the oldest known network of roads for everyday use; centuries before the Persian Empire, and over 2,000 years before the Incas, the Chinese had a fully developed system. Even before the Chou dynasty (*c.* 1122–221 BC) communications were controlled and roads maintained by a highways commissioner, with a separate budget of his own. During the Chou dynasty the volume of traffic necessitated the establishment of a uniform scale of size for wheeled vehicles, the prohibition of reckless driving, and traffic regulations for busy intersections. Roads were classified in five grades: pathways for men and pack animals; roads capable of taking narrow-gauge vehicles; roads that could accommodate larger vehicles; roads on which single vehicles could pass each other; and highways taking three wagons abreast.

Roads of the Persian Empire. The ruling dynasty in Persia, masters in their day (559–330 BC) of the entire Middle East, in order to maintain speedy communications with their provincial administrators, were forced to construct a road system. More accurately described as levelled and partly paved tracks, these roads were policed by guards posted at rest houses every 15 miles (24 kilometres). A continuous line of stations linked Sardis, on the Aegean shore, with Susa, the capital, 1,600 miles (2,600 kilometres) away; special messengers could cover the distance between Susa and Babylon (200 miles, or 320 kilometres) in two days.

The Roman road system. It was the Romans who brought the art of road building in antiquity to its highest pitch. The Romans may have taken their road-building techniques from the Etruscans. The roads built by the Greek colonists in southern Italy may also have had some influence.

The Appian and Flaminian ways

The first of the great Roman highways was the Via Appia, begun in 312 BC by the censor Appius Claudius. Built to link Rome with the military centre of Capua, it was later extended southeast to Tarentum (Taranto). The Via Flaminia, completed in 220 BC, gave Rome direct communications with the Po Valley.

By AD 200 the Roman system stretched from Hadrian's Wall in north Britain to the edge of the Sahara, and from Morocco to the Euphrates. Its primary purpose was to provide for speedy and safe military and civil contacts between the central seat of government and the capital cities of the imperial provinces. Horses that drew the two- or four-wheeled vehicles could be changed at stations along the road at intervals of six to 16 Roman miles. Rest houses were spaced at intervals of 20 to 30 Roman miles.

The Inca civilization. No account of the history of transportation would be complete without some mention of the astonishing achievements of the Incas in north and central South America. The Inca Empire reached its zenith under Pachacuti and Topa Inca (Tupac; 1438–93), when it stretched from the present Colombia–Ecuador border to central Chile, a coastal distance of over 2,500 miles (4,000 kilometres) and covering an area of approximately 380,000 square miles (984,000 square kilometres). From the capital, Cuzco, well constructed roads ran to all parts of the empire. Staging posts were frequent, and relay runners were stationed at them to carry messages and parcels quickly. The Incas knew something about bridging, and where necessary they carried their roads over canyons, using suspension bridges. (D.O'N.)

WHEELED VEHICLES IN THE MIDDLE AGES

In the early medieval period in the West, passenger vehicles such as the Romans used seem to have disappeared. Throughout the Middle Ages, Western men preferred travel on horseback. It was otherwise in eastern Europe, for the earliest description of a suspended carriage occurs in the 10th-century account of the travels of Ibrāhīm ibn Ya'qūb among the West Slavs. He said that the Slav kings travelled in great high wagons with four wheels and four tall posts from which a brocade-covered litter was suspended by strong chains, so that passengers would not feel the jolting of the wagon. The Slavs also used this wagon for the ill and wounded. Perhaps the earliest picture of a suspended vehicle is to be found in an 11th-century Anglo-Saxon manuscript. There, in a biblical illustration, Joseph is seen riding in a hammock suspended from two posts, each of which rises from the axle of a four-wheeled wagon. This vehicle looks like the imaginings of an artist who had heard of the Slav wagon but had never seen one. The suspension and body in this picture bear no relation to later illustrations of suspended vehicles.

The suspended carriage

During the later Middle Ages riding in vehicles in western Europe increased. In the 11th and 12th centuries, passenger vehicles were mostly two-wheeled, but in the 14th and 15th centuries they were almost invariably four-wheeled. The shift may have occurred because four-wheeled vehicles provided a steadier ride than the cart, which jerked as the horse raised or lowered his head. In the 13th century the four-wheeled chariot was the luxurious appointment of a great lady, and in 1294 Philip IV in a sumptuary ordinance forbade the use of *chars* to the wives of the bourgeoisie. In the 14th century the conveyance of a queen or duchess in England was called a whirlicote and in France a *char* or *curre.* Before the introduction into France in the 14th century of the *chariot branlant* ("trembling chariot"), the chassis of a lady's personal *char* was essentially no different from the chariot in which her baggage was transported. In either case the chariot's body rested directly on the axles. To the front axle were attached the supporting timbers (futchels), and pole, if two or four horses were to be attached in pairs, or the shafts, if horses were to be harnessed tandem. Chariots were ponderously built of wood and iron. The wheels, the pole connecting front and hind gear (perch), shafts, and body were of wood, but iron was necessary for the nails, cotter pins, axle spindles, strengthening pieces (hurters), chains, and bands around the futchels, the hub of the wheel, and frequently around the wheel as a tire. Such a chariot might weigh from 370 to 440 pounds (170–200 kilograms) and be pulled by as many as four or six horses. Pictures of vehicles drawn by one horse are uncommon.

The French *char*

By courtesy of the Zentralbibliothek Zurich; photograph, Paul Scheidegger

Figure 2: Drawing of a 14th-century carriage suspended longitudinally by straps. From Rudolf von Ems's *Weltchronik*. In the Zentralbibliothek Zürich.

A careful examination of pictures of 14th- and 15th-century *chars* makes clear their relationship to wagons (Figure 2). The superstructure of a medieval vehicle consisted of hoops supporting a leather or woollen covering, definitely resembling the American covered wagon. The body and chassis have a family relationship to the German farm wagon. For example, the latter has "standards" (*i.e.,* sticks), jutting vertically above each axle. These make it easy to convert the wagon from one with ladders at the sides for haying to one with solid sides for other purposes. From "standards" such as these the body of the passenger vehicle of the 10th-century Slavs and of the Breslau Froissart was hung, the latter by transverse chains. Longitudinal suspension by straps, the method of the future, is shown in a 14th-century German manuscript (Figure 2).

Wheels. Wheels on medieval vehicles seem to have been much the same as earlier ones, except that disk wheels were used at some places for farm carts and wagons, whereas most pictures show spoked wheels. Before the 15th century front and rear wheels were the same size. Technologically, wheels were the most sophisticated part of a medieval vehicle. They were commonly made by wheelwrights, whereas the rest of the work might be produced by nonspecialists. In the 13th century Villard de Honnecourt was acquainted with dishing. Wheels usually had composite felloes (the exterior rim); rims were studded with iron nails or had iron tires. Accounts show that movable parts of chariots were greased regularly.

Axles. It has been claimed on the basis of contemporary illustrations that medieval four-wheeled chariots had a rigidly fastened front axle. Since illustrators before the 14th or 15th centuries commonly drew vehicles without undercarriages (*i.e.,* vehicles that could not have functioned), it would be a mistake to take these pictures as precise representations of actual vehicles. The turning train is essential to wagons used for long distance transportation. The four-wheeled chariot was much used in medieval France for transporting the luggage of aristocrats and for commercial carriage of goods between Toulouse and Béarn, Paris and Melun, and Paris and Dijon. Had the wagon actually possessed rigidly fastened axles, it would have been simpler for carriers to have used carts.

COACHES

Hungarian coaches

In the early 15th century, Hungarian vehicles were admired for their lightness and comfortable ride. A light-wheeled covered chariot with rear wheels much higher than the front, such a vehicle held eight people and could be pulled by a single horse. In 15th- and 16th-century Germany, despite sharp criticism from advocates of the arduous military life, more and more noblemen rode in coaches. The word coach derives ultimately from the Hungarian town of Kocs between Raab and Buda. In the 16th century the Hungarian vehicle spread throughout Europe. There began to be a striking divergence between the farm wagon and the passenger vehicle. For one thing, the coach was a suspended vehicle. Furthermore, instead of the familiar arched tilt, the 16th-century coach had a new silhouette. Four corner posts held a rectangular roof from which leather curtains rolled down. Entrance was now from the side instead of the rear, and there was a coachman's seat in front. In his *Survey of London* (1598), John Stow complained of the danger to pedestrians when coachmen drove with reins and whip instead of having footmen lead the horses. This may have been the custom in town, but in medieval pictures when horses were hitched tandem, there was a postilion riding on one of the front horses.

The medieval *char* and whirlicote provided great elegance in ceremonial processions, as did their successors in the modern period. The first coach in England was in use in 1555; in 1564 Queen Elizabeth had a state coach that opened on all four sides, so her subjects could have a good view of her. It probably resembled the coach in which King Henry IV of France was riding when he was assassinated in 1610: a rectangular body with corner posts, a peaked roof, open sides capable of being closed with curtains when desired, and a leather screen hung across the doorway located in one side. In 1625 hackney coaches were for hire in London and in 1640, stage coaches in England. In 1650, in Paris, coaches for hire were called *fiacres,* after the Hôtel Saint Fiacre, where their owner lived. In 1662, Blaise Pascal introduced *carrosses à cinq sous,* omnibuses with scheduled routes and a timetable, but the project lasted only a few years.

Coaches were criticized as contributing to arrogance and effeminacy, blocking the streets, and taking fares away from the London wherrymen on the Thames. In the early 17th century John Taylor, the "Water Poet," called the coach a toy and trifle, "whose beginning is Folly, continuance Pride, and whose end is Ruine." The hackney coaches were competing with the watermen: "Against the ground we stand and knock our heeles,/Whilst all our profit runs away on wheeles."

By the 17th century on the Continent, coaches had superseded the litter for travel, but in town they still met stiff competition from sedan chairs, popular in Naples, France, Spain, and England. Sedans, some of them beautifully decorated, were large enough for only one occupant and were carried by two chairmen. Boasting a more comfortable ride than coaches, they continued in use until the end of the 18th century.

WAGONS

The Hungarian coach was not the only vehicle introduced into England in the 16th century from Europe. Both the word wagon and the four-wheeled vehicle itself were brought over at this time from Germany. In the Middle Ages the cart was ubiquitous. Pulled by horses or oxen, it was often hitched tandem, had disk or spoked wheels studded with nails, and could be fitted with ladders over the wheels to extend its capacity in harvest time. There were a few carts in the British Isles on which the wheels revolved with the axles, a form going back to 3000 BC. The medieval English cart was a farm cart pressed into service for hauling, but the new wagons were built for long distance haulage. By the end of the 17th century, stage wagons could transport eight tons of goods. These heavy wagons required modification to become suitable for farm use; in the 18th century the box wagon and the bow wagon were developed.

The cart

On the Continent the use of carts and wagons has continued in the modern period. In France, however, there are distinct differences between the medieval and modern vehicles. In the Middle Ages the capacity of the wagon, as recorded by toll charges, had been two to four times that of the cart, and the wagon was usually pulled by more horses. In the modern period, however, the capacity of the French *charrette* (cart) and *chariot lorraine* (wagon) are roughly equal. The former therefore exerts more pressure on two points (two very large wheels) and requires a harder surface than the latter, where the weight is distributed among four wheels, the rear ones being much higher than the front. The cart is more manoeuvrable (though less stable) than the *chariot lorraine.*

In France, Germany, and Sweden the distribution of carts and wagons goes by localities. Attempts to account for this distribution by ethnic backgrounds have failed, and even geography only partially explains it. Although the region of the wagon to a great extent covers the great plain from Siberia to Alsace, the Central Pyrenees use the four-wheeled *char* and the Eastern Pyrenees the two-wheeled cart. (M.N.B.)

THE REVIVAL OF ROAD BUILDING

During the medieval period responsibility for making and repairing the roads rested as a rule on the parishes and landowners through whose land the road passed; those employed on road work were usually farmers and forced labourers. The widespread use of bundles of faggots, erroneously supposed to improve the drainage of the subsoil and the carrying quality of the road, was harmful. But in the 16th century Italian architects and engineers gave attention to the scientific study of road building; a Reims lawyer, Nicholas Bergier, studied the remains of a Roman road that he found in his garden and with the aid of material collected from classical texts and archaeological data compiled a book, *Histoire des grands chemins de l'empire romain,* which attracted wide attention.

The emergence of the nation states of western and central Europe made possible the gradual development of strong, centralized administrative and technical bodies to train engineers and impose uniform standards of road building. The change began to take place at the end of the 16th century, in the France of Henry IV. In 1599 Henry created the post of chief road engineer, with local lieutenants in the provinces. Royal grants were made for new roads. By 1664 the state of the road system allowed for the establishment of a stagecoach service. Many country roads were paved with stone blocks (the *pavés du roi*).

After a decline in road building caused by the demands of the wars of Louis XIV (1643–1715), progress was resumed under Louis XV. The Corps des Ponts et Chaussées, created in 1716, was the first body of road and bridge experts and engineers in Europe to be financed by a government. The method of construction employed was, in general, to trench the road and then lay successive layers of smaller and smaller stones until a smooth surface was reached. By 1776 France had no fewer than 25,000 miles (40,000 kilometres) of highway completed or under construction, of which half were being reconstructed or aligned as avenues.

Another factor contributing powerfully to the pressure for more and better roads was the expansion of trade and commerce and the constant pressure of merchants and manufacturers for improved communications. The process was most marked in Britain, where the presence of large quantities of easily mined coal and iron ore gave that country a head start in the Industrial Revolution. Indeed, the rapid growth of industrial production from the middle of the 18th century onward made better communications not so much a desirable objective as a pressing and immediate necessity. Initially, priority was given to canals, known in those days as navigations; cheap labour imported from Ireland in large quantities dug these canals, and the workmen were known as "navigators," hence the modern use of "navvies" to cover any type of unskilled heavy labourers. Canals, however, could not possibly be built on a sufficient scale to meet the demands of industry; thus, the crying need for more and better roads. John Loudon McAdam was the best known of a number of self-taught engineers, of whom John Metcalf and Thomas Telford were also outstanding. They were fully aware of the necessity for a proper drainage system, and McAdam invented an inexpensive, self-sealing road surface, consisting of small stones, chips, or gravel, which could be applied directly to the soil or subsoil of a properly made roadbed. His first experiments in Bristol in 1815 were so successful that they set in motion a road-building explosion that has continued with increasing momentum for 150 years (see also PUBLIC WORKS: *Roads and highways*). (D.O'N.)

John Loudon McAdam's new road

WHEELED VEHICLES IN THE 17TH AND 18TH CENTURIES

At the opening of the 17th century, coaches were heavy vehicles, capable of carrying six to eight passengers. The boot, at this time a small seat on either side, between the wheels, later became a basket at the back of the coach for carrying luggage, and still later a seat at the rear for a groom.

Trends in coach design

During the 17th century, coaches tended to become smaller and lighter, to be enclosed, and to acquire improved springs. For example, in 1631, Mary, Infanta of Spain and consort of Emperor Frederick III, rode in a glass-enclosed coach accommodating only two persons. By the middle of the century most coaches had glass windows. Suspension received considerable attention. Although in 1625 a patent was granted in England "for hanging bodies of carriages on steel springs," nothing more is heard of this invention. Some 40 years later, however, Sir Harry Blount demonstrated to a committee of the Royal Society a chariot with four springs, which he claimed was "very easy." Samuel Pepys, the diarist, in 1668 bought one of the new coaches—"it being light, and will be very genteel and sober; to be covered with leather, but yet will hold four."

The most successful invention in the line of a light, fast coach was the Berlin, built by an Italian, Filippo di Chièse, in the city of Berlin about 1660 for use in distant travelling (Figure 3). It had two perches instead of one and was built with C springs and leather braces. The

Figure 3: French Berlin coach, *c.* 1780.
By courtesy of the Suffolk Museum and Carriage House at Stony Brook, Long Island, Melville Collection

bottom of the coach was curved and played up and down instead of swaying from side to side as before. There was a coachman's seat in front; the forward wheels were smaller than the rear, to permit sharp turns without scraping the carriage body. A hundred years earlier Queen Elizabeth's coach had been described as a "hollow-turning coach"; so the problem had long been under consideration. The first Berlins had glass doors, were narrow, and carried only two people. Berlins remained popular into the 19th century; their design was continually modified. For example, many later Berlins held four people.

Much more of a novelty was the development of two-wheeled carts for passengers, something hardly used since Roman times. About 1670 the *gig,* an English invention, was a light two-wheeled cart with a chair, the forerunner of the French *calèche,* the Norwegian *carriole,* the Neapolitan *calesso,* and the Cuban *volante.* The *calèche,* or *chaise* or chair, was known in America as a shay, the vehicle immortalized in the 19th century by Oliver Wendell Holmes in "The Deacon's Masterpiece, or the Wonderful 'One-Hoss-Shay'." The 18th-century American "cheer" was an open carriage hung upon springs made of wood with iron supports for the folding roof and with cloth curtains. A great advantage of the chaise was that it could be drawn by one horse between shafts. In the American colonies, coaches appeared in the last half of the 17th century, but before the Revolution the numbers were too small to support a local coachmaking industry.

The post-chaise

In France from 1664 and in England beginning in 1743, it became possible to travel post. The vehicle was a postchaise, and stations every few miles permitted the traveller to change horses and drivers. The early post-chaise was a two-wheeled vehicle suspended on leather braces, with shafts for one horse. Later post-chaises had four wheels. In France in the 18th century a two-wheeled post-chaise, drawn by three horses abreast and driven by a postilion, was called a diligence. In England, the name diligence was applied to John Palmer's Berlins, introduced in 1783, capable of a speed of seven miles an hour, while carrying four persons and the mail, but no luggage. The cumbersome stagecoaches with six passengers inside in addition to those outside were so slow that they could not compete with the mail coaches.

In the 18th century a landau was a four-wheeled carriage with a hood that could be opened and thrown back to allow the passengers to ride in the open air. The landaulet had the same distinguishing features but was smaller. After mid-century the most sporting carriage was the phaeton, a very high four-wheeled vehicle, renowned for its ability to negotiate sharp turns. Its reputation as a dangerous vehicle only added to its popularity with reckless drivers.

The vogue for lightness and speed did not extend to state coaches at this time. Such a heavy coach frequently carried in addition to a postilion and coachman (and of course the passengers) four to six grooms riding at the back, a supply of manpower frequently necessary to extricate the coach from country mudholes. Among the most famous of these coaches were that of the Lord Mayor of London (1757) and the English coronation coach (1761). The latter is 24 feet long, 8 feet 3 inches wide, and 12 feet high (7.3 by 2.5

Figure 4: English coronation coach, 1761.
Central Press Photos Ltd.

by 3.7 metres) and weighs four tons. It is hung upon steel C springs by leather braces. The elaborate gilded figures of tritons, boys, lions' heads, and seashells make it a very impressive rococo monument (Figure 4). By the end of the 18th century, taste in coaches, in common with costumes and furniture, had become much simpler.

19TH-CENTURY DEVELOPMENTS

Carriages. The 19th century brought two developments calculated to increase the use of carriages. One was the appearance of the macadam road in 1815, the other that of elliptical, steel springs, invented by Obadiah Elliott in 1804. With elliptical springs it was possible to build light carriages without the perch, or lower framework, and from this time on the varieties were not distinguished according to whether they were built with C springs or under springs (that is, elliptical springs) or with or without the perch. The basis for classification became the shape of the body.

The barouche was a four-wheeled open carriage with a high driving seat, and the phaeton evolved from a high and precarious vehicle to the respectability of the pony phaeton, later called the victoria, a hooded carriage drawn by one or two horses. The small britska (or Britzschka), originating in Austria, was popular as an open travelling carriage with a leather top and glazed front and sides. Among two-wheeled carriages, the curricle with two horses was popular in the early 19th century. The cabriolet was an advanced form of the one-horse shay. The dogcart was so arranged that the passengers sat sideways back to back, a form seen today in the Irish jaunting car.

Public transportation. Public transportation was furnished by vehicles for hire and by omnibuses, char-a-bancs, and coaches. The cabriolet, a two-wheeled vehicle, was used for hire (hence present-day "cab") and was faster than the old hackney coaches. The cabriolets were superseded by hansom cabs, designed by Joseph Aloysius Hansom beginning in 1834, with an enclosed square body and with a seat for the driver on the roof. Later there were four-wheeled cabs, and Lord Brougham had one constructed for his own use. A novel feature of his was that although it was a four-wheeled closed carriage, it was drawn by only one horse. The brougham ultimately became one of the more popular carriages.

The advent of the cab

Cabs felt competition inside cities from the omnibus, used under that name in Paris in 1828 and in London in 1829. Between towns in France there were char-a-bancs, with parallel benches, and in England coaches. When the coaches' long distance operations were curtailed by the railways, they nevertheless continued for a time as a supplement to rail travel until displaced by gasoline-driven vehicles. In England an interest in fast coaching inspired the founding of the Four-in-Hand Driving Club in 1856.

DEVELOPMENTS IN THE U.S.

The westward expansion, first of the American colonies and subsequently of the entire United States, encouraged concentration on production of rugged vehicles capable of carrying people and goods long distances. In the 18th century the movement of population beyond the Alleghenies stimulated the invention of the Conestoga wagon. This type, to be nicknamed the prairie schooner in the 19th century, carried freight over the Sante Fe Trail and transported settlers and their possessions to Oregon and to California. In some of these wagons the bed was 16 feet (4.9 metres) long, the rear wheels five to six feet high, and the hoops covered with white canvas rose 11 feet (3.4 metres) above the ground. The Conestoga was often pulled by as many as six horses, mules, or oxen. Concord coaches, first produced in 1825, were famous; their imitations, fast and durable, were still rolling over the Western plains in the 1880s.

Among other American vehicles were the buckboard, spring wagon, and a covered business wagon (1844), but what most impressed foreign visitors was the buggy. It was praised for its extreme lightness, ease of riding, and durability. There were two elliptical springs with four very large slender wheels and two steam-bent oak or hickory wood felloes per wheel. The iron, although cast, nevertheless possessed elasticity and was very thin. The buggy was built to travel over very difficult roads and was in demand in the British colonies as extremely serviceable and cheap.

The buggy

The U.S. also copied ideas and types of carriages from Europe. An omnibus line operated in New York City in 1831. Also in the 19th century adequate demand made for a thriving carriage-building industry, especially after the Civil War. One of these coachbuilders, the firm of Brewster & Company, produced carriages from the early 19th to the early 20th century. Although they exported vehicles to South America, their chief market was the American luxury trade. Their carriages took a gold medal at the Paris Exhibition in 1878. When it became obvious that the automobile was about to render the horse-drawn vehicle obsolete, the firm began to build bodies for automobiles in 1911, and in the 1920s the chassis was being produced by Rolls-Royce. The idea of mass production in the luxury trade was uncongenial to the head of the firm, William Brewster, however, and in 1927 he retired.

The case was different for the Studebaker Corporation of South Bend, Indiana, which around the turn of the 20th century claimed to be the world's greatest producer of horse-drawn vehicles. Studebaker wagons saw service in the Boxer Rebellion in China and in the South African War (Boer War). The company also produced carriages and, with the advent of the automobile, began in 1902 to make bodies for electric cars and in 1904 for gasoline-driven automobiles, which it successfully produced for more than half a century.

The horse had drawn vehicles for at least four millennia and oxen for more than five. When the animal-powered vehicle disappeared in much of the world, its influence nevertheless continued. The expertise of carriage makers was applied to automobile construction; examination of the silhouette of the earliest motor cars shows how much they owed to carriages. In addition, the technical vocabulary for parts of carriages and wagons was transferred to automobiles. Our ancestors, too, knew "cars," "rumbles," "dashboards," and "chassis." Automotive passenger cars and trucks have been found to do almost everything better than carriages and wagons. The one exception is that the coach is superior for true dignity and elegance in a ceremonial procession. (M.N.B.)

Sails and oars

ANCIENT SHIPS

Many of the most primitive types of ships still exist for special purposes. Log rafts are used in some regions in which seas are so rough that stiffer structures would be beaten to pieces. The efficiency of the outrigger canoe in giving the least possible frictional surface to the water for the most support against tipping under sail is still widely used by natives in the South Pacific and in Hawaii. Other surviving ancient types include the Arab dhow and the Chinese junk.

Egyptian and Minoan ships. From rock drawings dating from 6000 BC in Egypt and from descriptions in legends and stories, it is known that relatively large ships were developed in the eastern Mediterranean; and on the Nile River in Egypt, ships were built of bundles of reeds, the ends of which were bound together and bent upward to form the bow and stern of the ship so that in profile the ship was crescent shaped. This kind of construction was dictated not by choice but by the lack of large trees suitable for making dugouts or straight, heavy-strength members. Further to the east, across the Red Sea, where there were trees, early shipbuilders used a different method. They started with a canoe dug out from a stout log and graduated to building slanted sides fastened to a bow and stern boards to keep out the water and increase the carrying capacity. The result was a flat-keeled boat with square corners at the ends. These ships were also immortalized in rock drawings. By 3000 BC the reed boats of Egypt were venturing into the Mediterranean as far as Crete and Lebanon to bring back logs and other materials. Because these ships had no keel, they were held in shape by a taut cable, running on deck from the bow to the stern, which could be tightened as required. They were rowed and were steered by long oars over the stern. Later, sails were devised to move the ships when the wind was from the stern, which in the Nile was an advantage, because the wind normally blew upriver, so that the ships could sail up against the current and either pole or row down with the current. As successful and numerous as the Egyptian ships were, had not others invented a ship built around a sturdy log, ship development would have ceased, because without the strength and stiffness of a central structural member such as a keel or keels, larger and faster ships would have been impossible.

Flat-keeled boats

By about 2000 BC in Crete, the Minoans had developed ships using a log keel with ribs and planking on the sides joined at the stem and stern. To protect the bow against damage from waves, the heavy keel was bent upward and forward of the joint between the two sides of the ship, thus giving the ship a double, or bifid, bow.

During this period, nearly all ships were narrow beamed for their length to facilitate rowing. In the absence of navigational devices, the ships were restricted to moving on rivers, along coasts, or in narrow seas. Merchant ships and warships were very similar, although a warship development of the bifid bow became the sharpened ram projecting forward near the waterline. When the ram was used, it produced a great stress on the bow of the galley. In order to overcome this, heavy timbers were fastened lengthwise along the sides of the galley to help support the bow from damage. These timbers were known as whales (wales). Later, in addition to their original purpose of attacking other war vessels, it was found that they stiffened the ship so it did not have the unpleasant habit of bending in the middle when a wave passed under. In more modern times the strength members have been put inside the hull and are called longitudinals. To conserve the energy of the crew, these galleys included one or more large, square sails. Such galleys could not sail into the wind, and in battle the sail was never used; to set sail was a sign of defeat.

Phoenician merchant ships. The great merchants of the Mediterranean world, the Phoenicians of Tyre and Sidon, found that galleys were inefficient for trading voyages, because the large crews needed were expensive to feed, and the long narrow hull provided little space for cargo. The first merchant ships were descendants of the old Egyptian reed boats in that their hull form was broad and short, earning them the nickname of the round ship. They were built up from a heavy keel with ribs and a stem and stern post. A single large square sail furnished propulsion (see Figure 5). Such ships may have sailed around Africa. It is known that they sailed in the Atlantic as far north as Britain to trade for tin.

The Phoenician round ship

Greek and Roman ships. In the Greek era the galley developed from an open, undecked craft up to 100 feet (30 metres) long and driven by a single row of oars 25 on a side to the ships used in the Battle of Salamis in 480 BC, about 150 feet (45 metres) in length with an outrigger (*parado*) on which the oarlocks were fixed. Width including outrigger was 20 feet (six metres). The oars were arranged in two banks (biremes) or three banks (triremes). In the next few hundred years larger galleys were tried but were found to be too cumbersome to manoeuvre, and so the final development of the war galley produced a ship of

Figure 5: Model of a Phoenician ship, 13th century BC. In the Museum of The Philadelphia Civic Center.

By courtesy of the Museum of The Philadelphia Civic Center

about 150 feet with a full deck or decks and a strong ram. They were called quinquiremes, a term the meaning of which is still in dispute. Some authorities believe it refers to a ship having five banks of oars, and others interpret it to mean five men to each oar. While the galley was the predominant military ship, the vast Mediterranean commerce in the Greek era was carried on with the round ships of Phoenician design.

The Romans brought little change in ships except the addition of the corvus, a bridge at the bows of a war galley to accommodate boarding parties. Roman grain ships grew to new sizes, measuring some 90 feet (27 metres) in length and 28 feet (nine metres) in beam, capable of carrying about 250 tons of cargo and over 300 passengers. Such heavy oared ships required more sail to drive them as well as to help in manoeuvring. Though they could still not sail into the wind, they were able to hold a course with their sails hauled around to take the wind on the quarter (about 45° from dead astern), an important step forward. These ships proved their seaworthiness in regular commerce with the British Isles.

Oriental ships. While the peoples of the Mediterranean were developing ships from those of the Egyptians, at about the same time China, with its vast land areas and poor road communications, was turning to water for transportation. The development in China followed a slightly different pattern from that of the Mediterranean. Starting with a dugout canoe, the Chinese joined two canoes with planking, forming a square punt, or raft. Next, the side, the bow, and the stern were built up with planking to form a large, flat-bottomed wooden box. The bow was sharpened with a wedge-shaped addition below the waterline. At the stern, instead of merely hanging a steering oar over one side as did the Western ships, Chinese shipbuilders contrived a watertight box, extending through the deck and bottom, that allowed the steering oar or rudder to be placed on the center line, thus giving better control. The stern was built to a high, small platform at the stern deck, later called a castle in the West, so that, in a following sea, the ship would remain dry, and when hove to or anchored she would turn with her bow to the wind. Thus, in spite of what to Western eyes seemed an ungainly figure, the Chinese junk was an excellent hull for seaworthiness as well as for beaching in shoal (shallow) water. Her principal advantage, however, not apparent from an external view, was great structural rigidity. In order to support the side and the bow planking, the Chinese used solid planked walls (bulkheads), running both longitudinally and transversely and dividing the ship into 12 or more compartments, producing not only strength but also protection against damage.

The Chinese junk

In rigging the Chinese junk was far ahead of Western ships, with sails made of narrow panels, each tied to a sheet (line) at each end so that the force of the wind could be taken in many lines rather than on the mast alone; also, the sail could be hauled about to permit the ship to sail somewhat into the wind. By the 15th century junks had developed into the largest, strongest, and most seaworthy ships in the world. Not until about the 19th century did Western ships catch up in performance.

Meanwhile, in the island kingdom of Japan, little other than river or coastal dugouts and small ships were developed until about 81 BC, when the Emperor decreed that each province must build a ship. From this time until the early 17th century, when Japan closed its ports to the world, Japan developed its ships rapidly. From drawings in the 15th century, Japan had ships comparable to the best Western vessels. But soon after, the closure of Japanese ports halted progress until the mid-19th century, when Japan recommenced building ships.

Northern ships. In the European north, where the seas were cold and unfriendly, the peoples of the Scandinavian countries developed still another form of ship. Because they also started from the log, some authorities hypothesize that in early times Minoans fleeing invaders had taught the northern people how to build ships. In any case, the first northern ships were very similar to the Minoan ships with the bifid bow. Because these ships had to weather higher seas, the bifid was not developed into a ram, for in pitching in a heavy sea the ram put great stress on the ship and tended to break her back. Instead, the Vikings developed double-ended ships, having both a sharp bow and a sharp stern, built high against following seas. To survive in the strong gales of the northern waters, the single large square sail on the Viking ship was made of leather or cloth with reinforcing leather strips. Over the stern a long oar was suspended from one side, extending below the bottom of the keel, to improve stability. The hull form in the centre (amidships) was much broader than that of the galleys of the south, and overall there was a smooth, flowing curve from the high bow through the well-rounded midships to the high stern, a good design still used in lifeboats and whaleboats today. Another feature was the covering of the oar ports with sliding plugs to keep out the water when the oars were not in use. Many pictorial representations of Viking galleys show shields slung over the oar ports, which may be the locations they were placed when the ship was in port, but at sea this placement would have interfered with the operation of the oars. The planks were fastened to the ribs by lashings rather than by bolts or pegs, giving the ship a flexibility that reduced the stress in heavy seas. Even more important was a northern merchantman, the knorr, broader and deeper-hulled than the long ships and the first northern ships to sail into the wind. In about the 14th century the knorr developed into a standard merchant ship, the design of which governed north European shipbuilding for over 400 years. This later version, called the cog, was given a true stern rudder for better handling and a long spar extending forward called a bowsprit. Modified by a built-up castle in the stem or stern to provide a platform for soldiers, the cog became the standard man-of-war. (Ja.J.S.)

Viking ships

MEDIEVAL DEVELOPMENTS

The ships that carried William the Conqueror's army to England in 1066, as shown in the more or less contemporary Bayeux tapestry, are hardly distinguishable from Viking vessels of two centuries earlier. In northern European waters, ships continued to be clinker-built and double ended, with a single, central mast, for another 300 years. Some improvements were introduced, however, in the form of "castles," or fighting towers, at either end, at first temporary (for war only) and later permanent. Also a "fighting top," a square box from which men could fire or drop missiles on an enemy craft, was added to the mast. Its weight, together with the pull of the large square sail, made it necessary to add extra stays and shrouds to the standing rigging. At the start of the 13th century, or perhaps earlier, northern ships received a bowsprit, a large spar projecting over the stem (the timber to which the ship's sides are joined at the bow) to hold the bowline farther out and give the sail greater effect. Even so, the outsize oars, known as sweeps, were retained by every vessel as a standby precaution.

"Castles," or fighting towers

In the Mediterranean, where commerce was far ahead of that in northern regions, ships were better built and much larger in size. Instead of the overlapping clinker construction, Mediterranean ships, both Arab and European, had their planks fitted together edge to edge (carvel construction), nailed to the ribs, and caulked with pitch. By the mid-12th century, Genoese ships had two decks, three-deckers appearing in the late 13th century. Two masts were used, the forward, taller and slightly heavier and carrying three lateen-rigged, triangular fore-and-aft sails to two for the aftermast. The best sails, made of strong cotton or linen canvas, were of Genoese or Marseilles manufacture. Often, instead of a single castle at the stern, Italian ships had two castles, one atop the other. A combination galley and sailing ship, the *tarida,* was widely used throughout the high Middle Ages. One reason for the continued survival of the galley, in the face of competition from the sail, was that the large crew of a galley made it formidable in the event of attack by pirates.

Yet a significant advance in ship design, the stern rudder, first appeared not in the Mediterranean but in the north. The earliest picture of a stern rudder with the gudgeons (metal eyes or sockets attached to the sternpost to receive the rudder pintles, or pins) to form a hinge appears on an English civic seal dated 1200. At first the new rudder had to be curved to conform to the curving sternpost; later, ships were built with straight sterns. Despite the spread of the innovation in the north (a German seal shows a stern rudder in 1242), it did not appear in the Mediterranean until the 14th century. Possibly the larger Mediterranean ships, some of which were over 100 feet (30 metres) long in the mid-13th century, could be handled better with the existing technique of a pair of lateral rudders, one on either side, near the stern. In all other respects the Mediterranean shipbuilders remained in the vanguard of the world, their only serious competition being the Chinese junks, which Marco Polo admired. (D.P.C.)

The magnetic compass was first carried on ships in the Western world around 1000 and was in common use by the 12th century. Originally the magnetized needle floated on straw, but by the latter half of the 13th century it was mounted on a pivot. The use of charts for maritime navigation developed at the same time; the first recorded use of a chart aboard ship (*c.* 1280) relates to the Mediterranean and Black Sea area.

The higher standards of navigation made possible by the use of such instruments as the magnetic compass and the astrolabe, for angle measurement, extended the field of exploration. This in turn led to a sharp increase in the size of cargo vessels. Beginning about 1418 with Prince Henry the Navigator (inaccurately so named, as he apparently never voyaged personally farther afield than Tangier), a succession of captains probed farther and farther down the west coast of Africa to the Cape of Good Hope, opening the sea route to India and China. At the same time Columbus sailed from Spain to make his accidental but history-making discovery of the New World. The discovery of the extent of the Pacific Ocean by Magellan in 1519–21 completed a generation of titanic achievements in ocean exploration, though major details remained to be filled in. The most notable of the later explorers was Capt. James Cook, who in the 18th century explored the Pacific and Antarctic oceans and was the first of the truly scientific navigators. (D.O'N.)

The opening of the oceans

SAILBOAT DEVELOPMENT (15TH–17TH CENTURY)

At the start of the 15th century, three-masted ships were common in the Mediterranean, while in northern European waters the single mast remained the rule. But during the course of this century, the three-master became universal, with a short foremast forward of the tall mainmast and a mizzenmast aft. The foremast at first carried a single lateen sail; later, a square spritsail was rigged under a pole extending from the ship's bow, which made it practicable to move the foremast farther aft and increase its height. The additional shrouds (lines fixed to the sides of the ship to brace the mast) that were necessary found a secondary use: ratlines (short horizontal lines secured between shrouds) provided rope ladders, which replaced the wooden ladders used to climb the mast.

Three-masted ships

At this time a new fashion was being set by the carracks, the deep, broad vessels of Venice, Genoa, and Spain. These carracks had a high poop (stern) and a still higher forecastle thrusting out over the bow. Competing with the Italian and Spanish carracks, as the century progressed, were the simpler and lighter Portuguese caravels. Originally a fishing vessel, the caravel was not so deep and broad as a carrack. Named for the carvel method of construction, the caravel helped to popularize the fore-and-aft, lateen-rigged sail, which permitted a ship to take advantage of a beam wind. The two types of sails were often used in combination in an effort to allow for changing winds, but opinions varied on how the two sails should be mixed. One favoured rig had square sails on foremast and mainmast, possibly with a square topsail above the mainsail and the high, pointed lateen on the mizzen. Another class of caravels, however, kept to a complete lateen rig.

A few of the larger ships could carry three sails on the mainmast: from bottom to top, the course, the topsail, and the topgallant. Four-masters were also built, with square sails on the foremast and lateens on the other three masts.

There was now a standard method of shortening sail. A square sail was no longer reduced in area by reefing (folding and tying). Instead, a length of sailcloth called a bonnet, which had been added to its foot, could be unlaced and taken off. For increasing the sail area in light winds, there was a narrower strip called the drabbler, which could be laced to the bonnet. Both bonnet and drabbler remained in use until the 18th century.

Improvements in navigational equipment

Along with revolutions in the design, size, and rigging of ships came improvements in navigational equipment, notably the cross-staff, a 16th-century device that virtually replaced the astrolabe as a means of finding the altitude of a star or the sun and therefore the latitude of the ship. The mariner's compass had long been known in various forms. As early as AD 868 Norsemen are reputed to have used a lodestone (magnetic iron ore) compass during a voyage to Iceland. In the 13th century a lodestone that floated on a circular piece of wood in a bronze bowl was used in Scandinavian waters. Meantime, the instrument had arrived in the Mediterranean in the 12th century. In the latter part of the 15th century, the Portuguese sailed their caravels southward down the African coast and around the Cape of Good Hope, while Columbus sailed similar Spanish ships across the Atlantic.

Guns, galleons, and galleasses. The 16th century ushered in the era of the large carrack, which was followed by the galleon. In the early part of the century, there was an outburst of rivalry among six countries in the building of big carrack-type ships, with their triangular, overhanging forecastles. The "Santa Anna" of the Knights of Malta, the "São João" of Portugal, the "Great Michael" of Scotland, the French "Grand François," the Swedish "Stora Karfvel," and the English "Henri Grâce à Dieu" were all launched within a few years of one another.

The "Great Michael," built by James IV and launched in 1511, was 200 feet (61 metres) in length and 36 feet (11 metres) in beam. Its building exhausted the timber of Fifeshire, and extra lumber was brought from Denmark. Its canvas and cables came from France and its anchors from Spain. Its sides were protected along the waterline by a stout belt of timber five feet (1.5 metres) in thickness, an odd predecessor of the blisters that were added to the sides of British warships in World War I. Its crew is said to have included 300 mariners, 120 gunners, and 1,000 men-at-arms. After brief service at sea, when the king was killed in 1513, it was sold to the French.

Iron guns, sometimes lethal to their crews when they exploded, had been carried on board ships as early as the 14th century and were later placed in the forecastle and sterncastle. In the early 1500s an abrupt and universal change occurred. The clumsy iron guns gave way to heavy brass or bronze cannons, and these were mounted along the side to fire through holes cut in the ship's sides. The development of gunports is traditionally ascribed to a French shipbuilder in about 1501, and the idea was adopted in the "Great Michael," the builders of which lined its gunports with leather as precaution against fire.

Henry VIII laid down his "Henri Grâce à Dieu," known as the "Great Harry," in 1512. The first four-masted ship to be launched in England, it set square sails on the foremast and mainmast and lateen sails on the mizzen and bonaventure (the two masts aft of the mainmast). It had topsails on all of its masts and topgallants on the first three masts. After a major refit in 1540, it took gun mounting a step further by arranging some of its guns in two tiers, firing through ports in the side.

In the Mediterranean, oared galleys, with lateen sails as auxiliaries, continued to be used; but these were never a success in the rough, northern waters, although the English navy retained a few into the 16th century. The Spanish Armada (1588) included no galleys, but there were four galleasses, a hybrid type. More seaworthy than the galley, the galleass supplemented a crew of rowers with two or three high-peaked lateen sails.

The galleon

The galleon, which seems to have originated in Spain, was slimmer than the carrack that it was built to replace. Decked in a series of steps at each end and mounting high at the stern, it had a long, projecting beakhead, which was largely composed of open gratings instead of the carrack's overhanging forecastle. It may have looked topheavy with the towering stern; and, though its weaknesses became apparent to the Spaniards after the defeat of the Armada, it did much ocean voyaging. In the 16th and early 17th centuries the Spaniards, identifiable from afar by the large pictures of saints on their sails, as were the Portuguese by their huge crosses, brought gold and silver from the New World in "plate fleets" composed of such vessels. The whipstaff, a vertical lever that was pivoted through the poop deck, was invented to control the tiller. Though a clumsy contrivance by later standards, it greatly facilitated steering and lasted until early in the 18th century.

Another idea, originated by the English captain John Hawkins, was more effective. He had the topmast made separate from its lower mast, secured with a cap and supported by trestletrees (two horizontal timber crosspieces fixed fore and aft of the mast to support the crosstrees, which spread the shrouds at the upper section of a mast and the top, a platform at the lower crosstrees). Now topmasts could be struck and sent down on deck in threatening weather, making taller masts and more sails feasible. A Swedish warship of this era, the "Wasa" of 1627, which sank on first hoisting sail, was salvaged in astonishingly good state from the mud of Stockholm Harbour in 1962. It is now on view as a unique example of a 17th-century ship.

By the 17th century all English warships were rigged with square topsails on the mizzen. In addition to the regular spritsail under the bowsprit, a spritsail topsail was rigged on a small mast at the end of the bowsprit. A different kind of spritsail, one supported by a diagonal spar called a sprit and rigged as a fore-and-aft sail on the mainmast—in addition to the regular square sail—appeared on some coastal vessels. At the opposite extreme was the rigging of the huge "Sovereign of the Seas" of Charles I of England in 1637. Some idea of its size can be gathered from the fact that six men could stand upright inside the great lantern at its stern. The "Sovereign of the Seas" had three masts instead of the usual four. In order to spread something like the same amount of canvas on one less mast, she was rigged for a new sail above her topgallants on foremast and mainmast. This new sail was called a royal, possibly because it was set where the flagstaff for the royal standard had previously been placed. But royals were not seen again until they reappeared as fair-weather sails in men-of-war at the end of the century.

The junk

Sailing ships of the East. The Chinese junk, unwieldy and strange as it appears to Western eyes, is one of the most efficient vessels under sail; it has been said that it represents the ultimate in aerodynamic efficiency. Nobody knows how long junks have sailed the Far Eastern seas, but they were making prosperous voyages to India in the 9th century and for a time controlled the Indian Ocean. Through the Middle Ages Chinese merchantmen sailed regularly to Indonesia, Ceylon, India, the east coast of Africa, and even to Aden (Yemen). A good demonstration of the junk's seaworthiness was an 1848 voyage from China all the way to Boston, New York, and London.

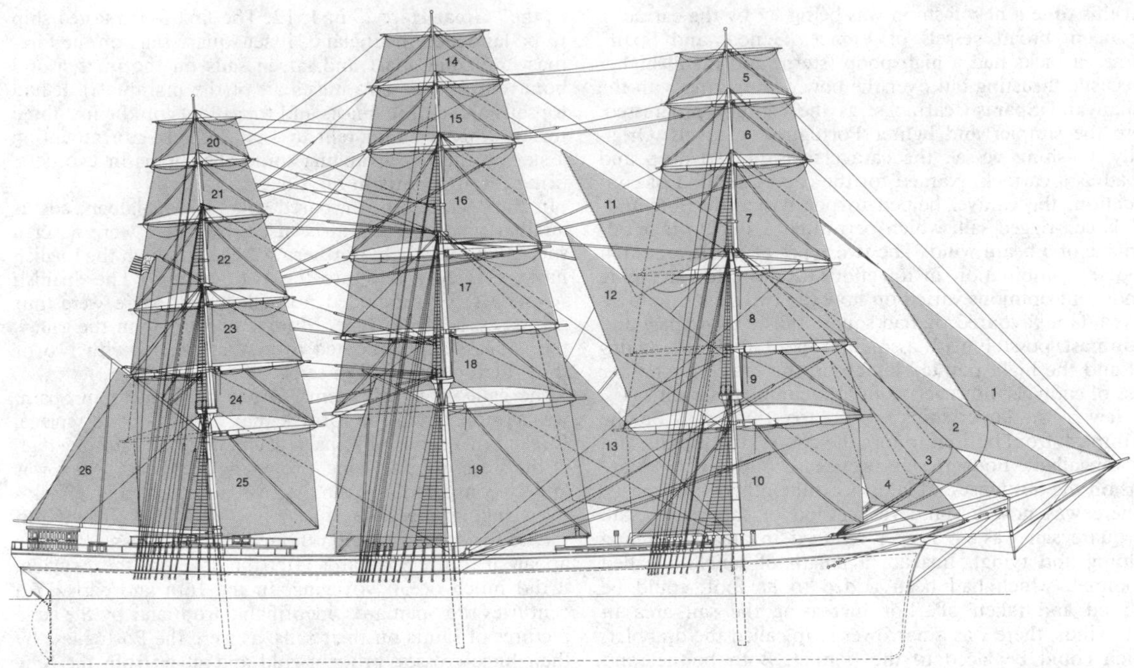

Figure 6: *Spars, sails, and rigging of a full-rigged ship.*
(1) Flying jib. (2) Outer jib. (3) Inner jib. (4) Jib. (5) Fore skysail. (6) Fore royal. (7) Fore topgallant sail. (8) Fore upper topsail. (9) Fore lower topsail. (10) Foresail. (11) Main royal staysail. (12) Main topgallant staysail. (13) Main topmast staysail. (14) Main skysail. (15) Main royal. (16) Main topgallant sail. (17) Main upper topsail. (18) Main lower topsail. (19) Mainsail. (20) Mizzen skysail. (21) Mizzen royal. (22) Mizzen topgallant sail. (23) Mizzen upper topsail. (24) Mizzen lower topsail. (25) Crossjack. (26) Spanker or driver.

There are, or were, upward of 70 different types of junks, oceangoing and riverine, varying in hull form and other respects. The number of masts vary from one to five (five-masters are uncommon, however); all share the same general characteristics. Usually, junks are highsterned, with outthrust bows. There is no keel, but the massive rudder, often mounted in a slot so that it can be raised and lowered, is deep enough to act as a centreboard to reduce drifting to leeward. The unique feature of the junk was the watertight compartment. The junks of the Huang Ho were built with four of these compartments, but the idea was not adopted in the West for centuries. A curiosity is the square lugsail. It is composed of a series of panels, of matting or linen, each panel stiffened and kept flat by a bamboo batten, which extends all the way across the sail. Each panel has its own parrel, or collar, around the mast and its own sheet leading to the mainsheet. Thus, all parts of the sail, from foot to head, can be close-hauled, enabling the junk to sail very close to the wind. These bamboo battens also act on the principle of a Venetian blind. When the halyard is let go, the panels fold up on top of one another, so that shortening sail is a matter of minutes for a practiced hand. Between one-third and one-sixth of each sail is forward of its mast. The mast itself is unsupported, having no stays or shrouds.

Invention of the compass

The Chinese invented the lodestone compass long before the 11th century, but by 1085 they were using the floating needle. The dry compass (with pivoting needle) was also devised in China, during the 13th century, but was not in general use until it was reintroduced in the 16th century by the Portuguese and the Dutch.

The Japanese junk, now rapidly passing from the sea, is different from the Chinese in nearly every respect. There is only one type, squat and heavy. The sails, made of matting or cloth, have no bamboo panels but are loosefooted and square. The rudder, while it can also be raised or lowered, is not enclosed but works in a well, open to the sea. Strangely enough, the Japanese junk has more than a hint of the old Roman artemon in the short foremast canted up in the bows to take the square sail.

To the south and southwest of Japan, in the Pacific and Indian oceans, there were and are myriad types of craft, each built to suit local conditions, and a host of varied rigs. There are mixtures of lateen and square sails, sails in parallelograms, sails like lobster's claws or leaves, and sails in inverted triangles. Outstanding among these craft for their ocean sailing were the big canoes of the Polynesians, who made voyages of several days' duration to other islands 200 to 300 miles (300 to 500 kilometres) distant. They are credited with having a corps of pilots trained in weather lore and the courses of the heavenly bodies for their own mysterious kind of navigation. Remarkable as these craft were, all that the West has borrowed from them—and that only recently—has been the modern catamaran and trimaran.

18TH-CENTURY AND LATER DEVELOPMENTS

East Indiamen and frigates. During the 17th and 18th centuries the finest merchantmen of six European countries—Portugal, France, the Netherlands, England, Denmark, and Sweden—traded in rivalry in India and the East Indies. Ships of the Dutch and British East India companies, similar in appearance, were built like men-of-war, apart from the fuller lines for their cargo carrying, which made them the "fat East Indiamen." They were well armed; English ships, for example, had more than 20 guns. These were used to cope with the normal hazards of Algerian and Malabar corsairs as well as rival European ships. The Dutch Indiaman "Amsterdam" (1749), found in the sand on an English south coast beach in 1970, was 150 feet (46 metres) in length and carried 56 guns.

Though the East Indiamen gave good service, they were not very speedy; the swiftest sailer of the era was a new class of warship, the frigate, designed for scouting, escort duty against privateers, and commerce raiding. Smaller, lighter, speedier than the massive ships of the line, frigates originated with the Spanish Navy; they were copied and redesigned by the French, and these French frigates were in turn copied by the British and U.S. navies. The first U.S. frigates were built during the Revolutionary War. A later class, which included the renowned "Constitution," still in existence at Boston, came into service in 1797. They were intended for the protection of American merchant ships in the Mediterranean against the piratical xebecs (or chebecs) of the Bey of Algiers and later of Tunis. The xebecs were very swift craft of shallow draft with high, triple lateen sails.

Refinements of hull and rigging. From 1765 to 1812, within the span of the active life of Nelson's flagship,

"Victory," large British men-of-war underwent a number of changes, which were copied in other navies. Forecastle and quarter deck had been linked by temporary gangways above the main deck guns; these gangways were gradually widened into a permanent decking, all but covering the waist of the ship. Bulwarks were added, low at first but heightened later. Instead of the old, beaklike prow, ships were given round bows, which allowed more guns to be brought forward and also helped to reduce the amount of water coming on board in a heavy sea. The square shape of the stern was altered to a curve, which allowed guns to be fired from each quarter, and, later, the curve became an ellipse. The stern gallery (balconies across the stern and around the quarters) returned after vanishing in Elizabethan times. The elaborate decorations of the 17th century nearly disappeared; only some gilding around the figurehead and fancy scrollwork at the stern remained. A method was found, at last, to protect the ship's bottom from the teredo worm by sheathing it below the waterline with copper, fastened by copper nails. The sheathing also had the effect of reducing marine growths on the bottom and so gave the ship more speed. This practice proved so successful that it was speedily adopted by merchant ships in the tropics.

New kinds of sail

Sails were undergoing a transformation that had begun in the 16th century, when the jib, a triangular headsail, was first used in some light craft. The staysail, also triangular and set on a stay (a line led forward and down from the upper part of a mast—to pull against the backstay to help support the mast—and set between masts) appeared in Dutch and then in British vessels late in the next century. Jibs began to be rigged on a jibboom (a spar extending from the bowsprit to which the foot of the jib was secured), at first on smaller ships, later by the big threedeckers. The jib's advantage over the old spritsail was that it was much easier to handle in heavy weather, and also it is a fore-and-aft sail. The pull of jib and forestaysail on the bowsprit was countered by a line or chain, the bobstay, leading from the tip of the bowsprit down to the ship's stem at the waterline. Another step was an overdue alteration to the lateen mizzen. Because the part of the sail forward of the mast had little effect, it was cut off. Eventually the cumbersome lateen yard was replaced with a gaff, and the sail, increased in length over the stern, was set on a boom to become the spanker or, as it was named in men-of-war, the driver.

For more than a century, ships had reefed or shortened sail by the use of reef points. These short, light lines, hanging down across both sides of the head of the sail (or across the foot, if a fore-and-aft sail), reefed it to smaller size by tying it up to its yard (or down to its boom, if fore-and-aft). In time, in place of the bonnet, reef points were added to the courses, the lowest sails. In 1805, however, a British naval captain maintained that if sails were reefed at the foot instead of, or as well as, at the head, it would save time and labour and would lessen risks to men's lives. Sails made to his specifications and tested in a dozen naval and merchant ships brought enthusiastic reports but failed to convince the Admiralty. Later, however, reef points were lowered among Western shipping.

In the 19th century the square-rigged ship had reached maturity. The mizzen had been lengthened, by addition of a mast, to take a topgallant sail, and in light winds royals were set above the topgallants. A pair of the light, additional studding sails (stuns'ls), extending wide of the mainsails on either side could be set on foremast and mainmast in a man-of-war. Merchant captains were even more ambitious. The mass of canvas they might spread when the wind served could verge on insanity. The most extravagant ever was probably the East Indiaman "Essex," with its capability of setting 63 sails. Taking only the mainmast and starting with the lowest sail, it could set eight sails: the course or mainsail, topsail, topgallant, royal, skysail, cloudscraper, moonraker, and stargazer; in addition, each of these, up to the skysail, could be extended on each side with studding sails. By 1880, however, stuns'ls had gone out of fashion, along with several of the topmost sails.

Schooners, clippers, and Cape Horners. Though the forerunners of the schooner were probably Dutch craft of the 17th century, the type was developed by American shipbuilders into a vessel designed for speed. The fame of these slim, fast schooners, called Baltimore clippers because the Baltimore yards specialized in them, spread quickly. As freighters down the American east coast, as light naval cruisers, as privateers, as fishing vessels on the Grand Banks, or as smugglers or slavers, they soon came into their own. Most of these Baltimore clippers had two masts and were rigged as topsail schooners, having two jibs, gaff-rigged foresails and mainsails, a square fore-topsail, and a gaff main-topsail. Others were rigged as brigs, brigantines, and hermaphrodite brigs—all of which are square-rigged on the foremast, with varying combinations of square or fore-and-aft sails, or both, on the mainmast (see Figures 6 and 7).

Soon shipbuilders, notably at Boston, turned to designing larger ships with more speed. These were the threemasted, ship-rigged American clippers that came into service in time for the California gold rush of 1849. Ship after ship was crowded with those who preferred the sea passage round Cape Horn to a hazardous overland journey. Two years later (1851) gold was discovered in Australia. The demand for shipping rocketed to such heights that British shipowners placed orders with yards in the United States.

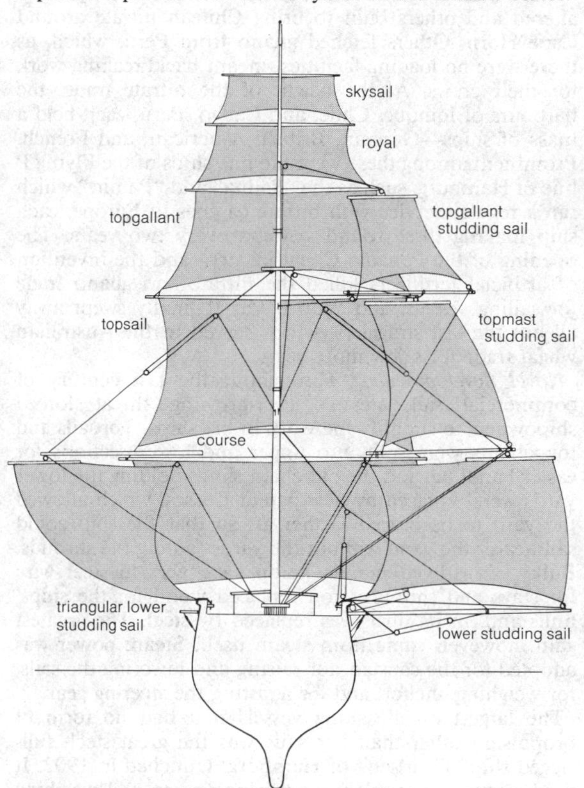

Figure 7: *Square sails.*
Studding sails shown astern with rigging.

The tea clipper

One eventual result was the tea clipper, first American- and then British-built. The British tea clippers were rather smaller than the American clippers and had a narrower beam; their registered tonnage was in most cases a little more than half that of the American ships. But they were just as fast and, in some cases, faster. Since the first consignment of the yearly crop of tea gained high prices and a rich bonus on the London market, speed was more important than the amount of cargo. The captains drove the ships hard. Their additional canvas in suitable weather went far beyond the normal style of stuns'ls, with such oddities as new-style bonnets, water sails, save-alls, and jib o' jibs. They made astonishingly good passages. The "Ariel," "Taiping," and "Serica," in their remarkable race of 1866, took 98 days from Foochow to London, while the "Fiery Cross" and "Taitsing," which had started later, took 101 days. The first three ships were in the English Channel together, and they sailed up the Thames at 13 knots (15 miles, or 24 kilometres, per hour) to dock on the same tide. The "Fiery Cross," however, had made the fastest day's run of all five, logging 328 nautical miles (378 statute miles, or 608 kilometres) in a single 24 hours. The most famous of all clipper ships, the "Cutty Sark," is now permanently in dock at Greenwich, England.

But the brief day of the great American clipper ship was over and was fading fast for the smaller English tea clippers. These were indeed the last days of sail, for improved steamships and the opening of the Suez Canal in 1869 drove the clipper from the China tea trade in the 1870s. Instead, a number began carrying wool from Australia, even though the trade was already flourishing with large, iron-hulled ships that had been specially built for the purpose. Although these iron ships were fast, they were straight stemmed and less graceful than the clippers. They had greater length and were able to carry huge cargoes but were slim enough to move easily through the water. Although they carried about the same square footage of sail as a clipper, modern improvements enabled them to get along with much smaller crews. Later vessels were still longer and rigged as four-masted ships or, as in the case of the typical Australian grain ship, a bark, with a fore-and-aft rig on the aftermast or jiggermast.

When wool cargoes dwindled after 1890, many ships were altered and others built to bring Chilean nitrate around Cape Horn. Others fetched guano from Peru, which, as there were no loading facilities, meant backbreaking work for their crews. At the height of the nitrate trade, the harbours of Iquique, Chile, and Callao, Peru, each held a mass of ships—German, British, American, and French. Prominent among these were the fine ships of the Flying P line of Hamburg, such as the "Padua" and "Pamir," which ran a regular service with nitrate cargoes to Europe, each ship making three round voyages every two years. The opening of the Panama Canal in 1914 and the invention of artificial fertilizers killed the nitrate and guano trade for sailing vessels, and World War II finally swept away all but the last stragglers, which served in the Australian wheat trade for a few more years.

Simplifying the big sailing ships

Novel developments. Throughout the last century of commercial sail, steam's ever-growing threat forced shipowners to simplify the work in big ships. Topsails and topgallants were split into upper and lower sections for easier handling, and the old chain slings holding the lower yards were replaced by new patent trusses, which allowed the yard to be braced farther aft so that the ship could sail nearer the wind without the yards fouling the shrouds. Bulky, short-lived manila hemp gave way to steel wire for stays and shrouds; iron replaced wood for the ships' hulls and, in its turn, was replaced by steel. The greatest gain, however, came from steam itself. Steam power was adopted for the capstan, for raising and lowering the sails, for weighing anchor, and for assisting the steering gear.

The largest of all sailing vessels that had no form of propulsion other than her sails was the great steel, full-rigged ship "Preussen" of Hamburg, launched in 1902. It used steam power solely for working cargo and weighing anchor. Its five steel masts were three feet (91 centimetres) in diameter, and its main yard was 100 feet (30 metres) long. The ship itself was 433 feet (132 metres) in length, with a beam of 54 feet (16 metres).

Among wooden sailing vessels the largest was the American "Great Republic" of 1853, with four decks. The first to use steam winches to hoist its yards and the first to have double topsails, it was built as a four-masted bark for the Australian trade but was gutted by fire on the eve of its maiden voyage. Partly rebuilt and drastically cut down in size and rig, it went into service carrying gold rush passengers around Cape Horn; later, after taking part in the guano trade, it returned to passenger carrying.

The "Great Britain," largest ship afloat when it was launched in 1843, was the first passenger vessel with a screw propellor to cross the Atlantic. It had a length of 322 feet (98 metres), a beam of 50.5 feet (15.4 metres), and a load draft of 18 feet (5.5 metres) with a displacement of 3,675 tons. It relied heavily on the schooner-rigged sails on its six masts. Three of the masts were removed later, but it continued as a mixed steam-sail vessel through a long career. It ended as a coal hulk in the Falkland Islands, but in 1970 it was towed back the 7,500 miles to England to be refitted and preserved.

Far more than twice its size was the "Great Eastern," launched in 1858. Its length was 692 feet (211 metres), beam 82 feet (25 metres), and draft 30 feet (nine metres), though it was of 18,914 tons. Also rigged as a schooner, it had both a propellor and paddle wheels. It was too large for its time and a commercial failure, though for a time it was usefully employed in laying an undersea telegraph cable across the Atlantic Ocean. It was last used as a floating fair.

The big steel-hulled American schooner "Thomas W. Lawson," of 5,218 tons, built in 1902, had seven masts, each 195 feet (59 metres) high. In spite of its size, it had a crew of only 16, with steam winches used for sail handling. It was in service only five years when it capsized off the Scilly Isles, southwest of England.

Flettner's rotor ship

In 1924 a wholly new kind of sailing vessel, the rotor ship, was extensively tested. Its German inventor, Anton Flettner, based his idea on the discovery that the wind pressure on a revolving cylinder was considerably greater than on a conventional sail. Flettner began by installing in a small freighter two cylinders 50 feet (15 metres) high, which were spun by an electric motor. Steering by controlling the spinning of the rotors, he reached a speed of nine and a half knots. He made further tests with three cylinders 60 feet (18 metres) high in a larger ship but found he could obtain satisfactory results only when all conditions were favourable. The idea was not pursued, and there seems to have been no other invention using wind power in such a radical way. (D.P.C.)

JETTIES AND HARBOUR IMPROVEMENTS

There is no conclusive evidence as to the dates of the first artificial harbour constructions, but it is known that the Phoenicians built harbours at Tyre and Sidon as early as the 13th century BC. Many other Mediterranean harbours, both natural and artificial, were of considerable commercial and military importance in Greek and Roman times.

In medieval times the prosperity of such cities as Venice, Genoa, and Alexandria (already a famous port in antiquity) required the building of harbour works for the protection and accommodation of their seaborne trade. The Pharos (lighthouse) of Alexandria was one of the seven wonders of the ancient world. Some of the early works at Venice and Genoa remain to this day. Natural harbours are more numerous in north Europe than in the Mediterranean. For many centuries these natural facilities, combined in some cases with rudimentary artificial harbour works, sufficed. From the late Middle Ages, Britain gave special prominence to the development of its port facilities. Artificial harbour works existed at Hartlepool (on the northeast coast) from about 1250 and at Arbroath in Scotland from about 1390. Dover lacked natural facilities but, because of its favourable situation on the English Channel, was a busy military and commercial port from the reign of Henry VIII (1509–47) onward, and a stone and timber breakwater was built there in his reign. Across the English Channel, Le Havre, Dieppe, La Rochelle, and Dunkerque were among the early ports to embark on harbour construction.

Harbour-building on the English Channel

The history of ports on the American continent followed the Mediterranean and northern European pattern. In the early days, natural havens offering protective anchorages were sufficient, but as the North American economy developed, ships became larger and of deeper draft, demanding larger and deeper harbours. Both natural and artificial harbours had to be dredged to maintain and increase the depth of water at quayside. All the great natural harbours in the world today have seen their native facilities improved, and in some cases transformed, by dredging, by the construction of breakwaters to enclose an area of protected water, and by running jetties into deep water to accommodate the giant tankers and bulk carriers that dominate their trades today.

Worldwide seaborne trade and the discovery of the New World brought new traffic to ancient ports but above all created a number of entirely new ones. Gorée (the predecessor of Dakar, on the West African coast) came into being before 1450. In the 16th century such famous ports as Havana (*c.* 1514), Lima (*c.* 1535), and Manila (*c.* 1750) were founded, to be followed in the next century by New Amsterdam (New York), Cape Town, and Calcutta, among many others.

This multiplication of ports was the outstanding feature of world port development in the period up to 1800. The chief engineering works on these "new" ports were devoted to fortifications against attack, particularly from the sea. Ships could be beached or worked at anchor within a defensible natural harbour. In the late 16th century the then small port of Rotterdam built an artificial harbour that served for two centuries. More typical, and certainly more expensive and elaborate, were the works of military engineering such as the late 16th-century fortifications of Valletta (Malta) or, on a smaller scale, the Morro Castle of Havana (1590–1640).

Military engineering rapidly developed, and by the late 17th century the lagoon-harbour of Dunkerque had been enclosed within the complex fortifications of the town and was approached from the sea between timber jetties armed with timber forts.

By the 18th century the increasing number of ships and quantities of cargo justified more expensive commercial facilities, at major ports at least. The earliest commercial wet docks (for example, Liverpool) date from the early 18th century. Near the end of the century there came the most remarkable work of harbour engineering of the century: the breakwater at Brest, constructed between 1783 and 1795. Over 9,800 feet (3,000 metres) long and built of stone and prefabricated timber units floated into position, it was built partly as a fortification.

The breakwater at Brest

All this activity, widely spread though it was, only faintly foreshadowed the spectacular development of port facilities that gathered momentum throughout the 19th century and matched in its complexity the equally spectacular growth in trade and industry. (See also PUBLIC WORKS: *Harbours and sea works.*) (D.O'N.)

THE END OF AN ERA

In 1775 the first successful trial of a boat driven by steam, on the Seine by Jacques Périer, foreshadowed the end of the age of sail. The sailing vessel fought long and hard, not admitting defeat for 100 years and more. One of the last rearguard actions was the struggle of a diehard Finnish skipper, Capt. Gustaf Ericson, who in the 1920s and 1930s built up a fleet of 16 sailing ships, ran them uninsured, except for their cargoes, and manned them with boys in training. The pride of Ericson's fleet, the four-masted bark "Herzogin Cecile," was finally wrecked on the rocks off the coast of Cornwall in 1936, and he died shortly afterward.

Yet there are plenty of schooners and similar fore-and aft-rigged vessels trading or pleasure cruising about the world today. Of the big square-riggers there are more than 80 sailing the seas. One or two serve as yachts or commercial pleasure ships, but nearly all the others are used to train youngsters for the navy or the mercantile marine of 18 different nations. The U.S.S.R. has the largest fleet, with the United States next but some way behind. The Scandinavian countries have quite a number, and Indonesia has a four-masted bark. Several have been launched since World War II, notably the German bark "Gorch Fock," built in West Germany in 1958 in the same yard and of the same design as four others (two of which are now Russian, one Portuguese, and another the training cutter of the U.S. Coast Guard). Britain has only two large schooners, owned by a private and highly successful sail-training association, and a brig built for sea scouts.

Two of the European barks have been tragically lost. In 1928–29 the five-masted "Kjøbenhavn," with 40 cadets in its crew, vanished mysteriously while at sea on passage. Then, in 1958, the four-masted German "Pamir" was overwhelmed in heavy weather, leaving only six survivors of its 35-man crew and 51 cadets. Yet in both Denmark and West Germany new vessels were soon built to replace them. Despite occasional losses of a lesser kind, large and small craft, ketches, schooners, and even a square-rigged ship or two are being launched in many parts of the world to carry on the long tradition of sea and sail. (D.P.C.)

THE AGE OF STEAM AND IRON

The railroad

EARLY DEVELOPMENTS

The first locomotives. The first reported self-propelled steam vehicle was created in Peking about 1681 by a Jesuit missionary named Ferdinand Verbiest. Nicolas-Joseph Cugnot, a French artillery officer, built a full-sized steam car in Paris in 1769. He intended it to haul army cannon or munitions, but it was demonstrated as a passenger carrier. Richard Trevithick, a Cornish engineer, demonstrated a steam car on hilly roads near Camborne, Cornwall, in 1801 and his second, bigger version in London in 1803, attaining a speed of six miles (10 kilometres) per hour. In 1804 Trevithick created a four-wheeled tramway locomotive that hauled a five wagon load of 10 tons of iron and 70 men at a speed of five miles per hour. The locomotive set several trends for the future; besides justifying Trevithick's preference for high-pressure instead of low-pressure steam used in stationary steam engines of the period, its single large cylinder was set horizontally and had a sliding crosshead, and exhaust steam was adapted for drafting the boiler to improve thermal efficiency.

In 1805 Trevithick's second locomotive was built at Gateshead, Northumberland, and in 1808 he laid down a circular track in London to demonstrate a third, "Catch-Me-Who-Can." The 10-ton machine achieved 10 miles per hour with an open coachload of passengers, but like its two predecessors it was eventually derailed by the flimsy track of the period, and Trevithick, discouraged, directed his talents elsewhere. (G.F.A.)

The Catch-Me-Who-Can

The first practical and successful locomotive was built in 1812 to the instructions of John Blenkinsop, an inspector at the Middleton colliery near Leeds. It ran on cast-iron rails and had two vertical cylinders driving two shafts geared to a toothed wheel that engaged a rack rail.

In 1813 the English inventor William Hedley built the "Puffing Billy," a simple adhesion locomotive that relied on friction between the wheels and the rails, dispensing with the toothed rack rail (the rack-rail system is now used only on a few mountain railroads with extremely steep gradients). Like John Blenkinsop's locomotives, "Puffing Billy" was used for hauling coal wagons between a mine and wharves, as was George Stephenson's first locomotive, the "Blücher," completed in 1814.

In 1823 Stephenson, one of the great pioneer railroad and locomotive builders, was invited to build and equip a railroad from Stockton to Darlington. The ceremonial opening of this landmark line took place on September 27, 1825. The Stockton and Darlington Railway was the first public railroad in the world to use locomotive traction and the first built to carry both freight and passengers. At first steam locomotives were used only for freight service; passenger service was provided by a contractor who used horse-drawn coaches. The first locomotive on the Stockton and Darlington was George Stephenson's "Locomotion." It and similar locomotives proved unreliable and expensive to maintain. They were suitable only for hauling low-speed mineral trains; their weight and tractive effort were limited by the relatively weak track. At times the railroad reverted to horses, but the situation was improved in 1827 with the introduction of the "Royal George," a six-coupled locomotive designed by Timothy Hackworth.

First public locomotive traction railroad

But the railroad era really began with the opening, on September 15, 1830, of the Liverpool and Manchester Railway. The Liverpool and Manchester incorporated all the features of modern public railroads. It was a public carrier of both passengers and freight, with all business

Figure 8: (Left) The "New Castle," built by Richard Trevithick in 1803, the first locomotive to do actual work. (Right) The "Rocket," built by George Stephenson; it won the 1829 trials by the Liverpool and Manchester Railway, England.
By courtesy of the Baltimore and Ohio Railroad Company

handled directly by the company itself; it used mechanical traction for all traffic.

Previous to its opening in 1829, the Liverpool and Manchester held a contest to determine the best type of motive power. The trials took place on the Rainhill level (Lancashire) from October 6 to 14, 1829. Three steam locomotives took part: George Stephenson's "Rocket" (Figure 8), Timothy Hackworth's "Sans Pareil," and the "Novelty," built by John Braithwaite and John Ericsson. On the last day of the trials the "Rocket" was awarded the £500 prize. The "Rocket's" superiority was due mainly to its use of a multiple fire-tube boiler rather than the single-flue boilers previously used. About this time, too, John Birkinshaw developed the fish-bellied (bellying out on the underside), rolled-iron edge rail. This was much stronger than the cast-iron rails previously used and enabled heavier locomotives to be run.

George Stephenson's "Rocket"

After the Rainhill trials, the steam locomotive became the dominant form of railroad motive power and was to remain so for over a century. The success of the Stockton and Darlington and the Liverpool and Manchester lines touched off widespread railroad building in Great Britain. In 1836 the London and Greenwich Railway opened, bringing the first public passenger service to London. In 1838 the London and Birmingham Railway was opened for its full length, and in 1840 the line from London to Southampton was completed. The Great Western Railway's line from London to Bristol was opened in 1841. By that time there were over 1,300 miles (2,100 kilometres) of rail line in the United Kingdom, and between 1844 and 1846 Parliament authorized the construction of more than 400 new lines, representing the height of the "railway mania" in Great Britain.

Unlike the other early British railroads, which used the four-foot-8.5-inch (1.435-metre) gauge, the Great Western line was built to a seven-foot (2.1-metre) gauge. The directors of the road adopted this broad gauge at the instigation of the line's brilliant chief engineer, Isambard Kingdom Brunel. There were, and still are, sound technical reasons for using a wide gauge; by 1835, however, when the Great Western directors adopted Brunel's seven-foot, it was already too late. The necessity for individual railroads to work together as an integrated network dictated a common gauge, and the 4-foot-8.5-inch width had already become the "standard gauge"; it remains so today. The Great Western continued to use the broad gauge until 1892, when the line was converted to standard gauge.

Continental Europe. Although the beginnings of railroads occurred quite early in most European countries, subsequent extension of rail lines was much slower than in Great Britain. Continental railroad practices soon diverged from those in Britain, though not as sharply as in North America. Standard gauge (or a width so close to it as to be compatible for through running) became dominant in all continental countries except Russia and Finland, where the width is five feet (1.5 metres), and Spain and Portugal, which use five feet six inches (1.680 metres). As compared with British railroads, continental railroads are also built to a much larger loading gauge, or clearance diagram, the dimensions above and outside the rails that rolling stock or loads must not exceed. This means that continental locomotives and cars are much bigger than those in Britain.

There was also more emphasis on state planning and control in the construction of early continental railroads. There, unlike the situation in Britain (and in North America), few competing railroads were built. In some cases the governments themselves built the lines; in other cases private companies received exclusive franchises to serve specific routes.

The first railroad in France, from Saint-Étienne to Andrézieux, went into use in 1827. It used horses and carried only freight until 1832, when steam locomotives were adopted. The Saint-Étienne–Lyon line was completed in 1832. The first international line, from Strasbourg to Basel, was completed in 1841, by which time France had 350 miles (about 550 kilometres) of railroads.

First railroad in France

The use of the steam locomotive in Germany began on December 7, 1835, with the opening of a railroad between Nürnberg and Fürth. A gauge of six feet (1.8 metres) was selected for the first public railroad in Russia, which was opened, with horse traction, in 1836. The original line in Russian Poland was of standard gauge, but Russia finally standardized on a width of five feet (1.5 metres). By 1850 there were only about 370 miles (600 kilometres) of railroad in all of Russia, but in 1851 the 404-mile (650-kilometre) link between St. Petersburg and Moscow was completed by the American engineer George Washington Whistler.

The first railroad in the Austro-Hungarian Empire, a 90-mile (140-kilometre) horse line between Linz and Budweis, was opened in 1832. By 1837, when the first steam locomotives were introduced, there were some 170 miles (270 kilometres) of horse-traction public railroads in the country.

North America. Interest in railroads in the United States developed almost as soon as in England. One of several horse-drawn tramways built early in the 19th century was Gridley Bryant's Granite Railway in Quincy, Massachusetts. This three-mile (five-kilometre) broad-gauge line carried the granite used in building the Bunker Hill Monument in Boston.

By 1813 the inventor Oliver Evans was proposing a railroad between New York and Philadelphia. Two years later, John Stevens received from the New Jersey legislature the first charter for a railroad ever granted in America. Stevens was ahead of his time: the chartered line, between the Delaware and Raritan rivers, was never built. But in 1825 he built and operated the first locomotive to run on rails in America; it ran on a half-mile circle of track at Stevens' home in Hoboken, New Jersey.

Success of the Stockton and Darlington in England spurred interest in railroads in the United States. On February 28, 1827, the Baltimore and Ohio Railroad Company was chartered. The line began carrying revenue traffic on January 7, 1830. The first 13 miles (21 kilometres) of line, from Baltimore to Ellicott's Mills (now Ellicott City), opened on May 24, 1830.

Baltimore and Ohio Railroad

The Baltimore and Ohio was the first railroad in the United States to be chartered as a common carrier of freight and passengers. Its promoters, looking beyond local needs, envisaged a line going all the way to the Ohio River to channel the commerce of the growing Middle West through the port of Baltimore. By 1834 the Baltimore and Ohio had built to Harpers Ferry, Virginia (now West Virginia), and on December 24, 1852, it reached the Ohio River at Wheeling. Subsequently, the company expanded, both by new construction and by acquiring other railroads, until it reached Chicago, St. Louis, and the Great Lakes.

Almost simultaneously, several other American railroads came into being. Construction of the five-foot- (1.5-metre-) gauge line from Charleston to Hamburg, South Carolina, by the South Carolina Canal and Rail Road Company began in February 1829. On December 25, 1830, this line became the first in the United States to start scheduled passenger operations using a steam locomotive. When the entire line to Hamburg was completed in 1833, it was the longest (136 miles [219 kilometres]) then operating in the United States. Ultimately, this line became part of the 10,000-mile (16,000-kilometre) Southern Railway System. Several other railroad systems that later grew into giants of the United States railroad industry had their beginnings in the decade of the 1830s. By 1840 there were 2,800 miles (4,500 kilometres) of line in the United States, and the country had entered its first great era of railroad building. Twenty years later, on the eve of the American Civil War, the country had 30,000 route miles (50,000 kilometres) of track.

With few exceptions, early railroads were designed to promote the commercial interests of local communities or areas. As growth progressed, however, many of the small roads were consolidated, forming through routes that served fairly large territories, and new railroad projects became more ambitious. The Pennsylvania Railroad Company (now Penn Central) completed its line from Philadelphia to Pittsburgh in December 1852, using 10 inclined planes to climb over the Allegheny Mountains. A little more than a year later, it completed an all-rail route.

The growth of Canadian railroads paralleled somewhat that of the United States. Construction of the first line, the Champlain and St. Lawrence Railroad, between Laprairie and St. John, Quebec, began in 1835; its first train operated on July 21, 1836. By 1860 there were about 2,000 miles (3,200 kilometres) of railroad line in Canada.

Social and economic consequences. The impact of the early railroads upon the societies in which they developed amounted to a social revolution. For the railroad represented the first big leap ahead in man's efforts to reduce the effects of time and distance on his travel and communications. As such, its effect on the society of the early 19th century was as profound in its day as was the effect later on of the development of the automobile, the airplane, and the radio. For the first time, farmers, manufacturers, merchants, and travellers had available a form of overland transportation that was fast, relatively inexpensive, little affected by weather conditions, and capable of moving large volumes of both goods and people.

Railroads compared to older forms of transport

The effect of the railroad upon the older forms of land transportation, the stagecoach and the canalboat, was immediate and often catastrophic. Though diehards opposed the railroads, few could afford not to use them once they were built. Typically, in 1841 a trip from London to Exeter, about 175 miles (280 kilometres), required about 21 hours by stagecoach, including meal stops. By 1846 an express train made the journey in $6^1/_2$ hours at less cost than by stage. (In 1970 express trains made this trip in two hours.) Newspapers and mail soon began to move by rail with dramatic time savings. On December 11, 1849, to publicize their joint route between London and Paris, the South Eastern and Nord railways of Britain and France dispatched copies of the morning *Times* from London at 7:00 AM and had them in Paris by 1:30 PM.

Established freight traffic quickly shifted to the new railroads; but just as railroads produced a vast increase in the total volume of passenger travel, so did they also present new opportunities for manufacturing and trade. They made it unnecessary for some types of factories to be located on canals or rivers; railroads could carry in the raw materials and take the finished products, at low cost, to much more distant markets than previously. Farmers could find a more ready market for their crops; coal and ore could be moved longer distances economically, thus making it feasible to work previously untapped resources.

So pervasive was the railroad's impact that great pressures developed on the part of both industries and communities to be served by rail transportation. Only a few towns and cities opposed the coming of railroads, and often they regretted their obstinacy when they saw growth and prosperity going to neighbouring communities that had welcomed the new form of transport. In both Europe and the United States, community leaders pushed hard to have main lines built through their towns, and if they could not get main-line status, they tried at least to get a branch-line connection.

In the United States, Canada, and other new undeveloped countries, the railroad proved to be the means of opening up new territory. Many towns and cities in the United States and Canada originally came into being as railroad "division points," where locomotives were changed, serviced, and repaired, and where operating crews were changed.

THE RAILROAD FROM 1850 TO 1900

The second half of the 19th century saw the railroad reach maturity and become a worldwide technical, economic, and social phenomenon. In the earlier part of the half century, railroad accidents became frequent and serious, as locomotive and car sizes grew rapidly, overstraining tracks and bridges. (T.C.S.)

Virtually the only important development in bridge building since Roman times had been the development of the elliptical masonry arch in place of the unnecessarily heavy and obstructive Roman circular arch. The advent of the railroad suddenly brought a demand for a vast number of bridges, many of great length, capable of carrying heavy loadings. The Stephensons were among the important pioneers of the railroad bridges in Britain; Robert Stephenson's unique box girder, the Britannia Bridge (over the Menai Strait, in Wales), through which trains ran completely enclosed, became a national landmark. The first steel rails were introduced in England in 1857, and a decade later (1867–73) Capt. James B. Eads built the first steel bridge, a powerful triple-arch, over the Mississippi at St. Louis. John Washington Roebling built a number of suspension bridges that were capable of taking railroad loadings, notably over the gorge at Niagara Falls (1851–55) and over the East River between New York and Brooklyn (1869–83) (see also PUBLIC WORKS: *Bridges*).

The timber-truss bridge, pioneered principally by a number of American inventors in the early 19th century, was adapted for railroad loadings in iron, in a number of designs.

The invention of the tunnelling shield by Marc Brunel for his tunnel under the Thames, the world's first subaqueous tunnel (1828–42), made it possible to carry railroad traffic conveniently into major cities. The Mont Cenis Tunnel in the Alps, driven by Germain Sommeiller with the aid of dynamite and compressed-air drills (1857–71), similarly pioneered long-distance rock tunnelling, indispensable to the crossing of mountain ranges by railroad lines.

(H.N.G.)

Other major technological advances of this period included automatic electric block signalling, telegraphic train dispatching, automatic coupling, and air brakes. Railroads learned to work together on common standards for brakes, couplers, and wheels, to permit interchange of equipment among different lines.

Britain. As the country where the railroad originated, Great Britain was the first to experience intensive building. Construction of new lines peaked there during the 1840s, when some 4,500 route miles (7,200 kilometres) were laid down, and remained at a high rate during the next two decades. By 1870 Britain had about 13,500 miles (21,700 kilometres) of railroad, largely double tracked. In the remaining three decades of the century the pace slowed down, but other important developments took place. Physical plant of the main lines was improved. In Scotland bridges were built over the two great firths of Tay and Forth. The first built over the Tay, on wrought-iron piers, was blown down in a gale (1879) and was replaced in steel. The Forth was bridged by the world's longest span bridge, a giant cantilever (1890). The world's longest underwater tunnel was driven under the Severn for the Great Western Railway (1886). First-class sleeping cars were introduced on trains between London and Scotland in 1873, and dining cars on the Great Northern's London to Leeds line in 1879. On August 22, 1895, competing trains of two lines raced from London to Aberdeen, Scotland, both completing the run at average speeds in excess of 60 miles (100 kilometres) per hour.

The United States. Railroad construction in the United States was on an even larger scale than in Britain in the 1850s, when more than 21,000 route miles (33,600 kilometres) were built. Construction was slowed down by the American Civil War (the first war, incidentally, in which railroads played a major role); but it resumed on a large scale immediately afterward, reaching a peak in the 1880s: in the year 1882 alone 11,500 miles (18,500 kilometres) were built, a record exceeded in 1887 with a total of 12,800 miles (20,600 kilometres). Altogether, more than 70,000 miles were built in the decade. Construction continued at a relatively high level through the 1900–10 decade.

The major thrust of American railroad development was westward. The first locomotive in Chicago, the "Pioneer" of the Galena and Chicago Union Railroad, now the Chicago and North Western Transportation Company, made its first run on October 25, 1848. The first railroad reached the Mississippi from Chicago in 1854. On May 10, 1869, the first transcontinental route was created when, at Promontory, Utah, the Union Pacific Railroad, building west from Omaha, Nebraska, met the Central Pacific Railroad, building east from Sacramento, California. Ultimately there were about nine major routes leading from the Midwest or South to the West Coast.

Government assistance to U.S. railroads

Although the United States railroad system, like that of other countries, was essentially a product of private enterprise, it received important government assistance, in the early years from state and local governments, and after the Civil War from the federal government in the form of land grants. Such grants, totalling about 131,000,000 acres (53,000,000 hectares) went to 29 railroads for about 18,000 miles (29,000 kilometres) of line (about 8 percent of total U.S. mileage). They made it possible for the railroads to push lines across prairies and mountains almost entirely undeveloped and very sparsely settled.

Railroad building becomes worldwide. Construction in western Europe followed that in Britain. In France six principal companies emerged, Nord, Est, Paris-Orléans, Paris-Lyon-Mediterranean, Midi, and Ouest. In 1878 the state took over a group of small companies in western France, creating the *État* (State) system. By 1902 the French rail network totalled 28,400 miles (45,700 kilometres). In Germany both private companies and the individual German states built railroads, but after 1876 the privately owned systems were gradually absorbed by the states. Germany's total route mileage had reached 35,625 (57,321 kilometres) by 1909.

Meanwhile, countries in other parts of Europe and throughout the world were getting their first railroads or expanding their small beginning networks to national proportions. In Canada the Canadian Pacific Railway Company tied Canada together just as the Central and Union Pacific lines had tied the United States together. One of the terms on which British Columbia entered the confederation in 1871 was the promise of this transcontinental route, which was completed in 1885. Two other Canadian transcontinentals, built with government assistance, reached the Pacific Coast in 1914 and 1915. India's first line, the East Indian Railway Company, was registered in 1849; the first line was opened between Bombay and Thana in 1853. By 1910 there were more than 32,000 miles (51,000 kilometres) of line in what are now India, Pakistan, and Bangladesh.

This period also saw the beginnings and rapid growth of railroads in Africa, Australia, and Japan. Railroad development was handicapped in Australia because each state laid track to the gauge it considered suitable for its own needs; as a result passengers and freight had to be transshipped from one line to another, and the railroad failed to play as strong a role in opening up the country as it did in the United States and Canada.

The Trans-Siberian Railroad

A notable achievement of this period in railroad development was the building by Russia of the Trans-Siberian Railroad, 5,787 miles (9,313 kilometres) long, linking Moscow and Vladivostok. Construction began in 1891, starting simultaneously from the east and west terminals. Originally, passengers could not make the entire journey by rail but had to travel by boat (or in winter, by sleigh) across Lake Baikal. By 1916 a line around the lake allowed the trip to be made without changing cars. (T.C.S.)

The steamship

GROWTH OF INLAND WATERWAYS

Throughout the centuries rivers have provided an obvious means of transport, but natural obstacles in the riverbeds and changes in water levels have hampered movement. With the invention of the lock, these could be overcome by lifting vehicles from one level to another and bypassing such hazards. Following the development of the lock in the 13th century, river navigation was improved and many artificial waterways were built.

To meet the demand for transport resulting from trade expansion, from the 16th century onward a network of canals was established linking Europe's navigable rivers. With technical improvements, and with further development of the mitre lock (see also PUBLIC WORKS: *Canals and inland waterways*), many canals incorporated unique engineering features including lock staircases, hydraulic lifts, and inclined planes that raised and lowered craft from one level to another. The expansion of trade created a need for the transport of raw materials and manufactured products that could not have been met by slow and hazardous road transport; as a result, canal construction was embarked upon on a grand scale. In the United Kingdom a series of canals joined the industrial Midlands to London and the ports, and links in the waterway system were forged in France to provide through navigation from the English Channel and the Atlantic to the Mediterranean. In Belgium and The Netherlands industrial expansion also led to the extension of canals that were more closely integrated with the French and German waterways. Russia provided through waterways from the Baltic to the Caspian Sea and interconnected its great rivers. In Greece, the Corinth Canal, abortively started by Nero to connect the Aegean and Ionian seas, was built. In the United States construction of canals contributed to the opening up of the West, with the Erie Canal, 363 miles (584 kilometres) long, joining the Hudson to Lake Erie and resulting in the establishment of New York as the predominant port on the Atlantic seaboard. Thus it was that apart from seagoing trade the main means for the transport of goods throughout the period of great industrial development of the late 18th and early 19th centuries was the river and canal.

Drawbacks in barge transportation

Transport by inland waterways did have some serious handicaps: goods were transported in dumb barges, drawn mostly by horse along towpaths, and the canal boats often had to be manually handled through the numerous locks and tunnels. Because of the large number of locks, transport was slow and the volume carried per unit was small. The railways, with their larger volumes, greater carrying power, and higher speeds, inevitably encroached upon the canals and brought the canal era to an end. In many countries, however, navigable rivers and canals continued to be used as a major means of transport; and with the coming of steam, tugboats supplanted the horse. Heavier loads could be carried at increased speeds. Heavy investment in ocean canals became worthwhile; the Suez Canal, joining the Mediterranean Sea to the Red Sea and thereby considerably reducing the voyage to India and the Far East, was opened in 1869, and the Panama Canal, connecting the Atlantic and Pacific, was completed in 1914. Meanwhile in North America navigation on the Mississippi was improved with the construction of link canals that joined this system with the St. Lawrence and the Great Lakes; thus an extensive and combined network of inland waterways was established. Development of this system continued, climaxed by the St. Lawrence Seaway, opened in 1959, providing a continuous deep waterway for oceangoing ships from the Atlantic to the Great Lakes. In Europe and the U.S.S.R., after World War II the inland waterway networks of canalized rivers and artificial waterways were being brought up to modern standards, and with the application of the latest technological skills larger loads could be carried at increased speeds. (E.A.J.D.)

POWER: FROM SAIL TO STEAM

The first steamboats. Though Robert Fulton is generally credited with the invention of the steamboat, it is well known that he had been preceded by several others. Salomon de Caus of France experimented with steam power for a boat as early as 1615, as did Denis Papin, a French Huguenot physicist, a century later. The first steam-powered boats to actually run followed James Watt's improvement of the steam engine in 1775. Among others, John Fitch demonstrated one in the United States in 1787 and by 1790 had built several. Fitch was unlucky in attracting backers and lacked the funds to continue development. His original model was powered by a set of six paddles suspended from either side of the boat and moved forward and aft by the action of the steam piston. He later built a craft with three paddles in the stern that attained a speed of eight miles (13 kilometres) per hour. All of these earliest steamboats used chains attached to ratchet wheels or other crude methods to convert the reciprocating motion of the piston rod of the single steam piston. In Scotland, however, William Symington aroused interest with his use of a crank, the capacity of which to convert linear to rotary motion is still the basic principle of reciprocating steam machinery. With the crank device, Symington built the 56-foot (17-metre) "Charlotte Dundas," named after the daughter of his financial backer, in 1801. Its piston developed ten horsepower and enabled it to act as a tug in the canals of Scotland, probably the first commercially successful steam-driven vessel.

John Fitch's paddle boat

Robert Fulton developed a steamboat that he demonstrated on the Seine in 1803 with indifferent success, but, undaunted, he had the "Clermont" built and shipped to the United States, where it was demonstrated on the Hudson River in 1807. The "Clermont," nearly three times the length of the "Charlotte Dundas," steamed up the Hudson under its own power at an average speed of five miles (eight kilometres) per hour. After a few improvements it was renamed the "North River Steamboat" and went into regular service between New York and Albany. Highly successful financially, it enabled Fulton to continue his work and produce many more ships.

A contemporary of Fulton's, John Stevens, in 1804 applied the principle of the Archimedes screw, a rotating helix, to drive a ship. His boat ran, but insufficient skill of the workmen who fabricated the propeller prevented him from perfecting his device. Stevens, however, formulated lasting principles in steam engineering. He said that a ship, to be successful, should have a multitube boiler, high-pressure steam, direct connection of the steam engine to the propeller, and a short, four-bladed, helical propeller. Although the number of blades has varied, Stevens' predictions have been remarkably accurate. While development continued in the United States, a number of shipbuilders on the Clyde River in Scotland, close to large foundries and machine works, led steamboat building in Europe.

For its first 50 years, steam power was looked on with mistrust, not totally unfounded in view of the wooden construction of the ships, yet the steam engines themselves were remarkably dependable, perhaps because of their simplicity. Nearly all ships of this period were equipped with sails as well as steam and relied mainly on sail to conserve their wood fuel supply. Such was the case with the "Savannah," built by Moses Rogers, a sea captain and engineer, who interested backers in Savannah, Georgia, in developing a steam-equipped ship to cross the Atlantic. Purchasing an unfinished sailing packet in New York, Rogers added a two-boiler reciprocating steam engine. The ship was about the size of a modern seagoing tug. The engine produced at most 75 horsepower, equalled by some modern outboard motors. Among noteworthy characteristics of the engine and propulsion system were the use of seawater for boiler feed; coal-fired instead of wood-fired boilers, collapsible paddle wheels to be stowed on deck in severe storms, and a full set of sails.

Moses Rogers' "Savannah"

Although the "Savannah" was especially outfitted for passenger comfort, people were apprehensive of taking passage in it, and in 1819 it sailed with no passengers and no cargo. Rogers took it all the way to Russia with no mechanical troubles reported, but the vessel remained a financial failure and in the end was stripped of its power plant and sold as a sailing packet. Despite its own fate, the "Savannah" was followed by many successors; by 1839 there were 776 steam-propelled ships registered in the British Isles alone. A series of Atlantic crossings under sail and steam culminated in 1827 in the all-steam crossing by the British-built Dutch ship "Curaçao," a ship of 438 tons with steam-driven paddle wheels capable of 50 horsepower each. A short time later the "Royal William," a Canadian ship of 830 tons and 200-horsepower engines, made regular scheduled crossings.

An important contribution to the success of the new ships came from Robert Napier, a British ship designer who observed that the bluff bows of old-fashioned sailing ships caused considerable turbulence. Experimenting in a model tank, Napier developed a sharp cutwater bow that allowed easier passage of the steamship, thus improving its speed. One of Napier's associates was a merchant named Samuel Cunard, who with several others formed a company that obtained a subsidy from the British government to carry mail. With this help they built the four ships that began the famous Cunard Line, the "Britannia," the "Acadia," the "Caledonia," and the "Columbia." They were not large, being about 200 feet (60 metres) long with 34-foot (10-metre) beam and displacing 1,150 tons. Their power of 750 horsepower enabled them to cross the Atlantic on a regular basis, the "Britannia" doing it in 14⅓ days.

In the United States in 1850, a new line called the Collins Line was formed with the purpose of surpassing the Cunard ships. This line built five large paddle-wheel steamers of 1,000 horsepower using a cylinder of eight-foot (2.4-metre) diameter with a nine-foot (2.7-metre) stroke. The Collins ships displaced 2,860 tons and carried extensive sail. Their speed of about 13 knots won them temporary dominance in the Atlantic trade.

Development of steam power. In all these early steamships the steam pressures were very low, at first as little as three to five pounds per square inch (2,100–3,500 kilograms per square metre) above atmospheric pressure. To grasp the problem confronting the marine engineers of the 19th century, a brief description of the low-pressure steam engine is necessary. In it, wood or coal was burned in proximity to water in a square boiler, causing the water to boil and form steam at a pressure above atmospheric. This steam was led into the cylinder, in which its expansive force pushed the piston to the end of the cylinder; valves then opened to allow the steam to escape to the condenser and be returned to the liquid state. The water, pressurized by pumps to a pressure slightly higher than that existing in the boiler, was reintroduced into the boiler to continue the cycle. Where water was plentiful, the cycle could be even further simplified by exhausting the steam from the engine directly to the atmosphere and pumping in new water to the boiler.

The expansive force, or pressure, of steam depends upon its temperature. In the low-pressure cylinder, during the stroke, the steam expanded to at or below atmospheric temperature and pressure. Because this represented only a relatively modest drop, the power generated was weak. After 50 years of steamboats, maximum steam pressure possible was about 20–30 pounds per square inch (14,100–21,000 kilograms per square metre) at the boiler. To increase power output, the size of the pistons was increased, or more were added. The largest pistons could deliver up to 1,000 horsepower. By the 1860s the boxlike low-pressure boiler had reached the limit of its potential. In the 1870s a new approach was tried. A British warship, HMS "Iris" was given a boiler built in the form of a cylinder. The experiment was a success; a much higher steam pressure was achieved without structural failure of the boiler. Within a decade, steam pressures multiplied six times.

With this increased pressure available, a further refinement could be introduced. The hot, high-pressure steam could be used more than once. It could be expanded through the original high-pressure cylinder and discharged to power a second, lower pressure but larger cylinder (double expansion) and even a third (triple expansion). Improved condensers brought the exhaust of the last cylinder to well below atmospheric pressure. With these improvements, the reciprocating steam engine approached the peak of its development by the turn of the 20th century, producing better than 20,000 horsepower per engine from an initial steam pressure of slightly over 200 pounds per square inch. Engines such as these drove the North Atlantic liners of the day, but the size of the reciprocating engine was placing a limit on its further development, because at these powers the lowest pressure cylinders were nearing 10 feet (three metres) in diameter, and, with their large structural foundations and braces to take the load of the tons of metal reversing every stroke, they were becoming extremely heavy.

The turbine. A continuing demand for greater speed and power brought the adoption of a newer form of engine, the turbine. Reciprocating machinery remained in vogue for moderate powered ships, however, and many still remain in service because of their simplicity of operation and maintenance, their long life, and dependability, ideal qualities for merchant ships relying on low-cost operation. One of the added advantages of the reciprocating engine was that it could be timed to turn at the relatively slow speed that is required of an efficient ship propeller, thus removing an added complication arising with the turbine.

The principle of the turbine, which is the reaction or impulse or both of a current of pressurized water, steam, or gas against a series of curved blades on a central rotating spindle, had been known for some time when, in 1884, an English engineer, Charles A. Parsons, patented a turbine in which the rotor wheel was driven by the reaction of a steam jet from its periphery (reaction turbine), and shortly afterward a Swedish inventor, Carl de Laval patented a turbine in which the jet of steam impinged on the turbine blade (see also ENERGY CONVERSION: *Turbines*). Because these turbines were inherently efficient devices that were not limited in size, they developed rapidly, and by the start of the 20th century they were in service. Initially, the real advantages of the turbines, high efficiency and light weight, were not exploited; directly connected to the relatively slow-turning propellers, they had to be made large and inefficient. The first solution for faster ships was to use several propellers (multiple screws) and turn them at higher than optimum speeds and to divide the turbines into several units, the lowest pressure units becoming very large in diameter.

The Parsons and De Laval turbines

Reduction gearing. About 1910 the real solution to the problem appeared in the form of new transmissions. These took three forms. The solution in Germany was to provide a hydraulic speed-reducing coupling in the propeller shaft so that the turbine could run at its more efficient high speed while the propeller could run at its slower optimum speed. In Britain a similar result was achieved by fitting mechanical reduction gearing between the turbine and the propeller shaft; and in the United States the turbines were used to drive electric generators, which in turn drove electric motors attached to the propeller shaft, and, by motor control, the best speed for each could be obtained. The net result of any of these systems was to open the way for rapid development of high-powered fast ships with improved range of operation, because these devices allowed the turbine and propeller designers to achieve about 25 percent improvement in overall efficiency. Ultimately, most ships adopted mechanical gearing. Electric drive, because of its lower efficiency and higher cost, is usually reserved for ships requiring very fine control of engines from the bridge or ships such as dredges in which there are high requirements for electric power. Because of poor efficiency, hydraulic couplings have almost disappeared except for certain specialized uses.

In the early cylindrical boilers the fire was still brought through the water in tubes, as in the old box types. The system was perpetuated in the so-called Scotch boiler widely used with reciprocating machinery in merchant ships requiring only moderate pressures; above a certain point such a boiler becomes too massive to be practical. Shortly after the introduction of the Scotch boiler, its successor, the water-tube boiler, was invented. Its perfection took several years because of difficulties in circulation and watertightness, but in the end it supplanted the fire-tube boiler in all high-powered ships. As the name implies, the water-tube boiler uses a furnace in which the fire is contained and through which water is passed in tubes between upper and lower cylindrical drums. Water-tube boilers originally employed natural circulation, using the lower density of hot water to keep the water flowing through the tubes. Later, in order to increase efficiency further and reduce size and weight, pumping was introduced to force circulation, thus achieving faster heating rates.

Scotch boiler and water-tube boiler

CONSTRUCTION: FROM TIMBER TO IRON

Hull materials and fabrication. From earliest times the custom was to build the hull from the most readily available natural material. In Egypt this meant reeds; in Crete it meant wood; and so it went for most of the shipping nations until the early and middle part of the 19th century. When iron first became available, the concept of putting to sea in a vessel built of a material heavier than water was not accepted by shipbuilders any more than by the general public. The fact that the ship is supported by the water it displaces rather than by the buoyancy of its material could not overcome the fear of sinking should the hull be ruptured. The beginning of iron shipbuilding was the construction by an iron founder in Scotland of an iron barge in 1787, a venture that met with ridicule. But in 1818 Thomas Wilson, also of Scotland, built an iron sailing ship, the "Vulcan," to haul coal in coastal and river traffic; the vessel proved so durable that it was still in service 60 years after its launching. In 1821 the "Aaron Manby," with a hull of iron, made the passage from Birmingham, where it was built, to France, where it entered service on the river Seine. There followed several smaller iron ships built in England and Scotland. Most were sailing craft and designed for service on inland waterways, a use that did not arouse popular apprehension over sinking so much as for oceangoing service. A significant event in 1834 helped to change the image of iron ships, when a number of wooden ships and one iron steamer, the "Garryowen," were driven ashore in a storm. After the storm the "Garryowen" was able to refloat itself and proceed, while the wooden vessels were either badly damaged or lost. This graphic demonstration of the superior hull strength of iron over wood quickly led to the widespread adoption of iron as a hull material. From 1850 through about 1880, iron was the principal material for ships' hulls.

Wood was finally abandoned for other reasons. In 1853 Russia first used explosive shells in warfare at sea, and the wooden ships that had resisted solid shot well splintered and came apart with exploding shells. Another reason was economic. The wooden ship cost more to build and maintain than her iron successor. Finally, because of difficulty in fastening and inherent strength, the size of ships built from wood was limited to about 300 feet (90 metres). Iron plates formed to the shape of the ship, joined by rivets to each other and to the frames of the ship, produced a more homogeneous structure than wooden hulls, which had a weakness wherever the ends of planks were connected. After 1880, steel offered superior ductility and strength to produce lighter and stronger hulls and soon replaced iron.

In the 20th century, engineers were long aware of the possible superior strength of welding over riveting, but the problems of incomplete welds or of cracking kept widespread use of welding for hulls from developing until nearly World War II, when welding's advantages in mass production became an overriding consideration. Great numbers of ships were then built with all of the connections in their hulls welded. During the latter part of the war and shortly thereafter, several mysterious ship losses occurred. In a few cases, tankers with all-welded hulls cracked in two while riding at anchor. The problem of welding ships was studied by metallurgists and shipbuilders, and it was found that some steels at low temperatures, such as are found in the wintertime in the North Atlantic, became very brittle and so sensitive to small cracks and notches that under the right conditions they cracked with almost explosive speed and violence. Remedies for these weaknesses were found by inserting riveted joints in these ships at critical points, a practice that stopped the running of cracks. For later ships a change in the composition and treatment of the steel was made to avoid the notch sensitivity. The episode was a good illustration of the unsuspected problems that have made shipbuilders and designers traditionally conservative.

Adoption of welding in ship construction

With the solution of the cracking problems, all-welded ships became the rule. As the search for higher speeds continued, newer hull materials were introduced. In the case of very high speed cutters and hydrofoils or air-cushion ships, almost exclusive use has been made of high-strength alloys of aluminum. Investigations continue in even higher strength materials, such as titanium, for highly stressed elements.

The screw propeller. From the introduction of steamships, both the paddle wheel and the screw propeller were available for propulsion, and at first the paddle wheel predominated. Of itself, the paddle wheel is a very efficient device and is competitive with even modern propellers. The drawbacks that led to its being replaced include its vulnerability to damage; its unhappy trait of coming out of the water when the ship rolls violently in a heavy sea, complicating steering; and the fact that, because it operates close to the surface of the water, it is susceptible to excessive slipping under heavy load at slow speed and high thrust (driving power). The propeller, on the other hand, is well submerged and if well designed can have good low-speed thrust as well as high-speed efficiency. Its disadvantages are underwater resistance of shafts and struts, the need to make the penetration of the hull by the shaft watertight, and vulnerability to underwater obstacles. In 1845 the British Admiralty staged a tug-of-war between HMS "Rattler," a screw-propelled ship designed and built by Isambard Kingdom Brunel, and a merchant ship equipped with paddle wheels, the "Alecto." Both ships were about 800 tons and about equal power. The event was held on a calm sea, and the "Rattler" towed the "Alecto" away at about two to two and a half knots. This test was hailed as a proof that the screw propeller was superior to the paddle wheel, because it was under those conditions of very slow speed and high thrust. Whether the paddle wheel would fare so badly at speed in an efficiency run was not determined, but from that day forward the screw propeller was favoured, and nearly all ships are fitted with propellers today, except for river steamers that are faced with shoal-water operation and some ships operating on sheltered lakes.

Drawbacks of the paddle wheel

Other forms of propulsion have developed to fill various specialized needs, such as the air propeller to supply thrust for high-speed boats designed to traverse swamps and for some air-cushion vessels. The simple air screw seems to have many advantages for propulsion, but its prohibitive size for larger powers at the relatively slow speed of ships has restricted its use. (Ja.J.S.)

MODERN TRANSPORTATION

The automobile and other road vehicles

An automobile is a self-propelled passenger vehicle designed to be operated on ordinary roads. In general, motor vehicles may be classified into several types, according to the service they render. Most numerous are the private passenger cars described in this section, intended usually to transport up to nine individuals; a subdivision of this type is formed by the so-called sports cars, which are designed primarily for speed and good road-handling characteristics, with passenger comfort a secondary consideration. Commercial passenger vehicles for carrying larger numbers of persons—buses and motor coaches—and commercial freight vehicles for carrying goods and materials are described below in the section *Trucks and buses.* The development of the relevant manufacturing technology is covered in the article INDUSTRIES, MANUFACTURING.

HISTORY OF THE AUTOMOBILE

Unlike many other major inventions, the original idea of the automobile cannot be attributed to an individual, and many individuals worked simultaneously on self-powered road vehicles. Certainly, the idea occurred long before it was first recorded in the *Iliad,* in which Homer (in Alexander Pope's translation) states that Vulcan in a single day made 20 tricycles, which

Wondrous to tell instinct with spirit roll'ed
From place to place, around the blest abodes,
Self-moved, obedient to the beck of gods.

Early experiments. Leonardo da Vinci considered the idea of a self-propelled vehicle. In 1760 a Swiss clergyman, J.H. Genevois, suggested mounting small windmills on a cartlike vehicle, their power to be used to wind springs that would move the road wheel. Genevois's idea probably derived from a windmill cart of about 1714. Two-masted wind carriages were running in the Netherlands in 1600, and a speed of 20 miles (30 kilometres) per hour with a load of 28 passengers was claimed for at least one of them. The first recorded suggestion of wind use was probably Robert Valturio's unrealized plan (1472) for a cart powered by windmills geared to the wheels.

Other inventors considered the possibilities of clockwork. Probably in 1748, a carriage propelled by a large clockwork engine was demonstrated in Paris by the versatile inventor Jacques de Vaucanson.

Clockwork carriage

The air engine is thought to have originated with a 17th-century German physicist, Otto Von Guericke. Guericke invented an air pump and was probably the first to make metal pistons, cylinders, and connecting rods: the basic components of the reciprocating engine. In the 17th century, a Dutch inventor, Christiaan Huygens, produced an engine that worked by air pressure developed by explosion of a powder charge. Denis Papin of France built a model engine on the vacuum principle, using the condensation of steam to produce the vacuum. An air engine was patented in England in 1799, and a grid of compressor stations was proposed to service vehicles. An air-powered vehicle is said to have been produced in 1832.

As early as the 16th century, steam propulsion was proposed, and in 1678, Ferdinand Verbiest, a Belgian Jesuit missionary to China, made a model steam carriage based on a principle suggestive of the modern turbine. Another early proponent of steam power encountered such skepticism, however, that he was certified insane.

In the 18th century a French scientist, Philippe Lebon, patented a coal-gas engine and made the first suggestion of electrical ignition. In Paris, one Isaac de Rivas made a gas-powered vehicle which he patented in 1807; his engine used hydrogen gas as fuel, the valves and ignition were operated by hand, and the timing problem appears to have been difficult.

The first automobile. The Royal Automobile Club of Great Britain and the Automobile Club de France now agree that Nicolas-Joseph Cugnot of Lorraine was the constructor of the first true automobile. Cugnot's vehicle was a huge, heavy, steam-powered tricycle, and his

Cugnot's steam tricycle

model of 1769 was said to have run for 20 minutes at 2.25 miles (3.6 kilometres) per hour while carrying four people and to have recuperated sufficient steam power to move again after standing for 20 minutes. Cugnot was an artillery officer, and the more or less steam-tight pistons of his engine were made possible by the invention of a drill that accurately machined cannon bores. A replica of the Cugnot vehicle, partially original, is preserved in the Conservatoire des Arts et Métiers in Paris.

By courtesy of the Montagu Motor Museum, Beaulieu, Hampshire

Figure 9: The 1769 Cugnot steamer, a three-wheeled artillery tractor with front-wheel drive, carried four passengers at a speed of 2¼ miles per hour.

Most authorities are inclined to honour Carl Benz and Gottlieb Daimler of Germany as the most important pioneer contributors to the gasoline-engine automobile. Benz ran his first car in 1885, Daimler his in 1886. Although there is no reason to believe that Benz had ever seen a motor vehicle before he made his own, he and Daimler had been preceded by a Frenchman, J.-J.-E. Lenoir, and an Austrian, Siegfried Marcus, in 1862 and 1864–65, respectively, but neither Lenoir nor Marcus had persisted. Benz and Daimler did persist—indeed, to such purpose that the firm of Daimler–Benz traces its origins back to 1895 and claims, with the Panhard firm of France, to be one of the oldest automobile-manufacturing firms in the world. Oddly, Benz and Daimler never met.

The four-stroke principle upon which most modern automobile engines work was discovered by a French engineer, Alphonse Beau de Rochas, in 1862, the year in which Lenoir ran his car from Paris to Joinville-le-Pont. The four-stroke cycle is often called the Otto cycle, after the German Nikolaus August Otto, who designed an engine on that principle in 1876. De Rochas held prior patents, however, and litigation in the French courts upheld him. Lenoir's engine omitted the compression stroke of the Otto cycle; fuel was drawn into the cylinder on the intake stroke and fired by a spark halfway on the next reciprocal stroke.

The idea for Siegfried Marcus' 1864–65 car apparently came to him by chance while he was considering the production of illumination by igniting a mixture of gasoline and air with a stream of sparks. The reaction was so violent that it occurred to him to use it as a power source. His first vehicle was a cart carrying a two-cycle engine geared to the rear wheels without any intervening clutch. It was started by having a strong man lift the rear end while the wheels were spun. It did run, however, a distance of about 200 yards (180 metres). In 1898 the Austrian Automobile Club arranged an exhibition of motor cars, and Marcus was a guest of honour. He denied interest in the entire idea of the automobile, however, calling it "a senseless waste of time and effort." Marcus' second model, the 1874–75 car, was sturdy and sufficiently well-preserved to make a demonstration run in the streets of Vienna on April 16, 1950, at a rate of three miles (five kilometres) per hour.

Other inventors have been put forward as originators of the internal-combustion automobile. In 1823 or 1826 an English mechanical engineer named Samuel Brown drove a self-powered road vehicle up Shooter's Hill in London. Brown's patent specifications and an eyewitness account of his drive both exist. His engine had separate combustion and working cylinders and apparently used carbureted hydrogen as fuel. Léon-Paul-Charles Malandin of France produced a four-wheel vehicle with a four-stroke, two-cylinder gasoline engine in 1883, and he, too, is sometimes cited as the first to run an automobile with a true internal-combustion engine. His claim, like the others, falters before the continuity of the Benz–Daimler efforts.

The age of steam. Before any internal-combustion engine had run, followers of Nicholas Cugnot were on the road, notably in England, although the first post-Cugnot steam carriage appears to have been that built in Amiens, France, in 1790. Steam buses were running in Paris about 1800. Oliver Evans of Philadelphia ran an amphibious steam dredge through the streets of that city in 1805. Less well known were Nathan Read of Salem, Massachusetts, and Apollo Kinsley of Hartford, Connecticut, both of whom ran steam vehicles during the period 1790–1800.

English inventors appear to have been active, and by the 1830s the manufacture and use of steam road carriages approached the status of a minor industry in the British Isles. James Watt's foreman, William Murdock, ran a model steam carriage on the roads of Cornwall in 1784, and Robert Fourness showed a working three-cylinder tractor in 1788. Watt was opposed to the use of steam engines for such purposes; his feelings were so strong that he inserted into the lease of a house he owned a clause stating that "no steam carriage should on any pretense be allowed to approach the house." Watt's low-pressure steam engine would have been too bulky for road use in any case, and all of the British efforts in steam derived from the earlier researches of Thomas Savery and Thomas Newcomen.

Richard Trevithick developed Murdock's ideas, and at least one of his carriages, with driving wheels 10 feet (three metres) in diameter, ran in London. Sir Goldsworthy Gurney, the first commercially successful steamcarriage builder, based his design upon an unusually efficient boiler. He could not, however, be convinced that smooth wheels could grip a roadway, and so he arranged propulsion on his first vehicle by iron legs digging into the road surface. His second vehicle was said to weigh only 3,000 pounds (1,400 kilograms) and to be capable of carrying six persons. He made trips as long as 84 miles (135 kilometres) in a running time of nine hours 30 minutes and once recorded a speed of 17 miles (27 kilometres) per hour. A rate of 32 miles (51 kilometres) per hour was later claimed by two other builders. To allay the public's fear of boiler explosions, Gurney designed a "drag," which was in effect a tractor, or locomotive, pulling one or more unpowered coaches.

Steam coaches on British roads

Gurney equipment was used on a regularly scheduled Gloucester–Cheltenham service of four round trips daily that at times did the nine miles (14 kilometres) in 45 minutes. Between February 27 and June 22, 1831, steam coaches ran 4,000 miles (6,400 kilometres) on this route, carrying some 3,000 passengers. The equipment was noisy, smoky, destructive of roadways, and admittedly dangerous; hostility arose, and it was common for drivers to find the way blocked with heaps of stones or felled trees. A minor accident occurred and finally aroused so much public feeling that the passenger service was ended. Nevertheless, many passengers had been carried by steam carriage before the railways had accepted their first paying passenger.

The most successful era of the steam coaches lasted from 1831 to 1838. Ambitious routes were run, including one from London to Cambridge. But by 1840 it was clear that the steam carriages had little future. They had had much to contend with, including the anti-machinery attitude of the public and the enmity of the horse-coach interests, which resulted in such penalties as a charge of £5 for passing a tollgate that cost a horse coach only 3*d.* The government was of small help: a select committee of Parliament recommended a research grant of £16,000 for Goldsworthy Gurney, but the treasury refused to pay it. The crushing blow was the Locomotives on Highways Act of 1865, which reduced permissible speeds on public roads to two miles (three kilometres) per hour within cities and four miles (six kilometres) per hour in rural areas. This legislation was known as the Red Flag Act because of its requirement that every steam carriage mount a crew of three, one to precede it carrying a red flag of warning. The act was amended in 1878, but it was not repealed until 1896, by which time its provisions had effectively stifled the development of road transport in the British Isles.

Inventors in other countries also experimented with steam carriages, and a few ran on roads in Europe and the United States.

The decline of the steam carriage did not prevent continued effort in the field, and much attention was given to the steam tractor for use as a prime mover. Beginning in about 1868, Britain was the scene of a vogue for light steam-powered personal carriages; if the popularity of these vehicles had not been legally hindered, it would certainly have resulted in the appearance of widespread enthusiasm for motoring in the 1860s rather than in the 1890s. Some of the steamers were designed to carry as few as two people and were capable of speeds on the order of 20 miles (30 kilometres) per hour. The public climate remained unfriendly, however.

Light steam cars were being built in the United States, France, Germany, and Denmark during the same period, and it is possible to argue that the line from Cugnot's lumbering vehicle runs unbroken to the 20th-century steam automobiles made as late as 1926. The grip of the steam automobile on the American imagination has been strong ever since the era of the Stanley brothers (one of whose "steamers" took the world speed record at 127.66 miles [205.4 kilometres] per hour in 1906), and in the 1960s it was estimated that there were still 7,000 steam cars in the United States, about 1,000 of them in running order.

The Stanley steamer

By courtesy of the Magic Age of Steam, Yorklyn, Delaware

Figure 10: Stanley, 1911, a four-passenger touring car.

Though the pollution crisis of the 1960s inspired a resurgence in steam-car research, the major Detroit companies were unwilling to finance a crash program, and of the individuals who attempted construction only the industrialist William Lear maintained a long-term program. In 1972 Lear demonstrated a steam-powered bus.

Benz and the gasoline car. Carl Benz was completely dedicated to the proposition that the internal-combustion engine would supersede the horse and revolutionize the world's transportation. He persisted in his efforts to build a gasoline-fuelled vehicle in the face of many obstacles, including lack of money to the point of poverty and the bitter objections of his associates, who considered him unbalanced on the subject.

Benz's day of triumph

Benz ran his first car, a three-wheeler powered by a two-cycle, one-cylinder engine, early in 1885, on a happy and triumphant day. He circled a cinder track beside his small factory, his workmen running beside the car, his wife running, too, clapping her hands; the little machine made four circuits of the track, stalling only twice, before a broken chain stopped it. Even Max Rose, Benz's skeptical partner, whose money had made the car possible, conceded that he was mildly impressed; but, like Siegfried Marcus, he remained convinced to the end of his association with Benz that there was no future in the horseless carriage.

In the autumn of 1885, when Benz attempted a public showing of a slightly improved model, he forgot to steer and smashed it against the brick wall surrounding the yard of his own house.

Figure 11: The first Benz, 1885, a three-wheeled vehicle with a steel frame in the shape of a horseshoe. This car was first driven in public in Mannheim on July 3, 1886, where a speed of 15 kilometres per hour was reached.

By courtesy of the Smithsonian Institution, Washington, D.C.

Benz made his first sale to a Parisian named Émile Rogers in 1887. Gradually, however, the soundness of his design and the quality and care that went into the material and the construction of his cars bore weight, and they sold well. By 1888 he was employing 50 workmen to build the tricycle car; in 1890 he began to make a four-wheeler.

In his way, Benz was almost as dogmatic and reactionary as Marcus had been; he objected to redesign of his original cars, and some authorities believe that he was never really convinced that his original concepts had been improved upon.

Development of the Daimler. Gunsmithing was Gottlieb Daimler's first vocation, and he showed marked talent, but he abandoned the trade to go to engineering school, studying in Germany, England, Belgium, and France. In Germany he worked for various engineering and machining concerns, including the Karlsruhe Maschinenbaugesellschaft, a firm that much earlier had employed Benz.

In 1872 Nikolaus A. Otto offered Daimler the position of technical director of his firm, then building stationary gasoline engines. Daimler was of notable utility to Otto during the next decade, when important work was done on the four-stroke engine. Daimler brought in several brilliant researchers, among them Wilhelm Maybach, but in 1882 both Daimler and Maybach resigned because of Daimler's conviction that Otto did not understand the potential of the internal-combustion engine. They set up a shop in Bad Cannstatt and built an air-cooled, one-cylinder engine. The first high-speed internal-combustion engine, it was designed to run at 900 revolutions per minute (rpm), while Benz's first tricycle engine had operated at only 250 rpm. Daimler and Maybach built a second engine and mounted it on a wooden bicycle, which first ran on

By courtesy of the Veteran Car Club of Great Britain

Figure 12: Panhard–Levassor, 1891, the first vehicle with an internal-combustion engine mounted at the front of the chassis.

The first Daimler

November 10, 1885. The next year the first Daimler four-wheeled road vehicle was made: a carriage modified to be driven by a one-cylinder engine. Daimler appears to have believed that the first phase of the automobile era would be a mass conversion of carriages to engine drive; Benz apparently thought of the motorcar as a separate device. Daimler's licensees in France were René Panhard and Émile Levassor. In 1889 they entered the field independently, and the Panhard-Levassor designs of 1891–94 are of primary importance. They were true automobiles, not carriages modified for self-propulsion.

Daimler's 1889 car was a departure from previous practice. It was based on a framework of light tubing, it had the engine in the rear, its wheels were driven by belt, and it was steered by tiller. Remarkably, it had four speeds. This car had obvious commercial value, and in the following year the Daimler Motoren-Gesellschaft was founded. The British Daimler automobile was started as a manufactory licensed by the German company but later became quite independent of it. (To distinguish machines made by the two firms in the early years, the German cars are usually referred to as Cannstatt–Daimlers.) Products of the Daimler–Benz company (the two firms were merged in 1926) are sold under the name Mercedes–Benz.

In France the giants were De Dion-Bouton, Peugeot, Renault (the last two are still in existence). The Italians were later in the field: the Steffanini-Martina of 1896 is thought of as the foundation of the industry in Italy, and Isotta-

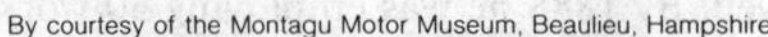
By courtesy of the Montagu Motor Museum, Beaulieu, Hampshire

Figure 13: Hammel, 1886, possibly the oldest automobile still in running order.

Fraschini was founded about 1898. Giovanni Agnelli founded Fiat (Fabbrica Italiana Automobili Torino) in 1899, saw it grow into one of the weightiest industrial complexes in the world, and maintained personal control until his death in 1945. Fabricators of lesser puissance but great repute were Lancia, Alfa Romeo, Maserati, and Ferrari, for years the standard against which other Grand Prix and Gran Turismo motorcars were judged.

The Grand Prix and Gran Turismo cars

The smaller European nations produced makes that were to remain less well known: the Belgian Minerva, Métallurgique, and Excelsior; the Swiss Martini; the Austrian Austro-Daimler, Steyr, Gräf, and Stift; and the Czechoslovakian Skoda and Tatra, the latter technically interesting for its big (V-8) rear-mounted engine. Spain had the Elizalde, and the classic Hispano-Suiza by the great Swiss designer Marc Birkigt was Spanish financed. Curiously, what some authorities believe to be the oldest automobile still in running order early in the 1970s was an 1886 Hammel, made in Denmark.

Early efforts in the United States. The Daimler–Benz claim to the invention of the automobile was attacked in 1895 when U.S. patent 549,160 was granted to George B. Selden as inventor of the automobile. Selden had filed on May 8, 1879, although he had not at that time built an automobile. He was successful in an effort to keep the patent pending for 16 years.

Some authorities credit Charles E. and J. Frank Duryea with creating the first American gasoline-powered automobile, in 1892–93. The idea for the car apparently

Figure 14: Duryea, 1893, a one-cylinder gasoline engine with electrical ignition.
By courtesy of the Montagu Motor Museum, Beaulieu, Hampshire

originated with Charles, and the machine was built by Frank. The Duryea consisted of a one-cylinder gasoline engine, with electrical ignition, installed in a secondhand carriage. It ran first on September 21, 1893. Driving a later model, J. Frank Duryea won the first automobile race in America in which more than two cars competed, the *Chicago Times-Herald* Race from Chicago to Evanston, Illinois, and return, in November 1895; the distance was 54.36 miles (87.47 kilometres). Duryea cars remained on the market until 1917. Despite this, many historians are convinced that the Duryea was not the first U.S. internal-combustion automobile and that this distinction should be assigned to a car built in 1890 and run in 1891 by John William Lambert of Ohio City, Ohio.

The Duryea was certainly not the first U.S.-built road vehicle. A number of steam carriages had been built after Oliver Evans' first example. In March 1863 the magazine *Scientific American* described tests of a vehicle that weighed only 650 pounds (about 300 kilograms) and achieved a speed of 20 miles (30 kilometres) per hour. Another American, Frank Curtis of Newburyport, Massachusetts, is remembered for building a personal steam carriage to the order of a Boston man who failed to meet the payment schedule, whereupon Curtis made the first recorded repossession of a motor vehicle.

The U.S. Patent Office issued patents in September 1889 and April 1893 for three-wheeled gasoline-engine carriages, and Gottfried Scholemer of Milwaukee, Wisconsin, in

By courtesy of the Lambert Corp.

Figure 15: The Lambert, 1891, a gasoline-driven, single-cylinder automobile with a maximum speed of 15 miles per hour.

1890 built a successful car that still exists. A machinist of Allentown, Pennsylvania, in 1899 produced an automobile that ran quite well despite its dependence on the most primitive possible carburetor: a wooden wick that delivered fuel to the cylinder by capillary attraction. Charles Black in 1891, aided by Elwood Haynes, constructed a car in Indianapolis, Indiana, and Haynes followed the Duryea brothers with a gasoline car demonstrated in Kokomo, Indiana, on July 4, 1894. Charles Brady King built a car in Detroit, the first of the millions to issue from the city, that first ran on March 6, 1896.

Ransom Eli Olds, whose name survives in the Oldsmobile, was active in gasoline-engine research in the 1890s, after initially being interested in steam; so were Alexander Winton and James Ward Packard. By 1898 there were more than 50 automobile companies in existence—although the name automobile had not been settled upon (also considered were motor fly, diamote, automotive, autometon, mocole, oleo locomotive, motorig, bolvite, locomotive car, autobaine, autokenetic, and electrobat).

The first commercially successful U.S. car

The three-horsepower, curved-dash Oldsmobile was the first commercially successful American-made automobile: 425 of them were sold in 1901 and 5,000 in 1904 (the model is still prized by collectors), and the firm prospered. Its prosperity was noted by others, and, from 1904 to 1908, 241 automobile-manufacturing firms went into business in the U.S. One of these was the Ford Motor Company, which was organized as a corporation in June 1903 and sold its first car on the following July 23; the company produced 1,700 cars during its first full year of business.

By courtesy of Oldsmobile Division

Figure 16: Oldsmobile, 1903, curved dash.

Electric power. At the turn of the century, 40 percent of U.S. automobiles were powered by steam, 38 percent by electricity, and 22 percent by gasoline. In the face of the gasoline car's unreliability, noise, and vibration and the steamer's complications and thirst, the electric offered attractive selling points: notably, instant self-starting, silence, and minimal maintenance. The first automobile to exceed 100 kilometres (60 miles) an hour was an electric (Camille Jenatzy's La Jamais Contente, 1899). An electric, also Jenatzy's, had been the easy winner in 1898 of a French hill-climb contest to assay the three forms of power.

Invention of the storage battery, by Gaston Planté of France in 1859–60, and its improvement by Camille Faure in 1881 made the electric vehicle possible, and what was probably the first, a tricycle, ran in Paris in 1881. It was followed by other three-wheelers in London, 1882, and Boston, 1888. The first American battery-powered automobile, built in Des Moines, Iowa, in 1890, could maintain a speed of 14 miles (23 kilometres) per hour.

The peak year of the electric's acceptance was 1912, when 20 companies were in the trade and 33,842 cars were registered in the United States, the country in which the electric car had maximum acceptance. It was another application of battery power, the electric self-starter, that did as much as anything to doom the electric car by eliminating the dreaded hand crank and making the internal-combustion engine car amenable to operation by women. Further, the electric had never been really suited to any but limited urban use because of low speed (15–20 miles [24–32 kilometres] per hour), short range (30–40 miles [50–65 kilometres]), and dependence on recharging equipment.

The electric came in for its share of attention during the general re-examination of the automobile following World War II; many variations on the theme were proposed, and a number of vehicles were constructed and marketed. The problems of battery weight, low speed, and short range were not notably diminished, however, and new forms of battery—tubular lead-acid, silver peroxide-zinc, cobalt, ceramic—were expensive, exotic, or dangerous. Manufacturers of gasoline-powered cars resisted proposals on electric propulsion on the grounds that, like the steam car, it posed technical problems of such complexity that solutions to them would require large expenditure and many years.

Resistance to electric cars

Universal changeover to the electric automobile, seriously proposed in some quarters as an antipollution imperative, would have vast effects on the world's economy. The electric car is extraordinarily durable, is mechanically almost trouble-free, cannot support a host of accessories, and uses almost no oil, but would impose a serious demand on the world's electric-power system, much of which is fossil fuelled.

Ford and the automotive revolution. Henry Ford produced eight versions of cars before the Model T of 1908, with which his name is synonymous; these were the models A, B, C, F, K, N, R, and S. They were not remarkable automobiles, but public response to the less expensive ones (the firm made some fairly costly cars at first) indicated the soundness of Ford's idea—to turn the automobile from a luxury and a plaything into a necessity by making it cheap, versatile, and easy to maintain.

Within two decades, the American automobile had won the revolution Henry Ford had begun. The country was on wheels, and the manufacture and sale of the automobile were a main prop under the U.S. economy. The closed car was no longer exclusively a rich's man possession. In 1920 most cars had been open models, the occupants protected from the weather by canvas-and-isinglass side curtains; 10 years later Detroit was producing closed models almost exclusively.

The 1920s saw also the emergence of the great European producers, Austin, Morris, Singer, Fiat, Citroën, companies founded between 1906 and 1919, as the Ford doctrine was carried forward on the Continent and elsewhere. Universal motor transportation was a long way off, but the concept of the small car that arose in the Austin Seven and the Fiat Topolino, to name two of the descendants of Ettore Bugatti's tiny Bébé Peugeot of 1911, was to have a profound effect.

Age of the classic cars. The decade 1925–35 was notable not only for the appearance of many new small automobiles; it also saw the building of many ultralarge ones. The years from 1925 to 1942 are cited by collectors of automobiles as the classic years, a period that saw the rise of the luxurious fast motorcar to a peak it seemed unlikely to reach again.

The first name in this field was Rolls-Royce, founded in 1904. Most Rolls-Royce chassis are designed for limousine and large sedan bodies, but the firm once made a comparatively light car (called the Twenty), and it has throughout its history produced fast models in addition to its regular

Rolls-Royce and Bentley

By courtesy of the Ford Motor Company

Figure 17: Ford, 1909 Model T, which featured a brass radiator, four-cylinder engine cast in one piece, and a detachable cylinder head.

line; *e.g.,* after World War II, the Continental, built under the Bentley Motors Ltd. label.

Other motorcars of this type included the Hispano-Suiza of Spain and France; Bugatti, Delage, Delahaye, Hotchkiss, Talbot (Darracq), and Voisin of France; the Duesenberg, Cadillac, Packard, and Pierce-Arrow of the United States; the Horch, Maybach, and Mercedes-Benz of Germany; the Belgian Minerva; and the Italian Isotta-Fraschini. These were costly machines, priced roughly from $7,500 to $40,000; fast, at 90 to 130 miles (140 to 210 kilometres) per hour and as comfortable as the state of the art would allow; and limited in luxury only by the purse of the purchaser. The great custom coach builders of England who furnished bodies for Rolls-Royce machines, unruffled by the whims of their clients, were prepared to satisfy any request, whether for upholstery in matched ostrich hide with ivory buttons or for a dashboard in rosewood.

The most expensive standard automobile of which there exists convincing record was the Type 41 Bugatti, produced in the 1920s by Ettore Bugatti, an Italian of extraordinary gifts who built cars in France, most of them racing and sports types, from 1909 to 1939. The Type 41 Bugatti, also called La Royale, was cataloged at a chassis price of 500,000 francs, about $20,000. Only six of the cars were built, and one of them, carrying a four-passenger convertible sedan body by a German coach maker, cost $43,000.

The market collapse of 1929 ended the era of the really luxurious motorcar. After World War II even Rolls-Royce abandoned its long-held policy of producing a standard chassis with custom-made bodies and offered a standard sedan that could be bought straight off the showroom floor. Custom bodies were still available to Rolls-Royce purchasers through the old-line suppliers, of course. In 1971 an overextension of Rolls-Royce's aeroengine division put the company into receivership and resulted in nationalization and a separate corporate entity for the profit-making automobile division, which continued in production without interruption.

The antique car

A few hundred persons in the 1930s were seriously interested in the collection of antique automobiles, purchasing pre-World War I specimens for $10, $25, $50—or the trouble of towing them away from a junkyard. Distaste for the mechanically dull and stylistically unpleasant 1946–50 U.S. cars attracted many Americans to the hobby, prices rose, and membership in concerned organizations such as the Antique Automobile Club of America increased. In 1951 the Museum of Modern Art in New York held an exhibition of the automobile as art object that notably influenced opinion molders. Publications devoted to the automobile proliferated; the old European idea of the *concours d'élégance* (competition in design elegance) began to be reflected in formal showings of fine pre-1939 motorcars. Shops specializing in the restoration of old automobiles were set up, and the best of them were soon booked months ahead. Collectors worked over primary sources so heavily that the discovery of a desirable car tucked away in a forgotten corner of a barn became rare indeed, and interest in the automobile as a hedge against inflation drove prices steeply upward. For example, a 1913 Mercer Raceabout, which had cost $1,250 in 1951, appreciated, in 20 years, to $45,000, and a 1936 Bugatti, $5,000 in 1954, fetched $59,000 at an auction in Los Angeles in June 1971. An offer of $50,000 for a 1933 Duesenberg was thought risible.

But rare motorcars were increasingly being taken off the market by museums; the first of which to do so may have been the Dangerfield Museum set up in England in 1912. The Harrah Collection in Reno, Nevada, became by far the largest, with about 1,350 vehicles, and, by many standards, incomparably the best of the world's 170-odd motorcar museums. The Montagu Motor Museum in England, the Museo dell'Automobile Carlo Biscaretti di Ruffia in Italy, and the Daimler–Benz Museum in Germany house superb collections, and there are many splendid smaller exhibits throughout Europe.

Developments after World War II. The effect of Italian ideas on the world's automobile-body designers was profound when manufacture began to be resumed in 1946. Pininfarina of Turin was the best known of the coach makers who established the characteristic Italian approach: grace, lightness in line and substance, and minimal use of decoration. Designs clearly derivative of those of Italian origin appeared everywhere, and manufacturers in France, England, and the United States contracted for the services of Italian *carrozzerie* (body factories).

The trend toward the small automobile in the United States, clear if not obtrusive after 1932, was strongly accelerated by World War II. A leading factor was the return from duty in Europe of servicemen who had previously not known of the existence of the sheer variety of automobiles the world afforded. The sports car, designed for pleasure, not transport, was particularly new to young Americans. The characteristics of automobiles such as the British sports two-seater M.G., plus their availability at a time of short domestic supply, made them attractive, and the importation of European-made models into the U.S. increased rapidly.

Auto racing as a major sport

At this time, automobile racing, which in the Vanderbilt Cup days around 1910 had drawn the biggest crowds in U.S. sports history, began to regain popularity. By 1954 motor racing had become a high-ranking American spectator sport, and by 1969 estimated attendance was 41,300,000, higher than that for baseball or football. Only horse racing showed a total higher than auto racing. In the 1950s and 1960s, U.S. manufacturers returned to racing as exploitation (a standard practice 1900–30); Ford was most successful, winning the Le Mans 24-hour Grand Prix d'Endurance race—the first U.S.-built car to do so—in 1966 and 1967 and producing, in a remarkably short time, a racing engine that dominated major U.S. tracks.

While the size of the standard U.S. motorcar increased steadily from the late 1940s to the early 1960s, and its design seemed to many to become even more bizarre, a small segment of the population was demonstrating a preference for smaller cars and for comparatively uncluttered styling. The success of the German Volkswagen and other small cars eventually led the major U.S. producers simultaneously to undertake the production of automobiles generically termed compact. At around 110-inch (280-centimetre) wheelbase, they were smaller than most U.S. cars, bigger than the average European models. By the mid-1960s a demand for more highly individualized luxury models of compact size had brought in the "fastback," a two-door coupé with roof line extending in a continuous curve to a rear bumper, a design reflecting the European tradition of simpler, cleaner lines. Not only in design but also in more basic engineering problems, much U.S. experimentation followed research begun by the European industry: development of gas turbine engines; experimentation with fuel-injection systems; disk brakes; return to body-and-frame assembly; introduction of rear-engine and later, conversely, of front-wheel-drive models.

In Europe and Japan, which became a major producer in the 1960s, the small car continued to dominate, though the number of larger automobiles increased. In the United States the market remained significantly influenced by European small-car design, and a new generation of "really small" cars appeared.

Another trend in popular taste discernible by the early 1970s was a fad among young people, especially in California. Young Californians, whose fads had often presaged trends, began to lose interest in the high acceleration and top-speed characteristics that had preoccupied them since the 1930s and were shopping the used-cars lots for vans, which they transformed into mobile recreation rooms and ran sedately at legal speeds. (K.W.P.)

MODERN AUTOMOTIVE SYSTEMS

The modern automobile is a complex technical system composed of more than 14,000 parts. The subsystems that comprise the complete vehicle have evolved over many decades and include the body, or passenger compartment; the engine, or power source; the chassis, or framework supporting the engine and body; a system of shafts and gears (transmission) for transmitting power from the engine to the wheels; braking and steering mechanisms; cooling and electrical systems; fuel and lubrication; and an increasingly sophisticated group of accessories.

Between 25,000,000 and 30,000,000 automobiles a year were being produced throughout the world in the 1970s. While the number of manufacturers was declining, the number of designs and models was proliferating. In an effort to increase effectiveness, cars were being engineered for longer production runs to utilize tooling more fully. Specific designs for individual segments of the market—subcompact, compact, sporty, intermediate, regular, and luxury—have been more successful. Firms with less capital have developed designs to meet particular needs. By late 1970 there were 243,000,000 cars, trucks, and buses in the world.

Motorists in the United States in the early 1970s numbered about half the world's total and drove about 1,000,000,000,000 miles each year, one-fifth of that total at speeds of 60 to 70 miles (100 to 110 kilometres) per hour on limited-access express highways linking major cities of the nation. Similar road networks and driving patterns were emerging in other industrialized nations. Vehicle stability and properly selected, manufactured, and assembled vehicle components are important in highway driving. Vehicle stability depends principally upon the distribution of weight between the front and rear wheels, the height of the centre of gravity and its position relative to the aerodynamic centre of pressure of the vehicle, suspension characteristics, and whether front or rear wheels are used for propulsion. Weight distribution depends principally upon the location and size of the engine. The common practice of front-mounted engines exploits the stability that is more readily achieved with this layout. The development of aluminum and magnesium engines and new manufacturing processes have, however, made it possible to locate the engine at the rear without necessarily compromising stability.

Stability and weight distribution

Bodies. Automotive body styles are frequently categorized according to the number of doors in the body and the manner in which the roof is supported. Automobile roofs are conventionally supported by three pillars on each side of the body. Convertible models with retractable fabric tops rely upon the pillar at the side of the windshield for upper body strength, as convertible mechanisms and glass areas are essentially nonstructural. Beginning in 1956, automotive stylists sought to increase the openness of conventional bodies by eliminating the side pillar behind the front door. This became known as hardtop styling, and the two-door hardtop was the most popular body style in 1970.

The high cost of new tools makes it impractical for manufacturers to produce totally new designs every year. New designs are usually programmed on three- to six-year cycles with generally minor refinements appearing during the cycle. As much as four years of planning and new tool purchasing is needed for a completely new design.

Automotive bodies are generally formed out of sheet steel. Elements are added to the alloy to improve its ability to be formed into deeper depressions without wrinkling or tearing in manufacturing presses. Steel is used because of its general availability, low cost, and good workability. For special applications, however, other materials, such as aluminum and fibre-glass-reinforced plastic, are used because of their special properties. Plastics have low ductility (are more brittle) in comparison with the same weight of steel or aluminum. Therefore, they are used in generally nonstructural areas.

To protect bodies from corrosive elements and to maintain their strength and appearance, special priming and painting processes are used. Bodies are first dipped in cleaning baths to remove oil and other foreign matter. They then go through a succession of dip and spray cycles. Enamel and acrylic lacquer are both in common use. Electrodeposition of the sprayed paint, a process in which the paint spray is given an electrostatic charge and then attracted to the surface by a high voltage, helps assure that an even coat is applied and that hard-to-reach areas are covered. Ovens with conveyor lines are used to speed the drying process in the factory.

Chassis. The chassis of the modern automobile is the main structure of the vehicle. In most designs a pressed-steel frame forms a skeleton on which the engine, wheels, axle assemblies, transmission, steering mechanism, brakes, and suspension members are mounted. The body is flexibly bolted to the chassis during the manufacturing process. The combination of body and frame absorbs the reactions from the movements of the engine and axle, receives the reaction forces of the wheels in acceleration and braking, absorbs aerodynamic wind forces and road shocks through the suspension, and absorbs the energy of impact in the event of an accident.

Since the 1930s there has been a trend toward combining the chassis frame and the body into a single structural element. In this arrangement the steel body shell is reinforced with braces that make it rigid enough to resist the forces which are applied to it. While this arrangement has been almost universally adopted for small cars, there has been a return to separate frames for other cars in order to achieve better noise-isolation characteristics and simplified tooling for body changes. The presence of a heavy-gauge frame member at the perimeter of the body also tends to limit intrusion in accidents.

Engines. A wide range of energy-conversion systems has been used experimentally and in automotive production. These include electric, steam, solar, turbine, rotary, and a variety of piston-type internal-combustion engines. The most successful for automobiles has been the reciprocating-piston internal-combustion engine, operating on a four-stroke cycle, while diesel engines are widely used for trucks and buses. The gasoline engine was originally selected for automobiles because it could operate more flexibly over a wide range of speeds and the power developed for a given weight engine was reasonable, it could be produced by economical mass-production methods, and it used a readily available, moderately priced fuel—gasoline. Reliability, compact size, and range of operation later became important factors.

Predominance of gasoline engines

Beginning in the 1960s there has been a reassessment of these priorities with new emphasis on the pollution-producing characteristics of automotive power systems. This has created new interest in alternate power sources, but by 1972 there were no commercially successful replacements for the gasoline engine, which had developed new emission-control devices to improve its emission performance.

The pollutants requiring control include hydrocarbons that are unburned fuel compounds, carbon monoxide, and oxides of nitrogen. It was estimated in 1970 that automotive emissions produced 39 percent of the national tonnage of pollution in the United States, a proportion that was being reduced as old cars were replaced by new ones with better control systems.

In the late 1940s a trend began to increase engine horsepower, particularly in United States models. Design changes incorporated all known methods of increasing engine capacity, including increasing the pressure in the cylinders to improve efficiency, increasing the size of the engine, and increasing the speed at which power is generated.

The higher dynamic forces and pressures created by these changes created engine vibration and size problems that led to stiffer, more compact engines with V and opposed cylinder layouts replacing longer straight-line arrangements. In passenger cars, V-8 layouts were adopted for all piston displacements greater than 250 cubic inches (four litres).

The advent of smaller cars brought a return to smaller engines, four- and six-cylinder designs rated as low as 80 horsepower, compared with the standard-size V-8 of large cylinder bore and relatively short piston stroke with horsepower ratings in the range from 250 to 350.

European automobile engines were of a much wider variety, ranging from one to 12 cylinders, with corresponding differences in overall size, weight, piston displacement, and cylinder bores. A majority of the models had four cylinders and horsepower ratings from 19 to 120. Several three-cylinder, two-stroke-cycle models were built. Most engines had straight or in-line cylinders. There were, however, several V-type models and horizontally opposed two- and four-cylinder makes. Overhead camshafts were frequently employed. The smaller engines were commonly air cooled

Multiplicity of engine types

and located at the rear of the vehicle; compression ratios were relatively low.

Fuel and lubrication. Gasoline is essentially the only fuel used for automobile operation, although diesel fuels are used for many trucks and buses and a few automobiles. The most important requirements of a fuel for automobile use are proper volatility, sufficient antiknock quality, and freedom from polluting by-products of combustion. The volatility is adjusted seasonally by refiners so that sufficient gasoline vaporizes, even in extreme cold weather, to permit the engine to be started but without being so volatile that vapour lock (a bubble of vapour that blocks gasoline flow) will prevent proper functioning of the fuel system at the highest outdoor temperatures encountered.

Antiknock qualities are controlled by refining processes that produce compact, stable molecules instead of long, straight-chain molecules. Antiknock compounds, principally tetraethyl lead, are added to some gasolines as a more economic way of attaining the same result. Small deposits of lead on such places as engine-valve seats serve to improve valve life. These same deposits, however, can contaminate certain emission-pollution-control systems such as catalytic converters. Antiknock quality is rated by the octane number of the gasoline. The octane-number requirement of an automobile engine depends primarily upon the compression ratio of the engine but is also affected by combustion-chamber design and deposits formed on the chamber walls. Various additives intended to minimize the effects of deposits are used in most automotive gasolines. No advantage is gained by using a fuel of octane number higher than that necessary to eliminate objectionable knock. In the early 1970s regular gasoline carried an octane rating of around 93 and high-test in the neighbourhood of 100. All moving parts of an automobile require lubrication. Without it, friction would increase power consumption and damage the parts. The lubricant also serves as a coolant, a noise-reducing cushion, and a sealant between engine piston rings and cylinder walls.

The engine lubrication system consists of an oil sump and a gear-type pump that delivers the oil under pressure to a system of drilled passages leading to various bearings. Drilled passages in the crankshaft conduct oil to lubricate the connecting-rod bearings, and leakage from these bearings sprays oil up into the cylinder bores to lubricate the pistons, piston pins, and piston rings. The spray also lubricates the cams and valve lifters. Usually the oil passes through a paper or cotton-waste filter before it enters the distribution passages; bypass filters sometimes are used to receive a small stream of oil from the system continuously and return it to the sump after removing any solids.

Engine oils

Engine oils may be identified by letters designating the severity of service for which the oil is suitable and by numbers indicating the viscosity range. Selection of the proper oil depends upon the conditions under which it will be used—for example, continuous high speeds, heavy loads, frequent starts and stops—and engine components such as hydraulic valve lifters that are sensitive to oil condition.

Wheel bearings and universal joints require a fairly stiff grease; other chassis joints require a soft grease that can be injected by pressure guns. Hydraulic transmissions require a special grade of light hydraulic fluid, and manually shifted transmissions use a heavier gear oil similar to that for rear axles. Hypoid gears used in most rear axles require oils that are compounded to resist heavy loads on the gear teeth. Gears and bearings in lightly loaded components, such as generators and window regulators, are fabricated from self-lubricating plastic materials.

Cooling system. The vast majority of automobiles employ liquid cooling systems for their engines. A typical automotive cooling systems comprises (1) a series of channels cast into the engine block and cylinder head, surrounding the combustion chambers with circulating water or other coolant to carry away excessive heat; (2) a radiator, consisting of many small tubes equipped with a honeycomb of fins to radiate heat rapidly, that receives and cools hot liquid from the engine; (3) a water pump, usually of the centrifugal type, to circulate coolant through the system; (4) a thermostat, which maintains constant temperature by automatically varying the amount of coolant passing into the radiator; and (5) a fan, which draws fresh air through the radiator.

For operation at outdoor temperatures below freezing, it is necessary to prevent the coolant from freezing. This is usually done by adding some compound to depress the freezing point of the coolant. Alcohol formerly was commonly used, but it has a relatively low boiling point and evaporates quite easily, making it less desirable than organic compounds with a high boiling point, such as ethylene glycol. By varying the amount of additive, it is possible to protect against freezing of the coolant down to any minimum temperature normally encountered.

Air cooling offers the important advantage of eliminating not only freezing and boiling of the coolant at temperature extremes but also corrosion damage to the cooling system. Control of engine temperature is more difficult, however, and the engine temperature is more likely to vary with the outside temperature. Air-cooled cylinders operate at higher, more efficient temperatures, but compression ratios (with the same fuels) must be lower, because combustion control is more difficult. In addition, it is more difficult to utilize engine heat to warm the car interior during winter. In spite of these disadvantages, in the early 1970s a sizable number of cars with air-cooled motors were being manufactured.

With the aim of eliminating seasonal draining of liquid cooling systems, manufacturers in the later 1950s and early 1960s introduced liquid coolants intended to replace water-antifreeze mixtures. These contained corrosion inhibitors that were designed to make it necessary to drain and refill the cooling system only once a year.

Permanent coolants

Other compounds under development in the early 1960s, some of which were organic silicates, contained no water and were permanent in characteristics. Such liquids permit the cooling system to be sealed and require no attention. The ultimate practicability of these permanent coolants depends upon their ability to carry heat away from the engine. All previously known liquids with appropriate boiling and freezing points were poorer than water in this respect and so were not as effective as engine coolants.

Pressurized cooling systems with operating pressures up to 14 pounds per square inch (10,000 kilograms per square metre) have been used to increase effective operating temperatures. Partially sealed systems using coolant reservoirs for coolant expansion if the engine overheats were introduced in 1970.

Electrical system. Originally, the electrical system of the automobile was limited to the ignition equipment. With the advent of the electrical starter on a 1912 model, electric lights and horns began to replace the kerosene and acetylene lights and the bulb horns. Electrification was rapid and complete, and by 1930 six-volt systems were standard everywhere. The electrical system comprises a storage battery, generator, or dynamo, starting (cranking) motor, lighting system, ignition system, and various accessories and controls.

Increased engine speeds and higher cylinder pressures of the post-World War II cars made it increasingly difficult to meet high ignition voltage requirements. The larger engines required higher cranking torque. Additional electrically operated features, such as radios, window regulators, and multispeed windshield wipers, also added to system requirements. To meet these needs, 12-volt systems generally replaced the six-volt systems in 1956 production.

The ignition system provides the spark to ignite the air–fuel mixture in the cylinders of the engine. In order to jump the gap between the electrodes of the spark plugs, the 12-volt potential of the electrical system must be stepped up to about 20,000 volts. This is done by a circuit that starts with the battery, one side of which is grounded on the chassis and leads through the ignition switch to the primary winding of the ignition coil and back to the ground through an interrupter switch, or circuit breaker. Interrupting the primary circuit induces a high voltage across the secondary of the coil. The high-voltage secondary terminal of the coil leads to a distributor that acts as a rotary switch, alternately connecting the coil to each of the wires leading to the spark plugs. The system consists of the spark plugs, contact breaker, coil, distributor, and battery.

The source of electrical energy for the various electrical devices of the automobile is a generator, or dynamo, that is belt driven from the engine crankshaft. The generator is usually a two-pole, direct-current type with a field controlled by a voltage regulator the function of which is to match the generator output to the electrical load and also to the charging requirements of the battery, regardless of engine speed. High-wattage electrical loads, resulting from the addition of many electrical accessories, has made it increasingly difficult to design direct-current generators with sufficiently high capacity to maintain the battery in a fully charged condition. Alternating-current generators, or alternators, with built-in rectifiers were introduced in 1958 to provide for these loads.

The generator

A lead-acid battery serves as a reservoir to store excess output of the generator by chemical changes in the sulfuric acid electrolyte and in the composition of the lead plates. Energy for the starting motor is thus made available along with power for operating other electrical devices when the engine is not running or when the generator speed is not sufficiently high to carry the load (see also ENERGY CONVERSION: *Batteries and fuel cells*).

The starting motor drives a small spur gear so arranged that it automatically moves into mesh with gear teeth on the rim of the flywheel as the starting-motor armature begins to turn. When the engine starts, the small gear is disengaged, thus preventing damage to the starting motor from overspeeding. The starting motor is designed for high current consumption and delivers considerable power for its size for a limited time.

Headlights that satisfactorily illuminate the highway ahead of the automobile for night driving without temporarily blinding approaching drivers have long been sought. Early dimming devices of the resistance type, which decreased the brightness of the headlights when meeting another car, gave way to mechanical tilting reflectors and later to double-filament bulbs with a high and a low beam, called sealed-beam units.

The double-filament headlight unit of necessity has only one of its filaments at the focal point of the reflector. Because of the greater illumination required for highspeed driving with the high beam, the lower beam filament was placed off centre, with a resulting decrease in lighting effectiveness. In the 1950s some manufacturers began equipping their models with four headlights to improve illumination. In most instances the outer lamps were double-filament types with a high-wattage low beam and a "soft" high beam for city driving. The inner lamps have a single-filament high beam of high wattage that produces a spotlight effect. The low beam of the two outer lamps is focussed slightly to the right and is used when overtaking or meeting other vehicles. The high beams of all four lamps are used on the open highway when there is no approaching traffic. Dimming is automatically achieved on some cars by means of an automatic photocell-controlled switch in the lamp circuit that is triggered by the lights of an oncoming car. Larger diameter double-filament lamps with improved photometrics permitted a return to two-headlamp systems on some cars. Total intensity of forward lighting systems in many places is limited by law to 75,000 candlepower.

Signal lamps and other special-purpose lights increased in usage in the 1960s. Amber-coloured front and red rear signal lights are flashed as a turn indication; all these lights are flashed simultaneously in the "flasher" system for use when a car is parked along a roadway or is travelling at a low speed on a high-speed highway. Marker lights that are visible from the front, side, and rear are also widely required by law. Red-coloured rear signals are used to denote braking, and, on some models, cornering lamps to provide extra illumination in the direction of an intended turn are available. These are actuated in conjunction with the turn signals. Backup lights provide illumination to the rear when backing up.

Transmission. The gasoline engine must be disconnected from the load (the rear wheels) when it is started and when idling. This characteristic necessitates some type of unloading and engaging device to permit gradual application of load to the engine after it has been started. In starting the engine, the crankshaft is rotated (cranked) by an electric motor; this in turn starts action in the cylinders. The torque, or turning effort, that the engine is capable of producing is low at low crankshaft speeds, increasing to a maximum at some fairly high speed representing the maximum, or rated, horsepower.

The efficiency of an automobile engine is highest when the load on the engine is high and the throttle is nearly wide open. At moderate speeds on level pavement the power required to propel an automobile is only a portion of the power the engine is capable of developing in its upper range of speeds. Thus, under normal driving conditions at constant moderate speed, the engine may operate at an uneconomically light load unless some means is provided to reduce its speed and power output.

Engine efficiency

The transmission is such a speed-changing device. It is installed in the drive train that connects the crankshaft of the engine to the driving wheels. This permits the engine to operate at a higher speed when its full power is needed and to slow down to a more economical speed when less power is needed. Under some conditions, as in starting a stationary vehicle or in ascending steep grades, the torque of the engine is insufficient, and amplification is desirable. Most devices employed to change the ratio of the speed of the engine to the speed of the driving wheels multiply the engine torque by the same factor by which the engine speed is increased.

The simplest automobile transmission is the sliding-spurgear type with three or four forward speeds and reverse. The desired gear ratio is selected by manipulating a shift lever which slides a spur gear into the proper position to engage the various gears. Early devices of this type required considerable skill on the part of the operator to shift the gears smoothly and without clashing the teeth. The shift from low to second gear was the most troublesome, because this shift required that two gears, moving at different speeds, be slid sidewise into tooth engagement. This problem was eliminated by a constant-mesh second gear in which the driven gear of the train is not keyed to the driven shaft of the transmission. Second gear is engaged by means of a toothed or jaw clutch, similar to that used to engage direct drive, arranged so that it can keep the driven gear from turning on the driven shaft.

Ease of shifting into second and high was further improved by the use of synchronizing clutches that engaged ahead of the toothed clutches and caused the two portions of the positive clutch to turn in unison before their engaging teeth touched each other. Another device, a blocker ring, was added later; its function was to block the two members of the clutch from contacting each other before their speeds were synchronized. The only difficulty remaining in the operation of the sliding-gear transmission was the need for simultaneously operating the accelerator pedal, the clutch pedal, and the gearshift lever. The automatic transmission was developed to eliminate this manipulation. Most automatic transmissions employ either a fluid coupling or a hydraulic torque converter, a device for transmitting and amplifying the torque produced by the engine. One manufacturer, DAF of The Netherlands, uses a mechanical linkage. Each type provides for manual selection of reverse and a low range that either prevents automatic upshifts or employs a lower gear ratio than is used in normal driving. Grade-retard provisions are also sometimes included to provide engine braking on hills. By 1970 the hydraulic torque-converter-type automatic transmission dominated its field. In hydraulic transmissions, shifting is done by a speed-sensitive governing device that changes the position of valves that control the flow of hydraulic fluid. The vehicle speeds at which shifts occur depend upon the position of the accelerator pedal, and the driver can delay upshifts until higher speed is attained by depressing the accelerator pedal further. Control is by hydraulically engaged bands and multiple-disk clutches running in oil, either by the driver's operation of the selector lever or by a speed-sensitive governor. Compound planetary gear trains with multiple sun gears and planet pinions have been designed to provide a low forward speed, an intermediate speed, a reverse, and a means of locking into direct drive. This unit is used with various modifications in almost all hydraulic-torque-converter transmissions.

Hydraulic transmissions

In hydraulic-torque-converter transmissions, torque is multiplied by means of gear trains and a hydraulic member with three or more elements.

As shown schematically in Figure 18, oil in the housing is accelerated outward by rotating vanes in the pump impeller and, reacting against vanes in the turbine impeller, forces them to rotate. The oil then passes into the stator vanes, which redirect it to the pump. The stator serves

Adapted from *Automotive Industry* (October 1970)

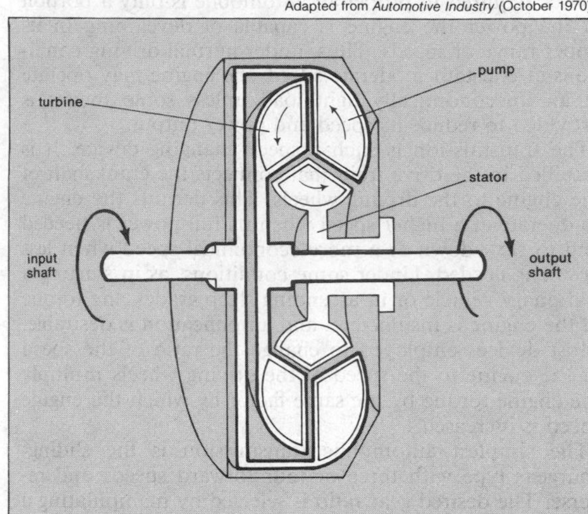

Figure 18: Torque converter.

as a reaction member providing more torque to turn the turbine than was originally applied to the pump impeller by the engine. Thus, it acts to multiply engine torque by a factor of up to $2^{1}/_{2}$ to 1.

Blades in all three elements are specially contoured for their specific function and to achieve particular multiplication characteristics. Through a clutch linkage, the stator is allowed gradually to accelerate until it reaches the speed of the pump impeller. During this period torque multiplication gradually drops to approach 1 to 1.

The hydraulic elements are combined with two or three planetary gear sets, which provide further torque multiplication between the turbine and the output shaft.

Automatic transmissions not only require no skill to operate but make possible better performance than is obtainable with transmissions that necessitate the release of a clutch during gear shifts. Power is applied to the driving wheels continuously whenever the accelerator pedal is depressed, and gears are shifted without closing the engine throttle or interrupting the drive.

Small, low-powered European cars usually have manually shifted, four-speed transmissions. Power-operated clutches are sometimes used in combination with pre-selective or semi-automatic transmissions. Fully automatic transmissions are used for the most part in larger cars with ratings above 60 horsepower.

Other mechanical subsystems. *Axles.* Power is conveyed from the transmission to the rear axle by a propeller shaft and universal joints. As body lines were progressively lowered, the floor level came closer to the propeller shaft, necessitating floor humps or tunnels to provide clearance. The adoption of hypoid or offset spiral bevel gears in the rear axle provided an increase in this clearance by lowering the drive pinion below the center of the axle shafts.

The differential

The ring gear of the rear axle surrounds the housing of a differential gear train that serves as an equalizer in dividing the torque between the two driving wheels while permitting one to turn faster than the other when rounding corners. The axle shafts terminate in bevel gears that are connected by several smaller bevel gears mounted on radial axles attached to the differential housing and carried around with it by the ring gear. In its simplest form this differential has the defect that one driving wheel may spin when it loses traction, and the torque applied to the wheel, being equal to that of the slipping wheel, will not be sufficient to drive the car. Several differentials have been developed to overcome this difficulty.

European manufacturers quite generally adopted a wide variety of articulated rear axles that provide individual wheel suspension at the rear as well as the front. Individual rear suspension not only eliminates the heavy rear axle housing but also permits lowered bodies with no floor humps, because the transmission and differential gears can be combined in a housing mounted on a rear cross member moving with the body under suspension-spring action.

In some instances, European manufacturers use articulated or swing axles similar to American rear axles except that the tubular housings surrounding the axle shafts terminate in spherical head segments that fit into matching sockets formed in the sides of the central gear housing. Universal joints within the spherical elements permit the axle shafts to move with the actions of the suspension springs. The gear housing is supported by a rear cross member of the chassis and moves with the sprung portion of the vehicle, as does the drive shaft. Other types eliminate the axle shaft housings and drive the wheels through two open axle shafts, each fitted with two universal joints. The wheels are then individually supported by radius rods or other suitable linkage.

The driving trains for rear engine, rear-wheel-drive cars and front engine, front-wheel-drive cars are simplified by individually supported wheels in that a combined transmission and differential assembly can form a unit with the engine. Two short transverse drive shafts, each having universal joints at both ends, transmit power to the wheels. In this case there is no axle as such, and the wheels may be individually suspended. Front-wheel-drive vehicles built in the United States since 1966 have, however, employed solid rear axles.

Brakes. Most automobile brakes are of the internally expanding shoe type, in which two nearly semicircular brake shoes are pressed against the inner surface of a drum attached to the wheel. Until the 1930s, most brake systems were of the mechanical type; *i.e.,* foot pressure exerted on the brake pedal was carried directly to the brake shoes by a system of flexible cables. Mechanical brakes, however, are difficult to keep adjusted so that equal braking force is applied at each wheel; and, as vehicle weights and speeds increased, more and more effort on the brake pedal was demanded of the driver.

Hydraulic brakes

Mechanical brakes have been almost universally supplanted by hydraulic braking systems, in which the brake pedal is connected to a piston in a master cylinder and thence by steel tubing with flexible sections to individual cylinders at the wheels. Front and rear hydraulic circuits are separated. The wheel cylinders are located between the movable ends of the brake shoes, and each is fitted with two pistons that are forced outward toward the ends of the cylinder by the pressure of the fluid between them. As these pistons move outward, they push the brake shoes against the inner surface of the brake drum attached to the wheel. The larger diameter of the piston in the master cylinder provides a hydraulic force multiplication at the wheel cylinder that reduces the effort required of the driver.

Further increases in vehicle weights and speeds in the 1950s made even hydraulic brakes difficult for drivers to operate effectively, and many of the larger automobiles consequently were equipped with power brake systems. These are virtually the same as the hydraulic system except that the piston of the master cylinder is operated by a vacuum piston and cylinder instead of by the pressure exerted on the brake pedal (see Figure 19). The master cylinder and vacuum power cylinder are formed in one unit. When the driver starts to depress the brake pedal, the control valve closes the atmospheric ports. Further movement of the valve opens the vacuum port connecting the vacuum inlet to the cylinder chamber at the left of the piston. The vacuum inlet pipe leads to the intake manifold, and, when the vacuum valve opens the port, a vacuum is formed on the left side of the power piston. Atmospheric pressure acting on the right side of the piston causes it to move to the left. Plungers in the master cylinder cover the compensating ports and place the hydraulic brake fluid under pressure in the wheel cylinders. As the brake-fluid pressure builds up, the control valve is pushed back. If the pedal is not depressed further, the vacuum port will close,

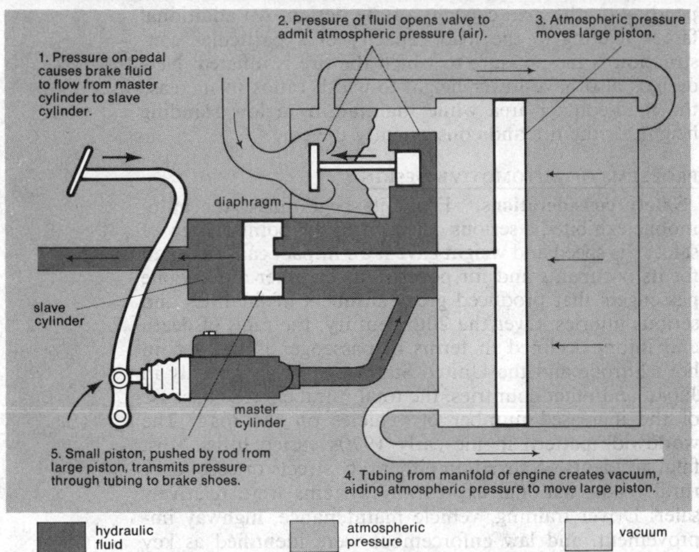

Figure 19: Schematic cross section of vacuum-actuated power brake.

By courtesy of F.E. Compton Co.

and the brakes will be held in application until the pedal is released. The amount of brake-fluid pressure depends upon how far the pedal is depressed; the driver feels a resistance to pedal movement proportional to the fluid pressure actuating the brakes. The force he must exert is much smaller, however, than is necessary with ordinary brakes, and no appreciable physical effort is necessary to apply the brakes fully.

Overheating of the brake drums and shoes causes the brakes to fade and lose their effectiveness when held in engagement for a considerable length of time. This problem has been attacked by the use of aluminum cooling fins bonded to the outside of the brake drums to increase the rate of heat transfer to the air. Vents in the wheels are provided to increase the air circulation for cooling.

Disk brakes, originally developed for aircraft, have been fitted to some automobiles. Although there are some four-wheel systems, usually disks are mounted on the front wheels, and conventional drum-type units are retained at the rear. Disk designs are somewhat more costly but have become increasingly popular. They were fitted on 56 percent of all new cars in 1970. Each wheel has a hub-mounted disk and a brake unit or caliper rigidly attached to the suspension. The caliper employs two friction-pad assemblies, one on each side of the disk. When the brake is applied, hydraulic pressure forces the friction pads against the disk. This arrangement is self-adjusting, and the ability of the disks to dissipate heat rapidly in the open airstream makes them practically immune to fading.

Parking brakes

Parking brakes usually are of the mechanical type, applying force only to the rear brake shoes by means of a flexible cable connected to a hand lever or pedal. On cars with automatic transmissions, an additional lock is usually provided in the form of a pawl that can be engaged, by placing the shift lever in the "park" position, to prevent the drive shaft and rear wheels from turning.

Steering. Automobiles are steered by a system of gears and linkages that transmit the motion of the steering wheel to the pivoted front wheel hubs. The gear mechanism, located at the lower end of the shaft carrying the steering wheel, is usually a worm-and-nut or cam-and-lever combination that rotates a shaft with an attached crank arm through a small angle as the steering wheel is turned. Tie rods attached to the arm convey its motion to the wheels. In cornering, the inner wheel must turn through a slightly greater angle than the outer wheel, because the inner wheel negotiates a sharper turn. The geometry of the linkage is designed to provide for this.

When the front wheels are independently suspended, the steering must be designed so the wheels are not turned as the tie rods lengthen and shorten as a result of spring action. The point of linkage attachment to the steering gear must be placed so that it can move vertically with respect to the wheel mountings without turning the wheels.

The distribution of weight between the front and rear wheels of automobiles shifted toward the front as the engine and passenger compartment were moved forward to improve riding comfort and road-handling characteristics. As the weight carried on the front wheels increased to more than half of the total vehicle weight, the effort necessary to turn the wheels in steering increased. Larger, heavier cars with wider tires and lower tire pressure also contribute to drag between tires and road that must be overcome in steering, particularly in parking. It was originally considered satisfactory to limit the pull on the rim of the steering wheel to 30 pounds (14 kilograms), but this limit proved to be too high, particularly for women drivers. Considerable reduction in the work of steering resulted from increased efficiency of the steering gears and better bearings in the front wheel linkage. Additional ease of turning the steering wheel was accomplished by increasing the overall steering gear ratio (the number of degrees of steering-wheel turn required to turn the front wheels one degree). Large steering gear ratios make high-speed manoeuvrability more difficult, however, because the steering wheel must be turned through greater angles. On the other hand, steering mechanisms of higher efficiency are also more reversible; that is, road shocks are transmitted more completely from the wheels and must be overcome to a greater extent by the driver. This causes a dangerous situation on rough roads or when a front tire blows out, because the wheel may be jerked from the driver's hands.

Power steering gear was developed to solve the steadily increasing steering problems. Power steering was first applied to heavy trucks and military vehicles early in the 1930s, and hundreds of patents were granted for devices to help the driver turn the steering wheel. Most of the proposed devices were hydraulic; some were electrical and some mechanical. A pump driven by the engine maintains the hydraulic fluid under pressure. A valve with a sensing device allows the fluid to enter and leave the power cylinder as necessary.

Suspension systems. The suspended portion of the automobile is attached to the wheels by elastic members designed to cushion the impact of road irregularities. The nature of the attaching linkages and spring elements varies widely among United States, European, and Japanese automobiles. Riding comfort and the handling qualities of the vehicle are greatly affected by the functioning of the suspension system. Mechanical simplification is gained by connecting the front wheels with a rigid front axle just as the rear wheels are connected by the conventional rear axle housing. Several important advantages, however, are gained by so-called independent-suspension systems that permit the wheels to move independently of each other. The unsprung weight of the vehicle is decreased, softer springs are permissible, and front-wheel vibration problems are minimized. Independent front suspensions entirely replaced the rigid-axle type after World War II, and numerous independent rear suspensions came into use, first on European cars. Spring elements used for automobile suspension members, in increasing order of their ability to store elastic energy per unit of weight, are leaf springs, coil springs, torsion bars, rubber-in-shear devices, and air springs.

Independent suspension systems

The leaf spring, although comparatively inelastic, has the important advantage of accurately positioning the wheel with respect to the other chassis components, both laterally and fore and aft, without the aid of auxiliary linkages.

Some cars equipped with rear leaf springs employ a drive in which the axle housing is rigidly attached to the spring seats so that the driving torque reaction, the brake torque, and the driving force are all imparted to the spring. Those using rear coil springs may have a torque tube enclosing the drive shaft that takes these forces to its point of attachment at the front of the axle housing. A diagonal transverse rod connecting one outer end of the axle housing to the chassis frame at the opposite side is provided to position the axle laterally. Other types with open drive shafts provide for these forces by radius rods and other linkages.

An important factor in spring selection is the relationship between load and deflection known as spring rate, defined as the load in pounds divided by the deflection of the spring in inches. A soft spring has a low rate and deflects a greater distance under a given load. A coil or a leaf spring retains a substantially constant rate within its operating range of load and will deflect ten times as much if a force ten times as great is applied to it. The torsion bar, a long spring-steel element with one end held rigidly to the frame and the other twisted by a crank connected to the axle, can be designed to provide an increasing spring rate.

A soft-spring suspension provides a comfortable ride on a relatively smooth road, but the occupants move up and down excessively on a rough road. The springs must be stiff enough to prevent a large deflection at any time because of the difficulty in providing enough clearance between the sprung portion of the vehicle and the unsprung portion below the springs. Lower roof heights make it increasingly difficult to provide the clearance needed for soft springs. Road-handling characteristics also suffer because of what is known as sway, or roll, the sidewise tilting of the car body that results from centrifugal force acting outward on turns. The softer the suspension, the more the outer springs are compressed and the inner springs expanded. Front-end "dive" under brake action is more noticeable with soft front springs. Air springs offer several advantages over metal springs, one of the most important of which is the possibility of controlling the spring rate. Inherently, the force required to deflect the air unit increases with greater deflection, because the air is compressed into a smaller space, and greater pressure is built up, thus progressively resisting further deflection.

A combination hydraulic-fluid-and-air suspension system has been developed in which the elastic medium is a sealed-in, fixed mass of air, and no air compressor is required. The hydraulic portion of each spring is a cylinder mounted on the body sill and fitted with a plunger that is pivotally attached to the wheel linkage to form a hydraulic strut. Each spring cylinder has a spherical air chamber attached to its outer end. The sphere is divided into two chambers by a flexible diaphragm, the upper occupied by air and the lower by hydraulic fluid that is in communication with the hydraulic cylinder through a two-way restrictor valve. This valve limits the rate of movement of the plunger in the cylinder, since fluid must be pushed into the sphere when the body descends and returned when it rises. This damping action thus controls the motion of the wheel with respect to the sprung portion of the vehicle supported by the spring.

The amount of hydraulic fluid in each spring unit is varied by front and rear levelling valves that transfer fluid to and from a central hydraulic system in which pressure is maintained by an engine-driven pump. These leveling valves serve to maintain constant clearance between the wheels and the sprung portion of the vehicle under varying passenger and luggage load.

Tires. The pneumatic rubber tire is the point of contact between the automobile and the road surface. It functions to provide traction for acceleration and braking and limits the transmission of road vibrations to the automobile body. Inner tubes within tires were standard until the 1950s, when seals between the tire and the wheel were developed, leading to tubeless tires, now used almost universally.

Tire-tread design

Tire-tread designs are tailored for the characteristics of the surface on which the vehicle is intended to operate. Deep designs provide gripping action in loose soil and snow, while smooth surfaces provide maximum contact area for applications such as racing. Current passenger car treads are a compromise between these extremes.

A typical tire casing is fabricated from layers, or plies, of varying proportions of rubber compounds reinforced with synthetic fibres or steel wire. The composition of the reinforcement and the angle of its application to the axis of the tread affect the ability of the tire to respond to sidewise forces created during cornering. They also affect harshness or vibration-transmission characteristics.

By 1970, longitudinal-, bias-, and radial-ply constructions were in use, with layers of two, four, or more plies, depending on the load capacity of the design. An additional factor relating to the load capacity of a particular construction is the pressure to which the tire is inflated. New designs also have lower height-to-width ratios to increase the road-contact area while maintaining a low standing height for the tire and consequently the car.

PROBLEMS OF AUTOMOTIVE DESIGN

Safety considerations. From its beginnings, the automobile exhibited a serious defect from the point of view of safety. Its speed and weight gave it an impact capacity both for its occupants and for pedestrians or other automobile passengers that produced great numbers of fatalities and serious injuries. Over the 20th century, the rates of death and injury declined in terms of passenger miles, yet, in both Europe and the United States and more recently in Japan and other countries, the total numbers rose because of the increased number of vehicles on the road. The worldwide pattern in the early 1970s varied little. Most fatal accidents occurred on either city streets or secondary rural roads; national expressway systems were relatively safer. Driver training, vehicle maintenance, highway improvement, and law enforcement were identified as key areas with potential for improving safety, but the basic design of the vehicle itself and the addition of special safety features were receiving increasing attention. Safety features of automobiles come under two distinct headings: accident avoidance and occupant protection.

Accident avoidance. Accident-avoidance systems are designed to help the driver maintain better control of his car. The dual-master-cylinder brake system is a good example. This protects the driver against sudden loss of brake-line pressure. Front and rear brake lines are separated so that if one fails the other continues to function. This system is sometimes coupled with an indicator lamp on the instrument panel to warn the driver if one section of the brake circuit has a failure.

Occupant protection. Systems to protect occupants in the event of an accident fall into four major classes: maintenance of passenger-compartment integrity, occupant restraints, interior-impact energy-absorber systems, and exterior-impact energy absorbers. Statistics indicate a far higher chance for survival among accident victims remaining inside the passenger compartment. Passenger-compartment integrity depends significantly on the proper action of the doors, which must remain closed in the event of an accident and must be sufficiently secure to prevent intrusion. Door-latch mechanisms have been designed to resist forward, rearward, and sideward forces and incorporate two-stage catches, so that the latch may hold if the primary stage fails. Reinforcement beams in doors are designed to deflect impact forces downward to the more rigid frame structure below the door. Forces are directed through reinforced door pillars and hinges.

Occupant restraints are used to help couple the passenger to the car. They permit decelerating with the car rather than free flight into the car structure or into the air. Combination lap- and shoulder-belt systems are the most common restraint system. These consist of web fabrics that are able to withstand 6,000-pound (2,700-kilogram) test loading and are bolted to the car underbody and roof rail. Button-type latch release mechanisms for buckles, together with belt-operation reminder systems that detect unlatched belts, became legal requirements for all cars in the United States in 1972. This is intended to help offset the major drawback of belt systems or any other arrangements that require active participation of the occupant to insure proper operation. A 1970 survey indicated that 60 percent of car occupants do not use lap belts, and shoulder-belt usage is less than 3 percent. Another line of research aimed at overcoming this problem has centred on passive restraints that do not require any action on the part of the occupant. Experimental air-cushion restraint systems have been developed; an inflatable fabric bag pops out of the instrument panel and is filled with high-pressure gas within 40 milliseconds after an impact. The system is triggered by a sensor that is automatically actuated at impact. The occupant flies forward into the inflated cushion, which then controls his further motion

Air-cushion restraint systems

and absorbs some of his energy. Energy is absorbed by forcing gas out of the cushion through a series of ports or orifices in the fabric. This system had not been accepted in the early 1980s because of developmental problems, including the possibility of inadvertent actuation, failure to actuate, the effect on occupants who are not sitting in the proper positions, the possible harmful effect on occupant hearing created by the high noise level of actuation, and the necessary safety precautions that must be taken when working with pyrotechnic devices and high-pressure gas cylinders.

Interior-impact energy-absorbing devices are designed to augment restraint systems by absorbing energy from the occupant while minimizing his injuries. The energy-absorbing steering column, introduced in 1967, is a good example of such a device (see Figure 20). In front-end collisions, the column resists being pushed rearward. The lower end compresses while the upper end is retained by U-shaped support brackets and bolts. A few milliseconds after impact the driver hits the steering wheel, and the support brackets break away, allowing the upper end of the column to move downward, absorbing energy by deforming a metal jacket surrounding the column. Instrument panels, windshield glass, and other surfaces that may be struck by an unrestrained occupant may be designed to absorb energy in a controlled manner.

By courtesy of General Motors Corporation

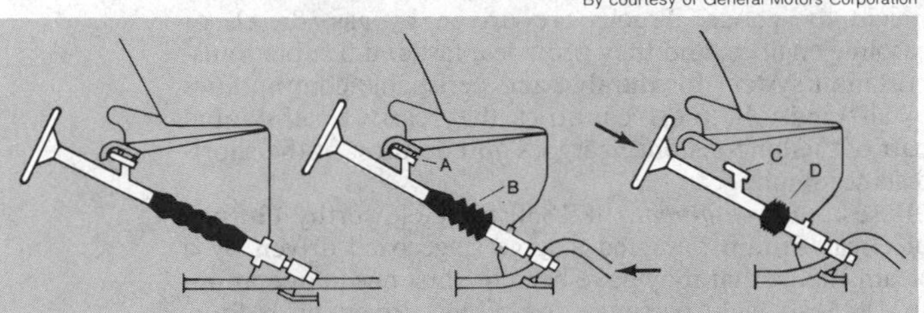

Figure 20: *Energy-absorbing steering column action* (see text). (Left) Assembly before impact. (Centre) An instant after impact. (A) Attachment bracket still holds; (B) lower steering column has started to collapse. (Right) An instant later. Impact of driver striking steering wheel breaks loose (C) attachment bracket and energy of impact is absorbed by further collapse of (D) lower steering column.

Exterior-impact-energy devices include the structural elements of the chassis and body, which may be tailored to deform in a controlled manner to decelerate the automobile more gradually and, as a result, leave less force to be experienced by the occupants. Stress risers in the form of section irregularities have been built into front frame members of some cars. These are designed to buckle under severe loads and absorb energy in the process. Retractable bumpers that have been developed absorb some of the impact energy of a collision as the bars move inward against the restraint of springs.

Pollution problems. Governments have also found a role in the automotive-air-pollution problem, to establish quality standards and to perform sample inspections to insure that standards are met. Standards have become progressively more stringent, and the equipment necessary to meet them has become more complex.

By courtesy of General Motors Corporation

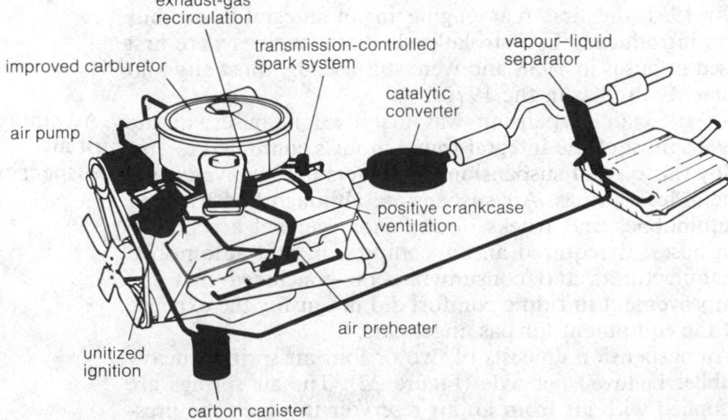

Figure 21: Emission-control systems for automobile engines (see text).

Positive crankcase ventilation (see Figure 21) was introduced in the United States in 1963, for the purpose of eliminating engine blow-by gas that formerly had been vented to the atmosphere as an emission source. This was achieved by routing the gas, along with crankcase-ventilation air, into the engine intake, where it could be recycled through the cylinders and properly burned. A small valve in the circuit was necessary to maintain the direction of flow. Beginning in 1966, cars increasingly were provided with air pumps to supply excess air to the exhaust stream near the exhaust valves. High gas temperatures in this zone promote thermal oxidation of hydrocarbons and carbon monoxide to form carbon dioxide and water.

Engine modifications to lower pollution

Various engine modifications that alter emission characteristics have been successfully introduced. These include adjusted carburetor air-fuel ratios, lowered compression ratios, retarded spark timing, reduced combustion chamber surface-to-volume ratios, and closer production tolerances. To improve drivability of some arrangements, preheated air from a heat exchanger on the exhaust manifold is ducted to the air cleaner.

The undesired evaporation of gasoline hydrocarbons into the air has been controlled by sealing the gas tank and venting the tank through a liquid-vapour separator into a canister containing activated charcoal. During engine operation these vapours are desorbed and burned in the engine.

The effect of these controls was well established by the early 1970s. The average hydrocarbon emissions from equipped vehicles was reduced by about 87 percent. A 65 percent reduction in carbon monoxide was also obtained. Controls to reduce the formation of oxides of nitrogen brought a 30 percent reduction result. The chemical conditions that tend to reduce hydrocarbon and carbon monoxide sometimes tend to increase the formation of undesirable nitrous oxide. This presents a formidable challenge to research scientists and engineers.

Among emission-control devices developed in the 1970s were catalytic converters (devices to promote combustion of unburned hydrocarbons in the exhaust), exhaust-gas-recirculation systems, manifold reactors, fuel injection, unitized ignition elements, and stratified charge combustion engines (see Figure 21).

A catalytic converter consists of an insulated chamber containing a porous bed of catalytic material through which hot exhaust gas must pass before being discharged into the air. The catalyst is in the form of pellets of a variety of metal oxides, which are heated by exhaust gas to about 900° F (500° C). At this temperature unburned hydrocarbons and carbon monoxide are further oxidized. Problems with catalysts involve their intolerance for leaded fuels and the need to prevent overheating.

Exhaust-gas recirculation is a technique to control oxides of nitrogen, which are formed by the chemical reaction of nitrogen and oxygen at high temperatures during combustion. Either reducing the concentrations of these elements or lowering peak cycle temperatures will reduce the amount of nitrous oxides produced. To achieve this, exhaust gas is piped from the exhaust manifold to the intake manifold. This dilutes the incoming fuel–air mixture and effectively lowers combustion temperature. The amount of recirculation is a function of throttle position but averages about 2 percent.

Manifold reactors are enlarged, insulated exhaust manifolds into which air is injected and in which exhaust gas continues to burn. The effectiveness of such units in experimental projects depends upon the amount of heat generated and the length of time the gas is within the manifold. Stainless steel and ceramic materials are used to provide durability at high operating temperatures (approaching 2,300° F [about 1,300° C]).

Fuel injection

Fuel injection, as a replacement for carburetion, has potential for reducing exhaust emissions. The precise metering of fuel for each cylinder provides a means of ensuring that the chemically correct air–fuel ratio is being burned in the engine. This eliminates cylinder-to-cylinder variations and the tendency of cylinders that are most remote from the carburetor to receive less fuel than is desired. A variety of metering and control systems are commercially available. A continuous-flow system was in use as early as 1957. Timed injection, in which a small quantity of gasoline is squirted into each cylinder or intake-valve port during the intake stroke of the piston, is employed on a number of European cars.

In one timed-injection system, individual pumps at each intake valve are regulated (timed) by an electronic controller. This controller monitors intake vacuum, engine temperature, ambient-air temperature, and throttle position and then adjusts the time and duration of injection accordingly.

Another direction of emission control involved ignition performance. Unitized or solid-state ignition circuitry was introduced on some cars in the late 1960s to improve starting and ignition reliability and durability.

Another approach is the stratified charge engine, a variation from conventional cylinder combustion. Fuel is injected into a combustion-chamber pocket, and the nonhomogeneous, stratified charge is spark ignited. Operation of the engine is possible at very lean fuel–air ratios, thus permitting high thermal efficiency at light engine loads. This provides excellent reductions in exhaust hydrocarbons, carbon monoxide, and oxides of nitrogen. The primary problem with the system is to make it function over a wide range of speeds and loads with good transient response.

Future systems. Expansion of the total potential automotive market in the future and concern for the environment may be expected to change cars of the future. Special-purpose vehicles designed for specific urban or rural functions, with appropriate power systems for each type of use, may be needed. Possibilities include electric, steam, gas-turbine, nuclear, and other power sources.

Electric propulsion is possible for relatively short-range vehicles, using power from batteries or fuel cells. Such systems have been used to power vehicles on the Moon. Conventional storage-battery systems do not have high power-to-weight ratios for acceleration or energy-to-weight ratios for driving range to match gasoline-powered general purpose vehicles. Special-purpose applications, however, such as urban delivery vehicles, may be practical because of the excellent low-emission characteristics of the system. Storage-battery systems may also be coupled with gasoline or other power sources to form a hybrid power plant with electric operation in cities and gasoline operation in less congested areas. Storage batteries that have high power-to-weight ratios are under development and may stimulate the increased production of electric cars in the future.

Steam power plants have been reexamined in the light of modern technology and new materials. The continuous-combustion process used to heat the steam generator offers potentially improved emission characteristics. Closed systems that use vapours other than steam are also under development, but further work is necessary to improve power-plant size, weight, and working fluid characteristics.

Gas turbines

Gas turbines have been tested extensively and are expected to power high-speed, long-haul trucks and buses. Turbines have good torque characteristics, operate on a wide variety of fuels, have high power-to-weight ratios, and offer quiet operation. Studies have shown that the advantages of the system are best realized in heavy-duty vehicles operating on long, nearly constant speed runs. Successful designs require regenerative systems to recover energy from hot exhaust gas and transfer it to incoming air. This improves fuel economy, reduces exhaust temperatures to safer levels, and eliminates the need for a muffler in some designs.

Nuclear energy offers the advantage of extremely low fuel weight. The obstacle for automotive use, however, is the great weight and volume of shielding required to protect the occupants from excessive nuclear radiation. This source can probably best be applied indirectly to produce stable chemical compounds or electricity, which could be converted to automotive uses.

A number of other energy-conversion systems have been studied for automotive applications. Many of these are variations of engine combustion cycles such as turbocharged four-stroke, two-stroke, and diesel (two- and four-stroke). Free-piston and other geometric configurations, including rotary engines, offer other possibilities. Great interest was shown in the Wankel, a type of rotary engine invented by Felix Wankel of West Germany in 1954, and several auto manufacturers were conducting tests on the motor in the late 20th century; at least one company (Japanese) was manufacturing Wankel-engined automobiles.

Because the automobile is likely to remain an important part of the overall mobility system, it requires continuing improvement in safety and emission control as well as in its older values of performance characteristics and economic contribution. (O.C.C./G.C.C.)

TRUCKS AND BUSES

A bus is a self-propelled road vehicle designed to carry a number of passengers, generally on a fixed route. In most cities buses have largely or entirely replaced electric streetcars, and they carry much intercity passenger traffic.

A truck, or lorry, is a motor vehicle designed to carry freight, or goods. Trucks are driven by gas, diesel, or gasoline engines, and they provide a fast and flexible transportation system for durable and perishable commodities of all kinds. In most countries they carry a substantial part of the long-distance cargoes and do most of the short-distance hauling.

Buses. *Development.* In 1830 Sir Goldworthy Gurney of Great Britain designed a large stagecoach driven by a steam engine that may have been the first bus in operation. In 1895 an eight-passenger omnibus, driven by a four- to six-horsepower (hp) single-cylinder engine, was built in Germany. In 1903 the Austro-Daimler firm built an omnibus that had a four-cylinder, eight-horsepower engine with a four-speed transmission. In 1904 an experimental route in Germany from Wendeburg to Braunscherg was begun, using a Büssing-built vehicle. In 1905 buses in Berlin pulled trailers carrying passengers, a practice that continued until 1962.

Until the 1920s the technical history of the bus was that of the motor truck, since the early bus consisted of a bus body mounted on a truck chassis. The majority of present-day school buses are made in this way. In 1922 the first vehicle with a chassis specifically designed for bus service was made in the United States by Fageol Safety Coach Company of Oakland, California. Its frame was about one foot lower than a truck frame, and it also had an extra-long wheelbase, a wide tread, and an engine in front. In 1926 the Fageol organization developed the first integral-frame bus, with twin engines mounted amidships under the floor. The integral frame utilized the roof, floor, and sides of the bus as structural members.

First vehicle designed as bus

Other early bus manufacturers were Mack and Yellow Coach in the United States, both of which built gasoline-electric models. In these buses, a gasoline engine drove a direct-current generator, and the output of the generator provided electrical power for the driving motors on the rear wheels. This electrical system performed the functions of a transmission; *i.e.,* it multiplied driving torque and provided a means of connecting and disconnecting the engine from the drive wheels. In 1928 the first transcontinental bus service was initiated in the United States.

In 1931 the first rear engine in an integral-frame bus was introduced. Two-stroke-cycle diesel engines were first used in buses in 1938 and were still used by most city and intercity models in the 1970s.

Advantage of air suspension

In 1953 air suspension was first used in buses; in the 1960s most of the integral-frame models continued to employ this type of suspension; the others used conventional metal leaf springs. Air suspension, although first tried on automobiles and trucks, found more general acceptance on buses. It required an air compressor, and automobile manufacturers and consumers soon concluded that the improvement in riding comfort did not justify the expense of the equipment for passenger cars.

Air suspension consists of two or four air springs (heavy rubber bellows) per axle (Figure 22). The air springs are supplied with air from an air reservoir in which the pressure is maintained at about 100 pounds per square inch (7 kilograms per square centimetre). An advantage gained

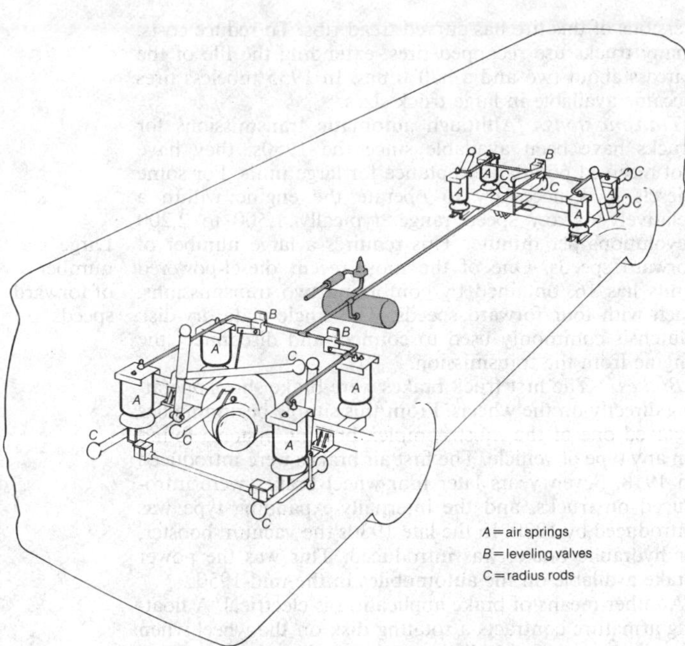

Figure 22: Air suspension for a modern bus or motor coach. The shaded area indicates the air lines.

from this type of suspension is that as the load increases or decreases the level and height of the vehicle remain constant. This is accomplished by valves that are actuated by the vehicle height between the body and the axle; as the load is increased, the air pressure is increased in the air spring. The increased unit pressure multiplied by a nearly constant area gives a greater load capacity. As the load is removed, the air is released from the air spring, reducing the pressure and load capacity.

Unlike the leaf spring but like the coil spring, the air spring is capable of withstanding only vertical forces. Consequently, braking and cornering forces must be absorbed by links or arms with one end attached to the axle and the other to the body by pin or ball joints.

Another interesting development in motor-bus transportation was the Scenicruiser introduced in the United States in 1954 for transcontinental use. It utilizes air suspension and has six wheels, two singles in the front for the steering axle and four doubles in the rear in a tandem arrangement (one axle directly behind the other with an interconnection to allow the equalization of the load). Thus, the weight of this vehicle, about 30,000 pounds (14,000 kilograms) empty, is supported by 10 tires, two on the front axle and four on each of the rear axles. The frame is of the integral type and provides two levels. The first level carries the driver, 10 passengers, and sanitary facilities; the upper level carries 33 passengers and has a windshield so that passengers can see forward. The Scenicruiser is powered by two four-cylinder two-stroke-cycle diesel engines of 133 horsepower each. Only a limited number of these vehicles were built because of cost.

Two-level design of Scenicruiser

Modern buses. In Europe, especially in England, the double-decker bus is used to minimize the street space occupied and to take advantage of the greater manoeuvrability of the shorter wheelbase without loss of passenger capacity. A typical bus of this type carries 26 passengers on the lower deck and 30 on the upper. In Germany, double-decker and 1½ decker buses are operated, as are trolley buses and articulated buses. An articulated bus is one in which a single-deck bus pulls a trailer, using a flexible joint. Consequently, unless it is turning a corner, the vehicle appears to be one continuous unit. In most of the world, however, the trend is toward one-unit singledeck vehicles, usually of large size. In Japan as late as 1963, 21-passenger buses were used in Tokyo and Kyōto, often mounted on a truck chassis. The improvement of roads and the building of expressways have triggered the rapid expansion of the automotive industry in Japan, which, in 1970, included eight bus manufacturers building buses ranging in size from small gasoline-driven units to large diesel-driven units.

There are four main types of buses: city or transit, suburban, intercity, and school. The city bus operates within the city limits and is characterized by low maximum speed, low-ride platform, provision for standing passengers, two entrances on the curb side, low-back seats, and no luggage space or racks. The suburban bus is designed for short intercity runs, with roof windows optional for sightseeing; back seats are high, some luggage space and luggage racks are provided, and there is a single, front entrance. The intercity type has a high-ride platform to provide maximum luggage space under the passengers, high-back seats, overhead luggage racks, individual reading lights, and a washroom. A typical intercity coach weighs about 26,000 pounds (12,000 kilograms), has a capacity of 47 passengers, a 285-horsepower two-stroke-cycle V-8 diesel engine, a four-speed manual transmission, and air brakes. School buses generally consist of a bus body mounted on a long-wheelbase truck chassis, but some integral-frame buses are now being manufactured.

Characteristics of the intercity bus

Gas-turbine engines were adopted for some types of buses. To provide wider, more comfortable bus seats, overall width has been increased on some new models.

Trucks. In 1896 Gottlieb Daimler of Germany built the first motor truck. It was equipped with a four-horsepower engine and a belt drive with two speeds forward and one in reverse. In 1898 the Winton Company of the United States produced a gasoline-powered delivery wagon with a single-cylinder six-horsepower engine.

In World War I motor trucks were widely used and in World War II largely replaced horse-drawn equipment on most fronts. A notable vehicle was the four-wheel-drive, quarter-ton-capacity, short-wheelbase jeep, capable of performing a variety of military tasks.

Types and definitions. Trucks can be classified as either straight or articulated. A straight truck is one in which all axles are attached to a single frame. An articulated vehicle is one that consists of two or more separate frames connected by suitable couplings. A truck tractor is a motor vehicle designed primarily for drawing truck-trailers and constructed to carry part of the weight and load of a semitrailer, which is a truck-trailer equipped with one or more axles, so constructed that the end and a substantial part of its own weight and that of its load rests upon a truck tractor. In contrast, a full trailer is so constructed that all of its own weight and that of its load rests upon its own wheels.

A device called a fifth wheel is used to connect a truck tractor to a semitrailer and to permit articulation between the units. It generally includes a lower half, consisting of a trunnion (pivot assembly) plate and latching mechanism, mounted on the truck tractor for connection with a kingpin mounted on the semitrailer. A semitrailer may be converted to a full trailer by a trailer-converter dolly, an auxiliary axle assembly equipped with the lower half of a fifth wheel, a drawbar, and other special parts.

Use of fifth wheel for articulated units

Axle assemblies of heavy trucks may be made up of two or more axles, any of which may be powered. Normally, they are so spaced that the distance between axle centres is not more than one and one-half times the overall diameter of the wheel and tire. If the axles are separated by a larger distance the assembly is called a spread tandem.

Shown in Figure 23 are several types of trucks and truck tractors in use, with a digit code to aid in identification of the vehicles. The first digit refers to the power unit and a second single digit refers to a full trailer. A digit with an S prefix refers to a semitrailer; for example, 2-S1 means a two-axle tractor and one-axle semitrailer; 3-2 means a three-axle truck with two-axle full trailer; 2-S1-2 means a two-axle tractor, one-axle semitrailer, and two-axle full trailer.

Frames. Truck and truck-tractor frames, except for the very small sizes, have remained separate from the cab and body. The frame is generally made of two channel sections of alloy steel with a standardized width of 34 inches (0.86 metre) overall. Semitrailers and tank trailers in many instances now employ the integral, or unitized, type of construction.

Suspensions. The most common form of front suspension is a drop-forged one-section front axle attached to the frame through leaf springs and shock absorbers. In 1960 individual front suspension was introduced.

The variations of rear suspensions for trucks and truck tractors are almost limitless. In the case of a truck with a single powered axle, the axle is generally attached to the frame by leaf springs. The axle is always full-floating; *i.e.*, all the weight is carried by the axle housing and none by the live or driving axle inside the housing. Thus, if a driving axle breaks, the load is still supported by the axle

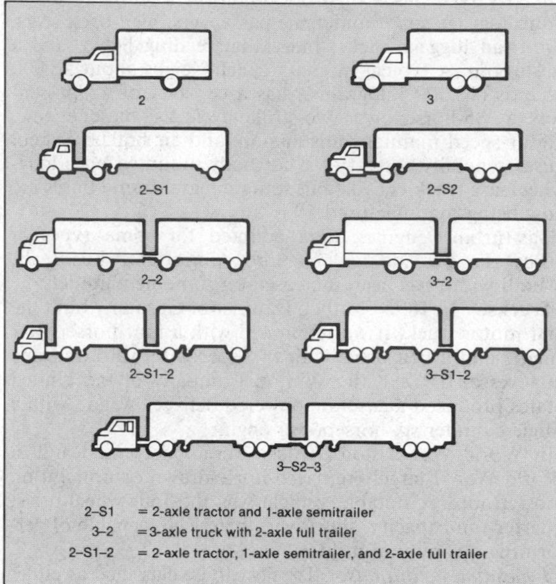

Figure 23: Truck types as designated by code based on axle arrangement.

housing. The axle may be a single reduction type, meaning that it has one-gear reduction, or double reduction. A two-speed axle is one in which there is a gear change built into the axle. This makes it possible to have two speeds for each transmission speed. The tandem-drive axle has two powered axles. There may be two drive shafts, one to each axle. There is always a system of levers between the two axles to equalize the load. A powered axle may be either the Hotchkiss type, in which all of the driving and braking thrust is taken by the leaf springs, or the torque-arm type, in which the thrusts are taken by the rods. Because the vertical movement of the body is only one-half that of the wheels in a tandem axle, this axle is used successfully with solid rubber springs, reducing maintenance to a minimum.

Ackermann steering system

Steering. Steering of trucks, with their relatively heavy loads, was a problem until power steering came into use in the early 1950s. Steering is always by the Ackermann system, which provides a kingpin for each front wheel. Maximum cramp angle of the front wheels is about 35 degrees. The minimum turning radius is dependent on the wheelbase. A few vehicles have been built with two steering axles in the front.

Engines and fuels. Until the 1930s the gasoline engine was widely used for trucks, especially in the United States, but since World War II the diesel engine has become increasingly favoured for trucks used for long-distance hauls. In 1950 the Boeing Company of the U.S. installed the first gas turbine in a truck; in the 1960s there was renewed interest in this type of engine. In 1952 an engine using liquid-propane gas was introduced. While the diesel engine has the disadvantage of high initial cost, the propane-burning engine has the disadvantage of lower output for a given engine displacement.

Tires. Although pneumatic tires appeared on automobiles as early as 1904, large trucks were equipped with hard rubber tires until World War I. Cotton was replaced by rayon in the carcass of truck tires in the 1930s, with wire and nylon appearing a decade later. Recent developments include the use of a single wide tire to carry the same load as a dual wheel. Tire chains first became available in 1904, knobby snow tires by 1936, and snow tires with embedded wire coils about 1950. One of the latest and most effective versions of this tire has curved tread ribs. To reduce costs, many trucks use recapped tires, extending the life of the carcass about two and a half times. In 1955 tubeless tires became available in large truck sizes.

Large number of forward speeds

Transmissions. Although automatic transmissions for trucks have been available since the 1950s, they have not received popular acceptance for large units. For some diesels it is necessary to operate the engine within a relatively narrow speed range, typically 1,500 to 2,200 revolutions per minute. This requires a large number of forward speeds. One of the most recent diesel-powered units has 16, obtained by combining two transmissions, each with four forward speeds. The single-plate dry-disk clutch is commonly used to connect and disconnect the engine from the transmission.

Brakes. The first truck brakes were brake shoes operating directly on the wheels. From this simple beginning has evolved one of the most complex braking systems found on any type of vehicle. The first air brakes were introduced in 1918. Seven years later four-wheel brakes were introduced on trucks, and the internally-expanding type was introduced by 1930. In the late 1930s the vacuum booster, or hydraulic brake, was introduced. This was the power brake available on the automobiles in the mid-1950s.

Another means of brake application is electrical. A floating armature contracts a rotating disk on the wheel when electric current is applied, and through a cam arrangement applies the shoes to the drums. Vacuum brakes working off the vacuum in the intake manifold of the spark-ignition gasoline engine have been used to apply the brakes on car carriers. Air-over-hydraulic brakes are also used in some vehicles.

Use of air brakes

Air, air-over-hydraulic, vacuum, and electrical brakes are all adaptable to articulated vehicles. Of these methods of application, air, or full air, as it is sometimes called, is the most widely used. The engine-driven compressor supplies air at a nominal pressure, regulated by an air governor. Air pressure is indicated by a pressure gauge and a low-pressure warning device, either audible or visual. Air is stored in the reservoirs and supplied to the brake valves; a foot valve supplies air to all brake chambers on the vehicle, including those being towed. Another brake valve is hand controlled and applies the brakes on the towed vehicle only. Both the foot pedal and hand valve supply air to the same service line, which extends back to the towed vehicles. The second, or emergency, line carries full air pressure when the vehicle is in operation. If this line is broken, the emergency brakes are applied on all towed vehicles from air reservoirs located on the towed vehicles. After reaching the brake chamber from the brake valves, the air acts on a diaphragm connected to a push rod, which in turn actuates a cam that moves the shoes against the brake drum. In the early 1970s the cam was being replaced by a wedge.

In recent years much attention has been given to the problem of brake failures that have resulted from loss of air pressure. The emergency system mentioned previously can be utilized in case of a failure in the service line by the use of the tractor protection valve and control valve. The driver can flip the lever of the control valve and apply all brakes on the towed vehicles.

There is another form of safety system that in normal use is a parking brake but in the event of loss of air can be used as an emergency system. It is known as a DD3 actuator. The driver has the option of using the axle on which the DD3 actuators are mounted as a parking system or as an emergency braking system by operating a push-pull button. Once this system is actuated, a mechanical lock holds the brake on, even if all air pressure is lost.

Another emergency system is the spring brake system, in which springs are used to apply the brakes if the air has been lost. As long as normal air pressure is available, the spring brake actuator is inactive and the normal brake chambers apply the brakes. The driver can place the emergency system in action at his option by means of a push-pull valve.

Athough air-cooled, disk-type hand brakes on the drive shafts of heavy-duty trucks have been used for some time, it was not until recent years that experimental models for the wheels were available. In the late 20th century there was increasing interest in antilocking brakes for articulated vehicles in order to reduce the possibility of jackknifing. (A.H.E.)

MODERN ROADS, BRIDGES, AND TUNNELS

Modern road-building

Modern road builders still use traditional materials, but quality is now closely controlled by scientific testing. Since World War II, machines have largely replaced hand labour; powerful diggers, scrapers, bulldozers, and graders handle the massive excavations needed in the cuttings and embankments of high-speed roads, and paving machines lay and surface both macadam and concrete roads. Modern pavers, guided by electronic sensors and preset alignment wires, can lay a mile of highway in a day. Firm foundations, efficient drainage, adequate thickness of base or slab, and strong antiskid surfaces are essential in good road building, as are adequate signs, markings, and lighting for the safe use of the finished road.

Bridge improvements during the past century stem from improved materials, new design concepts, more refined calculations, and better construction techniques. High strengths of concrete and steel, the development of steels resistant to brittle fracture at low temperatures, and, recently, the introduction of self-protecting steels to reduce maintenance costs have all helped to advance design. Computers have enabled engineers to save structural costs by quickly obtaining precise data. Wind effects on large structures are now better understood and can be confirmed by wind-tunnel tests.

Eugène Freyssinet's pioneer work in France on prestressed concrete, dating from 1928, marked a major advance in concrete construction, used in many notable bridges throughout the world. For the longest spans, steel suspension bridges are still favoured. This method was pioneered in the United States by John A. Roebling, whose greatest achievement, Brooklyn Bridge in New York City, was completed by his son in 1883. This was the first of many long suspension bridges constructed in the United States.

British engineers advanced the design of suspension bridges by substituting a shallow-plated box girder for the stiffening trusses and by inclining the suspenders for extra stability in the Severn Bridge linking England and Wales (1966). Steel box girders, acting on their own or compositely with concrete, have advanced the design of medium-span bridges (Tinsley Viaduct, Sheffield, England, 1968; and Europa Bridge, Austria), while box girders with cable stays can be used to attain spans of about 1,475 feet, or 450 metres (Severin, Cologne, West Germany, 1959).

The design of small bridges has been stimulated by their frequency on freeways, and, as more urban roads are built, refinements in elevated viaducts can be expected. In construction, rivetting has been almost entirely superseded by shop welding, and high-strength friction grip bolts are now used for site bolting. Foundation construction methods, especially in deepwater, continue to be improved (see also PUBLIC WORKS: *Bridges*).

Alpine tunnels for roads derive from the many 19th-century railway tunnels built throughout the world, but because tunnelling is very expensive and because motor vehicles can climb steep grades, there are as yet few major mountain-road tunnels. However, road traffic is now beginning to justify their cost on important routes as at Mont Blanc (7.8 miles [12.5 kilometres], 1965) between Italy and France and Great St. Bernard (four miles [6.4 kilometres], 1964) in the Swiss Alps and Straight Creek (1.6 miles [2.6 kilometres], 1971) in the Colorado Rockies.

Underwater tunnels for pedestrians, trains, and motor vehicles are to be found in many parts of the world. They avoid the use of high-level bridges over navigable waterways; and in populated areas, where they are usually found, they make less demand on surface space than bridges do. Since 1950 the trend has been toward the use of immersed tube tunnels, especially for estuarial crossings. Large prefabricated sections are built on shore, either of concrete or steel, then floated out and sunk into a trench in the riverbed. Urban tunnels, mostly short underpasses, are being built in many major cities to reduce traffic congestion (see also PUBLIC WORKS: *Tunnelling and underground excavation*). (H.N.G.)

Modern railroad technology

With the 20th century the railroad reached maturity. Railroad building continued on a fairly extensive scale in some parts of the world, notably in Canada, the Soviet Union, and in Africa. But in the more developed countries construction tapered off, except for improvements or refinements of existing systems. The technological emphasis shifted to faster operations, more amenities for passengers, larger and more specialized freight cars, safer and more sophisticated signalling and traffic-control systems, and new types of motive power. Railroads in many of the more advanced countries also found themselves operating

Table 1: Railway Systems of Selected Countries

	service began	ownership*	gauge†	mileage (track length)‡
Algeria	1862		standard	3,071
Argentina	1857	state	5 ft 6 in.	15,462
			metre	10,715
			standard	2,210
Australia	1854	state	standard	8,302§
			5 ft 3 in.	5,777§
			3 ft 6 in.	11,169§
Austria	1838	state	standard	6,998
Bangladesh	1861	state	metre	2,517
Belgium	1835	state	standard	7,754
Brazil	1854	state	metre	14,553§
Bulgaria	1866	state	standard	3,584§
Burma	1877	state	metre	2,400
Canada	1836	state	standard	35,147
		private	standard	29,321
Ceylon (Sri Lanka)	1865	state	5 ft 6 in.	1,236
Chile	1851	state	metre	3,844
			5 ft 6 in.	2,349
China	1881	state	standard	23,900§
Czechoslovakia	1839	state	standard	13,226
Denmark	1847	state	standard	3,395
East Africa (Kenya, Uganda, Tanzania)	1897	state	metre	4,370
Egypt	1854	state	standard	4,149
Finland	1862	state	5 ft	5,462
France	1828	state	standard	49,028
Germany (East)	1835	state	standard	18,179
Germany (West)	1835	state	standard	44,999
Greece	1869	state	standard	2,002
Hungary	1846	state	standard	8,442
India	1853	state	5 ft 6 in.	36,353
			metre	21,770
			2 ft 6 in.; 2 ft	3,513
Indonesia	1864	state	3 ft 6 in.	4,852
Iran	1917	state	standard	2,581§
Ireland	1834	state	5 ft 3 in.	2,282
Italy	1839	state	standard	20,649
Japan	1872	state	3 ft 6 in.	25,426
		private	3 ft 6 in.	5,733
Korea (South)	1899	state	standard	3,378
Malaysia	1885	state	metre	1,428
Mexico	1850	state	standard	30,613
Morocco	1911	state	standard	1,632
Mozambique	1886	state	3 ft 6 in.	2,551
The Netherlands	1839	state	standard	4,568
New Zealand	1863	state	3 ft 6 in.	4,499
Nigeria	1901	state	3 ft 6 in.	2,680
Norway	1854	state	standard	3,452
Pakistan	1861	state	5 ft 6 in.	7,664
Poland	1845	state	standard	16,540§
Portugal	1856	state	5 ft 6 in.	2,944
Rhodesia	1897	state	3 ft 6 in.	2,040
Romania	1869	state	standard	6,838§
South Africa	1860	state	3 ft 6 in.	19,648
Spain	1848	state	5 ft 6 in.	13,792
The Sudan	1900	state	3 ft 6 in.	3,379
Sweden	1856	state	standard	11,611
Switzerland	1844	state	standard	4,249
		private	metre	1,529
Taiwan	1891	state	3 ft 6 in.	1,061
Thailand	1893	state	metre	2,733
Tunisia	1876	state	metre	1,743
Turkey	1856	state	standard	5,874
Soviet Union	1837	state	5 ft	86,691§
United Kingdom	1825	state	standard	34,471
United States	1830	private	standard	305,179
Yugoslavia	1846	state	standard	9,433
Zaire	1911		3 ft 6 in.	3,702
Zambia	1905	state	3 ft 6 in.	1,000

*Predominant ownership is given; most countries have both private and state owned lines. †Gauge of the principal mileage; most countries have lines of several gauges: standard gauge = 4 ft 8½ in.; metre gauge = 3 ft 3⅜ in. ‡Data for early 1970s. §Route length.
Source: *Jane's World Railways* 1971–72.

in a new climate of intense competition with other forms of transport.

By mid-20th century, railroads in such countries as the United States, Britain, and Ireland, as well as in western Europe generally, were beginning to abandon secondary and branch lines that had become uneconomic. But in the Soviet Union, China, Japan, Australia, and Canada, important new lines were being built. In the Soviet Union the Trans-Siberian line was double tracked and, by 1970, had been largely electrified. At that time, additional construction had raised the Soviet system to a total of 86,691 route miles (139,511 kilometres), making it the largest single railroad system in the world. In China, a large-scale railroad building program was also launched. A recently completed trunk line links Tsining with Ulaanbaatar, the capital of Mongolia, which was already on a branch of the Trans-Siberian Railroad. Several other important Chinese lines have been built or are under construction. Some of the main lines are being double tracked and electrified. Two major bridges across the Yangtze River, one at Hankow and the other at Nanking, have been built; each is more than a mile (1,600 metres) long.

In Australia, considerable progress has been made in overcoming the handicap caused by the variety of gauges. The Commonwealth Railways has built several standard-gauge lines, the most important being the transcontinental link between Port Pirie and Kalgoorlie. Crossing the Nullarbor Plain, this line has one stretch of 300 miles (500 kilometres) without a curve, the longest straight track in the world. Standard-gauge rails also now link Perth with Sydney.

Australia's record straight-line track

As Canada entered a period of rapid economic growth, it built a number of railroad lines to open up new territory. Among them were the Great Slave Lake Railway, running from Peace River, Alberta, 432 miles (695 kilometres) to Hay River and Pine Point, Northwest Territories, and the Quebec North Shore and Labrador Railway Company, a 320-mile (510-kilometre) ore-carrying line from iron ore deposits near Schefferville, Quebec, to the St. Lawrence River at Sept Iles. The Pacific Great Eastern Railway (now the British Columbia Railway), completed from Vancouver, British Columbia, to Prince George in 1956, in 1958 reached Dawson Creek and Fort Saint John, 327 miles (526 kilometres) north of Prince George. In 1971 a further extension of 250 miles (400 kilometres) was completed to Fort Nelson, British Columbia, and another line from Fort Saint James to within 140 miles of the Yukon Territory border was planned.

In Japan, a major new railroad was built not to open new country but to enlarge the capacity of rail transportation between Tokyo and Ōsaka. The New Tōkaidō Line (see below) was built to standard gauge instead of the 3-foot-6-inch (1.07-metre) gauge commonly used in Japan. It has been so successful that a 100-mile (160-kilometre) extension, from Ōsaka to Okayama, was added in the early 1970s. Table 1 summarizes railway systems in selected countries.

In the period 1900 to about 1930, few apparent advances were made in railroad technolgy. Nevertheless, that period saw several developments that were later to have a profound effect on railroads everywhere. One was the first practical and reliable diesel-electric locomotive; another was the perfecting of centralized traffic control, a highly efficient system of controlling train operations; still another was the first use of continuous welded rail, a major contribution to smoother track that costs less to maintain.

After World War II these and other technological improvements began to take hold on many of the world's railroads. The diesel-electric locomotive completely superseded the steam locomotive in the United States in little more than a decade. The vastly improved efficiency of this type of locomotive was a major reason why railroads in that country were able to continue under private operation.

Another important trend became evident in the 1950s and 1960s: the electrification of major trunk lines in many countries. Electrification, though it requires a very heavy capital investment, is profitable wherever the traffic is extremely dense, as in Japan, parts of the Soviet Union, western Europe, and Great Britain.

LOCOMOTIVES

In normal practice a locomotive is a separate unit incorporating the machinery to generate (or, in the case of an electric locomotive, to convert) power and transmit it to the driving wheels. Motive power, however, can be incorporated into a car that also has passenger, baggage, or freight accommodations. Today there are three main sources of power for a locomotive: steam, oil, and electricity. Steam, the earliest form of propulsion, was in almost universal use until about the time of World War II; since then it has been largely superseded by the more efficient diesel and electric traction.

Modern locomotive power sources

The steam locomotive is a self-sufficient unit, carrying its own water supply for generating the steam and coal, oil, or wood for heating the boiler. The diesel locomotive also carries its own fuel supply, but the diesel-engine output cannot be coupled directly to the wheels; instead, a mechanical, electric, or hydraulic transmission must be used. The electric locomotive normally is not self-sufficient; it picks up current from an overhead trolley wire or a third rail beside the running rails. A few small battery-driven locomotives or railcars are used for special tasks.

The only other category of locomotive in use today is the turbine locomotive; although atomic-powered locomotives have been proposed, none has actually been built.

Steam locomotives. The basic features that made George Stephenson's "Rocket" of 1829 successful—its multitube boiler and its system of exhausting the steam and creating a draft in its firebox—continued to be used in the steam locomotive (Figure 24). The number of coupled drive wheels soon increased. The "Rocket" had only a single pair of driving wheels, but four coupled wheels soon became common, and eventually some locomotives were

From R. Ziel, *The Twilight of Steam Locomotives;* Grosset & Dunlap, Inc. Copyright © 1963, 1970 by Ron Ziel

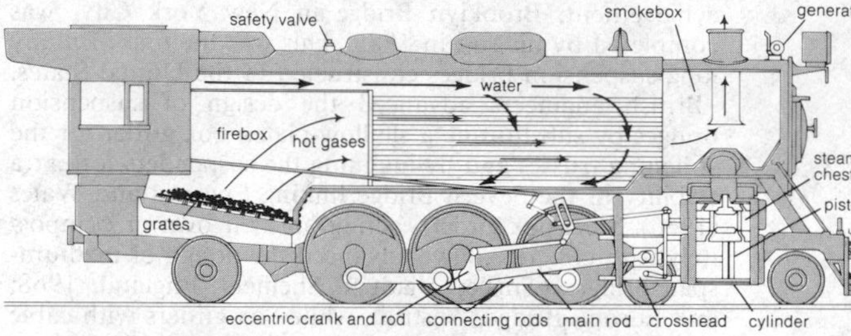

Figure 24: Cutaway diagram of steam locomotive.

built with as many as 14 coupled drivers. Smaller "pilot" wheels are often used ahead of the drivers. Their main function is to guide the coupled wheels around curves. Large locomotives may also have smaller wheels behind the drivers. These permit the locomotive to carry a larger, heavier firebox.

Steam-locomotive driving wheels are of various sizes, usually larger for the faster passenger engines. In Europe, the average was about 66- to 78-inch (1.7- to two-metre) diameter for passenger engines and 54 to 66 inches (1.4 to 1.7 metres) for freight or mixed-traffic types. Typical locomotives built in the United States just before the end of the steam era had drivers ranging from 60 to 84 inches (1.5 to 2.1 metres) in diameter.

Driving wheels

Supplies of fuel (usually coal but sometimes oil) and water can be carried on the locomotive frame itself (in which case it is called a tank engine) or can be carried in a separate vehicle, the tender, coupled to the locomotive. The tender of a typical European main-line locomotive had a capacity of ten tons (9,000 kilograms) of coal and 8,000 gallons (30,000 litres) of water. In the Soviet Union and on some African, Asian, and Australian systems, higher capacities were common. The tender of a typical large United States steam locomotive of the World War II period was carried on 14 wheels and had a capacity of 28 tons (25,000 kilograms) of coal and 25,000 gallons (95,000 litres) of water.

In the United States the steam locomotive quickly evolved to the general type that became known as the American Standard. It had a horizontal fire-tube boiler, a four-wheel pilot truck, and four coupled driving wheels.

This type, conventionally designated 4-4-0 to reflect the number of wheels, was used for all kinds of services; it dominated American railroading until well after the Civil War period.

To meet the special needs of heavy freight traffic, other types of locomotives with more (and usually smaller) drive wheels were developed. Among them were the Mogul (2-6-0), the Consolidation (2-8-0), and the Mikado (2-8-2). The Union Pacific used a three-cylinder 4-12-2, which had 12 coupled driving wheels. Still greater tractive effort was obtained by using two separate engine units under a common boiler. The front engine was articulated, or hinge-connected to the frame of the rear engine, so that the very large locomotive could negotiate curves. The articulated locomotive was originally a Swiss invention, with the first built in 1888. The largest ever built was the Union Pacific's "Big Boy," used in mountain freight service in the western United States (Figure 25). "Big Boy"

The articulated locomotive

By courtesy of the Union Pacific Railroad

Figure 25: The "Big Boy" of the Union Pacific Railroad, built in 1941. Considered to be the largest steam locomotive ever built, it was used for hauling freight in mountainous areas.

weighed nearly 600 tons (540,000 kilograms). It could exert 135,400 pounds (61,400 kilograms) of tractive force and developed more than 6,000 horsepower at 75 miles (120 kilometres) per hour.

One of the best known articulated designs is the Beyer-Garrett, which has two frames, each having its own driving wheels and cylinders, surmounted by water tanks. Separating the two chassis is another frame carrying the boiler, cab, and fuel supply. This type of locomotive is valuable on lightly laid track; it can also negotiate sharp curves. It is widely used in Africa.

In simple expansion locomotives (such as "Big Boy"), the steam from the boiler, after being used simultaneously in two (or more) cylinders, is exhausted to the atmosphere. With compound expansion, the steam goes first to one or two small high-pressure cylinders and then to two large low-pressure cylinders before being exhausted. This results in greater thermal efficiency, but with the disadvantage of higher maintenance costs.

Simple expansion locomotives with more than two cylinders were used in a number of countries; three- and four-cylinder locomotives were common in Britain. Compound locomotives were most popular in France, where for many years most locomotive designs were of this type.

Various further refinements gradually improved the reciprocating steam locomotive. Some included higher boiler pressures (up to 290–300 pounds per square inch [20–21 kilograms per square centimetre] for some of the last locomotives, compared with around 200 for earlier designs); superheating, feed-water preheating, roller bearings, and the use of poppet (perpendicular) valves rather than sliding piston valves.

Low efficiency of steam locomotives

Still, the thermal efficiency of even the best modern steam locomotives seldom exceeded about 6 percent. Incomplete combustion, heat losses from the firebox, stack, boiler, and cylinders, and other losses dissipated most of the energy of the fuel burned. For this reason the steam locomotive became obsolete, but only slowly, because it had compensating advantages, notably its simplicity and ability to withstand abuse.

By 1971 steam locomotives were virtually extinct in North America, Britain, and western Europe. They were still used to a declining extent in Africa, Asia, and Australasia. More than half the motive power in India (and in some smaller nations) was still steam, however.

Electric locomotives. Efforts to propel railroad vehicles using batteries date from 1835, but the first successful application of electric traction was in 1879, when an electric locomotive ran at an exhibition in Berlin. The first commercial applications of electric traction were for suburban or metropolitan railroads. One of the earliest came in 1895, when the Baltimore and Ohio electrified a stretch of track in Baltimore to avoid smoke and noise problems in a tunnel. One of the first countries to use electric traction for main-line operations was Italy, where a system was inaugurated as early as 1902.

By World War I a number of electrified lines were operating both in Europe and in the United States. Major electrification programs were undertaken after that war in such countries as Sweden, Switzerland, Norway, Germany, and Austria. By the end of the 1920s nearly every European country had at least a small percentage of electrified track. Electric traction was also introduced in Australia (1919), New Zealand (1923), India (1925), Indonesia (1925), and South Africa (1926). A number of metropolitan terminals and suburban services were electrified between 1900 and 1938 in the United States, and there were a few main-line electrifications. The advent of the diesel locomotive inhibited further electrification in the United States after 1938, but following World War II electrification was rapidly extended in Europe; in Switzerland 99 percent of the lines were electrified. There was also expansion of electrified operations in Africa, Asia, and Australasia. By 1972 electrified lines comprised a significant percentage of total route miles in such countries as Sweden (62 percent), Norway (57 percent), Italy (59 percent), France (26 percent), West Germany (33 percent), Soviet Union (22 percent), Japan (45 percent), and Great Britain (19 percent). By contrast, electrified route mileage in the United States was less than 1 percent.

Advantages and disadvantages. Electric traction is generally considered the most economical and efficient means of operating a railroad, provided that cheap electricity is available and that the traffic density justifies the heavy capital cost. Being simply power-converting, rather than power-generating, devices, electric locomotives have several considerable advantages. They can draw on the resources of the central power plant to develop power greatly in excess of their nominal ratings to start a heavy train or to surmount a steep grade at high speed. A typical modern electric locomotive rated at 4,000 horsepower has been observed to develop as much as 10,000 horsepower for a short period under these conditions. Moreover, electric locomotives are quieter in operation than other types and produce no smoke or fumes. Electric locomotives require little time in the shop for maintenance, their maintenance costs are low, and they have a longer life than diesels.

Extra power for starting and grades

The greatest drawbacks to electrified operation are the high capital investment and maintenance cost of the fixed plant—the trolley wires and structures and power substations—and the costly changes that may be required in signalling systems to make them compatible with electrified operation. A less important disadvantage is the lack of flexibility of electric locomotives, which cannot operate where there are no trolley wires.

Types of traction systems. Electric-traction systems can be broadly divided into those using alternating current and those using direct current. With direct current, the most popular line (*i.e.,* trolley or third-rail) voltages are 1,500 and 3,000, although there is a large mileage of 600 volts in southern England and several systems in the 600- to 700-volt range around New York City. The disadvantages of direct current are that expensive substations are required at frequent intervals, and the overhead wire or third rail must be relatively large and heavy.

The low-voltage, series-wound, direct-current motor is well suited to railroad traction, being simple to construct and easy to control. It was on a line electrified at 1,500 volts direct current that in 1955 two different French electric locomotives (Figure 26) achieved a speed of 205 miles (330 kilometres) per hour.

The potential advantages of using alternating instead of direct current prompted early experiments and applications of this system. With alternating current, especially with relatively high trolley-wire voltages (10,000 volts or above), fewer substations are required, and the special equipment needed to produce direct current for the locomotives is eliminated. Available alternating-current motors, however, were not suitable for operation with alternating current of the standard commercial or industrial frequencies (50 hertz [cycles per second] in Europe; 60 hertz in the United States). It was necessary to use a lower frequency ($16\frac{2}{3}$ hertz is common in Europe; 25 hertz in the United States); this in turn required either special railroad power plants to generate alternating current at the required frequency or frequency-conversion equipment to change the available commercial frequency into the railroad frequency.

By courtesy of the French Embassy, Press and Information Division

Figure 26: French C-C type electric locomotive, which operates on 1,500 volts direct current. This is one of the locomotives that set a world speed record of 205 miles (330 kilometres) per hour in 1955.

Nevertheless, alternating-current trolley wires at $16\frac{2}{3}$ hertz are widely used on European railroads, primarily those where electrification began before World War II. Several main-line electrifications in the eastern United States were built using 25-hertz alternating current (these comprise the present Penn Central and Reading railroad systems).

Interest in using commercial-frequency alternating current on the trolley wire continued, however; and in 1933 experiments were carried out in both Hungary and Germany. The German State Railways electrified its Höllenthal branch with a trolley wire at 20,000 volts, 50 hertz.

Electrification on the French railroads

In 1945 Louis Armand, former president of the French railroads went ahead with further development of this system and converted a line between Aix-Les-Bains and La Roche-sur-Foron for the first practical experiments. This was so successful that a network of lines in northeastern France was electrified using 25,000-volt, 50-hertz alternating current.

Subsequently, the 25,000-volt, 50- or 60-hertz system has become virtually the standard for new electrification systems; it is used in a number of countries, including Britain, Turkey, Portugal, the Soviet Union, India, China, Japan, and Argentina. In 1971 several major North American railroads were studying the feasibility of electrifying key main-line segments using alternating current at 50,000 volts, 60 hertz.

With commercial-frequency, alternating-current systems, there are three ways of taking power to the locomotive driving wheels: (1) by a rotary converter or static rectifier on the locomotive to convert the alternating-current supply into direct current at low voltage to drive standard direct-current traction motors; (2) by a converter to produce variable-frequency current to drive alternating-current motors; (3) by direct use of alternating-current traction motors. The first method, using silicon rectifiers or silicon-control rectifiers (thyristers), is by far the most satisfactory. It has the advantage that the locomotive designer, if he wishes, can use the same standard direct-current traction motors that are widely used in diesel-electric locomotives.

In Europe, the problem of international operation of electric locomotives is complicated by the variety of electrification systems in use. The solution is to use locomotives designed to operate on several different voltages or frequencies or both. In the United States, equipment of the former New Haven Railroad (now Penn Central) operating into Grand Central Terminal, New York City, is designed to run on two systems: 660-volt direct current and 11,000-volt, 25-hertz alternating current.

Diesel-electric locomotives. By the end of the 1960s, the diesel-electric locomotive (or simply the diesel) had almost completely superseded the steam locomotive as the standard railroad motive power in most parts of the world, except on the electrified lines. The change came first and most quickly in North America, where, during the 25 years 1935–60 (and especially 1951–60), railroads in the United States completely replaced their steam locomotives.

What caused the diesel to supersede the steam locomotive so rapidly was the pressure of competition from other modes of transport and the continuing rise in wage costs, which forced the railroads to improve their services and adopt every possible measure to increase operating efficiency. Compared with the steam locomotive, the diesel has a number of major advantages:

1. It can operate for long periods with no lost time for maintenance; thus, the diesel can operate through on a run of 2,000 miles (3,200 kilometres) or more and then, after brief servicing, start the return trip. Steam locomotives require extensive servicing after only a few hours' operation.

2. It uses less fuel energy than a steam locomotive, for its thermal efficiency is about four times as great.

3. It can accelerate a train more rapidly and operate at higher sustained speeds with less damage to the track.

In addition, the diesel is superior to the steam locomotive because of its smoother acceleration, greater cleanliness, standardized repair parts, and operating flexibility (a number of diesel units can be combined and run by one man under multiple-unit control). With diesels, too, there is no problem of supplying large quantities of boiler feed water; there is no loss of power capability in cold weather; and there is less standby cost, since the locomotive can be completely shut down when not in use, whereas a steam locomotive must have a fire under its boiler even when on standby at the roundhouse.

The diesel-electric locomotive is, essentially, an electric locomotive that carries its own power plant. Its use, therefore, brings to a railroad many of the advantages of electrification, but without the capital cost of the power distribution and feed-wire system. As compared with an electric locomotive, however, the diesel-electric has two important drawbacks: (1) because it is a more complex mechanism than the electric, it costs more to buy and maintain and (2) since its output is essentially limited to that of its diesel engine, it can develop less horsepower per locomotive unit. Since high horsepower is required for high-speed operation, the diesel is, therefore, less desirable than the electric for high-speed passenger services and very fast freight operations.

Drawbacks of the diesel

Diesel development. Experiments with diesel-engine locomotives and railcars began almost as soon as the diesel engine was patented by the German engineer Rudolf Diesel in 1892. Attempts at building practical locomotives and railcars (for branch-line passenger runs) continued through the 1920s. The first successful diesel switch engine went into service in 1925; "road" locomotives were delivered to the Canadian National and New York Central railroads in 1928. The first really striking results with diesel traction were obtained in Germany in 1932. There, a two-car, streamlined, diesel-electric train, with two 400-horsepower engines, began running between Berlin and Hamburg on a schedule that averaged 77 miles (124 kilometres) per

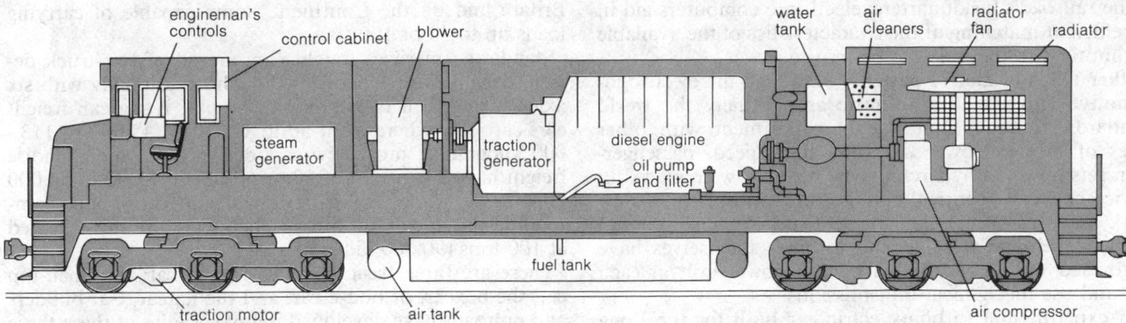

Figure 27: Cutaway of a modern diesel-electric locomotive.

hour. Diesel-electrics soon appeared elsewhere, notably in the United States.

The next step was to build a separate diesel-electric locomotive unit that could haul any train. In 1935 one such unit was delivered to the Baltimore and Ohio and two to the Santa Fe Railway Company. These were passenger units; the first road freight locomotive, a four-unit, 5,400-horsepower Electro-Motive Division, General Motors Corporation demonstrator, was not built until 1939.

By the end of World War II, the diesel locomotive had become a proven, standardized type of motive power, and it rapidly began to supersede the steam locomotive in North America. In the United States a fleet of 27,000 diesel locomotives proved fully capable of performing more transportation work than the 40,000 steam locomotives they replaced.

After World War II, the use of diesel traction greatly increased all over the world, though the pace of conversion was generally slower than in the United States. In Britain, steam-locomotive operation ended in 1968; by 1971 steam power had been largely superseded in most developed countries by diesels and electrification.

Elements of the diesel locomotive. Although the diesel engine (Figure 27) has been vastly improved in power and performance, the basic principles remain the same: drawing air into the cylinder, compressing it so that its temperature is raised, and then injecting a small quantity of oil into the cylinder. The oil ignites without a spark because of the high temperature. The diesel engine may operate on the two-stroke or four-stroke cycle and may have cylinders arranged in line, in V-formation, horizontally opposed, or vertically opposed. Rated operating speeds vary from 350 to 2,000 revolutions per minute and rated output may be from 10 to 3,600 horsepower. Railroads in the United States use engines in the 1,000-revolutions-per-minute range; in Europe and elsewhere, more compact but higher speed engines are common.

In the United States, early road units and most yard switching engines are equipped with diesels ranging from 600 to 1,500 horsepower. Road units commonly have engines ranging from 2,000 to 3,600 horsepower. Most builders use V-type engines, although in-line types are used on smaller locomotives (up to 1,200 horsepower).

Traction electrical system

With the nearly universal electric transmission, the diesel engine is directly connected to a main direct current generator that converts the mechanical energy produced by the engine into electrical energy. Through the appropriate control equipment, this is then used to drive the traction motors. The traction electrical system operates at a nominal 600-volts direct current, but the voltage varies greatly under operating conditions. The traction motors are of the series-wound type, each geared to the axle it drives. Most locomotives have a traction motor on each axle, although some passenger locomotives or units for light branch-line service may have six-wheel trucks (bogies) with the centre axle an idler.

In many recently built diesel-electric units, the engine drives an alternator (producing alternating current) instead of a direct-current generator. Static rectifiers convert the resulting alternating current to direct current for the traction motors. The reason for this design is that an alternator can produce more power and is less costly to maintain than an equivalent direct-current machine.

Other types of transmissions are also used in diesel locomotives. The hydraulic transmission has become quite popular in Germany. It employs a centrifugal pump or impeller driving a turbine in a chamber filled with oil or a similar fluid. The pump, driven by the diesel engine, converts the engine power to kinetic energy in the oil impinging on the turbine blades. The faster the blades move, the less the relative impinging speed of the oil and the faster the locomotive moves.

Mechanical transmission is the simplest type; it is mainly used in low-power locomotives. Basically it is a clutch and gearbox similar to those used in automobiles. A hydraulic coupling, in some cases, is used in place of a friction clutch.

Types of diesel motive power. There are four broad classes of railroad equipment that use diesel engines as prime movers:

1. The light railcar or rail bus (up to 180 horsepower) usually is four-wheeled and has mechanical transmission. It is often powered by a standard highway bus engine; it may be designed to haul a light trailer car.

2. The low-horsepower railcar (up to 1,000 horsepower) may have either mechanical or hydraulic transmission. Most railcars can haul additional trailer cars; some are designed mainly for this purpose, although they also have passenger and baggage accommodations.

3. Train sets (500 to 2,000 horsepower) are formations of more than one vehicle, usually designed to be worked from a single set of controls. The sets include one or more powered vehicles and usually have hydraulic or electric transmission.

4. Locomotives (ten to 6,600 horsepower) may have mechanical, hydraulic, or electric transmission, depending on power output and purpose. They are frequently designed to work in multiple-unit formations. Lower powered units (up to 600 horsepower) are usually designed for switching and light freight service. Medium-powered locomotives (600–1,200 horsepower) are normally used for freight, passenger, or heavy switching duties. Locomotives over 1,200 horsepower are required in main-line service in Europe and North America. In Europe locomotives in the 1,500- to 2,000-horsepower range are the most popular for express passenger work. In North America road freight units may range as high as 6,600 horsepower, and several units totalling as much as 15,000 horsepower may be used in multiple on heavy, fast trains.

Operating methods. Multiple-unit control and the operation of multiple diesel units in a train are almost universal in North America but much less common elsewhere. A number of railroads in the United States and Canada use "slave" locomotives; these are spotted in the middle of a long freight train and controlled automatically by radio from the locomotive cab at the front end of the train. Radio-controlled slave locomotives permit easier and more efficient handling of a very long freight train, up to as many as 250 cars in regular operations.

The "slave" locomotive

To take advantage of the diesel's special characteristics many railroads found it necessary to change both their operating techniques and their physical facilities. With diesels, many local and regional roundhouses and shops were closed, since diesels require much less frequent servicing than did steam locomotives. The scheduling of motive-power operations frequently has been centralized at the railroad's headquarters; electronic computers aid in the efficient matching of the characteristics of the available locomotives to the trains to be moved.

Other types of motive power. Although the electric locomotive and the diesel-electric are virtually the world standards, railroads continue to experiment with other types of motive power. In 1969 high-speed, passenger-train sets powered by aircraft-type turbines were placed in service between Montreal and Toronto and between New York and Boston. Though these "TurboTrains" are still in the development stage, the turbines themselves have performed well. These trains have a power unit at each end and use mechanical transmissions.

An experimental turbine-electric car built for the Long Island Rail Road in the U.S. proved sufficiently promising that additional units were planned. They are to be "dual powered" and operate from the third-rail electrification near New York City and under turbine power when outside the electrified zone.

The gas-turbine locomotive

In 1941 a gas-turbine locomotive was developed in Switzerland, and in the 1950s gas-turbine propulsion was tried in Britain and the United States. In France a two-car, gas-turbine-powered passenger train was tested at speeds up to 142 miles (228 kilometres) per hour and introduced in regular service on certain routes in 1970. British Rail was also studying gas turbines for passenger trains to operate at 150 miles (240 kilometres) per hour. The German Federal Railway used a gas turbine as a "booster" in one class of diesel-hydraulic locomotive.

Several attempts have been made to adapt the steam turbine to railroad traction. One of the first such experiments was a Swedish locomotive built in 1921. Other prototypes followed in Europe and the United States. They all functioned, but they made their appearance too late to compete against the diesel and electrification.

CARS

After the first crude beginnings, railroad-car design took divergent courses in North America and Europe, partly because of differing economic conditions and partly because of differing technological developments. Early cars on both continents were largely of two-axle design; but passenger-car builders soon began constructing cars with three and then four axles, the latter arranged in two four-wheel swivel trucks, or bogies. The trucks result in smoother riding qualities and also spread the weight of heavy vehicles over more axles.

Freight cars. European freight cars generally have two axles (four wheels), although there is a trend to two-truck, four-axle vehicles. Conventional British freight cars (goods wagons) have an average capacity of only about 13 tons, though many newer British cars are larger. On the Continent, the capacity of standard freight wagons varies from about 18 to 33 tons. The Soviet railroads use much larger, two-truck cars of up to 100 tons capacity. There is a growing trend toward higher capacity, four-axle cars in Britain and on the Continent, some capable of carrying loads up to 90 or 100 tons.

By courtesy of the Museum of Railway Traffic, Tokyo

Figure 28: Japanese double-deck car, especially designed for carrying automobiles; it can load up to 12 compact cars.

Standard American freight cars are all of two-truck design, usually with four axles though occasionally with six axles arranged in two three-axle trucks. American freight cars carry anywhere from 50 to 125 tons (45,000 to 113,000 kilograms); most new cars designed for merchandise freight have a capacity of 50 or 60 tons (45,000 to 54,000 kilograms), while new cars designed to carry bulk commodities, such as coal, ore, or chemicals, are mostly rated at 100 tons (90,000 kilograms).

There are three basic types of freight car: the open-top car, the boxcar, or house car, and the flatcar. Car builders and railroads have developed many varieties of these three basic types, plus many special types designed for efficiently carrying specific commodities.

Specialized freight cars

Among the special types of freight cars are double-deck cars for transporting automobiles (Figure 28), open cars with sliding roofs, pressurized tank cars for handling dry solids in bulk, hydraulically operating tipping cars for dumping bulk commodities, and boxcars with wide doors for easy loading and unloading of shipments on pallets.

Because of vertical-clearance limitations, highway trailers cannot be carried piggyback on conventionally designed flatcars on most European railroads. Ingenious special designs have overcome this problem. In France, for example, trailers are positioned on "kangaroo cars," which have pockets into which the trailer wheels are positioned, lowering the overall height. In West Germany highway trailers with their tractors are carried on certain fast intercity runs by special flatcars having small wheels to reduce the overall height.

On American railroads, in addition to the standard boxcar, the flatcar, and open-top "gondolas" and hopper cars (the latter equipped with doors for bottom unloading), the commonest specialized cars are tank cars, refrigerator cars, and livestock cars.

A growing trend is that of equipping cars with special internal fittings to accommodate specific products without the need for dunnage (*i.e.,* bracing or blocking of the load). Typical of these are the automobile-parts cars, which are often designed to carry certain automobile components, such as bodies, frames, or engines, of a single manufacturer. Among other special types of cars are those with "long travel" cushioned draft gear that absorb jolts and prevent damage to fragile commodities; extra-long flatcars with two- or three-level automobile racks; piggyback and container flatcars; 100- or 125-ton (90,000-or 113,000-kilogram) covered hopper cars for dry-bulk commodities; 100-ton gondolas for unit-train coal service; and 10,000-cubic-foot (280-cubic-metre) boxcars for light but bulky automobile parts.

Automobile-parts cars

The growing variety of specialized freight cars has complicated the problem of keeping each railroad shipper supplied with cars of the proper type. On the other hand, specialized cars usually run more miles and earn more revenue than standard cars. In the United States, so-called private car companies have played an increasing role. They acquire the cars and lease them to shippers or to the railroads themselves, a practice long followed with tank and refrigerator cars.

Passenger cars. The first passenger cars were simply road coaches with flanged wheels. Almost from the beginning, railroads in the United States began to use longer, eight-wheel cars riding on two four-wheel trucks, or bogies. In Britain and Europe, however, cars with more than six wheels were not introduced until the 1870s. Most cars of modern design, for both local and long-distance service, have an entrance at one or both ends of the car (some commuter-service cars also have additional centre doors), with centre aisle or a side corridor running the full length of the car. Flexible connections between cars give passengers access to any car of a moving train. In the United States modern passenger cars are usually 85 feet (25 metres) long and weigh from 60 to 80 tons (54,000 to 73,000 kilograms) or more. British and continental European cars are usually shorter and are always of lighter construction than cars in the United States. The standard British coach is 67 feet (20 metres) long; a modern, lightweight coach of the Swiss Federal Railways is 73 feet (22 metres) long. Recent continental designs, however, are up to 86½ feet (26 metres) in length and weigh 50 to 60 tons (45,000 to 54,000 kilograms). Narrow-gauge railroads impose weight and length restrictions. But even so, a 3.5-foot- (1.07-metre-) gauge coach of the South African Railways may be up to 63 feet five inches (19.3 metres) long and weigh up to about 48 tons (about 44,000 kilograms). Recent Australian cars follow American design and appearance.

Coaches. The interior arrangements and amenities on passenger cars vary widely. The most common type of car is the coach. In Europe the most favoured design has six- or eight-seat compartments, with the aisle, or corridor, along one side of the car. In the United States, two rows of double seats on either side of an aisle have long been standard; this design was appearing more frequently in Europe in the 1980s. Some American cars for local commuter runs have one row of triple seats and one row of double seats, with the centre aisle, permitting a 25 percent increase in the number of seated passengers. Several United States and Canadian railroads also use, for commuter runs, cars having an upper "gallery" in addition to the standard seating. These two-level coaches may seat up to 156 passengers. Luxury coaches in many countries have a small number of individual seats.

Sleeping cars. A crude sleeping car was operated in the United States as early as 1837; the first Pullman sleeper, named after its inventor and leased by the railroads, went into service in 1859. Sleeping cars were introduced in Europe and elsewhere beginning in the 1870s. Typical European sleeping cars have compartments with one, two, or more transverse beds (the trend is to more cars with single-berth compartments to meet the needs of business travellers). A typical modern American sleeping car has six bedrooms, each with two beds, and 12 "roomettes," with a single bed, giving a total capacity of 24 persons. Because the low capacity makes high fares necessary and so discourages patronage, the so-called slumbercoach was invented, with eight small double rooms and 24 single rooms, or a total capacity of 40.

"Feature" cars. Dining, or restaurant, cars became a feature of long-distance passenger trains almost from the beginning. A typical modern dining car has a kitchen at one end and tables seating 32 to 40 persons at the other. Such a car requires a large staff of waiters and kitchen personnel; thus, in recent years there has been a trend to "coffee-shop," or "lunch-counter," cars that provide limited, quick service and to food-service cars in which the passenger obtains his own food from vending machines.

The "coffee-shop" car

Another type of car often seen on long-haul trains is the lounge, or observation, car. It has a bar for beverage service and comfortable chairs for relaxation or reading. Dome cars, developed in the United States after World War II and popular on railroads having scenic routes, are also found in Canada and Europe. In a dome car passengers ride under a raised, glassed-in roof section that affords a wide-range view of the countryside.

Special types of cars. Besides the conventional freight and passenger cars already described, the world's railroads operate many special types of rolling equipment. Most numerous are the powered passenger cars and train sets mentioned previously. These may be operated by electricity on electrified railroads or have diesel engines or turbine engines mounted under the car floors. Such cars are usually designed to operate in multiple under the control of one driver and are used extensively for commuter service. The high-speed Metroliner trains (see below) operating on the electrified line between New York and Washington are of this type. Single or multiple diesel-powered passenger cars are used on light traffic lines.

Highly specialized, too, are a small number of freight cars designed to carry unusually heavy or oversized loads, such as large electrical transformers. One such car (Figure 29) carries a transformer suspended between two sets of high-capacity trucks. It has a total capacity of 375 tons (340,000 kilograms), carried on 28 wheels.

Among the many types of railroad "service vehicles" are the so-called office, or business, cars used by company officials while on inspection tours of the line, track-measuring cars and rail "detector" cars that automatically record the condition of the track surface alignment or locate internal flaws in the rails, and various types of instructional, or personnel-training, cars. "Camp cars" are often used to house the personnel of maintenance forces engaged in major projects, such as renewing rail or constructing a new line.

Figure 29: Specialized flatcar with low central section designed to carry electric power transformers while maintaining clearance in tunnels and under low bridges. The car is also unusual in its arrangement of eight axles.
UPI Compix

Rolling-stock standardization. Much of the commercial effectiveness of the railroad has derived from the standardization of basic rolling-stock components. Each railroad builds cars suited to its own needs; but cars can be interchanged freely among railroads (assuming that they use a common track gauge) only if such elements as wheels, wheel bearings, couplers, and brakes are standardized. The knuckle type of automatic coupler was adopted in North America beginning in 1882; a similar coupler is used in several other countries, notably Australia, Japan, and the Soviet Union. Screw-and-buffer couplers are used in western Europe, but a knuckle coupler compatible with that used in the Soviet Union is under development.

The Westinghouse air brake

There are two general types of continuous braking systems: the vacuum brake and the compressed-air brake. Of the two, the more popular is the air brake, patented in 1869 by George Westinghouse of the United States, where it was made compulsory equipment in 1893. The vacuum brake is used principally in Britain, where continuous brakes have been compulsory on passenger cars since 1889. With either system, application of the brakes on the locomotives applies the brakes throughout the entire train; and should the train become uncoupled, the brakes are automatically applied.

The brake itself takes the form of a single or double shoe that presses against the wheel tread. The disk brake has also been widely applied on high-speed passenger trains and some freight cars as well.

RAILROAD TRACK AND ROADWAY

Location and construction. Ideally, a railroad should be built in a straight line, over level ground, between large centres of trade and travel. In practice, this ideal is rarely approached. The location engineer, faced with the terrain to be traversed, must balance the cost of construction against annual maintenance and operating costs, as well as against the probable traffic volume and profit.

Thus, in areas of dense population and heavy industrial activities, the railroads were generally built for heavy duty, with minimum grades and curvature, heavy bridges, and perhaps multiple tracks. Examples include most of the main-line railroads of Britain and the European continent. In North and South America, and elsewhere, the country was sparsely settled, and the railroads had to be built at minimal costs. Thus, the lines were of lighter construction, with sharper grades and curves. As traffic grew, main routes were improved to increase their capacity and to reduce operating costs.

The gauge or distance between the inside faces of the running rails, can affect the cost of building and equipping a railroad. About 60 percent of the world's railroad mileage has been built to standard gauge, four feet 8 1/2 inches (1.435 metres). However, a considerable mileage of lines with narrower gauges has been constructed, mainly in undeveloped and sparsely settled countries. Use of a narrow gauge permits some saving in space. In addition, narrow-gauge cars and locomotives are generally smaller, lighter, and less costly than those used on standard gauge lines. Disadvantages of a narrow gauge include the limitation on speed because of reduced lateral stability and limitations on the size of locomotives and cars.

Eliminating adverse grades

The advent of modern high-capacity earth-moving machinery, developed mainly for highway construction, has made it economically feasible for many railroads to eliminate former adverse grades and curves through line changes. Graders, bulldozers, and similar equipment make it possible to dig deeper cuts through hillsides and to make higher fills where necessary to smooth out the profile of the track. Modern equipment has also helped improve railroad roadbeds in other ways. A number of railroads carried out ditching programs in which the drainage ditches along the roadbed were deepened. Where the roadbed is unstable, injecting concrete grout into the subgrade under pressure is a widely used technique. In planning roadbed improvements, as well as in new construction, railroads have drawn on modern soil-engineering techniques.

The first step in building a new railroad line, after the route has been surveyed and cleared of brush and trees, is to grade the right-of-way, much as is done when building a highway. Next, the crossties, or sleepers, are distributed and the rails laid and fastened to the ties. Then, ballast (usually crushed rock, slag, or volcanic ash) is applied. Finally, the track is aligned in both the horizontal and vertical planes, and the ballast is tamped, or compacted, around and under the ties.

In Canada, where much new railroad mileage was built after World War II, track-laying machines were often used (Figure 30). The machine is mounted on railcars. It feeds ties and rails ahead of the working crew, moving forward over the new track as soon as it is spiked down.

The inventors of the modern rail

Rail. The modern railroad rail has a flat bottom, and its cross section is much like an inverted T. An English engineer, Charles Vignoles, is credited with the invention of this design of rail in the 1830s. A similar design was also developed by Robert L. Stevens, president of the Camden and Amboy Railroad in the United States.

Present-day rail is, in appearance, very similar to the early designs of Vignoles and Stevens. Actually, however, it is a highly refined product in terms of both engineering and metallurgy. Much study and research have produced designs that minimize internal stresses under the weight of traffic and thus prolong rail life. Sometimes the rail surface is hardened to reduce the wear of the rail under extremely heavy cars or on sharp curves. After they have been rolled at the steel mills, rails are allowed to cool slowly in special boxes. This controlled cooling minimizes internal shatter cracks, which at one time were a major cause of broken rails in track.

In Europe a standard rail length of 30 metres (98 feet five inches) is common. The weight of rail, for main-line use, is from about 45 kilograms per metre (about 90 pounds per yard) to 75 kilograms per metre (150 pounds per yard). British Railways uses a flat-bottomed rail weighing 55 kilograms per metre (110 pounds per yard).

Railroads in the United States and Canada have used T-rails of hundreds of different cross sections. Many of these different sections are still in use, but there is a strong trend to standardizing on a few sections. In the 1970s most new rail in North America weighed 119 or 136 pounds per yard. The standard American rail section has a length of 39 feet (about 12 metres).

One of the most important developments is the welding of standard rails into long lengths. This continuous welded rail results in a smoother track that requires less maintenance. The rail is usually welded into lengths of about one-quarter mile (400 metres). Once laid in track, these quarter-mile lengths are often welded together in turn to form rails several miles long without a break.

Welded rail was tried for the first time in 1933 in the United States. It was not until the decade of the 1950s, however, that railroads turned to welded rail in earnest. By 1971 virtually all new rail, and much old rail taken up and relaid in new locations, was being laid in welded lengths. Welded rail was standard practice, or extensively used, in the United States, Japan, Canada, Germany, France, and Britain.

Controlling the temperature expansion of long welded rails proved not so difficult as first thought. It was found that the problem could be minimized by extensive anchorage of the rails to the ties to prevent them from moving when the temperature changes by the use of a heavy ballast section and by laying the rails when the ambient temperature is close to the mean temperature prevailing in the particular locality.

Rail fittings. Whether in standard or long lengths, rails are joined to each other and kept in alignment by fishplates or joint bars. The offset-head spike is the most used and least expensive way of fastening the rails to wooden crossties, but several different types of screw spikes and clips are also used extensively on heavy-traffic lines in many countries. The rails may be attached directly to wooden crossties, but on heavy-traffic lines it is common to seat the rail in a tie plate that distributes the load over a wider area of the tie. A screw or clip fitting must be used to attach rails to concrete ties. A pad of rubber or other resilient material is always used between the rail and a concrete tie.

Fastening rails to crossties

Crossties (sleepers). Timber has been used for railroad ties almost from the beginning, and it is still the most common material for this purpose. The modern wood crosstie is treated with preservative chemical to improve its life; the average life of crossties on main-line railroads is about 35 years. The cost of wood ties has risen steadily, creating interest in ties of other materials.

Steel ties have long been used in certain European, African, and Asian countries. Concrete ties, usually reinforced with steel rods or wires, have been gaining in popularity, as have ties consisting of concrete blocks joined by steel spacing bars. A combination of concrete ties and long welded rails produces an exceptionally solid and smooth-riding form of track. Concrete ties are extensively used in Britain, Europe, and Japan.

Track maintenance. Modern machinery enables a small

By courtesy of the Baltimore and Ohio Railroad Company

Figure 30: Moving work train laying quarter-mile lengths of continuous welded rail, which is positioned two strings at a time.

group of men to maintain a relatively long stretch of railroad track. Machines are available to do all the necessary track maintenance tasks: removing and inserting ties, tamping the ballast, spiking rail, tightening bolts, and aligning the track. Mechanized equipment also can renew rail, either in conventional bolted lengths or with long welded lengths; cranes are used to remove the old rail and lay the new.

Prefabricated track sections

Complete sections of track—rails and crossties—may be prefabricated and laid in the track by mechanical means. Rail-grinding machines run over the track to even out irregularities in the rail surface. Track-measurement cars, under their own power or coupled into regular trains, can record all aspects of track alignment and riding quality on moving charts, so that maintenance forces can pinpoint the specific locations needing corrective work. Detector cars move over the main-line tracks at intervals with electronic-inspection apparatus to locate any internal flaws in the rails.

The mechanization of track maintenance after World War II has constituted a technologic revolution comparable to the development of the diesel locomotive and electrification. In Europe in particular, highly sophisticated maintenance machines have come into use.

Auxiliary plant. Railroad fixed plant consists of much more than the track. The New Sanyo Line runs through tunnels for nearly half its total length. Railroad civil-engineering forces are concerned with constructing and maintaining thousands of buildings, ranging from switch tenders' shanties to huge passenger terminals.

Bridges. The designer of a railroad bridge must allow for forces that result from the concentrated impact that occurs as a train moves onto the bridge; the pounding of wheels, the sidesway of the train, and the drag or push effect as a train is braked or started on a bridge. These factors mean that a railroad bridge must be of heavier construction than a highway bridge of equal length.

As freight-train loads become heavier and train speeds higher, bridges need to be further strengthened. Another major objective in modern railroad-bridge construction is the need to minimize maintenance costs. The use of weathering steel, which needs no painting, all-welded construction, and permanent walkways for maintenance personnel contribute to this end. In the advanced countries there has been a widespread trend toward replacing timber trestles with concrete-slab structures or with concrete or steel-pipe culverts. The railroads also have sought ways to mechanize the maintenance of their bridges (see also PUBLIC WORKS: *Bridges*).

Buildings. Railroad buildings in the 20th century have become fewer and more functional. With paved highways running almost everywhere in the developed countries, it has become more economical to concentrate both freight and passenger operations at fewer but larger, strategically located stations. Only a few really modern passenger stations have been built. Notable among them are the highly efficient and functional stations on the New Tōkaidō Line in Japan, the new Euston station in London, and several of the new and rebuilt stations on the European continent, such as the main stations at Rome and Milan.

Diesel maintenance shops

Diesel and electric locomotives require few maintenance shops as compared with steam locomotives. Diesel shops are of three main types: small fueling, sanding, and light-maintenance centres at points where runs end or locomotives are changed; intermediate-maintenance shops, usually serving a region, that perform certain routine inspection and maintenance tasks; and heavy-repair shops, where locomotives undergo extensive repairing or rebuilding. Usually a single railroad requires only one of the latter type of shop.

Car shops, too, have been reduced in number and made more efficient through the use of process-line techniques. Terminal points and major classification yards usually have a shop for light repairs and maintenance of cars; a railroad also usually has one or more heavy-repair shops, where cars are completely overhauled or where new cars are manufactured.

It is usually more efficient to construct new shop buildings rather than convert old ones to handle modern types of rolling stock. Often, prefabricated buildings provide an economical solution to this problem. An important feature of new locomotive shops in particular is provision for collection and disposal of waste oil and other potentially polluting products of the shop or terminal operation.

Tunnels. Although very expensive, tunnelling provides the most economical means for railroads to traverse mountainous terrain or to gain access to the heart of a crowded city. Railroad tunnels, however, confront the construction engineer with some unique problems, particularly in the ventilation of tunnels on lines that are not electrified.

Some examples of famous tunnels and methods of construction are described in the article PUBLIC WORKS: *Tunneling and underground excavation.*

RAILROAD OPERATIONS AND CONTROL

Because a railroad's factory—its plant and train operations—may be spread out over thousands of miles and hundreds of communities, it has operating and service problems in some respects more complex than those of a major manufacturing installation. It is not surprising, therefore, that railroads have been among the pioneers in the use of improved methods of communication and control, from the telegraph to such present-day developments as the electronic computer and automation techniques.

Communications. Railroads were among the first to adopt the electric telegraph and the telephone, both for dispatching trains and for handling other business messages. Today, the railroads are among the larger operators of electronic communications systems.

Radio. Railroads began experimenting with radio at a very early date, but it became practical to use train radio on a large scale only after World War II, when compact and reliable very-high-frequency two-way equipment was developed. In train operations radio permits communication between the front and rear of a long train, between two trains, and between trains and the central dispatcher.

In terminals two-way radio greatly speeds yard-switching work. Through its use, widely separated elements of mechanized track-maintenance gangs can maintain contact with each other and with oncoming trains. Supervisory personnel often use radio in automobiles to maintain contact with the operations under their control.

Microwave communications

As the demand for more railroad communication lines has grown, more and more companies have begun to use broad-band radio beams (microwave) to supplement or replace the traditional lineside telegraph wires. As early as 1959, the Pacific Great Eastern Railway in western Canada began to use microwave radio for all communications, doing away almost entirely with line wires. Other railroads all over the world were turning to microwave in the 1970s and '80s.

Computers. A major reason for the growing use of microwave was the tremendously increased demand for circuits that developed from the railroads' widespread use of electronic computers.

Earlier, railroads had been among the leaders in adopting punched-card and other advanced techniques of data processing. In the 1970s and '80s there was a strong trend toward "total information" systems built around the computer. In such a system, each field reporting point, usually a freight-yard office or station, is equipped with a computer input device. Through this device, full information about every car movement (or other action) taking place at that point can be placed directly into the central computer, usually located at company headquarters. From data received from all the field reporting points on the railroad, the computer can be programmed to produce a variety of outputs. These may include train-consist reports (listing cars) for the terminal next ahead of a train, car-location reports for the railroad's customer-service offices, car-movement information for the car-records department, revenue information for the accounting department, plus traffic-flow data and commodity statistics useful in market research and data on the freightcar needs at each location to aid in distributing empty cars for loading.

Other pertinent data also may be integrated into the system so that the railroad's managers have a complete, up-to-the-minute picture of almost every phase of its operations. Such complete information and control systems promise to be a powerful tool for optimizing railroad operations and producing better service.

Signalling. Railroad signals are a form of communication designed to inform the train crew, particularly the engine crew, of track conditions ahead and to tell it how to operate the train.

The time-interval signal system

Methods of controlling train operations evolved over many years of trial and error. A common method in the early years was to run trains on a time-interval system; *i.e.,* a train was required to leave a station a certain number of minutes behind an earlier train moving in the same direction. It was common on single-track lines to program all operations in accordance with a timetable, which set up all the places trains were to meet and which could not be varied.

The development of distance-interval systems was a great improvement. In these so-called block systems, a train is prevented from entering a specific section of track until the train already in that section has left it.

The earliest form of railroad signal was simply a flag by day or a lamp at night. The first movable signal was a revolving board, introduced in the 1830s, followed in 1841 by the semaphore signal. One early signal consisted of a large ball that was hoisted to the top of a pole to inform the engineman that he might proceed (hence, the origin of the term highball).

The semaphore signal was nearly universal until the early years of the 20th century, when it began to be superseded, first by the colour-light signal and then by the searchlight type. The colour-light signal uses a separate lens and light bulb for each signal aspect, usually green, yellow, and red. The searchlight signal uses only a single, powerful lens and bulb; the different colours are displayed through the lens by means of roundels, or colour filters, that are rotated in front of the lamp. Two other types of signals are also used to a limited extent: the position light, in which rows of yellow lights duplicate the positions of semaphore arms, and the colour-position light signal, which uses coloured lights arranged in rows.

Most lines in Europe use a manual block system in which operations are controlled from wayside cabins or towers in conjunction with the wayside signals. Each tower controls a section; a train is not permitted to enter a section until the train ahead has left the section. Electric interlocking improves this system by making it impossible to give a "line clear" signal indication if the section is already occupied by a train.

The automatic block system

The basis of much of today's railroad signalling is the automatic block system, introduced in 1872 and one of the first examples of automation. It uses track circuits that are short-circuited by the wheels and axles of a train, putting the signals to the rear of the train, and to the front as well on single track, at the danger aspect. A track circuit is made by the two rails of a section of track, insulated at their ends. Electric current, fed into the section at one end, flows through a relay at the opposite end. The wheels of the train will then short-circuit the current supply and de-energize the relay.

Signalling on African, Asian, and Australian systems usually follows European practice in areas of heavy traffic. On light traffic lines, control is often via the telegraph or telephone.

Operation on the basis of a timetable alone, which was common on early lines in the United States, had the disadvantage that if one train were delayed, others would also be delayed, since it was impossible to change the meeting points. By using the telegraph, and later the telephone, the dispatcher could issue orders to keep trains moving in unusual circumstances or to operate extra trains as required. This "timetable–train order" system is still used on many lines in the United States and Canada. It is often supplemented with automatic block signals to provide an additional safety factor.

The first attempts at interlocking switches and signals were made in France in 1855 and in Britain in 1856. Interlocking at crossings and junctions prevents the signalman from displaying a clear signal for one route when he has already given clearance to a train on a conflicting route. Route-setting or route-interlocking systems are modern extensions of this principle. With them a towerman or dispatcher can set up a complete route through a complicated track area by simply pushing buttons on a control panel. This system allows a large area to be controlled from one point.

A logical development of the route-interlocking principle is centralized traffic control, a system in which trains are controlled entirely from a central point through remote operation of switches and signals (Figure 31). The operator sees the track layout in miniature on his control panel and directs the movement of trains over distances from a few miles to many hundreds of miles. Lights on the panel show the location and progress of all trains at all times.

By courtesy of the British Railways Board

Figure 31: Computerized signalling control centre at London Bridge Station, London.

In centralized traffic control, track circuiting is essential to ensure that the system always knows where each train is. Switches and signals are operated by coded electrical pulses that reduce the wiring required. Over long distances, centralized traffic control substantially increases track capacity by making more effective use of the trackage. Since it eliminates any need for written orders or manual operation of block signals, it permits closing telegraph or signal stations, another major economy.

The trend toward automation. A recent refinement in traffic control is to arrange the system for fully automatic operation. The machine will then set switches and clear signals for each train automatically; the dispatcher need exercise control only in unusual circumstances. This enables one dispatcher to control a still longer section of railroad. Completely automatic signalling activated by electronic program machines is used on some rapid-transit rail lines.

Automatic central traffic control

Automatic train control provides the locomotive engineman with audible (and sometimes visual) information on track conditions. Should he ignore a restrictive signal indication, the brakes are applied automatically to stop the train. A refinement of this system incorporates automatic control of train speed. A miniature signal in the cab repeats the aspects of the wayside signals (or it may take the place of wayside signals). Should train speed exceed that called for by the aspect being displayed, the brakes are applied and the speed reduced to the permissible level.

Only a slight further extension of this technique is needed to permit fully automatic operation of the train. By the early 1970s, a number of mining and industrial railroads were operated with crewless trains under full automation or remote control. On the high-speed New Tōkaidō Line in Japan, all trains operate under computerized automatic control throughout the entire 320-mile (510-kilometre) length of the line. The engineman, however, starts the trains, stops the train at station stops, and opens and closes the train doors. A similar system is used on the London Transport Victoria line, the Patco transit line in Camden, New Jersey, and the Bay Area Rapid Transit system in San Francisco.

Among other automatic aids to railroad operation is the

infrared "hotbox detector," which, located at trackside, automatically detects the presence of an overheated wheel bearing and alerts the train crew. Broken flange detectors are used in major terminals to indicate the presence of damaged wheels. Dragging equipment detectors set wayside signals to danger if a car's brake rigging or other component is dragging on the track. Slide detectors warn of rocks or earth that have dropped onto the track from an earth cutting; high-water detectors warn of flood conditions on the track; high-wide detectors alert the train crew of a freight load that may have shifted or of a load that is too high or wide to clear bridges or tunnels.

The automated marshalling yard

A major area for automation techniques in railroading is the large classification or marshalling yard. In such yards, freight cars from many different origins are sorted out and placed in new trains going to the appropriate destinations.

Most large classification yards have a "hump" over which cars are pushed. They then roll down from the hump by gravity and each is routed into a classification or "bowl" track corresponding to its destination.

By the 1970s, operations in the newer classification yards had reached a high degree of automation. The heart of such a yard is a digital computer, into which is fed information concerning all cars in the yard or en route to it. As the cars are pushed up the hump, electronic scanners confirm their identity by means of a light-reflective label, place the data (car owner, number, and type) in a computer, and then set switches to direct each car into the proper bowl track. Electronic speed-control equipment measures such factors as the weight, speed, and rolling friction of each car and operates electric or electropneumatic "retarders" to control the speed of each car as it rolls down from the hump. Every phase of the yard's operations is monitored by a computerized management control and information system.

Modern classification yards usually also use radio, telephone, teleprinter, pneumatic tube, and closed-circuit television. Repair shops adjacent to the yards are designed for quick, mechanized repair of cars found to be defective as they move over the hump.

Because such electronically equipped yards can sort cars with great efficiency, they eliminate the need to do such work at other, smaller yards. Thus, one large electronic yard may permit the closing or curtailing of a dozen or more other yards. Most modern electronic yards have quickly paid for themselves out of operating savings—and this takes no account of the benefits of improved service to shippers.

REGULATION, ECONOMICS, AND LABOUR RELATIONS

Regulation and public control. Although most of the early railroads were built and operated as private, profit-making businesses, railroads soon came under relatively intense public scrutiny and regulation. This was probably inevitable because of the far-reaching influence railroads quickly developed over the life and the commercial activities of the communities and countries they served. The history of regulation followed the same path with minor variations in all countries; beginning with regulation of railroad construction—that is, deciding whether to permit a new line to be built and approving its location—the government took an increasing interest in details of operation, especially in connection with safety. Railway acts were passed in country after country prescribing signal modes, brakes, track standards, employee training, and other aspects of railroad operation. At the same time, governments took an increasing interest in the financial side of railroads, regulating rates and fares and exercising licensing power over mergers and other financial operations. Degree of public regulation varied, but by the early 1970s in nearly every country in the world, with the notable exception of the United States, regulation had evolved into public ownership and operation. This resulted from the railroads' increasing financial difficulties in the course of the 20th century.

Post-war financial problems

Competition from other modes increased sharply after World War II for many of the world's railroads. Because of governmental and labour union restrictions, as well as the large investment required in railroad fixed plant (*i.e.,* track, bridges, buildings, stations), it was difficult for the railroads to adjust their operations to changing conditions. Unlike other kinds of businesses, a main-line railroad simply cannot cease operating when it gets into financial difficulties; its services are too essential to the economy of the area it serves. (Many secondary and branch-line railroads have, however, been pulled up, especially in Britain and the United States.) Thus, the solution has been to nationalize the railroad—to have the government provide the service. Operating deficits are then met out of tax revenues.

By 1971 only two large countries, the United States and Canada, had major railroads that were privately run. In Canada one large system, Canadian Pacific (CP Rail), remained a private enterprise, while the other line, Canadian National Railways, was a government-owned corporation. France nationalized its remaining privately owned railroads in 1938; Britain nationalized its four major companies (which had been formed out of 123 separate railroads after World War I) in 1948.

One result of growing financial difficulties in the United States was a wave of mergers during the 1950s and 1960s. Pushed through after protracted regulatory and legal delays were a number of important consolidations. Some of them were the merger of the Erie and the Delaware, Lackawanna and Western railroads to form Erie Lackawanna; Pennsylvania, New York Central, New York, New Haven and Hartford Railroad Company into the Penn Central; merger into the Norfolk and Western Railway of the former New York, Chicago and St. Louis and the Wabash railroads; merger of Atlantic Coast Line and Seaboard Air Line railroads to form Seaboard Coast Line Railroad; merger of Chicago, Burlington and Quincy Railroad, Great Northern Railway, Northern Pacific Railway, and Spokane, Portland and Seattle Railway to form Burlington Northern.

In 1970 the largest railroad in the United States, Penn Central, entered bankruptcy proceedings. After several attempts at reorganization had failed, the railroad's lines and equipment were acquired in 1976 by the new Conrail system (see below).

Innovations by nationalized railroads

While nationalization preserves services felt to be essential, it does not obviate the need for railroads to change, improve, and compete. Some of the most imaginative marketing innovations (for example, Freightliner, Trans-Europ Express, Japan's New Tōkaidō services) have come out of nationally run companies. In France the French National Railways have pioneered in freight-rate innovations. The French National Railways were reorganized to operate much like a privately run business, if possible at a profit. Other nationalized railroads, such as those in Sweden, Switzerland, The Netherlands, and Canada, also operate as much as possible under the incentives of a private business.

Competition and marketing. Planned as money-making enterprises, many early railroads were notably successful financially. Indeed, especially in Britain and the United States, railroad stocks were long highly regarded. Even today, a few of the more strategically located and well-managed American lines are notably good earners. In recent years, however, the picture has been much different.

The development of the internal-combustion engine and its application to highway vehicles and the invention of the airplane had far-reaching effects on railroad transportation. In the interval between the two world wars, buses, automobiles, and highway trucks were already cutting deeply into traffic that once had been exclusively the railroads'. World War II hastened the technological development of these new competitors as well as of air and pipeline transportation.

By the late 1950s, the inroads of competitors had reached serious proportions, from the railroad viewpoint, in the United States, Britain, and Canada; by 1970 the same situation was developing in western Europe and Japan. The loss of traffic extended to both passengers and freight and was especially pronounced on branch lines. By 1970, railroads in the United States had virtually abandoned the business of carrying intercity passengers, although they still moved much local commuter traffic in several large

Figure 32: (Left) Freightliner container train, a fast shuttle operated throughout the United Kingdom by British Railways. (Right) The "Fuel Foiler," a lightweight piggyback freight train of the Santa Fe Railway, which uses less fuel than conventional equipment for hauling piggyback trailers.

By courtesy of (left) the British Railways Board, (right) Santa Fe Railway

urban areas. A quasi-government company, the National Railroad Passenger Corporation (Amtrak), was formed in 1970 to take over and if possible improve the operation of about 200 intercity passenger runs thought to be essential to the national economy. Railroads in the United States were also suffering from the diversion of profitable freight traffic to trucks and pipelines. In 1973 another quasi-governmental body, the Consolidated Rail Corporation (Conrail), was established. It began operations in 1976 with major portions of the lines of six bankrupt railway companies in the northeast: the Central Railroad of New Jersey, Erie Lackawanna, Lehigh and Hudson, Lehigh Valley, Penn Central, and Reading.

In Britain, western Europe, and Japan, competitors were especially effective in diverting freight traffic from the railroads, although passenger traffic was also affected as the ownership of automobiles grew. Accustomed to competing, if at all, only with each other, the railroads found it hard to adjust their thinking and their operations to meet the challenge of competitors who could offer the public faster, more flexible, and in some cases cheaper service, and who in most cases were burdened much less by government regulation. Many railroads, however, began to fight back against their competitors with considerable success. In the passenger field, typical railroad responses to competition include much faster and more comfortable services, such as the TEE (Trans-Europ Express) services on the European continent, the Inter-City expresses in Britain, and the Metroliners in the United States.

In freight, considerable success has resulted from the "marketing approach," wherein railroads closely tailor their rates, services, and equipment to the particular needs of specific shippers. Typical are the "unit" or "block" trains operated for shippers of bulk commodities, such as coal, oil, ore, and grain. These trains are composed of large, modern cars designed for the commodity to be carried. They operate as a unit on fast schedules between one origin and one destination, bypassing all intermediate yards and terminals en route. With faster operation and larger cars, these trains are so productive that they permit the railroads to offer greatly reduced rates.

Another way in which railroads have responded to new competition is to offer shippers many special types of freight cars designed to load particular commodities quickly and at minimum cost, such as the trilevel autorack car, the 10,000-cubic foot (280-cubic metre) boxcar, and 100-ton (91,000-kilogram) covered hopper cars and gondolas.

The piggyback concept and containerization

Another significant competitive development was piggyback and containerized services (Figure 32). The piggyback idea, which actually dates from the 19th century, combines the flexibility of truck pickup and delivery with the economy of rail movement between cities. Along with piggyback development has come increasing interest among railroads (as well as other modes of transport) in container systems, by which merchandise could be loaded into large standard containers or boxes that could move via highway on a truck chassis, via rail on special container cars, in ships especially equipped to handle them, or even by air. A single shipment might use two or more modes of transport in the course of its trip. In western Europe special TEEM (Trans-Europ Express Merchandise) trains operate between major points, carrying only containers. In Britain, fast container shuttle trains now operate between about two dozen main cities and ports. This Freightliner system (Figure 32) has been highly successful and is said to be competitive with over-the-road trucking, even over relatively short distances. Canadian and Japanese railroads also have extensive container operations, mainly for import-export traffic.

Labour relations. Railroads were among the first industries to feel the effects of trade union activity. Railroad unions in the United States are organized along craft lines; in the early 1970s there were 19 railroad labour organizations. In most countries, however, a single large union embraces all railroad workers. Labour relations are governed by a variety of laws, which, in the democratic countries, guarantee the right of collective bargaining, usually with provision for mediation. Though railroad labour history includes many chapters of violence and bitterness in the past, its more recent era has been relatively peaceful. However, there was a discernible tendency toward an increase in work stoppages from the 1960s onward.

THE FUTURE OF RAILROADS

The railroad industry can look back over a proud history. Railroads were a vital element in the Industrial Revolution. They helped make Britain an industrial power, played similar roles in countries such as France and Germany, and went on to do much the same in Russia and Japan. Railroads almost literally built the United States and Canada; and they remained the economic backbone of most of the major world powers.

But as the last third of the 20th century began, the railroads in a number of countries, most notably Britain and the United States, were in serious trouble. The railroads' share of the total transportation business was dropping steadily. The railroads in most countries had long since come under state control, and the remaining privately owned lines were finding it difficult to operate at a profit. Some observers believed the end of railroading was in sight. Technology was evolving so rapidly that it was impossible to say, as of the early 1970s, that this could not happen, but it seemed unlikely. It was becoming clear, however, that the railroad of the future would have a different role to play than in the past.

Predictions of the end of railroading

For more than a century the railroad was the dominant form of land transportation in much of the world. It was, and remains, the one land carrier that can carry almost anything, anywhere the tracks go, and do it at a true cost lower than other types of land-air transportation.

Today, however, other modes of transportation have been developed to the point where they can do certain transportation jobs more effectively than the railroads. Pipelines can carry liquids and some solids over long distances economically. Airplanes, with their great speed, can carry some types of light, valuable freight at a saving; and trucks offer speed and flexibility, especially for the shorter hauls. The private automobile, operating over modern highways, and the airplane have taken over much passenger traffic formerly handled on rails. The motorbus is an effective competitor for the short-to medium-distance passenger business. The modern barge, operating on improved inland waterways systems, can move many commodities over specific routes at very low cost.

Undeniably, these competitors of the railroad can do a better job on some types of transportation tasks. The development of these newer modes, therefore, has changed the role of the railroad from that of the general-purpose carrier to that of a more specialized carrier, just as the other modes are specialized.

The future role of the railroad as a specialized carrier will vary in different nations. In general, however, the railroad is particularly strong in these areas:

1. It is especially effective in moving large volumes of bulk commodities, such as coal, ores, chemicals, and grain, over relatively long distances. It can also move large volumes of finished merchandise economically at relatively high speeds over long distances.

2. The railroad can efficiently handle containers in large volumes between major centres, and in some countries, trucks on "piggyback" trains. An efficient railroad container or piggyback shuttle system can be viable even over relatively short distance.

3. The railroad is the best mode for moving large numbers of commuters between big metropolitan centres and the outlying suburban areas.

4. Very high speed intercity passenger services can be successful when operated with modern equipment at distances of up to about 300 miles (500 kilometres).

In short, the railroad under modern conditions is at its best as a high-volume, medium- and long-distance carrier of both passengers and freight. There are, of course, many exceptions to this general rule.

The potential of the modern railroad

In looking at the future place of railroads, three other factors should be noted:

1. A railroad disturbs the natural environment far less than a highway or an air-transport system. It also produces less pollutants per unit of transportation performed than either highway or air transportation. These factors should become more significant as society increasingly concerns itself with the need to preserve the environment and to reduce air, water, and noise pollution.

2. A railroad is far more efficient in its use of fuel than are either highway or air transportation. It is probable that future concern over the best use of these resources will produce more emphasis on rail transportation.

3. While much public money has gone into technological research on the newer forms of transportation and into constructing facilities for them, relatively little has been spent to improve railroad technology. Thus, even the most advanced of today's railroad plants and services, with few exceptions, do not represent anything like the best that is possible from the railroad.

Modern passenger trains. *The New Tōkaidō Line.* In the early 1970s, perhaps the outstanding example of modern railroad technology was the New Tōkaidō Line of the Japanese National Railways (Figure 33). The Tōkaidō (Eastern Sea Route) Line between Tokyo and Ōsaka serves an area where 40 percent of Japan's population and 70 percent of its industrial output are concentrated. By the early 1960s the original double-track, 3-foot-6-inch-(1.07-metre-) gauge line between those points had reached capacity. The New Tōkaidō Line was opened in 1964 as a completely new, standard-gauge line, entirely separate from the original line, with its own right-of-way and stations, and handling high-speed passenger trains only.

Electrified with a trolley wire voltage of 25,000 volts, 60 hertz, the new line has no grade crossings, and its curves and grades permit operation at the maximum service speed of 131 miles (210 kilometres) per hour. The track was laid entirely on concrete ties, except at turnouts (switches). Sixteen-car electric trains provide the service. The express trains make the 322-mile (515-kilometre) Tokyo–Ōsaka

Figure 33: The New Tōkaidō Line train, developed by the Japanese National Railways. It achieves speeds of up to 131 miles per hour on its 322-mile run between Tokyo and Osaka. Comprised of eight two-car units, the train operates on electric power supplied by overhead wires.

By courtesy of the Museum of Railway Traffic, Tokyo

run in three hours and 10 minutes, at an average speed of 103 miles (166 kilometres) per hour, stopping at Nagoya and Kyōto. "Limited express" trains make 10 intermediate stops and cover the full distance in four hours and 10 minutes. The trains reach a maximum speed in normal operations of 131 miles per hour.

The New Tōkaidō Line proved outstandingly successful and highly profitable. In the late 1970s it carried an average of 339,000 passengers daily in 240 trains (120 each way). Its success prompted the Japanese National Railways to begin constructing a westward extension, the New Sanyo Line, from Ōsaka toward Hakata, about 346 miles (554 kilometres). This line was opened in 1975. In addition, planning was going ahead for a nationwide network of similar high-speed, standard-gauge trunk lines. Two additional lines—from Tokyo to Morioka and Niigata, respectively—were opened in 1982.

Successors to the New Tōkaidō

London–Manchester–Liverpool. Between 1960 and 1966, British Railways carried out a major project to electrify and upgrade its heavy-traffic main lines between London (Euston Station) and Birmingham, Manchester, and Liverpool. This involved electrifying 443 route miles (713 kilometres) or 1,467 track miles (2,360 kilometres) of line, using a trolley voltage of 25,000, 50 hertz, alternating current. Although this is a modernized existing line, not a completely new railroad as in the case of the New Tōkaidō, it has proved very successful. Passenger carryings on the line doubled in four years after the electrified operation made possible faster, more frequent service. On this line, trains operate regularly at 100 miles (160 kilometres) per hour. Electrification of this line is now being extended all the way to Glasgow.

High-speed trains in France. Electrification has also permitted very high-speed operation of passenger trains on major routes in France. The most famous of the high-speed French trains is the "Mistral," which has now been equipped with the most modern Trans-Europ Express type of equipment. This train makes a daily run between Paris and Nice, 676 miles (1,088 kilometres), at an average speed of 75 miles (120 kilometres) per hour. Another French Trans-Europ Express train, "Le Lyonnais," averages 85 miles (135 kilometres) per hour on its 320-mile (510-kilometre) run between Paris and Lyon. The "Capitole," which runs between Paris and Toulouse, is allowed a top speed of 125 miles (200 kilometres) per hour on some parts of the lines.

The United States Metroliners. In the United States, the strong emphasis on highways and air-travel facilities had, by the 1960s, caused most railroads in the United States to cut their passenger operations drastically. In the Northeast Megalopolis extending roughly from Boston through New

York and Washington to Richmond, Virginia, however, the dense population presented a market that could be exploited by a fast modern rail passenger service. In 1968 the Penn Central railroad, in conjunction with the United States Department of Transportation, began operating an experimental high-speed service on its existing electrified (11,000 volt, 25 hertz) main line between New York and Washington. Comfortable and modern electric multiple-unit train sets provide these services, which in 1971 were taken over by Amtrak (The National Railroad Passenger Corporation). Twelve Metroliner trains daily were operated in each direction as of 1972, with a running time of three hours for the 225-mile (360-kilometre) trip, including five intermediate stops. Average speed is 75 miles (120 kilometres) per hour, but trains are capable of running up to 160 miles (260 kilometres) per hour. The existing line, however, although it has been improved, has a number of highway grade crossings and restrictive curves; top running speed is currently held to 100 miles (160 kilometres) per hour.

Success of the Metroliner

Although the accommodations on the Metroliner trains are as advanced as any, the Metroliners cannot compare in frequency and speed with the high-speed passenger services of other countries described above. Nevertheless, they have reversed a long decline in patronage on the New York–Washington line; the trains consistently operate with large loads of passengers.

Modern freight trains. *Shuttle freight operations.* Perhaps the ideal freight railroad of the future would be one that is essentially a shuttle or "conveyor belt," carrying one commodity continuously between two points. Such a railroad would produce the maximum amount of transportation at the lowest cost. A few such railroads exist; they are mainly mineral railroads carrying coal or ore from mines to points of use.

One such line is an intraplant railroad, double-track, slow-speed, that carries taconite ore from mines 46 miles (74 kilometres) to a boat-loading dock. This relatively short line operates around the clock and carries some 30,000,000 tons of taconite annually; so efficient is the operation that it produces transportation at the rate of about 220,000 gross ton-miles per train-hour (a statistic derived by multiplying the weight of cars and contents by the number of miles hauled, and dividing this figure by the time required) even though half of the train-miles are run empty. This figure is about three times the average of the large general-purpose common carrier railroads in the United States and double the production of the most efficient of the general-purpose railroads.

A one-commodity, shuttle railroad is relatively rare; but similar gains in efficiency can be made on the common carrier railroads by operating unit trains. These are rarely as efficient as the example just cited; but they can be quite effective, especially when operated at fairly high speeds over long distances.

Advantages of the shuttle train

The shuttle-train principle is powerful because it obviates the delay and expense of moving trains through freight yards, since the trains operate directly from shipper to receiver; moreover, it greatly improves the utilization of costly locomotives and cars. Unit trains and similar applications of this principle are being tried by railroads all over the world.

Freightliner and Super C. The container shuttle train holds great promise for similar efficiencies in the hauling of general merchandise. In 1965 the first Freightliner container (Figure 32) shuttle trains began running on British Railways. By 1970 some 28 terminals and container ports were being served; the trains were operating over 80 different routes. More than 500,000 containers were being hauled annually.

The Freightliner system provides an integrated road-rail service direct from shipper to receiver, for both domestic and export-import business. Shippers may use their own containers if they conform to international standards. Space on the fast overnight trains is reserved in advance; the trains operate through to destination without intermediate reclassification in yards. Terminal handling cranes are designed for quick transfer of the containers from rail cars to truck chassis and vice versa. Freightliner service has proved competitive with over-the-road trucking even on many of the shorter runs prevailing in Britain.

Another glimpse of the railroad future is the Santa Fe (United States) railroad's Super C, a freight train carrying only containers or highway trailers. Super C runs 2,200 miles (3,500 kilometres) between Chicago and Los Angeles in less than 40 hours, at an average speed greater than that of the road's fast passenger trains. At this speed, the railroad is more than competitive with express trucks operating over highways.

The examples cited above are representative of some of the better achievements of present-day railroad technology. If they become typical instead of exceptional and if research can further improve existing technology, the railroad of steel rails and flanged wheels will remain viable for many years to come.

Advanced systems. In the 1960s and early 1970s, considerable interest developed in the possibility of building tracked passenger vehicles that could go much faster than conventional trains. Experiments conducted by the Japanese National Railways and others had indicated that the practical upper limit of speed for flanged-wheel railroad vehicles might be in the range of 150 to 200 miles (240 to 320 kilometres) per hour.

A tracked air-cushion vehicle

Several new types of guided vehicle systems have been proposed for possible ultra-high-speed operation. One of the more promising is the tracked air-cushion vehicle, as exemplified by the French Aerotrain (Figure 34). Air-cushion vehicles use a "cushion" of low-pressure air to "float" the vehicle away from the group or the guideway; they have no wheels and, when running, no contact with the guideway.

Technical development of the Aerotrain was completed in the late 1970s. The single vehicle or train of vehicles runs on an elevated beamway that has a vertical centre guide beam, using fans for both lift and lateral guidance. A prototype 80-passenger vehicle for intercity operations has been extensively tested on an elevated 11 miles (18 kilometres) of track north of Orléans (France). In its first version, the vehicle attained a cruising speed of 155 miles (250 kilometres) per hour by means of a shrouded propeller driven by two high-powered gas turbines. In a second version, propelled by a fan jet outfitted with a noise-reducing device, the same train body attained a record speed of 267 miles (430 kilometres) per hour while carrying more than 15,000 passengers. At lower speeds of 110 to 125 miles (180 to 200 kilometres) per hour, electrically driven vehicles have also been tested with both "pinched" wheels and linear induction motor propulsion.

By courtesy of the Societe de L'Aerotrain

Figure 34: The French Aerotrain running on an inverted-T-shaped concrete guideway near Orléans, France. Propelled by a fan jet, the train has attained record speeds.

A tracked air-cushion vehicle project is also under way in Britain. The vehicle, which will be tested at speeds up to 150 miles (240 kilometres) per hour, will be propelled by a linear induction motor. The linear induction motor could also be applied to conventional flanged-wheel vehicles; the United States Federal Railroad Administration is experimenting with this application.

Another proposed type of guided high-speed system is the magnetic-levitation, vacuum-tube system. Vehicles would run at very high speeds in underground tubes from which the air would be exhausted. They would be held away from the tube walls by magnetic force. So far, only small-scale experimental work has been done on this concept.

At their state of development in the early 1980s, none of these proposed systems seemed likely soon to displace the conventional railroad as an all-around high-volume, low-cost mover of both people and goods. They did, however, show promise as high-speed city-to-airport links and perhaps for certain high-speed intercity runs. Much depended on whether the costs of building and operating these still experimental systems could be made comparable to those of the proven flanged wheel, steel-rail system.

(T.C.S./Ed.)

Urban mass transportation

Urban transportation includes the movement of people and materials within any town or city but particularly within large metropolitan areas. In the last third of the 20th century, such movement was primarily by automobile and truck powered by internal-combustion engines, despite the fact that mass transit had long been recognized in all developed countries as desirable and necessary.

Before taking up the problems and possible solutions within the framework of urban transportation itself, it should be observed that solutions may come from technological advances outside the system. The picturephone, facsimile transmission, and other developments in communications may reduce the need for person-to-person contacts and eliminate many trips now considered necessary. Energy presently transported by railroads or trucks in the form of coal or oil can also be moved by pipelines. Generating plants can be built at mine mouths or other nonurban areas, and electricity can be transmitted by buried, high-voltage power lines to the urban area. Advances in building construction may also have large impact on transportation by facilitating development of more efficiently organized urban agglomerations.

HISTORY

While freight movement by water determined the location of many cities, major local transportation has rarely been by boat. Wheels have been paramount from the horse-drawn buggy and omnibus to the bicycle, streetcar, subway, and automobile. The first successful omnibus service was inaugurated in Paris in 1819; within a dozen years, London, New York, and other major cities had copied the idea. Electric traction was tried out in Richmond, Virginia, in 1888, followed by a rapid spread of electric transit first in the U.S. and then in Europe.

First subway

Meanwhile, London had pioneered the subway, or underground, as early as 1862 with a line of about four miles connecting the principal railroad terminals. The line was so successful that it was rapidly expanded, taking advantage of a tunnel driven under the Thames River a generation earlier by Marc Brunel; the tunnel had been intended for vehicular use, but suitable approaches had not been constructed. From this beginning the City and South London Railway grew, at first using steam traction and later (1890) electricity. Budapest, Boston, Paris, Berlin, New York, and other cities followed in rapid succession; within a few years hundreds of miles of subway were built, mostly by trenching streets and covering over (cut-and-cover method). A parallel development was the interurban system of electric surface traction, widely used in suburban areas and between small, neighbouring cities.

Like the subway the elevated railroad was conceived and built before electric traction, the first operating with a cable drive on Ninth Avenue, New York City, in 1867, and shifting in 1871 to steam locomotives. The first elevated to be equipped with electric power was the West Side Metropolitan Elevated Railroad in Chicago in 1895, soon followed by all other such railroads. The first use of multiple-unit cars, in which most units are powered but controlled from a single location, also came in Chicago, on the South Side Elevated, in 1897.

The last major component of the modern urban transportation system to arrive on the scene, but the one with the largest impact of all, was the automobile. As early as World War I, the automobile was an important user of city streets, especially in the U.S. but also in Europe; taxicabs were numerous enough in Paris in 1914 to be commandeered for a critical troop movement in the Battle of the Marne. Motor buses began to make a significant impact in the 1920s, especially in the U.S., where by mid-century they had nearly replaced electric streetcars. Buses received favoured treatment from government in the belief that they provided advantages, some of which, such as routing flexibility, subsequently proved illusory. Britain and France followed the U.S. lead, but other European countries generally retained their streetcars. In the U.S., the expectation that bus service could be upgraded through such devices as reserved lanes on freeways or preferential access at intersections was not widely borne out. In Detroit an experiment with operation of buses on freeways showed rider resistance and preference for the old surface-street routes. In Europe, efforts were made to separate tramlines from automobile traffic by placing them at the side of highways or on elevated tracks, by building grade separations at main intersections, and, especially in West Germany, by using special vehicles with high manoeuvrability.

The automobile's relationship to mass-transit systems proved complicated. As soon as commuter railroads developed in the late 19th century, isolated suburban clusters began to form. Streetcars and interurbans extended the reach of the railroads and filled in gaps in the system. The automobile, however, played the principal role both in extension and filling in, thus becoming indispensable to suburban living. The automobile thus created further demand for highways and expressways, both around and into the central business district. Expressway development both in the U.S. and Europe so accelerated growth in city and suburban areas that the word megalopolis was coined (or, more precisely, revived) to describe such areas as the chain of metropolitan regions along the northeast U.S. coast. The density of traffic in such areas had the effect of reducing the value of the automobile; by the 1960s, technologically innovative transportation modes were under consideration.

Planning land use

Possibly even more important in the changes in transportation thinking in the 1960s and 1970s was the growing conviction that land use must be planned. This concept was much more widely accepted in Europe than in the U.S., where the multiplicity of local and regional political units created a chaotic situation. In some small countries such as Sweden, it appeared possible to predict future land use, to design construction as transit lines were extended, to build roads to complement the transit lines, and thus to have appropriate facilities available when the suburb was developed rather than setting in motion an uncontrolled cycle of growth.

PROBLEMS OF URBAN TRANSPORTATION

The automobile's readiness and versatility has been the catalyst of spectacular suburban growth in almost all developed countries, making possible the exploitation of unused land areas farther out from the central city. The experience of Japan, Europe, and the U.S. has been the same; those who can afford new houses can afford automobiles to reach them.

Yet even apart from the inevitable pattern of overgrowth and congestion, public transit systems are indispensable for the large groups of persons who cannot drive autos, such as the poor, the very young or very old, and the disabled. In recent years a need for public transit has been shown in cities as small as 30,000.

Traditionally, transportation problems have been considered under the headings of cost and convenience, meaning primarily speed of travel. To these aspects have now been added such questions as pollution abatement and safety, the latter a question of increasing complexity.

High costs. In most countries the history of mass transit has been a history of maintenance problems versus rising fares. Lengthened trips combined with popular resistance to fare increases create maintenance problems; when these become acute, fares rise, often sharply. Flat fares discourage the short-distance rider, who may pay two or three times as much per mile as the long tripper. Zone fares are difficult and expensive to collect. Too often the result is a cycle of rising flat fares that discourages short-distance passengers and reduces revenue gains.

Another aspect of rising costs in mass transit is the substitution of subways for surface lines; a system such as the Montreal subway built in the 1960s cost 1,000 or 2,000 times as much per mile or kilometre as did the surface transportation that served the city at the turn of the 20th century.

While costs of both automobiles and highways have likewise risen steadily, apparent in Europe, the U.S., and Japan has been the willingness of the public to pay more for automobiles and to support highway construction through bond issues and toll collections while exhibiting marked resistance to paying more for improved mass transit. Signs of this public attitude have even become discernible in the Communist countries.

Social effects. The high cost of urban transportation has invariably fallen most heavily on the poorest classes, who pay a higher proportion of family income for transportation, and often cannot find adequate means of reaching employment. In modern industrial centres new jobs tend to be located away from the congested districts where the poor traditionally live.

Speed of travel. Normal walking speed for a man has remained at about 3.1 miles (4.9 kilometres) per hour since the beginning of recorded history. Horses and horse-drawn omnibuses raised the speed of travel to approximately 6 miles (10 kilometres) per hour. Buses and trolleys provide average speeds of 5 to 6 miles per hour in rush-hour traffic to 12–14 miles per hour on most city streets in other time periods. Speeds of up to 50 miles (80 kilometres) per hour are often reached by buses in outlying streets of large cities, but schedule speeds, which include stopping times, are much lower.

Studies of relative speeds of principal mid-20th-century urban-transit modes showed average automobile speeds of up to 19 miles (30 kilometres) per hour, compared with 16 miles (26 kilometres) per hour for suburban railroads, and substantially less for other mass transit. While doubtless valid statistically, such studies are misleading because of the different functions of the different types of transit. To gain a real picture of urban transit speeds in a city like Paris or New York would require a rationale that included the number of persons moved per mile, how near the centre of the city the movement took place, and also station spacing. Broadly speaking, it may be said that while speed of movement, especially during rush hours, still leaves something to be desired in most cities, it is not as critical a problem as that of costs.

Pollution. The relationship between air pollution and health began to be investigated in the 1950s, with London pioneering in research and abatement. The importance of automobile emissions in air pollution in urban centres was well established by 1970. The diesel engine, widely used in freight movement by truck and railroad both in Europe and the U.S., has been found to contribute a relatively minor amount as compared with the gasoline engine almost universally used on passenger vehicles. Because urban travel is largely start and stop and emissions are generally higher when vehicles are idling, it can probably be assumed that more than half of the motor-vehicle pollutants are concentrated in urban areas. Efforts were underway in the late 20th century to eliminate lead from gasoline and otherwise reduce emissions.

Another side effect of urban transportation is noise pollution, which takes the form of rumbling elevated railroads, aircraft takeoffs and landings, and trucks and autos in heavy concentrations on freeways and downtown streets. Such European cities as Rome, Florence, Genoa, Marseille, and Dijon, with ancient or medieval street layouts, are especially noisy.

So-called visual pollution by the urban transport system is another cause of urban blight. The abandoned automobile, for example, stripped of useful parts and not valuable enough as scrap to pay for removal, is a growing problem in the U.S. Another form of visual pollution is actually hazardous; many municipalities have done a poor job in maintenance of street hardware, permitting saturation of intersections with confusing directional signs that fight for space with commercial signs. Long delays in repairing broken street lights and even broken traffic signals are also dangerous as well as unsightly.

Many U.S. cities fail to keep streets adequately clean. Some European and Japanese cities set a better standard, despite high concentrations of vehicles and people.

Space pollution

Finally, the automobile has produced what might be termed space pollution, simply through its ubiquity. Parking lots now occupy squares and open spaces; in many cities, sidewalks have been reduced in width to accommodate extra traffic lanes for automobiles. In such European cities as Naples, and throughout the tropics, people normally overflow the sidewalks into the streets.

Several interesting experiments have been carried out to restrict or eliminate automobile traffic from certain sections or streets. Rome barred motor vehicles from one of its principal squares, the spacious Piazza Navona. Other Italian cities, such as Pisa, closed streets to auto traffic at certain hours. New York and other cities have temporarily or permanently closed some of their main avenues for the benefit of shoppers and strollers. Side streets may be closed for the benefit of children. These measures, however, have hardly counteracted the prevailing trend toward greater and greater domination of the city by the automobile.

Safety hazards. Though transportation in all ages has involved hazards to life and limb, the appalling toll in deaths and injuries brought by the automobile in the 20th century raises entirely new questions. Even if private automobiles can be shown to provide a substantially greater convenience, it is uncertain that a rationale can be supplied for their use in competition with safer public transit. The London underground, for example, had only one serious accident, in which 12 were killed, throughout the 1950s and 1960s. The Paris Metro had no deaths between 1930 and the late 1960s. The Tokyo subway had no deaths during the 1960s. The Toronto subway had no accidents in the 15 years following its opening in 1954.

Other types of urban mass transit, such as buses, have much less dramatic records but are still far ahead of the private automobile in safety.

Planning problems. Attempts by government agencies and others to plan systems to meet urban transit needs encounter chronic problems. The type and quality of transit systems that may be technically feasible a few years hence are difficult to predict safely; in addition, the public response even to improved versions of existing systems is difficult to determine. That people want a substantially improved urban-transit system in Tokyo, New York, and London cannot be doubted; how much they are willing to pay for what degree of improvement is uncertain. When the long lead time involved in planning a new or radically altered transportation system is taken into account, it becomes evident that considerable courage is needed on the part of planning authorities. In countries where public ownership or substantial government control over land use exists, some of the more obvious problems can be mitigated.

ELEMENTS OF URBAN TRANSPORTATION

Streets, expressways, and associated facilities. Since cities first developed, the construction and maintenance of urban streets have been almost exclusively a governmental function. Many methods of classification have been used in attempts to define street networks in a systematic way to provide for maintenance and expansion. One widely used method is based on volume of through traffic; those with nearly 100 percent through traffic are classed in the highest category, with high speeds and maximum traffic control required; those with the lowest percent of through traffic are placed in the lowest category. The classification is complicated by the obvious fact that most urban streets are in an intermediate role, carrying several kinds of traffic. This necessitates an attempt to classify on the basis of the predominant role of a given street, which may vary at different times of day and may change over a period of time.

Street planning

Street planning has always been a complex process, involving local commissions, intermediate agencies, and national governmental authorities. Land-use problems in metropolitan areas are particularly troublesome. Political agencies that let design contracts for new highways in urban areas permitted wide latitude to the engineers in determining location as well as design and construction details; this is done because intruding an expressway into the tightly congested metropolitan area involves major technological problems. A good illustration is furnished by the Arch of Triumph tunnel in Paris. The rotary traffic pattern, without traffic lights, at the twelve-way intersection that circles this famous monument was established in the early years of the century and served very well until the congestion of the 1950s and 1960s. The problem was defined as finding a route that would keep through traffic out of the rotary pattern. The solution undertaken in 1968 was an underpass of almost one-quarter mile capable of passing approximately 200,000 vehicles a day under the Arch of Triumph. The presence of five subway (Metro) tunnels, various pedestrian walkways and utility lines, and a large parking garage complicated the work, which also had to be carried out with minimum disturbance of existing traffic patterns. The crowns of three of the subway tunnels had to be removed to make room for the two-lane roadway.

Siting of roadways

Many other ingenious devices have served engineers attempting to reduce congestion and facilitate through traffic in cities. In several cities waterways have been used as sites, with a new expressway occupying the bed of a disused canal, or with an expressway built out over one side of a river. But for most expressway projects demolition and removal of residences and businesses is necessary, which creates problems much broader than the merely technological. Not only engineers, but sociologists, city planners, political scientists, and architects are commonly involved in the decision making.

Even after an urban expressway is completed, problems arise because of the difficulty of performing maintenance work on a road surface in constant use.

Parking. In recent years urban parking has gone increasingly underground, though above-ground, multilevel structures are still being built. In Europe and the U.S. it is becoming more and more common to integrate parking with new office and residential buildings by utilizing the lower several floors. Another trend is to reserve the surface above the underground structure for park space.

Traffic control. A complex traffic-control system embracing several transportation modes is inseparable from modern urban movement. Auto-traffic devices range from parking meters and signal lights to automatic scanners that measure traffic flow and adjust lane entrances. One problem is uniformity; a present goal is to establish worldwide sign standards. Western Europe has long employed an ingenious system of wordless signs, on which symbols indicate "no entrance," "one-way street," "stop," and other directives, thus overcoming the language barrier (see below *Traffic control*).

Surface transit. Many European and American cities abandoned electric trolley systems in favour of buses, which were believed to have certain advantages. Some of the advantages have proven illusory—for example, the greater flexibility of routing possible with buses. In addition, buses are contributors to air pollution, albeit primarily disagreeable odours. In the 1960s San Francisco, Philadelphia, and Boston, in the U.S., and Hamburg, Frankfurt, and other cities in Europe were maintaining and expanding their limited surface transit lines (tramlines). In some European cities, limited tramlines are being built in parkways or moved to one side of expressways or through road arteries.

Interurban lines

Interurban transit lines have also largely been abandoned in the U.S., despite remnants in Chicago, Philadelphia, and elsewhere. In Europe and Japan, several such lines survive, some in private ownership, most government operated. In the 1970s, however, the gasoline or diesel-powered bus had become the most ubiquitous form of mass transit for the whole world.

Subway and elevated transit. Subways are best adapted for carrying large numbers of people over short and medium distances into and through the central business district. The money savings achieved by building elevated lines has been shown to represent false economy in the long run because of the damaging effects of elevated structures on business and residential streets. Though arguments have been advanced that aesthetically pleasing and quiet monorail lines could be built in city streets, present experience is not favourable. Though most world fairs of recent years have had monorail systems, and Dallas has a short line connecting the airport parking area to one passenger terminal, no successful system has been built for a central business district.

Subways have continued to be built despite mounting costs and engineering problems because they are the most satisfactory solution to moving large numbers of people inside a city. They do no damage to streets and neighbourhoods overhead; and on the contrary they usually contribute to rising land values. The Toronto subway is a good example of the common effect of increasing population density along a new line.

The stations on the newest subway lines are much improved over those built early in the century; in some, as the Moscow and Rome subways, serious efforts have been made to create aesthetically pleasing as well as comfortable and convenient station facilities. The newer aluminum and stainless steel subway cars are also much improved, with easily cleaned plastic or plastic-covered seats, and increasingly, with air conditioning. Recorded vocal announcements and visual displays assist strangers and speed passenger loading and unloading. Higher rates

Table 2: Proposed Rail Transit Service Standards

service standards	subway-elevated	supersubway	suburban rapid transit	suburban railroad
Service territory (distance from Manhattan)	0–11 m	9–17 m	15–35 m	25–50 m
Average service speed	22 mph	35 mph	45 mph	45 mph
Peak-hour period passenger loading				
Passengers per track	48,000	40,000	30,000	30,000
Percent seated	30%	60%	100%	100%
Service frequency (outlying lines)				
Peak period	4 min	6 min	8 min	15 min
Off peak	8 min	12 min	15 min	30 min
Night-weekend	12 min	20 min	30 min	60 min
Fare level	$.15	$.25–$.45	$.50–$1.00	$.75–$1.40
Train characteristics				
Car type	standard rapid transit	modified rapid transit	modified rapid transit	standard suburban
Seats per car	50	80	100	125
Hourly trains per track	30	30	30	20
Hourly cars per track	300	300	300	240
Manhattan distribution	subway	subway	subway or terminal	terminal

Source: The City of New York, *Metropolitan Mobility.*

of acceleration in the all-powered-car trains further increase overall speeds.

Automatic systems control has been installed in some subways, including a variety of automatic fare collection devices. Television monitoring of stations by central observers is increasingly provided, along with radio communications, also widely used for bus spacing.

Commuter rail service. Suburban or commuter railroads grew out of the desire of 19th-century railroad management to increase the number of collection and distribution points in metropolitan areas for its long-range passenger service. With long-range rail service undergoing radical modification in most of the world and facing abandonment in some areas, notably in the U.S., this concept is far out of date, yet suburban rail service has become an increasingly indispensable component of metropolitan transit. The situation has led toward increasing participation in suburban rail management of governments and commuter groups, with ultimate results yet to be seen. In the U.S., public agencies formed for the purpose in various metropolitan areas have sought operational control of suburban lines.

The supersubway. One increasingly discernible tendency of the early 1970s, worldwide, was a blurring of distinction between rapid-transit lines and suburban railroads. In some cities, such as Philadelphia and Boston, in the U.S., standard subways have been extended over suburban railroad lines. In some cases the suburban rail lines have been abandoned by the former operators, and in some the subway trains are being integrated into an ongoing operation. In 1965 the New York City Planning Commission outlined what may be the shape of metropolitan rapid transit in the world's large cities in the later years of the century. The commission proposed that rail transit be differentiated by service standards only and suggested the plan shown in Table 2 for the differentiation.

The supersubway would have a higher fare than present subway–elevateds in New York, but would provide seating for 60 percent of the riders instead of 30 percent, thus giving better service for those more able to pay. Better service includes higher speeds, more seats, and transverse seats giving better support during acceleration and deceleration. The service would not operate as frequently, but its quality would be upgraded.

People movers. The moving stairway, or escalator, is one of the earliest examples of a people mover. Although initially provided inside retail establishments to replace the elevator, today such stairways facilitate the movement of people in railroad or subway stations as they move upstairs or down in the station or from station to street. Although fewer have been constructed, the moving sidewalk is similar to the moving stairway in concept. Generally, a moving sidewalk is a rubber belt approximately 30 inches (76 centimetres) wide, carried on rollers, and is equipped with a moving handrail. The belt is rigid enough to carry the load between rollers but flexible enough to turn around drums at each end. Other designs use a belt that is rigid in the centre with rollers at the edge. Entering and leaving requires some agility, so that people with slow reflexes, particularly the elderly, often find it difficult to utilize these facilities. Consequently, though speeds of 10 miles (16 kilometres) per hour are possible, present units rarely operate at more than one-fifth this speed.

Moving sidewalks

By courtesy of Ford Motor Company

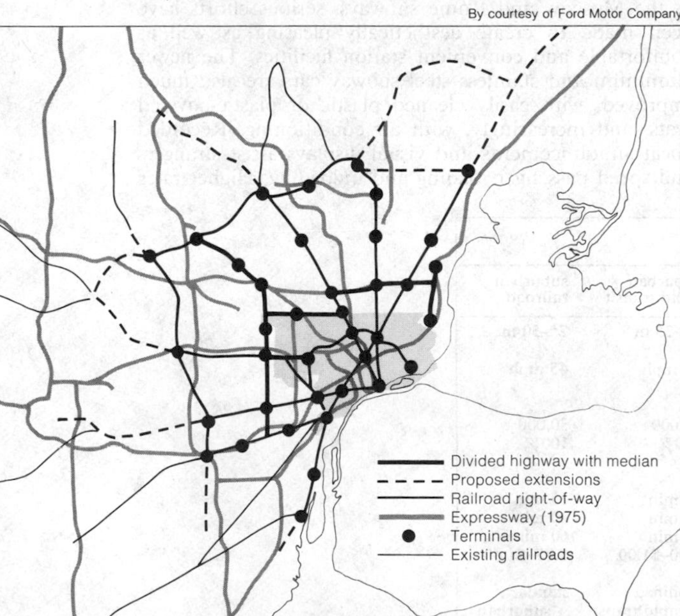

Figure 35: Artist's conception of a dual-mode guideway network superimposed on Detroit and its suburbs utilizing rail, air rights, and expressway median strips. The dots illustrate the location of local stations where ingress and egress can be made. In most cases, these are near shopping centres, airports, the central business district, as well as residential areas.

Mixed modes. In its broad sense, the term mixed modes simply refers to the use of more than one technology for a single trip; thus the Japanese and western European combination of bicycle and commuter railroad is a mixed mode. A narrower form of mixed mode is two kinds of public transportation, such as railroad or subway train and city bus. A possibility discussed in the 1970s was a cross of taxicab and bus to provide an on-call form of public transportation from suburban or metropolitan home to railroad or subway terminal. A computer would be programmed with appropriate data, and when a telephone call activated the system the computer would assign an available vehicle to pick up the passenger. The computer would further optimize the route of the vehicle for origins and destinations.

Another possibility is that small vehicles or buses could be designed to operate on both railroad tracks, or other types of guideways, and on city streets. These vehicles would pick up passengers along the street system, move to a guideway and travel off-street and out of congestion to their destination. Railroads have equipment permitting track supervisors to drive on-street to a section of track, drop steel-flanged wheels onto the track structure, and drive along the track for inspection purposes. Similarly, buses have been equipped with retractable flanged wheels and axles to permit operation on either streets or rails. Technical problems with this type of vehicle will require substantial sums of money and time to resolve, relating primarily to the truck design and quality of the ride. The vehicle must be light enough to travel easily over the roads but heavy enough to function on track or structure in moderate snow. Inadequate maintenance of lightly used track is a problem, and proponents of this system have rarely estimated the cost of upgrading and signalizing track for frequent use by small vehicles. Union conflicts can also be anticipated as the technique bridges transit and rail modes where different labour unions have contracts.

Road-rail vehicles

Just as trucks are being moved on flatcars, or containers on trucks and flatcars or both, it has been suggested that passenger containers be loaded in key sectors of a city and flown to airports by helicopter. When this proposal was evaluated in Los Angeles, investigators concluded that it was not feasible at the time. Special vehicles designed to move passengers from terminal to airplace, however, are being utilized at major airports in such cities as London and Washington, D.C.

NEW CONCEPTS AND NEW TECHNOLOGY

Increasing efforts are being put forward on many levels in all of the developed countries to untangle the urban transportation problem. These include both modes of conceptualization and technological innovations (Figure 35).

The systems concept. The systems approach, which has been used successfully in solving many complex engineering problems, has an obvious application to urban transportation. The systems engineer seeks to analyze a large problem by identifying its components and calculating the approximate effects of the trade offs that can be made among them. In viewing urban transportation, he asks such questions as these:

Is a cardinal aim the reduction of congestion in the central business district? Must congestion also be reduced on all links of the system or is there a tolerable level that can be permitted on some? Are these radial or circumferential to the central business district? How important is safety? Must the present automobile accident rate be radically reduced? How important are the transportation requirements of nondrivers? Must air and noise pollution be reduced? By how much?

Once the list of factors is determined and put in reasonable order of importance, engineers synthesize a design and analyze its performance, estimated cost, and socioeconomic attributes. The engineer can easily state the performance anticipated from the design in factors like acceleration and deceleration, overall speed, noise levels, and amount of pollutants from the engine. Cost of facilities can readily be estimated, especially for subsystems or components that have already been built. It is more difficult to evaluate the socioeconomic attributes and to weight the costs of externalities to the system. Externalities are those factors that affect third parties who have no direct connection with the system. How important is it to soundproof the track of a transit line that goes through a densely populated neighbourhood? What is it worth to reduce air pollution if emission meets the present public health standards but still has an adverse impact on health or increases the cost of laundry for citizens living nearby? As difficult as such evaluations are, they must be attempted.

Correcting design deficiencies

After making his evaluation, the engineer attempts to correct the deficiencies where the design falls below the established goals or the ranking of the criteria. Correcting the deficiencies may increase the cost, so cost estimates must be changed. When the new design is completed it is evaluated by the same process. Reiteration continues until the design is acceptable in terms of performance, cost, and socioeconomic effects.

Unfortunately, the decision-making process in respect to urban transportation is fraught with so many complications that the systems approach at present promises only limited benefits. Government authorities overlap; pressure groups abound. As an example of a problem that is likely to occur, a small town or village may block the development of an off-street transit line that would benefit a whole region. This is especially a problem in the U.S., but there are serious difficulties in applying the systems approach to metropolitan transit everywhere.

Technological innovations. Of the many directions of research on road transportation under active pursuit in the 1970s, perhaps that of most immediate interest for urban transportation is the automatically controlled vehicle. One imaginative concept involves completely relieving the driver of responsibility, substituting an electronic roadway control connected to a central computer system. The principal aim would be to increase safety. Cost estimates, however, run very high. Another possibility is to have the vehicle operate under its own power and driver on local streets but move onto a guideway with central power and control for longer distances. Among the many problems of such a system is the prospective overloading of ramps leading to and from guideways.

Another version, designed to eliminate the downtown parking problem, would provide an army of small vehicles that would be automatically controlled once the destination was identified. So ambitious a system probably will have applicability, even when technical problems are solved, only within a "new city," which can be designed with the system in mind or reconstruction of a very large area.

Gravity-vacuum tube system

In mass transit, several intriguing ideas have been put forward. One, the gravity-vacuum tube system (Figure 36), is a new model of a concept dating to the 19th century; a train that would be accelerated and braked by a combination of gravity and atmospheric pressure. The train would be circular in cross section and considerably longer than most trains, with the wheels located between the cars and inset so that the train could act as a seal while in the tunnel. The tube would descend from each station and rise toward the next. Gravity would reinforce the pressure from the atmosphere, exerted as air was evacuated from the portion of the tube in front of the train. The economy of power makes the idea attractive, but several problems

Figure 36: *Possible urban transportation system of the future.* In this system, streets are for pedestrian use. Underground, starting at left, is space for trains, truck traffic, automobile traffic, and special capsules directed by computer and capable of carrying four persons. At the lowest level is a pneumatic train, which travels between stations by means of gravity and air pressure (see text).

After a painting by Pierre Mion © 1969 National Geographic Society

remain, among which is the cost of the tunnel construction and the difficulty of precise braking.

Another old concept that has been tried with success in France and elsewhere is the linear-induction electric motor, in which the stator (magnetic coil) is attached to the vehicle while the "rotor" is stretched out flat to become the rail along which the train runs. High speeds have been attained; costs and reliability appear favourable. The possibility of combining linear induction with air-cushion support is promising.

Less innovative in detail is the Japanese National Railroad's new lines; the New Tōkaidō, opened between Tokyo and Ōsaka in the mid-1960s, has proved that conventional railroad technology, when fully exploited, can produce a highly satisfactory high-speed system.

In the air helicopters have a growing potential for many roles, and vertical takeoff and short takeoff aircraft (VTOL and STOL) may be useful within metropolitan regions as well as between cities, though existing forms present noise problems.

Research and development programs are under way in Europe, the U.S., Japan, and other countries on these and many other possibilities. The Railway Technical Research Institute of Japan, the British Railways Board, the French National Railways, and other national railroad systems, though concerned with the problem of rail transportation generally, produce valuable information for urban transit. Such national railroad systems have usually found government research grants easier to obtain than is the case with privately owned railroads.

Despite the efforts of these and many other agencies, public and private, the most important requirement of urban transportation in the 1980s remains funds for research and development. The cost of developing a system capable of meeting the needs of today's congested, pollution-plagued metropolis is fully comparable to that of a major space program. Only a public and government commitment on such a scale can produce favourable results. (J.A.Ba.)

Modern water transportation

The changes in the early steamships during the age of iron ships followed the developments in power, propulsion, and hull materials already discussed. A typical ship of the 1840s was the "Sarah Sands," 186 feet (57 metres) long, 33-foot (10-metre) beam, 1,400 gross tons, equipped with 300 horsepower in two cylinders. The Inman Line built a succession of ships of iron with screw propellers that set a new standard. For example, the "City of Washington" was 2,870 tons and 358 feet (109 metres) long with a 40-foot (12-metre) beam. In 1852 the last Cunard wooden ship was built, the "Arabia," with a sea speed of 13 knots (one knot = 1.15 miles or 1.85 kilometres per hour) on 3,250 horsepower.

DEVELOPMENTS IN SHIPBUILDING

The "Great Eastern." In nearly every development of ships, the fundamental motive that brought on the building of a better ship was economic need. So, too, was the case of the largest ship of its time and perhaps the most revolutionary single step in shipbuilding—the "Great Eastern." It was conceived in the mind of one of the great builders of his time, the "Little Giant," Isambard Kingdom Brunel, also an outstanding bridge and railroad builder. From his knowledge of naval architecture Brunel realized that, the larger a ship is, the less power it takes to drive it; or, stated another way, the longer the ship, the faster it will travel with about the same power. At the time, the mid-19th century, steamships were just beginning to come of age and compete with sailing ships. Their weakest feature was their lack of sufficient fuel for long voyages, and in the 1850s the most lucrative employment was the China tea trade, in which round-trip speed was important. Putting these factors together, Brunel sold the idea to a syndicate of building, with existing technology, a steamship five times as large as the largest ship then afloat. The result was a remarkable ship, over 690 feet (210 metres) long, of nearly 19,000 gross tons. To give adequate strength, it was fashioned out of 7/8-inch (22-millimetre) iron plates and was the first ship to have a double bottom. In addition, it was divided into 22 massive compartments by fore and aft- and transverse-subdivision bulkheads, making it comparable to modern ships in strength and capacity to survive damage. It was powered by three separate means of propulsion; these include a pair of 58-foot (18-metre) paddle wheels, a 28-foot (nine-metre) screw propeller that is driven by a separate steam engine, and, as an additional safety measure and to conserve fuel, the enormous spread of 6,500 yards of sail. Its fuel capacity gave it sufficient endurance to make the round trip of 22,000 miles (35,000 kilometres) from England to Ceylon and return without refueling.

Specifications of the "Great Eastern"

Launching a ship of such unprecedented size created unprecedented problems, and the launch effort ended in failure. The ship was stuck on the ways for almost four months, bursting some of the most powerful hydraulic jacks in the country before it was finally set afloat in 1858. By this time the original £780,000 cost of the project had been exceeded, and, because there was no government subsidy, the backers went bankrupt. After several changes of ownership and more difficulty, the "Great Eastern" finally went on an unprofitable voyage to the United States and was put on exhibition in several places to attempt to gain funds for its owners. It never was sent on the route for which it was designed, or it might have set records; but instead it gained a measure of fame for laying the transatlantic cable and the cable to India. The "Great Eastern" was certainly a technical marvel, but, because financing and other problems did not permit it to perform its design mission, it was an economic failure. Not approached in size or efficiency for more than 50 years, the "Great Eastern" led the way to the ship revolution of the second half of the 19th century.

The transatlantic liners. The rivalry for the record for the fastest passage of the Atlantic by steam spurred most of the developments in shipbuilding during this period, each company adopting new technology as fast as it was proved practical. By 1874 the ocean liners had reached the speed of 16 knots and had cut the Alantic crossing time to seven days. Their displacement had risen to over 5,000 tons. By 1881, ships of 7,000 to 8,000 tons and steam pressures of over 100 pounds brought speeds of 20 knots. Steel had arrived as a hull material, and double, triple, and quadruple expansion engines rapidly reduced fuel requirements by nearly 50 percent. Finally, in 1899 the "Oceanic" was built, measuring 704 feet (215 metres) in length, after a half century, the first ship to exceed the size of the "Great Eastern." German shipbuilders of this time took command of the Atlantic speed records with the "Deutschland," which raced across the ocean at from 22 to 23 knots.

Another event in this great change in the face and power of ships was the demonstration of Parsons' "Turbinia." Parsons experimented with a turbine-driven boat in secret, and, when he had achieved a reasonable balance between turbine speed and propeller speed, he took his boat to Queen Victoria's Diamond Jubilee Review of the Fleet. Before the large crowd of onlookers, he proceeded to weave his way in and out between the ships of the British fleet at a previously unheard of speed of 34½ knots. After this unorthodox demonstration, the turbine was accepted as a means of propulsion for the future high-speed ships. About the same time, Rudolf Diesel in Germany was discovering the principles of the diesel cycle, which eventually was to result in one of the most economical means of marine propulsion.

Between 1900 and 1914, all of the innovations in technology seemed to come into focus with the age-old principle that a larger, longer ship was easier to drive and more comfortable to ride. Ships grew to gigantic proportions. Geared turbines had made high powers easier to produce, and steam pressures were in the area of 300 pounds per square inch. The largest of the prewar monsters was the German "Vaterland," of 904-foot (276-metre) length and 54,000 tons.

The "Vaterland"

During World War I the "Vaterland" was seized by the United States, used as a troop transport, and later refurbished under the direction of William Francis Gibbs, a New York naval architect, who was to become for the United States what I.K. Brunel had been to the 19th century in England. The ship was converted to oil, and many structural changes were made in order to improve its resistance to damage. Renamed the "Leviathan," for years it dominated the Atlantic. Shortly after its refit, it set a new speed record of 27.48 knots average speed for over 25 hours.

In 1929–30 the Germans launched the "Bremen" and the "Europa," which, while moderate in size, had better engineering and hull design and thus gave them the transatlantic speed record. These ships exploited a new hull-design idea, the bulbous bow, in which the bow of the ship was made sharp at the waterline to cut the waves but flattened out further down, giving greater buoyancy, and easier changes of direction to the water. In addition, this greater buoyancy below the water reduced pitching of the ship and made it ride easier.

The next record holder was the giant 79,280-ton French liner "Normandie," which in 1935 reduced the transatlantic record to four days, three hours, and two minutes at an average speed of over 30 knots. It used a turbo-electric drive.

In the 1920s and 1930s the world's commerce was being hauled in many less glamorous ships, some with Scotch boilers and reciprocating engines, about 400 feet (120 metres) long and steaming at an economical 13 to 14 knots. The diesel engine had started to displace steam, because the fuel consumption and the crew requirements of the diesel made it more economical to operate, even though its maintenance costs were higher.

World War II ships. World War II, with its tremendous production of new tonnage of all types, brought several new standards. In steamships, superheated steam (600 pounds per square inch and 850° F [450° C]) became nearly a standard for high-powered ships, some going as high as 1,000 pounds per square inch (70 kilograms per square centimetre). In the light of boiler-maintenance problems, some engineers considered that a more modest pressure might have been more prudent, but "higher, lighter, and faster" was the watchword of the times. A military type of ship developed from a British prototype was introduced in several sizes during the course of the war. Its most widely used version was labelled the LST (landing ship tank), which could load or unload wheeled vehicles through a bow door, could transfer them to another deck through a ramp device, and could turn them around on a turntable. The great utility of this slow-moving, pedestrian-looking ship caused it to inspire many changes in ships of the postwar period.

In World War II, as in its predecessor, the momentum of war and the necessity of speed produced building programs that are unequalled in peacetime. Shortly after the start of the war, a British purchasing mission came to the United States to contract for 60 ships, 441 feet (134 metres) long, of 10,490 tons displacement, with reciprocating steam engines and coal-fired Scotch boilers, as simple and rugged a merchant ship as could be devised. Shortly afterward, the same designers redesigned this ship for the U.S. war effort, giving it oil-fired watertube boilers, but otherwise left them identical to the British vessels. The U.S. program to produce emergency ships got under way in April 1941, when the first keel was laid; the "Patrick Henry" was launched on September 27, 1941. In all, 2,610 Liberty (or Ec-2) ships were built. Many production records were set in this effort, including the launching of a ship within ten days of the laying of the keel, with completion and delivery four days later.

World War II Liberty ships

Altogether, the U.S. shipbuilding effort in World War II produced 5,874 merchant-type ships of 57,205,407 deadweight tons, over one-third of the world tonnage at the beginning of the war. As in World War I, the tonnage was of mixed types and quality. Barracks, barges, and drydocks were built of iron-enriched concrete. Few if any wooden ships were built during this time, but some older wooden hulls were converted to war service. Mass production of ships, the coming of age of welded steel as a hull material, standardization of machinery components and plants, and the many special-purpose ships and craft that were developed during the war left an important heritage in design and construction.

Postwar developments. After World War II, the arrival of fast, dependable air travel across the oceans signalled the beginning of the end of the era of the super passenger liners. The speed differential between a jet aircraft and even the swiftest liners made performance differences between ships somewhat irrelevant, but even toward the end of the superliner era new records were set. From 1961 the longest passenger ship in the world was the "France" (from 1979 the "Norway"). The "France" was 1,035 feet (315 metres) long; aluminum in its superstructure lightens its displacement, and it was equipped with fin stabilizers that protruded from its sides below the water in order to reduce roll. Its modern plant was powered by 1,000-pounds-per-square-inch steam at 1,052° F, and 175,000 horsepower drove it at a speed of slightly over 35 knots. This combination of improvements, however, did not gain for the "France" the speed record, which continued to belong to a ship that was ten years its elder, the 1952-launched "United States," the holder of the Atlantic records for both east and west crossings. The "United States," the personal project of noted designer William Francis Gibbs, on its maiden voyage established a record of three days, ten hours, and 40 minutes. The record was likely to stand, because the competition of air travel made it improbable that the expense and effort required to build a superliner to surpass it would be economically feasible (see Figure 37).

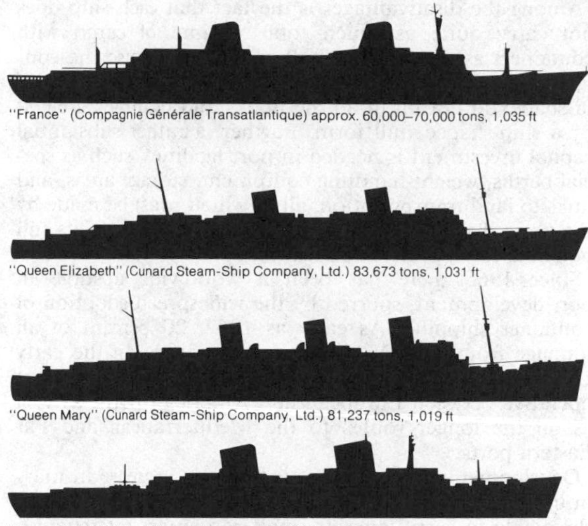

Figure 37: Silhouettes of several post-World War II passenger liners.
From Laurence Dunn, *Passenger Liners*

Two noteworthy technical developments of the postwar period were nuclear propulsion and hydrofoils (both discussed below). Far more significant in its impact on merchant shipping was the advent of containerization, a revolution in the transporting of freight that began in the late 1960s.

SPECIAL TYPES OF SHIPS

Container ships. The military success of prepackaged shipments to overseas points during World War II and the rising costs of stevedore services and labour in general stimulated consideration of the use of standardized containers for shipping materials. At first, the relatively poor volumetric efficiency in the stowage of the ship delayed acceptance of the concept. However, studies of the savings available in turnaround time, lower insurance rates because of reduced pilferage and damage, increased customer satisfaction, and the greater facility of transshipping from sea terminal to land transportation slowly made their weight felt.

Standard containers that fitted into cells created in container ships, on trailer trucks, and on rail cars were adopted (20 by eight by eight feet [about six by 2.5 by 2.5 metres]). The containers were fabricated of light, strong aluminum alloys, usually of corrugated construction in order to provide requisite stiffness. They were provided with lifting pads to allow easy hoisting and with fittings to permit them to be fastened to truck beds. Such containers became the unit of transit in a complete transportation system from point of origin to destination. Packed and sealed at the warehouse, a container is transmitted by road or rail to a port, at which specially designed high-speed lifting cranes take it from the carrier either to temporary pierside stowage or directly to the container ship. The ship is equipped with a cellular grid of belowdecks compartments opening to the weather deck; these are designed to receive the containers and hold them in place until unloading is achieved at the port of destination. The ship is filled to the deck level with containers, the hatches are closed, and one or two layers of containers, depending upon the size and stability of the ship, are loaded on the hatch covers on deck.

Upon arrival at the port of destination, specially designed lifting gear removes the containers from the ship in a matter of hours and loads them to trucks or trains or to temporary terminal stowage. In another few hours, the ship can be filled with containers destined for another port and can be under way. An additional economy is the low cost of the crew of the ship while in port awaiting loading or unloading. Further, because each ship can make more trips than before, container fleets require fewer vessels. There is also less pilferage and, hence, lower insurance rates and, finally, the assurance to the shipper that his shipment will not require any further handling until it arrives at its destination (see Figure 38).

Advantages of container ships

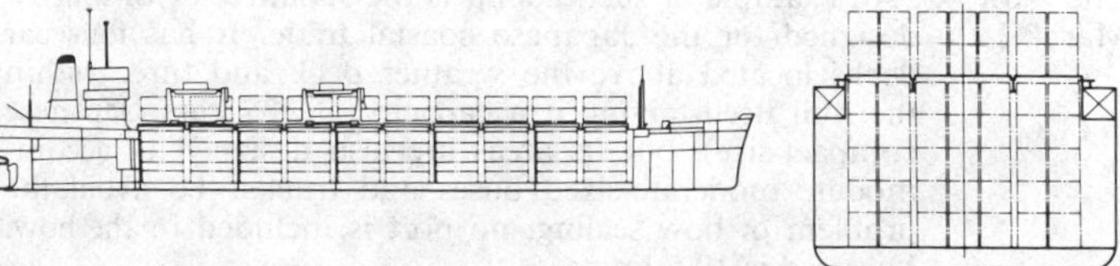

Figure 38: Profile and section of a typical container ship.

Among the disadvantages is the fact that each ship does not carry quite as much total volume of cargo with containers as with regular bulk stowage, because the containers themselves take space and, since they are square in shape, do not fill in all the nooks and crannies created by a ship-shaped hull form. Further, a rather substantial capital investment is needed in port facilities, such as special berths, weight-handling equipment, storage areas, and links to land transportation, all of which must be made by the ports that receive or ship via container ship if its full potential savings are to be realized.

Since 1965 there has been a worldwide upsurge in port development, spurred by the widespread adoption of container shipping. As early as 1967, 20 percent of all tonnage from New York was in containers. In the early 1970s several weekly scheduled container-ship lines were operative between European and American ports, as well as on the longer routes to the Mediterranean and Far Eastern ports.

Developments in containers include an increase in maximum size to 40 feet (12 metres) in length, with several ships able to carry large or small containers interchangeably. There are also refrigerated containers for perishables, open-top containers, and many other improvements.

The newer ships being built or converted to this service are moderate-sized merchant ships but of a higher average speed than in the past; in fact, few modern ships are built for speeds of less than about 20 knots. Greater use is being made of small, compact power plants to provide more space for containers. One new ship of the more common variety is the "Elbe Express." Built in 1969, it is equipped with fin stabilizers to help prevent damage to containerized cargo, and its nine-cylinder Diesel engine, giving 15,750 horsepower, drives it at 20 knots with good efficiency. It can carry either 786 standard 20-foot containers or 300 40-foot containers and 136 20-foot containers. Twenty-one 40-foot refrigerated containers can be accommodated. Special equipment includes six mooring winches to insure accurate positioning of the ship under cranes in port and special tanks to list (tip) and trim (level) the ship to permit a symmetrical loading or unloading without excessive list or trim. Its crew numbers only 33, including two stewardesses. Its route is from the continent of Europe via Britain to the United States East Coast ports.

The "Elbe Express"

Roll-on, roll-off. Another offspring of the specialized ships of World War II is the so-called roll-on, roll-off ship, which uses the general principles of the landing-ship tank but on a much larger scale. The ship is equipped with bow or stern openings (ports) and in most cases with side ports from which ramps can be extended to shore. Through these ports, vehicle traffic is efficiently ramped to the many decks within the ship. In essence, the inside of the ship is arranged to resemble a seagoing parking garage. Large sliding or folding watertight doors preserve the integrity of watertight bulkheads within the ship by giving sufficient compartmentation to withstand some flooding. Sealing the large doors that cover the openings in the hull offers a certain problem but one that modern mechanisms have satisfactorily solved. The general outline of the ship, in view of its relatively low density of cargo, is rather beamy, with a high deckhouse covering much of the ship's superstructure, to afford more parking decks. To ensure stability, fixed ballast is usually included in these ships, along with water ballast to adjust load and stability. The engineering plants of these ships are commonly twin engines of compact variety, such as geared diesel, and they are arranged so that the engine spaces are at either side of the ship, allowing valuable free space between them for vehicle passage.

The "Aoi Maru"

An example of such a ship is the Japanese "Aoi Maru," designed for the Japanese coastal trade. It has four car decks located above the weather deck and three within the hull itself, giving it a capacity of 737 cars (Japanese compact-size), but its areas are also designed to accommodate moderate-sized buses and trucks. To avoid the problem of bow sealing, no port is included in the bow. Its speed is 19.5 knots.

Ferryboats. A close kin to the roll-on, roll-off ship is the ferryboat, built for protected waters over a predetermined, usually short route. Ferries have been in existence for thousands of years. Some of the earliest were unpowered rafts towed back and forth across a stream by ropes that were pulled by men or horses. In other cases, the barges or rafts were towed by small boats or tugs. The modern powered ferryboat is usually relatively small—100 to 200 feet (30 to 60 metres) in length—and broad in the beam so that it can accommodate two to four lanes of vehicles located on either side of a narrow centre section containing access and exhaust systems. The ships are usually double-ended, with propellers and rudders at both ends and separate sets of controls in pilothouses at the top of both ends of the ship. At each terminal a specially devised slip is built so that the ship can, in any condition of tide or current, dock end first, with almost no manoeuvring required. A shore-based bridge is lowered to the deck to allow the vehicles to discharge and another load to come aboard.

Much larger ships have been used to carry trains across bodies of water such as the English Channel, although, because of their seaworthiness requirements, these might better be classed as seagoing ships than ferries. Ferries on longer inland routes, such as Puget Sound, in the northwestern United States, are of much more conventional hull form. In fact, the "Chinook," a Puget Sound ferry, somewhat resembles a destroyer; its propulsion plant is a wartime diesel destroyer escort plant, its bow is conventional, and with its 4,800-horsepower twin screws it makes over 17 knots.

Since World War II, construction of bridges over waterways that interrupt heavily travelled routes has considerably reduced the need for ferries. A notable example is the Mackinac Bridge connecting the upper and lower peninsulas of the state of Michigan.

Icebreakers. Many ports and harbours of the world are above the latitudes that provide ice-free navigation year around; consequently, ships that can break ice to provide lanes for other ships have been a necessity. These ships do not rush into ice and break it up by the impact of their hull against the edge of the ice, although this is possible with very thin ice of only a few inches thickness. Rather, the ship is designed to ride up over the ice as it proceeds along its path, and then, when the ice by a wedging action has picked up more of the weight of the ship than it can support by its shear strength, the hull falls through the ice, leaving a hole slightly larger than the ship's width. Thus, the hull lines of the icebreakers are broad, with very shallow draft at the bow and stern and gentle increases in draft to the midship section. The waterline of the ship must be reinforced with layers of plating and supported by a close-knit grill of stiffeners to protect against the constant collisions with solid ice. Because propeller damage is an obvious hazard, an icebreaker is usually provided with three screw arrangements, with the centre screw protected by a tunnel or flute in the bottom of the ship. It is also common practice to provide propellers at both ends of the ship, so that, if one end is imprisoned by ice, the other may be able to move the ship enough to get free. The propellers are built with large hubs to which each blade is individually bolted, so that single blades that are broken or bent can be replaced.

How an icebreaker operates

While sailing ships operated in ice at times, and some were strengthened to withstand the squeeze of the ice, the first genuine icebreaker that deserves the name was the "Ermak," built in Britain for the Russian government in 1899. It had 1½-inch (38-millimetre) steel plating on its waterline, displaced 10,000 tons, and had over 10,000 horsepower in steam engines. As today, it had three screws aft and an additional one in the bow. It was so successful at its task that it has served as a prototype of nearly all following icebreakers. One of the outstanding differences that has developed is in the propulsion. Modern ships have used electric drive extensively to obtain the fine control of the propellers needed, and, because the centre screw is the most protected, the propulsion system is so balanced that the centre screw carries 50 percent of the power, with the other 50 percent divided between the two outer propellers. Because many of their ports are icebound, the Russians are perhaps the world's leading

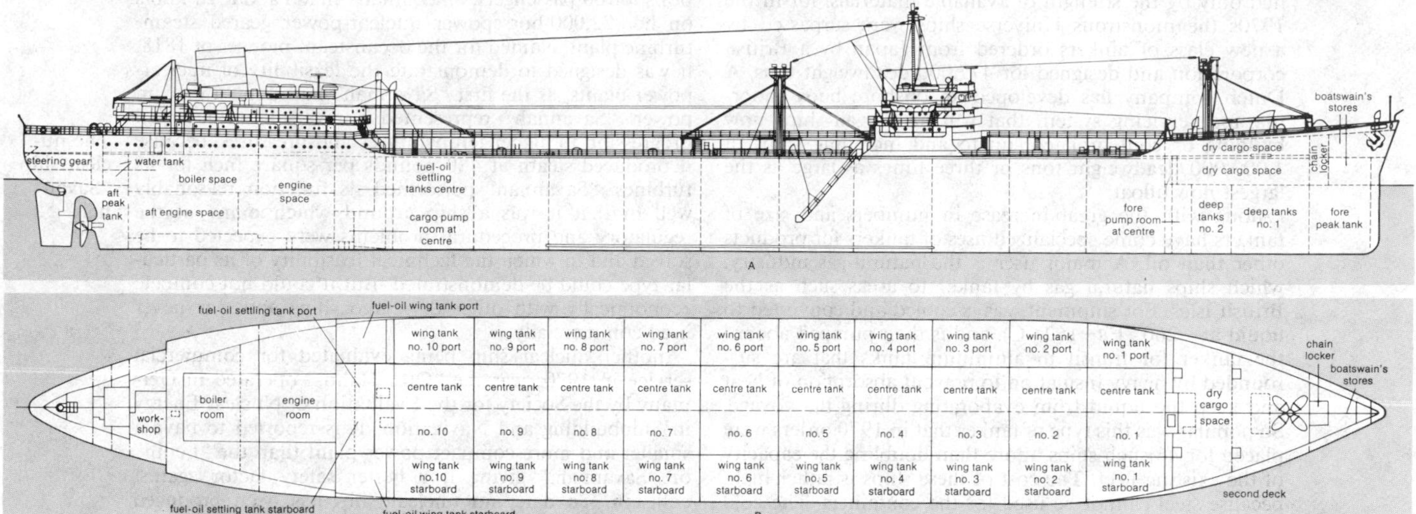

Figure 39: *Below-deck arrangement of a typical tanker.*
(A) Profile; (B) Plan view.
By courtesy of Newport News Shipbuilding and Dry Dock Co.

users and builders of icebreakers. The world's largest icebreaker is also the world's first nuclear surface ship—the "Lenin," built in Leningrad in 1957. Displacing 16,000 tons, it is 440 feet (134 metres) long and 90½ feet (27½ metres) in beam, with a maximum draft of 30 feet (nine metres). It has three screws with a total of about 44,000 horsepower from an atomic-steam-turbine-electric power plant. Its free route speed is 18 knots. It is protected at the sides by a stiffened ice belt of 1.5 to two inches (four to five centimetres) of high-strength steel. While the best weight-to-horsepower ratio would be obtained by using one large atomic reactor, the "Lenin" is fitted with three, two of which can carry the ship's load, leaving the third as a reserve reactor. The principal advantage of the nuclear reactor is that it imparts an almost unlimited cruising range to the ship. In heavy ice an icebreaker must do a huge amount of work, expending large amounts of fuel, to make a few miles a day. In conventional ships, the fuel supply is limited, and operations must at some times be curtailed to ensure that fuel will not be exhausted, while on the "Lenin," with for practical purposes an unlimited fuel endurance, power can be used in whatever amounts the situation demands. Next to the submarine, in which nuclear power makes possible almost an entirely new type of ship, the icebreaker represents the most advantageous marine use of nuclear power. The overall cost of nuclear-power installation, however, has discouraged construction of more such icebreakers.

The "Lenin"

Tankers. Perhaps the simplest ship to build and operate is the tanker. In essence, the tanker is a floating group of tanks contained in a ship-shaped hull, propelled by an isolated machinery plant at the stern. Each tank is substantially identical to the next throughout the length of the parallel-sided middle body of the ship. The tanks are fitted with heating coils to facilitate pumping in cold weather. Within the tanks are the main, or high-suction, pipes, running several feet from the bottom to avoid sludge. Below them, low-suction piping, or stripping lines, removes the lowest level of liquid in the tank. Tanks are filled either through open trunks leading from the weather deck or from the suction lines with the pumps reversed. Because tankers, except for military-supply types, usually move a cargo from the source to a refinery or other terminal with few manoeuvres en route, the machinery plant is called on only to produce at a steady rate the cruise power for the ship; consequently, considerable use of automatic controls is possible, thus reducing the size of the crew to a minimum. In view of the simplicity of inner arrangement, the tanker lends itself to mass production perhaps more than any other ship type. Because of the limited crew requirements and the low cost per ton for initial building and outfitting, the tanker has led the way in rapid expansion in the size of ships (see Figure 39).

Tanker crew requirements

For reasons already stated, larger ships are superior to smaller ones. The interaction of the wave train set up by the passage of the bow and that from the passage of the stern establishes a relationship between the speed of the ship and its length, such that, at a critical speed-to-length ratio, the addition of great amounts of power result in little if any increase in speed, while, below this ratio, the power requirements of a ship drop off radically, till, at low speed-to-length ratios, very small powers are required. Simply put, the longer the ship, the less power is required to drive it at a given speed. Hence, when ships of very high speed are desired, such as ocean passenger liners, lengths of up to 1,000 feet (300 metres) were used. In the case of the tanker, where economy is paramount, and speeds in the order of 15 to 18 knots are sufficient, the greater length of the ship reduces power requirements to very low amounts.

Early in the history of merchant ships, the carrying of oil was viewed with caution. Before the 1880s, oil that was transported across the seas was carried by loading it in barrels and stowing it in ordinary merchant ships. In 1886, however, a 300-foot (90-metre) German ship, the "Gluckauf," was launched, designed to carry oil in tanks that were situated against the ship's hull plating. By 1900 the idea of the tanker was so well established that 99 percent of the oil carried at sea was carried in such ships. Originally about the same size as other merchant ships, tankers were designed differently. For safety, the machinery was placed aft, with only enough superstructure forward to provide protection for the decks from water washing across and an elevated platform for ship control. The caution about the carrying of oil at sea has persisted to this day in that passengers are never carried in the same ship as cargo oil.

The first tanker

Gradually, the size of oil tankers increased as the demand for the service grew, and the need for economical operation to compete for cargo continued, until those of the 1970s and 1980s nearly stagger the imagination. The Universe-class tankers, built in Japan, the largest in service in the early 1970s, are of 326,000 tons deadweight. Dimensions are 1,132 feet (345 metres) in length and 175 feet (53 metres) in beam, with a loaded draft of 81 feet (25 metres), dwarfing the largest of the old-fashioned ocean liners. Such a ship is able to average over 15 knots on only 37,400 shaft horsepower. Complications arose with the introduction of such large ships; most of the harbours of the world are dredged to no more than 50 feet (15 metres) in the main channels, and special port facilities therefore had to be arranged. One solution that is used in Kuwait, where much oil is shipped, is to build an artificial island in deep water, connected to shore by a pipeline, to load and unload tankers.

Presumably, the length of tankers will ultimately be limited only by the strength of available materials, for in the 1970s the monstrous Universe ships were surpassed by a new class of tankers ordered from Japan by a British corporation and designed for 477,000 deadweight tons. A Dutch company has developed an offshore buoy mooring and servicing system that will handle all ships now building or contemplated, up to and including ships of 1,000,000 deadweight tons or three times as large as the largest now afloat.

Along with the great increase in numbers and size of tankers have come specialized uses of tankers for products other than oil. A major user is the natural-gas industry, which ships natural gas by tanker to areas such as the British Isles. For shipment, gas is cooled and converted to liquid at −260° F (−162° C), and is then pumped aboard the tanker for transit in aluminum tanks that are surrounded by heavy insulation to prevent absorption of heat and keep the liquid from evaporating during the voyage. So popular was this type of tanker that in 1970 orders were placed for 46 such ships, more than doubling the capacity of the existing fleet. The cost of these ships is rather high, because steel cannot be used for the containers. The cold liquid, in contact with steel, would make that material as brittle as glass. Aluminum is therefore used, sometimes backed by balsa wood, backed in turn by steel. A special nickel–steel alloy known as Invar has also been used in this application.

Other materials, such as iron ore, can be carried in a tanker in the form of slurry. The bulk dry cargo is mixed with high-velocity water jets, thereby forming a pumpable mixture to load the tanker; at the other end of the voyage, jets in the bottom of the tankers again mix the cargo with water in order to permit pumping the slurry ashore. The ships using this system have been reported to be much more economical to operate than are the ordinary dry bulk cargo ships.

Carrying dry cargo by tanker

Other cargo that has been shipped by tankers includes wine, molten sulfur, and methane gas. A novel type of tanker is the "Mobil Pegasus," by modern standards moderate-sized, only 1,017 feet (310 metres) long and 63 feet (19 metres) in draft for a total deadweight of 212,000 tons. The innovative feature of this ship is the fact that it is the first tanker to be built with a second bottom inside the hull. In this space is run all the piping to the tanks and to controls. The bottoms of the tanks above this are smooth so that no pockets of oil are formed when pumping out, and, since the tanks drain through a hole in the bottom, no stripping pipes are needed. In addition, the double bottom space allows what ballasting is necessary to be done outside the cargo oil tanks, reducing the possibility of polluting cargo.

A noteworthy tanker exploit was the voyage of "Manhattan," a 150,000-ton ship that had been refitted with a heavily reinforced bow. With the aid of two icebreakers the "Manhattan" was able to force her way through the Northwest Passage from Alaska to the Atlantic coast in 1969, breaking ice floes that were as thick as 15 feet and ridges as high as 40 in the process. This voyage, a first for a merchant ship, may foretell a new profitable route for transporting oil extracted from the newly discovered rich Alaskan fields later in the 1970s.

Nuclear ships. From the end of World War II, when the power generation capability of nuclear power was being developed, it was realized that, if a practical nuclear-power plant could be fitted into a submarine, a new type of ship could at last be realized—a true submarine instead of merely a short-term submersible. A large number of such submarines were ultimately built, with virtually unlimited underwater cruising range (see WAR, THE TECHNOLOGY OF: *Development of submarines*). A few nuclear-powered surface naval ships have also been built. Civil applications of marine nuclear power have so far been limited. As mentioned above, the Soviet Union built a successful icebreaker, the "Lenin," in 1957, and in 1962 the potential of nuclear power for an ordinary merchant ship was explored when the "Savannah," sponsored by the United States Atomic Energy Commission and Maritime Commission, was delivered. A modern shelter-deck ship of 12,220 gross tons with accommodations for 60 passengers, "Savannah" made about 20 knots on her 22,000-horsepower nuclear-power geared steam-turbine plant. Named for the oceansteam pioneer of 1818, it was designed to demonstrate the feasibility of nuclear-power plants, as the first "Savannah" had done for steam power. "Savannah" represented a reversal of the usual progression to higher temperatures and pressures, because it produced steam at 480 pounds per square inch for its turbines. "Savannah" performed its function reasonably well in that it was a ship around which many of the regulatory and procedural problems were expected to be solved and in which the technical feasibility of its particular type could be demonstrated. But it could not compete economically with other dry-cargo ships and was never used commercially.

The nuclear ship "Savannah"

Another nuclear ship being evaluated for commercial service in 1970s was the "Otto Hahn," operated in Germany by the Society for the Evaluation of Nuclear Energy in Shipbuilding and Navigation. It is reported to have a smaller and more compact power plant than the "Lenin" or "Savannah," giving it a better safety factor against collision. To date, no nuclear ship has been produced and operated by a commercial enterprise, because of the high initial costs and the difficulties in crew training. As nuclear cores become longer lasting and consequently reduce fuel costs and downtime (for overhaul and repair), and as other factors become more favourable, it is not considered impossible that this source of power could be important in ships.

Hydrofoils. The search for speed on water has been frustrated by the combination of the resistance created by the ship in making waves and by the friction of water flowing past the hull. The combination of these factors makes the power demands of a ship at very high speed prohibitive. One method of overcoming this situation is offered by the hydrofoil. This craft is so designed that the hull of the ship is lifted entirely out of the water as it gains speed and is supported on hydrofoils, wings shaped like those of an aircraft but made much stronger and smaller; because the density of water is about 600 times that of air, a relatively small lifting surface in water will lift as much as a large wing in air.

The mode of operation of these craft is for the hull to support its weight, either when at rest or steaming slowly, by means of its own buoyance. As speed is increased, the foils pick up more and more of the weight until at "takeoff" all of the weight is transferred to the foils and the ship is "flying."

The likeness to an aircraft is more than one of nomenclature. The problems of weight control are critical; because the same laws apply in foils as in aircraft, every pound of weight creates drag that must be supported by power. Thus, the hulls are built of light alloys and the foils of such materials as high-strength steel or titanium. Power is supplied by the lightest possible source, such as aircraft-type gas turbines.

Propulsion is a special problem for hydrofoils, because the power in a ship is normally generated in the hull and must be transmitted a considerable distance to the water. For this reason, several early hydrofoils used air-screw propulsion. Later, a water jet in which water is pumped out of the stern at high velocity was developed to provide low-weight propulsion.

Control and stability of foils is similar to that of aircraft, except that the control of altitude must be much more precise, for the range of motion can be only the distance from the surface of the water to the foil submergence, usually not over 10 feet (three metres). All of the early foils relied on their geometry for control. The most prevalent foil system is the surface system, in which the foil surface intersects the surface of the water at an angle, so that, when more lift is needed, the foil simply submerges farther and with more surface in the water produces enough lift to regain equilibrium. These types have been arranged in single Vs or in a ladder pattern, with several foils one above the other to increase the lift faster as more submergence is attained. All the early systems relied on the surface of the water for control and consequently produced a rather rough ride. Later developments produced electronic means of sensing the clearance of the hull from the water and signalling control-surface changes to fully submerged foils that operate nearly independent of the surface and hence provide both a smoother ride and greater seakeeping ability.

The first hydrofoil may have been described in 1897 by the Comte de Lambert in applying for a French patent on a catamaran hull that had been fitted with four transverse "hydroplanes." Authorities have expressed some doubt that this boat actually used the hydrofoil principle at all; it may instead have been only a specialized planing boat. The first true hydrofoil was operated by an Italian inventor, Enrico Forlanini, between 1898 and 1905 and was supported by a set of hydrofoils. While little is known of the performance of this craft, another Italian inventor is reported to have operated a craft of this type at 50 miles (80 kilometres) per hour.

Alexander Graham Bell's hydrofoil

Hydrofoils reached a pinnacle of performance and publicity when a boat built by Alexander Graham Bell and Casey Baldwin set the world's water speed record in 1918 with a speed of 60 knots. The craft, the HD 4, was powered by two Liberty aircraft engines of 350 horsepower each and was equipped with a set of ladder-type foils. While the boat was far ahead of its time, its efficiency by later standards was rather low. In the early 1930s several effective surface-piercing foil boats were developed, and World War II gave a major stimulus. In Germany, craft of up to 80 tons and speeds of nearly 60 knots were built, but Allied bombs prevented this effort from reaching operational status.

After the war the United States, Canada, the Soviet Union, Britain, and Germany all launched development efforts. A boat developed by a U.S. windmill builder was supported by four V foils, one located at each corner of the boat, that gave excellent stability.Because there was no supporting structure in the water, only lifting surface, it was most efficient, having the highest lift-to-drag ratio attained up to that time.

A breakthrough occurred in the early 1950s, when the laboratories of Massachusetts Institute of Technology in conjunction with the ship-designers firm of Gibbs and Cox developed a sonic device to measure the distance from the bow of the ship to the water and to use this measurement to control fully submerged foils. The new device was tried on a standard power yacht that had been converted to a set of tandem, fully submerged foils. The experiment proved a great success. The speed of the boat was more than tripled and its seakeeping ability in heavy seas greatly enhanced.

High-speed hydrofoils

By the early 1970s the technology was available to construct and operate hydrofoils of up to 500 tons with speeds from 40 to 50 knots. Several passenger ferries employed the hydrofoil principle; one in the Soviet Union, the "Meteor," had a capacity of 150. The U.S. Navy's "Plainview," of about 300 tons, had speed in excess of 40 knots, and test craft have reached speeds in excess of 80 knots on foils under controlled conditions.

The LASH ship. A recent development in shipping is the LASH (lighter-aboard-ship) vessel, designed to carry nearly any cargo in steel lighters or barges, each about 60 feet (18 metres) long and 30 feet (nine metres) wide and capable of handling 500 tons of cargo (see Figure 40). The hull of the ship is generally conventional except that its superstructure is dominated by a large travelling crane supported by legs from each side of the ship. At the stern the tracks for the crane extend well aft of the deck, so that barges that are picked up from the deck may be lowered directly into the water, or, in reverse, barges can be picked up directly from the water and placed in their stowage position aboard. The ship can also carry containers (for a complete description of LASH ships and some other recent developments in this area, see HANDLING, PACKAGING, AND STORAGE).

Ferrocement boats. Ferrocement construction, under development since 1965, involves the use of common waterproof cement or concrete applied over a metal rod or lath (wire-mesh) core to form the hull and subdivisions of a boat hull. The low cost of the materials (portland cement, metal lath, reinforcing rods, and wooden forms)

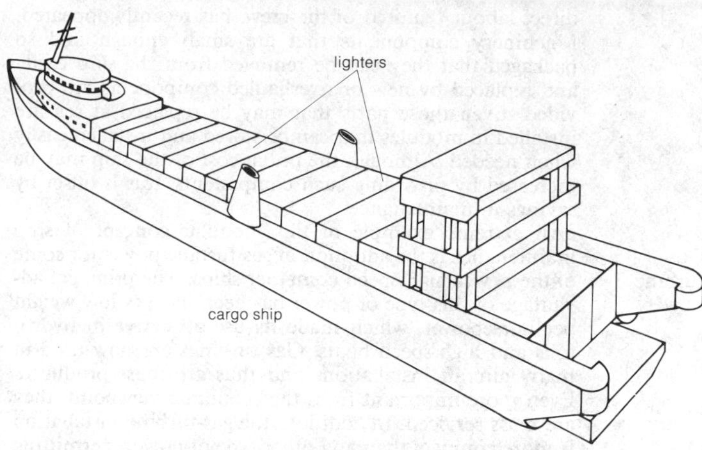

Figure 40: A group of lighters (small cargo vessels) loaded aboard a specially designed cargo ship. The combination is referred to as LASH (lighter aboard ship).
From *Business Abroad* (January 1971)

is somewhat offset by the relatively high amount of labour that is involved in plastering the successive layers required for the completed hull. In underdeveloped countries, however, where labour is plentiful and inexpensive, this material is widely used. Its resistance to rot and corrosion and ease of repair offer some of the advantages of plastic construction, while the weight of the hull is considerably greater than that of one built of aluminum or plastics. Its cost to the private boat builder who is furnishing his own labour is undoubtedly the lowest of any material now used. For further information on shipbuilding, see INDUSTRIES, MANUFACTURING.

SHIP MAINTENANCE

When ships were small, the ship's crew was able to perform not only routine maintenance but also major repairs. As ships grew larger and more complicated, they came to require specialized facilities. Such facilities are collectively called a shipyard. A shipyard consists of one or more dry docks or marine railways to expose the bottoms of the ships for cleaning and painting (normally every 18 or 36 months) and a series of long, high-reach cranes to take loads in and out of ships for repair. Waterfront facilities are supplemented by shops for shipfitting, machining, electric and electronic work, carpentry, pipe welding, painting, and rigging.

Shipyard facilities

Conventional ships are sent into shipyards on a regular schedule for purposes of bottom cleaning and overhaul. Though schedules vary among ship types and services, vessels are generally sent to shipyards once in every one to three years. A considerable amount of preplanning is required before the ship's entry to the shipyard. As a first step the operators of the ship and representatives of the shipyard meet, usually three to six months in advance of the overhaul, to determine the repairs and other work that will be needed. The owners and the repair yard then arrange the ordering of the necessary materials to perform the repairs.

Since modern ships have become more and more complicated advance planning in maintenance is vital. Electronic parts and control devices may need to be ordered several months in advance; the owner cannot afford to leave his vessel idle. In the case of submarines or nuclear-powered vessels, planning for repair may start from 18 months to two years in advance.

In addition to formal overhaul in the yard, ships require day-to-day servicing, such as cleaning, lubrication, adjustment, and minor repairs in order to continue to operate during their time at sea. This work is normally done by the crew, using onboard supplies. Because a ship at sea is dependent on itself for all such services as fresh water, heat, light, and refrigeration, the responsibility of the crew members is a great and personal one.

A new approach to maintenance, intended to increase the time that the ships are in service and to reduce the direct labour required of the crew, has recently appeared. Machinery components that are small enough and so packaged that they can be removed from the ship easily and replaced by new or overhauled components are provided. Even those parts that may be replaced at sea are installed in modules that can be stored and installed easily when needed. Although the initial cost of the ship may be increased by providing such components, this is offset by savings in maintenance.

Gas-turbine power

An extreme example of this modular concept of ship maintenance is the adoption of gas-turbine power for some of the newer high-speed container ships. The principal advantage of this type of power has been its very low weight per horsepower, which made its use attractive in hydrofoils and high-speed boats. Gas turbines are now used in many aircraft installations and thus are mass produced. Even more important from the economic viewpoint, they are mass serviced. In addition, the gas-turbine installation is more compact than any other type of power, permitting more room for cargo, and is light enough to be removable from the ship for servicing. Replacement of units, which can be accomplished in less than 12 hours in some installations, permits ships to remain in service without extended stays in port. In a container ship, for example, engines can be replaced while the ship is being loaded for her turn around, without any loss in time at sea. These advantages have overcome the disadvantages of higher fuel costs of gas turbines. The "Adm. William Callaghan," the largest roll-on-roll-off ship afloat in the early 1970s, was powered by a combination of gas turbines totalling 50,000 horsepower.

While the use of gas turbines increases the amount, weight, and cost of fuel needed, the reduction in crew and ease of maintenance (a gas turbine is so light and compact that it can be hoisted out of the ship and replaced in a few hours) tip the economic balance in their favour. The same procedure is used in modular electronic units, complicated control units, and even in the electrical-generating units themselves.

Of course, the new method of overhaul and repair by module requires a much more sophisticated planning and control system ashore to ensure that a new or repaired unit is available when and where it is needed without an excessive inventory of parts being accumulated. Computers are used to assist in such control. (Ja.J.S.)

SPECIALIZATION IN SHIPPING

The liner and the tramp ship. The two main types of ships are the liner, operating regular, scheduled services on a predetermined trade route, charging advertised rates, and the tramp ship, which is prepared to carry any suitable cargo from any port to any other on a negotiated contract basis. Liner services are of particular value for passengers and mails and for traders who are not dealing in entire shiploads of commodities. The bulk shipper finds it more economical to purchase transport services on the open market, offering his business to the lowest bidder. Thus tramp ships usually carry homogeneous cargoes, whereas liners transport small consignments of many different kinds of merchandise.

The principal bulk cargoes have varying characteristics. Liquids, for example, require specially designed ships and are considered as a separate branch of the industry. The normal dry-cargo tramp ship is designed for flexibility so that it can carry, as the occasion arises, commodities as different as iron ore, coal, grain, sugar, cotton, or copra. Because of the difference in stowage factors (*i.e.*, the iron by cubic capacity required per ton of cargo), for example, a ship that would be large enough to carry 10,000 tons of coal might be loaded to its maximum draft with less than 5,000 tons of ore; and if the same ship were to carry grain, interior partitions would be necessary to prevent the cargo from upsetting the stability of the ship that would result from their shifting when the vessel rolled.

Loading and unloading

Different methods are used for loading and discharging different types of cargo. Cargoes shipped in cases, bales, or bags must be handled by the ship's derricks or by shore cranes, and the same applies to cargoes of commodities like timber, steel, or scrap. Iron ore and coal are discharged by grab and grain by elevators or suction pipes. Bulk solids are gravity loaded by conveyers and chutes. Oil is often pumped from tankers directly into pipelines connected to storage tanks and refineries. With the trend toward larger bulk carriers, the installation of self-discharging gear has increased. A number of systems are in use, including various forms of conveyers and elevators.

Specialized carriers. Specialized ships such as ore carriers may still be divided into the two categories of liner and tramp. Some are constructed by tramp shipping companies to be hired out or chartered on a long-term basis to shippers or importers of ore, whereas others are built and operated by the shippers or consumers of ore themselves, mainly the large steelworks. Several other industrial consumers of raw materials in bulk, such as major importers of sugar, newsprint, molasses, gypsum, and chemicals, operate their own fleets of bulk carriers in a similar fashion and also hire ships from tramp shipowners on the open market.

Barge tows and barge carriers. Barges towed by high-powered tugs are another recent development; some of the units now being built are high-capacity carriers of around 10,000 tons. The tug and barge concept is mainly valuable when voyages are short; one tug can sometimes serve three barges—one loading, one discharging, and one in transit—providing the best possible utilization of the high-cost power unit and the labour required to man it.

Lighter aboard ship system

Even further advances in utilization have been made with the adoption of a so-called lighter aboard ship (LASH) system, which involves a mother ship carrying nests of lighters that are loaded and discharged by powerful stern cranes. This system permits the preloading and assembling of the cargo in the lighters and can be a particular advantage if the point of origin or destination of the cargo is not approachable by a larger vessel. Such ships now operate across the North Atlantic.

Tankers. The transport of petroleum products by sea has vastly expanded in the 20th century, particularly since World War II. In 1939 the world tanker fleet totalled 11,568,000 tons gross, comprising 16.9 percent of the total tonnage of all merchant ships. By 1970 the tanker fleet had reached a total of 86,140,000 tons gross, representing as much as 37.9 percent of the total world fleet. Accompanying this growth of total tonnage was a remarkable advance in the size of individual tankers, up to 300,000 tons deadweight, over 1,000 feet (300 metres) in length, 130 feet (40 metres) in breadth, and drawing up to 64 feet (20 metres) of water.

Tankers must be subdivided into compartments in order to restrict the movement of the cargo by the motion of the ship. No shipborne cargo-handling facilities are required; the oil is pumped on board and off.

Before World War II the greater part of the world tanker fleet was owned and operated by the major oil companies, operating as industrial carriers. Tramp tankers occasionally supplemented these vessels. After World War II, however, and despite the expansion of their own fleets, the oil companies came to rely also on tramp tankers. A particular feature of the tanker trade is that it is almost entirely a one-way traffic; since tankers are not suitable for carrying any other type of cargo without structural alterations, the outward journey must be made in ballast. An exception to this rule is made for iron ore. Sweden, an ore-exporting and oil-importing country, has evolved ships capable of carrying an inward cargo of oil and an outward cargo of ore. As a result of the exploitation of the Labrador ore fields, this combined oil and ore carrier was increasingly built after World War II. In the winter season, when the ore-loading ports of Labrador are closed by ice, these specially designed ships find alternative employment as oil carriers. Other liquid cargoes, such as molasses, caustic soda, asphalt, and wine, are also carried in bulk at sea.

Coastal and short-sea shipping. Most oceangoing ships have their smaller scale counterparts in coastal shipping, the function and extent of which varies in different parts of the world according to geographical conditions. Coastal shipping, also referred to as cabotage, is a separate branch of the shipping industry, generally confined to the coastal waters of a particular country. In countries with continental coastlines, such as the United States, Australia, and India, coastal shipping differs little operationally from oceangoing shipping; and in the United States the term is even extended to include the intercoastal trade between the Pacific and Atlantic coasts via the Panama Canal and the noncontiguous trade between continental America and outlying areas such as Hawaii. In Europe, where national coastlines are comparatively short, coastal shipping has a more international character.

British coastal trade

In the United Kingdom there can be distinguished the purely coasting trade, plying among the islands and along the coast of Great Britain; the home trades, which ply between the United Kingdom and the continent of Europe within the limits of Brest, France, and Hamburg; and the short-sea trade, between the United Kingdom and Scandinavia, the Baltic Sea, and the Mediterranean. Some shipping companies operate liners, tramps, or tankers in all of these trades, while others may specialize in any one.

In the coasting and short-sea trades there are also many specialized vessels, such as cross-channel passenger ships, train ferries, ramp-loading or roll-on, roll-off motor vehicle transport ships specially designed for container traffic, as well as colliers and tankers. These tend to be operated by companies specializing in particular routes over which traffic is heavy but localized. As these services often form sea links between, or extensions of, railway systems, the railway companies often operate them. Indeed, the coastal shipping industry may be regarded as complementary to the inland system of transport communications as well as a link with neighbouring countries; a useful characteristic of the coastal ship is its ability to load cargo directly from the oceangoing vessel for transshipment along the coast and distribution to smaller ports whose depth of water or lack of facilities precludes the direct approach of the larger ship.

Ancillary services. At the port, where the sea transport and inland transport systems meet, many ancillary services must be provided for ships. These include towage, stevedoring, warehousing, replenishment of stores, repair, and maintenance. Practice varies widely among different ports, the various services being provided by independent contractors, by the port authority, or by the shipping companies. In many ports, particularly those in which large liner companies operate, the companies have their own subsidiary organizations to provide such services not only for their own ships but also for others. Some of the larger shipping groups operate or control fleets of tugs, loading and discharging facilities and labour, warehouses and refrigerated stores, lighterage and land transport, and even provide for the building, repairing, equipment, and maintenance of ships for themselves and for other shipowners.

SHIPPING OPERATIONS

As the carrying performances of liners and tramps differ, so do the operational organization and methods of the companies that run them.

Liner operation. The operator of a liner service has special interests in the particular trade route on which he travels. The design and performance of his ships is directed toward fulfilling the requirements of shippers using his services in the most economical way possible. Since a liner may carry cargo from dozens or even hundreds of individual consignees, the company must maintain extensive facilities and staff, both at the loading port and at the port of discharge. In less active ports these functions may be carried out by agents acting for one or more liner companies. Furthermore, passengers and cargo must be solicited from inland centres often quite distant from the ports of shipment, and it must always be possible to arrange for the transshipment or onward movement of cargo and passengers from terminal ports to ultimate destinations.

The conference system. Liner companies provide regular and frequent carriage of all kinds of cargo in consignments large and small, at advertised fixed charges. They are enabled to do this by the liner conference system, which was first tried out on the Britain–Calcutta trade in 1875. The object of the conference system is to regulate uneconomic competition. Shipping companies of different ownership and nationality that service the same range of ports form a conference agreement to regulate rates for each type of freight; in some cases the agreement also allocates a specified number of sailings to each company. Coupled with this agreement there is generally a deferred-rebate system, by which regular shippers of goods by conference vessels receive a rebate of a percentage of the tariff freight rate, payable after a period of proved loyalty, provided they use conference vessels exclusively.

The shipping conference system has sometimes come under attack as tending to create a monopoly and to restrain competition against the public interest. It is, however, generally agreed that evidence is in favour of this system: it has been concluded that no realistically possible combination of shipping companies can force unreasonable rates and that shipping companies that provide regular sailings with good ships and maintain staffs and organizations in ports to handle and dispatch cargoes, irrespective of whether trade is good or bad, are entitled to some protection against the casual vessel that picks up an occasional cargo at cut rates. Advocates agree that through the system, the shipper can rely on a well-managed service, running vessels that will carry any desired quantities of his goods at predetermined rates.

Ship brokering and chartering. As mentioned above, tramp-ship sailings and rates are determined by negotiation. Most of the world's tramp-ship chartering business is carried out in the Baltic Mercantile and Shipping Exchange in London, commonly known as the Baltic Exchange. This exhange had its origins in the 17th century, when merchants and ships' captains were accustomed to meet in coffeehouses to arrange cargoes for ships. The Baltic and the Jerusalem were the two coffeehouses chiefly patronized by merchants and captains until the business was concentrated in the Baltic tavern in 1810. In 1823 the first rules and regulations of a "Baltic Club" were drawn up, limiting membership to 300 and providing for accommodations and refreshments. At that time tallow was the principal commodity in the Baltic trades, but with the repeal of the British protectionist Corn Laws in 1846, the buying and selling of grain cargoes became one of the chief activities.

The Baltic Exchange

On the floor of the Baltic Exchange brokers circulate daily, some of them representing the shippers of cargoes, such as grain, coal, or ores, who require shipping space for their movement, and others representing the owners of tramp ships wanting employment. When seeking a ship for the carriage of a cargo, the broker naturally looks for a ship of the right size and specifications, ready at the right time and in the right port and prepared to carry the cargo at the cheapest possible rate. Conversely, the owner's broker must attempt to anticipate the charterer's requirements by having his ship at the right place at the right time but must also try to obtain the highest freight rate possible without running the risk of losing the contract to a competitor. This constant interplay of supply and demand, of ships as well as of cargoes, has the effect of reducing sea transport costs to a minimum, although tramp rates fluctuate frequently and widely at times.

Speculation

These fluctuating rates also offer opportunities for speculation, as on a stock exchange. The shipper of grain, for example, may decide to charter a ship at what he considers to be a cheap rate even before he has sold the cargo, which he attempts to dispose of in the best market while it is still afloat. In this case the ship is chartered for a voyage from, say, the Río de la Plata to the English Channel "for orders," freight rates having been previously arranged to cover a variety of alternative destinations. Again, a shipper or owner may agree to charter a ship for a period of time at a certain rate, in the hope that he will later be able to "rent it" to another owner or shipper at a higher rate if the market improves. A good deal of "forward" chartering may also occur, in which a contract is entered into for performance at some specified time at a predetermined rate that both owner and hirer hope will prove favourable, according to their estimate of future market conditions.

Methods of charter

The four principal methods of chartering a tramp ship are voyage charter, time charter, bareboat charter, or on a contract or "lump sum" basis. The voyage charter, in which a ship is chartered for a one-way voyage between specified ports, with a specified cargo at a negotiated rate of freight, is most common. The charterer agrees to provide the cargo for loading within an agreed range of dates. Once the cargo has been delivered at the port or ports of destination, the ship is free to further employment at the owners' discretion. Sometimes, however, the arrangement is for a series of consecutive voyages, generally for similar cargoes over the same route. The freight rate is expressed in terms of so much per ton of cargo delivered.

On time charter, the charterer undertakes to hire the ship for a stated period of time or for a specified roundtrip voyage or, occasionally, for a stated one-way voyage, the rate of hire being expressed in terms of so much per ton deadweight per month. Whereas on a voyage charter the owner bears all the expenses of the voyage (subject to agreement about costs of loading and discharging), on time charter the charterer bears the cost of bunkers and stores consumed. On bareboat charter, which is less frequently used in ordinary commercial practice, the owner of the ship delivers it up to the charterer for the agreed period without crew, stores, insurance, or any other provision, and the charterer is responsible for running the ship as if it were his own for the period of the contract.

Contracts can also be arranged on a lump-sum basis, when an owner agrees to ship a given quantity of a stated cargo from one port to another for a stated sum. Sometimes large quantities of cargoes such as coal are arranged for on a contract basis. The shipowner agrees to undertake the shipment of a given quantity over a given period at a fixed price per ton of cargo, but not necessarily in any specified ship, although he generally uses his own ships if they are available. The question of substituted ships, however, often leads to disputes, and the terms of the contract may make special provisions for this eventuality. Once the owner's broker and the charterer's broker have agreed on the terms of contract, the ship is "fixed," although by word of mouth alone. The motto of the Baltic Exchange is "our word is our bond," and that code of ethics is observed by ship brokers throughout the world, whether they are members of the Baltic or not, for the simple reason that any ship broker who does not abide by it would be unable to transact further business. Legally, however, the final contract is the written "charter party," which for most transactions is accepted as a standard document and is agreed to by all parties normally concerned in a tramp-ship "fixture" for a particular trade. The standard form of a charter party covers all the main points that experience has shown might lead later to misunderstanding or disputes about the liabilities of each party, while the variable details, such as the particulars of the voyage, cargo, ship, loading and discharging conditions, ports, and rate of freight, can be inserted in accordance with the prior verbal agreement. The charter-party document is subject to scrutiny and interpretation by a court of law in the event of dispute, but in practice most disputes are submitted to arbiters (generally independent ship brokers appointed by each participant) for settlement, unless an important legal precedent is involved.

"Charter party"

Among the most important clauses in any charter party are those that lay down the number of days allowed for loading or unloading and those that determine who is to bear the expense involved. Normally a certain number of days are allowed for loading, and if the charterer fails to finish loading in the time specified, the shipowner is entitled to compensation. Quite often, on the other hand, the charterer receives dispatch money if the cargo is loaded in less than the time agreed in the charter party. Similar conditions usually apply in the port of discharge.

Many tankers, ore carriers, or other specialized bulkcargo carriers are operated by an oil company or a steel company or an ore exporter exclusively on company business, whether on a regular schedule or not, or they are owned by an independent tramp shipowner and taken on charter by an oil or steel company to fulfill its marginal transport requirements on terms similar to those employed in the dry-cargo tramp shipping market.

Shipowners' and seamen's associations. Shipowners are organized on a national and a regional basis, generally in Chambers of Shipping or their equivalent. The chambers deal with policy issues, recruitment, and training of seafarers and the supply of crews. Such associations have sections to look after the special interest of subgroups in the industry, such as tankers, liners, tramps, and bulk carriers. Chambers consult governments on matters of high policy and are concerned with a wide range of issues affecting the industry as a whole, such as port organization, international relations, technical research, marine safety, radio and navigation questions, marine pollution, maritime law, marine insurance, information, and fiscal policy. The chambers are the voice of the industry and the forum for discussing and deciding policy on whatever (except labour relations) affects the well-being of shipping.

On the international level, the chief shipowning organizations include the International Chamber of Shipping and the International Shipping Federation, whose offices and secretariats are housed in London. Formed in 1921, the International Chamber of Shipping excluded state shipping organizations of any kind. The ownership of the national fleet or of a substantial part of it had to be vested in private individuals or companies. Though the International Chamber of Shipping was suspended during World War II, shipowners representing 14 nations met in London in 1946 to reconstitute it, and in 1970 it had 19 member countries. To avoid the overlap of its functions with those of other organizations and to preserve the principles of private enterprise, it drew up a broad definition of its own purpose: to promote internationally the interests of the shipping industry; to coordinate expert advice on technical questions, in particular, with standards of safety and technical and scientific progress; and to provide a medium for the exchange of views and information on questions affecting the industry internationally.

To deal with more routine matters, other international shipping organizations exist. Prominent among these is the Baltic and International Maritime Conference, started in Copenhagen in 1905 as the Baltic and White Sea Conference to curtail cutthroat competition among tramp shipowners engaged in the Baltic and White Sea trades. The conference was organized primarily to secure minimum freight rates and negotiate uniform chartering terms between shipowners of different flags and the charterers. By 1969 the Baltic and International Maritime Conference consisted of shipowner and ship broker members from 75 different countries representing some 71,000,000 tons gross of shipping. The conference now embraces many kinds of trades in all parts of the world, and one of its principal functions is to inform members of changes in port expenses, in costs of loading and discharging cargoes, and in port labour conditions; but perhaps the most valuable part of its work consists of the drawing up of standard forms of charter party for use in a wide variety of tramp-shipping trades. There is also an International Committee of Passenger Lines and a Comité Maritime International and, on a regional basis, a Committee of European Shipowners, Committee of European National Shipowners' Association, and a Committee of Liner Operators: South America.

Government regulation agencies

On the governmental level, in the United States the Federal Maritime Commission carries out regulatory activities, as do government departments in most countries. Of the international governmental organizations, the United Nations' specialized agency, the Inter-Governmental Maritime Consultative Organization, is one of the most important and in the early 1970s was very much concerned with problems of oil pollution. Other bodies include the United Nations Conference on Trade and Development–Committee of Shipping and the Maritime Transport Committee of the Organisation for Economic Co-operation and Development.

INTERNATIONAL MARITIME LAW

International conventions. Ships operate in an international field, the high seas, and are subject not only to the laws of the country in which they are registered and to the laws of the country in whose territorial waters they may be but also to a series of international conventions, the principles of which are incorporated into the domestic legislation of most maritime countries. There has grown up, particularly in the years since the expansion of steam navigation, a body of international maritime law—"the common law of the sea"—that has been developed through international agreement. Nearly all the world's maritime nations, for example, have adopted the International Regulations for Preventing Collisions at Sea, originally based on British rules formulated in 1862 and made internationally effective after a series of international meetings culminating in a conference at Washington, D.C., in 1889. These rules specify in great detail how ships must navigate in respect of each other, what lights must be shown and what signals must be given in accordance with circumstances; any infringement of this international code of conduct is accepted in all maritime courts of law as prima facie evidence of liability in case of collision.

Similarly, the internationally accepted requirements for the protection and safety of life at sea, as far as the ship and its equipment are concerned, are embodied in the International Convention for Safety of Life at Sea. The sinking of the liner "Titanic" in 1912 gave rise to a general desire to raise the standards of safety of life at sea. Although a convention was drawn up in 1914 requiring certain minimum standards for passenger ships, it did not become fully operative because of the outbreak of World War I. A second Safety of Life at Sea Convention, drawn up in 1929, determined minimum standards for the construction of passenger ships engaged in international voyages and for the provision of lifesaving appliances and extended its rules for the safety of navigation to all ships on all voyages. The provisions regarding radio equipment were extended to cover cargo ships of more than 1,600 tons gross.

Improved techniques led to the convening of a third Safety of Life at Sea Conference in London in 1948, after which a third International Convention for Safety of Life at Sea was adopted. This convention came into force on November 19, 1952, having been ratified one year previously by the following countries in order of acceptance: United Kingdom, New Zealand, the United States, France, The Netherlands, Sweden, Norway, South Africa, Iceland, Portugal, Canada, Pakistan, Denmark, Yugoslavia, Italy, Belgium, Israel, Japan, and the Philippines. The scope of the 1929 convention was again extended to include, in several matters, cargo ships of 500 tons gross and above. Minimum requirements were laid down for construction of ships, provision of watertight bulkheads, closing of openings in hulls, lifesaving appliances, fire appliances, radio equipment and direction finders, grain divisions in ships carrying grain cargoes, precautions in carriage of dangerous goods, and emergency musters and drills. The 1948 convention also embodied the recommendations of governments associated with the World Meteorological Organization and provided for the continuance of the International Ice Patrol maintained by the United States Coast Guard in the North Atlantic. This convention was again revised in 1960. Whereas the Safety of Life at Sea Convention deals with the construction of ships from the safety point of view, particularly in respect of passengers and crews, the International Load Line Convention deals with the strength and seaworthiness of ships in normal operating conditions. This convention emerged from the British Merchant Shipping Act, 1875, providing the Plimsoll load line on the ship's side, indicating the maximum depth to which a ship could legally be loaded. In order to protect the competitive position of British ships, the Merchant Shipping Act of 1890 required all foreign ships leaving British ports to comply with the load-line regulations. This led to the adoption of load-line rules by most maritime countries, and the International Load Line Convention of 1930 was ratified by 54 nations. A new International Convention on Load Lines, drawn up in 1966, came into force in July 1968 and allowed for a smaller freeboard (vertical distance between the water and the deck) for large ships while calling for more stringent protection of openings in decks and superstructures.

International Load Line Convention

In 1958 the Inter-Governmental Maritime Consultative Organization, a specialized agency of the United Nations, came into existence. The purpose of this advisory organization is to promote international cooperation in maritime navigation. By mid-1971, membership had grown to 73 nations.

Commercial legislation. International agreements and international law are also concerned with the business dealings between maritime countries. In this connection, the International Maritime Committee (Comité Maritime International) and the International Law Association did invaluable work. Delegates to the International Conference on Maritime Law held at Brussels in 1921 recommended to their respective governments the adoption of a set of rules, known as The Hague Rules, which establish the responsibilities, rights, and immunities of carriers under bills of lading (documents acknowledging receipt of cargo for shipment and proving entitlement to the goods). The Hague Rules, which are generally also incorporated into the terms of a charter party, were given widespread legislative sanction by maritime countries.

The Hague Rules

Legislative sanction is not necessary to secure international agreement or observance. The York–Antwerp Rules of General Average, for example, differ in some respects from English law relating to marine insurance and contracts of affreightment. They were formulated by delegates from various maritime countries meeting at York, England, in 1864 and at Antwerp in 1877 and were revised at Stockholm in 1924 and at Amsterdam in 1950. They were so widely adopted by the maritime nations that for all practical purposes they have the force of law.

Ship classification. To ensure compliance with the various international safety and load-line and other maritime conventions as well as with the requirements of national legislation concerning the registry and construction of merchant ships, most maritime nations require ships to be built under the supervision of government surveyors or of surveyors belonging to recognized classification societies and in accordance with their standards.

Lloyd's Register of Shipping. The leading classification society, operating in almost every country in the world, is Lloyd's Register of Shipping, which began its work long before any national legislation existed for the performance of its purposes. The history of Lloyd's Register of Shipping can be traced back to 1760. The society was reconstituted in 1834 and again in 1914. The shipping community maintains it voluntarily, and its principal work is to supervise the survey and classification of merchant ships of all nationalities according to rigid standards. Through a worldwide organization of surveyors, initial classifications are made when ships are built, and maintenance surveys of such items as the hull, machinery, boilers, and refrigerating plant are carried out periodically or whenever the ship has suffered damage from collision or from any other cause. Lloyd's Register surveyors test and approve, during its manufacture, the steel intended for use in the ship's structure or in its engines and boilers; survey refrigerating machinery at sea or on land; supervise the testing of chains, anchors, and pressure vessels; and are competent authorities for the assignment of freeboard to all classes of ship in accordance with the provisions of merchant shipping acts or the load-line regulations.

The society publishes an annual multi-volume register book, which contains full details of all merchant ships in the world of more than 100 tons gross; this is kept up-to-date by means of regular supplements. Separate registers are kept of British and American yachts. The society also publishes annual and quarterly statistical summaries of shipping registered or under construction in the world.

Lloyd's Register of Shipping operates in most maritime countries, often in cooperation with classification societies established by other nations. These include the American Bureau of Shipping, originally established in 1867 and resuscitated as a result of the large volume of merchant ships built in the United States during World Wars I and II; the Bureau Veritas, which was founded in Antwerp in 1828 but moved its headquarters to Paris in 1832; the Norske Veritas, established in Norway in 1894; Germanischer Lloyd, founded in Germany in 1867; and Registro Italiano Navale, founded in Italy in 1861. Most of these and other national classification societies work in close conjunction with Lloyd's Register of Shipping.

Tonnage measurement. Classification societies largely agree on the strength requirements of different types of ship; the technical, legal, or commercial enactments of the conventions are almost universally accepted. On the other hand, complete international agreement on methods of interpreting the term tonnage measurement was slow to develop. The two chief reasons for this were, first, the possibility of interpreting the term tonnage itself in several senses and, second, the fact that a ship's tonnage is calculated by one of several methods, according to the standard of measurement required. In speaking of shipping, the term ton may be used not only to name a unit of weight in the usually accepted sense but also to name a unit of volumetric capacity.

Displacement tonnage and deadweight tonnage

As far as weight is concerned, the ton is the long ton of 2,240 pounds avoirdupois (1,016 kilograms, almost identical with the metric ton); this is used to measure the weight of the ship and its contents. According to Archimedes' law, the weight of a floating vessel and its contents is equal to the weight of water that it displaces. This weight is known as the displacement tonnage, and the term is used most commonly in comparing the size of warships. In a cargo-carrying ship it is obvious that the displacement varies according to the amount of cargo, bunkers, and stores that are in the ship; and as it is important to determine the amount of cargo that can be carried, the ship's displacement must be calculated both when it is in light condition and when it is loaded to find the difference, which represents the weight of cargo that can be carried. The lightweight displacement tonnage is equivalent to the weight of water displaced by the ship's hull, machinery, and equipment plus the weight of the crew and their effects, when no cargo or bunkers are carried. When the maximum admissible weight of bunkers and cargo is added, the ship has reached its full displacement tonnage. The difference between the full displacement tonnage and the lightweight displacement tonnage is called the deadweight tonnage, and this corresponds to the maximum weight of cargo and bunkers the ship can safely carry. Deadweight tonnage is the measurement ordinarily used to describe and compare the sizes of dry-cargo ships and tankers.

In many procedures, such as the assessment of harbour dues and canal transit dues, a different system of tonnage measurement, based on the volumetric ton, is required. The volumetric ton is a measure of the capacity of the enclosed space in a ship, one ton equalling 100 cubic feet (about 2.8 cubic metres) of enclosed space. The volume of the ship up to the tonnage deck (which is generally the uppermost continuous deck), excluding certain exempted spaces, such as the double-bottom tanks, the steering-gear compartments, the galley, and other spaces not used for the carriage of cargo, is called the underdeck tonnage and is expressed in terms of tons of 100 cubic feet. The internal volume of between-deck spaces and deck erections used for the carriage of cargo is added to the underdeck tonnage to give what is called the gross tonnage, again in terms of tons of 100 cubic feet. In merchant shipping statistics the gross registered tonnage is usually given. It is also given for passenger ships, whose deadweight tonnage is relatively unimportant as a means of comparing them in size. For the purpose of assessing dues payable for port, canal, pilotage, lighthouse, and other services, the freight-earning capacity of the ship is usually accepted as the criterion of measurement; this is commonly computed by deducting the space devoted exclusively to such items as machinery, bunkers, crew accommodation, and navigating quarters from gross tonnage, in order to calculate the net registered tonnage. It is apparent that the final tonnage measurement of a ship according to the volumetric reckoning depends much on the definition of the spaces exempted from computation.

The British system of tonnage measurement is the one most used by maritime nations, but in certain areas, notably the Suez and Panama canals, there are different systems of measurement for the assessment of tonnage on which dues are payable, and all ships have to be specially measured for the assessment of their dues when passing through these areas.

For the purpose of assessing freight rates on cargo, yet another form of volumetric tonnage is employed, known as the measurement ton. which is equivalent to 40 cubic feet (about 1.1 cubic metre) of capacity. This term has no connection with the tonnage measurements used for registration and for the assessment of dues. It derives from the fact that the charge made for carrying cargo is normally based either on the weight of the cargo or on the amount of space it occupies. Freight rates cannot all be fairly assessed by weight alone; a ton of feathers would occupy a far greater amount of the ship's hold than a ton of coal. Similarly, heavy machinery, although occupying much less space than coal, would prevent the extra space being used for the carriage of more cargo, for such a deadweight cargo would bring a ship down to its load-line limits with much of the cubic capacity of its holds still unfilled. Hence liner freight-rate tariffs are generally expressed in terms of so much per ton weight or measurement, the measurement ton being the equivalent of 40 cubic feet of capacity and the rate paid being the higher of the two.

The measurement ton

WORLD SHIPPING ROUTES AND FLEETS

Trade routes. Over the years a comprehensive pattern of worldwide liner services has been built up for both passengers and freight, linking all continents and countries, supplemented by the random movement of goods from one part of the world to another as occasion and demand has arisen. Despite the directional changes in world trade with the development of new areas, exploitation of new sources of supply, and different demands arising, these major routes have remained largely the same for the last century. An outstanding addition of new routes has been those served by the modern tankers, including those from the Persian Gulf to the United Kingdom and Europe; from the Persian Gulf to Japan; from the Caribbean to the United Kingdom and Europe; from the Caribbean to North Africa and Europe; from the Middle East to Japan; and from the Middle East to Europe and North America. While the worldwide trade routes are operated by liners and tramps, in the 1970s container services were extending further into the major deep-sea trade routes. Apart from the North Atlantic routes, which experienced the greatest expansion of capacity and hence intense competition, container services were operating between Japan and Australia and New Zealand; from the United Kingdom to Australia and New Zealand, the United States, and the Far East; between the United States and Australia; and on many short sea routes, such as between the United Kingdom and Ireland; the United Kingdom and near continental and Scandinavian ports; between Scandinavian and Baltic ports; and in United States coastal waters.

Merchant fleets of the world. By 1939, before the outbreak of World War II, world merchant shipping totalled 69,404,000 tons gross. Despite the enormous war losses, the world fleet reached 80,292,000 tons by 1948 and by 1955 exceeded 100,000,000 tons gross for the first time. In 1971 the world merchant fleet totalled 247,203,000 gross registered tons, over one-third (96,141,000 tons) of which consisted of tankers. Ore and bulk carriers totalled 53,797,000 tons and the fully cellular container tonnage 2,780,000 tons gross.

A significant feature of the development of the world merchant fleet after 1920 was the growth of the number of ships propelled by diesel engines. A simultaneous development was the replacement of coal by oil as fuel for steamships, a movement that reached its peak just after World War II. Motor ships totalled 145,425,000 gross registered tons and steamships 82,065,000 tons, of which only a negligible part was coal burning.

PROBLEMS OF THE SHIPPING INDUSTRY

As shipping entered the 1980s it faced a number of new problems, largely caused by the changing pattern and continual growth of world trade and the technological advances that brought larger, speedier, and otherwise improved vessels. The volume of cargo moving in international trade doubled between 1900 and 1950 and quadrupled between 1950 and 1970, from 500,000,000 tons to 2,000,000,000. During the same period—1900 to 1970—the merchant fleet increased sevenfold, most of it in the last 20 years. If past rates of increase in population, trade, and shipping are maintained, by the year 2000 the world fleet required to carry the seaborne proportion could be six times the level of today, or about 1,200,000,000 tons. Faced with this prospect, shipowners have striven for greater size, efficiency, and diversification. Shipping has become more specialized and more capital intensive. In the bulk trades, the trend has been increasingly away from spot charter of general-purpose ships toward longterm contracts, in which owners undertake to carry large volumes of a particular cargo over a period of years. This has led to owners cooperating in consortia to accumulate the necessary finance, tonnage, and management resources and to building specialized ships to meet the requirements of shippers. Between 1960 and 1970 the typical bulk-carrier size shot up from about 15,000 to 20,000 tons. For oil tankers the growth has been even greater, with the typical supertanker rising from about 50,000 tons in the late 1950s to 250,000 tons in the 1970s, with vessels up to 3,500,000 being constructed and vessels of 500,000 to 1,000,000 tons planned. Specialization in the carriage of liquid cargoes, such as chemicals and liquefied gas, to meet the growing demand has also required more costly and sophisticated ships. In general cargo, the major change has been in the development of containerization, with its certain advantages of speed, reliability, and control. But all these developments create new technical problems for the industry—in handling at sea and in port, in threatened pollution of the oceans and seacoasts, in an imbalance between the conventional liner and tramps and the bulk, unit load, container, and roll-on, roll-off ships. New international regulations are required, including those on pollution. This imbalance was particularly noticeable at the beginning of the 1970s, with an overcapacity of container ships, particularly on the North Atlantic routes, where container capacity exceeded cargo availability by some 50 percent. This led to withdrawal of some of the consortia from the trade. Equally, the ports of the world competing for the container trade were constructing the necessary facilities far in excess of requirements. At the same time the industry faced rising costs both in ship construction and operation. To help to meet these higher operating costs, automatic controls are being applied at every stage of a journey and the randomness of operation is being eliminated at the same time as the ratio of manpower to vessel size is being reduced.

Over-capacity problems

The passenger trade faced a more serious and longer lasting problem. Competition from air, particularly on the longer sea voyages, had drastically reduced demand for passenger accommodations. On the North Atlantic routes, in 1970, scheduled and chartered flights carried 2,202,000 passengers between North America and Europe, while ships carried only 249,000. To meet this challenge, growing with the advent of the jumbo jet, the passenger shipping companies were turning to car ferries and cruises. Their future appears to lie in the leisure and holiday field.

Meanwhile, many of the older problems of the shipping industry remain. Despite the large measure of international agreement and cooperation achieved in the shipping industry, competition among merchant fleets persists. Current problems and developments have driven several major lines to merge nationally or to cooperate through consortia at the international level.

The shipping industry is unique in that it has an economic and strategic as well as a commercial importance and is rarely free from political or strategic interference by governments. For internal political reasons, some states consider shipping services as a state monopoly. In practice, however, this is difficult to achieve since a state's jurisdiction does not extend beyond territorial waters. Nevertheless, various practices are observed from time to time to protect the domestic shipping industry and to discriminate against other flags. Higher port dues may be charged to foreign ships, or national flag ships may be favoured. In bilateral trade agreements it is sometimes stipulated that a fixed proportion of the cargoes must be carried in ships of the national flag. A common method of assisting the domestic shipping industry is to reserve coastal shipping to ships of the national flag, a policy that greatly assisted the expansion of the British mercantile marine until the policy was abandoned with the repeal of the Navigation Acts in 1849, except for the coastal trades, which were not brought into line until 1854. Several other nations, notably the United States, still follow this practice and strictly reserve their coastal trade for their own vessels. Assistance in the form of tax exemptions, preferential credit terms, direct subsidy of shipbuilding, or operating costs is often given to protect national fleets.

Although operating costs are much the same for ships of all flags, the rates of taxation vary, and after World War II heavy taxes, combined with a sharp rise in shipbuilding prices, caused the registration of more and more shipping companies under flags of convenience. Some 40,000,000 gross tons, over one-fifth of world tonnage, were so registered in the early 1970s.

Despite problems, the shipping industry has always proved itself resilient and, particularly in recent years, ready to adopt new technological aids to efficiency. Thus, it can be expected to meet the challenge of competition and changes in economic conditions. Its adaptation may be less through the increase of vessel sizes and the resultant economy of scale than through even greater specialization, rationalization of existing structures, and innovations through new types of vessels and services. (E.A.J.D.)

Air-cushion machines

Air-cushion vehicles, sometimes called ground-effect machines, are characterized by their movement, in which a significant portion of their weight is supported by forces arising from air pressures developed around the craft, as a result of which it hovers in close proximity to the Earth's surface. It is this proximity to the surface that chiefly distinguishes such craft from aircraft, which derive their lift from aerodynamic forces created by movement through the air.

Two main classes of air-cushion vehicles exist: those that generate their own pressure differential irrespective of forward speed; and those, more closely related to true aircraft, that require forward speed before the pressure differential can be generated. The former are classed as aerostatic craft (ACV's); the latter are called aerodynamic ground-effect machines (GEM's).

Aerostatic and aerodynamic machines

This section outlines the development of the air-cushion vehicle since the formation of its basic concept, indicating the wide range of uses to which it has been applied and the methods of construction and operation.

HISTORY

Perhaps the first man to research the air-cushion vehicle concept was Sir John Thornycroft, a British engineer who, in the 1870s, began to build test models to check his theory that drag on a ship's hull could be reduced if the vessel were given a concave bottom in which air could be contained between hull and water. His patent of 1877 emphasized that "provided the air cushion could be carried along under the vehicle" the only power that the cushion would require would be that necessary to replace lost air. Neither Thornycroft nor other inventors in following decades succeeded in solving the cushion-containment problem. In the meantime aviation developed, and pilots early discovered that when they were flying very close to land or water surface their aircraft developed greater lift than in free air. It was soon determined that the greater lift was available because wing and ground together created a "funnel" effect, increasing the air pressure. The amount of additional pressure proved dependent on the design of the wing and its height above ground. The effect was strongest when the height was between one-half and one-third of the average front-to-rear breadth of the wing (chord).

Practical use was made of the ground effect in 1929 by the German Dornier Do X flying boat, which achieved a considerable gain in performance during an Atlantic crossing when it flew close to the sea surface. World War II maritime reconnaissance aircraft also made use of the phenomenon to extend their endurance.

In the 1960s U.S. aerodynamicists developed an experimental craft, making use of a wing in connection with ground effect. Several other proposals of this type were put forward, and a further variation combined the airfoil characteristics of a ground-effect machine with an air-cushion lift system that allowed the craft to develop its own hovering power while stationary, then build up forward speed, gradually transferring the lift component to its airfoil. Though none of these craft got beyond the experimental stage, they were important portents of the future because they suggested means of using the hovering advantage of the air-cushion vehicle and overcoming its theoretical speed limitation of around 200 miles per hour (320 kilometres per hour), above which it was difficult to hold the air cushion in place. These vehicles are known as ram-wing craft.

In the early 1950s, engineers in the United Kingdom, United States, and Switzerland were seeking solutions to Sir John Thornycroft's 80-year-old problem. Christopher Cockerell of the U.K. is now acknowledged to have been the father of the Hovercraft, as the air-cushion vehicle is popularly known. During World War II he had been closely connected with the development of radar and other radio aids and had retired into peacetime life as a boatbuilder. Soon he began to concern himself with Thornycroft's problem of reducing the hydrodynamic drag on the hull of a boat with some kind of air lubrication.

Cockerell (later knighted) bypassed Thornycroft's plenum chamber (in effect, an empty box with an open bottom) principle (see Figure 41), in which air is pumped directly

By courtesy of T.E. Sweeney

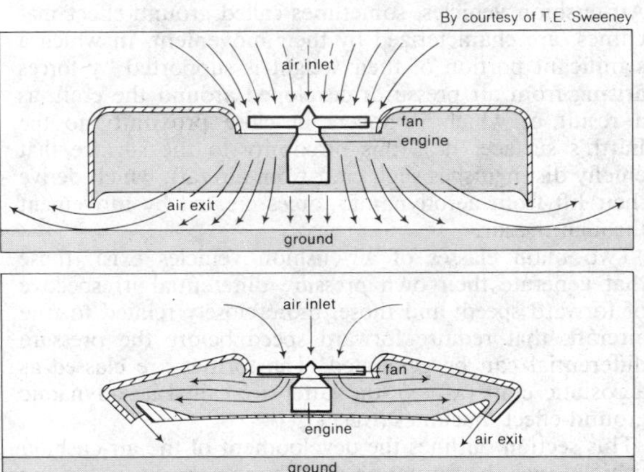

Figure 41: (Top) Plenum chamber. (Bottom) Peripheral jet.

into a cavity beneath the vessel, because of the difficulty in containing the cushion. He theorized that if air were instead pumped under the vessel through a narrow slot running entirely around the circumference, the air would flow toward the centre of the vessel, forming an external curtain that would effectively contain the cushion. This system is known as a peripheral jet. Once air has built up below the craft to a pressure equalling the craft weight, incoming air has nowhere to go but outward and experiences a sharp change of velocity on striking the surface. The momentum of the peripheral jet air keeps the cushion pressure and the ground clearance higher than it would be if air were pumped directly into a plenum chamber.

Cockerell's original Hovercraft design

To test his theory, Cockerell set up an apparatus consisting of a blower that fed air into an inverted coffee tin through a hole in the base. The tin was suspended over the weighing pan of a pair of kitchen scales, and air blown into the tin forced the pan down against the mass of a number of weights. In this way the forces involved were roughly measured. By securing a second tin within the first and directing air down through the space between, Cockerell was able to demonstrate that more than three times the number of weights could be raised by this means, compared with the plenum chamber effect of the single can.

Cockerell's first patent was filed on December 12, 1955, and in the following year he formed a company known as Hovercraft Ltd. His early memoranda and reports show a prescient grasp of the problems involved in translating the theory into practice. Such problems still concern designers of Hovercraft more than a decade later, and some of Cockerell's ideas have yet to be fully explored. He forecast, for example, that some kind of secondary suspension would be required in addition to the air cushion itself. Another of his ideas still to be developed deals with the recirculation of air in the peripheral jet so that part of it is used over and over, improving efficiency and reducing the power required.

Realizing that his discovery would not only make boats go faster but would allow the development of amphibious craft, Cockerell approached the Ministry of Supply, the British Government's defense-equipment procurement authority. The air-cushion vehicle was classified "secret" in November 1956, and a development contract was placed with a British aircraft and seaplane manufacturer. In 1959 the world's first practical ACV was launched. It was called the SR.N1.

Originally the SR.N1 had a total weight of four tons and could carry three men at a maximum speed of 25 knots (one knot = 1.15 miles or 1.85 kilometres per hour) over very calm water. Instead of having a completely solid structure to contain the cushion and peripheral jet, it incorporated a six-inch- (15 centimetre-) deep "skirt" of rubberized fabric. This development provided a means whereby the air cushion could easily be contained despite unevenness of the ground or water. It was soon found that the skirt made it possible to revert once again to the plenum chamber as a cushion producer. Use of the skirt brought the problem of making skirts durable enough to withstand the friction wear produced at high speeds through water. It was necessary to develop the design and manufacturing skills that would allow skirts to be made in the optimum shape for aerodynamic efficiency.

Skirts of rubber and plastic mixtures, four feet (1.2 metres) deep, had been developed by early 1963, and the performance of the SR.N1 had been increased by using them (and incorporating gas-turbine power) to a payload of seven tons and a maximum speed of 50 knots.

The first crossing of the English Channel by the SR.N1 was in 1959, symbolically on the 50th anniversary of Louis Blériot's first flight across the same water. Manufacturers and operators in many parts of the world became interested. Manufacture began in the United States, Japan, Sweden, and France; and in Britain, additional British companies were building craft in the early 1960s.

The sidewall craft

In 1963 the first major variation of the basic air-cushion vehicle theme was produced in the form of sidewall craft. This was a nonamphibious vessel that had a solid hull down each side, with a plenum chamber beneath the hull sealed by flexible skirts at the bow and stern. In the displacement mode, the central hull section floated in the water with the sidewalls well submerged, but when air was pumped into the plenum chamber, the hull was raised above the water and the sidewalls themselves were submerged for only some 12 inches (30 centimetres), considerably reducing the hydrodynamic drag.

The sidewall ACV has several advantages over the amphibious craft, although its use is confined to water: first, water propellers can be used, allowing a much greater freedom of control, especially at low speeds; second, the sidewalls themselves give the craft better stability and reduce the problems that are inherent in all-round flexible skirts. In the early 1970s sidewalls were once again coming into favour, especially among American manufacturers who saw a market for a high-speed marine freight carrier that would not need an amphibious capability.

The years 1962–64 were a peak period for worldwide interest in Hovercraft, but by the early 1970s only the British had produced what could truly be called a range of craft, and this against considerable odds. There were signs, however, that U.S., Soviet, and French manufacturers were seriously contemplating re-entry into the field, and that Australia and Japan also were becoming ACV-minded.

The stagnation of the intervening seven years can be explained by the failure of air-cushion vehicles to live up to what many people thought was their original promise. Cockerell and others had foreseen many of the difficulties, but some second-generation designers, builders, and, particularly, operators thought that the simple Hovercraft would be the answer to a variety of problems that at that stage of development were considerably beyond the scope of the craft available.

In the first place, amphibious craft generally needed to be air propelled. Directional control was imprecise, precluding their use on highways. As already mentioned, the design of and materials used in flexible skirts had to be developed from the first, and not until 1965 was an efficient and economic flexible-skirt arrangement evolved, and even then the materials were still being developed.

Problems of engine corrosion

Another major problem arose when aircraft gas-turbine engines were used in a marine environment. Although such engines, suitably modified, had been installed in ships with some success, their transition into Hovercraft brought out their extreme vulnerability to saltwater corrosion. By its very nature the air-cushion vehicle generates a great deal of spray when it is hovering over water, and the spray is drawn into the intakes of gas turbines in amounts not envisaged by the engine designer. Even after considerable filtering, the moisture and salt content is high enough to corrode large modern gas-turbine engines to such an extent that they need a daily wash with pure water and even then have a considerably reduced life span between overhauls.

The costs of engine overhauls and skirt maintenance and repairs have probably been the main factors retarding the advancement of air-cushion vehicles. Skirt development proceeded extremely rapidly in the first decade after SR.N1. Jet-engine corrosion may be solved by new materials or possibly by intake design to limit spray ingestion. In the meantime, some manufacturers are bypassing the gas-turbine difficulty by using high-speed marine diesel engines in multiple units. These are cheaper, more economical to run, and relatively free from corrosion problems but for a given power output are considerably heavier than their gas-turbine counterparts.

The history of the air-cushion vehicle principle also includes the use of air-cushion support in other applications, both for transportation and for support as such. These include air-cushion transporters, trains, and even beds.

DESIGN, CONSTRUCTION, AND OPERATION

Basic elements of the ACV

The basic elements of an air-cushion vehicle are a hull, beneath which a skirt system is attached and on which accommodation for passengers, crew, and freight is built; a propulsion system; and a lift system that feeds air into the plenum chamber below the craft in order to provide a cushion. The propulsion and lift systems can be driven by the same power plant or by separate units. If a common power plant is used, the system is known as an integrated lift-propulsion system. Some early craft had only one airflow generating system, which was used for both lift and propulsion, but optimum efficiency for both requirements was difficult to achieve simultaneously and separate systems are generally used.

The power-to-weight ratio is as critical at the design stage of an ACV as it is in an aircraft. In the ACV it not only determines the payload and performance of the craft but also the ground clearance between the surface and the skirt. The greater the ground clearance, the more efficiently the propulsion forces available can be used. Theoretical design operating weights are essential for comparison and evaluation purposes, but in practice it has been found that air-cushion vehicles can be overloaded by as much as 100 percent of the design payload and still operate.

To obtain the best power-to-weight-to-strength relationships, structural fabrication of air-cushion vehicles has been based more on aviation than on marine practices. Hull structures are of marine aluminum skin, welded or rivetted onto aluminum webs or frames. The enclosed spaces are usually sealed so that the airtight compartments thus formed provide natural buoyancy. More recent craft have aluminum honeycomb panelling separated by frames to provide the basic buoyancy raft, and considerable areas of glass-fibre structure have also been incorporated.

Early craft had a hole located near the centre of the buoyancy raft through which air was fed to the plenum chamber beneath, but the development of skirt and other techniques led to the ducting of fan air to the edge of the raft, where it was fed downward into the plenum chamber in the manner of a peripheral jet.

Skirt arrangements. Skirts themselves have developed from a simple curtain designed to enclose the cushion into complicated geometrical shapes that contain the cushion, duct the air, and, in some cases, provide a degree of secondary suspension. The simple curtain was quickly replaced by what is now known as a bag skirt. In the shape of a semicircle, this is fastened around the perimeter of the craft; the lower edge is taken inward and upward and is fastened inboard, below the hull. The inflated skirt forms a semicircular cross section. If air is fed through ducts in the top hull so that it inflates the skirt and then is allowed to escape through holes on the inside edge of the bag into the plenum area, the skirt acts as natural ducting, and by varying the size of the holes it is possible to vary the pressure ratio of bag inflation to plenum pressure.

The problem with bag skirts is that the lowest part of the bag quickly wears away and the bag itself tears, allowing air to escape and releasing the cushion pressure. In 1965 it was decided to lengthen the bag skirt by suspending a curtain-type skirt from it. But instead of a straightforward curtain arrangement, the skirt was split into small segments, each of which acted independently from the others. This segmented, or finger-type, addition to the basic bag skirt became the version most commonly used because worn segments could be replaced quickly and economically and because the independent action of each finger allowed the whole skirt to conform much more closely to the operating surface beneath, reducing drag and air-cushion losses.

Materials used in the skirts have varied from the original rubberized fabric, through pure rubber and nylon, to a lamination of nylon and a proprietary plastic known as neoprene. Bondings between the different layers have to be especially strong; otherwise the fabric delaminates under the severe conditions of wear and loses its tear resistance.

Power plants. Power plants used for air-cushion vehicles are generally gas-turbine engines; the output shaft is driven by a turbine that is not mechanically connected to the main compressor-turbine assembly. In this way the engine can be independent of the fan or propeller that it drives, and the free turbine will not begin to rotate until gas from the engine is allowed to pass over its vanes. This allows the craft to remain stationary and on the ground until the driver decides to move, even though the engines are delivering power. The fans used to provide air pressure for lift are usually of the centrifugal type, in which air is fed in through the centre and driven out at considerably higher pressure around the circumference. Propellers are generally similar to those used for aircraft, although because the air-cushion vehicles travel in the 0–60 knot speed range and can move in reverse, a standard aircraft propeller designed to operate best at higher speeds is inefficient. Hovercraft propellers can be fixed or mounted on swivelling pylons, which allow the craft to be manoeuvred quite accurately, independently of the rudders on which fixed propellers rely. Rudder effectiveness depends to some extent on the forward speed of the craft, and at very low speeds rudders are not efficient as a means of turning.

Propulsion

Other propulsion methods that have been tried in the past include ducted fans, which are quieter than normal propellers but tend to be large and cumbersome. Sidewall craft can be propelled by water screws or by water jets.

ACV operation. Operations on which air-cushion vehicles have been used have been largely confined to commercial passenger-carrying ferry services across stretches of water, varying between three and 25 miles (five to 40 kilometres) wide, and to certain military operations. Although scheduled services have been run for experimental periods in the United States, Canada, Sweden, and Italy, it is only in Britain and France that such services have survived longer than a season. By the early 1970s, a 170-ton car-carrying craft was so well established on routes across the English Channel that a considerable amount of traffic was being taken from sea ferries, and air services were virtually closed down.

Nonpassenger civil applications have also been found. Craft have been successfully used for seismic survey parties, either over shallow-water areas or in the desert, and in search-and-rescue operations from international airfields at Vancouver, British Columbia, at Auckland, New Zealand, and at San Francisco.

Military uses

Military uses have been more diverse. The main British use has been as a troop carrier during amphibious assaults and as a logistics follow-up craft during the post-assault period. The United States Army used the Hovercraft successfully in actual operations in Vietnam, both as a patrol craft and as a means of covering the vast area of marsh and paddy field that surrounds the Mekong Delta. Future military uses include mine-countermeasure work, antisubmarine work, aircraft carrying, and missile launching.

The mainstream of Hovercraft development as such has remained in Britain. Although United States firms built experimental craft in the mid-1960s, American interest declined as the pressure of the Vietnam War tended to encourage technologists to improve their established disciplines rather than develop new ones. Other countries also dropped out when the technical difficulties of skirts and the lift-propulsion system became too great for the financial or technical resources available.

The three British companies that pioneered ACV manufacturing merged their ACV interests in the 1960s into one company known as the British Hovercraft Corporation.

Cockerell's patent and other patents were taken up by a subsidiary of the National Research Development Corporation, a peculiarly British body set up to encourage the funding and backing of inventions. The subsidiary was known as Hovercraft Development Ltd., and, because of the patents that it held, could control the manufacture of skirted air-cushion vehicles in many countries of the world.

The line along which ACV's developed was:

SR.N1 (1959) 3½ to 7 tons, single engine, ducted fan propulsion, speeds between 25 and 50 knots.

SR.N2 (1962) 19 tons, four engines driving two pylon-mounted air propellers; speed about 73 knots.

SR.N3 (1963) 37½ tons, four engines driving two pylon-mounted air propellers; speed about 75 knots.

SR.N5 (1964) 3½ tons, one engine driving a fixed, variable-pitch propeller; speed about 50 knots. Capacity, 18 passengers.

SR.N6 (1965) 4½ tons, one engine driving a fixed, variable-pitch propeller; speed about 60 knots. Capacity, 38 passengers.

SR.N4 (1968) 177 tons, four engines driving four pylon-mounted air propellers; speed 65 knots. Capacity, 30 cars and 254 passengers.

BH.7 (1969) 48 tons, one engine driving a pylon-mounted airpropeller: speed about 65 knots. Capacity, 72 passengers and six cars (although the first three craft delivered were purely military versions).

Those somewhat bare statistics suggest the burst of creative energy in the Hovercraft field in the early 1960s and the subsequent slowing down and rationalization of craft into practical machines. In the period between 1960 and 1964, some six other companies in the world also were building their own prototypes or large-scale models, but because of technology problems many of these were never followed up by production models.

The exceptions were in the Soviet Union and France. Little is known about Soviet ACV development, except that after some five years of trials and experimentation large passenger-carrying craft were being operated on the Volga River in 1969 and that military craft were being tested in the Black Sea in 1970.

A French company, formed in 1965, built two amphibious craft that, carrying up to 90 passengers, operated a commercial service based at Nice in 1969. The French designs are basically the same as any other amphibious craft with the major exception of the skirts, which instead of forming one large plenum chamber are grouped together in a series of "mini-skirts" side-by-side along the length of the craft. Compartmenting the cushion in this way is said to improve stability and directional control. In the early 1970s it was announced that a larger craft, based on similar principles and carrying 32 cars and 260 passengers, would be put into production.

Non-amphibious Hovercraft

The development of nonamphibious Hovercraft along the sidewall principle began in 1962. For various reasons the manufacturer halted production, but the idea of a fast, essentially marine-oriented craft continued to appeal to designers, and a company known as Hovermarine was formed in 1965 to build a smaller sidewall craft, some 12 of which were sold. This is the HM.2, which carries about 65 passengers and is designed for short and medium ferry routes. Mechanical and skirt-design problems caused difficulties that led to liquidation of the parent British company, but in 1970 an American company took over the HM.2 and it appeared that its future would be assured. The basic advantage of sidewall craft is that since they are purely marine, it is possible to equip them with marine propellers and operate them in the same way as high-speed boats. Nevertheless, because a great part of their weight when under way is supported by an air-cushion, they can be classified as air-cushion machines.

It is along these lines (sidewall craft propelled by marine methods) that two United States manufacturers have designed much larger craft under government contracts. The first versions are 100-ton test craft, which will be used to evaluate the potential of multithousand-ton surface effect ships. The two models are somewhat similar in appearance; both are powered by six gas turbines. One craft uses propellers, the other water-jet propulsion. Another United States military application, an amphibious assault landing craft for the navy, offers potential uses in commercial operations.

OTHER APPLICATIONS

Air-cushion trains. Once air-cushion suspension was proved practicable in Hovercraft, the system was quickly applied to other forms of transport, and it soon became clear that a tracked vehicle, similar to a train or monorail, would benefit considerably from the lack of friction inherent in an air-cushion system. A French company was the first in the world to produce a practical device, and a later version of its machine was due to be in service as a high-speed link between Orléans and Paris by the mid-1970s. The system uses air-cushion pads above and at the side of a single concrete track to support the "aerotrain," while propulsion is via a large ducted fan mounted at the rear.

In Britain tracked air-cushion vehicle development is also under way, with a construction of a "Hovertrain," propelled by a relatively silent linear induction motor that has no moving parts and picks up current as it moves along the track.

Research is also proceeding in other countries. Air-cushion trains have speed potentials of up to 300 miles (480 kilometres) per hour; track costs are relatively low because of the simple concrete structure involved, which can be elevated on pylons, laid on the surface, or sunk in tunnels. Engineers in Britain, the United States, France, and Germany see this kind of high-speed surface transport as a means of connecting large urban centres with each other and with international airports.

Industrial applications. The other major area in which air-cushion technology has proved itself useful is in moving loads over surfaces that would be impossible for wheeled or tracked vehicles. One of the first of these applications was an air-cushion amphibious military vehicle. Another was an air-cushion truck built in France. Air-cushion load lifters for specialized applications were already in regular use in the early 1970s. One of the first was a British heavy-load carrier, designed specifically for the transport of large electrical transformers over bridges that were not stressed for the weights involved when normal wheeled transport was used. The transformers, weighing up to 300 tons, must be transported by road from the factory to the often remote power-station site. The costs of strengthening bridges sufficiently to take the load are far higher than those of fitting a special skirt and air-blower system to a conventional truck.

ACV load carriers

Similar systems on a smaller scale have been developed for transport of many types of unusual loads over awkward ground. They find particular application in the Arctic regions, where roads are often lacking and where oil-drill rigs are being constructed or where surveying is being carried out. Air-cushion vehicles have shown a large economic advantage over helicopters.

On an even smaller scale air-cushion pallets are used in many industries in the United States and Britain to carry heavy loads across factory floors or along production lines. Again the main benefit is the reducing of strain on floors and the ease of propulsion with reduced friction.

One unique form of air suspension may be employed in hospitals. The Hover-bed is a device on which a patient is supported with the minimum of body contact and surface pressure. The bed is being tested by the British Medical Research Council and is expected to be of particular use in cases in which the patient is burned over a large area of the body. Air support in such cases not only relieves pressure and pain but provides a film of sterile air that actually helps to heal the wound.

Sporting Hovercraft. Still another application promises to be that of recreation. In the mid-1960s enthusiasts in many parts of the world began to build their own Hovercraft, powered by automotive engines and using home-made propellers, fans, and skirts.

By the 1970s, Hover clubs existed in more than seven countries. The movement is probably most active in Britain, followed by the United States and Australia. Of the several hundred amateur-built craft, a few were capable of operating successfully over both land and water with more than one person aboard. Although power plants and other equipment are readily adaptable, the problem of providing sufficient lift was considerable. A craft capable of lifting 200 pounds (90 kilograms) needs a cushion area of 8 × 4 feet (1.3 × 2.4 metres). When weights of 1,000 pounds are involved, the area must be much greater. Another inhibiting factor in the sport's growth is the restrictions in most countries on operating air-cushion craft in public areas.

The future. Air-cushion vehicles have not yet fulfilled their original promise. Conventional skirted craft have not yet been shown to be completely economical in commercial use, although in certain military applications they are almost ideal. The ram-wing craft described earlier shows promise for over-water routes.

One area of research in which manufacturers were concentrating in the 1970s is that of secondary suspension systems to iron out skirt undulations and possibly reduce spray ingestion. (Jo.Be.)

Air transportation

It is a curious fact, but true, that man's age-long observation of birds in flight impeded, rather than accelerated, the development of man flight. All human attempts to fly on flapping wings led only to frustration or disaster, for what comes naturally to birds is almost certainly impossible for man to duplicate with his clumsy mechanisms. The only valid bird flight/man flight analogue appears to be in gliding and soaring. Wing flappers (ornithopters) have contributed little to man-flight history, and, although some research is still in progress, they seem likely to be of little significance.

Orni-thopters

In this section, the generic term man flight is used to describe any human navigation above the surface of the earth in any form of vehicle—balloon, airship, glider, powered aircraft, rocket, etc. "Aviation" refers generally to flight in heavier-than-air craft. "Aeronautics" is the science of aviation; "aerostatics" is the science of lighter-than-air flight; and "astronautics" the science of space flight. A fuller treatment of certain specialized areas of this subject will be found in WAR, THE TECHNOLOGY OF.

From a historian's point of view, exploring the development of man flight is a rewarding exercise. A substantial percentage of the significant events to be dealt with have occurred within the memory of persons still living in the 1980s, and many of the early experimenters were themselves articulate. Their notebooks and other records have been preserved, and a considerable amount of the actual hardware with which they worked still exists. Of greater importance, the invention and development of flight vehicles coincided historically with the development of photographic processes. Excellent visual records of many of the men, machines, and events that made flight history are available.

The subject has always attracted widespread coverage by the press, sometimes with dubious accuracy. Fortunately, it also engaged the serious attention of scholars concerned with separating fact from fancy. James Means of Boston, an early collector and compiler of aeronautical literature, made a notable contribution in this area with the publication of his *Aeronautical Annuals*—in 1895, '96, and '97. More recently, Charles Dollfus and Henri Bouché in France, J.E. Hodgson and Charles Gibbs-Smith in England, and Paul Garber of the Smithsonian Institution in the U.S. have established a firm and factual base for future air historians to build on. Other important contributors include V.M. Sokolsky in the Soviet Union, Ernst Klee in Germany, and Hidemasa Kimura in Japan. Their published works have provided prime sources of information for this condensed survey of flight history.

FLIGHTS OF FANCY

Had the early philosophers not been obsessed with the wing-flapping flight of birds, something resembling the gliders of the late 19th century might have evolved earlier. All the necessary materials—woods, fabrics, and cordage—were readily at hand, and skilled craftsmen were plentiful. What was lacking was the concept of air as a fluid and of its behaviour as it flows around three-dimensional bodies.

Practically all religions clothed their celestial beings in birdlike forms. Egyptian, Minoan, and Syrian deities were equipped with magnificent wings. The Greek and Roman gods and goddesses seemed to fly without visible means of support (except for Mercury with his winged heels), but the seraphim and cherubim of the Hebrews and the heavenly hosts of later persuasions were all provided with wings.

Flight in myth and legend

As time went on, earthly kings often assumed the role and perquisites of deities. Accordingly, magicians and court historians were called upon to create, if not the fact, at least the legend that their masters had been airborne. Thus, during the Han dynasty in China (206 BC to AD 220), the emperor was reputed to have travelled far in his flying chariot, while the throne of the Persian king Key-kāvūs was supposed to have been airborne by four eagles.

In Europe serious speculation about man flight occupied such thinkers as Roger Bacon (*c.* 1214–94) and Leonardo da Vinci (1452–1519). John Wilkins (1614–72), lord bishop of Chester and one of the founders of the Royal Society, summarized four possible ways in which man might fly: (1) with the spirits of angels, (2) with the help of fowls, (3) with wings fastened to his body, and (4) in a flying chariot. He questioned the practicability of the first three but forecast the evolution of the fixed-wing airplane thus:

> If fowl can so easily move itself up and down in the air without so much as stirring the wings . . . it is not improbable that when all due proportions of [a suitable apparatus] are found out, and when men by long practice have arrived to any skill and experience, they will . . . come very near unto the imitation of Nature.

During the next 100 years, science-fiction writers popularized the idea of flight—including space flight. Francis Godwin (1562–1633), Samuel Brunt (*c.* 1727), Cyrano de Bergerac (1619–55), and others described flights to the moon and elsewhere. Restif de la Bretonne (1734–1806) pictured explorers cruising over wilderness areas of Australia on a combination of batwings and umbrella-like devices.

The invention of the balloon in the 18th century brought the imaginative writers back to earth. Once a means had been found for man to leave the ground, fancy became somewhat related to fact; and for a time, fantastic adventures by balloon and airship were popular subjects.

Toward the end of the 19th century, the greatest of aviation fiction writers, Jules Verne (1828–1905), emerged in France. He himself was not an inventor and made only one balloon ascension in his life (with Godard at Amiens in 1873), but in imagination he developed an extraordinarily prophetic feeling for the future of the inventions of his day. He wrote of exploratory voyages around the world by airship and by helicopter and forecast a trip to the moon from a launching site in Florida. He even described in detail the weightlessness that space travellers were to experience in flight.

LIGHTER-THAN-AIR—EARLY SPECULATIONS

It took many years for man to realize that the air around him was a thing, not impalpable nothingness extending to the outer limits of the sky. The invention of the mercury barometer in 1643 provided the first proof that air was, in fact, a gas that not only had weight but that also responded (as do all gases) to changes in temperature and pressure. Once that was recognized, the way was opened for speculation as to why smoke rose through air. Eventually, as advancing scientific sophistication permitted the isolation of lighter-than-air gases, it was logical to think of a bubble of such gas floating like a cork in a sea of denser air. The first hint of the application of this concept occurs in the notes of the medieval philosopher Roger Bacon, after which, for many years, nothing further was recorded on the subject.

About 1670 a Jesuit monk, Francesco Lana, hit upon the same idea, but in reverse. He concluded that no air should be lighter than some air and, therefore, that a bubble of vacuum should rise through, and at some point of equilibrium, float about in the denser atmospheric air. He published a design for a man-carrying airship supported by four such vacuum balloons. The theory was good, but its realization was difficult. The thin copper spheres he proposed to evacuate would have collapsed under the external air pressure long before any measurable lifting force was developed. Impractical as it was, the concept was a notable philosophical achievement for the time. Lana abandoned any effort to develop it, however, on the ground that any attempt to fly would be regarded by the Creator as impious.

Later (*c.* 1755), after the structure of the Earth's atmosphere was better understood, another priest, Galien, in France, reasoned that a bagful of low-density air collected from the higher altitudes should float about at lower levels and could support a considerable load. In 1766 the isolation of hydrogen by the British chemist Henry Cavendish had a profound effect on lighter-than-air activity. Although the special properties of hydrogen had been known to scientists since 1766, its application to aeronautics (or, more properly, to aerostatics) did not occur to anyone for well over a decade. The honour of the first lighter-than-air demonstration and subsequently the first man flight went to a much more common gas—hot air.

BALLOONS AND BALLOONISTS (1783–1900)

The work of the Montgolfiers and J.-A.-C. Charles. The most important pioneers in balloon development were Joseph and Étienne Montgolfier, sons of a paper manufacturer of Annonay, in southeastern France. Watching smoke rise in the chimney, they had concluded that it possessed some mysterious property, which they called "levity." They made up a small silk bag, which they held over a fire. It filled with smoke and, when released, rose to the ceiling. After several other private experiments, they issued invitations to all the citizens of Annonay (including members of the Departmental Council, who happened to be meeting at the time) to assemble in the town square on June 5, 1783, to witness an ascension of their "Globe Aérostatique." This was a spherical bag about 35 feet (10.7 metres) in diameter (about 23,000 cubic feet, or 650 cubic metres), made up of light fabric backed by paper. Early prints show it as fastened together by rows of buttons and buttonholes. Held over a smoky fire fuelled by chopped wool and straw (it was assumed that "levity" was a special property of smoke), it rapidly inflated to its full spherical form and, to the great astonishment of the audience, rose rapidly (allegedly over a mile in the air) and drifted more than a mile and a half (2.4 kilometres) from its starting point before touching down.

The Montgolfiers' "Globe Aérostatique"

The excitement was great, and reports of the event spread rapidly throughout France. The Academy of Sciences asked for full information, and Étienne journeyed to Paris to report to that distinguished body.

Use of hydrogen. Even before Étienne arrived in Paris, the physicist J.-A.-C. Charles, with the assistance of two Robert brothers, Anne-Jean and Nicolas-Louis, sought to duplicate the Montgolfier performance. Not knowing then of the simple means used to inflate the balloon at Annonay, they adopted the newly isolated gas, hydrogen. (For some years thereafter, any hydrogen balloon in France was called a "Charlière.") They fabricated a balloon of varnished silk, some 15 feet (4.6 metres) in diameter, and produced hydrogen to fill it on a scale never before attempted. Released from the Champ de Mars, Paris, before an enthusiastic crowd, on the afternoon of August 27, 1783, it rose through a heavy rainstorm and descended some 15 miles (24 kilometres) away near the small village of Gonesse. The local peasants, alarmed by the apparition descending from the clouds, attacked the "monster" with scythes and pitchforks and tore it to pieces.

On September 12 Joseph Montgolfier appeared by invitation before the Academy (Benjamin Franklin was in the audience) to describe the work at Annonay. Montgolfier was invited to repeat his experiment before Louis XVI and his court at Versailles. A large aerostat was built but was destroyed in a storm four days before the scheduled event. A new one was hastily put together, and at about 1:00 PM on September 19, 1783, it was released from the Great Court at Versailles carrying a sheep, a rooster, and a duck as passengers. The objective was to determine whether or not high-altitude travel had any deleterious effects on living creatures. They survived the ordeal, and the stage was set for man's first venture into the air.

A new and enlarged aerostat—some 70 feet (21 metres) in height—was prepared. It differed from its predeces-

By courtesy of (right) the National Air and Space Museum, Smithsonian Institution, Washington, D.C.; photograph, (left) Brown Brothers

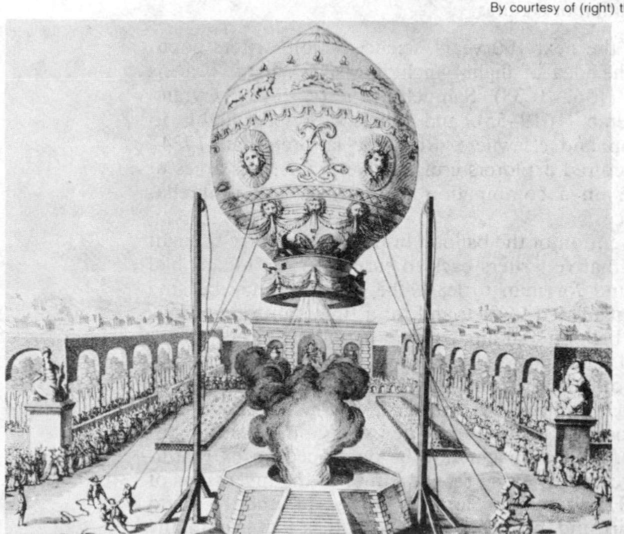

Figure 42: *Early lighter-than-air craft.*
(Left) Montgolfier balloon carrying Pilâtre and d'Arlandes on the first manned free balloon flight, November 21, 1783. (Right) Santos-Dumont airship, about 1900.

sors in having a circular gallery slung beneath it for the accommodation of the aeronauts, with arrangements for maintaining a smoky fire of straw and wool during flight. At first it was proposed that a pair of condemned criminals be used for the experiment. One Jean-François Pilâtre de Rozier, who had volunteered for the flight, however, protested that such were not worthy of the honour of being first to take to the air. In this he was joined by François Laurent, marquis d'Arlandes, who wished to share the adventure.

Louis XVI finally gave his consent, and after a number of tethered test flights (the longest of which lasted nine minutes at an altitude of 320 feet [98 metres]), Pilâtre and d'Arlandes took off in free flight from the Jardin de la Muette in the Bois de Boulogne. The date was November 21, 1783. Some 23 minutes later, after reaching an altitude of over 3,000 feet (900 metres) and an estimated distance of something short of ten miles (16 kilometres), they landed safely near Gentilly, to complete man's first aerial voyage (see Figure 42, left).

Man's first flight

Shortly thereafter (December 1, 1783), J.-A.-C. Charles, accompanied by Nicolas-Louis Robert, took off from the Tuileries Gardens in a large "Charlière." About two hours and 27 miles (43 kilometres) later, the balloon descended gently near the small town of Nesle, northeast of Paris. Robert climbed out of the car. The lightened balloon with Charles aboard promptly rose and continued the flight to land finally some miles away near Tour-de-Laye.

A comparison of notes by the aeronauts at once established the supremacy of the hydrogen balloon. Whereas Pilâtre de Rozier and d'Arlandes had remained airborne only by continuous labour to keep their smoky fire alive, Charles and Robert had drifted comfortably over the landscape without effort. The pattern for future development was thus set. The explosive nature of hydrogen gas was only learned later, over subsequent decades and at a cost of a number of lives. It was not until the loss of the German airship "Hindenburg" at Lakehurst, New Jersey, in 1937, that hydrogen was abandoned as a lifting gas.

Broadening interest. Meanwhile, the Paris flights stirred a worldwide interest in ballooning that carried into the 20th century. In the first 50 years following 1783, over 800 ascensions were made in England alone, and over 470 aeronauts (persons known to have made one or more flights) were recorded. Forty-nine of these were women.

Many names crowd the early records. Notable among them was Jean-Pierre Blanchard, who between 1784 and 1809 made flights in most European capitals. He crossed the English Channel by air on January 7, 1785, accompanied by a Boston physician, John Jeffries. He made the first balloon flight in America at Philadelphia on January 9, 1793, in the presence of George Washington and indoctrinated John Wise, the first American balloonist. Blanchard performed the earliest experiments in parachuting, using animals as subjects. He died in Paris in March 1809 after a fall from a balloon.

Jean-Pierre Blanchard

Among other experimenters of the period were the Sadlers, father and son, of Ireland; Lunardi and Zambeccari of Italy; Gay-Lussac and Biot in France; and Green and Coxwell in England. The latter four are credited with making the first scientific observations of meteorological phenomena and of human behaviour in the upper atmosphere.

Félix Nadar of France must be mentioned on two counts: (1) he made the first aerial photographs from a captive balloon in 1858 and many successful aerial photographs (1863) from a huge balloon, "Le Géant," fitted with a complete photographic laboratory; and (2) he was instrumental in organizing the *Ballon Poste,* which carried mail and passengers out of Paris during the siege in 1870.

Military balloons. The potential of the balloon in military situations had long been recognized. Francesco Lana, who had proposed the use of vacuum globes (1670) as noted, had foreseen the advantages of balloons in war but concluded that "God would not suffer such an invention to take effect, by reason of the disturbance it would cause to the civil government of men." In spite of such forebodings, the first balloon corps in history was formed in France in 1793. Captive observation balloons were used at the siege of Mainz in 1794, and free balloons took part in the Battle of Fleurus in June 1794.

During the American Civil War, observation balloons were in use by both sides. T.S. Lowe, a Connecticut Yankee and a pupil of John Wise, provided four balloons and their portable gas generators to the Union Army's Aeronautics Corps. These were used during the campaigns of 1862–63 for observation, and the westward movement of Lee's army from its Rappahannock camp to start the Gettysburg campaign was first detected by balloon observation. At one time, direct telegraphic communication was established between a balloon and the White House. The Confederacy made only two known attempts to launch observation balloons—one of the hot air variety and one filled with illuminating gas at Richmond—but neither was particularly successful.

Balloons in the Civil War

Ill-fated North Pole attempt. The last great ballooning adventure of the 19th century began when August Andrée and two companions, Strindberg and Fraenkel, set out July 11, 1897, from the island of Spitsbergen, in a free balloon, to attempt to drift across the North Pole. They vanished into the Arctic wastes. Some 33 years later (1930), a Norwegian exploring party discovered their frozen bodies, together with Andrée's journal and even photographic plates, which were developed and printed. The balloon had drifted eastward, off course, and gone down; Andrée and his crew had been able to survive the crash but had perished in their attempt to walk back to civilization.

AIRSHIPS PRIOR TO 1900

From earliest ballooning days, man sought to free himself from his dependence upon the uncertain winds. Truly to navigate the skies, propulsion was needed. Sails, oars, and paddle wheels for balloons were tried repeatedly. All failed. Not until the principle of the Archimedean screw was revived and applied to propulsion was any degree of success attainable.

The transformation of the spherical free balloon into a navigable airship required two things: adoption of the cigar shape, and invention of an adequate power plant.

Gen. J.-B.-M. Meusnier of the Engineer Corps of the French Army came close to many of the right answers—on paper—as early as 1783, but he was well ahead of the state of the mechanical arts and died before anything practical could be accomplished.

A century passed before the first airship capable of steady flight under control, able to return to its starting point at will, could be demonstrated. Meanwhile, many inventors tried, and some nearly made it. Sir George Cayley, the "father of British aeronautics" (see below *Heavier-than-air—the experimenters*), like Meusnier, committed his ideas on airship design to paper (1816–34) but never reduced them to practice.

Early power plants. The greatest drawback of the time was lack of a lightweight, self-contained power plant. A model airship driven by clockwork was demonstrated in London in 1843. Later (1850), a Parisian clockmaker, Pierre Jullien, built a model, "Le Précurseur" (also fitted with clockwork power), that incorporated all the elements of a modern, nonrigid airship.

In 1852, making use of the sketches of Meusnier and Cayley and inspired by Jullien's model, Henri Giffard built a steam-driven airship with a cigar-shaped gasbag some 144 feet (44 metres) in length with a capacity of 88,000 cubic feet (2,500 cubic metres). He took off from the Hippodrome in Paris on September 24, 1852, and flew under control to Elancourt, near Trappes. He did not attempt to fly against the wind nor to return to his point of departure, but the date establishes the beginning of man's practical conquest of the air. It also marked the introduction of the term dirigible, meaning steerable, as applied to airships. The terms airship and dirigible since then have remained almost synonymous.

The first dirigibles

Several attempts at airship design were reported from America between 1866 and 1870; *e.g.,* the Marriott steam-driven dirigible in San Francisco and a pedal-powered, elongated balloon of Solomon Andrews from Perth Amboy, New Jersey. Neither was a success.

In 1865 a German inventor, Paul Haenlein, filed a

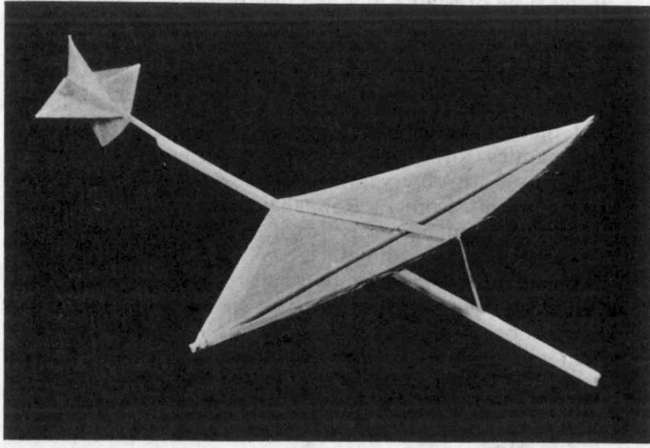

Figure 43: *Early gliders.*
(Left) Model of a glider by Sir George Cayley, of Yorkshire, England, about 1804. (Right) Biplane glider built by Otto Lilienthal of Germany, 1895.
By courtesy of (left) the National Air and Space Museum, Smithsonian Institution, Washington, D.C.; photograph, (right) Authenticated News International

patent for a semirigid airship to be driven by an internal-combustion gas engine. The machine, 164 feet (50 metres) long, was actually built in 1872 but lacked sufficient power for effective propulsion and control.

An interesting but abortive attempt to apply electric power to airships occurred in 1883. Gaston and Albert Tissandier, inspired by the Exposition d'Électricité in Paris in 1881, built a small, elongated dirigible powered by an electric motor and a large bank of lead storage batteries. The ship made a trial flight on October 8, 1883, but its heavy batteries and feeble power made it helpless in even the mildest breeze, and the Tissandiers shortly abandoned their effort.

Success finally came on August 9, 1884, when two French army captains, Charles Renard and A.-C. Krebs, flew the airship "La France" from Chalais-Meudon to Villacoublay and back in 23 minutes. "La France" was also electrically powered, but its large lifting capacity, coupled with redesigned and more efficient electrical motor and batteries, made the difference. A number of other successful flights were made in the months following. Although only little further work was done with electrical power, the day of controlled mechanical flight had finally arrived.

The closing years of the 19th century were marked by the appearance in Paris of one of the most colourful figures in flight history—the Brazilian-born sportsman-scientist Alberto Santos-Dumont. He built and flew his first small airship in 1898 and continued his experiments first in lighter-than-air and subsequently in heavier-than-air craft well into the first decade of the 20th century (see below *Aviation in adolescence; Balloons and airships*).

Beginning in 1896, Germany took an active interest in airships. Even before Graf von Zeppelin launched his first large, rigid airship in 1900 (see below *Balloons and airships*), two interesting developments appeared: the Wölfert dirigible, "Deutschland" (June 1897), and the Schwarz all-metal airship (November 1897). Neither was successful; both crashed during test flights. But Wölfert was the first to install a gasoline engine in any flight vehicle, and Schwarz pioneered the use of thin sheet aluminum (a relatively rare metal at the time) as a covering material for aircraft.

HEAVIER-THAN-AIR—THE EXPERIMENTERS

George Cayley. Throughout the years, the conflicting claims of inventors to priority have plagued aviation historians. On one point, however, there is clear consensus. The title of "father of British aeronautics" and, in fact, of all aeronautics rests with Sir George Cayley.

It is true that Leonardo had sketched wing-flapping devices and even a form of helicopter (*c.* 1500), and kites in many forms were commonplace prior to the 17th century. Also, the records of the 18th century contain accounts of many weird and wonderful machines for mechanical man flight. But at that time, as always, men's dreams far exceeded their scientific and technical capabilities.

It was in the early 1800s that George Cayley came upon the scene. Charles Dollfus characterizes Cayley as "the outstanding technical mind [in the field of flight] of the first third of the nineteenth century . . . the true inventor of the airplane . . . one of the most powerful geniuses in the history of aviation."

Cayley's active interest in man flight spanned the years from 1792 to his death in 1857. A perceptive theorist and an active experimenter with models (see Figure 43, left) and with full-scale gliders, he eventually had at his disposal all the aerodynamic theory required for the design of a man-carrying airplane. The problem, as he saw it, was "to make a surface support a given weight by the application of sufficient power to overcome the resistance of the air." Unfortunately, no light-weight, self-contained power plant was then available. That vital component was still half a century away.

The search for a suitable power plant

This was the problem that plagued all inventors who considered the flight of heavier-than-air craft up to the end of the 19th century. Until earthbound automobiles generated a requirement for a compact power plant that could operate on available liquid fuels, would-be aircraft designers saw no choice but to turn to the crude steam engines of the day. The best of engines, with the necessary boilers, fireboxes, condensers, fuel, and water, ran up the ratio of total weight to available power to an impossibly high figure for aeronautical use. Even now, with the advantages of light metals, high-energy fuels, and the most modern design techniques, no serious attempt is being made to apply steam power to aircraft, though in the 1800s some came remarkably close to configurations resembling successful 20th-century aircraft.

Gliders, models, and kites. In considering past achievements, it is apparent that those who concentrated on experiments with gliding flight made the most substantial contributions toward the final man-flight solution. They did not waste effort in attempts to solve the extremely difficult and costly task of combining crude and undeveloped mechanisms with light and fragile structures. Flights by Cayley and many others in the second half of the 19th century contributed much to basic knowledge of flight in machines without power.

Model makers and kite flyers also made important contributions, notably the mid-century collaboration of William Samuel Henson and John Stringfellow, which resulted in some far-reaching predictions on the format of a modern airplane and on future intercontinental airline operations—but only on paper. The invention of the box kite (1893) by Lawrence Hargrave in Australia had a positive influence on airplane design in the early 1900s.

Premature attempts at powered flight. The most conspicuous (and expensive) failures of the period were experienced by those courageous optimists who made premature attempts to take the giant leap to full-scale powered flight without intermediate steps. In 1857 Félix du Temple, a French naval officer, constructed a monoplane design fitted with a locomotive-like boiler and smokestack, but succeeded only in puffing his way down a long ramp without leaving the ground. In 1875 Thomas Moy, a British

Attempts to use steam power

engineer, in a tethered conglomeration of wires and fabric steamed his way around a circular track, rose briefly for a few inches, but never actually took off.

A more ambitious project took shape in Russia in 1884, when Aleksandr Mozhaysky designed and built a steam-driven monoplane. Launched down the ramp of a ski jump, and airborne for a few seconds before hitting the ground, it provided the basis for a subsequent Russian claim of the world's first airplane flight.

In France, also in 1884, M.-A. Goupil, encouraged by results obtained with a kite-glider prototype, built a bird-like monoplane and a steam power plant to install in it. He never put the two together, and no attempt to fly it ever took place. The construction, however, is of interest on two counts: (1) his design was the first to incorporate opposite-acting ailerons for lateral control, and (2) many years later (1917) Glenn Curtiss, in America, built and flew a reproduction of Goupil's airplane (powered, however, with a gasoline aircraft engine) as a part of his attempt to set aside certain Wright patents covering lateral control devices.

One near-miss of the period must be noted. A French self-made engineer and mechanical genius, Clément Ader, built a batlike steam-propelled monoplane that he christened "Eole." On October 9, 1890, on a friend's estate near Paris, he succeeded in leaving the ground in this craft under power. He was airborne for some 160 feet (50 metres). This achievement was substantiated by witnesses, but despite Ader's subsequent claims of "flight" the most that can be said is that he made a short-duration hop. It was in no sense a sustained, controlled, powered flight such as was made by the Wrights in 1903, and all subsequent investigations have established that "Eole" was totally incapable of such flight.

Moy's concept of testing tethered aircraft on a circular track appealed to other experimenters. His former associate, Horatio Phillips (who, in 1884 and the years following, patented the first designs for the thick wing sections, with curved upper and lower surfaces, now used on all airplanes), so tested (1893) a curious multiplane model whose wing system resembled a Venetian blind. Except to confirm his own wing theories, no other use was made of the device.

The most spectacular and certainly the most expensive test rig of this character was put together at Baldwyn's Park in Kent by Sir Hiram Maxim, inventor of the Maxim machine gun. Over many years his experiments in aviation, which were said to have cost him some £20,000, culminated finally in the design and construction of a huge steam-driven biplane with two propellers. It was tested in rails on a circular track, fitted with a restraining rail designed to prevent lifting off more than a few inches. During one of its trials, a guard rail broke; the machine swerved off the track and was extensively damaged. Discouraged, Maxim terminated the project.

Otto Lilienthal. Though the steamers held centre stage for a decade, they all huffed and puffed without results, and it fell to the gliders to cross the final gap—to provide the flight experience needed to take advantage of internal-combustion power when it became available. The greatest of them, and the man whose work provided the initial impetus to the Wright brothers, was Otto Lilienthal (1848–96) of Germany.

Lilienthal's early studies of bird flight had led him to experiment (1868) with wing-flapping devices (ornithopters), but shortly he turned to gliding and in this area made his greatest contribution. He built a number of batlike monoplane and biplane gliders (see Figure 43, right) and between 1893 and August 9, 1896 (the day of his fatal crash), made over 2,000 gliding flights from hilltops. On one occasion he covered over 1,000 feet (300 metres) in gliding flight. Eventually, he was able to fly in winds up to 15 miles (24 kilometres) per hour.

Glider stability and control

Lilienthal was primarily concerned with the stability and control of his machines. Originally, he did not use any movable aerodynamic control surfaces in flight but sought for an inherently stable machine that could be controlled by shifting his body weight. This proved to be unsatisfactory, and it was in the course of an experiment to test a movable elevator that his glider spun out of control and he sustained fatal injuries. He was convinced that it was essential to get the feel of flight in gliders before attempting powered flight—a lesson that was scrupulously followed by the Wrights five years later and that unquestionably contributed to their success.

Octave Chanute. Lilienthal's work was widely reported and came to the attention of a French-born, American-educated engineer, Octave Chanute, who was himself deeply interested in the problem of man flight. In 1896, when he was well over sixty years old, he and a group of assistants began gliding experiments on the sand dunes of Lake Michigan near Chicago. He wanted a better system of control than the Lilienthal body-shifting technique. He sought "an apparatus with automatic stability in the wind." During 1896–97 his group built and made over 1,000 flights in five different glider types. They kept careful records and were the first to use a series of single photographs (motion-picture cameras were not then available) showing consecutive phases of a single flight.

Chanute became a close friend and frequent correspondent of the Wright brothers as they began their gliding experiments in 1900. They adopted his bridge-truss biplane configuration and drew heavily on his gliding experience. On at least one occasion (1901) Chanute visited their camp at Kill Devil Hills near Kitty Hawk and made photographs of some of their glider flights.

INTRODUCTION OF THE GASOLINE ENGINE

By 1899 a number of lines of experimentation were converging. Vast sources of petroleum had been discovered and tapped, and chemists had found the means of unlocking its ancient sun-generated energy. Metallurgists could produce high-strength steels and the light metal aluminum. Toolmakers had evolved methods and machines to fabricate intricate mechanical devices, and scientists had harnessed electrical energy. All these in combination were essential to the development of the lightweight internal-combustion engine, the indispensable missing ingredient for man flight.

A requirement for such a source of power had already been established by the horseless carriage. In Europe and in America curious vehicles without harness and shafts (but usually with whip sockets still in place) were already churning up road dust to the gibes and guffaws of a skeptical public. So, by 1900, for the first time in history, the necessary power plant in a crude but usable form was waiting in the wings—for its wings.

During the first two years of the new century, while the Wrights were testing their gliders at Kitty Hawk, an Austrian piano maker turned engineer, Wilhelm Kress (1846–1913), was putting together a flying boat with three monoplane wings in tandem. The machine had two large propellers amidships, belt-driven by a Mercedes engine designed to produce 40 horsepower at a weight of 440 pounds (200 kilograms). Actually, however, the engine delivered only 30 horsepower with a total weight of 836 pounds—a combination that militated against successful flight. Kress, himself, then 68 years of age, made the first attempted takeoff (1901) from Lake Tullnerbach. The machine showed some signs of leaving the water but was wrecked when it ran aground. It was, however, notable for two innovations: (1) it marked the first attempted use of a gasoline engine in an airplane; and (2) it employed thin-walled steel tubing for its body structure. (Steel tubing for fuselage construction became commonplace only in the early 1920s.)

Kress's flying boat

SAMUEL PIERPONT LANGLEY (1834–1906)

The distinguished third secretary of the Smithsonian Institution, astronomer, mathematician, and inventor, spent the last twenty years of his life in active research in aeronautics. Few men before him pursued the subject more painstakingly or more scientifically, and none left as complete a record of experimental results. The *Langley Memoir on Mechanical Flight* (Smithsonian, 1911) is required reading for all serious students of man-flight history. But, in the end, Langley failed to fly. His only reward was ridicule and accusation of wasting public funds.

Aerodynamic research. He began his work (*c.* 1886) when he was professor of astronomy at the Western University of Pennsylvania (now the University of Pittsburgh). The wind tunnel as a tool for aerodynamic research had not appeared in America. Langley adopted a whirling arm device as his original test rig. This was a counterweighted 30-foot (nine-metre) beam, pivoted at one end, and arranged to rotate horizontally, sweeping a 60-foot-diameter circle. With a steam engine driving the central shaft, tip speeds up to 70 miles (112 kilometres) per hour could be attained. Models of wings and other shapes (including several stuffed birds) were mounted at the free end of the arm, and measurements made of their air resistance and other characteristics as the arm rotated. This was the first serious effort at systematic aerodynamic research in America. Appropriately, one of the principal U.S. government flying fields and its associated research laboratories bear Langley's name.

After his appointment to the Smithsonian (1887), Langley continued his aeronautical work. While still in Pittsburgh he had begun experiments with small models powered by twisted or stretched rubber bands. By 1891, in Washington, he had built and tested over 30 different configurations, keeping accurately detailed records of their characteristics and performance. Late in 1891 he realized that rubber-powered models had little practical future and began work to develop small steam power plants. At this time he coined the term aerodrome (Greek, "air runner") to describe his flying vehicles. By 1896 he had designed, redesigned, built, rebuilt, and tested Aerodromes numbers 0 to 6. This work involved literally thousands of changes and modifications to the hundreds of mechanical components involved. These are all carefully documented in his *Memoir*.

Langley's aerodromes

Between 1894 and early 1896 a number of launchings were attempted from a catapult device mounted on top of a small barge anchored in the Potomac River below Washington, D.C. Results were uniformly disappointing until May 6, 1896, when Aerodrome Number 5 went off successfully and flew some 3,200 (975 metres) feet in a series of wide circles. Recovered from the water, Number 5 made a second flight on the same day, this time covering some 2,300 feet (700 metres). On November 28, in the same year, a modified machine of the same general design (Number 6) made a stable flight of some 4,200 feet (1,280 metres) in one minute, 45 seconds. These flights were observed and photographed by the inventor of the telephone, Alexander Graham Bell, himself an active student and experimenter in aeronautics (see below *Glenn Curtiss and the Aerial Experiment Association*).

Charles Manly, later to become Langley's principal assistant, introduced Part II of the *Memoir* (1897–1903) as follows:

> Although in 1896 Mr. Langley had made a firm resolution not to undertake the construction of a large man-carrying machine . . . yet the longing to take the final great step of actually transporting a human being through the air, which the successful flights of the models had now for the first time in the history of the world actually proved to be possible, soon became irresistible.

At this point history took a hand. The United States was then involved in a war with Spain over Cuba. With unusual prescience, Pres. William McKinley and the War Department, intrigued by the possibilities of a flying machine as an instrument of warfare, granted Langley an allotment of $50,000 with which to build a man-carrying Aerodrome (December 1898).

Power-plant problems. Langley had no doubts of his ability to build the airframe, but he was gravely concerned, as were all experimenters before him, over the power plant. Steam was out of the question. Some form of internal-combustion engine was clearly indicated, but none of the automobile manufacturers of the time would undertake to build an engine to meet his specifications; *i.e.,* to develop 12 horsepower continuously at a total weight not to exceed 100 pounds (45 kilograms).

Finally, after communicating with all known sources in America and in Europe, he signed a contract (December 12, 1898) with one S.M. Balzer, an engine builder in New York City, to deliver an engine to the Langley specification by February 28, 1899. The engine proved to be a disappointment, and Langley went to Europe to search for a suitable power plant. Before his departure he turned the design problem over to his young engineering assistant, Charles M. Manly, recently graduated from Cornell. Langley returned empty-handed, but Manly's reworking of the Balzer engine was beginning to bear fruit. Actually, Manly abandoned most of the original design and built his own engine.

Manly's engine

It was a remarkable accomplishment. By the spring of 1903 the engine, with a weight of 187 pounds (85 kilograms), was developing over 50 horsepower. On a later occasion (August 1904, after the ill-fated flight tests), the Manly engine ran for ten consecutive hours at a rating of 52.4 horsepower. No other engine was to equal that record for many years.

Final attempts. While work was progressing on the large engine, a one-quarter scale Aerodrome was built, powered by a small, air-cooled, five-cylinder gasoline engine that developed just over three horsepower at 1800 rpm. Although work on the model was completed by October 1901, because of work priority given to the large machine it was not test-flown until August 8, 1903. Only one flight was made—1,000 feet (300 metres) in 27 seconds—but it demonstrated to Langley's satisfaction that the design of the large Aerodrome was fundamentally correct. This, incidentally, was the first flight of a heavier-than-air vehicle powered by a gasoline engine.

Shortly after the model flight, the full-scale machine was ready for test. By early October the necessary modifications had been made on the launching mechanism to accommodate the Aerodrome. On October 7, Charles Manly took his place at the controls, the engine roared, and the machine was released. Result: total failure. The Aerodrome plunged nose down into the river only a few yards from the boat. As a skeptical and disgruntled reporter described the incident in the next morning's *Washington Post,* "It simply slid into the water like a handful of mortar." Manly was unhurt and the wreckage salvaged. Two months later, December 8, the test was repeated. Immediately after launching, the rear wing structure collapsed and the machine went into the river, tail first. To the end of his life, Langley ascribed the accident to a failure of the launching mechanism. Again, Manly survived unhurt.

This was the end for Langley. He was subjected to a flood of ridicule and abuse in the press. Government funds were cut off, and a congressional investigation was threatened over wastage of public money "because, some man, perchance a professor wandering in his dreams, was able to impress [the War Department] that his aerial scheme had some utility." Langley never recovered, and he died two years later.

Only nine days after the Aerodrome's final crash, Orville Wright rose from the sands of Kitty Hawk on man's first successful airplane flight.

Curtiss and the Langley machine. There is a historical footnote to the Langley machine: in connection with a long and bitter legal controversy over claims of Glenn Curtiss and the Wright patents, the original Langley Aerodrome was lent to Curtiss by the Smithsonian Institution in 1914 and sent to his factory at Hammondsport, New York. There it was reconditioned, allegedly in accordance with the original plans, though significant structural modifications were made to enable the craft to operate off the water as a seaplane. It made one or two brief off-the-water hops (five seconds) with the original Manly engine, and later, after further stuctural changes, and with the substitution of a Curtiss aircraft engine and a propeller, it made several straightaway flights at low altitude over Lake Keuka, in New York. Returned to the Smithsonian, it was then labelled as "the first airplane capable of sustained free flight with a man," to the great annoyance of Orville Wright (Wilbur Wright had died in 1912).

Flights with Curtiss engine

The entrance of the United States into World War I, and the subsequent pooling of all aeronautical patents, ended the legal controversy, but the personal bitterness between Wright and the Smithsonian persisted for many years. In view of the institution's claims, Orville refused to deposit the original "Flyer" in the Smithsonian. In 1928 he sent the historic aircraft to the Science Museum in London, where it remained on display (except for the war years 1939–45, when it was placed underground for safety) until 1948. At that time, after due apologies by the then Smithsonian secretary, C.G. Abbot, the machine was returned to the United States aboard a U.S. aircraft carrier and, on December 17, 1948, formally installed in the Arts and Industries Building in Washington, D.C., where it is now displayed.

WILBUR AND ORVILLE WRIGHT

That the Wright brothers of Dayton, Ohio, were the actual inventors of the world's first practical powered airplane is unequivocally accepted by all serious aeronautical historians.

The notion that the Wrights were semi-literate bicycle mechanics who happened to stumble upon the secret of flight is fanciful. The fact is that, with limited formal education, they became research scientists in the most literal sense. Says Dollfus, "Brought up in austere simplicity, they shared the same character, combining the soul of the apostle with the spirit of practicality .... These qualities permitted them to triumph where all their forerunners had been halted." The Wrights first tried printing and publishing a newspaper, then built up a bicycle manufacturing and repair business in Dayton. This provided them with the tools, the mechanical knowledge, and the income on which their subsequent experiments in aviation were based. In 1899, after becoming interested in bird flight and reading of Lilienthal's experiments, they determined to make a serious study of aviation. A request to the Smithsonian in Washington, D.C., for a list of books and articles on flying was the starting point. Chanute's *Progress in Flying Machines,* published in 1894, became their basic text, but they absorbed everything else that was available. In a relatively short time their intensive studies transformed them into scientists. Their own contributions to the literature of flight are contained in over a thousand pages of the two-volume edition of *The Papers of Wilbur and Orville Wright,* edited by M.W. McFarland of the U.S. Library of Congress.

The Wrights did not make the mistake common to many of their predecessors; *i.e.,* to attempt powered flight without first learning to fly. They made their first tests on kites (1899–1900). From this they progressed first to tethered gliders (1900) and finally to gliders in free flight (1901–02). Only after becoming airmen in the true sense of the word were they ready in 1903 to attempt powered, man-carrying, controlled flight.

Early research of the Wrights

Between 1900 and 1903, they embarked on a remarkable program of research and development. The prior art had produced little but speculation and a record of unsuccessful experiments. Wilbur summarized the difficulties that then obstructed success as "(1) those which relate to the construction of sustaining wings; (2) those which relate to the generation and application of the power required to drive the machine through the air; (3) those relating to the balancing and steering of the machine after it is actually in flight." He conceded that some progress on items (1) and (2) had already been made, but considered that until item (3) could be resolved, "all other difficulties are of minor importance."

Methodically and persistently they set about finding solutions to all three, but in the end it was their work on the interrelated problems of flight stability and control that brought success.

Considering today's vast accumulation of aerodynamic, structural, and power-plant data in thousands of textbooks and hundreds of millions of informational bits stored in computers, the Wrights' technical resources were thin indeed. Step by step they had to test every wing and propeller shape, first by mounting crude measuring devices on the handlebars of a moving bicycle, later in a small wind tunnel of their own construction. Painstakingly, they recorded, tabulated, and applied these data. But it was on stability and control research that they concentrated their greatest effort.

Kites and gliders. They began with kites. They built the first in August 1899, a biplane of five-foot (1.5-metre) span of the Chanute type, fitted with control wires by which the wing cellule could be twisted—or warped—in flight. Wing-warping to achieve lateral control became the core of the subsequent Wright patents. The success of the kite led them to undertake a larger (17-foot [5.2-metre] span) man-carrying glider. It was completed in September 1900, and they moved their experiments to a site near Kitty Hawk, North Carolina, where the U.S. Weather Bureau had reported the existence of steady and reasonably constant winds and where the sand dunes offered cushioning for hard landings. (Secrecy was never a factor in the selection of Kitty Hawk, as has sometimes been asserted.)

The new machine was first flown as an unmanned kite, and after some skill had been acquired, it was flown with a man aboard but with ground control. The few attempts at free flight were disappointing (based on Lilienthal's data, the wing area appeared to be too small), and the brothers returned to Dayton to reconsider.

During that winter they built a larger (22-foot [6.7-metre] span) glider with an innovation—a front horizontal rudder (*i.e.,* elevator). Returning to Kitty Hawk in July 1901, the Wrights found that their revised calculations were still uncertain. At one point they almost duplicated Lilienthal's fatal crash. They did succeed, however, in overcoming some of the machine's erratic behaviour, and they eventually made a successful glide of some 300 feet (90 metres). Octave Chanute spent some time at the Kitty Hawk camp and made a number of photographs of the Number 2 machine in flight.

At this point, discouraged by the scarcity of reliable aerodynamic information ("Truth and error were everywhere so intimately mixed as to be indistinguishable," Wilbur wrote in the *Century* magazine in September 1908), they almost gave up. But building their own wind tunnel, they began systematic compilation of their own data. (The original wind tunnel and some of the experimental wing and propeller sections tested are now in the Franklin Institute in Philadelphia.) Here they became scientists. When they interpreted and applied their results to the construction of a practical flying machine, they became engineers.

Wind tunnel tests

In 1902 they turned the corner. In August and Septem-

By courtesy of (top) Air Force Central Museum, Wright-Patterson Air Force Base, Ohio, (bottom) National Air and Space Museum, Smithsonian Institution, Washington, D.C.

Figure 44: *The Wright brothers' aircraft.*
(Top) Modified Glider Number 3 in flight at Kill Devil Hills, near Kitty Hawk, North Carolina, 1902. (Bottom) Orville Wright piloting the "Flyer" at Kill Devil Hills, December 17, 1903.

ber 1902, they built Glider Number 3 (see Figure 44, top) which incorporated all their experimental findings. It retained the forward elevator but added a double fixed fin, which later was to become the rudder. Returning to North Carolina in September, they made over 1,000 glides on this machine. The early flights were unsatisfactory, but when the fixed tail fins were made steerable, so that banking and yawing (turning) could be coordinated (a characteristic common to all successful airplanes), the stability and control problem was solved. Gibbs-Smith writes, "After this vital step, the Wrights had a fully practical glider—the first in history—and with it made some hundreds of perfectly controlled glides." They applied for a patent in March 1903.

Powered flight. Back in Dayton, with this achievement behind them, they finally turned their attention to powered flight but like Langley, they could find no manufacturer to make an engine of the power and weight they could use. Like Langley, they designed and built their own in their bicycle shop, with the expert help of their assistant, Charles Taylor.

Wright "Flyer I" (later known as the "Kitty Hawk") was not a reconstruction of Glider Number 3, with engine attached. It was an entirely new machine. A biplane with a wing span of 40 feet four inches (12.3 metres) and a wing area of 510 square feet (47.4 square metres), it retained the front elevator and rear rudder configuration of 1902. The Taylor engine was a horizontal four-cyclinder type mounted in the centre of the lower wing, turning two chain-driven, counter-rotating, pusher propellers. The pilot, as in the gliders, lay prone on the lower wing beside the engine. It was designed to land on a pair of sledlike skids, and takeoff was accomplished from a simple droppable dolly running along a 60-foot monorail track.

The inevitable constructional and mechanical delays put off the trials until late in 1903. With winter almost upon them, the machine was finally ready for test by mid-December. On December 14, 1903, they tossed a coin for the first-flight honour. Wilbur won and made the attempt. Due to overcontrol of the elevator, the "Flyer" plowed into the sand at the end of the launching rail. Three days later, after repairs and a weather delay, Orville had his turn. At 10:35 AM, on December 17, into a 20–22-mph (32–35 kph) wind, he made a successful takeoff, flew for 12 seconds, and landed without damage—the first controlled man-carrying mechanical flight in history (see Figure 44, bottom).

History-making flight at Kitty Hawk

That morning, three more flights were accomplished, with alternating pilots. On the fourth, Wilbur flying, the machine was airborne for 59 seconds, covering 852 feet (260 metres) on the ground, the equivalent of a flight of one-half mile in still air. After the fourth flight, while the aircraft was being returned to the starting rail, a strong gust of wind overturned and damaged it beyond immediate repair.

Before breaking camp and starting back to Dayton, Orville sent a wire to his father: "Success four flights Thursday morning all against twenty-one mile wind started from level with engine power alone average speed through air thirty-one miles longest 57 seconds inform press home Christmas." The "57 seconds" was a telegrapher's error—59 seconds was correct.

Aftermath. Ten years later, Orville Wright, looking back on that day, said,

> With all the knowledge and skill acquired in thousands of flights in the last ten years, I would hardly think today of making my first flight on a strange machine in a twenty-seven mile wind, even if I knew that the machine had already been flown and was safe . . . Yet faith in our calculations and the design of the first machine, based upon our tables of air pressures, secured by months of careful laboratory work, and confidence in our system of control developed by three years of actual experiences in balancing gliders in the air, had convinced us that the machine was capable of lifting and maintaining itself in the air, and that, with a little practice, it could be safely flown.

Few editors paid any attention to the story, and those who used it embroidered it with facetious embellishments à la Jules Verne. Incredibly, almost five years went by before the citizens of the United States really accepted the fact that the Wrights had flown in 1903. Even their friends and neighbours in Dayton took the news very calmly. Wilbur and Orville were a pair of nice fellows, but who were they to make such claims when the most learned professors of the day had already proved mathematically that mechanical man flight was impossible!

Later flights. Wilbur and Orville also took the situation very calmly; in fact, it was exactly to their liking. They called no press conferences; they could not spare the time. During the winter of 1903–04 they built a new and larger "Flyer," with a much improved engine. In the spring of 1904 they rented a 90-acre (36 hectare) cow pasture, "Huffman Prairie," near Dayton. There they set up shop, assembled the new machine, and began to fly.

The Wrights were not secretive about their work. It was there in the open for anyone to see. When first ready to test the Number 2 "Flyer," they sent invitations to the press, but after one or two postponements of the promised flight due to weather, and unforeseen mechanical difficulties, the already skeptical reporters went off on more promising leads.

The summer of 1904 was employed in perfecting their flight techniques and eventually in learning to make turns in the air. On September 20, Wilbur made the first full circle in flight and returned to land at his starting point. This feat generated the first published eyewitness account in history of the flight of any airplane. It appeared, strangely enough, in the January 1905 issue of a small magazine called *Gleanings in Bee Culture,* published in Medina, Ohio. The editor, A.I. Root, had travelled to Dayton to see the Wrights fly and had observed the first circular flight. On November 9, Wilbur stayed in the air for over five minutes, making almost four complete circles of the pasture.

First full-circle flight

"Flyer" Number 3, incorporating all the improvements gained from the experience with Number 2, was first flown at Huffman Prairie on June 23, 1905. By October 16 some 49 flights had been completed, including several ranging in length from 11 to 24½ miles (18–39 kilometres), at average speeds of 38 mph (61 kph). Most flights were terminated only because of exhaustion of fuel. It could be said, and with confidence, that for all practical purposes the conquest of the air had been accomplished.

The Wrights' attitude toward publicity had also changed. The word had got around, and others, particularly abroad, were beginning to show interest in their work as possible competitors. Their basic patent had not yet been granted (it was not to be issued until 1906), and the Wrights were concerned about legal protection of, and financial reward for, their work. To avoid possibilities of military or commercial surveillance, they stopped all flights and prohibited any public inspection of their airplanes from October 16, 1905 until May 6, 1908. They then went back to Kitty Hawk with the greatly improved Number 3 machine to refresh their skill as pilots.

The changes in detail were many, but the most obvious were the upright positions of both pilot and engine. The prone pilot position was abandoned in favour of a seated configuration on the lower wing, facing forward. The flat engines of the No. 1 and No. 2 Flyers were replaced by a more powerful and more efficient vertical, in-line type.

Signal Corps project and European activities. Between 1907 and 1908 the Wrights entered into negotiations with the U.S. War Department for an experimental airplane for military use. Their original proposal was received with a notable lack of enthusiasm. The Signal Corps could see little value in a flying machine but finally drafted a specification that was designed to discourage, if not to eliminate, all bidders. Required was a machine capable of flying for one hour carrying a pilot and a passenger (combined weights not less than 350 pounds [159 kilograms]); top speed at least 40 mph (64 kph), and enough fuel on board for 125 miles (200 kilometres) of flight. In addition, the aircraft had to be readily demountable to be transferred from place to place in a standard horse-drawn army wagon. All this for a price of $25,000.

Although understandably discouraged by their own government's attitude, the Wrights went to work on the project. At the same time, however, they began to look for markets overseas.

A few experimental short-duration, straightaway hops had already been made in France by Santos-Dumont, Ferber, Blériot, and others, but nothing had been seen in Europe comparable to the by now routine performances at Dayton. When reports finally did filter through, the reaction abroad was total skepticism. A technical paper on the Wrights' work, read before the French Aéro-Club early in 1906, was covered by the *New York Herald* (Paris edition) under the headline "Flyers or Liars?"

In 1907 the brothers divided the field: Orville remained at home to develop the machine to meet the Signal Corps specification; Wilbur packed up a new and much improved "Flyer" and shipped it to France.

Orville was the first to get his machine into the air. (Wilbur's "Flyer" was unaccountably impounded by French Customs and was not released for many months after its arrival.) The army demonstrator was shipped to Ft. Myer, Virginia, and, beginning September 3, was put through public trials on the parade ground. With Orville Wright at the controls, it passed or exceeded all specifications. Suddenly the American press awoke to the realization of its mistake, and press reports became ecstatic and numerous.

But the triumph was short-lived. On September 17, with Lieut. Thomas E. Selfridge as passenger, a guy wire snapped, fouled a propeller, and the machine dove into the ground out of control. Selfridge was killed instantly, to become the first fatality in a powered airplane. Orville was seriously injured.

Wilbur Wright at Le Mans

In France, after many delays, Wilbur made his first flight at Le Mans on August 8, 1908. In the following months he proved to the world that both his piloting and his "Flyer" were far superior to anything that Europe could offer. On December 31 he established a world endurance record of two hours 20 minutes, covering a distance of 77½ miles (124 kilometres) to win the Michelin Prize. The European press and the technical community went wild. The Wrights were indeed flyers—not liars.

Orville, still suffering the effects of the Ft. Myer accident, joined Wilbur in France in mid-January 1909. After making demonstration flights in several European countries, they returned to the United States in May to prepare for renewed Signal Corps trials with a new machine. Orville again began test flights at Ft. Myer on June 28. By July 30 the army was satisfied that the specifications had been met (or exceeded), and the Signal Corps acquired its first airplane. This machine is now on display in the National Air and Space Museum in Washington, D.C. That fall, Wilbur set up the army's first flying school at College Park, Maryland.

Later years. Wilbur Wright contracted typhoid fever and died in 1912. For a few years Orville Wright carried on alone, manufacturing and testing his own aircraft and becoming involved in a bitter controversy with Glenn Curtiss over basic patents. He died in Dayton, Ohio, in 1948.

GLENN CURTISS AND THE AERIAL EXPERIMENT ASSOCIATION

Between 1908 and 1914 Curtiss had become the Wrights' greatest competitor. It was no friendly rivalry. Not only fame but potential fortunes were at stake, and the bitterness ran deep on both sides.

Curtiss was a natural competitor. Basically a mechanic and a showman, he was never a scientist nor even an engineer. He emerged first as a racer of motorcycles. His growing reputation as a designer and manufacturer of light-weight, high-speed gasoline engines brought him to the attention of Thomas Baldwin, then (1904–09) building and flying nonrigid airships (see below *Balloons and airships*). In 1907 his work with Baldwin attracted the notice of Alexander Graham Bell, experimenter with large tetrahedral kites and aspirant to the solution of the man-flight problem.

Aerial Experiment Association. Bell was the key figure and financial backer of the Aerial Experiment Association (AEA) with headquarters at Hammondsport, New York, and a test site at Bell's estate in Nova Scotia. He gathered around him a group of young, enthusiastic, and capable men, including Lieut. Thomas E. Selfridge (later killed in the crash of the Wright "Flyer" at Ft. Myer), F.W. Baldwin, J.A.D. McCurdy, and Glenn Curtiss. The association's objective was to conduct scientific research in heavier-than-air flight.

Wheeled landing gear

The AEA adopted the pusher-biplane configuration of Chanute and the Wrights, with the added advantage of more powerful and lighter engines, and a decided improvement in takeoff and landing gear, a three-wheeled undercarriage. The latter permitted operation from reasonably smooth fields without the somewhat clumsy launching rail and landing skid required by the Wright machines. (Gibbs-Smith considers the use by the Wrights of skids, after everyone else had shifted to wheeled landing gear, to have been one of their few serious mistakes.)

In turn, each of the association's members tried airplane design. Baldwin was first off, with Selfridge's "Red Wing." On March 12, 1908, he flew 319 feet from ice-covered Lake Keuka. A few months later (May 22, 1908), Baldwin's "White Wing," piloted by Curtiss, flew more than 1,000 feet (300 metres) in 19 seconds. Curtiss' own design, "June Bug," covered some 2,000 yards (1,830 metres) in one minute 43 seconds on July 4, 1908, to win a prize posted by *Scientific American* magazine. Later (November 1908), he mounted the aircraft on a pair of canoe-like floats, renamed it the "Loon," and attempted unsuccessfully to take off from the surface of the lake.

McCurdy's contribution, "Silver Dart," was tested at Bell's Nova Scotia estate. On February 23, 1909, he took off from the frozen surface of a nearby lake to record the first heavier-than-air flight in Canada.

During the next few years Glenn Curtiss became one of the leading figures in aviation both in the United States and abroad. In an improved machine, the "Gold Bug" (four-cylinder, 30-horsepower engine), he made the first public flights in New York City and won the second *Scientific American* prize at Mineola, Long Island, New York, on July 17, 1909, with a flight of 24.7 miles (39.5 kilometres) at 35 mph (56 kph). This also won for him official representation for the Aero Club of America at the Gordon Bennett Cup race at Reims, France, in August of that year. With a more powerful engine (eight-cylinder, 50-horsepower) and some structural modification, his "Golden Flyer" won the race at 47 mph (75 kph).

Back in the United States, Curtiss in 1910 won a $10,000 prize posted by the New York *World* for a flight from Albany to New York City. These successes established him as the principal competitor of the Wrights and led to the battle over patents that dragged through the courts for several years. Principal issue was the method of lateral control: wing warping (Wright), or opposite-acting ailerons (Curtiss). Finally, on January 13, 1914, the courts ruled in favour of the Wrights, by which time wing warping was a dead issue. Practicality and aerodynamic superiority had long since decided in favour of the aileron.

Seaplanes. While the Wright litigation was in full swing, Glenn Curtiss established a reputation in another vital area—he gave wings to the United States Navy by the development of successful hydro-airplanes and flying boats. Although the "Loon" of 1908 had not got off the water, the concept had been pursued.

Curtiss' work with U.S. Navy

Curtiss first cooperated with the navy in proving that an airplane could be launched from and landed upon a ship. The initial demonstration was a takeoff by Eugene Ely, a U.S. civilian pilot, from a platform erected on the bow of the cruiser USS "Birmingham" at Hampton Roads, Virginia, November 14, 1910. A little over two months later (January 18, 1911) Ely, in a similar machine, landed aboard the battleship USS "Pennsylvania" in San Francisco harbour, was turned around, and took off safely for a return flight ashore.

Shortly after Ely's flights Curtiss' research on properly shaped floats for seaplanes paid off. In the A-1 (a modification of the standard land plane) he made successful water takeoffs and landings. On February 17, 1911, he flew from the naval base at San Diego out to the USS "Pennsylvania" at anchor in the harbour, landed alongside, and was hoisted aboard by one of the ship's cranes. After paying his respects to the commanding officer, he and his plane were lowered into the water for a successful flight back to the base. For this, Curtiss was awarded the Collier Trophy for 1912 "for the greatest achievement in aviation in America . . . during the preceding year," and the navy became airborne.

With the navy's interest assured, Curtiss turned his attention to developing a truly integrated water aircraft. So far, his hydro-airplanes had been simply standard land types mounted on floats instead of wheels. In 1912 he built the "Flying Fish," the prototype for all true flying boats—a boatlike hull to accommodate pilot and passengers, to which wings, engines, and propellers were attached.

AVIATION IN ADOLESCENCE

Activities in Europe. While the Wrights were successfully flying circles and figure eights in America, aviation in Europe was only slowly coming to life. The hopes raised by Lilienthal and Pilcher in 1890 had faded. The dream of man flight had once more seemed out of reach. Gibbs-Smith summed up the situation between 1902 and 1905 as follows:

> No systematic, persistent and progressive study of the problems of glider control was made, hence no one came near to any kind of proficiency in gliding, let alone mastery . . . Europeans had available all the necessary facts and clues in Chanute's articles, and . . . in the two excellent Wright papers of 1901 and 1902, which were easily accessible. Yet, during the three years (1902–04) the total product of European endeavors amounted to only some four ineffectual gliders.

Ferber, Archdeacon, and Esnault-Pelterie tried so-called exact copies of Wright gliders with little success. Léon Levavasseur learned little from a full-sized bird-form machine (1903). They all failed to solve the basic stability and control problems.

Only little progress was made through 1905. A few tentative trials of float-mounted gliders towed behind motor boats were made in France by Archdeacon, Blériot, and Voisin. All followed Wright designs, or showed strong relationship to Hargrave's box kites, and the results were not promising.

The turning point in Europe came late in 1906. After two unrelated failures (one in France and one in Denmark), Alberto Santos-Dumont coaxed his awkward canard (tail first) 14-bis biplane off the ground at Bagatelle for six flights, the longest covering some 720 feet (220 metres) in 21 1/5 seconds, at a maximum altitude of six feet (two metres). It was a modest achievement compared with the Wrights' performances, but it earned him an Aéro-Club de France prize of 1,500 francs and the honour of having made the first powered airplane flight in Europe. His reputation as an airplane designer, however, rests more solidly on a subsequent machine, the fly-weight single-place "Demoiselle" of 1909.

English Channel crossing

During 1907 progress began to be made, but slowly. Of some 14 aircraft tested, only six showed any ability to get off the ground. Of these, only one, built by Gabriel and Charles Voisin for the French sportsman Henri Farman, remained airborne for more than a minute. Its nearest competitors were up only 55 and 45 seconds. Farman, in the course of his one minute-plus record, achieved the first full circular flight in Europe. Less spectacular, but possibly of greater importance, was the appearance (late in 1907) of Léon Levavasseur's eight-cylinder, 50-horsepower Antoinette engine, which was to power many of Europe's successful aircraft.

Finally, in 1908, European aviation got off the ground. Greatest impetus came from the performance of the imported Wright "Flyer" at Le Mans in August 1908. Wilbur Wright's mastery of the air astonished the European experimenters after their years of disbelief.

Even before the Wright demonstration, however, some progress had been made. Henri Farman and Léon Delagrange were rated the best of the European pilots. The former flew 12 miles (19 kilometres) in 20 minutes in July after having made a short hop with a passenger in May. By year's end Farman had doubled his July performance. Louis Blériot, in a monoplane of his own design, came close to Farman's records. Each made true cross-country flights of 11 and 20 minutes, respectively, in October. Elsewhere in Europe, England, Denmark, Germany, and Italy, dozens of curiously designed aircraft were making tentative hops.

Two major events marked the year 1909: (1) the crossing of the English Channel on July 25; and (2) the first great aviation meet at Reims in August. The Channel crossing ended the concept of political isolation by oceans, and the second established beyond all doubt that aviation was here to stay.

Circuit racing

The English Channel posed a challenge to aviation that could not be resisted. At midsummer three of Europe's best pilots, Hubert Latham, Louis Blériot, and the Count de Lambert, were encamped along the Pas-de-Calais preparing for the attempt. De Lambert was delayed by aircraft damage. Latham, in an Antoinette monoplane, got away first in early morning July 19. Halfway across his engine quit, and he landed in the water, to be rescued shortly by a French torpedo boat. Six days later, Blériot, in his Blériot XI monoplane, took off from Les Boraques near Calais and after a flight of 37 minutes landed on a hillside near Dover (see Figure 45, top).

The Blériot flight touched off a flurry of excitement all over Europe and focussed attention on the first of the great aerial circuses that marked the years 1910–12. The Grande Semaine d'Aviation, at Reims, sponsored by the local champagne industry, attracted not only the best airplanes and pilots of the world but also tens of thousands of people from all walks of life anxious to see for

By courtesy of (top) the U.S. Signal Corps, in The National Archives, (centre) the National Air and Space Museum, Smithsonian Institution, Washington, D.C., (bottom) the Ryan Aeronautical Co.

Figure 45: *Historic flights.*
(Top) Louis Blériot's Blériot XI plane, which flew the English Channel from Les Boraques, near Calais, to Dover, July 25, 1909. (Centre) The Curtiss NC-4, which flew from the U.S. to England via Newfoundland, the Azores, and Portugal, May 1919. (Bottom) The Ryan "Spirit of St. Louis," flown by Charles A. Lindbergh nonstop from Long Island, New York, to Paris, May 20–21, 1927.

themselves the miracle of man flight. Prizes totalled over 200,000 francs.

Meets and prizes. For the next few years prize money for record flights became plentiful, many of the donors being newspapers eager to profit from the attendant publicity. Race meets and aerial circuses brought keen competition among itinerant pilots.

From 1910 to the advent of war in 1914, the aviation carnival in America as in Europe became a "movable feast." The first important meet was held in Los Angeles in January 1910 with Curtiss and Louis Paulhan setting world speed and altitude records. In September, the Harvard–Boston Meet at Squantum, Massachusetts, attracted United States and European competitors, with thousands of spectators, including Pres. William Howard Taft. The biggest show was staged in Belmont Park, Long Island, New York, October 22–31. Some 40 aircraft, mostly of American or French design, participated. Thousands of New Yorkers turned out to witness speed runs (up to 61 mph [98 kph]), altitude records (over 9,700 feet [2,960 metres]), and a race around the Statue of Liberty. The newspapers of the country posted substantial prizes ($15,000–$30,000) for record flights to or from their respective cities. A manufacturer of a popular soft drink subsidized the first transcontinental flight. C.P. Rodgers, in a well-marked ("Vin Fizz") Wright biplane, accompanied throughout his journey by a special train carrying first-aid equipment, a mechanic, spare parts, and his wife, flew from New York to Los Angeles in a series of 68 hops (and almost as many crashes) between September 7 and November 5, 1911. His plane is now displayed in the Smithsonian Institution. In Europe the London *Daily Mail* put up £10,000 for a flight to be completed in less than 24 hours covering 183 miles (293 kilometres) between London and Manchester. Two pilots, Claude Grahame-White and Louis Paulhan, both in Farman biplanes, made a race for it on April 23–28, 1910, with Paulhan the winner in four hours two minutes.

The Italian Aviation Society offered 70,000 francs for the first pilot to cross the Alps. Jorge (or George) Chávez flew from Switzerland to Italy via the Simplon Pass on September 23, 1910, in a Blériot monoplane, but on landing his machine crashed, and he was killed.

Circuit racing

By 1911–12, racing from town to town, called "circuit racing," became popular in Europe, over courses up to 1,000 miles (1,600 kilometres). The temptation to fly in all kinds of weather in such contests left a long trail of wrecked machines and dead pilots. But stimulated by such competition, airplane and engine performance improved tremendously. Altitudes leaped to thousands of feet, speeds approached 100 mph (160 kph), and endurance flights were measured in hours rather than minutes.

France was still the aviation leader of Europe, but other countries were joining the sport: in January 1911 France had 353 certified pilots, England 57, Germany 46, Italy 32, Belgium 27. Rather amazingly, the United States, where heavier-than-air flight had begun, had only 26.

THE IDEA OF THE HELICOPTER

During the decade when the first airplanes were attracting wide public attention, the concept of vertical flight by direct action of Archimedean-screw propellers (envisioned by Leonardo and postulated by Cayley) was not entirely forgotten. A number of helicopter models had appeared at the London Aeronautical Exhibit of 1868, and flying models with steam and electric drives were demonstrated during the late 1870s. Also, Jules Verne's fictional hero, Robur le Conquérant (1886), cruised around the world in a remarkable craft airborne by 37 pairs of vertical propellers mounted atop 37 masts.

In 1904 Col. Charles Renard (who had piloted the first controlled airship) used an unmanned, twin-rotor, gasoline-powered helicopter as a part of his continuing researches in aerodynamics. About the same time, Paul Cornu tried a model of somewhat similar configuration. Encouraged by its performance, he tried a full-scale machine powered by a 24-horsepower Antoinette engine. On November 13, 1907, Cornu made several lift-offs of a few seconds' duration, the first by any helicopter. Once airborne, however, the machine proved uncontrollable and was shortly abandoned.

In America in 1908, Thomas Edison, after experimenting with vertical air screws driven by electric motors that were mounted on platform scales to measure lift, commented, "Whatever progress the airplane might make, the helicopter will come to be taken up by the advanced students of aeronautics." But more than 30 years were to pass before his prediction came true. A young Russian, Igor Sikorsky, at that time was making his first serious studies of the helicopter. During 1909 and 1910 he built two machines, each of which was powered by a 25-horsepower Anzani engine (see Figure 46, right). The most that either helicopter could do was to lift its own weight off the ground without a pilot. Many years later (November 1964) in a lecture before the New York Wings Club, Sikorsky said of his experiences in 1910,

> . . . by that time I had learned enough to recognize that with the existing general state of the art, engines, materials and . . . lack of experience . . . I would not be able to produce a successful helicopter at that time.

Nevertheless, several others tried. After Cornu gave up, a large and ungainly combination of airplane and helicopter (the Broquet–Richet No. II) managed to rise a few feet, only to crash on landing. Also, a persistent Danish experimenter, J.C.H. Ellehammer, in his twin-rotor helicopter attained a maximum altitude of about two feet (0.6 metre; 1912) but did not achieve flight. The real difficulty, then and for many years thereafter, was control. Until Juan de la Cierva (see below *Rotary wing aircraft*) designed independently articulated roto blades for his first autogiro, that problem remained unsolved.

BALLOONS AND AIRSHIPS AFTER 1900

With the advent of the steerable airship (dirigible), little interest remained in free ballooning until it became

By courtesy of (left) National Aeronautics and Space Administration, (right) the National Air and Space Museum, Smithsonian Institution, Washington, D.C.

Figure 46: *Early autogiro and helicopter designs.*
(Left) Autogiro Number 4, designed by Juan de la Cierva of Spain, about 1923. (Right) Helicopter attempt by the Russian Igor Sikorsky, 1909.

an important tool for upper-atmospheric research in the 1930s. Actually, scientific research of this sort had its beginnings very early. Blanchard and Jeffries made scientific observations on their cross-Channel flight in January 1785, and the French Academy of Sciences sponsored several upper-air research flights by Gay-Lussac and Biot in 1804. Coxwell and Glaisher in England (September 1862) recorded atmospheric data up to an altitude of approximately five miles (eight kilometres). On July 31, 1901, two German physics professors, A. Berson and A.J. Süring, made an atmospheric survey flight to an altitude of some 35,000 feet (10,670 metres), a record that stood for 30 years, when it was exceeded by Auguste Piccard.

Upper-air research

Ballooning. During the first decade of the 20th century ballooning was looked upon largely as a form of sport. The Aéro-Club de France encouraged competition by establishing rules for racing and by promulgation of records for distance, altitude, etc. Its Balloon Park at Saint-Cloud near Paris became a centre for amateur and professional aeronauts. During 1913 some 479 ascensions were recorded from this site alone.

Balloon racing became an international sport. Every year new records were made and broken, both in Europe and in America. But apart from such popular activities, limited use was made of free balloons as preliminary training for airship crews.

Airships. With the increasing availability of suitable engines (*c.* 1900), airship experimentation proliferated. New and improved designs emerged, and it became necessary to differentiate among three distinct categories: nonrigid, semirigid, and rigid airships.

Nonrigid airships consist simply of an elongated fabric gasbag (envelope), below which a car for the accommodation of crew and power plant is suspended by ropes or cables. The bag holds its shape solely because of the gas pressure inside. If the gas escapes, the whole apparatus collapses into a shapeless mass of fabric. All airships prior to 1900 were of this class.

Semirigid airships have a structural keel (or truss) fore and aft to which the envelope is directly attached. The keel provides housing for crew and power plant. If the gas escapes, only the envelope collapses. This type became popular in the 1900–20 period.

Rigid airships are characterized by an external structural skeleton covered by light fabric to preserve the overall shape surrounding a series of internal lifting-gas cells. Power plants, control surfaces, and passenger and crew accommodations are integrated into the main structure of the airship. The external appearance of the ship remains the same whether or not the gas cells are inflated. These make up the Zeppelin class of airship, which reached its developmental peak during World War I and persisted in both military and commercial form into the 1930s.

Nonrigid airships. Prior to 1904 when he turned his attention to heavier-than-air flight, Alberto Santos-Dumont was the world's greatest builder of nonrigid airships. A wealthy sportsman, Santos-Dumont flew largely for fun but created great public interest in aviation and contributed much to the technology of airship flight. Success came largely from his adoption for aeronautical purposes of the light gasoline engine then in popular use in small tricycle automobiles. His ships numbers 1–3 (1898–99) were not successful. None was able to return to the point of departure under its own limited power. Number 4, with a nine-horsepower engine (1900), did little better, but it established the configuration for Number 5, which, with installation of a 16-horsepower engine weighing only 215.6 pounds (98 kilograms), began to show positive results. The car was an elongated, open, triangular wooden framework with a single propeller at the rear and with engine and pilot located near the centre (see Figure 42, right). The engine was in the open, but the aeronaut rode in a small wicker balloon basket mounted some 20 feet (six metres) forward of the engine. The whole apparatus was suspended beneath an elongated fabric envelope by means of steel piano wire, the first use of metal instead of rope in nonrigid airship construction.

Santos-Dumont's airships

In this machine Santos-Dumont made his first attempts at the Deutsch de la Meurthe Prize established in 1900 for the first flight from the Aero Park at Saint-Cloud, around the Eiffel Tower, and return. His first several tries were unsuccessful and included one crash in the courtyard of the Trocadéro. That same evening he started construction of a new airship, Number 6, in which, after several more abortive efforts, he completed the flight to win the prize. During the following five years a series of 11 more of his airships appeared at Saint-Cloud, including one, Number 9, a small ship of only three horsepower, in which he landed and took off on the Champs-Élysées and in the Bois de Boulogne.

After Santos-Dumont turned to airplanes, interest in nonrigids tapered off in Europe. The French Société Zodiac built a series of small ships that were sold in limited numbers to the military services of France, The Netherlands, Russia, and Belgium, prior to World War I.

In America, exhibition flights in nonrigid airships (along with parachute jumps from hot-air balloons) became stock features at county fairs and expositions. A dozen or more pilots and their ships toured the racing circuits around the country from 1900 to 1910. Thomas Scott Baldwin, one of the prominent figures in this activity, in search of a suitable light-weight engine for his airship, discovered Glenn Curtiss, then building motorcycle engines, and started him on his career as an airplane designer and pilot. The Baldwin-Curtiss team produced the first U.S. military aircraft, the SC-1 airship, test flown at Ft. Myer, Virginia, in 1905 and subsequently purchased by the U.S. Army. Little further interest was shown in nonrigid ships by the military services of any country until the latter part of World War I, when both France and Britain built large numbers for offshore antisubmarine patrol work.

Semirigid airships. The success of a series of large semirigid airships built for the French government by Paul and Pierre Lebaudy (1903–07) focussed attention on this class of airship. "La Jaune" was the first (1902), followed in sequence by "La Patrie," "La République," and "La Liberté" (1908), each larger and more powerful than its predecessor. The latter two were 200 feet (60 metres) long, 33 feet (10 metres) in diameter, and powered by 70-horsepower engines. Each carried a crew of four. Ships numbers 2 and 3 were destroyed in accidents, but the performance of the fleet was so impressive that foreign governments became interested. Russia purchased two French airships, and England followed suit, taking delivery of one in September 1910 and another later in the year. The latter covered the 230 miles (368 kilometres) from the factory at Moisson, France, to Farnborough, England, in $5^{1}/_{2}$ hours.

Lebaudy airships

By 1902 Germany was committed to the development of rigid airships under Graf von Zeppelin but was also keeping a watchful eye on the French semirigids. Under the supervision of Maj. August von Parseval, several semirigid ships were built between 1906 and 1911. The largest and most successful was 224 feet (68.3 metres) long, 47 feet (14.3 metres) in diameter, and was driven by two 120-horsepower engines. It was demonstrated as a passenger carrier at the Frank-furt Aeronautical Exhibition in 1909 and later participated in military and naval exercises. But the performance of the Zeppelins was so far superior that by 1911 all other lighter-than-air programs were abandoned.

Only two American attempts at semirigids are recorded. In 1906 Walter Wellman, a journalist living in Paris, began construction of the "America"—185 feet (56.4 metres) long and powered by an 80-horsepower engine. His objective was to fly to the North Pole. Two attempts were made, in September 1907 and October 1909. Both failed. He then enlarged "America" (228 feet [69.5 metres] long, with two engines) for a transatlantic attempt. Wellman and his crew took off from Atlantic City, New Jersey, on October 15, 1910. Motor trouble developed almost immediately, and after drifting as a free balloon for two days to a point some 400 miles (640 kilometres) east of Hampton Roads, the ship descended. The crew was rescued by a passing steamer, and the ship was abandoned.

One of Wellman's crew, Melville Vaniman, decided to try again in the "Akron," a semirigid of his own design. While on a test flight off Atlantic City on July 2, 1912, it caught fire and crashed, killing Vaniman and his four companions. This was the end of semirigid development in the United States until a brief but abortive program was undertaken in 1923.

Rigid airships. Among all classes of lighter-than-air craft, the large rigid dirigible had the longest and most spectacular history. It began when Ferdinand, Graf von Zeppelin, launched his first ship from Lake Constance in 1900. It terminated when the "Hindenburg" exploded and burned on the naval air station at Lakehurst, New Jersey, in early May 1937.

Zeppelin's dirigibles

Zeppelin, as a military observer, had witnessed U.S. Army balloons in service during the American Civil War, and he made his own first ascent at St. Paul, Minnesota, in 1863. Around 1873 he became convinced that the future of lighter-than-air development lay in very large rigid ships. This concept was not wholly original. David Schwarz, a German, had built a ship with an external aluminum framework in Russia in 1897. It proved unsuccessful and was abandoned. Zeppelin patented his first design in 1898 and built LZ-1 (Luftschiff Zeppelin Nummer 1) during the next two years.

Assembled in a floating hangar on Lake Constance and launched from the water on July 2, 1900, the ship was 420 feet (128 metres) long with 38-foot (11.6-metre) maximum diameter. Its structure consisted of 24 longitudinal girders and 16 transverse rings, all of aluminum, tied together with a forest of diagonal bracing wires. The outside covering was smooth cotton cloth. Its 16 internal cells of rubberized fabric held a total of 338,410 cubic feet (9,584 cubic metres) of lifting gas. Two 16-horsepower gasoline engines were mounted in separate cars rigidly attached to the keel girder. Although all subsequent Zeppelins (up to and including LZ-129, the "Hindenburg") varied widely in size, shape, and mechanical detail, the basic pattern was established with LZ-1.

The first trials of LZ-1 were reasonably encouraging, but the following years (1900–10), in which LZ-1 to LZ-6 appeared, were marked by disasters and discouragement. The ships were continuously being improved and enlarged, but natural forces, mechanical failures, and financial difficulties almost brought the program to a standstill. But Zeppelin, foreseeing a commercial potential for his airships, organized Delag (Deutsche Luftschiffahrts-Aktien-Gesellschaft) in 1910 and began to carry passengers for hire. In the years remaining before the outbreak of World War I, Delag's five airships ("Deutschland," "Schwaben," "Viktoria Luise," "Hansa," and "Sachsen") spent over 3,000 hours in the air and carried 34,228 passengers a distance equivalent to four times around the Earth, without injury to passengers or crew. In late 1913, this remarkable safety record was marred when LZ-14 and LZ-18, both on military missions, were destroyed with a loss of 50 lives.

The onset of war changed the character of Zeppelin development. By 1918 some 100 airships had been built, primarily for the bombardment of London.

Britain was the only other country that, before the war, took any interest in rigid airships. One ship, at the time the largest in the world (510 feet [155.4 metres] long, 40 feet [12.2 metres] diameter, with two 200-horsepower engines), was constructed by Vickers Ltd., under Admiralty orders.

Christened "Mayfly," the aircraft was destined never to leave the ground. While being towed out of her hangar, she was caught in a severe crosswind and broken in two.

PARACHUTES (LEONARDO TO WORLD WAR I)

Though parachutes are not flight vehicles within the meaning of this article, their operation depends upon aerodynamic principles, and their association with man flight is intimate and of long standing. Even before any human being left the ground, Leonardo had sketched a fall-breaker in the form of a cloth pyramid and had discussed the aerodynamic factors involved (1514). Fausto Veranzio (1595) published a book containing a drawing of a man ("Homo Volans") descending from the top of a tower supported by a fabric panel stretched over a rectangular wooden framework. In 1632 Desmarets de Saint-Sorlin published a novel in Paris (*Ariane*) in which the hero escapes from a prison tower by jumping with a parachute made from a bed sheet.

Blanchard, the early balloonist, claimed to have experimented with parachutes as early as 1777. Prior to the invention of the hot-air balloon, Joseph Montgolfier is reported to have dropped a sheep, without damage, in a basket tied below a seven-foot (2.1-metre) parasol from a tower in Avignon. Several similar attempts were reported between 1785 and 1797, when the first manned parachute drop was accomplished.

Garnerin's parachuting

On October 22, 1797, André-Jacques Garnerin took off from the Parc Monceau in Paris in a basket attached to an umbrella-like parachute suspended beneath a balloon. At an altitude of about 3,000 feet (900 metres), he cut the suspension cord and descended without injury. Wilbur Wright later characterized this as one of the most courageous acts in aviation history.

Garnerin's original canopy-type set the pattern for virtually all subsequent parachutes. A conical parachute studied by Cayley and tested (July 1837), with fatal results, by Robert Cocking, attracted early attention but was shortly abandoned.

During the greatest period of free ballooning, hundreds of parachute drops were made, mostly to provide thrills for the public at county fairs. It was not until the latter part of World War I that the device began to be important as a means of saving the lives of pilots in disabled planes.

DEVELOPMENTS OF THE WORLD WAR I ERA

The circus-and-carnival era of man flight ended abruptly with the outbreak of World War I in 1914. The millions that belligerent governments were willing to pay aircraft designers suddenly made aviation big business on a scale no one had yet contemplated. Aircraft had found work to do, and the frantic competition of wartime brought, in a few years, performance improvements that might otherwise have required decades.

In the first weeks of the war, aircraft played a considerable role in reconnaissance; French aircraft spotting the movements of the German 1st Army led to the Battle of the Marne. But few thought that airplanes could be effectively armed.

In 1914 France mobilized some 150 military planes and several airships, Germany about 260 planes plus a fleet of 14 Zeppelins, and Britain fewer than 100 aircraft. The planes of course were flimsy kitelike structures powered by engines of uncertain power and longevity. At best, they could climb 2,000–3,000 feet (600–900 metres) and fly at 60–70 mph (96–112 kph), sometimes for as much as 200 miles. At worst, they could barely get off the ground. But four years later, 150–200-horsepower single-seat fighters, armed with two synchronized machine guns, were fighting each other at 15,000 feet (4,570 metres) or higher. Two-place reconnaissance machines were supplying hundreds of photographs of the ground action daily, and heavy bombers were penetrating deep into enemy territory both by day and by night. Airplanes had not only found jobs to do but had evolved into highly diversified forms to meet specialized requirements.

The production of aircraft, engines, and related material expanded tremendously to keep pace with combat needs. For the first time the need to manufacture large numbers of aircraft of identical types put builders on a production line rather than a jobbing basis. Also, mass training of pilots became a prime necessity. Flying had, indeed, ceased to be a game.

The following sections emphasize the status of aviation in the various belligerent nations. A more detailed description of the leading military aircraft and their armament appears in WAR, THE TECHNOLOGY OF.

Germany. In the immediate prewar period, German planes and pilots held world endurance (24 hours 12 minutes) and distance (1,178 miles [1,885 kilometres]) records. German aircraft appeared over Paris within weeks of the declaration of war. Germany produced military planes of standardized design for ease of maintenance and replacement, fitted with excellent engines by Benz and Mercedes. In a rapidly changing technology, however, too much standardization can be a liability. The air war rapidly became a seesaw affair with the better aircraft on one side soon outperformed by newer machines of the enemy.

Probably the greatest contributor to German aircraft development was a Dutch designer, Anthony H.G. Fokker, whose synchronized forward-firing machine guns restored combat superiority to the Germans in 1915 and whose excellent triplane fighter D.VII, used by Baron von Richthofen, could compete with anything put up by the Allies in 1917–18.

Fokker's fighter planes

By 1918 the imperial government's inventory included many well-known single-seat fighters—Albatros, Roland, Halberstadt, Pfalz—and a series of efficient two-place observation types—Aviatik, A.E.G., Rumpler, Albatros, etc. A number of seaplanes, largely twin-float, single-engined biplanes, were produced for fleet cooperation.

Airships. Germany's initial long-range heavy bombardment effort centred about its fleet of rigid Zeppelin-type airships. During the war over 100 were built by Zeppelin and some 20 more by the Schütte-Lanz Company. Many raids were launched against London and other cities, but by 1916 the Allied defenses had improved to the extent that airship missions became too costly in men and machines. During the latter phases of the war the big airships were used only for naval patrols at sea and for general over-land observation.

Performance, however, had improved tremendously. In the summer of 1917, LZ-120 made a 100-hour observation flight over the Baltic Sea. In November 1917, LZ-59 attempted a relief mission deep into German East Africa. Although the mission failed to reach its destination, the airship stayed in the air for more than 95 hours and covered over 4,000 miles (6,400 kilometres).

Large bombardment aircraft. With the blunting of the Zeppelin attacks against London and a need to provide an operational capability for night attack against other distant cities, German interest toward the end of the war centred on bombardment airplanes of very large size. Some 60 such aircraft were built in 1916–18. Most familiar were the Gotha biplanes of 1916, with a wingspan of nearly 90 feet (27 metres), powered by two Mercedes engines of 260 horsepower each. With a 2,000-pound bomb load they had an operating range of some 300 miles (480 kilometres). The largest of these giants, however, was the Siemens-Schückert R-VIII, with a wingspread of over 150 feet (46 kilometres) and powered by six 300-horsepower engines.

France. France entered World War I with the largest inventory of military aircraft and probably the largest cadre of aviators. Most of the machines were the immediate descendants of the 1910–12 racers (Blériot, Deperdussin, Nieuport, Morane, etc.), but production was under way on improved and specialized military types, including the R.E.P. monoplanes and the Farman, Voisin, and Caudron biplanes. Bréguet and Durand designs with fabric-covered fuselages were already in evidence.

French military aircraft improved tremendously under the pressures of war. The early birdcage Voisin and Caudron bombers and observation planes gave way to the more efficient long-range Bréguet and Letord day bombers. In the single-seat fighter category, France made great progress. In the end, French, British, and American fighter pilots flying single-seat Nieuports and Spads proved a match for the German Fokker, Pfalz, and Albatros squadrons. Of great importance was the mass production of reliable engines, particularly the eight-cylinder Hispano-Suiza, which was used in the Spads and in the British S.E. 5 fighters.

Ground-support aviation

Apart from combat operations, the French developed ground-support aviation to a high degree. Photographic missions over the lines provided ground commanders with needed battlefield information. Radio telegraphy and visual signals were also widely employed. For naval support, for scouting, and for bombing attack against submarines, a number of float-type seaplanes were in service.

In the early stages of the war the small fleet of nonrigid airships was used by the Army for reconnaissance and for bombardment, but these slow, low-flying machines were so vulnerable to ground and air attack that surviving specimens were turned over to the navy in 1917 for antisubmarine patrol use. Captive balloons were used in large numbers on all fronts for observation purposes.

The growth of the French aviation effort in the course of the war was enormous. As of November 1918, some 180,000 people were employed in the aircraft-manufacturing industry.

Great Britain. Of the three major western European powers, Britain went into World War I in the weakest position in the air. The Royal Flying Corps (RFC), organized in 1912, mustered only 1,800 officers and men and fewer than 150 flyable aircraft when war was declared in 1914. By November 1918, however, the corps consisted of some 300,000 officers and men, with 22,000 aircraft organized in over 200 squadrons.

Coincident with the formation of the RFC, a Royal Aircraft Factory had been established at Farnborough. Between 1912 and 1914 several experimental military machines were turned out from designs by De Havilland (first of the D.H. series); the British Experimental 2c; and the Sopwith Tabloid. The Tabloid was the ancestor of later high-performance fighters used by both American and British pilots—the Camels, Snipes, Kittens, Bullets, and Hawks—but the 70-horsepower, 75-mph (120 kph) B.E. 2c was the backbone of the RFC in 1912. By 1918, however, the Hispano-Suiza-powered British S.E. 5 performed with the best that Germany could put up.

The earlier British airplanes made use of French engines, Gnome and Clerget radial, and Renault in-line types. Later, the Hispano-Suizas were widely used. As the war progressed, however, excellent British-built engines—Rolls-Royce, Sunbeam, and Beardmore—became available in quantities. Such engines powered the D.H. 4 day bombers and the long-range Handley Page night bombardment types. Night operations began in 1916. By 1918 Handley Page bombers were being turned out in quantity in England and in America.

Naval aviation developed rapidly in Britain. Squadrons of seaplanes and flying boats were used for the protection of principal naval bases and for antisubmarine patrol offshore. Eventually, some 350 airplanes were assigned to the British Grand Fleet. During the last two years of the war, over 100 bombing attacks were made against German submarines at sea.

Naval aviation

The modern aircraft carrier had its genesis during this period. Experiments were conducted in launching small fighter planes from platforms built over battleship gun turrets, or from barges towed behind high-speed destroyers. At least one former passenger liner was fitted experimentally with a large landing platform above its superstructure.

Interest in nonrigid airships revived early in the war for antisubmarine convoy and coastal patrol work. Hundreds of blimps (from "British Class B airship" plus "limp"—*i.e.,* nonrigid) were built during the four-year period. In the last year of the war over 9,000 sorties against floating mines and submarines are recorded. Also, in spite of the disastrous experience with the rigid airship "Mayfly" in 1911, and based on designs of several Zeppelins shot down in England, construction was begun on several rigid ships. These had little significance during the war but did touch off a brief (and calamitous) postwar airship program (see below, *Developments from 1918 to 1930: Significant technical developments*).

Other countries. Only three other countries—Italy, Russia, and the U.S.—made significant contributions to aviation during World War I.

Italy. Italy was among the first to recognize the importance of aircraft in warfare. Beginning in 1911, its bombardment squadrons were active in Libya. Out of this experience emerged the multi-engined Caproni bombers. Italian manufacturers in 1914–18 produced a considerable number of trainers, observation planes, and single-seat fighters, but the most spectacular were the large two-, three-, and four-engined Capronis. Day bombing started in 1916. Night operations with larger types were begun early in 1917. Built originally as two-engined biplanes, the later Capronis (some of which were produced under contract in the United States, with Liberty engines) were three- and four-engined triplanes.

Caproni bombers

Russia. Russia's contribution to aviation development of the period was a giant four-engined bomber (1915) by Sikorsky. It was derived from the "Ilya Mourometz" of 1912. After Sikorsky had abandoned (temporarily) his work with helicopters, he designed and built the first successful multi-engined plane—a large biplane carrying 16 passengers in a closed cabin, powered by four 100-horsepower Mercedes engines. A bomber version of this machine with four 120-horsepower engines was used on the Russian front in 1915.

United States. When the U.S. entered the European war in April 1917, army aviation was still a section of the Signal Corps. It mustered 65 officers and 1,087 men and possessed not a single aircraft capable of combat. The naval air arm consisted of 38 naval aviators, some 160 enlisted men, and possibly a dozen hydro-airplanes and experimental flying boats, all based at a single air station at Pensacola, Florida. None of the flyable airplanes carried any armament.

An Aircraft Production Board was appointed by Pres. Woodrow Wilson, and the decision was made to manufacture British, French, and Italian planes and engines in quantity. The only fighting plane that came out of the program in time to see action was the American-built British D.H. 4. Some 1,370 were in Europe at the Armistice, but only 740 ever saw service at the front.

A major United States accomplishment, however, was the rapid design and production of the famous Liberty engines. By October 21, 1917, the first 12-cylinder Liberty was test-flown. At the Armistice, orders on the books totalled 52,000. Some 13,000 had already been delivered, and production was 150 engines a day.

AVIATION BETWEEN THE WARS

From 1914 to 1918 all aviation activities focussed on a single objective, the winning of a war. When that task ended, most of the machines and the thousands of people involved suddenly found themselves unemployed. Thousands of aircraft were simply piled up and burned. Manufacture of aviation equipment of all kinds halted. Former military pilots, trying to make a living by their war-acquired flying skill, revived the circus-and-carnival atmosphere of the prewar period. With a surplus "Jenny" or "Avro" or "Cannuck," the barnstormers provided thrills wherever they could get a crowd; they sustained popular interest in aviation, and, even more important, they sold rides to the public—the thin wedge that, a decade later, cracked open the air-transport market.

The barnstormers

A few found employment in flying the mail. In the spring of 1918 the U.S. Post Office Department had sought bids for special mail-carrying airplanes to operate between Washington and New York. With nonmilitary aircraft in short supply, the U.S. Army was requested to undertake the assignment. Flights were inaugurated in May, but by midsummer the army had found that with the heavy demands of the war in Europe it could not spare either planes or pilots for the mail service. On August 12, 1918, the Post Office took over the New York–Washington airmail run as a civil operation. On September 8, 1920, transcontinental airmail was inaugurated. At first, operations were restricted to daylight hours, but on February 22, 1921, day and night flights were started, marking the real beginning of commercial air transport in America and creating a new demand for more pilots and better airplanes.

One of the factors that limited technical development well into the mid-1920s was the great surplus of wartime engines that were in production at the time of the Armistice. The result was that for the first five or six years, in spite of far superior power plants on drawing boards, or actually running on test stands, economic necessity dictated that new airplane designs be laid out around wartime engines.

Toward the latter half of the 1920s substantial advances in design and construction of aircraft came into being. Concurrently, organized research laboratories, both governmental and private, were established to meet the needs of the scientifically oriented designers and engineers entering the industry.

Guggenheim Fund. In January 1926 an event occurred in America that had a profound effect on all subsequent development everywhere—announcement of the establishment of the Daniel Guggenheim Fund for the Promotion of Aeronautics. Daniel Guggenheim (1856–1930), who never in his life owned an airplane, nor derived any profit from participation in aviation, made grants totalling $3,000,000 (beginning January 16, 1926) for the following purposes: (1) To promote aeronautical education both in institutions of learning and among the general public. (2) To assist in the extension of fundamental aeronautical science. (3) To assist in the development of commercial aircraft and aircraft equipment. (4) To further the application of aircraft in business, industry, and other economic and social activities of the nation. By February 1, 1930, when the fund was completely liquidated, each of its objectives had been fulfilled many times over. Its greatest importance was in the fields of education and research. Beginning in 1926, several Guggenheim schools of aeronautics and Guggenheim aeronautical laboratories were established. These centres attracted such outstanding scholars and teachers as Alexander Klemin, Theodore von Kármán, Robert and Clark Millikan, and William F. Durand. Many of the most significant advances in aviation—and in space exploration since the 1940s—were the result of work by graduates of Guggenheim schools or by recipients of Guggenheim research grants.

Government-sponsored research. Government-sponsored aeronautical research in the United States lagged far behind that of other major powers in 1914. Since 1866 the Aeronautical Society of Great Britain had been stimulating research and experimentation and fostering the exchange of information in the aeronautical sciences. The Royal Aircraft Factory was actively engaged in development projects by 1912. France had several major experiment stations: Eiffel's two wind tunnels, one at the tower and one at Auteuil; an army laboratory at Chalais-Meudon; and the Institut Aérotechnique at Saint-Cyr. Germany supported research laboratories in universities and technical schools at Göttingen, Aachen, and Berlin and operated a national installation at Adlershof. Italy and Russia had well-organized laboratories before the United States took its first official steps in that direction.

Following a study of the United States position with respect to wartime aviation in Europe, the Smithsonian Institution in 1915 recommended to Congress the establishment of a National Advisory Committee for Aeronautics (NACA). In addition to other activities the committee was authorized to own laboratories and to conduct research. The enabling legislation was approved on March 3, 1915, and the first full committee meeting was held on April 23.

National Advisory Committee for Aeronautics

During the next decade the record of aeronautical research progress at Langley Field, Virginia, the site of the committee's first research laboratory, was phenomenal. From a standing start in 1917, with a handful of technical personnel and three or four test airplanes, it was recognized by 1930 as the greatest research centre in the world, with a large and growing scientific staff and a capability of testing virtually all forms of aircraft in all regimes of flight under controlled conditions in the laboratory.

Government coordination of aviation activities. Slowly but surely a market for new aircraft began to grow. Aircraft manufacture revived to meet the demand for new military types and to serve the needs of a growing airmail service. Intercompany competition for new customers benefited airplane and engine performance. Airplanes became more reliable, more comfortable, easier to fly. There was some preliminary activity in building larger planes to carry passengers and cargo for profit on regular schedules.

By 1925, however, it was apparent everywhere that the expanding manufacture and use of aircraft must be subject to some overall coordination and regulation if chaos was to be avoided. In the United States, a board was appointed by Pres. Calvin Coolidge to establish a national policy for the development of all aspects of aviation. The board's recommendations resulted in passage of the Air Commerce Act of 1926, the Navy Five Year Aircraft Program (1926), and the Army Five Year Aircraft Program (1926). These acts provided a relatively stable base for American aviation development for the next decade.

The same problems were attacked by governments everywhere. Britain, France, Italy, and other countries established air ministries at Cabinet level to coordinate their

Table 3: Principal Record Flights (1919–30)

1919	
February 21	U.S. Army, using Thomas Morse "Scout" with 300-hp Hispano-Suiza engine, sets American speed record of 164 mph.
May 6–31	A squadron of U.S. Navy Curtiss flying boats attempts first Atlantic crossing. NC-1 and NC-3 lost at sea off Azores, crews rescued. NC-4 completes crossing, (see Figure 4, center) via Azores, arriving at Plymouth, England.
June 14–15	Capt. John Alcock and Lt. Arthur Brown (ex-RFC) fly from Newfoundland to Ireland in Vickers "Vimy" 2-engined biplane.
July 2–13	British dirigible R-34 makes round-trip flight from England to New York with 6 officers and 21 men.
September 18	Roland Rohlfs in Curtiss "Wasp" sets 34,910-ft altitude record.
1922	
March 30–June 5	Two Portuguese officers, Capt. S. Cabral and Vice Admiral G. Coutinho, fly by stages from Lisbon to Rio de Janeiro in British-built Fairey seaplane to record first crossing of South Atlantic.
October 18	World speed record set by General William Mitchell in Curtiss racer at 222.96 mph.
1923	
May 2–3	U.S. Army pilots Kelly and Macready make first nonstop transcontinental flight (New York to San Diego) in Liberty-powered T-2 monoplane.
August–December	Former German Zeppelin L-72 acquired by France after war, renamed "Dixmude," makes series of five flights across Mediterranean into North Africa.
November 4	Lieut. A.J. Williams raises world speed record to 266.6 mph in Navy-Curtiss Racer.
1924	
April–September	Four U.S. Army Douglas "World Cruisers" attempt round-the-world flight. Two lost en route; two, "New Orleans" and "Chicago," complete 26,345-mi. trip.
May 21	Lieut. J.A. Macready, USAS, sets altitude record at 35,239 ft.
October 12–15	Zeppelin LZ1-1126 (ZR1-13) renamed "Los Angeles," crossed from Friedrichshafen (Ger.) to Lakehurst for delivery to U.S. Navy.
1925	
April–November	Italian Commander de Pinedo and mechanic in single-engined Savoia flying boat, fly from Italy to Australia, returning via Japan—30,000 miles.
November	Alan Cobham flies from London to Cape Town via Cairo—8,500 miles in 94 hours.
1926	
May 9	Commander Byrd and copilot Floyd Bennett fly from Spitsbergen over North Pole and return in 3-engined monoplane "Josephine Ford."
May 11–14	Amundsen and crew fly over North Pole from Spitsbergen to Pt. Barrow, Alaska, in Italian-built semirigid dirigible "Norge."
1927	
May 20–21	Charles A. Lindbergh, after a one-stop flight from San Diego to New York, in the Ryan-built monoplane "Spirit of St. Louis," makes first nonstop flight from New York to Paris (33 hours, 30 minutes) to win the Orteig Prize (see Figure 4, bottom).
June 4–5	Clarence Chamberlin and Charles Levine in a single-engine Bellanca monoplane, fly from New York City to Eisleben, Germany.
June 28	Lieuts. Maitland and Hegenberger (U.S. Army) in 3-engined Fokker fly from Oakland, Calif. to Honolulu, 2400 miles over open ocean.
June 29–30	Cmdr. Richard Byrd and crew of three fly from New York to France in 3-engined Fokker "America."
July 4	Lieut. C.C. Champion, USN, pushes world's altitude record to 37,995 ft over Washington, D.C., in a Wright "Apache."
July 14–15	Bronte and Smith fly 2340 miles from Oakland, Calif. to Molokai, Hawaii in 25 hours, 36 minutes.
October 14–15	Costes and Le Brix in Breguet biplane cross from Senegal, Africa, to Rio de Janeiro in 21 hours, 18 minutes.
November 6	Lieut. A.J. Williams in Schneider Cup Racer establishes an unofficial speed record of 322.6 mph.
1928	
February	Bert Hinkler makes solo flight London to Australia. Lady Mary Heath flies solo from Cape Town to London.
April 12–13	German Junkers monoplane "Bremen" makes first east-west Atlantic crossing.
May–June	Charles Kingsford-Smith and crew of three in Fokker "Southern Cross" fly from Oakland, Calif. to Sydney, Australia via Honolulu and the Fiji Islands.
June 17–18	Amelia Earhart with pilots Stultz and Gordon fly Atlantic in monoplane "Friendship."
October 11–15	Airship "Graf Zeppelin" flies from Friedrichshafen, Germany to Lakehurst, N.J. with 23 passengers.
1929	
January 1–7	U.S. Army Fokker C-2 "Question Mark" flies for 150 hours, 40 minutes over Los Angeles in first major air-to-air refueling test.
August 15–20	Mamer and Walker in single-engined Buhl monoplane "Spokane Sun God" make nonstop transcontinental round-trip from Spokane, Washington, in 115 hours, 45 minutes with 11 air-to-air refuelings en route.
August	"Graf Zeppelin" makes first round-the-world airship flight including nonstop distance record from Friedrichshafen to Tokyo of 6,980 miles.
November 28–29	Commander Byrd and crew of three fly over South Pole in Ford 3-engined monoplane "Floyd Bennett."
1930	
May–July	Kingsford-Smith in "Southern Cross" makes round-the-world flight.
July 4	Lieut. Apollo Soucek, USN, raises world altitude mark to 43,166 ft.
July 29–August 1	British airship R-100 flies from England to Canada in 78 hours, 51 minutes.
September 1–2	Costes and Bellonte make first Paris-New York City flight—4100 miles in 37 hours, 18 minutes.

civil and military aviation requirements. When international commercial flights became possible, international commissions were established to control traffic and to promulgate rules and regulations covering flight operations and passenger safety.

Record flights. With the growing improvement in performance and reliability, public interest focussed on long-range flights, both cross-country and intercontinental. Just as the English Channel had posed a challenge to Latham and Blériot in 1909, so ocean crossings and transpolar flights became the targets of many ambitions in the middle 1920s. Again, for their publicity value, newspapers and wealthy private citizens posted substantial prizes for such flights. The London *Daily Mail* offered £10,000 for a nonstop Atlantic crossing, and in 1919 Raymond Orteig established a $25,000 prize for a nonstop flight between New York and Paris. Later (1927) first and second prizes of $25,000 and $10,000 were posted by James Dole for a race from California to Hawaii.

Prizes for record flights

Although the military services of most countries were ineligible to compete for monetary prizes, many special long-range flights were organized for their value as military exercises. To illustrate the expanding capabilities of aircraft during the 1920s, a selection of successful transcontinent and transocean flights (both by airplane and by airship) is given in Table 3. Between 1927 and 1930, of 31 transatlantic attempts, only 10 succeeded, and 16 men and three women died in the failures. The Dole Race across the Pacific (August 1927) cost six planes and 10 lives. A few milestones in speed and altitude performance have been included in the table.

The decline of the airship. Development of nonrigid airships (blimps) in Europe halted at the end of the war. In the U.S., however, both the army and the navy carried on limited programs during the 1920s. Most interesting design innovation was the navy's all-metal ZMC-2, first tested in 1929. Only one was built.

The U.S. Army purchased the 400-foot (122-metre) semirigid airship "Roma" from Italy in 1921. It crashed and burned at Langley Field in 1922 with a loss of 34 lives. This ended the use of hydrogen as a lifting gas in U.S. airships.

As noted above, Britain had become actively involved in a rigid-airship construction program toward the end of the war. The successful transatlantic round trip of the R-34 induced the U.S. Navy to order a British-built ship (R-38), which was completed in mid-1921. During a test flight on August 21, however, she broke up in the air and crashed with a loss of 45 men.

Britain's construction program continued, however, and culminated in 1930 with the launching of two super-airships of the Zeppelin type, Barnes Wallis' R-100 and the R-101, designed for the transatlantic and the Far East trade. The R-100 made one round trip to Canada in July, but the R-101 crashed and burned on a French hillside on her maiden voyage to India, killing a number of high-ranking RAF and civil officials.

Meanwhile, the United States had some disastrous, home-grown experiences. Parallel with the construction of the ill-fated British R-38, the U.S. Navy built an airship at the Philadelphia Naval Aircraft Factory and assembled it at the Naval Air Station, Lakehurst, New Jersey. The 680-foot (207-metre) "Shenandoah" was the first rigid dirigible to be filled with helium rather than with hydrogen. She was commissioned in October 1923 and for two years participated in naval exercises over land and with the fleet at sea. In September 1925 she ran into a storm over southern Ohio and broke up in the air with a loss of 14 officers and men. Twenty-seven of her complement were saved by riding sections of the ship to the ground as free balloons.

The "Shenandoah" disaster

A month later the German-built LZ-126 (ZR1-13), acquired by the United States under reparations agreements, arrived at Lakehurst. Commissioned as the "Los Angeles," she was operated for nine years on missions of many kinds, in all weather conditions, without accident or serious incident, an all-time record for airships. Decommissioned in June 1932, she was kept intact for test purposes and was finally broken up in 1939.

On the strength of the experience with the "Los Angeles," the navy ordered construction of two much larger ships, the "Akron" and the "Macon," from the U.S. Goodyear-Zeppelin Corporation. The "Akron" went into service on October 27, 1931. After a year and a half of active service, including successful experimentation as a carrier for fighter aircraft, she went down in a storm at sea, losing 73 officers and men.

The "Macon" was well along when the "Akron" was lost. She went into service on June 23, 1933, and operated successfully until February 12, 1935, when, after what appeared to be a minor structural failure, she collapsed and was lost off Point Sur, California. Most of her crew were rescued.

Graf von Zeppelin had died in March 1917, and Germany's defeat had stopped all airship construction except for those due for delivery to the Allies under the reparations program. Restrictions on commercial airship construction were relaxed in 1926, and work was started on LZ-127, best known as the "Graf Zeppelin." She was launched in September 1928. Under the command of Hugo Eckener, Zeppelin's successor, she explored many areas of the world as a passenger carrier. Her successful performance encouraged the construction of a much larger ship, the "Hindenburg," in the early 1930s.

During the summer of 1936 the "Hindenburg" made 10 routine round trips between Friedrichshafen and Lakehurst, New Jersey. On her first trip the following year (May 5–6) as she was approaching the mooring mast at Lakehurst, for reasons that have never been fully explained, the ship exploded and burned. She, like all her European predecessors, was hydrogen-filled.

Rotary-wing aircraft. Interest in vertical mechanical flight lapsed during World War I except for an abortive effort by a young Hungarian scientist, Theodore von Kármán, to substitute a tethered helicopter for the conventional gas-filled military observation balloon. During the 1920s, however, an amazing variety of experimental vertical risers appeared in Europe and in America, all conspicuously awkward and complicated in configuration, all conspicuously unsuccessful as flying machines. Most of these machines, with a great deal of thrashing about, managed to rise a few feet off the ground but once airborne proved to be virtually uncontrollable.

It remained for a Spanish engineer, Juan de la Cierva, in a search for an airplane that could be slowed down in flight and landed vertically, to provide the key to practical rotary-wing flight. Between 1920 and 1923 he built a series of machines with conventional airplane fuselages (including engine and propeller) above which was mounted in a horizontal position a large multibladed windmill. The unpowered windmill was free to rotate under aerodynamic forces as the machine was driven forward by the action of its normal propeller. This autorotation of the wing system produced the required lift and gave the device its name—the autogiro.

The autogiro

Cierva's work was uniformly unsuccessful until in 1923 he hit upon the idea of articulating (or hinging) the rotor blades at the hub and allowing them to respond individually to the aerodynamic and centrifugal forces involved (see Figure 46, left). This arrangement not only solved the immediate problems of the autogiro but provided the experience that paved the way for helicopter development of 1930 and later.

During the early 1930s the autogiro created a great wave of popular interest everywhere, particularly in Britain and in America. Ninety autogiros were in service by 1932 in the United States alone, some in the hands of private owners, some for advertising and publicity purposes, a few under experimentation by the military services and the Post Office Department, which considered them for transferring mail from post office rooftops to airfields.

Although design improvements were continuous during the 1930s, and many new applications for autogiros were found, the type had virtually disappeared by 1940 and is unlikely to be revived in any appreciable numbers, simply because there is nothing that autogiros could do that helicopters cannot do better and more economically. (See below *Developments after 1945: General aviation.*)

Aircraft-carrier operations. Carrier operations were forecast as early as 1911 when Eugene Ely made the first landings and takeoffs from a U.S. Navy ship in a Curtiss biplane. During World War I the Royal Navy of Great Britain developed the first true aircraft carrier, the HMS "Argus," converted from a commercial vessel. In the early 1920s both the United States and Japan took active interest. The USS "Langley" (converted from the collier "Jupiter") and the Japanese "Hosho" both went into operation in 1922. The Washington Arms Limitation Treaty of 1922 put a size limitation on conversions and new construction. During the late 1920s a number of such vessels were under construction, including the USS "Saratoga" and USS "Lexington." These were the experimental ships on which were tested the carrier-based aircraft and operating techniques that were to play such dramatic and determining roles in World War II, a dozen years later.

The first aircraft carrier

Blind-landing research. By the mid-1920s it became obvious that all aircraft operations, both military and commercial, had to be made independent of weather. By that time, long-range flights over land areas were feasible, using rudimentary radio direction finders and lighted beacons at night, but the problem of landing and takeoff when the pilot could not see where he was or where he was heading was still unsolved. Instrument displays in cockpits had vastly improved over the improvised arrangements of wartime, but the pilots of rapidly moving airplanes required a reliable fix in three-dimensional space for landing and takeoff in conditions of limited visibility.

To deal with this problem, the Daniel Guggenheim Fund established a Full Flight Laboratory at Mitchel Field, Long Island, in cooperation with the Army Air Corps and the several manufacturers of aircraft instruments. Lieut. (later Lieut. Gen.) James H. Doolittle was selected to head the operation. On September 24, 1929, in a fully hooded cockpit, he made the first completely blind flight in history, taking off, flying over a predetermined course, and landing at the point of departure, all by instruments alone.

Rocket research. The idea of flying by rocket power goes far back into history. By 1920 it had captured the imagination of Robert H. Goddard, a young professor of physics at Clark University in Worcester, Massachusetts, who had made his first theoretical studies of a liquid-fuel rocket in February 1909. His basic patent for a rocket apparatus was granted in July 1914, and in 1918 he developed and patented a rocket missile, the forerunner of the shoulder-type rocket launcher of World War II known as the bazooka.

Robert H. Goddard

In September 1916 he applied to the Smithsonian Institution for a research grant to continue his work on rockets. He received $5,000, and in September 1919 the Smithsonian published his classic paper, "A Method of Reaching Extreme Altitudes." The first experimental liquid-rocket flight was made on March 16, 1926, from a farm near Auburn, Massachusetts. Three years later and after a number of spectacular and noisy rocket firings, the local fire and police authorities suggested that he move to some more remote place. By 1930, supported by a grant of $50,000 from the Guggenheim Foundation, Goddard's entire operation was moved to a desert site near Roswell, New Mexico.

Meanwhile, rocket research was going forward independently elsewhere in the world. Unpublished in the '20s (but amply documented in later years), active rocket research was under way in the Soviet Union under the direction of Konstantin Tsiolkovsky. Germany's official interest in rockets as weapons stemmed from the limitations imposed by the Treaty of Versailles on development of conventional artillery. As a by-product of the military-research program, an active society for space travel by rocket was formed in 1927. The first flight of a rocket-powered aircraft was made on September 30, 1929, by Fritz von Opel in a glider with a gunpowder rocket attached to the rear.

Gliders and sailplanes. Between 1910 and 1920 interest in gliders almost disappeared. The airplane had taken over. Beginning in 1919, however, and again as a direct result of the limitations in the building and use of powered aircraft imposed on Germany by the Treaty of Versailles, a renaissance of gliding and soaring occurred. It is still actively going on.

At first ostensibly a sport, gliding in Germany became a means of training fighter and bomber pilots to man future Luftwaffe squadrons. Furthermore, the design and construction of light and efficient sailplanes gave German scientists and engineers an opportunity for sophisticated research in aerodynamics and in the efficient use of light materials, which proved useful in the early 1930s when Hitler abrogated treaty limitations and began to rearm Germany in the air.

The first glider competition

The first motorless aircraft competition was held in the Rhön Mountains in 1920. Some two dozen machines participated. Best performance was a flight of 6,000 feet (1,830 metres) in about $2^1/_2$ minutes. Two years later, a permanent soaring centre had been established at the Wasserkuppe in Germany, and competitions were being staged frequently in France, Switzerland, and England. Thousands of young glider pilots were in training. By that time, as a result of improvements in design and in piloting techniques, the soaring record had been raised to over three hours.

By 1930 development was well under way in America. A number of soaring and gliding sites had been established, notably at Elmira, New York, and on the West Coast near San Diego, where wind and terrain conditions were favourable.

Periodic competitions at such centres attracted machines and pilots from all over the world. Using highly efficient sailplanes and taking advantage of mechanical updrafts (along mountain ridges) and thermal updrafts (in the vicinity of thunderstorms), by 1930 altitudes of over 17,000 feet (5,180 metres) had been reached, and flight ranges extended to nearly 300 miles (480 kilometres).

Amphibians. In the early 1920s interest developed in amphibious airplanes that could operate equally well from land or from water. Chief proponent of the idea was an American engineer, Grover Loening. As a successor to an experimental air yacht, his first amphibian was test-flown in June 1924. In appearance it was unique—a biplane powered with an inverted Liberty engine on a deep fuselage-hull combination with a long, slipper-like forebody to protect the propeller. A number of these machines were built for the military services and Coast Guard and were eventually sold to a number of airlines and to a few private owners.

A number of smaller amphibious types appeared in Europe in the late 1920s (Schrek, Savoia, etc.). By 1929 Pan American Airways Corporation had begun service to South America using Sikorsky S-38 and S-40 amphibians, but these were shortly replaced by large flying boats.

In the next ten years, however, interest in amphibious aircraft declined. High first cost and maintenance expense limited their acceptance by both military and civilian users. In addition, the greatly increased availability of suitable landing fields all over the world reduced the advantage of their dual operational capability.

The rise of commercial air transport. Commercial air transport, the carrying of paying passengers from point to point on preannounced schedules, began with the inauguration of Graf von Zeppelin's airship service, Delag, in 1912, and revived briefly in 1919. Since that time, however, the only commercial lighter-than-air operation (apart from sight-seeing flights by blimps at such places as Miami and Los Angeles) was that offered by the "Hindenburg" in 1936. All other commercial development has been based on the use of airplanes and (more recently) on helicopters.

The first regular passenger flights

Shortly after the close of World War I, international air transport services in Europe began to proliferate. By 1920 passenger flights on regular schedules were offered between many major cities. The equipment was war surplus, ranging from converted small craft with one or two seats up to modified Handley Page and Farman bombers. Seating accommodations were Spartan at best, usually a row of wicker chairs replacing the former military gear in the uninsulated, unheated fuselages. Such ships were noisy and uncomfortable, and the passengers had to make the best of their situation with very little attention from the crews. Operating procedures were sketchy. Air-to-ground communications were uncertain or lacking. There was little available in the way of ground equipment, either for servicing the aircraft or for flight information for pilots. Originally all such services were far from reliable, and accidents were not uncommon.

Major European governments early recognized the economic and political advantages of airline development under their own flags and gave official encouragement in the form of substantial subsidies to their nationals to extend their air services on the Continent and out to their colonial possessions. In the course of 10 years, Europe was crisscrossed with a regular air transport network. During this period the great airlines of Europe had their origins—Imperial Airways Ltd. (later BOAC and BEA), Air France, KLM (Royal Dutch Airlines), Lufthansa, Swissair, Alla Littoria. Also, with increasing competition for passengers, the earlier converted bombers disappeared, and especially designed passenger aircraft with more comfortable accommodations and better services for the customers (both on the ground and in the air) became standard equipment.

While the European countries were underwriting their passenger-carrying systems, the United States was expanding its airways and airway communications for the benefit of its rapidly growing airmail system, operated by the Post Office Department. It was not until 1925 that private companies were encouraged to handle U.S. airmail under contract, actually as a form of subsidy to encourage the development of passenger traffic. The present U.S. airline system can trace its origins to legislation passed in 1925 and designed to connect a large number of American cities and towns to the transcontinental mail routes operated by the Post Office. Passenger service supported by the system began on April 4, 1927, with a flight from Boston to New York City. Passenger demand was light until Lindbergh's flight in May of 1927. From 1927 to 1930, business began to boom, encouraged by Lindbergh's survey flights around the United States and his pioneering of new routes to South and Central America. Pan American Airways was already reaching out into the international market. Internally, new transcontinental and interurban lines were being formed by merger. New equipment, including the famous Ford and Fokker trimotors and the Sikorsky Clippers, was becoming available.

DEVELOPMENTS FROM 1930 TO 1945

To pinpoint the exact time when aviation turned a corner and won recognition as an important contributing factor to the world's economy would be difficult, but a definite breakthrough in this realm did occur in the early 1930s. Aeronautical research programs that had been developing in university- and government-supported laboratories both in Europe and in America in the late 1920s began to produce results. A rapidly accumulating body of experimental data became available to aircraft and engine designers. It became possible to make accurate mathematical forecasts of performance and flight behaviour and to check out calculations in wind tunnels (up to full-scale) before subjecting machines to the hazards of free flight. Much of this information was circulated in the form of scientific reports or technical publications.

Simultaneously a growing cadre of young, optimistic, and enthusiastic aeronautical engineers and scientists was coming out of the schools and universities in Europe and the United States, all eager to apply these data to new designs that would fly higher, farther, faster. Apart from purely military objectives, there now emerged a new and eventually more important idea: that aircraft could be designed to produce profit for their owners in commercial operations.

As a result, the external configurations and the inboard arrangements of virtually all categories of airplane underwent radical changes in the 1929–32 period. There were occasional exceptions, but the average pre-1930 airplane was only slightly distinguishable from its World War I prototype—a wood, fabric-covered, "stick and wire" braced biplane with fixed-pitch propellers and an open or only partially enclosed, pilot's cockpit. Passenger accommodations (if any) were primitive.

Streamlining

By 1932 the impact of research was clearly in evidence. Streamlining had become the order of the day. Again, there were exceptions, but the average airplane in all categories became an externally smooth, internally braced, low-wing, all-metal monoplane with air-cooled engine (or engines) and with controllable-pitch propellers (*i.e.,* the blade angle could be adjusted); landing gear retracted completely in flight, and pilots and passengers were housed in insulated and sound-proofed compartments. Except that jet engines have replaced the 1930–40 air-cooled engine-and-propeller combination, the same general description applies to most military and commercial configurations of the 1980s.

Commercial aviation. *Europe.* In Europe, commercial air transportation was well developed by the early 1930s. By then the converted bombers from World War I had largely been replaced by aircraft designed primarily for the handling of passengers and cargo. For the western European services, because city-to-city distances were short, comfort and convenience for the passengers were more important than high speed. On long colonial routes, however, conditions were reversed. Passenger comfort was compromised in favour of higher speeds and longer range.

Most of the aircraft in use were multi-engined (usually three-engined) monoplanes, such as the German Junkers G 24 (prototype of the Ju 52), the French Wibaut 210, the Italian Savoia Marchetti SM.73, etc. Britain, however, for many years retained the huge, four-engined Handley Page biplanes that lumbered between London and Paris at about 100 mph (160 kph). In the late 1930s Imperial Airways introduced the fast and efficient four-engined "Ensign"-class monoplanes on many of its services. This machine was useful as a troop carrier in World War II.

U.S. emphasis on airmail service

United States. In the United States commercial air transport got off to a slow start. Until 1927 developmental emphasis was focussed on the airmail service rather than on passenger carrying. This in the end proved advantageous, for when the commercial demand developed, the country was already laced together by a network of established airways, beacon-lighted for night operations and equipped with relatively reliable radio navigation and communication facilities.

The United States airways system was operated by the Post Office Department until September 1, 1927, when the mail routes were turned over to a group of private corporations under contract. Under the impetus of U.S. government subsidy for carrying the mail, many small companies combined into larger units, extended their range of operations to more distant cities, and began to think in terms of improving and standardizing both ground and airborne equipment. About this time (1928) Henry Ford's interest in aviation led to the production of the Ford trimotor all-aluminum plane as a competitor to the all-wood Fokker trimotor, which was a civil version of the U.S. Army's Fokker bombers.

During the first few years of the 1930s, airline passengers in Europe and the U.S. totalled only a few thousand annually. Accidents were common, the fatality rate being about one for every 8,000,000 passenger-miles. But a decade later several million passengers a year were riding the world's airlines, and the average fatal accident rate had dropped to less than three for every 100,000,000 passenger-miles.

The most apparent change (from the standpoint of the travelling public) was in the aircraft themselves. Almost overnight (1933–34) old planes vanished, and in their places came the streamlined, all-metal, efficient, and comfortable Boeing 247D's, the Douglas DC-2's and 3's, and the Lockheed 10's. These were to become the nucleus of most air-transport fleets in America and in Europe for many years. They and their direct descendants established performance standards that served the travelling public well for more than a decade; *i.e.,* until the introduction of jet aircraft in the 1950s.

Flying boats

Intercontinental service. For intercontinental commercial transport it first appeared that the flying boat was the logical vehicle. During the 1930s these reached the peak of their development, both in Europe and in America. A German-built Dornier WAL flying boat successfully explored the North Atlantic routes in 1930, and in the same year the world's largest flying boat, the 12-motored Dornier Do X, built for Lufthansa, left Friedrichshafen in November and, after a series of accidents and mechanical delays, finally reached New York nine months later (August 1931). It was shortly abandoned to end its days in a German museum. Meanwhile, France had established a service across the South Atlantic using Latecoeur-300 flying boats.

By the summer of 1939 French, German, and Italian air services were operating regularly between Africa and South America. Germany, in particular, was penetrating deep into South America with passenger and cargo operations. It had also piled up three years' experience with mail-carrying seaplanes catapulted from ocean liners in both the North and South Atlantic. All such activity terminated with the outbreak of World War II.

Britain's Imperial Airways and Pan American Airways of the U.S. cooperated in opening up passenger services between North America and Europe. Both were operating experimental services between New York and Bermuda in 1937. Shortly thereafter, flights were extended across the North Atlantic via Newfoundland and Ireland or the Azores.

Pan American World Airways

The history of America's intercontinental airlines was, for many years, largely the history of Pan American World Airways. Founded in 1928, the company originally operated between Florida and Cuba; by 1938 routes circled South America and reached across the Pacific to Manila and across the Atlantic to England. Large amphibians, then two- and four-engined flying boats were used.

In opening its Pacific routes in 1935, the company put into service the Martin M-130 four-engined flying boat (see Figure 47). It was replaced in 1938 by the still larger Boeing 314 Clipper, which performed service in both the Atlantic and Pacific through World War II.

But the flying boat had outlived its usefulness as a

By courtesy of Pan American World Airways, Inc.

Figure 47: The China Clipper, flying over the partially completed Golden Gate Bridge in San Francisco, on the first day of its service to the Orient, November 22, 1935.

commercial vehicle, and by 1950 virtually all overseas schedules by major airlines were being flown by the more economical and more flexible land-type aircraft.

U.S. government regulation. The development of air transportation in the United States was not without problems. Assignment of routes and regulation of rates, certification and licensing of airplanes and pilots, and the establishment of safety standards came under the general purview of the Aeronautics Branch of the Department of Commerce. In 1934 a scandal over allegedly illegal contract awards led to the sudden cancellation of all existing domestic mail contracts. Concurrently, the President ordered the Army Air Corps to take over the airmail services. Many problems ensued, and a temporary airmail law was rushed through Congress to enable the mail services to be returned to private contractors. The bill carried with it provision for the appointment of a Federal Aviation Commission to make a study of the overall aviation situation and to make recommendations for its future reorganization. This resulted in the Civil Aeronautics Act of 1938 and the creation of a Civil Aeronautics Authority. Later, in July 1940, the Civil Aeronautics Authority became a licensing and regulatory agency within the Department of Commerce, and a Civil Aeronautics Board (directly under the secretary of commerce) was established to control airline economic and safety functions. In 1968 these agencies were transferred to the newly created Department of Transportation.

Origin of Civil Aeronautics Authority

General aviation. All nonmilitary and non-airline airplanes and helicopters are considered to be engaged in general aviation activities.

Long-distance flights. Popular interest in spectacular long-distance flights was strong up until the outbreak of World War II. Whereas successful ocean crossings had been the prime objectives of pilots in the late 1920s, around-the-world attempts provided headlines for the 1930s. Since no nonstop, around-the-world capability then existed, such flights of necessity required numerous refuellings en route. Refuelling in the air had previously been tested by Sir Alan Cobham in England and by the Air Corps in America, but the logistics of an around-the-world refuelling system were beyond then-current capabilities.

Notable around-the-world attempts. Wiley Post and Harold Gatty left Roosevelt Field, New York, on June 23, 1931, in the single-engined Lockheed monoplane "Winnie Mae" and returned to their starting point on July 1 after covering 15,474 miles (24,898 kilometres) around the Northern Hemisphere in eight days 16 hours flying time. Wiley Post took off alone in the "Winnie Mae" from Floyd Bennett Field, New York, on July 15, 1933, and returned on July 22, after covering 15,596 miles (25,094 kilometres) on the same course.

Amelia Earhart (after her successful solo transatlantic and transpacific flights) made two attempts at a world flight in a twin-engined Lockheed Electra with Fred Noonan as navigator. In March 1937 they took off on a westbound course from San Francisco, but sustained takeoff damage in leaving Honolulu, which necessitated shipping the airplane back to the United States for repair. On a second attempt they departed from Florida, eastbound, on May 21, crossed the South Atlantic, traversed Europe and southern Asia, and started across the Pacific from Australia. Somewhere in the vicinity of Howland Island they disappeared. In spite of an extensive sea and air search no traces were found.

Howard Hughes, a motion-picture producer and sportsman pilot, took off from Floyd Bennett Field on July 10, 1938, in a twin-engined Lockheed 14 with a crew of four. Three days and 19 hours later they returned, having flown some 15,500 miles (24,800).

Other notable long-range flights

In 1933 and again in 1939 Commander Richard E. Byrd and the Arctic explorer Lincoln Ellsworth led separate expeditions into Antarctica, exploring huge unknown areas by air.

In the summer of 1931 Col. and Mrs. Charles A. Lindbergh flew a single-engined Lockheed Sirius monoplane on floats to Shanghai, China, via Canada, Alaska, and Japan. In 1933, in the same aircraft, they made a survey flight on behalf of Pan American Airways over the North Atlantic to England, across Europe, down the West Coast of Africa, over the South Atlantic to Brazil, thence to New York City, a cruise of over 30,000 miles (48,000 kilometres).

In July 1933 the Italian air minister, Italo Balbo, led a flight of 24 twin-engined Savoia Marchetti flying boats from Italy to Chicago via Iceland, Labrador, and Canada. The squadron returned to Italy via New York.

In 1937 the Soviet Union established an air-supplied navigation and communications base on the ice less than 15 miles from the North Pole. In June, two Soviet single-engined monoplanes (using this facility for navigation purposes) made nonstop flights from Moscow to the United States, the first landing in Oregon and the second in central California.

Races. A notable sporting event of the period was the MacRobertson International Race from England to Australia staged in 1934. The winners were the British pilots C.W.A. Scott and T. Campbell Black flying a specially built twin-engined De Havilland Comet racer. Second and third places were won by standard American transport planes: a Douglas DC-2 flown by a KLM (Royal Dutch Airlines) crew, and a Boeing 247D flown by an American pilot, Roscoe Turner. The result had some influence on the subsequent decisions by a number of European airlines to adopt American flying equipment.

Closed-course racing, popular in the 1910–14 period, was revived both in Europe and in America. In theory, at least, the point of the competition was to improve the equipment. The most spectacular and probably the most costly show of this sort was the international competition for the Schneider Trophy. Established in 1913, it was awarded for top speed in a free-for-all class. In the early 1930s, annual races were run in highly specialized, high-powered seaplanes developed and flown under government sponsorship. In 1931 Britain, after winning it the two previous years, won permanent possession of the trophy with a Supermarine S.6B at 340 mph (544 kph). Several years later an Italian Macchi raised the record to 440 mph (704 kph). Many of the competing machines were direct ancestors of single-seat fighters of World War II. By 1939 a stripped-down, super-powered German Messerschmitt fighter (not in a race) was officially clocked at 469 mph (750 kph).

The Schneider Trophy

In Europe during the prewar period a number of less spectacular race meets were established under civilian auspices, designed for amateur participation. Every year, British pilots raced for the King's Cup over a course around the British Isles. Germany not only encouraged competition among glider pilots but fostered interest in amateur powered flying in annual round-Germany races. In the United States the National Air Races at Cleveland became annual September events. The practical value of such events is open to question. Though they were originally thought to be good publicity for aviation, the fact is that participation by amateur pilots in home-built racers sometimes left a trail of wreckage and fatalities that had the opposite effect.

Private flying. Far more important for the development of aviation was the great upsurge in private ownership of aircraft for business and personal use that followed the Depression years. This trend was visible both in Europe and in the United States. Flying clubs and both private and municipal flying fields became centres of popular interest. By 1939 there were over 33,000 certified civilian pilots in the United States, and the records show that private owners were logging over 50,000,000 miles (80,000,000 kilometres) of flying annually for business and pleasure.

In spite of these impressive totals, however, private flying was not yet firmly established. Wartime demands of the early 1940s channelled development in other directions.

Military aviation. During the 1920s economic conditions and arms-limitation agreements reduced most military budgets to a minimum and left relatively little for new aircraft. Behind the scenes, some aeronautical research and development went on in government and university circles, but until Italy, Japan, and Germany began rebuilding their military establishments in the early 1930s, little that was radically new came into aviation inventories.

Two new strategic concepts put into practice during the

period had far-reaching effects on developments throughout the 1930s and well beyond World War II. The first was typified in U.S. Gen. William ("Billy") Mitchell's publicly expressed conviction, which cost him his job and his rank by court-martial, in favour of an air force completely independent of ground and naval forces. The other was the Italian Gen. Giulio Douhet's doctrine that wars of the future would be won in the air by huge formations of bombers striking deep into enemy territory against industrial targets and centres of civilian population to disrupt production and to destroy national morale.

Two innovative tactical concepts were fully developed and widely employed in World War II. The first was the massive assault by paratroops with air-dropped supplies, developed first by the Soviet Union as early as 1932. The second was the intensive development of carrier-based aviation by the navies of the major powers. This greatly increased range and striking power of waterborne fleets and eventually all but eliminated the heavy battleship as a major element of naval power.

Active aerial warfare was resumed with Japan's invasion of Manchuria (1931) and Italy's war against Ethiopia (1935). Most of the aircraft used were derived from World War I types, but by the mid-'30s the effects of research and development programs began to be in evidence. The Spanish Civil War (1936) and the Russian attack against Finland (1939) offered testing opportunities for German, Italian, and Soviet planes and pilots that subsequently participated in World War II.

Germany's rearmament program began in 1933 when Adolf Hitler came to power. Consistent with the beliefs of General Mitchell, Hitler established an independent Luftwaffe (air arm). Between 1934 and 1939 German factories produced 15,927 combat aircraft and 13,889 trainers and other types.

The Luftwaffe

After 1936 Hitler took few pains to conceal his program. A number of qualified observers from the United States were permitted to visit certain factories and research centres and reported what they saw. But Britain, France, and the United States were slow to react. It was only after the Munich crisis of 1938 that Britain inaugurated an emergency air-force expansion, and it was not until after more than a year of active warfare that British factories began to approach the German output of aircraft. The French situation was even worse, and the defeat of 1940 prevented its being remedied.

In the U.S., though the failure of the army's attempt to carry the mails in 1934 attracted public and congressional attention, air corps appropriations, only $25,000,000 in 1933, rose only to $74,000,000 in 1938. Under the impetus of the outbreak of war in Europe they jumped to $320,000,000 in 1939. Finally, the German blitzkrieg of May 1940 led Pres. Franklin D. Roosevelt to propose a combined active strength for the air corps and the navy of 50,000 airplanes, backed by a production capacity of 50,000 new planes per year. The cost of such a program was estimated at over $7,000,000,000. Though the proposal seemed fantastic at the time, the actual accomplishments of the next five years went far beyond it. The magnitudes of the efforts of the United States, Germany, and Japan are shown in =-0943212 Table 4.

Table 4: Military Aircraft Production

year	U. S.*	Germany†	Japan‡
1939	2,141	8,000	. . .
1940	6,019	10,000	. . .
1941	19,433	11,500	5,090
1942	47,838	14,500	8,861
1943	85,898	23,500	16,693
1944	96,318	38,500	28,180
1945	47,714	. . .	11,066

**Aviation Facts and Figures*, Aircraft Industries Association of America (1953). †*Overall Report—European War*, U.S. Strategic Bombing Survey (1945) (rounded numbers). ‡*Effects of Strategic Bombing on Japan's War Economy*, USSBS (1946).

Research. In periods of international tension and of actual warfare, research is seldom pure; *i.e.*, it is seldom a search for new knowledge with which to augment the general welfare. It inevitably becomes developmental research; *i.e.*, research for the improvement of weaponry. This was the principal characteristic of aeronautical research of the period. In Germany, the theoretical work of scientists at Aachen and Göttingen was put to practical application at the laboratories of the Deutsche Versuchsanstalt für Luftfahrt (DVL) at Adlershof, and at the rocket research station at Peenemünde. Although it was not realized at the time, extensive research in supersonic aerodynamics, essential for the development of the V-2s and other rockets, was assigned to Gudonia, Italy's great research centre near Rome.

In the U.S. during the early 1930s, the research programs of the National Advisory Committee for Aeronautics Laboratories at Langley Field were directed toward the general improvement of commercial aviation, but beginning in 1937 the emphasis shifted to research directly connected with improving military aircraft.

The paragraphs following outline only a few of the more important areas of research covered by this period, particularly those that have had a major influence on present-day aircraft.

Jet propulsion. The most radical developments of the period occurred in jet propulsion. In 1928 an Englishman, Frank Whittle, published his fundamental thesis on the use of gas turbines for aircraft, and by 1930 he took out his first patents on a jet engine. Hans von Ohain, in Germany, doing research in the same area, applied for a patent in 1935. The first flight of a jet-powered aircraft was made by a Heinkel He 178 at Rostock, Germany, on August 27, 1939. The first Whittle engine (W-1) was flown in a Gloster E.28/39 at Cranwell, England, on May 15, 1941 (see Figure 48). In June 1941 a prototype W-1X Whittle engine was flown to the United States,

The first jet flight

By courtesy of the Royal Aeronautical Society

Figure 48: A Gloster E.28/39, a pioneer jet-propelled plane.

where copies were quickly made by General Electric, and an experimental aircraft was designed by Bell Aircraft of Buffalo. On October 1, 1942, the Bell XP-59A, powered by two GE I-16 engines, made the first U.S. jet flight at Muroc Lake, California.

The idea spread quickly. By the end of the war the Junkers Jumo 004 engine was in full production for the Messerschmitt Me 262 fighters, of which some 1,400 were produced. The Gloster Meteor twin-jet fighter was in limited production by the end of the war, but only a few reached service status, and no combat is on record. The U.S. Lockheed XP-80 fighter prototype was test-flown on January 9, 1944, with a British-built engine.

These events marked a major breakthrough in aviation. From this point there was almost no limitation to the power that could be applied for man flight. Horizons, in fact, became unlimited.

Rocket research. The flight of the first rocket-powered Opel glider in Germany (1929) has been noted (see above *Developments from 1918 to 1930: Rocket research*). That same year (though it was not known abroad until some time later) the Soviet Union published the first section of a nine-volume encyclopaedia on interplanetary flight. The first demonstration of a rocket-assisted takeoff took place in Germany. In 1930 the Deutsche Verein für Raumschiffahrt set up a test site near Berlin, and the German Army Ordnance Corps established a rocket weapon experimental station at Kummersdorf. Later (1937) the Rocket Test Center at Peenemünde was opened. The Soviet Union had already established rocket research centres at Moscow, Leningrad, and Kazan.

The V-2 rockets

During 1942 initial test flights were conducted at Peenemünde on the A-4 rocket, later widely known as the V-2. After several disastrous failures, the first successful launching occurred in October of that year. Two years later, after the usefulness of the V-1 pulse-jet-powered flying bomb had been neutralized by the British defenses, the first V-2 rockets began to fall on London. Between November 1944 and March 1945 over 1,200 of these weapons landed in the London area. Another 800 were used against Antwerp.

Meanwhile, in the U.S., Robert Goddard continued his rocket research. Early in 1930 he had moved his operations to a desert site near Roswell, New Mexico. There, for the next ten years (with occasional interruptions when funds ran out) he continued to work on liquid-fuelled rockets. The results of his work were carefully studied by the German rocket experts at the time, and similarities between Goddard's designs and the later V-2s are unmistakable.

Resurgence of the helicopter. For almost a decade interest in the helicopter seemed to have disappeared. In Germany, however, designers had been quietly at work. In 1937, without prior notice, the Focke-Achgelis Company announced that it had built a helicopter that had all the desired qualifications; *i.e.,* vertical ascent and descent, the ability to hover, and a capability of flying forward, backward, or sidewise at the will of the pilot. Skepticism, particularly in the United States, was dispelled by repeated cross-country flights (including one from Bremen to Berlin at an average speed of 68 mph [109 kph]) and by spectacular public demonstrations by Hanna Reitsch inside the great Deutschlandhalle in Berlin (1938). In the following year Ewald Rohlfs set an altitude record of 11,700 feet (3,565 metres), but there was little evidence of further helicopter development. No available records indicate the use of helicopters by Germany during the war.

About that same time a spark of interest came alive in the United States. Igor Sikorsky, who had tried and failed to fly helicopters in Russia in 1910–11 (see above *Developments from 1900 to 1914: Helicopters*) and had then focussed his interest on airplanes, designed and built an experimental machine under the aegis of United Aircraft Corporation. The first flight of the VS-300, with Sikorsky at the controls, occurred on September 14, 1939. During 1940 he was able to stay in the air for 15 minutes at a time and in 1941 set an official world's endurance record of one hour 32½ minutes. Although the machine was demonstrated successfully for the NACA, the Air Corps, and the U.S. Navy, the increasingly heavy pressures of wartime put off further development of the helicopter until after 1945.

Balloon research. Despite the use of barrage balloons to protect cities against aerial bombardment, and an abortive attempt by Japan to bomb the United States mainland by drifting explosives in free balloons across the Pacific (1944–45), the most significant employment of balloons during the period was in the area of upper-atmosphere research.

Until 1931 the highest human penetration of the Earth's atmosphere had been at about 35,000 feet (10,700 metres) by A. Berson and A.J. Süring (1901). The limiting factor had been the inability of the aeronauts to survive low temperatures and pressures in an open balloon basket.

Auguste Piccard's ascensions

Early in 1930 Auguste Piccard, a Swiss physicist, conceived the idea of enclosing crew and scientific instruments in an airtight, pressurized, and air-conditioned spherical gondola suspended from a balloon. With such equipment he reached an altitude of 51,775 feet (15,781 metres) in May 1931, and 53,152 feet (16,201 metres) in August 1932. In 1933 three Soviet scientists (G. Profkoviet, F.N. Birnbaum, and K.D. Godunow) were reported to have reached 60,680 feet (18,495 metres) in a similar balloon.

In the United States, under the auspices of the air corps, the navy, and the National Geographic Society, a number of upper-atmosphere research flights were made between 1933 and 1935, the most successful of which took place on November 11, 1935, when Capt. A.W. Stevens and Capt. O.A. Anderson of the air corps set an altitude record at 72,395 feet (22,066 metres).

DEVELOPMENTS AFTER 1945

Early in 1944, when jet propulsion was familiar chiefly to readers of science fiction, the following prescient comment appeared (*Wings After War,* page 11, Duell, Sloan & Pearce Inc., N.Y. 1944):

> There is little reason to expect that the jet principle will have any appreciable effect on post-war commercial aviation of the next five years. Ten years from now the picture may be different.

By 1955 the picture had indeed changed. All major powers had adopted jet propulsion for combat aircraft. All major airlines were deeply involved in the design and procurement of jet-powered passenger and cargo planes and were watching with intense interest the performance of a four-jet De Havilland Comet (1952), a turbine propeller-driven Vickers Viscount (1953), first placed in service on Britain's airlines in 1953–54, and the French Caravelle with twin jets mounted at the rear of the fuselage.

Fifteen years later the revolution was complete. Research and development had solved the problem of speed with economy, and the conventional engine-plus-propeller combination that dominated the scene until the end of World War II virtually disappeared from both military and commercial aircraft. By 1970 this configuration was limited almost entirely to general aviation types.

Postwar expansion

Commercial aviation. Commercial air transport revived and expanded rapidly after the war. In 1939 U.S. air carriers had carried fewer than 2,000,000 passengers with a combined fleet of some 340 aircraft. A decade later, they handled over 16,700,000 passengers with an inventory of some 1,080 aircraft. In 1949, however, all these machines were direct descendants of prewar configurations, including DC-3s, DC-4s, DC-6s, Convair 240s, Martin 202s, and Lockheed Constellations. All were powered by two or four radial air-cooled engines with conventional propellers.

Between 1949 and 1959 the revolution came. The first jet airplane to appear on commercial routes was the British De Havilland Comet, which began service in 1952. Two serious accidents, later shown to have been caused by metal fatigue, led to the grounding of the aircraft. It was reintroduced into commercial service in 1958. In spite of this discouraging experience, the swing toward all-jet operation began.

America's first jet transport, the prototype four-engined Boeing 707, was first test-flown on July 15, 1954. It went into airline service in 1958. Other jet types soon began to appear. Boeing 720, Convair 880, McDonnell Douglas DC-8, Vickers VC10, the three-jet Boeing 727, the British Aircraft Trident, and the Sud-Aviation Caravelle, the twin-jet Boeing 737, BAC One-Eleven, McDonnell Douglas DC-9, and Dassault SE-20. By 1969 U.S. airlines were flying some 2,200 turbine-powered aircraft with fewer than 300 piston-powered machines remaining in their inventories. By the 1970s most of these had also disappeared.

During the 1950s and 1960s the Soviets, also starting from scratch, made great strides in their development of jet-powered and turboprop commercial air-transport equipment. Beginning with the post-World War II development of twin-engined propeller-driven machines (similar in size and performance to the U.S. DC-3's), they produced in a little over a decade a large fleet of pure jet and turboprop transports of a size and capability equal to any in the world. Typical are the Tu-104 pure jet and the large multiple turboprop transport the Tu-114.

Originally, jet-powered transports were accepted reluctantly by operators, who were dubious as to their technical and economic feasibility. Experience soon indicated, however, that maintenance and operating problems were not as formidable as had been anticipated, and the availability of fast, safe, comfortable transportation to virtually any point on the globe created a new travel demand that very quickly made airlines the dominant form of transportation. There was a comparable growth in cargo transportation.

In 1970 notably larger aircraft appeared. Besides longer versions of the DC-8 and 727 (stretched to increase their passenger capacity), a number of wide-bodied jets came into service. An example of these is the Boeing 747, a 720,000-pound (327,300-kilogram), four-jet aircraft 185 feet (56.4 metres) long, carrying, depending upon seating arrangement, between 365 and 490 passengers at 625 mph (1,000 kph). Several European designs for "Airbus" configurations were in prospect. All of these aircraft were subsonic.

Supersonic flying

Faster jet aircraft also were exhibited in the spring of 1970, when the British-French Concorde (see Figure 49) and the Soviet Tu-144 first flew at supersonic speeds. Both are Mach 2 aircraft, with approximately 1,200 mph (1,900 kph) maximum speed. Commercial transatlantic services were introduced in the late 1970s.

The possibility of adverse environmental effects was cited by opponents of supersonic aircraft in the United States. A government contract was awarded to the Boeing Company for a Mach 3 supersonic transport (SST). According to the original plans the plane was expected to fly in 1972, but in the spring of 1971 the U.S. Congress cut off all government funding for this purpose.

General aviation. Favourable economic conditions in the United States fostered an enormous postwar growth in non-airline flying. This category includes more than 50 times as many machines as are in the combined U.S. airline fleets, and they carry more passengers annually. Great interest in non-airline flying exists in many countries, but on a much smaller scale. (S.P.J.)

Business aircraft. The largest general aviation aircraft are those operated by international companies, which frequently use them for transoceanic flights. The aircraft employed may be current medium-range jet airliners that have been equipped with special interiors and fuel tanks for intercontinental range. Alternatively, they may be special-purpose business jet aircraft intended for as many as 15 passengers. Such aircraft are operated to airline standards in terms of flight crew, navigational equipment, all-weather capability and performance, and licensing standards. The next category consists of the smaller special-purpose jets capable of carrying six to 10 passengers in comfort at 450 miles (725 kilometres) per hour for distances of up to 1,200 miles (1,900 kilometres). In general, these aircraft are able to operate from hard runways of about 4,000 feet (1,200 metres). Next in size and performance are turboprop executive aircraft, which cruise at approximately 300 miles (480 kilometres) per hour over distances of at least 1,000 miles (1,600 kilometres), carrying up to 10 passengers. As might be expected from their lower speed, they are significantly cheaper than the pure jets in purchase cost and in the expense of operation. Aircraft in the above categories are invariably operated by full-time professional flight crews; for long hauls a relief crew may also be carried.

Use of airline standards in business aircraft

Transatlantic flights by business aircraft are commonplace, and at least one type of business aircraft can fly from New York to London nonstop. A small number of international corporations use such aircraft extensively for long-distance overseas flights of 2,000–3,000 miles (3,200 to 4,800 kilometres). Special high-frequency radio communication equipment is fitted in these aircraft as well as Doppler or inertial navigation systems. Special arrangements are often required for their servicing and maintenance if their stay abroad is lengthy. Flight planning, customs, and proof of airworthiness may necessitate special arrangements when planes visit foreign countries for the first time.

Despite the costs, a large corporation can achieve considerable savings in executive staff time, and even in travel costs by operating its own aircraft, if scheduled flights to necessary destinations are infrequent or nonexistent. Where plants are far apart, a company aircraft is almost essential for staff mobility and shipment of critical materials. Investment grants, depreciation, and tax allowances can often be used to reduce the funding and operating costs.

Smaller aircraft, usually below 6,500 pounds (2,950 kilograms) gross weight, are used extensively by smaller businesses and by larger firms to fill in for the bigger corporate aircraft on short flights. Planes of smaller firms are often flown by the owner or by company staff. With the advent of the small, supercharged piston engine, these aircraft may have pressurized cabins and be capable of ranges up to 1,200 miles at altitudes of over 20,000 feet (6,000 metres). They will have full radio and navigation systems, autopilots, and often anti-icing.

Further down the scale are the lighter, unpressurized twin- and single-piston-engine aircraft, with seating for four or more. These represent the minimum investment and, though usually fully equipped with radio and navigation aids, may lack full all-weather capability because of limited altitude performance. Typically, this category flies below 10,000 feet (3,000 metres) at between 160 and 230 miles per hour (260 and 370 kilometres) over ranges from 500 to 600 miles (up to 1,000 kilometres).

Business aviation costs

Capital cost is a major factor in purchasing a business aircraft, and it is reflected in depreciation, insurance, hangar costs, and, to some extent, crew salaries. Operating costs include these factors, together with fuel and oil, main-

The Press Association Ltd.

Figure 49: The Concorde, a British-French supersonic jetliner, taking off from Heathrow Airport, London, September 14, 1970.

tenance, landing, parking and navigation fees, handling charges, customs charges, and license fees. Some costs, such as fuel and oil, are directly related to the annual aircraft use (*i.e.,* the number of aircraft flying hours in a year). The greater the use, the lower the cost per flying hour, a common cost criterion for this class of aircraft. Utilizations of over 400 hours are desirable to make economic use of the capital cost of a large business aircraft. (A.H.St.)

Although their number were relatively small in the late 20th century, helicopters and STOL (short takeoff and landing) machines were increasingly popular. In the latter category, more interest was evidenced in Europe, where distances are generally shorter and local airports smaller. An increasing number of STOL transports for 10 to 20 passengers were available, including Canada's De Havilland, Britain's Britten-Norman, and the Short Brothers Skyvan, Germany's Dornier, and Switzerland's Pilatus Porter. In the U.S., Fairchild Hiller, Robertson, Helio, and Wren were developing similar machines designed to operate from runways less than 500 feet (150 metres) long.

Helicopter types. As with other forms of aircraft, the size and shape of helicopters relate to the missions that they are intended to perform. Their range and carrying capacity are of an order of magnitude less than that of present-day airplanes. The smallest are spiderlike devices built to carry one man. They consist of little more than a bare framework on tripod legs, fitted with a minimal seat for the pilot, a bracket to support a small gasoline engine, topped by a short pylon to carry a two-bladed rotor. A short tube attached to the pylon and projecting some six feet (two metres) aft carries the necessary vertical stabilizing rotor. Such machines have little civilian use, except for recreation, and only limited military application.

The most common helicopter type in civilian use is the two-, three-, or four-seat machine with single rotor, fitted with a bubble-like canopy or cabin over the pilot and passenger compartment in the nose. The tail rotor is usually supported on an open structural framework or on a light, tapered monocoque beam. Normal power plants are four- or six-cylinder, flat, air-cooled gasoline engines, but small turboprop engines have been used in some larger machines. Landing gear is usually a pair of simple ski-like skids.

Because of relatively high first cost and maintenance expense, few helicopters are privately owned. Business and commercial applications for the smaller machines are many, and the list is growing. Because of their manoeuvrability and hovering capabilities they lend themselves well to crop dusting, insect control, and conservation operations. Municipal and highway authorities, police and fire departments, ambulance operators, commercial photographers, and news agencies find increasing use for the two- to four-seat machines. Helicopter platforms are being installed in increasing numbers on or adjacent to municipal buildings, hospitals, and business centres.

Helicopter applications

Some of the larger single-rotor machines, designed originally for military use, are handling many unusual assignments. Oil companies operating wells far out in coastal waters or deep in inaccessible regions use fleets of helicopters to service and supply the drilling sites. Cross-country pipelines can be easily inspected and serviced by means of helicopters. Power companies transport cable, heavy hardware, even poles and steel towers by helicopter to sites that cannot be reached by road. Heavy machinery can be positioned on the tops of high buildings. The scope of such activities will undoubtedly be greatly extended.

Military helicopters are frequently employed for civilian disaster relief and in support of nonmilitary scientific activities. Thousands of tons of food and medical supplies were flown by helicopter into the devastated areas of East Pakistan (later Bangladesh) following the hurricane and tidal floods in the autumn of 1970.

For passenger transport in urban areas, particularly to shuttle passengers between airports and city centres, the larger, single- or twin-rotor machines are finding acceptance. They are powered by two interconnected turboprop engines. A crew of three and up to 25 passengers and their luggage can be carried in accommodations similar to those available in the smaller commercial planes. These machines operate from small spaces located on high buildings or at convenient waterfront sites and deposit their passengers alongside airline terminals for transfer to transport planes. They also serve to interconnect suburban and downtown centres on regular schedules. Such services have been offered for several years in leading European and U.S. cities.

Principles of modern helicopter operation. The principle of helicopter flight is very simple, but the practice proved considerably more difficult. Satisfactory control while hovering posed the greatest difficulty. As with an airplane propeller, thrust (in this case, lift) is developed by imparting velocity to a body of air flowing through the rotor. The lift is proportional to the change in momentum (mass times velocity) of the air. To limit the power required and to facilitate control in flight, all rotary-wing aircraft employ rotors of large diameter, turning at relatively slow speeds.

Rotor systems are normally composed of two to six blades connected to a single hub. Each blade is, in effect, an airfoil of very high aspect ratio (length to chord; *i.e.,* long and slender), which responds to aerodynamic forces developed by the airflow around it. For a given rate of revolution, however, airflow varies widely in velocity and direction from hub to tip; therefore, the lift and drag vary along each blade for each segment of a revolution. There is no steady-state condition along the blades, as is normal for an airplane wing in forward flight at a given speed.

When airflow induced by rotation is modified by edgewise translation (straight-line movement) of the rotor system, another complication develops. On the side where a blade is advancing into the airstream, the rate of flow over any blade element is the sum of the rotational and translational velocities. The lift is high. On the opposite side of the rotor, the blade is moving downwind, and its relative air speed is the difference between the two velocities. At some point on the blade the airflow and the resultant lift may be zero. In any case, it is clear that, unless some form of compensation is designed into the system, the total effect is an imbalance of the lift and drag forces acting on opposite blades, which would seriously affect rotor stability.

Imbalance of forces

The common method of compensation for lift variation is to make the blades quite flexible and sometimes to hinge them at the hub. Thus, in a single revolution each blade accommodates itself (within preset mechanical limits) to the loads imposed upon it, flapping up or down as the lift varies and speeding up or slowing down in the plane of rotation in accordance with variations in drag and torque (turning force). Articulation at the hub also relieves the severe bending stresses and stresses resulting from repeated application of loads (fatigue stresses) that normally would occur with rigid fastening. The mechanism is complicated, and its weight offsets some of the gain from the use of lighter primary structure in the blades. The availability of materials of improved fatigue resistance, however, makes feasible rigid hub assemblies that rely on blade flexibility to absorb the stresses.

Power to turn the rotor system may be derived from the aerodynamic reaction of airflow induced by motion through the air, as in an autogiro, or from power applied to the rotor shaft by a piston engine or a geared gas turbine. When power is applied to a helicopter rotor shaft, the turning reaction tends to rotate the vehicle as well as rotor but in an opposite direction. For single-rotor helicopters, an opposing turning moment (rotational force) is produced by a small, vertical tail rotor driven by gears and shafting from the main engine or turbine. By controlling the pitch of the tail rotor blades, thus increasing or decreasing its horizontal thrust, directional control of the vehicle is secured.

A balance in turning forces may also be secured by mounting two lifting rotors driven in opposite direction by the same power plant. A tandem arrangement is frequently used for large transport or cargo types in which long fuselages are needed. A smaller and more compact design utilizes twin rotors intermeshed as in an eggbeater.

Helicopters cannot depend on the usual devices provided

for airplanes for stability and control. In hovering and at low forward (or backward) speeds, little or no airflow exists to react with aerodynamic stabilizers, movable control surfaces, etc. Control comes from pitch changes in the rotor system, either collective (in which all blades are adjusted to the same pitch) or cyclic (in which the pitch of each blade varies throughout the 360 degrees of a revolution) or a combination of both. All flight manoeuvres, up, down, forward, backward, side-wise, or in any desired combination, can be accomplished by pitch changes and power setting. Collective pitch is usually controlled by a horizontal lever at the pilot's elbow ("up" to rise; "down" for descent). Cyclic pitch is generally controlled from a stick in front of the pilot, as in a fixed-wing airplane. Movement of the stick adjusts flight attitude and direction, fore and aft, laterally, or in any combination.

Pitch changes

A helicopter lacks the static stability and control damping (the tendency of controls to return to a neutral position) characteristic of fixed-wing aircraft. It is, therefore, inherently more difficult to learn to control. Sophisticated instrumentation has been developed to ease the problem for both the trainee and the experienced pilot.

The design of landing gear for helicopters is relatively simple. Because they touchdown normally at zero forward and vertical velocities, the dynamic loads imposed by airplanes during landings are eliminated. Simple wheels or skids or both, without complicated shock-absorbing devices, are generally all that is needed. Also, because of the relatively high drag of the overall system, there is little to be gained by retracting landing gear in flight.

Crop dusting. Substantial numbers of general-use aircraft are employed in agriculture, mainly for the spreading of insecticides over large farm areas. Crop dusting began in the late 1920s with surplus World War I airplanes fitted with powder-storage bins and crude distribution devices. These proved effective but hazardous because of the low-altitude flight requirement, including the need for frequent tight turns near the ground. Machines specially designed for low-level, highly controllable slow flight have become available that are effective in spreading large loads of powder or liquids, or both, accurately and evenly over large areas.

Private aircraft. On the strictly private, flying-for-fun side, less than 20 percent of the more than 500,000 licensed private pilots in the U.S. own aircraft. The majority rent planes on an hourly basis, or participate in flying clubs that own and service the planes to be rented to members at relatively low rates. (S.P.J.)

"Home builts"

The smallest aircraft in the private category are the "home builts" or "ultralights." Many of these are superb examples of ingenuity, workmanship, and aerodynamic efficiency. Design, construction standards, and licensing are usually controlled by national bodies, such as the Experimental Aircraft Association in the United States and the Popular Flying Association in the United Kingdom, which have the approval of the national aviation regulatory body. Home builts, often powered by automobile engines, have been produced for as little as $2,000.

Since the 1960s, motorized gliders have been produced commercially, particularly in Europe (140 in West Germany alone), and these represent a halfway step between the ultralights and the more conventional light aircraft. One- and two-seat versions are available, fully certificated, and because of their inherent aerodynamic efficiency, they offer excellent fuel economy at a cruise speed of about 100 miles (160 kilometres) per hour. Some private rotorcraft exist, the majority of which are autogiros. These are usually single-seat kit-built aircraft, with cruising speeds of 60 to 70 miles (95 to 110 kilometres) per hour and limited range. Landing and takeoff runs required are only about 50 feet (15 metres).

The next large category, one- to four-seat single-engined aircraft, is by far the most popular in every country, representing, for example, 83 percent of general aviation aircraft in the United States in 1968. These aircraft are fitted with engines of from 90 to 250 horsepower and cruise between 100 and 200 miles (160 and 320 kilometres) per hour over distances up to 1,000 miles (1,600 kilometres). This class of aircraft is manufactured principally in the United States, France, and Germany. Metal construction is almost universal, though reinforced plastic has also been used. Equipment varies enormously and may be extensive in the larger aircraft; the cost of equipment may well add 50 percent to the bare aircraft cost. A number of types can be fitted with floats for water operation or with skis for snow landing and takeoff. A few true amphibians, capable of landing on land or water, are also available. Aircraft in this size category are capable of operating from 2,000-foot (600-metre) strips, many requiring less than half this distance. Their unsupercharged engines, however, reduce their effective use in areas where the ground is 5,000 to 10,000 feet (1,500 to 3,000 metres) above sea level.

One minor category of private air transportation is the free balloon. A number are registered in Europe, particularly in Switzerland, and are normally of the hot-air type. Small private airships also exist, classified as business aircraft.

Private balloons

In less populous parts of the world, where distances are large, as in Australia, Africa, South America, and Canada, light aircraft have been a vital method of transportation for as long as 40 years. Casualty evacuation, transport of doctors, and freighting of vital supplies are among the uses remote regions make of such aircraft. In Canada, extensive use is made of the country's thousands of lakes to operate float planes.

Where landing is impossible, ingenious methods of air dropping and picking up are used. In most remote-area operations, funds, and consequently facilities, are at a minimum; the use of rotorcraft has not so far made a great impact except for exploration and survey work.

The regulation of private flying, both in terms of pilot licensing and aircraft certification, is similar to that employed for commercial aircraft. Efforts usually are made to simplify the procedures to reflect the less sophisticated requirements of the majority of lighter aircraft. (A.H.St.)

With increased interest in personal and private flying there has come a revival of sporting aspects of all kinds, including high-speed, closed-circuit racing, gliding and soaring competitions, parachute jumping, sky diving, model flying contests, and even hot-air balloon racing.

Military aviation after 1945. By early 1960 most military and naval combat aircraft had shifted to jet power. In the U.S. the rocket-powered Bell X-1 had demonstrated (October 1947) that the so-called sonic barrier was not impregnable. Soon the new fighter aircraft of all major powers were supersonic.

As flying speeds increased, the performance capabilities of the aircraft began to exceed the physical limitations of human pilots. More and more automatic electronic equipment was necessary for the detection, pursuit, and destruction of enemy aircraft. Some single-seat fighters began to approach the size and weight of some bombers of World War II.

External configurations also changed. Swept-back wings and delta plan forms replaced the straight or tapered wings of World War II types. The U.S. McDonnell Douglas F-4 Phantom series, the Anglo-French Jaguar swept-wing interceptor, and the Swedish Saab AJ 37 delta-wing tailless canard are good examples. Soviet fighters exhibited similar characteristics.

In the late 1960s several variable-geometry arrangements (with sweep or wing camber variable at will to achieve maximum efficiencies in slow-speed or high-speed flight regimes) were tested in the U.K. and U.S. The most novel fighter of the period was the Hawker Siddeley Harrier with both direct-lift capability at zero forward speed and Mach 2 capability in normal flight.

Bomber types have also undergone radical changes. Jet engines and aerodynamic improvements (*e.g.*, swept wings) have made higher speeds possible. In-flight refuelling from aircraft tankers has extended flight ranges.

In the early 1950s the prototypes of Britain's V series bombers were flying (Avro Vulcan, H.P. Victor, and Vickers Valiant) and the six-jet swept-wing Boeing B-47 was replacing the B-29s in the U.S. Strategic Air Command (SAC). In 1957 the B-47s were replaced by eight-jet Boeing B-52s. Also in 1957 SAC acquired the first Mach 2 bomber,

Modern bomber types

a four-jet delta-winged B-58 Hustler. More than 100 were built. Some were still in service in 1970, though production had been terminated in the early 1960s. In 1957 a contract was let for three experimental Mach 3 bombers. A prototype was built and flown in the fall of 1964, but the project was eventually abandoned (1968) in view of increasing intercontinental missile capability.

The military requirement for intelligence, both strategic and tactical, has forced the development of reconnaissance aircraft carrying extensive electronic and photographic gear. In the early 1950s surplus bombers and transport types were modified for the purpose, but as the Cold War progressed the need for sophisticated equipment for the collection of data over large areas of the world was recognized. Highly specialized aircraft were developed for such purposes; *e.g.,* naval, land, and carrier-based antisubmarine tracking and patrol machines; the much-publicized U-2 high-altitude reconnaissance and meteorological research plane of the late 1950s; and the long-range Mach 3 Lockheed SR-71 strategic reconnaissance aircraft in use by the USAF. In the 1960s much of this activity shifted to reconnaissance satellites.

Worldwide military and diplomatic operations require a capability to move officials, troops, and supplies rapidly over long distances on short notice. All major powers maintain transport fleets, ranging from luxurious high-speed jets and helicopters for official use to huge personnel and cargo carriers capable of delivering men, heavy equipment, and supplies to remote areas, sometimes by parachute. In 1969 the largest machine for such purposes, the Lockheed C-5 Galaxy, went into service with the USAF. This aircraft, with a gross weight of 728,000 pounds (330,900 kilograms), cruises above 400 mph (640 kph) over ranges up to 5,500 nautical miles (6,335 statute miles, or 10,190 kilometres).

The Skycrane

The most unusual items in the transport category are the large helicopter "Skycranes" designed to lift large and bulky loads over relatively short distances. Such machines have been under development in the Soviet Union and in the United States and are in active military service in a number of areas.

With the end of World War II, the aircraft-carrier fleets of the combatants were largely decommissioned or destroyed. The surviving naval powers, however, continued operational development with a limited number of aircraft carriers. Aircraft in service include carrier-based strike fighters, antisubmarine search and destroy aircraft, carrier- and land-based transports, helicopters, and a few amphibians. The strike and attack types are high-performance, catapult-launched jets with supersonic capability. The others, except for the helicopters, are generally propeller-turbine- or propeller-engine-powered.

For landing on carriers, naval aircraft (except helicopters) are provided with reinforced fuselage structures and retractable tail hooks to engage arresting gear on landing decks. The most unusual feature of ASW (antisubmarine warfare) types for tracking and early warning is a housing for a radar antenna resembling a large pie plate mounted over the midsection of the fuselage.

An outstanding development of the military actions in Korea and in Indochina was the use of helicopters in large numbers for transport of troops and supplies, for evacuation of wounded, and as gun ships firing both rockets and normal ordnance.

Research. During the course of World War II the emphasis in all countries was on aeronautical development; *i.e.,* accepting the best scientific data available and applying them to the improvement of existing aircraft to outperform those of the enemy. In the first postwar decade, as immediate pressures were removed and as general economic conditions improved, funds again became available for long-range scientific research in aeronautics. Although such work made considerable progress in the U.K. and Canada and revived in other countries, the most extensive and most widely reported research was performed by the then National Advisory Committee for Aeronautics (now the National Aeronautics and Space Administration, or NASA) at its laboratories at Langley Field, Virginia; Moffett Field, California; and at Cleveland, Ohio; and its Test Flight Centers at Edwards Air Force Base, California, and at Wallops Island, Virginia.

Some of the aircraft-oriented projects undertaken since World War II, indicating the scope and extent of the work, are trans-sonic wind-tunnel research that resulted in the so-called Coke-bottle shape for fuselages and swept- or delta-wing configurations for supersonic aircraft; flight tests on supersonic aircraft to determine stability and control characteristics; studies on variable-geometry wing configurations; analysis of structural flutter and vibration problems at high speeds; studies of helicopter stability and control; research in wind tunnels and in towing basins on high-speed submarines and on jet-powered flying boats; studies of arrested landing problems on carrier decks and on short runways; analyses of flexible-wing aircraft; studies of aerodynamic heating and the behaviour of aircraft materials at high temperatures; vertical takeoff and landing research; and research, development, and flight-testing the X-15 high-altitude Mach 6 airplane.

The X-15 airplane

Of these, the last is of particular significance, for the X-15 may represent the ultimate in airplane performance and bridge the gap between man flight in the Earth's atmosphere and man flight in space. Three of these special-purpose research machines were built under joint auspices of the U.S. Air Force, Navy, and NASA and flown by their pilots. First flight occurred on June 8, 1959, and in the following ten years (to September 28, 1968) a total of 197 flights were made. Speeds over 4,500 mph (7,200 kph) and altitudes of over 350,000 feet (106,700 metres) were attained.

PRINCIPLES OF AIRCRAFT DESIGN AND OPERATION

Aerodynamic principles. A stream of air blowing squarely against a flat plate exerts a dynamic pressure on the plate more or less proportional to its velocity. The faster the wind, the higher the pressure. This phenomenon may be easily demonstrated by holding a hand out of the window of a moving automobile. By inclining the hand with respect to the wind, upward or downward forces are experienced, roughly proportional to the angle of inclination and the speed of the vehicle.

Flat plates (or human hands) are poor aerodynamic shapes. They are not streamlined; that is, air does not flow smoothly around them. Because of this, irregular pressures and vortices (eddies) create a turbulent region behind them (Figure 50A), which absorbs considerable energy and results in high resistance, or drag. Also, the vertical reactions (lift) are irregular, unstable, and relatively small. The ratio of lift to drag is low.

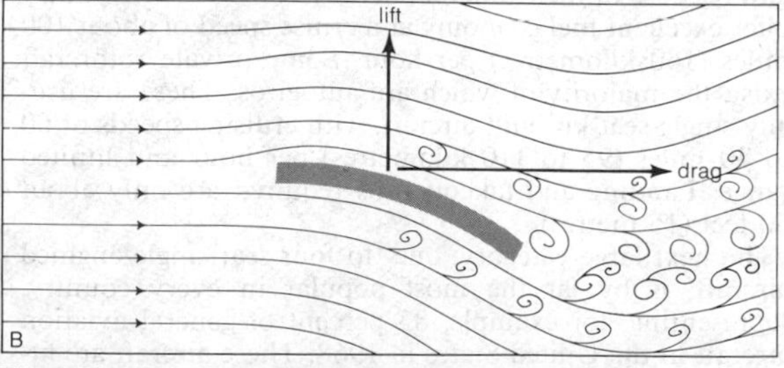

Figure 51: *Effect of airflow against a plate.*
(A) Airflow from left against flat vertical plate creates turbulence and severe drag. (B) Airflow over cambered plate creates drag, but also some lift. By modifying section shape (see Figure 51), the lift-to-drag ratio can be greatly improved.

Camber

Wing shape. Lift can be improved by putting a small degree of camber (curvature) in a thin, flat plate presented edgewise to the wind (Figure 50B). The flow of air at small inclinations becomes smoother. Up to a certain angle of attack, the turbulence is small, the lift increases, and the lift-to-drag ratio improves. Beyond the critical angle, however, the smooth flow breaks down, and the lift-to-drag ratio deteriorates rapidly.

In considering composite aerodynamic bodies (*e.g.,* an airplane with body, wings, tail surfaces, and other protuberances), drag comes, first, from the friction arising from motion through the air and the resulting turbulence and, second, from the horizontal component of the lifting force developed by the wing. Total drag is the sum of the two.

Aerodynamic research in wind tunnels early indicated that, by rounding and thickening the forward third of a curved plate and providing a smooth, curved taper to a sharp rear (trailing) edge, lift goes up and drag goes down. The lift-to-drag ratio is considerably increased. Such shapes are called airfoils. Many thousands of variations in thickness and in contour have been tested and the changes in lift and drag with angle of attack recorded. These tabulations provide the design data for airplane wings, propeller blades, helicopter rotor blades, and other streamlined bodies. There is no one best shape for all conditions. Each application requires detailed analysis to select the optimum shape to produce the desired aerodynamic performance.

It was first assumed that lift results from direct air pressure against the undersurface of a wing, as with kites. for this reason, fabric covering was applied to the lower wing surface only, leaving the structural framing exposed on top. Research soon revealed, however, that approximately two-thirds of the upward reaction comes from negative air pressure (suction) over the top of a wing and about one-third from the undersurface (Figure 51). Simple covering over the top surfaces greatly improved flight efficiency.

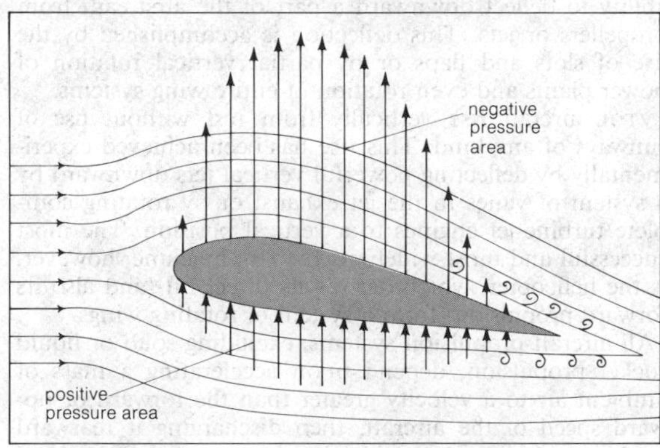

Figure 51: Relative lift developed by the upper and lower surface of an airfoil.

Advantage of monoplanes

Monoplanes have been almost universally adopted over multiplane configurations (*i.e.,* biplanes, triplanes, etc.) because airflow interference between adjacent planes reduces overall efficiency.

The planform of airfoils as aircraft wings also affects their overall characteristics. The pressure distribution with respect to span (length of wing) varies with aspect ratio (Figure 52), defined as the ratio of the span to the chord, the chord being the length of a straight line drawn from the leading to the trailing edge. The pressure distribution also varies with wing taper, with tip shape, and from interference effects between wing and fuselage or from other protuberances or attachments. There are many variables and many variations. Generally speaking, short-span, very tapered, low aspect-ratio (4–5 to 1) wings are associated with fast, highly manoeuvrable aircraft; long-span, high aspect ratios of 12–15 to 1 appear in long-range, relatively slow, high-altitude craft and in very efficient sailplanes.

Counteracting fore-and-aft instability. Most airfoils of interest to aircraft designers are inherently unstable fore and aft; *i.e.,* in pitch. The resultant upward pressures at normal angles of attack act as a centre of lift somewhat behind the centre of gravity of the section. Because these

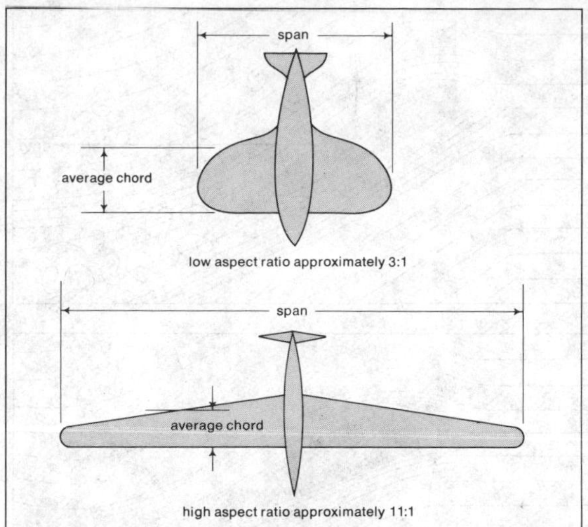

Figure 52: Aspect ratios of wings.

forces are offset from the centre of gravity, a negative moment (turning effect) is produced and tends to force the nose of the aircraft down. To compensate, a stabilizing force must be applied somewhere to create an equal and opposite moment. Canard (duck-like) configurations with a small lifting surface forward of the wing have been tried, but the normal arrangement is to provide a small horizontal surface (stabilizer) well aft of the main wing system (*i.e.,* at the tail of the aircraft) designed so that its lift reaction is downward to counteract the negative pitching moment of the wing (Figure 53). Pitch control is obtained by means of movable flaps (elevators) hinged to the trailing edge of the stabilizer.

Tailless designs have been tried in an attempt to reduce overall drag, but they have never been widely adopted. It is possible to compensate for the negative-pitching characteristic by altering wing planform (such as by twist or greatly increased sweepback), but the overall disadvantages generally outweigh the improvement.

Refinements in wing shape. Regardless of wing arrangements or planform, at some maximum angle of attack the smooth flow of air across the upper surface of any airfoil breaks down, and turbulence sets in. In most cases, the transition from smooth to turbulent flow is abrupt. Drag goes up rapidly, and lift is suddenly lost. The wing is said to stall (Figure 54A). (In aerodynamic terms, this phenomenon is in no way related to engine malfunction.) Under such conditions an airplane goes out of control, drops rapidly (usually with a disconcerting spinning motion), and, unless normal airflow over its wings and control surfaces can be restored, will crash. This reaction is what is called tailspin, which resulted in many fatal accidents until its cause was understood and effective recovery techniques applied.

Wing stall

Wing stall can be delayed and flight-speed range extended by the application of wing slots. A narrow spanwise slot of a properly designed contour near the leading edge of an airfoil (Figure 54B) allows a sheet of high-pressure air from the bottom surface to flow up and over the top surface.

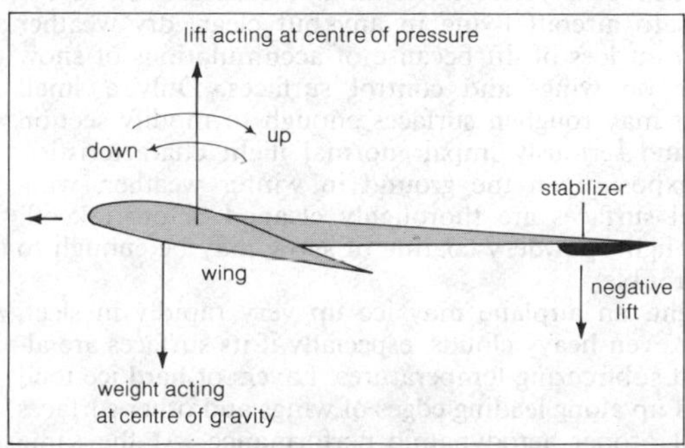

Figure 53: Stabilizer offsetting pitching action of the airfoil.

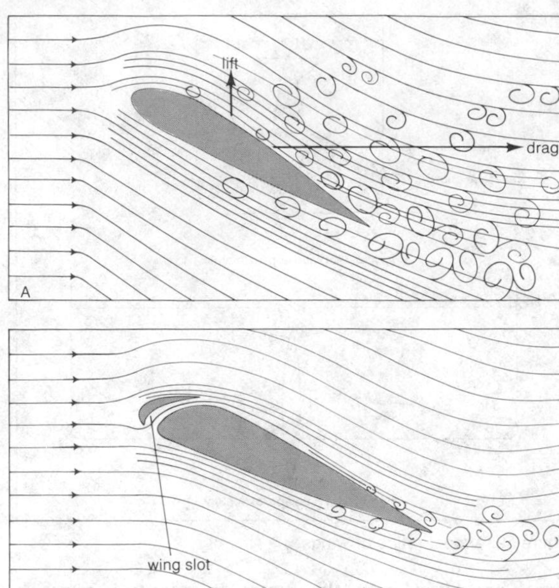

Figure 54: (A) Wing stall at high angle of attack. (B) Wing stall delayed by use of a wing slot.

This upward flow retards flow separation in the boundary layer and delays the onset of turbulence. A greater angle of attack can thus be maintained before stalling occurs and the lift-to-drag ratio increased.

Lift can also be increased by increased airfoil camber, or curvature. Because completely flexible wings (as in birds) are mechanically infeasible, hinged trailing-edge flaps provide a relatively crude but reasonably effective means of camber control (Figure 55A). Lift increases with increasing flap deflection, but so do turbulence and drag. Longitudinal stability also deteriorates.

The most effective arrangement is a combination of leading-edge slots and trailing-edge flaps. By interconnecting the activating mechanisms, it is possible to match varying effective camber with optimum slot openings to maintain relatively high lift over a range of flight speeds. As an added refinement, the flaps themselves may be slotted to smooth out local airflow (Figure 55B). Two points are obvious: (1) the analogy to the arrangement of certain feathers of a bird's wing and (2) the complicated structural and mechanical problems involved in application to aircraft.

Occasionally it is necessary quickly and effectively to reduce wing lift in order to lose altitude rapidly under control without excessive changes in attitude or to prevent aircraft on the ground from being inadvertently lifted off and damaged in high winds. For such purposes so-called spoilers are sometimes installed, either in the form of split trailing-edge flaps (one surface moving upward, the other downward, as in Figure 55C), or as narrow, spanwise slats or flaps that can be raised vertically from the top surface of the wing near the leading edge (Figure 55D) to deliberately generate turbulence and destroy lift.

Icing problems. Lift may be inadvertently and, sometimes, irrevocably lost from natural causes. One of the hazards to aircraft flying in any but clear, dry weather arises from loss of lift because of accumulations of snow and ice on wings and control surfaces. Only a small amount may roughen surfaces enough to modify section shape and seriously impair normal flight characteristics. After exposure on the ground in winter weather, wing and tail surfaces are thoroughly cleaned before takeoff. Even a light, powdery coating of snow may be enough to cause trouble.

In flight, an airplane may ice up very rapidly in sleet, rain, or even heavy clouds, especially if its surfaces are already at subfreezing temperatures. Layers of hard ice tend to build up along leading edges of wings and other surfaces to spoil proper aerodynamic performance. At the same time, the weight of the aircraft is materially increased. Many airplanes have gone out of control and have been lost under such conditions.

Early attempts to prevent icing by chemical pastes or coatings proved of no value. The more effective method has been provision of an inflatable rubber boot cemented spanwise along leading edges. By periodically inflating and deflating this boot with compressed air, ice accumulations are cracked loose and blow away as rapidly as they form. The system, however, involves considerable weight and mechanical complexity. In most aircraft of any size intended to operate in all weather conditions, wings are kept ice-free by application of heat. Hot air from engine exhaust heaters or from independent heaters is ducted inside metal leading edges and discharged at wing tips. A relatively small amount of heat applied continuously is sufficient for most flight conditions.

Propulsion systems. All conventional airplanes take off and climb because the propulsive system (engine- or turbine-driven propeller or turbine-generated jet) produces a forward thrust substantially in excess of the combined ground and total air-resistance effects. The resultant forward motion induces airflow over wings, which (because of cross-section shape and inclination) generates upward forces in excess of the total weight of the machine. Once in level, forward flight at uniform speed, the horizontal forces (thrust and drag) are equal and opposite, and the vertical forces (lift and weight) are also in equilibrium.

Equilibrium of forces

Unconventional aircraft, such as short-takeoff and -landing, or vertical-takeoff and -landing vehicles, make partial or complete use of vertical-thrust devices (jets or rotating wings) to get them off the ground quickly into steep or vertical climb.

Once off the ground and at an altitude to clear all obstacles safely, STOL airplanes (and some VTOL types) look like and behave like conventional airplanes. The ability of these aircraft to make steep takeoffs or landings on short runways (*e.g.,* in congested areas) is derived from an ability to deflect downward a part of the airstream from propellers or jets. This deflection is accomplished by the use of slots and flaps or by partial vertical rotation of power plants and even rotation of entire wing systems.

VTOL aircraft rise vertically from rest without use of runways of any kind. This rise has been achieved experimentally by deflecting powerful vertical jets downward by a system of vanes in the jet exhaust or by rotating complete turbine-jet engines to a vertical position. The most successful and most widely used VTOL machine, however, is the helicopter, which derives its direct lift (and also its forward propulsion) from a system of rotating wings.

All aircraft-propulsion systems, excluding solid or liquid rocket propulsion, depend upon accelerating a mass of ambient air to a velocity greater than the forward or upward speed of the aircraft, then discharging it rearward or downward. By increasing the momentum (mass times velocity) of the airstream, an equal but opposite momentum is applied to the aircraft. The resultant forward force is equal to the mass of air moved, multiplied by its acceleration.

The methods used to accelerate air for propulsion are piston-engine or turbine-driven screw propellers (or helicopter rotors) or gas-turbine generated jets.

Propellers. The theory and the application of the propeller for marine use was well known before 1900. Because of the great density difference (about 1:800) between air and water, however, an air propeller must move a much larger volume of air to produce a given reaction. This difference means relatively larger diameters and much nigher rotational speeds. Two-, three-, and four-bladed propellers are in common use. Most small aircraft use two blades; most large military and civilian multi-engined types use four-bladed propellers. Five-bladed units have been tried in an effort to reduce noise, but results were not sufficiently promising to offset structural and vibrational difficulties.

Multiple-bladed propellers

Each propeller blade is, in fact, an airfoil of high aspect ratio and varying planform. Every cross-section element (strip) produces its own increment of lift and drag, which, when integrated from blade root to tip, result in useful forward thrust plus resistance to rotation. The latter must be overcome by the application of power from an engine.

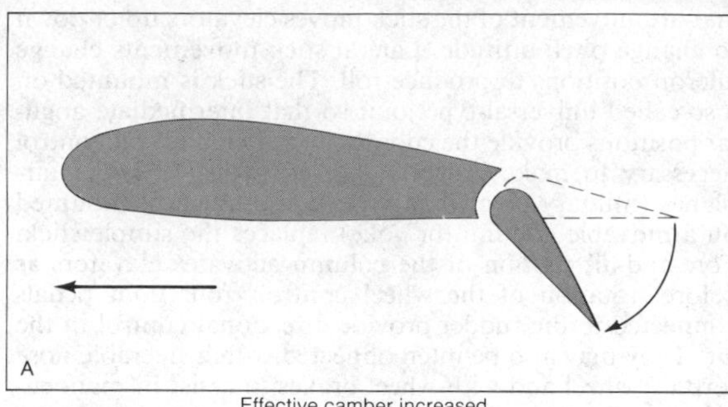

Effective camber increased by use of trailing edge flap.

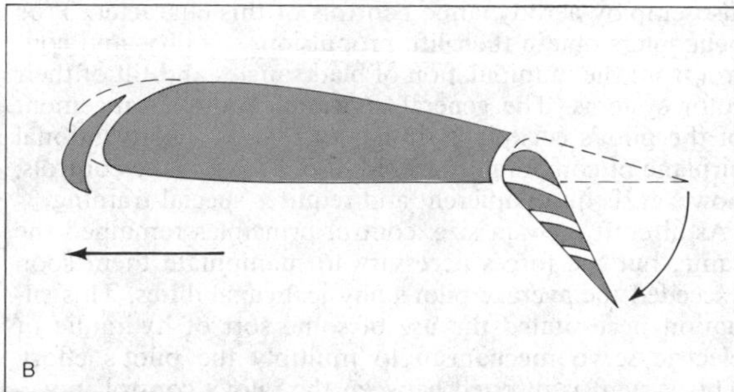

Combined wing slot and slotted flap for maximum camber effect.

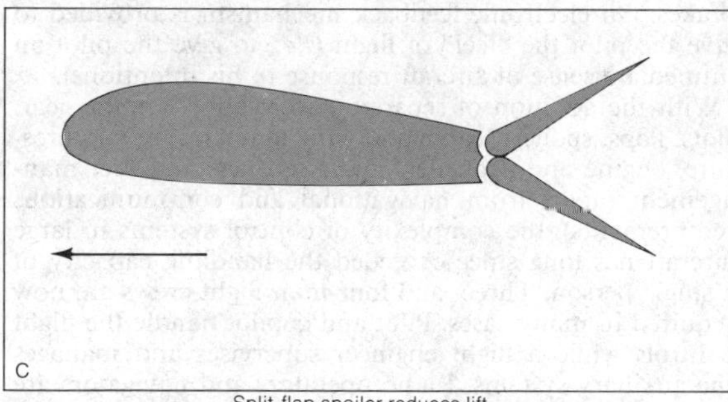

Split-flap spoiler reduces lift and greatly increases drag.

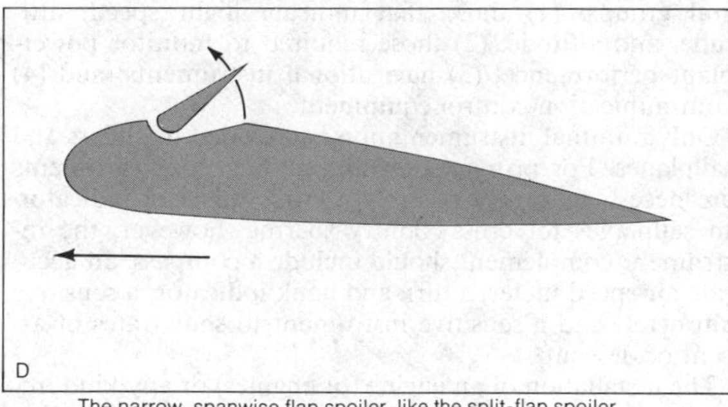

The narrow, spanwise flap spoiler, like the split-flap spoiler, is used to reduce wing lift.

Figure 55: Various flaps and wing slots.

Because the blade is rotating, the direction and velocity of air meeting each blade element varies widely from hub to tip. For maximum overall efficiency the angle of attack (pitch) of each element must be adjusted to produce the best local lift-to-drag ratio. For this reason, each propeller blade is twisted to make the geometrical pitch approximate the calculated optimum pitch at any point along the blade.

Solid, fixed-pitch aircraft propellers, carved from wood or machined from solid forgings, operate at maximum efficiency only at one specific air speed, air density rotational speed, and engine power. Departure from the design conditions reduces efficiency and impairs effectiveness. Every airplane flight, however, involves wide deviations from most of the preselected design criteria. As a result, performance is normally compromised. The obvious solution, overlooking the increased mechanical problems involved, is to manufacture hubs and blades separately so that some adjustment is possible after assembly. This accommodation has a further advantage in that high-strength steel can be used in the hub, where stresses are very high, with lighter forged aluminum for blades. The simple, variable-pitch propeller, which is adjustable only on the ground, gives an opportunity to optimize any selected flight situation without a complete propeller change. Many such propellers are in use on small airplanes for personal or general flying.

The next step, which first appeared in the early 1930s, was the two-position propeller, variable in flight under pilot control. A low-pitch setting is available for takeoff and climb with a higher pitch position for cruise and maximum speed. This improved airplane and engine performance, particularly for military and large transport types.

Continuously variable pitch

The ultimate configuration, which in various forms is in universal use on all large and high-performance commercial and military propeller-driven airplanes, is the continuously variable pitch propeller. Automatically or with pilot control, blade pitch can be incrementally changed in flight over a range of some 50 degrees to accommodate varying ambient and operating conditions. The pitch-changing mechanism is either hydraulic or electrical and is controlled electronically. To maintain optimum propeller-rotational speed, an engine-driven governor can be set to maintain the desired number of revolutions per minute of the engine.

Important additional features have been engineered into variable-pitch propellers; first, the ability to feather (change the angle of) a propeller on an engine stopped in flight. By turning blades edgewise to the airstream, windmilling (spinning in the airflow) of a dead engine is eliminated, and propeller drag is greatly reduced. In addition, blades may be completely reversed, from positive to negative angles, to produce negative thrust to help reduce ground roll after landing.

Piston engines and gas turbines. Steam or electric power to drive aircraft propellers has long since been abandoned as impractical. All modern propeller-driven aircraft are powered either with gasoline-fuelled piston engines or by kerosene-fuelled geared turbines. All are air-cooled.

Aircraft piston engines fall into two principal categories, depending on cylinder arrangement: (1) nine-cylinder, single-row or 18-cylinder, double-row radial engines used in business aircraft, commercial transport, and large military transport types; and (2) four- to six-cylinder, horizontally opposed flat types used in thousands of single or twin-engined light planes. In most flat engines and many of the smaller radials the propeller is connected directly to the engine crankshaft. The larger radials generally drive propellers through a train of gears.

All piston engines installed in conventional airplanes are completely cowled (housed in a removable metal covering that completely encloses the engine except for ventilating arrangements). This arrangement not only permits blending (fairing) engines into wing or fuselage contours to reduce overall airplane drag but also provides for internal ducting and baffling to produce optimum flow of air over and around all cylinders for efficient cooling. Adjustable cowl flaps are sometimes provided to expand or to restrict air flow to maintain uniform engine temperatures under varying flight conditions.

Turboprops

Turboprops (*i.e.,* propellers mechanically driven by gas-turbine engines) are in use in a few single-engined airplanes, in a number of two- and four-engined machines ranging from executive transports to medium commercial transports, and in certain large, specialized military aircraft. Their basic component is a gas turbine of the same type used to produce pure jet propulsion (see *Jet propulsion* below), consisting of air compressor, combustion chambers, and turbines. A turboprop engine, however, is designed to absorb most of the energy in the turbine. Because this arrangement provides much more power than is required to run the compressor, the excess is used to drive a propeller through a coaxial shaft and reduction gearing.

Machines of this type have good power-to-weight ratios. They operate most efficiently at low ambient temperatures and at high altitudes. They have been produced in units of more than 6,000 horsepower. For effective speed control, however, they must be fitted with fully automatic variable-pitch propellers. Because of their relatively small diameters, they may be easily shaped (faired) into aircraft structures to limit aerodynamic interference and drag.

Jet propulsion. The most effective way to produce large thrust reactions for high-speed flight is by turbojet engines, which, for a given thrust requirement at cruising speed, are much lighter than any piston-engine-propeller combination. Although, at very high forward speeds, propeller efficiency drops off rapidly, the efficiency of a jet remains high at high speeds.

Large thrust implies an ability to accelerate a large quantity of air to a high velocity. In a jet engine, ambient air taken in at the engine inlet is compressed 10 to 15 times in a compressor and discharged into a combustion section into which fuel is injected and burned to produce temperatures of the order of 1,400° to 1,900° F (760° to 1,040° C). The hot gases then pass through a multistage turbine, which drives the air compressor through a coaxial shaft, thence into a discharge nozzle at about two to three times the ambient air pressure, producing thrust from the high-velocity stream of hot gas ejected rearward.

To obtain considerably increased thrust for short periods of time, fuel may be injected into the hot jet stream after it leaves the turbine. The use period is short because the rate of consumption of supplementary fuel is very high. This so-called afterburning (reheat in British terminology) feeds on excess oxygen, which comes unconsumed through the combustion section of the turbine. Thrust for takeoff or for speed bursts in flight or for both may be increased by 50 percent or more by this procedure. Jet noise is also tremendously increased.

An intermediate form of engine, between the pure jet and the turboprop, came into use for long range transports in the late 1960s and early 1970s. The bypass, or fan-jet, engine includes a large low-pressure stage (or fan) ahead of the high-pressure compressor inlet. A large volume of low-pressure air is allowed to flow around (bypass) the compressor and turbine and to mix with the jet stream to increase the mass of accelerated air. This arrangement raises efficiency, reduces fuel consumption, and increases cruising range.

Deflection of jet flow

Reverse thrust to help decelerate large jet-powered aircraft after landing is obtained by introducing turning vanes or clamshell scoops into (or behind) the jet discharge nozzles to reverse the jet flow. This arrangement produces a negative thrust reaction which acts against the forward momentum of the plane to reduce the work load on mechanical wheel brakes and to shorten the stopping distance after landing.

Control systems. Airflow over movable control surfaces (elevators, ailerons, flaps, and rudder) supplies the forces necessary to change flight attitudes in conventional aircraft. Elevators and rudder are normally designed as part of the tail assembly (empennage). The former control vertical motions of the plane (climb or descent), and the rudder provides directional control (yaw) as in a surface ship. Ailerons are opposite-acting trailing-edge flaps mounted near wing tips. They control the lateral attitude (roll) of the aircraft. Inboard trailing-edge flaps lowered synchronously greatly increase lift and drag and are used principally to assist takeoff and to reduce speed in landing.

Air speed for a given flight path and control configuration is a function of thrust and is controlled by engine-throttle setting. Maximum available thrust is usually applied during takeoff and climb but is reduced in free flight as drag decreases. Reverse thrust, developed either by changing propeller-blade pitch from positive to negative angles or by introducing reversing vanes into jet-engine discharge nozzles, is used to retard speed on the ground and to shorten roll distance (in conjunction with wheel brakes) after touchdown. For airplanes that land at very high speeds, small (drogue) parachutes are sometimes deployed from the tail of the fuselage after landing to assist in shortening the roll-out.

Stick and rudder

The pilot's basic equipment (which evolved very early and is still in use in small civilian airplanes and in most single-seat military fighters) consists of a control lever, called a stick, and rudder bar (or pedals) for flight control and ignition switch and throttle for engine control. Fore-and-aft movement of the stick moves elevators up or down to change pitch attitude. Lateral stick movements change aileron positions to produce roll. The stick is mounted on a so-called universal-type joint so that intermediate angular positions provide the coordinated pitch and roll control necessary to make properly banked turns. In larger airplanes (military or civilian types), a handwheel mounted on a movable column (or yoke) replaces the simple stick. Fore-and-aft motion of the column activates elevators as before; rotation of the wheel controls roll. Foot pedals connected to the rudder provide directional control in the air. They may also be interconnected with a steerable nose (or tail) wheel and with wheel brakes to assist in manoeuvring on the ground.

Most nonconventional aircraft (except true helicopters) also employ aerodynamic controls of this character. True helicopters obtain their lift, propulsion, stability, and control from the manipulation of blade angles and tilt of their rotor systems. The general appearance and arrangement of the pilot's cockpit is similar to that of a conventional airplane of comparable size. Manipulation of the controls, however, is quite different and requires special training.

As aircraft grew in size, control principles remained the same, but the forces necessary to manipulate them soon exceeded the average pilot's physical capabilities. This situation necessitated the use of some sort of hydraulic or electric servo mechanism to multiply the pilot's effort. This system is inserted between the pilot's control movements and the aerodynamic control surfaces and operates in a way similar to automobile power steering and power brakes. An electronic feedback mechanism is provided to give the pilot the "feel" of flight (*i.e.,* to give the pilot an immediate sense of aircraft response to his intentions).

Flight crews

With the addition of separate controls for landing gear, slots, flaps, spoilers, cabin and wing temperature and pressure, engine and propeller power settings, and fuel management (apart from navigational and communications requirements), the complexity of control systems in large aircraft has long since exceeded the handling capacity of a single person. Three- and four-man flight crews are now required in many cases. Pilot and copilot handle the flight controls while a flight engineer supervises and manages the auxiliary systems. Radio operators and navigators are sometimes added for long flights.

Instrumentation. Aircraft instruments fall into four general groups: (1) those that indicate flight speed, attitude, and altitude; (2) those required to monitor power-plant performance; (3) navigational instruments; and (4) communication-control equipment.

Only minimal instrumentation is provided in gliders and sailplanes. For primary downhill gliding, no instruments are necessary, except possibly a crude airspeed indicator. In sailplanes for cross-country soaring, however, the instrument complement should include a compass, an accurate air-speed meter, a turn and bank indicator, a sensitive altimeter, and a sensitive instrument to show rates of ascent or descent.

The installation of an engine (or engines) or any kind immediately expands the instrument inventory. In addition to the minimal equipment required for flight, other instrumentation, such as fuel-tank gauges, fuel-flow meters, oil pressure and temperature gauges, engine-speed indicators, and manifold-pressure gauges, appear. For more sophisticated installations, separate cylinder-head temperature gauges, fuel-flow meters, and propeller-pitch indicators are added. For jet engines, thrust and jet-exhaust temperatures must be instrument indicated.

The total number of engine-control instruments increases with the number of engines installed and with the distribution and complexity of the fuel system and of other ancillary equipment on board, such as cabin pressure and temperature, landing-gear position, flap, trim tabs, and spoiler or thrust-reverse positions. The larger and more complicated the aircraft, the greater the number of specialized instruments required.

In addition to the supervision of aircraft and power-plant operations, complicated electronic devices are in everyday use for navigation and communication. Except for casual or sport flying in good weather in the vicinity of an airport, most business, commercial, and military flying is carried out on preplanned routes and fixed time schedules. This system presupposes an ability to identify in-flight positions accurately and to pinpoint destinations, regardless of weather or other unfavourable conditions. Further, aircraft must be safely guided onto the runway when landing in conditions of poor visibility.

A wide variety of systems and specialized equipment exists to carry out such operations. All are not yet completely reliable, but great progress has been made in improving the safety of all flight operations. The ultimate goal is routine, completely automated flight.

Detailed description of the electronics systems involved is beyond the scope of this discussion. The important point is that the amount and complexity of on-board instrumentation has multiplied tremendously. Care must be taken in the design and construction of aircraft to provide proper space for its use and maintenance.

Flight simulators. One of the most extensively instrumented aeronautical devices and one of the greatest contributors to flight safety never gets off the ground. First employed as an amusement-park device, the flight simulator taught the essentials of air navigation and blind flight to thousands of military pilots during World War II. It has since (in vastly more elaborate form) been widely adopted not only as a means of continually checking out and upgrading the competence of airline and military pilots under all normal and emergency conditions but also as a useful tool for aeronautical engineers to prove out the calculated in-flight behaviour of their aircraft without risk.

Concurrent with specifications for new aircraft destined for important commercial or military use, an order is usually placed for one or more complete flight-deck or cockpit simulators. These reproduce in complete detail all arrangements, instrumentation, and controls exactly as found in the aircraft. Through banks of computers and electronic circuitry, instruments respond to control movements as they would for all conditions of flight. Any desired flight plan can be set up and followed in detail, from engine start, takeoff, predetermined flight pattern, and landing through approach to engine shutdown. During the "flight," radio and visual navigation procedures can be followed and voice communication maintained with "the ground." Also, in many installations, the feel of actual flight is experienced by appropriate sound effects and physical movements; *e.g.,* engine noise corresponding with throttle settings or shaking and vibration as experienced in turbulence of various kinds. Visual landings may be made by watching film projections on a screen through cockpit windows.

Among the important features of simulator training are the ability to set up and to solve emergency situations of any kind that may be encountered in flight, without risk to flight crews or aircraft, and the group training of flight-deck personnel for coordinated action under all foreseeable conditions.

Materials and structures. The earlier type of aircraft construction, consisting of wooden beams, spars, ribs, and struts with fabric covering and tied together with steel wire and cables, virtually disappeared during the 1930s. Major exceptions were the expendable troop-carrying gliders of World War II and current small (generally single-engined) planes for personal and private use. For the latter, however, the primary structures are generally made of welded-steel tubes with plywood or fabric coverings.

The availability of strong, corrosion-resistant alloys of aluminum, magnesium, stainless steel, and titanium, in thin sheets, forgings and complicated extruded or rolled shapes, changed the approach to aircraft structural design. Monocoque construction (*i.e.,* thin shells, shaped and stiffened by internal stringers and ribs) is now universal for wings, nacelles and pods, fuselages, and tail surfaces. By careful design, extremely strong lightweight structures, combining smooth, aerodynamically acceptable contours of widely varying shape with ample internal space for passengers, ancillary machinery, cargo, and fuel, can be readily achieved.

In modern practice, subassemblies and major assemblies are fastened together by such methods as welding, bolting, and riveting, all of predictable strength and holding characteristics. Testing of sample components and assemblies in their final configuration is a routine requirement.

The advent of supersonic flight has imposed temperature as well as strength limitations on materials. The frictional resistance of air at high speeds generates heat that is transmitted to the aircraft structure. Below Mach 2 (twice the speed of sound, or approximately 1,200 miles (1,900 kilometres) per hour at medium altitude), the heat rise can be maintained at temperatures below which aluminum alloys begin to lose their strength. Before Mach 3 is reached, however, this temperature becomes critical, and materials with greater heat resistance must be substituted. Certain stainless steels and alloys of titanium and molybdenum qualify in this regard. Though their manufacture and fabrication are difficult and expensive, their use is mandatory for aircraft expected to fly at Mach 3 or beyond.

Materials problems above Mach 2

Fixed-wing aircraft configurations. The essential components of an airplane are a wing system to sustain it in flight, tail surfaces to stabilize the wing, movable surfaces (ailerons, elevators, and rudders) to control the attitude of the machine in flight, and a power plant to provide the thrust to push the machine through the air. An enclosed body (fuselage) to house the crew, passengers, and cargo must be provided, as well as controls and instruments for the pilots and navigators. Provision also must be made to support the machine when it is at rest on the ground (or on water) and during takeoff and landing.

Many hundreds of thousands of engineering man-hours go into specifications, design, construction, testing, and evaluation of a new airplane. After the basic configuration has been agreed upon, thousands of hours of detailed study must be spent upon the preliminary design before prototype construction can begin. Carefully built, geometrically and dynamically accurate scale models must be tested in wind tunnels to check the flying characteristics and to furnish information on the air-load distribution under different flight conditions. Vibration and flutter sources from fluctuating airflow on wing, body, and tail surfaces must be identified and evaluated.

Because designers are always pushing the state of the art to extreme limits and must work to the highest attainable strength-to-weight ratios in the use of materials, calculations must be exact. Margins for error are small. Rule-of-thumb methods cannot be applied to airplane structural design. Each part must be examined in detail and be designed for maximum efficiency. The problem is more difficult because of uncertainty in determining the magnitude and location of air loads on airplane structures. Often full-scale structural components must be built and tested to destruction to be certain that they will stand up under the dynamic and vibrational loads expected in flight. Such tests may be repeated many times before the final design is accepted and the first prototype built. In this process, modern high-speed computers have proven invaluable. The assembled airframe is then subjected to many complicated load and vibrational tests to be certain that it will meet overall strength specifications.

Testing components and airframes

After the power plants and all other auxiliary equipment are thoroughly tested for functional operation on the ground, the complete machine is ready for flight testing. A long series of well-engineered, well-instrumented test flights is usually required to guarantee that the original specifications for performance and safety have been met. For small, relatively simple machines the test stage may take days or weeks. Large and complicated transports or bombers may require a year or more of shakedown before being released for production.

Wings. Most modern airplanes are monoplanes. Their lift is derived from one horizontal, fixed-wing system; they are termed high-wing when the wing is attached at the top of the fuselage, midwing when it extends from or near the centre of fuselage section, and low-wing when the wing structure fastens to the fuselage structure at the bottom. Many of the smaller and lighter single-engine airplanes for private-owner use are of the high-wing configuration, as are most modern military aircraft, including bombers and the larger personnel and cargo carriers. Some high-performance fighters tend toward midwing variations. Virtually all multi-engined aircraft for executive and commercial transport service are low-winged monoplanes. The multiplane with two or more horizontal wing systems, one above the other, connected by a series of struts and wires, has virtually disappeared. The few biplanes still in service are used mainly for sport flying or for agricultural crop dusting.

Monoplanes may be characterized by the planform (top view) of their wings, which may be rectangular, tapered, swept-back, or delta. A so-called variable-geometry concept incorporating adjustable sweepback is a compromise to obtain good high- and low-speed characteristics from the same wing. For takeoff and landing, hinged wing panels are extended at right angles to the fuselage in order to utilize the advantages of long-span and high-aspect ratio. In flight, for maximum speed and manoeuvrability, the panels are swung rearward to make (with the tail surfaces) a delta configuration. A number of high-performance attack aircraft have been built to this configuration.

Fins and stabilizers. The normal location for stabilizers, fins, rudders, and elevators is well behind the wing, mounted on the tapered tail section of the fuselage. The standard arrangement (until the advent of jet engines) was a cruciform assembly, with vertical fins and rudders and horizontal stabilizer and elevators forming a cross, the axis of which is approximately coincident with the fuselage axis. In some large, high-wing airplanes with relatively short, large-diameter fuselages, airflow over the horizontal tail surfaces was disturbed to the extent that control effectiveness under some flight conditions was compromised. Also, in designs in which jet pods were to be mounted at the after end of the fuselage, it was necessary to relocate the horizontal surfaces to keep them clear of the jet blasts. The solution was the so-called T-tail configuration, in which the horizontal surfaces are mounted at the top of the vertical fin structure.

T-tail configuration

Where three jet engines are used, the fin structure may incorporate the air intake for the centre engine or the entire engine pod. The consequent increase in weight of the tail structure has changed the appearance of many airplanes. To maintain a viable relationship between centre of lift of the wings and centre of gravity of the entire machine, it has been necessary to move the wings aft and to extend the nose section of the fuselage far forward for proper balance.

Engines. For small machines, a single engine and propeller combination is usually mounted in the forward end of the fuselage. When two engines are used, they are normally mounted in nacelles joined into leading edges of wings.

In single turbojet trainers or fighters for military or naval use, the engine is usually mounted inside the fuselage behind the pilot's cockpit, with air intakes either in the nose or as scoops along the sides or in the wing roots. The turbine exhausts through an afterburner into a tailpipe, which extends slightly beyond the after end of the fuselage.

For two- or four-engined planes (either piston engine or turbine-propeller combinations or turbojets), the power plants are normally distributed outboard along the wings, either in nacelles projecting from wing and edges or in suspended pods. Jet pods are also attached to the rear of the fuselage, as indicated above. A combination of both systems (wing pods and tail pod) may be employed.

Landing gear. Landing-gear configuration depends on whether the aircraft is designed to operate from land airports or from water surfaces or from both. Very few current commercial operations are water based, however, except for those of the so-called bush pilots, who fly small seaplanes (usually twin-float) hundreds of thousands of miles per year from lake to lake in the subarctic regions of Canada and Alaska to keep the miners, hunters, and prospectors transported and supplied. All transcontinental and intercontinental airlines use land-based airplanes.

Float seaplanes and flying boats have been generally abandoned by the navies of the world. Fighters, bombers, and utility transports take off and land on aircraft-carrier decks. Larger transports and cargo planes operate from airport runways ashore. Amphibians, which can land and take off from the water as well as land, have become rare, as have seaplanes and flying boats. All these require considerable strength and bulk to be seaworthy. The hull shape must be modified in a number of ways to permit takeoff capability and on-the-water stability; these modifications add to the drag and militate against aerodynamic efficiency. Corrosion rates are high, and aluminum and magnesium must be given special treatment if used. Protection against corrosion is difficult, requires constant inspection, and is expensive. Further, suitable airports now exist in virtually every country, and landplanes can reach most of them safely from any point of departure.

Corrosion problems

Pneumatic-tired, wheeled landing gear has been used in most airplanes since the earliest days. Spring-loaded, hydraulically damped shock absorbers take up landing impact loads. For aircraft weighing thousands of pounds these devices become complicated and very heavy. Wheel brakes are generally hydraulically operated.

Until the late 1930s the common arrangement called for a pair of wheels well forward of the airplane centre of gravity with a skid, or tail wheel, aft. The airplane rested on the ground in a distinctly nose-up attitude. During takeoff, as speed increased, the tail was raised by the use of the elevators until the fuselage was rolling in a level position with respect to the ground. When flying speed was reached, the tail was depressed by pulling back on the stick, and the increased lift from the greater angle of attack on the wings lifted the machine off.

In landing the procedure was reversed. From an approach glide, the machine was levelled off a few feet off the ground, then, by use of the elevators (as speed decreased), the machine was stalled and dropped to a three-point landing on wheels and tail skid, the drag of the latter being used to reduce speed and shorten the ground roll after landing. This manoeuvre has always been considered the most difficult to learn. It requires good judgment and long practice. Many small, privately owned, sport and general-aviation types are still designed to perform in this way. In many cases the landing gear is exposed and contributes to the overall drag of the airplane in flight.

In the late 1930s, landing-gear design underwent significant changes. The undercarriage plan was reversed. For all large aircraft and most small ones, the main wheels were moved aft to a position well behind the aircraft centre of gravity and a nose wheel (steerable) installed well forward. The fuselage remains parallel with the ground at rest, during takeoff run, and on landing. The aircraft is never deliberately stalled. This arrangement, originally labelled tricycle landing gear, greatly simplifies ground handling, loading, and fuelling. The term is still applied, although very large aircraft may have double wheels or multiwheeled trucks at each of the three support points.

In another change, wheels and struts were made to retract into the fuselage, nacelles, or wings. This increases weight and mechanical complexity but pays off in greatly improved flight performance.

One special case requires comment; *i.e.,* takeoff and landing aboard aircraft carriers at sea. Although carriers are fast enough so that, under most conditions, a wind speed of 25–30 knots (29–35 miles [46–56 kilometres] per hour) can be maintained along the flight deck, modern heavily loaded aircraft do not have enough runway length to take off under their own power nor enough room to decelerate to a stop after touchdown.

Landing gear required for carrier-based planes

For carrier-based planes, landing-gear configurations are similar to those for land-based planes but must be strengthened to take the extra loads imposed by acceleration (from zero to flying speed in some 200 feet [60 metres]) by catapult. Also, fuselages must be modified and reinforced to permit installation of a tail hook to engage arresting gear cables strung crosswise on deck in the landing area.

Another necessary modification for carrier-based airplanes is the folding wing. To make it possible to accommodate a desirable number of machines in limited hangar-deck space and to permit handling on the elevators connecting flight deck and hangar deck, wings must be foldable. They are commonly hinged at each side of the fuselage and folded upward to reduce span. The hinges and operating mechanism add considerable weight and structural complexity. (S.P.J.)

AIRPORT DESIGN AND OPERATION

An aerodrome is described by the International Civil Aviation Organization as a defined area on land or water (including any buildings, installations, and equipment) intended to be used either wholly or in part for the arrival, departure, and movement of aircraft. The term airport has, however, come into common use and refers particularly to those aerodromes where air-transport movements occur on a considerable scale, and especially in the United Kingdom where full-time customs facilities are available. Airfield is used in reference to small aerodromes, generally without hard runways or facilities for handling large transport aircraft or their passengers and cargo.

Evolution of airports from early landing fields. The essential requirements for a landing field have expanded steadily since the earliest days of flying. Just before World War II, the landing and takeoff distance required was a maximum of 650 yards (600 metres), and the additional demands that could result from an engine failure were not clearly defined. In these terms the airfields at New York City, London, Paris, and Berlin were laid down, the area involved rarely exceeding 500 acres (200 hectares). London's airport at Croydon had no runway. Hard runways were rare. Tempelhof (Berlin), constructed in 1929, was one of the busiest airfields in prewar Europe; it became a major social centre with restaurants and rooftop observational areas. More than 750,000 visitors were recorded during its first year of operation. Le Bourget (Paris), Croydon (London), and La Guardia (New York City) likewise attracted many visitors. The aircraft and the air passenger at that time had made little impact upon the design of airfields or air terminals. Such a situation, in fact, still exists in the great majority of airfields throughout the world. In the overall world pattern, the small grass airfield with simple terminal building, rudimentary control tower, and negligible landing aids is still dominant.

Primitive airfields

A wide variety of airports and airfields has developed to accommodate the great range of modern aircraft types and the different kinds of facilities needed for passenger and cargo handling.

The increasing demand for air travel has created the need for the large transport aircraft, now almost exclusively of multi-jet design. The demands such aircraft make upon all kinds of ground facilities, runways and taxiways, fire-fighting and safety services, passenger and cargo-handling facilities, car parking, and lighting, navigational, and approach aids, are the principal determinants in the design of the large, sophisticated airports adjacent to the main centres of world population.

Of the 13 airports handling more than 8,000,000 passenger movements in 1969, 10 were located in the United States, a reflection of the fact that about 60 percent of the world's air transport occurs there. Chicago (O'Hare) heads the list. Of the non-U.S. airports, London (Heathrow) was sixth, Paris (Orly) was 12th, and Frankfurt (Rhine-Main) was 13th.

It should be noted that it is primarily at these large airports that the problems of noise, congestion in the air and on the ground, and conflicts in land use with other regional planning objectives have arisen. The difficulties of smaller airports have been largely those of economics.

Modern airports. *The elements of a major airport.* The four principal elements of a major airport are airport management and control; passenger and cargo terminals; the runway, taxiway, and apron systems; and airport services.

The airport management and control function embraces the day-to-day operation and long-term planning of the airport; the terminal; runway and taxiway system; local air-traffic control; the lighting, navigational, and aircraft approach guidance system; as well as fire-fighting, fuel supply, and all ancillary services, including customs facilities.

The passenger and cargo terminals provide for handling passengers, baggage, and cargo and the related activities.

The runway, taxiway, and apron systems are required to meet the needs of the aircraft for landing and takeoff, for positioning correctly for these manoeuvres, for aircraft location to receive and discharge loads, and for the operating and servicing crews to work.

Airport services related to the aircraft comprise the apron (the part of the airport surface adjacent to the terminal), the handling of aircraft, passengers' baggage, cargo, aircraft fuel supply, aircraft catering, cabin cleaning, and engineering services. Ground-related services include passenger-terminal catering and the concessionary facilities within the terminal (such as automobile rental), as well as the automobile parking and garage arrangements in the airport-terminal area for the travelling public and the airport staff.

Airport planning. There is no uniform pattern of airport layout and design. In the hierarchy from the great metropolitan airport to the small-town field with a single landing strip of tarmac, an immense variety of layouts has proved successful. The site itself is a critical factor. Runway orientation is the starting point for design, site selection being generally determined by its suitability for an appropriate runway system. Particularly important elements are the availability of level, well-drained land without approach-path obstruction or possible conflict with roads and access to existing major road systems. As in all exercises in technical development, conflicts arise at every stage in decision making, the most significant being that between noise and access to the urban community.

Site selection

It is important to note that airport layout and operation are keyed to development. The industry is dynamic and there are two sources of change: traffic growth and technological change. Most airports are in a period of dramatic growth, with passenger movements doubling every four to five years. In the major city airports such conditions are almost universal, but the small-town airport is often in a less favourable position. Technological change in aviation, however, is worldwide, being based on advanced aircraft and avionics industries in the United States, United Kingdom, France, Germany, Italy, The Netherlands, and Japan, with increasingly important contributions being made by Canada, Australia, Spain, Brazil, India, and Indonesia, particularly in medium-sized, short-haul aircraft. These industries are steadily promoting new types of aircraft, usually of increased size and performance, forcing modifications in airport design virtually each decade.

Runway, taxiway, and apron systems. The essentials of a runway and taxiway system for a given airport are related to the types of aircraft, the scale of traffic, and the prevailing meteorological conditions.

Modern types of jet aircraft can accept higher crosswinds than the aircraft of the immediate postwar years. Thus, in the late 20th century fewer runways were needed than formerly. Light aircraft may need to land and take off at an angle to the main runway because of limited handling capability in strong crosswinds, but the operation of such aircraft would not be sanctioned at major international airports. Indeed, considerable controversy exists concerning the use of large airports by executive and private aircraft.

Meteorological information is fully recorded and analyzed to determine the most desirable orientation for the principal runway(s), subject always to the suitability of the weather (visibility, cloud base, etc.) for an airport development in any region.

Experience in air operations has encouraged the International Civil Aviation Organization (ICAO) of the United Nations to establish standards of practice for the design and layout of airports and runway systems. These complex requirements have been incorporated in the Air Navigational and Air Terminal Regulations of most member governments of ICAO. Certain of these relate to the length, strength, and width of runways and taxiways, the limiting position of obstructions, and the lighting, navigational, communications, and approach aids.

Airworthiness standards are promulgated by the governments of aircraft-manufacturing nations to safeguard the operating standards, performance, and weight of aircraft in the various stages of flight, including takeoff and landing. Air-navigational regulations (based predominantly upon ICAO recommended practices) set down the runway specifications essential to allow the safe operation of transport aircraft.

Safety standards

Detailed requirements specify the many other critical design factors in runways, taxiways, and aprons. Runway length has probably reached a limit that is unlikely to be exceeded even with the development of larger jets. More stringent standards in design of equipment and layout for airfields are, however, gradually being incorporated by the licensing authorities.

Airport layout and terminal design. Different styles of airport layout and terminal design have developed since 1960 to meet the demands of the jet transport and the massive traffic increases.

The principal characteristic types of layout that have developed in this period are shown in Figure 56. The essential need is to deploy a large number of aircraft into positions for unloading and loading so that passengers can embark and disembark with minimum expenditure of time and effort and so that the other essential apron services can be performed. The essential terminal services must be provided, and a high order of access, especially for road traffic, must be arranged. Provision for expansion of all such facilities, with full retention of efficiency, must be built into the system.

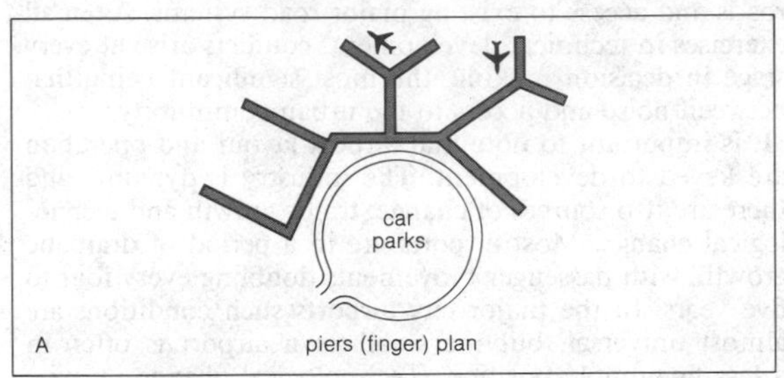

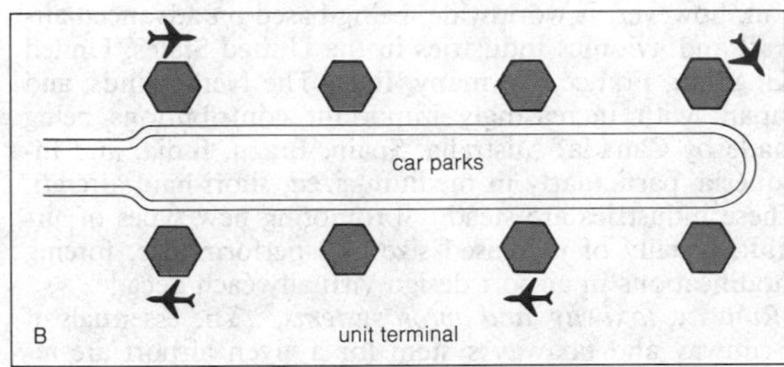

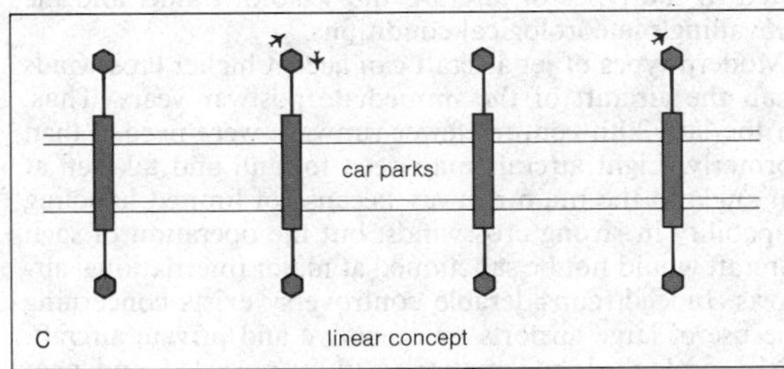

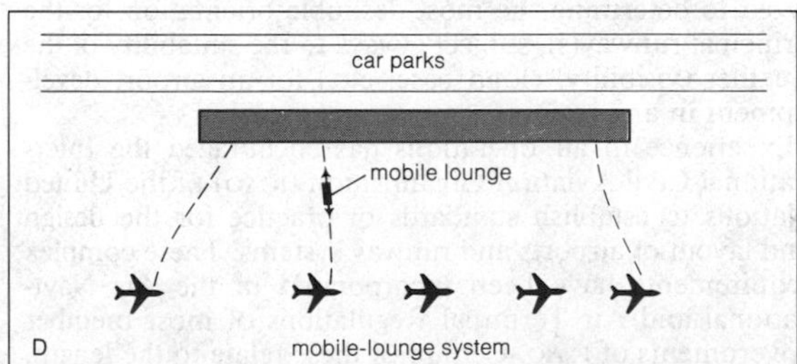

Figure 56: Typical airport terminal layouts.

The finger system (A), extensively developed during the 1960s and 1970s, is entirely suitable for medium-sized terminals with twin-jet aircraft and also the four-jet Boeing 707 and 747, the McDonnell Douglas DC-8, and the later DC-10, Tristar, and European Airbus. A major problem has been the long distances the passengers must travel from the reception areas to the aircraft. Passenger conveyor systems, called travelators, for horizontal transit were introduced during the 1970s.

Breaking the passenger flow into a number of units is effectively achieved in the unit terminal (B), which has the merits of shortening the passenger walk, allowing more space for expansion, and providing a convenient geometrical arrangement for the "nosing in" of large transports; the design has proved especially effective with the jumbo jets.

The linear concept (C) is also under active development and incorporates many of the basic features of the unit terminal. A new airport proposed for Louisville, Kentucky, was based on the linear concept. The British Airport Authority has described plans for the third London airport based on the linear concept.

The mobile-lounge system (D) has been applied at Dulles International Airport outside Washington, D.C. Mobile lounges transfer passengers between aircraft and terminal. This method offers a more intensive and flexible use of the apron space for the aircraft but at a high cost in motorized transfer and some congestion of vehicles on the apron when aircraft are being serviced at peak times.

Apron servicing

Terminals and aprons must be designed so that the aircraft is held for the shortest possible time in the turn around phase on the apron. This is most important in handling short-haul aircraft, for which ground time is a high percentage of operating time. A typical transit turn around time for a modern airbus type of aircraft is 25 minutes. A large number of vehicles are in circulation on the apron during the turn around, and marshalling of aircraft and vehicles is critical to the smooth operation of a large airport. During peak periods at O'Hare International Airport (Chicago), for example, an aircraft comes onto the apron or taxis out every 20 seconds.

Passenger and cargo terminals

The principal passenger and cargo areas should be related to the expected traffic flows. The limit of traffic through an airport may be determined by several factors, including aircraft landing and takeoff movements, congestion on the apron, or congestion in the air-traffic-control system. Limits may also arise in the passenger terminal or, less frequently, through congestion in the road or rail approaches to the airport buildings and parking areas.

The terminal areas may be self-contained and restricted, as originally on the central island site at Heathrow, or they may develop on the satellite principle, as at John F. Kennedy International Airport (New York City) and Aéroport Charles de Gaulle (Paris). More recent designs for large city airports have concentrated, however, on the linear concept, in which a continuous process of development and growth can be provided.

Factors in terminal size

The determining factors that fix the scale of the buildings are the standard busy rates of aircraft and passenger and cargo movements in the different categories of arrival, departure, domestic, and international movements. Standard busy rates are defined as submaximum movement rates, likely to be exceeded on about 20 occasions a year. With growth rates in passenger traffic in some cases exceeding 20 percent per annum, the need to make provision for the growth of all facilities becomes apparent.

Air-cargo movement on the apron is conducted in a variety of ways. At major airports automated systems can be justified by the high use achieved and the reduced manpower required. Lack of flexibility is inherent in such systems. Labour problems beset the early introduction of such arrangements (*e.g.,* at Heathrow). In smaller airports, truck transport from warehouse or freight shed to and from the aircraft is all that is required. Special accommodations for freight forwarders and bonded stores are provided at major international airports.

The airlines normally provide their own cargo-handling and storage facilities at the airport. Cargo is delivered to the terminal by the freight forwarder, agent, or shipper and is documented and located for loading or consolidating on a pallet or in a container for the next flight departure. Cargo aircraft tend to operate during the latter part of the day and at night; thus, it is generally true that cargo flights do not contribute greatly to congestion in the air or on the ground at major airports.

Congestion. At major airports, congestion has reached a high level both in the air and on the ground. Takeoff delays sometimes reach a point at which aircraft must return to the apron to refuel because of depletion of fuel while waiting to take off. It is largely because of the cost of such delays that an immense program of airport building was undertaken worldwide during the last quarter of the 20th century.

Some cities in the United States and Europe have sought to encourage general aviation use of the smaller aerodromes rather than the main air hub. Congestion in the air space, on aprons, and on runways becomes a matter for air-traffic control; it also arises in the terminal, in the automobile parking spaces, and on the access routes to and from the airport. Space at congested airports, such as Kennedy International and Heathrow, is at such a premium that ancillary services such as automobile parking, restaurants, and sales stands may need to be moved from the airport precincts. Off-airport parking has become a feature at the London airport; rates, including the transport of passengers by bus to the airport terminal, are considerably lower than on the airport.

Proposals to situate airports away from congested zones have found favour with some regional planners and with most conservationists. Air transport, however, must be accessible to its markets, and the offshore sites proposed for a London airport at Foulness as well as the Seadrome 10 miles (16 kilometres) west of Los Angeles in Santa Monica Bay were successfully resisted by the airlines.

Airport noise problem. A serious threat may exist to the development of aviation if action to curtail aircraft noise is not effective. Throughout the 1970s action took a number of forms. Restrictions on jet-aircraft movements were introduced, especially at night (*e.g.,* at London and New York City). Restraints on urban (particularly residential) development were imposed by many planning authorities within the zones having high noise ratings. Control of the flight path of aircraft (especially after takeoff) and in the use of runways (for landings and takeoff) was exercised to minimize noise nuisance in the airport environment and over a wider area. Airport development and new site selection were directed to minimize deterioration in the environment. Indeed, major airport projects in London and Munich were brought to a halt in the 1970s by disagreement over the noise nuisance issue. Aircraft noise certification standards for new types of jet transport aircraft were introduced, and intensive research has continued to produce quieter engines and auxiliary flight systems.

Airport links to local ground transportation. One aspect of an airport is that of a transport hub where different transport modes connect. Thus, access for surface vehicles is as critical a factor in airport design as in site selection.

The road traffic generated by the large air terminals is already on a scale that demands special consideration of the layout and width of roads and access routes to the city centres.

Highway congestion

The peak traffic in the airport approach roads tends to occur in the morning and evening, coinciding with other peaks of suburban traffic, so that journey times to and from an airport from the downtown areas are difficult to forecast in the rush periods. Because major airports have gradually moved farther away from the city centres, journey times to airports have increased. Road traffic congestion has accentuated the problem, and the cost of idle time has become critical in the economic comparison of air and surface transport. A major argument for vertical takeoff and short takeoff aircraft lies in their lesser requirements for airport space, promising sites close to the central city. (A.H.St.)

Traffic control

Traffic is the movement of people, goods, or vehicles between separated points, and traffic control involves the attempts to make these movements as fast, efficient, and safe as possible with minimum damage to the environment. Traffic control may thus involve planning automobile, truck, bus, and pedestrian movements through the congested streets of a large city; the design of navigation systems for aircraft takeoff, flight, and landing; and mechanized handling of freight for cargo ships. Inadequate control is characterized by congestion, pollution, and accidents.

The kinds of traffic present in a transportation system result from established patterns of activity. The principal land traffic systems, surface and underground, were over roads and railways, though other kinds are developing. Pipelines provide a unique continuous-flow means of moving an increasing variety of materials; though somewhat inflexible, often limited to single commodities, and directional in use, they have the important advantage of being practicable for almost any type of terrain. Cableway and conveyor systems are being developed for pedestrian use in high-density pedestrian traffic areas.

Sea and air transport are the other major types of transportation, but a number of hybrids are under development. Hovercraft (vehicles able to travel over land or water supported on a cushion of air), for example, have added a whole range of potential applications to vehicle technology since their development in 1955. Hovercraft control has aspects in common with both sea and land vehicles and, because of their high speeds, with air traffic (see above *Air-cushion machines*).

The main recent changes in air transport relate to the possible development of supersonic transports and, as in the case of shipping, increasing vehicle size. An especially promising development is the potential reduction in size of airports. Now requiring thousands of acres, they may be reduced in size by vertical-takeoff and associated aircraft types. In shipping there is more specialization of carriers: in some, the cargo is divided up into individual shipping units, as in barges; others unload from a parent ship in small self-propelled units; and others carry cargoes in submarine plastic containers.

The more mixed the traffic to be controlled is, either by type or performance, the greater are the control problems in maximizing vehicle flow and assuring safety. Control is usually exercised by a particular supervising agency for specific types of traffic; problems of competition and regulation arise between these agencies.

ROAD TRAFFIC CONTROL

The following discussion is limited to questions affecting traffic control. For a complete treatment of road design, construction, and maintenance, see PUBLIC WORKS: *Roads and highways.*

History. Traffic congestion, often bad enough to require drastic control measures, was a feature of city life at least as early as Roman times. A basic cause, then as now, was poor city planning, with roads laid out in such a way as to bring traffic from all quarters to a central crossing point. In the 1st century AD Julius Caesar banned wheeled traffic from Rome during the daytime, a measure gradually extended to cities in the provinces. Late in the 1st century AD the emperor Hadrian was forced to limit the total number of carts entering Rome.

The problem moderated with the decline of commerce in the early Middle Ages, but reappeared during the resurgence of city life in the high Middle Ages, when road maintenance and traveller safety were more paramount problems than traffic control. About 1500 Leonardo da Vinci, envisioning a revolutionary solution to urban traffic problems, then acute in the crowded and busy Italian cities, proposed separating wheeled and pedestrian traffic by creating routes at different levels. Except for the railways, however, very few segregated route systems were established before the 20th century.

Congestion was severe enough in European cities of the 17th century to require ordinances prohibiting parking on certain streets and establishing one-way traffic. The advent of the railroad brought temporary relief to the growing problem of road traffic control, though it created congestion at terminals inside cities. The automobile, with its increase, first in speed and then in numbers over horse-drawn transport, rapidly created a new situation that was to become one of the characteristic problems of urban industrialized society in the 20th century.

Traffic elements. Much motor traffic is still carried on roads that were conceived, if not used, for the horse-drawn vehicles of another age, though roads designed primarily and exclusively for motor traffic are not only easier, safer, and more efficient to drive on but facilitate the best form of traffic control. The essential features of major routes include separation of types of traffic and levels (grade separation), control of access, and design standards suited to the types of vehicle and drivers expected to use the routes.

"Free-flowing" traffic

Most of these characteristics are included to permit "free-flowing" traffic on autobahns (Germany), autostradas (Italy), autoroutes (France), freeways and expressways (U.S.), and motorways (U.K.). Early examples of such motor roads were the Avus in Berlin opened in 1919, the Bronx River Parkway in New York opened between 1921 and 1924, Lake Shore Drive freeway in Chicago in 1933, Frankfurt–Darmstadt autobahn in 1935, and several privately financed motor routes built around Milan between 1922 and 1930. The U.S. interstate system is now the most comprehensive highway network in the world.

The elements of road traffic and their various functions are many and often conflicting. In all countries, the needs of pedestrians are quite different from those of vehicles. Vehicles themselves may wish to move at high speed, to manoeuvre and circulate through congested areas, to stop frequently for loading and unloading. Policy makers try to plan traffic-control systems to minimize such conflicts.

Problems. The principal problems associated with road traffic are those which relate to its impact on city dwellers and on commuters while in the city (see above *Urban transportation*). Individual mobility and the desire for travel in the developed countries are increasing at such a rate that demand for roads invariably outstrips supply. Congestion and a continuous worsening of public transport facilities is the result, and this in turn tends to affect urban land use. Cities spread out in patterns determined more by the motor car than by human social needs. New areas lack a cohesive structure. Administration of these huge urban-suburban areas is a continuing problem. Of more immediate significance is the worldwide toll in death and injury that results partly from the failure of road users or their vehicles and partly from improper road design. Furthermore, the growing public awareness of the noise, atmospheric, and visual pollution caused by road vehicles makes it imperative to review vehicles, roads, and their relationship.

Government regulation. All nations regulate vehicles and drivers on their highways. Drivers are regulated by age, types of vehicle driven, and financial provisions; vehicles are controlled by specifications pertaining to registration, ownership, mechanical worthiness, required accessories, sizes, and weights. Further regulations determine the manner of operation of vehicles on the public highways. Uniform Traffic Acts and Model Municipal Ordinances have been developed to guide traffic legislation throughout the U.S. The nations of western Europe have cooperated effectively in highway and driver regulation. A notable success is the European system of road signs, which employs symbols instead of words to overcome the language barrier. In the underdeveloped countries, where roads and highways are now considered to be critical to economic progress, government takes an even larger role.

Conventional control techniques. Among the principal types of highway control are rules limiting the use of streets. The one-way street was one of the earliest measures and is still in widespread use. Traffic flow can be thought of as possessing properties analogous to frictional materials. The capacity of an undivided street is thus increased if traffic is allowed to move in only one direction. Furthermore, if side streets are used to handle complementary flows, the capacity of the traffic network is further increased. Other general benefits include a reduction in accidents and shorter journey times. Similar considerations apply to the banning of turns, particularly those which require crossing major traffic streams.

The traffic engineer attempts to ensure a homogeneous traffic flow in order to encourage a greater degree of consistency in traffic behaviour. Speeds can be limited with maximum allowable speeds established for specific locations. Another set of restrictions involves loading and unloading, and parking. Curbside parking seriously reduces the potential flow in a street and thus limits its capacity, and often increases the accident rate. Further, parked cars may block the way of public safety vehicles such as fire trucks. Loading, unloading, and parking are controlled by the designation of parking areas, no parking zones, loading zones, time limits on parking, etc. Increasingly important are control measures aimed at improving the flow and regularity of public transit vehicles, particularly in downtown areas.

Traffic-control devices

Traffic-control devices are often used to inform the driver of various conditions affecting road use. These can be divided into categories. Regulatory devices may be either prohibitory (no entry, speed limit, no waiting) or mandatory (stop, keep left, yield). Warning devices are used to warn the road user of hazardous conditions, unusual traffic movements, or special local conditions (children playing, junctions, slippery road surfaces). A final group is that of guidance or informative devices giving route and other pertinent information (destinations, parking and service areas, information offices). The principal devices are road signs and carriageway markings. To ensure effectiveness, these must compel attention and quickly convey their meaning and adequate time must be allowed for driver response. Signs must furthermore command respect and be sited to minimize accidental collision. Ensuring maximum performance is related to uniformity of siting and layout, and the development of correct habitual responses is important. Uniform national standards have been adopted in most countries and an international system in western Europe as noted above. International standards have been drawn up in a United Nations Protocol on Road Signs.

Road traffic signals have improved in effectiveness since their introduction 100 years ago. Their purpose is to promote the orderly movement of traffic and reduce the frequency of accidents. In large cities it is necessary to synchronize street networks in order to maximize traffic flow. Traffic signal controllers are either pre-timed or traffic-actuated. Pre-timed controllers, widely used in Europe and the U.S., allocate a specific time interval to each stream of traffic in an orderly repeating sequence. Extensively used in Britain for many years, traffic-actuated signals vary the time allocation and sequence in response to actual traffic demands as measured by traffic detectors. Individual signal units have an illuminated red, yellow (amber) and green lens mounted in a signal head, directionally sited on poles or wires. At least two signal heads are visible to a traffic stream. Pedestrian signals which indicate when to walk are often added. Today's designers, however, prefer to segregate pedestrians and vehicles by constructing overhead or underground walkways.

Cycle length, that is the time required for a complete sequence of signal indications, normally varies between 30 and 150 seconds. A short cycle length reduces the overall capacity of the intersection. The alternative, a long cycle, may provoke some impatience but a driver is not concerned merely with the time lost at a single junction as much as with the speed and smoothness of his whole journey. Considerable research in recent years has been aimed toward limiting delay in traffic control systems. Early coordinated movement patterns were developed with fixed-time signals to allow compact groups of vehicles to progress along a street together. This simultaneous system required that all colour indications be alike at the same time, and had the unfortunate effect of causing drivers to exceed speed limits without achieving high overall journey speeds. This disadvantage was overcome to some extent by an alternate system in which all signals changed indication simultaneously, but adjacent signals showed opposite colours. Problems arose because, since the greens and reds must be of approximately equal duration, the system is suited only to uniformly spaced blocks with cross flows approximately equal to those progressing down the street. A better compromise is the limited progression system which uses a master controller to offset the start of each green phase to enable a speed progression to be maintained by vehicles. A more advanced master controller can operate the flexible progressive system which permits a variation of progression plans by remote control, for example to cover peak hour operation, or to favour directional movements of traffic at particular times of day.

Area traffic control

Digital computers have made possible more complete and more extensive forms of control. Computer control of large networks of roads is generally called area traffic control (Figure 57). Information is obtained by a variety of traffic detectors installed in the street system, which measure the presence of vehicles, traffic flow rates, stopped

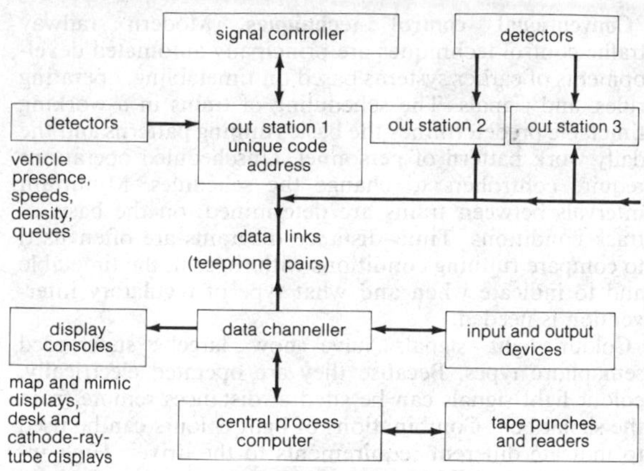

Figure 57: Relationship of elements in a road-traffic area-control system.

time, speeds, and turning movements. The greater the number of detectors and measurements being made the more complex and expensive the system becomes as items of data are fed over special lines, or are coded and carried on standard telephone cables. Information is processed by the central computer which can then determine settings for all the traffic signals in the network based on some optimization of time, speed, or flow for all traffic or for a particular segment of the flow.

Ideally, such control is dynamically responsive to all changes in the state of traffic flow. Few, if any, systems operate at this level. The more usual arrangement is for a computer to scan the data inputs and compare what it deduces of the current situation with past experience and then select the nearest suitable set of control plans, built up by trial and error over a time period and stored. The selected plan may be modified by further computation to fit a current traffic situation more precisely. Thereafter the computer directly or indirectly operates the switching system that controls the signals.

In the control centres information is printed out on teleprinters; often display diagrams indicate the current state of all signal settings, flows, and journey speeds along routes. These displays may be further supplemented by tabular information on cathode-ray (television) tubes and by closed-circuit television surveillance. This latter facility enables the controllers to monitor the smooth operation of the system and simultaneously, to recognize situations such as accidents which the computer cannot understand.

Electronic control on important high capacity routes of a freeway or motorway is becoming a normal feature of such roads. Its essential purposes are to facilitate traffic merging from entrance ramps into the available gaps of the main stream and to redistribute traffic to adjacent streets if the capacity of the route is being impaired by too many vehicles entering. It is also necessary to warn drivers of hazards and of the consequences resulting from emergencies. Information about gaps in the traffic stream, breakdowns, or hazardous weather are collected by surveillance systems and relayed to a local or central processing point. Detectors coupled with auxiliary equipment are capable of deducing traffic flow and speed. Radio telephones and closed-circuit television may be used as supplementary aids, the latter sometimes being triggered and directed to locations in the system when other types of detectors indicate unusual outputs. New types of signals, capable of displaying various messages such as lane closures, accidents, fog warnings, and speed control, can be set automatically and remotely from integrated control centres which maintain emergency services and receive information continuously from surveillance equipment and both ground and air police patrols.

New concepts in control. Several experimental automatic road-vehicle systems have been built in the U.S. and Europe. While a standard of exceptional reliability is a basic requirement of a practical system, and while present costs are high, improvements in micro-electronics and in solid-state microwave sources indicate that costs might be more than offset by reduced accident rates and more efficient use of highways. The latter characteristic may be achieved by a high-speed electronic guidance system which could achieve a fivefold increase in present lane capacity, from 2,000 to 10,000 vehicles per hour, at speeds from 60 to 75 miles per hour (96–120 kilometres per hour). One concept, involving electronically coupled automobiles moving like the cars of a railroad train, could raise highway capacity to 40,000 vehicles per hour.

Steering systems

Steering systems are operated by mounting two magnetic field detectors at the front end of the vehicle equidistant from the centre of its longitudinal axis. A guidance cable, installed in the road, sets up a surrounding circular magnetic field. Any movement of the vehicle, from the travel axis, is measured as a transverse error causing corrective operation of the electrohydraulic steering mechanism. For further control purposes a speed signal is emitted from a buried cable; deviations from correct speed cause either acceleration or braking of the car. Particular difficulties with these systems involve the design of transitions from manual control areas to fully automatic areas and the achievement of technical reliability. In addition, difficulties of unlocking traffic jams in which vehicle densities are five times those at present, may be extraordinary.

Several semi-automatic systems offer stepping stones to full automation. One of the principal problems, which both limits driver performances and increases road accidents, is the saturation of a driver's visual processes with a multiplicity of signs and signals. Improved methods of conveying the most important information have been developed in research programs. "Talking" signs for example, are activated by a signal from an approaching vehicle; their taped information is transmitted to the vehicle receiver for the driver's response. Receivers can be built so that they respond only to the roadside transmitters if the driver requires it but an override can be installed to permit the relay of important information such as traffic holdups ahead, accidents, changes in weather conditions, and information on parking.

Experiments have also been made with automatic routing systems. Traffic detectors linked to a computer measure flows and compute journey times on all parts of the road system. Control information is relayed to signs that display the most suitable routes to be used by approaching drivers to reach important destinations. One experimental project offers an individual route guidance system. The driver inserts a punched card, coded with destination and route requirements, into a transmitter which triggers a matching code transmitter at the approach to each intersection. A low-frequency response signal switch switches a visual display monitor on the vehicle's control panel indicating the turns required.

RAIL TRAFFIC CONTROL

History. The first slow and cumbersome horse-drawn rail traffic posed few control problems not resolved by follow-the-leader principles. It was only after the development of swifter steam-driven trains, in the early years of the nineteenth century, that more frequent trains and their proximity to each other created dangers of collisions. The smooth contact between tracks and iron wheels allowed higher speeds and greater loads to be hauled at the same time that the low friction necessitated long stopping distances. Engines were fitted with brakes and, later, manned brake vans, whose guard could apply the brakes when the engine driver signalled with a whistle.

Trackside control also developed slowly with the first signalman, or "railway policeman," located at passenger and goods depots, or stations, sited along the line. These men indicated, by means of hand signals, the state of the track ahead. Red taillights were mounted at the rear of trains at night to improve safety. Later, signal flags were often replaced by swivelling coloured boards, or disks, for daytime use and with coloured lights at night. Later, signals were located well ahead of stopping points, giving rise to the term "distant signal." As was the case with other modes of transport, the need for control increased with greater traffic movements and faster operating speeds; in the early period, elaborate signalling was unnecessary since the frequency of service was such as to still permit adequate train spacing. The first real method of control was the development of a time-interval system of train spacing. In the event of breakdown or accident, however, there were no means of delaying a following train from entering a section of track except by a physical check on entry and exit by sections; *e.g.*, a brakeman with a flag or lantern.

Telegraph communications

First introduced for railway use in England between Euston and Camden in 1837 the electric telegraph, permitted communication between fixed signal points. Each signalman was responsible for a portion of track known as a block section. Bell codes were used to describe the class and route of the train to be passed by the signalman to the next block section or to accept or reject a train from the preceding section. Generally, only one train was permitted in a section at one time; under poor visibility conditions a section was normally kept empty between every two trains. Many decisions of precedence were left to the individual signalman, and with only limited information at their disposal, signalmen often made incorrect decisions causing excessive delay. At the same time, standard codes and rules were established by most railway companies and safety was further improved by the introduction of Westinghouse air brakes about 1870.

Because concise and standardized information was needed by the engineer, mechanical semaphore arm signals, operated remotely by wires from a lever in a signal box, were developed in 1841 as a principal means of communication. The angle of the arm indicated stop, proceed with caution, or clear ahead. For night use coloured lenses, mounted near the pivot of the arm, are passed across a light source, thus displaying, for the different arm angles, either the familiar red for stop, yellow for caution (approach, reduce speed), and green for clear (proceed as authorized). Similarly the remote control and setting of points, in a block, was transferred from the trackside to the charge of the signalman. Interlocking devices were designed in the 1850s to prevent conflicting settings of points and signals. The time losses due to poor acceleration and deceleration characteristics of trains were obviated, to some extent, by the increasing use of presignals, informing the driver that the signal ahead might be at stop and requiring him to reduce speed or proceed slowly from a stop. Thus the more violent fluctuations were smoothed out; similar control arrangements have now been adopted for use in European cities to control road traffic.

Traffic elements. Railways in most countries are classified as either private or common carriers. Private carriers are in the minority, operating mostly in lumbering, industrial plants, and mining. Further operational classifications are made on the basis of the type of traffic carried. Principal subdivisions are intercity routes (linehaul), intracity route networks (commuter), switching services for warehousing and industrial plants, and general terminal operators.

Rail traffic is divided into passenger and freight, and, although both normally operate over the same system, there are special control problems particular to each. In recent years it has been clear that it is necessary to consider the total journey made by the rail passenger rather than simply the time he spends in the train. The integration of rail services with other forms of transport is essential, particularly in locating stopping points and in designing mainline terminals or commuter stations.

Freight is now a predominant factor in all rail operations. Although the heart of the freight control system is still the so-called marshalling yard, where individual wagons are collected for train makeup, recent years have seen the development of bulk trains, designed specifically for single train loads and running from a private siding to a similar destination siding. The rolling stock is often semipermanently coupled and the handling equipment at the terminals is usually designed for continuous operation of the system at a high capacity.

New systems management and control methods are still needed to improve the speed, regularity, and comfort of rail services while safeguarding established high standards of safe operation. The required resources are often beyond the capability of an outdated industry to provide; direct injection of capital, by national governments, is a worldwide phenomenon.

Conventional control techniques. Modern railway traffic-control techniques are principally automated developments of earlier systems based on timetabling, operating rules, and signals. The scheduling of trains in a working timetable predetermines the basic running patterns and the daily work pattern of personnel. Unscheduled operations require controllers to change the schedules. Minimum intervals between trains are determined, on the basis of track conditions. Time–distance diagrams are often used to compare running conditions with those in the timetable and to indicate when and what type of regulatory intervention is needed.

Colour light signals

Colour light signals have now largely superseded semaphore types. Because they are operated electrically, colour light signals can be sited at distances remote from the signal box. Combinations of light colours can be used to indicate different requirements to the driver. High intensity lights, visible over great distances, are particularly advantageous in poor weather. Searchlights use a single lens and bulb with different colours displayed by means of panels on colour filters rotated in front of the lamp. Lights can be more appropriately sited in relation to the driver's cab position and permit a greater variety of information to be efficiently displayed. With the development of hydraulic, pneumatic, and electrical methods of switching, the problems of distance are overcome and the displacement of mechanical devices from the local signal box enables many more sets to be controlled from a central point.

The basic element in automatic control is an electric circuit built into the track which operates track signals. When a train enters a section of track it causes the current to detour through the locomotive's wheels and axles, instead of completing its normal circuit, altering signals ahead.

When a train has passed a section, the signal behind it is automatically switched by a track circuit immediately ahead to indicate danger. As the train advances to the next section, the first signal can automatically be changed to a lower state of warning and so on until a full clearance signal is set at a given number of sections behind the train. The number of intermediate sections left behind a train is determined by train speeds and section lengths, and influences the capacity of a track.

Today, manual signal boxes have generally been replaced by a few centralized boxes controlling large areas of track. All operations are performed with pushbuttons and the system is designed with full interlocking plant preventing any mis-setting of switches, points, and signals. Each movement can be made only in a predetermined and safe way, eliminating the setting of conflicting routes and signals. Operation of all devices is monitored and relayed from the trackside to an illuminated display on a track diagram. Newer systems also monitor all train movements with individual identity and location indicated by lights supplemented by cathode-ray tubes.

Additional automation has been carried to the cab. Relays, tuned to the transmission of a particular frequency, feed back an activating signal rearward. Similarly each track circuit is set to control the signals. Coded circuits operate other train-borne devices by the installation of suitable receiving coils mounted, above the track, at the front of the locomotive. In this way trackside signal displays are transferred to the cab, reducing the risk of a crew missing a signal. Greater safety margins are provided by the addition of audio signals. Various methods of providing coded impulses include systems in which drivers must respond to audio warnings with an acknowledgment signal. Automatic train stopping is provided by the same means, and in addition, the brakes may be automatically applied if a driver fails to respond to track restrictions. Another form of visual display makes use of a moving map continuously indicating a spot position.

Radio communications

The first recorded moving train two-way radio was used by the New York Central Railroad in 1928. Radio offers a number of advantages in improving communications between train crews and control dispatchers or maintenance gangs on the track. It also establishes a direct link between trains and obviates the need for crews to use wayside telephones. Equipment failures can be reported directly and because of this and other advantages, particularly in automated marshalling yards, delay is reduced. Most railways throughout the world are equipped to some extent with two-way train radios.

A further development is the automation of route-setting procedures. These enable a controller to notify the computer at the beginning and end of the required route; thereafter, all intervening signals and points are automatically established. Storage of a working timetable in program form can be used to initiate the route settings for each subsequent track movement and as each train clears appropriate sections of the track. At the same time identities of trains may be transmitted from one control to another in the form of unique labels, known as head codes. Thus, in addition to changing the signals behind it to red as it proceeds from section to section, a train can remotely generate complete new control sequences.

The development of computer-controlled freight transit is incomplete until a corresponding organizational and documentation process for the dispatch and receipt of goods has been integrated within the total system. A customer may, for example, transcribe orders to the transport system, specifying commodity type, consignment identity, consignor and consignee information, payment instructions, priorities, etc. Information can then be relayed to and from the computer and prices indicated for a particular consignment. In the next stage, trains are made up after each wagon has been loaded and, if required, part-load consignments can be allocated a space number in a specified wagon. Train makeup takes into account engine types, routing, overall weights and lengths, numbers and types of cars, and braking power for all trains leaving a siding. The information is then relayed to points down the line by telephone, telegraph, or teleprinter for the reverse process of train breakup. The grouping of consignments for common destinations into single cars reduces transshipment costs and time losses. Where placement lists of all loads are stored in a computer, optimization programs can be developed to minimize subsequent trucking distribution movements.

Sorting freight cars is a complex operation. Various control systems have been installed in marshalling yards enabling cars to be pushed over a raised track, known as a hump, so that the car travels freely down a grade and over switching points to its correct berth. Automatic humping includes sensors to detect car speed and weight, from which car rolling resistance is estimated. Once the uncoupled car has been allocated a train and siding, automatic switching sets the points along its predetermined path. Simultaneously the computer calculates the speed required for the car to reach the end of the train. Automatic braking devices or boosters reduce or increase the car's speed off the hump to that needed to reach its train coupling point in the siding.

Other, more refined, methods remotely control the pushing locomotive. The spacing of cars rolling off the hump, the automatic control of the pushing speed, and the control of retarders or speed boosters are all directly controlled by computer. Identification of car destinations is an essential part of the process. Manual checking in the yard with radio links to the yardmaster have been displaced by closed-circuit television checking off the train against the makeup list forwarded by teleprinter.

The final scheduling and control of the freight train is integrated into the comprehensive rail control system, and computers permit the computation of alternative strategies with an assessment of benefits. Controllers finally impose their selection of priorities. In the 1970s many of these systems became universal.

Modern signalling systems

New concepts in control. Modern signalling systems have improved the safety, efficiency, and operating economics of railways by providing better track capacity and more flexibility. In West Germany alone more than 10,000 hand signal boxes in 1945 had been reduced to fewer than 3,500 in 1971, and the process is continuing throughout the world. Future control systems are largely developments of existing concepts, but wider area traffic control will be available as the reliability of components is improved and methods of optimizing large networks with multicommodity flows develop.

Difficulties occur when trains are run at different speeds under the same control system. The location of signals, for instance, is determined on the basis of the number of sections required for the fastest train to brake from full speed. This distance is excessive for slower moving trains and hence, because density cannot be maintained, line capacity is reduced. The greater the disparity, the more exaggerated the loss of efficiency will be. Because time is important to passengers, train speeds are rising; on the New Tōkaidō Line, a 310-mile (500-kilometre) section between Tokyo and Ōsaka carries 200 trains a day with more than 50 travelling at speeds up to 130 miles (210 kilometres) per hour.

A method of overcoming disadvantages of mixed traffic is the so-called moving block. In this system the fixed track block is replaced by a moving zone in the front and the rear of the train, the length of the zone determined by the speed of the train. If a train enters another train's zone, signals appear in the cab and at the same time automatically decelerate the train. The moving block system can be applied to express traffic while the conventional system is preserved for slower traffic.

Separating trains by an optimum minimum headway (distance between two trains moving in the same direction) requires the following train controller to have continuous information on the track ahead, including train positions and hazards. This information can be supplied by radar, overhead lines, and other methods.

These developments lead toward automation of the whole system, including driverless trains. A particularly interesting application of these principles is used in new urban rapid transit railways of which the Bay Area Rapid Transit railway in San Francisco is an example. A full system concept is being developed under complete surveillance, with computer processing and monitoring of all aspects ranging from automatic revenue collection to absolute traffic protection (insurance of no collisions) and automatic protection in case of computer failure. Operating speeds are up to 80 miles (130 kilometres) per hour at headways of 90 seconds.

Traffic control and communication is divided into three subsystems, line supervision, traffic protection, and automatic traffic operation. Unlike other control systems mentioned earlier, this system dispenses with central control and operates on the basis of car-carried traffic control, station and trackside control, central supervisory control, and the traffic telephone system.

Failure rates

Failure rates have been assessed for each subsystem based on component failure rates and, in turn, their failure consequences determined for the overall degradation of the system. Fail-safe operation and the minimization of delay were essential considerations. Maintainability has been the key to design of diagnostic apparatus. Other considerations have included a study of customer-created problems through the misuse of automatic ticket machinery.

AIR TRAFFIC CONTROL

History. In the early days of flying, man depended mainly on his own senses aided by primitive controls borrowed from the mariner. The penalties of failure were severe. The first step toward improvement was to end the basic hazard of the aircraft pilot's isolation by installing a communication system. After World War I commercial aircraft were regularly equipped with radios for communication between ground and air. Positioned information and estimated times of arrival were relayed to the ground. Ground stations, in turn, transmitted weather and instructions to the aircraft. With the development of regular routes, networks of ground stations were established so that positions could be determined with known direction-finding techniques: the beaming of an aircraft's radio signal was simultaneously plotted on maps at two or more ground stations, and the resulting positional intersect of the bearings was relayed to the aircraft's radio operator. This technique permitted course corrections to be made when the ground was obscured by clouds. In the late 1920s, the development of radio beams enabled a pilot to follow a track to his destination. (For a detailed discussion of this subject, see NAVIGATION.)

With all these methods, however, control still depended largely on the pilot and, in those early days of aircraft radio, interference, topography, and weather often obliterated the transmissions. Terminal control was limited to the use of light signals by the ground control officers. Later the radio link was added to the system.

While air travel expanded steadily, it was not until World War II that the need to handle large numbers of aircraft brought the development of much more sophisticated types of control. Night bombing led to the development of so-called en route control in which pilots were given time checkpoints along the flight path and at the target point. The problem of returning to a darkened home base many hours later and perhaps, in very different weather conditions, led to the use of the standard beam approach in which the pilot located himself once his aircraft entered a signal beam emitted by a ground transmitter. The wide, fan-shaped beam, tapering to a point at the end of the runway, was divided into two halves, one of which was dots, the other dashes. The plane followed the path where dots and dashes overlapped, forming a continuous note. As an aid to the pilot in determining his position and the point at which to begin a descent, additional transmitters, emitting a vertically directed signal of different intensity, were provided.

Improved ground control methods were also necessary in wartime because of the large number of aircraft returning to a base at the same time. Aircraft and bases exchanged radio identities and sequences of landing were established, including stacking, directing returning aircraft to circle at 1,000-foot (300-metre) altitude intervals. The lowest aircraft was designated the next in turn to land, with each higher aircraft descending through a one-thousand-foot step to its next altitude until the last had been accommodated by the controller on a specified runway. Ground controllers also established "talk-down" methods. One such system developed at the time was called controlled descent through cloud and has led to a modern version, ground-controlled approach.

Traffic elements. Aircraft are flown today for numerous purposes ranging from scheduled airliners to unscheduled airliners, military aircraft, bulk cargo carriers, and such independents as private business and sport planes, crop sprayers, weather craft, and traffic controllers. Operational control of aircraft depends primarily on their service use, on whether they fly near the ground or in adverse climates away from bases, and whether they operate from land, water, or ice. Aircraft have high operating costs and, with increasing sophistication, represent larger investment problems and fly from complex and costly ground bases. Helicopters and the newer generation of vertical-takeoff aircraft have somewhat different characteristics and, therefore, individual control problems.

Lengths and widths of runways are classified according to the type of traffic they handle. Principal types include private, secondary, feeder, continental, and intercontinental airports.

Collision avoidance

Problems. Collision avoidance remains a critical traffic control problem. Systems are developed and can act as a supplementary aid in terminal areas, as well as the principal sensor in airways lacking ground surveillance equipment. Considering the high closing (approaching) speeds of modern aircraft (20 miles, or 30 kilometres, per minute) the somewhat lower ascent or descent rates (two miles, or three kilometres, per minute and four miles, or six kilometres, per minute, respectively) and aircraft capability for rapid acceleration, it is necessary to be able to specify required avoidance manoeuvres quickly from among available options. Simple proximity warning indicators detect aircraft presence, within certain ranges, in the surrounding airspace and warn the pilot, but avoidance ultimately depends on visual sighting of the intruder. Newer types of instruments, operating on a common frequency, transmit regular interrogation pulses; other aircraft respond with an identity "label." This is in a digital code form, presenting such information as altitude and rate of change in altitude, together with range-finding signals. Extremely accurate atomic clocks are synchronized in order to measure the time elapsed between the sending and receiving of signals and to deduce the interval of time separating the two aircraft. Without directional location, avoidance options are limited to a vertical plane of escape, but both aircraft must make the correct decision relative to the other; generally one moves up and the other down.

Thunderstorms ahead of aircraft are readily detected by airborne radar, but ice particles and other turbulences in the upper altitudes are not. While airports are usually sited to avoid frequent fog situations, as many as one in fifty landings must be aborted because of visibility conditions. New electronic automatic landing systems, using radio altimeters in conjunction with a computer, have been perfected, and it is likely in the future that fog will be more of a hazard on the journey to and from the airport. Accidents and pollution problems, including smoke, turbulence, and noise, have grown increasingly important. (See above *Air transportation*.)

Regulation. Late in World War II a number of Allied and neutral nations convened in Chicago to determine the arrangements necessary for the safe and orderly development of international air transport. They established the International Civil Aviation Organization to study and report on customs facilities, traffic control, aircraft maintenance, and the important need for standardization. Air-transport terminals, unlike those of other transport modes, are likely to be used more frequently by the vehicles of another nation than those of the host country. Accordingly, standards have been laid down by member nations for all essential matters; factors of lesser import are subject to recommended practices. English has become the international language of control. The rules adopted are updated by regular conventions of the international organization.

Conventional control techniques. The purpose of air traffic control is to regulate flight movements, ensuring that collision courses are avoided and that safe distances are maintained between aircraft. The separation of aircraft is governed by International Civil Aviation Organization rules specifying lateral (angular distance), horizontal (distance or time interval), and vertical (different flight levels) intervals.

Airspace

Airspace is divided by flight levels into upper, middle, lower, and controlled airspace. Controlled airspace includes that surrounding airports and airways, which define the corridors of movement between them with minimum and maximum altitudes. The degree of control varies with the importance of the airway and may, for private light aircraft, be represented only by ground markings. Airways are usually divided by 1,000-foot (300-metre) and 500-foot (150-metre) levels with aircraft assigned specific operating levels, according to direction and performance. Normally all such movements are controlled by air traffic control centres. In upper airspace, above about 25,000 feet (7,500 metres) pilots may be allowed free route choices provided that flight tracks and profiles have been agreed on in advance. In middle airspace all pilots entering or crossing controlled airspace are obliged to accept control and notification must therefore be given to control in advance. Radar advisory services are often available in middle airspace but not generally below 5,000 feet (1,500 metres) in lower airspace. Besides vertical spacings, in airways, horizontal separations are important, usually taking the form of a minimum time interval of 10 minutes between aircraft on the same track and elevation with a lateral spacing, typically, of 10 miles (16 kilometres).

The simplest form of flight control is called the visual flight rule. Aircraft in controlled airspace must remain at least one nautical mile (1,852 metres) horizontally and 1,000 feet (300 metres) vertically away from all clouds and visibility must not be less than five nautical miles (9,260 metres). Outside controlled airspace, the aircraft must be flown clear of clouds and within sight of land or water. In congested airspace all pilots must obey the instrument flight rule; that is, they must depend principally on instruments for their safety. In poor visibility and at night instrument flight rules invariably apply. At airports, in control zones, all movements are subject to permission and instruction from Air Traffic Control when visibility is typically less than five nautical miles or the cloud ceiling is below 1,500 feet (450 metres).

Procedural control starts with the aircraft's captain receiving meteorological forecasts together with a briefing officer's listings of radio-frequency changes along the flight path and notices to airmen. Flight plans are checked and possible exit corridors from the flight path, in case of emergency, are determined. Flight plans are relayed to control towers and approach control centres. As the aircraft taxis out, under instructions from the ground-movement controller, the pilot awaits his turn to be fitted into the overall pattern of incoming and outgoing movements. Controllers allocate an outgoing track which enables aircraft separation to be maintained; this is determined from a check of the more recently used standard departure clearances. As the aircraft climbs to its initial altitude, on an instructed heading, the departure controller identifies the image caused by the aircraft on the radar screen before allowing any new takeoffs or landings. Further instructions clear the aircraft for its final climb to the en route portion of the flight and the pilots' first reporting point marked by radio devices. This portion of the flight may also be under radar surveillance.

Progress reports on the en route portion of the flight are required, and the aircraft may be tracked on radar. Pairs of transmitters define each leg of the airway. At several points along his route the captain reports altitude, time and the estimated time of arrival at the next listed reporting point.

Flight progress strips

Flight progress strips are made up on boards from the filed flight plans and include all traffic on an airway under that centre's control. Information includes call signs, flight details, and estimated times of arrival at reporting points. As each report is received actual times are entered and the estimated times of arrival are adjusted for subsequent reporting points; altitudes are also checked. Each aircraft has a separate strip for each reporting point. The progress of all aircraft is thus adjusted as the flights proceed, and updating estimates are made of the future state enabling the controller, in direct communication with the flight by radio, to maintain separations and to permit pilots a safe change of course or altitude if these are required.

Since the introduction of long-range tracking radar, the flight progress board has been used as a backup system immediately available in the event of instrument failures. Whereas tabulating reported information only represents a succession of reports on an aircraft's position, radar gives continuous coverage of flight movements allowing safe reductions to be made in separations and, thus, increasing capacity.

At a reporting point en route the receiving control centre takes over the flight from the departure centre, and all further reports and instructions are made to the new control centre. Descent instructions are relayed to arrange the incoming aircraft at separations of perhaps five miles (eight kilometres), in effect, on a slanting line. As the aircraft closes in speed adjustments or lengthening of flight paths may be necessary to maintain separations of three nautical miles over the airport boundary. Controllers determine the landing sequences and stacking instructions and may adjust takeoffs to handle surges in the incoming flights. The final stage is initiated by transfer of control to an approach controller. Under radar surveillance the final directions are given for landing. In the landing sequence, control passes to the control tower where precision radar is used to monitor the landing, and ground movement controllers issue taxiing instructions (Figure 58).

The control tower handles the initial and terminal parts of the flight. Other tower functions include the operational control of high-intensity approach lights, emergency services, taxiing movements, and continuous broadcasts of airport information on runways in use and weather details. Besides a clear viewing position of the whole runway area, immediate and direct communication is an important requirement, particularly in coordinating activities with area and approach control centres. Smaller airport towers, with fewer traffic movements, may combine the functions of approach and final control.

New concepts in control. Air traffic control is still a manual operation controlled by humans. Semi-automatic

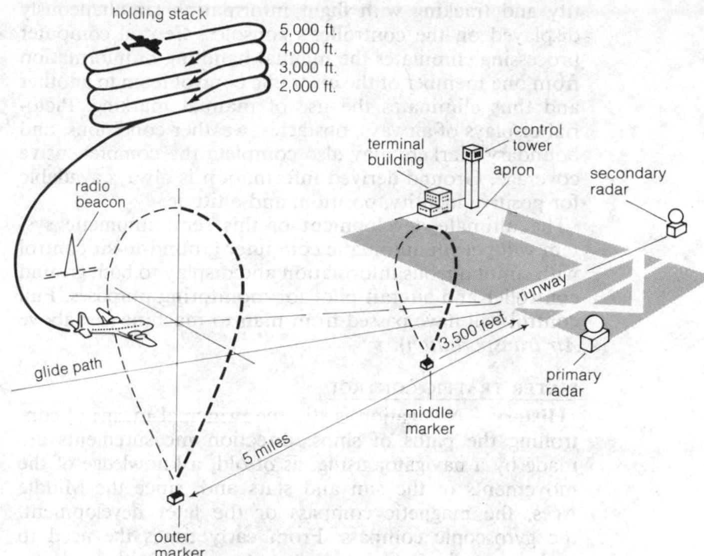

Figure 58: *Aircraft landing sequence.*
Control tower receives information on an airplane's approach via radar, allocates a runway, and issues final instructions so that the aircraft will intersect the glide-path beam of the instrument-landing system. Markers (dashed-line hoops) indicate to the pilot fixed distances from the runway.

systems are currently being installed, but if air travel is to continue its development, and effective airport and airway capacities with adequate safety are to be achieved, fully automatic systems will be required. Controllers are believed to be at, or near, the limit in the use of radar for aircraft surveillance and sequencing and voice communication for instructing aircrews and receiving information. Information is often limited and lacking in precision, both in terms of the ground controllers and the air crew and, furthermore, can be dangerously ambiguous. Because of this situation controllers and pilots may spend most of their time exchanging information. Decisions are thus in danger of being taken on the basis of incomplete data. The principal objective is to automate both the information and control systems, within a data-processing complex of specified reliability.

Flight data processing

The first essential component of an automated system is a means for processing flight data information. Flight plans, subsequent amendments, weather data, and notices to airmen may be entered directly into a central computer (Figure 59). Information from other centres is carried via data links to remote input devices of the central computer.

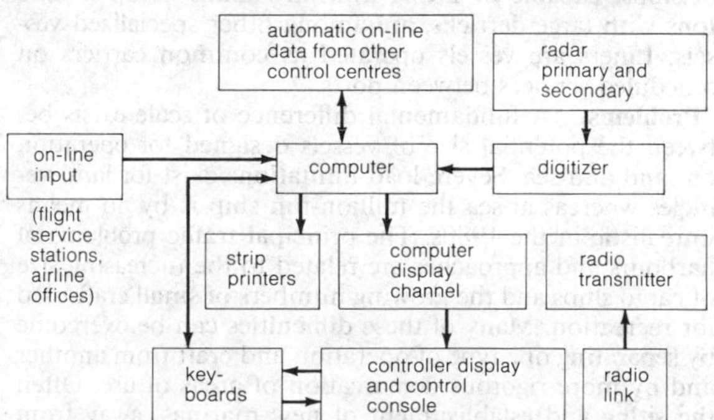

Figure 59: *Elements of an automated in-flight control system.*
The information from other control centres and from radar is entered in the computer, which already contains flight plan and weather data.

Operational data, from primary and secondary radar, is first processed into a digital form for onward transmission and subsequent computer processing. Data transfer and printout is available at equipped remote sites within a control centre or at other terminals. Target data and flight plan data can thus be correlated by developing suitable computer programs. Comprehensive information can be displayed to the controller giving automatic aircraft identity and tracking with flight information simultaneously displayed on the controller's consoles. Central computer processing eliminates the manual handling of information from one member of the air traffic control team to another and thus eliminates the use of manual marking. Pictorial displays of airways, obstacles, weather conditions, and boundary markers may also complete the comprehensive coverage. Ground-derived information is always available for positive identity, position, and altitude.

The ultimate development of this semi-automatic system will permit automatic computer ground-to-air control with simultaneous information and display to both ground controller and aircraft pilot for monitoring purposes. Full control will have passed from man to machine (see above *Air transportation*).

WATER TRAFFIC CONTROL

History. Navigation is still the principal means of controlling the paths of ships; direction measurements are made by a navigator using, as of old, a knowledge of the movements of the sun and stars and, since the Middle Ages, the magnetic compass or the later development, the gyroscopic compass. From early times the need to exchange information between ships and with land stations, led to the development of visual and audible signal systems. Markers were carried by ships and also laid in channels, and the transmission of messages was accomplished through flag, semaphore, horn, bell, whistle, and light signals leading to the establishment of first national and later international codes. The invention and use of radio, at the beginning of this century, brought a marked improvement in ship communication.

Considerable advances in mapping were made over the centuries; modern navigation charts show all coasts, submerged obstacles, sea depths, and navigational aids such as lighthouses, lightships, buoys, and radio beacons (see also MAPPING AND SURVEYING).

New forms of steam propulsion and the design of iron ships in the 19th century led to increased ship size. The growth in world trade brought to the fore the problem of establishing consistent avoiding action when vessels approached each other. International rules of the road at sea were laid down in 1863 and have since been periodically updated.

Traffic elements. Ships can be broadly divided into tramps, specialized vessels, and liners. Tramps are mostly conveyors of bulk cargo, trading internationally, and operating without fixed sailing schedules, generally committed on the basis of time, or for a specific voyage. Specialized carriers include tankers and a rapidly growing group of carriers designed for the movement of iron ore, sugar, and other bulk commodities. Container ships, ferries, and belships, capable of lifting awkward loads of up to 250 tons with large derricks, are among other specialized vessels. Liners are vessels operated as common carriers on scheduled services between ports.

Problems. A fundamental difference of scale exists between the potential size of vessels designed for operation on land and sea. Severe load limitations exist for land vehicles whereas at sea the million-ton ship is by no means unrealistic in the 1980s. The principal traffic problems of harbours and approaches are related to the increasing size of cargo ships and the growing numbers of small craft used for recreation. Many of these difficulties can be overcome by separating one type of operation and craft from another and by more rigorous demarcation of areas of use. Often the siting and establishment of new marinas, away from crowded shipping lanes and established ports, reduces the problems and permits the special needs of the leisure user to be fulfilled.

But a vast and urgent control problem has been created by the increasing pollution of the earth's water. At sea, improved sewage disposal methods and a reduction in air pollution can be effected by waste processing before discharge as required on land for other industrial operations. Reducing oil pollution is a more serious difficulty, long recognized by governments in legislation prohibiting oil discharge within 50 miles (80 kilometres) of land and in the designation and control of ocean dumping grounds. Such control is effected internationally through a United Nations agency, the Inter-Governmental Maritime Consultative Organization, and methods of instituting court proceedings against offenders have resulted from international conventions. Victims of pollution damage are also enabled to claim compensation from ship owners and insurers.

The redesign and development of control systems to prevent oil spillage are important in tanker design. Difficulties have arisen with some new systems due to the explosive dangers of residual vapour in the tanks. Apart from the "creeping" pollution arising from oil discharge during normal operations, the main problem is the danger of collision or shipwreck, in which massive quantities of crude oil or other harmful materials may be released to pollute vast coastal areas. New methods of treatment are being investigated and disaster procedures laid down, enabling authorities to undertake swift clearing operations.

Regulations, international and national. International regulations control ship construction and use. All important routes are now governed by regional agreements. Shipowners have developed the liner conference system that regulates sailings and ports of call and establishes a common tariff for freight and passenger movements. Postal administrations also contract with shipping companies, through the shipping conferences, for mail handled as a commodity on a tonnage basis. Coastal shipping is usually subject to governmental control. Tramp shipping is based on market chartering of ships or space therein, for the carriage of all types of cargo to and from all ports. The largest of these markets is the Baltic Mercantile and Shipping Exchange in London.

Generally there are obligations for ship constructors and owners to comply with rules, established nationally and internationally, governing classification of ships. These affect ship design, particularly elements concerned with safety standards, including lifesaving equipment, waterproof and fireproof bulkheads, gangways, navigational aids, and construction standards. The maritime nations regularly hold international conventions to consider the problems of safety at sea, including all aspects of navigation. National regulations impose survey systems to check vessels for seaworthy conditions, and societies, such as Lloyd's Register of Shipping (U.K.), American Bureau of Shipping (U.S.), Registro Italiano (Italy), Germanischer Lloyd (West Germany), and Bureau Veritas (France), today classify and survey most of the world's mercantile fleet.

Conventional control techniques. Control of ships on the open sea still remains exclusively with the master of the vessel; when other ships are met established rules of steering are practiced. This ancient arrangement, primitive by comparison with the sophisticated and centralized air traffic-control system, has survived thanks to the expanse of sea and the relatively few ships sailing upon it. Communication between ships is, therefore, vital in their control, both at sea and with the confined channels of inland waterways. The principal methods of transmitting a signal are visual (that is, by flag, semaphore, or light) or audible (by means of horns or radio). The revised International Code of 1934 includes alphabetic, numeral, and answering flags. Urgent messages can be communicated by single flags while three-letter groups are used for compass points, bearings, and times. Semaphore signalling employs hand flags, while Morse can be transmitted visually by searchlights equipped with horizontal control slats, or by radio. Ships also use sirens for "in sight" conditions, to indicate impending course changes and, generally, for warning purposes in bad visibility.

The control of ships near coasts is facilitated, both for warning and navigational purposes, by the use of lightships and lighthouses. Channels on the approach to ports are clearly marked by floating buoys, usually fitted with lights and equipped with sound signals (horns, bells, and whistles) for use in bad weather or at night. The proper provision of buoys and beacons, anchored in their correct position and their subsequent maintenance, is essential for control and safety purposes.

Buoys are classified by their functional role into categories denoted by shape, markings, and colour. The approach to an estuary for example, is marked by a landfall buoy and main channels by red can-shaped or black cone-shaped buoys. Where channels fork, at junctions, spherical buoys are used to indicate direction either to port or starboard. Other special buoys denote wreck positions, danger areas, and middle ground, the region near the centre of the channel where ships can safely move.

Marine and harbour radar was first developed during World War II in the United Kingdom. Subsequent developments have permitted much shorter wavelengths to be used, employing narrow beam scanners, that give an immediate measurement of bearing and range with accuracies better than 30 seconds and 20 yards (18 metres). Shipborne marine radar assists navigation and helps to reduce collisions at sea, providing map-type information both in darkness and fog of other objects, adjacent coastlines, icebergs, and some types of approaching storms. Harbour radar permits information to be radioed to ships to position themselves clear of channels in controlled anchorages and, entering or leaving port, allows determination of position relative to navigational markers. It also enables irregularities to be monitored by harbour masters and the movements of harbour vessels to be controlled by radio instructions to tug and other masters.

Collisions at sea

Collisions occur at sea even in cases in which vessels have clearly sighted each other. This happens when, despite radio and radar equipment, erroneous deductions are made. Some collisions result from the slow response and poor manoeuvrability of ships; this is particularly true of the new supersized ships. Furthermore, because of their great size, new ships congest the few deep channels near coasts or leading to harbours. The mechanization of cargo handling and docks has concentrated the huge new ships into a few ports and their narrow approaches. Such natural shipping lanes as the English Channel, where nearly 1,000 ships a day pass through straits less than 25 miles (40 kilometres) wide, and other heavily used manmade systems such as the Kiel Canal in Germany, which passes some 90,000 ships a year, create the need for new control systems.

The first type of physical control system to be applied after the establishment of a basic set of rules for a given area is to segregate opposing directions of movement. A working party from the various navigational organizations of Europe has agreed on a sea-lane three miles (five kilometres) wide, separated by a safety zone two miles (three kilometres) wide, at several European locations. As in all international developments where the rights of nations, or even individuals, have become established over the centuries, the pace and manner of changes are usually exceedingly slow.

Whereas navigational control of a ship refers to its position relative to natural features, operational control refers to the governing of its movements in relation to that of other vehicles and along prescribed channels. A return echo, received from the emission of pulsed radio energy and transmitted by the rotating aerial of a marine radar, is displayed on a cathode-ray tube in a plan position indicator. Ships and channel markers are thus displayed at various selected ranges, from about 1 to 100 nautical miles (1 nautical mile = 1,852 metres), dependent on the power radiated by the installation and aerial characteristics. Newer equipment provides for an automatic plotting of the data aligned to standard charts.

New concepts in control. The development of a new navigation system was based on the principle that if two radio stations transmitted different signals, a receiver, equipped to pick them up simultaneously, could compare the differences and obtain an estimate of its range from the two stations. Such a system has been designed and manufactured using a master station, transmitting two or three slightly different signals at frequencies around 100,000 cycles per second (see NAVIGATION). Over 30 chains of stations are being erected throughout the world's most crowded shipping areas, covering approaches to western Europe, the U.S. and Canadian western seaboards, the Persian Gulf and Indian Ocean areas, and the waters around Japan and South Africa. Other systems, operating over much greater oceanic distances, are being developed from early versions of long-range navigators, but lack the precision of the closer, lower frequency chains.

Control of lakes

While many of the problems of the control of inland waterways concern the maintenance of channels and locks, the increasing growth of traffic on major canals, inland seas, and lakes demands more advanced forms of traffic control than hitherto. Many of the most important waterways only offer single-lane operation for the larger ships, with carefully regulated speed control to inhibit erosion. An example of control is that maintained for the busy Kiel Canal, where a speed limit of nine miles (15 kilometres) per hour permits about 180 ships to be accommodated at one time in the canal, with control exercised by stations at either end. The stations monitor and log data on ships' movements, coordinating a flow of information from visual observations made at locks and sidings along the canal's length. By constructing time–distance diagrams, controllers attempt to optimize the traffic flow by using the sidings to organize priorities.

Currently research is being undertaken to test a digital computer system for making the control decisions. Favoured is a simulation technique in which each ship's movements would be forecast in advance; if a conflict threatened between two ships, signals would automatically be set to stop one or the other vessel, according to a minimum delay criterion, in the previous siding.

With the advent of nuclear-powered vessels the avoidance of collision at sea has become even more paramount in control development. For the present, while the automation of crew operations by the provision of monitoring and control systems is growing, it is likely that ships will remain primarily self-controlled at sea. But the improvement of satellite communications, for the tracking and control of air traffic over the oceans, will probably lead in future years to a joint-use system shared with ships at sea. (F.D.H.)

BIBLIOGRAPHY

General: CHARLES SINGER *et al.* (eds.), *A History of Technology,* vol. 1–5 (1954–58), an authoritative and standard work containing much material on the history of transportation; JOSEPH NEEDHAM, *Science and Civilization in China,* vol. 1–2 (1954), a history of the discovery, invention, and technological development in China through the centuries; EDWIN A. PRATT, *A History of Inland Transport and Communication in England* (1912); C.I. SAVAGE, *An Economic History of Transport,* rev. ed. (1966).

Carriages and wagons: Of the standard works on the history of this subject, the following are by carriage or wagon manufacturers: G.A. THRUPP, *The History of Coaches* (1877); E.M. STRATTON, *The World on Wheels* (1878); and W.B. ADAMS, *English Pleasure Carriages* (1837). R. STRAUS, *Carriages and Coaches: Their History and Their Evolution* (1912), is more popular but less original. C. SINGER *et al.* (eds.), *A History of Technology,* 5 vol. (1954–58), is very useful for ancient times, less so for medieval, and in the modern period for English carts and wagons only. See also V. GORDON CHILDE, "The First Waggons and Carts—From the Tigris to the Severn," *Proc. Prehist. Soc.,* n. s., vol. 17, pt. 2, pp. 177–194 (1951); L. TARR, *The History of the Carriage* (1969); FRANK E. HUGGETT, *Carriages at Eight: Horse-Drawn Society in Victorian and Edwardian Times* (1980); and RICHARD HEGEL, *Carriages From New Haven* (1975), a study of the industry's growth and decline.

Ships: EDWARD LEWIS, ROBERT O'BRIEN, and the EDITORS OF TIME–LIFE BOOKS, *Ships* (1970), a popular well-illustrated volume on ships and their design and use; A.C. HARDY, *The Book of the Ship* (1949), a brief but thorough description of various types of ships; CHRISTOPHER LLOYD, *Ships and Seamen from the Vikings to the Present Day* (1961), an excellent pictorial history of ships and the men who sailed them; HERBERT LEE SEWARD (ed.), *Marine Engineering,* 2 vol. (1942–44), a fundamental source of information on the design and use of marine power plants; HENRY B. CULVER, *Forty Famous Ships* (1936), on ships from the time of Christ to the Queen Mary; PHYLLIS FLANDERS DORSET, *Historic Ships Afloat* (1967), a tabulation of preserved ship relics; RUPERT SARGENT HOLLAND, *Historic Ships* (1926), a summary of facts and stories of famous ships; CHARLES GIBSON, *Wandering Beauties* (1960), an excellent compilation of tales, facts, and descriptions of sailing ships; FRANK O. BRAYNARD, *Famous American Ships,* rev. ed. (1978); ROBERT G. ALBION, *Five Centuries of Famous Ships* (1978), an excellent oceanic history.

More specialized studies include: J.S. MORRISON and R.T. WILLIAMS, *Greek Oared Ships, 900–322 B.C.* (1968); RICHARD

W. UNGER, *The Ship in the Medieval Economy, 600–1600* (1980); FRANK O. BRAYNARD, *By Their Works Ye Shall Know Them* (1968), a complete description of the life and ships of William Francis Gibbs, and *S.S. Savannah* (1963), the story of the first steamer across the Atlantic; WARREN TUTE, *Atlantic Conquest* (1962), good source on the Atlantic and its conquerors; ROBERT DOLLAR, *One Hundred-Thirty Years of Steam Navigation* (1931), a firsthand account of ships and shippers; WARREN ARMSTRONG, *Atlantic Highway* (1962), an interesting account of transoceanic ships and their adventures; HOWARD IRVING CHAPELLE, *The Baltimore Clipper: Its Origin and Development* (1965), an excellent account of a link in the chain leading to the Clippers; ALBERT COOK CHURCH, *Whale Ships and Whaling* (1960), a history with good illustrations; JAMES DUGAN, *The Great Iron Ship* (1953), the story of the "Great Eastern"; FREDERIC C. LANE, *Ships for Victory* (1951), a history of the shipbuilding programs of World War II; CHARLES BOSWELL, *The America* (1964), the story of the yacht "America"; CARLO M. CIPOLLA, *Guns, Sails and Empires: Technological Innovations and the Early Phases of European Expansion, 1400–1700* (1965), an exhaustive analysis of Oriental ships; JOHN D. HARBRON, *Communist Ships and Shipping* (1962), an overview of shipping developments behind the iron curtain; T.M. BUERMAN, P. LEEHEY, and JAMES J. STILLWELL, "An Appraisal of Hydrofoil Supported Craft," *Trans. Inst. Mar. Engrs.*, vol. 65, no. 8 (1954), a basic source document on the design and performance of hydrofoils; S.W. LANK and O.H. OAKLEY, *Application of Nuclear Power to Icebreakers* (1959), a tentative design analysis including a Russian description of the "Lenin."

Current information may be found in E.E. SIGWART (comp.), *Merchant Ships: World Built* (annual), a pictorial and descriptive catalog of each year's new ships; PATRICK FINLAY (ed.), *Jane's Freight Containers* (annual), a fascinating addition to the "Jane's Series" for those interested in modern shipping developments (see also *Jane's Merchant Ships*); the SOCIETY OF NAVAL ARCHITECTS AND MARINE ENGINEERS, *Transactions* (monthly); and the *Marine Engineering Log* (monthly).

Railroad: *Jane's World Railways* and the *Directory of Railway Officials and Yearbook* (both annual), comprehensive statistical data on operations of specific railroads (also lists of officers). A.M. WELLINGTON, *The Economic Theory of the Location of Railways,* 6th ed. (1904), a classic on location and operation principles; W.W. HAY, *Railroad Engineering*, 2nd ed. (1982), and *An Introduction to Transportation Engineering* (1961), on basic principles of design and operation; A.W. BRUCE, *The Steam Locomotive in America* (1952), a history of steam locomotive development in the 20th century; S.H. HOLBROOK, *The Story of American Railroads* (1947), a good popular history of railroads in the United States; R.S. HENRY, *Trains* (1954), a description of the organization and operation of American railroads. *Modern Railroads* (monthly); *Railway Age* (semimonthly); *Trains* (monthly); ASSOCIATION OF AMERICAN RAILROADS, *Railroad Facts* (annual); *Quiz on Railroads and Railroading* (irreg.); *A Review of Railway Operations* (annual), statistics on current American operations; *Moody's Transportation Manual* (annual), comprehensive financial and operating data on United States lines; BRITISH RAILWAYS BOARD, *The Reshaping of British Railways* (1963), the "Beeching Report" that influenced present policies; R. BELL, *History of British Railways During the War, 1939–45* (1946), an excellent account of railroads under wartime conditions; *Michael Robbins, The Railway Age in Britain* (1962), a highly readable account of British railroad history and development. *Railway Gazette International* (monthly); *Railway Magazine* (monthly); *Modern Railways* (monthly); INTERNATIONAL RAILWAY CONGRESS ASSOCIATION, *Rail International* (monthly); *Revue Générale des Chemins de Fer* (monthly); *Ingegneria Ferroviaria* (monthly); *International Railway Journal* (monthly); *Die Bundesbahn* (semimonthly); JAPANESE NATIONAL RAILWAYS, *Fact and Figures* (annual); *Japanese Railway Engineering* (quarterly). See also FREEMAN HUBBARD, *Encyclopedia of North American Railroading* (1981), covering 150 years of technology, history, and folklore; and DON BALL, *America's Railroads: The Second Generation* (1980), nearly 300 illustrations of post-1960 diesels from the U.S. and Canada.

Automobiles, trucks, and buses: G.N. GEORGANO (ed.), *The Complete Encyclopedia of Motorcars, 1885 to the Present,* 2nd ed. (1973), the definitive work on the subject, copiously illustrated, covering some 4,000 makes of automobiles; THE AUTOMOBILE QUARTERLY, *The American Car Since 1775* (1971), an exhaustive treatment of some 5,000 makes of cars produced or projected in North America; LAWRENCE J. WHITE, *The Automobile Industry Since 1945* (1971), based on critical, scholarly research; NEW ENGLISH LIBRARY, *History of the Motorcar* (1971), a lavishly illustrated, brightly written treatment of the self-propelled vehicle; DAVID BURGESS WISE, *The Motor Car: An Illustrated International History* (1979), a history of U.S. and European self-propelled vehicles since the 17th century; STEPHEN W. SEARS, *The American Heritage History of the Automobile in America* (1977), profusely illustrated; WILLIAM H. CROUSE, *Automotive Mechanics,* 7th ed. (1975), and *Automotive Engine Design* (1970), provide a complete introductory course on each subject and cover the theory of operation and construction, maintenance, repair, and adjustment of automotive components, as well as their design; M.W. STOCKEL, *Auto Mechanics Fundamentals* (1982), which contains basic information about various devices; C.F. and E.S. TAYLOR, *The Internal-Combustion Engine,* 2nd ed. (1961), provides analytical methods that lead to a basic understanding of engine behaviour; COLIN CAMPBELL, *The Sports Car: Its Design and Performance,* 4th ed. (1978), discusses the design and performance primarily of high-powered vehicles, sometimes called muscle cars, but includes also much broader fundamental information; and HARRIS E. DARK, *Auto Engines of Tomorrow: Power Alternatives for Cars to Come* (1975), reviews numerous possibilities, including the history of each and illustrations. G.N. GEORGANO (ed.), *The Complete Encyclopedia of Commercial Vehicles* (1979), provides comprehensive coverage from the 19th century through the late 1970s, and with C. DEMAND, *Trucks: An Illustrated History, 1892–1921* (1978), on European and American trucks of the period; A. INGRAM, *Off Highway and Construction Trucks* (1980), is a survey of specialized, heavy-duty trucks, well illustrated.

Urban transportation: Surveys of the status of urban transportation, including its economics, problems, and some proposed solutions, are presented in W. OWEN, *The Metropolitan Transportation Problem,* rev. ed. (1966); J.R. MEYER *et al., The Urban Transportation Problem* (1965); and G.M. SMERK (ed.), *Readings in Urban Transportation* (1968). R.L. CREIGHTON, *Urban Transportation Planning* (1970), outlines the planning process, drawing on the author's experience with the Chicago and Niagara Frontier studies. Origin–destination techniques, trip generation, and travel expenditures are discussed in W.Y. OI and P.W. SHULDINER, *An Analysis of Urban Travel Demands* (1962). E.N. THOMAS and J.L. SCHOFER, *Strategies for the Evaluation of Alternative Transportation Plans,* a report prepared for the National Cooperative Highway Research Program (1970), applies systems analysis to transportation decision making. STANLEY I. FISCHLER, *Moving Millions: An Inside Look at Mass Transit* (1979), deals with urban rail transportation.

Additional materials useful for review of urban transportation planning are UNIVERSITY OF CALIFORNIA INSTITUTE OF TRANSPORTATION AND TRAFFIC ENGINEERING, *Fundamentals of Traffic Engineering,* 7th ed. (1969), *Urban Mass Transit Planning* (1967); and WILBUR SMITH AND ASSOCIATES, *Transportation and Parking for Tomorrow's Cities* (1966), *Parking in the City Center* (1965). Pricing of streets, rather than the limitation of street use by congestion, is explored in G.J. ROTH, *Paying for Roads: The Economics of Traffic Congestion* (1967). C.D. FOSTER, *The Transport Problem* (1963), covers the economic criteria for transport investment.

Rail and bus transit are discussed in A. SCHEFFER LANG and R.M. SOBERMAN, *Urban Rail Transit: Its Economics and Technology* (1964); ORGANIZATION FOR ECONOMIC COOPERATION AND DEVELOPMENT, *Improvements and Innovations in Urban Bus Systems* (1969); WILBUR SMITH AND ASSOCIATES, *The Potential for Bus Rapid Transit* (1970), and *Motor Trucks in the Metropolis* (1969).

Concern for system environment and amenity is expressed in the GREAT BRITAIN MINISTRY OF TRANSPORT, *Traffic in Towns: A Study of the Long Term Problems of Traffic in Urban Areas* (1963); L. HALPRIN, *Freeways* (1966); H. BLUMENFELD, "Criteria for Judging the Quality of the Urban Environment," in H.J. SCHMANDT and W. BLOOMBERG, JR. (eds.), *The Quality of Urban Life* (1969); G.R. TAYLOR, "The Beginnings of Mass Transportation in Urban America," *Smithsonian Journal of History*, vol. 1, no. 2 pp. 35–50 and vol. 1, no. 3, pp. 31–54 (1966), traces the growth of urban transportation in Boston, New York, and Philadelphia between 1820 and 1860. B. RUDOFSKY, *Streets for People: A Primer for Americans* (1969); and D.N. LEWIS (ed.), *The Pedestrian in the City* (1965), consider city planning and pedestrian circulation.

Air transportation: C. DOLLFUS and H. BOUCHE, *L'Histoire de l'aéronautique* (1932), the classic and definitive history of flight to the early 1930s; C.H. GIBBS-SMITH, *The Aeroplane: An Historical Survey* (1968), a comprehensive and detailed compilation by a noted British historian; *Jane's All the World's Aircraft* (annual), specifications and photographs of all known aircraft and missiles; G. LOENING, *Our Wings Grow Faster* (1935), and *Takeoff into Greatness* (1968), a review of the development of the U.S. aeronautical industry by a pioneer and long-time participant; NATIONAL AERONAUTICS AND SPACE ADMINISTRATION, *Fifty Years of Aeronautical Research* (1968), a well-illustrated survey of aeronautical research progress; J.L. PRITCHARD, *Sir George Cayley* (1961), an in-depth biography of the father of British aeronautics; SMITHSONIAN INSTITUTION, *Langley Memoir on Mechanical Flight* (1902), a detailed and fully illustrated account of the aeronautical research of Samuel Pierpont Langley; H.S. VILLARD, *Contact: The Story of the Early Birds* (1968), personal reminiscences of planes and pilots of the pre-World War I era; WILBUR and ORVILLE WRIGHT, *Miracle at Kitty Hawk*, ed. by F.C. KELLY (1951), a compilation of the Wrights' research data; T. VON KARMAN, *The Wind and Beyond* (1967), a report on technical flight progress by an outstanding scientist. JOHN NEWHOUSE, *The Sporty Game* (1982), a study of the aircraft manufacturing industry.

Air-cushion machines: WILLIAM T. GUNSTON, *Hydrofoils and Hovercraft* (1970), is a comprehensive, easy-to-understand survey that is well-illustrated and includes a glossary of terms and a table of principal Hovercraft and ACV's. More technical, requiring some college-level mathematics, is G.H. ELSLEY and A.J. DEVEREUX, *Hovercraft Design and Construction* (1968), an excellent textbook, based on lectures given at the Isle of Wight Technical College, which deals with the theory and practice of ACV-building. ROBERT L. TRILLO, *Marine Hovercraft Technology* (1971), covers operational problems to a greater extent. See also *Jane's Surface Skimmers* (annual), a review of ACV's and hydrofoils giving technical details of craft available, operators, and consultants; and *Air-Cushion Vehicles* (bimonthly), a review of the state of the Hovercraft art including design, construction, and operation of ACV's of all sizes.

Transportation Law

Transportation law is a collective term for the branches of jurisprudence that govern the movement of passengers or goods from one place to another by means of carriers, as well as the activity and interaction of such carriers, on land or water or in the air. The first part of this article treats legal principles applying to the transportation of goods in general. In the second part, the laws governing marine transportation in particular are examined. The third part treats the law of civil aviation, including the special problems of airspace jurisdiction. For information on road and highway regulations, see PUBLIC WORKS: *Roads and highways.* For treatment of the larger context of transportation, see TRANSPORTATION.

The article is divided into the following sections:

The law of carriage of goods

HISTORICAL DEVELOPMENT

Until the development of railroads, the most prominent mode of transport was by water. Overland transportation of goods was relatively slow, costly, and perilous. For this reason, the law governing carriage of goods by sea developed much earlier than that governing inland transportation. The preclassical Greek city-states had well-developed laws dealing with the carriage of goods by sea, along with specialized commercial courts to settle disputes among carriers, shippers, and consignees. The sea laws of the island of Rhodes achieved such prominence that a part of them was carried, many centuries later, into the legislation of Justinian.

In Roman law the contract of carriage did not achieve the status of a distinct contractual form; jurisconsults (legal advisers) dealt with it in the framework of the contractual forms known to them, such as deposit and hire of services or of goods. There was special regulation only insofar as the responsibility of the carrier was concerned: shipowners (*nautae*), along with innkeepers and stable keepers, were liable without fault for destruction of or damage to the goods of passengers. Nevertheless, they could be relieved of responsibility by proving that the loss was attributable to irresistible force.

Early developments in common law

In English common law the principles applying to the relationship between the carrier and his customers go back to a time when neither railways nor canals existed. Whether influenced by Roman law or derived quite independently, early English decisions imposed on carriers the obligation not only to carry goods but to carry them safely and to deliver them in good condition to the owner or his agent. The carrier was always liable for the loss of the goods and also liable for any damage to the goods, unless he could prove that the loss or damage had resulted from an excepted cause. This duty of the carrier to deliver the goods safely was considered to exist without regard to obligations arising under any contract between the parties. It was imposed upon him by the law because he had been put in possession of another's goods. In legal language, this meant that the carrier was considered to be a bailee, who, in certain circumstances, was liable to the bailor if he failed to deliver the goods intact. This law of bailment developed in England long before the law of contract. The contractual element of bailment was not stressed until after the 17th century. Today, in common-law countries, the rights and liabilities of shippers, consignees, and carriers are in the large majority of cases based on a contract of carriage, whether express or tacit. The mere fact that, in the ordinary course of his business, a carrier accepts goods for carriage and delivery implies the making of a contract of carriage. The right of the carrier to claim the freight depends on this contract, and this contract is also the foundation of his duty to carry the goods safely to their destination. But there remain vestiges of bailment in the law of carriage of goods. Thus, the owner of the goods, though not a party to the contract of carriage between the shipper and the carrier, may sue the carrier for loss of or damage to his goods.

Early developments in civil law

In civil-law countries, the contract of carriage first achieved distinct form in the early 19th century. The French Civil Code of 1804, following the Romanist tradition, still dealt with the contract of carriage as a species of the contract for the hire of services and further subjected carriers to the same obligations as depositaries; but the French Commercial Code of 1807 established a special legal regime for professional carriers, making the contract of carriage a distinct contractual form. Subsequent civil and commercial legislation in civil-law countries gave expression to the same idea. Today, in the civil-law world, the contract of carriage may be regarded as a variation of the contract for the hire of services, namely, a contract whereby one of the parties engages to do something for the other party in consideration of a price agreed upon between them. Specifically, the contract of carriage of goods may be defined as the contract whereby a professional carrier engages to carry goods in accordance with a determined mode of transport and within a reasonable time, with the understanding that the carriage of the goods is the principal object of the contract.

In France and in a great number of countries following the French system, a contract of carriage requires the presence of three indispensable elements: carriage, control of the operation by the carrier, and a professional carrier. If any of these elements is missing, the contract is one for the hire of services rather than a special contract of carriage. The classification of a contract as a contract of carriage involves significant legal consequences. Exculpatory clauses in a contract of carriage are ordinarily null and void; receipt of the goods by the consignee and payment of the freight without protest within a designated period of time exclude all actions against the carrier; actions that may be brought against the carrier are subject to a short period of limitation, that is, one year; the carrier has a privilege, which corresponds to a common-law lien, on the things carried for the payment of the freight; and, finally, either party to a contract of carriage may demand that experts determine the condition of the things carried or intended to be carried.

CHARACTERISTICS OF CARRIAGE

Common carriers

Common-law common carrier. In English and American law, common carriers are distinguished from other carriers. A common carrier is one who holds himself out as being ready to carry goods for the public at large for hire or reward. In England carriers of goods by land that are not classified as common carriers are termed private carriers; carriers of goods by sea or by inland water that are not classified as common carriers may be public carriers, namely, professional carriers who do not hold themselves out as ready to serve the general public or persons who carry goods incidentally to their main business or for one consignor only. In the United States distinction is made among common carriers, contract carriers, and private carriers. A person who engages to carry the goods of particular individuals rather than of the general public is a contract carrier; a person who carries his own goods is a private carrier. Both a common carrier and a contract carrier are engaged in transportation as a business. The basic difference between them is that a common carrier holds himself out to the general public to engage in transportation, whereas a contract carrier does not hold himself out to serve the general public. The exact boundary between common carriage and contract carriage is not always clear.

A person may be a common carrier, although he limits the kinds of goods that he is ready to carry for the public, the mode of transport, or the route over which he is prepared to carry. He is a common carrier only to the extent that he holds himself out as ready to carry goods for the public. It is indispensable for the classification of a person as common carrier that he accepts reward for the carriage and that his principal undertaking is the carriage of goods. Ancillary carriage for purposes of warehousing does not make one a common carrier. Unless the law provides otherwise, a carrier may cease at any time to be a common carrier by giving notice that he is no longer ready to carry goods for the public at large.

The distinction between common carriers and carriers that are not classified as common carriers, such as private carriers or contract carriers, involves significant legal consequences in the light of both common law and legislation. Common carriers are everywhere subject to strict economic regulation. Thus, a common carrier is forbidden in the United States to charge unreasonably high rates or to engage in unjust discrimination, whereas a contract carrier may charge rates as high as he pleases and may discriminate among his customers, provided that none of his discriminatory rates in motor and domestic water transportation is unreasonably low. In both England and the United States, a common carrier must serve everyone who makes a lawful request for the services he offers, but a private or contract carrier may select his customers; a common carrier is liable for any loss or damage to the goods during carriage, unless the damage or loss is attributable to certain excepted causes, whereas a contract carrier or private carrier is only liable for damage or loss through his negligence; contractual clauses relieving the carrier from liability may have different effects depending on the status of the carrier as common carrier or private carrier; and, finally, the common carrier has a common-law lien on the goods, whereas other carriers may have none in the absence of contractual provision or may have a less extensive lien than that of the common carrier.

The civil-law counterpart of the common carrier

Civil-law public carrier. The concept of common carrier has no exact equivalent in civil-law systems. But, if one looks to substance rather than form or terminology, one may conclude that the concept of public carrier in civil-law systems is a functional equivalent of the concept of common carrier. A public carrier is a professional carrier of goods or passengers; he is distinguished from a private carrier who either carries his own goods exclusively or carries goods incidentally to his other business. Generally, the scope of private carriage is narrowly defined so that most carriage operations fall under the rubric of public carriage; this ensures maximum application of rules designed to safeguard the public interest in the carriage of goods. Public carriers, like common carriers in common-law countries, are subject to strict economic regulation and are under the supervision and control of administrative agencies. When a public carrier is also a professional merchant, normally an individual or a private corporation, he assumes all the duties, obligations, and liabilities attaching to merchants under applicable commercial codes or special legislation. Like a common carrier, a public carrier must accept the goods lawfully delivered to him for carriage, either because he is held to a permanent offer made to the public or because he is under obligation to carry by virtue of public legislation or administrative regulations. Unlike common carriers, public carriers are not liable for loss or damage to the goods without fault; this difference is more apparent than real, because carriers in civil-law systems are presumed to be liable, unless they prove that the loss or damage occurred without their fault.

Duties and liabilities of carriage. Common carriers and public carriers are under duty to carry goods lawfully delivered to them for carriage. The duty to carry does not prevent carriers from refusing to transport goods that they do not purport to carry generally. Carriers may indeed restrict the commodities that they will carry. Further, everywhere, carriers may refuse to carry dangerous goods, improperly packed goods, and goods that they are unable to carry on account of size, legal prohibition, or lack of facilities.

Liability for safety of the goods. Everywhere, carriers incur a measure of liability for the safety of the goods. In common-law countries carriers are liable for any damage or for the loss of the goods that are in their possession as carriers, unless they prove that the damage or loss is attributable to certain excepted causes. The excepted causes at common law include acts of God, acts of enemies of the crown, fault of the shipper, inherent vices of the goods, and fraud of the shipper. In maritime carriage perils of the sea and particularly jettison are added to the list of excepted causes. All these terms have technical meanings. An act of God is an operation of natural forces so unexpected that no human foresight or skill may be reasonably expected to anticipate it. Acts of enemies of the crown

Excepted causes of loss

are acts of enemy soldiers in time of war or acts of rebels against the crown in civil war; violent acts of strikers or rioters are not an excepted cause. Fault of the shipper as an excepted cause is any negligent act or omission that has caused damage or loss—for example, faulty packing. Inherent vice is some default or defect latent in the thing itself, which, by its development, tends to the injury or destruction of the thing carried. Fraud of the shipper is an untrue statement as to the nature or value of the goods. And jettison in maritime transport is an intentional sacrifice of goods to preserve the safety of the ship and cargo.

When goods are damaged or lost as a result of an excepted cause, the carrier is still liable if he has contributed to the loss by his negligence or intentional misconduct. In this case, however, the burden of proof of the carrier's fault rests on the plaintiff.

In civil-law countries the carrier under a contract of carriage is ordinarily bound as a warrantor for any damage to or loss of the goods carried, unless he proves that the damage or loss has resulted from irresistible force (*force majeure*), the inherent vice of the goods, or from the fault of the shipper or of the consignee. This contractual liability of the carrier under the general law is frequently modified by special legislation or by international conventions. In addition to his contractual liability, the carrier may, of course, incur liabilities that arise without contract. The carrier's contractual liability is often termed an "obligation of result," because the carrier, or a warrantor, is bound to make full restitution, unless he manages to exculpate himself in part or in whole.

Limitations of liability. In the absence of contrary legislation or decisions, carriers in common-law jurisdictions have been traditionally free to exclude or limit their liabilities by contract. In civil-law jurisdictions, as a rule, contractual clauses tending to limit liability for negligence or for willful misconduct have been considered null and void. Today, in most countries, municipal legislation and international conventions ordinarily limit the liability of certain carriers to a specified amount per weight, package, or unit of the goods carried. In this way, the liability of certain carriers has largely become standardized, at least in international carriage of goods. Parties are free to stipulate that the carrier shall be liable in excess of any statutory limitation, but clauses designed to reduce the liability of the carrier below statutory limits are ordinarily null and void. Statutory limitations cover both direct and indirect losses incurred by shippers or consignees. In most legal systems, the benefit of statutory limitation of liability is unavailable if the goods have been delivered to the wrong person or if the carrier is guilty of intentional misconduct or gross negligence.

International conventions limiting liability

The liability of a maritime carrier for loss or damage to goods carried under a bill of lading is limited in most countries to a specified amount per package or unit by application of the provisions of the Brussels Convention of 1924 or by municipal legislation containing rules similar to those of the convention. The liability of air carriers for loss or damage to goods carried in international trade is almost everywhere controlled by the provisions of the Warsaw Convention of 1929, as amended by the Hague Protocol of 1955. Air carriage in domestic trade is subject either to the rules of the international convention or to municipal legislation patterned after the model of the convention. In most countries the liability of railroad carriers is limited by legislation or administrative regulations that regularly become part of the contract of carriage. International carriage of goods by railroad is largely subject to the various Berne Conventions, the first of which was adopted in 1890. Most European nations, including Great Britain, Northern Ireland, and Communist countries with the exception of the U.S.S.R., have adhered to these conventions.

COMPONENTS OF THE CARRIAGE OF GOODS

The law of carriage of goods covers a variety of matters.

Goods in transit

Delay and misdelivery. In all legal systems, carriers incur liability for delay in delivering the goods to the consignee. Statutes, international conventions, administrative regulations, or even contractual agreements may fix the period of transportation with reference to the applicable means of carriage and determine the consequences of the delay. Under the law of contracts, failure of the carrier to deliver the goods within the prescribed period of time will be treated as a breach of contract.

In common-law jurisdictions, if the delay is caused by a deviation, the carrier is ordinarily answerable for damages. A deviation takes place when the carrier leaves the route that he has expressly or impliedly agreed to follow or when he goes past his destination. In civil-law jurisdictions carriers are not bound to follow any particular route in the absence of special legislation or contractual agreement. Thus, a deviation from the normal route does not itself constitute a fault of the carrier; if the deviation causes a delay, the carrier will be liable only if he is at fault.

Like delay, misdelivery engages the responsibility of the carrier. Misdelivery is the delivery of the goods by the carrier to the wrong person or to the wrong place.

Diversion and reconsignment; stoppage in transit. The terms diversion and reconsignment are used interchangeably to refer to a change in the destination or billing of a shipment before or after it reaches its original destination. Reconsignment is of considerable importance to the commercial world, because goods may be shipped from a distant source of supply toward a certain destination and then diverted to the most favourable market. Carriers are generally permitted to make a charge for the exercise of a diversion or reconsignment privilege. The number of diversions is generally limited in order to prevent the use of means of transport as places of storage.

The owner of the goods may, in all legal systems, change the carrier's instructions as to the place of destination or as to the person entitled to take delivery. The carrier must comply with this order, provided that he has satisfied himself that the person designating a new place of delivery or a new recipient is the owner of the goods at the time the order is given. In civil-law jurisdictions the person in possession of the title of transport, be it a bill of lading or other document, is ordinarily entitled to change the destination of the goods. This rule has been largely followed in international conventions, including the Warsaw Convention of 1929. At common law, in the absence of other provision, the consignee is regarded as the owner of the goods while they are in transit; therefore, it is ordinarily the consignee who is entitled to change the destination of the shipment.

Stoppage in transit is technically the right of an unpaid seller of goods to change their destination before they are delivered to the consignee. The seller has this right by virtue of directly applicable legislation even if he has not reserved the ownership of the goods in his transaction with the buyer. Indicatively, the British Sale of Goods Act of 1893, which codified the common-law rules, declares that the unpaid vendor may resume possession of the goods as long as they are in the course of transit and may retain them until payment or tender of the price. There are analogous provisions in civil-law jurisdiction.

Dangerous goods. Dangerous goods are those that, from their nature, are liable to cause damage to persons, to means of transport, or to other goods. In all legal systems, the carriage of dangerous goods has given rise to distinct problems and to the development of special rules.

In civil-law countries legislation or administrative regulations define categories of goods considered to be dangerous and either exclude their shipment by public carriers or determine the conditions under which they may be shipped. In common-law jurisdictions the shipper is liable to the carrier for all damage caused by dangerous goods delivered for shipment, unless he has declared the dangerous nature of the goods at the time of delivery, and the carrier has accepted them with knowledge of their nature.

Carriage by two or more carriers. Goods frequently reach their destination after they have passed through the hands of two or more carriers. This may happen when the shipper has contracted with several carriers, when the shipper has authorized one of the carriers to act as his agent with other carriers, or when the carrier, without authority, delivers the goods to another carrier.

If the carrier, without authority, delivers the goods to

another carrier, he is liable to the shipper for any misdelivery by the second carrier and for any loss or damage suffered by the owner of the goods while the goods were in the possession of the second carrier. This means that the carrier cannot relieve himself from liability by performing the contract through the services of an agent. Moreover, delivery of the goods to another carrier may be a breach of contract by virtue of an implied or express condition that the carriage shall be effected by the vehicles of the carrier. Such a condition is implied in maritime transports.

The carrier's assurance of payment

Carrier's liens. The law strives everywhere to secure payment of the freight to a carrier who has carried the goods to their destination. In common-law jurisdictions the carrier may have to this effect a common-law lien, a statutory lien, or even a contractual lien. In civil-law jurisdictions the carrier has, ordinarily, a privilege on the things carried.

A common carrier in common-law jurisdictions has a common-law lien under which he is entitled to retain possession of the goods until earned freight is paid to him. The carrier is not entitled to sell the goods or to use them; parties, however, may agree that the carrier shall have an active lien, namely, that he shall have the right to sell the goods. Thus, in maritime carriage in the United States, the shipowner is clearly entitled to seize and sell the goods carried by him in case of nonpayment of the freight. Parties may agree that the carrier shall have no lien at all or that he shall have a general lien on the goods carried, namely, a lien covering debts other than the pending freight. After the lien is exercised, the carrier has the rights and duties of a bailee. He may thus be liable for loss or damage occasioned by his negligence, and he may be entitled to recover expenses that were reasonably necessary for the preservation of the goods.

Carriers in civil-law jurisdictions ordinarily have a privilege on the goods carried by them for the payment of the freight and of incidental expenses. In France and in systems following the French model, this privilege is available only to professional carriers who carry goods by contract of carriage. The civil-law privilege differs from a common-law lien in that it confers on the carrier power and authority to sell the goods for the satisfaction of his claims. The privilege covers the whole shipment as determined by the documents of transport and is extinguished upon delivery of the goods to the consignee. Quite apart from the privilege, the carrier in civil-law jurisdictions may be entitled, under the general law of obligations, to refuse delivery of the goods until payment of the freight; moreover, he may secure payment of the freight by a variety of contractual arrangements.

Carrier's role as warehouseman and bailee. In all legal systems, the peculiar liabilities imposed on carriers extend only for the duration of the carriage, that is, from the time the goods are delivered to the carrier for shipment until the carrier has taken all reasonable steps to deliver them to the consignee. This means that the carrier is not under his liability as a carrier for the whole time during which the goods may be in his possession. Indeed, goods may be delivered to a carrier for safekeeping before the carriage begins or after it terminates in accordance with the terms of a special contract that may qualify as bailment in common-law jurisdictions and as a deposit in civil-law countries. Further, goods may be in the possession of the carrier because the consignee has unjustifiedly refused to take delivery, in which case the carrier may occupy the position of an involuntary bailee or depositary.

Goods not in transit

Generally, a carrier who is in possession of the goods before the beginning or after the end of the carriage is a warehouseman, and he is liable accordingly. In common-law jurisdictions the liability of a warehouseman is that of an ordinary bailee. In most cases a bailee, namely, a person entrusted with the goods of another, is not liable for the loss of or damage to the goods in his possession, unless the prejudice was caused by his intentional misconduct or negligence. In civil-law jurisdictions, if the parties agree that the carrier shall be in possession of the goods as a warehouseman before the beginning or after the end of the carriage, they form in effect a contract of deposit for reward, which is distinguishable from a contract of carriage. The elements of the contract of deposit and the rights and liabilities of the parties are dealt with in civil codes; exoneration clauses are valid under the conditions of the general law, and the period of limitation of actions is longer than one year. The depositary for reward is generally liable for intentional misconduct and negligence.

Measure of damages. Damages for the breach or nonperformance of a contract of carriage ordinarily are determined by application of the general rules of the law of contracts. Exceptional provisions applicable in case of breach of a contract of carriage are rare; they are mostly encountered in international conventions.

Bills of lading. Many shipments are made under bills of lading, issued by the carrier to the shipper upon delivery of the goods for shipment. The shipper is entitled to demand issuance of a bill of lading, unless his right is excluded by the contract of carriage. The bill of lading is, in the first place, an acknowledgment by a carrier that he has received the goods for shipment. Secondly, the bill of lading is either a contract of carriage or evidence of a contract of carriage. Thirdly, if the bill of lading is negotiable, as usually happens in carriage by sea, it controls possession of the goods and is one of the indispensable documents in financing the movement of commodities and merchandise throughout the world.

The bill of lading usually states the quantity, weight, measurements, and other pertinent information concerning the goods shipped. It frequently contains the statement that the goods have been shipped in apparent good order and condition. In this case, the carrier is not allowed to contradict the statement as to defects that were reasonably ascertainable at the time of delivery against an endorsee of the bill who relied on the statement. The bill of lading may be signed by the master or by a broker as agent of the carrier. As a receipt, the bill of lading is prima facie evidence that the goods have been delivered to the carrier; the burden of proof of nondelivery thus rests on the carrier.

In some jurisdictions the bill of lading is regarded as the contract of carriage itself. In other jurisdictions it is regarded merely as evidence of the contract of carriage; hence, oral testimony may be admissible to vary the terms of the contract evidenced by the bill of lading. When goods are shipped under a charter party or other document and a bill of lading is issued to cover the same goods, the bill of lading may ordinarily be regarded as a mere receipt. The terms of the contract are embodied in the charter party or other document, unless the parties intended to vary the terms of the agreement by the issuance of a bill of lading. A bill of lading that has been endorsed is ordinarily considered to contain the terms of the contract between the carrier and the endorsee.

Negotiable bills

At common law, a bill of lading functions as a semi-negotiable instrument. Delivery of the bill of lading to a transferee for valuable consideration transfers the ownership of the goods to the transferee, but the transferee cannot acquire a better title than that of the transferor. Under statutes, however, and under international conventions, bills of lading are in all legal systems fully negotiable instruments, unless they show on their face that they are not negotiable. When a bill of lading is negotiable, it confers a privileged status on the good faith purchaser, known as the holder in due course. A carrier who has issued a nonnegotiable bill of lading normally discharges his duty by delivering the goods to the named consignee; the consignee need not produce the bill or even be in possession of it. But a carrier who has issued a negotiable bill of lading will be discharged only by delivery to the holder of the bill, because, in a way, the goods are locked up in the bill of lading. The carrier who delivers goods without the bill of lading remains liable in common-law jurisdictions to anyone who has purchased the bill for value and in good faith, before or after the improper delivery. In civil-law jurisdictions, in case of an improper delivery, the carrier may remain liable to the endorsee of the bill of lading, even if the endorsee is himself not the legal owner of the bill but merely a finder or a thief.

Freight or forwarding agents. Shippers frequently engage the services of freight or forwarding agents, namely, persons who undertake for a reward to have the goods carried and delivered at their destination. The services of these persons are ordinarily engaged when the carriage of the goods involves successive carriers or use of successive means of transport.

A forwarding agent makes contracts of carriage for his principal. He may be a carrier or he may be merely a forwarding agent. When a carrier enters into a contract with the shipper by which he undertakes to carry goods in circumstances that involve an obligation on his part to hand over the goods to another carrier, he may be regarded as acting to some extent in the capacity of a forwarding agent. Conversely, when a forwarding agent carries the goods himself, he is to that extent a carrier and incurs the liabilities of a carrier.

Responsibilities of forwarding agents

In common-law jurisdictions a forwarding agent who is not a carrier is not responsible for what happens to the goods once they are handed over to a carrier with whom the forwarding agent has made a contract for his principal. By his transaction with the carrier, the forwarding agent establishes a direct contractual relationship between his principal and the carrier. Under the principles of the law of agency, the forwarding agent is under obligation toward his principal to conclude the contract on the usual terms. He is under no obligations, in the absence of an express contractual provision, to insure the goods. If, exceptionally, a forwarding agent acts as a carrier throughout the journey and uses other carriers on his own account, he is liable to the owner for any loss or damage to the goods during carriage. The extent of his liability depends on whether he is a common carrier or a contract carrier. If he is a common carrier, his liability to the owner of the goods may be heavier than the liabilities he can enforce against the carriers he has engaged.

In civil-law jurisdictions forwarding agents are clearly distinguished from carriers, and the contracts they make are clearly distinguishable from contracts of carriage. The profession of a forwarding agent, however, is not exclusive; thus, most frequently, carriers qualify as forwarding agents and vice versa. A forwarding agent has ordinarily a privilege on the goods under his control that is much broader and more effective than the privilege of the carrier. He has, in the absence of contrary contractual provision, freedom of choice of the means of transport and of particular carriers. His main obligation is to have the goods carried to their destination and delivered to the consignee. In the discharge of this obligation, he is generally entitled to engage the services of another forwarding agent. The forwarding agent is liable to his principal for any violation of his obligations resulting from negligence or intentional misconduct. He is relieved from liability if he proves that the loss or damage was occasioned by irresistible force. The liability of the forwarding agent for negligence may be excluded by contractual stipulations but not his liability for grave fault and intentional misconduct. A forwarding agent is considered as a carrier to the extent that he carries the goods himself, and to that extent he incurs the liabilities of a carrier. In contrast with the rule in common-law jurisdictions, the forwarding agent in civil-law countries is fully responsible for loss or damage suffered by the goods in the hands of carriers that the forwarding agent has engaged for the performance of the contract with his principal, unless the services of the particular carrier were requested by the principal. The liability of the forwarding agent does not exceed that of the carrier he has engaged, and, if the carrier is exonerated by virtue of an excepted cause, so is the forwarding agent.

Mixed-carrier transportation. The expression mixed-carrier transportation refers to situations in which goods are carried to their final destination by two or more means of transport, such as road and sea or rail, sea, and air. There are at least two possibilities. The successive carriers may have no common juridical link, as when the shipper has contracted with each carrier independently or when the shipper has contracted with a forwarding agent. In these cases, each carrier is subject to his own regime and has his own rights and duties toward the shipper or forwarding agent. A second possibility is that the successive carriers may be bound by a common juridical link toward the shipper or owner of the goods by virtue of directly applicable legal or contractual provisions or by virtue of the fact that the goods travel under a single document of transport, as a through bill of lading. In these cases, municipal laws in civil-law jurisdictions tend toward the irreconcilable aims of subjecting each carrier to his own regime and, at the same time, holding all carriers solidarily liable. In domestic carriage in common-law jurisdictions, the liability of each carrier is ordinarily determined by application of the rules governing carriage by two or more carriers.

The through bill of lading

Mixed-carrier transportation in international commerce under a through bill of lading or similar document has been dealt with in international conventions. A through bill of lading covers carriage of goods by two or more successive carriers or by two or more means of transport. It is issued by the first carrier and constitutes a single title to the goods. Under a purely maritime through bill of lading, successive carriers are equally bound, unless the contrary has been stipulated. Solutions differ, however, when carriage is effected by two or more means of transport. Under the Berne Railroad Conventions for the carriage of goods, carriage by rail and sea may be subject to the rules governing railroad carriage at the option of the contracting states, unless reservation has been made by them for application of certain rules of maritime law to the portion of sea carriage. Since these conventions may be entirely inapplicable to the portion of sea carriage, interested carriers and international organizations have concluded agreements for a uniform, legal regime of rail and sea carriage. In fact, accords have been concluded among United States and Canadian railway and ocean-shipping companies for application of the rules of the Brussels Convention of 1924 to goods carried under through bills of lading by rail and sea. The rules of the Warsaw Convention for carriage of goods by air apply always to the portion of air carriage and to that portion only, but the International Air Transport Association and the International Union of Railways have concluded agreements for carriage by rail and air under a single document. Only the Geneva Convention of 1956 has undertaken to establish rules applicable to all means of transport under a single document. The convention provides, however, that, if damage has been incurred in a portion of the journey other than road carriage, the carrier shall be subject to his proper law. This convention may conflict with the Berne Conventions and does conflict with the Warsaw Convention to the extent that carriage by air is subjected to the Brussels rather than the Warsaw Convention.

In the Western world, the transport of goods is divided between public and private enterprise. The basis of the legal relationship between a carrier and his customer is the same whether the carrier is a public corporation, a local authority, or a private corporation or individual. The law of carriage of goods governs the rights and duties of the shipper, carrier, and consignee.

NATIONAL AND INTERNATIONAL REGULATION

In all legal systems the law of carriage has been influenced by the idea that carriers enjoy a factual monopoly. The services that a customer may demand and the remuneration that a carrier may exact are generally regulated by legislation or administrative regulations. The growth of competition among carriers and means of transport in the Western world has led to a reduction in the scope of municipal legislation in a number of countries, but international conventions and administrative regulations have proliferated. The right to carry on a transport business is still everywhere regulated through elaborate licensing systems, and the operations of transport are subject to continuous supervision and control by appropriate agencies. The legal relation between the carrier and his customer is affected by this intervention of the public authorities, and public as well as private laws form the body of the law of carriage.

U.S. and British regulatory laws

Roads, railways, and inland waterways. Since the 19th century legislation has been enacted in most countries to safeguard the public interest in the movement of goods by road, railway, and inland waterway. In the United States a decisive step toward regulation of transportation was taken with the Act to Regulate Commerce of 1887. This act was made applicable to all common carriers by railroads engaged in interstate or foreign commerce and to common carriers transporting goods in part by railroad and in part by inland water when both were used under a common control, management, or arrangement for a continuous carriage. The act created the Interstate Commerce Commission, which today has wide powers to hear complaints against carriers concerning alleged violations of law, to investigate matters in dispute, to order carriers to cease and desist from unlawful practices, and to determine the amount of damages suffered as a result of violations. The commission also possesses rate-making power.

Since the time the 1887 act was adopted, new forms of transport have arisen, and older ones have been improved. The Interstate Commerce Commission now has jurisdiction over railroads, pipelines, motor carriers, and certain carriers by water. Other federal agencies that have been charged with regulation of transportation are the Civil Aeronautics Board and the Federal Maritime Commission.

In England the Carriers Act of 1830 was the first legislative intervention in the field of carriage of goods. The act originally applied to all common carriers by land, including both road and railway carriage. The Railways Act of 1921, however, made special provisions with regard to the railways, and the Transport Act of 1962 enacted that the Railways Board shall not be regarded as a common carrier. Consequently, carriage by railways is now regulated by the contract between the Railway Board and the shipper or other contracting party, as laid down in the Book of the Rules of British Railways. The Carriers Act has never been applicable to private carriers and to common carriers by sea or by inland waterway. If part of the carriage is by sea or inland water and part by road, the act applies to the land part only.

The Berne Conventions

For many decades the law governing the international carriage of goods by railway has been codified in a number of international conventions. These are frequently referred to as the Berne Conventions. The first international convention concerning the carriage of goods by rail was concluded in Berne in 1890 and came into operation in 1893; after World War I it was replaced by a new convention concluded in 1924, which was again amended by a convention signed in Rome in 1933. This in turn was replaced after World War II by the Berne Convention of 1952. A new convention was signed in Berne in 1961 and came into operation in 1965. The conventions apply whenever goods have been consigned under a through consignment note for carriage over the territories of at least two of the contracting states and on certain specified lines. They regulate mostly the form and conditions of the contract of carriage; its performance, including delivery and payment of the charges; its modifications; the liability of the carrier for delay, loss, or damage; and the enforcement of the contract by actions. Further, the conventions establish the obligation of the railways to carry goods and the rights and obligations of the various railway authorities of the contracting states. Most contracting states have incorporated into their municipal laws rules similar to those of the conventions for the regulation of the domestic carriage of goods by railway.

The Treaty of Rome of March 25, 1957, which created the European Economic Community, contains a number of provisions concerning matters of transport. Members of the Community are specifically bound to develop a common policy in matters of transport. The provisions of the treaty have been largely implemented by a number of international agreements. Since all members of the Common Market are members of the Berne Conventions, the mandate for uniformity of rules governing carriage of goods has been largely achieved as to carriage by railway.

Conflicts of laws

Sea carriage. Until the emergence of modern national states, the law governing maritime commerce had been largely uniform in the Western world. In the 18th and 19th centuries, however, legislative enactments and judicial decisions in pursuit of narrowly conceived national interests gradually displaced in various countries the venerable and uniform law of the sea and gave rise to sharp conflicts of laws. The movement of goods from country to country was thus hampered at a time when advancing technology and the spreading Industrial Revolution were about to lead to an expansion of maritime commerce on a world scale. Beginning with the last decades of the 19th century, it has become increasingly apparent that these conflicts of laws might be overcome by means of international conventions. The law of merchant shipping was quite naturally one of the first branches of private law to attract attention for possible international regulation.

The movement for uniformity culminated in the signing in 1924 of the International Convention for the Unification of Certain Rules of Law Relating to Bills of Lading. The convention was merely intended to unify certain rules of law relating to bills of lading and only with regard to damages occurring to hull cargo other than live animals. All bills of lading covered by the convention are subject to certain standard clauses defining the risks assumed by the carrier, which are absolute and cannot be altered by contrary agreement, and the immunities the carrier can enjoy, unless the parties agree otherwise. In general, clauses relieving the carrier from liability for negligence in loading, handling, stowing, keeping, carrying, and discharging the goods or that diminish his obligation to furnish a seaworthy vessel are declared null and void. The carrier, however, is relieved from liability for negligence in navigation or in the management of the vessel and from the absolute warranty of seaworthiness. The convention was originally intended to apply to all bills of lading issued in any one of the contracting states.

Most maritime nations, including the U.S.S.R., have ratified or adhered to the convention, and others, such as Greece and Indonesia, have enacted domestic legislation incorporating the rules agreed upon in Brussels. Some adhering nations, including Germany, Belgium, Turkey, and The Netherlands, have incorporated the rules of the convention into their commercial codes. Others, including the United States, Japan, Great Britain, and most members of the British Commonwealth, have enacted the rules in the form of special statutes known as Carriage of Goods by Sea Acts. Still others, including France, Italy, Egypt, and Switzerland, have given the convention itself the force of law and in addition have enacted domestic legislation modelled on the convention. The substantive standards governing bills of lading in maritime carriage have become largely uniform in most of the civilized world.

The Warsaw Convention

Air carriage. The Warsaw Convention of 1929, as amended by the Hague Protocol of 1955, exemplifies still another legislative approach to problems raised by the carriage of goods. It constitutes a major step toward international unification of the rules governing carriage of goods by air. The convention applies to international carriage of persons, luggage, and goods for reward, as well as to gratuitous carriage performed by an air-transport undertaking. It applies whether the aircraft is owned by private persons or by public bodies; but, as to aircraft owned by a state directly, application of the convention may be excluded by appropriate reservation. According to the convention, there is an international carriage when the points of departure and destination are located within different contracting states or within the same contracting state but stopping has been agreed upon in another state, even if that state is not a member of the convention. The convention applies during the time the goods are in the charge of the carrier in any aircraft, airfield, or other facility. It does not apply when goods are carried by a land, sea, or inland-water carrier. Most nations, including the United States, Great Britain, and the U.S.S.R., are members of the convention. Only a few nations in South and Central America and in the Middle East have remained outside the convention. Although the convention applies to international carriage only, a great number of contracting states, including France and Great Britain, have made its rules applicable to domestic carriage of goods as well.

The air carrier is liable under the convention for delay and for the loss of or damage to the goods, provided that the occurrence that caused the prejudice took place during the carriage by air. The carrier is relieved from liability if he proves that he had taken all the necessary measures to avoid the damage or that it was impossible for him to take such measures. Unlike carriers by land and by water, the air carrier is not bound to prove the actual cause of the damage and that the damage was not attributable to his fault. If the cause of the damage remains unknown, there is no recovery. Contractual provisions tending to relieve the carrier from liability are null and void, except those concerning limitation of liability for loss or damage attributed to the inherent vice of the goods. Provisions tending to increase the liability of the carrier, however, are valid.

The convention contains provisions as to the jurisdiction of courts in case action is brought against the carrier and establishes a two-year period of limitation for the bringing of actions. No provision is made for liability of the carrier in case of deviation, for a carrier's lien, or for stoppage in transit, as this term is understood at common law. Accordingly, these matters are governed by the municipal law of the contracting states.

Other international agreements. The international movement of goods may be regulated in certain countries by international agreements other than the Berne Conventions, the Brussels Convention on Limitation of Liability (1923), or the Warsaw Convention of 1929. The Communist countries in eastern Europe, including the U.S.S.R., have established a uniform regime for the movement of goods by railway that is comparable to that of the Berne Conventions. Since these nations, with the exception of the U.S.S.R., belong to the Berne Conventions as well, it is possible that conflicts may arise as to the scope of application of each convention.

Other agreements in the field include the Geneva Convention of 1956 for the carriage of goods by road. The convention became operative in 1961, and its original membership includes France, Austria, Italy, The Netherlands, and Yugoslavia. It applies to international carriage of goods by road for reward, with the exception of certain items, such as mail. Carriage is international if it involves two countries, one of which is a member of the convention. An original feature of the Geneva Convention is that it covers mixed-carrier transportation. It applies for the whole journey, even if the road vehicle has been carried, without being unloaded, by another means of transport, unless there is proof that the damage occurred in a portion of the journey other than that of carriage by road.

(A.N.Y.)

Maritime law

Maritime law is the term commonly employed to denote the branch of jurisprudence that governs ships and shipping. In English-speaking countries, "admiralty" is sometimes used synonymously, although in a stricter sense that term relates to the jurisdiction and procedural law of courts whose origins may be traced to the office of Admiral. Although etymologically maritime law and "law of the sea" are identical, the former term is generally applied to private shipping law, whereas the latter, usually prefixed by "international," has come to signify the maritime segment of public international law.

HISTORICAL DEVELOPMENT

Origins of maritime law

From the fact that the ancient Egyptians engaged in shipping on a wide scale, it can be inferred that they had at least rudimentary laws regulating that activity, although no trace of any has been found thus far. Nor is there anything known of any maritime laws of the Phoenicians, who succeeded the Egyptians as commercial leaders in the Mediterranean. That Rhodes was a major source of maritime law, however, is clearly indicated in two passages from the *Digest* (AD 533) of the Roman emperor Justinian. The first quotes the Emperor Antoninus (reigned AD 138–161) in a case of plunder following a shipwreck: "I am indeed lord of the world, but the Law is the lord of the sea. This matter must be decided by the maritime law of the Rhodians, provided that no law of ours is opposed to it." The second is a statement of the basic law of "general average," which the *Digest* attributes to the Rhodians. "Average" here means any loss sustained by a vessel or its cargo. When one segment of a maritime venture is sacrificed to save the others, the average is described as general, and the owners of the property saved must help make good the loss. Thus, if cargo is jettisoned in a successful effort to refloat a grounded vessel, the owners of the vessel and of the cargo saved are obliged to bear proportionate shares of the loss sustained by the owner of the cargo singled out for sacrifice.

Rome did not become a maritime power until the Punic wars of the third century BC. From the fact that the Romans were allies of the Rhodians and from the references in the *Digest,* it is logical to assume that Roman maritime law borrowed heavily from that of Rhodes. Acknowledging Rhodes as the birthplace of maritime jurisprudence, the maritime code of the later Eastern Empire, dating from the 7th or 8th century AD, was called the "Rhodian Sea Law."

The medieval maritime codes

Because the Mediterranean, under Roman control, was not only the centre of the Western world but also its principal commercial highway, European maritime law evolved as a uniform, supranational, comprehensive body of law—a characteristic which, though sometimes threatened by the spread of nationalism, has never been lost completely. The barbarian invaders who moved south were not seafarers, and the principal Mediterranean seaports were thus able to maintain their independence. Moreover, the conquered peoples were permitted to keep the Roman law to which they had become accustomed, and in the field of maritime jurisprudence the transition into the Middle Ages was therefore gradual. As certain Italian cities began to outstrip the Eastern Byzantine Empire commercially, they formulated their own maritime laws, some dating as early as 1063. Trani, Amalfi, Venice, and other Italian port cities all offered their own collections of laws. Nevertheless, the next widely accepted body of sea laws was the *Consolat de Mar,* or "Consulate of the Sea," originally compiled at Barcelona in the 13th century. More elaborate than the earlier codes, the *Consolat* was followed in Spain, Provence, and the Italian cities and had a significant effect on the development of modern maritime law.

The earliest code to emerge beyond the Mediterranean was the "Rolls of Oléron," named for an island in the Bay of Biscay and apparently dating from the 12th century. Whether the Rolls were of French or of Anglo-Norman origin, they became the nucleus of the maritime law not only of England and France but also of Scotland, Flanders, Prussia, and Castile; and they are still occasionally cited as authority, even by U.S. courts. The Rolls were closely followed in the Laws of Wisby, headquarters of the Hanseatic League until 1361.

The effect of nationalism

In continental Europe, loss of uniformity in the maritime law began with the late Renaissance and accelerated with the rise of nationalism in the 17th century, which witnessed adoption of the Maritime Code of Christian XI of Sweden (1667), the Marine Ordinances of Louis XIV of France (1681), and the Code of Christian V of Denmark (1683). Of these, the most significant were the Ordinances, prepared under Louis XIV's finance minister, Jean-Baptiste Colbert, as part of his comprehensive though unfulfilled plan for the codification of all French law. Established customs of the sea, revised to suit the times, were made part of the national law, enforceable in the French Admiralty Court, which was granted maritime jurisdiction to the exclusion of the old consular courts, whose judges had been elected by the mariners themselves.

The individuality of the maritime law—its "separation" from other types of law—was accentuated by the Ordinances, which gathered together in one code all of the criminal, private, procedural, and public laws relating to the sea. Although the French Admiralty Court failed to survive the Revolution that began in 1789, the substantive law embodied in the Ordinances was very closely followed in the *Code de Commerce,* whose adoption in 1807 meant that the maritime law was thereafter considered simply as a branch of commercial law, with consequent diminution of the weight previously given to custom and usage. Furthermore, abolition of the Admiralty Court resulted in the trial of maritime cases by the commercial courts, on which, in the smaller ports, maritime interests might not be represented. In countries with codes based directly or indirectly on the French commercial code, civil maritime cases, as well as nonmaritime commercial disputes, are heard and decided by commercial courts.

Although the *Code de Commerce* was widely adopted in the first half of the 19th century, in some cases by choice and in others by conquest, the German Commercial Code of 1861, revised in 1897, marked a departure from French law, and revisions of the Spanish and Italian codes showed the influence of the new German law. These, in turn, had their effect in countries under Italian and Spanish influence.

Early English maritime courts

Although the "Pied Poudre" courts, held primarily for the settlement of disputes at English fairs and markets, also had special jurisdiction of seamen's cases, it is probable that the first English tribunals to apply maritime law, with the Rolls of Oléron as a basis, were the courts of the Cinque Ports. The High Court of Admiralty, which sat at London, and the Vice Admiralty Courts set up in the other ports, were a later development. They were named after the admiral, an officer whose duties were at first solely administrative and military but were broadened early in the 14th century to include disciplinary proceedings in such matters as piracy. The Admiralty Court is considered as dating from 1360, when for the first time the admiral was expressly granted jurisdiction in civil maritime cases. By the end of the 16th century the admiralty courts had come to exercise an extremely wide jurisdiction, reaching far beyond saltwater transportation into many areas of commercial law. But during the first half of the 17th century, the judges of the common-law courts succeeded in divesting their competitors in the Admiralty of their commercial jurisdiction and in restricting them to the adjudication of "things done upon the sea."

The Admiralty was a royal court with valuable emoluments. It functioned without the aid of juries, following procedures borrowed from the Continent that were somewhat less dilatory and cumbersome than those of the common-law courts, and applied the laws and customs of the sea to the maritime controversies that came before it. For these reasons it was preferred by the merchants and favoured by the Crown, which depended to a considerable extent on taxation of the merchants for its revenues. Its jurisdiction therefore waxed and waned with the strength or weakness of the reigning sovereign. Thus, it enjoyed wide jurisdiction under the Tudors, but its powers were severely curtailed under succeeding monarchs and governments, and were never fully restored until the passage of the first of the Admiralty Court Acts in the 19th century.

Although the powers of the English Admiralty are today quite broad, in practice it is rare for cases other than those involving marine collisions and salvage to be brought before it. Controversies respecting charter parties, ocean bills of lading, and marine insurance, for example, are more generally brought before the Commercial Court.

In the United States, the federal district courts are by statute granted original jurisdiction, "exclusive of the courts of the States," of "Any civil case of admiralty or maritime jurisdiction, saving to suitors in all cases all other remedies to which they are otherwise entitled." This means, essentially, that if a maritime claimant wishes to have his claim litigated in accordance with admiralty procedure he must invoke the admiralty jurisdiction of the district courts. However, he is free to sue in a state court, unless the defendant is a citizen of another state, in which case the suit may be tried as an ordinary civil action in the district court.

COMPONENTS OF MARITIME LAW

Maritime liens. Although admiralty actions are frequently brought *in personam,* against individual or corporate defendants only, the most distinctive feature of admiralty practice is the proceeding *in rem,* against maritime property, that is, a vessel, a cargo, or "freight," which in shipping means the compensation to which a carrier is entitled for the carriage of cargo.

Proceedings *in rem* and *in personam*

Under American maritime law, the ship is personified to the extent that it may sometimes be held responsible under circumstances in which the shipowner himself is under no liability. The classic example of personification is the "compulsory pilotage" case. Some state statutes impose a penalty on a shipowner whose vessel fails to take a pilot when entering or leaving the waters of the state. Since the pilotage is thus compulsory, the pilot's negligence is not imputed to the shipowner. Nevertheless, the vessel itself is charged with the pilot's fault and is immediately impressed with an inchoate maritime lien that is enforcible in court.

Maritime liens can arise not only when the personified ship is charged with a maritime tort, such as a negligent collision or personal injury, but also for salvage services, for general average contributions, and for breach of certain maritime contracts.

In a proceeding *in rem,* the vessel, cargo, or freight can be arrested and kept in the custody of the court unless the owner obtains its release by posting a bond or such other security as may be required under the applicable law or as may be acceptable to the plaintiff. More frequently, however, the owner will post security to avoid a threatened arrest, and the property never has to be taken into custody. When the judgment is for the plaintiff in a proceeding *in rem,* there will be a recovery on the bond or other security if the owner of the property does not pay; or, if security has not been posted, the court will order the property sold, or the freight released, in order to satisfy the judgment. The sale of a ship by an admiralty court following a judgment *in rem* divests the ship of all preexisting liens—and not merely those liens sought to be enforced in the proceeding *in rem.* By way of contrast, the holder of an *in personam* judgment against a shipowner can, like any judgment creditor, have the ship sold in execution of the judgment; but such a sale, unlike the sale under an admiralty judgment *in rem,* does not divest existing liens; the purchaser at the execution sale takes the ship subject to all such liens. Thus, an *in rem* proceeding has decided advantages over a proceeding *in personam* in a case in which the shipowner is insolvent.

Ship mortgages

Efforts have been made from time to time to increase the security value of ship mortgages, in order to encourage lending institutions to finance vessel construction, but these efforts have not been very successful, largely because of differences in national laws respecting the relative priorities of mortgages and maritime liens. (Under general maritime law there is a complex hierarchy of maritime liens; that is to say, in a proceeding that involves distribution of an inadequate fund to a number of lien claimants, liens of a higher rank will be paid in full in priority over liens of a lower rank; and in most countries a ship mortgage ranks lower than a number of maritime liens.) Attempts were made to harmonize some of these conflicts by international conventions signed in 1926 and 1976, but the first failed to win widespread support and, as of the end of 1983, the second had been ratified by only half of the signatories required for the convention to enter into force.

Shipping charters. The function of ships, other than warships, pleasure craft, and service vessels of various types is of course transportation of cargoes and passengers. In the "jet age" the passenger-carrying segment of the shipping industry has lost much of its former importance, but the quantity of goods transported by water continues to grow as the world economy expands.

Charter parties and ocean bills of lading

The great majority of the contracts governing the carriage of goods by water are evidenced either by charter parties or by bills of lading. The term charter party (a corruption of the Latin *carta partita,* or "divided charter") is employed to describe three widely differing types of contracts relating to the use of vessels owned or controlled by others. Under a "demise" or "bareboat" charter, the shipowner delivers possession of the vessel to the charterer, who engages the master and crew, arranges for repairs and supplies, and, in general, functions in much the same way as an owner during the term of the charter. A much more common arrangement is the "time" charter, whereunder the shipowner employs the master and crew and the charterer simply acquires the right, within specified limits, to direct the movements of the vessel and determine what cargoes are to be carried during the charter period. Under both demise and time charters, the charterer pays charter hire for the use of the vessel at a specified daily or monthly rate.

The third type is the "voyage" charter, which is essentially a contract of affreightment, or carriage. Most voyage charters provide for the carriage of full cargoes on one voyage or a series of voyages, but occasionally a charterer contracts for the use of only a portion of the carrying capacity of the vessel, in which case the governing contract is described as a "space" charter. Under a voyage charter, it is customary for the master or his agent to issue a bill of lading to the shipper, who is usually the charterer, although as between shipowner and charterer the voyage charter remains the governing contract of carriage; the bill of lading serves only as a receipt and as a document of title to the goods. Ocean bills of lading are usually in order form; that is, they call for delivery to the order of the shipper or of some other designated party. Such a bill of lading may be negotiated in much the same way as a check, draft, or other negotiable instrument, which means that a bona fide purchaser of the bill of lading takes it free and clear of any defects not appearing on its face. Thus, if cargo is externally damaged on shipment but the damage is not noted on the bill of lading, the carrier will be barred from establishing that the cargo was in fact damaged before it came into the carrier's custody. Once a bill of lading issued under a voyage charter is negotiated to a bona fide purchaser, it becomes the governing contract between the carrier and the holder of the bill.

When a ship strands or collides with another vessel, substantial cargo loss or damage may result. If the casualty is found to have been caused by a sea peril or an error in navigation, there will be no liability if the goods are being carried under a statutory or contractual provision based upon the Brussels Convention on Limitation of Liability (1923), which incorporated the so-called "Hague Rules." If, however, the casualty was the result of the carrier's failure to exercise due diligence to make the ship seaworthy and to see that it was properly manned, equipped, and supplied, the carrier will be held responsible.

Limitation of liability. A distinctive feature of maritime law is the privilege accorded to a shipowner and certain other persons (such as charterers in some instances) to limit the amount of their liability, under certain circumstances, in respect of tort and some contract claims. In some countries, including the United States, the limit, except as to claims for personal injury and wrongful death, is the value of the ship and the earnings of the voyage on which it was engaged at the time of the casualty. On the other hand, in the United Kingdom and the other countries that have ratified the Brussels limitation of liability convention of 1957 or enacted domestic legislation embracing its terms, the limit is £28, or its equivalent, multiplied by the adjusted net tonnage of the vessel, regardless of its actual value. The basic condition of the privilege is that the party asserting it must be free from "privity or knowledge," in the words of the United States statute, or "actual fault or privity," in the words of the convention. This formula means, generally speaking, that the shipowner is entitled to limit his liability for the negligence of the master or crew, but not for his own personal negligence or that of his managerial personnel. In a sense the limited liability of shipowners may be compared to the limited liability that any investor may now achieve by incorporating his enterprise. The limited-liability idea in maritime law, however, long antedates the emergence or invention of the modern corporation or limited company; its early appearance in maritime law may be taken as a recognition of the extraordinary hazards of seaborne commerce and the need to protect the adventurous shipowner from the crushing burden of liability—that is, in the days before even the most primitive forms of insurance had become available. Some modern commentators have suggested that the peculiar features of maritime limitation of liability have outlived their usefulness, and that the development of insurance and of the modern limited-liability company has radically altered the conditions out of which the shipowners' privilege originally grew. Although no maritime country has yet gone to the length of abolishing limitation of liability, shipowning interests appear to have become concerned about the possibility of such a development.

Nature of limitation of liability

In most maritime countries the principle of limitation of liability was considered to be a part of the general maritime law. As it developed in continental Europe, the idea, generally stated, was that a shipowner entitled to limitation could satisfy his liability by abandoning the ship (and its pending freight) to claimants. Since the privilege of limitation was, and is, typically invoked following a large-scale maritime disaster, the abandonment theory meant that claimants got the value of the ship as it was following the disaster. If the ship had sunk or was a total loss with no freight pending, the claimants got nothing. This theory was carried over into the law of many South American countries.

Great Britain and the United States were once the only maritime countries that refused to admit the principle of limitation as part of the general maritime law. In both countries, however, the competitive needs of the shipping industry compelled its introduction by statute.

Foreign claims

In general, the limitation law of any country will be applied by its own courts in favour of foreign shipowners as well as of citizens. From the point of view of shipowning interests, however, a major weakness of limitation law has been the fact that limitation proceedings were not given international recognition. That has meant that a shipowner whose ships moved in international trade could find himself sued in several countries as a result of one disaster and forced to set up limitation funds in each country. The Brussels convention of 1957 makes limitation decrees delivered by admiralty courts in ratifying countries internationally effective; that is, a shipowner is required to set up only one limitation fund, out of which all claims are paid, no matter in how many countries proceedings might be instituted against him. Thus, the convention, which increases the liability of shipowners in most countries, does offer in return this considerable advantage to shipowners.

Collision liability. Under maritime law responsibility for collision damage is based upon the fault principle: a colliding vessel will not be held responsible for damage to another ship or to a fixed object such as a bridge, wharf, or jetty unless the collision is caused by a deficiency in the colliding vessel or by negligence or a willful act on the part of its navigators. It is not always necessary, however, to establish fault by positive evidence; there is a presumption of fault when a moving vessel collides with a fixed object or with another vessel that is properly moored or anchored, and the burden of proving freedom from fault will lie with the moving vessel.

In countries that have adopted the International Convention for the Unification of Certain Rules Relating to Collisions between Vessels, signed at Brussels in 1910, the rule of "comparative negligence" governs: if each of two colliding vessels is to blame, the total damages will be divided between their owners or operators in proportion to the respective degrees of fault. In certain countries that have not ratified the Convention, such as the United States, the law is such that, if both vessels are to blame, the total damages are equally divided, regardless of the respective degrees of fault. In certain other countries that have not ratified the Convention, including most of the Latin American states, the principle of "contributory fault" governs: if both vessels are to blame, each owner or operator bears his own damages.

Salvage and general average. Salvage and general average are doctrines peculiar to maritime law. Under the law of salvage, strangers to the maritime venture who succeed in saving maritime property from loss or damage from perils of the sea or other waters are entitled to an award for their efforts and have a maritime lien on the salvaged property therefor. Several elements will be taken into account in fixing the amount of the award, including the extent of the efforts required; the skill and energy displayed by the salvors, the amounts involved, including both the value of the vessel or other property employed by the salvors in rendering the service and the value of the vessel, cargo, or other property salvaged; the risks incurred by the salvors; and the degree of danger from which the property was rescued. General average (defined at the beginning of this article) is a principle still universally accepted, although there is some agitation for its abolition, principally because the accounting and other expenses incurred in administering a general average are often quite out of proportion to the amounts involved and because the same underwriters sometimes insure both hull and cargo.

Marine insurance. An appreciation of the part played by marine insurance is essential to an understanding of the shipping industry and the special law that governs it. Most shipowners carry hull insurance on their ships and protect themselves against claims by third parties by means of "protection and indemnity" insurance. Waterborne cargo is almost universally insured against the perils of the seas. It is impossible in a brief outline such as this to go into any of the special intricacies, which are many, of marine insurance law. Most cases of damage to a ship or its cargo resolve themselves into settlements between insurance carriers. Proposals for changes in the maritime law must always be evaluated against this background of insurance coverage, as the imposition of liabilities that cannot be insured against can discourage all but the wealthiest ocean carriers from engaging in the affected trades.

Insured perils

Marine insurance is the oldest known form of insurance. Indeed, the institution of general average, under which the participants in a maritime venture contribute to losses incurred by some for the benefit of all, may itself be looked on as a primitive form of mutual insurance. Hull and cargo insurance today, in fact, is usually written on forms whose wording has changed little since the 18th century. The so-called "perils" clause, enumerating the risks insured against, customarily includes not only the natural hazards to which a vessel is exposed but man-made perils such as capture or destruction by enemy forces as well. In 1898, however, Lloyd's of London underwriters inaugurated the practice of adding "Free of Capture and Seizure" (F.C.&S.) clauses to the basic policy forms, the effect of which was to remove war and similar risks from coverage. The practice has since become universal, with the result that the owner of a ship or cargo must either purchase separate war-risk insurance or else pay his marine underwriters an additional premium in return for deletion of the F.C.&S. clause.

An early type of marine liability insurance was against liability for damage that the insured vessel caused to other vessels. Such insurance was effected by the addition of a "running down" or "collision" clause to the basic hull policy insuring the owner or operator of a vessel against its loss or damage. On the theory that, if given full protection, owners and operators would not be encouraged to exercise proper care in the maintenance of their vessels and the selection of their masters and crews, hull underwriters at first refused to insure against more than 75 percent of the collision liability.

Protection and indemnity associations

With the advent of steam-driven vessels of iron and steel in the 19th century, the potential liabilities of shipowners increased substantially. To protect themselves, British owners banded together in "protection and indemnity" associations, commonly known as "P. and I. Clubs," whereby they insured each other against the liabilities to which they were all exposed in the operation of their vessels. These included liability for cargo damage, personal injury, and damage to piers, bridges, and other fixed objects, and also 25 percent of the liability for damage to other vessels against which the hull underwriters refused to insure. Foreign owners soon found the P. and I. Clubs attractive, and as of 1973 the operators of about 80 percent of the world's ocean tonnage were insured with the British clubs and their Scandinavian and Japanese affiliates.

INTERNATIONAL REGULATION

Maritime law is often thought of as being a species of international law rather than a branch of domestic or municipal law. It should not be denied that the international aspect of maritime law gives it a distinctive flavour; in doubtful cases courts of one country will often look to the precedents or statutes of another country for inspiration or guidance. Except to the extent that it may have bound itself by international conventions, however, each country has the right to adopt such maritime laws as it sees fit. Although many such laws are common to most maritime countries, others are not, though there is a growing tendency to restore the international uniformity in the maritime law achieved during the Middle Ages. In many areas, the lead has been taken by the International Maritime Committee, more commonly known by its French name, Comité Maritime International (CMI), which is composed of the maritime law associations of more than 30 nations. The work of the Comité consists principally of drafting international conventions relating to subjects of maritime law. When such a draft is prepared, it is submitted to the Belgian government, which then convenes a diplomatic conference at which the CMI draft is discussed and amended as the official delegates may decide. If the revised draft wins approval at the conference, it is then submitted to the national governments for possible ratification. Although many of these conventions have failed to be widely ratified, others have been highly successful.

International conventions

The international regulations for the prevention of collisions at sea, first adopted at an international conference held in Washington in 1889 and revised at maritime safety conferences held in London from time to time since 1914, are recognized by all of the maritime countries. The regulations are, in effect, an international code of navigation. In other fields much has been accomplished to ensure international uniformity through private agreements voluntarily adhered to by affected interests; the York-Antwerp Rules of General Average, first promulgated in 1890 and most recently amended in 1950, are the best known example of such agreements; although they do not technically have the force of law, nevertheless, by incorporation in charter parties and bills of lading, they determine the rights and obligations of the parties as effectively as any statute. (N.J.H.)

Air law

Air law is the body of law directly or indirectly concerned with civil aviation. Aviation in this context extends to both heavier-than-air and lighter-than-air aircraft. Air-cushion vehicles are not regarded as aircraft by the International Civil Aviation Organization (ICAO), but the practice of individual states in this regard is not yet settled. Because of the essentially international character of aviation, a large part of air law is either international law or international uniform law (rules of national law that have by agreement been made internationally uniform). The earliest legislation in air law was a 1784 decree of the Paris police forbidding balloon flights without a special permit. Insofar as international air law is concerned, it need hardly be mentioned that an international agreement or an amendment thereto is binding only on states that are parties to it.

AIRSPACE

Sovereignty. A basic principle of international air law is that every state has complete and exclusive sovereignty over the airspace above its territory, including its territorial sea. At the turn of the 20th century the view that airspace, like the high seas, should be free was sometimes advanced. But the principle of airspace sovereignty was unequivocally affirmed in the Paris Convention on the Regulation of Aerial Navigation (1919) and subsequently by various other multilateral treaties. The principle is restated in the Chicago Convention on International Civil Aviation (1944). Airspace is now generally accepted as an appurtenance of the subjacent territory and shares the latter's legal status. Thus, under the Geneva Convention on the High Seas (1958) as well as under international customary law, the freedom of the high seas applies to aerial navigation as well as to maritime navigation. Vertically, airspace ends where outer space begins.

Right to regulate the entry of foreign aircraft

It follows from the principle of airspace sovereignty that every state is entitled to regulate the entry of foreign aircraft into its territory and that persons within its territory are subject to its laws. States normally permit foreign private (*i.e.,* nongovernmental and noncommercial) aircraft to visit or fly through their territory without too much difficulty. Such aircraft registered in states that are parties to the 1944 Chicago Convention are, under the convention, allowed into the territories of all other contracting states without prior diplomatic permission if not engaged in the carriage of passengers, mail, or cargo for reward.

Commercial air transport is divided into scheduled air services and nonscheduled flights. Charter flights fall mostly, but not invariably, into the latter category. Under the Chicago Convention, contracting states agree to permit aircraft registered in the other contracting states and engaged in commercial nonscheduled flights to fly into their territory without prior diplomatic permission and, moreover, to pick up and discharge passengers, cargo, and mail, but in practice this provision has become a dead letter.

For scheduled air services, the privilege of operating commercial services through or into a foreign country was, at the time of the 1944 Chicago conference, split into five so-called freedoms of the air. The first is the privilege of flying across a country nonstop; the second, of flying across with a stop for technical purposes only. These two freedoms are also known as transit rights. A large number of ICAO members are parties to the 1944 International Air Services Transit Agreement, placing these rights on a multilateral basis. The other freedoms of the air are known as traffic rights, referring to passengers, mail, or cargo carried on a commercial service. The third of the five freedoms is the privilege of bringing in and discharging traffic from the home state of the aircraft or airline; the fourth is that of picking up traffic for the home state of the aircraft or airline; the fifth is that of picking up traffic for or discharging traffic from third states in the territory of the state granting the privilege. This fifth freedom is the main bargaining point in the exchange of traffic rights among states. Attempts have been made since 1944 to create other freedoms, but each new freedom usually represents in practice a new restriction.

Efforts to conclude a widely acceptable multilateral agreement on traffic rights were unsuccessful, and such rights have continued to be handled through bilateral international agreements. These agreements fix the routes to be served, the principles governing the capacity of the agreed services (frequency of the service multiplied by the carrying capacity of the aircraft used), and the procedures for the approval of fares and tariffs by the respective governments. Most agreements require that airlines operating the same routes consult among themselves before submitting their fares to the two governments concerned for approval, and many agreements specify the International Air Transport Association (IATA), an association of airlines, as the organ for such consultations. The right to carry domestic traffic between points within a state is normally reserved to that state's own airlines. A bilateral agreement signed at Bermuda in 1946 between the United Kingdom and the United States set a pattern that has generally been followed, although the formal Bermuda-type agreement is likely to be accompanied by confidential memoranda attaching various restrictions.

Private rights. The principle of airspace sovereignty in international law is probably well reflected in the maxim, *Cujus est solum ejus est usque ad coelum et ad inferos* ("he who owns the land owns what is above and below it"). In private law the acceptance of this maxim for a long time posed little difficulty, and the Code Napoléon of 1804 adopted it almost verbatim; in more recent times, however, it is more than questionable whether such a principle can be accepted without qualification. Both the German Civil Code (1896) and the Swiss Civil Code (1907), while recognizing the principle of *Cujus est solum,* adopted a functional approach, limiting the right of the owner to such a height and such a depth as are necessary for his enjoyment of the land. In common-law countries the courts have arrived at a broadly similar position. In France, too, both the doctrine and the courts have refused to take *Cujus est solum* literally. In one celebrated case, *Clément Bayard* v. *Coquerel* (1913), the Court of Compiègne, lending judicial authority for the first time to the theory of abuse of rights, awarded damages to a plaintiff whose balloon had been destroyed by "spite structures" erected by the defendant on his own land and ordered the offending spikes to be taken down.

In the course of the 1920s it became clear in most countries, either through judicial decisions or express legislation, that aircraft would be allowed to fly over the private properties of others in normal flight in accordance with aeronautical regulations. This immunity applies only to the mere passage of the aircraft and does not extend to damage caused by it or to other encroachments on the use or enjoyment of the land, such as excessively low flights.

AIRPORTS

In most countries airports may be privately, municipally, or nationally owned and operated, and the siting of an airport may be subject to town and country planning or zoning regulations. Whether or not the establishment of an airport requires special permission, aircraft leaving or entering a country will normally be required to do so at an airport having customs and immigration facilities. Airports that are open to public use are generally subject to some form of licensing or control in order to ensure compliance with minimum safety standards. Members of ICAO, in order to comply with their obligations under the Chicago Convention, have to make certain that such airports are open to aircraft of all other ICAO members under the same conditions as they are open to national aircraft. Restrictions may also be imposed on the noise level of aircraft taking off or landing, as well as the general level of noise, vibration, smoke, and so forth that may result from the operation of airports. In order to secure safety of flight, restrictions may be imposed on the use of lands adjoining an airport, such as the height of buildings or the planting of trees. Practice varies as to whether such restrictions are regarded as true measures of planning or zoning or as takings of private property for public use, which require the payment of compensation.

Some legal systems exempt the airport owner, operator, and users from liability for low flights over neighbouring properties, noise, vibration, or other forms of disturbance, provided that all the regulations and conditions laid down for the operation and use of the airport are complied with. In the absence of such immunity, granted by law or obtained privately from adjacent landowners, the owners, operators, and users of airports are basically liable, in much the same way as other occupiers of land, for any substantial impairment of the use or enjoyment of neighbouring lands.

AIRCRAFT

The channelling of rights and duties through the principle of nationality

Nationality. Among the most important points resolved in the 1919 Paris Convention were that aircraft should have a nationality, that they should have the nationality of the state in which they were registered, and that no aircraft could be validly registered in more than one state. The 1944 Chicago Convention retained these principles. While both conventions preclude dual or multiple registration, the ICAO Council in 1967 recognized the possibility of joint registration of aircraft by a number of states, and even "international registration"—without, however, specifying what the latter meant. The principle that every aircraft, at least every one that flies outside its country of origin, must have a nationality is of cardinal importance in air law, inasmuch as it enables a number of rights and duties to be either directly grafted onto the aircraft or channelled through the aircraft to a variety of persons. At the international level, moreover, it ensures that there will be no aircraft for which there is not a state answerable.

Under the 1944 Chicago Convention an aircraft, in order to benefit from the privileges conferred by the convention, must comply with its terms. Many of these terms are further elaborated in annexes to the convention. According to Article 20 of the convention, as among the contracting states, "every aircraft engaged in international air navigation shall bear its appropriate nationality and registration marks." Under Article 31, "every aircraft engaged in international navigation shall be provided with a certificate of airworthiness issued or rendered valid by the State in which it is registered"; in 1960 a number of European countries signed, at Paris, a multilateral agreement relating to Certificates of Airworthiness for Imported Aircraft, which is open to accession by other states, designed to facilitate mutual recognition of certificates of airworthiness for import and export purposes. Under Article 30(a) of the Chicago Convention, aircraft of [*i.e.,* having the nationality of] each contracting State may, in or over the territory of other contracting States, carry radio transmitting apparatus only if a licence to install and operate such apparatus has been issued by the appropriate authorities of the State in which the aircraft is registered.

As regards the operating personnel of the aircraft, the Chicago Convention provides that

the pilot of every aircraft and the other members of the operating crew of every aircraft engaged in international navigation shall be provided with certificates of competency and licences issued or rendered valid by the State in which the aircraft is registered.

When an aircraft registered in one contracting state is in or over the territory of other contracting states,

radio transmitting apparatus may be used only by members of the flight crew who are provided with a special licence for the purpose, issued by the appropiate authorities of the State in which the aircraft is registered.

In addition, the convention prescribes that

there shall be maintained in respect of every aircraft engaged in international navigation a journey log book in which shall be entered particulars of the aircraft, its crew and of each journey . . . .

All of the above documents must be carried by "every aircraft of a contracting State, engaged in international navigation," as well as the appropriate manifests if passengers and cargo are carried.

The fact that all of these rules concerning the aircraft and its crew are channelled through the state of registry can give rise to problems when an aircraft is leased or chartered for any length of time to operators of a different nationality ("interchange of aircraft"). These problems can sometimes be resolved by a temporary transfer either of de facto control or of registration of the aircraft to the state of the operator.

The provision and operation of ground and other air navigation facilities, as well as the establishment and enforcement of air navigation rules and air traffic control, are the responsibility of the territorial state. So is investigation of accidents, though among ICAO members, under the Chicago Convention the state of registry

shall be given the opportunity to appoint observers to be present at the inquiry and the State holding the inquiry shall communicate the report and findings in the matter to that State.

Among ICAO members, over the high seas the Rules of the Air established by ICAO apply. Enforcement rests primarily with the state of registry, which is also responsible for investigating accidents occurring over the high seas. A body known as Eurocontrol, established in 1960 by the Brussels Convention Relating to Co-operation for the Safety of Air Navigation, represents an attempt at international cooperation in air-traffic control by a number of western European states.

Private rights in aircraft

Registration of aircraft for nationality and public-law purposes is to be distinguished from registration for purposes of private law. Some legal systems treat aircraft simply as ordinary movable property. Others require all sales of, and other transactions relating to, aircraft, such as mortgages, to be effected in writing and recorded in a public registry before they may be invoked against third parties. Yet others regard only rights duly recorded as valid. If aircraft are to be used as security for credit or loans, a system of recording of rights with international recognition of the rights so recorded has obvious advantages. To this end, a Convention on the International Recognition of Rights in Aircraft was concluded in Geneva in 1948. Few states accepted it at first, but, with the rising cost of modern aircraft, interest in the convention increased. Its wide acceptance will have the side effect of bringing about much greater uniformity in rules of private law governing rights in aircraft.

Acts and occurrences on board aircraft. *Criminal jurisdiction.* Although some systems of national law still adhere to the view that ships and aircraft are part of the territory of the state the nationality of which they possess, this is merely a crude metaphor. In international law, a distinction has to be made between three types of state jurisdiction: territorial jurisdiction over national territory and all persons and things therein; quasi-territorial jurisdiction over national ships and aircraft and all persons and things thereon; and personal jurisdiction over all other nationals and all persons under a state's protection, as well as their property. In case of conflict, territorial jurisdiction overrides quasi-territorial jurisdiction and personal jurisdiction, while quasi-territorial jurisdiction overrides personal jurisdiction.

For a long time, the failure of states to extend their criminal laws to their aircraft while they were outside national territory posed a serious problem. As long as an aircraft is flying in the national airspace of some state, the law of that state is applicable. When a crime has been committed during an international flight, however, there may be difficulty in pinpointing when and where it occurred and hence in determining the state the law of which has been violated. Unless the criminal law and jurisdiction of the state of registry have been extended to the aircraft during the period it is outside the state of registry, there may be none applicable; over the high seas, for example, there would clearly be a gap in the law. This, together with the realization that with the constant increase in air traffic the incidence of offenses on board aircraft was bound to rise, led to the conclusion in 1963 at Tokyo of the Convention on Offences and Certain Other Acts Committed on Board Aircraft, obliging the contracting states to extend their criminal law and jurisdiction to aircraft of their registry when they are outside national territory. The convention furthermore gives the aircraft commander power to ensure law and order on board his aircraft and to disembark any offender in any contracting state in which the aircraft lands.

The Tokyo Convention

Civil jurisdiction. In most countries the general civil law applies, except as modified. In the interest of avoiding statelessness, most states confer their nationality on those born on aircraft of their registry; but there is in air law no general principle of the law of the flag (*i.e.,* the law of the state of registry) being applicable to every occurrence on board. There are, however, various international agreements that affect the exercise of civil jurisdiction by states. A few may be mentioned. The most important is doubtless Article 28 of the 1929 Warsaw Convention on International Carriage by Air, as subsequently modified by Article 8 of the 1961 Guadalajara Convention and amplified by Article 12 of the 1971 Guatemala City Protocol. Under Article 28, an action arising from an "international" carriage by air may be brought only before the courts of certain contracting states and no others. The 1933 Rome Convention on Precautionary Arrest of Aircraft, which has not been widely accepted, exempts aircraft actually used on government services or in commercial transport from precautionary attachment. In other cases, the giving of an adequate bond "shall prevent the precautionary attachment or give a right to immediate release." Among ICAO members, Article 27 of the Chicago Convention provides that, subject to certain conditions, aircraft of the contracting states on an international flight are exempt from seizure or detention on patent claims in the territory of other contracting states, without having to deposit a security. Under the 1952 Rome Convention on Surface Damage, in principle, actions may be brought only before the courts of the contracting state in which the damage occurred.

Crimes against aircraft. *Piracy.* The 1958 Geneva Convention on the High Seas intends to be declaratory of general international law when it defines the offense of piracy principally as

any illegal acts of violence, detention or any act of depredation, committed for private ends by the crew or the passengers of a private [*i.e.,* nongovernmental and not noncommercial] ship or a private aircraft, and directed: (a) on the high seas, against another ship or aircraft, or against persons or property on board such ship or aircraft; (b) against a ship, aircraft, persons or property in a place outside the jurisdiction of any State.

The convention defines the effect of piracy under international law as follows:

On the high seas, or in any other place outside the jurisdiction of any State, every State may seize a pirate ship or aircraft, or a ship taken by piracy and under the control of pirates, and arrest the persons and seize the property on board.

A state, having done so, may decide upon the penalties to be imposed and the fate of the ship, the aircraft, or the property. This definition of piracy deliberately excludes acts committed for political motives, as well as acts confined within a ship or aircraft, such as mutiny or the hijacking of an aircraft by its passengers or crew. Although some states, for example, the United States, have in their own laws categorized hijacking as aircraft piracy, this in itself is unable to bring about the consequences of piracy under international law.

Hijacking. Unlawful seizure is the legal name that states at the international level have given to aircraft hijacking. Thus, the 1963 Tokyo Convention obliges contracting states to take all appropriate measures to restore control of an aircraft hijacked in flight to its lawful commander, and obliges the state in which the aircraft lands to allow the passengers and crew to continue their journey, and to return the aircraft and its cargo to those lawfully entitled to possession. In response to a wave of hijackings that began in 1968, the 1970 Hague Convention for the Suppression of Unlawful Seizure of Aircraft was concluded in an effort to prevent hijackers from finding immunity in any of the contracting states.

Far more grievous than hijackings as regards the number of persons injured or killed and of aircraft damaged or destroyed have been the many acts of sabotage or violence committed against aircraft and civil aviation installations. This led to the conclusion at Montreal in 1971 of the Convention for the Suppression of Unlawful Acts Against the Safety of Civil Aviation, on roughly the same lines as the 1970 Hague convention dealing with the problem of unlawful seizure.

GOODS, PASSENGERS, SHIPPERS, AND OTHER PARTIES

Problems of liability arising from the international carriage of passengers, baggage, and cargo by aircraft are dealt with by the widely accepted Warsaw Convention on International Carriage by Air, which was concluded in 1929, amended in 1955 by the Hague Protocol, supplemented in 1961 by the Guadalajara Convention, and further amended in 1971 by the Guatemala City Protocol. The 1971 protocol was much influenced by the so-called Montreal agreement of 1966, which was an agreement among airlines accepting the terms of the United States government for withdrawing its denunciation of the Warsaw Convention. Not every party of the Warsaw Convention has accepted the 1955 or the 1971 amendment protocol; nor is a party that accepts either protocol required to denounce the treaty which the protocol amends. The result is that there are in fact three separate treaties (Warsaw, Warsaw–Hague, and Warsaw–Hague–Guatemala City) with a number of states being parties to more than one.

The contracting states to the Warsaw convention seek to reduce and eliminate problems of conflict of laws by agreeing to adopt uniform rules in their internal laws governing the international carriage of persons, baggage, or cargo by aircraft. The qualification "international" has the special meaning attributed to it by the convention and, in order to avoid ambiguity, carriage governed by the Warsaw Convention is often referred to as Warsaw carriage. Some states have extended the rules of the convention to carriage not governed by the convention. The rules established by the convention are mandatory in the sense that the parties to the contract of carriage cannot vary them, especially not to the detriment of the consumer. They are also exclusive in the sense that no additional claims can be brought against the carrier outside the terms of the convention.

In the event a passenger is injured or dies, or baggage or cargo is damaged or lost during "international" carriage, the convention makes the carrier prima facie liable. In order to avoid liability, the carrier has to prove that he and his servants and agents have not been at fault. His liability may also be excluded in whole or in part if the injured person is wholly or partly to blame for the damage. In return for the presumption of his liability, the carrier is given the benefit of limited liability, a benefit that he forfeits if it is proved that the damage resulted from his willful misconduct or that of his servants and agents. The convention lays down detailed rules on the issuance and contents of the appropriate documents of carriage (passenger ticket, baggage check, and air waybill) and enforces them with the penalty of absolute and unlimited liability.

For the carriage of passengers, the Guatemala City Protocol further lays down rules on possible supplementary compensation schemes and periodic increases of the liability limit. The rules concerning documents of carriage, which can have important effects on the carrier's liability, were substantially modified at The Hague and again at Guatemala City.

While aircraft may fly over private lands in normal flight, most national laws protect the landowner against excessively low flights and other undue interference with his possession and use of land, such as the performance of aerobatics and buzzing. In addition, normally, every system of national law allows third parties on the surface (of the Earth) to recover for damage done by an aircraft in flight, or by persons and things in or falling from it, though in some countries there are limits to the amount recoverable. Some national laws base liability on fault. The majority, however, hold the owner or the operator of the aircraft absolutely liable for any damage caused. Insurance against third-party liability is compulsory in many states.

Surface damage

In 1933 a convention was concluded in Rome on surface damage caused by foreign aircraft. This was supplemented by the 1938 Brussels Insurance Protocol. Both have since been superseded by the 1952 Rome Convention on the same subject. The convention applies only to surface damage caused in a contracting state by aircraft registered in another contracting state. It accepts the principle of absolute liability, subject to the exception of contributory negligence, providing however that

> there shall be no right to compensation . . . if the damage results from the mere fact of passage of the aircraft through the airspace in conformity with existing air traffic regulations.

The convention makes the operator of the aircraft liable. The main raison d'être of the convention is said to be its scheme of compulsory insurance; in return, the liability of the operator is limited according to the weight of the aircraft, unless the damage is caused by a deliberate act of the operator, his servants, or agents, done with intent to cause damage. An unauthorized user of the aircraft also incurs unlimited liability. Actions to recover compensation may be brought only in the state in which the damage occurred. An important element in the convention is the provision that judgments rendered under it are enforceable in all other contracting states. The convention came into force in 1958, but the number of states that have accepted it is not very high. The wording of Article 1(1) of the convention quoted above gives rise to doubt whether damage resulting from sonic booms is covered. In view of the treatment accorded to passengers by the Guatemala City Protocol, a revised convention establishing absolute, unlimited, and adequately secured liability for all damage caused by aircraft to third parties on the surface would seem indicated.

INTERNATIONAL REGULATION

Under the 1919 Paris Convention, an International Commission for Aerial Navigation (ICAN, or CINA) was created with headquarters in Paris. In 1937 an Inter-American Technical Aviation Conference decided on the creation of a Permanent American Aeronautical Commission (CAPA). Both were superseded by the establishment in 1947 of the International Civil Aviation Organization (ICAO) under the 1944 Chicago Convention. The Soviet Union joined in 1970, making ICAO membership almost universal.

Functions of the ICAO

ICAO is a specialized agency affiliated to the United Nations, with headquarters in Montreal. It has a plenary Assembly, which holds the budgetary power; a permanent Council elected triennially, which, among other things, adopts the Annexes to the Convention; an Air Navigation Commission; an Air Transport Committee; and a plenary Legal Committee, which discusses matters of air law of common interest to members and prepares draft conventions for their consideration and acceptance.

One of the most important functions of ICAO is the preparation and periodical revision of international standards and recommended practices relating to civil aviation. It has done much to standardize aeronautical regulations throughout the world. Among other functions of ICAO may be mentioned those in connection with joint support programs among members for financing air navigation facilities and its technical assistance program. The ICAO Council, under the Chicago Convention, may also function as either a conciliation body or a judicial organ in disputes between members. (Bi.C.)

BIBLIOGRAPHY. General works on transportation law include D. PHILIP LOCKLIN, *Economics of Transportation,* 6th ed. (1966); J.H. TEDROW, *Regulation of Transportation,* 6th ed. (1964); WILLIAM L. GROSSMAN, *Fundamentals of Transportation* (1959); FRANK M. CUSHMAN, *Manual of Transportation Law* (1951); and I.L. SHARFMAN, *The Interstate Commerce Commission,* 5 vol. (1931, reprinted 1969). Works dealing with the carriage of goods in general are HENRY N. LONGLEY, *Common Carriage of Cargo* (1967); JOHN MCKNIGHT MILLER, *Freight Loss and Damage Claims,* 3rd ed. (1967). Comprehensive works dealing with carriage of goods by a variety of means of transport are JASPER G. RIDLEY, *The Law of the Carriage of Goods by Land, Sea and Air,* 6th ed., ed. by GEOFFREY WHITEHEAD (1982); R. RODIERE, *Manuel de transports terrestres et aériens* (1969), and *Droit des transports,* 3 vol. (1953–62); PAUL SCAPEL, *Traité théorique et pratique sur les transports par mer, terre, eau, air et fer* (1958). On mixed carrier transportation, see GEORGES O. ROBERT-TISSOT, *Le Connaissement direct* (1957); on carriage of goods by road, rail, and inland water: OTTO KAHN-FREUND, *The Law of Carriage by Inland Transport,* 4th ed. (1965); EDGAR WATKINS, *Shippers and Carriers,* 5th ed., 2 vol. (1962); ALAN LESLIE, *The Law of Transport by Railway,* 2nd ed. (1928). Useful information can be found in numerous government documents, especially in the acts of such United States Congressional Committees as the Committee on Commerce, Science, and Transportation, and the Committee on Public Works and Transportation. Later monographs include MARVIN L. FAIR and JOHN GUANDOLO, *Transportation Regulation,* 8th ed. (1979); RICHARD J. PIERCE, JR., GARY D. ALLISON, and PATRICK H. MARTIN, *Economic Regulation: Energy, Transportation, and Utilities* (1980); KENNETH R. FEINBERG, *Deregulation of the Transportation Industry* (1981); JOHN GUANDOLO, *Transportation Law,* 4th ed. (1983); MALCOLM EVANS and MARTIN STANFORD (comps.), *Transport Laws of the World,* 5 vol. (1977–82). *Transguide: A Guide to Sources of Freight Transportation Information* (1980), is an informative, well-organized reference work.

Maritime law: E. BENEDICT, *The Law of American Admiralty,* vol. 1–4, 6th ed. by A.W. KNAUTH (1940–41) and vol. 5–6B, 7th ed. by A.W. and C.R. KNAUTH (1968–69), is the standard American text on admiralty practice. Included in *British Shipping Laws* are K. MCGUFFIE, P.A. FUGEMAN, and P.V. GRAY, *Admiralty Practice* (1964); N. SINGH, *International Conventions of Merchant Shipping* (1963); and the following standard British texts: SIR JOSEPH ARNOULD, *The Law of Marine Insurance and Average* 15th ed. by LORD CHORLEY and C.T. BAILHACHE, 2 vol. (1961); T. CARVER, *Carriage by Sea,* 12th ed. by R.P. COLINVAUX, 2 vol. (1971); R. LOWNDES and G.R. RUDOLPH, *The Law of General Average,* 9th ed. by J.F. DONALDSON, C.T. ELLIS, and C.S. STAUGHTON (1964); and R.G. MARSDEN, *The Law of Collisions at Sea,* 11th ed. by K. MCGUFFIE (1961). G. RIPERT, *Droit Maritime,* 4th ed., 3 vol. (1950–53), is the most respected modern French text on maritime law. G. GILMORE and C.L. BLACK, JR., *The Law of Admiralty* (1957), is the leading modern, single-volume text on American maritime law. SIR WILLIAM R. KENNEDY, *Civil Salvage,* 4th ed. by K. MCGUFFIE (1958), is the leading text on salvage law. J.W. GRIFFIN, *The American Law of Collision* (1949), is the standard American text on the law of marine collision. SIR THOMAS E. SCRUTTON, *Scrutton on Charter Parties and Bills of Lading,* 17th ed. by SIR WILLIAM L. MCNAIR, SIR ALAN A. MOCATTA, and M.J. MUSTILL (1964), is the best known work on the subject. M.J. NORRIS, *The Law of Seamen,* 3rd ed. (1970), is a widely used American text. F.R. SANBORN, *Origins of the Early English Maritime and Commercial Law* (1930), is an excellent inquiry into the sources of English maritime law. J.H. WIGMORE, *A Panorama of the World's Legal Systems* (1936), contains an account of the origins and early development of maritime law. T.L. MEARS, "The History of the Admiralty Jurisdiction," in *Select Essays in Anglo-American Legal History,* vol. 2 (1907), offers a fair survey. Later comprehensive studies include ANN L. HOLLICK, *U.S. Foreign Policy and the Law of the Sea* (1981); RODNEY P. CARLISLE, *Sovereignty for Sale: The Origins and Evolution of the Panamanian and Liberian Flags of Convenience* (1981); CHRISTOPHER HILL, *Maritime Law* (1981); R.P. ANAND, *Origin and Development of the Law of the Sea* (1983); D.P. O'CONNELL, *The International Law of the Sea* (1982); E. LANGAVANT, *Droit de la mer,* 3 vol. (1979–83); FRANK L. MARAIST, *Admiralty in a Nutshell* (1983); GEORGE S. ROUKIS (ed.), *The American Maritime Industry: Problems and Prospects,* 2 vol. (1983); RENÉ RODIÈRE, *Droit maritime,* 9th ed., (1982); EDWARD MILES *et al., The Management of Marine Regions* (1982); JOHN N. MOORE, *Ocean Law,* 2 vol. (1982); see also *The Law of the Sea: Official Text of the United Nations Convention on the Law of the Sea* (1983).

Air law: A comprehensive general work covering both international and English air law is *Shawcross and Beaumont on Air Law,* 3rd ed. by P.B. KEENAN, A. LESTER, and P. MARTIN, 2 vol. (1966), with its supplements. An introductory work for the student is G.A. SEABROOKE, *Air Law* (1964). A.D. MCNAIR, *The Law of the Air,* 3rd ed. (1964); and P.C. NATHAN and A.R. BARROWCLOUGH, "Civil Aviation," in *Halsbury's Laws of England,* 3rd ed., vol. 5, pp. 1–248 (1953), both deal with the subject from the standpoint of English law. For the United States, see A.J. MATHES and T. MATTERN, *Manual of Aviation Law* (1952), a booklet that commends itself by its scope and brevity. Much more elaborate are F. DE BILLYOU, *Air Law,* 2nd ed. (1964); and R.W. FIXEL, *The Law of Aviation* (1967). ROBERT R. WRIGHT, *The Law of Airspace* (1968), is on private rights and is not limited to air law, while D.H.N. JOHNSON, *Rights in Air Space* (1965), deals primarily with international law and is especially useful for its treatment of the historical evolution of the subject and the rules of air warfare. On the Chicago Convention, on ICAO, and on multilateral and bilateral agreements governing the operation of international nonscheduled flights and scheduled air services, see B. CHENG, *The Law of International Air Transport* (1962). H. DRION, *Limitation of Liabilities in International Air Law* (1954), a standard work, deals with both the Warsaw Convention and the Rome Convention. B. CHENG, "The Law of 'International' and 'Non-international' Carriage by Air," *The Law Society's Gazette* (1963–64), covers the Warsaw Convention, the Hague Protocol, and the Guadalajara Convention. A.F. LOWENFELD and A.I. MENDELSOHN, "The United States and the Warsaw Convention," *Harvard Law Review,* 80:497–602 (1967), is a more or less official apologia for absolute liability and the Montreal agreement. These were also the subject of two symposia: *Journal of the Royal Aeronautical Society* (1967); and "Symposium on the Warsaw Convention as Modified by the Montreal Agreement," *Journal of Air Law and Commerce,* 33:519–726 (1967). T. BUERGENTHAL, *Law-Making in the International Civil Aviation Organization* (1969); and J. SCHENKMAN, *International Civil Aviation Organization* (1955), are both works of great scholarly merit. U.S. LIBRARY OF CONGRESS, LAW LIBRARY, *Air Laws and Treaties of the World,* 3 vol. (1965), for the use of the Senate Committee on Commerce, is a mine of information. D.A. COOPER (ed. and trans.), *The Air Code of the U.S.S.R.* (1966; orig. pub. in Russian, 1961), has useful notes and explanatory comments. See also I.H. PH. DIEDERIKS-VERSCHOOR, *Introduction to Air Law* (1983); GERARD PUCCI, *Aviation Law,* 4th ed. (1981); STEPHEN COROVE (ed.), *United States Space Law: National & International Regulation,* 2 vol. (1982); and for the socialist countries, J.L. KNEIFEL, *Staatliches und internationales Luftverkehrsrecht der sozialistischen Staaten UdSSR, DDR, Polen, CSSR, Ungarn, Bulgarien, Rumänien, Kuba, Jugoslawien und der VR China* (1980), and *Fluggesellschaften und Luftverkehrssysteme der sozialistischen Staaten UdSSR, Polen, CSSR, Ungarn, Bulgarien, Rumänien, Kuba, Jugoslawien und der VR China* (1980). J. RAY FERGUSON, *Air Law: A Selected Bibliography of Articles, 1870–1980* (1982), is a useful reference source.

Trees

Although the concept of a tree as a growth form is useful and generally well understood, it is not possible to provide a precisely delimiting definition of a tree. There is an imperceptible merging of plants that obviously are trees into shrubs and of woody plants into herbaceous plants. To qualify as a tree a plant must be a perennial (*i.e.,* a plant that renews its growth each year); in addition, trees usually have a single self-supporting trunk that contains woody tissues. The trunk generally is dominant for some distance above the ground and commonly produces secondary limbs, called branches; in some species, however, the trunk divides at a low, sometimes even at ground, level into two or more trunks. Most palms have no branches. Although height is often considered a factor in defining trees—minimum limits of 15 or 20 feet (five to seven metres) being most commonly accepted—limits are an arbitrary measure of convenience; woody plants, like all others, are greatly influenced by environment, and the same species, and even specimens propagated by cuttings or some other means from the same stock of one species, may vary tremendously in size depending upon where they grow and the treatment they receive. Pines, spruces, birches, and many other trees, although reduced in size—in some cases to no more than a few inches tall—at the northernmost limits and the highest altitudes of their occurrence, may still have single woody trunks. Specimens of many species grown under adverse conditions of soil, moisture, exposure to wind, and other environmental factors may be similarly dwarfed. The Japanese, by manipulating natural factors that affect growth and by skillful pruning, practice bonsai, in which species that would be forest trees in nature are so dwarfed that they never exceed a few inches to three feet or so in height; such trees develop the proportions and appearance of their fully developed counterparts, however. This article discusses the botanical and popular classifications of trees, their importance to man, their structure and growth, and their origin and evolution.

The article is divided into the following sections:

TREE TYPES AND DISTRIBUTIONS

In 1948 the British botanist John Hutchinson, following a trend that had been gaining acceptance for several years, divided the traditionally recognized flowering plant class Dicotyledoneae into two classes: the Lignosae (containing all trees and shrubs as well as clearly related herbaceous plants) and the Herbaceae (all herbaceous plants in addition to some obviously related woody ones). This system stresses the woody characteristic of trees and shrubs more than do other modern systems of plant classification but is still very different from the arrangement put forward by the Greeks about 300 BC and accepted for 1,000 years; they separated plants according to their forms into such major groups as trees, shrubs, and vines.

Ancient system of classifying plants

An important objective of modern botanical classification has been to arrange species, genera, and other recognized groups phylogenetically; that is, according to their probable evolutionary lines of development and genetic relationships. In attempting such a classification, many factors are considered other than those concerned with plant form and gross morphology; *e.g.,* evidence from cytology, genetics, ecological behaviour, and indications of probable population migrations. Because of vast gaps in the knowledge of the actual evolutionary development that led to the Earth's present flora, phylogenetic systems of plant classification are based to a considerable degree on conjecture; in none of these systems, however, are trees treated as a discrete group.

Trees are represented in the major divisions and subdivisions of the plant kingdom called pteridophytes, gymnosperms, and angiosperms. To the first belong the tree ferns; to the second the cycads, the ginkgo, and the conifers; and to the third all flowering plants.

Tree ferns, which belong to the fern families Dicksoniaceae and Cyatheaceae, account for more than 300 of the approximately 10,000 species of ferns (*q.v.*). Many attain heights of 20 to 30 feet (seven to 10 metres); some are 50, 60, or occasionally 80 feet in height. These graceful trees, which are natives of humid mountain forests in the tropics and subtropics and of warm-temperate regions of the Southern Hemisphere, have huge lacy leaves; they are the remnants of a vastly more numerous flora that populated much of the Earth 280,000,000 to 345,000,000 years ago (the Carboniferous Period).

Cycads compose the Cycadaceae, a family consisting of nine genera and approximately 100 species. Natives of warm regions of the Eastern and Western Hemispheres, they also are remnants of a much larger number of species that in past geologic ages dominated the Earth's flora. (See GYMNOSPERMS.)

Ginkgo is the only living representative of the family Ginkgoaceae (order Ginkgoales). It is a relic that has been preserved in cultivation around Buddhist temples in China and elsewhere since the mid-18th century; the tree probably no longer exists in a wild state. It is believed to represent the last of a group of related genera that were most abundant in the Jurassic Period, some 165,000,000 years ago. (See GYMNOSPERMS.)

Conifers include trees and shrubs in seven families and more than 500 species. Familiar representatives are araucarias, cedars, cypresses, Douglas firs, firs, hemlocks, junipers, larches, pines, podocarpuses, redwoods, spruces, and yews. (See GYMNOSPERMS.)

Angiosperms (*q.v.*), or flowering plants, dominate the Earth's present flora; they are divided into about 300 families and approximately 220,000 species, among which are the majority of the world's trees. Angiosperms are divided on the basis of a group of characteristics into two classes: the Monocotyledoneae, or monocotyledons, and the Dicotyledoneae, or dicotyledons. The most numerous of the monocotyledonous trees are palms; others include agaves, aloes, dracaenas, screw pines (*Pandanus*), and yuccas. By far the greatest number of tree species are dicotyledons; they are represented by such familiar groups as apples, birches, elms, hollies, magnolias, maples, oaks, poplars, willows, and a host of others.

Popular tree classification systems. For nonscientific usage, trees have been grouped in various ways, some of which more or less parallel their scientific classification; *e.g.,* softwoods are conifers and hardwoods are dicotyledons. Hardwoods are also known as broadleaf trees. It is important to note, however, that the designations softwood, hardwood, and broadleaf do not indicate with precision the characteristics they imply. The wood of some hardwoods—for example, certain willows and poplars, and the softest of all woods, balsa—is softer than that of some softwoods; *e.g.,* the longleaf pine (*Pinus palustris*). Similarly, some broadleaf trees (tree heaths, *Erica,* and some kinds of *Tamarix*) have narrower leaves than do those of certain conifers (*Podocarpus*).

Evergreen and deciduous trees

A popular and convenient grouping of trees is evergreens and deciduous. This is most useful at the local rather than the worldwide level: whether a particular species retains its foliage throughout the year and thus qualifies as evergreen may depend on climate. At the northern limits or, in the Southern Hemisphere, the southern limits of their occurrence and at high elevations, species that under more favourable circumstances retain their foliage may become leafless for a period. Many tropical and subtropical species that in uniformly humid climates are never without foliage are deciduous in regions in which dry and wet seasons alternate. In northern North America the term evergreen is often used as a synonym for conifer and thus excludes foliage-retaining angiosperms. But five coniferous genera—*Larix* (larch), *Metasequoia* (dawn redwood), *Pseudolarix* (golden larch), *Taxodium* (swamp cypress), and *Glyptostrobus*—are composed of or include deciduous species.

Other tree groups are popularly recognized: tree ferns as tree ferns, palms as palms, and, among desert plants, the tree forms of agaves, aloes, cactuses, euphorbias, and yuccas. Sometimes the layman includes as trees plants that botanists cannot accept as such; for example, the banana. Such confusion arises from the fact that what appears to be the trunk of the "banana tree" is actually leafstalks rolled tightly around each other. The banana plant is entirely herbaceous, has no true trunk, and thus is not a tree.

The distribution of trees. The occurrence of trees in nature is largely determined by the length of the growing season and the availability of water. In areas in which the time between the thawing of the ground in spring and its freezing in fall is insufficient for woody plants to develop and mature their season's growth and to produce seeds, trees are not part of the natural vegetation. Except for a few desert and semidesert species, trees are less successful than many other plants in regions in which rainfall is scanty. In such regions, trees, for the most part, give way to grasses and other herbaceous plants or to low shrubs (chaparral), succulents (fleshy plants such as the cactuses), and other desert-adapted plants. Factors such as inhospitable soils, persistent winds, agricultural practices, and repeated burning of vegetation may also be responsible for the absence of trees. Trees usually inhabit regions in which the annual rainfall exceeds 30 inches (76 centimetres).

Northern cold-region evergreen forests consisting chiefly of conifers occupy a broad belt, occasionally extending northward to latitude 72° north, across North America, Europe, and Asia and with southward extensions in mountainous areas into the tropics. A moist temperate forest of chiefly conifers extends from central California to Alaska. In comparison with northern cold-region evergreen forests, this western North American forest experiences higher average temperatures and less violent seasonal changes. Temperate deciduous forests occupy or once occupied vast areas with marked seasonal changes of temperature in eastern North America, Europe, Australia, and southern South America. In parts of the Northern Hemisphere in which winter and summer temperatures are less extreme, subtropical broadleaf evergreen forests are found; they merge, wherever rainfall is adequate, into tropical rain forests, such as those that occupy vast areas in the Amazon and Orinoco drainage systems in South America; those of the Congo, Niger, and Zambezi rivers in Africa; and those in Madagascar, the Indo-Malayan region, Borneo, and New Guinea. Trees also occur as scattered individuals and groups in the savannas of South America, Africa, Australia, and elsewhere.

Forests of broadleaf evergreen trees

THE IMPORTANCE OF TREES

Forests are of immense importance in soil stabilization and erosion control, especially in mountainous and hilly regions; they also protect and conserve water supplies and prevent floods. Small groups of trees and even single trees have a similar role locally in preventing washouts and in holding stream banks. Trees can be considered guardians of soil and water; where they predominate, loss by erosion is compensated by the production of new soil resulting from the weathering of rocks and the accumulation of organic debris. Trees not only provide shelter, homes, and food for many animals but also, like all green plants, help to purify the atmosphere by absorbing carbon dioxide and releasing oxygen.

Economic importance. Without trees the world would be bleak, and life as it is known impossible. Carbonized and fossilized wood (coal) supplies fuel for energy needs; other fossilized products of trees include amber, which is formed from the gum of pines, and kauri gum, the product of *Agathis australis.* From earliest times wood has been employed for such purposes as homes, rafts, canoes, fuel, and weapons. Too often, however, so-called advanced civilizations have wantonly destroyed trees; great forests of cedars of Lebanon, for example, were virtually eliminated in lumbering operations during early historic times for such purposes as the construction of King Solomon's great temple and palace. Forests that covered much of the Mediterranean region and Middle East were extravagantly exploited by the Assyrians, Babylonians, Greeks, and Romans. Primitive peoples were dependent on trees for many materials in addition to wood. Fruits and nuts of many kinds were important foods for both man and animals. Leaves of palms and other trees were used for thatching roofs. Tapa cloth and woven fabrics made from bark, leaves, and other tree parts were used for clothing. Utensils were fashioned from calabashes, coconuts, and other fruits. Medicines, including quinine, the properties of which were long known to South American Indians, were obtained from trees, as were dyes, tanning materials, and spices. Seeds and other tree parts were used as charms and ornaments.

Modern civilizations are no less dependent upon trees. Although substitutes now are commonly used for some tree products—concrete, steel, glass, and plastics; synthetic drugs and dyes; and synthetic substitutes for natural rubber—the demand for tree products has vastly increased in the manufacture of newsprint, for example, and in the manufacture of other papers as well as cardboard and similar packagings. The plywood industry converts immense numbers of trees into useful building materials and, in so doing, makes more complete use of good lumber than can be done by other means.

Wood products

Many tree products other than wood and its derivatives are important. Edible fruits produced by trees include apples, cherries, peaches, pears, and others in temperate climates; avocados, figs, persimmons, and citrus fruits in warm-temperate and subtropical regions; breadfruit, coconuts, jackfruit, mangoes, and mangosteens in tropical regions; and the important fruit of desert regions—the date. The coconut (*Cocos nucifera*), the oil palm (*Elaeis guineensis*), and the olive (*Olea europaea*) are important sources of oils and fats used as food and for other purposes. From trees come such spices as cinnamon, cloves, and nutmeg; substances used in beverages, such as chocolate, coffee, and kola nuts; and chicle, the basis of chewing gum. Nonedible tree products exploited commercially include rosin, turpentine, tanbark, creosote, cork, and kapok fibre.

The aesthetic values of trees are generally appreciated. They are admired in their natural settings in forests, savannas, and along river courses; they are planted and cared for in gardens, parks, parkways, cemeteries, and city streets. They serve as screens to secure privacy and to reduce noise levels, and they provide shade.

Unusual trees of special interest. Mangroves, which consist not of one genus or species of tree but several, colonize tidal shores and brackish waters in the tropics and subtropics. In so doing they not only stabilize shore lines but also create new land by trapping debris, silt, and mud among their interlacing roots. Mangroves spread out into the water by sending from their branches roots that reach into the mud and develop into sturdy supporting props. A distinctive feature of mangroves is their large fruits, the seeds of which germinate and grow into sturdy seedlings before they leave the parent plant. When the seedlings fall, they either become fixed in the mud or float away, to be washed up at some site at which the opportunity to become established may occur.

Mangroves are not the only trees that spread by dropping prop roots from their branches. The habit is well developed in several tropical figs (*Ficus*), including one popular in small sizes as a houseplant—the rubber plant (*F. elastica*). Most noteworthy of the group is the banyan tree (*F. benghalensis*) of India; its numerous prop roots develop into secondary trunks that support the widespreading head of massive, constantly extending branches. One specimen 2,000 feet (600 metres) in circumference has been estimated as being capable of sheltering 20,000 people. The wonderboom (*F. pretoriae*) of Africa grows in a similar manner; a specimen at Pretoria has a spread of 165 feet. Because of their unusual growth habits these tropical ficuses are called strangler figs. Often they begin life high in a palm or some other tree in which a monkey, bat, or bird that has fed on the fruits deposits seeds that have passed through its alimentary tract. The seeds germinate, the roots growing into organic matter collected in crotches or crevices of the host tree. Under humid conditions the seedlings grow rapidly, sending roots down along the trunk of the host tree. Upon reaching the ground the roots branch and establish themselves. Above the ground the roots thicken until they form an interlacing cylinder around the trunk of the host.

Strangler figs

The ombu (*Phytolacca dioica*) is a remarkable South American relative of the pokeweed. A tree capable of attaining heights of 60 feet (20 metres) and a spread of 100 feet, it has a wide trunk; the branches contain as much as 80 percent water and very little wood tissue. From its base radiates a circle of rootlike outgrowths wide enough for a person to sit upon.

The traveller's tree of Madagascar (*Ravenala madagascariensis*) has a palmlike trunk up to 30 feet tall topped by a huge, symmetrical fan of long-stalked, paddleshaped leaves often much shredded by wind. The vernacular name alludes to the leaves having hollow bases from which, it has been reported, travellers could obtain potable water.

The talipot palm (*Corypha umbraculifera*) of tropical Asia may live as long as 75 years before it flowers and fruits just one time, then dies. The huge panicle (many-branched cluster) of creamy white blooms arises from the centre of the cluster of fan-shaped leaves topping the trunk, which may be 80 feet tall and three to four feet in diameter. Another palm of special interest is the double coconut (*Lodoicea maldivica*); a native of two tiny islands of the Seychelles group in the Indian Ocean, it has fruits that require about 10 years to mature, weigh up to 50 pounds (20 kilograms), and have the appearance of a pair of coconuts joined together. Long before their source was known, these fruits were washed up by the sea in India, and magical properties were ascribed to them.

The tallest trees are Pacific Coast redwoods (*Sequoia sempervirens*) specimens of which exceed 350 feet (105 metres) in height in an impressive grove in Redwood Creek Valley, California. The species is confined to a narrow coastal belt extending from southern Oregon to California. The next tallest trees are the Australian mountain ash (*Eucalyptus regnans*), specimens of which in Victoria, Australia, exceed 300 feet (90 metres), the greatest heights known for nonconiferous trees. A close relative of the redwood, the giant sequoia (*Sequoiadendron giganteum*) develops the greatest total bulk of wood, but not the biggest girth, among trees. This tree, which attains heights in excess of 300 feet and may have a trunk diameter of about 25 feet some distance above its flaring base, is restricted to a strip about 280 miles long and less than 20 miles wide in the region of the Sierra Nevadas, in California.

Records for tree girth are held by the baobab (*Adansonia digitata*) of Africa and the Mexican swamp cypress (*Taxodium mucronatum*). The baobab attains a maximum height of about 75 feet; its barrel-shaped trunk may be more than 25 feet in diameter a few feet above the ground. The most famous specimen of Mexican swamp cypress is "El Gigante," located at Tule, Oaxaca. The trunk of this massive tree is buttressed and not circular; if the bays and promontories of the buttresses are followed, the basal circumference is 150 feet.

The oldest living trees are bristlecone pines (*Pinus aristata*) in the western United States; some have been reliably reported to be from about 4,600 to 4,900 years of age. The species rarely exceeds a height of 35 feet.

Trees have been worshipped as gods, accepted as the

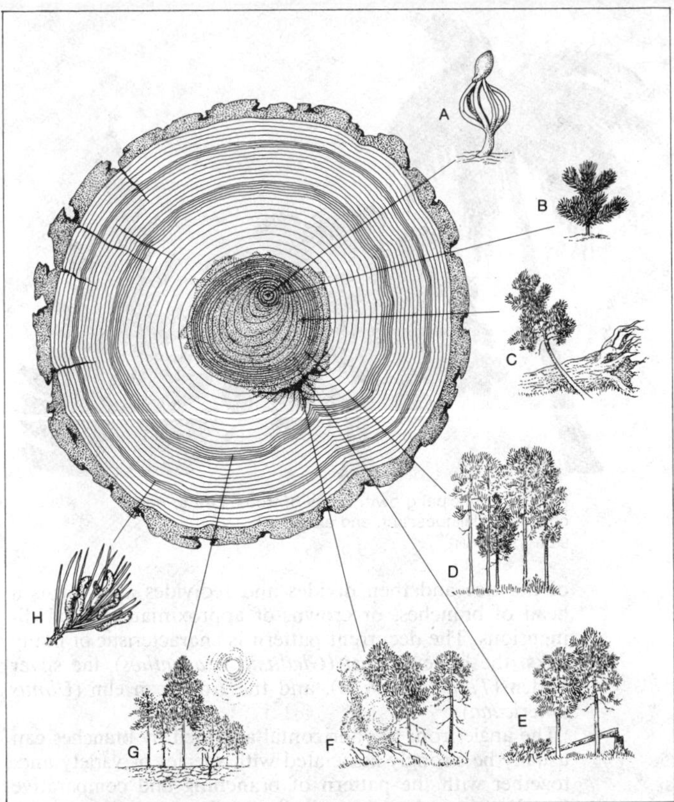

Figure 1: *Cross section of a tree trunk with events of its life indicated by growth patterns in wood.*
(A) A loblolly pine is born; (B) growth is rapid forming relatively broad, even rings; (C) "reaction wood" is formed to help support tree after something fell against it; (D) growth is straight but crowded by other trees; (E) competing trees are removed and growth is again rapid; (F) fire scars the tree; (G) narrow rings probably caused by prolonged dry spell; (H) narrow rings that may have been caused by an insect.
By courtesy of St. Regis Paper Company

dwellings of good and evil spirits, and revered. In some parts of the world some of these practices still exist. Sacred trees and holy groves have existed and still exist. The Bible makes early reference to the tree of knowledge, and the pomegranate was long held in reverence by Jews and Persians as the biblical forbidden fruit. The name of the Druid priests of ancient Britain is derived from that of the oak tree they venerated. The use of holly, the leaves of *Ilex* trees, is traceable to the pre-Christian practice of the Druids, who decorated altars with it in winter. The asoka, or sorrowless tree (*Saraca indica*), and the bo tree (*Ficus religiosa*) are held sacred by Buddhists, the first as the tree under which Gautama Buddha was born, the other as the one under which he mediated and received enlightenment. The Hindu divinity Vishnu (Viṣṇu) is also said to have been born under the bo tree. The banyan tree (*Ficus benghalensis*) is held sacred by Hindus, who believe that Brahmā was transformed into a banyan.

The role of trees in religion

THE STRUCTURE AND GROWTH OF TREES

In outward form trees vary greatly according to species, and individuals sometimes differ in response to the environment. Because of inherent similarities within related groups, recognition of species and even varieties is often possible from distances too great for observation of the distinctive characteristics upon which botanical separations are based.

External growth forms. The method of branching is highly significant. In some trees, including most conifers, the trunk forms a well-defined, dominant main axis, and the lateral branches are secondary in size and importance. Such a branching pattern, called excurrent, is characteristic of firs, spruces, larches, and most pines. In contrast is the decurrent, or deliquescent, branching pattern characteristic of many angiosperms, in which the trunk forms a well-defined central axis for the lesser part of the height

Figure 2: Principal growth forms of trees. Left to right: columnar, deliquescent, and excurrent.

Drawing by M. Pahl

of the tree and then divides and redivides as it forms a head of branches, or crown, of approximately equal dimensions. The decurrent pattern is characteristic of many oaks, the honey locust (*Gleditsia triacanthos*), the silver linden (*Tilia tomentosa*), and the American elm (*Ulmus americana*).

The angle from the horizontal assumed by branches can usually be strongly associated with species or variety and, together with the pattern of branching and comparative length of branches to trunk, is chiefly responsible for the form of the crown. The crown is usually strongly modified in trees growing in the forest as compared with those growing in open areas and thus not impeded by neighbours. In the consideration of tree forms presented here, specimens growing in the open are described. The Lombardy poplar (*Populus nigra* variety *italica*) is an upright form of strikingly columnar outline, very different from the vase-shaped American elm (*Ulmus americana*). The heads of both are shaped differently from that of the pin oak (*Quercus palustris*), which typically has a well-defined central trunk with downsweeping lower branches, horizontal middle branches, and upward-angling high branches. Globular or billowy globular heads are characteristic of many trees, including the Chinese scholartree (*Sophora japonica*), the London plane (*Platanus acerifolia*), the Norway maple (*Acer platanoides*), the saucer magnolia (*Magnolia soulangeana*), and the white oak (*Quercus alba*). Others, such as the sugar maple (*Acer saccharum*), have more oval heads. A very common form, usually called pyramidal, is more correctly described as conical; it is characteristic of the various types of conifers.

Distinctive landscape patterns are provided by "weeping" trees, the best known of which is the weeping willow (*Salix babylonica*). In weeping trees the younger and often the older branches are pendulous or markedly downsweeping. There are many others, however, most of which are horticultural varieties of species that typically are more upright in their branching, such as the weeping beech (*Fagus sylvatica* variety *pendula*).

Tree bark

A characteristic feature, useful in the identification of many trees, is the protective layer of bark covering the trunks and branches. Bark varies from smooth, copper-coloured covering of the gumbo-limbo (*Bursera simaruba*) to the thick, soft, spongy bark of the punk tree (*Melaleuca leucadendron*). Other types of bark include the commercial cork of the cork oak (*Quercus suber*) and the rugged, fissured outer coat of many other oaks; the flaking, patchy-coloured barks of sycamores (*Platanus*) and the lacebark pine (*Pinus bungeana*); and the rough shingle-like outer covering of shagbark hickory (*Carya ovata*).

The trunks of some tropical trees, such as the silk-cotton tree (*Ceiba pentandra*), are supported by great flangelike buttresses. The presence of thorns is often an identifying characteristic of trees, as are the arrangement, form, shape, texture, and colour of leaves, flowers, and fruits.

Growth and internal structure. The life-spans of trees, like those of all organisms, are limited. They originate in the fertilization of a female egg cell (ovule) by a male reproductive cell (pollen grain), and eventually they die. During their life-spans trees respire and carry on photosynthesis and other physiological processes, including growth. Except in their early years, trees usually produce reproductive bodies (seeds or, in the case of ferns, spores). Growth, which includes elongation throughout life, is commonly most rapid in young trees; it slows markedly after maturity and in old age may be almost infinitesimal. Nevertheless, as long as a tree lives, its stems lengthen each year, and those of conifers and angiosperms increase in diameter.

Structurally, trees consist of three systems of vegetative organs—roots, stems, and leaves—and, in addition, reproductive organs. The latter include flowers, fruits, seeds, and spores. Roots (except for small feeder roots) and stems are permanent for the life of the tree. The other organs are transient, remaining for periods ranging from a few hours to a few years. Even leaves of evergreens fall and are replaced.

Roots provide firm anchorage for the aboveground parts and absorb practically all water and essentially all of the required nutrients except carbon dioxide, which is obtained from the air. The stems (trunks, branches, and branchlets)

From (A) W.W. Robbins and T.E. Weier, *Botany: An Introduction to Plant Science*, © 1950 by John Wiley & Sons, Inc.; (B, D) *Biological Science: An Inquiry into Life*, 2nd ed. (1968); Harcourt Brace Jovanovich, Inc., New York; by permission of the Biological Sciences Curriculum Study; (C) E.W. Sinnott, *Botany: Principles and Problems*, 4th ed., copyright 1946; used with permission of McGraw-Hill Book Co.

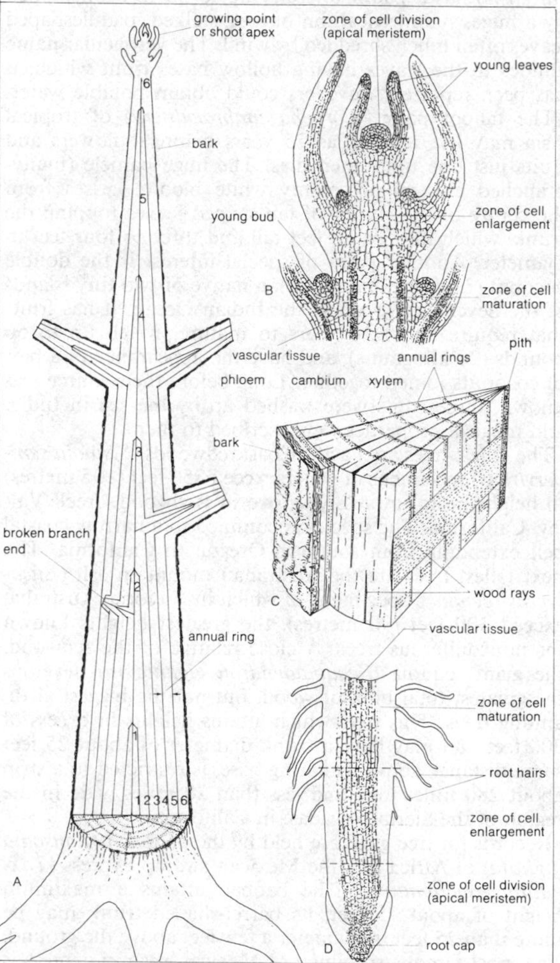

Figure 3: *Growth regions of a tree.*
(A) Longitudinal section of a young tree showing how the annual growth rings are produced in successive conical layers. (B) Shoot apex, the extreme tip of which is the apical meristem, or primary meristem, a region of new cell division that contributes to primary growth, or increase in length, and which is the ultimate source of all the cells in the above-ground parts of the tree. (C) Segment of a tree trunk showing the location of the cambium layer, a secondary meristem that contributes to secondary growth, or increase in thickness. (D) Root tip, the apex of which is also an apical meristem and the ultimate source of all the cells of the root system.

Bristlecone pine *(Pinus aristata)*, among the oldest known trees.

General Grant tree, a giant sequoia, or big tree *(Sequoiadendron giganteum)*, among the largest trees in total bulk.

Cedars of Lebanon *(Cedrus libani)*, known throughout ancient art and literature as symbols of power and longevity.

Leaves and fruit of the female ginkgo, or maidenhair tree *(Ginkgo biloba)*.

Tree ferns *(Alsophila australis)*, the largest of all ferns.

Cycas media, a treelike cycad that produces large terminal seed cones.

Plate 1: (Top left) Lola B. Graham—The National Audubon Society Collection/Photo Researchers, (top right, centre left) Bruce Coleman Inc., (top right) Gene Ahrens, (centre left) S. Wilhelm, (centre right) John Kohout from Root Resources—EB Inc., (bottom left) Walter Chandoha, (bottom right) G.R. Roberts

Bald cypress *(Taxodium distichum)*, showing emergent roots, or knees.

Joshua tree *(Yucca brevifolia)*, tallest of the yuccas, occasionally reaching 35 feet.

Screw pine *(Pandanus)*, showing prop roots.

Branches of the European larch *(Larix decidua)*, one of the few conifers that loses its leaves in autumn.

Talipot palm *(Corypha umbraculifera)* in bloom.

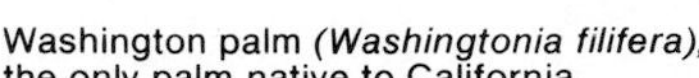

Washington palm *(Washingtonia filifera)*, the only palm native to California.

Plate 2: (Top left) Rudolf Schmid, (top right) Bucky Reeves—The National Audubon Society Collection/Photo Researchers, (centre right) Jim Annan—Annan Photo Features, (bottom left) D. Muench—Shostal/EB Inc., (bottom centre) Ingmar Holmasen, (bottom right) W.H. Hodge

Baobab *(Adansonia digitata)*, the trunks of which occasionally reach 30 feet in diameter and have many uses.

Strangler fig *(Ficus)* on host live oak *(Quercus virginiana)*.

Live oak *(Quercus virginiana)* draped with Spanish moss *(Bromeliales)*, which uses the tree for support.

Mangrove *(Rhizophora)*, showing (above) viviparous (germinating on parent) seedlings and (right) a thicket of tangled roots and stems spreading over a tidal estuary.

Plate 3: (Top left) Tierbilder Okapia, (top right) Dr. G.J. Chafaris—EB Inc., (centre left) Louise K. Broman from Root Resources—EB Inc., (bottom left) Rudolf Schmid, (bottom right) G.R. Roberts

Weeping willow *(Salix babylonica)*.

White birch *(Betula alba)*.

Bonsai of a Japanese maple *(Acer palmatum)*.

Australian gum tree *(Eucalyptus)*.

Magnolia denudata in flower.

Deciduous forest in fall coloration, Wasatch Mountains, Utah.

Plate 4: (Top left) G. Lord—Shostal/EB Inc., (top right) J.L. Watcham, (centre left) W.H. Hodge, (centre right) Ron Dorman—Bruce Coleman Inc., (bottom left) Dorothea W. Woodruff—EB Inc., (bottom right) Sven Samelius serve as a framework to support and dispose the leaves advantageously to the light needed in the process of photosynthesis; they also dispose and expose the reproductive parts to wind, insects, and other pollinating and dispersing agents. Also important is the pipeline function of stems by which water containing dissolved nutrients is moved from the roots to other parts, usually the leaves but sometimes leafless stems, in which photosynthesis takes place. Foods elaborated as a result of photosynthesis are translocated, or moved, to growing and storage tissues. The upward flow of water and solutes in conifers and angiosperms is almost exclusively through the tubular cells of the living xylem, or sapwood; the downward movement is through the phloem, or bast, which is a tissue layer that lies just beneath the bark.

Growth regions in trees

Increase in the size of trees results from the production of new cells, the enlargement of old ones, and sometimes the enlargement of the spaces between cells. New cells are formed by meristem tissues, regions of rapid cell division, which are located at the tips of stems and roots, and in secondary meristems, called cambium layers, which form a thin cylinder between the wood and the bark in conifers and dicotyledons; cambium occurs to a lesser extent in some monocotyledons and cycads. The meristems at the tips of stems and roots are responsible for increases in length and height, the secondary meristems for thickening. Tree ferns have no cambium; hence, no secondary thickening of the trunk takes place. In conifers and dicotyledons, the successive layers of wood, usually one each year, that are laid in concentric rings around previously developed wood comprise the annual rings so clearly seen when a trunk or branch of a tree is cut. The cells of the annual rings usually live for several years. During the time the cells are alive, the tissues they compose are called sapwood. As the tree ages, the older, inner portions of the sapwood undergo chemical changes and are infiltrated by oils, gums, resins, tannins, and other compounds. When the cells die, the sapwood has been converted to heartwood. Heartwood is often much darker in colour, denser, and contains less moisture than sapwood. Heartwood, although dead, persists for the life of the tree and affords structural strength unless invaded by disease organisms.

Trees that inhabit arid regions employ various devices to conserve moisture. Thick, succulent, water-storage tissues form a large bulk of the leaves of tree aloes and agaves and of the stems of tree cactuses. As additional protection from desiccation these parts are often coated with wax. Yuccas, including the Joshua tree (*Yucca brevifolia*), have tough, leathery foliage that transpires (loses water by evaporation) only to a limited extent. Some desert inhabitants, such as the tree euphorbias of Africa, the great columnar cactuses of North and South America, the boojum tree (*Idria columnaris*) of Baja California, and the paloverde (*Cercidium torreyanum*) of western North America, either have such meagre foliage—often in evidence only for short periods—or none, that it is not sufficient to photosynthesize the food they need. This deficiency of leaves is met in part or entirely by the chlorophyll-containing outer layers of the trunks and stems, which carry on photosynthesis. The roots of a few trees, notably the swamp cypress (*Taxodium distichum*) and mangroves, which live in watery habitats, produce pneumatophores, or "knees," that rise above the water level. It has behich live in watery habitats, produce pneumatophores, or "knees," that rise above the water level. It has been postulated that they are devices that ensure a supply of air to the cells of the roots, but this is by no means certain.

THE ORIGIN AND EVOLUTION OF TREES

After the initial invasion of land by plants, perhaps 500,000,000 years ago, the evolution of the first trees began; not until the Devonian Period (345,000,000 to 395,000,000 years ago) did the first vascular plants, including some treelike forms, appear. The Devonian was succeeded by the Carboniferous Period (280,000,000 to 345,000,000 years ago), during which the climate of most of the world was uniformly warm and moist. It favoured the growth of trees, and numerous kinds, many of gigantic size, evolved and populated the vast forests characteristic of that period. These trees formed the great accumulations of decaying organic matter that, after being innundated, buried under mud and silt, and subjected to immense pressures, were transformed into coal. The extent and thickness of the coal deposits of the world, some covering thousands of square miles, give silent evidence of the almost unbelieveable lushness, extent, and persistence of the Carboniferous forests. It has been estimated that 1½ inches (four centimetres) in the thickness of a seam of coal represent on the average 1,000 years of forest growth; some coal seams are hundreds of feet thick. A change in climate ended the vast Carboniferous forests and most of its plant forms, with the exception of a few descendants now called horsetails, club mosses, and ferns. The Permian Period (225,000,000 to 280,000,000 years ago) that succeeded the Carboniferous was by comparison cold, dry, and unfavourable to tree growth over much of the Earth.

Coal-age forests

None of the early trees had flowers or seeds. They reproduced, as ferns and other lower plants still do, by spores. Toward the end of the Devonian Period seed plants appeared. They were the seed ferns, which are now extinct; contemporary seed-producing plants now constitute by far the greatest portion of the vegetation of Earth. Seeds in effect are embryonic plants packaged with starter supplies of food. They enabled trees to colonize areas less moist and humid than those essential for the development of plants from spores. Seed ferns of tree dimensions became abundant during the Carboniferous Period. But they, too, vanished and were replaced, about 200,000,000 years ago, by a new breed of trees now called gymnosperms. Of the 750 species that survive, some—the cycads, ginkgo, and conifers—are abundant. None has flowers as that term is commonly accepted. Not until the latter part of the Cretaceous Period (65,000,000 to 136,000,000 years ago) did the first flowering plants appear, but their development and rise to ascendancy was remarkably rapid. The first flowering trees, having many of the characteristics of magnolias, appeared about the time the dinosaurs were becoming extinct.

BIBLIOGRAPHY. B.K. BOOM and H. KLEIJN, *The Glory of the Tree* (1966), on the beauty of trees, their uses, history, and folklore with 194 colour illustrations; ARTHUR CRONQUIST, *Introductory Botany,* 2nd ed. (1971), botanical facts and interpretation are stressed and new findings evaluated; THOMAS H. EVERETT, *Living Trees of the World* (1968), text and illustrations (many in colour) cover a wide range of tree subjects; ANDREAS FEININGER, *Trees* (1968), important facts on the history, structure, and uses of trees with magnificent photographs (many in colour); HILDERIC FRIEND, *Flowers and Flower-Lore,* 3rd ed., 2 vol. (1884), a plant lore classic; ALBERT F. HILL, *Economic Botany: A Textbook of Useful Plants and Plant Products,* 2nd ed. (1952), a concise, reference handbook on industrial, medicinal, and edible plants; PAUL J. KRAMER and THEODORE T. KOZLOWSKI, *Physiology of Trees* (1960), covers the role of physiological processes in tree growth; EDWIN A. MENNINGER, *Fantastic Trees* (1967), a popular treatment of unusual trees of the world; EUGENE P. ODUM, *Fundamentals of Ecology,* 3rd ed. (1971), concerned with interrelationships between plants and other organisms and the physical environment in which they exist; A.R. PENFOLD and J.L. WILLIS, *The Eucalypts: Botany, Cultivation, Chemistry, and Utilization* (1961), a simple, lucid survey of an important genus of trees; CARL L. WILSON, WALTER E. LOOMIS, and TAYLOR A. STEEVES, *Botany,* 5th ed. (1971), emphasis is placed upon plant diversity and the relation of plants to human affairs; ROBERT L. ZION, *Trees for Architecture and the Landscape* (1968), a well-illustrated work on landscaping with trees. *The Oxford Encyclopedia of Trees of the World,* ed. by BAYARD HORA (1981), is also well-illustrated.

(T.H.E./L.M.W.)

Trigonometry

Trigonometry is the branch of mathematics concerned with specific functions of angles and their application to calculations in geometry. For example, if a right-angled triangle contains an angle, symbolized here by the Greek letter alpha, α, the ratio of the side of the triangle opposite to α to the side opposite the right angle (the hypotenuse) is called the sine of α. The ratio of the side adjacent to α to the hypotenuse is the cosine of α. These functions are properties of the angle α, and calculated values have been tabulated for many angles. They are used in obtaining unknown angles and distances from known or measured angles in geometric figures. The subject developed from a need to compute angles and distances in such fields as astronomy, map making, surveying, and artillery range finding. Problems involving angles and distances in one plane are covered in plane trigonometry. Applications to similar problems in more than one plane of three-dimensional space are considered in spherical trigonometry.

This article is divided into the following sections:

HISTORY

Trigonometry among the early mathematicians was essentially a computational science based on geometrical theorems. What is now embodied in a formula earlier had to be described by words as a succession of computational steps, each justified by the citation of an appropriate geometrical theorem. The absence of negative numbers made necessary the discussion of many more cases in the solution of triangles. One or more steps in a solution was the passage from the length of an arc to the length of its chord (Greek) or the length of half the chord of the double arc (Hindu) or vice versa, a feat accomplished by means of a table. In the 12th century the Arabic word for the half chord of the double arc was confused with another word and translated "sinus" (sine). The difficulty of making tables with irrational entries (not expressible in ratios of integers) without decimals (first systematically introduced into arithmetic late in the 16th century) was met by selecting a circle so large that when the chords used were computed to the nearest integer the desired accuracy was attained. This unfortunately introduced into the discussions supporting the solutions the added complexity of proportionality between similar figures.

Trigonometry, uniting as it did aspects of the three disciplines of arithmetic, algebra, and geometry, progressed more slowly than did geometry. Astronomy, however, of great interest to the early Hindus and Arabs, required as a tool the solution of spherical triangles, a fact that drove them to master this art. It is, accordingly, not surprising that the development of spherical trigonometry preceded that of plane trigonometry. Not until about the 13th century did trigonometry divorce itself from astronomy and become an independent subject matter.

In the extant mathematical literature of the civilizations preceding the Greeks occur a few calculations suggestive of trigonometric calculations but no further evidence of the science. The early Greek writers appear to have advanced a step further by making calculations based on the proportionality of similar triangles. In the determination of a height by comparison of its shadow with the shadow of a known height can be seen the germ of the tangent function. Greek writers of the 4th century AD called Hipparchus, who lived in the 2nd century BC, the originator of the science of trigonometry. He was reputed to have calculated a table of chords in 12 books. To what extent he may have developed the uses of the table is unknown because the complete work is lost.

Early Greek trigonometry

Menelaus, about the end of the 1st century, is also reputed to have produced a treatment of the trigonometry of chords in six books, but this work is also lost. An extant work contains the important theorem of Menelaus and the corresponding theorem for the sphere upon which later writers based their work on trigonometry.

The first extant work on trigonometry is contained in the *Almagest,* a work on astronomy in 13 books, produced by Ptolemy of Alexandria around the middle of the 2nd century. In one section is a table of chords at intervals of 30′ (minutes), accurate to at least five places, and the method of computing the tables is explained. Another section is devoted to the solution of triangles, particularly spherical. Theorems are verified concerning chords that involve implicitly the equivalence of the addition formulas, the half-angle formulas, and the law of sines.

No Hindu work is extant, but it is known that Hindu mathematicians made tables of sines, the half chord of the double arc, at intervals of 3° 45′ using only the equivalent of $\sin^2 a + \cos^2 a = 1$; $\cos a = \sin (90 - a)$; and $1 - \cos 2a = 2 \sin^2 a$. These tables were used to solve right triangles, plane and spherical. This work was translated into Arabic about the last quarter of the 8th century.

Arab contributions

In the late 9th century the Arab al-Battānī added the law of cosines for oblique spherical triangles and introduced the sine for the chord into the work of Ptolemy and also into his tables. He brought into use the tangent and cotangent functions and constructed a table for them at intervals of 1°.

Abū al-Wafā' in the last half of the 10th century gave a more accurate method for computing sines and established the complete generality of the sine law for spherical triangles. He introduced the secant and cosecant (both definable in terms of the more familiar sine and cosine) and studied the interrelations of the six trigonometric lines associated with an arc. Credit for establishing the general sine law for plane triangles is given to the Persian al-Bīrūnī (973–1048).

Jabír of Seville, in the second half of the 11th century, added to the four formulas of Ptolemy the equivalent of the fifth formula for right spherical triangles. The systematization of plane and spherical trigonometry as a discipline independent of astronomy was finally achieved by the great Persian mathematician Naṣīr ad-Dīn aṭ-Ṭūsī in the second half of the 13th century. Essentially, the same work was done for the Western world independently by the Prussian astronomer Johann Müller (1436–76), known as Regiomontanus, the notions of the Arabic world having filtered into Europe over several centuries, that via the East coming much later than that via Spain. The development of arithmetic and algebra allowed the successors of Regiomontanus in Europe to unify and simplify the trigonometry of the triangle by substituting the angle for arc and the ratio for the trigonometric line, and by abstracting from the cumbersome treatment of Regiomontanus the essential formulas convenient for calculations. The cosine law for plane triangles appears for the first time in the work of a 16th-century French mathematician, François Viète.

The invention of logarithms (or powers of a fixed number such that a desired numerical result is obtained as the power of the given fixed number or "base") by Napier stimulated the development of formulas suitable to their use. The law of tangents appears in the writings of Viète and the half-angle formulas in the works of an Austrian mathematician, Rhäticus, in 1568 and an English mathematician, William Oughtred, in 1657. Napier's formulas called "analogies" appeared in 1619, while the Gauss-Delambre and Mollweide relations (trigonometric in nature) came later, in 1807–09. Abraham de Moivre and Leonhard Euler were among the first to open the field of analytic trigonometry. The work of Fourier on trigonometric series appeared in 1807.

TRIGONOMETRIC FUNCTIONS

For the purpose of trigonometry, a somewhat more general concept of angle is required than that used in geometry. An angle A with vertex at V, the initial side of which is VP and the terminal side of which is VQ, is indicated in Figure 1 by the solid circular arc. This angle is said to

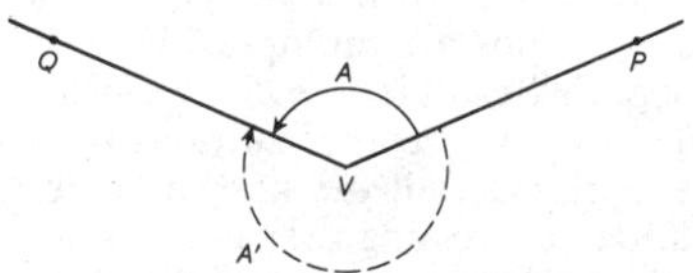

Figure 1: General angle (see text).

be generated by the continuous counterclockwise rotation of a line segment about the point V from the position VP to the position VQ. A second angle A' with the same initial and terminal sides, indicated in Figure 1 by the broken circular arc, is generated by the clockwise rotation of the line segment about the point V from the position VP to the position VQ. Angles are considered positive when generated by counterclockwise rotations, negative when generated by clockwise rotations. The positive angle A and the negative angle A' in Figure 1 are generated by less than one complete rotation of the line segment about the point V. All other positive and negative angles with the same initial and terminal sides are obtained by rotating the line segment counterclockwise or clockwise, respectively, about the point V one or more complete turns before coming to rest at VQ.

Positive and negative angles

Numerical values can be assigned to angles by selecting a unit of measure for angles. Besides the complete revolution and the right angle, the units commonly used are the degree and the radian. The degree is 1/90 of a right angle. There are 60′ (minutes) in a degree and 60″ (seconds) in a minute. In theoretical work, the radian is the most convenient unit. It is the angle at the centre of a circle that intercepts an arc equal in length to the radius. From these definitions, it follows that 1 revolution = 4 right angles = 360° = 2π radians.

Equal angles are angles with the same measure; *i.e.,* they have the same sign and the same number of degrees. Any angle $-A$ has the same number of degrees as A but is of opposite sign. Its measure, therefore, is the negative of the measure of A. If the angles A and B have the initial sides VP and VQ and the terminal sides VQ and VR, respectively, then the angle $A+B$ has the initial and terminal sides VP and VR, respectively (see Figure 2). The angle $A+B$ is called the sum of the angles A and B, and its relation to A and B when A is positive and B is positive or negative is illustrated in Figure 2. The sum $A+B$ is the angle the measure of which is the algebraic sum of the measures of A and B. The difference $A-B$ is the sum of

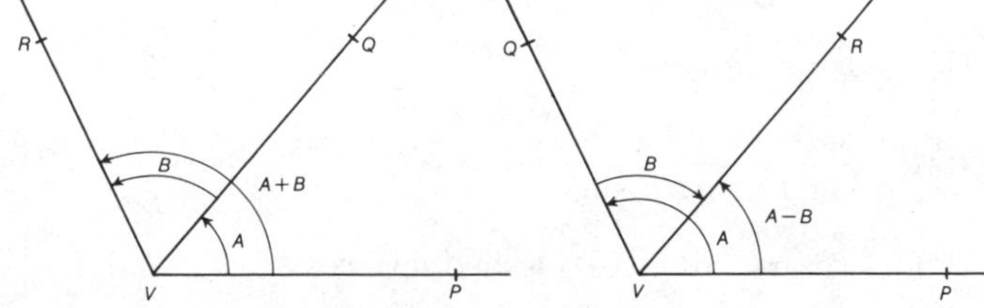

Figure 2: Addition of angles (see text).

A and $-B$. Thus all angles coterminal with angle A (*i.e.,* with the same initial and terminal sides as angle A) are given by $A \pm 360n$, in which $360n$ is an angle of n complete revolutions. The angles $(180-A)$ and $(90-A)$ are the supplement and complement of angle A, respectively.

Trigonometric functions of an angle. There are six functions of an angle commonly used in trigonometry. Their names and abbreviations are sine (sin), cosine (cos), tangent (tan), cotangent (cot), secant (sec), and cosecant (csc). To define these functions for any angle A, the angle is placed in position (Figure 3, left) on a rectangular coor-

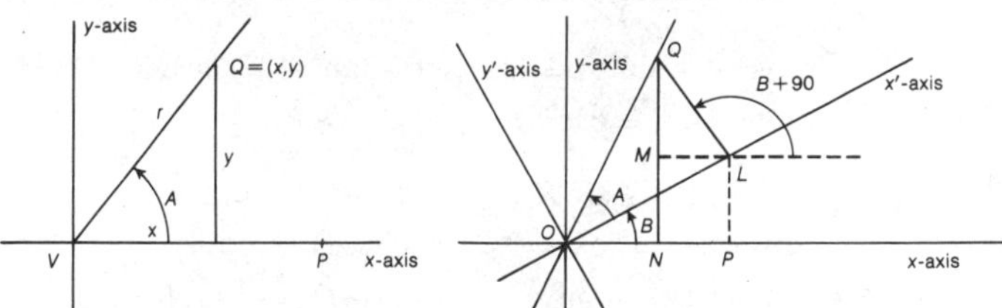

Figure 3: (Left) Angle in standard position. (Right) Rotation of axes (see text).

dinate system with the vertex of A at the origin and the initial side of A along the positive x-axis; r (positive) is the distance from V to any point Q on the terminal side of A, and (x, y) are the rectangular coordinates of Q. The six functions of A are then defined by six ratios (see 1). Because division by zero is not allowed, the tangent and secant are not defined for angles the terminal side of which falls on the y-axis, and the cotangent and cosecant are undefined for angles the terminal side of which falls on the x-axis. From these definitions follow three reciprocal relations for cotangent, secant, and cosecant (see 2) and the quotient identities for the tangent and cotangent (see 3). When the Pythagorean equality $x^2+y^2=r^2$ is divided in turn by r^2, x^2, and y^2, the three squared relations relating cosine and sine, tangent and secant, cotangent and cosecant (see 4) are obtained.

If the point Q on the terminal side of angle A in standard position has coordinates (x, y), this point will have coordinates $(x, -y)$ when on the terminal side of $-A$ in standard position. From this fact and the definitions are obtained further identities for negative angles (see 5). These relations may also be stated briefly by saying that cosine and secant are even functions, while the other four are odd functions.

It is evident that a trigonometric function has the same value for all coterminal angles. When n is an integer, therefore, $\sin(A \pm 360n) = \sin A$; there are similar relations for the other five functions. These results may be expressed by saying that the trigonometric functions are periodic and have a period of 360° or 180°.

When Q on the terminal side of A in standard position has coordinates (x, y), it has coordinates $(-y, x)$ and $(y, -x)$ on the terminal side of $A+90$ and $A-90$ in standard position, respectively. Consequently six formulas follow (see 6). The formulas display the fact that a function of the complement of A is equal to the corresponding co-function of A.

Of fundamental importance for the study of trigonometry are the addition formulas, or the functions of the sum or difference of two angles (see 7). These relations may be derived from formulas (see 8) for the rotation of the coordinate axes through the angle B about the origin, and these formulas are evident from Figure 3 (right), because $x = ON = OP + LM = OL \cos B + LQ \cos(B+90)$, which is the relation already expressed (see 8). Similarly, $y = NQ = PL + MQ = OL \sin B + LQ \sin(B+90)$, which is also an earlier expression (8). To obtain the addition formulas (7) it is only necessary to divide each equation in the given formulas (8) by $r = OQ$, and use the definitions of sine and cosine.

Sum and difference formulas

From the addition formulas are derived the double-angle and half-angle formulas (see 9). Numerous identities of lesser importance can be derived from the above basic identities.

Tables of natural functions. To be of practical use, the values of the functions must be readily available for any

$$(1)\quad \begin{cases} \sin A = y/r & \cot A = x/y \\ \cos A = x/r & \sec A = r/x \\ \tan A = y/x & \csc A = r/y \end{cases}$$

$$(2)\quad \begin{cases} \cot A = 1/\tan A & \sec A = 1/\cos A \\ \csc A = 1/\sin A \end{cases}$$

$$(3)\quad \tan A = \sin A/\cos A \qquad \cot A = \cos A/\sin A$$

$$(4)\quad \begin{cases} \cos^2 A + \sin^2 A = 1; & 1 + \tan^2 A = \sec^2 A \\ \cot^2 A + 1 = \csc^2 A \end{cases}$$

$$(5)\quad \begin{cases} \sin(-A) = -\sin A & \cot(-A) = -\cot A \\ \cos(-A) = \cos A & \sec(-A) = \sec A \\ \tan(-A) = -\tan A & \csc(-A) = -\csc A \end{cases}$$

$$(6)\quad \begin{cases} \sin(A \pm 90) = \pm\cos A & \cot(A \pm 90) = -\tan A \\ \cos(A \pm 90) = \mp\sin A & \sec(A \pm 90) = \mp\csc A \\ \tan(A \pm 90) = -\cot A & \csc(A \pm 90) = \pm\sec A \end{cases}$$

$$(7)\quad \begin{cases} \cos(A \pm B) = \cos A \cos B \mp \sin A \sin B \\ \sin(A \pm B) = \sin A \cos B \pm \cos A \sin B \end{cases}$$

$$(8)\quad \begin{cases} x = x' \cos B - y' \sin B \\ y = x' \sin B + y' \cos B \end{cases}$$

$$(9)\quad \begin{cases} \sin(2A) = 2 \sin A \cos A \\ \cos(2A) = \cos^2 A - \sin^2 A = 2\cos^2 A - 1 \\ \qquad = 1 - 2\sin^2 A \\ \sin^2(A/2) = (1 - \cos A)/2 \\ \cos^2(A/2) = (1 + \cos A)/2 \end{cases}$$

given angle. The identities $\sin(A \pm 360n) = \sin A$ as well as other identities (6) show that the values of the functions for all angles can readily be found from the values for angles from 0° to 45°. For this reason, it is sufficient to list in a table the values of sine, cosine, tangent, and cotangent of all angles from 0° to 45° that are integral multiples of some convenient unit (commonly 1′). Such tables are called tables of natural trigonometric functions.

For angles that are not integral multiples of the unit, the values of the functions may be interpolated. Because the values of the functions are in general irrational numbers, they are entered in the table as decimals, rounded off at some convenient place. For most purposes, four or five decimal places are sufficient, and tables of this accuracy appear in most texts. Simple geometrical facts alone, however, suffice to determine the values of the trigonometric functions for the angles 0°, 30°, 45°, 60°, and 90°. These values are listed in a table, which also illustrates the arrangement used in larger tables (see 10). The names at the head of sucha table are used for angles less than 45°, listed in the left-hand column; the names at the foot of the table are used for the complementary angles, larger than 45°, listed in the right-hand column. For example, from the table $\cos 30° = \frac{1}{2}\sqrt{3}$, and $\cot 60° = \frac{1}{3}\sqrt{3}$.

PLANE TRIGONOMETRY

In many applications of trigonometry the essential problem is the solution of triangles. If enough sides and angles are known, the remaining sides and angles as well as the area can be calculated, and the triangle is then said to be solved. Triangles can be solved by the law of sines and the law of cosines. To secure symmetry in the writing of these laws, the angles of the triangle are lettered *A, B,* and *C* and the lengths of the sides opposite the angles are lettered *a, b,* and *c,* respectively. An example of this standardization is shown in Figure 4.

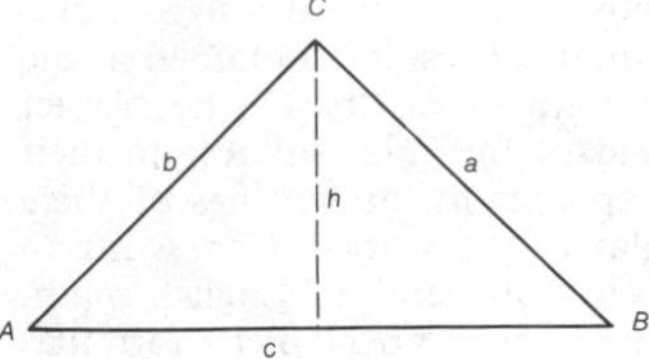

Figure 4: Standard lettering of a triangle (see text).

The law of sines

The law of sines or sine theorem is expressed as an equality involving three sine functions (11) while a law of cosines or cosine theorem is an identification of the cosine with an algebraic expression formed from the lengths of sides opposite the corresponding angle (see 12) with similar expressions for cos *B* and cos *C* obtained by cyclic permutation of the three letters. In Figure 4, $b \sin A = h = a \sin B$, from which the first equality follows (11). The second is shown by drawing a perpendicular from *A* to the opposite side of the triangle. Also $c = b \cos A + a \cos B$ and likewise $b = a \cos C + c \cos A$, $a = c \cos B + b \cos C$. When these three equations are multiplied by *c, b,* $-a$, respectively, and added, the result is $c^2 + b^2 - a^2 = 2bc \cos A$, which when divided by $2bc$ becomes an expression for cos *A* (12). To solve a triangle, all the known values are substituted into equations expressing the laws of sines and cosines (11, 12) and the equations are solved for the unknown values. The law of sines is employed when two angles and a side are known or when two sides and an angle opposite one are known. The law of cosines is appropriate when two sides and an included angle are known or three sides are known. The area of the triangle (see 13) may be found from a formula derived from the relations concerning area of a triangle and the sine of an angle.

Texts on trigonometry derive other formulas for solving triangles and for checking the solution, especially those suited to logarithmic calculation. With the advent of calculators and electronic computers, however, computation by logarithms has lost some of its advantage, and it is no longer so necessary to adapt formulas to logarithmic computation when machines are available.

SPHERICAL TRIGONOMETRY

The fundamental configuration of space to which the formulas of spherical trigonometry apply is the trihedral angle formed by three rays—half lines—radiating from a point. The point is the vertex, the rays are the three edges,

(10) Functions of 0°, 30°, 45°, 60° and 90°

	sin	cos	tan	cot	
0	0	1	0	—	90
30	$\frac{1}{2}$	$\frac{1}{2}\sqrt{3}$	$\frac{1}{3}\sqrt{3}$	$\sqrt{3}$	60
45	$\frac{1}{2}\sqrt{2}$	$\frac{1}{2}\sqrt{2}$	1	1	45
	cos	sin	cot	tan	

$$(11)\quad \frac{a}{\sin A} = \frac{b}{\sin B} = \frac{c}{\sin C}$$

$$(12)\quad \cos A = \frac{b^2 + c^2 - a^2}{2bc}$$

$$(13)\quad \text{area} = \tfrac{1}{2}bc \sin A$$

$$(14)\quad \frac{\sin\alpha}{\sin A} = \frac{\sin\beta}{\sin B} = \frac{\sin\gamma}{\sin C}$$

$$(15)\quad \cos\alpha = \cos\beta\cos\gamma + \sin\beta\sin\gamma\cos A$$

the planes and angles determined by the rays taken in pairs are the three faces, and the three face angles, symbolized by the Greek letters alpha, beta, and gamma, α, β, and γ, of the trihedral angle. The faces in pairs form three dihedral angles A, B, and C opposite, respectively, to the face angles. The formulas of spherical trigonometry relate the trigonometric functions of these six angles.

For the trihedral angle, there is the law of sines (see 14) that may be derived from Figure 5 (left) in which the planes

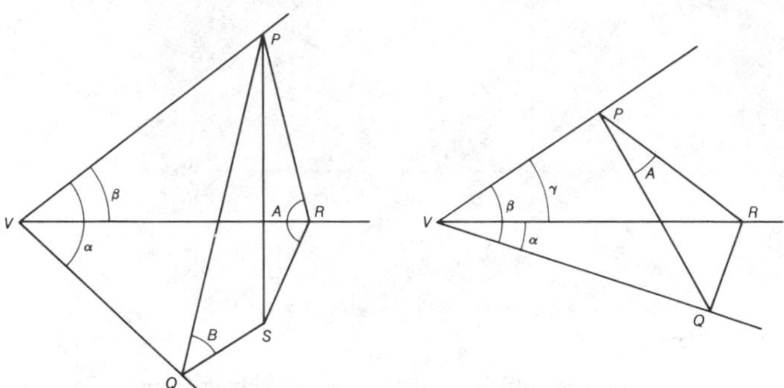

Figure 5: Trihedral angles for derivation of the laws of (left) sines and (right) cosines.

PQS and PRS are perpendicular to the edges VQ and VR, respectively. The first equality is a result of the relations $\overline{PS} = \overline{QP} \sin B = \overline{VP} \sin \alpha \sin B = RP \sin A = VP \sin \beta$ $\sin A$. The second equality may be verified in like manner.

The first law of cosines

There is a first law of cosines for the trihedral (see 15) with similar expressions for $\cos \beta$ and $\cos \gamma$ obtained by cyclic permutation of the letters. In Figure 5 (right), the plane PQR is perpendicular to the edge VP. The law of cosines applied to the plane triangles PQR and VQR gives $\overline{QR}^2 = \overline{PQ}^2 + \overline{PR}^2 - 2$ r $\overline{PQ}\ \overline{PR} \cos A = \overline{VQ}^2 + \overline{VR}^2 - 2$ $\overline{VQ}\ \overline{VR} \cos \alpha$. After transposing and using the Pythagorean theorem, $2\ \overline{VQ}\ \overline{VR} \cos a = 2\ \overline{VP}^2 +\ 2\ \overline{PQ}\ \overline{PR} \cos A$. When this relationship is divided by the value $(VQ)(VR)$,it becomes the first law of cosines for the trihedral (15) equation using the definitions of the trigonometric functions.

If at the vertex of a trihedral three rays are drawn perpendicular to the three inner faces of the trihedral, a second trihedral is obtained called the polar trihedral of the first. The first is also the polar of the second. The face angles α', β', and γ' of the polar trihedral are the supplements of the dihedral angles A, B, and C of the given trihedral, and hence the face angles α, β, and γ of the given trihedral are the supplements of the dihedral angles A', B', and C' of the polar trihedral.

The first law of cosines when applied to the polar trihedral and then simplified by the relations $\cos \alpha' = \cos (180 - A) = -\cos A$, and so on, yields the second law of cosines for the given trihedral (see 16) and two additional relations for $\cos B$ and $\cos C$, obtained by cyclic permutation of the letters.

When the vertices of a spherical triangle are joined to the centre of the sphere, there is formed a trihedral angle with vertex at the centre (Figure 6). The sides a, b, and c of the spherical triangle are the great circle arcs intercepted by the face angles α, β, and γ, and the angles of the spherical triangle are the dihedral angles A, B, and C of the trihedral. The faces of the polar trihedral intersect the

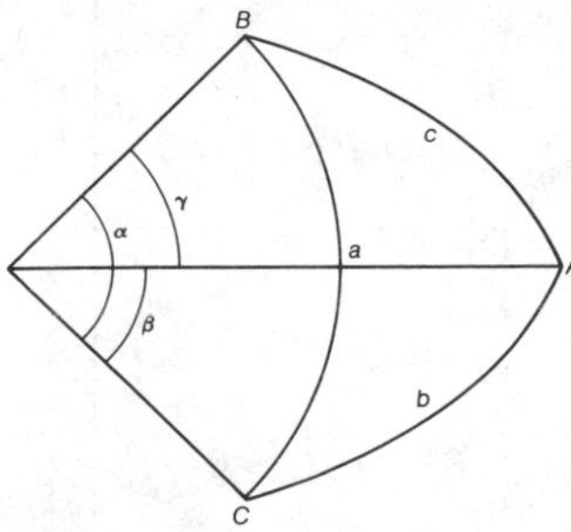

Figure 6: Spherical triangle and trihedral angle.

sphere in the polar triangle of the given spherical triangle. Because a trigonometric function of a central angle and of the intercepted arc have the same value, the law of sines (14) yields a law of sines for spherical triangles expressed in ratios of sine functions (see 17). Similarly, the first law of cosines (15) gives a law of cosines for the sides of the spherical triangle (see 18), and the second law of cosines (see 16) furnishes a law of cosines for the angles of a spherical triangle (see 19).

Solving the spherical triangle

To solve a spherical triangle, the known values are substituted in formulas, the laws of sines and cosines for the spherical triangle (see 17, 18, 19), and the resulting equations are solved for the unknowns. When three sides or two sides and the included angle are given, the law of cosines for the sides (18) is appropriate, and the law of cosines for the angles (19) is used when three angles or two angles and an included side are given. If two sides and an angle opposite one side or two angles and a side opposite one angle are given, the law of sines (see 17) is applied first, and the solution is completed by the use of a pair of equations (see 18, 19).

The area of the spherical triangle is given by the product of E and the square of r (see 20) in which r is the radius of the sphere, and E is the excess of $A + B + C$ over two right angles measured in radians. It should also be noted that a solution of a spherical triangle yields a solution of the polar triangle.

(16) $$\cos A = -\cos B \cos C + \sin B \sin C \cos \alpha$$

(17) $$\frac{\sin a}{\sin A} = \frac{\sin b}{\sin B} = \frac{\sin c}{\sin C}$$

(18) $$\begin{cases} \cos a = \cos b \cos c + \sin b \sin c \cos A \\ \cos b = \cos c \cos a + \sin c \sin a \cos B \\ \cos c = \cos a \cos b + \sin a \sin b \cos C \end{cases}$$

(19) $$\begin{cases} \cos A = -\cos B \cos C + \sin B \sin C \cos a \\ \cos B = -\cos C \cos A + \sin C \sin A \cos b \\ \cos C = -\cos A \cos B + \sin A \sin B \cos c \end{cases}$$

(20) $$\text{area} = Er^2$$

(21) $$\begin{cases} \sin a = \sin c \sin A = \tan b \cot B \\ \sin b = \sin c \sin B = \tan a \cot A \\ \cos c = \cos a \cos b = \text{ctn} A \cot B \\ \cos A = \cos a \sin B = \tan b \cot c \\ \cos B = \cos b \sin A = \tan a \cot c \end{cases}$$

(22) $$\begin{cases} \sin x = x - \dfrac{x^3}{3!} + \dfrac{x^5}{5!} - \dfrac{x^7}{7!} + \cdots \\ \cos x = 1 - \dfrac{x^2}{2!} + \dfrac{x^4}{4!} - \dfrac{x^6}{6!} + \cdots \end{cases}$$

Other relations between the sides and angles of a spherical triangle are derived in texts on spherical trigonometry. In particular, John Napier's analogies are formulas relating the half angles and half sides. Each formula contains five of the six parts and is well suited to logarithmic solutions of a spherical triangle. Other formulas of a similar character include the half-angle formulas, the half-side formulas, and the so-called analogies of Gauss-Delambre.

When angle C is 90°, the triangle is a right spherical triangle. Because $\sin C = 1$ and $\cos C = 0$, the relations in the spherical triangle (see 17, 18, 19) yield formulas (see 21) for the right spherical triangle.

ANALYTIC TRIGONOMETRY

Trigonometric functions of a real variable x are defined by means of the trigonometric functions of an angle. For example, sin x in which x is real is defined to have the value of the sine of the angle containing x radians. Similar definitions are made for the other five trigonometric functions of the real variable x. These functions satisfy the previously noted trigonometric relations (see 2–7 and 9) with A, B, 90, and 360 replaced by x, y, $\pi/2$, and 2π, respectively. The minimum period of tan x and cot x is π, and of the other four functions it is 2π.

Power series

In the calculus it is shown that sin x and cos x are sums of power series (see 22). These series may be used to compute the sine and cosine of any angle. For example, to compute the sine of 10°, it is necessary to find the value of sin $\pi/18$ because 10° is the angle containing $\pi/18$ radians. When $\pi/18$ is substituted in the series for sin x, it is found that the first two terms give 0.17365, which is correct to five decimals for the sine of 10°. By taking enough terms of the series, any number of decimal places can be correctly obtained.

Tables of the functions may be used to sketch the graphs of the functions, shown in Figure 7. The diagrams give the graph of each function for one period. To obtain the complete graph in each figure it is only necessary to extend the curve indefinitely in both directions by repetitions of the piece of graph shown in the figure.

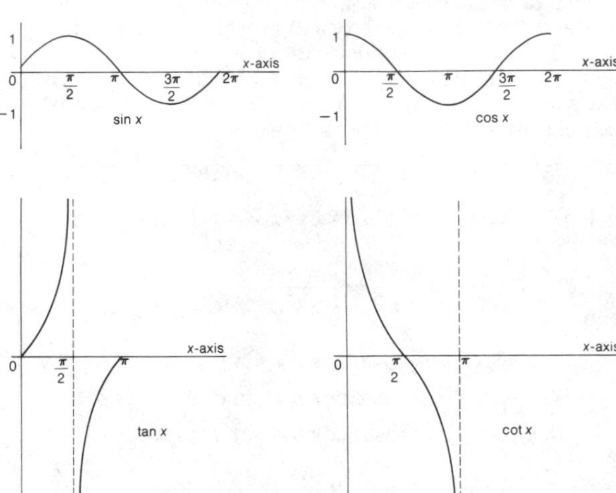

Figure 7: Graphs of some trigonometric functions.

Each of the trigonometric functions has an inverse. For instance, the inverse sine of x is the angle the sine of which is x. It is written $\sin^{-1} x$ or arc sin x. The other trigonometric functions also have inverses: arc tan x, arc cos x, etc.

COORDINATES AND TRANSFORMATION OF COORDINATES

Polar coordinates. For problems involving directions from a fixed origin (or pole) O, it is often convenient to specify a point P by its polar coordinates (r, θ), in which r is the distance OP and θ is the angle that the direction of r makes with a given initial line, which may be identified with the x-axis of rectangular Cartesian coordinates as shown in Figure 8. The point (r, θ) is the same as $(r, \theta + 2n\pi)$ for any integer n. It is sometimes desirable to allow r to be negative, so that (r, θ) is the same as $(-r, \theta + \pi)$.

Given the Cartesian equation for a curve, the polar equation for the same curve can be obtained by substituting the forms for x and y in terms of radius and angle as expressed throughout the trigonometric functions (see 23). For instance, the circle $x^2 + y^2 = a^2$ has the polar equation $(r \cos \theta)^2 + (r \sin \theta)^2 = a^2$, which reduces to $r = a$. (The positive value of r is sufficient, if θ takes all values from $-\pi$ to π or from 0 to 2π). Thus the polar equation of a circle simply expresses the fact that the curve is independent of θ and has constant radius. In a similar manner, the line $y = x \tan \alpha$ has the polar equation $\sin \theta = \cos \theta \tan \alpha$, which reduces to $\theta = \alpha$. (The other solution, $\theta = \alpha + \pi$, can be discarded if r is allowed to take negative values.)

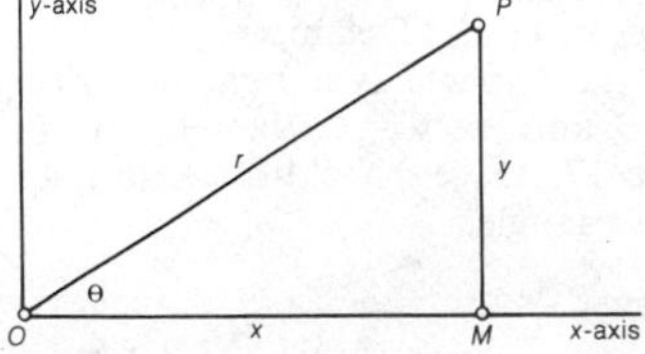

Figure 8: Cartesian and polar coordinates.

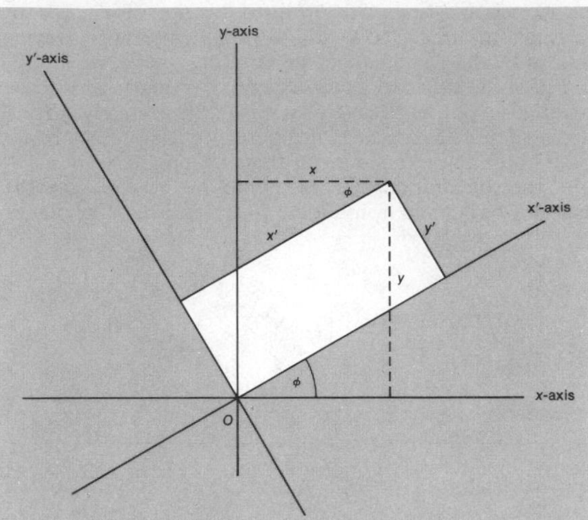

Figure 9: Rotation of axes.

Transformation of coordinates. A transformation of coordinates in a plane is a change from one coordinate system to another. A point in the plane will have two sets of coordinates giving its position with respect to the two coordinate systems used. The transformation expresses the relationship between a point or locus in one system and that in another.

One type of transformation is that just discussed: the transformation between polar and Cartesian coordinates with the same origin as in Figure 9. The equations giving the transformation are $x = r \cos \varphi$ and $y = r \sin \varphi$. Similarly, it is possible to accomplish transformation between rectangular and oblique coordinates.

In a translation of Cartesian coordinate axes, a transformation is made between two sets of axes that are parallel to each other but have their origins at different positions. If a point has coordinates (x, y) in one system and $(x',$

(23) $$x = r\cos\theta, \qquad y = r\sin\theta$$

(24) $$\begin{cases} x = x' + h \\ y = y' + k \end{cases}$$

(25) $$\begin{cases} 2x^2 + y^2 - 12x - 2y + 17 = 0 \\ x = x' + 3 \\ y = y' + 1 \\ x^2 + y^2/2 = 1 \end{cases}$$

(26) $$\begin{cases} x = x'\cos\phi - y'\sin\phi \\ y = x'\sin\phi + y'\cos\phi \end{cases}$$

(27) $$x^2 - y^2 = a^2$$

(28) $$Ax^2 + Bxy + Cy^2 + Dx + Ey + F = 0$$

(29) $$\Delta = \tfrac{1}{2}\begin{vmatrix} 2A & B & D \\ B & 2C & E \\ D & E & 2F \end{vmatrix}$$

(30) $$\begin{cases} B^2 - 4AC = 0, \qquad B^2 - 4AC > 0 \\ B^2 - 4AC < 0 \end{cases}$$

y′) in a second, then the transformation equations are linear including the constants h and k (see 24). Here (h, k) is the origin of the second system in terms of the first coordinate system. These transformation equations were used earlier to derive the general equation of a straight line. The common use of translations of axes is to simplify the equations of curves. For example, an equation that is quadratic with linear and constant terms (see 25) can be simplified with translations to an equation involving only squares of x and y and a constant term. In other words, the curve represents an ellipse with its centre at the point (3, 1) in the (x–y) coordinate system. The equation reduces to the standard form when the coordinates are translated to this point.

Rotation of coordinate axes

A rotation of coordinate axes is one in which a pair of axes giving the coordinates of a point (x, y) are rotated through an angle φ to give a new pair of axes in which the point has coordinates (x', y'). This is shown in Figure 9, from which it is apparent that the transformation equations are trigonometric in form (see 26). The application of these formulas to the rectangular hyperbola involving the difference of squares (see 27), with $\varphi = 45°$, leads to the equation $xy = c$, giving the form of the rectangular hyperbola when its asymptotes are used as the coordinate axes.

Discriminant of a conic. A conic is represented by a general equation of the second degree with the form that includes squared terms, cross product terms, and linear terms, as well as a constant (see 28). The discriminant is denoted by Δ (Greek delta) and is defined by a determinant in which constants of the general equation appear (see 29).

The discriminant and the expression ($B^2 - 4AC$) are invariants for rotational and translational transformations. They are used as criteria for the form of the curve represented by the general equation.

Three cases occur that are expressed in terms of numerical values for the above expression (see 30). In the first case the curve is a parabola if Δ is not zero, and if Δ is zero the curve is two parallel or coincident straight lines or there is no (real) curve. In the second case the curve is a hyperbola if it is not the case that $\Delta = 0$ and two intersecting lines if $\Delta = 0$. In the third case the curve is an ellipse if it is not the case that $\Delta = 0$ and becomes a single point if $\Delta = 0$.

The cases in which $\Delta = 0$ are limiting. A point is the limiting case of an ellipse in which the section of the cone is taken through its vertex. Similarly, an axial section of cones through the vertex gives two intersecting lines, a limiting case of the hyperbola. The parabola becomes a single line if the section plane is tangential to the cone and a pair of parallel lines when the vertex of the cone is at infinity (the "cone" is then a cylinder). These limiting cases are called degenerate conics. The general equation of a conic can be put in a form involving the discriminant (see 31).

(31) $$Ax^2 + Bxy + Cy^2 - \frac{\Delta}{B^2 - 4AC} = 0$$

(32) $$\frac{x_1t_1 + x_2t_2}{(t_1 + t_2)}, \quad \frac{y_1t_1 + y_2t_2}{(t_1 + t_2)}$$

(33) $$\begin{cases} \dfrac{x_1t_1 + x_2t_2 + x_3t_3}{t_1 + t_2 + t_3}, \quad \dfrac{y_1t_1 + y_2t_2 + y_3t_3}{t_1 + t_2 + t_3} \\ \dfrac{z_1t_1 + z_2t_2 + z_3t_3}{t_1 + t_2 + t_3} \end{cases}$$

(34) $$t_1 + t_2 + t_3 = 1$$

The centre of mass

Barycentric and areal coordinates. If two masses of magnitude t_1 and t_2 are placed at points P_1 and P_2, their total mass appears to act at point P on the line P_1P_2. P divides the distance P_1P_2 in the ratio t_2:t_1 and is known as the centroid or centre of mass. Its coordinates are rational functions of the $\{x_k\}$ and $\{t_k\}$ (see 32). For three masses in a plane at points P_1, P_2, P_3, the centroid has coordinates also rational functions of the $\{x_k\}$ and $\{t_k\}$ (see 33). Suitable values of t_1, t_2, t_3 will place the centroid P anywhere in the plane, and they are called the barycentric coordinates of the point (the centroid) with respect to the triangle of reference, $P_1P_2P_3$. They are homogeneous coordinates, because for any $k \neq 0$ masses kt_1, kt_2, and kt_3 have the same centroid as t_1, t_2, and t_3. The barycentric coordinates of P are proportional to the areas of the three triangles PP_2P_3, PP_3P_1, PP_1P_2. Accordingly, when normalized so that the sum of the $\{t_k\}$ equals 1 (see 34) they are called areal coordinates.

BIBLIOGRAPHY. ERNEST W. HOBSON, *A Treatise on Plane and Advanced Trigonometry,* 7th ed. (1957); MYRA MCFADDEN, *Modern Trigonometry* (1965); SISTER MARY CLAUDIA ZELLER, *The Development of Trigonometry From Regiomontanus to Pitiscus* (1946); JOHN F. SCOTT, *A History of Mathematics from Antiquity to the Beginning of the Nineteenth Century,* 2 vol. (1958); DAVID E. SMITH, *History of Mathematics,* 2 vol. (1923–25, reprinted 1958); HERBERT E. SALZER and NORMAN LEVINE, *Table of Sines and Cosines to Ten Decimal Places at Thousandths of a Degree* (1962); RUDOLF A. ZIMMER, *Basic Trigonometry with Applications in Technology* (1980).

(R.W.Bd./Ed.)

Turkey and Ancient Anatolia

Turkey (Türkiye in Turkish) is a country of the Middle East lying partly in Asia and partly in Europe. Its location in two continents has been a central factor in its history, culture, and politics; Turkey has often been called a bridge between East and West. The country's area of 300,948 square miles (779,452 square kilometres) includes the 9,175 square miles of European Turkey, consisting of a portion of Thrace (Turkish: Trakya), and the larger area (291,773 square miles) of Asian Turkey, called Anatolia (Turkish: Anadolu). İmroz (Imbros) and Bozca Ada (Tenedos) islands in the Aegean Sea also belong to Turkey.

Turkey is bounded on the east by Iran and the Soviet Union; on the south by Iraq, Syria, and the Mediterranean Sea; on the west by Bulgaria, Greece, and the Aegean Sea; and on the north by the Black Sea. The capital is Ankara. Turkey in Europe is separated from Anatolia by the Bosporus, the Sea of Marmara, and the Dardanelles Strait (called in ancient times the Hellespont), which form the only sea passage between the Black Sea and the Mediterranean. Turkmen tribes invaded the ancient region of Anatolia (a name derived from the Greek word *anatolē*, "sunrise"; *i.e.*, eastern land) in the 11th century AD and founded there the Seljuq Empire. Four centuries later the Ottomans began to spread their empire from a corner of Anatolia, and during the 17th century, when Turkish expansion was at its peak, the Ottoman Empire reached into central Europe to include what is now Romania and Hungary and most of present-day Yugoslavia. It also included what is now Syria, Iraq, Israel, Egypt, and North Africa as far west as Algeria.

This article covers the geographical, social, and political aspects of the contemporary Turkish state and the history of the region since prehistoric times.

The article is divided into the following sections:

PHYSICAL AND HUMAN GEOGRAPHY

The land

RELIEF

Turkey forms part of the belt of young mountain ranges that run from the Balkan Peninsula to Iran. The mean altitude of the country is more than 3,600 feet (1,097 metres), and it increases eastward to more than 6,560 feet. Lofty mountains are interspersed with depressions surrounded by steep slopes and high plateaus. Less than 9 percent of Turkey's area consists of level or gently sloping lands. Lowlands are mainly in the coastal areas. Turkey's rugged relief was formed in relatively recent geological times, and it is still a very active region of the Earth's crust, as is shown by frequent tremors and occasional destructive earthquakes.

The mountainous relief is dominated in the north and south by ranges of more than 10,000 feet that encircle the Central Anatolian Plateau and separate it from the narrow coastal lowlands. North of the central plateau the Pontic Mountains follow the contour of the southern shore of the Black Sea, their altitude increasing eastward to the highest peak in Kaçkar Dağı (12,900 feet [3,932 metres]), where traces of Quaternary glaciation (occurring during the last 2,500,000 years) are extensive and where even today small glaciers are found. South of the central plateau are the Taurus Mountains, composed of several ranges that extend in broad arches along the Mediterranean coast and north of Syria. Their highest points are Mor Dağı (12,490 feet [3,807 metres]) and the heavily glaciated Cilo Dağı (13,504 feet [4,116 metres]) in the eastern Taurus. The Taurus system is composed mainly of limestone and therefore is full of caves, potholes, and underground streams.

Central Anatolia

Central Anatolia is a semi-arid plateau with a core of older rocks overlain by horizontal or slightly tilted Tertiary deposits (formed from 65,000,000 to 2,500,000 years ago). It is divided into several basins, some of which were prehistoric lakes. Today the greater part of the region is an interior basin with a number of shallow salt lakes (*e.g.,* Tuz Gölü [Salt Lake], covering 579 square miles with a depth of only one or two feet) and extensive eroded areas—as around Ürgüp, near the middle course of the Kızıl Irmak (Kızıl River), where there are cave dwellings, underground churches, and subterranean villages. The region is rich in young volcanic features, like the glacier-crowned Erciyes Dağı (12,851 feet [3,917 metres]), the highest point of central Anatolia; many volcanic cones, crater lakes, and explosion pits lie between Konya and Kumköy.

Eastern Anatolia is composed of lofty ranges and recent volcanic cones, such as Mt. Ararat (Ağrı Dağı, the highest peak in Turkey with an altitude of 16,853 feet [5,137 metres]—the site where the legendary Noah's Ark came to rest) and Süphan Dağı (13,313 feet [4,058 metres]). These rise above high plateaus often covered by extensive lava flows. The plateaus are interrupted by basins, one of which is occupied by Lake Van (Van Gölü), a salt lake formed by the extinct volcano of Nemrut Dağı, which last erupted in 1441.

Western Anatolia, known as the Aegean region, has elongated mountain ridges separated by depressed floors: a system of young, roughly parallel fault lines running east and west. It includes, from north to south, the valleys of Bakır Çayı (ancient Caicus); Gediz (Hermus); Küçük Menderes (Cayster), with the ruins of Ephesus; and Büyük Menderes (Maeander), where there are the remains of several ancient towns, including Miletus. These valleys lead from the Aegean up to the plateau.

The landforms of northwestern Turkey around the Sea of Marmara are simple. Thrace is a large basin bounded by mountains of moderate height on the north (Istranca Dağları) and south (Ganos Dağı) and by low plateaus 300 to 500 feet in altitude around the Bosporus on the east. The semi-arid central part of Thrace, filled by recent deposits, forms a rolling plain. The plateaus around Istanbul are deeply dissected by valleys. One of these, the Bosporus, a former river valley drowned by the rising sea level after the last glaciers melted, is now the channel between the Sea of Marmara and the Black Sea. The Dardanelles, linking the Sea of Marmara at its other end to the Aegean, originated in the same way.

DRAINAGE AND SOILS

The rivers of Turkey

The water divide between the drainage basins of the Atlantic and Indian oceans runs obliquely through eastern Anatolia. The land east of the divide drains to the Caspian through the Kuruçay and Aras rivers and to the Persian Gulf through the Euphrates and Tigris rivers. The country west and north of the main divide drains to the Black Sea through the Kızıl Irmak (Halys) and Sakarya rivers. The Yeşil Irmak (Iris) also empties into the Black Sea. The western regions of the country drain to the Sea of Marmara through the Susurluk (Macestus) river and to the Aegean through the Gediz (Hermus) and the Büyükmenderes (Maeander) rivers. The principal rivers of the Mediterranean basin are the Göksu (Calycadnus), Seyhan (Sarus), Ceyhan (Pyramus), and the lower course of the Orontes (Asi). Approximately one-seventh of Turkey has no exterior drainage. Turkish rivers have generally irregular and shallow beds, and their seasonal changes in depth make them unsuitable for navigation.

The principal lakes of the country are Lake Van, 1,443 square miles, over 330 feet deep, and highly saline, in eastern Anatolia; Tuz Gölü, in central Anatolia; Keban, an artificial reservoir; and the freshwater lakes Beyşehir, Eğridir, and Burdur, northeast of the Gulf of Antalya.

Turkey has a variety of soil types, reflecting great differences in climate, geology, and vegetation. An outer belt of red and reddish-brown podzolic soils extends over the humid northern and southern marginal regions. The extremely humid eastern Black Sea coasts have strongly acid red soils, whereas the drier northwestern part of the country is covered by slightly acid brown and yellowish-brown podzolic soils. In the Mediterranean area, red and podzolic soil alternates frequently with patches of red clayey soil and in the northwest with rich limy soil. Most of the interior is covered by alkaline, brown and reddish-brown steppe soils. In the driest core of central Anatolia even patches of desertic gray soils occur, and saline soils cover considerable areas. The transitional regions between the dry interior and the humid margins are generally occupied by a belt of brown forest soils. Turkey faces a serious problem in soil erosion, resulting from extensive deforestation that began in the Hellenistic and Roman periods and continued in later times.

CLIMATE

The climate is varied, depending largely on geographic factors. The coastal areas are generally humid, while the interior is semi-arid because it is cut off from the rain-bearing winds by mountain ranges. The northern slopes of the Black Sea mountains receive heavy rain even during summer. Annual rainfall in the coastal areas is more than 27 inches (690 millimetres) and as much as 96 inches in the eastern Black Sea region. In most of central Anatolia average annual precipitation varies between 10 and 14 inches. Areas of moderate rainfall (15 to 24 inches) include the Marmara and Aegean regions and southeastern and eastern Anatolia.

The low coastal areas have relatively high annual temperatures and warm winters. Along the Mediterranean coast frosts are rare, and snowfall is almost unknown. In the interior, winter temperatures are often below freezing, and in the northeastern plateaus the winters are very cold. Snow cover lasts 20 to 40 days in central Anatolia and more than 120 days in the northeast. The regional differences are much less marked in summer. Four climatic regions can be distinguished. The south and west coasts have a Mediterranean climate with hot, dry summers and mild, rainy winters; the mean annual temperature is about 68° F (20° C) and ranges from 53° F (11° C) in the coldest month to 84° F (29° C) in the warmest month. The

Four climatic regions

Black Sea coast enjoys warm summers, mild winters, and a fair amount of rainfall throughout the year; the mean annual temperature is about 58° F (14° C), ranging from 44° F (7° C) in the coldest month to 73° F (23° C) in the warmest month. The high northeastern plateaus have fairly warm summers but severe winters, with maximum precipitation in the summer; the mean annual temperature is about 39° F (4° C), ranging from 10° F (-12° C) in the coldest month to 64° F (18° C) in the hottest. The semi-arid interior and southeast have cold, moist winters and hot, dry summers; the mean annual temperature is about 53° F (12° C), ranging from 32° F (0° C) in the coldest month to 74° F (23° C) in the warmest.

PLANT AND ANIMAL LIFE

Large areas in the south, west, and northwest are covered by a Mediterranean vegetation, consisting mainly of thick, scrubby underbrush in the lowlands and deciduous or coniferous forests at higher altitudes up to the timberline (6,000 or 7,000 feet). The humid northern margins of the country are the most densely wooded region of Turkey. On the eastern Black Sea there are subtropical forests. The Anatolian interior is a region of steppes. Forests, mostly oak and coniferous trees, occur only on the elevated parts.

Turkey is fairly rich in wild animals and game birds. The wolf, fox, boar, wildcat, beaver, marten, jackal, hyena, bear, deer, gazelle, and mountain goat are among the animals still found in secluded and wooded regions: Domestic animals include the buffalo, Angora goat (on the Central Plateau), and camel. Major game birds are partridge, wild goose, quail, and bustard.

GEOGRAPHIC REGIONS

The Black Sea coast. Extending along the northern margins of the country from the Soviet frontier in the east to the lower course of the Sakarya River in the west is a mountainous area with abundant precipitation at all seasons. It is densely wooded, comprising more than one-fourth of Turkey's forested areas. It also has the highest rural population density, in some local areas exceeding 500 inhabitants per square mile. The region is mainly agricultural, corn (maize) being the dominant field crop. Tea is grown in the eastern coastal strip, hazelnuts around Giresun and Ordu, and tobacco in Samsun and Trabzon. West of Sinop and south of the mountains, the transition toward the Marmara region and the Anatolian interior is marked by increasing acreage in wheat and fallow land. The principal mineral resources of the region are copper in the east (at Murgul) and coal in the west (the Ereğli-Zonguldak Basin). Samsun, Zonguldak, and Trabzon (site of a university) are the leading towns and ports.

The Marmara region. The areas adjacent to the Sea of Marmara, including Thrace, are the most heavily urbanized of the country. The principal cities are, in decreasing order of size, Istanbul (formerly Constantinople), Bursa, İzmit, Adapazarı, and Edirne. Istanbul, situated at the Bosporus, is Turkey's leading industrial, commercial, and cultural centre. The Marmara region is economically the most developed area of Turkey. Its agriculture is variegated, including tobacco, wheat, rice, sunflower, corn, olives, grapes, and natural silk. On the straits and coasts of the Sea of Marmara fishing is well developed. The leading manufacturing districts are around Istanbul and in a narrow coastal strip between Istanbul and İzmit.

The Aegean region. The coastal area from the Dardanelles on the north to the vicinity of Rhodes on the south is densely populated and economically one of the most advanced regions of the country. Its wealth rests on the production of several export crops, including tobacco (more than 50 percent of Turkey's total production), cotton (30 percent of the total), high-quality grapes suitable for drying, olives (more than 50 percent of the Turkish output), and figs. The main cities are İzmir (the leading export outlet of Turkey and site of a university), Manisa, and Aydın. The area draws many tourists with its beaches and historical sites (Pergamum, Ephesus, Miletus). Between the Aegean region and central Anatolia there is a high, thinly populated area specializing in grain and livestock production; in the 1960s it also produced much of the Western world's supply of opium. Following a two-year ban (1972–74), production resumed under strict controls.

Mediterranean region. Turkey's Mediterranean region extends from Rhodes to the Syrian frontier, and is occupied largely by the Taurus Mountains. Principal passes in the Taurus Mountains connecting the interior plateaus with the narrow coastal strip are the Külek Boğazı, leading to Tarsus and Adana; the Sertavul Pass, between Karaman and Silifke; and the Çubukboğazı pass, between the lake district and Antalya in the west. The Amanus Dağları (mountains) bordering the Gulf of Iskenderun are crossed by the Belen Pass. The region has several subregions: the sparsely populated limestone plateaus of Taşeli in the middle; the lake district in the west with its continental climate, where grain is grown; and the intensively cultivated, densely populated coastal plains. Principal cities of the region include Adana, an important commercial and industrial centre; Mersin; İskenderun (Alexandretta); Antalya; and Gaziantep. The coastal areas produce cotton (60 percent of Turkey's output), sesame, citrus fruits (more than 90 percent of the country's production), early vegetables, and bananas. The higher elevations have relatively little arable land; grain and livestock are produced, and there is pastoral nomadism among the Yürüks.

The Taurus Mountains

Central Anatolia. The middle of the Anatolian plain has a continental steppe climate and scanty rainfall. Grain occupies over 90 percent of the arable land (40 percent of the country's wheat production). One-third of Turkey's sheep and three-fourths of its Angora goats are raised there. The chief commercial and industrial centres are Ankara (capital of Turkey), Eskişehir, Konya, Kayseri, and Sivas.

Eastern Anatolia. The eastern part of the interior is a high and extremely rugged region with coniferous forests and mountain pastures in the northeast and wooded steppes in the south. Eastern Anatolia is the most thinly populated region of the country, with population densities as low as 13 people per square mile in some areas. Farming is difficult because of the long, severe winters, steep slopes, and eroded soil. Grain, chiefly summer wheat and barley, is the dominant crop. In the humid northeast, beef and dairy cattle are raised; in the south there are pastoral nomads who raise sheep and goats. Eastern Anatolia is rich in mineral resources (iron ore at Divriği, copper at Ergani, chrome at Guleman). The principal cities are Erzurum, Malatya, Elâziğ, and Van.

Southeastern Anatolia. At the foot of the Taurus Mountains is a barren plateau drained by the Tigris and Euphrates rivers. Agriculture is confined mainly to irrigated valleys and basins (wheat, rice, vegetables, grapes). Much of the population is nomadic or seminomadic. Turkey's principal oil fields extend westward from Raman and Garzan, linked by pipeline to the port of İskenderun. The principal urban centres are Gaziantep, Urfa, and Diyarbakır.

SETTLEMENT PATTERNS

Rural settlements. Turkey is essentially an agricultural country, and about 55 percent of its population lives in rural settlements. In physical form these differ from region to region: wooden houses are typical in the Black Sea area; sun-dried bricks and flat roofs prevail in the semi-arid interior, and stone is the dominant building material in the Taurus Mountains, the Aegean region, and parts of eastern Anatolia.

Types of rural settlements

Rural settlement types range from single-residence units and several types of temporarily occupied settlements to agglomerated villages. Single rural settlement units and dispersed settlements occur in the eastern and western Black Sea regions, in eastern Anatolia, and in the Taurus Mountains. In eastern Anatolia they are associated with stock raising, while in the eastern Black Sea region they are small farmsteads, based on a subsistence agriculture. In the karst (limestone sink) regions of the Taurus area, the scattered distribution of soil in small depressions accounts for the occurrence of dispersed settlements and single-residence units. In the Mediterranean coastal strip, single rural settlement units usually consist of a two-story dwelling surrounded by a large field in which cash crops such as bananas, citrus fruits, and early vegetables are cultivated; the lower story of the house is used for storage.

MAP INDEX

Cities and towns

Adana 37·01n 35·18e
Adapazarı 40·46n 30·24e
Adıyaman 37·46n 38·17e
Afyonkarahisar 38·45n 30·33e
Akçaabat 41·02n 39·34e
Akdağmadeni 39·40n 35·54e
Akhisar 38·55n 27·51e
Aksaray 38·23n 34·03e
Akşehir 38·21n 31·25e
Akseki 37·02n 31·48e
Alanya 36·33n 32·01e
Alaşehir 38·21n 28·32e
Amasra 41·45n 32·24e
Amasya 40·39n 35·51e
Anamur 36·06n 32·50e
Ankara 39·56n 32·52e
Antakya, see Antioch
Antalya 36·53n 30·42e
Antioch (Antakya) 36·14n 36·07e
Arapkir 39·03n 38·30e
Ardahan 41·08n 42·43e
Artvin 41·11n 41·49e
Avanos 38·43n 34·51e
Ayaş 40·01n 32·21e
Aydın 37·51n 27·51e
Ayvacık 39·36n 26·24e
Ayvalık 39·18n 26·41e
Bafra 41·34n 35·56e
Bâlâ 39·34n 33·08e
Balıkesir 39·39n 27·53e
Bandırma 40·20n 27·58e
Bartın 41·38n 32·21e
Batman 37·52n 41·07e
Bayburt 40·16n 40·15e
Bergama (Pergamum) 39·07n 27·11e
Beypazarı 40·10n 31·56e
Beyşehir 37·41n 31·43e
Bingöl 38·53n 40·29e
Bitlis 38·22n 42·06e
Bodrum 37·02n 27·26e
Bolu 40·44n 31·37e
Bolvadin 38·42n 31·04e
Bor 37·54n 34·34e
Bornova 38·27n 27·14e
Burdur 37·43n 30·17e
Bursa 40·11n 29·04e
Çanakkale 40·09n 26·24e
Çankırı 40·36n 33·37e
Çarşamba 41·12n 36·44e
Çatalca 41·09n 28·27e
Çetinkaya 39·15n 37·38e
Ceyhan 37·04n 35·47e
Cide 41·54n 33·00e
Çivril 38·18n 29·45e
Cizre 37·20n 42·12e
Çölemerik 37·34n 43·45e
Constantınople, see İstanbul
Çorlu 41·09n 27·48e
Çorum 40·33n 34·58e
Daday 41·28n 33·28e
Damar (Murgul) 41·15n 41·34e
Darende 38·34n 37·30e
Demirci 39·03n 28·40e
Denizli 37·46n 29·06e
Derik 37·22n 40·17e
Divriği 39·23n 38·07e
Diyarbakır 37·55n 40·14e
Duzce 40·50n 31·10e
Edirne 41·40n 26·34e
Edremit 39·35n 2·701e
Elâzığ 38·41n 39·14e
Elbistan 38·13n 37·12e
Erciş 39·02n 43·22e
Ereğli 37·31n 34·04e
Ergani 38·17n 39·46e
Ermenak 36·38n 32·54e
Erzincan 39·44n 39·29e
Erzurum 39·55n 41·17e
Eskişehir 39·46n 30·32e
Ezine 39·47n 26·20e
Fethiye 36·37n 29·07e
Finike 36·18n 30·09e
Garzan, see Zok
Gaziantep 37·05n 37·22e
Gediz 39·02n 29·25e
Gelibolu 40·24n 26·40e
Gemlik 40·26n 29·09e
Gerede 40·48n 32·12e
Gerze 41·48n 35·12e
Geyve 40·30n 30·18e
Giresun 40·55n 38·24e
Gökçekaya 40·50n 35·01e
Göksun 38·03n 36·30e
Gölcük 40·44n 29·48e
Gönen 40·06n 27·39e
Guleman 38·25n 39·54e
Güllük 37·14n 27·36e
Gümüşhane 40·27n 39·29e
Hadım 36·59n 32·28e
Hınıs 39·22n 41·44e
Hopa 41·25n 41·24e
Iğdir 39·55n 44·02e
Ilgın 38·17n 31·55e
İncesu 38·38n 35·11e
İnebolu 41·58n 33·46e
İnegöl 40·05n 29·31e
İskenderun 36·37n 36·07e
İskilip 40·45n 34·29e
İsparta 37·46n 30·33e
İspir 40·29n 41·00e
İstanbul (Constantınople) 41·01n 28·58e
Izmir 38·25n 27·09e
Izmit 40·46n 29·55e
Kadınhanı 38·15n 32·14e
Kadirli 37·23n 36·05e
Kalecik 40·06n 33·25e
Kangal 39·15n 37·24e
Karabük 41·12n 32·37e
Karaköse 39·44n 43·03e
Karaman 37·05n 29·20e
Karapınar 37·43n 33·33e
Kars 40·36n 43·05e
Kartal 40·53n 29·10e
Kas 36·12n 29·38e
Kasaba 39·19n 40·21e
Kastamonu 41·22n 33·47e
Kayseri 38·43n 35·30e
Keşan 40·51n 26·37e
Kilis 36·44n 37·05e
Kırıkhan 36·32n 36·19e
Kırıkkale 39·50n 33·31e
Kırklareli 41·44n 27·12e
Kirşehir 39·09n 34·10e
Konya 37·52n 32·31e
Korkuteli 37·04n 30·13e
Kozan 37·27n 35·49e
Kütahya 39·25n 29·59e
Lâpseki 40·20n 26·41e
Lice 38·28n 40·39e
Lüleburgaz 41·24n 27·21e
Malatya 38·21n 38·19e
Malazgirt 39·09n 42·31e
Malkara 40·53n 26·54e
Manavgat 36·47n 31·26e
Manisa 38·36n 27·26e
Maraş 37·36n 36·55e
Mardin 37·18n 40·44e
Marmaris 36·51n 28·16e
Mersin 36·48n 34·38e
Merzifon 40·53n 35·29e
Mesudiye 40·28n 37·46e
Midyat 37·25n 41·23e
Muğla 37·12n 28·22e
Murgul, see Damar
Muş 38·44n 41·30e
Mustafakemalpaşa 40·02n 28·24e
Mut 36·39n 33·27e
Nazilli 37·55n 28·21e
Nevşehir 38·38n 34·43e
Niğde 37·59n 34·42e
Nizip 37·01n 37·46e
Ödemiş 38·13n 27·59e
Oltu 40·33n 41·59e
Ordu 35·56n 36·01e
Osmancık 40·59n 34·49e
Osmaniye 37·05n 36·14e
Pergamum, see Bergama
Pınarbaşi 38·44n 36·24e
Polatlı 39·36n 32·09e
Raman 37·50n 40·45e
Rize 41·02n 40·31e
Salihli 38·29n 28·09e
Samsun 41·17n 36·20e
Sandıklı 38·28n 30·17e
Sarıkamış 40·20n 42·35e
Şarkışla 39·21n 36·26e
Şarköy 40·37n 27·06e
Savur 37·33n 40·53e
Şereflikoçhisar 38·56n 33·33e
Seydişehir 37·25n 31·51e
Siirt 37·56n 41·57e
Silifke 36·22n 33·56e
Sındırgı 39·14n 28·10e
Sinop 42·01n 35·09e
Sivas 39·45n 37·02e
Siverek 37·45n 39·19e
Sivrihisar 39·27n 31·34e
Söke 37·45n 27·24e
Sungurlu 40·10n 34·23e
Tarsus 36·55n 34·53e
Tasköprü 41·30n 34·14e
Tatvan 38·30n 42·16e
Tavşanlı 39·33n 29·30e
Tekirdağ 40·59n 27·31e
Tire 38·04n 27·45e
Tirebolu 41·00n 38·48e
Tokat 40·19n 36·34e
Tosya 41·01n 34·02e
Trabzon 41·00n 39·43e
Turgutlu 38·30n 27·43e
Turhal 40·24n 36·06e
Uluborlu 38·05n 30·28e
Ulukışla 37·33n 34·30e
Ünye 41·08n 37·17e
Urfa 37·08n 38·46e
Ürgüp 38·38n 34·56e
Uşak 38·41n 29·25e
Üsküdar 41·01n 29·01e
Van 38·28n 43·20e
Vezirköprü 41·09n 35·28e
Vize 41·34n 27·45e
Yalvaç 38·17n 31·11e
Yozgat 39·50n 34·48e
Zara 39·55n 37·46e
Zevker 40·00n 38·51e
Zile 40·18n 35·54e
Zok (Garzan) 38·02n 41·33e
Zonguldak 41·27n 31·49e

Physical features and points of interest

Ağrı Dağı, see Ararat, Mount
Akdağ, *mountain* 36·32n 29·34e
Akşehır Gölü, *salt lake* 38·30n 31·28e
Aksu, *river* 37·00n 30·50e
Aladag, *mountain* 37·44n 35·09e
Alexandretta, see Iskenderun
Anamur Burnu, *point* 36·03n 32·48e
Antalya, Gulf of 36·30n 31·00e
Ararat, Mount, (Ağrı Dağı), *mountain* 39·42n 44·18e
Aras, *river* 40·06n 43·39e
Asi Nehri, see Orontes
Bafra Burnu, *cape* 41·44n 35·58e
Bakır Çayı, *river* 38·55n 27·00e
Belkis, *historic site* 37·08n 31·12e
Beyşehir Gölü, *lake* 37·40n 31·30e
Black Sea 43·00n 34·00e
Bosporus (İstanbul Boğazı) *strait* 41·00n 29·00e
Bozca Ada, *island* 39·49n 26·03e
Burdur Gölü, *lake* 37·44n 30·12e
Büyükmenderes Nehri, *river* 37·28n 27·10e
Çanakkale Bogazı, see Dardanelles
Çekerek, *river* 40·34n 35·46e
Ceyhan, *river* 36·45n 35·42e
Cilician Gates (Külek Boğazı), *gorge* 37·17n 34·50e
Cilo Dağı, *mountain* 37·30n 44·00e
Çoruh, *river* 41·28n 41·42e
Çubukboğazı, *gorge* 37·09n 30·32e
Çukur Ova, *plain* 37·18n 35·55e
Dardanelles (Hellespont; Çanakkale Bogazı), *strait* 40·15n 26·25e
Demre, *ruins* 36·15n 29·54e
Dicle Nehri, see Tigris
Didyma, *ruins* 37·25n 27·20e
Eğridir Gölü, *lake* 38·02n 30·53e
Ephesus, *historic site* 37·55n 27·17e
Erciyas Dağı, *mountain* 38·32n 35·28e
Euphrates (Fırat Nehri), *river* 36·48n 38·02e
Gallipoli Peninsula 40·20n 26·30e
Ganos Dağı, *mountain* 40·47n 27·16e
Gediz Nehri, *river* 38·35n 26·48e
Göksu, *river* 36·20n 34·05e
Hasan Dağı, *mountain* 38·08n 34·12e
Hellespont, see Dardanelles
İmroz Adası, *island* 40·10n 25·50e
Iskenderun, Gulf of 36·30n 35·40e
İstanbul Boğazı, see Bosporus
Istranca Dağları, *mountains* 41·50n 27·30e
Kaçkar Dağı, *mountain* 40·50n 41·10e
Karaca Dağ, *mountain* 37·40n 39·50e
Kaz Dağı, *mountain* 39·42n 26·50e
Keban Gölü, *lake* 38·50n 39·15e
Kelkit, *river* 40·46n 36·32e
Kerempe Burnu, *cape* 42·01n 33·21e
Kerpe Burnu, *cape* 41·10n 30·11e
Kılınc, Tepesi, *mountain* 40·32n 38·10e
Kızıl, *river* 41·44n 35·58e
Köroglu Tepesi, *peak* 40·31n 31·53e
Kösdaği, *mountain* 40·59n 34·25e
Küçükmenderes, *river* 40·00n 26·11e
Külek Boğazı, see Cilician Gates
Kuruçay (Kura), *river* 41·18n 43·12e
Marmara, Sea of 40·40n 28·15e
Mediterranean Sea 35·00n 30·00e
Meriç, *river* 40·52n 26·12e
Miletus, *ruins* 37·30n 27·18e
Murat, *river* 38·52n 38·48e
Muratdagı, *mountain* 38·55n 29·43e
Nemrut Dağı, *mountain* 38·40n 42·12e
Nur Dağları, *mountains* 36·45n 36·20e
Nuruhak Dağı, *mountain* 38·04n 37·29e
Orontes (Asi Nehri), *river* 36·02n 35·58e
Pontic Mountains 40·30n 40·00e
Porsuk, *river* 39·42n 31·59e
Resülhınzır, *cape* 36·22n 35·45e
Sakarya, *river* 41·07n 30·39e
Seyhan, *river* 36·43n 34·53e
Simav, *river* 40·23n 28·31e
Süphan Dağı, *mountain* 38·54n 42·48e
Taurus Mountains (Toros Dağları) 37·00n 33·00e
Tigris (Dicle Nehri), *river* 37·05n 42·19e
Troy, *ruins* 39·57n 26·15e
Tuz Gölü, *lake* 38·45n 33·25e
Ulu Dağ, *mountain* 40·04n 29·13e
Van, Lake 38·33n 42·46e
Yeşil Irmak, *river* 41·24n 36·35e

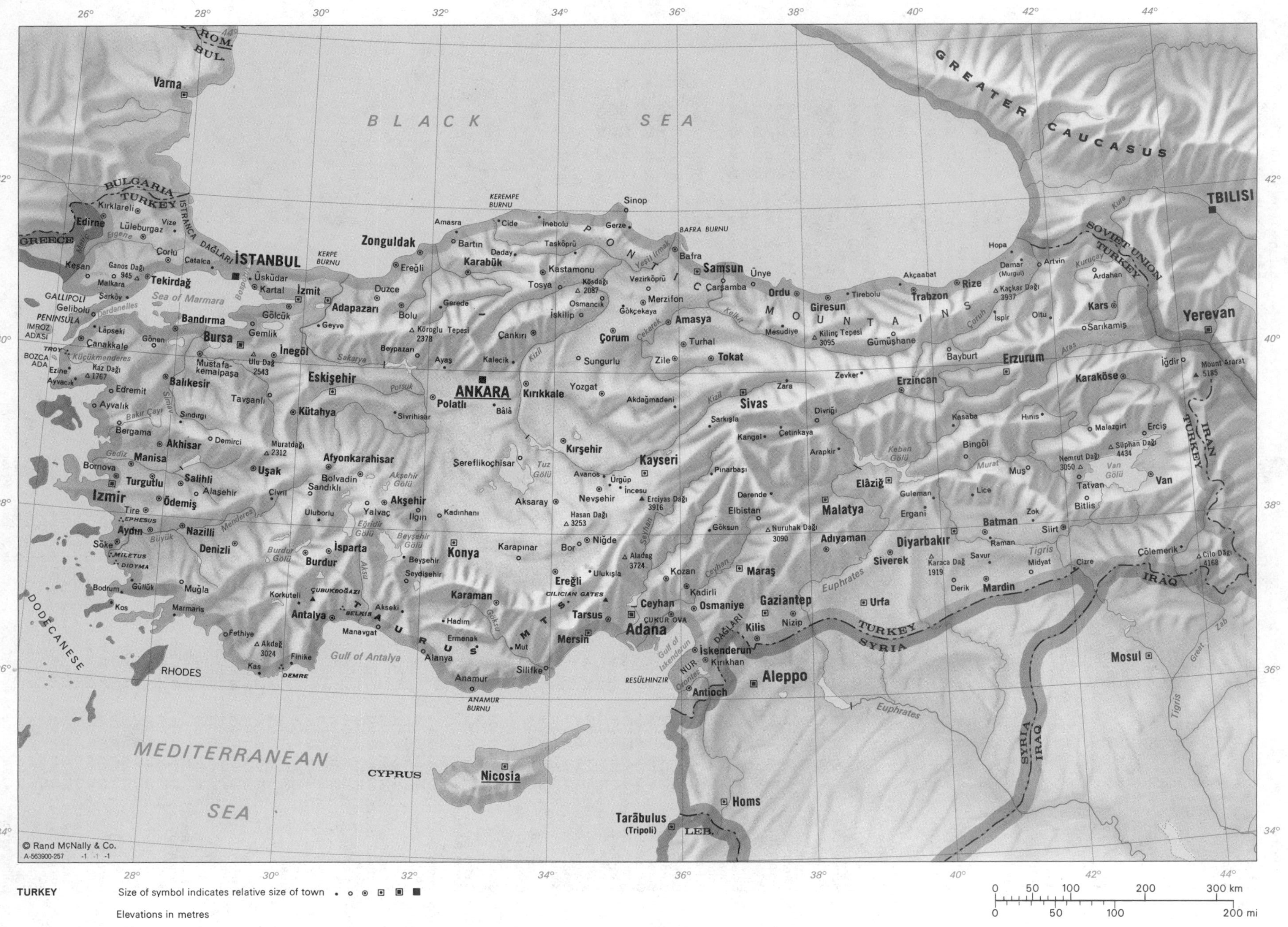
BLACK SEA
MEDITERRANEAN SEA
GREATER CAUCASUS
PONTIC MOUNTAINS
TAURUS MTS.
TBILISI
Yerevan
SOVIET UNION
TURKEY
IRAN
IRAQ
SYRIA
LEB.
BULGARIA
GREECE
ROM.
BUL.
Varna
Edirne
Kırklareli
Lüleburgaz
Tekirdağ
Çorlu
Sea of Marmara
GALLIPOLI PENINSULA
Gelibolu
Çanakkale
İSTANBUL
Üsküdar
Kartal
İzmit
Adapazarı
Zonguldak
Ereğli
Bartın
Karabük
Amasra
Cide
İnebolu
Sinop
Gerze
Kastamonu
Bafra
Samsun
Çarşamba
Ünye
Ordu
Giresun
Trabzon
Rize
Hopa
Artvin
Ardahan
Kars
Sarıkamış
Erzurum
Bayburt
Gümüşhane
Erzincan
Karaköse
Iğdır
Mount Ararat 5185
Van
Van Gölü
Tatvan
Bitlis
Muş
Siirt
Batman
Bingöl
Cizre
Midyat
Mardin
Diyarbakır
Siverek
Urfa
Elâzığ
Malatya
Adıyaman
Gaziantep
Kilis
Aleppo
Homs
Tarābulus (Tripoli)
Mosul
Euphrates
Tigris
Sivas
Tokat
Amasya
Çorum
Yozgat
Kayseri
Kırşehir
Nevşehir
Niğde
Aksaray
ANKARA
Kırıkkale
Polatlı
Eskişehir
Kütahya
Bursa
Bandırma
Balıkesir
Manisa
İzmir
Aydın
Söke
Denizli
Uşak
Afyonkarahisar
Akşehir
Isparta
Burdur
Antalya
Konya
Karaman
Ereğli
Adana
Mersin
Tarsus
Ceyhan
İskenderun
Antioch
Osmaniye
Maraş
Nicosia
CYPRUS
RHODES
DODECANESE
Tuz Gölü
Gulf of Antalya
© Rand McNally & Co.
TURKEY
Size of symbol indicates relative size of town
Elevations in metres
0 50 100 200 300 km
0 50 100 200 mi

Between the single rural settlement units and the more prevalent agglomerated villages, there are many transitional types. A *mahalle* consists of a group of single rural settlement units. *Divans* occurring mainly in northern Anatolia, comprise a number of *mahalles* organized into a single administrative unit. *Mezraas* are settlements founded on agricultural lands that were originally inhabited only temporarily during plowing and harvesting but later became permanently settled villages or towns. Among temporary settlements, *koms* are usually smaller than *mezraas*. *Yaylas* are temporary summer rural settlements, associated with nomadism. Every nomadic group in southeastern Anatolia or in the Taurus Mountains has its own *yayla,* used solely for pasture. The practice of migrating between summer-dry lowlands and humid mountain pastures has resulted in most permanently inhabited villages in many regions of Turkey possessing one or more *yaylas*. *Kişlas* (literally, "winter quarters") are the sheltered winter quarters of nomads or former nomads. A considerable number of *yaylas* and *kişlas* have in time been transformed into permanent settlements.

The growing towns

Urban settlements. About 45 percent of Turkey's population is located in municipalities of more than 10,000 inhabitants. The percentage of urban population is fairly high in the west and northwest, in northwestern central Anatolia, and around the Gulf of İskenderun. Most towns have fewer than 25,000 inhabitants. A majority of the larger towns are concentrated around the Sea of Marmara, in the western coastal region, and in the Adana subregion. Most are so old that they may be traced back to pre-Roman or Roman times. The great majority are commercial centres benefiting from a favourable location.

Istanbul, Ankara, İzmir, and Adana are the major urban centres. Istanbul, the largest city, includes adjacent urban communities extending 30 miles from the former village of Küçükçekmece on the west to Pendik on the east and 12 miles north along the Bosporus. The surrounding industrial area produces nearly one-third of the country's manufacturing output. Ankara, the capital and second largest city, was a flourishing trade centre and military base under Roman rule. The third largest city is İzmir, a busy commercial centre. Fourth in size, Adana serves as an important agricultural market centre.

The people

LANGUAGES, RACES, AND RELIGIONS

Linguistic groups. Turkish is the mother tongue of more than 90 percent of the country's population. Modern Turkish, one of the southwestern groups of the Turkic family of languages, has been derived from Ottoman Turkish through a long nationalistic effort to purify it of the Arabic and Persian words and idioms that invaded the literary language during the Ottoman Empire. Turkish is written in Latin script.

The principal linguistic minority groups are Kurds and Arabs. Kurdish (including the Zaza dialect), the mother tongue of about 7 percent of the country's population, is widely spoken by a predominantly rural population in the eastern and southeastern regions. Arabic is spoken by about 1 percent of the population, principally in parts of southeastern Anatolia. Greek, Armenian, and Yiddish are spoken by small groups in the larger cities, mainly in Istanbul. Most Turkish Jews are descendants of Jews expelled from Spain and speak a kind of Spanish mingled with some Turkish words; others speak Yiddish.

Ethnic groups. Turkey has been a melting pot of racially and culturally distinct groups since early prehistoric times. It was penetrated, settled, or ruled by Hittites, Phrygians, and Gauls from the north and northwest; by Greeks and Macedonians from the west; and by Parthians and Mongols from the east. The most decisive influence was the incursion of Turks from the east, who introduced a new element of mixed Mediterranean-Mongoloid origin into the country's ethnic composition. The rise and decline of the Ottoman Empire contributed to the racial mixture, particularly during the empire's decline, when many Muslim groups living in former Turkish territories in southeastern Europe and in countries around the Black Sea migrated

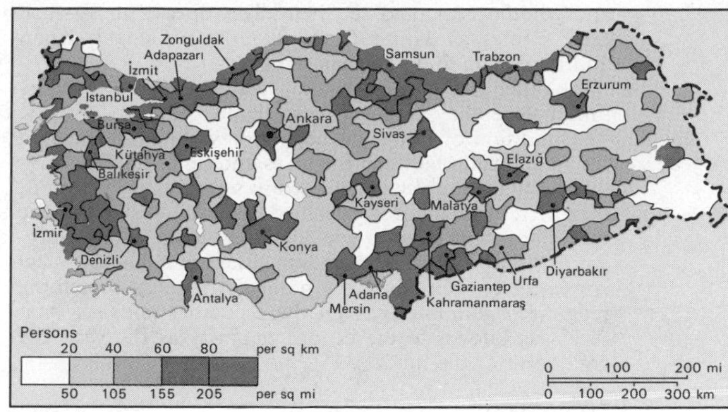

Population density of Turkey.

to the home country. (For further discussion, see below *Traditional cultures of Anatolia.*)

It is almost impossible to define an average Turk ethnically. He may be blond and blue-eyed; he may be of roundheaded alpine stock with dark hair and eyes; he may be of longheaded Mediterranean stock; or he may be Mongoloid with high cheekbones. The dominant stock seems to be Mediterranean-Turkic, giving way to Mediterranean in western and southern coastal areas and mixed with Alpine stock in the interior and the east.

Religious groups. More than 99 percent of the country's population are Muslims. The Sunnī rite is predominant, followed closely by the Shī'ite. Christians are few, and Orthodox Christians predominate over Roman Catholics. The Christian and Jewish minorities live mainly in Istanbul, Ankara, and İzmir. In the *il* of Mardin in southeastern Anatolia a community of Nestorians has survived. Religion and the state were strictly separated in Turkey after the foundation of the republic in 1923.

DEMOGRAPHIC TRENDS

Turkey has had one of the highest rates of population increase in the world. Total population, for example, almost tripled in the decades between 1930 and 1970. But despite a rapid increase in both population size and density, Turkey is not heavily populated in comparison with other countries. There are striking differences between the sparsely populated areas of Anatolia and the dense agglomerations in the northern and western parts of the country. The most densely inhabited area is the eastern Black Sea coastal strip; relatively high population densities also occur around the Sea of Marmara, in the Aegean region and around the Gulf of İskenderun.

Migration from rural areas to the cities has been another key demographic trend of the second half of the 20th century, associated with the increasing industrialization of the country. The general pattern of migration was from the rural eastern *iller* (provinces) toward the cities, including Istanbul, Zonguldak in the coal and metallurgical district in the northwest, Ankara in the interior, Adana and Mersin in the south, and İzmir in the west. (S.Er.)

Traditional cultures of Anatolia

REGIONAL CULTURE PATTERNS

Human settlement in Anatolia has been traced back well before 7000 BC. Much archaeological investigation has been devoted to the Hittite and other ancient empires, and Greek, Roman, Byzantine, Seljuq, Crusader, and Ottoman remains. (For the prehistory of the region, see below *History of Turkey and Anatolia.*) Indeed, Anatolia is one of the richest archaeological areas in the world. Genetically and culturally the resident peoples no doubt have influenced the waves of immigrants throughout history.

This complexity makes general statements somewhat hazardous, but the national characteristics and culture of the present peoples of Anatolia may be said to have two main strands. First, the Turks—and many of the minority ethnic groups—looking back to their nomadic forebears, are mindful of the people who came out of Central Asia, conquered the Arab and Byzantine empires of the Near and Middle East, and set themselves up as rulers—such great names as Timur (Tamerlane) and Genghis Khan and the Seljuq and Ottoman dynasties.

The other strand is Islām; the Asian invaders were Muslims before they reached Anatolia in the 11th century. The tradition of Islām has been a prevailing influence on the relationship between the sexes and on family life. Traditionally men and women lived in separate social worlds; men were unequivocally deemed superior, and it was the man's responsibility to see to the honour of his womenfolk. Traditionally, moreover, Islām has had political consequences. Government has been seen as something religiously guaranteed; even the secularist reformer Atatürk was known to the devout majority as the *gazi,* the conqueror of the infidels.

TECHNOLOGY

The village. As their main crop, most Turkish villages grow cereals—mostly wheat and barley but also, in some areas, corn (maize), rye, oats, and rice. In the mountains and coastal areas, however, there are many other crops: potatoes, cotton, tobacco, sugar beets, nuts, citrus fruit, grapes, figs, and tea. Dairy farming hardly exists as a separate activity, because cattle are bred for work as well as for meat and milk. Sheep and goats, found everywhere, are an important part of the rural economy, producing milk as well as meat and wool.

Agricultural and pastoral seasons

Each season has its tasks and activities. Except in the south and west, winter is a period of frost, snow, and social activities. Animals are often kept indoors and fed mainly on chopped straw. With the spring thaw, plowing and sowing are soon under way. After a month or so of less urgent work, the hay harvest is followed immediately by the main grain harvest, a period of intense activity lasting some six to eight weeks; everyone works, some people 16 to 20 hours a day. The crops are reaped, carted to the threshing floors, threshed, winnowed, and finally carted away to market or to storage.

The annual cycle of animal husbandry is even more variable. Sheep and goats that have been away for the winter return in the spring and may be sent away again to upland pastures—*yayla*—at the height of summer. How many, how far, and for how long depends on the particular village. In mountainous areas, many villagers are settled nomads, still owning upland pastures away from their main village. Cattle, water buffalo, horses, and donkeys are pastured on the village lands when they are not working.

Tools and housing

The tools used for these tasks resemble those found in other parts of the Middle East and are clearly very ancient in form. The light wooden plow, or *saban,* is drawn easily by one pair of oxen or buffalo. It has an iron-tipped share but no moldboard, so that it does not turn a furrow. Sowing traditionally is done by hand, reaping with a sickle or scythe. The crops are carried to the village for storage on four-wheeled horse-drawn carts or on the traditional two-wheeled oxcart, the *kağni.* Threshing involves driving an ox-drawn sledge about five feet long over the crops, round and round, day after day. Flint teeth on the underside of the sledge break the grain from the ears and chop the straw into chaff. This mixture is winnowed by hand with wooden forks and put into woollen sacks.

The typical Turkish village house is a rectangular, flat-roofed building, the colour of the local unbaked brick or stone from which it is made, one or two stories high. The poorest contain a single room to house family, livestock, and possessions; the very prosperous encompass joint households containing up to 20 people or so, living in large compounds off which lead many living rooms, stores, stables, and barns. The vast majority of homes fall between these extremes. The head of the household and his wife live and sleep in the main room of the household, which usually has a mud floor. This room contains the bedding, stacked away in the daytime, the cooking stove (in some areas a beehive-shaped oven built into the floor), shelves with cooking pots and implements, a gaily painted chest containing the woman's trousseau and personal possessions, and a chest for flour and grain. People sit on rugs or mats spread on the floor. Many homes also have at least one room fitted as a guest room, normally for the use of men only. It has built-in divans running along the walls and very often a stone or wooden floor. Tables and chairs, once rare, are now becoming more common. This description cannot possibly take into account the very great local variations. The most marked contrast occurs in the forests of the northern mountain ranges, where the village homes are made of timber with red roofs. Brick, cement, and, very recently, cinder block are also now becoming common, wherever people can afford them.

Village dress

Turkish men have adopted increasingly the styles and sombre colours of European male dress. Fezzes and turbans were abolished by law in 1925, and most peasants now wear cloth caps. The famous Turkish baggy trousers, exceedingly full in the seat, are still quite common, but the traditional cummerbund and colourful shift or waistcoat are rare. Shepherds, whose work may involve withstanding intense cold, wear a special large cloak made of felted wool and a hood with attached scarf that winds around the head and protects the ears. The village women still largely preserve traditional costume. They wear some locally customary combination of baggy trousers, skirts, and aprons. In many areas it is still possible to identify a woman's town or village and her marital status by her dress; village women in Turkey have never worn the veil, but they have traditionally covered their heads and mouths with a large scarf.

Most village areas contain weavers, masons, carpenters, and smiths and tinsmiths. Some villagers go to town for craft services, and a number of craftsmen travel around the villages—particularly specialists, such as sieve makers or sawyers.

Towns and cities. It is impossible to summarize in a few words the material culture of the towns and cities, which not long ago were the central part of a great empire and have since been profoundly influenced by European fashions and technology. Most towns, large and small, nevertheless, still contain markets where simple lockup shops stand side by side in rows. Usually these are arranged by craft or wares—coppersmiths, jewellers, cobblers, tailors, motor mechanics, and so on. Retailers also are grouped by commodity.

Traditional Anatolian town houses, still the normal thing in many Anatolian towns, were built in stone or wood, usually of two stories, with wooden floors and sometimes beautifully carved ceilings. The upper story often protrudes cantilever fashion into the street. With whitewashed walls and red tiled roofs, these small towns sometimes present a much more civilized appearance than most villages, though just as often the distinction between large villages and small towns is barely visible.

Although most townsmen wear Western dress, some townswomen still wear the *çarśaf,* which effectively conceals everything but the eyes.

Nomadic life. Traditionally, much of Anatolia, more especially the east, was peopled by nomads or transhumants, who migrated seasonally between upland and plain. A few of their descendants, herders of sheep and goats, move from plain to mountain, living in tents, while others possess houses in two or even three villages at different altitudes.

RELIGION AND BELIEFS

Central importance of Islām

Islām lay at the centre of the legal, political, and educational structure of the Ottoman Empire, formally defining religious minorities—and, by implication, the unorthodox Muslims—as second-class citizens but ignoring ethnic differences within religious communities. At this imperial level Islām, especially Orthodox Sunnī Islām, was a highly formalistic and demanding religion.

For the orthodox—and even the less orthodox—Islām imposes many duties. Men and women must keep themselves in a state of ritual purity, pray five times a day, fast for a month every year, and strive, if possible, to visit Mecca at least once in a lifetime. Islām provides basic ideas about the nature of morality, sin, and punishment, about relations between men and women, about cleanliness and impurity, and about political submission.

For centuries there has also existed within Islām a tradition of mysticism and holy men and teachers who founded orders explicitly distinct from, even opposed to, orthodox Islām. These orders were often known as dervishes. Some, for example, the Mevlevî (Mawlawīyah) and Bektaşî (Bektāshīyah) orders, were officially accepted and recognized in the Ottoman Empire; others existed at a popular level. Many of them incorporated ideas of love, passion, and salvation. These orders were in varying degrees secret societies, so that members often practiced the outward formalities of orthodoxy and kept their more heterodox beliefs and customs to themselves. The orders were sometimes sects or movements or institutions with urban branches, buildings, and monasteries that people might join; others were rural or tribal communities or parts of such communities.

Traditional beliefs

At the village level, a range of beliefs concerning magic and superhuman powers exists: the evil eye, the ancient belief that certain persons, consciously or unconsciously, can harm or kill with a glance; ritual healing and fortunetelling; and various personal and agricultural rites that are local versions of Islāmic belief and practice. It is, for example, still common to make offerings at the shrines and tombs of local holy men. People, houses, carts, and trucks carry amulets and religious texts to ward off evil, and people suspect each other of various forms of malicious magic, especially of inducing impotence on wedding nights. Pieces of paper with Qur'ānic verses written on them are thought especially potent in the performance of magic.

SOCIAL STRUCTURE

Traditionally, until World War I and after, Anatolian society could be roughly divided into four divisions. At the top were the rich or the rulers, mostly people who lived in or had close connections with the main cities, Istanbul and Izmir, and many of whom were increasingly westernizers and reformers. On the second level were the local townsmen, people who on the whole stayed in the towns—landowners, merchants, craftsmen, and also farmers—all of whom lived within and accepted the main political and legal system.

Third were the villagers, who formed the vast majority, about 80 percent, of the total population. Most villages were small, self-contained settlements, relatively isolated and economically self-sufficient and, to a large extent, autonomous with regard to their own internal political and social affairs. Although some villages or some lands around villages were owned by absentee landlords, most Anatolian villagers owned their own land and produced for their own needs. Generally, their only contacts with the central authorities involved paying taxes to the tax collectors or rents to the absentee landlords (who in turn paid the taxes); the government provided only minimal services in return. The villages that produced export products, such as cotton and tobacco, and thus had a more elaborate economic relation with the cities, were relatively few. In all cases, villagers were primarily concerned with power and prestige in their immediate social environment. The village looked inward.

Rights to land often depended more on the acceptance and recognition of kin and neighbours than on the legal rules of the state; moreover, in any case, landholding was not always very secure and depended on force or political influence. Quarrels over land were normal and permanent features of such a society, often involving violence.

The fourth division of Anatolian society consisted of the pastoralists in the mountainous areas, who were organized tribally, sometimes with powerful chiefs, and who held rights to the territories where they pastured their flocks. These tribes on the whole enjoyed even more political autonomy than the villagers did and were even more isolated from urban society. The large tribal organizations found in other areas of the Middle East, however, apparently did not exist in Anatolia.

This fourfold division is arbitrary. A detailed historical look at one area at one point in time would reveal that there are all kinds of complexities and that, within each of the divisions, there are great differences of power and wealth.

SOCIAL ROLES AND KINSHIP

Male and female roles. Anatolian men in the villages are responsible for the major agricultural work, for looking after the oxen, and for making all contacts outside the home, both official and economic, including shopping. Women—widows, for example—might do men's work, but men never undertake women's tasks. One consequence of this is that men are more dependent on women than women are on men, and a bereaved widower who has no other adult women in his household may remarry within a few days or weeks.

Women in Anatolia, as elsewhere, are concerned with the care of children and their houses and with the preparation and cooking of food. They are also responsible for the milking, for caring for the chickens, for making cakes of winter fuel from dung and straw, for weeding vegetable plots near the village, and for reaping barley and other short-stemmed crops.

The structure of social relationships is in innumerable ways profoundly affected by the sharp social segregation of men and women. Although women can and do exercise power and influence, not least by gossip and the control of reputations, they are seen and accepted by both sexes as inferior at every level, from religious and metaphysical reality to the details of the daily chores.

This segregation is related to attitudes toward sex and sexuality, which people treat as ritually impure and somewhat shameful. Women are measured by rigid standards of purity; sex is a forbidden topic between close kin; and a young couple is forbidden to show any interest in each other if anyone else, even a member of the household, is present. A man leaving on a trip does not say goodbye to his wife publicly, nor does he greet her publicly on his return.

Marriage and family life. Ideally, a traditional household consisted of a man, his wife, his adult sons and their wives, and his young children and grandchildren. On the death of the household head, this large household broke up into as many first-generation households as there were sons, each beginning the process again. The former high death rate among adult men, the lack of living sons, and, very rarely, quarrels between generations made these large households a minority of all households at any one time. Thus, although probably most villagers lived some part of their lives in such a household, most village households at any given time contained only parents and children, with perhaps other random relatives. The average size of a household was probably between five and six persons.

In most areas, household heads are grouped in patrilineal lineages or clans—that is, a group of men descended through males only from a common ancestor, usually a great grandfather, but perhaps an ancestor further back still. Such lineages are concerned primarily with mutual support and defense within the village, and the members often have adjacent houses and lands. In some areas in the past, lineages had wider political importance; and they were more important among tribal peoples.

Marriage is permitted between close kin under the incest rules of Islām. A man has a right to his brother's daughter as a bride for his own son; and this right has often been exercised. Men also sometimes marry their sons to more distant women of their lineages or to women related through marriage. Many marriages, however, involve completely unrelated persons. Whatever the precise arrangement, for societies of this kind marriage is of central importance. From the day of their own marriage every couple starts to consider and prepare for the marriage of their children. Marriage is thought of less in terms of personal choice and compatibility and more in terms of political and economic relationships.

Traditional village weddings involve elaborate ceremonies and last several days. Large transfers of wealth are often involved. Regional variations are considerable, but commonly a man must still make a marriage payment to the father of his son's bride and must also pay for the wedding, the total cost amounting to as much as or more than one year's total income for an average household, without counting the need to provide a new room or house.

Kinship carries strong obligations of mutual support and interest. People look to their kin for day-to-day sociability, for hospitality in other villages, for help in trouble, for cooperation in weddings and funerals, and for aid nowadays in urban migration, in finding jobs, or in getting official favours. Kinship and marriage ties have had important political and economic implications, both at higher levels of power in the towns and in links between towns and villages.

Roles of youth. Birth is surrounded by ceremonies and visits among the women. Very young children in crowded male-dominated households are not allowed to cry, and motherhood in the first months is more or less a fulltime job, day and night. Breast-feeding continues normally to the age of two or even later; weaning is sudden.

Small girls are expected to take charge of younger siblings from a very early age and to cooperate in women's work. After 10 or 11, they are progressively more secluded. Marriage was once thought possible at about 12 or 13 years of age and normal by about 16. No girl without severe handicaps remains single.

Boys have far more freedom in growing up, and from about the age of eight they are expected to pasture animals and take on other farming jobs. By 12 they have learned to plow. Boys are circumcised—often in groups—at any age from about six to 12. The actual operation is performed by recognized professionals, publicly and ceremonially. The fortitude shown by the boys reflects on the family reputation.

Deference to seniority

Seniority is the basic criterion for relationships of superiority and deference. Children are expected to be obedient and submissive, and on all public occasions sons defer to fathers, daughters to mothers and mothers-in-law, and younger siblings to elder siblings. A son, for example, should not smoke or even offer an opinion in his father's presence. The common word for elder brother in Turkish, *ağabey,* is a combination of two words for respected superiors, and the word for elder sister, *abla,* also carries strong overtones of respect. It is true that the villages have no formal age grades and that circumcision, though absolutely necessary for manhood, does not imply any specific admission to a grade. But the traditional deference patterns exclude personal intimacy between fathers and sons and encourage sociability among equals. Thus, informally, men do divide themselves into groups by age.

Marriage also is a rite of passage, since it changes many existing rights and duties, and for each partner it marks the passage from dependent youth to full adult status.

MODERN TRENDS

Social change. Change in Anatolian society has been rapid, complex, and extremely uneven. These changes, like those in many other developing countries, include rapid growth in population, communication, production, size of cities, and administration and education.

A vast increase in jobs available in towns and cities has attracted migrant labour in the form of men who work in urban centres although many still keep their families in the village tilling the land. It has also meant that many village households have uprooted themselves and moved to towns and cities, vastly increasing the urban populations.

At the same time, through political and administrative pressure and increasing efficiency, secularization and modernization have increasingly pervaded the rural areas and small towns. State schools have increased in numbers in the countryside, introducing more national or cosmopolitan ideas. Bureaucracy has introduced registration of births, deaths, and marriages and more complex systems of credit and law. Land disputes are now often settled by official and legal means rather than by local social pressures. Legal divorce has tended to replace socially recognized separation.

The range of social relationships has been widely extended. Village men need no longer deal with the world outside through their village leaders; they can deal themselves with merchants, salesmen, banks, government offices, employers, and fellow workers in the cities. Women, who twenty years ago hardly left the village except to visit neighbouring villages, now regularly visit their close relatives who are living in cities.

Changes in cultural traits. *Religion and beliefs.* Changes in religion in Turkey are controversial. The state is constitutionally secular, but it still controls the religious establishment. During the early republican period up to 1950 no religious teaching was permitted, but modern religious schools and theology faculties were later created, and religious lessons were allowed in state schools. Many courses and groups outside the state system have been set up to teach children religion, and the number of new mosques is large. Thus the deep attachment of the majority to Islām has been demonstrated. The Shīʿī Muslim minority are said to support firm official secularism, largely because they have tended to benefit from the weakening of orthodox institutions; they were never part of the national system, and thus were less directly affected by official secularism. In the long term, a decline in the range of activities influenced by Islām would seem probable, along with a decline in the numbers and devoutness of Muslims. But except for a small elite, the Turkish people remain deeply committed to their identity as Muslims and to an Islāmic world view.

Kinship and marriage. Changes in kinship, family, and marriage seem to stem from economic and demographic changes. Young men can now easily establish economic independence and the very large number of children who now survive creates new problems in large joint households. Far more men with living fathers are heads of independent households, though the proportion of village three-generation households has increased as well. Universal formal education and the possibilities of upward social mobility or migration for work have given young people a different view of the world from that of their fathers, but this generation gap is a recent phenomenon, and significant changes in customary behaviour are slow in developing. In some cases, the ties of kinship between households may be weakened, both by permanent migration and by the increase in other types of social relationships. The new situation, however, also provides new opportunities to exploit kinship ties—especially in finding jobs, in providing short-term hospitality to migrants, and in solving urban housing problems.

The economy

The Turkish economy, oriented to Europe and the Western world, has undergone rapid industrialization since 1950. At the same time, Turkey has close economic links with Iran and Pakistan within the framework of Regional Cooperation for Development (RCD), with other countries in the Middle East, and with eastern Europe.

RESOURCES

Turkey is believed to be rich in a wide variety of mineral deposits, but relatively few of these have been exploited on a large scale because of a lack of domestic capital for exploration and exploitation, political pressures that have discouraged wide-scale investment from abroad, a preponderance of large but inefficient state mining concerns, and inadequate processing facilities.

State enterprises dominate the production of hard coal, lignite, copper, sulfur, mercury, iron ore, lead, salt, and chrome; while private producers are the principal exploiters of asbestos, antimony, barites, boron minerals, zinc, meerschaum, manganese, emery, magnesite, marble, sodium sulfate, dolomite, and other minerals. Crude oil production began on a regular basis in the 1960s. Turkey's hard coal is of poor quality, and only negligible quantities are exported.

AGRICULTURE AND FORESTRY

The livelihood of many comes from agriculture, forestry, and fishing. Cereals, pulses, potatoes, grapes, citrus and soft fruits, olives, nuts, cotton, and tobacco are the major crops. The country's extensive forest lands—predominantly coniferous but also including beech, poplar, walnut, and oak—are almost entirely state owned. Forestry development has been given a high priority but provides only a small percentage of the national income.

INDUSTRY, FINANCE, AND TRADE

The textile industry has traditionally been Turkey's most important and has been considerably modernized. Motor-vehicle production (assembly and parts manufacturing) has grown in importance, along with chemicals, petroleum products, rubber and plastics, and iron and steel products. Other dynamic manufacturing industries include processed foodstuffs, paper, nonferrous metals, domestic appliances, beverages, and cement and building materials.

The Central Bank of the Republic of Turkey, set up in 1931, effectively controls the banking system. It is the only note-issuing bank, is the sole channel for the issue of import licenses (on behalf of the Ministry of Commerce), provides access to foreign currency, and plays a key role in the administration of the government's credit policies. There are several dozen commercial banks, a state-run Agriculture Bank, and a number of special-purpose, state-owned institutions, such as the Sümerbank (concerned with industrial enterprises), the Etibank (mining and electric power), and the Turkish Maritime Bank (Denizçilik Bankası). The main source of new finance for the numerous state enterprises is the State Investments Bank.

Agricultural products account for a majority of Turkish exports. Fruit and vegetables, cotton, and tobacco are among the leading sources of income. Minerals and textile fibres, both natural and synthetic, are also important exports.

ADMINISTRATION OF THE ECONOMY

Turkey's first ventures into industry were made in the 1930s, in the early years of the republic, when the state was of necessity the principal investor. A major portion of the country's economic resources remained state-owned for several decades, although the governments of the 1970s and '80s placed increasing importance on the role of private industry.

The State Planning Organization

The State Planning Organization, set up in 1960, became the arbiter of all foreign investment, as well as of all major Turkish private and state investment. Its five-year plans and annual programs set the guidelines for economic development. Through the Central Bank, the Agriculture Bank, and other state banking institutions, the government maintained a firm hold on all financial and investment operations. The railways, post office, airways, and internal sea passenger services were operated as government enterprises. (E.I.U./Ed.)

TRANSPORTATION

The Turkish Republic began very early to improve the transportation system as a means of integrating isolated regions and of developing the national economy. After World War II more emphasis was placed on road and harbour construction. The result was to give Turkey the best developed road and rail network in the Middle East. The heaviest traffic is between Istanbul and Ankara, followed by that of the Aegean region, with İzmir as its centre, the area around the Gulf of Iskenderun, with Adana as its centre, and the Ankara–Zonguldak route. Istanbul is the chief harbour; there are heavy flows of passengers and freight by sea between İzmir and Istanbul through the Aegean, between the southern coasts of the Sea of Marmara and Istanbul, and between Istanbul and the Black Sea ports of Zonguldak, Samsun, and Trabzon.

The main highways radiate from Ankara, in central Anatolia, from Istanbul and İzmir, in the west, from Adana, in the south, and from Erzurum and Diyarbakır, in the east.

The railroad pattern consists of a ring around the central Anatolian Plateau, from which branches radiate to the peripheral regions: two to Zonguldak and Samsun, on the Black Sea; three to the western ports of Istanbul, İzmir, and Bandırma; three to the east; and one to the south (via Adana to Syria and Iraq).

Turkey's merchant shipping fleet is relatively small. The ports of Istanbul and İzmir handle a major percentage of the country's imports and exports. Other principal ports are Mersin and İskenderun in the south and Zonguldak, Samsun, and Trabzon, in the north; all of these ports are located at the end of rail or land routes serving large hinterlands.

The state-owned Turkish Airlines (Türk Hava Yolları) flies from Ankara to Istanbul, İzmir, Adana, Erzurum, Van, Samsun, and Trabzon. While Ankara is the major junction of the domestic air routes, Istanbul is the busiest airport and the principal terminus of international lines. (S.Er./Ed.)

Administrative and social conditions

GOVERNMENT

Turkey is a republic, with its capital at Ankara. Under the constitution of 1961, political authority was centred in the Grand National Assembly, which had a lower chamber, the National Assembly, composed of 450 elected members, and a Senate made up of 165 members, 150 elected and 15 nominated by the president of the republic. There were also a few senators for life: army officers who carried out the 1960 revolution.

The head of state, the president of the republic, elected by the Grand National Assembly for a term of seven years, selected prime minister, who formed a government subject to approval by the National Assembly.

Under the 1982 constitution, drafted in the aftermath of a military takeover in 1980, Gen. Kenan Evren, head of the military junta, was automatically elected to a seven-year term as president. Provisions for an eventual return to civilian rule included the election of a 400-member, single-chambered parliament; members of the parliament, elected to terms of five years, are in turn to appoint the next president. A president serves for seven years and is not eligible for a second consecutive term. The powers of the president, greatly expanded, include the right to veto constitutional amendments, to call referendums, to dissolve the National Assembly, and to call for new elections. The president also selects judges of the military and civilian Supreme Courts.

The military

Young men are subject to two years of compulsory service at the age of 20. Turkey is a member of the North Atlantic Treaty Organization (NATO); headquarters of the Southeastern Command of NATO is at İzmir.

EDUCATION, HEALTH, AND WELFARE

At the time the Turkish Republic was formed, the population was estimated to be only 10 percent literate. Although the educational system underwent great expansion after World War II, many peasants were reluctant to send their children to school or could not afford to keep them there during planting and harvesting seasons. Religious instruction, forbidden in the early years of the republic, was permitted in primary schools and in the schools training religious personnel.

The Ministry of Health and Social Welfare carried out public health programs and operated a large number of hospitals and dispensaries. Others were run by the Ministry of Labour. State medical services are provided free to the poor. There are also private medical institutions run by philanthropic organizations and large business enterprises.

A basic law concerning labour and social insurance and regulating conditions of employment, passed in 1936, established the 48-hour week with paid holidays of 12 to 24 working days, depending upon length of service. Later legislation provided health and accident insurance and old-age pensions.

Housing conditions

Housing standards in general have been low, and overcrowded conditions in the cities have given rise to shantytowns (*gecekondu*) on the outskirts, put up by peasants migrating from the countryside. The Ministry of Reconstruction and Resettlement was established in 1958 to organize and direct this migration. All of the larger cities contain modern, middle-class residential areas that have expanded at a rapid rate.

The maintenance of internal security is the responsibility of the police, the gendarmerie, and the army. The police are organized on a national basis under the Ministry of the Interior but carry out their duties at the command of local civil authorities. In each province there is a directorate of security, divided into administrative, judicial, and political sections. The gendarmerie is a paramilitary force drawn from military conscripts and assigned to sectors not under police jurisdiction, notably rural frontier areas. It is attached to the Ministry of the Interior and subject to the same local authorities as the police.

Cultural life

Turkey has a long and various cultural heritage. When the Turks arrived in Anatolia in the 11th century they had already adopted Islām, and they soon fell under the influence of the highly developed Iranian and Arab civilizations. Another part of the Turkish inheritance came from the Byzantine civilization that had developed in the Eastern Roman Empire. As the Ottoman Empire expanded into Europe, it received cultural influences from the West, and, when the empire entered on its downward course in the 19th century, the cultural pressure of Europe became stronger. At the same time, European interest in Turkish language, history, and art inspired many educated persons in Turkey with a desire to strengthen and preserve the national culture. Among the most important of the reforms carried out after the national revolution were those aimed at reviving the Turkish language and breaking the hold of Islām upon the nation.

Modern Turkish culture has been dominated by nationalism. Writers, artists, and musicians have abandoned the long tradition of Islām and returned to the vernacular in literature, village scenes in painting, and folk ballads and other traditional forms in music. The theatre has become popular, and innumerable Turkish or foreign plays are performed. The Ankara State Opera was founded in 1940 and the Istanbul Opera in 1950; both perform classical Western works.

The popular arts flourish and are encouraged. Popular literature takes the form of narrative (*hikâye*) and poetry (*siir*), recited by minstrels known as *âşiks*. There are many popular dances and games, varying according to region. Folk instruments include drums, trumpets, flutes, pipes, tambourines, viols, and cymbals, along with some modern instruments. Popular drama includes shadow plays, performed by dolls reflected on a linen screen, and the *orta oyunu,* a type of improvised comedy.

Formal cultural institutions begin with the Ministry of Culture, set up in 1971. Various organizations are devoted to the sciences and arts, including three music conservatories, in Ankara, İzmir, and Istanbul; the Academy of Fine Arts, in Istanbul; the National Folklore Institute, in Ankara; the Turkish Folklore Society, in Istanbul; and a number of scientific and professional societies. Every province has museums of local culture. There are archaeological museums in Ankara, Istanbul, and İzmir and a Museum of Turkish and Islāmic Art in Istanbul. The National Library (Milli Kütüphane) is located in Ankara. (A.Te./Ed.)

HISTORY

Ancient Anatolia

PREHISTORIC CULTURES OF ANATOLIA

The earliest evidence of human occupation in Anatolia is at present confined geographically to a comparatively small area inland from Antalya on the Mediterranean coast. Of special significance are rock engravings of animals on the walls of caves, which suggest a relationship with the Upper Paleolithic art of western Europe. Associated with these are rock shelters, the stratified occupational debris of which may, after further study, finally clarify the transitional phases between cave-dwelling society and the Neolithic economy of the first agricultural communities.

Chronological summary

In the technical terms applied by archaeologists to these and subsequent phases of Middle Eastern prehistory, there is at present a confusing lack of uniformity, but for the present purposes they may be simplified as follows: the first indications of the beginning of the Neolithic Revolution (from food-gathering to food producing) are found in approximately 9000 BC; the two millennia that followed are often termed Proto-Neolithic to distinguish them from the Mesolithic or Terminal Paleolithic that preceded them; the true Neolithic begins in 7000 BC, by which time farming and stockbreeding were well established, and lasts until 5600 BC; the Neolithic is succeeded by the Chalcolithic, during which metal weapons and tools gradually took their place beside their stone prototypes, and painted pottery came generally into use; the Chalcolithic ends in the final centuries of the 4th millennium BC, when the great dynastic civilizations of Egypt and Mesopotamia were already foreshadowed by the invention of writing.

The Neolithic period. It was long understood that the origins of agriculture and stockbreeding should be sought in those areas of the Middle East where the wild ancestors of modern food grains and the natural habitats of domesticable animals were to be found. This line of inquiry pointed to the well-watered uplands around the fringe of the Fertile Crescent: Iraqi Kurdistan, northern Syria, and the Levant. There, indeed, the first discoveries were made of Neolithic farming communities. To the north in Anatolia, they extended to the great coastal plain of Cilicia, connected by easy routes with northern Syria, and to the eastern slopes of the Amanus Mountains. The plateau itself and the western provinces beyond Taurus, however, at first made little contribution to this investigation; and it was long thought that they had remained unoccupied until the beginning of the Chalcolithic period. Knowledge of the Anatolian Neolithic, then, depended for the time being upon sequences of pottery and small artifacts from exiguous soundings at such peripheral sites as Mersin, Tarsus, and Sakcagöz. Since the 1960s, however, the picture has been changed by British-sponsored excavations at two plateau sites: Hacilar, near Lake Burdur, and Çatalhüyük in the Konya Plain. Neither of these dated back as far as the Proto-Neolithic period, of which such striking evidence had been found at Jericho in Jordan. Hacilar, however, showed an earliest occupation of about 7000 BC by a people still unfamiliar with the use of pottery, though living in mud-brick houses with plastered walls and floors, painted and burnished like those in contemporary Jericho. Afterward abandoned for well over a thousand years, Hacilar was reoccupied in the latest phase of the Neolithic by villagers of a far more sophisticated culture. The houses were symmetrically arranged, and a striking collection of seminaturalistic figurines threw new light on Neolithic art and symbolism. The gap between these two widely separated periods was filled by the discovery (1961–63) at Çatalhüyük of a Neolithic settlement covering 32 acres and occupied from the mid-7th to the mid-6th millennium.

Hacilar and Çatalhüyük

The discoveries at Çatalhüyük not only amplified but transformed the whole conception of human behaviour in Neolithic times. In the town, houses were built of sundried brick, closely contiguous like the cells of a honeycomb, but each had several rectangular rooms similarly planned and was accessible only by a wooden ladder from its flat roof. The contiguous roofs provided space for the communal life of the inhabitants. Some of these buildings appear to have been religious shrines, elaborately ornamented with heads or horns of animals, either real or imitated in plaster. The walls were decorated with coloured murals, repeatedly repainted after replastering, and the designs closely resembled the cave paintings of the Paleolithic era. As a source of information about early man's activities, appearance, dress, and even religion, these paintings are of great significance. Other arts and crafts were well attested. Human and animal figurines were carved in stone or modelled in clay. Bone was used for tools and implements, sometimes with finely carved ornamentation. Weapons included polished maces, arrows, and lances with tanged obsidian heads. Impressions of mats and baskets were found, as well as implements used in spinning and weaving. Miraculously, fragments of actual textiles were recovered and preserved. The presence of Mediterranean shells and of metal ores and pigments not locally available suggested extensive trade. Undecorated pottery was in use throughout the life of the settlement, its shapes often imitating those of wooden vessels, examples of which were found intact.

Agriculture evidently formed the main basis of the economy at Çatalhüyük. The site, on a river subject to regular flooding, suggested that irrigation may have been practiced. No proof was found of domesticated animals, but the bones of wild cattle, deer, and boar confirmed the implications of the wall paintings that hunting was still widespread. Generally speaking, nothing suggests that this precocious culture had its origin elsewhere than in Turkey, and the peoples of the Anatolian plateau may well have played a leading part in the Neolithic Revolution.

The Anatolian origin of the Neolithic

The Chalcolithic period. The transition from the Neolithic to the Chalcolithic phase of cultural evolution is thought to have taken place gradually in the mid-6th millennium BC. At most sites where its progress can be traced, no perceptible break occurs in the continuity of occupation, and there is little reason to assume any major ethnographic upheaval. Archaeologically, the most conspicuous innovation is the decoration of pottery with coloured paint, the first clumsy attempts at which can be seen at Mersin. At Hacilar, however, expertise in this craft seems to have been born fully fledged, and the last four occupations of the village (designated Levels V-I) are characterized by some of the most competently and attractively decorated pottery in prehistoric Anatolia. Village architecture at this period is undistinguished, but it provides evidence for the necessity of communal defense. A line of contiguous houses created a peripheral fortification. Their heavy ground-floor chambers had no doorways and were evidently entered by ladders from a more fragile upper story. Metallurgy was beginning to be understood, and copper was used for pins and simple implements. For the later Chalcolithic, additional evidence is available from a deep sounding at Beycesultan, which produced a cache of more sophisticated copper tools and a silver ring, the earliest known use of that metal. For improvements in architecture at this period, however, one must return to Mersin, where one of its latest phases (Level XVI) is represented by a neatly planned and constructed fortress. The steeply revetted slope of the mound was crowned by a continuous defensive wall, pierced by slit windows and entered through a gateway protected by flanking towers. Inside, there was formally arranged accommodation for the garrison and other evidence of military discipline as conceived in 4500 BC.

Thus, in Anatolia, prehistoric man had emerged from the Neolithic having made much progress in social organization. He cultivated crops, herded livestock, lived in brick houses, made vessels of clay, stone, wood, or basketwork, and fashioned weapons of bone or flint. He traded for the raw materials to manufacture his weapons and personal ornaments, and his religious beliefs found expression in sculpture and painting. During the Chalcolithic period few improvements seem to have been made in this standard of living, save for the benefits inherent in the experimental use of metal. The most notable development during these two millennia was the growth and wide diffusion of agricultural societies.

Early Bronze Age. The period following the Chalcolithic in Anatolia is now generally referred to as the Bronze Age. In its earlier phases, the predominant metal was in fact pure copper, but the term Copper Age, at one time in vogue, created confusion and has since been discarded. Archaeological convention divides the Bronze Age into three subphases, early, middle, and late. Its beginning, toward the end of the 4th millennium BC, corresponded in Egypt to the Predynastic period and in Mesopotamia to the Protoliterate. It lasted until late in the 2nd millennium. In its earlier stages it is possible to recognize a number of well-defined cultural provinces, distinguished by slight disparities in their archaeological remains: a northwest province, represented by the excavations at Troy; a central Anatolian province, well-documented by the soundings at Alişar Hüyük, Alaca Hüyük, and elsewhere; an extensive southwestern province, best characterized at Beycesultan; and a Cilician province, represented by Mersin and neighbouring Tarsus. Other, less clearly defined provinces are found in the Konya Plain, connected with Cilicia by the Taurus passes, and in the Pontic area. The combined results of excavations in all of these localities have made possible a further chronological division of the Early Bronze Age alone into three successive phases, numbered from the earliest upward.

Subphases of the Bronze Age

Early Bronze Age I. In the stratigraphical sequence at Troy, for instance, Early Bronze Age I designates the earliest settlement—a small fortress, hardly more than 100 yards in diameter (Troy I). Supplemented by comparable finds at Poliochni and Thermi on the offshore islands of Lemnos and Lesbos, its contents reveal some characteristics of the new culture. Examples are found of houses built along a megaron plan—a rectangular hall with a central hearth and an open porch at one end. The toughening of copper by the admixture of tin was understood, at least in the Aegean and Mediterranean trading centres. The dead were buried in cemeteries outside the walls, often in large clay vessels. Pottery was invariably monochrome, black or red, and usually burnished to a slight shine.

Early Bronze Age II. The citadel at Troy, rebuilt on a more ambitious scale in the second phase of the Early Bronze Age (Troy II), is characterized by a more advanced metal industry and a more active commercial life. There, hoards of jewelry and other luxury objects were found by Heinrich Schliemann beneath the palace and christened by him "Priam's Treasure." Also purporting to have originated in the Troadic province at this period is the Dorak Treasure, of which only drawings are now available. These suggest an even higher standard of craftsmanship and a wider variety of precious materials. Nor was evidence of luxury restricted to the western peninsula. Contemporary with Troy II were the royal tombs discovered in the Early Bronze Age levels beneath the Hittite city at Alaca Hüyük. There, several generations of a ruling family were buried amid their funerary paraphernalia and private possessions. Men were buried with weapons, women with ornaments and toilet articles as well as domestic vessels and utensils, many of them in precious metals. The tombs themselves were rectangular pits enclosed by rough stone walls and roofed with timber. The tombs allotted sufficient space for wooden furniture, of which only the metal trappings and ornaments have survived. All-bronze furniture has since been found in a comparable group of tombs at Horoztepe, near Tokat to the northeast of Alaca Hüyük. The combined inventory of artifacts from these various cemeteries and treasures emphasizes the advances that were made in metallurgy and craftsmanship after the Chalcolithic period. Most of the technical processes later used by the Hittites seem already to have been familiar to the metalsmiths of the Early Bronze II period. They included casting in closed molds (the cire perdue, or lost-wax, process), metal inlay, sweating and soldering, hammering and repoussé, granulation, filigree, and even cloisonné. The metals used included copper, bronze, silver, gold, electrum, lead, and finally iron, which then was far more valuable than gold. All these metals are obtainable in Anatolia, but tin had to be imported. Semiprecious stones and other materials used in association with them included rock crystal, carnelian, jasper, nephrite, obsidian, and meerschaum—all native to Anatolia. Ivory, amber, lapis lazuli, and turquoise were imported.

Royal tombs

The constant warfare among the Anatolian states at this time is emphasized by the number and variety of weapons found—daggers, swords, spears, and battle-axes—and also by examples of military architecture. In Troy itself, the city walls, with their great towered gateway constructed of mud brick in a timber framework on a substructure of dressed stone, seem almost disproportionately substantial to the buildings they protect. The main public building—probably a communal assembly hall—is a vast megaron hall with a roof span of more than 30 feet (nine metres). The presumed residential palace, however, is a much less

Military architecture

pretentious building, and the whole enclosure is hardly 200 yards in diameter, giving the impression of a military fortress rather than a state capital. There are no obviously religious buildings. Such appear in the corresponding levels at Beycesultan, where they took the form of rectangular shrine chambers, arranged in pairs and perhaps dedicated to male and female deities. The ritual installations and accumulation of votive objects suggest an affinity with the tree, or pillar, cults of Crete.

Early Bronze Age III. The third phase of the Early Bronze Age (the final centuries of the 3rd millennium BC) appears to have been a time of major migrations. About 2300 BC a great wave of Indo-European invaders, speaking a Luwian dialect, seems to have swept over Anatolia from the west, occupying practically the whole southwestern part of the peninsula. Their progress was marked by widespread destruction, and for about a century, at sites where remains of this period have been found, there is every indication of a decline in prosperity. The northern and central provinces, however, remained unaffected. About 2200 BC, when contact with the Luwian-dominated southwest was re-established, profitable trade was resumed, particularly with Cilicia and the North Syrian markets beyond. At this point, at the beginning of the Middle Bronze Age, the attention of archaeologists returns to central Anatolia, particularly to the site of Kültepe (Kanesh), whose history was recorded by literate Assyrian colonists. The Assyrians occupied their own suburb outside Kanesh; but in the main city mound itself, Turkish excavations in the pre-*karum* levels have revealed some characteristics of the indigenous Anatolian population in this final phase of the Early Bronze Age. There is some impressive architecture, including a building thought to be a temple, which is planned around a square megaron hall with a huge circular hearth between four wooden columns, so much resembling the central feature of Mycenaean palaces a thousand years later that it is impossible to think of them as unrelated by tradition. For the rest, strange alabaster idols and fine polychrome pottery from Cappadocia seem purely Anatolian contributions, but other types of pottery and small objects suggest trade with Cilicia and even with Mesopotamia.

Indo-European invasion

Middle Bronze Age. The Middle Bronze Age, beginning in the first decades of the 20th century BC, seems to have inaugurated a period of cultural progress and prosperity in the Anatolian cities. Again, the discoveries at Kültepe are invaluable. The merchants from Ashur occupied a walled suburb that had apparently already existed before their arrival. Some scholars have disagreed as to the status of the colony in relation to the indigenous principality, but most are now satisfied that it was based on mutual agreement rather than vassalage. Certainly the foreigners lived on good terms with their Anatolian neighbours, for there was frequent intermarriage. The *karum* must have resembled a sort of chamber of commerce, with authority to fix prices, settle debts, and arrange transport.

The *karum* at Kültepe

The history of the *karum* falls into two periods, divided by some disaster that resulted in the destruction of the suburb by fire, after which it was rebuilt. Because written records were kept, the approximate dates of these two occupations may be calculated by correlating textual references to the names of Assyrian kings whose dates are already known. The Level II occupation, which was the longer and more productive of the two, must have covered the reigns of Erishum, Sargon I, and Puzur-Ashur (*c.* 1950–1850 BC), while Level Ib was contemporary with that of Shamshi-Adad I (*c.* 1813–1781 BC).

A new chronological system, now in use, divides the Middle Bronze Age into four subphases: the first covering the two pre-Assyrian occupations of the Kültepe suburb (Levels III and IV); the second corresponding to Level II; the third lasting until the destruction of the Level Ib *karum* by a fire that ended the colony; and the fourth phase representing the interval between this event and the foundation of the Old Hittite Kingdom.

The successive occupations of the suburb are paralleled in contemporary building levels in the main city mound, where the palaces of local rulers have occasionally produced vitally important cuneiform texts. In addition to writing on clay, Anatolian scribes in the city also adopted the use of the cylinder seal, which they decorated with designs of their own. The elaborate repertory of figurative symbolism used for this purpose has been one of the most revealing aspects of the finds at Kültepe, because it emphasizes the existence of an authentic and indigenous Anatolian culture persisting through the vicissitudes of migration and political change. A fully developed Anatolian iconography persisted into later centuries, reappearing almost unchanged in the art of the Hittites.

Anatolian iconography

THE RISE AND FALL OF THE HITTITES

The Hittite occupation of Anatolia. The first suggestion of the Hittites' presence in central Anatolia during the Middle Bronze Age is the occurrence in the Kültepe tablets of Indo-European personal names among pre-Indo-European texts. Pre-Indo-European languages then current

Anatolian languages

Adapted from S. Lloyd, *Early Highland Peoples of Anatolia* (1967); Thames and Hudson

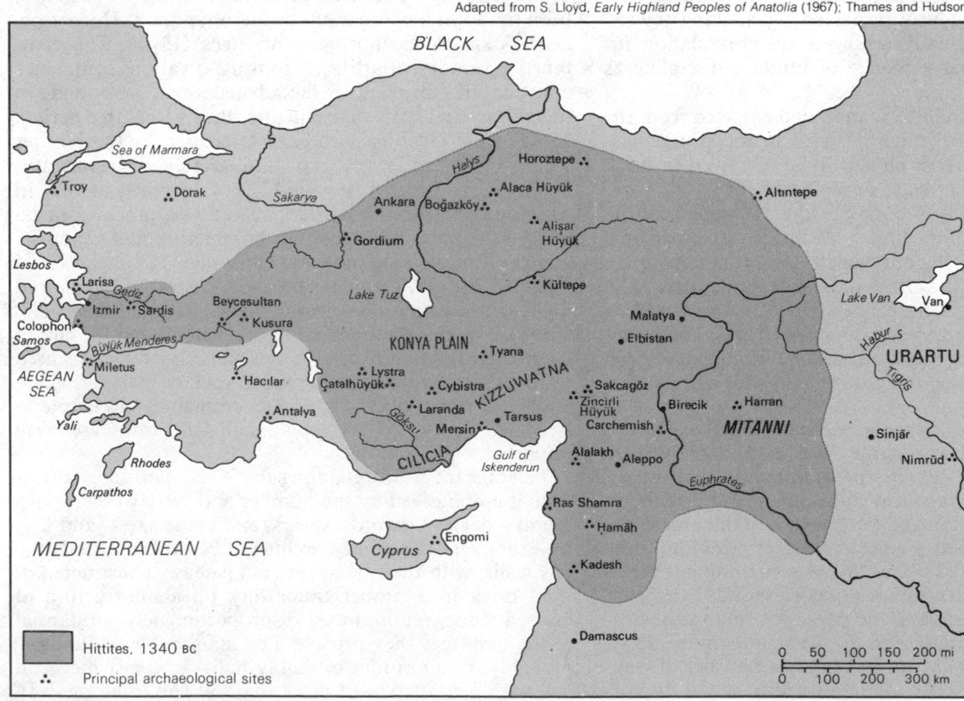

Principal archaeological sites of Anatolia and northern Syria to *c.* 1340 BC.

in Anatolia included Akkadian (Babylonian), the language of diplomacy in the Middle East, and the local dialects of the indigenous central Anatolian language now known as Hattic (Khattian, Khattic, or Hattian). The Indo-European name Kaneshite for the official language, now called Hittite, is a term literally meaning "the language of the town of Nesha" (= Kanesh, Kültepe). Besides Kaneshite, two other Indo-European dialects were found in Anatolia: Luwian (Luvian), spoken by immigrants into southwest Anatolia late in the Early Bronze Age and written with the pictographs commonly called Hittite hieroglyphs; and the more obscure Palaic, spoken in the northern district known in classical times as Paphlagonia.

The first knowledge of the Hittites, then, depends upon the appearance of typically Kaneshite names among the predominant Assyrian language of the texts. The problem of the origin of the Hittites has been the subject of some controversy and has not yet been positively solved. On linguistic grounds, some scholars were at first disposed to bring them from the west of the Black Sea, but it has been shown that this theory conflicts with much archaeological evidence. One authority argues for their arrival in Anatolia from the northeast, basing his theory on the burning or desertion during the 20th century BC of a line of settlements representing the approaches to Cappadocia from that direction. The evidence from the Halys cities and Cappadocia, however, does not support this picture of an invading army, destroying settlements in its path and evicting their inhabitants. The impression is rather one of peaceful penetration, leading by degrees to a monopoly of political power. From their first appearance among the indigenous Anatolians, the Hittites seem to have mingled freely, while the more flexible Neshian language gradually replaced Hattic.

More tangible evidence of the political events leading up to the foundation of the Hittite Kingdom is provided by the Hittites' own historical tradition recorded by them in later times. Only a few of the tablets of the Hittite archives found at Boğazköy can be dated earlier than the 17th century BC; nevertheless, certain historical texts of this period have survived in the form of more or less reliable copies made in the 14th or 13th centuries. One of these concerns two half-legendary kings of Kussara (Kushshar) named Pitkhanas and Anittas, whom the Hittites apparently associated with their heredity. The city called Kussara has yet to be identified, but the text gives an impressive list of cities that Pitkhanas had conquered, and among them appears the name of Nesha (Kanesh), which his son, Anittas, subsequently adopted as his capital. Also included in the list is Hattusa (Khattusha), known to be the ancient name of the later Hittite capital at Boğazköy, which Anittas was said to have destroyed. The fact that no direct connection could be inferred between these two kings and the subsequent history of the Hittites has been explained by later archaeological discoveries, which have shown them not only to have been authentic historical persons but native Anatolian (Hattian) rulers, whom the Hittites replaced at the end of the 18th century BC.

Kings of Kussara

The Old Hittite Kingdom. The two main periods of Hittite history are customarily referred to as the Old Kingdom (*c.* 1700–*c.* 1500 BC) and the New Kingdom, or Empire (*c.* 1400–*c.* 1180). The less well-documented interlude of about a hundred years is sometimes referred to as the Middle Kingdom. Among the texts from Boğazköy, preserved or recopied by the imperial archivists, those relating to the Old Kingdom are comparatively few. For many years historians of that period relied for the most part on a single remarkable document: the constitutional Edict of Telipinus, one of its last kings. In contrasting the prosperity of the nation under his earliest predecessors with the decadence into which it had fallen at the time of his own accession, Telipinus provides a useful though not always reliable summary of early Hittite history:

Edict of Telipinus

> Formerly Labarnas was Great King; and then his sons, his brothers, his connections by marriage, his blood-relations and his soldiers were united. And the country was small; but wherever he marched to battle, he subdued the countries of his enemies by night. He destroyed the countries and made them powerless [?] and he made the sea their frontier. And when he returned from battle, his sons went each to every part of the country, to Hupisna, to Tuwanuwa, to Nenassa, to Landa, to Zallara, to Parsuhanda and to Lusna, and governed the country, and the great cities were firmly in his possession [?]. Afterward Hattusilis became King . . . .

One would infer from this that the Hittites regarded their own history as beginning with a king called Labarnas (Labarnash); this inference is confirmed by the use in later times of his name and that of his wife Tawannannas as dynastic titles or throne names of subsequent rulers. A difficulty arises, however, because nothing else is known about this king, nor is it certain that he was the first of his line. The earliest contemporary texts date from the reign of his son Hattusilis (Khattushilish; mentioned by Telipinus), and the most important of them is a bilingual inscription in Hittite and Akkadian found in 1957. In the Akkadian version, his name is given as Labarnas, and it is implied that he is in fact the nephew of Tawannannas. In Hittite he becomes Hattusilis and is given the double title "King of Hattusa" and "Man of Kussara." This circumstance has given rise to the supposition that, whereas the original seat of his dynasty was at Kussara, at some time during his reign he transferred his capital to Hattusa (long ago destroyed by Anittas) and thus adopted the name Hattusilis.

The geographical identity of place-names in Hittite historical texts has always been a subject of controversy, but some of those mentioned in the Edict of Telipinus are known: Tuwanuwa (classical Tyana, near modern Bor); Landa (Laranda; modern Karaman); Hupisna (classical Cybistra); and Lusna (the Lystra of St. Paul's journeys). These and others are all located in the territory to the south of the Halys called by the Hittites the Lower Land, suggesting the first extension of the Hittite Kingdom from its restricted homeland in the bend of the Halys followed hard upon the establishment of the new capital at Boğazköy. The extent and direction of this expansion may have been unforeseen when the site was chosen. As a mountain stronghold dominating the northeastern corner of the plateau, Boğazköy may at the time have had much to recommend it; but later conquests left it on the periphery of the kingdom, and its security was consequently diminished. This possibility is reflected in the bilingual text, which gives a detailed account of events of six successive years of Hattusilis' reign.

Capital moved to Boğazköy

In the account of the first year's campaign, the obscure place-names give no more than a general impression of a localized operation, perhaps in Cappadocia. In the second year's records, however, the extent of Hittite conquests is more impressive, and there is some justification for Hattusilis' claim to have "made the sea his frontier." In fact, the very first place-name mentioned places Hattusilis beyond the Taurus passes in the plains of northern Syria. Alalkha can hardly be other than Alalakh, near Antioch, the ruins of which were excavated by the British archaeologist Sir Leonard Woolley from 1937–1949. The priority given to this town would suggest an approach to Syria through Cilicia and by the Belen Pass over the Amanus Mountains. Two other cities, Igakalis and Taskhiniya, remain unidentified, but Urshu, which Hattusilis destroyed and looted on his return journey, is known to have been located on the Euphrates above Carchemish. Rather curious in this account is the absence of any reference to the important city of Yamhad (modern Aleppo), of which the vassal state, Alalakh, may temporarily have been independent. For the rest of Hattusilis' reign, Aleppo apparently remained the principal power in North Syria, to whose armies and allies his own troops were to find themselves repeatedly opposed.

The third year's record introduces the names of two states later to play an important role in Hittite history. The first of these was Arzawa, a powerful kingdom with extensive territory in the southwest part of the peninsula, against which Hattusilis now organized a campaign. In doing so, he left unprotected his possessions in the south and southeast, and they were promptly annexed by the Hurrians, a people who now enter Anatolian history for the first time. During the preceding century, when the power of Assyria was temporarily in eclipse, the Hurrians had infiltrated

The Hurrians

into northern Mesopotamia and Syria from the east and soon constituted an important element in the population of both territories. On this occasion, having abandoned his attack on Arzawa, Hattusilis seems to have pressed them back and recovered his losses, but he spent the next two years in re-establishing his frontiers. In the sixth and last year of his recorded activities, he found himself once more opposed to the Hurrian armies in North Syria, this time supported by troops from Aleppo. His feud with Aleppo was never decided in his lifetime, for it is known from other sources that he returned, badly wounded, to his old residence at Kussara, anxious to appoint a successor who might continue the struggle. In this endeavour he was at first singularly unsuccessful, for three of his sons in succession proved unreliable to the point of treason; one of the most remarkable and humanly revealing documents of the period is a long and bitter lament in which he chided them for their infidelity and ingratitude. This text is, incidentally, one of the first examples of the Hittite language written in cuneiform, and it is thought that Babylonian scribes had been imported into the capital for the purpose of devising a formula by which this could be done.

Hattusilis eventually adopted his grandson Mursilis (Murshilish) as his successor, and he proved a wise choice. His first concern was to "avenge his father's blood" by settling accounts with Aleppo, which he destroyed after conclusively defeating the Hurrian armies. Following this victory, he launched an extraordinary expedition against Babylon and, according to Telipinus, destroyed the city. The fact that his army was able to advance almost 500 miles down the Euphrates and overcome the defenses of the Mesopotamian capital is one that historians have found it difficult to explain. His occupation of the city seems to have been extremely brief, because it was not the Hittites but the Kassites who afterward assumed control of the country and founded a dynasty in Babylonia. The Kassites had penetrated northern Mesopotamia from the east, on the heels of the Hurrians. It is by no means improbable that Mursilis had welcomed them as allies, and at least one authority suspects that the attack on Babylon may have been made possible by their support. Because it must have taken place just before or just after the death of Samsuditana, the last king of the 1st dynasty of Babylon, the event can be dated to 1595 BC. This date also may well have corresponded to the death of Mursilis, for, having returned to his own capital laden with booty, a conspiracy among his relatives resulted in his assassination. The succession of his brother-in-law Hantilis (Khantilish) marked the beginning of the catastrophic period referred to in the Edict of Telipinus, during which the Hittite Kingdom came near the verge of extinction.

Campaign against Babylon

A major disaster during this period, which eclipsed other military failures, was the conquest of Cilicia by the Hurrians. This great coastal plain to the south of the Taurus Mountains, hitherto described as the "land of Adaniya" (Adana), then acquired the name Kizzuwatna and became the seat of a Hurrian (Indo-Aryan) dynasty. The cities of North Syria were thus rendered inaccessible to the Hittite armies, except through the Antitaurus passes, and remained so until imperial times. When Telepinus himself approached the task of establishing defensible frontiers, he found it necessary to conclude a treaty with a king of Kizzuwatna named Isputakhsus, and he was also compelled to renounce his claims on the neighbouring country of Arzawa.

Of equal interest in the Edict of Telipinus is his program of political reforms. Citing examples of the political evils that had resulted in the past from aristocratic disunity at the death of a monarch, he laid down a precise law of succession, specifying an exact order of precedence to be observed in the selection of a new ruler. He further prescribed that in future

> the nobles must again stand united in loyalty to the throne, and if they are dissatisfied with the conduct of the king or of one of his sons, they must have recourse to legal means of redress and refrain from taking the law into their own hands by murder. The supreme court for punishment of wrongdoers must be the "pankus" or whole body of citizens.

The meaning of the word *pankus* (*pankush*) has been much discussed, for it has been taken to mean a general assembly in the democratic sense, composed of the fighting men and servants of the king. Because it is known to have been an essentially Indo-European concept and did not survive into imperial times, it has been thought to show that at this period the Indo-European aristocracy had not yet merged, as it did later, with the native Hattian population. There is in fact little other evidence to support this suggestion, and in the inscriptions no specific term or epithet is ever used to distinguish the non-Hittite indigenous population.

Hittite general assembly

The Middle Kingdom. Telipinus is ordinarily regarded as the last king of the Old Kingdom. His death marks the beginning of a more obscure period that lasted until the creation of the Hittite Empire. The Syrian provinces, which Telipinus had been compelled to abandon, fell for the time being into the hands of the Hanigalbat, one of the political units into which the Hurrians had become organized. The Hanigalbat, in turn, surrendered them to Egypt, after the successful eighth campaign of Thutmose III. This war also seems to be the first occasion on which the Hittites found themselves in alliance with Egypt, for it afforded an opportunity for them to attack Aleppo, which they once more managed to capture and destroy. The Hittite indebtedness to Egypt for their help may be inferred from an agreement between the two states, in 1471 BC, by which a Hittite king—presumably Zidantas or Huzziyas—paid tribute to the pharaoh in return for certain frontier adjustments. From 1471 to 1450 BC Syria was more or less dominated by Thutmose III, but this situation did not long survive his death. During these last years of his reign, the national unity of the Hurrians seems to have been revived by the imposition of an alien aristocracy and the foundation of a new Aryan dynasty. The Hittites now found themselves confronted on their southern boundaries by a powerful state, known from this time onward as Mitanni. Early in the reign of Amenhotep III, the Mitannians were able to recover Syria and establish their authority over Kizzuwatna. The profound penetration of Hittite civilization by Hurrian ideas, which became pronounced in later times, can be said to have been initiated at this period. For the moment, the situation was politically disastrous for the Hittite Kingdom, for a firm alliance was concluded between Mitanni and Egypt. This was sealed by a royal marriage between a daughter of the Mitannian king, Artatama, and the young Egyptian king, Thutmose IV. By the time of Tudhaliyas III, the formation of this alliance had encouraged a general revolt in all the Hittite provinces.

Mitannians

The Hittite Empire to c. 1180 BC. The Hittite king Suppiluliumas (Shuppiluliumash, Subbiluliuma) dominates the history of the Middle East for the greater part of four decades. He was the son of Tudhaliyas (Tudkhaliash) III, in whose company he had gained military experience before ascending the throne. He spent the first few years of his reign in consolidating the Hittite homeland and in improving the defenses of his capital, Hattusa. It may have been at this time that the greatly extended circuit of city walls was built, enclosing an area of more than 300 acres (120 hectares). He then applied himself to the task of settling accounts with Mitanni, the principal enemy of his immediate predecessors. After an abortive attempt to approach Syria by the conventional route through the Taurus passes and Kizzuwatna, Suppiluliumas next attempted a more carefully prepared attack from the rear by way of Malatya and the Euphrates Valley. Coming from this direction, he met little resistance and was able to enter and sack the Mitannian capital, Wassukkani (Washshuganni; not yet located). West of the Euphrates, most of the North Syrian cities hastened to offer their submission. The King of Kadesh put up some resistance but was defeated; and the Hittite armies penetrated southward almost to Damascus *c.* 1370 BC. The wholesale subjugation of the Mitannian kingdom seems on this occasion to have been a matter of indifference to its Egyptian allies, who, under the apostate pharaoh Akhenaton, had temporarily lost interest in imperial defense. Texts have survived of treaties made after this brilliant expedition that show, for instance, that Nuhassi (central Syria) and Amurru (including most

Conquest of Syria

of what is now Lebanon) and such cities as Aleppo and Alalakh then became part of the Hittite dominions. It is not easy to understand why Carchemish, which controlled the Euphrates crossings, was allowed to retain its independence and Wassukkani, somewhere to the east on the headwaters of the al-Khābūr River, to remain untenanted.

Suppiluliumas then returned to his capital, leaving his son Telipinus, "the Priest," to arrange the defense of the Syrian provinces. His task may have been complicated by a new situation that had arisen in the remnants of the Mitannian state. The Mitannian king, Tushratta, was assassinated, and his successor, King Artatama, unwilling to place any further reliance on Egypt, turned to Assyria for an alliance against the Hittites. Meanwhile, in 1340 BC, Suppiluliumas returned to complete his conquest of Syria, capturing Carchemish after an eight-day siege. Telipinus now became king of Aleppo and his brother, Piyasilis (Piyashilish), king of Carchemish. It remained only for Suppiluliumas to obtain control over the old Mitannian capital at Wassukkani; this he did, installing a son of the murdered Tushratta as vassal ruler of a buffer state between himself and the Assyrians.

During this last campaign an incident occurred that illustrates the elevated status then accorded the Hittite king as a result of his conquests. While he was encamped before Carchemish, a messenger arrived from Ankhesenamen (Ankhesenpaaten), the queen of Egypt, with a proposal that he should send one of his sons to become her husband. Suppiluliumas agreed to her request and sent her one of his sons, but, as it proved, he arrived too late; by the time he reached Egypt the Queen had been compelled to marry the ambitious courtier-priest Ay, who thus legitimized his usurpation of the throne. The son was murdered—an outrage that was never avenged, for shortly afterward Suppiluliumas himself died of a pestilence. His eldest son and successor, Arnuwandas (Arnuwandash) III, also died, and the throne descended to the young and inexperienced Mursilis II.

The first Hittite misfortune after the accession of Mursilis II was the loss of the small vassal kingdom based on Wassukkani, the last remnant of the once-powerful Mitannian state. It was invaded and occupied by the Assyrians under Ashur-uballit I, who thus was able to establish a frontier with Syria on the Euphrates. Carchemish and Aleppo, however, remained loyal to the Hittites, enabling Mursilis to face a new threat from the direction of his possessions in southwest Anatolia. Arzawa, with its satellites Mira, Kuwaliya, Hapalla, and the "Land of the River Seha," rose in revolt. A detailed account survives of the two-year campaign in which young Mursilis suppressed this insurrection, killing the Arzawan king and installing Hittite governors as rulers of the several kingdoms. Meanwhile, a threat from the north proved more difficult. The Kaska (Kashku) folk, who inhabited the remote mountain valleys between the Hittite homeland and the Black Sea, seem to have been continually in revolt. Their tribal organization and guerrilla tactics prevented the Hittites from conclusive conquest of the country despite Hittite yearly campaigns. Unrest in Kaska country seems also to have affected the rather nebulous state of Azzi-Hayasa, a client kingdom farther to the east on the upper Lycus River. Suppiluliumas had suffered a good deal of trouble from these people early in his reign, and, in the seventh year of Mursilis' reign they again revolted. The King, who was attending to his religious duties at Kummanni (Comana), entrusted their pacification to one of his generals. While the King was at Kummanni, he was joined by his brother, Shar-Kushukh, king of Carchemish, who was taken ill and died; his death sparked off a revolt in Syria. Fortunately, this was for the moment unsupported by Egypt or Assyria, and the appearance of the King himself at the head of his imperial army proved sufficient to suppress it. Mursilis reigned for 28 years (1334–1306) and bequeathed to his successor, Muwatallis, a substantial empire, securely surrounded by dependent states.

Anatolian revolts

Early in the reign of Muwatallis (Muwatallish), it became clear that Egypt, under its 19th-dynasty kings, was beginning to recover its imperialist ambitions. Seti I led his army into Canaan to restore the system of colonial administration relinquished in the time of Akhenaton and advanced as far as Kadesh on the Orontes. A confrontation between the two powers was avoided until the end of his reign. On the accession of Ramses II in 1304 BC, however, a clash between them became imminent, and Muwatallis enlisted the support of his allies. (The Hittite records at this time are fragmentary, but Egyptian scribes mention for the first time the Dardanians, familiar from Homer's *Iliad,* and the Philistines.) The Hittite and Egyptian armies met at Kadesh, and the battle that followed is one of the first in history of which tactical description has survived. The Hittite specialist O.R. Gurney summarizes the Egyptian text as follows:

Revival of Egypt

> The Hittite army based on Kadesh succeeded in completely concealing its position from the Egyptian scouts; and as the unsuspecting Egyptians advanced in marching order towards the city and started to pitch their camp, a strong detachment of Hittite chariotry passed round unnoticed behind the city, crossed the river Orontes, and fell upon the centre of the Egyptian column with shattering force. The Egyptian army would have been annihilated, had not a detached Egyptian regiment arrived most opportunely from another direction and caught the Hittites unawares as they were pillaging the camp. This lucky chance enabled the Egyptian king to save the remainder of his forces and to represent the battle as a great victory. (From O.R. Gurney, *The Hittites,* Penguin Books, 1952.)

Muwatallis subsequently advanced as far south as Damascus, and the Hittites maintained their ascendancy in Syria. The King then found it necessary to transfer his residence to Dattassa, a city somewhere in the Taurus area, and he assigned the government of his northern provinces to his brother Hattusilis. When Muwatallis died and was succeeded by his son, Urhi-Teshub (Urkhi-Teshub), the boy's uncle became a rival to the throne and, after a seven-year quarrel, was able to displace him forcibly and exiled him to Syria.

The accession of Hattusilis III in 1275 BC inaugurated a period of comparative peace and prosperity. Relations steadily improved between the Hittites and Egypt, perhaps as a result of their mutual interest in protecting themselves against Assyria. In 1269 Hattusilis negotiated a famous treaty with Ramses II, assuring the peace and security of the Levant state. Some years later, a further bond was created by the marriage of his daughter to the pharaoh. This girl's mother was Puduhepa (Pudu-Kheba), the daughter of a Kizzuwadnian priest whom Hattusilis had married 29 years previously. Puduhepa was evidently a woman of strong character who ably supported her husband. Together they reoccupied and rebuilt the old capital city at Hattusa, ordered the recopying of the national archives, and instituted a variety of constitutional reforms. Among the many surviving texts from this reign, one appears to be the King's personal apologia justifying his seizure of the throne and his displacement of Urhi-Teshub, the legitimate heir.

Puduhepa

After the death of Hattusilis, his son, Tudhaliyas (Tudkhaliash) IV, extended his father's system of reforms to include the structure and institutions of the Hittite state religion. In this he was much influenced by his mother, Puduhepa, who, surviving her husband, became coregent with Tudhaliyas. His reign was otherwise comparatively uneventful. In foreign relations the records do introduce two names of states hitherto barely mentioned: Assuwa, later corresponding to the Roman Province of Asia; and Ahhiyawa, a large and formidable country, the identity and geographical location of which have been the subject of a prolonged controversy. Some scholars identify the Ahhiyawans with the Achaeans of Homer, or at least with some subdivision of the Mycenaean world, while others place the country on the Anatolian mainland to the north of Assuwa, making the Ahhiyawans ancestors of the Trojans. There is no doubt, however, that a king of Ahhiyawa at this time interfered in the western Hittite dependencies and that Arnuwandas III, who succeeded Tudhaliyas, consequently found it necessary to reconquer Arzawa.

These final episodes in the saga of Hittite history are difficult to reconstruct; the Phrygian invasion of Asia Minor must already have started, and throughout the Near East a mass movement of peoples had begun that was destined

Phrygian invasion

not only to destroy the Hittite Empire but to sweep the Hittites out of their homeland on the Anatolian plateau and into Syria. (S.H.F.L.)

Hittite sculpture and architecture. The finest Hittite monuments date from the imperial period. The capital city, strategically placed astride a rocky gorge, has an inner enclosure, rising up to a high citadel rock (Büyükkale). Greatly extended in imperial times, the outer city has a four-mile circuit of powerful fortifications. The double walls, with their defensive towers and substructure of cyclopean masonry (large irregular blocks without mortar), stand upon a stone-faced rampart of earth, itself protected by a stone apron wall. The corbelled arches of its gates are flanked by portal sculptures—lions or sphinxes—anticipating those of the Late Assyrian palaces. Carved on the stone doorjamb of one arch is a famous relief of a warrior wearing the characteristically Hittite short kilt and conical helmet.

Elsewhere in the city there are four buildings recognizable as temples, the largest of which has been fully excavated. It is a huge building, surrounded by ranges of store chambers, planned around a wide courtyard with pillared colonnades and a small freestanding shrine in one corner. These features and the isolated position of the main sanctuary have no parallel in the temples of Mesopotamia or Syria.

Modern knowledge of Hittite sculpture is derived, first, from the portal sculptures of Hattusas itself, and, second, from rock sculptures, including those decorating the remarkable shrine called Yazılıkaya, some distance outside the town. Here, deep clefts in the limestone, open to the sky, form a setting for the cult; the reliefs are carved on the vertical faces of the rock. One of the recesses, or chambers, is decorated with a pageant of deities, some standing on their appropriate cult animal or identified by a hieroglyph inscription. These figures are carved with only average proficiency, and some of the iconography is borrowed from the Hurrians, with whom the Hittite royal family had intermarried. The figures in the second, or inner, sanctuary, however, are carved with an artistry inspired by religious fervor. The figure of a young king (Tudhaliyas IV) in the protective embrace of a god is hardly less impressive than the symbolism of a huge dagger thrust into the rock before him. The rock reliefs of this period elsewhere in Anatolia—Sirkeli, Gâvur Kalesi, and Fraktin, for example—are mainly of archaeological interest. They are inferior in carving to contemporary reliefs and to those of the Iron Age, of which there is a fine example at İvriz Harabesi in the Taurus Mountains, showing a local ruler of the 8th century BC paying homage to a fertility god.

Syro-Hittite period

Monuments such as that at İvriz Harabesi represent a curious aftermath of Hittite history. Although the empire was destroyed and the Hittites driven from their homeland on the Anatolian plateau by the Phrygians, in the 10th–8th centuries they reappear as part occupants of small city-states such as Malatya Samal (Zincirli Hüyük), and Carchemish, in the Taurus or north Syria, where they shared political authority with indigenous Aramaeans and other peoples. During this Syro-Hittite period their art and architecture was of a hybrid and rather inferior character, much influenced by Assyria, to which the Hittites frequently became subject, and also by Phoenicia and Egypt. Conspicuous in their buildings are the sculptured orthostats that line the bases of the walls, often of coarse, black basalt awkwardly alternating with white limestone. Columns are of wood, with bases and capitals of stone, and monolithic statues, more than life-size, are a common feature. Fortifications are still an important aspect of their cities. Those at Zincirli Hüyük enclose a circular town, a half mile in diameter, with a high-walled citadel in the centre, containing a complex of palaces. Like all Syrian palaces, these incorporate one or more *bit hilani* units, consisting of a columned portico, a long reception room, with an adjoining staircase to the roof, and a varying number of retiring rooms. A striking example of these *bit hilani* is the Kaparu Palace at Tall Ḥalaf, near the source of the Khābūr River. The almost barbaric array of sculpture shows the city to have been predominantly Aramaean.

ANATOLIA FROM THE END OF THE HITTITE EMPIRE TO THE ACHAEMENIAN PERIOD

With the end of the Hittite Empire, Anatolia and the whole of the ancient Middle East were severely shaken. Migratory groups of the Sea Peoples moving along the south coast of Anatolia and the seashore of Syria and Palestine caused great havoc and upheaval. The Sea Peoples followed the ancient trade route between the Greek Mycenaean world and the coastal cities of Syria, the commercial centres of the Middle East. The geographical characteristics of Anatolia facilitate the west–east connection, while the mountain ranges along the northern Black Sea coast and the southern Mediterranean hamper the traffic between north and south.

Anatolia has rightly been characterized as a bridge connecting the Greek world in the West with the great empires of the East. When in the course of a migration new groups passed over this bridge, part of them frequently remained and settled, as had been the case when the Hittites had entered Anatolia. The same happened to the Phrygians, either in connection with or after the fall of the Hittite Empire. The newcomers of the 12th century readily adapted themselves to an existing cultural pattern, and the geography of the country gave rise to the growth of a great number of small local powers and petty chieftains.

Political divisions after the fall of the Hittite Empire

Written records are few for the 12th through the 10th centuries, and the picture is not always clear; but the political divisions that emerged in Anatolia after the breakup of the Hittite Empire were roughly the following: A number of Greek city-states were established on the western (Aegean) coast, among them Miletus, Priene, and Ephesus. The southern part of this area became known as Ionia, the northern part as Aeolis. The early history of these cities is known mainly from archaeological finds and from scattered remarks in the writings of later Greek historians. Most of western and central Anatolia was occupied by the Phrygians. In the northeast were the Kaska, a people who had probably participated in the dismemberment of the Hittite Empire. In the southeast were the Luwians, who were related culturally and ethnically to the Hittites. They were organized in a number of small neo-Hittite states (including Carchemish, Malatya, Tabal, and Que) that extended into northern Syria. For the eastern region, archaeological evidence is supplemented by Assyrian texts and by neo-Hittite hieroglyphic inscriptions.

Phrygia from c. 1180 to 700 BC. The early Phrygians were probably not organized in one strong and centrally governed kingdom. Their origins and the affiliations of their language are still enshrouded in mystery. Greek tradition—and this is still in many cases the best source available—usually dates their migration into Anatolia from Europe around the period of the Trojan War (the early 12th century BC), and the Greeks were convinced that the Phrygians came from Macedonia and Thrace. It is possible, therefore, that the Phrygian language was related to Thracian or Illyrian. From the middle of the 8th century

Adapted from *Westermann Grosser Atlas zur Weltgeschichte*, Georg Westermann Verlag, Braunschweig

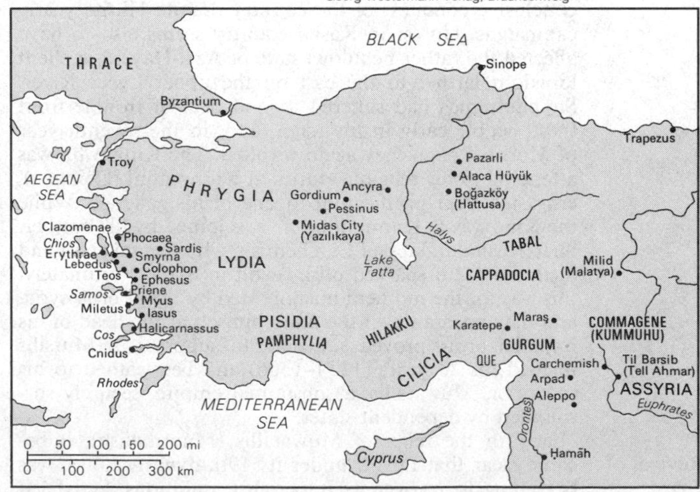

Anatolia and northern Syria, *c.* 1180 BC to the 6th century BC.

BC, the Phrygians are undoubtedly to be identified with the people called Mushki by the Assyrians, though it seems possible that the Assyrians had earlier used this name as a collective label for their northeastern neighbours. The area occupied by the Phrygians in this early period (12th and 11th centuries BC) is uncertain; many authorities believe they were confined to the area west of the Halys (Kızıl) River. Parts of the former Hittite capital, Boğazköy, were reoccupied well before 1000 BC. The new settlement was an open, unfortified collection of small, often one-room, houses. The occupants were apparently dissociated from and unaware of the great Hittite past, but it is not certain that they were Phrygians.

Areas of Phrygian settlement

By the 9th and 8th centuries, the Phrygians had formed a centrally organized kingdom in the west with its centres at Gordium and Midas City. Their three main areas of settlement were the hilly country between modern Eskişehir and Afyonkarahisar, the central regions around their capital, Gordium, and the region around Ancyra (modern Ankara), where Phrygian tombs and architectural remains of the 8th to the 6th centuries have been found. Such farther east settlements as Alaca Hüyük, Boğazköy-Hattusa, and Pazarlı temporarily belonged to the Phrygian sphere of influence. Alişar Hüyük and Çalapverdi were in a kind of no-man's-land between the Phrygians and their Luwian neighbours to the east. The Kaska had by this time probably penetrated into the region between the Halys and the upper Euphrates River. At the time of its zenith in the 8th and 9th centuries, the Phrygian kingdom comprised so large a part of Anatolia that geographically it could well be characterized as the political heir to the Hittite Empire. The invasion of the Cimmerians from beyond the Caucasus at the beginning of the 7th century BC prevented the full realization of this possibility. The American excavations in Gordium itself and in the neighbouring burial tumuli have provided evidence of the great wealth of the Phrygian rulers, reflected in the Greek legends about the Phrygian king Midas. For a later phase of Phrygian culture, the French excavations in Midas City are of prime importance.

Conflicts with Assyria

Phrygia's relations with Assyria are attested to by Assyrian documents. A letter of the late 8th century indicates collaboration between the two powers on an equal basis. Assyro-Phrygian relations, however, were not always friendly; between 715 and 709 BC the Assyrian provincial governor of Que (Cilicia) twice fought thc Phrygians before he was finally successful in 709. Before that King Sargon II (721–705 BC) himself had undertaken a campaign against them in 715. Between 718 and 709, a number of East Anatolian and North Syrian Luwian princes sought help from Phrygia in a vain attempt to protect themselves from Assyrian expansionism. The Luwian states, however, were one by one defeated and turned into Assyrian dependencies (see below *The neo-Hittite states*). In 709 King Midas himself sent an embassy to Sargon offering submission. During the reign of Sargon's successor, Sennacherib (704–681), the Cimmerians swept through Anatolia, bringing an end to the existence of Phrygia as a major political power. Tradition has it that Midas committed suicide when this happened, and some archaeologists have tried to identify a royal tomb excavated at Gordium as that of the legendary king. Evidences of the Cimmerian destruction of the city are unmistakable. After *c.* 690 the site was abandoned; late in the 7th or early in the 6th century BC it was reinhabited and a new city was built. This late Gordium functioned as the centre of a provincial district, limited probably to the upper valley of the Sangarius River.

Excavations at Gordium have shown that the building and fortification techniques of the Phrygians had reached a high level of perfection; the same is true of their woodcutting, metalwork, and ivory carving. The excellence of Phrygian textiles is known from ancient writings. Caldrons with bullhead attachments found at Gordium show the influence of Urartian craftsmanship, but the differences are significant enough to indicate an independent local school of bronze working. Other objects reflect the influence of Assyria. Bronze fibulae (clasps), traditionally held to have been a Phrygian invention, have been found in great numbers. According to Greek sources, King Midas was married to a Greek woman from Aeolic Cyme and was the first non-Greek ruler to send offerings to the oracle of Delphi. These traditions indicate that Midas had contacts with Greek coastal cities of western Anatolia. One of the principal ways of identifying an archaeological site is by the type of pottery it contains. Two main types of pottery have been found at sites associated with Phrygia: one polychrome with geometric designs and the other mainly gray or red monochrome. Some archaeologists believe that the polychrome variety, usually called Early Phrygian or Alişar IV in eastern Anatolia where it was first found, is actually Luwian. Whether or not this is true, there were certainly many cultural contacts between the eastern Phrygians and their Luwian neighbours. Geometric patterns typical of Phrygian sculpture appear in Luwian rock reliefs of İvriz Harabesi and Bor. On the other hand, Luwian influence is clearly present in Phrygian sculptures found at Ankara. There is at least a cultural, if not a political, division in this period between more purely native Phrygia in the west and the eastern Phrygians, with their neo-Hittite affiliations.

Phrygian-Luwian contacts

Around the middle of the 8th century BC the Phrygians adopted an alphabetic script, ultimately derived from the Phoenician alphabet. There is some question as to whether the Phrygians acquired their alphabet in the first instance from a Greek source in the west or south, or whether the Phrygian form of the alphabet was the parent of the Greek. The first supposition seems more likely, since the Greeks probably had more contact with the seagoing Phoenicians than did the inland Phrygians. The oldest Phrygian inscriptions found at Gordium date from the last quarter of the 8th century BC. Another inscription from the same period at Tyana may very well be an authentic document of King Midas, whose name is mentioned on the stone. Toward the end of the 8th century BC, Büyükkale, the citadel of Boğazköy-Hattusa, undoubtedly was a Phrygian settlement. In the early 7th century, perhaps as a result of the Cimmerian invasion, a new system of fortifications was added. Later in that century the settlement extended beyond the citadel to cover most of the area of the former Hittite capital. The Phrygian character of this city is clearly shown by graffiti (wall writing) in Phrygian script and especially by a cult image of Cybele, the main Phrygian goddess, found in a niche at the southeast gate of the citadel. Cybele, a goddess of the "Great Mother of Nature" type, was called Kubaba by the Luwians and, under that name, had played an important role in the religion of Carchemish. Her importance seems to have increased during the Phrygian period, and her statue at Boğazköy seems to show the influence of 6th-century Greek art, as do comparable cult statues from Gordium; from Ayaş, west of Ankara; and from Ankara itself.

The cult of Cybele

The neo-Hittite states (from c. 1180 to 700 BC). The Dark Age after the fall of the Hittite Empire lasted until between 1000 and 900 BC. Carchemish (on the modern border between Turkey and Syria) and Milid (Arslantepe, near present-day Malatya) were the most important Luwian strongholds of this intermediary age, and both were characterized by the same interaction of Luwian and Hurrian influences that had already prevailed during the New Empire period. Reliefs from Malatya, showing the king of that city making offerings to the gods, show a marked similarity to earlier Hittite reliefs at Yazılıkaya and Alaca Hüyük. During the 10th century Aramaean infiltration strengthened and transformed the indigenous Semitic population of Syria; the Aramaeans also penetrated into Luwian areas and sometimes managed to dominate them. Til Barsib (Tell Ahmar) in North Syria was an important Luwian stronghold taken by the Aramaeans in the second half of the 10th century. It became the centre of the Aramaean kingdom Bit-Adini until it was conquered by the Assyrian king Shalmaneser III (858–824). Samal, in the Amanus Mountains (Nur Dağları) of southern Turkey, became Aramaean *c.* 920 BC. Arpad fell shortly after 900 and belonged afterward to the Aramaean state Bit-Agusi. Still later Ḥamāh—the most southern Luwian city—became an important Aramaean power in combination with Aleppo (modern Ḥalab). Aleppo, already a famous capital in the 2nd millennium BC, probably had a numerous

Luwian population. The state of Hattina (sometimes called Amqa), which apparently managed to maintain its Luwian character for a very long time, occupied the region at the mouth of the Orontes River, on a site near later Antioch.

The North Syrian states

A great deal more is known about the neo-Hittite states of Syria in the 10th century than about those of inner Anatolia, because so much of the extant source material is Assyrian, and the Assyrian kings had not yet penetrated into Cilicia and Cappadocia.

Til Barsib and Gurgum (capital at modern Maraş) have provided texts from before 900 BC. Most important, however, are the texts from Carchemish, where the subject matter tends to be more diverse than in those of the Hittite imperial age, military exploits being added to the traditional religious subjects. The art of the neo-Hittite states is similar, perhaps under Mesopotamian influence, being more directed toward worldly affairs, frequently depicting hunting scenes and chariot fighting. The principal deities of Carchemish were the Luwian storm god Tarhun (Tarhundas, or Tarhus); Karhuhas, protector of nature's forces; and Kubabas-Cybele, the "queen of Carchemish." Their sacred animals were the bull, the stag, and the lion, respectively. A number of titles used by the kings of Carchemish (*e.g.,* Great King and Hero) are clearly relics of a more glorious Hittite past, but one (*tarwanas,* "judge") is entirely new, possibly reflecting a new political phenomenon. *Tarwanas* has been compared to the Semitic *shofet,* known from the Bible and especially from the Book of Judges, and also to the *tyrannos* of western Anatolia and the Greek world in general. It denotes the judicial capacity of its bearer as distinguished from his military leadership or priestly functions and probably reflects an enlarged concept of kingship resulting from the growing complexity of urban life. Neo-Hittite kings of the 9th century often bore the names of their imperial predecessors; an inscription at Boybeypınarı mentions both a Suppiluliumas and a Hattusilis; at Hattina, kings with the names Labarnas and Suppiluliumas are attested to by Assyrian sources; and during the long reign of a well-documentated dynasty in Gurgum three kings were called Muwatallis.

Assyrian expansion

Tiglath-pileser I of Assyria had invaded Syria *c.* 1200 BC. In the 9th century his successors renewed Assyrian attempts at westward expansion. Ashurnasirpal II (reigned 883–859) received tribute from Carchemish, penetrated into Hattina, reaching the Lebanon and the Mediterranean and returning to Mesopotamia by way of the Amanus Mountains (Samal, modern Zincirli Hüyük). Ambassadors from the Luwian regions of Hatti (Carchemish), Hattina, Gurgum, and Milid were among the foreign guests who took part in the celebrations for the inauguration of his new palace in Nimrūd (879 BC). Ashurnasirpal II and his successor, Shalmaneser III (reigned 858–824 BC), both attached great value to the fact that they were able to reach the Mediterranean, but they were unable to permanently subdue the Aramaeans in southern Syria. Included in the Luwian-Aramaean coalition that confronted Shalmaneser III at Qarqār in 853 were forces from the Luwian states of Anatolia, among them Que (the Cilician plain) and Hilakku, the mountainous region to the north of Que. Shalmaneser III made a serious effort to establish Assyrian control over that area; he led four expeditions against Que, one against Tabal (Tubal), and another to Milid (where the tribute of Tabal was brought to him). At this time Tuwatis, the king of Tabal (roughly coinciding with the Hittite Lower Land of the empire period—Lycaonia and Cappadocia south of the Halys), ruled over 20 (according to another text, 24) vassal kings. Apparently, however, the great military efforts of Assyria in this period overtaxed its strength. Toward the end of Shalmaneser's reign a rebellion broke out, and it took more than half a century before the Assyrians were able to renew their western expansion. Hieroglyphic inscriptions from Ḥamāh, the most southerly Luwian stronghold, show how extraordinarily complicated the ethnic situation in this region was. In a text from the middle of the 9th century a king with the Hurrian name Urhilinas—one of the leaders of the coalition against Assyria in 853—records in the Luwian language that he has built a throne and erected a monument for the Semitic goddess Bahalatis. Another contemporary of Shalmaneser III was Halpa-Rudas (Halpa-Rundas) of Hattina. His name has also been found in the hieroglyphic Luwian texts of Tell Tayinat and has helped in the dating of that site. It seems likely that Assyria's contacts with Que, Hilakku, and Tabal, though a threat to their independence, may also have been a strong stimulus to their internal development.

A great many texts from the various Luwian centres in northern Syria and southeast Anatolia shed light on the history of the 8th century BC. One of the most important of these is a bilingual (Luwian-Hittite and Phoenician) inscription at Karatepe; comparison with the Phoenician version greatly increased scholars' understanding of Hittite hieroglyphics.

The temporary setback in Assyria's westward expansion in the latter part of the 9th century provided a brief period of respite for the neo-Hittite states. This phase ended with the rise of the state of Urartu in the 8th century, at first a minor kingdom centred on Lake Van but later extended to include parts of what are now Soviet Armenia, Persian Azerbaijan, and Iraqi Kurdistan. Entrenched in a mountainous country, well organized with provincial capitals and a network of small fortress cities, it resisted aggression from the Assyrians in the south.

The rise of Urartu

Urartian culture was based upon that of Mesopotamia; yet, its architecture shows qualities that some consider superior to that of the Assyrians. For the monotonous mud-brick facades of the southern plains and valleys are here replaced by a pattern of crenellated stone towers and buttresses adapted to the natural beauty of a rocky landscape. The excavation of two fortress cities, Karmirblur and Arin Berd, in Armenia, together with many others in Anatolia itself, has also revealed some unique features of Urartian architecture, including a standard form of temple: a square, towerlike building anticipating the temple-towers of Achaemenian times in Persia.

Urartu became a serious threat to Assyria's northern border, and at the same time expanded in a westerly and southwesterly direction, eventually sharing a common border with Phrygia in northern Anatolia and asserting its hegemony over the Luwians. Milid (Malatya) was subdued by the Urartian kings Argishti I (reigned 780–756) and Sarduri II (reigned 755–735); the latter also conquered Kustaspi, king of Kummuhu (Commagene), and forced him to pay tribute around 745. At this time, a king named Asti-Ruwas ruled over Carchemish. A passage from one of his texts seems to indicate that he, too, was dependent on the Urartian king. At Carchemish, the sons of Asti-Ruwas were expelled by a usurper called Araras. In the introduction to one of his texts, Araras emphasizes his diplomatic relations with the state of Mira (on either the south or the west coast of Anatolia), the Mysians (on the northwest coast), the Mushki (Phrygians) and the "Syrians," which may perhaps mean the inhabitants of Cappadocia. In another text he distinguishes between the Luwian, "Syrian," Assyrian, and Aramaean languages. All this points to an active foreign policy in a world that is aware of its fundamental unity as well as of its political and linguistic distinctions. The archaeological evidence—demonstrating the existence of extensive international trade—supports this conclusion.

Under Tiglath-pileser III (reigned 744–727 BC), the Assyrians re-entered the political scene in the west. After Urartu had suffered severe setbacks, first in 743 (in a battle in southern Kummuhu) and afterward in 735, when the Assyrian king penetrated into the heart of Urartu itself, the Luwian and Aramaean kings began to suspect that Urartu was doomed. In 743 Milid, Kummuhu, Arpad, and Gurgum still belonged to the Urartian sphere of influence, but in 740 Tiglath-pileser conquered Arpad, and a large group of princes, among them the kings of Kummuhu, Que, Carchemish (where a King Pisiris reigned at this time), and Gurgum offered their submission to the Assyrians. King Tutammu of Hattina, who had been strategically safe as long as Arpad had not been conquered, was also defeated and his land turned into an Assyrian province. In 738, Samal, Milid, Kaska, Tabal, and Tuwanuwa (Greek Tyana) came to terms with the Assyrian King. The Assyrian influence had again reached the inner parts of

Anatolia. In 732 King Wasu-Srmas (Wasu-Sarrumas) of Tabal was deposed by the Assyrians, and it seems probable that Samal and Que were made into Assyrian provincial territory during the reign of Shalmaneser V (726–722). During the reign of his successor, Sargon II (reigned 721–705), Ḥamāh (720), Carchemish (717), Tabal (713), and Kummuhu (together with Malatya in 708) also ceased to exist as separate states, bringing the era of the independent neo-Hittite states to an end. Shortly afterward the Cimmerians destroyed neighbouring Phrygia.

The Cimmerians, Lydia, and Cilicia, c. 700–547 BC. During the last years of the 8th century BC and the first decades of the 7th century, the Assyrian kings had to fight various wars to maintain their positions in southeast Anatolia. In 705 BC Sargon II himself undertook a campaign in this region, and the unheard-of happened: the Assyrian King was killed in battle. Already in 704 or 703 and later again in 696, Sennacherib (704–681) sent his troops to Que and Hilakku to quell local revolts. On the whole, the Assyrians were not completely successful; while Que (the Cilician plain) remained in their possession, they lost their grip on the more northerly regions of Tabal, Hilakku, and Meliddu.

After the Cimmerians had sacked Gordium, the Phrygian capital (696 or 695), they withdrew to the countryside and confined themselves mostly to a nomadic existence in western Anatolia. So far it has proved impossible to assign any habitation levels or sites in Anatolia to Cimmerian occupation. According to the Greek historian Herodotus, they settled in the area of Sinope on the Black Sea. Herodotus may be right, for this same general area supported the Kaskan nomads of the 2nd millennium BC. Many scholars have concluded from indications in classical authors that a second wave of Cimmerians entered Anatolia from the west and that these western Cimmerians were reinforced by Thracian invaders.

The Lydians

Another new people that appeared in western Anatolia about this time were the Lydians. Their capital and earliest settlement was at Sardis, near present Izmir on the Aegean coast. According to ancient writers, they were the first people to coin money. Their ruling house in the 7th century were the Mermnads, founded by Gyges (reigned *c.* 680–648). The presence of Greek pottery in Sardis' early layers testifies to Lydian contact with the Greeks in this period. The Lydian language belonged to the Anatolian branch of Indo-European and resembled Hittite and Prabaic.

In 679 Esarhaddon of Assyria (reigned 680–669) defeated the Cimmerians under King Teuspa in the region of Hubusna (likely to be a variant of Hupisna-Cybistra), but the area did not thereby become tranquil. In the same year Esarhaddon's troops also fought a war in Hilakku, and a few years later they punished the Anatolian prince of Kundu (Cyinda) and Sissu (Sisium, modern Sis), who had allied himself with Phoenician rebels against Assyrian rule. Again and again the regions to the north of the Cilician plain caused trouble for Assyria. Early in the reign of Ashurbanipal (668–627), however, another Cimmerian invasion threatened the Anatolian states, arousing such alarm that not only Tabal and Hilakku but even Gyges of Lydia sought help from the Assyrians. According to the Assyrian texts, the god Ashur appeared to "Gugu" (Gyges) in a dream, advising him to turn to Ashurbanipal for help. On the same day that Gyges sent his messengers to Ashur, the Cimmerian invaders were indeed repulsed. When Gyges afterward failed to make these temporary relations permanent and instead formed an alliance with the Egyptian king Psamtik, however, Ashurbanipal prayed that "Gyges' body would be thrown down before his enemy," and this indeed happened. During a second attack in 652 Sardis, with the exception of the citadel, was taken by the Cimmerians, and the King was killed. The American excavators of Sardis have found a destruction layer that they connect with this event. Herodotus reports that, like the Phrygian Midas before him, Gyges dedicated offerings to the temple at Delphi, but also that he conducted campaigns against his Greek neighbours at Miletus and Smyrna (Izmir) and that he conquered the Greek city of Colophon. Ardys, his successor on the Lydian throne (651–*c.* 613), again attacked Miletus and took Priene. During his reign Sardis was taken a second time, this time by the Treres, the Thracian tribe mentioned above that operated in close connection with the Cimmerians. According to Assyrian sources, Ardys restored Lydia's diplomatic relations with Assyria. The Cimmerian forces were finally beaten by the Assyrians in Cilicia between 637 and 626. At that time the Cimmerian leader was Lygdamis (Tugdamme in the Assyrian sources), who is identified in Greek tradition as the victor over Sardis in 652 and is also said to have attacked Ephesus. The final defeat of Lygdamis is known both from Assyrian sources and from the later Greek geographer Strabo. The Lydian kings Sadyattes (d. *c.* 619) and Alyattes (reigned *c.* 619–*c.* 560) continued their attacks on Greek Miletus. Under Alyattes Lydia reached its commercial and political zenith. He attacked Clazomenae, in 590 took Smyrna, and also subjected many inland regions to Lydian rule. Sappho's poetry, with its references to faraway Sardis, is as eloquent in this respect as the results of modern excavations. The war described by Herodotus between the Lydians and the Medes, expanding out of Iran in the east, probably occurred between 590 and 585. From then on, the Halys River marked the border between the two powers, Lydia on the west and Media (later Persia) on the east.

The defeat of the Cimmerians

The growth of an independent Cilicia was one of the most important developments of the last decades of the 7th century BC. It did not include the southern Cilician plain, which came under the control of the Neo-Babylonian Empire after the fall of Assyria in 612. During the conflict between Lydia and the Medes, independent Cilicia and Babylonia acted jointly as mediators, no doubt as two important nonaligned powers of the region. The next and last king of Lydia was Croesus (reigned *c.* 560–546). Famous for his wealth, he ranks with Midas among the Anatolian rulers who made a deep impression on the imagination of the Greeks. Like Midas, Croesus sent offerings to such Greek sanctuaries as Delphi, Miletus, and Ephesus. A number of the relief-decorated pillars of the world-famous Temple of Artemis in Ephesus, one of the Seven Wonders of the World, were presented by him. Stories about his fabulous wealth find some support in the archaeological discovery at Sardis of gold-refining installations from the time of Alyattes and Croesus. Croesus completed the work of his predecessors by subduing the Greek cities of Anatolia. He planned to conquer the Greeks of the Aegean islands as well, but the growing threat from the Persians, who by this time had replaced the Medes as the dominant Iranian power, forced him to make an alliance with them instead. According to Herodotus, Croesus ruled all of Anatolia west of the Halys, although the Greek cities probably enjoyed a considerable measure of autonomy. Having secured the support of Egypt, Babylonia, and Sparta (Cilicia remained neutral), Croesus decided to make war against the Persians. Taking the initiative, he crossed the Halys River into Persian territory (547 BC). Both parties fought a battle into the region of Pteria (which may be identical with Boğazköy-Hattusa). Although the battle was indecisive, Croesus decided to return home to his capital, intending to reinforce his troops with allied forces and to renew the war in the following spring. Cyrus the Great, the Persian king, unexpectedly turned after him and took him by surprise. After a short siege, Sardis was taken, and Persian hegemony was established over Anatolia.

Lydian expansion under Croesus

Greek colonies on the Anatolian coasts, c. 1180–547 BC. Before the Greek migrations that took place soon after the end of the Bronze Age (*c.* 1200 BC), probably the only Greek-speaking communities on the west coast of Anatolia were Mycenaean settlements at Iasus and Müskebi on the Halicarnassus peninsula and walled Mycenaean colonies at Miletus and Colophon. The major Greek settlement of Anatolia's west coast belongs to the Dark Age (*c.* 1200–*c.* 1000). In contrast to the colonization of the Mycenaean period, this movement has all the characteristics of a migration. Aeolian territory stretched north of the Hermus (Gediz) River up to Pitane, with Cyme as the most important settlement. According to Herodotus, the Aeolians (coming perhaps from Boeotia and Thessaly or more generally from the eastern part of mainland Greece) once formed a league of 12 cities corresponding to those of

Ionia, but their number was reduced to 11 by the Ionian capture of Smyrna. The 12 Ionian cities of historical times were: (the isles of) Chios and Samos, and (from north to south) Phocaea, Clazomenae, Erythrae, Teos, Lebedus, Colophon, Ephesus, Priene, Myus, and Miletus. Among these, Ephesus (as the successor to Apasa, capital of the Luwian Late Bronze state of Arzawa) and Miletus had by far the best claims to historical fame. It is probable that the original number of towns of the 10th and 9th centuries was far larger. There may be a considerable element of truth in the tradition that makes Athens the departure point of the Ionians. Dorian Greeks settled on the Aegean islands of Rhodes and Cos before 900. After this, Cnidus and Halicarnassus were founded on the peninsulas of western Caria. The Dorians formed a league of six, later of five, cities. The Troas (Troy) region was colonized from Mytilene on the island of Lesbos early in the 8th century. By the 8th century, the city league (a group of cities with a common devotion to the same sanctuary) became the normal political institution among the Aeolians, Ionians, and Dorians. A certain measure of urbanization, which in turn was dependent on the development of both local industry and foreign trade, preceded the development of these larger units.

The Ionian cities

Much less is known about the non-Greek populations of the interior. The Mysians, an aboriginal people of the valley of the Caïcus (Bakir) River and the mountains to the north, are mentioned in an 8th-century Carchemish inscription. The Carians, from the hinterland of Miletus and Halicarnassus, enter history as mercenaries in the service of the Egyptian king Psamtik, along with their Ionian neighbours, in the 7th century BC. Of the Lycians, to the east of Caria, nothing definite is known before the 6th century, though archaeological evidence shows that the Greeks had commercial contacts with Lycia as early as *c.* 700. Curiously enough, it was under the aegis of Persian rule that Greek civilization really penetrated into this region. Among the peoples subject to Croesus, Herodotus mentions the Pamphylians, whose country lay in the south, between Lycia and Cilicia. A Neo-Babylonian text of the mid-6th century confirms this, indicating that the Lydian borderline was situated at Sallune (classical Selinus, the most westerly coastal city of Cilicia). There is evidence that the Mycenaean Greeks had contacts with Pamphylia even before 1200, and the name of the Greek hero Mopsus, who figures in the legends surrounding the Trojan War, is associated with the foundation of settlements in both Pamphylia and Cilicia. The appearance of the House of Muksas (Phoenician Mups) in the Karatepe bilingual inscription has suggested that there may be a historical kernel of truth in these traditions, which seem to be a heritage common to both the Greeks and the original Anatolian population. Archaeological finds indicate considerable Greek colonizing activity on the south coast of Anatolia in the 8th century BC and on the north coast in the 7th century. From the middle of the 8th century BC on, Greek merchants were active on the Cilician coast. An important evidence of this can be found in inscriptions of Sargon II (721–705), according to which their activities there began about a generation before his time. Such Greek place-names as Anchiale and Pityoussa occur repeatedly in Assyrian and Neo-Babylonian texts of the 7th and 6th centuries BC relating to the south coast of Anatolia. The North Syrian harbour of al-Mīnaʾ was also of great commercial importance to the Greeks. It is likely that Urartian and other west Asian influences visible in the art of the Greeks and the Italian Etruscans were the result of such commercial contacts. The neo-Hittite state of Hattina on the seacoast of which al-Mīnaʾ was situated probably played an important role in this respect. Of the two main Ionian cities, Ephesus and Miletus, Miletus was very active in colonization. At Ephesus, where the surrounding country produced enough grain and raw materials for the use of the city, there was less pressure for emigration and the founding of colonies. In the early 7th century, the Milesians settled Abydos and Cyzicus in the Propontis (Sea of Marmora) region; Greek tradition suggests that the Lydian king Gyges collaborated in the foundation of Abydos. Dascylium was named after Gyges' father and might be a foundation of the same period. Sinope on the Black Sea coast (founded *c.* 630) was another colony of Miletus. Destruction layers in the excavations of Miletus, Ephesus, and Smyrna, dating from the mid-7th century, suggest that the Ionian cities suffered heavily from the Cimmerian invasion. By the mid-6th century, as has already been mentioned, the cities had all been subjected to Lydian rule.

The Greeks in Cilicia

ANATOLIA IN THE ACHAEMENIAN AND HELLENISTIC PERIODS

Diversity of cultural influences. Between 546 and 334 BC, Anatolia was dominated politically by the Achaemenian Empire of Persia. Culturally, however, Greek influence continued to be strong and even increased. The coastal regions of Caria and Lycia on the one hand, and Pamphylia and Cilicia on the other, were Hellenized to a considerable degree under the aegis of Persian rule. At the same time, Iranian (Persian) cultural influence penetrated the regions of Armenia, Pontus, Cappadocia, and Commagene. The Persian deities Mithra and Anahita were honoured in Armenia. In Cappadocia, the influence of Iran is clearly visible in the names of the local rulers and in religious practices reported by classical authors. The religious life of eastern Anatolia during this period was characterized by a blend of Iranian, Greek, and indigenous Anatolian elements. The indigenous Luwian groups maintained their linguistic and cultural independence most clearly in such isolated areas as Lycia and western Cilicia, but they are also recognizable in such other southern provinces as Pamphylia, Pisidia, and Lycaonia. The Iranian influence was strong in the northeastern city of Dascylium, originally a Lydian settlement but chosen to be the administrative centre of the satrapy (province) of Hellespontine Phrygia. Aramaic was the official language in the western parts of the Achaemenian Empire, and Aramaic inscriptions in stone and on coins are relatively numerous for Anatolia in the 4th century BC. The Lydian and Phrygian languages continued to be used in their original homelands. The changing nomenclature and boundaries of satrapies and kingdoms throughout this general period present a confusing picture. Under the Persian king Darius the Great (reigned 522–486) Anatolia's original division was as follows: Armina (Armenia), Katpatuka (Cappadocia together with the territories of the Hellespont), Sea Peoples (the south coast together with Cyprus), Sparda (Lydia), and Yauna (the Greek west coast).

The Anatolian Greeks in the Achaemenian period. Of the Anatolian Greek cities, only Miletus had chosen the Persian side in the struggle with Lydia. A number of the others were subjected to Persian rule by force. During the ensuing period, many of these Greek towns maintained a semi-autonomous status, while recognizing Achaemenian overlordship. Outside the cities, occupation forces and military colonies preserved law and order. But in 499, Histiaeus, the Greek ruler of Miletus, led a revolt against Persia. This Ionian revolt was the opening phase of the Greco-Persian Wars. Although the rebels found wide support, not only in the Greek cities of the Propontis region and at the Bosporus but also in Caria, Lycia, and on Cyprus, they lost the decisive sea battle at Lade in 495 BC. In the following year Miletus, the heart of the insurrection, was taken and destroyed. In the last version of the list of satrapies of Darius, Karka (Caria) was added at the end. Apparently it had been brought under stronger control on account of its support for the Greek cause. During the Greco-Persian Wars, the Anatolian Greeks were compelled to contribute troops and ships to the Persian forces. After the Persian failure to subjugate Greece itself, the Athenians succeeded in pushing back the Persian sphere of influence from many of the coastal districts of Anatolia. A number of cities on the south coast joined the Athenian dominated Delian League. During the final phases of the Peloponnesian War (431–404), Persia gave support to the Spartan cause. Tissaphernes, satrap in Sardis, concluded a treaty with Sparta in the name of the Persian King (411): the Persians promised the Spartans both financial and naval support; all the Greek cities of Anatolia were to return to the Persian sphere. In spite of the fact that the growing internal weakness of their empire, and perhaps diplomatic reasons as well, restrained the Persians from exercising their full rights under this treaty, Sparta repudiated it and championed the Ionian cause in the early 4th century. After Spartan successes on the continent this war was lost at sea in the Battle of Cnidus (394). Later in the 4th century, however, Persian rule in Anatolia was severely shaken by an insurrection of the Persian satraps of the west (362–359), which subsequently resulted in a considerable measure of local autonomy for the area.

Caria, Lycia, and Cilicia in the Achaemenian period. In the 5th century Caria was ruled by tyrants and princes, some of whom chose the Greek and some of whom chose the Persian side at the time of the Ionian insurrection. Between the middle of the century and the end of the Peloponnesian War (404), Caria belonged to the Delian League. It seems to have been constituted as a separate Persian satrapy. The Carian satrap Mausolus (ruled 377–353) took part in the great insurrection of the western satraps but later changed sides and conquered Phaselis and western Lycia for the Persian King. He likewise profited from the defection of a number of Athens' allies (357), enlarging simultaneously both his own satrapy and the Persian sphere of influence: Rhodes and Cos were added to his possessions. Mausolus made Halicarnassus the metropolis of Caria. The architecture of the city, including the Satrap's tomb, the Mausoleum (another of the Seven Wonders of the World), showed strong Greek influence. The Mausoleum was planned by Mausolus himself but was actually built by his wife and successor, Artemisia (ruled 353–351). Later satraps were Artemisia's brother Idrieus (ruled 351–344), his wife and successor, Ada (ruled 344–341), and Pixodarus, brother of Ada (ruled 341–334).

Mausolus of Halicarnassus

Lycia was conquered by the Persian commander Harpagus after a stubborn resistance by the people of Xanthus. The Lycians had to make a contribution to the expeditionary force led by the Persian king Xerxes in his invasion of Greece (480), but they later sided with Athens. In the latter part of the 5th century, Lycia remained nominally under Persian rule but in practice was almost independent. Greek loanwords in Lycian, the influence of Greece on Lycian art, and the name Pericles, borne by a Lycian king of the 4th century, all attest to a cultural dependence on Greece. The rapid progress of Hellenization in the 4th century is illustrated by bilingual (Greek and Lycian) texts dating from that period. Around 400 BC the Persian grip on the country seems to have been strengthened. Persian rulers are named in inscriptions and on coins (*e.g.,* Artembares, governor of western Lycia). There is evidence that this same Artembares took part in the satrap rebellion. The above-mentioned King Pericles ruled over eastern Lycia between *c.* 380 and 362. Toward the end of his reign Pericles was at war with Mausolus of Caria, who, in all probability, was given western Lycia as a reward for his betrayal of the cause of the satraps. It is uncertain whether any part of Lycia regained its independence before the time of Alexander the Great (334).

Pamphylia under the Persians

During the 5th century, Pamphylia belonged to the satrapy of the Sea Peoples (and its successors), but its cities were allowed to issue their own coinage. After the Greek victory over the Persians at the Battle of the Eurymedon (fought in Pamphylia *c.* 469), Aspendus and one or two other cities of the south coast were incorporated for a time into the Delian League. In 449, by the terms of the peace concluding the Greco-Persian Wars, the Persians recovered control of Pamphylia; but they seem to have respected its autonomy. Inscriptions from the Pamphylian city of Side (modern Selimiye, Turkey) in a local Sidetan script (and language) together with the legends on Sidetan coins prove the existence in this city of a strong indigenous population group between the 5th and 3rd centuries BC.

The history of Cilicia under the Persians can be divided into two distinct periods: the period from 547 to 401, when it was a kingdom recognizing Persian overlordship, and the period between 401 and 334, when it was under the rule of a Persian satrap. During the first period the land was governed by an indigenous dynasty of kings, all of whom bore the name Syennesis. In the second period, the Persians probably actually controlled no more than a narrow coastal strip of western Cilicia, where there was a numerous Greek population.

Anatolia in the Hellenistic Age (334–c. 30 BC). In 334–333 BC the Macedonians under Alexander the Great conquered Anatolia from the Persians and proceeded to destroy the Achaemenian Empire. Alexander's empire was short-lived; quarrels among his successors brought about its fragmentation before 300, and by 275 three dynasties, descended from three of his commanders, had been established in various parts of the territory he conquered: the Seleucids were based in Syria, the Ptolemies in Egypt, and the Antigonids in Macedonia. Anatolia itself was divided: Lycia and Caria were governed by Ptolemaic Egypt, the Seleucids governed most of the other parts of the peninsula. Pamphylia changed hands frequently, but Cilicia, Hellespontine Phrygia, Phrygia, Lydia, southern Cappadocia, and Catonia were Seleucid satrapies. In the early 3rd century, the states of northern Anatolia (led by Heraclea, Byzantium, Pontus, and Bithynia) formed a league against the Seleucid king Antiochus I. In 278 three Celtic tribes that had migrated across Europe to the Dardanelles were taken as allies by Nicomedes I of Bithynia. The Celts invaded and ravaged Anatolia, until they were defeated by Antiochus in 275. Thereafter they were settled in northern Phrygia by Nicomedes and Mithradates, where they served as a buffer against the Seleucids. The district they occupied was thereafter called Galatia (from Galli, the Latin word for Celts).

The Celtic invasion

Adapted from W. Shepherd, *Historical Atlas;* Barnes & Noble Books, New York

Roman provinces of Anatolia in the 2nd century AD.

In the middle of the 3rd century, Cappadocia became an independent kingdom, and the rulers of Pergamum on the Aegean coast began to enlarge their territory. The Cappadocian leader Ariaramnes carved out a kingdom for himself by incorporating into his own possessions the territory of other local dynasts. Pergamum, originally a mountain fortress, became in the long run an important continental power through the careful manoeuvring of its rulers, Philetaerus and later his nephew Eumenes (ruled 263–241). Attalus I (ruled 241–197) took advantage of the growing weakness of the Seleucid kingdom to further expand his influence. He broke the power of the Galatians in two battles before 230, adopted the title of king, and for several years (228–223) ruled over the entire Seleucid territory north of the Taurus Mountains.

Antiochus III (reigned 223–187) temporarily restored Seleucid power in Anatolia. By 220, Attalus I was again restricted to practically the original borders of his kingdom. Disturbed by the renewed expansionism of the Seleucids, Egypt, Rhodes, and Pergamum appealed to Rome for help in 200, claiming that Antiochus had formed a pact with Rome's neighbour, Philip V of Macedonia. In 197 Antiochus conquered the entire coast of Anatolia from Cilicia to the Hellespont, while also attacking Pergamum in the interior. In 196 he crossed the Dardanelles and brought the conflict over to Europe. After some hesitation the Romans intervened against him in the Syrian War (192–189). After two defeats, first at Thermopylae and afterward in Magnesia (not far from Sardis), Antiochus was forced to accept the peace of Apamea, which definitely made Rome the predominant power in the Hellenistic East (188). Rome reorganized the Anatolian states: Lycia and Caria were allotted to Rhodes (when this period of Rhodian domination ended in 167, Lycia became a Roman protectorate); Antiochus III was forced to surrender all Seleucid possessions in Anatolia except the Cilician plain; the principal Anatolian powers were then Rhodes, Pergamum, Bithynia, Pontus, and Cappadocia.

Roman hegemony

A new and final stage of Roman involvement was reached when Attalus III (138–133), the last in the line of the Attalids, bequeathed the kingdom of Pergamum to Rome. All of western Anatolia was then reorganized as the Roman province of Asia. The remainder of the peninsula came under Roman rule in the 1st century BC and remained part of the Roman, and later the Byzantine, Empire, until the 11th century AD, when it was partially occupied by the Seljuq Turks. All of Anatolia was taken over by the Ottoman Turks in the 14th century. (For the later history of Anatolia, see below *The period of Seljuq domination,* and *The Ottoman Empire;* see also the *Macropædia* article BYZANTINE EMPIRE.)

(Ph.H.J.H.t.C.)

The period of Seljuq domination

ORIGIN AND EARLY CONQUESTS OF THE SELJUQS

The Seljuqs (Seljuks) were the ruling family of the Oğuz (Ghuzz) Turkmen tribes who invaded western Asia in the 11th century and founded a powerful empire, later to be divided into the principalities of Iran, Syria, and Asia Minor. The history of these invaders forms the first part of the history of the Turks in the Near and Middle East.

During the 10th century, in the course of the migrations and struggles of the Turkish peoples of Central Asia and southeast Russia, a group of nomadic Turks under a chief named Seljuq settled in the lower reaches of the Syr-Darya (Jaxartes) and later embraced Islām. They were incorporated in the frontier defense forces of the Sāmānids and moved to the vicinity of Bukhara *c.* AD 985. After the fall of the Sāmānids, they were established by Maḥmūd of Ghazna in the border regions of Khorāsān, but it was difficult to induce warlike nomads to live peacefully within a settled empire. While Maḥmūd's son Mas'ūd was busy waging war in northern India, the two grandsons of Seljuq, Chaghri (Chagri) Beg and Toghrïl (Ṭughril) Beg, saw the chance to win a realm of their own with the support of Persian nobles and religious leaders who were anxious to meet the threatening progress of heretic Shī'ite sects reinforced by the Būyid princes of western Iran and Iraq and the Fāṭimid Ismā'īlī caliphate of Egypt (see IRAN; EGYPT). When Mas'ūd saw the danger, it was too late: he was utterly defeated at Dendenkan (Dandānqān) near Merv in 1040. Thereafter Chaghri Beg remained in control of the greater part of Khorāsān while Toghrïl, with a mixed army of Turkmen and regular Mamlūk (slave) troops, set out to conquer new territories in the west.

Toghrïl Beg, a strong leader of men and a clear-headed statesman, achieved the creation of an empire that at his death (1063) included central and western Iran and Mesopotamia with Baghdad itself. There in 1055 Toghrïl undertook to deliver the caliph al-Qā'im from Būyid domination and to ally the house of Seljuq with the caliphate through marriage. Thereby the Seljuq conquests were identified with a restoration of the unity of the Muslim world under the Sunni caliphate. Alp-Arslan (1063 to 1072 or 1073), who succeeded both Chaghri and Toghrïl, and Malik-Shāh completed his conquering work. When Malik-Shāh I died in 1092, the Seljuq Empire included the whole of Iran, with the exception of the Ghaznavid realm of the Indian borderland, the whole of Mesopotamia, and Syria, including Palestine, to the frontier of Egypt. Furthermore, other Turkmen invaders closely akin to the Seljuqs had occupied the Asiatic provinces of the Byzantine Empire up to the Aegean Sea. The organization of the empire was the task of the vizier Niẓām al-Mulk, who remained in power during the reigns of both Alp-Arslan and Malik-Shāh.

The nature of the Seljuq Empire. The main problem facing the Seljuqs was to persuade the Turkmen invaders, to whom they owed their victory, to live within the framework of the bureaucratic Iranian-Iraqi state. This problem was never completely solved. The Turkmen tribesmen had no interest in victory over heretics if their lands were unsuitable for stockbreeding or if pillage was not allowed; but on the northwestern frontier of Iran lay the Byzantine Empire, including half of Armenia, which was lacking religio-national homogeneity and the kind of military force able to fight against nomadic invaders. Love of plunder and zeal for a holy war drew the Turkmens into Byzantine territory, and, to prevent them from becoming quite estranged from him, the sultan had sometimes to lead them himself. Thus Alp-Arslan won immortal fame in the Muslim world when he defeated a huge Byzantine army at Manzikert in 1071, capturing the Byzantine emperor Romanus IV Diogenes. Thenceforth the Turkmens were able to settle in Asia Minor undisturbed.

Surely the main feature of the Seljuq Empire was its religio-political character. The regime had to fight not only

Adapted from *Westermann Grosser Atlas zur Weltgeschichte,* Georg Westermann Verlag, Braunschweig (1965)

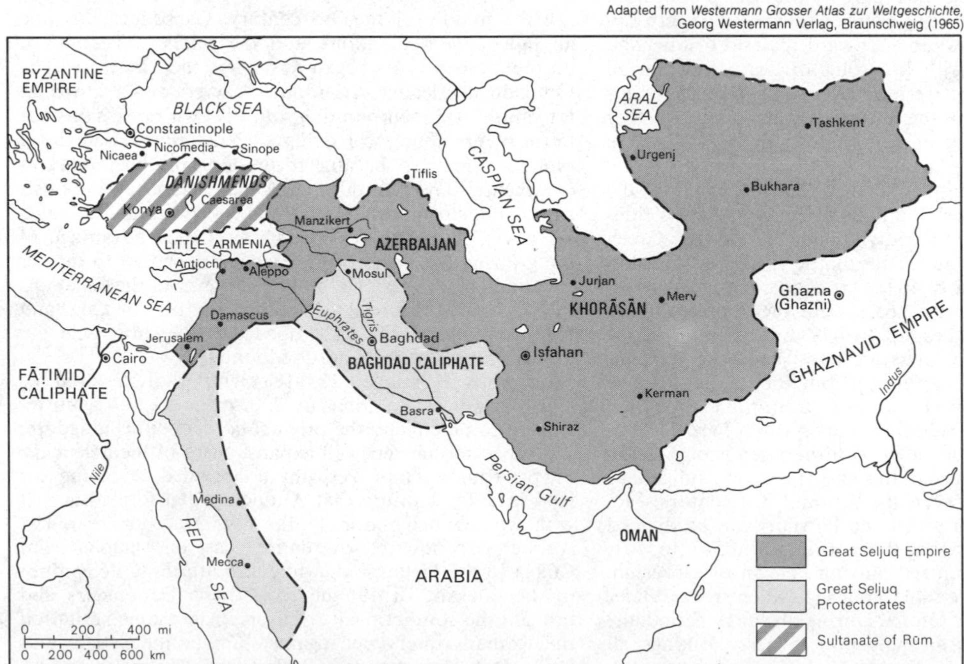

Seljuq Empire during the reign of Malik-Shāh (1073–92).

The significance of the Great Seljuq state

external wars but also wars against heretics within its frontiers, and to the Seljuqs Islām owes much of its later achievements. Although *madrasahs* (colleges) had been founded before the Seljuq period, Niẓām al-Mulk was the first official to establish a network of such institutions with the intention, presumably, of giving uniform training to administrators and religious scholars associated with the state. The head of orthodox Islām was the ʿAbbāsid caliph, but, though he was permitted a degree of veneration and independence in Baghdad, he had little real political power in the empire. The sultans as well as the caliph considered it their duty to promote religious works; for this reason as well as to show their power they built many mosques, including the Great Mosque of Iṣfahān (the Masjed-e-Jomʿeh).

Cultural developments. Strange as it may seem, the rule of the Turkish Seljuqs fostered rather than hampered the progress of Persian cultural autonomy. Before the Seljuq era a new form of Persian literature had developed in the Sāmānid territories of northeastern Iran and Transoxania. This was no longer written in the pure old language or in the alphabet of pre-Islāmic Iran but in the Arabic script with a number of borrowed Arabic words. At the same time the Būyids had favoured a form of Persian tradition that expressed itself in Arabic. Seljuq rule, on the other hand, led to the spread of literary Persian to the whole of Iran. The Turks had no cultural Islāmic tradition and almost no written literature. As the Iranians had been their instructors in Islām, they knew no cultural language other than Persian and showed no interest in the achievements of scholars or poets writing in Arabic. From the time of the Seljuqs onward, the Arabic language disappeared from the Iranian lands except in works of religious scholarship.

It is wrong to believe, as many have, that the pursuance of an Islāmic policy and of conquest in Anatolia led the Seljuqs to persecute the Christians. The plundering of the Turkmen armies in the Byzantine Empire no doubt caused much suffering and loss to Eastern Christianity, but inside the Seljuq Empire, as soon as order was restored, the lot of Christians was much the same as it had been before: the crusaders, who thought it must be otherwise, were judging conditions in Jerusalem by those prevailing in Anatolia (see also CRUSADES).

Weaknesses. Despite its successes there were weaknesses in the Seljuq Empire. It could not prevent the growth of the Assassins, a terrorist sect that began its activities with the murder of Niẓām al-Mulk (1092). Furthermore the Seljuqs, like the Būyids before them, could not rid themselves of the idea that sovereignty belonged to a family rather than to a single man; thus even the most powerful sultans thought it necessary to give provinces as appanages to their relatives. In the early years of the Seljuq conquests a practically independent principality had been founded in Kerman by a son of Chaghri Beg, Qāwurd (Kavurt), who extended his conquests to Oman on the Persian Gulf. Another independent but short-lived principality was created in Syria, partly for military reasons, by Malik-Shāh in favour of his brother Tutush.

The disintegration of the empire. When Malik-Shāh died, leaving several sons by different wives, all of them very young, the quarrels between them and their supporters resulted in a partition of the Seljuq heritage among Berk-yaruq, the eldest son; his brother Muḥammad, who received northwestern Iran; and a third brother, Sanjar, who was given charge of Khorāsān. When Berk-yaruq died in 1104, Muḥammad was able to establish only a measure of control in central and western Iran, and this broke down at his death (1118). Sanjar's realm in Khorāsān, however, attained a new power and glory, which were magnified in the eyes of posterity by the length of his reign and the disasters that befell him in his last years. It is necessary here only to recall his victories over the rival Turkish kingdom of the Qarakhanids in Transoxania and over the Ghaznavids of the Indian borderland. This was followed by his defeat in 1138 by new invaders from central Asia, the Karakitai, and by the revolt of his vassal in Khwārazm (Khorezmia). Finally came the general uprising of the Ghuzz (1153), which resulted in Sanjar's captivity, from which he escaped only to die in 1157. Years of disorder and misery ensued for Khorāsān until its final incorporation in a new Khorezmian empire in the reign of Tekish (Takash; 1172–1200).

Thereafter no territory was left in the former Seljuq Empire where a sultan could enjoy real power. When pretenders quarrelled they sought the help of high military officers, to whom they were obliged to abandon the government of whole provinces. This was especially so in the case of the *atabegs*, officers who were entrusted with a kind of tutorship over minor princes. Tribal chiefs also profited by the disorders to make themselves independent, and the caliph himself thought the time ripe, if not to recover the ancient power of the ʿAbbāsids over the whole of the Muslim world, at least to secure a principality of his own in Iraq.

The first of the Seljuq lines to disappear was that in Syria. There Tutush's sons, Riḍwān (Ruḍwān) of Aleppo and Duqāq of Damascus, had quarrelled and were weakened by the attacks of the crusaders. Tughtigin, son of Būrī, the *atabeg* of Duqāq, founded a dynasty of his own (the Būrids) when his master died in 1104. In Aleppo the general feeling was against "Easterners," and the dynasty scarcely survived Riḍwān's death (1113). *Atabeg*s also were governing upper Mesopotamia around Mosul, and one of them, Zangī, united this province and Aleppo under his sway in 1128, thus creating a new dynasty there. Another *atabeg* dynasty, which was to last until the beginning of the 13th century, came to power somewhat later in Azerbaijan. These *atabeg*s "protected" the last Seljuqs of the Iranian line, who resided in Hamadan but had no powers except those granted them by their all-powerful tutors.

In the mid-12th century, the caliph again became independent, and when the last of the Iranian Seljuqs, Toghrïl III, tried to recover some of his lost influence, the caliph appealed to the *shāh* of Khorezmia the (Khwārazm-Shāh) for help. As a result Toghrïl died on the battlefield in 1194. Meanwhile other parts of the Seljuq heritage had met their fate at the hands of tribal chiefs. Even Arab tribes, such as the Mazyadids on the Iraqi borders, had taken advantage of the situation to win at least temporary autonomy. The principality of Kerman did not long survive the death (1170) of its sultan Toghrïl-Shāh. His sons quarrelled and called in foreign aid, with the result that the country was utterly devastated and fell an easy prey to a band of Ghuzz from Khorāsān under their chief, Malik Dīnār (1185). Ten years later it was incorporated in the Khorezmian Empire. Only in Anatolia did Seljuq power survive, and there it did not reach its peak until the 13th century.

SELJUQ ASCENDANCY IN ANATOLIA

The invasion of Anatolia began as an uncoordinated movement of Turkmen tribesmen from Azerbaijan, and the expeditions of Toghrïl Beg and Alp-Arslan were aimed as much at controlling the tribesmen as at conquest. Alp-Arslan's victory at Manzikert (1071) destroyed the Byzantine frontier organization and enabled the Ghuzz to establish themselves in Byzantine territory, where they engaged as mercenaries in the struggles between the local commanders. Among a host of tribal chiefs the leading place was taken about 1075 by the sons of Toghrïl Beg's cousin Qutalmïsh (Kutlumush), who were violently hostile to Malik-Shāh. During the struggles of rival generals for the throne of Constantinople (1078–81), one after another of the contestants called for aid from the sons of Qutalmïsh and opened to them the gates of their cities, including Nicaea and Nicomedia (İzmit). By 1080 Sulaymān ibn Qutalmïsh held the greater part of Anatolia as the ally of the Byzantine emperor and rival sultan to Malik-Shāh. In 1084 Antioch (Antakya) was surrendered to him, but in 1086 he was killed near Aleppo in battle with Tutush and a coalition of Syrian princes. Malik-Shāh attempted to take advantage of Sulaymān's death, both by proposals for an alliance with the Byzantine emperor Alexius I Comnenus and by military expeditions into western Anatolia, but with little success; and on his death (1092), Sulaymān's son, Qïlïch (Kilij) Arslan (who had been captured by Malik-Shāh at Antioch), escaping from his captivity, reconstituted the sultanate. In the interval, however, northeastern Anatolia

Qïlïch Arslan I

had been occupied by a rival Turkmen chief, Dānishmend of Sivas, whose successors engaged in a prolonged conflict with the Seljuq sultans.

The new sultan was immediately confronted with the First Crusade. The first crusader bands, under Walter the Penniless, were defeated at Nicaea (1096), but the Turks were severely defeated before Nicaea and at Dorylaeum (Eskişehir) in 1097 and driven into the interior, while the emperor Alexius reoccupied western Anatolia. After his victory over the next wave of crusaders (1101), Qïlïch Arslan, tempted by the disorders that had weakened the Seljuqs in Iraq, made a bid for the greater sultanate. He succeeded in capturing Mosul but was defeated by the forces of his kinsman of Aleppo and drowned in the Khābūr (Habor) river (1107).

The Sultanate of Rūm. This event proved decisive in determining the future development of the Sultanate of Rūm (the name used by the Turks for the Byzantine Empire). The Seljuqs, hemmed in between Byzantines and the crusading states in Syria and increasingly isolated from the east, gradually established an organized and settled Anatolian kingdom. Qïlïch Arslan was succeeded by his son Malik-Shāh (1107–16), and he by his brother Masʿūd I (1116–55), who established his capital at Konya (Iconium). Masʿūd's long reign was occupied by resistance to the encroachments of the Byzantines and by engagements and negotiations with the Dānishmendids, the crusaders, and his Muslim neighbours. During the reign of his son and successor, Qïlïch Arslan II (1155–92), the Armenians established a principality in Cilicia, but the Dānishmendids were finally subdued and their territories annexed to the sultanate.

Qïlïch Arslan's numerous sons, each of whom held the command of a city of the empire, embittered his old age by their mutual rivalry; and the eldest Quṭb ad-Dīn, tyrannized over him in his own capital, exactly at the time that Frederick I Barbarossa entered the sultan's dominons on his way to the Holy Sepulchre (1190). Konya itself was taken, and the sultan was forced to provide guides and provisions for the crusaders. Qïlïch Arslan lived two years longer, finally under the protection of his youngest son, Kay-Khusraw (Kaikhosrau), who held the capital after him until 1196, when his elder brother, Rukn ad-Dīn Sulaymān II, having vanquished his other brothers ascended the throne and obliged Kay-Khusraw to seek refuge at the Byzantine emperor's court. Rukn ad-Dīn, who died in 1204, saved the sultanate from destruction and conquered Erzurum, which had been ruled for a considerable time by a separate dynasty; but Rukn ad-Dīn's son, Qïlïch Arslan III, was soon deposed, with Greek assistance, by Kay-Khusraw.

After the establishment of the Latin empire of Constantinople (1204), the Turks were the natural allies of the Greeks and the enemies of the crusaders and their allies, the Armenians. Kay-Khusraw, therefore, in 1207 took the important harbour of Attalia (Antalya) from the Italian Aldobrandini; but in 1211 he perished in battle with Theodore I Lascaris, emperor of Nicaea. His son and successor, Ḳay-Kāʾūs, made peace with Lascaris and extended his frontiers to the Black Sea by the conquest of Sinope (Sinop; 1214). On this occasion he took prisoner the Comnenian prince Alexius, who ruled the independent empire of Trebizond (Trabzon), and compelled him to acknowledge the supremacy of the Seljuqs, to pay tribute, and to serve in the armies of the sultan. Elated by this great success and by his victories over the Armenians in Cilicia, Kay-Kāʾūs attempted the capture of Aleppo, at this time governed by the descendants of Saladin, but the project was defeated by Ayyūbid resistance.

Kay-Kāʾūs' brother, ʿAlāʾ ad-Dīn Kay-Qubādh (Kaikobad) I (1219–37), was the most powerful and illustrious prince of this branch of the Seljuqs. He extended his rule as far as Seleucia and desisted from further conquest only on condition that the Armenian princes would enter into the same kind of relation to the Seljuqs as had been imposed on the Comnenians of Trebizond. But his greatest military fame was won by a war that, however glorious, was to prove fatal to the Seljuq Empire in the future; in conjunction with his ally, the Ayyūbid prince Ashraf, he defeated the Khwārazm-Shāh, Jalāl ad-Dīn, near Erzincan (1230). During this war Kay-Qubādh put an end to a collateral dynasty of the Seljuqs of Erzurum and annexed its possessions. He also gained the city of Khilāṭ with dependencies that had recently been taken from the Ayyūbids by Jalāl ad-Dīn. This acquisition, however, led to a new war, as Kay-Qubādh's ally, the Ayyūbid prince, contested it. Sixteen Muslim princes, mostly Ayyūbids, of Syria and Mesopotamia, under the leadership of al-Malik al-Kamil, prince of Egypt, marched with considerable forces into Asia Minor against him. Happily for Kay-Qubādh, the other princes mistrusted the power of the Egyptian, and it proved a difficult task to penetrate through the mountainous, well-fortified accesses to the interior of Anatolia. The advantage thus rested with Kay-Qubādh, who extended his power in upper Mesopotamia. This expansion was pursued by his son Kay-Khusraw II.

The Seljuq legacy to Turkey. The Seljuq sultanate of Anatolia can now be seen to have been one of the most important Muslim states of its age. Its population was a mixed one, including Christians, Armenians, Greeks, Syrians, and Iranian Muslims; but, when compared with the other Seljuq realms, of which the Turks had been only a small, if leading, element, it was really "Turkey" and was so called by its contemporaries. The Seljuqs of this line succeeded in establishing an administration largely based on the institutions of their Iranian-Seljuq neighbours, but it was modified by the Byzantine heritage and by its own evolution. With order and tolerance of all races and religions established, agriculture and mining activity revived, so that to foreigners Turkey seemed one of the richest of countries; meanwhile commerce was developed with the assistance of Italian merchants. In the cities beautiful buildings, several of which still survive, show the purity of an art related to, though not exactly identical with, the Iranian-Seljuq art of the same period. Literature, mostly in Persian, flourished, and, with it, mystical movements, such as that inspired by Jalāl aḍ-Dīn ar-Rūmī.

Yet this political organization and civilization were not really soundly based. The Seljuqs failed to tame, particularly in the frontier districts, the Turkmens, who, though partially settled, were impatient of centralized administration; they remained fond of petty wars against their Christian neighbours and still adhered to their traditional social and religious beliefs and practices. Newcomers from the countries invaded by the Khorezmians and Mongols added to their feeling of unrest. This helps to explain why, when the Mongol flood reached the frontiers of Turkey, which were no longer protected by the Khorezmian state, the Seljuq realm was no more able to resist than had been the Muslim principalities of Iran. At the Battle of Köse Dagh (1243), between Erzincan and Sivas, the independence of the Seljuqs was lost forever.

Seljuq defeat by the Mongols. The Mongols did not destroy the Seljuq state, but, in accordance with their plan, reduced it to vassalage. After the death of Kay-Khusraw II (1245) the quarrels between his sons led to a division of Asia Minor, ʿIzz ad-Dīn Kay-Kāʾūs II taking the part west of the Halys and Rukn ad-Dīn Qïlïch Arslan IV the part to the east. When the former intrigued with the Mamlūks of Egypt and the Byzantine emperor, however, he was driven out and fled to Constantinople. The unity of the realm was thus restored, but the financial requirements of the Mongols and the intrigues of the great chiefs with them against one another quickly brought about a breakdown of the Seljuq administrative system. In the central provinces and cities, the all-powerful minister, the *perwane* Muʿīn ad-Dīn Sulaymān, who had Rukn ad-Dīn executed *c.* 1265, succeeded in maintaining the Iranian-Islāmic civilization of the recent golden age; to this end he cooperated with the Muslim viziers of the Mongol Īl-Khān of Iran, the suzerain of Anatolia.

In the distant and mountainous districts, however, the Turkmen amirs, free from any form of government, established small principalities of their own: in the Taurus, on the Byzantine frontier; on the south Aegean coast, later even near the straits and the Black Sea. With their help and that of Baybars, the powerful Mamlūk sultan of Egypt, the most dreaded enemy of the Mongols, a group of Muslim nobles in Anatolia revolted during 1276–77 against the Mongol protectorate. The *perwane* himself had negotiated with them, and although he finally refused to join them, thus assuring the victory of the Mongols, he was executed. For a time the Seljuq sultanate was then no more than a Mongol province. Seljuq sultans, Kay-Khusraw II (died 1283), Masʿūd III, and Farāmurz, still reigned nominally, but in the first years of the following century the dynasty ended in obscurity.

Thereafter the power of the Turkish amirates increased and the control of the Mongol Īl-Khāns of Iran became less effective until it also finally disappeared, in the 1330s. (Ed.)

The Ottoman Empire

The Ottoman Empire spanned six centuries and came to an end only in 1922, when Turkey was proclaimed a republic. The empire, centred in Anatolia, varied greatly in extent during its history. At its height it included modern Albania, Greece, Bulgaria, Yugoslavia, Romania, and the islands of the eastern Mediterranean; parts of Hungary and Russia; Iraq, Syria, Palestine, the Caucasus, and Egypt; North Africa as far west as Algeria; and parts of Arabia. The term Ottoman is a dynastic appellation derived from the Arabic Uthmān (Turkish: Osman), the name of the warrior ruler who is regarded as the founder of both dynasty and empire. (In this discussion the most recent research into contemporary Ottoman sources is used to fix the major dates of the first century of Ottoman expansion. These replace dates traditionally accepted on the basis of inadequate non-Ottoman sources or limited research into conflicting Ottoman documents.)

THE OTTOMAN STATE TO 1481: THE AGE OF EXPANSION

The first period of Ottoman history was characterized by almost continuous territorial expansion, during which the Ottoman dominion spread out from a small northwestern Anatolian principality to cover an empire encompassing southeastern Europe, Anatolia, and the Arab world. At the same time, the political, economic, and social institutions of the Middle East were amalgamated with those inherited from Byzantium and the great Turkish empires of central Asia and re-established in new forms that were to be characteristic of the area into modern times.

The *gazis*

Ottoman victories under Osman and his successors, c. 1300–1402. In their initial stages of expansion, the Ottomans were leaders of the Turkish *gazis*, or fighters for the faith of Islām, against the shrinking Christian Byzantine state. The ancestors of Osman, the founder of the dynasty, were members of the Kayı tribe who had entered Anatolia along with a mass of Oğuz Turkmen nomads who overwhelmed Byzantium after the Battle of Manzikert in 1071 and came to occupy eastern and central Anatolia during the 12th century. The *gazis* fought against the Byzantines and then the Mongols, who invaded Anatolia following the establishment of the Il-Khanid Empire in Iran and Mesopotamia starting in the last half of the 13th century. Following the Mongol defeat of the Seljuq army at the Battle of Köse Dagh (1243), Osman I emerged as prince (*amīr*) of the border principality of Bithynia, in northwestern Anatolia, and was in command of the *gazis* leading the fight against the Byzantines in that area.

With the disintegration of Seljuq power and its replacement by Mongol suzerainty, independent Turkmen principalities emerged in parts of Anatolia not occupied by the Mongols, among which was that led by Osman. Hemmed in on the east by the more powerful Turkmen principality of Germiyan, Osman and his immediate successors concentrated their attacks on Byzantine territories bordering the Bosporus and the Sea of Marmara. The Ottomans became the main focus for the mass of nomads and urban unemployed then searching for means to gain their livelihoods and to fulfill their religious desire to spread Islām. The Ottomans were able to take advantage of the opportunity offered by the decay of the Byzantine Empire and, starting under Osman I and continuing under his successors Orhan (ruled 1324–60) and Murad I (ruled 1360–89), took over Byzantine territories, first in western Anatolia and then in southeastern Europe. It was only under Bayezid I (ruled 1389–1402) that the wealth and power gained by this initial expansion were used to assimilate the Anatolian Turkish principalities to the east.

By 1300 Osman ruled an area stretching from Eskişehir (Dorylaeum) to the plains of İznik (Nicaea), having defeated several organized Byzantine efforts to curb his expansion, and the Byzantine emperor's use of mercenary troops from western Europe caused more damage to the emperor's own territory than to that of the Turks. At the time, however, the Ottomans lacked effective siege equipment and were unable to take the major cities of Bithynia. Nor could they move against their increasingly powerful Turkmen neighbours at Aydın and Karası, in southwestern Anatolia. Orhan's capture of Bursa in 1324 provided the first means for developing the administrative, financial, and military power necessary to make the principality into a real state and to create an army. It was Orhan who began the military policy of employing Christian mercenary troops, thus lessening his dependence on the nomads as well as providing better fighting forces. Orhan soon was able to capture the remaining Byzantine towns in northwestern Anatolia: Nicaea (İznik; 1331), Nicomedia (İzmit; 1337), and Scutari (Üsküdar; 1338).

Capture of Bursa

He then moved against his major Turkmen neighbours to the south. Taking advantage of internal conflicts he annexed Karası in 1345 and gained control of the area between the Gulf of Edremit and Kapı Dağı (Cyzicus), reaching the Sea of Marmara. He thus put himself in a position to end Aydın's lucrative monopoly in providing mercenary troops to competing Byzantine factions in Thrace and Constantinople. In 1346 Orhan replaced Aydın as the principal ally of the Byzantine emperor John VI Cantacuzenus. The consequent entry of Ottoman troops into Europe gave them a direct opportunity to see the possibilities for conquest offered by the decline of Byzantium. The collapse of Aydın following the death (1348) of its ruler, Umur Bey, left the Ottomans alone as the leaders of the *gazis* against the Byzantines. Orhan helped Cantacuzenus take the throne of Byzantium from John V Palaeologus and as reward secured the right to ravage Thrace and to marry the emperor's daughter Theodora. Ottoman raiding parties began to move regularly through Gallipoli into Thrace. Huge quantities of captured booty strengthened Ottoman power.

Gallipoli as base for expansion

Starting in 1354, Orhan's son Süleyman transformed Gallipoli, on the European side of the Dardanelles, into a base for expansion into Europe and refused to leave, despite the protests of Cantacuzenus and others. From this base, his bands moved into the Balkans, up the Maritsa River, raiding as far as Adrianople. Cantacuzenus soon fell from power, at least partly because of his cooperation with the Turks, and Europe began to be aware of the extent of the Turkish danger.

It was only under Orhan's son Murad I that Gallipoli was used for permanent conquests. Constantinople itself was bypassed because its thick walls and well-organized defenses, despite the weakness and disorganization of its defenders, remained too strong for the rudimentary Ottoman army. Murad's initial conquests were northward into Thrace, culminating with the capture in 1361 of Adrianople—the second city of the Byzantine Empire; renamed Edirne, the city became the new Ottoman capital, providing the Ottomans with a centre for the administrative and military control of Thrace. As the main fortress between Constantinople and the Danube, it controlled the principal invasion road through the Balkan mountains, assured Ottoman retention of their European conquests, and gave them the means for further expansion to the north. Murad then moved through the Maritsa Valley and captured Philippopolis (Filibe) in 1363. Control of the main sources of Constantinople's grain and tax revenues enabled Murad to force the emperor to accept his suzerainty.

The death of the Serbian emperor Stefan Dušan in 1355 left his successors too divided and weak to defeat the Ottomans, despite an alliance with King Louis the Great of Hungary and Tsar Shishman of Bulgaria in the first European crusade against the Ottomans. The Byzantine emperor John V tried to mobilize European assistance

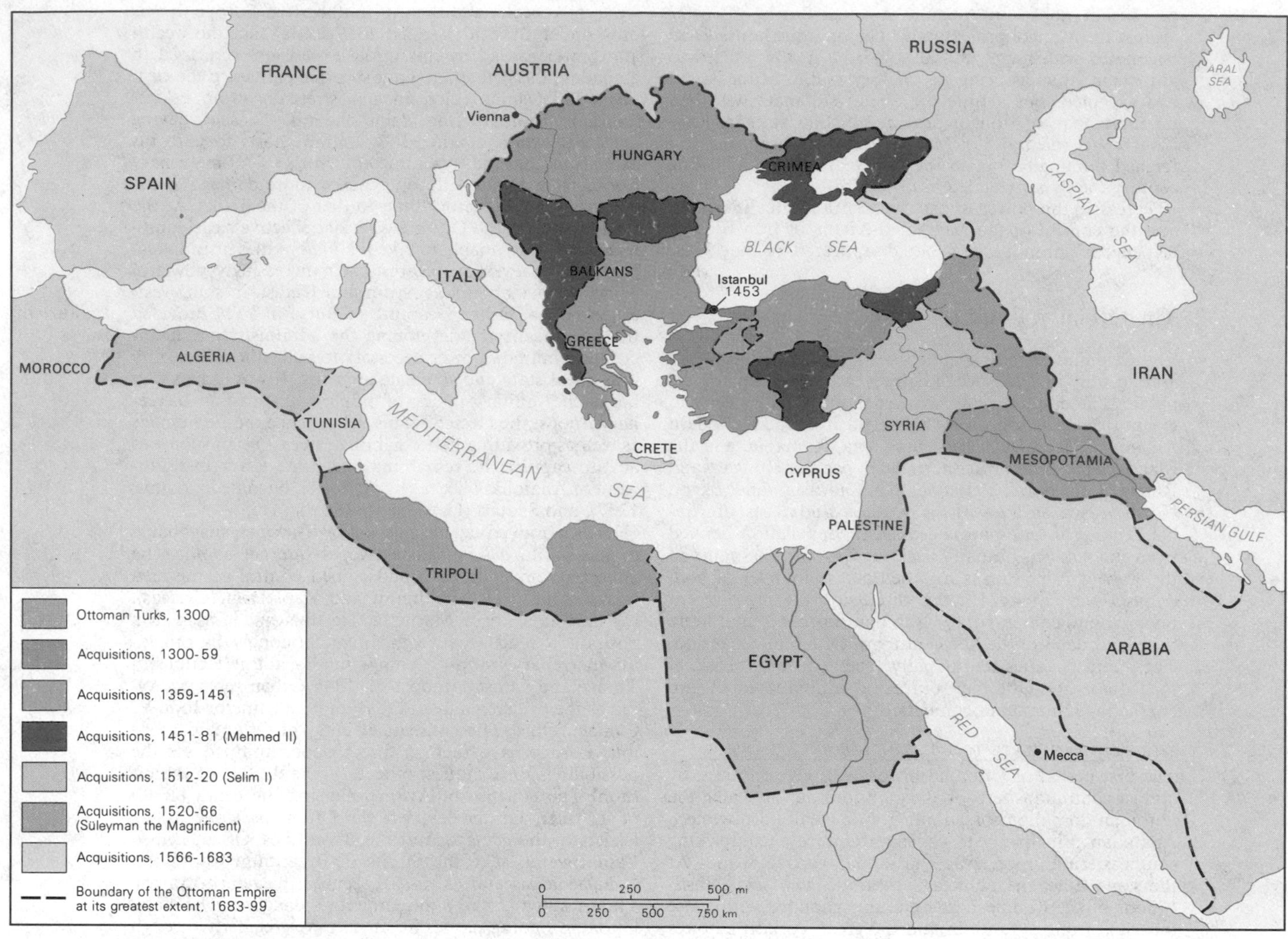

Expansion of the Ottoman Empire.
From S. Fischer, *The Middle East: A History* (1960); Alfred A. Knopf

by uniting the churches of Constantinople and Rome, but only further divided Byzantium without assuring any concrete help from the West. Murad was thus able to rout the allies at Chirmen, on the Maritsa in 1371, increasing his own confidence and demoralizing his smaller enemies, who rapidly accepted his suzerainty without further resistance. Murad next inaugurated an Ottoman empire of vassals in Europe. He retained local native rulers, who in return accepted his suzerainty, paid annual tributes, and provided contingents for his army when required to do so. This policy enabled the Ottomans to avoid a great deal of local resistance to conquest by assuring rulers and subjects alike that their lives, properties, traditions, and positions would be preserved if they peacefully accepted Ottoman rule. It also enabled the Ottomans to govern the newly conquered areas without building up a vast administrative system of their own or maintaining occupation garrisons.

Creation of European vassals

Moving rapidly to consolidate his empire south of the Danube, Murad captured Macedonia (1371–87), central Bulgaria (including Monastir (1382), Sofia (1385), and Niš (Nish) (1386), and Serbia, all culminating in the climactic defeat of the Balkan allies at the Battle of Kosovo (Kosovo Polje) in 1389. Walachia, Bosnia, Albania, Greece, and the Serbian fort of Belgrade remained outside Ottoman rule, and Hungary alone was in a position to resist further Muslim advances.

Bayezid's annexation of Anatolia and defeat by Timur. Murad was killed during the Battle of Kosovo. His son and successor Bayezid I was unable to take advantage of his father's victory to achieve further European conquest, and was, in fact, compelled to restore the defeated vassals and return to Anatolia to face the rising threat of the Turkmen principality of Karaman, created on the ruins of the Seljuq Empire of Anatolia, with its capital at Konya. Bayezid's predecessors had avoided forceful annexation of Turkmen territory in order to concentrate on Europe. They had, however, expanded by such peaceful means as marriage alliances and the purchase of territories. The acquisition of territory in central Anatolia from the amirates of Hamid and Germiyan had brought the Ottomans into direct contact with Karaman for the first time. Murad had been compelled to take some military action to prevent Karaman from occupying his newly acquired territories, but once this was accomplished he had turned back to Europe leaving the unsolved problem to his successor son. Karaman willingly cooperated with Serbia in stirring opposition to Ottoman rule among Murad's vassals in both Europe and Anatolia. It had strengthened the Balkan Union that was routed by the Ottomans at Kosovo, and had stimulated a general revolt in Anatolia that Bayezid was forced to meet by an open attack as soon as he was able to do so.

By the end of 1390, Bayezid had overwhelmed and annexed all the remaining Turkmen principalities in western Anatolia. He attacked and defeated Karaman in 1391, annexed several Turkmen states in eastern Anatolia, and was preparing to complete his conquest in the area when he was forced to turn back to Europe to deal with a revolt of some of his Balkan vassals, encouraged and helped by Hungary and Byzantium. Bayezid quickly smashed the rebels (1390–93), occupied Bulgaria and put it under direct Ottoman administration for the first time, and put Constantinople under siege. In response, Hungary organized a major European crusade against the Ottomans. The effort was beaten back by Bayezid at Nicopolis (Niğbolu) on the Danube in 1396. Europe was terrorized and Ottoman rule south of the Danube was so assured, and Bayezid's prestige in the Islāmic world was so extended that he was given the title of *sulṭān* by the shadow ʿAbbāsid caliph of Cairo—this despite the opposition of the caliph's Mamlūk masters, the rulers of Egypt, Syria, and the Holy Cities, who wanted to retain the title only for themselves.

Turning back to Anatolia to complete the conquests aborted by his move against the crusaders, Bayezid thoroughly overran Karaman, the last Turkmen principality, in 1397. His advances, however, now attracted the attention of Timur (Tamerlane), who had been building a powerful Turkic empire in Central Asia, Iran, Afghanistan, and Mesopotamia, and whose invasion of India in 1398 had been halted by his fear of the rising Ottoman power on his western flank. Encouraged by several Turkmen princes who had fled to his court when their territories were taken by Bayezid, Timur decided to destroy Bayezid's empire before resuming his campaigns in India and thus invaded Anatolia. As Bayezid and Timur moved toward battle, the former's Turkmen vassals and Muslim followers deserted him because he had abandoned the old Ottoman *gazi* tradition of advancing against the infidel. Left only with forces provided by his Christian vassals, Bayezid was decisively overwhelmed by Timur at the Battle of Ankara in 1402. Taken captive by the victor, he died within a year.

Battle of Ankara

Restoration of the Ottoman Empire, 1402–81. Timur's objective in Anatolia had not been conquest, and he followed his victory by retiring from Anatolia after restoring to power the Turkmen princes who had joined him. Even Bayezid's sons were able to assume control over the family's former possessions in western Anatolia, and the Ottoman Empire in Europe was left largely untouched. At this time a strong European crusade might have pushed the Ottomans out of Europe altogether, but weakness and division south of the Danube and diversion in other matters to the north left an opportunity for the Ottomans to restore what had been torn asunder without significant loss.

Disputed succession

But internal divisions were to hinder Ottoman efforts to restore their power. Bayezid's four sons fought for the right of succession. His eldest son Süleyman assumed control in Europe, with his capital at Edirne, and gained the support of the Christian vassals and those who had stimulated Bayezid to turn toward conquest in the East. The descendants of the Turkmen notables who had assisted the early Ottoman conquests in Europe supported the claims of Mehmed, who with the additional support of the Anatolian Muslim religious orders and artisan guilds was able to defeat and kill his brothers Mûsa Bey, who had established his capital at Bursa, and İsa Bey of Balıkesir, in southwestern Anatolia, as well as Süleyman, and so assume undisputed possession of the entire empire as Sultan Mehmed (Muḥammad) I. He was to reign from 1413 to 1420.

Under Mehmed and Murad II (ruled 1421–51), there was a new period of expansion in which Bayezid's empire was restored and new additions made. Mehmed restored the vassal system in Bulgaria and Serbia and promised the vassal princes that he would not undertake new European adventures and would restore his position within the state. Murad II was also compelled to devote most of the early years of his reign to internal problems, and particularly to the efforts of the *gazi* commanders and Balkan vassal princes in Europe, as well as the Turkmen vassals and princes in Anatolia, to retain the autonomy and even independence gained during the decade following the Battle of Ankara. In 1422–23, Murad suppressed the Balkan resistance and put Constantinople under a new siege that ended only after the Byzantines had provided him with huge amounts of tribute. He then restored Ottoman rule in Anatolia and eliminated all of the Turkmen principalities left by Timur with the exception of Karaman and Candar (Jandar), which he left autonomous though tributory so as not to excite the renewed fears of Timur's successors in the east. Murad then inaugurated the first Ottoman war with Venice (1423–30), which had maintained friendly relations with the sultans in order to develop a strong trade position in the Ottoman dominions and the Black Sea area. Venice, however, had accepted Salonica from Byzantium in order to prevent Ottoman expansion across Macedonia to the Adriatic, which it considered to be a Venetian lake. The war was indecisive for some time; Venice was diverted by conflicts in Italy, and the Ottomans needed time to build a naval force sufficient to compete with that of the Venetians. In addition, Murad was diverted by an effort of Hungary to establish its rule in Walachia, between the Danube and the Transylvanian Alps, a move which inaugurated a series of Ottoman-Hungarian conflicts that were to occupy much of the remainder of his reign. Murad finally built a fleet strong enough to blockade Salonica and enable his army to take it (1430), after which Ottoman naval raids against Venetian ports in the Adriatic and the Aegean compelled Venice in 1432 to make a peace in which it abandoned its efforts to prevent the Ottoman advance to the Adriatic, and was allowed to assume a role as the leading commercial power in the sultan's dominions.

Outbreak of Venetian War

Murad, who had been put on the throne by Turkish notables who had joined the Ottoman state during the first century of its existence, soon began to resent the power they had gained in return as well as in consequence of the great new estates they had built up in the conquered areas of Europe and Anatolia. To counteract their power, he began to build up the power of various non-Turkish groups in his service, particularly those composed of Christian slaves and converts to Islām, whose military arm was organized into a new infantry organization called the Janissary corps. To strengthen this group, Murad began to distribute most of his new conquests to its members, and to add new supporters of this sort he developed the famous *devşirme* system by which Christian youths were drafted from the Balkan provinces for conversion to Islām and life service to the sultan. With their revenues and numbers increasing, the *devşirme* men and their supporters achieved considerable political power. Because the new European conquests were being used by the sultan to build up the *devşirme* relative to the Turkish notables, the former wanted them to continue and expand, while the latter opposed them. Murad, wanting to return to aggressive policies of European expansion in order to help the *devşirme* reduce the power of the Turkish notables, renewed the struggle with Hungary in Serbia and Wallachia starting in 1434. He took advantage of the death in 1437 of the Hungarian king Sigismund to reoccupy Serbia, excepting Belgrade, and to ravage much of Hungary, and he then annexed Serbia in 1439, beginning a policy of replacing the vassals with direct Ottoman rule throughout the empire. Hungarian control of Belgrade was now the major bar to large-scale advances north of the Danube. Ottoman attacks on it and raids on Transylvania failed to move the Hungarians, largely because of the leadership of János Hunyadi, originally a leader of the Walachian border resistance to the *gazis* in 1440–42. Although Murad finally defeated Hunyadi at the Battle of Zlatica (İzladi) in 1443, the increased influence of the Turkish notables at Murad's court led the sultan to agree to the Peace of Adrianople in 1444. By its terms Serbia regained its autonomy, Hungary kept Wallachia and Belgrade, and the Ottomans promised to end their raids north of the Danube. In 1444 Murad also made peace with his main Anatolian enemy, Karaman, and retired to a life of religious contemplation, voluntarily passing the throne to his son Mehmed II who, still very young, already showed the qualities of leadership that were later to distinguish his long reign. The Byzantines and the pope sought to use the opportunity created by the existence of a youthful sultan to push the Ottomans out of Europe, organizing a new crusade joined by Hungary and Venice when the pope assured them that they were not bound to honour the peace treaty they had signed with Muslim infidels. A crusader army moved through Serbia across the Balkan Mountains to the Black Sea at Varna, where it was to be supplied and transported to Constantinople by a Venetian fleet, which was to sail through the Straits, at the same time using its power to prevent Murad from returning from Anatolia with the bulk of the Ottoman army. Though the crusaders reached Varna, a Serbian decision to remain loyal to the sultan, combined with Venetian reluctance to fulfill its part of the agreement for fear of losing its trade position should the Ottomans win, left the crusaders stranded. Fur-

Organization of the Janissary corps

New European crusade

ther quarrels among the crusade leaders gave Murad time to return from Anatolia and organize a new army. The Turkish victory at Varna on November 10, 1444, ended the last important European crusading effort against the Ottomans. Murad now reassumed the throne and brought back to power with him the *devşirme* party, whose insistent demands for conquest led him to spend the remainder of his reign eliminating the vassals and establishing direct rule in much of Thrace, Macedonia, Bulgaria, and Greece. In the process, he divided the newly acquired lands into estates the revenues of which further increased the power of the *devşirme* at the expense of the Turkish notables. Only Albania was able to resist because of the leadership of its national hero, Skanderbeg (George Kastrioti). He was routed by the sultan at the second Battle of Kosovo (1448). By the time of Murad's death in February 1451, the Danube frontier was secure, and it seemed that the Ottoman Empire was in Europe to stay.

Whereas the victory at Varna brought new power to the *devşirme* party, the grand vizier Candarlı Halil Paşa was able to retain a dominant position for the Turkish notables whom he led by keeping the confidence of the sultan and by successfully dividing his opponents. Prince Mehmed therefore became the candidate of the *devşirme,* and it was only with his accession that they were able to achieve the political and military power made possible by the financial base built up during the previous two decades. Under Sultan Mehmed II (1451–81), the *devşirme* increasingly came to dominate, and to press their desire for new conquests in order to take fuller advantage of the situation created at Varna. Constantinople became their first objective. To Mehmed and his supporters, the Ottoman dominions in Europe could never reach their full extent or be molded into a real empire so long as their natural administrative and cultural centre remained outside their hands. The grand vizier (the sultan's chief adviser) and other Turkish notables bitterly opposed the attack, ostensibly because it might draw a new crusade, but in fact because of their fear that the capture of the Byzantine capital might bring about a final triumph of the *devşirme.* The siege (April 6–May 29, 1453) and conquest of Constantinople and its transformation into the Ottoman capital of Istanbul marked an important new stage in Ottoman history. Internally, it saw the end of power and influence for the old Turkish nobility, whose leaders soon were executed or exiled and whose properties were confiscated, and the triumph of the *devşirme* and their supporters. Externally, the conquest made Mehmed II the most famous ruler in the Muslim world, even though the lands of the old caliphate still remained in the hands of the Mamlūks of Egypt and Timur's successors in Iran. Moreover, it was not long before possession of Constantinople stimulated Mehmed to nourish an ambition to place under his dominion not merely the Islāmic and Turkic worlds but also a re-created Byzantine Empire and, perhaps, the entire world of Christendom.

Final attack on Constantinople

Restoration of Istanbul

To pursue these objectives, Mehmed II developed various bases of power. Domestically, his primary objective was to restore Istanbul as the political, economic, and social centre of the area that it formerly had dominated. To this end, he worked to repopulate the city, not only with its former inhabitants but also with elements of all the conquered peoples of the empire, whose residence and intermingling there would provide a microcosm for a similar process that Mehmed hoped would weld the entire empire into a powerful and integrated whole. Special tax concessions were established to encourage the most active and skilled of his subjects to settle in the capital. The major religious groups were allowed to establish their own self-governing communities, called *millet*s, under the leadership of their religious chiefs, each retaining its own civil laws, traditions, and language under the general protection of the sultan. Mehmed also worked to restore the physical aspects of the city. Old buildings were repaired; streets, aqueducts, and bridges were constructed; sanitary facilities were modernized; and a vast supply system was set up to provide for the city's inhabitants. Great attention was paid to restoring Istanbul's industry and trade, with special concessions to attract merchants and artisans from all parts of the empire.

Mehmed also devoted much time in expanding his dominions in Europe and Asia in order to establish his claim to world leadership. To this end, he eliminated the last princes who might dispute his claims to be legitimate successor to the Byzantine and Seljuq dynasties, and replaced the remaining vassal princes with direct, Ottoman administration. In addition, he extended Ottoman rule far beyond the territories inherited from Murad II; from 1454 to 1463, he concentrated mainly on southeastern Europe, annexing Serbia (1454–55), conquering the Morea (1458–60), and eliminating in the process the last major claimants to the Byzantine throne. When Venice refused to surrender its important forts on the Aegean coast of the Morea, Mehmed inaugurated the second Venetian-Ottoman war (1463–79). At the same time he annexed Trebizond (1461) and the Genoese commercial colonies that had survived along the Black Sea coast of Anatolia, including Sinop and Kafa, and began the process by which the Crimean Tatar *khān*s were compelled to accept Ottoman suzerainty. In 1463 he occupied and annexed Bosnia, helped by the native Bogomils, an evangelical Christian sect that had been badly treated by the Catholic Hungarians. When Albania continued to hold out, helped by supplies sent by sea from Venice, Mehmed sent in large numbers of Turkmen irregulars, who in the process of conquering Albania settled there and formed a Muslim community. Whereas the papacy and Venice were unable to raise a new crusade, they were able to divert Mehmed by encouraging attacks by his Eastern enemies, the Turkmen principality of Karaman and the Ak Koyunlu ("White Sheep") dynasty, which under the leadership of Uzun Ḥasan, had replaced Timur's descendants in Iran. Mehmed, however, skillfully used dynastic divisions to conquer Karaman in 1468, extending direct Ottoman rule in Anatolia to the Euphrates. When Uzun Ḥasan responded by invading Anatolia in the company of many Turkmen princes, Venice intensified its attacks in the Morea, Hungary moved into Serbia, and Skanderbeg attacked Bosnia. Mehmed, however, was able to defeat these enemies, one after the other. In 1473 he routed Uzun Ḥasan, who acknowledged Ottoman rule in all of Anatolia and returned to Iran. This brought the Ottomans into conflict with the Mamlūk empire in Syria, which Mehmed neutralized, though he could not defeat it. He then turned to Venice, and several naval raids along the Adriatic coast finally led to a peace in 1479 whereby Venice surrendered its bases in Albania and the Morea and agreed to pay a regular annual tribute in return for restoration of its commercial privileges. Mehmed then used his new naval power to send a large force that landed at Otranto in southern Italy in August 1480, and to attack Rhodes. Success seemed within sight when his premature death in 1481 brought his effort to an end. But he had, indeed, laid the foundations for Ottoman rule in Anatolia and southeastern Europe that was to survive for the next four centuries.

Second Venetian war

In addition to conquering a large empire, Mehmed worked to consolidate it and to codify the political, administrative, religious, and legal institutions developed during the previous century in a series of law codes called *kanun-name*s. The immensity of the task, however, and his diversion in numerous campaigns delayed the process to such an extent that it was completed only during the mid-16th century. Nor was Mehmed overly successful in building the economic and social bases of his empire. His most important problem was securing sufficient money to finance his military expeditions and the new apparatus of government and society. The tax systems inherited from his predecessors did not provide the required money, particularly because most of the conquered lands were turned into estates whose taxes went entirely to their holders in return for military and administrative services. Mehmed therefore turned to a number of expedients that achieved their immediate objectives, but at the cost of grave economic and social difficulties. He regularly withdrew all coins from circulation and issued new ones with a larger proportion of base metal alloys. To enforce acceptance of the new issues, he sent armed bands around the empire with the right to confiscate without compensation all of the older and more valuable coins that had not been vol-

Financial difficulties

untarily exchanged for the new. The debasement of the coinage soon caused a rapid inflation, and this in turn greatly disturbed the industry and trade that the sultan had hoped to assist. In addition, in his search for revenues, Mehmed created monopolies over the production and use of essential goods, distributing them among the highest bidders, who in turn charged excessive prices and created artificial scarcities to secure their profits. Finally, Mehmed established the principle that all revenue-producing property belonged to the sultan. In pursuance of this, he confiscated much private property and religious foundation lands, creating tremendous resentment and opposition among those who lost their revenues, including members of the religious ‹*ulamā*› class, the Turkish notables, and even some *devşirme* men, whose discontent threatened to undermine both state and sultan. It was only by playing these groups off against each other that Mehmed was able to maintain his own position and power and to continue his conquests.

Ottoman institutions in the 14th and 15th centuries. Ottoman dynasts were transformed from simple tribal leaders to border princes (*uc bey*) and *gazi* leaders under Seljuq and then Īl-Khānid suzerainty in the 13th and early 14th centuries. With the capture of Bursa, Orhan had been able to declare himself independent of his suzerains and assume the title of *bey*, which was retained by his successors until Bayezid I was named sultan by the shadow ‹Abbāsid caliph of Cairo following his victory over the Christian crusaders at the Battle of Nicopolis (1396). These title changes were not immaterial in the position of the Ottoman ruler within the state and in the organization of the state itself.

Powers of Ottoman rulers

As *uc bey* and even *bey*, the Ottoman leader remained little more than a tribal chief, sharing administrative and military leadership with the Turkmen chiefs surrounding him. Like the tribal chiefs, he had the right to the loyalty and obedience of his followers only so long as he led them to victory, and only in relation to his military functions. Beyond this, he was only one among equals in the councils that decided general internal policies; the tribes and clans remained autonomous in their internal affairs. The *bey* was accessible to the tribe and clan leaders as well as to their followers. He could intervene in disputes among the clans, but jurisdiction was limited indeed. Muslim law and jurists had little influence, whereas Turkish tribal law and custom prevailed. In such a situation, the idea of rule was very limited; administration was conceived mainly in financial terms, with each clan or family or tribe accepting Ottoman military leadership largely for the financial rewards it could bring. Ottoman chiefs collected the booty in conquered lands, and following the conquest had the right to collect taxes from lands left in their possession. The only advantage that the *bey* had over the chiefs surrounding him was, as tribal war leader, the right called *pençik*, to collect an extra fifth of the booty taken by his followers. Because the *bey* was dependent for his power and revenues on the assent of his followers, his authority was limited in scope and in time.

Administrative offices. But as the territory of the Ottoman principality expanded, and the Ottomans fell heirs to the administrative apparatus left by the Byzantines, this simple tribal organization was replaced by a more complex form of government, so that by the time the Ottoman rulers became sultans, they already had far more extensive power and authority than had been the case a half-century earlier. The simple tribal organization of the Ottoman *bey* could suffice only for so long as the state was small enough for the individual tribal leaders to remain on their lands and fight the nearby enemy at the same time. But as the principality expanded and the frontiers and enemies became further removed from previously conquered territory, the financial and administrative functions at home had to be separated from the military. Taxes had to be collected to exploit the conquered territories and support the officers and soldiers while they were away. The treasury of the sultan had to be separated from that of the state so that each would have an independent income and organization.

Throughout the 14th and 15th centuries, the Ottoman state gradually evolved its institutions of government and the army to meet the needs of administering and defending an expanding empire. As this was done, it was natural that it should be influenced by those states that had preceded it, not only in the areas it came to rule, but also in the lands of its ancestors. So it was that the developing Ottoman state was influenced by the traditions of the nomadic Turkic empires of Central Asia, particularly in military organization and tactics. It was also influenced heavily by the classical High Islāmic civilization of the ‹Abbāsids, as passed through the hands of the Seljuqs, particularly in the development of orthodox Islām as the basis of its institutions of administration, religion, law, and education, and in the development of the *mukataa* as the basic unit of its administrative and financial systems. In the court hierarchy, the central financial structure, and the tax and administrative organizations developed in the European provinces, the Ottomans were influenced by the Byzantines and, to a lesser extent, by the Serbian and Bulgarian empires.

Influences of early states

Whereas conversion to Islām was not demanded of those conquered at this time, many Christians and Jews voluntarily converted to secure full status in the new empire. Most, however, continued to practice their old religions without restriction. A particularly important source of Christian influence during the 14th century came from the close marriage ties between the Ottoman and Christian courts. Sultan Orhan married Theodora, daughter of Byzantine emperor John VI Cantacuzenus. Theodora was the mother of Murad I, who in turn married Byzantine and Bulgarian princesses, whereas Bayezid I married Despina, daughter of the Serbian prince Lazar. Each of these marriages brought Christian followers and advisers into the Ottoman court, and it was under their influence that Bayezid I in particular abandoned the simple nomadic courts and practices of his predecessors and isolated himself behind elaborate court hierarchies and ceremonials borrowed primarily from the Byzantines. At the same time, the Greek and Serbian languages tended to dominate Ottoman court life, and to a lesser extent its administration.

The triumph of Sultan Mehmed I in 1413 was due at least in part to the support of the Turkish notables and Muslim religious orders of Anatolia who strongly resented the Christian predominance in Bayezid's court and attributed his abandonment of the *gazi* tradition and attacks in Turkish Muslim Anatolia to their influence. As a result, Turkish and Muslim influences dominated the Ottoman court during the 15th century, although the hierarchies, institutions, and ceremonies introduced in the previous century remained largely without change.

Growth of administration

The same process that isolated the sultans from their subjects also removed them from the daily administration of government. Formal institutions of administration therefore had to be evolved to take their place, with the rulers delegating more and more of their duties to executive ministers, to whom the Seljuq title *vezīr* (vizier) was given. The continued close connections of the Ottoman family with the urban guilds and orders of Anatolia, many of the members of which were descendants of officials of the Great Seljuq and Īl-Khānid empires, as well as the empire of the Seljuqs of Konya, provided continuity with the Islāmic Turkish traditions of government. With them came the basic unit of Islāmic administrative and financial organization, the *mukataa*, which intimately associated each office with a source of revenues and made each official the collector of his own salary, at the same time that it circumscribed his administrative powers within those tasks directly involved with the financial function. It was relatively simple for the Ottomans to preserve previous methods of taxing on the local levels in different parts of the empire while weaving them into a united whole through the veneer provided by the *mukataa* units in which the resulting tax revenues were assigned to Ottoman officials.

Office of grand vizier. As the central administration was divided into functional departments, a vizier was appointed to direct each. Most of the early viziers were former Turkmen princes who had entered Ottoman service, though some, particularly under Bayezid I, were Christians and Christian converts. State policy was discussed and decided in a council (*divan*) of these viziers, who were joined by religious, judicial, and military leaders under the direction and chairmanship of the sultan. As the duties of the state became more extensive and complex, the individual viziers gained increased financial and political power, and as the Byzantine influence caused the sultan to isolate himself, it was inevitable that the viziers would come to dominate. As if to emphasize his removal from the daily affairs of state, the sultan began to appoint one of his viziers as his chief minister, or grand vizier. From 1360 to the conquest of Constantinople, this powerful position was reserved for members of the Çandarli family, which came to lead and represent the powerful and assertative Turkmen notable families, who thus benefitted most from the 14th-century expansion of the empire.

Military organization. The first Ottoman army had been composed entirely of Turkmen nomads, who had remained largely under the command of their own tribe and clan leaders, and under the influence of the *şeyh*s of the heterodox and mystic religious orders that had converted most of them to Islām. Armed with bows and arrows and spears, these nomadic cavalrymen had lived mostly on booty, but those assigned as *gazi*s to border areas or sent to conquer and raid Christian lands had also been given more permanent revenues in the form of taxes levied on the lands they garrisoned. These revenue holdings were formalized as *mukata'a*s, with the tribal leaders and *gazi* commanders holding them and collecting their revenues to feed, supply, and arm their followers. It was this type of *mukataa* that developed into the Ottoman form of fief called *timar*, that was the basis of Ottoman military and administrative organization as the European portions of the empire were conquered from the vassals in the 15th century and placed under direct Ottoman administration.

These troops had predominated through Orhan's reign until he had seen that such mounted and undisciplined men were of limited use in besieging and taking large cities. In addition, once he had established his state, he had found it difficult to maintain order with such an army because the nomads still preferred to maintain themselves by the traditional forms of looting, in the lands of their commander as well as in those of the enemy. To replace the nomads, Orhan had organized a separate standing army of hired mercenaries paid by salary rather than booty or by *timar* estates. Those mercenaries organized as infantry were called *yaya*s, those organized as cavalry, *müsellem*s. Although the new force included some Turkmen who were content to accept salaries in place of booty, most of its men were Christian soldiers from the Balkans who were not required to convert to Islām as long as they obeyed their Ottoman commanders. As Murad I had conquered more and more of southeastern Europe these forces had become mainly Christian, and as they came to dominate the Ottoman army, the older Turkmen cavalrymen were maintained mainly as irregular shock troops, called *akincis*, who were compensated only by booty. As the *yaya*s and *müsellem*s expanded in numbers, their salaries became too burdensome for the Ottoman treasury, so in most cases the newly conquered lands were assigned to their commanders in the form of *timar*s. It was this new regular army that developed the techniques of battle and siege used to achieve most of the 14th-century Ottoman conquests, but because it was commanded by members of the Turkish notable class, it became the major vehicle for their rise to predominance over the sultans, whose direct military supporters were limited to the vassal contingents.

Growth of a regular army

Only late in the 14th century did Murad I and Bayezid I attempt to build up their personal power by building a military slave force for the sultan under the name *kapikulu* (pl. *kapıkullari*), or slaves of the Porte. Murad based the new force on his right to a fifth of the war booty, which he interpreted to include captives taken in battle. As these men entered his service, they were converted to Islām and trained as Ottomans, gaining the knowledge and experience required for service in the government, as well as the army, while remaining in the sultan's personal service. During the late 14th century, this force became the most important element of the Ottoman army, particularly its infantry branch, called *yeniçeri* ("new soldiers"), or the Janissary corps. The provincial forces provided by the timar holders comprised the Ottoman cavalry and were called *sipahi*s, while the irregular *akinci*s and salaried *yaya*s and *müsellem*s were relegated to rear-line duties and lost their military and political importance. But when Bayezid I abandoned the *gazi* tradition and moved into Anatolia, he lost the support of the Turkish notables and their *sipahi*s before his new *kapikulu* army was fully established. He thus had to rely only on the Christian vassal forces in the Battle of Ankara, and whereas they demonstrated considerable valour and fighting ability, they were not alone sufficient to resist Timur's powerful army.

When the Ottoman Empire was restored under sultan Mehmed I, the Turkish notables, in order to deprive the sultan of the only military force he could use to resist their control, required him to abandon the *kapikulu* as contrary to the Islāmic tradition that Muslims could not be kept in slavery. The European and Anatolian revolts that arose early in the reign of Murad II were at least partly stimulated and supported by members of the *kapikulu* as well as the Christian slaves and vassals who had been losing their power to the Turkish notables. But as soon as Murad II was established, he resumed earlier efforts to make the sultanate more independent, building up the strength of the Janissaries and their associates and playing them off against the notables. He distributed most of his conquests to members of the *kapikulu* force, occasionally as *timar*s, but more often as tax farms (*iltizam*s), so that the treasury could obtain the money it needed to maintain the Janissary army entirely on a salaried basis. In addition, in order to man the new force, Murad developed the *devşirme* system of recruiting the best Christian youths from southeastern Europe.

The *devşirme* system

System of status and rank. Whereas Mehmed II used the conquest of Constantinople to destroy the major Turkish notable families, and build up the power of the *devşirme,* he sought only to establish a balance of power and function between the two groups so that he could use and control both for the benefit of the empire. So it was that he enlarged the concept of *kapikulu* to include members of the Turkish nobility and their Turkmen followers as well as the products of the *devşirme.* Now only persons accepting the status of slaves of the sultan could hold positions in the Ottoman government and army. Persons of Muslim and non-Muslim origin could achieve this status, so long as they accepted the limitations involved, namely absolute obedience to their master and the devotion of their lives, properties, and families to his service. After this time, all important ministers, military officers, judges, governors, *timar* holders, tax farmers, Janissaries, *sipahi*s, and the like were made members of this class and attached to the will and service of the sultan. The salaried Janissary corps remained the primary source of strength of the *devşirme* class whereas the *sipahi*s and the *timar* system remained the bases of power of the Turkish notables.

Mehmed II thus avoided the fate of the great Middle Eastern empires that had preceded that of the Ottomans, in which rule had been shared among members of the ruling dynasty and with others, and rapid disintegration had resulted. The Ottomans established the principle of indivisibility of rule, with all members of the ruling class subjected to the absolute will of the sultan. To assure this, Mehmed II began the process of developing a firm law of succession, beginning the practice of executing all the brothers of the reigning sultan so that succession would be limited to one of his sons, preferably the ablest one.

THE PEAK OF OTTOMAN POWER, 1481–1566

Domination of southeastern Europe and the Middle East. During much of the century that followed the reign of Mehmed II, the Ottoman Empire achieved the peak of its power and wealth. New conquests extended its domain well into central Europe and throughout the Arab portion of the old Islāmic caliphate; and a new amalgam of political, religious, social, and economic organizations and traditions was institutionalized and developed into a living, working whole.

Bayezid II (ruled 1481–1512). The reign of Mehmed II's immediate successor, Sultan Bayezid II, was largely a period of rest. The previous conquests were consolidated, and many of the political, economic, and social problems caused by Mehmed's internal policies were dealt with, leaving a firm foundation for the conquests of the 16th-century sultans.

The economic stringencies imposed to finance Mehmed II's campaigns had led during the last year of his reign to a virtual civil war encouraged and participated in by the major factions in Istanbul—the *devşirme* party and the Turkish aristocracy. Bayezid was put on the throne by the Janissaries because of their military domination of the capital, whereas his more militant brother Cem fled to Anatolia, where he led a revolt initially supported by the Turkish notables. Bayezid managed to conciliate the latter, however, by exposing to them his essentially pacific plans, which he concealed from the Janissaries. Left without major support, Cem fled into exile to Mamlūk Syria in the summer of 1481. He returned the next year with the help of the Mamlūks and the last Turkmen ruler of Karaman, but his effort to secure the support of the Turkmen nomads failed because of Bayezid's heterodox religious policies. Cem remained in exile, first at Rhodes, then with the pope in Rome, until his death in 1495. European efforts to use him as the spearhead of a new crusade effort against Istanbul were unsuccessful.

Conciliation of Turkish notables

In the meantime, however, the threat that Cem might lead a foreign attack compelled Bayezid to concentrate on internal consolidation. Most of the property expropriated by his father was restored to its original owners. Equal taxes were established around the empire so that all subjects could fulfill their obligations to the government without the kind of disruption and dissatisfaction that had characterized the previous regime. Particularly important was the establishment of the *avâriz-i divaniye* (war chest) tax, which provided for the special expenditures of war without special confiscations or heavy levies. The value of the coinage was restored, and Mehmed II's plans for economic expansion were at long last brought to fruition. The vassal system was replaced by direct Ottoman administration throughout the empire. For the first time the central government was given a budget system in which expenditures were balanced against revenues on a regular basis.

Culturally, Bayezid stimulated a strong reaction against the Europeanizing trends of the previous half century. The Turkish language and Muslim traditions were emphasized. He worked to develop and establish the institutions of orthodox Islām in order to save the empire from the increasing menace of heterodox Shīʿism among the tribes of eastern Anatolia, until, late in his life, his own tendency toward mystic Ṣūfism led him largely to abandon the effort.

Though Bayezid preferred to maintain peace so as to have the time and resources to concentrate on internal development, he was forced into a number of campaigns by the exigencies of the time and the demands of his more militant *devşirme* followers. In Europe, he rounded off the empire south of the Danube and Sava by taking Hercegovina (1483), leaving only Belgrade outside Ottoman control. The Hungarian king Matthias Corvinus (ruled 1458–90) was interested mainly in establishing his rule over Bohemia and agreed to peace with the Ottomans (1484), and after his death, struggles for succession left this front relatively quiet for the remainder of Bayezid's reign. To the northeast, the sultan pushed Ottoman territory north of the Danube, along the shores of the Black Sea, capturing (1484) the ports of Kilia and Akkerman, which controlled the mouths of the Danube and Dniester, thus giving the Ottomans control over the major entrepôts of northern Europe's trade with the Black Sea and Mediterranean. Bayezid was there able to compel Moldavia to accept his suzerainty—an important step toward the incorporation of the Romanian principalities in his empire. Because these advances conflicted with the ambitions of Poland, war followed (1483–89) until the diversion of Poland by the threat of Muscovy under Ivan the Great (ruled 1462–1505) left this front quiet also after 1484.

Extension of the empire

Bayezid then turned to the East, where previous conquests as far as the Euphrates had for the first time brought the Ottomans up to the Mamlūk Empire. Conflict over control of the small Turkmen principality of Dulkadir (Dhū al-Qadr), which controlled much of Cilicia and the mountains south of Lake Van, and an Ottoman desire to share in the control of the Muslim holy cities of Mecca and Medina, led to an intermittent war (1485–91); but there were no concrete results, and Bayezid's disinclination to commit major forces to the endeavour led to dissension and criticism on the part of his militant followers. To counter this, Bayezid tried to use Hungarian internal dissention to take Belgrade; but he failed, and raiding forces sent into Transylvania, Croatia, and Carinthia were turned back.

In the same year that Cem died (1495) a new peace with Hungary left Bayezid's objectives unfulfilled, so he turned toward his other major European enemy, Venice, to rebuild his reputation. Venice had been encouraging revolts against the sultan in the Morea, Dalmatia, and Albania, which it had ceded to the Ottomans in 1479. It also gained control of Cyprus (1489), where it built a major naval base, which it refused to allow Bayezid to use against the Mamlūks, thus pointing up the strategic importance of Cyprus to the sultan. Bayezid also hoped to conquer the last Venetian ports in the Morea to establish the bases for complete Ottoman naval control of the eastern Mediterranean. All these objectives except control of Cyprus were achieved in the war that followed (1499–1503). The Ottoman fleet emerged for the first time as a major Mediterranean naval power, and the Ottomans became an integral part of European diplomatic relations.

Bayezid never was able to use this situation to make new conquests in Europe because the rise of revolts in eastern Anatolia occupied much of his attention during the last years of his reign. There the old conflict resumed between the autonomous, uncivilized nomads and the stable, settled Middle Eastern civilization—the Turkmen nomads resisted the efforts of the Ottomans to expand their administrative control to all parts of the empire. In reaction to the orthodox Muslim establishment, the nomads showed a fanatical attachment to the leaders of the Ṣūfī and Shīʿah mystic orders, of whom the most successful were the Ṣafavids of Ardabīl, who at this time used a religious-military appeal to conquer most of Iran. Under Shāh Esmāʿīl (ruled 1502–24), the Ṣafavids sent missionaries throughout Anatolia, spreading a message of religious heresy and political revolt, not only among the tribesmen but also to cultivators and some urban elements, who began to see in this movement the answers to their own problems. A series of revolts resulted, with Bayezid, because of his involvements in Europe, able to do little to suppress them. Finally, at the start of the 16th century, a general Anatolian uprising forced Bayezid into a major expedition (1502–03), which pushed the Ṣafavids and many of their Turkmen followers back into Iran; there the Ottomans turned from Ṣūfism to Shīʿism as a means of gaining the loyalty of the Persians to a Turkish dynasty. Shāh Esmāʿīl continued, however, to spread his message as Ṣūfī leader in Anatolia, leading to a second major revolt of his followers against the Ottomans (1511). All the grievances of the time coalesced into what was basically a religious uprising against the central government, and only a major expedition led by the grand vizier Ali Paşa could suppress it. But the conditions that had caused the uprising remained a major problem for Bayezid's successor. In the end, Bayezid's increasingly mystical and pacific nature led the Janissaries to dethrone him in favour of his militant and active son, Sultan Selim I.

The Ṣafavids

Selim I (ruled 1512–20). Whereas Bayezid, despite his pacific nature, had been put on the throne by the Janissaries, Selim I was their candidate because he shared their desire to return to an aggressive policy of conquest. But Selim did not wish to be dependent on, or under the control of, those who had brought him to power; he killed not only his brothers but also all seven of their sons and four of his own five sons, leaving only the ablest, Süleyman, as the sole possible heir to the throne. This deprived potential opponents of alternative leaders around whom they could coalesce. Selim was then able to leave the *devşirme* in control of the government; but with a single heir, and with the sultan establishing his personal control over the Janissaries, it was he who dominated, rather than the *devşirme*.

Selim's ambitions encompassed Europe as well as Asia; but Bayezid had left the European fronts relatively quiet, so the new sultan turned first to the East, and chose the Ṣafavids of Iran as his initial victims. Selim first launched a vigorous campaign against the Ṣafavid supporters in eastern Anatolia, massacring thousands of tribesmen and missionaries and espousing a strict defense of Islāmic orthodoxy as a means of regaining political control. In the summer of 1514 he launched a major expedition against the Ṣafavids, hoping to add Iran to his empire and finally to eliminate the threat of heterodoxy. Esmāʿīl employed a scorched-earth policy, retiring into central Iran and hoping that winter would force the Ottomans to retire without a battle. But the militant Kizilbâş (Kizilbash) followers of the Ṣafavids forced the *shāh* to accept battle by intercepting the Ottomans before they entered Azerbaijan. The Ottoman and Ṣafavid armies clashed at Chāldirān, on the eastern side of the Euphrates (August 23, 1514), and the Ṣafavids were routed by Ottoman superiority in weapons and tactics (particularly because of Selim's use of cannons and gunpowder, in contrast to Ṣafavid reliance on spears and arrows). Though Azerbaijan was occupied, the Ottoman victory led to neither the conquest of Iran nor to the collapse of the Ṣafavid empire. The Ottoman army became increasingly discontented under the impact of Ṣafavid propaganda among the already-heterodox Janissaries and because of a relative lack of booty and supplies compared to campaigns in Europe. Selim was compelled to retire, and the Ṣafavids regained their lost province without resistance. The major result of the Chāldirān battle was to convince Shāh Esmāʿīl and his successors to avoid open conflict with the Ottomans at all costs—a policy followed for the next century. This preserved the Ṣafavid army, but it enabled Selim to overcome the last independent Turkmen dynasties in eastern Anatolia (1515–17) and to establish a strong strategic position relative to the Mamlūk Empire, which was falling into internal decay and was ripe for conquest by either the Ottomans or the Ṣafavids.

Defeat of the Ṣafavids

With Shāh Esmāʿīl still busy restoring his army, Selim I was able to overwhelm the Mamlūks in a single year's campaign during the summer and winter of 1516–17. The Mamlūk army fell easily to the well-organized and disciplined Ottoman infantry and cavalry, supported by artillery. The conquest was aided by the support of many Mamlūk officials, who betrayed their masters in return for important positions and revenues promised by the conquerors. In addition, most of the major populated centres of Syria and Egypt turned out their Mamlūk garrisons, preferring the security and order offered by the Ottomans to the anarchy and terror of the prior century of Mamlūk dominion.

Control of the Arab world

Thus in a single sweep, Selim doubled the size of his empire, adding to it all of the lands of the old Islāmic caliphate with the exception of Iran, which remained under the Ṣafavids, and Mesopotamia, which was later taken by his successor. These acquisitions were of immense importance to the Ottomans. Under an efficient administration, the Arab world provided Istanbul with new revenues that solved the financial problems left from the 15th century and made the empire into one of the most powerful and wealthy states in the 16th century. Acquisition of the holy places of Islām cemented the position of the sultan as the most important ruler of Islām. The Ottomans had gained direct access to the intellectual, artistic, and administrative heritage of high Islāmic civilization, previously transmitted to them only indirectly. Now from the Arab world there came to Istanbul the leading Muslim intellectuals, artisans, administrators, and artists of the time. They penetrated every facet of Ottoman life and made the empire much more of a traditional Islāmic state than it ever had been before. Finally, the Ottomans replaced the Mamlūks in control of the Middle Eastern trade routes—part of the old international routes between Europe and the Far East.

One of the major reasons for the Mamlūk decline had been Portuguese discoveries in India and the establishment of an all-water route around southern Africa in place of that through the Middle East. It now remained for the Ottomans to restore the full prosperity of their Arab dominions by countering Portuguese naval activities in the Eastern seas. The Ottoman conquests in the East, combined with the Ṣafavid survival in Iran, ended the long period of political vacuum and anarchy that had followed the collapse of the universal ʿAbbāsid Empire, starting in the 11th century. Order and security finally were re-established, and the stability of Middle Eastern society was restored under the guidance and protection of powerful imperial orders. But the Islāmic world was left permanently divided, with Iran and Transoxania, once centres of the Islāmic caliphates, separated from the Arab world, to which Anatolia and southeastern Europe were for the first time added as integral parts of the Middle East.

Süleyman I (ruled 1520–66). Selim I's last years were spent in Istanbul solidifying the supremacy of the sultan, exploiting the prestige and revenues resulting from his Eastern victories. It was therefore only during the long reign of his son and successor Süleyman I (ruled 1520–66)—called the Magnificent in Europe and the Lawgiver among the Ottomans—that the foundations left by Selim were fully used to establish the classical Ottoman state and society and to make important new conquests in East and West. Süleyman assumed the throne with a position unequalled by any sultan before or after him. He was without opposition and with a great deal of control over the *devşirme* class as well as over the remnants of the Turkish notables. The conquest of the Arab world had doubled the revenues of the treasury without imposing important additional financial obligations, leaving Süleyman with wealth and power unparalleled in Ottoman history. Although Süleyman never took full advantage of the opportunities left him and, in fact, began a process of Ottoman decline, his reign still marked the peak of Ottoman grandeur, and it has always been regarded as the Golden Age of Ottoman history.

Expansion in Europe

The chief battlefields of Ottoman expansion in Europe now were Hungary and the Mediterranean. The weak southeastern European enemies of Süleyman's predecessors had been replaced by the powerful Habsburg Empire, bolstered by the appeals of the pope against the menace of Islām. Süleyman's main European ally was France, which sought to use Ottoman pressure in the East to lessen the pressure of the Habsburgs.

The land war with the Habsburgs centred in Hungary and was fought in three main stages. From 1520 to 1526 the independent Hungarian kingdom bore the direct brunt of the Ottoman attack and acted as a buffer between the two great empires; but a weak king, Louis II (ruled 1516–26) and feudal anarchy and misrule made a united defense impossible. A split among Hungarian nobles over the question of accepting Habsburg rule, combined with the social and national divisions stimulated by the Reformation, further weakened the opposition to Ottoman attack, and, as a result, Süleyman was able to take Belgrade in August 1521, opening the way for a large-scale advance north of the Danube. The only real army the Hungarian notables could muster was routed at the Battle of Mohács (August 29, 1526), and the death of Louis II ended the last hope for Hungarian unity and independence.

The second period of Ottoman-Habsburg relations (1526–41) was characterized by Hungarian autonomy under the anti-Habsburg prince of Transylvania, John Zápolya (ruled 1528–40), who accepted the suzerainty of the sultan in return for the right to continue native administration and military defense. The Habsburg prince Ferdinand, brother of the Emperor Charles V (ruled 1519–58), occupied the northern areas of Hungary with the support of the Hungarian nobles who desired Habsburg aid against the Turks, and for all practical purposes he annexed them to Austria before, in 1527–28, undertaking an effort to conquer the remainder of Hungary. In response Süleyman returned from Anatolia; drove the Habsburgs from all of Hungary; and besieged Vienna (1529), an effort that failed due to the difficulty of supplying a large force so far from the major centres of Ottoman power. Vienna thus was the chief remaining European bulwark against further Muslim advance. Under the existing conditions of supply, transport, and military organization, the Ottomans had reached the limit of their possible expansion in the West from a winter

Siege of Vienna (1529)

base that had to be maintained in Istanbul because of the constant threat of possible military needs in the East.

The siege of Vienna had important benefits for the Ottomans—it secured Süleyman's rule of Hungary, and it prevented Ferdinand from launching a new attack against Zápolya for some time to come. Although the siege frightened the other states of Europe sufficiently for them to agree to a temporary Catholic-Protestant truce (1532), the result was only temporary, and Ferdinand never was certain of the support of the independent German princes and of other European rulers who promised him help. Even Charles V was too preoccupied with the problems of the Reformation and with France to devote much attention to the Ottomans. Thus, when Süleyman went on a second Austrian campaign (1532), he was unable to draw the imperial army into conflict and had to content himself with devastating large parts of the Habsburg realm.

By the peace of 1533 Ferdinand abandoned his claims to central Hungary and recognized Zápolya's rule there as Ottoman vassal, whereas Süleyman agreed to accept Ferdinand as ruler of northern Hungary in return for the payment of an annual tribute. This arrangement lasted until 1540, when Zápolya died and left his dominions to Ferdinand in defiance of his agreement with the sultan. When Ferdinand tried to assume his heritage by force, Süleyman occupied and annexed Hungary (August 1541) under the guise of championing the cause of Zápolya's infant son, John Sigismund Zápolya. Thus began the third and final period of Ottoman-Habsburg relations, with the two great powers in direct contact and almost continuous border conflict; diversions on both sides, however, prevented long periods of open warfare.

Many historians have accused Francis I of France (ruled 1515–47) of encouraging Ottoman expansion into central Europe to relieve Habsburg pressure on him. But the Ottoman advances were due less to any French overtures than to Süleyman's own ambitions, together with his fears of a possible alliance among the Habsburgs, the Hungarians, and the Ṣafavids and of Habsburg rule in Hungary. The sultan regarded the French king largely as a supplicant for commercial favours, which were granted in the Capitulations of 1536—an agreement by which French subjects were given the freedom to travel and trade in the sultan's dominions, and subjects of other states wishing to do the same were required to secure French protection as a condition of the necessary permission. French and other merchants and travellers in the Ottoman Empire were allowed to remain under French laws and courts in cases concerning themselves and to have special privileges when involved with Ottoman law. Thus was established the foundation of the French predominance in the Levant, which remained to modern times. The Capitulations served as a model for later trade agreements between the Ottomans and the other European powers, who subsequently used them, during the centuries of Ottoman weakness, as means to dominate commerce within the Ottoman dominions and thus prevent the rise of a native commercial class.

The Mediterranean front

The stalemate between the Ottomans and Habsburgs in Hungary led their conflict to shift periodically from the land to the sea, with the Ottomans emerging as a major naval power for the first time. The decline of the Venetian navy led Charles V to try for complete control of the Mediterranean, enlisting as his naval commander a great Genoese seaman, Andrea Doria, and thus securing the support of the powerful Genoese fleet. Süleyman responded by driving the Knights Hospitallers—a Christian religious and military order—from Rhodes (1522), but Charles then established them on Malta (1530) and captured Tunis (1535). While Süleyman was busy in Anatolia, Doria captured a number of ports in the Morea (Peloponnese) and began to raid the Ottoman coasts, largely severing the sea lines of communication between Istanbul and Alexandria. To counter this, Süleyman in 1533 enrolled in his service as grand admiral Barbarossa (Khayr ad-Dīn), a Turkish captain who had built a major pirate fleet in the western Mediterranean and had used it to capture Algiers (1529) and other North African ports. The Ottomans annexed Algiers to the empire, but as a special province permanently assigned to the grand admiral to support the fleet. Ottoman land troops were sent to defend Algiers against Habsburg attacks—probably the main reason Barbarossa agreed to join the sultan.

Barbarossa built a powerful Ottoman fleet, able to meet the Habsburgs on equal terms. In 1537 he launched a major attack on southern Italy, expecting a promised French attack in the north, with the objective of a joint conquest of Italy. But France, fearing a hostile European reaction to its alliance with the infidel, withheld the diversion. Doria then organized and led an allied European naval force against the Ottomans; but it was routed at the Battle of Preveza (September 25–28, 1538), off the Albanian coast. Venice then surrendered its last possessions in the Aegean, the Morea, and Dalmatia, thus assuring Ottoman naval supremacy in the eastern Mediterranean, which remained unbroken for the next three decades.

The eastern front

Süleyman failed to pursue his ambitions in Europe after 1541, largely because of his increasing preoccupation with problems in the East. He ruthlessly suppressed Ṣafavid propagandists and supporters in eastern Anatolia and stimulated the Turkmen Özbek Empire of Transoxania to attack Iran from the East. Iran fell into disorder following the death of Shāh Esmāʿīl and the accession of his infant son Ṭahmāsp I (ruled 1524–76), but Süleyman was able to use this situation only during periods of peace in Europe. He personally led three campaigns into northwestern Iran—in 1534–35, 1548–50, and 1554—but although he captured Ṣafavid territories in the southern Caucasus, Azerbaijan, and Iraq on each occasion, he never was able to catch the Iranian army to defeat it; and supply problems invariably compelled him to retire to Anatolia during the winter months, allowing the Persians to regain their territories with little difficulty. Süleyman finally despaired of defeating his elusive enemies, so he agreed to the Peace of Amasya (May 29, 1555), by which he retained Iran and eastern Anatolia but renounced Ottoman claims to Azerbaijan and the Caucasus and agreed to allow Shīʿī Persian pilgrims to visit Mecca and Medina as well as their own holy places in Iraq. Thus the same geographical problems that had limited Ottoman conquests in central Europe made western Azerbaijan the viable limit of Ottoman expansion in the East; preventing the final elimination of the Ṣafavid danger.

Süleyman was somewhat more successful in restoring the old international trade routes through his Middle East possessions. To counteract the Portuguese fleet, supplied by the Ṣafavids from their Persian Gulf ports, he built major naval bases—at Suez (1517) and, as soon as he took Iraq, at Basra (1538)—establishing garrisons and fleets that not only resisted the Portuguese naval attacks but also went out against them in the Eastern seas. As a result the old trade route regained some of its former volume in the 16th century; the Ottomans never were able to fully restore it, however, because Portugal still was able to pay higher prices in the East and sell at lower prices in Europe because of their use of a sea route, which avoided the duties and local charges levied on goods sent through Ottoman territory. (It should be noted that it was the Ottomans who fought to keep the old Middle Eastern trade route open; the route was closed only when the Cape route was taken over from the Portuguese by the much more powerful fleets of Great Britain and Holland.)

Classical Ottoman society and administration. During the 16th century the institutions of society and government that had been evolving in the Ottoman dominions for two centuries reached the classical forms and patterns that were to characterize them until modern times.

Social divisions

The basic division in Ottoman society was the traditional Middle Eastern distinction between the small group of rulers who formed the ruling class, and the large mass of subjects. Possession of three attributes was essential for membership in the Ottoman ruling class: (1) profession of loyalty to the sultan and his state; (2) acceptance and practice of the Muslim religion and the system of thought and action that was an integral part of it; and (3) knowledge and practice of the complicated system of customs, behaviour, and language known as the Ottoman Way. Those who lacked any of these attributes were considered to be members of the subject class, *reayas (rayahs),* the "protected flock" of the sultan. There was a system of social mobility based on the possession of these definable and attainable attributes; *reaya*s able to acquire them could rise into the ruling class, and Ottomans who came to lack any of them would become members of the subject class.

Members of the Ottoman ruling class were considered to be the sultan's slaves, and thus acquired their master's social status. As slaves, however, their properties, lives, and persons were entirely at his disposition; and he could do with them as he wished. Their basic function was to preserve the Islāmic nature of the state and to rule and defend the empire. By Ottoman theory, the main attribute of the sultan's sovereignty was the right to possess all sources of wealth in the empire together with the authority necessary to exploit them. The function of enlarging, protecting, and exploiting that wealth for the benefit of the sultan and his state, therefore, was the main duty of the ruling class. The primary duty of the *reayas* was to produce the wealth—by farming the land or engaging in trade and industry—and then paying a part of the resulting profits to the ruling class in the form of taxes.

The Ottoman state encompassed organizations and hierarchies developed by the ruling and subject classes to carry out their functions in Ottoman society. The ruling class divided itself into four functional institutions: the Imperial (Mülkiye) Institution, led by the Sultan himself, provided the leadership and direction for the other institutions as well as for the entire Ottoman system; the Military (Seyfiye) Institution was in charge of expanding and defending the empire and keeping order and security within the sultan's dominions; the Administrative (Kalemiye) Institution, organized as the Imperial Treasury (Hazine-i Amire), was in charge of collecting and spending the imperial revenues; and the Religious/Cultural (İlmiye) Institution, which included the *ʿulamāʾ* (all Ottomans expert in the religious sciences), was in charge of organizing and propagating the faith and maintaining and enforcing the religious law (Sharīʿah), its interpretation in the courts, its expounding in the mosques and schools, and its study and interpretation.

To cover the areas of life not included within the scope of the ruling class, members of the subject class were allowed to organize themselves as they wished. As a natural manifestation of Islāmic society their organization was determined largely by religious and occupational distinctions. The basic class divisions within the subject class were determined by religion, with each important group organizing into a relatively self-centred autonomous community called a *millet,* under its own laws and forms of internal organization, directed by a religious leader who was responsible to the sultan for the fulfillment of the duties and responsibilities of the *millet* members, particularly those of paying taxes and security. In addition, each *millet* cared for the many social and administrative functions not assumed by the Ottoman state, concerning such matters as marriage, divorce, birth and death, health, education, internal security, and justice.

The *millet*s

Within the *millet*s, just as in Ottoman society as a whole, there was a social mobility, with persons moving up and down the ladder according to ability and luck. Individuals could pass from one *millet* to another if they wished to convert, but because all the *millet*s were extremely antagonistic toward those who left them to convert to another religion, the state discouraged such action as much as possible to preserve social harmony and tranquility, the main object of the system. The *millet* system succeeded for 500 years by keeping the different peoples of the empire as much apart as possible, thus reducing to a minimum the possible sources of conflict and keeping social order in a highly heterogeneous state.

All of the classes, institutions, and communities described above were, in essence, means by which the slaves and subjects of the sultan were divided and organized so as best to fulfill their functions. But there also were means by which they were related to one another and united into the whole of Ottoman society. The principal cement was the sultan, the keystone of the system who alone was the common focus of loyalty of the ruling and ruled subjects alike. But such loyalty was an abstract; it could not have held Ottoman society together without the help of the artisan and religious guilds, which cut across the boundaries and made members of different groups brothers in common organizations based not on class, rank, or religion but on mutually shared values and beliefs, economic activities, and social needs. Through contact and cooperation in such guilds, members of the different groups of Ottoman society were cemented into a common whole, performing many of the social and economic functions outside the scope of the ruling class and of the *millet*s, particularly those functions associated with economic regulation and social security, and receiving a more personal religious experience than that provided by the established religious organizations, whether Muslim or non-Muslim.

The *mukataʿa*

Within the Ottoman ruling class, the most important unit of organization and action was the *mukataʿa,* in which a member of the ruling class "cut off" a portion of the sultan's revenues and had sufficient authority to exploit it for purposes determined by the sultan. The exact nature of the —*mukataʿa* depended on the extent to which the holder remitted his revenues to the treasury and what portion he retained for himself. The *timar* type of *mukataʿa,* traditionally described as a fief, only marginally approached the concept of feudalism as it was known in Europe because it was part of a centralized system and did not involve the kind of mutual rights and obligations characteristic of Western feudalism. In return for services to the state, the *timar* holder was given the full profits of the source of revenue for his personal exploitation and profit, which were independent of, and in addition to, those connected with the exploitation of the *timar* itself. For many military and administrative positions, *timar*s normally were given in lieu of salaries, thus relieving the treasury of the trouble and expense of collecting revenues and disbursing them to its employees as salaries. Almost all the 14th- and 15th-century Ottoman conquests in southeastern Europe were distributed as *timar*s to military officers, who in return performed the tasks of administration in peacetime and provided soldiers and military leadership for the Ottoman army in war. Many of the officers of the central government also were rewarded with *timar*s in place of, or in addition to, salaries paid by the treasury.

The second principal form of the *mukataʿa* was the *emânet* (trusteeship), held by the *emin* (trustee, agent). In contrast to the situation of the *timar* holder, the *emin* turned all his proceeds over to the treasury and was compensated entirely by salary, thus being the closest Ottoman equivalent to the modern government official. The legal basis for this arrangement was that the *emin* did no more than administer the *mukataʿa;* he undertook no additional service, and so had no right to share in the profits of the *mukataʿa* that he held. This was the least common type of administrative position in Ottoman times, for the most part used for urban custom houses and market police, which were very close to, and under the supervision and control of, the central government and its agents, and which did not need the profit motive in order to assure efficiency on the part of the holders.

The most common kind of *mukataʿa,* and therefore the most prevalent type of administrative unit in the Ottoman system, was the tax farm (*iltizam*), which combined elements of both the *timar* and *emânet.* As in the former, the tax farmer (*mültezim*) could keep a part—but only a part—of the tax he collected, and, like the *emin,* had to deliver the balance to the treasury. This was because his service consisted only of his work in administering the *mukataʿa,* for which he was given a share of his collection instead of the *emin*'s salary. The tax farmer thus was given the inducement of profit to be as efficient as possible. Most of Anatolia and the Arab provinces were administered in this way because they were conquered at a time when the government's need for cash to pay the salaried Janissary infantry and to supply an increasingly lavish court required the treasury to seek out all the revenues it could find. As the *timar*-based *sipahi* cavalry became less important, and as the Turkish notables who held most of the *timar*s lost most of their political power during the time of Süleyman, the estates gradually fell into the hands of the *devşirme* class.

The legal and customary bases of organization and action in Ottoman society depended on a dual system of law—the Sharīʿah or religious law, and the *kanun,* or civil law. The former, the basic law of Ottoman society, as it was of all Muslim communities, was considered to be a divinely inspired corpus of political, social, and moral regulations and principles, which were supposed to cover all aspects of life for Muslims. But it was highly developed only in the fields of personal behaviour covered in detail in the early Muslim community and reflected in the Qurʾān and early Muslim tradition. It never was developed in detail in matters of public law, state organization, and administration. Its general principles left room for interpretation and legislation on specific matters by secular authorities; and the Muslim judges of the Ottoman Empire recognized the right of the sultan to legislate in civil laws, so long as he did not conflict with the Sharīʿah in detail or principle. The Sharīʿah, therefore, provided the principles of public law, and covered matters of personal behaviour and status in the Muslim *millet* in the same way that the members of the Christian and Jewish *millet*s were subject to their own religious codes. The Sharīʿah was interpreted and enforced by members of the Cultural Institution—the *ʿulamāʾ*—just as the laws of each non-Muslim *millet* were enforced by its leaders. Strictly speaking, the *ʿulamāʾ* members had the right to invalidate any law they felt contradicted the Sharīʿah, but they rarely did this because, as part of the ruling class, they were under the authority of the sultan and could be removed from their positions. The sultan therefore was relatively free to legislate changes in Ottoman institutions and practices to meet the needs of the time; this was a major factor in the long survival of the empire, even during centuries of decline. It must be noted, however, that with the restricted scope of the Ottoman ruling class and state and the large areas of power and function left to the religious communities and guilds as well as to the Ottoman officials who held the different kinds of *mukataʿas*, the sultans were never as autocratic as has been commonly assumed. It was only in the 19th century that Ottoman reformers centralized government and society on Western lines and restricted or ended the traditional autonomies, which had done so much to decentralize power in the previous centuries.

The dual system of law

DECLINE OF THE OTTOMAN EMPIRE, 1566–1807

Internal problems. The reign of Süleyman the Magnificent marked the peak of Ottoman grandeur, but elements of weakness crept in and began the slow but steady decline that followed. An important factor of decline was the increasing lack of ability and power of the sultans themselves. Süleyman tired of the long military campaigns and arduous duties of administration concentrated in his person, and withdrew more and more from public affairs to devote himself to the pleasure of his harem. To take his place, the office of grand vizier was built up to become second only to the sultan in authority and revenue, including the right to demand and obtain absolute obedience. But while the grand vizier was, indeed, able to replace the sultan in official functions, he could not take his place as the focus of loyalty for all the different classes and groups in the empire. The resulting separation of political loyalty and central authority led to a decline in the government's ability to impose its will.

Decline of the sultans

Triumph of the devşirme. The mid-16th century also saw the triumph of the *devşirme* over the Turkish nobility, which lost almost all of its power and positions in the capital and returned to its old centres of power in southeastern Europe and Anatolia. In consequence, many of the *timars* formerly assigned to the notables to support the *sipahi* cavalry were seized by the *devşirme* and transformed into great estates, for all practical purposes as private property, thus depriving the state of their services as well as of the revenue they could have produced if they had been transformed into tax farms. Whereas the *sipahis* did not entirely disappear as a military force, the Janissaries and the associated artillery corps became the most important segments of the Ottoman army.

Corruption and nepotism. Because the sultans no longer could control the *devşirme* by playing the Turkish notables off against them, the *devşirme* gained control of the sultans and used the government for its own benefit rather than for that of the sultan or his empire. In consequence, the evils of corruption and nepotism took hold at all levels of administration. In addition, with the challenge of the notables gone, the *devşirme* class itself broke into countless factions and parties, each working for its own advantage by supporting the candidacy of one or another of the imperial princes and each in close alliance with corresponding palace factions led by the mothers, sisters, and wives of each prince. Following Süleyman, therefore, accession and appointments to positions came less as the result of ability than as a consequence of the political manoeuvrings of the *devşirme*-harem political parties. Those in power found it more convenient to control the princes by keeping them uneducated and inexperienced, and the old tradition by which young princes were educated in the field, was replaced by a system in which all the princes were isolated in the private apartments of the harem and limited to the education its permanent inhabitants could provide. In consequence, few of the sultans after Süleyman had the ability to exercise real power even when circumstances might have enabled them to do so.

But the lack of ability did not end the sultans' desire for power; because they lacked the devices developed by their predecessors to achieve this end, they developed new ones. Selim II (ruled 1566–74), known as the Sot, and Murad III (ruled 1574–95) both gained power by playing off the different factions and by weakening the office of grand vizier, the main administrative vehicle for factional and party influence in the declining Ottoman state. As the grand viziers lost their dominant position following the downfall of Mehmed Sokollu (served 1560–79), power fell first into the hands of the women of the harem, during the "Sultanate of the Women" (1570–78), and then into the grasp of the chief Janissary officers, the *ağas* who dominated from 1578 to 1625. But no matter who controlled the apparatus of government during this time, the results were the same—a growing paralysis of administration throughout the empire and a pulling apart of the different groups into separate and hostile communities.

Economic difficulties. Under such conditions, it was inevitable that the Ottoman government could not meet the increasingly difficult problems that rose to plague the empire in the 16th and 17th centuries. Economic difficulties began in the late 16th century when the Dutch and British were able to completely close the old international trade routes through the Middle East. As a result, the prosperity of the Arab provinces declined and, in addition, the Ottoman economy was upset by inflation, started by the influx of precious metals into Europe from the Americas and by an increasing imbalance of trade between East and West. As the treasury lost more of its revenues to the depredations of the *devşirme,* it began to meet its obligations by debasing the coinage, heavily increasing taxes, and resorting to confiscations—all of which further worsened the situation. All those persons depending on salaries found themselves underpaid, and the result was further theft and corruption. Holders of the *timars* and tax farms started using them as sources of revenue to be milked as rapidly as possible, rather than as long-term holdings whose prosperity had to be maintained to provide for the future; political influence and corruption also enabled them to transform these holdings into private property, either as life holdings (*malikâne*) or as religious endowments (*vakf*), without any further obligations to the state. Inflation also hit the traditional industries and trades. Functioning under strict price regulations, the guilds were unable to provide quality goods at prices low enough to compete with the cheap European manufactured goods that entered the empire without restriction due to the capitulations agreements. In consequence, traditional Ottoman industry fell into rapid decline.

The decline of Ottoman industry

Social erosion. These conditions were exacerbated by a large increase of population during the 16th and 17th centuries—part of the general population rise that occurred in much of Europe at this time. The amount of subsistance available was not only unable to expand to meet the needs of the rising population, but in fact fell as the result of the political and economic conditions then prevalent in the Ottoman Empire; social distress increased, and upset resulted. Landless and jobless peasants fled from the lands as did cultivators subjected to confiscatory taxation at the hands of timariots and tax collectors, thus reducing food supplies even more. Many of them fled to the cities, where they added to the problem of food supply and reacted against their troubles by rising against the established order; many more remained in the countryside and joined rebel bands, known as *levend*s and Jelālīs (Celâlis), which took what they could from those who remained to cultivate and trade.

The central government became weaker; and as more peasants joined rebel bands, they were able to take over large parts of the empire, keeping all the remaining tax revenues for themselves and often cutting off the regular food supplies of the cities as well as of the Ottoman armies still guarding the frontiers. Under such conditions, the armies themselves broke up, with most of the salaried positions in the Janissary corps and other corps falling into the hands of urban investors, who used them simply as new sources of revenue, without performing any military services in return. Thus it was that the Ottoman armies came to be composed primarily of fighting contingents supplied by the vassals of the sultan (particularly the Crimean Tartar khans), together with whatever rabble could be dragged from the streets of the cities whenever required by campaigns. The Ottoman army still remained strong enough to curb the most pressing provincial revolts; but the latter proliferated through the centuries of decline, making effective administration outside the major cities still under the government's control almost impossible. In many ways the substratum of Ottoman society—formed by the *millet*s and various economic, social and religious guilds and buttressed by the organization of the Ottoman *ʿulamāʾ*—cushioned the mass of the people and the ruling class itself from the worst effects of this multisided disintegration.

External relations. Despite these difficulties, the internal Ottoman weakness was evident to only the most discerning Ottoman and foreign observers during much of the 17th century. Most Europeans continued to fear the Ottoman army much as it had been feared two centuries before; and whereas its ability was reduced, it remained strong enough not only to prevent the provincial rebels from assuming complete control but also to make a few more significant conquests in both East and West. Whereas the empire now suffered defeats for the first time, it still retained reserve strength sufficient for it to recoup when needed and to prevent the loss of any integral parts of the empire. Although the Ottoman navy was destroyed by the fleet of the Holy League at the Battle of Lepanto (1571), it was yet able to rebuild and regain naval mastery in the eastern Mediterranean through most of the 17th century, taking Tunis from the Spanish Habsburgs (1574), Fez from the Portuguese (1578), and Crete from Venice (1669). In consequence, so long as Europe continued to fear the Ottomans, no one tried to upset the precarious peace treaties concluded in Süleyman's later years; and the Ottomans were shielded from the results of their own weakness.

Superiority of Ottoman navy

Military campaigns. Despite the upsets then disturbing the Ottoman body politic, the Porte undertook new campaigns. When the rising Principality of Moscow conquered the last Mongol states in Central Asia and reached the Caspian, thus posing a threat to the Ottoman position north of the Black Sea and in the Caucasus, Murad II conquered the Caucasus and, taking advantage of anarchy in Iran following the death of Shāh Ṭahmāsp I in 1576, seized the long-coveted Azerbaijan. He thus brought the empire to the peak of its territorial extent and added wealthy new provinces whose revenues, for a half century at least, rescued the Ottoman treasury from the worst of its financial troubles and gave the empire a respite in which it could at least try to remedy its worst problems.

Reform efforts in the 17th century were undertaken by sultans Osman II (ruled 1618–22) and Murad IV (ruled 1623–40) and by a famous dynasty of Köprülü grand viziers who served under Sultan Mehmed IV (ruled 1648–1687)—Mehmed Köprülü (served 1656–61) and Ahmed Köprülü (served 1661–76). Each of these early reformers rose as the result of crises and military defeats that threatened the very existence of the empire. Each was given the power needed to introduce reforms because of the fears of the ruling class that the empire, on which its privileges depended, was in mortal danger.

Exposure of Ottoman weakness. In a war between the Ottomans and the Habsburgs (began 1593) the Austrians were able to take much of central Hungary and Romania, and only an accidental Ottoman triumph in 1596 enabled the Sultan to sufficiently recoup so that the Habsburgs agreed to the Treaty of Zsitvatorok (1606), by which agreement Ottoman rule of Hungary and Romania was restored. The treaty itself, however, like the events that led up to it, for the first time showed Europe the extent of Ottoman weakness and so exposed the Ottomans to considerable new dangers in subsequent years. In the East, anarchy in Iran was brought to an end by Shāh ʿAbbās I (ruled 1588–1629), who not only restored Iranian power but drove the Ottomans out of Azerbaijan and the Caucasus (1603), conquered Iraq (1624), and threatened to take the entire Ottoman Empire. Though Murad IV was able to retake Iraq (1638), Iran remained a major threat. Finally, a long war with Venice (1645–69), occasioned by Ottoman efforts to capture Crete, exposed Istanbul to a major Venetian naval attack. Although finally pushed back in a naval campaign culminating in the Ottoman conquest of Crete (1669), the Venetians still posed a major threat, which, like those that had occurred earlier in the century, stimulated the ruling class to accept needed reforms.

Reforms. The Ottoman reforms introduced during the 17th century were too limited in nature and scope to permanently arrest the Ottoman decline. Basically, they were no more than efforts to restore to the state the inherited system of government and society that had operated successfully in the past. Corrupt officials were executed. Efforts were made to restore the *timar* and tax-farm systems as the basis of the administration and army. Provincial revolts were suppressed, peasants were forced back to the lands, and cultivation was increased. Debased coins were replaced by coins of full face value. Industry and trade were encouraged, and corruption and insubordination were driven out.

Such reforms were sufficient to end the immediate difficulties. But they were successful only for the moment because the reformers were allowed only to act against the results of the decay and not its cause—the selfish rule of the ruling class—which continued. As soon as the worst consequences of decay had been alleviated, the old groups returned to power and resumed their old ways. Moreover, the reformers really did not understand that the Europe now faced by the Ottomans was far more powerful than that which the great sultans of the past had defeated; thus even if the reforms had been more permanently successful, they could not have corrected the increasing Ottoman weakness relative to the powerful nation-states then rising in Europe. Such an understanding was to come to the Ottoman reformers only in the 19th century.

Failure to assess new Europe

Military defeats, 1683–1792. The traditional 17th-century reforms did, however, produce at least a semblance of revival. By 1681 the Ottoman army seemed so strong that Grand Vizier Kara Mustafa Paşa (served 1676–83), brother-in-law of Ahmed Köprülü, was emboldened to move again into central Europe and besiege Vienna (July–September 1683). His effort quickly overextended the fragile bases of the Ottoman revival.

Anti-Ottoman coalition. The aroused defenders, stimulated by the Polish king Jan Sobieski (ruled 1674–96), not only held out but also built a major European coalition that moved to bring destruction to the Ottoman Empire during the subsequent century: the Habsburgs set out to reconquer Hungary, Serbia, and the Balkans; Venice hoped to regain its naval bases on the Adriatic and in the Morea and to resume its naval and commercial power in the Levant; Russia worked to extend its lands to the open seas. Only the enemies of the coalition in Europe, led by France and Sweden, tried to support the Ottomans; neutral Britain and Holland, to guard the commercial privileges they had secured from the sultan through the

Capitulations, worked to prevent any nation from gaining control of the entire Ottoman Empire and from becoming, thereby, preponderant in Europe.

Russia and Austria fought the Ottomans not only by direct military attack but also by fomenting dissatisfaction and revolt on the part of the non-Muslim subjects of the Sultan. Against such an attack, the Ottomans could only conciliate their subjects where possible and repress them when conciliation was rejected, taking advantage, at every opportunity, of every rivalry that arose between the Habsburgs and Russians for predominance in the Balkan provinces of the empire.

European wars. In consequence of this situation, the Ottoman Empire was at war with European enemies for 41 years between the second siege of Vienna (1683) and the Treaty of Jassy (1792). From 1683 to 1699 it fought the armies of the Holy League in a disastrous war culminating in the Treaty of Carlowitz (1699). In 1710 and 1711 it fought Russia again and at the Treaty of the Pruth (1711) regained some territories previously lost. The war of 1714–18 with Venice and Austria was concluded by the Treaty of Passarowitz (1718); and three wars with Russia and Austria—in 1736–39, 1768–74, and 1787–92—culminated in the treaties of Belgrade (1739), Küçük Kaynarca (1774), and Jassy (1792). As a result of these wars, the Ottomans lost Hungary, the Banat of Temisvar, Transylvania, and Bukovina in Europe, establishing their boundary on the Danube, where it had last been early in the 16th century. To Russia they lost all their possessions on the northern coasts of the Black Sea from the principalities to the Caucasus, including Bessarabia, Podolya, and the Crimea, the soldiers of which had provided the strongest element in the Ottoman army during the previous century. In addition, the Ottomans were compelled to allow the Russians and Austrians to intervene legally on behalf of the sultan's Christian subjects in a manner that opened the way to an increased European influence in internal Ottoman affairs.

Loss of territory

Imperial decline in the 18th and early 19th centuries. The manifestations of decline were only continuations and elaborations of earlier conditions. But a new factor of decline was added—the weakness of the central government resulted in the loss of control of most of the provinces to local rulers, called notables (*aʿyan*), who took more or less permanent control of large areas, creating a situation that in many ways resembled European feudalism much more than the traditional Ottoman *timar* system ever did.

Rise of local rulers. These notables were able to build up their power and maintain control not only because the Sultan's government lacked the military resources to suppress them but also because the local populations themselves preferred the notables' rule to that of the corrupt and incompetent Ottoman officials of the time. In the Balkans and Anatolia, local rulers solidified their positions by taking advantage of currents of local nationalism that were arising among the Balkan Christians and the Muslim Turks. The notables formed private armies of mercenaries and slaves, with which they sometimes provided important contributions to the Ottoman armies in return for recognition of their autonomy by the sultans. These rulers were able to exercise almost complete authority, collecting taxes for themselves and sending only nominal payments to the treasury, thus further increasing its problems. The central government maintained its position by playing off the local rebels against each other, using the leverage of Ottoman support to its own advantage, and securing considerable payments of cash and military contributions when needed. The treasury, therefore, did not suffer as much from these provincial revolts as might be imagined; but the revolts did disrupt the established food supplies of the empire sufficiently for large-scale famines to arise in the major cities on a regular basis. In response, the urban populace became a restless, misruled, and anarchic mass that broke loose at the slightest provocation, responding to unemployment, famine, the plague, and the like with riots and summary executions of the officials considered responsible. Such violence, while manifesting Ottoman difficulties, did not remedy them and, in fact, made things worse. Remedy lay only in the hands of the ruling class; but its reaction was quite different.

Urban anarchy

Resistance to change. Most Ottomans saw little need for the empire to change because they actually benefitted financially from the existing anarchy and lack of control by the sultan. In addition, the ruling class was completely isolated from developments outside its own sphere; it assumed that the remedies to Ottoman decline lay entirely within Ottoman practice and experience. This resulted from the basic belief of Ottoman society in its own superiority over anything the infidel could possibly produce—a belief that had far more basis in the 16th century, when it was developed, than in the 18th century. All of the developments in industrial and commercial life, in science and technology, and particularly in political and military organization and techniques that had occurred in Europe since the Reformation were simply unknown to the Ottomans. The only direct Ottoman contacts with Europe were on the battlefield, where most Ottomans still assumed that their military reverses were caused not by the superiority of Western armies as such but rather by Ottoman failure to apply fully the techniques that had worked so well in the past. So the 18th-century reforms largely paralleled those of the traditional Ottoman reformers of the 17th century, with only occasional efforts to add new military organizations and to make use of specific European weapons and techniques of undeniable superiority.

Contacts with the West. For a few Ottomans this isolation was at least partially broken down when some channels of contact opened with the West during the 18th century—a few Ottoman ambassadors went to Europe to participate in negotiations and sign treaties; more and more European merchants, travellers, and consuls came into the Ottoman Empire; a very few Ottoman men of science and philosophy began to correspond with their Western counterparts; members of the Ottoman minorities entered into correspondence with their relatives in the West. But such contacts had very limited effects; only a small number of Ottomans experienced them, and even when they did learn something, the effect was quite superficial because the resulting information did not fit into the patterns of thought of even the most educated Ottomans. Those few who did understand something of what they heard usually were only voices in the wilderness, and their efforts to apply and spread what they knew had little overall effect.

Such contacts did lead to changes in the modes of living of a few upper class Ottomans and to some military innovations, but to nothing more. Starting in the so-called Tulip Period (1717–30; see below) some Ottomans under the influence of Grand Vizier İbrahim Paşa began to dress like Europeans, and the palace began to imitate European court life and pleasures. Sultan Ahmed III (ruled 1703–30) built several lavish summer residences on the Bosporus and the Golden Horn (an inlet that forms the harbour of Istanbul), and these were imitated by members of his immediate entourage, who held frequent garden parties in imitation of the pleasures of Versailles. The sultan and his ministers were no longer confined behind the walls of the palace; and the new era was celebrated by Nedim, the court poet, who reflected a considerable awareness of his environment and an appreciation of nature. Growing tulips, as a mark of westernization, became an obsession with rich and poor alike, and the flower gave its name to the period. In 1727 Turkish language books were printed for the the first time in the empire by a Hungarian convert named İbrahim Müteferrika; and while the press was closed by the government at times, during the remainder of the century it provided a number of books on history and geography that further opened the minds of those who saw and read them.

The Tulip Period

Military reforms. As a result of contact with European armies and the influence of European renegades in Ottoman service, a few attempts were made during the century to adopt Western-type uniforms, weapons, and tactics. Because the members of the established military corps could not and would not surrender their old ways, entirely new corps were formed to handle the new weapons under the direction of European instructors. But the new corps had no effect at all on the Janissaries and the other older corps that continued to form the bulk of the army; the latter accurately saw that the new ways were threats to their privileges and security. The new corps were, therefore, no more than special mercenary bodies built up under the stimulus of individual Ottomans, lasting only so long as the latter remained in power. The most successful and lasting Ottoman military reform during this time came in the navy, which was modernized by Grand Admiral Gazi Hasan Paşa (served 1770–89), with the support and encouragement of Sultan Abdülhamid I (ruled 1774–89); this success came largely because the Ottoman naval establishment was wiped out at the Battle of Çeşme (1770) by a Russian fleet, and there was no such inbred resistance as that which stifled significant reforms elsewhere. Important reforms introduced into the army under Grand Vizier Halil Hamid Paşa (served 1782–85), with the help of Western technicians, were limited to new corps especially created for the purpose, while the bulk of the Ottoman army continued to remain without change.

Selim III (ruled 1789–1807). These 18th-century reform efforts culminated during the reign of Sultan Selim III, who is thought by some to have been the originator of modern reform in the Ottoman Empire. While still a prince, Selim developed plans for modernizing the Ottoman army. He came to the throne during the 1787–92 war with Austria and Russia and had to postpone serious reform efforts until its completion. Early efforts to modernize the janissary corps created such opposition that Selim thereafter concentrated on creating a new European-style army, called the *nizam-i cedid* ("new order"), using the modern weapons and tactics developed in Europe. This new force, never numbering more than 10,000 active soldiers, was trained in Istanbul and in certain Anatolian provincial centres by officers and military experts sent by the different European powers that were competing for the sultan's support at the time. So as not to disturb the established Ottoman institutions, it was financed by an entirely new treasury, called the *irad-i cedid* ("new revenue"), whose revenues came from taxes imposed on previously untaxed revenue sources and from the confiscation of some *timar*s whose holders were not fulfilling their military and administrative duties to the state. Under the guidance of European technicians, factories were constructed to manufacture modern weapons and ammunitions, and technical schools were opened to train Ottoman officers. Limited efforts also were made to rationalize the Ottoman administrative machinery, but largely along traditional lines.

Modern reform

The older military corps, however, remained intact and hostile to the new force, and Selim was therefore compelled to limit its size and use. At the same time, much of his energy was diverted by the rise of powerful autonomous notables in southeastern Europe, Anatolia, and the Arab provinces, as well as by a French Expedition to Egypt (1798–1801), which eventually drew him into alliances with Great Britain and Russia. The rise of nationalism among Ottoman subject peoples stimulated by agents of Russia, Austria, and Revolutionary France, and culminating in the beginning of a Serbian revolution (1804) and a new war with Russia (1806–12) also made it impossible for Selim to resist the wishes of the Janissaries, who still formed the bulk of his army. Finally, the sultan's personal weakness, which led him to desert the reformers and the new army whenever opposition became strong, left him with little significant support in 1807, when he was attacked and overthrown by a conservative coalition. While Selim was imprisoned in the palace, a conservative reaction under Sultan Mustafa IV (1807–08) ended the reforms and massacred most of the reformers. An effort to restore Selim led by the Bulgarian notable Bayrakdar Mustafa Paşa led to Selim's death and, after the short rule of Mustafa IV, the accession of his reforming cousin, Mahmud II (ruled 1808–39). Selim's reforms were largely abandoned for some time. But the greatly increased knowledge of the West in the Ottoman Empire, made possible by the schools established for the *nizam-l cedid* as well as by the increased numbers of Westerners present in Istanbul during the era of the French Revolution, began the process by which the old Ottoman isolation was finally and definitively broken. This set the stage for more significant reforms, which transformed the empire during the remainder of the 19th century. (S.J.S.)

THE EMPIRE FROM 1807 TO 1920

The triumph of the antireform coalition, which had overthrown Selim III, was interrupted in 1808 when the surviving reformers within the higher bureaucracy found

Adapted from R. Treharne and H. Fullard (eds.), *Muir's Historical Atlas: Ancient, Medieval and Modern*, 9th edition (1965); George Philip & Son Ltd., London

The dissolution of the Ottoman Empire, 1807–1924.

support among the *a'yan* (local notables) of Rumelia (Ottoman possessions in the Balkans), who were worried by possible threats to their own position. These were led by Bayrakdar (Standard Bearer) Mustafa Paşa. The forces of Mustafa and the grand vizier Çelebi Mustafa Paşa together recovered Istanbul; deposed Mustafa IV; set up Mahmud II, the son of Abdülhamid I; and recommenced some of the reforming policies that had been initiated by Selim.

Interruption of conservative rule

The *a'yan* took care to protect their own interests by securing in the Covenant of Union (Sened-i Ittifak) a definition and guarantee of their own rights against the central government. Their victory, however, was short-lived. A further Janissary uprising in November 1808 led to the death of the Bayrakdar and to the re-establishment of conservative rule.

Rule of Mahmud II (1808–39). The Ottoman situation at the end of 1808 appeared desperate. Within the empire the authority of the central government was minimal. Control of North Africa had long since faded. In Egypt, the Ottoman Viceroy Muḥammad 'Alī was laying the foundations for independent power. In Iraq the Georgian Mamlūk pashas paid only lip service to the authority of the Porte, as did various independent local governors in Syria. In Arabia the Wahhābīs mocked Ottoman pretensions. In all Anatolia only two provinces were really under central control, while in the European provinces power had fallen into the hands of such formidable local notables as Ali Paşa, who controlled southern Albania, and Osman Pasvanoğlu, who had dominated northern Bulgaria until his death in 1807. Serbia under the leadership of George Petrović (Karageorge) had been in revolt since 1804; at first the Serbs had risen in desperation against the terrorist policies of the Janissaries, who had usurped the power of the local governor, but they had subsequently demanded autonomy and, in 1807, allied with Russia.

The external threat to the empire was no less ominous. Selim III had hoped to enlist French aid in order to recover territory lost to Russia; as a result, the Ottomans found themselves at war with both Russia, which invaded the Principalities in November 1806, and Britain, which attempted to seize the Dardanelles with a naval force (February 1807) and invaded Egypt (March 1807). Meanwhile Napoleon, through the agreements of Tilsit (July 7, 1807) and Erfurt (October 12, 1808), had not only abandoned active opposition to Russia but had accepted its occupation of the Principalities.

The preoccupation of the European powers with other interests helped the Ottomans mend the international problems. Britain made peace on January 5, 1809 (Peace of the Dardanelles); and Russia, on May 28, 1812 (Treaty of Bucharest), by which the Principalities were returned to Ottoman rule although Russia retained most of Bessarabia.

Internal reform. Mahmud II was then able to concentrate on internal reform. The basic element in Mahmud's reforms was the reconstruction of the army to make it a fit instrument for preserving the Ottoman Empire against both the encroachments of European powers and the centrifugal ambitions of local potentates. This policy brought him into head-on collision with the Janissaries. In 1826 Mahmud set out his proposals for a new European style army; on June 15 the Istanbul Janissaries mutinied in protest and were promptly and efficiently massacred by the sultan—an episode known to later Ottoman historians as "The Auspicious Incident."

Reconstruction of the army

As a tactician, Mahmud proved to be superior to Selim. He had the support of most of the higher *'ulamā'*. Whereas in 1807 the Janissaries had enjoyed the approval of the population of Istanbul, in 1826 only two guilds gave them active help. Mahmud had built up a cooperative group among the Janissary officers and had carefully arranged to have loyal troops at hand. Perhaps most important of all, Mahmud presented his proposals not as dangerous and infidel innovations but as a restoration of the military system of the Ottoman golden age.

The destruction of the old army was completed in 1831 by the final abolition of the feudal (*timar*) system. The remaining fiefs were resumed by the government. Although the new army was dressed, equipped, and trained in the style of European armies and helped by a succession of European advisers (including the future chief of the German General Staff, Helmuth von Moltke), it differed from the former army in its greater loyalty to the sultan. It thus became an instrument of political centralization, and it provided the major motive for modernization. The continuing need to pay and equip the army and to train its officers and other specialized personnel in a sustained, but ultimately vain, attempt to keep pace with the European powers, stimulated reform of the political and economic institutions of the Ottoman Empire. The modernization of higher education began with the need to train officers, army doctors, and veterinary surgeons; that of the taxation system began with the need to pay the army; that of the administration, with the need to collect the taxes, and so on. Ultimately the entire system of minimal government—by which political, economic, and social decisions were left to local organizations—was replaced by one in which the state came to centralize decisions in its own hands.

Move toward centralization. Mahmud began by curbing the power of rival claimants. He undermined the influence of the *'ulamā'* and of popular religious organizations. He created a new directorate of *evkâf* (charitable endowments) in 1826, hoping to gain control of the hitherto independent financial base of *'ulamā'* power. To make his power more effective, he built new roads and, in 1834, inaugurated a postal service.

The central administration was reorganized. New European-style ministries were created to replace the ancient bottleneck of power caused by the universal administrative responsibility of the grand vizier. New councils were established to assist in long term planning; one—the Supreme Council of Judicial Ordinances (1838)—subsequently became the principal legislative body. Bureaucrats were given greater security by abolishing the practice of confiscating their property at death, while the opening of a translation bureau (1833) and the reopening of embassies abroad gave some the opportunity to learn European languages and encounter European ideas.

Administrative reorganization

The reformed army and administration became the agents by which the sultan extended his authority over the semi-independent governors, local notables, valley lords (*derebeys*), and other groups, that had wielded political power in various parts of the empire. This process had begun immediately after 1812. The Serbian revolt had been temporarily suppressed in 1813, although it broke out again in 1815. Firm Ottoman governmental control was established over Anatolia, Iraq, and much of Rumelia.

The only local ruler who succeeded in asserting his own authority, unaided against the Porte, was Muḥammad 'Alī of Egypt, who was carrying through a still more radical program of modernization. In 1831 Egyptian forces invaded Syria, routed the Ottomans at Konya (December 27, 1832) and threatened Istanbul. Mahmud was forced to seek Russian aid, and on July 8, 1833, he signed the Treaty of Hünkâr İskelesi (Unkiar Skelessi); Muḥammad 'Alī was, for a time, left in possession of Syria, but Mahmud had not abandoned his claims. In 1839 he attacked the Egyptians; once more the Ottomans were defeated (June 24, 1839). With the help of the European powers (except France) through the Treaty of London (July 15, 1840), the Ottomans recovered Syria and eventually consolidated their authority there; but Muḥammad 'Alī obtained recognition as hereditary ruler of Egypt (1841).

Attempts to extend Ottoman control in the European provinces, notably in Greece, Serbia, and the Principalities, were frustrated. The Greek revolt was the product of the economic prosperity of the Napoleonic Wars, exposure to western European ideas, and a reaction against Ottoman centralization. It had two sources. The first lay in the opposition of peasants and bandits; the second, in the plots of certain intellectuals organized through the Philikí Etairía (a political society) and led by Alexander Ypsilantis, who invaded Moldavia in March 1821. Ypsilantis was defeated, but a rising began in the Peloponnesus. A stalemate developed; but the Ottomans were reinforced, in 1825, by Egyptian troops and threatened to put down the revolt. The destruction of the combined Ottoman and Egyptian fleets by Russian, French, and British naval forces at Navarino, in the southwestern Peloponnese (October 20,

1827) prevented the Muslims from supplying their armies and made Greek independence inevitable. The Ottomans were forced to recognize first Greek autonomy (1829), and then independence (1832).

Similarly, Ottoman efforts to regain control of Serbia and the Principalities were obstructed by Russian opposition, leading to the Russo-Ottoman War (1828–29). By the Treaty of Edirne (Adrianople) on September 14, 1829, the Ottomans ceded to Russia the mouth of the Danube and important territories in eastern Asia Minor and conceded new privileges to the Principalities and Serbia. Serbian autonomy was recognized in 1830 and was extended over the full area of the state in 1833.

Changes in the empire

By the death of Mahmud II (July 1, 1839) the Ottoman Empire was diminished in extent; it was more consolidated and powerful but increasingly subject to European pressures, with Russia supporting and Britain opposing separatist movements and the other powers oscillating between. The cure, however, had begun. Mahmud had established the "respectability of change," and its symbol was the replacement of the turban with the fez (1828).

The Tanzimat reforms (1839–76). The Tanzimat is the name given to the series of Ottoman reforms promulgated during the reigns of Mahmud's sons Abdülmecid I (ruled 1839–61) and Abdülaziz (ruled 1861–76). The best known of these reforms are the Hatt-ı Şerif of Gülhane (Noble Edict of the Rose Chamber; November 3, 1839) and the Hatt-ı Hümayun (Imperial Edict, February 18, 1856).

Purpose of the Tanzimat. The Tanzimat has been the subject of much controversy. Many Western writers have dismissed the promises of reform as an Ottoman desire to win European diplomatic support at critical moments, and some features of the Tanzimat appear to support such a view. The promises of equality for Christian subjects were not always implemented—for example, it was proposed in 1855 to end the poll tax paid by non-Muslims and to allow them to enter the army; but the old poll tax was merely replaced by a new exemption tax levied at a higher rate, and Christians were still excluded from the army. It is also true that the timing of reform announcements coincided with crises—the 1839 edict came when the Ottomans needed European help against Muḥammad ʿAlī; the 1856 edict when the Ottomans needed European acceptance in the wake of the Crimean War; and the 1876 constitution when European pressure for reforms was mounting.

This view of the Tanzimat is based, however, upon a misconception of its purpose. Europeans, who were principally concerned with winning better conditions for Ottoman Christians, looked first at those elements of the Tanzimat that appeared to be directed toward this goal (*e.g.*, a proclamation in the 1839 edict of the principles of individual liberty, freedom from oppression, and equality before the law and a substantial section of the 1856 edict that was concerned with the rights of Christians). But to the Ottomans the purpose of reform was to preserve the Ottoman state. While it was necessary to make some concessions to European powers and to their own non-Muslim subjects, and, although some Tanzimat statesmen saw equality as an ultimate goal, it was preservation that required the mobilization of resources for modernization. The central reforms, therefore, were in the army (notably major reorganizations of 1842 and 1869, the latter following the pattern of the successful Prussian conscript system); in the administration, both at the centre and in the provinces; and in society, through changes in education and law.

Reform in education. Before the reforms, education in the Ottoman Empire had not been a state responsibility but had been provided by the various *millets*; education for Muslims was controlled by the *ʿulamāʾ* and was directed toward religion. The first inroads into the system had been made with the creation of naval (1773), military (1793), engineering, medical (1827), and military science (1834) colleges. In this way specialized Western-type training was grafted onto the traditional system to produce specialists for the army. Similar institutions for diplomats and administrators were founded, including the translation bureau (1833) and the civil service school (1859); the latter was reorganized in 1877 and eventually became the faculty of political science in the University of Ankara (1950) and the major training centre for higher civil servants.

Comprehensive education plan

In 1846 the first comprehensive plan for state education was made. It provided for a complete system of primary and secondary schools leading to university, all under the Ministry of Education. A still more ambitious educational plan, inaugurated in 1869, provided for free and compulsory primary education. Both schemes progressed slowly because of a lack of money, but they provided a framework within which development toward a systematic, secular pattern could take place.

By 1914 there were more than 36,000 Ottoman schools, although the great majority were small, traditional primary schools. The development of the state system was aided by the example of progress among the non-Muslim *millet* schools, in which the education provided was more modern than in the Ottoman schools; by 1914 these included more than 1,800 Greek schools with about 185,000 pupils and some 800 Armenian schools with more than 81,000 pupils. Non-Muslims also used schools provided by foreign missionary groups in the empire; by 1914 there were 675 U.S., 500 French Catholic, and 178 British missionary schools, with more than 100,000 pupils among them. These foreign schools included such famous institutions as Robert College (founded 1863), the Syrian Protestant College (1866; later the American University of Beirut), and the Université Saint-Joseph (1874).

Reforms in law. Law too, to a large extent, had been the responsibility of the various *millets.* The Capitulations exempted foreigners and those Ottoman citizens on whom foreign consuls conferred protection from the application of criminal law. The Tanzimat reformers had two objects in the reform of law and legal procedure—to make Ottoman law acceptable to Europeans so that the Capitulations could be abolished and sovereignty recovered, and to modernize the traditional Islāmic law. Their efforts resulted in the promulgation of a number of codes—a commercial code (effective in 1850), a commercial procedure (1861), a maritime code (1863), and a penal code (1858). French influence predominated in these, as it did in the civil code of 1870–76. Increasingly, the laws were administered in new state courts, outside the control of the *ʿulamāʾ*. Although they failed to achieve the purposes intended, they provided the basis for future success.

European interference

Obstructions to reforms. The Tanzimat reforms moved steadily in the direction of modernization and centralization. The reformers were handicapped by lack of money and skilled men; and they were opposed by traditionalists, who argued that the reformers were destroying the empire's fundamental Islāmic character and who often halted the progress of reform. Centralization, meanwhile, was slowed by European interference, which obstructed the Ottoman attempt to recover power in Bosnia and Montenegro in 1853; forced the granting of autonomy to Mount Lebanon in 1861; and considered, but eventually rejected, intervention to prevent the Ottomans from suppressing a Cretan revolt of 1868. Although Britain and France helped the Ottomans resist Russian pressure during the Crimean War (1853–56), the Ottomans derived no real benefits from the peace settlement; and new arrangements helped to bring about the unification of the Principalities (1859) and paved the way for the emergence of independent Romania.

The very success of the Tanzimat reformers revealed a novel weakness. The effect of centralization removed the checks on the power of the sultan. After the death of Ali Paşa, Abdülaziz so abused his unrestrained authority as to produce a major crisis in 1875–78.

The 1875–78 crisis. Drought in 1873 and floods in 1874 produced widespread discontent and even famine among an Ottoman peasantry already disturbed by its increased burdens under a landholding system that had spread in the Balkans in the 19th century and by increased taxation and greater liability to conscription as a result of the 1869 military reorganization. The burden of taxation had been aggravated by the Ottoman problems of debt repayment. The first Ottoman foreign loan was in 1854; by 1875 the nominal public debt was £200,000,000 with annual repayments and amortization taking £12,000,000, or more than half the national revenue, but the Ottomans could pay only half the interest due because a world financial crisis in 1873 had made new credit difficult to obtain.

Balkan discontent was fanned by nationalist agitation supported by Serbia and by émigré Slav organizations. It culminated in risings largely of Christian peasants against Muslim lords in Bosnia and Hercegovina (July 1875) and in Bulgaria (August 1876). Ottoman efforts to suppress the risings led to war with Serbia and Montenegro (July 1876) and to attempts by European powers to force Ottoman reforms.

Russo-Turkish War, 1877–78

Agreement among the European powers proved impossible; and when the Ottomans rejected its demands, Russia decided to act alone and declared war (April 24, 1877). The war ended in defeat for the Ottomans, but their unexpected resistance at Plevna (modern Pleven, Bulgaria; July–December 1877) allowed other European powers, led by Britain, to intervene. According to the Treaty of San Stefano (March 3, 1878), the Ottomans were to recognize the independence of Romania, Serbia, and Montenegro and cede territory to them; to concede autonomy to an extensive new state of Bulgaria; to cede territory to Russia in the Dobruja (west of the Black Sea) and eastern Asia Minor; and to introduce various administrative reforms and pay an indemnity.

Diplomatic pressure from other European powers led to the modification of these terms at the Congress of Berlin (June–July 1878). The major changes concerned autonomous Bulgaria, which was substantially reduced in size and divided into two parts—the northern part to have political and the southern (eastern Rumelia) to have administrative autonomy. The independence of Serbia, Montenegro, and Romania was recognized, but their territorial gains were much reduced. Russia retained its acquisitions of Kars and Batum in Asia Minor. Austria-Hungary was given control of Bosnia and Hercegovina and the strategic district of Novi Pazar, in Yugoslavia. By a separate convention Cyprus was put under British rule.

The settlement was a major defeat for the Ottomans. Eastern Rumelia was soon lost when it united with Bulgaria in 1885. The Ottoman territories in Europe were reduced to Macedonia, Albania, and Thrace, and European influence had attained new dimensions. Britain now proposed to supervise governmental reforms in the Asian provinces, although this was skillfully frustrated by Abdülhamid II (ruled 1876–1909). In addition, the Ottomans were soon forced to accept new financial controls. By the Decree of Muharrem (December 1881) the Ottoman public debt was reduced from £191,000,000 to £106,000,000, certain revenues were assigned to its service, and a European-controlled organization (the Ottoman Public Debt Administration—OPDA) was set up to collect them.

The OPDA subsequently played an important part in Ottoman affairs, acting as agent for the collection of other revenues and as an intermediary with European companies seeking investment opportunities. Its influence should not, however, be exaggerated. It remained under Ottoman political control, and its existence even enabled the Ottomans to add to the debt at the annual rate of £3,000,000 throughout the reign of Abdülhamid; nor was the burden of repayments a major drain on the country's resources. But taken in conjunction with the activities of European-controlled banks and with the tariff limitations imposed on the Ottomans by the capitulations, the result was a distinct restriction on Ottoman ability to guide the allocation of resources.

The Ottoman constitution, 1876. Perhaps more significant than external changes were the internal political developments that brought about the first Ottoman constitution, December 23, 1876. The Tanzimat had produced three types of criticism within the Muslim community. The first was a simple traditionalist opposition. The second was a more sophisticated critique elaborated by certain intellectuals, many of whom had bureaucratic training and some knowledge of Western ideas. The third was a determination to depose the sultan (see below).

The Young Ottomans

The intellectuals were known as the Young Ottomans. Although some had taken part in a secret society (the "Patriotic Alliance") in 1865 and had some similarity of background, the Young Ottomans were not an organized political party; they are considered as a group largely through the accident of their assembly in Paris and London in 1867–71. Their political views ranged from secular, cosmopolitan revolutionism to profoundly Islāmic traditionalism. Because his views occupied a middle ground among these intellectuals and because of his lucidity of expression, Namik Kemal (1840–88) has often been regarded as the representative figure, although he is no more representative than the others. His views, however, had the greatest effect on later reformers.

Kemal criticized the Tanzimat reformers for their indiscriminate adoption of Western innovations. While admiring much of Western civilization, he believed that the principles underlying its best institutions were to be found in Islām. In particular he derived from early Islāmic precept and practice the idea of a representative assembly that could check the unbridled power of the sultan and his ministers. He helped to form and popularize the idea of a constitution and of loyalty to the Ottoman fatherland. Like others, he was assisted by the development of an Ottoman press, which had its origins in the 1830s but began to express opinions, occasionally critical of the government, in the 1860s, which saw the establishment of the *Tercüman-i Ahval* (1860) and the *Tasvir-i Efkâr* (1862), both of which, along with later newspapers, became the vehicles for Young Ottoman ideas.

But it was the third line of criticism that was most important. Arising within the higher Ottoman bureaucracy itself, it was led by Midhat Paşa. Midhat and others became convinced by their own exclusion from power and by the disastrous results of Abdülaziz's policies that some check was needed upon the sultan's power. The traditional check was deposition, and this was accomplished (May 30, 1876) following a riot by theological students and the removal of the hated grand vizier Mahmud Nedim Paşa. A new Cabinet was formed, which included Midhat and other partisans of reform. A new sultan, Murad V (ruled 1876), with a reputation for liberalism was installed; but Murad became insane and was deposed in August and replaced by Abdülhamid II. The experience convinced Midhat of the necessity of a permanent check upon the power of the sultan, such as could be provided by a representative assembly that would give ministers a basis of support independent of the sultan. Accordingly, Abdülhamid was persuaded to agree to a constitution.

First Ottoman constitution

Although earlier documents had had constitutional implications and although the development of councils—particularly provincial councils with their elected elements—had had parliamentary aspects, the December 23 document was the first comprehensive Ottoman constitution and, except for a Tunisian organic law of 1861, the first in any Islāmic country. The constitution was derived entirely from the will of the ruler, who retained full executive power and to whom ministers were individually responsible. In legislation the sultan was assisted by a two-chamber Parliament—the lower indirectly elected and the upper nominated by the ruler. Rights of ruler and ruled were set out, but the system it established might best be described as attenuated autocracy. Midhat has been criticized for accepting certain amendments demanded by Abdülhamid, including the then notorious article 113, which gave the sultan the right to deport persons harmful to the state; but it is clear that the majority of Midhat's colleagues were content with these amendments, and that the amendments made little difference, so great were the sultan's powers within and outside the constitution. The Parliament summoned under the constitution in March 1877 was dissolved in less than a year and was not recalled until 1908. The liberals were exiled; some, including Midhat, were put to death.

Rule of Abdülhamid II (1876–1909). The reign of Abdülhamid II is often regarded as having been a reaction against the Tanzimat; but, insofar as the essence of the Tanzimat reforms was centralization rather than liberalization, Abdülhamid may be seen as its fulfiller rather than its destroyer. The continued development of the army and administration, the formation of a gendarmerie, the growth of communications—especially the telegraph and railways—and the formation of an elaborate spy system enabled the sultan to monopolize power and crush opposition. His brutal repression of the Armenians in 1894–96 earned him the European title red sultan. But Abdülhamid's reign also made positive advances in education (including the renovation of Istanbul University in 1900); in legal reform, led by his grand vizier Mehmed Said Paşa; and in economic development, through the construction of railways in Asia Minor and Syria with foreign capital and of the Hejaz Railway from Damascus to Medina with the help of international Muslim subscriptions.

Pan-Islāmism. The Hejaz Railway constituted one element in Abdülhamid's Pan-Islāmic policies. Political Pan-Islāmism had made its first appearance in Ottoman policy at the Treaty of Küçük Kaynarca (1774) with Russia, when the Ottoman sultan had put forward claims to religious jurisdiction over Muslims outside his territories (particularly those in the Crimea). Some years later the theory was elaborated by the addition of the baseless legend that in 1517 the ʿAbbāsid caliphate had been transferred to the Ottoman sultan. With the extinction of many independent Muslim states and their absorption into the empires of European powers, this myth of the caliphate became a useful weapon in the Ottoman diplomatic armoury and was exploited by Abdülhamid as a means of deterring European powers from pressing him too hard, lest he create dissension within their own territories. In addition, stress on popular Islām through the press and other publications and through the Sultan's patronage of dervish orders served to rally Muslim opinion within the empire behind him.

Power of the myth of the caliphate

Preservation of the empire. Abdülhamid had reasonable success in preserving the empire after 1878. Apart from eastern Rumelia, no further territories were lost until 1908 (Ottoman authority in Tunisia, occupied by France in 1881, and that in Egypt, occupied by Britain in 1882, was already insignificant). In Crete the Ottomans suppressed revolts and defeated Greece when it intervened in 1897 in support of the Cretans. The European powers, however, forced Abdülhamid to concede autonomy to Crete. He was more successful in obstructing the efforts of the powers to force the introduction of substantial reforms in Macedonia. In Arabia the Ottomans continued the expansion of their power that had begun in the early 1870s.

The Young Turk Revolution, 1908. Several conspiracies took place against Abdülhamid. In 1889 a conspiracy in the military medical college spread to other Istanbul colleges. These conspirators came to call themselves the Committee of Union and Progress (İttihad ve Terakki Cemiyeti). When the plot was discovered, some of its leaders went to reinforce Ottoman exiles in Paris, Geneva, and Cairo, where they helped to prepare the ground for a revolution by developing a comprehensive critique of the Hamidian system. The most noteworthy among these were Murad Bey, Ahmed Riza, and Prince Sabaheddin. As editor of *Mizan* ("Balance"), published first in Istanbul (1886) and later in Cairo and Geneva, Murad Bey preached liberal ideas combined with a strong Islāmic feeling; this last may have contributed to his defection and return to Istanbul in 1897. Ahmed Riza in Paris edited *Meşveret* ("Consultation"), in which he set out ideas of reform, strongly flavoured by positivism. His advocacy of a strong central government within the Ottoman Empire and the exclusion of foreign influence led to a major split within the Young Turk exiles at the 1902 Paris Congress; Ahmed Riza clashed with Sabaheddin, who, with Armenian support, favoured administrative decentralization and European assistance to promote reform. Sabaheddin set up the League of Private Initiative and Decentralization.

The émigrés could supply literary sustenance to dissidents, but Abdülhamid could not be overthrown so long as the army remained loyal. The real origin of the Young Turk Revolution of 1908 lay in the discontent within the 3rd Army Corps in Macedonia, where officers acted quite independently of the Committee of Union and Progress (CUP) in Paris. It is still unclear if a coordinated conspiracy existed in Macedonia or if a number of separate centres of disaffection, linked haphazardly through individuals, dervish orders, Freemason lodges, etc., coalesced in July 1908 under the banner of the CUP through the pressure of events. On July 3, 1908, Maj. Ahmed Niyazi (1873–1912), apparently fearing discovery by an investigatory committee, decamped from Resne with 200 followers, including civilians, leaving behind a demand for the restoration of the constitution. The Sultan's attempt to suppress this rising failed, and rebellion spread rapidly. Unable to rely on other troops, on July 24 Abdülhamid announced the restoration of the constitution.

The young officers who had made the revolution, like their civilian supporters, were primarily concerned with preserving the Ottoman Empire; they feared that Hamidian policies and European interventions were endangering its existence. Personal grievances concerned with pay, promotion, etc., also played a part. Though some writers have argued that a new type of officer of lower than usual social origins influenced this discontent, there is little evidence to support such a theory. It is clear, however, that the officers had not thought much beyond their demand for the restoration of a constitution that had proved ineffectual in 1877–78. They had no program of action and were content to leave government to the established bureaucrats.

Goals of rebel leaders

In April 1909, however, an army mutiny in Istanbul (known because of the Julian calendar as the "31st March Incident") exposed the weakness of the CUP and at the same time gave it a new opportunity. The mutiny resulted from the discontent of ordinary soldiers arising from their conditions and their neglect by college-trained and politically ambitious officers, and from what they regarded as infidel innovations. They were encouraged by a religious organization—the Mohammedan Union. Government weakness allowed the mutiny to spread; and although order was eventually restored in Istanbul and more quickly elsewhere, a force from Macedonia (the Action Army) led by Mahmud Şevket Paşa marched on Istanbul and occupied the city (April 24).

Dissolution of the empire. Abdülhamid was deposed and replaced by Sultan Mehmed V (ruled 1909–18), son of Abdülmecid. The constitution was amended to transfer real power to the Parliament. The army, and particularly Şevket Paşa became the real arbiters of Ottoman politics.

Rise of the CUP. Although the removal of many of its political opponents had allowed the CUP to move into a more prominent position in government, it was still weak. It had a core of able, determined men but a much larger collection of individuals and factions that wore the Unionist label so lightly that they easily merged into other parties. Although the CUP won an overwhelming majority in the election of April 1912, its support rapidly melted away following military losses to Italy. Evidence of army hostility finally forced the CUP out of office in July 1912, to be succeeded by a political coalition called the Liberal Union.

The Liberal Union, too, lost support following defeats in the Balkans. This provided the opportunity for a small group of CUP officers and soldiers to stage a coup (January 23, 1913), known as the Sublime Porte Incident, to force the resignation of the grand vizier Mehmed Kâmil Paşa and establish a new cabinet under Şevket. Şevket, however, was not a Unionist and it was only after his assassination (June 11, 1913) that the CUP at last succeeded in establishing a Unionist-dominated government under Said Halim Paşa.

The Sublime Porte Incident

Internal developments. The disastrous results of the Young Turks' external policies have overshadowed the important internal developments of the years 1908–18. Further administrative reforms, particularly of provincial administration in 1913, led to more centralization, although by European standards the central Ottoman government remained relatively weak, particularly in the provinces distant from Istanbul. The burden of taxation was well below that of European powers.

The Young Turks were the first Ottoman reformers to promote industrialization, with a Law for the Encouragement of Industry (1909, revised 1915). Although they had little success, they did build a framework for later state-directed economic planning. Considerable attention was given to education, especially to the neglected area of primary education. The process of secularization of the law was carried much further. A major development in national journalism took place, and the position of women improved. The whole period was one of intense social and political discussion and change.

Turkish nationalism. The basic ideologies of the state remained Ottomanism and Islām, but a new sense of Turkish identity began to develop. This new concept was fostered by educational work of the Turkish Society (1908) and the Turkish Hearth (1912). A political twist was given by the adherents of Pan-Turkism and Pan-Turanianism. Pan-Turkism, which aimed at the political union of all Turkish-speaking peoples, began among Turks in the Crimea and on the Volga. Its leading exponent was Ismail Bey Gasprinski (Gaspirali; 1851–1914), who attempted to create a common Turkish language. Many Pan-Turkists migrated to Ottoman lands, especially after 1905. One of them, Yusuf Akçuraoğlu, argued in *Üç tarz-ı siyaset* (1903; "Three Kinds of Policy") that Turkism provided a better basis for the Ottoman Empire than either Islām or Ottomanism. Pan-Turanianism developed from a now much-disputed 19th-century theory of the common origin of Turkish, Mongol, Tungus, Finnish, Hungarian, and other languages; in certain very limited circles it looked forward to a great political federation of speakers of these languages, extending from Hungary to the Pacific.

Pan-Turkism and Pan-Turanianism

These ideas, however, found little support within the Ottoman government. The accusation that the Young Turks pursued a deliberate policy of Turkification within the empire so as to alienate non-Turks and promote the rise of Arab and Albanian nationalism is an oversimplification. The extension of government activity inevitably brought with it the language of government—Turkish. This produced some reaction from speakers of other languages, but the evidence suggests that it did not override basic feelings of Muslim solidarity, except among some small minorities. It was among the Christian groups that distinct separatist ideas were developed.

Foreign relations. The foreign relations of the Ottoman Empire under the Young Turks led to disaster. The 1908 revolution provided an opportunity for several powers to press home their designs upon the empire. On October 5, 1908, Austria annexed Bosnia and Hercegovina and Bulgaria proclaimed its independence. Italy seized Tripoli and occupied the Dodecanese, a group of Aegean islands; by the Treaty of Lausanne (October 18, 1912) Italy retained the former but agreed to evacuate the Dodecanese. In fact, however, it continued to occupy them.

The two Balkan Wars (1912–13) almost completed the destruction of the Ottoman Empire in Europe. In the first (October 1912–May 1913), the Ottomans lost almost all of their European possessions, including Crete, to Bulgaria, Serbia, Greece, Montenegro, and the newly created state of Albania (Treaty of London, May 30, 1913). In the second (June–July 1913), fought between Bulgaria and the remaining Balkan states, including Romania, over the division of Macedonia, the Ottomans intervened against Bulgaria and recovered part of eastern Thrace including Edirne (Adrianople). The Ottomans had lost 83 percent of the territory and 69 percent of the population of their European provinces.

The people. In 1914 the total population of the Ottoman Empire was approximately 25,000,000, of which about 10,000,000 were Turks; 6,000,000, Arabs; 1,500,000 each, Kurds and Greeks; and between 1,000,000 and 1,500,000 Armenians. The population of the empire (excluding such virtually independent areas as Egypt, Romania, and Serbia) in the period immediately prior to the losses of 1878 is estimated to have been about 26,000,000. Natural increases and Muslim immigration from Russia and the Balkans virtually made up the losses, and in 1914 the population was more homogeneous in religion and, though less so, in language.

Population of the empire

World War I, 1914–18. The Ottoman entry into World War I resulted from an overly hasty calculation of likely advantage. German influence was strong, but not decisive; Germany's trade with the Ottomans still lagged behind that of Britain, France, and Austria and its investments, which included the Baghdad railway, were smaller than those of France. A mission to Turkey led by the German military officer Otto Liman von Sanders in 1913 was only one of a series, and Liman's authority was much more limited than contemporaries supposed. Except for the interest of Russia in Istanbul and the Straits, no European power had really vital interests in the Ottoman Empire. The Ottomans might have remained neutral, as a majority of the cabinet wished to do, at least until the situation became clearer. But the opportunism of the minister of war Enver Paşa, early German victories, friction with the Triple Entente (France, Russia, and Great Britain) arising out of the shelter given by the Ottomans to German warships, and basic hostility to Russia combined to produce an Ottoman bombardment of the Russian Black Sea ports (October 28, 1914) and a declaration of war by the Entente against the Ottoman Empire.

The Ottomans made a substantial contribution to the Central Powers' war effort. Their forces fought in eastern Asia Minor, Azerbaijan, Mesopotamia, Syria and Palestine, and at the Dardanelles, as well as on European fronts, and they held down large numbers of Entente troops. In September 1918 they dominated Transcaucasia. During the war the Young Turks also took the opportunity to attack certain internal problems—the Capitulations were abolished unilaterally (September 1914), the autonomous status of Lebanon was ended, a number of Arab nationalists were executed in Damascus (August 1915 and May 1916), and the Armenian community in eastern Asia Minor and Cilicia was massacred or deported to eliminate any domestic support for the pro-Christian tsarist enemy on the Eastern Front. Possibly a million Armenians either fled or were killed (principally by Kurdish irregulars) or deported.

From the end of 1916 army desertions took place on a massive scale, and economic pressures became acute. The surrender of Bulgaria (September 28, 1918), which severed direct links with Germany, was the final blow. The CUP Cabinet resigned on October 7, and a new government was formed under Ahmed Izzet Paşa (1864–1937) on October 9. On October 30 the Ottomans signed the Armistice of Mudros.

Allied war aims and the proposed peace settlement. Entente proposals for the partition of Ottoman territories were formulated in a number of wartime agreements. By the Istanbul Agreements (March–April 1915) Russia was promised Istanbul and the Straits; and France, a sphere of influence in Syria and Cilicia. Britain had already annexed Cyprus and declared a protectorate over Egypt. By the Anglo-French Sykes-Picot Agreement (January 3, 1916) the French sphere was confirmed and extended eastward to Mosul in Iraq. A British sphere in Mesopotamia as far north as Baghdad, control of Haifa and Acre, and a linking sphere of influence were recognized. Palestine was to be placed under an international régime. In compensation, the Russian gains were extended (April–May 1916) to include the Ottoman provinces of Trabzon, Erzurum, Van, and Bitlis in eastern Asia Minor. By the London Agreement (April 26, 1915) Italy was promised the Dodecanese and a possible share of Asia Minor. By the Agreement of St.-Jean-de-Maurienne (April 1917) Italy was promised a large area of southwestern Anatolia, including Izmir (Smyrna) and a further sphere to the north. Britain made various promises of independence to Arab leaders, notably in the Ḥusayn-MacMahon correspondence, 1915–16, and, in the Balfour Declaration (November 2, 1917), promised to support the establishment of a national home for the Jewish people in Palestine.

Partition of Ottoman territories

The Russian withdrawal in 1917 and postwar bargaining led to some modifications of these agreements, and the Allied terms were not finally presented until 1920. By the Treaty of Sèvres (August 10, 1920) the Ottomans retained Istanbul and part of Thrace, but lost the Arab provinces and a large area of Asia Minor to a newly created Armenian state with access to the sea, surrendered the islands of İmroz and Bozcaada to Greece, and accepted arrangements that implied the eventual loss of Izmir to Greece. The Straits were internationalized, and strict European control of Ottoman finances was established. An accompanying tripartite agreement between Britain, France, and

Italy defined the extensive spheres of influence of the latter two powers. The treaty was ratified only by Greece and was abrogated by the Treaty of Lausanne (July 24, 1923) as the result of a determined struggle for independence waged under the leadership of the outstanding Ottoman wartime general Mustafa Kemal, later known as "Atatürk."

The emergence of the modern Turkish state

KEMAL AND THE WAR OF INDEPENDENCE, 1919–23

Although the legal Ottoman government in Istanbul, under the 36th, and last, Ottoman sultan Mehmed VI Vahideddin (ruled 1918–22) had decided that resistance to Allied demands was impossible, pockets of resistance remained in Asia Minor after the armistice. These included bands of irregulars and deserters, certain intact Ottoman forces, and various societies for the defense of rights. Resistance was stimulated by the Greek occupation of Izmir (May 15, 1919). At this time Mustafa Kemal was sent on an official mission to eastern Asia Minor, landing at Samsun on May 19. He immediately began to organize resistance, despite official Ottoman opposition. Through the Association for the Defense of the Rights of Eastern Anatolia (founded March 3, 1919), he summoned a congress at Erzurum (July–August), followed by a second congress at Sivas (September) with delegates representing the whole country. A new Association for the Defense of the Rights of Anatolia and Rumelia was established, and an executive committee with Mustafa Kemal as chairman was created to conduct resistance.

Congress at Erzurum

The official government yielded to Kemalist pressure. The unpopular grand vizier, Damad Ferid Paşa, resigned and was replaced by the more sympathetic Ali Riza Paşa. Negotiations with the Kemalists were followed by the election of a new parliament, which met in Istanbul in January 1920. A large majority in parliament was opposed to the official government policy and passed the "National Pact," which embodied the political aims of independence roughly within the October 1918 armistice lines and which had been formulated at Erzurum and Sivas. The Allies countered by extending the occupied area of Istanbul (March 16, 1920) and by arresting and deporting many deputies. Damad Ferid became grand vizier again on April 5 and, with religious support, set out to crush the Kemalists.

The Fundamental Law and abolition of the sultanate. The Kemalists were now faced with local risings, official Ottoman forces, and the Greeks. The first necessity was to establish a legitimate basis of action. A parliament (the Grand National Assembly) met at Ankara on April 23 and asserted that the sultan's government was under infidel control and that it was the duty of Muslims to resist foreign encroachment. In the Fundamental Law of January 20, 1921, the assembly declared that sovereignty belonged to the nation and that the assembly was the "true and only representative of the nation." The name of the state was declared to be "Turkey" ("Türkiye"); and executive power was entrusted to an executive council, headed by Mustafa Kemal, who could now concentrate on the war.

The uprisings and Ottoman forces were both defeated, principally by irregular forces, who at the end of 1920 were brought under Kemal's control. In 1920–21 the Greeks made major advances, almost to Ankara, but were defeated at the Battle of the Sakarya River (August 24, 1921) and began a long retreat that ended in the Turkish occupation of Izmir (September 9, 1922).

The Kemalists had already begun to gain European recognition. On March 16, 1921, the Soviet-Turkish Treaty gave Turkey a favourable settlement of its eastern frontier by restoring Kars and Ardahan. Domestic problems induced Italy to begin withdrawal from the territory it occupied; and, by the Treaty of Ankara (Franklin-Bouillon Agreement, October 20, 1921), France agreed to evacuate Cilicia. Finally, by the Armistice of Mudanya the Allies agreed to Turkish reoccupation of Istanbul and eastern Thrace.

A comprehensive settlement was eventually achieved at the Lausanne Conference (November 1922–July 1923). The Turkish frontier in Thrace was established on the Maritsa river, and Greece returned the islands of İmroz and Bozcaada. A compulsory exchange of populations was arranged, as a result of which an estimated 1,300,000 Greeks left Turkey in return for 400,000 Turks. The question of Mosul was left to the League of Nations, which in 1925 recommended its retention by Iraq. The Lausanne Treaty also provided for the apportionment of the Ottoman Public Debt, for the gradual abolition of the Capitulations (Turkey regained tariff autonomy in 1929), and for an international régime for the Straits. Turkey did not recover complete control of the Straits until the 1936 Montreux Convention.

New Turkish frontier

The result of the war and the peace settlement created a state in which the great majority spoke Turkish. Though there has been a tendency to see this as the almost inevitable consequence of the rise of Turkish and Arab nationalisms, it seems in fact to have been the accident of war that broke off the Arab provinces. Whatever the views of Mustafa Kemal himself, it is clear that the majority of his followers thought of themselves primarily as Muslims; in the elaborate religious ceremony that preceded the opening of the Grand National Assembly there was no word of Turks or Turkey but only of the need to save "religion's last country." The creation of a sense of Turkish nationhood was the product of a long effort in which Mustafa Kemal played the dominant role.

Construction of a new political system began with the abolition of the sultanate and the declaration of a republic. Loyalty to the Ottoman dynasty was strong even among Kemalists; but Vahideddin's identification with the Allies weakened his support. An Allied invitation to the sultan to nominate representatives to Lausanne aided Kemal—a split Turkish delegation would be self-defeating. With a brilliant mixture of threats and persuasion, Kemal was able, therefore, to induce the Assembly to abolish the sultanate (November 1, 1922). Vahideddin left Turkey, and his cousin Abdülmecid (died 1944) was installed as the first and last Ottoman caliph who was not also sultan.

Declaration of the Turkish republic. The caliphate was finally abolished on March 3, 1924, and all members of the Ottoman dynasty were expelled from Turkey. Before that the assembly had declared Turkey to be a republic and had elected Mustafa Kemal as first president (October 29, 1923). A full republican constitution was adopted on April 20, 1924; it retained Islām as the state religion, but in April 1928 this clause was removed and Turkey became a purely secular republic.

TURKEY UNDER KEMAL

Government. The assembly was the instrument of Kemal's will. The first assembly had contained large factions hostile to his policies, including religious conservatives, merchants, and former members of the CUP. In opposition to his 197 acknowledged supporters, who were known as the "First Group," there were 118 opponents, members of a "Second Group." The first Assembly was dissolved on April 16, 1923, and Mustafa Kemal took care to keep his opponents out of the second assembly; only three of the Second Group were returned. Kemal's own party, which became the Republican People's Party (RPP), dominated all assemblies until 1950; this period saw a heavy preponderance in the Assembly of urban professional men and of officials with university education. With an outlook different from that of the illiterate Turkish peasant they carried out a revolution from the top.

Opposition. There was little opposition to Mustafa Kemal—the small Progressive Republican Party (founded, November 17, 1924; dissolved, June 5, 1925) had only 29 members and was suppressed because Kemal feared that its leading members, who included some of his most notable associates in the war of independence, might have too much influence in the army; the short-lived Liberal Republican Party (August 12–December 18, 1930) was an abortive attempt by Kemal to organize a moderate opposition to his own party. Otherwise Kemal ruled quite autocratically. A plot against his life in 1926 gave him the chance to deal with his rivals, who were tried by a special court and many of them sentenced to death, imprisonment, or exile. Opposition outside the assembly, of which the most dangerous were the Kurdish revolts of 1925, 1930, and 1937, was suppressed vigorously.

Kemalist policies. The bases of Mustafa Kemal's policies were enshrined in the Republican People's Party program of 1931 and subsequently (February 1937) written into the Turkish constitution. These were the six principles of republicanism (the creation of the republic), nationalism, populism, statism (*devletçilik*), secularism, and revolution. Revolution was implicit in the whole radical reorganization of the political, social, and economic systems. Populism was the effort to mobilize popular support from the top through such characteristic devices as the People's Houses (1931–51), which spread the new concept of a national culture in provincial towns, and the village institutes, which performed the same educational and proselytizing role in the countryside. The creation of a sense of nationalism was encouraged by changes in school curricula, by the rewriting of history to glorify the Turkish past, by the "purification" of the language by a reduction of the number of words of foreign origin (sometime later, this effort appeared to be redundant in the light of a promulgation that all languages were descended from Turkish), and by the renunciation of Pan-Islāmic, Pan-Turkish, and Pan-Ottoman goals in foreign policy.

Mustafa Kemal's six principles

Statism was the movement toward state-controlled economic development; the shortage of skilled labour and entrepreneurs (particularly owing to the reduction of the Greek and Armenian communities, which in 1914 had controlled 80 percent of Ottoman finance, industry, and commerce), the lack of capital, and the intense nationalist desire for industrial self-sufficiency that would banish foreign influence, all stimulated a movement in the 1930s towards state ownership or control. This was achieved through investment banks, monopolies, state industrial enterprises, and planning. A five-year plan was instituted in 1934. Although the immediate results were disappointing, the policy of state-inspired economic growth was important for future economic advance.

Under secularism is included the reform of law, involving the abolition of religious courts and schools (1924) and the adoption of a purely secular system of family law. The substitution of Latin for the Arabic alphabet in writing Turkish was a significant step toward secularism and made learning easier; other measures included the adoption (1925) of the Gregorian calendar that had been jointly used with the Hijrī calendar since 1917; the replacement of Friday by Sunday as the weekly holiday (1935); the adoption of surnames (1935); and, most striking of all, the abolition of the fez (1925). The wearing of clerical garb outside places of worship was forbidden in 1934.

These changes, coupled with the abolition of the caliphate, and the elimination of the dervish orders after a Kurdish revolt in 1925, dealt a tremendous blow to Islām's position in social life, completing the process begun in the Tanzimat. With secularism there came a steady improvement in the status of women, who were given the right to vote and to sit in the parliament.

Vital as the changes made were, in many cases they were primarily matters of appearance and style. Structural changes in society took longer. At the first census, in 1927, the population was put at 13,600,000, of which 24 percent was urban. In 1940 the population was 17,800,000, but the urban percentage was almost unchanged. In 1938 the per capita income and literacy were both below comparable figures for developed countries.

Foreign policy was subordinated to internal change. The loss of Mosul was accepted (June 5, 1926). Hatay, however, was recovered. It was given internal autonomy by France in 1937, occupied by Turkish troops in 1938, and incorporated into Turkey in 1939. Turkey followed a neutralist policy, supported the League of Nations, which it joined in 1932, and sought alliances with other minor powers, leading to the Balkan Entente (1934) and the Saʿdābād Pact with Iran, Iraq, and Afghanistan (1937).

Neutralist policy

TURKEY AFTER KEMAL

World War II and the postwar era, 1938–50. Atatürk's autocratic, dominating, and inspiring personality had directed and shaped the Turkish republic. At his death in 1938, his closest associate İsmet İnönü was elected president. With the approach of war, foreign affairs assumed greater importance. An alliance with Britain and France (October 19, 1939) was not implemented because of Germany's early victories. After Germany's invasion of Russia (June 22, 1941), there was popular support for an alliance with Germany, which seemed to offer prospects of realizing old Pan-Turkish aims. Although a nonaggression pact was signed with Germany (June 18, 1941), Turkey clung to neutrality until an Axis defeat was seen to be inevitable, when it entered the war on the Allied side (February 23, 1945). The great expansion of Soviet power exposed Turkey, in June 1945, to demands that control of the Straits be given to Black Sea powers and for the cession of territory in eastern Asia Minor. It was also suggested that a large area of northeastern Anatolia be ceded to Soviet Georgia and a more democratic government established in Turkey. This caused Turkey to seek U.S. assistance; it received U.S. military aid beginning in 1947 (providing the basis for a large and continuing flow of military aid) and economic assistance beginning in 1948.

The war also brought changes in domestic policy. The army had been kept small throughout the Atatürk period, and defense expenditure had been reduced to 28 percent of the budget. The army was rapidly expanded in 1939, and defense expenditures rose to between 50 percent and 60 percent of the budget for the duration of the war. Substantial deficits were incurred, imposing a severe economic strain, which was aggravated by shortages of raw materials. By 1945 agricultural output had fallen to 70 percent of the 1939 figure; per capita income, to 75 percent. Inflation was strong; official statistics show a rise of 354 percent between 1938 and 1945, but this probably understates the fall in the value of money, which in 1943 was less than one-fifth its 1938 purchasing power. One means chosen by the government to raise money was a capital levy introduced in 1942, arranged to fall with punitive force upon the non-Muslim communities and upon the Dönmes (Jewish converts to Islām). The war did provide some stimulus to industry, however, and enabled Turkey to build up substantial foreign credits, which could be used to finance postwar economic development.

The most notable change in the postwar years was the liberalization of political life. The investment in education was beginning to show some return, and literacy had risen to 29 percent by 1945. A growing class of professional and commercial men demanded more freedom. The Allied victory had made democracy more fashionable; accordingly, the government made concessions allowing new political parties, universal suffrage, and direct election.

Political liberalization

From a split within the Republican People's Party (RPP), the Democrat Party (DP) was founded in 1946 and immediately gathered support. Despite government interference, the DP won 61 seats in the 1946 general election. Some elements in the RPP, led by the prime minister Recep Peker (served 1946–47), wished to suppress the DP, but they were prevented by İnönü. In his declaration of July 12, 1947, İnönü stated that the logic of a multiparty system implied the possibility of a change of government. Prophetically, he renounced the title of "National Unchangeable Leader," which had been conferred upon him in 1938. Peker resigned and was succeeded by more liberal prime ministers in Hasan Saka (served 1947–49), and Şemseddin Günaltay (served 1949–50).

Other restrictions on political freedom, including press censorship, were relaxed. The period saw the establishment of the first mass circulation, independent newspapers. Trade Unions were permitted in 1947, although they were not given the right to strike until 1963. A far-reaching measure of land redistribution was passed in 1945, although little was done to implement it before 1950. Other political parties were established including the conservative National Party (1948); Socialist and Communist activities, however, were severely repressed.

In the more open atmosphere the DP was able to organize in the villages. The RPP, despite its Village Institutes, had always been the government party and had had little real grass-roots organization. The Democrats were much more responsive to local interests. The DP won a massive victory in the 1950 elections, claiming 54 percent of the vote and 396 out of 487 seats. The RPP won 68 seats; the National Party, one. The DP victory has been attributed variously to U.S. influence, to social change, to a desire for economic liberalization, to better organization, to religious hostility to the RPP, and to a bad harvest in 1949. Perhaps the basic reason was that in 27 years the RPP had made many enemies.

Turkey under the Democrats, 1950–60. In the DP government Celâl Bayar became president; Adnan Menderes, prime minister (a post which for the first time came to surpass that of the president in importance).

The economy. The Democrats were pledged to a program of economic growth, to be achieved through a reduction of state interference. At first they had much success. Good harvests in 1950 and 1953 and the Korean War boom assisted. But problems appeared after 1953. In 1954 a poor harvest obliged Turkey to import wheat again. A shortage of foreign exchange limited the purchase of essential materials and parts, which handicapped industry. After a sudden favourable surge in the early 1950s, the terms of trade moved steadily against Turkey. Inflation, which averaged 15 percent or more annually, became a serious problem. The government attempted unsuccessfully to check the price rise by legislation, but its policies contributed to inflation as the result of a continued rise in public expenditure. Despite the problems, the DP achieved considerable success over the decade 1950–60.

Political repressions. The political fortunes of the Democrat government closely reflected the economic changes. In the 1954 elections—the Democratic peak—the DP took 57 percent of the vote and gained 503 out of 541 seats; the RPP took 35 percent and 31 seats. Subsequent economic difficulties led to mounting criticism within and outside the DP, to which the government replied with increasing repression. In 1953 much of the property of the RPP was confiscated, forcing the closure of the People's Houses. The RPP newspaper presses in Ankara were seized. In 1954 the National Party was dissolved because of its opposition to Kemalist principles (it was immediately reformed as the Republican Nation's Party and united in 1958 with the Peasants' Party to form the Republican Peasants' Nation Party). Laws passed in 1954 provided for heavy fines on journalists who damaged the prestige of the state or the law; several prominent journalists were prosecuted under this law, which was made more severe in 1956, in which year other laws substantially abridged the independence of civil servants (including university teachers) and judges. In October 1955 critics within the DP were expelled; these critics subsequently formed the Freedom Party (December 1955), which later (1958) merged with the RPP. In 1956 limitations were placed upon public meetings.

Seizure of RPP newspaper presses

The DP's loss of popularity was reflected in the elections of October 1957, when they won only 48 percent of the vote and 424 out of 610 seats. The RPP took 41 percent and 178 seats. The three opposition parties had attempted to form an electoral coalition, but a law passed that September had declared such coalitions illegal. The combined opposition vote was 52 percent of the total, and many persons believed that this government action had deprived them of victory. Opposition attacks upon the DP became stronger, and it was accused of unconstitutional action. At the same time, the Democrats, fearing a revolution, redoubled control. In December 1959 an alleged plot (the so-called Nine Officers' Plot) was unearthed; some of the accused were so clearly innocent that punishment fell upon the accuser, but it appears that there had been a conspiracy of some sort.

A charge on which the RPP laid great stress was that the DP was reversing the principles of secularism and favouring conservative religious organizations. The DP had relaxed some of the secularist policies of pure Kemalism, following in the steps of the RPP in the years 1945–49. Religious instruction in schools had been extended and the organization of religious schools permitted. Arabic had been reinstated for the call to prayer, and radio readings of the Qur'ān had been allowed. These, however, were modest concessions in themselves, and the Democrats had clearly demonstrated their unwillingness to tolerate religious influence in politics by suppressing the activities of dervish orders in 1950–52.

The years 1958–60 saw a further worsening of the economic situation as the government reluctantly introduced restrictive measures. Returns on new investment fell and inflation continued. Serious problems of housing, unemployment, etc., were emerging in the large towns, whose population had been growing annually at the rate of about 10 percent, so that by 1960 the proportion of urban population to the whole had risen, to 32 percent. RPP attacks became more bitter, and the government's response stronger. In April 1960 the government ordered the army to prevent İnönü from campaigning in Kayseri and followed this by forming a committee to investigate the affairs of the RPP. It was widely believed that the next action would be to close the RPP. Student demonstrations followed, and martial law was declared on April 28. The army had been brought directly into the political arena.

Growth of economic problems

THE MILITARY COUP OF 1960

Relatively neglected from 1923 to 1939, the army during the war had undergone a rapid expansion and a considerable modernization subsequently with the aid of U.S. advisers. Many officers feared that the DP threatened the principles of the secular, progressive Kemalist state. Some younger officers saw the army as the direct instrument of unity and reform. On May 3, 1960, the commander of the land forces, Gen. Cemal Gürsel, demanded political reforms, and resigned when they were refused. On May 27 the army acted; an almost bloodless coup was carried out by officers and cadets from the Istanbul and Ankara War colleges. The leaders established a 38-man "National Unity Committee" with Gürsel as chairman. The Democrat leaders were imprisoned.

The National Unity Committee, 1960–61. From the outset, a clear division existed among the officers who had carried out the coup. One group, predominantly of younger officers, believed that to restore national unity and carry out major social and economic reforms it was necessary to retain power for some years; this group included both those who supported a nationalistic and Islāmist policy and those who favoured accelerated secularization. Another group, which included most of the senior officers, wanted to withdraw the army from politics as soon as possible. In November 1960 the dispute was decided against the first group, and 14 were expelled from the committee and sent into diplomatic exile.

The main work of the National Unity Committee was to destroy the DP and to prepare a new constitution. Substantial purges took place—5,000 officers including 235 out of 260 generals were dismissed or retired; 147 university teachers left their jobs; 55 wealthy landowners were banished from eastern Anatolia, their lands confiscated. The DP was abolished (September 29, 1960), and many Democrats were brought to trial at Yassi Ada (October) on charges of corruption, unconstitutional rule, and high treason. Of 601 tried, 464 were found guilty. Three former ministers, including Menderes, were executed; 12 others, including Bayer, had their death sentences commuted to life imprisonment.

Work of the National Unity Committee

Constitution of 1961. Work on the new constitution began immediately after the coup, when a committee of five law professors was appointed to prepare a draft. This was submitted to the National Unity Committee on October 18. The Committee appointed a second committee to redraft the constitution; the new draft was presented to a Constituent Assembly, which met in January 1961. The constitution was completed in May and approved by 61 percent of the voters at a referendum in July.

The new constitution established a two chamber parliament—consisting of the Senate and the National Assembly. A separate electoral law provided for proportional representation. The president was elected by the Senate and National Assembly together. The constitution also provided for a Constitutional Court and a State Planning Organization. The first elections were held in October 1961. The army then withdrew from direct political involvement, although the members of the National Unity Committee retained some influence as life members of the Senate.

PERIOD OF POLITICAL MODERATION, 1961–65

No party won a majority in October 1961. The RPP won 38 percent of the votes and 173 of the 450 Assembly seats. The newly formed Justice Party (JP), led by retired general Rağıp Gümüşpala, received 35 percent and 158 seats. The remaining seats were divided between two smaller parties—the Republican Peasants' Nation Party, which took 54 seats, and the liberal New Turkey Party, which gained 65. The results demonstrated the enduring popularity of the old Democrat Party. Its votes had been divided among the three smaller parties, the majority of them going to the Justice Party, which had also emerged as the largest party in the Senate. The RPP had failed to hold all of its 1957 vote and had suffered by identification with the army coup.

The new Grand National Assembly elected General Gürsel as president. The RPP leader İnönü formed a coalition government with the JP, but the coalition survived only until June 1962, when it broke up over the question of an amnesty for the imprisoned Democrats. After some delay and splits within the parties (which led to the formation of the Nation Party by dissidents who withdrew from the Republican Peasants' Nation Party), the RPP formed a coalition with the two smaller parties. This accelerated the tendency for former Democrat voters to turn to the JP.

In the local elections of 1963 the JP made extensive gains at the expense of the two smaller parties. This led to the breakup of the coalition, and, because the JP was unable to form a government, İnönü formed a minority government from his own party alone, but with voting support from the New Turkey Party. The RPP government resigned after a defeat on the budget in February 1965 and was replaced by a coalition of all the other parties under the leadership of an independent, Suat Hayri Ürgüplü; this coalition acted as caretaker until the elections of October 10, 1965.

The national remainder principle

In December 1964 a new electoral law had introduced the principle of "the national remainder," by which a certain number of seats were distributed to parties according to their proportion of the vote. The law had been intended to operate in favour of the smaller parties and against the JP, but in the election the JP won a surprising majority with 53 percent of the votes and 240 seats. The RPP received 29 percent and 134 seats; and the smaller parties, 76 seats. The new JP leader, Süleyman Demirel, a former engineer, was able to form a government.

Political moderation had triumphed in the years 1961–65. The army had stood aloof while power came gradually to a party that drew its main support from the same groups and areas as the Democrats and that espoused a similar philosophy. Attempts to restore army rule had failed. Intervention proposed by senior officers in October 1961 had been rejected by others. Two projected coups had been foiled in February 1962 and May 1963. Members of a secret society within the army—the Young Kemalists—were arrested in April 1963. Criticism of the 1960 revolution was made illegal in 1962; army leaders contented themselves with occasional warnings.

The political trends were liberal: the Democrat prisoners were released (1962–64); the labour law of 1963 made strikes legal and promoted a great expansion of trade unionism; workers became more active in politics through the left-wing Confederation of Reformist Workers' Unions, or DISK, and through the Marxist Turkish Workers (or Labour) Party (TWP; founded in 1961).

COALITION GOVERNMENTS

Political development, 1965–71. The victory of the Justice Party in 1965 did not lead to strong government mainly because the JP was itself a coalition of disparate elements—modernizers and traditionalists, secularists and religious conservatives. Prime Minister Demirel showed considerable skill in balancing factions and holding his party to a moderate line. He concentrated on fostering rapid economic growth through foreign investment (thus avoiding the need for tax reform) and on suppressing the increasingly violent hostility of the radical left, notably of the Federation of the Revolutionary Youth of Turkey (Türkiye Devrimci Gençlik Federasyonu; short form, Dev Genç), a Marxist student organization, founded in 1969, that adopted terrorist methods. The leftists clashed with the newly emerging radical right.

Election of 1969

In the election of 1969 the JP won with a reduced majority. The national remainder system, which favoured the smaller parties, was dropped in favour of simple proportional representation. The result was that the two major parties, JP and RPP, increased their share of seats in the National Assembly, although they secured a smaller share of the vote. The JP won 47 percent of the vote and 256 seats, and the RPP won 27 percent and 143 seats, while the extremist parties of left and right performed poorly.

The loss of votes weakened Demirel's hold on the JP. His power was challenged by the rightists, led by his chief rival, Sadettin Bilgiç. Excluded from the new Cabinet, they retaliated by defeating Demirel's government in February 1970. Demirel was reappointed prime minister, but his authority was considerably weakened; some rightists seceded from the JP in December 1970 to form the Democratic Party (DP), led by Ferruh Bozbeyli. The Demirel government was unable to deal with the increasing disorders in Turkey. The army leaders became disturbed by the situation and by their own identification with Demirel's policies. On March 12, 1971, possibly to anticipate a takeover of government by more radical junior officers, the senior military commanders, led by the chief of staff, Gen. Memduh Tağmaç, presented a memorandum calling for the resignation of the government on the grounds that it had proved itself incapable of dealing with the crisis that threatened civilization in Turkey. Demirel immediately resigned.

Political development from 1971 to 1980. Beginning in 1971, Turkey was governed by coalition governments—led successively by Nihat Erim (March 1971–April 1972), Ferit Melen (to April 1973), and Naim Talu (to January 1974)—which claimed to be above party politics and included several technocrats and bureaucrats as well as politicians, enjoyed the support of the army leaders, and obtained the consent of the National Assembly. Their main aim was to restore law and order. On April 26, 1971, martial law was established in 11 provinces; there were many arrests and trials before military courts and armed clashes between the security forces and the radical guerrillas (called the Turkish People's Liberation Army). The Islāmic-based National Order Party (founded January 1970) was suppressed in May 1971 and the TWP in July. In September 1971 the constitution was amended to reduce personal freedoms. Martial law was not completely lifted until September 1973, when the military courts were replaced by special security courts.

The crisis of 1971 accelerated an important change in the RPP. Its failure to attract popular support after 1961 had led to a re-examination of its policies and the adoption in 1965 of a "left of centre" policy. The party's failure in the election of 1965 sharpened divisions between the radicals (led by Bülent Ecevit) and the conservatives (led by Turhan Feyzioğlu). The party leader, İnönü, favoured the Ecevit group, and in 1967 Feyzioğlu and others seceded to found the Reliance Party (renamed National Reliance Party in 1969). Many conservatives remained in the RPP, however, and the conflict broke out again after the party's defeat in 1969; it was brought to a head by the army's intervention in March 1971. Ecevit opposed İnönü's acceptance of the army's action and in May 1972 defeated him in a battle for control of the party. Other conservatives then formed a Republican Party, which merged with the National Reliance Party in March 1973 to form the Republican Reliance Party (RRP). Because the RPP had largely shed its eastern and central Anatolian landowner element, it could present itself as a social democratic party.

No party secured a majority at the general election in October 1973, but the RPP emerged as the largest single party, with a third of the vote and 185 seats. The right-wing vote was much larger (more than 60 percent) but was divided among several parties, mainly the JP (29.8 percent and 149); the DP (11.9 percent and 45); the religiously based National Salvation Party (NSP), founded in October 1972 in succession to the banned National Order Party and led by Necmettin Erbakan (11.8 percent and 48); the RRP (5.3 percent and 13); and the National Action Party (NAP), until 1969 the Republican Peasants' Nation Party, a right-wing nationalist party led by Alparlan Türkeş (3.4 percent and 3).

An uneasy coalition government was eventually formed by the RPP and NSP in January 1974 with Ecevit as prime minister. In September 1974 it was dissolved by Ecevit. There followed a long ministerial crisis and an above-party caretaker government under Sadi Irmak. This was succeeded by a right-wing coalition of the JP, NSP, RRP, and NAP (the Nationalist Front) led by Demirel. During this period the internal security situation again deteriorated; there were numerous conflicts in universities between leftists and rightists and clashes between security forces and guerrillas in eastern Turkey.

Nationalist Front coalition

At the National Assembly election in June 1977, the swing to the smaller parties that had characterized the elections of 1973 was reversed. The RPP gained 41.4 percent of the vote and 213 seats, the JP 36.9 percent and 189 seats. Only two of the smaller parties secured more than 2 percent of the vote: the NSP (8.6 percent and 24) and the NAP (6.4 percent and 16). The DP was virtually obliterated, and the reformed Turkish Workers Party gained only 0.1 percent of the vote. Demirel's ineffective coalition returned to office until the end of the year. In January 1978 Ecevit formed a new coalition with the RRP, DP, and independents, mainly defectors from the JP. Ecevit's coalition government was also unable to curb inflation, unemployment, and political violence, all of which increased rapidly and led to the re-imposition of martial law in 13 provinces. He was again forced to resign, and Demirel formed a minority JP government in November 1979.

THE MILITARY COUP OF 1980

By 1980 the military, which had watched the growing violence and the government's ineffectiveness with alarm, intervened. They precipitated a bloodless coup on September 12, after the National Assembly had failed to elect a successor to President Korutürk. A National Security Council composed of the military high command took over government duties, naming Gen. Kenan Evren head of state, and quickly dissolved the Assembly, political parties, and trade unions; suspended the constitution; and imposed martial law. Thousands of dissidents were jailed and, as later revealed, tortured. The immediate result of these measures was a substantial drop in the number of terrorist killings, from about 3,700 in 1979–80 to fewer than 300 in 1981. In July 1982 the government published a draft of a new constitution that won overwhelming approval in a national referendum held the following November. In 1983 the National Security Council transferred power to an elected parliament. The exclusion of some parties from the 1983 parliamentary elections suppressed the factionalism that had crippled the Turkish government before the coup. Local elections in 1985 confirmed popular support for the ruling Motherland Party and also gave opposition parties the opportunity to reorganize and gain support on the local level. Martial law was gradually lifted from all the provinces except those where Kurdish rebel groups remained active. Growing international concern over reports of torture in the prisons after the coup prompted condemnation from the Europeans and led to the government granting on-site observation of prison conditions by international human rights organizations.

FOREIGN POLICY AFTER 1950

Until about 1964 Turkish foreign policy was wholly based upon the Western alliance. Turkey sent troops to Korea, joined NATO (1952), joined the Baghdad Pact, later Central Treaty Organization, or Cento (1955), joined the Organization for European Economic Co-operation (OEEC) and the Council of Europe, and applied for membership in the European Economic Community (1959). This policy was based on fear of the Soviet Union, on dependence upon U.S. military and economic aid, and on the conviction that Turkey's destiny was as a secular European state. From 1960 the suitability of this policy was increasingly questioned, and from 1964 Turkish policy, while retaining its Western inclination, was more attuned to Turkey's own regional interests. The principal causes of this change were the general East–West détente; the growing importance of Middle Eastern countries; and discontent with the fruits of Turkey's cultivation of the United States. Turkish doubts were brought to a head by the problem of Cyprus.

During the 1950s Greek Cypriot demands for independence from Britain and union with Greece led to strife involving the Turkish Cypriot community, which looked to Turkey for help. Tension between Turkey and Greece ensued, although this was reduced by the Zürich and London agreements of 1959, providing for the independence of Cyprus under certain conditions. Disputes between Greek and Turkish Cypriots in independent Cyprus led to civil war in December 1963, and Turkish public opinion demanded intervention in support of the Turkish Cypriots. The crisis passed, but in November 1967 Turkey again threatened military intervention. War was then averted by U.S. and UN pressure, which procured the withdrawal of Greek regular forces that had been introduced into Cyprus. In July 1974, however, a major crisis occurred when, following a coup against President Makarios of Cyprus that had been supported by the Greek government, Turkish forces occupied the north of the island. Turkey's action led to an embargo on military aid to Turkey, imposed by the U.S. Congress from February 1975 (relaxed in October 1975 and May 1977). In retaliation Turkey denounced the U.S.–Turkish defense agreement of 1969 and closed U.S. defense installations on July 25, 1975. A new defense agreement was negotiated (March 26, 1976) by which the bases passed under Turkish control and the United States guaranteed $1,000,000,000 in military aid to Turkey over four years. In September 1978 the arms embargo was lifted, and the next month Turkey responded by giving the United States permission to reopen four installations.

The Cyprus dispute and indifferent relations with the United States were important factors in Turkey's decision to respond to Soviet overtures for friendship, which had been frequently repeated since 1953. In 1964 the Turkish foreign minister visited Moscow in the first of a series of high-level visits that led to economic and cultural agreements and, on June 23, 1978, a political agreement couched in broad terms of friendship. Turkey also set out to improve relations with the Balkan states (other than Greece), which had languished since the Balkan Entente (Greece, Yugoslavia, and Turkey) of 1954. Relations with Greece suffered not only from the Cyprus problem but also from disputes over rights in the Aegean Sea.

Soviet–Turkish accords

Turkey also endeavoured to improve its relations with other states. China was recognized in 1971. A movement toward the Arab position in the dispute with Israel and the cultivation of Islāmic bonds led to better relations with the Arab world. Relations with Iran and Pakistan, which had been close, were markedly reduced by the Iranian revolution and the dissolution of Cento in September 1979, but Turkey remained neutral in the Iran–Iraq war. Turkey's overall commitment to the West, however, was shown by its close ties with western European countries and by its attainment of associate status in the European Economic Community. Turkey's recognition of the Turkish Cypriot assembly's unilateral declaration of independence in November 1983 once again strained relations with Europe.

For later developments in the political history of Turkey, see the *Britannica Book of the Year* section in the BRITANNICA WORLD DATA ANNUAL. (M.E.Y./Ed.)

BIBLIOGRAPHY

Turkey. A general introduction that contains a useful bibliography is RICHARD F. NYROP (ed.), *Turkey: A Country Study* (1979). Another useful work is BERNARD LEWIS, *The Emergence of Modern Turkey,* 2nd ed. (1968). For geography, see W.C. BRICE, *South-West Asia* (1966); and GEORGE B. CRESSEY, *Crossroads: Land and Life in Southwest Asia* (1960). For the economy, see Z.Y. HERSHLAG, *Turkey: The Challenge of*

Growth (1968); UNION OF CHAMBERS OF COMMERCE, INDUSTRY, AND COMMODITY EXCHANGES OF TURKEY, *Investment Guide to Turkey* (1964); ORGANIZATION FOR ECONOMIC COOPERATION AND DEVELOPMENT, *Annual Survey of the Turkish Economy;* and the annual publications of the Economic Research Department, Ankara, and of the Industrial Development Bank of Turkey, Istanbul. The State Planning Organization, Ankara, has issued four five-year development plans (1964, 1969, 1972, and 1979). See also WILLIAM M. HALE, *The Political and Economic Development of Modern Turkey* (1981), covering the years since 1923; and BINNAZ TOPRAK, *Islam and Political Development in Turkey* (1981), a study of the role of religion in Turkey's development.

Traditional cultures of Anatolia. Perhaps the most comprehensive work on this subject, although in French and quite out of date, is VITAL CUINET, *La Turquie d'Asie,* 4 vol. (1890–95). A vast range of specific studies, travel books, and histories is available in Turkish, French, or German—especially, for example, on nomads. One excellent work is XAVIER DE PLANHOL, *De la plaine pamphylienne aux lacs pisidiens, nomadisme et vie paysanne* (1958), a human geography of the region of Anatalya. SETON LLOYD, *Early Anatolia* (1956), summarizes pre-classical archaeology up to that date. FREDERICK W. HASLUCK, *Christianity and Islam Under the Sultans,* 2 vol. (1929), emphasizes popular cults and the transition to Islām. MARY GOUGH, *The Plain and Rough Places* (U.S. title, *Travel into Yesterday;* 1954), is a readable personal account of modern Turkey. For Istanbul traditions, see HALIDE EDIB ADIVAR, *Memoirs of Halidé Edib* (1926); for a study of Turkish villagers, see PAUL STIRLING, *Turkish Village* (1965). On 20th-century changes, see EDWIN COHEN, *Turkish Economic, Social and Political Change* (1970), a general optimistic appraisal; and JAN HINDERINK and M.B. KIRAY, *Social Stratification As an Obstacle to Development* (1970), a sociological account of drastic changes in four villages near Adana. A useful introduction to modern Turkey is GEOFFREY L. LEWIS, *Turkey,* 3rd ed. (1965).

Ancient Anatolia. *Anatolia to c. 1180 BC:* The main body of information on this subject with full bibliographies relevant to the various periods is contained in the following fascicles of the new *Cambridge Ancient History:* J. MELLAART, *Anatolia: before c. 4000 B.C. and c. 2300–1750 B.C.* (1964), and *Anatolia: c. 4000–2300 B.C.* (1962); HILDEGARD LEWY, *Anatolia in the Old Assyrian Period* (1965); O.R. GURNEY, *Anatolia: c. 1750–1600 B.C.* (1962), and *Anatolia: c. 1600–1380 B.C.* (1966); A. GOETZE, *Anatolia: From Shuppiluliumash to the Egyptian War of Muwatallish* (1965). The following two sources are earlier and semipopular summaries: O.R. GURNEY, *The Hittites,* rev. ed. (1961), dealing with Hittite history; and SETON LLOYD, *Early Anatolia* (1956), archaeology from the prehistoric to the Phrygian periods. More recent popular summaries, fully illustrated and based on more recent archaeological evidence are: J. MELLAART, *Earliest Civilizations of the Near East* (1965); and SETON LLOYD, *Early Highland Peoples of Anatolia* (1967). A very fully illustrated account of excavations at a prehistoric site of paramount importance to world prehistory is J. MELLAART, *Catal Hüyük: A Neolithic Town in Anatolia* (1967). A recent and temporarily definitive treatise on the subject is JOHN GARSTANG and O.R. GURNEY, *The Geography of the Hittite Empire* (1959). A standard work until the postwar period but now quite outdated is JOHN GARSTANG, *The Hittite Empire* (1929). An article on a vital and controversial aspect of religious iconography relating to the intrusion of Hurrian ideas into Hittite culture is E. LAROCHE, "Le Panthéon de Yazilikaya," *Journal of Cuneiform Studies,* 6:115–123 (1952). An article pioneering some new ideas about the arrival of the Hittites in Anatolia is J. MELLAART, "The End of the Early Bronze Age in Anatolia and the Aegean," *American Journal of Archaeology,* 62:9–33 (1958). See also J. MELLAART, *The Archaeology of Ancient Turkey* (1978), an introduction to the period between the Neolithic and Iron Ages; and JOHANNES LEHMANN, *The Hittites* (1977; originally published in German, 1975), a popularly written history.

Anatolia from c. 1180 BC to the Roman conquest: (*Phrygia from c. 1180 to 700 BC*): A brilliant survey of archaeological material on the Cimmerians and Phrygians may be found in K. BITTEL, "Kimmerier, Phryger und Skythen in Kleinasien," ch. 3 of *Kleinasiatische Studien* (1942). The results of the new American excavations at Gordium have appeared in the Preliminary Reports by R.S. YOUNG in the *American Journal of Archaeology* since 1955. M.J. MELLINK edited the acta of an important archaeological conference on the nomadic impact in both Anatolia and Iran during the Iron Age under the title *Dark Ages and Nomads c. 1000 B.C.* (1964). R.D. BARNETT recently dealt with this general period in fasc. 56 of the new *Cambridge Ancient History—Phrygia and the Peoples of Anatolia in the Iron Age* (1967). Although in fact devoted to Hattusa, the Hittite capital, K. BITTEL, *Hattusha, the Capital of the Hittites* (1970), also contains much information on the Phrygian parts of Anatolia, especially in ch. 6. (*The Neo-Hittite states of Anatolia from c. 1180 to 700 BC*): B. LANDSBERGER, *Sam'al: Studien zur Entdeckung der Ruinenstätte Karatepe* (1948), is a brilliant study of southeast Anatolia during the beginning of the 1st millennium BC, based not only on all of the Assyrian and northwest-Semitic texts that are relevant to this region but also on the results of the excavations. P.H.J. HOUWINK TEN CATE, "Kleinasien zwischen Hethitern und Persern," ch. 2, in E. CASSIN, J. BOTTERO, and J. VERCOUTTER (eds.), *Die altorientalische Reiche,* vol. 3 (1967), is a general account of Anatolian history between *c.* 1180 and 547 BC. (*The Cimmerians, Lydia, and Cilicia, c. 700–547 BC*): G. RADET gave an exhaustive collection of all the data on Lydian history found in classical authors in *La Lydie et le monde grec au temps des mermnades, 687–546* (1893). The archaeological results of the new American excavations at Sardis are regularly presented by G.M.A. HANFMANN in the *Bulletin of the American Schools of Oriental Research* since 1959. (*The Greek colonies, Mysia, Lycia, Pamphylia, etc. from c. 1180 to 547 BC*): The history of these regions in the first half of the 1st millennium BC can only be written by archaeologists on the basis of archaeological evidence. H. METZGER, *Anatolie,* vol. 2 (1968; Eng. trans., 1969), gives an account of these archaeological data with a marked emphasis on the indigenous population. On Greek colonization and commercial adventures in the East, see J.M. COOK, *The Greeks in Ionia and the East* (1962); and J. BOARDMAN, *The Greek Overseas* (1964). (*The Anatolian Greeks in the Achaemenian period*): A recent treatment is H. BENGTSON, *Griechen und Perser* (1965; Eng. trans., *The Greeks and the Persians,* 1969). (*Caria, Lycia, and Cilicia in the Achaemenian period*): G. BOCKISCH, "Die Karer und ihre Dynasten," *Klio* 51:117–175 (1969), is based on full use of all the Greek evidence, both from classical authors and from inscriptions, but the study disregards the few available data from Persian sources. O. TREUBER, *Geschichte der Lykier* (1887), is the old, but by no means antiquated, collection of all the evidence on Lycian history before it became possible to incorporate evidence from indigenous sources such as inscriptions and coins. P.H.J. HOUWINK TEN CATE, *The Luwian Population Groups of Lycia and Cilicia Aspera during the Hellenistic Period* (1961), contains an introductory historical chapter, based on both the Greek and the indigenous evidence. (*Anatolia between 334 BC and the Roman period*): W.W. TARN, *Hellenistic Civilisation* (1947), gives a general survey of the Hellenistic period with full emphasis on historical evidence. A trustworthy study of the intricate geographical problems connected with the Hellenistic history of the Anatolian states is E. MEYER, *Die Grenzen der hellenistischen Staaten in Kleinasien* (1925). A storehouse of information, also for the preceding periods, is D. MAGIE, *Roman Rule in Asia Minor,* 2 vol. (1950).

The period of Seljuq domination. Three works have been published in recent years that to a great extent supersede previous studies of the Seljuqs. The *Cambridge History of Iran,* vol. 5, *The Seljuq and Mongol Periods,* ed. by J.A. BOYLE (1968), contains chapters on all aspects of Seljuq history—government, religion, institutions, literature, and art. CLAUDE CAHEN, *Pre-Ottoman Turkey: A General Survey of the Material and Spiritual Culture and History, c. 1071–1330* (1968), covers the same topics for the sultanate of Rūm. Finally, GEORGE MAKDISI, *Ibn 'Aqīl et la résurgence de l'islam traditionaliste au XIe siècle* (1963), is of great importance for its analysis of politics and religion under the early Seljuqs.

The Ottoman Empire. *General studies:* For the nonspecialist, LORD KINROSS, *The Ottoman Centuries* (1977), is a very readable general history; KEMAL H. KARPAT (ed.), *The Ottoman State and Its Place in World History* (1974), contains seven stimulating and wide-ranging essays; a comprehensive history is STANFORD J. SHAW and E.K. SHAW, *History of the Ottoman Empire and Modern Turkey,* 2 vol. (1976–77), which has an excellent bibliography, as has L.S. STAVRIANOS, *The Balkans Since 1453* (1958), for the European provinces. Two classic histories are J.F. VON HAMMER-PURGSTALL, *Geschichte des osmanischen Reiches,* 10 vol. (1827–35, reprinted 1963; French trans., 18 vol., 1835–43); and J.W. ZINKEISEN, *Geschichte des osmanischen Reiches in Europa,* 7 vol. (1840–63, reprinted 1962), the first based largely on Turkish, the second on European sources.

The rise of the Ottoman Empire to 1566: PAUL WITTEK, *The Rise of the Ottoman Empire* (1938, reprinted 1965), is a classic study of Ottoman origins; CLAUDE CAHEN, *Pre-Ottoman Turkey* (1968), based on extensive research in Turkish and Greek sources, emphasizes the economic and social background; HALIL INALCIK, *The Ottoman Empire: The Classical Age, 1300–1600* (1973), is a scholarly survey of the early period; on the 15th century an important study is FRANZ BABINGER, *Mehmed der Erober und seine Zeit,* 2nd ed. (1959; Eng. trans., *Mehmed the Conqueror and His Time,* 1978), which is based mainly on European sources; D.M. VAUGHAN, *Europe and the Turk: A Pattern of Alliances, 1350–1700* (1954), describes diplomatic, economic, and cultural relations between the Ottoman Empire and Europe; the excellent articles in the *New Cambridge Modern History* relating to the Ottoman Empire are conveniently assembled in M.A. COOK (ed.), *A History of the Ottoman Empire to 1730* (1976); S.N. FISHER, *The Foreign Relations of Turkey, 1481–1512* (1948), considers Ottoman relations with Venice, Hungary, the papacy, and Iran; G.W.F. STRIPLING, *The Ottoman Turks and the Arabs, 1511–1574* (1942, reprinted 1968), describes the Ottoman conquest of Egypt and Syria; and S.A. FISCHER-GALATI, *Ottoman Imperialism and German Protestantism, 1521–1555* (1959), describes the effect of the Ottoman threat on the development of the Reformation. A very wide-ranging study of the whole Mediterranean area in the 16th century is FERNAND BRAUDEL *La Méditerranée et le monde méditerranéen à l'époque de Philippe II*, 2nd rev. ed., 2 vol. (1966; Eng. trans., *The Mediterranean and the Mediterranean World in the Time of Philip II*, 2 vol., 1972–73). See also PAUL COLES, *The Ottoman Impact on Europe* (1968); and R.C. ANDERSON, *Naval Wars in the Levant, 1558–1853* (1952). On Ottoman administration and society, see ALBERT HOWE LYBYER, *The Government of the Ottoman Empire in the Time of Suleiman the Magnificent* (1913); A.D. ALDERSON, *The Structure of the Ottoman Dynasty* (1956); and, at a more popular level, BERNARD LEWIS, *Istanbul and the Civilization of the Ottoman Empire* (1963), and RAPHAELA LEWIS, *Everyday Life in Ottoman Turkey* (1971).

The decline of the Ottoman Empire, 1566–1807: A good study of social organization is H.A.R. GIBB and HAROLD BOWEN, *Islamic Society and the West*, 1 vol. in 2 pt. (1950–57, reprinted 1965), which deals primarily with the 18th century but includes material from earlier periods. An exhaustive study of Ottoman political, economic, and social life in the 17th century is ROBERT MANTRAN, *Istanbul dans la seconde moitié du XVII*[e] *siècle* (1962). T.M. BARKER, *Double Eagle and Crescent* (1967), is a detailed study of the Eastern question in the late 17th century; LAVENDER CASSELS, *The Struggle for the Ottoman Empire, 1717–1740* (1966), discusses a similar topic in readable fashion. On internal events, W.L. WRIGHT, JR., *Ottoman Statecraft* (1935), is an analysis of 17th-century Ottoman imperial decline; LADY MARY WORTLEY MONTAGU, *The Complete Letters of Lady Mary Wortley Montagu*, ed. by ROBERT HALSBAND, 3 vol. (1965–66), is a travel classic as well as an amusing description of Ottoman life during the early 18th century. M.L. SHAY, *The Ottoman Empire from 1720 to 1734* (1944, reprinted 1968), is a description of Ottoman life during the Tulip Period, based on the reports of Venetian consuls in Istanbul. S.J. SHAW, *Between Old and New: The Ottoman Empire Under Sultan Selim III, 1789–1807* (1971), is a detailed study of the Ottoman reform program with an account of the diplomatic problems of the Revolutionary and Napoleonic period.

Foundation of the Turkish republic. *The Ottoman Empire and Turkey (from 1807 to the present):* The best general history covering this period is B. LEWIS, *The Emergence of Modern Turkey*, 2nd ed. (1968). N. BERKES, *The Development of Secularism in Turkey* (1964), covers similar ground but concentrates on the development of ideas. R.E. WARD and D.A. RUSTOW (eds.), *Political Modernization in Japan and Turkey* (1964), has valuable essays on general themes. For diplomacy the best outline is M.S. ANDERSON, *The Eastern Question, 1774–1923* (1966). Useful for the European provinces is L.S. STAVRIANOS, *The Balkans Since 1453* (1958), which has an excellent bibliography. For the Tanzimat, see R.H. DAVISON, *Reform in the Ottoman Empire, 1856–1876* (1963). Although old, E.P. ENGELHARDT, *La Turquie et Le Tanzimat*, 2 vol. (1882–84), is still a valuable source of information. R. DEVEREUX, *The First Ottoman Constitutional Period: A Study of the Midhat Constitution and Parliament* (1963), is a careful study of the 1876 crisis and the establishment of the first Ottoman Parliament. For the Young Ottomans, see S. MARDIN, *The Genesis of Young Ottoman Thought* (1962); and for the Young Turks, E. RAMSAUR, *The Young Turks: Prelude to the Revolution of 1908* (1957); and F. AHMAD, *The Young Turks: The Committee of Union and Progress in Turkish Politics, 1908–14* (1969). DAVID KUSHNER, *The Rise of Turkish Nationalism, 1876–1908* (1977), considers ideological aspects. The Ottoman public debt is considered in D.C. BLAISDELL, *European Financial Control in the Ottoman Empire* (1929). AHMED EMIN, *Turkey in the World War* (1930), is still the only account, although relations with Germany can be followed in U. TRUMPENER, *Germany and the Ottoman Empire, 1914–1918* (1968). CHARLES ISSAWI (ed.), *The Economic History of Turkey: 1800–1914* (1980); and DONALD QUATAERT, *Social Disintegration and Popular Resistance in the Ottoman Empire, 1881–1908: Reactions to European Economic Penetration* (1983), are good economic histories.

Several books consider aspects of Allied war aims in the Near East. Although outdated in parts, H.N. HOWARD, *The Partition of Turkey: A Diplomatic History, 1913–1923* (1931, reprinted 1966), is comprehensive. On the Kemalist movement, see E.D. SMITH, *Origins of the Kemalist Movement and the Government of the Grand National Assembly, 1919–1923* (1959). LORD KINROSS, *Atatürk: The Rebirth of a Nation* (1964), is a good biography. On political developments in Turkey and particularly the rise of the Democrat Party, see K.H. KARPAT, *Turkey's Politics* (1959). R.D. ROBINSON, *The First Turkish Republic* (1963), is a good general account, strongest on economic aspects. F.W. FREY, *The Turkish Political Elite* (1965), is an illuminating and detailed analysis of the membership of the Grand National Assembly. For the 1960 military coup, see W.F. WEIKER, *The Turkish Revolution, 1960–1961* (1963); for the period from 1961–65, C.H. DODD, *Politics and Government in Turkey* (1969); and for the postwar period generally, FEROZ AHMAD, *The Turkish Experiment in Democracy, 1950–1975* (1977). On recent political movements see JACOB M. LANDAU, *Radical Politics in Modern Turkey* (1974), and ERGUN OZBUDUN, *Social Change and Political Participation in Turkey* (1977). The chronologies by G. JASCHKE are very useful for Turkish history since 1918; the earlier ones appeared mostly in *Die Welt des Islams* and subsequent are *Die Türkei in den Jahren 1935–1941* (1943), *Die Türkei in den Jahren 1942–1951* (1955), and *Die Türkei in den Jahren 1952–1961* (1965). For economic developments see M.W. THORNBURG, GRAHAM SPRY, and GEORGE SOULE, *Turkey: An Economic Appraisal* (1949); Z. Y. HERSHLAG, *Turkey: The Challenge of Growth* (1968); and ANNE O. KRUEGER, *Foreign Trade Regimes and Economic Development*, vol. 1, *Turkey* (1974). A wide-ranging collection of articles is NERMIN ABADAN-UNAT, *Turkish Workers in Europe, 1960–1975* (1976). For education, see A.M. KAZAMIAS, *Education and the Quest for Modernity in Turkey* (1966). A fine study of Turkish foreign relations is KEMAL H. KARPAT *et al., Turkey's Foreign Policy in Transition, 1950–1974* (1975). There are good bibliographies of works in Turkish in the books by Lewis, Karpat, Dodd, Ahmad, and Hershlag. See too WALTER F. WEIKER, *The Modernization of Turkey: From Ataturk to the Present Day* (1981), an optimistic account; and BERCH BERBEROGLU, *Turkey in Crisis: From State Capitalism to Neocolonialism* (1982), a Marxist critique of Turkey's political economy in the 20th century.

Union of Soviet Socialist Republics

By area the world's largest country, the Union of Soviet Socialist Republics (U.S.S.R., or, popularly, the Soviet Union) covers a vast segment of the Northern Hemisphere: one-sixth of the world land surface and two-fifths of the Eurasian continent. Its 8,650,000 square miles (22,400,000 square kilometres) are seven times the area of India, two and one-half times that of the United States, and 60 times that of Japan. It covers 11 of the 24 world time zones; while citizens of the Soviet Far East are greeting the dawn, their fellows in Moscow, the capital, are sitting down to dinner.

The Soviet Union has the world's longest frontiers, and no other country is bounded by so many nations. Norway, Finland, Poland, Czechoslovakia, Hungary, and Romania lie to the west; Turkey, Iran, Afghanistan, China, Mongolia, and North Korea lie to the south; the eastern and northern frontiers are coastal. Conventional lines linking the Rybachy Peninsula and Big Diomede Island to the North Pole form the boundaries of the Soviet sector of the Arctic. Twelve seas, belonging to three oceans (Arctic, Atlantic, and Pacific), wash the country's coast.

The Soviet Union was formed on December 30, 1922, and it now comprises, in addition to the 15 union republics, 20 autonomous republics, 8 autonomous regions, 10 autonomous districts, 6 territories, and 123 regions. Under the constitution adopted October 3, 1977, the political foundation of the Soviet Union is formed by the Soviets (Councils) of People's Deputies, with the Communist Party of the Soviet Union (CPSU) the "leading and guiding force of Soviet society and the nucleus of its political system." The economic foundation is "Socialist ownership of the means of production."

The varied terrain of the Soviet Union harbours a wealth of raw material, fuel, and power resources. The Soviet period has seen the accelerated development of these resources and the emergence of the country as an advanced industrial power. The proportion of the population living in cities has risen from 18 to about 65 percent.

The following article offers a survey of the Soviet Union and of its predecessor, the Russian Empire. It is divided into the following major sections and subsections:

PHYSICAL AND HUMAN GEOGRAPHY

The land

RELIEF

As a result of the country's enormous territorial extent, the complexity of its relief, and the wide range of climatic, drainage, and soil conditions, the natural landscapes of the Soviet Union exhibit exceptional variety. Broad plains and depressions occupy the western half of the Soviet territory, while plateaus and mountain ranges prevail in the east; an almost continuous belt of high mountains runs along the southern border of the country. Altitudes range from the 24,590-foot (7,495-metre) Communism Peak in the Pamirs to the bottom of the Karagiye, a depression that lies 433 feet (132 metres) below sea level in the Mangyshlak Peninsula.

Range of altitudes

Plains and plateaus. The plains—subdivided into the enormous Russian (or East European), West Siberian, and Turan plains—stretch from the Baltic Sea in the west to the Yenisey River in the east and from the shores of the Arctic Ocean to the foothills of the southern Kopet-Dag Range.

The average altitude of the Russian Plain is about 560 feet (170 metres), but elevations rising to 1,000–1,300 feet above sea level alternate with depressions. In the northern half of the plain, formerly covered by glaciers, the relief between the river valleys is strewn with lakes and swamps. In the south, however, watersheds are higher and cut into by valleys and ravines. The ancient wind-blown deposits known as loess are widespread and locally deep in the Ukraine and in the Don River Basin. In the northwest, near Scandinavia, the ancient uplands of Karelia and the mountains of the Kola Peninsula (maximum height 3,907 feet [1,191 metres]) abut on the Russian Plain, while in the south it is bounded by the moderately high (maximum 6,762 feet [2,061 metres]) mountain ranges of the Carpathians and the Crimea and the great barrier of the Caucasus. The last named, stretching from the Black Sea to the Caspian, rises to 18,510 feet (5,642 metres) at Mt. Elbrus. In the east, the moderate relief of the Ural Mountains extends for more than 1,200 miles (2,000 kilometres) from north to south, forming part of the traditional dividing line between Europe and Asia.

The Russian Plain

The upland ridges of the Urals also separate the Russian Plain from the West Siberian Plain, an area of monotonous, low relief and one of the largest lowlands in the world. In the south this is bounded by the Turgay Plateau and the Kazakh Uplands, which rise to a maximum of 5,134 feet (1,565 metres). South again, the Turan Plain occupies the greater part of Central Asia. Its relief is varied; troughs lying below sea level alternate with extensive low plateaus.

Between the Yenisey and Lena rivers lies the Central Siberian Plateau, mainly at heights of 1,500–3,000 feet (450–900 metres). This is bounded on the north by the North Siberian, or Khatanga, Lowland, beyond which the uplands of the Taymyr Peninsula rise to 3,760 feet (1,146 metres), while to the east, in the middle basin of the Lena, lies the Central Yakut Plain.

The mountainous belts. Regions with markedly dissected mountainous relief lie in the south and east of Soviet Asia. The highest ranges occur in the Uzbek, Tadzhik, Kirgiz, and Kazakh republics and in southwest Siberia, where the Pamir, Alai, Tien Shan, and Altai have crest lines well above 10,000 feet (3,000 metres). Numerous somewhat lower ranges, together with extensive plateaus and uplands, occupy a large area on either side of Lake Baikal. Farther east, the Stanovoy Range forms the watershed between the Aldan River, which flows toward the Arctic, and the Zeya, draining to the Pacific via the Amur. Southeast of the Stanovoy lie the mountain ranges of the South Primorye and the region around the Amur River. North from the Amur region, on the shores of the Sea of Okhotsk, stretches the Dzhugdzhur Range, and beyond it the mountains of northeast Siberia and the Chukchi Peninsula begin.

The Kamchatka Peninsula is also mountainous; it harbours a group of volcanoes, including the Klyuchevskaya Volcano, at 15,584 feet (4,750 metres) the highest summit in all Siberia and the Far East. The Kuril group of some 30 rather large and markedly rugged islands is part of the East Asian volcanic arc. In these islands are found more than 100 volcanoes, almost 30 of which are active. West of the Sea of Okhotsk, Sakhalin Island forms a major feature running north–south for more than 560 miles (900 kilometres) but with an average width of only about 60 miles (100 kilometres).

CLIMATE

Latitudinal climatic belts are superimposed on the patterns of physical relief. The Far North, with most of its offshore islands, lies in the Arctic climatic belt; the northern European Soviet Union, Western Siberia above the Arctic Circle, and Central and Eastern Siberia between 70° and 60°–64° north latitude are in the sub-Arctic climatic belt; the remainder of Soviet Europe and Siberia, as well as Central Asia as far south as 40° north latitude, are in the temperate belt; and parts of Transcaucasia and southern Central Asia lie in the subtropics.

Latitudinal climatic belts

As most Soviet territory lies far from the oceans, the climate almost everywhere is markedly continental, with a clear division of the year into cold and warm periods. Continentality increases eastward and is especially pronounced in Central Asia and Eastern Siberia, where the average temperature difference between the warmest month (July) and coldest month (January) ranges from 81° F (45° C) to 117° F (65° C). The most westerly regions on the Black Sea coast and the south Crimean coast are much milder than the rest of the country. The southern Far East is subject to Pacific Ocean influences, having a monsoon climate.

Atmospheric circulation above Soviet territory depends upon the seasons. In winter, when there is a negative heat radiation balance (that is, the Earth's surface is losing heat), a region of high pressure known as the Asian anticyclone is formed in Inner Asia. West of it, a ridge of high pressure (the "Voyeykov axis") stretches over the northern edge of Central Asia and the southern Russian Plain. The northern half of Soviet Europe is then under the influence of recurrent Atlantic cyclones that bring west and southwest winds, relative warmth, and rain and snow. In the Far East, meanwhile—a region reached by air formed in the Asian anticyclone—the winter monsoon is under way, and cold, dry west or northwest winds prevail.

A cold continental air mass, formed as a result of the cooling of the land, nevertheless dominates the greater part of Soviet territory in winter; it is cold almost everywhere, and precipitation is relatively small. Average January temperatures along a line from the southwest to the northeast fall from 43° F (6° C) at Batumi, on the Black Sea coast, to a remarkable −58° F (−50° C) in the vicinity of Verkhoyansk, in the Far East region. The Murmansk coast, Kaluga, Volgograd, and Kyzyl-Orda, situated in widely different latitudes, have the same January mean of 14° F (−10° C). There are particularly severe January frosts (down to −85° F [−65° C] or below) in the Yakut A.S.S.R., while the absolute minimum of −90° F (−68° C) recorded at Verkhoyansk is the lowest temperature ever recorded on the Earth's surface outside Antarctica. Relief as well as anticyclonic conditions contributes to this "pole of cold" in the Verkhoyansk district; the heavier cold air lingers in hollows, which are much colder than the surrounding mountain slopes. The highest winter temperatures occur in southern Central Asia, but even here the January mean is only a few degrees above freezing.

Minimum temperatures at Verkhoyansk

In the cold half of the year up to eight to 12 inches (200 to 300 millimetres) of precipitation occurs in the Soviet west, but this decreases toward the east, falling to only two to four inches (50 to 100 millimetres) in Central Asia and Eastern Siberia. Winter precipitation falls mostly as snow, which lies for a few days in the Crimea, Transcaucasia, and Central Asia but covers the ground for 260 days or more in the Taymyr Peninsula and on the Arctic islands. The thickness of the snow cover is also uneven. In the steppes of the southern Ukraine and northern Caucasus and in the Central Asian deserts it is rarely as much as four inches. Snow cover is thin on the Baltic coast and in Belorussia, where there are frequent thaws, and also in the Volga region and Kazakhstan, where there is little winter precipitation. It generally thickens to the north and east to reach 40 inches or more on the east coast of Kamchatka Peninsula.

In summer, because of the intense heating of the land surface (the radiation balance is now positive everywhere), a broad region of low pressure is formed over Asia and covers almost all Soviet territory except the southern Russian Plain, where pressure remains high. Westerly winds prevail in Soviet Europe, northerlies in Northern Siberia and in Central Asia; meanwhile, the east and southeast summer monsoon dominates the Far East. Summer air temperatures are above freezing everywhere (except in the mountains) and generally decrease toward the north; only on the northeast Pacific coast, under oceanic influence, is a fall in temperature observed from west to east. Average July temperatures in southern Central Asia are, in places, above 86° F (30° C). The absolute Soviet maximum temperature, recorded in the town of Termez in the Uzbek S.S.R., is 122° F (50° C). The central Soviet Union has considerably lower July temperatures—from 59° to 70° F (15° to 21° C)—while the Arctic coasts experience even lower readings. Conversely, the frost-free period increases from 45–60 days in the Siberian tundra to 270 days in Transcaucasia.

Maximum temperatures at Termez

Most precipitation falls in the warm half of the year; in the central Soviet Union, totals drop from 20 inches (500 millimetres) in the west to less than half that amount in Eastern Siberia. The heaviest rain (up to 47 inches, or about 1,200 millimetres) falls in the western Caucasus region, the least (less than 4 percent of that) in the southern Turan Plain.

DRAINAGE

Rivers. There are more than 150,000 rivers in the Soviet Union that are more than six miles (10 kilometres) long; their total length is about 2,000,000 miles (3,200,000 kilometres), one-sixth of which is suitable for navigation or floating logs. Soviet waterpower resources are the world's greatest. The density of the river system, however, ranges from 0.40–0.56 mile per square mile (0.25–0.35 kilometre per square kilometre) in the European forest zone to a fraction of this amount in the deserts and semideserts of the Caspian Depression.

The majority of rivers drain to the Arctic Ocean. The largest of these northward-draining rivers are the Northern Dvina, Pechora, Ob and Irtysh, Yenisey, Khatanga, Lena, Indigirka, and Kolyma. The Pacific Ocean takes in all the Far Eastern rivers, including the Amur, Anadyr, Penzhina, and Kamchatka. The Atlantic Ocean ultimately receives the waters of the rivers that discharge into the Black Sea (the Danube, Dnestr, Dnepr, Kuban, and Rioni), the Sea of Azov (the Don), and the Baltic Sea (the Neva and the Western Dvina).

Arctic rivers

The eastern Caucasus, part of the Russian Plain, the Tien Shan, and the Pamirs, as well as the semideserts and deserts of Central Asia and Kazakhstan, comprise the extensive internal Aral–Caspian drainage region, more than 60 percent of which is drained by rivers flowing into the Caspian Sea. These are the Volga, Ural, Emba, Kura, and Kuma rivers. The Syrdarya and Amu Darya drain to the Aral Sea Basin, while many rivers in this region, such as the Ili, Chu, and Zeravshan, either end in lakes or vanish into the desert sands.

Climatic variety is reflected in riverflow characteristics, or regimes. The differing climatic zones offer varying sources of nourishment to the associated rivers and affect annual distribution of flow. Thus a distinction is made between rivers fed mainly by melted snow (the Volga, Don, Dnepr, Pechora, Ob, Yenisey, and Lena), by rain (the Amur), by glacier and snow melt (the high mountain rivers of the Caucasus, the Central Asian mountains, and the Altai), and by subterranean groundwaters (in the foothill regions of Central Asia).

Soviet rivers may be divided into three groups, depending on flow characteristics: those with spring high water (the most numerous); those with spring and summer high water (the rivers of the Far East, the Yana–Indigirka Basin, Transbaikalia, and the high mountains of the Caucasus and Central Asia); and those with a flood regime (the mountain rivers of the Crimea, the northern slope of the Great Caucasus, the Carpathians, and the Black Sea coast of the Caucasus). The rivers with the largest discharge are those in the Arctic Basin (three-fifths of the annual total Soviet river discharge), especially the Yenisey, which has an annual discharge of 150 cubic miles (624 cubic kilometres).

Most Soviet rivers are at times covered with ice; the period varies from eight to nine months in the Siberian north to one to two months in the extreme south.

Lakes and reservoirs. An abundance of lakes—they number about 270,000—includes five of the world's largest, each with an area exceeding 4,000 square miles (10,000 square kilometres): the Caspian and Aral seas, Lake Baikal (at 5,315 feet [1,620 metres] also the world's deepest), Lake Balkhash, and Lake Ladoga. An additional 14 lakes—including Onega and Issyk-Kul—have areas of more than 400 square miles (1,000 square kilometres). The lakes are very unevenly distributed, being particularly numerous in the regions of surplus moisture in the Soviet north and the Western Siberian steppes. In Karelia and the Lena–Vilyuy plain, they occupy more than 10 percent of the surface area, whereas in the forest–steppe of the Russian Plain they are almost nonexistent.

Largest lakes

As a rule, there is a flow of river water through the large northern lakes, while in some regions (notably Karelia and the Kola Peninsula) there are many rivers that start from lakes, run through lakes, and sometimes even end in lakes. Nonflowing lakes are scattered through the Soviet south; each lies in a hollow from which there is no water discharge, gathers atmospheric and groundwater from the whole region, and then expends it mainly by means of evaporation.

Soviet lakes also vary greatly in their content of mineral salts, and there are freshwater, brackish, and salt lakes. In Soviet Asia, especially in the Kulunda Steppe of Western

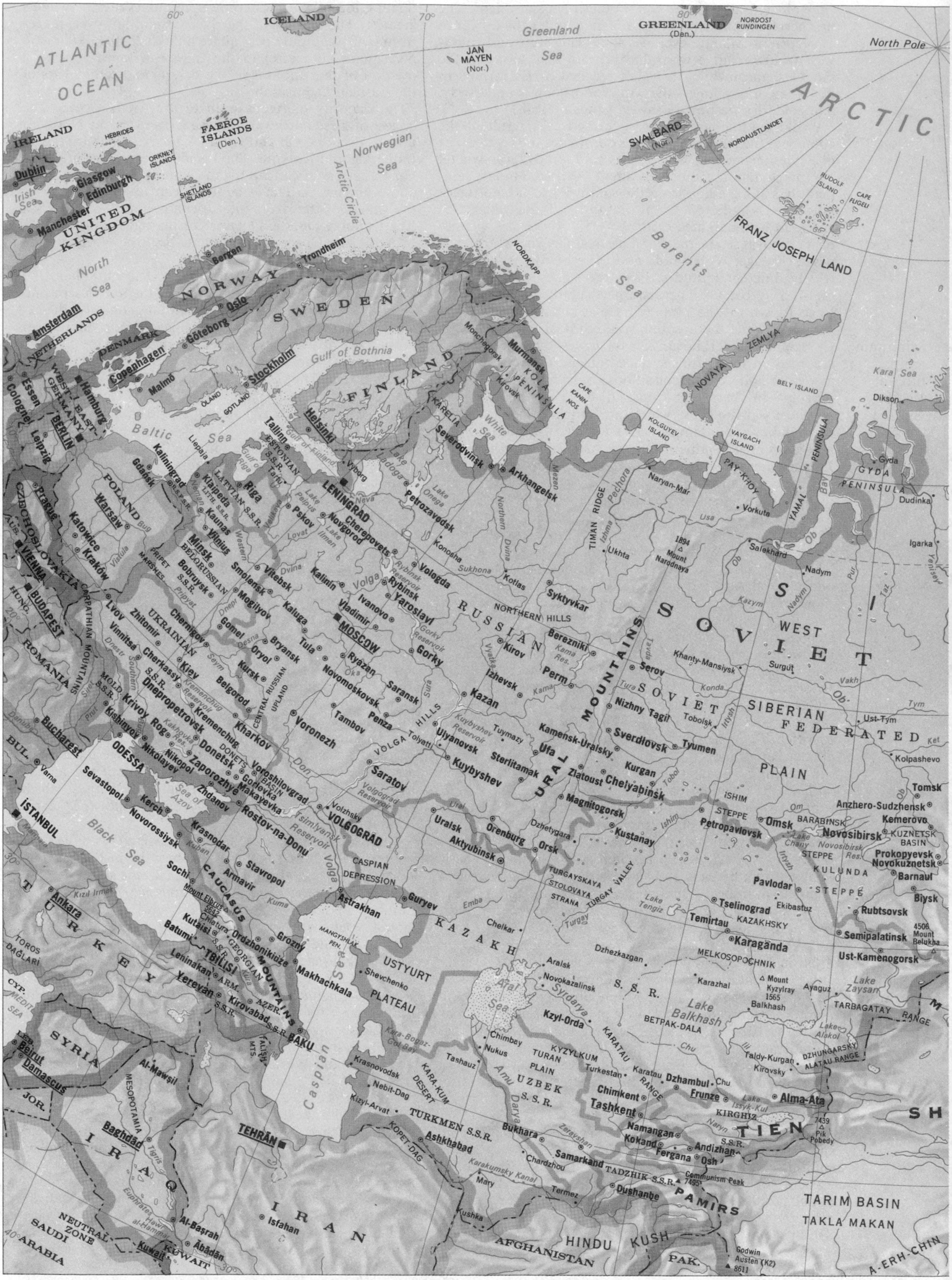

SOVIET UNION

Size of symbol indicates relative size of town

Elevations in metres

UNITED STATES
Norton Sound
Nome
POINT HOPE
Bering Strait
DIOMEDE ISLANDS
NUNIVAK ISLAND
CAPE DEZHNEV
Chukchi Sea
Enurmino
CHUKOTSK PENINSULA
Provideniya
WRANGEL ISLAND
ALEUTIAN ISLANDS
Vankarem
Gulf of Anadyr
Egvekinot
Uelkal
Long's Strait
OCEAN
Beringovsky
CAPE NAVARIN
Anadyr
Velikaya
Bering Sea
Ust-Chaun
ANADYR PLATEAU
Arctic Circle
AYON ISLAND
Ambarchik
East Siberian Sea
NEW SIBERIAN ISLANDS
KOTELNY ISLAND
Markovo
Khatyrka
KORYAK RA.
Gora Ledyanaya 2562
Yeropol
Shcherbakovo
Penzhina
Slautnoye
Kavacha
CAPE OLYUTORSKY
SEVERNAYA ZEMLYA
CAPE CHELYUSKIN
Laptev Sea
Tabor
Alazeya
Kolymskaya
YUKAGIR PLATEAU
Omolon
Gizhiga
Korf
KARAGIN ISLAND
KAMCHATKA PENINSULA
COMMANDER ISLANDS
Indigirka
Druzhina
Srednekolymsk
Kazachye
GREAT BEGICHYOV ISLAND
TAYMYR PENINSULA
Lake Taymyr
Nordvik
Tiksi
Buolkalakh
Saskylakh
Olenyok
Zyryanka
Mount Pobeda 3147
Kolyma
Omsukchan
Gulf of Shelikhov
Palana
Ust'
SREDINNY RANGE
Klyuchevskaya Volcano 4750
Selennyakh
CHERSKY RANGE
Kadykchan
Yana
NORTH SIBERIAN LOWLAND
Khatanga
Anabar
Dzhardzhan
Verkhoyansk
Myakit
Palatka
Yamsk
Magadan
Moroshechnoye
Petropavlovsk-Kamchatsky
Milkovo
Agapa
Kheta
Kotuy
VERKHOYANSK RANGE
Sartang
Ust-Nera
Oymyakon
Volochanka
Sukhana
Muna
YAKUTIYA
Norilsk
Zhigansk
Lena
Aldan
Khandyga
Okhotsk
Sea of Okhotsk
Kirovsky
CAPE LOPATKA
PUTORAN MTS.
Yessey
CENTRAL YAKUT PLAIN
SETTE-DABAN RANGE
Sholgontsy
SIBERIAN
Batamay
Vilyuy
Ekonda
CENTRAL PLATEAU
Yakutsk
Turukhansk
DZHUGDZHUR RANGE
CAPE YELIZAVETY
Okha
KURIL ISLANDS
Nikolayevsk-na-Amure
SAKHALIN ISLAND
Markha
Amga
Nelkan
Tomptokan
Ayan
SHANTAR ISLANDS
Nizhnyaya Tunguska
Mirny
Tommot
ALDAN PLATEAU
Bakhta
UNION
Lensk
Dushekan
Chona
Chumikan
Uda
Aleksandrovsk-Sakhalinsky
Poronaysk
CAPE TERPENIYA
Podkamennaya Tunguska
Vanavara
Macha
REPUBLIC
Olyokma
Gonam
STANOVOY RANGE
Guga
Komsomolsk-na-Amure
Amgun
Tatarsk Strait
Uglegorsk
Sovetskaya Gavan
Kholmsk
Yuzhno-Sakhalinsk
Korsakov
Bodaybo
Ust-Nyukzha
Nagorny
Bomnak
Ekimchan
SOCIALIST
Kirensk
Chara
Vitim
Skovorodino
Zeya
Shimanovsk
Svobodny
SIKHOTE-ALIN
Angara
Chuna
Zheleznogorsk-Ilimsky
STANOVOY UPLAND
Mogocha
Amur
Belogorsk
Birobidzhan
Maklakovo
Bratsk
Bratsk Reservoir
Bagdarin
Blagoveshchensk
Raychikhinsk
Svetlaya
La Perouse Strait
Krasnoyarsk
Kansk
Oka
YABLONOVY RANGE
Shilka
Khabarovsk
Sapporo
HOKKAIDO
EASTERN SAYAN
MINUSINSK BASIN
Abakan
Cheremkhovo
Lake Baikal
Chita
Borzya
Argun
GREATER KHINGAN RANGE
MANCHURIAN PLAIN
Lesozavodsk
Terney
Tetyukhe
Angarsk
Irkutsk
Ulan-Ude
Khilok
Lake Khanka
Spassk-Dalny
Ussuriysk
Artyom
Nakhodka
SAYAN MOUNTAINS
WESTERN SAYAN
Kyzyl
Slyudyanka
Petrovsk-Zabaykalsky
BORSHCHOVOCHNY
Zabaykalsk
Selenga
HARBIN
Sungari
Vladivostok
Yenisey
Ulaanbaatar
Sea of Japan
HONSHU
NORTH KOREA
MONGOLIA
ALTAI MOUNTAINS
MUKDEN
TOKYO
JAPAN
Nagoya
Kyoto
OSAKA
P'yongyang
SEOUL
SOUTH KOREA
Pusan
Hiroshima
GOBI
PEKING
TIENTSIN
Dairen
Lü-ta
Gulf of Chihli
Huang Ho
KYUSHU
T'ai-yüan
Yellow Sea
PACIFIC OCEAN
CH'I-LIEN SHAN-MO
Grand Canal
SHAN-MO
TSAIDAM BASIN
CHINA
Yün Ho
EAST CHINA SEA
Lan-chou
Sian
Nanking
SHANGHAI
© Rand McNally & Co.
A-570000-257
0 200 400 600 800 km
0 200 400 600 800 mi

MAP INDEX

Political subdivisions

Armenian S.S.R..........40·00n 43·00e
Azerbaidzhan S.S.R..........40·30n 47·30e
Belorussian S.S.R..........53·30n 28·00e
Estonian S.S.R..59·00n 26·00e
Georgian S.S.R.42·00n 44·00e
Kazakh S.S.R...48·00n 68·00e
Kirghiz S.S.R...41·30n 75·00e
Latvian S.S.R...57·00n 25·00e
Lithuanian S.S.R..........56·00n 24·00e
Moldavian S.S.R..........47·00n 29·00e
Russian Soviet Federated Socialist Republic......60·00n 100·00e
Tadzhik S.S.R...39·00n 71·00e
Turkmen S.S.R..40·00n 60·00e
Ukrainian S.S.R.49·00n 32·00e
Uzbek S.S.R....41·00n 64·00e

Cities and towns

Abakan.........53·43n 91·26e
Agapa..........71·27n 89·15e
Aktyubinsk.....50·17n 57·10e
Aldan..........58·37n 125·24e
Aleksandrovsk-Sakhalinsky....50·54n 142·10e
Alma-Ata........43·15n 76·57e
Ambarchik......69·39n 162·20e
Anadyr.........64·45n 177·29e
Andizan........40·45n 72·22e
Angarsk........52·34n 103·54e
Anzhero-Sudzhensk.....56·07n 86·00e
Aralsk..........46·48n 61·40e
Arkhangelsk....64·34n 40·32e
Armavir.........45·00n 41·08e
Artyom.........43·22n 132·13e
Ashkhabad.....37·57n 58·23e
Astrakhan......46·21n 48·03e
Ayagus.........47·58n 80·27e
Ayan...........54·43n 110·55e
Bagdarin.......54·26n 113·36e
Bakhta.........62·28n 89·00e
Baku...........40·23n 49·51e
Balkhash.......46·49n 74·59e
Barnaul........53·22n 83·45e
Batamay........63·31n 129·27e
Batumi.........41·38n 41·38e
Belgorod.......50·36n 36·34e
Belogorsk.......50·57n 125·28e
Berezniki......59·24n 56·46e
Beringovsky....63·03n 179·19e
Birobidzhan....48·48n 132·57e
Biysk...........52·34n 85·15e
Blagoveshchensk......50·16n 127·32e
Bobruysk.......53·09n 29·14e
Bodaybo........57·51n 114·10e
Borzya.........50·24n 116·31e
Bratsk.........56·05n 101·48e
Bryansk........53·15n 34·22e
Bukhara........39·48n 64·25e
Buolkalakh......72·56n 119·50e
Chara..........56·54n 118·12e
Chardzhou......39·06n 63·34e
Chelkar.........47·50n 59·36e
Chelyabinsk....55·10n 61·24e
Cheremkhovo...53·09n 103·05e
Cherepovets....59·08n 37·54e
Cherkassy......49·26n 32·04e
Chernigov......51·30n 31·18e
Chiatura........42·19n 43·18e
Chimbay........42·57n 59·47e
Chimkent.......42·18n 69·36e
Chita...........52·03n 113·30e
Chu............43·36n 73·42e
Chumikan.......54·42n 135·19e
Dalnegorsk.....44,35n 135,35e
Dikson..........73·30n 80·35e
Dnepropetrovsk.48·27n 34·59e
Donetsk........48·00n 37·48e
Druzhina.......68·14n 145·18e
Dudinka........69·25n 86·15e
Dushanbe......38·35n 68·48e
Dushekan......60·39n 109·03e
Dzhambul......42·54n 71·22e
Dzhardzhan....68·43n 124·02e
Dzhetygara.....52·11n 61·12e
Dzhezkazgan...47·47n 67·46e
Egvekinot.......66·19n 179·10w
Ekibastuz.......51·40n 75·22e
Ekimchan.......53·04n 132·58e
Ekonda.........65·47n 105·17e
Enurmino.......66·57n 171·49w
Fergana........40·23n 71·46e
Frunze.........42·54n 74·36e
Gizhiga.........62·03n 160·30e
Gomel..........52·25n 31·00e
Gonam.........57·21n 131·12e
Gorky..........56·20n 44·00e
Gorlovka.......48·18n 38·03e
Grozny..........43·20n 45·42e
Guga...........52·43n 137·35e
Guryev..........47·07n 51·56e
Igarka..........67·28n 86·35e
Irkutsk..........52·16n 104·20e
Ivanova.........57·00n 40·59e
Izhevsk.........56·51n 53·14e
Izhma..........65·02n 53·55e
Kadykchan.....63·02n 146·50e
Kalinin..........56·52n 35·55e
Kaliningrad.....54·43n 20·30e
Kaluga..........54·31n 36·16e
Kamensk-Uralsky........56·28n 61·54e
Kansk..........56·13n 95·41e
Karaganda.....49·50n 73·10e
Karatau.........43·10n 70·28e
Karazhal.......48·02n 70·49e
Kaunas.........54·54n 23·54e
Kavacha........60·16n 169·51e
Kazachye.......70·44n 136·13e
Kazan..........55·49n 49·08e
Kemerovo......55·20n 86·05e
Kerch..........45·20n 36·26e
Khabarovsk.....48·27n 135·06e
Khandyga......62·40n 135·36e
Khanty-Mansiysk......61·00n 69·06e
Kharkov.........50·00n 36·15e
Khatanga.......71·58n 102·30e
Khatyrka.......62·03n 175·15e
Khilok..........51·21n 110·28e
Kholmsk........47·03n 142·03e
Kiev............50·26n 30·31e
Kirensk.........57·46n 108·08e
Kirov...........58·33n 49·42e
Kirovabad......40·40n 46·22e
Kirovsk.........67·37n 33·40e
Kirovsky........54·18n 155·47e
Kirovsky........44·52n 78·12e
Kishinyov......47·00n 28·50e
Kizyl-Arvat.....38·48n 56·15e
Klaipeda........55·43n 21·07e
Kokand.........40·33n 70·57e
Kolpashevo....58·20n 82·50e
Kolymskaya.....68·44n 158·44e
Komsomolsk-na-Amure.........50·35n 137·02e
Konosha........60·58n 40·15e
Korf............60·19n 165·50e
Korsakov.......46·38n 142·46e
Kotlas..........61·16n 46·35e
Krasnodar......45·02n 39·00e
Krasnovodsk....40·00n 53·00e
Krasnoyarsk....56·01n 92·50e
Kremenchug....49·04n 33·25e
Krivoy Rog.....47·55n 33·21e
Kurgan.........55·26n 65·18e
Kursk..........51·42n 36·12e
Kushka.........35·16n 62·20e
Kustanay.......53·10n 63·35e
Kutaisi.........42·15n 42·40e
Kuybyshev......53·12n 50·09e
Kyzyl...........51·42n 94·27e
Kzyl-Orda......44·48n 65·28e
Leninakan......40·48n 43·50e
Leningrad......59·55n 30·15e
Lensk..........60·43n 114·55e
Lesozavodsk....45·28n 133·27e
Liepaja.........56·31n 21·01e
Lvov...........49·50n 24·00e
Macha..........59·54n 117·35e
Magadan.......59·34n 150·48e
Magnitogorsk...53·27n 59·04e
Makayevka......48·02n 37·58e
Makhachkala...42·58n 47·30e
Maklakovo......58·16n 92·29e
Malka..........53·20n 157·30e
Markha.........61·49n 122·20e
Markovo........64·40n 170·25e
Mary...........37·36n 61·50e
Minsk..........53·54n 27·34e
Mirny..........62·33n 113·53e
Mogilyov........53·54n 30·21e
Mogocha........53·44n 119·44e
Monchegorsk...67·56n 32·58e
Moroshechnoye.56·24n 156·12e
Moscow.........55·45n 37·35e
Murmansk.......68·58n 33·05e
Myakit..........61·24n 152·09e
Nakhodka.......42·48n 132·52e
Nadym..........65·35n 72·42e
Nagorny........55·58n 124·57e
Nakhodka.......42·48n 132·52e
Namangan......41·00n 71·40e
Naryan-Mar.....67·39n 53·00e
Nebit-Dag......39·30n 54·22e
Nelkan.........57·40n 136·13e
Nikolayev.......46·58n 32·00e
Nikolayevsk-na-Amure.........53·08n 140·44e
Nikopol.........47·34n 34·24e
Nizhny Tagil....57·55n 59·57e
Nordvik.........72·02n 111·32e
Norilsk.........69·20n 88·06e
Novgorod.......58·31n 31·17e
Novokazalinsk...45·50n 62·10e
Novokuznetsk...53·45n 87·06e
Novomoskovsk..54·05n 38·13e
Novorossiysk....44·45n 37·45e
Novosibirsk.....55·02n 82·55e
Nukus..........42·50n 59·29e
Odessa.........46·28n 30·44e
Okha...........53·34n 142·56e
Okhotsk.........59·23n 143·18e
Omsk...........55·00n 73·24e
Omsukchan.....62·32n 115·48e
Ordzhonikidze..43·03n 44·40e
Orenburg........51·54n 55·06e
Orsk............51·12n 58·34e
Oryol...........52·59n 36·05e
Osh............40·33n 72·48e
Oymyakon......63·28n 142·49e
Palana..........59·07n 159·58e
Palatka.........60·06n 150·54e
Pavlodar........52·18n 76·57e
Penza..........53·13n 45·00e
Perm...........58·00n 56·15e
Petropavlovsk..54·54n 69·06e
Petropavlovsk-Kamchatsky...53·01n 158·39e
Petrovsk-Zabaykalsky....51·17n 108·50e
Petrozavodsk...61·47n 34·20e
Poronaysk......49·14n 143·04e
Prokopyevsk....53·53n 86·45e
Provideniya.....64·23n 173·18w
Pskov..........57·50n 28·20e
Raychikhinsk...49·46n 129·25e
Riga............56·57n 24·06e
Rostov-na-Donu..........47·14n 39·42e
Rubtsovsk......51·30n 81·15e
Ryazan.........54·38n 39·44e
Rybinsk.........58·03n 38·52e
Salekhard......66·33n 66·40e
Samarkand.....39·40n 66·58e
Saransk........54·11n 45·11e
Saratov.........51·34n 46·02e
Saskylakh.......71·55n 114·01e
Semipalatinsk..50·28n 80·13e
Sevastopol.....53·08n 65·44e
Serov...........59·29n 60·31e
Severodvinsk...64·34n 39·50e
Shcherbakovo...65·15n 160·30e
Shevchenko....43·35n 51·05e
Shilka..........51·51n 116·02e
Shimanovsk....52·00n 127·42e
Shologontsy....66·13n 114·14e
Skovorodino....53·59n 123·55e
Slautnoye.......63·00n 167·59e
Slyudyanka.....51·38n 103·42e
Smolensk.......54·47n 32·03e
Sochi...........43·35n 39·45e
Sovetskaya Gavan.........48·58n 140·18e
Spassk-Dalny...44·37n 132·48e
Srednekolymsk.67·27n 153·41e
Stavropol.......45·02n 41·59e
Sterlitamak.....53·37n 55·58e
Sukhana........68·45n 118·00e
Surgut..........61·14n 73·20e
Sverdlovsk.....48·05n 39·40e
Svetlaya........46·33n 138·18e
Svobodny.......51·24n 128·07e
Syktyvkar......61·40n 50·46e
Syrdarya.......40·52n 68·38e
Tabor...........71·16n 150·12e
Taldy-Kurgan...45·00n 78·23e
Tallinn.........59·25n 24·45e
Tambov.........52·43n 41·25e
Tartu...........58·23n 26·43e
Tashauz........41·50n 59·58e
Tashkent.......41·20n 69·18e
Tbilisi..........41·42n 44·45e
Temirtau.......50·05n 72·56e
Termez.........37·14n 67·16e
Tiksi...........71·36n 128·48e
Tobolsk.........58·12n 68·16e
Tolyatti.........53·31n 49·26e
Tommot.........58·58n 126·19e
Tomptokan.....57·06n 133·59e
Tomsk..........56·30n 84·58e
Tselinograd.....51·10n 71·30e
Tula...........54·12n 37·37e
Turkestan......43·18n 68·15e
Turukhansk.....65·49n 87·59e
Tuymazy........54·36n 53·42e
Tyumen.........57·09n 65·32e
Uelkal..........65·32n 179·17e
Ufa............54·44n 55·56e
Uglegorsk......49·02n 142·03e
Ukhta..........63·33n 53·38e
Uka............57·50n 162·06e
Ulan-Ude.......51·50n 107·37e
Ulyanovsk......54·20n 48·24e
Uralsk.........51·14n 51·22e
Ussuriysk......43·48n 131·59e
Ust-Chaun......68·47n 170·30e
Ust-Kamenogorsk .49·58n 82 38e
Ust-Nera........64·34n 143·12e
Ust-Nyukzha....56·34n 121·37e
Ust-Tym.........59·26n 80·08e
Vanavara.......60·22n 102·16e
Vankarem.......67·51n 175·50w
Velikaya........64·04n 176·12e
Verkhoyansk....67·35n 133·27e
Vilnius..........54·41n 25·19e
Vinnitsa........49·14n 28·29e
Vitebsk.........55·12n 30·11e
Vladimir........56·10n 40·25e
Vladivostok.....43·08n 131,54e
Volochanka.....71·00n 94·28e
Volgograd......48·44n 44·25e
Vologda........59·12n 39·55e
Volzhsky........48·49n 44·44e
Vorkuta........67·27n 63·58e
Voronezh.......51·40n 39·10e
Voroshilovgrad..48·34n 39·20e
Vyborg..........60·42n 28·45e
Warsaw.........52·15n 21·00e
Yakutsk........62·13n 129·49e
Yamsk..........59·35n 154·10e
Yaroslavl.......57·37n 39·52e
Yerevan........40·11n 44·30e
Yeropol.........65·15n 168·40e
Yessey.........68·29n 102·10e
Yuzhno-Sakhalinsk.....46·58n 142·42e
Zabaykalsk.....49·38n 117·19e
Zaporozhye.....47·50n 35·10e
Zhdanov........47·06n 37·33e
Zheleznogorsk-Ilimsky........56·37n 104·08e
Zhigansk.......66·45n 123·20e
Zhitomir........50·16n 28·40e
Zlatoust........55·10n 59·40e
Zyryank.........65·45n 150·51e

Physical features and points of interest

Alakol, Lake, *salt lake*.......46·10n 81·45e
Alazeya, *river*...70·51n 153·34e
Aldan, *river*.....63·28n 129·35e
Aldan Plateau, *upland*.........57·00n 127·00e
Altai Mountains.....48·00n 90·00e
Amga, *river*.....62·38n 132·32e
Amu Darya, *river*...........43·40n 59·01e
Amgun, *river*....52·56n 139·40e
Amur, *river*.....52·56n 141·10e
Anabar, *river*...73·08n 113·36e
Anadyr Plateau.........67·00n 174·00e
Anadyr, *river*....64·55n 176·05e
Anadyr, Gulf of..64·00n 179·00w
Angara, *river*.....58·06n 93·00e
Aral Sea.........45·00n 60·00e
Arctic Ocean...85·00n 90·00e
Argun, *river*.....53·20n 121·28e
Ayon Island.....69·50n 168·40e
Baikal, Lake.....53·00n 107·40e
Balkhash, Lake..46·00n 74·00e
Baltic Sea.......57·30n 20·00e
Barabinsk Steppe, *plain*...55·00n 79·00e
Barents Sea....74·00n 36·00e
Belukha, Mount, *mountain*......49·48n 86·40e
Bely Island.....73·10n 70·45e
Bering Sea.....58·00n 180·00
Bering Strait....65·30n 169·00w
Betpak-Dala, *plain*..........46·00n 70·00e
Black Sea......43·00n 35·00e
Bolshoy Begichyov Island..........74·20n 112·30e
Borshchovochny Range, *mountain range*..........52·00n 117·00e
Bratsk Reservoir......56·10n 102·10e
Carpathan Mountains.....48·00n 23·00e
Caspian Depression....48·00n 52·00e
Caspian Sea....42·00n 50·30e
Caucasus Mountains.....42·00n 45·00e
Central Russian Upland, *mountain*......52·00n 38·00e
Central Siberian Plateau, *upland*.........65·00n 105·00e
Central Yakut Plain...........65·00n 124·00e
Chany, Lake, *salt lake*......54·50n 77·30e
Chelyuskin, Cape..........77·45n 104·20e
Chersky Range, *mountain range*..........52·00n 114·00e
Chono, *river*....62·54n 111·06e
Chu, *river*.......45·00n 67·44e
Chukchi Peninsula.....66·00n 175·00w
Chukchi Sea....69·00n 171·00w
Chuna, *river*.....57·47n 95·26e
Chunya, *river*...61·36n 96·30e

MAP INDEX (continued)

Commander Islands 55·00n 167·00e
Communism Peak 38·57n 72·01e
Desna, *river* 50·33n 30·32e
Dezhnev, Cape 66·06n 169·45w
Diomede Islands 65·45n 169·30w
Dnepr, *river* 46·38n 32·18e
Dnestr, *river* 46·18n 30·17e
Don, *river* 47·04n 39·18e
Donets Basin 48·30n 38·30e
Dvina, *river* 57·04n 24·03e
Dzhugdzhur Range, *mountains* 58·00n 136·00e
Dzhungarsky Alatau Range, *mountain range* 45·00n 80·00e
East Siberian Sea 74·00n 166·00e
Elbrus, Mount, *mountain* 43·21n 42·26e
Emba, *river* 46·38n 53·14e
Finland, Gulf of 60·00n 27·00e
Fligeli, Cape 81·50n 59·20e
Franz Joseph Land, *islands* 81·00n 55·00e
Gorky Reservoir 57·00n 43·10e
Gyda Peninsula 70·50n 79·00e
Ili, *river* 45·24n 74·08e
Ilmen, Lake 58·17n 31·20e
Indigirka, *river* 70·48n 148·54e
Irtysh, *river* 61·04n 68·52e
Ishim, *river* 57·45n 71·12e
Ishim Steppe, *plain* 55·00n 71·30e
Issyk-Kul, Lake 42·25n 77·15e
Japan, Sea of 42·00n 135·00e
Kakhovka Reservoir 47·25n 34·10e
Kama, *river* 55·45n 52·00e
Kama Reservoir 58·52n 56·15e
Kamchatka, *river* 56·15n 162·30e
Kamchatka, Gulf of 55·35n 162·21e
Kamchatka Peninsula 56·00n 160·00e
Kanin Nos, Cape 68·39n 43·16e
Kara-Bogaz-Gol Bay 41·00n 53·15e
Karagin, Gulf of 58·50n 164·00e
Karagin Island 58·50n 164·00e
Kara-Kum Desert 39·00n 60·00e
Karakumsky Kanal, *canal* 37·35n 61·50e
Kara Sea 76·00n 80·00e
Karatau Range, *mountain range* 43·50n 68·30e
Karelia, *historic region* 64·00n 32·00e
Kazakh Uplands, *hills* 49·00n 72·00e
Kazym, *river* 63·54n 65·50e
Ket, *river* 58·55n 81·32e
Khanka, Lake 45·00n 132·24e
Khatanga, *river* 72·55n 106·00e
Kheta, *river* 71·54n 102·06e
Klyuchevskaya Volcano 56·04n 160·38e
Kola Peninsula 67·30n 37·00e
Kolguyev Island 69·05n 49·15e
Kolyma, *river* 69·30n 161·00e
Konda, *river* 60·40n 69·46e
Kopet-Dag, *mountains* 37·50n 58·00e
Koryak Range, *mountain range* 62·30n 172·00e
Kotelny Island 75·45n 138·44e
Kotuy, *river* 71·55n 102·05e
Kremenchug Reservoir 49·30n 32·30e
Kuban, *river* 45·20n 37·22e
Kulunda Steppe, *plain* 53·00n 79·00e
Kuma, *river* 44·55n 46·32e
Kura, *river* 39·24n 49·19e
Kuril Islands 46·10n 152·00e
Kuybyshev Reservoir 53·40n 49·00e
Kuznetsk Basin 54·00n 86·00e
Kyzylkum, *desert* 42·00n 64·00e
Kyzylray, Mount, *mountain* 48·27n 75·32e
Ladoga, Lake 60·08n 30·01e
La Perouse Strait 45·45n 142·00e
Ledyanaya, Gora, *mountain* 49·28n 142·45e
Lena, *river* 72·25n 126·40e
Long's Strait 70·20n 178·00e
Lopatka, Cape 50·52n 156·40e
Lovat, *river* 58·14n 31·28e
Mangyshlak Peninsula 44·18n 51·00e
Mezen, *river* 66·11n 43·59e
Minusinsk Basin 53·30n 92·00e
Muna, *river* 67·52n 123·06e
Nadym, *river* 66·12n 72·00e
Narodnaya, Mount, *mountain* 65·04n 60·09e
Navarin, Cape 62·16n 179·10e
Neman, *river* 55·18n 21·23e
Neva, *river* 59·57n 30·20e
New Siberia Island 75·00n 149·00e
New Siberian Islands 75·00n 142·00e
Nizhnyaya Tunguska, *river* 65·48n 88·04e
Northern Dvina, *river* 64·35n 40·30e
North Siberian Lowland, *plain* 73·00n 100·00e
Novaya Zemlya, *islands* 74·00n 57·00e
Novosibirsk Reservoir 54·35n 82·35e
Ob, *river* 66·45n 69·30e
Ob Bay 69·00n 73·00e
Oka, *river* 56·20n 43·59e
Oka, *river* 56·03n 101·50e
Okhotsk, Sea of 53·00n 150·00e
Olenyok, *river* 73·00n 119·55e
Olyokma, *river* 60·22n 120·42e
Olyutorsky, Cape 59·55n 170·27e
Om, *river* 54·59n 73·22e
Onega, Lake 61·30n 35·45e
Onon, *river* 51·42n 115·50e
Pamirs, *mountains* 38·00n 73·00e
Pay-Khoy, *mountains* 69·00n 63·00e
Pechora, *river* 68·13n 54·10e
Peipus, Lake 58·45n 27·30e
Penzhina, *river* 62·28n 165·18e
Pobeda, Mount, *mountain* 65·12n 146·12e
Pobedy, Pik, *peak* 42·02n 80·05e
Podkamennaya Tunguska, *river* 61·36n 90·18e
Pripet Marshes, *physical region* 52·00n 57·00e
Pripyat, *river* 51·21n 30·09e
Prut, *river* 45·28n 28·12e
Pur, *river* 67·31n 77·55e
Putoran Mountains 69·00n 95·00e
Pyasina, *river* 73·50n 87·10e
Riga, Gulf of 57·30n 23·35e
Rudolf Island 81·45n 58·30e
Rybinsk Reservoir 58·30n 38·30e
Sakhalin Island 51·00n 143·00e
Sartang, *river* 67·44n 133·12e
Sayan Mountains 52·45n 96·00e
Sea of Azov 46·00n 36·00e
Selenga, *river* 52·16n 106·16e
Selennyakh, *river* 67·48n 144·54e
Sette-Daban Range, *mountains* 62·00n 138·00e
Severnaya Zemla, *islands* 79·30n 98·00e
Severnye Hills, *mountains* 59·30n 49·00e
Seym, *river* 51·27n 32·34e
Shantar Islands 55·00n 137·36e
Shelikhov, Gulf of 60·00n 158·00e
Shilka, *river* 53·22n 121·32e
Siberia, *historic region* 60·00n 100·00e
Sikhote-Alin, *mountains* 48·00n 138·00e
Sredinny Range, *mountains* 56·00n 158·00e
Stanovoy Range, *mountains* 56·20n 126·00e
Stanovoy Upland, *mountains* 56·00n 114·00e
Sukhona, *river* 60·46n 46·24e
Sura, *river* 56·06n 46·00e
Syrdarya, *river* 46·03n 61·00e
Talish Mountains 38·42n 48·18e
Tarbagatay Range, *mountain range* 47·12n 83·00e
Tatarsk Strait 50·00n 141·15e
Tavda, *river* 57·47n 67·16e
Taymyr, Lake 74·30n 102·30e
Taymyr Peninsula 76·00n 104·00e
Taz, *river* 67·32n 78·40e
Tengiz, Lake 50·25n 69·00e
Terpeniya, Cape 48·39n 144·44e
Tien Shan, *mountains* 42·00n 78·00e
Timen Ridge, *mountains* 65·00n 51·00e
Tobol, *river* 58·10n 68·12e
Tsimlyansk Reservoir 48·00n 43·00e
Tura, *river* 57·12n 66·56e
Turan Plain 42·00n 61·00e
Turgay, *river* 48·00n 62·45e
Turgay Valley 52·00n 64·30e
Turgay Tableland, *plateau* 51·00n 64·00e
Tym, *river* 59·25n 80·04e
Uda, *river* 54·42n 135·14e
Ural, *river* 47·00n 51·48e
Ural Mountains 60·00n 60·00e
Usa, *river* 54·00n 28·55e
Ustyurt Plateau 43·00n 56·00e
Vakh, *river* 60·45n 76·45e
Vaygach Island 70·00n 59·30e
Velikaya, *river* 64·40n 176·20e
Verkhoyansk Range, *mountains* 67·00n 129·00e
Vilyuy, *river* 64·24n 126·26e
Volga, *river* 45·55n 47·52e
Volga Hills, *mountains* 52·00n 46·00e
Volgograd Reservoir 49·20n 45·00e
Vostochny Sayan, *mountain range* 53·00n 97·00e
Vytaka, *river* 55·36n 57·30e
Western Dvina, *river* 57·04n 24·03e
West Siberian Plain 60·00n 75·00e
White Sea 66·00n 40·00e
Wrangel Island 71·00n 179·30e
Yablonovy Range, *mountain range* 53·50n 115·00e
Yakutiya, *historic region* 65·00n 130·00e
Yamal Peninsula 70·00n 70·00e
Yana, *river* 71·31n 136·32e
Yelizavety, Cape 54·27n 142·42e
Yenisey, *river* 71·50n 82·40e
Yukagir Plateau 66·00n 155·00e
Yuzhny Bug, *river* 46·59n 31·58e
Zapadny Sayan, *mountain range* 53·00n 94·00e
Zaysan, Lake 48·00n 84·00e
Zeravshan, *river* 39·32n 63·45e
Zeya, *river* 50·13n 127·35e

Siberia, there are lakes whose water has a high sulfate content, from which chemicals are produced.

Lake temperatures are subject to sharp variations. In summer, the water in shallow lakes is intensely heated, while in the deep lakes the temperature falls with depth to a low of 39° F (4° C); in winter the water temperature rises with depth as the lower levels retain summer heat.

As a result of the construction of hydroelectric plants and navigation canals, there are many very large artificial lakes in the valleys of the major rivers. These include the Kakhovka, Kremenchug, and Kiev reservoirs on the Dnepr, Tsimlyansk on the Don, Rybinsk, Kuybyshev, and Volgograd on the Volga, Novosibirsk on the Ob, and Bratsk on the Angara. The Kayakkum, Chardzhou, and other lakes in Central Asia have been created by irrigation projects.

Groundwaters and marshes. The groundwaters of the Soviet Union are not homogeneous. In much of Soviet territory—from the tundra to the northern steppes—they have a relatively high content of calcium bicarbonate and dissolved silica and are also marked by abundant underground discharge, thus helping to feed rivers. In the dry steppes, semideserts, and deserts, groundwaters with high chloride and sulfate content are formed, which in places are unsuitable for drinking. In the loamy deserts of Central Asia the groundwaters lie at great depth and are usually bitterly salty. In the sand deserts the water lies nearer the surface and is not so mineralized. In the foothill zone of Central Asia, groundwaters are abundant and slightly mineralized.

Marshes occupy nearly 10 percent of Soviet territory, and they are an important element of the landscape in several regions. They are found mainly in the northern half of the country, in the forest and tundra zones, where precipitation exceeds evaporation. In central and northern Karelia they amount to 40–50 percent of the land surface, and they occupy nearly 80 percent in parts of the Western Siberian taiga. Farther south the marshland area falls off, and marshes are concentrated in such depressions as that called (in the West) the Pripet Marshes (in Belorussia and the Ukraine) and the Meshchera (near Moscow and Ryazan). In the forest-steppe zone, marshland diminishes sharply, and south of this zone it becomes quite insignificant; it covers about 1.5 percent of the Ukrainian steppes.

SOILS

The Soviet plains are characterized by several distinct latitudinal (zonal) soil belts.

In the Arctic islands and on the Arctic coast, relatively infertile (and often permanently frozen) Arctic and tundra soils are dominant. The latter are thin, with a low organic content (1–2 percent) and coarse composition, and are boggy.

About a third of Soviet territory is covered by the soils of the forest zone. These include podzols and (in Eastern Siberia) frozen taiga soils (both developed under taiga-type forests), together with turf–podzol soils and huge areas of peat bog and gley-podzol soils, "gley" being a sticky clay formed in waterlogged soils. All varieties of podzols and podzolic soils are characterized by intense leaching, as a result of which easily soluble substances are washed out of the upper strata. The top stratum is gray or brown with 1–4 percent of humus, or organic matter. The underlying stratum is ashy ("podzol" comes from Russian *zola,* "ashes") and consists of the finest quartz sand grains; nutrient substances are completely washed out. Below this is a third layer, which in fully developed podzols has an accumulation of humus and leached mineral nutrients; in podzolic soils the humus is lacking, and in gley–podzols there is only an accumulation of clay minerals. In the extreme southwest (in Transcarpathia) and southeast (the central Amur and South Primorye) of the podzol soil zone, there appear brown forest soils, formed under broad-leaved and partially mixed forests. These are characterized by an accumulation of clay minerals and ferrous oxides, which impart the brown colour; a "clotty" structure; and a fairly well-developed humus stratum (3–7 percent).

Podzols

South of the zone of podzol and marshland soils stretches a narrow strip of gray forest soils, developed under leafy forests of the northern forest steppe. Gray forest soils have a distinctly formed stratum of humus, and there is no uninterrupted podzolic stratum.

Still farther south stretch the black-earth, or chernozem, lands, occupying 9 percent of Soviet territory and comprising almost half the world area of this soil type. Black-earth soil is formed under the grassy vegetation of the steppe and forest–steppe, in conditions of adequate warmth and a negative or near neutral balance of moisture. This prevents intense leaching and assists the accumulation of organic substances. In addition, meadow–black-earth soil is also widespread in the steppes. The greater part of the black-earth belt is now under the plow.

In the dry steppes and semideserts of the southeast Russian Plain and of Kazakhstan are found chestnut soils, marked by a rather low humus content, a tendency toward saltiness, and a feeble structure. The meadow–chestnut soils are formed in hollows and estuaries in conditions of heightened surface or ground moisture.

Continuing the southward succession, chestnut soils give way to other semidesert types and then, in the deserts themselves, to brownish-gray and gray-earth soils (sierozems). These are all very poor in humus and are often salty (solonetz and solonchak) and are broken by extensive salt marshes. A unique type of desert soil is the *takyr,* a clay soil found in depressions, which creates impassable mud during rain and a brick-hard crust in dry periods. These soils are so barren that they are often devoid of all vegetation except meagre lichens.

Red-earth soils

Red-earth soils in their typical form are found only on the lower mountain slopes of the Kolkhida plain (in the Caucasus). These, the most ancient of Soviet soils, are soils of humid subtropical forests, very thick, and rich in iron and aluminum oxides. Abkhaziya and the Talish Mountains are the sites of other humid subtropical forest soils, the yellow-earth soils, distinguished from the red-earth by their paler yellow tint and their inconsiderable depth. In addition to the typical gray-earth soils, brown soils are widespread in the dry subtropics, notably on the slopes of the mountains of Central Asia and the Caucasus, being found under low-growing, broad-leaved forests, sparse forests, and thickets.

Finally, in the mountain regions, comprising 31 percent of Soviet territory, the soils form a series of vertical belts. A particularly full selection of high-altitude soil belts is represented in the Caucasus, where the soils vary from black-earth to mountain pasture, subalpine, and alpine. The mountain soils are stony, well drained, and not very thick. The alluvial soils of the river floodplains also should be mentioned, because they are the youngest of Soviet soils, still being formed.

PLANT LIFE

About 17,000 plant species and almost half of all the families of higher plants known in the world are found in the Soviet Union, which lies entirely in the area known to botanists as the Boreal kingdom. The vast Soviet plains are characterized (as in the case of soils) by clearly marked latitudinal vegetation zones. Successively, these are Arctic waste, tundra, forest–tundra, forest, forest-steppe, steppe, semidesert, and desert.

The latitudinal belts. The Arctic wastes include most of the Arctic islands and the north coast of the Taymyr Peninsula; mosses, lichens, and a variety of grasses cover scarcely half of the soil surface.

The tundra zone—divided into subzones of Arctic, moss–lichen, and scrub tundra—stretches in a continuous belt along the northern border of Eurasia, including some Arctic islands and the Commander Islands of the Pacific.

To the south lies the zone of forest–tundra, in which the barren tundra landscapes alternate with marshes and sparse forests of birch and fir (in the west) and larch (in the east).

The forest zone

Farther south stretches the broad belt of the forest zone, extending from the western borders of the country to the Pacific coast. Coniferous taiga forests of fir, pine, silver fir, cedar, and Siberian larch are most widespread to the west of the Yenisey River, while in Central and Eastern Siberia the forests are predominantly of larch. Marshes are very common, especially in the taiga of Western Siberia, and various types of meadows are also found.

Large areas of birch and aspen groves, growing on the site of former coniferous forests destroyed by felling or fire, are common in the southern taiga of the Russian Plain and in the West Siberian Plain; they do not last long, because shoots of conifers gradually appear under their canopy and choke the young trees. Mixed (coniferous and broad-leaved) and broad-leaved forests occur in the southern half of the Russian Plain forest zone. Unlike the conifers, the broad-leaved forests have many tiers, the uppermost usually consisting of crowns of oak, lime, ash, and maple. Below these come bird cherry and mountain ash, then a thick, shrubby undergrowth, perhaps of hazel; the whole is underlain by grass. Beech and hornbeam appear in broad-leaved forests in the southwest of the zone. Mixed forests are also widespread in the southern Far East, where most of the conifers are pine or whole-leaf silver fir, and common broad-leaved trees include oak, Amur linden, maple, and hazelnut. The depressions and lower mountain slopes are covered with broad-leaved forests of oak with a striking admixture of black birch.

The forest–steppe zone extends in a narrow latitudinal belt across the Russian Plain and the West Siberian Plain. Meadow steppe with various grasses alternates with small areas of oak (in Soviet Europe) or birch and aspen (in Western Siberia). Farther east, forest–steppe is encountered only as isolated islands in taiga forests.

To the south, forest–steppe gives way to mixed-grass and grassy steppe, and the forests remain only along river valleys and ravines. The herbaceous covering of the grassy steppes consists of needlegrass (*Stipa* sp.) and such other perennial turf grasses as fescue.

Farther south lies a semidesert zone extending in a continuous belt from the Yergeni hills (in the southeast of the Russian Plain) to the mountain systems of the Altai and Tien Shan. Grasses that like dryness (such as *Stipa rubens* and fescue) and semishrubs (such as saltwort and wormwood) predominate in the thin, patchy, vegetation covering.

The desert zone

Finally, the southernmost desert zone occupies the southern third of the Caspian Depression and the Central Asian plain. It is distinguished by a very sparse and poor covering of vegetation, composed of saltwort, wormwood, and grasses. Saltwort (*Salsola richteri*) and sand acacia are found in relatively light sandy soils and in river valleys. An abundance of ephemeral plants is typical of the southern part of the zone, where sand deserts, notably the Kara-Kum and Kyzylkum, predominate; in addition *Haloxylon* "forests" are common, alternating with salt-marsh wastes overgrown with saltwort.

The subtropical, Mediterranean, and mountain regions. The humid subtropics of the Kolkhida and Lenkoran depressions have a unique vegetation as well as soils; they are clothed in dense broad-leaved forests that include oak, beech, hornbeam, chestnut, and alder, with an undergrowth of evergreen plants and lianas.

Vegetation of the Mediterranean type makes a strong showing on the Black Sea coast. Forests of oak, juniper, and pine are common.

In mountainous regions, vegetation is distributed in altitudinal belts, particularly in the Caucasus, the Carpathians, and the mountains of the Primorye. Thus the steppes of the foothills of the northern Caucasus give way to mountain forest–steppe, broad-leaved forests of oak and beech, and then pine (in the west) and fir (in the east). Above the forest belt lie sparse high mountain forests, thickets of rhododendron, and subalpine and alpine meadows. In arid regions the middle mountain belt of vegetation is in some places composed of turf-grass steppes, related thickets, and sparse juniper forests. High mountain steppe and meadow are widespread in Central Asia, with turf-grass steppe giving way to areas of dark coniferous forests of spruce or to mixtures of steppe, meadow, shrub thickets, and sparse juniper forests. Coniferous taiga forests cover the Siberian mountains, with tundra above; the higher Altai, however, exhibits subalpine and alpine meadows.

ANIMAL LIFE

The Soviet Union lies entirely in what zoologists call the Palaearctic subregion of the Holarctic faunal region, in which animal life is characterized by five distinct sectors of varying size and natural conditions.

The Arctic sector embraces both Arctic and tundra landscape zones. The Arctic zone (the islands and the mainland seacoasts) is poor in animal species; such mammals and birds connected with the sea as the polar bear, sea hare, seal, walrus, eider, gull, and loon are found. In summer the coastal rocks are covered with nesting colonies of seabirds. The tundra is inhabited by animals adapted to cold climate and open spaces that are under snow for long periods. They include the Arctic fox, reindeer, alpine hare, lemming, and—among its birds—ptarmigan and snowy owl. Geese, swans, and ducks migrate into the region in summer. Lizards, frogs, and other reptiles and amphibians are found only in the extreme southwest of the zone and in the forest–tundra.

The European–Siberian forest sector (covering the Russian Plain, Siberia, and much of the Far East) possesses a much richer and more varied animal life. The northern taiga harbours elk, brown bear, reindeer, lynx, sable, and alpine hare, with such birds as the crossbill, nutcracker, cuckoo, owl, and woodpecker. There are few reptiles or amphibians. Representative fauna of the broad-leaved forests are wild pig, deer, and mink, and the most typical birds are the hawfinch, oriole, owl, and nightingale. Various snakes, lizards, and tortoises are the common reptiles.

The steppe environment

In the steppes, the abundance of plant food allows such rodents as the marmot, jerboa, and hamster to predominate. Birds include the kestrel, crane, eagle, and lark; hooved animals include the occasional steppe antelope; the masked (or steppe) polecat and Tartar fox represent beasts of prey. There are few amphibians but more reptiles than in the north.

Animal life in the Mediterranean sector, found in the Caucasus and mountainous Crimea, is very varied as a result of the great landscape variety and also of the fact that the fauna was originally connected with that of the Mediterranean, Central Asia, and south and southeast Europe. The Caucasus harbours the wild goat, bison, chamois, bezoar goat, Caucasian deer, wild pig, porcupine, leopard, hyena, jackal, Persian squirrel, brown bear, and roe deer. Birds include species characteristic of both mountain (Caucasian black grouse, turkey, and stone partridge) and forest (nuthatch, jay, crossbill, woodpecker, and bullfinch). Reptiles and amphibians are numerous, ranging from cobra to tortoise.

The semideserts and deserts of Central Asia and Kazakhstan form the Central Asian sector, whose animals are specially adapted for existence in conditions of high summer and low winter temperatures, lack of water, and poor vegetation. Many of them are nocturnal. Typical desert dwellers are the Persian gazelle, sand cat, and ground squirrel; birds include the bustard, pheasant, raven, and sparrow. Spiders, including tarantulas, are also present. Several northern forest species are widespread in the eastern part of the Tien Shan; the Kopet-Dag harbours fauna of the fore-Asian type (leopard, stone marten, partridge, and others); and the remaining part of the mountains is inhabited by animals of Central Asian and even (in insignificant measure) Indian origin: the argali (a wild sheep), snow leopard, wild goat, red wolf, bear, turkey, and others. (V.M.St./J.C.D.)

TRADITIONAL REGIONS

Traditional names for large sections of the Soviet Union, such as the North, Western Siberia, and the Far East, are well established. Some of these names have been applied to the present-day official economic regions into which the country is divided for planning purposes, but the traditional regional divisions do not constitute natural or economic entities; it would be more correct to define them as natural historic regions, differing in both their geography and their economy and also in the density and composition of their populations. Their borders are quite arbitrary, following sometimes natural and sometimes administrative boundaries.

The traditional regions of the European Soviet Union are the North (or European North), Centre, Volga Lands, West, Southwest, and Urals. The Caucasus is a distinctive region abutting the European Soviet Union on the south. The Asian part includes Central Asia and Kazakhstan, which occupy the vast area south of Western Siberia and east of the Caspian Sea; the huge territory of Siberia, traditionally subdivided into Western Siberia and Eastern Siberia; and the Far East.

The North. The European North (also long known as the Russian North and equivalent to the present-day Northwestern economic region) corresponds closely to the ancient lands of Novgorod and covers a much greater area than the other European Soviet regions. Bordered by Finland on the west and the Urals on the east, it comprises the northern slopes of the Russian (or East European) Plain, running toward the Arctic Ocean and to the Gulf of Finland of the Baltic Sea. It also includes such major Arctic islands as Novaya Zemlya and the Arctic archipelago Franz Josef Land. Administratively, the North lies within the Russian Soviet Federated Socialist Republic and is composed of the Arkhangelsk, Leningrad, Murmansk, Novgorod, Pskov, and Vologda *oblasti* (regions) and the Karelian and Komi Autonomous Soviet Socialist republics. It covers some 640,000 square miles (1,660,000 square kilometres)—about one-third of Soviet Europe—and is the home mainly of Russians, with Komis (or Zyryans), Karelians, and Nenets (or Yuraks) leading the minority nationalities.

Regions of the North

The physical geography of such a huge area is naturally varied. The main overall character, however, is molded by forest and sea; the whole landscape is marked by a northern severity, and transitions are generally gradual.

A characteristic feature is the extremely uneven distribution of population and economic development. The east and north consist of taiga and swampy tundra and are thinly populated; settlement is concentrated principally in valleys of the main rivers, the Northern Dvina and Pechora. The most important resources here are timber, petroleum, and coal in the northeast and various minerals in the Kola Peninsula. The largest cities are Arkhangelsk, the country's oldest timber port and a centre of industry, and Murmansk, a major ice-free port and fishing centre.

In the southwest, conditions are less severe, and settlement was already quite dense in early times, for here such old Russian cities as Novgorod arose, as the economy developed. Here, too, is Leningrad, the second Soviet city in population and economic importance and one of the largest cultural and scientific centres.

The European North today is one of the Soviet Union's most important industrial regions and the main base of the timber industry.

The Centre. Central Russia (all of it within the Russian S.F.S.R.), with an area of 350,000 square miles (900,000 square kilometres), occupies the whole central belt of the Russian Plain as far south as the Ukraine and from Belorussia eastward to the Volga Lands. Low hills alternate with broad lowlands, and the greater portion lies in a forest zone (taiga in the north, mixed and then broad-leaved forests farther south). The far south is in fact in the forest-steppe zone, noted for its black-earth soil; fields of wheat, sugar beets, and sunflowers occupy the open expanses.

The Russian nucleus

Ever since the formation of the Russian state in the 15th century, central Russia, as the nucleus of that state and the hearth of Russian national culture, has played a primary role in national growth. More than 17 percent of the Soviet population is concentrated here, in little more than 4 percent of the national area. Its proportionate share of industrial production, of scientific manpower, and of the training for the professions generally is even greater.

There are three distinct economic subregions: the Central Industrial region, the Black-Earth Belt, and the Volga–Vyatka region.

The Central Industrial region. This subregion (called the Central region in the official economic classification and composed of Bryansk, Ivanov, Kalinin, Kaluga, Kostroma, Moscow, Oryol, Ryazan, Smolensk, Tula, Vladimir, and Yaroslavl *oblasti* and the city of Moscow) stands out sharply for its level of economic development. The region produces more than half the country's textiles and a large percentage of the total output of, among others, the products of engineering and chemistry. Among the urban centres (which contain the great majority of the population), Moscow, the Soviet capital and leading political, industrial, scientific, and cultural centre, is of exceptional importance. Here the natural scenery has charm and variety deriving from its undulating expanses, the bright, neat birch groves, and the broad valleys of deep rivers on whose banks communities of various sizes lie amid meadows and copses.

The Black-Earth Belt. To the south, abutting the Ukraine, lies the Black-Earth Belt (officially the Central-Black Earth region and including the Belgorod, Kursk, Lipetsk, Tambov, and Voronezh *oblasti*), notable both for its extremely fertile black-earth (chernozem) soil and for the unique iron-ore deposits of the Kursk Magnetic Anomaly. The landscape has many features of the transition from northern forest to southern steppe; it is lent character by fields, oak groves, and villages strung out along river valleys and ravines or occupying flat watersheds. With only 0.75 percent of the country's area, this region nevertheless provides 6 percent of its agricultural produce and is of growing industrial significance. The largest town is Voronezh, and nearly half the population is urban.

The Volga–Vyatka region. This region (its name is the same in the official classification) occupies the eastern part of central Russia, covering the Gorky and Kirov *oblasti* and the Chuvash, Mari, and Mordvinian A.S.S.R.'s. The regional landscape is given character by its great rivers,

The Upper Volga landscape

the Volga and its tributary the Vyatka. Steep river banks, wide bands of water, and water meadows lend variety to the plains. Here the Volga flows from west to east along the boundary of the forest and forest–steppe zones. On its precipitous right bank rise the "mountains," as the local people say, while on its left bank, beyond the water meadows, stretch forested lowlands. This area was often celebrated in the works of Aleksandr Herzen and Maksim Gorky, who were born there. The Volga–Vyatka region is known as the land of forests and factories. Timber is its principal natural wealth, but industry (particularly engineering) accounts for the greater part of economic output. A majority of the population is urban, and the largest industrial centre is Gorky.

The Volga Lands. Near Kazan the Volga sharply changes direction to flow southward. Here the Tatar, Kalmyk, and Bashkir A.S.S.R.'s, together with six *oblasti* of the Russian S.F.S.R., form the Volga Lands, called the Povolzhye region officially. It has an area of some 260,000 square miles (680,000 square kilometres).

Stretching a thousand miles from north to south, the region extends across a series of natural landscape zones from the southern fringe of the forest zone to the semidesert bordering the northern Caspian. Its principal natural resources are fertile land, pastures, the country's most important oil fields, and, not least, two rivers, the Volga and its tributary the Kama. As the largest waterway and the most important source of hydropower in Soviet Europe, the Volga is of enormous economic importance, and, with the building of hydroelectric stations at Kuybyshev, Saratov, and Volgograd, the Volga Lands have become the principal link in the Soviet unified power grid. After World War II the area became the country's main oil base and the main centre of the chemical industry. Agriculture, too, is important; the Volga Lands provide more grain than any other region of the Russian S.F.S.R., and Saratov wheat is among the best in the country. At the same time the region is one of the Soviet Union's main suppliers of meat, wool, vegetables, and melons. The curse of agriculture here is drought and dry winds, but the area of irrigated lands increases every year.

The Lower Volga landscape

More than two-thirds of the population is urbanized; the largest towns and industrial centres are Kazan, Kuybyshev, Saratov, and Volgograd (formerly Stalingrad).

The West. Composed of Belorussia, Moldavia, the three Baltic republics (Estonia, Latvia, and Lithuania), and the Kaliningrad *oblast* of the Russian S.F.S.R., the West occupies an area of more than 166,000 square miles (430,000 square kilometres). The five union republics have vigorous national traditions.

The natural features here are lent character by the residual influence of ancient glaciers; the climate is relatively mild and humid, and many forests, especially pine forests, flourish on the sandy soil. Southwest Belorussia contains the world's oldest nature reserve, the Belovezhskaya (Belavezhskaya) Pushcha. The morainic ridges of residual glacial debris lend variety to the landscape, which changes imperceptibly every few miles from plain to hilly country, woods alternating with fields, meadows with marshes. Rivers connect hundreds of scattered lakes. In the Baltic republics a special element is introduced by the ruins of medieval castles that are often found on high ground, while the Baltic coastal resorts are very popular.

Effects of ancient glaciers on the landscape

The region as a whole embraces three major economic regions: the Baltic region (Estonia, Latvia, Lithuania, and the Kaliningrad *oblast*), Belorussia, and Moldavia. Fishing is highly developed (the Baltic republics provide more than 20 percent of the total national catch), as is engineering. Agriculture, specializing in raising livestock, is noted for its butter and bacon. The main type of fuel produced in Belorussia is peat, together with small quantities of oil, natural gas, and lignite. Belorussia also produces flax and potassium fertilizers and is the main source of heavy trucks and tractors. About half of the population of the West is urban; the biggest urban centres are the republic capitals—Minsk, Kishinyov, Riga, Vilnius, and Tallinn—and Kaunas and Kaliningrad (formerly Königsberg).

The Southwest. Covering an area of 233,000 square miles (604,000 square kilometres), the Southwest is coterminous with the Ukrainian S.S.R. (though in some classifications the region includes also Moldavia and the Rostov *oblast* of the R.S.F.S.R.). In the official Soviet pattern of economic regions, the Ukraine is divided into the Donets–Dnepr, Southwestern, and Southern regions. The Black Sea and the Sea of Azov are on the south, and it is through their ports that the Soviet Union maintains its trade with Asia, America, and southern Europe. The southern coast of the Crimean Peninsula and the area around Odessa are noted for their holiday resorts.

Forest–steppe and steppe occupy the greater part of the land area; both (but especially the latter) possess the fertile black-earth soil, which has attracted dense settlement from ancient times. The soils are almost entirely plowed to such crops as wheat, maize (corn), sugar beets, and sunflowers. There are also many orchards and vineyards there, especially in the Crimea, the southern coast of which forms the northern fringe of the subtropical zone.

Mineral resources of the Southwest

Topographically, the Southwest is predominantly a plain (though the western Ukraine contains a portion of the Carpathians, and the Crimean Mountains rise in the south). The plain is divided into right bank and left bank regions by the Dnepr, the republic's largest river, as it flows south to the Black Sea.

The Ukraine is rich in coal (the largest coalfield being the Donets Basin, or Donbass, which extends into the adjacent Rostov *oblast* of the R.S.F.S.R.), iron ore (the Krivoy Rog and Kerch deposits), manganese (the largest deposit in the world is at Nikopol), natural gas, and other mineral resources. Hydropower is also significant, chiefly on the Dnepr.

Covering but 3 percent of Soviet territory, the Southwest contains about one-fifth of the total Soviet population. Of the region's population, more than two-thirds live in urban areas. The largest Ukrainian cities are Kiev (the capital of the republic), Kharkov, Odessa, Dnepropetrovsk, and Donetsk. There are more than a dozen other cities with populations over 250,000, most of them in the Donets–Dnepr industrial zone.

The Urals. The Urals region contains the mountains that give it its name. These run southward from the Arctic shores to form the traditional boundary between Europe and Asia. The name is also given to the economic region. The region includes the Udmurt A.S.S.R. and five *oblasti* of the R.S.F.S.R., a total area of 260,000 square miles (680,000 square kilometres).

Divisions of the Urals

The Ural Mountains themselves consist of many medium ridges and rises, covered with forest. Customarily divided into the Polar, Nether-Polar, Northern, Central, and Southern Urals, they rise to a high point of 6,214 feet (1,894 metres). Natural features of the mountain region and the adjacent plains are unusually varied. The tundra and "alpine" peaks of the Polar and Nether-Polar Urals give way to the rolling taiga plains of the Northern Urals, while the fertile plowed steppes of the Central and Southern Urals are succeeded by the lake-dotted forest plains of the far (Siberian) side. The region is rich in minerals, notably metallic ores and precious and semiprecious stones. The Urals region has long played an outstanding role in the Russian economy because of its mineral wealth. In its industrial development it is surpassed only by central Russia and the Ukraine; it produces just under one-third of all Soviet iron, steel, and rolled steel. It is also a major petroleum-producing region and a base for the industrialization of the Soviet eastern regions.

The Central and Southern Urals are urbanized and contain such major industrial cities as Sverdlovsk and Chelyabinsk, metallurgical and chemical centres such as Magnitogorsk and Perm, and many settlements by mines, factories, and power stations. At the same time, old timber villages are to be found in the heart of the mountains. Most of the population is Russian, though there are many minority nationality groups, ranging from Tatars to the oldest inhabitants, the Komi-Permyaks.

The Caucasus. The Caucasus is the isthmus between the Black Sea and the Sea of Azov in the west and the Caspian Sea in the east. The northern boundary is the Kuma-Manych Depression, while the southern is the frontier with Turkey and Iran. The region is subdivided into the North Caucasus (predominantly plain), the Great Caucasus range, and Transcaucasia, containing the Kolkhida and Kura-Araks lowlands, the mountains of the Little Caucasus, and the Armenian Highland. The Caucasus is often alternatively divided (as it is in the formal Soviet classification of economic regions) into only two parts, the North Caucasus and Transcaucasia; the whole Caucasian sector of the Russian S.F.S.R. is included in the former, while Transcaucasia takes in the Georgian, Azerbaijan, and Armenian S.S.R.'s.

Extremes of the Caucasus landscape

The natural conditions of this comparatively small region (about 209,000 square miles [541,000 square kilometres]) are exceptionally varied, for it contains fertile steppe plains and high mountains covered with glaciers and snow (the highest point is Mt. Elbrus, at 18,510 feet [5,642 metres]); the hot and humid lowlands of Kolkhida and the dry steppes of the Kura-Araks; lava plateaus, alpine pastures, and forests on the mountain slopes of the humid west.

The Great Caucasus is an important natural boundary. North of it stretches the temperate zone of the Russian Plain, and to the south lie subtropical zones. A wide range of crops is cultivated.

The Caucasus has various minerals, notably petroleum, gas, copper, and manganese, which have contributed to the development of industry in several parts of the region. At the same time, the Caucasus is the main Soviet resort area, boasting a mild climate, warm seas, muds believed to be curative, and, most important of all, numerous mineral springs. The latter support such spas as Kavkazskiye and Mineralnye Vody in the northern foothills of the Great Caucasus, near which are the major resort towns of Kislovodsk, Yessentuki, Pyatigorsk, and Zheleznovodsk. On the Black Sea coast are numerous health and holiday resorts, of which Sochi is the largest in the Soviet Union. The Caucasus—especially around Mt. Elbrus—is also a major centre for hiking and mountaineering.

The Caucasus is unrivalled in the Soviet Union for the number of its nationalities; the Dagestan A.S.S.R. alone has at least 20 ethnic groups. More than half the total population lives in cities, the largest of which are Baku, Tbilisi, and Yerevan, the capitals, respectively, of the Azerbaijan, Georgian, and Armenian S.S.R.'s.

The Caucasus is the home of the most ancient cultures in the Soviet Union. Numerous architectural monuments of past centuries are found, and the ruins of temples and fortresses witness to the distant past. As a consequence of this great age and the region's ethnic diversity, several distinctive local cultures may be distinguished.

Central Asia. In the heart of Eurasia, stretching from the Caspian eastward to the Altai and from the Urals and Western Siberia southward to the frontiers with Iran, Afghanistan, and China, the region known as Central Asia and Kazakhstan covers 1,550,000 square miles (4,000,000 square kilometres). This is the Soviet Union's hottest and driest region, full of striking contrasts: immense plains, with desert and semidesert depressions below sea level; very high mountains permanently covered with snow and ice; and thickly populated oases surrounded by empty deserts.

Desert and semidesert

All the Soviet deserts and almost all the semideserts (occupying in all about one-seventh of the national area) are found here. To the south and east, the desert expanses are bordered by mountain ranges, culminating in the Pamirs and the Tien Shan. To the north of the desert belt, low hills and isolated mountain ridges—the Kazakh Uplands—extend for hundreds of miles in central Kazakhstan. Many of the hills are covered with pine forests, while semideserts predominate in the depressions. North again stretches the West Siberian Plain; the north Kazakhstan portion is a zone of forest–steppe and steppe, with black-earth and dark chestnut soils.

Central Asia. In the political, administrative, and economic sense (and in terms of natural history), the term Central Asia embraces, properly, the four Central Asian republics—Uzbekistan (including the Kara-Kalpak A.S.S.R.), Turkmenistan, Tadzhikistan, and Kirgiziya. These republics cover almost 6 percent of the total Soviet area. Apart from the four nationalities for which the union republics are named, Central Asia is now the home of Russians, Ukrainians, Tatars, Kazakhs, Uighurs, and other people who have settled there at various times.

Settlement in the Central Asian republics is almost entirely concentrated where irrigation potential is high, in a narrow belt between the desert plains and the mountains and also in the valleys of the major rivers. The rivers of Central Asia not only irrigate the fields (the area contains more than half of all Soviet irrigated land) but also, with the area's hydroelectric resources, serve as an important source of power. Oasis agriculture specializes in fruit, grapes, silk, vegetables, rice, and cotton and other fibre crops. Central Asia provides most of the cotton grown in the Soviet Union and much of its dried fruit and raw silk. The deserts and mountains are areas of natural pasture for sheep and lesser numbers of cattle, horses, camels, and—in the Pamirs—yaks. Central Asia is of importance as a supplier of petroleum, natural gas, mercury, antimony, iodine, bromine, and gold and rare metals. Engineering is mainly directed to the production of cotton-picking and textile machinery and oil and chemical equipment.

Cities of the Central Asian region

The largest cities and industrial centres are the capitals of the union republics—Tashkent, Frunze, Dushanbe, and Ashkhabad—and also the oldest city of Central Asia, Samarkand, which was an important place in the 4th century BC. These ancient lands are replete with traces of the great civilizations of the past and cherish distinctive contemporary ways of life.

Kazakhstan. Lying to the north, the Kazakh S.S.R., with an area of 1,050,000 square miles (2,700,000 square kilometres), is the second largest union republic and ranks third in population. Situated between the Urals, Siberia, and the Central Asian republics, Kazakhstan finds much of its geographical and economic character molded by those of its neighbours; cold Siberia and hot Central Asia, forest and desert, broad plains and great mountain ranges meet, as it were, in Kazakhstan. It also contains important deposits of iron, copper, lead, zinc, and rarer minerals, as well as coal, oil, phosphorites, and rare metals. Industry dominates the republic's economy, but its agricultural importance increased greatly during the 1950s, when nearly 100,000,000 acres (40,000,000 hectares) were brought into cultivation in north Kazakhstan and southwest Siberia under the Virgin and Idle Lands Campaign. As a result, Kazakhstan now produces more cereals than the Ukraine, ranking second only to the R.S.F.S.R. in this respect.

The indigenous people, the Kazakhs, constitute only about a third of the republican total; Kazakhstan is also the home of representatives of almost all the major peoples of the Soviet Union, including Russians, Ukrainians, Germans (deported from the Soviet west in 1941), Tatars, Uzbeks, Belorussians, Uighurs, Dungans, Koreans, and others. More than half of the population lives in towns and cities, of which the largest are the capital, Alma-Ata, and the industrial centre of Karaganda.

Siberia. Siberia (all of which is part of the Russian S.F.S.R.), the giant among Soviet regions, stretches 4,300 miles (7,000 kilometres) from the Urals in the west to the mountain ranges of the Pacific watershed in the east; from north to south it extends 2,200 miles (3,500 kilometres) from the shores of the Arctic Ocean to the dry steppes of Kazakhstan and the Mongolian frontier. It occupies an area of 2,500,000 square miles (6,550,000 square kilometres), or 30 percent of all Soviet territory. Siberia lies in the Arctic, sub-Arctic, and temperate climatic belts, and its climate is sharply continental. The outlying northern parts of the region are covered by tundra and forest-tundra, with the taiga zone occupying the greater part. In the south there are zones of forest–steppe and steppe, and it is here that settlement is thickest.

Economic resources of Siberia

Siberia contains up to 90 percent of Soviet coal resources, petroleum, about half the natural gas, 70 percent of the peat, and deposits of iron and polymetallic ores and minerals. Siberia has more than 50 percent of all Soviet hydropower resources, more than two-thirds of its timber, and 230,000 square miles (600,000 square kilometres) of arable and pasture lands. Its forests contain a wealth of furbearing animals.

With each five-year plan the population of Siberia increases, new towns are built, and production expands. The overwhelming majority of the people are Russians, who began to settle among the Ostyaks (Khants), Voguls (Mansis), Evenks, Buryats, Yakuts, Khakass, and other indigenous peoples in the late 16th century. There are several autonomous *oblasti* (regions) and autonomous (formerly national) *okruga* (districts) in which one of these peoples constitutes the chief element in the population.

Western Siberia. Western and Eastern Siberia—separated by the Yenisey River—may be differentiated (as they are in the official Soviet economic regional scheme) in respect of their physical geography and their degree of economic development. Three-fifths of Siberia's people live in the predominantly flat lands of Western Siberia (the West Siberian Plain), which cover 940,000 square miles (2,400,000 square kilometres). The greater part of Siberia's industrial and agricultural output comes from this region, the most important cities of which are Novosibirsk, Omsk, Novokuznetsk, and Barnaul.

Eastern Siberia. Eastern Siberia is predominantly plateau and mountain. It provides the country with diamonds, gold, aluminum, nickel, and other minerals, and its forests supply timber and furs. The world's largest hydropower stations are found on the Eastern Siberian rivers. The most important towns are Krasnoyarsk and Irkutsk.

The Far East. The Soviet Far East (which in some classifications is considered part of Siberia) stretches for 2,700 miles (4,300 kilometres) along the Pacific coast. It is composed of seven administrative entities: the Yakut A.S.S.R., the Primorye and Khabarovsk *kraya* (territories), and the Amur, Kamchatka, Magadan, and Sakhalin *oblasti.* Its area is 2,400,000 square miles (6,200,000 square kilometres).

The highest point—the Klyuchevskaya Volcano (15,584 feet [4,750 metres])—is less than 200 miles (320 kilometres) from the north end of the Kuril Trench, which at its lowest point is 34,586 feet (10,542 metres) deep. The Far East is mountainous: ridges, highlands, and plateaus are found in more than three-quarters of the region, and plains are found only between mountains and along the rivers and seacoasts. There are more than 250 volcanoes (almost 70 active) in the Kamchatka Peninsula and the Kuril Islands. The Far East is a source of gold, lead, tin, zinc, and other minerals. The customary power resources are here supplemented by the force of high ocean tides and heat generated by volcanoes and hot springs.

Most of the maritime region has a monsoon climate, with severe winters and cool summers. Because of abundant summer rainfall, the rivers, notably the Amur, are generally full. Landscapes are varied: in the north, tundra extends over large expanses; farther south lies taiga, giving way to broad-leaved forests. The Far East is second only to Siberia in its timber resources. In the south is a variety (and rare mingling) of southern and northern flora and fauna: lianas wind round the trunks of fir trees, and the northern deer meet the Siberian tigers.

Ethnic variety

Russians—who began to inhabit the region in the 17th century—constitute the majority of the population in the south. Next in numbers come Ukrainians, Belorussians, and Jews, and there is a great variety of very small indigenous population groups. Slightly more than three-quarters of the population lives in cities, the most important of which are Vladivostok, Khabarovsk, and Komsomolsk-na-Amure, the last named largely constructed by members of the All-Union Leninist Communist League of Youth, or Komsomol.

The Far East provides almost one-third of the total Soviet catch of fish and other seafoods and produces one-third of the canned fish. The region also takes a leading place in the extraction and smelting of ores, in the production of paper, and in the supply of timber. It is becoming of increasing importance as a base for Soviet exports.

SETTLEMENT PATTERNS

The mass of the Soviet population is concentrated in the so-called Main Belt of Settlement, which coincides with the main zone of grain production. Its base stretches along the western border from Leningrad to Moldavia; the northern edge of this belt passes through Cherepovets, Vologda, Kirov, and the north of the metallurgical and mining district of the Urals; the southern edge passes along the shores of the Black Sea and the Sea of Azov and then proceeds through Rostov-na-Donu, Volgograd, and Kuybyshev, to Chelyabinsk. Beyond the Urals the Main Belt of Settlement narrows, and to the east of Novosibirsk it becomes a narrow strip along the Trans-Siberian Railroad, spreading out only in a few places (in the Kuznetsk Basin, Minusinsk Basin, and elsewhere). This ribbon of denser population then stretches to the Pacific. To the south of this belt are important areas of denser population in Central Asia and the Caucasus.

Rural settlement. Of the total Soviet population, about 65 percent now lives in urban settlements. Before World War II more than two-thirds was still rural, but even then industrialization had brought about both a relative and an absolute reduction in the rural population. Rural dwellers were first outnumbered by urban in 1961, but, since urban settlements occupy only about 1 percent of the country's total area, it is rural forms of settlement that chiefly mold the character of the landscape visible to the transcontinental traveller.

Most of the rural settlements are connected with agricultural production. The remainder include small settlements at railway stations, at individual small mines, at centres of timber felling, at small or medium-sized processing enterprises, and also at resort settlements, inhabited localities at sanatoriums and hospitals sited in rural areas, and so on. Agricultural settlements are either old, formerly separate hamlets and villages whose inhabitants now work on collective farms, or the communities of state farms.

Collective and state farm structure

As a rule, each collective and state farm (respectively, *kolkhoz* and *sovkhoz*) has a central principal farmstead with its own settlement. At collective farms this is usually the largest (or the most conveniently sited) village in the area; at state farms, the largest farm settlement is the centre that houses machinery, fuel, and produce. These central settlements contain the collective farm board or the state farm directorate and such services as a club, one or more shops, a secondary school, clinics, and so on. Peripheral settlements contain primary schools, simple shopping facilities, and medical posts (without permanent staff) and the individual collective farm brigade (or state farm section) leadership.

Soviet Europe. In the Far North of Soviet Europe the rural population is very sparse, a reflection of the unfavourable environment. Tundra is used only as pasture for reindeer and as hunting and trapping grounds; fishing settlements are found along the rivers and the Arctic coast. The habitations (*stanovishcha*) are small in size. Several clusters of mining and port settlements have nevertheless sprung up, and railways (with their station settlements) have consequently reached these remote parts.

Farther south, in the northern taiga, the population is somewhat denser; agriculture acquires significance, and small villages of perhaps 100 inhabitants, centres of cleared patches of land, are strung along the fertile river valleys. Timber felling and occasionally timber processing are still the economic mainstays and have caused the creation of a great number of small settlements (populations 100–500) surrounded by felled areas; some of these lie along rivers (floating timber by raft to processing centres is common), others along railway lines and their timber-hauling (sometimes narrow-gauge) branch lines, or at ports.

In the middle belt of the European Russian S.F.S.R. (home of up to a quarter of the total Soviet rural population) settlement is still denser, and the landscape becomes one of continuous cultivation, with arable land comprising 30–60 percent of the total area; southward are fewer and fewer forests, and at about the latitude of Kuybyshev they survive as mere islets or strips of pine forest. Overlying the comparatively dense village network are strings of settlements at railway stations and also whole clusters of settlements at industrial enterprises situated outside the towns. Fairly evenly distributed medium and occasionally large villages nevertheless continue as the basic structure. From northwest to southeast there is a marked regularity in the increasing size of rural settlements, reflecting the growth in general density of the agricultural population and the associated fall in the proportion of uncultivable land. Historical circumstances—the widespread earlier distribution of large farms—were also important in the south. The predominant rural building material in this region (and also to the north of it) continues to be wood. From this, one-family houses and the necessary auxiliary structures are constructed. Apartment buildings of the modern urban type, however, are gradually appearing. The systematic enlargement of rural settlements—especially in the northwest, where villages average only 10–20 households—is an important precondition for spreading urban amenities and for raising the level of services, a process that, it is thought, requires an average settlement population of 1,500 to 3,000.

Taken together, the Ukraine, southern Belorussia, and Moldavia contain nearly 30 percent of the total Soviet rural population. The forms of population distribution—a close village network—are similar to those that have arisen in the middle belt of the R.S.F.S.R., but, reflecting greater densities, villages are generally larger and closer together. They are especially dense in the western Ukraine and in Moldavia. Nonagricultural rural settlements are mainly connected with processing agricultural raw materials, occasionally with mining, and also (on the seacoast, especially in the Crimea) with resort functions. In Belorussia and the northern Ukraine wood is still the major building material, but bricks, clay, and stone are used elsewhere; multifamily structures are spreading very rapidly.

Stanitsy and *auly*

Especially large rural settlements—Cossack villages, or *stanitsy,* numbering several thousand and sometimes 10,000–15,000 inhabitants—are typical of the plains of the North Caucasus; in the past these were Cossack communities guarding the southern frontiers. Villages are also large in the neighbouring Lower Volga region. The *auly,* settlements of the indigenous peoples in the foothills and mountains of the North Caucasus, are also quite large, their size depending on the economic capacity of the valleys in which they are situated. While the population distribution in the plains is fairly even, in the foothills and mountains it is in ribbons following the rivers flowing from the mountains. Population distribution has also been affected by the plowing up of steppe and by the building of irrigation systems linked to, for example, the Nevinnomyssky Kanal and the Volgo–Donskoy Kanal reservoirs.

In Transcaucasia, too, the rural population is distributed in generally large villages; their siting is largely determined by the terrain, and stone is widely used in construction. In the plains, villages are evenly distributed, locally reflecting aridity and irrigation patterns, while in areas characterized by ravines the villages keep to the valley roads, and surrounding valley land is intensively utilized for vineyards, tea plantations, and other crops. The Black Sea coast is marked by a string of health resorts.

Urals and Siberia. In the Urals and Siberia, including the Far East, where only one-eighth of the total rural population is to be found, population distribution in the Far North differs substantially from that in the more settled part of the Main Belt of Settlement adjoining the Trans-Siberian Railroad. In the Far North the population distribution is similar to that referred to above in the description of the European North, and the rural settlements are even smaller and more widely dispersed (mainly following the rivers). A greater proportion of settlements is connected with mines. Ordinary villages of the same type as those in the middle zone of the R.S.F.S.R. predominate within the boundaries of the Main Belt of Settlement; but they are more widely separated and, within them, houses are spaced farther apart, reflecting the large Siberian expanses.

The young rural settlements of Siberia

There are more young settlements here (particularly in the state farm communities of the steppes), and settlements connected with industry and transport are common. Farmsteads are virtually nonexistent; in the recent past small groups of farmsteads were traditional for the Yakuts, but in the Soviet period rural dwellers have been concentrated in settlements of medium size, where it is easier to provide public services and to direct the collective economy. Although the rural population is denser near the railways and large towns, only a fraction of the whole territory is intensively utilized, and cultivated areas are separated by large areas of taiga and forest–steppe.

Central Asia. In Central Asia and in southern and central Kazakhstan (rural settlement in north Kazakhstan is similar to that of southern Siberia) live about one-seventh of the Soviet rural population. The size and disposition of rural settlements are determined by the configuration and size of the areas used for agriculture, which are mainly irrigated.

*Qishlaq*s and *auly*

In the thickly populated oases, where water makes intensive farming possible, rural settlements (*qishlaq*s and *auly*) often are composed of several hundred households. The *qishlaq*s whose population is engaged in unirrigated agriculture or who specialize in livestock (raising Karakul sheep in the semideserts or raising free-ranging livestock in alpine and dry plain pastures) are much smaller. The appearance of *qishlaq*s is unique. The flat-roofed houses are built of raw bricks (occasionally of packed clay or reeds and clay); many of them have no windows onto the street,

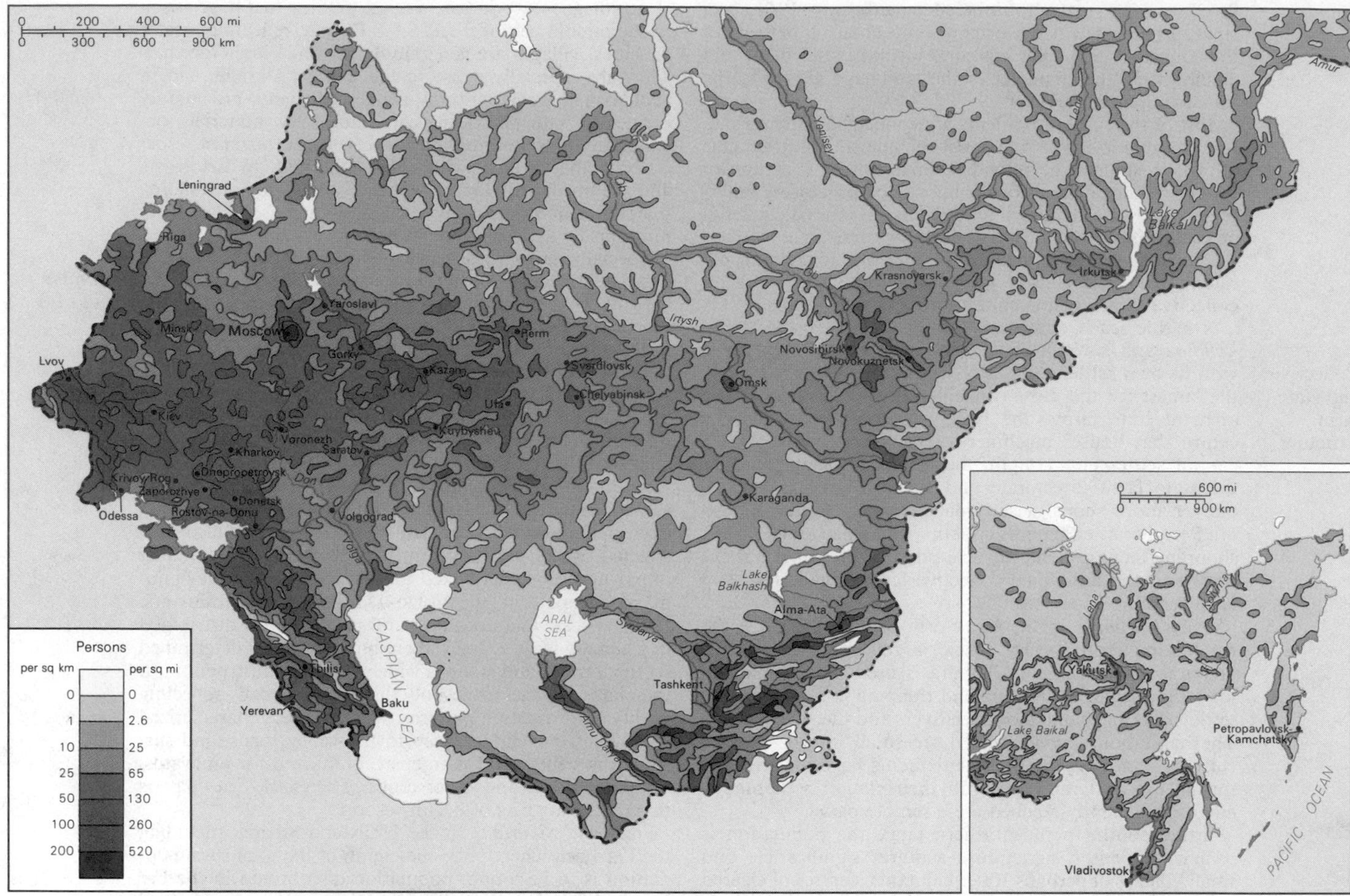

Population density of the Soviet Union.

but the inner courtyard, which gives way to the orchard, usually has an open platform with an awning that is a place for dining, welcoming guests, and so on. There is often a small pond in the courtyard. The walls surrounding the house are thick. Because of the packed clay construction and the absence of windows, a village street in this region looks like a narrow clay corridor. New building, however, is in the main made to follow standard plans, with single-family dwelling houses of European type. Public buildings are new, meeting modern technical requirements but taking note of national architectural motifs.

Urban settlement. More than three-quarters of the total urban population is to be found in a half dozen highly urbanized zones: (1) the Moscow region together with the adjacent cities on the Upper Volga from Kalinin through Yaroslavl and Kostroma to Gorky; (2) the zone stretching from Leningrad southwestward across the Baltic republics and into northern Belorussia, including Riga, Vilnius, Tallinn, Klaipėda, Kaliningrad, and the Belorussian cities of Minsk, Vitebsk, and Mogilyov; (3) the cluster of cities on the Donbass coalfield, where the urban population of two *oblasti*—Donetsk and Voroshilovgrad—totals nearly 7,000,000; (4) the cluster of cities around the Dnepr bend, with a total population of 4,000,000; (5) the Urals group of metallurgical and mining cities, notably Sverdlovsk, Chelyabinsk, Perm, Ufa, Nizhny Tagil, and Magnitogorsk; and (6) the cities of the Kuznetsk basin, including those in the Kemerovo *oblast* together with nearby Novosibirsk. The great bulk of the cities and towns therefore fall within the Main Belt of Settlement and the outlying population concentrations of Central Asia and Transcaucasia. Quite a few urban nuclei, however, including some of considerable size (*e.g.,* Murmansk, Arkhangelsk, Norilsk, Bratsk, and Komsomolsk-na-Amure in the north and Karaganda, Astrakhan, Orsk, and Semipalatinsk in the south), lie in isolated situations outside these zones.

The administrative centre of the *oblast* or the capital of the union or autonomous republic is nearly always the largest city—there are only isolated exceptions in the entire country. The fact that they are administrative centres attracts to these cities institutions of higher education, public bodies, associations, and so on, all of which contribute to increasing their population. Thus most of the largest cities combine many functions—productive, administrative, and social. Cities with only one predominant function rarely grow to considerable size. Smaller urban settlements may serve only one function (sometimes connected with a single enterprise—a mine or a fish-processing plant, for example). There are also smaller settlements that act as the centres of subordinate administrative units; they have several functions, housing the bodies concerned with administration and communications within the district and also serving the surrounding rural area, processing local raw material and producing consumer goods.

Role of administrative centres

The people

ETHNIC COMPOSITION

The Soviet population is composed of more than 100 distinct national groups. Soviet ethnographers and demographers generally consider it inaccurate to assign national-ethnic affiliation on the basis of mother tongue, since cases of persons using as their basic everyday language the language not of their own people but of the people among whom they live, though at the same time preserving awareness of their own national identity, are fairly common; according to the 1979 census, 6.9 percent of the Soviet people indicated the language of another nationality as their mother tongue. Accordingly, Soviet censuses establish nationality and mother tongue as separate and independent indexes (according to the awareness of the person interviewed, as he declares it). Provision is also made for the recording of any second language spoken fluently.

On the basis of ethnic territories occupied (and in most cases occupied since ancient times), the Soviet Union is composed of one Soviet Federated Socialist Republic (the

Russian), which includes 16 Autonomous Soviet Socialist republics, five autonomous *oblasti,* and 10 autonomous *okruga* (districts); and 14 Soviet Socialist republics, which include four A.S.S.R.'s and three A.O.'s. Yet the total of such entities does not coincide with the total number of Soviet nationalities; there is much overlap of one kind or another. The Dagestan A.S.S.R., for example, in the R.S.F.S.R., is inhabited by no fewer than 20 nationalities, within which are consolidated many smaller national groups. The ethnic diversity of the Soviet population is, however, officially recognized in the composition of these political entities.

The eponymous nationalities of (*i.e.,* those that give their name to) the union republics comprise 90 percent of the total Soviet population. The most numerous are Russians, followed by Ukrainians, Uzbeks, Belorussians, Kazakhs, and numerous other smaller groups of less than 2½ percent. Even smaller but still administratively distinct nationalities include the Nenets, who, scattered over huge tundra areas, are grouped in three autonomous districts. Nationalities without a distinct ethnic area and hence without administrative status include Koreans, Poles, Bulgarians, Greeks, and Gypsies.

It is Soviet practice to classify nationalities according to their affinity with language families and groups within families. The Slavic language group predominates: about three-quarters of the population speaks Slavic languages (not counting those who speak one of these languages fluently as a second language). Ability to speak Russian is necessary for career advancement for non-Russians. The Turkic language group, spoken by about one-eighth of the total population, ranks next in number of speakers.

Language families and groups

Since 1918, the official Soviet policy has been to eradicate religion, viewed by doctrinal Communism as the "opiate of the people." In that year, by decree, church and state were separated and all church property was confiscated. A church has no legal status, and believers who wish to have a place to worship must sign a contract with the local soviet, which has discretionary power to permit such use of a building. Private instruction in religion is hemmed round with restrictions.

Church membership

No official statistics on church membership or religious belief are published, but Western scholars have estimated that believers make up about 40 percent of the population of the Soviet Union; many of them, however, because of the official attitude, never attend services. The religionists include Russian Orthodox, Muslims (mainly Turkic peoples and some in the North Caucasus), Roman Catholics (chiefly Lithuanian), Eastern-rite Catholics (Ukrainians and Belorussians), Lutherans (Latvians and Estonians), Baptists, Jews, and Buddhists. The supreme catholicos of the worldwide Armenian Church resides in Echmiadzin, in the Armenian S.S.R.

DEMOGRAPHY

In the absence of large-scale immigration or emigration, the rate of growth of the Soviet population as a whole is attributable almost entirely to natural increase (*i.e.,* the excess of births over deaths). Regional population growth rates, however, are influenced not only by regional variations in the rate of natural increase but also by interregional migrations, which occur on a large scale.

Natural rates of increase. Social factors have had a considerable influence on the natural increase of the Soviet population. The most important factors have been a substantial decline in the average birth rate as a result of rapid urbanization (fertility is appreciably lower in the towns than among the rural population); the widespread employment of women, on the same terms as men, in nearly all branches of economic activity, including a rise in the percentage of trained female professional workers, which has also contributed to a fall in the birth rate; provision of state aid for mothers to assist them in the raising of children, which has tended to check birth rate decline; and, not least, a progressive rise in standards of health. This last factor has influenced the natural rate of increase in a number of ways: the decline in infant mortality has not only reduced the overall death rate but has also reduced the psychological "insurance" attained by giving birth to additional children and thus has tended to reduce the birth rate; in addition, reduced mortality at all ages and a subsequent increase in life expectancy have increased the proportion of the older, non-childbearing element in the population. The net result has been a long-term decline in both birth and death rates.

Birth rate

The Soviet demographic model was greatly distorted by the enormous population losses incurred during World War II. Direct losses, both in the ranks of the military forces and among the civilian population (especially in the Nazi-occupied territories), exceeded 20,000,000. If the indirect losses—fewer births than usual as well as greatly increased mortality associated with poor living conditions—are taken into account, then the total population deficit resulting from World War II may be put at approximately 50,000,000. These war losses greatly deformed the age and sex structure, with results still visible in the late 20th century. In addition, the accelerated decline in the birth rate that occurred during the 1960s was in part caused by the arrival at marriageable age of the small wartime generation.

The role of migration. Some of the results of the movement of population from rural areas to towns and cities are considered above in connection with the marked trend of urbanization (see above *Settlement patterns: Urban settlement*). The largest and most rapidly growing towns, including those at the sites of new construction projects, have attracted people not only from localities nearby but also from remote regions. Thus, country-to-town movement is accompanied by interregion and even interrepublican migration. The motive force in such a widespread redistribution of population is the creation of new jobs in economically developing regions; the state offers incentives (particularly in the Far North) to draw potential migrants to areas with manpower shortages. The regions that most attracted settlers in the late 20th century were, above all, Kazakhstan and Central Asia, where, although the natural local population growth is already high, several million migrants (mainly from the R.S.F.S.R.) settled. Migration also took place to the Baltic republics, where high economic potential brought about a shortage of manpower. The regions providing settlers were mainly the Volga–Vyatka region (where the numbers of emigrants almost reached the amount of the natural growth), the Black-Earth and Central Industrial regions, and Belorussia. In the Ukraine, internal movement was from the Southwest to the Donets–Dnepr area and to the South. The characteristic link between migratory influx and a higher level of natural growth and between efflux and a lower level of natural growth is explained by the fact that it is mainly young persons that migrate.

Regions of out-migration

The demographic outlook. Soviet scientists expect the population to reach 333,000,000 (±25,000,000) by the year 2000. The overall natural reproduction will probably be marked by a not very high birth rate, a very low death rate, and a moderate net growth. Life expectancy will rise to 80–85 years, and three-quarters of the population may be urban. According to published Soviet forecasts, by the time the total population rises to 300,000,000 there will be 205,000,000 town dwellers (almost 70 percent); moreover, almost one-quarter of the population will be concentrated in the largest cities (those with more than 500,000 inhabitants) and almost one-third in large cities (100,000–500,000 inhabitants). The most rapid growth is forecast for this last category. A redistribution of the population in certain regions—specifically, a growth in the share of the eastern and southern regions—may also be anticipated. In rural areas, the size of inhabited localities will continue to increase, while their numbers will be reduced; by the year 2000 the bulk of the remaining rural population will probably be concentrated in well-equipped settlements with populations of at least 1,500 to 3,000 and with living conditions close to those in towns. Such an abolition of the substantial differences between urban and rural settlements is, at least, one of the major long-term Soviet goals. (V.V.P./J.C.D.)

Moderate net growth

The economy

Although considerable economic development took place between the 1860s and World War I, the economy of tsarist Russia lagged behind those of the western European industrialized nations and the United States. Since the early 1920s, the economy of the Soviet Union has developed into the most powerful in the world after that of the United States. Since 1928 the course of economic development has been guided by a series of ambitious five-year plans.

The agricultural sector has become one of the world's principal sources of cereals and of a number of other farm, forestry, and fisheries products. Western specialists nevertheless regard the sector as relatively inefficient and underdeveloped, and Soviet authorities admit that they are far from satisfied with the level of some farms and some branches of agriculture.

Minerals and industry

In the world economy, however, the Soviet Union is more important for its mineral resources and industrial production. The country produces a very wide range of minerals and boasts huge reserves of coal, iron ore, copper, petroleum, and natural gas. Geography and climate make many of these reserves difficult to work, but the development of several new fields has placed the nation among the leading producers of iron ore, coal, oil, natural gas, and manganese. In the latter part of the 20th century, the value of Soviet industrial production was estimated to be second only to that of the United States. The country manufactures an immense range of products, although large quantities of technologically advanced equipment are imported from capitalist countries. The nation is also among the world's three top manufacturers of a large number of basic and heavy industrial products. As a result of historical factors that made emphasis on consumer industries a relatively recent development, however, it tends to lag behind in the output of light industrial products and consumer durables. One result of this has been that consumer demand is only partially satisfied and that the quality of the goods available is, in some cases, poor when judged by Western standards.

Despite a rapid increase in industrial investment in the past, productivity and industrial technology are still judged to be below the level of the most advanced capitalist countries.

Role in world trade

Judged in Western terms, the role played by the Soviet Union in world trade is considerably smaller than its economic strength would justify. It has been estimated that it exports only some 3 percent of its national production and accounts for about 4 percent of total world trade—figures that would be more than halved if its trade with other Communist countries were excluded. Although the country has extensive influence—heightened by its foreign-aid program—in some developing countries, the principal international effects of Soviet economic power are felt in the Communist world. The eastern European economies in particular are closely integrated with that of the Soviet Union, which is the source of more than two-thirds of their imports and accounts for an even larger share of their raw material purchases.

In spite of rapid economic development in the past—a process carried out against a scarcely propitious internal and external background—Soviet living standards in the late 20th century were lower than in some capitalist and certain Communist countries. Western economists estimate that the Soviet per capita national income puts the country somewhere between 20th and 30th place in the world. Soviet authorities aver that such a reckoning is somewhat misleading as it does not take into account the low rate of income tax, the low rents (generally about 5 percent of family income), and the provision of such free services as medicine and education.

RESOURCES

Mineral resources. The U.S.S.R. is abundantly supplied with mineral resources. Almost every commercially exploited mineral occurs somewhere in the country, and, for most, the deposits are large enough to supply the Soviet Union's requirements in the foreseeable future. The basic geological survey of the whole country has been completed since World War II, and intensive mineral prospecting is continuing throughout the U.S.S.R. There is every probability that further deposits will be discovered. Even in the event that certain minerals are relatively scarce, it must be remembered that such a handicap can be overcome by substitution of minerals that occur in quantity.

One of the most important of Soviet mineral resources is coal. The country's coal output is more than enough to meet domestic requirements, and large quantities are exported, mainly to nations of eastern Europe. Reserves are widely scattered, but about a third of total output comes from three main producing areas: the Donets Basin (Donbass) region; the Kuznetsk Basin region; and the scattered fields of the Urals. Other important coal-producing areas include Eastern Siberia, Karaganda and Ekibastuz in Kazakhstan (producing large quantities of coking coal), and the Pechora field in the Arctic, centred on the town of Vorkuta.

Donbass

The U.S.S.R. is one of the oldest oil-producing countries in the world. The largest producing area is the Volga–Urals region, which accounts for more than half of total production. Other important fields are situated at Baku in Azerbaijan, in the North Caucasus, and in Western Siberia.

Production of natural gas has increased even more rapidly than that of oil. The principal gas fields are situated in the Volga–Urals region, the Ukraine, Central Asia, the North Caucasus, and the West Siberian Plain. Shale oil is produced in relatively small quantities around Lake Peipus in Estonia and is also found in the Volga Valley and eastern Kazakhstan.

Ores for iron and steel

Soviet reserves of iron are estimated to account for about 40 percent of the world's total. Iron ore is mined in a number of different places, but a large percentage comes from two areas, the Ukraine (especially the fields at Krivoy Rog) and the Urals. Small quantities of ore are also derived from scattered sites elsewhere.

The Soviet Union is the world's leading producer of manganese, mined in two principal areas—Nikopol in the Ukraine and Chiatura in Transcaucasia. Output is more than adequate to meet domestic demand, and large quantities are exported, especially to eastern Europe but also to some Western countries. The Soviet Union has large reserves of ores of several other important components of steels, including nickel, cobalt, molybdenum, vanadium, tungsten, and, in the Urals, chromium (sufficient to allow substantial exports). There are also large copper resources in several parts of the country. The principal producer is Kazakhstan, but there are also important mines in parts of the Urals as well as in Uzbekistan and Armenia. The Soviet Union is not particularly rich in bauxite; there are several rather low-grade deposits in Asia (mainly in Kazakhstan) and in the European northwest. Aluminum production, while relying to some extent on imported bauxite (from the Balkans) and alumina (from Hungary), is chiefly supported by the use of alternative ores—nephelite from the Kola Peninsula, nephelite and alunite from Transcaucasia, and kaolinite from Central Asia. Titanium is produced in the Ukraine and in the Urals; and uranium is derived from Uzbekistan, Tadzhikistan, and Kirgiziya. The country is thought to be the world's second largest producer of gold, and a large number of other metals—including, among others, platinum, beryllium, niobium (columbium), and mercury—are also produced on a significant scale.

Ores for nonferrous metallurgy

Among nonmetallic minerals, there are large phosphate deposits at Kirovsk in the Kola Peninsula, at Karatau in Kazakhstan, in the Donbass, and around Moscow. Potash is mined in the Urals, and there are also a number of pyrite deposits. The Urals area also yields large quantities of asbestos (especially north of Sverdlovsk) and some graphite. Other important nonmetallic minerals include kaolin, mica, fluorspar, and salt.

Biological resources. Taking the vast expanse of Soviet territory as a whole, much of the soil is unsuitable for agriculture, and the climate—characterized by long, cold winters, poor water distribution, and much unpredictability in most parts of the country—is also adverse. The northernmost belt, stretching from the Kola Peninsula eastward toward Kamchatka, consists of economically unimportant barren tundra, where the subsoil is permanently frozen.

Timber resources

The northern part of European Russia, much of Western Siberia, and most of the area east of the Yenisey River is covered with forests (see above *The land: The natural landscape: Vegetation*). All in all, about 40 percent of the country's total land area is covered by forests. The Soviet Union is the world's leading timber producer, with Siberia and the Far East accounting for about one-third of the total output.

Agricultural activities are concentrated in an irregular and narrowing belt stretching from the Ukraine, Belorussia, and the Baltic lands toward Omsk, Karaganda, Novosibirsk, and Barnaul, and extending into Eastern Siberia. All in all, agricultural land accounts for 27 percent of Soviet land territory. Approximately 40 percent of the agricultural area consists of arable land; the remainder is made up of meadows and pastures.

AGRICULTURE AND FISHERIES

Contrary to the practice in several other Communist countries, farming in the Soviet Union is fully socialized, the two basic agricultural units being the collective and the state farm (*kolkhoz* and *sovkhoz,* respectively). The only obligation that the collective farm has is to meet a delivery quota. It makes its own decisions on profit sharing. Weak and unprofitable collectives are being amalgamated into larger collectives or turned into state farms. The collectives as a whole (which provide pasture and feed for the individual plots) concentrate, Soviet sources emphasize, on the production of grain and cotton, sugar beets, and related industrial crops.

State farms are owned and operated by the state, and their employees are paid a regular wage which is not usually significantly affected by their performance. Since the mid-1950s, the number and importance of state farms have progressively increased. Their size varies considerably, but on average they employ some 550 workers and have about three times as much farmland as the average for the collectives. State farms account for rather less than 50 percent of the output of most agricultural products, and in a number of cases (notably cotton, sugar beets, and sunflower seeds) their share is very much smaller than that of the collectives.

As in most other countries of the Communist bloc, agriculture, in the opinion of Western experts, has been the Achilles' heel of the Soviet economy. Growth in agriculture has not kept up with that of the rest of the economy. Among agriculture's principal problems have been the lack of adequate resources, the absence of effective material incentives, and the low level of earnings. Despite undoubted improvements, the farming sector is still relatively underdeveloped if compared with those of many other—including some Communist—countries. Soviet use of mineral fertilizers is still one of the lowest among the members of Comecon (the east European trade group), and agricultural machinery is still in short supply and, in some areas, relatively poor in quality. Notwithstanding a spectacular rise in productivity, labour is still inefficiently used, especially in the collectives. As a result, and as a consequence of poor climatic conditions, yields tend to be low. Productivity in livestock also leaves much to be desired; the difficulties here are aggravated by an almost permanent shortage of high-grade fodder.

Of the total crop area, about 60 percent is devoted to grain, nearly half of it sown to wheat. Fodder crops occupy another 30 percent, and the area devoted to industrial crops—mainly cotton, sugar beets, and sunflower seeds—constitutes only about 7 percent of the total.

The Soviet Union accounts for about 14 percent of the world fish catch.

INDUSTRY

Because of its wealth of mineral resources and its long-standing policy of giving priority to industrial development, the Soviet Union is among the world's foremost industrial powers. Although international comparisons of industrial production are always subject to qualifications, it is estimated that, in absolute terms, Soviet total industrial output is second only to that of the United States, and it exceeds that nation in production of some individual items. The country's industrial strength is also illustrated by its ranking as the second or third world producer of a wide range of important industrial products.

Although Soviet industry can claim a number of spectacular technical achievements in certain fields, including space exploration, it is still well behind the leading capitalist countries in terms of productivity and overall industrial technology. Several industries—including computers, metallurgy, chemicals, and engineering—rely on relatively unsophisticated and outdated equipment and are incapable of producing sufficient quantities of the more advanced products. While imports of advanced machinery account for a large share of total Soviet purchases from the West, sales of such products are insignificant in relative terms.

The industrial sector (including mining) contributes nearly two-thirds of the country's net material product and employs more than a third of the economically active population. Growth in this sector has been extremely rapid; among the developed countries only Japan recorded a better performance during the late 20th century. As a result of the past emphasis on heavy industry, however, production facilities in consumer goods are generally outdated and inadequate, and labour productivity is considerably lower than in most other branches of industry.

Within the capital goods sector, which makes up approximately three-quarters of total industrial production, the principal emphasis has been on the development of machinery building (defined as producing the means of production), metalworking (*i.e.,* using a semi-finished metal product such as plate or tube to make a component or finished product), metallurgy, and the chemical industry. Collectively these branches form the backbone of Soviet industry, accounting for about half the total industrial production.

Chemicals

In the pre- and early post-World War II periods, the chemical industry was one of the less well-developed branches of Soviet manufacturing industry. From the late 1950s onward, however, helped by the rapid growth in the production of oil and natural gas, particular attention was paid to this sector of manufacturing, and in the late 20th century it was a rapidly expanding branch. During the phase of most rapid expansion, the main emphasis was on ensuring an adequate supply of such basic chemicals as soda ash, sulfuric acid, caustic soda, and chemical fertilizers and on the establishment of large-scale artificial fibres and plastics industries. This growth was aided by heavy imports of Western equipment and technology, including a large number of complete plants.

Metallurgy

Since the beginning of the Soviet era, a strong metallurgical industry has been looked upon as one of the main preconditions of industrial growth and has, on the whole, been given priority in the allocation of investment funds. Its share of total capital spending, although subject to some recent limitations, has been significantly higher than its share of industrial output. Although the increase in both productivity and production has fallen well below the average for industry as a whole, output has managed to keep up with the growth of domestic demand, and steel, manganese, and a number of other metals are exported in substantial quantities. Other important manufacturing branches include the building materials, timber, woodworking, and paper industries.

The bulk of the country's industrial output comes from relatively large production units, and the average size of industrial plants is steadily increasing.

ENERGY

Throughout the Soviet period, the energy sector has been given high priority by economic planners; partly in response to Lenin's dictum that "Communism equals Soviet power, plus the electrification of the whole country," particular attention has been paid to the development of the electric power industry. Although hydroelectricity production has seen a rapid increase, its share of the total has declined from a peak of nearly 20 percent in the late 1950s. This change marks a realization of the greater returns obtainable from coal-, oil-, and gas-fired thermal stations in consuming areas and some lessening of the emphasis on grandiose hydroelectric projects in remote districts (though these continue to be built). The Soviet Union's first nuclear power plant came into operation in the mid-1960s, and several others were built, but their combined output remains a minor proportion of the total.

Oil and natural gas fuels

A major development in the energy sector since the mid-1950s has been a rapid growth in the production of oil and natural gas, which are now the leading fuels. Whereas in 1955 oil and gas accounted for only about a quarter and coal for some two-thirds of the country's energy supplies, by the late 20th century the contribution of coal was down to less than a third and that of oil and gas had reached 65 percent (the small balance came from such minor sources as peat, oil shale, and firewood).

The development of Soviet energy resources, particularly oil, gas, and hydroelectricity, has involved problems resulting from their highly uneven distribution and the great distances that separate resources from consuming areas. These difficulties are being attacked by a large program of oil and gas pipeline construction and the creation of an integrated electric power grid and by bringing the geographical pattern of demand nearer to that of supply.

FINANCE

Gosbank

As in other Socialist countries, the banking sector is owned and controlled by the state. This control is exercised through the powerful Gosbank (Gosudarstvenny Bank S.S.S.R., or State Bank of the U.S.S.R.), which not only fulfills most of the functions of a Western central bank but also acts as a clearing bank and is used as one of the principal instruments of control over state enterprises. It is responsible for note issue, for controlling the currency circulation, for foreign trade and other overseas transactions, and for executing the government's financial and credit policy. It administers tax receipts, pays out much of the state's current expenditure, monitors the performance of state enterprises, holds their accounts, handles their receipts and payments, and provides them with short-term credit.

A number of specialist transactions, however, are handled by other banking institutions, notably the Bank for Foreign Trade (called Vneshtorgbank, from Bank Dlya Vneshney Torgovli) and the Stroybank (Vsesoyuzny Bank Dlya Finansirovaniya Kapitalnykh Vlozheny, or All-Union Bank for the Financing of Capital Investments; the common name is derived from *stroytelstva,* "construction," which the bank finances), which is the source of much long-term credit to state enterprises and organizations. The most widely spread banking institution is the State Savings Bank (Sberegatelnye Kassy). It has branches distributed all over the country and provides a wide range of banking services to the general public, collectives, and other organizations. The Soviet Union also maintains a number of banks in the West.

TRADE

Although the Soviet Union's foreign trade increased in the late 20th century, the country is still a very small foreign trader in relation to its size and economic power. In value terms its exports and imports are small even when compared with that of other Communist countries. The country's rather poor showing in world trade is attributable in part to its wealth of mineral resources, which obviate the need for large purchases of raw materials, and in part to a marked lack of interest in specialization.

In effect, Soviet policy appears to be to attain virtual self-sufficiency in as many fields as possible and to use foreign trade as a means of making good some gaps that cannot otherwise be filled by domestic producers and to mitigate occasional shortages. As is the case in most other countries of the Communist bloc, great care is taken to maintain a balance between exports and imports or to earn a surplus.

In contrast to the healthy surplus maintained in most years in the Soviet Union's trade with Communist and developing countries, trade with several of the developed capitalist countries (*e.g.,* West Germany and the United States) has often yielded a deficit. This is covered by exports of gold, of which the Soviet Union is one of the world's leading producers.

Imports

In view of the country's abundant mineral resources, it is not surprising, as noted above, that raw material imports make up a relatively small part of its purchases abroad. About a third of these purchases are accounted for by a wide and growing range of machinery and equipment. The second largest import group is consumer products, followed by foodstuffs and ores, concentrates, and metal products. The composition of Soviet imports from the developed Western world is more than half accounted for by machinery and transport equipment items, while a further quarter is taken up by shipments of manufactures, especially iron and steel and textile yarns.

Principal exports

Nearly a quarter of the Soviet Union's export earnings is derived from sales of machinery and allied products, mainly to fellow Communist and some developing countries. The advanced Western world takes only a minute portion of the total. Much of Soviet machinery sales is made up of complete plants. Vehicles and transport equipment, communications equipment, lifting machinery, agricultural equipment, and a wide range of electrical machinery are also important. In second place come sales of metallic ores and concentrates, and fuel and electricity sales—mostly of oil and petroleum products—rank third.

The structure of Soviet sales to the West, however, differs sharply from the overall pattern. A large proportion of these is made up of inedible crude materials (hides and skins, textile fibres, metallic ores) and oil. Manufactured products account for about a quarter.

Overall, the Soviet Union is a net importer of machinery, consumer goods, and chemical products and a net exporter of fuels, ores and metals, and timber products. Exports and imports of foodstuffs are usually small and in most years cancel each other out. On a number of occasions in the late 20th century, however, large imports of grain were necessary to offset poor harvests at home.

(E.I.U./J.C.D.)

TRANSPORTATION

In a country the size of the Soviet Union—where great distances separate industrial resources from manufacturing centres and manufacturing centres from markets—transport costs, both capital and recurrent, assume a much greater scale and significance than they do in smaller geographic entities. This is particularly so where heavy industry has received priority and requires the movement of enormous quantities of bulky materials over long distances; in addition, long-distance movement of foodstuffs, particularly grain, takes place on a very large scale. It is not surprising, therefore, that the development of the Soviet economy has involved a vast increase in the volume of freight movement and, to a lesser extent, of passenger travel. The various transport media have been developed as a single coordinated system, avoiding the competition between various modes of transport that occurs in the capitalist world.

Rail transport. Though it is declining, first place in volume of operations is still taken by rail transport; the explanation for this is the country's immense overland expanses and the spread of the principal production zone over several thousand miles from west to east. Only rail transport can effect long-distance mass carriage of freight and passengers all the year and this despite the severe climatic conditions of the eastern and northern regions.

The total length of the rail network has roughly doubled during the Soviet period. Railway construction in the European sector has been mainly confined to rebuilding old lines and building shortcuts to reduce the length of many of the more circuitous routes between the cities of the European plain; the only completely new route is the Vorkuta–Kotlas line, constructed in the 1940s to provide an outlet for the Pechora coalfield. Most of the new routes built since the Revolution are to be found in the economically expanding middle zone of the country, embracing the Volga, Urals, West Siberian Plain, Kazakhstan, and Central Asian regions. In this zone, the Novosibirsk–Novokuznetsk main line linked the main Trans-Siberian line with the Kuzbass; the Artyshta–Barnaul–Tselinograd–Magnitogorsk line linked the Kuzbass with the Urals via north Kazakhstan; the Petropavlovsk–Karaganda–Chu line linked the Trans-Siberian with the Central Asian system, while the latter was drawn together by the completion of the Turkistan–Siberia (Turksib) route from Kransnovodsk on the Caspian via Tashkent, Alma-

Ata, and Semipalatinsk to Barnaul. The busiest and most important main lines have been reconstructed, notably the Moscow–Donbass, Moscow–Sverdlovsk, Yaroslavl–Arkhangelsk, and Chelyabinsk–Vladivostok sections. The largest single project constructed in the late 20th century was the Baikal–Amur Mainline, linking existing railheads at Bratsk and Komsomolsk-na-Amure. Running about 250 miles (400 kilometres) north of the Trans-Siberian line for a distance of some 2,000 miles (3,200 kilometres), this line was designed to tap a variety of new industrial resources in Eastern Siberia and the Far East. It was also intended to lessen reliance on the Trans-Siberian line, which, over much of its length, runs very close to the border with China.

Railway modernization

Traffic on many sections of the Soviet railway system is the heaviest in the world, and the growth of traffic during the 1960s necessitated the replacement of steam by diesel and electric traction, along with other technological improvements. Several major routes were electrified, notably those from Moscow to Leningrad, the Donbass, northern Ukraine, Caucasus, and Urals, together with the Trans-Siberian as far as Irkutsk. Virtually all other lines are operated by diesel locomotives.

Sea transport. Sea transport plays an increasingly important role. In addition to its dominance in Soviet foreign trade, sea traffic is of considerable importance in freight movement between the various regions, particularly where, as in northern Siberia and much of the Far East, no alternative form of communication is available. The great length (30,000 miles [48,000 kilometres]) of the Soviet coastline favours this, though the winter freeze in northern regions limits its growth potential.

First place in internal traffic volume is taken by the Caspian and Black Sea–Sea of Azov basins, followed by the Far Eastern, Baltic, and Arctic basins. The northern sea route, through the seas of the Arctic and Pacific oceans, has, since 1935, played an important role in ensuring regular communications between regions of the European North and Siberia and the Far East.

Foreign traffic nevertheless predominates, with a well-equipped Soviet merchant fleet. The main emphasis in technological development in the Soviet fleet is toward containerization of freight and expansion of regular freight and passenger line services.

Transport by inland waterways. Inland waterways are an important component part of the unified system. The majority of waterways (of which about a fifth are artificial) lie off the main lines of communication, a factor that helps to explain the relatively small percentage of river freight traffic. But wherever the river networks coincide with the main transport routes or wherever other forms of transport are insufficiently developed, the proportion of inland waterways traffic increases. The Volga area, the northwest of Soviet Europe, the Far East, and Eastern Siberia are such regions.

Most of the freight carried is oil, timber, and bulk materials such as stone, gravel, ores, coal, and grain. More than half the freight is carried on the rivers of the Volga–Kama Basin. Other important areas are the Northern Dvina, Dnepr, and Don in the European part of the country; the Ob and Irtysh, Yenisey and Angara, Lena, and Amur and its tributaries in Siberia and the Far East, and the Amu Darya in Central Asia.

The most important navigation canals are the Moskovsky Kanal (a short but vital link between the Moskva and Volga rivers), the Volgo--Donskoy Kanal, the White Sea–Baltic Waterway, and the Volga--Baltic Waterway (a system of canals linking the Baltic Basin and the Volga).

Pipelines. One of the most economic forms of transport, pipelines, became of major importance only after World War II. The oil pipeline network is most highly developed in the European Soviet Union and the Caucasus. Oil is carried from the Volga–Urals field to the major cities of the European plain, to exporting ports on the Baltic and Black seas, and, via the Druzhba (Friendship) pipeline, to the Communist countries of eastern Europe as well as to West Germany, France, and Italy. A major oil pipeline from the Volga–Urals region (Tuymazy–Omsk–Angarsk) traverses Siberia; lines from the Tyumen oil field of Western Siberia connect to the trans-Siberian pipeline, which then pumps Siberian oil westward as well as eastward. Oil pipelines also connect the Mangyshlak field of eastern Kazakhstan with the European system and carry oil from Sakhalin to Komsomolsk-na-Amure.

Oil pipelines

The first big gas pipeline, running 524 miles (843 kilometres) from Saratov on the Volga to Moscow, began to function in 1947. Since then an extensive system has been laid in the western part of the Soviet Union carrying gas from the Ukraine, Caucasus, and Central Asia to the Central Industrial region, the Urals, and other industrial zones.

Road transport. Road transport, second only to that of the railways, is limited largely to movements over relatively short distances.

The densest network of improved roads is in the Baltic region, the western Ukraine, the Crimea, Transcaucasia, and the region around Moscow. The oil field areas of Tatariya and Bashkiriya are also well provided with hard-surfaced roads. On the whole, the European part of the country is better provided with roads than the east. In Siberia and the Far East, roads are the main means of communication in a number of areas remote from railways.

Bus services

In the towns, buses account for about 40 percent of all passenger transport. The greatest use of buses is in the suburban zones of Moscow and Leningrad.

Air transport. Air transport is most widely used for passenger movement. Internal airline routes reach more than 3,500 towns and inhabited localities. Air travel is very popular as the fastest form of transport over the country's immense distances. Soviet international air routes link the nation with countries in Europe, Asia, Africa, and America; Soviet air transport, by volume of traffic, accounts for more than 25 percent of the world total.

Urban passenger transport. Electric systems for the conveyance of passengers in urban areas are of major importance and include both tram services and trolley bus services. Five great cities—Moscow, Leningrad, Kiev, Tbilisi, and Baku—have underground railway systems.

(V.N.D./J.C.D.)

MANAGEMENT OF THE ECONOMY

The role of government. In this, the prototype Communist economy, the government's role is all-important. Industry and most service trades are owned and controlled by the state, and agriculture is in the hands of the collective and state farms. In effect, there is no private sector; in the countryside, private enterprise is tolerated only in respect of farmers' small individual plots, while in other sectors of the economy only artists, a few artisans, etc., can earn a living without being formally employed by the state.

This means that the government is in full control of the economy. It formulates economic policy, prepares long- and short-term plans, lays down a large number of detailed targets, controls investment, determines wages and incomes, and fixes the prices of most commodities and products. It is in control of foreign and internal trade, banking, and almost every other branch and sector of the economy.

The structure of state planning

Under the system the top planning position is occupied by Gosplan (Gosudarstvenny Planovy Komitet, or State Planning Committee), the authority of which extends right down the line through a number of regional Gosplans. Detailed control over industrial activities is exercised by all-union ministries and ministries of the union republics, which look after industries of national significance. There are also some republican ministries that control local industries and certain construction activities. In addition, there are a number of state committees, the most important of which are the State Committee for Science and Technology and the State Committee for Material and Technical Supplies. The latter works through regional supply authorities and shares the task of material and resource allocation with Gosplan. There is also a State Committee for Prices, but this comes under Gosplan rather than under the Council of Ministers. Agriculture is the responsibility of the Ministry of Agriculture, while credit, finance, banking, and foreign exchange are under the control of the Ministry of Finance and the Gosbank.

At the top of the planning mechanism is the Council of Ministers, determining the broad lines of economic policy and the principal plan priorities. These guidelines are passed down to Gosplan, which is charged with incorporating them into a fairly detailed draft plan, setting out the principal tasks for the various sectors and branches of the economy. The plan is then passed on to the appropriate ministries, the local Gosplans, and other regional authorities, where—after extensive consultations with individual enterprises—more detail is added. The draft plan, suitably embellished, then goes back to Gosplan, which—after the necessary checking, coordination, and balancing—works out a detailed program. This is then submitted to the Council of Ministers and thence, after amendments, to the Supreme Soviet. After any further amendments, it becomes the all-important official current plan.

Taxation. The two most important taxes are the turnover tax and the tax or levy handed over to the government by state enterprises. The latter is made up of the difference between the enterprises' profits and the amount they are allowed to keep, as well as a charge on their capital assets. Turnover tax is collected at the factory or the wholesale distribution centre and is levied on a wide range of consumer goods.

Turnover tax

Among other taxes, the most important group covers direct levies on the general public. Most of the amount raised in this way is derived from income tax, which is payable on incomes in excess of roughly two-thirds of the average wage. Another direct levy is the tax imposed on collective farmers in respect of the area of their private plots. The rate of this tax is fairly low but is increased by a significant margin if the farmer fails to reach a stated work-day quota in the collective. This regulation is designed to ensure that farmers do not neglect their work in the collective in favour of their private activities.

(E.I.U./J.C.D.)

Administrative and social conditions

GOVERNMENT

In view of the domination exercised over political, economic, social, and cultural life in the Soviet Union by the ruling, monopolistic Communist Party, constitutions and other legal documents are subordinate to the policies of the party and its leadership, centred in the Politburo. The party, however, desires to project an aura of constitutional legitimacy. Hence, it is important that finally, after many years of a somewhat shadowy existence, the Constitutional Commission, appointed in 1962, produced in May 1977 a draft of a new constitution, which, after several months of well-organized discussion in the controlled press, was enacted unanimously into law by the Supreme Soviet in October 1977.

Comparison of the Stalin Constitution—as the "fundamental law" enacted in 1936 was usually called by the Soviet communications media—and the constitution of 1977 reveals no essential changes. The new document is far longer than the old one and in some ways more candid. It much more openly proclaims the ruling and all-penetrating role of the Communist Party of the Soviet Union (CPSU; Kommunisticheskaya Partiya Sovetskogo Soyuza), for example, describing it (Article 6) as "the nucleus of [the] political system." It describes more fully the various legal rights of citizens than did its predecessor. In emphasizing that all rights are accorded by the authorities in return for exemplary performance of duties, however, it in effect limits the rights of citizens more severely than did even the Stalin Constitution.

The fundamental point, however, is that, to a far greater extent than is the case in Western democracies, the Soviet constitution of 1977, like that of 1936, will have meaning only to the extent that the leadership desires and allows it.

The economic foundations. The economic life of the Soviet Union and all other aspects of social activity are dominated by the CPSU. Its Politburo determines economic policy and sees to it that its decisions are enforced by the Soviet government. The CPSU penetrates and guides the government by a system of interlocking membership of party and governmental executive bodies and by many other means. The Soviet economy is held to be "socialist" because its basic principle is state ownership, established by Lenin in 1918 insofar as the main elements (industry, transport, finance, etc.) were concerned and extended by Stalin to agriculture, which Lenin had for pragmatic reasons left largely in the hands of smallholder peasants. Despite state domination of the Soviet economy, not all property is directly administered by state agencies. The state owns and administers land, minerals, water resources, forests, industrial enterprises, banks, large state agricultural enterprises (known as *sovkhozy,* or state farms), means of transport and communication, municipal enterprises, and basic housing funds. In addition to state property, there are two other kinds of property in the Soviet Union, namely cooperative property, predominant in agriculture, and personal property. Most farmers are members of cooperative, or collective, farms, known as *kolkhozy.* Nominally, the land farmed by the collective farmers is assigned to them in perpetuity, but, as is indicated by government-ordered consolidations of collective farms into larger units since the late 1950s, the collective farms in fact exercise whatever control they have over their land within a framework of policies determined by the political authorities.

Ownership of property

As for personal property, it includes articles of clothing, household objects, electronic goods, automobiles (in the case of citizens who can afford them, at prices several times higher than in the West, and only after waiting several years), and many other types of goods, including (again for upper-income persons) country cottages, or dachas. Soviet inheritance law with respect to personal property is fairly liberal.

Social and political aspects. According to offical doctrine, there are two "friendly" classes in Soviet society, the working class and the collective farm peasantry. There is also a rapidly growing "stratum," the intelligentsia, which, Western observers agree, is by far the most privileged of the three. This does not mean that all members of the intelligentsia are better off than the workers or even, perhaps, than the peasants. Highly skilled workers earn considerably more than the more poorly paid members of the intelligentsia, which roughly corresponds to the professional classes in Great Britain or America. However, the highest ranking writers, scientists, and other professionals are, next to highly placed party and state bureaucrats, the most privileged of Soviet citizens.

As implied by the official slogan, "From each according to his ability, to each according to his work," Soviet society is not egalitarian. However, there is a considerable degree of equality of opportunity. Generally, life is very competitive, and the unofficial guiding principle of distribution of rewards might be described as that of the career open to talents. This is modified by the requirement that to achieve success a person must be not only professionally competent but also politically reliable.

The CPSU dominates the political life of the country. The party rules through the formal structures of government, which include the pyramid of soviets ("councils") extending down from the Supreme Soviet of the U.S.S.R. to village soviets, and the system of ministries, headed by the Moscow-centred Council of Ministers and extending down to local representatives of ministries. Nominally, the deputies and presiding officers of the soviets at all levels are elected, but there is only one candidate for any office in those elections, and the selection of candidates is controlled by the CPSU. Party, soviet, and ministerial posts—as well as other positions of influence and power—are allocated in accordance with a "nomenclature" (*nomenklatura*) system, which is operated by the central authorities of the CPSU.

Soviets

The federal structure. The Soviet Union, in fact a highly centralized state, is nominally a federal republic. Its federal aspect derives from the fact that it consists of 15 theoretically equal republics, each of which has equal representation in the Soviet of Nationalities, the upper chamber of the bicameral Supreme Soviet, the national legislature. The republics, as well as lower ranking autonomous republics, autonomous regions, and autonomous (formerly national) districts, constitute a means by which symbolic political representation is granted to the numerous ethnic groups of which the Soviet Union is composed. All of the people of the Soviet Union, however, share common federal citizenship. Federal laws have equal force in the territories of the union republics. The federal legislature, under the guidance of the CPSU and the State Planning Committee (Gosplan), determines the federal budget, which includes the budgets of the union republics. Thus the central government in Moscow dominates the economics of the union republics.

This dominance by Moscow is fortified by features of the Soviet system more fundamental than constitutional provisions. Perhaps the most important instrument of central control is the hierarchical, centralized structure of the CPSU. Party headquarters in Moscow, through its centralized control over personnel assignments, can appoint, promote, demote, or transfer even the heads of the party organizations of republics.

The tight control exercised by the Moscow leadership over local economic, political, and cultural life engenders keen resentment among many members of the non-Russian minority nationalities residing in the republics that are named for them. Resistance to Moscow's control has been manifested in a variety of ways; at its mildest it takes the form of anti-Russian jokes and other innocuous verbal behaviour (though even these have at times been punished harshly) or—as after Soviet conquest of the western Ukraine as a consequence of the Nazi–Soviet pact of 1939 and Soviet victory over Germany in 1945—it may be manifested in sanguinary guerrilla warfare. Needless to say, the right of secession from the Soviet Union granted by the constitution (both that of 1936 and that of 1977) has never been exercised. Indeed, any suggestion of dissatisfaction with Moscow's rule on the part of members of non-Russian nationalities is usually regarded as grounds for the imposition of draconian penalties. Of all of the many forms of dissent or opposition to Soviet rule with which the Soviet authorities have had to contend over the years, nationality dissent has aroused the deepest anger and has been punished most severely.

Resistance to Moscow

Organs of state power and government. *The Supreme Soviet.* Formally, the Supreme Soviet is the highest organ of state power in the Soviet Union. In keeping with this status, affirmed in the constitution, only the Supreme Soviet can make laws for the entire country. In practice, however, the Supreme Soviet enacts only such legislation as has already been initiated by the CPSU; this is indicated by the fact that the CPSU Central Committee meets before the Supreme Soviet does and lays down the policies that are subsequently endorsed by the latter. It is also clear that the Council of Ministers, nominally appointed by the Supreme Soviet, is in fact a more powerful body than the latter. Despite its limitations, however, the Supreme Soviet is an important body. Its legislative commissions, each of which specializes in a given field of legislation, have been playing an increasingly larger role in bringing to bear on the legislative process the expert knowledge of lawyers, economists, and other kinds of specialists. Thus the competence of the Supreme Soviet to perform its legislative functions has increased. Certainly the Supreme Soviet is not the mere rubber stamp it was in the Stalin era, as is indicated by the increased regularity with which it has met since Stalin's death and by the increased length of its sessions, which, however, are still extremely short by Western standards.

Role of the CPSU

Nonetheless, the Supreme Soviet is far from being a parliament of the Western democratic type. Among the many striking differences, for example, is the fact that in the Supreme Soviet all legislation, including crucially important budgetary legislation, passes unanimously. Quite apart from this, and from the unfailing correspondence between CPSU directives and Supreme Soviet legislation, much law is made, despite the apparent lack of constitutionality, by governmental bodies other than the Supreme Soviet, such as the Council of Ministers. There are even many secret laws, not passed by and unknown to the Supreme Soviet.

In form, the Supreme Soviet is bicameral. Members of both chambers are elected (in one-party, one-candidate elections) for four-year terms. One chamber, called the Soviet of the Union, represents, with one deputy for every 300,000 inhabitants, constituents regardless of national origin. The other chamber, the Soviet of Nationalities, is so organized as to take at least symbolic account of the multinational composition of the Soviet population; it has 32 deputies from each of the 15 union republics and for the lower units, designated in descending order as autonomous republics, autonomous regions (*oblasti*), and autonomous districts (*okruga*), respectively 11, five, and one each. The Supreme Soviet normally assembles for regular sessions twice a year. It passes all legislation introduced by its leading members (who are also leading members of the CPSU) unanimously and expeditiously. It sometimes holds special sessions.

The two chambers

The Presidium of the Supreme Soviet. The Presidium of the Supreme Soviet has 37 members, elected by the Supreme Soviet itself and, like the parent body, serving for four years. Between sessions of the Supreme Soviet, which last for only about a week, the Presidium acts for it, performing such functions as convening and dissolving the Supreme Soviet, receiving ambassadors of foreign states, selecting and recalling Soviet diplomats, removing and appointing ministers, instituting and awarding honorary titles, etc. It may also order mobilization of the armed forces and may declare war.

It is obvious that the Presidium is a more powerful body than the Supreme Soviet, although probably somewhat less powerful than the Council of Ministers, which it appoints, and vastly less powerful than the Politburo and Central Committee of the CPSU. Of the 37 members of the Presidium, only its chairman is normally a major party leader and a significant national political figure. Fifteen vice chairmen, one from each of the union republics, serve under the chairman of the Presidium, symbolizing the nominally federal structure of the Soviet state. There are 20 additional members and a secretary.

Both the Supreme Soviet and its Presidium symbolize but do not really exercise power. They legitimize the power of the real ruling force in the Soviet polity, the CPSU. The Presidium also provides an instrument through which the CPSU can deal with foreign states in a manner more understandable and acceptable to the latter than direct transactions with the party would be. With regard to very important business, however—such as negotiations in the area of arms control—the general secretary of the CPSU has dealt with presidents of the United States, dramatically displaying the superordination of party to state in the Soviet Union.

The Council of Ministers. Nominally subordinate to the Supreme Soviet and, between Supreme Soviet sessions, to its Presidium, the Council of Ministers is in fact the most important governmental and administrative agency in the country; in fact, it is designated in the constitution as the "government" of the Soviet Union. According to the constitution, the decrees and ordinances issued by the Council of Ministers must conform to law as promulgated by the Supreme Soviet, but the Supreme Soviet has never overruled any decree of the Council of Ministers. This is not really surprising, since both bodies are dominated by the most powerful leaders of the CPSU.

Ministries

Working under the direction of the council are ministries of two kinds, the extremely centralized all-union ministries and the slightly less centralized union republican ministries, so-called because in addition to their Moscow headquarters they have local headquarters in the capitals of the union republics. In addition, there are under the council various state committees and special agencies, some of which wield enormous power; one of these is the Committee of State Security (KGB), which controls the Soviet political police and is probably, with the exception of the CPSU itself and perhaps the regular armed forces, the most powerful organization in the country. Both the state committees and the special agencies have ministerial status.

Republican and local state organs. The political structure of republics and autonomous republics is almost identical to that of the country. To a somewhat lesser degree this is also true in the local administrative subdivisions, which are called, respectively, *kray* ("territory," very large in area), *oblast* (variously translated into English as "region," "province," etc.), *okrug,* and *rayon;* the last two subdivisions (both translated as "district") may be either rural or urban in character.

The essential element in this system of units is its hierarchical, pyramidal character; the whole constitutes a unified structure. There is no counterpart in the Soviet system to the independent unit of local government such as the American state, county, or city government, each with lawmaking and taxing powers.

The union republics have their own supreme soviets, but they are unicameral rather than bicameral like the Supreme Soviet. Like the federal Supreme Soviet, the supreme soviets of the repblics (both union and autonomous) are elected for five-year terms; *oblast* and *rayon* soviets are elected for two and a half years. The soviets elect executive committees, in whose hands most of their power is concentrated. As at all levels of the system, CPSU groups in the local soviets see to it that these bodies carry out party policy.

It is possible that the highly developed "mass participation" in the working of this vast machine affords some satisfaction to some citizens. Official sources, such as speeches by party leaders, and a steady stream of articles on socialist democracy in the controlled press assert that the participation of citizens in local government constitutes a special advantage of the Soviet political system. It is impossible, because of official secrecy, either to confirm or refute such claims by direct investigation, but enough is known about the reality of political life in the Soviet Union to cast doubt on them. It is clear that participation is so hedged about with controls and limits that for most of its alleged beneficiaries it must be more a burden than a privilege.

The electoral system. Little needs to be said about Soviet one-party, one-candidate elections. They are so carefully managed that the official candidates—who are said to represent the bloc of party and nonparty voters—invariably receive virtually 100 percent of all possible votes. All citizens 18 years of age or older may vote, except for the certified insane and criminals confined by court sentence. In fact, voting, though not formally compulsory, is obviously regarded by the authorities as the duty of all citizens; enormous pressure and great fanfare are resorted to in getting people to vote.

The judicial system. The Soviet judicial system is highly centralized, hierarchical, and subject to supervision and control by the CPSU. Although far less arbitrary and coercive than it was under Stalin (whose police officials arrested, deported, and did to death millions of persons without anything remotely resembling due process of law), today's system is, by Western and especially by Anglo-American standards, exceedingly defective. There is no equivalent of habeas corpus, no trial by jury, no presumption of innocence, no real independence of the judiciary from ideological and political pressures. Indeed, judges, prosecutors, attorneys, and all others involved in dispensing justice are required to propagate CPSU policy in the judicial field.

Political crimes

Moreover, although the Soviet authorities deny the existence of political crimes in the Soviet Union, they obviously do exist and are dealt with by very special, severe methods. The criminal code of the Russian Soviet Federated Socialist Republic, largest of the 15 union republics, contains provisions for prosecuting "especially dangerous state crimes" that are clearly political in nature; there are parallel provisions in the codes of the other republics. Loosely drafted, catchall statutes in effect make any publicly expressed criticism of official policy or ideology a crime. Thus, circulating or even having in one's possession written statements that "slander" the state or social system is punishable by long terms in concentration camps, euphemistically described as corrective labour camps. In several important categories of cases, judicial investigation is carried out not by the regular prosecutors but by officials of the security police (KGB). Outside the political sphere there is a system of courts, prosecutors, and attorneys that functions fairly well, subject to the limitations referred to above. In evaluating this system, however, it is necessary to bear in mind that it is subject to CPSU policies, which can change arbitrarily from time to time.

At the apex of the system is the Supreme Court of the U.S.S.R., whose judges are appointed by the Supreme Soviet. Below the Supreme Court (the only national court, apart from military tribunals) stand supreme courts of the union and autonomous republics, provincial, territorial, and city courts, courts of autonomous regions and national areas, and, at the lowest level, the people's courts, the last of which try the overwhelming bulk of all cases. The members of people's courts include a professional judge, who is elected, and two lay "assessors," who theoretically represent the people in the administration of justice at this level. Another so-called popular feature of the people's courts is the openness of their proceedings, though this is restricted in cases involving state security or intimate personal or family matters. Judges at the levels higher than the people's courts are legally trained professionals, appointed rather than elected. There is no institution of judicial review in the Soviet Union, though there is a well-developed system of appealing the verdicts of lower to higher courts.

An important role is played in Soviet justice by the institution of the procuracy. The procurator general of the U.S.S.R. is appointed for a seven-year, renewable term. He in turn appoints lower level procurators for five-year terms. The system of procurators has two main functions. The most unusual of these, in terms of U.S. practice, is supervision of the actions of government officials, with a view to preventing and if necessary prosecuting illegal actions taken by officials. The procurators also conduct criminal investigation and prosecute accused thieves, embezzlers, counterfeiters, and other violators of law. To be sure, prosecution of violators of certain Soviet laws (for example, that of "speculators" for engaging in private trade or other types of prohibited economic activity) is unfamiliar to Westerners.

The armed forces. In the Soviet Union military service is compulsory for all male citizens: two years for the army, three for the navy. There are a very large professional Soviet Army, Soviet Navy, Long Range Air Force, Air Defense Command (established 1955), and Strategic Rocket Force (1960). Most of the armed forces are under the direction of the Ministry of Defense, but the KGB also has several hundred thousand men under arms in such services as the Border Troops, which are equipped with patrol boats, helicopters, aircraft, trained dogs, etc. There is also a vast paramilitary organization known as DOSAAF (Vsesoyuznoye Dobrovolnoye Obshchestvo Sodeystviya Armii, Aviatsii i Flotu S.S.R., or All-Union Voluntary Society for Assistance to the Army, Air Force and Navy of the U.S.S.R.), which, among other functions, provides military training and patriotic indoctrination for schoolchildren. Of great importance also is the GlavPU SA i VMF (Glavnoye Politicheskoye Upravleniye Sovetskoy Armii i Voyenno-Morskogo Flota, or Main Political Directorate of the Soviet Army and Navy), an agency of the CPSU Central Committee, whose task is political supervision and indoctrination of the military forces.

DOSAAF

The police systems. As in the administration of justice, two administrative systems maintain public order. The rough Soviet equivalent of Western police systems is the Ministry of Internal Affairs (Ministerstvo Vnutrennikh Del, or MVD), which controls the militia, or ordinary police, as well as prisons, labour camps, fire prevention services, road safety services, registration of births, marriages, and deaths, etc. The more political aspects of order maintenance are administered by the KGB (Komitet Gosudarstvennoy Bezopasnosti, or Committee of State Security), which performs espionage and counterespionage, guards high officials and state frontiers, and also exercises surveillance over foreign diplomats and press correspondents and in general safeguards the power of the regime.

MVD and KGB

There is an auxiliary police system known as the *druzhina,* whose more than 5,000,000 members, called *druzhinniki,* normally serve a few hours once a month. Wearing red arm bands, they patrol streets and other public places; they may apprehend violators of public order and turn them over to the militia.

The Communist Party of the Soviet Union. The CPSU is the driving and integrating force and the main control mechanism of state and society in the Soviet Union. This fact is registered in article 6 of the constitution (1977), which states that the party is the "leading and guiding force of Soviet society . . . , of all state organizations and public organizations." Article 100 of the constitution also mentions the CPSU first in a list of organizations having the right to nominate candidates for election to the soviets. Of course these articles suggest only feebly the overwhelming initiatory, mobilizing, and penetrating capacities of the CPSU. Although official doctrine characterizes the party as a public organization, it is in fact the collective ruler of the country, containing within its ranks the men and women who make and enforce national policy. It, not the state through which it rules, dominates all Soviet life.

Although CPSU membership numbers in the millions, only about 100,000 of those members enjoy some measure of executive authority, and only a few hundred have much power. These are the people who head the republic and main *oblast* party organizations and the party organizations of major economic and other enterprises and institutions, those who edit leading newspapers, and those who hold high military or police positions or head Central Committee departments and, on the basis of such status, are full members of the Central Committee or full or alternate members of the party's Politburo (Political Bureau).

The dominance of the party's central headquarters over the rank and file is effected by many means. One of the most important is the nomenclature (*nomenklatura*) system of centralized personnel selection, according to which only party members who pass the screening tests imposed from above by appropriate levels of the party leadership can be promoted to a given post. There are lists of positions for which only Moscow headquarters can clear aspirants; lower levels of the party hierarchy screen candidates for positions at their levels, and so on down the line. Another important principle of party organization that enhances centralized control is known as democratic centralism, the most important components of which are strict party discipline and subordination of the minority to the majority (in practice, of lower to higher ranking organizations) and the obligatory nature of the decisions of higher organs for lower. In addition, Moscow headquarters dominates the Soviet mass media of communication. The CPSU Central Committee's newspaper, *Pravda,* and other Central Committee organs such as the magazine *Kommunist,* set the tone of the national press. Central control is also strengthened by the ladderlike system of political schools (in their role as hurdles for promotion somewhat similar to military academies in the United States armed forces), through which party leaders must pass in order to get to the top.

Nomenclature system

The All-Union Leninist Communist League of Youth (Vsesoyuzny Leninsky Kommunistichesky Soyuz Molodyozhi, or VLKSM), better known as the Komsomol, includes youth between the ages of 14 and 28. The Komsomol has grown very rapidly, a growth that reflects in large part the continuing urbanization and industrialization of the country, since Komsomol recruitment is far more successful in the cities than in rural areas. The Komsomol's organizational structure is modelled on that of the CPSU, and many former Komsomol leaders have risen to high posts as executives of the party. The Komsomol is regarded by the party as its reserve and helper, terms that convey some sense of the organization's role as an agency of indoctrination in the official ideology and as a channel for dissemination of CPSU propaganda on domestic and international issues. The Komsomol issues a number of publications, the best known of which is the mass circulation newspaper *Komsomolskaya Pravda* ("Komsomol Truth").

There is general agreement among Western experts on the Komsomol that it has by no means achieved its officially imposed objective of creating a "new Soviet man," imbued with Leninist zeal and self-sacrificing devotion to the ruling party's goals. This verdict is based, in part, on frequent Soviet press reports indicating political apathy, cynicism, and even widespread delinquency among Komsomol members. On the other hand, the Komsomol is a useful device for mobilizing Soviet youth for such drives as the Virgin and Idle Lands Campaign of 1954–56, to settle virgin lands especially in Siberia and Central Asia.

The Komsomol also performs other functions for the party, such as assistance in the work of the Pioneers (All-Union Lenin Pioneer Organization, or Vsesoyuznaya Pionerskaya Organizatsiya Imeni V.I. Lenina), an organization the membership of which embraces Soviet schoolchildren between the ages of nine and 14. Vastly larger in membership than the Boy Scouts and Girl Scouts in the U.S., and, unlike them, an organ of the state, the Pioneers assist the schools in ideological and patriotic indoctrination of children. Pioneers wear a three-cornered red scarf, which according to Soviet sources symbolizes the unity of the Communist, Komsomol, and Pioneer generations. Under the guidance of the CPSU and the Komsomol, the Pioneers seek to instill in children disciplined work habits, love of learning, and identification with Soviet ideology and the social and political system. Children's summer camps and educational and recreational centres aid in the pursuit of these goals.

Pioneers

The trade unions. Soviet trade unions are organized according to broad branches of the economy, covering employees of all ranks within a particular branch, such as medicine or engineering. Collective farmers are not covered. Membership is not compulsory but appears highly advisable on both economic and political grounds. Among the largest unions are those for state farm and allied employees and educational institutions.

The basic units are the enterprise and factory unions, most of which are run by small committees. The activities of the enterprise and factory unions are coordinated by town, provincial, or republican union councils, which are elected at the conferences of the basic unit representatives. At the top is the All-Union Trade Union Congress, which is supposed to be convened every four years. The principal task of the congress is to elect the All-Union Central Council of Trade Unions (or VTsSPS; Vsesoyuzny Tsentralny Sovet Professionalnykh Soyuzov), the Presidium of which is responsible for broad policy and activities. Detailed administrative work is handled by the Secretariat. Individual unions, the structure of which follows this pattern, are closely controlled by the central union authorities.

Unlike the situation in Western countries with market economics, where the function of trade unions is to advance the economic and other interest of workers in relation to employers, labour unions in the Soviet Union are agents of the state. Strikes are forbidden, if not in law certainly in practice. Worker protests and even brief spontaneous labour stoppages occur now and then, but the outside world learns of these only by word of mouth reports that reach foreigners; they are not reported in the controlled Soviet press. From such reports as have reached the West, it appears that military force has been used to put down labour disturbances and that very severe measures were taken against some of their participants.

Union function

The main function of the trade unions is to stimulate workers to increase their productivity. Among the methods used to achieve this, perhaps the best known is "socialist emulation," in which factory is pitted against factory, industry against industry, in nationwide production contests; winning enterprises are awarded banners and receive much praise in the press. Another important function of the unions is the administration of the social insurance system. They also operate an extensive system of rest homes and sanatoriums and generally play an important role in providing services to workers who are in good standing. Like the other Soviet mass organizations, the unions operate an extensive publications network, which of course functions within the framework of overall directives laid down by the CPSU Central Committee but focusses on matters of special interest to employees, including teachers and other professionals as well as industrial workers. The most important trade union publication is the newspaper *Trud* ("Labour").

SOCIAL CONDITIONS AND SERVICES

The basic principle of distribution of goods and services in the Soviet Union is stated in the constitution as "From each according to his ability, to each according to his work." The interpretation and application of this slogan is of course determined by the supreme leadership of the CPSU and is not subject to public discussion. There is abundant evidence, even in Soviet official sources—guarded though they are on such matters as the existence of pronounced inequality and privilege—that this constitutional principle is interpreted so as to permit very wide differences in income, perquisites, opportunities for domestic and foreign travel, access to quality education, and status and power. The existence of such differences is emphasized in statements by dissidents and by many former Soviet citizens now émigrés. In terms especially of power, but also in access to the best vacation and medical facilities, foreign travel, and many other values, high-ranking party and police executives, military officers, and government officials are at the upper end of the scale, while office workers, unskilled labourers, and collective farmers are at the bottom. Also exceptionally well off, in comparison with ordinary citizens, are writers and performing artists in good standing with the political authorities. Favoured novelists and playwrights receive enormous royalties. Scientists who rise to the coveted status of membership in the Academy of Sciences of the U.S.S.R. are perhaps the most honoured citizens of the Soviet Union. Not only do they enjoy, by Soviet standards, very comfortable incomes, superior recreational and medical facilities, and preferential access for their children to the best institutions of higher education, but they also receive substantial additional emoluments by virtue of their academy membership, in addition to their salaries as directors of scientific laboratories. Individual party officials who abuse their positions—for example, by building for their personal use excessively luxurious private homes, using materials illegally obtained at bargain prices—are from time to time sharply criticized or even severely punished, but, according to statements by leading Soviet dissidents, the traditional practice of regularly distributing special pay envelopes to party officials persists.

Privileged persons

Soviet society is thus far from being egalitarian. The people are also, by the standards of advanced Western industrial nations, rather poor. Though rents are low, and housing, though still of very poor quality, is increasingly abundant, the prices of food and clothing are far higher, in proportion to income, than they are in the West. Both husband and wife usually must work in order to make ends meet, though it should also be said that the overwhelming majority of women apparently want to work at paying jobs. In certain respects, women have achieved much in the Soviet economy, as is exemplified by the dominant role of women in the medical profession. Most of the best jobs in all fields, however, and particularly in industry, politics, and public administration, are occupied by men.

Standard of living

Since Stalin's death, the Soviet authorities have made great efforts to raise the standard of living above the very low level of the Stalin era. Perhaps even more important is the program, begun under N.S. Khrushchev, to raise the incomes of the lowest paid categories of workers and in general to improve the economic situation of the workers and collective farmers. This has involved, among other measures, the extension of social security coverage to the collective farm peasantry, who until the mid-1960s remained outside the social security system. Since the mid-1950s there has been a fairly steady rise in Soviet living standards, though this has not necessarily increased the contentment of the mass of the population and has been interrupted by bad harvests in some years. There has been substantial improvement in a previously dire housing and very poor food situation. There has also been rapid progress in availability of basic consumer goods—excellent in terms of refrigerators, quite good in terms of washing machines and even of television sets, but still very poor in terms of private automobiles. The Soviet population, however, was still at a standard of life far below that of all of the developed capitalist countries and of several of the eastern European Communist nations.

Health services. Public health and education are perhaps the areas in which Soviet achievements have been greatest, especially in quantitative terms. The official Soviet claim is that medical services are "free and accessible." It is also asserted in Soviet sources that the Soviet Union has about a quarter of all the physicians in the world and that it has more than 3,000,000 hospital beds. Even if these claims are somewhat exaggerated and, in any case, say nothing about the quality of medical care, there is no doubt that the Soviet Union's record in this field has been impressive, particularly in view of the backward conditions that prevailed in the tsarist period and the difficulties that had to be overcome along the way. It is also apparent, however, that Soviet medical services—which are administered centrally by the Ministry of Health—suffer from the evils common to overcentralized, bureaucratically administered programs: excessive time is spent by both doctor and patient in record keeping and patients often experience long delays in getting treatment. Nor can it be said that the Soviet Union has a record of innovation in medical research and development even remotely comparable to that of the United States and other advanced Western nations, and the quality of care available to Soviet citizens (so far as it can be judged on the limited information to which foreign students have access) is not equal to the best offered by Western medicine. There is no doubt, however, that death rates have been substantially reduced, and the health of the population compares well with that of citizens of other industrial countries.

Education. An objective Western observer cannot fail to be impressed by the achievements of the Soviet Union in the field of education, especially quantitatively, since the Revolution. At the same time, he will also be struck by the peculiarities of the vast Soviet program as it is viewed from the perspective of Western traditions.

Politics and education

The Soviet educational system is characterized by extreme centralization and uniformity in structure and curriculum and by heavy-handed political control and political indoctrination. Especially (but not only) in the humanities and social sciences, textbooks and classroom instruction are permeated by Marxist–Leninist propaganda. Applicants for higher education must pass examinations in political subjects and must continue to devote several hours a week to the study of political subjects even after admission to medical or other professional schools.

Even in quantitative terms, however, Soviet education has thus far by no means achieved the goals set by the CPSU leadership. Universal secondary education (10 years of schooling) has not been attained, despite many years of predictions in the official press that it was imminent. Certainly the country is far from having made education equally available to all of its youth. Rural, as contrasted to urban, youth are still at a great disadvantage in access to secondary and still more to higher education. As for access to the best universities, such as the state universities of Moscow and Leningrad, or to the best specialized scientific, economic, and other institutes, children of workers and peasants are at an almost hopeless disadvantage in comparison with children of professional people, administrators, and officials. The advantages of the intelligentsia in this respect are apparently so great that many students of the Soviet Union believe that a hereditary class, or caste, system may be forming, if indeed it has not already taken shape. Great efforts are made to provide opportunities to work toward higher education, by evening or correspondence study, etc., for young people who have chosen or have been forced to take jobs in industry upon graduation from primary or secondary school. It is generally agreed, however, that, useful though such efforts may be to the economy, they come nowhere near to equalizing opportunities for higher education.

Education in the Soviet Union is a formidable instrument of national policy. It provides the national economy, the armed forces, science and engineering, and the communications media with an abundance of reasonably well-trained man- and womanpower. These young people have acquired basic skills in a highly organized setting, in which discipline and conformity to authority are stressed. Also, though almost half of the Soviet population belongs to non-Russian national minorities, an apparently successful effort is made to teach all graduates (at least of the secondary schools and of course of higher educational institutions) to read and speak Russian effectively. Indeed, for non-Russians, mastering Russian—in addition to a "sound" political outlook—is a prerequisite for career advancement. Certainly the educational system is one of the sinews of the Soviet state. It is possible, however, that its successes, by providing for some individuals at least a basis for critical thought, may cause trouble for Soviet rulers in the future. (F.C.B.)

Cultural life

The roots of Soviet literature and arts lie deep in folk traditions. The vast extent, multinational nature, and varied history of the area that was to become the Soviet Union produced an exceptionally rich and diverse folk culture that continues to manifest itself in oral poetic forms, songs, dances, folk instrumental music, and various forms of decorative and applied art. The Russian Revolution and the establishment of the Soviet Union introduced fundamental changes into the cultural milieu. The process of change has been helped by the reduction of illiteracy and by expansion of education; by an immense growth in the output of printed matter; and by increasing the number of cultural institutions of all kinds, especially in the rural areas.

Multinational culture

One of the distinguishing features of creative life in the Soviet Union is its multinational character. Russian literature, music, and art had achieved international significance in the 19th century and were not without influence on the cultural life of all the peoples of the Russian Empire. Despite their somewhat lower overall level of economic and cultural evolution, many of the minority peoples—from the Baltic to Armenia, from the Ukraine to Central Asia—also had highly distinctive cultures and art forms. During the Soviet period, these have, in the majority of cases, been preserved and developed, within the official Soviet policy that all art should be "national in form and Socialist in content." The annual festivals of the arts and literature of the union republics (held in Moscow), together with republican festivals of the arts of other republics, help to assist the understanding of the cultures of the many different peoples of the Soviet Union. Annual competitions in the various arts further the same aim. All these events enjoy great popularity, as attested by large attendance figures.

Socialist Realism

Specifically Soviet culture, as distinct from Russian or any other national culture, is characterized by what is known as "Socialist Realism," and all national cultures are expected to conform to this approved artistic style. It consists of an emphasis on a Communist approach; "revolutionary humanism"; a popular spirit and appeal; an optimistic vision of the future; and a close connection with what is viewed as actual life. The characters portrayed are to embody what is conceived as the reality of contemporary Soviet life and the ideals of Soviet society, both nationally and internationally.

Soviet culture has also become known internationally (often through exhibitions, film distribution, and performances by leading individuals and cultural bodies) and has had a considerable influence, particularly in the other Communist countries. Internally, the highest recognition of creative work is indicated by award of the Lenin and State prizes and by republican prizes. Soviet cultural work is under the direction of the all-union Ministry of Culture; related union and autonomous republican bodies; and the cultural organs of the local soviets. Many mass organizations are also involved in cultural life.

THE ARTS

Literature. Belles lettres occupy a leading place in Soviet cultural life, drawing on a multinational tradition that has produced acknowledged world masterpieces. The great poets of Central Asia—Neẓāmī, Fuzûlî, and ʿAlī Shīr Navāʾī—were writing in the Middle Ages. Shota Rustaveli's 12th-century Georgian poem *The Knight in the Tiger's Skin* is another landmark in world literature, and the major Transcaucasian poets of the 18th century, Sayat-Nova and Vagif, together with their contemporary the Ukrainian poet and philosopher Hryhoriy Skovoroda, also contributed much to this tradition.

19th-century Russian achievements

But it was 19th-century Russian literature that acquired the greatest world standing. Giants of this period include Aleksandr Pushkin, the "father of Russian literature," whose masterpiece, *Eugene Onegin,* is a verse novel that achieved an encyclopaedic portrayal of Russian life; Mikhail Lermontov, whose *Hero of Our Time* is a brilliant novel in a Caucasian setting; Nikolay Gogol, whose unfinished masterpiece, *Dead Souls,* was a remarkable portrayal of the ruling class of the time; Aleksandr Herzen, whose memoirs, *My Past and Thoughts,* offered a penetrating commentary on Russian society; Ivan Turgenev, whose major novel *Fathers and Sons* produced much discussion among Russian youth and their parents alike; Ivan Goncharov, whose *Oblomov* is an acknowledged triumph of psychological portrayal; and, perhaps most famous of all, the great novelists Leo Tolstoy (*War and Peace*) and Fyodor Dostoyevsky (*Crime and Punishment*). There were also many other figures of major status active at the time, ranging from the dramatist Anton Chekhov to the poet and novelist Ivan Bunin, who in 1933 became the first Russian recipient of the Nobel Prize.

Their ranks also included figures in what became the union republics. Among them were Taras Shevchenko and Ivan Franko (the Ukraine); Yanka Kupala and Yakub Kolas (Belorussia); Akaki Tsereteli and Ilia Chavchavadze (Georgia); Jānis Rainis and Andreijs Upīts (Latvia); Julija Žymantienė-Žemaitė (Lithuania); Eduard Vilde (Estonia); Khachatur Abovyan and Ovanes Tumanyan (Armenia); and many others.

20th-century achievements

The foundations of Soviet literature were laid by the great working class writer Maksim Gorky, whose *Mother* (1906) initiated a series of the first classics of Socialist Realism; and by the major early Soviet poet Vladimir Mayakovsky. Contemporary Soviet literature is marked by a wealth of forms and genres, which, although multilingual and multinational, are integrated by the common Communist ideological content. In prose fiction, Soviet opinion ascribes major significance to the work of Aleksey N. Tolstoy (*The Road to Calvary, Peter the Great,* and other novels), whose attitude to life may be indicated by the statement in his autobiography that he loved life and opposed every kind of abstraction with all the power of his temperament. Mikhail Sholokhov, a Nobel Prize winner, created in his novels *The Silent Don* and *Virgin Soil Upturned* epic accounts of the struggle to construct the new society. Aleksandr Fadeyev was the author of *The Rout* and *The Young Guard,* novels that deal realistically with partisan and guerrilla activities in the Civil War and World War II; he was for three decades head of the Union of Soviet Writers. Aleksandr Serafimovich's *Iron Flood,* completed in 1923 when the author was 60, was one of the first significant novels about the Revolution. Dmitry Furmanov's novels *Chapayev* and *Mutiny* were among the first and best on the Civil War. Nikolay Ostrovsky, who died in 1936 at the age of 32, yet produced, in *How the Steel Was Tempered,* a classic autobiographical statement of the revolutionary generation. There are many other major figures, including Aleksandr Blok, the great poet of the Revolution; Ilya Ehrenburg; Boris Pasternak, a Nobel prize winner, lyric poet, and translator of Georgian, German, and English poets; Konstantin Fedin; and Leonid Leonov. The great poet Anna Akhmatova incurred the displeasure of the authorities but was "rehabilitated" in 1959. Another major poet, Osip Mandelstam, perished in the Great Purge of the 1930s. The Tadzhik author Sadriddin Ayni; the Uzbek poet and dramatist Niyazy; the Tatar poet and writer Musa Dzhalil; the Kazakh author Mukhtar Auezov; and writers from the Baltic republics also have achieved national and in some cases international fame.

Oral folk traditions are continued in the work of such outstanding bards as Jambil Jabayev (called Jambil) in Kazakhstan, Suleyman Stalsky in Dagestan, and Toktogul in Kirgiziya.

Contemporary literature

In contemporary Soviet literature, Soviet opinion ascribes significance to such authors as Galina Nikolayeva, Mikhail Bubennov, and Sergey Sartakov, whose novels have described post-World War II agricultural and industrial life; Konstantin Simonov (*The Living and the Dead, They Were Not Born as Soldiers, The Last Summer,* and other works), Aleksandr Chakovsky (*Blockade*), and

Vadim Kozhevnikov (*Shield and Sword*), who, with many others, have written of the war years; the Kirgiz author Chingiz Aytmatov, whose novel *Dzhamilya* is about a young woman who breaks away from traditional ways of life; and a host of others. The Nobel prize-winning novelist Aleksandr Solzhenitsyn was exiled in 1974. The poets Yevgeny Yevtushenko, Andrey Voznesensky, Stepan Shchipachov, Nikolay Tikhonov, Rasul Gamzatov (of Dagestan), Vsevolod Rozhdestvensky, Leonid Martynov, Bella Akhmadulina, among many others, have achieved great contemporary popularity. Soviet children's literature—prominent writers of which include Korney Chukovsky, Agniya Barto, and Sergey Mikhalkov—is well-known at home and abroad.

Visual arts. Paleolithic and Neolithic art has been discovered in the Caucasus, in Central Asia, in Siberia, and on the northern Black Sea coast. In the Middle Ages the most notable work was done by the great icon painters of the Novgorod and Moscow schools, among whom the finest were Theophanes the Greek, Andrey Rublyov, and Dionisy. In the 19th century the modern realistic schools of Ivan Kramskoy, Ilya Repin, and Isaak Levitan were founded.

Major works of the revolutionary art of the Soviet period include the scenes from Revolutionary history associated with Isaak Brodsky, Valentin Serov, and Kuzma Petrov-Vodkin; the genre painting of Nikolay Kasatkin and Yury Pimenov; and the portraits of Mikhail Nesterov and Aleksandr Gerasimov. Artists from minority nationalities, including Ural Tansykbayev of Uzbekistan, Martiros Saryan of Armenia, and others, have recorded the varying scenery of the country. Yevgeny Lansere and Aleksandr Deyneka have produced monumental works, while the graphic arts, represented by Viktor Deni, Dmitry Moor, and "Kukryniksy" (a nickname of Mikhail Kupriyanov, Porfiry Krylov, and Nikolay Sokolov) are marked by great variety. Vera Mukhina's group "Worker and Collective Farm Woman" and the memorial ensembles created under the direction of Yevgeny Vuchetich in East Berlin and at Volgograd, as well as works by Sergey Konenkov and Sergey Merkurov, are regarded as masterpieces of monumental sculpture.

Monumental and decorative art

In the decorative and applied arts field, there is great demand for the products of factory and folk industries, which include pottery, glassware, and carpets; carving on wood, stone, bone, and horn; silverware; and delicate lacquer miniatures.

Persons working in the fine arts, as well as theatre designers, film cartoonists, and art scholars, are members of the Union of Artists and the Academy of Arts.

Music. The works of the classics—including those of Mikhail Glinka, Modest Mussorgsky, Aleksandr Borodin, Nikolay Rimsky-Korsakov, Peter Ilich Tchaikovsky, and Sergey Rachmaninoff—remain very popular. Soviet music is regarded as embodying important modern themes as well as those of the past: an example is provided by the symphonies of Dmitry Shostakovich, particularly his *Seventh (Leningrad), 11th* (dedicated to the Revolution of 1905), and *12th* (dedicated to the October Revolution of 1917). Soviet opera reflects both national epics (as in Uzeir Hajjibekov's *Ker-Ogly*) and historical and modern themes, respectively illustrated by Sergey Prokofiev's *War and Peace* and *Semyon Kotko.* Soviet ballet music ranges from Prokofiev's *Romeo and Juliet* to Aram Khachaturian's *Gayane.* There is a union of Soviet composers.

Soviet performing artists have traditionally won international recognition, and to such well-known names as those of the pianist Emil Gilels and the violinist David Oistrakh have been added those of a brilliant new group including, among many others, the pianist Svyatoslav Richter, the cellist Mstislav Rostropovich (who, however, while serving as conductor of the National Symphony Orchestra in Washington, D.C., was deprived of Soviet citizenship), and the conductor Kiril Kondrashin.

Music festivals

Large folk-song choirs from differing national backgrounds have also won fame at home and abroad, and professional musical activities generally blend into and enrich amateur and folk music of all sorts, from balalaika orchestras to brass bands. Each summer, song festivals are held in public parks and squares, with individual performers and choirs participating. The international P.I. Tchaikovsky Competition for pianists, violinists, cellists, singers, and ballet dancers is held every four years in Moscow. At the first competition, in 1958, the young American pianist Van Cliburn won first prize.

Theatre and ballet. Soviet theatre, embodying the principles of Socialist Realism, has inherited much from the past, notably the tradition of Russian Realist theatre. By the second half of the 19th century and the turn of the 20th, this tradition included the Maly Theatre of Moscow (founded in 1824) and the renowned Moscow Art Theatre, founded in 1898 by the theatrical innovator Konstantin Stanislavsky, often characterized as the founder of modern acting, and his colleague V.I. Nemirovich-Danchenko.

Soviet theatrical growth was marked by the interaction of the old-established Bolshoi ("Large"), Maly ("Small"), and Art theatres in Moscow and the Aleksandrinsky, Mariinsky, and Mikhaylovsky theatres in St. Petersburg (now Leningrad), with the new Soviet theatres. Major Soviet drama producers have used a variety of forms and methods, often based on those of Stanislavsky. In similar fashion, the great traditional Russian actors passed on their skill to the newer generations of the Soviet period.

Of particular interest are the developments outside the leading centres, Moscow and Leningrad; such peoples as the Uzbeks, Kazakhs, Turkmens, and Kirgiz, who had no professional theatre before the Revolution, have created vigorous national theatre based on traditional performing arts forms.

In addition to Soviet drama, the country's theatres put on many plays from the world and Russian literary traditions, from Chekhov to Shakespeare, Molière to Schiller. Modern foreign playwrights—Bertolt Brecht, Jean Anouilh, and Arthur Miller among them—are also often performed. These contemporary developments have been associated with the emergence of a young school of producers and actors.

Contemporary Soviet ballet theatres strive to preserve all that is regarded as the best of the great pre-Revolutionary era while creating a repertory that conforms to Soviet reality and the interests of new audiences. Thus, new, heroic qualities appeared in the dancing of such stars as Yekaterina Geltser, A.N. Yermolayev, and S.M. Messerer, and the 1930s saw the development of many-act ballets with highly developed plots. That decade also saw the flowering of the talents of Galina Ulanova, the first Soviet prima ballerina *assoluta.* Ballet companies were also organized with striking results in the constituent republics. In later decades a new generation of performers—including Maya Plisetskaya, Yekaterina Maksimova, Vladimir Vasilyev, and many more—has emerged. Ballet in the West has been enriched by the emigration of several Soviet-trained dancers, among them the great Rudolf Nureyev and Mikhail Baryshnikov. Russian ballet has of course had a major influence on world dance, and Soviet companies continue to give many well-received performances abroad. There are almost 20 ballet schools, the best known being located in Moscow and Leningrad. Amateur ballet is also well developed.

Ballet stars

The major Soviet theatres include the Gorky Moscow Art Theatre (MKhAT), whose curtain bears a sea-gull emblem as a symbol of the theatre's close links with Chekhov; the Maly Theatre in Moscow, one of the country's oldest; the Pushkin Academic Drama Theatre in Leningrad (the Aleksandrinsky Theatre from 1832 to 1920), after the Maly the great centre of Russian Realism; and the Academic Gorky Bolshoy State Drama Theatre in Leningrad, founded in 1919. In Kiev are found the Leslya Ukrainka and Ivan Franko theatres.

Opera and ballet theatres, in addition to the renowned Bolshoi Theatre (formally, the State Academic Bolshoy Theatre of the U.S.S.R., or GABT; founded in 1772), include the Kirov State Academic Theatre of Opera and Ballet in Leningrad (formerly the Mariinsky Theatre, founded 1836) and the same city's Maly Theatre (formally, Leningrad Academic Maly Theatre of Opera and Ballet), as well as the Academic Musical Theatre in Moscow, named after Stanislavsky and Nemirovich-

Danchenko. The Shevchenko Theatre of Opera and Ballet is in Kiev. The Moscow Operetta Theatre is the major musical comedy stage.

Children's theatre

Almost all the country's theatres present special performances for children, and there are more than 150 theatres for children and young people, including puppet theatres. The most important include the Moscow Central Children's Theatre, the Moscow Young Spectators Theatre and its equivalent in Leningrad, and youth theatres in the major cities. The unique State Central Puppet Theatre in Moscow, founded and directed by Sergey Obraztsov, has delighted patrons of all ages in many countries.

Actors and producers are trained at the Lunacharsky Theatre Art Institute (GITIS), the Shchepkin and Shchukin theatre schools, the Moscow Art Theatre School, and many other institutions. Actors belong to the All-Russian Theatrical Society and analogous republic organizations.

Variety and circus. Both the variety stage and the circus are extremely popular in the Soviet Union, and the Soviet Folk Dance Ensemble, the Red Army Song and Dance Ensemble, and national groups have achieved world fame. Illusionists, acrobats, jugglers, and others appear in variety performances and also in circuses, which are well known for the variety of their performances and their high level of technique. Entertainments range from performances by the animals trained by V.L. Durov, noted for his scientific approach, to the clowning of Oleg K. Popov and others, much of which has a satirical, topical character.

Motion pictures. The cinema is undoubtedly the most popular form of Soviet art, the first Russian film having appeared in 1907. Historical themes and the developing Soviet experience provided the major subject matter of earlier films, and landmark productions of international renown include *The Battleship Potemkin* (1925; director Sergey Eisenstein), regarded as one of the world's great films; *Mother* (1926; director Vsevolod I. Pudovkin), from Gorky's novel, with Nikolay Batalov in the main role; *Earth* (1930; director Aleksandr P. Dovzhenko); and *Peter the Great* (1937–38; director Vladimir M. Petrov), from A.N. Tolstoy's novel.

Postwar films

Later years were characterized by a change of artistic emphasis to contemporary themes, notably the upheavals of World War II. Films include *The Cranes Are Flying* (1957; director Mikhail K. Kalatozov), *Ballad of a Soldier* (1961; director Grigory N. Chukhray), and *The Fate of a Man* (1959; director and leading actor Sergey F. Bondarchuk). There has also been a considerable output of biographical, documentary, and semidocumentary films. Films based on Russian and world classics include the *Hamlet* and *King Lear* of Grigory Kozintsev, several dramatizations of the novels of Dostoyevsky, and epics in several parts based on Tolstoy's *War and Peace* and Sholokhov's *Silent Don.* Other works popular with Soviet audiences include *The Living and the Dead, Soldier's Father,* the five-part epic *Liberation, The Belorussian Terminal,* and many others. International film festivals, held biennially in Moscow and Tashkent, are also very popular. There is a union of film workers (founded 1957).

Amateur activities. Folk art and mass nonprofessional art are widely developed. They include the production and performance of artistic works by dancers, ballad singers, singers of *chastushki* (rhymed couplets), and instrumentalists. There are many crafts workers. Clubs, palaces of culture, houses of folk art, and similar centres are the main base for a host of amateur organizations. Professionals may take part in amateur activities, and vice versa. Regular festivals, reviews, and competitions help raise the level of skill, and many professional groups and performers were originally amateur.

CULTURAL AND EDUCATIONAL INSTITUTIONS

Cultural and educational institutions include clubs, the institutions known as people's universities, libraries, lecture halls, museums, and parks of rest and culture. The stated basic object of these bodies is to spread political and scientific knowledge; to propagate the achievements of science and technology, of the arts, and of literature; and to organize the cultural leisure of the population. The Soviet authorities favour communal rather than individual leisure activity.

Clubs. There are clubs all over the country, but mostly in rural areas. These are attached to and organized by individual state economic enterprises and collective farms, which are obliged to devote part of their income to the cultural and recreational functions carried out by the clubs. Membership is voluntary, but there are often strong social pressures on the individual to join, given the Soviet ethos. The clubs organize recreational evenings, concerts, lectures, and so on and provide facilities for amateur organizations such as dramatic, choral, dance, and musical societies.

Lecture halls and people's universities of culture. Lecture halls are to be found at many factories, farms, and other enterprises. They are important centres for the propagation of the state ideology as well as for the dissemination of cultural and scientific knowledge. A leading role is played by the all-union Znaniye (Knowledge) society, which organizes lectures, often providing travelling lecturers on particular topics in science and culture. The voluntary people's universities of culture have the aim of broadening people's political and cultural horizons through part-time courses of one to three years' duration on such topics as Soviet and foreign literature, aesthetics, and the sciences.

Libraries. A considerable portion of the output of books, magazines, and newspapers enters the state library system. The Lenin State Library in Moscow is the country's largest. Other leading libraries are found in Leningrad at the Saltykov-Shchedrin Public Library and at the U.S.S.R. Academy of Sciences; in Kiev at the Ukrainian S.S.R. Academy of Sciences; and in Moscow at the Moscow State University (MGU), which houses the Gorky Scientific Library.

Museums and galleries. Museum attendance in the Soviet Union is high. Most museums and galleries of art are state institutions, administered by the Ministry of Culture, but there are also museums established by volunteer enthusiasts, often found in small towns and rural areas. Famous museums include (in Moscow) the Central Lenin Museum, the Central Museum of the Revolution, the Armoury Museum in the Kremlin, the State Historical Museum, the Polytechnic Museum, the State Pushkin Museum of Fine Arts, and the State Tretyakov Gallery. Leningrad has the Hermitage and the State Russian Museum, while Kiev is the home of a historical museum, the Kiev State Museum of Ukrainian Art, and the Kiev State Museum of Russian Art. A unique place is occupied by the permanent Exhibition of National Economic Achievements, in Moscow.

Parks of rest and culture. Parks are administered by the state and by trade unions. The largest include the Gorky Central Park of Culture and the Sokolniki and Izmaylovsky parks in Moscow and the Kirov Central Park of Culture and Rest in Leningrad. Parks are the scene of many cultural events and lectures, including open-air chess matches in the spring and summer.

COMMUNICATIONS MEDIA

The press. Soviet citizens are noted for their devotion to reading, and the Soviet Union produces more printed material than any other country. It takes first place internationally both in the number of books published and in the number of translations. About a quarter of the total output deals with political, economic, and social matters, and one-tenth of the titles (and one-third of the copies) are belles lettres. About 30 percent of the books printed are educational literature, and books for children have become increasingly important. There are more than 200 book and some 15 newspaper and magazine publishing houses attached to a variety of state bodies.

The CPSU and the press

Newspapers include universally available Russian language dailies, regional dailies in the languages of the constituent republics, and papers of smaller circulation published by individual ministries, economic enterprises, collective farms, and other organizations. Newspapers are owned and published by the Communist Party organization of the area or enterprise within which they circulate.

The main all-union dailies are *Pravda* ("Truth"), the organ of the Central Committee of the CPSU; *Izvestiya* ("News"), the government newspaper, published by the Presidium of the Supreme Soviet; *Komsomolskaya Pravda,* published by the Central Committee of the Komsomol; and *Trud* ("Labour"), the organ of the All-Union Central Council of Trade Unions. *Pionerskaya Pravda,* the children's newspaper, is published thrice weekly, also by the Central Committee of the Komsomol. *Krasnaya Zvezda* ("Red Star"), the organ of the Ministry of Defense, is published six times a week. Other papers published two or three times a week are owned by the appropriate industrial ministry or trade union or by both jointly; these include, among others, special newspapers for workers in the railway, timber, and construction industries and for cultural workers, teachers, the medical profession, and athletes.

Content of all newspapers is closely scrutinized by party officials, and deviations from official policy are either eliminated by the editorial board or vigorously criticized after publication. On the other hand, newspapers often publish and investigate complaints by individual citizens and in this sense do provide a medium for the expression of public opinion. Criticism of the political and economic system as such, however, does not appear in the Soviet press. While content of individual newspapers varies according to the special interests of their readers, there is much common material supplied by official press agencies, of which by far the largest are TASS (the Soviet Telegraph Agency, founded in 1925) and APN (the Novosti Press Agency, founded in 1961).

Magazines

The number and circulation of weekly and monthly magazines increased greatly during the late 20th century, though all are subject to the same restraints as the newspapers and are controlled by party organizations. Among the weeklies, two of the most important are *Literaturnaya Gazeta* ("Literary Gazette"), published by the Union of Soviet Writers, and *Ekonomicheskaya Gazeta* ("Economic Gazette"), published by the Central Committee of the CPSU, which deals particularly with problems of industrial organization. There are monthly publications for teachers, literary monthlies, and a variety of scholarly journals.

Radio and television. Soviet radio and television, like the press, are closely controlled by the state and party, and transmissions on ideological, political, economic, and social affairs, to which much time is devoted, reflect official policies. In addition to such aspects there is an increasing volume of light entertainment and special programs directed at, for example, preschool children, collective farmers, and the armed forces. Internal broadcasts are conducted in some 70 languages, external broadcasts in about 60 languages.

Although the first Soviet television transmissions began in 1931, it was not until the 1960s that a nationwide system was developed. By use of communications satellites, the peoples of Central Asia, Siberia, the Far North, and the Far East receive programs originating in Moscow as well as the transmissions of their local stations. The Moscow television centre is the nerve centre of the Soviet system, from which the great majority of programs, whether live or filmed, originate. (I.V.Ko./J.C.D.)

HISTORY OF RUSSIA AND THE SOVIET UNION

The term Russia properly refers only to the empire that occupied approximately the present area of the Soviet Union in the 18th, 19th, and early 20th centuries. In the title of this section, however, it is used very loosely to describe the European part of the Soviet Union from ancient times as well.

From the beginnings to c. 1700

PREHISTORY

Indo-European and Ural-Altaic peoples have occupied what is now the European territory of the Union of Soviet Socialist Republics (U.S.S.R.) since the second millennium before Christ, but little is known about their ethnic identity, institutions, and activities. In ancient times, Greek and Iranian settlements appeared in the southernmost portions of what is now the Ukrainian S.S.R. Trading empires of that era seem to have known and exploited the northern forests, particularly the Permian triangle formed by the Kama and Volga rivers, but these contacts seem to have had little lasting impact. Between the 4th and 9th centuries, the Huns, Avars, Goths, and Magyars passed briefly over the same terrain, but these transitory occupations also had little influence upon the East Slavs, who during this time were spreading south and east from an area between the Elbe River and the Pripet Marshes. In the 9th century, as a result of penetration into the area from north and south by north European and Middle Eastern merchant adventurers, their society was exposed to new economic, cultural, and political forces.

Ancient trading empires

Exploration and the rise of the Rus. The scanty written records tell little of the processes that ensued, but archaeological evidence—notably, the Oriental coins found in eastern Europe—indicates that the development of the East Slavs passed through several stages.

From about 770 to about 830, commercial explorers began an intensive penetration of the Volga region. From early bases in the estuaries of the rivers of the eastern Baltic region, Germanic commercial–military bands, probably in search of new routes to the East, began to penetrate territory populated by Finnic and Slavic tribes, where they found amber, furs, honey, wax, and timber products, all of which provided generous rewards for the hardy and fortunate. The indigenous population, unlike that of western areas where the Vikings were becoming active, offered little resistance to their incursions, and there was no significant local authority to negotiate the balance among trade, tribute, and plunder. From the south, trading organizations based in northern Iran and North Africa, seeking the same products, particularly slaves, became active in the Lower Volga, the Don, and, to a lesser extent, in the Dnepr region. The history of the Khazar state (see below *The Khazars*) is intimately connected with these activities.

Around 830 commerce appears to have declined in the Don and Dnepr regions. There was increased activity in the north Volga, where Scandinavian traders who had previously operated from bases on Lakes Ladoga and Onega established a new centre, near present-day Ryazan. Here, in this period, the first nominal ruler of Rus (called, like the Khazar emperor, *khaqan* or *kagan*) is mentioned by Islāmic and Western sources. This Volga Rus kaganate may be considered the first direct political antecedent of the Kievan state.

Within a few decades, these Rus, together with other Scandinavian groups operating further west, extended their raiding activities down the main river routes toward Baghdad and Constantinople, reaching the latter in 860. The Scandinavians involved in these exploits are known as Varangians; they were adventurers of diverse origins, often led by princes of warring dynastic clans. One of these princes, Rurik of Jutland, is considered the progenitor of the dynasty that ruled in various portions of East Slavic territory until 1598. Evidences of the Varangian expansion are particularly clear in the coin hoards of 900–930. The number of Oriental coins reaching northern regions, especially Scandinavia, indicates a flourishing trade. Written records tell of Rus raids upon Constantinople and the northern Caucasus in the early 10th century.

The Varangian expansion

In the period from about 930 to 1000, the region came under complete control by Varangians from Novgorod. This period saw the development of the trade route from the Baltic to the Black Sea, which established the basis of the economic life of the Kievan principality and determined its political and cultural development.

The degree to which the Varangians may be considered the founders of the Kievan state has been hotly debated since the 18th century. The debate has from the beginning borne nationalistic overtones. Recent works by

Russians have generally minimized or ignored the role of the Varangians, while non-Russians have occasionally exaggerated it. Whatever the case, the lifeblood of the sprawling Kievan organism was the commerce organized by the princes. To be sure, these early princes were not "Swedes" or "Norwegians" or "Danes"; they thought in categories not of nation but of clan. But they certainly were not East Slavs. There is little reason to doubt the predominant role of the Varangian Rus in the creation of the state to which they gave their name.

The Khazars. In the mid-7th century, the Khazars, a nomadic confederation of Turkic and Iranian tribes in the North Caucasus, rapidly expanded their power, pressing the Hunnic Bulgars northward and westward and confronting Byzantine and Arab power to the south. Khazar relations with Constantinople became very close (a son of Emperor Leo III was married to a daughter of the Khazar Kagan in 731) but could not forestall a terrible defeat by the Arabs in the Caucasus in 737, at which time the Khazar capital was destroyed. The centre of Khazar activities shifted north to a new capital at Itil on the Lower Volga, and by the end of the century the Khazars had recovered and surpassed their previous power. The Khazar state was multinational, based upon the military might of Turkic and Iranian nomadic horsemen and the skills of Iranian and Jewish traders. The Khazars seem to have retained their importance through the 9th century, in spite of competition from the Rus and the Hungarians, but were eclipsed in the 10th century.

KIEV

The first East Slavic state

Rise of Kiev. The consecutive history of the first East Slavic state begins with Prince Svyatoslav (died 972), the greatest of the Varangian princes. His victorious campaigns against other Varangian centres, the Khazars, and the Volga Bulgars and his intervention in the Byzantine–Danube Bulgar conflicts of 968–971 mark the full hegemony of his clan in Rus and the emergence of a new political force in eastern Europe, similar in some ways to the princely dynasties of the Piasts in Poland and the Árpáds in Hungary. But Svyatoslav was neither a lawgiver nor an organizer; and on his death he left, in true Varangian style, only his sword and that which had been gained by it. The role of architect of the Kievan state fell to his son Vladimir (*c.* 980–1015), who established the dynastic seniority system of his clan as the political structure by which the scattered territories of Rus were to be ruled. He also promulgated the first code of law and invited or permitted the patriarch of Constantinople to establish an episcopal see in Rus in 988. Vladimir's reign inaugurated the golden century of Kievan life, and he has remained in later tradition a figure of heroic stature.

Vladimir extended the realm to its natural limits (the watersheds of the Don, Dnepr, Dnestr, Neman, Western Dvina, and Upper Volga), destroyed or incorporated the remnants of competing Varangian organizations, and established regular relations with neighbouring dynasties. The successes of his long reign made it possible for the reign of his son Yaroslav (ruled 1019–54) to produce a flowering of cultural life. But neither Yaroslav, who gained control of Kiev only after a bitter struggle against his brother Svyatopolk (1015–19), nor his successors in Kiev, however, were able to provide lasting political stability within the enormous realm. The political history of Rus is one of clashing separatist and centralizing trends inherent in the contradiction between local settlement and colonization, on the one hand, and the hegemony of the clan elder, ruling from Kiev, on the other. As Vladimir's 12 sons and innumerable grandsons prospered in the rapidly developing territories they inherited, they and their retainers acquired settled interests that conflicted both with one another and with the interests of unity.

The conflicts were not confined to Slavic lands: the Turkic nomads who moved into the southern steppe in the 11th century (first the Torks, later the Kipchaks—also known as the Polovtsy, or Cumans) became involved in the constant internecine rivalries, and Rurikid and Turkic princes often fought on both sides. In 1097 representatives of the leading branches of the dynasty, together with their Turkic allies, met at Liubech, north of Kiev, and agreed to divide the Kievan territory among themselves and their descendants, although, later, Vladimir Monomakh made a briefly successful attempt (1113–25) to reunite the land of Rus.

The Kievan Rus in the 10th and 11th centuries.

Adapted from *Westermann Grosser Atlas zur Weltgeschichte* Georg Westermann Verlag, Braunschweig

Decline of Kiev. The hegemony of the prince of Kiev depended upon the cohesion of the clan of Rurik and the relative importance of the southern trade, both of which began to decline in the late 11th century. The primary reason for this decline was a major shift of trade routes in the eastern Mediterranean, which can conveniently be associated with the First Crusade (1096–99). The reestablishment of the traditional east–west routes, together with other factors, made the route from the Baltic to the Black Sea superfluous and less profitable. Moreover, much of the trade that had followed that route now began moving over land routes through central Europe. At the same time, conflicts among the Rurikid princes acquired a more pronounced regional and separatist nature, reflecting new patterns in export trade along the northern and western periphery. Novgorod, in particular, began to gravitate toward closer relations both with the cities of the Hanseatic League, which controlled the Baltic trade, and with the rapidly developing hinterland in Suzdalia, between the Oka River and the Upper Volga. Smolensk, Polotsk, and Pskov became increasingly involved in trade along western land routes, while Galicia and Volhynia established closer links with Poland and Hungary. The princes of these areas still contested the crown of the "grand prince of Kiev and all of Rus," but the title became an empty one; when Andrew Bogolyubsky of Suzdal won Kiev and the title in 1169, he sacked the city and returned to the Upper Volga, apparently seeing no advantage in establishing himself in the erstwhile capital. (Roman Mstislavich of Galicia and Volhynia repeated these actions in 1203.) By the middle of the 12th century, the major principalities, thanks to the prosperity and colonization of the Kievan period, had developed into independent political and economic units, some as large as modern European nation-states.

Social and political institutions. The paucity of evidence about social and political institutions in Kievan Rus suggests that they were rudimentary. The East Slavs had no significant tradition of supratribal political organization before the coming of the Varangians, who themselves, until well into the 10th century, had little interest in institutions more elaborate than those necessary for the exploitation of their rich, new territory. Nor did the Varangians soon acquire any attachment to Rus as a second homeland: archaeology and the sagas agree in portraying the "East" as a theatre of heroic adventure and freebootery, not of colonization. The territory of Rus, moreover, was immense and sparsely settled. The scattered towns, some probably little more than trading posts, were separated by large primeval forests and swamps.

The adoption of Christianity

Thus, although the campaigns of Svyatoslav indicate the extent of the political vacuum that his clan filled, he construed his domains as a clan possession rather than as a territorial or national state. His successor Vladimir, however, seems to have been conscious of one political element—organized religion—that distinguished both the contemporary empires and the newly established principalities in Poland and Hungary from his own. The church provided the concepts of territorial and hierarchical organization that made states out of tribal territories; its teachings transformed a charismatic prince into a king possessing the attributes and responsibilities of a national leader, judge, and first Christian of the realm.

Once Vladimir had adopted Christianity in 988, his rule was supported by the propagation of Byzantine notions of imperial authority, and there is ample evidence that Kievan princes after him styled themselves as autocrats in the Byzantine tradition. The political traditions and conditions of Rus, however, required that the actual workings of the political system and some of its style be derived from other sources. The succession system, probably a vestige of the experience of the Rus khaganate in the Upper Volga, was based upon two principles: the indivisibility of the basic territory of Rus (the principalities of Kiev, Chernigov, and Pereyaslavl) and the sovereignty of a whole generation. Seniority passed through an ascension by stages from elder brother to younger and from the youngest eligible uncle to the eldest eligible nephew. Such a system was admirably suited to the needs of the dynasty, because, by providing a rotating advancement of members of the clan through apprenticeships in the various territories of the realm, it assured control of the key points of the far-flung trading network by princes who were subject to traditional sanctions, and it gave them experience in lands over which they could someday expect to rule from Kiev. This system served well for a century after it was given final form by Vladimir and was revived by Monomakh (Vladimir II, ruled 1113–25), but it could not survive the decline of Kiev's importance.

The boyars

Each of the princes had a retinue composed of boyars (upper nobility), who gave personal allegiance and military service to the prince in return for grants of income from specified territories. Some of these boyars were originally Scandinavians—perhaps members of dynasties defeated by the Rurikids. Others may have been leading members of local tribal units. The princes and their retinues drew their most significant revenues from the tribute or taxes collected annually in kind from the various territories and disposed of in the export trade.

Some slaves were apparently employed in princely and boyar households, but their number was not large. The main group of dependent peasants consisted of indentured freemen, while most people were apparently free peasants organized in communes, who paid tribute to the prince but not to a landlord.

Very little is known of law in this period; it may be assumed that juridical institutions had not developed on a broad scale. The earliest law code (1016), called the "Russian Law," was one of the "Barbarian" law codes common throughout Germanic Europe. It dealt primarily with princely law—that is, with the fines to be imposed by the prince or his representative in the case of specified offenses; it was later modified by the inclusion of ecclesiastical and moral law from Byzantine and Slavic sources.

Soviet scholars have adhered to a rather literal Marxist view of the nature of the Kievan state, holding that, since land was in the hands of the boyar class, who exploited the labour of slaves and peasants, Kievan society should be termed feudal. The meagre sources indicate, however, that Kiev experienced nothing like the complex and highly regulated legal and economic relationships associated with feudalism in western Europe. Kiev's political system existed primarily for and by international trade in forest products and depended upon a money economy in which the bulk of the population scarcely participated. The rich and powerful doubtless exploited the tillers of the soil. The subsistence agriculture of the forest regions, however, was not the source of Kiev's wealth, nor was it the matrix within which law and politics and history were made.

Formal culture came to Rus, along with Christianity, from the multinational Byzantine synthesis, primarily through South Slavic intermediaries. A native culture, expressed in a now lost pagan ritual folklore and traditions in the arts and crafts, existed before the Kievan period, and then persisted alongside the formal culture, but its influence on the latter is conjectural. Authorities often speak of the imitative nature of Kievan culture, especially of its literature, and of Kiev's "silence." There were no heresies or great disputes in the Kievan church; Christianity came to virgin territory, where there were no native religious or philosophical traditions vital enough to force a confrontation or synthesis such as occurred elsewhere. The Kievan achievement, however, was none the less remarkable: within a few generations, an enormous population was brought within the embrace of Western culture and introduced to the artistic, philosophical, and literary treasures of the contemporary Christian world.

No single one of the regional (or, later, national) cultures, perhaps least of all that of Muscovy, can be called the heir of Kiev, although all shared the inheritance. The strands of continuity were everywhere strained, if not broken, in the period after Kiev's decline. But "Golden Kiev" was always present, in lore and bookish tradition, as a source of emulation and renascence.

THE LANDS OF RUS

The decline of Kiev led to the disintegration of Rus into its component principalities. Regional developments are so striking in the subsequent period that it has often been called the Period of Feudal Partition. This is misleading: "feudal" is hardly more applicable to the widely varying institutions of this time than to those of the Kievan period. "Partition" implies a former unity for which there is no historical evidence. The distinct character and historical fortunes of each of the major East Slavic regions is clear even in the Kievan period and has persisted into the 20th century. The following is a brief coverage of the most important states.

The commercial centre of Novgorod

Novgorod. The town of Novgorod arose in the 9th century as one of the earliest centres of the exploitation of the forest hinterland and remained the most important commercial centre of the Kievan period. The changes of the latter Kievan period did not diminish Novgorod's importance, for it benefitted both from the increased activity of the Hanseatic League and from the development of the Upper Volga region, for which it was a major trade outlet. Although Novgorod was the first base of the Rurikids, from which Kiev was repeatedly captured and to which Kievan princes often returned to recruit Varangian retinues during their struggles for the Kievan throne, the princely traditions characteristic of Kiev and other post-Kievan centres never developed in Novgorod. During the height of Kiev's power, Novgorod was usually ruled by a son of the grand prince rather than by a member of the "generation of brothers," who held decidedly less important towns. When Kiev declined, Novgorod soon (1136) declared its independence from princely power, and, although it accepted princely protectors from various neighbouring dynasties, it remained, until conquered by Muscovy (Moscow), a sovereign city.

During the 13th century, Novgorod's burghers easily found an accommodation with the invading Mongols. In the Mongol period, its energetic river pirates pushed farther north and east toward the Urals and even down the Volga, and Novgorod's prosperity was generally unbroken until the commercial revolution of the 16th century. Its absorption by the growing principality of Muscovy in 1478 ended its political independence and changed its social structure, but Novgorod's characteristic economic and cultural life did not end with that catastrophe.

Novgorod is notable for its sociopolitical institutions, similar in some ways to those of north European towns but almost unique in East Slavic territory. Novgorod was governed by an oligarchy of great trading boyar families who controlled the exploitation of the hinterland. They chose (from among themselves) a mayor, a military commander, and a council of aldermen, who controlled the affairs of the city and its territories. The town itself was divided into five "ends," which seem to have corresponded to the "fifths" into which the hinterland was divided. There was, in addition, a *veche* ("council"), apparently a kind of town meeting of broad but indeterminate composition, whose decisions, it would appear, were most often controlled by the oligarchy. A major role in politics was played by the archbishop, who after 1156 controlled the lands and incomes previously owned by the Kievan princes and who appears throughout Novgorod's history as a powerful, often independent figure.

The northwest. During this period, much of the territory of the principalities of Smolensk, Polotsk, Turov, and Pinsk was controlled by the grand principality of Lithuania, which was essentially an international or nonnational formation, led by a foreign dynasty (of east Lithuanian pagan origins) ruling over predominantly Belorussian and Ukrainian populations. By the 15th century, the dynasty had become Slavic in culture (a version of Belorussian was the official language of the realm), and at its height under Vytautas (1392–1430) it controlled all of the old Kievan territory outside of Great Russia proper—that is, most of the present-day Lithuanian, Belorussian, Moldavian, and Ukrainian Soviet Socialist Republics. In 1385 the grand principality joined the Kingdom of Poland, and the union was sealed shortly thereafter by the marriage of Grand Prince Jogaila (Jagiełło) to Jadwiga, the Polish queen.

Early Moscow

The northeast. The region bounded by the Oka and Volga rivers, later to be the heartland of the grand principality of Moscow, was settled before the arrival of Slavs from Novgorod and the Baltic area by a Finnic tribe with whom the Slavic newcomers intermingled. Rostov, the earliest princely centre, was from Vladimir's time included in the princely rotation system. In the 12th century, it became the patrimony of the younger branch of Vladimir Monomakh's family (who founded the new princely centre Vladimir in 1108). Under his son Yury Dolgoruky (1125–57) and grandson Andrew Bogolyubsky (1157–74), the principality reached a high political and cultural development, which it retained through much of the succeeding century. Early in the 13th century, the principality of Moscow was created as an appanage (royal grant) within the grand principality of Vladimir, and this new seat grew in importance when Michael Khorobrit, brother of Alexander Nevsky, conquered Vladimir (1248) and made himself prince of both centres. Daniel, Nevsky's son and the progenitor of all the later Rurikid princes of Moscow, had a long and successful reign (1276–1303), but at his death the principality still embraced little more than the territory of the present Moscow *oblast* (an area of 140 miles [225 kilometres] in length and width). The beginning of Moscow's rise to its later preeminence came in the reign of Daniel's son Ivan (1328–41), who, by cooperating with Öz Beg, khan of the Golden Horde, and also by his shrewd purchases (probably of tax-farming rights), greatly expanded the influence of his principality.

The southwest. The lands of Galicia and Volhynia were always ethnically and economically distinct from the Kievan region proper, as well as from more distant regions. Agriculture was highly developed, and trade, particularly in the valuable local salt, tended to take westward and overland routes. Galicia, already a separate principality by 1100, grew as Kiev declined. Later, Roman Mstislavich of Volhynia (ruled 1199–1205) conquered Galicia and united the two principalities. Under his son Daniel (1201–64), difficulties with the Galician landed magnates and the interference of the Hungarians weakened the principality, and it was subjugated in 1240 by the Mongol invasion. Eventually, this region came under the domination of Lithuania (Volhynia) and Poland (Galicia).

THE MONGOL PERIOD

The Mongol invasion. In 1223, when the first Mongol reconnaissance into former Kievan territory led to the disastrous defeat of a Volhynian–Galician–Polovtsian army on the Kalka River, the various Rurikid principalities had for generations been intermittently at war, usually in complex alliances with equally disunited groups of Polovtsian clans. Kiev was in ruins, Novgorod was preoccupied with commerce and with its northern neighbours, Galicia was being torn internally and drawn increasingly into Polish and Hungarian dynastic affairs, and Vladimir-Suzdal, apparently the leading principality, was unable to resist the finely organized and skillful mounted bowmen of the steppe, the greatest military force of the age.

Pious tradition, born of the works of monkish annalists

From A. Hermann, *An Historical Atlas of China*

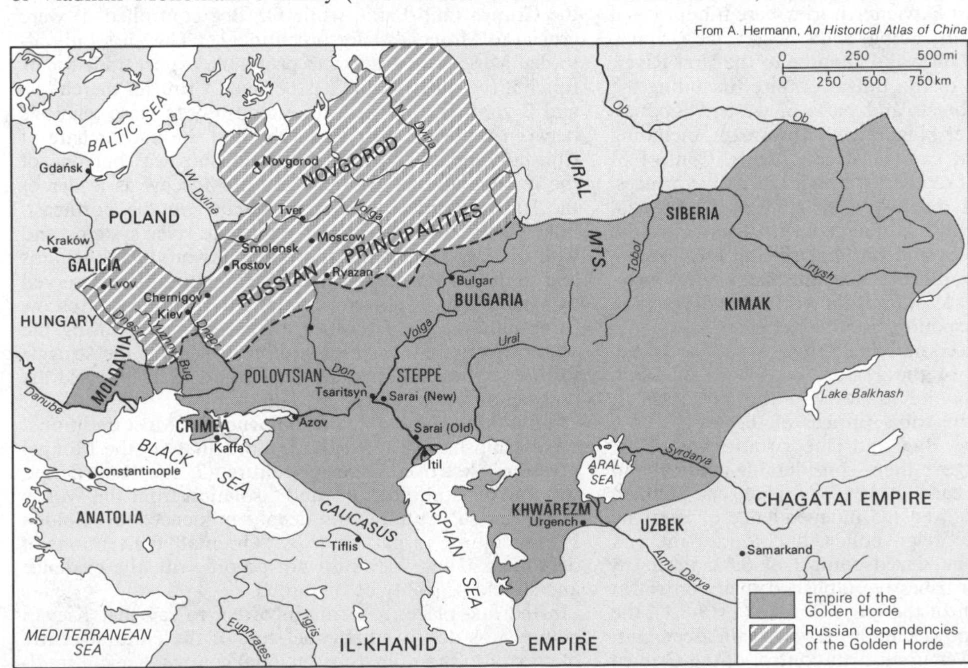

The empire of the Golden Horde at its greatest extent.

Impact of Mongol victories

and court panegyrists, has exaggerated both the destructiveness of the first Mongol conquests and the strength of the resistance. The Mongols aimed to revive, under a unified political system, the trade that had traditionally crossed the central Asian steppe and vitalized the economy of the pastoral nomads. As they moved westward, they easily gained the collaboration of groups of Turkic nomads and the predominantly Iranian and Muslim traders in the towns of the old silk route; they encountered the greatest resistance in sedentary political centres and among land-owning elites. The lands of the Rus presented numerous similarities with the central Asian areas the Mongols had already conquered. Here, too, a former commercial empire had fallen apart into an aggregation of warring principalities. Here, too, ready recruits were to be found in the Polovtsians, who controlled the lower Dnepr and Volga and Don, and in the Muslim merchants, who dealt in the towns of the Crimea and the Upper Volga. These merchants showed the way, first (1223) to the Crimea and up the Volga to the old centre of Bulgar, later (1236) to Bulgar a second time, then to Ryazan, Rostov, and the Suzdalian towns, and still later (1240) to Kiev and Galicia.

Many of the conquered cities made a striking recovery and adjustment to the new relationships. Some towns, such as Kiev, never fully recovered in Mongol times, but the cities of the Vladimir-Suzdal region clearly prospered. New centres, such as Moscow and Tver (modern Kalinin), hardly mentioned in any source before the Mongol period, arose and flourished in Mongol times.

Thus, the Mongol invasion was not everywhere a catastrophe. The local princely dynasties continued unchanged in their traditional seats; some princes resisted the new authority and were killed in battle, but no alien princes ever became established in Slavic territory. Few Mongols remained west of the Urals after the conquest; political and fiscal administration was entrusted to the same Turkic clan leaders and Islāmic merchants who had for generations operated in the area. The whole of the Novgorodian north remained outside the sphere of direct Tatar control, although the perspicacious burghers maintained correct relations with the khans.

The Mongol commercial empire

Tatar rule. After a brief attempt to revive the ancient centres of Bulgar and the Crimea, the Jucids (the family of Jöchi, son of Genghis Khan, who inherited the western portion of his empire) established a new capital, Itil. (It was moved to New Sarai, near the site of Tsaritsyn, modern Volgograd, in about 1260.) These towns became the commercial and administrative centres of what was later to be called the "Golden Horde" (the term is probably a Western invention). Its East Slavic territories were tributaries of an extensive empire, including, at its height, the Crimea, the Polovtsian steppe from the Danube to the Ural River, the former territories of the Bulgar empire (including the fur-rich Moldavian forests and parts of western Siberia), and in Asia the former kingdom of Khwārezm, including Urgench, the cultural capital of the Jucids. Control of the Slavic lands was exercised through the native princes, some of whom spent much of their time at the Mongol capital, and through agents charged with overseeing the activities of the princes and particularly the fiscal levies. The meagre evidence indicates that the Tatar rulers were, for the first century at least, more interested in developing commerce than in despoiling their subjects.

This multinational commercial empire was unstable. Early in the history of the Horde, the khans of Sarai, who tended to reflect the interests of the Volga tribes, were challenged by the tribal princes of the west, whose control of the Danube, Bug, and Dnepr routes and of the access to the Crimea gave them considerable political and economic power. As early as 1260, Nokhai, one of these western chieftains, showed his independence of Sarai by establishing his own foreign policy, and toward the end of the 13th century he seized control of Sarai itself. At his death, the eastern tribes reestablished their control in Sarai, but in the reign of the great Öz Beg (1313–41), the high point of Horde power, the west was again ascendant. Öz Beg based his power upon firm control of the Crimea and had extensive relations with the Genoese and Venetians, who controlled the main ports there. After the death of Öz Beg's son Jani Beg (died 1357), however, the empire began to reveal serious internal strains. The tribes of the west paid little heed to the khans who appeared in dizzying succession in Sarai; the north Russian princes fell to quarrelling and to manoeuvring for their own advantage in the internecine politics of the Horde; the Volga Bulgar region was detached by a dissident Tatar prince; and the lands of the east were drawn into the orbit of the Turkic conqueror Timur (Tamerlane).

The Horde's last cycle of integration and dismemberment was closely linked with events in Timur's domains. Tokhtamysh, son of a minor Tatar prince, had been unsuccessfully involved in the skirmishes around the throne of Sarai in the 1370s and had fled to the court of Timur, with whose aid he returned to Sarai and vanquished the tribal leaders who had opposed him. Having defeated and made peace with them, he now turned to defeat Mamai (1381), who had the previous year been defeated by Prince Dmitry Donskoy ("of the Don"; grand prince of Moscow, 1359–89). Mamai's western tribal allies went over to Tokhtamysh, and, for a brief time, the major components of the tribal structure of the Horde were reunited. Tokhtamysh successfully attacked Moscow (just as Mamai had hoped to do) and set about consolidating his gains. As his power grew, however, Tokhtamysh was drawn into a struggle with Timur, who had conquered much of Iran, the south Caucasus, and eastern Anatolia. After a number of encounters in the northern Caucasus, Timur, who apparently was intent upon diversion of east–west trade through his own Transoxanian and North Iranian territories, set out to destroy Tokhtamysh and the latter's commercial centres. In 1395 and 1396, Timur's armies systematically annihilated Sarai, Azov, and Kaffa and marched through the Lower Volga to the borders of the Russian principalities. The Horde never recovered; its subsequent history is a record of struggles among its erstwhile subjects for supremacy and attempts to find some new *modus vivendi* that would restore political and commercial stability to the steppe.

The rise of Muscovy. From the beginning of the Tatar period, the Rurikid princes displayed much disunity. During the reign of the Tatar khan Öz Beg there was a shift of alignments. The princes of Moscow and their allies, together with Öz Beg and his Crimean supporters, generally opposed the princes of Tver, Pskov, and, intermittently, Novgorod. The major punitive measures directed by Öz Beg against Tver with Muscovite support were a part of this pattern.

Factors favouring Moscow

The links forged in the 14th century between Moscow and the Crimea (and Sarai, while Öz Beg controlled it) were crucial to Moscow's later preeminence. They not only afforded Moscow a steady and profitable export trade for its furs but (because of contacts between Crimean merchants and Byzantium) also led quite naturally to close relations between the Muscovite hierarchy and the patriarchate of Constantinople. This special relationship was but one of the reasons for the eventual rise of Moscow as leader of the Russian lands. Admirably situated in the northeast, linked with all of the major navigable river systems and with the steppe, close to the major fur-producing regions and to the most intensely settled agricultural lands, served by a succession of shrewd and long-lived princes, Moscow came naturally to a position of preeminence during the 14th century and was best equipped to enter the struggle for the political inheritance of the Horde that followed the destruction of its capitals by Timur.

Cultural life and the "Tatar influence." Most traditional scholarship has accepted the notions that (1) the Mongol invasion "destroyed" Kievan culture; (2) the Tatar period was one of "stultification" and "isolation from the West"; (3) "Russian" culture was deeply influenced by Golden Horde culture, in particular by "Oriental" conceptions of despotism. These views do not accord with the evidence and should probably be discarded.

In the first place, it seems incorrect to say that Kievan culture was destroyed. In the shift of the cultural centre of gravity to the numerous regional centres, Kievan traditions were in the main continued and in some cases (*i.e.*,

Galician literature, Novgorodian icon painting, Suzdalian architecture) enjoyed remarkable development.

Similarly, the notions of stultification and isolation from the West cannot be supported. The enormous Novgorodian culture sphere, the Upper Dnepr territories that eventually came under Lithuanian control, and the principalities of Volhynia and Galicia all had, if anything, closer contacts with western and central Europe than in the previous period. Each of these areas, in its own way, acted as a repository of the Kievan traditions and produced some features that later were to be incorporated into the new Muscovite culture.

As to "Tatar influence," in the areas of religion and intellectual life, it was practically nonexistent. Control of formal culture by the Orthodox clergy and Muslim divines and limited contact between the Slavic and Turkic populations prevented it. There is no evidence that any single Turkic or Islāmic text of religious, philosophical, literary or scholarly content was translated directly into Slavonic or any East Slavic vernacular during the period.

Concerning the secular culture of the court and counting house, the situation was radically different. These spheres were controlled by very pragmatic princes, merchants, and diplomats. Here, Slavs and Tatars elaborated together an international subculture whose language was Turkic and whose administrative techniques and chancellery culture were essentially those of the Golden Horde. Slavic merchants took full part in this culture, and the princes of Muscovy, in particular, developed their original court culture and chancellery practices within its context. These borrowings, however, were not of a theoretical or ideological nature, and to ascribe later despotism—and its theoretical basis—to "Oriental" influence is to misunderstand the development of Muscovite absolutism. The phenomenon and its justification spring from other sources (see below).

The post-Sarai period. The collapse of the Golden Horde saw a growth in the political power of the old sedentary centres—Muscovy, Lithuania, the Volga Bulgar region (which became the khanate of Kazan), and the Crimea. This growth was accompanied by dynastic struggles. This period of recovery also saw cooperation among the emerging dynasties against their internal enemies and toward the stabilization of the steppe.

Even by the end of the 14th century, Moscow's position was by no means as dominating as the cartographers' conventions or the historians' hindsight make it seem. Other centres—Lithuania, Tver, Novgorod—were as rich and powerful as Moscow; many of the areas nominally subject to the Muscovite princes retained their own dynasties, whose members often broke away and sided with one of Moscow's rivals. Only after a series of dynastic conflicts in the early 15th century did Moscow emerge as the leader of the Great Russian territory.

The struggle began at the death of Vasily I, a son of Dmitry Donskoy, in 1425. The succession of his ten-year-old son Vasily II was challenged by his uncle Yury, prince of the important Upper Volga commercial town of Galich. Although the ensuing conflict was conducted in the name of the right succession to the grand princely throne, the underlying issues were regional and economic. After many turns of fortune, Vasily II succeeded, with the help of Lithuanian and Tatar allies, in establishing his house permanently as the rulers of Muscovy.

RURIKID MUSCOVY

Ivan III. Ivan III (ruled 1462–1505), known to history as the Great, consolidated from a secure throne the gains his father, Vasily II, had won in the saddle. Although little is known of Ivan, an exceptional intelligence is apparent behind the consistent and brilliantly effective military and diplomatic campaigns of his time.

The gathering of the Russian lands

The "gathering of the Russian lands," as it has traditionally been known, became under Ivan a conscious and irresistible drive by Moscow to annex all East Slavic lands, both the Great Russian territories, which had traditionally had close links with Moscow, and the Belorussian and Ukrainian regions, which had developed under distinctly different historical and cultural circumstances. In 1471 Ivan mounted a simultaneous attack upon Novgorod and its Upper Volga colonies, which capitulated and accepted Moscow's commercial and political demands. The trading republic, however, retained considerable de facto independence and became involved with the Lithuanian princes in an attempt to resist Moscow. Ivan, using these dealings as a pretext, attacked again, and in 1478 Novgorod was absorbed by Moscow. A Muscovite governor was installed, and 70 Novgorodian boyar families were deported and assigned estates elsewhere to hold in service tenure, being replaced by members of the Moscow military-service class.

Tver suffered a similar fate. Ivan had agreed with Prince Michael Borisovich of Tver to conduct foreign relations in concert and by consultation, but, when the Tverite complained that Ivan was not consulting him on important matters, Ivan attacked him and annexed his lands (1485). By the end of Ivan's reign, there were no Great Russian princes who dared conduct policies unacceptable to Moscow.

The success of Ivan's expansion was determined by his skillful dealings with the Polish–Lithuanian state, which had expanded down the Dnepr Basin and into Slavic territories on the south flank of Moscow. After 1450 a competition developed for control of the numerous semi-independent principalities of the Dnepr and Upper Donets regions. In the early 1490s, some minor East Slavic princes defected from Lithuania to Moscow. The first phase of the conflict, confined to border skirmishes, ended in 1494 with a treaty ceding Vyazma to Moscow and with the marriage of Ivan's daughter Yelena to Alexander, grand duke of Lithuania. In 1500, on the initiative of Lithuanian defectors, Ivan's armies seized a number of important border towns; this began a war that ended somewhat inconclusively in 1503 with a truce that extended Ivan's border considerably to the west.

The third major element of Ivan's foreign policy comprised his relations with the various Tatar confederations. In the 1470s, the Crimean khan Mengli Giray came into increasing conflict with Khan Ahmed of the Horde and became interested in an alliance with Moscow against Ahmed and Lithuania. Ivan, eager to dissolve the connection between Lithuania and the Crimea, but not wanting to alienate Ahmed, stalled for time. In 1481, when Ahmed died, Ivan was able to forge an alliance with the Nogais, Mengli Giray, and Kazan. The security provided by this system became the cornerstone of his later policies. Ivan was the first Muscovite prince to have an integrated foreign policy, but he did not "cast off the Tatar yoke" as he is traditionally supposed to have done. The yoke—if such it was—had long since fallen of itself.

In addition to problems of war and diplomacy, Ivan was faced with a number of challenges from within his own family and court. In 1472 his eldest brother, Yury, died childless, and Ivan appropriated his entire estate. This action antagonized the two eldest surviving brothers, Andrey and Boris, whose grievances were further increased by Ivan's refusal to give them a share of conquered Novgorod. In 1480 they rebelled, at a time when he was threatened by a Tatar invasion, and only with difficulty were they persuaded to remain loyal. A more serious conflict arose (1497–1502) in the form of an open and murderous struggle among Ivan's relatives for succession to the throne. Ivan had originally named as his heir his grandson Dmitry, son of his deceased son Ivan and the Moldavian princess Yelena, but a group close to Ivan's second wife, Sofia (Zoë) Palaeologus, opposed this; her son Vasily threatened and perhaps attempted an insurrection, and Ivan was forced to accept Vasily. Historians have long pondered the causes of this struggle, in which most of the strands of Ivan's politics are brought together, but the motives and actions of the prince and his family remain obscure. For all its obvious achievement, Ivan's reign was nevertheless full of conflict and contradiction.

The entrance into Europe

Ivan made the first effort on the part of a Muscovite ruler to become involved in the diplomacy of western Europe. He and his advisors realized the need for a counterpoise to the Polish–Lithuanian power, while the diplomats of Rome and Vienna were interested in the possibility of flanking the growing empire of the Ottomans with a Muscovite–Tatar force. In the 1470s and 80s, there was an unprecedented traffic between these capitals and Moscow. It was through these channels that Ivan arranged his marriage to Sofia Palaeologus, a niece of the last Byzantine emperor. Sofia has been credited with considerable influence over Ivan, in particular with urging him to adopt the Byzantine political style (*e.g.*, autocracy, state domination of the church, etc.), but in fact she probably had little influence over Ivan's policies. His reign ended on a note of failure, with his overtures to the west and his brief rapprochement with Lithuania both disrupted by the intractable territorial and religious conflicts of the Slavic east and by the opportunism of the local magnates. Moscow's situation was worsened after Ivan's death by the collapse of the alliance with the Crimean khan Mengli Giray upon the Khan's death in 1515, opening a new period of chaos and readjustment in the steppe.

A similar appraisal must be made of Ivan's domestic policies. Although his reign was notable for the annexation of the rich Novgorodian provinces, for the establishment of a regular bureaucracy and a land-tenure system, and for certain improvements in agriculture, these achievements created new problems for his successors. The system of land grants to military servitors led to a major struggle over monastic landowning and hastened the enserfment of the free peasantry in the central lands. His territorial annexations were to be the seeds of future administrative and political problems.

Vasily III. Ivan's son Vasily, who came to the throne in 1505, greatly strengthened the monarchy. He completed the annexation of Great Russian territories with the absorption of Pskov (1510) and Ryazan (1521) and began the advance into non-Great Russian territories (Smolensk, 1514). He also undertook to limit the scale of monastic and lay landholdings, as well as the juridical immunities attached to them. In these measures he relied upon the growing crops of bureaucrats and service gentry, rather than upon the great boyars, whose power subsequently declined.

Faced with a continuing Lithuanian war and with the breakdown of his father's Tatar policy, Vasily carefully temporized in order to avoid uniting his enemies. Once he had secured peace in the west, he was able to deal directly with the khan of the Crimean Tatars. In the end, however, much of what Vasily accomplished was undone by his failure as a procreator: divorcing his first wife for her apparent barrenness, he married Yelena Glinskaya, who bore him only two children—the congenitally retarded Yury and the sickly Ivan, who was three years old at Vasily's death, in 1533.

Ivan IV the Terrible. Vasily had been able to appoint a regency council composed of his most trusted advisors and headed by his wife Yelena. The grievances created by his limitation of landholders' immunities and his antiboyar policies soon found expression in intrigue and opposition. The bureaucracy he had relied upon could not function without firm leadership. Although Yelena continued Vasily's policies with some success, on her death, in 1538, various parties of boyars sought to gain control of the state apparatus; a decade of intrigue followed, during which affairs of state, when managed at all, went forward because of the momentum developed by the bureaucracy. Foreign policy was moribund, in spite of considerable opportunities presented by the continuing decay of the khanate of Kazan, and domestic policy vacillated so wildly that scholars cannot agree upon an appraisal of its main directions.

Toward the end of the 1540s, however, there emerged a strong coalition of bureaucrats, clergy, and old Muscovite boyars. Apparently inspired by a common awareness of the needs of the state, they ended the debilitating intrigues and embarked upon a thoroughgoing program of reform. The first important step was the reestablishment of the monarch (for the first time to be officially designated tsar), accomplished through the coronation of the 16-year-old Ivan in unprecedented solemnity and pomp. Shortly afterward, he was married to Anastasia Romanovna Zakharina, of the leading boyar family.

Although there is a voluminous literature devoted to Ivan, almost nothing is known of his personality, his political views, or his methods of rule. There is little reliable biographical information about him aside from the facts of his six marriages, his lifelong ill health, and his mercurial temper. It is not even known when he began to rule in fact or which of the policies of his reign can be considered his.

Power of politicians over Ivan

Ivan was doubtless a puppet in the hands of the leading politicians long after his coronation. The major reforms of the middle 1550s, which produced a new law code, a new military organization, a reform of local government, and severe restrictions upon the powers of hereditary landowners (including the monasteries), were probably the work of the bureaucrats and clergy, their objective being to modernize and standardize the administration of the growing state. The immediate goal was to strengthen the state and military apparatus in connection with major campaigns (the first undertaken in 1547) against the khanate of Kazan, and to prepare for the major colonization of the new lands that that conquest and others were expected to secure. Toward the end of the 1550s, Ivan seems to have gained the support of certain groups opposed to these policies and to have seized control of the government. The issue was evidently foreign policy. The planned conquest of the Volga and steppe region had been delayed in execution, and the Kazan campaigns had been enormously costly. By 1557, when the campaigns against the Crimea began, there was much opposition in the highest military circles. Ivan took the dissidents' part and for the first time emerged as an independent figure.

Ivan was a disastrously bad ruler, in part because no one had ever anticipated that he would rule. His lifelong ill health and the idiocy of his brother made it quite natural for the regency and the politicians to ignore him and to neglect his education. In his adulthood, he contracted a painful and incurable bone disease, from which he sought relief in potions provided by a succession of foreign doctors and quacks and in alcohol. Once he had acquired full power, he set about destroying those who had ruled during the interregnum, as well as the machinery of government they had built up.

Ivan's famous *oprichnina,* an aggregate of territory to be separated from the rest of the realm and put under his immediate control as crown land, established in 1564, was the device through which he expressed his hatred and misunderstanding of the established government. As his private domain, a state within the state, he took into it predominantly northern and commercial territories that had enjoyed a special prosperity in preceding decades. Specific towns and districts all over Russia were included in the *oprichnina,* their revenues being assigned to the maintenance of Ivan's new court and household. He established a new, much simplified officialdom and a court composed of sycophants and mercenaries, prone to rule through terror, accompanied by persecution of precisely those groups that had contributed so much to the modernization of the state. As trained statesmen and administrators were replaced by hirelings and cronies, the central government and military organization began to disintegrate. The destructiveness of the *oprichnina* was heightened by Ivan's involvement in the costly and ultimately disatrous Livonian Wars throughout this period (indeed, some historians have viewed the *oprichnina* as a device for the prosecution of these taxing campaigns). Even before they had ended, Ivan was forced by the utter incompetence of his special *oprichnina* army to reintegrate it (1572) with the regular army and to revert, in theory at least, to the previous institutions of government. By the time he died, in 1584, the state that he had wanted to reclaim from its makers was in ruins.

Boris Godunov. Ivan had murdered his eldest son, Ivan, in a fit of rage in 1581, and his only legitimate heir, Fyodor, was an idiot. Power passed to those who were at Ivan's deathbed, among whom Boris Godunov, who had capped a rapid rise in court circles by the cynical marriage of his sister Irina to the pathetic Fyodor, soon emerged as the leading force. Godunov's judicious combination of chicanery, vision, and force enabled him to disarm his most dangerous enemies and to have himself proclaimed tsar after Fyodor's death in 1598. His policies during Fyodor's reign had been consistently restorative and concilia-

The struggle for Ivan's succession

tory, and he had apparently succeeded in repairing much of the damage done to the state in Ivan's time. He conducted a cautious and generally successful foreign policy: the 20 years of his reign were, except for a short, successful war against Sweden, peaceful. In domestic policy, he returned to the modernizing and standardizing policies of the mid-century. He reorganized the land-tenure system, commerce, and taxation.

For a number of his problems Godunov could find no solution. Chief among these were the depopulation of the central Muscovite lands and the discontent among small landholders in the territories recently acquired in the south and southwest. Added to these problems was the continuing opposition of the boyars.

The first False Dmitry

In spite of these difficulties and widespread famine caused by crop failures in 1601–02, Godunov remained well in control of the situation until the appearance of the so-called first False Dmitry, a defrocked monk who had appeared in Poland in 1601 claiming to be the son of Ivan IV. (The true Dmitry had died during an epileptic seizure in 1591.) The False Dmitry found some supporters in Poland—notably, Jerzy Mniszech, to whose 15-year-old daughter, Maryna, he became engaged. As the impostor moved northeast toward Muscovy, he acquired growing support among the disaffected petty gentry and Cossacks (peasants who had escaped from serfdom to a nomadic life) of the regions through which he passed, and border cities throughout the south opened their gates to him. Godunov's troops easily defeated the ragtag force, which apparently had many secret supporters among Muscovite boyars, but a few weeks later Godunov died. The boyars staged a coup against Godunov's family and declared Dmitry tsar. The pretender entered Moscow in triumph, was crowned, and married Maryna Mniszchówna.

The Time of Troubles. The events of 1606–13 cannot be captured in a few words. Chaos gripped most of central Muscovy; Muscovite boyars, Polish–Lithuanian–Ukrainian Cossacks, and assorted mobs of adventurers and desperate citizens were among the chief actors. In May 1606, a small-scale revolt supported by popular indignation at the foolishly insulting behaviour of Dmitry and his Polish garrison brought the overthrow and murder of the pretender. The boyars gave the crown to Prince Vasily Shuysky, a leader of the revolt against Dmitry, with the understanding that he would respect the special rights and privileges of the boyars. While the new tsar had the support of most boyars and of the northern merchants, he could not, however, end the disorders in the south or the adventures of the Polish and Swedish kings, who used Muscovy as a battlefield in their continuing conflict with each other. In 1608 a number of boyars, led by the Romanovs, went over to a second False Dmitry, who had ridden a wave of discontent and freebootery from the Cossack south into the centre of Muscovy. A kind of shadow government was formed in the village of Tushino, nine miles (14 kilometres) west of Moscow, in which the boyars and bureaucrats of the Romanov circle took leading posts. It managed to gain Cossack support and to manipulate Dmitry's pretensions while dealing with the Polish king Sigismund III over terms on which his son Władysław IV might become tsar. Shuysky, in desperation, turned to Sweden for aid, promising territorial concessions along the Swedish–Muscovite border. At this, the Polish king invaded Muscovy and besieged Smolensk (September 1609). The Tushino coalition dissolved, and Dmitry withdrew to the south. The position of the Shuysky government deteriorated, and in 1610 the tsar was deserted by his army and his allies. The boyars formed a seven-man provisional government with the aim of installing a Polish tsar. This government proved unable to settle its affairs and to restore order to the country. A new insurgent army, financed by northern merchants and staffed with Swedish troops, marched on Moscow with the intention of ousting the Polish garrison and of bringing the various Cossack bands under control. It nearly gained Moscow but fell apart because its leadership could make no arrangement with the Cossack leaders.

Cossack capture of the Kremlin

A year later, a second force, raised in the same northern cities and supported by Cossacks who had been part of the Tushino camp, was able to take possession of the Kremlin. A call was issued for the election of a new tsar.

Social and economic conditions. In the flux of social and economic life in the 15th and 16th centuries, three interconnected processes may be observed: a steady economic growth, mainly from colonization and trade but also from the productivity of agriculture; an expansion in the power of the central government; and the encroachment of the nobility upon the lands previously held by the free peasantry, accompanied by the reduction of the bulk of the peasantry to serf status.

In the middle of the 15th century, society and the economy were still organized along traditional lines. The land was sparsely settled. Life for most of the population was simple and probably close to the subsistence level. Serfdom did not yet exist. Most of the peasantry lived on state lands and paid whatever taxes could be extracted from them by their prince or his bailiff.

A number of changes occurred in this pattern in the latter part of the 15th century. Around 1460, measures were taken to bring the peasantry under more regular control of the state and the landlord. Peasant registration appeared at this time, and also the requirement spread that peasants might renounce the tenancy of the land they were working only at the end of the agricultural cycle, in the week of St. Yury's Day (November 26). The growing controls upon the peasantry received impetus from the large-scale deportations and colonizations that accompanied the annexations of Novgorod, Tver, Pskov, and Ryazan, when the old nobility were replaced with nobility owing service to the prince of Muscovy. The nationwide promulgation of the restriction on movement to St. Yury's Day was contained in the law code of 1497, which added the stipulation that peasants leaving a former situation must pay the landlord all arrears in addition to a departure fee. All of the measures, together with the expansion of the state apparatus for tax gathering and adjudication of disputes over land and peasants, were associated with the growing complexity and power of the central government.

The law code of 1550 repeated the stipulation of 1497 limiting peasant departure, but with much more specific provisions and stronger sanctions. Other reforms put an end to local administration by rotating military governors and limited monastic landholding and the juridical rights of landlords over their peasants. The events and policies of the latter half of the reign of Ivan IV destroyed many of the beneficial results of the reforms. The Livonian Wars imposed unprecedented burdens on the tax-paying population and required such long absences by the landed nobles that their estates fell into ruin. Ivan's *oprichnina* caused the breakup of the great independent boyar holdings, in which the vitality of the peasant commune had been preserved, and replaced them with smaller service estates, often too small to be operated efficiently, whose masters needed to exploit serf and indentured labour in order to meet their obligations of service to the grand prince. These burdens led to the mass flight of the peasantry from the central agricultural regions, resulting in serious economic difficulties and a sharp fiscal crisis. Godunov's government attempted to deal with the problems through remission of taxes, avoidance of war, and harsher measures to keep the peasants on the land; but the country entered the Time of Troubles weakened by decades of economic chaos.

The crystallization of Great Russian culture

Cultural trends. This period also saw the crystallization of that complex of forms and ideas that can, for the first time, be identified as Great Russian culture. There was a gathering and integration of the Novgorodian, Tverite, and Suzdalian cultural traditions. Moscow began to attract the artists, craftsmen, and learned monks who built the eclectic but "national" churches of Ivan III's otherwise Italianate Kremlin and who wrote the revised national, pro-Muscovite versions of the chronicles that had been kept in Rostov, Ryazan, and Novgorod. The regional traditions were not always easily reconciled. Novgorodian attitudes, in particular, clashed with those of Muscovy.

The reign of Ivan III saw a marked turning toward the West. Ivan surrounded himself with Italian and Greek diplomats and craftsmen. His palace of 1487, his Kremlin with its Latin inscription over the main gate, and his churches, the original aspect of which has been altered by successive russifying restorations, were clearly in the Italian style, as contemporary foreign visitors noted. His marriage to Sofia, the niece of the last Byzantine emperor, Constantine Palaeologus, had, in addition to its diplomatic significance, a symbolic function of bringing Ivan into the circle of Western princes. This was the time of the "Third Rome" theory, when Muscovy supposedly regarded itself as the heir of Byzantium and as the spiritual leader of the Orthodox world. It may be that the church leadership, militantly anti-Roman, thought of itself in this light. Ivan and many around him viewed the Byzantine heritage as Western, by contrast with the Ottoman and Tatar world, and were at pains to associate Muscovy with Western traditions and interprincely relations. This striving to be accepted in the Western world marked most of the changes in regalia and style of Ivan's reign, although these were later to be buried in the lore of Muscovite Byzantinism.

Three significant causes can be discerned for the evolution of Muscovite culture in the 16th century. The first was the growth and prosperity of the Great Russian population, united under a stable and increasingly centralized monarchy, which produced the conditions for the rise of a national culture. The second was the diplomatic and cultural isolation in which Muscovy found itself, particularly in the first half of the 16th century, as a result of hostile relations with increasingly powerful Lithuania and Poland, a cause that, more than any other, brought an end to Ivan III's westward turn and to the revolutionary adjustments of the age of exploration. The third cause was the resolution of church–state relations, in the course of which the church submitted to the power of the princes in politics but gained control over the culture, style, and ideology of the dynasty, producing the peculiar amalgam of nationalistic, autocratic, and Orthodox elements that became the official culture of high Muscovy. This new synthesis was reflected in the great undertakings associated with the name of Metropolitan Makary of Moscow: St. Basil's Cathedral in the Kremlin; the encyclopaedic Menolog, or calendar of months, which contained all of the literature, translated and original, permitted to be read in the churches; and the *Illustrated Codex,* a compilation of East Slavic and Greek chronicles in an official Muscovite version.

ROMANOV MUSCOVY

Michael Fyodorovich. The military drive that finally expelled the Poles from Moscow led to the election of Michael, the sickly 16-year-old son of Fyodor Romanov, as the new tsar. The composition of the coalition that elected him is not clear, but he evidently represented a compromise among the Cossacks, the boyars (especially the Tushino boyars), and the leaders of the northern army. It would be difficult to imagine circumstances less favourable for the beginning of the reign of the adolescent monarch and a new ruling coalition. The military campaigns had left much of the central and southwestern portions of the country in ruins. In many areas, populations had fled, land lay fallow, and administration was in disarray. Significant portions of the Novgorod, Smolensk, and Ryazan regions were occupied by Swedish and Polish armies and by sundry insurrectionary forces, who threatened to renew hostilities.

Establishment of the Romanovs

The Romanov government required more than a decade to establish itself politically and to restore economic and social order. Few had expected the election of a new tsar (the fourth in eight years) to bring an end to the turmoil. But the election of Michael reflected a resolution of political forces that permitted the coalition government to address itself to the problems of reconstruction. Another cause was the survival of the central bureaucracy; the civil servants in Moscow had served all successive governments without much interruption and were ready to restore administrative regularity as soon as political order was established. Fortunately, the new government refrained from involving itself in the Polish–Swedish conflicts, which reached their height at this period. This restraint was a most important element in the success of the 1613 settlement, for the international situation was, if anything, grimmer than the domestic. Polish–Swedish differences permitted Muscovite diplomats to bring the two countries to separate truces (Poland, 1618; Sweden, 1617); although these left substantial territories under the control of Poland and Sweden, they provided a needed interlude of peace. The Romanov government wisely avoided any significant participation in the Thirty Years' War, in which most European states engaged. At the death of the Polish king Sigismund III in 1632, Muscovy made an ill-advised attempt to regain Smolensk that ended in military disaster; but, in 1634, it obtained Władysław's formal abjuration of the Polish king's questionable claim to the title of tsar.

After the failure of the Smolensk campaign, the government refrained from further military involvement with Poland for nearly a generation. It concentrated instead upon the extension and fortification of its southern borders, where the incursions of Crimean Tatars were an impediment to colonization. Moscow, however, was not prepared to go to war with the Ottomans, who were the protectors of the Crimean khan; when in 1637 the Don Cossacks, Muscovy's clients, captured the critical port of Azov and appealed to Moscow for aid in holding off a counterattack, a *zemsky sobor,* or national assembly (see below *Trends in the 17th century*), decided not to intervene, and the port was lost.

Alexis Mikhaylovich. The reign of Michael's son Alexis, whom later generations considered the very model of a benevolent and gentle tsar, began badly. Like his father, Alexis came to the throne a mere boy. Immediately, the boyar who controlled the government, Boris Ivanovich Morozov, embarked upon policies that brought the government to the brink of disaster. Morozov cut government salaries; he also introduced a tax on salt and a state monopoly of tobacco, the first of which caused widespread hardship and discontent, while the second brought the church's condemnation. At the same time, he alienated boyar groups close to the throne by his interference in his ward's marriage.

Domination of Morozov

Morozov's actions exacerbated an already dangerous situation in the country. The city populations and service gentry, in particular, were heavily burdened by taxes and other obligations and were increasingly angry at the growing wealth and power of the ruling clique. During a riot in Moscow in May 1648, a mob surrounded the 19-year-old tsar, demanding the execution of Morozov and the leading officials. Some of the latter were thrown to the mob, and a brief protective exile was arranged for Morozov. Morozov's boyar enemies, who may have abetted the riot, took control of affairs and carried out a series of reforms. The salt tax and tobacco monopoly were ended, and a commission was established for the drafting of a new law code. Serious disorders continued in the cities of the north, particularly in Pskov and Novgorod, where force was required to reimpose authority.

In Novgorod, the principal actor in the government's interest was the metropolitan Nikon, an energetic and authoritarian monk who had made influential friends in Moscow while archimandrite at the Romanov family church and continued assiduously to cultivate the tsar and his relations while in Novgorod. In 1652 his solicitations earned him the patriarchate. Tradition has it that, before accepting the position, Nikon demanded a declaration of full obedience in religious and moral matters from the tsar. In the first years of Nikon's tenure, his relations with Alexis and the court were good; the patriarch, with official support, carried out a number of liturgical and organizational reforms; he surrounded himself with an impressive bureaucracy modelled upon the state apparatus. Relations with the tsar became strained in 1658, however, and, after he was publicly snubbed by Alexis, Nikon announced that he was abandoning the patriarchate. He later held that he had simply gone into temporary seclusion, but his effective power and influence were at an end.

The main event of Alexis' reign was the annexation of the eastern Ukraine. His government had continued the previous policy of avoiding entanglements in the West while expanding eastward but could not resist the opportunity offered, in 1654, when the leader of a Cossack revolution against Polish rule in the Ukraine appealed to Moscow for the help he had been unable to obtain from Sweden and the Turks. Moscow accepted his allegiance in return for military assistance and thus became involved in a protracted struggle with Poland and Sweden for the Ukrainian, Belorussian, and Baltic territories. At first, the war went well, but the differing objectives of the Ukrainian and Muscovite allies soon revealed themselves; when Charles X of Sweden entered the fray against Poland, Alexis made peace, in 1656; he feared a strong Sweden as much as a strong Poland. Muscovite forces plunged into war with Sweden for the Estonian, Livonian, and Karelian territories along the Baltic coast. The situation in the Ukraine became increasingly confused and dangerous for Moscow, and it was necessary to end the war with Sweden in 1661, even at the cost of yielding, once again, the Baltic coast.

Territorial expansion in the 17th century

In the Ukraine, the war took on a new aspect when, in 1664, Peter Doroshenko, a new leader, put himself under the protection of the Ottomans. The Turks joined in a number of major military operations, alarming both Poland and Moscow sufficiently to bring them to a truce at Andrusovo (1667). Poland recognized Moscow's control over eastern Ukraine and Kiev, while Moscow yielded most of Belorussia and the Ukraine west of the Dnepr.

The peace did not greatly improve the government's position, for the same year saw the beginning of a threatening movement among the Don Cossacks and peasants of the Volga region, led by Stenka Razin, and a political battle within the inner circles at court, caused by the death of Alexis' wife. After two years, Alexis was married to Nataliya Naryshkina. In 1676, however, Alexis himself died, and Fyodor, a sickly son of his first wife, Mariya Miloslavskaya, succeeded him. A struggle began between the rival Naryshkin and Miloslavsky families. The Naryshkins were exiled, and the Miloslavskys, with their clients and supporters, took over. In 1682, however, Fyodor died, and the Naryshkin faction sought to place his half-brother Peter on the throne instead of Fyodor's full brother, the ailing Ivan. The elite corps of *streltsy* (a hereditary military caste) revolted and established Ivan's elder sister Sophia as regent. (For the accession and reign of Peter the Great, see below *The 18th century: The reign of Peter I.*

Trends in the 17th century. Economic reconstruction was slow, particularly in agriculture and in the old central lands, but it was accompanied by a growth of trade and manufacturing. The state revenues profited from the expansion eastward beyond the Urals and southward into the black-soil region. In the north, the port of Archangel handled the export of forest products and semimanufactures (naval stores, potash) to the English and Dutch, and its merchants took a leading role in the early exploitation of Siberia. The government itself became deeply involved in the development of trade and commerce, both through its monopolistic control of certain areas and commodities and by its efforts to build up such strategic industries as metallurgy. The economy grew at unprecedented speed during the 17th century. By 1700 Russia was a leading producer of pig iron and potash, and the economic base upon which Peter's military successes were to depend had been firmly established.

The political recovery of the Russian state after the Time of Troubles was due largely to the survival of the central bureaucracy and ruling oligarchy. The lines of subsequent development were determined by the growth, consolidation, and almost unimpeded self-aggrandizement of these groups in the 17th century. The expansion of the bureaucratic apparatus can be measured in various ways. In 1613 there were 22 *prikazes,* or departments; by mid-century there were 80. At the beginning of the period, the jurisdiction of the bureaucracy included primarily fiscal, juridical, and military matters; by the end of the century, it also covered industrial, religious, and cultural life. At the close of the Time of Troubles, the bureaucracy's functions were exercised by leading boyars and professional administrators; by Peter's time, the mercantile class, the whole of the nobility, and the clergy had become part of its ubiquitous network. This bureaucracy was the buttress—indeed, the substance—of an absolute monarchy whose prerogatives knew no internal bounds.

The expansion of central authority

The ease with which the extension of central authority overwhelmed all other political and social forces is to be explained by the frailty of local institutions and by the absence of independent ecclesiastical or social authority. The Muscovite administration was extended first into the devastated areas, where local institutions had been swept away, and then into new territories that had no significant political institutions, until it became a standardized and centralized mechanism powered by the colossal wealth generated by its own expansion.

These processes were reflected in the great law code of 1649, the first general codification since 1550, which was to remain the basis of Russian law until 1833. Its articles make clear the realities of Muscovite political practice: the rule of the bureaucrats and the extension of the powers of the state into all spheres of human activity. It was based in large measure upon the accumulated ad hoc decisions of the officials and was intended for their guidance. It made ecclesiastical affairs a matter of state jurisdiction; it gave legal expression to the practice of serfdom; and, in an important new article, it enumerated crimes "of word and deed" against the "Sovereign"—by which were to be understood the state and all its agents.

Social development paralleled and was determined by the developments just described. The great families of hereditary princes, still rich and powerful at the turn of the century, were systematically reduced, first through direct repression by the Romanovs, who feared them, and later through fiscal and administrative measures. By the end of the century, only those families that had made new careers in the state apparatus through service as generals, ministers, and ambassadors remained at the apex of society; they were joined by numerous parvenu families that had risen in government service. Particularly striking was the prosperity of the *dyak* class of professional administrators, which had become a closed hereditary estate by a decree of 1640; this class had become a new and powerful "nobility of the seal" that was to survive into modern times.

During much of the 17th century, the government was run, for all practical purposes, by high officials in cooperation with relatives and cronies of the reigning tsar. Nineteenth-century historians, eager to find constitutional traditions in Russia's past, have stressed the role of the *zemsky sobor*—an assembly of dignitaries that from the time of Ivan IV had been called together when matters of crucial importance had to be decided. In the period after 1613, it was in almost continuous session for some years. After 1619, however, the services of these assemblies were no longer required. It is questionable whether they ever had, in law or in fact, any power beyond that of a crowd of military and administrative leaders. They were summoned by the government, and their composition was determined by the government.

Cultural life. No period of Russia's cultural history has been as full of change, turmoil, creativity, failure, and sheer destructiveness as the 17th century. Russian society emerged from the Time of Troubles shattered and unsure of itself, disoriented and impoverished. This shaken society was then subject to wrenching social and economic change and strong external influences.

The old culture, in its formal aspects, had been the culture of the monasteries. Art, literature, architecture, and music remained, until the end of the 16th century, traditional, canonical, and orthodox.

The emergence of a new elite

The 17th century produced, first among the officials and boyars, later among the merchants and middle classes, a new elite that was increasingly interested in European culture and that had mainly secular interests. Yet the government of these same officials and boyars worked to stifle native cultural development, and many of these merchants and nobles were drawn into movements opposed to westernization.

The reasons for this paradoxical development were three. First, Western culture had reached Muscovy largely through Polish and Roman Catholic mediation, which rendered it unacceptable to all but those sophisticated enough to take a very broad view of the events of the Time of Troubles. In the Ukrainian and Belorussian territories, the Polish counter-reformation had brought a national cultural revival. The books and ideas and men flowing from these lands into Muscovy in the 17th century, however, were hardly less suspect than those of Catholic Poland, and, as these "aliens" acquired a dominant position in Muscovite cultural affairs, resentment was added to suspicion.

A second reason for the character of Muscovite cultural development in the 17th century was the preponderant role of the church and, later, of the state, which took over at last the assets, liabilities, and responsibilities of the ecclesiastical establishment. From 1620, when the patriarch Philaret pronounced an anathema upon "books of Lithuanian imprint" (in effect the only secular books in print for the Russian reader) until the end of the century, when the government turned to imposing Greek and "Lithuanian" (*i.e.,* Ukrainian and Belorussian) views upon a resisting populace, the state and its ecclesiastical adjunct had a repressive and stultifying influence.

Finally, indigenous cultural forces were, for various reasons, unable to assert themselves. They were physically dispersed, socially diverse, and set at odds by cultural and political disaffection. The development of a vernacular literature, which can be seen in the synthetic "folk songs," pamphlets, tales, and imitations produced for and by the growing educated class, remained an underground phenomenon; they were unpublished because of the ecclesiastical monopoly of the press, and they were anonymous out of fear. The promising experiments of a group of noble writers who worked within the formal Slavonic tradition were ended by exile and repression. The gay and expressive architecture and painting of the northern regions, which continued certain Novgorod traditions, fell victim to official discrimination against this region and its predominantly Old Believer population.

Despite these negative influences, the court, especially in the time of Alexis, was a centre of literary and artistic innovation, and many of the leading men of the realm were considered cultured and cosmopolitan by Westerners who knew them.

The great schism. The contradictions of the age were reflected in the great schism within the Russian church. The doctrinal debate began over obscure and petty matters of ritual, but larger, unarticulated issues were at stake. Religion in the Time of Troubles had taken two directions, which were at first closely associated: the reformation of religious life (with stress on the pastoral functions of the clergy and the simplification of the liturgy), and the correction and standardization of the canonical books (which had, over centuries of regional mutation and textual degradation, come to vary widely from the Greek originals). The government had at first supported these linked objectives, but the supporters of "Old Russian piety" fell into opposition to the reforms as they were officially promulgated. When, in the 1650s, the patriarch Nikon began to enforce the reforms in the parishes, where they had been generally ignored, the discontent developed into a massive religious and regional insurrection. Towns and parishes of the north were riven by warring "old" and "new" bishops. The Old Believers were either crushed by government force, driven to self-destruction, or reduced to silent resistance.

Enforcement of religious reforms

In the end, the Western secular culture fostered at the court and the new religious culture and education, spread by Ukrainians and Belorussians, who came to dominate church life, submerged and displaced the disparate beginnings of a modern synthesis within native matrices and cleared the way for Peter's cultural policies, which erected a Western facade over the ruins of the native culture.

(E.L.K.)

The 18th century

THE REIGN OF PETER I (1689–1725)

Peter's youth and early reign. The accession of Peter I ushered in and established the social, institutional, and intellectual trends that were to dominate Russia for the next two centuries. Both Russian and Western historians, whatever their evaluation of Peter's reign, have seen it as one of the most formative periods of Russia's history. The seminal nature of the reign owes much to Peter's own personality and youth. The child of his father's second marriage, Peter was pushed into the background by his half brother Fyodor and exiled from the Kremlin during the turbulent years of the regency (1682–89) of his half sister Sophia. He grew up among children of lesser birth, unfettered by court etiquette. Playing at war and organizing his young friends into an effective military force, he could manifest his energy, vitality, and curiosity almost untrammeled. He also came into close contact with the western Europeans who lived in Moscow; the association kindled his interest in navigation and the mechanical arts—at which he became a skilled practitioner—and gave him the experience of a socially freer and intellectually more stimulating atmosphere than he might otherwise have had. He resolved to introduce this more dynamic and "open" style of life into Russia, a goal he pursued after the overthrow of Sophia in 1689 and that he erected into a policy of state after he became sole ruler following the death of his mother in 1694. (His half-witted half brother, Ivan V, remained co-tsar but played no role and died in 1696.)

Peter's first political aim was to secure Muscovy's southern borders against the threat of raids by Crimean Tatars supported by the Ottoman Empire. For lack of adequate sea power, his initial attempt in 1695 failed to gain a foothold on the Sea of Azov. Undaunted, Peter built up a navy—the first Russian ruler since early Kievan times to do so—and succeeded in capturing Azov a year later. The experience convinced him of the necessity of extending his own technical knowledge and of securing tools and personnel from the West. To this end Peter travelled to western Europe, something no Muscovite tsar had ever done; he spent almost a year in Holland and England acquiring mechanical and maritime skills, hiring experts in various fields, purchasing books and scientific curiosities, and carrying on diplomatic negotiations for a crusade against the Turks. In the course of negotiations with Poland-Saxony and Denmark, an alliance was formed, not against Turkey but against Sweden. The alliance led to the Great Northern War (1700–21), which became Peter's major concern for almost the remainder of his reign.

Western influence in Russia

Not only did the war absorb the country's resources and energies, but the war's requirements—defensive at first, and offensive after Peter's decisive victory over Charles XII at Poltava in 1709—determined most domestic policy measures as well. Only when victory was well in sight could Peter devote more of his attention to a systematic overhaul of Russia's institutions. The hastiness and brutality of steps taken under the stress of war had an effect on subsequent history. Historians have debated whether Peter's legislation was informed by an overall plan based on more or less clearly formulated theoretical considerations, or whether it was merely a series of ad hoc measures taken to meet emergencies as they occurred. Pragmatic elements predominated, no doubt, over theoretical principles. Yet the struggle against Sweden's modern military machine, together with the prevailing intellectual climate and administrative practices of Europe, contributed to orient Peter's thinking.

The Petrine state. Formally, Peter changed the tsardom of Muscovy into the Empire of All Russias, and he himself received the title of "emperor" from the Senate at the conclusion of the peace with Sweden (Treaty of Nystad, 1721). The title not only aimed at identifying the new Russia with European political tradition, it also bespoke the new conception of rulership and of political authority that Peter wanted to implant: that the sovereign emperor was the head of the state and its first servant, not the patrimonial owner of the land and "father" of his subjects (as the tsar had been). Peter stressed the function of his office rather than that of his person and laid the groundwork of a modern system of administration. Institutions and officials were to operate on the basis of set rules, keep regular hours and records, apply laws and regulations dispassionately, and have individual and collective responsibility for their acts. Reality, of course, fell far short of this ideal, because Muscovite traditions and conditions could not be eradicated so rapidly. Furthermore, there was a great shortage of educated and reliable persons imbued with such rationality and efficiency (a problem that

Peter I's new administration

bedevilled the imperial government until its end). They were mainly to be found in the military establishment, where officer and noncommissioned ranks acquired the requisite outlook, experience, and values in the army and navy established by Peter. The Russian bureaucracy thus acquired a preference for uniformity and militarism that did not foster respect or concern for the individual needs of the various regions and peoples of the far-flung empire.

In the new administration, performance was to be the major criterion for appointment and promotion. Peter wanted this principle to apply to the highest offices, starting with that of the emperor himself. As a result of his bad experience with his own son, Alexis (who fled abroad, was brought back, and died in prison), Peter decreed in 1722 that every ruler would appoint his own successor. He did not have the opportunity to avail himself of this right, however, and the matter of regular succession remained a source of conflict and instability throughout the 18th century. Peter's concern for performance lay at the basis of the Table of Ranks (1722), which served as the framework for the careers of all state servants (military, civil, court) until the second half of the 19th century. In it, the hierarchy was divided into 14 categories, or ranks; theoretically one had to begin at the bottom (14th rank) and proceed upward according to merit and seniority. Throughout the 18th century the 8th rank (1st commissioned officer grade) automatically conferred hereditary nobility on those who were not noble by birth. In a sense, therefore, the Table of Ranks opened all offices to merit and thus democratized the service class; but because service was contingent on good preparation (*i.e.,* education), it was accessible only to the few—nobility and clergy—until later in the 18th century.

Policies toward the social classes

The same need for qualified personnel that had brought about the Table of Ranks also determined Peter's policies toward the several social classes of his realm. The traditional obligation of members of all estates to perform service to the state, each according to his way of life (*i.e.,* the nobleman by serving in the army and administration, the peasantry and merchants by paying taxes, the clergy by prayer), was given a modern, rational form by Peter. Paradoxically, the reform helped to transform the traditional estates into caste-like groups from which—except in rare instances of clergy and rich merchants—it became impossible to escape. The nobility was most directly affected by the change, not only in Peter's lifetime but under his successors as well. The nobleman's service obligation became lifelong, regular, and permanent. The staffs of military and government institutions were no longer recruited on the basis of regional origin or family ties, but strictly according to the need of the state and the fitness of the individual for the specific task at hand. The serviceman was transferred from one assignment, branch, or locality to another as the state saw fit. The office of heraldry within the Senate kept the service rosters up to date and decided on appointments and transfers. Peter also introduced single inheritance of real estate (1714), attempting in this way to break the traditional inheritance pattern that had led to the splintering of estates. In so doing he hoped to create a professional service nobility unconnected with the land and totally devoted to the state; but the resistance the law met in its application forced its revocation in 1731. He also required the nobility to be educated as a prerequisite for service. Schooling, whether at home or in an institution, became a feature of the nobleman's way of life. Until the late 18th century, a nobleman was not considered to have attained his majority and did not have the right to marry unless he had passed a government examination in basic subjects. Schooling was a radical innovation, at first resented and resisted; but within a generation it was accepted as a matter of course and became the decisive element in the status and self-image of the nobility.

The peasantry had been enserfed during the 17th century, but the individual peasant had retained his traditional ties to the village commune and to the land that he worked. To prevent tax evasion through the formation of artificial households, Peter introduced a new unit of taxation, the "soul"—*i.e.,* a male peasant of working age—and the lords were made responsible for the collection of the tax assessed on each of their souls. The peasant thus became a mere item on the tax roll who could be moved, sold, or exchanged according to the needs and whims of his master—whether a private landlord, the church, or the state. The serf became practically indistinguishable from a slave. The noble landlord, on the other hand, was turned into an agent of the state; he stood in the path of the peasantry's traditional personal relationship with the sovereign and thereby contributed to the sense of alienation that the ordinary Russian felt toward the new, rational, but remote, Petrine state.

As befitted a secular-minded autocrat who saw his main task as enlightening and leading his people to "modernity," Peter had little regard for the church. He recognized its value only as an instrument of control and as an agent of modern education. When the patriarch died in 1700, Peter appointed no successor; finally in 1721 he gave the church a bureaucratic organization: a Holy Synod composed of several appointed hierarchs and a lay representative of the emperor; the latter, called the chief procurator, came to play the dominant role. Ecclesiastic schools turned into closed institutions with a narrowly scholastic curriculum. Membership in the clerical estate became strictly hereditary; the priesthood was transformed into a closed caste of government religious servants cut off from the new secular culture being introduced in Russia and deprived of their traditional moral authority. One of the priests' main tasks was to assist the state in enforcing its laws, in particular those directed against the Old Believers, so that the clergy became an instrument of persecution and oppression. Both on economic and religious grounds, therefore, the reign of Peter I appeared particularly oppressive to the common people. It seemed unnatural and contrary to tradition; for many it clearly was the reign of Antichrist from which one escaped only through self-immolation (practised by some of the Old Believers), open rebellion, or flight to the borderlands of the empire.

Reform of the church

Resistance and flight were made possible by Peter's failure, despite all his modernizing and rationalizing, to endow the government with effective means of control on the local level. The noble landlords might have acted as police agents; but Peter removed them from the local scene by forcing them into permanent and lifelong service. Regular officials were short in number and experience and could not be easily spared for local administration. Peter tried to have the officers of the regiments that were garrisoned in the provinces double as local officials; but the experiment failed because of the necessities of war and because regular officers proved incompetent to administer peasants. The attempts at copying Western models were also unsuccessful, for the Russian nobility lacked (and was not allowed to develop) a local corporate organization that could serve as the foundation for local self-government.

Peter concentrated his attention almost entirely on the central administration, an area in which his reforms provided the basic framework within which the imperial government was to operate until its fall in 1917. To prosecute the war, the Petrine state had to mobilize all the resources of the country and to supervise practically every aspect of national life. This required that the central executive apparatus be extended and organized along functional lines. Peter hoped to accomplish this by replacing the numerous haphazard *prikazy* (administrative departments) with a coherent system of functional and well-ordered colleges (their number fluctuating around 12 in the course of the century). Each college was headed by a board for more effective control; it had authority in a specific area such as foreign affairs, the army, the navy, commerce, mining, finances, justice, etc. The major problems of this form of organization proved to be the coordination, planning, and supervision of the colleges. Peter endeavoured to cope with these defects pragmatically through the creation of a Senate, which came to serve as a privy council as well as an institution of supervision and control. In addition, he set up a network of espionage agents (*fiskaly*), who acted as tax inspectors, investigators, and personal representatives of the emperor. Internal security was vested in 1689 in the chancery of the Preobrazhensky Guards, the tsar's own military group, which became a much dreaded organ of political police and repression. Under different names the police apparatus remained a permanent feature of the imperial regime. The police were also the instrument of the ruler's personal intervention, an essential function for the preservation of the autocracy as a viable political system.

The needs of war, as well as the desire to modernize Russia, led Peter to promote and expand industry, particularly mining, naval construction, foundries, glass, and textiles. The Emperor aimed at maximizing the use of all potential resources of the country to heighten its power and further its people's welfare; these goals were pursued in mercantilist fashion through discriminatory tariffs, state subsidies, and regulation of manufactures. Peter hoped to involve the rich merchants and the nobility in economic enterprise and expansion. As a class, however, the merchants failed to follow his lead; many were Old Believers who refused to work for the Antichrist. Nor did Peter's urban legislation provide the townspeople with the incentives and freedom necessary to change them into an entrepreneurial class; as a matter of fact, the municipal reforms were simply means to collect taxes and dues in kind. As to the nobility, only a few had the necessary capital to become entrepreneurs, and their time and energies were completely taken up by their service obligations. The shortage of capital could be, and in some specific cases was, overcome by direct government grants. But the equally serious shortage of labour was not so easily resolved. Peter permitted the use of servile labour in mines and manufactures, with the result that thousands of peasants were moved and forced to work under unfamiliar conditions, in new places, at very difficult tasks. Resentment ran high and the productivity of this forced labour was very low. Most of the enterprises established in Peter's lifetime did not survive him. But the impetus he had given to Russian industrial development was not altogether lost; it revived with new vigour—under different policies—in the middle of the 18th century.

Petrine economy

Among the important factors in Russia's economic development under Peter was the building of St. Petersburg (now Leningrad) on the then inhospitable shores of the Gulf of Finland. Its construction cost an estimated 30,000 lives (lost from disease, undernourishment, and drowning) and engulfed vast sums of public and private monies. Nobles who served in the central administration and at court were required to settle in the new city and to build townhouses.

The location of the new capital symbolized the shift in the empire's political, economic, and cultural centre of gravity toward western Europe. After two decades of war, during which the survival of Russia seemed at times to hang in the balance, Peter emerged victorious. The Treaty of Nystad gave him control of the Gulf of Finland and of the eastern shore of the Baltic Sea and put under his sceptre several provinces having Western constitutions, social structures, and cultural traditions. This acquisition was to create constitutional and administrative problems for the multinational empire; but in the meantime trade and social intercourse with western Europe became easier, and the icebound peripheral ports of what is now Murmansk and Archangel were abandoned for the more convenient harbours of Riga, Revel (now Tallinn), and the new St. Petersburg. Secure on the Baltic, Russia could now take an active part in the diplomatic and military affairs of the comity of European states, although sometimes this was to its disadvantage because it became embroiled in dynastic and political conflicts not involving its own interests. After 1721 Peter also extended the borders of the empire in the south along the Caspian Sea as a result of a successful war against Persia (Treaty of St. Petersburg, 1723).

The changes that made Peter's reign the most seminal in Russian history were not the administration reforms and the military conquests, significant as those were, but the transformation in the country's culture and style of life, at least among the service nobility. Foreign observers made much of Peter's requirement that the nobility shave off their beards, wear Western clothes, go to dances and parties, and learn to drink coffee. These were only the external marks of more profound changes that in a generation or so were to make the educated Russian nobleman a member of European polite society. The common people, especially the peasantry, were not so immediately and positively affected, although by the end of the 18th century most peasants, and all inhabitants of towns, had moved a considerable distance from the values and habits of their 16th- and 17th-century forebears.

Change in Russia's culture and life-style

Most important of all, perhaps, the reign of Peter I marked the beginning of a new period in Russian educational and cultural life. Peter was the first to introduce secular education on a significant scale and to make it compulsory for all state servants. (More significant than the limited quantitative results during Peter's lifetime was the fact that education eventually became indispensable to membership in the upper class.) First, Peter tried to use the church to establish a network of primary schools for all children of the free classes; this plan failed largely because the clergy were unable to finance and staff schools for secular learning. But the specialized technical schools Peter founded, such as the Naval Academy, struck roots and provided generations of young men with the skills necessary for leadership in a modern army and navy. Although he did not live to see its formal inauguration, Peter also organized the Academy of Sciences as an institution for scholarship, research, and instruction at the higher level. The Academy's beginnings were quite modest—German professors lectured in Latin to a handful of poorly prepared students—and its development was not free from difficulties; but at the end of the 18th century it was a leading European centre of science and enlightenment, preparing and guiding Russia's scientific and technological flowering in the 19th century.

Assessment of Peter's reign. Contemporaries as well as later historians have given first place among Peter's accomplishments to his conquest of the Baltic provinces and areas on the Caspian Sea. More important was the fact that during his reign Russia became a major European power, in regular intercourse with the major trading powers and especially with Holland and Great Britain. This status of European power, however, burdened Russia with the maintenance of a large and up-to-date military establishment, which became involved in many costly conflicts. The weakening of Poland during the Northern War with Sweden led ultimately to Poland's partitioning, which proved a heavy burden for the Russian body social. Finally, the cultural, religious, and linguistic diversity of the empire was increased by the incorporation of national and social groups that were not easily assimilated. The new institutional forms that Peter introduced helped to shape a less personal and more modern (*i.e.,* routinized and bureaucratized) political authority. This led to an ambiguous relationship between the autocratic ruler and his noble servants and also to a sense of alienation between the common people and the ruler.

Russia as a major European power

Contemporaries and later generations alike shared the feeling that Peter's reign had been revolutionary—a radical and violent break with the centuries old traditions of Muscovy. To some extent this was the consequence of Peter's ruthless manner, his dynamism, his harsh suppression of all opposition, and his obstinate imposition of his will. From a historical perspective, Peter's reign may appear to have been only the culmination of 17th-century trends rather than a radical break with the past. But men are more conscious of changes in manners and customs than of deeper transformations that require a long time for their working out. Thus Russia's cultural Europeanization in the early 18th century produced works of literature in a new manner, using foreign styles and techniques, such as the treatises and sermons of Feofan Prokopovich, Peter's main assistant in church matters, and the satires and translations of Prince Antiokh Kantemir, the first modern Russian poet. These writers, and many anonymous ones, praised Peter's work, stressing its innovative and necessary character; and the educated elite, reared on the cultural elements introduced by Peter, perceived his reign as the birth of modern Russia. This fact in itself became the source of critical thought and raised the question of whether the break with the past was desirable or a betrayal of the genuinely national patterns of development of Russian culture. It appeared that forcible imposition of foreign elements had led to an alienation between the elite and the Russian people. This debate as to the nature and value of the reign of Peter I served as the main stimulus to a definition of Russian national culture and to the elaboration of competing political and social philosophies in the 19th century (*e.g.*, those of the Slavophiles and the westernizers). Peter's reign has been at the centre of all debates over Russian history, since any attempt to define its periods and to assess Russia's development in modern times requires a prior judgment of the reign and work of Peter I.

PETER I'S SUCCESSORS (1725–62)

Peter's unexpected death in 1725 at the age of 52 left unresolved two major institutional problems. The first was the succession to the throne, which remained unsettled not only because Peter did not choose his own successor but also because during the remainder of the century almost any powerful individual or group could disregard the choice of the preceding ruler. The second problem was the lack of firm central direction, planning, and control of imperial policy; closely related to it was the question of who would have the determining role in shaping policy (*i.e.*, what would be the nature of the "ruling circle" and its relationship to the autocrat). The failure to solve these problems produced a climate of instability and led to a succession of crises in St. Petersburg and Moscow that make it difficult to give unity and meaning to the period from 1725 until the accession of Catherine the Great in 1762.

Instability and crisis

Normal and peaceful succession to the throne was thwarted by a combination of biological accidents and palace coups. At Peter's death his chief collaborators, headed by Prince A.D. Menshikov and with the help of the guard regiments (the offshoots of the play regiments of Peter's youth), put on the throne Peter's widow—his second wife, Catherine I, the daughter of a Lithuanian peasant. Quite naturally, Menshikov ruled in her name. Soon, however, he was forced to share his power with other dignitaries of Peter's reign. A Supreme Privy Council was established as the central governing body, displacing the Senate in political influence and administrative significance. Catherine I's death in 1727 reopened the question of succession; Peter's grandson (the son of Alexis who had perished in prison) was proclaimed emperor Peter II by the Council. An immature youngster, Peter II fell under the influence of his chamberlain, Prince I. Dolgoruky, whose family obtained a dominant position in the Supreme Privy Council and brought about the disgrace and exile of Menshikov. It looked as if the Dolgorukys would rule in fact because Peter II was affianced to the chamberlain's sister; but Peter's sudden death in January 1730 crossed the plans of that ambitious family.

Anna (1730–40). Under the leadership of Prince Dmitry Golitsyn—scion of an old Muscovite boyar family and himself a prominent official under Peter I—the Supreme Privy Council elected to the throne Anna, dowager duchess of Courland and niece of Peter I (daughter of his co-tsar, Ivan V). At the same time, Golitsyn tried to circumscribe Anna's power by having her accept a set of conditions that left to the council the decisive voice in all important matters. This move toward oligarchy was foiled by top level officials (the *generalitet; i.e.,* those with the service rank of general or its equivalent), in alliance with the rank-and-file service nobility. While the former wanted to be included in the ruling oligarchy (and Golitsyn seemed to have been ready to concede them this right), the latter opposed any limitation on the autocratic power of the sovereign. Indeed, the ordinary service nobles feared that an oligarchy, however broad its membership, would shut them off from access to the ruler and thus limit their opportunity to rise in the hierarchy of the Table of Ranks.

Role of Ernst Biron

Anna left most of her authority to be exercised by her Baltic German favourite, Ernst Johann Biron, who acquired a reputation for corruption, cruelty, tyranny, and exploitation and who was felt to have set up a police terror that benefitted the Germans in Russia at the expense of all loyal and patriotic Russians. Recent scholarship has modified this image and shown that Biron's bad reputation rested on his inflexibility in applying the law and collecting taxes, rather than on malevolence. The Supreme Privy Council was abolished upon Anna's accession in 1730, and the functions of coordination, supervision, and policy planning were vested in a cabinet of ministers composed of three experienced high officials, all Russians.

Elizabeth (1741–62). Anna was childless; she appointed as successor her infant nephew, Ivan Antonovich, under the regency of his mother, Anna Leopoldovna. Biron, who had at first retained his influence, was overthrown by Burkhard Christoph, Graf von Münnich, who had made his fortune in Russia. The continuing domination of a few favourites—many of whom were Germans—much displeased the high officials, whose position was threatened by the personal caprices of ruler or favourite, and incensed even more the rank and file of the service nobility, who could not obtain rewards or favours from the sovereign without the approval and help of the favourites. The malcontents banded together around Peter I's daughter, Elizabeth, whose easygoing and open ways had gained her many friends; she was also popular because of her Russian outlook, which she emphasized, and because she shared the aura of her great father. With the help of the guard regiments and high officers, and with the financial support of foreign diplomats (in particular the French envoy), Elizabeth overthrew the infant Ivan VI and the regent Anna Leopoldovna in 1741. Her 20-year reign saw the rise of certain trends and patterns in public life, society, and culture that were to reach their culmination under Catherine the Great. On the political plane, the most significant development was the restoration of the Senate to its earlier function of chief policy-making and supervising body. At the end of her reign Elizabeth also established a kind of permanent council or cabinet for planning and coordination—the Special Conference at the Imperial Court.

Stabilization under Elizabeth

During this period Peter's administrative reforms began to bear fruit. The Table of Ranks became the framework for a class of servicemen whose lives were devoted to the interests of the state. In principle, entry to this class of officials was open to anyone with the required ability and education, including the sons of priests and non-Russian landowners. In fact, however, promotion in the Table of Ranks was possible only if the individual's merit and performance were recognized by the ruler or, more likely, by high officials and dignitaries who had access to the ruler. The personal element, bolstered by family and marriage ties, came to play an important role in the formal system of promotion; most significantly, it determined the makeup of the very top echelon of the administrative and military hierarchies (which were interchangeable), the so-called *generalitet.* This group constituted an almost permanent ruling elite, co-opting its own membership and promoting the interests of the families most directly connected with it; in order to solidify its influence and function it aimed at bringing as many routine government operations as possible under a system of regulations that would make appeal to the ruler unnecessary. The latter's autocratic power could not be infringed however, because his authority was needed not only to settle special cases but to promote, protect, and reward members of the ruling group and their clients. The greatest threat to the system was the interference or interposition of favourites—"accidental people"—and to guard against this, the oligarchy entered into an alliance with the rank-and-file service nobles who wanted to join its ranks and could hope to do so with the help of the dignitaries' patronage; this alliance permitted successful palace coups against favourites. The system benefitted both the high and low nobility; but it worked only with the help of a strong autocracy in which the ruler could easily fend off any attempt at limiting his power, as Anna had demonstrated in 1730. The system worked well enough to allow the consolidation of Peter's reforms, some success in foreign policy, and a general increase in the power and wealth of the state, despite the low calibre of the rulers and the mismanagement of favourites.

The service nobleman

The system rested on the availability to all nobles of the minimum education necessary for entrance and promotion in service; this created a desire to go through rapidly, or omit altogether, the most arduous and tedious lower echelons of the Table of Ranks. As a consequence, cultural policy became a major concern of the government and the nobility alike; the members of the service class demanded that institutions of learning be set up to prepare the nobility for better careers, skipping the lowest ranks. The demand was fulfilled in 1731 with the creation of the Corps of Cadets. In the course of the following decades, the original corps was expanded and other special institutions for training the nobility were added. General education became accessible to a large stratum of the rank-and-file nobility with the founding of the University of Moscow in 1755, although the lack of automatic preferment for its graduates kept it from being popular among the wealthier nobles until the end of the century. The Corps of Cadets and similar public and private institutions also acted as substitutes for the local and family bonds that had formerly given cohesion to the Muscovite service class but which Petrine practices had destroyed; these schools were also the seedbeds for an active intellectual life, and their students played a leading role in spreading the literature and ideas of western Europe in court circles and in the high society of the capitals.

The service nobleman was a landlord and serf owner; he was very poor for a number of reasons, chief among which were the low productivity of Russian agriculture and the continual splintering of estates through inheritance. As a rule his estates provided him only with the minimum necessary for his maintenance in service. But as long as he remained in service and away from his estates, he could do little to improve his property. He thus depended on the ruler for additional income, either in the form of a salary or as grants of land (and serfs) in reward for service. The salary was not very large, it was often in kind (furs), and it was paid out rather irregularly; lands and serfs could be obtained only from the ruler, and most went to favourites, courtiers, or high dignitaries. Service, it is true, provided the nobleman with some extras such as uniforms, sometimes lodgings, and—most important—greater accessibility to court, cultural life, and education for his children. Thus, he remained in service, took less and less direct interest in his estates and serfs, and became almost a rootless, permanent serviceman.

Shuvalov's gifts to the nobility

Elizabeth's chief advisor, Pyotr Shuvalov, had the government grant exclusive privileges and monopolies to some of the nobility, hoping to involve them in the development of mining and manufacturing. Shuvalov also initiated a gradual loosening of state controls over economic life in general. He began to dismantle the system of internal tariffs, so that local trade could develop; he strengthened the landlord's control over all the resources on his estate; and he gave the nobles the right to distill alcohol.

At the same time, the landlords were obtaining still greater power over their serfs. The full weight of these powers fell on the household serfs, whose number increased because their masters used them as domestics and craftsmen in their town houses to make Western-style objects with which they surrounded themselves. When noblemen established factories or secured estates in newly conquered border areas, they transferred their serfs to them without regard for family or village ties. The operation of most estates was, in the absence of the landlord, left to the peasants. This only perpetuated the traditional patterns of agriculture and made the modernization and improvement of agricultural productivity impossible.

THE REIGN OF CATHERINE II THE GREAT (1762–96)

Elizabeth, too, was childless, and the throne passed to the heir she had selected—her nephew the Duke of Holstein, who became Peter III. Intellectually and temperamentally unfit to rule, Peter III made himself personally unpopular with St. Petersburg society; in addition, he allowed his entourage (mainly his Holstein relatives and German officers) to take control of the government. The regular hierarchy of officials—particularly the Senate—was pushed into the background; power passed into the hands of the emperor's favourites, while a modernized police, under the personal control of a general who was one of the emperor's minions, spread its net over the empire. The pro-Prussian foreign and military policy pursued by Peter III (who abruptly ended Russia's victorious involvement in the Seven Years' War) and his treatment of his wife Catherine provoked much resentment. As a result, the Emperor lost all support in society. It was easy for Catherine, with the help of the senators, high officials, and officers of the guard regiments (led by her lover Grigory Orlov and his brothers) to overthrow Peter III on July 9 (June 28, old style), 1762. Thus began the long and important reign of Catherine II, whom her admiring contemporaries named "the Great."

The daughter of a poor German princeling, Catherine had come to Russia at the age of 15 to be the bride of the heir presumptive, Peter. She matured in an atmosphere of intrigue and struggle for power. She developed her mind by reading contemporary literature, especially the works of the French Encyclopaedists and of German jurists and cameralists. When she seized power at the age of 33 she was intellectually and experientially prepared, as the more than 30 years of her reign were to show.

Assessment of Catherine's reign

The historiography of Catherine's reign has been dominated by two main approaches: a dramatization and romanticization of her personal life, which was indeed colourful for the number and variety of her lovers; and the viewpoint of 19th-century liberalism, which took literally her self-description as a "philosophe on the throne." Marxist and Soviet historians, to the extent that they have dealt with her reign at all, see it primarily in terms of the pressures put on the state by the serf-owning nobility faced with the demands of an expanding market economy. In recent years, scholars have come to think of Catherine's government as working to further the formation of a modern civil society in which social classes and groups pursue their own interests rather than serving the needs of the state exclusively.

Even before she seized power, Catherine wrote that the task of good government was to promote the general welfare of the nation by providing for the security of person and property; to that end, government should operate in a legal and orderly fashion, furthering the interests of individual subjects and giving groups and classes as much autonomy in the pursuit of their normal activities as possible. All the same, Catherine believed that the autocratic state had important functions; she had no intention of relinquishing or limiting her authority, even though she was willing to withdraw from those areas of national life that could be safely administered by an educated elite.

Expansion of the empire. Catherine's reign was notable for imperial expansion. The expansion had been prepared by military and political efforts since the reign of Peter I; in particular, an important process of incorporating and settling empty land (especially in the south, corresponding roughly to the modern Ukraine) had been initiated in the reign of Elizabeth. This continued with the partitions of Poland, in which Catherine played a leading role, with the result that all eastern Poland and the former Grand Duchy of Lithuania came under Russian rule. A disadvantage of this was that Russia became a partner in the alliance of the three partitioning powers and had to mind its common border with Prussia. An additional source of difficulty was that the Roman Catholic Poles, proud of their cultural and political traditions and resentful of their loss of independence, proved less easy to assimilate and draw into Russian society than had the Baltic Germans. Also, the large number of Jews in the formerly Polish and Lithuanian provinces created special problems for the imperial government.

Of greater immediate importance for the empire were the securing of the northern shore of the Black Sea (Treaty of Küçük Kaynarca, 1774), the annexation of the Crimea (1783), and the expansion into the steppes beyond the Urals and along the Caspian Sea. This permitted the adequate protection of Russian agricultural settlements in the south and southeast and the establishment of trade routes through the Black Sea and up the Danube. On the other hand, these gains involved Russia more and more in the political and military struggle over the crumbling Ottoman Empire in the Balkans (the Treaty of Küçük Kaynarca, for example, allowed intervention on the pretext of protecting the Christian populations under Turkish

The expansion of Russia, 1300–1796.
From W. Shepherd, *Historical Atlas*; Barnes & Noble Books, New York

rule). Russian sovereignty was extended over these territories through traditional means of war and diplomacy, but their incorporation into the Russian polity and their economic integration showed the hand of Catherine.

G.A. Potemkin, Catherine's favourite in the 1770s, may be considered the chief architect of her imperial policy. He promoted large-scale foreign colonization and peasant resettlement in the south—with only mediocre success so far as agricultural settlements went but with great success in the foundation and rapid growth of such towns and ports as Odessa, Kherson, Nikolayev, Taganrog, and Mariupol (now Zhdanov). Within a generation or two these became lively cultural centres and major commercial cities for all of southern Russia, contributing to the reorientation of Russia's pattern of trade with the development of agricultural exports from the Ukraine. Local society was transformed on the Russian pattern: the landlords became imperial service nobles with full control over their peasants; vast new lands were parcelled out to prominent officials and made available for purchase by wealthy Russian nobles, who also received the right to resettle their own serfs from the central regions. Thus, serfdom, along with elements of the plantation system, was extended to still more people and over whole new provinces. If this expansion benefitted the state and a small and already wealthy part of the Russian nobility, it increased the misery and exploitation of the Ukrainian and Russian peasantries. The traditional military democracies of the Cossack hosts on the Dnepr, Don, Ural, Kuban, and Volga rivers lost their autonomy and special privileges; the wealthier officers became Russian service nobles, receiving the right to own and settle serfs on their own lands, while the rank-and-file Cossacks sank to the level of state peasants with special military obligations.

Policies toward new nationalities

Integration of the new territories required the absorption of a large number of non-Russian, non-Christian, nomadic peoples. The approach of Catherine's ministers, which prevailed until the late 19th century, was based on the idea, taken from Enlightenment writings, that there is a natural progress of society from primitive hunting and fishing groups through the stage of nomadism to settled agriculture, trade, and urbanization. Accordingly, the government sought to bring the nomadic peoples up to what it considered to be the Russian peasantry's higher way of life; this policy had the advantage also of producing uniformity in administrative and legal structures. Catherine's government was quite willing to let religious, cultural, or linguistic differences stand, although it did not feel committed to protect them actively. Inevitably, however, its effort to change the ways of the nomads affected their culture and religion and, through these, their social equilibrium and sense of national identity. While Catherine's policy led some peoples to accept (more or less under duress) changes in their way of life, thus facilitating the extension of Russian agricultural settlements onto the open steppes, it also gave rise to a new national self-consciousness and to a growing sense of identity based on cultural, linguistic, and religious traditions. These nationalistic sentiments clashed with the outlook and practices of officials accustomed to thinking in universal categories. The government found it difficult to rely upon native elites to operate the institutions it imposed on the new territories. Russian officials had to be sent in, strengthening uniformity and centralization in contradiction to the professed aim of furthering autonomy in local affairs. The policy thus defeated its own aims: it handicapped the economic development of the empire's border regions (*e.g.,* in Siberia) and worked against the social and cultural integration of the natives into the fold of the dominant Russian culture (although russification did take place on a significant scale in the case of some native elites, as in the Caucasus and the Crimea).

Reforms of local government

Government administration under Catherine. The reforms of local government carried out by Catherine also contained contradictions. The successors of Peter I had not solved the problem of local administration. St. Petersburg relied on appointed officials, too few in number and much given to abuse and corruption, and on the informal control exercised by individual landowners and village communes; but a great peasant rebellion, led by Ye.I. Pugachov in 1773–74, demonstrated the inadequacy of this system. Taking up suggestions of various officials and mindful of the information and complaints offered by the deputies to the Legislative Commission (1767–68), Catherine shaped the local administration into a structure that remained in force until the middle of the 19th century and also served as a foundation for the *zemstvos* (local elected councils), established in 1864. The basic pattern was established by the statute on the provinces of 1775 and complemented by the organization of corporate self-administration contained in the charters to the nobility and the towns (1785). Essentially, the reforms divided the empire's territory into provinces of roughly equal population, disregarding historical traditions and economic ties; each of these units (*guberniya*) was put under the supervision and responsibility of a governor or governor general acting in the name of the ruler, with the right of direct communication with him. A governor's chancery was set up along functional lines (paralleling the system of colleges) and subordinated to and supervised by the Senate. The regular provincial administration was assisted by officials who were elected from among the nobility for the countryside and from the higher ranks of townspeople for the cities; these elected officials took care of routine police matters in their jurisdictions, helped to enforce orders received from the central authorities, and assisted in the maintenance of law and the collection of taxes. Other elected personalities (marshals of the nobility and heads of city councils) protected the interests of their respective classes and helped to settle minor conflicts without recourse to regular tribunals. This delegation of some administrative functions to the local level (albeit under the strict control of St. Petersburg) not only relieved the bureaucracy of much burdensome detail and multiplied the number of its agents on the local level but also fostered a sense of responsibility among the active and cultured members of the local upper classes. On the other hand, the serfs and the lower classes in the towns found themselves without anyone to protect their interests.

The central government under Catherine

Catherine made no fundamental changes in the administration of the central government. The system of colleges was retained; but the authority of the presidents increased at the expense of the boards, initiating an evolution that culminated in the establishment of monocratic ministries in 1802. The Senate supervised all branches of administration, regulating the orderly flow of business. The Senate was also involved—albeit indirectly—in coordination, mainly because its procurator general, Prince A. Vyazemsky, held the office for a quarter of a century with the full trust of the empress. At the same time, the judicial functions of the Senate as a high court of appeal and administrative review were widened.

The major institutional weakness of the Petrine system remained—namely, the lack of a body to coordinate the jurisdictions and resolve the conflicts of the colleges and to plan policies and control their implementation. A ruler as energetic, hard-working, and intelligent as Catherine could perform these tasks almost single-handedly, as had Peter I; but with the growing complexity of administration even Catherine felt the need for such a body, if only to reduce her involvement in every small detail or contested matter and to provide a wider scope for government by permanent laws and uniform regulations. Eventually, she set up a council of state as a kind of cabinet but without giving it any specific authority or jurisdiction.

A major need of the empire was an up-to-date code of laws. The last code, issued in 1649, had become largely inoperative as a result of Peter's reforms and the transformation of society. Peter and his successors had recognized this need by appointing commissions to prepare a new code; none of the several efforts having reached a successful conclusion, Catherine tried to tackle the job again, but in a different manner. In 1767 she convoked a commission of representatives elected by all classes except private serfs. For their guidance she drafted an instruction largely inspired by Western political thinkers; but, far from providing a blueprint for a liberal code, it emphasized the need for autocracy and strong central institutions. In its civil part the instruction owed much to German political philosophy and natural-law jurisprudence, putting the individual's duties before his rights emphasizing the state's responsibility for the welfare of the nation, and encouraging the pursuit of material self-interest within the established order. Although not implemented by the commission (which was dissolved in 1768), the instruction stimulated the modernization of Russian political and legal thought in the early 19th century.

Catherine's social policy

In her social policy Catherine aimed at steering the nobility toward cultural interests and economic activity so as to reduce their dependence on state service. (They already had been freed from its compulsory character by Peter III [February 18, 1762].) To this end she made a general land survey that fixed clearly and permanently the boundaries of individual estates, and she granted the nobility the exclusive right to exploit both the subsoil and surface resources of their land and to market the products of their estates and of their serfs' labour. The nobles also obtained a monopoly of ownership of inhabited estates, which, in fact, restricted ownership of agricultural serfs to the noble class. Catherine hoped to stimulate agricultural expansion and modernization by providing easy credit and by disseminating the latest techniques and achievements of Western agriculture through the Free Economic Society founded in 1765. She also fostered the nobility's corporate organization. The Charter to the Gentry, 1785, gave the corps of gentry in every province the status of a legal entity. The corporation's members gathered periodically, in the provincial and district capitals, to elect a marshal of the gentry, who represented their interests before the governor and the ruler himself; they also elected a number of officials to administer welfare institutions for the gentry (schools, orphanages, etc.), to help settle disputes, and to provide guardianships for orphans. The corporate life of the gentry did not develop as well as expected, however, and the gentry never became the class it was in Prussia or England; but the charter did foster a sense of class consciousness and afforded legal security to the members and their property. The periodic electoral meetings stimulated social intercourse, led to a livelier cultural life in the provinces, and helped to involve the gentry in local concerns.

Turning the gentry's interests toward economic activity brought the return home of many landowners to supervise the operation of their estates. Interested in obtaining greater income, they not only intensified the exploitation of serf labour but also interfered in the traditional routine of the village by attempting to introduce new agricultural techniques. In most cases this meant increased regimentation of the serfs. The secularization of the monasteries and episcopal sees in 1764 had brought a considerable amount of land into the possession of the state. To reward her favourites and to encourage the gentry to economic activity, Catherine gave away large tracts with many peasants, who now had to work for ambitious and capricious masters.

Serfdom had never been acceptable to the Russian peasant; it now became particularly burdensome and unjust, the more so since the lord's extensive police powers removed his serfs from the state's protection, and the new local officials enforced strictly the prohibition against appealing for relief to the sovereign. There were also the specific grievances of the Cossacks, whose traditional liberties had been sharply curtailed and their social organization undermined, and the discontent of the nomadic peoples forced to accept a new way of life. Peasant misery erupted in rebellion that engulfed all of eastern European Russia in 1773–74, led by the Cossack Yemelyan Pugachov. The peasant forces captured a number of towns and cities before they were finally defeated by government armies. The revolt demonstrated the inadequacy of local controls and was thus partly responsible for the reform of provincial administration mentioned above. It also brought the educated elite to a new awareness of the profound alienation of the peasantry from the culture of St. Petersburg.

Town planning and building

The reign of Catherine II was a period of active town planning and building. The number and size of the urban centres grew slowly but steadily. Along with new cities in the south, many old towns were rebuilt and developed. The renaissance of the old provincial centres was in part due to the administrative reforms of 1775 and 1785, which brought an influx of officials and nobles. Along with them came craftsmen, artisans, and merchants. An act of Peter III, which permitted peasants to trade in neighbouring towns without passports or controls at the gates, gave impetus to the emergence of a class of small merchants from among the peasantry. This trend received support from the administrative reorganization of the towns and the limited degree of corporate self-administration granted by the Charter of 1785.

EDUCATION AND SOCIAL CHANGE IN THE 18TH CENTURY

Secular education had been actively propagated by Peter I. At first it focussed on technical subjects—those directly related to the prosecution of a war, the building of a navy, and the running of the government. This was also the original emphasis of the Academy of Sciences and the school connected with it. But as education became the prerequisite for advancement in service and as Western ways of life spread among the upper classes, the focus of education gradually broadened. A class of nobles grew up who were interested in culture for the sake of their own development, as well as for cutting a good figure in society. Beginning in the 1760s the demand for western European artistic and cultural works grew in the salons of St. Petersburg increasingly. By the 1780s the major classics of European literature had become easily available in translation to any educated person. Private boarding and day schools proliferated, as did the number of tutors hired by wealthy nobles for their children (and for less fortunate neighbours and relatives). The Academy of Sciences took its place among the major academies of Europe. The University of Moscow and the chief schools of the military, naval, and civil services had become regular institutions.

There were also ecclesiastical schools. Paradoxically, the instruction they gave was almost irrelevant for the future priest but quite useful for the future official or scholar; it emphasized the rhetorical arts and logic and gave a solid foundation in scholastic philosophy, natural-law doctrine, the classical languages, and mathematics. The seminaries and theological academies not only trained future members of the episcopate and officials of the Holy Synod but also staffed government bureaus on the middle and higher levels and produced the first native Russian academics, scholars, and scientists. Russia's lack of professional experts in such fields as jurisprudence, civil and military engineering, astronomy, and geophysics brought a great influx of foreigners. Peter I imported large numbers of engineers and technicians from Holland and England, and the practice continued on a reduced scale after his death, so that foreign scholars, scientists, and experts staffed the Academy of Sciences and the University of Moscow and supplied the requirements of the state for such purposes as geological surveys. They brought with them French and German philosophy: the metaphysics and epistemology of René Descartes and the natural-law doctrines of the German school of Gottfried Leibniz, Samuel von Pufendorf, and Christian Wolff. These emphasized social obligation and the individual's dependence on the community. Stressing his duties to the group, they laid the foundation for a critique of society. The critique was at first directed against the moral inadequacies of individuals—the vain courtier, the superficially westernized fop, the corrupt official—but it soon broadened into the view that the educated man had an obligation to help his fellowmen improve themselves. In the Russian context the class most obviously in need of improvement was the peasantry. Moral progress, it was quickly realized, was not possible without material progress, and this led quite naturally to an advocacy of practical philanthropy and social action.

Western intellectual influences

German natural-law doctrines furthered the dissemination of German Pietism, with its emphasis on spiritual progress and on the need to serve man and the community. Similar tendencies underlay the most influential branch of Freemasonry; the Freemasons devoted themselves to disseminating knowledge, relieving hunger, and caring for orphans and other destitutes. The publisher Nikolay Novikov carried the Pietist and Masonic messages to the public in his satirical journals and periodicals for women and children. All would-be reformers were concerned about the serf, especially since the Pugachov revolt had shown the degree of the peasantry's alienation. The major writers of Catherine II's reign (including the empress herself, who dabbled in journalism and drama) produced satires, fables, and comedies of manners attuned to the belief that moral and spiritual progress would lead to social improvements. A similar approach was noticeable in education, which stressed the development of moral feeling in the conviction that a good heart would guide the well-filled head in the proper direction. This was the context in which the writings of the French philosophes (*e.g.,* Jean-Jacques Rousseau, Guillaume Raynal, Claude Helvétius, Paul-Henri Holbach) struck a response in the Russian educated elite. The Russians had been prepared by natural-law teachings, Pietism, and Freemasonry for a more radical criticism of contemporary society looking to the perfectibility of man through education and social change.

Growth of national pride

All of these intellectual currents combined to awaken among educated Russians a sense of national pride and a feeling that, thanks to the impetus given by Peter I, Russia had managed to lift itself to the cultural and political level of a great European state. The educated Russian was no longer a servile and mute slave of the tsars; he had made himself into a gentleman, a man of heart and honour, a "true son of the fatherland," concerned about his fellow men. Nor was this regarded simply as imitation of the West; it was the fruit of Russian history, which was not to be scorned or neglected. A revived interest in Russian history led to the first important native works of modern Russian historiography.

The response of the empress and her entourage to these intellectual developments was ambivalent. The new sense of national pride and personal dignity enhanced the government's prestige and was in line with Catherine's own aspirations for the nobility. But the spread of these new interests and ideas was also dangerous, for the moral criticism of abuses could easily turn into criticism of Russia's social and political system. The outbreak of the French Revolution made Catherine II particularly anxious. She felt that large-scale private philanthropic and educational activities without government guidance and control were trespassing on her own prerogatives as an enlightened autocrat. By the end of the 18th century the ideal of service to the state, which had underlain the Russian nobility's value system, had been transformed into one of service to the people; this meant the elite's separation from the state, which Catherine II could not accept. A dramatic illustration of Catherine's concern occurred after the appearance in 1790 of Aleksandr Radishchev's *Journey from St. Petersburg to Moscow.* A member of the nobility, Radishchev had returned from Germany to rise to a prominent position in the government service. He depicted social conditions as he saw them, particularly the dehumanization of the serfs and the corruption of their masters, warning that these threatened not only the stability of the existing order but also Russia's survival as a nation. Incensed by the book, Catherine had Radishchev arrested and banished to Siberia. He became the first political martyr of the Russian elite; his book and his fate foreshadowed the antagonism between the intelligentsia and the government that was to dominate Russia's history in the 19th century.

THE REIGN OF PAUL I (1796–1801)

Catherine died in 1796 and was succeeded by her son Paul. A capricious, somewhat unstable individual, Paul had a passion for military order that conflicted with the basic values of the developing civil society; he felt that the nobility should again become a service class (or withdraw completely into agriculture) and help the ruler in implementing his reform program, even at the expense of its private interests. In trying to reestablish compulsory state service, he made it more rigid, harsh, and militaristic. He sought to promote the welfare of the serfs, but the manner of his approach—a decree permitting a maximum of three days of labour service a week—was clumsy and high-handed; it did nothing to help the serfs and angered their lords. Paul also made the same mistake as his father, Peter III: he wanted to govern with his own minions, disregarding both tradition and the administrative patterns that had developed during his mother's 30-year reign. Paul's hatred of the French Revolution and of everything connected with it led him to impose tight censorship on travel abroad and to prohibit foreign books, fashions, music, etc. He thereby earned the enmity of upper society in St. Petersburg. On March 23 (March 11, O.S.), 1801, he was murdered by conspirators drawn from high officials, favourites of Catherine, his own military entourage, and officers of the guard regiments. The accession of his son, Alexander I, inaugurated a new century and a new period in the history of imperial Russia. (M.Ra.)

Russia from 1801 to 1917

THE REIGNS OF ALEXANDER I AND NICHOLAS I

General survey. When Alexander I came to the throne in March 1801, Russia was in a state of hostility with most of Europe, though its armies were not actually fighting; its only ally was its traditional enemy, Turkey. The new emperor quickly made peace with both France and Britain and restored normal relations with Austria. His hope that he would then be able to concentrate on internal reform was frustrated by the reopening of war with Napoleon in 1805. Defeated at Austerlitz, the Russian armies fought Napoleon in Poland in 1806 and 1807, with Prussia as an ineffective ally. After the Treaty of Tilsit (1807), there were five years of peace, ended by Napoleon's invasion of Russia in 1812. For further information see EUROPE: *Napoleon in power.* From the westward progress of its arms in the next two years of heavy fighting, Russia emerged as Europe's greatest land power and the first among the continental victors over Napoleon. The immense prestige achieved in these campaigns was maintained until mid-century. During that period, Russian armies fought only against weaker enemies: Persia in 1826, Turkey in 1828–29, Poland in 1830–31, and the mountaineers of the Caucasus during the 1830s and 1840s. When Europe was convulsed by revolution in 1848, Russia alone among the Great Powers was unaffected; and in the summer of 1849 the Tsar sent troops to crush the Hungarians in Transylvania. Russia was not loved, but it was admired and feared. To the upper classes in central Europe, Nicholas I was the stern defender of monarchical legitimacy; to democrats all over the world, he was "the gendarme of Europe" and the chief enemy of liberty. But the Crimean War (1853–56) showed that this giant had feet of clay. The vast empire was unable to mobilize, equip, and transport enough troops to defeat the medium-sized French and English forces under very mediocre command. Nicholas died in the bitter knowledge of general failure.

Russian victories against weak enemies

Alexander I as a young man had longed to reform his empire and benefit his subjects. His hopes were disappointed, partly by the sheer inertia, backwardness, and vastness of his domains but chiefly because Napoleon's aggressive enterprises diverted Alexander's attention to diplomacy and defense. Russia's abundant manpower and scanty financial resources were both consumed in war. The early years of his reign saw two short periods of attempted reform. During the first, from 1801 to 1803, the Tsar took counsel with four intimate friends, who formed his so-called Unofficial Committee, with the intention of drafting ambitious reforms. In the period from 1807 to 1812, he had as his chief adviser the liberal Mikhail Speransky. Both periods produced some valuable administrative innovations, but neither initiated any basic reform. After 1815 Alexander was mainly concerned with grandiose plans for international peace; his motivation was not merely political but also religious, for the years of war and national danger had aroused in him an interest in matters of faith to which, as a pupil of the 18th-century Enlightenment, he had previously been indifferent. While he was thus preoccupied with diplomacy and religion, Russia was ruled by conservatives, among whom the brutal but honest Gen. Aleksey Arakcheyev was outstanding. Victory in war had strengthened those who upheld the established order, serfdom and all. The mood was one of intense national pride: Holy Russia had defeated Napoleon, the Corsican Antichrist, and therefore it was not only foolish but also impious to copy foreign models. Educated young Russians, who had served in the army and seen Europe, who read and spoke French and German and knew contemporary European literature, felt otherwise. Masonic lodges and secret societies flourished in the early 1820s. From their deliberations emerged a conspiracy to overthrow the government, inspired by a variety of ideas: some men looked for a model to the United States, others to Jacobin France. The conspirators, known as the Decembrists because they tried to act in December 1825 when the news of Alexander I's death became known and there was uncertainty about his successor, were defeated and arrested; five were executed and many more sentenced to various terms of imprisonment in Siberia. Nicholas I, who succeeded after his elder brother Constantine had finally refused the throne, was deeply affected by these events and set himself against any major political change, though he did not reject the idea of administrative reform. After the revolutions of 1848 in Europe, his opposition to all change, his suspicion of even mildly liberal ideas, and his insistence on an obscurantist censorship reached their climax.

The sections that follow cover the development, under Alexander I and Nicholas I, of the machinery of government; of social classes and economic forces; of education and political ideas; of the relations between Russians and other peoples within the empire; and of Russian foreign policy.

Government. The discussions of Alexander I's Unofficial Committee were part of an ongoing debate that was to remain important until the end of the imperial regime. This may be called the debate between enlightened oligarchy and enlightened autocracy. The proponents of oligarchy looked back to a somewhat idealized model of the reign of Catherine II. They wished greater power to be placed in the hands of the aristocracy for the purpose of achieving a certain balance between the monarch and the social elite, believing that both together were capable of pursuing policies that would benefit the people as a whole. Their opponents, of whom the most talented was the young Count Pavel Stroganov, were against any limitation on the power of the tsar. Whereas the oligarchs wished to make the Senate an important centre of power and to have it elected by senior officials and country nobility, Stroganov maintained that, if this were done, the sovereign would have "his arms tied, so that he would no longer be able to carry out the plans which he had in favour of the nation." In the event, neither enlightened oligarchs nor enlightened absolutists had their way: Russia's government remained autocratic but reactionary. Alexander, however, never quite abandoned the idea of representative institutions. He encouraged Speransky to

The debate between oligarchy and autocracy

prepare in 1809 a draft constitution that included a pyramid of consultative elected bodies and a national assembly with some slight powers of legislation. In 1819 he asked Nikolay Novosiltsev, a former member of the Unofficial Committee who had made a brilliant career as a bureaucrat, to prepare another constitution, which turned out to be rather similar. Neither was ever implemented, though Alexander took some features of the first and used them out of their intended context.

In 1802 Alexander instituted eight government departments, or ministries, of which five were essentially new. The organization of the departments was substantially improved in 1811 by Speransky. In the 1820s, the ministry of the interior became responsible for public order, public health, stocks of food, and the development of industry and agriculture. Inadequate funds and personnel and the dominant position of the serf-owning nobility in the countryside greatly limited the effective power of this ministry. There was no question of a formal council of ministers, or of anything corresponding to a cabinet, and there was no prime minister. A committee of ministers coordinated to some extent the affairs of the different departments, but its importance depended on circumstances and on individuals. When the tsar was abroad, the committee was in charge of internal affairs. Aleksey Arakcheyev was for a time secretary of the committee, but he did not cease to be the strongest man in Russia under the tsar when he ceased to hold this formal office. The committee had a president, but this office did not confer any significant power or prestige.

Under Nicholas I the committee of ministers continued to operate, but the individual ministers were responsible only to the emperor. The centre of power to some extent shifted into the emperor's personal chancery, which was built up into a formidable apparatus. The Third Department of the chancery, under Count Aleksandr Benckendorff, was responsible for the security police. Its head was also chief of gendarmes, and the two offices were later formally united. The task of the security force was to obtain information on the state of political opinion and to track down and repress all political activity that might be considered dangerous to the regime. The Third Department was also considered by the tsar as an instrument of justice in a broad sense, the defender of all those unjustly treated by the powerful and rich. Some of the department's reports show that there were officials who took these duties seriously, but as a whole it showed more talent for repressing opposition and stifling opinion than for redressing the grievances of the powerless. This was the case notwithstanding the fact that the department was often on the worst of terms with other branches of the public service.

Rule by bureaucracy

Russia under Alexander I and Nicholas I was ruled by its bureaucracy. The efforts of successive sovereigns after Peter the Great to establish a government service of the European type had had partial success. The Russian bureaucracy of 1850 combined some features of a central European bureaucracy of 1750 with some features of pre-Petrine Russia. One may speak of a "service ethos" and trace this back to 16th-century Muscovy. But the foundation of this ethos was, for the great majority of Russian officials, servile obedience to the tsar and not service to the state as that phrase was understood in a country such as Prussia. The notion of the state as something distinct from and superior to both ruler and ruled was incomprehensible to most government servants. Russian bureaucrats were obsessed with rank and status. Indeed, this was the only incentive that the government could give, as salaries were very meagre. Rank was not so much a reward for efficient service as a privilege to be grasped and jealously guarded. In order to prevent able persons, especially of humble origin, from rising too quickly, great emphasis was laid on seniority. There were exceptions, and outstandingly able, cultured, and humane men did reach the top under Nicholas I, but they were few.

The rank and file of the bureaucracy was mediocre, but its numbers steadily increased, perhaps trebling in the first half of the century. It remained poorly paid. The government's poverty was caused by the backward state of the economy, by the fact that no taxes could be asked of the nobility, and by the cost of waging wars—not only the great wars but also the long colonial campaigns in the Caucasus. Government officials were badly educated. They lacked not only precise knowledge but also the sort of basic ethical training that competent officials need. They were reluctant to make decisions: responsibility was pushed higher and higher up the hierarchy, until thousands of minor matters ended on the emperor's desk. Centralization of responsibility meant slowness of decision, and delays of many years were not unusual; death often provided the answer. There were also many antiquated, discriminatory, and contradictory laws. Large categories of the population, such as Jews and members of heretical Christian sects, suffered from various legal disabilities. Since not all of those discriminated against were poor and since many small officials were unable to support their families, bending or evasion of the law had its market price, and the needy official had a supplementary source of income. Corruption of this sort existed on a mass scale. To a certain extent it was a redeeming feature of the regime: if there had been less corruption the government would have been even slower, less efficient, and more oppressive than it was.

Social classes. No significant changes were made in the condition of the serfs in the first half of the century. Alexander I, perhaps from fear of the nobility and with the memory of his father's fate in mind, approached the problem with caution, though with a desire for reform, but first war and then diplomacy diverted him. His successor, Nicholas, disliked serfdom, but there were political hazards in eliminating it. The power of the central government extended down to the provincial governors and, more tenuously, down to the *ispravnik,* or chief official of the district, of which each province had about three or four. The *ispravnik* was elected by the local nobility. Below the level of the district, the administration virtually ceased to operate: the sole authority was the serf owner. If serfdom were to be abolished, some other authority would have to be put in its place, and the existing bureaucratic apparatus was plainly inadequate. The Decembrist conspiracy in 1825 had greatly increased the tsar's distrust of the nobility. He was determined to avoid public discussion of reform, even within the upper class.

Problems of the countryside

The one important exception to the general picture of bureaucratic stagnation was the creation of the Ministry of State Domains, under Gen. Pavel Kiselev. This became an embryonic ministry of agriculture, with authority over peasants who lived on state lands. These were a little less than half the rural population: in 1858 there were 19,000,000 state peasants and 22,500,000 private serfs. Kiselev set up a system of government administration down to the village level and provided for a measure of self-government under which the mayor of the *volost* (a district grouping several villages or peasant communes) was elected by male householders. There was also to be a *volost* court for judging disputes between peasants. Kiselev planned to improve medical services, build schools, establish warehouses for stocks of food in case of crop failure, and give instruction in methods of farming. Something was done in all these fields, even if less than intended and often in a manner that provoked hostility or even violent riots; the personnel of the new ministry was no more competent than the bureaucracy as a whole.

Opposition to serfdom

Only minor measures were taken to benefit the serfs on private estates. Opposition to serfdom grew steadily however, not only among persons of European outlook and independent thought, but also among high officials. It seemed not only unjust but intolerable that in a great nation men and women could be owned. Serfdom was also obviously an obstacle to economic development. Whether serfdom was contrary to the interests of serf owners is a more complex question. Those who wished to abolish it argued that it was, since their best hope of getting the nobility to accept abolition lay in convincing them that their self-interest required it. Certainly in parts of southern Russia where the soil was fertile, labour was plentiful, and potential profits in the grain trade with Europe were high, a landowner would do better if he could replace his serfs by paid agricultural labour and be rid of obligations to those peasants whom he did not need to employ. In other regions, where the population was scanty, serfdom provided the landowner with an assured labour supply; if it were abolished, he would have to pay more for his labour force or see it melt away. In large parts of northern Russia where the land was poor, many serfs made a living from various crafts—in cottage industry or even in factories—and from their wages had to pay dues to their masters. The abolition of serfdom would deprive the serf owner of this large income and leave him with only what he could make from farming and from tenants with rather poor economic prospects. On balance, it seems likely that the short-term interests of the great majority of serf owners favoured the maintenance of serfdom, and, in any case, there is no doubt that this is what most serf owners believed.

Industry and trade made slow progress during these years. In the latter part of the 18th century, Russia had been, thanks to its Urals mines, one of the main producers of pig iron. In the next 50 years, it was left far behind by Great Britain, Germany, and the United States. In cotton textiles and sugar refining, Russia was more successful. Count Ye.F. Kankrin, minister of finance from 1823 to 1844, tried to encourage Russian industry by high protective tariffs. He also set up schools and specialized institutes for the advancement of commerce, engineering, and forestry. Russia's exports of grain increased substantially, though its share of total world trade remained about the same in 1850 as in 1800. The first railways also appeared; rail traffic between St. Petersburg (now Leningrad) and Moscow was opened in 1851. The road system remained extremely inadequate, as was demonstrated in the Crimean War.

The urban population grew significantly. There were a few prosperous merchants, well protected by the government. Some centres, such as Ivanovo, in central Russia, with its textile industry, had the beginnings of an industrial working class. The rest of the inhabitants of the cities consisted of small tradesmen and artisans, together with serfs living in town with their owners' permission as household servants or casual labourers.

Education and intellectual life. Alexander I's School Statute (1804) provided for a four-tier system of schools from the primary to the university level, intended to be open to persons of all classes. Under its provisions, several new universities were founded, and gymnasiums (pre-university schools) were established in most provincial capitals. Less was done at the lower levels, for the usual reason of inadequate funds. In the latter part of Alexander's reign, education was supervised by Prince A.N. Golitsyn, head of the ministry of education and spiritual affairs. In an effort to combat what he believed to be dangerous irreligious doctrines emanating from western Europe, Golitsyn encouraged university students to spy on their professors and on each other; those who taught unacceptable ideas were frequently dismissed or threatened with prison. Under Nicholas I there was some improvement. Count Sergey Uvarov, minister of education from 1833 to 1849, permitted a much freer intellectual atmosphere, but he also began the practice of deliberately excluding children of the lower classes from the gymnasiums and universities, which was continued under his successors.

Nevertheless, in increasing numbers the children of minor officials, small tradesmen, and especially priests, were acquiring education. Together with the already Europeanized nobility, they began to form a new cultural elite. Direct political criticism was prevented by the censorship of books and periodicals. Petty police interference made life disagreeable even for writers who were not much concerned with politics. Aleksandr Pushkin, Russia's greatest poet, got into trouble with the police for his opinions in 1824; he was also a friend of some leading Decembrists. After 1826 he lived an unhappy life in St. Petersburg, tolerated but distrusted by the authorities, producing magnificent poetry until he met his death in a duel in 1837. The writers Mikhail Lermontov and Nikolay Gogol were also objects of suspicion to the bureaucrats.

The censorship was not always efficient, and some of the censors were liberal. It became possible to express political ideas in the form of philosophical arguments and literary criticism. Thus, it was partly in intellectual periodicals and partly in discussions in the private houses of Moscow noblemen that the controversy between "westernizers" and "Slavophiles" developed. It began with the publication of a "philosophical letter" by Pyotr Chaadayev in the periodical *Teleskop* in 1836. One of the most penetrating essays ever written about Russia's historical heritage, it argued that Russia belonged neither to West nor to East, neither to Europe nor to Asia:

Westernizers and Slavophiles

> Standing alone in the world, we have given nothing to the world, we have learnt nothing from the world, we have not added a single idea to the mass of human ideas; we have made no contribution to the progress of the human spirit, and everything that has come to us from that spirit, we have disfigured. . . . Today we form a gap in the intellectual order.

Nicholas declared that Chaadayev must be mad and gave orders that he should be confined to his house and regularly visited by a doctor. This humiliating but relatively mild treatment silenced him.

It is misleading to represent the westernizers as wishing slavishly to copy all things Western or the Slavophiles as repudiating Europe and rejecting reform. The chief Slavophiles—Aleksey S. Khomyakov, the brothers Ivan and Pyotr Kireyevsky, and the brothers Konstantin and Ivan Aksakov—were men of deep European culture and bitter opponents of serfdom. Indeed, as landowners they knew more about the problems and sufferings of the serfs than many westernizers. The leading westernizers—Aleksandr Herzen, Vissarion Belinsky, and Mikhail Bakunin—were for their part profoundly Russian. Belinsky was ill at ease with foreigners, and Herzen and Bakunin, despite many years' residence in France, Germany, England, and Italy, remained not only hostile to the world of European bourgeois liberalism and democracy but also strangely ignorant of it.

The difference between westernizers and Slavophiles was essentially that between doctrinaire radicals and empirical conservatives, a familiar theme in the history of most European nations. It was the difference between those who wished to pull the whole political structure down and replace it by a new building, according to their own admirable blueprints, and those who preferred to knock down some parts and repair and refurnish others, bit by bit. Another basic difference was that the Slavophiles were Orthodox Christians and the westernizers either atheists or, like the historian T.N. Granovsky, deists with their own personal faith. Belinsky described the Orthodox Church, in his famous "Letter to Gogol" (1847) as "the bulwark of the whip and the handmaid of despotism." He maintained that the Russian people was "by its nature a profoundly atheistic people," and that they viewed the priesthood with contempt. These were but half-truths: the church was indeed subject to the government and upheld autocracy, and priests were often unpopular; but this did not mean that the peasants and a large part of the upper and middle classes were not devoted to the Orthodox faith.

The Slavophiles idealized early Russian history. They believed that there had once been a happy partnership between tsar and people: the tsar had consulted the people through their elected spokesmen in the *zemsky sobor.* This had been changed by Peter the Great when he sought to copy foreign models and interposed an alien bureaucracy, staffed largely by Germans, between himself and his people. The Slavophiles held that Russia should return to the way from which it had strayed under Peter. They asked not for a legislative body of the Western type, still less for parliamentary government, but for a consultative assembly to advise the emperor. This was quite unacceptable to Nicholas, who was proud of Peter the Great and believed himself his political heir. To the westernizers, on the other hand, Peter the Great was a symbol of radical change, not of autocracy.

The Russian Empire. Russia in the 19th century was both a multilingual and a multireligious empire. Only about half the population were at the same time Russian by language and Orthodox by religion. The Orthodox were to some extent privileged in comparison with the other Christians; all Christians enjoyed a higher status than Muslims; and the latter were not so disadvantaged as the

The multilingual and multireligious empire

Russian expansion in Asia.

From M. Florinsky, *A Short History of Russia*, © copyright, Michael T. Florinsky, 1964; published by the Macmillan Company

Jews. The basis of legitimacy was obedience to the tsar: Nicholas expected all his subjects to obey him, but he did not expect non-Russians to become Russians. Admittedly, he detested the Poles, but that was because they had been disloyal subjects and revolted against him.

The idea that Russians, as such, should have a status superior to that of other peoples of the empire was distasteful to Nicholas. Russian nationalism nevertheless received some support from Count Uvarov, who, in his famous report to the tsar in 1832, proclaimed three principles as "truly Russian": autocracy, Orthodoxy, and the national principle (*narodnost*). In 1833 Uvarov set up a new university in Kiev, to be the centre for a policy of spreading Russian language and culture through the schools in the western provinces, at the expense of the Polish. Nicholas approved of this, for the Poles had been guilty of rebellion. But when the attempt was made to russify the Germans of the Baltic provinces, he objected. The Baltic Germans were loyal subjects and provided admirable officers and officials: they must be allowed to preserve their German culture and to maintain their cultural and social domination over the Estonians and Latvians. The young Slavophile and landowning nobleman Yury Samarin, a junior official in Riga, was severely reprimanded by the Emperor for his anti-German activities.

The most revolutionary of the Decembrist leaders, Pavel Pestel, had insisted that all non-Russian peoples of the empire except the Poles should "completely fuse their nationality with the nationality of the dominant people." Another group of Decembrists, however, the Society of United Slavs, believed in a federation of free Slav peoples, including some of those living under Austrian and Turkish rule. In 1845 this idea was put forward in a different form in the Brotherhood of SS. Cyril and Methodius, in Kiev. This group, among whose members was the Ukrainian poet Taras Shevchenko, believed that a federation of Slav peoples should include the Ukrainians, whom they claimed were not a part of the Russian nation but a distinct nationality. The society was crushed by the police, and Shevchenko was sent as a private soldier to the Urals; Nicholas himself gave orders that the great poet should be forbidden to write or draw. But Ukrainian national consciousness, though still confined to an educated minority, was growing; and nothing did more to crystallize Ukrainian as a literary language than Shevchenko's poetry.

Russian victories in Asia

During the first half of the century Russia made substantial conquests in Asia. In the Caucasus, the kingdom of Georgia united voluntarily with Russia in 1801, and other small Georgian principalities were conquered in the next years. Persia ceded northern Azerbaijan, including the peninsula of Baku, in 1813 and the Armenian province of Erivan (Yerevan) in 1828. The mountain peoples of the northern Caucasus, however, proved more redoubtable. The Chechens, led by the Shaykh Shāmil, resisted Russian expeditions from 1834 until 1859, and the Circassians were not finally crushed until 1864. In the 1840s, Russian rule was established over the pastoral peoples of Kazakhstan. In the Far East, Russian ships explored the lower course of the Amur River and discovered the straits between Sakhalin and the mainland of Asia in 1849. The Russian-American Company, founded in 1799, controlled part of the coast and islands of Alaska.

Foreign policy. At the beginning of the 19th century, Russian foreign policy was essentially concentrated on the three western neighbour countries with which it had been preoccupied since the 16th: Sweden, Poland, and Turkey. The policy toward these countries also determined Russian relations with France, Austria, and Great Britain.

Russo-Swedish relations were settled during the Napoleonic era. When Napoleon met with Alexander at Tilsit, he gave the latter a free hand to proceed against Sweden. After two years of war, in which the Russians did not always fare well, the Swedish government ceded Finland to the Tsar in 1809. Alexander became grand duke of Finland, but Finland was not incorporated into the Russian Empire, and its institutions were fully respected. In 1810, when Napoleon's former marshal, Bernadotte, was elected heir to the Swedish throne, he showed no hostility to Russia. In 1812 he made an agreement recognizing the Tsar's position in Finland in return for the promise of Russian support in his aim to annex Norway from Denmark. Bernadotte achieved this in the Treaty of Kiel of 1814, and thereafter the relations between Russia and Sweden, now a small and peaceful state, were not seriously troubled.

Alexander I, influenced by his Polish friend Prince Adam Czartoryski, had plans for the liberation and unity of Poland, which had ceased to exist as a state in the 18th century, when it had been partitioned among Russia, Prussia, and Austria. After his defeat by Napoleon in 1805, he abandoned those plans in favour of an alliance with Prussia. In 1807 Napoleon established a dependency called the Grand Duchy of Warsaw and in 1809 increased its territory at the expense of Austria. Alexander's attempts to win the Poles to his side in 1811 and to persuade Austria to make concessions to them failed; when Napoleon invaded Russia in 1812, he had 100,000 first-class Polish troops fighting for him. After Napoleon's defeat Alexander was not vindictive. He protected the Poles against the demands of Russian nationalists who wanted revenge, and sought once more to create a large Polish kingdom comprising the territories annexed by Russia and Prussia in the partitions of the 18th century. He was opposed at the Congress of Vienna in 1814–15 by Austria and Britain, and the ensuing kingdom of Poland, which, though nominally autonomous, was to be in permanent union with the Russian Empire, consisted of only part of the Prussian and Russian conquests. Alexander was popular in Poland for a time after 1815. But real reconciliation between Poles and Russians was made impossible by their competing claims for the borderlands, which had belonged to the former Grand Duchy of Lithuania. The majority of the population of this region was Belorussian, Ukrainian, or Lithuanian; its commercial class was Jewish; and its upper classes and culture were Polish. Neither Russians nor Poles considered Belorussians, Ukrainians, or Lithuanians to be nations, entitled to decide their own fates: the question was whether Lithuania was to be Polish or Russian. Russians could argue that most of it had been part of "the Russian land" until the 14th century, and the Poles that it had been Polish since the 16th. Alexander had some sympathy for the Polish point of view and allowed the Poles to hope that he would reunite these lands with Poland, but the effective political forces in Russia were strongly opposed to any change. The disappointment of Polish hopes for Lithuania was probably the most important single cause of the growing tension between Warsaw and St. Petersburg in the late 1820s, which culminated in the revolt of the Poles in November 1830 and the war of 1831 between Polish and Russian armies. It ended in the defeat of the Poles and the exile of thousands of political leaders and soldiers to western Europe. Poland's constitution and, thus, its autonomy were abrogated; and there began the policy of russification of Poland.

Defeat by Napoleon

International reactions to the Russo-Polish war were of some importance. There was much public sympathy for the Poles in France and Britain, but this had no influence on Russian actions. On the other hand, the governments of Prussia and Austria strongly supported Russia. It is arguable that the cooperation among the three monarchies, which continued over the next two decades and was revived from time to time later in the century, had less to do with their eloquently proclaimed loyalty to monarchical government than with their common interest in suppressing the Poles.

Balkan problems

Turkey had long been the main object of Russian territorial expansion; through a certain inertia of tradition, the Turkish policy had become almost automatic. It was to some extent reinforced by religious motives—by the romantic desire to liberate Constantinople, the holy city of Orthodoxy—but more important in the mid-19th century was the desire to assure the exit of Russian grain exports through the Black Sea. During certain periods, Russia sought to dominate Turkey as a powerful ally: this was its policy from 1798 to 1806 and again from 1832 to 1853. When this policy was successful, Russia supported the integrity of the Ottoman Empire and made no territorial demands. When it was not successful, Russia sought to undermine Turkey by supporting rebellious Balkan peoples or, more directly, by war: this was the case from 1806 to 1812, from 1828 to 1829, and from 1853 to 1856.

The periods of cooperation were more profitable for Russia than those of conflict. In the first period, a promising foothold was established in the Ionian Islands, which had to be abandoned after the Treaty of Tilsit. In the second period, Russia achieved a great success with the 1833 Treaty of Hünkâr İskelesi, which in effect opened the Black Sea Straits to Russian warships. It achieved a more limited but more durable gain by the Straits Convention of 1841, signed by all the Great Powers and by Turkey, which forbade the passage of foreign warships through either the Dardanelles or the Bosporus as long as Turkey was at peace, thus protecting Russia's position in the Black Sea unless it was itself at war with Turkey.

In the periods of hostility between Russia and Turkey, the main object of Russian expansion was the area later known as Romania—the Danubian principalities of Moldavia and Walachia. In 1812 Moldavia was partitioned between Russia and Turkey: the eastern half, under the name of Bessarabia, was annexed to Russia. In the war of 1828–29, Russian armies marched through the principalities and afterward remained in occupation until 1834. In 1848 the Russians returned, with Turkish approval, to suppress the revolution that had broken out in Bucharest. It appeared to be only a matter of time before the two Romanian principalities were wholly annexed to Russia. This did not occur, however, because of Russia's defeat in the Crimean War.

The Crimean War (1853–56) pitted Russia against Great Britain, France, and Turkey. It arose from a series of misunderstandings and diplomatic errors among the powers in their conflict of interests in the Near East, particularly over Turkish affairs. It has been called "the unnecessary war." The fact that it was fought in the Crimea was due to Austrian diplomacy. In June 1854 the Russian government accepted the Austrian demand that Russian troops be withdrawn from the Danubian principalities, and in August Austrian troops entered. It is arguable whether, on balance, the presence of Austrian troops benefitted Russia by preventing French and British forces from marching on the Ukraine or whether it damaged Russia by preventing its troops from marching on Constantinople. The tsar resented the Austrian action as showing ingratitude toward the power that had saved Austria from the Hungarian rebels in 1849. When the British and French were unable to attack in the principalities, they decided to send an expedition to the Crimea to destroy the Russian naval base at Sevastopol. It was here that the war dragged out its course. The war showed the inefficiency of Russia's top military command and of its system of transport and supply. The Russian armies, nevertheless, won victories over the Turks in the Caucasus; and the defense of Sevastopol for nearly a year was a brilliant achievement.

FROM ALEXANDER II TO NICHOLAS II

Emancipation and reform. Defeat in the Crimea made Russia's backwardness clear, and the first step toward modernization was the abolition of serfdom. It seemed to the new tsar Alexander II (reigned 1855–81) that the dangers to public order of dismantling the existing system, which had deterred Nicholas I from action, were less than the dangers of leaving things as they were. As the Tsar said to the nobility of Moscow in March 1856, "it is better to abolish serfdom from above than to wait until the serfs begin to liberate themselves from below." The main work of reform was carried out in the ministry of the interior, where the most able officials, headed by the deputy minister Nikolay Milyutin, were resolved to get the best possible terms for the peasants. In this they were assisted by a few progressive landowners, chief among whom was the Slavophile Yury Samarin; but the bulk of the landowning class was determined, if it could not prevent abolition of serfdom, to give the freed peasants as little as possible. The settlement, proclaimed on March 3 (February 19, old style), 1861, was a compromise. Peasants were freed from servile status, and a procedure was laid down by which they could become owners of land. The government paid the landowners compensation and recovered the cost in annual "redemption payments" from the peasants. The terms were unfavourable to the peasants in many, probably most, cases. In the north, where land was poor, the price of land on which the compensation was based was unduly high: in effect this served to compensate the landowners for the loss of their serfs and also for the loss of the share that they had previously enjoyed of the peasants' earnings from nonagricultural labour. In

The emancipation of the serfs

the south, where land was more valuable, the plots given to the peasants were very small, often less than they had had for their use when they were serfs.

It is arguable that the main beneficiary of the reform was neither peasant nor landowner, but the state. A new apparatus of government was established to replace the authority of the serf owner. From the *ispravnik,* the chief official of the district, who in 1862 ceased to be elected by the nobility and became an appointed official of the ministry of the interior, the official hierachy now stretched down to the village notary, the most powerful person at this level, who was assisted by an elder elected by an assembly of householders. The lowest effective centre of power was the village commune (*obshchina*), an institution of uncertain origin but great antiquity, which had long had the power to redistribute land for the use of its members and to determine the crop cycle, but which now also became responsible for collecting taxes on behalf of the government.

Introduction of the *zemstvos*

Further important reforms followed the emancipation. A new system of elected assemblies at the provincial and county levels was introduced in 1864. These assemblies, known as *zemstvos,* were elected by all classes including the peasants, although the landowning nobility had a disproportionately large share of both the votes and the seats. The *zemstvos* were empowered to levy taxes and to spend their funds on schools, public health, roads, and other social services, but their scope was limited by the fact that they also had to spend money on some of the tasks of the central government. In 1864 a major judicial reform was completed. Russia received a system of law courts based on European models, with irremovable judges and a proper system of courts of appeal. Justices of the peace were instituted for minor offenses; they were elected by the county *zemstvos.* A properly organized, modern legal profession now arose, and it soon achieved very high standards. The old system of endless delays and judicial corruption rapidly disappeared. There were, however, two important gaps in the system: one was that the ministry of the interior had power, regardless of the courts, to banish persons whom it regarded as politically dangerous; the other was that the courts for settling disputes between peasants were maintained and operated on the basis of peasant custom. Their institution by Kiselev in the 1840s had been a well-intentioned reform, but their continuation after emancipation meant that the peasants were still regarded as something less than full citizens.

During the first years of Alexander II's reign there was some demand from a liberal section of the nobility for representative government at the national level—not for full parliamentary rule, still less for a democratic suffrage, but for some sort of consultative assembly in which public issues could be debated and which could put before the Emperor the views of at least the educated section of the Russian people. The tsar and his bureaucrats refused to consider this. The principle of autocracy must remain sacred. Such was the view not only of bureaucrats but of such men as Nikolay Milyutin and Yury Samarin, both of whom rested their hopes for the progressive reforms they so ardently desired on the unfettered power of the Emperor. Their attitude was essentially that of Pavel Stroganov at the beginning of the century, that the sovereign must not have "his arms tied" and so be prevented from realizing "the plans which he had in favour of the nation." The decision against a national assembly in the early 1860s was a negative event of the greatest importance: it deprived Russia of the possibility of public political education such as that which existed, for example, in contemporary Prussia, and it deprived the government of the services of hundreds of talented men.

Revolutionary activities. The emancipation was received with bitter disappointment by many peasants as well as by the radical intellectuals. The serfs' view of their relationship to the landowners had been traditionally summed up in the phrase: "We are yours, but the land is ours." Now they were being asked to pay for land that they felt was theirs by right. During the 1860s small revolutionary groups began to appear. The outstanding figure was the socialist writer N.G. Chernyshevsky; the extent of his involvement in revolutionary action remains a subject of controversy, but of his influence on generations of young Russians there can be no doubt. In 1861 and 1862 revolutionary leaflets were distributed in St. Petersburg, ranging from the demand for a constituent assembly to a passionate appeal for insurrection. The Polish uprising of 1863 strengthened the forces of repression. An unsuccessful attempt on the tsar's life in 1866 led to a certain predominance, among Alexander's advisers, of extreme conservatives. Nevertheless, there were still some valuable reforms to come. In 1870 the main cities of Russia were given elected municipal government (on a very narrow franchise), and in 1874 a series of military reforms was completed by the establishment of universal military service. This was the work of Dmitry Milyutin, the brother of Nikolay and like him a liberal, who was minister of war from 1861 to 1881.

From reform to terrorism

In the 1870s revolutionary activity revived. Its centre was the university youth, who were increasingly influenced by a variety of socialist ideas derived from Europe but adapted to Russian conditions. These young people saw in the peasantry the main potential for revolutionary action. In 1873 and 1874 hundreds of the youth, including women, "went to the people," invading the countryside and seeking to rouse the peasants with their speeches. The peasants did not understand, and the police arrested the young revolutionaries. Some were sentenced to prison, and hundreds were deported to remote provinces or to Siberia. It became clear that no progress could be expected from overt action: conspiratorial action was the only hope. In 1876 a new party was founded that took the title of Land and Freedom. Some of its members favoured assassination of prominent officials in reprisal for the maltreatment of their comrades and also as a means to pressure the government in order to extract Western-type political liberties. Experience also had shown them that while the peasants were physically too scattered to be an effective force, and in any case too apathetic, the workers in the new industrial cities offered a more promising audience. This faction was opposed by others in the party who deprecated assassination, continued to pay more attention to peasants than to workers, and were indifferent to the attainment of political liberties. In 1879 the party split. The politically minded and terrorist wing took the name People's Will and made its aim the assassination of Alexander II. After several unsuccessful attempts it achieved its aim on March 13 (March 1, O.S.), 1881, when the tsar was fatally wounded by a bomb while driving through the capital. All the main leaders of the group were caught by the police, and five of them were hanged.

Attempts at repression

Shortly before his death the Tsar had been considering reforms that would have introduced a few elected representatives into the apparatus of government. His successor, Alexander III (reigned 1881–94), considered these plans. Under the influence of his former tutor, Konstantin Pobedonostsev, the procurator of the Holy Synod, he decided to reject them and to reaffirm the principle of autocracy without change. In 1882 he appointed Dmitry Tolstoy minister of interior. Tolstoy and Pobedonostsev were the moving spirits of the deliberately reactionary policies that followed. Education was further restricted, the work of the *zemstvos* was hampered, and the village communes were brought under closer control in 1889 by the institution of the "land commandant" (*zemsky nachalnik*)—an official appointed by the ministry of interior, usually a former officer or a local landowner, who interfered in all aspects of peasant affairs. The office of elected justice of the peace was abolished, and the government was authorized to assume emergency powers when public order was said to be in danger. By this time Russian public officials were better paid and educated, and less addicted to crude corruption, than they had been in the reign of Nicholas I, but they retained their arrogant contempt for the public and especially for the poorer classes. The discriminatory laws against Jews and members of dissenting Christian sects remained a source of widespread injustice, hardship, and resentment.

The repressive policies of Dmitry Tolstoy worked for a time. But the economic development of the following decades created new social tensions and brought into existence new social groups, from whom active opposition once more developed. The *zemstvos* were in growing conflict with the central authorities. Even their efforts at social improvement of a quite unpolitical type met with obstruction. The ministry of the interior, once the centre of Russia's best reformers, now became a stronghold of resistance. In the obscurantist view of its leading officials, only the central government had the right to care for the public welfare, and *zemstvo* initiatives were undesirable usurpations of power. Better that nothing should be done at all than that it should be done through the wrong channels. This attitude was manifested in 1891, when crop failures led to widespread famine and relief work by *zemstvo* officials met with government obstruction. The revival of political activity may be dated from this year. It was accelerated by the death of Alexander III in 1894 and the succession of his son Nicholas II (reigned 1894–1917), who commanded less fear or respect but nevertheless at once antagonized the *zemstvo* liberals by publicly describing their aspirations for reforms as "senseless dreams." In the late 1890s moderate liberalism, aiming at the establishment of a consultative national assembly, was strong among elected *zemstvo* members who were largely members of the landowning class. A more radical attitude, combining elements of liberalism and socialism, was to be found in the professional classes of the cities, including many persons employed by the *zemstvos* as teachers, doctors, engineers, or statisticians. The growth of an industrial working class provided a mass basis for socialist movements, and by the end of the century some interest in politics was beginning to penetrate even to the peasantry, especially in parts of the Middle Volga Valley.

Economic and social development. Liberation from serfdom was a benefit for the peasants that should not be underrated. The decades that followed brought a growth of prosperity and self-reliance to at least a substantial minority. In 1877, when about four-fifths of the land due to be transferred to the former serfs was actually in their possession, this "allotment land" constituted about half of the arable land in 50 provinces of European Russia. A further one-third of the arable land was still owned by the nobility, and the rest belonged to a variety of individual or collective owners. In 1905 substantially more than half the arable land was in allotment land and another 10 percent belonged to individual peasants or to peasant associations; the nobility's share of arable land had fallen to a little more than 20 percent. Peasant land had increased by more than 99,000,000 acres (40,000,000 hectares) between 1877 and 1905, of which more than half had been obtained by purchase from landowners and the remainder by the completion of the transfer of allotment land. Peasant purchases had been assisted by loans from the Peasants' Land Bank, set up by the government in 1882. The Nobles' Land Bank, set up in 1885, made loans to landowners at more favourable rates of interests; it may have retarded, but did not prevent, the passage of land from landowners to peasants. In 1894 the rate of interest charged by the two banks was equalized.

Difficulties in agriculture

Though many peasants improved their position, agriculture remained backward, and poverty increased more rapidly than prosperity. One of the main reasons for this was the indifference of the government to agriculture. The government's economic policy was motivated by the desire for national and military power. This required the growth of industry, and great efforts were made to encourage it. Agriculture was regarded mainly as a source of revenue to pay for industry and the armed forces. Exports of grain made possible imports of raw materials, and taxes paid by peasants filled the state's coffers. The redemption payments were a heavy charge on the peasants' resources, though a gradual fall in the value of money appreciably reduced it with the passage of years. Consumption taxes, especially on sugar, tobacco, matches, and oil, affected the peasants, and so did import duties. In 1894 the government introduced a liquor monopoly that drew enormous revenues from the peasants, to whom vodka was a principal solace in a hard life. The techniques and tools of agriculture remained extremely primitive, and farm output low; virtually nothing was done to instruct peasants in modern methods.

The second main cause of peasant poverty was overpopulation. The vast landmass of Russia was, of course, sparsely populated, but the number of persons employed in agriculture per unit of arable land, and relative to output, was extremely high as compared to western Europe. There was a vast and increasing surplus of labour in the Russian villages. Outlets were available in seasonal migration to the southern provinces, where labour was needed on the great estates that produced the grain that Russia exported; and peasants could move permanently to new land in Siberia, which at the end of the century was absorbing a yearly influx of 200,000; or they could find seasonal work in the cities or seek permanent employment in the growing industrial sector. These alternatives were not enough to absorb the growing labour surplus, which was most acute in the southern part of central Russia and in the northern Ukraine, in the provinces of Kursk and Poltava. Peasants competed with each other to lease land from the landlords' estates; this drove rents up; the existence of the large estates became more and more resented; and class feeling began to take the form of political demands for further redistribution of land.

The difficulties of agriculture were also increased by the inefficiency of the peasant commune, which had the power to redistribute holdings according to the needs of families and to dictate the rotation of crops to all members. In doing so, it tended to hamper enterprising farmers and protect the incompetent. In defense of the commune it was argued that it ensured a living to everyone and stood for values of solidarity and cooperation that were more important than mere profit and loss. Russian officials also found it useful as a means of collecting taxes and keeping the peasants in order. The 1861 settlement did provide a procedure by which peasants could leave the commune, but it was very complicated and was little used. In practice, the communal system predominated in northern and central Russia, and individual peasant ownership was widespread in the Ukraine and in the Polish borderlands. In 1898, in 50 provinces of European Russia, about 198,000,000 acres (80,000,000 hectares) of land were under communal tenure, and about 54,000,000 were under individual tenure.

The dispute over the peasant commune divided the ranks both of officialdom and of the government's revolutionary enemies. The ministry of the interior, which stood for paternalism and public security at all costs, favoured the commune in the belief that it was a bulwark of conservatism, of traditional Russian social values, and of loyalty to the tsar. The Socialist Revolutionaries favoured it because they took the view that the commune was, at least potentially, the natural unit of a future socialist republic. The ministry of finance, concerned to develop capitalism in town and country, objected to the commune as an obstacle to economic progress; it hoped to see a prosperous minority of individual farmers as a basis of a new and more modern type of Russian conservatism. The Social Democrats agreed that the commune must and should be replaced by capitalist ownership, but they saw this only as the next stage in the progress toward a socialist revolution led by urban workers.

Industrial growth

The emancipation of the serfs undoubtedly helped capitalist development, though this began rather slowly. A rapid growth of railways came in the 1870s, and in the same decade the exploitation of petroleum began at Baku in Azerbaijan. There was also progress in the textile and sugar industries. Only in the 1890s did the demand for iron and steel, created by the railway program and by military needs in general, begin to be satisfied on a large scale within Russia. By the end of the century there was a massive metallurgical industry in the Ukraine, based on the iron ore of Krivoy Rog and the coal of the Donets Basin. The iron industry of the Urals, which lost a large part of its labour force when the serfs became free to leave, lagged far behind. Poland was also an important metallurgical centre. Textiles were concentrated in the central provinces of Moscow and Vladimir; by the end of the century they were drawing much of their raw cotton from the newly conquered lands of Central Asia. Baku was also booming, especially as a supplier of petroleum to the Moscow region. St. Petersburg had begun to develop important engineering and electrical industries. Count Sergey Witte, minister of finance from 1892 to 1903, was able to put Russia on the gold standard in 1897 and to encourage foreign investors. French and Belgian capital was invested mainly in the southern metallurgical industry, British in petroleum, and German in electricity.

Industrial growth began to produce an urban working class, which seemed fated to repeat the history of workers in the early stages of industrial capitalism in Western countries. The workers were unskilled, badly paid, overworked, and miserably housed. Uprooted from the village communities in which they had at least had a recognized place, the peasants' sons who flocked into the new industrial agglomerations suffered both physical and moral privation. This was especially true of central Russia, where the surplus of labour kept wages down to the minimum. It was in St. Petersburg, where employers found it less easy to recruit workers, that the transformation of the amorphous mass of urban poor into a modern working class made the most progress. St. Petersburg employers were also less hostile to government legislation on behalf of the workers. In 1882, Finance Minister N.Kh. Bunge introduced an inspectorate of labour conditions, and limited hours of work for children. In 1897, Count Witte introduced a maximum working day of 11½ hours for all workers, male or female, and of 10 hours for those engaged in any night work. Trade unions were not permitted, though several attempts were made to organize them illegally. The ministry of the interior, being more interested in public order than in businessmen's profits, occasionally showed some concern for the workers. In 1901 the head of the Moscow branch of the security police, Col. S.V. Zubatov, encouraged the formation of a workers' society intended to rally the workers behind the autocracy; but it became largely infiltrated by Social Democrats. Strikes were strictly forbidden but occurred anyway, especially in 1885, 1896, 1902, and 1903.

A Russian business class also developed rapidly under the umbrella of government policy, benefitting especially from the high protective tariffs and the very high prices paid for government purchases from the metallurgical industry. Russia's industrial progress took place under private capitalism, but it differed from classical Western capitalism in that the motivation of Russian industrial growth was political and military, and the driving force was government policy. Russian and foreign capitalists provided the resources and the organizing skill, and they were richly rewarded. The richness of their rewards accounted for a second difference from classical capitalism: Russian capitalists were completely satisfied with the political system as it was. English and French capitalists had material and ideological reasons to fight against absolute monarchs and aristocratic upper classes; Russian businessmen accepted the principle and the practice of autocracy.

Education and ideas. At the time of the first modern census in Russia, in 1897, there were 104,000 persons who had attended or were attending a university—less than 0.1 percent of the population—and 73 percent of these were children of nobles or officials. The number who had studied or were studying in any sort of secondary school was 1,072,977, or less than 1 percent of the population, and 40 percent of these were children of nobles and officials. In 1904 primary schools managed by the ministry of education had rather more than 3,000,000 pupils, and those managed by the Orthodox Church not quite 2,000,000. The combined figure represented only 27 percent of the children of school age in the empire at that time. Persistent neglect of education could no longer be explained by sheer backwardness and lack of funds: the Russian empire of 1900 could have afforded a modern school system if its rulers had thought it important.

The Russian intelligentsia

In the last half of the 19th century the word intelligentsia came into use in Russia. This word is not precisely definable, for it described both a social group and a state of mind. Essentially the intelligentsia consisted of persons with a good modern education and a passionate preoccupation with general political and social ideas. An uneducated or stupid man could not be a member of the intelligentsia, but not all educated and intelligent men could belong to it either; for example, a brilliant scientist devoted solely to his science would not be reckoned a member of the intelligentsia. Its nucleus was to be found in the liberal professions of law, medicine, teaching, and engineering, which grew in numbers and social prestige as the economy became more complex; yet it also included individuals from outside those professions—private landowners, bureaucrats, and even army officers. The intelligentsia was by its very nature opposed to the existing political and social system, and this opposition coloured its attitude to culture in general. In particular, the value of works of literature was judged by the intelligentsia according to whether they furthered the cause of social progress. This tradition of social utilitarianism was initiated by the critic Vissarion Belinsky and carried further by N.A. Dobrolyubov in the late 1850s. Its most extreme exponent was Dmitry I. Pisarev, who held that all art was useless and that the only aim of thinking people should be "to solve forever the unavoidable question of hungry and naked people." In the last decades of the century the chief spokesman of social utilitarianism was the sociological writer Nikolay K. Mikhaylovsky, a former supporter of the terrorist group People's Will. It is hardly an exaggeration to say that Russian literature was faced with two censorships—that of the official servants of the autocracy and that of the social utilitarian radicals. Yet the great writers of this period—Leo Tolstoy, Fyodor Dostoyevsky, Aleksandr Blok, and the symbolist poets of the early 20th century—though profoundly concerned with social issues, did not conform to these criteria.

The intelligentsia did not consist of active revolutionaries, although it preferred the revolutionaries to the government; but it was from the intelligentsia that the professional revolutionaries were largely recruited. The lack of civil liberties and the prohibition of political parties made it necessary for socialists to use conspiratorial methods. Illegal parties had to have rigid centralized discipline. Yet the emergence of the professional revolutionary, imagined in romantically diabolical terms in the "Revolutionary Catechism" of Mikhail Bakunin and Sergey Nechayev in 1869 and sketched more realistically in *What Is To Be Done?* by Vladimir Ilyich Ulyanov, better known as Lenin, in 1902, was not entirely due to the circumstances of the underground political struggle. The revolutionaries were formed also by their sense of mission, by their absolute conviction that they knew best the interests of the masses. For these men and women, revolution was not just a political aim; it was also a substitute for religion. It is worth noting that a remarkably high proportion of the young revolutionaries of the late 19th century were children of Orthodox priests or persons associated with religious sects. It is also worth noting that the traditional Russian belief in autocracy, the desire for an all-powerful political saviour, and the contempt for legal formalities and processes had left its mark on them. The autocracy of Nicholas II was, of course, odious to them, but this did not mean that autocratic government should be abolished; rather, it should be replaced by the autocracy of the virtuous.

The socialists

Russian revolutionary socialism at the end of the century was divided into two main streams, each of these being subdivided into a section that favoured conspiratorial tactics and one that aimed at a mass movement to be controlled by its members. The Socialist Revolutionaries (founded in 1901 from a number of groups more or less derived from People's Will) first hoped that Russia could bypass capitalism, and when it became clear that this could not be done, they aimed to limit its operation and build a socialist order based on village communes. The land was to be socialized but worked by peasants on the principle of "labour ownership." The Social Democrats (founded in 1898 from a number of illegal working-class groups) believed that the future lay with industrialization and a socialist order based on the working class. The Socialist Revolutionaries were divided between their extreme terrorist wing, the "Fighting Organization," and a broader and looser membership that at one end merged imperceptibly with radical middle-class liberalism. The Social Democrats were divided between Lenin's group, which took the name Bolshevik (derived from the Russian word for "majority," after a majority won by his group at one particular vote during the second congress of the party, held in Brussels and London in 1903), and a number of other groups that were by no means united but that came to be collectively known as Menshevik (derived from the word for "minority"). The personal, ideological, and programmatic issues involved in their quarrels were extremely complex, but it is a permissible oversimplification to say that Lenin favoured rigid discipline while the Mensheviks aimed at creating a mass labour movement of the west European type; that the Mensheviks were much more willing to cooperate with nonsocialist liberals than were the Bolsheviks; and that Lenin paid much more attention to the peasants as a potential revolutionary force than did the Mensheviks.

The repression of nationalities

Russification policies. After the Crimean War the Russian government made some attempt to introduce in Poland a new system acceptable to the Polish population. The leading figure on the Polish side was the nobleman Aleksander Wielopolski. His pro-Russian program proved unacceptable to the Poles. Tension increased and in January 1863 armed rebellion broke out. This was put down, being suppressed with special severity in the Lithuanian and Ukrainian borderlands. In order to punish the Polish country gentry for their part in the insurrection, the Russian authorities carried out a land reform on terms exceptionally favourable to the Polish peasants. Its authors were Nikolay Milyutin and Yury Samarin, who genuinely desired to benefit the peasants. The reform was followed, however, by a policy of russification intended to separate the Polish peasants from their own culture. In the 1880s this went so far that the language of instruction even in primary schools in areas of purely Polish population was Russian. At first, all classes of Poles passively accepted their defeat, while clinging to their language and national consciousness; but in the 1890s two strong, though of course illegal, political parties appeared—the National Democrats and the Polish Socialist Party, both fundamentally anti-Russian.

After 1863 the authorities also severely repressed all signs of Ukrainian nationalist activity. In 1876 all publications in Ukrainian, other than historical documents, were prohibited. In Eastern Galicia, however, which lay just across the Austrian border and had a population of several million Ukrainians, not only the language but political activity flourished. Here the great Ukrainian historian Mikhail Hrushevsky and the socialist writer Mikhail Drahomanov published their works; Ukrainian political literature was smuggled across the border. In the 1890s small illegal groups of Ukrainian democrats and socialists existed on Russian soil.

In the 1890s the government began to adopt a general policy of russification. It was no longer enough that the subjects of the tsar should obey him loyally: they were required to become Russians. The social driving force behind this policy was the growing bureaucracy, comprised mainly of children of landowning families who no longer owned estates. The Orthodox Church played an active part, since russification and imposition of Orthodoxy went naturally together. It must be recognized that russification had considerable support among all classes of the Russian population except the intelligentsia. Part of the large-circulation conservative press in particular was intensely nationalistic.

The main victims of russification were the very peoples that had shown consistent loyalty to the empire and now found themselves rewarded by being pressed to abandon their own culture. The Germans of the Baltic provinces were deprived of their university and their ancient secondary schools were russified. The Latvians and Estonians did not object to action by the government against the Germans, whom they had reason to dislike as landowners and rich burghers; but the prospect of the German language being replaced by the Russian had no attraction for them, and they strongly resented the pressure to abandon their Lutheran faith for Orthodoxy. The attempt to absorb and russify Finland united the Finns in opposition to St. Petersburg in the 1890s. In 1904 a Finnish terrorist murdered the Russian governor-general, and passive resistance to Russian policies was almost universal. Effective and widespread passive resistance also occurred among the traditionally Russophile Armenians of the Caucasus when the Russian authorities began to interfere with the organization of the Armenian church, and to close the schools maintained from its funds.

Resistance to russification

Of the Muslim peoples of the empire, those who suffered most from russification were the most economically and culturally advanced, the Tatars of the Volga Valley. Attempts by the Orthodox Church to convert Muslims, and the rivalry between Muslims and Orthodox to convert small national groups of Finno-Ugrian speech who were still pagans, caused growing mutual hostility. The Tatars had developed a substantial merchant class by the end of the century and the beginnings of a national intelligentsia. Modern schools, maintained from merchants' funds, were creating a new Tatar educated elite that was increasingly accessible to modern democratic ideas. In Central Asia, on the other hand, modern influences had barely made themselves felt. In those newly conquered lands, Russian colonial administration was paternalistic and limited: like the methods of "indirect rule" in the British and French empires, it made no systematic attempt to change old ways. Here there was no russification.

The position of the Jews was hardest of all. As a result of their history and religious traditions, as well as of centuries of social and economic discrimination, the Jews were overwhelmingly concentrated in commercial and intellectual professions. They were thus prominent both as businessmen and as political radicals, hateful to the bureaucrats as socialists and to the lower classes as capitalists. In the 1880s legal discrimination against them became more severe both in education and in economic life. It was at this time that the police began the practice of pogroms, or officially sponsored riots that led to the destruction of Jewish shops and to physical assaults on Jews—in some cases to killings. These were deliberately used by the authorities as a means of diverting popular discontent to a convenient scapegoat in order to diminish popular hostility to the government.

Foreign policy. During the second half of the 19th century, Russian foreign policy gave about equal emphasis to the Balkans and the Far East. The friendship with Germany and Austria weakened; and in the 1890s the Triple Alliance of Germany, Austria-Hungary, and Italy stood face to face with a dual alliance of France and Russia.

The Balkans

The demilitarization of the Black Sea coast that had resulted from the Crimean War was ended by the London Conference of 1871, which allowed Russia to rebuild its naval forces. In 1876 the Serbo-Turkish War produced an outburst of Pan-Slav feeling in Russia. Partly under its influence, but mainly in pursuit of traditional strategic aims, Russia declared war on Turkey in April 1877. After overpowering heavy Turkish resistance at the fortress of Pleven in Bulgaria, the Russian forces advanced almost to Constantinople. By the Treaty of San Stefano of March 1878 the Turks accepted the creation of a large independent Bulgarian state. Fearing that this would be a Russian vassal, giving Russia mastery over all the Balkans and the straits, Britain and Austria-Hungary opposed the treaty. At the international Congress of Berlin, held in June 1878, Russia had to accept a much smaller Bulgaria. This was regarded by Russian public opinion as a bitter humiliation, for which the German chancellor Bismarck was blamed. In 1885–87 a new international crisis was caused by Russian interference in Bulgarian affairs, with Britain and Austria-Hungary once more opposing Russia. Once more, Russia suffered a political reverse. In the 1890s, despite the pro-Russian sentiment of many Serbs and Bulgarians, neither country's government was much subject to Russian influence. In the crises that arose in connection with the Turkish Armenians and over Crete and Macedonia, Russian policy was extremely cautious and on the whole tended to support the Turkish government. In 1897 an Austro-Russian agreement was made on spheres of influence in the Balkans.

The attempt of Bismarck to restore Russo-German friendship through the Reinsurance Treaty of 1887, with a view to an ultimate restoration of the alliance of Russia, Germany, and Austria, did not survive Bismarck's fall from power in 1890. The Russian government, alarmed by indications of a closer cooperation between the Triple Alliance and Britain and by some signs of a pro-Polish attitude in Berlin, reluctantly turned toward France. The French needed an ally against both Germany and Britain; the Russians needed French capital, in the form both of loans to the Russian government and of investment in Russian industry. The Franco-Russian alliance was signed in August 1891 and was supplemented by a military convention. Essentially the alliance was directed against Germany, for it was only in a war with Germany that each could help the other.

Russia established diplomatic and commercial relations with Japan by three treaties between 1855 and 1858. In 1860, by the Treaty of Peking, Russia acquired from China a long strip of Pacific coastline south of the mouth of the Amur and began to build the naval base of Vladivostok. In 1867 the Russian government sold Alaska to the United States for $7,200,000. The Treaty of St. Petersburg between Russia and Japan in 1875 gave Russia sole control over all of Sakhalin and Japan all the Kuril Islands.

The systematic Russian conquest of Turkistan, the region of settled population and ancient culture lying to the south of the Kazakh steppes, began in the 1860s. This was watched with distrust by the British authorities in India, and fear of Russian interference in Afghanistan led to the Anglo-Afghan War of 1878-80. In the 1880s, Russian expansion extended to the Turkmen lands on the east coast of the Caspian, whose people offered much stiffer military resistance. The Russian conquest of Merv in 1884 caused alarm in Calcutta, and in March 1885 a clash between Russian and Afghan troops produced a major diplomatic crisis between Britain and Russia. An agreement on frontier delimitation was reached in September 1885, and for the next decades Central Asian affairs did not have a major effect on Anglo-Russian relations.

War with Japan

Much more serious was the situation in the Far East. In 1894–95 the long-standing rivalry between the Japanese and Chinese in Korea led to a war between the two Oriental empires, which the Japanese won decisively. Russia faced the choice between collaborating with Japan (with which relations had been fairly good for some years) at the expense of China, or assuming the role of protector of China against Japan. The tsar chose the second policy, largely under the influence of Count Witte. Together with the French and German governments, the Russians demanded that the Japanese return to China the Liaotung Peninsula, which they had taken in the treaty of peace. Russia then concluded an alliance with China in 1896, which included the establishment of a Russian-owned Chinese Eastern Railway to cross northern Manchuria from west to east, linking Siberia with Vladivostok, and administered by Russian personnel and a Russian police force with extraterritorial rights. In 1898 the Russian government went still further and acquired from China the same Liaotung Peninsula of which it had deprived the Japanese three years earlier. Here the Russians built a naval base in ice-free waters at Port Arthur. They also obtained extraterritorial rights of ownership and management of a South Manchurian railroad that was to stretch from north to south, linking Port Arthur with the Chinese Eastern Railway at the junction of Harbin. When in 1900 the European powers sent armed forces to relieve their diplomatic missions in Peking, besieged by the Boxer Rebellion, the Russian government used this as an opportunity to bring substantial military units into Manchuria. All of this bitterly antagonized the Japanese. They might have been willing, nonetheless, to write off Manchuria as a Russian sphere of influence provided that Russia recognize Japanese priority in Korea, but the Russian government would not do this. It was not so much that the tsar himself wished to dominate the whole Far East; it was rather that he was beset by advisers with several rival schemes and could not bring himself to reject any of them. The British government, fearing that Russia would be able to establish domination over the Chinese government and so interfere with the interests of Britain in other parts of China, made an alliance with Japan in January 1902. Negotiations between Russia and Japan continued, but they were insincere on both sides. On the night of February 8/9, 1904, Japanese forces made a surprise attack on Russian warships in Port Arthur, and the Russo-Japanese War began.

THE LAST YEARS OF TSARDOM

Revolutionary disturbances of 1905

Defeat and disorder. The Russo-Japanese War brought a series of Russian defeats on land and sea, culminating in the destruction of the Russian Baltic fleet in the Straits of Tsushima. Political discontent grew steadily at home. The efforts of the moderate *zemstvo* liberals to organize help for the war effort were discouraged by the authorities, and criticism of the government in the press and at public banquets grew bolder. On Sunday, January 22 (January 9, O.S.), 1905, a large crowd of workers, led by a priest named Georgy Gapon, who was active in one of the officially sponsored workers' societies, marched to the square in front of the Winter Palace. Troops opened fire and several hundred were killed or injured.

Bloody Sunday was followed by disorders in gathering momentum. There were strikes, workers' demonstrations, street fighting, peasant insurrections, and mutinies in both the army and navy. The disorders were especially violent in regions inhabited by non-Russians: in Poland, Latvia, Georgia, and parts of the Ukraine. There were also numerous pogroms, not only of Ukrainians and Russians against Jews but also of Tatars in Azerbaijan against Armenians. Armed bands of townsmen of various social origin, led by men of the extreme right, in many cases by policemen or priests, formed to fight against left-wing bands. These groups, known as Black Hundreds, were a prototype of the fascist gangs of central Europe in the 1930s. The revolutionary movement of 1905 reached its climax in October with a nationwide railway strike and the formation in St. Petersburg of a Soviet (council) of Workers' Deputies. Faced by the threat of collapse, the Tsar issued a manifesto promising to convoke a national Parliament. Count Witte, who had just successfully conducted peace negotiations at Portsmouth (New Hampshire), saving for Russia the northern half of Sakhalin and the Chinese Eastern Railway but ceding Port Arthur and the South Manchurian Railway, became Russia's first prime minister. In the following weeks a series of laws established the powers of the Parliament, called the State Duma, and the procedure for its election.

Popular sentiment and the Dumas

The Dumas. The election, held in April 1906 on a rather broad franchise, produced a Duma with a left-wing majority even though the Social Democrats and Socialist Revolutionaries had for the most part boycotted the election. The largest party, the Constitutional Democrats (Kadets), were the heirs to the earlier Union of Liberation (a group of nonsocialist radicals formed in 1903). The second largest, the Labour Group (Trudoviki), may be described as moderate socialists. The non-Russian peoples returned a large number of deputies, among them 40 Ukrainians and 30 Muslims. Russian conservatives were a tiny minority. Cooperation proved impossible between this assembly and the tsar's ministers, who were responsible to him only and could not be overthrown by Duma majorities. The reforms demanded by the Duma—redistribution of landowners' estates to peasants with or without compensation, amnesty for political prisoners, equal rights for Jews and for religious dissenters, autonomy for Poland—were unacceptable to the government. After two months of deadlock the tsar dissolved the Duma in July. For the next eight months the new premier, Pyotr Stolypin, ruled by decree. Peasant riots were ruthlessly suppressed, with hundreds executed by specially established courts-martial. By the beginning of 1907 the last stirrings of revolution were over; the discipline of the armed forces was restored, and the police functioned effectively. In February 1907 elections were held for a second Duma. This time the Social Democrats put up official candidates and won 65 seats, giving them the third largest representation after the Trudoviki (101) and the Kadets (92). Conservative groups had 63 seats, and the Octobrists, heirs to the moderate *zemstvo* liberals of the 1890s, had 32. The political centre of gravity thus lay still further to the left than it had in the first Duma. Cooperation again proved impossible. In June 1907 the tsar dissolved the second Duma and Stolypin changed the electoral law, restricting the franchise in favour of the upper classes against the peasants and in favour of the Russians as against the other nationalities.

The third and fourth Dumas were accordingly more conservative in their composition; the Kadets, the Socialists, and the non-Russians had a total of about a quarter of the seats. The regime that followed from 1907 to 1914 was, however, substantially different from that before 1905. On the one hand, the principle of autocracy was officially upheld: the tsar had complete control over military affairs and over the appointment of ministers; while many bureaucrats, from provincial governors down to local police officials, continued to treat the public with contempt, and even flouted the laws that they were supposed to administer. On the other hand, political parties now existed, with public meetings and open political debate in the Duma. The press was relatively free. Workers were able to form trade unions, although strikes were illegal. The central government no longer obstructed local governments; it even made substantial money grants to them for social services. Primary education was improving in quantity and quality. The government was less positive in its attitude toward the universities, and there were massive disorders accompanied by resignations of teachers in the University of Moscow in 1911. Though conditions and prospects did improve, there was still plenty for educated men and women to resent; and the alienation of the intelligentsia from the regime was only marginally reduced.

Stolypin's reforms

Stolypin's main concern, apart from restoring order, was to improve agriculture. He introduced measures facilitating the dissolution of peasant communes and the formation of individual farms, with scattered strips consolidated in economically viable holdings. The events of 1905–06 had shattered the view, formerly held by ministry of interior officials, that the commune was a bulwark of conservative feeling. Since the political arguments in favour of the commune were no longer considered valid, the economic arguments against it carried more weight. The extent to which Stolypin's reforms benefitted the Russian peasants, or would have done so if the war had not come, is debatable. The Stolypin policy was, however, a recognition that it was worthwhile to put money, effort, and education into agriculture and that the countryside could no longer simply be milked for the benefit of other parts of the economy. The assassination of Stolypin in September 1911 deprived the regime of its one outstanding leader; thereafter the government reverted to the old pattern of a weak and irresolute tsar surrounded by intriguing bureaucrats and flatterers. In these years the religious adventurer Grigory Rasputin obtained great influence over the empress through his ability to check by some hypnotic power the hemophilia that afflicted her only son Aleksey.

These years also saw continued progress in industry and a marked tendency toward the formation of large concentrations of capital. In June 1912 the Duma introduced health insurance for industrial workers. In Siberia land of first quality was brought under cultivation, and a self-reliant farmer class began to grow up using modern machinery and efficient marketing cooperatives.

While the non-Russian peoples had made political and cultural gains in 1905 and 1906, these were reversed after 1907. Russification was one of the most important features of the policy of Stolypin and his successors. The Finns and the Volga Tatars suffered especially, though they resisted stubbornly. Ukrainian nationalism gained ground despite the efforts to repress it, and extended from its nucleus in the intelligentsia to embrace a growing section of both peasants and workers. In Central Asia the increasing colonization of the lands of the Turkic peoples by immigrants from European Russia caused bitter resentment.

War and the fall of the monarchy. After 1906 Russia pursued a policy of cooperation with Japan in the Far East. Conflicts with Great Britain in Persia, Afghanistan, and Tibet were mitigated by the Anglo-Russian Convention of 1907. The alliance with France was reaffirmed after massive French loans had been received in return for Russian diplomatic support to France in its conflict with Germany over Morocco. Russian policy became absorbed by Balkan affairs after the Bosnian crisis of 1908–09, in which Russia was publicly humiliated by Germany and forced to abandon its support for Serbia. In the ensuing years Russian diplomacy tried to organize an anti-Austrian block of Balkan states, including Turkey. This failed, but the organization of the Serbian–Greek–Bulgarian alliance against Turkey in 1912 was a success for Russia. The second Balkan War of 1913 again placed Bulgaria in the Austrian camp. When Austria made demands upon Serbia in the summer of 1914, Russia was faced by a terrible dilemma. If it abandoned Serbia, it would lose the whole of the Balkans, raising doubt as to its usefulness as an ally of France; in that event Russia would be likely to drift into the status of a satellite of Germany. The alternative was to escalate the Balkan conflict. By the conventional wisdom of 1914, Russia's choice of the second alternative must be considered reasonable; but it destroyed the imperial regime.

Outbreak of First World War

In 1914 the Franco-Russian alliance proved its value. The German Army could have crushed either France or Russia alone, but not both together. The Russian invasion of East Prussia was a failure, and in two unsuccessful battles the Russians lost nearly 150,000 as prisoners. It did, however, enable the French to win the First Battle of the Marne. In Galicia the Russian armies advanced far into Austrian territory. The entry of Turkey into the war as an ally of Germany was a major disaster, since it not only created a new front in the Caucasus (where the Russian armies did rather well), but, by closing the straits, enormously reduced the amount of supplies the allies could deliver to Russia. The Russian armies were seriously short of munitions. The failure of the British and French campaign in the Dardanelles and the entry of Bulgaria into the war on the German side meant that no relief could come from the south. In May 1915 the central powers launched their offensive in Poland and made enormous gains of territory. By the autumn Russia had lost more than 1,000,000 men.

These disasters aroused bitter discontent. A demand was raised, both in the Duma and in the press, for a "government commanding the confidence of the nation." The tsar ignored the demand; he insisted on assuming the supreme command of the armies in the field and left in the capital a collection of ministers of second-rate ability that could hardly be said to constitute a government at all. Economic conditions deteriorated. The mobilization of manpower disorganized both industry and agriculture; transport was overloaded; the military authorities interfered arbitrarily with civilian needs; prices rose much faster than wages; and there were serious shortages of goods, even of food. Working class discontent grew.

Political collapse

During 1916 the military situation improved. Gen. A.A. Brusilov advanced in Galicia and captured nearly 400,000 Austrian prisoners. Public discontent, however, increased. The official bureaucracy and the leaders of the *zemstvos* and municipalities wasted much energy in fighting each other. The ministers chosen by the tsar—in some cases probably on the advice of the empress and Rasputin—were exceptionally incompetent and unpopular. The murder of Rasputin in December 1916 probably made matters still worse by further demoralizing the emperor. In January 1917 the food supply in the capital worsened. At the beginning of March (February, O.S.) strikes, demonstrations, and food lines filled the streets with aimless crowds. Mutinies took place in some barracks—their origin remains obscure—and it became clear that the troops were not going to fire on crowds. The tsar refused for several days to appoint a "government of public confidence." In Petrograd (formerly St. Petersburg), a Soviet of Workers' and Soldiers' Deputies was formed; a standing committee was also set up by the Duma, which the tsar had prorogued. By agreement between the Soviet and the Duma committee, a Provisional Government was formed, composed principally of Kadets and Octobrists, headed by Prince G.Ye. Lvov. On March 15 its emissaries reached Pskov, where the tsar had been held up in a vain attempt to return from military headquarters to Petrograd. Here he handed to them his abdication: the thousand-year-old Russian monarchy had come to its end. (H.S.-W.)

The U.S.S.R. from 1917 to 1939

THE GOVERNMENTS OF 1917

Results of the February (March) Revolution. To fill the vacuum left by the collapse of the ancient Russian monarchy, the leaders of the recently dissolved Duma set up a Provisional Committee to maintain order and establish democratic reforms. The same day, March 12 (February 27, old style), leaders of the Petrograd workers and the rebellious garrison created the Petrograd Soviet of Workers' and Soldiers' Deputies, an unofficial but representative body elected by the factories and regiments and dominated at the outset by the Menshevik and Socialist Revolutionary parties. Similar soviets were quickly set up all over Russia on the Petrograd model. Unsure of their strength and convinced that Russia was still in the stage of the bourgeois revolution, the leaders of the soviet refrained from any claim to exercise governmental power.

Establishment of the soviets

Prodded by the potential challenge of the soviet, the Duma Committee on March 15 (March 2, O.S.) established the Provisional Government. Prince Georgy Lvov was designated prime minister; Pavel Milyukov, leader of the Constitutional Democratic Party, was foreign minister and the strong man of the Cabinet; Aleksandr Guchkov, leader of the conservative Octobrist Party, became war minister. Aleksandr Kerensky, a Duma deputy of the moderately socialist Labour Group, became minister of justice and the unofficial liaison man with the soviet.

The Provisional Government. The Provisional Government was faced with a series of difficult and controversial problems. The food shortages and worsening economic crisis that led to the fall of the tsar were no nearer solution. Russia's participation in World War I, underlying these difficulties, raised agonizing questions—whether to fight or make peace and on what terms. Above all, the circumstances of the revolutionary overthrow of the monarchy released the latent grievances and demands of every sector of a frustrated population. As the year wore on, the political mood of the masses grew more and more radical, with the increasingly insistent demands of the peasants for land, of the workers for food and for control of the factories, of the soldiers for an end to the war, and of the national minorities for independence.

The first serious crisis of the Provisional Government was occasioned by foreign policy. Foreign Minister Milyukov wanted to continue the war for the territorial gains promised by the Allies, despite growing popular sentiment for a "democratic peace without annexation or indemnities." The release of a note from Milyukov promising Russian solidarity with Britain and France precipitated the mass demonstrations of the "April Days." Milyukov and Guchkov were compelled to resign, and the Cabinet was reshuffled to strengthen its popular base. Kerensky took over the war ministry, and Mikhail Tereshchenko, a businessman of moderate persuasion, became foreign minister. Several leaders from the soviet were brought in, including the Socialist Revolutionary Viktor Chernov as minister of agriculture and the Menshevik Irakli Tsereteli as minister of posts and telegraphs.

The "April Days": demonstrations against the war

This first coalition cabinet made no more progress than its predecessor toward solving the country's fundamental problems, despite the convening in June of the First All-Russian Congress of Soviets, designed to permit the delegates from the local soviets all over the country to define their program. Major decisions were postponed until a Constituent Assembly could be elected to draft a democratic constitution for Russia. (The election was finally scheduled in September and held in November, after the Bolshevik Revolution.) Meanwhile, at the prodding of War Minister Kerensky, the Provisional Government turned to the prosecution of the war, which had been more or less dormant on the eastern front since the outbreak of the revolution. In June, Kerensky ordered an offensive; at first, the Russians were successful, but in July they were routed by the counterattacking Germans. Russian discipline and morale then began to disintegrate rapidly, desertions mounted, and, by the time of the Bolshevik Revolution, the army was scarcely a fighting force.

The rise of the Bolsheviks and the crisis of the Provisional Government. At the time of the March Revolution, the Bolshevik Party was small (fewer than 30,000 members) and disoriented. Most of its leaders, including Lenin, were in exile abroad or in Siberia. Initially, the Bolsheviks in Petrograd were hostile to the Provisional Government; then, higher ranking leaders returning from Siberia, including Lev Kamenev and Joseph Stalin, endorsed the Soviet's conditional acceptance of the Provisional Government. Lenin, in Switzerland, denounced the Provisional Government as a bourgeois, imperialist regime, and was independently echoed by Leon Trotsky in New York (though he was not not a member of the Bolshevik Party). Refused passage by the Allied powers, Lenin secured permission to travel across Germany (and thence, via Sweden and Finland, to Petrograd) in the famous "sealed train" (actually one car to which Lenin and his party were confined while in transit).

Lenin's return to Russia

There has been much controversy over Lenin's relations with the German government. It seems certain from the German archives that the Germans facilitated Lenin's journey in the hope that he would help undermine the war effort of the Provisional Government and that they also made funds available to the Bolsheviks and other extremist groups for the same purpose. On the other hand, the allegations that Lenin was literally a German agent, after, as well as before, the Bolshevik Revolution, are without foundation. Documents published to this effect have proved to be forgeries.

Upon his arrival in Petrograd at the Finland Station on April 16 (April 3, O.S.), 1917, Lenin issued an open call for the overthrow of the Provisional Government and "All Power to the Soviets" (his so-called April Theses). He quickly brought the Bolshevik Party around to this position and launched it on a campaign of organization and propaganda to win the allegiance of the increasingly radical Russian masses. He was joined in this by Trotsky and a number of other people formerly in the left wing of the Menshevik Party. Rank and file Bolshevik membership grew rapidly, until, on the eve of the Revolution, it stood at around 200,000. The party rapidly attracted popular support at the expense of the Mensheviks and Socialist Revolutionaries, reflected in increasing Bolshevik representation in the soviets.

The first test of strength between the Bolsheviks and the Provisional Government came in the violent mass demonstrations of the "July Days" in Petrograd. Sparked by sailors from the Kronstadt naval base, the Petrograd mob started to act on the Bolshevik appeal for a new revolution. The Bolshevik leadership drew back, however, and the Provisional Government was able to restore order with loyal troops and outlaw the Bolshevik Party. Trotsky was arrested, and Lenin went into hiding in Finland, where he composed his principal theoretical work, *The State and Revolution.* In the aftermath of this setback for the Bolsheviks, Kerensky replaced Prince Lvov as prime minister in the second coalition cabinet.

The "July Days": the abortive revolt and the new Kerensky government

The next two months witnessed a temporary swing toward the right. Conservatives, rallying around the appeal for discipline and the war effort, looked to Kerensky's chief of staff, Gen. Lavr Kornilov, as the man who could restore order and check the course of the revolution. The State Conference held by Kerensky in Moscow in August only underscored the gulf between the right and the moderate left. Finally, late in August, on the pretext of supporting the government against the soviet, General Kornilov ordered troops to march on Petrograd in what Kerensky, at least, perceived to be a right-wing plot to overthrow him. Kerensky turned at this point to the forces of the left, even relaxing the ban on the Bolsheviks. Kornilov's troops deserted him, and the attempted counter-revolutionary coup collapsed. The consequence of the attempt was to drive the country further to the left and imbue it with an acute fear of counter-revolution.

The October (November) Revolution. Following the Kornilov affair, popular support for the Provisional Government dissipated rapidly, as the country polarized toward the extremes of left and right. The revolutionary mood of the masses, accentuated by rampant inflation and worsening shortages of goods, reached the stage of direct action. Peasants, impatient with the legal delays of the government, began seizing and plundering the landlords' estates. Strikes mounted, and workers began imposing "Workers' Control" in the factories through elected factory committees. Nationalist leaders in Kiev and Helsinki made the Ukraine and Finland virtually independent. The army began to crumble as peasant troops deserted to return home and share in the land seizures. The reserve units in the cities, fearful of being sent to the front, came under increasing Bolshevik influence.

Against this setting of growing turmoil, the Bolsheviks, with their slogan "Peace, Land, and Bread," were the only party (along with their allies, The Left Socialist Revolutionaries) ready to acknowledge the most extreme popular demands. They scored a series of political victories in the soviets, winning control of the key Petrograd and Moscow soviets by mid-September. Trotsky, released from jail at the time of the Kornilov affair, was elected chairman of the Petrograd Soviet.

At this juncture, Lenin (still hiding in Finland) concluded that the time had come for the Bolshevik Party to attempt the armed seizure of power, overthrow the Kerensky government, and make the soviets the official organs of power. He so instructed the Bolshevik leaders in Petrograd, but the latter, convinced that power was coming to the party more or less democratically, at first resisted his instructions. Against Lenin's wishes, they participated in the Democratic Conference convoked by the Provisional Government to speed consideration of Russia's political future.

The conference merely registered the deepening political cleavages in Russia, between Kerensky and the moderate left, as well as among the government, the right, and the far left. To continue its work until the Constituent Assembly could be convoked, the conference authorized the establishment of a provisional parliament, the Council of the Republic, or Pre-Parliament, composed, like the Democratic conference, of representatives nominated by the various parties and interest groups. When the Pre-Parliament convened early in October, the Bolsheviks walked out in a gesture of revolutionary defiance. The Second Congress of Soviets had been scheduled for later on in the month, and the Bolsheviks made it clear that they expected this body to resolve the question of power.

Lenin's advocacy of armed insurrection

This was not sufficient for Lenin. On October 20 (October 7, O.S.) he returned secretly to Petrograd to urge the policy of armed insurrection, and on October 23 (October 10, O.S.) the Bolshevik Central Committee voted in principle (with only Kamenev and Grigory Zinoviev in opposition) to "place armed insurrection on the agenda." Meanwhile plans by the government to move the capital to Moscow stirred up rumours that Kerensky meant to surrender Petrograd to the Germans in order to defuse the revolution. Utilizing the consequent state of panic, the Bolsheviks persuaded the soviet to assert emergency authority over the garrison through the Military Revolutionary Committee, finally activated on November 2 (October 20, O.S.). Although it is generally believed (and asserted by the official Soviet historians) that by this time the Bolsheviks were actively planning an armed uprising to coincide with the Congress of Soviets on November 7 (October 25, O.S.), there is no documentation of such planning, and the preponderance of evidence indicates that the Bolshevik leaders were concentrating on defensive measures to prevent another Kornilov-style coup and to protect the Congress of Soviets while it voted itself into power. This was contrary to Lenin's demands, but he was sidetracked by polemics against the more openly expressed opposition of Zinoviev and Kamenev.

The actual revolution was precipitated by an abortive government crackdown. Angered by the soviets' claim to control the garrison, Kerensky sent troops on the morning of November 6 (October 24, O.S.) to close the Bolshevik newspapers. This was seen by the Bolsheviks as the opening of the expected counter-revolutionary coup. They called out sympathetic troops and the workers' Red Guards to defend the soviet, only to find that effective government forces were almost nonexistent. With most of the city in their hands by evening, the Bolshevik leaders then began a more deliberate take-over of public utilities and government buildings. It is not clear from the evidence whether this preceded or followed Lenin's midnight return from his hiding place to soviet headquarters in the Smolny Institute. On the morning of November 7 (October 25, O.S.), the Bolsheviks proclaimed the overthrow of the Provisional Government. The virtually bloodless siege and capture of the Cabinet members in the Winter Palace that night came as an anticlimax.

The Bolshevik Revolution

The circumstances of the Bolsheviks' armed insurrection turned out, in part by accident, to be close to the strategy Lenin had demanded. Retrospectively, the Bolsheviks' victory can be attributed to a combination of factors—superior organization, skillful manipulation of the mood of the masses, and Lenin's single-minded leadership—but, on balance, their success was more a matter of good fortune and of default, thanks to the dissension and mistakes on the government side.

The Bolshevik coup was quickly ratified by the Second Congress of Soviets, where the Bolsheviks and their allies, the Left Socialist Revolutionaries, had a substantial majority. The soviets were proclaimed to be the ruling organs in Russia, headed by the Soviet Central Executive Committee as a quasi-parliament and by the Council of People's Commissars as the Cabinet. Lenin was designated chairman of the Council of People's Commissars—in effect, prime minister; Trotsky took the post of commissar of foreign affairs; Stalin, in line with his Georgian origin, was made commissar of nationalities. An abortive attempt by Kerensky to return to power with loyal troops and military cadets was quickly put down, and the new Soviet government of the Bolsheviks proceeded to consolidate its hold. Kerensky went into hiding and the following year fled to England and thence to the United States.

The consolidation of the Soviet government. The revolutionary seizure of power by the Bolsheviks in Petrograd in the name of the soviet was quickly followed by similar moves on the part of the local soviets in most other parts of Russia. In Moscow alone there was serious fighting for about a week, before the Soviet forces prevailed over conservative military units. The Soviet takeover was resisted in southern Russia, where the Ukrainian nationalists and the Don Cossacks under General Kaledin established autonomous regimes. Thus, a state of civil war existed from the outset of Soviet rule. As to Finland, its independence was recognized by the Soviet regime in December 1917, in anticipation of a take-over by pro-Bolshevik Finnish revolutionaries.

The revolutionary decrees

The Soviet government lost no time in proclaiming its revolutionary intentions in a series of sweeping decrees. The decree on land abolished private property and ordered the distribution of the land to those who worked it, thus ratifying the peasants' land seizures. The decree on peace called for an immediate armistice and a peace "without annexations or indemnities" among all the warring powers, on pain of unleashing the forces of world revolution. These two basic steps were soon followed by decrees legitimizing workers' control in industry; nationalizing the banks; abolishing the old courts and police in favour of revolutionary tribunals and a workers' militia; removing legal class privileges and titles and abolishing inheritance; separating church and state; and establishing the legal equality of the sexes. Calendar reform was proclaimed in order to bring Russia into line with the new-style Western dates in February 1918.

Aside from these initial steps, there arose a basic disagreement among the Bolshevik leaders over the future shape of the regime. A hard-line faction headed by Lenin and Trotsky insisted on one-party Bolshevik rule, representing the dictatorship of the proletariat. Zinoviev and Kamenev, joined by several of the new people's commissars and seconded by the Left Socialist Revolutionaries, argued for a coalition government in order to avoid violence and defeat. Negotiations among the parties broke down, and only the Left Socialist Revolutionaries joined the Council of People's Commissars.

Suppression of opposition

Meanwhile, the Soviet government was suppressing the Constitutional Democrats and other conservative groups. In December the Cheka (All-Russian Extraordinary Commission for Combatting Counterrevolution and Sabotage—or secret police) was established to root out opposition to the government. The elections to the Constituent Assembly, held as scheduled in November, were disappointing for the Bolsheviks: they won around 25 percent of the seats against an absolute majority for the Right Socialist Revolutionaries, with the rest scattered among the other moderate socialist and conservative groups. The Soviet government allowed the Assembly to convene in January 1918 for one day only; it was then closed down as a counter-revolutionary body.

The appeal for peace by the new Soviet government was rejected by the Allied powers as a betrayal of the war effort. On the other hand, Germany and its allies quickly took advantage of the Soviet proposal, agreed to an armistice on the eastern front, and commenced peace negotiations in the city of Brest-Litovsk in Russian Poland. Confronted with a Soviet determination to turn the negotiations into a forum for revolutionary propaganda, the Germans broke off the talks and resumed their offensive in February 1918, meeting virtually no resistance. Lenin, faced with an imminent threat to his regime, called for acceptance of the German peace terms, assuming that a proletarian revolution was due soon in Germany anyway. He was bitterly resisted by the left wing of the Bolshevik Party, led by Nikolay Bukharin, and by the Left Socialist Revolutionaries, who called for guerrilla war against the Germans as an example to inspire revolutionaries elsewhere. Trotsky took the position "No war, no peace" and abstained on the final vote in the Central Committee, which backed Lenin by a narrow margin. The Soviet delegates thereupon signed the Treaty of Brest-Litovsk on March 3, surrendering the Baltic provinces, Poland, the Ukraine, Finland, and the Caucasus to German, Austrian, and Turkish occupation. At the cost of a major part of Russia's population and economic resources, Lenin had won a "breathing space" for the consolidation of his rule.

Treaty of Brest Litovsk

WAR COMMUNISM

The civil war and intervention. The period of relatively peaceful consolidation for the Soviet government was ended by the outbreak of civil war in May 1918, triggered by a clash between Soviet forces and the troops of the Czechoslovak Legion who were being evacuated from Russia via the Trans-Siberian Railway. Anti-Communist Russians, called the "Whites" and led by officers of the old army, seized this opportunity to take control of most of the country from the Volga River to the Pacific Ocean. Bitter fighting ensued between White units and the Red Army, newly organized by Trotsky (as Commissar of Military Affairs since Brest-Litovsk), and a White thrust on Moscow was barely turned back in August.

Meanwhile, the Allied powers had begun to intervene militarily in Russia. With the original aim of keeping Allied munitions shipments out of German hands, British forces had landed in Murmansk in March by arrangement with the Soviet government. Following the Czech revolt, Great Britain, France, and the United States landed troops in northern Russia, while the U.S. and Japan landed forces in eastern Siberia, all in support of the Whites. The Allied motives were mixed, with Britain and France impelled by the hope both of getting Russia back into the war against Germany and of suppressing the Communist Revolution. Japan was interested in annexing Russian territory, and the United States was concerned mainly to restrain the Japanese and help rescue the Czechoslovaks.

The collapse of Germany and the end of World War I in November 1918 terminated the original excuse for intervention and, at the same time, appeared to herald the world revolution anticipated by the Communists. Intervention now assumed an avowedly counterrevolutionary aim. U.S. Pres. Woodrow Wilson proposed a peace conference on Russia to be held on the Turkish island of Prinkipo (Büyükada), but the Whites, backed by French Premier Georges Clemenceau and British War Secretary Winston Churchill, rejected the idea. The British and French landed additional forces and stepped up their logistical support of the White armies, despite sharp cleavages of opinion at home over the Russian Revolution.

Stiffened by their foreign backing, the Whites launched a series of determined offensives toward Moscow in 1919—from Siberia under Adm. Aleksandr Kolchak, from the Don region under Gen. Anton Denikin, and from the Baltic region under Gen. Nikolay Yudenich toward Petrograd. Though militarily formidable, the White cause was weakened politically by its authoritarian tendencies, its unwillingness to leave the peasants in possession of the land, and its harsh treatment of non-Russian minorities, particularly the Jews. The Communists had the advantage of interior communications and a spirit of national resistance against foreign intervention. Allied intervention was not sufficiently massive or resolute to be decisive. One by one, the White thrusts were turned back, and, by early 1920, with the capture and execution of Kolchak, the serious challenge of counterrevolution was at an end. Acknowledging the futility of intervention, all the Allied powers, except the Japanese, now withdrew their forces.

Reoccupation of lost territories

In the course of its victories, the Red Army reoccupied much of the territory that had been lost under the Treaty of Brest-Litovsk. Where independent states had been set up under the aegis of the Central Powers—in the Ukraine and in Georgia, Armenia, and Azerbaijan in the Caucasus—local Communists were installed in power to form new soviet republics, linked to Russia by treaty. A similar republic was set up for the area of Belorussia ("White Russia," as distinguished by language, not to be confused with the White Russians in the political sense). In the Baltic region, the Communists were not able to take power; and the republics of Estonia, Latvia, and Lithuania, which had proclaimed their independence when the Armistice ended the German occupation, survived with Allied backing.

Poland, which had similarly proclaimed independence, uniting Polish-speaking territory formerly under German or Austrian rule with German-occupied Russian Poland, was soon at odds with Soviet Russia over the undefined frontier between them. The Poles rejected the Curzon Line proposed by British Foreign Secretary Lord Curzon as Poland's eastern frontier and attacked in the Ukraine in the spring of 1920. The Russians pushed back and very nearly took Warsaw, before a Polish counter-offensive with French staff and logistical support routed the Red Army. In the Treaty of Riga of March 18, 1921, the Russians accepted a frontier leaving considerable Belorussian- and Ukrainian-speaking territory under Polish rule. This region was the object of Soviet annexation in 1939 and again at the close of World War II.

The last White offensive against the Soviet regime was led by Baron P.N. Wrangel from his base in the Crimea in mid-1920. The Red Army, once a settlement with the Poles was in prospect, turned its full force against Wrangel and easily drove him and his army into exile. There remained only the Japanese and White Russian forces in eastern Siberia, with which Moscow dealt through a nominally independent government known as the Far Eastern Republic. In the fall of 1922, the Japanese finally withdrew, the Whites went into exile (mainly in Manchuria), and the Far Eastern Republic was absorbed into Soviet Russia.

The Communist dictatorship. The passions and desperation of the Russian Civil War rapidly transformed the Communist regime into a terroristic one-party dictatorship. With the dissolution of the Constituent Assembly and the suppression of the conservative parties, it was clear that the Bolsheviks (renamed Communists at the Seventh Party Congress in March 1918) would brook no serious challenge to their own power. The Left Socialist Revolutionaries resigned from the Council of People's Commissars in protest against the Treaty of Brest-Litovsk, thus leaving a one-party Communist executive. For a time, along with the Mensheviks and Right Socialist Revolutionaries, they continued to function as opposition parties in the local soviets and in the Central Executive Committee (both of which were given legal sanction as the official organs of government by the first constitution of the Russian Socialist Federated Soviet Republic in July 1918). The outbreak of civil war and the sympathy of the Right Socialist Revolutionaries for the anti-Communist cause led to the prompt outlawing of that party. The Left Socialist Revolutionaries sealed their own doom by an abortive uprising against the Soviet government in July 1918 (intended mainly to provoke a resumption of war with Germany by assassinating the German ambassador). Only the Mensheviks remained, sharply curtailed despite their neutrality in the civil war, until they were finally suppressed and their leaders exiled in 1920. By this time, Lenin had made one-party rule by the Communists a cardinal principle in his doctrine of the dictatorship of the proletariat.

The Civil War and the suppression of opposition parties were accompanied by a rising tide of political violence. Socialist Revolutionaries, true to their terrorist tradition, assassinated a number of Communist leaders and wounded Lenin in August 1918. The Communists replied with an avowed campaign of Red Terror, designed to extirpate or terrorize any opposition to the regime within the territory they held. Among both Reds and Whites, the murder of hostages and prisoners and the execution of suspected enemies without trial became the rule. The number of victims probably reached a figure of 100,000 on the two sides. A far greater number of persons, perhaps 2,000,000, mainly of the educated upper and middle classes, were lost to Russia by emigration to escape Communist rule. Russian social life has never recovered the element of sophistication and westernization that these groups represented.

The Red Terror

The suppression of opposition parties was paralleled by the development of progressively more authoritarian practices within the Communist Party itself. Though formally democratic in structure and reasonably so in practice in 1917, the party rapidly tightened its internal organization in order to wage civil war and deal with the staggering problems of the Soviet government. The leadership structure was more sharply delineated in 1919 by the creation, in addition to the Central Committee, of a political bureau (Politburo) for policy decision making, an organizational bureau (Orgburo) to supervise the party organization, and a Secretariat to superintend the assignments of individual party members. At the same time, Lenin's principle of "democratic centralism" was affirmed—that party decisions once arrived at had to be obeyed with "iron discipline" by the members and that the decisions of higher party organizations were automatically binding on the local organizations. Utilizing this authority, the party Secretariat commenced the practice of transferring dissidents out of positions of influence and of appointing the secretaries of local organizations to impose party discipline. The stage was thus set for the development of personal control over the party organization by Joseph Stalin after he became general secretary in 1922.

The experiment of War Communism. With the onset of civil war and the emergence of the one-party dictatorship in mid-1918, the Communists abandoned the relatively gradual approach that they had taken in economic and social matters since the October Revolution, an approach characterized by Lenin as "one foot in socialism." Beginning with the sweeping nationalization of large-scale industry in June 1918, an attempt was made to transform Russian society directly into the classless communist ideal. At the same time, a pattern of centralization and coercion was adopted to channel the country's efforts and resources into victory in the civil war. Economic conditions deteriorated rapidly, and by 1921, amid a crisis of opposition within the Communist Party as well as outside, the experiment of War Communism had to be admitted a failure.

Nationalization and centralization

Nationalization, initiated ostensibly to forestall German influence, was eventually extended to practically every enterprise of consequence, including small-scale as well as large-scale industry and trading and service enterprises. Workers' control was now rejected by Lenin as an impediment to production; instead, he pressed for one-man management by paid experts, with the tight centralization of overall administration of each industry in the *glavki* ("chief administrations") in Moscow. Nevertheless, industrial production, already declining in 1917 as a result of the disruptions of war and revolution, continued to sag. Transportation (mainly the railroads) was in a critical state, which contributed further to the paralysis of industry. Steel production, for example, fell from a level of 4,200,000 tons in 1913 to a mere 200,000 tons in 1920.

To finance the costs of government and the Civil War, the Soviet regime relied mainly on the printing press (a practice already begun by the tsarist government during the war years), with the inevitable consequence of accelerating inflation. By 1922 the ruble was worth approximately 1/200,000 of its prewar value. Some Communists welcomed the result as a victory over the capitalist economic system, and increasingly the government relied on measures of a "natural economy," rewarding workers with rations in kind, free streetcar tickets, confiscated apartments, and so forth. The breakup of the large landholdings and the propensity of the peasants to consume their produce or curtail production rather than sell it for worthless money caused a catastrophic drop in the food available for the urban sector and the army. The Soviet government responded by having grain "requisitioned" by armed detachments, aided by "committees of the Village poor." The consequence was further disruption of food production and a severe alienation of the majority of the peasants, to the point of armed insurrection against the Soviet authorities in some districts of central Russia.

The practices of War Communism—above all the centralizing trend in political life and in industry—evoked within the Communist Party a series of protests by left-wing idealists. These included the "Democratic Centralist" group led by Valerian Osinsky and the "Workers' Opposition" group led by Aleksandra Kollontay and Aleksandr Shlyapnikov (commissars of welfare and of labour, respectively, in 1917–18). With the end of the pressure of civil war in 1920, these groups temporarily made considerable headway.

Soviet Russia experienced its most severe internal crisis after the cessation of civil war. By the end of 1920, the experiment of War Communism, coupled with the wartime disruptions, had brought industry almost to a standstill. The countryside was seething with unrest over the requisitioning of food. Strikes, though outlawed by the Soviet government, erupted in the major cities.

Within the Communist Party, bitter controversy broke out in the winter of 1920–21 over the future of Soviet society, focussed on the test issue of the trade unions. In this controversy, the ultraleft groups, with a goal of democratic communism in mind, called for control of industry by the unions; Trotsky and Bukharin and their followers wanted to absorb the unions into the government and press toward communism by strict discipline and central authority; Lenin, backed by Zinoviev, Kamenev, and Stalin, took the less ambitious stand that industry should be run by qualified managers and that the function of the unions was only to protect the workers. This was a harbinger of the retreat from communism soon to be announced in the New Economic Policy (NEP).

As the delegates of the Communist Party were assembling in March 1921 to resolve their deep disagreements at the Tenth Party Congress, the Soviet regime was confronted by armed challenge in the mutiny of the sailors and garrison at the Kronstadt naval base. The Kronstadt Rebellion was bloodily put down, though it professed to represent the true goals of the revolution. Kronstadt made it clear to Lenin and most of the Communist leadership that a continuation of War Communism would endanger the existence of the Soviet regime. There was virtually no opposition when Lenin called a halt to War Communism and, as a "strategic retreat" of the revolution, introduced the New Economic Policy.

The Kronstadt mutiny

THE NEW ECONOMIC POLICY

The decisive step marking the end of War Communism and the beginning of the era of the New Economic Policy was the suspension of food requisitioning and the introduction of a tax in kind specifying the amounts that each peasant had to contribute. From this there followed a series of measures putting the government on a more legal and orderly basis, while temporarily sacrificing the collectivist and equalitarian goals of the Communist Party. In the perspective of the history of revolution, the NEP had many of the characteristics of a Thermidorean reaction on the model of France in 1794 after the overthrow of the Jacobins. Although the revolutionary party remained in power in the Soviet case, there was a marked psychological relaxation and a turning away from revolutionary extremism.

The policies of the NEP. The NEP was described frankly by Lenin as a retreat from the momentarily unattainable goal of Communism to state capitalism. The monetary system and the market economy were restored. The peasants were allowed to dispose of their produce freely after meeting their tax obligations. Most trading enterprises and much small-scale industry were denationalized, permitting the rise of a new class of small businessmen, the Nepmen. On the other hand, large-scale industry, transportation, public utilities, the financial system, and major natural resources—the so-called "commanding heights"—were kept under state ownership.

State capitalism: denationalization and decentralization

Within the state-owned sector, there were further steps back toward capitalistic economic arrangements. Individual, professional management became the rule, and profit-and-loss accounting was restored. State-owned enterprises traded with each other and sought to grow by earning profits. Wages and salaries were set to reflect effort and responsibility, an acknowledged reversion from the Marxist goal of equality. Economic planning was reduced to a modest effort at forecasting resources, rehabilitating war-torn plants, and building up the infrastructure, particularly electric power.

The NEP quickly achieved a recovery in both agricultural and industrial production, although a drought in 1921 on top of the ravages of War Communism caused a devastating famine in the Volga region in 1921–22 (the occasion of a major international relief effort headed by the U.S. relief administrator Herbert Hoover). By the mid-1920s, most branches of the economy reached prewar levels. A major issue then developed over the manner of future development—an issue between the proponents of gradual growth in the pattern of market socialism, on the one hand, and the advocates of more deliberate planning for a high tempo of industrialization, on the other. The issue was ultimately decided by the political succession struggle that characterized the years of the NEP.

The politics of succession. The leadership of the Communist Party was nominally collective, although Lenin enjoyed such personal force and prestige that his will was seldom resisted successfully by his colleagues. Lenin's illness and then his death, on January 21, 1924, which invited a contest for ultimate control of Soviet Russia, put the system of collective leadership to a test that it could not withstand. By 1928, when the period of the NEP came to an end, the Soviet Union was well on the way to the unrestricted personal dictatorship of Joseph Stalin.

A critical step toward a monolithic system of rule within the Communist party was taken at the Tenth Party Congress in 1921, when it was resolving the crisis of War Communism. At Lenin's behest, the congress condemned the ultraleft factions of the Democratic Centralists and the Workers' Opposition as "petit-bourgeois deviations" and banned any further existence of organized factions within the party. Thus, while Lenin was making economic concessions to the general public on the right and curtailing secret-police terror (the Cheka was curbed and renamed State Political Administration, or GPU), he was cracking down on idealistic sentiment within the party of the left. To underscore this shift of emphasis, the party Secretariat, composed of ideologically oriented friends of Trotsky, was replaced by a more discipline-oriented group (including Vyacheslav Molotov) under the influence of Stalin. A systematic purge of the party membership was instituted in the fall of 1921, expelling individuals guilty of such sins as corruption, incompetence, alcoholism, or opposition; the membership was cut from some 700,000 before the purge to around 400,000 in 1922. Finally, to tighten the organization further, Lenin decided to install Stalin in the new post of General Secretary of the party in April 1922.

The 1921 purge and the rise of Stalin

In May 1922, Lenin fell ill with the first of a series of cerebral hemorrhages. Although Trotsky was clearly the party's second-ranking figure in terms of prestige, he was opposed by all the other members of the Politburo and most of the Central Committee, who backed instead a temporary troika, or triumvirate, of Zinoviev, Kamenev, and Stalin. Recovering briefly in the fall of 1922, Lenin found serious fault with the leadership of the troika, particularly Stalin. In a series of articles and letters, Lenin attacked the reappearance of traditional bureaucratic habits and the lack of systematic economic policy (particularly in the foreign-trade area). He took Stalin particularly to task for his heavy-handed approach in forcing the non-Russian soviet republics to accept formal federation with the Russian Republic in the Union of Soviet Socialist Republics (established in December 1922). Finally, in his so-called "Testament" written December 23–26, 1922, Lenin recognized the personal power that Stalin was accumulating through the party Secretariat and concluded,

> Stalin is too rude, and this deficiency, fully tolerable in the milieu and dealings among us Communists, becomes intolerable in the office of General Secretary. Therefore I propose to the comrades to think up a means of transferring Stalin from that position.

Felled by new attacks of arteriosclerosis in December 1922, Lenin turned to Trotsky to lead the attack on Stalin. Trotsky temporized, possibly hoping that he could enlist Stalin against Zinoviev, until then his chief personal antagonist. Stalin continued to tighten his control through the appointment of local party secretaries and the handpicking of congress delegates, and at the Twelfth Party Congress in April 1923 he had effective control of the selection of new members for the expanded Central Committee. By this time, a final stroke had rendered Lenin speechless and removed him from the political scene altogether.

In the fall of 1923, a coalition of Trotsky supporters and former Democratic Centralists launched an open attack on the leadership of the troika, charging economic mismanagement, neglect of the industrial workers, and violation of the principle of democracy within the party. In this "New Course" controversy (so termed from a pamphlet by Trotsky), the opposition was overwhelmed by the organizational machinery of the party and was condemned in January 1924 for factionalism and anti-Marxist deviation. Lenin's death a few days afterward came as an anticlimax; Stalin's leading role at the funeral was symbolic of the advantage that he had already won in the contest for power.

Death of Lenin and final triumph of Stalin

In December 1925 the succession struggle took a new turn, when Zinoviev and Kamenev, alarmed at Stalin's accretion of power, tried to unseat him at the Fourteenth Party Congress. Stalin easily turned back the challenge and removed the Zinoviev supporters from their Leningrad power base.

Early in 1926, Zinoviev and Trotsky finally joined forces in the "United Opposition," waging a desperate battle of polemics with the party leadership for a year and a half. They re-echoed the themes of party democracy and economic mismanagement, criticized the trend toward "State capitalism" and favouritism for the peasants as against the workers, and called for the institution of vigorous planned industrial development to strengthen the proletarian base of Communist rule. In foreign policy, they alleged that the leadership was abandoning the world revolution.

To defend himself from these charges, Stalin appealed to the theory of "Socialism in one country," which he had first suggested in 1924. This was the argument, based on a statement made by Lenin in 1915 and taken out of context, that the Soviet Union could build socialism by itself without waiting, as the Communists had earlier assumed, for the victory of the proletarian revolution in the more advanced countries of the West. The "Socialism in one country" issue is often interpreted to mean that Trotsky and Zinoviev believed in promoting world revolution, whereas Stalin was a Russian nationalist, but in practice there was little difference between the two groups. The significance of "Socialism in one country" lay first of all in the attempt of the opposition to argue that the Party leadership was deviating in an unsocialist direction because of the isolation of the revolution and should therefore be removed. Secondly, the controversy represented a landmark in the manipulation of party doctrine and history by Stalin, who was able to make a palpably false interpretation of Lenin and compel the party to accept this by organizational pressure. This manoeuvre established the pattern, still followed, of ideological reinterpretations imposed by the party leadership to suit the political needs of the moment, with the consequent necessity of strict control over all ideological discussion within the party.

The 1927 purge

Beginning in the fall of 1926, Trotsky, Zinoviev, and their followers were progressively stripped of their party and governmental positions, with the vacancies going to Stalin's followers. At the Fifteenth Party Congress in December 1927, the entire opposition group was expelled from the Communist Party. The Zinoviev–Kamenev group recanted and shortly afterward won temporary readmission to the party. Trotsky and his supporters were exiled, tsarist fashion, to remote parts of the country, Trotsky himself being sent to Alma Ata in Central Asia. A year later, in January 1929, Trotsky was deported from the Soviet Union altogether. After periods of residence in Turkey, France, and Norway, during which he organized the "Fourth International" of anti-Stalinist splinter groups from numerous Communist parties around the world, Trotsky settled in Mexico. He was assassinated in 1940, most probably on orders from Stalin.

Foreign policy during the NEP. Along with their relinquishment of utopian goals in internal affairs, the Soviet leaders were compelled to recognize that the forces of international revolution had subsided. By 1921 Lenin had made it clear that the survival of the Soviet state—if necessary, through accommodation with the major capitalist powers—took precedence over any momentary gains for international revolution.

In 1921 the Soviet Union concluded treaties of peace or nonaggression with its immediate neighbours Poland, the Baltic states, and the Middle Eastern tier of Turkey, Persia, and Afghanistan, where the Soviets endeavoured to align themselves with nationalist sentiment against the European powers. Also in 1921, a trade agreement with Great Britain opened the way to normalization of commercial relations with most of the world.

Treaty of Rapallo and the ally-seeking policy

On April 16, 1922, the U.S.S.R. scored a major diplomatic breakthrough by concluding the Treaty of Rapallo with the Weimar Republic of Germany, providing for diplomatic recognition and secret military collaboration, despite the fact that the German Communists were still attempting revolution. As a sequel to Rapallo the Soviet Union secured diplomatic recognition by Great Britain early in 1924 (by the first Labour government), and soon afterward by most other countries. The United States remained the major holdout—over the issue of repudiated tsarist debts and Communist propaganda—until the advent of the Franklin D. Roosevelt administration in 1933; commercial relations, including the award of business concessions to U.S. firms, nevertheless became active in the 1920s.

Following the achievement of recognition, the U.S.S.R. continued its quest for allies, particularly in the European labour movement and among Asian anti-Western nationalists. In Europe, the Communist parties were brought under tight Soviet control but were directed to curtail revolutionary activity in the interest of collaboration with reformist groups. In Asia, the Soviets vested their hopes in the Chinese Nationalist Party (Kuomintang) of Sun Yat-sen and Chiang Kai-shek, then struggling to extend its power from Canton to the whole of China. The U.S.S.R. supplied advisors, directed the small Chinese Communist Party to work within the Nationalist movement, and helped Chiang organize a Leninist-style one-party system of political controls. Nevertheless, as soon as Chiang had achieved national power in 1927, he purged the Communists from his ranks and abandoned the Soviet alliance. The end of the NEP period saw the U.S.S.R. almost as bereft of allies as the beginning of the era.

Society and culture during the NEP. As in the "Thermidorean" periods of earlier revolutions, Soviet social and intellectual life during the NEP swung back substantially toward the pre-revolutionary norm, far more so than during War Communism or after 1928. In literary and cultural matters the regime was generally content to suppress overt political opposition, allowing a variety of artistic schools to work out their ideas. The same held true for social thought—economic, educational, and philosophical—among representatives of the regime itself. No attempt was made to control the conclusions of scientists. Strictly speaking, the Soviet regime, while dictatorial, was not yet totalitarian; nonpolitical areas were not subjected to the positive and exclusive dictates of official controllers.

Experimentalism and freedom in the arts and sciences

Literature and the arts during the NEP were distinguished by the emergence of a variety of extreme leftist groups, experimenting radically in their respective media and contending for the right to represent the proletariat and the new society. Most notable were the poets Sergey A. Yesenin and Vladimir V. Mayakovsky (both suicides after official controls began to close in), the theatrical directors Konstantin Stanislavsky and Vsevolod Meyerhold (the latter purged in 1938), and the film director Sergey M. Eisenstein. The "proletarian culture" movement of Aleksandr Bogdanov was suppressed, however, in favour of the doctrine that former bourgeois artists and writers could be induced to create in the service of the proletarian state. Overall, Russia's leading role in the international artistic revolution of modernism, begun in the decade before World War I, was sustained.

In education as well as in the arts, a doctrine of service to the proletariat was combined with serious attempts at experimentation. Radical educators, encouraged by Anatoly Lunacharsky, the commissar of education, borrowed from American theories of progressive education and pressed further, in their reaction against discipline, to the doctrine of the "withering away of the school." At the same time, great strides were made in expanding the basic primary and secondary school system, creating the machinery that, by the end of the following decade, substantially wiped out illiteracy among the younger Soviet generation. In higher education, class principles required admission preference for children of workers and peasants, regardless of preparation, to the great detriment of the universities. Much was achieved, however, in the education of the working class (and of many future Soviet leaders) through the so-called rabfak, or workers' night courses.

A liberating attitude toward social mores generally prevailed. The family was regarded as a bourgeois anachronism by many Communist leaders (notably Aleksandra Kollontay, an outspoken exponent of free love). Abortion was legalized and divorce made a matter of request (the so-called postcard divorce). Children were encouraged to inform on anti-Soviet parents. The effect of social change among the mass of the population, however, was probably not as great as during the industrialization era that followed.

Religion continued to be actively discouraged, though not persecuted violently as it had been before 1922. Patriarch Tikhon of the Russian Orthodox Church, elected in 1917 when the office was restored, was arrested in 1922 and thereupon abandoned political opposition to the Soviet regime. After his death in 1925, however, the government kept the office vacant until World War II.

THE STALIN REVOLUTION

In 1928 the relatively relaxed and pluralistic character of Soviet life came abruptly to an end. Joseph Stalin, having made himself to all intents and purposes the unchallenged ruler of the Communist Party, proceeded to impose the controls of the Party on every aspect of life in the Soviet Union, and to use those controls to drive the country through an unprecedented experience of violent economic transformation.

The character and origins of Stalinism

The Stalin revolution had its origins in the circumstances of internal political struggle within the Communist Party. After Stalin had destroyed the Left Opposition of Trotsky and Zinoviev, his next concern was to isolate and discredit the people with whom he had shared the leadership during the NEP—particularly Nikolay Bukharin (editor of the official Party newspaper *Pravda* and chairman of the Comintern, or Third International of Communist parties), Aleksey Rykov (chairman of the Council of People's Commissars after Lenin's death), and Mikhail Tomsky (chairman of the trade unions). In an adroit series of political manoeuvres, Stalin shifted to leftist lines of policy that his colleagues were bound to oppose. Then he brought into play the organizational machinery of party discipline to condemn them for factionalism and deviation.

Stalin's "left turn" began early in 1928, with moves for a more militant stance by the Comintern and with pressure on the peasantry who were failing to sell their grain in the needed amounts. By virtue of Stalin's shift and his evident determination to get rid of them, Bukharin, Rykov, and Tomsky found themselves the leaders of the Right Opposition. There was an open rupture in the Central Committee in July, followed by a decisive battle in the Moscow provincial party organization in the fall, when Stalin's control of the central Secretariat proved decisive. In 1929 and 1930, after they had lost effective power, Bukharin, Rykov, and Tomsky were removed from their posts and relegated to minor jobs. Rykov yielded the chairmanship of the Council of People's Commissars to Molotov in 1930. Tomsky was replaced by Nikolay Shvernik, who served as trade union chief (with an interruption as chief of state after World War II) until 1956. Meanwhile, the policies that Stalin had adopted as a political vantage point for fighting the Right Opposition became permanent commitments, the foundations for a violent and profound transformation of Soviet society.

The Five-Year Plans. The concept of a planned economy—in particular, planned industrial development through investment of governmental funds—was not new with Stalin, though, on the other hand, there was little clear background for it in Marxist or pre-revolutionary Russian thought. Mainly it had its origins in the improvised central industrial administration of War Communism, encouraged by Lenin's admiration for the "war socialism" of German economic controls during World War I. The first substantial steps toward economic planning had been the creation of the State Commission for the Electrification of Russia (Goelro) in 1920 and the State Planning Commission (Gosplan) in 1921.

Gosplan and the growth of centralized economic controls

During the NEP, Gosplan built a highly competent staff of economists studying various planning approaches, some relying more on market mechanisms (the "geneticists") and some stressing the role of deliberate governmental action (the "teleologists"). The planning controversy became deeply involved in the factional struggle within the Communist Party, as the Trotskyists called for an aggressive industrialization drive, while the Stalin–Bukharin leadership held to the virtues of gradualness. Nevertheless, the leadership accepted the concept of comprehensive planning, and the Fifteenth Party Congress in 1927 directed Gosplan to prepare a five-year plan.

During 1928 Stalin repeatedly raised his expectations for the targets of the plan and resorted to the Supreme Economic Council under Valerian Kuibyshev to prepare a more ambitious version. Bukharin vainly supported the caution expressed in the work of Gosplan, which was purged and restaffed early in 1929. In April 1929 the Central Committee adopted the most optimistic variant of the plan, backdated to October 1928. The plan called for more than quadrupling the output of heavy industry and at the same time substantially increasing the output of agriculture and consumer-goods industries.

Implementation of the five-year plan entailed the imposition of much tighter controls over the Soviet economy. The managers of state-owned enterprises lost most of their autonomy; rather than produce for the market as they saw it, they were placed under intense pressure to fulfill specific output plans. The relative autonomy of the trade unions was brought to an end, and their function was redefined from the protection of the workers to the promotion of productivity. All small-scale industry and trade that had been left in private hands during the NEP were renationalized and subjected to the same system of central planning.

The manner in which the five-year plan was adopted precluded the practice of careful, scientific planning. The five-year plan was rather a set of politically prescribed targets, demanding maximum effort. Given the limitations of existing resources and trained manpower, the plan as a whole was unrealizable. As shortages appeared, decisions were made according to the implicit primacy of heavy industry, sacrificing consumer goods and agriculture. Although money incomes rose, particularly with the influx of peasants into industrial jobs, a very substantial inflation caused a serious net decline in consumer real income. To absorb excess purchasing power, the "Turnover" tax—actually a sales tax with high rates depending on the supply of each item—was instituted and still remains the basic Soviet governmental revenue. While the industrialization drive stimulated rapid urbanization all over the country, inadequate provision was made for housing, a chronic Soviet problem ever since.

In December 1932, Stalin proclaimed the First Five-Year Plan completed. Actually it had been in effect only three years and eight months. In the area of heavy industrial construction the results were impressive: steel output up 40 percent, electrical power up 150 percent, machinery output multiplied significantly. On the other hand, the targets for consumer goods production were far underrealized, and agricultural production was woefully inadequate, thanks to collectivization. Statistically, the achievements of the plan were exaggerated by the tabulation of new products at higher prices, a practice that has distorted Soviet economic claims ever since.

The Second Five-Year Plan

The Second Five-Year Plan, initiated in January 1933, ran full term. Consumer needs were more favourably reflected than in the actual conduct of the First Five-Year Plan, and the standard of living recovered appreciably. At the same time, many of the new plants begun in 1929–32 only now went into production, so that output of certain commodities such as steel scored their most spectacular increases during this period. With the Third Five-Year Plan, begun in 1938, the rate of increase sagged again—partly because of the shift of expenditures to armaments and partly because of the impact of the Great Purge (see below) on industrial management. Nevertheless, with all their defects, the five-year plans had accomplished their purpose of turning the Soviet Union into a first-class industrial power and providing the technological foundation for modern war.

Collectivization. The forcible reorganization of the Soviet peasantry into collective farms was the second great accomplishment of the Stalin revolution, closely related to the first, as the economic foundation on which the industrialization drive was based. Like forced-tempo industrialization, compulsory collectivization was hit upon by Stalin as a political expedient, but it answered his economic need for a guaranteed farm surplus and became a permanent commitment of his regime, regardless of cost.

Marxism offered little guidance for the organization of the peasants under socialism, having assumed that capitalism would already have converted them into proletarians or hired labourers. Non-Marxist Russian revolutionary thought stressed the maintenance of the peasant commune as well as the distribution of all land to those who tilled it. This was the program accepted by Lenin in 1917. During the NEP the Soviet peasants were fully individual proprietors, not altogether equal; the class of kulaks—those peasants with above average landholdings and hired labour—grew distinctly stronger. Only a few voluntary communal experiments and a few large-scale state-owned demonstration farms were maintained.

Until 1928 the government induced the peasantry to join cooperatives voluntarily, while meanwhile satisfying their economic needs in return for the sale of food for the urban market. This approach was inherently unsatisfactory, largely because of the propensity of the peasants to consume the produce of confiscated estates that had been the source of a major part of the marketable food supply before the Revolution. There was still enough surplus to feed the cities, but the prospects for supplying a growing industrial labour force were uncertain, and the prewar grain surplus for export and earning foreign exchange had been lost altogether. Faced with this problem, the Trotskyists called openly for exploitive taxation of the peasants to finance the "primary socialist accumulation" of capital for industrial construction.

In the course of his struggle with the Right Opposition in 1928–29, Stalin opted for a more and more ambitious program of collectivization, first couched in voluntary terms, but by the fall of 1929 implemented by force in many parts of the country. The program called for the complete socialization of the peasants' land, tools, and animals. Actual residence was not affected, since the new collective farms were generally based on the villages in which most of the peasantry were concentrated. Legally, each collective farm (*kolkhoz*) was regarded as a cooperative, using land allotted to it by the state, and in return paying taxes and meeting obligatory deliveries of food at prices favourable to the state. Peasants were to be remunerated with a share of the produce in proportion to the amount and skill of their work. Mechanization was supposed to accompany collectivization and to constitute one of its major advantages; in fact, the availability of tractors fell far short of meeting the loss in horses eaten by the peasants. Machinery was not assigned to the *kolkhozy* but was concentrated in "machine-tractor stations" (MTS), which also functioned as centres of political indoctrination and control in the countryside. For special crops and agricultural experiments, the state-owned-and-managed farms (*sovkhozy*) were retained, with labour paid on an industrial basis.

Forced collectivization: the *kolkhozy* and *sovkhozy*

There was widespread peasant resistance to collectivization, not only among kulaks but also among "middle" (that is, self-sufficient) peasants. A significant element in the passive resistance that followed was the slaughter and consumption of livestock rather than surrendering it to the collective; in consequence, over half the national livestock resources were lost in most categories. Resistance was most severe in the major grain-surplus-producing regions (the Ukraine, the Volga region, and the North Caucasus), where the peasants were more prosperous and traditionally more independent, and where the government pushed collectivization earliest and most vigorously to get control of the grain surplus. Active resisters were branded as kulaks; kulaks were denied membership in the collectives and were subjected to "liquidation as a class," that is, deportation en masse to Siberia and central Asia. The toll is unknown, but probably some millions of lives were lost in the deportation process and in the labour camps, where many were incarcerated.

Early in 1930 Stalin criticized the excesses of collectivization and permitted partial decollectivization. The following winter, however, the drive was resumed again and pursued steadily, until by 1936 virtually 100 percent of peasant households were incorporated in some form of collective enterprise. The cost in terms of disruption to agriculture was a serious decline in production, although at the same time the farms proved their efficacy as a tax-collecting device for the government by delivering steadily larger amounts of grain to the state. The peasants, doubly pinched, were stricken further by the disastrous drought and famine of 1932–33 in the Ukraine and Volga regions. Unlike the famine of 1921–22, the government now refused to admit the existence of the famine and allowed no disaster relief for the suffering areas. As in the dekulakization, the exact loss of life is not known, but it probably reached several million.

The famine crisis prompted the government to make certain concessions in the collective farm system. Each peasant household was allotted a small plot with the right to raise vegetables and livestock for its own use and to sell the surplus in the free *kolkhoz* markets established for this purpose. Certain chronic limitations remained in the system: investments of machinery and fertilizer were inadequate; centralized instructions were inappropriate to the local requirements of farming; and the peasants lacked incentive to work more than a minimum on the collective fields. Collective agriculture remains the weakest single aspect of the Soviet economic system, though it does represent a system of effective political control over the peasantry, and it has assured a minimum grain supply for the cities and the troops in time of war or famine.

Chronic problems in agriculture

Social and cultural policies. The Stalin revolution embodied as its third major aspect, along with industrialization and collectivization, the imposition of totalitarian regimentation in practically all realms of life. With the rise of Stalin, the Communist Party had been subjected to strict centralization of authority within its ranks; after 1928, using the party as his primary agent of control, Stalin extended this pattern to most aspects of Soviet social, cultural, and intellectual life.

The social pattern of the period of the Stalin revolution was based above all on the subordination of the individual to the collective organization. This was most apparent in the elimination of individual economic enterprise among Nepmen and peasants, but it also became the rule among writers, scholars, and scientists. At the same time, the old revolutionary impulse toward collective equality was suspended. Stalin put heavy emphasis on the development of individual responsibility, on the strengthening of the authority of organizers and managers, and on the expansion of wage and salary differentials on the basis of skill and effort. This was no longer represented as a postponement of the Marxian ideal but as a permanent aspect of it.

The educational experimentation of the 1920s was abruptly suspended in 1929 with the replacement of Lunacharsky by Andrey Bubnov as commissar of education. The new emphasis, under the label "polytechnicism," was heavily toward practical industrial skills. In this realm, the challenge of training uneducated peasants for the tasks and responsibilities of industrial life was a monumental one, but, through a complex network of technical schools and institutes and on-the-job training, the Soviet government made a substantial breakthrough in the modernization of its population.

Suppression of freedom in the arts and sciences

In 1929 the power of the party was turned on Soviet intellectual life, until then the freest aspect of the system. Beginning with crackdowns on the philosophers and historians, every academic and artistic field was subjected to the dictates of extreme Marxism and the imposition of strict party controls. Typically, the party found a leader in each particular field who represented the doctrinaire Marxist view—notably, the historian Mikhail Pokrovsky and the literary critic Leopold Averbakh—and gave them authority to impose the party line on their colleagues. "Bourgeois" (that is, nonconformist) thinkers and artists were silenced or, in many cases, imprisoned. Immediate technological or propaganda contributions to production were the overriding demand. Few artistic works of merit were produced, with the notable exception of Mikhail Sholokhov's novels. Overall, the doctrine of *partiynost*—party spirit—was stressed, entailing party judgments in every field as to the ultimate truth and the appropriateness of any piece of work. Party judgment, in turn, ultimately meant Stalin's personal judgment.

Foreign policy in the "third period." During War Communism, Soviet foreign policy had been characterized by defiance of the outside world; during the NEP it had involved a search for allies. During the period of the Stalin revolution Soviet foreign policy took still another turn in consonance with the domestic radicalism of the period. Essentially, the years 1928–34 witnessed a resumption of revolutionary rhetoric and a tendency in practice to withdraw into diplomatic isolation, although trade with the West and the solicitation of Western engineering services were pursued vigorously in support of the Five-Year Plan.

Commencing in 1928, the so-called left turn was enjoined on the parties of the Comintern, with emphasis (particularly in Germany) on hostility toward the Social Democrats and reformist governments (labelled "Social Fascism"). In consequence, the Soviet Union did nothing to prevent the rise of Hitler, hoping he would pave the way for Communist revolution in Germany. Hitler's victory and his avowed plans to expand eastward soon made it clear that the U.S.S.R. needed a new diplomatic approach.

In Soviet–Far Eastern relations much the same crisis developed even earlier. Relations with China had degenerated to the point of armed clashes in Manchuria in 1929. In 1931, with the rise of Japanese militarism and the Japanese occupation of Manchuria, a new and more serious threat emerged. By 1933, the Soviet Union was confronted with the spectre of aggressive enemies both to the West and to the East and an absence of any allies at all. The stage was thus set for the fundamental change in Soviet foreign policy characteristic of the period of collective security.

THE PURGES AND THE CONSOLIDATION OF STALINISM

The Great Purge. By 1934 the essential framework of Stalinist society had been laid down in the economic and political structure of the Soviet Union. The country was nevertheless in a state of severe tension and unrest, not only among the masses who had experienced the privations of collectivization, famine, and forced industrialization, and among the intellectuals newly subjected to severe regimentation, but within the party hierarchy as well, where misgivings about the rigours of Stalin's approach had never been entirely overcome. These were the circumstances in which Stalin launched the Great Purge, involving the arrest, exile, or liquidation of some millions of persons, mainly Communists and officials in Soviet government and industry.

Although the Right Opposition had been hopelessly defeated by 1929, occasional manifestations of opposition by small groups in the party continued, mainly over the issue of collectivization. These critics were uniformly denounced as counter-revolutionary, expelled from the party, and turned over to the police. The rank and file of the party were subjected to a purge in 1929 similar to the purge of 1921, directed officially at personal inadequacies but also at opposition sympathies. In 1933 the purge was renewed, in the course of re-issuing party cards. Meanwhile, the practice of staging show trials with elaborate confessions was begun with a series of groups accused of "wrecking" and sabotage. In all cases, the culprits—mainly managers and economists of bourgeois background—were found guilty and sentenced to long terms.

The purges of 1929 and 1933

The critical event signalling the advent of the Great Purge was the assassination of Sergey Kirov, Leningrad party secretary and Politburo member, in December 1934. Kirov was thought to be Stalin's chosen second-in-command, but he had recently become associated with the protests against collectivization; he apparently figured in moves to alleviate the lot of the peasants and consumers. There is some evidence that Stalin had the secret police (absorbed into the Commissariat of Internal Affairs, or NKVD, under Genrikh Yagoda in 1934) arrange or allow the assassination of Kirov in order to eliminate a potential challenger.

In any event, Kirov's murder was taken as the pretext for a sweeping roundup of old oppositionists in Leningrad, including Zinoviev and Kamenev and most of their known sympathizers. Zinoviev and Kamenev were put on trial in 1935 on charges of abetting the assassination and were sentenced to long terms. The following year, in the first of the "Moscow trials," Zinoviev and Kamenev and their principal followers were tried again for conspiring to assassinate the entire Soviet leadership; they confessed to the charge, were condemned to death, and were shot.

The Zinoviev–Kamenev trials opened the most familiar aspect of the purges—namely, the show trials of the old Communist oppositionists. The 1936 trial was followed early in 1937 by the trial of the principal supporters of Trotsky, including Karl Radek and G.L. Pyatakov. The charges were extended to include conspiring with Germany and Japan to partition the U.S.S.R. Again the defendants confessed and were condemned to death or long prison terms.

The third trial, in 1938, was the most bizarre. The leaders of the Right Opposition, including Bukharin and Rykov, were accused along with additional Trotskyists and physicians and with Yagoda, who as head of the NKVD had prepared the first trial. The charges included the medical murders of Maksim Gorky and others, and a plot in 1918 to depose and assassinate Lenin. All confessed again (with the exception of the former Trotskyist party secretary Nikolay Krestinsky), and most were shot.

There has been much speculation over the reasons for the uniform confessions to clearly absurd charges. Most probably it was a combination of torture, psychological pressure, and promises of leniency for the accused or their families. A number of former oppositionists were not brought to trial but simply liquidated without publicity, and it can be presumed that this was the fate of individuals who could not be induced to confess.

Alongside the spectacular liquidation of the old opposition leaders, a sweeping, though unpublicized purge of the newer, Stalinist party leaders was conducted in 1937 and 1938. The reasons are generally obscure, but, in any event, members of almost the entire party hierarchy below the rank of the Politburo and over the age of 35 were secretly arrested and executed; two members of the Politburo, five of the six candidate members, and over two-thirds of the Central Committee elected at the Seventeenth Party Congress in 1934 were liquidated. The purge was particularly severe in the non-Russian Soviet republics, where virtually the entire party and government leadership were liquidated on the charge of "bourgeois nationalism."

Purges of the newer party leaders

Simultaneously with the purge of the party hierarchy, the "Yezhovshchina" (the "Yezhov business," named for the new head of the NKVD) extended down into the government bureaucracy, industrial management, cultural circles, and the army. The chief of staff, Marshal Mikhail Tukhachevsky, and seven other Red Army commanders were brought to trial in June 1937 on charges of conspiring with Germany and were executed. Most of the upper-grade officers of the army were likewise liquidated or committed to labour camps (from which many returned in the hour of need in 1941). Numerous intellectual figures who had incurred Stalin's ire also perished, usually without mention. Altogether, in the dragnet of forced confessions and fabricated incriminations, some millions of Soviet officials, high and low, with members of their families, were caught up and executed, jailed, or exiled.

The reasons for the Great Purge remain obscure and controversial. The official charges of wrecking, espionage, and counter-revolutionary activity were repudiated by Nikita S. Khrushchev in 1956, when he "rehabilitated" all the victims except those accused in the Moscow trials. Some authorities hold that periodic mass purging is inherent in the maintenance of totalitarian personal control over the bureaucracy. Others believe that the purges of the late 1930s were a distinct aberration, as the secret police instrument got temporarily out of hand. Still others see the period as the manifestation of a psychotic state of paranoid suspicion on the part of Stalin himself. It does seem clear, in view of the damage done to Soviet administration, industry, and the army, that the purge was an irrational phenomenon, detracting from, rather than adding to, the strength of the dictatorship. No further purge of similar scale has occurred, although lesser purges of the same nature continued, particularly in the late 1940s.

The Stalin constitution. Simultaneously with the onset of the purges, Stalin took steps to improve the democratic appearances of his regime, notably by introducing the Stalin Constitution in 1936. Reportedly drafted by Bukharin shortly before he was arrested, the constitution abolished the structure of local soviets, indirectly elected and class-based, which had constituted the formal basis of government since 1917. The new soviets were directly elected by universal suffrage, culminating at the top in the Supreme Soviet, a directly elected, parliamentary-style body, bicameral in composition (the Soviet of the Union and the Soviet of Nationalities). Nominally, the Council of People's Commissars was responsible to the Supreme Soviet. The chairman of the Presidium of the Supreme Soviet functioned as ceremonial chief of state (Mikhail Kalinin, from 1919 to 1946). The individual rights traditional in democracies were guaranteed, along with the right to work and other economic rights. In practice, the constitution was vitiated by the de facto power of the Communist Party, which controlled all nominations, and the practice of treating any manifestation of opposition as a criminal and anti-Soviet act.

Establishment of a parliamentary and democratic facade

The constitution continued the formal federal structure of the U.S.S.R. and even accorded union republics the right of secession. Five new republics had meanwhile been added, for a total of 11, by partitioning the Turkic and Iranian-speaking areas of Central Asia from the Russian Republic—the Uzbek, Turkmen, and Tadzhik republics in 1929, and the Kazakh and Kirgiz republics in 1936. On the other hand, the actual autonomy of the union republics was strictly limited by the centralized authority of the Communist Party, which subordinated all of them to Moscow. Cultural and linguistic autonomy of the non-Russian nationalities had been encouraged in the 1920s, but in the purge period it yielded to a renewed Russification effort in many regions. Accompanying this was the severe shake-up of the republic governments and Communist Party organizations in the purge itself.

New doctrine and theory resting on the permanency of the state

In line with the more conventional appearances of the Stalin constitution, Soviet legal doctrine and political theory were fundamentally revised during the later 1930s. Older revolutionary notions, expressed in the formulas, "the withering away of the state" and "the withering away of law"—conceiving government and law as essentially transitional devices to combat the remnants of capitalism—were rejected in favour of emphasizing the permanent or very long-term functions of the state and law in the development and protection of the communist society. The legal theoreticians of the old school were purged, and Andrey Vyshinsky, prosecutor at the Moscow trials, became the chief spokesman for the new "socialist law." Subsequently, a reasonably orderly legal procedure, both civil and criminal, has prevailed, except in the case of political crimes. In political theory Stalin himself made the basic pronouncements at the Eighteenth Party Congress in 1939, stressing the positive role of the state, the armed forces, and the police even after the presumed attainment of the communist society.

The culture of Stalinism. A remarkably consistent shift, analogous to Stalin's new legal and political interpretations, characterized most fields of Soviet thought and culture after 1934. Using the machinery of Communist Party control imposed on Soviet cultural life in the service of extreme Marxist doctrines during the period of the First Five-Year Plan, Stalin and his lieutenants now ordered a shift in the party line in one field after another, away from the revolutionary mode and toward traditional and conservative models, though all in the name of Marxism. Writers, artists and scholars who attempted to adhere to earlier, more obviously Marxist ideas were swept away in the purges. By 1939 Soviet cultural life was cast in the mold that has essentially contained it ever since—restrictive in form, conservative in substance, revolutionary in labels.

Control of arts and sciences

The writers were the first to feel the new strictures, beginning as early as 1932 with the manifest failure of proletarian propagandistic writing. The Russian Association of Proletarian Writers (RAPP), which had controlled the field since 1929, was dissolved and replaced by the Union of Soviet Writers. The new line was enunciated in 1934—Socialist Realism, meaning in practice artistic work that was traditional in form, accessible to the masses, hortatory, and optimistic. Similar standards were enjoined on all other fields of artistic creation during the next few years. Modern art and literary experimentation were condemned as "bourgeois formalism," and their dissemination was altogether banned.

The sciences were affected less severely and somewhat later. Work in the physical sciences generally proceeded without interference, except when philosophical issues were involved. The theory of relativity, for example, was condemned as a bourgeois idealist doctrine. Biology, and particularly genetics, was subjected to increasingly severe political interference, as the party gave official sanction to Trofim Lysenko and his theory of acquired characteristics. The eminent Soviet geneticist Nikolay Vavilov was purged and perished in a labour camp.

In historical teaching and research, ultra-Marxism was condemned in 1934 in favour of a more conventional approach stressing nationalism and great leaders, though still couched in Marxist language. A related reversal was imposed on the behavioral sciences, dismissing modern deterministic and analytical approaches to the study of man and emphasizing the traditional model of rationality, will power, and incentives. Freudian psychology was condemned as "reactionary idealism."

Soviet educational policies shifted similarly. Beginning in 1934, traditional discipline, examinations, and the like were restored. The polytechnic approach was dropped in favour of a classical secondary school curriculum, heavily oriented toward language and science, for those who could master it. Educational preference for children of proletarians was abandoned in the late 1930s in favour of a combination of merit and political reliability.

Stalin's concern for order

Changes in the area of social policy reflected the Stalin regime's paramount concern with order and discipline. The loose family legislation of the 1920s was abolished; in 1936, new laws banned abortion and made divorce difficult and expensive. Leniency toward crimes on the part of juveniles and the insane yielded to much stricter definitions of responsibility. Labour regulations put a premium on discipline, punctuality, and incentives. In 1935 there was launched the "Stakhanovite" movement (named after a Donets coal miner, Aleksey Stakhanov, whose team had speeded up output remarkably); it rewarded "shock brigades" and "innovators" with higher pay and other privileges and dramatized the stress on individual productive effort in the service of the state. Overall, the regime acquired an aura of grim puritanism, compared by some commentators with the Protestant ethic that earlier spurred the forces of industrial revolution in the West.

Soviet foreign policy in the era of collective security. The external threats that Soviet Russia faced by 1933 as a diplomatically isolated and internally hard-pressed power were sufficient to compel a basically new approach in foreign policy. The architect of this shift was Maksim Litvinov, commissar of foreign affairs from 1931 to 1939. Under Litvinov, and with Stalin's implicit backing, the Soviet Union commenced a pragmatic search for allies and supporters, in the Comintern in the form of the Popular Front and diplomatically in the policy of collective security.

The Popular Front movement

In the international Communist movement, by 1934, the ultraleft stance of the "third period" had given way to the quest for political accommodation with socialist, reformist, or nationalist groups and governments. The new strategy was formalized by the Seventh (and last) Congress of the Communist International in 1935, with the doctrine of the Popular Front allying Communists with any other anti-Fascist elements.

In 1936 the Popular Front tactic succeeded in bringing Communist-supported governments to power in France and Spain. The ensuing Spanish Civil War constituted a severe test of collective security, as the Soviets endeavoured to expand their influence in Spain while restraining the extremist revolutionaries so as not to alarm the potential allies of the Soviet Union.

Meanwhile, the Soviet Union concluded an agreement for diplomatic recognition by the United States in 1933, joined the League of Nations in 1934, and entered into defensive military alliances with France and Czechoslovakia in 1935. Litvinov became a familiar figure in the League of Nations, espousing disarmament and collective security against aggression. Collective security finally collapsed in 1938, however, when Britain and France came to terms with Nazi Germany at Munich. Stalin apparently interpreted the Munich agreement as a free hand for Hitler in the East. He thereupon replaced Litvinov with Molotov early in 1939 and began to explore possibilities of accommodation with the Germans. (R.V.D.)

The U.S.S.R. since 1939

PRELUDE TO WAR

Military and diplomatic preparations for war

As the year 1939 opened, the storm clouds of an impending war cast their shadow over Soviet life. The rising power of Hitler's Germany posed dangers that could not be ignored. During the Second Five-Year Plan (1933–37), Soviet defense industries expanded about two and a half times as rapidly as industry as a whole. The military and naval budget rose from 1,420,700,000 rubles in 1933 to 23,200,000,000 rubles in 1938, and by 1940 it had reached 56,800,000,000 rubles. New industrial centres were erected beyond the Urals, and military industries were dispersed with the contingency of war in mind. The size of the standing army was greatly increased; the Universal Military Service Act of 1939 made service in the armed forces obligatory for all citizens of the U.S.S.R. The draft age was lowered to 19, the age limits for reservists increased from 40 to 50, and the terms of service substantially lengthened in the air force, the navy, and other branches with special technical requirements.

Despite these intensive military preparations, the state of

the Soviet armed forces left much to be desired. The purge of the officer corps following the execution of Marshal Mikhail Tukhachevsky and other high-ranking generals in 1937 for alleged "treason to the Fatherland" and Stalin's decision to keep the army under the closest political supervision weakened the authority of the military command structure and deprived it of some of its most professional and experienced leadership. The damaging effects of the Great Purge were also registered in a slowing up in the rate of industrial growth and in a lag in technical innovation in weaponry. Although desperate efforts were made to modernize the military equipment of the Soviet Army during the middle and late '30s—advanced designs in tanks and aircraft were on the drawing board and in prototype—the existing stock, except for artillery, did not compare in quality or performance with the equipment the Nazis already had available in 1939.

Clearly the Soviet leaders were not ready for war, though this did not deter them from proclaiming their invincibility. Hitler, after disposing of Austria and Czechoslovakia, turned his energies eastward, hurling threats against Poland. If Poland succumbed, or joined with Germany, and if the Western powers stood aside, the Soviet Union would be left alone. The British declaration of March 31, 1939, concurred in by the French, that they would "lend the Polish government all support in their power" in the event of a Nazi attack, gave Moscow room to manoeuvre. If it joined in the British–French guarantee and concerted its military plans with the western Allies, there was the possibility that Hitler might be deterred; but there remained the great risk that Hitler would persevere in his invasion plans and that the Soviet Union would then find itself embroiled in a war in which it would receive the main brunt of Nazi military action. If, on the other hand, it held off from participation in the British–French guarantee, with its implicit commitment to join in a war against Hitler, and banked on the possibility that Hitler wished to avoid a two-front war, it might extract concessions from the Nazis as the price of Soviet neutrality. In the event, Hitler proved ready to bargain. The result was the German–Soviet Nonaggression Pact of August 23, 1939, with its secret protocol providing for the partition of Poland between Germany and the Soviet Union, reserving Lithuania to the German sphere of influence and giving the Soviet Union a free hand in Estonia, Latvia, Finland, and Bessarabia. On September 1 the German armies marched into Poland, and two days later France and Britain declared war on Germany.

WORLD WAR II

The uneasy truce with Hitler

Consolidation in eastern Europe. The outbreak of World War II seemed at first to represent a triumph of Soviet diplomacy. Vast territorial gains were achieved with virtually no effort. The expectation that Germany and the western Allies would wear each other out in a bloody and prolonged war of attrition opened up the prospect that the Soviet Union would emerge as the arbiter of Europe's destinies. But unfolding events betrayed Stalin's calculations. The quick collapse of Polish resistance and the decision of the French high command not to advance against the Germans aroused the most acute apprehensions in Moscow. Stalin undertook to ease possible friction with Germany in Poland by yielding the provinces of Lublin and Warsaw to Hitler in exchange for most of Lithuania. Meanwhile, Moscow moved swiftly to consolidate its new-found gains and improve its defensive posture. The Polish territories assigned to it were occupied by the Soviet Army and absorbed into the White Russian and Ukrainian Soviet republics. The fate of the three Baltic states was settled, first by military occupation and then, in August 1940, by annexation to the Soviet Union. Finland proved more difficult. When the Finns refused to cede territories and yield naval bases that the Soviets deemed vital to the defense of Leningrad, the Soviet Army invaded Finland. The so-called Winter War, which lasted from the end of November 1939 to March 1940, proved costly to the Russians. The Finns offered fierce resistance, attracting worldwide sympathy and support for their cause. Although the Soviet Army finally succeeded in breaching the Mannerheim line, Soviet casualties were large and the army's performance was unimpressive. Hitler concluded that the U.S.S.R. was militarily weak and that he could afford to press his aggressive designs without much concern for Soviet reactions.

The German occupation of Denmark and Norway in April 1940, and the crushing defeat of the Anglo-French armies in June, reinforced Soviet fears and apprehensions. All Europe appeared to be at Hitler's feet. The question was no longer who would win a war of attrition in western Europe but rather which way the Nazi juggernaut would turn next—against Britain or the Soviet Union. The Soviet response was fourfold. First, it accelerated its efforts to strengthen its armaments industry, modernize its military equipment, and prepare its armed forces for war. Second, it sought to expand its borders, particularly at the expense of Romania, and to limit Nazi penetration into Finland, eastern Europe, and the Balkans. Third, it undertook to protect its Far Eastern flank by concluding a neutrality and nonaggression pact with Japan. Finally, it did what it could to placate Hitler by giving trade concessions and abstaining from anti-German propaganda or other provocatory gestures.

The Soviet seizure of the Romanian territories of Bessarabia and Bukovina in late June 1940 exacerbated Nazi–Soviet relations. Hitler's reply was to move German troops into what remained of Romania. By late July, Hitler had reached a tentative decision to invade the Soviet Union, though the official directive for "Operation Barbarossa" was not signed until December 18, 1940. Other preparatory moves were made. German armed forces were granted the right of passage through Finnish territory. On September 27, 1940, Germany, Italy, and Japan concluded a Tripartite Pact proclaiming the "leadership of Germany and Italy in the establishment of a new order in Europe" and according a similar status to Japan in Greater East Asia. In November Vyacheslav M. Molotov, then head of government as well as foreign commissar, was invited to Berlin, where Hitler offered the Soviet Union a chance to share in the spoils of the "bankrupt" British Empire by expanding in the direction of the Indian Ocean. The Soviet reply was to accept the offer, provided German troops were withdrawn from Finland and the Soviet Union was permitted to establish military bases in Bulgaria. Hitler's response was to move troops into Bulgaria and later into Yugoslavia and Greece. His determination to consolidate his hold on the Balkans and strengthen his ties with Finland foreshadowed the coming invasion. In this increasingly ominous situation Stalin scored at least one diplomatic coup. The negotiation of the Soviet–Japanese Neutrality Pact of April 13, 1941, held out the hope that Japan would not join in a strike against the Soviet Union.

By late spring German preparations for the onslaught on the U.S.S.R. became so obvious that it seemed impossible to ignore them: German troops were massing on the Soviet frontier; German overflights of Soviet territory were virtually a daily occurrence; intelligence reports testified to Nazi intentions. Yet Stalin persisted in behaving as if war could be averted. Large-scale shipments of Soviet materials to Germany continued. The Soviet press derided the idea that there might be a war with Germany. Soviet frontiers were poorly defended. Front-line troops were ordered not to respond to Nazi provocations. There seems to have been no carefully drawn plan of defense against a surprise attack. One can only speculate that Stalin believed to the end that Hitler would not march, or that he could be appeased by concessions. Hitler made no demands. In the early dawn of June 22, 1941, the German divisions crossed the borders and advanced rapidly, meeting little resistance.

The German offensive. The first phase of the war was a Soviet disaster. The Luftwaffe dominated the air, destroying some 2,000 Soviet planes in the first two days of the war and subjecting the retreating troops to incessant bombing and machine-gunning. German tank columns contributed to the disorganization of the Soviet Army. Hundreds of thousands of Soviet soldiers were killed during the early days of the war, and many more hundreds of thousands were encircled and taken prisoner. By mid-November the German army was at the gates of Leningrad, had penetrated into the suburbs of Moscow, had captured Kiev, and was in occupation of the whole of the eastern Ukraine and most of the Crimean Peninsula.

Leningrad and stiffening of Soviet resistance

As the Germans began to outrun their supply lines, Soviet resistance stiffened. Leningrad held firm. In early December the Soviet command, with the aid of fresh troops hurriedly brought from Siberia, launched a counteroffensive on the Moscow front that pushed the Germans back as much as 200 miles in some areas. Soviet forces also recaptured the Kerch Peninsula in the Crimea.

By the end of 1941 it was already clear that the quick victory on which Hitler was counting had eluded him. Soviet losses had been huge, but German casualties were also heavy (1,250,000 in the first 12 months). The Russian winter was hard on German troops and equipment. Supplying them was becoming increasingly difficult because of long lines of communications, poor roads, shortages of railway rolling stock, and guerrilla attacks in rear areas. The Soviets had recovered from their early panic and were beginning systematically to rebuild their army, reorganize their armaments industries, and gird their forces for a long war. Over 1,500 factories, including 1,360 armaments plants, were evacuated with their workers from European U.S.S.R. to the east. During the next years they were to contribute significantly to the mounting supply of planes, tanks, and munitions; together with British and American Lend-Lease aid, they helped turn the tide of battle.

Stalingrad. After the grim winter of 1941–42 the Germans returned to the attack. In May they recaptured the Kerch Peninsula and routed three Soviet armies that sought to liberate Kharkov; in early June they completed their occupation of the Crimea by overwhelming the defenders of Sevastopol. Toward the end of June they launched a major offensive in the direction of Voronezh. Halted there, they turned south toward Stalingrad (now Volgograd), where they again met stubborn resistance. Farther to the south they scored a series of victories, occupying the rich Donets Basin, capturing Rostov, and overrunning the Kuban granary. Turning in the direction of the Caucasus, they seized the Maykop oil fields and drove toward Baku, but they were finally stopped in the mountains that stood between them and their objective. By this time the German armies were dangerously dispersed, and the Soviet high command began preparations for a new counteroffensive. Hitler's insistence that the Battle of Stalingrad be fought to a successful finish and that no retreat be tolerated provided the Russians with their opportunity.

Victory at Stalingrad

Marshalling fresh reserves, the Soviet forces under the command of Gen. Georgy Zhukov encircled the German 6th Army in Stalingrad and barred the way to German columns sent to relieve it. In Stalingrad more than 200,000 German soldiers perished. On February 2, 1943, the remaining 91,000 men of the 6th Army surrendered after their commanding general, Friedrich Paulus, and 23 other generals had been taken prisoner. The German defeat at Stalingrad marked the turning point of the war. Although many bitter battles remained to be fought, the U.S.S.R. had reason to be confident that it would emerge victorious.

In the aftermath of Stalingrad the German armies began to yield ground. Fearing that their forces in the Caucasus would be cut off, they managed an orderly withdrawal, but with the Soviet Army in hot pursuit they abandoned Rostov and retreated into the Ukraine. In mid-February Soviet troops fought their way into Kharkov, but the German general Erich von Manstein staged a successful counterattack, pushing the Soviets back across the Donets River and reoccupying Kharkov on March 12, 1943. Meanwhile, however, the Germans were forced to withdraw from the Vyazma salient near Moscow; and Soviet forces in the Leningrad area broke through the blockade lines over a seven-mile front and established a precarious railway link with the rest of the U.S.S.R. Hitler's final bid for victory—the July battle for the Kursk salient, in which he hoped to trap and annihilate four Soviet armies—proved a fiasco. The Germans were thrown back with heavy losses, and the Soviet Army advanced on a wide front, recapturing Kharkov, Kiev, and Smolensk. By the end of 1943 the Soviet Army had liberated nearly two-thirds of the vast areas seized by the Nazis.

The advance into Europe. Soviet military historians describe 1944 as the "Year of the Ten Blows." The first, which came in January, freed Leningrad from encirclement. The second, struck in the Ukraine in February and March, forced a German retreat to the old Polish and Romanian borders. The third, in April and May, resulted in the recapture of the Crimea. The fourth was directed against the Karelian Isthmus and forced the Finns out of the war. The fifth, in June–July, was aimed at German Army Group Centre and resulted in the capture of 30 German divisions, the seizure of Minsk and Vilnius, and the clearing of the road to the Vistula and Warsaw. The sixth hammered German forces in Galicia and resulted in the capture of Lvov on July 25 and a march to the San and Vistula rivers and the Carpathian passes. The seventh was directed against the German and Romanian armies along the Dnestr River. It produced the unconditional surrender of Romania on August 23 and opened the road to Hungary and the Balkans. The eighth carried the Red Army to Yugoslavia and Hungary. The ninth cleared the Baltic states, cutting off a number of German divisions in Courland. The final blow was directed against the Petsamo region and northern Norway.

Final drive toward Berlin

By January 1945, when the Soviet Army launched its final drive toward Berlin, it possessed a decisive superiority in troops, aircraft, tanks, artillery, and munitions. The Soviet advance was rapid. In the north, two army groups invaded East Prussia. In the centre, General Zhukov drove from the Vistula directly toward Berlin. To the south, I.S. Konev's armies cleared Upper Silesia. Farther south, Gen. R.Ya. Malinovsky and Gen. F.I. Tolbukhin occupied Austria and Slovakia. In early March, Soviet forces established bridgeheads across the Oder, and by April 25 Berlin was completely surrounded. On April 30 Hitler committed suicide. By May 2 the last pockets of Nazi resistance in Berlin were eliminated, and a joyful Soviet nation celebrated victory.

The cost of the war

The war had entailed bitter sacrifices for the Soviet people. Some 15,000,000 to 20,000,000 soldiers and civilians were killed, and many millions more were maimed, wounded, or weakened by malnutrition. The material losses were equally staggering. Officially estimated at 679,000,000,000 rubles, they spelled destruction on so vast a scale as to pose a colossal task of reconstruction. The stoicism with which the Soviet populace endured its suffering had few parallels in history. After the panic and disorganization of the first phase of the war, the will to resist stiffened. Stories of brutal treatment of Soviet prisoners of war and Nazi atrocities in occupied areas contributed to a deep hatred for the German invaders. As the armed forces drained factories and farms of manpower, the women, old men, and children who replaced them worked all the harder because they were bound to the front by the knowledge that the fate of husbands, brothers, and sons depended on them. The reservoirs of patriotic sacrifice on which the regime was able to draw helped to ensure its survival.

Stalin, in his first broadcast to the nation on July 3, 1941, was wise enough to identify himself with this patriotic upsurge and to exploit it to the full. The war became the Great Patriotic War, the Great Fatherland War, and a National War of Liberation. The cult of Stalin fused with the new patriotism. Slogans of class struggle were put aside, at least temporarily. Anti-religious propaganda was subdued, church leaders were wooed, the patriarchate was restored, and the church faithful joined in defense of their country. A new national anthem replaced the "Internationale." The Army was glorified, and patriotic slogans dominated the mass media. The nationalist revival that Stalin led was an important key to victory.

Perhaps equally significant was the ruthless determination of the Soviet leadership to gear the economy to the needs of the front. Beginning in 1942, the industries evacuated to the east and new factories and mines began to lift the tempo of production. In 1943 tank production totalled 19,500 and included such advanced models as the T-34, one of the best medium tanks used in the war. In the same year, 35,000 planes were produced, an increase of 37 percent over 1942. During the next years, production of all types of arms continued to increase. Soviet production was supplemented by a mounting flow of supplies from Britain and the United States. By the end of the war, U.S. Lend-Lease aid to the Soviet Union totalled $9,100,000,000; U.S. trucks and Jeeps had contributed significantly to the mobility of the Soviet Army.

The war alliance. The Soviet–British–U.S. alliance during the war proved a troubled partnership. Relations were poisoned by Stalin's deep-seated suspicion that the delay in opening a second front in the west represented a deliberate effort to bleed and weaken the Soviet Union. Once the tide of battle had turned and victory appeared inevitable, the conflicting interests of the Allies came more sharply into focus. The initial clashes centred on the future of Poland. For Stalin, security considerations dictated the installation of a "friendly" regime in Poland, and in his eyes the only friendly regime was a Communist-dominated one. The British and Americans pressed instead for a freely elected Polish government. The disposition of the Soviet forces at the end of the war made certain that Stalin would have his way, but at the price of the war alliance. His diplomatic moves at the conferences of Teheran, Yalta, and Potsdam, and his actions in the closing days of the war and in the immediate postwar period, revealed that he was determined to assume a dominant position in eastern Europe and to regain the Far Eastern territories lost in the Russo-Japanese War of 1904–05. But his claims extended farther. They included a military base on the Turkish straits, which would enable the Soviet Union to control access to the Black Sea; trusteeship of one of the former Italian North African colonies, which would establish the Soviet Union as a Mediterranean power; participation in control of Germany's industrial Ruhr area as well as unilateral control of the eastern occupation zone of the country; and a continued Soviet occupation of Iranian territory. These demands met increasing resistance from the United States and Britain, who became determined to contain what they regarded as Soviet expansionist tendencies.

By the end of the war the Soviet Union could justly claim that its military triumph over Germany entitled it to the status of one of the world's two great powers. To the territories it had seized during the German–Soviet pact were now added a slice of East Prussia taken from Germany, the Western Ukraine taken from Poland, the Carpatho-Ukraine taken from Czechoslovakia, and the Far Eastern outposts yielded by Japan. Soviet armies of occupation extended from Germany and Poland through Czechoslovakia and the eastern section of Austria to Hungary, Romania, and Bulgaria. But the imposing military establishment also concealed serious internal weaknesses: the economic base on which it rested had been ravaged by the war, and Soviet industry and agriculture were in a sorry condition.

POSTWAR POLICY TO STALIN'S DEATH

The task of rehabilitation

Reconstruction. With the end of hostilities, the Soviet Union faced difficult problems of demobilization, reconversion, and reconstruction. The pattern of industrial location had shifted to the east during the war, and areas nearer the front lines had been neglected. In the war-devastated areas of European U.S.S.R., enormous tasks of rehabilitation presented themselves. As early as 1943, a special committee attached to the Council of People's Commissars was established to work on the restoration of the economy in regions liberated from the Germans. The first of the postwar five-year plans was announced early in 1946. Its proclaimed objective was to reach and surpass the prewar levels of output in industry and agriculture. Because of the deterioration of relations with the United States, Stalin could no longer count on American aid in postwar reconstruction. He exploited to the utmost such war booty and reparations as were available to him.

Table 1: Total Livestock in the Soviet Union (000,000)

	cows	cattle (including cows)	hogs	sheep and goats	horses
1916	28.8	58.4	23.0	96.3	38.2
1928	33.2	66.8	27.7	114.6	36.1
1941	27.8	54.5	27.5	91.6	21.0
1950	24.6	58.1	22.2	93.6	12.7
1951	24.3	57.1	24.4	99.0	13.8
1952	24.9	58.8	27.1	107.6	14.7
1953	24.3	56.6	28.5	109.9	15.3

Source: Report of Khrushchev to the Plenary Session of the Central Committee, Sept. 3, 1953, *Pravda*, September 15, 1953, and *Vestnik Statistiki*, No. 5 (May 1961).

The Five-Year Plan gave priority to heavy industry, and in this area its goals were by and large reached and even exceeded. The first Soviet atomic bomb was exploded in September 1949, much sooner than many knowledgeable Western scientists had anticipated. If the progress made in heavy industry and military technology was impressive, the same could not be said of consumer goods and agriculture. In these low-priority areas even the relatively modest targets set by the plan were not met. The situation was particularly critical in agriculture. In 1946 a devastating drought in the Ukraine and other grain-producing areas resulted in a famine of major proportions. Despite Stalin's efforts to force the collective farms to increase their production, Soviet agriculture remained backward and stagnant. Inadequate incentives and meagre capital investment contributed to low agricultural productivity. The full dimensions of the agricultural crisis were not publicly revealed until after his death. Tables 1 and 2, based on official data, show how little progress agriculture had made.

Table 2: Gross Physical Output for Selected Food Items*

year	grain	potatoes	vegetables	milk	meat (dressed weight)	eggs
1940	83.0	75.9	13.7	33.640	4.695	12.214
1950	81.4	88.6	9.3	33.311	4.867	11.697
1951	78.9	59.6	9.0	36.154	4.671	13.252
1952	92.0	68.4	11.0	35.702	5.170	14.399
1953	82.5	72.6	11.4	36.475	5.822	16.059

*All values are in millions of tons, except for eggs which are given in billions of units.
Source: Joint Economic Committee (86th Cong., 1st sess.), *Comparisons of the United States and Soviet Economies* 1959.

Stalin's harsh postwar policies

The return to Stalinism. The postwar years were also marked by intensive political mobilization. During the war the party leadership had sought to broaden its appeal to the army and the nation by muting its Marxist–Leninist ideology and stressing the great unifying theme of patriotism. Early in the war, when the army was undergoing vast expansion, the party also expanded its ranks to include many members of the armed forces, particularly front-line fighters. Glorification of the army and the high command formed part of the wartime pattern, but as the war drew to a close the party reasserted its ascendancy. The organs of mass communication put increasing emphasis on the role of Stalin and the party as the major architects of victory; the heroic exploits of Soviet marshals were painted in more subdued colours. When there were signs at the end of the war that Marshal Zhukov was becoming too prominent, he was removed from the limelight and relegated to a less conspicuous military command in the Ukraine. Ideological indoctrination of the army, which had been relaxed during the war, was revived and intensified. The ranks of the party were purged.

A series of authoritative pronouncements by party leaders at the end of the war reasserted the historical perspectives of Marxism–Leninism. Stalin's election speech of February 9, 1946, restated the basic Communist analysis of capitalism and imperialism, as well as the dangers they posed for the Soviet Union. The increasingly strong Western resistance to Soviet expansion aroused an equally strong Soviet reaction. Gen. Andrey A. Zhdanov's blunt speech at the organizing conference of the Cominform in September 1947 allowed no doubt as to the Soviet position. The world, Zhdanov declared, was divided into two camps, the imperialist camp led by the United States and the anti-imperialist camp led by the Soviet Union. The Communists of the world were summoned to join in the battle against the "imperialist aggressors." All Soviet party members were called upon to alert the population to its peril and to discipline the masses for new sacrifices.

Soviet patriotism, as Stalin propounded it in the postwar years, fused Russian nationalism with an ideological commitment to Marxism–Leninism. In one of its aspects, it stressed the leading position of the Great Russian people in the Soviet family of nations. In another aspect, it proclaimed the superiority of the Soviet social and political order over capitalism.

Under the cover of Soviet patriotism, Stalin also attempted to ignite a xenophobic hatred for the capitalist world. By making "cosmopolitanism" equivalent to treason, he sought to destroy pro-Western sentiment among the people; in doing so he virtually sealed off the Soviet populace from contact with the outside world. History, literature, drama, music, and art were purged of every trace of "bourgeois objectivism" and noncommitment. *Partiynost* (devotion to the party) became the new watchword; in fact, it meant complete subservience to Stalin.

The cult of Stalin reached its apogee in the postwar period. In theory, the party ruled the state. In practice, Stalin ruled the party and through it dominated every other sector of Soviet life. His colleagues in the party's Politburo functioned as administrative henchmen and assistants on a high level; the Central Committee of the party went into a shadowy eclipse, meeting rarely; no party congress was held between 1939 and 1952. The party ranks (members and candidates) expanded from 3,876,885 in February 1941 to 6,882,145 on October 1, 1952, but as the party grew its influence diminished because of the undisputed personal authority that Stalin exercised. His method of governance was shaped to a very considerable extent by his own personality—his paranoiac suspicion, his fear of rivals, his distrust of those around him, and his insistence on holding all the strings of power in his own hands. In his drive to safeguard his own authority, he evolved a system of competing and overlapping bureaucratic hierarchies in which he depended on the party apparatus and the security police to penetrate and watch each other and made use of both to control the administrative organs of government as well as all other parts of Soviet life. The same pattern of rule was imposed on his East European Communist partners, at least as far as his power could reach. In the postwar years Poland, Czechoslovakia, Hungary, Romania, Albania, and Bulgaria were all transformed into Soviet satellites, completely subservient to Stalin's will. Only Tito's Yugoslavia managed a successful resistance; leaders elsewhere in eastern Europe who might have sought to imitate Tito were executed or purged.

The intrigues of the leaders

The system of calculated insecurity in which Stalin enveloped his henchmen carried over to the postwar years. At the end of the war the two chief rivals for Stalin's favour were Georgy M. Malenkov and Andrey A. Zhdanov. Malenkov's primary area of jurisdiction was the party apparatus. Immediately after the war his prestige suffered a temporary eclipse, and in 1946 he ceased to be listed as a party secretary. Meanwhile, Zhdanov, who had been recalled to Moscow from his post as Leningrad first party secretary, occupied the limelight as the ideological spokesman of the party and exercised his influence to promote members of his Leningrad entourage to leading party and governmental posts. If Nikita S. Khrushchev's later testimony is to be believed, Malenkov conspired with Lavrenty P. Beria, who had charge of the security police, to curb Zhdanov and to fan Stalin's distrust of the Leningraders. On July 21, 1948, the party newspaper *Pravda* revealed that Malenkov had been restored to his secretarial authority. The death of Zhdanov on August 31, 1948, was followed by a ruthless purge of his dependents in the apparatus, most of whom were executed for their alleged involvement in a conspiracy called the Leningrad Affair. According to Khrushchev, the case was fabricated from beginning to end. Among its victims were N.A. Voznesensky, a Politburo member; A.A. Kuznetsov, the Central Committee secretary who had been entrusted by Stalin himself with the supervision of state security organs; P.S. Popkov, first secretary of the Leningrad party organization; and many others. Malenkov seized the opportunity to fill many of the vacancies with his supporters, although after 1949 his own authority was somewhat diluted by Stalin's appointment of Khrushchev as Central Committee secretary with some jurisdiction over party organizational affairs. Until Khrushchev's transfer from the Ukraine to Moscow in 1949, A.A. Andreyev had served as the chief Politburo spokesman on agricultural policy. Khrushchev replaced him in that role in the following year, when Andreyev was publicly attacked and discredited for championing the link, or small team, method of organizing agricultural production in preference to reliance on the larger brigade unit then coming into favour. Khrushchev in turn soon found himself in troubled waters because of the radical and overambitious character of his proposals for the limitation of peasants' private plots and for the resettlement of the rural population in large *agrogorods*, or rural towns. But Khrushchev, unlike Andreyev, remained a member of Stalin's inner circle.

During the last years of Stalin's life, according to Khrushchev, "Stalin became even more capricious, irritable and brutal"; his distrust extended even to his closest associates. A mass purge of the party organization in the republic of Georgia was apparently directed against Beria. The anti-Semitic campaign of the years 1948–52, which began with a sweeping denunciation of rootless cosmopolitans and culminated in the execution of several dozen Jewish writers, even extended into the Kremlin: Foreign Minister Vyacheslav Molotov's Jewish wife was sent to Siberia to live. The 19th Party Congress (1952), with its reiterated call for vigilance, suggested that there were still more purges to come. According to Khrushchev, Stalin had plans "to finish off the old members of the politburo." Andreyev was expelled from it. Marshal Kliment Ye. Voroshilov was forbidden to attend meetings, was spied upon, and was accused by Stalin of being an English agent. Molotov and Anastas I. Mikoyan, then a deputy prime minister, were under suspicion, and the decision after the 19th Congress to create a Presidium of 25 members and 11 alternates to replace the Politburo was intended, according to Khrushchev, as a cover "for the future annihilation of the old Politburo members." The arrest of the Kremlin doctors (a majority of them Jews) for allegedly having cut short the lives of Zhdanov and Politburo member Aleksandr S. Shcherbakov and having conspired to destroy the health of leading Soviet military personnel, evoked grim memories of the earlier "doctors' plot" during the great purge of the late 1930s and seemed to portend its repetition on a mass scale. If Khrushchev's testimony is to be credited, only Stalin's death averted a blood-bath reaching into the very highest Kremlin circles. Indeed, the cloud of fear that Stalin projected cast its shadow over the whole of Soviet society.

The struggle with the West

The Cold War. The fear and tension evident inside the Soviet Union were reflected in its foreign policy. Deeply suspicious of his wartime capitalist partners, Stalin failed to utilize the goodwill that the Soviet Union had acquired in the West. Instead, he chose to pursue the most brutal policies of power, assuming that the withdrawal of U.S. military forces would leave the Soviet Union dominant in Europe. At the same time he did not overestimate his strength and sought to avoid confrontations that might lead to war. Urged by Tito to help drive the Anglo-Americans out of Trieste, he gave the Yugoslavs diplomatic support but stopped short of military action. In a revealing exchange with the Yugoslavs, he declared:

> Since all other methods were exhausted, the Soviet Union had only one other method left for gaining Trieste for Yugoslavia—to start war with the Anglo-Americans over Trieste and take it by force. The Yugoslav comrades could not fail to realize that after such a hard war the U.S.S.R. could not enter another.

Stalin did not hesitate to press hard where he thought substantial Soviet interests were at stake. The U.S. atomic monopoly in the immediate postwar years did not deter him from consolidating his position in eastern Europe. But stiffening Anglo-U.S. resistance led him to withdraw his troops from Iran in 1946, and he did not challenge the program of U.S. military and economic aid to Greece and Turkey that began in March 1947. Another barrier to the expansion of Soviet influence arose in western Europe, where the economic assistance program known as the Marshall Plan, put forward by the United States in June 1947, succeeded in restoring those countries to economic viability.

The main battlefront between the Soviets and the West in the postwar years lay in Germany. The breakdown of cooperation over the matter of reparations, the transformation of the eastern zone of occupied Germany into a Soviet satellite, the decision of the Western powers to unify the three western zones, and their introduction of a currency reform in 1948 set the stage for the Berlin crisis of 1948–49. Berlin had been divided into sectors by the occupying powers, and it lay far within the Soviet-occupied part of Germany. The Soviet blockade of West Berlin, which appeared primarily designed to prevent a West German state from coming into being, was answered by an Anglo-U.S. airlift. The blockade was finally lifted in May 1949. Its de facto result was the division of Germany into two states: the Federal Republic of Germany, aligned with the West; and the German Democratic Republic, incorporated into the Soviet satellite system. Stalin then sought unsuccessfully to prevent or impede the rearmament of West Germany.

Difficulties in Yugoslavia and Korea

Meanwhile, Stalin was encountering problems with Tito. Not only did Tito seem to have his own expansionist plans in the Balkans, but he also insisted on running the affairs of his party and state without interference. When Tito refused to subordinate himself to Stalin's dictates and showed himself powerful enough to make his defiance effective, he and his party were expelled from the Cominform and denounced as counterrevolutionary agents of American imperialism. Facing the possibility of Soviet invasion, Tito turned to the West for aid and demonstrated that a Communist regime could survive without Moscow's support or approval. Tito's successful assertion of national independence opened the first crack in the international Communist monolith. Stalin moved to tighten his hold over the rest of eastern Europe by purging some of the leading Communists in Poland, Bulgaria, Hungary, and Czechoslovakia.

Far Eastern problems. While Stalin sought to contain Titoism in eastern Europe, a far more formidable threat was beginning to take shape in Asia. The victory of the Chinese Communists in 1949 was saluted as a great triumph for the world Communist movement, but friction between Peking and Moscow began almost at once. The Chinese leader, Mao Tse-tung, proved a hard bargainer. A treaty concluded between the Soviet Union and China on February 14, 1950, provided for the return to China of the Manchurian Railway and the Soviet-held base of Port Arthur no later than 1952. The ultimate disposition of Dairen was to be settled after the conclusion of a peace treaty with Japan; meanwhile, its administration was transferred to China.

There was also Korea. At the end of World War II Soviet troops had occupied Korea north of the 38th parallel of latitude, the area south of the parallel being occupied by U.S. forces. The withdrawal of Soviet and U.S. troops in early 1949 set the stage for conflict between the Soviet-sponsored Korean National Democratic Republic in the north and a regime established in the south with the help of the Americans. Both claimed to represent the Korean nation. Stalin, perhaps impressed by the American failure to intervene on behalf of Chiang Kai-shek on the Chinese mainland and misled by authoritative U.S. pronouncements that South Korea was outside the sphere of U.S. defense commitments, either allowed or encouraged the North Koreans to invade the south on June 25, 1950, and apparently counted on a quick victory. Operating under United Nations auspices, U.S. forces intervened to aid the South Koreans and in their march north threatened for a time to eliminate Stalin's North Korean satellite altogether. The intervention of Chinese "volunteers" drove the Americans back to the 38th parallel, where the front remained more or less stabilized. Negotiations for a truce began in July 1951, but sporadic fighting continued over the next two years, and the conclusion of an armistice had to await Stalin's death. While the Soviet Union managed to avoid direct involvement in the conflict, the Korean War set off a formidable American rearmament drive and hardened American attitudes, in Europe as well as in Asia. As a direct result of the Korean conflict, the United States concluded a peace treaty and security pact with Japan in September 1951.

Stalin's legacy. The patrimony that Stalin handed on to his successors was in many respects impressive. The territorial gains achieved as a result of World War II, and the consolidation of control in eastern Europe, testified to the Soviet Union's status as a major power. The industrialization drive launched by Stalin had made the Soviet Union second only to the United States in heavy industry and military power. To this end Stalin invested heavily in elementary and higher education; pushed the training of engineers, technicians, and scientists; reorganized the incentive system to reward skills essential to the production process; and assigned great prestige to the new industrial elite in Soviet society. But forced-draft industrialization had exacted its toll. Its cost could be measured in the millions Stalin consigned to forced-labour camps or killed in mass purges, and in the chronic shortages of food, consumer goods, and housing that resulted from the priority accorded to heavy industry.

Heavy investment in education

Stalin left a legacy of suppressed aspirations with which his successors had to reckon. First, there was a widespread desire for improvement in the standard of living. The most disadvantaged groups were the collective farmers and the unskilled and semiskilled workers, but the pressure for improvement extended well beyond these groups into the middle and even relatively privileged strata of Soviet society.

Second, there was an equally widespread yearning for greater personal security, for a life of stable expectations free from the numbing uncertainties of arbitrary arrest, police surveillance, denunciation by one's associates, or sentencing to forced labour.

Third, there was the desire for greater freedom—not necessarily freedom in the Western political sense, but freedom to use one's talents and capacities without fearing the consequences. These aspirations found their sharpest focus in the new Soviet intelligentsia. Their dreams of greater autonomy did not necessarily involve an overt challenge to the ruling ideology; many of those who harboured thoughts of greater independence and authority operated within a framework of loyalty to the Soviet system and envisaged such developments as strengthening a regime of which, after all, they were an integral part.

THE KHRUSHCHEV ERA

Stalin's successors had to deal with these aspirations. The first response of Stalin's lieutenants upon his death on March 5, 1953, was to submerge their differences. Two facts quickly became apparent: first, that none of Stalin's former colleagues had the strength immediately to assume the position of undisputed leadership that Stalin had commanded; second, that all of them were at least temporarily agreed on the necessity of presenting a united front to the nation and the world. Faced with the uncertainties of the transitional period and the necessity of stabilizing their authority, they embarked on a policy of concessions and relaxation of tensions at home and abroad. Amnesties, reductions in the prices of consumer goods, and promises to raise living standards showed a new disposition to seek popular support. The ending of the Korean War helped to ease tensions with the West.

The transition. But the issue of the succession remained to be resolved. The leading figures were Georgy M. Malenkov, who served as head of government; Lavrenty P. Beria, who had the formidable police weapon in his hands; Vyacheslav M. Molotov, who headed the foreign ministry; Nikita S. Khrushchev, who had succeeded Malenkov as the senior party secretary; and Nikolay A. Bulganin, the minister of defense. The threat posed by Beria's control of the police was eliminated with his arrest in July and execution in December 1953.

The rise of Khrushchev

At the September 1953 session of the Central Committee, Khrushchev was elected first secretary of the party, and his star began to rise. His report on the agricultural situation contained a remarkable acknowledgment of the seriousness of the agricultural crisis and initiated a series of measures to raise production, particularly by offering the collective farmers a higher return for their efforts. His propensity for bold and daring ventures was manifest in early 1954, when he obtained Central Committee approval for his Virgin Idle Lands Campaign. This sought to bring new areas into cultivation, mainly in western Siberia and northern Kazakhstan. The hope was to obtain a vast increase in grain output with minimal capital investment, but success depended on favourable weather in areas that were climatically marginal and subject to drought. Khrushchev was gambling his political future on harvests that might not materialize. Fortune favoured him in the early years, but later there were failures that contributed to his downfall.

Except for the innovations that Khrushchev sponsored in agriculture, his first public pronouncements followed a conservative course. There was a settlement of accounts with various Beria henchmen, and a number of Stalin's victims were discreetly rehabilitated. Friction with Malenkov became evident. Khrushchev's militant speech at Prague on June 12, 1954, with its boast of Soviet leadership in developing the hydrogen bomb and its declaration that a nuclear war would spell the end of capitalism, contrasted sharply with Malenkov's earlier declaration that nuclear war would mean the destruction of civilization. In a series of speeches he clearly dissociated himself from Malenkov's alleged "consumerism" and reasserted the priority of heavy industry over light industry. The denouement came on February 8, 1955, when Malenkov resigned as head of government and was replaced by Bulganin.

It is not clear whether the positions taken by Khrushchev at this time represented his deep convictions or whether they were designed to undercut Malenkov among the more conservative elements in the party. Subsequently, however, Khrushchev adopted Malenkov's formulation on the danger of nuclear warfare, wavered on the issue of heavy versus light industry, and became a strong partisan of the consumer.

With the downgrading of Malenkov, Khrushchev's field of manoeuvre widened and he began to place his personal stamp on foreign as well as on domestic policy. One of his most dramatic initiatives was the effort to woo Tito back into the fold by flying to Belgrade in May 1955. The expedition, undertaken against the opposition of Molotov, was apparently inspired by Khrushchev's faith that shared ideological commitments would serve to transcend all past difficulties. Although the visit did result in improved relations, Tito wrung heavy concessions from the Soviet leadership, including recognition of Yugoslavia's independence in both domestic and international affairs. The ultimate consequences for the unity of the Soviet bloc were to be less than happy.

Overtures toward Tito

At the same time, Khrushchev moved toward an easing of relations with the West. The conclusion of the Austrian State Treaty with the Western powers in May 1955 put an end to the occupation of Austria and neutralized that country, marking the first significant withdrawal of Soviet power in Europe. Against this background of a negotiated settlement, Khrushchev met with U.S. Pres. Dwight D. Eisenhower in July 1955 in Geneva. No agreements of substance emerged from the conference, but the very fact that the sessions took place in an atmosphere of relative cordiality raised hopes for peace throughout the world. The "spirit of Geneva," as it came to be called, provided Khrushchev with a useful theme for his peace-seeking stance.

Khrushchev also undertook to strengthen Soviet influence among the new nations of Asia and Africa. Abandoning Stalin's postwar policy of encouraging local Communists to struggle for power in these countries, Khrushchev wooed their nationalist leaders with offers of aid and trade, sought to weaken their ties with the West, and tried to influence them to adopt a policy of positive neutrality favourable to Soviet interests. The campaign began with Khrushchev's and Bulganin's trip to India toward the end of 1955. A more ominous note was struck by an agreement to supply large quantities of arms to Egypt, thus aligning the Soviet Union with the anti-Israeli and anti-Western forces of Arab nationalism.

The 20th Party Congress. While the new dynamism thus introduced into Soviet foreign policy reflected a departure from the Stalinist legacy, it remained for the 20th Congress of the party, held in February 1956, to define the content of what has since come to be described as de-Stalinization. Khrushchev made a "secret speech" to the delegates in which he combined a wide-ranging condemnation of Stalin's methods of rule with sensational disclosures of his crimes. Khrushchev's motivation in making the speech is not known, but it can be seen as a bold manoeuvre in the struggle for the succession, freeing him to pursue new policies of his own. In repudiating Stalin's terrorist excesses, he in effect offered his personal guarantee that they would not be repeated.

Khrushchev's denunciation of Stalin

The Congress also brought a number of ideological innovations designed to make Communism more attractive abroad. The doctrine that Lenin had formulated and Stalin had often reiterated—that war between the Soviet Union and the so-called imperialist states was inevitable—was now amended to read that war was not "fatalistically inevitable." This new formulation laid the groundwork for a reaffirmation of the theory of peaceful coexistence, this time without the usual qualification as to its temporary character. Khrushchev's effort to present communism in a more attractive guise was particularly evident in his theses on ways of building socialism. In defending the proposition that there were different roads to socialism, he went so far as to include the Yugoslav road in his approved list. Even more startling was his statement that the parliamentary road to power was now open to the working class "in many capitalist countries," though he added that victory would be possible only under Communist leadership and that the use or non-use of violence would depend on the resistance offered by the capitalists.

The de-Stalinization campaign and the ideological reformulations announced at the 20th Congress were intended both to broaden the appeal of the Communist movement and to strengthen Khrushchev's own position within it. In the event, they came close to destroying Khrushchev, and they released divisive forces within the Communist world that have not yet run their full course. In the Soviet Union, the ferment stirred up by Khrushchev's secret speech—which did not long remain secret—infected wide circles of the intelligentsia and the youth and inspired a protest literature that went beyond denunciation of Stalin to criticism of the Soviet system itself. The demoralization elsewhere assumed proportions serious enough to threaten the Soviet hold over eastern Europe. The gathering unrest came to a climax in October 1956, when large contingents of Soviet troops had to be rushed into Hungary to suppress a revolution in which native Communists were leading workers into battle against the Soviet Union. In Poland, direct military intervention was narrowly averted when a last-minute modus vivendi was worked out with Władysław Gomułka, who had reassumed leadership in the Polish party over Soviet objections. The bloody repression in Hungary and the reimposition of cultural curbs within the Soviet Union tarnished the image of Khrushchev as a liberalizer. In the aftermath of Hungary, his prestige declined sharply. His handling of Hungarian events also exacerbated relations with Yugoslavia. The Chinese party leaders gave him public support, but subsequent disclosures showed that they were privately highly critical of his de-Stalinization campaign, of his ideological initiatives, and above all of his failure to consult with them. Within the Soviet party leadership his opponents began to organize a cabal to unseat him, and by May 1957 they were able to mobilize a seven-to-four majority against him in the Presidium, where they confronted him with a demand for his resignation.

Decline of Khrushchev's prestige

It is a measure of the power concentrated in the office of the first secretary, as well as of Khrushchev's capacity to turn adverse developments to his own advantage, that he was able to triumph even in these circumstances. By appealing from the 11-member Presidium to the several-hundred-member Central Committee, in which his followers were strongly installed, he turned the tables on his opponents and emerged victorious. Molotov, Malenkov, and L.M. Kaganovich were expelled from both the Presidium and the Central Committee. In October of the same year he further consolidated his position by removing his erstwhile supporter Zhukov from the Presidium. (M.F.)

Khrushchev's position as party leader appeared unassailable. He had surmounted the crisis in eastern Europe, where the political structure seemed to have been stabilized. The world now saw a startling demonstration of Soviet accomplishments in rocketry. On August 26, 1957, the Soviet government announced the successful firing of an intercontinental ballistic missile. On October 4 the Soviet Union launched the first space satellite, Sputnik 1, followed on November 3 by Sputnik 2, with the dog Laika aboard as passenger. These developments lifted the Soviet Union's world prestige to new heights. They also enhanced the prestige of its political leadership. The space ventures had obvious military implications, and Khrushchev was not slow to claim that they indicated a significant shift in the balance of power. He initiated a drive to translate Soviet rocket superiority into diplomatic gains, and in a militant speech on November 10, 1958, ignited a new Berlin crisis by demanding that the occupation regime in West Berlin be terminated.

There were limits to the pressure that Moscow could apply on the West. The United States was still a formidable thermonuclear power with larger resources than the Soviet Union, and any confrontation that imperiled vital American interests might have disastrous consequences for both sides. As long as relations remained tense and difficult, they fostered an expensive arms race that diverted resources from domestic development and required continual sacrifices from the Soviet people. An easing of relations with the United States, by contrast, would offer hope of more rapid economic development and better living standards. But obstacles to even a partial détente remained formidable. Khrushchev's visit to the United States in the fall of 1959 was made in the hope both of easing tensions and of winning concessions in Berlin and Germany, but no concessions were forthcoming. On May 1, 1960, a U.S. high-altitude reconnaissance airplane, a U-2, was shot down deep in Soviet territory and its pilot was captured. This was followed by the collapse of a Paris summit conference scheduled for that month. Further deterioration in Soviet–American relations was manifest in connection with the civil war in the Congo in the early 1960s, the building of the Berlin Wall in 1961, and finally in the Cuban Missile Crisis in October 1962.

Cuban Missile Crisis

The Cuban Missile Crisis seemed to bring the two great nuclear powers to the brink of war. Under the guise of providing Cuba with defensive weapons, the Soviet government was found to be trying to establish launching sites on the island for medium- and intermediate-range missiles. The U.S. government's rapid deployment of a naval blockade around Cuba and an exchange of letters between Pres. John F. Kennedy and Khrushchev resulted in the latter's agreement to withdraw the "aggressive" weapons.

The rift with China. Khrushchev also faced increasing difficulties in his relations with China. At the root of the Sino-Soviet dispute lay the fact that the Soviet Union and China were two great nations with different destinies, each with its own defined set of interests. Khrushchev saw as his main tasks the building up of Soviet power, minimizing the risks of thermonuclear war, demonstrating the superiority of the Soviet system, and at the same time exploiting the vulnerabilities of the non-Communist world by means of nuclear stalemate. For the Chinese leaders, termination of the Kuomintang regime in Taiwan was a prime objective. Involved with this, however, and going well beyond it, was the need for Soviet military and economic support to help overcome Chinese backwardness.

Growing dissension with China

Khrushchev's reluctance to challenge the U.S., as well as his insistence on giving priority to Soviet interests, became evident as the Sino-Soviet dispute developed. Faced with a choice between providing broad economic and military assistance to the Chinese or concentrating on the homeland, he chose the latter. Fearing that the Chinese might embroil him in a war with the West, he denied them nuclear weapons and gave them only token support in their campaign to win Taiwan. He imposed more and more severe sanctions on the People's Republic, reducing trade and military and economic assistance, withdrawing specialists, and demanding the repayment of debts. His attempt to persuade the Chinese to desist from attacks on the Soviet leadership, however, failed. Faced with defiance and with Chinese efforts to mobilize support within the international Communist movement, he moved to close up his own ranks and to expel the Chinese and their allies from the movement as heretics who had broken away from the true faith of Communist internationalism.

In the wake of the Cuban missile crisis of 1962, with its sobering reminder of how close the world had come to thermonuclear extinction, Khrushchev demonstrated renewed eagerness to improve his relations with the United States and the West. He signed, with the U.S. and the U.K., the Nuclear Test Ban Treaty (August 1963); joined in establishing better communications between Moscow and Washington; undertook in cooperation with the United States to prohibit missiles in orbit and to cut back the production of fissionable material; pressed restraints on the regime of Fidel Castro in Cuba; and relaxed tension over Berlin and undertook to improve relations with West Germany. All these efforts to "normalize" relations with the West were received by the Chinese as additional confirmations of Khrushchev's apostasy from true Marxism–Leninism. The rift was rapidly becoming unbridgeable.

Domestic strains and difficulties

Economic problems. Khrushchev's decision to seize the "peace issue," even at the cost of further alienating China, won support among Communists as well as non-Communists who feared nuclear war. But perhaps the most compelling reasons for seeking a détente with the West were domestic strains and difficulties. The efforts of the post-Stalin leadership to raise the low living standards in the U.S.S.R. had whetted the appetite of the people but failed to satisfy it. Their deeply felt need for more and better food, clothing, and housing could not be met without a diversion of investment from armaments and heavy industry to light industry and agriculture. The situation in agriculture was particularly troublesome. The good harvest of 1958, largely attributable to uniformly favourable weather, was followed by a series of mediocre harvests. Disaster struck in 1963, when bad weather and widespread drought combined to cause a greatly reduced output and compelled the government to purchase abroad approximately 12,000,000 tons of grain to meet consumer needs. While there were several reasons for the decline in agricultural output, one important factor was the failure to invest adequate capital in agriculture.

In a belated effort to meet the problem, Khrushchev announced a program to expand the chemical industry (including fertilizer production), increase output of agricultural machinery, extend irrigation, and other measures that required substantial new capital investment. This would mean less rapid expansion in heavy industry, as well as reduced funds in other sectors, including the military. The proposed shift in priority, of course, met resistance from others in the leadership.

Nor were Khrushchev's problems limited to agriculture. Industrial progress also lagged. The industrial slowdown and the fall in agricultural output combined to produce a serious decline in the overall economic growth rate in 1962–63.

Khrushchev's efforts to cope with these problems by periodic reorganizations of the state and party machinery created more confusion. His division of the party organization into separate industrial and agricultural branches in November 1962 antagonized many regional leaders and eroded his support in that section of the party apparatus where he had previously commanded the strongest loyalty. His increasing disposition to announce important changes in policy without consulting his colleagues in the Politburo tended to antagonize them. These domestic developments, taken together with his unsuccessful efforts to dislodge the Western powers from Berlin and the rebuff he received during the Cuban Missile Crisis, helped set the stage for his removal.

THE BREZHNEV ERA

Collective leadership. On October 16, 1964, the Soviet press announced that the Central Committee had met two days earlier and granted Khrushchev's request that he be released from his responsibilities "in view of his advanced age and deterioration in the state of his health." *Pravda* the next day charged him with:

> harebrained schemes, halfbaked conclusions and hasty decisions and actions divorced from reality; bragging and bluster; attraction to rule by fiat; unwillingness to take into account what science and experience have already discovered.

The new collective leadership was led by Leonid I. Brezhnev, the new first secretary of the CPSU, and Aleksey N. Kosygin, who succeeded to the chairmanship of the Council of Ministers (*i.e.,* head of government). Public polemics with Peking ceased. The parallel industrial and agricultural hierarchies that Khrushchev had introduced into the party and governmental structure were combined. The new leaders announced the removal of "unwarranted limitations" on the size of household plots of land in the collective farms and on private livestock holdings by collective farmers. The party apparatus was assured that it could count on stability; the industrial managers were told that more rational economic policies would be pursued.

Brezhnev and Kosygin

The style of the new Brezhnev–Kosygin leadership was much less dramatic than that of Khrushchev, and there was renewed emphasis on collective leadership. De-Stalinization was arrested, and indeed reversed, despite sharp opposition from liberal intellectual circles. Brezhnev took the lead by stressing Stalin's leadership during World War II and his achievements as an industrializer and builder of Soviet power. Khrushchev vanished from the public eye.

Within the new collective leadership, Brezhnev became increasingly prominent, until at length the notion of collectivity was simply dropped. His position was strengthened when in December 1965 N.V. Podgorny, one of the party secretaries, was elevated to the largely ceremonial post of chairman of the Presidium of the Supreme Soviet (*i.e.,* head of state) in place of Anastas I. Mikoyan. Another potential rival was eliminated when A.N. Shelepin lost his post as deputy premier and secretary of the Central Committee of the CPSU. At the 23rd Party Congress in March–April 1966, Brezhnev's title of first secretary was changed to general secretary, a title that had last been used by Stalin. During the next years Brezhnev's became the most authoritative voice on issues of domestic and foreign policy. In 1977 he became the first Soviet party leader to hold also the post of chairman of the Presidium, and at his death in 1982 he had held the party secretaryship longer than any predecessors.

Unbinding the economy. Among the economic problems inherited by Khrushchev's successors, the most serious were in agriculture. In March 1965 Brezhnev promised relief to the collective and state farmers: higher prices for grain and livestock; stable delivery quotas; decreased tax burden on collective farms; and doubling of investments in farm machinery, trucks, tractors, fertilizer, and land improvement. The promises came too late to prevent a poor harvest in 1965, but the harvest in 1966 was very good, apparently confirming the measures Brezhnev had taken. That year the prices of trucks, tractors, and agricultural machinery were reduced for collective and state farms, rural electricity rates were reduced, and retail prices on certain consumer items in rural stores were lowered to the level of prices in the cities. Collective farms were authorized to introduce guaranteed monthly pay for their members based on rates of corresponding categories of state farm workers.

Reforms in agriculture and industry

Poor harvests in 1967 and 1969 alternated with good harvests in 1968 and 1970. But even the harvest of 1970, estimated at more than 160,000,000 tons of grain, fell short of the projected goal for that year of 190,000,000–200,000,000 tons. If the overall performance of agriculture in the period 1966–70 compared favourably with that of the preceding five-year period, it was still far from satisfactory.

Khrushchev's successors also confronted difficult problems in industry. While space and weapons technology and the iron and steel industry matched the best that the West had to offer, technological progress in such new industrial fields as automation, computers, petrochemicals, and industrial research and management techniques lagged well behind that of the United States, Japan, and western Europe. Many industries, particularly those producing consumer goods, also were far less developed technologically. The slowing of the industrial growth rate and the difficulty of resolving increasingly intricate and complex planning and management problems aroused deep concern in the party and government leadership.

Industrial reforms announced in September 1965 represented an effort to come to grips with the management problem by giving managers of enterprises greater discretion in decision making and by establishing an incentive system designed to reward the efficient use of resources. Hand in hand with these changes went complete repudiation of Khrushchev's administrative reforms. The whole system of regional, republican, and all-Soviet economic councils was abolished, and the ministerial system that had prevailed before 1957 was reestablished. Each ministry was made responsible for a sector of the economy, while central planning functions were concentrated in the State Planning Committee (Gosplan), and responsibility for the allocation and distribution of supplies was entrusted to a new State Committee for Material and Technical Supplies.

These industrial changes were hailed by economic reformers as a modest step in the right direction, but enterprise managers complained that they were still hemmed in by rigid supply restrictions. The economy continued to function much as it had eariler—the bureaucratic machinery resisted change and innovation.

The Five-Year Plan for 1966–70, which was presented at the 23rd Party Congress in April 1966, represented a considerable reduction of the targets Khrushchev had originally set for 1970. Even the relatively modest new goals for 1970, however, turned out in many cases to be impossible of fulfillment.

Cultural controls. In cultural affairs the Brezhnev regime, after some tentative liberalization, became increasingly conservative and regressive. Innovations in the arts and literature had been greatly stimulated by Khrushchev's de-Stalinization program. The problem for Stalin's heirs was that of defining the limits of cultural freedom. It was perhaps inevitable that Khrushchev should find himself increasingly out of sympathy with the bolder spirits who wanted greater freedom of expression and found his cultural outlook oppressive. Nevertheless, his experiments in controlled relaxation provided the liberals with a field of manoeuvre, and it was Khrushchev himself who authorized the publication of Aleksandr I. Solzhenitsyn's powerful concentration-camp novel, *One Day in the Life of Ivan Denisovich.*

The regressive trend in culture

Khrushchev's successors were less tolerant. The arrests on September 13, 1965, of Andrey Sinyavsky and Yuly Daniel, for publishing abroad (under the pseudonyms Abram Tertz and Nikolay Arzhak, respectively) works allegedly slandering the Soviet Union, introduced a period of increased repression. Over the next years many other dissident writers and their sympathizers were also arrested, imprisoned, or consigned to forced-labour camps. After the Arab defeat by Israel in the Six-Day War of 1967, attacks on Israel and Zionism took on anti-Semitic overtones. The events in Czechoslovakia in 1968 (see below) also had repercussions within the Soviet Union. After the invasion of Czechoslovakia, Soviet cultural policy hardened. The treatment of Solzhenitsyn was symbolic: even before Czechoslovakia the police had seized all his unpublished manuscripts and withdrawn his few published works from circulation; in November 1969 he was expelled from the Writers' Union, and the Nobel Prize for Literature that was awarded to him the next year only intensified the attacks on him. Even such a moderate party spokesman as Aleksandr T. Tvardovsky, editor of the literary magazine *Novy Mir,* found himself deprived of his seat as an alternate member of the Central Committee in 1966; he was subjected to increasing harassment culminating in a purge of the staff of the journal in 1970 that forced him to relinquish his editorship.

The repressive measures did not go unchallenged. After the sentencing of Sinyavsky and Daniel to seven and five years' hard labour, respectively, 63 well-known Moscow writers joined in an appeal for their release. On the eve of the 23rd Party Congress, 25 distinguished figures in Soviet public life, including some leading nuclear physicists, signed an open letter to Brezhnev registering their opposition to Stalin's rehabilitation.

Foreign policy. The Brezhnev regime also had to contend with difficult problems in foreign affairs. The most troublesome was that of relations with China. After an initial effort to lower tensions, the quarrel flared into violence, culminating in clashes along the Ussuri River in March 1969 and along the Soviet–Sinkiang border in August. Subsequently the two sides agreed to negotiate their differences, but friction persisted. The Soviet Union strengthened its military formations along the Chinese border and continued to provide military aid to India as well as to Pakistan in an effort to counter Chinese influence in those countries. Even the extensive military and economic aid supplied to North Vietnam during the Indochina war could be viewed not only as a demonstration of Soviet willingness to assist a fellow Communist state but also as an effort to decrease North Vietnamese dependence on China.

In eastern Europe, Khrushchev's successors found an increasing spirit of independence. Romania had begun to take an increasingly nationalist position, proceeding with plans for all-around industrialization despite Soviet insistence that Romania's economic role should be based on division of labour with other countries in eastern Europe. Over the next years Romania continued to display independence by reorienting its foreign trade away from the Soviet bloc, concluding a trade treaty with the United States (1964), and expanding contacts with the West.

Czechoslovakia was less fortunate. The downfall of the party leader, Antonín Novotný, and his replacement by Alexander Dubček in January 1968 was followed by the "Prague Spring," a period of remarkably free political expression. Past abuses were attacked, and demands for democratization of the system were made. Fearful that the Dubček leadership had lost control of the situation and that the challenge to party authority under Dubček might spread to other Communist countries, the Soviet leaders decided on military intervention. On August 20, 1968, Soviet forces occupied Czechoslovakia. The invasion was justified by what later came to be called the Brezhnev Doctrine: in essence, that the Soviet Union reserved the right to intervene militarily in the affairs of any of its eastern European Communist neighbours whenever it believed that its interests or the security interests of its allies were significantly threatened. The effect of Soviet intervention was to force Czechoslovakia back on a more orthodox Communist course and to warn other Communist states in eastern Europe that there were limits to the degree of autonomy Moscow would tolerate.

Brezhnev doctrine

Soviet policy in the Middle East was directed toward protecting the interests of its Arab clients, expanding Soviet influence, and eliminating residual Western influence. While the failure of the Soviet Union to come to the aid of the Arabs in the Six-Day War in 1967 tarnished its prestige, the Soviet decision to rearm its Arab clients won it renewed favour.

The primary objective of Soviet policy in western Europe continued to be to weaken U.S. influence. A special relationship was cultivated with France, which had withdrawn its forces from the North Atlantic Treaty Organization. A substantial increase in trade with several western European countries emphasized mutual needs and dependencies. At the same time, the Soviet Union remained determined to keep Germany divided and to press for general recognition of East German sovereignty.

Relations with the United States

Soviet attacks on "American imperialism" became increasingly vigorous following the U.S. bombing attacks on North Vietnam in February 1965. The cooling of relations did not, however, prevent agreement on specific questions of mutual interest. On January 27, 1967, both the U.S. and the Soviet Union became parties to the International Treaty on the Peaceful Uses of Outer Space, which prohibits the orbiting of nuclear weapons. The Middle East crisis of May 1967, which culminated in the Six-Day War in June, brought a new clash of Soviet and U.S. interests; but both sides joined in efforts to stop the fighting in order to prevent the war from broadening into a direct Soviet–American military confrontation. (M.F./Ed.)

Détente. The Cuban missile crisis taught the Soviet leadership that its military might at that time was no match for that of the United States. Also, throughout the 1960s it became apparent that the Soviet economy was far behind Khrushchev's goal of catching up with the West by 1970. The policy of détente (Russian *razryadka napryazhyonnosti;* "spacing" or "easing of tension") was formed out of the recognition that improving the economic and diplomatic position of the Soviet Union required some sort of rapprochement with the West. Brezhnev enunciated this policy in 1969 when he committed the Soviet Union to a "struggle for peace" and to a greater range and number of contacts with the West.

The first step in normalizing relations with western Europe was resolving the German problem. The election in October 1969 of Willy Brandt as chancellor of West Germany was helpful in this respect because he declared his readiness to establish good relations, on a realistic basis, with the Soviet Union, Poland, and East Germany. On August 12, 1970, in Moscow and on December 7 in Warsaw Brandt initialled with the Soviet and Polish premiers, respectively, separate treaties by which West Germany recognized the inviolability of the existing frontiers. On June 3, 1972, in a quadripartite agreement, the foreign ministers of the United States, the United Kingdom, France, and the Soviet Union declared that West Berlin was not a constituent part of West Germany but that the existing links between that city and West Germany must be maintained and developed. Finally, on December 21, in East Berlin, the two German states concluded a basic treaty establishing formal relations between them that cleared the way for the entry of both into the United Nations.

On May 26, 1972, U.S. Pres. Richard M. Nixon and Brezhnev signed in Moscow the first SALT (Strategic Arms Limitation Talks) agreement, a document embodying acceptance on both sides that nuclear war had ceased to be a reasonable option. In June 1973 Brezhnev travelled to Washington, D.C., where he signed with Nixon an agreement designed to avert nuclear war between the U.S. and the U.S.S.R. or between one of them and any other country. At the same time, some of the restrictions on Jewish emigration—which had become a major source of criticism—were relaxed. The number of Jews leaving the Soviet Union rose throughout the decade, reaching a peak in 1979, when more than 50,000 emigrated.

Since the 1950s the Soviet Union had called for a conference to legitimize the postwar border arrangements in Europe. This goal was finally achieved at Helsinki on August 1, 1975, when the heads of the 33 European governments and those of the United States and Canada signed the Final Act of the Conference on Security and Cooperation in Europe. The Helsinki Accords recognized as inviolable the existing frontiers of all states in Europe. The Soviet Union and its allies conceded that human rights in each European country were a matter of all-European concern, but the accords were hailed in Moscow as a major success for détente in Europe, since the frontiers of its eastern European satellites were now secured. In response to complaints from the NATO countries about human rights restrictions, the Soviet Union insisted that, while it was fulfilling all the provisions of the Helsinki Accords, it would not submit to outside scrutiny of matters that fell within the competence of the Soviet state.

The Helsinki Accords

In fact, dissidence within the Soviet Union over the denial of basic human rights was a cause of anxiety to the Soviet authorities during the entire period of détente. In 1976 the security police began to put pressure on the members of the Public Group to Promote the Fulfillment of the Helsinki Accords; by 1982 the group had been effectively dissolved. Meanwhile, the Soviet press attacked Pres. Jimmy Carter of the United States for introducing the human rights theme in his inaugural address (January 20, 1977) and the U.S. Department of State for its warning to Moscow against trying to silence Andrey Sakharov, a leading critic of political repression.

On March 24, 1977, Brezhnev submitted to the Central Committee the draft of a new Soviet constitution, which showed no basic differences from the Stalin Constitution of 1936; it was approved by the Supreme Soviet on October 7, 1977.

Trade agreements with the West

Trade with the West prospered, particularly the import of grain and technology. In July and August 1972 the first massive purchase, on easy credit terms, of wheat and feed grains from the United States took place. In October 1974 West Germany arranged to sell the Soviet Union pipe for a Siberian natural gas pipeline. Other western European countries, the United States, and Japan supplied additional pipe as well as pipe-laying equipment and compressor turbines.

Reporting to the 25th Party Congress in February 1976 on main economic guidelines for the 10th Five-Year Plan (1976–80), Kosygin stated that during the 1971–75 plan total industrial output had increased by 43 percent, and he announced a target of 36 percent for 1980.

The economic gains of détente were accompanied by a series of foreign-policy victories. In 1975 North Vietnam completed its conquest of South Vietnam, and by the next year Soviet-backed revolutionaries had come to power in Angola and Mozambique. In 1977 Soviet military advisers were expelled from Somalia, but the Soviet Union promptly sent arms and Cuban soldiers to Ethiopia to help fight Somali-backed secessionists. On the Arabian Peninsula, Yemen (Aden) was becoming a close Soviet ally. And in 1978 a bloody coup in Afghanistan established a government that signed a 20-year treaty of friendship with the Soviet Union.

These foreign advances alarmed the NATO allies, particularly the United States, where fears of the growth of Soviet military power were becoming more vocal. Indeed, during the time of détente the Soviet Union had become a global power, with military capacities rivalling those of the United States in nearly all categories. Nevertheless, on June 18, 1979, after six and a half years of arduous negotiations, Carter and Brezhnev met in Vienna and signed the SALT II, which limited each country to a ceiling of 2,250 strategic missiles by 1981.

SALT II

On December 27, 1979, the Soviet Union invaded Afghanistan after a year of coups and rebellions had threatened its influence in that country. Within months about 100,000 Soviet troops had dug in for a long, bitter war of attrition against Muslim fighters in the mountains. In retaliation, President Carter withdrew the SALT II treaty from consideration for ratification in the U.S. Senate; he also announced that 17,000,000 metric tons of grain ordered by the Soviet Union would not be delivered. The landslide election of Ronald W. Reagan—long an opponent of SALT II—to the U.S. presidency in November 1980 signalled the demise of détente in the Brezhnev era.

Tension over nuclear weapons expanded to the European theatre. In 1979, in response to Soviet deployment of SS-20 intermediate-range ballistic missiles aimed at western Europe, NATO decided to deploy ground-launched cruise and Pershing II ballistic missiles starting in December 1983. Negotiations with the Soviets to reduce or to eliminate deployment began in November 1981 in Geneva, and strategic arms reduction talks (START) opened the following June. Gambling that popular disapproval would prevent deployment of the NATO weapons without negotiations, the Soviet Union insisted that their installation would mean the end of the talks. The gamble failed, and when the first missile components arrived on November 23, 1983, the Soviets broke off negotiations. On December 8 they suspended START. (K.M.S./Ed.)

AFTER BREZHNEV

Andropov and Chernenko. By 1979 Brezhnev's health had begun to fail. The end of his long tenure marked the passing of an entire generation of leaders. In 1980 Kosygin died and was replaced as premier by his 75-year-old deputy, Nikolay Tikhonov. In 1982 the party ideologue Mikhail Suslov died and was succeeded by Konstantin Chernenko. The most momentous death was that of Brezhnev himself, on November 10, 1982. He was succeeded as general secretary of the Communist Party two days later by Yury V. Andropov, who had been head of the KGB from 1967 until May of that year. By June 1983 Andropov had become president and chairman of the Defense Council. This rapid accumulation of all of Brezhnev's titles was not unopposed. Brezhnev had clearly favoured Chernenko, a loyal protégé and party bureaucrat, as his successor and had been supported in his choice by many of the older leaders. Andropov was part of a new generation of party technocrats that included Mikhail S. Gorbachev, Central Committee Secretary for agriculture since 1978 and full member of the Politburo since 1980.

Death of Brezhnev

Soon after taking office, Andropov began a crackdown on corrupt officials and a public campaign against alcoholism and worker absenteeism. However, his failing health prevented him from dealing with the nation's paramount problem: the shrinking economy and, in particular, the deplorable state of agriculture, exemplified by another series of disastrous harvests beginning in 1979. The 1976–80 Five-Year Plan had achieved industrial growth of about 25 percent, much lower than the expected 36 percent, prompting officials to lower the planned growth figure for the 1981–85 period to 26 percent.

Andropov died of kidney failure on February 9, 1984, and was succeeded by the ailing 72-year-old Chernenko, the last of the older generation. Faced with unexpected unified resistance from NATO, as well as President Reagan's plan for a 20-year, multibillion-dollar Strategic Defense Initiative, Chernenko agreed to resume nuclear disarmament talks. The original Soviet demand that NATO withdraw its Pershing II and cruise missiles as a precondition of the talks was dropped.

Gorbachev. Chernenko died on March 10, 1985, and Gorbachev was made general secretary the next day. At age 54, he was the youngest man to become leader since Stalin. He immediately overhauled the party and state bureaucracies, securing the election of supporters to full membership in the Politburo. Nikolay Ryzhkov replaced Tikhonov as premier, and Eduard Shevardnadze replaced Andrey Gromyko as foreign minister. Gromyko was appointed president. By the end of the year Gorbachev had replaced more than 40 percent of the party first secretaries at the *oblast* or *kray* level and had carried out the most rapid turnover at the top of the Soviet military since the end of World War II.

At the 27th Party Congress in February 1986 Gorbachev stressed the need for economic and structural reforms (*perestroika*) and more openness (*glasnost*) in Soviet society. The Soviet handling of the explosion of a nuclear reactor at the Chernobyl nuclear power station on April 26, 1986, drew world attention to *glasnost.* After waiting 18 days before revealing the extent of the disaster, Gorbachev announced that thenceforth there would be more openness in the reporting of formerly taboo subjects, such as drug abuse, crime, and disasters.

A law on individual enterprises became effective May 1, 1987, allowing citizens to set up part-time businesses. Many Soviet citizens remained skeptical of the reforms, however, preferring the security of the old system to the uncertainties of *perestroika.*

On April 14, 1988, the Soviets signed accords in Geneva, agreeing to begin withdrawal of all troops from Afghanistan on May 15. This decision marked a dramatic shift away from the Brezhnev Doctrine: for the first time the Soviet Union abandoned a Communist regime in danger of being overthrown. Withdrawal began as scheduled, and on February 15, 1989, the last Soviet soldier left Afghanistan.

Arms control talks between the Soviet Union and the United States resumed in March 1985. Later that year a series of Reagan–Gorbachev summit meetings began. A treaty calling for the reduction of intermediate-range nuclear forces was signed at a Washington summit in 1987, and the two leaders exchanged documents of ratification the following year in Moscow.

In June 1988 the Soviet Communist Party held its first conference in more than 40 years. Addressing the 4,991 delegates at the opening session, Gorbachev proposed a new presidential system of government that would reduce the role of the Communist Party and shift much of the day-to-day power to the soviets. In keeping with this plan, Gorbachev was elected Soviet president at the Central Committee plenum on October 1, replacing Gromyko, who retired. Elections for the new Congress of People's Deputies began on March 26, 1989, the first popularly contested national legislative elections since 1917. Two-thirds of the delegates were directly elected by the Soviet people; the remaining delegates were elected by the Communist Party and party-affiliated organizations (100 seats were reserved for members of the Communist Party). Members of the congress then chose 542 of their number to serve on the restructured Supreme Soviet. (Ed.)

For later developments in the history of the Union of Soviet Socialist Republics, see the *Britannica Book of the Year* section in the BRITANNICA WORLD DATA ANNUAL.

RUSSIAN SOVIET FEDERATED SOCIALIST REPUBLIC

In terms of territory, population, and economic development, the Russian Soviet Federated Socialist Republic is preeminent among the 15 republics that make up the Soviet Union. It covers 76 percent of that nation's area and—following it—is the second largest political unit in the world; with 6,592,800 square miles (17,075,400 square kilometres), it is almost twice the size of either China or the United States. The "Russian" of its title (often abbreviated R.S.F.S.R., otherwise known as the Russian Federation, or simply Russia) derives not from *russkaya*—"pertaining to the Russian nationality"—but from *rossiyskaya*—"pertaining to the country Russia," and the vast territory is the home of some 60 nationalities. This situation is reflected in the republic's complex administrative system.

The character of the R.S.F.S.R.

Extending halfway round the northern portion of the globe and covering much of eastern and northeastern Europe and all of northern Asia, the Russian S.F.S.R. displays an enormous variety of landforms and environments. These form great bands across its territory: Arctic deserts lie to the north, giving way toward the south to the wastes of tundra and the forest that covers two-thirds of the entire republic and accounts for much of its character. In the far south, beyond belts of open steppes, portions of the land assume a subtropical and even a hot semidesert character. The republic's position, in latitudes in which evaporation can scarcely keep pace with the accumulation of moisture, engenders abundant rivers (including a number of the world's largest), lakes, and swamps.

Most of the people are found in a great triangle in the western, or European, portion of the republic, but since World War II there has been a great flow of population to the Siberian Basin of the east, where deposits of minerals are being exploited.

The republic itself was set up immediately after the October Revolution of 1917 and became a union republic on December 31, 1922, when the federal state of the Soviet Union was created. Its capital, Moscow, is also the capital of the Soviet Union.

The Russian S.F.S.R.'s maritime border, longer than the Equator, meets the Arctic and Pacific oceans. The land borders touch Norway, Finland, and Poland on the northwest and west and the People's Republic of China, the Mongolian People's Republic, and North Korea on the south. They also touch eight constituent Soviet republics: to the west Estonia, Latvia, Lithuania, and Belorussia, to the south the Ukraine, Georgia, Azerbaijan, and Kazakhstan.

Historically, the republic was the core of the expanding Russian state and suffered onslaughts ranging from that of the Mongol hordes in the 13th century to the Nazi invasion of World War II. (For historical coverage, see the section above *History of Russia and the Soviet Union.*) This historical heritage, together with a vast area and great natural wealth, has given Russia a unique place among the Soviet republics. Its brooding landscapes and the complexities of the old society have been celebrated in prose and in music by such giants of world culture as Pushkin, Tolstoy, and Tchaikovsky, while the October Revolution and enormous transformations engendered in the Soviet period have been recorded by such people as the novelists Maksim Gorky and Mikhail Sholokhov, the poet Vladimir Mayakovsky, and the composers Dmitry Shostakovich and Sergey Prokofiev.

Physical and human geography

THE LAND

Relief. The Russian S.F.S.R. is divided basically into plains and mountains and, using these and other natural characteristics as criteria, may be subdivided into nine physical regions.

The Kola–Karelian region. The Kola–Karelian region lies in the northwest of the European Russian S.F.S.R. To the west, beyond the Finnish (and, in the north, a small portion of the Norwegian) frontier, it continues as Scandinavia. Karelia is a plateau marked by ridges and knolls and dotted with many lakes, the largest being Ladoga, Onega, Segozero, Pyaozero, Imandra, Umbozero, and Lovozero (*ozero,* "lake"). Ancient glaciation is evident everywhere, both in the scoured landscape of the glaciers' advance and in the mask of drift left on their retreat.

Karelian lakes

Taiga and swamps cover the southern part. The Kola Peninsula is mainly hills and plateaus, though Mt. Khibini rises to 3,907 feet (1,191 metres).

Despite the Arctic location, the climate here is temperate continental, averaging 12° F (−11° C) in January and 57° F (14° C) in July, with annual precipitation of 14–20 inches (350–500 millimetres). The principal rivers are the Ponoy, Vodla, Kem, and Suna. There is a narrow band of tundra in the northern Kola Peninsula and a zone of taiga forests on rocky podzolic soil in the south.

The Kola region has deposits of nickel, copper, iron, valuable types of mica, apatite, and nepheline as well as raw materials for the construction industry and peat.

Animal life depends on the character of the natural zones. The Arctic fox, northern reindeer, and snowy owl are characteristic of the tundra; elk, wolverine, brown bear, lynx, hare, and fox are found in the taiga and forest zones.

The Russian Plain. The Russian Plain, one of the great lowland areas of the world, extends east from the western border to the Ural Mountains and from the Arctic Ocean south to the Caucasus and the Caspian Sea. The topography is varied; there are elevations of up to 1,300 feet (400 metres) in the Valdai Hills west of Moscow, in central Russia stretching south of Moscow, and in the Volga Hills (just west of the Volga, southeast of Moscow), alternating with the vast lowlands of the Oka–Don and the Caspian littoral, part of which lies below sea level. The Oka–Don lowland, passing imperceptibly into the Volga Hills, ends sharply at the Volga, where the Zhiguli Mountains begin, sometimes rising to 1,200 feet.

The climate is mainly temperate continental, with January temperatures varying from 29° F (−1.5° C) in the southwest to −8° F (−22° C) in the northeast. July temperatures average 48° F (9° C) in the north and 77° F (25° C) in the southeast. Annual precipitation ranges from around 24 inches (600 millimetres) in the west to five inches (125 millimetres) in the southeast. Many great rivers flow across the plain, most of them—for instance, the Volga, Dnepr, Don, and Western Dvina—originating in the centre. They are fed mainly by snow and freeze for about two months in the south and seven in the northeast. The Volga is the principal river, its basin encompassing nearly half the Russian Plain. In the north there are many lakes and swamps.

The European triangle is nearly devoid of exploitable natural resources. The soil is very thin podzol, which historically has yielded poor crops and much of which has been allowed to return to forest, where the Russians like to hunt mushrooms. The situation for the homeland of the Great Russians is desperate in regard to underground minerals, for there are none. Prior to the 18th century, iron, copper, and more precious metals had to be imported into Muscovy. The situation changed when the Russians began to exploit the Urals during the reign of Peter the Great and subsequently moved to develop Siberia, the Ukraine, and other regions outside their homeland. The absence of

Absence of natural resources

local natural resources explains much of Russia's geopolitics for the past quarter millennium.

A significant part of the Russian Plain is covered with forests: taiga (spruce, fir, and Siberian spruce), mixed, and broad-leaved (oak, birch, beech, and linden). In the north of the plain are tundras; on the southeast fringes, steppes and semideserts.

Animal life varies: Arctic fox, northern reindeer, snowy owl, and willow ptarmigan are found in the tundras; white elk, brown bear, lynx, wolverine, squirrel, sable, hare, and fox in the forests. In the forest steppes and steppes are rodents—suslik (ground squirrels, genus *Spermophilus*), jerboa, and marmot—and birds—bustard, eagle, and *strepet* (related to the bustard).

The Caucasus. The Russian S.F.S.R. includes the northern part of the Great Caucasus (Bolshoy Kavkaz), extending north-northwest to south-southeast from the Black Sea to the Caspian, containing the Kuban–Azov and Terek-Kuma lowlands, separated by the Stavropol Upland, about 2,300 feet high. Alpine and moderate-altitude relief prevails, and the region's climate is temperately continental; January temperatures average 21° F (−6° C) and July 76° F (24.5° C). In parts of the east the climate is arid. Maximum annual precipitation is 16 inches (400 millimetres). The mountaintops have permanent snow and glaciers, feeding the numerous rivers, which can flood for up to six months in warm years. Tundra vegetation and, on the lower slopes, alpine meadows are found. Pine, spruce, and fir grow to elevations of 6,500 feet (2,000 metres), and oak, hornbeam, ash, beech, and wild fruit trees are found to 5,000 feet (1,500 metres).

The foothills form sloping plateaus, sometimes intersected by spurs rising 5,000 feet. Fields, vineyards, and orchards are numerous, and in the subtropical southwest are laurel, palm, bamboo, and boxtree. The seaward slopes of the Caucasus Mountains, with their extremely fertile *zheltozem* (yellow-earth) soils, luxuriant vegetation, and subtropical climate, make good sites for health resorts, rest homes, Pioneer camps, and tourist centres.

Mountain animals of the Caucasus

Mountain animals include species from temperate forests, semideserts, and high mountains: tur (wild goat), chamois, stag (red deer), brown bear, lynx, fox, and leopard, and, among the birds, eagle, Caucasian grouse, and pheasant. (See also *Caucasus* below.)

The Urals and Novaya Zemlya. The great north–south spine of the Urals and of their continuation, Novaya Zemlya (a group of islands in the Arctic Ocean), separates Europe from Asia. The Urals extend about 1,250 miles (2,000 kilometres) north–south and are extended an additional 600 miles into the Arctic Ocean by Novaya Zemlya; their landscapes vary from tundra to steppes. Tundra and forest tundra cover Novaya Zemlya and the Polar and Nether-Polar Urals, culminating in Mt. Narodnaya at 6,214 feet (1,894 metres). Shrubs are the commonest vegetation, but there are leaf-bearing trees in the south. The animal life is sparse, mostly reindeer, Arctic fox, willow ptarmigan, duck, and goose. An extremely harsh climate and permafrost inhibit the development of this northernmost area.

The Northern Urals and the northern part of the Central Urals form a taiga zone, rich in forests and potash minerals, predominantly carnallite and sylvite. The Central Urals and much of the Southern Urals are forest steppes and steppes, including extensively eroded massifs and high plains. The Southern Urals' highest point is 5,374 feet (1,638 metres), and it has a continental climate; coniferous, mixed, and broad-leaved forests are found on the slopes, with forest steppe and steppe in the foothills. The area's favourable climate and topography, valuable iron, copper, nickel, asbestos, gemstone, construction stone, and petroleum deposits, and comparative proximity to areas of dense population have caused it to become highly industrialized.

Siberia. For a discussion of this vast region between the Ural Mountains and the Far East, see the section *Siberia* below.

The Far East. The Far East, traditionally regarded as a distinctive region, extends from the Chukchi Peninsula in the north to Vladivostok in the south, including the Kamchatka Peninsula and the Commander, Kuril, and Sakhalin islands. It is of medium elevation, the highest ranges being the Dzhugdzhur, Stanovoy, Burein, and Sikhote-Alin in the southwest and the Koryak Mountains and the Sredny (Central) and Vostochny (Eastern) ranges on Kamchatka in the northeast.

The region has many active volcanoes, and severe earthquakes are common. There are more than 250 volcanoes on Kamchatka and the Kuril Islands, of which 67 are active, including Klyuchevskaya Sopka (15,584 feet [4,750 metres]). There are small lowlands—the Anadyr, Central Amur, Lower Amur, and Khanka lowlands. The climate is monsoonal, with cold, fairly snow-free winters and moderately warm, wet summers. Precipitation ranges from eight inches in the north to 30–40 inches (760–1,000 millimetres) in the Primorye (the southeasterly mainland coast) and southwest Kamchatka.

Monsoonal climate of the Far East

The northern Far East consists mainly of plains and mountain tundras, while in the forest zone are stony birches and Dahurian larches (*Larix gmelini*) on Kamchatka and spruce and firs around the Sea of Okhotsk. In the south grow Dahurian larch, Sayan spruce (*Picea ajanensis*), stony birch, oak, hornbeam, ash, maple, Korean cedar, Manchurian nut (*Juglans mandshurica*), and fir, with some relict vegetation, such as Amur cork and the vine *Actinidia.*

The Lower Amur Basin has a dry winter and rainy summer; 85–96 percent of the annual precipitation falls from mid-April to September, causing many floods.

The Primorye area, with its Sikhote-Alin mountain complex parallel to the coast and its intermontane and coastal plains, is economically well developed. The deeply indented coast provides many convenient inlets.

Sakhalin Island, lying between the Tatar Strait and the Sea of Okhotsk, is the largest island in the east Russian S.F.S.R. Its north is lowland, with tundra vegetation; the remainder is forest. The climate is fairly warm in the intermontane plains of the south and on the coast, the soil is fertile, and there are waterpower and timber resources. In the forests are many furbearing animals and medicinal plants. Iron, tin, molybdenum, antimony, polymetallic ores, gold, coal, and oil have been discovered there, and Siberian salmon, humpback (Pacific) salmon, carp, and bream are found in the sea and river waters.

The Kamchatka–Kuril Ridge is made up of young folded mountains, covered by Arctic tundra on the Koryak Mountains (north of the Kamchatka Peninsula) and by tundra–taiga vegetation on the Kamchatka Peninsula, where turf-podzolic soil predominates. The southern islands of the archipelago are washed by the warm Soi Current. Coal, oil, gold, copper, and sulfur have been discovered in the Kamchatka–Kuril Ridge, but only coal is mined in the Kamchatka Peninsula. It was there that Soviet engineers first harnessed the hot subterranean waters for electric power and heating.

The sealing industry is important, as is fishing for Pacific herring, cod, *Eleginus navaga,* Pacific and Siberian salmon, smelt, and crab.

Drainage. The Russian S.F.S.R. contains some of the world's largest rivers: the Ob–Irtysh system (3,362 miles, or 5,410 kilometres), Amur (1,755 miles [2,800 kilometres]), Lena (2,650 miles [4,240 kilometres]), and Yenisey (2,543 miles [4,069 kilometres]). There are about 100,000 rivers more than six miles (10 kilometres) long. They flow into the Arctic Ocean—such as the Northern Dvina, Pechora, Ob, Yenisey, Lena, Indigirka, and Kolyma; to the Pacific Ocean—such as the Amur, Anadyr, and Kamchatka Peninsula rivers; and to the Atlantic Ocean, by way of the Baltic and Black seas—such as the Neva, Don, Dnepr, and Kuban. The Volga and Ural rivers flow into the Caspian Sea. Most rivers are fed by snow and rain, while ice lasts from a month in the south of the European section to nine months in Northern Siberia. There are more than 200,000 lakes, particularly in the Kola–Karelian region. Large artificial reservoirs include Rybinsk, Gorky, Kuybyshev, and Volgograd on the Volga, Kama on the Kama, Tsimlyansk on the Don, and Ob on the Ob.

Reclaimed land

Russia has the largest amount of artificially drained land in the Soviet Union, mostly in the European part. Such drainage is also widespread in the Baraba Steppe beyond the Urals and along the Upper Angara, the Lower Selenga, and the Amur. Artificial irrigation occurs in the Northern Caucasus, in the Middle and Lower Volga region, in the Oka River Basin around Moscow, in the Tuva Trough, east of Lake Baikal, and near Yakutsk.

THE PEOPLE

Ethnic composition. The ancient group of peoples known as the Slavs developed in eastern Europe between the 3rd and 8th centuries AD, and the first Slav state, Kievan Rus, arose in the later 9th century, laying the foundation of three related nationalities: Russian (the national backbone of the Russian S.F.S.R.), Ukrainian, and Belorussian.

The Russia that emerged from this historic nucleus has since had to ward off the Pechenegs (a Turkic people from an area north of the Black Sea) and Polovtsy (or Kipchak; a tribe from the steppe north of the Black Sea) in the 10th–12th centuries, Mongol hordes in the 13th–15th centuries, Teutonic Knights and Swedes in the 13th century, Poles and Swedes in the 17th, Napoleon's army in the 19th, the intervention of 14 governments from 1918 to 1920, and Nazi Germany from 1941 to 1945. This heritage has strongly molded the national character.

The multiplicity of peoples

The multiplicity of peoples in the contemporary republic is reflected in 16 Autonomous Soviet Socialist republics (A.S.S.R.'s) within the Russian S.F.S.R., as well as the five autonomous regions and the 10 autonomous (until 1977 national) districts (see Table 3). The rest of the republic is administratively divided into six *kraya* (territories) and 49 *oblasti* (regions).

Table 3: Minority Republics, Regions, and Districts of the Russian S.F.S.R.

Autonomous Soviet Socialist republics	autonomous *oblasti* (regions)
Bashkir (Bashkiriya)	Adygey
Buryat (Buryatiya)	Gorno-Altay
Chechen-Ingush (Chechen-Ingushetiya)	Karachay-Cherkess
Chuvash	Khakass
Dagestan	Yevreyskaya (Jewish)
Kabardino-Balkar (Kabardino-Balkariya)	
Kalmyk (Kalmykiya)	**national *okruga* (districts)**
Karelian (Karelia)	Agin-Buryat
Komi	Chukchi
Mari	Evenk
Mordvinian (Mordviniya)	Khanty-Mansi
Severo-Ossetian (Severo-Ossetiya)	Komi-Permyak
Tatar (Tatariya)	Koryak
Tuvinian	Nenets
Udmurt (Udmurtiya)	Taymyr
Yakut (Yakutiya)	Ust-Ordynsky Buryat
	Yamalo-Nenets

The population of the Russian S.F.S.R. is overwhelmingly Russian but also contains small minorities of Tatars, Ukrainians, Chuvash, Bashkirs, Mordvins, Dagestani nationalities, Belorussians, Jews, Germans, Udmurts, Chechens, Kazakhs, Cheremis (or Mari), and many others, more than 60 in all. Most of the nationalities have deep historical roots, and communities speaking different languages have long-established economic and cultural ties, facilitating communication among them.

Main language groups

Linguistically, the people can be divided into the Indo-European group, comprising East Slavic- and Iranian-speakers; the Altaic group, including Turkic, Mongolian, and Manchu-Tungus; the Uralic group, with the Finno-Ugric and Samoyedic; and the Caucasian group, comprising Abkhazo-Adyghian and Nakho-Dagestanian.

The Slavic group. The Russian language, together with Ukrainian and Belorussian, constitutes the East Slavic group of the Indo-European languages. Despite the fact that the Russians cover an expanse from the Baltic Sea to the Pacific Ocean, the Russian language's main features are homogeneous.

The Altaic group. Another major group of languages, the Altaic, includes the Turkic-speaking people of the Altai–Sayan foothills, the Altaics, Khakass, Shors, Tuvinians, and Tofalars (or Karagasy). Various groups of Siberian Tatars live in the forest steppe regions of Western Siberia and on the Upper Ob, while many Yakuts have settled in the basin of the Lena River and Dolgans in the northern Krasnoyarsk area. The Bashkirs live in the Southern Urals.

The Turkic cluster also includes the Chuvash and Tatars living along the Middle Volga, and there are Turkic peoples in the Northern Caucasus, among them the Kumyks, Nogay, Karachay, and Balkars. The Evenks and Evens speak Manchu-Tungus languages and the Buryats and Kalmyks Mongolian tongues.

The Uralic group. The Uralic-speaking group, widely disseminated along the Eurasian forest and tundra zone, has complex origins. Finnic people inhabit the European part of the Russian S.F.S.R.: Mordvins, Cheremis (or Mari), Udmurts (or Votyaks), and Komi (or Zyryans) and the closely related Komi-Permyaks are found along the Volga and in the Urals, while Estonians, Karelians, Finns, and Veps inhabit the northwest. The Mansi (or Vogul) and Ostyak (or Khant) peoples, few in number and living beyond the Urals and in the Ob Basin, belong to the Ob-Ugric group.

The Samoyedic group likewise has few members but is dispersed over a vast territory: the Selkups on the Middle Ob and on the Taz; the Nenets in the forest tundra and tundra from the Yenisey to the Yamal Peninsula and from the Urals to the Kola Peninsula; the Enets (Entsy) along the Lower Yenisey; and the Nganasans mainly on the Taymyr Peninsula.

The Caucasian group. The Caucasian-speaking aggregate, which includes people of the Abkhazo-Adyghian, Nakh, and Dagestani groups, is remarkable in its complexity. In the Northern Caucasus, the Abkhaz, Abaza, Kabardian (or Circassian), and Adyghian languages are similar to each other but differ sharply from the languages of the Nakh group (Chechen and Ingush) and of the Dagestani group (Avar, Lezgian, Dargin, Lakk, Tabasaran, Andi, Tzez, Archi, and about 20 others).

Minority peoples

Other groups. There are in Siberia a few Paleo-Asiatic peoples, having much of their way of life and culture in common but differing in origin and also, largely, linguistically. Some of these peoples are nevertheless related by language, so that the Chukchi, Koryaks, and Kamchadals (Itelmens) belong to a group known as Luorawetlan, while the Eskimos and Aleuts belong to the Eskimo-Aleut group. The languages of the Gilyaks (or Nivkhs) on the Lower Amur and Sakhalin Island and the Yukaghirs of the Kolyma area are quite isolated, while the language of the Kets, a small population living along the Middle Yenisey, is likewise unique.

Demography. The distribution of population in the republic is not uniform, depending both on the opportunities offered or denied by the environment and on the equally varied potential of various eras of history. Regions in the central band of European Russia are of long settlement and economically well developed. Here the population is densest in an area between a line linking Leningrad–Cherepovets–Vologda–Kirov in the north and the Caucasus Mountains in the south. In the Urals region the people live mainly between Sverdlovsk and Chelyabinsk, the population tailing off to the east. The Trans-Siberian Railroad forms an axis along which Siberia's agricultural colonization has proceeded since the mid-19th century. The narrow population belt widens around Novosibirsk (because of the Kuznets Basin and its coalfield) and along the Yenisey to the south of Krasnoyarsk (around the Minusinsk Basin). To the east of Lake Baikal the population band narrows further, stretching along the railway to the Pacific Ocean and terminating in the Suyfun-Khanka Plain near Vladivostok.

Migration from the crowded central portion of European Russia is traditional. Immigrants traversed the Urals with the first caravans as the Russian government extended its boundaries. The Soviet period has seen rapid economic development of the eastern Russian S.F.S.R., stimulating the flow of population there. Migration has not been solely across the Urals but also to other union republics, as economic development accelerated, natural resources were exploited, and capital was invested in industry and urban construction. More than two-thirds of the population is urban.

THE ECONOMY

The Russian S.F.S.R. since World War II has been transformed into a powerful, highly developed, industrial-agrarian republic. Natural resources have undoubtedly been significant in this development. Hundreds of deposits of mineral wealth have been discovered: more than 70 percent of Soviet coal reserves are concentrated in the Russian S.F.S.R., exceptionally large deposits having been discovered in Eastern Siberia and the Far East. There are also large deposits of iron ore as well as copper, zinc, lead, nickel, aluminum, tin, molybdenum, gold, platinum, and other nonferrous metals. The world's largest petroleum and natural gas reserves are located in the republic, in the northern part of Western Siberia, and the petroleum reserves have been estimated as second only to those of the Persian Gulf region.

Mineral reserves

The republic can be divided into 10 economic regions: Northwest, Central, Volga-Vyatka, Central-Chernozem, Volga, Northern Caucasus, Urals, Western Siberia, Eastern Siberia, and Far East. Industry is the principal component of the republic's economy, its structure hardly differing from that of the industry of the Soviet Union as a whole. Food and light industries account for about 12 percent of industrial production.

Heavy industry. Heavy industry plays a decisive role in the Russian S.F.S.R.'s economy, particularly the fuel and power sectors.

Fuel. More than half the fuel sector is engaged in the processing of petroleum; a third produces coal; and the remainder exploits natural gas. Western Siberia has become the largest petroleum centre in the country. Expansion of the oil refinery at Komsomolsk-na-Amure (in the Far East) was completed during the Five-Year Plan of 1971–75, and new factories were set up in the Far East and in the Arkhangelsk region (around the White Sea, an inlet of the Arctic Ocean).

Pipelines from the oil and gas areas in Western Siberia were extended to the Central region via the Urals and across Siberia to the Far East, and underground gas reservoirs were significantly enlarged in European Russia near the main industrial centres. A centre for gas extraction and processing was built near Orenburg.

Power. Electrical energy occupies a special place in the complex fuel and power economy of the Russian S.F.S.R., with thermal power plants supplying about 80 percent of the total electric energy. Construction of hydroelectric power plants, providing generating power, with simultaneous provision of water supply and water for irrigation and development of river navigation and fishing, was also being pressed forward. The main centres of activity were on the Volga and Kama and the rivers of the Northern Caucasus. Atomic power plants were also increasing in number.

Metallurgy. About half the ferrous metallurgy plants existed before the Revolution, and they have since been fundamentally reconstructed. A large proportion of the products of ferrous metallurgy is supplied by plants built after the Revolution. The latter include the complexes at Magnitogorsk (in the Southern Urals) and Kuznetsk (in Western Siberia) and the plants at Novotulsky, Novylipetsk, Tagil, and Petrov-Transbaikalia. The Amurstal, Komsomolsk-na-Amure, and Chelyabinsk metallurgical plants and the Orsk-Khalilovo and Cherepovets complexes began production during World War II. The first unit of the large West Siberian Iron and Steel Works, near Novokuznetsk, was constructed during 1966–70.

Nonferrous metallurgy

Most of the nonferrous metallurgical plants have been installed under the Soviet administration, whether in the Northern Caucasus (at Nalchik and Ordzhonikidze) or in the subpolar region (at Monchegorsk, Kandalaksha, and Norilsk). The Urals, Western Siberia, and the Far East are the centres of nonferrous metallurgy.

Machine building. The Russian S.F.S.R.'s machine-building industry provides most of the Soviet Union's total requirements for steam boilers, grain-harvesting combines, automobiles, and main-line electric locomotives and much of its metal-cutting machine tools, instruments, means of automation, and spare parts.

There are important automobile factories in Moscow, notably the Likhachyov plant and the MZMA (Moscow low-powered car works), and in Gorky, Miass, Yaroslavl, Ulyanovsk, and Izhevsk (in the Udmurt A.S.S.R.). A factory at Tolyatti (near Kuybyshev) manufacturing the Zhiguli car was completed and a heavy-truck factory was being built in the same period in Naberezhnye Chelny, in the Tatar A.S.S.R. The Russian S.F.S.R. also manufactures high-power hydraulic and steam turbines and electrical generators with unit capacity of 500,000 and 800,000 kilowatts.

Automobile manufacturing

Chemicals. The chemical industry was developing along with manufacturing, with coal, wood, and foodstuffs providing raw materials for most of its branches. Accordingly, synthetic-rubber factories are found at Yaroslavl, Yefremov, and Voronezh, in the potato-growing centres; sulfuric acid factories at Krasnouralsk, Kirovograd, Karabash, Mednogorsk, Chelyabinsk, and Ordzhonikidze, where nonferrous metallurgy was developed; and potassium and phosphorus fertilizer plants at Solikamsk, Berezniki, Perm, Voskresensk, Bryansk, and Krasnouralsk, near deposits of potassium salts and phosphorites.

At the end of the 1950s the chemical industry was able to make use of new natural and by-product gas and by-products of the petroleum industry and therefore no longer needed to appropriate to itself valuable raw materials that could be used for food processing instead. The result was an immediate shift in the location of newly erected chemical enterprises, which gravitated toward the Urals–Volga zone and the Northern Caucasus. Siberia, too, offers favourable conditions for chemistry involving large amounts of electrical energy. Factories manufacturing synthetic rubber, nitrogenous fertilizers, automobile parts and accessories, and various plastic goods are already in operation there.

Forestry and wood pulp. The forest, paper, and wood industries are important, since more than 90 percent of Soviet wood resources are in the Russian S.F.S.R.; indeed, the republic has the largest forest reserves in the world. Most forest areas contain matured and overmatured trees, which are of the greatest value.

Coniferous trees, including pine, are important, and the Russian S.F.S.R. is the world's richest area in this valuable species, though other coniferous trees, such as spruce, cedar, and especially larch, are equally important.

Within the Soviet period the forest industry has extended even to the trans-Urals forests. Eastern Siberia has overtaken the Urals in terms of timber output, and the tempo is increasing in Western Siberia and the Far East.

Construction materials. During the Soviet period, rapid growth in the production of structural materials has taken place. The structural-materials industry has aimed at producing materials and implements ready for the factory, widening the assortment of finished materials and sanitary equipment, and increasing production of ceramic drainage and irrigation pipes.

The industry is helped by utilizing intermediate products from other branches of industry, such as slag and cinders.

Light industry. Light industry, which is concentrated in the Central region, provides much of the nation's cotton fabric, linen, silk and woollen fabrics, knitted wear, and leather footwear.

The republic accounts for 70 percent of the Soviet Union's total catch of fish, whales, and seals and its utilization of other sea products. In addition, it produces sausage and ham products, soap, whole-milk products, candy, meat, animal oil, canned food, vegetable oil, and sugar.

Agriculture. The Russian S.F.S.R. accounts for half the total agricultural production of the Soviet Union. The main product of farming in the Russian S.F.S.R. has always been grain, and 60 percent of the farmlands are devoted to wheat, rye, barley, oats, and groat (hulled) crops. Fodder crops come second, grown on 30 percent of the arable land and including annual and perennial grasses and corn (maize). The Volga area, the Urals, the Northern Caucasus, the Central and Central-Chernozem regions, and Western Siberia are the main grain producers of the Russian S.F.S.R., supplying most of the total grain yield. European Russia has always been the leading producer of the main commercial crops, such as sunflower seeds,

Grain and subsidiary crops

sugar beets, and flax fibre, as well as potatoes, vegetables, and melons.

Livestock breeding is the second main agricultural feature and includes cattle, pigs, sheep, and goats. Animal products include meat, milk, eggs, and wool.

European and Asiatic Russia differ in livestock breeding. Intensive processes such as raising of beef and dairy cattle take place in the European part; raising of distant pasture sheep takes place in Asia. Reindeer graze on moss and lichens in the north.

Transportation. The railroads, the most widely used form of transport, are responsible for about three-quarters of the freight turnover in the republic. The density of the modern railroad network is by no means uniform, being high in the Central and Central-Chernozem regions, low in Western Siberia, and meagre in Eastern Siberia and the Far East.

River navigation plays an important role in regions in which there are no other means of communication.

Motor transportation accounted for about five percent of the republic's annual freight turnover.

Pipelines for petroleum, petroleum products, and gas are carrying vast quantities of petroleum and products each year. The Druzhba (Friendship) is the longest pipeline—2,900 miles (4,700 kilometres)—beginning on the shores of the Volga and ending in the socialist countries of central Europe. Lines have also been built to transport gas to Italy and West Germany.

The merchant fleet plays a great role in establishing ties within the republic, especially between regions on the Arctic seaboard, despite the seasonal nature of Arctic shipping. The port of Murmansk is open 365 days a year, partly by means of icebreakers; Arkhangelsk is open 175 days and Nizhnyekolymsk 110 days. Merchant shipping is also very important in foreign trade.

Air transport is widely used for bulk goods and for passengers. Aviation is important in the extreme north, in parts of Siberia, and in the Far East, being nonseasonal and the only means of long-distance transport to some areas.

ADMINISTRATIVE AND SOCIAL CONDITIONS

Government. The Russian Soviet Federated Socialist Republic is, according to its current constitution, a sovereign socialist state, the power of which derives from workers and peasants. The socialist economic system and the socialist ownership of tools and means of production form the economic basis of the republic. Even before the Russian S.F.S.R. had been formed, the Second All-Russian Congress of Soviets had created the Soviet government and promulgated decrees on peace and on land, which ultimately took Russia out of World War I and transferred land to the peasants.

Creation of the R.S.F.S.R.

The Third All-Russian Congress of Soviets, which sat from January 23 to 31, 1918, announced the creation of the Russian S.F.S.R., and the republic's first constitution dates from the fifth congress, which assembled in July 1918. During and after the Civil War (1918–20) the Russian S.F.S.R. was organized to include Autonomous Soviet Socialist republics, the first of which was the Bashkir A.S.S.R., on March 23, 1919.

The Russian S.F.S.R. entered the Soiet Union, then being formed, in 1922.

The Soviet dictator Joseph Stalin, during the purges of the 1930s, advanced a new constitution, established by the Extraordinary 17th All-Russian Congress of Soviets on January 21, 1937. A new constitution was adopted in 1978.

As described above (see *The people*), the Russian S.F.S.R. is composed of A.S.S.R.'s, autonomous *oblasti* and *okruga* for the larger non-Russian nationalities, as well as administrative *oblasti* and *kraya* (territories), the latter incorporating such national administrative subdivisions as autonomous *oblasti*.

Autonomous republics. The autonomous republics enjoy a form of political independence; each has its own constitution, higher organs of state power, legislature, and higher judicial bodies. Each autonomous republic, being a federated part of the Russian S.F.S.R., is represented in the Presidium of the Supreme Soviet of the Russian S.F.S.R. by a vice chairman of the Presidium.

Autonomous regions and districts. Another administrative form of autonomy—the autonomous *oblast* and *okrug*—extends only to self-government in internal affairs. While non-Russians participate extensively in the administration of both units, the needs of the Russian Communist Party to control the given nationality are always paramount.

Autonomous *oblasti* and *okruga* send deputies directly to the Soviet of Nationalities of the Supreme Soviet of the U.S.S.R.

Legislative and executive bodies. The highest organ of state power is the unicameral Supreme Soviet of the Russian S.F.S.R. Between sessions the Presidium of the Supreme Soviet of the Russian S.F.S.R. is the highest organ of state power, embodying all the rights accorded to the Russian S.F.S.R. by the constitution. It is elected by the Supreme Soviet of the Russian S.F.S.R. and includes a chairman, 16 vice chairmen (one for each autonomous republic), a secretary, and 13 members.

Supreme Soviet

The Presidium in all its activity is subordinate to the Supreme Soviet. The latter confirms the border and regional division of the autonomous republics, autonomous *oblasti,* territories (or *kraya*), and regions; confirms the economic plan and state budget of the Russian S.F.S.R.; reports on its implementation; and chooses the government of the republic—the Council of Ministers of the Russian S.F.S.R.

The Council of Ministers is the highest executive and administrative organ of state power. It coordinates and directs the work of the ministries of the republic and other bodies subordinate to it, adopts measures to carry out the economic planning and state and local budgets of the Russian S.F.S.R., ensure social order while defending the interests of the state and protecting the rights of citizens, directs and inspects the work of the councils of ministers of the autonomous republics, and supervises and inspects the work of the executive committees of the territorial and regional soviets of workers' deputies.

A unicameral Supreme Soviet with its Presidium is the highest organ of state power in each autonomous republic. The Supreme Soviet of the autonomous republic chooses the governing body of the republic—the Council of Ministers.

The local bodies of state power in the *oblasti, okruga, kraya, rayony,* cities, and other localities are the corresponding soviets of workers' deputies.

Electoral procedure. The Supreme Soviet of the Russian S.F.S.R. is elected, from a single list of candidates, by the citizens of the Russian S.F.S.R. for a term of four years; the Supreme Soviet of an autonomous republic is elected by the citizens of that republic only, also for a term of four years.

The Soviet of Workers' Deputies of an autonomous *oblast* is elected, also from a single slate, by its citizens for a two-year term. The regional and territorial soviets of workers' deputies, soviets of workers' deputies of autonomous *okruga,* towns, the regions of large cities, settlements, villages, farmsteads, and *auly* (North Caucasian villages) are elected (under the same circumstances as other elections) for a term of two years.

Any citizen of the Russian S.F.S.R. over the age of 21 may be elected a deputy to the republic's Supreme Soviet or to that of an autonomous republic, regardless of racial and national affiliation, sex, religion, educational attainments, social origin, place of settlement, property holdings, or past activity. Citizens over the age of 18 may be elected to local organs of power.

Franchise qualifications

Judiciary. The Supreme Court of the republic, chosen by the Supreme Soviet for a five-year term, is the highest judicial body of the Russian S.F.S.R., supervising the activities of all other judicial bodies. The main task of the supreme courts of the autonomous republics, and courts of territories, provinces, and autonomous *oblasti* and *okruga* lies in controlling the activities of the people's courts.

Judicial proceedings in the Russian S.F.S.R. are carried on either in Russian or in the language of the prevailing nationality; persons not knowing the language of the court, however, have full access to an interpreter and the right to testify in their native language.

According to the constitution, justice in the courts is based on the equality of citizens before the law and the court and in exact accordance with the law. Judges are independent and subordinate only to the law. Trials are open, and the accused is guaranteed a defense. These ideals, however, have been violated in the extreme since their promulgation. In the 1930s millions suffered from official illegality, in the late 20th century thousands. The unconstitutional use of psychiatric institutions and drugs as coercive and control instruments has remained part of the Soviet judicial process since Stalin's time.

The Communist Party. The organizations of the Communist Party of the Soviet Union (CPSU) direct political life. They are guided by the Central Committee of the Communist Party and by its regional and territorial committees.

The republic's Komsomol (Young Communist League) organizations accomplish political and educational work with people between 14 and 25 years of age.

Labour organization. Trade unions in the Russian S.F.S.R. were charged with looking after labour protection, industrial safety, labour legislation, and social-insurance funds. They were also prominent in business efficiency and investment and were part of an effort to enhance the popularity of socialist competition and the Communist-labour movement.

Wages

Social conditions. The average monthly wages of workers and serving personnel were considerably enhanced by benefits from public-welfare funds. Wages depend on the type, chiefly the heaviness, of the work, working conditions, and importance of the branch of industry. Wages higher than average are paid to labour engaged in construction work, transportation, and mining. Collective farm wages are paid after all other commitments (taxes, compulsory investments, seed reserves) have been met.

Public-welfare funds from the state budget, enterprises, and trade unions are used substantially to improve the condition of workers in the Russian S.F.S.R., both materially and socially. A major portion of public-welfare funds goes for free medical service, training, pensions, and scholarships.

With free and universal education, the rise in the workers' cultural and technological level, and mechanization and automation, distinctions between intellectual and physical labour are being reduced, and material and cultural differences between population groups are, it is hoped, disappearing.

All workers and professionals in the Russian S.F.S.R. receive paid vacations of up to one month. Advances in health care and material well-being have led to a sharp decline in mortality, especially among children, the disappearance of the more dangerous infectious diseases, and an increase in the average life-span.

CULTURAL LIFE

Russian cultural life is discussed mainly in the introductory section above on the Union of Soviet Socialist Republics as a whole. Here, only a few distinguishing features of the Russian S.F.S.R. are treated.

The Russians' modern culture differs markedly from that of the non-Slavic nations in the Russian S.F.S.R. After the October Revolution, village planning, the peasant household, dress, national cuisine, holidays, and folklore underwent substantial changes as a result of the complete reorganization of individual agriculture, cultural innovation, and the availability of medical aid in the villages, as well as of other factors that the republic shared with the rest of the world: development of various rapid modes of transport, radio, and television. Particularly great changes came about in dress and the arts, while several holidays, although closely related to Russian traditions, took on a new colour, such as New Year's Day, End of the Russian Winter, and Harvest Festival. The centuries-old culture, with its regional variations, nonetheless still finds wide, colourful, and vigorous expression.

Innovations have also come about in the case of non-Slavic people living in the Russian S.F.S.R., though individuality is preserved and reflected in architecture, interior decoration, festivals, and folklore. The peoples of the Northern Caucasus, for example, have adopted urban attire without completely abandoning their traditional dress: Circassian coat (*cherkeska*) with cartridge belt, quilted jacket (*beshmet*), sheepskin hat (*papakha*), felt cloak (*burka*), with silver-ornamented belts, shirt (*rubakha*), and long, wide trousers (*sharovary*) for men and, for women, a dress fitting loosely at the waist, high headdress, and shawl and ornamented belt. There are also many unique features in the headdress and in the style, colours, and ornaments of clothing of the nationalities along the Volga, such as the Tatars, Chuvash, Mari (Cheremis), Kalmyks, and Mordvins.

Traditional costumes

Significant changes, too, have occurred in the customs of the Siberian people, especially in the far north. The nomadic life that prevailed before the Revolution has been replaced by a settled one; now only reindeer herders and hunters are nomadic. The log house has remained, but urban dress has replaced traditional clothing, except among the reindeer herders, who still prefer clothing made of warm reindeer skins, the most comfortable for their occupation. The ancient art of the Siberian people is preserved and encouraged, as in the case of the masterly bone carving of the Chukchi, the birch-bark carving of the Khants (Ostyaks), and the colourful fur appliqué work of the Nenets.

Dance and theatre

Theatres in Russia that are of world renown include, in Moscow, the Bolshoi Theatre, Moscow Art Theatre, Maly (Small) Theatre, Vakhtangov Theatre, and State Central Puppet Theatre; in Leningrad, the Kirov State Academic Theatre of Opera and Ballet and the Leningrad Bolshoi Dramatic Theatre; and in Novosibirsk, the Novosibirsk Theatre of Opera and Ballet. Creative artists from the theatre belong to the All-Russian Theatrical Society in Moscow.

Music has always flourished in Russia; the symphonic and chamber works, oratorios, and songs of Dmitry Shostakovich, Sergey Prokofiev, V.P. Solovyov-Sedoy, and Georgy Sviridov are performed throughout the world, while the Pyantnitsky, Voronezh, and Northern chorus troupes, the Siberian Omsk Folk Choir, the Aleksandrov Song and Dance Troupe of the Soviet Army, and the State Academic Folk Dance Ensemble are also popular.

Authors are united in a collective, the Union of Writers of the Russian S.F.S.R. Artists and sculptors belong to the Union of Artists of the Russian S.F.S.R., architects to the Union of Architects of the Russian S.F.S.R.

Among recent sculptural and architectural monuments, the best known are the Piskarevskoye Memorial Cemetery to those who died during the siege of Leningrad in World War II, the memorial to the soldiers who perished at Stalingrad, and the Tsiolkovsky State Museum of Cosmonautical History in Kaluga.

Russian achievements in science, literature, music, and fine arts have received international recognition. Mikhail Lomonosov, Dmitry Mendeleyev, Klement Timiryazev, Ivan Michurin, Konstantin Tsiolkovsky, Ivan Sechenov, and Ivan Pavlov are famous in Russian science; Aleksandr Pushkin, Mikhail Lermontov, Leo Tolstoy, Anton Chekhov, and Maksim Gorky in literature; Ilya Repin and Vasily Surikov in art; and Mikhail Glinka and Peter Ilich Tchaikovsky in music.

In Soviet times their successors in various fields have included Gleb Krzhizhanovsky, Igor Kurchatov, Nikolay Semyonov, Sergey Korolyov, Boris Petrovsky, Vladimir Mayakovsky, Boris Pasternak, Mikhail Sholokhov, Aleksandr Solzhenitsyn, Aleksandr Tvardovsky, Isaak Brodsky, and Tikhon Khrennikov.

There are more than 600 museums in the republic, some of them world renowned: the Central Lenin Museum, the Central Museum of the Revolution, the State Historical Museum, and the State Tretyakov Gallery in Moscow; the Hermitage and the State Russian Museum in Leningrad; the museum-estate of Leo Tolstoy, Yasnaya Polyana, near Tula; and the Mikhaylovskoye A.S. Pushkin Museum in Pushkin.

Publishing

The Russian S.F.S.R. leads the Soviet Union in book, newspaper, and journal publication. The Sovetskaya Rossiya (Moscow), Tatarskoye Izdatelstvo (Kazan), Bashkirskoye Izdatelstvo (Ufa), and Lenizdat (Leningrad) are the leading publishing houses. The universities of Moscow, Leningrad, Voronezh, Rostov, Saratov, and Tomsk also have their own presses.

More than 5,100 journals are published in the republic. The literary journals *Novy Mir* ("New World"; Moscow), *Neva* (Leningrad), *Ural* (Sverdlovsk), and *Sibirskiye Ogni* ("Siberian Lights"; Novosibirsk) are the most widely read.

The Russian S.F.S.R. publishes more than 4,400 newspapers, *Sovetskaya Rossiya* ("Soviet Russia") being the most widely read. There are also newspapers published in the native languages of the autonomous republics, autonomous regions, and national districts. Newspapers are also published directly by industrial enterprises, schools, and large collective and state farms.

The Russian S.F.S.R. also encourages sports. New stadiums, playing fields, and sporting camps and centres are built each year, the largest being the Lenin Central Stadium in Moscow and the Kirov Stadium in Leningrad. Large physical-fitness organizations have grown up in factories, plants, schools, and collective and state farms. The Russian S.F.S.R. national athletic games are held every four years. (S.A.V./R.He.)

History

Above, in the section *History of Russia and the Soviet Union,* the main body of Russian and Soviet history is treated. Here is offered only a sketch of the territorial development of the Russian S.F.S.R. since its inception.

Originally, Russian Soviet Federated Socialist Republic was the name of the whole Soviet state upon its founding in 1917. It became officially the name of the constituent republic on the basis of the agreement of December 30, 1922, in the formation of the U.S.S.R. Thereafter, the republic's area changed many times. In 1923 it covered about 7,945,900 square miles, or 94.6 percent of the whole. Later, it was successively reduced by the creation of the Uzbek and Turkmen republics in 1924, of the Tadzhik republic in 1929, and of the Kazakh and Kirghiz republics in 1936. On the eve of World War II the Russian S.F.S.R. had an estimated area of 6,374,700 square miles (77.3 percent of the U.S.S.R.); about 24 percent of the Russian S.F.S.R. was then in Europe and the rest in Asia.

The annexations of 1939–45 and certain changes in the administrative divisions within the U.S.S.R. caused new variations in the area of the Russian S.F.S.R. In 1940 it was further reduced when the Karelian A.S.S.R., with the area ceded by Finland, became the Karelo-Finnish S.S.R. In 1944 the Tannu Tuva People's Republic, formerly part of China, was included in the Russian S.F.S.R. In 1945 the northern part of East Prussia, southern Sakhalin, and the Kurile Islands were added to the Russian S.F.S.R., while in 1946, when the Karachay Autonomous Region and the Chechen-Ingush A.S.S.R. were suppressed, parts of them were included in Georgia; finally, in 1954, the Crimea was "ceded" by Russia to the Ukraine. At that time the total area of the Russian S.F.S.R. was 6,523,524 square miles, or 76 percent of the U.S.S.R. In December 1953 a new region (*oblast*), Magadan, was formed from part of the Khabarovsk territory (*kray*); in January 1954 five new *oblasti* (Arzamas, Balashov, Byelgorod, Lipetsk, and Kamensk) were formed in European Russia by revising the boundaries of the existing ones. On July 16, 1956, the Karelo-Finnish S.S.R. was reestablished as the Karelian A.S.S.R. and incorporated into the Russian S.F.S.R. This action, along with other annexations since 1940, increased the area to 6,592,800 square miles.

Siberia

Extent of Siberia

Siberia (Russian Sibir) is a vast region of the U.S.S.R. composed of the whole of northern Asia between the Ural Mountains (west) and the Far East on the Pacific Ocean (east) and extending southward from the Arctic Ocean (Kara Sea, Laptev Sea, and East Siberian Sea) to the hills of central Kazakhstan and the frontiers of the U.S.S.R. with China and Mongolia. Within the Soviet Union a small part of Siberia in the southwest (Tselinn Kray and Semipalatinsk and East Kazakhstan *oblasti*) is administratively incorporated into the Kazakh S.S.R., while the rest of the region belongs to the Russian Soviet Federated Socialist Republic. Two regions no longer considered officially a part of Siberia are the administrative areas adjacent to the Ural Mountains (Tyumen, Sverdlovsk, Chelyabinsk, and Kurgan *oblasti*) and those along the Pacific coast (Khabarovsk and Primorsky *kraya* and Amur, Magadan, Kamchatka, and Sakhalin *oblasti*) together with the Yakut A.S.S.R.

Siberia proper is divided into western and eastern Siberia by a line running meridionally somewhat west of the Yenisey River. The administrative divisions of West Siberia are the Altai Kray, Kemerovo, Novosibirsk, Omsk, and Tomsk *oblasti.* The administrative divisions of East Siberia are the Krasnoyarsk Kray, Irkutsk, and Chita *oblasti* and the Buryat and Tuva Autonomous Soviet Socialist republic. The total area of Siberia in the wider sense is 5,330,896 square miles (13,807,037 square kilometres), or more than a quarter of the Asian continent and more than 60 percent of the territory of the U.S.S.R.; in the narrower sense, it is 4,374,475 square miles (11,330,600 square kilometres). The population is sparse, chiefly concentrated in the west and south, more than half urban, and, in modern times, overwhelmingly Russian. (Ed.)

PHYSICAL AND HUMAN GEOGRAPHY

The land. *The West Siberian Plain.* The West Siberian Plain, between the Urals (west) and the Yenisey River (east), is a subdivision of the Siberian Basin, the taming and exploitation of which is forming what may be the greatest developing region in the world today. The area is a plain, marshy in the north and with marked differences encountered in proceeding from tundra to steppe. The climate is continental, with prolonged winter; January's temperatures average −18° F (−28° C) in the north and 3° F (−16° C) in the south, while July's average is 37° F (3° C) in the north and 73° F (23° C) in the south. Precipitation varies between about 18 inches (450 millimetres) in the taiga and about half that amount in the tundra and steppes.

The rivers belong to the Ob and Yenisey systems (both of which traverse the plain from the south to north and empty into the Kara Sea of the Arctic Ocean), and there are various lakes: Chany, Ubinka, and Kulunda. Tundra and forest tundra with peat bogs cover the north, under which vast oil and natural gas deposits have been discovered. The Urengoy natural gas deposits (some 100 miles [160 kilometres] up the Pur River, which lies about halfway between the Yenisey and Ob) are considered to be the world's largest.

Peat, oil, and gas

Taiga prevails in the central West Siberian Plain, to the north growing spruce and cedar, in the centre cedar and pine, and to the south fir, spruce, and cedar. Precipitation is, as noted above, twice that of the tundra, and the climate is kinder. Large oil and natural gas deposits have been discovered in the Ob region, and deposits of brown iron ore lie along the Yenisey River. Great expanses are covered with peat.

Western Siberia's southern stretches include the Ishim (west of Lake Chany), Baraba, and Kulunda (south of Lake Chany) steppes. This area is one of the Russian S.F.S.R.'s most important granaries. The vegetation and animal life are meagre: fir and cedar, the large-eared hedgehog, the migratory and striped hamsters, and the chestnut and red-cheeked suslik. The Kulunda Steppe has many ill-drained lakes with high mineral content.

Central Siberia. Central Siberia is a vast territory between the Yenisey River, on the west, and the mountains of northeastern Siberia, on the east. The region includes the Byrranga and Severnaya Zemlya mountains (in the far north), the North Siberian Plain, and the Central Siberian Plateau (farther south), the peaks of which reach 5,600 feet (1,700 metres). In the east, along the Lena and Vilyuy rivers, lies the Central Yakut Lowland. The climate is harshly continental, January temperatures dropping to −47° F (−44° C), though summer, when 68° F (20° C) may be recorded in the south, is benign. Annual precipitation is eight to 20 inches (200–500 millimetres). Permafrost is virtually ubiquitous. There is a dense river network, the largest river being the Lena, with its tributary the Vilyuy, and the Yenisey, with its tributaries the Angara, Podkamennaya Tunguska, and Nizhnyaya Tunguska.

Pine forests cover about 60 percent of the Central Siberian terrain; in the north there are Arctic deserts and mountain and plain tundras and in the south small strips of forest steppe and steppe, as in the areas around Achinsk, Krasnoyarsk, Irkutsk, and Kansk.

The Central Siberian Plateau is a high plain, marked by fracture zones along the edges and mountainous in places. The northern borders are covered by tundra and forest tundra, the southern by forest steppe. The remainder is taiga, with stone outcrops covered by mountain tundra sometimes rising to 2,600 feet (800 metres). In the taiga area are dark-coned forests below 1,300 feet and cold-resistant larch forests—the preponderant form of arboreal vegetation in Central Siberia—above.

The climate becomes increasingly continental eastward, while precipitation diminishes, with a long, cold, almost snowless winter and a short, mild summer.

Hydroelectric power of Central Siberia

The rivers are numerous, swift, and full of rapids, providing sources of energy complementing the rich deposits of lead and iron ores, nephelines, and coal. The Irkutsk and Bratsk hydroelectric power plants on the Angara River, which flows northwest from Lake Baikal, and the Ust-Ilimsk hydroelectric power plant, which, though not completed, began generating power in 1974, augur well for the future development of the Russian S.F.S.R.

To the north of the Central Siberian Plateau extends the Taymyr Depression. The Byrranga Mountains—an isolated, compact upland some 1,800 feet (550 metres) high—break into separate ridges near the Laptev Sea, in the east. In the southwestern Taymyr Depression are deposits of copper, nickel, and rare-earth metals.

Southern Siberia's mountains, which include the Altai, Salair, Kuznets Alatau, Sayan, and Stanovoy ranges, are part of the belt forming the southern border of the Soviet Union and average 1,100 feet (335 metres). The climate is sharply continental, January temperatures averaging −13° F (−25° C), with mild summers. Intermontane basins receive about six inches in precipitation; the windward western slopes gather 60–80 inches (1,500–2,000 millimetres). The region contains the sources of the Ob, Yenisey, and Lena rivers as well as Lake Baikal, the deepest lake in the world. Soil and vegetation vary greatly: a widespread mountain-taiga belt, with subalpine and alpine meadows and mountain tundras in the high mountains, steppes in the intermontane hollows and foothills, and semideserts in the south.

The greatest elevations are in the Altai Mountains, particularly the Katun, where Mt. Belukha, the highest point in the entire Asiatic Russian S.F.S.R., rises 14,783 feet (4,506 metres). Snow and glaciers cover the peaks—numbering more than 1,000—all year.

In the intermontane hollows are steppes: Uymon, Abay, and Kansk, the highest of which, at around 6,000 feet (1,830 metres), are reminiscent of the deserts of neighbouring Mongolia. The soil, vegetation, and animal life differ with altitude, though mountain taiga vegetation predominates.

The Altai Mountains are crossed by rivers that, with their rapids, are large reserves of energy. Near Mt. Belukha is the source of the Katun River, which joins the Biya to form the Ob. There are more than 3,500 mountain lakes, the principal being Lake Telets.

Extreme climate of the Tuva Trough

To the east of the Altai stretch the Zapadny Sayan (West Sayan) Mountains, well broken up, and on the border with the Mongolian People's Republic are the broad Tannu-Ola Mountains. Between them is the Tuva Trough, at about 2,000 to 3,000 feet (600–900 metres) above sea level. The climate here is harshly continental—severe winters with little snow, and hot, dry summers. To the northwest of the Altai and Sayan mountains extend three nearly parallel ranges: the Salair Ridge, Vostochny Sayan (Eastern Sayan), and Kuznets Alatau. In the west of this latter chain is the Kuznetsk Basin, or Kuzbass, where high-quality coal is mined. In the east is the Minusinsk Basin, an important agricultural region. The Sayan-Shushenskoye hydropower station, one of the world's largest, is being developed there, along with a number of power-consuming industrial plants. By the end of the 1970s the region is expected to be well developed industrially and agriculturally.

The Baikal area. The Cisbaikalia area, west of Lake Baikal, and Transbaikalia, east of it, lie between Southern Siberia's mountains and the Central Siberian Plateau on the west and the Yakutsk Basin on the north. The climate is harshly continental—hot, dry summers and severe, almost snowless winters. Annual precipitation is only eight to 12 inches (200–300 millimetres), occurring chiefly in short spring cloudbursts.

Through the Yakutsk Basin, surrounded by mountains, pass the Middle Lena as well as the Lower Vilyuy and Aldan rivers. Again the climate is harshly continental, with winter temperatures reaching −76° F (−60° C) and a short, dry, hot summer. Annual precipitation is less than 16 inches (400 millimetres).

Northeastern Siberia. Northeastern Siberia is the area east of the Lena River and west of the Kolyma Mountains. Moderately high mountain ranges alternate with vast plateaus, such as the Alazeya and Yukagir, and swampy lowlands, such as those of Yana–Indigirka and Kolyma. The highest ranges—the Verkhoyansk, Chersky, Sarychev, and Suntar-Khayata—reach more than 10,000 feet (3,000 metres).

The climate of the region is, once more, harshly continental, January's temperature sometimes sinking to −94° F (−70° C). The summer is moderately warm, except in maritime and extremely mountainous parts, with an average July temperature of 63° F (17° C) in the south. The Yana, Indigirka, and Kolyma rivers belong to the Arctic Basin.

Lichen tundra, forest tundra, and thin forests predominate in the north, sparse mountain-taiga larch forests in the south.

The swampy, lake-studded East Siberian Lowland extends along the shores of the East Siberian and Laptev seas. The Anadyr Plain, extending in a broadening path to the Bering Sea, never rises above 660 feet (200 metres). The extreme eastern part is occupied by the Chukchi Highlands, covered with mountain tundra and cedar.

Northeastern Siberia has an extremely severe climate, wide expanses of mountain tundra, and extreme permafrost (up to 2,000 feet [600 metres] deep); possesses large deposits of gold and tin; and is still remarkably little settled. Its indigenous peoples, like those of much of the less developed regions of Siberia, retain a vigorous folk culture with roots deep in antiquity.

(S.A.V./R.He.)

The people. Before the large-scale influx of Russians from in the mid-17th century on, Siberia was inhabited by a large number of ethnic groups, most of them very small. The culture of these peoples was adapted to the natural and climatic conditions of three major zones: a fringe of arid or semi-arid steppe on the south; a wide forested belt in the middle; and, along the northern edge, a band of tundra subject to permafrost and with numerous tidal rivers and lakes. In the south were pastoral nomads with herds of sheep and horses. In the forest areas lived hunters and gatherers of wild foods. Most of the latter groups kept some reindeer of a large and sturdy breed for purposes of transport and occasionally milked them but consumed them as food only in case of absolute necessity. The nomads of the northern tundra kept fairly large herds of domestic reindeer, which provided them with their principal means of sustenance and which they drove along fixed routes according to the season. Other parts of the tundra were inhabited by still more primitive nomadic groups who hunted wild reindeer and fished. Finally, the shores of the Arctic Ocean and of the Sea of Okhotsk were settled by groups of maritime hunters living off whales, walruses, and seals.

Hunters, gatherers, and nomads

Agriculture was unknown in Siberia until the beginning of massive Russian colonization in the mid-17th century, and it is even now possible only on the West Siberian plain (Omskaya, Tomskaya, Kemerovskaya, and Novosibirskaya *oblasti* [regions]) as well as in a relatively few favoured locations in other places—the Khabarovsky and Primorsky (Maritime) *kraya* (territories), for example. Animal husbandry—dairy farming, beef cattle, and the raising of the Siberian stag, or maral, for meat—is more widely distributed. The Yakuts, who are the largest indigenous ethnic group, are raisers of cattle and horses; they represent an incursion of Central Asian pastoral nomads into the northern Siberian environment.

The indigenous population of Siberia before the coming of Europeans was divided into a large number of usually small ethnic groups, the boundaries between which shifted over time and were often arbitrary. The important social unit under Siberian conditions was probably not the tribe but the clan. Instances are known in which members of the same clan belonged to two or even three different tribes but considered themselves bound to each other by clan obligations in respect of marriage and mutual aid. The Siberian ethnic groups belong to a number of different linguistic stocks, the most important of which are: Turkic (Yakut, Siberian Tatars, and a number of small groups along the southern fringe); Manchu-Tungus (the numerous and widely scattered groups of Evenks and Lamuts); Finno-Ugric (Khanty [Ostyaks], Mansi [Voguls]); Mongolic (Buryats); and the so-called Paleosiberian family (Koryaks, Yukaghirs, Gilyaks [Nivkhi], and some others) consisting of a number of languages that do not fit elsewhere but whose interrelationship has yet to be demonstrated. The shifting and fluid nature of ethnic boundaries resulted in parts of one tribe often engaging in types of economic activity and assuming other cultural patterns characteristic of another tribe. Hence the older ethnographic sources frequently speak of "Yukaghirized Tungus" or the like. Such assimilated groups often acquired a different name from either the main body of their former tribe or from the one to which they were assimilated.

Traditional social organization. Except for the Yakuts, who are considered by Soviet scholars to have been in a stage of incipient feudalism at the time of the first intensive European contact, the Siberian peoples were without exception small, extremely primitive, and loosely organized. The major organizational unit over large parts of the year was the camp group, similar in constitution to the horde among the Australian Aborigines in that it consisted of a core of members of one descent group, with the addition of women from other groups and some male hangers-on. The overall kinship pattern was patrilineal, but Russian and Soviet scholars have identified numerous phenomena that, in their opinion, show the previous existence of a matrilineal pattern. These phenomena include not only the kinship terminology itself but also important elements in the religion, such as the fact that the shaman wore modified female dress and had in certain respects a hermaphrodite personality. The camp group cooperated in economic activity on a regular basis and controlled the important economic resources. The concept of private property in the Western sense was lacking, except among the Yakuts and in regard to domestic reindeer.

Kinship patterns

Social stratification was rudimentary, with one significant exception. For administrative convenience, the Russian authorities appointed certain members of the local ethnic groups to represent these groups in dealings with the Russians. These individuals, referred to in the Russian sources as "princelings," gained opportunities for enrichment and came to form a kind of incipient nobility. In addition, Soviet scholars point to the existence, just prior to the Revolution, of individuals who controlled large herds of reindeer and who could call upon the services of their poorer fellow clansmen—that is, people who were on their way to becoming feudal lords. It is difficult to determine from the sources whether this development was the result of a natural evolution or was due entirely to Russian contact.

As among primitive peoples, the nuclear family (parents and children) among the Siberian tribes was not clearly separated out in its economic and child-rearing functions from the larger kin group. Children were introduced early to economic activities and were taught the basic skills by older relatives. The same skills were also inculcated by special games and contests, some of which are still being used for the same purposes. Such games were a common feature of the rites of passage for both boys and girls. The professions of shaman and blacksmith, which were the only separate professions among most Siberian groups, were acquired by apprenticeship to older practitioners, but these professions called in addition for evidence of special aptitude and election on the part of the apprentice.

Traditional technology and economy. The technology and applied art of the Siberian peoples relied heavily on such materials as horn, mammoth ivory, wood, and the skins of birds, mammals, and fish. The latter were processed in various ways and either tailored into garments or used whole as containers. Iron was obtained by trade with groups close to the sources of supply in the south, or with the Russians. The smelting of iron from ore was unknown, but some groups used a small portable forge to produce such items as smoking pipes (from old gun barrels), stands for storing women's jewelry, and various pieces of harness. The standard weapons before the introduction of firearms were the bow and arrow and barbed spear with a head of mammoth or walrus ivory. The bow in common use was compound, since the wood available was not in sufficiently large pieces to permit the making of a simple bow. Fire was made by the bow-drill method, in which a shaft was spun in a socket by means of tightly wound cords, friction igniting the tinder. In addition to the skin containers mentioned above, many Siberian groups made vessels of wood or birch bark decorated with natural colouring in intricate patterns. Pots for cooking were made of metal and were bought from the Russians. The same was true of small griddles, which were used for preparing unflavoured pancakes of wheat flour; these were considered a delicacy. Clothing was made of cured skins with or without the fur and was elaborately decorated. In certain areas capes and boots were made from fishskin, processed so as to be waterproof. Skins were also used to cover boats and to make bags for clothing and small pieces of equipment.

Aboriginal hunting methods included the use of nets made out of rawhide strips in which reindeer became tangled, to be dispatched with spears. Another favourite device of the reindeer hunter was a movable blind behind which a hunter on skis concealed himself, shooting through a small hole. Nets of rawhide, gut, or string were used for fishing, along with hooks and lines similar to those used by the European peoples.

Means of transport were adapted to the tundra or forest environments: sleds drawn by dog teams, with runners of walrus ivory or metal, sleighs drawn by reindeer, skis, snowshoes, and riding reindeer. In the summer, boats, either of birch bark or covered with skins, were important.

Types of dwellings

Dwellings were generally portable and made of poles and skins, or (among the more southerly groups) of poles covered with brush and a layer of sod. These latter dwellings were of semi-dugout form. A distinctive type of house was the *balagan,* constructed on runners and moved by means of reindeer. Finally, the maritime sea mammal hunters had more or less permanent dwellings the structures of which were supported on the rib bones of whales. Such houses are very ancient, going back to Paleolithic times.

With the gradual exploration and conquest of Siberian territory by the Russians, various changes took place in the economy of the native peoples. The introduction of firearms, steel spring traps, metal utensils, and the like, led to more efficient hunting and fishing technology. The native peoples were drawn into the ambit of the fur trade and were subject to a special tax, first in furs and later in money. The effect of European contact at this stage, however, was limited and did not affect the basis of the subsistence economy. Other than hunting equipment and supplies needed for the fur trade, only luxury goods—vodka, tobacco, cloth, salt, sugar, tea, and flour in very small quantities—reached the native inhabitants through the trade network.

Religious belief and practice. The religious system of the Siberian peoples was firmly anchored to their subsistence activities. The central figure of their religious life, at least as far as the society as a whole was concerned, was the shaman, who acted as intermediary between the natural and supernatural worlds. The shaman was at once a physician, a counsellor of the community in regard to subsistence activities, and a defender of it by magical means against the attacks of other groups. The shamanistic ritual was embellished with the full skills of the shaman in poetry, song, ventriloquism, and magic. The ritual took the form of a dramatic representation of the shaman's journey to the world of the spirits and his return.

The mythical world of the Siberian peoples was conceived of as being on three levels, which were connected either by a "world tree" or by a river, or both (the parallel with ancient Norse mythology is striking). The position of shaman was acquired through a "call," usually during adolescence, that was manifested through a peculiar illness from which the victim could only recover by agreeing to assume the role of shaman. Certain characteristics of a shaman—his hermaphrodite personality, for example, and the fact that he was thought to have organs other than the natural ones implanted in his body—have close parallels among other primitive peoples in widely scattered parts of the world and even in the residual religious phenomena found in more complex societies.

Besides the rites and ceremonies performed by the shaman on behalf of the group at large or of individuals, there were also private ceremonies conducted by individuals in connection with hunting and fishing activities or with important milestones in personal life. On such occasions, the shaman was often not present—perhaps because his participation would have involved an additional expense.

Traditional arts. The folklore of the Siberian peoples includes an origin myth, shamanistic songs, proverbs, and some rudimentary epics. Many groups have a rich tradition of graphic art, in terms both of sculpture in the round and incised drawing on mammoth or walrus ivory. The assortment of musical instruments is meagre: besides the drum (or more accurately tambourine) used by the shaman and as an accompaniment for dancing, there are only a small Jew's harp of wood and metal and a few bone and reed pipes. Some of the Far Eastern peoples have primitive stringed instruments, the idea of which was apparently borrowed from the Chinese people.

Early Russian influence

Russian cultural influence (apart from the mere availability of Western trade goods) was present in various places but was neither universal nor profound. On the southern fringes of the Siberian area—on the Altai upland and in the vicinity of Lake Baikal—there were considerable settlements of Russian peasants, and the native population had begun to acquire agricultural skills. Certain groups—some of them, like the Yakuts, fairly large—had been nominally Christianized, and a few individuals attended schools sponsored by the Russian Orthodox Church. Western medicine was available in a few places, but the mortality rate remained extremely high, especially among children. A factor the importance of which was certainly considerable was the tsarist government's policy of exiling political dissidents to remote areas. This affected the type of Russians with whom the native population in many places came into contact. In addition, there were long-established Russian peasant societies in certain parts of Siberia, in many cases the descendants of exiled religious dissidents. Such people, known as Sibiryaks or "local Russians," have a culture and an outlook differing markedly from those of the people of European Russia. Physical and cultural hybridization with the native population has given rise to a wide range of intermediate groups, some of which still retain their own ethnic identity.

Contemporary Siberian peoples. After the Revolution of 1917, the Soviet government adopted in principle the goal of comprehensive economic and social development of the Siberian area. Approximately the first 15 years subsequent to the Revolution were devoted chiefly to exploration and planning, and the area was exempted from the requirements of the first five-year plan for the development of the Soviet national economy. Considerable progress was made in education and public health, but these measures were of limited effectiveness among the peoples whose way of life had been and remained nomadic. Institutions such as the Northern Division of the Leningrad Institute of Living Eastern Languages (established in 1926 and later transformed into the Institute of the Peoples of the North), however, performed an important function, despite the very small numbers of persons involved, in training the first professional cadres of physicians, paramedical workers, and teachers for the northern peoples.

During the 1920s and early 1930s, the languages of a number of small Siberian peoples were reduced to writing for the first time, and elementary school books were published in these languages. In connection with this and other practical tasks, a considerable amount of ethnographic research was undertaken. The publication of books in the languages of some very small groups, and instruction in these languages in the elementary schools, were later abandoned as being uneconomical, or as working counter to the general policy goal of integration of the population of the Soviet Union into a single and unified whole.

Until the end of World War II, however, the basic economic patterns of Siberian native life remained largely unchanged. Collectivization of the hunting, fishing, and reindeer economies (agriculture had been collectivized in the rest of the country during the early 1930s) was hardly even attempted until the end of World War II in most areas, or until the early 1950s in the more remote places. Small cooperative production units of a traditional type, using the native technology and often based on kinship groups, had existed up to that time but represented no sharp break with the pre-Revolutionary situation.

The Soviet policy and practice with regard to the peoples of the Siberian North represent a unique experiment in the integration of small, primitive, formerly tribal groups into a complex modern industrial state. The severity of the climate and the former backwardness of the people, both in a social and a technological sense, are such stubborn factors in the story of cultural change that no serious student of the Soviet Union can fail to admire what has been achieved, notwithstanding serious shortcomings in the planning and implementation of government policy.

Indigenous population and ethnic affiliation

In surveying the present situation, a few statistics are in order. According to 1979 census data, there are 158,000 indigenous peoples of the North, Siberia, and the Far East (as against 151,000 in 1970). Native language may be used as an index of ethnic affiliation: in 1979, 61.7 percent of these peoples considered the language of their nationality to be their native language (67.4 percent in 1970). In addition, 54 percent were fluent in Russian, and 5.2 percent were fluent in the language of another nationality. There are 26 ethnic groups, all increasing in size, a change from the pre-Revolutionary situation in which most were dying out. There has been a consistent attempt throughout the Soviet period to foster ethnic awareness among the Siberian peoples, even, in some cases, when the awareness had to be created. "National in form, socialist in content" was the slogan created by Soviet premier Joseph Stalin to describe the kind of culture the regime thought appropriate for the Soviet system, and even though Stalin has been discredited, the idea still remains.

Particularly since World War II, the Siberian peoples have been developing under conditions of unprecedented industrialization, almost all of it with labour and tools imported from European Russia. The total population of the Soviet North has risen to 3,000,000. Well into the 1960s, however, the small peoples of the North were predominantly rural, and even urban residency was likely to mean that the family had moved into a large fishing cooperative, or that many young people were away attending school, where for the most part they became doctors, teachers, and cultural or government workers. In some instances the large-scale influx of Europeans has irreparably damaged the traditional way of life of the Siberian peoples, not least because educated young people are unwilling and often physically unable by training or capacities to carry on the occupations of their forefathers. Technological means exist by which reindeer can be herded and waters fished more easily, but the skill to operate and maintain the equipment must be acquired, not, as previously, within the family group but in schools of a radically different type. Change of this type has been slow in coming to the North but will increase in proportion to capital investment in the area.

Soviet policy for the peoples of the Siberian North, particularly with respect to education, faces a dilemma that in the long run is inescapable. This dilemma can be baldly stated as follows: to dismantle the traditional economy, turn the small peoples into an industrial labour force, and supply the North completely from the outside, or to develop the traditional economy and pursue the industrialization of the North exclusively with an imported labour force. No clear choice has yet been made between these two alternatives, and the result is that the educational system is ill-adapted to either one. It goes without saying that if the first alternative is chosen, there will soon be little left of the traditional culture of the small Siberian peoples, and the slogans that have been prevalent up to now will lose their meaning.

Which elements of native Siberian culture can be expected to survive industrialization, urbanization, and the changes in status which accompany them? Certain aspects of material culture will certainly persist for many years to come—native clothing, for example, which is warmer than present synthetics and more readily available. Kinship ties will continue to be important, although the increasing number of mixed marriages may alter the traditional patterns. Other elements of the native culture will have to be nurtured, perhaps artificially. In 1970, for example, there was the premiere of the first Kamchadal (Itelmen) ballet, *Emem Kutkh,* based on a Kamchadal legend of a battle between good and evil and staged in Petropavlovsk-Kamchatsky; the ballet was subsequently sent on tour to the Mongolian People's Republic. The Kamchatka Kamchadals (also called Itelmen) numbered 1,400 by the 1979 census. It should be noted that aside from the ballet's value as an example of Soviet cultural policy, the theme itself is universal enough to appeal to a wide variety of people. Ideally, the unique culture of the Siberian peoples will not be lost but will blend with and enrich Soviet culture as a whole. (S.P.D./E.D.D.)

HISTORY

Early history. It is still not established whether humans came to Siberia from Europe or from Central and Eastern Asia. The earliest Paleolithic finds, in the Altai area of Southern Siberia, are of the Mousterian type. Finds of the later Paleolithic Period are numerous and are concentrated, apart from the Altai area, along the upper reaches of the Yenisey (the Minusinsk Basin) and near Lake Baikal. The Neolithic Period has been mainly studied in two areas: near Lake Baikal, which was then the centre of a hunting culture stretching from the Yenisey to the middle reaches of the Amur; and along the lower Amur and the Pacific coast, where a totally different fishing culture existed, connected with Manchuria, China, and Korea. About 2000 BC the inhabitants of the Altai–Minusinsk area first began to make use of copper. The people of this culture were of the Europoid race, while those living to the east and to the north were predominantly Mongoloid. Soon the tribes of the Baikal–Lena area, who are regarded as the ancestors of the Paleo-Asiatic Yukaghir, also started using copper and bronze—possibly under Chinese influence—though they remained primarily hunters. They were later partly displaced and partly assimilated by the Tungus tribes, which, coming from the Amur area, sprad over a vast territory in Eastern Siberia and probably brought with them the use of reindeer. The bronze culture that centred in the Altai–Minusinsk area and reached as far west as the Urals shows not only a further development of animal husbandry but also the beginnings of agriculture. The working of bronze was stimulated by the existence of rich local ores and attained high technological and artistic levels.

Chinese influence

About 1000 BC Chinese influence began to be felt. Subject to strong influences from China and Central Asia, Southern Siberia developed rapidly both economically and politically, while the Paleo-Asiatic and Tungus tribes of the northern forests and tundra lagged far behind. In the 7th–2nd century BC the Minusinsk Basin was the home of an advanced sedentary culture involving complicated systems of irrigation developed by the people who are tentatively identified as the Ting-Ling of the Chinese chronicles; they were the first users of iron in Siberia. The rest of Southern Siberia was at this time inhabited by nomadic tribes, probably Iranian (Scythian) in the west, belonging to the large belt of similar cultures stretching from the steppes north of the Black Sea to Mongolia and characterized by the "animal style" of ornamentation. The famous Pazyryk burial mounds of the Altai area, on the right bank of the Bolshoy Ulagan River, show strong signs of Persian influence.

From the 3rd century BC the whole of Southern Siberia belonged in turn to the Turkic–Mongol Huns and to the various Turkic states centred in Mongolia. From the 6th century AD, when the local Altaic Turks established their khanate, the Turks also predominated ethnically, partly assimilating the neighbouring Samoyed and partly driving them north. The central part of Southern Siberia, around the Minusinsk Basin, was the home of the Kirgiz, ancestors of the present-day Khakass and Altaic peoples as well as of the Kirgiz of Contral Asia. Farther east, in the Baikal area, lived the Kurykans, perhaps the ancestors of the Yakuts, while the steppes of northern Kazakhstan were inhabited by the nomadic Kipchaks (Kumans), who later became the chief ethnic component of the Kazakh people. From the 10th century the Turks were overpowered by the Mongols, whose states, however, remained unstable until the creation of the great Mongol Empire by Genghis Khan. Almost the whole of Siberia was incorporated into this empire, at least nominally. The primitive peoples in the far north were scarcely affected, but for the comparatively high civilization of Southern Siberia the Mongol conquest had fatal consequences. The larger part of Siberia belonged to the domain of Genghis Khan himself, but Western Siberia was included in the domain of his son, Jöchi, and commonly known as the Golden Horde. The Mongol conquest strengthened the Turkic element in the Ob River area, hitherto predominantly Ugrian, where the Turks later became known as Siberian Tatars. They were the dominant element in the Sibir khanate that emerged after the breakup of the Golden Horde in the mid-15th century.

Russian colonization (1581–1890). Siberia is first mentioned in Russian sources in the 11th century, and from the 12th century the merchants of Novgorod traded with the tribes of the lower Ob area, the main attraction being furs. In 1581 a small band of Cossacks under Ermak Timofeyevich, a mercenary in the service of the Stroganov family (merchants who had large property in the western Urals), undertook an expedition to Western Siberia and within a year conquered the Siberian khanate. From then on, the opening up and annexation of Siberia by the Russians proceeded rapidly. Small Cossack units, using the river systems of the Ob, Yenisey, and Lena, spread throughout the whole of Northern Siberia and parts of the south, establishing fortified towns in strategic positions (Tyumen in 1585, Tobolsk in 1587, Tomsk in 1604, Kuznetsk in 1617, Krasnoyarsk in 1628, Yakutsk in 1632, Okhotsk on the Pacific coast in 1649, Albazino [Albazin] on the Amur in 1651, and Irkutsk in 1652) and imposing their administration upon the surrounding areas for the purpose of collecting tribute for Muscovy. There was a major reverse in the Amur area, where the Russian advance met with Chinese resistance; and, according to the Treaty of Nerchinsk in 1689, most of the area was declared Chinese, though in fact it remained a no-man's-land between Russia and China.

Cossack conquest

Kamchatka Peninsula was annexed in 1699, but only by the Aigun and Peking treaties in 1858 and 1860, respectively, did China renounce all claims to the Amur area and the Pacific coast between the mouth of the Amur and Korea. In the southwest the khan of the Kazakh Middle Hundred exchanged Dzungarian (Kalmyk) suzerainty for Russian in 1740, and the Altai area was annexed in 1756, when the Dzungarian state, to which it had belonged since the breakup of the Mongol Empire, passed under Chinese rule.

Cossack officers, Muscovite officials, monks, and merchants were the first Russian explorers of Siberia, and the Cossack Semen Dezhnev was the first to sail through the Bering Straits in 1648. The exploration was put on a systematic and more scientific basis in the 18th century, when the Russian Academy of Sciences organized several expeditions, mainly to northern Siberia and the Far East. In the 19th century, the task of studying Siberia's physical and human geography was largely taken over by the Imperial Russian Geographical Society.

The administration of annexed Siberia was directed by the Siberian office in Moscow (later in St. Petersburg) from 1614 until 1763. Several provinces were formed during the 18th century, and, as a result of the administrative reform of 1822 prepared by Count M.M. Speransky, two governors general were appointed: one for Eastern Siberia with his seat in Irkutsk and another for Western Siberia with his seat first in Tobolsk and then, from 1838, in Omsk. The Western Siberian provinces of Tobolsk and Tomsk were in 1882 exempted from the jurisdiction of the governor general in Omsk, who retained authority only over the Kazakh steppe. Finally, a viceroy was appointed in 1884 for the newly annexed territories in the Far East together with the old Russian possessions on the Pacific coast.

At first Russian economic activity was limited to the collection of tribute, which was paid by the local inhabitants in furs as it had been paid to the Mongols; Siberian furs were one of the main assets of the Muscovite state's trade with western Europe. Russian agricultural colonization on a small scale went on parallel with the military occupation in the late 16th century and throughout the 17th, however, its primary aim being to feed the military and administrative personnel. An extensive network of stagecoach and mail routes was developed by the government, and many settlers were employed in this service.

Mining and industry

Silver mining on a small scale was started in 1698, and in the next century two important industrial areas developed in Siberia: the Altai, where silver and copper were mined and smelted; and the Nerchinsk area in Transbaikalia (Zabaykalye), with silver and lead mining. With the decline of the fur trade, mining became the main economic activity in Siberia, the principal entrepreneurs being the state and the imperial household. The supply of labour was largely guaranteed by a system of bondage that tied workers permanently to the mines and metal plants. Forced labour by convicts was also persistently practiced by the government, though it was highly unproductive and many convicts managed to escape, usually to become bandits. Gold mining, in contrast, which developed in many areas from the 1830s, was mainly in the hands of private enterprise employing free labour.

The emergence of an indigenous class of industrialists and the banishment to Siberia of large numbers of revolutionary intellectuals (beginning with the Dekabrists in 1826 and participants of the Polish insurrection of 1830–31) combined to produce a small but vocal Siberian intelligentsia and the development of a Siberian regional consciousness. The regionalists demanded the removal of all discriminatory measures arising from Siberia's colonial status, with regional self-government.

Many indigenous Siberian peoples had resisted Russian conquest, but resistance was not great except, briefly, from the Buryats and, for a much longer period, from the most warlike and least accessible of the Siberian peoples, the Chukchi, who considered themselves independent until they were subdued in the 1930s. The impact of the Russians upon the indigenous peoples was two-fold. The smaller and more primitive tribes succumbed to exploitation by merchants and corrupt officials, to poverty, and to diseases brought by the colonists. On the other hand, larger peoples such as the Yakuts, Buryats, and Kazakhs adjusted themselves to the new situation and began to profit from the material benefits of the colonization. The internal institutions and way of life of the indigenous peoples were generally not interfered with by the Russian authorities, and there was remarkable religious tolerance, which led to the spread in the 17th and 18th centuries of Buddhism among the Buryats and Islām among the Kazakhs, while most of the other peoples became at least nominally Christian.

The Trans-Siberian Railroad

The modern period. The great event that marked the transition of Siberia (with its vast natural resources) from a traditionalist to a modern economy was the construction of the Trans-Siberian Railroad. The original line was begun at both ends, at Chelyabinsk and at Vladivostok, in 1891 and was completed in 1905. It facilitated the influx of new colonists, first in connection with the construction itself, then under the colonization plan introduced by P.A. Stolypin, president of the Council of Ministers, to reduce the rural overpopulation in European Russia. Siberian agriculture, which had never known peasant serfdom or large private estates, quickly developed American-type farming methods, specializing in grain and, particularly, in butter, the production and marketing of which were largely in the hands of cooperatives. Coal mining was started in several places along the line to supply the needs of the railway, and the railway repair shops were the first engineering plants in Siberia.

Siberia took an active part in both the 1905 and 1917 revolutions, and events of the Russian Civil War there were most dramatic. An autonomous Siberian government was formed after the overthrow of the Soviet power in the region early in 1918 but was soon superseded by the government of Adm. Aleksandr Vasiliyevich Kolchak, in Omsk, who was proclaimed the supreme ruler of Russia by the leaders of the "White" armies. After the defeat of Kolchak, the Far Eastern Republic was set up in 1920 in the area east of Lake Baikal as a buffer state between Soviet Russia and Japan; in reality, however, this was one of the first "people's democracies" and was incorporated into the Soviet state as soon as the Japanese interventionists left Vladivostok in 1922. Indigenous authorities set up by the Kazakhs, Buryats, and Yakuts during the Civil War were suppressed, and several ostensibly autonomous republics and regions were established instead with the purpose of remolding the population's way of life according to the general Soviet pattern.

Industrial development, interrupted by revolution and civil war, was resumed during the First Five-Year Plan period (1928–32), when the Ural–Kuznetsk coal-mining and iron-and-steel combine was built in southwestern Siberia, largely by the forced labour of deported peasants. Forced-labour camps spread throughout Siberia during the 1930s, the most important being the Dalstroy (Far Eastern Construction Trust) system in the extreme northeast and the Norilsk area on the lower Yenisey, both concerned with the mining of nonferrous and precious metals. World War II gave new impetus to industrial development; many enterprises were evacuated from the west, and Sibera, together with the Urals, became the industrial backbone of the Soviet war effort.

Agriculture, on the contrary, suffered greatly from collectivization in 1930–33 and was largely neglected until the Virgin Lands Campaign of 1954–56, when the southwest of Siberia (including northern Kazakhstan) was the principal area to be cultivated together with areas in the Minusinsk Basin and the Far East.

During the late 1950s and 1960s major industrial developments took place, notably the opening up of large oil and gas fields in West Siberia, centred on Surgut, and the construction of a series of giant hydroelectric stations—such as at Bratsk and Ust-Ilim on the Angara, Krasnoyarsk and Sayan on the Yenisey, and Novosibirsk on the Ob. A network of gas and oil pipelines was built between the new fields and the Urals and eastward to Angarsk. Mining of lignite near Kansk and Achinsk and of diamonds in Yakutiya was developed. New industries were established, such as aluminum and cellulose pulp-making at Bratsk. The Trans-Siberian Railroad was electrified as far east as Lake Baikal. Nevertheless, during the late 20th century, migration out of Siberia and the Urals was considerable, and population growth was slow. At the same time, the late decades saw a tense political situation with China over boundary disputes, culminating occasionally in minor armed clashes along the Ussuri River. (S.V.U.)

Russian Steppe

The Russian steppes are vast, open, treeless expanses of predominantly grassy, drought-resistant vegetation on rich chernozem (black earth) and chestnut-brown soils. They extend across Eurasia in a vast wedge, running over the south of the Soviet Union from the southernmost part of the Moldavian S.S.R. across the southern Ukraine, the Don Basin, northern Caucasia, the Volga Basin below the Kama confluence, the lowlands north of the Caspian Sea, and northern Kazakhstan into southwestern Siberia, beyond which—east of the Altai—they break up among the mountains. Covering an area of about 1,400,000 square miles (3,500,000 square kilometres), they have been of immense importance in the historical and economic development of a huge area and have been a constant theme in Russian literature and art.

PHYSICAL AND HUMAN GEOGRAPHY

The land. Those parts of the steppe that escaped glaciation during the early Quaternary Period of the Cenozoic Era (2,500,000 years before present [BP]) are mostly covered with loose carbonaceous rock loesses (soft porous rocks of a pale yellowish or buff colour) and loess-like loam. These deposits, together with the absence of forests and the presence of occasional torrential rain, have contributed to the formation of a water-eroded relief. Within the river valleys, which are wide and asymmetrical, some two to four terraces may often form, of which the lowest are usually of sand.

Relief

The plateaus between the rivers are also asymmetrical and are interrupted by ravines through which water flows only during the spring thaw and summer storms. In many places the steep sides of both valleys and ravines are scoured by recent gullies, the majority of which occur in the highlands rising successively west of the Dnepr, west of the Don, and west of the Volga. (In order to limit the spread of gullies, which reduce the economically exploitable potential of the steppe lands, trees have been planted and grass has been sown on them; grazing has been restricted, and surface water has been drained.)

Shallow interfluvial areas are spotted with round depressions, or "steppe saucers"; caused by subterranean collapse, they rarely exceed six feet (two metres) in depth but are generally more than five times (and sometimes even 50 or more times) this measure in diameter. In the Ukrainian steppes nearest to the Black Sea, larger depressions, *pody*, are found. Between the depressions the country is drained by long, winding channels with shallowly slanting sides—the products of superficial erosion. Sometimes the uniformity of the interfluvial area's relief is broken by mounds—barrows or lookout points that reach a height of from 16 to 20 feet—or by erosion-denudation residual outcrops. Rather less conspicuous are the little mounds thrown up by burrowing marmots.

Topographic saucers and mounds

Drainage. The rivers are fed mostly by snow. They overflow their banks during the spring thaw and in summer become very shallow. A high rate of evaporation reduces river flow to insignificance. The network of rivers is not dense, and those belonging properly to the steppe (as distinct from those rising outside, such as the Volga and the Ob) are shallow; the Don, with a length of 1,160 miles (1,856 kilometres) and a catchment area of 163,000 square miles (422,000 square kilometres), has an average discharge of only 33,000 cubic feet (935 cubic metres) per second at low water.

Climate. The climate is continental, with warm, sunny summers, fairly cold winters in the east, and milder winters in the west, with a stable but shallow covering of snow. Temperatures for July are about 70° F and 75° F (21° C and 24° C), while those of January are wider ranging, −22° F (−30° C) in the east, 28° F (−2° C) in the west. Most precipitation takes the form of snow. Toward the end of winter the snow cover of the Ukrainian steppe and that of northern Caucasia is from four to eight inches deep—though it may reach from eight to 16 inches or even 19 inches (200 to 400 or 480 millimetres) elsewhere—and drops sharply over the trans-Bailkalian steppe. Rainfall is comparatively sparse, with 18–24 inches (460–610 millimetres) of rain in the northwest and ten to 12 inches (250–300 millimetres) in the southwest. It is heaviest at the end of spring and at the beginning of summer. The degree of humidity varies. Every third year is arid, with strong dry winds blowing in spring and summer, and dust storms.

Plant and animal life. Among the turf grasses, of which the steppe is mainly composed, bunchgrass (*Stipa*), fescue (*Festuca*), bluegrass (*Poa*), and agropyron (*Agropyrum*) are most characteristic. Mixed perennial grasses include sage (*Salvia*), pinks (*Dianthus*), vetch (*Astralagus*), bedstraw (*Galium*), and yarrow (*Achillea*). Mosses are often found among the turf grasses, with lichens and blue-green algae also in the south. Annual and perennial plants with a short vegetational period occur—particularly in the south. Grassy plants of various species, collectively known to the Soviet people as *perekati-pole,* take on a spherical brushwood shape with their seasonal maturing; then, breaking off easily in the wind, they roll along the steppe to mass along the edges of the forests and ravines. Thick clumps of shrubs and bushes—including karageny, steppe cherry, blackthorn, dwarf almond, and spirea—occur in the steppes of the east European plain and in the foothills of the Urals and of the Altai.

Though to the north of the steppe a dry climate, saline soils, and proliferation of various grasses, and the uninterrupted relief discourage forests, they do sometimes occur on interfluvial plateaus and in complicated relation to expanses of meadow and grass. Most paleo-botanists and paleo-zoologists agree that the forest was advancing over the steppe before the advent of man and cite as evidence those studies that show that in postglacial times the boundary between forest and steppe was little changed and that their natural interrelation was disturbed by man, who, with axe, fire, and grazing cattle, was responsible for the destruction of many forested areas.

The advancing forest

The absence of natural shelter on the steppe conditions the kind of animals that inhabit it. Typical rodents include various types of marmot and other such burrowing animals and various species of mouse. The skunk, fox, and wolf are common—as was the tarpan (or small wild horse) until the second half of the 19th century. Antelopes are found in the south. The commonest birds are bustards, steppe eagles, steppe kestrels, larks, and gray partridges. Insects are many and various.

Types of steppe. The amount of moisture in the soil conditions both the composition and the structure of the steppe, so that, from north to south, marked changes in vegetation and soil occur.

This northern region of the steppe is humid and is characterized by a thick vegetation, mainly of thick grasses, and a solid or almost solid ground cover of soil. Forty or 50 different species of plants may be found in every 10-foot (three-metre) square. As the alternate masses of mixed grass bloom, the steppe repeatedly changes colour. In spring and early summer it begins to shade from lilac to golden yellow, then to pale blue, and finally to white. In late summer the burned-out steppe takes on a buff-coloured hue.

Steppe coloration

Tracts of forest break up the grass-meadow steppe along the floodplains and depressions, occurring also on the sandy areas and on outcrops of close-grained bedrock between the rivers. Under the grass meadows lie granular chernozems—soils rich in humus and in ash and very fertile. Around the saucer-like depressions de-alkalized, less fertile clays (de-alkalized solonetz) have formed by draining and leaching their silty upper layers. Meadow chernozem soils occur near underground water.

A drought-resistant variety in which clumps of grass or turf predominate, the grass steppe is characterized by feather grass (*stipa*), fescue, *Koeleria,* the perennial oat, and wheat grass. Ground cover is not continuous, and bare soil is visible between the clumps of grass. In the interfluvial areas, forests are extremely rare. (Tidal forests tend to proliferate in flood-river valleys or to spring up on the slopes and tops of gullies in times of flood.)

This most southern variety of steppe, ending in desert, abounds in drought-resistant shrubs and such herb species as *Artemisia, Kochia,* and *Matricaria.* Various species of bluegrass are also present, as are tulips. In general, vegetation is mainly sporadic, and various combinations of different species occur according to accidents of relief and soil (including irregular salinity). Chestnut-coloured soils, in which solonetz soils and meadow-chestnut soils are interspersed, predominate. (Their fertility is considerably lower than that of the chernozem and dark-chestnut soils.)

The nature of the steppe changes significantly from west to east. In the west, the East European Plain is characterized by an uninterrupted relief, a relatively mild climate, and little of the sage-and-grass vegetation common to the east. Feather grass and fescues predominate in the grass steppe, and oaks and broad-leaved species of tree dominate the forest. Soils are chernozems. Many species of animals and plants common to western Europe occur.

The steppe of eastern Kazakhstan and Western Siberia has a more complicated relief—flat lowlands typical of Western Siberia in the north, and in the south, low, rounded, isolated hills common to Kazakhstan—and a more continental climate. The vegetation, in general, resembles that of the East European Plain, but local Kazakh species of feather grass may also occur. Broadleaved trees appear less frequently than in the east, and island birch forests predominate. The proportion of rocky and alkaline soil increases, and the chernozems, though rich in humus, are shallow and unstable.

In Central and Eastern Siberia the Russian steppe gravitates toward the steppes of Mongolia. The climate is harsh, with winters in which little snow falls but which are characterized by sharp frosts that may last for several months. Average temperatures in January are about −22° F (−30° C). *Diplachne* and *Stipa capillata* are typical grasses, and in trans-Baikalia *Stipa capillata* and tansy also occur.

The economy. Mixed grass-and-meadow steppe and grass steppe have long served as the country's granary, for they produce most of the wheat, sugar beets, sunflowers, corn, millet, and cucurbitaceous (cucumber family) cultures, and to the west they support both horticulture and viticulture. Agricultural products include cattle, sheep, and poultry, and there is also horse breeding. To the west some 70 or 80 percent of the steppe has been tilled, and in Kazakhstan and Siberia all suitable land has been put to the plow. On sage-and-grass steppe less soil is tilled, but cattle and sheep are raised, horses are bred, and agriculture is pursued with the help of artificial irrigation. Windbreaks and strips of forest have been planted over wide areas to prevent soil erosion—particularly on the banks at the Don, Volga, and Ural rivers and on several interfluvial plateaus. Ponds and reservoirs have been built in ravines, and small river valleys and dams have been constructed across many rivers.

Agricultural products

Few natural expanses of mixed grass-and-meadow and grass steppe remain, save in the state national forests (the most important of which is the V.V. Alekhin Central Chernozem National Forest, south of Kursk) and on the shores of the Black Sea, where certain rare species of animals are also preserved. (F.N.M.)

HISTORY

The history of the Russian Steppe is found in the context of the separate article STEPPE. (Ed.)

WESTERN REPUBLICS

Belorussia

Lying in the western portion of the Soviet Union, the Belorussian (or Byelorussian) Soviet Socialist Republic (Belorussian S.S.R., or, more popularly, Belorussia, formerly often referred to in English as White Russia) combines a high density of settlement in its central portion with virtually unpeopled expanses of swamp and forest. One of the 15 constituent republics of the Soviet Union, the Belorussian S.S.R. was set up on January 1, 1919, in response to and counteraction against the Belorussian Democratic Republic, established and proclaimed independent on March 25, 1918.

On the northwest, the Belorussian S.S.R. adjoins the Latvian and Lithuanian S.S.R.'s; the Russian S.F.S.R. and the Ukrainian S.S.R. lie to the north and east and south, respectively, and the frontier with Poland is on the west. The total area of the republic is 80,200 square miles (207,600 square kilometres), or about half of the total area occupied primarily by Belorussians in the Soviet Union. Its capital, the ancient city of Minsk, is now the industrial powerhouse of the western Soviet Union.

PHYSICAL AND HUMAN GEOGRAPHY

Low relief

The land. *Relief.* Belorussia gives an impression of flat and sometimes monotonous landscapes, with extensive but low hilly tablelands alternating with plains and lowlands. The highest point, Dzerzhinsky (Dzyarzhynskaya; the spellings given in parentheses are Belorussian) Mountain, is only 1,135 feet (346 metres) above sea level, and the elevation of more than half of the republic is less than 330–660 feet (100–200 metres). In the north, gently sloping ridges formed from glacial debris are separated by lake-dotted lowlands. The largest of these ridges, the Belorussian Ridge (Belaruskaya Hrada), runs from the northwest into the centre of the republic, where it widens into the Minsk Upland (Minskaye Ŭzvyshsha), a region covered with sandy loam and light soils. The large Central Berezinskaya Plain (Tsentralna-Byarezinskaya Raŭnina) is well drained and suitable for agriculture.

In the southwest, along the Pripyat (Prypyats) River, there are tracts of marshy land known as the Belorussian Lowland (Belaruskaye Palesse) merging with the swampy Dnepr Lowland (Prydnyaproŭskaya Nizina) in the east (all of which, with adjoining areas in the Ukraine, are commonly called the Pripet Marshes in the West). The structural trough of the Belorussian Lowland collected meltwater from the glaciers of the Pleistocene Epoch together with great quantities of glacial outwash, which were deposited as sands, lake clays, etc. These deposits and the overall lack of relief caused the formation of the extensive swamps of southern Belorussia and adjoining areas of the Ukraine.

Drainage. Rivers and lakes, major features in the Belorussian S.S.R., are used for shipping, floating timber, and generating power. The streams number about 20,800, with a total length of about 56,300 miles (90,600 kilometres), and the lakes total about 10,800, mostly in the north. The southward-flowing Dnepr River and its tributaries—the Pripyat, Berezina (Byarezina), and Sozh—dominate; a small portion of the Bug drains the extreme southwest; and in the north and west, respectively, the Western Dvina and the Neman (Nyoman) flow to the Baltic. The largest lakes are Narach, 31 square miles (80 square kilometres), Osveyskoye (Asveyskaye), and Drisvyaty (Drysvyaty).

Soils. Swamp and marsh soils cover about 10 percent of the republic's surface; because these soils are very fertile when drained (having high contents of both phosphorus and decomposed organic matter), land reclamation has high priority with Belorussian agricultural planners. The largest part of the republic, about 60 percent, is a region of podzols, parts of which are still covered by the postglacial coniferous and mixed forests beneath which they formed. The best soils in the podzol zone for agricultural purposes are those of the Central Berezinskaya Plain and the region around Orsha and Mogilyov. Between the podzol and swamp soils in the south is a zone of sandy soils that are utilized principally in the cultivation of potatoes.

Plant and animal life. The forests known as *pushchy,* covering almost a third of the Belorussian S.S.R., not only are of exceptional importance in its economy but also lend variety and character to the flat relief. In the north, conifers abound, pine and fir predominating, interspersed with birch and alder. The silver trunks of the birch trees stand out against the darker background formed by the conifers. Farther south, deciduous trees—oak, hornbeam, and ash—make an appearance, lending further variety to the landscape.

Belovezhskaya Pushcha

The Belovezhskaya (Belavezhskaya) Pushcha, the scenic forest, is a remnant of the forest that covered much of prehistoric Europe. The Belovezhskaya Pushcha Reserve is remarkable as an exceptionally successful example of international cooperation, comprising 185,000 acres (75,000 hectares) in Belorussia and 155,000 acres in Poland; the reserve is administered jointly by the two countries. The oldest preserve on the continent, it harbours rare animals and birds that have long since vanished elsewhere. The European bison, or wisent (sometimes mistakenly referred to as the aurochs), is the pride of the reservation. The animal life of the republic as a whole is also rich, including elk, deer, boar, hare, and squirrel, with occasional wolf, fox, badger, ermine, and marten, and, near water, such valuable fur animals as otter and mink, as well as beaver.

Game birds include black and hazel grouse, partridge, duck, woodcock, and snipe. Numerous fishes are found in the Dnepr Lowland, with carp prevailing in the lakes of the Baltic Basin. Some fish are raised for food in "farms," and lakes are stocked with food fish.

Climate. The proximity of the Baltic influences the climate of the republic, which varies from maritime to continental. The average July temperature is about 64° F (18° C) with humidity high. The winter is mild, with frequent thaws; the average January temperature is 21° F (−6° C). The average annual precipitation amounts to 22–28 inches (550–700 millimetres) and is occasionally excessive; the temperature range, however, is favourable for all temperate-zone crops. Except in the southern swamps, soils are generally fertile, especially in the river valleys.

The people. Ethnically, the people living in the republic are comparatively homogeneous, Belorussians making up more than four-fifths of the total. Other peoples included Russians, Ukrainians, Poles, and Jews and smaller numbers of Tatars, Lithuanians, Gypsies, and Latvians. The overall density of population is relatively high, the central areas being most densely settled and the southern swamplands thinly peopled.

Patterns of settlement

As a result of industrialization, city dwellers accounted for about half of the population in the late 20th century, as compared with less than 25 percent in 1940. Ancient cities such as Minsk, Brest, and Grodno (Hrodna) have been joined by such entirely new centres as Soligorsk (Salihorsk), Novopolotsk (Navapolatsk), and Svetlogorsk (Svetlahorsk). Most cities cluster around centres of heavy industry and main communication routes in central and eastern Belorussia.

The economy. As a result of the devastation of World War II, agriculture and industry were almost wiped out; an intensive postwar drive was required to restore the economy. The main industries are now engineering, chemicals, woodworking, light manufacturing, and food processing. The main agricultural activities include the raising of cattle (for meat and dairy products), pigs, and poultry and the production of potatoes and flax fibre.

The Belorussian S.S.R. receives from other Soviet republics coal, oil, natural gas, metals, cotton, synthetic rubber, and a variety of machinery. In its turn, it supplies vehicles, agricultural machinery, timber products, and agricultural goods, which are also exported by the Soviet Union to foreign countries.

Resources. Traditionally, Belorussia was considered to be poor in mineral resources. Intensive prospecting, however, has revealed minerals, notably high-quality petroleum, now extracted in the south. The southeastern part of the Belorussian Lowland section of the Pripet Marshes has the largest oil reserves. The western part of the Belorussian Lowland and the centre of the republic have peat deposits. Coal, brown coal, and combustible shale un-

Salt deposits

derlie the Pripet Marshes. Salt deposits in the Belorussian Lowland are the second largest in Europe; the reserves are considered sufficient to meet the needs of neighbouring regions as well as of Belorussia itself. Other deposits include limestone, dolomite, marl, and sand, with the quartz sands of the Gomel (Homel) region a major component in the manufacture of high-quality glass. Refractory clays—used for pipes and tiles—are found near Brest, and deep mineral springs lie around the Minsk, Mogilyov (Mahilyoŭ), and Bobruysk (Babruysk) areas. There are also phosphate reserves and ferrous and nonferrous metal supplies.

Industry. Almost two-thirds of the republic's income is provided by industry. Although some industries are based on local resources—agricultural raw materials, timber, oil, peat, and potassium salts—most industrial plants work, at least partly, on imported raw materials and semi-manufactured goods. The post-World War II years have witnessed major changes in the industrial pattern. New industries, including tool and instrument making, oil extraction and refining, and synthetic fibre production, have sprung up, and the geographic distribution of industry has been affected.

Production of heavy engineering equipment is an important industry in the republic, the largest manufacturing centres being Minsk, Gomel, and Mogilyov. The republic's heavy-duty trucks, tractors and other agricultural machinery, and metal-cutting tools are used throughout the Soviet Union. More specialized products include computers and such consumer goods as wristwatches, radios, television sets, pianos, bicycles, motorcycles, and sewing machines.

The republic's important chemical industry produces, among other products, some 40 percent of Soviet potassium fertilizers, with Soligorsk, Grodno, and Gomel as the main centres. A growing number of factories works on the by-products of oil refining; others turn out various rubber products, paints, and plastics. The Belorussian S.S.R. was the first Soviet republic to produce dimensionally stable glass pipes for transporting hot and cold liquids and gases.

The woodworking industry, drawing on the republic's forest reserves, notably pine, produces matches, plywood, pressboard, and furniture. It also supplies timber for the coal mines of the Donets Basin. The Belorussian S.S.R. also manufactures various types of paper and paperboard and sections of prefabricated houses.

Belorussian textile mills produce linen, woollen, cotton, and silk fabrics. Linen mills in the flax-growing areas of the north and northwest are responsible for 10 percent of Soviet linen fabric. Synthetic fibres are also manufactured. Starch, syrup, alcohol, canned foods, and yeast are produced, and many river- and lake-based plants process fish.

Petroleum deposits were discovered in the Belorussian Lowland in 1964. Oil from the Rechitsa (Rechytsa) and Ostashkovichi (Astashkavichy) fields is pumped, via the Druzhba pipeline, to refineries in Polotsk and Mozyr (Mazyr).

Power generation is based on local peat and petroleum, as well as on coal and natural gas that are largely imported from the Ukraine.

Agriculture. The Belorussian environment is favourable to crop production, especially fodder crops. The main commodity crops are grain (predominantly rye and oats), flax, potatoes, and sugar beets. The temperate climate of northern Belorussia is particularly suited to flax, which predominates among industrial crops and accounts for one-fourth of Soviet production. Hemp, grown mainly in the south, is also important, and large areas are given over to tobacco as well. Crops

Livestock production, based on good pasturage and a substantial acreage in fodder crops, accounts for more than half of the value of Belorussian agricultural output. Cattle raising accounts for about two-thirds of the total and hog production for most of the remaining third. Meat and poultry production predominates in the central regions, with dairying carried on in suburban areas. Potatoes being their chief feed, hogs are raised in central and southern potato-growing regions. Fur farming—Arctic fox, silver fox, and mink—is carried on, and beekeeping is traditional in Belorussia.

Agriculture in the Belorussian S.S.R. is fully collectivized.

Economic regions. The Minsk region, an advantageously situated region, is the industrialized heart of Belorussia; with more than half of its population city dwellers, it harbours a wide variety of industries. The regional centre, Minsk, on the banks of the Svisloch (Svislach) River, accounts for a third of the republic's total industrial output, mostly in heavy industry. Woodworking is also important in the region and includes the production of furniture in Minsk and Molodechno (Maladzechna) and matches in Borisov (Barysaŭ). Textile mills and dairying are also significant. The city of Minsk is the hub of rail, road, and air routes of national and international significance and is a major centre of Belorussian culture, having a dozen institutions of higher education.

Situated in the northeast, across the upper reaches of the Dnepr and Western Dvina, the Vitebsk region is notable for its toolmaking, textile production, and oil refining. It also leads the republic in flax production.

About a third of the Mogilyov region, which lies in the east, is forested, crossed by the Dnepr, Berezina, and Sozh rivers. The main industrial centres are at Mogilyov and Bobruysk, and the region has engineering, chemical, woodworking, and building industries. Agricultural products include flax, grain, and potatoes, and cattle are raised.

A third of the Gomel region (second to Minsk in size) is covered with peat bogs and swamplands, and one-fifth is occupied by forests. Its health and recreation spas are known throughout the Soviet Union. The region's industry includes production of machinery for land reclamation. Horticulture is carried on, and agricultural products include grain, hemp, flax, and milk. Gomel is the main urban centre.

The flat and largely swampy Brest region lies in the extreme southwest of the republic and is crossed by transport routes linking the Russian S.F.S.R. and the Ukraine with Poland, the German Democratic Republic, and other central European countries. There is specialization in woodworking, light manufacturing, and building. The region's agriculture, aided by a mild climate, emphasizes flax, sugar beets, potatoes, grain, cattle, and hogs.

Lying in the Neman River Basin in the northwest, the Grodno region is the smallest in the Belorussian S.S.R. A quarter of the area is forested, and timber is floated down the Neman. The region's flatlands produce sugar beets, and cattle and hogs are raised. Fertilizers and leather are also produced.

Transportation. The flat Belorussian landscape has facilitated development of a transportation network. The main railways are the Moscow–Minsk–Brest and Gomel–Minsk–Vilnius lines, as well as a section of the Odessa–Leningrad route. The road networks and waterways, too, are extensively used. Among several canals is the Dnepr–Bug link, important for the hauling of freight from the German Democratic Republic.

Air transport plays an important role, with regional and international links. In addition to passenger, mail, and freight traffic, planes serve remote areas as ambulances.

Administrative and social conditions. *Government.* The Belorussian S.S.R. is formally an independent republic with a constitution that came into force on February 19, 1937. It is also a charter member of the United Nations, a status it shares only with the Ukraine among the Soviet republics. The highest body of state power is the Supreme Soviet, which is elected for a four-year period and selects from its ranks a Presidium consisting of a president, two deputy presidents, a secretary, and 11 members who carry on its functions between sessions of the Supreme Soviet. The Supreme Soviet also chooses the government, or Council of Ministers, the highest executive and administrative body. The Belorussian S.S.R. is represented by deputies in the federal Soviet of the Union and Soviet of Nationalities. The highest judicial organ in the republic is the Supreme Court, elected by the Supreme Soviet for a five-year period. The procurator general of the Soviet Union appoints the chief procurator of the Belorussian S.S.R. for a five-year term.

Communist Party

The Communist Party of Belorussia is the only political party in the republic, controlling its government and all political, economic, and cultural life. Part of the Communist Party of the Soviet Union (CPSU), it is guided by that body's program and statutes. Trade unions do not function as bargaining agents between workers and management but do have giant memberships.

Education. Literacy is universal and eight-year schooling obligatory. Ten-year secondary obligatory education has been introduced in general and professional schools. Institutions of higher learning include the Belorussian V.I. Lenin State University, the Gomel State University, the Belorussian Agricultural Academy in Gorky (Horki; in Mogilyov *oblast*), and medical, pedagogical, technological, and agricultural institutes. The Belorussian S.S.R. Academy of Sciences coordinates the work of scientific research centres and research workers. The academy has an atomic reactor and a computer centre engaged in economic planning and management.

Housing and medical services. World War II caused the destruction of 74 percent of urban housing (and some 1,200,000 village dwellings) and almost all industrial buildings and schools. The situation was restored to normal after the war. Housing construction in cities and towns consists mainly of multi-story prefabricated units, while individual dwellings predominate in the villages.

Health services

Medical services have shown a steady improvement since the war, and there has been a planned growth in the number of places in hospitals, sanatoriums, convalescent centres, and dispensaries.

Cultural life. Belorussia is a land of ancient and rich culture. Architectural monuments of the early period include the 11th-century Cathedral of St. Sophia in Polotsk, while local architects of the 14th–16th centuries evolved (at Maloye Mozheykovo, or Maloye Mazheykava, and Synkovichi, or Synkavichy) an original design for a church-fortress. The 17th and 18th centuries are notable for the Baroque style of the Jesuit church in Grodno and for a remarkable variety of wood sculptures. Belorussia was also known for original items of applied art, including the 18th-century Slutsk belts, decorated with gold and silver threads.

Literature. Literary activity in Belorussia dates back to the 11th century. In the 12th century, Cyril of Turov preached and wrote his sermons and hymns and was deeply venerated among all the Orthodox Slavs as "the second Chrysostom." Frantsysk Skaryna of Polotsk in the 16th century translated the Bible into Belorussian, publishing lavish editions in Prague (1517–19) and Vilnius (1522–25), the first printed books not only in Belorussia but in all of eastern Europe. The Belorussian poet Simeon Polotsky (Polatsky; Symeon of Polotsk) was the first to bring Baroque versification and the Baroque sermon to Moscow (after 1655).

The classics of modern Belorussian literature include works of the poets Maksim Bahdanovich, Ales Harun, Yanka Kupala, and Yakub Kolas and the fiction writer Maksim Haretski. The last three lived long enough to contribute to Belorussian literature in the Belorussian S.S.R. This contribution includes, among others, such remarkable works as Kupala's collections of poems titled *Heritage* (1922), *The Nameless* (1925), and *1918–1928* (1930) and his play *Natives* (1924); Kolas' long narrative poems *The New Land* (1910–23) and *Symon the Musician* (1911–25) and his trilogy of novels, *On the Crossroads* (1921–54); and Haretski's short novel *The Quiet Current* (1918–30), his diary, *On the Imperialistic War* (1926), and his collection of short stories, *Before the Dawn* (1926).

The literary upheaval of the 1920s brought into Belorussian literature outstanding poets and writers, whose influence is felt in many respects to this day. Among these were the poets Uladzimir Dubouka and Yazep Pushcha, the novelist Kuzma Chorny, and the fabulist, satirist, fiction writer, and playwright Kandrat Krapiva. Their most notable works are Dubouka's trilogy of long poems ("combines," in his terminology), *Circles* (1927), *And the Purple Sails Unfurled* (1929), and *Storm the Outposts of the Future* (1930); Pushcha's long poems *Song of the War* (1927), *Shadow of the Consul* (1928), and *Gardens of the Winds* (1929); Chorny's novels *Sister* (1927), *The Soil* (1928), and *Lyavon Bushmar* (1929); and Krapiva's *Fables* (1927), long poem, *Shkiruta* (1928), collection of short stories, *Folks, Neighbours* (1928), novel, *Myadzvedzichy* (1933), and play, *Who Laughs Last* (1939).

After the re-annexation of western Belorussia from Poland in 1939, the poet Maksim Tank entered Belorussian literature in the Belorussian S.S.R. and became one of its most outstanding contemporary poets; his best works include the long poems *Narach* (1937), *Kalinouski* (1938), and *Yanuk Syaliba* (1943). Among contemporary Belorussian fiction writers the most outstanding are Vasil Bykau, whose short novels *Alpine Ballad* and *The Ordeal* have been translated into English (1966 and 1972, respectively), as have some of the short stories of Yanka Bryl (*Short Stories,* 1957?).

Contemporary writers

The poets Pyatrus Brouka, Arkadz Kulashou, and Pimyen Panchanka, along with the novelists Ivan Shamyakin and Ivan Melezh and the playwright Andrey Makayonak, are the best representatives of Socialist Realism in Belorussian literature.

Music. The years since World War II have witnessed the intensive development of music in the Belorussian S.S.R. Notable composers include Dzmitry Lukas (the opera *Kastus Kalinouski,* 1947), Ryhor Pukst (the operas *Masheka,* 1947, and *Marynka,* 1955, and several symphonies), Yaŭhen Hlebaŭ (the opera *Your Spring,* 1963, and the ballet *Alpine Ballad,* 1967), Yaŭhen Tsikotski (the operas *Mikhas Padhorny,* 1939–57, and *Alesya,* 1944–67), and Yury Semyanyaka (the operas *Thorny Rose,* 1960, *When the Leaves Fall,* 1968, and *Star Venus,* 1970). The republic has a conservatory of music and a philharmonic society. Belorussian folk-music companies have made traditional music popular both in the republic and farther afield, the ensemble Pyesnyary (Songsters) being especially popular.

Theatre, film, and broadcasting. The Belorussian State Theatre of Opera and Ballet in Minsk and two Belorussian state dramatic theatres, in Minsk and Vitebsk, are functioning, as well as a dozen professional drama companies and a film studio. A television centre began operating in Minsk in 1956. (M.I.R./A.Ad.)

HISTORY

The Belorussian region has long been settled by man. Archaeology provides evidence of prehistoric cultures as early as the Magdalenian, while Neolithic remains are widespread. The area was one of the earliest to be settled by Slavs, between the 6th and the 8th century AD. The early Slavic tribes, the Dregovichi, Radimichi, Krivichi, and Drevlyane, had formed petty princedoms by the 8th–9th century, such as those of Pinsk, Turov, Polotsk, Slutsk, and Minsk. These all came, in time, under the general suzerainty of Kiev. The economy of the period was based on primitive, shifting agriculture on burned-over forestland, as well as on honey collecting. Along the rivers, trade developed, particularly on the Dnepr, part of the "water road" from Kiev to Novgorod, and towns began to appear. Most of the Belorussian towns were founded by the end of the 12th century. Polotsk and Turov are two of the earliest mentioned towns of Slavic foundation—862 and 980. Brest is first recorded in 1017 and Minsk in 1067.

Lithuanian rule. With the overthrow of Kiev by the Tatars in 1240, Kievan Rus broke up. Many of the Belorussian towns were laid waste. Almost all this area passed to the control of Lithuania. Although most of the aristocracy was Lithuanian and pagan, a number of Russian and Orthodox nobles remained as feudatories of the grand duke. Throughout the 13th and 14th centuries the power of Lithuania increased, encompassing Smolensk and Kiev and even reaching the shores of the Black Sea. In 1386 the Lithuanian and Polish ruling houses were united under the Jagiellon dynasty, and Roman Catholicism became the official religion of Lithuania. Between Lithuania–Poland and the rising power of Muscovy there was an incessant and bitter struggle for this area. Although during the 15th and early 16th centuries the steppe areas and the region around Smolensk were lost to Moscow, Belorussia remained under Lithuanian control. During the 16th century a code of laws was drawn up, known as the Lithuanian Statutes, defining civil and property rights. Only the aristocracy and merchants derived any advantage, however. In 1557 the *voloka* agrarian reform was instituted, introducing the three-field system of agriculture and transforming the patterns of fields and of settlements. Under the new system, the condition of the peasants became increasingly that of serfs.

Agrarian reform and the peasantry

In 1569 the Lublin Union made Poland and Lithuania one state, although Lithuania retained its title of grand duchy and its code of laws. In Belorussia a mainly Polish-speaking, Roman Catholic aristocracy developed, though the peasants on the whole remained Orthodox. In 1596 the Union of Brest established the Uniate Church, but this made relatively little headway among the Orthodox. The rule of the Polish landowners was not popular and gave rise to a large-scale revolt in 1648–54, but Belorussia remained under Poland until the reign of Catherine the Great. Economic development was slight, and the Belorussian population was almost entirely engaged in primitive agriculture. Trade lay in the hands of Poles and Jews. Conditions were particularly backward in the swamps of Polesye.

Russian and Soviet rule. By the first partition of Poland, in 1772, Catherine II the Great acquired eastern Belorussia, including the towns of Vitebsk, Mogilyov, and Gomel. The second partition (1793) gave Russia Minsk and all the central part, and in 1795 the third partition united the remainder of present-day Belorussia to the Russian Empire. The area was divided administratively among the governments (*i.e.,* provinces) of Minsk, Mogilyov, Vilnius, and Vitebsk. Under tsarist rule the Uniate Church was persecuted, and many of its members became Orthodox. In 1812 Napoleon crossed Belorussia in his advance on Moscow and again during his retreat. The forcing of the Berezina River was one of the heaviest battles of the campaign.

The 19th century saw the beginning of industrial growth in the towns of Belorussia, largely based on local supplies: timber working, glassmaking, and boatbuilding along the rivers. Following the emancipation of the serfs in 1861, the tempo of industrialization increased, particularly with the coming of the railways, from the 1880s on. Nevertheless, the area remained economically backward to 1917, particularly in rural areas. This resulted in considerable emigration, nearly 1,500,000 persons leaving Belorussia during the 50 years before the Russian Revolution. Most of the emigration was to the United States or to Siberia: between 1896 and 1915 more than 600,000 persons migrated to Siberia. In 1898 a small congress to form the Russian Social-Democratic Workers' Party was held in Minsk, the first attempt to establish the Marxist party in Russia.

Emigration

In World War I heavy fighting took place in Belorussia, with great destruction. The peace treaty between the Soviet revolutionary government and the Germans was signed in Brest-Litovsk (now Brest) on March 3, 1918. On January 1, 1919, the revolutionaries proclaimed the founding of the Belorussian Soviet Socialist Republic, but fighting continued between the Soviets and the Poles. In 1919 the Poles advanced east to the Berezina, only to be thrown back again. Peace was finally achieved on March 18, 1921, by the Treaty of Riga, which divided Belorussia between the U.S.S.R. and Poland. The frontier was the same as that following the first partition. In 1924 the regions of Polotsk, Vitebsk, Orsha, and Mogilyov were added to the original Belorussian S.S.R., and in 1926 Gomel was included.

In 1939, after the German attack on Poland, the U.S.S.R. entered Poland from the east, occupying all Belorussia up to the Bug River and including the Bialystok region. In June 1941 the German attack on the Soviet Union rapidly overran Belorussia, although the garrison of the Brest fortress made a prolonged and courageous atand. Heavy fighting once more devastated the area during the German retreat, and a number of major engagements took place, notably at Vitebsk, Minsk, and Borisov. During the war years, 74 percent of the housing and more than 10,000 industrial undertakings were destroyed. After the war, in 1945, a treaty between the U.S.S.R. and Poland left western Belorussia, except the Bialystok region, in Soviet hands. The Polish population of this area was transferred en masse to Poland. With the establishment of the United Nations, the Belorussian S.S.R. was given a seat in the General Assembly. (R.A.F.)

Moldavia

The hilly land of Moldavia (formally the Moldavian Soviet Socialist Republic) lies in the extreme southwest of the European portion of the Soviet Union, surrounded by the Ukraine on the north, east, and south and bordered on the west by the Prut River, forming the Soviet frontier with Romania. Occupying an area of 13,000 square miles (33,700 square kilometres), it is the second smallest of the 15 constituent union republics. The capital is at Kishinyov.

The greater part of the republic lies between the great, meandering rivers Prut and Dnestr (Dniester), as they flow to their Black Sea estuaries. This region was formerly known as Bessarabia. It was an integral part of the Romanian principality of Moldavia until 1812, when it was ceded to Russia by the suzerain Ottoman Empire. It remained a province of the Russian Empire until 1918, except for the southern districts along the Danube River, which were joined to Romania after the Crimean War in 1856, only to be retroceded to Russia in 1878. In 1918 Bessarabia became part of Greater Romania, and in the interwar period it was gradually integrated into the political and economic structure of that country. The Soviet Union did not recognize this cession of territory, and in 1924 it established the Moldavian Autonomous Soviet Socialist Republic, a small strip of territory on the left bank of the Dnestr. In June 1940 the Soviet Union obliged Romania to cede Bessarabia, and in August it established the Moldavian S.S.R. Between 1941 and 1944, while Romania and the Soviet Union were at war, Bessarabia again became part of Romania. In 1944 Soviet troops retook the territory, and the Moldavian S.S.R. was re-established. The territory has been fully incorporated into the Soviet political and economic system, but in the late 20th century Bessarabia was still a subject of controversy between Romania and the Soviet Union.

PHYSICAL AND HUMAN GEOGRAPHY

The land. *Relief.* Moldavia lies beyond the great arc of the Carpathian Mountains, mostly on deep sedimentary rocks covering the southwest portion of the ancient structural block known as the Russian Platform. Harder crystalline rocks outcrop only in the north. Its surface is a hilly plain, with an average elevation of 482 feet (147 metres), cut by a deep network of river valleys, ravines, and gullies.

Kodry Hills

The uplands of the centre of the republic, the Kodry Hills, lie at an average elevation of about 1,150–1,300 feet (350–400 metres), and the highest point, Mt. Balaneshty in the west, reaches 1,409 feet (430 metres). These uplands are interlaced by deep, flat valleys, ravines, and landslide-scoured depressions, separated by sharp ridges, and steep, forest-clad slopes account for much of the terrain. The Dnestr uplands, their eastern slopes forming the high right bank of the Dnestr River, border the central uplands on the east and northeast.

The northern Moldavian landscape is characterized by the level plain of the Beltsy steppe (500 to 650 feet, or 150 to 200 metres, in elevation) and also by uplands averaging twice this height, culminating in the 1,053-foot (321-metre) Vysokaya Hill. The northern uplands include the strikingly eroded Medobory-Toltry limestone ridges, which border the Prut River.

In the south, the extensive Budzhak Plain is broken by numerous ravines and gullies, while in the east, left-bank Moldavia includes spurs of the Volyn-Podolsk Upland, cut into by tributaries of the Dnestr.

Climate. Moldavia's climate, warm and moderately continental, is characterized by a lengthy frost-free period, a comparatively mild winter, considerable temperature fluctuations, and, in the south, long dry periods.

Average annual temperature reaches 45.9° F (7.7° C) in the north and 49.8° F (9.9° C) in the south, but the July averages rise to 67° and 73° F (19.5° and 23° C), respectively, and the mercury drops to as low as 23° and 27° F (−5° and −3° C) in January. Absolute temperatures recorded range from a record low of −31° F (−35° C) and a high of 106° F (41° C). Moldavia experiences a very variable rainfall, with the average figures of 18 to 22 inches (450 to 550 millimetres; the figure is a little lower in the south) concealing variations that may double the figure in some years and result in prolonged dry spells in others. Most rainfall occurs in the warmer months, and heavy summer showers, coupled with the irregular terrain, cause erosion problems and river silting. Winter snow cover is thin. Winds tend to come from either the northwest or the southeast.

Drainage. Moldavia has a well-developed network of about 3,000 rivers, all draining south to the Black Sea, but only 246 of these exceed six miles (10 kilometres) in length, and only eight exceed 60 miles. The Dnestr, the rapidly flowing main artery, is navigable almost throughout the republic and has an average discharge of about 10,000 cubic feet (300 cubic metres) per second, swollen by spring snowmelt from the Carpathians and by heavy summer rains. In the warmer winters, it is not frozen. The other, smaller, main artery, the Prut, is a tributary of the Danube, which it joins at the extreme southern tip of the country. The Yalpukh, Kogilnik, and other small southern rivers drain largely into the Danubian estuary in the nearby Ukraine.

Underground water, extensively used for the republic's water supply, includes about 2,200 natural springs. The terrain favours construction of reservoirs.

Soils. Moldavian soils are varied and very fertile, with chernozem—rich, black soils—covering three-quarters of the republic. The best developed chernozem, fostering the growth of grain, tobacco, and sugar beets, is found in the north, in the low-lying parts of the central Moldavian and Dnestr uplands, as well as in the left-bank regions. Chernozem quality diminishes southward, but grapes and sunflowers can still be grown. Woodland soils characterize the uplands: 40 percent are covered by forests, the rest by orchards, vineyards, and fields of grain. Floodplain soils characterize the riverside areas, while the lower reaches of the Prut and southern river valleys have saline and marshland soils.

Chernozem soils

Plant and animal life. Northern and central Moldavia is a forest zone, while a steppe belt crosses the south. There are more than 1,500 species of plants in the republic, with scenic expanses of forests, covering about 1,150 square miles (3,000 square kilometres), of particular importance, especially in the central Kodry Hills region. The commonest trees are hornbeam and oak, followed by a rich variety including linden, maple, wild pear, and wild cherry. There are beech forests at the sources of the Ikel and Byk rivers. Large-scale reforestation projects have been carried out in the republic.

Moldavia's steppes were originally grass covered, but most of them are now cultivated. Lush meadows and reed growths occur in the floodlands of the Dnestr and portions of the Prut, while salt-marsh grasslands flourish in the saline valleys of the Kogilnik, Yalpukh, Botna, and lower Prut.

Moldavian animal life is rich, despite the republic's small size. Mammals include boar, roe deer, hare, wolf, fox, badger, wildcat, ermine, and polecat. Siberian stag, fallow deer, spotted deer, and muskrat have been successively introduced and are firmly established. Roe deer, hares, foxes, and muskrats are of commercial importance.

There are many species of birds, both resident and migratory. The marshy lower reaches of Moldavia's rivers provide sanctuary for wild geese, migratory ducks, and herons, while white-tailed sea eagles are to be found in the floodland forests. The wood lark, jay, song thrush, blackbird, hawk, and long-eared owl frequent the republic's forests. Plentiful fish supplies include carp (raised in artificial reservoirs), perch, bream, ruff, and pike.

The people. Of the total population, almost two-thirds are Moldavian, the remainder comprising Ukrainians, Russians, Gagauzi (a Turkic people), Jews, and Bulgarians.

Ethnic composition

Moldavia has a higher average population density than any other Soviet Union republic. The urban population has increased as a result of industrialization: more than a third of the people live in towns. Moldavian villages, moreover, are large, most of them having a thousand and more inhabitants; all are supplied with electricity, and the gas network is being extended.

The economy. A diversified industry has been established in Moldavia, agriculture has been modernized, and transport and the building industry have been overhauled. Moldavian industrial and agricultural products are supplied to all the union republics and are exported to some 50 foreign countries.

Industry. The leading branch of the Moldavian economy, industry concentrates in the main on food processing, with the machine-building, power-engineering, consumer-goods, and building-materials industries undergoing development as well.

The food industry has numerous branches: wine making, canning, sugar refining, and oil pressing, as well as

The food industry

production of essential oils, are of all-union significance. In particular, Moldavia is an important supplier of wine, including champagne and brandy, and is responsible for one-fifth of the Soviet output. Moldavia holds the third place in Soviet sugar production, the sugar-refining industry being located in the north. For local needs the republic has flour and other mills and well-developed meat, dairy, and confectionary industries.

Machine building, established in the mid-1950s and centred on Kishinyov, Beltsy, Tiraspol, and Bendery, has acquired importance. Tractors made in Moldavia, specially equipped for use in orchards and vineyards, are supplied to other Soviet republics.

Light industry includes the production of furs at Beltsy, garments and knitwear at Kishinyov and Tiraspol, footwear at Kishinyov, and silk fabrics at Bendery.

Building materials produced in Moldavia include bricks, limestone, tiles, cement, slate, and concrete blocks. Rybnitsa is the leading centre of this industry.

Thermoelectric power plants are located in Kishinyov, Beltsy, and Tiraspol, and there are hydroelectric stations in Dubossary on the Dnestr and in the town of Dnestrovsk. The republic provides electricity to the southern regions of the Ukraine and also to Bulgaria through a transmission line. The republic's power system is connected to the unified southern power system of the Soviet Union.

Agriculture. There is no large-scale private farming, but collective farmers do have small plots for their own use. Collective farms (*kolkhozy*) cultivate four-fifths of the area under grain crops and are generally engaged in mixed farming. On an average a collective farm has 7,000 acres (2,800 hectares) under crops and more than 1,200 acres (500 hectares) of vineyards and orchards. The state farms (*sovkhozy*) usually specialize in cultivating and processing a particular crop, some of them producing grapes and wines, others growing aromatic plants and producing essential oils.

Agriculture is highly mechanized, almost all of agricultural jobs being carried out by machines. All collective and state farms are provided with electricity, and use is made of chemical means of pest control and mineral fertilizers.

Since 1940 the area used for vegetables, orchards, berries, and vineyards has undergone significant expansion. Viticulture, fruit and vegetable growing, and other specialized farming are particularly important, comprising 90 percent of the commodity output of arable farming. The largest vineyards are to be found in the southern and central regions, and most of the orchards are situated in northern and southeastern Moldavia. Walnuts are also significant.

Sunflower seed is the most important industrial crop, and, though it is grown all over Moldavia, the southeastern regions have the largest plantations. Sugar beets, a relatively new crop in Moldavia, are cultivated in the north. Moldavia is also the major Soviet tobacco grower. Vegetables are grown mainly in the southeast.

The chief grain crops are winter wheat and corn (maize). Wheat is used for the republic's own needs, and corn is supplied as seed to other republics. Most of the grain is grown in the north.

Dairying and cattle breeding are also important, as is pig farming. The sturdy Karakul and *tsigayk* breeds constitute a large portion of the sheep, raising of which is particularly important in southern Moldavia.

Economic subregions. The Moldavian S.S.R. is divided into four subregions: Northern, Central, Southern, and Southeastern. Each of the subregions has distinct natural and economic features, possessing unique problems of development.

The Northern region stretches from the northern border to the central Moldavian upland. Its area constitutes about a third of the total area of the republic and the same proportion of the total population. Agriculture dominates the economy: the subregion produces grain, sugar beets, tobacco, fruit, sunflowers, and animal-husbandry products. A diversified industry has been established and includes all the cement and sugar production and most of the processed tobacco. Instrument making and electrical engineering are important industries. Beltsy is a prominent industrial centre, and Soroki and Rybnitsa are also developing industrial towns.

The Central region lies in the middle of Moldavia, between the Dnestr and the Prut. It occupies about a quarter of the republic's territory and is the home of a third of the population. Engineering and light industry are of great importance, alongside the food industry. The region also has a developed agriculture, concentrating on viticulture, fruit, and dairy and poultry farming. Kishinyov, the Moldavian capital, is the largest industrial centre of the region and of the republic. The urban complex produces engineering products, light industry commodities, building materials, and food industry products.

Kishinyov

Occupying 20 percent of the republic's territory, the Southern region is predominantly agricultural. There are no large cities, and the most important town is Kagul, on the Prut River, which has wine-making and building-materials industries.

The Southeastern region occupies about 18 percent of the republic's territory and has about the same proportion of the population. It is noteworthy for its highly developed intensive agriculture and industry, specializing in the production of vegetables, fruits, grapes, and sunflower seeds and in animal husbandry. It also has silk-manufacturing, canning, oil-pressing, meat-packing, and heavy industrial plants, with Tiraspol and Bendery the main industrial centres.

Transportation. Railway and motor transport are the basis of the Moldavian transport system. The railway network contains two lines—one linking Tiraspol, Kishinyov, and Ungeny and the other linking Tiraspol and Reni—that are of importance in the Soviet Union as a whole. Incoming freight goods include coal, petroleum products, iron and nonferrous metals, timber, mineral fertilizers, and machines and equipment. Agricultural goods and products of the food industry prevail among the outgoing commodities, although a growing quantity of machines and light industrial goods is sent to other parts of the Soviet Union. Motor transport generally carries freight inside the republic, over a road network of which somewhat less than half is asphalt covered. River transport is of local importance, and air transport links Moldavia with other parts of the Soviet Union, Kishinyov being the site of the main airport.

Administrative and social conditions. *Government.* According to the constitution of the Soviet Union and the constitution of the Moldavian Soviet Socialist Republic (adopted in February 1941), Moldavia is a sovereign socialist state of workers and peasants. Its political foundation is the Soviets of Working People's Deputies, and its economic foundation is the socialist ownership of the means of production. It has a coat of arms, flag, and national anthem.

A one-chamber Supreme Soviet, elected for a four-year period, is the highest organ of state power, supplemented, between sessions, by the Presidium of the Supreme Soviet, which it elects. The Supreme Soviet appoints the government—namely, the Council of Ministers, which is the highest executive and administrative organ.

The organs of state power in districts, cities, and rural localities are the Soviets of Working People's Deputies, which are elected for two-year periods. The Supreme Soviet also appoints, for a five-year period, the Supreme Court, which is the highest judicial establishment of the republic. The general procurator of the Soviet Union appoints for a five-year period the chief procurator of Moldavia, who is responsible to him.

The Communist Party

The Communist Party of Moldavia, part of the Communist Party of the Soviet Union (CPSU), is the only political party allowed to function. There is no organized political opposition. So-called nonparty candidates may run for election to the Supreme Soviet and other bodies, but only on a single list with Communist candidates approved by the Communist Party. Nonparty deputies do not pursue policies distinct from those of the Communist Party. As in the other union republics, the party employs the various state organs mentioned above to carry out its policies in all spheres of activity. The primary purpose of elections and the various public bodies is, consequently, to rally mass support for party policies. The Young Communist League (Komsomol) of Moldavia is in close collaboration with, and under the leadership of, the Communist Party of Moldavia.

The trade unions of the republic, as in other socialist countries, concern themselves with the recreational and working conditions of their members, the stimulation of fulfillment of various economic goals, and the organization of the emulation process known as socialist competition. The trade unions have little independence or power of initiative. No strikes in Moldavian industry have been recorded since the end of World War II.

Education. Significant changes have occurred in Moldavian society during the years of Soviet power. Illiteracy was eradicated, and, as in other union republics, emphasis has been placed upon technical education in order to satisfy the steadily growing needs of agriculture and industry for specialists and a highly skilled work force. Before 1940 Moldavia had only one institution of higher education, a teacher-training college. In the late 20th century there were several higher educational institutions and specialized middle schools.

Academy of Sciences

At the highest level, the Moldavian S.S.R. Academy of Sciences, established in Kishinyov in 1961, coordinates the activities of some 20 scientific institutions. An additional 50 or so research centres in the fields of viticulture, horticulture, beet growing, grain cultivation, and wine making have been set up, and Moldavian scientists have won international acclaim in these fields.

Social services. The monthly income of the average Moldavian is enhanced by a third or so by the provision of social services from the republic's national income. In addition to free education in elementary, secondary, and high schools, this "social consumption fund" is used for medical help, for pensions and stipends to students, for free stays in sanatoriums and the like, for kindergartens and nurseries, and for Pioneer camps for younger children. Social insurance funds created for agricultural workers are used to provide medical assistance during sickness and temporary disability. All payments for education and social services come out of the state budget.

Cultural life. Because of the historical ties between Bessarabia and Romania and the ethnic identity of Moldavians and Romanians, the culture of the Moldavian S.S.R. to a considerable extent still reflects these primordial sources. Although the Moldavian language, as it is officially called, employs the Cyrillic alphabet, the differences between it and literary Romanian are of little significance and are confined to phonetics and vocabulary. Soviet scholars, mainly for political reasons, have insisted since the 1920s that Moldavian is an independent Romance language distinct from Romanian, a view rejected in the West.

Since World War II the development of Moldavian culture and literature has followed the prevailing pattern of the Soviet Union as a whole. Moldavian literature experienced the vicissitudes of Soviet literature generally during the Zhdanov era of the late 1940s and early '50s. Nonetheless, some notable work was done by the poets Emilian Bucov and Andrei Lupan, among the older generation, and by the dramatist and prose writer Ion Druța, whose novel *Frunze de dor* (1957; "Leaves of Yearning") marks the coming of age of literature in Romanian in the Moldavian republic.

Particular attention has been given to the expansion of cultural opportunities for the general population. There are numerous amateur theatres and musical and art groups. The Doina choir and the Zhok popular ballet company have won international reputations. (F.N.S./K.A.H.)

HISTORY

Bessarabia

Bessarabia—the name often given to the region of Moldavia between the Dnestr and Prut rivers—has a long and stormy history. Part of Scythia in the first millennium BC, it later came marginally under the control of the Roman Empire as part of Dacia. Lying on the great routeway into Europe, it was invaded by successive waves of barbarians, and the area knew many masters. Gradually, under varying influences, the Vlach (or Walachian) nationality developed. Part of the area came under Kievan Russia in the 10th–12th century AD and passed later to the Galician princes. From 1240 to the 14th century Moldavia was vassal to the Tatars.

Old Moldavia. The Genoese, founding fortified commercial outposts on the Dnestr in the 14th century, paved the way for contact with Western civilization, but Bessarabia's history did not take shape until the end of that century, with the rise of the principalities of Moldavia and Walachia, which soon expanded to include the territory. The southern area, which fell originally into the Walachian sphere, probably took its name from the Basarab dynasty. The whole province became part of Moldavia in the 15th century but was soon exposed to the Turkish onslaught; the key points of Akkerman and Chilia were captured in 1484, and this conquest was ratified by treaty (1503, 1513). The southern part of Bessarabia was again detached and organized by the Turks into two sanjaks of the Ottoman Empire.

Russia entered the scene with the rise of Peter I the Great, and Moldavian princes more than once sought Russian support against Turkey. Russia, in its drive toward the mouths of the Danube, occupied Moldavia five times between 1711 and 1812 and finally secured Turkey's cession of Bessarabia proper, with half of Moldavia, in the Treaty of Bucharest (1812). The name of Bessarabia was then extended to the whole area.

The Russian administration (1812–1917). In 1829, in the Treaty of Adrianople, Russia pushed the frontier south to include the Danube delta. After the Crimean War the Treaty of Paris in 1856 restored Danubian Bessarabia (at that time divided into three districts, namely Izmail, Kagul, and Bolgrad) to Moldavia; but in 1878, despite Romania's having fought on the Russian side against Turkey, the Treaty of Berlin assigned these three districts once more to Russia, giving Romania the inadequate compensation of Dobruja.

Treaty of Berlin

The Russian administration had at first been liberal. Autonomy had been granted in 1818 and had remained in force until 1828; a Moldavian boyar had been made governor and a Moldavian archbishop installed. Nevertheless, many Moldavian peasants fled across the Prut fearing the introduction of serfdom. The introduction of the zemstvo system in 1869 provided a measure of local autonomy, but a policy of Russification in both civil and ecclesiastical administration was thereafter pursued, with little effect on the largely illiterate peasantry. The founding of the kingdom of Romania (1881) formed a centre of attraction for Moldavian nationalism, but no lively movement developed in Bessarabia until after the Russian Revolution of 1905. Its strength was drawn not from the boyars (largely Russified) but from schoolteachers and parish priests. Bessarabia achieved some prosperity under Russian rule, the empire forming a good market for its agricultural produce, which was dispatched by river or by the railway system built to link the country with the north–south main line to Odessa. Kishinyov was a relatively flourishing town, though its large Jewish population suffered severely in the pogrom of 1903.

World War I and the Russian Revolution. In World War I the Central Powers tempted Romania to their side with offers to restore Bessarabia; but the scales were tipped in favour of the Allies by counteroffers of Transylvania and Bukovina, as well as by the Francophile sentiment of the Romanian people, so that by 1916 Romania was fighting as Russia's ally. The revolutionary and nationalist ferment in the Russian Empire spread quickly to Bessarabia, which proclaimed support for A.F. Kerensky in March 1917. In April a National Moldavian Committee demanded autonomy, land reform, and the use of the Romanian language; similar rights were claimed for the Moldavians, about 400,000 in number, settled east of the Dnestr. A move toward complete independence was encouraged by events in the Ukraine, and in November 1917 a council known as Sfatul Țării was set up on the model of the Kiev rada. It had originally 84 Moldavian deputies and 36 from the minorities chosen by military and professional organizations and a peasants' congress. On December 2, 1917, the Sfat proclaimed Bessarabia an autonomous constituent republic of the Federation of Russian Republics. Disorders caused by the revolutionary Russian soldiery led the Sfat to appeal to the Allies' representatives and to the Romanian government at Iaşi for military help, whereupon the Bolsheviks occupied Kishinyov on January 5, 1918. They were driven out by a Romanian division on January 13; and on January 24 the Sfat, again following Kiev, proclaimed Bessarabia an independent Moldavian republic, renouncing all ties with Soviet Russia. Recognizing the economic impossibility of isolation and alarmed by the pretensions of the German-sponsored Ukrainian government, the Sfat voted for conditional union with Romania on March 27, 1918. With the defeat of the Central Powers and the creation of greater Romania, reservations were abandoned, and unconditional union was voted at the final session of the Sfat on December 9, 1918. The union of Bessarabia with Romania was recognized by the Treaty of Paris of October 28, 1920, signed by Great Britain, France, Italy, and Japan. Great Britain ratified this treaty in 1922 and France in 1924; Italy delayed ratification until 1927, and Japan never ratified it. The U.S.S.R. never recognized Romania's right to the province. The frontier along the Dnestr was closed; but the railway bridge at Tighina was opened in 1936, two years after the resumption of diplomatic relations.

Union with Romania

The Romanian administration (1918–40). The Romanian government immediately put through a drastic land reform, initiated by Sfatul Ţării, whereby the maximum holding allowed was 247 acres (100 hectares). Despite this, the province languished economically. The uncertainty caused by the continued pretensions of the U.S.S.R. hindered development; Romania had little need of Bessarabia's fruit, corn, and wine; roads were inadequate; the railway system was geared to that of Russia; and the closing of the Dnestr and the loss of the natural outlet, Odessa, had a disastrous effect. The province was put under a centralized regime, at times military in character; in 1938 King Carol II attempted to break up the historic unity by dividing it among newly created regions. Some tardy concessions to the minorities were made in 1939.

World War II. After the German–Soviet pact of August 1939, the U.S.S.R. revived claims to Bessarabia; and the collapse of the western front in 1940 precipitated action. On June 27 a Soviet ultimatum to Romania demanded the cession of Bessarabia and of northern Bukovina as "compensation for Romanian misrule in Bessarabia." The Romanian government had to submit, and Russian troops marched in (June 28). On July 11 the districts of central Bessarabia inhabited predominantly by Moldavians were joined to part of the Moldavian Autonomous Soviet Socialist Republic across the Dnestr (an autonomous republic of the Ukraine set up in 1924) to form, in August, a Moldavian Soviet Socialist Republic, with Kishinyov as capital. The Khotin district in the north was incorporated in the Ukrainian Soviet Socialist Republic as were the southern districts of Cetatea Albă and Izmail. Further land was expropriated, and collectivization launched. Many Moldavians left, some Jews entered, and the whole German population was removed to western Poland under an agreement between Germany and the U.S.S.R. In July 1941 Romania, having entered the war as Germany's ally against the U.S.S.R., reoccupied Bessarabia; and by December 1942 it was fully governed as Romanian territory, though a formal decree of annexation was postponed until the end of hostilities. Some Moldavian peasants from Transnistria, the newly organized Romanian province between the Dnestr and the Bug, were settled on the farms of departed Germans, and many Jews were killed or deported.

Soviet occupation

Reincorporation into the U.S.S.R. The Russians reoccupied Bessarabia in the course of 1944, and, by the peace treaty of February 10, 1947 (ratified in September), Romania had once more to yield Bessarabia and northern Bukovina to the Soviet Union. The Soviet territorial arrangements of August 1940 were restored, the Communist system was introduced, and Bessarabia lost its administrative identity. (B.Br.)

Ukraine

The Ukrainian Soviet Socialist Republic (or the Ukraine) lies in the southwest of the European Soviet Union, bordered by the Belorussian S.S.R. on the north; the Russian S.F.S.R. on the east; the Sea of Azov, the Black Sea, the Moldavian S.S.R., and Romania on the south; and Hungary, Czechoslovakia, and Poland on the west. With an area of 233,100 square miles (603,700 square kilometres), it is one of the largest geographical entities in Europe, third in size after the Soviet Union and the Russian S.F.S.R. Nonetheless, it constitutes only 2.7 percent of Soviet territory, though it produces more than 20 percent of the Soviet industrial and agricultural output and one-fourth of its grain. It became a union republic of the Soviet Union in 1924.

Three-quarters of the population consists of Ukrainians (formerly also called Ruthenians, or Little Russians). The Ukrainian language belongs to the East Slavic group, of which Russian and Belorussian are also members.

PHYSICAL AND HUMAN GEOGRAPHY

The land. *Relief.* The Ukraine, consisting almost entirely of level plains at an average elevation of 574 feet (175 metres) above sea level, occupies a considerable portion of the East European Plain. Such mountainous areas as the Ukrainian Carpathians and Crimean Mountains occur only on the borders and account for barely 5 percent of the area. The landscape is nevertheless diverse, and the plains are broken by highlands—running in a continuous belt from northwest to southeast—as well as lowlands. The rolling plain of the Dnepr Plateau, which lies between the middle reaches of the Dnepr (Dnipro; alternative spellings given in parentheses are Ukrainian) and Yuzhny (Southern) Bug (Boh, or Buh) rivers, is the largest highland area, broken up by many river valleys, ravines, and gorges, some more than 1,000 feet (300 metres) deep. From the west, the plateau is abutted by the characteristically rugged Volyn–Podolsk (Podilian) Upland, which rises to 1,549 feet (472 metres) at its highest point, Mt. Kamul. On the left bank of the Dnepr the Azov Upland, the highest point of which is Mt. Mogila-Belmak (1,070 feet [326 metres]), stretches gently away from the mountains to the Donets Ridge on its northeastern edge, which is surmounted by Mt. Mogila-Mechetnaya (1,204 feet [367 metres]). The northeastern portion of the Ukraine is a spur of the Central Russian Upland, but it reaches an elevation of only 774 feet (236 metres) at its highest point.

In the northern part of the republic lie the Pripet Marshes, crossed by numerous river valleys. In the central Ukraine is the Dnepr Lowland, flat in the west and gently rolling in the east. The Black Sea Lowland extends along the shores of the Black and Azov seas, its level surface, broken only by low rises and shallow depressions, sloping gradually toward the Black Sea. In the Crimean Peninsula it becomes the North Crimean Lowland. In the Transcarpathian region of the western Ukraine, the Tisa Lowland lies in the valley of the Tisa (Tysa) River and its tributaries. Toward the south it becomes the Pannonian Basin. In the west the parallel ranges of the Carpathian Mountains—one of the most picturesque areas in the Ukraine—extend for more than 150 miles (240 kilometres). Easily accessible, the mountains range in height from about 2,000 to 6,500 feet, rising to 6,762 feet (2,061 metres) in Mt. Hoverla, the highest point. A number of passes through the mountains provide routes for both highways and railroads.

The Carpathian Mountains

About 90 miles long and 30 miles wide (145 by 48 kilometres), the Crimean Mountains lie in three low, parallel ranges, with fertile valleys between them. They form the southern coast of the Crimean Peninsula, the belt of land between the Black Sea and the Sea of Azov; Mt. Roman-Kosh, at 5,069 feet (1,545 metres), is their highest point. The shores of the two seas are low, characterized by narrow, sandy spits of land that jut out into the water.

Climate. The Ukraine lies in a temperate climatic zone, influenced by moderately warm, humid air from the Atlantic Ocean. Winters in the west are considerably milder than those in the east, which is strongly affected by the northern high-pressure belts, or anticyclones. In summer, on the other hand, the east often experiences higher temperatures than the west. Average annual temperature ranges from 42°–45° F (5.5°–7° C) in the north to 52°–55° F (11°–13° C) in the south. The average temperature in January, the coldest month, is 26° F (−3° C) in the southwest and 18° F (−8° C) in the northeast. The average in July, the hottest month, is 73° F (23° C) in the southwest and 66° F (19° C) in the northeast.

Precipitation

Precipitation is uneven, with two to three times as much rainfall in the warmer seasons as in the cold. Maximum rainfall generally occurs in June and July, minimum in February. Snow falls mainly in late November and early December, varying in depth from a few inches in the Steppe region to several feet in the Carpathians.

The southern shore of the Crimea has a warm, gentle, Mediterranean-type climate. Winters are mild and rainy, with little snow, and the average January temperature is 39° F (4° C). Summers are dry and hot, with an average July temperature of 75° F (24° C). Precipitation totals 16 to 24 inches (400 to 600 millimetres) per year.

Drainage. Inland waters of the Ukraine include rivers, lakes, reservoirs, ponds, and marshes, as well as underground water sources. Almost all of the major rivers flow through the plains toward the Azov–Black Sea Basin; only 3 percent of drainage enters the Baltic Sea Basin. Nearly 23,000 rivers and streams are found within the republic's borders; some 3,000 of these are at least six miles (10 kilometres) long, and 116 exceed 60 miles in length. Of the total course of the Dnepr, 748 miles (1,204 kilometres) is in the Ukraine, making it by far the longest river in the republic, of which it drains more than half. Like the Dnepr, the Yuzhny Bug, with its major tributary, the Ingul, flows into the Black Sea. To the west and southwest, partly draining Ukrainian territory, the Dnestr (Dnister) also flows into the Black Sea; among its numerous tributaries, the largest in the Ukraine are the Stry and the Zbruch. The Danube River flows along the southwestern frontier of the Ukraine, and one of its tributaries, the Tisa, flows through Transcarpathia. The middle course of the Donets River, a tributary of the Don, flows through the Ukraine and is an important source of water for the Donets Basin. The largest river in the Crimea, the Salgir (Salhyr), flows into the Sea of Azov.

The rivers are most important as a water supply, and for this purpose a series of canals has been built, such as the Donets–Donets Basin, the Dnepr–Krivoy Rog, and the Kakhovka Reservoir–Crimea. Several of the larger rivers are navigable, including the Dnepr, Danube, Dnestr, Pripyat (Prypiat), Donets, and Yuzhny Bug (in its lower course). Mountain rivers are also used for rafting timber, and hydroelectric plants are situated on all of the larger ones.

Lakes and reservoirs

The Ukraine has a few lakes, all of them small and most of them very old, scattered over the river floodlands. One of the largest is Lake Svityaz (Svytiaz), 11 square miles (28 square kilometres) in area, in the northwest. Small saltwater lakes occur in the Don Basin and the Black Sea Upland. Lakes in the Carpathians are of the small, deep, alpine type. Some artificial lakes have been formed, the largest of which are reservoirs at hydroelectric dams. The Lenin Reservoir of the Lenin hydroelectric station on the Dnepr near Zaporozhye (Zaporizhia) is the best example, but other large reservoirs are found in the Donets and Krivoy Rog (Kryvyi Rih) basins near Zhdanov, Kharkov (Kharkiv), and other industrial centres. Almost 3 percent of the Ukraine is marshland, primarily in the northern river valleys and in the lower reaches of the Dnepr, Danube, and other rivers. Underground water is exceptionally important for agriculture, especially in three large artesian basins: the Volyn–Podolsk (Lvov), the Dnepr–Donets, and the Black Sea.

Soils. From northwest to southeast, the soils of the Ukraine may be divided into three major aggregations—a zone of sandy podzolized soils (a podzol is a soil having an acidic surface of forest humus, a light gray zone of leaching beneath it, and a bottom layer of accumulation); a central belt consisting of the famous Ukrainian chernozems (black-earth soils); and in the southeast a zone of chestnut and salinized soils surrounding the Black Sea.

The podzolized soils of the forested steppe, occupying about 21 percent of the republic's area, mostly in the northwest, were formed by the extension of postglacial forests into regions of grassy steppe; most of these soils may be farmed, although they require the addition of nutrients leached by the podzolizing process to obtain good harvests.

The chernozems of the centre are among the most fertile soils in the world, occupying about 65 percent of the republic's area; they may be divided into three broad groups: in the north a belt of the so-called deep, or thick, chernozems (the most fertile; about 5–6½ feet [1.5–2 metres] thick and rich in humus); south and east of the former, a zone of degraded (podzolized) chernozems, lean (eroded) chernozems, and podzolized mountain soils; the southernmost of these southwest–northeast-trending belts consists of ordinary steppe, or prairie, chernozems and the southern chernozems (both of the latter types are thinner than the deep chernozems, about 3 feet [1 metre], and high in humus, the southern less so than the ordinary). About 9 percent of the republic is covered by mixed gray and black-earth soils. Almost all soils in this belt are very fertile when enough water is available.

The remaining 5 percent of the soil cover consists of the chestnut soils of the south and east, similar in chemistry to the chernozems but lower in calcium and higher in sodium; they become increasingly salinized as they approach the Black Sea, where highly saline solonets and solonchak soils are found.

Plant life. Plant life exists in great variety. In the north the abundant rainfall and moderate temperatures provide favourable conditions for forest vegetation. Woodlands alternate with areas of steppe in the central region. Forest usually covers river valleys and the slopes of ravines and gorges. The total area of forested land, however, is only about 19,800,000 acres (8,000,000 hectares), and nearly one-third of this has been planted by man. Most of the rich forest lands are in the Transcarpathian region, with very little woodland in the south.

Polesye, Lesostep, and Steppe

Three natural zones of vegetation are distinguishable: the Polesye (woodland and marsh), the Lesostep (woodland–steppe), and the Steppe.

The Polesye zone lies in the northwest and north, with an area of about 44,000 square miles (114,000 square kilometres), of which 35 percent is arable land. Nearly one-quarter of this land is covered with mixed woodland, including oak, elm, birch, hornbeam, ash, maple, pine, linden, alder, poplar, willow, and beech. About 5 percent is peat bog, a substantial portion is marshland, and the river valleys are floodplains. Swamp drainage is a primary project in the Ukraine's program of land reclamation; in the 1970s about 7,500 square miles (19,400 square kilometres) of marshland were being reclaimed annually, most of it in the Polesye.

The 78,000-square-mile (202,000-square-kilometre) Lesostep extends south from the Polesye. Arable land covers about 67 percent of this agricultural region, forests only about 12 percent. Farther south, near the Black and Azov seas and the Crimean Mountains, the Lesostep joins the Steppe zone (92,500 square miles, or 240,000 square kilometres). The natural vegetation of the Steppe is protected in nature reserves, the largest being the Askaniya-Nova reserve in Kherson *oblast.* The lack of moisture makes necessary widespread irrigation, which in the mid-1970s was carried out on about 5,000 square miles (12,950 square kilometres) of the Ukraine's arid land, mostly in the Steppe zone.

Three other natural regions are found near the borders of the republic: the Carpathians, the Crimean Mountains, and the southern coast of the Crimean Peninsula. In the mountainous areas the lower slopes are covered with mixed forests, the intermediate slopes (4,000–5,000 feet, or 1,200–1,500 metres) with pine forests; these give way to grassland and alpine meadows at higher altitudes. A narrow strip of land, only six miles wide, along the southern coast of the Crimea constitutes a unique natural region where both deciduous and evergreen grasses and shrubs grow. Near the city of Yalta is located the Nikitsky Botanical Garden, in which plants from almost every country in the world are found. An exceptionally beautiful environment, a warm climate, and the sea make the southern shore of the Crimea one of the finest vacation areas in the world.

Animal life. The animal life of the Ukraine is diverse, with more than 350 species of birds, about 100 of mammals, and more than 200 of fish. The commonest predators are wolf, fox, wildcat, and marten, while hoofed animals include the roe deer, wild pig, and sometimes elk and mouflon (a wild sheep). The wide variety of rodents includes gophers, hamsters, jerboas, and field mice. The major bird species are black and hazel grouse, owl, gull, and partridge, as well as many migrating birds, such as wild goose, duck, and stork. Among the fish are pike, carp, bream, perch, sturgeon, and sterlet. Introduced and well-acclimatized wildlife includes muskrat, raccoon, beaver, nutria, and silver fox. Common insect pests are the meadow butterfly, sugar beet weevil, and cabbage butterfly.

Nature reserves. The conservation of the biological heritage of the republic is given high priority, and considerable manpower is expended on it. The republic established its first nature reserve, Askaniya-Nova, in 1921, three years before it entered the Soviet Union. This reserve, occupying about 25,900 acres (10,500 hectares), preserves a portion of virgin steppe, with characteristic fescue and feather grasses. Some 40 different mammals, including the onager and Przewalski's horse, have been introduced as part of a successful program of breeding endangered species; even ostriches have been successfully introduced.

Among the other important reserves is the Black Sea (established 1927; area 90,400 acres [36,600 hectares]), including protected areas of the sea. It is among the most visited reserves in the Ukraine, the attractions including many species of waterfowl, and is the only breeding ground in the Soviet Union of the gull *Larus melanocephalus.*

The Ukrainian Steppe reserve is discontinuous, comprising four separate sections, each of which preserves a special type of steppe: the Mikhaylovsk (Mykhailiv; virgin meadow steppe), the Strelets (Striletsky; a *stipa,* or grass steppe), the Khomutovsky (chernozem, or black-earth, steppe), and Kammeniye Mogily (Kamiani Mohyly, "Stone Tombs"; a stony steppe). This reserve was established in the period 1925–37. Other major reserves include the Crimean (established 1923, area 65,700 acres [26,590 hectares]), the Azov-Sivash (established 1927, area 21,000 acres [8,500 hectares]), and the Kanev (Kaniv; established 1931, area 2,570 acres [1,040 hectares]).

The people. The Ukraine ranks as the second most populous Soviet republic, after the Russian S.F.S.R. The great majority are Ukrainians, who are the second most numerous ethnic group in the Soviet Union, after Russians. Although more than 100 different nationalities live in the Ukraine, almost all the people are linguistically classified as Slavs, including Ukrainians, Russians, Poles, Belorussians, and Bulgarians. Jews account for a tiny percentage of the total, and there are small numbers of Greeks, Romanians, Armenians, Gypsies, Hungarians, Tatars, Chuvash, Lithuanians, Bashkirs, and Kazakhs.

Population density

The population density is among the highest in the Soviet Union, most notably in the highly industrialized Donets Basin and Dnepr Lowland. These two regions account for most of the total urban population. The major cities are Kiev, Kharkov, Odessa, Donetsk, Dnepropetrovsk, Zaporozhye, Krivoy Rog, and Lvov (in Ukrainian, Kyiv, Kharkiv, Odessa, Donetske, Dnipropetrovske, Zaporizhia, Kryvyi Rih, and Lviv). The rural population is distributed among the villages and some 10,000 other settlements, such as *sovkhozy* (state farms), *kolkhozy* (collective farms), and so on. More than 50 percent of the rural population lives in large villages (1,000 to 5,000 inhabitants), most of them located in the Lesostep area.

The economy. The complex industrial–agrarian economic structure of the Ukraine is integrally related to that of the entire Soviet Union. In its rate of economic development it ranks second among the Soviet republics (after the Russian S.F.S.R.). The effects of the devastation of the Nazi invasion in World War II have been completely overcome.

Resources. The Ukraine has many kinds of mineral resources. Iron-ore reserves are located in the Krivoy Rog, Kerch, Belozyorka, Kremenchug, and Mariupol regions. The Ukraine is one of the richest areas in the world in manganese-bearing ores. Anthracite and bituminous coal reserves are largely in the Donets Basin (called Donbass), and reserves of brown coal are mostly in the Dnepr Basin.

The three major petroleum-producing areas in the Ukraine are the Ciscarpathian, Dnepr–Donets, and Crimean regions.

Among the most important deposits of other minerals are the Irsha titanium ores, the Smela and Vysokopolye bauxite deposits, nephelites from the Oktyabrskoye and Yelanchitsa deposits near the Sea of Azov, the Beregovo and Began deposits of alunites, and the Nikitovka mercury (cinnabar, or mercuric sulfide) ores in the Donets Basin. The largest deposit of ozokerite (a natural paraffin wax) in the Soviet Union is near the city of Borislav. Ciscarpathia possesses potassium salt deposits. That region and the Donets Basin have very large resources of rock salt. Some phosphorites exist, notably in the Izyum and Krolevets deposits, as well as natural sulfur in the Ciscarpathian and Dnepr regions and in the Crimea. In Transcarpathia and near the cities of Lvov, Kiev, Vinnitsa (Vinnytsia), Poltava, Khmelnitsky (Khmelnytsky), and Kharkov are health spas noted for their mineral springs; spas near the Black Sea and the Sea of Azov specialize in mud baths.

Health spas and mineral springs

Industry. The Ukrainian S.S.R. has a major ferrous-metal industry, producing a good percentage of the Soviet Union's cast iron, steel and rolled steel, and steel pipe. Mining output is also a very high proportion of the Soviet total, the main products being coal, natural gas, and iron ore. Manufactured goods include metallurgical equipment, diesel locomotives, tractors, and television sets. The Ukrainian chemical industry produces coke, mineral fertilizers, and sulfuric acid. The food industry produces granulated sugar, grain, sugar beets, sunflower seeds, potatoes, vegetables, meat, eggs, and milk. Diversified industry, in more than 150 fields, is the most important sector in the economy in terms of productivity and revenue earned.

Railway locomotives and freight cars, seagoing vessels, hydroelectric and thermal steam and gas turbines, electrical generators, and automobiles are made in Ukrainian factories. Expanded residential and industrial construction demands hoisting and transportation equipment and other machinery for the building trades. The Ukraine is also the principal centre of production of giant airliners.

Plants for the production of equipment for food-processing and other light industries are scattered throughout the republic. The Ukraine, one of the great agricultural regions of the world, also has more than 50 factories engaged in the production of a wide range of agricultural equipment, the chief centres of production being Kharkov, Odessa, Lvov, and Kherson. Machine-tool and instrument-manufacturing industries are being developed. The growing importance of consumer goods is reflected in the increasing output of, among other items, cameras, television sets, refrigerators, and washing machines.

The Ukrainian chemical-equipment industry, accounting for one-third of Soviet production, is mainly concentrated in Kiev, Sumy, Fastov (Fastiv), and Korosten. The chemical industry includes coking and the manufacture of coke products, as well as the manufacture of mineral fertilizers, sulfuric acid, synthetic fibres, caustic soda, petrochemicals, photographic chemicals, and pesticides.

The larger divisions of the Ukrainian food-processing industry—sugar refining, processing of meat, fruit, and dairy products, wine making, and distilling—are important to the entire Soviet Union. Of the approximately 2,000 products, one of the most important is sugar. Production of vegetable oil, mainly from sunflower seeds, is also significant. Nearly 30 percent of all the wine made in the Soviet Union comes from the Ukraine—in the south, in the Transcarpathian region, and in the Crimea, where the vintners of the Massandra group are established near Yalta. In the coastal cities, such as Odessa, are found local industries processing fish.

Some of the principal products of light industry are textiles, both knitted and woven, ready-to-wear garments, and shoes.

Energy. Almost all the energy for industrial processes in the Ukraine is provided by fossil fuels, hydroelectricity accounting for only a tiny percentage. Thermal power stations are found in all parts of the republic, though the largest are in the Donets Basin and along the Dnepr. A third electric energy-producing area is in the vicinity of the Lvov–Volyn coal basin, and in the Ciscarpathian region there is a group of six hydropower stations.

Agriculture. Although the German occupation in World War II almost completely destroyed Ukrainian agriculture, recovery was achieved by 1955. The Ukraine today accounts for more than 20 percent of the Soviet Union's agricultural produce and, in particular, grain. Four-fifths of Ukrainian agricultural production is represented by grain, potatoes, vegetables, fodder crops, fruit, and grapes. Sugar beets are the most important industrial crop, primarily in the Lesostep region. Sunflower seeds are the principal oil crop. In the northwest a considerable acreage is allotted to flax. Potatoes are grown in the northern and central regions. In the southern steppes, especially where irrigation is practiced, vegetables are grown; truck farming, or market gardening, takes place in the Donets Basin and along the Dnepr River and on the outskirts of the cities of Kiev, Kharkov, and Lvov. Fruit is grown throughout the Ukraine but especially in the Crimea, Transcarpathia and Ciscarpathia, and the Lesostep.

Beef and dairy cattle, pigs, sheep, and goats are raised throughout the republic. Bees are kept chiefly in the Lesostep and the Polesye, and silkworms are raised in Transcarpathia.

Almost 8,000 collective farms (*kolkhozy*) and 1,700 or so state farms (*sovkhozy*) raise most of the cattle, cereals, and sugar beets. These highly mechanized enterprises employ agronomists, zoologists, veterinarians, engineers, and other specialists.

Fishing. The Black Sea estuaries are the main fishing grounds, although the Sea of Azov, rivers, lakes, ponds, and reservoirs also contribute to the fish catch. Among the major rivers for fishing are the Dnepr, Danube, Dnestr, Yuzhny Bug, and Donets.

Transportation. The flat relief of most of the Ukraine presents few obstacles to transportation, and the republic thus utilizes almost every means of modern transport. The heaviest concentration of railroad trackage is in the Donets Basin and near the Dnepr River, especially its right bank; the largest railroad centres are Kharkov, Kiev, Dnepropetrovsk, Bakhmach, Yasinovataya, Debaltsevo, Kovel, and Kupyansk.

Ukrainian docks on the Black Sea and the Sea of Azov handle more than a fifth of the Soviet Union's ocean freight, mainly at the ports of Odessa, Ilyichevsk (Illichevske), Nikolayev (Mikolayiv), Kherson, Feodosiya (Feodosia), Kerch, and Zhdanov. Ships of the whaling fleet Sovetskaya Ukraina (Soviet Ukraine) sail from Odessa to the Antarctic.

River shipping

River shipping is conducted primarily on the Dnepr and its tributaries (the Pripyat and Desna), on the Yuzhny Bug, and on the Danube, important in trade with other European countries. Ships on the Danube call at the port of Izmail, which is accessible to oceangoing freighters and passenger liners. Through the Dneprovsko–Bugsky (Dnepr–Bug) Kanal, in Belorussia, the inland waterways of the Ukraine are joined to the Vistula Basin of Poland and to the Baltic. Efforts to transform the Dnepr into a continuous, deep waterway have been furthered by the creation of large reservoirs at hydroelectric stations. The largest ports on the Dnepr are Kiev, Dnepropetrovsk, Zaporozhye, and Kherson.

A network of good highways connects all the regions and large industrial centres. The links between Kiev and Moscow, Kiev and Leningrad, Moscow–Kharkov–Simferopol (Symferopol), and Kharkov and Rostov-na-Donu are of importance to the whole Soviet Union.

Kiev is connected by air with all the regional centres of the republic and with major cities throughout the Soviet Union. Major airports include Borispol (Boryspil), near Kiev, and those at Kharkov and Odessa.

The exploitation of petroleum and natural gas has brought about the creation of a pipeline transport system. The major natural gas lines connect Mukachevo and Kiev; Shebelinka (Shebelynka) and Kharkov; Shebelinka, Poltava, and Kiev; Shebelinka, Dnepropetrovsk, Krivoy Rog, and Odessa; and Shebelinka and Slavyansk. The chief petroleum pipelines are the Dolina–Drogobych (Dolyna–Drohobych) and Gnedintsy–Priluki lines and a 420-mile (670-kilometre) segment of the trans-European Druzhba (Friendship) line, which supplies Soviet oil to other eastern European countries.

The Ukrainian transportation system makes industrial and agricultural products available to the entire Soviet Union. By this same network, the Ukraine receives petroleum and petroleum products from the Trans-Volga region, nonferrous metals from Kazakhstan and the Urals, and several types of machinery, fabric, footwear, and printed material from the central Soviet regions. By sea, bread, sugar, iron ore, coal, manganese, and machinery are exported, and coffee, tea, cocoa, fruit, jute, machinery, and equipment are imported.

Administrative and social conditions. *Government.* The government of the Ukrainian Soviet Socialist Republic is organized according to the 1937 constitution. As amended in 1944, the constitution (like the constitutions of the other union republics, as well as that of the Soviet Union) gives the Ukraine the right to "enter into direct relations with foreign states, to conclude agreements, and to exchange diplomatic and consular representatives with them" and to maintain its own military forces. The only real expression of these constitutional prerogatives in international affairs is the Ukraine's membership in the United Nations (it was one of the founding members), a distinction it shares with Belorussia, the two being the only UN members that are not fully sovereign countries. It is also a member of some 70 other international organizations.

Ukrainians abroad

These international contacts are more direct and of longer historical standing than those of most Soviet republics, and, because there are large communities of Ukrainians in Europe and North America, official institutions display considerable nationalism. There is, for example, a society specifically created to maintain cultural relations with foreign organizations and individuals, and two weekly newspapers on events in the Ukraine are published for distribution overseas.

In the main, however, contacts permitted by the central authorities of the Soviet Union between the Ukraine and foreign countries are not of great importance. While the Ukrainian Ministry of Trade is permitted to establish agreements (especially exchanges) overseas, usually these are limited to the Socialist countries of eastern Europe and are not of great enough value or volume to affect the promulgation of national policy either domestically or internationally.

The Supreme Soviet

The highest legislative unit is the unicameral Supreme Soviet of the Ukrainian S.S.R., whose members are elected for four years from a single slate of candidates. The Supreme Soviet meets twice a year for a few days to approve, generally unanimously, budgetary and other proposals made by the central government in Moscow and legislation passed by its Presidium and Council of Ministers. The Presidium of the Supreme Soviet, selected by that body and composed of a chairman, two vice chairmen, a secretary, and 15 members, acts for the Supreme Soviet between sessions, exercising both executive and legislative powers.

The highest executive and administrative organ is the Council of Ministers, which is equivalent to a cabinet; its chairman is the counterpart of a premier in the West. Most legislation introduced to the Supreme Soviet comes from the Council of Ministers, which is responsible for carrying out policy decisions made in Moscow.

The highest court in the judicial system is the Supreme Court of the Ukrainian S.S.R., consisting of five judges elected for five-year terms by the Supreme Soviet. The court's function is to supervise judicial activities; it does not rule on constitutional questions (a function of the Presidium). On the local level, justice is dispensed by "people's courts."

The only political party is the Communist Party of the Ukraine (CPU), a branch of the Communist Party of the Soviet Union (CPSU) formed in 1918. Most of the major legislation approved by the Supreme Soviet originates in, or is approved by, the CPU.

Education. In 1917 more than 70 percent of the population was illiterate. Within the next half century, illiteracy was practically wiped out, and 99 percent of the population can now read and write. Ukrainian is the main language of instruction, although there are schools in which Russian, Moldavian, Polish, Bulgarian, Hungarian, French, German, Spanish, or English is dominant. Great emphasis is placed on general and correspondence schools, as these institutions allow young industrial and agricultural workers to receive an education without interrupting their work.

Further education for workers

An extensive system of higher education includes the state universities at Kiev, Kharkov, Odessa, Dnepropetrovsk, Lvov, Chernovtsy (Chernivtsi), Uzhgorod (Uzhhorod), and Donetsk (Donetske). The largest single scientific organization is the Academy of Sciences of the Ukrainian S.S.R., which governs a host of research institutions and scientific workers. Founded in 1919, the academy received the Order of Lenin in 1969 for its contributions to science and Soviet life. After the Academy of Sciences, the largest concentration of scientific and technical workers is in the universities. Among the specialized scientific facilities available in the republic are a half dozen oceanographic research vessels, which are the basis of a substantial concentration of scientific manpower in the areas of mineral resources, biology, and, with the cooperation of schools of chemistry and technology, desalinization of seawater.

Elsewhere in the republic can be found one of the finest experimental nuclear reactors in the world, five computer centres, four astronomical observatories, and seven major botanical gardens. Ukrainian scientists and technicians have made important discoveries and advances in the fields of cybernetics; nuclear and plasma physics; foundry, blast furnace, and powder metallurgy technology; and welding methods. In medicine they have made contributions in the areas of tissue therapy and brain biochemistry.

Social services. Medical help is available in hospitals and also in medical centres in such places as factories and schools. There are sanitation-epidemiological centres, institutions staffed by paramedical personnel and midwives, gynecological outpatient clinics, children's clinics, and sanatoriums and rest homes. More workers are sent annually to sanatoriums, rest homes, resorts, camps, and boardinghouses. Many workers get accommodations at one-third of the cost or free of charge. The residue is paid by trade unions from social consumption funds at their disposal. All the funds originally derived from a turnover tax and from various taxes levied on individuals, collective farms, and others.

Standard of living

The standard of living of the Ukrainian people is rising. More than three-quarters of the republic's income is used for individual workers' funds and collective benefits, such as public health, education, and pension funds. The major supplements to wages from public funds include free medical care and education, pension and stipend payments, vacation benefits, and the maintenance of kindergarten and child-care facilities.

During World War II, 714 cities and towns and 26,000 villages were devastated, and reconstruction was a long project.

Cultural life. *Visual arts.* Over the centuries Ukrainians have evolved a varied folk art. Embroidery, wood carving, ceramics, and weaving are highly developed, with stylized ornamentation in many regional styles. Intricately designed Easter eggs (*pysanky*) have become popular in many countries that have Ukrainian immigrant populations.

With the introduction of Christianity in the 10th century, the various forms of Byzantine art (architecture, mosaics, frescoes, manuscript illumination, icon painting) spread rapidly and remained the dominant art forms through the 16th century. The mosaics and frescoes of the churches of Kiev, notably the Cathedral of St. Sophia (11th–12th century), and the icons of the more distinctively Ukrainian school in Galicia (15th–16th century) are particularly noteworthy. Western European influences in the 17th and 18th centuries affected iconography and stimulated portrait painting, engraving, and sculpture. From the Ukraine the Western trends penetrated into Russia, where many Ukrainian artists worked, especially after the Ukraine lost its autonomy to Russia in the 18th century. During the late 18th and early 19th centuries the portraitists Dmytro Levytsky and Volodymyr Borovykovsky were among the leading figures of the St. Petersburg Classical school of painting.

The Classicism and the emergent Realism of the 19th century are best exemplified by the poet-painter Taras Shevchenko. New movements—Impressionism, Expressionism, Futurism—affected the work of such 19th-century painters as Ivan Trush and Oleksandr Novakivsky. Modernism and experimentation ended in the Soviet Ukraine in the 1930s, however, when Socialist Realism became the only officially sanctioned method in the arts.

A number of Ukrainian artists have won considerable renown in the West, among them the painter Alexis Gritchenko (Hryshchenko). The sculptor Alexander Archipenko, one of the pioneers of Cubism, who later experimented in Constructivism, Expressionism, and Surrealism, was a major figure of 20th-century European art.

Music. Folk music in the Ukraine retains great vitality to this day. Ritual songs, ballads, and historical songs (*dumy*) were sung *a cappella* or accompanied by folk instruments, of which the multi-stringed *bandura* is the most popular. Church music was patterned on Byzantine and Bulgarian models with local variations evolving in Kiev in the early period. Polyphonic singing developed by the 16th century and was subsequently in the 17th transmitted to Russia, where Ukrainian singers and musical culture soon won a dominant position. Ukrainian choral music reached its peak in the 18th and early 19th centuries in the works of Maksym Berezovsky, Dmytro Bortnyansky, and Artem Vedel.

Choral music

Secular music became ascendant in the 19th century. The opera *Zaporozhets za Dunayem* ("A Cossack Beyond the Danube"; 1863) by Semen Hulak-Artemovsky gained great popularity, as did *Kateryna* by Mykola Arkas and the compositions of Petro Nishchynsky. At the turn of the century, Ukrainian musical life was dominated by Mykola Lysenko, whose output encompassed vocal and choral settings, piano compositions, and operas, including *Natalka Poltavka* (1889), *Utoplena* ("The Drowned Girl"), and *Taras Bulba.* Other major composers of the period were Kyrylo Stetsenko and Mykola Leontovych.

In the early years of the Soviet period several composers produced works of high artistic merit, particularly Lev Revutsky and Borys Lyatoshynsky and their contemporary in Polish-occupied Galicia, Stanyslav Lyudkevych. From the mid-1930s, however, political regimentation dampened individual expression and innovation in musical language. Typical among contemporary composers of the Soviet Ukraine are Kostyantyn Dankevych, Yuliy Meytus, and the brothers Yuriy and Platon Maiboroda.

The Ukraine has six opera theatres, numerous symphony orchestras, academic and folk choirs, and other performing ensembles.

Theatre and motion pictures. The theatre originated in the Ukraine under Western influence in the 17th century Verse dialogue (*intermedia*) rapidly developed into a specific genre, the school theatre, whose repertory expanded to encompass dramatization of Christian legends, historical drama, and a puppet play (*vertep*) performed on a stage of two levels. The best example of the Cossack Baroque theatre was Feofan Prokopovich's historical play *Vladimir* (1705). After a period of decline, a Ukrainian ethnographic theatre developed in the 19th century. Folk plays and vaudeville were raised to a high level of artistry by such actors as Mykola Sadovsky and Maria Zankovetska in the late 19th and early 20th centuries. The lifting of censorship in 1905 permitted a significant expansion of the repertory to include modern dramas by Lesya Ukrainka, Volodymyr Vynnychenko, and Oleksandr Oles, as well as translated plays.

The real flowering of the Ukrainian theatre occurred between 1917 and 1933. The Berezil Theatre (1922–33) in Kharkov, under the artistic director Les Kurbas, was the most distinguished troupe. Preeminent among the playwrights was Mykola Kulish, whose *Patetychna Sonata* ("Sonata Pathétique") combined Expressionist techniques with the forms of the Ukrainian *vertep.* Since the mid-1930s, however, the theatre in the Ukraine has been dominated by Socialist Realism. Oleksandr Korniychuk (Korniichuk) has been the most favoured of the playwrights writing in the approved manner.

There are about 60 professional theatres in the Ukraine, notably the Ivan Franko Theatre in Kiev and the Maria Zankovetska Theatre in Lvov.

Film

Ukrainian film has achieved some marked successes. The director and scenarist Aleksandr (Ukrainian Oleksandr) Dovzhenko (who died in 1956) was an important innovator in world cinematography. Among his works, *Zvenygora* (1928), *Arsenal* (1929), and especially *Zemlya* (1930; "The Earth") have become classics of the silent-film era. In later years, *Tini zabutykh predkiv* ("Shadows of Forgotten Ancestors"), directed by Serhii Paradzhanov, won critical acclaim in the West. The Ukrainian motion-picture industry is centred on the O. Dovzhenko Studio in Kiev and on the Odessa studio.

Literature. Oral literature in the Ukraine can be traced back to pre-Christian times. Pagan ritual songs were subsequently much modified by association with various church feasts (*e.g., koliadky* with the Christmas cycle). The heroic epics of the early medieval period (*byliny*) may have survived in the Ukraine until the 16th century, but they were then wholly superseded by historical songs (*dumy*) based on events in the 16th and 17th centuries in the Cossack Ukraine.

Written literature began with Christianization and the introduction of Church Slavonic as a liturgical and literary language, later increasingly influenced by vernacular Ukrainian. Only with the school theatre of the 17th–18th century and with Ivan Kotlyarevsky's *Eneida* (1798) did vernacular Ukrainian begin to develop as an independent literary language.

The earliest works of the Kievan period (10th century and following) were the historical annals: *Povest vremennykh let* ("Tale of Bygone Years"), the Hypatian (Kievan) chronicle, and the Galician–Volhynian chronicle. The 12th-century *Slovo o polku Igoreve* ("Lay of Igor's Campaign") is a unique historical epic, written in the ornamental style. Sermons, tales, and lives of the saints comprised the major genres.

After the Mongol invasions (13th century), literature suffered a period of decline. Revival began in the late 16th century with the introduction of printing, the Reformation ferment, and the advance of the Counter-Reformation into Polish-dominated Ukrainian lands. The Union of Brest-Litovsk (1596), which united several million Ukrainian and Belorussian Orthodox with Rome, stimulated an exceedingly rich polemical literature, with the *Apocrisis* ("Reply"; 1598) of the pseudonymous Khrystofor Filalet and the anonymous *Perestoroha* ("Warning"; 1605) on the Orthodox side and the *Antirizis* ("Refutation"; 1599) of Ipatii Potii in the Uniat camp. The most distinguished and prolific polemicist was the Orthodox Ivan Vyshensky, whose ornate style combines Church Slavonic with vernacular elements.

The major current in Ukrainian literature of the 17th and 18th centuries, as in all of Europe, was the Baroque, with its love of adornment and originality. Among the major figures of this age were Kassian Sakovych and Ivan Velychkovsky in verse, Yoannikiy Galyatovsky in homiletics, and Feofan Prokopovich in the drama. Historical writing is best represented by the Cossack chronicle of Samoil Velychko (*c.* 1720). Of interest for their content and their literary qualities were the 18th-century writings of the philosopher Hryhoriy Skovoroda, styled the "Ukrainian Socrates." (I.A.Y./Ed.)

HISTORY

Kievan Rus. In the territory known in the 20th century as the Ukraine there existed in the 9th century a political organization called Rus, which belongs to the history of both the Russian and Ukrainian nations. It originally covered the areas of Kiev (Kyiv), Chernigov, and Pereyaslavl, under the suzerainty of a duke of Varangian origin. These Varangians were called Rus by the surrounding Slavonic tribes, a name borrowed from the Finns, for whom the people from the other side of the Baltic were Ruotsi. The conquerors became Slavicized. St. Vladimir, who accepted the Christian faith from Byzantium in 988–989, was no longer a Varangian *koning,* or king, but a Slavonic *knyaz,* or prince. This Kievan state extended westward and northward during the 11th and 12th centuries but was destroyed in the Tatar invasion of 1237–41.

St. Vladimir

A century before the fall of the Kievan state two principalities existed with capitals at Wlodzimierz (Vladimir Volynski, or Volodymir) in Volhynia and Halicz (Galich, or Halych) on the Dnestr River. Prince Roman of Volhynia, a direct descendant of St. Vladimir, united the two principalities in 1199 and founded a local dynasty, which became extinct in 1323. The succession passed, by family ties, to a Polish prince of the Piast dynasty, Bolesław of Mazovia, and, in 1340, to King Casimir the Great, who in 1349 incorporated into his kingdom the principality of Galiciae et Lodomeriae.

Polish expansion. Meanwhile, Lithuania was extending rapidly eastward and southward. The dynastic union of Poland and Lithuania in 1386 opened up the Ukraine to Polish expansion. The frontier moved steadily eastward across the vast, sparsely populated *ukraina* (*u-,* "at"; *-kraj,* "land," or "border"). A new social order was also being created, for the peasants were subject to their local lords for whom they were obliged to work. But it was easy for men to escape farther southeast into the great no-man's-land, and such a fugitive was called *kozak,* an adaptation of the Turkic word *kazakh,* meaning "outlaw," or "adventurer." These Cossacks were escaping "beyond the cataracts" (*za porohy*) on the lower Dnepr River. Thus was born the Zaporizhska Sich, or Zaporozhian clearing.

At the beginning of the 16th century, to protect their states against the incursions of the Tatars, both the Polish kings and the Muscovite grand princes started to organize military colonies manned by the Cossacks; at the end of that century both the Dnepr and Don Cossacks alike owned land and led a settled life. When the Polish–Lithuanian union became a real one in 1569, the Ukrainian territory was separated from Lithuania and incorporated into Poland. The Cossacks believed that as warriors they were free from all serfdom. But for the Polish estate owners, Cossacks escaping to Zaporozhe were rebels, and by trying to enforce obedience the landowners aroused resentment. This social antagonism had also a religious foundation, for landlords, sheriffs, and magistrates were almost exclusively Roman Catholics. Slowly, a national separatism was being born.

This evolution was not stopped by the religious union achieved by the synod that met at Brzesc (Brest-Litovsk) in June 1595 and October 1596. Nine out of 10 Orthodox bishops recognized in matters of doctrine the full primacy of the Holy See, but they retained the ancient Eastern rite. As a result of the union of 1596 the population of the Ukraine became divided into three religious groups: the Roman Catholics of the Latin rite, who were generally identical with Poles; the Uniate Roman Catholics now known as Eastern Catholics; and the Orthodox—*i.e.,* the Cossacks. The last two groups often called themselves *gente Rutheni, natione Poloni* ("people of Ruthenians, nation of Poles").

Religious union and division

From 1578 there existed a small standing force of "registered" Cossacks in Polish service, while all others were either counted among the feudal peasantry or formed the so-called self-governing Zaporozhian Cossacks. In 1630 the registered Cossacks were increased to 8,000, and the claims of the Orthodox population were in part fulfilled by dividing the high offices of the church between Uniates and Orthodox. But when Poland built the fortress of Kudak at the cataracts (its site is currently included in the town of Dnepropetrovsk) to keep the Sich in dependence, rebellions broke out between 1635 and 1638. All of these rebellions were suppressed. The Polish Sejm (Diet) in 1638 passed an act reducing the number of registered Cossacks to 6,000 and aiming at the suppression of self-governing Cossacks.

The Khmelnytsky insurrection. An officer of registered Cossacks, Bohdan Khmelnytsky (or Chmielnicki), who had suffered injustice at the hands of a local Polish official, went "underground" in 1647 and a year later was elected hetman (commander in chief) of the Zaporozhian

Cossacks, gathered several thousand men, took Kudak by surprise and destroyed it, obtained help from the Tatars, and in May 1648 defeated the Poles in the battles of Zhovti Vody and Korsun. Khmelnytsky moved into Poland, won a victory on September 23 at Pilawce, took Lvov (Polish Lwow), and besieged Zamosc. The slaughter of landlords, the Latin and Uniate clergy, and the Jews spread throughout the conquered countryside. Meanwhile, the King of Poland promised that he would send a commission of inquiry to the Ukraine. The Hetman stopped fighting and in October entered Kiev where he was greeted as liberator.

Meanwhile, in Warsaw, the party of conciliation was opposed by all the Ukrainian magnates, who were for repression by force. In March 1649 Khmelnytsky resumed operations. The Poles again suffered defeat, and on August 18, at Zborow, the King reached an agreement with Khmelnytsky by which the number of registered Cossacks was raised to 40,000 and all officials of the crown in the provinces of Kiev, Chernigov, and Bratslav were to be Orthodox. The Zborow agreement was criticized by both the Polish gentry and the Cossacks, the former objecting to the creation within the frontiers of Poland of what amounted to an autonomous Ukrainian principality and the latter resenting the return of Polish landlords to their estates. Because a ferment was spreading among the Cossacks against Khmelnytsky's statesmanship, he started another campaign in the spring of 1651; but on June 29–30 he was defeated at Berestechko. On September 28, at Bila Tserkva, the Hetman was compelled to accept a new agreement: the registered Cossacks were reduced to 20,000, and the provinces of Chernigov and Bratslav ceased to be Cossack territory. The Cossack Rada (Council) also rejected the new agreement, resolving in May 1652 to renew hostilities against Poland and to ask Tsar Alexia (Aleksey Mikhaylovich) for protection.

Search for a protector. The second Romanov saw his chance to regain the Kievan Rus, which the Muscovites called Malo-Rossiya (Little Russia). On October 11 (October 1, old style), 1653, the Moscow Council of State decided to grant Khmelnytsky's request and to declare war on Poland. A deputation headed by Vasili V. Buturlin met Khmelnytsky and the secretary general of the Rada, Ivan Vyhovsky, at Pereyaslavl. On January 18 (January 8, O.S.), 1654, took place the act of submitting the Ukraine to "the tsar's hand," with the general reservation "of all rights and privileges" for the Cossacks. A Russo-Polish war, complicated by Swedish aggression, followed and was ended by an armistice in 1656. On Khmelnytsky's death in 1657 Vyhovsky succeeded him as hetman. The new hetman decided to throw off Russian protection. On September 16, 1658, an agreement was signed at Hadziacz (Hadyach) that created a commonwealth of the Poles, Lithuanians, and Ruthenians. A second Russo-Polish war followed. It lasted eight years and was ended on February 9 (January 30, O.S.), 1667, by the Treaty of Andruszow (Andrusovo), under which the Ukraine was partitioned between Poland and Russia along the Dnepr River, and the two governments outlawed Petro Doroshenko, the then hetman, whom neither trusted.

Cossack-Russian alliance

Doroshenko conceived the plan that the Ukraine should form a vassal state of the Ottoman Empire, and in December 1668 Sultan Mehmed (Mohammed) IV took the Ukraine under his protection. In 1672 a Turkish army marched against Poland, took Kamieniec (Kamenets) Podolski, and on October 18 imposed the Peace of Buczacz (Buchach) by which the "right-bank," or Polish, Ukraine came under Ottoman suzerainty. This treaty was never ratified by the Polish Sejm, but not until 1684, a year after his spectacular victory of Vienna, was John III Sobieski able to clear the Polish Ukraine of the Turks; they remained at Kamieniec until the Treaty of Carlowitz (Karlowitz, or Karlovci; January 26, 1699).

In the "left-bank," or Russian, Ukraine, Ivan Mazepa became hetman of the Cossacks in 1687. He served Tsar Peter I the Great but planned to unite the two parts of the Ukraine. In 1708 he concluded an alliance with Charles XII of Sweden according to which the Ukraine was to become an independent state with Mazepa as ruler. Peter's victory over the Swedes at Poltava on July 8 (June 27, O.S.), 1709, put an end to this new Ukrainian orientation. There were three further hetmans, all of them Russian nominees. Kyrylo Razumovsky, the last, was the younger brother of the empress Elizabeth's favourite. Catherine II the Great forced him to resign in 1764.

Under tsarist rule. In 1775 the Sich was suppressed, the Cossacks were disarmed, and the Russian Ukraine was divided into three *guberniyi.* In 1793, at the second partition of Poland, the Ukraine was again united, but as part of Russia. Not only its political autonomy but even its name disappeared. In 1846 Ukrainian nationalism was reborn when about 30 Ukrainian patriots founded in Kiev the secret Brotherhood of SS. Cyril and Methodius. The brotherhood's most prominent members were two historians, Mykola Kostomariv (1817–85) and Panteleimon Kulish (1819–97), along with the poet Taras Shevchenko (1814–61), who in his poem "The Dream" accused Peter I of "crucifying" the Ukraine and Catherine II of "finishing off his victim." The brotherhood was discovered the following year, and its members were arrested and deported to other parts of Russia. In 1861, however, *Osnova* ("The Outset"), a periodical in Ukrainian, was authorized to appear in St. Petersburg, with Kulish and Volodymir Antonovich (1834–1908) as principal contributors. Two years later they returned to Kiev, where a society called Hromada (Group) was formed. Their historical research led them to certain contradictory conclusions. Antonovich believed that, placed between an autocratic Russia and an aristocratic Poland, the Ukrainians represented a true democracy. Kulish, however, maintained that the Cossacks were anarchist rather than democratic. In 1876 the tsarist government forbade the use of the Ukrainian language in schools and for the printing of journals or books. Myhailo Dragomaniv (1841–95), a professor at Kiev University, moved to Geneva, where between 1878 and 1883 he published five volumes of the Ukrainian periodical *Hromada.*

Brotherhood of SS. Cyril and Methodius

Galician "Piedmont." After 1876, Lvov became the centre of Ukrainian nationalism. It was the capital of Galicia, annexed to Austria in 1772 at the time of the first partition of Poland, and the name was thus extended far to the west, to include Kraków; in eastern Galicia, however, the rural population was mainly Ruthenian. The Vienna government had to recognize Polish supremacy in Galicia, but it also supported the Ruthenians. In 1868 the educational society Prosvita (Enlightenment) came into being in Lvov. Four years later a Shevchenko Scientific Society was founded there. In 1890 a chair for the history of southeastern Europe was instituted at Lvov University, and Myhailo Hrushevsky (1866–1934), a Russian subject and a pupil of Antonovich, was appointed to the post. In 1898 he started publication of his 10-volume *History of the Ukraine-Rus,* in which he defended the view that the Kievan Rus was the cradle of the Ukraine-Rus, while Moscow was the centre around which the Russian state was built. After 1905 the publication of journals and books in Ukrainian was again permitted in Russia, and Hrushevsky returned to Kiev.

World War I and after. In the eyes of the tsarist government the population of eastern Galicia and sub-Carpathian Ruthenia was "Russian." Count Georgy Bobrinsky, the newly appointed governor general, affirmed this in Lvov in September 1914, when the Russian Army entered the city. But tsarist Russia was defeated and plunged into revolution. The Ukrainians felt that once more history was presenting them with a chance to achieve unity and independence. A National Ukrainian Congress met in Kiev in April 1917 and elected a Rada (Council) headed by Hrushevsky. On June 23, in its first universal (the name of the proclamation issued by the hetmans of the Ukraine in the 17th century), the Rada proclaimed that an autonomous Ukrainian republic had come into being with Hrushevsky as president. On July 16 a government, called the General Secretariat, was formed with Volodymir Vinnichenko (1880–1951) as premier and Symon Petlyura (1879–1926) as war minister. On November 20, the Rada announced the convocation of a freely elected Ukrainian Constituent Assembly. The Russian Communist government replied to

Proclamation of the republic

this on December 26 by forming a Ukrainian Soviet government in Kharkov. On January 22, 1918, in its fourth universal, the Rada proclaimed a "free and sovereign" Ukrainian republic.

On February 9, 1918, the Central Powers concluded a separate peace with this republic at Brest-Litovsk. On the previous day the Communists had captured Kiev, and the Rada had fled to Zhitomir. The German and Austrian armies occupied the Ukraine and soon came into conflict with the Rada, which was too democratic for their liking. On April 24 they staged a coup d'etat, appointing Pavlo Skoropadsky hetman of the Ukraine. After the collapse of the Central Powers, a directorate of five, with Vinnichenko as chairman and Petlyura as commander in chief, assumed power in Kiev.

Meanwhile, on November 1, 1918, in Lvov, the last Austrian governor, Count Huyn, had armed the Ukrainians, who proclaimed an independent Republic of the Western Ukraine. The Poles freed the town on November 22, and the Ukrainian government, headed by Evhen Petrushevych, retreated to Stanislawow (now Ivano-Frankovsk). There, on January 22, 1919, the union of the two Ukraines was proclaimed; but on the same day, the Red Army reoccupied Kiev. While the directorate, now headed by Petlyura, moved to Vinnitsa, Khristian Rakovsky formed in Kiev, on March 14, a government of a Ukrainian Soviet Socialist Republic. In May 1919 the whole of eastern Galicia was in Polish hands, and in the summer the Russian White Army of Gen. A.I. Denikin started to advance toward Moscow. On September 1 the White Russians and the Petlyurians entered Kiev, and the directorate suggested a common struggle against the Communists, but Denikin refused to negotiate with "separatists." Denikin was subsequently defeated, and on December 20 Kiev was evacuated and almost the whole of the Ukraine was in the hands of the Red Army.

Treaty of alliance

On December 28, 1919, Lenin addressed an open letter to the workers and peasants of the Ukraine in which he recognized the equality of the Russian and Ukrainian peoples and suggested a treaty of alliance between the two. Such an alliance was concluded in Moscow on December 28, 1920, and was signed by Lenin and Rakovsky; it was an act of incorporation.

Petlyura retreated with the remnant of his army to Kamieniec Podolski and went to Warsaw to ask Marshal Józef Piłsudski, head of the Polish state and commander in chief, for help. On April 21, 1920, Piłsudski signed a treaty of alliance with Petlyura, and three days later a Polish offensive started in the Ukraine. On May 7 the Poles occupied Kiev. Piłsudski dreamed of building a commonwealth of Polish, Lithuanian, and Ukrainian nations and hoped that the Ukraine would answer Petlyura's call. It soon was obvious that it would not. The fortunes of war forced Poland to sign the Treaty of Riga (March 18, 1921) with the Communist Russian and Ukrainian governments. Eastern Galicia and Volhynia were recognized as part of Poland. On May 25, 1926, in Paris, Petlyura was assassinated.

Ukraine in the U.S.S.R. On December 30, 1922, the first All-Union Congress of the Soviets voted a plan of federation between the four original soviet socialist republics—the Russian, Belorussian, Ukrainian, and Transcaucasian. The final constitution was published on July 6, 1923. This was the period of the New Economic Policy (NEP) and, in the Ukraine, the period of Ukrainization. A Language Act of August 1, 1923, proclaimed the priority of Ukrainian over Russian, and many Ukrainian émigrés decided to go home to help the process of Ukrainization. Hrushevsky had shown the way and was appointed president of the Ukrainian Academy of Science, founded in 1918. In 1928 Stalin abandoned the NEP, stopped the policy of Ukrainization, and introduced Russian as the second official language of the republic. In 1930 the first Ukrainian political trial took place in Kharkov: 45 intellectual leaders, headed by Serhiy Efremov, were accused of high treason; 13 were sentenced to death, and the rest were deported. Hrushevsky was not tried but was deported and died in 1934. In 1931 the trial of the "National Centre" was staged; this time the accused were politicians headed by Vsevolod Holubovych, and all were sentenced to death. Another trial followed in 1933, when the OGPU (Soviet secret police) purported to have discovered a military conspiracy. Yury Kotsiubinsky, deputy premier of the Ukrainian Communist government, and many others were shot, while Mykola Skrypnik, another deputy premier, committed suicide. None of their accusers nor any of the Ukrainian Communists who helped Moscow to purge the Ukraine of "bourgeois nationalism" survived. Two successive Ukrainian premiers, Panas Lyubchenko and Vlas Chubar, were shot in 1937 and 1939, respectively. In January 1934 the capital of the Ukraine was transferred from Kharkov to Kiev.

Stalinist purges

World War II and after. Between World Wars I and II there existed in Poland an underground Ukrainian Military Organization (UVO), and the Organization of Ukrainian Nationalists (OUN), both with Col. Evhen Konovalets as leader. On May 23, 1938, he was killed in Rotterdam by a Soviet agent and was succeeded by Col. Andriy Melnyk. When Germany started World War II, differences of opinion as to the best tactics to employ created a split in the OUN. Stefan Bandera became the leader of the majority, and Roman Shukhevych (Lieut. Gen. "Taras Chuprynka") was appointed chief of the UVO. For years the Ukrainian nationalists had looked to Germany for the realization of an independent Ukraine. Now they hoped to provoke a Ukrainian revolution in the Soviet empire.

On June 30, 1941, after the occupation of Lvov by the German Army, the OUN proclaimed the "restoration of the Ukrainian state" and formed a government headed by Yaroslav Stetsko, with the idea of waging war against the U.S.S.R. But Bandera, Stetsko, and most of the "ministers" were arrested by the Germans, who did not wage a war of liberation. Walther Funk, German minister of economics, declared in December 1941 that the Ukraine, this "promised colonial land," had become accessible to "European" exploitation.

In 1943 Shukhevych formed an underground Ukrainian Insurgent Army (UPA). He remained in the Polish Ukraine after the Soviet occupation and on March 4, 1950, was killed by the Soviet security forces at Bilohorshcha, near Lvov. (Bandera was killed on October 15, 1959, in Munich by a Soviet agent.)

As a result of World War II, the Ukrainian S.S.R. considerably enlarged its territory. The Soviet Army occupied the eastern parts of Poland on September 17, 1939. On October 22 a plebiscite was organized in the "Western Ukraine" by Nikita Khrushchev, then first secretary of the Ukrainian Communist Party. According to Soviet sources, 92.83 percent of the electorate went to the polls, and 90.93 percent voted for the official candidates to the People's Assembly. The assembly met in Lvov on October 28 and unanimously voted for the incorporation of eastern Galicia and Volhynia into the Ukrainian S.S.R. After the war, a Soviet–Polish treaty, signed in Moscow on August 16, 1945, confirmed the new frontier. Sub-Carpathian Ruthenia had to be ceded to the U.S.S.R. by the Soviet–Czechoslovak treaty of June 29, 1945. Romania was forced to accept a Soviet ultimatum of June 27, 1940, and cede Bessarabia and northern Bukovina to the U.S.S.R. The new frontier was confirmed by the Romanian peace treaty signed in Paris on February 10, 1947. Northern Bukovina and the Bessarabian districts of Hotin and Izmail were incorporated into the Ukraine. The most unexpected addition to the Ukraine was the transfer to it of the Crimea. This Russian gesture was made on February 19, 1954, to mark the 300th anniversary of the Russo-Ukrainian union and to strengthen the unity of the Russian and Ukrainian peoples. After these annexations and additions the area of the Ukrainian S.S.R. increased between 1939 and 1954 from 171,930 square miles (445,300 square kilometres) to 232,046 square miles (601,000 square kilometres). On December 16, 1965, the Moscow *Pravda* accused a group of academics in the western Ukrainian region of Lvov (Lviv) of being apologists for the "so-called" independent Ukrainian state proclaimed in November 1918.

In May 1970 monuments were erected in Kiev to Chubar and to G.I. Petrovsky, also a prominent Ukrainian Communist and a victim of the Stalinist purges in the 1930s. (K.M.S.)

BALTIC STATES

Diverse backgrounds of the Baltic peoples

The Baltic states comprise the present-day Soviet republics of Lithuania, Latvia, and Estonia, on the extreme eastern shores of the Baltic Sea. While, in some respects, they have a common history, they are ethnically and linguistically diverse. The Lithuanian and Latvian languages belong to the Baltic branch of the Indo-European linguistic family. The Estonian people, on the other hand, belong to the Finno-Ugric family of peoples. More anciently, the area included such provinces as Courland (Kurland), Livonia, Selonia, and East Prussia. Under Russian imperial rule from the 18th century, Estonia, Latvia, and Lithuania were independent from 1917–18 until 1940, when, during World War II, they were overrun by the Soviet Union and incorporated as constituent soviet socialist republics.

Physical and human geography

THE LAND

The region is a section of the great North European Plain stretching from the Baltic Sea to the Ural Mountains. The coastal areas are flat and low lying, with few places rising above 300 feet (90 metres); inland there is some hilly land, but, except for Gaizins Hill (1,027 feet [313 metres]), no surface is higher than 950 feet (290 metres). The territory so described applies to the modern Baltic states. Historic Lithuania covered a far larger territory, comprising the whole of Belorussia and, for a time, part of the Ukraine. East Prussia, on the southern and southeastern shores of the Baltic Sea, was overtaken by German expansion in the late Middle Ages.

The Baltic region is crossed by a multitude of rivers emptying into the Baltic, including the Neman and the Western Dvina, and is dotted by more than 6,000 lakes. Almost a quarter of the area is forested. Because of the long occupation by man, animal life is restricted mainly to the smaller animals; but elk, bear, roe deer, wolves, and wild boar do occur, as well as hares and badgers.

Until 1945 the Baltic states were predominantly agricultural, but since then industrial production has increased considerably. Industry includes fishing and forestry as well as mining and manufacturing.

THE PEOPLE

A group of nations speaking languages of the Indo-European family, the Balts live on the southeastern shores of the Baltic Sea and include the Lithuanians and Latvians (Letts) and several other peoples now extinct—such as the Prussians, who were Germanized at the beginning of the 18th century; the Curonians, who were Lettonized in the 16th century; and the Semigallians and Selonians, who died out in the 14th century. The eastern Baltic tribes, scattered in what are now Belorussia and western Russia, were Slavonized after the northward expansion of the Slavs between the 7th and 13th centuries AD. (The name Balts is derived from the Baltic Sea; it is a neologism, used since the middle of the 19th century.)

The Estonians belong to the Finno-Ugric family of peoples and constitute the core of the southern branch of the Baltic Finns, the other constituents of that group being the Livs and the Votes. The Livs occupy the northern tip of Courland and number fewer than 1,000. The Votes are still less numerous and live in a few villages in the vicinity of Narva. Formerly, they were said to have inhabited the whole of Ingermanland (Ingriya), whereas the expansion of the Livs along the Baltic shores to the south reached Kurisches Haff (Kursky Zaliv) toward the end of the 9th century. They were later absorbed by the Latvians.

The Estonians and Livs intermarried with the early Germans and also with the Lapps, but the extent of the admixture is not known. Culturally, the Estonians were strongly influenced by the Germans, and traces of the original Finnish culture have been preserved only in folklore. The Latvians were also considerably Germanized, and the majority of both the Estonians and Latvians belong to the Lutheran Church. The great majority of Lithuanians, historically long associated with Poland, are Roman Catholic. (Ed.)

History

FROM EARLIEST TIMES TO THE 18TH CENTURY

In prehistoric times, the Finno-Ugric tribes formed a long belt in northern Europe from the Urals to northern Scandinavia and south into Latvia. The predecessors of the modern Balts formed an equally long belt further south from a region west of the Urals to the Vistula region, including sizable territories of Russia, the Baltic region, eastern Prussia, and portions of northern Poland. About 1250 BC, during the Bronze Age, the western Baltic region was known throughout the civilized portions of Europe and the Near East as the land of fabulous amber. From the 1st to the 6th century AD, the Baltic peoples experienced their Golden Age, characterized by remarkable cultural progress and vigorous trade with the Roman Empire and the German lands. Western histories praised their industry, humanity, personal integrity, and warlike qualities. The Baltic trade diminished during the years of the decline of the Roman Empire and of the Great Migrations of Germanic tribes. The Balts then engaged alternately in trading and warring with the expanding Scandinavian tribes (from the 8th century) and the Slavs (from the 11th century).

The Baltic Golden Age

At the dawn of written history the Estonians had eight independent districts and four smaller ones. The Livs had congregated in four major areas of northern Latvia and northern Courland. Among the Balts, the westernmost, or Prussian, group had formed 10 principalities. Yotvings (or Sudavians) and Galinds were considered as separate Baltic groups; they reached far into Slavic territories and were possibly related to the Neuri. Ancient Lithuanians were divided into two major groups, the Samogitians (or Zhemaitians) and the Augshtaitians, later united under one king or grand duke. The Curonians (Kurs), the westernmost Latvian group, had five to seven principalities that were sometimes united under one king, as were the principalities of the Zemgals (Semigallians). Further east were the Latvian Selonians and Latgals (or Latgallians), the latter divided at least into four major principalities ruled by local kings or chieftains.

The religion of the Balts was dominated by a friendly and benevolent god, called Dievs (Dievas), assisted by a number of lesser deities. The Estonians had their own major epic poem, the *Kalevipoeg,* while the Lithuanians, and especially the Latvians, had an immense collection of folk songs called *dainas* (singular, *daina*); their subject matter was the totality of human life, revealing strong individualism, high ethical standards, and a love of work and nature. Archaeological excavations have revealed a high level of artistic expression.

Conquest of Latvia and Estonia. In the 9th century, the Scandinavian vikings ravaged the Curonian and Estonian coastal areas and established strongholds and trading posts along the Baltic waterways to Russia. The Curonians managed to destroy a Danish fleet *c.* 853, and from *c.* 1040 to *c.* 1230 the Estonians and Curonians often attacked Danish and Swedish lands. In the east, the Slavs partly destroyed and partly assimilated the Yotvings and Galinds, the remnants of these people being mentioned in Russian chronicles as late as the 15th century. As early as 1030 the Russians took over the southeastern portion of Estonia, but the struggle continued throughout the next century. In 1132 the Estonians defeated a Russian Army and in 1177 even attacked the Russian stronghold of Pskov. From time to time Latgallian lands were also invaded by the Russians, but in 1106 the Zemgals defeated two Russian armies.

Christianization of Baltic peoples

The Slavic tribes were successful in bringing the Eastern Orthodox religion to eastern Latvia and in establishing alliances with local leaders. One of the oldest (1270) extant Gospels in Russia was written by Georgius, the son of a

Lithuania and the lands ruled by the Teutonic Order in the 14th and 15th centuries.
Adapted from *Westermann Grosser Atlas zur Weltgeschichte;* Georg Westermann Verlag, Braunschweig

Latvian priest. The first attempt of the Roman Catholics to bring Christianity to Prussia dates to 997. The first Danish church in Courland was built *c.* 1070, and the first Danish missionary was sent to Estonia *c.* 1171. In 1219–22, the king of Denmark, Baldemar II, conquered all of northern Estonia. The Germans conquered the rest of Estonia and Latvia from 1198 to 1290. In 1236 the Order of the Brothers of the Sword, founded in 1202 by Bishop Albert of Buxhoevden, was defeated by the combined forces of the Lithuanians and Zemgals at Saule, and in 1260 its successor, the Livonian Order (a branch of the Knights of the Teutonic Order), was badly defeated by the Lithuanians and Curonians at Durbe. The Teutonic Order conquered all Prussian lands from 1236 to 1283. (By the end of the 17th century the Baltic Prussians had become completely assimilated by the introduced German population.) Livian territories were conquered by 1207, three of the Latgallian territories by 1214, and Estonia by 1227. Courland lost its independence in 1263, Zemgalia in 1290. The Zemgalian army retreated to Lithuania, and their envoys continued a diplomatic struggle in Rome as late as 1300. In 1343 the northern Estonians freed themselves from the yoke of Denmark, only to be subjugated by the Livonian Order in 1346.

The old order along the Baltic coast was replaced by a number of small feudal ecclesiastical states dominated by German knights and burghers: the State of the Livonian Order, the Archbishopric of Riga, the bishoprics of Courland (Kurzeme), Dorpat (Tartu), and Ösel-Wiek (Saaremaa-Läänemaa), and the free city of Riga. Although loosely united in a Livonian confederation from 1418, the states often fought each other and suppressed the native population. The Confederation of Livonia was considered to be the bulwark of the Western world in the East and the intermediary between western Europe and Muscovy, but it was internally weak and a cultural desert, thus allowing the colourful native civilizations to survive.

Independent Lithuania. The Lithuanians succeeded in maintaining their independence and were united in 1236 under Mindaugas, who was crowned king of Lithuania in 1253, after accepting Christianity. Ten years later he was assassinated and Lithuania rejected Christianity. The country was not unified again until 1290, when the grand duke Vytenis was recognized as absolute ruler. He was succeeded in 1316 by his younger brother, Gediminas, who ruled until 1341. Gediminas extended Lithuania's territories from the Baltic Sea southward almost to the Black Sea and eastward to the Dnepr. Lithuania became a major power. Under Gediminas' sons Algirdas and Kęstutis, the Grand Duchy expanded to include Kiev in the east, and in 1370 the Lithuanians besieged Moscow. The Tatar conquest of Kiev had destroyed the influence of the Kievan Russian state over the other Russian principalities. This gave Lithuania an opportunity to expand to the east and southeast, while at the same time fighting off the Teutonic Order on its western frontiers. That a small non-Christian state was able to conquer and maintain control over such an extended area was partly the consequence of the skillful diplomacy of the Lithuanian leaders. The conquered Russian principalities were allowed to keep their autonomy and their Orthodox religion. The business of the state was conducted in Belorussian Slavonic.

The Lithuanian Empire

In 1385 Jogaila, the son of Algirdas, concluded an agreement to unite Lithuania and Kievan Russia. He then went to Kraków, was baptized on February 15, 1386, married the Polish Queen Jadwiga, and on March 4 was crowned king of Poland, receiving the name Władysław II Jagiełło. The Lithuanians were baptized in 1387, and Władysław's cousin Bytautas, son of Kęstutis, became grand duke of Lithuania. On July 15, 1410, the Polish-Lithuanian forces inflicted a crushing defeat on the Teutonic Order at Tannenberg-Grünwald. Vytautas renewed the policy of eastward expansion, and during this time Lithuania reached its largest expansion (350,000 square miles; 906,-

500 square kilometres). When Vytautas the Great died in 1430, the heroic epoch of medieval Lithuania ended.

With the acceptance of Roman Catholicism, Lithuania was drawn culturally toward the West. The Teutonic Muscovy posed a threat to Lithuania's Belorussian conquests. The Federal union between Lithuania and Poland was of no advantage to the Lithuanian peasantry. The culturally more advanced Polish nation tended to assimilate the Lithuanians, and after the equalization of the aristocracy of the two countries in 1413, the Lithuanian nobility became polonized. The Lithuanian and Belorussian peasantry now met with a fate like that of the Latvian and Estonian peasantry before them; under the rule of a foreign aristocracy, they were restricted to farming and sank into serfdom. On July 1, 1569, at Lublin, the personal union between the dynasties of Poland and Lithuania was changed to a union of the two countries, and Lithuania was reduced to a subsidiary land under the Polish crown. When Poland was partitioned among Prussia, Austria, and Russia in 1772, 1793, and 1795, Lithuania was annexed by Russia.

Livonia, Estonia, and Courland from the 16th to the 18th century. While the internal strength of the Confederation of Livonia was gradually weakening, the importance of the corporations of the landed nobility and of the free cities increased. The towns enjoyed prosperity through the commercial activity of the Hanseatic League, predominantly in the trade with Russia. At the same time, the Latvian and Estonian populations, both rural and urban, were methodically deprived by their German overlords of their remaining rights and privileges. The Latvian and Estonian nobility had been exterminated long before, and only a few pockets of free peasantry remained. As early as 1522–24, Lutheranism began to gain ground among the German ruling classes. This was important to the non-German population, for the evangelical ministers did much to foster written literature in the Estonian and Latvian languages. With the establishment of Lutheranism in Latvian and Estonian lands, the Catholic ecclesiastical states became anachronisms.

Partition of Livonia in the 16th century

When the Russian tsar Ivan IV the Terrible advanced claims on Livonia in 1558 in order to secure access to the Baltic Sea, the Confederation of Livonia broke down before the violent onslaughts of the Russian troops. The last able grand marshal of the Livonian Order, Walter von Plettenberg, who had managed to forestall the Russian advance in 1502, had no worthy successors, and the Germans had disarmed the Latvians and Estonians at the most crucial moment. The German leaders were forced to apply for protection to the kings of Sweden, Denmark, and Poland-Lithuania. During the Livonian War, Livonia broke up into three duchies of Livonia, Estonia, and Courland, Denmark holding the island of Saaremaa until 1645. The borders of the new entities were different from the original Estonian and Latvian settlements, but they remained the administrative divisions until 1917. Estonia, with its capital, Reval (Tallinn), came under Swedish rule; Livonia, with its capital, Riga, became a part of Lithuania; while Courland became a hereditary duchy nominally under Polish suzerainty. The nobility and the magistrates of the free cities retained their privileges; German was recognized as the official language; and German law and German administration remained.

In 1592, the Baltic lands became the object of the first Swedish-Polish war and of the struggle between Lutheranism and Catholicism. In 1629 Poland was forced to cede Livonia with Riga to Sweden, retaining only the southeastern province of Latgale.

The Swedish kings, particularly Gustavus II Adolphus (reigned 1611–32) and Charles XI (reigned 1660–97), accustomed to a free peasant class in their own country, sought to raise the Estonian and Latvian peasants from serfdom. Compulsory elementary education was introduced, the Bible was translated into Latvian and Estonian, a high school was opened in Riga in 1631, and a university was founded at Dorpat in 1632. Numerous Swedish administrative, judicial, and ecclesiastical reforms in favour of the peasantry fell short, however, of their intended accomplishments because of the frequent, devastating wars. The Estonians and most of the Latvians still regard the

Baltic States from 1561 to 1721.

Adapted from *Westermann Grosser Atlas zur Weltgeschichte*; Georg Westermann Verlag, Braunschweig

association with the Swedish Empire as one of the better periods of their history.

In Courland the last master of the Teutonic Order of Livonia, Gotthard Kettler (ruled 1559–61), had preserved the duchy's relative independence with himself as duke (Herzog). His grandson, Jacob (sole ruler, 1642–82), the ablest duke of Courland, developed local industry, fostered foreign trade, and created a formidable navy. He also acquired two colonies, the island of Tobago in the West Indies and The Gambia on the West African coast, as well as an ocean station and several mining and agricultural settlements in Norway. His ships sailed to Brazil, Iceland, Sierra Leone, Liberia, and Indonesia, and in 1651 he planned to colonize Australia, then newly discovered. His son, Frederick Casimir (ruled 1682–1737), attempted to make his capital of Mitau (Jelgava) into a northern Paris; the Academia Petrina was founded there in 1775. When the Kettler dynasty became extinct, the Biron dynasty was founded in Courland by Ernst Johann von Biron. He ruled intermittently until his son, Peter, became duke in 1769, only to lose his duchy to Russia in 1795.

THE BALTIC COUNTRIES UNDER RUSSIA (UNTIL 1918)

With his victory over Sweden in the Great Northern War (1700–21), the Russian tsar Peter I the Great gained both Livonia and Estonia. He thus fulfilled an age-old Russian dream of "opening the window to the seas." The other Baltic lands passed into Russian hands from 1772 to 1795, except for a small portion of Lithuania, which was incorporated into Prussia. For the Germans of the Baltic lands their incorporation into Russia opened up great opportunities for increasing their privileges and power over the peasants and for advancement in the service of the tsar. For the great majority of Latvians and Estonians, and, later, the Lithuanians, it brought a deterioration of their legal status and increased exploitation.

Social changes under the tsars

Not until the 19th century did a process of social and national emancipation begin. Under the tsar Alexander I the Estonian and Latvian peasants were given their personal freedom (1816–19), but without the right to own land. By the middle of the century, however, they were allowed to acquire leased land as their personal property. The Baltic provinces thus began to develop an agrarian structure quite different from that in Russia. However, as the big landed estates remained untouched, most of the peasants were not able to acquire enough land to be self-supporting. In consequence, thousands of Latvians and Estonians migrated to the Russian interior, where land was available for settlement. In Lithuania the peasantry was not liberated until 1861—when the emancipation of

Russian's own serfs took place. Tens of thousands of Lithuanians emigrated to the United States, Canada, and Brazil, followed by thousands of Latvians and hundreds of Estonians.

Advances in education

Considerable progress was made in education. By the end of the century there was almost no illiteracy in Estonia and Latvia, in contrast to Russia proper. A German-language university was reopened in Dorpat (Tartu) in Estonia in 1802. By the middle of the 19th century it had become a focal point for national revival among the Estonians and Latvians. A Polish-language university restored in Vilnius (Vilna) in 1803 served in a similar way for the Lithuanians. Educated Latvians, Estonians, and Lithuanians began to grow conscious of their national origins. Starting with an interest in the past and with the study of the national languages, folklore, and ethnography, the movement developed political aims.

The Lithuanians and Latgals had to fight particularly hard. They took part in the Polish rebellions of 1830–31 and 1863–65 and suffered considerable repression afterward. From 1864 to 1905 the policy of Russification extended to every part of their public life: it was forbidden to publish newspapers, periodicals, or books in Polish, while books in Lithuanian or Latgallian could be printed only if the Russian alphabet was used. Russian was the only language of teaching in the schools, and the Roman Catholic religion was persecuted. The Lithuanian resistance was able to capitalize on the fact that Lithuanian was also spoken in the eastern part of East Prussia, and the national movement flourished there under the leadership of Lutheran clergymen and teachers. On German territory the first Lithuanian daily newspaper was published, and Lithuanian books were printed to be smuggled into Russia. Beginning in the 1880s, the Lithuanian resistance to Russification also received strong support from the Catholic clergy.

In the Baltic provinces, the Russian government introduced a series of liberal reforms during the 1860s and 1870s, but after 1881 a general strategy of systematic Russification began that lasted until 1905. It extended to the whole educational system, the courts, and local administration. At the same time, however, it did much to strengthen the Baltic nationalities, especially the Latvians and Estonians. Railroad lines were built from the Baltic seaports to the Russian hinterland. A considerable merchant fleet was built and manned by Latvians and Estonians, and Riga became a world port, its population growing from more than 250,000 in 1900 to about 500,000 in 1914. Riga, Tallinn, and Narva also became important industrial centres. These developments changed the character of the urban population. The Baltic Germans, who had never comprised more than 10 percent of the population, declined in number and importance. Although the German influence remained strong in the sciences, as well as in the Lutheran Church, in the large landed estates, and in wholesale trade, industry, banking, and the professions, the advancing Estonians and Latvians crowded the Germans out of the trades, business, and civil service. Many of the German academicians, artists, and writers emigrated to Germany. The percentage of Estonians in the population of Tallinn rose from 51.8 in 1867 to 88.7 in 1897, and the percentage of Latvians in the population of Riga rose in the same period from 23.5 to 41.6.

Displacement of Germans

Marxism appeared in the Baltic provinces in the 1880s, at first known as the "New Current." The Latvian Social Democratic Party was founded in 1904, and an independent Estonian sister party was established in 1906. Both parties maintained connections with the Russian and German Social Democratic parties. A Lithuanian Social Democratic Party was founded in 1895.

The Russian Revolution of 1905 was felt strongly in Latvia and Estonia. Bourgeois politicians, together with radical revolutionaries, raised the demand for national autonomy. When revolutionary forces spread into the countryside, looting and burning the manor houses, the government sent troops to put down the uprising. About 1,000 Latvians and Estonians were shot, and thousands of revolutionaries were sent to Siberia or fled abroad. The Revolution was followed by concessions from the Tsar in the way of liberal reforms in all three Baltic regions, and the Baltic regions were allowed to send elected representatives to the new imperial Duma (legislature).

LIBERATION AND INDEPENDENCE (1917–40)

Estonian liberation. The Russian Revolution of March (February, old style) 1917 overthrew the Tsar and brought a brief period of political autonomy for Estonia. On April 12 the Russian provisional government allowed all Estonian districts to be united into one province, and elections to the Estonian National Council (Maapäev) took place in June. After the October Revolution, the bourgeois majority parties of the Maapäev decided to break away from the Russian Empire, but the Bolsheviks appointed a Communist administration for Estonia. In February 1918 German forces advanced to Estonia. The Communists fled from Tallinn, and on February 24 the Maapäev declared Estonia's independence and formed a provisional government, which collapsed the following day when German troops entered Tallinn. On March 3, 1918, by signing the Treaty of Brest-Litovsk, the Soviet Russian government effectively transferred sovereignty over the Baltic countries to Germany.

Germany capitulated on November 11, 1918, and the Estonian provisional government renewed its activities. The Soviet Russian government declared the Treaty of Brest-Litovsk null and void and, on November 28, Soviet troops began an invasion of Estonia, which had been denuded of all arms by the retreating Germans. The government of Konstantin Päts was successful in obtaining weapons and war materiel from the Allies. With the aid of a British naval squadron and a Finnish voluntary force, the commander in chief, Johan Laidoner, was able to open a counteroffensive in January 1919. By the end of February all of Estonian territory had been freed, and the Estonian Army penetrated into Soviet and Latvian territories.

Repulse of the Red Army

Latvian liberation. In Latvia, the struggle for independence was even more difficult than in Estonia. The Latvian Provisional National Council in the Soviet-held portion of Latvia had proclaimed the autonomy of Latvia as early as November 30, 1917. The Latvian People's Council, representing peasant, bourgeois, and socialist groups, proclaimed the independence of Latvia on November 18, 1918. A government was formed by the leader of the Farmers' Party, Kārlis Ulmanis. The Soviet Russian government established a Communist government for Latvia, headed by Pēteris Stučka. The Red Army, which included Latvian units, took Riga on January 3, 1919, and the Ulmanis government moved to Liepāja (Libau), where it was protected by a British naval squadron. There were also German troops whom the Allies expected to defend East Prussia and Courland against the advancing Red Army. Their commander, Gen. Rüdiger, Graf von der Goltz, however, intended to transform Latvia into a German base of operations against the Soviets, the Allies, and the new Social Democratic government of Germany by building his own anti-Communist German-Russian force, supplemented by Baltic German volunteers, and to form Baltic regimes faithful to imperial Germany and Russia. On November 9, 1918, the Baltic German barons had created a short-lived Duchy of the Baltic. While some Latvian nationalist troops fought alongside the Estonians, other units were temporarily forced to fight alongside the Germans, who took Riga on May 22, 1919. Pushing northward, the Germans were stopped near Cēsis (Wenden) by the Estonian Army and 2,000 Latvian troops. The head of the Allied military mission, the British general Sir Hubert Gough, negotiated an armistice. The defeated Germans had to abandon Riga, to which the Ulmanis government returned in July. In the meantime, the Red Army, finding itself attacked from the north by the Estonians, from the west by the Latvians, and from the south by the Lithuanians, had withdrawn from most of Latvia.

In July, General Gough demanded that the German troops retreat to East Prussia. In the meantime, however, General von der Goltz managed to organize an anti-Communist West Russian army, reinforced by units of German monarchist volunteers and headed by an obscure adventurer, Pavel Bermondt-Avalov. On October 8,

Bermondt attacked the Latvian Army and occupied the suburbs of Riga. By November 11, however, the Latvians, assisted by an Anglo-French naval squadron, defeated Bermondt's army, which was also later attacked by Lithuanian troops. By December 15, all German troops had finally abandoned Latvia and Lithuania. Latgale remained in Red hands; but this Latvian province, too, was cleared by Latvians, Poles, and Baltic Germans, who in February 1920 were placed under the command of the British.

Lithuanian liberation. During World War I the Germans occupied a great part of historic Lithuania. On December 11, 1917, the Lithuanian National Council (Taryba), with tacit German approval, proclaimed the restoration of the independent state of Lithuania. On March 15, 1918, the German emperor, William II, recognized the "independence" of the former duchy of Courland, on March 23 of the "Kingdom" of Lithuania, and on September 22 of the entire Baltic area, to remain in close association with Germany. Because the Lithuanians were not allowed by Germany to act independently, they again proclaimed their independence on February 16, 1918, severing the ties with Germany. On November 11, 1918, a republican government was formed under Augustinas Voldemaras but, as the German armies withdrew, the Red Army occupied Vilnius on January 5, 1919, and installed a Communist government. The Germans remained in western Lithuania until December 1919. The Lithuanian Army took the offensive against the Reds in February 1919, and by the end of August the country had been cleared of Soviet troops.

The contest for Vilnius

A dispute with Poland had developed, however, over the possession of the Lithuanian capital city of Vilnius and the surrounding area. The city was largely Polish in population, while the district of Vilnius was predominantly Lithuanian. The head of state of Poland, Józef Piłsudski, himself a former resident of Vilnius, took Vilnius from the Red Army on April 19, 1919. Although the Lithuanians were able to regain the region in July 1920, the Poles took it back on October 7. For the next 18 years this region remained the principal trouble spot in northeastern Europe. As a theoretical state of war existed between Lithuania and Poland, northeastern and eastern European countries could not form a bloc between the Soviet Union and Germany. Relations between the two countries were normalized only on March 17, 1938, after a Polish ultimatum, but on October 10, 1939, the Soviet Union granted Vilnius to Lithuania.

Soviet Baltic governments. The Estonian Soviet government had been established on November 29, 1918; the Latvian Soviet government on December 17, and the Lithuanian Soviet government on December 15. The three were "recognized" by the Soviet Russian government on December 7 and December 22, 1918, but were dissolved in January 1920, when Lenin decided to sign peace treaties with the democratic governments of the Baltic states. The treaty with Estonia was signed on February 2, 1920, that with Lithuania on July 12, and that with Latvia on August 11, recognizing their independence "in perpetuity." At the same time, the Soviet Baltic agencies were converted into the nuclei of the Baltic Communist parties, with the aim of launching underground activities in the Baltic states in order to convert them into Soviet republics at a later date. Eight Latvian rifle regiments that had kept the German Army at bay near Riga from 1915 to 1917 had retreated to Russia at the time of complete German occupation of the Baltic region, and had become a sort of "praetorian guard" for Lenin. The Latvian (and Estonian) rifle divisions had played a crucial role in major battles during the Russian civil war against the tsarist forces; of these men, about 12,000 Latvian riflemen later returned to Latvia. Thousands of remaining Baltic Communists acquired important positions in the Soviet Russian administration, military forces, and economic life; almost all of them became the victims of Stalin's purges in the late 1930s.

Consolidation. There were serious internal problems faced by all three Baltic republics after the war: to reorganize their semifeudal, basically German and Polish, agrarian structures; to adapt their economies to the new conditions; and to establish constitutions. In Estonia and Latvia the governments had promised the distribution of land parcels to the landless combatants during the war. Now both republics solved their agrarian problems with the expropriation of all the holdings of large estates, thus destroying the economic and political power of the Baltic German nobility, whose corporations were dissolved. Tens of thousands of the rural proletariat were given land, thus effectively eliminating Communist influence in Estonia and Latvia. The expropriated forest lands remained the property of the state and became an important source of income from lumber exports. In Lithuania, the large estates were mainly in the hands of Poles and polonized Lithuanian aristocrats. The land reform there was less radical than in Estonia and Latvia. The governments sponsored cooperatives to handle the collection and marketing of farm produce.

Agrarian reform

Constitutional reform. Constitutional reorganization in all three countries was radically parliamentarian in character, the legislative body clearly predominating over the executive branch. In Estonia, for example, there was a single-chamber parliament (Riigikogu) with a system of proportional representation, and the prime minister was also the chief of state. In both Latvia and Lithuania, a president of the republic was elected by the parliament (in Latvia, called Saeima; in Lithuania, Seimas). In all three countries there were numerous political parties and groups (up to 36 in some elections), but in Latvia and Estonia the dominant organizations were the Social Democrats, the farmers' unions, and some nationalist and liberal groups, while in Lithuania there was a strong conservative Christian Democratic Party. The membership in the outlawed Communist parties in Latvia and Lithuania never exceeded 1,000. In Estonia the Communist Party was outlawed after a Soviet-supported coup d'etat failed on December 1, 1924.

The economy. In seceding from the Russian Empire, the Baltic states had lost their economic hinterland. The situation was worsened by a wholesale destruction of industrial enterprises in Latvia and the waste of agricultural resources in all three countries during the war. They were also burdened with war debts. With the exception of Estonia in 1926, the Baltic states did not receive any financial assistance from the West despite the fact that, for instance, Latvia was one of the countries most devastated during the war.

Economic recovery

Their economic recovery was a miracle, thanks mainly to the hard work, thriftiness, and perseverance of the Balts themselves. Estonia developed an entirely new industry with the opening of rich oil shale fields. The timber and related industries increased slowly in importance, as did the export of meat, dairy, and poultry products. Great Britain became the principal market for all three countries, and Germany a close second. Trade with the Soviet Union remained slight.

Education and culture. Freed from outside restrictions, cultural life expanded. Schools of all kinds increased. Each country had its own university, conservatory of music, academy of arts, and various types of higher technical schools. Literature, music, and the fine arts reached the level of the rest of Europe. Cultural policy was strongly Western in orientation; English was the first foreign language taught in the schools, German or French usually taught as the second foreign language. Germans, Russians, Jews, Poles, Belorussians, and other minorities had their own state-supported schools, churches, theatres, and cultural organizations, something the Baltic peoples had never enjoyed before the war.

Political tendencies in the 1920s and 1930s. The Baltic republics were admitted to the membership of the League of Nations on September 22, 1921. They subscribed to all conventions of a humanitarian, social, and cultural nature and to all schemes and conventions intended to maintain the status quo and keep the world free of war. They also attempted to form a bridge between the Western world and the Soviet Union. Schemes to establish regional security were actively supported by the Baltic states, but did not materialize because of the unwillingness of Germany, Poland, and the Soviet Union to subscribe to them and the hesitation of Great Britain and France to support them. In October 1936, Latvia was given a nonpermanent seat on the Council of the League of Nations, and in 1938 the Latvian foreign minister served as the president of the 101st meeting of the Council. The Soviet Union, Nazi Germany, and Poland attempted to alienate the Baltic states from each other. France at first tried to dominate them through Poland, and Great Britain supported the unsuccessful idea of a Scandinavian-Baltic bloc until the end of 1922. Serious problems emerged because political experience and democratic traditions were lacking, as were institutions that would have protected the interests of the state against those of particular groups. On December 16–17, 1926, an authoritarian presidential regime was established in Lithuania.

The numerous political parties in Estonia and Latvia prevented the formation of stable coalitions and led to frequent governmental crises during the 1920s. The life-span of the governments of Estonia during the years 1919–33 averaged eight months and 20 days. The political problem became even more pronounced in 1930, when the world economic crisis brought financial difficulties and unemployment that emphasized the need for stable government. Voices demanding constitutional reform were heard in both countries. Some small groups looked to Fascist Italy for guidance, and the Baltic German minority was infiltrated by Nazi agents. In Estonia the movement was led by the "Vaps" (Vabadussõjalaste Liit, or League of Freedom Fighters), which had grown from a group of war veterans into an anti-Communist and anti-parliamentary mass movement. The proposal of the Vaps won a majority of 72.7 percent in a referendum of October 1933. The acting president, Konstantin Päts, was expected to prepare for the election of a new president. Instead, he declared a state of emergency on March 12, 1934; the Vaps was dissolved, its leaders were arrested, and the parliament was soon also dissolved. After that Päts ruled by decree until 1938.

The Vaps movement

In Latvia a similar development occurred on May 15, 1934. After attempts at constitutional reform had failed and the country had become increasingly polarized between the far right and the far left, the prime minister, Kārlis Ulmanis, declared a state of emergency. He formed a government of national unity from representatives of almost all the important parties. From then on he governed without the parliament.

In neither Estonia nor Latvia was there any significant resistance to the suppression of parliamentary government. The new authoritarian regimes drew their main support from the well-to-do and the peasants, from the army, and the home guard. Both heads of state based their coups d'etat on the need to prevent the interference of foreign powers in state affairs and to strengthen the position of the Estonian and Latvian peoples in their own countries. Both were quite successful in diminishing the power of the radical right as well as the influence of the radical left. Both strove to reorganize the society by setting up representative bodies of the professions, called chambers, patterned after the Italian Fascist model.

There were, however, marked differences in their styles of leadership. The Estonian president regarded his authoritarian regime as a regency for the restoration of the endangered democracy and worked for a conservative reform of the state. He legalized his regime by a referendum in 1936 in order to elect a constituent assembly to draft a new constitution. The candidates were chosen mostly from the ranks of the Patriotic League that he had founded in February 1935. The new parliament that convened on April 21, 1938, had in its lower chamber 63 members of the Patriotic League and a token opposition of 17. On April 23, 1938, Päts was elected the first president of the republic, and in May a new government was sworn in, headed by a separate prime minister.

In Latvia the dynamic "leader of the people," Ulmanis, did not bother to legalize his regime by popular referendum or even to organize a unified following. On April 11, 1936, he combined the office of prime minister with that of the president of the state and adopted the nationalistic theme of a "strong and Latvian Latvia." He also enlarged the state-run sector of the economy. The Germans felt themselves to be losing out to the Latvian majority, and German National Socialism found an increasing number of supporters among them. On the other hand, both Socialism and Communism lost their appeal among the population. Under the new regime no one was killed, and only a few hundred persons were temporarily imprisoned. The rural population and the business interests favoured the authoritarian regime because it brought prosperity; foreign trade showed a steady increase. In Latvia an entirely new electronics industry came into existence and made surprising progress.

Rise of the one-party state in Lithuania

In Lithuania a nationalistic one-party state emerged. The dictatorial tendencies of Prime Minister Voldemaras aroused opposition among conservative-ecclesiastical circles, which led to his removal by the president, Antanas Smetona, on September 19, 1929. Smetona now cast himself as a "people's leader" with the small Nationalist Party in full control of the state. His regime had the support of the army, the home guard, and the state-sponsored youth organization, Young Lithuania. The obvious model for the regime was Fascist Italy, and it led to the alienation and dissolution of other parties. Two unsuccessful attempts were made to return Voldemaras to power, and there were peasant strikes and workers' demonstrations. These events, coupled with the dispute with Germany over control of Klaipėda (Memel), forced Smetona to broaden his power base. On September 1, 1936, the President summoned the rump parliament to draft a new constitution, which was promulgated on May 12, 1938; it provided for a single-chamber Diet elected for five years by democratic suffrage, and for a strong head of the state elected for seven years by delegates of the nation.

The end of independence. The Baltic states had won their independence at a time when both Russia and Germany were defeated in war. They retained it as long as the two powers remained weak. Proposals for closer ties with Finland and Poland ran aground on the irreconcilable differences between Lithuania and Poland and on the refusal of Finland from 1922 to engage in affairs south of the Gulf of Finland. An Estonian-Latvian defense alliance was formalized in 1923 and renewed in 1934. When Lithuania joined the alliance in 1934 it became known as the Baltic Entente. All three Baltic states signed nonaggression pacts with the Soviet Union, which were renewed in 1934. They also signed nonaggression pacts with Germany in 1939. In the summer of 1939 the Baltic question was one of the issues in the ill-fated Anglo-French negotiations with Moscow. The Baltic states attempted to maintain absolute neutrality in the power struggle.

The geographic plight of the Baltic states

In a secret protocol to the German-Soviet pact of August 23, 1939, however, Estonia and Latvia were recognized as belonging to the Soviet sphere of interest, and on September 28, after the German victory over Poland, Lithuania was put in the same category. Moscow then demanded that the Baltic states should sign mutual assistance pacts with the Soviet Union and allow Soviet military bases on their territory. Completely isolated, the governments of the Baltic states realized that military resistance was useless. The agreement between Berlin and Moscow for a resettlement of Baltic Germans in Germany on September 28 made it clear to the Balts that Hitler had left their states at the mercy of Stalin. On September 28, October 5, and October 10, 1939, Estonia, Latvia, and Lithuania signed mutual assistance treaties with the Soviet Union and admitted Soviet troops that exceeded in numbers those of their own armies. The Soviets at first were satisfied to observe the limits of their bases, concentrating their attacks on Finland.

When the Germans took Paris on June 14, 1940, Stalin demanded that the governments of the Baltic states admit more Soviet troops and establish pro-Soviet regimes. On June 15, Lithuania was completely occupied by Soviet forces, and on June 17 Latvia and Estonia experienced similar fates. Soviet emissaries organized elections on July 14–15 in which only a single list of Soviet-sponsored candidates was allowed to stand. The new "parliaments," disregarding the constitutions of the Baltic states, immediately "voted" by a show of hands for incorporation of their countries into the Soviet Union; the requests were accepted by the Supreme Soviet on August 3, 5, and 6, 1940, respectively.

Arrests and deportations

Many Baltic political leaders were arrested, deported to Siberia, or killed, or were able to flee to the West. Beginning on June 14, 1941, there were mass deportations of the Balts, including women and children, to the polar or desert regions of the Soviet Union. In one year, Estonia lost more than 60,000 people; Latvia more than 34,000; and Lithuania about 35,000. Another, even larger, deportation of Baltic citizens was scheduled for July, but it did not materialize because of the German invasion.

After the Lithuanian revolt of June 23, 1941, and the subsequent German occupation of the Baltic region, the Baltic states and Belorussia were combined in July 1941 into a new territorial unit, Ostland, scheduled to be Germanized and added to the German Reich at a later date. Many Balts at first considered the Germans as their liberators and were willing to cooperate with them. They soon found out, however, that such a stance would not help them to regain their national independence or most of their nationalized property. All the Balts were considered by the German occupation authorities as second-class citizens, Lithuanians receiving the worst treatment. Whereas the Soviets had sought to annihilate the upper classes, the Nazis at first tried to wipe out the Jews and other "undesirable" elements among the Balts themselves. They killed at least 14,000 Lithuanians and 136,000 Lithuanian Jews. About 90,000 Jews were killed in Latvia and 4,500 in Estonia. Hundreds of Latvians and Estonians also lost their lives, and about 95,000 Lithuanians and 30,000 Latvians were sent to concentration camps.

On July 17, 1941, Alfred Rosenberg became the *Reichs minister* for the occupied eastern territories. Under him, the *Reichs kommissar* for Ostland resided in Riga and *Gebiets kommissars* in the capitals of each of the former Baltic States and in Belorussia. As was the case in the Soviet Union, the *Sicherheitsdienst* (SD) of the Nazis often wielded greater power than the administrative agencies. Indigenous, but generally powerless, self-governments were also formed in each of the Baltic countries. Disregarding international conventions, the German Reich proclaimed the compulsory draft of Baltic men and women into labour service and the German armed forces (camouflaged as *Schutzstaffel* (SS) "voluntary" units and police battalions). One Estonian division and one brigade, along with two Latvian divisions and a large number of other units, were sent to fight against the Soviets. At least 146,000 Latvians, 47,000 Lithuanians, and 50,000 Estonians were enlisted in military units of various kinds.

In May 1944, 4,000 mobilized Lithuanians clashed with the Germans. There were also sizable nationalist and Communist guerrilla movements in the Baltic countries, and more than 3,000 Estonians fled to Finland and enlisted in the Finnish Army and Navy. A Lithuanian provisional government, proclaimed on June 23, 1941, was disbanded by the German authorities on August 5 of the same year. On November 25, 1943, an underground nationalist Supreme Committee for the Liberation of Lithuania started its activities. A similar underground Central Council of Latvia came into existence on July 13, 1943, and on March 23, 1944, an underground Republican National Council of Estonia was founded. These bodies cooperated with each other and established ties with the Western powers through Finland and Sweden. In April, May, and July 1944, many of the Baltic nationalist leaders were arrested and sent to concentration camps, where a number of them perished. The Latvian underground nationalist armed force was annihilated by German forces in Courland in November–December 1944. On September 18, 1944, a short-lived Estonian nationalist government started its activities, and on May 4, 1945, a similar Latvian government was founded.

Underground resistance

The Baltic countries were again devastated. Latvia, which had lost 650,000 people during World War I, lost another 450,000 during World War II. Estonia lost 200,000 and Lithuania 473,000 people. In the fall of 1944, as the Germans retreated and the Soviet Russians returned, large numbers of people were evacuated or fled before the advancing Soviet armies. Courland held out until the end of the war. About 33,000 Estonians, 115,000 Latvians, and 70,000 Lithuanians were deported or managed to flee to western Germany; about 30,000 Estonians and 5,000 Latvians reached Sweden. During World War II, 18 Latvian vessels, a few Lithuanian ships, and more than 30 Estonian vessels served the interests of the Western Allies; most of these ships were victims of German submarines and airplanes. One Lithuanian, two Estonian, and two Latvian divisions fought with the Soviets, the soldiers, however, being partly or mostly non-Balts.

After the Soviets restored the Communist regimes in the three countries, they faced a nationalist guerrilla war that lasted until 1951. The Communists tried to eradicate the last vestiges of the private economy and faced considerable opposition among the rural population. New waves of deportations followed. Estimates of the numbers of those deported in the years 1941–49 run to about 570,000, including large numbers of peasants who resisted the collectivization of their farms. About 25–30 percent of these persons are said to have returned home after Stalin's death in 1953 and a general amnesty in 1955.

THE BALTIC STATES AS SOVIET UNION REPUBLICS

Soviet policies

After the victory over Germany the Soviet authorities resumed their previous efforts to integrate the Baltic states into the Soviet Union. Most of the Communist leaders of the early days were replaced by officials who had grown up in the Soviet Union or been trained there.

Baltic republics since 1945.

Collectivization and industrialization. The rural population was forced into the *kolkhozy,* or collective farms, without regard for the consequences to agriculture. Resistance by partisans or guerrillas, which had persisted longest in Lithuania, was ultimately broken by special forces of the security police. Collectivization eliminated the independent farming class, which had been the political basis of the Baltic states. The Baltic region concentrated on dairy farming and cattle breeding; in the 1950s and 1960s Estonia and Latvia held first place among the union republics of the Soviet Union in milk production per cow.

The economies of the Baltic republics were integrated into the Soviet system of economic planning and development. This resulted in considerable growth in production, as a result of Soviet investment in the Baltic region. Some outstanding projects of the postwar period included the development of the Estonian oil shale industry, which supplies gas for Leningrad and Tallinn. Five giant power stations generate large quantities of electricity. Industrial establishments produce textiles, synthetic fibre, microbuses, electric trains, radio and television sets, refrigerators, and fine electronic equipment for the entire Soviet Union and foreign countries. There is also a large fishing and canning industry. Living standards remain relatively low, but they are higher than the average standard for the Soviet Union as a whole. Soviet citizens of other regions feel as if they are abroad while in the Baltic countries, and tens of thousands of them have attempted to settle there.

Demographic changes. Postwar political, industrial, and agricultural policies of the government of the Soviet Union have made fundamental changes in the social structure of the Baltic republics. From predominantly rural societies they became predominantly urban. In 1939, 65 percent of the Latvians lived in rural areas, as did 66 percent of the Estonians and 77 percent of the Lithuanians, but 40 years later the ratio was reversed, and 70 percent of the Latvians, 71 percent of the Estonians, and 64 percent of the Lithuanians were urban dwellers; Latvia and Estonia had achieved the highest rate of urban population in the Soviet Union.

Russian immigration

Another demographic change was the immigration of Russians and other non-Balts. By the late 20th century almost half of the population of Riga was estimated to be Russian. The Russians manned the large military force stationed in the Baltic; they took over many of the top positions in government and most of the administrative posts; hundreds of thousands of them came in with newly created large industrial enterprises; they took over most of the shipping and transportation, commerce, trade, and customer services; and they penetrated the professions and even larger agricultural enterprises. Many fields of enterprise were subordinated directly to union ministries in Moscow. Feeble attempts by indigenous Baltic Communists to curb enforced Russification in the 1950s ended in their removal from top positions and their replacement by Balts from Russia and Russians themselves.

Religion, education, and culture. Under Soviet rule, the activities of the formerly influential Lutheran and Roman Catholic churches have been severely limited. Church attendance has declined markedly.

Education and culture in the Baltic republics have been "national in form, socialist in content." The native languages and literature, theatre and music, popular customs and national histories have all been promoted, but as part of a multinational Soviet culture and in terms of Soviet ideology. The severance of ties between the Baltic states and Russia after 1919 is explained as the work of Western imperialism, and the forced integration into the Soviet Union as a "liberation from the yoke of imperialism." In the new histories, the periods of independence of the Baltic peoples have been either ignored or condemned, but the ties with the Russians and the periods of Russian rule have been emphasized. The Balts are reminded daily that they are Soviet people, and they are encouraged to use the Russian language as their "second mother language." Most of the Baltic technical literature is now published only in the Russian language.

In 1980 the incorporation of the Baltic states into the Soviet Union had still not been recognized by the United States and many other countries, although some governments did accord it de facto recognition. Prewar Baltic legations are still active in Washington, D.C., and in several other Western capitals. (E.An.)

Estonia

The Estonian Soviet Socialist Republic, one of the 15 republics of the Soviet Union, was proclaimed on July 21, 1940, and became a member of the Soviet Union on August 6, 1940. On the north and west the republic is bounded by the Baltic Sea and on the east by Lake Peipus (Chudskoye Ozero) and the Narva River; in the south it borders on Latvia and the Russian S.F.S.R.

Estonia has an area of 17,400 square miles (45,100 square kilometres), of which 9 percent is made up of some 800 islands and islets. The larger islands are Saaremaa (1,048 square miles [2,714 square kilometres]) and Hiiumaa (373 square miles [966 square kilometres]). The capital is Tallinn.

PHYSICAL AND HUMAN GEOGRAPHY

The land. *Relief.* The Estonian landscape bears traces of glacial activity; the south is covered with moraine (glacial deposit) hills, and the central part abounds in elongated hills with flat tops. They are usually arranged in groups in the direction of glacial movement, for the most part from the northwest to the southeast. The northern part of Estonia is characterized by long narrow swells consisting of deposits left by glacial rivers that formed during the melting of ice. Extensive sandy areas mark what was once the glacier's edge.

Glacial landforms

The Estonian relief is thus generally undulating, with small hills and numerous lakes, rivers, and forests lending the scene mildness and picturesqueness, particularly in the south.

The mean absolute altitude is 160 feet (49 metres), only one-tenth of the territory lying at altitudes exceeding 300 feet (90 metres) above sea level. In the southeast is the Haanja elevation containing Mt. Munamägi (1,042 feet [318 metres]), which is the highest point in Estonia.

During the postglacial period a considerable part of Estonia was flooded by the Baltic Sea. Later, large areas emerged from under water as a result of the elevation of the mainland—a process still observable, particularly in the northwest, where a rise of approximately five feet (1.5 metres) in a hundred years has been recorded.

In northern Estonia is a low limestone plateau that falls abruptly to the sea. The sheer cliff stretches along the southern shore of the Gulf of Finland from Tallinn and continues beyond the republic's borders. It rises to its maximum height (544 feet, or 166 metres, above sea level) at Pandivere.

Rivers and lakes

Estonia abounds in rivers, which carry their water to the gulfs of Finland and Riga and into Lake Peipus. The longest rivers are the Pärnu (88 miles, or 142 kilometres) and the Pedja (81 miles). Lakes occupy about 5 percent of the republic's territory. The largest lake is Peipus, with a surface area of 1,370 square miles (3,548 square kilometres).

Climate. The temperate and humid climate of Estonia differs sharply from the climates of many regions of the Soviet Union situated at the same latitude but in the depth of the continent. The republic lies in the path of air masses brought in by cyclones born in the northern Atlantic that carry warm air in winter and cool air in summer. The mean temperature in February is 23°–43° F (−5° to +6° C) and in July 61°–63° F (16°–17° C). Annual precipitation is 24–28 inches (610–710 millimetres), which, coupled with negligible evaporation and plain relief, leads to waterlogging. The Estonian climate is generally favourable to agriculture.

Plant and animal life. Mixed forests, with about 90 species of trees and shrubs, cover almost one-third of Estonia's territory. Most widespread are pine, fir, birch, and aspen; less common are oak, lime, maple, elm, and ash. Meadows occupy a considerable area, as do marshes and swamps.

About 60 species of mammals live in Estonia. The elk is the largest; roe deer, red deer, and wild pigs are also found. In the deep forests of the northeast, bear and lynx are encountered. Foxes, badgers, otters, rabbits, hares, and—along the riverbanks—mink and nutria (coypu) are fairly common. Among the sea animals, seals and fishes (cod, salmon, eel, plaice, and others) are of commercial importance. Birds are very numerous; 295 species have been identified, of which 60 are year-round residents.

Minerals. The most important mineral is bituminous shale; the output of Estonia accounts for 80 percent of the shale produced in the Soviet Union. Reserves and production of peat also are substantial, and large deposits of high-quality phosphorites, limestone, dolomites, marl, and clay exist.

The people. Estonians belong ethnically and linguistically to the Baltic-Finnish group of Finno-Ugric peoples.

The development of Estonia's economy has been attended by a considerable internal migration. The population in the northern, industrially advanced part of the republic has increased appreciably since the mid-1950s at the expense of the southern and western regions, which are basically agrarian. There has also been extensive immigration from other territories of the Soviet Union, particularly the Russian S.F.S.R. The major towns are Tallinn, Tartu, Kohtla-Järve, Narva, and Pärnu.

Towns

The economy. Estonia is basically an industrial region, with agriculture also making a contribution.

Fuel and power. About 20 percent of the industrial workers of Estonia are employed in producing bituminous shale and phosphorites or in the power industry. Estonia, the only area of the Soviet Union that has a large shale processing industry, produces a great percentage of the Soviet Union's artificial gas, much of which is transported by pipelines extending from Kohtla-Järve to Leningrad.

Most of the electricity produced in the republic is generated by thermal power plants fired with bituminous shale. One station near Narva, the Estonskaya, which began to operate in 1968, accounts for much of the electricity produced in the Soviet Baltic republics. Other major power plants include a hydroelectric station at the Narva falls and a peat-fired plant at Ellamaa. The electrical power industry has great significance both for the economy of Estonia and for the whole northwest Soviet Union.

Manufactures. Estonia's industry uses both local resources and imported raw materials. About 20 percent of the industrial labour force is engaged in engineering and metalworking activities that provide oil-refining equipment, agricultural implements, mining machinery, gas pipes, and excavators. Technical and scientific instruments and electronic apparatus are also produced.

The chemical industry

Shale processing underlies a developing chemical industry centred in Tallinn and Kohtla-Järve. Such products as benzene, adhesives, tanning agents, resins, formaldehyde, and detergents are made.

Estonia's natural resources provide a base for the production of building materials, including cement, mural blocks, and panels made either from shale ash or reinforced concrete. The main centres of this industry are Tallinn, Kunda, Tartu, and Aseri.

Timber and woodworking make up one of the oldest industries of Estonia. As a result of a disorderly exploitation of woodlands in former times the total wooded area decreased considerably. Many thousands of acres of new trees have been planted, but in order to satisfy its needs Estonia is nevertheless obliged to import from the northwestern regions of the Soviet Union about one-fourth of its requirements. Paper, pulp, plywood, matches, and furniture are among the republic's wood products. The main centres of production are Tallinn, Tartu, Narva, Pärnu, Kehra, Kuressaare (Kingissepp), and Viljandi.

Among consumer goods industries, textiles are the most developed. Seventy percent of all cotton cloth produced in the Soviet Baltic republics is manufactured in Estonia. The republic also produces wool, silk, and linen. Knitted and woven garments and shoes are also produced.

Agriculture. After 1945 Estonia's agriculture was collectivized. Instead of the former 120,000 small peasant farms there were by the late 20th century more than 140 collective farms and about 150 state farms. Agriculture accounts for 20 percent of the gross national product and engages a quarter of the labour force.

The land is generally fairly difficult to farm. Large areas have to be cleared of stones, and 70 percent of the natural pastures require draining. Cattle and pigs account for about two-thirds of the Estonian S.S.R.'s agricultural production.

Fodder crops for animal husbandry account for almost half the total crop production. Grain crops, legumes, and potatoes represent most of the balance.

An increased level of mechanization and the application of more advanced methods of work in agriculture have resulted in a considerable increase in labour productivity and in agricultural incomes.

Transport and communications. Transport systems in Estonia include railways, roads, rivers, and pipelines. Most of the republic's freight is carried by railways. River transport is of local significance only.

Estonia is connected by air with Moscow, Leningrad, the capitals of the union republics, and the Black Sea resorts.

Administrative and social conditions. *Government.* Estonia has a state emblem, flag, and national anthem. It is a socialist republic, and its constitution (1940) declares it to be a sovereign entity, though in fact it has no power to carry on relations with foreign countries. The highest organs of state power are the Supreme Soviet, elected for a four-year term, and the Presidium, selected by the Supreme Soviet. The highest executive and administrative organ of government is the Council of Ministers. In the provinces government is effected through local soviets.

Communist Party of Estonia

All political life in the republic is under the direction of the Communist Party of Estonia. The party concerns itself with the political and ideological education of the population, establishes policy for the development of the economy, and directs the activities of the Young Communist League of Estonia (Komsomol; created in 1921).

Trade unions do not, as in the West, represent the workers in negotiations with management; their efforts are directed more to providing incentives for increased production, maintaining labour discipline, and serving as an instrument of Communist Party policy.

Welfare and education. As a result of the development of industry and agriculture, the economic and social welfare of the population has increased substantially compared to the period immediately after World War II.

Scientific research in the republic is centred on the Academy of Sciences of the Estonian Soviet Socialist Republic (founded in 1946), which has three departments: physics, mathematics, and technical sciences; chemistry, geology, and biology; and social sciences.

More than 40 newspapers are published in Estonia, some with a circulation of more than 1,000,000 copies. Book publishing also flourishes.

Estonian radio broadcasts diversified programs. The system possesses a mixed chorus, a symphony, and a variety orchestra. The republic has had a television centre since 1955, and television broadcasts from Moscow and Leningrad are also received in most areas.

Literature

Cultural life. The scope and importance of Estonian literature has steadily increased since the period of national awakening in the 19th century. The greatest achievements in the first half of the 20th century were made in the genres of realistic novel (Anton Tammsaare) and imaginative poetry (Marie Under, Betti Alver). Open to cultural and literary influences of western Europe, Estonian literature developed a diversity of styles, ranging from Neoclassicism to bold experimentation. Since World War II, the dominant theme has been Soviet reality, expressed in the form of Socialist Realism especially in the prose writings of Soviet Estonian authors (Juhan Smuul). During the 1960s, a younger generation of exceptionally talented poets (Paul-Eerik Rummo, Jaan Kaplinski) brought about a revival of Estonian poetry that continued into the '70s (Jüri Üdi). A new and sophisticated genre, the so-called short novel, deals primarily with psychological problems (Enn Vetemaa, Mati Unt), sometimes projecting them into history (Jaan Kross). New developments can also be found in drama and short story. Both Estonian classics and the works of contemporary authors have been translated into many languages.

The beginning of professional theatrical art in Estonia is closely connected with the creation of the Vanemuine Theatre in Tartu in 1870. Tallinn has five theatres, including an opera and ballet theatre, a drama theatre, a youth theatre, and a puppet theatre. There are also professional theatres to be found in Pärnu, Viljandi, and Rakvere.

Tallinn is famed for its song festivals. There is an enormous stage for popular mass performances, and tens of thousands of singers and up to 200,000 spectators come to take part in these events. (A.A.Ke./V.J.T./Ed.)

HISTORY

The Estonians are first mentioned by the Roman historian Tacitus (1st century AD) in *Germania,* in which he wrote of the keepers and tillers of the soil. Their political system was patriarchal, based on clans headed by elders. The first invaders of the country were Vikings, who from the mid-9th century AD passed through Estonia and Latvia on their way to the Slavonic hinterland. These Vikings were soldiers and merchants, and there is much evidence to

Viking invasions

show that the Estonians learned from them: apart from ornaments, many of local make, archaeological finds in Estonia include Arabic, Byzantine, German, and Anglo-Saxon coins as evidence of trade. In the 11th and 12th centuries, the Danes and the Swedes tried to Christianize the Estonians, whithout success. Between 1030 and 1192 the Russians made 13 campaigns into Estonia but failed to establish supremacy there.

German conquest. Meinhard, a monk from Holstein, landed in 1180 on what is now the Latvian coast and for 16 years preached Christianity to the Livs, a Finno-Ugric tribe. His successor, Berthold of Hanover, appointed bishop of Livonia, decided that the sword must be used against the recalcitrant pagans. He was killed in 1198 in the first great battle. Albert of Buxhoevden, who succeeded him as bishop, proved himself a shrewd colonizer, pacifying the "treacherous Livs" and forcing them to build the fortress of Riga. To popularize recruitment for his army, Albert dedicated Livonia to the Virgin Mary. In 1202 he established the Order of the Knights of the Sword.

By 1208 the knights were firmly established on both banks of the Daugava (Western Dvina), and Albert felt strong enough to proceed northward to the conquest of Estonia. In the following years the Estonians lost steadily in manpower while the knights replenished theirs with new crusaders from Germany. The Russian princes of Novgorod and Pskov also raided Estonia on many occasions, penetrating especially deep in 1212 and 1216. Finally, in a major battle in 1217, the knights defeated the Estonians and killed their commander, Lembitu. Northern Estonia and the islands, however, remained free for another 10 years. To complete the conquest, Albert concluded an alliance with King Valdemar II of Denmark, who in 1219 landed with a strong army on the northern coast, on the site of Tallinn. Moreover, in the summer of 1220, Swedes conquered part of western Estonia, but the garrison they left there was wiped out shortly afterward. The Danes landed on the island of Saaremaa two years later, but, after their castle was bombarded with catapults, they surrendered on a safe conduct. Prompted by this victory, fighting flared up all over Estonia, and the Estonians raided as far as Sweden in 1226.

German domination

In 1237 the Knights of the Sword joined the Teutonic Order, which assumed control of Livonia. Northern Estonia and the islands were under Danish rule; Livonia (*i.e.,* southern Estonia and Latvia) was shared between the Teutonic Order and the bishops. The terms under which the Estonian localities submitted were not severe, but the conquerors violated them as their position became stronger, thus provoking a series of revolts. After major risings in 1343–45, the Danish crown sold its sovereignty over northern Estonia to the Teutonic Order in 1346. The Germans became the masters in the "Land of the Virgin" and, with minor exceptions, formulated its history in colonization, commerce, and the church for centuries to come. The Estonians, the Latvians, and the Livs became the serfs of their conquerors, with little to sustain their national feeling save their folklore and traditional crafts. In agriculture, however, the Germans made an improvement by introducing the three-field instead of the two-field system, and the towns enjoyed prosperity through the commercial activity of the Hanseatic League.

Swedish period. By the end of the 15th century two major powers were emerging around Livonia: Poland-Lithuania, already united in the south; and Muscovy, which had conquered Novgorod, in the east. A third factor, the Reformation, was to produce disunity and strife in this quarter, as in many others. More by diplomacy than by victory in batlle, Poland gained Livonia on the dissolution of the Teutonic Order in 1561. Three years before, northern Estonia had capitulated to the King of Sweden. The Muscovite tsar Ivan IV the Terrible had captured Narva in 1558 and penetrated deep into Estonia, bringing devastation with him, and it was not until 1581 that the Russians were expelled by the Swedes. In 1559 the Bishop of Saaremaa had sold the Estonian islands to Denmark, but in 1645 they became part of the Swedish province. By the Truce of Altmark (1629), which ended the first Polish–Swedish War, Poland surrendered to Sweden the major part of Livonia, so that all Estonian lands then came under Swedish rule.

Prolonged wars left the country devastated, and many farms were unoccupied. The vacancies were partly filled by foreign settlers who were soon assimilated. This also gave the German nobility the opportunity to enlarge their estates, increase taxes, and exact more unpaid labour. The Swedish kings attempted to curb the power of the nobility and improve the lot of the peasants. Soon after Charles XI of Sweden came of age (1672), the nobles of Livonia were forced to show their title deeds, and those who failed to do so became tenants of the crown.

The Russian conquest. The "good old Swedish days" for Estonia were more a legend than reality, but they ended with the Great Northern War. The Russian tsar Peter I the Great was finally able to achieve the dream of his predecessors and conquer the Baltic provinces. After the defeat of Charles XII of Sweden at Poltava (1709), Russian armies seized Livonia. The barons did not resist, angered as they were against the Swedish crown for its policy of reversion of estates. By the Peace of Nystad in 1721 Sweden ceded to Russia all its Baltic provinces. The old Land of the Virgin was divided into the three *guberniya*s (provinces) of Estonia, Livonia, and Kurlandia (Courland). In 1740 a famous lawsuit by an Estonian peasant, Jaan the Miller from Vohnja, against his landlord ended in a decision by the College of Justice in St. Petersburg that the peasants had no right to sue their landlords. The peasants' lot became worse than ever.

Abolition of serfdom

In 1804, however, under the emperor Alexander I, the peasants of Livonia were given the right of private property and inheritance; a bill abolishing serfdom was passed in Estonia in 1811 and in Livonia in 1819. Other agrarian laws followed, in particular that of 1863 establishing the peasants' right of free movement; that of 1866 abolishing the landowner's right of jurisdiction on their estates, including the right to flog; and that of 1868 abolishing the corvée.

Estonian national awakening. The Estonian peasants benefitted by these reforms, and at the end of the 19th century they possessed two-fifths of the privately owned land of the country. With the growth of urban prosperity as a result of industrialization, the population increased. Improvement in education was such that by 1886 only about 2 percent of the Estonian recruits were unable to read. National consciousness increased too.

The accession of Alexander III marked the beginning of a period of more rigid Russification. The Russian municipal constitution was introduced in 1882; Russian criminal and civil codes replaced the old Baltic ones; in 1887 Russian was made the language of instruction, instead of German and Estonian. In 1893 the University of Tartu (Dorpat), which was then an important centre of German learning, was Russified. The first reaction of the Estonians was that poetic justice was being administered to their age-long oppressors, but they also feared the reactionary Pan-Slavism. In 1901, in Tallinn, Konstantin Päts founded the newspaper *Teataja,* in which moderately radical ideas were expressed. In 1904, thanks to Päts, the Estonians won a clear victory on the Tallinn town council.

In January 1905 a revolution started in Russia and spread immediately to Estonia. Tônisson founded a National Liberal Party and organized its first congress in Tallinn on November 27. The 800 delegates soon split into a Liberal and a Radical wing, but both voted resolutions demanding political autonomy for Estonia. In December, Päts summoned a peasant congress in Tallinn, but martial law was proclaimed. Parties of workers scattered into the countryside and began to loot and burn the manor houses. Troops were drafted and repression started: 328 Estonians were shot or hanged. Päts and the Radical leader Jaan Teemant fled abroad, both being sentenced to death *in contumaciam.* At the elections to the first and the second Russian Duma, the Estonians returned five deputies.

Independence. The Russian Revolution of March 1917 brought autonomy to Estonia. An Estonian National Council, which came to be known as the Diet Maapaev, met on July 14 and on October 12 appointed a provisional government with Päts as premier.

The November coup d'etat that brought the Communists into power in Petrograd made itself felt in Estonia. On November 28, 1917, the Estonian Diet decided to break away from the Russian state, but on December 8 the Russian Council of People's Commissars appointed a puppet Communist government headed by Jaan Anvelt, who seized power in Tallinn but never obtained control of the whole country. (He was shot in Moscow in 1937.) In February 1918 German forces advanced. The Communists fled, and on February 24 the provisional government declared Estonia independent. The following day German troops entered Tallinn. Estonian leaders, except Päts, who was arrested, went abroad or underground. On March 3 the Treaty of Brest-Litovsk was signed, and, by a protocol signed in Berlin on August 27, sovereignty over the Baltic countries was transferred from Russia to Germany.

Germany capitulated on November 11, 1918. The Estonian provisional government again proclaimed the independence of Estonia. But the Soviet government declared the Treaty of Brest-Litovsk null and void. On November 28 the Red army took Narva and started the invasion of Estonia, which had been denuded of all arms by the retreating Germans. The government of Konstantin Päts obtained weapons and war materiel from the Allies. With the aid of a British naval squadron and a Finnish voluntary force of 2,700 men, the commander in chief Col. (later General) Johan Laidoner opened a counteroffensive in January 1919. By the end of February all of Estonian territory had been freed, and the Estonian Army penetrated into Soviet and Latvian territory.

Repulse of the Red army

On June 15, 1920, the constituent assembly (elected in April 1919), with August Rei as president, voted the new constitution with a single-chamber Parliament (Riigikogu) of 100 members elected for three years, with a system of proportional representation, and a chief of state (*riigivanem*), who was also the premier. Because no party had an absolute majority, government by coalition became the rule, and from May 1919, when the first constitutional Cabinet was formed, to May 1933, Estonia had 20 coalitions headed by 10 statesmen.

On December 1, 1924, 300 conspirators, mostly Russians working on the transit base at Tallinn or smuggled in, tried to seize communications and to call in Soviet troops but failed ignominiously. The Communist Party was outlawed, and the movement became virtually extinct. The world depression of the early 1930s caused unemployment and the falling off of agricultural prices. The strong government action necessary to cope with the situation was precluded under the 1920 constitution. A new constitution in 1933 gave sweeping powers to the president. Päts became acting president and was expected to prepare the ground for the first presidential election. Instead, he proclaimed on March 12, 1934, a state of emergency; opposition leaders were arrested and the political activities of all parties forbidden. For three years Päts ruled as a benevolent dictator. In December 1936 a new constituent assembly was elected. It prepared a third constitution with a chamber of 80 deputies elected by the majority system and a national council of 40 members. The election was held in February 1938. In April Päts was elected president for a term of six years.

Independence lost. The fate of Estonia was decided by the so-called Nonaggression Treaty of August 1939 between Nazi Germany and the U.S.S.R. A secret protocol to this treaty assigned Finland, Estonia, Latvia, and eastern Poland to the Soviet orbit. After the defeat of Poland this arrangement was revised on September 28, and a secret supplementary clause extended the Soviet sphere of influence to Lithuania. On the same day, the Soviet government imposed on Estonia a treaty of mutual assistance that conceded to the U.S.S.R. several military bases on Estonian territory, which were manned forthwith. A broadly based nonpolitical government under Juri Uluots was appointed. On June 16, 1940, a Soviet ultimatum demanded a new Estonian government, "able and willing to secure the honest application of the Soviet–Estonia mutual assistance treaty." The following day, Soviet armed forces occupied the whole country. On July 21 the Chamber of Deputies was presented with a resolution to join the U.S.S.R.; it was unanimously adopted the following day in spite of being contrary to constitutional procedure. On August 6 the Moscow Supreme Soviet incorporated Estonia into the U.S.S.R. Meanwhile, Päts, Laidoner, and many political leaders were arrested and deported to the U.S.S.R. In the first 12 months of Soviet occupation, more than 60,000 persons were killed or deported: more than 10,000 were removed in a mass deportation during the night of June 13–14, 1941.

Soviet ultimatum

On June 22, 1941, Germany attacked the U.S.S.R. Large areas of Estonia were freed from Soviet forces by improvised Estonian units before the German front reached Estonia. For three years Estonia was under German occupation. It became part of the Ostland province. By February 1944, however, the Russians were back on the Narva front. A few thousand Estonian youths, who had escaped to Finland to fight the Reds in the Finnish Army rather than with the Germans, returned but of course could not save the situation. About 30,000 Estonians escaped by sea to Sweden and 33,000 to Germany; many thousands perished on the sea. On September 22, 1944, Soviet troops took Tallinn. It is estimated that about 20,000 Estonians were deported in 1945–46. The third large deportation took place on March 24–27, 1949, and comprised about 40,000 persons, mostly farmers who resisted collectivization.

After restoration of the Soviet regime, Estonia became nominally the 15th union republic of the U.S.S.R., subject to the laws and practices of the union. The Communist party and the administration were both permeated by ethnic Russians or by Russified Estonians.

(K.M.S./E.Ar./Ed.)

Latvia

Latvia, which had been an independent republic since 1920, was constituted as one of the 15 republics of the Soviet Union on July 21, 1940, and was proclaimed a Soviet Socialist republic on August 5. Situated in the Soviet west on the shores of the Baltic Sea and the Gulf of Riga, it covers an area of 24,600 square miles (63,700 square kilometres). In the north it borders on the Estonian Soviet Socialist Republic, in the east on the Russian S.F.S.R., and in the south on the Lithuanian S.S.R. The overall length of Latvia's borders is 1,120 miles (1,800 kilometres), of which 307 miles (494 kilometres) are coastal. The capital is Riga (Rīga in Latvian).

PHYSICAL AND HUMAN GEOGRAPHY

The land. *Relief.* Latvia is essentially an undulating plain, with fairly flat lowlands alternating with hills. The eastern part is more elevated, the most prominent feature being the central Vidzeme (Livonia) elevation, which reaches a maximum height of 1,020 feet (311 metres). In the southeast the highest point is 948 feet (289 metres). The Kurzeme (Courland) elevation in the west is cut by the Venta River into western and eastern parts. Between the central Vidzeme and Latgalē (Latgallian) elevations lies the East Latvian Lowland, partly crossed by moraine ridges that impede drainage; there are many peat bogs in this area.

The shores of the Baltic and the Gulf of Riga are only slightly indented, and there are considerable stretches of excellent sandy beaches.

Drainage and soils. Latvia contains a multitude of rivers belonging to the Baltic drainage area. The largest are the Western Dvina, locally called the Daugava (with a total length of 224 miles [358 kilometres] in Latvia), the Gauja (Russian Gauya), the Venta, and the Lielupe. Amid the hills, many of which are forested, are numerous lakes, ranging from a few acres up to 12 square miles (30 square kilometres) in area. Soils are predominantly podzolic, though calcareous soils characterize the Zemgale Plain. Swampy soils are found in some areas, particularly the East Latvian Lowland. Erosion is a problem in the more intensely cultivated hilly areas.

The Daugava River

Mineral resources are confined to gravel, sand, dolomite, limestone, clay, and peat. Oil has been discovered in the Courland Peninsula, but reserves have not yet been explored.

Climate. The climate is influenced by the prevailing air masses coming from the Atlantic. Humidity is high, and the skies are usually somewhat cloudy; there are only 30 to 40 days of sunshine per year and 150 to 180 completely overcast days. Average precipitation is 22–24 inches (about 550–600 millimetres) on lowlands and 28-31 inches (about 700–800 millimetres) on elevations. Southwesterly and southerly winds prevail. The frost-free season lasts from 125 to 155 days. Summers are cool and rainy more often than not. The mean air temperature in June is 63° F (17° C) with occasional jumps to about 93° F (34° C). Winter sets in slowly and lasts from the middle of December to the middle of March. The mean January temperature ranges from 28° F (−2° C) on the coast to 19° F (−7° C) in the east. There are occasional drops to −40° F (−40° C).

Plant and animal life. About two-thirds of Latvia is covered with forests, meadows, pastures, swamps, and wasteland. Forests, which account for more than a third of the total area, are a dominating feature of the republic's natural scene; about 10 percent of the forests are cultivated. The larger forest tracts are to be found in the northern part of the Courland Peninsula, along the left bank of the Daugava, and in the northeast. Conifers (pine and spruce) predominate. Of the deciduous species, birch, aspen, and alder occur more commonly. Meadows are found everywhere, both in the river valleys and among the hills.

Forest animals

Latvia's fauna is typical for a region with mixed forests; there are squirrel, fox, hare, lynx, and badger. Somewhat less common are ermine and weasel. Conservation measures have resulted in an increase in the number of deer and elk and reintroduced beaver.

The numerous birds include the nightingale, oriole, blackbird, woodpecker, owl, grouse, partridge, finch, tomtit, quail, and lark. Storks and herons are found in the marshes and meadows.

The people. The bulk of the people are Latvians and Russians. The Latvians, or Letts, speak one of the two surviving Baltic languages, the other being Lithuanian. In 1935 about 68 percent of them were Lutheran, 26 percent Roman Catholic. The ancestors of the present-day Latvians were the Latgals (Latgallians), who in the 9th century lived in the northeastern part of the present republic and who absorbed the Kurs (Cours, Couronians) and Livs. Two other early Latvian tribes were the Selonians and the Zemgals (Semigallians).

The economy. Industrialization in Latvia began in the latter part of the 19th century, and by the late 20th century it was the most heavily industrialized republic of the Soviet Union.

Energy. Latvia produces approximately half of its own energy requirements, the remainder being derived from imported fuel and from the unified power system of the northwest regions of the Soviet Union. On the Daugava River stand the major hydroelectric stations—Pļaviņas, Ķegums, and Riga. There are thermoelectric stations in Riga and other cities. All the stations are integrated in a single power grid, which in turn is incorporated in the power grid of the Soviet northwest.

Industry. Machine building and metal engineering are the leading manufacturing activities. Labour-intensive goods—that is, items utilizing small quantities of raw materials and much labour—such as radios and scientific instruments, are produced in quantity. Durable consumer goods, such as refrigerators, washing machines, motorcycles, and motor scooters, are also produced. The heavy engineering sector turns out ships, rolling stock, streetcars, power generators, diesel motors, and agricultural implements. The light consumer goods industry, concentrating on textiles, shoes, and hosiery, is sufficiently well developed that its products can be exported to other Soviet republics. There are many food-processing enterprises.

Agriculture and fisheries. Agricultural specialization is in dairy farming and meat production. Of the agricultural land, some two-thirds is used for crops, the remainder mainly for pasture. Of the crops, grain is the most important, industrial crops (sugar beets and flax) occupying only a tiny percentage of the total crop area.

Collective and state farms

Collectivization of agriculture was accomplished, against resistance, in 1947–50. In the late 20th century there were some 300 collective farms and 240 state farms. Agriculture is mechanized, permitting intensive farming.

Latvia accounts for a small percentage of the Soviet Union's fish catch.

Transportation. All types of transport are found in Latvia, which ranks first among the union republics in the density of its rail network. Much Soviet foreign trade is conducted via the seaports of Riga and Ventspils, which are open the year round. Riga has air links with Moscow and other large cities of the Soviet Union, and there is some internal air service.

Administrative and social conditions. *Government.* The highest formal organs of government in Latvia are the Supreme Soviet, members of which are elected for a period of four years, and the Presidium. The Supreme Soviet appoints the Council of Ministers and elects the Supreme Court and the Presidium. The latter exercises power between sessions of the Supreme Soviet. Administration is the responsibility of the Council of Ministers, which drafts economic development plans and oversees their implementation. For administrative purposes the republic is divided into *rayony* (districts) and cities. At the local level, government is exercised by district, city, and village soviets, elected for terms of two years.

Justice is administered by people's courts, the judges of which are elected for terms of two years.

The Communist Party of Latvia

The Communist Party of Latvia, like its counterparts in the other union republics, is in fact the only source of political power, under the Communist Party of the Soviet Union. Western students of the Soviet Union conclude that the party is dominated by non-Latvians (mainly Russians and other Slavs) and by Russified Latvians who have lived in Russia for large parts of their lives.

Education. General literacy was achieved in Latvia in the 1890s. Teaching in the general schools is in Latvian or Russian or both. In Latvian-language schools the study of Russian is compulsory.

Scientific work is carried on at the institutes of the Latvian Academy of Sciences (founded in 1946), in higher educational establishments, and in research institutes.

Cultural life. Amateur art thrives in Latvia. Clubs and individual enterprises have drama groups, choirs, ensembles, orchestras, and dance companies. The song festivals that have been held in Latvia since 1873 are still very popular; every five years the local districts and towns hold their own festivals and then send their best choirs, orchestras, and dance companies to the national festival, held at a park in Riga. The republic has a conservatory of music, an academy of arts, and a number of specialized secondary educational establishments for students of music, painting, and the applied arts.

Noted Latvian composers include Jāzeps Medins, Jānis Medins, and Emēlis Melngailis.

Modern Latvian literature dates from the late 19th century; the national epic, *Lāčplēsis* ("Bear Slayer"), by Andrejs Pumpurs, was published in 1888. Jānis Rainis, who died in 1929, is generally considered to be the most important Latvian writer. Three houses now publish literature in Latvian, Russian, and other languages. Newspapers and magazines are published in Latvian and Russian. Like the other Baltic republics, Latvia is better supplied with radio receivers than the rest of the Soviet Union and receives foreign broadcasts. Television broadcasts are part local, part from Moscow; a large part of television transmission is in Russian. The Riga Film Studio produces full-length feature films as well as documentaries, short subjects, cartoons, and newsreels.

An important national tradition is the festival of Midsummer Eve (St. John's Eve, or Janu Naktis) and Day, which, though officially abolished by the government in 1960, continues to be observed. (P.V.G./Ed.)

HISTORY

Amber trade of the Aestii

The Latvians constitute a prominent division of the ancient group of peoples known as the Balts. The first historically documented connection between the Balts and the civilization of the Mediterranean world was based on the ancient amber trade: according to Tacitus, the Aestii (predecessors of the Old Prussians) developed an important trade with the Roman Empire. This trade, with Germanic tribes as middlemen, reached its peak in the first two centuries AD and was maintained, precariously, when the migrations of the Germanic peoples began. What isolated the Balts from direct contact with the Mediterranean world was the large expansion of the Slavs over central and eastern Europe. Trade routes then shifted farther to the east or to the west, and the eastern Baltic countries had to rely on their Scandinavian neighbours for trade and cultural relations.

The Varangian, or Viking, expansion southeastward to the steppes north of the Black Sea was along the Western Dvina and Dnepr rivers and so passed across the Latvian lands. During the 10th and 11th centuries these lands were subject to a double pressure: from the east there was the Russian penetration; from the west came the Swedish push toward the shores of Courland.

German rule. During the crusading period, German, or, more precisely, Saxon, overseas expansion reached the eastern shores of the Baltic. Because the people occupying the coast of Latvia were the Livs, the German invaders called the country Livland, a name rendered in Latin as Livonia. In the mid-12th century, German merchants from Lübeck and Bremen were visiting the estuary of the Western Dvina; and these visits were followed by the arrival of German missionaries. Meinhard, a monk from Holstein, landed there in 1180 and was named bishop of Üxküll (Ikškile) in 1186. Berthold of Hanover, who succeeded Meinhard as bishop in 1196, was killed in 1198 because he used force against the "treacherous Livs" resisting Baptism. Then, the third bishop, Albert of Buxhoevden, with Pope Innocent III's permission, founded the Order of the Knights of the Sword in 1202. Before they merged in 1237 with the Knights of the Teutonic Order, they had conquered all the Latvian tribal kingdoms. The history of the country as written by the Germans is thus a conqueror's account.

The Livonian confederation

After the conquest, the Germans formed a so-called Livonian confederation, which lasted for more than three centuries. This feudalistic organization was not a happy one, its three components—the Teutonic Order, the archbishopric of Riga, and the free city of Riga—being in constant dispute with each other. Moreover, the vulnerability of land frontiers involved the confederation in frequent foreign wars: the network of German strongholds testifies to the lack of security no less eloquently than the earlier system of castle mounds builts by the Latvians. The Latvians, however, benefitted from Riga's joining the Hanseatic League in 1282, as the league's trade brought prosperity. In general, however, the situation of the Latvians under German rule was that of any subject nation. The indigenous nobility was extinguished, apart from a few of its members who changed their allegiance; and the rural population was forced to pay tithes and taxes to their German conquerors and to provide corvée, or statute labour.

The rise of Lithuania in the 14th century and the union of the Lithuanian and Polish crowns (1386) created a power that could wage long and devastating wars with the fast-growing Muscovite state in the east; but these wars were partly fought out on Livonian soil, so that the Latvian people's sufferings increased. As the fortunes of the Teutonic Order declined, the knights exploited their subjects more and more ruthlessly, and by the 16th century the Latvian peasants were reduced to virtual slavery as the chattels of their landlords.

The Poles, the Swedes, and the encroachment of Russia. In 1561 the Latvian territory was partitioned: Courland, south of the Western Dvina, became an autonomous duchy under the suzerainty of the Polish crown; and Livonia north of the river was incorprated into Poland under the name Inflanty. Riga was likewise incorporated into Poland in 1581 but was taken by the Swedish king Gustavus II Adolphus in 1621; Vidzeme—that is to say, the greater part of Livonia north of Livonia north of the Western Dvina—was ceded to Sweden by the Truce of Altmark (1629), though Latgale, the southeastern area, remained under Polish rule.

Conquest by Peter the Great

The rulers of Muscovy had so far failed to reach the Baltic shores of the Latvian country, though Ivan III and Ivan IV had tried to do so. The Russian tsar Alexis renewed the attempt without success in his wars against Sweden and Poland (1653–67). Finally, however, Peter I the Great managed to "break the window" to the Baltic Sea: in the course of the Great Northern War he took Riga from the Swedes in 1710; and at the end of the war he secured Vidzeme from Sweden under the Peace of Nystad (1721). Latgale was annexed by the Russians at the first partition of Poland (1772), Courland at the third (1795). By the end of the 18th century, therefore, the whole Latvian nation was subject to Russia.

Russian domination. In the period immediately following the Napoleonic Wars the Russian emperor Alexander I was induced to grant personal freedom to the peasants of Courland in 1817 and to those of Vidzeme in 1819. This was remarkable insofar as it preceded the abolition of serfdom in Russia by more than 40 years; but it did not imply any right of the peasant to buy the land that his ancestors had tilled for centuries, so that the Latvian peasant's freedom was compared by wits to that of a bird. Consequently, there was unrest in the Latvian lands until the emancipation of the serfs throughout the Russian Empire (1861) brought the right to buy land in ownership from the state and from the landlords, who were still mostly German.

In step with the growing economic strength of the local peasantry came a revival of national feeling. This movement was led by idealistic, strong-willed men who soon saw how difficult and dangerous it would be to steer a course between the German aristocracy and merchant groups on the one side and the Russian administration on the other. During those years of intermittent hope and despair, the idea of political self-rule was conceived; and moreover, in order to meet the rapidly increasing intellectual demands of the people, educational establishments and other national institutions were required. The idea of an independent Latvian state was openly put forward during the Russian Revolution of 1905. This revolution, evoked as it was simultaneously by social and by national groups, bore further witness to the strength of the Latvian reaction to economic and political German and Russian pressure. Nine years later, World War I broke out.

Independence. After the Russian Revolution of March 1917 the Latvian National Political Conference, convened at Riga, asked in July for complete political autonomy. On September 3, however, the German Army took Riga. After the Bolshevik coup of Noverber 1917 in Petrograd, the Latvian People's Council, representing peasant, bourgeois, and Socialist groups, proclaimed independence on November 18, 1918. A government was formed by the leader of the Farmers' Union, Kārlis Ulmanis. The Soviet government established a Communist government for Latvia at Valmiera, headed by Pēteris Stučka. The Red Army, which included Latvian units, took Riga on January 3, 1919, and the Ulmanis government moved to Liepāja (Libau), where it was protected by a British naval squadron. But Liepāja was still occupied by German troops whom the Allies wished to defend East Prussia and Courland (Kurzeme) against the advancing Red Army. Their commander, Gen. Rüdiger Graf von der Goltz, demanded control over the Latvian units as well. He intended to build a German-controlled Latvia and to make it a German base of operation in the war against the Soviets. This intention caused a conflict with the government of independent Latvia supported by the Allies. Von der Goltz had at his disposal—besides his German troops—the *baltische Landeswehr,* a combat-ready unit of predominantly Baltic-German volunteers including also Latvian units. On May 22 these forces took Riga. Pushing northward, the Germans were stopped near Cēsis by the Estonian army which included 2,000 Latvians. The British general, Sir Hubert de la Poer Gough, head of the Allied military mission, negotiated an armistice. The Germans had to abandon Riga, to which the Ulmanis government returned in July. In the meantime, the Red Army, finding itself attacked from the north by the Estonians, had withdrawn from Latvia.

Red Army actions

In July Gough demanded that the German troops should retreat to East Prussia. But von der Goltz now raised a "West Russian" army, systematically reinforced by units of German volunteers. These forces, headed by an adventurer, Col. Bermondt-Avalov, were to fight the Red Army, co-operating with the other "White Russian" armies of Kolchak, Denikin, and Yudenich, supported by the Allies. But on October 8 Bermondt attacked the Latvian troops and occupied the suburbs of Riga south of the river. By November 10, however, the Latvians, helped by the artillery of an Anglo-french naval squadron, cooperating with Estonian forces, defeated von der Goltz's and Bermondt's troops, attacked finally also by the Lithuanians. Until December 1919 all German troops had abandoned Latvia and Lithuania. Only Latgale remained in Red hands; but this province was cleared by 33,000 Latvians under Gen. Jānis Balodis, 20,000 Poles under Gen. Édward Smigły-Rydz, and 6,000 men of the *Landeswehr,* which had been put under the command of the British Lieut. Col. H.R.L.G. Alexander (later Earl Alexander of Tunis).

A Latvian constituent assembly, elected in April 1920, met in Riga on May 1; and on August 11 a Latvian-Soviet peace treaty was signed in Riga, the Soviet government renouncing all claims to Latvia. The Latvian constitution of February 15, 1922, provided for a republic with a president and a unicameral parliament, or *saeima,* of 100 members elected for three years.

The multiplicity of parties in the Saeima (22 in 1922 and 24 in 1931) made it impossible to form a stable government; and in 1934 Ulmanis, prime minister for the fourth time since 1918, proposed a constitutional reform. This was angrily opposed by the Social Democrats, the Communists, and the national minorities. The German minority became Nazified, and Ulmanis had to suppress the Latvian branch of the Baltischer Bruderschaft (Baltic Brotherhood), whose program was the incorporation of the Baltic state into the Third Reich; but a Latvian Facist organization called Perkonkrust (Thundercross) developed a fierce propaganda. On May 15, 1934, Ulmanis and Balodis issued a decree declaring a state of siege. The Saeima and all the political parties were dissolved. On April 11, 1936, on the expiry of the second term of office of Pres. Alberts Kviesis, Ulmanis succeeded him. The country's economic position improved considerably.

Fascist organizations

The Soviet occupation and incorporation. When World War II started in September 1939, the fate of Latvia had been already decided in the secret protocol of the so-called German-Soviet Nonaggression Treaty of August 23. In October Latvia had to sign a dictated treaty of mutual assistance by which the U.S.S.R. obtained military, naval, and air bases on Latvian territory. On June 16, 1940, Latvia was invaded by the Red Army. On June 20 the formation of a new government was announced; on July 21 the new Saeima voted for the incorporation of Latvia into the U.S.S.R.; and on August 5 the U.S.S.R. accepted this incorporation. In the first year of Soviet occupation about 35,000 Latvians, especially the intelligentsia, were deported to Russia.

After the German invasion of the U.S.S.R., from July 1941 to October 1944, Latvia was a province of a larger Ostland, in which Estonia, Lithuania, and Belorussia were also included. After the reconquest of Latvia by the Soviet Army, the Soviet regime was restored with August Kirchensteins as chairman of the Presidium of the Supreme Soviet. About 65,000 Latvians fled to Germany and to Sweden before the arrival of the Soviet forces, while during 1945–46 about 105,000 were deported to Russia. The extreme northeastern section of Latvia with its predominant Russian population was ceded to Pskov Oblast of the Russian S.F.S.R. in 1945. In March 1949, when collective farming was forcibly introduced, the third mass deportation took place, in which about 70,000 Latvians were sent to northern Russia and Siberia. In 1952 Kirchensteins was succeeded by Karlis Ozolins, who was dismissed in November 1959 as the leader of the "Nationalist Communist" faction that opposed Russian influence in Latvia. From then on, Latvia was subjected to increasing Russification. (Ar.Sp./K.M.S./Ed.)

Lithuania

The Lithuanian Soviet Socialist Republic, more popularly known as Lithuania (Lithuanian Lietuva, Russian Litva), was proclaimed on July 20, 1940, and became a member of the Soviet Union on August 3, 1940. It is bounded on the north by the Latvian S.S.R., on the east and south by the Belorussian S.S.R., and on the southwest by the Kaliningrad *oblast* (region) of the Russian Soviet Federated Socialist Republic and by Poland. The waters of the Baltic Sea to the west add an important maritime element to the natural environment of the republic. Lithuania has an area of 25,200 square miles (65,200 square kilometres).

PHYSICAL AND HUMAN GEOGRAPHY

The land. *Relief.* Underlying rock structures are of little significance for the contemporary Lithuanian terrain, which, basically, is a low-lying plain scraped by Ice Age glaciers that left behind thick, ridgelike terminal deposits known as moraines. The Baltic coast area is fringed by a region characterized by geographers as the maritime depression, which rises gradually eastward. Sand dunes line an attractive coast, and the Kuršių Maries (Kurisches Haff), a lagoon almost cut off from the sea by a thin, 60-mile (100-kilometre) sandspit, forms a distinctive feature. This is bounded on the east by the Žemaičių (Samogitian) Hills, which give way to the flat expanses of the central Lithuanian lowland.

The central lowland

The lowland consists of glacial lake clays and boulder-studded loams and stretches in a wide band across the republic from north to south; some portions of it are heavily waterlogged. The lowland is bordered in the southeast by the narrow Žiežmariai Plain, which was formed from an ancient glacial valley filled with sandy, gravelly, and pebbly deposits. The sandy portions have often been whipped up into dunes, which have become overgrown with pine trees. The elevated Baltic Ridge thrusts between these two lowland areas into the eastern and southeastern portions of the republic; its rumpled glacial relief includes a host of small hills and numerous small lakes. The Švenčionių-Naročiaus and the Ašmenos Hills—the latter containing Juozapinė, at 964 feet (294 metres) above sea level the highest point in the republic—are located in the extreme east and southeast.

Lithuanian soils range from sands to heavy clays. In the northwest, the soil is either loamy or sandy (and sometimes marshy) and is quite heavily podzolized, or leached out. In the central region, weakly podzolized, loamy peats predominate, and it is there that the most fertile, and hence most cultivated, soils are found. In the southeast, there are sandy soils, somewhat loamy and moderately podzolized. Sandy soils, in fact, cover a quarter of Lithuania, and most of these regions are blanketed by woodlands.

Lithuanian rivers drain to the Baltic and generally have the slow, meandering characteristics of lowland rivers. The Neman (Nemunas), cutting north and then west through the heart of the country, is the largest. Its main tributaries are the Merkys, Neris, Nevėžís, Dubysa, Jūra, Minija, and Šešupė. The rivers have a total length of some 1,700 miles (2,720 kilometres), nearly a fifth of which is navigable. Most of them can be used for floating timber rafts and for electric-power generation. A distinctive feature of the Lithuanian landscape is the presence of about 3,000 lakes, mostly in the east and southeast. The boggy regions produce large quantities of peat that, dried by air, is used in both industry and agriculture.

Climate. The climate of the republic is transitional between the maritime type of western Europe and the continental type found farther east. As a result, damp air masses of Atlantic origin predominate, alternating with continental Eurasian and, more rarely, colder Arctic air or air with a southern, tropical origin. Baltic Sea influences dominate a comparatively narrow coastal zone. The mean temperature for January, the coldest month, is 23.4° F (−4.8° C), while July, the warmest month, has an average temperature of 63° F (17.2° C). Average annual rainfall is 25 inches (630 millimetres), diminishing inland. Rainfall reaches a peak in August, except in the maritime strip, where the maximum is reached two to three months later.

Plant and animal life. The natural vegetation cover of Lithuania falls into three separate regions. In the maritime regions, pine forests predominate, and wild rye and various bushy plants grow on the sand dunes. Spruce trees add their colour to the hilly eastern portion. The central region is characterized by large tracts of oak trees, with elegant birch forests in the northern portions, as well as distinctive black alder and aspen groves. Pine forests again prevail in the south; indeed, about a quarter of the whole republic is forested, with a further quarter taken up by meadowlands. Swamps and marshlands account for about 7 percent of the total area.

Three distinctive vegetation zones

Wildlife is very diverse, with about 60 mammalian species. There are wolves, foxes, otters, badgers, ermines, wild boars, and many rodents. The deep forests harbour elk, stag, deer, beaver, mink, and water rats. Common birds include delicate white storks, a variety of ducks, geese, and swans, cormorants, herons, hawks, and even an occasional bald eagle. There are many types of grouse and partridge, and the total number of bird species recorded approaches 300. The more than 50 species of fish include salmon, eel, bream, carp, and trout, with cod, plaice, and herring common off the coast.

The people. Ethnically, about 80 percent of the population are Lithuanians, but there are also Russians and Poles and lesser numbers of Belorussians, Ukrainians, Jews, Latvians, Tatars, Gypsies, and others. Urban dwellers make up over half the total population.

Natural increase, rather than any inward migration, has accounted for most of the recent population growth. Internally, however, there has been a modest but steady movement of people to the cities, accentuated in the case of the planned regional centres of Alytus, Kapsukas, Utena, Plungė, and Mažeikiai.

The economy. *Resources.* Lithuania possesses a good range of useful mineral resources, including sulfates, notably gypsum; chalk and chalky marl; limestones; dolomites; various clays, sands, and gravels; peat; some iron ore and phosphorites; and mineral waters. Oil deposits have been detected in the offshore regions. The power potential of the many rivers and the traditional resources of the great forests and the rich agricultural areas have added to the basic wealth of the republic, which is well placed geographically for trade purposes.

Planning goals

During the Soviet period, economic policy has emphasized industrialization; and, since the end of World War II, the machinery, shipbuilding, electronic, electrical- and radio-engineering, chemical, cement, and fish-processing industries have been completely overhauled. Traditional industries such as food processing and various branches of light industry have also expanded considerably. Since 1961 the Lithuanian power system has been part of the unified network covering the northwestern Soviet Union. Two major plants, one a hydroelectric station on the Neman and the other a thermal station at the town of Elektrėnai, increased output. Local resources have also stimulated building materials and construction industries to meet the demands of a growing and urbanizing population.

Agriculture. Lithuanian agriculture has maintained something of its traditional importance, with almost one-fourth of the economically active population still engaged in farming the approximately 740 collective and 310 state farms. The development of agriculture has been closely linked to land reclamation and swamp-drainage schemes. The chief agricultural trend is toward the production of meat and milk, together with the cultivation of flax, sugar beets, potatoes, and vegetables. Half the total production is made up of fodder crops; a large percentage consists of grain and leguminous crops; and most of the rest consists of potatoes and vegetables. Livestock breeding is still the leading branch of agriculture, however, with emphasis on dairy cattle and pigs. One feature of the Soviet period has been the injection of technology into agriculture, and most crop cultivation is mechanized, although at autumn harvest time large amounts of manual labour are still required.

Emphasis on livestock breeding

Economic regions. Lithuanian planners, using as criteria environmental, economic, and transportational indexes, have divided the republic into four economic regions.

Occupying almost 30 percent of the total area, Eastern Lithuania, containing the capital, Vilnius, is characterized by a diversified and rapidly growing industry (primarily metalworking and mechanical engineering, woodworking, and branches of light industry) centred on the main cities and by a substantial rural economy. It also contains a number of well-sited health resorts, including Trakai and Ignalina, and is crisscrossed by highways linking the area with major Soviet cities.

Occupying slightly more than one-fourth of the republic's territory, the southern portion of central Lithuania contains more than half of the republic's developed water-power resources. Metalworking, mechanical-engineering, and food-processing industries predominate; farming is intensive, with a concentration on stock raising and the growing of sugar beets. Kaunas, Alytus, and Kapsukas are the main centres.

Sprawling over the northern portion of the middle Lithuanian lowland and the eastern slopes of the ŽemaiciųHills, Northern Lithuania occupies almost 30 percent of the republic and is noted for its fertile soils and its dolomite, gypsum, and limestone reserves. Farming is intensive, with almost half the winter-wheat sowing and most of the sugar-beet and flax crops located here. Industry is not very well developed. The main centres are Šiauliai, Panevėžys, and Rokiškis.

Occupying the remaining 15 percent of the republic, Western Lithuania lies along the Baltic Sea shores and has a distinctive maritime quality. Shipbuilding, ship repairing, fish processing, and oil refining are the main industries, with Klaipėda, Telšiai, Plungė, and Mažeikiai the main centres. There are many pastures, and horse breeding and the raising of dairy cattle and pigs, together with poultry farming and fishing, are well developed.

Transportation. Railways continue to be the main means of transport in Lithuania. Motor transportation has nevertheless increased sharply, and cars and buses account for almost all of the total number of people carried. Sea transport is an important factor, with freight transportation showing a rapid increase since World War II. River transport is also significant.

Vilnius is the main air-transportation centre, with links to other important Soviet cities and resort areas. The transportation network also includes a natural-gas pipeline that carries gas from the Ukraine and an oil pipeline that carries crude from Western Siberian oil fields to the refinery at Mažeikiai.

Administrative and social conditions. *Government.* The constitution of the Lithuanian Soviet Socialist Republic, adopted on August 25, 1940, states that political power resides in the workers and peasants of the republic, acting through the local soviets, or councils of workers' deputies. This political foundation rests on a socialist economic system, with communal ownership of the means of production.

The Supreme Soviet, elected for four years and acting through a Council of Ministers, is the highest legislative body of the republic. Its Presidium exercises executive power between sessions. Locally, power is vested in various levels of soviets, down to the smallest village unit; all are elected for two-year periods.

Justice is administered through the Supreme Court and a local network of people's courts, with members elected for five and two years, respectively. Law enforcement is in the hands of the Lithuanian S.S.R. procurator, who is appointed for five years.

The Lithuanian Communist Party

The Lithuanian Communist Party, a constituent of the Communist Party of the Soviet Union, is the political organization of the republic. Its members and candidates for membership are supported by the activities of the Komsomol youth movement. As elsewhere in the Soviet Union, the trade unions play social and economic roles in formulating and implementing state policy.

Social services. Lithuanian society has benefitted from emphasis on the production of consumer goods and the improvement of social services, as well as on the building up of heavy industry. As a result, both average monthly income and the proportion of the national income set aside for social purposes have showed a steady expansion.

The latter provisions were important, as they augmented the standard of living by providing free education and medical services, as well as a range of ancillary services. The latter included the upkeep of kindergartens and day nurseries, sick leave, pension payments, and help in providing vacation and sanatorium accommodations. The urbanization process has meant a constant struggle to keep up with housing needs, and new techniques, including prefabrication, have been introduced.

Cultural life. As elsewhere in the Soviet Union, there is a high level of public interest in various forms of cultural life, exhibited in public libraries, museums, amateur cultural centres, theatres, and cinemas. The works of contemporary Lithuanian writers, poets, and playwrights are evolving in a milieu that blends a very old cultural tradition with the new social factors introduced over a relatively short period of Soviet life. Many Lithuanian critics feel that the poetry of Eduardas Mieželaitis, especially his collection *Žmogus* (1962; "Man"), illustrates a deep and optimistic human, as well as social, vision. Related concerns animate historical writing, as in the case of *Parduotos vasaros* (1957; "Bartered Summers"), a novel by Juozas Baltušis, and also the writings about the World War II invasion, notably the heroic poem *Kraujas ir pelenai* (1960; "Blood and Ashes"), by Justinas Marcinkevičius.

The great majority of Lithuania's newspapers and magazines, which enjoy high circulations, are published in Lithuanian, and there are a number of broadcasting services, including a television service that is part of the East European Intervision network. Yet, in spite of such modern incursions, Lithuanian folklore continues to hand down a rich and original heritage from generation to generation. Lithuanian songs and a remarkable collection of fairy tales, legends, proverbs, and aphorisms have their roots deep in a language and culture that are among the oldest in Europe. The folk songs—*dainos*—are melodious and lyrical, while the communal folk dances, often related to everyday activities, are characterized by an elegant symmetry of design and motion. Lithuanian folk art is mainly embodied in ceramics, leatherwork, wood carving, and textiles; its colouring (which tends to avoid gaudiness) and its original geometric or floral patterns are characteristic features.

The country's folk heritage

The Vilnius drawing school, founded in 1866, has had a strong influence on the republic's fine-arts traditions, while the composer and painter M.K. Čiurlionis, who died in 1911, also had a considerable influence on contemporary forms. During the Soviet period, a realistic note has been introduced into sculpture and painting, and Lithuanian contemporary drawing, noted for the use of natural colour and a highly refined technique, has won international acclaim. The republic's architecture has been affected by a rich heritage in rich monuments and old buildings and by styles, ranging from the Gothic to the Neoclassical, that have acquired a distinctive local character. While much attention is given to preservation of historical monuments, much of the energy of Lithuanian architects goes into the designing of new buildings, both industrial and domestic, and especially to cultural and educational centres.

Music, too, has a strong tradition in the republic, a special feature being the dances and singing festivals held in the towns and villages every summer. These build to a climax every five years in national singing festivals during which as many as 40,000 persons may compete.

(K.A.M./Ed.)

HISTORY

Early history. Lithuanians belong to the Baltic group of nations, which included also the Prussians to the west and the Latvians to the north. The Prussians were exterminated by the Teutonic Order in the 13th century. The Latvians, together with the Finno-Ugrian Estonians, were conquered during the first three decades of the 13th century by the German Knights of the Sword, who in 1237 joined the Teutonic Order. The Lithuanians, protected by the primeval forest that almost entirely covered their land, resisted the German pressure. Samogitia (Lithuanian Zemaitija), the cradle of the Lithuanian people, lying between Prussia and Livonia, two lands already in the hands of the Teutonic Order, was an object of German covetousness, however. Under this threat the Lithuanian tribes united in the middle of the 13th century under Mindaugas. He and his family were baptized in 1251, and two years later, in his capital (probably at Kernave on the Neris), he was crowned the first (and only) king in Lithuanian history by the authority of Pope Innocent IV. Mindaugas and his two sons were assassinated in 1263, and Lithuania remained officially pagan.

The first and only king

Traidenis, ruler of Lithuania from 1270 to 1282, was probably the founder of the dynasty known as that of Gediminas, who began to rule in 1315. Although shortly after the destruction of Kievan Russia by the Tatars Lithuania had already begun to expand eastward and southward to the lands inhabited by Belorussians, it was Gediminas who really built the empire later known as historic (as opposed to ethnic) Lithuania. He made Vilnius the capital, as his letters of 1323 show. When he died in 1341, Lithuania's frontiers extended across the upper Dvina in the northeast, to the Dnepr in the southeast and to the Pripet Marshes in the south. the warlike but small Lithuanian nation could not colonize this vast territory but maintained control over it because the ruling class had shown an undoubted political talent and a spirit of religious toleration.

Gediminas divided his empire among his seven sons. Soon, however, only two remained to continue their father's policy of expansion: Algirdas, with Vilnius as his capital, succeeded to the title of grand prince and undertook the defense of Lithuania against the Tatars and Muscovy; and Kestutis, with his seat at Trakai, reigned over ethnic Lithuania and defended it against the Teutonic Order. When Algirdas died in 1377 he left to his son Jogaila (Jagiello) an empire including Kiev, which had come under Lithuanian suzerainty in 1362; but Kestutis drove Jogaila from Vilnius in 1381 and proclaimed himself grand prince of Lithuania. Jogaila, however, captured Kestutis and his son Vytautas in 1382, and Kestutis died in prison; but Vytautas escaped and found sanctuary in the territory of the Teutonic Order. The German danger had become, moreover, especially serious because the knights had taken Kaunas in 1362, and Jogaila had promised them the whole of Samogitia to the Dubysa River in 1382. His Orthodox elder brothers tried, therefore, to convince him that Lithuania's interests lay in alliance with Muscovy and accession to the Orthodox Church, but his pagan younger brothers recommended a pro-Polish policy with acceptance of Roman Catholicism.

Polish-Lithuanian union. On August 14, 1385, at Kriavas (Krewo), Jogaila concluded with Polish ambassadors an agreement that he would forever unite Lithuania and Kievan Russia with the Polish crown if he could marry the 12-year-old queen Jadwiga of Poland and become king of Poland himself. He went to Kraków, was baptized on February 15, 1386, receiving the name Władysław, married Jadwiga, and, on March 4, was crowned king of Poland.

The Lithuanians outside the German-devastated Samogitia were baptized in 1387, and Jogaila granted the newly baptized boyars, or gentry, great privileges. In 1392 a reconciliation took place between Jogaila and Vytautas, who became lieutenant governor of Lithuania.

The claim of the Teutonic Order to be combating Polish-Lithuanian "pagans" deceived many a western European knight into moving east to save Christianity; but in the decisive Battle of Grunwald (Tannenberg), on July 15, 1410, the Polish-Lithuanian forces inflicted a crushing defeat on the Order. German supremacy in the Baltic countries was broken, though the first Treaty of Torun (Thorn), concluded on February 1, 1411, was a moderate one. Samogitia was returned to Lithuania until the death of Jogaila and Vytautas. On September 27, 1422, however, the Order was forced to agree that Samogitia, by then Christian, was Lithuanian forever.

Battle of Grunwald

In the meantime, at Horodlo, on October 2, 1413, a new pact of union was concluded between Poland and Lithuania. The principles of the union remained unchanged, but the autonomy of the grand principality was made permanent. Later in the century a crisis arose in Polish-Lithuanian relations because the Lithuanian boyars elected one Alexander as grand prince, while the Poles chose his brother John Albert. The Polish-Lithuanian personal union lapsed, but, on the death of John Albert in 1501, the Lithuanians insisted that their grand prince should be king of Poland too. The Poles agreed, and the senates of the two countries decided at Piotrkow that thenceforth the king of Poland should always be grand prince of Lithuania. The Teutonic Order was no longer a menace, but in the east there appeared another and greater danger. Ivan III, the grand prince of Muscovy, in 1480 assumed the title of sovereign of all Russia; and the major part of historic Lithuania was Belorussian-speaking.

On July 1, 1569, at Lublin, a common Polish-Lithuanian Sejm, or Parliament, transformed the personal union into a real one. In the course of the ensuing two centuries, both the Lithuanian and Belorussian nobilities of historic Lithuania became Polonized, but the two peasantries continued to use their own languages.

Russian rule. While at the first (1772) and the second (1793) partitions of Poland only the Belorussian lands of the grand principality of Lithuania were annexed by Russia, at the third partition (1795) ethnic Lithuania suffered the same fate, the only exception being the province of Suvalkai (Suwalki), the northern part of which was Lithuanian-speaking, which became part of the Kingdom of Prussia. In 1806 Suwalki was incorporated into the Duchy of Warsaw, which in 1815 was annexed by Russia. The Congress of Vienna added to the style of the Russian emperors the titles of king of Poland and grand prince of Lithuania.

When the Poles rose against Russia in 1830–31 the insurrection extended to the Lithuanian provinces before it was suppressed. The Polish rising of 1863 also spread into Lithuania, and its repression there was particularly severe, 180 insurgents being hanged and 9,000 deported to Siberia.

On March 25, 1839, the Uniates were forced to join the Orthodox Church, and the next year the Lithuanian statute was replaced by Russian codes. The tsarist government treated the Territory of the Northwest—as historic Lithuania was called after 1832—as an integral part of Russia. From 1864 to 1905 the policy of russification extended to every domain of public life. It was forbidden to publish newspapers, periodicals, or books in Polish or Belorussian, while books in Lithuanian could be printed only if the Russian alphabet was used. Russian was the only language of teaching in the schools. The Roman Catholic religion was persecuted.

Russification

When the manifesto of October 30, 1905, granted freedom of speech to the peoples of the Russian Empire, two daily newspapers appeared at Vilnius, one Polish (*Kurjer Litewski*) and one Lithuanian (*Vilniaus Zinios*). On December 4–5, 1905, a congress of about 2,000 delegates was held in Vilnius. The congress demanded territorial autonomy for Lithuania with a democratically elected *saeima.* The frontiers of the national Lithuanian state were to be drawn according to the freely expressed wish of the peoples concerned. Soon afterward, the teaching of the Lithuanian language in schools was permitted.

Independence. During World War I the Germans occupied a great part of historic Lithuania. On September 18, 1915, the German armies entered Vilnius. The German government authorized the gathering at Vilnius, on September 18–22, 1917, of a congress of 214 Lithuanian delegates and the election of the 20-member Lietuvos Taryba, or Council of Lithuania. The congress called for an independent Lithuanian state within the ethnic frontiers and with Vilnius as capital. On February 16, 1918, the Taryba proclaimed an independent Lithuanian state and the dissolution of all political connections that had existed with other nations.

Lithuania was still under German occupation when, on November 5, Augustinas Voldemaras was chosen prime minister of independant Lithuania. After the German troops had evacuated Vilnius, the city was entered on January 5, 1919, by the Red Army, and a Communist Lithuania government, appointed by the All-Russian Central Executive Committee on December 23, 1918, was installed. It was headed by Vincas Mickevicius-Kapsukas. The Voldemaras government moved to Kaunas, which, on January 17, however, was also occupied by the Red Army. The Germans remained in western Lithuania, which from the end of October to December 15, 1919, was controlled by the German Army under Rüdiger von der Goltz.

The Polish-Lithuanian dispute. Józef Piłsudski, the head of the restored Polish state, proposed two alternatives for Lithuania. Either an independent state might be set up within purely ethnographic frontiers (that is, without Vilnius and its region, which was largely Polish), or a larger state might be set up including Vilnius; but in the latter case, some sort of a federal link with Poland would be indispensable. On April 20, 1919, the Polish Army led by Piłsudski took Vilnius from the Red Army, which enabled the Lithuanians to reenter Kaunas. In the following summer the Polish forces moved to the Western Dvina River in the north and to the Berezina in the east. Against Lithuania they occupied the demarcation line fixed by the Inter-Allied Committee presided over by Marshal F. Foch. This Foch line, "adopted by the Supreme Council on July 27, 1919, ran to the west of the Grodno–Vilnius–Daugavpils railways and more or less coincided with the eastern ethnic frontier of Lithuania. On July 12, 1920, when the Polish Army was retreating, the Kaunas government concluded in Moscow a peace treaty by which the Soviet Union "ceded" to Lithuania not only Vilnius but also Lida and Grodno. After Piłsudski's final victory, the Red Army, which occupied Vilnius on July 14, left it on August 26 while the Lithuanian Army entered the city. On September 5, 1920, the Warsaw government appealed to the League of Nations. A Polish-Lithuanian conference met at Suvalkai, and a partial armistice was signed on October 7. Nevertheless, Piłsudski ordered Gen. Lucjan (Lucien) Zeligowski to seize Vilnius, and this was done on October 9. Zeligowski set up a government of central Lithuania. A new armistice, restoring the Foch line, was signed on November 29, 1920.

The Foch Line

Meanwhile the Council of the League of Nations had made many attempts to settle the Polish-Lithuanian dispute and, at last, on February 3, 1923, adopted a final resolution fixing a Polsih-Lithuanian line of demarcation almost identical with the Foch line, leaving the decision as to the frontier to the Conference of Ambassadors in Paris. On March 15, 1923, the Conference of Ambassadors recognized the line of February 3 as the final frontier between the two states. Lithuania, however, refused to accept this decision.

Foreign and domestic relations, 1919–39. Lithuania was received into the membership of the League of Nations on September 22, 1921. On September 28, 1926, a Soviet-Lithuanian treaty of nonaggression was signed in Moscow. On September 12, 1934, at Geneva, a treaty of good will and cooperation was concluded by Lithuania, Latvia, and Estonia. Lithuania's relations with Germany were jeopardized by Nazi propaganda in the Klaipeda (Memel) territory.

In March 1935, at a trial of Klaipeda Nazis, most of the accused were found guilty of high treason. On March 17, 1938, Poland demanded of Lithuania the immediate opening of the frontier, acceptance of the cession of Vilnius, and the establishment of normal diplomatic relations. Lithuania yielded to these demands. In February and May 1938 the Lithuanian government released the convicted Nazis and in October abolished martial law in the Klaipeda territory. On December 11, at the election of the Klaipeda Landtag, the Nazis won 25 seats out of a total of 29. On March 21, 1939, Lithuania was presented with another ultimatum, which meant the loss of its only port.

Meanwhile, the period of 1927–38 was that of restricted democracy. A new constitution, adopted on February 12, 1938, was to provide the basis for a return to parliamentary institutions. A coalition government was formed with the inclusion of the Christian Democrats and Liberals, but it had not enough time to reorganize the republic on a more solid basis.

Independence lost. A secret protocol to the German-Soviet treaty of nonaggression of August 23, 1939, stipulated that in the event of a territorial and political rearrangement in the areas belonging to the Baltic states, the northern boundary of Lithuania should represent "the

German-Soviet protocol

boundary of the sphere of influence of Germany and the U.S.S.R." When they began World War II, the Germans made frantic efforts to induce Lithuania to attack Poland so that the former might thus become their ally and protégé. Lithuania chose to remain neutral, and the secret protocol to the German-Soviet treaty of September 28, 1939, revised the previous agreement by deciding that the territory of Lithuania fell within the sphere of influence of the U.S.S.R.

On October 10, 1939, a mutual assistance treaty was signed in Moscow, in accordance with which Lithuania was compelled to admit Soviet garrisons and to grant air bases. On June 15, 1940, Lithuania was confronted with an ultimatum demanding immediate formation of a "friendly" government. On the same day, the country was occupied by the Soviet Army. Many Lithuanian leaders either fled to the West or were arrested and deported to Siberia. An obscure journalist, Justas Paleckis, became premier. On July 21, a subservient Parliament unanimously requested the incorporation of Lithuania into the Soviet Union. On August 3, 1940, the Moscow Supreme Soviet readily acceded to the request, and Lithuania was declared a constituent republic of the U.S.S.R. In the night of June 14–15 the next year, 30,455 members of the Lithuanian intelligentsia (members of the national guard, civil servants, etc.) were deported to Siberia. Including other deportees and about 5,000 political prisoners executed at the time of the hasty departure of the Soviet forces, the country suffered during the first Soviet occupation a loss of about 45,000 people.

A few days after the German attack on the Soviet Union (June 22, 1941), the whole of Lithuania was in German hands. On July 17, 1941, Hitler announced the creation of the Ostland province including the three Baltic states and Belorussia.

Soviet occupation

Vilnius was taken by the Soviet Army on July 13, 1944, and Lithuania was again under Soviet occupation by the middle of October. All non-Communist organizations were immediately dissolved. The period of methodical Sovietization and russification started. Fleeing before the Soviet armies, about 80,000 Lithuanians reached the western zones of Germany, but about 60,000 were rounded up in the eastern zone and sent to Siberia. In Lithuania, during 1945–46, about 145,000 Lithuanians were removed from their native land. The third mass deportation, ordered in connection with the forced collectivization of agriculture, took place on March 24–27, 1949, when about 60,000 Lithuanians were sent to northern Russia or Siberia. Lithuania had become a Soviet Socialist republic.

(K.M.S./M.G./Ed.)

CAUCASUS

The great historic barrier of the Caucasus Mountains rears up across the wide isthmus separating the Black and Caspian seas, at that extreme southern portion of the European section of the Soviet Union where Europe and Asia converge. If the ranges are placed in Europe, then Mt. Elbrus, at 18,510 feet (5,642 metres) their highest peak, is also the highest point in Europe; but the environment of the whole region is so subject to Asian influences that there is a good case for assigning the Caucasus to southwestern Asia. Traditionally, the watershed of the Great Caucasus Range (Bolshoy Kavkaz), the backbone of the system, is regarded as part of the line dividing the continents.

The name Caucasus is a Latinized form of "Kaukasos," which the ancient Greek geographers and historians used, and the Russian "Kavkaz" is of the same origin. The ultimate derivation is thought to be from "Kaz-kaz," the Hittite name for a people living on the southern shore of the Black Sea. This ancient nomenclature reflects the historical importance of the region: the Greeks made the mysterious range the scene of the mythical sufferings of Prometheus, and the Argonauts sought the Golden Fleece in the land of Colchis, nestling against the range on the Black Sea coast. The ranges also filtered cultures of the ascendant civilizations of the Middle Eastern "fertile crescent" through to the north, besides nurturing their own distinctive societies. The peoples of the region have exhibited an extraordinary variety since early times: the Colchians, for example, as described by the 5th-century-BC Greek historian Herodotus, were black skinned, and the subsequent centuries witnessed successive waves of peoples migrating across Eurasia, adding to, and being molded by, the Caucasian cultural heritage. Not surprisingly, a larger quantity of different languages is spoken in Caucasia than in any other area of similar size in the world.

The ethnic and linguistic heritage

Caucasia is defined as the region including not only the soaring mountain ranges of the Caucasus proper but also the country immediately north and south of them. The northern country is called Ciscaucasia (Predkavkaz; *i.e.,* Hither Caucasia); the southern is Transcaucasia (Zakavkaz, or Farther Caucasia). The whole region, which has an area of 170,000 square miles (440,000 square kilometres), is nevertheless predominantly mountainous. It extends from the lowlands of the Kuma and Manych basins southward to the political frontiers separating the Soviet Union from Turkey and from Iran and so comprises the southernmost divisions of the Russian S.F.S.R. (including Dagestan), the Georgian S.S.R., the Armenian S.S.R., and the Azerbaijan S.S.R., besides several minor administrative units constituted on an ethnic basis.

Physical and human geography

THE LAND

Relief. The Great Caucasus extends for approximately 750 miles (1,200 kilometres) southeastward across the Caucasus from the Taman Peninsula (Tamansky Poluostrov) thrusting between the Black Sea and its northern extension, the Sea of Azov, to the Apsheron Peninsula (Apsheronsky Poluostrov), which juts into the Caspian past the oil-rich port of Baku. The vast plains and uplifted areas of Ciscaucasia stretch from its northern foothills to the Kuma-Manych depression lying west of the huge Caspian delta of the Volga. Western Ciscaucasia consists largely of plains: from the lowland north of the Kuban River, the delta of which adjoins the broad, low ridges of the Taman Peninsula, a plain slopes gradually southward up to the foothills of the mountains. Central Ciscaucasia comprises not only the Stavropol Highland (Stavropolskaya Vozvyshennost), mainly characterized by tablelands of limestone or sandstone and by deep valleys, but also the Mineralnye Vody-Pyatigorsk zone to the southeast (where Mt. Beshtau rises to 4,593 feet [1,400 metres] from a surrounding plateau) and, still farther southeastward, beyond the middle Terek River, the highlands backing the Terek and the Sunzha, with the Alkhan Churt Valley between them. Eastern Ciscaucasia is lowland traversed by the lower Terek and, to the north beyond the sands of the vast Nogay Steppe, by the Kuma. Both rivers flow into the Caspian.

The northern slopes of the Great Caucasus are not as steep as the southern. The middle of the system is comparatively narrow, but its western and eastern ends have widths of 100 miles (160 kilometres) or more. The watershed and a lateral range to the north of it, which together constitute the axis of the system, contain, in addition to Mt. Elbrus itself, such magnificent lofty peaks as Mt. Dombay-Ulgen, 13,274 feet (4,046 metres), in the western sector; Mts. Shkhara, Dykhtau, and Kazbek, all well over 16,000 feet (4,875 metres), in the central sector; and Mt. Tebulos-Mta and Mt. Bazar-Dyuzi, both over 14,000 feet (4,265 metres), in the east. Spurs tonguing north and south from the main axis in places reach heights approaching 10,000 feet (3,000 metres).

The Great and Little Caucasus

South of the Great Caucasus, on the Black Sea coast, lies the alluvial plain of Kolkhida (ancient Colchis). On the Caspian side, in the basin of the Kura River, plains and such uplands as the long Shirak Steppe (Shirakskaya Step) succeed one another till the level falls sharply into an extensive depression, in the centre of which the Kura receives

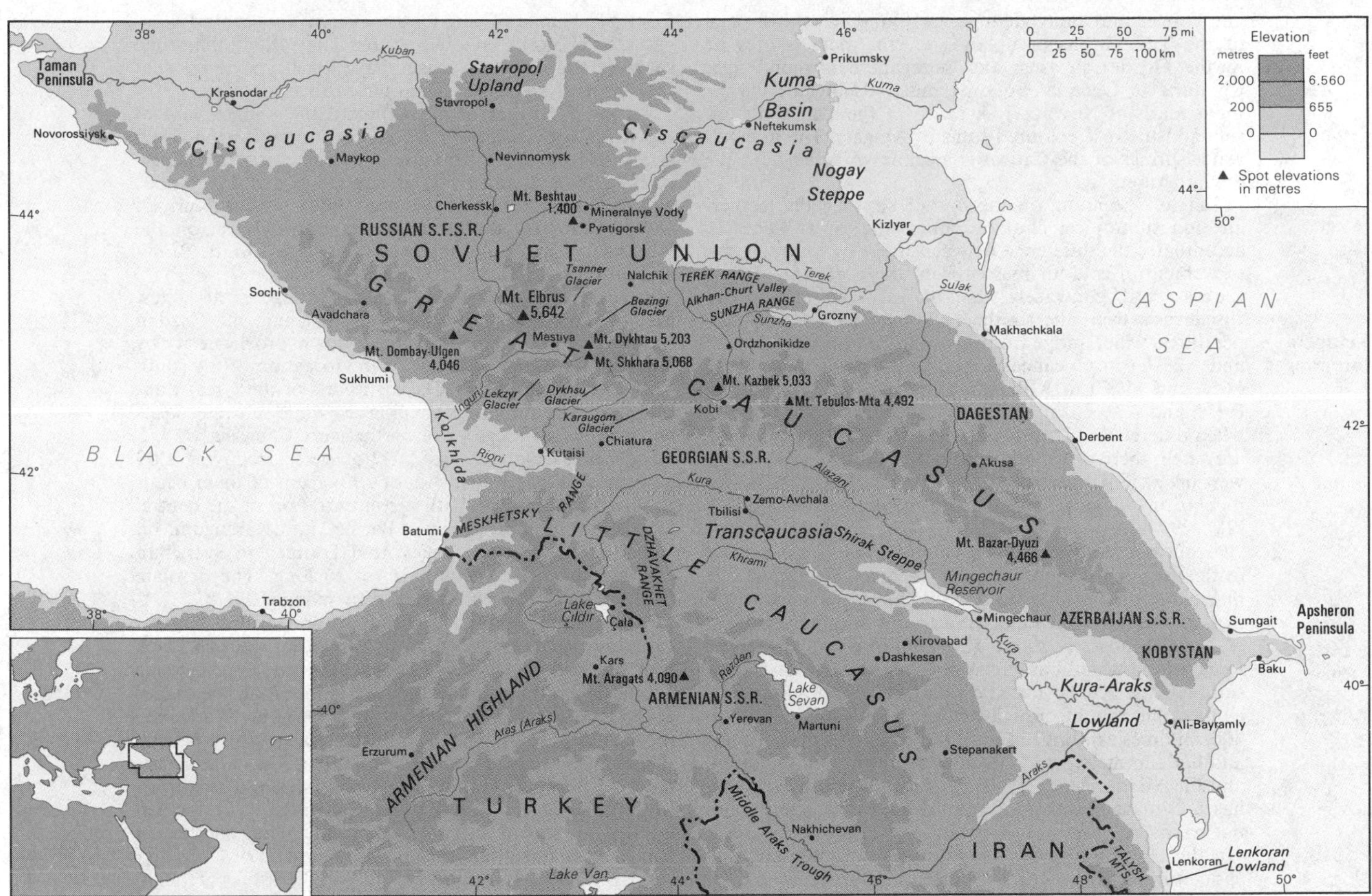

The Caucasus Mountains.

its major right-bank tributary, the Araks. To the northeast, the hills of southeastern Kobystan separate the Kura-Araks Lowland (Kura-Araksinskaya Nizmennost) from the Apsheron Peninsula. From the extreme southeast of the Kura-Araks Lowland, the narrow Lenkoran Lowland (Lenkoranskaya Nizmennost) extends southward between the Caspian Sea and the Talysh Mountains, which reach heights exceeding 8,000 feet (2,440 metres).

West of the Kura-Araks Lowland rises the Little Caucasus, which is continued southward by the Dzhavakhet mountain range and the Armenian Highland, the latter straddling the Soviet–Turkish frontier. East of Lake Sevan, the highest peaks rise to 12,000 feet (3,660 metres) or more, while Mt. Aragats (Alagez), west of the lake, rises another 1,000 feet (300 metres). From their western sources in the Armenian Highland, the Kura and the Araks both flow round the Little Caucasus, the one north of it, the other south, before their confluence in the east.

The greater part of Caucasia originated in the vast structural downwarp in the earth's crust known as the Alpine Geosyncline, dating from about 25,000,000 years ago, and thus reflects the mountain-building movement that produced the younger mountains of Europe. Northern and central Ciscaucasia has a platform-like construction, with a foundation of folded structures dating from Hercynian times, about 345,000,000 years ago. Southwestern and southeastern Ciscaucasia lie on the margins of the vast downfold in the earth's surface that rose later in the Alpine mountain-building movement, with the collapse deepest on the lower courses of the Kuban and Terek rivers. The surface of Ciscaucasia is composed essentially of Tertiary and Quaternary rocks less than 65,000,000 years old; on the Stavropol Highland there are layers of various ages in folded, platform-like structures.

Rocks of the Great Caucasus

Structurally the Great Caucasus represents a great upfold, or anticline, thrown up at the margin of the Alpine Geosyncline about 25,000,000 years ago and subsequently altered by fresh cycles of erosion and uplift. Hard, crystalline, heat-altered rocks such as schists, gneisses, and granites, of pre-Jurassic origin (more than 190,000,000 years old), have been exposed at the core of the western sector, while somewhat softer, clayey schists and sandstones of Lower and Middle Jurassic origin have emerged in the east. The spurs of the Great Caucasus are composed of younger limestones, sandstones, and marls.

Kolkhida and the Kura-Araks Lowland are both structural depressions linked to the Alpine Geosyncline; the former is related to the formation of the Black Sea, the latter to that of the Caspian. In Kolkhida, the overall surface of Quaternary deposits laid down less than 25,000,000 years ago is broken, at the foot of the mountains, by the emergence of slightly earlier sedimentary rocks. Late Tertiary and Quaternary rock also underlies the Kura-Araks Lowland.

The structures of the Little Caucasus, of the Talish Mountains, and of the Dzhavakhet–Armenian ranges likewise reflect folds uplifted from the Alpine Geosyncline. While the western sector of the Little Caucasus and the Talish are formed chiefly of deposits of Tertiary Age (about 50,000,000 years ago) laid down in the great former downwarp of the geosyncline, the intervening eastern sector of the Little Caucasus consists, north of Lake Sevan, of layers of Jurassic and Cretaceous sedimentary and intruded volcanic rock, which are at least twice as old. Volcanism and the intrusion of heat-altered rock have everywhere played a great role: the folded base of the Dzhavakhet Range and of the Armenian Highland is masked by debris from eruptions of Tertiary–Quaternary date. Much older rocks emerge largely between the middle course of the Araks and the latitude of Lake Sevan.

The geologically recent rock layers around the Great Caucasus, notably in the Kura-Araks Lowland and beneath the Caspian Sea, contain oil-bearing deposits. These also occur, together with fuel gases, among the earlier rocks of Ciscaucasia, while, in Dagestan, oil, fuel gas, and coal deposits are found. Metallic ores are associated with magmatic rocks thrust up from deep in the crust: magnetite iron occurs near Dashkesan, in Azerbaijan; copper and molybdenum are found in several parts of the Transcaucasian upland; several metallic ores lie in the Great Caucasus; and manganese is found near Chiatura, in Georgia. Building materials include the cement marls of Novorossiysk south of the Taman Peninsula and the rose-coloured tufas of Aragats. The mineral-water springs of the Caucasus are known throughout the Soviet Union.

Climate. Standing on the border between the temperate and subtropical climatic zones, the Great Caucasus accentuates the difference between them by impeding the movement of cold air masses from the north into Transcaucasia and, conversely, that of warm air masses into Ciscaucasia from the south. Thus average January temperatures, which range from between 23° and 28° F (−5° and −2° C) in Ciscaucasia, are between 40° and 43° F (4.5° and 6° C) in Kolkhida and between 34° and 38° F (1° and 3.3° C) in eastern Transcaucasia. In summer, when differences of temperature between north and south are small, there is a more noticeable contrast between the west (average temperatures 73°–79° F [23°–26° C]), with its maritime climate, and the continental east (77°–84° F [25°–29° C]).

Tempera-ture ranges

Ciscaucasia has a moderately continental steppe climate in the west and a more continental, drier, semidesert one in the east. In Transcaucasia, Kolkhida has a humid, subtropical climate with mild winters and an annual rainfall of 47 to 71 inches (1,200 to 1,800 millimetres); as does the Lenkoran Lowland but with a dry season at the start of the summer; the Kura-Araks Lowland has a dry subtropical climate, an annual rainfall of eight to 16 inches (200 to 400 millimetres), but lower in the east, and mild winters and hot summers, which favour the cultivation of cotton; and the Middle Araks Trough in the Armenian Highland has a climate like that of the lowland downstream, but not so warm.

In the Great Caucasus, temperatures naturally fall, and agricultural seasons become shorter, as altitude rises; more rain falls on the mountain slopes than on the neighbouring plains. From the altitude of approximately 6,500 feet (1,980 metres), a westerly air current prevails, strengthening maritime influences: average air temperatures reach 18° F (−8° C) in January and 55° F (13° C) in August. As the Great Caucasus stands at an angle to the westerly air currents, the heaviest precipitation, reaching a maximum of no less than 160 inches (4,000 millimetres), accumulates on the south-southwest-facing slopes. Higher up, a cold climate with severe humidity prevails, and perennial snow shrouds the highest crests. In the northern Black Sea coast region, the climate is Mediterranean, with humid winters and dry summers.

The slopes of the Little Caucasus facing toward those of the Great Caucasus have a climate similar to that of the latter at corresponding altitudes, with rainfall concentrated in the west. On the slopes of the Talysh Mountains, the climate is humid, with yearly precipitation up to 68 inches (1,700 millimetres). The Armenian Highland has a climate more continental than that of the Great Caucasus at corresponding altitudes (at 6,500 feet the average temperature 10° F [−12° C] in January, 64° F [18° C] in July). Snow cover lasts for four or five months. Annual precipitation averages 20 inches (500 millimetres), with a spring maximum. The climate of the upland steppe plateaus is moderately cold and continental, whereas that of the heights is more humid and Alpine, with cool summers and cold, prolonged winters.

Drainage. The Kura (with its tributary the Araks), the Sulak, the Terek, and the Kuma rivers flow into the Caspian Sea, the Rioni and the Inguri, into the Black Sea; and the Kuban, into the Sea of Azov. In the warm season, when snow and ice begin to melt, rivers of the Great Caucasus and some of those of the Little may be in flood for six months; and other Transcaucasian rivers are characterized by spring flooding. The rivers of the southern slope of the Great Caucasus generally have summer floods also. The rivers of Ciscaucasia, except those flowing from the Great Caucasus, flood in spring and freeze in winter but become very shallow and sometimes even dry up in summer, while the Stavropol area is artificially irrigated from the Kuban River. In the eastern and central Caucasus, brief storm flooding occurs. The soluble limestone spurs of the Great Caucasus have karst-type rivers that intermittently plunge beneath the earth.

Flood perils

The lower reaches of the Kura, of the Kuban, and of the Rioni are navigable. Water from many of the rivers serves to irrigate the arid zone of Ciscaucasia, the Kura-Araks Lowland, and the lands around the Middle Araks. Hydroelectric stations have been built on the Kura at Mingechaur and at Zemo-Avchala, near Tbilisi; on the Khrami (a right-bank tributary of the Kura); on the Rioni; and on several rivers of the Great Caucasus.

Ozero Sevan in the Transcaucasian Range is the largest lake of Caucasia. Its overflow, draining into the Razdan tributary of the Araks, is exploited for hydroelectricity by a chain of stations and also for the irrigation of the south of the Armenian S.S.R. The high parts of the Great Caucasus contain numerous small lakes, while saltwater lakes occur in the arid regions of northeastern Caucasia.

The Great Caucasus has 2,047 glaciers, occupying 1.09 percent of its total area. About 70 percent of them occur on the northern face, with a concentration in the centre. The largest, notably Dykhsu, Bezingi, and Karaugom, on the northern face, and Lekzyr and Tsanner, in Svanetian Georgia, are often eight miles or so long. The desolate flanks of Mt. Elbrus are streaked by many glaciers.

Plant and animal life. In western and central Ciscaucasia, steppe vegetation used to prevail on the rich black soils but has now largely been plowed up. Forest-steppe vegetation, with oaks and beeches, is found on the higher ground of the Stavropol Highland, around Pyatigorsk, in the west sector of the Sunzha Range (Sunzhensky Khrebet), and at the foot of the Great Caucasus. Eastern Ciscaucasia is semidesert, with grasses and sagebrush (*Artemisia*) on chestnut soils and saltworts where the soil is salty. *Artemisia,* saltworts, and ephemeral species on gray soils characterize the arid Kura-Araks Lowland; and similar vegetation occurs in the Middle Araks Trough. In Kolkhida and in the Lenkoran Lowland, subtropical broad-leaved forest has given way before the advances of agriculture.

In the mountains themselves, at altitudes between 2,000 and 3,000 feet, arboreal brushwood and broad-leaved forest predominates. On the Black Sea slopes of the Great Caucasus and in the mountainous hinterland of Kolkhida, there are mixed forests—beech, oak, hornbeam, chestnut, and alder—with evergreen undergrowth and lianas on red and on yellow soils. In the Talysh Mountains, forests of chestnut-leaf oak and *Parrotia persica* flourish on yellow soils likewise. On the heights backing the Kura-Araks Lowland, there are xerophytic (adapted to a limited water supply) leaf-bearing forests and brushwood. On the northern face of the Great Caucasus, oak forests and secondary brushwood occur.

In the next zone, at altitudes up to 6,500 feet, both the Great and the Little Caucasus sustain forests of oak and hornbeam and of beech on brown soils; but these trees are superseded at the higher levels by Caucasian elm and Nordmann fir in the west and in the southwest and sometimes by pine farther east. Feather grass and needlegrass cover the black soil of the steppes on the lava plateaus and plains of the Armenian sector. Steppes and meadow steppes are widespread also among the mountains of Dagestan.

Above 6,500 feet in the Great Caucasus and in the Transcaucasian Range, mountain-meadow vegetation covers three belts, sub-Alpine, Alpine, and subnivean, up to the lonely zone of glaciers and perpetual snow—which begins at about 10,000 feet.

The animal life of the Great and of the Little Caucasus includes certain indigenous species—the West Caucasian and the Dagestanian mountain goat, or tur, the Caucasian black grouse, and the Caucasian mountain turkey, or ular—and even indigenous genera, such as the long-clawed mole-vole (*Prometheomys schaposchnikowi*). It also includes chamois, red deer, bear, lynx, and fox. Ciscaucasia's fauna is connected both with eastern Europe's and with Central Asia's; and the latter connection is also evident in the Kura-Araks Lowland, which has the Persian

Indigenous animals

gazelle (*Gazella subgutturosa*), the long-eared hedgehog, the jerboa, and the reed cat (*Felis chaus*). The fauna of the Talish Mountains, which includes leopard and porcupine, is related to that of more southerly territories, while that of the Armenian Highland is related to that of Anatolia, with the ground squirrel, or suslik (*Citellus*), and the mountain jerboa (*Allactaga williamsi*). (N.A.G.)

THE PEOPLE

The most densely populated area is on the Black Sea coast; the Rioni Valley and several smaller valleys in Transcaucasia are intensively cultivated; and the foothills of the mountains also have a considerable density of population. The rural population is unevenly distributed. The Alpine regions of the Caucasus and the arid steppes and lowlands of the Caspian littoral are sparsely populated.

Caucasia has long played a major role as a link between Europe and Asia, and through it the culture of ancient Mesopotamia spread northward. Indigenous cultures also arose; in particular, Caucasia was one of the most ancient centres of bronze working from the first half of the 2nd millennium BC. Autochthonous peoples of the Caucasus are mentioned by Herodotus and by later writers such as Strabo. In the centuries between pre-Classical antiquity and the 14th century AD, Caucasia underwent successive invasions by various peoples, including Scythians, Alani, Huns, Khazars, Arabs, Seljuq Turks, and Mongols; and contacts were also maintained with the Mediterranean world. All this history has left its imprint on the culture of the Caucasian peoples: Near Eastern and Middle Eastern influences, in particular, disseminated Iranian languages on the one hand and Islāmic and Christian religion on the other. The later history, beginning with a long period of rivalry between Ottoman Turkey and Iran, is marked by the advance of Russian culture, which penetrated farther and farther into Caucasia from the 16th century onward. Throughout this process, individual ethnic groups, under pressure from stronger neighbours, took refuge in the ravines of the mountain ranges to preserve themselves in isolation.

Ethnic succession

More than 50 different peoples inhabit Caucasia. Russians and Ukrainians, who constitute more than 80 percent of the total population of Ciscaucasia, speak Slavic languages of the Indo-European family. The Armenians also speak an Indo-European language, but one that stands by itself. The Ossetes, the Kurds, the Tats, and the Talysh speak Indo-European languages of the Iranian branch. The majority of the peoples, however, speak tongues that are sometimes tentatively classed together as belonging to a Caucasian language "family," although not all the languages in this "family" are genetically related to one another. The most important Caucasian language is Georgian, spoken by a nation into which numerous tribes have long been amalgamated. Georgian and its many dialects belong to the Kartvelian group of Caucasian, the the other groups being the Adyghian and Abkhazian, the Nakhian, and the Dagestani. Adyghian and Abkhazian comprise the languages of Kabarda, of the Adygei, and of the Cherkess, or Circassians (all three of them closely related), as well as those of the Abaza and of the Abkhaz (who have both been strongly influenced by the neighbouring Georgians); Nakhian comprises Shishan (Chechen) and Ingush; and the Dagestani group of the "family" is chiefly represented by the languages of the Lezgian, of the Tabasaran, of the Dargante, and of the Laki peoples, together with those of the 15 minor nationalities collectively described as Avarian. The Dagestani group of "Caucasian" languages is of course quite distinct from the Turkic languages spoken in Dagestan, namely those of the Kumyk and of the Nogay. Other Turkic languages of Caucasia include Karachay and Balkar—besides the extensive Azerbaijani. If Caucasia is the world's best stocked linguistic museum, Dagestan is Caucasia's.

High up in the Caucasus, the people can only raise cattle, grow some mountain crops, and pursue a few domestic crafts. On the plains and on the foothills, viticulture is traditional. The Soviet governments promote heavy or light industry wherever practicable.

(S.I.B.)

History

Food-gathering cultures of Mesolithic type, as represented by the discoveries at Nalchik in the Central Caucasus, continued in this region until quite late. They were replaced in the later part of the 3rd millennium BC by the Kuban culture, which left its remains in many thousands of burial mounds, or kurgans, on the steppes of Ciscaucasia. This Kuban culture, which lasted through the Late Bronze Age into Early Iron Age times, was undoubtedly stimulated by contact with the higher civilization of Mesopotamia. The grave funiture of the kurgans, as in the famous royal grave of Maikop, included metalwork of great refinement, often ornamented with animal motifs. A common weapon was the shaft-hole battle-ax of copper, of a type also found in central and northern Europe. There is evidence that the distribution of this weapon resulted from a migration of horse-riding folk, the so-called Battle-Ax people, who spread Indo-European speech. Their place of origin is not certain, but it was more probably in the east than in the west of their area of spread.

The Kuban culture

A South Caucasian, or Kura-Araks, culture, again associated with rich metalwork and characterized also by tholoi, cyclopean masonry and burnished black pottery with incised spiral decoration, dates from the late 3rd millennium BC. It has been found particularly in the kurgans of the Trialeti cistrict, notably that of Beshtasheni. Pottery comparable with that of this culture has been found at Karaz near Erzurum (Turkey), at Geoy Tepe in Iranian Azerbaijan, in the ʿAmūq plain near Antioch in Turkey, and as far away as Khirbet Kerak in Palestine.

Transcaucasia contains some fine church architecture dating from the 4th century onward, including some very early pendentives. Ashlar masonry was used there instead of the bricks more common in Byzantine architecture. The most extensive remains of this kind are in the ruins of the city of Ani in the Armenian Soviet Socialist Republic.

EARLY HISTORY

The Caucasian isthmus—or, more precisely, the road that passes across it along the shores of the Caspian—is one of the two great routes along which nomadic peoples have moved at various times from Central to Southwestern Asia. The other route runs from Merv over the Elburz to Meshed or Herat. The chief significance of the Caucasus in Asian history, therefore, is as a gateway of migration. It also plays the part of an ethnic museum, for very many of the peoples who have passed this way have left detachments in the remoter parts of the mountains, particularly in Dagestan. Like Afghanistan farther east, Caucasia, along with Armenia, has often appeared in the role of a buffer zone between rival empires, Roman and Parthian, Byzantine and Arab or Ottoman, Persian and Russian.

The two greatest and longest lived of the many semi-independent states of the Caucasus in classical and medieval times were Georgia (earlier, Iberia) in the north and Armenia in the south. The culture and ethnic character of both can be traced back to the period of the breakup of the Hittite Empire in the 12th century BC, and both were converted to Christianity quite early.

Greek contact with the Caucasus region dates from the colonizing period between the 8th and the 6th century BC, when many settlements, like the Milesian outpost of Dioscurias, were set up on the Caucasian coasts of the Black Sea. In legend, Prometheus was said to have been chained in the Caucasus Mountains, and Colchis was the setting for the Argonauts' search for the Golden Fleece. The conquests of Alexander the Great freed Georgia from Persian Achaemenid suzerainty, and despite Pompey's (Pompeius') imposition of Roman control in 65 BC, after his defeat of Mithradates, the incursions of the Khazars in the 3rd century AD, and Arab occupation of Tiflis (Tbilisi) in the 8th century, the state survived to reach its golden age between the 10th and the 13th century. The country was overrun and devastated by the Mongols in 1234 and the following years and again by the hordes of Timur at the end of the next century. Thus weakened, it was on many occasions obliged to submit in the later Middle Ages to Islāmic rule, Persian or Ottoman. In 1783 the King

Greek influences

of Georgia concluded an alliance with Russia in the hope of gaining protection from Islāmic expansion. Russian demands became increasingly importunate, however, and in 1801 it annexed the Georgian state. From that time, the history of Transcaucasia in the 19th century is one of ever-expanding Russian conquest.

RUSSIAN PENETRATION

Russian interests in the Caucasus began early. In AD 943 Varangian, or Russified Norse, adventurers had sailed down the Caspian from the Volga and captured the fortress of Barda in Caucasian Albania. Subsequently, certain marriage alliances were concluded between the Russian and Georgian royal families, and in the 17th century Caucasian rulers were on several occasions constrained to ask for Russian help against their enemies. Peter I the Great was the first to take advantage of the opportunities thus afforded to take possession of Caucasian territory. He occupied Derbent in 1722 and Baku in the following year. In 1770 Russian troops for the first time crossed the Caucasus range and took possession of Kutaisi. By 1785 all the northern region of the Caucasus was designated as a Russian province; and, as already mentioned, Georgia was absorbed at the opening of the next century.

Two large groups of tribes in the middle Caucasus then acknowledged their subjection to the Russians, the Ossetes in 1802 and the Lezgians in 1803. Mingrelia fell in 1804 and the kingdom of Imereti in 1810. By the Treaty of Gulistan in 1813, Persia ceded to Russia a wide area of the khanates of the Eastern Caucasus, from Lenkoran northward to Derbent. Russia had little difficulty in acquiring by conquest from Persia in 1828 a stretch of the northern Armenian plateau, including the entire plain of Yerevan, and was able to take over more territory in the same area from Turkey in the following year.

Resistance of mountain tribes

The resistance of the mountain tribes, particularly of the Circassians of Abkhasia and the Lezgians of Dagestan, was more fierce and protracted. During 30 years, from 1815 to 1845, the Russians could do little more than hold these mountain peoples at bay. Some were sustained by patriotic feelings, others by religious fervour. The Circassians of the Western Caucasus were largely quelled between 1832 and 1839, but farther east in Dagestan resistance by the Muslim tribes was carried on longer. A holy war was declared by the sheikh Kasi-Mullah, and, after he was killed by the Russians, the struggle was continued by his son Shamil. Shamil was finally captured in a remote fortress of Dagestan in 1859, though the main fighting had ceased four years before. The country was completely pacified by 1864, after which almost the entire Circassian nation, numbering perhaps 400,000, preferring exile to subjection, emigrated into Ottoman territory, leaving the Western Caucasus empty and desolated.

Without doubt, the protracted resistance of the peoples of the Caucasus delayed Russian plans for an attack on the Turks of Asia Minor. When these nations eventually came to conflict in the Russo-Turkish War of 1877–78, the Russian lines of communication in Armenia were ill prepared, and the Turks were able to support an attempt by Circassian exiles to reoccupy their homeland. But this failed, and, by the Peace of Adrianople, Russia succeeded in adding to its Transcaucasian territories the districts of Kars, Batumi, and Ardahan. During the next 40 years the peoples of the Caucasus—particularly the Armenians—endured Russian rule with increasing discontent; and, after the October Revolution of 1917, they cherished strong hopes for an independent Armenian republic and a federal republic to be governed by a Transcaucasian Diet. These ambitions were thwarted after the Turks reoccupied late in 1920 the districts of Batumi and Kars, and the Russians hurried to counter by entering Yerevan.

POST-REVOLUTIONARY PERIOD

Under the Soviet system Transcaucasia was administered until 1936 as a single unit, the Transcaucasian Soviet Federated Socialist Republic. Under the new constitution of that year, it was subdivided into the three major partitions of the Armenian, Azerbaijan, and Georgian Soviet Socialist republics. Lesser nationalities, such as the Abkhaz, Adzhar, and Ossete, are administered as autonomous Soviet Socialist republics or as *oblasti*.

The district of Ciscaucasia is included in Soviet geography in the regional complex known as the Lower Don and Northern Caucasus. Except in its western part, in Dagestan, the population of Ciscaucasia is predominantly Russian and Ukrainian, elements that entered the territory during its rapid period of development after the building of the Rostov–Baku railway line late in the 19th century. Throughout the 25 years after the arrival of the railroad, the population of the Kuban district doubled and the area under cultivation increased fivefold. The great cities of Ciscaucasia also largely grew up or expanded during this period, particularly after the Revolution, as the oil fields of the area increased their output.

Railroad and development

At the extreme limit of their penetration into Russia, in the autumn of 1942, the German armies overran parts of Ciscaucasia; and, in a drive toward the oil fields, they had by the end of October of that year reached the Georgian military highway leading to Tbilisi. The tide turned in November, when the Germans began to pull out of Caucasia to strengthen their forces on other sectors of the Russian front.

The attack left its mark on the economic geography of Ciscaucasia; in particular, there was much destruction in the oil fileds of the Maikop district. More serious were its repercussions on the political geography of the area. Unlike the Crimea and the Lower Don, which are each administered as a single unit (the Crimean and Rostov *oblasti,* respectively) the Northern Caucasus is composed of several Russian and autonomous non-Russian regions. These were reorganized as a result of the alleged collaboration with the German troops of four ethnic groups, which by way of punishment were deprived of their identity and deported to other parts of the U.S.S.R. Thus, the autonomous *oblast* of the Karachai was partitioned in 1943 between the Stavropol *krai* and the Georgian S.S.R. In the same year, the Balkar part of the Kabardino-Balkar A.S.S.R. was handed over to the Georgian S.S.R., and the name Balkar was deleted from the title of the republic. Also, the Chechen-Ingush A.S.S.R. was dissolved, most of its territory becoming part of the newly established Grozny *oblast.* All these were subsequently restored. (W.C.B.)

Armenia

Occupying a landlocked area just south of the great mountain range of the Caucasus, and fronting on the northwestern extremity of Asia, the Armenian Soviet Socialist Republic, or Armenia, is the smallest of the 15 republics that make up the Soviet Union. Its area—11,500 square miles (29,800 square kilometres)—is no more than 0.13 percent of the national territory. To the north and east, Armenia is bounded by the Georgian and Azerbaijan Soviet Socialist republics, while its neighbours to the west and southeast are, respectively, Turkey and Iran. Armenia lies in the southern portion of the Transcaucasian region.

Modern Armenia is part of ancient Armenia, one of the world's oldest centres of civilization, whose peoples have long inhabited the highlands of the area. With the loss of autonomy in the 14th century AD, Armenia was subjected to constant foreign incursions, which, together with the centuries-old rule of Ottoman and Persian conquerors, imperilled the very existence of the Armenian people. The portion of Armenia lying within the former Russian Empire achieved its current political status on November 29, 1920.

Turkish Armenia, with an area of about 57,000 square miles (147,630 square kilometres), unlike Soviet Armenia, has no political designation. It is the location of Mt. Ararat, the highest point in the region; and the historic Tigris, Euphrates, and Aras (Russian, Araks; classical, Araxes) rivers have their sources there.

PHYSICAL AND HUMAN GEOGRAPHY

The land. *Relief.* The Armenian Soviet Socialist Republic is a mountainous country, characterized by a variety of scenery. Its average altitude is 5,900 feet (1,800 metres) above sea level. There are no lowlands: half the territory

Mountainous terrain

lies at altitudes of 3,300 to 6,600 feet (2,000 metres); a mere 10 percent lies below the 3,300-foot mark.

The northwestern part of the Armenian highland—containing Mt. Aragats, the highest peak (13,418 feet, or 4,090 metres) in the republic—is a combination of lofty mountain ranges, deep river valleys, and lava plateaus dotted with extinct volcanoes. To the north and east, the Somkhet, Bazum, Pambak, Areguni, Sevan, Vardenis, and Zangezur ranges of the Little Caucasus lie across the northern sector of Armenia. Elevated volcanic plateaus (Lory, Shirak, and others), cut by deep river valleys, lie amid these ranges.

In the eastern part of the republic, the Sevan Depression, containing Lake Sevan (525 square miles, or 1,360 square kilometres) and hemmed in by ranges soaring to a height of 11,800 feet, lies at an altitude of about 6,200 feet (1,900 metres). In the southwest, a large depression—the Ararat Plain—lies at the foot of Mt. Aragats and the Gegam Range; the Aras River cuts this important plain into halves, the northern half lying in the Armenian S.S.R. and the southern in Turkey and Iran.

Climate. Armenia's climate, because of its position in the deep interior of the northern part of the subtropical zone, enclosed by lofty ranges, is dry and continental. Regional climatic variation is nevertheless considerable. Intense sunshine occurs on many days of the year. Summer, except in high-altitude areas, is long and hot, the average June and August temperature in the plain being 77°F (25° C); sometimes it rises to 108°F (42°C). Winter is generally not cold; the average January temperature in the plain and foothills is about 23°F (−5°C), whereas in the mountains it drops to 10°F (−12°C). Invasions of Arctic air sometimes cause the temperature to drop to −22°F (−30°C): the record low is −51°F (−46°C). Winter is particularly inclement on the elevated, windswept plateaus. Autumn, long, mild, and sunny, is the pleasantest season.

The ranges of the Little Caucasus prevent humid air masses from reaching the inner regions of the republic. On the mountain slopes, yearly rainfall approaches 315 inches (8,000 millimetres), while the sheltered inland hollows and plains receive only 80 to 160 inches (2,000 to 4,000 millimetres) of rainfall a year.

The climate changes with elevation, ranging from the dry subtropical and dry continental types found in the plain and in the foothills up to a height of 3,000 to 4,300 feet (900–1,300 metres), to the cold type above the 6,600-foot mark. The plains and foothills are sufficiently well warmed to permit cultivation of such cold-sensitive fruits as figs, pomegranates, peaches, and grapes. Higher up, tobacco, cereals, and some fruits are raised; and grain crops, potatoes, and fodder grasses are found up to 6,600 to 8,200 feet (2,000–2,500 metres).

Drainage. Of the total precipitation, some two-thirds is evaporated, and one-third filters into the rocks, notably the volcanic rocks, which are porous and fissured. The many rivers in Armenia are short and turbulent with numerous rapids and waterfalls. The water level is highest when the snow melts in the spring and during the autumn rains. As a result of considerable difference in altitude along their length, some rivers have great hydropower potential; the total for the republic is nearly 22,000,000,000 kilowatt-hours a year.

Aras River

Most of the rivers fall into the drainage area of the Aras (itself a tributary of the Kura River of the Caspian Basin), which, for 300 miles (480 kilometres), forms a natural boundary between the Soviet Union and Turkey and Iran.

The Aras' main left-bank tributaries, the Akhuryan (130 miles [208 kilometres]), the Razdan (Hrazdan; 90 miles [144 kilometres]), the Arpa (80 miles [128 kilometres]), and the Bargushat (110 miles [176 kilometres]), serve to irrigate most of Armenia. The tributaries of the Kura—the Debet (57 miles [91 kilometres]), the Agstev (80 miles [128 kilometres]), and others—pass through Armenia's northeastern regions. Lake Sevan, holding over nine cubic miles (39 cubic kilometres) of water, is fed by dozens of rivers, but only the Razdan leaves its confines.

Armenia is rich in springs and wells, some of which possess medicinal properties.

Plant and animal life. The broken relief of Armenia, together with the fact that its highland lies at the junction of various biogeographical regions, has produced a great variety of landscapes; though a small country, it boasts more soil types (over 15) and plant species (over 3,000) than the vast East European Plain. There are five altitudinal vegetation zones: semidesert, steppe, forest, alpine meadows, and high-altitude tundra.

The semidesert landscape, ascending to a height of 4,300–4,600 feet (1,300–1,400 metres), consists of a slightly rolling plain covered with scanty vegetation, mostly sagebrush. The vegetation includes drought-resisting plants such as juniper, sloe, dog rose, and honeysuckle. The boar, wildcat, jackal, adder, gurza (a venomous snake), scorpion, and, more rarely, the leopard inhabit this region.

Steppes

Steppes predominate in the republic. They start at altitudes of 4,300–4,600 feet, and in the northeast ascend to altitudes of 6,200–6,600 feet. In the central region they reach 6,600–7,200 feet and in the south are found as high as 7,900–8,200 feet. In the lower altitudes the steppes are covered with drought-resistant grasses, while the mountain slopes are overgrown with thorny bushes and juniper.

The forest zone lies in the southeast of Armenia, at altitudes of 6,200–6,600 feet (1,900–2,000 metres), where the humidity is considerable, and also in the northeast, at altitudes of 7,200–7,900 feet (2,200–2,400 metres). Occupying nearly 10 percent of the republic's entire territory, the northeastern forests are predominantly beech. Oak forests predominate in the southeastern regions, where the climate is drier, and in the lower part of the forest zone hackberry, pistachio, honeysuckle, and dogwood grow. The animal kingdom is represented by the Syrian bear, wildcat, lynx, and squirrel. Birds—woodcock, robin, warbler, titmouse, and woodpecker—are particularly numerous.

The alpine zone lies above 6,600 feet, with stunted grass providing good summer pastures. The fauna is rich; the abundant birds include the mountain turkey, horned lark, and bearded vulture, while the mountains also harbour the bezoar goat and the mountain ram, or mouflon.

Finally, the alpine tundra, with its scant cushion plants, covers only limited mountain areas and solitary peaks.

The Ararat Plain

Regions. One of the more important of the distinctive regions of Armenia is that including the Ararat Plain and the surrounding foothills and mountains. This is a prosperous and densely populated area, the centre of Armenia's economy and culture, and traditionally the seat of its governmental institutions.

The other regions are the Shirak Steppe, the elevated northwestern plateaus, the republic's granary; Gugark, high plateaus, ranges, and deep valleys of the northeast, covered with forests, farmlands, and alpine pastures; the Sevan Basin, the hollow containing Lake Sevan, on whose banks are farmlands, villages, and towns; and Syunik, the two parts of which—the northern (Vayk) and the southern (Zangezur)—lie in the southeast. This last region is a maze of gorges and river valleys cutting through high ranges. It is an area rich in ores, with fields and orchards scattered here and there in the valleys and on the mountain sides.

The people. Armenians constitute nearly 90 percent of the republic's population. The remainder include Azerbaijanis, Russians, and a small number of Kurds, Ukrainians, and other groups.

The Russian campaigns against the Persians and the Turks in the 18th and 19th centuries resulted in large emigrations of Armenians under Muslim rule to the Transcaucasian provinces of the Russian Empire and to Russia itself (Erivan, Tiflis, Karabakh, Shamakhi, Astrakhan, Bessarabia). At the time of the massacres in Turkish Armenia in 1915, some Armenians found asylum in Russia.

The Armenians were converted to Christianity *c.* AD 300 and have an ancient and rich liturgical and Christian literary tradition. Believing Armenians today belong mainly to the Armenian Apostolic (Orthodox) Church or the Armenian Catholic Church, in communion with Rome.

The population density is highest in the Ararat Plain. The river valleys in the southeast and northeast are the next most densely populated area. Half the population is in fact concentrated in the zone marked by an upper altitudinal limit of 3,300 feet (1,000 metres), which makes up only about 10 percent of the entire territory. Many people also live in the foothills, at altitudes of 3,300–4,900 feet, and in the mountains (4,900–6,600 feet [1,500–2,000 metres]). These regions account for a further third of the entire population. The high ranges and mountains are scantily peopled; no one resides above 7,700 feet (2,350 metres).

Fundamental changes in the distribution of Armenia's population are being caused by the urbanization resulting from economic growth, particularly the republic's industrialization. Before the Revolution, the republic's four cities—Erivan (now Yerevan), Aleksandropol (Leninakan), Nor-Bayazet (Kamo), and Geryusy (Goris)—accounted for 10 percent of the total population. In the late 20th century the urban population numbered about two-thirds of the total population.

The rural population of the Armenian S.S.R. has grown much less rapidly than the urban population. The high country to the north of Shirak and in Syunik has small hamlets that lie in secluded glens, on riverbanks, and near springs; in the plain, such settlements cluster around mountain streams and irrigation canals, amid orchards and vineyards.

The economy. Armenia has become an industrial country with an important agricultural element. The share of industry in the country's economy—14 percent in 1913 in value terms—reached 73 percent by 1970.

This rapid economic advancement—unparalleled among the Soviet republics—is attributable to national financial investments that made possible the creation of a diversified industry, the reconstruction of agriculture, and the development of transport. Formerly a supplier of copper, certain farm products, and brandy, Armenia is now a major supplier of chemicals, nonferrous metals, machines, equipment, precision instruments, textiles and clothing, wines, brandies, and canned goods. The republic also has mineral resources, especially metal ores.

Electricity

At the initial stage of industrialization, the creation of a power base utilizing the hydraulic potential of mountain streams was of decisive importance. Production of electricity was combined with the building of irrigation works and water-supply systems for industries and cities. The Sevan–Razdan series of hydraulic power stations became a first-priority project that used not only the waters of the Razdan but also those of Lake Sevan. This project made possible the electrification of agriculture and helped to build numerous industries. In the 1960s emphasis shifted to thermal electric power stations, which, within a decade, accounted for most of the power produced in the republic.

Industry. Mechanical engineering, machine tools and electrical power machinery, electronics, and the chemical and mining industries hold a prominent place in the republic's heavy industry, but light and food industries are also fairly well advanced. Yerevan, Leninakan, and Kirovakan are machine-building cities. The centres of the chemical industries are Yerevan, Kirovakan, and Alaverdi.

Nonferrous metallurgy—in Gugark and Zangezur—includes the mining and dressing of copper, molybdenum, and other ores; the smelting of copper; and the extraction of precious and rare metals.

The food industry processes various farm products, meets domestic demand, and supplies other parts of the Soviet Union. The most advanced branches are involved in the primary processing of grapes and production of high-quality cognacs, wines, canned fruits, and vegetables for export.

Light industry—a modern innovation—specializes in the production of woollen, silk, and cotton fabrics; knitted goods and clothes; carpets; and footwear.

Yerevan is the foremost industrial centre, accounting for nearly three-fifths of the total industrial output in the republic; but other industrial centres and regions are developing, notably in the north, where Leninakan and Kirovakan are now major industrial centres.

Agriculture. Agriculture still plays a major role in the Armenian economy, even though industry has taken precedence; and it engages nearly half the population, located on state farms (*sovkhozy*) and collective farms (*kolkhozy*). Many items are shipped to other republics, and farm products provide raw materials for a number of industries.

Agriculture in Armenia has to contend with many difficulties. Arable land is scarce; cultivated lands (plowland, orchards, and vineyards) occupy only 20 percent of the republic's total area. Pastures and meadows mowed for hay cover a larger area, approaching 28 percent of the territory. Farmlands in mountain regions form a mosaic of cornfields, orchards, vineyards, and pastures. Considerable tracts of arable land also are found in the Ararat Plain, the Shirak plateau, and the southern part of the Sevan basin.

The extensive irrigated lands in the low, sunny Ararat Plain and cultivated stretches in the northeastern and southern river valleys yield high-quality grapes and fruits. Storage lakes, dams, and pumping stations have been built and irrigation canals dug. More than half the total arable land area is irrigated. Farming, above an elevation of 3,300 feet (1,000 metres), also combines with cattle raising; grain crops are cultivated and cattle raised in the mountains, while tobacco and potatoes are raised in the lower, warmer part of the mountain belt.

The leading branch of agriculture is viticulture. Among the many orchard crops, peaches and apricots are commonest. Apples, cherries, mazzards (sweet cherries), and pears are cultivated in the colder climate, and walnuts, hazelnuts, almonds, pomegranates, and figs are also produced in this area. Vegetables are grown in the main agricultural regions, potatoes in the cooler mountains. Quality tobaccos are widely cultivated.

Cotton and sugar beets, formerly grown in the Ararat Plain, are being succeeded by more valuable crops, such as grapes. The area under grain crops has been sharply reduced.

Extensive alpine pastures raise the productivity of animal husbandry, whose main branches are the raising of beef and milk cattle and sheep. Pig and poultry raising, as well as sericulture and apiculture, play subsidiary roles.

Transportation. Mountains are a serious impediment to the construction of land transport routes of any kind, although distances between towns and regions are not great. A railway line, leading to Tbilisi in the north and Baku in the east, runs through the northern, western, and southern regions of the Armenian S.S.R. Yerevan is linked with the Sevan basin by a line running along the Razdan River. Clustered along the rail routes are major industrial centres.

Road network

The network of motor roads is much denser, with Yerevan as the main hub. Road transport—whose role in freight and passenger traffic is growing—carries many times as much cargo as the railways, and buses remain the chief mode of travel between towns and villages.

Local air transport is being used increasingly. Air routes link Yerevan with many towns in the republic, and planes carry fresh fruits and grapes to Moscow, Leningrad, and other Soviet cities. Gas pipelines link Armenia with the Azerbaijan and Georgian S.S.R.'s.

These transportation facilities enable the other union republics to supply Armenia with coal, petroleum products, metals, timber, grain, industrial raw materials and equipment, while Armenia, in turn, exports lighter but more valuable products.

Administrative and social conditions. *Government.* The state structure of the Armenian S.S.R., defined by the constitution adopted in 1937, is similar to those of the other union republics.

The highest organ of state power is the Supreme Soviet of the Armenian S.S.R., elected for a four-year term from a single list of candidates. The Supreme Soviet designates its Presidium to administer the state in the periods between its own brief sessions, and it appoints the Council of Ministers and enacts laws.

The organs of state power in the districts, cities, and rural areas are the soviets of working people's deputies, elected by the population for two years.

The Supreme Court of the republic, whose members are elected by the Supreme Soviet for five years, is the highest judicial body. The procurator of the Armenian S.S.R. is appointed, for five years, by the procurator general of the Soviet Union. The Armenian S.S.R. has a coat of arms, a state flag, and a national anthem.

Political life is under the direction of the Communist Party, part and parcel of the Communist Party of the

Communist Party

Soviet Union. It was founded in 1920 through the unification of Armenia's Bolshevik organizations. The Young Communist League (Komsomol) of Armenia was formed in 1921 in close contact with the party.

The trade unions of Armenia operate 60-odd clubs and palaces of culture, nearly 100 public libraries, nearly 300 sports facilities, sanatoriums, and rest homes.

Education. Countrywide eight-year schooling has become the standard. There are trade schools, secondary specialized educational establishments, and institutes and colleges. Establishments of higher learning include Yerevan State University; polytechnical, medical, agricultural, pedagogical, and theatrical institutes; and a conservatory.

The public libraries include the A.F. Myasnikyan State Public Library of the Armenian S.S.R. and the Matenadaran archives in Yerevan containing 10,000 Armenian manuscripts, the largest collection in the world. There are also about 1,200 clubs and 35 museums, including a comprehensive State Historical Museum of the Armenian S.S.R.

Social services. Medical treatment in hospitals and clinics is free of charge for all citizens, being supported, like education, by taxation.

Cultural life. Armenian written literature began in the 5th century AD, and monasteries became the principal centres of intellectual life. The earliest works were historical, Moses of Khoren's *History of Armenia* being representative. The masterpiece of classical Armenian is Eznik Koghbatsi's *Refutation of the Sects.* The first great Armenian poet (10th century) was St. Gregory Narekatzi, renowned for his mystical poems and hymns. During the 16th–18th centuries, popular bards, or troubadours, called *ashugh,* arose, outstanding among them being Nahapet Kuchak and, especially, Aruthin Sayadian, called Sayat-Nova (died 1795), whose love songs are still popular. In the 19th and early 20th centuries, Hakob Paronian and Ervand Otian were outstanding satirical novelists, and Grigor Zohrab wrote Realist short stories. Paronian was also a comic playwright, whose plays still entertain Armenian audiences. The most celebrated novelist was Hakob Meliq-Hakobian, called Raffi, and perhaps the best dramatist of recent times was Gabriel Sundukian (died 1912).

Among Armenian composers, Aram Khachaturian achieved world-wide renown.

The broadcasting system has been operating since 1926 and the Yerevan television centre since 1956. Broadcasts and telecasts are conducted in Armenian, Russian, Azerbaijani, and Kurdish.

The republic boasts a State Academic Theatre of Opera and Ballet, several drama theatres, theatres for children, orchestras, a national dance company, and the Yerevan film studios, which produce feature, documentary, and popular science films. The traditional folk arts, especially singing, dancing, and artistic crafts, are thriving.

Armenian science, like its culture, has its roots in antiquity, but research institutions are a 20th-century development. The Armenian Academy of Sciences is composed of a number of institutes engaged in research problems in natural and social sciences. (A.A.M./Ed.)

Academy of Sciences

HISTORY

The Armenians, an Indo-European people, first appear in history shortly after the end of the 7th century BC. Driving some of the ancient population to the east of Mount Ararat, where they were known to the Greeks as Alarodioi ("Araratians"; *i.e.,* Urartians), the invaders imposed their leadership over regions which, although suffering much from Scythian and Cimmerian depredations, must still have retained elements of a high degree of civilization (*e.g.,* walled towns, irrigation works, arable fields, and vineyards) upon which the more primitive newcomers might build. The Hayk, as the Armenians name themselves (the term Armenian is probably due to an Iranian or Greek confusion of them with the Aramaeans), were not able to achieve the power and independence of their predecessors and were rapidly incorporated first by Cyaxares into the Median Empire and then annexed with Media by Cyrus II the Great to form part of the Achaemenian Empire of Persia (*c.* 550). The country is mentioned as Armina and Armaniya in the Bīsitūn inscription of Darius I the Great and, according to the 5th-century Greek historian Herodotus, formed part of the 13th satrapy (province) of Persia, the Alarodians forming part of the 18th. Xenophon's *Anabasis,* recounting the adventures of Greek mercenaries in Persia, shows the local government *c.* 400 BC to have been in the hands of village headmen, part of whose tribute to the Persian king consisted of horses. Armenia continued to be governed by Persian or native satraps until its absorption into the Macedonian empire of Alexander the Great (331) and its successor, the Seleucid Empire (301).

The Artaxiads. After the defeat of the Seleucid king Antiochus the Great by Rome at the Battle of Magnesia (winter 190–189), his two Armenian satraps, Artashes (Artaxias) and Zareh (Zariadres), established themselves, with Roman consent, as kings of Greater Armenia and Sophene, respectively, thus becoming the creators of an independent Armenia. Artashes built his capital Artashat (Artaxata) on the Aras River near modern Yerevan. The Greek geographer Strabo names the capital of Sophene as Carcathiocerta. An attempt to end the division of Armenia into an eastern and a western part was made about 165 BC when the Artaxiad ruler sought to suppress his rival, but it was left to his descendant Tigranes I the Great (*c.* 94–*c.* 55 BC) to establish, by his conquest of Sophene, a unity that was to last almost 500 years. Under Tigranes, Armenia ascended to a pinnacle of power unique in its history and became, albeit briefly, the strongest state in the Roman east. Extensive territories were taken from the kingdom of Parthia in Iran, which was compelled to sign a treaty of alliance. Iberia (Georgia), Albania, and Atropatene had already accepted Tigranes' suzerainty when the Syrians, tired of anarchy, offered him their crown (83 BC). Tigranes penetrated as far south as Ptolemais (Acre). Deeming Artaxata too far north to serve as the capital of his new empire, he founded a new one, Tigranakert (Tell Armen/Kızıl Tepe? or Silvan?), nearer the centre. Although Armenian culture at the time of Tigranes was Iranian, as it had been and as it was fundamentally to remain for many centuries, Hellenic scholars and actors found a welcome at the Armenian court. The Armenian Empire lasted until Tigranes became involved in the struggle between his father-in-law, Mithradates VI of Pontus, and Rome. The Roman general Lucullus, capturing Tigranakert in 69 BC, failed to reach Artashat, but in 66 the legions of Pompeii, aided by one of Tigranes' sons, succeeded, compelling the King to renounce Syria and other conquests in the south and to become an ally of Rome. It has been the fate of Armenia throughout a long and turbulent history to be a small state struggling to preserve its independence between two powerful neighbours; it now became a buffer state, and often a battlefield, between Rome and Parthia. Their natural self-interest gave the Armenians a reputation for deviousness; the Roman historian Tacitus called them an *ambigua gens.*

Strongest state in the east under Tigranes I

The Arsacids. Both Rome and Parthia strove to establish their own candidates on the Armenian throne until a lasting measure of equilibrium was secured by the treaty of Rhandeia, concluded in AD 63 between the Roman general Corbulo and Tiridates (Trdat), whereby an Arsacid occupied the throne of Armenia, but as a Roman vassal. A dispute with Parthia led to the country's annexation by the emperor Trajan in 114, but his successor, Hadrian, withdrew the frontier of the Roman Empire to the Euphrates. A similar dispute resulted in the destruction of Artashat by Marcus Aurelius' general Priscus in 163 and in the building of a new capital, Kainepolis (Vagharshapat, modern Echmiadzin). After Caracalla's capture of King Vagharshak and his attempt to annex the country in 216, his successor, Macrinus, recognized Vagharshak's son Tiridates II (Khosrow the Great in Armenian sources) as king of Armenia (217). Tiridates II's resistance to the Sāsānids after the fall of the Arsacid dynasty in Persia (224) ended in his assassination by their agent Anak the Parthian (*c.* 238) and in the conquest of Armenia by Shāpūr I, who placed his vassal Artavazd on the throne (252). Under Diocletian, the Persians were forced to relinquish Armenia, and Tiridates III, the son of Tiridates

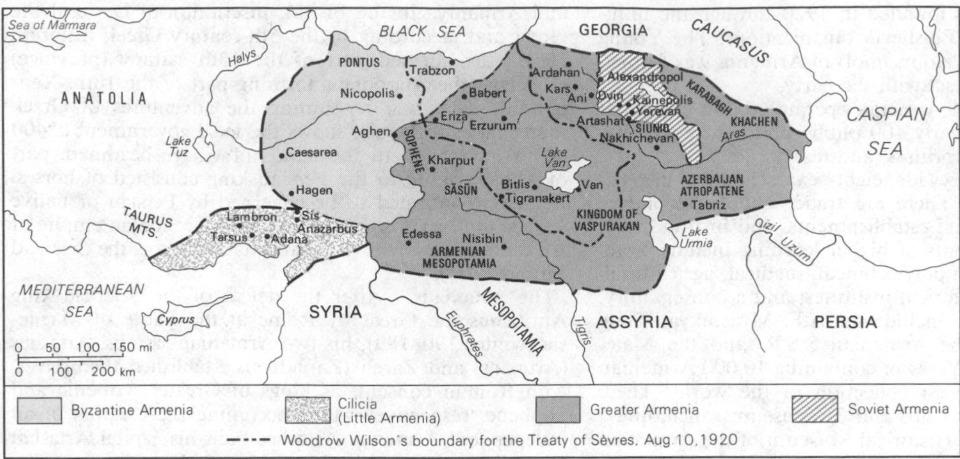

Historical divisions of Armenia.

II, was restored to the throne under Roman protection (*c.* 287). The reign of Tiridates III determined the course of much of Armenia's subsequent history. His ultimate conversion by St. Gregory the Illuminator and the adoption of Christianity as the state religion (*c.* 300) created a permanent gulf between Armenia and Persia, and the Armenian patriarchate became one of the surest stays of the Arsacid monarchy while it lasted and the guardian of national unity after its fall. The Mamikonian family, which played a similar role, came to the fore in his reign. Tiridates' assassination by his own chamberlain in league with the *nakharar*s (clan chiefs, barons; Parthian *n.ḥwd.r*, "Nohodares") of Siuniq underlines the disloyalty of many of the local nobles, whose revolts and jealous quarrels fill the pages of Armenian historians.

Christianity's adoption as the state religion

The dissatisfaction of the *nakharar*s with Arshak II led to the division of Armenia into two sections, Byzantine Armenia and Persarmenia (*c.* 390). The former, comprising about one-fifth of Armenia, was rapidly absorbed into the Byzantine state, to which the Armenians came to contribute many emperors and generals. The latter continued to be ruled by an Arsacid in Dvin, the capital after the reign of Khosrow II (330–339), until the deposition of Artashes IV and his replacement by a Persian *marzpan* (governor) at the request of the *nakharar*s (428). Although the Armenian nobles had thus destroyed their country's sovereignty, the cause of national unity was furthered by the development of a national Christian literature; culturally, if not politically, the 5th century was a golden age.

The marzpans. The Persians were not as successful as the Byzantines in their efforts to assimilate the strongly individualistic Armenian people. The misjudged attempt of Yazdegerd II to impose the Zoroastrian religion upon his Armenian subjects did much to reunite them as a nation. In the war of 451, which resulted from this policy, the Armenian commander St. Vardan Mamikonian and his companions were slain at the Battle of Avarayr (June 2?, 451), but the Persians renounced their plans to convert Armenia by force and deposed their *marzpan* Vasak of Siuniq, the archtraitor of Armenian history. The revolt of 481–484 led by Vahan Mamikonian secured religious and political freedom for Armenia in return for military aid to Persia, and with the appointment of Vahan as *marzpan* the Armenians were again largely the arbiters of their own affairs. Their independence was further asserted in 554, when the second Council of Dvin rejected the dyophysite formula of the Council of Chalcedon (451), a decisive step that cut them off from the West as surely as they were already ideologically severed from the East.

Byzantine Armenia

In 536 Justinian I reorganized Byzantine Armenia into four provinces, and, by the suppression of the power of the Armenian nobles and by transfers of population, he completed the work of hellenizing the country. In 591 its territory was extended eastward by the emperor Maurice as the price of reestablishing Khosrow II on the throne of Persia. After transporting many Armenians to Thrace, Maurice (according to the Armenian historian Sebeos) advised the Persian King to follow his example and to send "this perverse and unruly nation, which stirs up trouble between us" to fight on his eastern front. During the war between the emperor Phocas and Khosrow, the Persians occupied Byzantine Armenia and appointed a series of *marzpan*s, only to be ousted by the emperor Heraclius in 623. In 628, after the fall of Khosrow, the Persians appointed an Armenian noble, Varaztirotz Bagratuni, as governor. He quickly brought Armenia under Byzantine rule but was exiled for plotting against Heraclius (635).

The Mamikonians and Bagratids. The first, unsuccessful, Arab raid into Armenia in 640 found the defense of the country in the hands of the Byzantine general Procopius and the *nakharar* Theodor Rshtuni. Unable to prevent the pillage of Dvin in 642, Theodor in 643 gained a victory over another Arab army and was named commander in chief of the Armenian army by Constans II. In 653, after the truce with Mu'āwiyah, then governor of Syria, Constans voluntarily surrendered Armenia to the Arabs, who granted it virtual autonomy and appointed Theodor as governor (*ostikan*).

Theodor's successor, Hamazasp Mamikonian, sided with Byzantium, but after 661 Arab suzerainty was reestablished, although Byzantine-Arab rivalry, Armenian nationalism, and reluctance to pay the tribute made the region a difficult one to govern. An unsuccessful revolt led by Mushegh Mamikonian (771–772) resulted in the virtual extinction of the Mamikonians as a political force in Armenia and in the emergence of the Bagratunis and Artsrunis as the leading noble families. The Arabs' choice in 806 of Ashot Bagratuni the Carnivorous to be prince of Armenia marked the establishment of his family as the chief power in the land. The governor Smbat Ablabas Bagratuni remained loyal to the caliph al-Mutawakkil when he sent his general Bugha al-Kabir to bring the rebellious *nakharar*s to submission, although he too was dispatched in 855 with the rest of the captive nobles to Samarra. The election by the nobles of Smbat's son Ashot I the Great, who had been accepted as "prince of princes" by the Arabs in 862, to be king of Armenia in 885 was recognized by both Caliphi and Emperor. Throughout the 10th century art and literature flourished. Ashot III the Merciful (952–977) transferred his capital to Ani and began to make it into one of the architectural gems of the Middle Ages.

The Bagratids of Ani, who bore the title of *shāhanshāh* ("king of kings"), first conferred upon Ashot II the Iron by the Caliph in 922, were not the sole rulers of Armenia. In 908 the Artsruni principate of Vaspurakan became a kingdom recognized by the Caliph; in 961 Mushegh, the brother of Ashot III, founded the Bagratid kingdom of Kars; and in 970 the Prince of East Siuniq declared himself a king.

By the time of the Seljuq invasions in the 11th century the Armenian kingdoms had already been destroyed from the west. The province of Taron had been annexed to the Byzantine Empire in 968, and the expansionist policy of Basil II finally extinguished Armenian independence. The possessions of David of Tayq were annexed in 1000 and

Byzantine conquest

the kingdom of Vaspurakan in 1022. In the latter year, the Bagratid king of Ani, Yovhannes-Smbat, was compelled to make the Emperor heir to his estates, and in 1045, despite the resistance of Gagik II, Ani was seized by Constantine IX Monomachus. The Byzantine conquest was short-lived: in 1048 Togrul led the first Seljuq raid into Armenia, in 1064 Ani and Kars fell to Alp-Arslan, and after the Battle of Manzikert (1071) most of the country was in Turkish hands. In 1072 the Kurdish Shāddādids received Ani as a fief. A few native Armenian rulers survived for a time in the Kiurikian kingdom of Lori, the Siunian kingdom of Baghq or Kapan, and the principates of Khachen (Artzakh) and Sasun. In the 12th century many former Armenian regions became part of Georgia, and between 1236 and 1242 the whole of Armenia and Georgia fell into the hands of the Mongols. Armenian life and learning, centred around the church, continued as best it could.

Lesser Armenia. On the collapse of Greater Armenia many Armenians emigrated to Georgia, Poland, and Galicia, while others crossed into Cilicia, where some colonies had already settled at the end of the 10th century. One of Gagik II's lieutenants, a certain Ruben, established himself about 1080 at Bardzrberd in the Taurus, and another noble named Oshin at Lambron: the former became the founder of Rubenid dynasty of barons and kings who ruled Cilicia until 1226, and the latter was the ancestor of the Hethumid dynasty, which succeeded them and ruled until 1342. The barons Constantine I (1092–1100), Thoros I (1100–29), and Leo I (1129–39) enlarged their domains at the expense of the Byzantines, and by 1132 Vahka, Sis, Anazarbus, Mamistra, Adana, and Tarsus were under Rubenid rule. Although the Byzantine emperor John II Comnenus succeeded in annexing the whole of Cilicia during 1137–38, Thoros II (1145–68) and Mleh (1170–75) restored Armenian rule, with some Turkish aid. Leo II (I) the Great (1187–1219), an ally of the German emperor Frederick I Barbarossa, received the royal crown from the latter's son Henry VI and Pope Celestine III and was crowned king of Armenia in Tarsus in 1199 by the cardinal Conrad von Wittelsbach. The Byzantine Emperor lost no time in sending a crown also, but Little Armenia was now firmly allied to the West.

Influence of the crusaders

Intermarriage with Frankish crusading families from the West was common, and Frankish religious, political, and cultural influence, though resisted by the more nationalistic barons, was strong. Leo reformed his court and kingdom on Western models, and many French terms entered the language. Little Armenia played an important role in the trade of the Venetians and Genoese with the East, and the port of Lajazzo (on the Gulf of Iskenderun) rivalled Alexandria. Leo II left no son, and the throne passed to his daughter Zabel. Her first husband, Philip of Antioch, who refused to accept the Armenian faith—Leo II's lip service to Rome as the price of his coronation being largely ignored—was deposed by the barons, and the regent Constantine, baron of Lambron, a descendant of Oshin, arranged the marriage of Zabel to his son Hethum (Hayton) I (1226–69), the first of the Hethumid dynasty. Hethum conceived the idea of employing the Mongols against the growing menace of the Mamlūks of Egypt and was present with the Mongol army that entered the Syrian cities of Aleppo and Damascus in 1260. His successors followed the same policy, but the Mongols weakened and, after their defeat in 1303 near Damascus, were unable to protect Cilicia.

On the death, without heir, of Leo V, the crown passed to Guy de Lusignan, the eldest son of Hethum II's sister Zabel and her husband Amaury de Lusignan (Amalric of Cyprus). He was assassinated by the barons in 1344 for doctrinal reasons, and the next two kings, Constantine IV and V, were elected from their own ranks. On the assassination of Constantine V, the crown passed again to a Lusignan, to Guy's nephew Leo VI (V) (1374–75). By this time, as a result of the Mamlūk advance, little remained of Armenia except Sis and Anazarbus; Lajazzo had finally fallen in 1347, followed by Adana, Tarsus, and the Cilician plain in 1359. In 1375 the capital of Sis fell to the Mamlūks, and the last king of Armenia was captured; ransomed in 1382, he died in Paris in 1393. The title "king of Armenia" passed to the kings of Cyprus, thence to the Venetians, and was later claimed by the house of Savoy, but from the end of the 14th century the history of Armenia as a separate state is replaced by the history of Armenians under foreign domination.

The Turkish conquest. After the capture of Constantinople by the Ottoman Turks, the Armenian bishop of Bursa, transferred in 1461 to the capital, was appointed leader of the Armenian *millet* in the Ottoman Empire. Although as non-Muslims they were greatly disadvantaged, the Armenians of Turkey retained, as *zimmî*s (Arabic, *dhimmī*) or "people of the Book," the management of their own affairs. Their numbers were increased at the beginning of the 16th century by the conquest of Cilicia and Greater Armenia.

On the death of Timur in 1405, the eastern Armenian regions had passed into the hands of the Turkmen rival confederacies, the Black Sheep and the White Sheep, until the defeat of the latter by the Persian Shāh Esma'īl I in 1502. Armenia again became the battlefield between two powerful neighbours, and in 1514–16 the Ottomans wrested it from Persian rule. During the war that broke out in 1602, Shah 'Abbās I strove to regain the lost territories, and in 1604–05, with the aim of stimulating trade in his dominions, he forcibly transferred thousands of Armenians from Julfa to Isfahan, where those who survived the march settled in the quarter named New Julfa. At the peace of 1620, while the greater part of Armenia remained in Ottoman hands, Persia regained the regions of Yerevan, Nakhichevan, and Karabagh. In the mountainous region of Karabagh a group of five Armenian *malik*s (princes) succeeded in conserving their autonomy and maintained a short period of independence (1722–30) during the struggle between Persia and Turkey at the beginning of the 18th century; despite the heroic resistance of David Beg, the Turks occupied the region but were driven out by the Persians under Nāder Qolī (the future Nāder Shāh) in 1735.

Armenian settlement in New Julfa

In New Julfa the Armenian merchants served as links between Europe (including England, Spain, and Russia) and the East, exporting Persian silk and importing glass, clocks, spectacles, paintings, etc. In the course of the 17th century they amassed great wealth and built many magnificent churches and mansions, thereby attracting Persian envy, and from the beginning of the 18th century, when Nāder Shāh (1736–47) penalized them with excessive taxation, they began the gradual decline that continues at the present day.

Armenia and Europe. At the beginning of the 19th century the Russians advanced into the Caucasus. In 1813 the Persians were obliged to acknowledge Russia's authority over Georgia, northern Azerbaijan, and Karabagh, and in 1828 they ceded Yerevan and Nakhichevan. Contact with liberal thought in Russia and western Europe was a factor in the Armenian cultural renaissance of the 19th century. In Turkey, the Armenians benefitted with the rest of the population from what measures of reform there were, and in 1863 a special Armenian constitution was recognized by the Ottoman government. But social progress in Turkey was slow and the Armenians in Anatolia were subject to many abuses. After the Russo-Turkish War of 1877–78, in which Russian Armenians had taken part, Russia insisted in the Treaty of San Stefano that reforms be carried out among the Sultan's Armenian subjects and that their protection against the Kurds be guaranteed. This demand was reiterated at the Congress of Berlin, and the "Armenian question" became a factor in international politics in which Great Britain took a special interest.

Russian repression and Turkish atrocities

The socialist Hënchak ("Handbell") party was founded in 1887 and the nationalist Dashnaktzutiun ("Confederacy") party, commonly called Dashnaks, in 1890, and in the face of increasing Armenian demands for much needed reforms both the Turkish and Russian governments grew more repressive. In 1895, after Abdülhamid II had felt compelled to promise Britain, France, and Russia to carry out reforms, large-scale systematic massacres took place in the provinces. In 1896, following the desperate occupation of the Ottoman Bank by 26 young Dashnaks, more massacres broke out in the capital. In 1897 Nicholas II closed hundreds of Armenian schools, libraries, and newspaper offices, and in 1903 he confiscated the property of the Armenian Church. The greatest single disaster in the history of the Armenians came with the outbreak of World War I. In 1915 the Young Turk government, regarding the Turkish Armenians, despite pledges of loyalty by many, as a dangerous foreign element conspiring with the pro-Christian tsarist enemy to upset the Ottoman campaign in the east, resolved to deport the whole Armenian population of about 1,750,000 to Syria and Mesopotamia.

The chances of survival in these ill-prepared desert regions were slight: it may have been a death sentence, a "final solution" that Adolf Hitler was to emulate consciously in Germany. Hundreds of thousands of Armenians died or were massacred en route. Many of those who survived or escaped settled in Syria or emigrated to France and the United States.

The republic of Armenia. In 1916 the Turkish Armenian regions fell to the Russian army, but in March 1918 Russia was forced by the Treaty of Brest-Litovsk to cede all Turkish Armenia and part of Russian Armenia to Turkey, though some Armenians continued to hold out against the advancing Turks. On April 22, 1918, Armenia, Georgia, and Azerbaijan formed the Transcaucasian Federal Republic, but their basic diversity caused them to split into separate republics on May 26, 1918. Though short-lived, this Armenian republic was the first independent Armenian state since the Middle Ages. On June 4, 1918, Armenia was forced to sign the Treaty of Batum with Turkey, acknowledging the pre-1878 Russo-Turkish frontier along the Arpa and Aras rivers as its boundary, but after the Allied victory the Armenians reoccupied Alexandropol (Leninakan) and Kars. A short war with Georgia ensued for the possession of Borchalu and Akhalkalaki, and with Azerbaijan for the Karabagh region; despite temporary military success, these regions were destined to remain outside Armenia. On January 15, 1920, the Allies recognized the de facto existence of the three Transcaucasian republics. Pres. Woodrow Wilson hoped to persuade the U.S. to accept a mandate for an independent Armenia, but the Senate refused the responsibility (June 1, 1920). On August 10, 1920, Armenia, now recognized de jure, signed the Treaty of Sèvres by which Turkey recognized Armenia as a free and independent state. On November 22, 1920, Wilson, as instructed, announced projected boundaries that ceded to Armenia most of the vilayets of Erzurum, Trabzon, Van, and Bitlis. Already in the summer of 1919, however, the Turkish government of Ankara, under Mustafa Kemal, had repudiated Constantinople's treaties with Armenia. In September 1920 the Turks attacked, seizing Kars and Alexandropol by November 7; at the treaty of Alexandropol on Dec. 2, 1920 Armenia renounced all pre-1914 Turkish territories and Kars and Ardahan, recognized that there were no Armenian minorities in Turkey, and accepted that the region of Nakhichevan should form an autonomous Turkish state. The next day a new Armenian government at Yerevan, a coalition of Communists and Dashnaks (nationalists), proclaimed Armenia a Soviet republic; the Dashnaks were quickly eliminated, provoking an abortive revolt in February 1921. In March 1922 Armenia joined Georgia and Azerbaijan to form the Transcaucasian Soviet Federated Socialist Republic, which became part of the U.S.S.R. on December 30, 1922. The Nakhichevan enclave was awarded to Azerbaijan, sandwiching the southern part of Armenia between Turks and remaining a constant cause of friction between Armenia and Azerbaijan. Irrigation and hydroelectrical work began immediately, and though industry developed slowly at first, by 1935 the value of the gross industrial product was six times that of 1928. Yerevan State University was founded in January 1921. Under the new Soviet constitution (December 5, 1936) Armenia, Georgia, and Azerbaijan became separate constituent republics of the Soviet Union. (C.J.F.D.)

Proclamation of the Soviet republic

Azerbaijan

One of the 15 union republics of the Soviet Union, the Azerbaijan Soviet Socialist Republic, or Azerbaijan, is the easternmost of the three such entities—the others are Armenia and Georgia—that occupy the area fringing the southern flanks of the Caucasus Mountains. To the south lies Iranian Azerbaijan, to the east the waters of the Caspian Sea. In addition to a variegated and often strikingly beautiful natural environment, the Azerbaijan of the later 20th century offers a blend of traditions and modern development. The proud and ancient people of its remoter areas retain many distinctive folk traditions, but the lives of its inhabitants have been touched by an accelerating modernism characterized by industrialization, the development of power resources, and the growth of the cities, in which half the people now live. Industry dominates the economy, and more diversified pursuits have supplemented the exploitation of oil, which made Azerbaijan the world's leading producer at the beginning of the 20th century. Fine horses and caviar continue as some of the more distinctive traditional exports of the republic.

Administratively, the Azerbaijan S.S.R., which was established on April 28, 1920, now includes the geographically separate Nakhichevan Autonomous S.S.R., which, with its capital, Nakhichevan, lies beyond an intervening strip of Armenian territory. The Nagorno-Karabakh Autonomous Oblast, of which Stepanakert is the administrative centre, is also an administrative division. The territory of Azerbaijan covers 33,400 square miles (86,600 square kilometres), larger than Sri Lanka and about the same size as Portugal. Its capital is the ancient and economically important city of Baku, whose harbour is the best on the Caspian Sea.

Iranian Azerbaijan (or Azarbaijan), formerly the Northwestern Province, was subdivided in 1938 to form the Third and fourth *ostāns* (provinces), later East and West Azerbaijan, with capitals at Tabriz and Rezaiyeh, respectively. With a combined area of 42,762 square miles (110,754 square kilometres), Iranian Azerbaijan is bounded on the north by the Aras River, separating it from the Soviet republics of Azerbaijan and Armenia.

PHYSICAL AND HUMAN GEOGRAPHY

The land. *Relief.* As a result of its broken relief, its drainage patterns, and its climate, Azerbaijan is characterized by a variety of landscapes. More than 40 percent of its territory is taken up by lowlands, about half lies at 1,300 to 4,900 feet (400 to 1,500 metres), and areas above 4,900 feet occupy a little more than 10 percent of the total area.

The highest peaks are Bazardyuzi, Shakhdag, and Tufan, all part of the Great Caucasus, which forms a natural northern boundary for the republic. Magnificent spurs and ridges, cut into by the deep gorges of mountain streams, make this part of Azerbaijan a region of great natural beauty.

Forests and wildlife

The slopes of the mountains are covered with beech, oak, and pine forests, and the animal life includes Caucasian deer, roe deer, wild boar, brown bear, lynx, European bison (wisent), chamois, and leopard, though the latter is rare. Typical birds include the Caucasian grouse and the stone partridge.

The spurs of the Little Caucasus, in southwest Azerbaijan, form the second important mountain system, which includes the Shakhdag, Murovdag, and Zangezur ranges and also the Karabakh upland. The large and scenic Lake Gyoygyol lies at an altitude of 5,138 feet (1,566 metres).

The southeast part of Azerbaijan is bordered by the Talysh Mountains, with Kyumyurkyoy as the highest.

The Kura-Aras (Araks) Lowland is named after the main river and its tributary. The Shirvan, Milskaya, and Mugan plains are part of this lowland and have similar soils and climate, the difference in names reflecting purely historical considerations. Plant life is that of the steppe and semidesert, and gray soils and saline solonchaks and, in higher regions, gray alkaline solonetz and chestnut soils prevail. A well-developed network of canals between the Kura and Aras rivers makes it possible to irrigate a major part of the lowland. The Upper Karabakh Canal, 109 miles (175 kilometres) long, provides a vital link between the Aras River and the Mingechaur Reservoir on the Kura River. The reservoir, constructed in 1953, contains 565,000,000,000 cubic feet (16,000,000,000 cubic metres) of water and has a surface area of 234 square miles (606 square kilometres) and a maximum depth of 246 feet (75 metres). The Upper Karabakh Canal alone irrigates about 250,000 acres (100,000 hectares) of fertile land, and in addition supplies the Aras River with water during dry summer periods.

The Upper Shirvan Canal, the second most important, is 75 miles (120 kilometres) long and also irrigates about 250,000 acres.

Climate. The dry subtropical climate prevailing in central and eastern Azerbaijan is characterized by a mild winter and a long (four to five months) and very hot summer, with an average temperature of 81° F (27° C) and a maximum temperature of 109° F (43° C).

Southeast Azerbaijan is characterized by a humid subtropical climate and has the highest precipitation in the republic, reaching 47–55 inches (1,200–1,400 millimetres) a year, most of which falls in the cold months.

A dry continental climate, with a cold winter and a dry, hot summer, prevails in the Nakhichevan Autonomous S.S.R. at altitudes of 2,300 to 3,300 feet (700 to 1,000 metres). Moderately warm, dry or humid types of climate are to be found in other parts of Azerbaijan. The mountain forest zone has a moderately cold climate, while an upland tundra climate characterizes the altitude of 10,000 feet (3,000 metres) and above. Frosts and heavy snowfalls make the passes at such altitudes inaccessible for three or four months of the year.

Cosmopolitan ethnic heritage

The people. Today's Turkic Azerbaijanis, who comprise about three-quarters of the republic's population, combine in themselves the predominantly Turkic strain, which flooded Azerbaijan especially during the Oğuz Seljuq migrations of the 11th century, with mixtures of older inhabitants—Iranians and others—who had lived in Transcaucasia since ancient times. In the Nakhichevan A.S.S.R., almost all of the inhabitants are Azerbaijanis, whereas more than 80 percent of the population of the Nagorno-Karabakh Autonomous Oblast are Armenian. These subunits of the union republic were established to minimize friction between the two nationalities. Russians make up the largest minority in Azerbaijan. Urban population constitutes half the republic's total.

The economy. Azerbaijan is a developed industrial and agrarian republic, with the balance between the gross output of agriculture and that of industry gradually tilting in favour of the latter. The emphasis on heavy industry has considerably expanded two traditional industries—petroleum and natural gas—but engineering and light and food industries are also of growing importance.

Resources. At the turn of the 20th century Azerbaijan was the world's leading petroleum producer, and it was also the birthplace of the oil-refining industry. In 1901, for example, Azerbaijan produced 11,400,000 tons of oil, more than the United States; it accounted for 95 percent of Russian and 50 percent of the world production. As the 20th century progressed, however, Azerbaijan's role in oil production decreased as the industry developed in other regions of the Soviet Union and the world, though by the late 20th century the annual output of oil in Azerbaijan was still considerable.

Azerbaijan also has other natural resources, including gas, iodo-bromide waters, lead, zinc, iron, and copper ores, nepheline syenites utilized in the production of aluminum, common salt, and a great variety of building materials, including marl, limestone, and marble.

Fuel and power. The development of Azerbaijan's industry created a demand for fuel and power supplies. Almost 90 percent of the electricity is produced at thermoelectric power stations, which have been built throughout the republic.

Industry. Azerbaijan has a diversified industrial base, with heavy industry and its leading branches—power, manufacturing, and chemicals—predominating.

Branches of the processing industry, producing mineral fertilizers, gasoline, and kerosene, herbicides, industrial oils, synthetic rubber, plastics, etc., are developing. Sumgait has emerged as the major centre of this industry, as well as of ferrous metallurgy.

The republic's share in the total output of Soviet manufacturing has increased considerably in the late 20th century. Azerbaijan manufactures equipment for the oil and gas industry, electrical equipment of all kinds, and many appliances and instruments. Some of these goods are exported to other countries. This type of industry is located mostly in Baku, Kirovabad, and Mingechaur.

Light industrial manufactures include cotton and woollen textiles, knitwear, traditional household items and souvenirs, footwear, and other consumer goods. The cities of Sheki, Stepanakert, Kirovabad, Mingechaur, and Baku are the main centres of this industry. Food processing plants are distributed fairly evenly throughout the republic. Azerbaijan fisheries are of particular importance because of the sturgeon of the Caspian Sea; sturgeon roe is made into caviar of world renown.

Agriculture. Azerbaijan's agriculture has also been developing: although arable land in Azerbaijan constitutes only 7 percent of the total, the republic accounts for 10 percent of the gross agricultural output of the Soviet Union. Raw cotton is the leading agricultural product; tobacco is the second most valuable crop. Favourable conditions for grapes have contributed to the development of this branch of agriculture. Most of the grape varieties grown in Azerbaijan are used for wine making. Vegetables, particularly early varieties, fruit, walnuts, and hazelnuts are also promising crops. Some districts, particularly those of Sheki, Zakataly, and Geokchay, are—as they have been traditionally—engaged in silkworm breeding.

Development of viticulture

High commodity output is not characteristic of Azerbaijan's animal husbandry.

Economic regions. The Apsheron region includes the Apsheron Peninsula and several other areas of eastern Azerbaijan. As a result of its advantageous geographical position, it is crossed by freight routes connecting Azerbaijan and the whole of Transcaucasia with the North Caucasus and Central Asia. Numerous highways also run from the peninsula to every corner of the republic.

On the shores of the Caspian Sea, the Apsheron region nevertheless remains one of the most arid parts of Azerbaijan. Its main natural wealth is mineral, including oil, natural gas, iodo-bromide waters, and limestone, used in building and cement production.

Such cities as Baku, the capital of the republic, Sumgait, and other industrial centres make the Apsheron region one of the most highly industrialized and densely populated areas of Azerbaijan.

Baku

Baku itself owes its modern growth to the development of the oil industry; oil derricks encircle the city, and it acts as a magnet to workers from many areas. Contemporary Baku is one of the largest and most attractive cities in the Soviet Union. Situated on natural terraces running down to a gulf of the Caspian Sea, the city has a two-mile (3.2-kilometre)-long picturesque boulevard and many historic sites.

Modern Sumgait, 22 miles (35 kilometres) northwest of Baku, is currently a centre of the iron and steel, nonferrous metallurgical, and chemical industries, although the development of light engineering is envisaged.

The Lenkoran region of southern Azerbaijan is well endowed by nature, with evergreen vegetation and thick beech and oak forests. Warm climate crops, such as tea, feijoa (a fruit-bearing shrub), rice, grapes, tobacco, and citrus trees, flourish there. The region is one of the largest producers of spring and winter vegetables in the Soviet Union.

Mild winters draw many birds to the Caspian coast, and a reservation provides a resting home for flamingos, swans, pelicans, herons, and buzzards.

The towns of Lenkoran, Astara, and Masally are small, and the Talysh, or Talīshī—Iranian people who form the bulk of the local population—have preserved their old customs and traditions. Industry is mostly concerned with the processing of agricultural goods, while in the mountains the Talysh make colourful rugs and carpets.

The Kuba-Khachmas region lies to the north of Apsheron. Its coastal lowlands specialize in grain and vegetable production, while vast orchards surround the towns of Kuba and Kusary. The mountain slopes are used for grazing. Special kinds of sheep are bred in order that their skins may be utilized in the fur industry.

The Shirvan region, an industrially and agriculturally developed part of Azerbaijan, is centred on the Shirvan Plain. The Mingechaur hydroelectric station is located here. The area also has a well-developed network of highways. Industry is generally engaged in the processing of such agricultural products as cotton, grapes, and fruit. The most important vineyards lie in the vicinity of Shemakha, a town famed for its wines, notably Matrasa and Shemakha, respectively dry red and sweet. In Kyurdamir a fragrant dessert wine of the same name is produced. The best varieties of pomegranates are grown near Geokchay.

The Mugano-Salyany region, lying south of the Kura River and within the boundaries of the Mili and Mugan plains, specializes in cotton growing, producing about 70 percent of the gross cotton output of the entire republic. Cotton-ginning plants are located in Barda, Salyany, and Ali-Bayramly, all of which, in addition to being located on the Kura River, have the advantage of being junctions of railways and motor roads. A thermal power station stands near Ali-Bayramly.

Cotton production

The Southwestern region includes the Nagorno-Karabakh Autonomous Oblast, as well as Lachin, Fizuli, and Kubatly administrative districts. Because the average altitude is 4,900 feet (1,500 metres), it is one of the areas in the republic where broken relief impedes the development of transport, industry, and agriculture. Agricultural production is concentrated in the mountain valleys. Animal husbandry constitutes a large percentage of the gross agricultural output, the leading branches being sheep and pig raising. Grapes, tobacco, and grain are the main crops.

Armenians form the greater part of the population. The Nagorno-Karabakh Autonomous Oblast is well known in the Soviet Union for the longevity of its people; many have a life-span of more than 100 years.

The Kirovabad-Kazakh region is situated in the centre of Transcaucasia at the junction of the Azerbaijan, Armenian, and Georgian republics. The region has conditions favourable both for human life and for intensive agriculture. Trade routes have crossed this part of Azerbaijan from time immemorial, and the ancient town of Ganja (now Kirovabad) was founded here. It is an important industrial centre, with light, food, engineering, chemical, and nonferrous metallurgical industries. Naftalan is a health resort.

The Sheki-Zakataly region includes the towns of Sheki (formerly Nukha), Zakataly, and Belokany. Its territory borders on the Great Caucasus, which shields it from cold northern winds. Numerous mountain rivers provide it with an ample supply of water, and the region is densely populated. Agricultural products include tobacco, aromatic plants (mint, basil, and roses), rice, corn (maize), and various fruits. The area is also the largest Soviet producer of hazelnuts and walnuts.

The Nakhichevan region is a typical semi-desert, although a system of irrigation makes it possible to cultivate grapes, cotton, and grain. There are several sources of mineral water in the foothill areas of the Nakhichevan A.S.S.R.

Transportation. Most of the rivers of Azerbaijan are not navigable, and most freight—including that sent out of the republic—is carried by rail. Considerable portions of the rail network are electrified. The principal goods carried are oil products, building materials, timber, and grain. The major railway lines go through the Kura Valley and connect Baku with Tbilisi and Batumi in the Georgian S.S.R.

Railways

Motor transport is used extensively for both freight and passengers within the republic. Highways connect various parts of the republic and are often the only means of land communication between some of the remote mountain districts and the administrative centres and large cities.

Baku, on the Caspian, is one of the busiest seaports in the Soviet Union, handling such important and vital goods as oil, timber, grain, and cotton. A ferry link (1962) between Baku and Krasnovodsk (also on the Caspian, in the Turkmen S.S.R.) increased considerably the amount of cargo passing through Azerbaijan.

Administrative and social conditions. *Government.* The Azerbaijan constitution (1937) declares it to be one of the 15 constituent republics forming the Soviet Union. Though sovereignty and equality are claimed for it, both are limited by the fact that the republic lacks independence in foreign affairs, military matters, economic planning, domestic political control, and cultural and ideological questions, in all of which it must defer to the central Soviet authorities in Moscow. At the top of the governmental structure within Azerbaijan today are the republic's Supreme Soviet, selected from a single slate of candidates for a four-year term, and its Presidium, selected by the Supreme Soviet. The duties of both are largely ceremonial rather than legislative. The highest executive and administrative body of the republic's government is the Council of Ministers. Local branches of government are the *oblast* and city soviets. The judicial system includes a Supreme Court and lower courts.

The Communist Party of Azerbaijan, a subordinate branch of the Communist Party of the Soviet Union (CPSU), is the only authorized political organization. Closely connected is the Azerbaijan Komsomol (Young Communist League). Labour unions are not concerned with relations between workers and management except with regard to such matters as incentives to increase production.

Communist Party

Social services. The republic has a well-established health service with large specialized clinics and medical research institutes. Medical service, provided without direct charge to patients, is supported by general taxation on individual employees and workers and by taxes from income of factories and other firms.

Cultural life. In the course of its long history, Azerbaijan has given the world a number of outstanding thinkers, poets, and scientists. Among the medieval scientists and philosophers, Abul Hasan Bakhmanyar (11th century), the author of numerous works on mathematics and philosophy, and Abul Hasan Shirvani (11th–12th centuries), the author of *Astronomy,* may be noted. The poet and philosopher Neẓāmī, called Ganjavī after his place of birth, Ganja (now Kirovabad), was the author of *Khamseh* ("The Quintuplet"), composed of five romantic poems, including "The Treasure of Mysteries," "Khosrow and Shīrīn," and "Leyli and Mejnūn."

The people of Azerbaijan have kept their ancient musical tradition. The art of *ashug*s, who improvise songs to their own accompaniment on a stringed instrument called a *kobuz,* remains extremely popular. *Mugam*s, vocal and instrumental compositions, are widely known, the town of Shusha being particularly famous for this art.

In the Soviet period, illiteracy has been virtually eradicated, and a network of institutes of higher education, research centres, theatres, and similar bodies has been established. By 1983 there were 18 institutes for higher education in Azerbaijan with more than 110,000 students. The largest is the Azerbaijan Institute of Petroleum and Chemistry, in whose six faculties more than 16,000 students attend classes.

Education at all levels is supported by taxes levied upon working people and firms and is available without direct tuition charge.

The Azerbaijan Academy of Sciences, established in 1945, coordinates the activity of research centres, including institutes of cybernetics, physics, theoretical problems of chemical technology, petrochemical processes, and genetics.

Since World War II a number of new cultural institutions have been established, such as theatres, clubs, museums, and libraries. The opera and ballet are widely attended. Some of Azerbaijan's composers, notably Uzeir Hajjibekov (the operas *Ker-Ogly* and *Leyli and Mejnūn* and the operetta *Arshin Mal ʾAlan*) and Kara Karayev (the ballets *Seven Beauties* and *The Path of Thunder*), have international reputations. The latter's symphonic music is also well known abroad.

Azerbaijan has no private publishing; several government firms publish scientific books and magazines as well as books and magazines about art and literature in Azerbaijani, Russian, and other languages.

Publishing

The magazines *Literaturny Azerbaidzhan* (in Russian), *Azerbaijan Gadïnï* ("Azerbaijan Woman," in Azerbaijani), and *Azerbaidzhanskoye neftyanoye khozyaistvo* ("Azerbaijan Petroleum Economy," in Russian) have the highest circulation.

Baku has several radio stations, a television studio, and a film studio. (E.D.S./E.Al.)

HISTORY

The Azerbaijan S.S.R. and the Iranian provinces of Azerbaijan adjoin each other, and the origin of the peoples of both regions is broadly the same. They have never been united politically, however, except in the sense that from the 11th century up to 1723 and again from 1735 to 1813 the whole territory was either under Persian (Iranian) suzerainty or actually part of the Persian Empire. Known to the Romans as Albania and to the Arabs as Aran, Azerbaijan was conquered by the Arabs in AD 642. The population originally had been Iranian but became Turkicized by the 9th century. Under the Arabs the various khanates—Shirvan, Aran, and Mughan—became prosperous, but they deteriorated after the collapse of the Arab empire. During the Mongol domination (1236–1498) and the Ṣafavid dynasty of Persia, the khanates, especially that of Shirvan (Shemakha), recovered some of their former prosperity. The 18th century saw the military rise of Russia and its territorial expansion at the expense of Turkey and Persia. As a result of long wars of aggression, Russia acquired by the Treaty of Gulistan (1813) the khanates of Derbent, Baku, Shirvan, Sheki (Nukha), Ganja (or Gandzha; now Kirovabad), and Lenkoran and by the Treaty of Turkmanchai (1828) Nakhichevan and the southern part of Talish. Thenceforward, Azerbaijan was divided between Russia and Iran by the present-day frontier, the majority of the Azerbaijanis remaining in Iran. Under Russian rule the Azerbaijanis were called Tatars or Musulmans, and they were administered in the *gubernii* of Baku and Elizavetpol.

After the 1905 Revolution some political activity developed, and the Musavat (Equality) Party was formed in 1911. The March 1917 Revolution and the presence of the Turkish Army in Transcaucasia brought about an alliance between the Musavat and Turkey. At the same time, an attempt was made to found an independent Transcaucasian federation consisting of Azerbaijan, Georgia, and Armenia. Racial and religious animosity caused this to fail, and an independent republic of Azerbaijan was formed in May 1918, its capital being at Gandzha until Baku, which had been under the control of a Communist council, was captured with the help of the Turkish Army in 1918. A small British force that had originally occupied Baku in August 1918, but had withdrawn on the arrival of the Turks, returned after the collapse of Turkey in November and was virtually in control of the republic's affairs until it was finally evacuated in August 1919. The new republic was recognized de facto by the Allied powers on January 15, 1920. In April 1920 Azerbaijan was invaded by the Red Army and the government surrendered to the Communist authorities. The Azerbaijanian S.S.R. was created in the same month. In 1922 it was incorporated into the Transcaucasian Soviet Federated Socialist Republic until 1936, when it became a union republic.

Turkish alliance

Although the economy of the republic developed greatly after the Soviet regime took over, it is difficult to speak of its political stability with precision. (G.E.Wh./An.Sh.)

Georgia

Lying at the eastern end of the Black Sea just to the south of the great barrier formed by the Caucasus Mountains, the Georgian Soviet Socialist Republic, or Georgia, lies in the southernmost region of the European section of the Soviet Union, at the same latitude as Rome. Formed in 1921, it has been since 1936 one of the 15 Soviet union republics. With the notable exception of the fertile plain of Kolkhida—ancient Colchis, where the legendary Argonauts sought the Golden Fleece—the Georgian terrain is largely mountainous (85 percent of the total area) and a third is covered by forest or brushwood. There is a remarkable variety of landscape, ranging from the subtropical Black Sea shores to the ice and snow of the crest line of the Caucasus. Such contrasts are made more noteworthy by the relatively small size of the republic, which, at 26,900 square miles (69,700 square kilometres), ranks 10th among the union republics.

The roots of the Georgian people are deep in history. Their cultural heritage is equally ancient and rich. During the 20th century Georgia has experienced a major transformation from an economically backward outpost of the tsarist Empire to a modernized and diversified economy.

The republic is bounded to the north, at the Caucasian crests, by the Russian Soviet Federated Socialist Republic. Azerbaijan and Armenia lie to the east and southeast, and a portion of the Soviet frontier with Turkey is to the south. Georgia includes two autonomous Soviet Socialist republics, the Abkhaz (principal city Sukhumi) and the Adzhar (principal city Batumi), as well as the Yugo-Ossetian Autonomous Oblast, a unit centred on Tskhinvali. The Georgian capital is at Tbilisi (Tiflis).

Autonomous S.S.R.'s and *oblast*

PHYSICAL AND HUMAN GEOGRAPHY

The land. *Relief.* The rugged Georgia terrain may be divided into three bands, all running from east to west.

To the north lies the wall of the Great Caucasus Range, consisting of a series of parallel and transverse mountain belts, rising eastward, and often separated by deep, wild gorges. Spectacular crest line peaks include Shkhara (16,627 feet [5,068 metres]), Rustaveli (16,273 feet [4,960 metres]), Tetnults (15,918 feet [4,852 metres]), and Ushba (15,420 feet [4,700 metres]). The cone of the extinct Kazbek (Mqinvari) volcano dominates the northernmost Bokovoy Range from a height of 16,512 feet (5,033 metres). Farther south, the central range thrusts out a number of important spurs, including those of the Lomissky (Lomisi) and Kartliysky (Kartli, Kartalinian) ranges at right angles to the general Caucasian trend. From the ice-clad flanks of these desolately beautiful high regions flow many streams and rivers.

The southern slopes of the Great Caucasus merge into a second band, consisting of central lowlands formed on a great structural depression. The Kolkhida lowlands, near the shores of the Black Sea, are covered by a thick layer of river-borne deposits, accumulated over thousands of years. Rushing down from the Great Caucasus, the major rivers of western Georgia, the Inguri, Rioni, and Kodori, flow over a broad area to the sea. The Kolkhida lowland was formerly an almost continually stagnant swamp. In a great development program, drainage canals and embankments along the rivers have been constructed and afforestation plans introduced; the region has now become of prime importance through the cultivation of subtropical and other commercial crops. To the east, the structural trough is crossed by the Meskhetsky (Meskheti) and Likhsky (Likhi) ranges, linking the Great and Little Caucasus and marking the watershed between the Black and Caspian Sea basins. Beyond, in central Georgia, between the cities of Khashuri and Mtskheta (the ancient capital), lies the inner high plateau known as the Kartalinian Plain. Surrounded by mountains on all sides and covered for the most part by deposits of the loess type, this plateau extends along the Kura (Mtkvari) River and its tributaries.

Kolkhida

The southern band of Georgian territory is marked by the ranges and plateaus of the Little Caucasus, which rise beyond a narrow, swampy coastal plain to reach 10,830 feet (3,301 metres) in the peak of Didi-Abuli.

Climate. The Caucasian barrier protects Georgia from cold air intrusions from the north, while the republic is open to the constant influence of warm, moist air from the Black Sea. Western Georgia has a humid subtropical, maritime climate, while eastern Georgia has a range of climate varying from moderately humid to a dry subtropical type.

Altitudinally, too, there are marked zones. The Kolkhida lowland, for example, has a subtropical character up to about 1,600–2,000 feet (500–600 metres), with a zone of moist, moderately warm climate lying just above; still higher is a belt of cold, wet winters and cool summers. Above about 6,600–7,200 feet (2,000–2,200 metres), there is an alpine climatic zone, lacking any true summer; above 11,200–11,500 feet (3,400–3,500 metres), snow and ice reign perpetually. In eastern Georgia, farther inland, temperatures are lower than in the western portions at the same altitude.

Altitudinal zones

Western Georgia has heavy year-round rainfall, totalling 40 to 80 inches (1,000 to 2,000 millimetres) and reaching a maximum in autumn and winter. Southern Kolkhida receives the most rain, and humidity decreases to the north and east. Winter in this region is mild and warm; in regions below about 2,000–2,300 feet (600–700 metres), the mean January temperature never falls below 32° F (0° C), and warm, sunny winter weather persists in the coastal regions, where temperatures average about 41° F (5° C).

In eastern Georgia, precipitation decreases with distance from the sea, reaching 16 to 28 inches (400 to 700 millimetres) in the plains and foothills but, nevertheless, increasing to double this amount in the mountains. The southeastern regions are the driest areas, and winter is the driest season; the rainfall maximum occurs at the end of spring. The highest lowland temperatures occur in July (about 77° F), while average January temperatures over most of the region range from 32° to 37° F.

Plant and animal life. The republic's location and its diverse terrain have given rise to a remarkable variety of landscapes. The luxuriant vegetation of the moist, subtropical Black Sea shores is relatively near to the eternal snows of the mountain peaks. Deep gorges and swift rivers give way to dry steppes, and the green of alpine meadows alternates with the darker hues of forested valleys. Soils, too, present a great variety, ranging from gray-brown and saline semi-desert types to richer red earths and podzols, with man-made improvements adding to the diversity.

Forests

About a third of the republic is covered by forests and brush. In the west, relative constancy of climate over a long period has preserved many relict and rare items, including the Pitsunda pines (*Pinus pithyusa*). The forests include oak, chestnut, beech, and alder, as well as Caucasian fir, ash, linden, and apple and pear trees. The western underbrush is dominated by evergreens (including rhododendrons and holly) and such deciduous shrubs as Caucasian bilberry and nut trees. Liana strands entwine some of the western forests. Citrus groves are found throughout the republic, and long rows of eucalyptus trees line the country roads.

Eastern Georgia has fewer forests, and the steppes are dotted with thickets of prickly underbrush, as well as a blanket of feather and beard grass. Herbaceous subalpine and alpine vegetation occurs extensively in the highest regions. Animal life is very diverse. Goats and Caucasian antelope inhabit the high mountains; rodents live in the high meadows; and a rich birdlife includes the mountain turkey, the Caucasian black grouse, and the mountain and bearded eagles. The clear rivers and mountain lakes are full of trout.

Forest regions are characterized by wild boar and roe and Caucasian deer, brown bear, lynx, wolf, fox, and jackal, and hares and squirrels. Birds range from the thrush to the black vulture and hawk. Some of these animals and birds also frequent the lowland regions, which are also the home of introduced raccoon, mink, and nutria. The lowland rivers and the Black Sea itself are also rich in fish.

The Georgians

The people. The likelihood is great that the Georgians (whose name for themselves is Kartveli, "Georgian" having been derived from the Persian name for them, Gorj) have always lived in this region, known to them as Sakartvelo. Ethnically, contemporary Georgia is not homogeneous but reflects the intermixtures and successions of the Caucasus region. Two-thirds of the people are Georgians; the rest consist of Armenians, Russians, Azerbaijanis, and smaller numbers of Ossetes, Greeks, Abkhaz, and other minor groups.

The republic is one of the first among the union republics in terms of population density. About 90 percent of the population lives below 3,300 feet (1,000 metres); the density decreases sharply with increasing altitude.

The Georgians, a proud people with an ancient culture, have through the ages been noted as warriors as well as for their hospitality, their love of life, and their lively intelligence and sense of humour. Physically, they tend to be taller than average, with athletic, wiry bodies, complexions ranging from fair or ruddy to sallow, and generally dark hair, though fair-haired persons are seen. Their eyes are commonly hazel, with some blue and some gray. The nose shape varies, those in the east tending to be hooked, those in the west straight and thin. The standard of looks is high, and the beauty of Georgian women is legendary; many of them graced the harems of the Ottoman sultans and the shahs of Iran. The Georgians are often also remarkably long-lived.

During the Soviet period the Georgian population has not only increased but has also shown a marked trend toward urbanization. Further, a considerable portion of the population that is defined as rural is, in fact, engaged in the urban economy of nearby cities. Enterprises for primary processing of agricultural products have been constructed in the villages, while ore-processing plants and light industry are also increasing in number. As a result, many of the slow-paced traditional villages have developed into distinctly modern communities. The number of rural inhabitants remains high because of the wide distribution of such labour-intensive branches of the economy as the tea and subtropical crop plantations.

Tbilisi, the capital, an ancient city with many architectural monuments mingling with modern buildings, lies in eastern Georgia, partly in a scenic gorge of the Kura River. Other major centres are Kutaisi, Sukhumi, Batumi, and Tskhinvali.

The economy. Georgia has a well-developed industry alongside a diversified and mechanized agriculture. It stands out as a region of waterpower, mineral extraction, and developing machine production. A hundred or more different products are now exported all over the world.

Resources. The interior of Georgia has coal deposits (notably at Tkvarcheli and Tkibuli), petroleum (at Kazeti), and a variety of other resources ranging from peat to marble. The manganese deposits of Chiatura rival those of India, Brazil, and Ghana in quantity and quality. Its waterpower resources are also considerable. The deepest and most powerful rivers for hydroelectric purposes are the Rioni and its tributaries, the Inguri, Kodori, and Bzyb. Such western rivers account for three-quarters of the total capacity, with the eastern Kura, Aragvi, Alazani, and Khrami accounting for the rest.

Waterpower

Industry. The fuel and power foundation developed in Georgia has served as the base for industrialization. Dozens of hydroelectric stations, including the V.I. Lenin Zemo-Avchala, Rioni, and Sukhumi plants, as well as many stations powered by coal and natural gas, have been constructed. All are now combined into a single power system, an organic part of the Transcaucasian system.

The coal industry is one of the oldest mineral extraction industries, centred on the restructured Tkibuli mines. Deposits found in Tkvarcheli and Akhaltsikhe have increased production.

Manganese and nonmetallic minerals, ranging from talc to marble, supply various industries throughout the Soviet Union. The Rustavi metallurgical plant, located near the capital, produced its first steel in 1956. Its laminated sheet iron and seamless pipe products are used throughout the Soviet Union. Zstafoni is the second major metallurgical centre.

The machine-building industry now turns out a diverse range of products, from electric railway locomotives, heavy vehicles, and earth-moving equipment to lathes and precision instruments. Specialized products include tea-gathering machines and anti-hail devices for the republic's plantations. The industry is centred in the major cities.

The chemical industry of Georgia produces mineral fertilizers, synthetic materials and fibres, and pharmaceutical products. The building industry, using local raw materials, supplies the republic with cement, slate, and many prefabricated reinforced-concrete structures and parts.

Commonly used manufactured goods were previously imported, in large part, from other union republics, but a ramified system of light industries set up in major consumption areas in Georgia now produces cotton, wool, and silk fabrics, as well as items of clothing.

Products of the food industry include tea, wine, and tobacco, as well as canned foods. Georgia leads the Soviet Union in labelled table and dessert wines. Brandy and champagne production is also well developed. Other food-industry activities include dairy products and canned foods.

Agriculture. A distinctive feature of the Georgian economy is that agricultural land is both in short supply and

Difficulty of cultivation

difficult to work; each patch of workable land, even on steep mountain slopes, is valued highly. The relative proportion of arable land is less than that in almost any other union republic. The importance of production of labour-intensive (and highly profitable) crops, such as tea and citrus fruits, is a compensatory factor, however. The introduction of a system of collective farms (*kolkhozy*) and state farms (*sovkhozy*) has radically altered the traditional structure of landowning and working (though a considerable portion of Georgia's agricultural output still comes from private garden plots). Contemporary agriculture uses modern equipment supplied under a capital investment program, which also finances the production of mineral fertilizers and herbicides, as well as afforestation measures.

The harvest of tea plantations accounts for around 95 percent of all Soviet tea production. The vineyards of the republic constitute one of the oldest and most important branches of Georgian agriculture, and perhaps the best loved. Centuries of trial and error have produced more than 500 varieties of grape.

Orchards now occupy 310,000 acres (125,500 hectares) throughout the republic. Georgian fruits are varied, even slight differences in climate and soil affecting the yield, quality, and taste of the fruit.

Sugar beets and tobacco are especially significant among other commercial crops. Essential oils (geranium, rose, and jasmine) are also grown to supply the perfume industry. Grains, including wheat, are important, but quantities insufficient for the republic's needs are raised and wheat must be imported. Growing of vegetables and melons has developed in the suburbs.

Livestock raising is marked by the use of different summer and winter pastures. Sheep and goats, cattle, and pigs are raised. Poultry, bees, and silkworms are also significant.

Transportation. Georgia has a dense transportation system. Most freight is carried by rail, but in the mountainous regions road transport remains the principal means of moving both passengers and freight.

The seaports of Batumi and Poti are of major economic importance for the whole of Transcaucasia, and air-route links with major Soviet centres have become increasingly important.

Administrative and social conditions. *Government.* The unicameral, 400-member Supreme Soviet, elected for four years from a single list of candidates, is the highest government organ; the Presidium, its working organ, consists of a chairman, two vice chairmen, a secretary, and 11 members. Local authorities are the councils of deputies in, respectively, the cities, the *raionebi* (districts), and the *aulebi* (villages).

The Supreme Court is the highest judicial organ, supported by regional and city people's courts. Criminal codes taking fuller account of the national characteristics of the republic were adopted in 1960, and their observance is supervised by a republican procurator, who serves for five years.

The Communist Party of Georgia is the only political party and, under the Communist Party of the Soviet Union, establishes policy. Georgians are dominant in the party, constituting more than three-fourths of its membership (while constituting only two-thirds of the total population).

Social services. Payments from public funds (a large part of which are derived from a turnover tax on consumer goods) provide free education, medical services, pension grants, and stipend payments and free or reduced-cost accommodation in rest homes and sanatoriums, as well as holiday pay and the maintenance of kindergartens and day nurseries.

Health facilities

Georgia ranks high in the level of medical services. The republic is famed in the Soviet Union as a health centre, a reputation stemming from the numerous therapeutic mineral springs, the sunny Black Sea coast climate, the pure air of the mountain regions, and a wide range of resorts. The Tskhaltubo baths, with warm radon water treatment for rheumatism sufferers, are especially noted.

Educationally, Georgia also ranks high in the Soviet Union. Tbilisi State University was founded in 1918; the Academy of Sciences (founded 1941) is made up of several scientific institutions, which conduct research throughout the republic. This educational system is backed up by an extensive library system.

Cultural life. Georgia is a land of ancient culture, with a written language that was developed in the early 5th century AD. Kolkhida (Colchis) early housed a school of higher rhetoric in which Greeks as well as Georgians studied. By the 12th century, academies in Ikalto and Gelati, the first medieval higher-education centres, disseminated a wide range of knowledge. The national genius was demonstrated most clearly in *Vepkhis-tqaosani* (*The Knight in the Tiger's Skin*), the epic masterpiece of the 12th-century poet Shota Rustaveli. Major figures in later Georgian literary history include a famed 18th-century writer, Sulkhan-Saba Orbeliani; the novelist and poet Ilia Chavchavadze, author of *Do You Call This a Man?*; the lyric poet Akaki Tsereteli; Alexander Qazbegi, novelist of the Caucasus; the nature poet Vazha Pshavela; Mikheil Javakhishvili, Paolo Iashvili, and Titsian Tabidze, all executed during the Stalin era; and Giorgi Leonidze and Irakli Abashidze. Important workers in other arts include the painters Niko Pirosmani (Pirosmanashvili), Irakli Toidze, Lado Gudiashvili, and Sergo Kobuladze; the composers Zakaria Paliashvili and Meliton Balanchivadze, and the founder of Georgian national ballet, Vakhtang Chabukiani. Georgian theatre, in which outstanding directors of the Soviet period are Kote Mardzhanishvili and Sandro Akhmeteli, has had a marked influence in the Soviet Union and beyond. Amateur theatre and other art forms are also very popular. There is an active Georgian film industry, and a Georgian film, *The Wedding,* directed by Mikheil Kobakhidze, won the Grand Prix for best short film at the Cannes festival in 1966.

The ancient culture of the republic is reflected in the large number of architectural monuments, including many monasteries and churches; indeed, Georgian architecture (with Armenian) played a considerable role in the development of the Byzantine style.

Maintained by preservation schemes, these buildings are attracting an increasing number of Soviet and foreign tourists.

(M.L.D./Ed.)

HISTORY

The latest findings of archaeology make it possible to trace the origins of human society on the territory of the modern Georgian S.S.R. back to the early Paleolithic and Neolithic periods. A number of Neolithic sites have been excavated in the low-lying Kolkhida (Colchian) Basin, in the Khrami Valley in central Georgia, and in South Ossetia; they were occupied by settled tribes engaged in cattle raising and agriculture. The cultivation of grain in Georgia during the New Stone Age is attested by finds of saddle querns and flint sickles; the earth was tilled with stone mattocks. The Caucasus was regarded in ancient times as the primeval home of metallurgy. The start of the 3rd millennium BC witnessed the beginning of Georgia's Bronze Age. Remarkable finds in Trialeti show that central Georgia was inhabited during the 2nd millennium BC by cattle-raising tribes whose chieftains were men of wealth and power. Their burial mounds yielded up finely wrought vessels in gold and silver; a few are engraved with ritual scenes suggesting Asianic cult influence.

Neolithic agriculture and metallurgy

Origins of the Georgian nation. Early in the 1st millennium BC, the ancestors of the Georgian nation emerge in the annals of Assyria and, later, of Urartu (Armenia). Among these were the Diauhi (Diaeni) nation, ancestors of the Taokhoi, later domiciled in the southwestern Georgian province of Tao, and the Kulkha, forerunners of the Colchians, who held sway over large territories at the eastern end of the Black Sea. The fabled wealth of Colchis early became known to the Greeks and finds symbolic expression in the legend of Medea and the Golden Fleece.

Following the influx of tribes driven from the direction of Anatolia by the Cimmerian invasion of the 7th century BC and their fusion with the aboriginal population of the Kura Valley, the centuries immediately preceding the Christian Era witnessed the growth of the important kingdom of Iberia, the region that now comprises modern

Kartalinia and Kakhetia, with Samtskhe and adjoining regions of southwestern Georgia. Colchis to the west was colonized by Greek settlers from Miletus and subsequently fell under the sway of Mithradates the Great, king of Pontus. The campaigns of Pompey led in 65 BC to the establishment of Roman hegemony over Iberia and to direct Roman rule over Colchis and the rest of Georgia's Black Sea littoral.

Medieval Georgia. Georgia embraced Christianity about the year 330; its conversion is attributed to a holy captive woman, St. Nino. During the next three centuries, Georgia was involved in the conflict between the Byzantine and Persian empires. Lazica on the Black Sea (incorporating the ancient Colchis) became closely bound to Byzantium. Iberia passed under Iranian control, though toward the end of the 5th century, a hero arose in the person of King Vakhtang Gorgaslani, a ruler of legendary valour who for a time reasserted Georgia's national sovereignty. The Sāsānian monarch Khosrow I (reigned 531–579) abolished the Iberian monarchy, however. For the next three centuries, local authority was exercised by the magnates of each province, vassals successively of Iran, of Byzantium, and, after 654 AD, of the Arab caliphs, who established an amīrate in Tbilisi (Tiflis).

Christianization

Then came a national revival leading ultimately to the unification of all the lands inhabited by peoples of Georgian and related Ibero-Caucasian stock. This movement was led by the Bagrationi (Bagratids), a princely dynasty long prominent in the affairs of Armenia. Toward the end of the 8th century, the Bagratid Ashot I the Great settled at Artanuji in Tao (southwestern Georgia), receiving from the Byzantine emperor the title of *kuropalates* ("guardian of the palace"). In due course, Ashot profited from the weakness of the Byzantine emperors and the Arab caliphs and set himself up as hereditary prince in Iberia. King Bagrat III (975–1014) later united all the principalities of eastern and western Georgia into one state. Tbilisi, however, was not recovered from the Muslims until 1122, when it fell to King David II Aghmashenebeli ("the Builder"; reigned 1089–1125).

The zenith of Georgia's power and prestige was reached in the reign (1184–1213) of Queen Tamara, whose realm stretched from Azerbaijan to the borders of Cherkessia, from Erzurum to Gandzha (Kirovabad), forming a pan-Caucasian empire, with Shirvan and Trabzon as vassals and allies.

The invasions of Transcaucasia by the Mongols from 1220 onward, however, brought Georgia's golden age to an end. Eastern Georgia was reduced to vassalage under the Mongol Il-Khans of the line of Hulagu, while Imeretia, as the land to the west of the Suram Range was called, remained independent under a separate line of Bagratid rulers. There was a partial resurgence during the reign (1314–46) of King Giorgi V of Georgia, known as "the Brilliant," but the onslaughts of Timur between 1386 and 1403 dealt blows to Georgia's economic and cultural life from which the kingdom never recovered. The last king of united Georgia was Alexander I (reigned 1412–43), under whose sons the realm was divided into squabbling princedoms.

Turkish and Persian domination. The fall of Constantinople to the Ottoman Turks in 1453 isolated Georgia from western Christendom. In 1510 the Turks invaded Imeretia and sacked the capital, Kutaisi. Soon afterward, Shāh Esmāʿīl I of Iran invaded Kartalinia. Ivan IV the Terrible and other Muscovite tsars showed interest in the little Christian kingdoms of Georgia, but the Russians were powerless to stop the Muslim powers from partitioning the country and oppressing the inhabitants. In 1578 the Turks overran the whole of Transcaucasia and seized Tbilisi, but they were subsequently driven out by Shāh ʿAbbās I (reigned 1587–1629), who deported many thousands of the Christian population to distant regions of Iran. There was a period of respite under the viceroys of the House of Mukhran, who governed at Tbilisi under the aegis of the shahs from 1658 until 1723. The most notable Mukhranian ruler was Vakhtang VI, regent of Kartalinia from 1703 to 1711 and then king, with intervals, until 1723. Vakhtang was eminent as a lawgiver and introduced printing to Georgia; he had the Georgian annals edited by a commission of scholars. The collapse of the Ṣafavid dynasty in 1722, however, led to a fresh Ottoman invasion of Georgia. The Turks were expelled by the Persian conqueror Nāder Shāh, who gave Kartalinia to Tʿeimuraz II (1744–62), one of the Kakhian line of the Bagratids. When Tʿeimuraz died, his son Erekle II reunited the kingdoms of Kartalinia and Kakhetia and made a brave attempt at erecting a Caucasian multinational state based on Georgia. Imeretia under King Solomon I (reigned 1752–84) succeeded in throwing off Turkish domination.

House of Mukhran

Raids by Lezgian mountaineers from Dagestan, economic stringency, and other difficulties impelled Erekle to adopt a pro-Russian orientation. On July 24, 1783, he concluded with Catherine II the Great the Treaty of Georgievsk, whereby Russia guaranteed Georgia's independence and territorial integrity, while Erekle accepted Russian suzerainty. Russia soon left her new ally in the lurch. Erekle and his Georgians had to face alone the firece hordes of the Persian eunuch Āghā Moḥammad Khān Qājār. Tbilisi was sacked in 1795, and Erekle died brokenhearted in 1798. His invalid son Giorgi XII sought to hand over the kingdom unconditionally into the care of the mad Russian emperor Paul I, but both rulers were dead before this could be formally implemented. In 1801 Alexander I reaffirmed Paul's decision to incorporate Kartalinia and Kakhetia into the Russian Empire. Despite the treaty of 1783, the Bagratid line was deposed and replaced by Russian military governors, who deported the surviving members of the royal house and behaved in such a way as to provoke several popular uprisings. The western Georgian kingdom of Imeretia was annexed in 1810, while Guria, Mingrelia, Svanetia, and Abkhazia were finally swallowed up in 1829, 1857, 1858, and 1864, respectively. The Black Sea ports of Poti and Batumi, as well as areas of southwestern Georgia long under Ottoman rule, were wrested from Turkey in successive wars, culminating in the campaigns of 1877–78.

Russian annexation

National revival. By waging war on the Lezgian clansmen of Dagestan and on Iran and Turkey, the Russians ensured the corporate survival of the Georgian nation. Under Prince M.S. Vorontsov, who served with distinction as viceroy (1845–54), commerce and trade began a rapid upswing, and a theatre and other institutions and amenities were opened in Tbilisi. Following the liberation of the Russian serfs in 1861, the Georgian peasants also received freedom 1864 onward, though on terms regarded as burdensome. The decay of old patriarchal ways was accelerated by the spread of education and European influences. A railway linked Tbilisi with Poti from 1872; and mines, factories, and plantations were developed by Russian, Armenian, and Western entrepreneurs. Peasant discontent, the growth of an urban working class, and the deliberate policy of Russification and forced assimilation of minorities practiced by Emperor Alexander III (reigned 1881–94) fostered radical agitation among the workers and nationalism among the middle-class intelligentsia. The tsarist system permitted of no organized political activity, but social issues were debated with verve in journals, works of fiction, and local assemblies.

The leader of the national revival was Prince Ilia Chavchavadze, leader of a literary and social movement dubbed Pirveli Dasi, or the First Group. The Meore Dasi, or Second Group, led by Giorgi Tseretʿeli, was more radical in its convictions, but it paled before the Mesame Dasi, or Third Group, an illegal Social Democratic party founded in 1893 and led by Noe Zhordania, Karlo Chkheidze, and others. The Third Group professed Marxist doctrines; from 1898 it numbered among its members Joseph Dzhugashvili (Stalin). When the Mensheviks under Zhordania gained control of the group, Stalin left the Caucasus and threw in his lot with Lenin.

The 1905 Revolution in Russia led to widespread disturbances and guerrilla fighting in Georgia, later suppressed by Cossacks with indiscriminate brutality. After the Revolution of March 1917 the three Transcaucasian nationalities—Georgians, Armenians, and Azerbaijanis—were ruled by a committee controlled by Petrograd and known as the Ozakom. The Bolshevik coup later in the year forced the predominantly Menshevik politicians of Transcaucasia to secede from Russia, though with reluctance, and form a new body, the Transcaucasian Commissariat. The stresses of local nationalisms, combined with a Turkish advance from the west, brought about the breakdown of the federation. On May 26, 1918, the Georgians set up an independent state and placed themselves under German protection, but the collapse of the Central Powers at the end of 1918 led to a British occupation. The Georgians viewed Anton Denikin's White Russians, who enjoyed British support, as more dangerous than the Bolsheviks themselves. They refused to cooperate with a movement designed to restore the tsarist imperial order, and British forces evacuated Batumi in July 1920.

Short-lived independence

Although the independence of Georgia had been recognized de facto by the Allies in January 1920, the country's fate was now sealed. The Russo-Georgian treaty of May 7, 1920, enabled a Soviet mission under S.M. Kirov to be sent to Tbilisi in order to undermine the Georgian regime and prepare the way for a Bolshevik coup there.

Incorporation in the U.S.S.R. In January 1921 the Georgian republic was recognized de jure by the Allies, after having been refused admission to the League of Nations. Within a month the Red Army, acting under the orders of two Georgian Bolshevik leaders, Stalin and G.K. Ordzhonikidze, entered Georgia, and on February 25 a Soviet regime was installed in Tbilisi.

After the establishment of a Soviet republic in their native country, Stalin and Ordzhonikidze incorporated Georgia in a Transcaucasian Soviet Federated Socialist Republic, abolishing the country's autonomy. A period of the severest repression began, with the aim of destroying "the hydra of nationalism" and consolidating the country within the Soviet framework. Active nationalists and others were executed, the Georgian Church was subjected to persecution, and even the Georgian Communist Party itself had to be vigorously purged of local patriots.

The transition to the new order was to some extent eased by the Socialist policies pursued by the Georgian Mensheviks, who had nationalized all important industries. But the Georgian peasantry rose against the Communists on several occasions. Particularly violent was the rising that broke out in 1924 under the leadership of Kaikhosro Choloqashvili, which had to be put down by the Red Army.

On December 5, 1936, the Transcaucasian Federated Republic was dissolved. The Georgian Soviet Socialist Republic became a full-fledged member of the U.S.S.R. Many of the original local Bolshevik leaders were executed as Trotskyite deviationists during the purges of 1936–37. L.P. Beria, a Georgian who had played a prominent part in bringing his fellow countrymen to heel, became head of the Soviet secret police, the NKVD. Industrialization and collectivization of agriculture were pressed on apace. Public institutions, including a Georgian Academy of Sciences, were set up, and much progress was made in public health and education. In spite of social regimentation and political conformity, Georgia has shared in the growing material prosperity of the U.S.S.R. (D.M.La.)

SOVIET CENTRAL ASIA

Central Asia comprises the inland part of Asia, furthest removed from the world oceans, in the midst of the greatest land mass on earth. Because of its geographic location, prevailing winds, and drainage, it is a zone of great aridity, extending from the Caspian Sea in the west to northwestern China and Mongolia in the east, and from southern Siberia in the north to northern Iran and Afghanistan in the south.

Physical and human geography

THE LAND

Natural zones

Relief. There are four major natural, or ecological, zones of Central Asia: steppe, steppe-desert, desert, and mountain. Only recently and in a minor way have human beings disturbed the ecological processes in the area. These ecological zones run in broad bands from east to west across Eurasia. The northernmost zone is the steppe, a belt of grassland covering Mongolia and northern Kazakhstan, extending into southern Siberia and eastern Europe. The terrain is flat, almost featureless, with few rivers and mountains. The grass cover is denser toward and within the European parts, where there is somewhat more rainfall; in eastern Kazakhstan the grass cover thins out, becoming the dry steppe. Mongolia is a high-altitude steppe, averaging about a mile above sea level; Kazakhstan is low-altitude steppe, lying at sea level. Steppe-desert (semidesert), too, is grassland, drier than the steppe, lying at low altitude and not extending into Europe or Siberia. There the grass cover is thinner than in the steppe, with patches bare of plant cover increasing in size and number toward the south. It is likewise flat terrain with few watercourses and no mountains. In the desert, grasses give way to dry vegetation. There lie the innermost parts of Asia, south of the steppe and steppe-desert, farthest from the moisture-bearing winds and the seas, with most intensive water evaporation. The Central Asian deserts are vast, spreading from the Red Sands (Kyzylkum) of Turkmenistan to the Black Sands (Kara-Kum) of southern Kazakhstan, to Sinkiang, and to the Gobi. The mountain zone lies in the southeast of Soviet Central Asia, the Pamirs rising to nearly five miles as part of the highest mountain systems in the world.

The few rivers are shallow, narrow, and shifting and many are dry in summer. They flow only inland, some into the Caspian, Aral, Balkhash, and lesser lakes of the region; others lose themselves in the sands of the desert. They are of limited usefulness for transport and navigation, but they irrigate bands of fields along the rivers.

Transportation is chiefly overland, hence the importance of the domesticated animals. The historical significance of Central Asia to the world was that it served in the manner of a great inland sea, connecting China, India, Iran, and Europe by means of camel, ass, and horse caravans that moved goods and peoples, permitted military invasions, and spread technology, religions, ideas, and science through and across its breadth.

Climate. Throughout the region rainfall never exceeds 12 inches (300 millimetres) in an average year, far too little to grow grain; parts of Central Asia receive less than four inches (100 millimetres) of rain per year. The exception is near mountain ranges, where there is higher rainfall and a more rapid change from one climatic and ecological zone to the next. The prevailing winds blow from west to east, losing their moisture before reaching the inland parts of Asia. Consequently all agriculture requires artificial irrigation.

Plant and animal life. Cereal grasses, including forms of wheat, are native to the region, being found wild even at present. They were domesticated by the early farmers and have been continuously grown since. Other crops, such as rice and cotton, are historically recent imports. The grasses of the steppe and steppe-desert provide good livestock fodder. Animals native to the steppe include the wild horse and wild cattle, the camel, and the wild goat. The wild yak is native to the mountains of Tibet and Mongolia, and other mountain fauna include wild sheep and goats. All these animals, when domesticated, play roles in the herding economy and are raised for food, trade, and transport.

Irrigation and pastoralism

The vegetation and fauna of the arid zone made possible two great indigenous economic specializations. First, irrigation agriculture developed near the valleys of the Amu Darya, the Syrdarya, the Ili, and the Zeravshan rivers and in such mountain valleys as the Fergana. Second, specialization in pastoralism occurred in the steppe and steppe-desert belts where grasses and water provide sustenance for livestock. Herding communities living in the deserts take their flocks there in the spring when the desert briefly flowers. The agricultural and pastoral economies, were mutually supportive, each being dependent on the products of the other.

THE PEOPLE

The peasants lived in permanent settled villages, in houses of sun-dried brick. The herding families lived in tents of felt stretched over lattice frames that they could collapse and pack into carts as they moved from pasture to pasture. Their communities were always mobile, each family having a camel or two to pull the family cart, its tent, and possessions; horses to transport goods and carry the herdsmen to, from, and around the pastures; mares and cows for breeding and milking; sheep and goats for milk and wool. The herders owned many sheep and goats but small numbers of the other stock.

The languages of the region are members of the Altaic and the Indo-European families. The Altaic family comprises three major divisions, two of which, Turkic and Mongol, are represented in Central Asia and neighbouring parts of Siberia and China. The Turkic speakers include Kazakhs, Kirgiz, Uzbeks, Kara-Kalpaks, and Turkmens. The Mongol speakers include the Khalkhas of Mongolia, Buryats of southern Siberia, Kalmyks of the Volga, and several groups in the neighbouring provinces of China (*e.g.*, Daghur and Monguor). The Indo-European speakers are the Tadzhiks, speaking an Iranian language; in ancient times Central Asia was inhabited by a number of other Iranian-speaking groups (Scythians, Massagetai, Parthians). Central Asia has in recent centuries received new migrants speaking Russian and Ukrainian.

The Turkic, Mongol, and Iranian speakers of Central Asia were encountered in antiquity, and modern peoples in the region are their descendants, mixed together with the later immigrants, invaders, settlers, and resettlers. None are pure races.

Traditional culture patterns. *The economy.* The historical period in Central Asia began about 500 BC with the rise of the traditional cultures. These cultures flourished about AD 500 down to the 20th century, when the region was absorbed in the great revolutionary movements emanating from Russia and China.

Pastoral culture patterns

The cultural pattern of the herdsmen grew rapidly, and, according to Chinese reports, these peoples by the 3rd century BC had already formed the herding communities that they now have. The Chinese reported that their country "is the back of a horse," meaning that the communities were nomadic.

The herding village community moved as a single unit across pastoral tracks that they owned and defended, for if others used their tracks their own herds would die for lack of grass or water on the way from pasture to pasture. Herds and men spread out in the summer pasture, gathering in closely during the winter encampment. The herdsmen defended the herds from predacious beasts, such as wolves and snow leopards, and helped the herds to forage beneath the snow. They helped the mares to foal, the cows to calve, and the lambs and kids to find the teats of their mothers beneath the woolly undercoats. The herds provided food (mainly milk, rarely meat) and materials for clothing and housing. The pastoralists were traditionally nomadic; that is, they moved about in small communities together with their herds in fixed annual round, from winter camp to spring and summer pastures, and back to the winter camp. The Kazakhs, Kirgiz, Turkmens, Uzbeks, and Kara-Kalpaks raised herds of horses, cattle, sheep, goats, camels, and asses; the Mongols raised all of these except the ass; in the east, the Mongols of Mongolia also raised the yak.

The cultural pattern of the Central Asian irrigation-cultivators differed little from that of the great agricultural civilizations neighbouring them in China, Iran, India, and the Middle East. Water was scarce, and thus life depended on careful maintenance of the soil and water systems by village communities that collectively coordinated their labour and managed their resources. The result was an ability to support great populations in dense concentrations, ranging up to hundreds of persons per square mile. Harnessed to the needs of their livestock, the pastoral peoples stood in sharp contrast: they spread out thinly over the landscape, their average density being no more than two or three people per square mile.

Irrigation required a collective and planned effort and a peaceful inner regime so that the peasants could work together. War disturbed these efforts both by preventing peaceful labours and by drawing the peasants away to military defense and attack. When wars came, the irrigation channels deteriorated, and civilizations raised upon them disappeared rapidly.

The Tadzhiks had an old tradition of agriculture in Central Asia; the Turks, their neighbours, originally herdsmen, gradually developed an agricultural wing to their village economies. Over centuries agriculture became increasingly important among the Uzbeks, somewhat less so among the Turkmens, Kazakhs, and Kirgiz. The agricultural peoples grew grain (rice and wheat), cotton, and vegetables and raised fowl. Central Asia, together with Iran and Sinkiang, is still a world centre of melon growing; many fruits and nuts such as the peach, pistachio, and almond originated there.

Exchange systems

Mongols and Turks became highly specialized herders and undertook little or no agriculture. They traded for most of their agricultural needs with farmers who were likewise specialized. The Mongols traded with the northern Chinese, who spared no land for pasture; and the Turks traded with the neighbouring cultivators, some of whom were Turks, some Chinese, and some Iranian (Tadzhiks, Persians). Neighbouring Chinese, Iranians, and the farmers of Central Asia similarly depended on the herders for pastoral products, being bound together in great institutional networks of economic exchange, their products distributed in the bazaars and caravan trade and collected and offered as political tribute—actions of great economic significance. Marriage ceremonies also were occasions for ritual presentations and gifts in localized exchanges. The great institutional networks embraced the entire Asian continent, as well as parts of Europe and North Africa during the period of the nomadic empires in the Middle Ages. The most highly specialized relation was that of the Mongols and the Chinese; the former monopolized the herding, the latter the farming of east Asia. Their symbiotic system was not a smoothly working mechanism; it broke down frequently, accompanied by wars and unrest among the great economic wings and civilizations.

Social organization. The Central Asian Turks and Mongols had the same kinship system, founded upon the principle of common descent reckoned patrilineally, from father to son. The founding father and his son or sons formed a kin-village community, together with their wives, children, more distant collateral kin, dependents, and clients. The villages were maintained by the direct male descendants over a number of generations, forming new ones as the population grew and the need for land increased. Families related by descent and marriage lived in a common household, raised the crops or herds together, and maintained a common economy. Several such great families, whose founders were related as brothers or close cousins, formed a village. Each family owned stock and land in common; the agricultural village was the unit of management of the cultivated land and the irrigation channels; the nomads' village was the unit of range (pasture, camp, and track) management.

Marriage rules

A son brought his wife to the paternal household; the daughter joined that of her husband and his father. Marriage with several wives was practiced, but it was costly and rare. In arranging marriages, elders would trace ancestry back to the sixth generation and even further. In theory, a marriage was permitted only if there was no common male ancestor in or nearer than the sixth generation. This restriction meant that a marriage partner had to be found not only out of the village, but out of the neighbouring villages or districts, because these villages were generally composed of kinsmen descended from a common male ancestor only four or five generations removed. The kin-community clusters formed a local district and had a number of economic functions, managing the pastoral range land, maintaining local resources and pasture tracks, and fending off incursions. They also provided troops of horse to the imperial armies when levies of men were made.

The village of the sedentary agricultural peoples of Central Asia was likewise composed of patrilineal extended families, but the long lineage organization of the herdsmen was not found there. Marriage outside the peasant village community was nevertheless required; the husband took his wife to the father's household; and the daughter left the family into which she was born to join that of the husband, under the patriarch, his father. The peasant villages were bound to the political system of the Oriental empires, which centred on the great cities.

Political organization. At the base of the Mongol empire of Genghis Khan, which flourished in the 13th and 14th centuries, stood the nomadic kin communities that were clustered in groups, tracing descent through the male line from a common male ancestor and living on a common territory. These descent groups formed a clan ruled by a chief. The clan chief was a relative in the father's line of every member of the clan. He was a minor nobleman and the senior member of the highest line traced back according to the principle of primogeniture to the founding ancestor. The differentiation into aristocracy and commoners began at this point. The clans were grouped into clan confederations, and these in turn into principalities, with the nobility becoming ever grander. At the peak stood the emperor, who was related in theory to every Mongol in the first to 20th degree or even higher. He was, however, also surrounded by courtiers and retainers, warriors who respected neither kinship nor grandeur in carrying out the imperial commands. The Mongol empire ruled briefly over most of Asia and eastern Europe when the strength of the herding peoples prevailed over the agricultural empires whose leadership was broken down. Life in the villages below went on as before.

The peasant villages were linked in local exchange systems with the herding communities; the empires of herdsmen and agriculturists were linked in great, continent-wide exchange institutions. When these institutions of trade, tribute collection, and exchange broke down, one side would sweep in and conquer the other. Thus Genghis Khan and his dynasty prevailed during the 13th century. China then was using its soldiers to maintain internal order and could not keep the nomads out. The horsemen came to trade, but instead they took the agricultural produce they wanted and retained the stock they had intended to exchange. The nomad chief returned from the encounter doubly enriched, and this attracted further braves to his standard. The increased wealth and armed might enabled him to extend his conquests further. The pattern on different scales and with some variations in products is encountered again in the west of Asia, between Kazakhs, Uzbeks, Tadzhiks, Turkmens, and Iranians.

Relationship between the city and peasantry. The agricultural principalities centred on the great cities of Central Asia, such as Samarkand, Bukhara, and Khiva, all known for their magnificence. Their wealth was based on the labour of the peasantry. At times their hegemony embraced the surrounding pastoral peoples; at times the pastoral dynasties swept in and conquered the city-based empires. The cities usually tempered and civilized the nomad conquerors, so that after a few years their dynasties were no different from any other.

City centres

The cities were the centres of rulership over the agricultural domains, at times over those of the pastoralists as well, alternating between dynasts of one or the other provenience. The cities served as the centres of trade and exchange between the products of the herdsmen and the soil cultivators; also, they served as the centres for the great transcontinental exchange between China, India, and the West; hence their wealth. They were also local manufacturing centres, particularly of the sumptuary ware of the courts: the jewels, silks, brocades, rugs, tiles, and metalwork that were the wonder of the world. The separation between town and countryside was not so pronounced as in the modern day, and the opposition between peasants and townsmen was not so deep as that found, for instance, in European history. The peasants engaged in manufacture and in cottage industries such as spinning and weaving. The nomads worked in leather, felt, and other pastoral products. All brought their goods to the bazaars and caravanseries of the cities for trade. The cities were also international trade centres, typically for the medieval Silk Road linking China and the Mediterranean across Central Asia. Gardens and orchards were cultivated by the urban populations within and immediately without the city walls. During the 14th to 16th centuries there were no greater centres for astronomy, mathematics, medicine, history, theological doctrine, metaphysical speculation, and poetry.

The great Oriental monarchies were built around the urban centres. Land was cultivated by the peasantry living in the village communities. The monarchs taxed the peasants heavily, but solely to maintain themselves, their court, and their army. Nothing was spent on the health, education, or welfare of the subjects. The only other enterprise in which the monarchic power and the peasantry interacted occurred when the central power mobilized the peasantry to clean the irrigation canals.

Religions of Central Asia. The religious leaders of the Turks and Mongols were shamans. The shaman is a figure who induces a state of trance in himself, wherein he believes that he communicates with the spirits of the supernatural world. He then performs rites of divination and makes oracular pronouncements about the outcome of a hunt or of battles; and he dispels the evil spirits that cause disease and bring misfortune to men and beasts. As the Turks and Mongols came into increasing contact with the great civilizations of Asia, their shamanist practices and beliefs became intermingled with those of the great world religions, particularly Buddhism and Islām. Buddhism, originating in India, became implanted in Tibet and then in Mongolia. It gained influence among the Mongols as their relations to the Chinese and Tibetans were intensified and diminished when the contacts faded. The Mongols were converted in some degree to Buddhism in the 13th and 14th centuries; its role among them retreated in the 15th and 16th centuries; but they were converted again in the 1590s, and its influence remains among them today.

Buddhism and Islām

The forms of Buddhism are many. The Mongolian form is that of Tibet, founded on the existence on earth of the perpetual reincarnation of the Buddha. The Dalai Lama is the "Living Buddha," the head of the cult. His chief officers are manifestations on earth of the lesser members of the Buddhist pantheon, who intercede on behalf of the salvation of the devout. The entire cult centres on a system of monasteries governed by abbots and staffed by monks who perform the rituals of the faith and in turn are supported by its followers. It is now a state church in the Mongolian People's Republic.

Islām came to western and Central Asia within a few decades of the *hijrah,* or emigration, of the Prophet Muḥammed in AD 622. It has been the traditional religion of the Turks and Tadzhiks for more than 1,200 years. Most of the Muslims are Sunnī, as opposed to the Shīʿa of Iran and to the Ismāʿīlīs, a sect represented by a few small tribes in the mountains of Tadzhikistan, but more importantly in Afghanistan and Pakistan. The tradition of Islām was rigidly followed in the cities and sedentary villages of central Asia and more liberally or freely observed in the nomadic communities. Women went veiled in the cities, less so in the villages, and not at all in pastoral encampments. The doctrine was fully debated in the cities, but superficially, if at all, among the peasants and herdsmen; there were many mullahs, or clerics, in the cities, but few in the villages, and fewer still among the nomads. The great urban mosques and *ʿulamā*'s (religious colleges) were centres not only of prayer but also of learning—primarily theology and, to some extent, philosophy and of the sciences.

The religious systems of Buddhism and Islām involved Central Asia in a great set of institutions and institutional relations that bound the area to similar institutions of east and south Asia (in the case of Buddhism) and to the Middle East (in the case of Islām). These institutional networks of the Buddhist monasteries and of the Islāmic mosques and religious foundations (*waqf*) and orders (brotherhoods of monks and preachers) traced out paths across the entire continent similar to the economic and political networks of institutions. In addition to religious conversions of entire countries and transfer of cults and belief systems from one part of the world to another, the widespread movement of people, ideas, world views, science, and technology resulted. Whole populations were brought from the Middle East to Central Asia in the wake of the Islāmic conquest and conversion. Primitive peoples in the refuge areas of the mountains and the Arctic were brought into contact with the literate civilizations to the south, east, and west. And the great literate civilizations were brought into contact with one another, Central Asia serving as the zone of contact. The means for bringing this active contact was not any vague process of diffusion; instead, it was the network of trade routes, the institutions of political rulership, and those of the world religious systems.

The contemporary cultures. The Turks and Mongols of Central Asia are all parts of the Soviet Union and of the Peoples' Republics of China and Mongolia. The traditional ways of life have been radically changed by the revolutionary processes of the 20th century. Since the 1920s, millions of Russians and other peoples from different parts of the U.S.S.R. have been settled in Central Asia, continuing a process begun in the 19th century. The surviving remnants of older regimes, such as the khanates of Bukhara and Khiva, have been replaced by the Soviet political system. As a consequence, the profound divergencies and symbiosis between cultivators and pastoralists have been virtually eradicated. The two great cultural wings have been caught in a single institutional system emanating from the Soviet regime.

Modern agriculture

Central Asian agriculture continues to require artificial irrigation, and the same crops are raised: the cereal grains (wheat, rice), cotton (of improved sorts), vegetables, hemp and other fibres, fruits and melons. The agricultural production of Soviet Central Asia today, however, is carried on not by the family or the village but by a system of state and collective farms. Tractors and trucks have advanced the mechanization of agriculture. The agricultural population still lives in villages of sun-dried brick, but electric power is everywhere. The pastoral practices of Central Asia and Mongolia have been rationalized. The herds now consist of great flocks or herds of one type of animal, instead of mixed combinations as of old, because the family no longer maintains the old pastoral practices; teams of herders are now employed. The family used to need animals in a definite proportion; now the herding family lives in a settled village and the herders go off to ranges with the animals for pasturing (transhumance). They no longer live in tents but in the same kinds of houses and villages as the tillers of the soil.

The Islāmic faith is much restricted, the number of colleges and mosques reduced, and the brotherhoods and foundations absolutely banned. The Buddhist monastic system is sharply reduced in Mongolia: at one time, it is guessed, the monasteries included one-third of all the males of the country; today there are only two major monasteries, numbering together but a few score monks. Religious proselytization is restricted throughout the region.

Soviet Central Asia is organized into the union republics of Uzbekistan, Tadzhikistan, Kirgiziya, and Turkmenia; the Kara-Kalpak A.S.S.R. is a part of Uzbekistan. Each republic bears the name of one of the major peoples of the region. Kazakhstan is included with these republics in the ethnographic accounts. Russians form the majority of the population of Kazakhstan, and they are second in number to the native people in each of the other republics. The Russian migration into the area has accompanied a vast effort, begun in the 1930s, to collectivize the agriculture and the herding according to the Soviet pattern, and to nationalize all the land for farming and herding and all the manufacturing and mining industry. The cities have been built up along modern lines, and transportation has been modernized. The Russian population has been closely associated with the new developments, as well as with the Soviet administration. The capitals and other cities of the region are at once administrative centres of the Soviet system and centres of industry, trade, education, the arts, and public entertainment. The natural resources of Central Asia are intensively exploited, including oil, iron ore, coal, and nonferrous metals. Railroads and airfields have replaced the caravans of old.

Modern social forms

The ancient lineage and clan systems have been entirely forgotten. The genealogies are no longer kept up because their function in social organization, marriage, and military and economic activities is no longer applicable in modern Central Asia. The great extended families, under a patriarch's dominion, have been replaced by the new forms of the family, small in size and composed of parents and their children. The father of the family is typically a wage earner in a factory or state farm. The children now go to school in the Soviet educational system, rather than, as before, in the schools run by the Islāmic or Buddhist clergy. Modern technology is being introduced throughout the region, and modern medical, educational and welfare practices have been instituted. The desire of parents to have many children in order to have someone to take care of them in old age is no longer a deeply felt social incentive; medical practices have reduced infant mortality so that the need to have many children in the hopes that a few would survive to care for the parents has likewise been reduced as a social force in child breeding. These trends hold equally for pastoralists and cultivators, for the old differences in institutional organization between them have been eradicated by the broad trends of modernization and collectivization. (L.Kr.)

History

In its historical application the term Central Asia designates an area that is considerably larger than the heartland of the Asian continent. Were it not for the awkwardness of the term, it would be better to speak of Central Eurasia, comprising all those parts of the huge Eurasian landmass that have not developed a distinctive, sedentary civilization of their own. Europe, the Middle Eastern civilizations (both Semitic and Iranian), India, and East Asia surround Inner Asia, limited in the north by the Arctic, its only natural boundary. But because the hearts of men stake out frontiers more clearly than do mountains, streams, or deserts, the real boundaries of Central Asia are determined at any given time in history by the relationship between the "civilized" and the "barbarian"—the two opposed but complementary. The equation so often propounded—of the civilized with the sedentary and the barbarian with the nomad—is misleading, however, and does not correspond to historical reality. The most significant distinction between the two groups in Eurasia lies probably in the successful attempt of the civilized to alter and command his physical environment, whereas the barbarian simply uses it, often in a masterly fashion, to his own advantage. In its essence, the history of Central Asia is that of the barbarian, and its dominant feature is the sometimes latent, sometimes open conflict in which he clashes with the civilized. Following the tides of history, the area of Central Asia is subject to fluctuations. In the rhythm of expansion and contraction, it is possible to detect the two basic patterns of conquest: that of the barbarian—accomplished with arms and ephemeral in his results—and that of the civilized—slow, rather unspectacular, achieved through absorption and assimilation.

The principal difficulty for the historian of Central Asia lies in the paucity and relative lateness of indigenous written sources. The first aboriginal sources—written in a Turkic language—date from the 8th century AD, and source material of similar value does not become available again until the 13th century. Most of the written sources dealing with Central Asia originate in the surrounding sedentary civilizations and are almost always strongly prejudiced against the barbarian; the most important among them are in Chinese, Greek, Latin, Arabic, and Persian.

Without a sufficient number of indigenous written sources, the language of a given Central Asian people is difficult to determine. It is, however, reasonable to suppose that many of them spoke a Uralic or an Altaic language, and it can be taken for certain that Paleo-Asiatic languages were in wider use in early times than they are now. While it seems likely that the principal languages of many great nomadic empires were Turkic or Mongol,

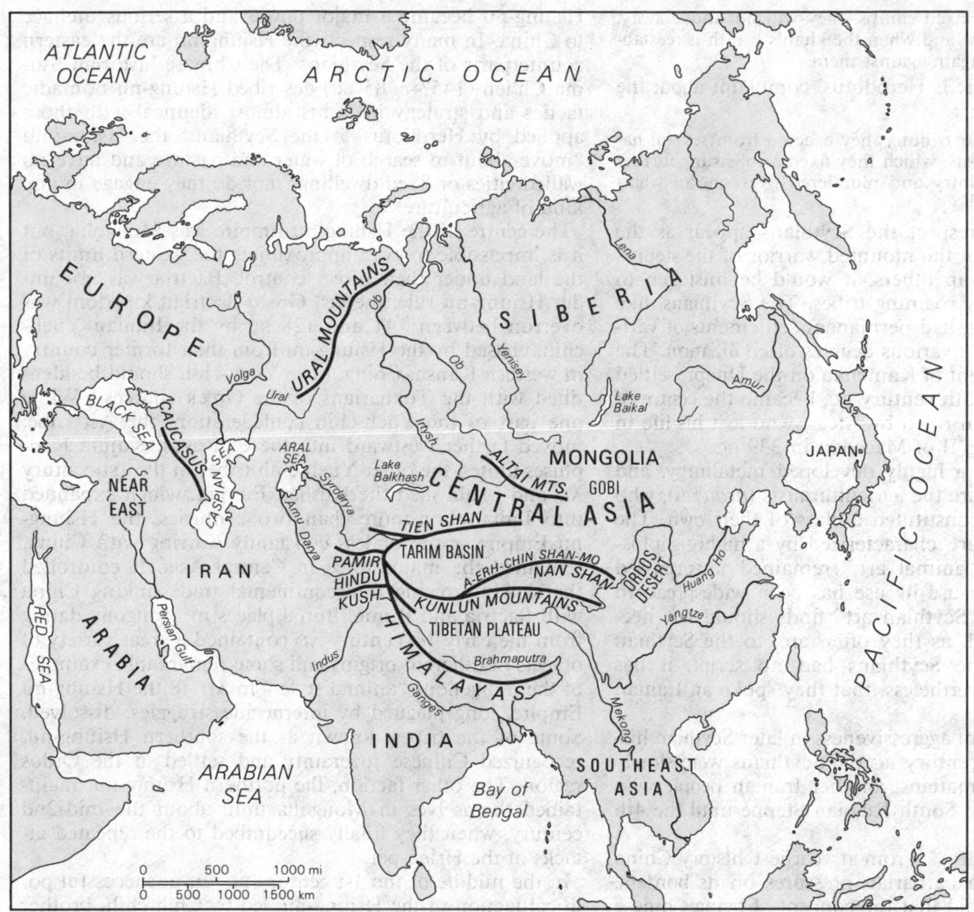

Major physical features of Central Asia (Central Eurasia).

the attribution of such languages to peoples about whose speech insufficient linguistic evidence exists—as in the case of the Hsiung-nu or the Avars—is unwarranted and misleading; it is wiser to confess ignorance.

Role of the forest belt and the steppe

Two of the natural vegetation zones of Central Asia have played a prominent part in history: the forest belt, 500 to 1,000 miles (800 to 1,600 kilometres) wide, and, south of it, the steppe, a vast grassland extending from Hungary to Mongolia, facilitating communications and providing grass, the only raw material absolutely essential to the creation of the great nomad empires. The northern frozen marshes and the southern deserts played a minor role in Central Asian history.

PREHISTORY AND ANTIQUITY

The beginnings of human's history in Central Asia date back to the late Pleistocene Epoch, some 25,000 to 35,000 years ago, which includes the last full interglaciation and the last glaciation period, the latter being followed by the interglaciation that now exists. The Aurignacian culture of the Upper Paleolithic coincided with the last glaciation period, which was much less severe in northern Asia than in Europe. At a period when ice covered northern France, Siberia below 60° latitude was ice-free. The Paleolithic Malta site, 28 miles (45 kilometres) northwest of Irkutsk, is clearly Aurignacian, and it is safe to assume that in this period Siberia and the sub-Arctic areas of Europe belonged to the same civilization. The differentiation between Central Asia and the surrounding civilization did not begin until Neolithic times, marked by tremendous technical progress and a wide diversification of cultures. This article does not deal with their development or indicate their contacts with eastern, southern, and western cultures; most of the archaeological results, however important, are controversial and are subject to different interpretations in the light of new finds.

Early western peoples. The first human groups to emerge at the dawn of history that are identifiable by name rather than by their artifacts are the Cimmerians and the Scythians, both located in the western half of Central Asia and reported on by the Greeks.

The Cimmerians. The Cimmerians, whose name appears in the *Odyssey* of Homer, occupied the South Russian Steppe from about 1200 BC. Their civilization, which belongs to the Late Bronze Age, is barely distinguishable from that of other peoples with whom they mingled.

The Scythians. From the second half of the 8th century BC, the Cimmerians were replaced by the Scythians, who used iron implements. The Scythians created the first known typical Central Asian empire. The chief thrust of their expansion was directed against the south rather than the west, where no major power existed and which thus offered little chance for important booty. In the late 8th century BC, Cimmerian and Scythian troops fought against the Assyrian king Sargon II; and, at the end of the 6th century BC, a violent conflict arose between the Scythians and the Achaemenid king Darius I.

Herodotus' description of the Scythians

Darius' expedition (516?–513? BC) against the Scythians in south Russia was described in great detail by the Greek historian Herodotus, who provided the first and perhaps the most penetrating description of some characteristics of a great nomad empire. His praise of the Scythian horse, "which always put to flight the horse of the enemy," and his description of Scythian reluctance to engage in direct, open combat and of their preference to harass the enemy are, among others, *loci classici,* applicable to virtually all nomad empires. Herodotus showed the essential conservatism of Central Asian civilization. The Scythian argument against towns, allegedly put to Darius and reported by Herodotus, "We Scythians have neither towns nor cultivated lands, which might induce us, through fear of their being taken or ravaged, to be in any hurry to fight with you," has its counterpart in Mongol thinking of the 13th century AD. When, in AD 1226, because of Genghis Khan's illness the Mongols hesitated to attack the Tanguts of China, the campaign was postponed on the ground that

The Tangut people have cities surrounded with earthworks and fixed camps. They will not pick up and carry away their

> walled-in cities, their fixed camps, they will not move away. Let us leave them now and when the khan's health is reestablished we will move again against them.

Equally characteristic is Herodotus' complaint about the Scythians' "insolence":

> For besides the regular tribute, they exacted from several nations additional imposts, which they fixed at pleasure; further they scoured the country and plundered everyone of whatever they could.

In more than one respect the Scythians appear as the historical prototype of the mounted warrior of the steppe; yet in their case, as in others, it would be mistaken to see in them aimlessly roaming tribes. The Scythians, like most nomad empires, had permanent settlements of various sizes, representing various degrees of civilization. The vast fortified settlement of Kamenka on the Dnepr, settled since the end of the 5th century BC, became the centre of the Scythian kingdom ruled by Ateas, who lost his life in a battle against Philip II of Macedon in 339 BC.

The Scythians had a highly developed metallurgy, and in their social structure the agriculturalists (*aroteres*), who grew corn for sale, constituted a class of their own. The quality of Scythian art, characterized by a highly sophisticated style called "animal art," remained unsurpassed in Central Asia. Because its use has been widespread in time and in space, "Scythian art" finds should not necessarily be attributed, as they often are, to the Scythian people. Although the Scythians had no script, it has been established, nevertheless, that they spoke an Iranian language.

There is little trace of aggressiveness in later Scythian history. From the 4th century BC the Scythians were slowly absorbed by the Sarmatians, another Iranian people who were to dominate the South Russian Steppe until the 4th century AD.

Early eastern peoples. From its earliest history China had to contend with barbarian pressures on its borders. In fact, it could be said that the concept of being Chinese was created in opposition to the concept of the barbarian. The group of barbarians called the Hu thus played a considerable role in early Chinese history, leading to the introduction of cavalry and the adoption of foreign clothing, more suitable than its traditional Chinese counterpart for new types of warfare. Around 200 BC a new and powerful barbarian people emerged on China's western borders, the Hsiung-nu. Little is known of T'ou-man, founder of this empire, beyond the fact that he was killed by his son Mao-tun, under whose long reign (*c.* 209–174 BC) the Hsiung-nu became a major power and a serious menace to China. In many respects the Hsiung-nu are the eastern counterparts of the Scythians. The Chinese historian Ssu-ma Ch'ien (145?–*c.* 85 BC) described Hsiung-nu nomadic tactics and strategy in terms almost identical with those applied by Herodotus to the Scythians: the Hsiung-nu "move about in search of water and pasture and have no walled cities or fixed dwellings, nor do they engage in any kind of agriculture."

Emergence of the Hsiung-nu

The centre of the Hsiung-nu Empire was Mongolia, but it is impossible to even approximate the western limits of the land under their direct control. Bactria was not under Hsiung-nu rule; the last Greco-Bactrian kingdom was overrun between 141 and 128 BC by the Iranian Yüeh-chih, chased by the Hsiung-nu from their former country in western Kansu, China. (The Yüeh-chih should be identified with the Tokharians of the Greek sources.) While one part of the Yüeh-chih confederation, the Asi tribe, moved farther westward into the Caucasus, Kujūla Kadphises united the other Yüeh-chih tribes in the 1st century AD and established the Kushan Empire, which expanded into India.) For more than two centuries, the Hsiung-nu Empire, more or less constantly warring with China, remained the major force in Central Asia. It controlled the slowly growing transcontinental trade linking China with Bactria and Rome. Burial places in Mongolia dating from the early 1st century AD contained a great variety of objects of different origins and some remarkable examples of the indigenous "animal style." In AD 48 the Hsiung-nu Empire, long plagued by internecine struggles, dissolved. Some of the tribes, known as the southern Hsiung-nu, recognized Chinese suzerainty and settled in the Ordos region. The other faction, the northern Hsiung-nu, maintained themselves in Mongolia until about the mid-2nd century, when they finally succumbed to the repeated attacks of the Hsien-pei.

In the middle of the 1st century BC, an unsuccessful political faction of the Hsiung-nu, led by Chih-chih, brother and rival of the ruler, moved westward. With the death of Chih-chih in 36 BC, this Hsiung-nu group disappeared from sight; but, according to one theory that has been put forth, the Huns who appeared on the South Russian Steppe (*c.* AD 370) were descendants of these fugitive tribes.

THE MIDDLE AGES

The last decades of the 4th century AD saw the formation of a new, powerful empire in Mongolia, the political heartland of Central Asia. The Juan-juan had stepped into

Adapted from A. Hermann, *An Historical Atlas of China*

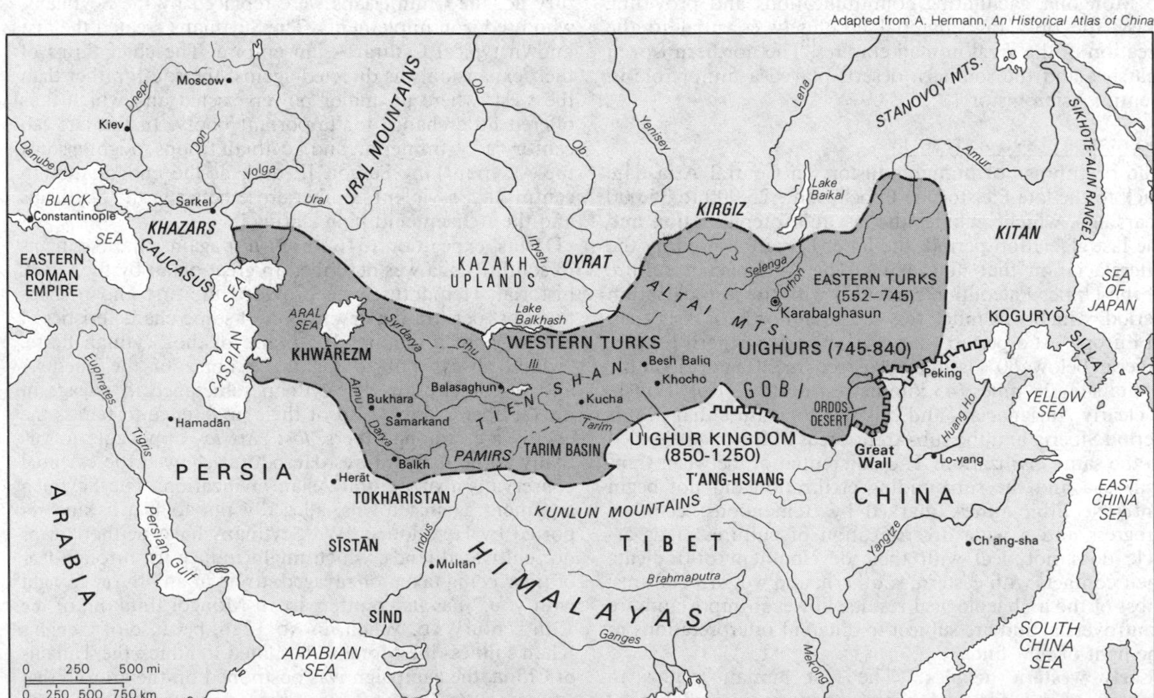

Central Asia in the Middle Ages.

the place vacated by the Hsiung-nu. Chinese descriptions barely distinguish them from their predecessors. Their history is an incessant series of campaigns against their neighbours, especially the Chinese.

The Turks. In 552 the Juan-juan Empire was destroyed by a revolution of considerable consequences for world history. The tribe of the Turk (T'u-chüeh in Chinese transcription), living within the Juan-juan Empire and apparently specializing in metallurgy, revolted and seized power. It established an empire that for about two centuries remained a dominant force in Asia. The Turks are the first people in history known to have spoken a Turkic language and the first Central Asian people to have left a written record. Inscribed funerary stelae still standing in Mongolia, mostly near the Orhon Gel (Orhon River), are invaluable from both a linguistic and a historical point of view. These inscriptions give a Turk view of the creation and provide insights into the internal stresses of a pastoral nomad state that, at the height of its power, stretched from the borders of China to those of Byzantium.

Division of the empire. The founder of the Turk Empire, Bumin—who bore the title of khagan—died shortly after his victory. Soon afterward the empire split into two halves. The eastern part, ruled by Bumin's son Muhan (ruled 553–572), centred on Mongolia; the seat of the western part, ruled by Bumin's brother Ishtemi (ruled 553–573?), lay in Ektagh, an unidentified place, possibly in the Ili or Chu valley. In alliance with the Sāsānids, the Turks attacked and destroyed the Hephtalite Empire (560), thereby gaining control over an important portion of the Silk Road leading from China to Byzantium. Persian reluctance to allow free passage to the Sogdian merchants, who on behalf of the Turks handled the transcontinental trade, led the Turks to seek direct contacts with Byzantium. In 567 a Turk embassy led by the Sogdian Maniakh arrived in Constantinople and was received by the emperor Justin II, who was interested in possible allies situated east of his enemies, the Sāsānids. A series of embassies and counterembassies followed, but they failed to bring about an effective military alliance against the Sāsānids. Under Ishtemi's successor, Tardu (ruled 573–603), the western Turk Empire continued to thrive and, in its westward expansion, reached the borders of Byzantium. In a letter to the emperor Maurice in 598, Tardu refers to himself as "the chief of the seven races and lord of the seven climates of the world." Indeed, by that time the eastern Turk Empire was facing grave difficulties caused partly by internal strife and partly by the vigorous Central Asian policies of the Chinese Sui dynasty. While the weakening of eastern Turk power gave preponderance to the western Turks, it would seem that basic solidarity between the two parts of the Turk Empire was maintained. They both fell victim to Chinese attacks. In 630 the T'ang emperor T'ai Tsung occupied Mongolia, and in 659, under Kao Tsung, Chinese forces penetrating as far west as Bukhara and Samarkand subdued the western Turks.

Turk revolt against the Chinese

Reunification. In 683 the Turks revolted. The Turk Empire was reborn and reunified under the khagan Eltérish (ruled 683–692). Temporary setbacks notwithstanding, the Turk Empire was now centred on Mongolia, and it prospered under the rules of Kapaghan (ruled 692–716) and Bilge (ruled 716–734) but disintegrated soon afterward. In spite of the relatively short duration of their state, the historical role of the Turks is considerable. They linked China, Iran, India, and Byzantium and gave their name to all the Turkic-speaking peoples. The solidarity that exists between these peoples to this day goes back to the Turks.

The Uighurs. The replacement of the Turks by the Uighurs in 745 was little else than a coup d'etat. There was virtually no difference between the Turk and Uighur languages, and the bulk of the Turks, although no longer the ruling stratum, probably remained within the boundaries of the newly formed Uighur state.

The Uighur Empire. This new empire comprised many tribes and seems to have been headed by a smaller tribal confederation standing under Uighur leadership. This federation is referred to in Chinese sources as the Nine Clans, whereas Islāmic sources and the inscriptions of the Orkhon call it the Nine Oğuz (Tokuz Oğuz). There are some indications that the Uighur Empire stood under dual leadership, the khagan belonging to one tribe and the prime minister, in whose hands much of the effective power rested, to another.

Relations with China were the dominant factor in Uighur foreign affairs. The Uighurs proved somewhat less cumbersome for the Chinese than had the Hsiung-nu or the Turks. Their help to the Chinese, plagued by the An Lushan Rebellion and by repeated Tibetan incursions, was appreciated and paid for through trade conducted on terms unfavourable to China. In exchange for Uighur horses, often of dubious quality, the Chinese were expected to provide the Uighurs with much-coveted riches. The third Uighur khagan—Mou-yü by his Chinese name (ruled 759–780)—visited Lo-yang in China, where he was converted to an Iranian religion, Manichaeism. Its adoption brought to the Uighur land many Sogdians, whose growing influence on state affairs was resented by the Turkic Uighurs and led to Mou-yü's assassination.

The Uighur Empire was governed from a city, Karabalghasun, the foundations of which were probably laid under the Turks and can still be seen. A Muslim traveller, Tamīm ibn Baḥr, who visited the city around 821, speaks in admiring terms of this fortified town lying in a cultivated country—a far cry from the traditional picture of the pastoral nomad existence.

The Kirgiz invasion. In 840 another Turkic people, the Kirgiz, put an abrupt end to Uighur rule in Mongolia. Coming from the upper reaches of the Yenisey, the Kirgiz represented a lower degree of civilization than the rather sophisticated Uighurs. Their political ambitions did not lead them into campaigns against China, and thus virtually no records exist concerning their activities. Content to stay in the backwaters of history, the Kirgiz are among the very few peoples to have survived the Mongol tide; today theirs is one of the constituent republics of the Soviet Union.

End of Uighur rule in Mongolia

The Uighur kingdom. The Kirgiz invasion, while putting an end to Uighur power, did not annihilate the people. Fleeing Uighur groups settled on the Chinese border in Kansu Province and in Eastern Turkistan in the Turfan region, which had been an Uighur protectorate since the end of the 8th century. Falling back now on the Turfan oases and setting up their capital city in Khocho (Kao-ch'ang, today Karakhoja), the fugitive Uighurs created a remarkably stable and prosperous kingdom that lasted four centuries (*c.* 850–1250). Because of the dry climate of the region, many buildings, wall paintings, and manuscripts written in a great variety of languages have been preserved. They reveal a complex, refined civilization in which Buddhism, Manichaeism, and Christianity lived side by side, practiced by Turks as well as by Tokharians, Sogdians, and other Iranian peoples in the region.

When the time of the Mongol conquests came, the Uighurs lived up to their best cultural traditions. Realizing that resistance would be vain and would only lead to the destruction of his country, Barchuk, the ruler of the Uighurs of Khocho, of his own free will submitted to the Mongols. Uighur officials and scribes were the first "civil servants" of the Mongol Empire and exerted a beneficial civilizing influence on the conquerors. The Sogdian script used by the Uighurs was adopted by the Mongols, who in turn passed it on to the Manchus. Side by side with the Cyrillic alphabet it is still in use in Mongolia.

The Khitans. The first people known to have spoken a Mongol language were the Khitans. Mentioned from the 5th century AD, this people, living in the forests of Manchuria, had contacts with the Turks as well as with the Uighurs. In 924 their leader, A-pao-chi, defeated the Kirgiz and offered the Uighurs the possibility of a resettlement in their former country. The Khitans conquered northern China, which they ruled under the dynastic name Liao (907–1125) until they were ousted by the Tungus Juchen, also originating in Manchuria, who founded the Chin dynasty (1115–1234) of northern China, which was in turn replaced by that of yet another Altaic people, the Mongols. Cathay, an early western denomination of China, goes back to the name Khitan (variant: Kitai). The spread of this name, still used in Russian for China, is but one sign of the Khitans' extraordinary impact on history.

The Khitans' impact on history

Driven from China by the Juchen, in 1124 some Khitans moved westward under Yeh-lü Ta-shih's leadership and created the Karakitai (Black Kitai, or Western Liao) state. Its centre lay in the Semirechye and the Chu Valley, where the city of Balāsaghūn was located. Founded by the Sogdians, Balāsaghūn was by then occupied by the Muslim Qarakhanids —a Turkic people descended from the Karluks and closely related to the Turks and Uighurs—who, in the middle of the 8th century, had moved west to the Semirechye. In Balāsaghūn, in 1070, the *Kutadghu Bilig* was written, a lengthy didactic poem, the first product of Turkic literature to show Islāmic influence.

The Seljuqs were another Turkic people on whose land the Karakitai set their eyes. An Oğuz tribe, the Selijuqs moved to the Syrdarya Valley during the 10th century, took the name of their leader, and converted to Islām. They soon became a major factor in the history of the Muslim world. In 1137 Yeh-lü Ta-shih received the submission of the Qarakhanid ruler Maḥmud, and in 1141, in a battle fought near Samarkand, he decisively defeated the Seljuq sultan Sanjar. The Karakitais thus established themselves in Transoxania, whence they exerted considerable political influence on Khwārezm. Their rule was shattered in 1211 through the joint action of Küchlüg, a Naiman prince fleeing from the Mongols, and ʿAlāʾ ad-Dīn Muḥammad, ruler of Khwārezm.

The Mongol epoch. The creation of the Mongol empire by Genghis Khan was a great feat of political and military skill that left a lasting imprint on the destinies of both Asia and Europe. The geographical basis of Genghis' power, the northwestern parts of which later became known as Monglia, had been the centre of such Turkic empires as those of the Turks and Uighurs. There are no indications of the time and the manner in which the Mongols took over this region.

Creation of the Mongol Empire. It is probable that Turks were incorporated in the nascent Mongol Empire. In a series of tribal wars that led to the defeat of the Merkits and the Naimans, his most dangerous rivals, Genghis gained sufficient strength to assume, in 1206, the title of khan. Acting in the tradition of previous nomad empires of the region, Genghis' aggressive policies were directed primarily against China, then ruled in the north by the Juchen Chin dynasty. His western campaigns were set in motion quite accidentally by a senseless attack on Mongol forces by the fugitive Naiman prince Küchlüg, and they maintained their momentum through the pursuit of ʿAlāʾ ad-Dīn Muḥammad of Khwārezm, who, in 1218, ordered the execution of Mongol envoys seeking to establish trade relations. As a result, many of the flourishing cities of Khwārezm, Khorāsān, and Afghanistan were destroyed, and by 1223 Mongol armies had crossed the Caucasus. Although an important Russo-Kipchak force was defeated May 31, 1223, at the Battle of the Kalka, the Mongols did not make a definite thrust into eastern Europe until the winter of 1236–37. The fall of Kiev in December 1240—with incalculable consequences for Russian history—was followed by a Mongol invasion of Hungary in 1241–42. Though victorious against the forces of King Béla IV, the Mongols evacuated Hungary and withdrew to southern and central Russia. Ruled by Batu (died *c.* 1255), the Mongols of eastern Europe (the so-called Golden Horde) became a major factor in that region and exerted a decisive influence on the development of the Russian states.

Mongol thrust into eastern Europe

Simultaneously with these western campaigns, Genghis' successor Ögödei (reigned 1229–41) intensified Mongol pressure in China. Korea was occupied in 1231, and in 1234 the Chin dynasty succumbed to Mongol attacks. The establishment of the Mongol Yüan dynasty in China (1206–1368) was accomplished by the great khan Kublai (ruled 1260–94), a grandson of Genghis.

Mongol rule. The great khan Möngke (ruled 1251–59), who had sent his brother Kublai to conquer China, entrusted another of his brothers, Hülegü, with the task of consolidating the Mongol hold on Iran. In 1258 Hülegü occupied Baghdad and put an end to the ʿAbbāsid caliphate. He laid the foundations of a Mongol state in Iran, known as that of the Il-Khans, which, under Abagha (ruled 1265–82), Arghun (ruled 1284–91), Ghāzān (ruled 1295–1304), and Öljeitü (ruled 1304–15), became both powerful and highly civilized. Although practically independent, the Il-Khans of Persia remained loyal to Möngke and Kublai, but with the passing of Kublai—the last of the great khans still rooted in Mongol soil—the Persian drift toward full independence grew stronger. With Ghāzān's decision to make Islām the state religion—a gesture intended to gain the confidence of the majority of his subjects—a big step toward integration in the purely Iranian (as opposed to Mongol) tradition was taken. A lengthy conflict that opposed the Il-Khans to the Mamlūks of Egypt was not resolved until 1323, when a peace was concluded between the sultan al-Malik an-Nāṣir and Abū Saʿīd (ruled 1316–35), the last of the Il-Khans. After Abū Saʿīd's death the Il-Khanid state, no longer held together by Mongol efficiency, disintegrated.

In Iran and China, the Mongol states that linked their destinies to those of "major" civilizations were gradually losing their identity. But in the steppes of Central Asia, the descendants of Chagatai and Ögödei, sons of Genghis, maintained an old-fashioned, steppe-oriented policy, increasingly opposed to the "progressive" wing represented in China and Iran by the descendants of Genghis' youngest son, Tolui. After Möngke's death, the steppe candidate Arigböge lost his bid for supreme power to Kublai; further attempts to re-establish the centre of Mongol power in the steppe also failed. The most active and successful protagonist of this policy was Kaidu, a grandson of Ögödei, who made several attempts to carve out an empire for himself from lands ruled by other Mongol princes; he extended his control over Transoxania, the Ili region, and Chinese Turkistan, and in 1269 he even assumed the title of great khan. The Chagataid khans, to some extent victims of this policy, for lack of better alternatives lent some support to Kaidu; but, after Kaidu's death in 1301, the Chagataid khan Duwa hastened to make his peace with his Mongol kin in both Iran and China. In a letter written to Philip the Fair of France in 1305, the Il-Khan Öljeitü referred to this peace as a portent for universal peace—an overly optimistic statement in view of the many conflicts in the Mongol world, let alone elsewhere.

The Golden Horde

Development within the Golden Horde was on different lines. Its Islāmization, begun under Batu's successor Berke (ruled 1257–67), led to tensions with the Il-Khans but created strong links with the Mamlūks of Egypt, themselves of Kipchak origin. The prosperity of the Golden Horde under ʿAbd Allāh Khan Özbeg (Uzbek; ruled 1313–41) stands in sharp contrast to the disintegrating Il-Khanid state, yet it had its own problems, both internal and external. From within, the growing and unavoidable antagonism between a ruling class that was Muslim-Mongol, but de facto largely Turkic speaking, and the local Christian-Russian elements was aggravated by dissensions within the ruling class. In foreign policy the peace concluded in 1323 between the Il-Khans and the Mamlūks weakened the Golden Horde's influence in Egypt, and the establishment of Ottoman power in the Dardanelles (1354) put a virtual end to the commercial relations between the Volga and the Nile valleys. Perhaps the gravest political mistake of the rulers of the Golden Horde was their failure to recognize that the West—with which, through the Russians, they had excellent links—offered a more fertile ground for further development than the sunbaked deserts of Turkistan. The khans of the Golden Horde, instead of ruling over Russian and Lithuanian princes, were increasingly relying on their help in internal struggles that were rending the state asunder. While their eyes were turned southward, they allowed the rise of dangerous enemies—Russians and Lithuanians—in their rear. The policies of the khan Tokhtamysh (ruled 1377–95) differed from those of his opponents; he enlarged his power base by uniting the Golden Horde with the so-called White Horde, situated farther eastward in West Siberia and on the lower reaches of the Syrdarya. He thus introduced some fresh "steppe power" into the relatively stale, unimaginative military machinery of the Golden Horde. Furthermore, instead of seeking the help of petty eastern European princes, he hitched his wagon to the rising star of Timur, with whose support Tokhtamysh reasserted Mongol supremacy in Russia.

The aftermath of Mongol rule. Probably Turkic-speaking, and yet claiming to restore the empire of Genghis, Timur emerged from the general anarchy that characterized Central Asia in the second half of the 14th century. Not certain of his own legitimacy, Timur enthroned puppet emperors, on whose behalf he pretended to act. His whole life was spent in campaigns, among which those against his former protégé Tokhtamysh (defeated in 1395), the Delhi sultanate (1398–99), and Anatolia (1400–02) stand out. Timur's victory over the Ottoman sultan Bayezid I in a battle near Ankara (July 20, 1402) gave much-needed respite to Byzantium and eastern Europe, seriously menaced by the Ottomans. Timur's death in 1405 ended an era of almost two centuries characterized by Central Asian attempts to create huge if not universal empires. Yet, by the end of the 14th century, the dismemberment of the Mongol Empire was almost complete. After the fall of the Il-Khanids (1335) and the Yüan (1368), only the Golden Horde survived of Genghis' heritage. Itself torn by internal dissensions, the Golden Horde disintegrated in the 1430s, its place taken by the successor khanates of Kazan, Astrakhan, and the Crimea.

Dismemberment of the Mongol Empire

The khanate of Kazan, a multinational and multilingual state, had a relatively short span of life. Its rulers—among whom Mahmutek (ruled 1445–66) was particularly successful—did their best to maintain Kazan's independence in the face of Crimean and Muscovite pressures. When, in 1521, the Crimean Giray dynasty obtained that one of its members, Sahib Giray, be enthroned in Kazan, Ivan IV the Terrible, of Russia, thought the time had come to put an end to Tatar (Mongol) rule in central Russia. In 1552 he occupied Kazan, and, only four years later, he established his rule over Astrakhan, securing thereby for himself the waterway to the Caspian Sea. Under the rule of the Girays, the khanate of Crimea survived until 1783, when it was absorbed by Russia. Moscow continued to pay an annual tribute to the Tatars until 1681.

The 15th century was relatively peaceful on the borderland between Iran and Central Asia. Timur's son Shāh Rokh Mīrza (ruled 1407–47) in Herat and Shāh Rokh's son Ulugh Beg in Samarkand established centres of civilization that continued to flourish until at least the end of Husain Baykara's (ruled 1469–1506) beneficent rule in Herat. The Timurids, turned sedentary, now constituted a protective layer defending Iran from the barbarians still beyond the pale—the Uzbeks united by Muḥammad Shaybānī. Muḥammad was killed in battle in 1510, but his descendants maintained their grip on Transoxania until the end of the century. The reserves of nomadic power represented by the Uzbeks, however cumbersome, no longer constituted a serious menace to the existence of strong, sedentary states such as those of the Ṣafavids of Persia or the Ottomans, both capable of repulsing attacks coming from the steppe. Ottomans and Ṣafavids, bitterly opposed to one another, clashed in the Battle of Chāldirān (August 23, 1514); the use of firearms gave the former a decisive victory. Thus appeared in the wings of the Central Asian scene the faceless protagonist of centuries to come: the gun.

THE MODERN PERIOD: THE AGE OF DECADENCE

From the beginnings of recorded history, pastoral nomadism, practiced on a grandiose scale, was the economic basis of the great Central Asian empires. Once the domestication of the horse was sufficiently advanced to allow for its use in warfare, the superiority of the mounted archer over the foot soldier or the war chariot was never effectively challenged.

The waning of nomadic military power. When headed by capable leaders, well-trained and disciplined mounted troops were almost invincible. The sedentary civilizations could not, by their very nature, put aside for breeding purposes pastures sufficiently large to sustain a cavalry force that could equal that of the pastoral nomads; hence the latter's military superiority remained a constant for about 2,000 years of Eurasian history.

At its highest degree of development, Central Asian nomad society constituted a very sophisticated and highly specialized social and economic structure, advanced but also highly vulnerable because of its specialization and the lack of diversification of its economy. Geared almost entirely to the production of war material—*i.e.*, the horse—when not engaged in warfare it was unable to provide the people with anything but the barest necessities of life. To ensure their very existence, Central Asian empires had to wage war and obtain through raids or tributes the commodities they could not produce. When, owing to circumstances such as severe weather decimating the horse herds or inept leadership, raids against other peoples became impossible, the typical Central Asian nomad state had to disintegrate to allow its population to fend for itself and secure the necessities for a subsistence. Hunting and pastoral nomadism both need vast expanses to support a thinly scattered population that does not naturally lend itself to strong, centralized political control. The skill of an Central Asian leader consisted precisely in the gathering of such dispersed populations and in providing for them on a level higher than they had been accustomed to. There was but one way to achieve this: successful raids on other, preferably richer, peoples. The military machinery was dependent on numbers, which then precluded self-sufficiency. In case of prolonged military reverses, the nomadic aggregation of warriors had to disband because it was only in dispersion that, without recourse to war, they were economically autonomous.

Social and economic structure of nomad society

In the course of the 15th century, the steppe territory suitable for great horse herds began to shrink. In the east the Yung-lo emperor of the Ming led five major campaigns against the Mongols (1410–24), all successful but none decisive. Yet when, under the leadership of Esen Khan (1439–55), the Mongol Oirats pushed as far as Peking, they found the city defended by cannons, and they withdrew. In the Middle East, as noted above, the Ottoman and Ṣafavid states barred the road to the no longer invincible nomad cavalry, and, along the western borders of Central Asia, the Russians were soon to start on their decisive and irresistible march across Central Asia to the borders of China, India, and Iran.

The Russian conquests. Their most spectacular advance into Central Asia carried the Russians eastward through the forest belt, where the hunting and fishing populations offered little resistance and where the much-coveted fur of Siberia could be found in abundance. Acting on behalf of the merchant family Stroganov, in 1578 or 1581 the cossack Yermak moved across the Urals and defeated the Shaybānīd prince Kuchum, who alone represented organized political power in Siberia.

The Russian advance from west to east across Siberia, motivated by commercial rather than political considerations, remains unparalleled in history for its rapidity. The native Finno-Ugric—Samoyed or Tungus hunters accustomed to paying their fur tribute—were little concerned with the nationality of the tax collectors and found dealing with the Russians no more unpleasant than with Turks or Mongols. Russian penetration was marked by the building of small forts, such as Tobolsk (1587) near the former capital of Kuchum, Tara (1594) on the Irtysh, and Narym (1596) on the upper Ob. The Yenisey was reached in 1619, and the town of Yakutsk on the Lena was founded in 1632. Around 1639 the first small group of Russians reached the Pacific in the neighbourhood of present-day Okhotsk. About 10 years later, Anadyrsk was founded on the shores of the Bering Sea, and, by the end of the century Kamchatka was annexed. When advanced Russian parties reached the Amur around the middle of the 17th century, they entered the Chinese sphere of interest; although some clashes occurred, restraint on both sides led to the signing of the treaties of Nerchinsk (1689) and Kiakhta (1727), which remained in force until 1858. To this day the border delineated at Kiakhta has not been altered substantially. It is important to note that Russian occupation of Siberia did not entail the extinction of the native population. Although outnumbered by the colonists as early as the beginning of the 18th century, it continued to grow and, at an estimate, quadrupled since the beginning of the Russian conquest. Many of these peoples have kept their language and their distinctive national identity and, within the framework of the Soviet system, are autonomous.

The thorniest question to be dealt with in the early Russo-Chinese negotiations concerned the Mongols—wedged between the two great powers—who, in the course of the 16th and 17th centuries, reasserted their control over most of the steppe belt. In the 15th century the western Mongols, or Oirats, had become quite powerful under Esen Khan; but, under the strong leadership of Dayan Khan (ruled 1488–1507) and his son Altan Khan (1507–82), the eastern Mongols—and more precisely the Khalkha tribe—gained ascendancy. In 1552 Altan took possession of what was left of Karakorum, the old Mongol capital. Altan's reign saw the conversion of a great many Mongols to the tenets of the Yellow Hat sect of Tibetan Buddhism, a religion that, until the 1920s, played a major role in Mongol life. Ligdan Khan's (ruled 1604–34) attempts to unite the various Mongol tribes failed not only because of internal dissensions but also on account of the rising power of the Manchus, to whom he was forced to surrender. The active Central Asian policy of China's Manchu Ch'ing dynasty brought a lasting transformation in the political structure of the region.

Mongol resurgence

More distant from China, the Oirats could pursue a more independent course. In 1616 one of their tribes, the Torguts, moved westward and settled on the lower reaches of the Volga, where they became known by the name of Kalmyk. The land on which they settled was nominally under Russian control, and the Kalmyks, jealously guarding their independence, were ready to serve the Tsar in his undertakings against the Kazakh and other Turkic tribes. Losing ground to the steady advance of Russian settlers, some Kalmyks tried to return to their former territory, by then under Chinese rule. After a gruelling journey begun in 1770 or 1771, about half of those who set out reached China and were settled in the Ili Valley.

During the century and a half that had elapsed since the Torgut emigration to the Volga, their Oirat brethren had had an eventful history. One of their tribes, the Dzungars, under the leadership of Galdan (ruled 1676–97), created a powerful state that remained a serious menace to China until 1757, when the Ch'ien-lung emperor defeated their last ruler, Amursana, and thus put an end to the last independent Mongol state prior to the creation, in 1921, of Outer Mongolia (the Khalkha princes had submitted to the Manchus in 1691).

The treaties of Nerchinsk and Kiakhta established the northern border of the Chinese zone of influence, which included Mongolia. In the wars against the Dzungars, the Chinese established their rule over Eastern Turkistan and Dzungaria. China's western boundary remained undefined, but it ran farther west than it does today and included Lake Balkhash and parts of the Kazakh Steppe.

Wedged between the Russian and Chinese empires, unable to break through the stagnant but solid Ottoman and Ṣafavid barriers, the Turkic nomads of the steppe lying east of the Volga and the Caspian Sea and south of Russian-occupied Siberia found themselves caught in a trap from which there was no escape. If there is cause for surprise, it lies in the lateness rather than in the fact of the ultimate Russian conquest.

Muḥammad Shaybānī's death did not end Uzbek supremacy in the territories to the south and the east of Lake Aral. Three small, independent Uzbek khanates—from west to east: Khiva, Bukhara, and Kokand—shared the land and vied with one another and with outside foes. To the west of them, between Lake Aral and the Caspian Sea, were the nomad Turkmens, notorious robbers who roamed the inhospitable land. In many respects similar to the Turkmens but better organized, the Kazakhs, since the 17th century divided into three "hordes," nomadized between the Volga and the Irtysh. During the 16th and 17th centuries, they fought Oirats and Dzungars but succeeded in holding their own, and in 1771 Ablay, ruler of the "central horde," located west of the Balkash, was confirmed as ruler both by China and Russia. Yet Russian expansion, motivated by the urge to get closer to the Indian Ocean, forced the Kazakhs to yield. Although some Kazakh leaders, such as the sultan Kinesary, put up spirited resistance (1837–47), the line of the Syrdarya was reached by the Russians toward the middle of the 19th century.

The Uzbek khanates

The Uzbek khanates, militarily less significant and farther from Moscow, survived until the 20th century. Khiva, under the rule of Abulghazi Bahadur Khan (ruled 1643–63), a learned and beneficial ruler, knew a prosperity that was not to return. It became a Russian protectorate in 1873, although the local Kongrat dynasty was not removed until 1920. After the time of the Shaybānīds, Bukhara was ruled successively by two dynasties, the Astrakhanids (1599–1747) and the Mangits (1747–1868). The latter had to recognize Russian suzerainty in 1868 but remained in charge of some local affairs until 1920. Of the three khanates, only Kokand was annexed by Russia (1876).

The passing of the three Uzbek khanates should not lead to an underestimation of the real achievements of Central Asia. Although their destruction was the direct result of foreign military intervention, the time was ripe for their demise. Insignificant and narrowminded, they were not worthy of the finest Central Asian tradition. The 14th-century Chinese scholar Wang Li, in his remarks about the Mongol Empire, characterized it well:

> All the territory within the Four Seas had become the domain of a single family, civilization had spread throughout, and all barriers were removed. . . . Fraternity among the races had reached a new zenith.

(D.Si.)

Under Russian rule. The Russian conquests in Central Asia had given the tsars control of a vast area of striking geographical and human diversity, acquired at relatively little effort in terms of men and money. The motives for the conquest had not been primarily economic; peasant colonization of the virgin steppes and the systematic cultivation of cotton were later developments. The factors that determined the Russian advance into the area were both complex and interrelated. They included the historic pull of the frontier, the thirst for military glory on the part of the officer corps, and the fear of further British penetration into Central Asia from across the Indus, as well as the infectious rhetoric of imperialism common to the age. From the outset, Russia's objectives as a colonial power were strictly limited: to maintain "law and order" at minimum cost and to disturb as little as possible the traditional way of life of its new subjects. Such an approach was favoured by the remoteness of the area and its isolation even from the rest of the Muslim world. It was improbable that an almost wholly illiterate population, its prejudices formed by a venal and obscurantist *'ulamā'* (class of Muslim theologians and scholars), could offer any concerted resistance to the Russian presence; and such, indeed, proved to be the case. The Russians, like other colonial powers, did experience an occasional uprising, generally of a very localized character, but the overwhelming military superiority displayed by the Russians at the time of the initial conquest, the inability of the inhabitants

Motives for conquest

From P. Holt, A. Lambton, and B. Lewis (eds.), *Cambridge History of Islam*, vol. 1 (1970); Cambridge University Press

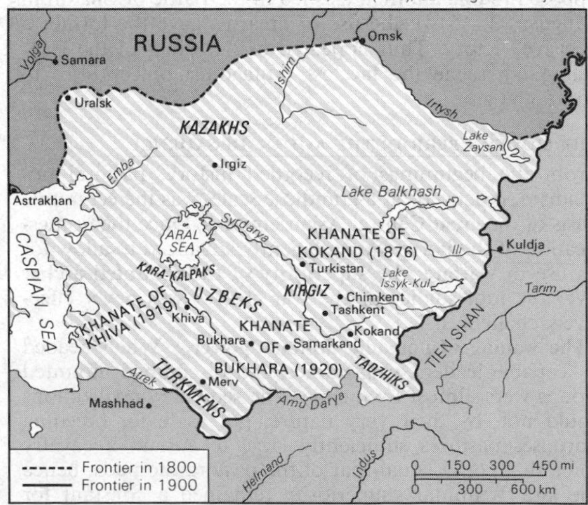

Russian penetration of west Central Asia in the 19th and 20th centuries.

of the khanates to offer effective resistance, and the heavy-handedness with which subsequent insurrection or insubordination was dealt with ensured minimal opposition. Finally, by preserving the titular sovereignty of the emir of Bukhara and the khan of Khiva, they left a substantial part of the population, especially the urban classes, most deeply devoted to the Islāmic way of life, under traditionally minded Muslim rulers.

Tsarist rule. Yet the Russians, whether intentionally or not, became agents of change throughout the area in much the same way as any other colonial power. The economy was gradually realigned to meet the Russian need for raw materials and new markets. This required the construction of railroads: by 1888 the Trans-Caspian Railroad had reached Samarkand; between 1899 and 1905 the Orenburg-Tashkent Railroad was completed; the Turkistan-Siberian Railroad came later, begun just before World War I and not completed until 1930. In Tashkent and Samarkand new European suburbs were laid out at a distance from the walled native cities, but as in the case of the newly established garrison towns, such islands of European life required local services and supplies. Nor did the Russians wholly ignore the welfare of their new subjects. An effort was made, halfheartedly at first, to put down the indigenous slave trade; irrigation projects were initiated; and bilingual elementary education was cautiously introduced. As elsewhere in colonial Asia, the work of Russian scholars studying the literature, history, and antiquities of the Central Asian peoples aroused upon the part of a numerically small but influential Russian-educated elite, especially among the Kazakhs, nostalgic awareness of a colourful past and a sense of national, or cultural, identity.

Kazakh response to Russian rule

Of the major racial groups in Central Asia—Uzbeks, Kazakhs, Turkmens, Tadzhiks, and Kirgiz—the Kazakhs were the first to respond to the impact of Russian culture. Their early contacts with their new masters had in the main been carried out through intermediaries—Kazan Tatars, who, paradoxically, had contributed to strengthening the Kazakhs' awareness of being part of a greater Muslim world community and their sense of being a "nation" rather than a welter of tribes and clans. Moreover, through the Tatars they were exposed to current Pan-Turkish and Pan-Islāmic propaganda. In the 1870s the Russians countered Tatar influence by establishing bilingual Russian-Kazakh schools, from which emerged a westernized elite of considerable distinction. The time seemed ripe for a meaningful process of cultural interchange, made more credible by the fact that, despite the growing sense of Kazakh national identity, the Kazakhs were too much on the peripheries of the Islāmic world to feel strongly the pull of Pan-Islāmic or even Pan-Turkish sentiment.

This Russo-Kazakh "dialogue" was, however, doomed to founder on the rock of the government's policy of settling peasants from European Russia and the Ukraine on the Kazakh steppe, where agricultural settlement on an extensive scale could be undertaken only by curtailing the area available for grazing by the nomads' livestock and by restricting their seasonal migrations. As early as 1867–68 the northwestern fringes of the Kazakh steppe had been the scene of violent protests at the presence of colonists; but it was not until the last decade of the century that the movement got fully under way with the arrival of upward of 1,000,000 peasants, resulting in the inevitable expropriation of Kazakh grazing grounds and in savage conflict between the Kazakhs and the intruders. Finally, in 1916, during World War I, the Kazakhs, driven to desperation by the loss of their lands and by the ruthlessness of the wartime administration, rose up in protest against a decree conscripting the non-Russian subjects of the empire for forced labour. The rebellion assumed the character of a popular uprising, in which many colonists and many more Kazakhs and Kirgiz were massacred. The revolt was put down with the utmost savagery, and more than 300,000 Kazakhs are said to have sought refuge across the Chinese frontier.

With the collapse of tsarist rule, the westernized Kazakh elite formed a party, the Alash-Orda, as a vehicle through which to express their aspirations for regional autonomy. Having found during the Russian civil war that the anti-Communist "Whites" were implacably opposed to their aspirations, the Kazakhs cast in their lot with the "Reds." After the war the Kazakhs were granted their own republic, in which, for the first few years, the leaders of the Alash-Orda maintained a fairly dominant position and were active in protecting Kazakh interests; after 1924, however, direct confrontation with the Communist Party became more intense, and in 1927–28 they were liquidated as "bourgeois nationalists."

The Kazakh republic

The history of the Kazakhs in the first half of the 20th century was bleak indeed—expropriation of their grazing lands under the tsars, the bloody uprising and reprisals of 1916, the losses in the civil war and in the famine in 1921, purges of the intelligentsia in 1927–28, collectivization during the 1930s, and further peasant colonization after World War II.

In Transoxania, divided between the administration of the Russian governor general of Turkistan, based on Tashkent, and that of the emir of Bukhara and the khan of Khiva, opposition to colonial domination was centred in the most conservative elements of a profoundly Islāmic society—the ʿ*ulamā*ʾ and the inhabitants of the bazaar. Nonetheless, the Russian favoured, for reasons of expediency, the preservation of the traditional social framework and endeavoured, with only partial success, to insulate the inhabitants of the region from contact with the more "advanced" Muslims of the empire—the Volga and Crimean Tatars. In this they were aided by the fact that the virtual absence of European colonization provided no fuel for popular resentment comparable to that felt by the Kazakhs; and, in consequence, the westernized products of the bilingual Russian–Uzbek educational system, primarily concerned with reform of the Islāmic way of life, regarded the Muslim "ultras" as their most dangerous opponents.

If the main influence in shaping the outlook of the Kazakh intelligentsia was the educational system imported from European Russia, the catalyst in the case of the Uzbeks was knowledge of the educational reforms and the Pan-Turkish ideology of the Crimean Tatar renaissance of the late 19th century. The Uzbek reformers, known as Jadidists, advocated the introduction of a modern educational system as a prerequisite for social change and cultural revitalization; and despite intense opposition from the clerical classes, they opened their first school in Tashkent in 1901 and by 1914 had established more than 100. After 1908, influenced by the Young Turks of the Ottoman Empire, the Young Bukharans and the Young Khivans worked for a program of radical institutional change in the ramshackle governments of the khanates. By 1917, however, it may be doubted whether the Uzbek intelligentsia had made any substantial impact outside a fairly narrow circle of like-minded persons.

Soviet rule. Neither before nor after the Russian Revolution of 1917 were the nationalist aspirations of the Muslims of Central Asia compatible with the interests of the Russian state or those of the European population of the region. This was demonstrated once and for all when the troops of the Tashkent Soviet crushed a short-lived Muslim government established in Kokand in January 1918. Indeed, the Soviet authorities in Central Asia regarded the native intelligentsia, even the most "progressive" of them, with lively and (from their point of view) justifiable apprehension. At the same time there was the problem of an active resistance on the part of conservative elements, which was anti-Russian as much as anti-Communist. Having extinguished the khanate of Khiva in 1919 and that of Bukhara in 1920, local Red Army units found themselves engaged in a protracted struggle with the Basmachis—guerrillas operating in the mountains in the eastern part of the former khanate of Bukhara. Not until 1925 did the Red Army gain the upper hand.

In time, however, the Soviet Union came to realize that armed insurrection was far less dangerous to the new regime than the adherence to local Communist parties of members of the Muslim intelligentsia—former nationalists turned Marxists, suspected of harbouring separatist and Pan-Turkish designs. This indigenous leadership was therefore systematically liquidated during the 1930s.

Elimination of local leaders

Thereafter, the Soviets continued to reinforce the administrative and cultural autonomy of Kazakhstan, Uzbekistan, Turkmenistan, Tadzhikistan, and Kirgizia with a view to eliminating Pan-Turkish or Pan-Islâmic sentiment through a policy of "divide and rule." It would be unwise, however, not to recognize the positive advantages accruing to the inhabitants of Russian Central Asia as a result of the Soviet Union's federal structure or to underestimate the scope that it has allowed for the cultural development of each individual republic. (G.R.G.H.)

Kazakhstan

Stretching across the rolling tablelands of the heart of the Eurasian landmass, the Kazakh Soviet Socialist Republic (or Kazakhstan) has been since December 5, 1936, one of the 15 constituent republics of the Soviet Union. It is bounded by the People's Republic of China on the east; by the Kirgiz and Uzbek S.S.R.'s on the south; by the Caspian Sea and a small portion of the Turkmen S.S.R. on the west; and by the Russian S.F.S.R. on the north. It covers 1,049,200 square miles (2,717,300 square kilometres), an area larger than that of Algeria. It stretches about 1,200 miles (1,900 kilometres) from east to west and 800 miles (1,300 kilometres) from north to south. The capital is at Alma-Ata.

The ancient nomadic way of life in this part of the world has been changed greatly during the Soviet period. Industry, particularly the extractive industries, now plays the major role in the economy of Kazakhstan, the republic functioning as an important supplier of raw materials for the entire Soviet Union. Agriculture, however, continues to be of significance. The transformation was accompanied by an influx of settlers—the Kazakhs themselves now form only slightly more than a third of the population. Urbanization, too, is increasing, but many traditional customs have been preserved, side by side with such incursions of modernity as the Soviet cosmodrome, or space-launching centre, Baykonyr, near Leninsk.

PHYSICAL AND HUMAN GEOGRAPHY

The land. *Relief.* Although it exhibits a variety of relief forms, Kazakhstan is essentially a tableland. Lowlands account for more than a third of the total area, hilly plains and plateaus for nearly half, and mountainous regions make up barely 20 percent. The highest point is Khan-Tengri Peak, on the border between Kazakhstan and Kirgiziya. The lowest point in the whole Soviet Union is found in the Karagiye salt depression of the east Caspian region.

The Caspian Depression

The western and southwestern portions of the republic are dominated by the Caspian Depression (Prikaspiyskaya Nizmennost), south of which lies the Ustyurt Plateau and, on the Mangyshlak Peninsula, the Karatau and Aktau mountains. Farther east, the Ural Plateau and its extension, the Mugodzhar Hills, separate the Caspian Depression from the extensive Turan Plain, while the Aral Sea lies to the south. The rivers that lose themselves in this region have deposited vast amounts of sand, forming the Greater and Lesser Barsuki deserts in the north, the Aral region of the Kara-Kum Desert in the centre, and the sandy Kyzylkum desert in the south. Most of the deserts retain some vegetative cover, fed by subterranean groundwater.

Central Kazakhstan is an undulating upland, having depressions filled by salt lakes, the water of which has largely evaporated. In the north, the mountains reach about 5,000 feet (1,500 metres), and there are similar high areas in the west (the Ulutau Mountains) and in the east (the Chingiz-Tau Range).

In the east and southeast, high mountain massifs are furrowed by valleys. The Altai mountain complex to the east sends three ridges—the Listvyaga, Kholzun, and Tigirek—into the republic, and, farther south, the Tarbagatay Range is a similar offshoot of the Narym-Kolbin complex.

Another range, the Dzhungarian Alatau, penetrates the republic to the south of the depression containing Lake Balkhash. The Tien Shan rises along the southern frontier with the Kirgiz S.S.R., and, to their northwest, the much lower Chu-Ili Mountains and the Karatau Range are penetrated by the Muyunkum Desert.

Drainage. The republic has more than 7,000 streams and rivers, most of them part of the inland drainage systems of the Caspian and Aral seas and lakes Balkhash and Tengiz. The major exceptions are the Irtysh, Ishim, and Tobol, which flow across Kazakh territory and ultimately drain to the Arctic. Many of the other rivers cease to flow in summer or wander through salty lagoons. In addition to the Irtysh in the northeast, the major rivers include the Ural in the west and the Syrdarya in the south.

The Irtysh River

Every year the Irtysh discharges some 988,000,000,000 cubic feet (28,000,000,000 cubic metres) of water into the vast West Siberian catchment area, and the Irtysh-Karaganda Canal will ultimately divert 8 percent of this mass of water into central Kazakhstan. The only major tributary of the Irtysh is the Bukhtarma. The Ural winds its way along a wide, flood-prone valley dotted with lakes; the Syrdarya, rising in the Tien Shan, is vital to Kazakh agriculture, several dams having been built to prevent floods and aid irrigation. Its major tributary, the Arys, irrigates more than 500,000 acres (200,000 hectares).

The rivers of the east and southeast are swollen by melting snow and by glaciers, of which there are more than 1,500, covering more than 800 square miles (2,070 square kilometres). Kazakhstan also contains about 48,000 small lakes, most of which have variable water levels, and some of which dry up periodically. The Caspian Sea is the largest inland body of water in the world, and Kazakhstan has 1,450 miles (2,320 kilometres) of its coastline. The other large bodies of water are the Aral Sea and Lake Balkhash, followed by Zaysan, Alakol, Tengiz, and Seletytengiz.

Climate. The climate is sharply continental, especially in the plains and valleys, with hot summers alternating with equally extreme winters. Temperatures fluctuate remarkably: the average January temperature in northern and central regions ranges from 3° to −2° F (−16° to −19° C), and in the south from 23° to 29° F (−5° to −1.4° C), while the average July temperatures range from 68° F (20° C) in the north to 84° F (29° C) in the south. Absolute temperatures have been recorded at −49° F (−45° C) and 113° F (45° C), with desert-sand temperatures occasionally reaching 158° F (70° C). Precipitation ranges from eight to 12 inches (200 to 300 millimetres) in the north and centre to 16 to 20 inches (400 to 500 millimetres) in the southern mountain valleys, although it rises to twice the latter figures in the high ranges and falls to one-fifth in the deserts.

Strong, dry winds are common in the northwest and in the centre of the country, and mountain valleys (*e.g.*, the Dzungarian Gate) are often hit by hurricane-like winds.

Plant and animal life. The rich, black chernozem soils of the north account for about 7 percent of the total area; farther south they are replaced by fertile chestnut-brown soils and steppe areas (about 26 percent), and these give way to infertile alkaline soils (35 percent) consisting of sands and saline clays; there are also saline solonchak soils. Wind-blown loess soils are found in the Dzhambul and Chimkent regions. Kazakhstan has 74,000,000 acres (30,000,000 hectares) of arable land, with cultivation most highly developed on the chestnut-brown soils of the northern steppes. Other cultivated areas fringe the mountains on the south and east, and, where irrigation and reclamation are feasible, extend along river valleys into the deserts.

Plant life

Steppes and deserts dominate the landscape, the vegetation of the latter including wormwood and tamarisk. Wormwood is also found in the drier steppes, along with feather grass. The wooded area is very small (about 3 percent of Kazakh territory).

The fauna of Kazakhstan includes 155 mammal species, including antelope, elk, and, in the mountains, wolf, bear, and snow leopard. Ermine and sable have commercial importance. The rivers and lakes contain many fish species, including carp, perch, pike, and white salmon, and sprats and trout have become acclimatized. The fishing industry also makes use of the sturgeon, herring, and roach of the Caspian.

Settlement patterns. Kazakhstan's varied historical heritage has given rise to distinct regional patterns of settlement. Large villages, centres of collective and state farms (*kolkhozy* and *sovkhozy,* respectively) characterize the northern steppes, forming green oases separated by wheat fields, often situated along a stream or on a lake shore. The more arid steppes, semideserts, and deserts also contain large villages, housing the state farms of sheep breeders, while *chabany,* or herdsmen, live in temporary settlements made up of yurts, tents made of felt. The foothills are fringed by a string of village settlements, clustering along highways and surrounded, in the north, by fields of wheat and sugar beets and, in the south, by orchards, vineyards, and fields of melons.

Urban settlements are of two types: older communities such as Alma-Ata, Semipalatinsk, Petropavlovsk, and Uralsk, which have one- and two-storied houses and whole districts of modern multistoried buildings; and entirely new, planned towns such as Karaganda, Ust-Kamenogorsk, and Rudny, with wide, straight thoroughfares, tall buildings, and fringing industrial areas.

The people. The Kazakh people—Muslims, who speak a Turkic language but are Mongol in physical type—were never the exclusive inhabitants of Kazakhstan; and in the late 20th century they made up only about one-third of the total population, the Russians outnumbering them. There are also Ukrainians, Germans (deported from the Soviet west to Central Asia in 1941), Tatars, Uzbeks, Belorussians, Uighurs, Dungans, Koreans, and others. About half of the total population live in urban areas.

Immigration

About 400,000 Russians arrived in Kazakhstan before 1897. Some Uighur and Dungan settlers (both Muslim) also appeared there in the last third of the 19th century (after Russia conquered Kazakhstan) and settled in the south and in the Alma-Ata and Taldy-Kurgan regions, to the east. Some Uzbeks and Kirgiz also inhabited the Chimkent and Dzhambul regions in the south. The main immigration, however, took place in the first third of the 20th century. More than a million had come to the area by 1916 and remained. Large numbers of Russians, Ukrainians, Belorussians, Mordvins, Germans, Bulgarians, Poles, Jews, and Tatars, most of them non-Muslim, moved in, first from the tsarist and then from the Soviet west. Koreans were transported by Joseph Stalin's orders from the Soviet Far East to Central Asia. Immigration by additional settlers occurred mainly between 1954 and 1956, as a result both of industrialization and of the Virgin and Idle Lands program.

The population is very unevenly distributed, with highest densities in the developed agricultural regions of the north and southeast. Since World War II, as a consequence of rapid industrialization, there has been a great movement to the urban areas. This process occasioned an urban housing problem, which was attacked by the development of a building industry, using industrialized methods, and an intensive regional planning program.

A notable feature of the urbanization process has been the fact that it involved an influx of people from other republics rather than a movement (of young people, for example) from the countryside. Major factors in this respect have been the virtual monopolizing of urban and industrial employment by Russians and other outsiders and, to some extent, the modernization of agriculture, which demands skilled, well-educated manpower. During the mid-1950s, there was even an exodus from the towns to the Virgin Lands areas.

Like its neighbouring Central Asian republics, Kazakhstan has one of the highest birth rates in the Soviet Union.

The economy. During the Soviet period, the economy of Kazakhstan has become characterized by industry and mechanized agriculture, and the republic acts as a major supplier of raw materials for other parts of the Soviet Union.

Resources. The development of the economy has been determined largely by the availability of natural resources. More than 90 different minerals have been discovered in the republic. Copper, in central Kazakhstan and the Aktyubinsk *oblast;* lead, zinc, and silver in the Rudny Altai, the Dzhungarian Alatau, and the spurs of the Karatau; tungsten and tin in the Kolbin Ridge and the southern Altai; chromite, nickel, and cobalt in the Mugodzhar Hills; titanium, manganese, and antimony in the central regions; vanadium in the south; and gold in the north and east are the most important.

Mineral wealth

Iron ore is worked in the Karaganda and Kustanay *oblasti,* and an extensive iron-ore basin has been prospected in the east; phosphorite deposits lie beneath the Karatau Mountains, and borates and other salts are worked in the deposits at Inderborsky. The leading coalfields lie in the Karaganda, Turgay, Ekibastuz, and Maykuben basins, while the Mangyshlak Peninsula and the Caspian Depression are promising regions for oil and gas. The republic also contains other reserves, ranging from asbestos to molybdenum, while its building materials include marble and limestone.

Industry. Industry is now the leading branch of the Kazakh economy, though it engages less than one-tenth of the indigenous Kazakhs, most industrial manpower being supplied by Russians and other Slavs. Cast iron, steel, rolled metal, cement, and mineral fertilizer are manufactured, as well as consumer goods. There are steelworks in Temirtau and Karaganda. Kazakhstan's nonferrous industry, concentrated in the east, holds first place in the Soviet Union for lead production and second for copper.

Fuel production is on the increase; the main coalfields include those in the Karaganda Basin and Ekibastuz. The discovery of petroleum deposits in the Mangyshlak Peninsula stimulated oil production from the late 1960s onward.

The building industry is vital, and prefabricated construction has become as important as traditional methods. Manufacturing was stimulated during World War II, and Kazakhstan's plants now range from the automatic press factory at Chimkent to the X-ray equipment centre at Aktyubinsk.

Meat-packing plants are widespread; creameries are found chiefly in the north and east, and sugar refineries in the Alma-Ata, Dzhambul, and Taldy-Kurgan *oblasti.* Grain milling, brewing, and wine making are also important, as are fruit- and vegetable-canning plants. Newer industries include a synthetic-fibre plant at Karaganda and pharmaceutical manufacturing at Chimkent.

Agriculture. Agriculture still occupies almost half the population, and the republic has about 2,100 state and about 390 collective farms, most of the former in the central and northern regions, and the latter in the south and east. Grain-growing state farms represent more than a third of these farms, and another third are occupied in sheep raising. Also raised are cattle, goats, pigs, and poultry.

Arable farming, not introduced until the 1880s, is now very important, with grain crops alone accounting for almost two-thirds of Kazakhstan's gross agricultural output. The republic is also a leading Soviet producer of fodder and industrial crops, potatoes, vegetables, and melons. The principal grain-producing areas are the rolling plains of the north, which produce up to a third of all wheat grown in the Soviet Union. In the south, fruits, vegetables, melons, sugar beets, rice, and grapes predominate.

Granary regions

Transportation. The great distances, scattered industrial centres, and developing extractive industries of Kazakhstan mean that transportation plays a critical role. The railways take most of the total freight turnover. Kazakhstan is crossed by long sections of the Trans-Siberian, South Siberian, and Turkistan–Siberian trunk lines, among others, while the Orenburg–Tashkent line serves the west and south.

Some traffic is also carried on highways and rivers. The bulk of passenger traffic is by air, and air transport provides a vital link between Kazakhstan and the rest of the Soviet Union. There is also an air network connecting regional centres and minor settlements, including individual collective and state farms.

Kazakhstan also possesses an extensive network of pipelines, including the Guryev–Orsk and the Uzen–Zhetybay–Shevchenko oil pipelines. Important sections of Soviet trunk oil pipelines also cross the republic.

Administrative and social conditions. *Government.* According to the constitution of the Kazakh Soviet Socialist Republic, adopted on March 24, 1937, all power in the republic belongs to working people, with a socialist system, based on state ownership of the means of production, forming its economic foundation. The highest legislative

The socialist state

body, which possesses no real power in the Soviet political system, is the Supreme Soviet of the Kazakh S.S.R., selected (no opposing candidates compete with a single list) every four years and meeting for a short period semiannually. Its members select a Presidium, composed of a chairman, three deputy chairmen, a secretary, and 15 members, to function between the widely spaced sessions of the Supreme Soviet.

Local government operates through *oblast,* district, city, village, and *aul* (Kazakh village) soviets, selected for two-year terms.

The republican Supreme Soviet also generates the Council of Ministers, which coordinates and supervises the work of republican ministries and agencies. The chairman of the Supreme Soviet of the Kazakh S.S.R. serves also as a vice chairman of the union-wide Supreme Soviet, which meets in Moscow, and the chairman of the republican Council of Ministers also serves in the Council of Ministers of the Soviet Union.

Political life in the republic is largely determined by the Communist Party authorities in Moscow, acting via the Communist Party of Kazakhstan, a republican branch (there is no Kazakh Communist Party as such) of the CPSU (Communist Party of the Soviet Union). Half the membership is Kazakh. The Komsomol (Young Communist League) of Kazakhstan includes many Slavs and other non-Kazakhs.

The trade unions do not, as in the West, have the right to strike, to picket, or otherwise energetically to protect labour's interests in relations with management.

Education. All forms of education are provided tuition-free, the institutions being supported mainly by turnover and business taxes affecting most employees and enterprises in the republic. Languages of instruction are mainly Russian and Kazakh but include minority tongues. In sparsely populated areas, there are boarding-type secondary schools for pupils whose homes are far away. Evening secondary schools for young workers and farmers are widely attended. Vocational education is also available at numerous specialized secondary and technical schools.

Multilingual instruction

Major establishments of higher education are the Kazakh S.M. Kirov State University, the Abay Teachers College, and polytechnical, agricultural, veterinary, and other institutions in Alma-Ata; and the medical and teachers' institutes in Karaganda. Other regional centres have at least one institution of higher learning. Many Kazakhs study in other Soviet cities.

Scientific research is under the auspices of the Academy of Sciences of the Kazakh S.S.R., founded in 1945. The work of Kazakh scholars on the history of the Kazakh language and literature, on the history and ethnography of the Kazakh people, and in industrial and agricultural research has been widely acclaimed.

Social services. Urbanization and population growth have been accompanied by a housing boom. Living conditions in heavily industrialized regions such as Karaganda, however, have been said by visitors to be largely substandard, with considerable attendant ethnic friction resulting from overcrowding and competition for adequate living space. As industry has developed, anti-pollution measures have been introduced.

Health standards are high. There are hospitals and infant and maternal care centres everywhere. Sanatoriums of different types are scattered through the republic, the best known being those for treatment of respiratory diseases with koumiss (fermented mare's milk), which are often situated in settings of woods and lakes. Hospitals for rheumatics have been built around mineral springs, and mud cures are also available.

Cultural life. Cultural traditions are deeply rooted in the distinctive ways of life found in Kazakhstan. This heritage is evident in clothes, food, and interior decoration. The national costume style is best preserved in women's clothes: long, wide dress with a stand-up collar and bloomers gathered at the ankle, supplemented by a kerchief or cotton headdress with a face slit, bracelets, and earrings. Young girls wear both European clothes and such national styles as wide, white gowns, brightly coloured velvet waistcoats, and beads. Elderly men usually wear wide, white shirts, wide trousers, and woollen or cotton robes. Kazakh homes are decorated with carpets and *qoshmas,* felt rugs in gay colours. Kazakh ornamentation (stucco work and wall facing) is widely used in building.

Kazakh folklore has roots deep in the past. Abay Ibragim Kunanbayev, a late 19th-century humanist, poet, man of letters, and translator, gave a strong start to the development of modern Kazakh written literature and literary language. Most important to the development of Kazakh as a national written language in the first decades of the 20th century was the work of Aqmet (Ahmed) Baytursinuli, reformist politician, author, intellectual leader, and editor of the influential Kazakh newspaper *Qazaq,* published intermittently between 1913 and 1918 in Orenburg and Troitsk. The *aqïn* (bard) Jambil Jabayev gained major recognition from the Soviet authorities as a folk poet.

Kazakh literature

One of the first Soviet Kazakh playwrights, the academician Mukhtar Auezov, also wrote a long novel, *Abay,* the first part of which won a Stalin Prize in 1949; on completion, it was awarded the Lenin Prize for literature in 1959. *Abay,* translated into English and many other languages, is an encyclopaedic but nevertheless somewhat psychological representation of Kazakh steppe life in the late 19th century; its main characters are based upon real historical counterparts. This tradition is actively continued by Kazakh writers and poets as well as through the observance of such traditional Kazakh rites as the recital of folk lyrics and epic poems, the performances of popular comedians, and the competitions between *aqïns,* any of which events may turn into grand theatrical performances. There is also a large number of modern theatres of all types, including Uighur and Korean musical show houses, as well as opera, ballet, and a puppet theatre. The Kazakh film studio, founded in 1944, has released many feature films and a great number of documentaries, popular science films, and newsreels.

There are many art schools, and Alma-Ata has a national picture gallery; museums and libraries are numerous. Amateur art, drama, musical groups, and dance ensembles abound.

Kazakhstan has a multilingual radio centre, in Alma-Ata, and local broadcasting stations in the regional centres. Many collective farms, state farms, and large plants have their own relay systems. Television relay systems enable the viewers to watch programs from Moscow and Alma-Ata and, in the south, from Uzbekistan and Kirgiziya.

Every year many thousands of families find accommodation at rest homes, tourist and skiing camps, and the Young Pioneer summer camps. Many people also take part in physical culture and sports, including horseback riding, and the network of sports facilities includes a world-famous ice skating rink at Medeo, near Alma-Ata. (V.F.Ko./E.Al.)

HISTORY

It is impossible, with any certainty, to trace the separate existence of the Kazakhs before the 15th century. The word Kazakh occurs in Turkic-language historical records from the 11th century onward, but simply as meaning "riders of the steppe" and not with reference to any particular people. The first mention of the Kazakhs as living in Central Asia appeared in Russian writing in 1534. After the Russians established contact with the Kazakhs at the end of the 17th century, they habitually referred to them as Kaisak-Kirgiz or simply as Kirgiz, to avoid confusion with the Cossacks (in Russian, Kazaky), with whom the Kazakhs had no ethnic connection whatever. The most reliable theory of the origin of the Kazakhs seems to be that they were formed from the Kipchak tribes making up part of the Golden Horde.

Kazakh khanates. During the late 15th century and throughout the 16th century the Kazakhs were able to consolidate a nomadic empire stretching across the steppes east of the Caspian and north of the Aral Sea as far as the upper Irtysh and the western approaches to the Altai. The time was peculiarly favourable: the Oyrat Empire, formidable during the 14th and early 15th centuries, had passed into temporary eclipse; the Chagatai khanate bestriding the Tien Shan range was moribund; the Noghay

Kazakh consolidation

Horde between the mouths of the Volga and the Ural rivers was in a similar condition; and the Uzbeks were preoccupied with the conquest of Transoxania and with raiding Khorāsān. Under Burunduk Khan (reigned 1488–1509) and Kasym Khan (reigned 1509–18) the Kazakhs were the masters of virtually the entire steppe region, reputedly able to bring 200,000 horsemen into the field and feared by all of their neighbours. Under Kasym Khan's sons—Mamash (reigned 1518–23), Tagir (reigned 1523–33), and Buydash (reigned 1533–38)—there was, however, a partial weakening of the khan's authority, accompanied by a trend, later to become more pronounced, for the khanate to disintegrate into three separate "hordes." These were, from east to west: the Great Horde, in the Semirechiye north of the Tien Shan; the Middle Horde, in the central steppe region east of the Aral Sea; and the Little Horde, between the Aral Sea and the Ural River. In each horde the authority of the khan tended to be curtailed by the de facto power exercised by tribal chieftains known as sultans and perhaps even more by the beys and batyrs (the heads of the clans that were the components of each tribe). Nominally, the khans commanded a formidable force of mounted warriors, but, in reality, they depended upon the loyalty of the sultans, who, in turn, were dependent upon the loyalty of the beys and batyrs. The last son of Kasym Khan to rule the Kazakh steppes, Ḥaqq Naẓar (reigned 1538–80), overcame these obstacles and, having succeeded in reuniting the three hordes, embarked upon systematic raiding into Transoxania, a trend that continued under his immediate successors down to the reign of Tevkkel Khan (1586–98), who even temporarily occupied Samarkand.

During the 17th century the Kazakhs lost ground, although even in the last quarter of the century Tauke Khan (reigned 1680–1718) was still able to hold the tribes together in a single confederacy. By then, however, the Kazakhs were already in decline, having suffered from the ceaseless depredations of the revived Oyrat Empire in Jungaria. These Oyrat raids began as early as 1643 but reached their peak during the reign of the Oyrat ruler Cevang Rabdan (1697–1727), when the Kazakh steppes were ravaged again and again without the Kazakhs being able to offer any effective resistance. Not until the Oyrats were finally overthrown by the Manchu rulers of China in 1757 were the Kazakhs released from this scourge, which had for so long decimated their manpower and appropriated their livestock.

The reverses experienced by the Kazakhs at the hands of the Oyrats undoubtedly retarded the emergence of a unified Kazakh state and further depressed the prevailing level of Kazakh cultural life. It also rendered the Kazakhs even less able to resist the encroachments of Russia from the north. The Russian advance onto the Kazakh steppe began with the construction of a line of forts—Omsk in 1716, Semipalatinsk in 1718, Ust-Kamenogorsk in 1719, and Orsk in 1735—which was then steadily advanced southward. Some Kazakhs believed that the Russian presence might at least provide some security against Oyrat raids, and in 1731 the Little Horde accepted Russian protection, followed by the Middle Horde in 1740 and by part of the Great Horde in 1742, although its effect upon the Oyrats was to prove minimal. During the second half of the 18th century the Kazakhs found themselves threatened not only by Russian encroachments from the north but also by the Manchus from the east, who considered themselves the heirs of the Oyrats in Jungaria and who, in 1771, demanded the submission of the khan of the Great Horde. But, in reality, the Manchu Empire was too remote to intervene effectively; it was the Russians alone who were in a position to exert severe pressure on the Kazakhs. Finally, after a series of ineffectual uprisings, of which the most extensive was that of Batyr Srym in 1792–97, Russia resolved to suppress such autonomy as the Kazakh khans still possessed. In 1822 the khanate of the Middle Horde was abolished; in 1824, the Little Horde; and in 1848, the Great Horde.

Russian advance onto the Kazakh steppe

Russian and Soviet rule. Russian encroachment on Kazakh lands began in the early 18th century with the establishment of forts on the Irtysh River and, later, a continuous fortified line from the Irtysh to the Ural River. In the meantime, the Little Horde in 1731, the Middle Horde in 1740, and part of the Great Horde in 1742 expressed their allegiance to Russia to obtain protection from the Dzhungarians threatening them in the east. They remained beyond the fortified line, which they often attacked, however, until the 1820s, when Russia abolished the authority of the khans of the Middle and Little Hordes and pushed farther into the steppe. This resulted in a series of resistance movements, the most important being that led by Kenesary Kasymov (1837–47). The khanate of the Great Horde was suppressed in 1848. In 1853 the Russians took Ak-Mechet (now Kzyl-Orda) and in 1854 founded the fortress of Verny (now Alma-Ata). The country was known as the steppe region and was divided into four provinces: Uralsk, Turgay, Akmolinsk, and Semipalatinsk. At this time the Russians referred to the Kazakhs as Kirgiz in order to distinguish them from the Cossacks, while the real Kirgiz were described as Kara-Kirgiz. There was large-scale Russian peasant settlement in the north from the latter part of the 19th century.

Under the tsarist government there was no question of eventually granting self-determination to the Kazakhs; but a small nationalist movement started at the beginning of the 20th century, and, after the 1905 Revolution, Kazakh deputies were elected to the first and second Duma (Parliament). The first Kazakh newspaper, *Aykan,* appeared in 1910, followed by *Kazakh* in 1913. When in 1916 the government ordered the mobilization of all males between 19 and 43 for auxiliary army service, the Kazakhs rose under Abdulghaffar and Amangeldy Imanov. The revolt was suppressed by Russian troops with heavy loss of life.

Kazakh revolt

In November 1917, after the Revolution, Kazakh nationalists led by Ali Khan Bukei (Bukeikhanov) demanded full autonomy for Kazakhstan, and in 1917 a nationalist government known as the Alash Orda was formed. In 1919–20 the Red Army defeated the White Russian forces and occupied Kazakhstan; on August 26, 1920, a Kazakh (still erroneously described as Kirgiz) Autonomous Soviet Socialist Republic was formed with a temporary capital at Orenburg. In 1925 the name of the republic was changed to Kazakh, and the capital was moved first to Kzyl-Orda and in 1929 to Alma-Ata. From 1927 onward the Soviet government pursued a vigorous policy of transforming the nomads into a settled population and of colonizing Russians and Ukrainians. Kazakh protests against the latter led to the execution of Kulumbetov, a Kazakh deputy premier, and 18 other leading Kazakhs for "bourgeois nationalism."

In 1936 Kazakhstan became a Soviet Socialist republic, and in June 1937 the Kazakh Republican Communist Party, then numbering 51,440 members, held its first congress. During World War II a Kazakh, Zhumabay Shayakhmetov, was appointed first secretary of the Kazakh Communist Party. He was replaced in 1954 by a Slav, P.K. Ponomarenko, because of his unsatisfactory attitude toward the Virgin Lands campaign launched in that year. L.I. Brezhnev was associated with this campaign as second and, later, first secretary of the Communist Party of Kazakhstan in 1954–56. It involved a further large influx of Russians and Ukrainians into Kazakh territory and was a major event in Kazakh history. Also of great significance was the selection of the flinty desert of central Kazakhstan near Baykonur in Karaganda *oblast,* about 150 miles (240 kilometres) northeast of the Aral Sea, as the site of the cosmodrome for launching space vehicles. (Ed.)

Kirgiziya

Located in the heart of the Asian landmass, the Kirgiz (or Kirghiz) Soviet Socialist Republic (Kirgiziya, or Kirgizistan) has an area of 76,600 square miles (198,500 square kilometres). Somewhat less than half the population is composed of Kirgiz, a Turkic people, former nomads whose known history dates back at least to 200 BC. Kirgiziya became an autonomous *oblast* under the Russian Soviet Federated Socialist Republic in 1924 and an autonomous soviet socialist republic in 1926. It was made a constituent republic only in 1936, with its capital at Frunze (until 1925 named Pishpek).

By the late 20th century Kirgiziya had become transformed into a rapidly industrializing state, with the former nomads settled under a collectivized agricultural system. Though urbanization is accelerating, many of the old ways of life, nevertheless, survive.

To the north and northwest, Kirgiziya is bounded by the Kazakh S.S.R. On the southwest lies the Uzbek S.S.R., and on the south, beyond the Turkistan and Zaalay ranges, the Tadzhik S.S.R. On the southeast, the Kokshaal-Tau Range, part of the Tien Shan, forms the border with China. Most of Kirgiziya's borders run along mountain crests, and the few lowland areas—the Chu and Fergana valleys—occur near the places where the borders dip down to meet the plains and deserts that lie to the west and north. A deep hollow in the northeast holds Lake Issyk-Kul, one of the finest natural features in all of Central Asia.

PHYSICAL AND HUMAN GEOGRAPHY

The land. *Relief.* Kirgiziya is, above all, a mountainous country. At its eastern extremity, on the Chinese border, rise Victory Peak (Pik Pobedy), the second highest in the entire Soviet Union, and Pik Khan-Tengri, the fourth highest. This region is the core of the massive Tien Shan system, which thrusts on eastward into China; from it, mountainous belts spread westward over most of Kirgiziya. On the republic's southern border appear the Kokshaal-Tau, Alay, and Zaalay ranges, the last named influenced geologically by the vast structural knot of the Pamirs lying to the south in the adjoining Tadzhik Soviet Socialist Republic.

Mountain peaks

In the southwest lies the Fergana Valley. A similar huge hollow lies in the northeast, comparatively close to Khan-Tengri; bounded by the westward-thrusting arms of the Kungey-Alatau and Terskey-Alatau ranges, it contains Lake Issyk-Kul, the clear and deep waters of which are backed by snow-clad peaks. The rugged mountain and basin structure of much of the country, and the high alpine plateau of the central and eastern regions, are separated from the Fergana Valley on the west by the Fergana Range, running southeast to northwest, which merges into the Chatkal Range. The last named is linked to the Issyk-Kul region by a final enclosing range, the Kirgiz.

Apart from the Fergana Valley, the only important lowland areas are the Chu and Talas valleys near the northern border of the republic, the former containing the capital, Frunze. These lowland areas, occupying 15 percent of the total area, are of immense significance for settlement.

Drainage. The crests of the ranges are mantled in perpetual ice and snow. The total area thus clad exceeds 2,500 square miles (6,475 square kilometres) and includes the 37-mile (59-kilometre)-long southern branch of the Inylchek glacier, one of the world's greatest. Numerous short rivers, with many rapids, pour from the mountains into the inner basins. The Naryn River, running down into the Fergana Valley and continuing northwestward as a tributary of the Syrdarya, is of major significance, as is the Chu, running parallel to, or forming part of, the northern boundary with Kazakhstan.

Climate. Important influences on the climate are the remoteness of Kirgiziya from the oceans and the sharp change of elevation from neighbouring plains. The republic is surrounded by the Central Asian plains and deserts to the north, west, and southeast, making the contrast with the climate and landscape of its mountainous interior all the more striking. The lower parts of its fringing ranges lie in belts of high temperature and experience the hot, moisture-consuming winds from the deserts beyond. Conditions in the transitional zone above this hot desert region but below the cold high deserts vary greatly according to relief patterns: westward- and northward-facing slopes generally receive more moisture, which increases with altitude. Summer in the valleys is hot and dry, and the mean temperature in July is 82° F (28° C), while the average January temperature is −0.5° F (−18° C). Absolute temperatures have an even wider range, from a high of 109° F (43° C) to a low of −65° F (−54° C). Annual precipitation varies from 7.1 inches (180 millimetres) in the eastern Tien Shan to 30–40 inches (750–1,000 millimetres) in the Kirgiz and Fergana mountains. In the most populous valleys, it ranges from four to 20 inches.

Precipitation

Plant and animal life. Except at the highest altitudes, the elevated landscapes of Kirgiziya are characterized by flower-strewn alpine and subalpine pastures. Woodlands are found along the lower valleys and on the slopes of the north-facing ranges; occupying 3 to 4 percent of the total area of the country, they are coniferous and include the striking Tien Shan white spruce. Animal life in the forests is a varied mixture of European and Asian species that includes brown bear, wild pig, lynx, gray wolf, and ermine. The wooded ravines and the valleys of the mountainous steppe regions are the abode of the *arkhar*—a mountain sheep—mountain goats, deer, and snow leopards. Birds are plentiful in the mountains; rock partridges are found on cliffs and around water sources, and jackdaws and the snow, black, and bearded varieties of vulture live in the alpine areas. By comparison, animal life in the desert regions is scanty: rodents—yellow gophers and jerboas—hares, and a large-eared hedgehog are typical; birds include the desert bullfinch and red starling, and among reptiles are the steppe turtle and some snakes.

Settlement patterns. The pattern of settlement has changed considerably, with large immigration and industrialization. Cities have grown remarkably, with more than a third of the population clustered in large cities and other urban communities. The modern buildings and planned layout of the new cities contrast with rural life, which differs according to ethnic background. Russian and Ukrainian villages are scattered in the north, together with communities of Dungans, or Hui (Chinese Muslims). There are old fashioned Uzbek settlements, known as *qishlaq*s, in the south. The Kirgiz *kyshtak*s, villages built during the Soviet period to speed the transition from a nomadic to a settled existence, are scattered everywhere, as are collective and state farms.

The development of a modern transportation network is breaking down much of the old isolation. Frunze was formerly linked with the Fergana region only by a railway that made a long detour over the lowlands to the west, through Kazakhstan and Uzbekistan, but since 1965 traffic has flowed along the direct Frunze–Osh highway that cuts through the mountains and halves the distance. Alpine terrain still presents a great impediment to the construction of railways, but a network of highways is gradually replacing the winding paths along which people travelled for centuries by horse or camel or on foot.

The people. Kirgiziya's population is made up mainly of Kirgiz, Russians, Uzbeks, Ukrainians, and Germans (the last deported to Central Asia from the Soviet west in 1941). The first Kirgiz tribes settled in the Tien Shan region in ancient times and had a long history as one of the great nomadic groups of Central Asia. During the Soviet period, the almost complete abandonment of nomadic life under compulsion, and the replacement of individual farming by state collectivization in agriculture, have caused great changes in Kirgiz society.

The early Kirgiz

The economy. Kirgiziya was formerly wholly agricultural, and stock raising was prevalent. By the late 20th century the republic was a source of nonferrous metals, notably antimony and mercury ores, and a producer of machinery, instruments, hydroelectric power, and the products of light and food industries. The mineral wealth of the mountains—lead, zinc, and other metals—is being discovered. Kirgiziya has large coal reserves and some deposits of petroleum and natural gas. Extensive irrigation makes possible the expansion of agriculture and represents part of a large capital investment in the republic. During the years of the pre-World War II five-year plans, this investment produced plants for the extraction of antimony and for the processing of agricultural products, and the first metal-manufacturing plants and modernized blast furnaces were introduced. Large sugar factories were built, and emphasis was given to the primary processing of cotton and other fibre crops. During World War II, manufacturing expanded, and in ensuing decades the industries producing machines, building materials, and electric power were developed.

Industry. Coal mining continues to be of basic importance. But food-processing and light industries, utilizing local agricultural raw materials, are also important and include the production of meat, canned meat, fruits and vegetables; woollens, cotton, and silk fabrics; and leather goods. Cotton spinning and cleaning and enterprises producing worsted cloth, knitted garments, and leather and sheepskin coats are particularly significant.

Energy resources

The considerable energy resources of the republic are essential for industrial development. More than half the electric energy comes from waterpower.

Agriculture. Industrialization has stimulated the mechanization of Kirgiz agriculture, and many types of machines necessary to cope with the rugged terrain are now manufactured in the republic. Irrigation has been most important in increasing agricultural output; in the Fergana region, for example, where the republic's cotton is produced, the network of canals and reservoirs has been completely restructured.

The leading branches of agriculture are pasture-based stock raising and the cultivation of cotton, sugar beets, tobacco, and opium poppies. Most of the total agricultural land is taken up by pastures and by fields used to grow hay. Under the collectivized, state-owned system, the always important stock raising of the Kirgiz is being linked with the cultivation of cereals and industrial crops, silage, and seed grasses. This process is encouraged on every *kolkhoz* (collective farm) and *sovkhoz* (state farm) but is most fully developed in the valleys on the republic's borders.

Livestock

Livestock includes sheep, goats, and milk and beef cattle—especially in the Chu Valley and the Issyk-Kul region. Around Lake Issyk-Kul and in other mountain regions, the breeding of fine racehorses has been developed, as well as the raising of swine, bees, and rabbits.

Horses are also important in the mountain *kolkhozy;* not only are they used as draft animals, but also their meat is eaten, and fermented mare's milk, known as koumiss, is the favourite nourishing beverage of the Kirgiz and is also used as part of the treatment at mountain health resorts.

In the Naukat Valley in the south and also in the Talas Valley of the north, tobacco is cultivated. Horticulture and viticulture are developed in the Chu Valley and the Fergana area, with the mulberry trees of the latter supporting the raising of silkworms.

Hunting and fishing. The sparsely populated interior valleys contain almost inaccessible regions suitable for valuable fur-bearing species of animals. Kirgiz are enthusiastic hunters; indeed, five of the months in the Kirgiz calendar are named after game animals. Although modern firearms and traps have been introduced, there is still a preference for using the trained golden eagles to search out rabbits, foxes, and even wolves.

Lake Issyk-Kul, in spite of a paucity of plankton, is rich in fish. The catch is brought to the shoreline communities almost year round, the exception being in winter, when the fish descend to great depths. Artificial stocking of the lake has included the introduction of trout from Lake Sevan in Armenia, and fish-breeding farms are also used.

Transportation. Before 1924 the only railways in Kirgiziya were two narrow-gauge lines leading from the borders to the coal deposits of Kok-Yangak and Sulyukta. The construction of a line from Frunze across the Chu Valley and over the border to Lugovaya in Kazakhstan joined the north of the republic to the Turkistan–Siberian main railway line and, through it, to the south of the republic and the entire Soviet railway network. In 1948 a link extended the line up-valley from Frunze—it reached heights of 5,000 feet (1,525 metres) along the remote Boam Canyon—to Rybachye at the western tip of Lake Issyk-Kul. New southern lines reached the coal mines at Tash-Kumyr and Kyzyl-Kiya.

The road system

Highways nevertheless have been developed as the basic answer to the topographic problems confronting land transportation. One main route climbs from Frunze to Rybachye (with extensions along the north and south shores of Issyk-Kul), then swings south across difficult central terrain to Naryn, and then through the high Torugart Pass across the frontier with China and down to the city of Kashgar, in the Sinkiang Uighur Autonomous Region. The other major artery, the "route beyond the clouds," from Frunze to Osh, crosses the Kirgiz Alatau crest through a 10,500-foot (3,200-metre) tunnel. An important southern link is provided by the road joining Osh, via the Alay Pass, to the Pamir region of Tadzhikistan. An offshoot runs eastward through Irkeshtam to Kashgar.

Cargo-carrying and passenger vessels ply Lake Issyk-Kul, whose waters, although surrounded by peaks clad with snow, remain unfrozen in winter. Very strong local winds, raising waves and waterspouts, are an ever-present hazard, and travellers, not unexpectedly, generally prefer to use the modern lakeside highways.

Administrative and social conditions. *Government.* The republican constitution dates from March 23, 1937. All significant state functions are subordinated to the central government in Moscow, the capital of both the Russian S.F.S.R. and the Soviet Union. Though sovereignty is claimed for the Kirgiz S.S.R. by Soviet authorities, in fact it exercises no independent control over cultural, economic, social, political, military, or foreign affairs affecting it.

The highest governmental body in the republic is the Supreme Soviet, selected from a single slate of nominees for a four-year term. The Supreme Soviet, which exercises only ceremonial functions, generates an executive and administrative Council of Ministers. Local soviets are selected every two years. The chief legal officer of the Kirgiz S.S.R., the procurator, is appointed by the central government in Moscow.

The Communist Party

The sole authorized political organization and centre of power in Kirgiziya is the Communist Party, a branch of the Communist Party of the Soviet Union (CPSU). Kirgiz constitute a disproportionately small part of the membership throughout the Soviet Union as well as within their own republic. The Komsomol (Young Communist League) is closely tied to the CPSU.

Labour unions exert little influence upon protecting the interests of workers in relations with management. In effect, they serve the government by leading campaigns for higher labour productivity and by supervising granting of vacations to working people as well as access to resorts, sanatoriums, and other facilities.

Education. Education is provided without direct tuition charge, the institutions being supported by turnover taxes, touching most working people, and levies upon factories and other firms.

Academy of Sciences

The Academy of Sciences, established as a branch of the central body in Moscow in 1954, has three departments and about a dozen research institutes, and there are 50 other scientific and other research establishments.

Social services. With the concentration of a growing immigrant population from outside the republic in the cities, housing development has had to undergo great expansion, as have hospitals, maternity and child welfare centres, and other public health bodies.

Cultural life. Newspapers and magazines are published in both Russian and Kirgiz. Radiobroadcasting also is carried out in both languages, and most of the larger cities and all the districts have studios. There are republican television centres and studios in Frunze and regional studios in nearly all regional capitals. A network of relay lines connects the stations, enabling them to receive programs from Moscow, as well as those of the European Intervision and Eurovision networks.

Kirgiz cultural life has been greatly influenced by the rich oral literary tradition (including epic cycles and lyric poetry) of the region; by the development of a modern literary language and the change from the Arabic alphabet to Roman and finally to Cyrillic (with diacritical markings added) beginning in 1940; by imposition of Marxist-Stalinist-Leninist ideology in all fields of thought and the arts; and by persistent official attacks upon Islām (to which the Kirgiz were converted long ago) and the practice of religion.

A leading figure in drama and the novel today is the Kirgiz writer Chingiz Aytmatov, whose work, especially *Tales of the Mountains and Steppes,* which was widely circulated in English translation, won him a Lenin Prize in 1963. Although Aytmatov writes in both Kirgiz and Russian, the easy accessibility of his prose makes both originals and translations of the stories and longer writings extremely popular. His play, *The Ascent of Mt. Fuji,* written with the Kazakh playwright Kaltay Muhamedjanov, with its discussion of moral compromises made under Stalin, was a sensation when it first appeared on stage in Moscow in 1973 and has since been performed in English in Washington, D.C., and elsewhere. Kirgiz poets strive to accommodate their tradition to the new ideology and its literary guidelines known as Socialist Realism. Folk legacies are handed on by the bards, who recite the long Kirgiz verse epic *Manas,* expressing the fiercely independent outlook of the earlier Kirgiz.

In music, older traditions are represented in ensembles of the three-stringed *komuz,* plucked like a lute, and there is a Kirgiz Philharmonia. There are vigorous folk dance groups, and theatres perform Kirgiz and Russian plays as well as plays translated from other languages.

The Kirgiz motion-picture studio, which was established in 1942, produces feature films as well as newsreels, documentaries, and popular scientific films. (S.N.R./E.Al.)

HISTORY

The origin of the Kirgiz has not yet been fully determined. Chinese chronicles of the Han epoch speak of a Kirgiz people as neighbours of the Usun. Some historians have believed that these Kirgiz must have inhabited the upper reaches of the Yenisey River. There is also mention of them in the 8th-century Orkhon Inscriptions. In the 11th century Mahmud Kashgari wrote of them as the most easterly of the Turkic people "living near China." The Russians encountered them in the Yenisey Valley during the 16th century, but nothing was heard of the Yenisey Kirgiz after 1703 when they were forced by the Oyrat (Kalmyk) invasion to immigrate to Dzungaria. An earlier theory that this immigration was in fact to the Tien Shan, where the majority of the Kirgiz now live, has been discarded, since records of the existence of the Tien Shan Kirgiz date back to the beginning of the 16th century. Soviet ethnographers now quote archaeological evidence that from the 12th century Mongoloids predominated over Caucasoids in the Tien Shan, and they incline to the view that the present-day Kirgiz originated from the arrival in Kirgizia of the Khara-Khitais in the 12th century. This was the first big incursion of Mongolian peoples into Central Asia, and it is thought that the Khara-Khitais brought some Kirgiz with them from the upper Yenisey and that these were the precursors of the present inhabitants of Kirgiziya. This theory is supported by the fact that the modern Kirgiz language strikingly resembles that of the Orkhon Inscriptions.

Origin of the Kirgiz

In the first half of the 19th century the people occupying Kirgiziya were mainly nomadic. They preserved some degree of tribal independence but were partly under the control of the Kokand khanate. During the second half of the 19th century, Kirgizia was overrun by the Russians and eventually became a major area of Russian colonization. Most of the best land was given to Russian settlers, and this was a major cause of the revolt in 1916, in the suppression of which the Kirgiz suffered very heavily. Before the Revolution of 1917 the Kirgiz were not recognized as a national or political entity. The present territory of Kirgiziya was divided between the provinces of Semirechye and Fergana. Before the Revolution—and indeed until 1926—the Kirgiz were wrongly known as the Kara-Kirgiz, in order to distinguish them from the Kazakhs, who were always called Kirgiz by the Russians to distinguish them from the Cossacks (in Russian, Kazaky). After the Revolution, Kirgiziya was the scene of much guerrilla opposition to the Soviet regime. On October 14, 1924, Kirgizya (until then a part of the Turkistan A.S.S.R.) became an autonomous *oblast* of the Russian Soviet Federated Socialist Republic. On February 1, 1926, it became the Kirgiz Autonomous Soviet Socialist Republic of the Russian S.F.S.R.; and only on December 5, 1936, was it proclaimed the Kirgiz Soviet Socialist Republic.

Isolation of Kirgizia

During its existence as a constituent republic of the Soviet Union, Kirgizia has never been given a voice in international affairs. Similarly, no Kirgiz has made an impact on Soviet affairs, except, perhaps, during the great political purge of 1937, when the prime minister and the chairman of the Kirgiz planning commission disappeared. There has been considerable progress in the republic's economy, in the standard of living, and in education. Apart from Frunze, the capital, the republic has not been readily accessible to visitors from non-Communist countries. (Ed.)

Tadzhikistan

The Tadzhik (or Tajik) Soviet Socialist Republic (Tadzhikistan in Russian, or Tojikistan in the Tadzhik language) lies in the mountainous heart of Asia and is one of the 15 constituent union republics of the Soviet Union. It is in the extreme south, bounded by China to the east, Afghanistan to the south, and the Uzbek and Kirgiz S.S.R.'s to the west and north. Its area is 55,250 square miles (143,100 square kilometres), and its capital is Dushanbe, known from 1929 until 1961 as Stalinabad. The republic includes the Gorno-Badakhshan Autonomous Oblast, with its capital at Khorog. Tadzhikistan was first constituted as an autonomous republic within the Uzbek S.S.R. in 1924; it became a union republic in 1929.

As in the other Central Asian republics, an economic and social transformation has taken place during the Soviet period: industry now provides a large share of the republic's income, although cotton growing is still a mainstay of the economy. This change has been accompanied by considerable immigration and a high birth rate. Much of the old way of life nevertheless survives, and the republic's ancient cultural traditions are preserved.

PHYSICAL AND HUMAN GEOGRAPHY

The land. *Relief.* Tadzhikistan is a mountainous country, more than half its territory lying above 10,000 feet (3,000 metres). The western Tien Shan reaches into the north, with the Kuramin and Mogoltau ranges. In the central portion of the republic are found the massive ranges of the southern Tien Shan: the Turkistan Range and the slightly lower Zeravshan, Gissar (Hissar), and, in part, Alay ranges. The southeast contains the ice-clad peaks of the Pamir–Alay mountain system, which is made up of the Pamir Upland and, extending westward, the Peter I and Darvaz ranges. The Soviet Union's highest peaks—Lenin Peak (23,405 feet [7,134 metres]) and Communism Peak (24,590 feet [7,495 metres])—are found in the northern portion of the Pamirs. The relief of the southwestern portion of the republic, lying between the Gissar range and the Pyandzh (Panj) River (Ab-e Panj in Afghanistan), is made up of a series of transverse ranges interspersed by wide river valleys and structural depressions.

The valleys, although important on Tadzhikistan's human geography, comprise less than 10 percent of the total area of the republic; the largest are the western portion of the Fergana (Fergnana) Valley in the north and the Gissar, Vakhsh, Yavansu, Obikiik, Lower Kafirnigan (Kafirnihan), and Pyandzh valleys to the south. The whole country is in an active seismic belt, and severe earthquakes are common.

Most of the few lakes in Tadzhikistan are found in the Pamir region. Lake Kara-Kul, salt and devoid of life, lying at an altitude of about 13,000 feet (3,960 metres), is the largest; Lake Sarez was formed in 1911 during an earthquake, when a colossal landslide dammed the Murgab River. The Zeravshan range contains Iskanderkul, of glacial origin like most Tadzhikistan lakes.

Rivers

Drainage. The republic has a dense river network, the largest courses being those of the Syrdarya and the Amu Darya, together with their tributaries, notably the Vakhsh and the Kafirnigan. Upstream from the Vakhsh–Amu Darya junction, the latter river is known as the Pyandzh and forms a good portion of the southern boundary of the republic. Other rivers include the Zeravshan (Zarafshān), which runs through the central part of the republic. Most of the rivers drain into the Aral Sea Basin, although a few of the small streams running down from the Pamirs empty into Lake Kara-Kul, which has no outlet. The rivers have two high-water periods each year: in the spring, when the mountain snows melt and rainfall occurs, and in the summer, when the glaciers begin to melt. The summer flow is particularly helpful for irrigation purposes.

Climate. The climate of Tadzhikistan is sharply continental and changes with altitude. In the subtropical valley areas, summer is very hot and dry; the mean July temperature is 81.3° F (27.4° C) in Leninabad and 86.5° F (30.3° C) in Kulyab, farther south. The corresponding January figures are 30.4° F (−0.9° C) and 36.1° F (2.3° C), respectively. In very severe winters, the mercury has been known to drop to −4° F (−20° C), and even lower. Annual precipitation is slight, ranging between six and 10 inches (150 and 250 millimetres), but is higher in the Gissar Valley. In the highlands the situation is different; the mean January temperature in Murgab is −3.3° F (−19.6° C), and the temperature sometimes drops to −51° F (−46° C), with the record standing at −81° F (−63° C). Precipitation is scant, barely reaching two to three inches (60 to 80 millimetres) a year, mostly falling in summer.

Precipitation

The long, wide valleys that separate the ranges of the Tien Shan and the Pamir-Alay join in the Turgay Valley in the southwest, but in the east the high mountain barriers form dead ends. As a result, moist air masses from the west move up the valleys and suddenly reach low temperature areas, with heavy precipitation (30–60 inches [800–1,500 millimetres] or more annually), falling mostly as snow. Not all this snow melts in the summer heat, and there are large ice fields in the higher regions.

Plant and animal life. This topographic and climatic variation has given Tadzhikistan an extremely varied plant life, with more than 5,000 kinds of flowers alone. Generally, grasses, bushes, and a variety of shrubs predominate. Animal life, too, is rich and varied. The great gray lizard, jerboa, and gopher are typical inhabitants of the desert regions. In wooded areas deer and tigers are still sometimes seen, and jackals and wildcats live and hunt in reed thickets. In the mountains, the brown bear is found at the lower levels, and the goat and the golden eagle frequent higher altitudes.

The soils of the republic are mostly gray soils, poor in organic humus but rich in mineral nutrients. In unirrigated areas, there are dark gray steppe soils and brown mountain loess. About two-thirds of the surface is covered by sand, shingle, scree, bare rock, and permanent snow and ice. Those desert and semidesert areas suitable for irrigated farming have been turned into flourishing oases, with cotton plantations, gardens, and vineyards, by means of an extensive irrigation network. Population density is also high in the large villages strung out in clusters along the foothill regions.

The Pamir region

The landscapes of the Pamir region are quite distinctive, especially in the east, where there is sparse vegetation and the underbrush, known as *teresken,* supplies the only fuel. The high-altitude semidesert regions manage to provide year-round food for sheep. There are also narrow valleys with small villages (*qishlaq*s) surrounded by apple orchards, apricot trees, mulberry groves, and small cultivated fields.

Tadzhikistan may be divided into a number of regions: Northern Tadzhikistan, the southern boundary of which is the northern slope of the Turkistan Range; Central Tadzhikistan, or Kukhistan (*kūhistān,* "mountain country"), containing the Turkistan, Zeravshan, and Gissar ranges; low-lying Southwestern Tadzhikistan, containing two-thirds of the country's people and stretching to the south of the Gissar Range; and the Pamirs. The last may be subdivided into the East Pamirs—which, in its structure, resembles Tibet—and the deeply cleft West Pamirs.

The people. The name Tadzhik (Tajik) did not acquire its present definition until very recent times. Not until the 1920s did an official Tadzhik administrative unit come into being under that name. The area's population is ethnically extremely mixed, as it has been for centuries; but more than half the population are deemed to be ethnically Tadzhik.

On the basis of language, customs, and other traits, the Tadzhiks can be subdivided into a number of distinct groups. The Pamir Tadzhiks include minority people speaking Wakhī, Shughnī, Rōshānī, Khufī, Yāzgulāmī, Ishkashmī, and Bartang, grouped in the Gorno-Badakhshan Autonomous Oblast. Another distinct group is formed by the Yaghnābīs, direct descendants of the ancient Sogdians, who live in the Zeravshan River basin.

So closely are the Tadzhiks mixed with their Muslim coreligionists the Uzbeks that the Soviet partition of the area in 1924 failed to segregate the two nationalities with any degree of thoroughness. Uzbeks constituted the second largest ethnic group in Tadzhikistan, making up nearly a quarter of the population. Other groups include Russian immigrants and descendants of earlier Russian immigrants, Tatars, Germans, Kirgiz, Ukrainians, and Jews.

Like the other Central Asian republics, Tadzhikistan has a high rate of population increase. The natural population growth rate is three times the overall Soviet figure and is even higher in the Gorno-Badakhshan region. Half the population is under 20 years of age.

Urban life

The two largest cities are Dushanbe and Leninabad (formerly Khojand). Russians dominate Dushanbe's ethnic mixture, constituting somewhat less than half of the inhabitants. The more important of the smaller urban centres are Kulyab, Kurgan-Tyube, and Ura-Tyube. Kayrakkum, Ordzhonikidzeabad, Kalininabad, Nurek, and Regar are new creations.

The larger part of the population continues to live in the rural *qishlaq*s. Such a settlement usually consists of 200 to 700 one-family houses built along the banks of a river or an irrigation ditch. Traditionally, the house is surrounded by a mud fence. Many houses have flat roofs, and every household has an orchard or vineyard. In the mountains, the *qishlaq*s, sited in narrow valleys, form smaller settlements, usually 15 to 20 households. On the steep slopes, the flat roof of one house often serves as the yard for the house above it. There are schools, clinics, shops, and cultural centres in most *qishlaq*s. Settlements in newly developed areas have a more urban aspect; they cluster together and often include two-story houses and a community service centre.

The economy. Tadzhikistan is a major producer of long-staple cotton. The main industries are nonferrous metallurgy, cotton processing, oil production, fruit canning, and wine making.

Resources. The republic is rich in mineral deposits, including iron, lead, zinc, antimony, mercury, gold, tin, and tungsten. Nonmetals include common salt, carbonates, fluorite, arsenic, quartz sand, asbestos, and precious and semiprecious stones. The major mineral fuel is coal. There are also considerable deposits of petroleum and natural gas. Tadzhikistan's natural wealth also includes medicinal mineral springs. Finally, there is great potential electric power in the republic's rivers, most of it concentrated in the south.

Industry. Soviet authorities classify Tadzhikistan as an industrial-agrarian republic, with both sectors versatile.

The chief mining and ore-dressing area is in the north. Oil extraction and coal mining are among the oldest industries in the republic, the latter the more significant. Gas extraction began in the Kyzyl-Tumshuk and Komsomol fields (the latter near Dushanbe) in the mid-1960s, but, because of its small scale, local supplies have to be augmented by natural gas from Afghanistan, delivered by means of a pipeline built in 1974. Major power stations include the Kayrakkum on the Syrdarya and the Nurek and Golovnaya on the Vakhsh. An important thermal power station operates near Dushanbe.

Electric power

Light industry includes a dozen cotton-cleaning mills and two silk factories. The Dushanbe textile mill complex is the republic's largest enterprise in the cotton industry. Other branches of light industry include manufacture of knitted goods and footwear, sewing, and tanning. The Soviet Union's largest carpet-making factory is in Kayrakkum. The food industry concentrates on processing local agricultural products, which include fruit, grapes, various natural oils, and tobacco. The republic is the main Soviet producer of geranium oil, used in perfumery.

Engineering and metalworking products include looms, power transformers, cables, and agricultural and household equipment. The chemical industry includes a nitrogen fertilizer plant in Kalininabad (built in 1967).

Agriculture. Cotton growing is the leading branch of Tadzhik agriculture. Other important branches are cattle raising and the growing of fruit, grain, and vegetables; sericulture is also widespread, except in the Pamirs. Wheat and barley are the predominant grains, and rice cultivation has been expanded. Horticulture has been significant in Tadzhikistan since ancient times: apricots, pears, apples, plums, quinces, cherries, pomegranates, figs, and nuts are all grown. Dried apricots, nuts (particularly almonds), and grapes are important exports. There are also long-horned cattle, sheep (Gissar sheep), and goats.

The role of irrigation

Agriculture in Tadzhikistan would be severely limited without extensive irrigation. Emulating the technique widely practiced in Central Asia since ancient times, two main canals, the Vakhsh and the Gissar, were built at the end of the 1930s, followed by two joint Tadzhik–Uzbek projects, the Great Fergana and North Fergana canals. After World War II the network was expanded by construction of the Dalverzin and Parkhar–Chubek irrigation systems; the Muminabad, Kattasay, and Selbur reservoirs; the Hungry Plains irrigation system; and a tunnel through which water is brought from the Vakhsh to the Yavansus Valley.

Transportation. The railway net in Tadzhikistan is not extensive. Just under half of the total freight turnover is handled by rail, the rest by motor transport. About half of the highways are surfaced. Regular air service connects Tadzhikistan with Moscow, Tashkent, and other Soviet cities, and there is much internal air traffic. Dushanbe is the air transport centre, and there is an airport in Leninabad. A small amount of freight is carried by water, mainly between the river port of Termez (in the Uzbek S.S.R.) and Faizal-Kala (160 miles [256 kilometres] up the Amu Darya).

Administrative and social conditions. *Government.* The constitution of the Tadzhik S.S.R., adopted on March 1, 1937, states that the republic has all the rights of a sovereign state, including its national emblem and anthem. In practice, this republic, like the other 13 non-Russian union republics, does not possess and cannot exercise independence from Moscow in any vital matter, whether economic, social, cultural, political, or military.

Supreme Soviet and Council of Ministers

The republic has a Supreme Soviet, selected every four years, which ordinarily meets briefly twice each year to provide *pro forma* sanction to acts and decisions taken elsewhere. The Council of Ministers is the administrative organ and, though formally accountable to the republic's Supreme Soviet, takes its direction from executive bodies in Moscow. Local administration is carried out by regional, district, city, and village bodies, selected from a single list of candidates every two years. Judges are selected in a similar manner every five years; the courts include the Supreme Court of the Tadzhik S.S.R., the court of the Gorno-Badakhshan Autonomous Oblast, and district and city courts.

The Communist Party of Tadzhikistan is the true centre of power in the republic, but it, too, takes its direction in all respects from the party headquarters in the Russian S.F.S.R. Moreover, within the Communist Party of Tadzhikistan, Tadzhiks have remained in minority status. The Young Communist League (Komsomol) is another party organization. Tadzhik trade unions represent party and state rather than workers' interests.

Education. The educational level of Tadzhiks has risen greatly in the 20th century, initially under the impetus supplied by the Jadid (New Method) schools in Bukhara, Samarkand, and elsewhere, opened or taught by intellectual leaders such as Shakuri, Behbudi, and Ayni. In the late 19th century and early 20th there were also a few tsarist schools offering secular learning to indigenous pupils. The educational establishment was dominated until the 1920s, however, by the network of Muslim *mekteb*s and *medrese*s for which Central Asia was well known. Literacy for Tadzhikistan's inhabitants is now high.

There are several institutions of higher learning and about 60 research institutes, 16 of them under the auspices of the Tadzhik Academy of Sciences, founded in 1951. This emphasis on education and research keeps Tadzhikistan supplied with young specialists. The chronic Central Asian problem of placing indigenous graduates in employment commensurate with their advanced training besets the Tadzhiks, for most urban and industrial jobs are held by outsiders such as Russians, Tatars, and Ukrainians.

Social services. There is an extensive modern medical system. Housing construction and community services have also been developed. Electricity has been brought to every settlement, and the gas network has been extended. The amenities, however, benefit principally the urban centres, with their large non-Tadzhik populations.

Cultural life. Tadzhikistan has an ancient culture, and over the centuries it has given the world poets, philosophers, and scientists. Many of the popular traditions and customs have been retained, including the costumes worn by both men and women and such ancient festivals as the New Year celebration of the tillers of the land, known as Navrūz, which takes place on March 21, the period of the vernal equinox. A festival celebrated after the gathering of the cotton crop is another. These festivals are colourful affairs, incorporating horse races and horsemanship and wrestling contests. The Muslims (mostly Sunnī) continue regular mosque worship and observe religious holidays where possible, though religion is actively persecuted.

Festivals

The national cuisine includes flat cakes, the equivalent of bread, made in special ovens; *manti,* a kind of large dumpling; *laghmān,* a stew of chopped meat and noodles; *kaurdak,* fried meat and potatoes; and fermented milk. Fruit is an important dietary item, as are black and green tea.

Languages

The principal language of Tadzhikistan, Tadzhik (known to its speakers as Tojikī), with distinct northern and southern dialects, belongs to the southwest group of Iranian languages, in the Indo-European family; it is very close to the language used widely in neighbouring Afghanistan, where it is known as Farsī. The language of the Pamir Tadzhiks belongs to the east Iranian group. Tadzhik was formerly written in a modified Arabic and later in the Roman alphabet but since 1940 has used a modified Cyrillic script. Writers from this region have made notable contributions to Persian literature since the 10th century AD, and a vigorous folk literature is still being collected.

A number of Tadzhik poets and novelists have achieved fame in the Soviet Union and beyond. They include Abdalrauf Fitrat, whose *Last Judgment* has been reprinted many times in Tadzhik, Russian, and Uzbek, and Sadriddin Ayni, known for his novels *Slaves* and *Dokhunda* and for his autobiography, *Bukhara.* Abū ol-Qāsem Lāhūtī's poems *We Won* and *Crown and Banner,* and Mirzo Tursunzade's poem *Hasan the Arab* respond to the changes of the Soviet period; the latter's lyric cycle *The Voice of Asia* won him the Lenin Prize in 1960, followed by a number of other major awards noting his contribution to Soviet Tadzhik poetry and his influence on younger poets.

For centuries, songs, dances, and theatrical and circus performances have been a distinctive popular tradition in the region: singers, tightrope walkers, conjurers, musicians, and other performers continue to entertain audiences. In addition, festivals are now held for amateurs working in both traditional and modern fields.

The Tadzhik National Theatre, which was established in 1929, has nine separate theatres presenting opera, ballet, musical comedy, and puppetry. The cinema is developing, with Tadzhik studios producing feature films and documentaries as well as dubbing films from elsewhere. Radio and television services are increasing, and Dushanbe has had a television centre since 1960. (A.I.I./E.Al.)

HISTORY

The Tadzhik peoples descended from Persian-speaking Iranian stock and were included in the empires of Persia and of Alexander the Great of Macedonia. In the 8th century the Arabs crossed the Amu Darya (river); conquered Sogdiana (Transoxania), which was inhabited by the Tadzhiks; and called it Mā Warāʾ an-Nahr (That Which Lies Beyond the River). Two centuries later the first Turkic invaders (from the northeast) seized this area of Transoxania; and, in time, because both conquered and conquerors were Muslim, many Tadzhiks, especially those in the valleys of the Syrdarya and Amu Darya, became Turkicized. They gave up their Persian language and adopted Turkish.

Until the mid-18th century the Tadzhiks were part of the *amīrate* of Bukhara, but then the Afghans conquered

Turkish, Afghan, and Russian conquests

lands south and southwest of the Amu Darya with their Tadzhik population, including the city of Balkh, an ancient cultural Tadzhik centre.

Russian conquests in Central Asia in the 1860s and 1870s brought a number of Tadzhiks in the Zeravshan and Fergana valleys under direct Russian rule, while the *amīrate* of Bukhara in effect became a Russian protectorate in 1868.

After the Russian Revolution of 1917 a considerable part of the Tadzhik people was included in the Turkistan Autonomous Soviet Socialist Republic established in April 1918. On August 23, 1920, the Revolution was extended to the khanate of Bukhara, which embraced most of the territory occupied by the modern Tadzhik S.S.R. In October 1920 the Bukharan People's Soviet Republic was declared, and early in 1921 the Soviet Army captured Dushanbe and Kulyab. From 1922 until the summer of 1923 Tadzhikistan was the scene of the Basmachi revolt, and rebel banks under Ibrahim Bek operated in Eastern Bukhara until 1931. In 1924 the Tadzhik Autonomous Soviet Socialist Republic was created as part of the Uzbek S.S.R.; in January 1925 a Special Pamirs Oblast was created out of the Kara-Kirgiz and Tadzhik parts of the Pamirs; and in December 1925 this *oblast* was renamed the Gorno-Badakhshan Autonomous Oblast. Tadzhikistan was thus composed of the following former administrative units: Eastern Bukhara, seven *volosts* (rural districts) of the Samarkand *uyezd* (county), the five southern *volosts* of the Khodzhent (later Leninabad) *uyezd,* and six *volosts* of the Pamirs region.

On December 5, 1929, the status of the republic was raised to that of a Soviet Socialist republic.

Collectivization of agriculture was carried out in 1928 and 1929 in the face of considerable opposition. There were later periodical purges of the council of ministers and the party apparatus, including one in 1961. (Ed.)

Turkmenistan

A sun-beaten land of deserts and oases, the Turkmen Soviet Socialist Republic (also known as Turkmenistan, or Turkmeniya), is situated on the same latitude as the Mediterranean but deep in the heart of the Asian continent, as the southernmost Soviet territory. Its area is 188,500 square miles (488,100 square kilometres). It was formed on October 27, 1924, and on May 13, 1925, formally became one of the constituent republics of the Soviet Union; its capital is at Ashkhabad. Its Central Asian neighbours are the Kazakh S.S.R. to the north, the Uzbek S.S.R. to the east, and Iran and Afghanistan to the south, while the Caspian Sea forms its western boundary.

PHYSICAL AND HUMAN GEOGRAPHY

The land. *Relief.* Deserts occupy 90 percent of Turkmenistan's territory. The Kara-Kum (Black Sand) is one of the world's largest sand deserts, taking up the entire central part of Turkmenistan and extending into Kazakhstan. Topographically, four-fifths of Turkmenistan is plains—the southern part of the Turan Plain. Mountains and foothills rise mainly in the southern part of the republic, the Kugitangtau and Kopet-Dag ranges being spurs of the Pamir-Alay mountain ranges. The Kopet-Dag is geologically young, its instability indicated—as in 1929 and 1948—by intermittent earthquakes of great destructive force.

Climate. Turkmenistan's position deep inside Asia, the resultant unique air-mass circulation, and the character of the relief are responsible for a strongly continental climate, which exhibits great fluctuations in temperatures during the day and the year. The average annual temperature is 57°–61° F (14°–16° C), but this figure masks an extremely wide range. The temperature is seldom lower than 95° F (35° C) during summer days, and the absolute maximum high temperature in the southeast Kara-Kum reaches 122° F (50° C) in the shade. By contrast, in winter, the temperature in Kushka drops to −27° F (−33° C). Humidity is very low and rainfall meagre. Precipitation occurs mainly in the spring and ranges from about three inches (80 millimetres) per year in the northwest desert to as much as 12 inches (300 millimetres) in the mountains.

Temperature extremes

Drainage. Turkmenistan's main rivers are the Amu Darya (the Oxus of classical times), flowing along its northeastern border toward the Aral Sea, and the Tedzhen, Murgab, and Atrek; there are also numerous small mountain rivers. Unfortunately, however, the geographical position of the rivers and the direction of their flow do not coincide with the location of cultivable lands; the most fertile—and still insufficiently used—lands lie chiefly in the south, northeast, and west, whereas the principal rivers run mostly in the east. A great number of canals and reservoirs has been built. The construction, across the Kara-Kum, of the world's largest irrigation and shipping canal, the Karakumsky Kanal (Kara-Kum Canal), began in the mid-1950s.

Plant and animal life. Turkmenistan's soils are varied. A unique feature is that there is no definitely formed soil layer in most of the desert region. In the northern and western Kara-Kum, on raised areas, the sand gives way to sandy loam and sandy and clay soils, sometimes mixed with broken rock. In the oases, a layer suitable for irrigated cultivation has formed.

The biological resources are varied but not abundant. Except in the oases and mountain valleys and plateaus, vegetation is of a pronounced desert character. In the mountain valleys of the Kopet-Dag, wild grape, almond, fig, and walnut are found, while juniper and pistachio trees grow on the open slopes. On the riverbanks and islands, chiefly in and along the Amu Darya, stand *tugai* forests of black poplar, willow, reed, and cane.

The animal world is represented mainly by desert creatures: steppe and Persian fox, wildcat, Kara-Kum gazelle, and tortoise. The wildlife of the mountains includes mountain rams and goats; such wild cats as the cheetah, lynx, and snow leopard; and the porcupine. Jackals, wild boars, and birds frequent the *tugai.* Rare pink deer are also found along the Amu Darya, and wild donkeys roam the Badkhyz and Karabil plateaus in the southwest. The eastern coast of the Caspian Sea is the winter home of vast flocks of ducks, geese, and swans.

In the waters of the eastern Caspian, various kinds of herring, sprat, roach, and sturgeon (including the beluga, prized for caviar) are widespread; the Amu Darya and its lakes, and other rivers, contain carp, barbel, and pike.

Settlement patterns. There is much variety in the different regions of Turkmenistan, but two broad divisions may be seen: an oasis region—characterized by adequate water supply, cultivated lands, and developed industry—composed of the Kopet-Dag, Tedzhen, Murgab, Middle Amu Darya, and Lower Amu Darya oases; and a desert region, subdivided into Western Turkmenistan, with a well-developed industry, and the Kara-Kum, with cattle raising and resources of natural gas and petroleum under the sands.

The Kopet-Dag Oasis

The Kopet-Dag Oasis stretches along the northern foothills of the Kopet-Dag Range, the slopes of which offer large areas for nonirrigated farming; both the mountains and foothills are also rich in mineral resources. The economic and cultural centre of the oasis is Ashkhabad, the republic's capital, with about 340,000 inhabitants. The development of the capital has stimulated industry, turning an agrarian oasis into the industrial-agrarian core of the republic. The Central Asian Railway, linking Tashkent, in the Uzbek S.S.R., with Krasnovodsk, via Ashkhabad and other cities of Turkmenistan, runs between the foothills and the Kara-Kum. The Firyuza and Chuli mountain valleys, rich in water and with a mild climate, have become known as health resorts.

The Murgab Oasis is famous for its fine-staple cotton, silk, handmade carpets and rugs, and Karakul sheep. The Murgab River, now that its lower reaches are crossed by the Karakumsky Kanal, can supply more water for irrigation. Mary (formerly Merv) is the centre of the oasis and the surrounding region, and one of the most attractive towns in the republic.

Separated from the Murgab by a stretch of the Kara-Kum, the Tedzhen Oasis formed along the Tedzhen River. Because of the scarcity of water, only small areas of wheat, barley, and melons could be cultivated. After the oasis was crossed by the Karakumsky Kanal, however, and the Khauz-Khan Reservoir was built, large areas were irrigated, thus making possible the cultivation of long-staple cotton and the construction of cotton-processing plants. The economic and cultural centre is the town of Tedzhen. South of the oasis lies the Badkhyz National Reserve, with unique pistachio tree woodlands strongly resembling African savanna.

The Middle Amu Darya Oasis, in contrast to other oases, stretches almost without interruption for hundreds of miles and is almost entirely cultivated. The Amu Darya waters are very rich in silt, an excellent natural fertilizer. Raising of cotton and silkworms has long been widespread in that area. It is an important producer of kenaf and other fibre crops and the only supplier of wild licorice in the Soviet Union. The adjoining deserts provide fodder for Karakul sheep. Industries processing agricultural products and mineral raw materials have been developed in the oasis and the adjoining Gaurdak-Kugitang district. The Soviet Union's largest deposits of sulfur as well as deposits of potassium and other salts are found here, together with building materials. The economic and administrative centre of the oasis and the region is Chardzhou, the second largest city and industrial centre in Turkmenistan.

The Lower Amu Darya Oasis lies in the ancient delta of the Amu Darya; Turkmenistan's northernmost oasis, it is one of the most important agricultural regions of the republic. The oasis is cut by a dense network of old riverbeds as well as by irrigation channels and ditches beginning in the neighbouring Uzbek S.S.R. The climate is more continental than that of other oases, but it is warm enough to grow medium-staple cotton and alfalfa. Rice, sweet sorghum, beans, kenaf, sesame, grapes, vegetables, and melons are also grown, and cattle and silkworms are raised. Most industrial enterprises are concentrated in the regional centre, the town of Tashauz.

The desert of Western Turkmenistan is an enormous and almost waterless expanse, with only a small oasis irrigated by the Atrek River in the extreme southwest. The mountainous part of Western Turkmenistan, a continuation of the Caucasus Mountains, has mineral and fuel resources. The unique deposits of mirabilite in the Kara-Bogaz-Gol Gulf of the Caspian Sea, petroleum (with natural gas and iodine-and bromine-containing waters), and rock salt and common lake salt are of great importance.

Western Turkmenistan

Western Turkmenistan is one of the most developed regions of the republic industrially, emphasizing oil extraction and refining, chemical and mining industries, and fisheries and fish processing. The rural population in Western Turkmenistan is less dense than that in the east. People are mostly engaged in raising sheep, goats, and camels and, to a lesser extent, grains and melons.

In the southern part of the Krasnovodsk Plateau, overlooking a bay of the Caspian Sea, stands the city of Krasnovodsk. Nebit-Dag lies inland, east of Krasnovodsk.

The three parts of the Kara-Kum and the other featureless deserts—occupying the greater portion of the republic—enter, in part, all of the above-mentioned areas. They are distinguished by the same desert landscape, lack of surface water, exceptionally meagre precipitation, and high summer temperatures. At the same time, the desert is a zone of fuel and mineral resources, and its richest pastures can be used all the year round for sheep, goats, and camels.

The people. It is a multinational republic with Turkmens the predominant nationality, followed by Russians, Uzbeks, Kazakhs, and small numbers of Tatars, Ukrainians, Armenians, Azerbaijanis, and Kara-Kalpaks. The Turkmens living in the republic make up almost all the Turkmens in the Soviet Union; the remaining few live mainly in Uzbekistan, Tadzhikistan, and the Northern Caucasus and the Astrakhan *oblast* of the Russian S.F.S.R.

Population distribution

The population is distributed unevenly, with few people in the Kara-Kum and mountain regions but large numbers in the oases. With the development of the Turkmenistan economy, numbers of non-Turkmen skilled workers and scientific and technical intelligentsia—with a large proportion of youth and women—immigrated to the republic.

There is a large urban population (about half the total); the rest of the people live in rural settlements and villages. The urban population consists mainly of outsiders, those from the Soviet west and the Russian S.F.S.R. being concentrated in the principal centres.

For centuries the Turkmens were divided into numerous tribes and clans, the largest being the Tekke, Ersari, and Yomut, whose total number exceeded 500,000. The number of people in other tribes (the Salor, Sarïq, Goklan, and Chaudar) fluctuated between 20,000 and 40,000.

Up to the time of the Russian Revolution (they had come under Russian domination in the 19th century) most of the Turkmens were pastoral nomads, though during the 18th and 19th centuries many had settled in the oases and become agriculturalists. Their tribal organizations and loyalties were strong. They had always been warlike and had commonly hired themselves out as mercenaries to various rulers in Central Asia. The establishment of the Turkmen S.S.R.—which was not done without a struggle, in which Turkmens joined with Bukharan Uzbeks and others in a protracted battle to throw off Russian domination—had the effect of bringing greater unity to the Turkmen tribes and of giving them the beginning of a sense of nationhood.

The economy. The republic specializes in cotton growing and in oil and gas extraction. Although it occupies a relatively small place in overall Soviet industrial and agricultural output, the republic turns out considerable quantities of certain products, such as iodine, bromine, and sodium sulfate.

Resources. Turkmenistan is rich in various minerals and in petroleum and natural gas. Chemical resources are also extensive, especially those of mirabilite and other similar salts in the Kara-Bogaz-Gol area of the Caspian. Deposits of sulfur, potassium, and sodium chloride and oil-field waters containing iodine and bromine are also considerable. Dolomites, limestone, and marl are found in the mountains and foothills, and the Kara-Kum supplies sands used in making glass and bricks.

Industry. The radical reconstruction of the economy was finished by 1930. Old branches (cotton ginning, oil pressing, and carpet making) were retained, and new ones (heavy and light industry, and food processing) made their appearance. The net result has been a huge increase in gross industrial output during the Soviet period.

Petroleum deposits and the associated oil industry are centred in the Caspian plain in Western Turkmenistan and in the offshore oil fields to the west of the Cheleken Peninsula in the Caspian Sea. In oil extraction Turkmenistan holds third place among the Soviet republics, after the Russian S.F.S.R. and Azerbaijan. Turkmenistan oil is of a very high grade, both as a fuel and as a chemical raw material. A network of natural gas pipelines links gas deposits in Western Turkmenistan with Ashkhabad, Krasnovodsk, Cheleken, and the central regions of the republic.

Significant in the chemical industry are the Chardzhou superphosphate plant, mirabilite from the vicinity of the Kara-Bogaz-Gol, sulfur from Gaurdak, iodine and bromine factories on the Cheleken Peninsula, and production of detergents at the Krasnovodsk oil refinery.

Electrical power

Turkmenistan has a number of thermal power stations, using liquid fuel, at Nebit-Dag, Ashkhabad, Bezmein, Krasnovodsk, and elsewhere; a station near the town of Mary uses natural gas. Hydropower stations include the Hindu Kush plant, as well as plants at Kaushtubent and at the Tashkeprin Reservoir on the Murgab River.

Engineering and metal-processing enterprises include repair shops for diesel locomotives, railway cars, and agricultural machinery. In Ashkhabad and in Mary there are plants producing, among other products, equipment for extracting and refining oil. Textile and cotton-ginning industries are also important; there are silk-winding and silk-weaving mills, as well as cotton, cotton-wool, and worsted mills. Artificial furs, leather footwear, and sewn goods are also produced.

The most important branches of the food industry are vegetable oil, fish, meat, and flour production and wine making. The republic exports oil, butter, wine, fish, and salt to other parts of the Soviet Union.

Domestic industries, especially carpet and rug making, occupy an important place in the republic's economy.

Turkmen carpets and rugs, long renowned for their durability and unique designs, are exported to more than 50 countries. Among Turkmen carpets well known in the West are those made by the Tekke, Yomut, Salor, and Ersari Turkmens and called by those names.

Agriculture. The growing of cotton and the raising of Karakul sheep, horses, and camels are the most important branches of agriculture. Turkmenistan is the largest producer of fine-staple cotton in the Soviet Union.

Agricultural enterprises are large and include collective farms (*kolkhozy*) and state farms (*sovkhozy*).

Kenaf is a new industrial crop, and sesame is important among oil-bearing plants. Wheat and barley account for much of the area sown in grain crops; areas under millet and rice are as yet insignificant. Fodder crops (corn [maize], alfalfa, and others) occupy one-sixth of the sown area. Turkmenistan melons have long been famous, and the republic's grapes are also well known.

The republic produces Karakul pelts, including black *arabi,* golden *sur,* and silver-gray *shirazi,* all very beautiful, durable, and in great demand in the world market; indeed, Karakul sheep account for more than 70 percent of all sheep in the republic.

Horse-breeding traditions

Over the centuries, Turkmens have also evolved the horses of the Akhal Tekke and Yomut breeds, valued for their physical endurance, speed, and beauty. Camels—mainly Arabian, and indispensable in the desert as a means of transport for sheep herders, for getting water from desert wells, and as a source of meat, wool, and milk—are also traditional Turkmen livestock. Turkmenistan leads the Soviet Union in the production of silkworm cocoons.

Transportation. The basic means of transport is the railways, though the density of the rail network is much below the Soviet average. The main trunk line is between Krasnovodsk and Tashkent (in the Uzbek S.S.R.), with branch lines from Mary to Kushka and from Nebit-Dag to Vyshka. In the 1950s a line was built to link Chardzhou, and areas as far northwest along the Amu Darya as Kungrad, to the central regions.

Motor transport is developing more rapidly than rail, and trucks handle most freight traffic within the republic. The main highways pass near railway lines and supplement them, especially in short-distance deliveries, but roads are also being constructed in more remote regions.

There is a merchant fleet, and the Krasnovodsk–Baku ferry provides a 210-mile (336-kilometre) link across the Caspian Sea; the electrically powered ferries are each capable of handling a freight train and making two trips daily. River transport, in seasonal operation on the Amu Darya and the Karakumsky Kanal, is of local importance.

Passenger planes and helicopters connect Ashkhabad, the capital, with many towns in the republic and elsewhere in the Soviet Union, as well as with remote geological prospectors' camps.

A network of pipelines connects the oil fields and gas deposits with transportation or consumption points. Natural gas is taken to central regions of the Russian S.F.S.R. and to the Urals through a two-pipe line, each pipe being up to five feet in diameter.

Administrative and social conditions. *Government.* The republic has its own flag, emblem, and anthem; its official languages are Turkmen and Russian. According to the 1937 constitution, all power in Turkmenistan derives from the workers; however, there are no democratic elections, hence no effective channels for exercising the will of an electorate.

The Supreme Soviet

The highest body of republic government is the one-chamber Supreme Soviet of the Turkmen S.S.R., which is elected for a four-year term. All citizens of the republic reaching the age of 18 are eligible to vote, and those over 23 years of age can be elected deputies. The Supreme Soviet of the Turkmen S.S.R., however, exercises no real power. It meets for only a short time at six-month intervals, and deputies are selected from a single list of persons provided by the authorities without primary contests. The ethnic makeup of the Supreme Soviet is mixed, though there are no specifically stated protections for the various nationalities, nor are selections for the single list of candidates organized ethnically. Rather, candidates appear as designees from precincts, though often they are neither residents of the given precinct nor even permanent residents of the Turkmen S.S.R. (high-ranking Russian generals of the Soviet Army, for example, often emerge from the list as deputies to both the republic and unionwide supreme soviets). The Turkmen S.S.R., along with all other constituent republics, is represented in the national Supreme Soviet, the country's highest organ of state power. The Presidium of the Supreme Soviet consists of a chairman, two vice chairmen, a secretary, and 11 members.

The highest executive and administrative body in the republic is the Council of Ministers, formed by the republican Supreme Soviet; it organizes and supervises the activity of all ministries and other accountable departments. The chairman of the Council of Ministers of the republic is ex officio a member of the Council of Ministers of the Soviet Union.

Local government is carried out through district, town, rural settlement, and village soviets, elected for terms of two years.

The highest judicial body is the Supreme Court of the republic; in districts and in cities there are people's courts, with judges and people's assessors elected from one list of candidates provided by the authorities.

Communist Party

The Communist Party in Turkmenistan (there is no Turkmen Communist Party or party division) is a branch of the Communist Party of the Soviet Union (CPSU) and the real centre of organized power in the republic.

Education. Until the collapse of the Khanate of Bukhara in 1920, Turkmens not attending schools in the Khanate of Khiva (also terminated the same year) largely received their education from the *mekteb*s (primary schools) and *medrese*s (seminaries) of Bukhara, that ancient, multi-ethnic Muslim centre, as well as in a scattering of New Method (Jadid) schools established by Muslim reformers in the early 20th century in towns such as Kerki and Chardzhou. A great extension of Turkmenistan's educational facilities has occurred since 1924, though the beginnings were relatively ineffective, compared with the best years of the late 19th-century revival in the Muslim educational system.

There were in the late 20th century general primary and secondary schools serving pupils of all ethnic groups. There are also six institutions of higher learning—the Turkmen State University (located in Ashkhabad), a teachers' training college, and medical, agricultural, and polytechnical institutes.

Education is supported from turnover taxes affecting most employees and from levies upon factories and other firms. It is provided tuition-free to students, and those selected for higher education receive stipends from the republic budget.

In the scientific field, the major institution is the Academy of Sciences of the Turkmen S.S.R., set up in 1951. It incorporates 16 research institutes of various kinds employing highly qualified staffs.

Cultural life. The intellectual and cultural life of Soviet Turkmenistan, led initially by the outstanding graduates of Bukharan seminaries such as Abdulhekim Qulmuhammed-oghli (died about 1937)—once active in the resistance movement, later a Communist, and influential as writer, editor, researcher, and cultural organizer—passed into the hands of Soviet-educated persons after the Stalinist purges of the 1930s "liquidated" men such as Qulmuhammed-oghli.

Turkmen literature

The widespread Turkmen traditional practice of composing poetry orally gave way, after printing became well established in Turkmen centres in the 1920s, to writing and to the dissemination of verse and prose in book form. Though written Turkmen literature dates back at least to the 18th-century poet Mahtum Quli (Magtim Guli), it underwent a burst of growth when the literary publications of the new republic began to appear in the late 1920s and '30s.

A film studio in the capital produces features and documentaries, and Ashkhabad and Krasnovodsk have television stations. Films, television, radio, and theatre, however, are largely carried on in the Russian language and for Russian constituents rather than in Turkmen for the eponymous nationality. Further, even the few Turkmen-language programs included many devoted to translations from Russian or about Russian subjects and themes. (V.B.Z./E.Al.)

HISTORY

Ethnologically, the Turkmens are the most distinctive of the Turkic peoples of Central Asia. One Turkmen tradition traces their origin to a legendary Oğuz Khan, probably a personification of the Oğuz, a powerful tribal union mentioned in the Orkhon Inscriptions as occupying the lower reaches of the Syrdarya. Toward the end of the 10th century the Oğuz started to move south, and the part that accepted Islām was called Turkmen. One branch of them was the Seljuqs.

Another Turkmen tradition makes the Mangyshlak Peninsula on the Caspian Sea the homeland of the Turkmens; but the Soviet ethnographer S.A. Tokarev considered that it would be a mistake to regard the Turkmens as pure descendants of Turkic nomads who moved into their present habitat from the north and northeast. Their language belongs to the southwestern group, thus connecting them more with the Osmanli (Ottoman) and Azerbaijani Turks than with the Turkic peoples of Central Asia. Further, their dolichocephalic skulls, not found elsewhere in Central Asia, suggest intermingling with an ancient non-Turkic population, most probably the Massagetae.

Until 1924 the Turkmens had never experienced even nominal political unity. Their organization was exclusively tribal, and the tribes were either nomadic and independent or subject to the neighbouring states of Persia, Khiva, and Bukhara. During the 16th and 17th centuries, the Chaudor tribe led a powerful tribal union in the north, while the Salor tribe was dominant in the south. During the 17th and 18th centuries, the ascendancy passed to the Yomuds, Tekes, Ersaris, and Saryks, who began to move out of the desert into the oases of Khorezm and to the Atrek, Tedzhen, and Murghab rivers and to adopt a settled way of life. There was bitter rivalry among the tribes, particularly between the Tekes and Yomuds, while the Goklans, inhabiting part of the Khiva oasis, were opposed to both. Thus, while the Tekes were the principal opponents of the Russian invasion in the 1860s and 1870s, the other tribes either failed to support them or helped the Russians.

Tribal rivalries

The first notable expedition under Prince Aleksandr Bekovich-Cherkasski in 1717 met with failure, but in 1869 a Russian military force landed on the eastern coast of the Caspian and founded the port of Krasnovodsk. In 1874 the Transcaspian military district was established, and in 1881 this became the Transcaspian *oblast,* which in 1899 was made part of the governorate general of Turkistan. There was fierce resistance to Russian encroachment, but this was finally broken by Gen. Mikhail Dimitrievich Skobelev at the Battle of Geok-Tepe (1881). Turkmens took an active part in the revolt of 1916 against Russian rule, particularly in the town of Tedzhen, where many Russian settlers and officials were murdered.

After the Russian Revolution, during the Civil War (1918–20), Turkmenistan was the scene of sporadic fighting between the Social Revolutionary Transcaspian Provincial Government and the Bolshevik troops trying to penetrate from Tashkent. The Social Revolutionaries were for a time supported by a small British force of 1,200 men with its headquarters in northeastern Iran, sent there to forestall a German-Turkish thrust in the direction of southern Iran and Afghanistan, made possible by the military collapse of Russia in 1917. The British force was withdrawn in April 1919, and Red troops captured Ashkhabad in July 1919 and Krasnovodsk in February 1920. Bolshevik rule was thereafter established.

Up to 1924 the Transcaspian (after 1921 called the Turkmen) *oblast* formed part of the Turkistan Autonomous Soviet Socialist Republic, while the remaining districts of Turkmenistan were embodied in the Bukharan and Khorezmian Soviet Socialist republics formed in 1920. In 1924 the Turkmen S.S.R. was formed out of the Turkmen *oblast,* together with the Turkmen *rayony* of the former Khorezmian Republic (Tashauz, Takhta, Ilyata, Kunya-Urgench, and Porsa) and of the Bukhara Republic (Chardzhui, now Chardzhou, Kerki, and part of Sherabad).

In 1948 severe damage was caused by an earthquake in the regions of Ashkhabad and Geok-Tepe, the capital being largely destroyed. (Ed.)

Uzbekistan

A land of desert landscapes and fertile oases clustering around the foothills of high mountain ranges, the Uzbek Soviet Socialist Republic (or Uzbekistan) lies in the heart of Central Asia, largely between the region's major rivers, the Amu Darya on the southwest and the Syrdarya on the northeast. One of 15 republics of the Soviet Union, it is bounded on the north and northwest by the steppes of the Kazakh S.S.R.; on the east and southeast by the mountainous Kirgiz and Tadzhik S.S.R.'s; on the southwest by the predominantly desert Turkmen S.S.R.; and, for a short distance in the south, by Afghanistan. It was founded in 1924, and its capital is at Tashkent. The republic—which since 1936 has included the Kara-Kalpak Autonomous Soviet Socialist Republic, on the southern shores of the Aral Sea—has an area of 172,700 square miles (447,400 square kilometres).

PHYSICAL AND HUMAN GEOGRAPHY

The land. *Relief.* The flat, sun-baked, western portion of Uzbekistan, almost four-fifths of the total area, has an often monotonous appearance. In the northwest, the alluvial Turan Plain stretches around the Aral Sea at heights of about 200 to 300 feet (60 to 90 metres) above sea level, merging in the south with the barren wastes of the Kyzylkum. In the extreme west lies the Ustyurt Plateau, with a slightly undulating flat surface up to 650 feet (200 metres) above sea level. The region is characterized by low ridges and internal drainage basins, the latter dotted with salt marshes, and by sinkholes and caverns that mark intermittent stream courses.

The many-branched delta of the Amu Darya (the Oxus River of the ancients) lends character to the region immediately south of the Aral Sea. The western portion of the delta is furrowed by ancient riverbeds; the modern delta originates at the town of Nukus and spreads out over the central portion of the Kara-Kalpak A.S.S.R. The plain thus formed is covered with alluvial deposits and is broken by scattered hills on the lower Aral Sea side and also by the Sultan-Uizdag Mountains, which attain heights of 1,600 feet (500 metres).

Delta of the Amu Darya

To the southeast, the wastes of the central Kyzylkum are broken by the slopes of the Altyntau, Tamdytau, Kuldzhuktau, and Bukantau hills, fringed for up to 20–30 miles (30–50 kilometres) by flat surfaces that usually end in basins. The latter include the Mynbulak, which, at 39 feet (12 metres) below sea level, is the lowest point of the Kyzylkum. The southern Kyzylkum is part of an ancient plateau cut into by an old delta of the Zeravshan River; it continues in the Sundukli sand deserts that extend along the right bank of the Amu Darya upstream from the lower Zeravshan.

Mountainous eastern Uzbekistan is marked by a diverging cluster of mountain chains thrusting in from the east and separated by valleys and basins. The spurs belong, respectively, to the western Tien Shan—the Karzhantau, Ugam, Pskem (with the 14,104-foot [4,299-metre] Beshtor Peak), Chatkal, and Kuramin ranges. Across the Fergana Valley lie the Gissar and Alay ranges. The intermontane and foothill basins, forming thickly populated oases, are covered with a network of canals and contain fields, orchards, and vineyards.

The Tashkent–Golodnaya steppe lies between the Tien Shan spurs to the north and the Turkistan, Malguzar, and Nuratau ranges to the south and is divided by the Syrdarya into the flat, southern Golodnaya Steppe and the southeastern Dalverzin Steppe. The narrow Sanzar–Nuratau Basin is a continuation of the Golodnaya Steppe plateau and is bounded on the south by the Chumkartau and Aktau mountains. Farther south again, the valley of the Zeravshan broadens westward. An ancient cultural centre, it is graced by the cities of Samarkand and Bukhara. Toward the east, the fertile Fergana Valley, the largest in Central Asia, is densely settled, with new urban communities, a product of industrialization, contrasting with the traditional rural patterns. To the south of the Zeravshan Valley, the Kashkadarya Basin forms a triangle between the western spurs of the Zeravshan and Gissar ranges, merging into a flat, sandy desert on the west. Much of its ancient plain is now irrigated. The Surkhandarya Basin lies in southeastern Uzbekistan, between the Gissar (Surkhantau) and Babatag ranges. Its terraced surfaces are covered with loess deposits.

The soils of Uzbekistan reflect the topographic diversity: gray desert soils in the flat desertlands, a variety of brown and meadow soils in the mountains, and meadow, bog, marshy, and even saline soils in the river valleys.

Plant and animal life. The republic's vegetation falls into marked bands depending largely on altitude. The western lowlands and the basins have a thin natural cover of desert sedges and grasses. Low foothills have a semidesert cover, and high foothills are characterized by mixed grass and grass steppe. Hills (defined as up to 9,200 feet, or 2,800 metres) have wood and brushwood plants, with forests, in fact, covering 12 percent of the republic's total area. The peaks of the high mountains rise above subalpine and alpine meadows.

Fauna

Uzbekistan's fauna is dominated by desert forms, including a variety of snakes and such lizards as geckos. Rodents are common in the desert areas, where foxes and wolves and the occasional gazelle and antelope are also found. There are few birds, apart from the desert warbler, jay, and turtledove. In the east, in the plains and foothills, live lizards and snakes, including the cobra in the south, along with gazelle, fox, and wolf. The steppe tortoise and mottled polecat are also found here, and badgers live close to the foothills. Birds include the tufted lark, rock pigeon, and eagle.

Animal life is much more abundant in the irrigated regions, where the oriole, goldfinch, woodpecker, and common swallow are found. In the mountain forests live boars and a few roe deer. Bears and wolves, the Siberian goat, and a few lynx are found in the high mountains, as are many birds, from nightingales to vultures and eagles.

The rivers and the Aral Sea are rich in fish, with giant catfish weighing up to 330–370 pounds (150–170 kilograms) being taken from the Amu Darya; such lakes as Aksykent, Tuzkan, and Dengizkul, although poor in fish, are known for their therapeutic muds.

Climate. Located as it is in the far south of the Soviet Union, Uzbekistan enjoys an abundance of warmth and sunshine and a climate that overall is very dry and markedly continental. In winter the relatively moist temperate latitude air masses are carried into Central Asia. In summer, warm, dry tropical air intrudes. The temperate air masses of Atlantic origin arrive heated and dried out by their long journey inland, while the tropical air masses bring only heat; the combined effect is one of marked aridity. Rainfall averages only eight inches (200 millimetres) a year, mostly falling in winter and spring, with amounts up to three times the averages occurring in the mountains and a corresponding drop over the desert surfaces.

From May to October, a long, hot, dry, cloudless summer descends on Uzbekistan, with the mean July temperature reaching 90° F (32° C) in the south. Daytime air temperatures frequently exceed 104° F (40° C). The winter is short, with considerable cloudiness and frequent severe frosts; mean temperatures in the north are as low as 10° F (−12° C), and individual days can register temperatures as low as −36° F (−38° C).

Drainage. Uzbekistan lies almost entirely in an internal drainage basin; in few other parts of the world is drainage so strongly influenced by climate or the contrast between highland and lowland regions rendered so sharply. All Uzbekistan rivers, large and small, originate in the mountains; as they move into the dry lowlands, their waters are gradually lost to irrigation, filtration, and evaporation, and the rivers are mostly lost in the sands. There are more than 600 streams in the republic, all lying in the Aral Sea drainage basin, although the two major arteries, the Syrdarya and the Amu Darya, originate far away in the mountains of the Kirgiz and Tadzhik S.S.R.'s.

The Amu Darya

The Amu Darya, Central Asia's greatest river, runs along or near to much of Uzbekistan's southwestern boundary with the Turkmen S.S.R. Its lower reaches are extensively tapped for irrigation, and the rivers of southern Uzbekistan—the Surkhandarya and the Sherabaddarya—are essentially the last lower tributaries of the Amu Darya. The Zeravshan and the Kashkadarya, in theory, are also tributary to the Amu Darya, but, since they do not reach it, trickling instead to nothing in the desert, they are considered independent entities. The Syrdarya, Central Asia's second largest river, is formed in Uzbekistan by the confluence of the Naryn River and the Karadarya; downstream from this confluence, many would-be tributaries are, in fact, captured for irrigation purposes before they reach the main riverbed. The desert is slowly receding before irrigation.

The people. Contemporary Uzbekistan has around 60 different ethnic groups. Uzbeks make up a little more than two-thirds of the population. Russians, Tatars, and Kazakhs make up notable percentages, with lesser numbers of Tadzhiks, Kara-Kalpaks, and a host of others.

The Uzbek nationality is second in size among non-Russian groups throughout the Soviet Union, having surpassed the Belorussians between 1959 and 1970.

The cities and towns

Although urbanization has increased, about three-quarters of the republic's Uzbeks remained rural in the late 20th century, Russians, Tatars, Ukrainians, Jews, and Armenians making up the bulk of the urban population. Russians are the largest ethnic group in the capital city, Tashkent (Central Asia's largest metropolis), followed by Uzbeks, Tatars, Jews, Ukrainians, Koreans, Kazakhs, Armenians, and others. Samarkand is the oldest and second largest Uzbek city, dating back at least 2,500 years. Tashkent and Samarkand, like the other ancient cities of Bukhara, Khiva, and Kokand, developed in irrigated regions or on the caravan trade routes. Younger towns—Chirchik, Angren, Bekabad, Almalyk, Navoi, and others—were established in places rich in mineral resources. Yangiyul, Gulistan, and Yangiyer developed as cotton, silkworm, or fruit-processing centres on more recently developed lands.

The economy. Uzbekistan is the chief source of the Soviet Union's cotton and the third largest cotton producer in the world. It is also one of the leading centres of the Soviet natural gas industry and the most important region for the raising of Karakul sheep and silkworms. It is also known for its orchards and vineyards. Industry has become the leading branch of the republican economy, however. Heavy industry received its first impetus during the early five-year plans but at that time was mainly designed to serve cotton growing; today it is much more diversified.

Resources. Uzbekistan has large reserves of natural gas, petroleum, and coal, while its mountain streams offer potential hydroelectric development. In addition to pipeline links with neighbouring republics, a natural gas pipeline stretches from Bukhara to the central regions of the European Soviet Union and the Urals, and gas powers much of the local industry. Petroleum resources are also great; fields are exploited in the Fergana Valley, in the south, in the Bukhara region, and in the Kara-Kalpak A.S.S.R. Coal was barely worked at all until World War II, but the Angren field has since gained regional as well as republican significance. Power stations fuelled by natural gas and by oil are supplemented by hydroelectric projects, notably at Kayrakkum on the Syrdarya, Uchkurgan on the Naryn River, and Charvak on the Chirchik. The power stations are connected to a single Central Asian grid system.

Industry. Uzbekistan is the main producer of machines and heavy equipment in Central Asia. The republic is also the main Soviet producer of machinery for cotton cultivation and harvesting (as well as processing), and some machines are exported by the Soviet Union to other countries. Machines for irrigation projects and for road construction are also prominent, as are machines for the textile industry.

This emphasis on machinery necessitates, in turn, emphasis on ferrous and nonferrous metallurgy, although the republic's first metallurgical plant, that at Bekabad, did not begin operations till 1946. Uzbekistan has a variety of metallic ores, and the Almalyk mining belt in the Kuramin Range has deposits of copper, zinc, and lead. Tungsten and molybdenum are also mined, and there are prospects for the development of an aluminum industry. Gold is found at Muruntau in the Kyzylkum.

Chemical industry

The chemical industry of the republic—centred in the Fergana region, Navoi, Kokand, Namangan, and Andizhan—is closely connected with cotton production; not only are fertilizers for the cotton fields produced, but many chemical products are derived from by-products and waste materials of the cotton industry itself.

In the construction industry, plants using local raw materials and producing prefabricated, reinforced-concrete structures (including those used in irrigation projects) are found in all the large cities. Uzbekistan marble, notably Gazgan marble from the Nuratau, is known for its beauty and durability and was used in the facades of the Moscow subway system.

The various agricultural raw materials are processed by light industry. Both cotton fabric and silk fabric are important products. The food industry processes animal products, vegetables, fruits, and fish, the last concentrated in Muynak on the Aral Sea, where canned items, caviar, and dried, smoked, and salted fish are the chief products.

Agriculture. With warmth and sunlight, mild, short winters, fertile, irrigated soils, and good pastures, Uzbekistan is well situated for cattle raising and for growing cotton and related crops. The centuries-old struggle for water has been attacked by large, state-directed irrigation projects. Canals include the Great Fergana, North Fergana, and Tashkent; reservoirs include the Kattakurgan on the Zeravshan River (the "Uzbek Sea"), the Kuyumazar near Bukhara, the Kassansay in the Fergana Valley, and the Tyuyabuguz on the Akhangaran (the "Tashkent Sea"). Modern irrigation schemes are thoroughly mechanized.

Farming and cotton growing are supported by mechanical equipment, enabling good use to be made of the diverse natural conditions. There is a high and stable yield of cotton, though the region is the most northerly of the great cotton regions of the world. Silkworm breeding is another branch of agriculture with a long tradition behind it: silkworms were raised in the Fergana Valley as early as the 4th century AD, and today the streets and irrigation ditches of most settlements are lined with mulberry trees, the leaves of which are fed to silkworms. The republic accounts for more than half the Soviet cocoon production.

Uzbekistan orchards produce apricots, peaches, figs, apples, pears, and other fruits. The republic's raisins and table and wine grapes are widely known beyond the republic's borders. The major fruit-growing regions are the Fergana Valley, the Zeravshan Oasis, and the Chirchik and Agren valleys.

Fur production

Livestock raising is distinguished by an unusual feature: Karakul sheep, which produce a very beautiful fur, are native to the Bukhara region and constitute one of the major branches. Many varieties of lamb are raised, producing furs ranging in colour from black, or black with gold- or silver-tipped tufts, to red and white. Broadtail fur, from very young or unborn Karakul lambs, which is flat and has a shimmering, moiré appearance, has won special acclaim.

Fur farming has been developed in the republic; muskrats, introduced to the lower reaches of the Amu Darya, have become well acclimatized and are prized for their thick, soft fur. Silver-black fox, blue fox, and mink are also bred in the same region.

Transportation. The development of the Uzbek economy has been closely connected with the development of a transportation network. Railroad and truck transport account for almost all of the freight carried. Major roads include the Great Uzbek Highway, running from Tashkent to Termez; the Zeravshan Highway, linking Samarkand and Chardzhou; and a road between Tashkent and Kokand. The Fergana Ring, connecting the major settlements of the valley, is also important. The use of the Amu Darya for water transportation has declined relatively from the days when it formed virtually the only link with regions to the north and west, though the lower reaches remain important. Air transport is vital, and Tashkent international airport is a major link in routes between Europe and the countries of South and Southeast Asia. The pipeline network, particularly that used for natural gas, is also well developed.

Uzbekistan's exports include machine equipment, fertilizers, coal, cement, oil, natural gas, nonferrous metals, and textile products, as well as the traditional cotton, Karakul pelts, silk, and fruit. Imports include wood and wood materials, coke, metal, petroleum products, chemical products, sugar, and bread.

Administrative and social conditions. *Government.* The governmental structure of the Uzbek Soviet Socialist Republic operates under the terms of the constitution ratified on February 14, 1937. As in other constituent union republics, the constitution stipulates that Uzbekistan is a sovereign nation. In fact, however, Uzbek and Uzbekistan sovereignty is severely if not totally curtailed through the subordination to the central government in Moscow of all matters concerning economic development and social, political, cultural, foreign, and military affairs. The governmental administrative and executive bodies are the Supreme Soviet of the Uzbek S.S.R., made up of deputies selected from a single slate of nominees for a four-year term, and that body's Presidium, together with a Council of Ministers. The Supreme Soviet, which seats deputies from many ethnic groups, exercises only ceremonial functions in the Soviet system of power. Local administration consists mainly of a network of lower level soviets, selected for two-year terms. There is a Supreme Court with subsidiary *oblast* and lower level courts. The chief legal officer in the republic is appointed for a five-year period by the central government in Moscow.

The Communist Party

The Communist Party of Uzbekistan, a branch of the Communist Party of the Soviet Union, is the only authorized political organization and the main power centre in the republic. Labour unions, which had more than 2,413,000 members, play an active role in carrying out the party's economic policies rather than representing the interests of workers and employees in relations with management or other state agencies.

Social services. The state budget allocates large capital sums for social and domestic needs, particularly housing, a continuing problem in the presence of a substantial immigration of people from the Soviet west and especially the Russian S.F.S.R., who add mainly to the population of the cities.

Hospital care has improved greatly since 1914. Mortality rates have fallen two and a half times since the 1920s, and there has been a great reduction in infant mortality (which formerly was as high as 30 per 100 births within the first year of life) and an extension of the life-span.

Education. Central Asian Uzbek cities were famed for centuries as educational centres. Students in the thousands annually came from many parts of the Muslim East to attend the hundreds of seminaries in Bukhara, Khiva, Samarkand, Tashkent, and the Fergana Valley.

The leading research body of the republic is the Uzbek Academy of Sciences, established in 1943 as a branch of the central academy in Moscow. It includes some 200 scholarly institutes and centres.

Cultural life. The ancient national heritage of the Uzbek people is clearly evident in their customs, traditions, cuisine, and styles of interior decoration. The Uzbek national costume (often seen, especially on holidays) is, for men, a robe striped with bright colours, tied with a kerchief, with a finely embroidered skullcap adding to the effect; for women, it includes bright silk dresses with a coloured or white shawl over the head, often with a silk-embroidered skullcap. Houses are often decorated with magnificent rugs patterned on both sides and with ancient works of folk art. Distinctive foods include *läghman* (meat with pastry or rice in strong broth); *mänti* (chopped meat and flavourings wrapped in a thin dough); and *plov* (rice with meat, carrots, and onions, sometimes with dried apricots and spices). The favourite beverage is green tea, drunk everywhere, but especially in a *chäykhanä* (teahouse). The national cultural tradition is also seen in the observance of the Näwroz, the spring festival; Lalä Bäyrämi, the tulip festival; Äshulä Bäyrämi, the song festival; and Päkhta Bäyrämi, the cotton harvest festival, as well as more conventional Soviet holidays. Increasingly, again, Friday worship is taking place in and around certain mosques; the Uzbeks were already Muslims (of the Sunnī branch)

National festivals

when they migrated to Central Asia. Traditional horse racing and various games and tests of strength, dexterity, and skill remain very popular.

Over the centuries, Uzbekistan has produced great scholars, poets, and writers whose heritage has enriched the general culture of modern man. The scholar and encyclopaedist al-Bīrūnī, who lived in the 11th century, created a series of geographic works about India, as well as a wide range of writings in natural sciences and the humanities. In the 15th century the astronomer and mathematician Ulūgh Beg founded a famous observatory in Samarkand. The world-renowned ʿAlī Shīr Navāʾī was a late 15th-century scholar, poet, and writer who greatly advanced Turkish literature and was also a talented artist and composer.

The major writers of the early 20th century broke from the Navāʾī tradition in their style but continued to revere it in their literary history. Among the foremost modern poets and prose writers were Abdalrauf Fitrat, Mahmud Khoja Behbudi, and Sadriddin Ayni, all bilingual in Turkī and Farsī (later called Uzbek and Tadzhik). Abdullah Qadiri, best known today for his first two Uzbek-language historical novels, *Days Gone By* and *Scorpion from the Pulpit*, published in the second half of the 1920s, wrote drama, poetry, and short prose before 1917. Like Fitrat, he was killed in the great Soviet purges of the late 1930s. Behbudi died in 1919 at the hands of the executioners of the Emir of Bukhara. Hamza Hakim-Zada Niyaziy was also an early 20th-century playwright and poet later much favoured by Soviet authorities for his simplified, class-oriented plots and subjects.

Since World War II, and especially since Stalin's death, the period of relative calm has seen a flourishing of tendentious ideological poetry and prose together with some genuinely musical and interesting lyrical verse, plays, and, occasionally, extended artistic prose. Among the young poets, especially, there is a true revival of Central Asia's most popular genre, the short lyric poem. Ghafur Ghulam, an older poet, was widely admired, though his work was often heavily tendentious, and Kamil Yashen's many plays deal with political conflict. Sharaf R. Rashidov, writer and politician, composes simple prose pieces about unbelievably devoted collective farmers. Among this older generation of contemporary authors, Asqad Mukhtar, whose Socialist Realist novel *Sisters* (1955) appeared in English and other languages, has been especially effective in encouraging the efforts of the new Uzbek poets, a group much less burdened by sloganeering and extraliterary influences than their elders.

Uzbek musical tradition, like that of much of southern Central Asia, includes a distinctive classical form of composition in the great cycles of *maqom*s handed on from master performer to apprentices. The Uzbek cultural heritage includes magnificent monuments in the national architectural tradition: the mausoleum of the Sāmānid ruler Esmāʿīl I (9th and 10th centuries) in Bukhara, the great mosques and mausoleums of Samarkand, constructed in the 14th and 15th centuries, and many other fine buildings. The ancient practices of ornamental wall painting, coin making, wood carving, and fabric printing have been augmented by modern graphic arts (Uzbek lithographed books first appeared in Khiva in 1874) and sculpture. Ornamental murals decorate schools, clubs, and tearooms.

Dramatic arts

Though privately organized drama and theatre were very active in Samarkand, Margilan, Tashkent, and other cities before 1917, permanent troupes scarcely existed. State-supported theatres, such as the Navoi Theatre of Opera and Ballet in Tashkent, have won international attention. Uzbekistan also has its own film studio and television, radio, and publishing establishments. Like the theatres, most of these media use both Uzbek and other languages, mainly Russian. (G.V.K./E.Al.)

HISTORY

Traces of human habitation in what is now Uzbekistan date as far back as the Old Stone Age, some 55,000 to 70,000 years ago, and the great states of Bactria, Khwārezm, and Sogdiana existed there as early as the 1st millennium BC. A succession of invaders then swept over the area: the troops of King Darius of Persia in the 6th century BC; the troops of Alexander the Great in the 4th century BC; and Arab forces in the 8th century AD. Following the devastating Mongol invasion of the 13th century, the area became part of the empire of Timur (Tamerlane) and his successors until the early 16th century.

The Uzbek khanates. The early history of the Uzbek people is wrapped in obscurity; but at the time of the establishment of the khanate of Kipchak (the Golden Horde), Genghis Khan's grandson Shibaqan (Arabic: Shaybān) was given as his inheritance the area stretching east of the Urals toward the upper waters of the Irtysh. His tribes were at that time pagan shamanists; but early in the 14th century, presumably during the reign of the greatest of the rulers of Kipchak, Uzbek (or Özbeg; reigned 1313–40), they were converted to Islām and perhaps assumed the name of Uzbeks in honour of their distant sovereign. (By the late 14th century these tribes were already known by that name.) They began to move southeastward during the first half of the 15th century; and under their ruler Abū al-Khayr Khan they reached the north bank of the Syrdarya, whence they threatened the Timurid possessions across the river in Transoxania (Mā Warāʾ an-Nahr) but whence they were also threatened, in turn, by the depredations of the Buddhist Oyrats, now advancing steadily westward out of Jungaria (western Mongolia).

Assumption of the name Uzbeks

Before Abū al-Khayr Khan could undertake a full-scale invasion of Transoxania, however, he was defeated in battle and killed in 1468 by two kinsmen—Karay and Jani Beg—who, refusing to recognize Abū al-Khayr's paramount position, had defected, together with their tribal followers, and had placed themselves under the nominal suzerainty of the Chagatai khan of Mughalistān. Their descendants were to become the Kazakh hordes of later centuries.

With the death of Abū al-Khayr Khan, the fortunes of the Uzbeks declined, only to revive under the leadership of his grandson Muḥammad Shaybānī, who was an empire builder cast in the ancestral Genghiskhanid mold. By 1500 he had seized the whole of Transoxania, including the metropolis of Samarkand, and was threatening the remaining Timurid rulers in Khorāsān. Although he himself was killed at Merv (1510), he had changed the course of Central Asian history. By the time of his death all the lands between the Syrdarya and the Amu Darya were in Uzbek hands, and so they were to remain.

The Shaybānid dynasty ruled Transoxania down to 1598, with a separate line reigning in Khwārezm. Like the Timurids, the Shaybānids followed Turko-Mongol tradition in selecting as their paramount chieftain the senior member of the ruling family and in dividing their territory into separate appanages for the brothers, sons, and nephews of the khan—a practice tending toward instability. Transoxania under the Shaybānids appears to have declined in prosperity by comparison with the preceding century of Timurid rule, partly because of a falling off in the importance of the transcontinental caravan trade. In other respects the Shaybānids followed the precedents set by the Timurids, especially in regard to their patronage of literature and the arts, although neither in architecture nor in miniature painting did the output of the Shaybānid period compare favourably with the best Timurid work. Unlike the Timurids, however, the Shaybānids strove to establish a reputation for impeccable orthodoxy. This was especially the case with the greatest of Shaybānid rulers, ʿAbd Allāh Khan II (reigned 1583–98).

On the extinction of the Shaybānid line, Transoxania passed into the hands of a family related by marriage to the preceding dynasty, the Janids or Astrakhanids (descended from the former khans of Astrakhan on the Volga). Under the Janids there was a marked decline in material prosperity and in the general level of cultural life; and such pretensions to sovereignty as the dynasty still possessed by the early 18th century vanished with the invasion of Transoxania by the Iranian warlord Nāder Shāh, who, in 1740, entered Bukhara as a conqueror before passing on to attack the khanate of Khiva, the name used hereafter for Khwārezm. During the second half of the 18th century the last Janid ruler, Abū al-Ghāzī Khan (reigned 1758–85), lost much of his power to chieftains of the Mangit tribe, who, in the person of Shāh Mūrad (reigned 1785–1800), eventually usurped the throne.

Dominance of the Bukhara, Khiva, and Kokand khanates

At the beginning of the 19th century the area between the Amu Darya and the Syrdarya was dominated by three khanates—Bukhara, Khiva, and Kokand. Not one of these states had defined frontiers with its neighbours; not one was able to keep recalcitrant chieftains permanently in check; and not one could trust its neighbour not to intervene in times of difficulty or crisis. In addition, the emir of Bukhara and the khan of Khiva exercised a nominal suzerainty over the Turkmen tribes of the Karakum Desert, whose slave-raiding proclivities in the direction of Iran they encouraged—to provide labour in the oases of Khiva and Bukhara—but over whose movements they exercised not the slightest control. Paradoxically, however, all three khanates were probably better administered in the first half of the 19th century than at any time during the preceding century: in Kokand both Muḥammad ʿUmar Shaykh (died 1822) and his son Muḥammad ʿAli (died 1842) were talented rulers, while in Bukhara the ferocious Naṣr Allāh (Nasrullah; reigned 1827–60) aspired to the role of a second Timur.

Russian and Soviet rule. Yet nowhere in the Muslim world during the 19th century were there regimes less prepared to face the challenge of European expansion than the khanates of Central Asia; and it was their geographical isolation alone that impeded the otherwise inexorable advance of Russia, especially in the case of Khiva, ringed by desert, against which Russia mounted unsuccessful expeditions in 1717 and 1839. The Russian conquest began in earnest, however, with the acquisition from Kokand in 1855 of the fort of Ak-Mechet on the Syrdarya. Kokand was attacked in 1864–65, Chimkent and Tashkent taken, and a treaty extracted from Khudāyār Khan in 1866. In 1868 Bukhara was invaded, and the emir was compelled to accept the status of a Russian vassal. The same happened with Khiva in 1873. In 1875 there was an uprising in Kokand, which was swiftly suppressed, and the khanate was formally annexed in 1876.

At the outbreak of the Russian Revolution in 1917, the Uzbeks were distributed in Russian Turkistan mainly in the Syrdarya, Samarkand, and Fergana *oblasti* and in the semi-independent khanates of Bukhara and Khiva. They had no national status and were not recognized as a distinct nationality for administrative purpose. In Tashkent, power passed first to a Turkistan Committee of the Provisional Government and then to a Communist-controlled Council of Workers', Soldiers', and Peasants' Deputies. In these, the Uzbeks and other Muslims played virtually no part, although a Muslim Council (Shurayi-Islām) and a Muslim reformist movement, the Jadid-ul-Islām, were active, the former having come into existence about 1902. In December 1917 the Muslims convoked a National Congress in Kokand, and a Muslim government under Mustafa Chokayev was formed. This was liquidated in February 1918 by a military force sent from Tashkent, which in turn provoked a resistance movement, known as the Basmachi Revolt, against the new regime. This is sometimes represented as a positive Turkistani nationalist movement aiming at independence from Soviet rule; but it is also possible that it was more the reaction of the people to inefficient and oppressive authority.

The Basmachi Revolt

In April 1918 the Autonomous Soviet Socialist Republic of Turkistan was proclaimed. For most of the period from the outbreak of the October Revolution until September 1919, Turkistan was cut off from European Russia by White forces, and power was in the hands of Russian settler elements in Tashkent, who resisted Moscow's efforts to persuade them to include Muslims in the government.

Disturbed at the way in which the potential sympathy of the Turkistan peoples for the Soviet regime had been alienated, Lenin dispatched the Turkistan Commission in autumn 1919, which took over the authority of the Tashkent government and introduced a number of palliative measures designed to humour the Muslims. The overthrow of the khans of Khiva (Khwārezm) and Bukhara by the Red Army in 1920 and the establishment of the nominally independent but Communist-controlled Khwārezm and Bukharan People's Soviet republics (which became Soviet Socialist republics in 1923 and 1924) led to an extension of the Basmachi Revolt, particularly in the eastern part of the former emirate of Bukhara. When the Turkistan Commission introduced a number of real reforms in 1922, the revolt began to collapse.

In 1924 a fundamental redrawing of the administrative boundaries of Central Asia and Kazakhstan on ethnic lines was carried out. The republics of Turkistan, Khwārezm (Khiva), and Bukhara were abolished and the whole area divided into five republics: Uzbekistan, Tadzhikistan, Kirgiziya, Turkmenistan, and Kazakhstan. Tadzhikistan was an Autonomous Soviet Republic within Uzbekistan until December 5, 1929, when it became a Soviet Socialist republic. In December 1936 Uzbekistan was expanded by the incorporation of the Karakalpak Autonomous Soviet Socialist Republic, which had belonged to Kazakhstan until 1930 and afterward had come under direct control of the Russian Soviet Federated Socialist Republic. In 1956 and 1963 parts of southern Kazakhstan, including the Hungry Steppe, were transferred from the Kazakh to the Uzbek S.S.R. In 1971 some of this territory was returned.

In 1937–38, during the Great Purge, a nationalist plot was said to have been discovered and a number of Uzbeks were executed, including the prime minister, Fayzullah Khodzhayev, and the first secretary of the Uzbek Communist Party, Akmal Ikramov. Both were "rehabilitated" after Stalin's death. (Ed.)

BIBLIOGRAPHY. The following reference titles may be recommended as sources of general information: *СССР: Энциклопедический справочник* (1982), an illustrated handbook giving extensive information on natural features, population, political structure, history, economic conditions, science and technology, and cultural life; *Die Union der Sozialistischen Sowjetrepubliken: Handbuch* (1979), a similar handbook published in the German Democratic Republic; *Soviet Union: Political and Economic Reference Book* (1977), a Soviet book published for English-language users; *Советский энциклопедический словарь* (1980), another Soviet publication, containing 1,600 pages of text with almost 1,000 illustrations, charts, and maps, providing about 80,000 entries of encyclopaedic nature, including biographical information; VADIM MEDISH, *The Soviet Union* (1981), a comprehensive introduction to practically all aspects of contemporary Soviet life, with the constitution of the U.S.S.R. appended.

Physical and human geography: English-language studies of the land and people include LEV S. BERG, *Natural Regions of the U.S.S.R.* (1950; originally published in Russian, 2nd ed., 1938), an important, authoritative work on the physical geography of the U.S.S.R. by a scientist who had an outstanding reputation; VIKTOR BUNAK *et al.*, *Contributions to the Physical Anthropology of the Soviet Union* (1960); JOHN P. COLE and FRANK C. GERMAN, *A Geography of the U.S.S.R.*, 2nd ed. (1970); JOHN C. DEWDNEY, *A Geography of the Soviet Union*, 3rd ed. (1979); INNOKENTY P. GERASIMOV *et al.*, *Natural Resources of the Soviet Union, Their Use and Renewal* (1971); *Man, Society, and the Environment: Geographical Aspects of the Uses of Natural Resources and Nature Conservation* (1975), a translation from Russian of research papers of the INSTITUTE OF GEOGRAPHY of the U.S.S.R. ACADEMY OF SCIENCES; PAUL E. LYDOLPH, *Geography of the U.S.S.R.*, 3rd ed. (1977), *Geography of the U.S.S.R.: Topical Analysis* (1979), and *Climates of the Soviet Union* (1976); WILLIAM H. PARKER, *An Historical Geography of Russia* (1968), and *The Soviet Union* (1969); V.V. POKSHISHEVSKY, *Geography of the Soviet Union: Physical Background, Population, Economy* (1974); PHILIP R. PRYDE, *Conservation in the Soviet Union* (1972); НИКОЛАЙ А. ГВОЗДЕЦКИЙ and НИКОЛАЙ И. МИХАЙЛОВ, *Физическая география СССР, Азиатская часть*, 3rd ed. (1978); EUGENE K. KEEFE *et al.* (eds.), *Soviet Union: A Country Study* (1971, reprinted 1980); JUDITH PALLOT and DENIS J.B. SHAW, *Planning in the Soviet Union* (1981), a treatment of economic planning from the aspect of physical factors; ROY E.H. MELLOR, *The Soviet Union and Its Geographical Problems* (1982); LESLIE SYMONS *et al.* (eds.), *The Soviet Union: A Systematic Geography* (1982).

Useful introductory works on the Soviet economy include MORRIS BORNSTEIN and DANIEL FUSFELD, *The Soviet Economy: A Book of Readings*, 4th ed. (1974); ALEC NOVE, *An Economic History of the U.S.S.R.* (1969, reprinted 1982); MORRIS BORNSTEIN, *The Soviet Economy, Continuity and Change* (1981); GEORGE R. FEIWEL, *The Soviet Quest for Economic Efficiency: Issues, Controversies, and Reforms*, 2nd ed. (1972). Studies of the growth and development of the Soviet economy include ABRAM BERGSON, *The Real National Income of Soviet Russia Since 1928* (1961); ALASTAIR MCAULEY, *Economic Welfare in the Soviet Union* (1979), a complement to the Bergson work; ROBERT W. CAMPBELL, *The Soviet-Type Economies: Performance and Evolution,* 3rd ed. (1973; originally published as *Soviet Economic Power: Its Organization, Growth, and Challenge,* 1960); RAYMOND HUTCHINGS, *Soviet Economic Development* (1971); VLADIMIR G. TREML, *Studies in Soviet Input-Output Analysis* (1977); TIMOTHY DUNMORE, *The Stalinist Command Economy: The Soviet State Apparatus and Economic Policy 1945–53* (1981); PAUL R. GREGORY and ROBERT C. STUART, *Soviet Economic Structure and Performance,* 2nd ed. (1981). Economic resources and their development are treated in JOHN C. DEWDNEY, *The USSR* (1976); A.N. LAVRISHCHEV, *Economic Geography of the USSR* (1969; originally published in Russian, 1965); RAYMOND S. MATHIESON, *The Soviet Union: An Economic Geography* (1975); НИКОЛАЙ П. НИКИТИН *et al.* (eds.), *Экономическая география СССР,* 4th ed. (1973); LESLIE DIENES and THEODORE SHABAD, *The Soviet Energy System: Resource Use and Policies* (1979); THEODORE SHABAD and VICTOR L. MODE, *Gateway to Siberian Resources (The BAM)* (1977). Organization and output in various branches of the economy are treated in IAIN F. ELLIOT, *The Soviet Energy Balance: Natural Gas, Other Fossil Fuels, and Alternative Power Sources* (1974); G.W. HEMY, *The Soviet Chemical Industry* (1971); JORDAN A. HODGKINS, *Soviet Power: Energy Resources, Production and Potentials* (1961, reprinted 1975); GEORGE MARKON, *Mineral Industries of Eastern Europe and the U.S.S.R.* (1978); CECIL RAJANA, *The Chemical and Petro-Chemical Industries of Russia and Eastern Europe, 1960–1980* (1975); ROBERT W. CAMPBELL, *Soviet Energy Technologies* (1980); HARRY G. SHAFFER, *Soviet Agriculture: An Assessment of Its Contributions to Economic Development* (1977); ARTHUR E. ADAMS and JAN S. ADAMS, *Men Versus Systems: Agriculture in the U.S.S.R., Poland, and Czechoslovakia* (1971); LESLIE SYMONS, *Russian Agriculture: A Geographic Survey* (1972); LESLIE SYMONS and COLIN WHITE, *Russian Transport: An Historical and Geographical Survey* (1975). A valuable compendium of economic statistics for the Soviet period is ROGER A. CLARKE, *Soviet Economic Facts 1917–1970* (1972). Regional economic studies include ALLEN S. WHITING, *Siberian Development and East Asia: Threat or Promise?* (1981); VIOLET CONOLLY, *Siberia Today and Tomorrow: A Study of Economic Resources, Problems, and Achievements* (1976); E. STUART KIRBY, *The Soviet Far East* (1971); ALEXANDRE A. BENNIGSEN and S. ENDERS WIMBUSH, *Muslim National Communism in the Soviet Union: A Revolutionary Strategy for the Colonial World* (1979). Soviet economic planning is the subject of a large literature, among which may be recommended ABRAM BERGSON, *The Economics of Soviet Planning* (1964, reprinted 1980), and *Productivity and the Social System: The U.S.S.R. and the West* (1978); CONSTANTIN A. KRYLOV, *The Soviet Economy: How It Really Works* (1979); *Soviet Economy in a Time of Change: A Compendium of Papers Submitted to the Joint Economic Committee, Congress, October 10, 1979* (1979); GEORGE J. DEMKO and ROLAND J. FUCHS, *Geographical Perspectives in the Soviet Union* (1974); JANE DEGRAS and ALEC NOVE (eds.), *Soviet Planning: Essays in Honour of Naum Jasny* (1964, reprinted 1981). MICHAEL ELLMAN, *Soviet Planning Today: Proposals for an Optimally Functioning Economic System* (1971), and *Socialist Planning* (1979); JOHN P. HARDT *et al.* (eds.), *Mathematics and Computers in Soviet Economic Planning* (1967); MOSHÉ LEWIN, *Political Undercurrents in Soviet Economic Debates: From Bukharin to the Modern Reformers* (1974); HOWARD J. SHERMAN, *The Soviet Economy* (1969); NICHOLAS SPULBER, *The Soviet Economy: Structure, Principles, Problems,* rev. ed. (1969); JOZEF WILCZYNSKI, *Socialist Economic Development and Reforms* (1972), and *The Economics of Socialism: Principles Governing the Operation of the Centrally Planned Economies in the U.S.S.R. and Eastern Europe Under the New System,* 3rd ed. (1977); ALFRED ZAUBERMAN, *Mathematical Theory in Soviet Planning* (1976); ARON KATSENELINBOIGEN, *Soviet Economic Thought and Political Power in the U.S.S.R.* (1980). Foreign economic relations are discussed in V.F. GRUZINOV, *The U.S.S.R.'s Management of Foreign Trade* (1980; originally published in Russian, 1975), describing organization of foreign trade in the Soviet Union and some theoretical issues of foreign trade management; PHILIP HANSON, *Trade and Technology in Soviet-Western Relations* (1981), a comprehensive work on economics of foreign trade and technology transfer; E.G. FEUCHTWANGER and PETER NAILOR (eds.), *The Soviet Union and the Third World* (1981), an overview of political, ideological, military, and economic factors, with an especially informative chapter on trade; GIUSEPPE SCHIAVONE, *The Institutions of Comecon* (1981), an important source work on the Council for Mutual Economic Assistance; JOZEF M. VAN BRABANT, *Socialist Economic Integration: Aspects of Contemporary Economic Problems in Eastern Europe* (1980), a discussion of central planning and its political and technical issues.

Works on administrative and social conditions include JOHN A. ARMSTRONG, *The Politics of Totalitarianism: The Communist Party of the Soviet Union from 1934 to the Present* (1961); DONALD R. KELLEY (ed.), *Soviet Politics in the Brezhnev Era* (1980); FREDERICK C. BARGHOORN, *Politics in the U.S.S.R.,* 2nd ed. (1972), and *Detente and the Democratic Movement in the U.S.S.R.* (1976); L.G. CHURCHWARD, *Contemporary Soviet Government,* 2nd rev. ed. (1975); ROBERT CONQUEST, *Power and Policy in the U.S.S.R.: The Struggle for Stalin's Succession, 1945–1960* (1967); MARGARET DEWAR, *Labour Policy in the U.S.S.R., 1917–1928* (1956, reprinted 1979); PHILIP HANSON, *The Consumer in the Soviet Economy* (1968), and *Advertising and Socialism* (1974); A. INKELES, *Social Change in Soviet Russia* (1968, reissued 1971); ROBERT G. KAISER, *Russia: The People and the Power* (1976), and *Russia from the Inside* (1980); MOSHÉ LEWIN, *Russian Peasants and Soviet Power* (1968, reprinted 1975; originally published in French, 1966); MERVYN MATTHEWS, *Class and Society in Soviet Russia* (1972), and its sequel, *Privilege in the Soviet Union* (1978); JAMES MILLAR (ed.), *The Soviet Rural Community: A Symposium* (1971); W.H. PARKER, *The Russians* (1973); HARRISON E. SALISBURY (ed.), *Soviet Society Since the Revolution* (1979); HEDRICK SMITH, *The Russians* (1976); ARCADIUS KAHAN and BLAIR A. RUBLE (eds.), *Industrial Labour in the U.S.S.R.* (1979); LEONARD SCHAPIRO and JOSEPH GODSON (eds.), *The Soviet Worker: Illusions and Realities* (1981). JERRY F. HOUGH and MERLE FAINSOD, *How the Soviet Union Is Governed,* rev. ed. (1979); JOHN N. HAZARD, *The Soviet Legal System: Fundamental Principles and Historical Commentary,* 3rd ed. (1977), *The Soviet Legal System: Selected Contemporary Legislation and Documents* (1978), and *The Soviet System of Government,* 5th rev. ed. (1980); ANDREA LEE, *Russian Journal* (1981); JIRI ZUZANEK, *Work and Leisure in the Soviet Union: A Time Budget Analysis* (1980); JENNY BRINE *et al.* (eds.), *Home, School and Leisure in the Soviet Union* (1980); DONALD D. BARRY *et al.* (eds.), *Contemporary Soviet Law* (1974); R.W. MAKEPEACE, *Marxist Ideology and Soviet Criminal Law* (1980); WOLFGANG LEONHARD, *The Kremlin Since Stalin* (1962, reprinted 1975; originally published in German, 1959); WESLEY A. FISHER, *The Soviet Marriage Market: Mate-Selection in Russia and the U.S.S.R.* (1980); BERNICE Q. MADISON, *Soviet Income Maintenance Programs in the Struggle Against Poverty* (1978), and *Soviet Social Welfare System* (1982); KLAUS MENHERT, *Soviet Man and His World* (1962, reprinted 1976; originally published in German, 1959); ELIZABETH POND, *From the Yaroslavsky Station: Russia Perceived* (1981); ALEC NOVE, *Political Economy and Soviet Socialism* (1979); ANTON REFREGIER, *Sketches of the Soviet Union* (1978); ALBINA TRETYAKOVA, *Labor and Capital in the Soviet Union by Republics* (1977). Russian political tradition is discussed in NICHOLAS P. VAKAR, *The Taproot of Soviet Society* (1962), the exposition of the author's theory of the peasant character of Soviet rule. This theory is balanced by several later titles, including ROBERT E.F. SMITH (ed.), *The Russian Peasant, 1920 and 1984* (1977); THEODORE H. FRIEDGUT, *Political Participation in the U.S.S.R.* (1979); and THOMAS H. RIGBY *et al.* (eds.), *Authority, Power and Policy in the U.S.S.R.* (1981), which deal with the interaction between personalities and political, legal, cultural, ideological, and economic institutions. A valuable set of social statistics appears in ELLEN MICKIEWICZ (ed.), *Handbook of Soviet Social Science Data* (1973).

The official Soviet exposition of social, economic, and foreign policies is found in an illustrated book specially published for foreigners: BORIS KROTKOV, *The Soviet Union in the '80s: The 26th CPSU Congress Declares, Our Main Aims, Prosperity at Home, and Peace in the World* (1981). For a broader look at the Communist Party and its activities, see LEONARD B. SCHAPIRO, *The Government and Politics of the Soviet Union,* 6th rev. ed. (1978), and *The Communist Party of the Soviet Union,* 2nd rev. ed. (1971), the latter being a well-known history of the CPSU; RONALD J. HILL and PETER FRANK, *The Soviet Communist Party* (1981), concentrates on the party's structure, functioning, and membership.

Soviet education is discussed in NIGEL GRANT, *Soviet Education,* 4th ed. (1979); MERVYN MATTHEWS, *Education in the Soviet Union: Policies and Institutions Since Stalin* (1982); KITTY D. WEAVER, *Russia's Future: The Communist Education of Soviet Youth* (1981); N. NORMAN SHNEIDMAN, *The Soviet Road to Olympus* (1979); SEYMOUR M. ROSEN, *Education in the U.S.S.R.: Recent Legislation and Statistics* (1975), *Education in the U.S.S.R.: Research and Innovation* (1978), and *Education in the U.S.S.R.: Current Status of Higher Education* (1980), a series of government reports; and YUSHIN YOO, *Soviet Education: An Annotated Bibliography and Readers' Guide to Works in English, 1893–1978* (1980), an extensive bibliographic survey.

Cultural life is treated in ARTHUR VOYCE, *Moscow and the Roots of Russian Culture* (1964, reprinted 1972); BERNHARD J. STERN and SAMUEL SMITH (eds.), *Understanding the Russians: A Study of Soviet Life and Culture* (1947, reprinted 1971); ELLEN PROPPER MICKIEWICZ, *Media and the Russian Public* (1981); ANGELICA ZANDER RUDENSTINE (ed.), *Russian Avant-garde Art: The George Costakis Collection* (1981); and VINCENZO GOBELLI, *Musicisti di oggi nell'U.R.S.S.* (1972), which includes information on composers of the smaller national areas. Soviet literature can be sampled in several collections and translations: THOMAS P. WHITNEY (ed. and trans.), *The New Writing in Russia* (1964), and *The Young Russians* (1972), both collections of short stories by post-World War II authors; VASILY M. SHUKSHIN, *Snowball Berry Red & Other Stories* (1979; trans. by DONALD M. FIENE *et al.*); ALEXANDER GREEN, *Scarlet Sails* (1967; trans. by THOMAS P. WHITNEY); and YURY V. TRIFONOV, *The Long Goodbye* (1978; trans. by HELEN P. BURLINGAME and ELLENDEA PROFFER). Sources of scholarly literary criticism are VLADIMIR V. NABOKOV, *Lectures on Russian Literature* (1981); and HAROLD B. SEGEL, *Twentieth-Century Russian Drama: From Gorky to the Present* (1979).

History to c. 1700: The best brief survey of early Russian history in English is SERGEI F. PLATONOV, *History of Russia* (1925, reprinted 1964; originally published in Russian, 1910; French trans. 1929). A judicious survey is NICHOLAS V. RIASANOVSKY, *A History of Russia,* 3rd ed. (1977). Other useful surveys include V.O. KLIUCHEVSKY, *A History of Russia,* 5 vol. (1911–31, reissued 1960; new trans. of vol. 3, 1970; originally published in Russian, 1904–10); and PAVEL N. MILIUKOV, *Outlines of Russian Culture,* 3 vol. (1942; originally published in Russian, 1898–1903). On the history of Kiev, see BORIS D. GREKOV, *Kiev Rus* (1959; originally published in Russian, 1953); M.W. THOMPSON, *Novgorod the Great* (1967); and GEORGE VERNADSKY, *Kievan Russia* (1948, reprinted 1973), and *The Origins of Russia* (1959, reprinted 1975). The Mongol period is treated in GEORGE VERNADSKY, *The Mongols and Russia* (1953). For the history of Muscovy, see JOHN L.I. FENNELL, *The Emergence of Moscow, 1304–1359* (1968), and *Ivan the Great of Moscow* (1961); SERGEI F. PLATONOV, *The Time of Troubles: A Historical Study of the Internal Crises and Social Struggle in Sixteenth- and Seventeenth-Century Muscovy* (1970; originally published in Russian, 1923); GEORGE VERNADSKY, *Russia at the Dawn of the Modern Age* (1959), and *The Tsardom of Moscow, 1547–1682,* 2 vol. (1969).

1700–1801: A topical interpretive synthesis, with a comprehensive bibliographical guide, is MARC RAEFF, *Imperial Russia 1682–1825: The Coming of Age of Modern Russia* (1971). It is complemented by MARC RAEFF (ed.), *Catherine the Great: A Profile* (1972). For imperial institutions, see the indispensable ERIK AMBURGER, *Geschichte der Behördenorganisation Russlands von Peter dem Grossen bis 1917* (1966). For the reforms and reign of Peter the Great, a very brief summary is BENEDICT H. SUMNER, *Peter the Great and the Emergence of Russia* (1950, reprinted 1972); while the only comprehensive survey is REINHARD WITTRAM, *Peter I, Czar und Kaiser,* 2 vol. (1964). The standard economic history of Russia is PETER I. LYASHCHENKO, *History of the National Economy of Russia to the 1917 Revolution* (1949, reprinted 1970; originally published in Russian, 2 vol., 1947–48). For an introduction to a history of the nobility, both as social class and matrix of the intelligentsia, see MARC RAEFF, *Origins of the Russian Intelligentsia: The Eighteenth-Century Nobility* (1966). For the Russian Church, see JAMES CRACRAFT, *The Church Reform of Peter the Great* (1971). For an insight into the dissident Old Believers, see ROBERT O. CRUMMEY, *The Old Believers and the World of Antichrist: The Vyg Community and the Russian State, 1694–1855* (1970). On education, cultural life, and the emergence of radical thought among the intelligentsia, see HAROLD B. SEGEL (comp.), *The Literature of Eighteenth-Century Russia,* 2 vol. (1967). Sources of philosophy and social thought may be found in JAMES M. EDIE, JAMES P. SCANLAN, and MARY-BARBARA ZELDIN (eds.), *Russian Philosophy,* 3 vol. (1965, reissued 1976); and MARC RAEFF (ed.), *Russian Intellectual History: An Anthology* (1966, reprinted 1978). For a comprehensive survey of philosophical trends, see V.V. ZENKOVSKY, *A History of Russian Philosophy,* 2 vol. (1953, reprinted 1967; originally published in Russian, 1948–50). On educational and scientific institutions, see A.S. VUCINICH, *Science in Russian Culture,* vol. 1, *A History to 1860* (1963), and its sequel, *Science in Russian Culture, 1861–1917* (1970); the seminal revolt of Radishchev is discussed by ALLEN MCCONNELL in *A Russian Philosophe: Alexander Radishchev* (1964, reprinted 1981); and in RADISHCHEV's *Journey from St. Petersburg to Moscow,* trans. and ed. by LEO WIENER and RODERICK PAGE THALER (1958). On the influence of the German Enlightenment and Russia's relations with the West, see MARC RAEFF, "Les Slaves, les Allemands, et les 'Lumières,' " *Revue Canadienne d'Études Slaves,* 1:521–551 (1967).

1801–1917: General surveys of Russian history in the 19th century include: MICHAEL T. FLORINSKY, *Russia: A History and an Interpretation,* 2 vol. (1953–54, reprinted 1960); and HUGH SETON-WATSON, *The Russian Empire, 1801–1917* (1967). The best work in English on the reign of Alexander I is MARC RAEFF, *Michael Speransky, Statesman of Imperial Russia, 1772–1839,* 2nd rev. ed. (1969, reprinted 1979). The best work on the reign of Nicholas I is NICHOLAS V. RIASANOVSKY, *Nicholas I and Official Nationality in Russia, 1825–1855* (1959, reprinted 1969); intellectual life during the reign of Nicholas I is described in his *A Parting of Ways: Government and the Educated Public in Russia, 1801–1855* (1976). A useful addition is JOHN S. CURTISS, *The Russian Army Under Nicholas I, 1825–1855* (1965), a general description of the army's performance; a highly detailed operational account as seen by the Russian high command is found in ALBERT SEATON, *The Crimean War* (1977). In *Black Night, White Snow: Russia's Revolutions, 1905–1917* (1978, reprinted 1981), HARRISON E. SALISBURY grapples with a large subject and emerges on top. For the general economic development of Russia in the 19th century, see G.T. ROBINSON, *Rural Russia Under the Old Régime* (1932, reprinted 1969). The industrialization drive of the 1890s is treated in THEODORE VON LAUE, *Sergei Witte and the Industrialization of Russia* (1963, reprinted 1974). Economic and political trends at the turn of the 20th century are discussed in D.W. TREADGOLD, *The Great Siberian Migration* (1957, reprinted 1976). Biographical studies that do much to explain the interplay of cultural and political factors in the 19th century are M. MALIA, *Alexander Herzen and the Birth of Russian Socialism, 1812–1855* (1961, reprinted 1965); and RICHARD PIPES, *Struve: Liberal on the Left,* vol. 1, *1870–1905* (1961), and *Struve: Liberal on the Right, 1905–1944* (1980). For the earlier revolutionary movement and the development of so-called Populism, the classical description and interpretation is FRANCO VENTURI, *Roots of Revolution* (1960, reprinted 1966; originally published in Italian, 1952, reissued 1972), and his later work, *Studies in Free Russia* (1982), describes 19th-century Socialist movements. An absolutely essential source for the history of revolutionary activity up to 1917 are the earlier volumes of Lenin's *Works* (available in English in many editions). Three useful books on individual non-Russian peoples in this period are MICHAEL HRUSHEVSKY, *A History of the Ukraine* (1941, reprinted 1970; originally published in Ukrainian, 1918); S.A. ZENKOVSKY, *Pan-Turkism and Islam in Russia* (1960, reprinted 1967); and GEOFFREY WHEELER, *The Modern History of Soviet Central Asia* (1964, reprinted 1975). Four studies of important moments and problems in Russian foreign policy, which thoroughly examine the Russian point of view, are MARIAN KUKIEL, *Czartoryski and European Unity, 1770–1861* (1955, reprinted 1981); MICHAEL B. PETROVICH, *The Emergence of Russian Panslavism, 1856–1870* (1956); B.H. SUMNER, *Russia and the Balkans, 1870–1880* (1937, reprinted 1962); and A. MALOZEMOFF, *Russian Far Eastern Policy, 1881–1904* (1958, reprinted 1977). On the final collapse of tsardom, MICHAEL T. FLORINSKY, *The End of the Russian Empire* (1931, reprinted 1973), remains the best general survey. RICHARD PIPES, *Russia Under the Old Regime* (1974), is a historical overview of prerevolutionary Russia from the 9th century to the 1880s, with an analysis of the principal social groups—peasantry, nobility, bourgeoisie, and clergy.

1917–1939: General works on the period include: GEORG VON RAUCH, *A History of Soviet Russia,* 6th ed. (1972; originally published in German, 1955), a critical survey; EDWARD HALLETT CARR, *A History of Soviet Russia,* 14 vol. (1950–78), a detailed history of the years 1917–29; RAPHAEL R. ABRAMOVITCH, *The Soviet Revolution, 1917–1939* (1962), the Menshevik viewpoint; B.N. PONOMAREV *et al.* (eds.), *History of the Communist Party of the Soviet Union,* 2nd rev. ed. (1963), translation of an official Soviet textbook that has since been updated (the 5th enlarged edition of the Russian original was published in 1978 and reprinted in 1980); MAURICE DOBB, *Soviet Economic Development Since 1917,* 6th ed. (1966), sympathetic though critical; and DONALD W. TREADGOLD, *Twentieth Century Russia,* 5th ed. (1981), a substantial overview, with 30 pages of bibliography. Biographies of the Bolshevik leaders include: ADAM B. ULAM, *The Bolsheviks* (1955, reprinted 1976), on Lenin; ISAAC DEUTSCHER, *The Prophet Armed: Trotsky 1879–1921* (1954, reprinted 1980), *The Prophet Unarmed . . . 1921–1929* (1959, reprinted 1980), and *The Prophet Outcast . . . 1929–1940* (1963, reprinted 1980); BORIS SOUVARINE, *Stalin* (1939, reprinted 1972; originally published in French, 1935); and ROBERT CONQUEST, *The Great Terror,* rev. ed. (1973), an exhaustive account of the purges of the 1930s. Outstanding works on Soviet foreign relations include: MAX BELOFF, *The Foreign Policy of Soviet Russia, 1929–1941,* 2 vol. (1947–49, reprinted 1966–68); LOUIS FISCHER, *The Soviets in World Affairs,* 2 vol., 2nd ed. (1951, reprinted 1975), and *Russia's Road from Peace to War: Soviet Foreign Relations* (1969, reprinted 1979); GEORGE F. KENNAN, *Russia and the West Under Lenin and Stalin* (1961), a critical analysis of the period 1917–45; and ADAM B. ULAM, *Expansion and Coexistence: Soviet Foreign Policy, 1917–73,* 2nd ed. (1974).

1940 to the present: (*World War II*): ALEXANDER DALLIN, *German Rule in Russia, 1941–1945: A Study of Occupation Policies,* 2nd ed. (1981); ALBERT SEATON, *The Russo-German War, 1941–45* (1971); HARRISON E. SALISBURY, *The 900 Days: The Siege of Leningrad* (1970), and *The Unknown War* (1978); Г.А. КУМАНЕВ, *1941–1945: Краткая история, документы, фотографии* (1980), a short history, with documents and photographs. (*Domestic politics*): *History of the U.S.S.R. in Three Parts,* 3 vol. (1977; trans. from Russian), a comprehensive Soviet work covering the period from the early days of Russia to the Soviet Union of the mid-1970s; RUSSIAN INSTITUTE, COLUMBIA UNIVERSITY (ed.), *The Anti-Stalin Campaign and International Communism* (1956), the text of Khrushchev's secret speech at the 20th Party Congress and related documents; CARL A. LINDEN, *Khrushchev and the Soviet Leadership, 1957–1964* (1966), an analysis of leadership conflicts; ARCHIE BROWN and MICHAEL KASER (eds.), *The Soviet Union Since the Fall of Khrushchev,* 2nd ed. (1978); JOHN A. ARMSTRONG, *Ideology, Politics, and Government in the Soviet Union,* 4th ed. (1978); MERVYN MATTHEWS (comp.), *Soviet Government: A Selection of Official Documents on Internal Policies* (1974); HENRY W. MORTON and RUDOLF L. TÖKÉS (eds.), *Soviet Politics and Society in the 1970's* (1974); JOHN LÖWENHARDT, *Decision Making in Soviet Politics* (1981); MARTIN MCCAULEY, *The Soviet Union Since 1917* (1981), a work that traces major developments in the history of Russia from the March Revolution of 1917 to Soviet activities in Angola and Afghanistan in the middle and late 1970s; DOROTHY ATKINSON *et al.* (eds.), *Women in Russia* (1977); ALISTAIR MCAULEY, *Women's Work and Wages in the Soviet Union* (1981); VLADIMIR G. TREML, *Alcohol in the U.S.S.R.* (1982); ADAM B. ULAM, *Russia's Failed Revolutions: From the Decembrists to the Dissidents* (1981); ABRAHAM BRUMBERG (comp.), *In Quest of Justice* (1970), commentaries and documents of protest and dissent in the Soviet Union; SIDNEY BLOCH and PETER REDDAWAY, *Psychiatric Terror* (1977), a work by a psychiatrist and a student of Soviet politics. MARSHALL S. SHATZ, *Soviet Dissent in Historical Perspective* (1981); НАТАЛИЯ ГОРБАНЕВСКАЯ (ed.), *Память: Исторический сборник* (1976–), a historical compendium on political persecution in Russia in the 20th century; ANDREI D. SAKHAROV, *Sakharov Speaks* (1974); AMNESTY INTERNATIONAL, *Prisoners of Conscience in the U.S.S.R.: Their Treatment and Conditions,* 2nd ed. (1980); S.P. de BOER *et al.* (eds. and comps.), *Biographical Dictionary of Dissidents in the Soviet Union, 1956–1975* (1982), containing almost 3,400 concise biographies of Soviet citizens of various social, religious, and political backgrounds who have opposed the government.

(*International relations*): N.I. LEBEDEV, *Great October and Today's World* (1981; originally published in Russian, 1978), a work on Soviet foreign relations—interesting as an indicator of official thinking—written by the rector of the Moscow Institute of International Relations, which trains Soviet diplomats; RAYMOND J. SONTAG and JAMES S. BEDDIE (eds.), *Nazi–Soviet Relations, 1939–1941: Documents from the Archives of the German Foreign Office* (1948, reprinted 1976); И.Н. ЗЕМСКОВ, *Дипломатическая история второго фронта в Европе* (1982), a history of diplomacy covering the period 1939–44; ODED ERAN, *The Mezhdunarodniki: An Assessment of Professional Expertise in the Making of Soviet Foreign Policy* (1980), a historical survey of institutions and personnel involved in Soviet foreign policy; KAREN DAWISHA and PHILIP HANSON (eds.), *Soviet–East European Dilemmas: Coercion, Competition, and Consent* (1981), a survey of politics within the Eastern bloc; FRED H. EIDLIN, *The Logic of "Normalization": The Soviet Intervention in Czechoslovakia of 21 August 1968 and the Czechoslovak Response* (1980); TUFTON BEAMISH and GUY HADLEY, *The Kremlin's Dilemma: The Struggle for Human Rights in Eastern Europe* (1979); RAYMOND W. DUNCAN (ed.), *Soviet Policy in Developing Countries,* 2nd ed. (1981).

DONALD S. ZAGORIA (ed.), *Soviet Policy in East Asia* (1982); GEORGE GINSBURGS and CARL F. PINKELE, *The Sino-Soviet Territorial Dispute, 1949–64* (1978); ALASTAIR BUCHAN, *The End of the Postwar Era: A New Balance of World Power* (1974); WALTER LaFEBER, *America, Russia, and the Cold War, 1945–1980,* 4th ed. (1980), a view of the origins and history of the Cold War; WILLIAM TAUBMAN, *Stalin's American Policy: From Entente to Detente to Cold War* (1982); LAWRENCE CALDWELL and WILLIAM DIEBOLD, *Soviet–American Relations in the 1980s: Superpower Politics and East–West Trade* (1980), an assessment of Soviet foreign policy; RICHARD PIPES, *U.S.–Soviet Relations in the Era of Detente* (1981). (*The economy*): ALEC NOVE, *The Soviet Economic System* (1977), an excellent introduction to the Soviet economy; DAVID GRANICK, *Managerial Comparisons of Four Developed Countries: France, Britain, United States, and Russia* (1972); NICHOLAS LAMPERT, *The Technical Intelligentsia and the Soviet State: A Study of Soviet Managers and Technicians 1928–1935* (1979), a work on the place of the technical intelligentsia in Soviet society; JAN S. ADAMS, *Citizen Inspectors in the Soviet Union* (1977), a discussion of the role of the People's Control Committees in the Soviet economy; HOLLAND HUNTER (ed.), *Future of the Soviet Economy: 1978–1985* (1978); STEVEN A. GRANT (ed.), *Soviet Housing and Urban Design* (1980); LAZAR VOLIN, *A Century of Russian Agriculture: From Alexander II to Khrushchev* (1970), a scholarly treatment of both pre-Soviet and Soviet agricultural policies and problems; EVERETT M. JACOBS (ed.), *The Organization of Agriculture in the Soviet Union and Eastern Europe* (1982); MARSHALL I. GOLDMAN, *The Spoils of Progress* (1972), a survey of environmental pollution in the Soviet Union. (*Military problems*): SERGEI M. SHTEMENKO, *The Soviet General Staff at War, 1941–1945* (1975; originally published in Russian, 1968), the memoirs of the head of the general staff under Stalin; HARRIET FAST SCOTT and WILLIAM F. SCOTT, *The Armed Forces of the U.S.S.R.* (1979), a factual compendium on almost all aspects of the Soviet defense establishment, including the relationship between the Communist Party and the military; EDWARD L. WARNER III, *The Military in Contemporary Soviet Politics* (1979), a discussion of the role of the military in the formation of Soviet policy; MARK E. MILLER, *Soviet Strategic Power and Doctrine* (1982), an analysis of the Soviet quest for superiority; JOSEPH D. DOUGLAS, JR., *Soviet Military Strategy in Europe* (1980), a study based on translations of official Soviet literature on military science; HERBERT GOLDHAMER, *The Soviet Soldier* (1975), a Rand Corporation research study on Soviet military management at the troop level; JOHN E. MOORE, *The Soviet Navy Today* (1976); and BRADFORD DISMUKES and JAMES M. MCCONNELL (eds.), *Soviet Naval Diplomacy* (1979), works on the use of the Soviet Navy for political purposes and on its deployment. (*Biographies*): ISAAC DEUTSCHER, *Stalin,* 2nd ed. (1966, reprinted 1978), a well-written biography; EDWARD CRANKSHAW, *Khrushchev: A Career* (1966, reissued 1971), a standard biography; ALBERT SEATON, *Stalin as Warlord* (1976), the first comprehensive and analytical military biography of the Soviet dictator; *Leonid Ilyich Brezhnev: A Short Biography* (1977), English translation of an official Russian text. (*Cultural issues*): PRISCILLA JOHNSON and LEOPOLD LABEDZ (eds.), *Khrushchev and the Arts: The Politics of Soviet Culture, 1962–1964* (1965), a useful collection of documents on political control of the arts; HAROLD SWAYZE, *Political Control of Literature in the USSR, 1949–1959* (1962), a historical analysis of literary controls; L.G. CHURCHWARD, *The Soviet Intelligentsia* (1973), an essay on the social structure and roles of Soviet intellectuals; ROY A. MEDVEDEV, *An End to Silence: Uncensored Opinion in the Soviet Union* (1982), a collection of materials from Medvedev's underground magazine, *Political Diary,* which contained constructive suggestions for improving life in the Soviet Union; ROY A. MEDVEDEV (ed.), *The Samizdat Register* (1977), and *The Samizdat Register II* (1981), a collection of writings originally included in another underground magazine, *XX Century;* JOSEPHINE WOLL and VLADIMIR TREML (comps.), *Soviet Unofficial Literature—Samizdat* (1978), an annotated bibliography of works published in the West; RONALD HINGLEY, *The Russian Mind,* rev. ed. (1978), an analysis of the Russian character and psyche by an eminent student of Russian literature, and *Russian Writers and Soviet Society, 1917–1978* (1979), a treatise on a multitude of aspects of the life of this segment of the Soviet intelligentsia.

Siberia: Detailed discussions of Soviet development policy in the Far North, its ethnographic background, and sociological effects may be found in STEPHEN P. and ETHEL DUNN, "The Transformation of Economy and Culture in the Soviet North," *Arctic Anthropology,* 1:1–28 (1963); ETHEL DUNN, "Educating the Small Peoples of the Soviet North: Further Thoughts on the Limits of Culture Change," and "Education and the Native Intelligentsia in the Soviet North: The Limits of Culture Change," *ibid.,* 5:1–31 (1968), *ibid.,* 6:112–122 (1970); and in a Soviet book on the topic, ИЛЬЯ С. ГУРВИЧ (ed.), *Этногенез народов Севера* (1980). VLADIMIR I. BOIKO, "Direction and Motivations of Potential Migration of Peoples of the Lower Amur," *Soviet Sociology,* 9:567–578 (1971), and his Russian-language publication, ВЛАДИМИР И. БОЙКО (ed.), *Городское население Тувинской АССР* (1968), provide data on urbanization among small peoples of the Far East. TERENCE ARMSTRONG, *Russian Settlement in the North* (1965), and "The Administration of Northern Peoples: The USSR," in RONALD ST. J. MACDONALD (ed.), *The Arctic Frontier,* pp. 57–88 (1966), are historical and political studies by a Canadian scholar, one of the few Westerners dealing with technological development in the Soviet North; these are supplemented by VIOLET CONOLLY, *Siberia Today and Tomorrow* (1975), which is a study of economic resources of the region and its development problems and achievements; and V. IANOVSKII, "Man in the North," *Soviet Sociology,* 7:16–26 (1969), which gives interesting impressions of "the northern experience" by a prominent Soviet journalist. I.S. GURVICH, "Directions to be Taken in the Further Reorganization of the Economy and Culture of the Peoples of the North," *Soviet Anthropology and Archeology,* 1:22–30 (1962), provides an interesting and important discussion of technical problems and limitations of cultural change for northern peoples. Statistical data on Siberian population is offered in ЕВГЕНИЙ Д. МАЛИНИН and А.К. УШАКОВ, *Население Сибири* (1976). VILMOS DIÓSZEGI and MIHÁLY HOPPÁL (eds.), *Shamanism in Siberia* (1978), gives information on traditional ethnography, especially religion and magic. VLADIMIR G. BOGORAZ, *The Eskimo of Siberia* (1913, reprinted 1975) and *The Chukchee*, 3 pt. (1904–09, reprinted 1975), are classic ethnographies of small Siberian groups, reflecting mainly the situation before intensive Russian contact. Another historical treatise of value is ALEKSEI OKLADNIKOV, *Yakutia Before Its Incorporation into the Russian State* (1970). Strategic aspects of economical and social development of Siberia are discussed in ALLEN S. WHITING, *Siberian Development and East Asia* (1981).

Baltic states: CLARENCE A. MANNING, *The Forgotten Republics* (1952, reprinted 1971), a historical survey of Latvia, Lithuania, and Estonia; GEORGE VON RAUCH, *The Baltic States* (1974; originally published in German, 1970), a survey of 1918–40, the years of independence; BRONIS J. KASLAS, *The Baltic Nations: The Quest for Regional Integration and Political Liberty* (1976); ARVIDS ZIEDONIS *et al.* (eds.), *Problems of Mininations—Baltic Perspectives* (1973), and *Baltic History* (1974), which discuss economic and social conditions in particular; MARIJA GIMBUTAS, *The Balts* (1963, reprinted 1968), a research study devoted to the ancient population of the territories of the Baltic states; SUNITI K. CHATTERJI, *Balts and Aryans in Their Indo-European Background* (1968), which discusses Baltic languages and mythology; ARNOLDS SPEKKE, *The Ancient Amber Routes and the Geographical Discovery of the Eastern Baltic* (1957, reprinted 1976); HENRICUS LETTUS, *The Chronicle of Henry of Livonia* (1961), a 13th-century historical chronicle, originally published in Latin, the English translation being based on the 19th-century version; WILLIAM L. URBAN and J. SMITH (trans.), *The Livonian Rhymed Chronicle* (1973); WILLIAM L. URBAN, *The Baltic Crusade* (1975), concerned mainly with Livonia and Estonia; WALTHER KIRCHNER, *The Rise of the Baltic Question* (1954, reprinted 1970); JILL LISK, *The Struggle for Supremacy in the Baltic: 1600–1725* (1967), a history of the Baltic Sea region; AUGUST REI (ed.), *Nazi-Soviet Conspiracy and the Baltic States: Diplomatic Documents and Other Evidence* (1948), and *The Drama of the Baltic Peoples* (1970, reprinted 1972), deal with political and social conditions in the World War II period; STANLEY W. PAGE, *The Formation of the Baltic States* (1959, reprinted 1970), a study of the influence of the politics of the great powers on the emergence of Lithuania, Latvia, and Estonia; M.W. GRAHAM, *The Diplomatic Recognition of the Baltic States,* 3 vol. (1935–39); ADOLF SPRUDZS and ARMINS RUSIS (eds.), *Res Baltica* (1968), a collection of essays on politics and governments of Baltic states; ALBERT N. TARULIS, *American-Baltic Relations, 1918–1922* (1965), and *Soviet Policy Toward the Baltic States, 1918–1940* (1959), discuss the problems of political recognition of the independent Baltic states; ROYAL INSTITUTE OF INTERNATIONAL AFFAIRS, *The Baltic States* (1938, reprinted 1970), a survey of the political and economic structure and the foreign relations of Estonia, Latvia, and Lithuania in the period before World War II; HUGH I. RODGERS, *Search for Security: A Study in Baltic Diplomacy 1920–1934* (1975); VYTAS S. VARDYS and ROMUALD J. MISIUNAS (eds.), *The Baltic States in Peace and War, 1917–1945* (1978); ALFREDS BERZINS, *The Unpunished Crime* (1963), a book on the incorporation of Latvia into the U.S.S.R. I. KAVASS and A. SPRUDZS (eds.), *Baltic States: A Study of Their Origin and National Development, Their Seizure and Incorporation into the USSR* (1972); JOHN A. SWETTENHAM, *The Tragedy of the Baltic States* (1952, reprinted 1981), a source on the events of the early 1940s, compiled from official documents and eyewitness reports; ADOLFS SILDE, *The Profits of Slavery: Baltic Forced Laborers and Deportees Under Stalin and Khrushchev,* rev. and enlarged ed. (1958; originally published in Latvian, 1956); EDWARD ALLWORTH (ed.), *Nationality Group Survival in Multi-Ethnic States: Shifting Support Patterns in the Soviet Baltic Region* (1977); EDGARS DUNSDORFS, *The Baltic Dilemma* (1975), discusses the recognition of incorporation of Baltic states into the Soviet Union. REINHARD WITTRAM, *Baltische Geschichte* (1954, reprinted 1973), is a work on the history of the Baltic provinces covering the period from 1180 to 1918. For the official Soviet treatment of the events of 1940 in the Baltic states, see И.И. МИНЦ *et al.* (eds.), *Социалистические революции 1940 г. в Литве, Латвии и Эстонии: восстановление Советской власти* (1978).

The separate states: (*Estonia*): JOHN H. JACKSON, *Estonia* 2nd ed. (1948, reprinted 1979); EVALD UUSTALU (ed.), *Aspects of Estonian Culture* (1961); ARTHUR VÖÖBUS, *Studies in the History of the Estonian People,* 3 vol. (1969–74); JUHAN KAHK and K. SIILIVASK, *History of the Estonian SSR* (1979); *Estonia: Story of a Nation* (1974); IVAR PAULSON, *The Old Estonian Folk Religion* (1971); TONU PARMING and ELMAR JARVESOO, *A Case Study of a Soviet Republic: The Estonian SSR* (1978); TONU PARMING, *The Collapse of Liberal Democracy and the Rise of Authoritarianism in Estonia* (1975); OLAF KUULI, *Six Years of Fascist Dictatorship in Estonia* (1975); ARTHUR VADER, *Equal Among Equals* (1974); АРВЕД КАЛВО, *Изгнание фашистов из Южной Эстонии* (1976), a history of the German occupation of Estonia and the military campaigns of August–September 1944; MARJU R. PARMING and TONU PARMING, *A Bibliography of English-Language Sources on Estonia* (1974). (*Latvia*): ALFREDS BILMANIS, *A History of Latvia* (1951, reprinted 1970), and *Latvia as an Independent State* (1947); ANDREW EZERGAILIS, *The 1917 Revolution in Latvia* (1974); ADOLFS BLODNIEKS, *The Undefeated Nation* (1960); GEORGE B. CARSON (ed.), *Latvia,* 2 vol. (1956); EDGAR ANDERSON, *Latvia—Past and Present,* 2nd rev. ed. (1969); JANIS RUTKIS *et al.* (eds.), *Latvia: Country and People* (1967); GUNDAR J. KING, *Economic Policies in Occupied Latvia* (1965); С.И. ПОРТНОВ (comp.), *В сражениях за Советскую Латвию* (1975), a collection of military memoirs, describing German occupation of Latvia and military campaigns in its territory; ВАСИЛИЙ И. САВЧЕНКО, *Латышские формирования Советской Армии на фронтах Великой Отечественной войны* (1975), a study of military history, focussing on Latvian divisions in the Soviet Army during World War II; *Latvian Soviet Socialist Republic* (1972), for foreign readers, a general, illustrated survey published by the Soviets. МИХАИЛ КОЖИН, *Латышская деревня в 50–70е годы XIX века* (1976), a history of rural conditions and agriculture in Latvia; R. EKMANIS, *Latvian Literature Under the Soviets 1940–1975* (1978). (*Lithuania*): OWEN J.C. NOREM, *Timeless Lithuania* (1943, reissued 1967); CONSTANTINE R. JURGELA, *History of the Lithuanian Nation* (1948), *Tannenberg* (*Eglija-Grunwald*) *15 July 1410* (1961), and *Lithuania: The Outpost of Freedom* (1976); JACK J. STUKAS, *Awakening Lithuania: A Study on the Rise of Modern Lithuanian Nationalism* (1966); URIAH KATZENELENBOGEN (ed.), *The Daina: An Anthology of Lithuanian and Latvian Folk Songs* (1935); ALFRED E. SENN, *The Emergence of Modern Lithuania* (1959, reprinted 1975), and *The Great Powers: Lithuania and the Vilna Question 1920–1928* (1966); LEONAS SABALIUNAS, *Lithuania in Crisis: Nationalism to Communism 1939–1940* (1972); BRONIS J. KASLAS (ed.), *The USSR-German Aggression Against Lithuania* (1973); K.V. TAURAS, *Guerilla Warfare on the Amber Coast* (1962); BENEDICT V. MACIUIKA (ed.), *Lithuania in the Last 30 Years* (1955); VYTAS S. VARDYS (ed.), *Lithuania Under the Soviets: Portrait of a Nation 1940–65* (1965), and *The Catholic Church: Dissent and Nationality in Soviet Lithuania* (1978); BRONIUS AKSTINAS, *Glimpses of Lithuania,* 2nd ed. (1978); ALBERTAS GERUTIS (ed.), *Lithuania: 700 Years,* 2nd rev. ed. (1971); *Encyclopedia Lituanica,* 6 vol. (1970–78); ANTANAS BARKAUSKAS, *The Lithuanian Countryside: Past, Present, and Future* (1976), a Moscow Novosti (News) Press Agency publication; JUOZAS MANIUSIS, *Soviet Lithuania: Achievements and Prospects* (1977; trans. from Lithuanian); *Lithuanian Soviet Socialist Republic* (1972), a Soviet publication for foreign readers, from a series devoted to the 50th anniversary of the Soviet Union; MICHAEL BOURDEAUX, *Land of Crosses: The Struggle for Religious Freedom in Lithuania, 1939–78* (1979), illustrated, with a foreword by Franz Cardinal König; ROMAN SZPORLUK (ed.), *The Influence of East Europe and the Soviet West on the USSR* (1975); STEPHEN P. DUNN, *Cultural Processes in the Baltic Area Under Soviet Rule* (1966).

Belorussia: English-language sources on Belorussia are scarce. NICHOLAS P. VAKAR, *Belorussia: The Making of a Nation* (1956), is a detailed work on traditions, origins, and the history of the population and territory; M. DUBENETSKII, *Soviet Byelorussia* (1973), is a brief survey of modern Belorussia published in the Soviet Union for foreign readers; MARCELI KOSMAN, *Historia Białorusi* (1979), is a history in Polish, with a bibliography. Intellectual life in the republic and its popular culture are discussed in ИВАН Е. МАРЧЕНКО, *Культурное строительство в Белорусской ССР, 1946–1958 гг.* (1979). И.М. ИГНАТЕНКО *et al.* (eds.), *История Белорусской ССР* (1977), is an academic history of the Belorussian Soviet Republic. *Белорусская Советская Социалистическая Республика: энциклопедический справочник* (1978), is an encyclopaedic handbook; ВИКТОР Ф. БОРУШКО, *Белоруссия: люди, события, факты* (1977), is a book of general facts. Economic conditions of the 1960s are discussed in ВАЛЕНТИН И. ДРИЦ, *Развитие экономики Белоруссии в 1961–1970 гг.* (1978).

Caucasus: НИКОЛАЙ А. ГВОЗДЕЦКИЙ, *Кавказ* (1963), discusses the wealth and diversity of the nature of the Caucasus; special attention is given to the economic value of the natural resources. DOUGLAS W. FRESHFIELD, *Exploration of the Caucasus,* 2 vol., 2nd ed. (1902), is the classic work of the famous English alpinist about his investigations of the alpine Caucasus. For Armenia, see HARRY F.B. LYNCH, *Armenia: Travels and Studies,* vol. 1, *The Russian Provinces,* vol. 2, *The Turkish Provinces* (1901, reprinted 1965), an excellent account (with well-informed historical details) of two journeys to Armenia in 1893–94 and 1898, comprising scientific descriptions of geographical and architectural features, with numerous photographs of the monuments and inhabitants, many plans, a large bibliography, and the best physical map of Armenia available; RENÉ GROUSSET, *Histoire de l'Arménie des origines à 1071* (1947, reissued 1973), an excellent general history of Armenia from prehistoric times to the Seljuq conquest, with chapters on the geographical background, a brief history of Urartu, full and up-to-date documentation, and historical maps; HRANT PASDERMADJIAN, *Histoire de l'Arménie depuis les origines jusqu'au traité de Lausanne,* 3rd ed. (1971), a patriotic political history of Armenia, useful for the periods of Ottoman and tsarist domination; SIRARPIE DER NERSESSIAN, *The Armenians* (1969), a short cultural history of Armenia, with well-illustrated chapters on literature, architecture, sculpture, and painting, and *Armenian Art* (1978; trans. from French), a useful survey with many excellent colour illustrations, maps, and an impressive bibliography; DAVID M. LANG, *The Armenians, a People in Exile* (1981), a work on one of the most tragic and revealing aspects of Armenian history, and his *Armenia, Cradle of Civilization,* 3rd ed., corrected (1980), an illustrated work on Armenian history and Armenia's role in the history of mankind. For Georgia, see CHARLES A. BURNEY and DAVID M. LANG, *The Peoples of the Hills* (1972), which gives a survey of the history of Georgia to 1801; it is supplemented by DAVID M. LANG, *A Modern History of Soviet Georgia* (1962, reprinted 1975), as well as by his *Lives and Legends of the Georgian Saints,* 2nd rev. ed. (1976), which is a source for both biography and mythology. For information on Azerbaijani life, see FIRUZ KAZEMZADEH, *The Struggle for Transcaucasia, 1917–1921* (1951, reprinted 1981); EDWARD ALLWORTH, "La Rivalité entre lc Russe et les langues orientales dans les territoires asiatiques de l'U.R.S.S.," *Cahiers du Monde Russe et Soviétique,* vol. 7, no. 4 (1966), pp. 531–563; DAVID M. LANG, "Religion and Nationalism; A Case Study: The Caucasus," *Survey: A Journal of East and West Studies,* No. 66 (January 1968), pp. 33–47; ALEC NOVE and J.A. NEWTH, *The Soviet Middle East: A Communist Model for Development?* (1967); ZEV KATZ *et al.* (eds.), *Handbook of Major Soviet Nationalities* (1975). Additional information can be found in STEPHEN P. DUNN and ETHEL DUNN (eds.), *Introduction to Soviet Ethnography,* 2 vol. (1974), a collection of 17 translations of Soviet ethnographic studies; ROBERT CONQUEST, *The Nation Killers* (1970), which deals with population transfers and deportation of whole nationalities in the Soviet Transcaucasia and Crimea; GEORGE W. SIMMONDS (ed.), *Nationalism in the USSR and Eastern Europe in the Era of Brezhnev and Kosygin* (1977); and GREY HODNETT, *Leadership in the Soviet National Republics* (1978), a study of recruitment policies and social conditions.

Soviet Central Asia: General surveys of the peoples and culture of Soviet Central Asia may be found in LAWRENCE KRADER, *Peoples of Central Asia,* 3rd ed. (1971); and in GEOFFREY WHEELER, *The Peoples of Soviet Central Asia* (1966). General histories of Mongolia and of Soviet Central Asia have been prepared by CHARLES R. BAWDEN, *The Modern History of Mongolia* (1968), and GEOFFREY WHEELER, *The Modern History of Soviet Central Asia* (1964, reprinted 1975). The cultural background of the Turks and Mongol pastoralists are given in LAWRENCE KRADER, "The Cultural and Historical Position of the Mongols," *Asia Major,* 3:169–183 (1952); "Feudalism and the Tatar Polity of the Middle Ages," *Comparative Studies in Society and History,* 1:76–99 (1958); and "Pastoralism," *International Encyclopedia of the Social Sciences,* vol. 11, pp. 453–461 (1968). WILLIAM F. ALBRIGHT, *From the Stone Age to Christianity,* 2nd ed. (1957, reprinted 1967), contains an attack on the notion of geographic determination of Central Asian history and culture. FRANÇOIS BERNIER, *Travels in the Mogul Empire A.D. 1656–1668,* rev. ed. (1891, reprinted 1976; originally published in French, 1699), is an early report on Oriental despotism. KARL A. WITTFOGEL, *Oriental Despotism* (1957, reprinted 1981), is a recent statement of the same subject. JOHN A. BOYLE (trans. and ed.), *History of the World Conqueror,* 2 vol. (1958), is the medieval account of Genghis Khan by ʿAla-ad-Din ʿAta-Malik Juvaini. RENÉ GROUSSET, *The Empire of the Steppes: A History of Central Asia* (1970; originally published in French, 1939), is the best general history but does not reflect our present knowledge. DENIS SINOR, *Inner Asia: History—Civilization—Languages,* 2nd ed. (1971, reprinted 1979), is a syllabus for use in college teaching, to which can be added his collection of topical research materials, *Inner Asia and Its Contacts with Medieval Europe* (1977). BERTOLD SPULER, *The Mongols in History* (1971), and *History of the Mongols, Based on Eastern and Western Accounts of the Thirteenth and Fourteenth Centuries* (1972); as well as GAVIN HUMBLEY (ed.), *Central Asia* (1969), are comprehensive history books. Some of the great issues of Central Asian history are admirably treated by OWEN LATTIMORE in *Inner Asian Frontiers of China,* 2nd ed. (1951, reprinted 1962), *Studies in Frontier History* (1962), and *The Desert Road to Turkestan* (1972). A detailed, heavily annotated bibliographical guide is DENIS SINOR, *Introduction à l'étude de l'Eurasie centrale* (1963). Soviet nationality policy is examined in WILLIAM O. MCCAGG and BRIAN D. SILVER (eds.), *Soviet Asian Ethnic Frontiers* (1979), with conclusions on the substantial material progress in Soviet Central Asia. Other governmental policies and social conditions are dealt with in MICHAEL RYWKIN, *Moscow's Muslim Challenge: Soviet Central Asia* (1982).

For further information on Kazakh life, see НИКОЛАЙ А. ГВОЗДЕЦКИЙ and В.А. НИКОЛАЕВ, *Казахстан: очерк природы* (1971), an overview of the geography and natural history of the area; THOMAS G. WINNER, *The Oral Art and Literature of the Kazakhs of Russian Central Asia* (1958, reprinted 1980); EDWARD ALLWORTH (ed.), *Central Asia: A Century of Russian Rule* (1967); GEORGE J. DEMKO, *The Russian Colonization of Kazakhstan, 1896–1916* (1969); EDWARD ALLWORTH (ed.), *The Nationality Question in Soviet Central Asia* (1973); and *Canadian Slavonic Papers (Russian and Soviet Central Asia),* vol. 18, no. 2 and 3 (1975). On specific political problems of the area, see GREGORY J. MASSELL, *The Surrogate Proletariat: Moslem Women and Revolutionary Strategies in Soviet Central Asia, 1919–1929* (1974); and ALEXANDRE A. BENIGSEN and S. ENDERS WIMBUSH, *Muslim National Communism in the Soviet Union: A Revolutionary Strategy for the Colonial World* (1979). HÉLÈNE CARRÈRE D'ENCAUSSE, *Decline of an Empire: The Soviet Socialist Republics in Revolt* (1979, reprinted 1981), is a historical survey of Soviet nationality policy in Central Asia, with discussion of demographic trends affecting various nationality groups and their relationships to economic developments, language, and political and religious institutions.

For modern Kirgiziya, extensive reference lists appear in RICHARD A. PIERCE, *Soviet Central Asia: A Bibliography,* 3 vol. (1966), as well as in the following publications, which also cover recent developments in the Kirgiz S.S.R. in detail: EDWARD ALLWORTH (ed.), *Central Asia: A Century of Russian Rule* (1967), and *The Nationality Question in Soviet Central Asia* (1973); and ZEV KATZ *et al.* (eds.), *Handbook of Major Soviet Nationalities* (1975).

Various aspects of Tadzhik life are dealt with in the following works: JIRI BECKA, "Tajik Literature from the 16th Century to the Present," in JAN RYPKA, *History of Iranian Literature* (1968); TERESA RAKOWSKA-HARMSTONE, *Russia and Nationalism in Central Asia: The Case of Tadzhikistan* (1970); LAWRENCE KRADER, *Peoples of Central Asia,* 3rd ed. (1971); and EDWARD ALLWORTH (ed.), *The Nationality Question in Soviet Central Asia* (1973).

For further information on Turkmen life, see EDWARD ALLWORTH, *Central Asian Publishing and the Rise of Nationalism* (1965); EDWARD ALLWORTH (ed.), *Central Asia: A Century of Russian Rule* (1967); ZEV KATZ *et al.* (eds.), *Handbook of Major Soviet Nationalities* (1975); *Canadian Slavonic Papers (Russian and Soviet Central Asia),* vol. 17, no. 2 and 3 (1975).

Extensive bibliographies concerning recent developments among the Uzbeks, as well as analyses of such developments, are to be found in EDWARD ALLWORTH, *Uzbek Literary Politics* (1964); ALEC NOVE and J.A. NEWTH, *The Soviet Middle East: A Communist Model for Development?* (1967); WILLIAM K. MEDLIN *et al., Education and Development in Central Asia: A Case Study on Social Change in Uzbekistan* (1971); and EDWARD ALLWORTH (ed.), *The Nationality Question in Soviet Central Asia* (1973). ТАТЬЯНА А. ЖДАНКО (ed.), *Этнография каракалпаков, XIX-начало XX века* (1980), and *Хозяйство Каракалпакии в девятнадцатом-начале двадцатого века* (1972), are materials for a historical atlas of Central Asia, giving a comparative historical overview of population developments and economic conditions in the pre-Soviet period. For information on social life and customs in the Soviet Central Asian republics, ELIZABETH BACON, *Central Asians Under Russian Rule* (1966, reprinted 1980), remains an interesting, if not current, source. EDWARD ALLWORTH, *Soviet Asia, Bibliographies* (1975), is a list of sources on the Iranian, Mongolian, and Turkic nationalities of the U.S.S.R. and includes an essay on controversial topics in Soviet nationality policies.

Moldavia: English-language sources are very scarce. DUMITRU KOVAL and G. MARIN, *Moldavia; Years of Development* (1978), is an overview of the republic, consisting chiefly of illustrations, and though this Soviet book is published with an English title, the text is in Russian and Moldavian, with only summaries and a list of illustrations in English, French, and German. Another survey of history and of economic and social conditions of Soviet Moldavia is ИВАН И. БОДЮЛ, *Советская Молдавия* (1978). Н.П. ФРОЛОВ *et al.* (eds.), *История народного хозяйства Молдавской ССР 1959–1975 гг.* (1978), is a history of the republic's economy in the Soviet period. Statistical information for the Soviet period can be found in a handbook, published for the 60th anniversary of the November Revolution, *Советская Молдавия к 60-летию Великого Октядря* (1977). ВЛАДИМИР М. ИВАНОВ, *Конституционное развитие Молдавской ССР* (1979), is a book on the constitutional history of the republic.

Ukraine: MYKOLA P. BAZHAN *et al.* (eds.), *Soviet Ukraine* (1969), is a Soviet reference work in English, translated from one of the volumes of the encyclopaedia originally published in Ukrainian in 1959–68. The most extensive Western reference work is VOLODYMYR KUBIJOVYČ (ed.), *Ukraine: A Concise Encyclopaedia,* 2 vol. (1963–71; originally published in Ukrainian, 1949). Physical geography is treated in КАЛЕНІК І. ГЕРЕНЧУК (ed.),

Географічні ландшафти України (1966); and В.П. ПОПОВ *et al.* (eds.), *Физико-географическое районирование Украинской ССР* (1968), the first of which is in Ukrainian, the second in Russian, and both of which contain extensive bibliography. The economic life of the republic is examined in МАКСИМ М. ПАЛАМАРЧУК, *Украинская ССР: экономико-географическая характеристика* (1970), and *Экономическая география Украинской ССР с основами теории* (1977); and IWAN S. KOROPECKYJ (ed.), *The Ukraine Within the USSR: An Economic Balance Sheet* (1977). Details of the demographic and ethnic characteristics of the Ukrainian people can be found in the reports of the 1970 census of the Soviet Union, including information on ethnic makeup, households, education, and so on. For treatment of historical and ideological questions, see ROMAN SZPORLUK, *Ukraine, a Brief History* (1979); ARTHUR E. ADAMS, *Bolsheviks in the Ukraine: The Second Campaign, 1918–1919* (1963, reprinted 1973); JOHN A. ARMSTRONG, *The Soviet Bureaucratic Elite: A Case Study of the Ukrainian Apparatus* (1959); GEORGE LIBER and ANNA MOSTOVYCH, *Nonconformity and Dissent in the Ukrainian SSR, 1955–1975: A Select Bibliography* (1977); KENNETH C. FARMER, *Ukrainian Nationalism in the Post-Stalin Era: Myth, Symbols and Ideology in Soviet Nationalities Policy* (1980); and LESYA VERBA and BOHDAN YASEN (eds.), *The Human Rights Movement in Ukraine: Documents of the Ukrainian Helsinki Group 1976–1980* (1980). For political, administrative, and cultural affairs in the contemporary Soviet Ukraine, see ROBERT S. SULLIVANT, *Soviet Politics and the Ukraine, 1917–1957* (1962); YAROSLAV BILINSKY, *The Second Soviet Republic: The Ukraine After World War II* (1964), and, with TONU PARMING, *Helsinki Watch Committees in the Soviet Republics: Implications for the Soviet Nationality Question* (1980); JOHN A. ARMSTRONG, *Ukrainian Nationalism*, 2nd ed. (1963, reprinted 1980); and ROMAN SZPORLUK, "The Ukraine and the Ukrainians," in ZEV KATZ *et al.* (ed.), *Handbook of Major Soviet Nationalities* (1975). KONSTANTYN SAWCZUK, *The Ukraine in the United Nations: A Study in Soviet Foreign Policy* (1975), treats the Ukrainian S.S.R.'s role in international affairs. The most comprehensive study of Ukrainian art is МИКОЛА БАЖАН (ed.), *Історія українського мистецтва*, 6 vol. (1966–70). SVIATOSLAV HORDYNSKY, *The Ukrainian Icon: The Twelfth to the Eighteenth Centuries* (1973), covers Ukrainian schools of icon painting. The most exhaustive surveys of early Ukrainian literature are МИХАЙЛО С. ВОЗНЯК, *Історія української літератури*, 3 vol. (1920–24, reprinted 1970); and МИХАЙЛО ГРУШЕВСЬКИЙ, *Історія української літератури*, 5 vol. (1923–27; facsimile ed. 1959–60). In English, see DMYTRO ČYŽEVS'KYJ, *A History of Ukrainian Literature, From the 11th to the End of the 19th Century* (1975); CLARENCE A. MANNING, *Ukrainian Literature: Studies of the Leading Authors* (1944, reprinted 1971); and YEVHEN SHABLIOVSKY, *Ukrainian Literature Through the Ages* (1970; trans. from Ukrainian).